Chronicle of the 20th CENTURY

Chronicle of the 20th Century

Dorling Kindersley

LONDON • NEW YORK • STUTTGART • MOSCOW

Editor-in-Chief: Derrik Mercer

Executive Editor: Jerome Burne

Picture Editor: Colin Jacobson
Associate Editors: Robert Carvel, Peter Lewis
Foreign Correspondents: Frank Barber, Christopher Dobson, Godfrey Hodgson, John Miller, Ronald Payne
Specialist Correspondents: Muriel Bowen, Hugh L'Etang, Liz Gill, Nicholas Mason, Bryan Silcock, Hugh Stephenson, David Wallen
Senior Writers: Peter Bently, Robert Jones, Denis Pitts
Additional Writers: Hazel Bedford, Harry Fieldhouse, David Gould, Jonathan Green, Laurence Joffre, Michael Johnstone, John May, Andrew Moger, Carol Price, Tony Scott
Editorial Research: Danny Gittings, Henrietta Heald
Picture Manager: Susanna Harrison
Additional Picture Research: Mary Corcoran, David Brownridge, Sue Cranmer, Ann-Marie Ehrlich, Caroline Metcalfe, Peter Brogan (Hulton Picture Library); Ruth Twyman and Chris Coupeland (Mary Evans Picture Library); Siobhan Hewitt and Gerry Conrad (Photo Source); Liz Moore and Dawn Wyman (Popperfoto); Robert Opie; Mike Hollingshead (Topham Picture Library)
Production: Bronwen Lewis (Manager), Didier Camal, Claire Gannaway, Laura Hicks, Maxine Lee Fatt, Christine Remonte
Computer Systems: Catherine Legrand (Manager), Dominique Klutz (Software Engineer), Pascal Wauters de Besterfeld
Art: Henry Marganne (Manager), Christian Baude, Michel Colley

Created and produced by Jacques Legrand

Acknowledgements
The publishers would like to thank the following for their special contributions to the *Chronicle of the 20th Century:* Peter Ball, John Bently, Stephen Clackson, Chris Ellis and Jonathan Glancey whose work either appears in these pages or shapes the content; *The Daily Telegraph* for enabling us to have access to their back numbers; The British Library Newspaper Library; the Media Resources Library at City University and the Hans Tasiemka Archives.

We also express our gratitude to the following institutions for their assistance:
The Automobile Association; Amstrad Consumer Electronics plc; Association of British Travel Agents Ltd; British Broadcasting Corporation; Britoil plc; Barclays Bank plc; British Petroleum plc; British Airways plc; British Airports Authority plc; British Coal; British United Provident Association Ltd; Bank of England; Boots Company plc; Building Societies Association; British Aerospace plc; British Steel Corporation; J. Barbour and Sons Ltd; Bejam Group plc; Confederation of British Industry; Civil Aviaton Authority; Cunard Line Ltd; Courtaulds plc; Consumers' Association; Electricity Council; Family Planning Association; Filofax plc; Ford Motor Company plc; Halifax Building Society; Habitat plc; Independent Broadcasting Authority; Jaguar Cars Ltd; Laura Ashley plc; London Regional Transport; Lloyds Bank plc; Metropolitan Police; Midland Bank plc; Mothercare plc; National Theatre; National Westminster Bank plc; National Farmer's Union; Oxfam; Prudential Assurance; Rover Group plc; Rowntree plc; Royal Shakespeare Company; J. Sainsbury plc; Save the Children Fund; Selfridges Ltd; Stock Exchange; Trustee Savings Bank; Vauxhall Motors Ltd; Vickers Group plc; Virgin Group plc; and Wembley Stadium Ltd.

Published in 1995 by Dorling Kindersley Limited, 9 Henrietta St, London WC2E 8PS
First edition in 1988

ISBN 0 7513 3006 X

Printed in Belgium by Brepols

1900-1909

These illustrations are used to introduce each change of decade throughout the volume. In them the artists of the time have caught the flavour of their time. "Salon Des Artistes Français" is by Jules-Alexandre Grun, a scene typical of the salon painters who flattered the rich, self-assured **beau monde** of turn-of-the-century Paris, the world that Marcel Proust was to conjure up in his great novel. It was not much different from the upper middle class society in England that John Galsworthy was to depict in the Forsyte Saga.

1910-1919

Otto Dix: "Flanders". This was where the **beau monde** and the **Belle Epoque** ended when the lights went out all over Europe. The devastation of No Man's Land, the tree-stumps, the water-filled shell holes, the misery and the mud, are seen here from the German side on which Otto Dix fought. The men who had eagerly volunteered on both sides did not long retain any illusions about the chivalrous art of war as it had once been fought. This was slaughter on an inhuman scale by creeping barrage, machine guns and mustard gas.

1920-1929

Dix survived the war to record the fever of defeated Germany. Here, in "The Night Bird", is the desperate gaiety of the Berlin cabaret nights of the Weimar Republic. In 1928, when this was painted, the party had not much longer to run. In Munich the seeds of National Socialism were ripening; on Wall Street, even the lift-men were speculating on a boom that was about to burst. The Roaring Twenties, with their emancipated girls dancing the Charleston and Black Bottom, were ended by a combination of both.

1930-1939

Richard Oelze: "Expectation". When this was painted, Hitler had been in power for two years. The Nazis seemed, in Germany, to be on the course for an ever-expanding future watched by a mesmerised Europe that still clung to peace at any price. Britain and America were pole-axed by their own Depression. But the artist sees beyond the present to the approaching storm which these pallid, trilby-hatted civilians are powerless to avert. "A low, dishonest decade" is what W.H. Auden called it as it ended in 1939.

1940-1949

"Drawing from the Shelter Notebooks". In 1940, Henry Moore found himself travelling at night on the London Underground, whose platforms had been taken over by those who had no adequate shelter from the air raids. Confronted by so extraordinary a human predicament, he returned with his sketchbooks again and again to produce with his sculptor's eye not only a record, but a symbol of that predicament. Human beings, huddled together for comfort, sleep in the bowels like mummies in their shrouds.

1950-1959

Fernand Leger. “Country Party”. After years of suffering and dcpri vation, now comes freedom and prosperity. Fernand Leger knew how to reproduce splendidly the relaxation and pleasure enjoyed by the labouring classes, exemplified by a family excursion to the country in the luxury of the automobile – symbol of emerging well-being of society at large. Grim war time memories fade and the reconstruction of Europe is completed. People devoured the fruits of industry and commerce and relished their new leisure time.

1960-1969

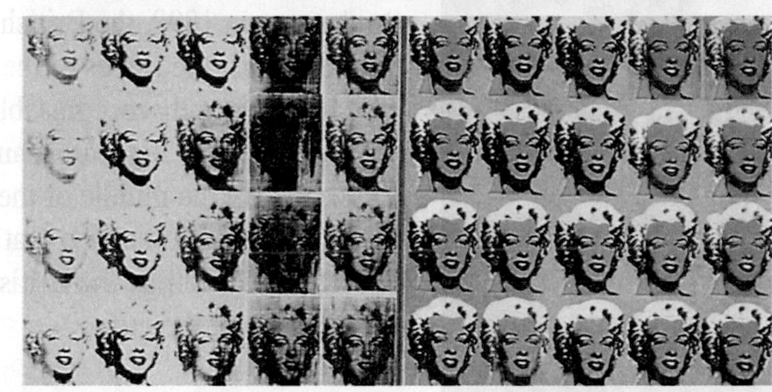

Andy Warhol: “Marilyn Monroe”. In the Sixties, the Media Age dawned. Advertisements, newspapers, magazines, cinema and television screens needed a supply of instantly readable images. No-one was quicker to comment on this than Andy Warhol. In helping to invent Pop Art, he turned posters, packaging, even soup cans, into pictures, using mechanical processes of repetition to mirror the contemporary worship of mass consumption. As subjects he took the Pop icons themselves like Elvis Presley and Marilyn Monroe.

1970-1979

David Hockney: “Mr and Mrs Clark and Percy”. After the lurid images of Pop, the Seventies found a more inward-looking style. Hockney did not tax the onlooker with profound emotion but offered the naive enjoyment of the good life in decorative environments like the California of sunshine and swimming pools. Ossie Clark and his wife Celia Birtwell were at that time leading London fashion designers. Their chosen self-image is as cool and *soigné* as Percy, their immaculate cat.

1980-1989

November 1989: The Berlin Wall falls. The oil crises of 1973 and 1980 signalled the end of 30 years of prosperity and led industrialized society to rethink its objectives. They also heralded the beginning of a period of profound social upheavals. The disintegration of the Communist regimes of Eastern Europe, symbolized by the fall of the Berlin Wall, was the most unexpected of these changes. 1989 also saw the Soviet army’s withdrawal from Afghanistan and the merciless crushing of the pro-democraty movement in China.

1990-1999

Towards the information superhighway and the millenium. The world’s maps are redrawn. Borders vanish and conflicts break out following the disintegration of the USSR and Yugoslavia. Some borders, such as the one between Kuwait and Iraq, are restored by force, while others are created. The Gaza Strip becomes Palestinian. However, the 30 million users of the Internet web know no borders. As the new computer-based networks spread from Los Angeles to Timbuctu, the age of global, real-time communication dawns.

Foreword
by Jeremy Paxman

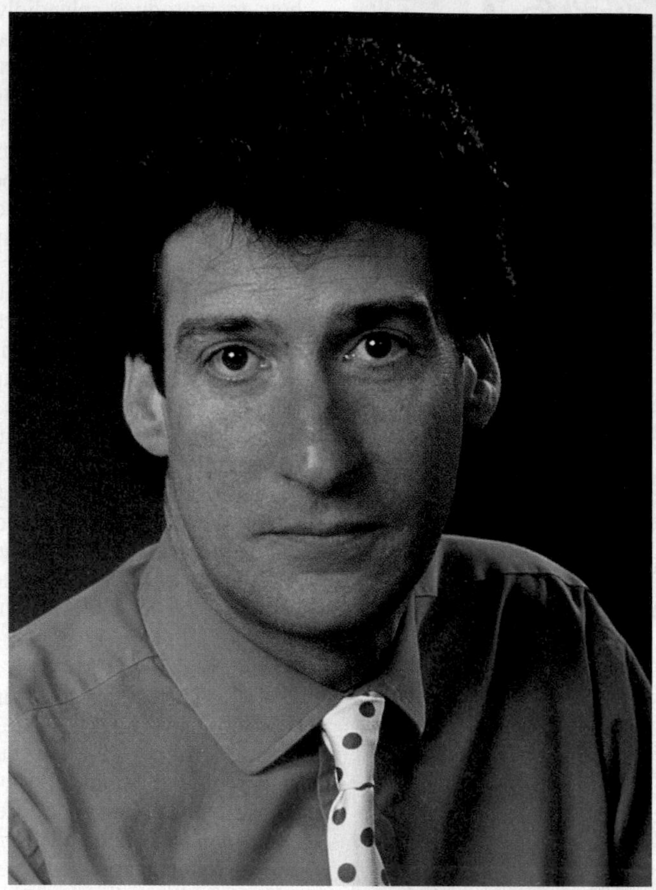

The 20th century really ought to have lasted 500 years. That way, history would have advanced at the same pace it always had.

As it is, in these hundred years the clocks started to run at double, treble and then quintuple time. Two years before the century began, at the battle of Omdurman in 1898, the British army made a cavalry charge against the forces of the Mahdi which would have been instantly recognisable to any soldier who had fought in any big European army in the previous 300 years. By the middle of the 20th century, one of the subalterns who had led that charge, Winston Churchill, was telling the British people that the Allies had split the atom.

The huge destructive potential of the Bomb changed the rules of international politics and recast the post-war map of the world. But in every area of life, science has transformed the experience of everyday living. We live longer, in greater comfort and in greater freedom from life-threatening diseases than our grandparents could have imagined.

Yet the British experience of this helter-skelter century has been of more-or-less constant fall, like the final trajectory of a shell blasted from one of the great Dreadnoughts with which the British Empire expected to dominate the world in 1897, when the streets of London were packed for Queen Victoria's Diamond Jubilee, the grandest spectacle of imperial power ever seen. A quarter of the world, the greatest domain ever assembled under a single flag, trembled to the tap of a morse key in London. Twenty years later, the notions of hierarchy, honour and sacrifice which had given the British Empire its apparent moral purpose were left hanging on the barbed wire of the Somme and Passchendaele. The Second World War finally drew the lees from the bank account of a nation which could no longer afford the rent for its imperial pretensions. A power which had controlled a quarter of the world's population was left with one or two tropical islands and a few sheep farmers in the South Atlantic.

British politicians have been pretty inept at adjusting to our changed circumstances. It isn't entirely their fault: high culture is a product of wealth and self-confidence and so much of Britain's image of itself was created in the years of imperial purple. As the British have failed conspicuously to dream up anything newly reassuring, they continue endlessly refighting the old battles about where they belong in the world.

If the era of British greatness belongs to the 19th century, the 20th century has been the property of America and there is something instructive to be learned about why. It is not merely that the United States is the one remaining Superpower, capable of putting half a million men into the Gulf while maintaining fleets in the Far East and without jeopardising its ability to wipe any world city off the map in a nuclear strike. It is also because America has captured something much more elusive. For the first time, a way of life has captured the imagination of the world. The elites of Edwardian India may have wanted to become English gentlemen, but America offers something for the dreams of Everyman.

This is not to rerun the French nightmare in which all the world's culture is determined by a bunch of manipulative Californians with improbably perfect teeth and resculpted jawlines. That battle is already largely lost, as a quick glance at the baseball hats in McDonalds restaurants from Tallinn to Tokyo will show. The paradox is that in the midst of this uniformity, the American dream thrives on belief in the individual.

Those who talk about "Cultural Imperialism" miss the point. America is merely the conduit through which the promise of the 20th century has been brought about. If we stop looking at the world in terms of maps and armies, we see the great change of these hundred years has been the empowerment of the individual. The most far-reaching changes to our lives have not been made by politicians but by scientists.

Of course it helps that the great inventions of the century were arrived at in democracies. But the inherent thrust of science in capitalism is to create opportunities for the individual. The television, telephone, washing machine, dishwasher and the rest are designed to provide individual freedom. All the secret policemen in Eastern Europe could not keep the post-war tyrannies in power when people knew that all around, freedom was on the march.

So, the true heroes of the 20th century are not the strutting leaders but the scientists, designers and engineers who have reinvented our world. No question, the monsters of the century had political ambition - Hitler, Stalin, Pol Pot and their little brothers Amin, Stroessner, and Bokassa. But the dreams of the politicians, the "White Man's Burden" in colonial Africa, "The Thousand Year Reich", Communism's claim to the West that "We will bury you", have turned out to be bluster. We cannot plot a course into the future on the basis of any grand claims by men with their eyes on grace-and-favour mansions or statues erected at public expense.

At the start of the century, suffragettes were fighting to win the vote for women. But what really changed women's lives was not the vote but the Pill. We owe our health, comfort, mobility and comparative longevity to chemists, physicists, doctors and engineers. We increasingly depend upon machines whose functioning we cannot understand, a chasm which will only become deeper. The capacities of computers are doubling every 18 months and as they develop, the complexities beneath our apparently simple life choices are going to multiply at a comparable rate. The great workplaces of the post-war years, huge factories employing thousands have gone forever, replaced by societies comprised of individuals and small groups in ad-hoc arrangements.

As societies atomize, governments seem increasingly irrelevant. *Their* real challenge is to see that everyone gets a share in the benefits.

JEREMY PAXMAN
Television journalist and author

1900 – 1909

1900

JANUARY

Su	Mo	Tu	We	Th	Fr	Sa
	1	2	3	4	5	6
7	8	9	10	11	12	13
14	15	16	17	18	19	20
21	22	23	24	25	26	27
28	29	30	31			

1. Nigeria becomes British protectorate (→25/4).

2. New York: First electric omnibus installed in New York City.

3. Southampton: New Royal Yacht, Victoria and Albert, capsizes as soon as it undocks.

4. Belgium and Germany: Strikes lead to riots in mining areas.

5. Baltimore: Dr Henry A. Rowland of Johns Hopkins University discovers the cause of the earth's magnetism.

5. Ireland: Nationalist leader John Redmond calls for uprising against the British.

6. S. Africa: General White repels fierce Boer attack on Ladysmith (→10).

9. Egypt: The first through train runs from Cairo to Khartoum in the Sudan.

12. India: Three and a quarter million people are receiving famine relief.

15. London: The Hippodrome theatre opens in the Charing Cross Road.

17. US: Mormon Brigham Roberts is refused a seat in the House of Representatives because of polygamy.

23. Austria: 5,000 miners go on strike.

24. S. Africa: The Boer government of the Transvaal holds peace talks with the British.→

24. S. Africa: British under General Warren take Spion Kop.

27. China: Foreign legations demand that the Imperial Government discipline the rebellious Boxer sect (→7/4).

DEATHS

20. British art critic and social theorist John Ruskin, at Coniston in the Lake District (*18/2/1819).

20. British novelist Richard D. Blackmore (*7/6/1825).

31. British peer the 8th Marquess of Queensberry, author of boxing's Queensberry Rules (*1844).→

High hopes greet the new century

Jan 1. As the new century was rung in last night the extent of Britain's imperial powers have never been greater. "The Empire, stretching round the globe, has one heart, one head, one language, one policy" stated one newspaper report.

There is of course the matter of the Boer War which started a few months ago, but no one is in any doubt that the fight with this "stubborn breed of Dutch peasants revolting against the just sovereignty of the Queen" will soon end in victory. The relief of Ladysmith, for instance, one knowledgeable war correspondent has declared, is only days away.

Certainly looking back to the beginning of the previous century the picture then was far gloomier – America recently lost, war with Dutch, Spain and France in progress, mutinies at the Nore and Spithead and Napoleon's meteoric rise just beginning. Yet such an inauspicious start was, as we all know, followed by a century of unparalleled success and expansion. So, it seems not unreasonable to speculate that the next hundred years might well be even more glorious.

The New Year's honours list, besides ennobling Sir John Lubbock who, among other things, gave us the Bank Holiday, also features Crown servants from around the globe. Knighthoods are bestowed on administrators as far apart as Bengal, Melbourne and Trinidad.

The "Dawn of the Century" march, with inventions of the 19th century.

The financial outlook is buoyant on both sides of the Atlantic. Total British revenue is up £4 million on last year, while on Wall Street the Americans are pleased with themselves and the bankers are talking of a "prosperity panic." They are also delighted with the Boer War which they regard as being good for trade.

New chief for army in Boer War

Jan 10. Field Marshal Lord Roberts, hero of the Afghanistan expedition to relieve Kandahar, has arrived at Cape Town to assume supreme command of British forces in South Africa.

Since the outbreak of hostilities last October, when Boer commandos invaded Natal, the British have suffered a series of defeats, despite the gallant way the troops fought at Ladysmith. Before leaving London Lord Roberts received news of the death of his only son in battle during the "Black Week" defeats of December.

Thousands hit by influenza outbreak

Jan 9. Fifty people a day are now dying from the influenza epidemic in London. Other major cities in Britain have also been hit badly by the outbreak of an illness which was regarded as something of a fashionable malady when it occurred seven years ago. But grave-diggers are now working night and day as the epidemic worsens.

There is also a shortage of nurses and some wards have had to be closed. Requests for trained nursing staff cannot now be met and London hospitals are having trouble coping with the epidemic.

Marquess of Queensberry, father of boxing rules, died this month.

1900

FEBRUARY

Su	Mo	Tu	We	Th	Fr	Sa
				1	2	3
4	5	6	7	8	9	10
11	12	13	14	15	16	17
18	19	20	21	22	23	24
25	26	27	28			

2. Paris: First performance of Gustave Charpentier's opera "Louise".

3. Europe: Strikers in Aachen, Vienna and Brussels demand an 8-hour day and higher pay (→ 3/3).

5. Washington: Britain and the US sign a treaty for the building of a Central American shipping canal through Nicaragua (→ 2/5).

6. London: Commons vote of censure over the government's handling of the Boer War is defeated by majority of 213 (→ 11).

6. Washington: The Senate ratifies the 1899 decree of the Hague Peace Conference, creating an international court of arbitration at The Hague.

9. US: Dwight F. Davis creates the Davis Cup tennis tournament (→ 10/8).

11. S. Africa: Col. Hannay begins invasion of Orange Free State with march from Orange River to Ramdam (→ 12).

12. London: Meeting held at Mile End to protest against the Boer War ends in uproar (→ 28).

16. London: Appearance of "Savrola", the first novel of Winston Spencer Churchill.

18. US: Harry Vardon becomes world golf champion.

18. San Francisco: A man claims X-rays have cured his cancer.

19. Germany: Minister of the Navy Alfred von Tirpitz says the German fleet "must be strong enough to ensure its mastery of the North Sea".

26. London: The Grand Theatre, Islington, is destroyed by fire.

BIRTHS

1. US actor Clark Gable (†16/11/60).

4. French poet and writer Jacques Prevert (†11/4/77).

5. US politician Adlai Stevenson (†14/7/65).

22. Spanish film director Luis Bunuel (†29/7/83).

Ladysmith relieved after long siege

Boer scouts camping out on the veldt near Ladysmith.

Feb 28. In late afternoon a detachment of cavalry, appearing on the hills above the town and being called on by a sentry to identify itself, responds with the triumphant cry: "The Ladysmith relief column".

So, after 118 days, the siege of this garrison town and rail junction is over. General Sir Redvers Buller has received a telegram from the Queen "Thank God for news you have telegraphed to me. Congratulate you and all under you with all my heart VRI".

The garrison commander, General Sir George White, also received a royal message, to which he replied: "Any hardships and privations are a hundred times compensated for by the sympathy and appreciation of our Queen."

In his dispatch to the Secretary of State for War, General Buller says the victory has been more complete than he had dared to hope. The Boers packed their wagons and retreated, taking most of their guns, but leaving behind vast quantities of ammunition.

For General Buller the victory is particularly gratifying. After defeats at Stormberg, Magersfontein and Colenso, all in one week in December, he failed again at Spion Kop, leaving 1,200 casualties in the hills seven miles from Ladysmith.

Though accused of indecisiveness, failing to gather adequate intelligence of enemy positions and fatally dividing his forces, Buller was allowed to stay as field commander in Natal.

Along with news of his victory, it was revealed that Lord Roberts had visited Mr Cecil Rhodes, the financier, in Kimberley, where the siege was lifted a fortnight ago. After receiving the surrender of General Piet Cronje at Paardeberg, near Kimberley, Roberts has launched a drive towards the Orange Free State capital of Bloemfontein. General Cronje has been exiled to St. Helena.

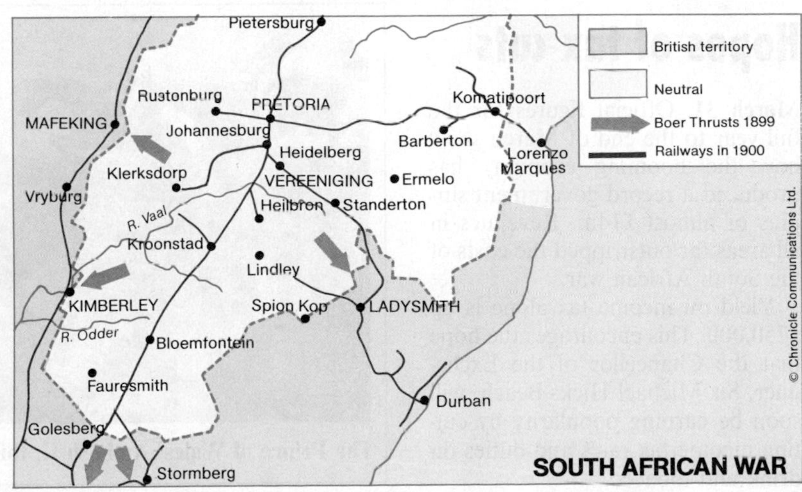

Trade unions create Labour Party

Feb 27. The Labour Representation Committee was born today. In the Memorial Hall, Farringdon Street, London – on the site of the old Fleet Prison – 129 delegates from 65 trade unions and three Socialist societies resolved to establish "a distinct Labour Group in Parliament". Organising the committee as its secretary will be James Ramsay MacDonald. They represented 568,000 workers – less than half the total in unions affiliated to the Trades Union Congress which sponsored the meeting.

The outcome was an uneasy compromise between rival factions. A proposal by the Marxist-orientated Social Democratic Federation for a full-blooded Socialist Party-based upon recognition of the class war was defeated. So was another that the Labour Movement in Parliament should be represented only by members of the working classes and be concerned only with trade union questions.

Delegates did not quarrel about their goal, just how best to reach it and how long it might take. After day-long debate they accepted a proposal by the Scottish miner James Keir Hardie, for seven years now a leading light in the Independent Labour Party, that the aim must be a party in Parliament with flexibility for development. This satisfied the Fabians, most union men and the SDF despite reservations. Keir Hardie said: "It has come. Poor little child of danger, nursling of the storm. May it be blessed." Delegates left the hall to face the future. Outside it rained.

Ramsay MacDonald.

1900

MARCH

Su	Mo	Tu	We	Th	Fr	Sa
				1	2	3
4	5	6	7	8	9	10
11	12	13	14	15	16	17
18	19	20	21	22	23	24
25	26	27	28	29	30	31

2. Rome: Pope condemns Boer War bloodshed.

3. Germany: Striking miners return to work.

5. US: Two cruisers are sent to Central America to protect US interests in a dispute between Nicaragua and Costa Rica.

6. London: "Baby-farmer" Ada Williams is hanged at Newgate prison for murdering a 19-month old girl.

7. London: Fire at Buckingham Palace destroys part of the roof.

8. London: Rejoicing as Queen Victoria makes one of her rare visits to the capital.

9. Germany: Women petition the Reichstag for the right to sit state examinations and to attend university (→31).

13. South Africa: Lord Roberts takes Bloemfontein (→14).

14. Holland: The botanist Hugo de Vries rediscovers Mendel's laws of heredity.

15. London: Prime Minister Lord Salisbury rejects US President McKinley's offer to mediate in the Boer War.

19. London: Public subscription for new Government Boer War loan is £335m – 11 times amount asked.

27. Far East: Arrival of a Russian fleet in Korea causes concern to Japanese government.

31. France: Law passed limiting the working day for women and children to 11 hours.

BIRTHS

2. German composer Kurt Weill (†3/4/50).

23. German-born US psychoanalyst Erich Fromm (†18/3/80).

DEATHS

6. German pianoforte maker Carl Bechstein (*1/6/1826).

6. German motor car designer and builder Gottlieb Daimler (*17/3/1834).

Excavation of Knossos begins in Crete

March 19. Sir Arthur Evans, the archaeologist, has begun to reveal the ancient wonders of the palace of Knossos, on Crete.

Evans discovered the palace in 1899, on a site which the great German archaeologist Schliemann had earlier refused to buy as being of poor archaeological value. An extremely short-sighted man, Evans has microscopic vision at short range, and his ability to discern tiny hieroglyphs on Cretan seal stones convinced him that an ancient, undiscovered civilisation existed on Crete even before the Homeric age unearthed by Schliemann at Mycenae.

Almost as soon as he started to dig on the Kephala, legendary site of the palace of Knossos, Evans uncovered a huge labyrinth of some ancient pre-Mycenaean palace. He calls the newly-found culture "Minoan" after the King Minos of Cretan legend.

King Minos was said to have kept the terrible Minotaur, half-man and half-bull. Fascinatingly, one of Evans' first finds were signs everywhere that the "Minoans" worshipped bulls.

Sir Arthur Evans.

Millions starving in Indian famine

March 27. Millions of starving Indians are turning to the colonial government for help as their meagre food supplies dry up in the widespread famine. India's British Viceroy, Lord Curzon, said today that relief officials were now distributing food to more than five million people hit by drought and by disastrous crop failures.

He told the Vice-Regal Council in Calcutta that the government planned to spend a total of £8.5 million on famine relief in the next year, and another £1.3 million on irrigation projects to protect India against future famine. Lord Curzon warned, however, that military spending would not be cut to free more money for famine relief. "I am not going, for the sake of the one, to neglect the other," he declared. In London, a fund set up by the Lord Mayor to aid famine victims has raised £155,500 (→4/5).

President McKinley goes for gold

March 14. The US dollar went formally onto the gold standard today as President William McKinley signed the bill declaring that the gold dollar is now to "be the standard unit of value". The signing puts a symbolic seal on the President's election victory four years ago over William Jennings Bryan, his Democrat opponent, who had championed a much looser monetary policy based on the unlimited mining of silver.

Britain rejects Boers' surrender offer

March 14. In the wake of recent Boer defeats at the hands of British forces, it has been disclosed in London that the two Boer presidents, Paul Kruger of the Transvaal, and Marthinus Steyn of the Orange Free State, have put forward a proposal for peace "in the sight of the true God".

They suggest that both sides should withdraw their armies to positions within their own borders, and that the Boer republics be given full independence. These terms have been summarily rejected by British ministers, who argue that the re-emergence of the republics would simply revive the threat to the British position in South Africa that had existed before the war.

The Boer overtures became known to the British public the day after the burghers of Bloemfontein surrendered the Free State capital to Lord Roberts, whose troops were greeted by cheering crowds and decorated streets. President Steyn escaped by train before General French's cavalry could cut the railway line.

Hopes of tax cuts

March 31. Official figures for the full year to the end of March show how the booming economy has produced a record government surplus of almost £14m. Revenues in all areas far outstripped the costs of the South African war.

Yield on income tax alone is up £750,000. This encourages the hope that the Chancellor of the Exchequer, Sir Michael Hicks-Beach, will soon be earning popularity by cutting income tax rates and duties on drink and tobacco.

The Prince of Wales' Ambush II, this year's Grand National winner.

1900

APRIL

Su	Mo	Tu	We	Th	Fr	Sa
1	2	3	4	5	6	7
8	9	10	11	12	13	14
15	16	17	18	19	20	21
22	23	24	25	26	27	28
29	30					

1. France: New law authorises police to carry revolvers.

1. Greece: Prince George becomes absolute monarch of Crete.

3. Rome: Left-wing agitation leads to adjournment of the Italian parliament for three weeks.

4. Ireland: Queen Victoria arrives in Dublin on a rare visit.

9. S. Africa: Boers defeat British troops at Kroonstadt (→17).

14. Brussels: Gaston Peuchot is arrested and confesses to instigating attempt on Prince of Wales' life.

16. US: World's first book of stamps is issued.

17. London: Government publishes Lord Roberts' criticisms of Generals Buller and Warren over handling of Spion Kop battle (→15/5).

21. France: Dugardin announces he has made major advances in colour photography.

24. Johannesburg: Explosion at engineering works kills 10 people.

25. Gold Coast: Several thousand Ashanti rebels surround and attack Kumasi fort.

26. Canada: Huge fire reduces the cities of Ottawa and Hull to ashes in 12 hours, leaving 12,000 people homeless.

28. London: Bury beat Southampton 4-0 in the FA Cup Final at Crystal Palace.

29. Paris: The collapse of a footbridge at the great world exhibition kills ten people.

30. Pacific Ocean: Hawaii, formerly the British Sandwich Islands, becomes a US Territory.

BIRTH

5. US actor Spencer Tracy (†10/6/67).

DEATH

30. US railway engineer Casey Jones (*1864).

World Exhibition opens in Paris

April 14. The President of France, M. Loubet, opened the spectacular Paris International Exhibition today with a plea for world peace. The exhibition, covering 547 acres, is the biggest of its kind in European history and features "palaces" from every major nation on a site along the Rue des Nations and the Quai d'Orsay.

The electrical illuminations in the Chateau d'Eau and the Hall of Illusions were a particular attraction to the thousands who heard the President declare sonorously that the "meeting of the governments of the world will not remain without fruit". The exhibition is seen as a determined effort by the French to restore the international image of their Empire (→1/5).

Fountains outside the Palace of Electricity, Champ de Mars.

Allies urge Chinese to suppress Boxers

April 7. Faced by a growing threat posed by the Boxer Rebellion to the lives of foreigners living in China the European powers here presented an ultimatum giving the Chinese government two months to suppress the uprising.

In a joint note, the British, American, German and French ministers threatened that if this were not done they would land troops in China in order to ensure the safety of foreign residents there. Concentrated action was decided upon in face of the new and dangerous developments among the Boxers.

It began as a patriotic society of discontented Chinese, then turned into a popular movement against foreign, and especially Christian, influence. Recently the Boxers, who originally confined their enthusiasm to boxing, have been observed openly drilling in military style in Peking. They are being joined by disaffected soldiers.

Until now many officials have held aloof from the movement, but recently there have been signs that many high Manchus, including members of the Imperial Clan, are joining. Others are still trying to keep in favour with the party of the Dowager Empress (→31/5).

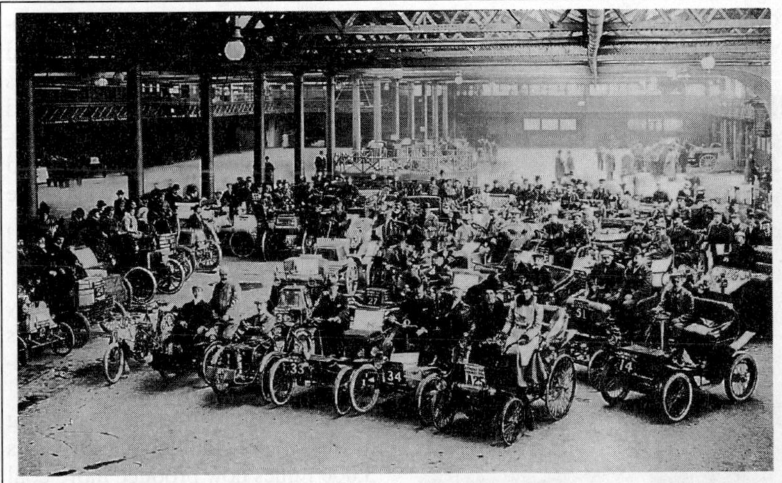

Motorists gather at the Waverley Market in Edinburgh, for the start of the Automobile Club's 1,000-mile trial around Britain.

Prince of Wales survives shooting

The attempt on the Prince's life.

April 4. The Prince of Wales escaped uninjured today when a 16-year-old anarchist fired two shots at him from point-blank range on a Brussels railway station. Jean-Baptiste Sipido stepped onto the footboard of the train which was due to take the Prince and Princess on a trip to Copenhagen but his shots somehow missed.

Brussels has been a centre of opposition to the British role in the Boer War for some time, with much of the protest directed at the Royal Family. Anarchist literature was found on Sipido, and he told police he wanted to kill the Prince who had so many men killed in South Africa (→14).

1900

MAY

Su	Mo	Tu	We	Th	Fr	Sa
		1	2	3	4	5
6	7	8	9	10	11	12
13	14	15	16	17	18	19
20	21	22	23	24	25	26
27	28	29	30	31		

1. US: Explosion in Utah coal mine kills 200.

2. US: Bill passed by Congress for the building of the Nicaraguan canal (→ 1/8).

4. India: Viceroy receives famine relief donation from Kaiser Wilhelm II.

4. Germany: Austrian Kaiser Franz Josef I meets Kaiser Wilhelm II, reaffirms friendship.

8. Manchuria: Russians and Chinese clash on route of new Russian railway (→ 21).

9. US: Striking tramway workers blow up tramcar during riots in St. Louis.

11. Spain: Riots close all shops and theatres in Madrid.

14. India: 27 rioters are shot dead by police at Vizagapatam.

14. Paris: Start of "World Amateur Championships", known as the Olympic Games (→ 22/7).

15. S. Africa: General Buller reoccupies Dundee and Glencoe (→ 20).

19. Britain annexes Tonga, formerly the Friendly Islands.

21. Russia annexes Manchuria, taking advantage of the Boxer rebellion in China.

21. US: Secretary of State John Hay tells Boers US will keep strictly neutral in the South African war (→ 28).

27. Belgium: World's first experiment in proportional representation is made in the general election.

28. S. Africa: Britain formally annexes the Orange Free State and Utrecht, Transvaal, surrenders to the British.

28. UK: Eclipse of the sun.

30. UK: The Prince of Wales's Diamond Jubilee wins the Derby.

DEATH

29. British musicologist Sir Charles Grove, first director of the Royal College of Music and founder of Grove's Dictionary (*13/8/1820).

Violent Boxer uprising rocks China

May 31. As the Boxer rebellion engulfed the southern provinces, British and Belgian residents poured into Peking to escape massacre. Yesterday rebels waving the heads of murdered missionaries occupied the nearby city of Tientsin.

Although the Imperial Government has banned Boxer activity it is ignored. Indeed, there are reports of imperial troops joining the rebels. The Boxers, who call themselves the "Fists of Righteous Harmony", are members of what started as a patriotic society devoted to martial arts; fiercely secretive, they have become inspired by a hatred of "foreign devils", especially missionaries.

Foreign diplomats in China have described the attitude of the Government as highly unsatisfactory, and are attempting to pressure it to restore order. For the Western Powers to intervene would need hundreds of thousands of troops.

A detachment, consisting of 340 British, American, Russian, Italian and Japanese marines, arrived in Peking this evening. That they had been hastily scraped together was demonstrated by the fact that the Americans wore winter uniforms and the Russians had come without their cannon.

In the US, religious groups have been exerting heavy pressure upon the McKinley administration to order military intervention. The State Department in Washington said that the US would act with other nations if the Chinese government failed to suppress Boxer outrages.

Future Chinese officers at school in Tientsin.

Champion Jeffries KO's Corbett

May 11. Jim Jeffries of the United States, who won the world heavyweight boxing title last June by defeating the British-born champion Bob Fitzsimmons, retained his title in New York today. After a punishing 23 rounds he knocked out the former holder James J. Corbett with a right to the jaw.

Champion Jim Jeffries.

New age limit for British boy miners

May 22. The House of Lords gave a second reading today to a bill restricting the right of mine-owners to employ young boys underground.

Restrictions on the use of children in mines, most commonly in coal mines, began in the first half of the 19th century with the philanthropic campaigning of Lord Shaftesbury, known as the "Miner's Friend". In 1842, he pushed through Parliament a bill outlawing the employment below ground of women and girls of any age. The bill, which became the Mines Act, also banned the employment underground of boys younger than 10.

Legislation later in the century raised the age threshold for boys slightly. The bill raises the minimum age again – from 12 to 13.

Despite this gradual tightening of the law on child labour, Britain's 3,000 mines now produce more coal than ever: some 170 million tons a year, of which 70 million are exported.

Lillie Langtry wows Washington

May 4. Mrs Lillie Langtry caused a sensation in Washington with her portrayal of a dissolute courtesan in "The Degenerates". She packed the theatre here as in London, where the play was attended by Edward, Prince of Wales. Mrs Langtry took out US citizenship on a previous visit.

Actress Lillie Langtry.

Rejoicing as Mafeking siege relieved

May 20. At last, the comparative calm of Sunday has descended on London after two tumultuous nights and a day of celebrations for the lifting of the seven month siege of Mafeking, the small town on the railway line to Rhodesia.

At times the entire metropolis seemed given over to the surging crowds, singing and dancing, waving flags and setting off coloured flares. The enthusiasm spread to the provinces, where brass bands turned out and factory sirens wailed. Not even a War Office refusal to confirm the news could dampen the people's mood.

It appears that late on Friday evening a portrait of the Mafeking commander, Colonel Robert Baden Powell, appeared outside the Mansion House, with a placard saying in large letters: Mafeking is Relieved. The news spread rapidly, but in the House of Commons Arthur Balfour, speaking for the government, said it was unconfirmed.

However, the source of the sensational intelligence became known when special newspaper editions appeared with a Reuters news agency message. At Covent Garden the news was shouted from the gallery as the curtain came down on Lohengrin; in his box the Prince of Wales beat time when the audience broke into song.

The relief of the town, on the evening of May 16, was effected by a flying column riding up from Kimberley and joining forces with a second one, reinforced with Canadians, and pressing south. Boer resistance was quickly broken.

On the central front Lord Roberts continued his march across the Free State, forcing President Steyn to flee his new capital, Kroonstadt; Boer prisoners of war were disarmed and allowed to return to their farms. The frenzied scenes witnessed in London are seen as a spontaneous response, not only to the news of Mafeking, but also to the realisation that a war that had brought such humiliations for Britain was now going well.

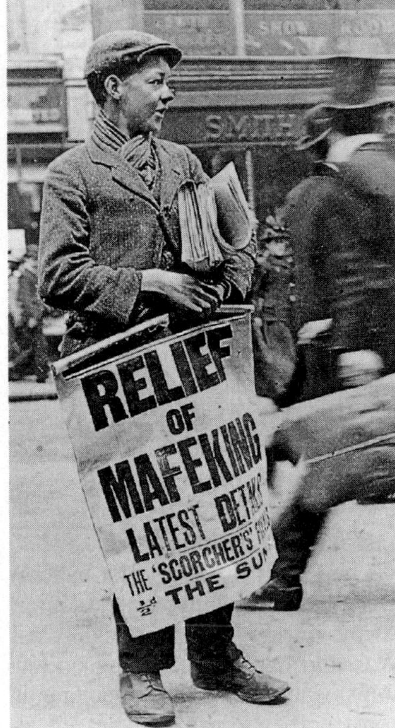

Mafeking, and Britain, relieved.

Baden-Powell: victorious.

Universal joy at the news.

1900

JUNE

Su	Mo	Tu	We	Th	Fr	Sa
					1	2
3	4	5	6	7	8	9
10	11	12	13	14	15	16
17	18	19	20	21	22	23
24	25	26	27	28	29	30

1. France: The government introduces a bill to grant amnesty to all concerned in the Dreyfus Case (→ 19/9).

4. Paris: Great exhibition of sculptures by Auguste Rodin opens at the Pont de l'Alma.

5. Atlantic Ocean: German liner "Deutschland III" sets new speed record of 23.61 knots (→ 13/8).

7. China: Boxer rebels cut off railway links between Peking and Tientsin (→ 10).

10. China: Admiral Seymour leaves Tientsin for Peking with 2,000 mostly British troops (→ 16).

16. China: German ambassador Baron Klemens von Ketteler is murdered by Boxer rebels in Peking (→ 17).

17. US: Troops are ordered to China (→ 18).

18. China: Chinese forces fire on international fleet at Taku (→ 24).

19. US: William McKinley and Theodore Roosevelt win the Republican election nominations for President and Vice-President.

22. London: The Wallace Collection of art opens.

23. Paris: Opening of the dome of Sacre Coeur.

24. China: All foreign embassies except the British, French and German destroyed by Boxers (→ 27/7).

27. London: Central Railway "Tuppenny Tube" opens from Shepherd's Bush in west London to the Bank.

28. London: New weekly river and sea itinerary to Paris is opened, taking 72 hours.

29. UK: Massive Dictionary of National Biography is completed.

BIRTHS

25. British military commander and last Viceroy of India Lord (Louis) Mountbatten (†27/8/79).

29. French writer and aviator Antoine de Saint-Exupery (†31/7/44).

Germans announce naval build-up

June 12. The Reichstag today approved a second new law allowing Germany's naval expansion to continue with the building of 38 battleships over 20 years. The German fleet would then be one of the largest in the world.

Admiral von Tirpitz, Kaiser Wilhelm II's naval minister, who was the driving force behind the passage of the first German naval law in 1898, has argued that Germany needs a bigger and stronger fleet to help protect its colonies and trade routes.

MacArthur offers Filipinos amnesty

June 21. General Arthur MacArthur, the United States Military Governor of the Philippines, has offered an amnesty to the Filipino rebels in an attempt to end an insurgency which began in opposition to Spanish rule. The amnesty grants a full pardon to all Filipinos who have taken part in the rebellion – on condition that they take an oath of allegiance and acknowledge the sovereignty of the American government. The Philippine Islands came under US rule during the course of the Spanish-American war, after the Spanish fleet was sunk in Manila Bay in 1898.

The Cakewalk, an American dance, now all the rage.

1900

JULY

Su	Mo	Tu	We	Th	Fr	Sa
1	2	3	4	5	6	7
8	9	10	11	12	13	14
15	16	17	18	19	20	21
22	23	24	25	26	27	28
29	30	31				

1. Austria: Archduke Franz Ferdinand, heir to Kaiser Franz Josef, marries Countess Sophie Chotek (→ 28/6/14).

2. Brussels: Jean-Baptiste Sipido, alleged assassin of the Prince of Wales, goes on trial (→ 5).

3. Russia: Czar signs law abolishing exile to Siberia as a punishment for dissent.

4. S. Africa: British troops join forces at Vlakfontein, dispersing Boer troops (→ 1/9).

5. US: William Bryan gets the Democratic nomination for the presidential election.

5. Belgium: Sipido acquitted of attempt on Prince of Wales' life.

7. Wimbledon: Reginald Doherty beats Sydney Smith for the Men's Singles championship; Blanche Hillyard beat Charlotte Cooper for the Ladies' title.

9. London: Royal Assent given to act creating federal Commonwealth of Australia.

12. London: Puccini's "Tosca" is first performed in the U.K., at Covent Garden (→ 31/12).

13. Earl of Hopetoun appointed first Governor-General of Australia.

19. Paris: Opening of the Metropolitain, or metro, underground system.

22. London: 11 killed when steamer "Campania" hits smaller boat.

23. Canada: The federal government forbids immigration of paupers and criminals.

30. Rome: Prince Victor Emmanuel Ferdinand Marie Janvier is proclaimed King Victor Emmanuel III.→

BIRTH

4. US jazz trumpeter Louis Armstrong (†6/7/71).

DEATHS

30. Alfred, Duke of Edinburgh, Queen Victoria's second son, (*1844).

30. Italian King Umberto I (*14/3/1844).→

Count Zeppelin takes to the skies

Slowly, but surely, airship LZ1 rises above Lake Constance.

July 1. Count Ferdinand von Zeppelin's airship today flew for the first time near Friedrichshafen. A small crowd of observers looked on as the huge airship, built in a floating hangar on Lake Constance, was wheeled out and its engines started up. It moved forwards, backwards and sideways, then rose to a height of about 12 feet before being returned to its hangar an hour and a half later. Count Zeppelin said he was well satisfied with the result.

The Count made his first balloon ascent while serving with the Union Army during the American Civil War and has been working on airships since 1891. His machine is constructed from a wire-braced aluminium hull covered with a cotton cloth. It contains 16 gas cells each filled with hydrogen. Two 16-horsepower engines give it a potential speed of 14 mph.

Italian King shot dead by anarchist

July 30. The much-loved King Umberto I of Italy was shot dead by an anarchist, Angelo Bresci, late last night at Monza, where the King had attended the award of prizes at the city's Gymnastic Society. The assassin, elegantly dressed in a dark suit and carrying a pair of white gloves, fired four times as the King entered his carriage.

Three bullets struck home, one piercing his heart, and he died almost immediately. Bresci was seized before the crowd could harm him and the carriage was driven at speed to the Palace where Queen Margaret, refusing to believe her husband was dead, implored the doctors to revive him.

The 31 year old Prince of Naples, Victor Emmanuel, who is cruising off Greece, succeeds to the throne. It is believed that the motive for the murder was revenge for the events of 1898 when King Umberto used the army to crush a workers insurrection in Milan (→ 29/8).

1,500 Europeans are massacred in fresh Boxer outrage

July 27. After fierce fighting, Allied forces have stormed Tientsin and managed to hold the city despite determined counter-attacks by 100,000 Boxer rebels and renegade Chinese soldiers.

It is reported that 1,500 foreigners have been brutally massacred, including missionaries, traders and diplomats. The Allied force, which involved British, American, German and Japanese troops, lost 400 men in the victorious assault.

Vice-Admiral Sir Edward Seymour signalled the Admiralty that British bluejackets and Japanese infantry had succeeded in a flank movement, and that their cavalry completed a rout of the Boxers, killing a large number of them. The Allies were handicapped by the fact that the Chinese had artillery superiority.

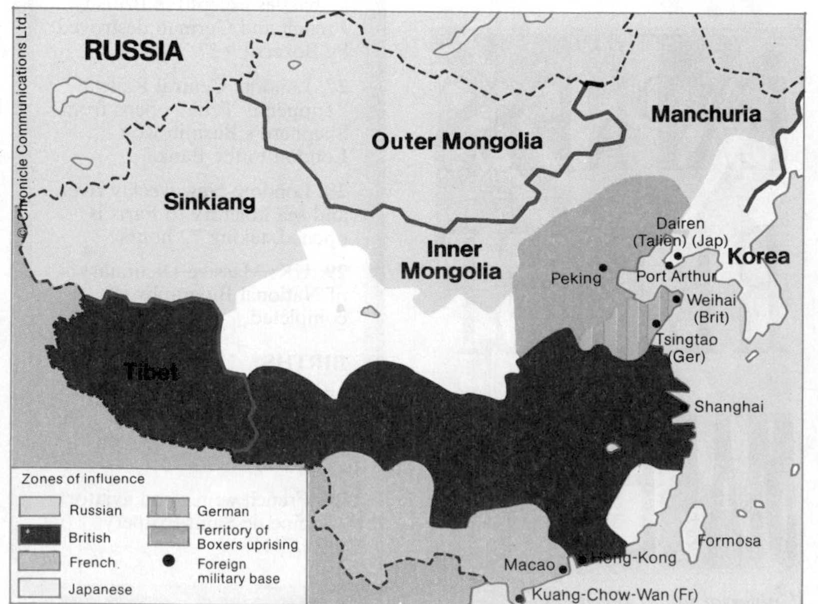

Despite their defeat there is no sign that the Boxers are giving in. Reports from the capital say that at least 300,000 are massed around the city, making up in numbers what they lack in military training, while hordes of Boxer reinforcements, supported by cavalry and soldiers from the Chinese Imperial army continued, to move into the region.

A news agency correspondent reports: "It is difficult to overestimate the magnitude of the task the Powers have before them. It is all China against the foreigner."

Great anxiety is still felt about the fate of missionaries and other Europeans living in isolated areas. Many hundreds are known to have been slain. The Boxers have also slaughtered large numbers of Chinese Christian converts (→ 14/8).

1900 Paris

First woman Olympic gold medallist, Charlotte Cooper (GBR).

July 22. The second Olympic Games of the modern era closed in Paris today with yet another victory for the United States team, Walter Tewsbury's 200 metres win giving them a total of 16 gold medals from the track and field events. Of the other 13 nations competing, Great Britain stood out with four athletics gold medals from their outstanding middle-distance runners – the 800m, 1500m, 4000m steeple-chase and 5000m team race. France, the hosts, with a team of 884 competitors, dominated the minor sports, and with women competing for the first time (they were barred from the Athens Games four years ago) Britain's Charlotte Cooper became the first woman Olympic champion in winning the tennis singles.

The Olympic Committee for this year's games, with Baron Pierre de Coubertin (standing, r.). The ancient festival of sport was revived in 1896.

Men Athletics

100m		
1. Frank Jarvis	USA	11.0
2. Walter Tewksbury	USA	11.1
3. Stanley Rowley	AUS	11.2

200m		
1. Walter Tewksbury	USA	22.2
2. Norman Pritchard	IND	22.8
3. Stanley Rowley	AUS	22.9

400m		
1. Maxey Long	USA	*49.4
2. William Holland	USA	49.6
3. Ernst Schulz	DEN	

800m		
1. Alfred Tysoe	GBR	2:01.2
2. John Cregan	USA	2:03.0
3. David Hall	USA	

1500m		
1. Charles Bennett	GBR	*4:06.2
2. Henri Deloge	FRA	4:06.6
3. John Bray	USA	4:07.2

Marathon		
1. Michel Théato	FRA	2:59:45
2. Emile Champion	FRA	3:04:17
3. Ernst Fast	SWE	3:37:14

110m Hurdles		
1. Alvin Kraenzlein	USA	*15.4
2. John McLean	USA	15.5
3. Fred Moloney	USA	

400m Hurdles		
1. Walter Tewksbury	USA	57.6
2. Henri Tauzin	FRA	58.3
3. George Orton	CAN	

2500m Steeplechase		
1. George Orton	CAN	7:34.4
2. Sidney Robinson	GBR	7:38.0
3. Jacques Chastanié	FRA	

High Jump		
1. Irving Baxter	USA	*1.90
2. Patrick Leahy	GBR-IRL	1.78
3. Lajos Gonczy	HUN	1.75

Pole Vault		
1. Irving Baxter	USA	3.30
2. Michael Colket	USA	3.25
3. Carl-Albert Andersen	NOR	3.20

Long Jump		
1. Alvin Kraenzlein	USA	*7.185
2. Meyer Prinstein	USA	7.175
3. Patrick Leahy	GBR-IRL	6.95

Triple Jump		
1. Meyer Prinstein	USA	*14.47
2. James Connolly	USA	13.97
3. Lewis Sheldon	USA	13.64

Shotput		
1. Richard Sheldon	USA	*14.10
2. Josiah McCracken	USA	12.85
3. Robert Garrett	USA	12.37

Discus		
1. Rudolf Bauer	HUN	*36.04
2. Frantisek Janda-Suk	CZE	35.25
3. Richard Sheldon	USA	34.60

Hammer		
1. John Flanagan	USA	49.73
2. Truxtun Hare	USA	49.13
3. Josiah McCracken	USA	42.46

200m Hurdles		
1. Alvin Kraenzlein	USA	25.4
2. Norman Pritchard	IND	26.6
3. Walter Tewksbury	USA	

4000m Steeplechase		
1. John Rimmer	GBR	12:58.4
2. Charles Bennett	GBR	12:58.6
3. Sidney Robinson	GBR	12:58.8

5000m Team		
1. Great Britain/Australia		15:20.0
2. France		

Standing High Jump		
1. Ray Ewry	USA	*1.65
2. Irving Baxter	USA	1.52
3. Lewis Sheldon	USA	1.50

Standing Long Jump		
1. Ray Ewry	USA	3.21
2. Irving Baxter	USA	3.135
3. Emile Torcheboeuf	FRA	3.03

Standing Triple Jump		
1. Ray Ewry	USA	10.58
2. Irving Baxter	USA	9.95
3. Robert Garrett	USA	9.50

Tug-of-War
1. Sweden/Denmark
2. France

Men Fencing

Foil Individual	
1. Emile Coste	FRA
2. Henri Masson	FRA
3. Jacques Boulanger	FRA

Epée Individual	
1. Ramón Fonst	CUB
2. Louis Perrée	FRA
3. Léon Sée	FRA

Sabre Individual	
1. Georges de la Falaise	FRA
2. Léon Thiébaut	FRA
3. Siegfried Flesch	AUT

Foil for Fencing Masters	
1. Lucien Mérignac	FRA
2. Alphonse Kirchhoffer	FRA
3. Jean-Baptiste Mimiague	FRA

Epée for Fencing Masters	
1. Albert Ayat	FRA
2. Emile Bougnol	FRA
3. Henri Laurent	FRA

Epée for Amateurs and Masters	
1. Albert Ayat	FRA
2. Ramón Fonst	CUB
3. Léon Sée	FRA

Sabre for Fencing Masters	
1. Antonio Conte	ITA
2. Italo Santelli	ITA
3. Milan Neralic	AUT

Men Swimming

200m Freestyle		
1. Frederick Lane	AUS	*2:25.2
2. Zoltán Halmay	HUN	2:31.4
3. Karl Ruberl	AUT	2.32.0

1500m Freestyle		
1. John Jarvis	GBR	13:40.2
2. Otto Wahle	AUT	14:53.6
3. Zoltán Halmay	HUN	15:16.4

200m Backstroke		
1. Ernst Hoppenberg	GER	2:47.0
2. Karl Ruberl	AUT	2:56.0
3. Johannes Drost	NETH	3:01.0

200m Obstacle Event		
1. Frederick Lane	AUS	2:38.4
2. Otto Wahle	AUT	2:40.0
3. Peter Kemp	GBR	2:47.4

4000m Freestyle		
1. John Jarvis	GBR	58:24.0
2. Zoltán Halmay	HUN	1:08:55.4
3. Louis Martin	FRA	1:13:08.4

60m Underwater Swimming	
1. Charles de Vandeville	FRA
2. A. Six	FRA
3. Peder Lykkeberg	DAN

200m Team
1. Germany
2. France
3. France

Water polo

1. Great Britain
2. Belgium
3. France

Shooting

Pistol – Rapid-Fire Pistol		
1. Maurice Larrouy	FRA	58
2. Léon Moreaux	FRA	57
3. Eugène Balme	FRA	57

Free Pistol 50m		
1. Karl Roderer	SUI	503
2. Achille Paroche	FRA	466
3. Konrad Staheli	SUI	453

Live Pigeon Shooting		
1. Léon de Lunden	BEL	21
2. Maurice Faure	FRA	20
3. Donald MacIntosh	AUS	18

Military Rifle (3 positions)		
1. Emil Kellenberger	SUI	930
2. Anders Peter Nielsen	DEN	921
3. Ole Ostmo	NOR	917
3. Paul van Asbroek	BEL	917

Military Rifle Team 300m	
1. Switzerland	4399
2. Norway	4290
3. France	4278

Military Revolver Team	
1. Switzerland	2271
2. France	2203
3. Netherlands	1876

Archery

Au Cordon Doré-50m		
1. Henri Herouin	FRA	31
2. Hubert van Innis	BEL	29
3. Emile Fisseux	FRA	28

Au Chapelet-50m	
1. Eugène Mougin	FRA
2. Henri Helle	FRA
3. Emile Mercier	FRA

Au Cordon Doré-33m	
1. Hubert van Innis	BEL
2. Victor Thibaud	FRA
3. Charles Frédéric Petit	FRA

Au Chapelet-33m	
1. Hubert van Innis	BEL
2. Victor Thibaud	FRA
3. Charles Frédéric Petit	FRA

Sur la Perche à la Herse	
1. Emmanuel Foulon	FRA
2. Serrurier	FRA
3. Druart jun.	BEL

Sur la Perche à la Pyramide	
1. Emile Grumiaux	FRA
2. Louis Glineux	BEL

Men Gymnastics

Individual All-around Competition		
1. Gustave Sandras	FRA	302
2. Noël Bas	FRA	295
3. Lucien Démanet	FRA	293

Football

1. Great Britain
2. France
3. Belgium

Rowing

Single Sculls		
1. Henri Barrelet	FRA	7:35.6
2. André Gaudin	FRA	7:41.6
3. George Saint Ashe	GBR	8:15.6

Coxed Pairs	
1. Netherlands	7:34.2
2. France	7:34.4
3. France	7:57.2

Coxed Fours – First Final	
1. France	7:11.0
2. France	7:18.0
3. Germany	7:18.2

Coxed Fours – Second Final	
1. Germany	5:59.0
2. Netherlands	6:33.0
3. Germany	6:35.0

Eights	
1. USA	6:09.8
2. Belgium	6:13.8
3. Netherlands	6:23.0

Yachting

Open	
1. Great Britain	Scotia
2. Germany	Aschenbrödel
3. France	Turquoise

Class 0.5t	
1. France	Quand-même
2. France	Baby
3. France	Sarcelle

Class 0.5t-1.0t	
1. Great Britain	Scotia
2. France	Crabe II
3. France	Scamasaxe

Class 1-2t	
1. Switzerland	Aschenbrödel
2. France	Lerina
3. France	Marthe

Class 2-3t	
1. Great Britain	Ollé
2. France	Favorite
3. France	Mignon

Class 3-10t	
1. France	Bona Fide
2. France	Gitana
3. Netherlands	Frimousse

Class 10-20t	
1. France	Estérel
2. France	Quand-même
3. Great Britain	Lauréa

Cycling

1000m Sprint		
1. Georges Taillandier	FRA	2:52.0
2. Fernand Sanz	FRA	
3. John Henry Lake	USA	

Equestrian Sports

Individual Jumping Competition		
1. Aimé Haegeman	BEL	2:16.0
2. Georges van de Poele	BEL	2:17.6
3. M. de Champsavin	FRA	2:26.0

High Jump		
1. Dominique Maximien Gardères	FRA	1.85
2. Gian Giorgio Trissino	ITA	1.85
3. Georges van de Poele	BEL	1.70

Long Jump		
1. Constant van Langhendonck	BEL	6.10
2. Gian Giorgio Trissino	ITA	5.70
3. de Bellegarde	FRA	5.30

Tennis

Men – singles	
1. Hugh Doherty	GBR
2. Harold Mahony	GBR/IRL
3. Reginald Doherty	GBR

Men – doubles
1. GBR
2. USA/FRA
3. FRA

Women – singles	
1. Charlotte Cooper	GBR
2. Hélène Prevost	FRA
3. Marion Jones	USA

Mixed doubles
1. GBR
2. FRA/IRL
3. BOH/GBR

Cricket

1. GBR
2. FRA

Croquet

Singles – 1 ball		
1. Aumoitte	FRA	45
2. Johin	FRA	21

Singles – 2 balls	
1. Waydelick	FRA
2. Vignerot	FRA
3. Santereau	FRA

Doubles
1. FRA

Golf

Men		
1. Charles Sands	USA	167
2. Walter Rutherford	GBR	168
3. David Robertson	GBR	175

Women		
1. Margaret Abbott	USA	47
2. Pauline Whittier	USA	49
3. Daria Pratt	USA	53

Polo

1. GBR/USA
2. GBR/USA
3. FRA/GBR

Rugby

1. FRA
2. GER
3. GBR

(Key to symbols and abbreviations p. 1456)

1900

AUGUST

Su	Mo	Tu	We	Th	Fr	Sa
			1	2	3	4
5	6	7	8	9	10	11
12	13	14	15	16	17	18
19	20	21	22	23	24	25
26	27	28	29	30	31	

1. Managua: Nicaraguan government cancels the shipping canal concession (1/12).

2. Paris: Francois Salsou, an anarchist, tries to assassinate the Shah of Persia.

5. Russia: Anti-Jewish riots break out in Odessa (→29/4/01).

9. China: German Count von Waldersee is appointed commander-in-chief of the European forces fighting the Boxer rebels (→13).

10. US: Americans Dwight Davis and Holcombe Ward win the first Davis Cup tournament.→

11. US: 26 die in record high temperatures of up to 107 degrees F.

13. China: Russians occupy Meduchei in Manchuria (→21).

14. New York: Sixty blacks are injured in race riots.

17. US: Nikolai Tesla patents a new method of electrical insulation.

20. Sudan: British explorer Major Gibbons has traced the course of the Zambesi River.

21. China: Allies capture inner city in Peking.→

27. UK: First long distance bus service: the weekly 200-mile journey from London to Leeds takes a total of two days.

29. Italy: The assassin of King Umberto, Bresci, is sentenced to penal servitude for life (→30/7).

30. Glasgow: Bubonic plague has broken out (→3/9).

31. South Wales: End of a 10-day strike by railway workers in Taff Vale.

BIRTH

6. Austrian composer Ernst Krenek (†23/12/91).

DEATHS

7. German social democrat Wilhelm Liebknecht (*29/3/1826).

25. German philosopher Friedrich Nietzsche (*15/10/1844).

Allies storm Peking, Empress flees

Aug 14. Troops of the Allied forces in China today entered Peking to end the 56 day long siege of Europeans in the capital by forces of the Boxer rebellion. Final success came after a long fighting advance from Tientsin, captured by them last month. The Allied column of 10,000 men met fierce and determined resistance from the Chinese who were well equipped with modern field guns.

Whole sections of the railway line linking the two cities had been destroyed by the rebels, but once the advancing force had taken Ho Si Wu five days ago they detected signs of enemy despair.

Small pockets of Boxer resistance still remain in the capital and surrounding countryside, but once the allies have consolidated their positions they intend to attack these enemy nests. It is reported that the losses in the international force are light.

The Allied advance guard found that foreigners in the besieged legations were in a desperate plight. All women and children had gathered in the British Embassy, a large building, which had been under heavy, though intermittent, attack throughout the siege. When the troops arrived they had less than a week's supply of food.

Both the Emperor and the Empress Dowager are reported to have fled the city with a vast amount of treasure only two days ago.

A French view of the Allies' advance on Peking.

America wins the first Davis cup

Aug 10. The British pairing of A.W. Gore and Roper Barrett was unable to adapt to the conditions at Longwood Cricket Club in Boston, Massachusetts, today, and succumbed to the United States in a decisive 3-0 defeat. They were competing for the new International Lawn Tennis Trophy, established earlier this year by the Harvard player Dwight F. Davis.

The winning team, with Davis (c.).

German liners set two speed records

Aug 13. The Hamburg American liner Deutschland is now the quickest way of crossing the Atlantic from America to Europe.

Just a day after a new east-west Transatlantic speed record was set by the steamer Kaiser Wilhelm der Grosse of the North German Lloyd Line, the Deutschland steamed home at an average of 23.32 knots to knock eight hours off the Kaiser Wilhelm's time of five days, 19 and three-quarter hours.

But prospective passengers of the Kaiser Wilhelm should not be over hasty in switching their bookings to its rival. The liner landed at Cherbourg in France, further from New York than Plymouth, the Deutschland's destination.

So the Hamburg American ship's achievement, while remarkable, is perhaps not quite as brilliant as it seems.

The previous fastest crossing from New York to Plymouth was five days 14 hours and 50 minutes, set only a month ago – by the Deutschland (→17/7/01).

Britons get their first taste of Coke

Aug 31. Coca-Cola arrived in Britain, 14 years after it went on sale in the United States. Charles Candler, eldest son of Cola company founder Asa Candler, visited Britain with a jug of Cola syrup in hand, and it proved so popular that five more gallons were immediately ordered from the US.

The real thing comes to Britain.

1900

SEPTEMBER

Su	Mo	Tu	We	Th	Fr	Sa
						1
2	3	4	5	6	7	8
9	10	11	12	13	14	15
16	17	18	19	20	21	22
23	24	25	26	27	28	29
30						

1. S. Africa: General Roberts annexes the Boer republic of Transvaal (→ 5).

2. Ireland: At a demonstration in Dublin, nationalists demand freedom from British rule.

3. Glasgow: Bubonic plague outbreak is still spreading in the city.

4. Belgium: Glass workers at Charleroi go on strike.

5. S. Africa: Siege of Ladybrand raised.→

6. London: The Trades Union Congress resolves to champion old age pensions as a fundamental human right.

7. Austria: Kaiser Franz Josef dissolves parliament because of a campaign of disruption by the Czech faction.

7. Arctic: Italian Duke of Abruzzi reaches latitude of 86 degrees 33 minutes, beating Nansen's record for furthest north reached.

10. Berlin: German colonies officially given status of Protectorates of the Empire.

11. Philippines: Filipino rebels kill US troops on Maranduque Island.

11. US: Pennsylvania coal miners go on strike.

13. Austria: Kaiser Franz Josef threatens to withdraw nominal Polish autonomy if Poles continue to press for further demands.

15. Germany: Socialist Rosa Luxemburg calls for a popular front to oppose Germany's Chinese policies.

19. France: President Loubet pardons Jewish army captain Alfred Dreyfus, after a second court martial upheld his previous wrongful conviction for spying for Germany.

23. Far East: Russia formally annexes all occupied parts of Manchuria.→

25. London: Parliament is dissolved as Lord Salisbury calls a general election (→ 17/10).

30. China: Allies begin to withdraw from Peking.

Boer War is over, claims Roberts

A Boer gun team opens fire during fighting close to Tugela.

Commander-in-chief Lord Roberts.

Sept 30. The war that began less than a year before is over, Lord Roberts has assured London. Since May, the British commander-in-chief has marched his men three hundred miles from Bloemfontein to Pretoria, and then as far again along the Delagoa railway in pursuit of the Boers and their fleeing presidents, Kruger and Steyn.

Resistance seems to have been reduced to scattered bands derailing trains. Roberts has proclaimed the annexation of the Transvaal and Orange Free State (formerly Orange River Colony). But he has only broken up the Boer forces, not captured them; and Steyn remains at large on the high veld with a loyal band and gold bullion worth half a million.

But the British insist things are returning to normal. In Johannesburg, the big mining companies are taking tenders for 300 railway wagons, worth about £150,000, from British and American firms.

Slump puts cotton industry in a spin

Sept 12. Gloom gripped the Lancashire cotton industry today, as reports came in by telegraph of the damage caused by the hurricane that hit Galveston, Texas, on September 8. The cotton shortage is already the worst since the end of the American Civil War, nearly four decades ago.

The cotton price has now risen to a level which makes spinning and weaving uneconomic. Almost all mills are already on short time, and there are regular reports that mills in Blackburn and Oldham are having to close indefinitely. Unemployed members are making heavy calls on trade union funds.

Without precise information on the extent of the crop damage, intense speculation has swept the Cotton Exchanges in Liverpool and Manchester this week. In Liverpool some spinners holding cotton were selling it in order to cash in on the high price.

World's socialists gather in Paris

Sept 23. The fifth congress of the Socialist International is meeting in Paris with delegates from 21 countries. They have decided to create an international socialist bureau whose task will be to organise against militarism and war. Other topics on the agenda are workers' rights and colonialism. A sharp row broke out over the issue of alliance with bourgeois parties to take power. Karl Kautsky, a colleague of the writer Friedrich Engels, settled the row with his diplomatic line that each socialist party must take its own decision.

Czar's troops move to annex Manchuria

Sept 3. Russia has moved to tighten the Czar's grip over areas occupied by his troops in Manchuria. After a campaign lasting several weeks General Gribsky, military governor of the huge Amur district, announced regulations putting occupied areas under Russian laws and authority.

Several areas along the Amur river, including a number of towns and settlements, have been annexed, and the Chinese people were forbidden to live there any more. General Gribsky said the annexation of Manchuria was punishment for the Chinese attack on Blagovestchensk, and was therefore a warning to the population of Manchuria to respect the power of Russia.

Early last month, on August 3, Russian troops relieved Harbin, which had played an important role in the Manchurian operations. Ten days later Cossacks clashed heavily with a Chinese force estimated at 7,000 and put them to flight.

A biscuit tin showing an ever more popular mode of travel.

1900

OCTOBER

Su	Mo	Tu	We	Th	Fr	Sa
	1	2	3	4	5	6
7	8	9	10	11	12	13
14	15	16	17	18	19	20
21	22	23	24	25	26	27
28	29	30	31			

1. Germany: The Reichstag passes a new act to provide workmen's compensation in case of accident or illness.

5. Paris: Peace congress condemns British government policy in the Transvaal; asserts Boer right to self-determination (→ 19).

6. Belgium: Arrests in Brussels following the discovery of an anarchist plot against Prince Albert.

8. Germany: Socialist Maximilian Harden sentenced to six months hard labour for attacking the Kaiser in an article "The fight against the dragon".

9. China: Imperial Government sentences officials guilty of provoking Boxer rebellion; Prince Tuan exiled (→ 10).

10. India: 10,000 Indian Army troops are requisitioned for fear of uprising in South China (→ 15).

15. China: Anti-imperial forces under Sun Yat-Sen capture Mu-chan (→ 16).

16. China: Britain and China agree that the waters of the Yang-Tse River will be international if China controls the land along its banks (→ 20).

17. Russia: Plot to murder the Czar is uncovered.

18. Germany: Count Bernhard von Bulow succeeds Prince von Hohenlohe as Imperial Chancellor.

19. S. Africa: Paul Kruger flees on a Dutch cruiser for fear of being attacked by Boers fiercely opposed to a peace plan. →

24. UK: The National Union of Women Workers meets to discuss problems of health and intemperance.

28. UK: Many are killed in severe floods in the north of England.

30. US: National census reveals that the population stands at 72.3 million.

BIRTH

7. German Nazi leader and SS chief Heinrich Himmler (†23/5/45).

Tories win election

Oct 17. Lord Salisbury's government has been re-elected with another huge majority. With general election results declared by today from 669 constituencies, and only one still to come next week, the Tories and their Unionist allies have 401 MPs against 268 for the opposition parties.

Polling has been taking place on different dates since Sept 28. Overall there has been little change in party strengths. The election has been notable for the large number of uncontested returns – 243. There is a Tory majority in Scotland for the first time in the Imperial Parliament.

The Boer War issue dominated a splenetic campaign. The Government attacked the Opposition for lack of patriotism and the Opposition accused the Government of exploiting war fever. In the new parliament there will be 116 lawyers and 85 gentry and landowners.

The third Marquess of Salisbury.

The oldest member will be an 82-year-old Tory with brewery family connections who won Mile End. The Government proposes to delay the opening of Parliament until February.

Anglo-German pact on China is signed

Oct 20. Great Britain and the Imperial German government today announced that they had concluded an alliance to ensure continuation of the open door policy towards China after the suppression of the Boxer rebellion.

Lord Salisbury, the Prime Minister, and the German Ambassador, Baron von Hartzfelt, agreed three days ago to ensure that the rivers and seaports of China remain open to international trade and to "every other legitimate form of economic activity, for nationals of all countries".

The alliance also agreed to maintain the territorial integrity of the Chinese Empire, promising that neither party would make use of the present complications to obtain for themselves any territorial advantages in China. Were any others to attempt to get advantages from the confusion, Britain and Germany would then discuss what to do to protect their own interests.

Both governments undertook to communicate the contents of their agreeement to other interested countries, notably France, Italy, Austria-Hungary, Japan, and the USA, all of whom were invited to accept its principles.

Diplomats were quick to note that no mention was made of Russia as one of the interested powers. The omission was seen, especially by the French, as reproof for what is regarded as Russia's reluctance to co-operate in the successful campaign against the Boxers.

Freud unlocks secrets of dreams

Oct 14. Dreaming will never be the same again. Sigmund Freud, a well-known Austrian psychiatrist and neurologist, has published a book which looks likely to revolutionise the way we regard our sleeping hours, entitled "The Science of Dreams". Freud seeks to show that sleep is never just a continuation of life when we are awake.

He refuses to recognise sleep as a simple physiological event, and argues that dreams express the frustrations and resentments of our waking hours. In this way, argues Freud, dreams are a means of satisfying our desires. One important factor, he says, is that sometimes our wishes are socially unacceptable and so suppressed by day.

By bringing suppressed material into consciousness, a patient with psychomosomatic symptoms can better understand his mental conflict and the symptoms may then disappear.

Soldiers return from Boer War to a heroes' welcome

Oct 29. Britain's first troops to return from the Boer War came home in triumph today. So dense were the crowds that the procession of the City of London Imperial Volunteers took five hours to cross from Paddington station to St. Paul's for a thanksgiving service.

The Prince of Wales viewed the procession from Marlborough House as it wound its way towards the Guildhall in the City where the troops were welcomed by the Lord Mayor. A number of people were injured in the crush. Celebrations went on late into the night.

Volunteers line up outside St. Paul's on their return from South Africa.

1900

NOVEMBER

Su	Mo	Tu	We	Th	Fr	Sa
				1	2	3
4	5	6	7	8	9	10
11	12	13	14	15	16	17
18	19	20	21	22	23	24
25	26	27	28	29	30	

3. Madrid: Arrests and suppression of Carlists, supporters of Don Carlos, pretender to the Spanish throne.

4. Switzerland: Referendum rejects electoral reform proposed by the Social Democrats.

6. S. Africa: British defeat De Wet at Bothaville (→ 24).

8. Canada: Liberals under Sir Wilfrid Laurier win general election.

9. China: Russia completes occupation of Manchuria with 100,000 troops.

10. Germany: Social Democrat August Bebel condemns German policy on China.

12. Paris: The World Exhibition closes, after having had more than 50 million visitors.

13. British Somaliland: Deputy commissioner Jenner is murdered during a native uprising.

14. US: Noah Roby of New Jersey claims he will be 128 on 1/4/01, and that he has smoked for 120 years.

15. France: Madrid to Paris express train derails, killing 17, including the Peruvian ambassador.

16. Germany: Woman hurls an axe at Kaiser Wilhelm but fails to hit him.

23. Paris: Exhibition of paintings by Claude Monet at the Durand-Ruel gallery.

24. France: Boer leader Paul Kruger is warmly welcomed on arrival in Marseilles (→ 2/12).

30. Germany: Front-wheel drive mechanism is patented.

BIRTHS

8. US writer Margaret Mitchell (†16/8/49).

14. US composer Aaron Copland (†2/12/90).

DEATHS

22. British composer Sir Arthur Sullivan (*1842).→

30. Irish-born poet Oscar Wilde (*16/10/1854).→

McKinley is re-elected President

Nov 6. Republican William McKinley has been re-elected President of the US, together with Vice-President Theodore Roosevelt, who won fame as one of the Rough Riders in Cuba during the recent Spanish-American war.

Republicans also won increased majorities in the Senate and the House of Representatives. The defeated Democratic candidate, as in 1896, was William Jennings Bryan of Nebraska. Adlai Stevenson of Illinois was his running-mate.

Once again the issue of the gold versus the silver standard dominated the campaign, though the Spanish war also made imperialism an issue, which, on balance, helped the Republicans. McKinley beat Bryan by over one million votes, and almost 100,000 voted for the socialist candidate, Eugene Debs.

Supporters marched to the McKinley home in Canton, Ohio. Bands played and rockets lit up the cloudy sky. Mr McKinley came out on the porch and greeted the crowd with the words: "Fellow citizens, I thank you for the great compliment of this call on this inclement night and at this late hour."

Election returns were relayed from around the country via the telegraph office in the local railroad station three miles away to the Vice-President's home on Long Island. Governor Roosevelt declared in response: "Isn't that fine? It shows what the American people are. It shows they want the good times to continue." (→4/3/01).

McKinley: back to Washington.

Oscar Wilde dies disgraced in Paris

Oscar Wilde: fame or notoriety?

Nov 30. The death is reported in Paris of the writer, Oscar Wilde, who had been living there since his release from prison under the name of Sebastian Melmoth. Wilde's career crashed in ruins when he was convicted of homosexual offences in 1895 and sentenced to two years penal servitude, which he described in "The Ballad of Reading Gaol", published under the pseudonym C.33, his prison number. His stage successes, such as "The Importance of Being Earnest", have remained unperformed since his disgrace. He died in poverty, dependent on the charity of his friends, and had become a Roman Catholic.

New century calls for new fashion

Nov 13. Should the modern woman abandon her skirts in favour of the knickerbocker? The Rational Dress League thinks so, and keen cyclists will have no doubts on the matter. Women's dress today reflects their growing freedom at work and play. Strait-laced corsets and stuffy bustles are being consigned to the dustbin, while hemlines are slowly creeping above the ankle.

Different types of blood are discovered

Nov 14. Three different blood groups have been identified by a Viennese scientist. This discovery could explain why different people react differently to blood transfusions. Dr Karl Landsteiner, of the Pathological and Anatomical Institute in Vienna, made his discovery while investigating how blood agglutinates.

He had thought that the ability of serum to agglutinate other red cells was more pronounced in some diseases because of the more powerful effect of such serum on what had been regarded as normal red blood cells, but he has found significant and characteristic differences between blood serum and red blood cells in healthy people.

In his experiments, Doctor Landsteiner found that blood serum could be divided into three groups: A, B and C. In group A, for instance, the serum reacts with the red blood cells from group B, but not with those of group A. The detailed findings suggest two different types of agglutinin in groups A and B, with both present in group C. The red cells do not react to agglutinins in the same serum.

Corsets: not for the strait-laced.

▷

World's largest battleship launched

Nov 9. The largest and most powerful warship ever built slid down the Vickers' Barrow-in-Furness slipway today, flying the Rising-Sun flag of Japan. The 15,150 ton "Mikasa", similar to British battleships now being built, carries four 12-inch guns protected by 14 inches of armour. Add to that 14 six-inch guns and a range of smaller weaponry and you have an impressive war machine which can fire 11 and a half tons of shells a minute.

The Japanese minister present expressed the hope that the the new ship would strengthen the close ties between Japan and Britain, and that they would co-operate in the Far East.

The "Mikasa" in Vickers' shipyard.

Sullivan, loved operetta composer, dies

Sir Arthur Sullivan.

Nov 22. Sir Arthur Sullivan, composer of the famous Savoy Operas with librettos by W.S. Gilbert, died today at the age of 58. Their partnership began in 1875 with "Trial by Jury" and continued through 12 more operettas, the most popular being "HMS Pinafore" and "The Mikado".

Songs, cantatas and oratorios poured from Sullivan's pen. Gilbert quarrelled with him in 1890 over the cost of a carpet for the Savoy Theatre – built especially for them – and their partnership broke up to national dismay. They resumed it in 1893 with "Utopia Ltd" but they never recaptured their original sparkle.

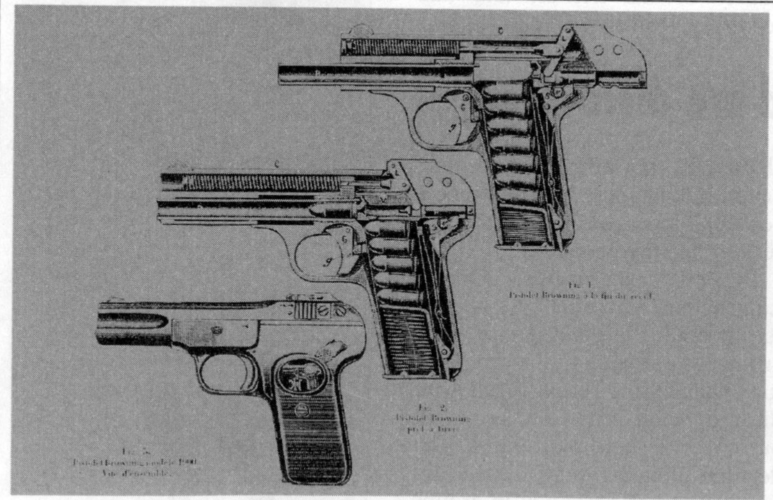

The new Browning automatic pistols are the very latest in modern small arms engineering, as these diagrams demonstrate.

1900

DECEMBER

Su	Mo	Tu	We	Th	Fr	Sa
						1
2	3	4	5	6	7	8
9	10	11	12	13	14	15
16	17	18	19	20	21	22
23	24	25	26	27	28	29
30	31					

1. C. America: Nicaragua sells US canal rights for $5 million (→ 11/3/01).

1. Germany: Census shows that the population is 56.3 million.

2. Germany: Paul Kruger is refused access to Kaiser, but is welcomed by ordinary citizens (→ 11).

3. Philippines: 2,000 rebels surrender to US troops in northern Luzon.

4. London: Government asks for £16 million.

4. Paris: The National Assembly rejects a proposal by ultra-nationalist Gen. Mercier to prepare for the invasion of England.

7. London: First British delegates appointed to the International Court of Arbitration in The Hague.

9. Paris: First performance of "Nocturnes" by Claude Debussy.

10. China: Peking-Tientsin railway is reopened.

11. S. Africa: Lord Roberts leaves Cape Town for England (→ 12).

19. London: Report on poisoned beer says glucose supplied to brewers contained arsenic (→ 8/1/01).

19. France: The National Assembly passes bill to grant amnesty to all involved in the Dreyfus Affair.

22. China: Preliminary peace terms signed by China and the Allies.

30. UK: Over 50 people are dead as gales and flooding lash the country.

HITS OF 1900

I'm only a bird in a gilded cage.

Goodbye Dolly Gray.

QUOTE OF THE YEAR

"Though cowards flinch and traitors sneer,
We'll keep the Red Flag flying here". Attributed to **James Connell**, from the song The Red Flag.

First Australian cabinet is formed

Dec 31. There is great excitement in Sydney as preparations are made to celebrate the birth tomorrow of the Commonwealth of Australia. The Prime Minister, Mr Barton, has announced the formation of the first Federal Cabinet in which he also holds the post of Foreign Minister. The city is filling with leaders from the capitals of all the states and some 50,000 people are thought to have arrived for the celebrations.

Arrangements are under way for the inaugural procession, which will be two miles long and include detachments of British troops, whose bearing is exciting great admiration here. The sense of being involved in a great occasion is heightened by good news of the economy. The only sad note is that Countess Hopetoun, wife of the Governor-General, is indisposed (→ 1/1/01).

France and Italy share out Africa

Dec 16. An exchange of letters between France and Italy has committed both countries to respect each other's rights in North Africa. Under the terms of this agreement, reached in negotiations of the utmost secrecy, France recognises that Libya falls within Italy's sphere of influence, while, in return, Italy promises not to interfere in France's ambitions with respect to Morocco. This arrangement, satisfying as it is to the two parties, is unlikely to please their European rivals.

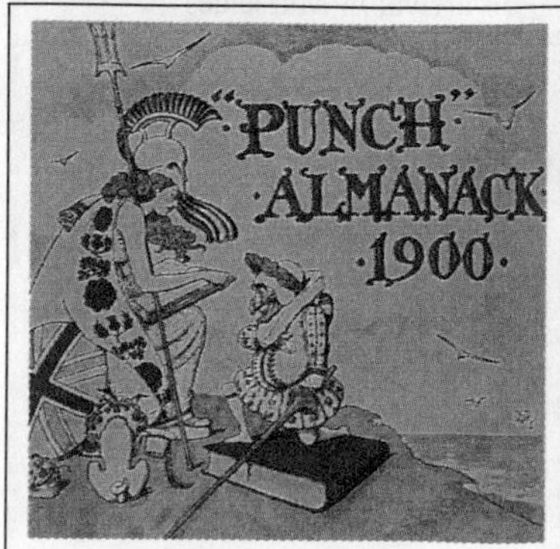

"Punch" offers its own view of the state of things in 1900.

Private viewing of moving pictures is increasingly popular

Arts: The moving picture has acquired sound in France where the private viewer can hear as well as see an artist on the screen. The phonograph beside the screen is controlled by the projectionist in his booth who synchronises it with the picture.

The "sound film" may be the entertainment of the future but it was in the traditional opera house that the artistic triumph of the year occurred, when **Puccini's** "Tosca" was premiered in Rome last January and at Covent Garden in July. The story of the singer who offers herself to a villainous police chief to save her lover's life aroused as much passionate enthusiasm in both capitals as "La Boheme" did four years ago.

In Paris the great Universal Exhibition was dominated by the genius of **M. Rodin**, who set up his pavilion and displayed therein his life's work in sculpture. Among the figures shown for the first time was "The Kiss". The sculptor has been besieged with requests for copies of this work in marble.

Elsewhere in Paris the 60 year-old Impressionist, **Claude Monet**, has surprised his public with a new subject, the water lilies in the water garden that he has built at his country home at Giverny. The lily ponds are crossed by a white Japanese bridge of great charm. M. Monet visited London this year to paint the river view from his room at the Savoy Hotel.

A sound-cinema. New devices let projectionists match sound and picture.

In Britain music lovers were stirred by the first hearing of **Edward Elgar's** mighty oratorio, "The Dream of Gerontius", given at Birmingham. Following last year's "Enigma Variations", this sublime work confirms that in Mr Elgar Britain has a composer of the first European rank.

The year also saw the death of **John Ruskin**, a giant among Victorian critics and social reformers, who was unhappily in his last years reduced to periods of mental unbalance. He championed Turner and the Pre-Raphaelites when they were spurned by the art establishment and attacked the injustice and squalor which he saw resulting from capitalism.

Giacomo Puccini whose "Tosca" premiered in London in July.

Max Planck unveils Quantum Theory

Dec 14. Energy comes in minute indivisible packets, analagous to the indivisible atoms of matter. That is the basis of a new theory unveiled today by Professor Max Planck of Berlin University. He calls his atom-like packets of energy "quanta", so his proposal has been named the "Quantum Theory".

Its implications are revolutionary, for it has been one of the basic assumptions of science that energy, unlike matter, is infinitely divisible, and physicists have hardly begun to consider them.

It does, however, solve an important problem (first posed by Planck's teacher and predecessor at Berlin, Gustav Kirchoff) that has been puzzling physicists for years: how can theory be reconciled with the observed pattern of intensity and colour in the light radiated by incandescent bodies? Conventional theory cannot do so; in fact it actually predicts an unreal situation known as the violet catastrophe.

Planck's theory leads to no violet catastrophe, and it explains the observations neatly. The crucial question is whether quanta have physical reality. Planck himself has not ruled out the possibility that quanta may be a kind of mathematical sleight of hand. Testing the Quantum Theory directly is going to be difficult: a quantum of energy is unimaginably small.

British deaths in Boer War top 11,000

Dec 12. Over 11,000 men have died in South Africa in the first fourteen months of campaigning, according to War Office figures issued today. Little more than one-third of the deaths were caused by enemy action; over 7,000 men died of dysentary, enteric fever and other diseases.

This pattern has persisted, despite the changed character of the war, with the Boers avoiding pitched battles and resorting to guerrilla tactics. Their commando raids are beginning to reach down into the Cape Colony, to the alarm of the British there, who fear an uprising of Dutchmen, as the Boers are referred to in the Colony.

The great majority, however, remain loyal to the Crown, though Dutch newspapers in Cape Town daily publish stories of alleged British outrages.

Lord Kitchener, who succeeded Roberts as C-in-C last November, has sent an urgent demand to London for 30,000 new mounted troops. In response, practically every trained soldier in Britain is being shipped out.

A royal gift for the troops.

Britons threatened by poisoned pint

Dec 1. Thousands of gallons of beer are being poured into the sewers of Liverpool and Manchester following an outbreak of arsenic poisoning which has killed at least four people and left 2,000 suffering from nervous illnesses.

The cause of the outbreak has been traced to sulphuric acid supplied by a Liverpool company and used to treat brewing sugar. Hospitals in the area continue to admit cases of peripheral neuritis, a form of paralysis of the hands and feet.

Kent and Sussex hop-growers have condemned the use of chemical substitutes in brewing in a campaign for "pure beer" (→ 19/1/01).

A Christmas card for the first festival of the 20th century.

1901

JANUARY

Su	Mo	Tu	We	Th	Fr	Sa
		1	2	3	4	5
6	7	8	9	10	11	12
13	14	15	16	17	18	19
20	21	22	23	24	25	26
27	28	29	30	31		

1. Australia: The Commonwealth of Australia comes into being with Lord Hopetoun as governor-general and Edmund Barton as first prime minister (→9/5).

3. US: Census Commissioner predicts a US population of at least 300 million by 2001.

4. South Africa: Sir Alfred Milner is appointed Governor of Transvaal and Orange River Colony.

7. China: It is reported that Russia and China signed a secret deal over Manchuria in December 1899.

8. Manchester: 12 retailers are prosecuted for selling beer containing arsenic.

9. South Africa: Morgendal, the burghers peace envoy, is shot on the orders of De Wet.

10. US: The Automobile Club of America meets to discuss signposts on main highways.

11. China: Russia and Britain agree on the partition of China (→21/2).

14. Manchester: An explosion in a hat factory kills 12 people.

16. Paris: Exhibition of Camille Pissaro's works at Durand-Ruel gallery.

18. South Africa: 800 Boers are routed near Ventersburg by Australasian troops.

19. Osborne House, Isle of Wight: Queen Victoria is gravely ill and stricken with paralysis.→

21. Nigeria: Rebel emirs of Kontagora and Bida defeated by British.

23. London: King Edward VII makes his accession speech.

27. London: King Edward VII appoints his nephew, the German Kaiser, a field-marshal in the British army.

31. Moscow: Anton Chekhov's play "Three Sisters" is first performed.

DEATHS

22. Queen Victoria (*24/5/1819).→

27. Italian composer Giuseppe Verdi (*10/10/1813).

Queen Victoria dies: an era ends

Jan 22. Queen Victoria is dead. She died today at Osborne, her seaside home in the Isle of Wight. She was 82 and had reigned for 64 years, a lifetime in which industry transformed Great Britain and which saw a growth of the British Empire to all corners of the globe. Her children and some of her many grandchildren were at the Queen's bedside when she died. Among them was the Prince of Wales, now the King of an Empire "on which the sun never sets".

Victoria was the first British Queen to reign since Anne, more than a century earlier. She was only 18 when she ascended the throne. Victoria was born and brought up at Kensington Palace, the daughter of the impoverished Duke of Kent. In 1840 she married Prince Albert from the German duchy of Saxe-Coburg-Gotha. They had nine children, several marrying into other royal and noble families, so that the Queen was known as the "grandmother of Europe" as well as the "mother of Empire". Six monarchs in Europe, excluding Britain, are linked to Victoria.

The Queen was devoted to Albert and devastated by his death, in 1861, of typhoid. She had wanted to make him King Consort, but ministers advised that this was unconstitutional. Later, as Prince Consort, he became deeply involved in helping his wife with government business. This, plus his German origins, stirred some public criticism, but the Queen never wavered in her loyalty, and for 40 years wore the black clothes of mourning. For many years she remained busy but avoided ceremonial duties.

During her reign she saw 12 Prime Ministers come and go, some of them several times. Disraeli was thought to be her favourite, while Gladstone ranked lower in royal favour.

One cause of tensions between Downing Street and the Palace was the sheer length of her reign. This experience, contrasting with frequent changes in administrations, was allied with many relatives in high places throughout Europe. The combination gave her unprecedented insight into government at home and abroad – and the Queen did not hesitate to give advice to her ministers, particularly in her later years.

Her years of public withdrawal after Albert's death were forgotten by 1887, when Victoria's Golden Jubilee became the focus of a national celebration. The Queen had travelled to more parts of Britain than her predecessors, using the steam railways which linked the rapidly-growing cities. Her death, coming at the dawn of the new century, marks the end of an era and she will be widely mourned.

The late Queen with Disraeli, who devised her title Empress of India.

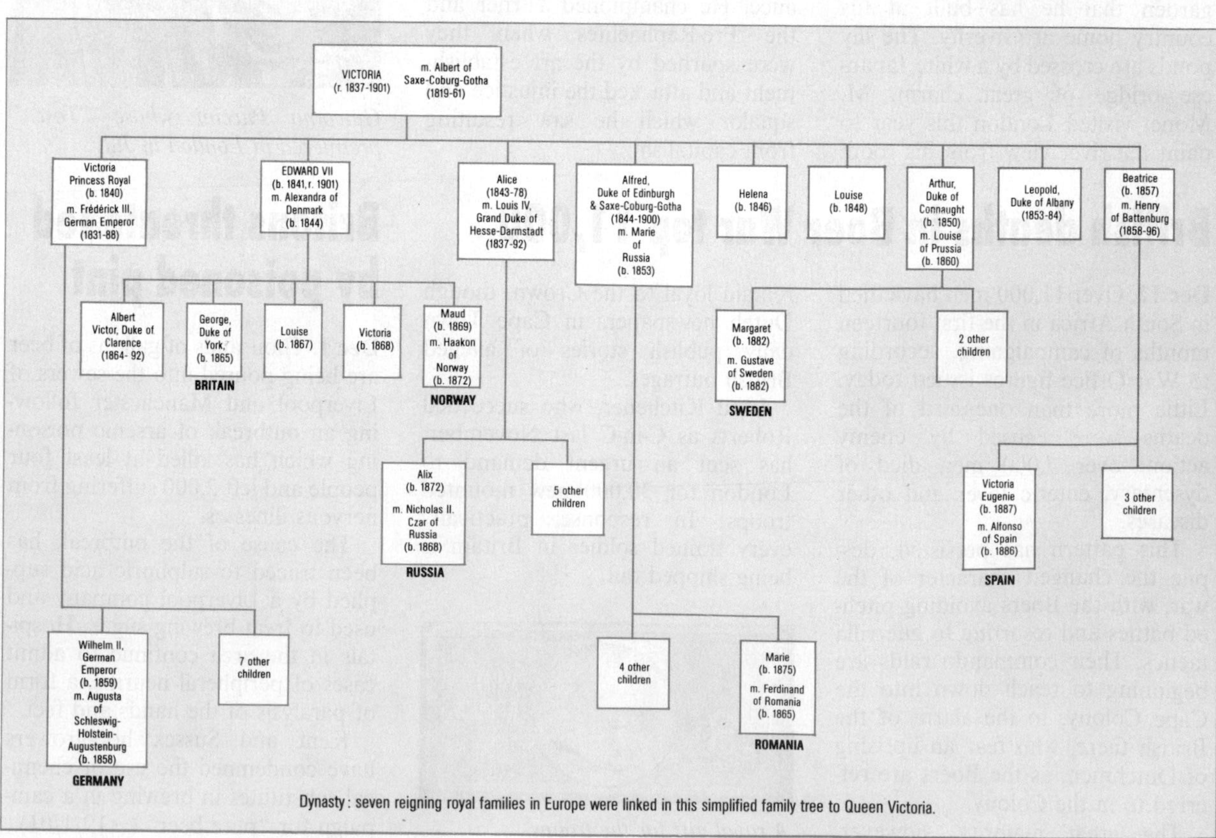

Dynasty: seven reigning royal families in Europe were linked in this simplified family tree to Queen Victoria.

Monarch of an Empire where the sun never sets

One of the last pictures of Queen Victoria, seen here surrounded by members of her family in the grounds of Balmoral.

Queen Victoria gazes up at her beloved husband, Prince Albert. A touching photograph taken in July 1859, two years before his untimely death.

Four generations: Queen Victoria with her son, now King Edward VII, her grandson Prince George and her great-grandson Prince Edward.

1901

FEBRUARY

Su	Mo	Tu	We	Th	Fr	Sa
					1	2
3	4	5	6	7	8	9
10	11	12	13	14	15	16
17	18	19	20	21	22	23
24	25	26	27	28		

2. London: Funeral of Queen Victoria.

5. London: Kaiser Wilhelm II, in England for the funeral of his grandmother Victoria, is warmly greeted in London.

5. Panama: Signature of Hay-Pauncefote Treaty on new shipping canal by Britain and US (→ 11/3).

6. Paris: First public telephones appear at railway stations.

11. Spain: Anti-Jesuit riots sweep the country.

14. Germany: Presentation of a plan to build a 125mph railway between Berlin and Hamburg.

15. London: King Edward VII resigns as Grand Master of Freemasons.

15. US: Nikola Tesla declares that transatlantic telegraphy without wires is at hand (→ 14/10).

21. London: The Apollo Theatre opens in Shaftesbury Avenue.

21. China: Allies agree that no more territorial concessions will be obtained without international consent.→

22. US: Pacific mail steamer sinks in Golden Gate harbour, killing 128.

23. Africa: Germany and the United Kingdom agree on the boundary between German East Africa and the British colony of Nyasaland.

25. Germany: King Edward VII arrives in Frankfurt to visit his nephew, the Kaiser.

27. South Africa: Middelburg peace conference fails as Boers continue to demand autonomy (→ 19/3).

27. Turkey: The Sultan orders 50,000 troops to Bulgarian frontier because of unrest in Macedonia.

BIRTHS

1. US film actor Clark Gable (†16/11/60).

2. Russian-born US violinist Jascha Heifetz (†10/12/87).

28. US chemist Linus Carl Pauling (†19/8/94).

Boxer leaders are publicly executed

Illustration showing how the captured Boxer rebels were executed.

Feb 26. Two leaders of the Boxer Rebellion, Chi-hsui and Hsu-cheng-yu, were today publicly executed in Peking. Found guilty of rebellion, they were beheaded by a court executioner. Both of these senior officials were dressed in mandarin uniform, from which all badges of rank and decorations had been removed in advance.

There was a marked contrast in the way they behaved up to the moment of execution. Chi-hsui met his fate in a calm and dignified manner, walking with little assistance from the cart to the place of execution. On the other hand his colleague, Hsu-cheng-yu, presented a very different picture, appearing to be stupefied by the effects of opium. Japanese troops escorted the men to the execution while American, French and German troops guarded the streets.

Curzon creates new frontier for India

Feb 12. Lord Curzon, the Viceroy of India, has decided to create a new Frontier Province in the North of the Punjab, bordering on Afghanistan. The new province will include the tribal areas of Peshawar, Khyber and Waziristan where so much fighting has taken place recently, to keep the Pathans under control.

According to the communique announcing this move, Lord Curzon has visited the frontier and has decided that the tribal areas needed to come more under the control of the central government. The administrative arrangements, under which the Punjab will lose more than a tenth of its area and nearly a twentieth of its people, are now being made.

It is expected that the legal and financial details will be completed in a few months. The new system of government for this troublesome area of warring tribes in their mountainous strongholds has been widely welcomed by both the public and the army.

First billion dollar business deal

Feb 5. J. Pierpont Morgan, already one of the largest steel owners in America, today pulled off the biggest business deal ever when he bought up a billion dollars worth of mines and steel mills. Never one for competition, preferring secret cooperation between supposedly competing corporations, Morgan now has a virtual monopoly of the steel industry.

The turning of the century was used to sell even biscuits.

Edward VII opens his first Parliament

Feb 14. To the enthusiastic acclaim of crowds lining London's streets, England's new monarch drove today in full state splendour from Buckingham Palace to Westminster, where the King opened the first parliament of his reign.

It was a cold but sunny morning as King Edward and Queen Alexandra processed in the magnificent state coach, which has not been seen in public since the death of Prince Albert in 1861.

Despite the splash of colour provided by the coach and the soldiers' uniforms, the prevailing colour was black, in mourning for Queen Victoria.

King Edward VII and Queen Alexandra open their first Parliament.

1901

MARCH

Su	Mo	Tu	We	Th	Fr	Sa
					1	2
3	4	5	6	7	8	9
10	11	12	13	14	15	16
17	18	19	20	21	22	23
24	25	26	27	28	29	30
31						

1. China: Britain, Germany and Japan protest at Sino-Russian agreement on Manchuria (→ 3/4).

2. US: Congress passes Platt amendment, limiting Cuban economy in return for the withdrawal of US troops.

4. US: Inauguration of President McKinley and Vice-President Roosevelt.

5. London: Police eject jeering Irish Nationalists from the House of Commons.

6. Germany: Anarchist attempts to assassinate Kaiser Wilhelm, who escapes with face wounds.

11. Panama: Britain rejects amended Hay-Pauncefote Treaty on Central American canal.

12. London: The Whitechapel Art Gallery opens.

15. Berlin: Chancellor von Bulow declares that an agreement between China and Russia over Manchuria would not violate the Anglo-German accord of October 1900.

19. S. Africa: Government announces that Louis Botha has rejected Kitchener's peace terms (→ 23).

23. S. Africa: The world learns of Boer starvation in British concentration camps (→ 22/4).

24. France: Census shows that the population stands at 38.9 million.

25. UK: The first Diesel motor goes on show.

29. UK: B. Bletsoe's Grudon wins the Grand National at Aintree.

31. Russia: 72 revolutionaries are arrested and two printing presses seized by police (→ 3/4).

BIRTH

18. Russo-German dancer Tatiana Gsovsky (†24/1/82).

DEATH

13. 23rd US President Benjamin Harrison (*20/8/1833).

Rioters set Russian cities alight

March 17. Student unrest in several cities in Russia in the past week took a particularly ugly turn in St. Petersburg today with a riot in Kazan Cathedral. Over 800 students were arrested after clashes with two regiments of Cossacks.

The demonstrations were the worst for several years, and were ostensibly the result of new regulations over student behaviour issued by the Minister of Public Instruction before he was assassinated by a youth suspected of being a member of a Nihilist group. But other reasons for the unrest were the excommunication of the writer, Leo Tolstoy, by the Holy Synod and the anniversary of the death of a girl student in the St. Peter and Paul prison.

Some 500 students marched to Kazan Cathedral on Nevsky Prospect where they tried to stop a Mass. They jeered and threw objects at icons. The students were driven out of the cathedral into the street where they handed out leaflets calling for freedom and the downfall of the Czar.

The authorities called in 1,500 Cossacks who charged at the students and split them into small groups.

A state of siege was declared in Moscow last week, in which Tolstoy took an active part, when work stopped at four factories and thousands of workers joined students in setting up barricades. There have also been serious disturbances in a number of other towns including Odessa, Kiev, and Kharkov (→ 16/4).

Rioters and Cossacks clashing outside the Governor's palace in Moscow.

United States scents victory

March 27. Emilio Aguinaldo, leader of the Philippine rebels, has been captured by the Americans. It is believed in Washington that this means that the long rebellion in the islands may now be over.

Aguinaldo was only taken by means of a ruse on the part of the US General Frederick Funston who disguised himself as a prisoner captured by the rebels, and so tricked Aguinaldo into giving away the whereabouts of his headquarters.

Before leading the insurrection against American annexation of the islands, Aguinaldo, who was persuaded to return from exile by US Admiral Dewey, was America's ally in the war against Spain and then president of the Visayan Republic in the Philippines.

Many Americans felt uneasy at the way he has been treated, and he has become a hero to Filipinos who agree about little else (→ 15/4).

Daimler has built the first Mercedes car

March 31. A revolutionary high-performance car has been made for Emile Jellinek, Consul-General of the Austro-Hungarian Empire in Nice. Called Mercedes after his daughter, it is an improved version of a model delivered to him by Daimler in 1899.

The appearance of this striking new car is quite unlike a horse-drawn carriage.

The four cylinders of the 5.9 litre engine, which is cooled by water circulating through a honeycomb radiator, are capable of generating 35 brake horsepower.

The remarkable new Mercedes 53 mph motor car which was built by Daimler for Emile Jellinek, who named it after his daughter.

1901

APRIL

Su	Mo	Tu	We	Th	Fr	Sa
	1	2	3	4	5	6
7	8	9	10	11	12	13
14	15	16	17	18	19	20
21	22	23	24	25	26	27
28	29	30				

1. US: Texas oil companies form a $1 billion trust (→ 7/4/02).

3. Russia: Attempted assassination of Interior Minister Sipiagin.

3. China: The Imperial Government refuses to sign the Manchuria Treaty with Russia for fear of alienating the great powers (→ 10).

4. Belfast: Harland and Wolff launch the world's largest ship, the "Celtic".

8. Belgium: Social democratic conference adopts policy of universal suffrage.

10. Japan: The government accepts Russian declaration of good faith over Manchuria, averting conflict.

14. US: Actors are arrested in New York at the Academy of Music for wearing costumes on a Sunday.

15. Rome: Pope Leo XIII condemns trend toward state regulation of Catholic Church throughout Europe.

16. Russia: Arrests continue in all parts of the empire, with 1,500 in Odessa alone.

21. London: Lillie Langtry opens as Marie Antoinette in "A Royal Necklace" at the Imperial Theatre.

25. Germany: 200 people are killed as chemical factory near Griesheim explodes.

27. London: Non-league Tottenham Hotspur wins the Football Association Cup, beating Sheffield United 3-1 at Crystal Palace.

29. Hungary: Clashes in Budapest between Jewish and anti-Semitic student groups (→ 4/12).

30. Philippines: General Tinio, a prominent rebel leader, surrenders to United States Army.

30. UK: Beginning of the commercialisation of the indoor game of table tennis, or "Ping-Pong", created by James Gibb.

BIRTH

29. Crown Prince Hirohito (†6/1/89).

Pledges made on Boer camp conditions

April 22. Responding to widespread concern in Britain and abroad, over conditions in the concentration camps for Boers, Mr St. John Broderick, Secretary for War, has told the House of Commons that the High Commissioner, Sir Alfred Milner, is giving his personal attention to improving conditions, and that every provision has been made for medical treatment and the education of children.

The reassurance has been received with scepticism by critics, inside the House and beyond. The camps accommodate over 75,000 Boers, most of them women and children made homeless by the British destruction of farms.

Baron von Richthofen, the Foreign Secretary, told the Prussian Diet that the British Government had refused to allow a German-Austrian medical mission to visit the camps, but would accept food, clothing and other articles for distribution. German newspapers have attacked Colonial Secretary Joseph Chamberlain for saying the British have behaved no worse than the Germans in past wars (→ 17/6).

The French view of the way the British treat Boer prisoners.

Rodin's Victor Hugo outrages public

April 21. Auguste Rodin's sculpture of Victor Hugo was unveiled at the Grand Palais in Paris today to the gasps of outraged critics and art patrons. The renowned French novelist had been portrayed as a semi-nude reclining figure, apparently growing out of rough-hewn rock like some pagan deity.

This is not the first time that Rodin's sculptures have shocked. A few years ago, in 1897, his interpretation of another French literary giant, Honore de Balzac, encountered scorn and hostility for trying to fuse the form of the man with scenes from his multi-volume masterpiece "The Human Comedy". It was clumsy and unfinished, declared the critics.

The-60-year-old sculptor must sometimes feel that he can't win. His first major work, "The Age of Bronze", was accused of being too life-like not to have been cast directly from a model.

Horse-drawn trams are on their way out. Here workmen are erecting overhead wires to electrify the trams in Portsmouth.

1901

MAY

Su	Mo	Tu	We	Th	Fr	Sa
			1	2	3	4
5	6	7	8	9	10	11
12	13	14	15	16	17	18
19	20	21	22	23	24	25
26	27	28	29	30	31	

1. London: National Conference of Miners recommends strike action unless the coal export tax is reduced.

2. Glasgow: International Exhibition opens.

7. London: Education Bill is introduced in the House of Commons, under which county councils will take charge of all state education.

8. India: Britain says 1.25 million people have died from famine since 1899; India's overpopulation is blamed for the dramatic situation.

9. Australia: The first Federal parliament meets in Melbourne.

9. Ireland: Authorities seize copies of the "Irish People" newspaper following its virulent attack on King Edward VII (→ 13).

14. China: Following a fortnight of talks, the Imperial Government agrees to pay war indemnity demanded by the Allies (→ 7/9).

15. London: The Admiralty decides to build three 18,000 ton battleships – the biggest in the world.

18. London: Alexandra Park and Alexandra Palace open to the public.

23. Rome: Angelo Bresci, the assassin of King Umberto of Italy, commits suicide in prison.

25. Norway: Men and women paying more than 300 crowns tax per year in the country and 400 crowns in towns are enfranchised for local elections.

28. Persia: William Knox D'Arcy is granted a concession by the government to explore for oil (→ 26/6/08).

30. London: Alfred Dreyfus's own account of the Dreyfus Case is now available in the United Kingdom, as well as France, Germany and the United States.

BIRTH

7. US actor Gary Cooper (†13/5/61)

Salisbury vows to keep Ireland British

May 13. The Prime Minister, Lord Salisbury, today firmly ruled out self-government for Ireland. He said that Britain's military power could be undermined if Home Rule were ever conceded. Speaking to the Non-Conformist Association, he reflected on how a free and hostile Ireland might have blunted the Government's recent war effort in South Africa.

He said: "There is no power but knows that if it defies the might of England it defies one of the most formidable enemies it could possibly encounter." However, there was a lesson to be drawn from experience with modern weapons. This was that, if some Irish leaders were left with the chance of making preparations, "We should have to begin by conquering Ireland".

Lord Salisbury's audience included politicians who backed Mr Gladstone's Home Rule Bill eight years ago. "They were once the backbone of the Liberal Party", he said. The Prime Minister hailed this as proof that the tide of public opinion is running inexorably against the Irish Nationalists and their Liberal allies. This view was broadly endorsed by many of the government MPs.

Darkness at noon with eclipse of the sun

May 18. British astronomers have successfully photographed all stages of a total eclipse of the sun from the Indian Ocean island of Mauritius. Many pictures were taken with the help of instruments from Greenwich Observatory. Now scientists are waiting to see whether the eclipse causes a cyclone.

British and Dutch expeditions in Sumatra were less successful. Early cloud cleared partially, enabling the Dutch to photograph the corona, but conditions were never really satisfactory. During the six and a half minute period of totality Mercury and Venus were seen.

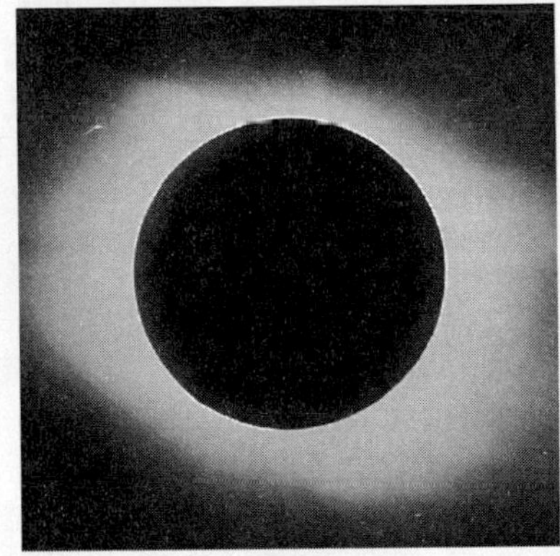

Land of the midday night: the corona is clearly visible in this photograph of the eclipse.

Kitchener's new tactics in war

May 9. At the start of the South African winter, Lord Kitchener, in supreme command for six months, has a force of 240,000 men, one third mounted, to deal with the enemy's mounted strength estimated at 44,000.

Kitchener gained immense popularity for his reconquest of the Sudan after the killing by dervishes of General Gordon at Khartoum led to the withdrawal of the British and Egyptians from the country. In South Africa, though, Kitchener is grappling with a resourceful and elusive adversary whose commandos repeatedly avoid capture after delivering damaging blows at the slow-moving British columns.

Kitchener has responded by erecting blockhouses and barbed wire along the railways and across the veld; reinforcements can thus be called up by telegraph at the first sighting of an enemy force.

Boer morale is falling as their numbers are worn down by these tactics; but appeals for peace at a recent council of war were opposed by those who still hope Britain will agree to independence.

Kitchener gravely embodies Britain.

Miners entombed by pit explosion

May 24. At least 78 men were buried alive by a series of gas explosions early this morning in a Welsh coal mine near Caerphilly. The bodies of three other miners were brought out by rescuers. The Universal Mine at Sengenydd – the first to be dug in the Aber Valley – went into production only four years ago.

The disaster happened at about 5.30am as the night shift was leaving the pit. Three explosions, which could be heard 3.5 miles away, shattered the top of the shaft. As relatives gathered at the pithead, rescuers reported that gas and huge rockfalls at the shaft bottom were preventing them from reaching the trapped men.

Census reveals population boom

May 9. Britain's population is growing faster than ever, say the results of last month's national census published today. The figures reveal that 32,525,716 people now live in England and Wales, three and a half million more than during the last census ten years ago.

The population boom is biggest in the Northern industrial towns, such as Bradford and Leeds, and in the Home Counties, which are fast becoming London's suburbs, linked to the capital by better train services. Elsewhere in Britain people have been moving off the land and in 12 counties, including Oxfordshire, Norfolk and Devon, the population has fallen since the last census in 1891.

Racing yacht wrecked with King aboard

May 22. King Edward VII had a narrow escape this afternoon when Shamrock II, the challenger for the America's Cup, was badly damaged by a squall during trials off the Isle of Wight.

The yacht was hit by the storm as it manoeuvred alongside Shamrock I, the unsuccessful entrant in the last America's race. Almost without warning, the ship's masts snapped and collapsed, bringing down the rigging and sails. Shamrock I lost its own topsail as it rushed to the scene, but Sybarita, another yacht in the area, immediately sent a rescue dinghy to transfer the King and his party to the Sir Thomas Lipton's steam yacht, the Erin. Miraculously, no one was hurt.

His Majesty had been invited aboard Shamrock II as the guest of Sir Thomas Lipton, and other members of this aristocratic party included the Marchioness of Londonderry (→26/9).

The biggest camera in the world, weighing over 1400 lbs, is used to photograph high-speed trains. Its plates measure 8 x 5 feet.

1901

JUNE

Su	Mo	Tu	We	Th	Fr	Sa
						1
2	3	4	5	6	7	8
9	10	11	12	13	14	15
16	17	18	19	20	21	22
23	24	25	26	27	28	29
30						

2. South Africa: Jamestown surrenders to Boers under Kruitzinger (→ 17).

5. UK: C. W. Whitney's Volodyovski wins the Derby in record time.

6. London: Committee suggests reform of the War Ministry (→ 9/5).

9. Somaliland: British Colonel Swayne defeats the Mad Mullah.

10. Brussels: The Belgian parliament decides to postpone the annexation of the Congo.

13. Arabia: The whole of Yemen is reported to be in a state of revolt.

16. Atlantic: Wireless telegraphy at sea is tried for the first time aboard the liner "Lucania".

17. London: Welsh Member of Parliament David Lloyd George speaks out against the alarming death rate among Boer women and children in the South African concentration camps (→ 24/7).

19. Berlin: Kaiser says in a speech that Germany's future "lies on the water".

20. London: Liberal MP Herbert Asquith distances himself from anti-war policy of fellow MP Sir Henry Campbell-Bannerman.

25. London: The London County Council adopts new tramways scheme presented by the Highways Committee.

26. Canada: The liner "Lusitania" is wrecked off Cape Ballard, Newfoundland; 350 rescued.

26. Paris: Professional chauffeurs protest at a move to prevent them from wearing moustaches.

27. London: The Admiralty rejects a bill before the House of Lords to extend Gibraltar at Spain's expense.

29. Berlin: Henri Fournier wins 750-mile motor race from Paris to Berlin.

BIRTH

6. Akhmed Sukarno, first president of Indonesia (†21/6/70).

Paris critics acclaim first Picasso show

Pablo Picasso stares with grave self-assurance from his self-portrait.

June 24. There is much talk in Paris this week of an exhibition by a 19-year-old artist from Barcelona. Pablo Ruiz Picasso set up his studio in Montmartre this year, and is known because of his Andalusian hat as "Le Petit Goya".

The subjects of his pictures vary from children to prostitutes, from race meetings to the dancers of Le Moulin Rouge. "Everything can be a subject for Picasso," writes the critic of "La Revue Blanche".

He addeds: "He is capable of using any idiom and is in such a feverish hurry that he is able to do three canvases a day, which could easily lead to facile virtuosity. However, we shall hear more of P.R. Picasso."

Becquerel presents radium discoveries

June 12. Atoms, thought for almost a century to be the ultimate units of matter, may contain smaller particles still. That is the startling implication of a discovery just announced by French physicist Henri Becquerel.

In 1896 Becquerel found that salts of the metal uranium emitted rays. He has now shown that these rays behave like the artificially produced cathode rays, recently shown by Professor J.J. Thomson to consist of electrons which weigh only a fraction of the lightest atom.

Becquerel's rays can only have come from uranium atoms. The inescapable conclusion is that these atoms, and probably all other atoms, contain still smaller particles: electrons.

Becquerel in his sparse laboratory.

Punch's famous cartoonist quits

June 12. The leading names of politics, the arts and the stage gathered at the Hotel Metropole last night for a dinner in honour of Sir John Tenniel, to mark his retirement from "Punch".

The famous illustrator of "Alice" was on the staff for fifty years and drew the main weekly cartoon on more than two thousand occasions; the most celebrated was entitled "Dropping The Pilot", when Prince Bismarck resigned over the policies of the Kaiser. The audience, which included playwrights Arthur Pinero and J.M. Barrie, heard cabinet minister Arthur Balfour praise Sir John for "giving us week by week a picture of what Englishmen were thinking".

Sir John Tenniel.

Rhodesia said to make a profit

June 17. In a speech delivered in the country to which he gave his name, Cecil Rhodes, the statesman, financier and philanthropist, predicted that, within four years, Rhodesia will join South Africa in a self-governing federation within the British Empire.

Rhodesia now earns £700,000 a year from its produce and would, he said, be self-supporting but for the burden of its contribution to the Boer War. However, he added, everybody knew perfectly well that the war was practically over, even though Dutch politicians and some newspapers in the Cape were still encouraging Boer commandos to invade the colony.

1901

JULY

Su	Mo	Tu	We	Th	Fr	Sa
	1	2	3	4	5	6
7	8	9	10	11	12	13
14	15	16	17	18	19	20
21	22	23	24	25	26	27
28	29	30	31			

1. France: Law restricting public activities of religious groups goes into effect amid protests from the Catholic Church.

1. China: British-occupied parts of Peking are handed back to the authorities.

2. New York: Nearly 400 people die in one day during heat wave, with temperatures up to 110 degrees F (43.33 degrees C) in the shade.

3. Wimbledon: Arthur Gore beats Reginald Doherty for the Men's Singles Championship; Charlotte Sterry (nee Cooper) beats Blanche Hill for the Ladies' title.

4. Manila: William Howard Taft is installed as Civil Governor of the Philippines, in succession to Military Governor, Gen. Arthur MacArthur.

8. France: The speed limit for cars in towns is set at 10 km/h (6 mph).

10. Opening of first completed section of London Electric Tramway from Shepherd's Bush to Southall.

12. Berlin: Reichstag members unsuccessfully attempt to outlaw duelling.

13. France: Brazilian aviator Santos-Dumont crashes his dirigible at Boulogne after circling the Eiffel Tower.

17. Atlantic Ocean: The liner "Deutschland" sets new east-west transatlantic speed record of five days, 11 hours and five minutes.

22. UK: British Congress on Tuberculosis opens.

23. Germany: Dr Robert Koch advances theory that bubonic plague may be due solely to rats.

24. London: Statistics reveal that around 86,000 whites and 23,000 blacks are being held in South African concentration camps (→ 7/8).

DEATH

7. American Pierre Lorillard, owner of Tuxedo Park, who made the "tuxedo" dinner jacket fashionable in the US (*1833).

Liberals rocked by Boer War rows

July 9. At a special meeting in the Reform Club Sir Henry Campbell-Bannerman demanded and got a vote of confidence as Liberal leader. He claimed that personal antagonism, rather than differences over the conduct of the Boer War, was responsible for paralysing the party in Parliament. This interpretation was endorsed by Mr. Lloyd George but contested by Mr. Asquith.

After the meeting the rival Radical and Imperialist factions continued to wrangle over the peace terms to offer the Boers. The Tories saw this as strengthening their own electoral position.

Leopold holds on to Congo State

July 17. King Leopold has successfully fought off an attempt by the Belgian government to annex his Congo Free State, which he established in 1885, with the agreement of the European colonial powers. Because of foreign and domestic criticism of the King's administration for its harsh treatment of the indigenous African population, the Belgian government wanted to take the territory away from him and administer it directly as a colony. But under the new deal Leopold is left with a freer hand than before – at a time when both the production of Congo rubber (6,000 tons last year) and its market price is rising.

Radio messages on the move.

1901

AUGUST

Su	Mo	Tu	We	Th	Fr	Sa
				1	2	3
4	5	6	7	8	9	10
11	12	13	14	15	16	17
18	19	20	21	22	23	24
25	26	27	28	29	30	31

1. London: House of Commons votes additional £12.5 million for the naval and war budgets.

1. US: A black mother and her two children are lynched after a white couple are murdered at Carrollton, Mississippi.

4. S. Africa: Important gold strike is made in the Rand.

7. S. Africa: British supremo Lord Herbert Kitchener says all Boer leaders must surrender by September 15 or face banishment.

8. S. Africa: Boer Commandant de Villiers surrenders to the British at Warmbaths (→ 2/9).

9. S. America: Colombian troops invade Venezuela.

12. London: Government suffers surprise defeat of Factory Bill to limit textile workers' hours.

14. Bridgeport, Connecticut: It is claimed that G. Weisskopf has flown a motor-powered vehicle designed by Wright brothers.

15. Munich: Opening of an exhibition by the group "Phalanx" organised by the Russian Wassily Kandinsky.

21. US: New motor car company is founded in Detroit, named after 18th century French explorer Antoine de la Mothe Cadillac (→ 17/10/02).

26. Austria: Newspapers in Vienna and Budapest warn of the Russian army's Balkan manoeuvres.

BIRTHS

3. Polish primate Cardinal Stefan Wyszynski (†28/5/81).

20. Salvatore Quasimodo, Italian writer (†14/6/68).

25. Danish playwright Kjeld Abell (†5/3/61).

DEATH

5. Empress Victoria of Germany, mother of Wilhelm II and eldest child of Queen Victoria (*21/12/1840).

White lottery for Red Indian land

Aug 9. The United States territory of Oklahoma has grown overnight by two million acres in a great allotment sale of former Red Indian lands to 6,500 white settlers. More than 170,000 people applied for a stake.

Federal agents bought the land from the Comanche, Kiowa and Apache tribes for $2 million. Ranchers had pressed for more grazing lands while railway owners for their part wanted to increase traffic in the area.

At the same time, the new lands are believed to hold considerable coal reserves and the soil to be good for wheat and cotton.

World bike record set for one mile

Aug 26. Americans saw cyclist Robert Walthour shatter numerous world records yesterday. He notched up a mile in 1 minute 37.4 seconds just a week after Jimmy Michaels of Wales had broken the previous record with a 1 minute 52.4 second mile.

Walthour outsped his opponent, John Nelson of Chicago, in a 15-mile race round Madison Square Garden in New York. Two miles into the race Nelson, who was suffering from flat bicycle tyres, was 50 yards behind Walthour who, having set a new mile time, went on to break other records.

Doctor W.G. Grace scores hot sponsor.

1901

SEPTEMBER

Su	Mo	Tu	We	Th	Fr	Sa
1	2	3	4	5	6	7
8	9	10	11	12	13	14
15	16	17	18	19	20	21
22	23	24	25	26	27	28
29	30					

1. South America: Venezuelan General Davila and 10,000 men are ready to invade Colombia (→8).

2. London: Dr Krause, former Boer governor of Johannesburg, is arrested for high treason (→11/10).

7. China: The Allies finally sign the peace protocol with the Chinese.→

8. South America: Colombia reported to be invaded by Venezuela, Ecuador and Nicaragua.

9. Austria: Kaiser Franz Josef restores diplomatic relations with Mexico, cut off since the execution of Mexican Emperor Maximilian, a Habsburg, in 1867.

10. US: Anarchist Emma Goldman arrested for part in plot to kill President McKinley.→

17. China: Allies complete formal evacuation of Peking.

18. Grimsby: Torpedo boat "Cobra" wrecked with the loss of 59 lives.

24. US: Leon Czolgosz is sentenced to death for President William McKinley's assassination (→29/10).

25. Africa: Britain annexes Ashanti kingdom as part of Gold Coast.

26. US: The yacht "Columbia" beats "Shamrock II" in the first America's Cup race (→ 4/10).

26. London: Reported outbreak of smallpox is spreading.

30. France: Registration becomes compulsory for cars capable of speeds of more than 20 mph.

BIRTH

29. Enrico Fermi, Italian nuclear physicist (†28/11/54).

DEATHS

9. French painter Henri de Toulouse-Lautrec (*24/11/1864).→

14. US President William McKinley (*29/1/1843).→

McKinley shot: Roosevelt is President

Sept 14. President William McKinley died early today in Buffalo, New York, of wounds inflicted by a Polish anarchist, Leon Czolgosz, on September 6 while he was opening an exhibition.

At first the President's wounds were thought not to be serious. But yesterday a runner reached the Vice-President as he was returning from a holiday climb in the Adirondacks and handed him a telegram. "The President's condition," it read, "has changed for the worse."

Mr Roosevelt covered the 440 miles to Buffalo at high speed by horsedrawn buckboard and special locomotive and took the oath of office only about twelve hours after President McKinley died.

His last words, before going into a coma, were those of his favourite hymn, "Nearer, my God, to thee". McKinley is the third President to have been assassinated. President Roosevelt is 42 (→24).

Artist's impression of the moment of President McKinley's assassination.

Peking treaty ends Boxer rebellion

Sept 7. The Boxer uprising officially ended today when China signed the peace protocol drawn up by a dozen foreign powers. Diplomats and Chinese plenipotentiaries were present at the Spanish Legation to hear an exchange of friendly speeches. Prince Ching, who had arrived in a chair, escorted by cavalry, solemnly declared that China intended to carry out all her pledges and hoped that China and the powers would never clash again.

Under the terms of the protocol the Chinese will pay an indemnity of $739 million and will permit the stationing of troops from the allied nations both in Peking and in the main ports. The Chinese Government also undertakes to honour commercial agreements made with American and European governments. The Allies agreed to leave in ten days (→19/01/03).

Toulouse-Lautrec dies, aged thirty-six

Sept 9. The great French painter Henri de Toulouse-Lautrec has died at Malrome in the Gironde at the early age of 36.

Best known for his portrayals of the entertainers and other bohemian characters haunting Montmartre in Paris, Toulouse-Lautrec first drew the public's attention in the mid-1880s, and shot to fame with his 1891 poster, "Moulin Rouge – La Goulue".

The artist was never in the best of health throughout his short life. In adolescence he broke both thighbones in the space of a year, leaving him a cripple.

Lautrec at work in his studio.

Taff Vale ruling alarms unions

Sept 4. Trade unions are liable for the financial losses of companies affected by industrial action, the House of Lords ruled today. The interpretation of the law until now has been that each side in an industrial dispute pays its own costs.

The Lords' judgement, arising out of a walkout a year ago by workers at the Taff Vale Railway Company in South Wales, is a major setback for the trade union movement. In South Wales, it means that the Amalgamated Society of Railway Servants, which organised the strike, must pay £23,000 in damages to the firm.

But the Trades Union Congress has pledged fiercely to fight the decision. It fears the risk of bankruptcy will deter most of the trade unions from striking.

The Lords' decision follows a High Court ruling that the Taff Vale strikers picketed unlawfully by trying to "molest and injure" employees who continued to work. Mr Justice Willis said that picketing was only lawful near the workplace or an employee's home for information to be passed on.

1901

OCTOBER

Su	Mo	Tu	We	Th	Fr	Sa
		1	2	3	4	5
6	7	8	9	10	11	12
13	14	15	16	17	18	19
20	21	22	23	24	25	26
27	28	29	30	31		

2. UK: Vickers launches "Holland 1", the Royal Navy's first submarine; four more are planned.→

4. London: Winston Churchill says situation in South Africa is no better.

6 London: Sir Henry Irving and Ellen Terry depart for a tour of the US.

9. China: Prince Ching demands withdrawal of foreign businesses from Peking.

11. S. Africa: Boer Commandant Lotter is executed (→14/11).

14. London: It is reported that Italian Guglielmo Marconi has successfully sent wireless messages over 350 miles (→11/12).

14 UK: 174 people receiving treatment for smallpox (→31/01/02).

16. China: Russians sign new agreement with Imperial Government over Manchuria.

19. France: Brazilian aviator Alberto Santos-Dumont flies a dirigible airship for 30 minutes and wins the $50,000 Deutsch de la Meurthe award.

20. Belgium: Fund for the unemployed is established by Parliament.

22. Mexico: Second Pan-American conference.

23. London: General Buller is relieved of his command for "indiscretion" and "lack of military discipline" in speech given October 10.

25. Edinburgh: Colonial Secretary Joseph Chamberlain gives anti-German speech in which he also defends Boer camps.

28. UK: Vickers launch the "King Alfred", the world's fastest cruiser.

28. US: 34 people are killed in race riots sparked by Booker T. Washington's visit to the White House.

29. US: Leon Czolgosz, assassin of President William McKinley, is executed (→14/9).

BIRTH

15. German author Bernard von Brentano (†29/12/64).

Britain's first submarine launched

Oct 2. There was a marked lack of ceremony when Britain's first submarine was launched at Barrow today. The 63 foot Holland Class submarine carries torpedoes but, although the Americans have tested them, there is considerable doubt in the Admiralty as to what use they may be. An Admiralty memorandum has noted: "What the future value of these boats may be in naval warfare can only be a matter of conjecture."

The submarine is powered by a petrol engine while on the surface where she can reach nine knots. When submerged an electric motor, running off batteries, allows her to make seven knots for up to four hours.

Outside her hull shape is smooth to reduce the resistance of the water and to prevent catching on ropes or underwater obstacles. Inside she is lit by electricity and her crew breathe compressed air.

Holland I, Britain's first submarine, has a petrol engine and 9 man crew.

First negro dines at White House

Oct 16. President Roosevelt broke with tradition and angered his southern opponents last night by inviting a black man to dine in the White House. The President's guest was Booker T. Washington, the noted reformer and teacher and president of the first university for coloured people in the USA at Tuskeegee, Alabama (→28).

Booker T. Washington in black tie.

Britain fails again in America's Cup

Oct 4. The America's Cup was once more successfully defended by its perennial holders today, as the United States yacht "Columbia" completed a 3-0 clean sweep over Sir Thomas Lipton's "Shamrock II" off Sandy Hook, New York.

It was the closest of all the races in the current series, with "Shamrock" actually crossing the line two seconds ahead of the New York Yacht Club's defender, only to be defeated by her 43-second handicap. Sir Thomas's courage and sportsmanship in sustaining his challenge (the grocery millionaire's "Shamrock I" went down to "Columbia" by an equally decisive 3-0 only two years ago) was roundly cheered even by the partisan American support on the quayside.

Though this is the eleventh successive challenge to fail since the yacht "America" first took the trophy at Cowes in 1851, Sir Thomas still plans to mount another attack in two years' time.

Eastman firm will manufacture Kodak

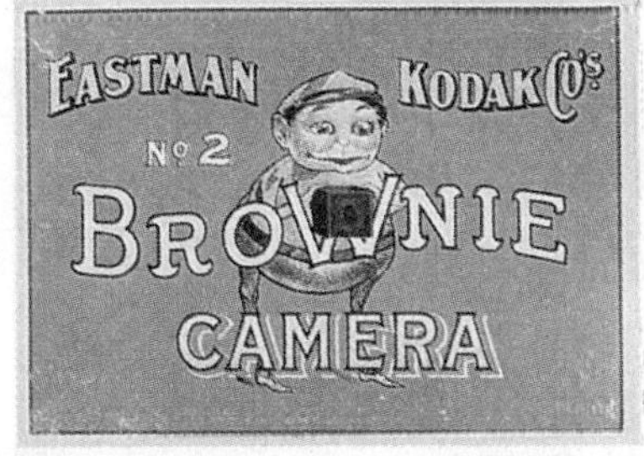

Brownie cameras cost one dollar.

Oct 24. Kodak's founder George Eastman has set up an international camera company following the success of his one dollar Brownie camera.

Formally incorporated in New Jersey, the Eastman Kodak Company amalgamates existing camera and supply companies on both sides of the Atlantic.

Educated in New York, Eastman originally worked in banking and insurance before turning to photography. After a period of working out of a garage he perfected a process for making dry film plates, then invented transparent film, and in 1884 founded the Eastman Dry Plate and Film Company.

At 4.23pm on October 24, aged 43, Mrs Ann Edson Taylor went over the Niagara falls in a padded barrel and survived unharmed. She did it because she could not pay her mortgage and wanted the notoriety.

1901

NOVEMBER

Su	Mo	Tu	We	Th	Fr	Sa
					1	2
3	4	5	6	7	8	9
10	11	12	13	14	15	16
17	18	19	20	21	22	23
24	25	26	27	28	29	30

1. Chicago: Dr J.E. Gillman announces an x-ray treatment for breast cancer.

1. South Africa: British troops suffer heavy losses at Brakenlaagte.

4. US: New terms of Hay-Pauncefote Treaty are approved (→4/1/02).

7. Turkey: French navy, occupying the island of Mytilene, forces the Turks to pay compensation for 1896 losses.

10. India: Formal inauguration of the new North-West Frontier Province created out of the Punjab.

12. UK: Great gales lash the country; nearly 200 people are killed and many ships are lost.

14. S. Africa: Boers repulsed at Piquetburg.→

19. London: The new telephone system for the capital is completed.

19. London: Liberal MP Sir Henry Campbell-Bannerman condemns the extension of martial law to Cape Town and the other main ports of South Africa.

20. South America: US troops intervene as rebels take Colon, Colombia.

22. Dresden: First performance of Richard Strauss's opera "Feuersnot".

25. Russia: Prince Ito visits Russia to seek concessions on Korea (→30/1/02).

26. Africa: Britain signs an agreement with Italy fixing the frontier between Eritrea and the Sudan.

29. South America: Colombian liberals surrender at Colon to Dr. Alban, Governor of Panama.

BIRTHS

3. Belgian King Leopold III (†26/9/83).

3. French author and politician Andre Malraux (†23/11/76).

18. US journalist and statistician George Gallup (†27/7/84).

Goat dung tea for Boer camp kids

Nov 15. The death rate in the refugee camps for Boer families in South Africa is still rising, especially among children, but urgent action is under way to improve conditions, according to an official report published today in London.

The effects of a severe measles epidemic sweeping through the camps have been worsened by what the report calls the insanitary habits of many refugees and the refusal of Boer mothers to accept medical advice. The military governor is quoted as saying the mothers insist on treating their children's measles with a tea made of goat's dung, "with deplorable results".

In addition to the 77,000 white people in camps in the Transvaal, Orange River and Natal, there are some 21,000 non-whites, most of them the Boers' servants and farmworkers. Last month in the Transvaal camps, of 37,000 inmates, 335 died, 252 of them children. Overall, for every three white people joining the camps, one can expect to die. There are no figures for the non-white death rate.

While the report supports many of the allegations, it rejects charges in the continental press of deliberate neglect and brutality. It claims the Boers' mortality rate is often just as high on their farms.

First hearing-aid offers hope to deaf

Nov 30. A mechanical hearing aid known as the Akouphone is the most powerful sound reproducer yet developed. Designed by Miller Reese Hutchinson, an electrical engineer, it is a telephone with a battery fitted to the body and a transmitter in the lap or on a table. The receiver on the ear can be controlled by adjustment of a switch on its handle.

Britain agrees to US canal rights

Nov 18. Britain and the US today agreed terms for the building of a new shipping canal through Central America.

US Secretary of State John Hay and British ambassador Lord Pauncefote signed a treaty, modelled on the Suez Canal agreement, giving the US extensive rights over the new canal in return for a guarantee of its neutrality.

Life below stairs may be less luxurious than that enjoyed in the drawing room but some products are found on both sides of the baize door.

1901

DECEMBER

Su	Mo	Tu	We	Th	Fr	Sa
1	2	3	4	5	6	7
8	9	10	11	12	13	14
15	16	17	18	19	20	21
22	23	24	25	26	27	28
29	30	31				

2. Washington: The Supreme Court decides that Puerto Ricans do not qualify for US citizenship (→4/1/01).

4. Germany: The Bavarian parliament permits the appointment of Jewish judges but will not allow their proportion to exceed that of Jews in the whole population.

18. Birmingham: Lloyd George is forced to flee pro-Boer meeting as riots break out (→13/2/02).

19. London: Anglo-German talks about alliance are suspended following Joseph Chamberlain's anti-German remarks (→8/1/02).

21. Norway: Women are allowed to vote for the first time, but only in local elections (→18/2/02).

26. Sweden: First performance of "Dance of Death" by playwright August Strindberg.

27. Switzerland: Zionist Congress reports that the movement is making great progress.

29. UK: Woman house surgeon in Macclesfield resigns after male colleagues refuse to work with her because of her sex.

BIRTHS

5. American cartoonist and animator Walt Disney (†15/12/66).

16. American anthropologist Margaret Mead (†15/11/78).

27. German actress and entertainer Marlene Dietrich, born Magdalena von Losch (†6/5/92).

HITS OF 1901

Just a-wearyin' for you.

Mighty lak' a rose.

QUOTE OF THE YEAR

"A European war can only end in the ruin of the vanquished and the hardly less fatal commercial dislocation and exhaustion of the conquerors." **Winston Leonard Spencer Churchill**, speaking to the House of Commons on 13/5/1901.

Sweden awards first Nobel Prizes

Dec 10. The first Nobel laureates received their awards today, for outstanding contributions in the fields of literature, chemistry, physics, peace and medicine. They were distributed in Oslo by the Norwegian Nobel Committee, and by the King of Sweden in Stockholm.

The awards, funded by a legacy from the former Swedish chemist Alfred Nobel will be "annually made to those who, during the preceding year, shall have conferred the greatest benefit on mankind" in the appropriate fields, according to the terms of Nobel's will.

This year's Nobel Peace Prize is shared by Red Cross founder Jean Henri Dunant of Switzerland and economist Frederic Passy, founder of the French Society of the Friends of Peace. Wilhelm Roentgen of Germany received the Physics prize for his discovery of X-rays, Emil von Behring of Germany the Medicine prize for his work on serum therapy, Jacobus Henricus Van't Hoff of the Netherlands the Chemistry prize for his laws of chemical dynamics, and Sally Prudhomme of France the Literature award for his poetry.

From now on the laureates will be chosen by one Norwegian and three Swedish institutions, and the ceremonial presentation of the prizes will take place on December 10, which is the anniversary of Nobel's death in 1886. The prizes are funded by the annual interest on the scientist's bequeathed fortune, administered by the independent Nobel foundation.

Originally stereotyped as a "mad scientist", Alfred Nobel made his fortune by inventing dynamite. He hoped that the destructive power of his invention would help bring wars to an end.

Physics Prizewinner Roentgen.

Gillette to market a replaceable razor

Dec 2. It was announced today in America that a replaceable razor would be going on sale some time next year. It is the invention of King Camp Gillette, a businessman who actually patented it in 1895. Shaped like a hoe, the double-edged blade is designed to be used just once, or until blunt, and then thrown away. As well as being a safety razor, Gillette claims that it will be more efficient than existing models.

The delay in marketing the new razor has been due to manufacturing problems but these have been solved by William Nickerson – the company's only employee. With the decreasing popularity of beards, it should find a ready market.

Using the Gillette safety razor.

Marconi wireless message spans Atlantic

The young Marconi soon after his arrival in England from Italy.

Dec 11. The feasibility of global communication by wireless was demonstrated beyond all possible doubt today, when a signal transmitted from Cornwall was detected in Newfoundland, over 2,000 miles away.

The Italian wireless pioneer, Guglielmo Marconi, planned and carried out the experiment. At Poldhu on the Lizard he set up an aerial 164 feet high. At St. John's in Newfoundland a kite took an aerial even higher. At 6pm GMT Poldhu started to transmit the three dots of the letter S in Morse code at five minute intervals. Faint but clear signals were detected almost immediately on the other side of the Atlantic.

Today's triumph is the culmination of a series of experiments with wireless by Marconi. He started at home in Italy in 1895 attempting to transmit messages from his house to a receiver in the garden.

Lack of interest in his work in Italy brought Marconi to England, where Sir William Preece, the Postmaster General, has provided support. The Royal Navy, too, is taking a keen interest.

Mystery author intrigues Paris

All Paris is intrigued by a new novel, "Claudine à Paris" sequel to last year's "Claudine à l'école". Both books are somewhat shocking and betray every sign of female authorship. Yet the author's name is given as "Willy", the nom de plume of a well-known Paris journalist and man-about-town, Henri Gauthier-Villars.

In the preface, "Willy" thanks his wife for the help she has given him. She is a woman in her twenties whose maiden name is **Colette**. There are rumours that this account of a young girl's education in the arts of love is Colette's work entirely. "Claudine" is a "succes fou". Hats, collars, perfumes, even cigarettes, are being named "Claudine".

In England the literary year has been dominated by the new tale from the pen of the poet of our empire in India, **Rudyard Kipling**. "Kim" is an urchin boy of the streets of Lahore, Irish by birth but passing as a native. He is a character of irresistible boyish charm and mischief. His pilgrimage as the guide of an ancient Buddhist monk steeps the reader in all the colour, mystery, duplicity and fascination of India. It has been hailed as Kipling's masterpiece.

The death of **Giuseppe Verdi** in January removed the foremost Italian opera composer at the age of 88. Although it is half a century since "Rigoletto" and "La Traviata" were first heard, Verdi's genius was astonishingly reaffirmed less than ten years ago when, at nearly 80, he produced two more mature masterpieces, "Otello" and "Falstaff".

Colette alias "Willy".

1902

JANUARY

Su	Mo	Tu	We	Th	Fr	Sa
			1	2	3	4
5	6	7	8	9	10	11
12	13	14	15	16	17	18
19	20	21	22	23	24	25
26	27	28	29	30	31	

1. Madrid: First exhibition in modern times of the works of Domenikos Theotokopoulos, known as El Greco.

4. Malta: Protests at new taxes and the substitution of English in place of Italian as the official language.

4. US: The Carnegie Institution is formed in Washington to promote study and research.

7. China: The Imperial Court returns to Peking; the Empress Dowager rules again.

8. Germany: Chancellor von Bulow makes aggressive reply to anti-German speech by Joseph Chamberlain.

9. US: New York State introduces a bill to stop public flirting.

10. London: Irish MPs pass resolutions protesting at interference in meetings and suppression of free speech (→14/2).

14. UK: Over 300 trade unions declare themselves in favour of universal state pensions.

16. Turkey: Germany is granted the right to build a railway between Konia and Baghdad.

17. Mexico: An earthquake in Mexico City kills more than 300 people.

18. US: Isthmian Canal Commission shifts support to Panama for new shipping canal (→25/6).

20. Switzerland: Referendum opposes separation of Church and State.

25. St. Petersburg: Russia abolishes the death penalty (→4/2).

28. UK: Census shows the population of Greater London is 6,581,372.

31. UK: First French soccer team plays in England; Paris loses 4-0 to Marlow Football Club.

BIRTHS

8. Soviet politician Georgi Malenkov (†14/1/88).

15. Saudi Arabian King Ibn Saud (†23/2/69).

Britain clinches Pacific deal with Japan

Jan 30. Britain and Japan today signed a treaty of alliance. It is essentially an arrangement for the defence of their parallel interests in China and Korea, with each side agreeing to respect the other's position in the area. In addition, both powers contracted not to make a treaty with third party countries without consultation.

When it became known that the treaty had been signed it was put down in Europe as the most outstanding diplomatic coup for years. Britain has pursued an expansionist policy in China, both commercially and otherwise, ever since the Opium War of 1839-42. But at a time when the Government feels that its interests are threatened by other European powers, the presence of an ally is reassuring.

Japan, too, has ambitions in China and the fact that, after the war she fought there in 1894-95, the combined might of Russia, France and Germany forced her to hand back the territory she had conquered in Southern Manchuria, reinforced the truth that she needed a European ally. Japan also felt alarmed after the Boxer Rebellion in China when Russia occupied southern Manchuria.

Thousands hit by smallpox outbreak

Jan 31. The number of smallpox victims today rose to 2,273 as doctors in London warned that only public support for a vaccination programme would halt the epidemic. The latest figure includes 878 patients still receiving care on special quarantine ships or at remote treatment centres on the banks of the River Thames.

Health authorities have opened vaccination clinics for the capital's population and ordered suspected cases to udergo further tests.

Infected homes will also be fumigated in an attempt to check the eight-month-old outbreak, which is said to be one of the worst in medical history.

Irish League links with US supporters

Jan 8. The United Irish League has decided at its annual convention in Dublin to give new emphasis to its cause in America. The League, which is the largest group in Ireland pushing for independence from Britain, is sending two of its leaders on a tour of America to argue the cause of Irish home rule.

The League's chairman, John Redmond MP, told the convention that the League was "growing like wildfire". With 1200 branches in Ireland, it is now looking to set up branches among Irish emigrants in America. At home, the Irish are urged to boycott businessmen who do not support the League's campaign (→14/2).

This year saw the launch of the Preussen, the only five-masted, full-rigged sailship ever built.

1902

FEBRUARY

Su	Mo	Tu	We	Th	Fr	Sa
						1
2	3	4	5	6	7	8
9	10	11	12	13	14	15
16	17	18	19	20	21	22
23	24	25	26	27	28	

1. China: Imperial decree abolishes binding of women's feet and ends the ban on mixed Chinese-Manchu marriages.

1. China: US protests at Russian privileges in China, saying they breach the open door policy.

4. Australia: England score 769 runs in a single test innings against Australia.

5. France: Miners' working day fixed at nine hours (→5/4).

6. Bulgaria: Education minister Kanchev is murdered by a Macedonian.

9. Paris: The Barnum and Bailey Circus siamese twins are successfully separated.

13. London: Government refuses to allow a German Boer relief committee to visit South African concentration camps.

14. Liverpool: Lord Rosebery makes speech saying he would never grant independence to Ireland (→1/9).

14. Italy: Martial law is declared in Trieste as strikes for reduced working hours lead to clashes.

15. Berlin: Underground railway is inaugurated.

18. London: 37,000-signature petition is presented by women textile workers to Parliament, demanding votes for women.

19. France: Vaccination against smallpox becomes obligatory.

20. Spain: 500 reported dead in Barcelona strike clashes (→31/5).

24. London: Post Office opens its telephone system to subscribers.

24. S. Africa: Heavy British defeat near Klerksdorp (→1/3).

25. US: Hubert Cecil Booth founds Vacuum Cleaner Co Ltd.

BIRTHS

4. US avaiator Charles Lindbergh (†26/8/74).

27. US author John Steinbeck (†20/12/68).

Yellow fever is carried by mosquitos

Feb 22. Major Walter Reed and Dr James Carroll of the United States Yellow Fever Commission published a report today confirming that the disease so endemic to the tropics is transmitted by a species of mosquito. On the commission's advice, the city of Havana is now instituting a programme to combat the virulent effect of mosquitos in the Cuban capital.

A Cuban doctor, Carlos Finlay, first advanced the theory that yellow fever was spread by a species of mosquito as far back as 1881. The Yellow Fever Commission then began investigations. In its preliminary report in 1900 the commission found that, in a two-month period, there were only three cases of yellow fever in 1400 non-immune Americans. In two cases, the victims had been bitten within five days of their illness.

Tragically, the investigation cost the life of one doctor, Jesse Lazear. Dr Lazear was bitten by an infected mosquito while collecting blood from yellow fever patients. He had been bitten before, without ill-effects, but died within a fortnight.

In their new report Major Reed, the president of the commission, and his colleague show that yellow fever can also be produced by the injection of both blood or filtered blood serum from infected patients. The organism introduced into the blood by the mosquito is able to pass through a fine porcelain filter and is smaller than any known bacteria. It may therefore be an ultra-microscopic organism known as a virus.

Rosebery forces split in Liberal Party

Feb 26. Lord Rosebery, former Liberal Prime Minister, announced today that he will head a new organisation called the Liberal League. Its aims are to revitalise the party and give it a fresh identity after a debilitating period of internal squabbling over policies and personalities.

Lord Rosebery, returning to public life after an absence of five years, referred in a letter to The Times to his "definite separation" from the the views of the party leader Sir Henry Campbell-Bannerman. He said that he wants "a clean slate" re-launch of Liberalism. His supporters include Herbert Asquith and Sir Edward Grey. David Lloyd George indicated that he continues to back Sir Henry. So the lines are drawn for a battle for the soul of the party between its Imperialist and Radical wings – in personality terms, between the rising stars Asquith and Lloyd George.

Parliamentary lobby talk was about a possible ultimate realignment of the main parties in British politics, with Lloyd George flirting even more than ever with the rising Labour group.

New ladies fashion, even adopted by elegant women.

Russian students go on strike

Feb 4. Russian students are now leading the political opposition to the Czarist government. More than 30,000 are now on strike throughout the country, supported by many among the more liberal of their professors. They are protesting at "temporary rules" giving the government new powers to curb the activities of student organizations. These were introduced by General Vannovsky, the Czar's Minister of Education, on December 22 1901. The government fears that revolutionaries among the students are planning acts of violence.

Boer commandos elude British troops

Three generations of Boers, from 15-year-old grandson to 65-year-old grandfather, personify a solidarity undimmed by military setbacks.

Feb 24. The roaming Boer commandos, who invaded Cape Colony last October and came within fifty miles of Cape Town, are being steadily pushed back, though the necessity for martial law in the colony remains. In his latest dispatch to London, Lord Kitchener says the Boers are in small scattered parties "very difficult to catch."

Several reports suggest that the most successful of the Boer leaders operating in the Cape is the young lawyer, Jan Smuts, who was Kruger's State Attorney. Smuts grew up in the Cape and thus is on familiar ground; he is believed to have persuaded several thousand Cape Dutch, who owe allegiance to the Crown, to become rebels.

By tying up a British force three times their own strength, Smuts and other commandos in the Cape have diverted forces Kitchener badly needed for his pursuit of better known Boer leaders, Steyn, de la Rey and (most sought after of all) Christian de Wet.

In the latest British sweep in the north eastern Orange River Colony, de Wet and his force appeared to be completely enclosed; once again, though, he escaped, although his son was captured.

The sophisticated Magneto Exchange of the National Telephone Company in London.

1902

MARCH

Su	Mo	Tu	We	Th	Fr	Sa
						1
2	3	4	5	6	7	8
9	10	11	12	13	14	15
16	17	18	19	20	21	22
23	24	25	26	27	28	29
30	31					

1. S. Africa: Over 900 Boers killed or captured during Kitchener's "great drive" on de Wet.

3. US: Supreme Court rules that dealing in financial "futures" is illegal speculation.

4. US: Creation of the AAA, American Automobile Association.

5. Paris: National miners' congress decides to strike for an eight-hour day (→ 22/5).

6. London: Army order gives soldiers the right to wear spectacles on or off duty.

7. London: Reported that Welsh colonists in Patagonia fear descendants will lose British characteristics.

7. S. Africa: Boers' victory over the British at Tweebosch (→ 10/4).

10. Turkey: Earthquake wipes out entire town of Tochangri.

11. Germany: Foreign Minister von Richthofen urges more sympathy towards the British.

12. London: Bill to limit miners' hours to eight a day is defeated on second reading.

13. Poland: Schools are shut as pupils refuse to sing Russian imperial anthem.

18. China: Rebellion in the southern regions reported to be spreading.

21. UK: A. Gorman's Shannon Lass wins the Grand National at Aintree.

22. Persia: The Shah signs an agreement with Britain to build a telegraph link between Europe and India.

23. S. Africa: Acting Transvaal President Schalk arrives at Pretoria under a white flag (→ 10/4).

23. Italy: Minimum working age raised from nine to 12 for boys, from 11 to 15 for girls.

28. Turkey: 90,000 troops mobilise in the face of Macedonian agitation.

DEATH

26. British colonial statesman Cecil Rhodes (*5/7/1853).→

Rhodes, architect of Empire, is dead

Rhodes: the visionary of an empire.

March 26. Cecil Rhodes, who gave his name to vast territories twice the size of France, died today in his seaside cottage near Cape Town aged 48. He had used his great wealth to advance the interests of the British Empire, and to establish Oxford scholarships for students from the Empire and America.

His huge fortune stemmed from his skill in consolidating all South African diamond mining under his direction. Prime Minister of the Cape for five years from 1890, he was brought down by the disastrous raid into the Transvaal, led by his friend, Dr Jameson.

Rhodes expressed a wish to be buried in the Matopos Hills in his beloved Rhodesia. Shortly before his death he was heard to inquire, "They don't change the names of countries, do they?" (→ 3/4)

Schools to be taken over by councils

March 23. Sweeping new powers for local councils over Britain's schools were outlined in the House of Commons today. For the first time, county councils and the larger urban councils will be responsible for all education in primary and secondary schools in their area.

Council education committees will also fund the voluntary or church schools in their area. This has angered liberals and nonconformist church leaders. They object to financial responsibility without powers to run the schools and plan to fight the bill.

1902

APRIL

Su	Mo	Tu	We	Th	Fr	Sa
		1	2	3	4	5
6	7	8	9	10	11	12
13	14	15	16	17	18	19
20	21	22	23	24	25	26
27	28	29	30			

1. France: Working day for women and children cut from 11 to 10.5 hours, but pay is also cut accordingly.

2. London: Edward German's opera "Merrie England" first performed at the Savoy Theatre.

3. S. Africa: Funeral of Cecil Rhodes.

4. S. Africa: Cecil Rhodes' will gives £6 million to fund scholarships to Oxford University for British Empire, US and German citizens.

7. US: Foundation of Texas Oil Company, or Texaco.

8. China: Treaty with Russia signed over Manchuria; Russia promises to withdraw troops.

9. London: The Underground Electric Railways Co. is incorporated.

10. S. Africa: Boers accept British terms of surrender (→ 31/5).

10. Rome: Italy breaks off diplomatic relations with Switzerland, which it accuses of fostering anarchist agitation.

12. London: Foundation stone laid of the Institute of Journalists.

13. France: M. Serpollet sets new motor car speed record of 74.5 mph at Nice.

14. London: Budget puts a penny on income tax, twopence duty on cheques and higher duty on grain.

15. Russia: Sipyagin, the head of the secret police, is murdered by socialist revolutionaries.

20. Paris: Exhibition opens at the Societe Nationale des Beaux-Arts of "modern style", or "Art Nouveau".

21. US: Morgan Steamship Co. announces it will provide a daily transatlantic service.

22. Glasgow: Magistrates require men to replace barmaids on licensed premises (→ 12/5).

26. London: Sheffield United beat Southampton 2-1 in the FA Cup Final.

Sino-Russian treaty over Manchuria

April 4. Russia and China have reached an agreement over Manchuria which should lead to the withdrawal of Russian troops within six months.

The Manchurian Treaty, which was drawn up after talks between the Russian minister Lessar and Prince Ching, has yet to be signed. But it has been accepted in principle by other interested powers such as Britain, the United States and Japan.

Essentially, the draft treaty says Russia will now overlook the Chinese attacks on Russian citizens living in three Manchurian provinces and along the Russian border during the disturbances in 1900. In response to these attacks Russia had sent troops in to occupy large areas of Manchuria. These regions will now be restored to Chinese authority.

But Russia is insisting on having a say in the number of Chinese troops to be kept in the three provinces and must be told of any increases in forces along the border, while for its part China has agreed to observe the 1886 Manchurian railway contract (→ 8).

Sir Henry Irving known as the "bishop actor" and seen here as Wolsey in Henry VIII, currently stars in Wills' Faust as Mephistopheles at the Lyceum.

Massive blaze strikes City of London

Horse-drawn fire appliances fight the blaze which gutted the Barbican.

April 22. A massive blaze destroyed several acres of the Barbican in the City of London last night, lighting up much of the metropolis in a lurid spectacle not seen in London for many years. A fierce wind swept through the narrow streets of the City centre, whipping up flames, visible over four miles away, which destroyed over 30 factories, warehouses and shops, despite the heroic efforts of nearly 400 firemen.

There were no serious casualties although several firemen were taken to hospital suffering from smoke inhalation. The blaze attracted hundreds of thrilled spectators, many of whom were on their way home from the theatre. Damage is estimated at over £1 million, and hundreds of workers now find themselves out of work.

State of emergency declared in Ireland

April 16. Twenty thousand people protested at a rally in Dublin's Phoenix Park today over proposals by the British government to impose tough new laws in Ireland. The Criminal Law and Procedure (Ireland) Act will enable courts to move to different venues and juries to be changed. British politicians hope that this will make it easier to secure convictions against members of the United Irish League currently leading boycotts against farmers and businessmen who do not support their campaign for a united Ireland.

Juries have been acquitting defendants, seeing them as "agitators against injustice". Under the new law, agitation will be classed as "lawlessness". Parts of Dublin are among the areas of Ireland where, in effect, what amounts to a state of emergency has been declared.

Twenty die as football stand collapses

April 5. Twenty people died and 200 others were badly hurt today when a stand collapsed at the Ibrox Park stadium in Glasgow during an England-Scotland football match, attended by 70,000 supporters.

Many of the dead were crushed as panicking fans fled onto the pitch. Other victims plunged 50 feet to the ground when the wooden northwest terracing gave way. Mounted police, unaware of what had happened, rode into the fleeing crowd, so play continued despite the disaster. Witnesses described how the screams of the injured, carried aloft on broken planks, became mixed with the partisan cheers at the Glasgow Rangers Football Club ground.

1902

MAY

Su	Mo	Tu	We	Th	Fr	Sa
				1	2	3
4	5	6	7	8	9	10
11	12	13	14	15	16	17
18	19	20	21	22	23	24
25	26	27	28	29	30	31

1. India: 416 die in Dacca tornado.

2. US: An estimated 200,000 miners go on strike in Pennsylvania for more pay, shorter hours and the recognition of their union (→15/10).

5. Germany: The Prussian government denies women the right to form political associations.

7. New Orleans: US rabbis discuss moving Jewish sabbath from Saturday to Sunday.

10. Germany: The Kaiser abolishes the dictatorship in Alsace-Lorraine.

15. Paris: Publication of "Claudine en menage" by Colette and of Alfred Jarry's "Le Surmale".

20. Cuba: US troops withdraw.

21. Germany: A bill is put before the Prussian parliament to hasten and intensify "Germanisation" of Polish territories (→5/6).

22. Paris: International Miners Congress votes for nationalisation of all mines.

22. US: President Roosevelt Theodore asks the new International Arbitration Court at The Hague to settle the United States' debt dispute with Mexico.

27. South America: Argentina and Chile sign bilateral armaments and arbitration treaties.

28. East Africa: Colonel Swayne leads a punitive raid against the Mad Mullah (→27/7).

29. London: Lord Rosebery opens The London School of Economics and Political Science.

30. Spain: King Alfonso XIII suspends the Madrid Cortes (Parliament) amid growing unrest.

31. Glasgow: Dr A.C. Faulds claims he can cure diabetes with eucalyptus leaves.

31. Spain: King Alfonso XIII declares martial law to quell spreading protests by Spanish workers.

British celebrate victory in Boer War

May 31. After two years and seven months the war that began with a string of British defeats is over. The Boer leaders arrived in Pretoria to meet Lord Milner, the High Commissioner, and Lord Kitchener, the Commander-in-Chief. Less than an hour before the expiry of the British deadline, at midnight on the last day of May, they signed the terms of surrender.

Though the Boer submission had been anticipated, the news did not become public in London until the next day, Sunday, when most people were attending church. At one service the vicar came back to the pulpit to make the announcement. In St. Paul's, the Bishop of Stepney read out Lord Kitchener's telegram and called on the congregation to sing hymn 279: "Now thank we all our God ...". Special editions of newspapers have been selling at six pence and a shilling.

To the last the Boers had hoped Germany would come to their rescue; but when the Boer leader Paul Kruger visited Germany the Kaiser refused to meet him. So, "with grief" the Boer commanders, meeting (under British protection) at the Transvaal border town of Vereeniging voted to accept the British terms: British colonial rule, with a promise of self-government later; £3 million British grant to assist reconstruction; question of votes for natives not to be decided before self-government granted.

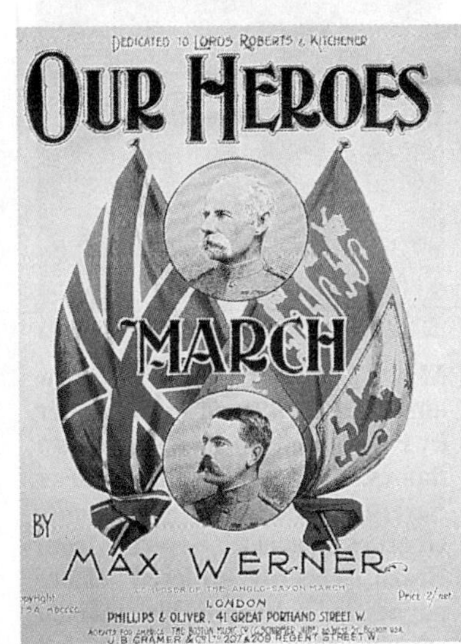

Victory inspired patriotic music like this march.

Melies makes first special effects movie

A scene from "A Trip to the Moon", produced by Georges Melies.

May 1. Entertainment by moving pictures has reached a new sophistication in Paris with the latest production of the astute M. Georges Melies, the former stage magician who has already made more than 100 short films at his studios.

The latest, "A Trip to the Moon", depicts a voyage into space by rocket, as well as fantastic forms of life on other planets. This latest example of Melies, "special effects" has attracted large crowds. Last year he showed "The India Rubber Head" in which he appeared to inflate his head to such a size as to dwarf everything else on the screen.

These tricks and effects, not possible in any other medium, are an advance on those of the pioneering Lumiere Brothers, who were content to record a train pulling into a station or workers leaving a factory. The great interest which was aroused by such scenes five years ago, when audiences were happy to sit and watch surf breaking on the screen, has much abated now that the novelty of the moving picture is wearing off.

May 12. The first flight of a new airship, Pax, turned into disaster in Paris today when it burst into flames, killing its pilot, Auguste Severo, and his mechanic, Georges Sachet. Severo, from Brazil, cheerily ordered champagne to celebrate his maiden voyage, then minutes later fell 1,600 feet to his death.

Barmaids win sex battle in Glasgow

May 12. Barmaids in Glasgow won a victory today when the appeal court reversed a ban on women bar staff and granted a licence to leading restaurateur Daniel Brown.

Last month Glasgow magistrates ruled that the services of all the city's barmaids should be dispensed with, to preserve good order, morality and propriety. It was said that barmaids are exposed to improper language, jests and suggestions, and that the average respectable life of a barmaid is only three years. The court decided not to renew the licences of employers who failed to comply with the ban. Only one employer, Daniel Brown, appealed. The magistrates said the decision had been taken for the benefit of certain susceptible young men, and old men too, but the appeal was sustained.

Volcano wipes out Martinique capital

May 8. The whole town of St. Pierre, capital of Martinique, has been wiped out by the massive eruption of Mount Pele, the largest mountain on the island.

About 30,000 people lived in St. Pierre, the largest town in the French West Indies and a major commercial centre. Only one person survived, a M. Cyparis, who was in prison for drunkenness at the time of the eruption.

Reports state that all buildings in the town were destroyed. Eyewitnesses report that most deaths were caused by asphyxiation from poisonous volcanic fumes (→ 1/9).

Thomas Edison invents battery

May 28. The American inventor Thomas Alva Edison today announced the invention of a new electrical storage battery which is lighter than the lead-acid type of batteries and also lasts longer.

The battery is made up of nickel and iron in an alkaline solution, and according to Edison its applications are greater than those of the older type, and will enable the electric motor car to remain a viable competitor for the petroleum-powered vehicle.

Edison numbers the phonograph and the electric light bulb among his long list of inventions.

Corsets designed for active women in sports.

1902

JUNE

Su	Mo	Tu	We	Th	Fr	Sa
1	2	3	4	5	6	7
8	9	10	11	12	13	14
15	16	17	18	19	20	21
22	23	24	25	26	27	28
29	30					

3. Zurich: International textile workers' congress votes to abolish piecework.

4. UK: Ard Patrick wins the Derby.

5. Germany: Kaiser Wilhelm calls for "Germanisation" of Slav subjects (→ 13/9).

7. Belgium: Mass strikes begin in favour of electoral reform.

9. S. Africa: 10% tax is imposed on the profits of goldmines in the Transvaal.

10. London: Ellen Terry and Herbert Beerbohm Tree open in "The Merry Wives of Windsor" at His Majesty's Theatre.

13. Finland: Russia intensifies the process of "Russianisation" by imposing Russian as the official language.

14. S. Africa: 16,500 Boer troops have now surrendered.

19. London: Royal Commission recommends the creation of a single dock authority for London.

23. The Triple Alliance (Germany, Austro-Hungary and Italy) is renewed for 12 years, although it may be cancelled after six (→ 1/11).

23. Switzerland: Albert Einstein starts work as a Confederal Patent Office functionary.

25. US: Nurse Jane Toppan is committed to a Massachusetts asylum after confessing to the murder of 31 people with poison.

27. France: Government closes more than 2,500 religious schools (→ 15/8).

27. UK: Near riot at Watford following postponement of coronation.

BIRTH

28. US musical composer Richard Rodgers (†30/12/79).

DEATH

18. English satirist Samuel Butler (*4/12/1835).

US pays $40 million for Panama Canal

June 28. The US Congress voted today to pass the bill introduced by Sen. Spooner. This authorises President Roosevelt to pay up to $40 million to buy the concession of a French Company which had tried for thirty years to build a canal across the Panama isthmus, between the Atlantic and Pacific Oceans.

In recent years Congress has been the battleground for two rival groups: the French company, promoted by the engineer Ferdinand de Lesseps, and an American group who wanted to build a canal across Nicaragua, farther to the north.

The Panama company is thought to have owed much of its success to the considerable lobbying skills of a New York lawyer, William Nelson Cromwell. He got the French company to drop its price to $40 million and shrewdly contributed $60,000 to Republican Party funds.

Concern about volcanoes was aroused after the eruption of Mount Pele in Martinique last month. When the Nicaraguan government denied that there was any active volcano on its route, Panama lobbyists sent to each Senator a Nicaraguan postage stamp depicting a volcano in eruption. Roosevelt is enthusiastic about the canal, which will shorten the distance of the sea route between the US coasts by 8,000 miles (→22/1/03).

Emergency operation delays Coronation

June 24. King Edward VII came safely through an emergency operation for appendicitis today in a hastily constructed operation room in Buckingham Palace. Afterwards it was announced that the Coronation, due to take place in Westminster Abbey in two days time, was being postponed indefinitely.

A medical bulletin issued by Buckingham Palace said that the King was recovering satisfactorily. He was in less pain and had taken some food. But the doctors warned: "It will be some days before it is possible to say that the King is out of danger."

When news of the delay broke the Bishop of London was rehearsing the ceremony at Westminster Abbey. With great presence of mind he promptly held a service of intercession for the King's complete restoration to health.

The postponement had widespread and unexpected repercussions. In London hotels, coronation visitors, invited from as far away as India and the African colonies, started to pack for the long journey home by sea (→9/8).

Edward VII at Sandringham before illness delayed his coronation.

Renault wins first Paris-Vienna race

June 29. The French car maker, Marcel Renault, roared into the Austrian capital today, the winner of the first Paris-Vienna motor race. Six other cars made by Renault Freres, the company he set up with his brother Louis, who also competed, followed him across the finishing line, taking second and third places in the light car class.

The race's decisive stretch came on the third day, when the 148 competitors tackled the 5912ft high Arlberg peak in western Austria. The descent was particularly dangerous; motorcar brakes had never before been put to such a test.

Marcel's final time of 26 hours, 10 minutes, 47 seconds even beat Europe's fastest train, the Arlberg Express. Its record for the run is 33 hours 43 minutes.

Sarah Bernhardt back in triumph

Sarah Bernhardt, successful in Paris and America, returns to London.

June 16. Madame Sarah Bernhardt, who first appeared on the London stage over 20 years ago, returned to triumph once again last night in her best-known role, Marguerite Gautier in "La Dame Aux Camelias".

London has seen her as Tosca, as Cleopatra, as Hamlet and only last year as the young Napoleon II. On each occasion she makes the audience forget her age (58), never more so than as the consumptive courtesan Marguerite. "She moves and lives before us as a weak, impulsive, passionate, but true woman," writes the critic of the Daily Telegraph. "The dry sobs which shake her whole frame, the tears which will not come, the heartbroken despair with which she writes her farewell letter to Armand are the indubitable proofs of Mme Bernhardt's mastery over our emotions."

Key conference prefers Empire

June 30. Representatives of the Dominions from all over the world gathered at the Colonial Office yesterday for the opening of the third Imperial Conference under the presidency of Joseph Chamberlain, the Secretary of State for the Colonies.

This conference will be of great importance to the economic development of the Empire, and the visiting premiers have made it plain that they expect the British government to protect their trade against foreign tariffs. It is anticipated that the subjects of "Empire Preference" and defence will dominate the conference (→11/8).

I'm looking out for you at Southend-on-Sea.

Southend is known as "East-London-by-the-Sea" as day-trips boom.

1902

JULY

Su	Mo	Tu	We	Th	Fr	Sa
		1	2	3	4	5
6	7	8	9	10	11	12
13	14	15	16	17	18	19
20	21	22	23	24	25	26
27	28	29	30	31		

1. Washington: Congress passes the Philippine Government Act, under which Filipinos will be ruled by a US Presidential commission.

3. London: House of Lords committee decides that betting will be restricted to the sites of sporting events.

5. Wimbledon: Hugh Doherty beats Arthur Gore in the Men's Singles Final; Muriel Robb beats Charlotte Sterry in the Ladies' Singles Final.

7. London: Colonial Secretary Joseph Chamberlain suffers deep head wound in a hansom cab accident.

8. S. Africa: Announced that Basuto chief Joel will be tried for high treason for helping the Boers.

9. Germany: Formula patented for barbituric acid, used for sleeping pills.

10. UK: Irish Nationalists renew their charges of jury packing.

11. London: King Edward VII confers the Order of the Garter on Archduke Franz Ferdinand, heir to Habsburg Empire.

12. London: Lord Kitchener given triumphal welcome on return from S. Africa (→ 4/10).

15. Paris: International conference opens for the suppression of white slavery.

16. London: 8 Bills for the building of London underground lines receive their second reading.

18. St. Petersburg: Russia announces its intention to restore Manchuria to China.

25. US: Heavyweight champ James Jeffries knocks out Robert Fitzsimmons.

27. Africa: Reported that the British have defeated the Mad Mullah in Somaliland (→ 5/11).

BIRTHS

7. Italian actor and film director Vittorio de Sica (†13/11/74).

28. Austrian-born British philosopher Karl Popper.

Dramatic collapse of Venice bell tower

Devastation in Venice, shortly after the Campanile tower collapsed.

July 14. The Campanile of St. Mark's Cathedral in Venice, one of the oldest and most celebrated gothic towers in Italy, today collapsed as architects carried out a safety inspection. Dating back to the year 902, and 322 feet high, the tower was reduced to rubble in less than a minute.

The belfry, topped by a bronze statue of an angel, had been weakened by a bolt of lightning nearly 160 years ago. Troops later stood guard on the ruins.

Fresh riots flare in Russia

July 3. In an effort to halt bloody riots spreading through southern Russia, Czar Nicholas today offered to confer with representatives of the people. The Czar said he was ready to hold private audiences with more than 200 Russians from all walks of life, including professors, editors and political prisoners.

The riots have centred on Rostov-on-Don, where clashes with troops have led to the death and injury of thousands. The public has been confused by fanatical worker organisations destroying factories and machinery while claiming they have the approval of the Czar. At the same time they have managed to persuade peasants that their poverty is the result of the government's drive for industrialisation.

Opposition to the Czar's offer of talks has come from his ministers, apparently because they fear for his safety. But there was agreement that something had to be done to prevent more rioting.

Balfour takes over as Prime Minister

July 12. Arthur James Balfour, already First Lord of the Treasury, became Prime Minister today. He has been Leader of the House of Commons for the past seven years. With peace restored in South Africa, the King felt he could at last allow Lord Salisbury to relinquish the Premiership – a move which he has wished to make for the past two years.

Taking over: Arthur Balfour.

London's poor eat the King's dinner

July 6. King Edward treated the poor of London to dinner tonight, with music and singing to celebrate his accession to the throne. In all, it is estimated that 456,000 people sat down to dinner as guests of the King.

The dinners took place at over 700 venues and, in all its long history, it seems unlikely that London had ever seen such a feast. It cost the King £30,000 but many others chipped in with contributions, notably the brewers. Over 1500 entertainers were booked for the occasion, with pianists moving round from one hall to another, all giving their services free. Family pianos were offered so that no dinner would be without a singsong, and thousands volunteered to act as helpers. At the Inns of Court, barristers rolled up their sleeves and washed the potatoes, before waiting on some of the King's less prosperous subjects.

Everywhere buildings were transformed, none more so than in Covent Garden where the big hall was bedecked with flowers and Chinese lanterns. In Lambeth, no fewer than 6,000 people were fed plum puddings cooked over a fire in a trench.

The King himself, from his sickbed in Buckingham Palace where he is recovering from an operation, sent a message to each local mayor, regretting that he could not be present. But some of his family did turn up. The Prince and Princess of Wales visited more than a score of dinners in the East End of London.

Dinner party: RSVP to the Palace.

1902

AUGUST

Su	Mo	Tu	We	Th	Fr	Sa
					1	2
3	4	5	6	7	8	9
10	11	12	13	14	15	16
17	18	19	20	21	22	23
24	25	26	27	28	29	30
31						

1. Australia: 100 miners killed in explosion at Wollongong.

3. London: The Post Office sends its first parcel mail to the US on the White Star liner "Teutonic" (→ 26).

4. London: Report is issued on the alleged dislike of Southern Rhodesian natives for regular and prolonged work.

11. London: King Edward VII gives Osborne House, favourite residence of Queen Victoria, to the nation.

12. S. America: Venezuelan rebels sack consulates in Barcelona province (→ 18/10).

14. London: Formation of the Imperial Vaccination League, which aims to eradicate smallpox.

15. France: 15,000 people demonstrate against the planned closure of convent schools in Brittany.

16. London: Britain, Germany, the United States and Japan sign the Chinese Tariff Protocol (→ 5/9).

18. London: Shah of Persia begins a visit to the United Kingdom.

21. Belfast: Harland and Wolff shipyard launch the 21,000-ton "Cedric", world's largest ship.

25. New York: The intrepid Harry de Windt successfully completes his 248-day trek from Paris to New York via Siberia.

26. London: It is announced that the General Post Office and the American Express Company have agreed to carry parcels between the UK and the US.

29. Egypt: 5,540 deaths reported in cholera epidemic (→ 21/9).

30. London: Labour MP James Keir Hardie addresses London meeting protesting at House of Lords' Taff Vale decision (→ 3/9).

BIRTHS

6. German opera singer Margarete Klose (†14/12/68).

8. British physicist Paul A.M. Dirac (†1984).

Vivat Rex: Edward VII is crowned

Aug 9. King Edward VII was crowned at Westminster Abbey today. After 64 years, and before most of the monarchs of Europe, the crown has passed to a sovereign already in his sixtieth year.

The streets of London were packed on a bright sunny day to see the royal procession. The women wore dresses studded with diamonds, and adding to the colour of the scene were the uniforms of the military inside and outside the abbey. There were loud cheers for Sir Alfred Gaselee, who led British troops in China, and Lord Kitchener, fresh from successes in the Boer War. The ministers of the crown were there too, headed by Arthur Balfour, the prime minister. Then came the King's Danish-born wife, Alexandra, greeted by shouts of "Vivat Alexandra ! Vivat". Finally, there was the King himself, striding purposefully to the altar flanked by the Bishop of Durham and the Bishop of Bath and Wells.

Before the Coronation there had been concern expressed about the King's health, as it was less than two months since the operation to remove the king's appendix. It was therefore decided to shorten the ceremony. So the King did not carry the heavy sword of state to the high altar, and the walk to different points of the altar to make declarations to the four points of the compass was also dropped. Instead, the King made the declarations standing beside his chair.

After years as heir apparent, Edward at last is crowned king.

Although he appeared in good health, nobody was taking any chances. The two nurses who attended him during his illness were in a gallery above the coronation chair, each ready with a black bag of medicines in case the King should need assistance.

However, it was not the King but the Archbishop of Canterbury who needed medical attention. He felt faint and had to retire to St. Edward's Chapel to rest. He returned to the high altar, but was clearly far from well. Having sworn allegiance to his new sovereign on behalf of the clergy of the Church of England, the archbishop had to be helped to his feet.

Threatened American buffalo saved by law from extinction

Aug 23. The American buffalo is thriving, compared, that is, to the state it was in thirteen years ago when there were only 551 buffalo in the country and it seemed the breed was on the verge of extinction. However, the stricter Federal game laws enacted in 1889 have had the desired effect, and now there are two herds of more than 1000 head in Yellowstone Park and Canada.

In 1800 there were vast herds of about 60 million buffalo roaming the Great Plains; they were hunted by the Indians, who depended on them for food and clothing. However, they were ruthlessly slaughtered by European settlers, and almost wiped out.

Once common on the Great Plains, the buffalo almost became extinct.

1902

SEPTEMBER

Su	Mo	Tu	We	Th	Fr	Sa
	1	2	3	4	5	6
7	8	9	10	11	12	13
14	15	16	17	18	19	20
21	22	23	24	25	26	27
28	29	30				

1. Dublin: State of emergency declared (→ 14).

3. Austria: A huge landslide in Transcaucasia kills 700 people.

5. London: Britain and China sign commercial treaty.

8. South America: Colombian rebels defeat government troops in several clashes.

9. East Africa: British and Italians plan joint offensive against the Mad Mullah in Somaliland.

10. London: Royal commission is appointed to investigate British military preparations for the Boer War.

13. Germany: Nationalist group "The German Union of the Eastern Marches", meeting at Danzig, demands harsher measures to suppress Polish culture and language.

14. UK: 20,000 people demonstrate in Phoenix Park, Dublin, against the British government's strict measures to maintain law and order (→ 23/10).

17. South Africa: Martial law is lifted in Cape Colony (→ 4/10).

19. London: Stanley Spencer makes 30-mile flight in an airship of his own invention.

21. Egypt: The current cholera epidemic, which has claimed 26,554 lives, is now reported to be abating.

22. Finland: Czar abolishes nominal Finnish autonomy and appoints a Russian governor general.

25. Italy: Hundreds die as a tornado strikes the Catania region of Sicily.

28. South Africa: A total of 15,000 applications for gold mining licences have been received in a single week.

30. UK: The shipping company Cunard agrees to hold its entire fleet at disposal of UK government for an annual fee.

DEATH

29. French writer Emile Zola (*12/4/1840).→

Unions launch drive for Labour MPs

Sept 3. The Trades Union Congress meeting in Holborn Town Hall voted today to form a central organisation to get Labour candidates into Parliament and to advise them after winning seats. Congress was urged to nurture the infant Labour Representation Committee because it is the TUC's own child. Delegates reported that constituency deals with the Liberal Party are proving unsatisfactory. "I would prefer to let a Tory in sooner than bargain with the Liberals", one said. It was agreed that Labour candidates should fight independently from other parties whenever possible.

A fraternal delegate from the American Federation of Labour advised his British bretheren to respect the motto "Reason, not force" and said that putting up union candidates in the United States had been a failure.

Liberal MP David Lloyd George was allowed to address the TUC "to beg bread for the thousands of Penrhyn quarrymen" now in a two-year-long dispute over union recognition in a remote Welsh valley. He was cheered when he cried: "They are standing firm as the rock they have hewn for Lord Penrhyn". However, the quarrymen and their families are now reported to be totally destitute.

Keir Hardie: pioneering the way.

Automobile club begins reliability trials

Sept 1. A total of 63 motor cars took part in reliability trials driving from Crystal Palace to Folkestone and back today, and showed to everyone's satisfaction that they are now almost as reliable as railways as a means of transport.

The trials, organised by the Automobile Club, were designed to see how each vehicle performed over the 139 mile route fully laden with passengers and keeping firmly to an eight miles per hour speed limit through towns.

A maximum of two hours was allowed to prepare each car before they set off at 20 second intervals. Most managed to complete the course without mishap, although there were some unfortunate incidents of horses annoying motorists along the way.

Five for the road in 1902 with cricketer Dr W.G. Grace next to driver.

Zola, who defended Dreyfus, is dead

Sept 29. Emile Zola, the great French writer and valiant champion of Captain Dreyfus, has died at his home in Paris, suffocated by fumes from a blocked chimney, only a day after returning from the countryside.

A servant found M. Zola and his wife after hearing groans from their bedroom at around nine o'clock this morning. Mme Zola was revived but the author of "Germinal" and "Therese Raquin" was beyond help, and had probably died a few minutes earlier.

Zola made enemies through his defence of Dreyfus. But with the emergence of the truth about the Jewish officer's trumped up crimes and his eventual pardon, Zola won only respect. All France is shocked by his death (→ 5/10).

Emile Zola, campaigning author.

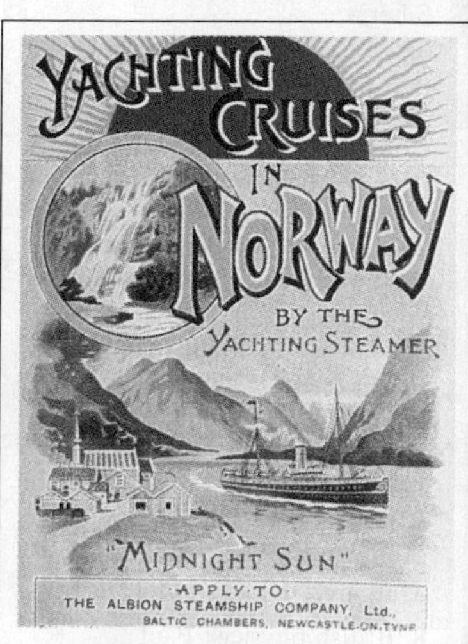

Sea cruises to the fjords offered alternatives to sun further south.

1902

OCTOBER

Su	Mo	Tu	We	Th	Fr	Sa
			1	2	3	4
5	6	7	8	9	10	11
12	13	14	15	16	17	18
19	20	21	22	23	24	25
26	27	28	29	30	31	

2. Switzerland: Immigrant workers expelled as strikes lead to rioting.

4. S. Africa: Martial law repealed in Natal (→4/12).

5. Paris: Author Anatole France tells congregation at Emile Zola's funeral: "He was a moment of the human conscience".

6. South Africa: 2,000 mile railway between Cape Town and Beira in Mozambique is completed.

7. UK: It is announced that Windsor Castle will be open to the public when the court is absent.

7. Indochina: France and Siam sign a treaty to settle Siamese frontier and Mekong basin.

9. France: Two-thirds of all French miners go out on strike.

11. Boston: Decision announced to establish a steamship service between Canada and the UK.

12. Egypt: 32,000 people are now reported dead from cholera.

15. US: Coal strike ends when President Roosevelt threatens to send troops in to work the mines.

17. US: The first Cadillac motor car is made in Detroit and sold in Buffalo, New York State.

18. South America: President Castro of Venezuela defeats rebels after a week-long battle.

19. Far East: The Royal Navy is removing all stores to Hong Kong, now the sole UK naval base along China's coast.

24. Paris: French cyclist Henri Contenet achieves new speed record of 48 mph (pulled by motorcycle).

30. South America: Colombian revolt is contained to Panama isthmus as General Marjarres defeats General Uribe-Uribe.

31. Pacific: UK-Australia cable reaches Fiji.

BIRTH

2. British author Roy Campbell (†22/4/57).

Irish passions disrupt Commons

Oct 23. Arthur Balfour, the Prime Minister, narrowly escaped assault during violent scenes in the House of Commons today. An Irish member, O'Donnell, suddenly went berserk and broke loose from colleagues trying to restrain him. He dashed shrieking across the floor of the House to the Government front bench. There he repeatedly shook his fists within inches of the Prime Minister's face. There were shouts of "Send for the police", and other ministers gathered around Mr Balfour to protect him.

Mr O'Donnell was eventually exhausted by his own disorderly behaviour and went back to his own seat. There was just sufficient time to cancel a request for the constabulary to enter the debating chamber to restore order. Mr O'Donnell unexpectedly disappeared before the House voted to suspend him from its service. Passions had flared in the first place when Mr Balfour calmly declared that it was neither necessary nor desirable for the House to debate the condition of Ireland during this particular sitting.

Passions flare in the House: a French view of parliamentary strife.

Theodore Roosevelt settles coal strike

Oct 15. At 2.20 a.m. today the White House in Washington was able to announce the end of the damaging five-month strike in the Pennsylvania anthracite coalfield. President Roosevelt intervened by appointing a commission of inquiry to "inquire into, consider and pass upon all questions at issue between the operators and the miners". The miners, led by John Mitchell, the young President of the United Mine Workers, sought a wage increase, recognition of the union, and a nine-hour day.

The coal operators are mainly railroad companies, like the Pennsylvania and Reading Railroad, whose President, George F. Baer, said working men should trust, not in "labour agitators, but (in) the Christian men to whom God ... has given control of the property interests in this country". The end of the strike is a victory for the union and for President Roosevelt.

Crowds protest over school reforms

Oct 14. The great debate about the future of Britain's schools came to London tonight with a rally of opponents to the government's Education Bill. This followed the demonstration in Leeds, when over 80,000 people were estimated to have protested about proposals to make councils fund church schools without any power to run them. "No rate without control" was the cry again of the self-styled "progressives". Other critics have opposed the principle of sectarian schooling as such, but ministers argue that most people want some form of religious instruction for their children. They do not accept that this means indoctrination, as has been alleged by some nonconformist churchmen and their political supporters.

How the Rhino got his Skin: one of the illustrations by Rudyard Kipling from his "Just So Stories" written for children and published this year with great popular success.

1902

NOVEMBER

Su	Mo	Tu	We	Th	Fr	Sa
						1
2	3	4	5	6	7	8
9	10	11	12	13	14	15
16	17	18	19	20	21	22
23	24	25	26	27	28	29
30						

1. London: 15,000 Liberals demonstrate against the Education Bill at Alexandra Palace.

1. Paris: France tries to sign a secret agreement with Italy in which both countries agree to remain neutral in Africa.

4. London: J.M. Barrie's "The Admirable Crichton" is first performed at the Duke of York's Theatre.

5. Somaliland: The Mad Mullah and 17,000 men are reported to be advancing on British troops at Bohodle.

8. London: Kaiser Wilhelm II begins a 12-day visit to try to improve Anglo-German relations.

12. Italian tenor Enrico Caruso's recording of "Vesti la Gubbia" has sold one million copies.

13. North Africa: Royal Navy cruisers are sent to Tetuan following the outbreak of a rebellion.

15. Belgium: Attempted assassination of King Leopold II by anarchist Gennaro Rubino (→ 10/2/03).

24. Paris: World's first professional photography conference opens.

25. South America: Colombia rejects US canal offer (→ 4/12).

26. New Zealand: Fifth consecutive general election victory for the Progressive Party.

27. US: President Roosevelt says skin colour is no bar to public office.

29. Copenhagen: Carl Nielsen's opera "Saul and David" is first performed.

BIRTHS

9. British film director Anthony Asquith (†21/2/68).

29. Italian author Carlo Levi (†4/1/75).

DEATH

22. Germany's wealthiest man, steel magnate Friedrich Krupp (*17/2/1854).→

Tennyson appointed Australian governor

Nov 20. Lord Tennyson, the son and biographer of the Victorian Poet Laureate, was appointed Governor-General of Australia today. Lord Tennyson – who, though trained as a lawyer in London, is something of a poet himself – has been Governor of South Australia since 1899. At his own request, the appointment will be for one year only.

He replaces the Earl of Hopetoun, Australia's first Governor-General, who has resigned after a row over expenses. Lord Hopetoun spent heavily on entertaining the Duke and Duchess of York when they visited Melbourne for the opening of the first federal Parliament in May 1901. Despite being awarded £10,000 by the House of Representatives, he declares he is still £15,000 out of pocket. Lord Tennyson has now agreed favourable financial arrangements with the Australian government.

Poet in politics: Lord Tennyson.

Steel magnate Krupp dies of apoplexy

Friedrich Krupp, who expanded his father's existing steel business.

Nov 22. The shocked Krupp steel family was in mourning today after the sudden death from apoplexy of Friedrich Krupp, aged only 48. He had taken over as head of Germany's largest manufacturing firm in 1887 when his father Alfred had died.

The firm expanded massively in the last century, largely thanks to Bismarck's incessant wars, and had a reputation for providing the best wages and welfare conditions in Germany. Under Friedrich, despite fierce competition, the company continued to expand, adding armour plating and shipbuilding to making guns.

Nov 22. Fire destroyed the Williamsburg Bridge across the East River in New York today. The bridge had not been completed when sparks set alight the wooden walkway. Nearby riverside houses were evacuated.

1902

DECEMBER

Su	Mo	Tu	We	Th	Fr	Sa
	1	2	3	4	5	6
7	8	9	10	11	12	13
14	15	16	17	18	19	20
21	22	23	24	25	26	27
28	29	30	31			

1. Vienna: Austria and Russia agree joint supervision of reforms in Macedonia.

3. South Africa: The British South Africa Company decides to spend £2 million on railways in Rhodesia.

7. Venezuela: The United Kingdom and Germany ask the government to compensate for losses incurred during President Cipriano Castro's 1899 coup (→ 9).

9. Venezuela: British and German warships seize the Venezuelan navy, demanding settlement of compensation claims (→ 19).

9. Switzerland: The Swiss parliament approves the construction of a railway through Simplon.

13. London: First meeting of the Committee of Imperial Defence.

16. Central Asia: A huge earthquake in Turkestan kills 4,000.

18. Moscow: Premiere of "Les bas-fonds" by Maxim Gorki.

19. Venezuela: The UK and Germany are joined by Italy in a naval blockade of Venezuelan ports (→ 31).→

21. Canada: Guglielmo Marconi sends first transatlantic telegraph message, to King Edward VII in London.

24. London: W.W. Astor makes a gift of £50,000 to the Great Ormond Street Children's Hospital.

30. Spain: The Spanish government sends battleships to Tangiers and prepares to invade Morocco.

HITS OF 1902

Bill Bailey won't you please come home.

In the good old summer time.

QUOTE OF THE YEAR

"Perhaps it is God's will to lead the people of South Africa through defeat and humiliation to a better future and a brighter day." Boer leader **Jan Smuts** at the Vereeniging peace talks.

Peter Rabbit makes his literary debut

One of the smallest yet most charming books for young children to appear for many years is "The Tale of Peter Rabbit" by a new author, **Beatrix Potter**, who also paints the delightful watercolour illustrations. These depict Peter and his friends and relations in the rabbit world dressed in becoming human clothes, but the effect is wonderfully natural because of the artist's delicate taste. The tale, told in a few sentences per page, is mercifully unsentimental.

How the camel got its hump and why cats like to walk by themselves are two of the piquant tales for children which **Mr Kipling** calls "Just So Stories" and which are perfect for reading aloud.

Beatrix Potter, with dog.

Sir Arthur Conan Doyle has luckily been coaxed into allowing us one more Sherlock Holmes story, although that ingenious gentleman is defunct. "The Hound of the Baskervilles", which comes from an earlier era in his career, is a story which it is not advisable to read on a dark night, especially on the moors.

It has been a rich year for fiction with **Arnold Bennett's** "Anna of the Five Towns" and more prophetic visions from **H.G. Wells'** in "The First Men on the Moon". But the most effective and disturbing work of fiction to appear is **Joseph Conrad's** "Heart of Darkness" which goes up the Congo in search of a Mr Kurtz, and into the depths of the human soul.

Aswan dam finally tames the Nile

The Aswan dam: harbinger of an agricultural revolution in Egypt.

Dec 10. After four years of construction with a workforce of 11,000, the massive Nile dam at Aswan, 590 miles south of Cairo, was declared completed today.

The dam is one and a quarter miles long and 130 feet high. It has been built to contain the annual flood waters of the Nile for gradual release throughout the dry period of the Egyptian year. Already, a 200-mile lake is beginning to build up behind the new dam, which is expected to revolutionise Egyptian irrigation methods and to reclaim vast areas of arid land for agricultural use.

Despite archaeologists' concern at the submersion of ancient monuments, the practical applications of the new dam have been generally welcomed.

British gunboats bombard Venezuela

Dec 31. Venezuela's president, Cipriano Castro, has agreed to abide by any ruling of the Hague Tribunal over the international dispute which has paralysed his nation this month. Venezuela seeks removal of the British and German fleets from its harbours, plus the dismissal of debts allegedly owed to these two nations. Both European powers will appear before the Hague Tribunal to demand payment of these arrears.

The crisis flared on December 7 when British and German ambassadors sought immediate repayment of losses suffered during the 1899 Venezuelan coup. Some of those losses were incurred when railways previously owned by Europeans were taken over by Venezuela. President Castro claims neither he nor the appropriate congressional committee were aware of any liabilities. But two days later, the British and German fleets sailed into La Guayvra harbour and seized the entire Venezuelan navy – four battleships. Since then, both sides have engaged in brief skirmishes. After its fleet was taken, Venezuela arrested Britons and Germans in Caracas. The two foreign navies replied by bombarding a fortress. America's President Roosevelt declined to mediate, so now the peace moves will switch to The Hague (→ 13/2/03).

European ships on the attack.

Army doctor wins a Nobel Prize

Dec 10. Major Ronald Ross was awarded this year's Nobel Prize for Medicine for his work on the causes of malaria. His discovery that the deadly disease is transmitted by the bite of a female mosquito is a major advance in the search for a cure.

The Peace prize is shared by Elie Ducommun and Swiss statesman and peace bureau founder Charles Gobat. The other laureates are German historian Theodor Mommsen, chemist Emil Fischer for his carbohydrates research, and the Dutch scientists Hendrik Lorentz and Pieter Zeeman for their electromagnetic radiation work.

Ross: prize-winner for medicine.

Half a million buys 82 acres of London

Dec 1. Cheers broke out in the great hall of Winchester House last night when 82 acres of land around Earl's Court were sold at auction for £565,000. Although this is the most valuable London estate to come under the hammer, the auctioneer, before banging his gavel, urged the bidders, "Do consider what you are missing. This property is honestly worth a million."

The estate, which was bought by an agent for an anonymous bidder, was part of the property of Lord Kensington and consists of 1450 town houses, flats, shops and other buildings yielding a ground rent of £18,000. Not long ago it was a market garden.

1903

JANUARY

Su	Mo	Tu	We	Th	Fr	Sa
				1	2	3
4	5	6	7	8	9	10
11	12	13	14	15	16	17
18	19	20	21	22	23	24
25	26	27	28	29	30	31

1. Germany: New orthography rules introduced throughout German-speaking world, replacing *c* by *k*, and *th* by *t*, for example.

2. US: President Roosevelt closes post office in Missouri, for refusing to employ a black postmistress (→ 14).

4. E. Africa: British General Manning lands at Obbia to prepare an attack on the Mad Mullah (→ 24/2).

10. S. America: Argentina and Chile sign a treaty of disarmament.

11. Turkey: Russian torpedo boats reported to have passed through the Dardanelles secretly.

12. Paris: First meeting of the Goncourt Academy (→ 21/12).

13. Polynesia: Tidal wave sweeps through Society and Tuamoto Islands, causing thousands of deaths.

13. Morocco: The Sultan flees from Fez; Pretender's army defeats Sultan's troops (→ 1/2).

14. Washington: Blacks demand pensions for ex-slaves (→ 30/6).

16. Paris: The government is condemned in the Assembly for forbidding the use of Breton in churches (→ 18/3).

19. Paris: A new bicycle race is announced for 1903, called the "Tour de France" (→ 19/7).

19. China: The Imperial Government announces it is unable to meet reparations for the Boxer Rebellion (→ 10/2).

20. Vienna: Talks about equal status for Czechs in Bohemia-Moravia collapse after opposition from German-speakers.

24. Washington: US and UK create joint commission to determine Alaskan frontier (→ 16/10).

27. UK: 51 die at a fire in a mental hospital at Colney Hatch, north of London.

BIRTHS

10. British sculptress Barbara Hepworth (†21/5/75).

11. South African author Alan Paton (†12/4/88).

India acclaims Edward VII as Emperor

The Viceroy Lord Curzon, and his wife, lead the procession into the Indian capital, Delhi.

Jan 1. The proclamation of Edward VII as Emperor of India took place today on the great plains near Delhi. At a signal from the Viceroy, Lord Curzon, who was seated on a glittering gold and white dais, the trumpets sounded and a lone horseman rode up and read a proclamation. Lord Curzon then read a message from the new Emperor and announced that there would be a remission of interest on British loans for those states suffering from famine.

Next, 100 potentates and princes of Indian states went in procession to the dais with messages for the new Emperor, led by the Nizam of Hyderabad in blue frock coat and yellow turban.

There was fantasy as well when the Shans who guard the frontier on the Mekong performed a walking version of a pagoda.

US signs treaty for Panama Canal

Jan 22. The US and the Republic of Colombia today signed a treaty which will allow the construction of a Panama Canal. The signatories were the Secretary of State, John Hay, and the Charge d'Affaires of Colombia, Tomas Herran.

The exact terms of the treaty are not known, but it is believed that the Colombian government has ceded to the United States the right to build a canal and a strip of land six miles wide in exchange for an annual rental and a sum in gold.

The treaty must be ratified by the US Senate. The idea of building a canal over the isthmus of Central America, either at Panama or in Nicaragua, is an old one. The last attempt, by the French, ended in disaster, with 20,000 workers dead of fever, and political scandals in Paris. An isthmian canal will have great strategic value to the United States, and has the keen support of President Roosevelt (→ 14/3).

Report offers new deal for Irish tenants

Jan 3. The two persistent Irish problems of land ownership and high farm rents took a step nearer to solution today with the publication of the report of the Irish Land Conference. Supported by both Unionists and Nationalists, it suggests that tenants should be helped by reordering rental payments. The report says that a first payment of one-third of the capital, as set down by the Gladstone government in 1869, was much more than most Irish tenants could afford. It further recommended that landlords whose property was purchased by the government should also be compensated.

Wizard flies in

Jan 20. New York is buzzing with talk of the latest musical spectacular to hit Broadway. The show they all want to see is an adaptation of L. Frank Baum's highly popular children's book "The Wonderful Wizard of Oz", published in 1899.

A modern fairy-tale, it recounts the adventures of Dorothy, a farm girl from Kansas, who is blown to the magical land of Oz by a cyclone. In Oz, she meets a Tin Man, a Scarecrow and a Cowardly Lion, who accompany her on her journey to the Wizard.

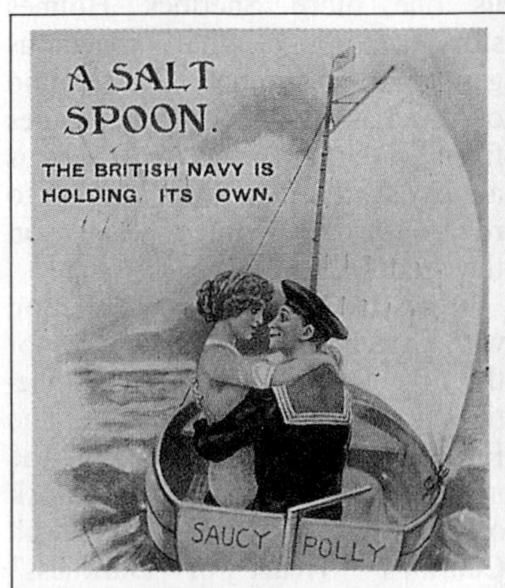

Jolly Jack Tar: the popular view of a life on the ocean wave.

1903

FEBRUARY

Su	Mo	Tu	We	Th	Fr	Sa
1	2	3	4	5	6	7
8	9	10	11	12	13	14
15	16	17	18	19	20	21
22	23	24	25	26	27	28

1. Morocco: Pretender's army is routed (→22/4).

3. Nigeria: British under General Morley occupy Kano (→15/3).

4. London: New headquarters of the National Society for the Prevention of Cruelty to Children opens.

7. Turkey: The Sultan orders the mobilisation of 240,000 troops for Macedonia (→23).

10. Brussels: Rubino, would-be assassin of King Leopold, is sentenced to life imprisonment.

10. London: The County Council names two new streets: Kingsway (after King Edward VII) and Aldwych.

12. UK: Dr Randall Davidson becomes Archbishop of Canterbury.

13. Washington: Envoys sign British peace protocol lifting blockade of Venezuela (→22/3).

19. Vienna: The government decrees a two-year conscription period for the Austrian army.

20. Berlin: Kaiser Wilhelm II declares his faith in Christian orthodoxy to reassure church leaders.

21. S. Africa: Chamberlain makes an important speech in Cape Town regarding the future of the colony.

23. Turkey: The Sultan accepts Austrian and Russian proposals for reforms in Macedonia (→14/4).

26. London: The Commons debates call to restrict immigration into the UK.

BIRTHS

13. Belgian novelist Georges Simenon (†4/9/89).

21. French author Raymond Queneau (†25/10/76).

26. Italian chemist Giulio Natta (†2/5/79).

DEATHS

22. Austrian composer Hugo Wolf (*13/3/1860).

26. US inventor of the rapid-fire gun, Richard Gatling (*12/9/1818).→

Traffic problems force official inquiry

Feb 6. The Board of Trade today announced the appointment of a Royal Commission, under the chairmanship of Sir David Barbour, to report on ways of improving the capital's rail and tramway facilities. It will also look at how road and pedestrian traffic should best be organized to ease increasing traffic congestion in London.

Schemes requiring Parliament's permission to extend the tube and other means of locomotion are unlikely to be approved until the commission submits its findings.

The Prime Minister, Mr Balfour, is known to believe that London's transport problems could be eased if a network of roads was built extending from the centre to the suburbs, for the exclusive use of rapid transport. No doubt his views will be sympathetically considered by the commission (→14/7).

Early 20th century rush hour: horsepower is no match for shanks's pony.

Porcelain set to replace gold fillings

Feb 16. How porcelain could be used to restore teeth was disclosed to 2,000 American dentists today at the 15th anniversary meeting of the Orthontographic Society of Chicago. Porcelain can be used to replace the more expensive gold, silver or amalgam of other metals when filling teeth.

The new method of fitting porcelain faces to broken crowns has also been expounded within the last month by Carl Schelling, a British dentist. Despite the obvious advantages of using a cheaper material for dental repairs, some reservations have been expressed. These arose partly because the first patient still had gold backing the porcelain face.

Man who gave his name to a gun dies

Feb 26. The inventor of the gun which changed the face of modern warfare, Dr. Richard Gatling, died yesterday in New York aged 84.

Early Gatling guns developed during the American Civil War fired only 250 shots a minute compared to the current 3,000 shots and Dr Gatling hoped that because the gun could be fired by one man alone it could save a complete army from indiscriminate enemy fire.

Dr. Gatling sold his interest in the machine gun to the Colt Firearms Company after 30 years and although he made a lot of money from this and other inventions he lost a lot by investing in American railways.

He was born on a farm and helped his father design a device for thinning cotton. He went on to invent a machine for sowing rice and at the time of his death was designing a new plough.

March on the Mad Mullah begins

Feb 24. A detachment of the British field force operating against the "Mad" Mullah in Italian Somaliland struck from the Indian Ocean port of Obbia today. Commanded by General Manning, who is accompanied by Count Lovateli, the Italian representative, the flying column includes the Punjab Mounted Infantry and the Camel Corps.

The Mullah, Mohammed bin Abdullah, who claims to possess supernatural powers, first caused trouble when he began raiding tribes friendly to the British. Calling himself Mahdi, or Messiah, he believes he is destined to convert others to Islam.

After clashes with the British he fled into Italian territory and lay low for two years until the raids began again recently. Though General Manning's force is driving west into the interior, the Mullah's present whereabouts are unknown.

A transport arrived at Obbia a fortnight ago with 600 camels, but more are urgently needed and it is reported that the Red Sea ports are being scoured for the animals at any price (→8/3).

Newspaper at sea

Feb 22. The Cunard liner Etruria arrived in New York today with a copy of the first newspaper ever published in the middle of the Atlantic Ocean. It features news reports transmitted from Britain by wireless while the ship was at sea. Guglielmo Marconi, the inventor of wireless telegraphy, was among the ship's passengers (→29/3).

From pillar to post by Royal Mail.

1903

MARCH

Su	Mo	Tu	We	Th	Fr	Sa
1	2	3	4	5	6	7
8	9	10	11	12	13	14
15	16	17	18	19	20	21
22	23	24	25	26	27	28
29	30	31				

3. US: A man is arrested in St. Louis for spitting.

5. Turkey: Agreement on the building of a railway from Constantinople to Baghdad.

8. Africa: 10,000 Abyssinians are supporting General Manning's advance on the Mad Mullah (→ 22/4).

10. Paris: The Academy of Medicine issues a report denouncing alcohol as detrimental to health.

12. St. Petersburg: Czar issues manifesto concerning important reforms, including freedom of religion (→ 17).

14. Washington: Senate ratifies treaty with Colombia giving US right to build a canal through Panama (→ 12/8).

17. Russia: Arrests follow discovery of anarchist plot against the government (→ 8/5).

18. France: Government refuses all applications to teach from religious orders (→ 29/4).

20. Paris: Exhibition of paintings by Matisse, Derain and de Vlaminck at the Salon des Independants.

22. New York: The US side of the Niagara Falls runs dry.

22. Washington: Coal Commission recommends shorter hours and higher pay for US miners.

24. Scandinavia: Sweden and Norway agree to create separate consular systems (→ 13/8/05).

26. Helsingfors: Czar appoints Russian General Bobrikov virtual dictator of Finland.

27. UK: J.S. Morrison's Drumcree wins the Grand National at Aintree.

29. London: Regular news service between London and New York begins using Marconi's wireless.

BIRTHS

4. US painter Adolph Gottlieb (†4/3/74).

10. US jazz musician Bix Beiderbecke (†7/8/31).

18. Italian politician Galeazzo Ciano (†11/1/1944).

US slams the door on "undesirables"

March 3. A bill seeking to ban undesirables from entering the United States was passed today by Congress. This latest move to curb immigration will place a two dollar head tax on all aliens arriving at US ports. The new law will exclude from admission altogether idiots, felons, anarchists, polygamists, the insane, and women of "bad repute".

This is not the first time Congress has sought to limit immigration. Yet it marks an historic shift in US immigration policy. The US used to welcome all comers. By 1900 35 million aliens had immigrated. Until some twenty years ago, the majority came from the British Isles, Scandinavia, and Germany.

They were therefore predominantly Protestants and of similar ethnic origin to the existing US population. Recently the total number of immigrants each year has grown to around 1 million a year and the proportion coming from southern and eastern Europe, mostly Roman Catholic or Jewish, has increased from 7 per cent in the 1870s to about 70 per cent today.

La Vita Nuova: Italian immigrants arriving at Ellis Island, New York.

This new wave has drawn protests not only from social workers concerned at the immigrants' poor living conditions, but also from unions worried about their willingness to work for low wages.

Big boost for Royal Navy announced

March 6. The Government today announced the building of a major new naval base in the Firth of Forth, within good striking range of the Continent, designed to ease pressure on other ports caused by the build up in the Royal Navy.

The new base near the Forth Bridge faces directly onto the North Sea, through which £200 million of trade passes annually. It will be only 560 miles from the German port of Hamburg; the Government plans that in war men from the warship building yards on the Clyde could be brought over to the new base.

There is concern within the Admiralty about the growth of the German navy but the Royal Navy is still by far the largest with 42 battleships against the 19 of France and 12 of Germany (→ 23/7).

The Royal Navy: steering to glory.

Sultan flees as British take city

March 15. Troops of the West African Frontier Force led by British officers today entered Sokoto after a brief skirmish; the rebellious Sultan has fled. Sir Frederick Lugard, Britain's High Commissioner for Northern Nigeria, told the people that the Fulani empire, founded a century ago after a holy war, was dead. "All the things which the Fulani by conquest took the right to do now pass to the British", he said.

Sir Frederick then appointed the fleeing Sultan's brother as the new Sultan. With the fall of Sokoto, after Kano last month (the only cities offering resistance), Sir Frederick is free to implement his policy of indirect rule (→ 17/2/04).

Scott and Shackleton set new Antarctic record for Britain

March 3. Commander Robert Scott and his fellow explorers, Lt. Ernest Shackleton and Dr Edward Wilson, have achieved an Antarctic record by travelling further towards the South Pole than any other explorers. In an epic journey to the 80th latitude from McMurdo Bay in Victoria Land, the three men were forced to pull their own sledges after their dogs died. Lt. Shackleton came close to death.

Several new mountain ranges have been discovered during the expedition, on which one young seaman has died.

Go south young man: explorer Scott with Dr. Wilson on the ice.

1903

APRIL

Su	Mo	Tu	We	Th	Fr	Sa
			1	2	3	4
5	6	7	8	9	10	11
12	13	14	15	16	17	18
19	20	21	22	23	24	25
26	27	28	29	30		

2. Spain: Bloody clashes as students are confronted by police in Madrid, Saragossa and Salamanca.

6. Paris: Revealed that nationalist army officers forged documents relating to the Dreyfus Affair (→ 5/3/04).

7. London: Education Bill introduced to make London County Council the education authority for London.

9. Holland: The government passes a bill punishing civil service and railway strikes with imprisonment (→ 13).

12. France: President Emile Loubet embarks on a visit to Algeria.

13. Holland: National Strike Committee of 40 unions decides to abandon week-old general strike.

14. S. Africa: Bill published making males from 17 to 50 liable for militia service.

15. Germany: International Congress on Alcohol opens in the port of Bremen.

17. Ireland: Irish Nationalist Convention gives approval, with qualifications, to Irish Land Purchase Bill (→ 1/8).

18. UK: Bury beat Derby 6-0 in the FA Cup final.

22. Morocco: Muldi Mohammed is proclaimed the new Sultan of Morocco (→ 13/5).

23. Africa: Mad Mullah's forces suffer heavy losses in clashes with British (→ 11/1/04).

23. London: Government reveals that the Boer and Boxer wars cost one-third of the national budget (→ 7/11).

25. Venice: The Foundation stone laid of new Campanile.

28. Peking: China rejects Russia's demand to evacuate Manchuria (→ 8/5).

29. Turkey: Earthquake in Van kills 860.

29. Balkans: Many die in bomb attacks on Turkish official buildings in Salonika (→ 6/5).

Peasants slaughter Jews in Russia

April 16. A mob running wild in Kishinev, Bessarabia, savagely murdered scores of Jews during a two-day pogrom that started on Easter morning. Police were called to the area but made no effort to stop frenzied peasants raping and murdering as well as setting fire to homes. There are reasons to believe that the pogrom was incited by the authorities.

The massacre is the first of its kind since 1881 but the ten-year reign of Czar Nicholas II has been marked by persecution of Jews, of which there are some five million in Russia. The Czar is said to be angered by the belief that Jews were responsible for 500 strikes this year, and organising revolutionary terrorism. It is certainly beyond dispute that local police have been encouraged to turn a blind eye to outbreaks of anti-Semitism.

The slaughtered victims of superstitious peasant anti-Semitism.

Almost half of the 100,000 population of Kishinev, which Russia seized from Turkey in 1812, are Jewish. The death of a Christian boy during the winter angered peasants who believed he was killed by Jews. The reason for the killing, according to them, was that they needed his blood to celebrate the Passover feast.

Their anger was further inflamed by the death of a Christian girl just before Easter. Leaflets appeared in the streets on Easter Day stating that the Czar had approved Christians wreaking "bloody havoc" on the Jews. Within hours the Jewish sector was alight (→ 4/6).

Dissolution of French monasteries starts

April 29. Soldiers on horseback moved in today on a French monastery high in the Alps to expel all the residents. The move against the Chartreuse monastery is the latest example of the power of the anticlerical movement which has been growing steadily in France since the Dreyfus Affair nine years ago.

The government has been trying to limit the religious influence on education and only last month the House of Deputies denied 21 groups of monks the right to teach. Protests from the right, and the Chartreuse monks' own offer to pay two million francs to avoid expulsion, have not had any effect on the government's determination to make any religious teaching – even if it involves only one teacher in a school – subject to formal government authorisation.

Ironically, President Combes was a seminarian before he embarked on a political career (→ 5/8).

Bulgarians massacre 165 in single village

April 14. The situation in the Balkans is growing more dangerous every day. In the latest incident a band of Bulgarians razed a small Moslem village near Monastir in Macedonia, killing in a frenzy of blood letting 165 men, women and children.

It seems that all the inhabitants in the region, Turks, Albanians, Bulgarians and others, are determined upon massacre as Turkish authority crumbles. The Sultan has been greatly embarrassed by the murder of the Russian Consul Stcherbina, who has died after being shot by an Albanian soldier in Mitrovitza. The agitation continues and, despite the reforms promised by the government, it is now plain that the Bulgarians and the Albanians will be satisfied with nothing short of freedom from Turkish domination (→ 6/5).

Stepping out in style.

1903

MAY

Su	Mo	Tu	We	Th	Fr	Sa
					1	2
3	4	5	6	7	8	9
10	11	12	13	14	15	16
17	18	19	20	21	22	23
24	25	26	27	28	29	30
31						

1. Paris: King Edward VII arrives on a visit aimed at improving Anglo-French relations.

3. Rome: Kaiser Wilhelm II visits Pope Leo XIII.

5. London: Foreign Secretary Lord Lansdowne declares that the Persian Gulf is one of the frontiers of India.

6. Turkey: Italian and Austrian warships are sent to Salonika to help Turks quell Macedonian uprising (→5/8).

7. London: Treaty on customs signed between United Kingdom, Italy and Germany.

8. Manchuria: Russians re-occupy and fortify Niu-Chwang (→3/7).

10. Vienna: Government says Innsbruck University will stay German, Italy insists on an Italian university at Trieste.

11. London: Government says new Transvaal loan is 40 times oversubscribed: £1,174 million has been offered.

15. London: Joseph Chamberlain appeals for customs reform to give UK colonies advantages over foreign powers (→21).

15. Australia: Striking railway workers in Victoria submit unconditionally after only five days.

18. S. Africa: British Commissioner Lord Alfred Milner favours letting educated and prosperous non-whites vote in local elections.

20. London: Kew Bridge over the Thames is opened.

26. France: Paris to Madrid motor race is banned after deaths on opening day.→

27. UK: Sir James Miller's Rock Sand wins the Derby at Epsom.

28. Constantinople: An earthquake kills 2,000 people.

30. Paris: First performance of "Danses-Idylles" by Isadora Duncan.

DEATH

8. French painter Paul Gauguin (*7/6/1848).→

League formed to boost Empire trade

One view of Chamberlain's preference for the Empire.

May 21. The Tariff League was launched today at a meeting of MPs and manufacturers to promote a preferential trading system within the Empire. Joseph Chamberlain, the Colonial Secretary, is its chief sponsor and he hopes for support across party lines.

About 3,000 businessmen have already signed a petition demanding rearrangement of Empire fiscal duties. This follows Chamberlain's recent Birmingham speech in which he called for consolidation of the Empire through strengthening the colonies. His argument is that the self-governing lands overseas will then be sure to rally behind the Mother Country in the event of attack on Britain by a coalition of hostile European nations.

MP Winston Churchill was doubtful, however, about Chamberlain's tariff reform ideas. While praising the colonies, he warned against upsetting "the elaborate machinery by which Britain's great wealth was produced". It was important, he said, not to disregard the people at home (→1/9).

Six killed in 65mph French motor race

May 24. Fatal accidents marred the opening day of the road race from Paris to Madrid. Six died, among them four spectators. A British casualty was Mr Nixon of Belfast, killed at a level crossing when the Wolseley in which he was competing struck the keeper's cottage. The race, in which average speeds reached 65 mph, has been stopped at Bordeaux, and may be banned. The French Minister of the Interior gave special permission for the race, stipulating safety precautions. But enforcement was erratic and spectators strayed too close (→26).

King Edward VII inaugurated London's first electric trams on 15 May.

Gauguin, painter of Tahitian idylls, dies

May 8. News has reached Paris of the death of the painter, Paul Gauguin, in the Marquesas Islands. M. Gauguin, 54, gave up a prosperous life as a stockbroker on the Bourse to devote himself full-time to painting although he had no formal training. He could not support his wife and family whom he abandoned.

With Vincent Van Gogh, he rejected the conventions of Impressionism for Primitivism. Painting, he declared, needed "rejuvenation through barbarism". On visits to Martinique and Tahiti he discovered a new style using simplified forms and areas of flat and exotic colour which stimulated several other artists.

He left Paris for Tahiti for the last time in 1895. He ended his life at odds with the colonial administration and the church because he lived like a native.

Artist Paul Gauguin, as he saw himself in this self-portrait.

Morocco in revolt

May 13. Rebel tribesmen, who refuse to accept Abd al-Aziz as Sultan of Morocco, have encircled Tetuan, according to messages reaching Paris. After a Cabinet meeting yesterday, it was reported that the French are considering a police operation against the rebels, since the Sultan seems powerless. French troops and convoys in Algeria have been attacked by marauders crossing the border. French and British postmen have been seized by the rebels and told not to try to deliver letters.

1903

JUNE

Su	Mo	Tu	We	Th	Fr	Sa
	1	2	3	4	5	6
7	8	9	10	11	12	13
14	15	16	17	18	19	20
21	22	23	24	25	26	27
28	29	30				

1. US: A tornado kills 100 people and destroys Georgia town of Gainsville.

2. Italy: Anti-Austrian agitation is reported throughout the country.

4. Australia: Government approves British proposals for preferential tariff system with the Empire.

4. Russia: An Imperial decree forbids Jews from owning property or land outside the area in which they live (→15).

7. France: 100 people die when steamship "Liban" sinks off Marseilles.

9. Germany: Daimler motor factory at Cannstadt is destroyed by fire.

11. Scotland: Harry Vardon wins his fourth open golf championship, at Prestwick.

14. Belgrade: Prince Peter Karageorgevitch is confirmed King of Serbia.→

15. Russia: 5,000 Jewish workers holding pro-socialist demonstration are attacked by police and Cossacks (→26).

16. Germany: Socialists make large gains in elections to the Reichstag.

16. US: The year-old Pepsi-Cola Company registers its trade name, "Pepsi-Cola".

18. London: 16 people killed in an explosion at Woolwich Arsenal.

26. Russia: Czar Nicholas II rejects US protests at the treatment of Jews in Russia (→19/8).

29. London: The government protests to Belgium about Congo atrocities (→7/12).

30. US: Government committee reports on treatment of blacks in southern states (→2/6/04).

BIRTHS

6. Russian-Armenian composer Aram Khachaturian (†1/5/78).

25. British writer Eric Arthur Blair, alias George Orwell (†21/1/50).

King and Queen shot in cupboard

June 11. King Alexander and Queen Draga of Serbia were murdered in their bedroom in the early hours of this morning. A group of disaffected army officers, led by Colonel Misches and Colonel Mashin, a brother of the Queen's first husband, forced their way into the Royal Palace in Belgrade, shooting down the bodyguards.

They burst into the royal bedroom where they discovered the royal couple hiding in a cupboard. It is said that 30 shots were fired into the King and Queen. Queen Draga died immediately, but King Alexander lingered until four o'clock this morning.

The immediate reason for the assassination is believed to be the King's plan to move the War School from Belgrade but the real causes of the army's disaffection go much deeper than that.

There was much scandal when the King married Draga Mashin three years ago. Rumour had it that she had a shady and promiscuous past, but the King would not listen to advice and enraged the nation by marrying her.

The King, who succeeded to the throne on the abdication of his father in 1889, had previously made himself unpopular by abolishing the liberal constitution of 1888 and restoring the reactionary one of 1869. Prince Peter Karageorgevitch has been proclaimed King by the army (→14).

The murdered king and queen.

Henry Ford forms a motor company

June 16. A group of Detroit investors today formed the Ford Motor Company. It represents the industrial ambitions of Henry Ford, son of a Dearborn farmer, who has been experimenting with "horseless carriages" since he moved to Detroit as a teenager.

Mr Ford has worked on petrol driven cars since 1893, inspired by the inventions of Carl Benz in Germany in the mid-1880s. The recent success of the one-cylinder Oldsmobile, now being produced at the rate of 4,000 a year, was a major factor in persuading Alexander Malcolmson, a Detroit coal merchant, to put together a group of investors to back the venture. Mr Ford owns about a quarter of the new company's shares and will be its vice president as well as its chief engineer (→23/7).

Ford: looking for market share.

Mussolini watched by Swiss police

June 19. According to police sources, a young Italian teacher who goes by the name of Benito Mussolini has today been put under special investigation by the police in Berne, Switzerland. He arrived in the country from his homeland just under a year ago and was soon able to find himself a job working as a stonemason.

A Swiss police spokesman gave the reason as being that Mussolini, the son of socialist blacksmith, had been spending time with revolutionary friends and studying the works of Karl Marx.

Cinema makes crime pay for the "Great Train Robbery"

June 15. Audiences are packing into showings all over the US of "The Great Train Robbery", an eight-minute film in which a gang of bandits take over a train and are pursued and hunted down by the sheriff's posse. Edwin Porter, who made the film for the Edison company, has cut it directly from one scene to the next, dispensing with captions, achieving a thrilling, break-neck pace.

At the climax the moustachioed bandit chief fires a pistol point-blank at the audience. Patrons are returning again and again to experience this curious effect (→21/9).

Sensational and startling hold-up of the Gold Express by outlaws.

1903

JULY

Su	Mo	Tu	We	Th	Fr	Sa
			1	2	3	4
5	6	7	8	9	10	11
12	13	14	15	16	17	18
19	20	21	22	23	24	25
26	27	28	29	30	31	

1. Wimbledon: Laurence Doherty beats Frank Risely for the Men's Singles title; Dorothea Douglass beats Ethel Thompson for Ladies' title.

2. Ireland: Belgian Camille Jenatzki wins the Gordon Bennett motor-racing trophy in a Mercedes.

3. London: UK and Japan demand Russian evacuation of Manchuria (→ 12/8).

6. London: Official visit of French President Loubet and Foreign Minister Delcasse to UK (→ 4/8/04).

7. London: Announcement of a fall in the birth rate that will lead to a standstill in population growth in 18 years.

11. Ireland: World's first powerboat race takes place, organised by the Royal Cork Yacht Club.

16. Berlin: International monetary conference decides to set a fixed scale between gold and silver-indexed currencies.

17. Brussels: Russian Social Democratic Labour Party meets, led by exiles including Vladimir Lenin (→ 29).

17. Paris: France and Spain say they will keep Moroccan status quo (→ 15/8/04).

20. London: The Government announces it intends to increase the number of troops stationed in India.

21. Ireland: King Edward VII and Queen Alexandra arrive on a visit (→ 1/8).

23. US: Ford Motor Co. sells first production car, two-cylinder Model A.

27. Glasgow: 15 die and many are injured in a train crash.

29. Russia: Strikes and unrest occur at Kiev, Odessa and Tiflis (→ 17/11).

BIRTH

2. Norwegian King Olav V (†17/1/91).

DEATHS

17. US painter James McNeill Whistler (*10/7/1834).→

20. Italian churchman Vincenzo Pecci, Pope Leo XIII (*2/3/1810).→

A bill to catch up with cars and drivers

The motor car: freedom for some but a menace to others?

July 14. Parliament resumed its consideration today of a new law to regulate motor vehicles and drivers. Since the last legislation traffic has multiplied. The President of the Institute of Civil Engineers counted, in 11 minutes on the Brighton road near Horsham, 209 cars, motor cycles, and motor tricycles – a total of 1200 vehicles an hour.

But much of the bill is "of a speculative character", admitted its Commons sponsor, Walter Long. The bill requires private cars to be registered and numbered. Cars used commercially would also have to be licensed.

A new speed-limit procedure would shift the responsibility for this controversial area to county councils. The Government is rejecting proposals for driving tests, vehicle inspection or penalties for drunk drivers (→ 11/8).

Labour scores by-election victory

July 25. Labour has narrowly won the Barnard Castle by-election by pushing the Liberals into third place behind the Tories. The Liberals had held the seat in the general election three years ago.

The result announced today means that the Labour Representation Committee, led by James Keir Hardie, now has three MPs. It was Labour, rather than the Liberals, who reaped the benefit of the big anti-Tory swing in this Durham coal-mining constituency.

The new MP, Arthur Henderson, was, until recently, Liberal agent in the area. "The workers are becoming alive to their own interests", he said, explaining his shift of allegiance (→ 3/11).

Pope who aimed to end class war dies

The late Pontiff and Bishop of Rome, Pope Leo XIII.

July 20. Pope Leo XIII died quietly today at the age of 93. He will be mourned by millions of Catholics worldwide who have been impressed with the unifying aspects of his 25-year period in office. He worked unstintingly to unite Christendom and to reduce class warfare. He first made his mark in the field of education after he was made a Cardinal in 1853. Born Vincenzo Gioacchino Pecci he was admitted to Holy Orders in 1837 and became Bishop of Perugia in 1846. He succeeded Pius IX in 1878 (→ 4/8).

American painter Whistler dies

July 17. James McNeill Whistler, American painter who made London his home, died today aged 69 after a lifetime of what he called "the gentle art of making enemies". His pictures aimed at creating harmonies of only two predominant colours. The portrait of his mother is entitled "Arrangement in Grey and Black". Art critic John Ruskin attacked one of his "nocturnes" of the Thames, as "flinging a pot of paint in the public's face". Whistler won a farthing's damages but the case bankrupted him.

J.A.M. Whistler, by Whistler.

Finish of first Tour de France

July 19. Maurice Garin today won the first Tour de France in fine style, arriving back in Paris 2hrs 49 minutes ahead of his closest rival, the unknown Pothier, "the butcher of Sens". Only 20 of the 60 entrants finished the gruelling race, the creation of journalist and promoter Henri Desgrange. It took them 19 days to cross France in six stages travelling from Paris through Lyons, Marseilles, Toulouse, Bordeaux and Nantes.

1903

AUGUST

Su	Mo	Tu	We	Th	Fr	Sa
						1
2	3	4	5	6	7	8
9	10	11	12	13	14	15
16	17	18	19	20	21	22
23	24	25	26	27	28	29
30	31					

1. Ireland: At the end of his tour, King Edward VII speaks of hope that "a brighter day is dawning upon Ireland" (→11).

3. Vienna: Emperor Franz Josef vetoes the election of new pope to succeed Leo XIII (→4).

4. Rome: Outcome of Papal election; orthodox Patriarch of Venice, Giuseppe Sarto, becomes Pope Pius X (→9).

5. France: Teachers' congress in Marseilles welcomes government's abolition of religious instruction in schools (→21/3/04).

9. Rome: New Pope Pius X is crowned at the Vatican before a crowd of 70,000 people (→8/1/04).

11. Paris: 84 people die in metro fire.

12. Russia: Czar declares Amur and Kwantung regions a vice-royalty, effectively annexing Manchuria (→31/12).

12. Central America: The Colombian senate refuses to ratify the treaty with the US on a canal through Panama (→2/11).

15. New York: Joseph Pulitzer gives $2 million to Columbia University to start a school of journalism.

16. Balkans: Turks say many officials have been punished for murder of Russian consul in Monastir (→31).

19. Washington: President Roosevelt favours a law to make large monopolies pay for social improvements.

22. Manchester: Report says a shortage of cheap cotton has forced many mills to close down.

25. London: Royal Commission into Boer War slams poor campaign planning, and reveals 100,000 British dead (→7/11).

31. Vienna: King Edward VII arrives on a visit to Emperor Franz Josef I.

DEATH

22. British statesman Robert Arthur Talbot Gascoyne Cecil, 3rd Marquess of Salisbury (*3/2/1830).→

Death of Lord Salisbury

Aug 22. The Marquess of Salisbury, three times Tory prime minister and world-renowned statesman, died at Hatfield House today on the 50th anniversary of his first election to Parliament. The King and the Royal Family led the nation's profound expression of sorrow.

Lord Salisbury, who was 73, has suffered from heart weakness since retiring from the premiership last year. His nephew and successor Arthur Balfour was near the bedside when he passed away. Telegrams of tribute to Robert Cecil, the third Marquess and direct descendant of Queen Elizabeth's famous Secretary of State, arrived in London from all over Europe.

Lord Salisbury's long public career spanned a half-century in the development of Britain's Imperial power. As Foreign Secretary and Disraeli's one-time lieutenant, he was at the hub of Europe's turbulent history-making.

In home affairs he was a forthright champion of the Anglican Establishment and a strenuous opponent of reforms which could place power in the hands of the least educated and responsible classes.

Four times PM, 1885-1902.

Offer to site Jewish state in Uganda

Aug 19. Delegates to the sixth Zionist Congress in Basel, Switzerland, clashed over proposals to set up a Jewish state in Uganda. The suggestion came from the British Colonial Office who had just given approval to a commission to look into the possibility.

Theodor Herzl, founder of the Zionist movement, declared that although he considered Palestine was the best place for a Jewish state, he was prepared to consider Uganda and certainly would not refuse the offer. He pointed out that attempts to get a charter of colonization from the Ottoman Empire had been fruitless and Uganda could provide a haven for persecuted Jews.

But it soon became clear that many flatly refused to consider East Africa. Russian delegates from Kishinev which was recently the centre of violent persecution said that they would refuse to go anywhere but Palestine, the ancient home of the Jews.

Horror at details of Balkan atrocities

Aug 31. The details of the atrocities perpetrated on all sides in the anarchy sweeping the Balkans continues to horrify the civilised world. The terrible stories emerging from the mountains tell of whole villages being put to the sword, of women raped and even of small children being bayoneted.

The murder of officials has become commonplace, government is breaking down. Order is kept only by the army but the soldiers themselves are in a parlous state. With their uniforms worn out and without supplies they are living off the land and bringing further misery to the inhabitants. Atrocity follows atrocity. No one is safe in the Balkans today (→1/9).

Macedonian boot-blacks cleaning the boots of the troops.

Operation for eyes

Aug 8. The development of a new operation for cataracts – or opacity of the eye's lens – is revealed today by Lt-Colonel Henry Smith of the Indian Medical Service. He has produced good vision in 99.4 per cent of the 1023 operations performed in the first four months of this year by extracting the capsule containing the opaque lens.

The latest bathing fashions.

1903

SEPTEMBER

Su	Mo	Tu	We	Th	Fr	Sa
		1	2	3	4	5
6	7	8	9	10	11	12
13	14	15	16	17	18	19
20	21	22	23	24	25	26
27	28	29	30			

1. London: Imports of sugar from Denmark, Russia and Argentina are banned as part of imperial preference policy (→ 6).

1. Turkey: Macedonian rebels blow up a Hungarian steamer, killing 29 passengers and crew (→ 8).

3. New York: US yacht "Reliance" beats British entry "Shamrock" to win the America's Cup.

4. Brussels: Belgian King Leopold II has talks with French President Loubet over the situation in the Congo.

6. Moscow: Russia increases import duties on Indian and Ceylon tea, in retaliation for British import policies (→ 8).

7. Vienna: Opening of the Inter-Parliamentary Conference on Arbitration (→ 10/12).

8. London: The Trades Union Congress opposes the Government's tariff policy (→ 17).

10. UK: Great storm in the south of England causes deaths and widespread damage.

14. Bulgaria: The government issues a note to the great powers saying they must intervene in Macedonia (→ 17).

17. Turkey: Turkish troops destroy town of Kastoria, killing 10,000 people (→ 30).

20. Vienna: German Kaiser Wilhelm II arrives on visit to Emperor Franz Josef.

22. S. Africa: Commission appointed to look into question of native Africans.

25. London: Government says it will back Russian and Austrian plans for a settlement of the Macedonian problem (→ 4/10).

26. US: Connecticut gives women the vote in state elections.

30. Vienna: Czar Nicholas II arrives on visit to Emperor Franz Josef; the Balkan crisis is discussed (→ 2/10).

BIRTH

25. US artist Mark Rothko (†25/2/70).

Turks butcher 50,000 in Bulgaria

Sept 8. An appalling massacre of Bulgarian men, women and children has been carried out by Turkish troops in the village of Monastir. Some reports speak of 50,000 people being killed as the Turks persue what can only be described as a policy of extermination against the rebellious Bulgarians.

Dispatches from Monastir say that every Bulgarian village in the area has been destroyed. The surviving inhabitants have fled to the forests but the Turks are setting fire to the undergrowth, forcing the people into the open and shooting them. Where the people have not been shot, they are starving in their thousands, without food or shelter.

The harshness of the Turkish action seems to have sprung from the decision by the Macedonian Central Revolutionary Committee to mount a revolt against Turkish rule. The uprising was due to start on August 31, but the Turks learnt of the plot and consequently built up an army of 300,000 men in Macedonia, more than enough to put down the revolt.

Further news may be difficult to obtain as all European correspondents have been ordered to leave the country (→ 14).

Macedonian troops have breakfast after a night's raiding.

"Kit Carson" is first Wild West movie

Sept 21. The first film to capture some of the derring-do of the "Wild West" years opens in the US today. Called "Kit Carson", it is a 21-minute account of the life of the Kentucky farmer's son, born in 1809, who guided traders and fur trappers across the Rockies, battled with Apaches, Mexicans and rival trappers, married an Indian and died a brigadier-general in 1868. The film aims to exploit the success of Edwin S. Porter's "Life of an American Fireman" in January.

Fun for all the family on a British beach in 1903.

Chamberlain quits over Empire trade

Sept 17. The resignation from the Cabinet of Joseph Chamberlain, the Colonial Secretary, after eight years in the post was announced from 10 Downing Street today. He has quit office in order to have greater freedom in advocating preferential tariff treatment for Empire countries.

Arthur Balfour, the Prime Minister, said they both agreed that it was politically impossible at present to support even the small new taxes on non-Empire food imports which Imperial Preference would involve. In an exchange of letters both men also deplored what Mr. Chamberlain called the unscrupulous use for electoral purposes of a "dear loaf" cry which their Liberal opponents will make their chorus in the next general election and are already rehearsing with relish (→ 1/10).

1903

OCTOBER

Su	Mo	Tu	We	Th	Fr	Sa
				1	2	3
4	5	6	7	8	9	10
11	12	13	14	15	16	17
18	19	20	21	22	23	24
25	26	27	28	29	30	31

1. London: Balfour makes important speech on fiscal policy, says there will be no tariff war (→5).

2. London: Parts of the ancient Roman city wall are discovered during demolition of Newgate prison in the City.

4. Vienna: Austro-Russian note to Turkey indicates that both powers intend to control Turkish actions in Macedonia (→3/11).

4. Moscow: Report reveals 45 per cent illiteracy in the city.

5. London: Austen Chamberlain becomes Chancellor and Alfred Lyttelton Colonial Secretary in reshuffle after resignation of Joseph Chamberlain (→6).

5. Berlin: Siemens electric train reaches 125 mph.

6. Glasgow: In a speech, Joseph Chamberlain explains the general principles of Imperial Reciprocity (→12/12).

7. US: Professor Samuel Langley fails in his attempt to fly a heavier-than-air machine in Virginia (→17/12).

11. Spain: Seven die and 33 are hurt in violent clashes between Catholics and Republicans in Bilbao.

12. UK: Amalgamation announced of shipbuilders Cammell and Laird.

16. London: Commission to arbitrate in UK-US Alaskan boundary dispute decides in favour of US.

22. London: The National Temperance Manifesto is published.

23. Portsmouth: Battleship rams Nelson's "HMS Victory", causing severe damage.

26. London: The Foundation stone is laid of the Royal Waterloo Hospital for Women and Children.

BIRTHS

17. US author Nathanael West (†22/12/40).

28. British novelist Evelyn Waugh, born Evelyn Arthur St. John (†10/4/66).

Mrs Pankhurst forms new group

Oct 10. A number of women met in a house in Nelson Street, Manchester, today and agreed to form a new militant movement to gain the vote for their sex with the motto "Deeds, not Words". The leader of the society – The Women's Social and Political Union – is Mrs Emmeline Pankhurst who said that membership would be limited exclusively to women, free of party affiliation and satisfied with nothing but action.

The new approach favoured by Mrs Pankhurst suggests a radical change in future tactics. Previous suffragists have met regularly with sympathetic members of Parliament to plead their cause but have inevitably been frustrated by Parliament's refusal to debate the subject or even consider the idea of female emancipation.

Plants lure Alpine climbers to death

Oct 18. More than 130 mountaineers are now known to have lost their lives in the climbing season that has just ended. Many of the 136 who died were making assaults on previously unscaled peaks on attempting to beat existing records. But it is the popular desire to collect Alpine plants, many of which bloom on inaccessible ledges, that lured most of the casualties to the precarious crags from which they plunged.

The perils and pitfalls of the piste.

1903

NOVEMBER

Su	Mo	Tu	We	Th	Fr	Sa
1	2	3	4	5	6	7
8	9	10	11	12	13	14
15	16	17	18	19	20	21
22	23	24	25	26	27	28
29	30					

1. Russia: Administrative centre in the Far East moved from Port Arthur to Vladivostok (→24).

2. Washington: Roosevelt orders three US warships to Panama isthmus (→6).

3. Holland: Willem Einthoven describes electro-cardiograph, his new invention for monitoring the heart.

3. Turkey: The government agrees to Balkan reforms, but refuses to appoint non-Turkish civil servants.

6. Washington: Government recognises the Republic of Panama, which declared independence from Colombia earlier this week (→18).

7. London: Lord Esher creates committee to reform War Office after criticisms of Boer War Commission (→31/1/04).

12. China: 10,000 Chinese troops are moved into Manchuria.

15. Balkans: Bulgaria admits the existence of army plot to provoke war with Turkey.

18. Washington: US and Panama sign a treaty to build the Panama Canal (→4/5/04).

20. New Zealand: Parliament approves of the preferential trade agreement with the UK (→15/12).

22. Philippines: Gen. Leonard Wood wins a five-day battle against rebels, 300 of whom were killed.

24. Far East: Port Arthur is opened to international trade.

29. Washington: Official report into the US postal service reveals the loss of millions of dollars through fraud.

BIRTHS

1. French author Jean Tardieu (†27/1/95).

7. Austrian naturalist Konrad Lorenz (†27/2/89).

DEATHS

1. German historian Theodor Mommsen (*30/11/1817).

12. French artist Camille Pissarro (*10/7/1830).→

Leading French painter dies

Pissarro by Pissarro, painted 1903.

Nov 12. Camille Pissarro, the great French painter, has died in Paris at the age of 73. A friend of Claude Monet and Paul Cezanne, Pissarro belongs to the "Impressionist" group of artists and took part in the famous "Salon des refuses" exhibition of 1863.

Nature and the countryside inspired some of Pissarro's best works, especially between 1872 and 1884 when he was living at Pontoise. "The harvest at Montfoucault", "Red roofs" and "Spring in Pontoise" are examples. Camille Pissarro also painted in the "Pointilliste" style after meeting Georges Seurat in 1885.

Russian Socialists split by Lenin

Nov 17. Russia's Socialist Democrats have formalised their split into two groups at a meeting in London. At the end of a stormy congress of the Russian Social Democratic Labour party Vladimir Lenin obtained a majority after several delegates had left.

His supporters are called Bolsheviks ("majority") and they believe a revolution must be led by a single centralised party of professional revolutionaries. The opposing Mensheviks ("minority") are led by Yuly Martov and they advocate a broad proletarian party. The congress took place in London because most of the leaders of Russian socialism are exiles.

1903

DECEMBER

Su	Mo	Tu	We	Th	Fr	Sa
		1	2	3	4	5
6	7	8	9	10	11	12
13	14	15	16	17	18	19
20	21	22	23	24	25	26
27	28	29	30	31		

3. Russia: Police arrest protesting students in the Ukrainian capital of Kiev.

7. Africa: British consul in Belgian Congo confirms reports of widespread massacres (→ 10/2/04).

9. Christiania: The Norwegian Storting (parliament) rejects attempts to give women the vote.

12. Germany: The Reichstag approves a bill to extend by two years preferential treatment for British imports.

14. Australia: England batsman R.E. Foster scores record Test innings of 287 against Australia.

15. London: Australian Chamber of Commerce in the capital approves preferential trade with UK .

20. S. Africa: Mass meeting in Cape Town condemns the decision a week ago to import Chinese labour.

23. US: at least 60 people die in a head-on train collision in Pennsylvania.

31. Chicago: Five employees at the destroyed Iroquois Theatre are arrested for manslaughter.→

BIRTH

17. US writer Erskine Caldwell (†11/4/87).

DEATH

8. British philosopher Herbert Spencer (*27/4/1820).

HITS OF 1903

Ida.

The Kashmiri Song.

Sweet Adeline.

QUOTE OF THE YEAR

"If civilisation is to advance at all in the future, it must be through the help of women, women freed of their political shackles, women with full power to work their will in society."

Mrs Emmeline Pankhurst, on the foundation of the Women's Social and Political Union, October 1903.

Orville Wright flies heavier-than-air

Orville Wright coaxes his craft off the end of its wooden launch-rail, while his brother Wilbur looks on.

Dec 17. Two inventors from Dayton Ohio, Wilbur and Orville Wright, today flew a curious-looking, heavier-than-air machine over the beach at Kitty Hawk, North Carolina. The two brothers claim they made four flights in all, the longest lasting almost a minute and covering 850 feet. The Wrights managed to get their aircraft to fly when so many have failed before by using moveable wingtips to control the machine. They also developed their own lightweight 25-horse-power engine providing a higher power-to-weight ratio than any previous models.

The "Flyer", as the Wrights call their machine, weighs 605 pounds and was launched off a trolley rolling along a greased 60-foot launching track. The two propellors on the aircraft began moving soon after 10.30 am and Orville Wright, 32, four years younger than Wilbur, climbed into a cradle-like harness slung beneath the lower of two wings. The controls of the aircraft were designed so that he could move the rudder and wing flaps by changing the position of his body while his hands controlled the engine throttle and other controls.

The aircraft hit the ground after 12 seconds on the first flight but later in the day Orville managed to keep it in the air for longer. The brothers have been working secretly on the machine for several years and began by testing models in a wind-tunnel they built near their home.

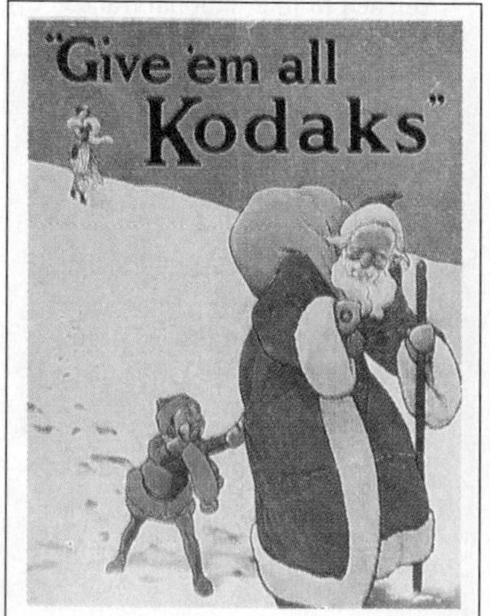

Chicago theatre in flames: 578 dead

Dec 31. New Year celebrations in Chicago were suspended by the city's Mayor today in the wake of last night's devastating fire at the Iroquois Theatre. The death toll now stands at 578 after what began as a night of fun and laughter between Christmas and the New Year turned into tragedy. One moment the audience of 2,000 people was enjoying an octet singing "Pearly Moonlight". Just 10 minutes later the theatre was consumed by flames. Many who escaped the flames were trampled to death in the rush for safety. Comedian Eddie Foy appealed for an orderly exit, but to no avail. In the panic, people inside the theatre jumped from the balcony to the stalls below while outside others jumped from fire escapes to their deaths.

Preliminary investigations have revealed that the theatre violated numerous local safety laws. Fatally, the asbestos stage curtain jammed, allowing the uncontained backstage blaze to rage through the theatre to make it Chicago's worst fire since 1871.

Madame Curie becomes first woman to win a Nobel Prize

Dec 10. Marie Curie, the French scientist, today became the first woman to receive the Nobel Prize. She shares the award for physics with her husband, Pierre, and Henri Becquerel for the work all three of them have done to explore the mystery of radio-activity.

It was Becquerel who first discovered that materials containing uranium emit rays able to fog photographic plates. Mme Curie became interested in the phenomenon and named it radio-activity. By measuring the amount of radiation emitted by different materials (using an earlier discovery of her husband's to do so) she showed that it was always related to the amount of uranium present. In other words, radio-activity is an inherent property of uranium atoms themselves.

In 1898 Mme Curie discovered a second radio-active element, thorium. That same year radiation from a sample of ore too great to be accounted for by uranium alone led her to discover a third substance, hundreds of times more radioactive than uranium. She named it polonium after her native Poland.

Physics Prize winner Marie Curie.

Peacemaker Sir William Cremer.

The Curies' greatest triumph was the discovery of an element even more radio-active, and rarer, than polonium, now known as radium.

Scandinavians dominated this year's other Nobel prize-winners: Svante Arrhenius (Sweden, Chemistry); Niels Finsen (Denmark, Medicine); Bjornsterne Bjornson (Norway, Literature). The Nobel Peace Prize goes to British Liberal MP Sir William Cremer, Secretary of the Inter-Parliamentary Union and a tireless champion of peace and arbitration.

Japanese army dispatched to Korea

Dec 31. Japan has taken firm action to deal with rioting Korean labourers by landing marines at Mok-Pho seven miles from the mouth of the Yellow River. In view of present strained relations between Japan and Russia this action threatens to bring increased tension to the area.

Japan is suspicious of Russian ambitions in Korea but her diplomats said they still hoped for a peaceful solution. The marines who went ashore on December 14 opened fire on the mob and killed a number of rioters when the situation got out of hand.

Mok-Pho is a small walled town at the south-western tip of the Korean peninsula (→5/1/04).

Test record set

Dec 14. R.E. 'Tip' Foster, the Worcestershire amateur who has won six full football caps for England, made a sensational start to his international cricket career today. He scored a superb 287, the highest individual score ever made in a test match, out of England's formidable total of 577 against Australia in Sydney.

Fashionable Gibson Girls with their characteristic "curved and coy" demeanour.

From garden city to squalid slums

Britain's first "garden city" has been begun at Letchworth, Hertfordshire, by **Ebenezer Howard**, author of the visionary and influential book, "Garden Cities of Tomorrow".

His principle is to combine the best of urban and rural life in a new town for 30,000 people. Industry will be kept in a separate zone from the housing and shopping areas and a permanent belt of agricultural land will surround the town.

A corporation owns all the land which will be let on behalf of the community. Mr Howard believes that the England of the future will boast of many more garden cities.

In contrast with these utopian conditions, the completion this year of **Charles Booth's** "Survey of Life and Labour in London" reveals the extent of poverty and the squalor of living conditions among the working population of the capital. "Those who can afford it move out and those who cannot escape crowd in", he concludes.

Isadora Duncan dances to success.

Even more dramatic is the picture given by the American writer, **Jack London**, who disguised himself as an East End tramp to give the searing descriptions in his book, "The People of the Abyss".

A postscript from the Victorian era: the late **Samuel Butler's** novel, "The Way of All Flesh", is a savage exposure of the oppressions of Victorian family life.

1904

JANUARY

Su	Mo	Tu	We	Th	Fr	Sa
					1	2
3	4	5	6	7	8	9
10	11	12	13	14	15	16
17	18	19	20	21	22	23
24	25	26	27	28	29	30
31						

2. South-West Africa: An uprising by Herero tribesmen threatens Windhoek and Okahandja.→

4. Washington: US Supreme Court says Puerto Ricans can enter US freely, but stops short of granting citizenship (→2/3/17).

5. Korea: British, US and Russian marines land to protect legations in Seoul (→31).

7. Rome: Joan of Arc is dubbed Blessed by the Pope, second stage to canonisation (→1/5/20).

11. Somaliland: British troops massacre 1,000 Dervishes.

12. US: Henry Ford sets new land speed record of 91.37 mph in his motor car "999" on frozen Lake St. Clair.

13. Russia: Foreign Minister Lambsdorff tells Japan that Manchuria concerns only China and Russia (→31).

17. Moscow: "The Cherry Orchard", a play by Anton Chekhov, Russian playright, is first performed.

18. Germany: Crimmitschau textile workers' strike is called off as employers refuse to concede demands.

22. Norway: Fire destroys the city of Alesund; 12,000 people are left destitute.

25. US: Two hundred miners are buried alive in an explosion in a Pennsylvania mine; many more feared dead.

25. Chicago: Inquest into Iroquois Theatre fire finds city Mayor Carter Harrison responsible for the tragedy.

27. US: W.K. Vanderbilt sets new motor speed record, covering a mile in 39 seconds.

31. London: King approves War Office reforms, including abolition of office of Commander-in-Chief and creation of German-style General Staff.

BIRTHS

14. British photographer Cecil Beaton (†18/1/80).

18. British-born US film actor Cary Grant (†29/11/86).

Tribesmen murder 123 German settlers

Jan 11. Rebellious Herero tribesmen today systematically massacred 123 German settlers in South-West Africa. The massacre occurred near Okahandja, seat of the Herero Paramount Chief, Samuel Maharero, who ordered that, while English and Dutch missionaries were to be spared, every German must be killed.

However, it is understood that with three exceptions all the women and children were spared and are making their way to military forts in the region.

The tribesmen are said to be angry at the loss of their grazing grounds and water holes to German settlers. The land, with the water supplies, was legally purchased by the Germans, but the people do not appear to have appreciated that they were losing the right of access to what to them is an inalienable tribal possession.

The Hereros, whose lands are in the centre of the territory, struck while the main German forces, under Major Theodor Leutwein, were in the south, quelling an uprising by the Namqua, which broke out after a German official was shot. So the central forts are only lightly garrisoned (→11/8).

Overwhelmed: a German garrison.

Russia and Japan spoiling for fight

Jan 31. War between Japan and Russia seemed imminent today as Russian warships sailed to reinforce cruisers shadowing a Japanese squadron reported off Korea. The army and navy went on the alert after a meeting in Tokyo of the military council and the government also took control of private railways for military use. A Russian battalion is on its way to Port Arthur. However, the St. Petersburg government said that it still hoped for a peaceful solution to the current clash of interest.

Pope orders female frontal cover-up

Jan 8. Pope Pius X added to the controversial actions of his first year of office by hitting out at low-cut evening gowns. No woman who wishes to be thought of as a good Catholic should wear such a gown whenever cardinals or other high Church dignitaries are present, according to his latest instruction to the diplomats accredited to the Holy See. Some diplomatic wives are threatening to stay at home. Others are already planning a new fashion to maintain their allure and their papal fealty.

High fashion in patent leather – for less than 10 shillings.

1904

FEBRUARY

Su	Mo	Tu	We	Th	Fr	Sa
	1	2	3	4	5	6
7	8	9	10	11	12	13
14	15	16	17	18	19	20
21	22	23	24	25	26	27
28	29					

1. London: UK agrees with France that it will remain neutral if Japan and Russia go to war (→4).

3. London: Irish Nationalist leader John Redmond makes renewed call for Home Rule in Ireland.

4. St. Petersburg: Czar offers Japan a free hand in Korea if Japan will leave Manchuria to the Russians.→

6. US: Maryland joins the other southern states and disenfranchises its black voters (→7/3).

7. US: Mine guards at Coal Creek, Tennessee, kill four miners during industrial dispute.

10. Africa: British Consul Roger Casement publishes an account of the Belgian atrocities against Congo natives (→25/3).

11. London, Washington: The UK and US governments declare their neutrality in the Russo-Japanese war (→23).

13. Balkans: Turkish troops clash with 16,000 Albanian insurgents at Djakova (→18).

17. Africa: Uprising by "Silent Ones", aimed at overthrowing white rule, breaks out in Asaba, Nigeria.

18. Macedonia: Turks kill 800 Albanians in the siege of Shemsi Pasha (→22/11/05).

22. The Hague: Arbitration tribunal settles the amount due from Venezuela to powers involved in 1902 blockade.

23. Far East: Japan guarantees the sovereignty of the Korean Empire in exchange for military aid in the war against Russia (→4/3).

25. South-West Africa: Herero rebels are defeated by the Germans near Omaruru (→14/3).

29. London: White Paper shows that the colonies would prefer metric to imperial system of weights and measures.

BIRTH

20. Soviet politician Alexei Kosygin (†18/12/80).

Japanese night attack stuns Russians

Feb 10. A surprise night raid by Japanese torpedo boats crippled the Russian fleet at Port Arthur and plunged the two countries into undeclared war. Two battleships, the "Retivizian" and the "Czarevich", together with the cruiser "Pallad" were badly damaged by torpedos and sank in the channel, trapping other Russian warships. Two more cruisers, "Variag" and "Korietz", were disabled by Japanese ships at Chemui Po on the west coast of Korea. The Japanese claim they captured seven other warships.

When the victory at sea, and the fact that the Japanese squadron suffered only slight losses, was announced in Tokyo thousands of flag-waving students demonstrated in the streets. Only after news of the raid became public did the Emperor officially declare war – "to ensure the safety of our realm".

He blamed Russian imperial ambitions in Korea and Manchuria for causing the conflict. So completely were the Russians taken by surprise that first news of the Port Arthur disaster was rushed to the Czar in St. Petersburg while he was at the opera. Officials waited until the end of the performance before informing him so as not to spoil his evening. The Japanese were quick to exploit their startling success and yesterday, 8,000 infantry disembarked to begin their march on Seoul, capital of Korea. The Japanese can now land where they like and there is little the Russians can do to stop them (→ 11).

Battle cries: Russian naval power was crippled by the raid on Port Arthur.

Victory cheers: Japanese officers toast the success of their surprise attack.

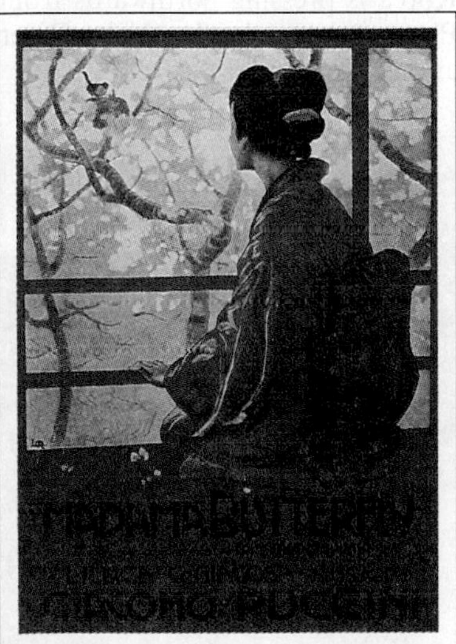

Tragedy: Puccini's new opera.

America ends its occupation of Cuba

Feb 5. The American occupation of Cuba ended today when the US flag was lowered and the Cuban flag raised in a ceremony in La Havana, which ended with a 21-gun salute for the new republic. Then the last battalion of American troops sailed for home on the "USS Sumner".

Thomas Palma, the President of the new Cuban Republic, expressed thanks for American friendship. In 1898, when Cubans rose against the rule of Spain, the US first helped them achieve independence. Then it occupied Cuba itself.

Tidal wave wreaks havoc in England

Feb 3. A freak tidal wave swept up the Channel today leaving a trail of devastation in its wake. Worst hit were the coastal towns of Sandgate, Portsmouth, St. Leonards (where huge waves ripped a 200-foot gash in the sea wall) and Hallsands in Devon where six cottages were washed out to sea.

Elsewhere gale force winds and heavy rain have caused considerable damage to property and wide spread flooding has brought work to a standstill on farms all over the country.

Caruso makes first recording in US

Feb 1. The New York Metropolitan Opera is currently at the feet of Enrico Caruso, the great tenor from Naples, who is now appearing in "L'Elisir d'Amore". Caruso, at 30, is a rich man. He is paid nearly $1000 for each performance and has just made his first American recording, a ten-inch disk of "La Donna e Mobile". This will surely outdo even his million-selling English record of "Vesti la Giubba" ("On with the Motley") from "I Pagliacci".

He will be the first opera star of the first rank whose voice will be heard by generations to come, thanks to the wonders of the phonograph. Caruso's fame began with his performance in Milan as Rodolfo in Puccini's "La Boheme" in 1898. He made his Covent Garden debut two seasons ago. Besides being acknowledged as the leading tenor of the day, he is also a highly talented caricaturist.

Caruso is unmarried but has two sons born to an Italian soprano. He smokes two packets of cigarettes a day and never takes exercise. He has even gone before the curtain at the Met to acknowledge the applause patting his ample stomach. He then implores the audience to go home "because I'm hungry and want my supper".

Triumph: Caruso's new recording.

1904

MARCH

Su	Mo	Tu	We	Th	Fr	Sa
		1	2	3	4	5
6	7	8	9	10	11	12
13	14	15	16	17	18	19
20	21	22	23	24	25	26
27	28	29	30	31		

1. Russia: Opening of stretch of Trans-Siberian Railway over frozen Lake Baikal (→ 7/21).

3. Germany: Kaiser Wilhelm makes the first political recording, on an Edison cylinder.

4. Far East: Russian troops retreat towards Manchurian border as 80,000 Japanese land in Korea (→ 15).

7. US: Mob in Springfield, Ohio, bursts into local prison and shoots dead black man accused of murder (→ 2/4).

8. Berlin: The Reichstag lifts the ban on Jesuits practising in Germany.

12. UK: First mainline electric train runs from Liverpool to Southport.

14. South-West Africa: Reinforcements are sent to back up Leutwein in fight against Herero tribesmen (→ 11/8).

15. Far East: 300 Russians die in Japanese bombardment of Port Arthur (→ 31).

16. London: End of festival of music by Edward Elgar, during which the composer received a knighthood.

22. US: The "Daily Illustrated Mirror" carries the first colour photographs in a newspaper.

22. London: Coal Smoke Abatement Society calls for smokeless capital at its fifth annual meeting.

25. UK: Spencer Gollan's Moifaa wins the Grand National; only nine out of 23 horses finished the course.

25. Liverpool: Formation of Congo Reform Association by Roger Casement and Edmund Morel (→ 9/6).

29. London: King Edward VII opens Richmond Royal Park to the public.

BIRTHS

1. US bandleader Glenn Miller (†16/12/44).

7. German Nazi Reinhard Heydrich, key figure in Adolf Hitler's "Final Solution" (†4/6/42).

Pressure forces new look at Dreyfus case

March 5. The criminal chamber of France's court of appeal, known as the Court of Cassation, today ordered a supplementary inquiry into the Dreyfus Affair. The case will now go to the Supreme Court and the conviction of Captain Alfred Dreyfus for treason in 1894 could be finally quashed.

Dreyfus was originally found guilty of selling military secrets to the German military attache – and served four years in the infamous Devil's Island penal colony – on the basis of two papers allegedly written by him. There is real doubt whether he wrote the first, while Major Henry, who confessed to forging the second, committed suicide.

The real significance of the case, however, is the political passion it generates, which has split France into bitterly warring camps. The Dreyfusards include radicals and anticlericals. The anti-Dreyfusards include anti-Semites, and those afraid Dreyfus' acquittal may harm the prestige of the army and of France. There was a second court-martial in 1899, at Rennes, partly as a result of passionate lobbying by novelist Emile Zola. Found guilty but pardoned, he reluctantly accepted it but has always pressed for total vindication (→ 29/6).

Scorned: Dreyfus (2nd from right).

British kill many hundreds in Tibet

March 31. Some 300 Tibetans, including their top general, were killed today when they attempted to halt the British Mission to Tibet and its accompanying force under Brigadier-General Macdonald.

About 2,000 Tibetans took up positions in sangars and behind a high wall commanding the road to Guru and ordered the British to turn back. At the request of Colonel Younghusband, General Macdonald ordered his men not to fire but manouevred so that the Tibetans were outflanked behind the wall. One of them, believed to be their general, opened fire with a pistol, blowing away a Sikh soldier's jaw.

The Tibetans then rushed the British with great bravery, some with eight or nine wounds, but faced by a Maxim gun and mountain guns, they stood little chance. Only half escaped unharmed and the road was opened (→ 10/4).

British sub lost

March 18. One of the six submarines now taking part in trials off Portsmouth was run down by a liner and lost with all 11 crew today. They were engaged in manoeuvres and the accident comes just days after the Royal Navy showed its confidence in the new craft by taking the Prince of Wales on an underwater trip around Portsmouth Harbour.

High roller: fashion on wheels.

Japanese torpedo Russian hopes

March 31. Russian forces in the Far East are now in a desperate position. Admiral Togo has sunk block ships in the approaches to Port Arthur which cannot hold out for long. His ships have bombarded the naval base at Vladivostok.

It is now known that Russian naval losses in the first Japanese raid were higher than originally reported. Two battleships and one cruiser were a total loss; a further battleship was sunk and yet another completely disabled. This week, for the first time, the commander of the beleaguered force in Port Arthur attempted a counter attack.

He sent six torpedo boats in an unsuccessful sortie against bombarding warships. The Russians claim to have sunk one Japanese torpedo boat but lost one of their own.

Meanwhile, the 80,000-strong Japanese force which landed in Korea is pressing northwards from Pingyan towards the Yalu River and the border (→ 5/4).

Eastward bound: Russian priests bless troops on their way to the front.

1904

APRIL

Su	Mo	Tu	We	Th	Fr	Sa
					1	2
3	4	5	6	7	8	9
10	11	12	13	14	15	16
17	18	19	20	21	22	23
24	25	26	27	28	29	30

1. Manchester: Henry Royce's engineering firm produces its first motor car, a 10-hp 2-cylinder model (→ 4/5).

2. US: 14 blacks lynched in race riots at St. Charles, Arkansas (→ 3/6).

3. East Indies: Dutch kill 541 Achinese in Sumatra revolt.

5. London: King Edward VII offers to mediate in Russo-Japanese War; Czar Nicholas is interested (→ 13).→

9. UK: Train runs non-stop from Plymouth to London in record time of under four and a half hours.

10. Tibet: British kill 190 Tibetans at Gyangtse (→ 6/5).

12. Spain: Premier Maura wounded in assassination attempt.

14. London: First attempt at "talking pictures" at Fulham Theatre, using cinematography and phonograph.

18. Paris: First edition of "L'Humanite" appears.

19. London: Austen Chamberlain's first budget raises income tax and duties on tobacco and tea.

23. London: Manchester City beat Bolton Wanderers 1-0 in the FA Cup at Crystal Palace.

24. Hungary: Riots follow collapse after five days of strike by 60,000 railway workers.

26. London: G.B. Shaw's "Candida" opens at the Court Theatre.

30. US: President Theodore Roosevelt opens World Fair in St. Louis.

BIRTHS

14. British actor John Gielgud.

22. US physicist J. Robert Oppenheimer (†18/2/67).

24. US painter Willem de Kooning.

DEATHS

9. Isabel II, former Queen of Spain (*10/10/1830).

24. Friedrich Siemens, German industrialist (*8/12/1826).

Pact aids cordial feelings for France

April 8. Great Britain and France this morning signed a historic agreement aimed at resolving all outstanding differences between them. The crucial pact was initialled by Paul Cambon, on behalf of Paul Delcasse, the French Minister of Foreign Affairs, and by Lord Lansdowne, the British Foreign Secretary.

The agreement is nothing less than a global deal. Issues which have troubled relations between the two powers, in one instance for centuries and in others for decades, are resolved so that no major causes of conflict remain.

The longest-standing dispute concerns Newfoundland, where fishing rights and French rights on shore have been disputed since the Treaty of Utrecht in 1714.

France has agreed to surrender shore rights in return for confirmation of fishing rights and the end of an ancient dispute over whether a lobster is a fish. The French accept that it is. In return, Britain has made small territorial concessions to France in West Africa.

The two powers have also made two declarations, one about Egypt and Morocco, the other about Thailand and the New Hebrides. France will be given a free hand in Morocco if the Sultan's rule should break down. In return, France will respect British primacy in Egypt.

The agreement caps months of delicate negotiations. The initiative for the conference came from His Majesty King Edward VII when he visited Paris last year.

Spirit of friendship: a souvenir postcard celebrates the Entente Cordiale.

Russia loses flagship and 600 men

April 13. In an ill-fated sortie from Port Arthur, the Russian fleet yesterday suffered yet another great blow with the loss of the battleship "Petropavlovsk". She went down under the telescopes of Admiral Togo and the Japanese fleet.

The ship, flying the flag of Admiral Makaroff, sank within two minutes after striking a mine. The commander-in-chief went down with his ship along with 600 other officers and ratings. Among the 37 survivors was the first officer, Grand Duke Cyril. In addition to this disaster the battleship "Pobieda" was badly damaged (→ 15/5).

Sunk: battleship Petropavlovsk.

New union rights

April 22. By a majority of 39, the House of Commons approved a bill which allowed for "peaceful picketing" by trade unionists and amended the present law on conspiracy and the protection of union funds. The Prime Minister, Arthur Balfour, said that he had twice attempted to form a commission on the matter but that trade unions had refused to co-operate. He rejected claims that the Government was supporting employers against the trade union movement.

Higher tobacco tax sparks protests

April 26. The threepence per lb duty on tobacco announced by the Chancellor in his Budget last week was rounded upon by members of the United Kingdom Tobacconists' Alliance at a meeting held in London today.

Retailers who fear that they will have to bear the brunt of the tax changes cheered when their president declared that he did not know of a more harassed trade than theirs. The last six years, he said, had been enough to drive Britain's tax-hit tobacconists into the lunatic asylum.

A resolution calling for the proposed tax to be withdrawn and replaced with large increases in the duty levied on imported cigars and cigarettes was carried by an enthusiastic majority.

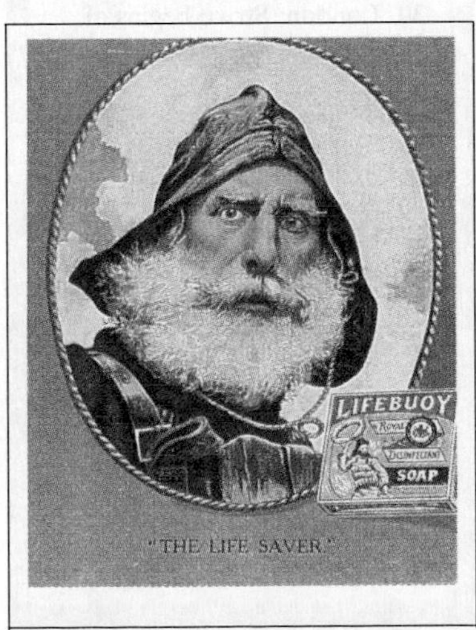

1904

MAY

Su	Mo	Tu	We	Th	Fr	Sa
1	2	3	4	5	6	7
8	9	10	11	12	13	14
15	16	17	18	19	20	21
22	23	24	25	26	27	28
29	30	31				

4. Panama: US engineers start work on the Panama Canal.

7. Germany: Reported that steam trains can now do 85 mph.

9. Paris: Exhibition opens at the Galerie Durand-Ruel of 37 "Views of the Thames at London" by Claude Monet.

11. Turkey: 900 Armenian rebels die in clashes with the Ottoman troops.

13. London: Anglo-Chinese Labour Convention signed, permitting the introduction of "coolies" to the colonies.

14. Vienna: Emperor Franz Josef asks for a massive increase in the military budget.

15. Far East: 450 die as a Japanese battleship is destroyed by a mine (→25).

17. Paris: The first performance of "Sheherazade" by Maurice Ravel.

21. Paris: France recalls its ambassador from the Vatican (→29/7).

23. Chicago: Republican Convention nominates President Roosevelt to stand for reelection (→8/11).

25. Far East: 4,500 Japanese and 3,000 Russians die at Nanshan; Gen. Oku seals off Port Arthur by land and sea (→24/6).

29. Vienna: King Edward VII is made honorary field-marshal of the Austro-Hungarian army by Emperor Franz Josef.

30. London: Strike begins of 3,000 cabbies.

BIRTHS

2. US singer and actor Harry L. Crosby, alias Bing Crosby (†14/10/77).

11. Spanish painter Salvador Dali (†23/1/89).

21. US jazz musician Fats Waller (†15/12/43).

DEATHS

1. Bohemian composer Antonin Dvorak (*8/9/1841).→

9. British explorer Sir Henry Morton Stanley (*28/1/1841).→

Mr Rolls and Mr Royce to make cars

At the wheel: Charles Rolls.

One of Royce's first three cars, built last month, a 10hp 2 cylinder model.

May 4. An agreement was reached today between the Hon. Charles Rolls, whose company C.S. Rolls sells and repairs cars from Conduit Street, London, and Henry Royce, the driving force behind F.H. Royce, the well-known Manchester electrical engineers. Under the provisional agreement, which stops short of a merger, Rolls will sell Royce cars under the name "Rolls-Royce".

The two men met at the Midland Hotel, Manchester, having been introduced by Henry Edmunds, a director of the Royce company and a former rival of Rolls in motor rallies. In the Thousand Mile Trial of 1900, which first popularised motoring in Britain, Charles Rolls was the overall winner in a 12hp Panhard. Last year Rolls, the third son of Lord Llangattock, set the world land speed record of 93 miles an hour at Phoenix Park, Dublin.

He seems to have struck up an instant rapport with Mr Royce, a self-made engineer with an established reputation for perfectionism in engineering. The son of a miller, Royce started work as a telegraph boy in Mayfair. But after an engineering apprenticeship with the Great Northern Railway, he eventually set up his own workshops in Manchester.

Last year he turned his attention to cars with his first model, 10hp two-cylinder, being praised for its "excellent running" when it made its debut last month. Three other models are planned.

Britain goes to war on the rooftop of the world and kills 400

May 6. A brisk battle was fought today high up in the Karo Pass between the column protecting the British Mission to Lhasa and a force of some 3,000 Tibetans. At one stage the affair took a dangerous turn with the British force held up by riflemen positioned behind the wall and in two flanking stone-built native forts. Captain Bethune and his small assault party had been killed rushing the wall and the guns made no impression on the forts.

The day was saved by Major Row's Gurkhas, who climbed the face of a nearly sheer precipice and fired down on the Tibetans. At the same time the Sikhs climbed to the edge of the glacier and flanked the forts. The Tibetans then fled, pursued by the Mounted Infantry. They lost 400 dead (→3/8).

Summit conference: British and Tibetan representatives meet beside a hilltop town to discuss peace terms, after torrid fighting in the Karo Pass.

Stanley is dead, one presumes

May 9. Sir Henry Morton Stanley, the illegitimate son of a Welsh butcher's daughter who became the most famous explorer of his time, died in London today, aged 63. He achieved fame and made a fortune with his account of his seven-month 1,500-mile safari into Central Africa in search of Dr David Livingstone in 1871. He later expressed regret at having greeted the missionary with what was to become a catch phrase, for wherever he went he was met with: "Mr Stanley, I presume?" He traced the course of the Congo River and helped King Leopold of the Belgians form the Congo Free State.

Livingstone's finder: Stanley.

Dvorak, old world composer, dies

May 1. Antonin Dvorak, the Bohemian butcher's son who rose to rank with the immortals of music, has died at the age of 62.

Dvorak is recognised as a master of most forms of composition. His "Dumky" trio and "American" quartet are among the finest written, but it is perhaps for his orchestral music that he will be best remembered. His symphonies and tone-poems won Dvorak the admiration of Brahms. The glorious seventh symphony matches Brahms for quality, while the great ninth, "From the New World", has been a hit since it was first written in New York in 1892.

1904

JUNE

Su	Mo	Tu	We	Th	Fr	Sa
			1	2	3	4
5	6	7	8	9	10	11
12	13	14	15	16	17	18
19	20	21	22	23	24	25
26	27	28	29	30		

1. UK: Leopold de Rothschild's St Amant wins the Derby at Epsom in a thunderstorm.

2. Paris: Exhibition of paintings by Matisse at the Galerie Vollard.

3. US: President Roosevelt names a black Senator, Charles Warren Fairbank, to second his presidential nomination (→7/9).

9. London: The House of Commons debates alleged Belgian atrocities in the Congo (→19/9).

10. UK: Jack White wins the Open Golf Championship with the record lowest ever score of 296.

15. S. America: UK and Brazil sign an arbitration convention to settle the disputed border of British Guyana.

17. UK: The Gordon Bennett motoring cup is won by Gustave Thery in a Richard-Brasier.

18. S. Africa: First Chinese labourers arrive.

19. London: Admiral Sir John Fisher is appointed First Sea Lord.

23. Finland: The Russian governor-general, General Bobrikov, is assassinated.

24. UK: First meeting of the International Salvation Army Congress.

28. New York: Inquiry into "General Slocum" disaster finds ship's owners guilty of negligence.

28. UK: Over 700 Scandinavian emigrants die when steamer Norge is wrecked off Ireland.

29. Wimbledon: Laurence Doherty beats Frank Riseley in Men's Singles final; Dorothea Douglass beats Charlotte Sterry for Ladies' Singles title.

BIRTHS

2. US swimmer and actor Johnny Weissmuller (†20/1/84).

26. Hungarian-born actor Peter Lorre (†23/3/64).

Pleasure cruise to nightmare: 693 dead

The wrecked ship "General Slocum" in New York harbour.

June 15. In the sheltered waters of New York harbour, a church outing took a calamitous turn today when a fire broke out aboard a paddle-steamer, the "General Slocum". So far 693 bodies have been recovered but 1,000 are estimated dead.

The outing was an annual event for St. Mark's German Lutheran Church in New York City. Most of the casualties were women and children. The boat was an hour into its trip, with the band playing, when fire struck with terrifying suddenness. Its cause is unknown.

The steamer was opposite 135th Street in the East River and the New York shoreline was no more than 300 feet away. The captain, however, chose to steer for North Brother Island and the vessel burned to the waterline. Trapped women threw babies overboard. Life belts were rotten (→28).

Russia reels under Japanese attacks

June 24. Japanese forces in Korea have inflicted a major defeat on the Russians at Telissu, completely routing two divisions under General Stackelberg. His relief column was engaged by the Japanese as it marched south in a forlorn attempt to break the siege at Port Arthur.

Reports from the front today indicate that 2,000 Russian soldiers were killed and that their total losses, including prisoners, amount to more than 10,000; the Japanese only lost 1,000. It was the fiercest battle of the war, fought in a huge thunderstorm, along the vital Port Arthur-Muckden railway.

The attempt to relieve Port Arthur totally failed and the shattered Russian force, which lost 24 guns, is now threatened by three Japanese armies (→1/8).

Roosevelt named for the presidency

June 23. Sweltering in the heat of a Chicago summer, the Republican Party today unanimously nominated President Theodore Roosevelt for another term in office. Waving flags and banners as they noisily paraded through the aisles of the vast coliseum, the convention delegates cheered lustily when the president's name was placed in nomination. There were cheers, too, for Senator Charles Warren Fairbanks of Indiana, who was chosen as Republican candidate for vice-president (→9/7).

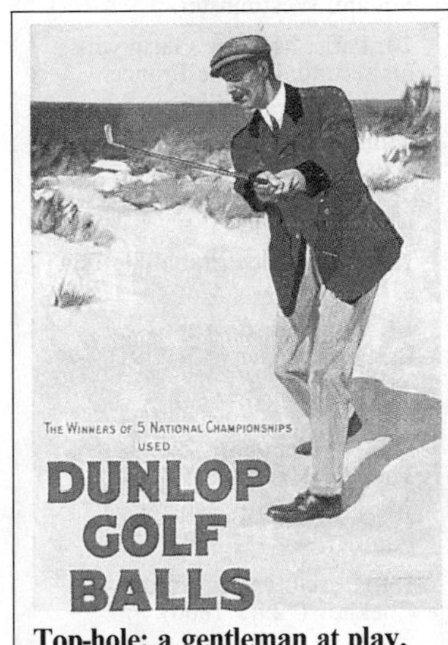

Top-hole: a gentleman at play.

1904

JULY

Su	Mo	Tu	We	Th	Fr	Sa
					1	2
3	4	5	6	7	8	9
10	11	12	13	14	15	16
17	18	19	20	21	22	23
24	25	26	27	28	29	30
31						

1. US: Third summer Olympic Games of modern times open at St. Louis (→29/8).

5. Finland: Prince Ivan Obolenski is appointed governor-general in succession to Bobrikov (→16/8).

9. US: Democratic convention at St. Louis nominates Judge Alton B. Parker as presidential candidate (→8/11).

9. US: Willie Anderson wins third US Open Golf Championship.

12. London: UK signs five-year treaty with Germany to resolve disputes through arbitration.

13. Far East: Japan occupies Niuchwang (→1/8).

14. London: Joseph Chamberlain is elected president of the Liberal Unionist Council.

18. Tehran: The cholera epidemic is reported to be killing as many as 900 people daily.

19. Middle East: UK sends warships to protect its shipping from harassment by the Russian navy looking for Japanese (→21).

21. London: Crisis in Anglo-Russian relations as Russia sinks one British ship and seizes another (→16/8).

22. London: The Royal Horticultural Society opens new headquarters in Vincent Square, Westminster.

24. Paris: Maurice Garin wins his second Tour de France.

28. Russia: The Interior Minister Viacheslav von Plehve is assassinated (→22/10).

BIRTHS

12. Chilean poet Pablo Neruda (†23/9/1973).

14. US Yiddish writer Isaac Bashevis Singer (†24/7/91).

DEATHS

3. Hungarian-born Zionist Theodor Herzl (*2/5/1860).

14. S. African Boer leader Paul Kruger (*10/10/1825).→

15. Russian writer Anton Chekhov (*29/1/1860).→

Railway crosses Siberia

All aboard! Russians marvel at their new railway.

July 21. The long-awaited Trans-Siberian railway – stretching 4,607 miles from Chelyabinsk to Vladivostock – has been completed after 13 years of construction. The decision to build the railway was made in 1891.

The Trans-Siberian railway represents a landmark in railroad engineering. The Russians had to overcome massive problems: wide rivers, steep gradients around Lake Baikal, permafrost in Eastern Siberia and extremes of temperatures. Now there are more than 1,000 stations along the route of the railway.

The Russian government sees the new railway as a valuable asset in "opening up" Siberia and promoting trade with China and the Orient (→1/1/05).

Chekhov, chronicler of Russian life, dies

July 15. Anton Chekhov, known in Britain for his deceptively simple but guileful short stories published here last year, has died in Germany at 44 of tuberculosis. He began writing comic pieces as a medical student and continued his short stories as a country doctor.

His early efforts at play-writing were failures but in 1897 "The Seagull", which had flopped in St. Petersburg, was produced at the Moscow Arts Theatre with success. It was followed by "Uncle Vanya", "The Three Sisters" and, earlier this year, "The Cherry Orchard". Its leading role, an ageing actress, was played by Olga Knipper, whom he married in 1901. His plays have not been seen here.

Writer's circle: Chekhov (with book) beside actor-producer Stanislavsky.

Ex-Boer president dies in exile

June 14. Stephanus Johannes Paulus Kruger, four times President of the Transvaal Republic, three times married and known to his people as Oom ("Uncle") Paul, died today in exile at Clarens on Lake Geneva aged 79.

He stubbornly resisted the spread of British influence in South Africa and his denial of equal voting rights for uitlanders (foreigners working in the Transvaal) led to the Boer War. As a boy of 10 his parents took him on the Great Trek north from Cape Colony to escape British rule; at 13 he fought alongside his parents against the Zulus.

Uncle of a nation: Paul Kruger.

France breaks off links with Vatican

July 29. France severed its final diplomatic links with the Vatican today by recalling its Charge d'Affaires – the ambassador was recalled in May. This is the latest move in the battle between the increasingly anti-clerical French government and the church.

Simultaneously the Pope's man in Paris was called to the French foreign office and told to leave. The anti-clerical movement in France has always been strong but under the present government it has won the support of the President, Emile Combes, a former cleric.

1904

AUGUST

Su	Mo	Tu	We	Th	Fr	Sa
	1	2	3	4	5	6
7	8	9	10	11	12	13
14	15	16	17	18	19	20
21	22	23	24	25	26	27
28	29	30	31			

1. Far East: Russian General Count Keller killed as Russians defeated near Liao-Yang.→

4. UK: First Atlantic weather forecast is received by wireless telegraph.

7. US: 125 people die when railway bridge collapses at Pueblo, Colorado.

8. Austria: Oil workers' revolt at Borislav is ended by a reduction in working hours and an improvement in sanitation.

9. Paris: International Miners' Congress calls for minimum wage and eight-hour day.

11. S.W. Africa: Hereros tribesmen defeated near Waterberg by German colonial troops.

14. London: The National Gallery buys Titian's "Portrait of Aristotle" for £150,000.

16. London: Government officially protests to Russia over seizure and sinking of neutral merchant ships.

16. St. Petersburg: Russian government says Jewish aggression is responsible for the massacres of Jews in Poland (→4/9).

17. US: Mob invades courthouse, seizes two blacks on trial for murder, and burns them at the stake (→7/9).

19. Persia: It is reported that 40,000 people have died from cholera.

24. Germany: Duchy of Baden establishes direct universal suffrage.

25. UK: First ocean-going turbine steamer, the "Victoria", is launched in Belfast.

BIRTHS

12. Russian imperial heir Czarevich Alexis, son of Czar Nicholas II (†29/7/18).

21. US jazz musician Count Basie (†26/4/84).

26. British author Christopher Isherwood (†4/1/86).

DEATH

25. French painter Henri Fantin-Latour (*14/1/1836).

Japanese deploy new war technology

Aug 30. The Japanese army today captured Liao-Yang, 250 miles north-east of Port Arthur. It is the last big town on the Trans-Siberian railway before the Korea-Manchuria border.

In heavy fighting both sides made lavish use of artillery and a Russian war correspondent describes "greedy shrapnel" waylaying terrified troops. At Port Arthur, the other critical sector of the front, most of the outlying forts are now in Japanese hands. The Russians have little chance of holding out and their only chance is to attempt a desperate last sortie.

In the harbour lies the wreckage of three Russian battleships. At sea, Admiral Togo's battle-fleet destroyed the Russian squadron attempting to relieve Port Arthur. One badly mauled battleship managed to limp into port, but Admiral Witgeft was killed.

Japanese successes are partly attributed to their use of modern devices such as wireless telegraphy. In night attacks they employ powerful searchlights to blind enemy troops.

On to victory: Japanese troops.

"We were wrong to call them little Japs," writes a Russian war correspondent. "We have never before had to deal with such skilful opponents" (→3/9).

Britain takes Lhasa as Dalai Lama flees

Aug 3. The British mission to Tibet arrived before the capital, Lhasa, at midday today with no further opposition being offered to General Macdonald's force. The inhabitants of this extraordinary city are quiet at the moment and the Dalai Lama has left for a monastery some miles away.

It is not yet known if he will receive Colonel Younghusband and the members of his mission or if he will continue to refuse to negotiate. In the meantime a number of dignitarics have called on Colonel Younghusband at the British camp on the Pota-la road two miles outside Lhasa.

The dignitaries, who include representatives from China and Nepal and the Great Abbot, confidant of the Dalai Lama, have been assured by Colonel Younghusband that the British force will leave as soon as a treaty is signed settling relations between Great Britain and Tibet (→7/9).

Champ wins again

He's a knockout: James Jeffries.

Aug 27. James Jeffries remains the undisputed world heavyweight champion. Today he knocked out the latest challenger, miner Jack Munroe, only 45 seconds into the second round. The 7,000 San Francisco crowd who paid £4,360 booed angrily at Munroe's poor performance. Munroe was knocked down four times before the referee stopped the fight.

Postcards prove popular: 25% increase

Aug 17. The country is in the grip of a mania for postcards, according to the latest report from the Postmaster-General. They have been very popular on the Continent for the last two years but now they have caught on here with a vengeance and last year their use increased by 25%. The craze reached its height in Scotland where the increase was a remarkable 35%.

This growth was all the more impressive when compared with the fact that in London, at least, the number of letters delivered actually decreased. In terms of total numbers, however, the letter is still very much king with 2,597,600,000 delivered last year as against 613,000,000 postcards.

The report also noted some extraordinary examples of absent-mindedness: 379,426 packets were posted without any address on them at all, 4,190 of which contained a total of over £10,000.

Just in time
to catch the
post

Postcards are popular with holidaymakers, but letters remain supreme.

1904 St. Louis

Aug 29. The third modern Olympic Games ended today with American domination virtually unchallenged. Americans won all but two of the 23 track and field titles. However, a series of events spread over several weeks and ignored by many European nations evoked little interest outside the World Fair city of St. Louis. The very slow marathon (three hours and 28 minutes in 90 degree heat and stifling dust) provided the main excitement. The first American home was disqualified for taking a lift in a lorry, and the eventual winner, English-born Thomas Hicks, was fed alternate doses of strychnine and brandy on his painful route to victory.

Golden swimmer: Emil Rausch.

The barrel-jump, an unusual newcomer to the list of Olympic sports.

Men Athletics

100m
1. Archie Hahn USA 11.0
2. Nathan Cartmell USA 11.2
3. William Hogenson USA 11.2

200m
1. Archie Hahn USA *21.6
2. Nathan Cartmell USA 21.9
3. William Hogenson USA

400m
1. Harry Hillman USA *49.2
2. Frank Waller USA 49.9
3. Herman Groman USA 50.0

800m
1. James Lightbody USA *1:56.0
2. Howard Valentine USA 1:56.3
3. Emil Breitkreutz USA 1:56.4

1500m
1. James Lightbody USA *4:05.4
2. Frank Verner USA 4:06.8
3. Lacey Hearn USA

Marathon
1. Thomas Hicks USA 3:28.63
2. Albert Corey USA 3:34.52
3. Arthur Newton USA 3:47.33

110m Hurdles
1. Fred Schule USA 16.0
2. Thaddeus Shideler USA 16.3
3. Lesley Ashburner USA 16.4

200m Hurdles
1. Harry Hillman USA *24.6
2. Frank Castleman USA 24.9
3. George Poage USA

400m Hurdles
1. Harry Hillman USA 53.0
2. Frank Waller USA 53.2
3. George Poage USA

3000m Steeplechase
1. James Lightbody USA 7:39.6
2. John Daly IRL 7:40.6
3. Arthur Newton USA 25 m

High Jump
1. Samuel Jones USA 1.803
2. Garret Serviss USA 1.778
3. Paul Weinstein GER 1.778

Pole Vault
1. Charles Dvorak USA *3.505
2. Leroy Samse USA 3.43
3. Louis Wilkins USA 3.43

Long Jump
1. Myer Prinstein USA *7.34
2. Daniel Frank USA 6.89
3. Robert Stangland USA 6.88

Triple Jump
1. Myer Prinstein USA 14.35
2. Fred Englehardt USA 13.90
3. Robert Stangland USA 13.365

Shotput
1. Ralph Rose USA 14.81
2. William Coe USA 14.40
3. Leon Feuerbach USA 13.37

Discus
1. Martin Sheridan USA *39.28
2. Ralph Rose USA *39.28
3. Nicolaos Georgantas GRE 37.68

Hammer
1. John Flanagan USA *51.23
2. John DeWitt USA 50.265
3. Ralph Rose USA 45.73

Decathlon
1. Thomas Kiely GBR/IRL 6036
2. Adam Gunn USA 5907
3. Truxton Hare USA 5813

60m
1. Archie Hahn USA *7.0
2. William Hogenson USA 7.2
3. Fay Moulton USA 7.2

Team Cross Country
1. New York A.C. 21:17.8
2. Chicago A.A.

5000m Team
1. Great Britain
2. France

Standing High Jump
1. Raymond Ewry USA 1.60
2. Joseph Stadler USA 1.45
3. Lareison Robertson USA 1.45

Standing Long Jump
1. Raymond Ewry USA *3.476
2. Charles King USA 3.28
3. John Biller USA 3.26

Standing Triple Jump
1. Raymond Ewry USA 10.54
2. Charles King USA 10.16
3. Joseph Stadler USA 9.60

56lb. Weight Throw
1. Etienne Desmarteau CAN 10.46
2. John Flanagan USA 10.16
3. James Mitchel USA 10.13

Tug-of-War
1. USA (Milwaukee Athletic Club)
2. USA (St. Louis Southwest Turnverein No. 1)
3. USA (St. Louis Southwest Turnverein No. 2)

Golf

Men Individual
1. George Lyon CAN
2. Chandlier Egan USA
3. Burt McKinnie USA

Men Team
1. USA (Western Golf Association)
2. USA (Trans Mississippi Golf Association)
3. USA (United States Golf Association)

Lacrosse

1. CAN (Shamrock Lacrosse Team, Winnipeg)
2. USA (St. Louis Amateur Athletic Association)
3. CAN (Mohawk Indians, Brantford)

Roque

1. Charles Jacobus USA
2. Smith Streeter USA
3. Charles Brown USA

Men Swimming

100m Freestyle
1. Zoltán Halmay HUN 1:02.8
2. Charles Daniels USA
3. J. Scott Leary USA

200m Freestyle
1. Charles Daniels USA 2:44.2
2. Francis Gailey USA 2:46.0
3. Emil Rausch GER 2:56.0

400m Freestyle
1. Charles Daniels USA 6:16.2
2. Francis Gailey USA 6:22.0
3. Otto Wahle AUT 6:39.0

1500m Freestyle
1. Emil Rausch GER 27:18.2
2. Géza Kiss HUN 28:28.2
3. Francis Gailey USA 28:54.0

100m Backstroke
1. Walter Brack GER 1:16.8
2. Georg Hoffmann GER
3. Georg Zacharias GER

High Diving
1. George Sheldon USA 12.66
2. Georg Hoffmann GER 11.66
3. Alfred Braunschweiger GER 11.33

50 m Freestyle
1. Zoltán Halmay HUN 28.0
2. J. Scott Leary USA 28.6
3. Charles Daniels USA

400m Breaststroke
1. George Zacharias GER 7:23.6
2. Walter Brack GER 20 m
3. H. Jamison Handy USA

880 yards Freestyle
1. Emil Rausch GER 13:11.4
2. Francis Gailey USA 13:23.4
3. Géza Kiss HUN

Plunge for Distance
1. William Dickey USA 19.05
2. Edgar Adams USA 17.53
3. Leo "Budd" Goodwin USA 17.37

200 Yards Team Relay
1. New York A.C. 2:04.6
2. Chicago A.C.
3. Missouri A.C.

Waterpolo
1. New York A.C.
2. Chicago A.C.
3. Missouri A.C.

Platform Diving
1. George Sheldon USA 12.66
2. Georg Hoffmann GER 11.66
3. Alfred Braunschweiger GER 11.33

Boxing

Flyweight
1. George Finnegan USA
2. Miles Burke USA

Bantamweight
1. Oliver Kirk USA
2. George Finnegan USA

Featherweight
1. Oliver Kirk USA
2. Frank Haller USA
3. Fred Gilmore USA

Lightweight
1. Harry Spanger USA
2. James Eagan USA
3. Russell Van Horn USA

Welterweight
1. Albert Young USA
2. Harry Spanger USA
3. Joseph Lydon USA
3. Jack Eagan USA

Middleweight
1. Charles Mayer USA
2. Benjamin Spradley USA

Super Heavyweight
1. Samuel Berger USA
2. Charles Mayer USA
3. William Michaels USA

Weightlifting

All-around dumbbell (10 tractions)
1. Oscar Paul Osthoff USA 48 points
2. Frederick Winters USA 45 points
3. Frank Kungler USA 10 points

Super Heavyweight 2 hand lift
1. Periklės Kakousis GRE 111.70 kg
2. Oscar Osthoff USA 84.37 kg
3. Frank Kungler USA 79.61 kg

Freestyle Wrestling

Light Flyweight
1. Robert Curry USA
2. John Hein USA
3. Gustav Thiefenthaler USA

Flyweight
1. George Mehnert USA
2. Gustave Bauers USA
3. William Nelson USA

Bantamweight
1. Isidor Niflot USA
2. August Wester USA
3. Z.B. Strebler USA

Featherweight
1. Benjamin Bradshaw USA
2. Theodore McLeer USA
3. Charles Clapper USA

Lightweight
1. Otto Roehm USA
2. R. Tesing USA
3. Albert Zirkel USA

Welterweight
1. Charles Erickson USA
2. William Beckmann USA
3. Jerry Winholtz USA

Heavyweight
1. Bernhuff Hansen USA
2. Frank Kungler USA
3. Fred Warmbold USA

Men Fencing

Foil Individual
1. Ramon Fonst CUB
2. Albertson van zo Post CUB
3. Charles Tatham CUB

Epée Individual
1. Ramon Fonst CUB
2. Charles Tatham CUB
3. Albertson van zo Post CUB

Sabre Individual
1. Manuel Diaz CUB
2. William Grebe USA
3. Albertson van zo Post CUB

Single Sticks
1. Albertson van zo Post CUB
2. William Grebe USA
3. William Scott O'Connor USA

Men Rowing

Single Sculls
1. Frank Greer USA 10:08.5
2. James Juvenal USA 2 lengths
3. Constance Titus USA 1 length

Double Sculls
1. USA (Atalanta Boat Club, New York) 10:03.2
2. USA (Ravenswood Boat Club, Long Island)
3. USA (Independent Rowing Club, New Orleans)

Coxless Pairs
1. USA (Seawanaka B.C., Brooklyn) 10:57.00
2. USA (Atalanta B.C., New York)
3. USA (Western Rowing Club, St. Louis)

Coxless fours
1. USA (Century Boat Club, St. Louis) 9:05.8
2. USA (Mound City Rowing Club, St. Louis)
3. USA (Western Rowing Club, St. Louis)

Eights
1. USA (Vesper Boat Club, Philadelphia) 7:50.0
2. Canada (Argonaut R.C. Toronto)

Men Archery

Double York Round (100 yards-80 yards-60 yards)
1. Phillip Bryant USA 820
2. Robert Williams USA 819
3. William H. Thompson USA 816

Double American Round (60 yards-50 yards-40 yards)
1. Phillip Bryant USA 1048
2. Robert Williams USA 991
3. William H. Thompson USA 949

Team Round (60 yards)
1. Potomac Archers, Washington, D.C. 1344
2. Cincinatti Archers 1341
3. Boston Archers 1268

Women Archery

Double National Round (60 yards-50 yards)
1. Lida Howell USA 620
2. Jessie Pollock USA 419
3. Emma Cooke USA 419

Double Columbia Round (50 yards-40 yards-30 yards)
1. Lida Howell USA 867
2. Emma Cooke USA 630
3. Jessie Pollock USA 630

Team Round
1. Cincinatti A.C. 506
2. Potomac Archers, Washington

Men Gymnastics

Individual All-around Competition
1. Adolf Spinnler GER 43.49
2. Wilhelm Weber GER 41.60
3. Hugo Peitsch GER 41.56

Team Combined Exercises
1. USA

Parallel Bars
1. George Eyser USA 44
2. Anton Heida USA 43
3. John Duha USA 40

Long Horse Vault
1. Anton Heida USA 36
1. George Eyser USA 36
3. William Merz USA 31

Pommelled Horse
1. Anton Heida USA 42
2. George Eyser USA 33
3. William Merz USA 29

Horizontal Bar
1. Anton Heida USA 40
1. Edward Henning USA 40
3. George Eyser USA 39

Flying Rings
1. Hermann Glass USA 45
2. William Merz USA 35
3. Emil Voigt USA 32

Rope Climb
1. George Eyser USA 7.0
2. Charles Krause USA 7.8
3. Emil Voigt USA 9.8

Club Swinging
1. Edward Hennig USA 13.0
2. Emil Voigt USA 9.0
3. Ralph Wilson USA 5.0

Triple Competition (Parallel Bars, Horizontal Bar, Vault Horse)
1. Adolf Spinnler SUI 43.49
2. Julius Lenhart AUT 43.00
3. Wilhelm Weber GER 41.60

Triathlon
1. Max Emmerich USA 35.70
2. John Grieb USA 34.00
3. William Merz USA 33.90

Combined Competition (4 apparatus)
1. Anton Heida USA 161
2. George Eyser USA 152
3. William Merz USA 135

Basketball (demonstration)

1. USA 4 (Buffalo German YMCA)
2. USA 3 (Chicago Central YMCA)
3. USA 0 (Xavier A.C. New York)

Football

1. Canada (Galt F.C. Ontario)
2. USA (Christian Brothers College)
3. USA (St Rose, St Louis)

Tennis

Men singles
1. Beals Wright USA
2. Robert LeRoy USA
3. Alonzo Bell USA

Double
1. USA – 2. USA – 3. USA

1904

SEPTEMBER

Su	Mo	Tu	We	Th	Fr	Sa
				1	2	3
4	5	6	7	8	9	10
11	12	13	14	15	16	17
18	19	20	21	22	23	24
25	26	27	28	29	30	

1. US: Helen Keller, deaf and blind since age of two, graduates with honours from Radcliffe College.

3. London: American cyclist Robert Walthour wins 100km (62.5 miles) race at Crystal Palace.

3. Far East: General Kuropatkin's army is routed at Liao-Yang (→25).

4. Russia: Imperial decree defines residence rights of Jews (→10/1/05).

5. Korea: Japanese force Russians to give up Mukden (→25).

6. Scotland: The Salvation Army's General Booth ends his crusading trip from Land's End to Aberdeen.

7. US: Alabama mob of 2,000 burns black man accused of murder.

7. Tibet: Anglo-Tibetan treaty gives UK trading posts and forbids Dalai Lama to make cessions to foreign powers.

16. Switzerland: Italian aeronaut Spelterini flies over the Alps in a balloon.

18. Italy: General strike called by the Socialists ends after four days (→12/3/05).

21. Belgrade: King Peter is crowned.

24. US: 62 people die in head-on train crash in Tennessee.

25. Russia: Czar orders reorganisation of Manchurian Army, replacing Kuropatkin with General Grippenberg (→15/10).

28. US: Woman arrested for smoking on New York's Fifth Avenue.

30. China: Republican unrest is reported in the south of the country.

BIRTHS

16. Finnish writer Arvo Turtiainen (†8/11/80).

17. Sir Frederick Ashton, founder of the British Royal Ballet (†19/8/88).

21. Franco-German painter Hans Hartung (†8/12/89).

British pressure forces establishment of board to investigate Congo cruelties

Sept 19. Responding to intense pressure from the British government, Leopold II, the King of the Belgians, has appointed an international commisssion which sailed today to investigate conditions in his Congo Free State.

Concern about the ill-treatment of natives employed by concessionaires to collect ivory and rubber has been widespread for several years, but Leopold always defended his administration. Events moved swiftly, however, after the British government published the report by their consul Roger Casement. The report corroborated evidence, already given by missionaries, that in many districts Africans were living in conditions of forced labour and that they were often assaulted by their supervisors, both black and white.

A Congo pressure group was formed in London and MPs raised the issue in the Commons. Leopold's appointment of three lawyers – Belgian, Swiss and Italian – to investigate goes some way towards meeting his critics.

Army sees no use for Wright plane

Sept 20. The two Wright brothers have won over sceptics who did not believe their aircraft could actually fly with a display in front of a crowd near their home town of Dayton, Ohio, but the American Army still believes the heavier-than-air machine has no military value.

Orville and Wilbur Wright only received limited recognition last year when they made their first flight from Kitty Hawk, North Carolina. Soon after they returned to Dayton they began to build a new machine, the "Flyer No. 2", which was completed this spring.

Again, the first trials with this machine proved difficult and when they invited the Press along for a demonstration the aircraft failed to take to the air, due in part to lack of headwinds. To overcome that problem the brothers have now added a catapult to their launching platform and have made short hops in the aircraft for some weeks.

Today the aircraft succeeded in circling the field they have rented for trials, just outside the city, for the first time. "Flyer 2" has a more powerful engine than the Wrights' first model but it still retains the system of moveable wingtips which was the secret of their aircraft's successes. They seem certain soon to be granted a patent, if not official recognition.

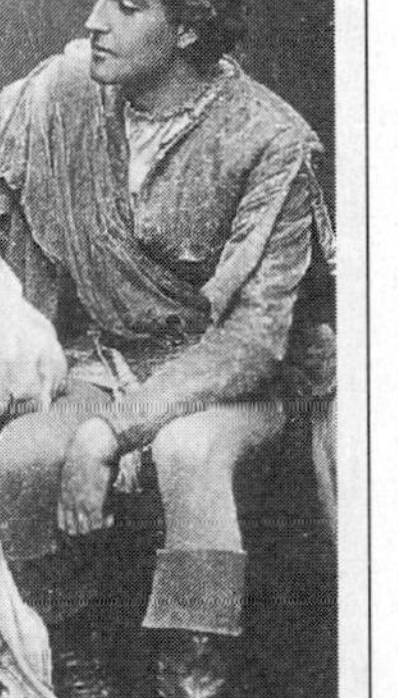

Double act: Basil Gill and Nora Kerin as Ferdinand and Miranda in a London production of Shakespeare's play, "The Tempest".

Motor cars are more reliable

Sept 21. Reliable light cars are now on the market at prices from £150 to £200. Half a dozen or so makers like Siddeley, De Dion and Oldsmobile offer models of the voiturette type, featuring low upkeep costs and virtually trouble-free operation.

Business users report that these machines are an improvement on the horse. In the city they are considerably faster and for going out of town they save all the waiting around associated with railways. Until now there has been a doubt about breakdowns, but simple design and robust construction have cut this hazard, so that drivers no longer need to be mechanics.

Hot wheels: new cars from Olds.

Fingerprint bank at Yard tops 70,000

Sept 23. Detective Inspector Collins of Scotland Yard said today at Mansion House police court that he would stake his life that a fingerprint, taken at the scene of a burglary in the Ludgate Circus area, was that of a man who had been arrested recently after a break-in at Whitefriars.

The officer, who was giving evidence against William Simpson, a 20-year-old clerk of no fixed address, said that Scotland Yard's collection of fingerprints now numbers more than 70,000 and that no two were identical. The detective inspector was congratulated on his evidence by the magistrate, who committed William Simpson for trial.

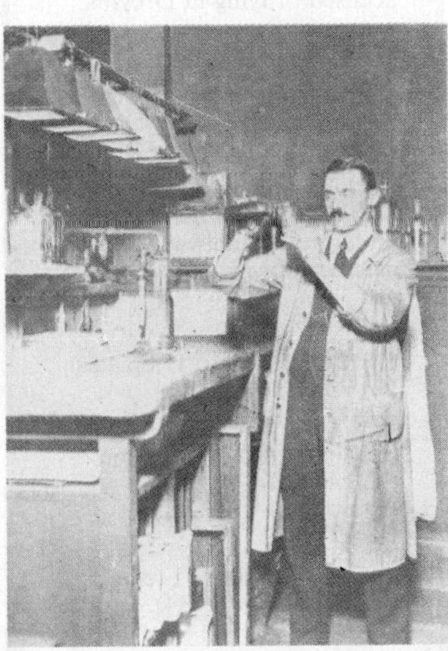

Police science: in the laboratory.

1904

OCTOBER

Su	Mo	Tu	We	Th	Fr	Sa
						1
2	3	4	5	6	7	8
9	10	11	12	13	14	15
16	17	18	19	20	21	22
23	24	25	26	27	28	29
30	31					

3. S.W. Africa: Hottentot chief Hendrik Witbooi declares war on Germany rather than see his soldiers disarmed (→9).

4. Netherlands: Treaty with Portugal delineating the colonial frontiers of the East Indies island of Timor.

8. Berlin: Germany signs a treaty with Rumania to improve trade relations.

9. S.W. Africa: Hottentot uprising is spreading (→12/11).

10. Central Asia: Many Armenians massacred by Kurdish tribesmen near Van (→20/2/05).

15. Russia: Baltic fleet under Admiral Rozhdestvenski leaves Libau for Port Arthur to help lift the siege (→18).

17. UK: Briton Joe Bowker beats American Frankie Neil to become world bantamweight boxing champion.

18. Far East: Russians win a 13-day battle on river Sha-Ho, but lose 40,000 troops against 20,000 Japanese dead (→22).

22. St. Petersburg: Reservists leave for the Far East to cries of "Down with the Czar" and "Long Live Japan" (→23).

23. Far East: General Kuropatkin, victor of Sha-Ho, is appointed Russian commander-in-chief in war with Japan (→7/11).

24. France: Four officers appear before War Council accused of lying in Dreyfus case.

27. North Sea: Royal Navy ships surround the Russian Baltic Fleet following Dogger Bank incident (→15/11).

27. New York: Mayor McLellan opens the New York underground railway. 150,000 use the subway on its first day.

BIRTHS

1. Ukrainian-born US pianist Vladimir Horowitz (†5/11/89).

2. British novelist Graham Greene (†3/4/91).

DEATH

4. French sculptor Frederic Bartholdi (*2/4/1834).

Russia sinks British boats in North Sea

Disaster: Japan on the brain?

Oct 22. The fishing community of Hull was stunned to learn today that two of its trawlers had been sunk and their captains killed in an astonishing attack by ships of the Russian Baltic fleet.

The trawlers were part of a fleet steaming off Dogger Bank when they were fired on by vessels heading for Japan. The Russians claim two torpedo boats approached their ships, which is strongly contradicted by witnesses (→27).

New valve heralds radio breakthrough

Oct 31. A new device which acts like a valve for electricity, allowing it to flow in one direction but not another, will have a big future in wireless. Among other uses it can replace the unreliable crystal and cat's-whisker combination which makes the operation of many wireless receivers so frustrating.

Invented by John Fleming, of London University, it looks a bit like an electric light bulb. A heated filament boils off negative electric particles, which are collected by a positively charged plate.

1904

NOVEMBER

Su	Mo	Tu	We	Th	Fr	Sa
		1	2	3	4	5
6	7	8	9	10	11	12
13	14	15	16	17	18	19
20	21	22	23	24	25	26
27	28	29	30			

1. London: Premiere of G.B. Shaw's play "John Bull's Other Island" at the Court Theatre.

7. Poland: Reserve troops in Warsaw are mobilised as the revolutionary movement gathers pace (→13).

12. S.W. Africa: As Hottentot revolt continues, Gen. Adolf von Trotha takes over from Theodor Leutwein as governor of the German colony (→28).

13. Warsaw: 49 people are killed or wounded in riots against Russian government of Poland (→19).

15. London: The Board of Trade inquiry opens into the Dogger Bank clash between British trawlers and Russian ships (→22/12).

16. Brazil: Martial law is declared in Rio de Janeiro following the violent riots.

17. Southampton: The first underwater journey of a submarine, across the Solent to the Isle of Wight.

18. Rhodesia: Large important gold discovery is made 200 miles south of Salisbury.

19. St. Petersburg: Representatives of zemstvos (local elected councils) call for a Russian parliament.

21. East Indies: 30,000 people reported destitute after a typhoon near the Philippine island of Mindanao.

28. S.W. Africa: German colonial troops beat Hottentots at Warmbad (→2/6).

29. Russia: Many cities witness student riots in protest at the Russo-Japanese War (→30).

30. Far East: Japan takes the last hill surrounding Port Arthur, despite loss of nearly 12,000 troops (→5/12).

30. Paris: Cornet is declared winner of the Tour de France after the commission disallows the first results.

BIRTHS

14. British churchman Michael Ramsey (†23/4/88).

21. US jazz saxophonist Coleman Hawkins (†19/5/69).

Roosevelt romps back to power

Nov 8. President Roosevelt won a full four-year lease on the White House today, carrying most of the northern and western states in the presidential elections. Democrat Alton B. Parker, his challenger, sent the president a telegram, congratulating him on his overwhelming victory.

In a statement issued from the White House, Roosevelt thanked the voters and assured the nation that "under no circumstances will I be a candidate for or accept another nomination". Under the constitution, he could run again in 1908. Roosevelt became president in 1901 when, as vice-president, he took over after the assassination of William McKinley.

The Philadelphia Inquirer

A WONDERFUL LANDSLIDE FOR ROOSEVELT

Trumpeted: Republican victory.

Troop moves spark riots in Moscow

Nov 7. The call-up and treatment of reservists has led to trouble in several Russian cities. The worst incidents appear to have taken place in Moscow when a detachment of over a thousand reservists were passing through the city on board a train.

Most of the men were more or less drunk. They left the station and tried to break into the state liquor shops and restaurants. Police were called out and some shots fired. Other reports said reservists had caused trouble elsewhere through heavy drinking (→29).

Greater numbers of the poor receive relief in Britain than ever before

On the parish: a child of London's overcrowded and festering slums.

Nov 29. Figures released today show that there has been a dramatic increase in the number of people receiving poor relief: there are now over 122,000 in London alone and nearly 800,000 in England and Wales. At the end of last month there were about 250,000 in workhouses and more than 520,000 getting outdoor relief.

This is 26,982 more on indoor relief than two years ago and more outdoor paupers than at any time since 1888. If the total population is considered to be around 33,000,000 it means that one out of every 41 people in the country is getting some sort of aid from the local parish.

Conditions are at their worst in the eastern counties – such as Essex, Suffolk and Norfolk – with the northern ones – Durham, Northumberland and Cumberland – being next. The increase is at its smallest in the southwest.

In London, the increase has been least in northern areas such as Hampstead and Hackney, and greatest in eastern boroughs like Shoreditch and Whitechapel. With the coming cold weather numbers can only increase and charities have been told to prepare themselves.

US buys up French Panama concession

Nov 16. The United States today removed one of the last obstacles to a Panama canal by buying from a French company its concession to build a canal across the isthmus. The firm, led by Philippe Bunau Varilla, has agreed to sell the existing workings, plus a library of surveys and plans, for $40 million. Last February the US bought sovereignty over the Canal route from the new Panamanian republic for $10 million.

Just over a year ago, US marines landed to stop Colombian troops defeating the rebels who set up the Republic of Panama.

Digging for victory: Uncle Sam.

1904

DECEMBER

Su	Mo	Tu	We	Th	Fr	Sa
				1	2	3
4	5	6	7	8	9	10
11	12	13	14	15	16	17
18	19	20	21	22	23	24
25	26	27	28	29	30	31

1. US: The World's Fair closes at St. Louis.

2. Berlin: Germany signs a commercial treaty with Italy (→25/1/05).

5. Far East: The Japanese destroy the Russian fleet at Port Arthur, leaving only torpedo boats afloat (→22/1/05).

10. Stockholm: Nobel Prizes awarded to Lord Rayleigh (UK, Physics); Sir William Ramsay (UK, Chemistry); Ivan Petrovich Pavlov (Russia, Physiology); Frederic Mistral and Jose Echegaray y Eizaguirre (France, Literature) and the Institute of International Law (Belgium, Peace).→

11. St. Petersburg: The police clash with an anti-government demonstration (→26).

12. London: Government signs a treaty of arbitration with the United States.

13. Budapest: The interior of the Hungarian parliament building is wrecked by government opponents.

22. Paris: The international inquiry into the Dogger Bank incident opens (→23/2/05).

24. London: The Coliseum opens in St. Martin's Lane.

27. Russia: Czar's reform proposals are greeted with disappointment; agitators will continue demonstrations (→19/1/05).

28. London: The first weather forecasts by wireless telegraphy are published.

30. London: The Post Office says it will now accept wireless telegrams to be sent to ships at sea.

HITS OF 1904

Give My Regards To Broadway.

Meet Me In St. Louis, Louis.

QUOTE OF THE YEAR

"If the American nation will speak softly and yet keep at a pitch of the highest training a thoroughly efficient navy, the Monroe Doctrine will go far."
Theodore Roosevelt.

Chamberlain steps up trade battle

Dec 15. Calling himself "a missioner of the British Empire", the ex-Colonial Secretary Joseph Chamberlain took his campaign to a working-class audience tonight for the first time. Addressing an enthusiastic 4,000-strong rally in London's East End, "Radical Joe" – as he is now widely nicknamed – denounced duty-free imports and called for preferential tariffs for the Empire. He also demanded curbs on immigration from Europe which he said is disproportionately responsible for crime and disease.

Radical Joe: Keep Europeans out.

Monroe Doctrine to cover economics

Dec 6. President Roosevelt may invoke the Monroe Doctrine to make the debt-ridden Dominican Republic repay its creditors in Europe. In his annual message to Congress President Roosevelt said today that "the Monroe Doctrine may force the United States, however reluctantly, to the exercise of an international police power". He said that the economic situation in the Dominican Republic might let countries such as Germany gain a foothold in the Caribbean if they try to recover their debts. This would violate the Monroe Doctrine against colonial expansion in America, and threaten the new Panama Canal. ▷

Czar offers liberalising reforms, but warns that strikes and riots must stop

Outlook bleak: Russia plods onward, bowed down by despotism and war.

Dec 26. Czar Nicholas II today pledged himself to improve the conditions of the population, particularly the peasants, but warned that law and order would be maintained. The Czar's decree, addressed to the Senate, follows months of unrest and increasing demands for major reforms of the government as well as an end to the war with Japan.

The government has been especially concerned by serious rioting involving university students, including a large number of women, in the centre of St. Petersburg a fortnight ago. More than 50 people were hurt when the mounted police made numerous charges and there were many arrests.

The decree said conditions of the peasants were being urgently examined. The role of local authorities would be expanded (→27).

Peter Pan flies into children's hearts

Arts: James Barrie's new play, "Peter Pan – or The Boy Who Wouldn't Grow Up", which opened last night at the Duke of York's, is the unquestioned hit of the season. With Nina Boucicault as Peter and Gerald du Maurier as Captain Hook, it proved that today's audiences do indeed believe in fairies.

"A capital entertainment full of droll imaginings, of such originality, tenderness and daring that no shade of doubt regarding its complete success was discerned at the fall of the curtain," said one critic.

The year saw two notable new buildings. On July 19 the King laid the foundation stone in Liverpool for the first cathedral to be built in the north of England since the Reformation. The architect, **Giles Gilbert Scott**, was only 22 when he won the competition to design it. It is not expected to be completed until 1940.

In London the first building to be erected on a steel frame has opened – the Ritz Hotel. Its luxurious interior in the French style includes a "Palm Court" where tea is served round a gilded fountain.

Peter Pan soars off with Wendy to Never-Never Land.

Salivating dogs win Nobel Prize for Russian Ivan Pavlov

Dec 10. The Russian physiologist, Ivan Pavlov, received the Nobel Prize today for his researches into how the digestion works. However, some scientists believe that his other experiments, not cited, may turn out to be more significant.

The prize was awarded for the discovery that nerve messages transmitted via the brain play an important part in the digestive process. Thus when Pavlov severed a dog's gullet, so that food it chewed never reached its stomach, digestive juices still flowed. Conversely, when he cut appropriate nerves, no juices were produced, although food reached the dog's stomach normally. Pavlov has moved on to other experiments. He has found that if a bell is regularly rung when a dog is fed, the animal eventually comes to salivate at the sound alone. This conditioned reflex, as Pavlov calls it, could be of major importance in understanding how we learn.

Reflex action: Dogs normally salivate in the presence of food, but not at the mere sound of a bell. Pavlov found that, by producing food when a bell was rung, he could eventually train the dogs to salivate at the sound alone. This learned reaction could still be triggered even six months later.

Lord Rayleigh: prize for physics.

London's first tube goes electric

Dec 13. At three o'clock today, a train labelled "No. 1" glided quietly out of Baker Street station in London bound for the suburb of Uxbridge. It was the first train operated by the Metropolitan Railway to use electricity instead of steam. Eventually all Metropolitan trains will use electricity, including the presently smoke-filled stretch from Paddington to Farringdon Street which in 1863 became the first of what are now known as "underground railways".

The new trains are quieter than their predecessors and move more quickly away from stations. With the new system has come a new design of coach, with a central corridor so that more people can be carried. Also, there are only two classes of travel instead of the usual three.

1905

JANUARY

Su	Mo	Tu	We	Th	Fr	Sa
1	2	3	4	5	6	7
8	9	10	11	12	13	14
15	16	17	18	19	20	21
22	23	24	25	26	27	28
29	30	31				

1. Russia: The Trans-Siberian Railway officially opens, allowing travel from Paris to Vladivostok in a mere 21 days.

1. Italy: Belgian Henri Oedenkoven founds the world's first vegetarian organisation.

4. UK: Seven die in a Midland Railway crash near Barnsley.

7. Washington: The US Senate reluctantly approves Roosevelt's choice of a black man as head of South Carolina customs service, most senior official US post ever held by a black.

8. Bethlehem: Greeks celebrating the Orthodox Christmas clash with Roman Catholic clergy.

10. Germany: Jewish newspaper complains of a rising tide of German anti-Semitism (→26/5).

11. London: Transatlantic liner tickets are increasing; it now costs £6 to travel third class to the US.

17. Norway: 59 die at Bergen when a rock-fall into fjord causes 20-foot waves.

19. Russia: 75,000 workers strike amid growing unrest led by Father George Gapon.→

21. Washington: The US signs an agreement to run the affairs of the Dominican Republic.

25. St. Petersburg: Czar Nicholas promises reforms (→27).

25. Poland: Striking workers fire at troops and bomb several buildings in Warsaw (→29).

27. Russia: Students and professors demonstrate against the imprisonment of Maxim Gorky (→2/2).

28. Far East: Japanese drive Russians out of Hei-kou-tai (→3/2).

29. Poland: Unruly troops and mob loot Warsaw as protests continue against Russian rule (→1/5).

BIRTH

21. French fashion designer Christian Dior (†24/10/57).

Bloody Sunday: Czar's troops kill 500

Jan 22. Loyal strikers marching through St. Petersburg to petition Czar Nicholas II for better conditions were shot down today, leaving more than 500 dead and many more wounded.

The slaughter, on what is already being called "Bloody Sunday," arose from a march led by Father George Gapon, a youthful priest who has been the impetus behind several strikes.

Gapon spent last week rallying workers for a mass march to the Winter Palace where he hoped to deliver a petition to the Czar. The march, which began at midday, was headed by the priest wearing his vestments and carrying a cross. Others carried icons, flags and the Czar's portrait.

Lines of infantry backed by Cossacks blocked the way but the procession had not expected what happened when they moved forward. The troops had been given firm orders to disperse any crowds although the Czar was not actually at the Winter Palace. Without warning, and at a distance of only 30 yards, the troops opened fire on men, women and children. The hardpacked snow was stained by crimson blotches. Gapon survived and escaped, but other leaders of the march were seized.

The events appear to have struck a death blow to the ancient legendary belief that the Czar and the people were one. He has been presented as the "Little Father" but after today it will be difficult to preserve the fiction. Nor will they further believe he was kept ignorant of their problems (→25).

Popular faith in Czar dies in a hail of bullets as troops fire on workers.

Port Arthur falls to massive Japanese assault: thousands die

Jan 2. After a cruel seven-month siege, the 20,000-strong Russian garrison at the great Korean naval fortress of Port Arthur surrendered to the Japanese today. At 4.30pm General Anatoly Stossel, the Russian commander, presented the documents of capitulation to Japanese general, Nogi Maresuke.

General Nogi reported to the Emperor today that after occupying the last remaining forts he had suspended all operations. Almost all warships in the port were blown up and scuttled by the Russians before they gave in.

Precise terms of surrender are not yet known but it is expected that Russian officers will be freed on parole. Because of the heroic defence, the Mikado seems likely to accord liberal terms permitting the entire surviving garrison to return to Russia on parole with their arms.

Today the Emperor signalled the chief of staff that military honours must be shown to General Stoessel who had rendered commendable services to his country. It is believed that of the garrison some 15,000 are wounded or sick with dysentery and other illnesses. Crowds, wild with joy, gathered in Tokyo streets shouting "Banzai". In St. Peterburg there was gloom in the Russian official classes who are the only ones so far aware of the disaster in the Orient (→28).

A Russian cartoonist's vision of victory that never was (date unknown).

1905

FEBRUARY

Su	Mo	Tu	We	Th	Fr	Sa
			1	2	3	4
5	6	7	8	9	10	11
12	13	14	15	16	17	18
19	20	21	22	23	24	25
26	27	28				

2. Russia: Maxim Gorky is released from prison (→ 12).

3. Far East: Reported that Japan has ordered four new battleships and other armaments from the UK (→ 13).

5. Chicago: Polar bear freezes to death in the zoo after three nights of -15 degrees F.

7. Germany: 215,000 miners return to work after six-week strike for shorter hours and better conditions.

7. Washington: Congress passes Statehood Bill admitting Oklahoma and New Mexico to the Union.

8. Paris: Court declares all gramophone recordings of published music to be in breach of copyright.

9. UK: The Board of Education calls for the encouragement of greater thrift among children.

10. US: Wisconsin passes a tax on bachelors over 30.

11. London: Two Frenchmen land in a balloon at Crystal Palace after crossing the English Channel.

12. Russia: The nobility asks the Czar to consider reforms; the Czar orders an investigation into people's living conditions.→

13. Far East: Japanese lay siege to Vladivostock (→ 21).

17. London: An outbreak of typhus reported in the East end of the city.

20. Central Asia: Hundreds of unarmed Armenians are massacred at Baku as the authorities look on (→ 22/6).

21. Russia: Peace terms to end the disastrous Far East conflict are presented to Japan (→ 10/3).

23. Paris: The International inquiry into the Dogger Bank incident blames Russia (→ 9/3).

24. St. Petersburg: Agriculture Minister Alexei Yermolov presents the Czar with a proposed new constitution (→ 3/3).

BIRTH

6. Polish leader Wladyslaw Gomulka (†2/9/82).

Grand Duke killed by bomb dropped in lap

Feb 17. An assassin's bomb blew Grand Duke Sergei to pieces in Moscow today. The Grand Duke was an uncle of Czar Nicholas II and one of his most influential advisers. It happened as his carriage passed through the gates of the Kremlin. The Grand Duke had just left his apartment when the bomb, filled with nails, was thrown into his lap from a distance of about 15 paces.

The Grand Duchess heard the massive explosion and rushed to the scene. The force of the explosion ripped her husband into unrecognisable pieces of flesh, bleeding into the snow. Parts of the carriage were found 200 hundred yards away. She eased the last moments of the dying coachman by telling him the Grand Duke had survived the explosion.

The youth who threw the bomb was also carrying a revolver. He refused to give his name, but his identity should soon be known. News of the assassination was given to the Czar at the Winter Palace in St. Petersburg where he was entertaining Prince Frederick Leopold of Prussia.

Grand Duke Sergei with his wife.

The Czar went white and bowed his head in silence for some moments. Finally he said, "But how can that be? Everything is so quiet – the strikes are ceasing. The excitement is subsiding. Whatever do they want?" (→ 24)

Anti-motoring brigade concedes defeat

Feb 11. This year's Motor Show, the biggest yet, brought crowds to Olympia in London. Two early enthusiasts were the Prince and Princess of Wales, who had a preview yesterday.

For today's opening the Prime Minister, Arthur Balfour, was there along with the Foreign Secretary, Lord Lansdowne. The presence of such notables and the unflagging eagerness of the throng confirm the decline of anti-motoring prejudice. When the Prince of Wales asked to see British cars he was shown the two-cylinder Siddeley, which had just made a 5000-mile reliability run.

A Rover model on display at the Motor Show at Olympia.

1905

MARCH

Su	Mo	Tu	We	Th	Fr	Sa
			1	2	3	4
5	6	7	8	9	10	11
12	13	14	15	16	17	18
19	20	21	22	23	24	25
26	27	28	29	30	31	

1. London: 350% increase in spending on the Royal Navy announced.

3. St. Petersburg: Government rejects strikers' demands, but the Czar agrees to create a consultative assembly (→ 7/4).

4. Washington: President Roosevelt declares "No weak nation should have cause to fear us ... no strong power can attack us" in inaugural speech.

6. London: Chief Secretary for Ireland, Wyndham, resigns over problems of creating coherent Irish policy (→ 13).

9. UK: Russia agrees to pay the UK £65,000 compensation for the Dogger Bank incident.

9. Africa: Belgian vice-governor of the Congo commits suicide following findings of international commission on Congo (→ 18/5).

10. UK: 32 die in pit disaster in South Wales.

13. London: Walter Long succeeds Wyndham as Chief Secretary for Ireland (→ 30/12).

13. Far East: General Kuropatkin asks the Czar to recall his army (→ 14).

14. St. Petersburg: Czar refuses to abandon war with Japan; orders 400,000 more troops to the front (→ 30).

15. UK: 23 drown off Land's End and 100 mph gales lash Edinburgh as storms grip the country.

17. London: Commons gives second reading to bill to give miners under 18 maximum eight-hour day (→ 8/9).

18. New York: President Roosevelt gives away his niece Eleanor Roosevelt at her wedding to her cousin Franklin Delano Roosevelt.

25. UK: Kirkland wins the Grand National at Aintree.

30. Washington: President Roosevelt is chosen to mediate in the Russo-Japanese War (→ 4/4).

DEATH

24. French writer Jules Verne (*8/2/1828).→

200,000 Russians routed at Mukden

March 10. In a 12-day battle Japan has inflicted an historic and unprecedented defeat on the Russian army of Manchuria. General Kuropatkin's army of 200,000 men no longer exists as a fighting force.

The only question now is what proportion of his battered units can be got to safety in Tie-ling. Total destruction or surrender are the grim alternatives now facing the surrounded Russian soldiers

It is now two days since the Russian centre was smashed by an irresistible infantry assault which followed a formidable barrage from massed artillery. General Kuropatkin was forced to make a stand with his right wing at Fushun where the Russian troops conducted an obstinate but doomed defence.

Marshal Oyama, the Japanese commander, reported last night that the enemy was surrounded and in full retreat. Casualties on both sides are estimated to be as many as 200,000 dead. The battle is without doubt the bloodiest engagement of the war to date.

In a gesture towards the native Chinese population, Marshal Oyama ordered his troops not to occupy the ancient capital near Mukden, which is the birthplace of the imperial dynasty. Steps were taken to protect its imperial tombs.

From the front today there are reports that Japanese forces are pursuing the enemy and have forced them into retreat towards the Tie pass, three days' march to the north. Fleeing troops have abandoned more than 100 artillery pieces, including all heavy guns and other equipment.

So great is the scale of the disaster that the Russian commanders can no longer conceal it. General Kuropatkin finally had to report to St. Petersburg that he was compelled to retreat. Although the Czar's government still claims it has no intention of ending the war, there have been anti-war demonstrations in the capital and news from the front will no doubt increase their scale. From the provinces now come reports of disturbances.

A priest leads troops in a makeshift service for their dead comrades.

An officer despairs over defeat.

French are angry at Kaiser's Africa trip

March 31. European rivalry in North Africa has been heightened by the visit of the German Emperor to Morocco. France, which claims a "special standing" in Morocco has been provoked by the Kaiser's remarks to his subjects that they were "devoted pioneers of German industry who are helping me in the task of always upholding the interests of their motherland".

Kaiser Wilhelm II said that he had come to protect German economic interests, but added: "The sovereignty and integrity of Morocco will be maintained". This appeared to put the French position in some doubt, but the French Foreign Ministry countered by saying that "France does not pretend to base her interests on disregard for the interest of others".

Sherlock returns

March 31. Brought back from the dead by public demand, Sherlock Holmes' new adventures from the Strand magazine have just been issued in volume form as "The Return of Sherlock Holmes". His explanation to an astonished Watson of how he escaped going over the precipice of the Reichenbach Falls with his arch-enemy, Moriarty, is laconic in the extreme.

Readers rejoiced at news of his return but, says the Daily Telegraph, "It is to be feared realisation is not up to expectation".

Holmes struggling with Moriarty.

Cheering crowds greet Roosevelt

March 4. Huge crowds greeted President Roosevelt today as he was inaugurated for his first full term of office since succeeding the assassinated William McKinley in 1901. Accompanied by a large military escort, the President rode in splendour from the White House to the Capitol to take the oath of office.

Later, he reviewed the biggest parade ever staged in Washington. President Roosevelt is quoted as saying the ceremonies "touched me to the heart".

Father of science fiction, Jules Verne, dies

Around the world with Jules Verne.

March 24. Jules Verne, the inventor of the scientific novel, died in Amiens, France, today at the age of 77, having delighted at least two generations with such adventure stories as "Around the World in 80 Days" and "Twenty Thousand Leagues Under the Sea".

Born in Nantes in February 1828, he went to Paris to study for the legal profession but began writing plays and librettos. His first big success came in 1863 with the novel "Five Weeks in a Balloon."

He never travelled but lived a very quiet and happy life at Amiens writing two novels a year.

1905

APRIL

Su	Mo	Tu	We	Th	Fr	Sa
						1
2	3	4	5	6	7	8
9	10	11	12	13	14	15
16	17	18	19	20	21	22
23	24	25	26	27	28	29
30						

1. Canada: World's first turbine steamer "Victorian" arrives in Halifax, Nova Scotia, at end of maiden voyage.

2. Switzerland: Simplon rail tunnel through the Alps is officially inaugurated.

4. Far East: Japanese occupy Kai-Yuan (→ 19/5).

7. Russia: The Pan-Slavic Congress of Soviets demands a democratic constitution (→ 11).

8. Madrid: 400 die when reservoir collapses.

11. St. Petersburg: Government lifts censorship on private telegrams (→ 18).

16. Algiers: King Edward arrives on official visit (→ 30).→

18. London: London County Council decides to build new £1.7 million headquarters opposite Parliament.

18. St. Petersburg: Secret "parliament" votes to abolish the aristocracy and settle ethnic grievances within the Russian Empire (→ 30).

19. UK: Judge decides the public have no right of way to Stonehenge.

21. Turkey: Crete's elective assembly votes for union with Greece (→ 26/6).

23. Paris: The government creates an Algerian office within the Ministry of the Interior.

25. S. Africa: Former Boer republic of Transvaal given new constitution by UK; Boers condemn it (→ 4/7).

29. London: Aston Villa beat League champions Newcastle United 2-0 in the FA Cup Final at Crystal Palace.

30. St. Petersburg: Czar abolishes religious restrictions and arrears on famine loans to peasants; guarantees freedom of conscience (→ 1/5).

BIRTH

2. Serge Lifar, Russian-born French dancer (†16/12/86).

DEATH

4. Belgian artist and sculptor Constantin Meunier (*12/4/1831).

Massive Indian earthquake: 10,000 dead

April 4. More than 10,000 people are feared to have perished in an earthquake which hit the north-east Indian province of Lahore during the night. The town of Dharmsala was almost completely razed to the ground with the entire population rendered homeless and sleeping out in icy conditions.

Five hundred Gurkha soldiers were buried alive when their stone-built barracks collapsed on them. Major General Walter Kitchener is preparing a relief train from Lahore to the stricken town. The towns of Kangra and Palampur have also been levelled to the ground by the worst natural disaster to hit the sub-continent in centuries.

Serious damage and loss of life is reported from Kashmir, Dalhousie and other centres. In Lahore, where 70 Indians were killed, Mohammedan inhabitants are parading in the streets, weeping and offering up prayers with ceremonial rites. Several British administrators and missionaries are known to have been killed or injured. At Simla, Lady Curzon, wife of the Viceroy, had a close escape from death when a chimney crashed into the room in which she was sleeping.

The ruins of the town of Kangra.

Frenchman invents intelligence tests

April 31. Tests which, it is claimed, measure intelligence rather than knowledge have been devised by a French psychologist, Alfred Binet. The tests, based on things like following instructions and identifying patterns, are designed to measure the ability of the brain to reason rather than the factual knowledge it has absorbed. Binet hopes that his tests will measure intelligence independently of education, and he suggests that, although children perform better as they age, their ranking compared to others of the same age will remain similar.

Advert for Brasso polish.

King courts French in visit to Paris

April 30. King Edward VII had three hours of discussions with President Emile Loubet today as part of a brief stop-over visit to Paris on His Majesty's return from a trip to Algeria.

His Majesty and the president discussed a wide range of topics during the talks at the Elysee Palace. Following this, M. Loubet called on the King at the Hotel Bristol in the afternoon and was later host to a gala dinner in the King's honour at the Elysee. The King hopes to remain incognito for the remainder of his short stay.

Liege expo opens

April 27. A huge international exhibition opened today at Liege, to celebrate the 75th anniversary of Belgian independence. More than 17,000 exhibitors from 39 lands are represented on the 175-acre site, and the organisers are hoping to draw up to seven million visitors. The Belgian Tourist Office expects the show to boost the country's tourist trade.

1905

MAY

Su	Mo	Tu	We	Th	Fr	Sa
	1	2	3	4	5	6
7	8	9	10	11	12	13
14	15	16	17	18	19	20
21	22	23	24	25	26	27
28	29	30	31			

1. New York: Radium tested as cure for cancer.

1. Poland: 100 people die when troops fire into the May Day demonstrators in Warsaw (→ 2).

2. Poland: General strike called following the May Day massacre (→ 6).

8. Russia: Paul Miliukov forms the Union of Unions, calling for a parliament and universal suffrage (→ 16).

8. Switzerland: International Conference of Workers' Protection in Berne debates night shifts for women workers (→ 12).

13. Paris: Dancer Mata Hari is highly acclaimed (→ 15/10/17).

14. Philippines: Seven American troops and 300 Moro tribesmen die when 600 Moros launch an attack.

16. Russia: General Sokolovski, Governor of Ufa Province, is assassinated (→ 24).

19. Far East: Admiral Rozhdestvenski is replaced by Admiral Birilev as commander of the Russian forces (→ 28).

23. London: G. B. Shaw's "Man and Superman" opens at the Court Theatre.

24. Poland: Many Jews die in Warsaw anti-Semitic riots as authorities look on (→ 30/7).

24. Russia: Prince Nakashidze, Governor of Baku, is assassinated (→ 3/6).

25. France: The first flight of a motorised aeroplane in Europe.

29. UK: Atlantic yacht race for the Kaiser's Cup is won by US yacht "Atlantic" after 15-day crossing from New York.

31. UK: Lord Rosebery's Cicero wins the Derby, the former Prime Minister's third winner.

31. Paris: Attempted assassination of Emile Loubet, the French President and King Alfonso of Spain (→ 7/6).

BIRTH

16. US actor Henry Fonda (†12/8/82).

Russian navy wiped out at Tsushima

Russian dreams of a great victory.

Russian battleship "Navarin" ravaged by Japanese torpedoes at Tsushima.

May 28. In the greatest naval battle ever fought, Admiral Togo's warships yesterday annihilated the Russian Baltic fleet, which had sailed halfway round the world to save Russia's Asian imperial dream.

In a daring manoeuvre in the Strait of Tsushima, Admiral Togo brought his battlefleet about and reversed direction to engage the Russians coming out of the fog. His aim was to prevent them breaking through on the final stage of their 18-month voyage towards the Manchurian base at Vladivostock.

Out of a total of 38 ships which entered the Strait at 1.30 pm, all but three have been sunk or disabled or captured. Some 4,800 officers and ratings, half of the fleet's complement, perished in the encounter. Japanese losses amounted to only three torpedo boats and 117 sailors.

The main engagement began in mid-afternoon with a determined attack on the line of four Russian capital ships. Within an hour the formation was in total confusion as all were hit by enemy shellfire. The first battleship sunk was the "Oslyabya" which rolled over and sank after the crew abandoned ship.

Shortly afterwards the flagship "Suvorov", crippled by an explosion near the bridge, dropped out of the line. Four hours later the "Alexander III" fell out and went down with all 900 hands. Finally, early this morning the Russian Admiral Nicholas Nebogatow, who had taken over from the injured fleet commander Admiral Zinovi Rozhdestvenski, raised the flag of surrender.

Japan's victorious Admiral Togo.

Matsushima
Sea of Japan
KOREA
Ush
Sisoi Veliky
Pusan
Navarin
Tsushima
Takeshili
Vladimir Nakhimov
Korea Strait
Tsushima Strait
Kyúshú

Position of the major Russian battle ships on the eve of battle.

Libau
RUSSIAN EMPIRE
Departure of Rozhdestvenski on Oct. 15, 1904.
Departure of Nebogatov on Jan. 15, 1905.
Vladivostock
Vigo
Port Arthur
Tangier
EMPIRE OF CHINA
JAPAN
Suez Canal
The "Sisoi Veliky", "the Navarin", and several destroyers pass through the Suez Canal.
Van Fong
Meeting of Nebogatov and Rozhdestvenski in the Bay of Cam Ranh on May 9, 1905.
Dakar
Djibouti
Cam Ranh
Libreville
Pacific Ocean
Moçâmedes
Madagascar
Luderitz
Indian Ocean

The long journey of the Baltic fleet from Russia's western coast, around the Cape of Good Hope and via Suez, towards the Strait of Tsushima.

New socialist group founded in Geneva

May 6. Following the Czar's savage response to unrest in Russia and Poland, seven eastern European socialist parties have joined together to plan a common strategy. The parties, which include those from Poland, Georgia, Finland and Armenia, have set up a general fighting committee with headquarters in Geneva, Switzerland.

Among the demands is one for constituent assemblies in Poland, Armenia and Russia itself. However, the weak link in this revolutionary chain may prove to be Poland. Following a Warsaw May Day strike, Polish Socialists urged workers to return to work, explaining that the time was not yet ripe for revolution (→21/8).

Americans sail to transatlantic win

May 29. No other competitors were in sight at 18 minutes past nine this evening, when the schooner "Atlantic" sailed through the winning mark off the Lizard to take the German Kaiser's Cup for the New York Yacht Club.

"Atlantic" and the other 10 yachts in this great ocean race sailed from Sandy Hook in Connecticut shortly after noon (local time) 12 days ago.

Captain Barr, the winning ship's skipper, was delighted with the average speed of 10.5 knots and said that all on board had enjoyed the crossing.

Suffrage bill fails

May 12. A bill to give women the vote was "talked out" by MPs at Westminster today. Under the rules of Parliament, if MPs are talking when the House is due to adjourn, a bill is automatically lost – and this is what happened today after a debate marked by much laughter by MPs and one noisy interruption from the gallery. One MP said that "men and women differed in mental equipment with women having little sense of proportion". Giving women the vote would not be safe, he said.

1905

JUNE

Su	Mo	Tu	We	Th	Fr	Sa
				1	2	3
4	5	6	7	8	9	10
11	12	13	14	15	16	17
18	19	20	21	22	23	24
25	26	27	28	29	30	

1. Far East: Kaiser Wilhelm puts pressure on Czar to end the disastrous war with Japan (→ 2).

2. Washington: President Roosevelt says he will mediate in the Russo-Japanese War (→ 10).

3. St. Petersburg: Cossacks charge crowds in attempt to put down serious riots (→ 23).

7. Dresden: Formation of "Die Brucke" ("The Bridge") group of artists.

7. Norway: The Norwegian parliament refuses to recognise Swedish king and declares independence from Sweden (→ 13/8).

8. Plymouth: 14 people drown when the submarine A8 sinks.

8. France: Frenchman Gabriel Voisin experiments with an aeroplane on floats on the Seine.

10. Washington: Diplomatic triumph for Roosevelt as Russia agrees to peace conference with Japan (→ 15).

13. Athens: Greek premier Delyannis is assassinated outside the Greek parliament.

15. Washington: Russia and Japan agree to hold peace talks in the US capital, as Japanese troops continue to advance on Vladivostock (→ 8/7).

20. Hungary: Opposition Nationalists begin campaign of non-payment of taxes and refusal to be conscripted.

22. Turkey: Moslems massacre 170 Armenians (→ 5/9).

23. St. Petersburg: Czar Nicholas repudiates an earlier promise to give Russia an elected assembly (→ 27).→

27. Berlin: Germany tells France there is no immediate prospect of talks over their interests in Morocco (→ 16/1/06).

29. London: House of Lords rejects the bill for compulsory Sunday trading.

BIRTH

21. French writer and philosopher Jean-Paul Sartre (†15/4/80).

Potemkin mutineers kill their officers

June 27. Mutinous sailors have seized the "Potemkin", Russia's most powerful battleship in the Black Sea, thrown their officers overboard and raised the red flag. Reports from Odessa, where the ship is anchored off-shore, described the city as being gripped by a general strike with shooting and bomb explosions.

The trouble on the "Potemkin" arose when a sailor complained about bad food being served to the crew. He was shot by the first lieutenant. With that, the crew mutinied. Inflamed by speeches and shouts of "liberty, liberty", they threw the commander and several other officers overboard. Eight officers joined the mutiny.

The crew of two Russian torpedo boats were also said to have sided with the sailors. A steamer laden with coal was seized and the fuel transferred to the "Potemkin".

The news caused consternation in Odessa where the authorities were trying to cope with street rioters under the shadow of the guns of a battleship. Dozens of buildings were set on fire along the water-front.

The main squadron of Russia's Black Sea fleet is expected to engage the "Potemkin" soon (→ 20/7).

The officers and men on the deck of the "Potemkin" before the mutiny.

Automobile Association is founded

June 29. Car owners, concerned at popular prejudices against motoring and police hostility, founded the Automobile Association today. Its main task will be helping motorists avoid the increasingly widespread speed-traps, in which policemen often use conventional stop-watches to estimate car speeds. Anyone driving faster than the 20 mph legal speed limit is arrested, although motorists claim the tests are wildly inaccurate.

The new association's objectives were defined as "the protection and advancement of the legitimate interests of motorists and opposition to restriction on the use of roads" by the 50 drivers at today's inaugural meeting at the Trocadero restaurant in London's West End. Among them were the racing driver and general manager of Dunlop Tyres, Selwyn Edge, and London Palladium founder Walter Gibbons. All agreed to pay an annual subscription of two guineas to support the association.

An early AA patrolman checks the road for police speed-traps.

First American lady to win Wimbledon

Tennis champion May Sutton.

June 26-July 8. For the first time in the history of the Wimbledon lawn tennis championships, one of the titles has gone abroad. In the tournament's biggest surprise Dorothea Douglass of Great Britain, Ladies' Singles champion in both 1903 and 1904, was beaten in the final 6-3, 6-4 by talented 17-year-old American May Sutton.

1905

JULY

Su	Mo	Tu	We	Th	Fr	Sa
						1
2	3	4	5	6	7	8
9	10	11	12	13	14	15
16	17	18	19	20	21	22
23	24	25	26	27	28	29
30	31					

1. London: Colonial Office considers a plan for resettling surplus urban population in the Empire.

1. Australia: Salvation Army General Booth buys 20,000 acres of land on which to settle poor immigrants (→9/10).

3. Russia: 50,000 troops kill 6,000 to restore order in Odessa; a general strike is declared in St. Petersburg (→8).

4. S. Africa: Boers protest at new electoral laws which give new privileges to British.

6. London: Commons give second reading to bill to provide London with electricity.

8. Wimbledon: Laurence Doherty beats Norman Brookes for the Men's Singles title; May Sutton beats Dorothea Douglass for the Ladies' Singles crown.

8. Russia: The crew of the ship "Potemkin" surrender to the Rumanians, who say they will not be extradited because the mutiny was a political act (→20).

9. Brest: Royal Navy vessels arrive for a visit (→7/8).

10. London: Government's proposed redistribution of parliamentary seats would mean 22 fewer MPs for Ireland.

10. London: First UK performance of Puccini's "Madame Butterfly", at Covent Garden.

11. Milan: Discovery of documents revealing the identity of the original Othello.

11. UK: 124 die in Glamorgan pit disaster.

16. US: Commander Peary sets sail on second expedition to North Pole (→6/4/09).

20. St. Petersburg: The nobility protest to the Czar over the proposal for a "Duma" (→19/8).

27. Liverpool: 23 die in crash of an electric train.

30. Basel: Zionist Congress in Basel rejects offer by UK premier Balfour of Jewish homeland in Uganda, calls for one in Palestine (→8/11).

Emperors agree on pact

Kaiser Wilhelm II offers a friendly greeting to Czar Nicholas II.

July 24. German Kaiser Wilhelm II and Russia's Czar Nicholas II met today and concluded a treaty of alliance between their two countries. The treaty was signed after two days of talks on board the Imperial yachts "Hohenzollern" and "Standart" anchored in a fjord at Bjorko, Finland.

The meeting is widely seen as a move by the Kaiser to break Russia's long-standing alliance with France. But it was also clear that its immediate origins lay in the furore arising from the incident at Dogger Bank when Russian ships fired on British fishing boats.

Russia has so far not apologised and the matter will now go to the International Court. The Kaiser is furious at demands in the British press for the Royal Navy to prevent German ships fuelling the Russian navy and believes that the treaty will "teach the British a lesson".

It is thought that the Czar may face opposition to his treaty from his ministers who see the French alliance as the cornerstone of Russian foreign policy.

Time and speed relative, says scientist

July 1. Ideas about the universe accepted since the time of Newton more than two centuries ago are now being questioned in the light of a new theory proposed by a German-born physicist. According to the "Theory of Relativity" of Albert Einstein there is no such thing as absolute time or absolute motion. Everything – even the order in which events happen – depends on the observer. The most striking implication of the theory is that matter and energy are interconvertible, minute quantities of matter being equivalent to vast amounts of energy. Physicists speculate that radioactivity may arise through the conversion of mass to energy.

Albert Einstein: revolutionary.

In Einstein's universe, one absolute is the speed of light. Nothing can travel faster than it does and curious things happen as it is approached: masses increase, distances contract.

France separates church and state

July 3. The anti-clerical movement in France won its greatest victory with big majorities in both houses of parliament today for a bill to separate Church and State. The Chamber of Deputies voted 341 for and 233 against while the Senate voted decisively 179 to 103.

The move overturns the Concordat of 1801 in which Napoleon agreed to restore much of the influence of the Church which had been eroded during the French Revolution. The essence of the new bill is that while it grants religious freedom to all it removes all public funding for religious establishments, except for specific exceptions like hospitals, asylum chaplains and certain colleges.

Russians close to suing for peace

July 31. General Liapunoff, the Russian Governor of Sakhalin Island, off Siberia's coast, surrendered to the Japanese today, after his 3,270-strong garrison ran out of bandages and medicines needed for their wounded. Russia's defeat on the island came three weeks after 7,000 Japanese soldiers landed there in the first invasion of Russian territory this century.

This latest defeat, coupled with those at Mukden and Tsushima and the increasing internal opposition to the war, will intensify pressure on Russia to sue for peace.

Matsushenko, alleged ringleader of the mutiny on the Russian battleship "Potemkin".

1905

AUGUST

Su	Mo	Tu	We	Th	Fr	Sa
		1	2	3	4	5
6	7	8	9	10	11	12
13	14	15	16	17	18	19
20	21	22	23	24	25	26
27	28	29	30	31		

1. London: Field Marshal Roberts claims UK forces are less prepared now than at outbreak of Boer War.

2. US: Russian and Japanese delegates open peace talks at Portsmouth navy base, New Hampshire (→ 10).

6. Germany: Newspaper Reichsbote predicts war with UK and future naval supremacy of the US (→ 26/10).

7. Cowes: French naval ships arrive on an official visit, welcomed by Edward VII.

8. Leicester: Australian swimmer B.B. Kieran swims half-mile in record 11 mins 28 seconds.

10. US: Japan demands cession of Sakhalin Island and an indemnity as condition of peace with Russia (→ 29).

13. Norway: Referendum votes 80 per cent in favour of dissolving union with Sweden (→ 25/9).

16. Russia: 52 die in unrest at Riga in Latvia (→ 19).

21. Warsaw: General strike begins in protest at disregard for Polish rights in manifesto creating Russian Duma (→ 22).

22. Poland: The Russian governor declares a state of emergency in the face of the general strike (→ 1/9).

24. Japan: 127 Japanese troops returning from the Russian war die when their steamer collides with a British ship.

25. Russia: Eight crew of the "Potemkin" are sentenced to death after a court martial for mutiny (→ 2/9).

27. Ireland: Severe storms and flooding hit the country.

29. US: Russia and Japan finally agree on peace terms; an armistice is arranged for August 31 (→ 5/9).

31. US: Figures reveal that one million immigrants arrived in 1904, compared with 0.8 million in 1903.

BIRTH

2. German composer Karl Amadeus Hartmann (†5/12/1963).

Curzon quits as Viceroy

Two rulers of India: Viceroy Lord Curzon with the Maharajah of Patiala.

Aug 20. Lord Curzon has resigned as Viceroy of India and is to be replaced by the Earl of Minto. Lord Curzon's departure from his exalted office comes as no great surprise and the reasons for it are made plain in a White Paper issued earlier today.

His quarrel with the Government centres on the reorganisation of the Indian Army. Specifically, he wished to appoint Major-General Barrow as Military Supply member of his council, but he was refused by the Cabinet who, according to the Secretary of State for India, "are not willing to appoint General Barrow".

The exchange of telegrams between the Governor-General and the Secretary reveals that Lord Curzon fought hard but the Cabinet was adamant. He therefore felt resignation was the only option.

God's general begins 2000-mile crusade

Aug 1. The streets of Dover were packed today for the first stage of the latest crusade by the leader of the Salvation Army, General Booth. The motor car crusade, accompanied by newspaper reporters, will last a month and nine days. Its aim is to encourage the troops and spark a new countrywide wave of religious enthusiasm.

Salvation Army founder William Booth addresses his eager followers.

Czar creates Duma but retains power

Aug 19. Russia took a half-hearted step towards a constitutional monarchy today with the publication of a manifesto establishing a representative assembly. The new body will be called the Duma, the Russian word for "deliberation".

It is not expected to infringe on the powers enjoyed at present by Czar Nicholas II since it will be a strictly consultative body with no independent right to pass laws. At the same time the Czar will rule absolutely when the Duma is not in session and he can dissolve it at will.

To ensure that it will not assume a revolutionary role, election laws give disproportionate representation to the peasants who are considered more conservative than urban residents and more likely to follow the Czar.

The publication of the manifesto has been greeted coolly. There were a few isolated "Hurrahs" when the news became known, but for the most part it was met by a stony silence. A special meeting of the Senate held to hear the manifesto read was attended by only six members.

The new proposal was described by one commentator as a "miserable makeshift", which could lead to further division. The Union of Liberation, a liberal group calling for a genuine national body, said it was "unsatisfactory".

Train trips: now very popular.

1905

SEPTEMBER

Su	Mo	Tu	We	Th	Fr	Sa
					1	2
3	4	5	6	7	8	9
10	11	12	13	14	15	16
17	18	19	20	21	22	23
24	25	26	27	28	29	30

1. Germany: Imperial decree makes German compulsory for religious instruction in occupied Poland (→ 20/10).

2. Russia: Worst famine reported since 1891 (→ 5).

5. Central Asia: Hundreds killed as Moslem Tartars fight Christian Armenians (→ 7).

7. Japan: Martial law is declared as riots against the peace treaty with Russia continue (→ 12).

7. US: A mob in Dallas, Texas, burns a black man to death.

8. UK: The TUC says 1.5 million Britons are in unions, and calls for free trade and eight-hour day (→ 25/10).

9. Italy: Thousands feared dead in an earthquake in the Calabria region.

11. London: Government figures show an increase in rural lunacy owing to the tedium of country life.

12. Tokyo: 544 die when the Japanese Navy's flagship Mikasa catches fire and sinks (→ 14/10).

12. London: Anglo-Japanese treaty provides for Japan to help safeguard India (→ 11/10).

19. Europe: British and German armies hold simultaneous, but unrelated, war manoeuvres.

25. Stockholm: Terms of the independence of Norway announced (→ 26/10).

26. Moscow: Zemstvo congress calls for an elected popular assembly with real powers (→ 1/10).

27. Bradford: Lord Londonderry says it is parental duty to feed children and school meals are unnecessary.

BIRTHS

5. Hungarian-born British writer Arthur Koestler (†3/3/83).

18. Swedish actress Greta Garbo (†15/4/90).

DEATH

19. Irish-born doctor, Thomas John Barnardo, (*4/7/1845) →

Russia pays high price for peace

Sept 5. The long war fought out in Korea and Manchuria by Russia and Japan officially ended today with the signing of a peace treaty at Portsmouth, New Hampshire.

President Roosevelt had helped to mediate and it will be known as the Treaty of Portsmouth. As a 19-gun salute was fired, Sergei Witte of Russia and Baron Komura of Japan shook hands after signing.

Under the terms of this agreement the Japanese will achieve almost all their war aims and the Russians are paying the price of defeat. The Czar's government has agreed to evacuate troops from Manchuria, to recognize the exclusive rights of Japan in Korea, and guarantees not to intervene there again.

Japan has effectively won control over the Laotung Peninsula which includes Port Arthur, finally conquered by her troops after a long siege, as well as the southern half of Sakhalin Island.

In addition, Russia has agreed to pay a huge war indemnity. Furthermore, Japan will also gain access to fishing rights in Russian territorial waters in the Sea of Japan.

Despite these favourable terms, the Japanese are still not entirely satisfied. In Tokyo a protesting crowd of 100,000 gathered in Hibiya Park; they threw stones and destroyed ten churches (→ 7).

Muscovites are anxiously reading the news.

Dr Barnardo dies, but his homes for orphans live on

Sept 19. The death was announced today of Thomas John Barnardo, the Irish-born doctor and philanthropist who founded over 112 institutions for deprived children during the latter half of the last century. As a medical student in the East End of London, Barnardo was so affected by the plight of homeless children that he gave up missionary ambitions and created a simple shelter and school in a former stable. No child in need was ever turned away from a Barnardo home, it was claimed. Through the Barnardo organisation, over 17,000 boys and girls have emigrated to Canada and thousands more have been saved from lives of misery and privation in Great Britain.

Dr Barnardo with some of the orphans whose lives he tried to improve.

Tartars and Armenians battle as Baku oil fields blaze

Russian oil goes up in smoke in the Middle East.

Sept 7. A dense pall of smoke hangs over the blazing oilfields of Baku in the Caucasus where for the past week there has been fighting between the Armenians and the Tartars. Over 1,000 people have been killed and the area looted.

Although the battle has yet to reach the centre of the city, many of the residents have already fled. Both the Russians and the Turks have been blamed for not doing enough to damp down the conflict. The Turks are said to have distributed religious and racial propaganda about each side.

1905

OCTOBER

Su	Mo	Tu	We	Th	Fr	Sa
1	2	3	4	5	6	7
8	9	10	11	12	13	14
15	16	17	18	19	20	21
22	23	24	25	26	27	28
29	30	31				

1. Russia: Widespread strikes grip the country (→ 26).

2. Berlin: 40,000 striking electricians are locked out (→ 26).

5. US: Wright brothers make longest flight yet of 38 minutes three seconds.

9. Australia: Salvation Army abandons General Booth's plan to resettle poor immigrants.

11. Japan: Visiting Royal Navy ships are given an enthusiastic welcome on arrival in Yokohama harbour (→ 3/11).

14. St. Petersburg: The Emperor of Japan and the Czar sign the final peace treaty ending all hostilities in the Far East (→ 20).

16. London: King and Queen lay foundation stone for new General Post Office (→ 18).

18. London: King Edward VII opens Kingsway and Aldwych, two new roads to ease congestion between Holborn and the Strand.

19. London: Prince and Princess of Wales leave on an official visit to India.

20. Russia: Czar permits the teaching of Polish in Polish schools after a 15-year ban (→ 28).

23. Chile: 550 people die as workers' unrest sweeps the country.

25. UK: Lord Rosebery calls for a future Liberal government to challenge the power of the House of Lords (→ 3/11).

26. St. Petersburg: Typographers create a workers' council with Leon Trotsky as vice-president (→ 30).

26. Sweden: King Oscar II formally abdicates the Norwegian crown (→ 16/11).

28. Warsaw: Russian Governor-General imposes eight o'clock curfew to counter the growing strike (→ 6/11).

31. Finland: General strike begins across the whole country.

DEATH

13. English actor Sir Henry Irving (*6/2/1838).

Czar's concessions fail to stem unrest

Kronstadt's streets littered with the remains of the popular uprising.

Oct 30. With all Russia paralysed by a general strike, Czar Nicholas II today transformed the country from an absolute autocracy into a semi-constitutional monarchy. An Imperial Manifesto promised Russians such civil rights as "freedom of conscience, speech, assembly and association". It extended suffrage, granted an elected parliament, the Duma, and pledged that no laws would be enforceable without its consent.

The Czar's agreement to grant the people the constitutional rights they have been demanding for the past year is the work of the Count Sergei Witte, who has been appointed President of the Council of Ministers.

But the fact is that Russia has been in a state of open revolt for months. From Warsaw to the Urals there are 1,500,000 men on strike; trains have stopped running, ships are idle, factories shut down. In St. Petersburg and Moscow there is little food and schools and hospitals are closed.

Law and order has gone by the board with vast crowds marching through the streets cheering orators while revolutionary red flags can be seen flying from hundreds of buildings. Latest reports from the countryside speak of peasants burning estates and stealing cattle.

Earlier this month Leon Trotsky, the leader of the St. Petersburg Soviet of Workers' Deputies, urged other workers' councils to begin arming themselves in preparation for a revolution.

Critics scorn new art group – the "wild beasts" of Paris

Oct 1. This year's Salon d'Automne in Paris is a sensation thanks to a group of artists who have thrown restraint to the winds and exhibit pictures painted with primary colours straight from the tube. They have been dubbed by one critic "Les Fauves" – the wild beasts. They have accepted the nickname.

Leader of the group is Henri Matisse, a painter from northern France. His clashing, lurid colours bear no relation to the colours found in nature. In his wife's portrait there is a green stripe across her forehead and down her nose, which has scandalised onlookers.

Andre Derain shows a portrait of Matisse smoking a pipe in which half the face is bright turquoise while the beard is a series of daubs of crimson and black. Maurice de Vlaminck, a racing cyclist turned painter, shows landscapes with trees of the wildest pink and Raoul Dufy fills his pictures with flags.

Georges Braque and Georges Rouault are two other painters exhibiting with the group. These artists believe that colour in itself is a primary means of expression, and unleash its energy in its most intense form. "Violence on the walls" has provoked such violent reactions among the more conservative members of the public that Mme Matisse has been advised not to attend by her husband.

Andre Derain's "Collioure, le village et la mer," (1905).

1905

NOVEMBER

Su	Mo	Tu	We	Th	Fr	Sa
			1	2	3	4
5	6	7	8	9	10	11
12	13	14	15	16	17	18
19	20	21	22	23	24	25
26	27	28	29	30		

1. St. Petersburg: Czar signs amnesty for political prisoners as unrest continues.→

3. London: Sir Claude MacDonald is appointed first UK ambassador to Japan.

3. London: Joseph Chamberlain attacks the concept of universal old age pensions.

6. Poland: Riots in Warsaw mark renewed calls for Polish autonomy (→12).

7. Japan: Famine spreads after failure of rice crop (→29/12).

8. Chicago: Fund launched to aid Russian Jews.→

9. Russia: Troops and sailors mutiny at Kronstadt (→10).

10. Russia: Imperial decree closes all universities until further notice (→1/12).

12. Poland: Martial law declared in Russian-occupied Poland (→26/10/06).

13. Portsmouth: The King of Greece arrives on a state visit to the UK.

16. Norway: Referendum shows 78% want Danish Prince Carl, second son of Frederick VII, as king (→18).

17. Japan: Treaty with Korea recognises Japanese rule but guarantees "dignity and honour" of Korean Emperor.

18. Norway: Prince Carl of Denmark accepts Norwegian throne, taking name Haakon VII.

19. France: 128 die when British steamer "Hilda" is wrecked off St. Malo.

19. Glasgow: 39 people perish in a fire at a lodging-house.

22. Liverpool: The world's largest turbine liner, Cunard's "Carmania", leaves on maiden voyage to New York.

27. London: First performance of W. B. Yeats' play "On Baile's Strand" at St. George's Hall.

28. Vienna: 250,000 Austrians celebrate as the government grants universal suffrage in Austria.

Henry Irving, first theatrical knight, dies

Sir Henry Irving: born in Somerset, buried in Westminster Abbey.

Oct 13. Sir Henry Irving is dead and the English stage is in mourning for the monarch who has been at its head for 35 years. Irving was 67 and still near the height of his powers as the first member of his profession to be knighted. His reign at the Lyceum Theatre began in 1871 and his partnership there with Ellen Terry conquered all hearts on both sides of the Atlantic.

Max Beerbohm writes today of "his incomparable power of stirring up a sense of mystery and horror." It was nowhere more thrillingly seen than as the haunted murderer of "The Bells", which Irving gave again and again by public demand. His wife believes the strain of it hastened his end.

First suffragettes go to prison

Oct 14. Two young members of the militant women's suffrage movement elected to go to prison rather than pay fines. Christabel Pankhurst, daughter of Emmeline Pankhurst, founder of the Women's Political and Social Union, was sentenced to seven days and her colleague, Annie Kenney, to three days for assaulting police at a meeting addressed by the leading Liberal politician, Sir Edward Grey, at the Free Trade Hall in Manchester.

Aspirin goes on sale for first time

Oct 30. After High Court action over its trademark, Aspirin for the relief of pain is now available in Britain. The drug was developed by Bayer, a German chemical firm, and first used there in 1899. Although there have been reports of stomach trouble, sweating and sickness after its use, Professor N. Tizard of King's College Hospital, London, says it is useful in countering headaches due to anxiety or overwork.

London's underground:one of the new deep lines known as "tubes".

Queen launches appeal for jobless

Nov 12. Queen Alexandra today launched an appeal for the jobless. Her Majesty opened it with a personal donation of £2,000. In a statement issued through Earl de Grey, the Treasurer of her Household, she called on "all charitably disposed people in the Empire, both men and women, to assist me in alleviating the suffering of the poor starving unemployed this winter".

The Queen appears to be responding to a call by the Prime Minister, Arthur Balfour, in his speech last week for help for the deserving poor – "victims mainly of economic causes". It was immediately welcomed, though several, like Will Crooks, MP for Poplar, warned against demoralising people "by giving them charity without work".

More details about the Queen's Fund may become known later this week, but today Earl de Grey said he knew no more than was contained in the announcement, and that Buckingham Palace was probably the place to send money. Recently the Queen has also shown interest in the work of General Booth's Salvation Army and the Church Army, which are known for their work with the poor.

Actors in Shaw's play prosecuted

Nov 1. "Mrs Warren's Profession", which has twice been refused a licence by the Lord Chamberlain, was presented in a New York theatre this week and promptly closed by the police. Mr Arnold Daly and his actors were arrested for offences against public decency. The magistrate adjourned the case in order to read Mr Bernard Shaw's notorious play. Tickets for it had changed hands at high prices.

Mr Shaw wrote the play as long ago as 1893 but it has had only two private performances in London at a club theatre in 1902. Yesterday his comments on these events was: "I have no wrath but a very great pity for all those foolish people. Prostitution is a permissible subject on the stage only when it is made agreeable. Why didn't they arrest the whole audience?"

Russian peasants "urged to massacre Jews": Britain launches an appeal

Some of the Jews massacred by Russian peasants in Odessa.

Nov 8. Recently, a new round of violence has erupted in Russia with much of it directed against Jews and including a horrific pogrom in Odessa where 1,000 people may have been killed.

The pogrom got underway within a few days of Czar Nicholas II announcing his manifesto granting greater political rights. Observers believe the fact that local police were stripped of many of their powers may have prompted the recent bloodshed.

Leaflets appeared in Odessa last week with the words "Death to the Jews". Next a mob appeared carrying icons and pictures of the Czar and the Czarina and yelling "Down with the Jews". Soon Jewish shops and houses were being smashed and looted. Eventually a howling, armed mob of 50,000 roamed the city shooting Jewish men and stabbing, strangling or cutting to pieces Jewish women and children. More than 5,000 were injured, and 6,000 Jewish families made homeless. Involved in the massacre were peasants, policemen, reactionary army officers and government officials. The mob had lists of specific Jewish homes, and an inexhaustible supply of bullets.

In other towns and villages of the Ukraine and White Russia bands calling themselves "Black Hundred" have also attacked Jews.

Keeping fit – the latest craze.

Russian troops mutiny in East

Nov 12. Soldiers and sailors based at Vladivostock, Russia's only Pacific port, mutinied today and hundreds are reported dead. The mutiny arose after two soldiers murdered a shopkeeper in the Chinese quarter. A detachment was sent to arrest them but they killed their own officer instead. Other officers and soldiers took to the streets and there was confused fighting. Some 40,000 men were said to have joined the mutineers while 10,000 soldiers are still loyal. The town is described as being in flames while frightened foreign residents are demanding protection.

1905

DECEMBER

Su	Mo	Tu	We	Th	Fr	Sa
					1	2
3	4	5	6	7	8	9
10	11	12	13	14	15	16
17	18	19	20	21	22	23
24	25	26	27	28	29	30
31						

1. St. Petersburg: 20 officers and 230 guards are arrested after plot to kill the Czar is uncovered (→5).

3. British Guyana: British troops quell a riot at Georgetown.

4. New York: 125,000 Jews march in sympathy with the plight of Jews in Russian Empire (→4/1/06).

5. London: The roof of Charing Cross Station collapses, killing six and destroying the Avenue Theatre.

6. Dublin: John Redmond opens the Irish National Convention with a call for Home Rule (→21/5/07).

7. Russia: Revolutionaries occupy the fortress at Kiev in the Ukraine (→30).

9. Dresden: Richard Strauss's opera "Salome", based on Oscar Wilde's play, is first performed.

10. Stockholm: Nobel Prizes awarded to Philipp von Lenard (Germany, Physics); Johann von Bayer (Germany, Chemistry); Robert Koch (Germany, Physiology); Henryk Sienkiewicz (Poland, Literature) and Bertha von Suttner (Austria, Peace).

14. UK: Trades unions call for universal suffrage, old age pensions and an eight-hour day.

29. Japan: 680,000 reported to be starving as famine worsens.

BIRTH

24. US industrialist Howard Hughes (†5/4/76).

HITS OF 1905

How'd You Like To Spoon With Me, Jerome Kern's first hit.

Wait Till The Sun Shines, Nellie

QUOTE OF THE YEAR

"In a country economically backward, the proletariat can take power earlier than where capitalism is more advanced." **Leon Trotsky** revolutionary pamphlet.

Scottish Liberal is new Prime Minister

Dec 5. Sir Henry Campbell-Bannerman, the Liberal leader, today accepted the King's commission to form a new government. This follows the resignation of Arthur Balfour, the Tory Premier, whose party is now in disarray over tariff reform. Sir Henry told the King he needs several days to complete a new cabinet. It is assumed that this is on account of a clash of personalities within his party hierarchy.

Liberal critics of Sir Henry would have preferred Herbert Asquith as Premier but he is to be Chancellor of the Exchequer.

Sir Henry Campbell-Bannerman.

Explorer Amundsen finds magnetic pole

Dec 6. Norwegian explorer Roald Amundsen has landed at Fort Egbert, Alaska, after a perilous two-and-a-half-year voyage along America's frozen Arctic coast from Atlantic to Pacific. The search for the North West Passage has claimed many sailors' lives over the centuries and few thought Amundsen would survive in his small 47-foot cutter, which was ice-bound for nearly two years.

Not only did the Norwegian survive, but he found the magnetic North Pole en route. It is on King William Island, slightly shifted from the spot located by Briton John Ross 60 years ago.

Czar's troops brutally crush revolt

Dec 30. A revolt in Moscow by workers and students is being crushed by government forces, with several thousand casualties. After a week of bitter street fighting across barricades in parts of old Moscow, which included the use of artillery, it is clear that the battle has begun between order and anarchy, revolution and the government.

The first shots were fired by the insurgents who assembled in a school and proclaimed a new "provisional government". Their original plan was to get hold of weapons, provoke a mutiny in St. Petersburg and establish a revolutionary government there. When their plans were foiled they raised the red flag in Moscow where there were fewer troops, many dissatisfied workers and a terrain of narrow streets which was wellsuited to barricades.

One report says that between 9,000 and 11,000 people have been killed or wounded, but this estimate could be on the high side. Some have been civilians, in particular droskhy drivers and a number of curious spectators.

Czarist generals enjoying themselves after crushing the Moscow uprising.

Tubercular bacillus wins prize for Koch

Dec 10. Robert Koch, the German bacteriologist, today received the Nobel Prize for identifying the germ that causes that most dreaded of diseases: tuberculosis.

This discovery, made in 1882, was only one highlight in a career that has established Koch as one of the greatest of all bacteriologists. He also discovered the germs that cause anthrax and cholera, and more recently he has proved that bubonic plague is transmitted by rat lice and sleeping sickness by the tsetse fly.

Koch also developed many now standard techniques of bacteriology, among them the use of aniline dyes for staining bacteria to aid recognition and ways of growing them outside the body. He also established the classic rules for proving that a particular germ causes a disease, which have contributed greatly to the enormous strides made by medicine.

Motor car victims to get ambulances

Dec 19. The London County Council today decided to set-up the capital's first-ever motorised ambulance service for traffic accident victims. Currently ambulances are only used to isolate those suffering from infectious diseases, while accident victims have to rely on stretchers or vehicles commandeered by the police, and many suffer further injuries on their way to hospital. The LCC plan, which has still to be approved by Parliament, is to have wheeled litters and two ambulances which can be summoned using roadside telephones.

One of the first ambulances used for rushing accident victims to hospital.

Shaw is Superman of London stage

Arts: This year there has been no escaping **George Bernard Shaw**, whose star in the theatre has risen as never before. His comedy of Anglo-Irish relations, "John Bull's Other Island", was the first success of the new management at the Court Theatre. When the King attended a command performance in March he laughed so heartily that he broke his chair.

In May came the first production of "Man and Superman", in which **Granville Barker** as the hero who advances the idea of creative evolution was made up to resemble Shaw himself. Then "Major Barbara" in November dramatised the plight of the poor through the Salvation Army heroine's attempt to do something about it. "Even my cleverest friends confess that the last act beat them. Their brains simply gave way under it", Mr Shaw claims.

George Bernard Shaw.

In a lighter vein the year saw the huge popular success of "The Scarlet Pimpernel", Baroness Orczy's disdainful aristocrat who puts the French Revolutionaries to scorn. "They seek him here, they seek him there" is a current catchphrase following the stirring exploits of "the damn'd elusive Pimpernel" in print and on stage.

However, like a letter from beyond the grave has appeared "De Profundis", the long, anguished, accusatory letter that **Oscar Wilde** composed in his prison cell to Lord Alfred Douglas, the man whose fateful friendship had ruined him.

1906

JANUARY

Su	Mo	Tu	We	Th	Fr	Sa
	1	2	3	4	5	6
7	8	9	10	11	12	13
14	15	16	17	18	19	20
21	22	23	24	25	26	27
28	29	30	31			

1. Berlin: Head of armed forces, Gen. von Schlieffen, retires; succeeded by Lt. Gen. von Moltke (→ 18/11/07).

2. France: New Darraq racing motor car achieves new speed of 108 mph (→ 26).

4. Berlin: Police forbid "obscene" Isadora Duncan to dance in public.

4. Russia: Government interferes with the distribution of $3m in international Jewish relief (→ 21/6).

6. US: The US Army in the Philippines is boosted in anticipation of unrest in China.

7. US: Wright brothers' aeroplane flies 24 miles in 38 minutes at 38 mph, 75 to 100 feet altitude (→ 3/3).

8. US: Debut in New York of pianist Arthur Rubinstein.

11. UK: David Lloyd George prevented by violent crowds from speaking at election rally (→ 13).

13. UK: Voting begins in the general election; ex-Tory PM Arthur Balfour loses his seat (→ 7/2).

17. France: Radical senator Armand Fallieres is elected President in succession to Emile Loubet (→ 4/5).

22. Liverpool: Tram accident kills 30.

22. Germany: "Red Monday" Socialist reform rally attracts 250,000 people.

24. Canada: 120 drown when steamer "Valencia" runs aground off Vancouver, British Columbia.

26. US: New motor speed record for the mile of 28.2 seconds achieved in Florida (→ 10/6/07).

27. London: River Thames catches fire as oil on the surface ignites.

BIRTH

20. Greek shipping tycoon Aristotle Onassis (†15/3/75).

DEATH

29. Danish King Christian IX (*8/4/1818).

Conference to settle Moroccan question

Jan 16. The conference to settle the Moroccan question, which Germany has been seeking for the past several months, opened in the Spanish seaport of Algeciras today, with the Germans virtually isolated.

The French have shown great firmness in upholding their claim to a special role in Morocco, not least because of the long frontier French Algeria shares with that country. Britain, Italy and Spain have given their support, while Germany is backed only by Austria, which has a minor role here today.

Germany stepped up her efforts in Morocco after the 1904 treaties France signed with Britain and Italy, under which the French gave up their interests in Egypt and Libya in return for recognition of their place in Morocco.

The French are still bitter at the memory of the Kaiser's intervention in Moroccan affairs last year, when he made his spectacular visit to Tangier and obtained from Moroccan ministers the concession to build the port of Tangier, which had already been promised to France (→ 31/3).

Officials take a break from talks.

Czar orders army on punitive raids

Jan 7. Czar Nicholas II has ordered a crackdown against opposition and sent army units to deal with trouble. So-called punitive expeditions are concentrating on the Baltic provinces where the situation was "critical". A major uprising against the Czar was put down in Moscow last month. But trouble spread to the countryside where the army is ruthlessly dealing with peasants who have burnt down landowners' homes (→ 2/3).

Britain shuts out mad and the poor

Jan 1. Potential immigrants, in particular political refugees from Russia and Central Europe, found themselves under close scrutiny as they arrived in Britain today when the new Aliens Act came into force. Ships arriving at Gravesend, Grimsby and other ports were met by launches and the occupants questioned about their finances before being subjected to a series of stringent tests for both physical and mental health (→ 5/3).

Men and machines having a rest during work on the Simplon Tunnel.

1906

FEBRUARY

Su	Mo	Tu	We	Th	Fr	Sa
				1	2	3
4	5	6	7	8	9	10
11	12	13	14	15	16	17
18	19	20	21	22	23	24
25	26	27	28			

1. London: Government drops plans to build a fast motor highway between London and Brighton.

2. Paris: 570 injured in riots as government officials gather inventory of Church property (→ 10/12).

3. Japan: Government decides almost to double size of Japanese navy by 1908.

7. Pacific: Many killed as a cyclone with 120-mph winds and 65 ft waves strikes the Cook Islands (→ 8).

8. London: Jobless marchers from the Midlands get a cool reception on arrival in the capital.

9. US: Doctor claims that fresh air and cold are best treatment for pneumonia.

12. London: Keir Hardie elected leader of new Labour MPs in the House of Commons (→ 27).

15. Austro-Hungarian Empire: Workers revolt at the port of Fiume.

19. US: William S. Kellogg forms the Battle Creek Toasted Corn Flake Company, to market the cereal his brother, John Harvey, invented as a therapy for mental patients.

20. Africa: Two companies of British troops sent to quell native revolt in northern Nigeria.

23. US: Chicago "Bluebeard" Johann Koch, said to have murdered at least one of his 50 wives, is executed.

27. UK: Former Tory PM Arthur Balfour, who lost his seat in the election, is reelected to Commons (→ 1/11).

28. US: One person is killed and many are injured in racial rioting at Springfield, Ohio.

28. London: Government announces UK Navy budget is to be £1.5 million lower than 1905.

BIRTHS

4. US astronomer Clyde Tombaugh.

4. German theologian Dietrich Bonhoeffer (†9/4/45).

Liberals sweep to landslide victory

Feb 7. The Liberals were formally confirmed in power today after a landslide General Election victory of astonishing size. They have 399 MPs in the new Parliament compared with only 183 elected in 1900. The Tories now have 156 MPs, instead of 401 last time.

Equally remarkable is the success of the Labour Representation Committee. Led by James Keir Hardie it won 29 seats, a gain of 27, and trebled its share of the total popular vote.

Excitement has mounted over this political earthquake and for several nights now crowds have gathered in London streets at hoardings showing the latest election results. These have been provided by searchlights flashing the news in morse from newspaper offices.

Sir Henry Campbell-Bannerman has begun reshaping the Liberal government which he has led since the Tories surrendered office in December without first going to the polls. Jubilant Liberals dubbed the new administration as the "Ministry Of All The Talents", with Messrs Asquith, Lloyd George and Churchill featuring as the party's brightest stars.

Labour's fruits: MP Keir Hardie.

The election campaign, which lasted a month, has been notable for the participation of women. They have been much more prominent as speakers and canvassers as well as persistent hecklers demanding female suffrage. Nonetheless, free trade has been the dominant issue.

It is generally agreed that the Liberals, reunited after the divisions caused by the Boer War, have won so decisively because many voters feared there would be dearer food if the Tories were re-elected and imposed tariffs on foreign goods in order to boost trade with the Empire.

The industrial working-classes appear to be more anti-Tory than ever before. The number of constituencies where there were unopposed returns was dramatically down – from 243 in 1900 to 114 this time (→12).

Biggest and fastest battleship in the world built in 4 months

Feb 10. "HMS Dreadnought", the most powerful warship the world has ever seen, was launched today, immediately placing the Royal Navy years ahead of its potential adversaries. She is the largest, fastest battleship afloat and is armed with ten 12-inch guns so revolutionnary in design that eight of them can fire on either side of the ship at one time. Experts claim this means she will be capable of taking on older battleships with a superiority of 10 to four.

The great range and effectiveness of torpedoes now means close range engagements with six-inch guns are doubly dangerous. Only 12-inch barrels give the long range sufficient to avoid hits from torpedoes. Work on the ship began just four months ago and when she is completed later this year she will have cost in excess of £3 million.

"HMS Dreadnought", helping Britannia to rule the waves.

"HMS Dreadnought's" launch by the King today is the result of action following an Admiralty report last year which stated that no matter what number of ships Britain produced they could not guarantee the safety of the United Kingdom from potential aggressors on the opposite side of the North Sea without a change in quality of design as well. First Sea Lord Admiral Sir John Fisher immediately ordered the new ship. He had been worried for some time that the quality of British vessels was being placed second to their quantity.

He scrapped 154 old vessels a year ago and pressed ahead with the current building programme under which 50 warships and submarines are now under construction.

Naval experts believe "Dreadnought" will render all others ships obsolete, but many in the Admiralty believe she may only serve to fuel the naval building race between Britain and Germany (→12/6).

Typhoon hits Tahiti: 10,000 feared dead

Feb 8. At least 10,000 people are thought to have been killed by a fierce cyclone which has hit Tahiti and neighbouring Pacific islands. Winds of 120 miles an hour whipped up 65-foot high waves, forcing people living near the coast to abandon their homes. Not only have villages been wiped out but even islands have disappeared completely. Tahiti's city of Papeete was inundated by the storm; about 75 buildings were destroyed including the American consulate. Other islands badly hit by the cyclone were the Society, Tuamoto and Cook islands.

Pope tells French: stop persecuting us

Feb 21. Pope Pius X today condemned the French government for its new law separating Church and State. "We pray to God that the enemies of religion will stop persecuting us," the Pope declared. "We shall fight hate with love, fallacy with truth and intimidation and humiliation with forgiveness."

The new French law guarantees freedom of religion but imposes severe restrictions on church property and religious education. The Pope's denunciation of the government for trying to destroy religious sentiment in the country follows the failure of attempts by French church leaders to fight the law (→10/8).

A German view of alpine fun.

1906

MARCH

Su	Mo	Tu	We	Th	Fr	Sa
				1	2	3
4	5	6	7	8	9	10
11	12	13	14	15	16	17
18	19	20	21	22	23	24
25	26	27	28	29	30	31

2. St. Petersburg: Czar grants legislative power to Duma and Council, but retains his right of veto (→ 20).

3. France: The first trials of an aeroplane with tyres take place at Montesson, Seine-et-Marne (→ 6/4/07).

4. France: Latest census shows the country has a population of 39.2 million.

5. London: A government committee expresses grave concern at what it calls the "vagrant army" of the poor (→ 7/6).

5. S. Africa: British troops kill 60 Zulus in fierce clashes (→ 2/4).

7. Finland: Men and women over 24 are given the vote, except those state-supported or not paying tax (→ 15/3/07).

10. London: Underground railway opens from Baker Street to Waterloo, and is dubbed the "Bakerloo" line (→ 10/6).

11. France: 1,200 miners die in mine explosion at Courrieres.

14. London: Parliament approves the principle of old age pensions paid for by taxation (→ 10/5/07).

20. Sicily: The island of Ustica is devastated in massive volcanic eruption.

20. Russia: Mutiny and massacre of officers take place at Sevastopol in the Crimea (→ 8/4).

21. S. Africa: The UK pays £9.5 million in compensation for the damage caused in the Boer War (→ 9/8).

22. Paris: England win the first rugby international against France by 35 to eight.

24. UK: The Grand National at Aintree is won by Ascetic's Silver.

28. New York: The State Meteorological Office says that the science of forecasting the weather is "within our grasp".

DEATH

27. French painter Eugene Carriere (*17/1/1849).

Land of Hope and Glory spans globe

March 8. The British Empire occupies one-fifth of the land surface of the globe and has a population of 400,000,000, according to a Government Blue Book of 300 pages, published today and on sale at three shillings and five pence. Statistics were collected and analysed by the English Local Government Board: India reported some 300,000,000 people, while the Falkland Islands counted a mere 2,253 inhabitants.

The survey shows the rapidity with which the Empire expanded in the latter part of the last century. At the time of the last census in 1861, the Empire occupied eight and a half million square miles. For twenty years there was little change; then between 1881 and the end of the century more than three million square miles were added, chiefly in west, east and southern Africa.

In some territories, notably western Australia, Malaya and Hong Kong, a shortage of white women is reported. In India, there is an excess of Indian males, but this may be because the men "regard the women as of no importance" for census purposes.

Wider still and wider shall thy bounds be set: Peoples of the Empire.

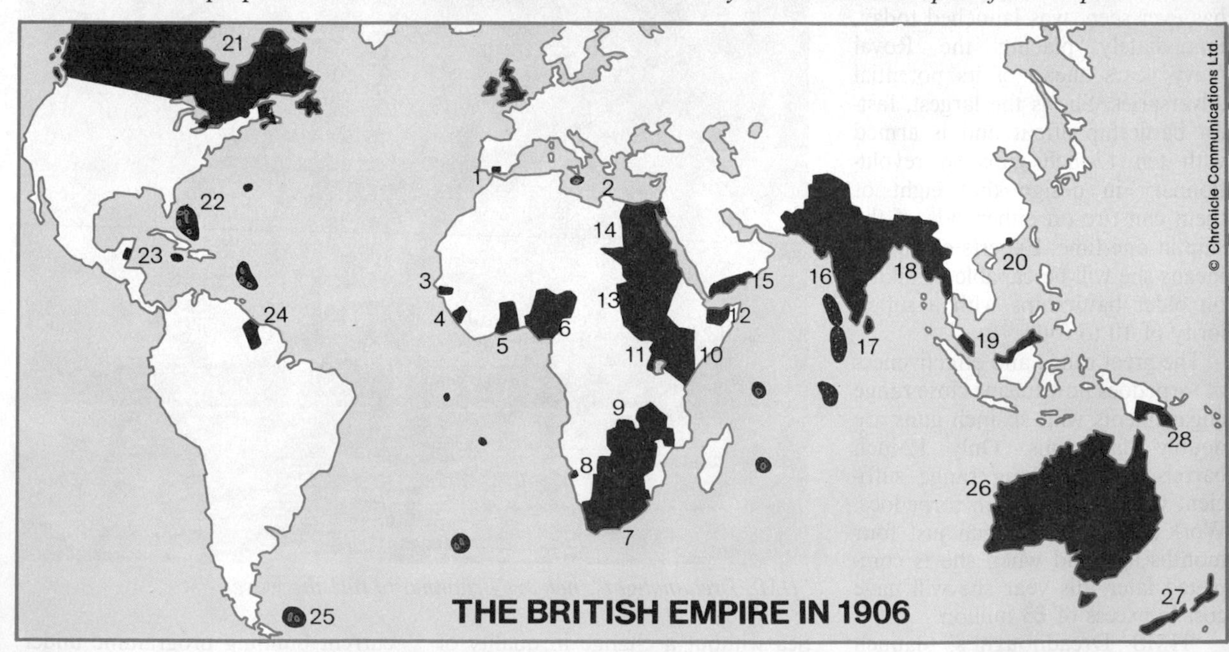

EUROPE
1 Gibraltar
2 Malta and Cyprus

AFRICA
3 Gambia
4 Sierra Leone
5 Gold Coast
6 Nigeria
7 Cape Colony
8 Bechuanaland
9 Rhodesia and Nyasaland
10 Kenya
11 Uganda
12 British Somaliland
13 Anglo-Egyptian Sudan
14 Egypt

ASIA
15 Aden
16 India
17 Ceylon
18 Burma
19 Malayan States
20 Hong Kong

AMERICA
21 Dominion of Canada
22 Bahamas and Bermuda
23 British West Indies and Honduras
24 British Guiana
25 Falkland Isles

AUSTRALASIA
26 Australian Commonwealth
27 New Zealand
28 British New Guinea

SEAS AND OCEANS
Many islands of the world

Women urged to shun rough sports

March 30. The increase in women playing contact sports came under fire tonight in a speech by Dr Dudley Sargent, physical director of Harvard University. Hockey and lacrosse, now widespread in English colleges, are gaining ground in the US, and netball, or women's basketball, is growing fast. Dr Sargent, however, advises women to leave the rougher sports to men. "Let woman rather confine herself to the lighter and more graceful forms of gymnastics and athletics and make herself supreme in those," he said (→ 14/6).

Keeping fit: damaging to health?

Morocco talks end

March 31. The conference on Morocco closed today at Algeciras with both France and Germany claiming satisfaction after two months of hard negotiations. Moroccan independence under the Sultan is upheld, German demands for equal access for all countries have been accepted and France's "special position" is recognised.

The conference almost foundered on the question of control of the police, but reached a compromise under which a senior officer will report to both the Sultan and the diplomatic corps in Tangier. But both France and Spain will police Morocco's ports (→ 4/8/07).

1906

APRIL

Su	Mo	Tu	We	Th	Fr	Sa
1	2	3	4	5	6	7
8	9	10	11	12	13	14
15	16	17	18	19	20	21
22	23	24	25	26	27	28
29	30					

2. Russia: Voting begins in the Duma elections (→ 8).

8. Russia: Peasants vote the Progressives to new Duma (→ 11).

9. Persia: Europeans attacked in anti-Christian riots.

11. Russia: Social Democrats murder Father Gapon, who led "Bloody Sunday" march on 22/1/05 (→ 10/5).

12. New York: Mark Twain speaks in favour of Russian revolution at dinner for visiting Maxim Gorky.

14. Washington: Roosevelt declares wish for inheritance tax on large fortunes.

14. US: Mob burns two blacks to death in front of cheering crowd of 3,000 at Springfield, Ohio (→ 7/8).

16. Washington: Supreme Court rules against inter-state divorce.

17. UK: The Independent Labour Party calls for female emancipation (→ 25).

19. S. Africa: 7,000 troops are called out to suppress Zulus (→ 6/5).

21. UK: Everton beat Newcastle United 1-0 in FA Cup final at Crystal Palace.

22. Athens: "Interim Olympics" open in the presence of King Edward VII.

26. London: Headmaster tells House of Commons Select Committee school meals are not necessary (→ 8/3).

27. Italy: King Edward VII visits the scene of the Vesuvius eruption.

30. US: State troopers shoot dead 20 striking miners in Pennsylvania.

BIRTHS

9. British Labour Party leader Hugh Gaitskell (†18/1/63).

13. Franco-Irish playwright Samuel Beckett (†22/12/89).

DEATH

19. French physicist Pierre Curie, in a road accident (*15/5/1859).

Vesuvius erupts: lava flow engulfs town

History repeats itself as Mount Vesuvius blows its top.

April 7. Lava from the erupting volcano Mount Vesuvius in Italy has destroyed the town of Ottaiano leaving hundreds dead and injured. The river of fire is now heading unchecked towards other communities. In nearby Naples more than 100 people died when the weight of cinders on roofs caused buildings to collapse. The air, thick with choking ash and fumes, was filled with pitiful cries for help, mingling with the noise of frenzied rescue work.

For miles around the volcano danger zone, villages and towns are cut off. Elsewhere in the region thousands of people have joined a mass exodus to escape the showers of ash and sand. Boats and trains are at a standstill and the military authorities are distributing emergency food and supplies (→ 9).

Britain to control all access to Tibet

April 27. China, which claims suzerainty over Tibet, has reluctantly signed a treaty proposed by Britain following the occupation of the capital, Lhasa.

Under its terms Britain will control all roads into Tibet. No foreign power may send representatives into the country. They are forbidden transportation and mining concessions and they may not occupy, buy or lease territory in Tibet without British permission.

The main aim of the treaty is to stop the Russian march south and it is worth noting that the treaty was agreed without the participation of Tibet's ruler-priest, the Dalai Lama, who fled when the British arrived (→ 23/2/10).

US President raps muckraking press

April 14. President Roosevelt today criticized those investigative journalists whom he called "muckrakers". He had in mind such recent exposes of municipal corruption and business eithics as Lincoln Steffens' "The Shame of our Cities" or Ida Tarbell's history of the Standard Oil Company.

Speaking at the opening of a new office building for the House of Representatives in Washington, the president quoted John Bunyan's "Pilgrim's Progress", and the character in it who never looked up at the stars, but steadily plied his rake in the muck, and so lost his chance of a celestial crown. Muckrakers are needed, Roosevelt said, but they must know when to stop.

Thousands flee as quake devastates San Francisco

And the walls came tumbling down: Grant Avenue, after the quake.

April 19. The full agony of San Francisco was revealed at first light today after a major earthquake destroyed most of the city, killing at least 1,000 people and causing a firestorm which reduced hundreds of damaged buildings to ashes. Martial law has been declared and looters have been shot in the streets with military units assisting police in keeping order.

Thousands of citizens have spent the night sleeping in parks. Thousands more have fled in ferries and trains as fires continue to rage and more shock waves hit the city. San Francisco's business district and industrial areas have been wiped out. The fashionable Nob Hill district is threatened by advancing flames, even though gas and electricity supplies have been cut off.

Firefighters are using dynamite in desperate efforts to contain the fires which have destroyed newspaper offices and other commercial buildings. The city's water mains were destroyed in the 30-second earth tremor which has caused an estimated $200 million worth of damage.

Most of the fatalities are believed to have been burned to death or killed by falling debris. Hundreds more are being treated in local hospitals (→18/8).

Weary San Franciscans view the destruction of their city.

Olympic spirit is rekindled as Games come home to Athens

The Olympic Games, back in Greece after around 2,600 years.

April 27. After the disappointments of the Paris and St. Louis Games, the Olympics returned to Athens with an "Interim Games" to celebrate the 10th anniversary of the start of the modern era.

Performances were unremarkable, but for the first time the Americans competed as a team rather than individually, and the Finns participated, albeit under the Russian flag. After the sparse attendances in 1900 and 1904, Athens rekindled the enthusiasm that launched the Games in 1896.

The Olympics has clearly regained its early popularity and at short notice London has agreed to stage the 1908 Games.

Women protesters halt Parliament

April 25. A group of women were today thrown out of the House of Commons after their noisy protests halted a debate. The outcry came when they feared that a motion by Keir Hardie in their favour was going to be talked out. At this point the angry demonstrators began shouting "We won't be treated this way" and "Give us votes". Fists were shaken at members and a white flag with the words "Justice for Women" was waved through the grille of the Ladies' Gallery. The police were called to remove the women. The debate later closed without a vote (→23/6).

1906

MAY

Su	Mo	Tu	We	Th	Fr	Sa
		1	2	3	4	5
6	7	8	9	10	11	12
13	14	15	16	17	18	19
20	21	22	23	24	25	26
27	28	29	30	31		

1. Europe: 3,000 workers arrested during Paris May Day demonstrations; in Germany, 6,000 strikers are sacked (→ 20).

4. Paris: President Fallieres meets King Edward VII.

6. S. Africa: British troops kill 60 Zulus at Durban, Natal (→ 23/7).

8. London: MP Sir W. Anson calls Education Bill "tyrannical imposition of knowledge" in Commons debate (→ 11).

11. London: Massive protest against the Education Bill held at Royal Albert Hall (→ 19/7).

12. St. Petersburg: Duma clashes with Czar by calling for amnesty for political prisoners (→ 14).

14. Russia: Murders of Czarist officials mark May Day in the Russian calendar (→ 24).

19. Italy: Official opening of the 12-mile Simplon rail tunnel between Switzerland and Italy, the world's longest.

20. France: Leftist bloc victorious in parliamentary elections.

22. Canada: Departure of the last British troops based in the Dominion.

24. St. Petersburg: Czar concedes universal suffrage but refuses amnesty for political crimes (→ 28).

26. New York: Lewis Nixon announces the invention of the sonar.

26. London: Vauxhall Bridge opens.

28. Russia: Government decides to redistribute 25 million acres of land to peasants (→ 21/6).

30. UK: The Derby at Epsom is won by Major E. Loder's Spearmint.

BIRTHS

6. French mathematician Andre Weil.

8. Italian film director Roberto Rossellini (†3/6/77).

DEATH

23. Norwegian dramatist Henrik Ibsen (*20/3/1828).→

Duma opens with splendour and security

May 10. Russia's first elected Parliament, the Duma, began work today after a ceremony of great splendour in St. Petersburg and a speech from Czar Nicholas II on the necessity for freedom, order and justice. There was unprecedented security for the event with thousands of police and troops present.

The Czar's speech was coolly received by the deputies who were disappointed by his failure to announce an amnesty for political prisoners. He wrote it himself after rejecting three drafts.

The Czar described the deputies as the "best men" of Russia but in the ensuing debate he was frequently criticised over the amnesty. Another resolution called for an end to death sentences being passed by military and civil tribunals.

It was noticeable that government ministers are not taking part in the debate and are ignoring the Duma's proceedings (→ 12).

The Czar and Czarina attend the birth of Russia's parliament.

Playwright Ibsen gives up the ghost

Ibsen, great Norwegian dramatist.

May 23. Henrik Ibsen, whose plays so often outraged audiences ten years ago, has died in his native Norway at the age of 78. He had been unable to write since having a stroke in 1900. Of his 26 works for the stage, it was the "problem plays" of the 1880s that caused the trouble, controversial works like "A Doll's House", "Ghosts", "Rosmersholm" and "Hedda Gabler".

The first English production of "Ghosts" was declared by the critic Clement Scott to be "an open drain, a loathsome sore unbandaged, a dirty act done publicly" and a Daily Telegraph editorial described it as bestial, cynical, disgusting, poisonous, sickly, delirious, indecent, loathsome and fetid. Meanwhile Bernard Shaw championed Ibsen as a social reformer who had restored the play of intelligence and ideas to the theatre.

Ibsen himself claimed, "I have been more of a poet and less of a social philosopher than people seem to want to believe. My task has simply been to create human beings."

Assassin fails to kill Spanish King

May 31. King Alfonso of Spain and his bride Queen Victoria narrowly escaped assassination on their wedding day. As they drove in an open carriage to the Royal Palace in Madrid, a bomb hidden in a bridal bouquet was hurled at them from a balcony on the route. A splinter from it struck the King, but he was saved from injury by the decorations he was wearing. "This is infamous" he said. The bomb, which exploded under the horses, was powerful enough to kill 18 people and injure 30 others. Fifteen anarchists have been arrested (→ 2/6).

Oil giant challenged

May 10. One of America's leading oil giants, the Standard Oil Company, was accused today of stifling competition through intrigue and trickery. These charges were made in Chicago at a court hearing of the Interstate Commerce Commission which will report to the US Congress.

Witnesses, including former employees of Standard, alleged that the company bribed workers with smaller, independent companies to obtain information to help drive them out of business (→ 8/9/07).

1906

JUNE

Su	Mo	Tu	We	Th	Fr	Sa
					1	2
3	4	5	6	7	8	9
10	11	12	13	14	15	16
17	18	19	20	21	22	23
24	25	26	27	28	29	30

2. Spain: Would-be assassin of King Alfonso XIII commits suicide.

3. Rome: Discovery of plot to blow up the Italian King, Victor Emmanuel III.

5. St. Petersburg: Peter Stolypin is appointed Prime Minister.→

6. Europe: Italy reaffirms its Triple Alliance with the Austro-Hungarian and German Empires (→30/7/07).

7. UK: Inquiry opens into the alleged extravagant spending on caring for the poor in Poplar, East London (→8/11).

7. Glasgow: The world's largest and fastest passenger liner, Cunard's "Lusitania", is launched (→20/9).

12. London: British actress Ellen Terry celebrates 50 years on the London stage.

12. UK: 322 warships start exercises involving mock attacks on British ports (→1/10).

13. France: Scientists claim they have successfully immunised cattle against tuberculosis.

14. London: Bill banning women from dangerous sports following the death of a woman parachutist (→23).

17. Russia: Officials admit that a massacre of hundreds of Jews at Bielostock was planned by officials in advance.→

22. Washington: Roosevelt sues John D. Rockefeller's Standard Oil Co. for operating monopoly (→8/9/07).

27. France: The first circuit motor race held at Le Mans is won by the Hungarian, Ferenc Szisz in a Renault (→26/5/23).

BIRTHS

3. US-born French dancer and jazz singer Josephine Baker (†11/4/75).

22. Austrian born US film director Billy Wilder.

DEATH

29. French historian Albert Sorel (*13/8/1842).

Battle for suffrage gathers strength

June 23. A deputation representing half a million women met the Prime Minister to press their claims for the vote. Representatives of 20 political, trade and professional societies and their supporters gathered appropriately at Boadicea's statue on the Embankment before moving off to the Foreign Office.

Miss Emily Davies, a member of the Women's Suffrage Societies, reminded Sir Henry Campbell-Bannerman that she had handed a petition to John Stuart Mill 40 years ago. Since then great change had taken place but women were still without the vote.

In reply, the Prime Minister said they had made out a conclusive and irrefutable case but they must be patient: "It is more likely you will succeed if you wait than if you act now in a pugnacious spirit." As he left, Miss Annie Kenney, wearing traditional Lancashire clogs and shawl, stood on a chair and cried: "We are not satisfied".

Later in the day Emmeline Pankhurst told a 6,000 strong crowd in Trafalgar Square "We have been patient too long. We will be patient no longer." Similar feelings were expressed at a demonstration by Lancashire and Cheshire women in Hyde Park and at a crowded meeting in Exeter Hall.

Suffragist passions have been ignited across the country, meetings interrupted and speakers heckled. Herbert Asquith, regarded as an arch enemy, was howled down by women, protests marred Liberal victory celebrations and government candidates in by-elections were harassed (→24/10).

Champion brothers bow out in triumph

Tennis champion Laurence Doherty.

June 25-July 7. After dominating British tennis for a decade, the Doherty brothers, Reginald and Laurence, announced their retirement from competitive tennis after this year's Wimbledon championships. Both have recently been dogged by ill-health and are likely to spend more time abroad.

"Reggie", the elder by two years, won Wimbledon in four successive years from 1897 while "Laurie", who lost to his brother in the 1898 final, has won every year since 1902, culminating in his fifth triumph this year. Between them, they have won the doubles eight times, and four times secured the Davis Cup for Great Britain.

Massacres and mutiny wrack Russia

June 21. Russia is gripped by a new crisis promoted by a vicious pogrom against Jews and the outbreak of unrest among troops at several garrisons. The murders of Jews and destruction of Jewish property has occurred at Bielostock, a town of some 60,000 people, in west Russia.

Hundreds of Jews have been killed in several days of rioting which some eye-witnessess said was planned by the authorities and connived at by the police. Jewish shops in four main streets were wrecked and afterwards a stream of Jewish refugees arrived at the border with East Prussia.

The governor of the area was quoted as telling a Jewish deputation that he believed "a little bloodletting" would be useful. He said that last year 40 Jews were killed "and we had peace for half a year".

Mutinies by soldiers and sailors took place at Sevastopol, the Kronstadt garrison, and in other towns. Speaking in the Duma, Peter Stolypin, the Prime Minister, was heckled by deputies when he defended the police against charges of brutality as well as organising pogroms. Stolypin, who successfully suppressed peasant uprisings last year as governor of Saratov province, said the government would use every weapon it had to stop the unrest.

There was an extraordinary speech from Prince Urusov who was loudly applauded for saying that massacres had been provoked by police spies (→2/7).

Two stations rolled into one: Pimlico's new Victoria terminus for Brighton and the South Coast one side, Kent and the Continent the other.

1906

JULY

Su	Mo	Tu	We	Th	Fr	Sa
1	2	3	4	5	6	7
8	9	10	11	12	13	14
15	16	17	18	19	20	21
22	23	24	25	26	27	28
29	30	31				

1. London: The University of London reports a drop in upper-class births and a higher birth rate among the poor (→8/11).

1. UK: 27 die in a railway accident near Salisbury.

2. St. Petersburg: Duma proposes abolition of the death penalty (→21).

3. London: London County Council warns of the spread of tuberculosis through infected milk.

5. Wimbledon: Dorothea Douglass beats May Sutton for the Ladies' Singles championship.

7. London: Seven balloons take part in the UK's first hot-air balloon race (→30/9).

12. London: 10 Londoners on a day trip to Brighton are killed in a bus crash.

15. London: House of Commons agrees to create a separate government ministry for Wales.

17. Russia: 50 regiments reported to have mutinied (→21).

18. Egypt: More British troops sent as unrest follows execution of murderers of army officer.

19. London: A Commons select committee recommends introduction of school meals, despite opposition from local authorities (→20/12).

21. St. Petersburg: Duma dissolved and martial law declared (→23).

23. Finland: Duma meets in exile and calls on Russians to refuse to join the army or pay taxes.→

23. S. Africa: 1,047 rebels, including reputedly 106-year-old Zulu chief Sigananda, surrender to the British troops (→12/12).

30. France: Gabriel Lippmann presents a new method of colour photography to the Academie des Sciences.

BIRTH

18. US writer Clifford Odets (†14/8/63).

Duma deputies hit back at Czar

A revolutionary view of how the Romanovs run the Russian Empire.

July 31. The dissolution of Russia's first democratic institution, the Duma, has led to widespread resentment with deputies calling on Russians to refuse to pay taxes and serve in the army. Within hours of the Duma being shut down nearly 200 deputies, most of them from the Constitutional Democratic and Labour parties, travelled to Vyborg in Finland where they were out of reach of Russian police.

A manifesto issued in the name of the Imperial Duma warned that it could be seven months before a new Duma was convened and meanwhile the government could be expected to act in an arbitrary fashion. It called on Russians not to give a kopek to the throne nor a soldier to the army. Government attempts to raise money from loans would be invalid without the consent of the people, the deputies said.

The Duma, which met for 73 days, had limited power over financial and other matters and was dissolved by the Prime Minister, Mr Peter Stolypin, leading to a crash on the European stock exchanges but so far not to any riots in Russia.

Meanwhile there is increasing concern in government and military circles over disaffection existing in some of the country's finest regiments. An inquiry has been set up to look into the morale of the troops.

Several senior secret police officers have been reprimanded following the assassination of General Kozlov and security has been strengthened around the Peterhof Palace (→25/8).

Claude Johnson at the wheel of Charles Rolls' and Henry Royce's latest automobile, the elegant six-cylinder "Silver Ghost".

Legion of Honour vindicated Dreyfus

July 21. At long last, the French Republic today made the "amende honorable" to Captain Alfred Dreyfus in a ceremony at the Ecole Militaire, where he was publicly disgraced after his conviction on charges of treason and espionage 11 years ago. In front of ranks of troops drawn up just as on that earlier day when Dreyfus's badges were torn from his uniform and his sword snapped, General Guillain pinned a cross on Major Dreyfus's coat and dubbed him lightly on the shoulders with a sword, saying: "In the name of the President of the Republic, I make you knight of the Legion of Honour". The ceremony ends the Dreyfus Affair; its violent anti-Semitism bitterly divided France but in the end it strengthened the Republic.

J'excuse: Dreyfus back at camp.

Treaty brings peace to Central America

July 20. A peace treaty was signed today, ending the war between Guatemala on the one side and El Salvador and Honduras on the other. The war began in May, when Guatemala invaded both of her neighbours after a change of government. On July 14 the Guatemalan army was beaten with the loss of 2,000 killed, wounded and captured. The governments of the United States and Mexico both helped to negotiate peace.

1906

AUGUST

Su	Mo	Tu	We	Th	Fr	Sa
			1	2	3	4
5	6	7	8	9	10	11
12	13	14	15	16	17	18
19	20	21	22	23	24	25
26	27	28	29	30	31	

4. Spain: Italian passenger boat "Sirio" wrecked off Cape Palos, with the loss of more than 200 lives.

7. US: North Carolina mob lynches five blacks (→23/9).

8. UK: Winston Churchill and 100 other eminent people protest at street noise caused by vehicles (→2/11).

9. London: Boer War Commission says corruption and incompetence in the war cost over £1 million (→14/9).

9. Berlin: Government reports that Kiel Canal will be widened to allow the passage of larger battleships.

10. Rome: Pope Pius X protests to French bishops against the secularisation of France (→9/12).

15. Warsaw: 27 die in widespread revolutionary unrest against Russian rule (→9/9).

19. Warsaw: The Russian Governor-General escapes an assassination attempt by revolutionaries.

23. Spain: Martial law declared in Bilbao as nationwide general strike spreads.

24. Toronto: Kidney transplants are performed on cats and dogs at a medical conference.

25. St. Petersburg: Premier Stolypin survives bomb attack at his home which kills 30, including his daughter (→26).

26. Hamburg: Police discover a bomb factory run by Russian revolutionaries (→5/9).

28. Washington: President Roosevelt proposes producing all federal documents in simplified spelling.

30. UK: First express train runs from London to Dublin, via Fishguard in Wales.

31. London: Current heat wave brings temperatures as high as 93 degrees Fahrenheit in the shade (→4/9).

BIRTH

5. US film director John Huston (†28/8/1987).

Edward VII enjoys cordial visit to Kaiser

Aug 15. King Edward VII arrived at Kronberg to spend a pleasant day with his nephew Kaiser Wilhelm II, Emperor of Germany. A train with ordinary third class coaches attached to the King's saloon car took the party from Frankfurt to the rural station there.

The Kaiser, in excellent spirits, was proudly wearing the striking uniform of his new regiment, the Posen Cavalry Jaegers. Its main feature is an imposing steel helmet. He greeted his uncle by throwing his arms around his neck, and kissing him warmly on both cheeks.

It was a warm and informal family occasion and none of the English party wore uniform. The King himself arrived in the regulation frock coat and later, after breakfast, he changed into a grey tweed suit to inspect Kronberg Castle. Hearty cheering from the townspeople greeted the party as it drove into town.

In the afternoon the two monarchs drove by motor car to the beautiful spa of Homburg, which is a favourite of the King (→3/2/07).

Bank Holiday Britain basks in heatwave

The clifftop at Folkestone, Kent, is an ideal spot to enjoy the heatwave.

Aug 6. The 90-degree heatwave made this Bank Holiday one of the busiest ever. London's parks did record business. At the London Pavilion, the beautiful Australian Patsy Montague delighted crowds with her "tasteful" impersonation of a living marble statue. Twopence took trippers on the horse-drawn tram to Hampstead Heath where cockney girls in feathers and purple skirts bought song sheets, and ate bread and fish for a penny. In the wilds of West Kensington, a "Tyrol village" with yodelling singers was packed (→31).

George Hirst: record 200 wickets and 2,000 runs this season.

Large Chile quake leaves many dead

Aug 18. The port of Valparaiso, Paradise Valley, is stricken with horror at the effects of a massive earthquake that has left hundreds dead and destroyed two-thirds of this beautiful Chilean city.

Martial law is in force to stop looting after the earthquake, reckoned even more powerful than the one that recently razed San Francisco, struck at night during a violent rainstorm (→22/1/07).

1906

SEPTEMBER

Su	Mo	Tu	We	Th	Fr	Sa
						1
2	3	4	5	6	7	8
9	10	11	12	13	14	15
16	17	18	19	20	21	22
23	24	25	26	27	28	29
30						

2. Alaska: Roald Amundsen reaches Nome, completing the North-West Passage round Canada (→2/11).

3. Liverpool: Biggest ever TUC conference opens, with 490 delegates representing 1.5 million union members.

4. London: Huge downpour ends the heat-wave.

5. St. Petersburg: Premier Stolypin issues new policies aimed at repressing unrest with limited reforms (→3/10).

8. UK: Robert Turner announces the invention of automatic carriage return on typewriters.

8. London: Cambridge beat Harvard by two lengths in international university boat race.

9. Poland: 100 Jews are massacred in Siedlce (→12).

11. Spain: Spanish bishops denounce civil marriages.

12. Poland: Revealed that the Russian authorities instigated Siedlce massacre of Jews (→1/3/07).

15. Durham: 25 miners die in a pit disaster.

18. Hong Kong: Typhoon leaves hundreds dead.

19. UK: 12 passengers are killed when London to Scotland express train is derailed.

20. UK: Launch of the Cunard liner "Mauretania" and of the White Star liner "Adriatic" (→1/8/07).

22. London: Thousands help recapture Life Guards' mascot bear, which escaped in transit to London Zoo.

23. US: 3,000 state troopers fail to quell race riots in Atlanta, Georgia (→24).

24. US: Blacks kill two whites in reaction to race riots in Atlanta (→8/4/08).

30. Paris: First international hot-air balloon race sets off (→1/10).

BIRTH

25. Russian composer Dmitri Shostakovich (†9/8/75).

Lloyd George hits drink and poverty link

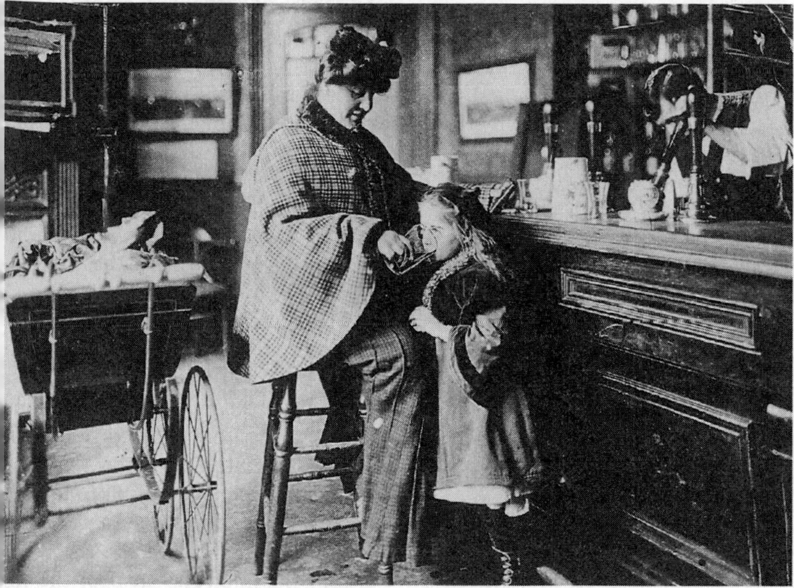

One mother has few scruples about encouraging early alcoholism.

Sept 25. Britain is the richest country under the sun yet it has 10 million workmen living in conditions of chronic destitution, David Lloyd George declared today in an address to the Society for Social Service of North Wales Wesleyans.

The imprudent habits of gambling and drink cause 60% of the poverty, he went on. "Drink is the most urgent problem of the hour for our rulers to grapple with. Next year the government will wrestle with it in earnest and tackle the potent forces that profit from this degradation." (→27/2/08)

British Army to follow German model

Sept 14. The German army was last night singled out by Britain's War Secretary, Mr Haldane, as the model on which British forces should be reorganised. The Army Council has been working on the new structure for nine months, following recommendations drawn up two years ago by a report analysing what went wrong during the Boer War. Mr Haldane wants to modernise the army and centralise control under a new general staff and he admitted to having talks about his ideas with German army officers (→13/1/07).

Real charmer: Ruth St. Denis.

US steps into Cuba power vacuum

Sept 28. US War Secretary William Taft has intervened to fill the Cuban power vacuum left by the resignation of President Palma last month, in a bid to end fighting between government and rebel forces. Taft has declared himself provisional governor of Cuba until peace is restored and fresh elections are held, probably within a fortnight. Palma's supporters are pleased with the US move. It is thought that Palma resigned to force Taft's intervention, rather than give way to the rebels (→1/10).

1906

OCTOBER

Su	Mo	Tu	We	Th	Fr	Sa
	1	2	3	4	5	6
7	8	9	10	11	12	13
14	15	16	17	18	19	20
21	22	23	24	25	26	27
28	29	30	31			

1. UK: US Army Lieutenant Frank Lahm wins first international balloon race, landing at Whitby, Yorkshire.

1. UK: In its trials, the battleship "Dreadnought" reaches a record speed of 21.5 knots (→6/2/07).

3. Berlin: First wireless telegraphy conference agrees to the adoption of SOS as international distress signal (→17).

5. Russia: Report estimates that 1,000 political prisoners a day are being sent to exile in Siberia (→2/11).

5. France: Rehabilitated Major Alfred Dreyfus is made Commander of the artillery at St. Denis (→12/7/07).

6. Cuba: 900 US troops arrive to quell unrest (→27/4/07).

12. S.W. Africa: German troops crush an uprising by native Hottentot tribesmen (→28/11).

15. Berlin: The Social Democratic Party creates schools of political instruction for workers.

16. Australia: British New Guinea becomes part of Australia.

19. Paris: Premier Ferdinand Sarrien hands in his resignation to President Fallieres (→25).

22. US: Henry Ford succeeds John S. Gray as president of the Ford Motor Company.

25. Paris: Georges Clemenceau succeeds Ferdinand Sarrien as premier.

26. Poland: Pupils in German Poland strike against compulsory use of German for religious instruction.

BIRTHS

9. Senegalese politician Sedar Senghor.

10. Indian writer Rudi K. Narayan.

16. US literary critic Cleanth Brooks.

DEATH

22. French painter Paul Cezanne (*19/1/1839).

"We'll go to prison rather than pay" say suffragettes

Oct 24. Eleven suffragettes were jailed today for their part in the rowdy demonstrations during the opening session of Parliament yesterday. The accused included the daughter of the late Richard Cobden, and Adela and Sylvia Pankhurst whose mother heads the Women's Social and Political Union. The women, many of whom refused even to acknowledge the court, chose prison rather than be bound over for the sum of £10.

From Holloway, Mrs Emmeline Pethick Lawrence said: "Women of England, we are going to prison for you and therefore we do it gladly. We call upon you to take up the standard, ... and bear it on to victory." (→6/11)

One suffragette won't come quietly.

German professor telegraphs pictures

Oct 17. Newspapers may soon be able to publish pictures taken only hours before on the other side of the Atlantic. Today a picture was transmitted by telegraph over more than a thousand miles by German professor Arthur Korn. Korn has built on an invention of Italian physicist Luigi Cerebotani, for taking a photograph a small part at a time and producing from each part an electrical current corresponding to its shade of grey. Today's success is the culmination of several years' work (→3/11).

1906

NOVEMBER

Su	Mo	Tu	We	Th	Fr	Sa
				1	2	3
4	5	6	7	8	9	10
11	12	13	14	15	16	17
18	19	20	21	22	23	24
25	26	27	28	29	30	

1. Paris: England football team beat France 15-0; Woodward of Tottenham and Harris of Corinthians star.

2. Russia: Leon Trotsky is exiled for life to Siberia.

3. Berlin: International telegraphy conference agrees on making exchange of information between boats and coastal stations compulsory.

6. London: Sylvia Pankhurst is released from Holloway Prison (→ 8).

6. US: Republicans make clean sweep in all states but one in national elections.

8. London: Keir Hardie introduces a bill in the House of Commons providing for female emancipation (→ 25/12).

8. London: Inquiry slams Labour politician George Lansbury and others for "municipal extravagance" in looking after Poplar's poor.

9. Belgium: Prince Albert declared successor to King Leopold as sovereign of the Congo.

11. Europe: Two Italians make balloon crossing of the Alps, from Milan to Aix-les-Bains.

15. Japan: Launch of the world's biggest battleship, the "Satsuma" (→ 11/12).

20. London: First performance of G. B. Shaw's "The Doctor's Dilemma".

21. Glasgow: Man killed when a deluge of 200,000 gallons of hot whisky bursts from vats.

23. New York: Enrico Caruso fined $10 for sexual harassment.

25. Russia: New law grants concessions to peasants and abolishes compulsory village communes (→ 5/12).

28. Berlin: Centre party joins with Socialists in the Reichstag to oppose funding of war in South West Africa (→ 13/12).

BIRTHS

2. Italian film director Luchino Visconti (†17/3/76).

18. German author Klaus Mann (†21/5/49).

Roosevelt first President to leave US

Hail to the Chief: Roosevelt lends a hand to dig the Panama Canal.

Nov 26. President Theodore Roosevelt returned to Washington today from an historic trip. It is the first time that an American president has ever left the territory of the United States while still in office.

He visited Panama, where he inspected the canal which he has done so much to promote. It is four years since the administration recognized the junta of Panamanian rebels who seceded from Colombia, then sold to the US the concession to build the canal.

President Roosevelt sailed on board the battleship "Louisiana" to "see how the ditch is getting on". He inspected the canal and Marine barracks and personally operated a 95 ton steam shovel (→ 10/12).

Noisy buses banned from London roads

Nov 2. Many London buses are off the road, banned as too noisy. The police are applying, with sudden strictness, the licensing law requiring no "undue noise". This follows calls for curbing the growing din of London, where some 750 motor buses now ply the streets, with 400 more on order.

The new rigour, say bus firms, is unreasonable, and threatens to drive some of them out of business. Bus chiefs also tell of outrageous delays at the understaffed police inspection centre, where repaired buses may be kept waiting for clearance for days on end. There is no appeal from a Scotland Yard decision. Bus interests suspect the influence of powerful lobbyists, not least London County Council and its trams (→ 13/11/08).

Typical traffic in Regent Street.

Labour gains push out Liberals

Nov 1. The Liberals are on the slide again just nine months after their massive general election victory. There was evidence of a large Tory recovery in today's voting for London and provincial borough council seats. The trend was clear despite confusion over party labels.

The drop in Liberal (Progressive) support was fairly general. While the main beneficiaries were the Tories (Municipal Reformers) it was significant that Labour (also describing themselves as Socialist) knocked out Liberals in some places where previously there was no contest between them.

The growing split in the working-class vote is most obvious in the more industrialised areas and amply justifies anxiety expressed by some Liberal leaders in recent months about erosion of their party's social base. During today's counting of the votes there were charges and counter-charges about misuse of party colours in efforts to bamboozle the voters.

Cartoons – sometimes of a scurrilous nature – and dogs with pictorial cards and mottoes fastened to their collars were again widely used in the campaign (→ 12/2/07).

Leon Trotsky (2nd from l.) and comrades en route to Siberian exile.

1906

DECEMBER

Su	Mo	Tu	We	Th	Fr	Sa
						1
2	3	4	5	6	7	8
9	10	11	12	13	14	15
16	17	18	19	20	21	22
23	24	25	26	27	28	29
30	31					

4. US: Wireless messages are sent 1200 miles from Port Loma to Puget Sound, the furthest ever transmitted.→

5. Russia: Admiral Niebogatov goes on trial for surrendering ships to Japanese (→15/2/07).

9. Rome: Pope Pius X tells French priests to remain in churches till driven out (→13).

10. Stockholm: Nobel Prizes awarded to Sir Joseph Thomson (UK, Physics); Ferdinand Moissan (France, Chemistry); Camilio Golgi and Santiago Ramon y Cajal (Italy and Spain respectively, Medicine); Giosue Carducci (Italy, Literature) and President Roosevelt (US, Peace).

10. Belgium: King Leopold denies Congo atrocities (→1/5/07).

12. S. Africa: Transvaal given autonomy with white male suffrage (→23/2/07).

14. Germany: First German submarine, U1, enters service.

15. UK: Education Bill withdrawn after amendments by House of Lords.

24. Canada: First radio programme broadcast by Reginald Aubrey Fessenden.

25. London: Suffragettes in Holloway Prison refuse to eat Christmas dinner (→14/2/07).

28. Scotland: 13 die when a train is derailed by snow on the track north of Dundee.

BIRTHS

5. US film director Otto Preminger (†23/4/86).

19. Soviet leader Leonid Brezhnev (†10/11/82).

HIT OF 1906

Waiting at the church

QUOTE OF THE YEAR

"Mankind will possess incalculable advantages and extraordinary control over human behaviour...when the human mind will contemplate itself not from within, but from without."
Ivan Pavlov.

Arts: Shaw writes his first death scene

Dec 31. France has lost the man who has been recognised as perhaps its greatest living painter – **Paul Cezanne**, who died in October, a recluse at his family's mansion in Aix-en-Provence. Only two years ago a whole room at the Salon d'Automne was devoted to his work, a conspicuous mark of homage. He was 67.

Cezanne had exhibited with the Impressionists until 1877 but then broke away in order to explore a means of painting not the immediate sensations of nature but its "objective reality". His aims were, he said, "to make Impressionism solid and enduring like the Old Masters" or to paint "a living Poussin in the open air with colour and light".

He was a slow, laborious worker who reworked his favourite motifs - still life with apples and oranges, groups of bathers, the Provencal countryside, especially Mont Ste. Victoire - over and over again.

Cezanna wrote recently that one should seek "the cylinder, the sphere and the cone" in nature.

The success of the London stage has been another **Shaw** play at the Court, "The Doctor's Dilemma", which mocks the pretentions of the medical establishment and contains the author's first death scene. The critic William Archer had maintained that he would be unable to write one.

Shaw's rejoinder is to create an unprincipled artist with tuberculosis who proclaims as his dying creed, "I believe in Michaelangelo, Velasquez and Rembrandt" - which some critics held to be blasphemy.

John Galsworthy's novel, "A Man of Property" introduces the Forsytes, an upper middle class family possesive of their wealth, which has begun a vogue for the documentary saga.

Cezanne, as he saw himself.

Conan Doyle's Sir Nigel.

Radio buffs soon to be receiving louder

The year of 1906 will go down as an historic one in the development of wireless: the one in which the American scientist **Lee De Forest** invented a device called the triode valve. The triode amplifies without distortion the feeble electric currents in wireless equipment.

This makes possible more powerful transmitters and the detection of weaker signals, implying communication over longer distances, as well as those signals being louder. The triode consists of three elements, sealed in a vacuum into a device like an electric light bulb. It can also act as a detector for wireless signals, like the two element diode invented two years ago.

Another important event of 1906 was an idea, advanced in a lecture by **Dr Gowland Hopkins** of Guy's Hospital in London, which could explain a range of human diseases. For over a century we have known that fresh fruit can prevent scurvy. In the last few years it has been shown that a diet of polished rice leads to beri beri, which can be cured by eating rice with husks.

Hopkins suggested that rice husks and fruit contain still unidentified materials essential for human nutrition, through only in minute quantities. Without them diseases like scurvy and beri beri develop; supply them and the diseases disappear. Rickets may also have a similar cause. So a bad dict, as well as germs, may cause serious diseases (→17/10/07).

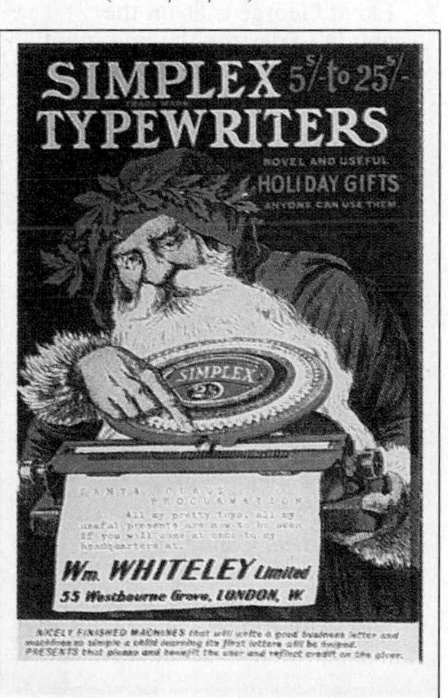

Piccadilly goes down the "Tube"

Dec 15. David Lloyd George, the President of the Board of Trade, today opened a new underground railway line between Finsbury Park and Hammersmith, crossing the heart of London's West End underneath Piccadilly Circus. Like the line opened earlier this year between Baker Street and Waterloo, the Piccadilly trains run in a circular tunnel or "tube" at far greater depths than the older "cut and cover" tunnels.

Catholic priests defy French law

Dec 13. There was little sign in the churches today of any let-up in the battle between the French government and the Catholic Church. As the law requiring church services to be registered as public meetings came into effect, police served notices to the clergy who are boycotting the law. The services went on, but 69 priests who defied the order have been charged. The Papal Agent has also been expelled from France (→2/1/07).

1907

JANUARY

Su	Mo	Tu	We	Th	Fr	Sa
		1	2	3	4	5
6	7	8	9	10	11	12
13	14	15	16	17	18	19
20	21	22	23	24	25	26
27	28	29	30	31		

1. China: Four million people are feared to be starving owing to heavy rains and crop failure.

1. London: Senior diplomat Sir Eyre Crowe says Britain must stand up to Germany's wish to dominate Europe (→ 8).

2. France: Latest anti-clerical law comes into force, which forbids the crucifix in schools (→ 11).

8. Berlin: Colonial policy committee under Gustav von Schmoller demands greater colonial expansion (→ 25).

11. Rome: Pope Pius X says French government policies aim to de-Christianise France (→ 20).

11. Europe: People living in the German-Danish frontier zone are guaranteed citizenship of either country.

14. West Indies: Massive earthquake strikes Jamaica (→ 17).

17. London: Fund opened to aid Jamaica earthquake victims; the King and Queen each give £1,000.→

20. Switzerland: National referendum votes against splitting Church and State (→ 6/4).

22. Dutch East Indies: About 1,500 people are reported killed in a massive tidal wave.

23. Newcastle-upon-Tyne: Lloyd George calls on the nation to destroy the powers of the House of Lords (→ 6/5/07).

24. Europe: Arctic weather grips the Continent; it is -30 degrees Fahrenheit in Austria.

25. Germany: Socialists opposed to colonial expansion suffer losses in first round of national elections (→ 5/2).

26. New York: The Metropolitan Opera House bans Richard Strauss's opera "Salome" as obscene.

28. Germany: 164 are killed in a mine explosion at Saarbrucken.

30. France: Chamber of Deputies votes to abolish the law requiring notice of all public meetings.

Hundreds die as quake hits Jamaica

Despondent Jamaicans survey the earthquake's work.

Jan 22. Hundreds are now feared dead in an earthquake which devastated the Jamaican capital of Kingston eight days ago. Buildings in a ten-mile radius were badly damaged, leaving thousands homeless.

Large areas of the city were flattened and the quake set off numerous fires. It has been compared to the great earthquake which levelled San Francisco eight months ago. Despite the extent of the destruction the British Governor, Sir J. A. Sweetenham, has rejected an offer of medical and food aid from a visiting American fleet.

The decision has caused widespread indignation in the US. Two British relief ships were brought in instead (→ 4/3).

I say, I say, I say we're striking today

Jan 22. A new show-stopper has hit the London stage. It is called the "Music Hall War" and stars many of London's music hall artistes opposite the hall owners.

The artistes claim they are getting a raw deal from the hall managers. For two nights running halls have been hit by strikes, disrupting programmes at such famous venues as Mr. Walter Gibbons' Tivoli and East Ham Palace and Mr. Adney Payne's Holborn Empire, Clapham Junction Grand and the Balham Duchess. Some managers, such as Mr. Blyth Pratt of the Oxford theatre, used amateurs to stay open.

Marie Dainton pulled out of a show at the Ealing Hippodrome in sympathy. She said some artistes did 20 shows a week for no more money than they would get for 12.

But with employers claiming that their performers are the highest paid in the world, there is little sign of a denouement (→ 15/2).

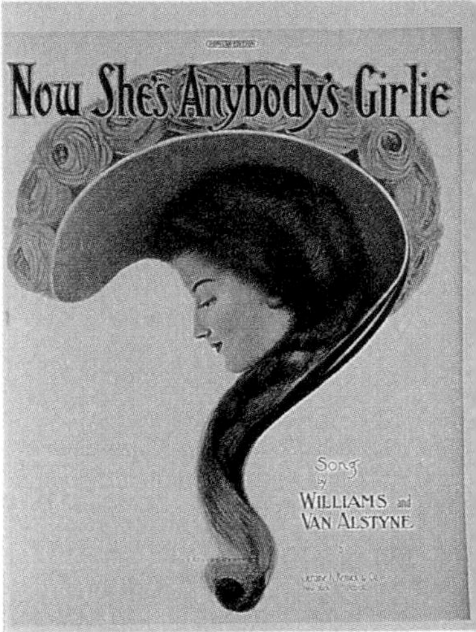

Mohammad Ali is the new Shah of Persia

Jan 19. With great pomp and ceremony Mohammad Ali Mirza was today crowned Shah of Persia in the Royal Palace in Tehran. After the coronation, attended by a glittering assembly of princes, holy men and the diplomatic corps he ascended to the Peacock Throne, richly adorned with emeralds.

Mohammad Ali succeeds his father, Muzaffar ad-Din, who died recently aged 54, with a reputation for being enlightened. Like his father before him he was intent on liberalisation. He framed a constitution, established a parliament and turned his attention to education for his people, including women.

To prevent intrigue, it has been established that the heir apparent is the dead Shah's second son, Sultan Ahmed (→ 11/2/07).

War Office creates expeditionary force

Jan 13. The first part of the reorganisation of the British Army has been unveiled with the creation of a new expeditionary force designed to strike deep into the heart of enemy territory overseas. There was considerable concern within the War Office about weaknesses in the way the Boer War was run and and this is intended to prevent a repeat. The new force will be made up of 160,000 men (→ 1/4/08).

England thrashes France at rugby

Jan 7. England, as expected, easily defeated France at Richmond this afternoon in the first meeting between the two countries over here. France's inexperience was exposed by the dazzling Harlequin trio of Lambert, who scored 5 tries, Stoop and Birkett as England won 41-13. But the visitors were not disgraced, a 7,000-strong crowd cheering off their full-back Isaac.

1907

FEBRUARY

Su	Mo	Tu	We	Th	Fr	Sa
					1	2
3	4	5	6	7	8	9
10	11	12	13	14	15	16
17	18	19	20	21	22	23
24	25	26	27	28		

2. Argentina: Revolution breaks out.

3. Paris: King Edward VII and Queen Alexandra arrive on a state visit (→ 13/4).

5. UK: Alarm at an epidemic of meningitis in Glasgow, Edinburgh and Belfast.

5. Germany: Socialists routed in final round of Reichstag elections, losing to parties loyal to the Kaiser (→ 19).

6. Atlantic: "HMS Dreadnought" sails from Gibraltar to Trinidad at record speed of 17 knots (→ 2/4/08).

11. Teheran: New Shah Mohammad Ali Mirza recognises constitutional government of Persia (→ 19/1).

12. London: Parliamentary programme outlined, including Irish Home Rule and better public housing (→ 2/3).

15. London: Music hall pay dispute is settled after mediation; halls to reopen.

15. New York: Ex-Duma member says famine is widespread in Russia (→ 20).

19. Berlin: Kaiser opens first session of Reichstag (→ 3/8).

20. Russia: Opposition Radicals make large gains in elections for the new Duma (→ 5/3).

21. Holland: 144 drown when steamer "Berlin" is wrecked.

23. S. Africa: General Louis Botha appointed Premier.

26. Washington: President Roosevelt says the US Army will take charge of building the Panama Canal (→ 10/10/13).

28. London: Government says it will spend less on the Navy this year, but is ordering three more dreadnoughts.

BIRTH

21. British poet Wystan Hugh Auden (†29/9/73).

DEATHS

2. Dmitri Mendeleev, Russian chemist (*8/2/1834).

10. British journalist Sir William Howard Russell (*28/3/1821).→

Women and police in Commons clash

Feb 14. A record number of suffragettes – 57 – plus two men appeared in court today following bitter clashes with the police last night. The struggles between the women and the officers, many on horseback, lasted for more than five hours and marked the most ferocious battle yet in women's war for the vote. The trouble happened after a decision by what the movement calls "its parliament", which has been set up in Caxton Hall, to present a resolution to its male counterpart in Westminster.

As the women marched through the streets at dusk, mounted police rode into the procession to break it up. The women were scattered. Some had their clothes torn and their bodies bruised but still they fought to get to the House. Fifteen of them reached the Strangers' Lobby where they tried to hold a meeting before being arrested.

In court the first defendant, Christabel Pankhurst, said they had wanted a peaceful march. She claimed that the disturbance was the fault of the authorities who had instructed the police to use strong measures.

Christabel Pankhurst gestures defiantly at authority after her arrest.

Miss Pankhurst added: "The women who asked for votes were in danger of their lives. We do not come here in any way to excuse our conduct. We feel yesterday was a great day for our movement". She then vowed: "There can be no going back for us and more will happen if we do not get justice."

The court room itself was packed to overflowing for the hearing and crowds who could not get in lined the street outside. When the prisoners were driven off to Holloway, the crowd broke into loud cheers and waved their handkerchiefs wildly at the women they see as modern martyrs (→ 8/3).

Final deadline for war correspondent

Giant of journalism: Sir William.

Feb 10. Prince Albert called him "that miserable scribbler" for exposing Britain's military failures in the Crimea War. But Sir William Howard Russell, who died today aged 86, is now regarded as the first and greatest of war correspondents.

King opens courts on old prison site

Feb 27. The King and Queen drove down a flower-lined route, loyally cheered by large crowds, to open the new Criminal Courts of Justice at Old Bailey today. It was a magnificent spectacle as the King, in uniform, and the Queen, in a costume of black velvet, greeted Judges, Bishops and City dignitaries all in full robes. Work began on the new court – built on the site of Newgate Prison – in 1902. Designed by Mr E.W. Mountford, it is both dignified and beautiful; the cost was met by the City of London. In his speech the King said that the noblest purpose of justice was that the criminal should be reformed.

"Mr Lazy" gets up

Feb 15. The laziest man in the world has got up after 29 years in bed. James Thompson, who hasn't been seen outside his home in the Ulster village of Clare since 1877, was forced out of bed earlier this month when his 80-year-old mother became too ill to look after him. Doctors now examining him say he suffers from a severe case of chronic lethargy which they have been unable to cure even by the use of electric shocks and irritating plasters.

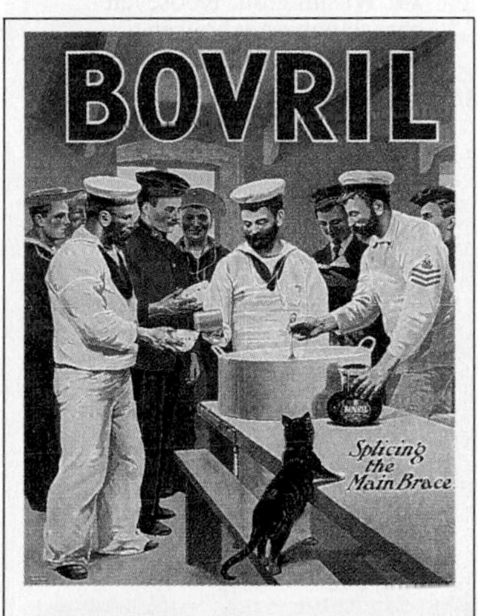

1907

MARCH

Su	Mo	Tu	We	Th	Fr	Sa
					1	2
3	4	5	6	7	8	9
10	11	12	13	14	15	16
17	18	19	20	21	22	23
24	25	26	27	28	29	30
31						

1. Russia: Only 15,000 Jews remain in Odessa as anti-Semitic attacks continue.

1. Spain: Royal decree bans civil marriages.

1. New York: Salvation Army sets up an anti-suicide bureau.

2. London: Progressive candidates defeated in London County Council elections, losing 44 seats.

2. Paris: Premier of Georges Feydeau's "La Puce a l'oreille".

2. Hamburg: 2,000 British port workers brought in by German shipowners as local workers strike in protest at night shifts.

4. Jamaica: Sir A. Sweetenham, the governor, resigns after mismanagement of earthquake disaster.

5. St. Petersburg: New Duma opens; 40,000 demonstrators broken up by troops.

8. London: Keir Hardie's Women's Enfranchisement Bill defeated in the Commons, despite support of Campbell-Bannerman.

11. Bulgaria: The Bulgarian premier Nicholas Petkov is assassinated in Sofia by an anarchist; Josef Gudev succeeds.

12. France: 118 die when the French battleship "Iena" explodes at Toulon.

14. Bulgaria: 50 arrested for Petkov's assassination; riots break out (→ 5/4).

14. Washington: Roosevelt bars Japanese labourers.

19. Vienna: Bread shortage begins as 12,000 bakers join 7,000 tailors on strike.

21. London: Campbell-Bannerman expresses Government opposition to Channel Tunnel Bill.

22. London: 72 suffragettes refuse to pay fines for demonstrating outside Parliament and are sent to prison.

DEATH

18. Marcelin Berthelot, French chemist (*25/10/1827).

3-D art causes surprise

New perspectives: Picasso's revolutionary "Les demoiselles d'Avignon".

March. Even the avant-garde painters of Montmartre have been baffled by the latest canvas from Pablo Picasso's studio entitled "Les demoiselles d'Avignon". It breaks all accepted rules of composition, perspective and truth to nature.

The five figures (the subject is women in a house of ill-fame) are reduced to visual shorthand of dislocated shapes seen simultaneously from different angles. Some of the demoiselles sport masks resembling the African carvings shown in Paris this year. Some see in it the solid geometry that the late Paul Cezanne was seeking in nature. Others believe it is a joke.

Leading lady: actress Ellen Terry and her new husband.

Finns are first to elect women as MPs

March 15. As women in Britain continue their struggle for the vote, women in Finland had a real taste of political power today when they won their first seats in the Finnish parliament. The deputies-elect belong mostly to the majority Social Democratic Party, but come from all social classes. They will be sworn into their new seats shortly.

Finland became the first European country to give women the vote last year. The Finnish women's triumph is expected to add momentum to the suffragettes' campaign in countries like Britain and America (→ 25/5).

Gandhi begins civil disobedience battle in South Africa

March 22. The passage of the "Asiatic Law Amendment Ordinance" has incensed the Indian population of the Transvaal and their leader, the lawyer Mohandas Gandhi, has declared a campaign of "Satyagraha" or civil disobedience.

They say that they will refuse to register under the terms of the new law when it comes into power on July 1, when all Indians will be required to submit to being finger-printed and receive a certificate of registration which they must carry with them at all times. Failure to comply means loss of right of residence in the Transvaal and possibly a fine, imprisonment or even deportation.

Mr Gandhi, who served as a sergeant-major in the Ambulance Corps during the Zulu revolt last year, recently pleaded his cause in London where he received a sympathetic hearing from Winston Churchill, the Colonial Under Secretary, and the new law was refused assent. But Transvaal became self-governing on January 1 and is insisting on finger-printing the "Asiatics" (→ 1/7).

Gandhi: opposed to new race laws.

1907

APRIL

Su	Mo	Tu	We	Th	Fr	Sa
	1	2	3	4	5	6
7	8	9	10	11	12	13
14	15	16	17	18	19	20
21	22	23	24	25	26	27
28	29	30				

3. London: Royal Commission on Vivisection recommends humane restrictions on the practice.

3. Russia: 20 million reported starving in the worst famine on record (→9).

5. Bulgaria: Troops clash with 10,000 peasant insurgents.

6. Paris: Louis Bleriot flies his new monoplane ten yards (→27).

6. Rome: Italian government pays the Vatican £360,000 for seizure of Church property in 19th century (→4/7).

9. Russia: Statistics show that 1,242 people were assassinated and 1,080 executed in the last seven months (→16/6).

10. Paris: French doctors announce the discovery of a new serum to cure dysentery.

11. New York: Opening of the Carnegie Institute in Pittsburgh.

13. Malta: King Edward VII and Queen Alexandra arrive on a visit (→13/11).

14. Budapest: First performance of Jozsef Nabadi's opera "Kossuth" sparks anti-Austrian demonstrations.

15. Rome: Pope Pius X officially condemns separation of the French Church and State.

16. London: Visit of colonial heads of government, including old adversary General Louis Botha, Transvaal premier.

17. London: Bill introduced in parliament to create Court of Appeal against criminal sentences.

19 Paris: Georges Clemenceau orders sacking of striking civil servants; army mobilised for fear of May Day unrest (→1/5).

20. London: Sheffield Wednesday beat holders Everton 2-1 in the FA Cup Final at Crystal Palace.

24. London: Liberal MP Winston Churchill is appointed a Privy Councillor (→12/4).

27. Berlin: The Wright Brothers arrange to demonstrate their flying machine to German officials (→13/11).

Manchuria handed back to Chinese

April 15. Manchuria is today once again under Chinese rule. The last detachments of Japanese troops, which had been stationed in the region of Mukden since the Japanese army inflicted humiliating defeats on the Russians there, are leaving.

The evacuation is being carried out under the terms of the Treaty of Portsmouth, signed in New Hampshire, USA, which brought the four year Russo-Japanese War to an end. Chinese troops will move to keep order during what is expected to be a rapid changeover of administration. China thanked Japan for leaving and the Russians left a month early (→3/6).

Hands off: the Japanese bow out.

Channel Tunnel Bill killed in Commons

April 25. Today, three months after the War Office declared its opposition, the bill to facilitate the construction of a railway tunnel under the Channel was withdrawn from parliament. One of its sponsors blamed government hostility for the proposal's lack of popular support.

He was convinced that had the plan been fully discussed by a parliamentary committee the merits of the scheme would have become greatly appreciated. But in view of the widespread fear that the tunnel is a threat to the nation's defences, the sponsors realized they had little chance (→24/10).

1907

MAY

Su	Mo	Tu	We	Th	Fr	Sa
			1	2	3	4
5	6	7	8	9	10	11
12	13	14	15	16	17	18
19	20	21	22	23	24	25
26	27	28	29	30	31	

1. Paris: Government rebukes King of the Belgians, declares support for British interests in the Congo (→28/11).

1. Canada: Death reported of Neil Brodie, nation's dirtiest man, who only bathed when ordered by law.

2. India: Riots break out in Rawalpindi and East Bengal, spreading to the Punjab (→9).

6. London: Lord Newton proposes a reform of House of Lords but is told the Government plans its own move (→14/6).

7. France: 100 feared dead when a passenger ship is wrecked 30 yards from land.

9. India: Troops ordered into Lahore as unrest continues, to mark 50th anniversary of Indian Mutiny (→6/6).

10. London: Second reading of bill providing an old-age pension of 5/- a week to people over 65.

15. Austria: Socialists gain in the first elections under universal, direct and equal suffrage (→18).

16. Africa: Nairobi is chosen as capital of British East Africa.

17. France: Several thousand riot in support of local wine growers at Beziers.→

18. London: Women's Labour League holds first conference, chaired by Mrs Ramsay MacDonald (→25).

19. Russia: 100 Jews hurt in anti-Semitic riots at Odessa (→7/7).

25. Helsingfors: Opening of Finnish Diet, world's first parliament with women members (→12/6).

30. Glasgow: Launch of King Edward VII's new turbine yacht, "Alexandria".

BIRTHS

13. British novelist Daphne du Maurier (†19/4/89).

22. British actor Lord Olivier, born Laurence Kerr Olivier (†11/7/89).

22. Belgian creator of "Tintin" Georges Remi, alias Herge (†3/3/83).

Irish Bill faces a two-pronged assault

May 21. An Irish Council Bill proposed by the British government would go further than any of its predecessors in giving a measure of self-government to Ireland. The new council would administer education and other local government services, although Irish MPs will continue to sit at Westminster.

However, the bill is under attack from two sides. In the House of Commons today Sir Edward Carson, for the Unionists, said it would mean "the swallowing of loyal Ulster in the government of Ireland". In Dublin, nationalists passed a resolution saying Irish MPs should oppose the bill and "stick out for full rights" (→3/6).

Wine growers in a ferment in France

May 20. Thousands of wine growers rioted in the streets of Perpignan last night, burning down the town hall and police station in a protest at high taxes and the adulteration of wine by producers in other regions. Twelve people, including three policemen, are reported seriously injured during the demonstration which began peacefully. More protests are planned for the coming days. The growers are angry at over-production and the French government's refusal to cope with the crisis (→20/6).

Wrathful: leader Marcelin Albert.

1907

JUNE

Su	Mo	Tu	We	Th	Fr	Sa
						1
2	3	4	5	6	7	8
9	10	11	12	13	14	15
16	17	18	19	20	21	22
23	24	25	26	27	28	29
30						

3. London: Government abandons Irish Council Bill after Nationalist opposition (→13).

5. UK: The Derby at Epsom is won by Orby.

6. London: Government declares UK will not withdraw from India under any circumstances.

9. Paris: Aviator Santos-Dumont's combined aeroplane and airship is wrecked on its first trial.

10. London: First performance of John M. Synge's "The Playboy of the Western World".

12. London: Second reading of bill to allow women to sit on county and borough councils (→30/8).

13. London: Tory ex-PM Arthur Balfour tells Unionists that Ireland now has choice of union or disintegration (→4/8).

14. London: Government announces plans to curb powers of House of Lords (→3/12/08).

15. The Hague: Second International Peace Conference opens (→22/8).

16. London: UK, France and Spain form a loose Triple Alliance or Entente.

19. Athens: A bomb is hurled into the Greek Chamber of Deputies but fails to explode.

20. France: Wine war continues; many killed when troops fire on crowd in Narbonne.

22. London: David Lloyd George opens new Hampstead Tube line (→16/7/08).

24. Wimbledon: Prince of Wales made first President of All England Club on opening day of tennis meeting (→5/7).

26. Oxford: US author Mark Twain receives honorary Doctorate of Letters from the University.→

28. France: Georges Clemenceau wins a majority in the Chamber of Deputies.

30. Switzerland: Government votes to split Church and State (→20/1).

Duma dissolved amid treason charge

Closing order: Czar Nicholas II.

June 16. Russia's second Duma, or parliament, was dissolved today with the Prime Minister, Peter Stolypin, accusing 55 Socialist deputies of plotting against the monarchy of the Czar. The Duma, which had met for 102 days, was closed by an Imperial manifesto which was published in the government press very soon after it had adjourned.

At the same time the Ministry of Justice issued indictments against the deputies for conspiring to use violence to set up a republic. Several deputies have already been arrested while others have fled.

St. Petersburg has received the news of the dissolution of the Duma calmly. The city is full of troops and there is practically no possibility of serious rioting. The move against the Duma had been widely expected, despite official insistence that relations between the Duma and the government had been improving.

But it has always been apparent that both the first and the second Dumas would fail. It was hoped by the government that the majority of the representatives would be conservative. In fact they were mainly liberal and socialist and their demands for reform were almost totally unacceptable to the government.

Elections for a third Duma will take place in September. The franchise is expected to be restricted with a big reduction in non-Russian representation (→8/8).

Chinese fears delay Peking-Paris race

June 10. The Peking to Paris motor race got off to a flying start today, despite bureaucratic hitches. The Chinese government put off the issue of safe-passage papers to the drivers, apparently because it believes the race is a plot to discover how to invade China.

But the competitors can expect a friendlier reception from the Mongolians, who are reported to be very excited by rumours of machines that run by themselves faster than a galloping horse (→10/8).

Jolly good Fellow: US writer Mark Twain in Oxford robes.

Socialism on Sundays upsets councillors

June 11. Four London Sunday schools accused of being a front for the teaching of socialism are to close after a bitter three-hour debate today at County Hall, headquarters of the London County Council.

The motion to end Sunday tenancies of LCC schools in Islington, Fulham and Hammersmith was moved by Mr R.A. Robinson. He said that when the council decided in 1904 to let schoolrooms for Sunday schools, they were clearly meant for religious teaching to young persons only. But in the four schools under scrutiny it was clear that "nothing in the form of the truths of religion was taught," he said, and one school was found on February 3 to have "144 persons present, many of them adults". Instead of religion it taught "Socialist hymns", including one called "The Red Flag", he said.

Mr Robinson was accused of being moved more by his opposition to socialism than his concern for LCC regulations. One leading Socialist, Sidney Webb, said he "was embarking on a path of extraordinary danger" while another compared the move to the Czar "dragooning the Duma". But the motion was carried by 68 votes to 42, anyhow.

Movie pioneers claim colour breakthrough

June 10. A new process, which is said to be practical enough to make colour photography "commonplace", has been developed by those pioneering brothers of moving pictures, Auguste and Louis Lumiere.

The process, devised at the family business in France, is based on taking three separate pictures of a scene, through filters of the three primary colours, red, yellow and blue.

Screens consisting of thousands of microscopic dots are laid over the three negatives. A full colour image of the original scene can be produced by superimposing the negatives and screens and shining lights through them.

The Lumieres' is not the first colour photography process. The eminent physicist James Clerk Maxwell demonstrated one at the Royal Institution in London as long ago as 1861.

But Maxwell's process and its successors have all been too complicated and expensive for everyday use. The Lumieres say that theirs is different, and is more important than their moving picture camera developments (→11/2/08).

1907

JULY

Su	Mo	Tu	We	Th	Fr	Sa
	1	2	3	4	5	6
7	8	9	10	11	12	13
14	15	16	17	18	19	20
21	22	23	24	25	26	27
28	29	30	31			

1. S. Africa: The Orange River Colony gains autonomy as the Orange Free State (→30/1/08).

4. Italy: National celebrations mark the 100th anniversary of birth of Giuseppe Garibaldi (4/7/1807-2/6/1882).

5. UK: Labour's Pete Curran wins Jarrow from the Liberals in a by-election; the Liberal candidate comes third.→

5. Wimbledon: Norman Brookes beats Arthur Gore for the Men's Singles title; May Sutton beats Dorothea Chambers for the Ladies' Singles championship.

6 London: Tom Reece ends billiards break of 499,135, begun June 3rd when two balls stuck in pocket opening.

12. Paris: Major Alfred Dreyfus resigns from the army, one year after his complete rehabilitation (→4/6/08).

14. Paris: President Armand Fallieres narrowly escapes an assassination attempt.

15. Munich: Experimental train reported to average 81 mph and reach 98 mph maximum.

19. Korea: Emperor abdicates, succeeded by Crown Prince; riots in Seoul against the Japanese.→

20. Japan: 471 miners lost in mine disaster.

27. Portsmouth: Princess Henry of Battenberg launches dreadnought, "HMS Bellerophon".

28. St. Petersburg: Treaty signed with Japan for the protection of seals and sea lions.

29. London: Robert Baden-Powell forms Boy Scouts after Brownsea camp (→16/1/08).

29. St. Petersburg: Russo-Japanese entente guarantees Chinese territorial integrity and freedom of trade (→8/9).

30. Belfast: Troops sent in following unrest (→4/8).

30. Europe: Germany, Austria and Italy renew Triple Alliance for a further six years (→1/12/08).

Boy Scouts go camping for first time

July 25. Twenty boys from widely different backgrounds were ferried across Poole Harbour to Brownsea Island today. They will spend the next few days in the woods there being "Boy Scouts".

The lads, who come from Eton, Harrow, London's East End and the Poole area, will be taught outdoor skills such as woodcraft, fire-making and tracking, as well as life-saving and first aid.

The man behind the project is Sir Robert Baden-Powell, hero of the defence of Mafeking. Since he returned to England in 1903 he has been considering ways of encouraging a sense of discipline, duty, unselfishness and good citizenship in British boys. He believes that this can be achieved by introducing youngsters to the ways of the army scouts who impressed him so much during his tours of duty in India and Africa.

His memorandum "Boy Scouts: A Suggestion", in which he set out his ideas, was circulated to many leading public figures last year. The response has been so encouraging that Sir Robert is determined to press ahead with his plans, hence this first experimental camp to see what happens in practice (→29).

Blazing a trail: Baden-Powell.

First MP elected on socialist ticket

July 19. The West Riding of Yorkshire sent the first MP elected on a pure Socialist ticket to Parliament today. Victor Grayson, a 25-year-old schoolteacher, won a by-election in Colne Valley, where the Liberals were unopposed last year, on a programme of total state ownership and control.

The result – a narrow majority over the Liberals with the Tories a close third – surprised all parties and shook the Stock Exchange. "It marks an epoch," said Mr Grayson who fought without help from the 31-strong Labour group in Parliament whose members are not all Socialists. "Socialism is losing its terrors," he said.

Shocked Liberal spokesmen predictably said that this result was only a temporary reverse but a fortnight ago Labour captured another seat from the Liberals at Jarrow.

The Liberals called this an aberration. However, there is a feeling that a realignment of the non-Tory vote is now under way (→1/11).

Pope fears secular threat to Church

July 4. Pope Pius X struck a further blow today against modernism which he believes is threatening the traditional values and practices of the Catholic Church. In a papal decree, "Lamentabili", he introduced strict censorship over publications right down to the parish level. Congresses, in which some priests have gathered together to discuss new ideas, are to be banned. Committees of censorship are to be set up in every diocese. Even bishops are not immune and several who have voiced modernist sentiments have already been removed. The Pope wants all Catholics to return to the traditional religious practices of the mass, confession and bible-reading (→7/9).

Koreans resent new Japanese rule

July 25. Rioting is expected in Korea in reaction to the signing in Seoul of new agreements, which give absolute power over all local administration to the Japanese resident general in Seoul.

The Korean government will be compelled to follow his guidance in all administrative matters. He will recruit Japanese officials to reorganise courts of justice in a country where no legal code exists.

Rioting began after the Japanese insisted upon the abdication of the Emperor of Korea. It was harshly suppressed and ringleaders executed, which only increased hatred of the Japanese for their occupation of Korea.

Girls, girls, girls: "The Follies of 1907" is the first revue staged by the US impresario Florenz Ziegfeld.

1907

AUGUST

Su	Mo	Tu	We	Th	Fr	Sa
				1	2	3
4	5	6	7	8	9	10
11	12	13	14	15	16	17
18	19	20	21	22	23	24
25	26	27	28	29	30	31

1. Liverpool: New Cunard turbine liner "Lusitania" completes 1,200 miles in 48 hours (→ 6/9).

1. US: Establishment of Signal Corps Aeronautical Division, first US military air force.

3. Germany: Kaiser Wilhelm meets Czar at Swinemunde; Baghdad railway and Anglo-Russian ties discussed (→ 16).

4. Belfast: Strikes and rioting continue.→

6. Holland: Dockers strike at Antwerp; 250 British dockers are brought in by management to replace strikers (→ 2/9).

8. Russia: Representatives of provincial councils call for compulsory schooling throughout the country (→ 20).

16. London: Puccini's "Madam Butterfly" first performed in English at the Lyric Theatre.

16. Germany: Visiting King Edward VII and Kaiser Wilhelm exchange cordial speeches at a banquet (→ 18).

18. Germany: Women's Socialist Congress at Stuttgart denounces German militarism and colonial policy.

20. St. Petersburg: Trial opens of 18 charged with plotting to assassinate Czar Nicholas (→ 14/10).

22. The Hague: International Peace Conference proposes creation of International High Court of Justice (→ 7/9).

23. Rumania: Amnesty is granted to 8,000 political prisoners.

24. New York: The uncompleted Singer Building is the world's tallest building.

29. Quebec: 80 drown when a section of the new bridge across the St. Lawrence River collapses.

30. Vienna: Women allowed to be lecturers and assistants in universities and hospitals on same terms as men (→ 12/10).

DEATH

15. Austrian violinist Joseph Joachim (*28/6/1831).

French gunships shell Casablanca

Aug 4. Some 2,000 French troops made an unopposed landing at Casablanca this afternoon after a naval bombardment lasting 48 hours. An earlier attempt to land had encountered heavy fire from the town's batteries and some firing on French blue-jackets from a minaret, killing one man and wounding another. French warships then shelled the town, demolishing the minaret. Over 1,000 Moors were killed or wounded.

The French government has been under pressure from public opinion to take action after the killing last month by a mob of Moorish fanatics of nine Europeans, five of them French, employed on the Casablanca harbour works.

Though the English have for years taken the lead in developing trade with Casablanca, it is the French who have been the chief target of Moorish resentment at the intrusion of European ways. Conditions in the town are appalling, with dead and injured lying about everywhere. The French recognise that their task of pacification is likely to prove bigger than was anticipated (→ 27).

Carnage in Casablanca.

Doctor warns of child "cigarette fiends"

Aug 2. The evils of smoking and chewing tobacco were attacked at the annual meeting of the British Medical Association in Exeter today. Dr Herbert Tidswell, a GP from Torquay, singled out what he called the poisonous habit of smoking among Britain's children for particular concern. Claiming that the nation was deteriorating because of smoking, Dr Tidswell said every boy and girl should be encouraged to sign a pledge never to take up the habit. The difficulty of giving up smoking was so great that it was clearly foolish to start.

Dangers of smoking, according to Dr Tidswell, include cancer of the tongue and lip. But other doctors argued that no clear case had been put forward against the moderate use of tobacco.

Smoking by Britain's youngsters is giving doctors cause for concern.

Four killed by Belfast troops

Aug 13. Four civilians were killed last night when troops opened fire on crowds in Belfast. Fierce fighting had flared in the city after two men were arrested. Troops and police used rifle butts to break up the crowds and mounted cavalry galloped down streets in the Falls Road area of the city, but the crowds soon reformed elsewhere. Women and girls surrounded one army barracks with their upturned aprons full of stones and bricks for their menfolk; every window in the barracks was broken.

The order to fire was given by Captain Welsh, a military magistrate. Several people were wounded in addition to the four killed. Priests, who came on to the streets to give the last rites, joined with James Larkin, a trade union leader, to try to persuade people to go home (→ 27).

Peking to Paris in a gruelling 62 days

Aug 10. Prince Borghese of Italy has beaten five other competitors to win what has probably been the most gruelling motor race ever staged. He covered the 8000 miles of rugged terrain between Peking and Paris in 62 days, overcoming swamps, a brushfire and a Belgian policeman who stopped him for speeding (→ 8/6/08).

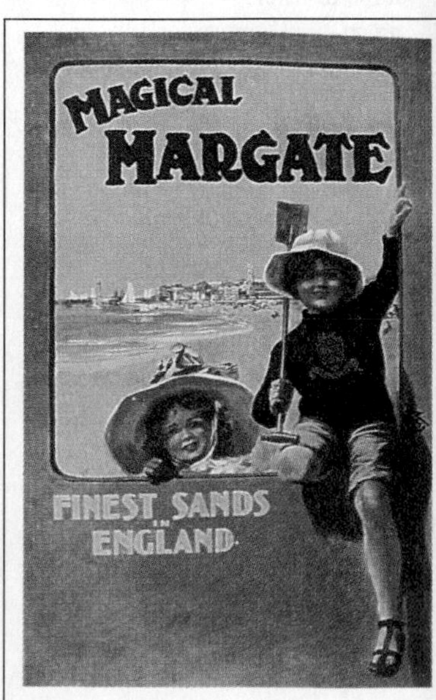

1907

SEPTEMBER

Su	Mo	Tu	We	Th	Fr	Sa
1	2	3	4	5	6	7
8	9	10	11	12	13	14
15	16	17	18	19	20	21
22	23	24	25	26	27	28
29	30					

2. Holland: British "blacklegs" fired upon during Antwerp dock strike.

3. New Zealand: Court declares all strikes to be illegal (→ 13).

6. Liverpool: The "Lusitania" embarks on her official maiden voyage (→ 13).

7. The Hague: Peace conference adopts rule that all powers must give notice of war (→ 7/10).

8. US: Investigation uncovers Standard Oil contribution of $100,000 to Roosevelt's 1904 election campaign.

8. China: Establishment of the Kuomintang, Chinese republican movement, by Dr Sun Yat-Sen (→ 28/12/11).

10. Farnborough: UK's first military airship, the "Nulli Secundus", flies successfully (→ 5/10).

10. London: New Zealand gains autonomy from UK as a Dominion within the British Empire.

13. New York: "Lusitania" arrives after a record five day, 54 minute Atlantic crossing at an average 23 knots (→ 11/10).

14. Berlin: Germany agrees with the Vatican that the state will control non-religious teaching in occupied Poland.

17. France: Louis Bleriot flies 184 metres in his aeroplane "Libellule" before crash-landing (→ 27/10).

20. Morocco: French troops resume fighting with rebels in Casablanca after breakdown of peace talks (→ 16/4/08).

25. Spain: Severe floods cause widespread devastation in the city of Malaga.

29. India: Labour MP James Keir Hardie accuses UK of running India "like the Czar runs Russia" (→ 4/10).

BIRTH

25. French film director Robert Bresson.

DEATH

4. Norwegian composer Edvard Grieg (*15/6/1843).→

Methodists unite at first conference

Sept 18. The chapel of John Wesley in Islington, London, was packed today for the first conference of the United Methodist Church. The faithful had started queueing at 5.40am more than four hours early. The seeds of the union were planted at the 1901 Ecumenical Conference and it represents a major step towards the unification of all British methodism. It is a three-way merger of the United Methodist Free Churches, the Methodist Connexion and the Bible Christians, but many other Methodist groups have expressed support. The new church has some 184,000 members and 908 ministers.

Norway mourns death of Grieg

Grieg: his melodies linger on.

Sept 4. Edvard Hagerup Grieg, Norway's most eminent composer, has died in Bergen at the age of 64. Grieg's piano concerto and "Peer Gynt" suite have assured his place in the world's concert halls. But it is perhaps in his smaller pieces that Grieg's best music can be found, especially the solo piano works, which often draw upon traditional Scandinavian melodies. As Rachmaninov put it: "Grieg may be a 'petit maitre' but there is no doubt about the 'maitre'."

1907

OCTOBER

Su	Mo	Tu	We	Th	Fr	Sa
		1	2	3	4	5
6	7	8	9	10	11	12
13	14	15	16	17	18	19
20	21	22	23	24	25	26
27	28	29	30	31		

1. Germany: The army buys Count Zeppelin's dirigible (→ 9/1/08).

2. London: Lord Mayor unlocks the door of the first house in new Hampstead Garden Suburb.

5. London: Dirigible circles St. Paul's in first UK public display of an airship (→ 14/8/08).

7. The Hague: Peace conference accepts compulsory arbitration proposal of UK and US (→ 18).

10. London: Labour MPs propose a general strike if railways reject workers' pay demands.

11. India: Nationwide ban on public meetings of 20 or more is imposed (→ 1/11).

12. Germany: Socialist Karl Liebknecht is jailed for 18 months for publishing anti-militarist book.

14. St. Petersburg: The Czar's third Duma, conservative and pro-Stolypin, is created (→ 11/11).

15. Shrewsbury: 19 die when an express train ignores danger signal and crashes.

15. US: The town of Fontanet is almost entirely destroyed when a gunpowder factory explodes.

16. Philippines: US civil governor William Taft opens the Filipino assembly but says independence must wait.

17. Canada: Guglielmo Marconi opens a transatlantic wireless service from Nova Scotia to Ireland (→ 8/11).

22. Berlin: Protests at supposed "Americanisation" are voiced in the Reichstag (→ 14/4/08).

24. London: Lloyd George approves plans for a Channel ferry from Dover to Calais.

27. Paris: Henri Farman flies 470 yards in record 31 seconds (→ 13/11).

29. Ottoman sultan complains to Western powers of Bulgarian, Greek agitation in Macedonia.

Serious Indian riot: Keir Hardie blamed

Oct 4. Riots are raging through Calcutta tonight and much of the trouble is being blamed on the British Labour leader Mr Keir Hardie who has given a number of interviews in which he is understood to have compared the situation in India to that in the Balkans.

The paper "The Englishman" roundly declares: "Mr Keir Hardie visits the most disaffected town in Bengal. He there speaks of Armenian horrors ... No wonder people at home are disgusted. The sooner he leaves India the better."

Mr Hardie's explanation of his reference to Armenian horrors is that he was alluding to outrages by Moslems on Hindu widows.

Another view is taken by the "Amrita Bazar Patrika" which says that the sweepers looted the shops in the presence of police and asks: "Is it possible that this situation has been created in order to throw discredit on Mr Keir Hardie?"

Whatever the cause, there is no doubt of the seriousness of the disturbances which have now lasted for two days. They started at a meeting to honour students who were recently punished for assaulting the police. Stones were thrown at the police and the rioting then spread through the streets where Europeans in cars were singled out for attack (→ 11).

Off to the races: a well-dressed English sporting gentleman.

Giant liners battle for speed record

Oct 11. Cannons boomed, sirens shrieked and thousands waved flags today as the new Queen of the Seas, the "Lusitania", broke all records for crossing the Atlantic and regained for England the supremacy of this key passenger route.

She took just 4 days 19 hours 52 minutes to beat the Hamburg-American line's "Deutschland", the previous holder of the Blue Riband, by 11 hours 46 minutes – an average speed of just over 24 knots. Even more amazing is that the monthold liner was not even out for the record. Her captain had been instructed not even to bother to try for it in the face of high seas and head winds.

The giant Cunard ship left Liverpool with 400 first and 473 second class passengers aboard on Saturday night and passed the Daunt's Rock, Queenstown, the point from which Atlantic crossings are officially timed, at 10.25 am on Sunday. Her best day's steaming was between noon on Tuesday and noon on Wednesday when she covered 617 miles, 16 more in a day than the "Deutschland" has ever managed.

Today's success comes in only the second West-bound voyage of the new liner but her master, Captain J.B. Watt, believes she can do better still using the full strength of her 70,000 horse power steam turbines. The "Lusitania" was described on her maiden voyage last month as "the most brilliant thing in ships the world has ever seen". Capt. Watt praised her too. "She's a daisy," he said (→16/11).

Heroine's welcome: the "Lusitania" steams triumphantly into New York.

Sister ship: Cunard's "Mauretania" which is even bigger and faster.

Secret plans for new International Court

Oct 18. The secret text of a proposal to establish the International Court of Justice, drawn up at the International Peace Conference at The Hague, was revealed to the public today.

Drafted by British, American and German delegates, it proposes 26 articles to govern the composition and duties of this court designed to further the cause of arbitration.

It is intended to be "easily accessible, free of charge, with judges representing the various legal systems of the world". Sitting in The Hague, it will be composed of 17 high court judges of equal rank, who will enjoy diplomatic privileges and immunity.

The conference also managed to renew the conventions governing the conduct of wars, although it failed to reach agreement about armaments. In addition, eleven new rules were added to the list formulated at the 1899 conference also held in The Hague.

This year's conference, initiated by President Theodore Roosevelt, was attended by delegates representing 44 nations.

King creates medal for heroic miners

Oct 18. King Edward VII has announced that a new medal is to be awarded to miners "who endanger their own lives in saving, or endeavouring to save, the lives of others from perils in mines or quarries". There will be two classes of medal: First, made of silver, and Second, made of bronze. Both will consist of a circular medal with the King's head on the front and on the back "a design representing the rescue of a miner with the inscription 'for courage' " (→27/2/08).

1907

NOVEMBER

Su	Mo	Tu	We	Th	Fr	Sa
					1	2
3	4	5	6	7	8	9
10	11	12	13	14	15	16
17	18	19	20	21	22	23
24	25	26	27	28	29	30

1. UK: Widespread Labour losses in municipal elections (→22/1/08).

1. India: Provincial authorities granted powers to ban all public meetings in bid to curb unrest (→5).

2. Christiania: UK, France, Russia and Germany agree to guarantee Norway's independence.

5. India: Special commissioner appointed to deal with famine conditions (→26/12).

6. UK: Railway dispute settled without a strike.

8. Paris: The first newspaper photograph is transmitted by cable, from "L'Illustration" to the London "Daily Mirror".

11. St. Petersburg: The first session of the third Duma is formally opened (→26).

15. Oxford: Kaiser Wilhelm is awarded an honorary degree.

16. Liverpool: The world's biggest liner, the "Mauretania", leaves on her maiden voyage (→22).

18. Berlin: Announced that the German navy will build three more battleships (→7/3/08).

22. New York: The Cunard liner "Mauretania" arrives at the end of her maiden voyage (→13/12).

23. US: Standard Oil boss John Rockefeller gives $2.6m towards a medical institute.

24. Berlin: Chancellor von Bulow introduces a bill to expropriate land belonging to Poles in German Poland.

26. St. Petersburg: Duma claims that Czar Nicholas II has renounced autocracy (→5/12).

29. London: King Edward VII appoints 87-year-old Florence Nightingale to the Order of Merit.

BIRTH

28. Italian author Alberto Moravia (†26/9/90).

DEATH

1. French author Alfred Jarry (*8/9/1873).

Asquith shouted down by women

Nov 16. Militant suffragettes chanting slogans and hurling insults disrupted a speech by the Chancellor of the Exchequer, Herbert Asquith, at Nuneaton today.

The shouting began almost immediately and became so loud that it drowned the chairman's calls for order. No sooner had one group of women been forcibly removed by stewards than another took up the cry.

Thirty women were carried out and the rough way they were treated brought strong protests from some of the men present (→13/12).

Campaign song: written by a man.

London crowds cheer Kaiser on state visit

Nov 13. The crowds watched with a tremendous sense of occasion as the Kaiser and King drove in procession to lunch with the Lord Mayor of London at the Guildhall. Several of Europe's sovereigns have made the same journey in recent years, but this one today was special – the state visit of the most powerful military monarch in the world – and the crowds looked on with curiosity and, perhaps, a slight apprehension.

The Kaiser, a big, strongly-built man, was in the black uniform, laced with gold, of Ziethen's Hussars. Alongside was the Kaiserin in mauve, with ostrich feathers in her hair. The bright sunshine not only added sparkle, but was a relief. Yesterday the Kaiser was four hours late arriving at Portsmouth because of dense fog. There were anxious moments as for 14 hours nobody knew the location of the royal yacht or its escorting naval warships.

In Guildhall's library, the Lord Mayor Sir John Hall welcomed the Kaiser to the City of London. He recalled the Kaiser's last visit to the Guildhall 16 years earlier. Now Gladstone had gone and so had Bismarck. In more than one continent, the map had been recast.

Relatives: King (l) and Kaiser (r).

The Kaiser – introduced as "His Imperial Majesty, Emperor of Germany, and King of Prussia" – spoke in his reply of something he had seen on his drive from Buckingham Palace. "I saw an inscription, "Blood is thicker than water". May this ever be so between our two countries and may the great City of London successfully develop under the reign of King Edward, my beloved uncle" (→18/12).

Belgian state takes Congo from King

Nov 28. King Leopold of Belgium has at last given up his Congo independent state, which he has ruled as absolute monarch for the past 22 years. After lengthy debates in parliament, the Belgian government received a vote in favour of annexation and today a treaty was concluded under which Leopold surrenders the vast Central African territory, 80 times the size of Belgium itself.

Pressure from abroad, particularly from the British government, backed by public opinion, horrified by accounts of the cruelties inflicted on the natives, was the determining factor in the Belgian action.

For the first time the Congo question became an issue in a Belgian election. The Socialists campaigned violently against annexation, saying it would mean "sending your soldier sons to their death". But the Catholics, who favoured annexation, were returned to power and immediately opened negotiations with Leopold even before the parliamentary vote.

Leopold has held on to the "Fondation de la Couronne", which allows him to exploit the Congo resources for public works in Belgium; but there is much opposition to this concession and he can expect pressure to surrender this, too, in the very near future (→26/2/08).

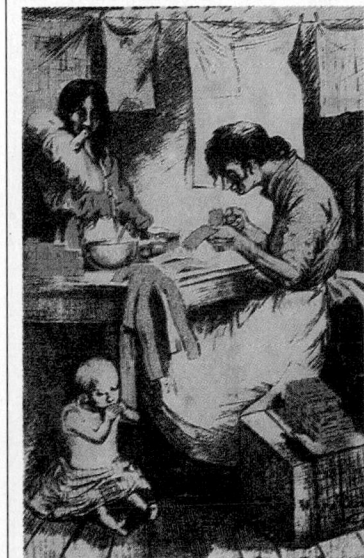

Match girls: sweated labour in an East End matchbox factory.

Frenchman's first aeroplane to take off vertically, briefly aloft

Nov 13. A French inventor, Paul Cornu, today achieved a first flight in a new type of aircraft which lifts off vertically from the ground powered by two motor-driven propellors or rotors above the pilot. He wants to win a 50,000-franc prize on offer to the first Frenchman to complete an aerial circuit of one kilometre even though today he only managed to get one and a half metres off the ground.

However, his brother did not help today's flight by jumping onto the aircraft as it took off, fearful that it was going out of control. Cornu proved his machine would fly by demonstrating a model of the aircraft in a field near his home town of Lisieux in Normandy. This so impressed the spectators that recently they raised 12,500 francs so he could continue flying when funds ran out (→18/12).

Pedal power: the world's first working helicopter, invented by Paul Cornu, a French bicycle-maker.

1907

DECEMBER

Su	Mo	Tu	We	Th	Fr	Sa
1	2	3	4	5	6	7
8	9	10	11	12	13	14
15	16	17	18	19	20	21
22	23	24	25	26	27	28
29	30	31				

2. Canada: 730 people are rescued from the shipwrecked liner Mount Temple off Nova Scotia.

5. St. Petersburg: One day strike is called to protest against prosecution for treason of members of first Duma.→

10. Stockholm: Nobel Prizes awarded to Albert Michelson (US, Physics); Eduard Buchner (Germany, Chemistry); Charles Laveran (France, Medicine); Rudyard Kipling (UK, Literature) and Ernesto Moneta and Louis Renault (Italy and France respectively, Peace).→

11. London: The German Kaiser and Kaiserin leave at end of state visit (→ 6/6/08).

12. New York: New rules force women to sign affidavits of their age and good character before they marry.

13. Liverpool: The "Mauretania" runs aground (→ 12/1/08).

14. St. Petersburg: 38 soldiers jailed for life for surrendering to Japan at Port Arthur.

18. France: Louis Bleriot's demonstration of his new aeroplane at Issy ends in its destruction into seven pieces.

25. St. Petersburg: Duma Speaker says "restriction of the rights of Jews is incompatible with justice"(→ 13/2/08).

26. India: First Indian National Congress session is suspended after moderates and extremists clash (→ 15/3/08).

DEATH

17. British physicist William Thomson, Lord Kelvin (*26/6/1824).

HIT OF 1907

If those lips could only speak

QUOTE OF THE YEAR

"I have seen thousands of boys and young men, ... hunchedup, miserable specimens, smoking endless cigarettes, many of them betting."
Sir Robert Baden-Powell, explaining why he formed the Boy Scouts.

Arts: "Jungle Book" author wins Nobel

For the first time a Nobel prize for literature has gone to an English writer, **Rudyard Kipling**. There is no disputing the correctness of the choice – Mr Kipling is the foremost story writer in English and the acknowledged poet of the Empire. When he came to London in 1889, he was already famous in his native India for his "Plain Tales from the Hills". His first collection of stories published here made him the toast of literary London at 26.

In 1892 came his "Barrack Room Ballads" of Danny Deever, Gunga Din and Fuzzy Wuzzy, and the Road to Mandalay, full of his close identification with the lot of the common soldier. But Kipling's imagination also identifies with children as he showed in the two classic "Jungle Books", which delight young and old, followed by the "Just So Stories" written to be read aloud, and which he illustrated very capably himself.

Kipling's early years as a journalist and his extensive travels in both East and West (he set up home in New England with his American wife Caroline for a period) give his work that exotic and compulsive flavour which is most memorable in "Kim", the finest novel yet written about British India.

It has been a hectic year for Dublin's new Abbey Theatre, founded three years ago by W.B.Yeats in order to revive Irish drama.

Kipling's award: Just-so deserts.

J.M. Synge's play, "The Playboy of the Western World" caused a week of riots and the arrest of playgoers by the police, provoked by the hero's boast that he has killed his father and the respect it brings him in a West of Ireland village, which was held to be slander on Ireland. "A vile and inhuman story told in the foulest language," declared "Sinn Fein".

Meanwhile in London Lily Elsie entrances as "The Merry Widow".

Leader of the Zulu uprising surrenders

Soldier king: rebel chief Dinizulu.

Dec 12. With several hundred of his loyal followers, Dinizulu, King of the Zulus, yesterday surrendered without bloodshed to Colonel Sir Duncan Mackenzie, commandant of the Natal forces. Dinizulu was brought from his Kraal and was told by Colonel Mackenzie: "There is a great deal of unrest in the country. Many murders have been committed, both of whites and your own chiefs. The troops are here to restore order."

It is hoped Dinizulu's surrender will bring to a close the two years of unrest which began after the Natal government imposed a poll tax of £1 on every European and native over 18 years. Dinizulu did not at first support the rebels but joined later.

Duma "MPs" jailed on treason charge

Dec 31. A St. Petersburg court has sent to prison 167 deputies of the Duma, the Russian parliament, after they issued a revolutionary manifesto to mark the body's dissolution. The deputies were found guilty of treason and sentenced to three months' imprisonment. Two of the deputies had died since signing the manifesto.

The sentence carries with it the loss of all political rights, which bars the deputies from standing in elections for the next Duma. Most of them were members of the Constitutional Democratic party, the Cadets and the Labour Party.

When the Duma was shut down by Czar Nicholas II, the deputies travelled to Vyborg in Finland where they met in a forest and called on Russians not to pay taxes or serve in the army until the Duma was restored (→ 8/2/08).

British worried by Japanese rivals

Dec 11. British shipbuilders are increasingly worried about unfair competition from Japan. The industry notes that Japanese shipbuilders now get subsidies worth £2 per ton for ships over 1,000 tons and 10/- per horse power for engines. While her fleet which defeated the Russians three years ago was built mainly in the United Kingdom, Japan is now building ships for others as well as for herself.

1908

JANUARY

Su	Mo	Tu	We	Th	Fr	Sa
			1	2	3	4
5	6	7	8	9	10	11
12	13	14	15	16	17	18
19	20	21	22	23	24	25
26	27	28	29	30	31	

1. New York: Gustav Mahler makes US conducting debut at the Metropolitan Opera.

1. US: Georgia introduces a law prohibiting alcohol (→26/5).

6. Oldham: 2,000 cotton-mill workers go on strike (→24).

6. London: "The Times" is bought by Arthur Pearson from the Walter family.

8. Paris: Opening of an exhibition of paintings by Van Gogh at Bernheim Gallery.

9. London: The Road Car Company dismisses 800 striking bus drivers.

9. Berlin: Count von Zeppelin announces he is building an airship capable of carrying 100 passengers (→27/4).

10. Berlin: Chancellor von Bulow rejects universal suffrage, in a speech to the Prussian parliament (→30).

11. Barnsley: 16 children die when a staircase collapses at a children's show.

14. Panama: Chief Panama Canal engineer George Goethals says the project will cost around £60 million.

16. UK: First issue of "Scouting for Boys", journal of the scouting movement.

22. Hull: Labour Party Conference decides by a narrow margin to adopt socialism (→12/4).

22. New York: Katie Mulcahey is the first arrested under new city law forbidding women to smoke in public.

24. Oldham: Cotton workers strike is settled after negotiation.

28. London: Playhouse Theatre opens.

BIRTH

9. French writer Simone de Beauvoir (†14/4/86).

DEATHS

9. German illustrator and poet Wilhelm Busch (*15/4/1832).

25. British writer Marie-Louise de la Ramee, alias Ouida (*1/1/1839).

Gandhi freed by Smuts

Jan 30. Mohandas Gandhi, leader of the Indians in Transvaal, was released from prison in South Africa today on the direct orders of General Smuts. He had been sentenced to two months' imprisonment without hard labour on January 10 for refusing to register and have his fingerprints taken as required by the new "Asiatic Law".

Mr Gandhi, who had led the protest against the law, was lodged in Johannesburg jail where he spent most of his time reading. However, it is understood that he was taken secretly by train and automobile yesterday to meet General Smuts in Pretoria.

The meeting began at noon and two hours later they had reached a compromise under which, in return for some minor amendments to the law, Mr Gandhi agreed to register and to call off the protest. The Indian leader then waited while General Smuts held a cabinet meeting to discuss this development.

At seven o'clock the General returned and told Mr Gandhi "You are free this very moment". Despite the secrecy surrounding the meeting, a group of his followers were waiting for him. They were much puzzled and it is believed that Mr Gandhi will have some difficult explaining to do.

England's Test win a close run thing

Jan 7. Amid rising tension in the closest Test Match yet played overseas, England's final pair of Arthur Fielder and Sydney Barnes put on the 39 runs needed to beat Australia by one wicket in Melbourne.

An accurate throw from cover at the very last minute as the pair scampered home for the winning run would have given Test cricket its first-ever tie.

Suffrage demo hits ministers' houses

Jan 30. Nine suffragettes were arrested today following incidents at the homes of six cabinet ministers. The raids, carried out simultaneously, were part of a new strategy to harass prominent politicians who oppose their cause. Other examples of the policy include attempting to hand a petition to the King and chaining themselves to railings in Downing Street (→12/2).

Transatlantic liners in price-cutting war

Jan 12. The price of travel across the Atlantic is falling sharply as the two main shipping lines, White Star and Cunard, battle it out to attract more passengers. Both lines have recently cut their fares twice so that second class tickets have fallen by as much as 45 shillings and third class by 30 shillings.

The prize in the battle is the third class passenger market now dominated by Cunard who carried 86,000 such passengers across the Atlantic last year (→10/2).

Life afloat: steaming to the US.

Frenchman makes first circular flight in heavier-than-air craft

Jan 13. Henri Farman, the flying Frenchman, today won the coveted £5,000 prize for the first heavier-than-air aircraft to cover a circuit of at least one kilometre. He took off from a large field in Issy-les-Moulineaux, five miles south of Paris, in a biplane weighing 300 lbs powered by a 50 hp engine.

He flew around a pylon 500 metres away and returned but because of the distance covered while turning it seems he may have flown as much as one and a half kilometres. Farman flew at 24 miles an hour, at a height of about 25 feet and the whole flight took just one minute 28 seconds. It is being heralded as proof that the new aircraft will in future replace steerable balloons in air travel (→21/3).

Round trip: at 24mph, French aviator Henri Farman roars towards the finish line – and a £5,000 prize.

1908

FEBRUARY

Su	Mo	Tu	We	Th	Fr	Sa
						1
2	3	4	5	6	7	8
9	10	11	12	13	14	15
16	17	18	19	20	21	22
23	24	25	26	27	28	29

3. Lisbon: Dictator Joao Franco and his cabinet resign following the King's assassination (→5).

5. Lisbon: Franco flees Portugal, his dictatorship is abolished, decrees annulled and political prisoners released.

8. Russia: The Czar orders army to the Persian border, following Turkish incursions into Persia (→17).

10. London: Transatlantic passenger fares nearly double as the main carriers agree to end price-cutting war (→12/3).

12. London: "Women's Parliament" meets to discuss important women's issues (→18).

12. London: Children's Bill published, which would penalise anyone allowing children to smoke.

13. Berlin: Jewish Relief League says the Czar regards anti-Semitic pogrom leaders as heroes (→9/6).

17. Persia: Russia and Turkey settle dispute over Persian border incursions by Turks (→28).

20. St. Petersburg: Gen. Stossel is sentenced to death for surrendering at Port Arthur (→18/3).

26. Brussels: The Belgian government agrees to pay King Leopold £5 million for the Belgian Congo (→20/8).

27. London: Licensing Bill introduced, which would cut the number of drinking licences by a third (→26/9).

27. Washington: Oklahoma becomes the 46th state of the US.

28. Teheran: The Shah of Persia survives an assassination attempt.

29. Holland: Dutch scientists succeed in producing solid helium.

BIRTHS

6. Italian politician Amintore Fanfani.

11. British geologist and explorer Sir Vivian Ernest Fuchs.

Pankhurst reveals misery of jail life

Feb 18. An inside view of the horrors of prison life has been revealed by the leading suffragette, Emmeline Pankhurst, 50-year-old founder of the Women's Social and Political Union. Her vivid account of the drudgery and misery of Holloway jail follows her imprisonment there on charges of obstructing the police within the proscribed area of parliament.

In a letter from her bleak cell Mrs Pankhurst writes powerfully of the meagre rations, the coarse clothing with its convict's arrows, the stark surroundings and the dreadful unhappiness of her fellow inmates "all so sad and weak and feeble".

"All the hours seem very long in prison. The sun can never get in ... and every day so changeless and uninteresting. One grows almost too tired to go through to the exercise yard and yet one has a yearning for the open air."

Mrs Pankhurst, who has since been moved to hospital, had been sentenced to six weeks', imprisonment after refusing to find sureties for her good behaviour.

She claimed she was acting legitimately and added: "Whatever happens to me, the agitation will go on until those rights are obtained." In another incident 50 suffragists were arrested when they tried to enter the Commons by concealing themselves, Trojan horse style, in a large furniture van (→18/2).

Campaigner Emmeline Pankhurst.

Edison and film companies win right to projector monopoly

Thomas Alva Edison with the first motion picture projector.

Feb 11. Thomas Alva Edison, the prolific American inventor, has settled a long-running dispute over one of his most ingenious devices, the motion picture projector.

The inventor of the phonograph, the carbon telephone transmitter and the light bulb claimed that other companies were infringing the 1891 patent for his "Stereo-projecting kinetoscope".

The courts have finally decided to uphold Edison's complaints, which were backed by major US film producing companies who say the new patent rights agreement will put competitors out of business (→2/3).

Assassin shoots Portuguese King in back

Feb 1. King Carlos I and Crown Prince Luiz were assassinated in Lisbon today. They were shot at point-blank range by assailants whose leader, later identified as a cavalry sergeant, was killed in the melee following the murders.

King Carlos received two bullets in the back while his son was killed by a rifle bullet. As they slumped dead in their carriage, one of the assassins also tried to murder the Queen but he was beaten off by a guard at sword-point. Panic gripped the crowd when the shots rang out. "Women and children were trampled underfoot," said one witness, "some were seriously injured and the police fired at random." The assassination comes in the wake of last month's failed revolution.

King Carlos, a cultured and urbane oceanographer, looked to his premier, the dictatorial Joao Franco, to run the country. He will be succeeded by 19-year-old Don Manuel (→7/4).

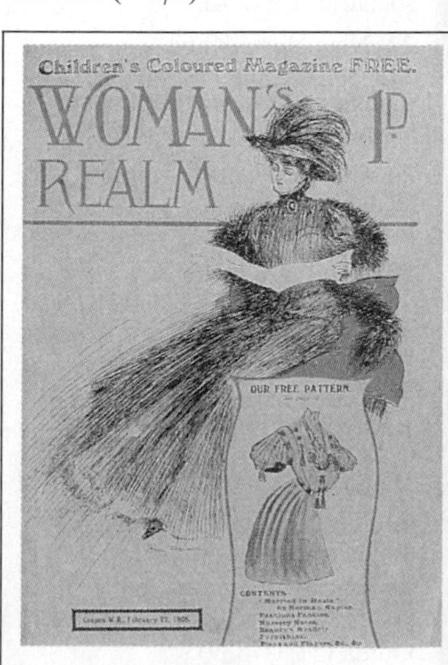

A penny for female thoughts.

1908

MARCH

Su	Mo	Tu	We	Th	Fr	Sa
1	2	3	4	5	6	7
8	9	10	11	12	13	14
15	16	17	18	19	20	21
22	23	24	25	26	27	28
29	30	31				

2. Paris: Gabriel Lippmann introduces colour photography process at the Académie des Sciences (→ 10/12).

4. New York: Board of Education bans the whip as a means of corporal punishment in schools.

12. UK: The "Mauretania" sets new record time for eastbound Atlantic passage of five days, five minutes (→ 21/5).

15. India: Police shoot four people dead in rioting (→ 2/5).

16. London: Freedom of the City of London is conferred on 87-year-old Florence Nightingale.

16. London: The High Court agrees to Lord Northcliffe taking control of "The Times" from Arthur Pearson.

18. St. Petersburg: Port Arthur veterans Generals Smirnoff and Fock fight a pistol duel (→ 13/9).

21. London: Sir John Hare suggests the creation of a National Theatre as a monument to Shakespeare (→ 19/5).

21. Paris: Henri Farman makes the first aeroplane flight with a passenger (→ 8/5).

25. Venice: Kaiser Wilhelm II of Germany pays an official visit to King Victor Emmanuel III.

25. London: Serious fire destroys the stage of the Drury Lane Theatre.

26. US: The US Thomas Flyer car sails for Alaska at the head of motor race from New York to Paris.

28. UK: Rubio wins the Grand National at Aintree.

31. US: 250,000 coal miners in Indianapolis strike for higher wages.

BIRTH

7. Italian actress Anna Magnani (†26/9/73).

DEATH

11. British humanitarian and NSPCC founder Reverend Benjamin Waugh (*20/2/1839).→

German battleship rivals dreadnought

March 7. Just two years after the Royal Navy's first dreadnought battleship was launched, Germany's own version of the revolutionary vessel, the "Nassau", was sent down the slipway today by the Grand Duchess of Baden with a bottle of German champagne, giving a further boost to the naval rivalry between the two countries.

Considerable secrecy surrounds the "Nassau", which was only laid down once the Germans had aquired some details of the Royal Navy's own vessel, but it is thought she has at least a dozen 11-inch guns and six torpedo tubes.

Britain is still ahead in naval development, though. By the end of this year the Royal Navy will have seven dreadnoughts in service and still outnumber the Germans two to one in large ships (→ 6/8).

Child's protector Rev. Waugh dies

March 11. The death has been announced of the Rev. Benjamin Waugh, founder of the National Society for the Prevention of Cruelty to Children, after a long illness.

Having served on the first School Board for London he launched the Society in 1884. As director he was a tireless champion of children's rights, despite frequent illness, and became known as the children's protector.

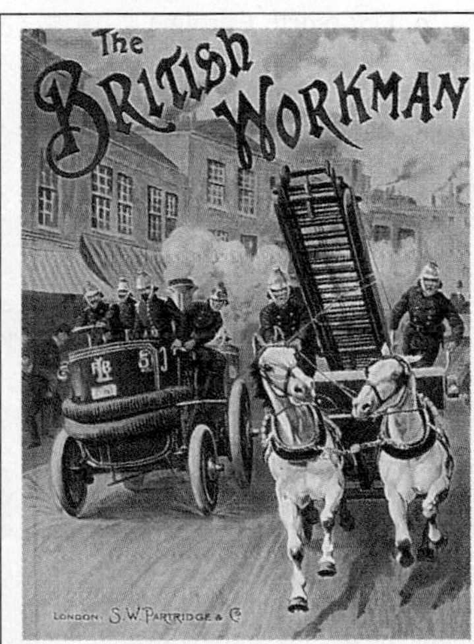

Fetch the engine! But will horse or horsepower get there first?

1908

APRIL

Su	Mo	Tu	We	Th	Fr	Sa
			1	2	3	4
5	6	7	8	9	10	11
12	13	14	15	16	17	18
19	20	21	22	23	24	25
26	27	28	29	30		

2. Isle of Wight: 35 die when destroyer "HMS Tiger" sinks after collision with cruiser "HMS Berwick" (→ 8/7).

4. France: Rene Jeannel announces discovery of prehistoric cave paintings at Louhans.

6. Berlin: The Reichstag authorises women to create their own associations (→ 14).

7. Portugal: Monarchists sweep to victory in general election.

8. Washington: Roosevelt issues an injunction to let blacks use same train carriages as whites in the South.

9. Somerset: Ten miners die in Norton Hill pit explosion.

13. China: 2,000 die in widespread flooding.

14. Copenhagen: The Danish Parliament adopts universal suffrage for taxpayers over 25 (→ 1/5).

20. India: British troops are sent to confront 10,000 frontier tribesmen following their killing of a British soldier.

23. Berlin: Six powers including the UK sign a treaty guaranteeing North Sea status quo (→ 3/6).

25. London: Wolverhampton Wanderers beat Newcastle United 3-1 in the FA Cup Final at Crystal Palace.

27. Berlin: Count von Zeppelin announces new airship capable of 47mph (→ 1/7).

27. Salzburg: Opening of the first International Congress of Psychoanalysis.

29. US: The US Steel Corporation manufactures the first car wheels made entirely of steel.

BIRTHS

5. Austrian conductor Herbert von Karajan (†16/7/89).

5. US actress Bette Davis (†6/10/89).

DEATH

22. British statesman Sir Henry Campbell-Bannerman, Liberal Prime Minister 1905-8 (*7/9/1836).→

The Foreign Legion puts Moors to flight

An artist's view of the conflict.

April 16. Troops of the French Foreign Legion went into action at dawn yesterday when Moorish irregulars, including 300 horsemen, swept across the border into Algeria and attacked French outposts. The Moors soon fled, leaving 125 dead; the French lost 28 dead. Clashes with the Moors have been increasing as the French fight to strengthen their position along the vague Moroccan border (→ 23/8).

Haldane forms the Territorial Army

April 1. The new Territorial Army came into existence today, one of the final steps in the planned reform and modernisation of the British army brought about by the Liberal War Secretary, Mr Haldane.

King Edward VII himself has spoken in favour of the move which has merged the Yeomanry, a volunteer cavalry corps, formed at the time of the French Revolution to maintain internal order, with the Volunteers. The force will be split into 14 infantry divisions and the same number of cavalry brigades.

There has been concern for some time about the lack of good organisation in all sections of the army, and some have accused parts of the Yeomanry of being little more than a decorative honour guard. It has also been seen as representing only the landed classes.

The training of the new Territorial Army will be linked to that of the regular army commanded by the General Staff (→ 23/11).

Asquith takes over as Prime Minister: Winston Churchill joins the cabinet

April 12. Herbert Henry Asquith was received by the King at Biarritz today and kissed hands on his appointment as the new Prime Minister. This follows the resignation of Sir Henry Campbell-Bannerman for reasons of health. After seeing the King, Mr Asquith walked on the golf-course and took tea with non-political friends before continuing with forming the government. The King will continue with his holiday in France.

The changeover at 10 Downing Street has been anticipated for some time and Mr Asquith is understood to have reached broad agreement with leading colleagues about the allocation of posts before being summoned to see the King. It was explained in the parliamentary lobbies that the team changes are aimed at giving new impetus to the social reform programme.

The most significant new appointments are David Lloyd George as Chancellor of the Exchequer and Winston Churchill joining the Cabinet as President of the Board of Trade. It is now up to Mr Lloyd George to decide exactly how the extra revenue needed for the new state pensions will be raised. The new Chancellor's reputation is as a man for radical action and there was immediate speculation that there may now be one or two Budgets with tax increases for the wealthier classes.

It is understood that there is to be no delay in asking Parliament to approve the five shillings a week old age pension at the age of 70. Mr Asquith was at work on this proposal before leaving his post at the Treasury. As for foreign affairs, Sir Edward Grey's reappointment to head the Foreign Office indicates no policy changes there (→7/5).

New PM Asquith, by Spy.

Rising star: Winston Churchill.

US doctors try to mend a broken heart

April 5. Surgeons at St. Joseph's Hospital in New York carried out an emergency operation early today on Robert Inglis, aged 23, after he had received a stab wound in his chest and heart. Dr Edward Duffy and Dr Philip McKormick removed two ribs and successfully sutured the wound in his heart. Mr Inglis is reported to be feeling strong.

Such an operation succeeds only once every 14 years, the two surgeons said later. However, an article in the British Medical Journal this year suggested the operation had a 46 per cent success rate since a human heart was first sutured 11 years ago.

1908

MAY

Su	Mo	Tu	We	Th	Fr	Sa
					1	2
3	4	5	6	7	8	9
10	11	12	13	14	15	16
17	18	19	20	21	22	23
24	25	26	27	28	29	30
31						

2. India: Police in Calcutta discover a cache of explosives, for use in alleged anarchist plot (→2/10).

5. US: Circuit court Judge Lacombe declares that moving pictures come under copyright law.

8. US: The Wright Brothers make ten flights to test new design of aircraft steering gear (→22).

9. London: J.J. Duveen makes gift of new wing to the Tate Gallery.

11. London: New Official Secrets Bill is postponed owing to press objections.

15. Paris: Painter Claude Monet destroys paintings valued at £20,000, saying they were unsatisfactory.

15. Berlin: Law comes into force reaffirming the unification of the German Empire.

21. New York: The "Lusitania" sets new record for westbound Atlantic passage of four days, 20 hours and 12 minutes.

22. Washington: Wright Brothers patent their "flying machine" (→27).

23. Uganda: 4,000 deaths from severe famine in Usoga region.

25. London: French President Armand Fallieres arrives to visit the Anglo-French Exhibition.

26. US: North Carolina introduces prohibition of alcohol.

27. Rome: Leon Delagrange makes record aeroplane flight of 5.5 miles (→30).

28. Canada: The Civic Dam on the Current River bursts, causing great devastation.

29. Turkey: 150 die as Samos islanders revolt against the Turkish garrison.

30. Rome: Leon Delagrange flies for a record 15 minutes 30 seconds (→8/6).

BIRTHS

20. US actor James Stewart.

28. British writer Ian Fleming (†12/8/64).

Meeting calls for a UK national theatre

May 19. The growing demand for a national theatre in Britain took a stride forward at the Lyceum Theatre in London yesterday with a mass meeting of some 2,000 people representing drama, literature and Parliament. They voted unanimously in favour of combining the two campaigns – for a national and for a Shakespeare memorial theatre – in one.

Lord Lytton presided over the meeting, which included such celebrities as Bernard Shaw, H.G. Wells, G.K. Chesterton, John Masefield, Rider Haggard and Jerome K. Jerome. He called for a theatre to be built by 1916 so as to commemorate the 300th anniversary of Shakespeare's death.

Budget gives single OAPs 5/- a week

May 7. In the budget debate, well received on both sides of the House, Mr Asquith today announced the government's intention to introduce an old age pension at a rate of five shillings a week for everybody over 70 or 7/6 for married couples. Everybody, that is, with sufficient exceptions to rebut charges of feather-bedding. So excluded are people who have failed to work according to their ability, prisoners, the insane and paupers (→10/6).

1908

JUNE

Su	Mo	Tu	We	Th	Fr	Sa
	1	2	3	4	5	6
7	8	9	10	11	12	13
14	15	16	17	18	19	20
21	22	23	24	25	26	27
28	29	30				

2. Turkey: Baghdad Railway Company signs contract to build from Constantinople to Halif, 500 miles.

3. UK: 100-1 outsider Signorinetta wins the Derby at Epsom, only the fourth filly to win since 1780.

4. US: Government announces two cents post to UK from 1/10, matching UK penny post to US from same date (→1/10).

5. UK: The Miners' Federation decides to affiliate to the Labour Representation Committee (→7/10).

6. France: New law grants automatic divorce after three years' legal separation.

8. Paris: Robert Pelterie makes a flight in a monoplane, over a distance of a mile at 120 feet (→8/7).

10. London: Parliament passes the Invalid and Old Age Pensions Act (→24/9).

11. London: Opening of the Rotherhithe Tunnel under the River Thames.

11. London: The Prince and Princess of Wales join 1,000 children from East End slums on a trip to Epping Forest.

12. Vienna: Half a million people watch celebrations of Emperor Franz Josef's Diamond Jubilee.

14. Berlin: The Reichstag passes new Navy Bill, which aims to boost the size of the German fleet.

22. US: Six blacks accused of murder in Houston, Texas, are lynched.

24. Spain: 85 people are feared drowned when the steamer Larache sinks in thick fog off Muros.

29. Paris: Physicist Henri Becquerel is elected permanent secretary of the Academie des Sciences (→25/8).

DEATHS

21. Russian composer Nikolai Rimsky-Korsakov (*18/3/1844).→

24. US statesman Grover Cleveland, President 1885-9 and 1893-7 (*18/3/1837).

"White City" celebrates the Entente

The great White City, centrepiece of the Franco-British Exhibition.

May 14. The wealth of two great nations went on display to the world today when the Prince of Wales opened the Franco-British Exhibition which includes the 70,000 capacity stadium for the coming Olympic Games. Despite a driving rainstorm which had thousands of Londoners and foreign visitors sheltering under umbrellas and turning much of the newly planted grass into a quagmire, the scale of the exhibition, covering 200 acres of West London with 25 palaces and halls, is clearly unprecedented in Britain.

The excellent relations between the two countries, four years after the signing of the Entente Cordiale, were demonstrated in an anthem composed by Sir Stanford including the lines: "Jolly Britons, advance – here's a health to old France. Welcome! Welcome! Welcome!"

Exhibits range from British shipbuilding to the cuisine of France with the fine arts of India housed in a graceful white building of Saracen design. French imperial power is represented by exhibits from Algeria and her West African colonies. Canada is well represented with a display of furs.

A complete reproduction of an Irish village, Bally Maclinton, is a popular attraction. It includes an exact replica of "McKinley Cottage" – where the ancestor of the late American president was born.

Making friends: exhibition poster.

The Olympic Games, revived in Athens 12 years ago, begin in July and today's spectators were given a foretaste by hundreds of British and foreign athletes competing in difficult conditions in the heavy rain.

The stadium – said to be big enough to contain seven buildings the size of the Albert Hall – is the biggest sporting arena in the world. The 109-yard long swimming pool is equally impressive.

Royal Naval reservists will be on duty throughout the Olympics to hoist the flags of the winning nations (→31/10)

Military journalist shoots at Dreyfus

June 4. An attempt was made today to murder Major Alfred Dreyfus during a ceremony honouring his great defender, the novelist Emile Zola.

Two shots were heard which were first thought to be an attempt on the life of the president, Mr Fallieres. Then Dreyfus was seen looking pale, with a slight wound in the arm.

An elderly man was holding a still-smoking revolver. He is Sosthene Gregory, aged 65, a journalist who works for two army newspapers. Gregory claimed that he meant to hit "Dreyfusism". Ironically, he was saved from the fury of the crowd by Dreyfus's brother, Mathieu Dreyfus.

Gregory is led away from the scene.

Shah's army riots

June 23. The Shah's Cossack guard and other troops finally succeeded at dawn yesterday in surrounding the parliament building where armed reformists are still holding out on the roof. When the troops first entered Tehran they ran amok, looting, raping and behaving with savage cruelty.

Artillery fire badly damaged public buildings in the capital. Twenty-two leaders of the Liberal party, which supports the anglophile Prince, Zill-es-Sultan, have been arrested. ▷

First visit of English King to Russia

June 9. On a beautifully bright sunny morning King Edward VII of Britain and Czar Nicholas II of Russia, monarchs of the two largest empires on earth, met today in Russian waters off Reval on the Baltic Sea. The little Estonian town had seen nothing like it since Czar Peter the Great captured it from Sweden 198 years ago.

The friendliness of the place was demonstrated when the Czar and his family stepped out of their train at the quayside. Hundreds of children sang; there were no police or military guards. The Czar, wearing naval uniform, met the King on board the royal yacht, "Victoria and Albert". In addition to two days of talks, there are plans for family banquets and balls, for the two royal families are related.

The friendly, family atmosphere of the meeting was a relief to those accompanying the King. The visit had led to noisy scenes in the House of Commons with one Labour MP calling the Czar "a common murderer". Keir Hardie, the Labour leader, attacked the government for allowing the visit, claiming the King was condoning atrocities in going to see the Czar. Nor did the massive display of German naval power, as the "Victoria and Albert" steamed through the Kiel Canal en route to Reval, ease the tensions surrounding the visit.

The King refused to have a cabinet minister accompany him during his meeting with the Czar. But a senior Foreign Office official accompanying the King did raise the persecution of Jews and was told by the Russian Prime Minister, Mr Stolypin, that new legislation is contemplated.

King Edward VII with his nephew-in-law, Czar Nicholas II.

200,000 support London's largest-ever suffragette demo

June 21. Huge crowds jammed Hyde Park today in a Votes for Women rally, at one of the biggest demonstrations seen in London.

Bugles blew and banners waved and leading speakers on the 20 different platforms wore sashes in the campaign colours of purple, green and white. Though most of the crowd appeared sympathetic to the cause, there were several ugly moments when trouble flared and police had to come to the rescue. One of the chief speakers was Miss Christabel Pankhurst. She claimed the demonstration would convince the government that public opinion was on their side. Another, Annie Kenney, said it showed they had the support of men as well as women. A resolution calling on the government to bring in an official women's suffrage bill without delay was passed overwhelmingly.

Votes for women: Christabel Pankhurst (second from left) leads the demonstrators at Hyde Park.

Taft is nominated by the Republicans

June 18. There was a last-minute scare at the Republican Convention here in Chicago yesterday, when for a moment it looked as though William Howard Taft was not going to get the nomination.

Everyone thought he was going to walk it. He was, after all, the hand-picked successor to the popular outgoing President, Theodore Roosevelt. But on the eve of the nomination the delegates had a sudden change of heart and for fifty minutes they demonstrated on behalf of the former president chanting "Four more years, four more years". However by the first ballot this morning order had been restored and the delegates dutifully voted for Taft (→3/11).

Finale for Russian musical pioneer

Nikolai Rimsky-Korsakov.

June 21. Nikolai Rimsky-Korsakov the Russian composer, has died near St. Petersburg at the age of 64. He belonged to the nationalist strain of Russian composers like Borodin and Mussorgsky rather than to the traditional European symphonic school. But his best music transcends any extra-musical programme through its sheer inventiveness and brilliant orchestration. "Scheherazade" is firmly in the repertoire, and Rimsky's operas, including "Mozart and Salieri", and "Le Coq d'Or", enjoy acclaim, especially in Russia.

1908

JULY

Su	Mo	Tu	We	Th	Fr	Sa
			1	2	3	4
5	6	7	8	9	10	11
12	13	14	15	16	17	18
19	20	21	22	23	24	25
26	27	28	29	30	31	

1. Wimbledon: Arthur Gore beats Herbert Barrett in Men's Singles Final; Charlotte Sterry beats Agnes Morton for the Ladies' Singles title.

3. Turkey: Revolt of the "Young Turks" breaks out in Monastir.→

4. Russia: 228 die in Jusovka pit disaster; 150 missing.

6. Rome: Papal decree says that the UK, US, Canada and Holland are no longer missionary lands.

8. UK: Scotsman George Davidson invents a "gyropter", a flying machine with two rotary fans (→ 5/9).

8. UK: New list of world navies shows Germans catching up Royal Navy in number of vessels (→ 10).

10. London: The Admiralty reveals a new torpedo with a four-mile range and speed of four knots (→ 6/8).

13. London: Controversy over why Labour MP Keir Hardie was not invited to the royal garden party for MPs.

15. Germany: Count von Zeppelin's new airship is badly damaged; further experiments postponed (→ 8/10).

16. London: Fire breaks out in Moorgate tube station.

17. London: The first criminal appeal, against a murder conviction, is turned down at the Central Criminal Court.

18. Bombay: 14,000 mill workers go on strike.

22. S. Africa: De Beers mines announce they will close until US trade revives.

27. Russia: The Czar meets French President Armand Fallieres at Reval.

29. Teheran: The Shah of Persia decides to reform the Persian parliament along the lines of the Russian Duma.

BIRTH

26. Chilean President Salvador Allende Gossens (†11/9/73).

DEATH

3. US author Joel Chandler Harris (*9/12/1848).→

Young Turks force changes on Sultan

July 24. The success of the Young Turk revolutionary movement in spreading disaffection throughout the army has forced Sultan Abdul Hamid II to restore Turkey's constitution.

Telegrams have been sent to all districts ordering the authorities to hold elections for parliamentary representatives. The constitution of 1876 is thus restored. It provides for a responsible Cabinet and Senate and guarantees the freedom of religion, education and the press.

The previous attempt to make the constitution work failed dismally. The meetings of the Senate were described as "pure comedy" and it soon ceased to sit. From then until now, there has been no talk of a parliament in Turkey.

However, the situation is different today for the Young Turk movement is gaining support in the army. Even the Albanian troops on whom the Sultan could normally depend to crush any revolt have thrown in their lot with them.

What remains to be seen now is whether these changes will prove sufficiently radical to appease the Young Turks.

Caricature of Abdul Hamid II.

Marathon runner loses race, wins hearts

July 30. Dorando Pietri, the courageous Italian runner, has been presented with a gold cup by Queen Alexandra in recognition of his dramatic efforts in the Olympic marathon. Only exhaustion, leading to his subsequent detention in hospital, prevented his winning the gold medal.

He entered the stadium after the 26-mile run from Windsor well in the lead, only to take a wrong turning, correct himself, stumble four or five times, fall, and receive medical attention and a helping hand from well-meaning stewards before crossing the finishing line still ahead of the rest of the pack. His disqualification was inevitable, but the crowd's, and the country's, admiration meant some gesture had to be made.

Pietri collects his prize.

Pietri crosses the finishing line after his valiant marathon effort.

Second car home wins first prize

July 26. The German car, Protos, was first to reach Paris in the race from New York, but there were no celebrations. The "winner" was the American Thomas car because the Protos had been penalised for travelling part of the way by train.

When the Protos was delayed by repairs in America it was shipped by rail to Seattle in order to sail with the Thomas car to Russia. The Protos was not disqualified, but received an ultimately decisive 15-day penalty. Its driver, Lt. Koeppen, said: "I wish the roads in America were as nice as the people."

Author of Uncle Remus stories dies

July 3. The author of the Brer Rabbit stories, American Joel Chandler Harris, died today from cirrhosis of the liver. His Uncle Remus stories, animal fables in which the hero was regularly doused with tar or pitched into briar patches, proved popular here.

A major influence on his style was "The Vicar of Wakefield" by Oliver Goldsmith, which he came across at the age of six. Harris' animals shared the same wistfulness and resignation that characterised Goldsmith's parson.

1908  London

Competitors line up for the Olympic 1500 metres final.

The greatest sporting festival ever seen in the British Isles provided a fitting climax to two years of building and planning in and around London. Most impressive was the new White City stadium where the athletic events were held – cycling, fencing, gymnastics and wrestling – as well as swimming, in a specially constructed temporary pool inside the arena.

The spectators were treated to 21 different sports at the various venues which included, inevitably, Henley for the rowing and Wimbledon for the tennis.

For the first time the organisers agreed to include the winter sport of ice skating in which the British veteran Madge Syers won the women's figures. Britain alone made a significant challenge to the USA in the athletic events and the host country dominated the rowing and the boxing.

Despite the undoubted success of the organisation there were many technical disputes between competitors and the (exclusively British) judges. It is hoped that the resulting breach, which has caused considerable acrimony between the athletic associations of Britain and the USA, will soon be healed.

Men Athletics

100m
1. Reginald Walker SAF *10.8
2. James Rector USA 10.9
3. Robert Kerr CAN 11.0

200m
1. Robert Kerr CAN 22.6
2. Robert Cloughen USA 22.6
3. Nathaniel Cartmell USA 22.7

400m (only 3 runners in Final)
1. Wyndham Halswelle GBR 50.0

800m
1. Melvin Sheppard USA **1:52.8
2. Emilio Lunghi ITA 1:54.2
3. Hanns Braun GER 1:55.2

1500m
1. Melvin Sheppard USA *4:03.4
2. Harold Wilson GBR 4:03.6
3. Norman Hallows GBR 4:04.0

Marathon
1. John Hayes USA *2:55:18.4
2. Charles Hefferon SAF 2:56:06.0
3. Joseph Forshaw USA 2:57:10.4

110m Hurdles
1. Forrest Smithson USA **15.0
2. John Garrels USA 15.7
3. Arthur Shaw USA

400m Hurdles
1. Charles Bacon USA **55.0
2. Harry Hillman USA 55.3
3. Leonard Tremeer GBR 57.0

3000m Steeplechase
1. Arthur Russell GBR 10:47.8
2. Archie Robertson GBR 10:48.4
3. John Eisele USA

4x400m Relay
1. USA 3:29.4 (William Hamilton, Nathaniel Cartmell, John Taylor, Melvin Sheppard)
2. Germany (Arthur Hoffmann, Hans Eicke, Otto Trieloff, Hanns Braun)
3. Hungary (Pal Simon, Frigyes Mezey-Wiesner, Jozsef Nagy, Odon Bodor)

High Jump
1. Harry Porter USA *1.905
2. Con Leahy GBR-IRL 1.88
3. István Somodi HUN 1.88
4. Géo André FRA 1.88

Pole Vault
1. Edward Cooke USA *3.71
2. Alfred Gilbert USA *3.71
2. Ed Archibald CAN 3.58
3. Charles Jacobs USA 3.58
3. Bruno Söderström SWE 3.58

Long Jump
1. Francis Irons USA *7.48
2. Daniel Kelly USA 7.09
3. Calvin Bricker CAN 7.085

Triple Jump
1. Timothy Ahearne GBR-IRL 14.915
2. J. Garfield MacDonald CAN 14.76
3. Edvard Larsen NOR 14.39

Shotput
1. Ralph Rose USA 14.21
2. Dennis Horgan GBR 13.62
3. John Garrels USA 13.18

Discus
1. Martin Sheridan USA *40.89
2. Merritt Giffin USA 40.70
3. Marquis Horr USA 39.445

Hammer
1. John Managan USA 51.92
2. Matthew McGrath USA 51.18
3. Cornelius Walsh USA 48.51

Freestyle Javelin
1. Erik Lemming SWE *54.445
2. Michel Dorizas GRE 51.36
3. Arne Halse NOR 49.73

Javelin
1. Erik Lemming SWE 54.825
2. Arne Halse NOR 50.57
3. Otto Nilsson SWE 47.105

5 miles (8046m)
1. Emil Voigt GBR 25:11.2
2. Edward Owen GBR 25:24.0
3. John Svanberg SWE 25:37.2

3 miles Team (4828m)
1. Great Britain 6
2. USA 19
3. France 32

Standing High Jump
1. Ray Ewry USA 1.575
2. Konstantin Tsiklitiras GRE 1.55
3. John Biller USA 1.55

Standing Long Jump
1. Ray Ewry USA 3.335
2. Konstantin Tsiklitiras GRE 3.23
3. Martin Sheridan USA 3.225

Discus, Ancient Style
1. Martin Sheridan USA 38.00
2. Marquis Horr USA 37.325
3. Werner Järvinen FIN 36.48

Tug-of-War
1. GBR – 2. Great Britain

3500m Walk
1. George Larner GBR 14:55.0
2. Ernest Webb GBR 15:07.4
3. Harry Kerr NZ 15:43.4

10 mile walk (16,093m)
1. George Larner GBR 1:15:57.4
2. Ernest Webb GBR 1:17:31.0
3. Edward Spencer GBR 1:21:20.2

Swimming

100m Freestyle
1. Charles Daniels USA **1:05.6
2. Zoltán Halmay HUN 1:06.2
3. Harald Julin SWE 1:08.0

400m Freestyle
1. Henry Taylor GBR 5:36.8
2. Frank Beaurepaire AUS 5:44.2
3. Otto Scheff AUT 5:46.0

1500m Freestyle
1. Henry Taylor GBR **22:48.4
2. Thomas Battersby GBR 22:51.2
3. Frank Beaurepaire AUS 22:56.2

100m Backstroke
1. Arno Bieberstein GER **1:24.6
2. Ludvig Dam DEN 1:26.6
3. Herbert Haresnape GBR 1:27.0

200m Breaststroke
1. Frederick Holman GBR **3:09.2
2. William Robinson GBR 3:12.8
3. Pontus Hanson SWE 3:14.6

4x200m Freestyle Relay
1. GBR **10:55.6 (John Derbyshire, Paul Radmilovic, William Foster, Henry Taylor)
2. HUN 10:59.0 (Jozsef Munk, Imre Zachár, Béla Las Torres, Zoltán Halmay)
3. USA 11:02.8 (Harry Hebner, Leo "Bud" Goodwin, Charles Daniels, Leslie G. Rich)

Springboard Diving
1. Albert Zürner GER 85.5
2. Kurt Behrens GER 85.3
3. George Gaidzik USA 80.8

Platform
1. Hjalmar Johansson SWE 83.75
2. Karl Malström SWE 78.73
3. Arvid Spångberg SWE 74.00

Water-Polo

1. Great Britain
2. Belgium
3. Sweden

Boxing

Bantamweight
1. A. Henry Thomas GBR
2. John Condon GBR
3. W. Webb GBR

Featherweight
1. Richard Gunn GBR
2. Charles W. Morris GBR
3. Hugh Roddin GBR

Lightweight
1. Frederick Grace GBR
2. Frederick Spiller GBR
3. H.H. Johnson GBR

Middleweight
1. John Douglas GBR
2. Reginald Baker AUS
3. W. Philo GBR

Heavyweight
1. Albert L. Oldham GBR
2. S.C.H. Evans GBR
3. Frederick Parks GBR

Greco-Roman Wrestling

Lightweight
1. Enrico Porro ITA
2. Nikolai Orlov RUS
3. Arvid Lindén FIN

Middleweight
1. Frithiof Märtensson SWE
2. Mauritz Andersson SWE
3. Anders Andersen DEN

Light Heavyweight
1. Verner Weckman FIN
2. Yrjö Saarela FIN
3. Carl Jensen DEN

Heavyweight
1. Richard Weisz HUN
2. Aleksandr Petròv RUS
3. Sören Marius Jensen DEN

Freestyle Wrestling

Bantamweight
1. George Mehnert USA
2. William Press GBR
3. Aubert Côté CAN

Featherweight
1. George Dole USA
2. James Slim GBR
3. William McKie GBR

Lightweight
1. George de Relwyskow GBR
2. William Wood GBR
3. Albert Gingell GBR

Middleweight
1. Stanley Bacon GBR
2. George de Relwyskow GBR
3. Frederick Beck GBR

Heavyweight
1. George Con O'Kelly GBR/IRL
2. Jacob Gundersen NOR
3. Edmond Barrett GBR/IRL

Men Fencing

Epée Individual
1. Gaston Alibert FRA
2. Alexandre Lippmann FRA
3. Eugène Olivier FRA

Epée Team
1. FRA – 2. GBR – 3. BEL

Sabre Individual
1. Jenö Fuchs HUN
2. Béla Zulavsky HUN
3. Vilém Goppold von Lobsdorf BOH

Sabre Team
1. HUN – 2. ITA – 3. BOH

Rowing

Single Sculls
1. Harry Blackstaffe GBR
2. Alexander McCulloch GBR
3. Bernhard von Gaza GER

Coxless pairs
1. Great Britain 9:41.0
2. Great Britain 2.5 lengths

Coxless fours
1. Great Britain 8:34.0
2. Great Britain 1.5 length

Eights
1. GBR – 2. BEL – 3. CAN – 3. GBR

Yachting

6m: 1. GBR – 2. BEL – 3. FRA
7m: 1. GBR
8m: 1. GBR – 2. SWE – 3. GBR
12m: 1. GBR – 2. GBR

Cycling

1000m Sprint (No winner, time limit exceeded)

2000m Tandem
1. France 3:07.6
2. GBR – 3. GBR

4000m Team Pursuit
1. Great Britain 2:18.6
2. Germany 2:28.6
3. Canada 2:29.6

One Lap Race
1. Victor L. Johnson GBR 51.2
2. Emile Demangel FRA (in the wheel)
3. Karl Neumer GER (one wheel)

5000m Track
1. Benjamin Jones GBR 8:36.2
2. Maurice Schilles FRA (in the wheel)
3. André Auffray FRA

20km Track
1. Charles B. Kingsbury GBR 34:13.6
2. Benjamin Jones GBR (in the wheel)
3. Joseph Werbrouck BEL

100km Track
1. Charles H. Bartlett GBR 2:41:48.6
2. Charles H. Denny GBR (in the wheel)
3. Octave Lapize FRA

Shooting

Free Rifle, 3 positions
1. Albert Helgerud NOR 909
2. Harry Simon USA 887
3. Ole Saether NOR 883

Free Rifle Individual
1. Jerry Millner GBR 98
2. Kellogg Kennon Casey USA 93
3. Maurice Blood GBR 92

Free Rifle Team
1. Norway 5055
2. Sweden 4711
3. France 4652

Small-Bore Rifle (prone)
1. A.A. Carnell GBR 387
2. Harry Humby GBR 386
3. Georges Barnes GBR 385

Small-Bore Rifle Individual Moving Target
1. J.F. Fleming GBR 24
1. M.K. Matthews GBR 24
1. W.B. Marsden GBR 24

Disappearing Target
1. William Styles GBR 45
1. H.I. Hawkins GBR 45
1. Edward J. Amoore GBR 45

Miniature Rifle Team
1. Great Britain 771
2. Sweden 737
3. France 710

Pistol-Rapid Fire
1. Paul Van Asbroeck BEL 490
2. Reginald Storms BEL 487
3. James Gorman USA 485

Clay Pigeon Shooting Team
1. Great Britain I 407
2. Canada 405
3. Great Britain II 372

Military Rifle Team
1. USA 2531
2. Great Britain 2497
3. Canada 2439

Running Deer Shooting (Single Shot) Individual
1. Oscar Swahn SWE 25
2. Ted Ranken GBR 24
3. Alexander E. Rogers GBR 24

Running Deer Shooting (Single Shot) Team
1. Sweden 86
2. Great Britain 85

Running Deer Shooting (Double Shot) Individual
1. Walter Winans USA 46
1. Ted Ranken GBR 46
2. Oscar Swahn SWE 38

Military Revolver Team
1. USA – 2. BEL – 3. GBR

Mixed Shooting
1. Walter Henry Ewing CAN 72
2. George Beattie CAN 60
3. Alexander Maunder GBR 57

Men Archery

York Round (100 yards-80 yards-60 yards)
1. William Dod GBR 815
2. R.B. Brooks King GBR 768
3. Henry B. Richardson USA 760

Continental Style (50m)
1. E.G. Grisot FRA 263
2. Louis Vernet FRA 256
3. Gustave Cabaret FRA 255

Women Archery

National Round (60 yards-50 yards)
1. Queenie F. Newall GBR 688
2. Lotti Dod GBR 642
3. A. Hill-Lowe GBR 618

Men Gymnastics

Individual All-around Competition
1. Alberto Braglia ITA 317.0
2. S.W. Tysal GBR 312.0
3. Louis Ségura FRA 297.0

Team All-around Competition
1. SWE – 2. NOR – 3. FIN

Football

1. GBR – 2. DEN – 3. HOL

Field Hockey

1. GBR – 2. IRL – 3. GBR

Tennis

Men's singles
1. Josiah Ritchie GBR
2. Otto Froitzheim GER
3. Wilberforce Vaughan Eaves GBR

Men's singles (indoors)
1. Arthur Gore GBR
2. George Caridia GBR
3. Josiah Ritchie GBR

Men's doubles
1. GBR – 2. GBR/IRL – 3. GBR

Men's doubles (indoors)
1. GBR – 2. GBR – 3. SWE

Women's singles
1. Dorothy Chambers GBR
2. Dorothy Boothby GBR
3. Joan Winch GBR

Women's singles (indoors)
1. Gwendoline Eastlake-Smith GBR
2. Angela Greene GBR
3. Märtha Adlersträhle SWE

Jeu de Paume

1. USA – 2. GBR – 3. GBR

Lacrosse

1. CAN – 2. GBR

Motor boating

Open: 1. FRA 2:26.53
8m: 1. GBR 2:28.26
Under 60': 1. GBR 2:28.58

Polo

1. GBR – 2. GBR – 3. GBR/IRL

Rackets

Men's singles
1. GBR – 2. GBR – 3. GBR

Men's doubles
1. GBR – 2. GBR – 3. GBR

Rugby

1. AUS – 2. GBR

1908

AUGUST

Su	Mo	Tu	We	Th	Fr	Sa
						1
2	3	4	5	6	7	8
9	10	11	12	13	14	15
16	17	18	19	20	21	22
23	24	25	26	27	28	29
30	31					

1. Cuba: The first elections under supervision of the US are held.

2. Canada: 100 die as forest fires sweep parts of British Columbia.

3. UK: "HMS Indomitable" sets new steamship speed record of 26 knots carrying the Prince of Wales to Cowes Week.

6. London: The Admiralty claims new German dreadnoughts will be most heavily armed in the world (→ 11).

12. Austria: King Edward VII meets Emperor Franz Josef II at his country retreat at Bad Ischl (→ 31/10).

13. London: The wife of tenor Enrico Caruso runs away with another man; Caruso says "it was the very thing I desired".

14. London: One person dies when a dirigible airship blows up at the Anglo-French Exhibition.

15. Constantinople: New government issues its proposals for liberal reforms (→ 14/12).

15. London: Winston Churchill announces his engagement to Clementine Hozier (→ 12/9).

19. Brussels: The Belgian Parliament finally votes for the annexation of the Congo from King Leopold II.

21. Berlin: UK Liberal MP David Lloyd George arrives to study Germany's old-age pension system.

23. Morocco: Sultan Abd-el Aziz flees after defeat by Mulai Hafid, who declares himself Sultan (→ 17/9).

31. UK: 20 drown off South Wales when the barque "Amazon" sinks in gales.

BIRTHS

27. US statesman Lyndon Baines Johnson, President 1963-68 (†22/1/73).

31. US author William Saroyan (†18/5/81).

DEATH

25. French physicist Henri Becquerel (*15/12/1852).

"Model T" ready to roll

Aug 12. Ford's first new Model T was produced in Detroit today. It replaces the existing Model A, made for the past five years, and fulfils Henry Ford's promise last year to produce "a motor car for the great multitude".

His aim has been to produce a car cheap enough for anyone on a good salary to buy, but made from the best materials and on "the simplest designs that modern engineering can devise" and employing the latest manufacturing methods.

"Mass production" techniques, based on an "assembly line", will eventually produce over 18,000 cars a year to sell at a retail price of around $900. The new model, which will be produced initially in three colours, has already been nicknamed the "Tin Lizzy".

Ford's production techniques have created the first "mass-produced" car.

Coming years will be without Grace

Grace the Great pads up for play.

Aug 31. The first class cricket season that has just ended will be remembered as the last, in an unbroken sequence that began in 1865, to feature Dr W. G. Grace as a player.

Despite the imminence of his 60th birthday the doctor, whose beard, bulk and sheer artistry have been synonymous with the game for nearly half a century, took the field for the Gentlemen of England against Surrey in the first game of the season on Easter Monday and scored 15 and 25 despite snow on the pitch. That turned out to be his last first class game, although he later scored a century in a minor game at Crystal Palace. In all, he scored 54,211 runs in first-class cricket and took 2,808 wickets.

Monarchs meet in shadow of naval race

Aug 11. King Edward VII of Britain and Kaiser Wilhelm II of Germany met at Friedrichshof Castle, Kronberg, today and talked completely alone without their staffs for three hours. The British government backed the King's desire to meet the Kaiser – his nephew – to ease the growing tension between the two countries.

Ministers are anxious to learn more about the build-up of German forces, especially the navy. This is happening at a time when spending on British forces was cut by £2 million in the last budget. Officials accompanying the King are also expected to raise the forthcoming disarmament conference at The Hague. So far Germany, unlike Britain, has shown no interest in attending the talks.

73 miners trapped

Aug 18. Seventy-three miners were killed today in an underground explosion at a Lancashire pit. Only three miners out of an entire shift of men and boys escaped the blast and the roof collapse which followed.

In the explosion, ventilation gear was destroyed and a rescue team had to wait four hours before entering the Maypole Collieries pit network near Wigan. Once underground they were hampered by lethal gases, flooding and fire. Many victims were severely burned and others were found suffocated, lying where they had fallen next to their dead pit ponies.

Teatime on an outing for old ladies at Loughton, near London.

1908

SEPTEMBER

Su	Mo	Tu	We	Th	Fr	Sa
		1	2	3	4	5
6	7	8	9	10	11	12
13	14	15	16	17	18	19
20	21	22	23	24	25	26
27	28	29	30			

1. Dresden: Opening of an exhibition of paintings by the group "Die Brucke".

3. London: Premiere of James Barrie's play "What Every Woman Knows" at the Duke of York's Theatre.

5. France: Leon Delagrange sets new flight record by staying aloft in his aeroplane for 29 minutes 54 seconds.

7. London: Botany Professor Harold Wager claims plants have eyes and can see.

9. Poland: Russia orders the sacking of teachers who oppose unification of the Russian and Polish school systems.

10. Nottingham: The TUC conference says motor cars should have fixed maximum speeds of 15 mph (→13/11).

11. US: Orville Wright establishes new flight record of 70 minutes aloft.→

12. London: Prime Minister Asquith prevents the display of the Blessed Sacrament during the visit of the Papal Legate.

13. France: Crop failure feared to cut 1908 champagne production to 88,000 gallons, normal for one vineyard.

15. Russia: 3,000 people are reported dead from cholera.

16. Detroit: William Crapo Durant merges his Buick and Oldsmobile firms into a new car company, General Motors.

21. Cologne: In his thesis "Space and Time", Hermann Minkowski defines time as the "Fourth Dimension".

24. UK: "Pensions Day"; old people around the country apply for Old Age Pensions under new Act (→1/1/09).

26. London: 500,000 demonstrate in Hyde Park against the new Licensing Bill.

29. Switzerland: International Conference on Workers' Protection bans night shifts of children under 14.

BIRTHS

9. Italian writer Cesare Pavese (†27/8/50).

30. Russian violinist David Oistrakh (†24/10/1974).

First man dies in US plane crash

Bystanders rush to the aid of Wright and Selfridge, trapped in the wreck.

Sept 17. A United States army officer died today in an aircraft piloted by Orville Wright. Lieutenant Thomas E. Selfridge, 26, of the US Army Signal Corps is the first person to have died in a crash involving an aircraft since the two Wright brothers proved such flight was possible in 1903. Wright was seriously injured in the crash but is expected to recover.

The tragedy occurred as the lieutenant and Mr Wright were flying one of the brothers' biplanes on army trials at Fort Myer, Virginia. The pair climbed onto the aircraft before a crowd of around 2,000 spectators and took off from the centre of the army base at 5.14 pm.

At first all seemed fine as the twin engined aircraft slowly climbed after take off. Then as it turned suddenly a blade on the left propellor broke. This unbalanced the opposite good blade which tore loose the wires holding the rudder outriggers on the wings that controlled the aircraft.

The aircraft fell from a height of 75 feet and the lieutenant suffered a fractured skull and never regained consciousness before he died. Wright had been conducting a series of flight trials in front of senior army officers to demonstrate that the aircraft meets all the requirements set by the War Department. The US Secretary of War, Luke Wright, says the accident will not stop the Army's trials.

Sept 12. Winston Churchill arrives at the church for his wedding to Clementine Hozier.

France and Spain back new Sultan

Sept 17. France and Spain yesterday delivered notes to Britain and other European powers seeking support for their decision to recognise Moulay Hafid as Sultan of Morocco after his overthrow of Abd el-Aziz last June.

The French and Spanish say they have demanded undertakings from Hafid that he will observe all international treaties and financial obligations, disavow the jihad, or holy war, called by tribes, and impose strict security around ports and along main roads. Abd al-Aziz's position had been weakened by repeated tribal uprisings against foreign influence.

1908

OCTOBER

Su	Mo	Tu	We	Th	Fr	Sa
				1	2	3
4	5	6	7	8	9	10
11	12	13	14	15	16	17
18	19	20	21	22	23	24
25	26	27	28	29	30	31

1. Detroit: Model T Ford goes on sale for first time; it is the first motor car with left-hand drive.

1. UK: The penny post to the US starts today; also the start of the US two cents postage to the UK.

2. India: Hundreds reported dead in severe flooding at Hyderabad.

5. Balkans: Austria annexes Bosnia and Herzegovina, with Russian approval.

5. Balkans: Prince Ferdinand of Bulgaria declares his country independent of the Ottoman Empire (→6).

6. Crete: Following Bulgaria's example, Crete declares independence from Turkey and union with Greece (→9).

8. Berlin: Government councillor prophesies massive fleet of 200,000 Zeppelin airships to invade England.

9. Malta: Royal Navy fleet sails for Aegean as Balkans crisis deepens (→10).

10. Balkans: Italy, France and Russia put pressure on Balkan countries to hold a congress to settle the crisis.

10. Balkans: The Serbian Parliament votes against war with Austria (→12).

12. London: Russia persuades the UK to participate in a congress on the Balkan situation (→21).

15. UK: New harbour is opened at Dover, considered vital to UK defences.

17. Paris: Professor Lannelongue announces his development of a new tuberculosis serum.

21. Vienna: The Government bans the export of arms and equipment to Serbia (→15/11).

23. Cairo: Tory MP Sir Eldon Gorst tells the Egyptians they are "unripe" for self-government.

31. London: The Franco-British Exhibition closes.

BIRTH

16. Albanian leader Enver Hoxha (†11/4/85).

Amazement as Kaiser knocks Britain

Oct 31. The furore caused by Kaiser Wilhelm's II interview with the "Daily Telegraph", in which he expressed more than usually indiscreet opinions on foreign affairs, continues to cause much excitement throughout Europe.

The Chancellor, Prince von Bulow, is being heavily criticised in the German press for allowing the interview to be published. It is understood that he passed it to the Foreign Office without reading it.

The interview, discussing as it did Anglo-German relations and the secret talks that took place between Russia, France and Germany on finding a way to end the Boer War and to "humiliate England to the dust", is called "The Catastrophe" in the German press.

While the burden of the interview was the Kaiser's efforts to improve relations with England, it is felt in Germany that it will have the opposite effect. His assertion that the prevailing sentiment among middle and lower-class Germans was anti-British is considered particularly inept and it seems that his remarks have also succeeded in enraging Holland and Japan.

The Kaiser's remarks so astonished the Germans that some newspapers suggested they had been invented.

Cartoon view of the German peril.

Wilbur Wright sets new flight record

Oct 6. Wilbur Wright topped a series of record-breaking flights today by staying aloft more than an hour with a passenger, and won himself a $100,000-patent deal with a French group who have already ordered 50 of his aircraft.

The flight at Le Mans was Wright's second record breaker since August during which time he has been demonstrating in front of the syndicate of French backers.

He set one record on September 21, when he made a flight of one hour, and 32 minutes covering a distance of 61 miles and then another on October 3 when he stayed in the air for 55 minutes with a journalist as passenger.

Pankhurst calls Ministers in her defence

Mrs Emmeline Pankhurst and Christabel in the dock at Bow Street court.

Oct 24. The Suffragette leaders, Emmeline Pankhurst and Christabel, her daughter, were imprisoned today at the end of a sensational trial which saw two cabinet ministers in the witness box for the defence. The two women were found guilty of conduct likely to cause a breach of the peace by inciting the public to 'rush' the House of Commons.

The Chancellor of the Exchequer, David Lloyd George, and the Home Secretary, Henry Gladstone, although originally reluctant witnesses, attested to the orderliness of the night of October 13, as did a succession of others. One woman said she had been more jostled at society weddings. Mr Gladstone, however, resisted Miss Pankhurst's repeated suggestions that they should be treated as political prisoners.

Despite a spell-binding speech from Mrs Pankhurst and tears from both women, the magistrate remained unmoved. Their protests meant 5,000 police were needed to keep order that night. If they would not be bound over they must go to jail.

One woman, Travers Symonds, who did reach the floor of the Chamber that evening said afterwards: "I have made my first speech on the floor of the House of Commons and I hope it will not be the last a woman will make."

Emergency measures to cut jobless total

Oct 21. In reply to a question today Herbert Asquith, the Prime Minister, announced several steps to reduce the number of those out of work from the present unacceptable level. Local authority loans and grants are to be increased to encourage councils to take on the men needed to start work on public utility projects earlier than had been planned and on some that had been deferred.

Amid cheers from both sides of the House, Mr Asquith said that 8,000 temporary workers are to be hired by the Post Office to help cope with the seasonal increase in mail. The War Office is to start recruiting a further 24,000 men into Special Reserve as soon as possible, and 2,100 more dockyard workers are to be employed by the Board of Admiralty to work on repair projects.

The Prime Minister said that he was aware that these were only temporary measures and that he hoped that the real causes of high unemployment will be tackled by this Parliament.

Down but not out: The unemployed on the march for jobs.

1908

NOVEMBER

Su	Mo	Tu	We	Th	Fr	Sa
1	2	3	4	5	6	7
8	9	10	11	12	13	14
15	16	17	18	19	20	21
22	23	24	25	26	27	28
29	30					

2. India: 50 years after the start of direct rule, Edward VII talks of "prudently extending" democracy (→11/12).

5. Amsterdam: The Cullinan Diamond is cut into eight stones, seven for a necklace for Queen Alexandra.

6. Lancashire: Cotton strike ends after seven weeks with workers agreeing to lower wages.

7. London: Professor Ernest Rutherford announces he has detected a single atom of matter (→10/12).

7. Devonport: Launch of "HMS Collingwood", the Navy's biggest battleship.

10. Berlin: Chancellor Bernhard von Bulow retracts part of Kaiser's interview with "Daily Telegraph" (→17).

12. Germany: 360 miners die in a pit explosion at Hamm, Westphalia.

12. Australia: Andrew Fisher becomes Labour Prime Minister.

13. London: Opening of the International Motor Exhibition.

14. Switzerland: Professor Albert Einstein presents his "quantum" theory of light.

15. Balkans: Austria sends troops to the Serbian frontier (→1/12).

17. Berlin: Kaiser Wilhelm endorses retraction of London interview; promises to be more constitutional in future.

19. Germany: Dr. Anschutzkampfe exhibits his "gyroscope", a compass without a magnetic needle.

23. London: Field Marshal Earl Roberts warns the Lords that Germany is capable of invading the UK (→29).

27. London: House of Lords throws out the Licensing Bill.

29. Berlin: In response to Earl Roberts, Chancellor von Bulow says no-one wants to attack the UK.

BIRTH

28. French anthropologist Claude Levi-Strauss.

Taft wins the US presidential race

Republican William Howard Taft, 27th President of the US.

Nov 3. William Howard Taft, the Republican candidate, was today elected as the 27th President of the United States. His margin in the electoral college was handsome: 321 votes to 162. His Democratic opponent, William Jennings Bryan, sustained his worst defeat.

Although President Taft will command safe Republican majorities in both the Senate and the House, certain aspects of the election returns are disturbing for the Republicans. For one thing, their margin in the popular vote fell from more than 2.5 million to 1.3 million, reflecting growing political conflict between the party's regular wing and the Progressives.

Although President Taft, who weighs more than 350 pounds, combines the joviality traditionally attributed to men of his size and girth with the dignity of his profession as a judge, the political atmosphere is unusually tense. Taft was chosen by Roosevelt to succeed him but delegates at the Chicago convention nearly stampeded for a third term for Roosevelt.

Empress of China dies: foul play?

Nov 15. Rumours of foul play surround the death of the Dowager Empress of China, Yehonala, here today. Her long career was marked by ambition and cruelty so there is no shortage of candidates. The fact that her nephew, Emperor Kuang-Hsu, died the previous day is seen as added evidence.

She began her career as one of Emperor Hsien Feng's concubines. When he died in 1861 her young son became Emperor and she rose to Dowager Empress. In 1875 he died and her infant nephew ascended to the throne. She was a staunch conservative who opposed her nephew's modernisation programme and supported the abortive Boxer Rebellion.

Unions banned from funding Labour MPs

Nov 28. The Court of Appeal today ruled that trade unions cannot use their funds for political activities. The decision created consternation within the Labour Party since most of its MPs depend on sponsorship by the trade unions.

The case began in an action by Mr W.V. Osborne, a branch secretary of the Amalgamated Society of Railway Servants. He claimed a political levy to support candidates for parliament was illegal. Mr Osborne initially lost, but the appeal court has backed his view on the grounds that no provision for political activities had been made in the Trade Union Act of 1876. However, the political battle over the case now begins.

1908

DECEMBER

Su	Mo	Tu	We	Th	Fr	Sa
		1	2	3	4	5
6	7	8	9	10	11	12
13	14	15	16	17	18	19
20	21	22	23	24	25	26
27	28	29	30	31		

1. Rome: The Italian Parliament asks Austria to pay compensation for annexing Bosnia-Herzegovina.

2. China: Child Emperor Pu Yi accedes to the throne as Hsuan Tung.

3. London: House of Lords select committee recommends hereditary peers be elected to the upper house.

4. London: Prime Minister announces scrapping of Education Bill.

9. Vienna: Resumption of talks between Austria and Turkey aimed at easing the Balkan crisis.

10. Stockholm: Nobel Prizes awarded to Gabriel Lippmann (France, Physics); Ernest Rutherford (UK, Chemistry); Ilya Mechnikov and Paul Ehrlich (Russia and Germany respectively, Medicine); Rudolf Eucken (Germany, Literature) and Klas Arnoldson and Fredrik Bajer (Sweden and Denmark respectively, Peace).

11. India: New law suspends trial by jury and increases penalties for "sedition" (→17).

14. Constantinople: Opening of the first "reformed" Turkish parliament, with "Young Turks" in majority.

16. St. Petersburg: Premier Komiakov resigns.

24. Paris: World's first international aviation show is opened by President Armand Fallieres.

BIRTHS

10. French composer Olivier Messiaen (†28/4/92).

11. US composer Elliott Carter.

HITS OF 1908

Shine on harvest moon.

Oh Oh Antonio.

QUOTE OF THE YEAR

"America is God's crucible, the great Melting Pot where the races of Europe are melting and reforming." **Israel Zangwill** in his book "The Melting Pot".

Quake reduces Sicilian city to rubble

Dec 28. The festive season has come to an abrupt, horrific end for the wretched citizens of Messina. The horrors of San Francisco and Valparaiso are doubled in Messina, smashed in the most violent and cataclysmic earthquake ever recorded in Europe.

Of the 150,000 inhabitants of Sicily's second largest town perhaps fewer than half are still alive, while thousands more have perished in the surrounding countryside and across the Straits of Messina in Calabria, the toe of Italy.

Reports say the earthquake let loose a massive tidal wave, adding to the chaos, and it is feared that Reggio, across the Straits, may have suffered even greater devastation than Messina.

Thousands left homeless in cataclysmic Sicilian earthquake.

First black wins heavyweight title

World Champion Jack Johnson.

Dec 26. Texan boxer Jack Johnson became the first Negro to hold the world heavyweight champion's title when he defeated Tommy Burns in Sydney, Australia, today. The fight was so severe that police stopped the match in the 14th round after Burns was knocked out for eight seconds, and the referee declared Johnson the winner. Johnson, who has lost only two of his last 63 matches, said he was confident of victory from the start. Burns, the defeated champion who won his title two years ago, admitted "I was in bad shape when the police stopped the fight".

Arts: crowning glory of Sir Edward Elgar

The musical event of the year has been the first symphony of **Sir Edward Elgar**, our foremost composer. Since its premiere in Manchester at the Free Trade Hall, it has proved so popular that it has been performed many times.

But all Elgar's works have the gift of appealing to the widest public, from his "Introduction and Allegro for Strings" of three years ago to his ever-popular "Pomp and Circumstance Marches" of which the fourth appeared last year. It was the first of these marches that caught the ear of the King, who suggested that words should be set to it. They duly were, by **A.C. Benson,** and the result, performed in Coronation year, was virtually a new national anthem, "Land of Hope and Glory". It was in recognition of this, among other works, that he received a knighthood.

The novel many people have been talking about is **Arnold Bennett's** "The Old Wives' Tale", which takes us back to the Five Towns of the Potteries. This tale of two sisters, Constance and Sophia, is his finest to date.

But the book of the year is surely the delightful fantasy from the pen of the Secretary of the Bank of England, **Kenneth Grahame**. Everyone who has fallen under the spell of "The Wind in the Willows" says it will become a classic.

The modern gramophone, bringing music into people's homes.

Rutherford wins a Nobel Prize for his radio-activity work

Dec 10. Professor Ernest Rutherford of Manchester University received the Nobel Prize for Chemistry today for his work on radioactivity and the nature of the atom.

Rutherford's first contribution was to show that the three kinds of radiation involved in radioactivity were: positively charged "alpha" particles, negatively charged "beta" particles, and pure radiation, related to X-rays and light – gamma rays.

In the last two years Rutherford has added to his reputation with a dramatic discovery about the structure of the atom. It emerged from his studies of how alpha particles are scattered by thin gold foil.

Prize-winner Ernest Rutherford.

He found most of the particles passed straight through, but that every now and then one was strongly deflected, sometimes through as much as a right angle. He concluded that atoms were mostly empty space, but with a tiny dense core – the nucleus – containing virtually all the atom's mass and carrying a positive electric charge.

It was the occasional alpha particle that encountered a nucleus that was deflected in the experiments. The rest of the atom is, to all intents and purposes, empty space, though it must have a negative charge to balance the nucleus. Probably this is in the form of the light particles which are known as electrons.

1909

JANUARY

Su	Mo	Tu	We	Th	Fr	Sa
					1	2
3	4	5	6	7	8	9
10	11	12	13	14	15	16
17	18	19	20	21	22	23
24	25	26	27	28	29	30
31						

1. London: Astronomers report they may have sighted another planet beyond Neptune (→ 18/3/30).

3. US: Reported that the motion picture industry employs 100,000 people and is already worth $40m.

5. Colombia: The government recognises the independence of the Republic of Panama.

5. India: Serious riots take place between Hindus and Moslems in Calcutta.

9. Paris: First performance of Maurice Ravel's "Gaspard de la Nuit".

11. France: Four murderers are publicly guillotined at Bethune.

12. US: 105 miners die in a pit explosion at Wheeling, West Virginia.

12. Balkans: Turkey accepts Austrian offer of 2.5 million Turkish pounds for Bosnia and Herzegovina (→ 24/2).

14. London: Winston Churchill calls England "the best country in the world for rich men".

18. New Zealand: Brewers decide to abolish barmaids and mostly ban women from buying alcohol in bars.

21. US: Tennessee state legislature passes a bill prohibiting manufacture of alcohol from 1/1/10 (→ 21/2).

23. London: New direct 7,000-mile telegraphic link with India is hailed as a great achievement.

25. Dresden: First performance is given of Richard Strauss's opera "Elektra".

27. Cuba: The US governor leaves the island as Jose Gomez is sworn in as President of the republic.

BIRTHS

1. US politician Barry Goldwater.

16. US entertainer Ethel Merman, born Ethel Zimmerman (†1984).

22. Burmese statesman Sithu U Thant (†25/11/74).

Messina razed in Europe's worst quake

Jan 15. A massive international rescue operation is under way in southern Italy as the full horror of the Messina earthquake becomes known. At least 200,000 people are now feared to have died in the disaster. Thousands more are homeless, many of them starving, many more desperately ill with pneumonia and other diseases.

The city of Messina has been almost totally destroyed and countless villages not only in Sicily but also on the mainland of southern Italy in Calabria have been razed to the ground. At least 1,500 people are thought to be alive under the wreckage.

Martial law has been declared in Messina and troops are still digging frantically through the debris, calling frequently for silence in attempts to trace survivors.

Ships of six navies are anchored off the coast, taking off hundreds of refugees, while an armada of small boats ferries food and drugs to the disaster zone.

Malta-based British ships are in the forefront of the operation bringing doctors and army nurses. Four American battleships are also steaming at speed from Suez.

Survivors are living in tented villages, many of them still numbed and dazed. Several suicides have been reported. Convicts, freed by the powerful earth tremor, are looting the hundreds of dead who remain unburied.

Rescue workers recovering bodies.

Shackleton closest-ever to South Pole

Jan 9. A British expedition, led by Lieutenant Edward Shackleton, has reached a point closer to the South Pole than any other explorers. After an epic journey through storms and blizzards in which they scaled the 13,120 feet Mount Erebus and charted eight new mountain chains, the party came to a halt less than 111 miles from the elusive target. Another party, led by Professor Edward David, reported reaching the magnetic Pole and planting a Union Jack given to the expedition by the Queen.

It took the main party 126 days to traverse 1,708 miles of icecap, dragging their sledges themselves after some of their ponies were lost in crevasses.

Ernest Shackleton's expedition ship, as seen by Player's Cigarettes.

First pensioners polite on payday

Jan 1. This was an especially happy New Year for thousands of Britons over 70 who went to the Post Office to draw their first weekly pension of five shillings.

The whole process went smoothly and the claimants were nearly all very neat, especially the women; they were also very polite and patient. Many expressed delight that the payments were not like poor relief, but were pensions like those paid by the state to soldiers and sailors only in their cases they were veterans of industry. But one ex-soldier had just received his pension in Bishop's Stortford, Essex, when he dropped down dead.

A Londoner draws his first pension.

Three die chasing Russian bandits

Jan 23. Three people are dead and 17 injured after a dramatic chase of two robbers across five miles of streets and fields from Tottenham to Chingford, north of London.

At 10.15 this morning two armed Russians made off with a payroll in Tottenham, hotly pursued by the police. Ralph Joscelyn, aged ten, was tragically felled by a stray bullet. Soon after, PC Tyler was shot dead. Then one of the robbers killed himself when cornered after a high-speed tram chase along Chingford Road. The second Russian also attempted suicide, but failed, when finally apprehended at a cottage in Hale End.

1909

FEBRUARY

Su	Mo	Tu	We	Th	Fr	Sa
	1	2	3	4	5	6
7	8	9	10	11	12	13
14	15	16	17	18	19	20
21	22	23	24	25	26	27
28						

4. US: The Californian lower house passes a bill segregating immigrant Japanese schoolchildren (→ 8).

5. Vienna: Czech nationalists disrupt proceedings in the Austrian parliament, forcing its adjournment.

8. US: Roosevelt warns California that its anti-Japanese legislation breaches agreements with Japan (→ 10).

8. London: The Government announces that the Navy will get six new dreadnoughts (→ 21/3).

9. London: Court rules that a wife is not entitled to a divorce, even if her husband has deserted her (→ 26/4).

9. Morocco: Franco-German agreement recognises French hegemony in Morocco.

10. US: California's state legislature rejects the anti-Japanese.

17. London: Royal Commission reports that conditions in London produce a "degenerate race, morally and physically enfeebled".

19. Washington: President Roosevelt calls for a world conference on conservation.

20. Paris: Filippo Tommaso Marinetti publishes "The Futurist Manifesto of Poetry" in "Le Figaro".

22. London: Prime Minister Asquith tells the Commons that the Government must act against the Lords' powers (→ 17/9).

24. Brighton: Colour films are screened in public for the first time.

28. Balkans: Russia tries to defuse Austro-Serbian crisis by advising Serbia to drop claims for compensation (→ 2/3).

BIRTHS

3. French philosopher Simone Weil (†24/8/43).

28. British poet Stephen Spender.

DEATH

17. Chiricahua Apache chief Geronimo (*1829).

Poor laws are criticized

A poor family in London's East End with no money for food.

Feb 17. No more children would stay in workhouses, if proposals suggested by a Royal Commission on Britain's poor laws are accepted. Help would also be given for the "unemployed of good character". And, in a lengthy and radical report published today, the commission calls for the boards of guardians to be scrapped and powers to pass to counties and county boroughs.

Although the commission was united in its condemnation of the present system, its 18 members disagreed over the remedies. Four members, including Mrs Beatrice Webb from the Fabian Society and George Lansbury, produced a minority report which outlines a detailed programme including the creation of a Ministry of Labour to help people find work. The minority report also calls for public money to be spent on work such as coastline protection.

The majority report does not go this far, but wants more help for the sick and elderly. Controls on boys working below the age of 15 should also be tightened, it says.

Serbs are urged to reject Austro-Hungarian rule

Feb 24. The age-old national rivalries of the Balkans are threatening to plunge this blood-soaked area into war yet again. The Serbs, who lost control of neighbouring Bosnia and Herzegovina 600 years ago, are now demanding them back from the Austro-Hungarian Empire, which annexed them fully only last year.

The European powers, alarmed at the prospect of another Balkan war which could spread with unforeseeable consequences, are trying to prevent hostilities by suggesting that Serbia renounce its territorial claims in return for an economic treaty with Austria.

The Serbs, imbued with Prime Minister Stojan Novakovic's ideal of a Pan-Slavic nation, refuse to listen and are demanding the independence of all ten million Slavs under Austro-Hungarian rule.

The Austrians are countering by making military preparations and talking of a "war of extermination". The Serbs are also arming and declare they would rather fight and die than yield. But they will look to their fellow Slavs in Russia for help, if the shooting starts.

Saloons shut as US drink ban spreads

Feb 1. The temperance army is on the march in the United States with increasing numbers of states and counties adopting laws which ban the sale of alcohol. The prohibition movement, as it is known, would eventually like a nationwide ban.

At the moment the law varies widely. Some states have outlawed all alcoholic sales while others have adopted local option plans under which counties can act. In New York state, for example, 315 towns have banned saloons. In Ohio, saloons have been closed in 57 out of the state's 66 counties.

But the "wets" are fighting back, claiming that prohibition will result in fraud and drinkers switching to drugs such as cocaine. They also say most people spend no more on drink than on tobacco.

King Edward VII in German military uniform with his nephew, Kaiser Wilhelm II, in front of the Brandenburg Gate. The King, accompanied by Queen Alexandra, arrived in Berlin on February 9 on an official visit. King and Kaiser reaffirmed their friendship and pledged to work for lasting good relations between their countries.

1909

MARCH

Su	Mo	Tu	We	Th	Fr	Sa
	1	2	3	4	5	6
7	8	9	10	11	12	13
14	15	16	17	18	19	20
21	22	23	24	25	26	27
28	29	30	31			

1. London: David Lloyd George tells MPs that the Old Age Pension is more popular than expected (→ 29/4).

2. Balkans: Russia, France, Italy, Germany and the UK urge Serbia to drop claims to Bosnia and Herzegovina (→ 8).

3. US: Aviators Herring, Curtiss and Bishop announce that they will manufacture aeroplanes commercially (→ 19).

5. London: MPs are told that daylight-saving would check people's "physical deterioration".

5. Birkenhead: Dam bursts, drowning 11 workmen.

8. Balkans: New crisis as Austria rejects Russian mediation in its dispute with Serbia (→ 28).

15. Berlin: Start of six-day European bicycle race.

17. France: Postal and telegraph workers strike.

19. London: First international exhibition of aircraft opens; most expensive is £1,440.

20. UK: Mr J Hennessy's Lutteur III wins the Grand National at Aintree.

23. New Zealand: Ernest Shackleton arrives after record polar expedition.

24. Washington: President Taft approves a bill imposing income tax.

25. Russia: Madame Popova is arrested for committing 300 murders.

28. Balkans: Great powers agree a formula for Serbia to renounce claims on Bosnia and Herzegovina (→ 31).

29. London: Motion censuring the Government's naval policy is defeated.

31. Balkans: Crisis is defused as Austria accepts Serbian dropping of compensation claims for Bosnia and Herzegovina (→ 27/4).

DEATH

24. Irish playwright John Synge ("The Playboy of the Western World") (*16/4/1871).

Panic at German dreadnought threat

Caricature of the Kaiser and navy.

How British and German battleships will compare in 1910

BRITAIN

GERMANY

Pre-dreadnoughts

Dreadnoughts

March 21. Controlled panic swept the Commons today at the revelation that Germany may soon overtake Britain in naval might. Just two years ago such a suggestion would have been laughed at.

The First Lord of the Admiralty, Reginald McKenna, told MPs that the Government had underestimated German naval growth. New assessments were that 13 German dreadnoughts may be completed in 1911 alone, on top of those already in service.

Although MPs agreed plans to build new cruisers and heavily armoured destroyers along with six dreadnoughts, the Royal Navy will only have 11 of the ships by 1911.

Tory leader Arthur Balfour described the position as "so dangerous that it is difficult to realise all its import" while in Berlin Admiral Tirpitz denied a British government statement saying that the UK wanted talks to control this naval race (→ 29).

British workers better off than Europeans

March 12. British workers are better off than their French or German counterparts, according to a new survey presented to Parliament. The survey shows that while average wages in France are 75 per cent of British wages, French rents are only fractionally cheaper than British. And Germans can expect to pay up to a quarter more in rent than Britons on only 83 per cent of the earnings. Worse, the French and Germans work longer hours. But British is not always best: French milk, at 1d farthing a pint, is two farthings cheaper.

The fantastic landscape of the Niagara Falls, frozen in action.

Selfridge's brings US style to the UK

G. S. Selfridge: shopping in style.

March 15. All your shopping under one roof – that is the slogan of Selfridge's, the American "store" which opens today in London's Oxford Street. The latest in Transatlantic shopping means no fewer than six acres of departments, with restaurants and lounges, plus a bargain basement.

1909

APRIL

Su	Mo	Tu	We	Th	Fr	Sa
				1	2	3
4	5	6	7	8	9	10
11	12	13	14	15	16	17
18	19	20	21	22	23	24
25	26	27	28	29	30	

3. Rome: Opening of Keats and Shelley memorial.

4. Switzerland: The Canton of Lucerne adopts proportional representation.

5. London: Formation of the Aerial League of the British Empire, to promote British supremacy in the air (→ 3/5).

9. Widnes: The town corporation introduces the first closed-top double-decker buses.

10. Persia: British forces land at Tabriz as fear of famine causes widespread unrest.

14. New York: Singer Enrico Caruso sails for Europe to be operated on for rheumatism of the throat.

14. London: The Anglo-Persian Oil Company is formed to operate the D'Arcy concession in Persia.

18. Rome: Joan of Arc is beatified.

19. Balkans: Turkey recognises independence of Bulgaria (→ 27).

21. Rome: Pope Pius X issues encyclical "Communium rerum", condemning modernism.

22. London: Bill to abolish censorship of plays is introduced in the Commons.

23. Turkey: Moslem fanatics backed by the Sultan have butchered at least 30,000 Armenians in the last week.→

24. London: Manchester United beat Bristol City 1-0 in the FA Cup Final.

26. London: International Women's Suffrage Convention opens, chaired by American Carrie Pratt (→ 29/6).

27. Balkans: The Triple Alliance (Germany, Austria, Italy) recognises Bulgarian independence.

BIRTH

30. Queen Juliana of the Netherlands.

DEATH

10. British poet and literary critic Algernon Charles Swinburne (*5/4/1837).

Lloyd George raises taxes to pay for pensions in the "People's Budget"

Lloyd George: the giant awakes.

April 29. David Lloyd George, Chancellor of the Exchequer, today introduced the most radical budget in the nation's history.

Its purpose is to finance rearmament and the new old age pensions simultaneously through higher taxation. The budget was instantly condemned by the Tory Opposition as attacking the propertied classes on whom the prosperity and stability of the country depend.

A new "supertax" of 6d in the pound will be levied on the 10,000 people with incomes over £5,000 a year. The standard rate of tax on earned income stays at 9d in the pound up to £2,000 and 1 shilling above that level.

Unearned income will be taxed at 1/2d in the pound. Taxes on alcohol, tobacco and petrol rise, death duties double and motor car duties increase.

In introducing what he is calling the "People's Budget", Mr Lloyd George argued that social reform cannot be postponed until rearmament is completed. He described his strategy as "Liberalism, not lunacy" and said that the Government is already considering schemes for state pensions and unemployment insurance.

The Opposition warns that the new death duties may well lead to economies on large estates to the detriment of tradesmen and the working classes. This budget signalled implacable resistance to the Chancellor's proposals in both Houses.

Joy as Young Turks topple old Sultan

April 27. There is much joy in the streets of Constantinople as the Turks celebrate the downfall of their Sultan, Abdul Hamid, who called himself "the shadow of God" but was more popularly known as "the old spider".

The decision to depose him was taken in unanimous votes in both houses of the Parliament he was forced to set up by the Young Turks last year. The statement announcing his replacement by his brother, Mahmud Reshad, accused him of squandering the wealth of the Ottoman Empire, breaking the laws and burning holy law books and committing massacres.

The Sultan's abdication came after heavy fighting when the troops of the Young Turks marched into Constantinople to put down an uprising by Islamic zealots demanding an end to the new secular ideas. Unwisely the Sultan had supported the zealots.

The man who had tyrannised 200 million subjects was arrested in his exotic palace of Yildiz Kiosk. He pleaded abjectly for his life and was taken to the Cheragan palace. "I was born there" he said "there let me die."

Peary triumphs in North Pole bid

Peary: sixth time lucky

April 6. The North Pole was finally conquered today by Commander Robert E. Peary of the United States Navy. The "Roosevelt", his ship, sailed from the United States to Greenland from where the party traversed 90 miles of mountain terrain before making a final 36-day trek to the Pole.

Peary approached this final attempt in military fashion, with members of the party turning back when they had blazed their share of the trail. By the time he reached the Pole, he was accompanied only by his Negro assistant, Matthew Hensen, and four Eskimos. This was Peary's sixth attempt at the Pole since 1902 when he was beaten by frozen seas.

BATHING COSTUMES LENT FREE
"THEY MAY BE A BIT TIGHT MISS BUT I'LL LEND YOU A SHOE-HORN"
AT BLACKPOOL

Britain's holiday resorts are spawning a new breed of humour in the form of saucy seaside postcards, such as this one from Blackpool.

1909

MAY

Su	Mo	Tu	We	Th	Fr	Sa
						1
2	3	4	5	6	7	8
9	10	11	12	13	14	15
16	17	18	19	20	21	22
23	24	25	26	27	28	29
30	31					

2. Turkey: New Sultan Mehmet V promises "liberty, equality and justice" for all his subjects.

3. London: The Aeronautical Society presents the Wright brothers with its gold medal for achievement (→ 19/7).

5. Persia: The Shah accepts the principle of a constitution (→ 26/6).

6. Italy: King Edward VII, Kaiser Wilhelm II and the dowager Czarina of Russia discuss possible alliance.

11. S. Africa: The National Convention in Bloemfontein agrees a draft constitution for a unified South Africa (→ 12/6).

13. Germany: Invention announced of a wireless system that can overcome atmospheric disturbances.

14. Paris: The Chamber of Deputies votes in favour of banning civil servants from going on strike.

18. Paris: Diaghilev's Ballets Russes perform for the first time, starring the dancer Nijinsky.

22. US: White firemen on Georgia Railroad strike in protest at the employment of blacks (→ 28).

23. New York: Police break up a lecture by anarchist Emma Goldman.

25. Russia: Court jails publisher of Tolstoy's "Thou Shalt Not Kill", but refuses to prosecute Tolstoy himself.

25. London: The Indian Councils Act is passed giving more power to local Indian legislative councils.

28. US: Mob attacks black crew of a Georgia Railroad mail train as strike by white firemen continues.

BIRTHS

15. British actor James Mason (†27/7/84).

30. US jazz clarinettist Benny Goodman (†13/6/86).

DEATH

18. British writer George Meredith (*12/2/1828).

Fierce Tory attack on People's Budget

May 21. The line-by-line Tory onslaught on the so-called People's Budget began today. The former Prime Minister Arthur Balfour told the House of Commons that the Government is being pushed by David Lloyd George into equating robbery with democracy.

Mr Lloyd George retorted that the Government is spreading taxes fairly. "The rich are more powerful than ever," he added scornfully.

As for the Budget raising more from motor car tax, he promised this money will be used for coping with bumps, holes and big stones on the roads. Village by-pass routes may in the future also be provided so that children can play more safely on the roadsides. He hoped that the Opposition would agree with his wish to reduce the accident total caused by motor vehicles.

Record flight ends up a pear tree

May 31. A record-breaking flight by a Zeppelin airship ended in near disaster today when it crashed into a pear tree on the side of a mountain as it came in to refuel. Count Zeppelin had been flying for a record 37 hours when he tried to bring it in to land near Stuttgart. The tree tore a 28 foot hole in the craft, preventing him reaching Berlin and a reception with the Kaiser.

May 26. The King watches his horse Minoru win the Derby.

1909

JUNE

Su	Mo	Tu	We	Th	Fr	Sa
		1	2	3	4	5
6	7	8	9	10	11	12
13	14	15	16	17	18	19
20	21	22	23	24	25	26
27	28	29	30			

1. US: Opening of the World's Fair in Seattle.

2. Paris: The Ballets Russes give the first performance of the ballet "Les Sylphides" based on music by Chopin.

4. Morocco: The Sultan forbids the Jews of Fez from seeing his new palace; offenders will be shot.

7. London: Chamberlain and Lloyd George clash in a fierce Commons budget debate (→ 21/8).

7. Paris: The French government announces it will spend £120 million on new ships (→ 21/7).

11. France: 60 people die in an earthquake that destroys five villages in Provence.

12. S. Africa: Natal votes overwhelmingly in favour of South African union (→ 27/7).

13. Dover: Lt. Shackleton arrives back in England after his Antarctic expedition.

17. Finland: Kaiser Wilhelm meets the Czar at Pitpikas.

19. US: Industrialist and philanthropist Andrew Carnegie proposes a world disarmament conference in England.

22. London: First UK performance of Ethel Smyth's opera "The Wreckers" at His Majesty's Theatre.

23. Cambridge: Opening of the Darwin Museum to commemorate the centenary of Darwin's birth.

26. Persia: The Shah annuls new law providing for elections and postpones promised constitution indefinitely (→ 16/7).

26. London: King Edward VII opens the Victoria and Albert Museum in South Kensington.

29. London: 120 suffragettes are arrested outside Parliament and 10 Downing Street (→ 28/9).

BIRTHS

6. British philosopher Sir Isaiah Berlin.

28. British writer Eric Ambler.

No to workhouses for sick children

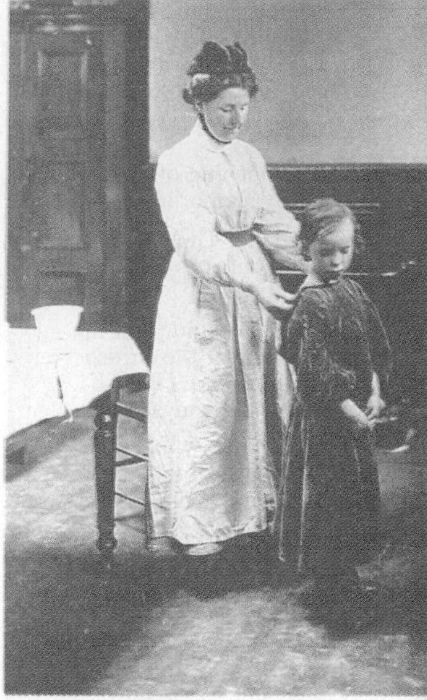

Free check ups for children.

June 17. During a debate in the House today on the Local Government Board it was agreed by both sides that workhouses were not fit places for children. While agreeing, the President of the Board, Mr Burns, pointed out that Britain spent more than any country in the world on children in care (between 8s 6d and 25s 2d a week each).

Even so, they had already sent 1,000 of the 2,500 sick children in workhouses to an institution "on the healthy, breezy Downs of Surrey". To cheers, he added that he would not rest content until all sick children had been transferred.

We never speak
as we pass by.

1909

JULY

Su	Mo	Tu	We	Th	Fr	Sa
				1	2	3
4	5	6	7	8	9	10
11	12	13	14	15	16	17
18	19	20	21	22	23	24
25	26	27	28	29	30	31

1. London: Prominent Anglo-Indian Sir Curzon Wyllie is murdered by an Indian at the Imperial Institute.

5. Wimbledon: Arthur Gore, at 41 the oldest ever men's champion, beats Major Ritchie in the Men's Singles Final; Penelope Boothby beats Agnes Morton for the Ladies' title.

7. China: US protests against the Sino-Russian treaty, saying it will give Russia too much power.

8. London: King Edward VII says that the nation's prosperity depends on scientific training.

9. London: Public performance of George Bernard Shaw's censored play "Press Cuttings" (→ 20/8).

11. Berlin: Bill raising £25 million in extra taxes is passed; Chancellor von Bulow is expected to resign.→

13. Persia: Nationalist forces opposed to the Shah capture Teheran.→

15. Paris: Dr Alexis Carrel demonstrates the organ transplants he has carried out on animals.

18. Greece: 116 people are killed in an earthquake.

19. French aviator Hubert Latham fails in the first attempt to fly the Channel.→

23. London: Two banks merge to form the London, Country & Westminster Bank.

24. Paris: Aristide Briand takes over as premier.

27. London: MPs give second reading to South African Union Bill, but criticise denial of vote to blacks (→ 16/8).

30. France: Czar Nicholas II arrives on an official visit en route to England (→ 2/8).

31. Germany: Count von Zeppelin makes a 220-mile flight at 21 mph in his latest airship.

BIRTHS

18. Soviet statesman Andrei Gromyko (†2/7/89).

28. British writer Malcolm Lowry (†27/6/57).

Bleriot flies 43 minutes into history

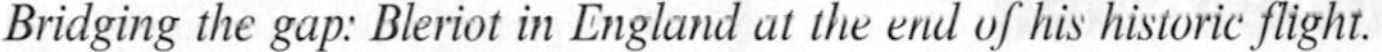

Bridging the gap: Bleriot in England at the end of his historic flight.

Mme Bleriot greets her husband.

July 25. Frenchman Louis Bleriot became aviation's latest hero today when he flew across the Channel. He landed at Dover Castle 43 minutes after taking off from Sangatte, near Calais, to win the £1,000 prize offered by the "Daily Mail".

Bleriot, 36, flew a monoplane driven by a three cylinder engine, attached to a two bladed propeller. His intention was to set off immediately he arrived at the coast five days ago but weather conditions delayed him until today when he took off at 5.00 am. The only mishap was when he suffered a slight injury on landing.

The French government laid on a destroyer in mid-Channel in case of mishap but Bleriot soon left it behind. He was lost for a while in cloud and almost came down near Deal. Then he felt a severe buffeting from the wind as he approached the White Cliffs, but a French journalist was on hand to guide him down to a suitable landing spot by waving the French tricolour flag. His flight took 43 minutes at an average speed of 40 miles an hour over a distance of 31 miles.

Bleriot carried neither compass nor watch for the flight, which other expert aviators had warned against making today because of the windy conditions. He believes that had he flown in a biplane it would not have withstood the sort of buffeting he eventually received.

"I saw an opening and I found myself over dry land," he said, describing the flight. "I attempted a landing, but the wind caught me and whirled me round two or three times. At once I stopped my motor and instantly my machine fell straight on the ground."

The tricolour greets Bleriot: how a French artist saw the triumph.

The Channel flight has been the goal this summer of three of Europe's top aviators, Bleriot, the Count de Lambert and Hubert Latham.

Bleriot's wife watched the flight from the destroyer. Now he has promised to stop (→ 22/8).

Top-level changes in Paris and Berlin as von Bulow and Clemenceau step down

July 21. The French cabinet, led by Georges Clemenceau, resigned today after being defeated in the Chamber of Deputies by 36 votes. The fall of the government, which lasted longer than any under the Third Republic except one, was the result of a dramatic debate on the condition of the French navy. The deputies were swayed by a violent exchange between Clemenceau and Theophile Delcasse.

The fall of the government in Paris follows that of the German government five days ago, when Kaiser Wilhelm II replaced Prince Bernhard von Bulow as Chancellor with Theobald von Bethmann Hollweg. By coincidence, von Bulow was largely responsible for Delcasse's fall during the Moroccan crisis of 1905; on the day Delcasse fell the Kaiser created von Bulow a prince. But Wilhelm lost confidence in his Chancellor when he failed to protect his sovereign from embarrassment over a "Daily Telegraph" interview last October. When von Bulow was defeated in the Reichstag by a coalition of industrialists and junkers, Kaiser Wilhelm replaced him with Bethmann Hollweg, a friend from their student days in Bonn.

Prince, aged 12, replaces ousted Shah

July 16. The 12-year old Crown Prince of Persia, Sultan Ahmed Mirza, was yesterday proclaimed Shah to enthusiastic cheers from crowds in Majlis Square. The move followed four days of widespread fighting in the streets of Tehran.

The boy Shah, with Azad-ul-Mulk as Regent, will rule in place of his elder brother, Mohammad, who was deposed after a turbulent two years by a revolution of the Nationalist Party which resented his despotic behaviour. The former Shah sought protection in the Russian Legation following the surrender of his Persian Cossack forces.

Sultan Ahmed Mirza.

They're off! The contestants get under way at the start of the relay race that took place on July 31 this year at Brooklands motor racing circuit.

1909

AUGUST

Su	Mo	Tu	We	Th	Fr	Sa
1	2	3	4	5	6	7
8	9	10	11	12	13	14
15	16	17	18	19	20	21
22	23	24	25	26	27	28
29	30	31				

1. Spain: An anti-government revolt in Catalonia leaves as many as 1,000 dead.

2. UK: Many workers stage demonstrations in protest at the official visit of the Russian Czar.→

5. London: Thousands of slum children leave for a fortnight's free holiday in the country, organised by charity.

8. Turkey: The four protecting powers in Crete meet in Therapia to plan a settlement of the island's problems (→17).

11. Nigeria: 12 British colonial policemen are killed by poisoned arrows in an attack by natives.

15. London: Reported that wife desertions are up annually by a third; higher prices blamed.

16. London: Tory leader Arthur Balfour tells MPs that giving equal rights to South Africa's blacks would threaten white civilisation (→20/9).

17. Turkey: International fleet arrives off Crete.

19. Hungary: Decree imposes Hungarian as the official language of religious instruction in Rumanian schools.

21. UK: Arthur Henderson says the Labour movement is eager to do battle with the Lords (→4/9).

22. France: First international air race meeting opens at Rheims, with most big names, except the Wrights (→28).

22. US: Five die in riots of striking steelworkers.

25. Dublin: Bernard Shaw's play "The Sewing Up of Blanco Posnet" is performed despite censor's ban.

25. US: Publication by the Simplified Spelling Board of "Nu Spellin" dictionary of 3,261 words needing reform.

28. Rheims: American Glenn Curtiss wins first Gordon Bennett Cup for flying 12.42 miles in 15 minutes 50.6 secs.

30. Mexico: 1,400 are feared to have died after nearly a week of floods in the city of Monterrey.

Top dramatists join blue pencil battle

Hardy: no to censorship.

Aug 20. The Lord Chamberlain's powers to censor stage plays are being challenged before a select committee of both Houses of Parliament. The public is crowding in to hear famous authors declaim against the system. Bernard Shaw, three of whose plays have been banned, declared: "The censor has my livelihood and good name absolutely at his disposal, without any law to administer – a control past the last pitch of despotism."

Henry James, Thomas Hardy, Joseph Conrad, H.G. Wells, Arnold Bennett and John Galsworthy all argued that censorship deters men of letters from writing for the English stage (→25).

Girls prefer curls, they say.

Whisky report spots real McCoy

Aug 9. The report of the Royal Commission on Whisky and other Potable Spirits published today says that the authorities can do little to stop licensed victuallers selling inferior whisky by the glass and charging for a quality blend. Labels afford no protection. The remedy lies with the customer. If he does not like what he buys in one place, he must go elsewhere.

But it is recommended that only spirits distilled in Scotland from a mash containing at least 30 per cent malt can legally be called "Scotch Whisky".

"FIRST OVER THE BARS"
TAKE IT NEAT
HUNTER RYE
THE GENTLEMAN'S WHISKY.

Keep up the spirits with scotch.

Czar greeted with pomp and pageant

Aug 2. King Edward VII gave his nephew-in-law Czar Nicholas II a spectacular welcome at Spithead today, honouring him with a formal review of the Royal Navy. In brilliant sunshine the Czar inspected the world's mightiest armada of battleships and dreadnoughts.

Thousands watched the two royal yachts steam slowly between the warships as saluting cannons boomed, bands played the two countries' anthems and seamen cheered. The mind recalled descriptions of another famous review when Peter the Great visited Portsmouth in 1698.

1909

SEPTEMBER

Su	Mo	Tu	We	Th	Fr	Sa
			1	2	3	4
5	6	7	8	9	10	11
12	13	14	15	16	17	18
19	20	21	22	23	24	25
26	27	28	29	30		

4. Leicester: Winston Churchill warns of a fight to the finish with Lords if they veto the budget (→ 10).

4. London: First Boy Scout parade takes place, at Crystal Palace.

7. London: Lord Northcliffe, owner of "The Times", claims Germany is rapidly preparing for war with UK.

9. Boston: Professor Lovell claims there is oxygen on Mars.

10. London: Liberal ex-PM Lord Rosebery resigns presidency of Liberal League over "People's Budget".→

13. Geneva: Congress of Egyptian Youth demands the British withdrawal from Egypt.

16. Spain: Spanish newspaper editors call on the king to lift the press censorship and guarantee the constitution (→ 10/10).

20. London: Parliament approves South African constitution, making English and Dutch official languages (→ 20/11).

21. London: Catholic Truth Conference labels socialism a "subtle and powerful evil".

24. New York: Peary claims he found remains of tropical animals in polar zone.→

25. London: Captain Robert Scott acquires the "Terra Nova" for South Pole expedition (→ 13/12).

26. Spain: Government announces the defeat of the Moors in Morocco.

30. London: The first performance of W. Somerset Maugham's comedy "Smith", at the Comedy Theatre.

BIRTHS

7. US film director Elia Kazan.

18. Ghanaian statesman Kwame Nkrumah, first president 1960-1966 (†27/4/72).

DEATH

9. US industrialist Edward H. Harriman (*25/2/1848).

Explorers clash over North Pole claims

Sept 30. Was Brooklyn doctor Frederick A. Cook the first man to reach the North Pole? Or did he falsify information to win international acclaim? Cook and the explorer Commander Robert E. Peary are the central figures in a major controversy which is intriguing their fellow Americans.

Peary arrived in Labrador earlier this month to announce that he had reached the Pole on April 21, 1909 - to be told that Cook claimed that he had raised the Stars and Stripes at the Pole on April 21, 1908.

Cook accompanied Peary on one of his previous five expeditions to the Pole. His attempt was a "low key" affair which started as a hunting expedition.

Peary has dismissed Cook's claim and says that he interviewed two Eskimos in the doctor's party who said that Cook turned back a long way from the Pole. Significantly, it has been Peary whom the Royal Geographical Association has invited to address them, rather than Cook (→ 28/11).

Cartoon view of Polar row.

"People's Budget" faces Lords' veto

Sept 17. Rejection by the House of Lords of the "People's Budget" could put the country on the road to revolution, so Herbert Asquith, the Prime Minister, said tonight. This follows indications that a majority of peers will oppose the government's proposals as socialistic. He said: "We are eager to take up this challenge" and hinted at abolition of the Lords (→ 9/10).

Suffragettes are being "force fed"

Sept 28. It was confirmed in the House of Commons today that several of the nine suffragettes in prison in Birmingham have been force fed. The announcement came in response to a question by Labour MP James Keir Hardie, who was told the Home Office authorised the action to prevent the women killing or harming themselves through self-starvation (→ 12/10).

Australian swimmer Annette Kellerman and a friend are arrested in Boston for indecent exposure for wearing men's bathing costumes.

1909

OCTOBER

Su	Mo	Tu	We	Th	Fr	Sa
					1	2
3	4	5	6	7	8	9
10	11	12	13	14	15	16
17	18	19	20	21	22	23
24	25	26	27	28	29	30
31						

2. Berlin: Orville Wright flies at a record 1,600ft (→6).

2. China: First railway built entirely by Chinese opens, from Peking to Kalgan.

6. Switzerland: US aeronaut E.W. Mix wins Gordon Bennett International Balloon Race (→19).

9. Newcastle-upon-Tyne: Lloyd George calls peers "500 men chosen accidentally from the unemployed" (→24/11).

9. New York: Newspaper owner William Randolph Hearst announces he will run for mayor.

10. Spain: Execution of anarchist leader Professor Francisco Ferrer triggers a wave of protest all over Europe.→

15. Finland: Russia exempts Finns from military service, but orders them to pay army costs of £4 million.

16. US: President Taft meets Mexican President Porfirio Diaz at El Paso, Texas.

19. Paris: 20,000 people watch the Comte de Lambert fly over the Eiffel Tower (→4/1/10).

22. Mansfield: Army intervention with 8,000 strikers.

23. The Hague: International Court of Arbitration decides Swedish and Norwegian territorial waters.

26. Austria: Tax on bachelors proposed as nation struggles with deficit caused by annexation of Bosnia and Herzegovina.

28. Brussels: Government announces major liberalising reforms in the Congo.

31. UK: 26 miners have died in South Wales pit explosion two days ago.

BIRTHS

19. Pakistani politician Mohammed Ali (†23/1/63).

28. British painter Francis Bacon (†28/4/92).

DEATH

26. Japanese statesman Prince Hirobumi Ito (*16/10/1841).→

Courts order force feeding inquiry

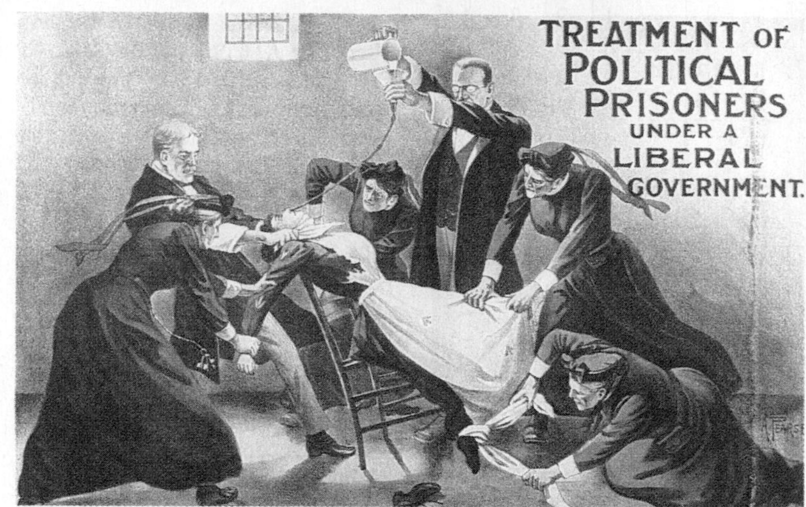

The policy of force feeding hunger strikers has caused much outrage.

Oct 12. A full inquiry is to be held into the treatment of a suffragette in Winson Green prison after allegations that she was repeatedly force fed.

The order came today from the High Court at the end of an action brought by Laura Ainsworth, who was given 14 days for obstructing the police during the Prime Minister's visit to Birmingham last month. In jail she adopted the now widespread suffragist tactic of going on hunger strike.

In her affidavit Mrs Ainsworth, who is now recovering in a nursing home, said that the attempt to feed her by force came after she had been three days without eating. She had been held down by wardresses and the prison doctor had tried first to push a feeding cup through her teeth and when that failed had attempted to insert a tube up her nostrils. Her nasal passages were blocked, however, by an injury.

She says: "I was raised into a sitting position and a tube about two feet long was produced. My mouth was prised open with what felt like a steel instrument. I felt a choking sensation and a cork gag was placed between my teeth to keep my mouth open. It was a horrible feeling altogether."

Medical evidence to the court claimed the treatment had caused an inflamed throat and nervous prostration. The procedure carried a very grave risk (→9/11).

"Bismarck of Japan" assassinated

Ito, the Japanese Bismarck.

Oct 26. Japan has lost its senior statesman, Prince Ito, to an assassin's bullet. The Prince, who once came to Britain to study weapons, was shot by a Korean nationalist at Harbin in Manchuria. He was 68.

Some have seen him as Japan's Jefferson and Bismarck rolled into one: the former because of his leading role in framing the constitution and the latter because of his success in building Japan into a world power.

Just before his death he had been the Governor-General of Korea. Japanese rule is not popular there and it is fairly certain that the shooting was an act of revenge for his harsh repression of Korean insurgents.

Anarchist's death sparks Paris riots

Oct 14. Fighting went on for several hours near the Spanish embassy in Paris last night as police with drawn swords fought off a mob trying to storm the Spanish embassy. The rioters, many of them anarchists, were protesting at the execution in Barcelona of Professor Francisco Ferrer on charges of taking part in an uprising against the Spanish government, even though he was in London during the violence.

One French policeman was killed and M. Lepine, the prefect of police, was grazed by a bullet during the violence. Eyewitnesses speak of motor buses being set on fire, revolver shots ranging out in the darkness and a charge by the Republican Guards as the mob, allegedly swollen by gangs of criminals, advanced up the Boulevard de Courcelles, shouting "death to the assassins".

The battle swayed to and fro in streets lit by gas escaping from the broken lamp standards until rioters gave way leaving behind streets littered with debris (→8/11).

"The World's Sweetheart", Mary Pickford, who starred this year in "Her First Biscuits".

1909

NOVEMBER

Su	Mo	Tu	We	Th	Fr	Sa
	1	2	3	4	5	6
7	8	9	10	11	12	13
14	15	16	17	18	19	20
21	22	23	24	25	26	27
28	29	30				

1. Paris: The Chamber of Deputies asks for a colonial army of 100,000 blacks in case of a European war.

2. London: Labour suffers setbacks in municipal elections.

8. Spain: Constitutional rights restored and state of emergency lifted.

9. London: Suffragettes throw stones at the Guildhall during the Lord Mayor's banquet.

12. US: Mob lynches a black and a white man in Cairo, Illinois.

13. India: Two bombs thrown at Viceroy in an assassination attempt.

14 Brussels: European powers meet to discuss regulation of arms market in Africa.

19. St. Petersburg: Court is adjourned when public prosecutor refuses to work with Russia's first woman barrister.

20. London: Herbert Gladstone agrees to be first Governor-General of Union of South Africa (→7/12).

24. London: Bishops announce they will abstain in Lords budget vote.→

27. London: Thomas Lewis of University College Hospital describes auricular fibrillation of the heart.

28. New York: Sergey Rachmaninov gives world premiere of his third piano concerto under Walter Damrosch.

28. Paris: The Assembly passes a law to allow pregnant women eight weeks' leave from work.

28. New York: Robert Peary's rival North Pole claimant, Frederick Cook, disappears mysteriously (→21/12).

29. Russia: Maxim Gorky is expelled from Revolutionary Party for his "bourgeois" high living on Capri.

BIRTH

14. US politician Joseph McCarthy (†5/2/57).

People's Budget thrown out by Lords

Nov 30. The House of Lords tonight rejected the "People's Budget" after seven months of splenetic party struggle. At the end of a six-day debate the peers voted overwhelmingly to refuse endorsement of Mr Lloyd George's tax package "until it has been submitted to the judgment of the country".

So the Liberal Government's challenge to the Lords has been accepted and there will now be a general election in the New Year. Before the peers voted there was a threat in the closing speech from Lord Chancellor, Lord Loreburn. He said: "Clearly it is to be war to the death. If the Government fails, it will be only the beginning of the struggle. If it succeeds, it will not flinch from its duty."

In saying that, he reflected the views of his Prime Minister, Herbert Asquith. The Liberals are now bracing themselves for the constitutional crisis which is inevitable in the process of trying to destroy the power of the nonelected upper House of Parliament. Mr Asquith accepts that this must embarrass the King.

There have been glittering attendances throughout their Lordships' debate, which appears to have been watched by the eyes of the world. Peeresses packed the galleries and room was also found for the ambassadors of the major powers. A place was kept for the King of Portugal who listened attentively in the closing stages.

The Battle of the Budget: Chancellor Lloyd George addresses the House.

Sally Army salvages "human wrecks"

Police and Sally Army members with a man who fainted in the soup queue.

Nov 23. Londoners are becoming increasingly aware of the problem of homeless and unemployed down-and-outs who congregate on the Embankment, making it such an unpleasant place. The men and women who crowd the area at night are attracted there because they know it offers their one chance of food and shelter. The Salvation Army said today it feeds as many as 640 vagrants every night and also provides some shelter during the early hours of the morning.

Police at Scotland Yard which is only a few yards from the squalor could disband the queues but, not unmoved by the pitiful scenes on their doorstep, their attitude is one of kindly tolerance.

Navy base planned for Pearl Harbor

Nov 14. President William Taft has settled a row between his Army and Navy over the best site for a new naval base to defend the US from a Japanese attack.

Taft has decided in favour of a naval station at Pearl Harbour in the Hawaiian Islands. This should please the Army, who argued that the Navy's preferred spot for a base, Subic Bay in the Philippines, was indefensible. The President followed the Army's wish for a site closer to home because of the greater ease with which the fleet could intercept Japanese ships heading for the US West Coast. Equally importantly, the decision reflects Taft's concern to protect the Panama Canal.

People's capitalism takes off in US

Nov 7. America now has more than two million shareholders, making its economy more dependent than ever before upon the health of Wall Street where at least $40 billion, a third of the nation's wealth, is now invested.

Playing the stock market has become a favourite pastime for all social classes, from bell-boys to businessmen, and many have been made rich by the large rises in share values. Railway dividends, for example, have trebled during the last ten years, while about $1 billion is now paid out annually in stock dividends and only slightly less in bond earnings.

This growth in popular capitalism has provided many corporations with a ready source of much needed finance to help fund their expansion and this has helped trigger the industrial boom of the last decade. But the rapid rise in the number of small shareholders the John D. Rockefeller Corporation, for instance, now has 5,000 partners – has created an administrative headache for the company officials responsible for sending out the annual dividends.

At the Carnegie Steel Corporation, which now has 100,000 shareholders compared with just 63 a decade ago, it is estimated that all the dividend cheques sent out to shareholders every year would stretch for 50 miles if they were placed end to end.

No trace of verdict in miracle libel trial

Nov 23. The Munich Law Courts today refused to deliver a verdict as to whether the cures effected at the shrine of Our Lady of Lourdes are the work of God or natural causes.

The case arose from a libel action brought by one, Dr Aigner, who believes that any Lourdes cures are of nervous not physical illnesses. He sued a Catholic paper which had roundly attacked him. Experts supported both sides so the Court declared a draw. But the Catholic editor was fined £15 for using strong language.

Is a footballer legally a worker?

Nov 23. Crystal Palace football club today appealed against an award for compensation for match injuries given to a player called Walker, under the Workman's Compensation Act. Their grounds were that he wasn't engaged in work but was just playing a game.

Walker's lawyer, however, said that his client had surrendered to the club the bodily labour of his arms and legs and that he was a servant in that he had to obey the club's orders. The appeal was dismissed.

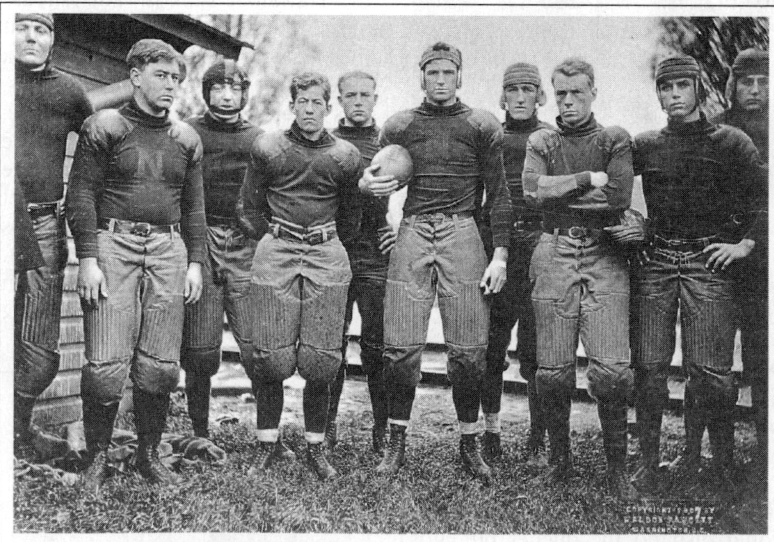

An American football team in a typical line up. Questions have been raised recently about whether the game is too rough and potentially dangerous.

1909

DECEMBER

Su	Mo	Tu	We	Th	Fr	Sa
			1	2	3	4
5	6	7	8	9	10	11
12	13	14	15	16	17	18
19	20	21	22	23	24	25
26	27	28	29	30	31	

1. London: The Cabinet calls Lords' opposition to the Budget unconstitutional (→ 3).

1. US: Mob burns a black preacher in Cochran, Georgia.

3. London: Lloyd George calls peers "broken bottles stuck on a park wall to keep off poachers".

3. London: King Edward VII dissolves Parliament; taxes on beer, spirits, tobacco and cars lifted because no Budget has been passed (→ 10).

4. Nicaragua: President Jose Zelaya invites US, which backs revolutionaries, to see conditions in the country (→ 16).

10. London: Asquith puts Irish home rule and abolition of Lords' veto at centre of election campaign (→ 1/1/10).

11. Africa: 2147-mile section of the Cape-to-Cairo Railway is completed by a link up at the Sudan-Congo border.

13. South Polar explorer Ernest Shackleton is knighted (→ 6/1/10).

16. Nicaragua: President Jose Zelaya resigns under pressure from US Marines (→ 21).

20. London: Eight die in a fire at Arding and Hobbs department store, Clapham Junction.

21. Nicaragua: Dr Jose Madriz is elected to succeed the ousted President Zelaya.

22. Greece: The army and parliament struggle for power.

29. Constantinople: The Grand Vizier resigns.

DEATH

17. Belgian King Leopold II (*9/4/1835).

HITS OF 1909

Moonstruck.

I wonder who's kissing her now.

Has anybody here seen Kelly?

QUOTE OF THE YEAR

"Any colour you like, as long as it's black."
Henry Ford,
advertising slogan for the new Ford Model T.

Peary's North Pole triumph confirmed

Dec 21. Dr Frederick Cook, the New York doctor and explorer, was publicly disgraced today when experts rejected his claim to be the first man to reach the North Pole. The honour goes to Commander Robert E. Peary who succeeded on his sixth attempt.

While Peary was presented last week with a gold medal by the National Geographic Society, Cook was further humiliated when his claim to be the first man to climb Mount McKinley – the highest mountain in the USA – was also proved false by one of the mountain guides.

Cook's colourful descriptions of his alleged journey to the Pole have raised knowledgeable eyebrows throughout the world of exploration. Among his supplies were said to be "two barrels of wine gums because the Eskimo has a very sweet tooth".

His Eskimo companions were his downfall, however, when they testified that Cook did not come within 20 miles of the Pole.

A committee appointed by the University of Copenhagen found that documents provided by Cook "do not contain certain observations and information which can be regarded as proof that Dr Cook reached the North Pole". Some committee members hinted that Cook may have forged some of his evidence.

Frederick Cook: experts reject his claims of Polar victory.

Arts: Russian ballet transforms dance

This year's Ballets Russes programme, and one of Bakst's costume designs.

Ballet has been revolutionised by the season of the Ballets Russes presented in Paris by **Serge Diaghilev**. The technical brilliance of the Russian dancers, led by **Vaslav Nijinsky** and **Anna Pavlova**, has electrified audiences with the Polovtsian Dances from "Prince Igor", and "Les Sylphides".

The choreography by **Michel Fokine** goes far beyond the vocabulary of classical steps and stresses the male dancer's role. Nijinsky defies gravity in his airborne leaps. Critics describe him as "the power of youth, drunk with rhythm, terrifying in his muscular energy".

Just as sensational as the dancing are the decor and costume designs of **Leon Bakst** and **Alexandre Benois**, which have amazed the world of fashion by their boldness and brilliant, exotic colours.

Death has removed two last great Victorians of literature, the poet **Swinburne** and the novelist **George Meredith**. In place of their world, **H.G.Wells** has called up a critical panorama of present English society in "Tono-Bungay", where a fortune is made out of a worthless patent medicine of that name. In "Ann Veronica" he has drawn an emancipated modern woman, a suffragist, quite prepared to live with a man she cannot marry. Mr Wells calls this "a modern love story" and it will shock not a few readers.

A very much more charming tale of girlhood is told by **Miss L.M. Montgomery** in "Anne of Green Gables", whose heroine is an orphan brought up in Avonlea, Canada, by an elderly brother and sister. It is a simple tale of homely things in a tranquil village but Anne charms all who read of her.

In South Kensington the King opened the **Victoria and Albert Museum**.

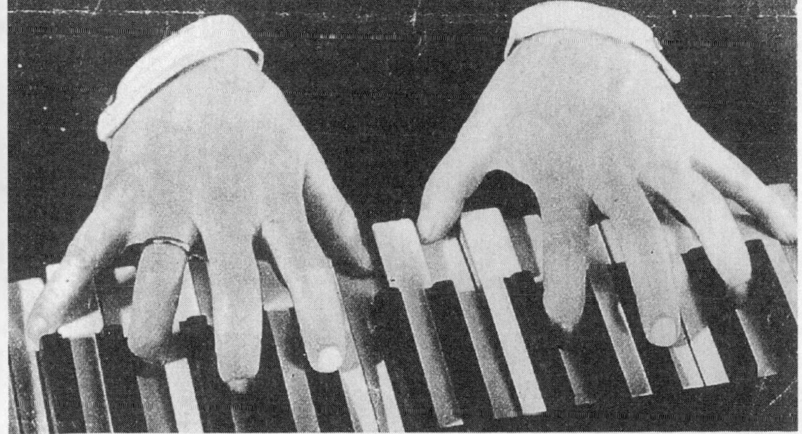

The hands of Rachmaninov who premiered his third concerto in New York.

Marconi wins Nobel Prize for wireless

Dec 31. A novel and promising new material made its appearance this year: Bakelite. Its inventor, the Belgian chemist Leo Baekeland, was actually looking for a substitute for shellac when he happened to produce a sticky resinous mass by reacting together phenol and formaldehyde.

It was no shellac substitute, but Baekeland found that under the right conditions of temperature and pressure it would flow into a mould like a liquid and then set to a hard material which did not soften with heat. Bakelite is light, reasonably strong, does not corrode, and is a good electrical insulator. It seems probable that a number of uses will be found for it.

Among this year's Nobel Prize winners were Guglielmo Marconi of Italy and K. F. Braun of Germany (Physics) for their contributions to wireless and F. W. Ostwald of Russia (Chemistry) for his work on the theory of catalysis, which has important implications for the future of the chemical industry.

Ban on union funds for MPs confirmed

Dec 12. The House of Lords today unanimously upheld the appeal court's decision last year that it was illegal to use trade union funds for political purposes, such as sponsoring Labour MPs. The judgment, in what has become known as the Osborne case, will renew efforts by the Labour Party and the Trades Union Congress to persuade the Liberal government to bring in a new act to change the law.

The case began two years ago in the claim by Mr Osborne, branch secretary of the Amalgamated Society of Railway Servants, that a political levy was illegal. Today Lord Halsbury, delivering the leading judgment, said: "There is nothing in any of the Trades Union Acts from which it can be reasonably inferred that trades unions, as defined by parliament, were ever meant to have the power of collecting and administering funds for political purposes."

The Union of South Africa proclaimed

Louis Botha, PM of the Union.

Dec 7. A royal proclamation creating the self-governing Union of South Africa was read from the steps of the Royal Exchange in the City of London today. The Union brings together the four colonies of the Cape of Good Hope, Natal, Transvaal and Orange River.

Creation of the Union, promised by Britain at the end of the Boer War, was made possible by concessions by the Liberal Government in London, notably in accepting Boer demands that the Cape electoral system, which allows qualified Natives and Coloureds of mixed race to vote, should not apply in Union elections.

Britain's submarine fleet comes up for air as it passes the Houses of Parliament on a trip down the friendly waters of the Thames.

1910 – 1919

1910

JANUARY

Su	Mo	Tu	We	Th	Fr	Sa
						1
2	3	4	5	6	7	8
9	10	11	12	13	14	15
16	17	18	19	20	21	22
23	24	25	26	27	28	29
30	31					

1. Reading: Lloyd George says the budget will "drive hunger forever from the hearths of the poor" (→ 8).

1. New York: First wireless broadcast of opera is made from the Metropolitan Opera, with tenor Enrico Caruso.

2. UK: 12 die when the ship "Arcadian" collides with another vessel in the Irish Sea.

3. Germany: Prussian social democratic congress calls for universal suffrage (→ 11).

4. France: Leon Delagrange dies in a flying accident at Bordeaux (→ 8/3).

6. Germany: The German Society of Geography honours Ernest Shackleton for South Polar explorations (→ 1/6).

8. UK: The German military threat becomes an election issue.→

10. Milan: Publication of the "Futurist Manifesto" of painting.

11. Berlin: Kaiser Wilhelm pledges suffrage reform (→ 6/3).

13. Manchuria: Russia and Japan agree to neutrality of Manchurian railway.

13. India: Five provinces are banned from holding "seditious meetings" (→ 24).

15. Africa: France reorganises French Congo as French Equatorial Africa.

18. Berlin: The German government tells the US it is ready for a tariff war.

18. London: New comet becomes visible (→ 12/5).

19. Constantinople: The Turkish parliament burns down.

24. India: Anarchist shoots dead a policeman in a Calcutta court (→ 11/1/11).

26. London: Police rescue Asquith when he is mobbed by suffragettes (→ 22/6).

31. Persia: Russia and UK decide to intervene as political unrest sweeps the country.

31. London: The wife of Dr Crippen, an American, vanishes from their home in Camden Town (→ 31/7).

Floods threaten Louvre art treasures

The flooding of the Seine means unconventional modes of transport.

Jan 26. The rains which have been falling unrelentingly on Paris for several days now have brought devastating floods to parts of the city. Thousands have been forced to leave their homes and seven soldiers drowned while trying to rescue stricken families.

Communications throughout in the city are badly hit with few trains running on either the railway or Metro. The River Seine was today reported to be running at more than three times its normal 7ft level.

The authorities fear that if it rises much more, the Louvre's Sculpture Gallery could be inundated with flood water. If this does happen the Venus de Milo and the other priceless art treasures on display in the gallery could be damaged beyond repair.

Empire trade rings up massive sales

Jan 10. The latest trade figures for the British Empire show that it is still a rapidly expanding market of now almost 350 million. Board of Trade figures show that its total trade has more than doubled in the last fifteen years, from £346 million a year to £698 million.

The United Kingdom alone still accounts for over half this total, but our share of the market is falling steadily. Since 1894 the annual value of trade business done by foreign countries has risen by £154 million, while trade with the empire is only up £138 million. This has spurred the campaign to give colonies trading advantages.

Free trade: could it lead to a free-for-all for foreign manufacturers?

Tories take early lead in election

Jan 18. Results declared so far in the general election suggest a strong swing to the Tories. Following the usual practice, voting is taking place on different days in different places and it will be another three weeks before the final score is known. But today's tally of 266 constituency figures and 404 still to come shows the Liberal Government with 41 net losses, pointing to a close finish.

Meanwhile Herbert Asquith, the Prime Minister, is holidaying in Lucerne and Cannes, but he plans to return to London before polling ends (→ 14/2).

Women: still no vote in 1910.

Miners strike for eight-hour day

Jan 21. Violence erupted today in the Northumberland and Durham coalfields. The coal strike is spreading and the men are angry that their officials have agreed to the proposed system of eight-hour shifts and round-the-clock working. A resolution has been proposed calling for the resignation of the entire Durham Miners' Association executive.

The worst rioting was at the Murton Colliery where 200 police, 120 of them drafted in from surrounding districts, battled with stone-throwing miners. Several of the policemen suffered head injuries. Some 1,000 tons of coal were stolen.

1910

FEBRUARY

Su	Mo	Tu	We	Th	Fr	Sa
		1	2	3	4	5
6	7	8	9	10	11	12
13	14	15	16	17	18	19
20	21	22	23	24	25	26
27	28					

1. Paris: The Red Cross starts providing assistance to flood victims.

1. Turkey: Army reservists called up as fears grow of clash with Greece over Crete.

1. UK: First 80 labour exchanges open under new act; they are inundated with job-hunters.

3. Turkey: Government warns Greece against accepting Cretan delegates in the Greek parliament (→9/5).

4. India: New press censorship bill announced; government says repressive measures necessary to halt unrest.

7. Africa: Belgium, the UK and Germany fix frontiers of Congo, Uganda and German East Africa respectively.

8. US: William Boyce founds Boy Scouts of America, inspired by UK Boy Scouts.

9. Glasgow: Launch of destroyer "Parramatta", first ship of the Australian Navy.

10. Newport: Labour Party Conference demands the abolition of the Lords and a right to work bill (→15).

13. China: 6,000 foreign-led troops mutiny and loot Canton, killing 100.

15. London: Failure to pass budget has left the Treasury £10 million in arrears (→28).

18. Germany: 300 are injured in clashes between socialists and police over the new suffrage reform bill.

19. Alps: Switzerland, Germany and Italy agree to build a railway through the St. Gothard Pass.

20. UK: Hurricane-force winds cause several deaths and severe damage.

22. London: First performance of Delius' opera "A Village Romeo and Juliet" under Thomas Beecham.

21. Egypt: Christian premier Butros Ghali is assassinated by a nationalist fanatic.

28. London: Asquith says the government will not pass the budget until it has abolished the Lords' veto (→8/3).

Labour props up Liberals

Feb 14. With the last general election result now in, the complete score-card reads: Tories 273 seats, Liberals 273, Nationalists 82 and Labour 42. So there is a dead heat between the major parties. Mr Asquith and his government stay in power, fairly certain of the support of Labour, if not of the much bigger Irish contingent.

There has been much behind-the-scenes horse-trading in the past 72 hours. Labour said today that it expects to back the Government in whatever action it takes over reintroducing the Budget rejected by the House of Lords and in trying to strip the upper House of all effective power. The Irish are demanding that Mr Asquith should get guarantees from the King that he will co-operate in moves to abolish the Lords' veto.

Mr Asquith is understood not to have made Royal agreement immediately to curb the Lords a condition of continuing in office himself; however, there is some mystery over what the King and the Prime Minister have agreed.

In this situation, lobby correspondents reported that Labour MPs plan to use all possible leverage to force another election once they have given the Liberals help with relaunching the budget.

They quoted a senior Labour man as saying "We should soon be ready to throw in our lot with the Irish". Government Whips however, reckoned that there was an element of bluff in this and currently little likelihood of any full-scale withdrawal of both Nationalist and Labour support. But the new parliament is brittle (→15).

X-rays guide removal of nail from lung

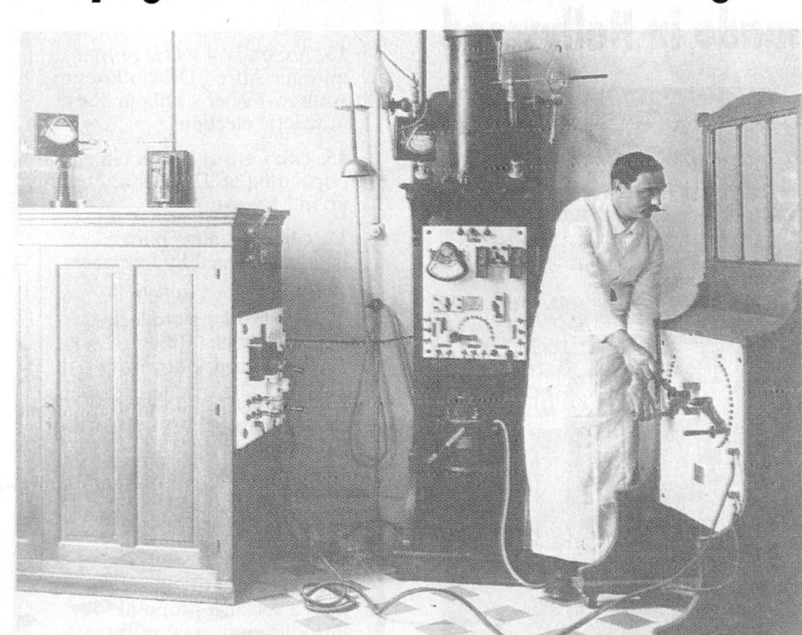

One of the latest X-ray machines, a modern aid for the modern surgeon.

Feb 27. An X-ray machine guided a surgeon's forceps to a nail in the lung of a nine-year-old boy in an operation at Beth Israel Hospital in New York.

The boy, Jacob Miller, had swallowed the nail but, fearing punishment, had been afraid to confess to what he had done. He started to lose weight and doctors were baffled at first. Then Jacob's father took him to the hospital where Dr Francis Huber of the children's ward took X-ray plates of the boy's stomach, which revealed the inch-long nail.

For the operation to remove the nail, Dr Huber used an X-ray machine with a fluorescent screen. This produced a moving picture as he inserted forceps through an incision in Jacob's neck and, guided by what he saw on the screen, removed the nail.

Dalai Lama flees as Lhasa falls

The Dalai Lama in India.

Feb 23. A Chinese army has occupied and is reportedly looting Lhasa, forcing the Dalai Lama to flee to India. He returned from exile in Peking only two months ago, having fled there after the arrival in Tibet of British troops in 1904. It appears that he reached an arrangement with the Chinese over their future role in Tibet, but could not sustain it (→1/3).

Forces lack horses

Feb 2. Britain could face a serious shortage of horses should war break out, it was reported today. The National Horse Supply Association was told that 170,000 would be needed immediately on the outbreak of hostilities, the same number being replaced every six months. Despite this, Britain exported more horses than any other country. Germany and Austria spent £200,000 each annually on horse breeding, Britain less than £5,000.

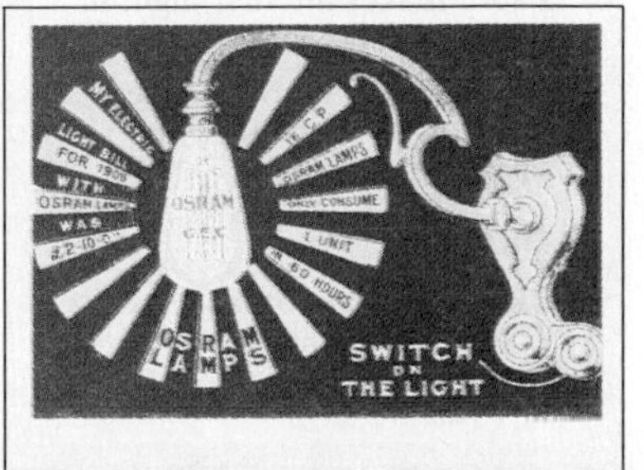

1910

MARCH

Su	Mo	Tu	We	Th	Fr	Sa
		1	2	3	4	5
6	7	8	9	10	11	12
13	14	15	16	17	18	19
20	21	22	23	24	25	26
27	28	29	30	31		

1. India: The Dalai Lama is welcomed in Darjeeling.

6. Berlin: Socialists are shot and sabred during a suffrage demonstration (→ 10/4).

8. London: Government says it will have to borrow to make up lost budget revenue of £29 million (→ 19).

8. France: The Baroness de Laroche becomes the first woman to receive a pilot's licence (→ 28).

9. Norway: The Storting (parliament) votes to pay its members.

10. China: The Imperial Government abolishes slavery.

11. Wales: 500 children are swept away when a dam bursts in the Rhondda Valley; 494 are rescued.

11. Manchester: US cotton magnate J. A. Patton is mobbed by protesters angry that his high prices have slashed demand for cotton.

18. New York: Banker Otto Kahn pays a record price for a painting of £103,000 for a Frans Hals.

19. Manchester: Churchill says if Government fails to beat Lords it "is the fortune of war; but we will win" (→ 21).

21. London: Government introduces its bill to abolish the House of Lords' power of veto (→ 4/4).

21. Budapest: Government ministers are assaulted during the final session of the Hungarian parliament.

26. UK: S. Howard's Jenkinstown wins the Grand National at Aintree.

27. Italy: Mount Etna erupts, causing widespread destruction (→ 6/4).

28. France: Aviator Henri Fabre makes the first flight in a seaplane at Martigues (→ 7/7).

29. Monaco: World's largest oceanographic museum is opened.

DEATH

21. French photographer Felix Tournachon, alias Nadar (*6/4/1820).

Commission probes cost of divorce

March 8. The high cost of divorce and evils of separation orders came under attack at the Royal Commission on Divorce today. Experts claimed that an average £80 for an undefended case and £121 for a defended one was beyond the reach of the poor.

Separation orders, now running at 2,000 a year and designed to protect women from a husband's cruelty, caused problems because the courts had ruled that they prevented subsequent divorce.

A spokesman for the Divorce Law Reform Union pointed out that these factors contributed to the large number of couples living immorally and an illegitimate birth rate of about 36,900 a year. It is a law that "punishes the innocent", the spokesman said (→ 22/10).

The first movie is made in Hollywood

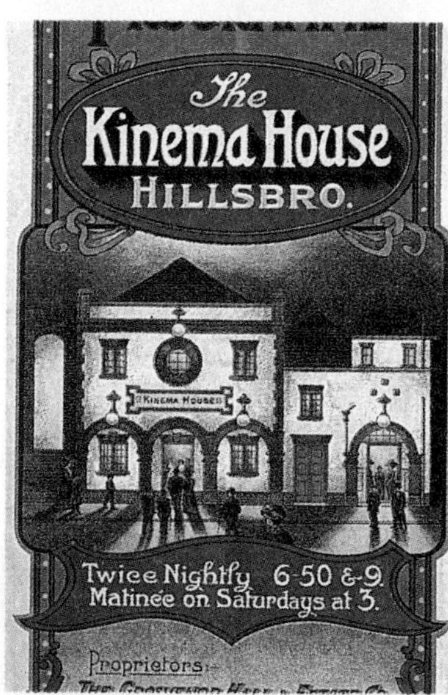

Movies: catching on in California.

March 10. D.W. Griffith's film "In Old California" goes on release today. It is the first film to be made in Hollywood, near Los Angeles in Southern California, and tells of a Spanish maiden's liaison with a future Governor of California.

Hollywood, with its wide variety of landscapes, could prove popular as a venue for the large number of film companies moving into the Los Angeles area.

1910

APRIL

Su	Mo	Tu	We	Th	Fr	Sa
					1	2
3	4	5	6	7	8	9
10	11	12	13	14	15	16
17	18	19	20	21	22	23
24	25	26	27	28	29	30

2. Berlin: Prof. Karl Harries announces he has perfected a process for the artificial manufacture of rubber.

4. London: Commons gives first reading to bill abolishing House of Lords' power of veto.→

5. France: Kissing is banned on French railways because of claim it delays trains.

6. Italy: Etna's eruption now the longest for 200 years.

9. Glasgow: Launch of HMS Colossus, Royal Navy's biggest battleship to date.

10. Berlin: Anti-government demonstration is attended by 250,000 socialist supporters (→ 21/9).

12. Turkey: Albanian rebel force of 15,000 is crushed by Turkish troops (→ 25).

13. Australia: Liberal prime minister Alfred Drakin loses to Andrew Fisher's Labour Party in federal elections.

15. US: Census shows US population at 92 million, 21% up in 21 years.

15. China: Rioters burn buildings owned by foreigners.

15. Germany: 250,000 building workers are locked out as pay talks with employers break down.

23. Brussels: King Albert of the Belgians opens the World Exhibition.

25. Turkey: Heavy fighting is reported between Turkish troops and up to 30,000 Albanian rebels.

27. Belgium: Parliament rejects a socialist proposal to introduce universal suffrage.

27. S. Africa: Louis Botha and James Herzog found South African Party, calling for independence and equality for Boers (→ 21/5).

28. London: Newcastle United beat Barnsley 2-0 in the FA Cup Final replay at Crystal Palace.

DEATH

21. US writer Samuel Langhorne Clemens, alias Mark Twain (*30/11/1835).→

PM urges King to create new peers

April 14. In a state of great uproar the House of Commons tonight approved resolutions for abolishing the power of the House of Lords to veto legislation passed by MPs. In the parliamentary lobbies it is recognised that this bring a constitutional crisis closer.

Mr Asquith, the Prime Minister, expects the Lords to reject the formal Commons decision to clip their wings. No attempt is being made any longer on the Government side to disguise the fact that he has already talked with the King about creating enough new peerages – maybe 300 of them – to swamp the anti-government majority in the upper House. In government circles, there are hints that the King will agree but may want another election first (→ 11/7).

No exaggeration in Twain dead report

April 21. There was no doubt about it this time – the reports of Mark Twain's death at the age of 74 were not, as he once said of an erroneous report, "greatly exaggerated".

Samuel Langhorne Clemens, America's best-loved humorous writer, became a Mississippi river pilot before turning author of "Huckleberry Finn". His nom-de-plume came from the call "mark twain", indicating two fathoms.

Novelist and wit Mark Twain.

1910

MAY

Su	Mo	Tu	We	Th	Fr	Sa
1	2	3	4	5	6	7
8	9	10	11	12	13	14
15	16	17	18	19	20	21
22	23	24	25	26	27	28
29	30	31				

1. US: Foundation of National Association for the Advancement of Colored People, pledged to black equality.

4. London: Reported that King Edward VII is seriously ill (→ 6).

4. London: At the Albert Hall, Commander Robert Peary receives a gold medal for discovery of the North Pole.

5. Nicaragua: Earthquake around Cartago kills 500.

5. Christiania: Ex-US President Theodore Roosevelt collects Nobel Peace Prize for his mediation in the Russo-Japanese War (→ 12/06).

6. London: King Edward VII dies of pneumonia (→ 7).

7. London: George V takes his oath as King.→

9. Crete: Violent scenes in the National Assembly as union with Greece is pledged (→ 27/7).

12. France: Halley's Comet causes widespread concern and fears it is responsible for bad weather.→

18. Paris: First conference on air traffic opens.

19. London: Westminster court decides that cabbies who ask for tips can be prosecuted.

21. Cape Town: General Louis Botha will be the first prime minister of the new Union of South Africa (→ 14/6).

23. London: King George V gives his first address to the Empire.

26. English Channel: 27 die when French submarine "Pluvoise" hits a steamship.

28. Russia: Government orders thousands of Jews to leave Kiev (→ 9/6).

31. London: Theodore Roosevelt receives the freedom of the City of London.

DEATHS

6. Albert Edward of Saxe-Coburg-Gotha, King Edward VII (*9/11/1841).→

27. German bacteriologist and 1905 Nobel Prize winner Robert Koch (*11/12/1843).

Nation mourns death of Edward VII

The last photograph of Edward VII, about to board his yacht at Calais.

George V with his Queen and heir.

May 21. The toll of a single bell on the Curfew Tower above the battlements of Windsor Castle announced the arrival of the royal train today bringing the body of King Edward VII for burial.

It was a day of high drama and sadness from early morning when the first funeral procession of the day formed at Westminster Hall. The King's coffin, made from one of the oak trees in Windsor Great Park, was placed on a gun carriage and pulled by members of the Bluejackets. The procession wound its way to Paddington station through silent streets watched by crowds estimated at 500,000 people.

The King was buried in the family vault at St. George's Chapel. The coffin was placed beside that of his eldest son, the late Duke of Clarence. It was the last homecoming for a man who loved the town where he spent much of his boyhood. He was both christened and married there, too.

King George V, wearing the uniform of a field marshal, rode on horseback behind his father's coffin. Among the mourners were the kings of Belgium, Bulgaria, Denmark, Greece, Norway, Spain and Portugal. Archduke Ferdinand of the Austro-Hungarian Empire was among more than 50 dukes, princes and princesses.

The biggest change since the funeral of Queen Victoria, nine years ago, was the international atmosphere with its emphasis on the Empire. Servicemen from all parts of the Empire were in the Guard of Honour today and the processions included exotically-garbed men of foreign regiments of which the late king was colonel-in-chief, among them Hussars from Russia and Prussia.

At St. George's Chapel, Windsor, the King led the mourners, walking to his place with a hand on that of his mother, Queen Alexandra. Queen Mary was escorted by a rigid-faced Kaiser Wilhelm. The German Emperor had complained about having to give precedence to a dog – the late King's fox terrier, Caesar, led by a servant, had pride of place behind the coffin.

King George V and Kaiser Wilhelm II, united in grief for father and uncle. ▷

Halley's Comet at closest to Earth

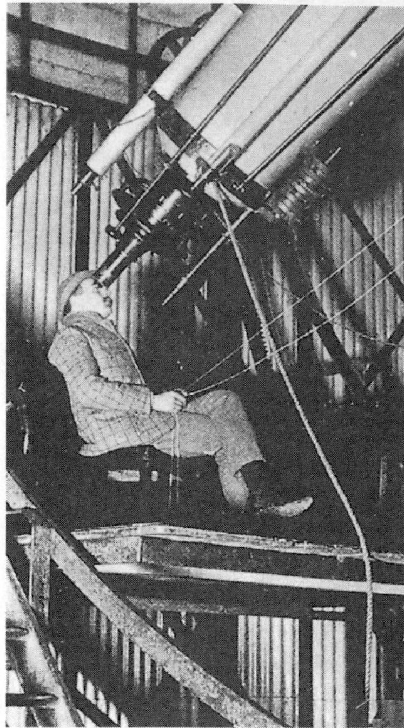

On the look-out for the Comet.

May 20. Halley's Comet today passed within about 13 million miles of the earth, the closest it will get on its present visit. It is expected to be a spectacular object in the evening sky for the next few days.

Recently the comet's tail has been going through some striking changes. At the end of last month it was observed to have taken on a twisted appearance, as though there had been an explosion.

Girl Guides' birth

May 31. A youth movement which encourages girls to be obedient, clean-living and resourceful is being formed by Sir Robert Baden-Powell and his sister Agnes. The Girl Guides will run along the lines of the Boy Scouts, who were established three years ago.

Scouting: growing popularity.

1910

JUNE

Su	Mo	Tu	We	Th	Fr	Sa
			1	2	3	4
5	6	7	8	9	10	11
12	13	14	15	16	17	18
19	20	21	22	23	24	25
26	27	28	29	30		

1. UK: A.W. Cox's Lemberg wins the Derby at Epsom.

2. East Indies: British explorers find pygmies in Dutch New Guinea mountains.

3. Russia: Duma decides to abolish Finnish autonomy.

4. Berlin: Reichstag approves cremation, against Catholic, conservative and Polish opposition.

8. Naples: 30 people are killed in an earthquake.

9. Washington: Delegation appeals to the President for aid for Russian Jews (→11/9).

11. UK: Dr Wilfred Harris injects the ganglion of the fifth cranial nerve to relieve the pain of facial neuralgia.

11. Spain: King Alfonso proclaims freedom of belief (→9/8).

14. S. Africa: Premier General Louis Botha calls for closer ties with UK (→1/7).

17. Central Europe: Severe floods in many countries; 1,000 die in Hungary alone.

22. London: Suffragette Mrs Fawcett tells Divorce Commission that men and women should be on equal terms.

22. Germany: Count von Zeppelin's new airship "Deutschland" is first to fly with paying passengers (→28).

23. London: The King's eldest son is created Prince of Wales on his 16th birthday.

25. Paris: New season of Diaghilev's Ballets Russes opens with new ballet "Firebird" by Igor Stravinsky.

28. Germany: Zeppelin "Deutschland" is wrecked in a gale in the Teutoburg Forest.

29. Munich: Russian ambassador insists on removal of a painting of the Kiev pogrom from an exhibition.

BIRTHS

7. Italian artist Pietro Annigoni (†29/10/88).

23. French playwright Jean Anouilh (†4/10/87).

Scott sets out in race to find South Pole

June 1. Captain Robert Falcon Scott's ship, the "Terra Nova", steamed from the East India Dock today on the first stage of a new attempt to reach the South Pole. A large crowd of Londoners lining the quay heard Lady Bridgeman, wife of the expedition's patron, wish Scott and his party "good luck and a safe return".

Heavily laden with supplies – packed, ironically, in several tons of ice – and carrying 1,120lbs of tobacco and 30,000 cigars, "Terra Nova" is bound for Port Lyttleton in New Zealand. Scott will use motorised transport and ponies for the 1,800mile journey across Antarctica, killing the ponies for food.

In 1904, Scott and his party failed to reach the Pole, but travelled further south than any others had then managed. Norwegian explorer Roald Amundsen will be making a similar attempt on the Pole later this year.

Captain and Mrs Scott share a joke with a friend aboard the Terra Nova.

Scourge of syphilis yields to new drug

June 22. A new treatment for syphilis has been put forward by the Nobel Prize winner Dr Paul Ehrlich, of Germany. Details of the treatment, which uses a drug known as salvarsan, were revealed in Berlin today.

The drug was first patented by Dr Ehrlich in 1907 – it was his 606th to be patented. So far all patients treated with the drug have improved, with their syphilitic ulcers healing rapidly. Dr Ehrlich, who directs two research institutes in Frankfurt, won the Nobel Prize for medicine in 1908.

One of the first motor-cycles displayed by its proud owner in Swansea.

1910

JULY

Su	Mo	Tu	We	Th	Fr	Sa
					1	2
3	4	5	6	7	8	9
10	11	12	13	14	15	16
17	18	19	20	21	22	23
24	25	26	27	28	29	30
31						

1. Baltimore: Duncan Black and Alonzo Decker found a tool company.

1. S. Africa: Union of South Africa becomes a dominion of the British Empire (→15/9).

2. Wimbledon: Anthony Wilding beats Arthur Gore for the Men's Singles title; Dorothea Chambers beats Penelope Boothby for the Ladies' Singles crown.

4. Far East: Russia acknowledges Japan's occupation of Korea in return for a free hand in Manchuria.

6. Berlin: Premiere of the opera "Kobold" by Richard Wagner's son Siegfried.

7. France: French aviator Hubert Latham reaches a record height of 5000ft during trials at Rheims.

9. Egypt: Discovery of a tablet describing the fall of Jerusalem.

11. UK: In a speech in Wales Lloyd George says Lords' reform has priority over women's suffrage (→18/11).

12. France: The King and Queen of the Belgians arrive on an official visit.

14. London: Police launch a hunt for Dr Crippen after a woman's remains are found in his cellar.→

15. Poland: Ceremonies to commemorate the battle of Tannenberg are marked by anti-Russian demonstrations.

16. Spain: Rioting breaks out in Bilbao as miners go on strike.

19. Newcastle-upon-Tyne: 30,000 railway workers come out on strike.

20. London: Churchill announces prison reforms including lectures for inmates in various subjects.

27. Turkey: The government threatens war on Greece if it accepts Cretan representatives in the Greek parliament.

DEATH

12. British aviator and motorist Charles Stewart Rolls (*28/8/1877).

Radio link captures Dr Crippen at sea

July 31. Dr Hawley Harvey Crippen, wanted for murder, was arrested on a ship off Canada today – the first criminal suspect to be caught by radio. Crippen and his 27-year-old mistress, Ethel Le Neve, disappeared from his home in London, on July 9. Police who later searched the house in Camden Town found the mutilated and dismembered body of his wife buried beneath the cellar floor.

Le Neve and Crippen, a US-born dentist, fled to Belgium. Then, posing as "Mr Robinson and son", they booked passage on the "SS Montrose", which sailed from Antwerp for Quebec on July 20.

The ship's captain, Henry Kendall, had read newspaper descriptions of the couple before leaving port. After the ship sailed, his suspicions were aroused when he saw the two "men" holding hands. He also noticed Mr Robinson had recently shaved off a moustache, and that though he wore no spectacles he had a mark on the bridge of his nose from them – both Crippen trademarks. Kendall radioed Britain. Chief Inspector Walter Dew of Scotland Yard caught a faster boat, the "Laurentic", and overtook the "Montrose". Disguised as a St. Lawrence River pilot, he boarded the "Montrose" this morning and arrested "Robinson" when he arrived at the captain's cabin at Kendall's invitation to meet the pilot. When Dew – who had interviewed Crippen before his flight – revealed himself, Crippen quivered, according to Kendall. Then he said: "Thank God it's over. The suspense has been too great. I couldn't stand it any longer" (→29/8).

Crippen in custody: the alleged murderer is led down the gangway.

Flyer Rolls breaks neck in plane crash

July 12. Aviation claimed its first British victim today when the Hon. Charles Stewart Rolls died as his aircraft crashed during a flying competition at Bournemouth.

Mr Rolls, aged 33, the son of Lord and Lady Llangattock, was flying his French-built Wright biplane when the rudders appeared to break as he tilted the aircraft, sending it plummeting to the ground. An eye witness said: "There was a crack, a wooden strut fell, the tail bent upward, and the whole machine came head forward to the ground with a heart rending crash."

The tragedy occurred during a competition in which the flyers were supposed to bring their aircraft to rest on a bull's eye marked out on the field. He was still sitting in his seat after the crash with his crumpled aircraft beneath him, but attempts to bring him round failed.

Mr Rolls, described by a friend as a "modest unassuming hero" was a distinguished aviator in his own right; only last month he became the first person to fly both ways across the Channel without stopping. He was also a renowned pioneer motorist, winning the 1,000-mile trial in 1900, and a partner in the Rolls-Royce car manufacturing company which bears his name.

Rolls after his Channel round-trip.

Riots break out as Johnson keeps title

Johnson (right) and Jeffries.

July 4. Jack Johnson, the first black world heavyweight champion, crushed a comeback attempt by the former title-holder Jim Jeffries in Reno. His knock-out victory in the 15th round sparked off race riots.

1910

AUGUST

Su	Mo	Tu	We	Th	Fr	Sa
	1	2	3	4	5	6
7	8	9	10	11	12	13
14	15	16	17	18	19	20
21	22	23	24	25	26	27
28	29	30	31			

1. Paris: Arrival of 23-year-old Russian Jewish artist Marc Chagall.

3. Palestine: Druze sect Moslems massacre 100 Jews.

5. Hamburg: 10,000 dockers come out on strike.

9. Rome: Vatican announces imminent break with Spain over Spanish plans to clamp down on religious orders.

12. London: Electric street lamps are replaced by 3,000 high-pressure gas lamps giving more light in fog.

13. Russia: Cholera epidemic reported to have killed 3,330 people in a week (→26).

14. Panama: First eight miles of the Panama Canal are opened, eastward to the Caribbean.

14. Brussels: Fire destroys a large part of the World Exhibition, including priceless works of art.

17. Japan: 800 die in severe flooding.

22. Korea: 18 drown when the British naval cruiser "HMS Bedford" sinks.

28. Russia: Cholera death toll now reported to have reached 60,000.

28. Balkans: Montenegro declares full independence from the Ottoman Empire under King Nicholas I.

29. London: Dr Crippen and Ethel Le Neve charged at Bow Street Court (→22/10).

31. US: Ex-President Roosevelt outlines his ideas of a "New Nationalism".

BIRTHS

4. US composer William Schuman (†15/2/92).

20. Finnish architect Eero Saarinen (†1/9/61).

DEATHS

13. British nursing pioneer Florence Nightingale, first woman to hold Order of Merit (*12/5/1820).→

16. Chilean President Pedro Montt, on an official visit to Germany (*1846).

Florence Nightingale's lamp goes out

Aug 20. Soldiers and citizens from all over Britain paid quiet tribute today to the Lady of the Lamp – Florence Nightingale, the founder of nursing, who died last week at the age of 90. They packed St. Paul's Cathedral for a solemn memorial service held at noon in her honour. And hundreds more stood bareheaded as her hearse, drawn by two horses, rolled through the streets of London.

The coffin was covered with a white pall almost hidden beneath flowers. Among the tributes was one from Alexandra, the Queen Mother, a huge white floral cross from the matrons and nurses of the London hospitals, a cushion of flowers sent by the survivors of the charge of the Light Brigade, and a wreath shaped like an Army lantern of the type she carried on her rounds in Scutari hospital during the Crimean War.

Nightingale, great humanitarian.

At Waterloo, the coffin was put onto a special train for the journey to her family's home in Hampshire, where she was buried beside her parents in the churchyard at East Wellow.

Talking pictures: a major breakthrough

Aug 27. Talking motion pictures were demonstrated today by the gifted American inventor Thomas Alva Edison at his laboratory in West Orange, New Jersey. His process uses a device which is part camera and part phonograph, enabling picture and sound to be recorded simultaneously.

Furthermore, the actors are able to move about freely. Both these features mark a major advance on the attempts by other pioneers at producing talking pictures. Two years' work have gone into Edison's device. He hopes that it will be in use in theatres in another two. He also hinted at the possibility of motion pictures in colour as well as with sound.

Edison's track record as an inventor suggests that he may be successful in both aims. He already has to his credit the phonograph, the carbon microphone now used in most telephones, and the first commercially successful incandescent electric light.

Treaty completes Japanese control of Korean life

Aug 24. The threat of street rioting hangs over Seoul today following the announcement that within a week Japan intends to carry out the formal annexation of Korea. Japan is already in control of every aspect of Korean public life, but the decision to annex the territory is bound to lead to fresh troubles.

Ever since the "Hermit Kingdom" became a protectorate as a result of the Russo-Japanese war Koreans have demonstrated fierce hatred of their new masters. Rebellions have been suppressed by the Japanese with an iron hand. Japanese concern about the consequences of annexation in Korea is evident from the fact that Tokyo newspapers have agreed to censor publication of unauthorised news under existing conditions. The annexation convention was signed three days ago but only today were its contents communicated to diplomatic missions in Tokyo.

There is a long history of Japanese interference in the affairs of the Korean Peninsula which has resulted in rivalry and conflict with the Russians because they, too, have been expanding their interests in Korea from territory they controlled in southern Manchuria. That culminated in the Russo-Japanese war in which Russia was heavily defeated. The ensuing peace treaty in 1905 sanctioned Japanese domination of Korea.

Young bathers enjoying the late summer sunshine on the beach at an English seaside resort.

1910

SEPTEMBER

Su	Mo	Tu	We	Th	Fr	Sa
				1	2	3
4	5	6	7	8	9	10
11	12	13	14	15	16	17
18	19	20	21	22	23	24
25	26	27	28	29	30	

1. Spain: Rioting occurs in Bilbao after a general strike is proclaimed.

2. UK: 10,000 Welsh miners come out on strike in sympathy with dockers.→

8. Rome: Pope Pius X condemns modernism, warns clergy not to be distracted by newspapers.

9. UK: Striking dockers reject compromise as cotton workers prepare to strike in sympathy (→1/10).

11. Germany: 12th Zionist Congress raises 100,000 marks to establish a Jewish colony in Palestine.

12. UK: Figures show that 300,000 workers went on strike in 1909, four times the number for 1908.

14. Germany: Airship "Zeppelin VI" is destroyed by fire at Baden-Baden while on hire to Baron Rothschild.

15. South Africa: Boer nationalists win first parliamentary elections with 67 seats.→

17. London: Doctor asserts that if lunacy increases at present rate insane will outnumber sane in 40 years.

19. Germany: British workers imported to help employers best dock strike.

21. Germany: Rosa Luxemburg is shouted down at German Socialist congress in Magdeburg.

23. Europe: Aviators Chavez, de Brigue and Domodossola make the first powered flight over the Alps (→29).

27. Italy: 100,000 flee Naples as cholera epidemic breaks out.

29. Europe: French aviator M. Tabuteau makes the first flight across the Pyrenees (→25/10).

30. Constantinople: Turkey signs a military convention with Rumania.

DEATHS

2. French painter Henri "le Douanier" Rousseau (*21/5/1844).

7. British artist William Holman Hunt (*2/4/1827).→

Bosses lock out dockers

Sept 2. In a move that took shipbuilding unions completely by surprise, the employers today gave 24 hours notice of a national lock-out. The move by the Shipbuilding Employers' Federation is aimed at the boilermakers' union, whose leaders have so far been unable to stop continual unofficial strikes.

Some 40,000 boilermakers, out of a national membership of 68,000, work in federation yards. But other crafts linked to boilermaking, such as riveters, platers, caulkers and iron workers, are also being laid off. The 19 shipyard unions have some 70,000 members in federation yards. With labourers and non-unionists, over 100,000 men are likely to be out of work because of the dispute.

The employers are digging in for a long fight. They have decided to use the 24-hour notice clause in their new national agreement with the Boilermakers' Society, citing two current "wild cat" strikes at yards on the Clyde and Tyne.

Mr F.N. Henderson, chairman of the employers' federation, said today that the present situation must now be ended once and for all. The boilermakers claim that employers are using the national agreement to cut rates of pay for specific jobs (→1/10).

Striking dockers leave after being sacked by their employers.

Botha loses seat but stays as PM

Sept 19. General Louis Botha, hero of the Boers' fight against the British, and caretaker Prime Minister in the newly-launched Union of South Africa, lost his seat in the first Parliamentary election last week. But his Nationalist Party, with a safe majority in the Assembly, has now decided he should remain in office until a new seat is found for him.

Though policy differences between the mainly Dutch-speaking Nationalist Party and the English-language Unionists are minimal, bitter resentment has been caused by a hard-line wing of the Nationalists, led by General James Barrie Hertzog, which is seeking to impose Dutch on reluctant English speakers in schools (→7/10).

Pure radium is new Curie discovery

Sept 7. The first pure sample of radium has been isolated by Marie Curie, who with her late husband Pierre discovered the element 12 years ago. Hitherto it has been studied only in the form of its salts.

Mme Curie and a colleague obtained radium by an electrolytic process which produced an amalgam of radium and mercury. The mercury was then distilled off at 7,000C to leave a tiny quantity of pure radium, a white metal that oxidises quickly in air so that the only way to retain any of it is to keep it sealed in a vacuum tube.

Their success coincides with the announcement that a new institute for the study of radio activity, now being built in Paris, is to be named after the Curies.

Holman Hunt goes to join Raphael

Hunt's "Light of the World".

Sept 7. The last of the Pre-Raphaelites, William Holman Hunt, who founded the Brotherhood with Rossetti and Millais, died yesterday long after his work had gone out of fashion. It is more than 50 years since he painted "The Light of the World" and paid his first visit to the Holy Land.

One of the fruits of his journey was the morbid picture of "The Scapegoat" painted on the unhealthy shores of the Dead Sea. Four goats he obtained as models died in its service.

Sarah Bernhardt, making her music hall debut this month.

1910

OCTOBER

Su	Mo	Tu	We	Th	Fr	Sa
						1
2	3	4	5	6	7	8
9	10	11	12	13	14	15
16	17	18	19	20	21	22
23	24	25	26	27	28	29
30	31					

1. Manchester: 100,000 cotton workers are locked out as 700 mills are shut down.→

1. Paris: Opening of an international conference on cancer.

5. Egypt: Discovery of the mummy of Red Sea pharaoh.

7. S. Africa: General Botha returns to the South African parliament as member for Losberg (→4/11).

7. Portugal: Provisional Government orders expulsion of all nuns and monks within 24 hours (→17).

12. Birmingham: First performance of Ralph Vaughan Williams Symphony No. 1, "A Sea Symphony".

12. France: Nationwide rail strike paralyses western European railways.

15. London: Premiere of Somerset Maugham's "Grace" at the Duke of York's Theatre.

17. Portugal: Provisional Government banishes the royal family and abolishes nobility (→9/11).

18. UK: Frenchman Baudry lands at Wormwood Scrubs in London after first airship Channel crossing from France.

20. UK: Launch of the White Star liner "Olympic", biggest vessel afloat (→31/5/11).

25. Italy: Severe storms and a tidal wave lash the Bay of Naples, killing 1,000.

25. Europe: Figures show that 20 aviators have been killed so far in 1910, compared with four in 1909 and one in 1908.

27. Persia: 160 British troops land at Lingah in the Gulf to protect British interests amid local unrest.

BIRTH

13. US jazz pianist Art Tatum (†4/11/56).

DEATHS

17. US women's campaigner Julia Ward Howe, who wrote "The Battle Hymn of the Republic" (*27/5/1819).

30. Swiss philanthropist Henri Dunant (*8/5/1828).→

Revolution ousts Portuguese monarchy

Revolutionary sailors arrest a supporter of the deposed King Manuel.

Oct 4. King Manuel of Portugal has been deposed by a well-planned revolution and has fled to Gibraltar on board the royal yacht "Amelia". The revolution is the culmination of a decade of turmoil during which King Manuel came to power after the assassination of his father and elder brother.

Troops loyal to the King were overpowered after sporadic but brisk exchanges of rifle and artillery fire while sailors who had joined the revolt shelled strategic points. Casualties are heavy, but the main fighting in Lisbon was over by breakfast time when columns of soldiers and sailors marched through the streets shouting "long live the republic" (→7).

Guilty: Dr Crippen is sentenced to death

Oct 22. Dr Crippen, brought back from Canada to face a murder trial at the Old Bailey, was convicted today of poisoning his wife, a former music-hall performer. The jury took just half an hour to reach their verdict. Crippen, who had seemed unmoved during the trial, looked dazed. He said only: "I still protest my innocence." Then the Lord Chief Justice donned the traditional black cap to pronounce the death sentence – and Crippen, white-faced, was led away (→23/11).

Crippen and his lover Ethel Le Neve under questioning in the dock.

Swiss founder of Red Cross dies

Oct 30. Jean-Henri Dunant, a Swiss philanthropist who was spurred to action by the horrors of warfare, died today, aged 82. His legacy to mitigating man's inhumanities to man, the Red Cross, lives on.

M Dunant shared the first Nobel Peace Prize in 1901 for his work in organising the Red Cross. He had been appalled when he saw injured soldiers left writhing on the battlefield in the Franco-Austrian war of 1859.

He recorded his impressions in a book called "Memories of Solferino". The book was later retitled "The Origin of the Red Cross" after M. Dunant had helped to organise an international conference in 1863 which created the health group. Based in his native Switzerland, it has taken its symbol from the Swiss national flag.

Minister intervenes in cotton crisis

Oct 6. The 700 Lancashire cotton mills, shut down by the employers' federation four days ago to assert their absolute "right to manage", will open again next week. A compromise settlement with the Card Room Workers' Union, achieved by Mr George Askwith, the Board of Trade's conciliator, ends the dispute which started at the Fern Mill in June, when a worker was fired for insubordination.

The latest in light technology.

1910

NOVEMBER

Su	Mo	Tu	We	Th	Fr	Sa
		1	2	3	4	5
6	7	8	9	10	11	12
13	14	15	16	17	18	19
20	21	22	23	24	25	26
27	28	29	30			

1. France: The cabinet of premier Aristide Briand resigns.

4. S. Africa: Opening of the first parliament of the new Union of South Africa in Cape Town.

5. Germany: Czar Nicholas II agrees to drop objections to Baghdad Railway if he has a free hand in north Persia.

8. US: Democrats win control of Congress in elections.

9. Portugal: Republic is recognised by the UK, France, Germany, Russia, Spain, Norway and Belgium (→24/8/11).

10. London: First performance of Elgar's violin concerto by German violinist Fritz Kreisler, under the composer.

11. Sandringham: Asquith asks King George if he will create peers to allow passage of Lords reform bill.→

12. Russia: Count Leo Tolstoy retreats to an ancient monastery, saying he wishes to die in solitude.

14. UK: Welsh miners accept a pay rise and call off strike (→26/3/11).

18. London: 119 arrested in suffragette attack on the House of Commons (→9).

19. London: Churchill orders charges against 100 suffragettes to be dropped (→23).

21. London: Lloyd George says "Out with the Lords" in radical speech at Mile End (→26).

22. London: Asquith promises to counter effects of House of Lords' Osborne Judgement in next Parliament.

23. London: Suffragettes mob ministers, leaving one Cabinet member confined to bed (→17/3/11).

23. London: Dr Crippen is hanged.

26. London: Balfour warns that "behind the single chamber conspiracy lurks socialism and home rule".

DEATH

20. Russian writer Count Leo Tolstoy (*9/9/1828).→

Leo Tolstoy finds peace

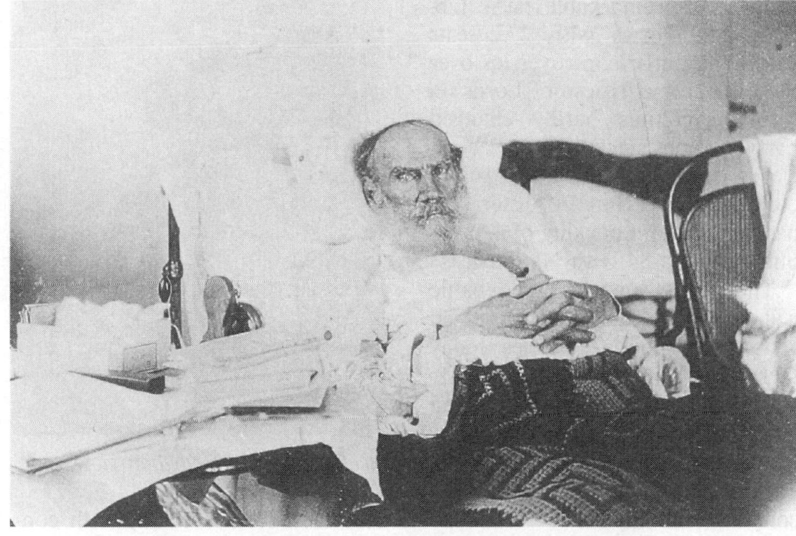

Count Leo Tolstoy, the great Russian author, on his sickbed.

Nov 21. Extraordinary scenes are reported from the railway station at Astopov, where Leo Tolstoy died today after lying ill there ever since his secret flight from his estate at Yasnaya Polyana. Peasants are flocking to pay homage.

It appears that Count Tolstoy had quarrelled with his wife, Countess Sophie, to whom he had made over his fortune while he lived in peasant style on his estate. He took with him his daughter, Tatiana, to whom his last words were spoken.

Pushing aside the doctors, he said to her: "there are millions of people suffering in the world. Why are so many of you looking after me?" He died unreconciled to the church and refusing to see his wife.

Crisis over Lords veto forces an election

Nov 18. Herbert Asquith, the Prime Minister, announced today that the King will dissolve Parliament and the second general election this year will be over before Christmas. Mr Asquith told MPs that failure of recent inter-party talks about House of Lords reform means "we revert to a state of war". The Prime Minister refused to be drawn on plans to create a huge number of peers to scupper Tory opposition. The constitutional crisis has arisen over the Lords' veto of the 1909 budget. But it will still be a ballot confined to men, so suffragettes plan to protest during the campaign (→ 21).

Street lobby: Prime Minister Herbert Asquith harassed by suffragettes.

Cavalry ride out to restore order in Welsh coalfields

Nov 9. General Macready, the officer in command of troops at Cardiff, yesterday ordered a squadron of the 18th Hussars to Pontypridd in a bid to restore order in Rhondda coalfield. A second army squadron is due to arrive today, together with two infantry battalions of the north Lancashire Regiment and the Lancashire Fusiliers from Tidworth.

Earlier the Home Secretary, Winston Churchill, had hoped that police reinforcements would be enough. 70 mounted and 200 foot constables of the Metropolitan Police went by train to Wales after the Chief Constable of Glamorganshire called for help against strikers in Tonypandy (→14).

Carson hurls down Orange gauntlet

Carson: Unionist challenge.

Nov 16. Sir Edward Carson, the new leader of Irish Unionist MPs, today warned that Ulster would fight proposals for Irish home rule. "By that means we can maintain our civil and religious liberty," he told the Ulster Unionist Association. Ulster Protestants want to remain part of the United Kingdom, governed by Westminster.

1910

DECEMBER

Su	Mo	Tu	We	Th	Fr	Sa
				1	2	3
4	5	6	7	8	9	10
11	12	13	14	15	16	17
18	19	20	21	22	23	24
25	26	27	28	29	30	31

1. Germany: Census shows population has grown by four million in five years to 64.9 million.

3. Morocco: France occupies the port of Agadir.

5. Russia: Barge convoy on River Volga sinks with loss of 300 workmen.

9. Palestine: Turkish troops suppress an Arab uprising.

10. New York: Toscanini conducts the first performance of Giacomo Puccini's "The Girl of the Golden West".

12. Greece: Eleutherios Venizelos wins legislative elections, remaining as premier.

13. Russia: Students protest at use of corporal punishment for political prisoners.

14. Palestine: Turkish troops are sent to suppress an uprising of 20,000 Bedouin Arabs.

16. London: Robbers shoot dead three policemen.

21. Leipzig: Trial opens of two British Army officers accused of espionage (→22).

22. China: Russia presents China with a project for a railway from Lake Baikal to Peking via the Gobi Desert.

22. Leipzig: British officers Lieutenant Trench and Captain Brandon are found guilty of espionage.

BIRTHS

1. British ballerina Dame Alicia Markova, born Lilian Alicia Marks.

19. French writer Jean Genet (†15/4/86).

HITS OF 1910

Ah! Sweet mystery of life.

Chinatown, my Chinatown.

QUOTE OF THE YEAR

"Four spectres haunt the poor: old age, accident, sickness and unemployment. We are going to exorcise them."
David Lloyd George, Chancellor of the Exchequer, after the Liberal victory.

General election results in dead-heat

Dec 20. The general election has produced a remarkable tie – Liberals and Tories with 272 seats each. The fierce controversies over the Budget and House of Lords reform have thus hardly changed party fortunes since the last election eleven months ago. Mr Asquith continues as Prime Minister. He has the reluctant backing of 42 Labour MPs and 84 Irish Nationalists.

The Peers versus People battle will now be fought with increased venom. In political circles today there was no doubt that Mr Asquith considers that by holding an election the Liberals have satisfied the King's condition for co-operation in solving the constitutional crisis.

There has been great turbulence on the hustings. The campaign ended with an infuriated mob preventing Winston Churchill, the Home Secretary, from breaking with convention and making a polling day speech in Lincoln. He yelled: "Keep your places. Somebody will be killed."

Neck and neck: a cartoon view.

344 feared dead in pit disaster

Dec 22. Up to 350 men and boys are believed dead following an explosion below ground at a Lancashire pit today in Britain's second worst mining disaster. Only one 16-year-old has so far been brought out alive. Messages of sympathy from around the world have been flooding in to Hutton Colliery, near Bolton, where rescue teams say there is now little hope of anyone else surviving.

The cause of the blast at Hulton Colliery, previously regarded as one of the safest and best-equipped, could have been a forgetful pitman striking a match below ground. About 1,000 children have been orphaned and one mother has lost her husband and four sons out of her family of fourteen.

Artist calls for art without representation

"Father Juniet's Cart" by Rousseau: typically primitive in style and subject.

A Russian painter called **Wassily Kandinsky**, working in Paris, has has written a treatise which claims that painting should be "purified" of all representation of nature.

Kandinsky now paints works that are termed "abstract" which depend entirely on the emotional effect of meaningless forms and arbitrary colours, chosen to "make close contact with the human soul".

Meanwhile French painting has lost an eccentric figure, **Henri Rousseau**, better known as "Le Douanier" because he began painting when he was a customs official. Naive and untaught, his fresh, primitive vision was admired by Renoir and Picasso, who gave a dinner in his honour.

The composer, **Igor Stravinsky**, who is 28, has caused a sensation with his score for Diaghilev's ballet "The Firebird". The leading role, half bird, half woman, is danced by **Tamara Karsavina** and the costumes by **Leon Bakst** are an oriental orgy of colour.

Germans are top in Nobel prize awards

Dec 10. Germany has walked away with three of the five prizes presented this year by the Nobel Committee in Stockholm.

Paul Heyse wins the Nobel Prize for Literature, while the Chemistry prize goes to Otto Wallach. Their compatriot Albrecht Kossel carries off the prize for Medicine for his work on albumins.

A Dutchman, Johannes Diderik van der Waals, is this year's Physics laureate for his work on fluids and gases. The Peace prize goes to the International Peace Bureau in Berne, Switzerland.

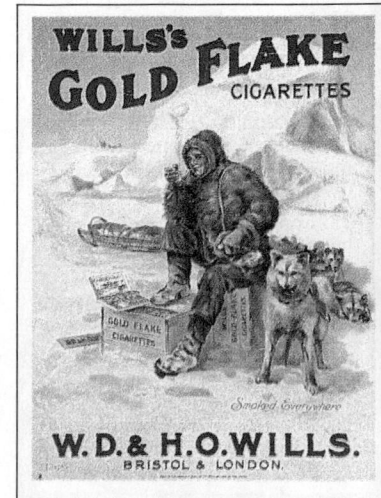

1911

JANUARY

Su	Mo	Tu	We	Th	Fr	Sa
1	2	3	4	5	6	7
8	9	10	11	12	13	14
15	16	17	18	19	20	21
22	23	24	25	26	27	28
29	30	31				

1. London: Russian Jew Leon Beron is found murdered on Clapham Common – anarchist link suspected (→8).

2. Nicaragua: President Taft acknowledges the new government of Jose Estrada and orders withdrawal of troops (→31/5).

4. Paris: The Academie des Sciences debates the admission of women as Marie Curie is a candidate for election (→23).

8. London: Police arrest Beron murder suspect in the East End (→30).

10. London: Automobile Association and Motor Union amalgamate.

11. India: 18 people killed and 11 injured in Bombay riots.

17. Paris: Attempt made on the life of French premier Aristide Briand.

18. London: Inquest on two deaths in Sidney Street siege returns verdicts of justifiable homicide and suffocation.

18. Japan: 25 condemned to death for plotting to kill the Mikado.

19. London: Author Pinero's "Preserving Mr Panmure" opens at the Comedy Theatre.

23. Paris: The Academie des Sciences votes to admit Jean Becquerel rather than a woman, Marie Curie.

24. Rhodesia: Whites protest at commutation of death sentence on black guilty of assaulting a white woman.

26. Dresden: Triumphant premiere of Richard Strauss's opera "Der Rosenkavalier".

27. UK: Airship Beta sends the first wireless messages from the air.

29. Vienna: A £39 million boost for the Austrian navy is announced over the coming ten years (→1/2).

30. London: Beron murder inquest returns wilful murder verdict on Stinie Morrison (→15/3).

BIRTH

22. Austrian statesman Bruno Kreisky (†29/7/90).

Anarchists burn in Sidney Street siege

Jan 3. A house in the East End of London burned to the ground today with three anarchists trapped inside after a gun battle with over 1,000 troops and armed police. "Who could have imagined a scene like this in England," declared Winston Churchill, the Home Secretary, who soon took command.

The battle began at 4am when armed detectives arrived at No 100 Sidney Street, off the Mile End Road, looking for anarchists who had already killed three policemen.

They were met with concentrated pistol fire which badly wounded one of them so reinforcements were called for, including Scots Guards from the Tower of London who arrived with a Maxim gun. Later a contingent of Royal Horse Artillery from St. John's Wood came with two 13-pounders.

All morning pistol and rifle fire was poured into the house, with the anarchists replying vigorously with their automatics. In all ten people were injured, including a few of the onlookers, but the anarchists seemed unharmed.

Then, at 12.50pm, some smoke appeared from the chimney. The fire brigade was called and soon galloped up, but Mr Churchill refused to allow them to intervene. By 1.50 pm the house was fiercely ablaze and it seemed impossible that anyone could have survived.

Afterwards two charred bodies were found, but one of the men, "Peter the Painter", is believed somehow to have escaped (→18).

Top-hatted Winston Churchill (l.) at the scene of the anarchist siege.

Policemen at the scene, armed with shotguns on Churchill's orders.

Cancer found to be caused by a virus

Jan 21. An important advance in the study of cancer is reported today by Dr Francis Peyton Rous of the Rockefeller Institute in New York. He has shown how a tumour can spread, possibly by a virus.

Last September Dr Rous described how he was able to transplant a cancerous growth from a chicken into healthy hens and produce – in some cases – fairly rapid spread of the malignancy. In his latest experiments he has used a special variety of chicken cancer which was bred in the laboratory.

After the cancer had been ground, it was thought that the fluid, free from any obvious cancerous growth after passage through a special filter, would be harmless. But this was not so: cancer was caused by not only by the watery filtrate but also fluid extracted from the main cancerous residue.

In Dr Rous's view, spreading of disease by filtrates free of any cancerous cells is of exceptional importance. There is no clear sign yet of the factor responsible, but as it is capable of slipping through a fine filter it could be the smallest of all micro-organisms, a virus. A chemical or microbe may also be considered.

Large oil strike made in Borneo

Jan 16. A rich oil strike has been made in Borneo. The drillers of the Anglo-Saxon Petroleum Co. hit oil 860 feet down opening a new well which is to be developed immediately. The drillers say the importance of the strike cannot be overrated.

A pipeline, refinery and tank farm will be built to handle the flow of oil, creating an industry which will add considerably to the prosperity of Sarawak, the jungle state ruled by the Brooke family, the "White Rajahs".

1911

FEBRUARY

Su	Mo	Tu	We	Th	Fr	Sa
			1	2	3	4
5	6	7	8	9	10	11
12	13	14	15	16	17	18
19	20	21	22	23	24	25
26	27	28				

1. London: Edward Mylius is sentenced to one year's imprisonment for libel, accusing King George V of bigamy.

1. London: Launch of first Thames-built dreadnought, "HMS Thunderer" (→24).

1. Manchuria: 1,000 people are reported to be dying daily from plague.

2. US: Minnesota doctors claim tetanus can be cured by spinal injection of Epsom salts.

2. St. Petersburg: Dr Patchenko, "Poison Doctor," confesses to murder of 40 for profit.

4. Rolls-Royce, appalled by mascots on owners' cars, commission "Spirit of Ecstasy" statuette.

5. Germany: 750,000 attend funeral of socialist leader Paul Singer.

6. London: George V opens his first new Parliament.→

6. Turkey: Large area of Constantinople is devastated by fire.

6. UK: Labour Party elects Ramsay MacDonald chairman.

14. France: 13 people are killed in a railway accident near Chartres.

22. Canada: Parliament votes to remain within the British Empire.

24. Berlin: Reichstag votes to increase the German standing army by 515,000 (→8/3).

27. Paris: Aristide Briand's cabinet resigns again.

28. UK: Air Battalion of the Royal Engineers is created.

28. Washington: Senate defeats constitutional amendment proposal for direct election of senators (→12/6).

BIRTH

6. US actor and 40th President (1980-88) Ronald Reagan.

DEATHS

4. Boer War leader General Piet Cronje (*1835).

25. German painter Fritz von Uhde (*22/5/1848).

New Labour leader makes his debut

MacDonald, workers' champion.

Feb 21. At Westminster today, James Ramsay MacDonald, who was elected as Labour Party chairman a fortnight ago in succession to James Keir Hardie, made an effective start in his leadership career.

Other party leaders listened attentively to his Commons speech in the momentous "Battle of the Constitution" debate. Mr MacDonald supported the Liberal Government's bill to curb the powers of the House of Lords.

However, he agreed with the Tories in opposing the idea, now being floated, of having an elected Upper House. That, he said, would make the Lords think that with a new respectability they could still compete with the Commons for power. "I want a single Chamber," he said (→2/3).

The New Year has brought in new modes for modern women.

1911

MARCH

Su	Mo	Tu	We	Th	Fr	Sa
			1	2	3	4
5	6	7	8	9	10	11
12	13	14	15	16	17	18
19	20	21	22	23	24	25
26	27	28	29	30	31	

1. US: President Taft sends 30,000 US soldiers to the Mexican frontier in case of revolution (→1/4).

2. London: The Government's Lords' Veto Bill gets second Commons reading after a stormy debate (→3/4).

2. Paris: Ernest Monis succeeds Aristide Briand as premier.

5. France: Figures show that France's population has grown by 350,000 in five years, the lowest rate in Europe (→3/4).

8. London: Foreign Secretary Edward Grey says Britain will not support France if it is attacked (→9).

9. London: The Government announces programme to build five more battleships for the Royal Navy (→4/4).

10. France: Time is set on Greenwich Mean Time.

12. New York: Dr Fletcher of the Rockefeller Institute discovers the cause of infantile paralysis.

15. London: Stinie Morrison sentenced to death for murder of Russian Jew Leon Beron.

17. Norway: Anna Rogstadt takes her seat as the country's first woman member of parliament (→4/4).

19. New York: Booker T. Washington, black rights leader, is assaulted by a white man.

20. St. Petersburg: Premier Peter Stolypin resigns.

24. UK: F. Bibby's Glenside wins the Grand National after a race in which only four out of 26 runners finished.

24. Denmark: The government abolishes corporal punishment.

26. Wales: Mid-Rhondda miners vote to continue their strike which began September 1910.

27. Antarctica: Captain Robert Scott discovers Roald Amundsen is also in race to reach the South Pole (→14/12).

BIRTH

26. US playwright Tennessee Williams (†25/2/83).

Shop workers to win 60-hour week

March 31. A 60-hour maximum working week for shop assistants is proposed by the Government in its new Shops Bill. Winding up the second reading debate in the Commons, the Home Secretary Winston Churchill, said that the 1904 Shops Act had failed to dea with the social evil caused by 80 and 90-hour working over a seven-day week.

Meal times are not to be included in the limit, which is the same for women as under the Factory Acts It can also be exceeded where the assistant is given one or two weeks holiday with full pay. The government will also "stir up" loca authorities to make half day "early closing" orders, when supported by a majority of local traders.

Shop staff: busiest at sale times.

Moroccan uprising terrifies Europeans

March 30. All the European consuls in the besieged town of Fez have called for assistance. The road to Tangier is blocked and English and German travellers have been stopped and robbed. Traders have failed to turn up for the weekly market and food is running out.

The revolt among tribesmen which began last October has continued to spread and the Sultan himself is said to be considering asking the French for help.

1911

APRIL

Su	Mo	Tu	We	Th	Fr	Sa
						1
2	3	4	5	6	7	8
9	10	11	12	13	14	15
16	17	18	19	20	21	22
23	24	25	26	27	28	29
30						

1. Mexico: President Porfirio Diaz promises great reforms in view of growing rebellion (→15).

2. Paris: First performance of Ravel's ballet "Daphnis et Chloe".

3. London: King George waives royal prerogative on Lords' reform issue (→26).

3. London: UK and Japan sign a commerce treaty.

4. US: Massachusetts state legislature refuses women the right to vote (→30).

4. London: Lords adopts Earl Roberts' motion on "inadequate arrangements for defence of the Empire" (→1/8).

6. Rome: The Italian government establishes a state life assurance scheme.

7. India: British Assistant Political Officer at Sadiya, Noel Williamson, and 50 others murdered by Abar tribesmen.

10. London: Marriage Law Amendment Bill introduced.

12. London: Stinie Morrison's death sentence is commuted to life imprisonment.

13. France: Furious rioting in Epernay and Rheims areas; thousands of bottles of wine smashed.

15. Mexico: US troops cross Rio Grande, begin fighting rebels under Francisco Madero (→20).

19. Portugal: Provisional government separates Church and State (→30).

20. Mexico: Rebel leader Madero refuses cease-fire until President Diaz resigns (→1/5).

26. London: Amendment to Lords' Reform Bill, for referendum when two Houses disagreed, is beaten (→22/7).

26. London: Bradford City beat Newcastle United 1-0 to win the FA Cup Final.

30. Portugal: Constitutional Court establishes female suffrage (→17/6).

BIRTH

10. French statesman Maurice Schumann.

French march to aid Moroccan Sultan

April 23. A special Sunday evening meeting of the French Cabinet, after endorsing measures taken by the War Ministry to suppress the revolt in Morocco, decided that more reinforcements are necessary. These will consist of French and Algerian troops from Algeria, Negro troops from Senegal and several battalions of the home army.

The French action, ostensibly in response to an appeal from the Sultan and to protect Europeans in Casablanca as well as Fez, has led German newspapers to give warning that a permanent French military occupation would violate the 1906 Algeciras conference accords on Morocco's independence.

Heads of rebels make a ghoulish display at Traitor's Gate in Fez.

Writers get 50-year copyright period

April 7. Authors and musicians were delighted today when the House of Commons gave a second reading to the Copyright Bill.

The Bill provides for the application of copyright throughout an author's lifetime and for 50 years after an author's death, unless the copyright is bequeathed, thus ending unchecked plagiarism and reproduction dating back to 1774. Before then authors had perpetual copyright to their works, which were treated as their own property. But this was changed on the basis that authors wrote for posterity and not the "miserable pittance" of royalties.

Russian and US populations boom: France drops behind UK

April 3. Britain's population is still growing and has now overtaken that of France. Germany continues to grow rapidly, but the rate of growth is even greater in the United States and Russia. America has been swelled by large-scale immigration from Europe and, to a lesser extent, Japan.

Within Britain the greatest growth in the last ten years has again been in the conurbations. It is understood that this year's census will show that the population in London's outer ring of suburbs has soared by a third, so that the capital now houses more than seven million people – roughly one in five of the entire population of England and Wales.

How populations have grown

millions	1880	1900	1910
RUSSIA	97.1	132.1	160.7
UNITED STATES	50.2	76.0	92.0
GERMANY	45.2	56.4	64.9
GREAT BRITAIN	35.1	41.8	45.0
FRANCE	37.7	39.0	39.6

Old Etonians bewail the abolition of the birch in upper school

April 4. The Duke of Marlborough joined several other former pupils of Britain's top public school today in expressing his support for the birch, and his disappointment that it may no longer be used in his old school. The duke is all for birching. "Better than writing out lines!" he said.

Although some Old Etonians are known to be in favour of the proposal, most agree with the duke. The Earl of Winterton said that writing lines could hurt the eyes and "is far more harmful than corporal correction".

Eton birching swansong: will lines attack the seat of indiscipline?

1911

MAY

Su	Mo	Tu	We	Th	Fr	Sa
	1	2	3	4	5	6
7	8	9	10	11	12	13
14	15	16	17	18	19	20
21	22	23	24	25	26	27
28	29	30	31			

1. Mexico: Durango falls to rebels in worst government defeat of rebellion.→

1. US: Supreme Court orders dissolution of Standard Oil Co. and American Tobacco Co., found guilty of restraint of trade under monopoly laws.

4. UK: First British airship is wrecked at Aldershot.

10. London: General Omnibus Co., United Tramways Co. and underground railway companies provisionally agree on joint operations.

12. London: King and Queen open the Festival of Empire at the Crystal Palace in south London.

15. London: King George V and his visiting cousin, Kaiser Wilhelm II, reassert mutual friendship.

16. London: The King unveils the Queen Victoria Memorial outside Buckingham Palace.

16. London: Budget proposes paying MPs a salary, of around £400 a year.

21. France: War Minister Maurice Berteaux is killed and premier Ernest Monis injured when an aeroplane crashes at Issy-les-Moulineaux.

24. London: Sir Edward Elgar conducts the first performance of his Symphony No. 2 in E flat at the Queen's Hall.

30. US: Ray Harroun wins first Indianapolis 500 motor race in Marmon Wasp at an average 74.59 mph.

31. Belfast: Launch of White Star liner "Titanic"; she and sister "SS Olympic" are largest vessels afloat (→15/5/12).

31. UK: J.B. Joel's Sunstar wins the Derby at Epsom.

BIRTH

15. Swiss writer Max Frisch (†4/4/91).

DEATHS

18. Austrian composer and conductor Gustav Mahler (*7/7/1860).

29. British writer and Sir Arthur Sullivan's librettist Sir William Schwenk Gilbert (*18/11/1836).→

Mexican rebels victorious: Diaz ousted

Mexico: revolutionary fervour.

Rebel leader Pancho Villa.

May 25. After almost 45 years, the Mexican dictator, Porfirio Diaz, today fell from power. Yesterday mobs thronged the streets of Mexico City, demanding Diaz's resignation. Though troops loyal to Diaz fired into the crowd today Diaz resigned as president.

He has held office for all but four years since 1876 and last year celebrated the centennial of Mexican independence with great solemnity. Although Diaz achieved considerable successes in the economic field, in recent years there has been widespread unrest both among intellectuals in the capital and among landless peasants in the provinces.

Last autumn, while Diaz was feting the centennial with great luxury, rebels like Zapata in the south and Pancho Villa in the north were in arms against his government. But it was the man who now takes over as provisional president, Francisco Madero, who set off the explosion which has now swept Diaz away. In October, from Texas where he was in exile, he published a "plan" calling for the removal of Diaz (→21/6).

London and General Omnibus Company drivers at a garage for the growing number of motor-buses to be seen on London's streets. These days the horse-drawn omnibus is an increasingly rare sight for travellers although traditionalists will certainly regret that it is no longer here.

Plans unveiled for national insurance

May 4. Mr Lloyd George today unveiled the Liberal Government's revolutionary Insurance Bill, designed to deal with sickness and unemployment. The Chancellor of the Exchequer's two-hour 20-minute speech to the Commons was warmly welcomed by Ramsay MacDonald, the Labour leader, who described the bill as "a big thing".

The Chancellor's surprise announcement that £1 would be made available to local authorities to build sanatoria to "stamp out the scourge of consumption" was particularly welcomed by the whole House.

The sickness scheme will cover the estimated 15 million workers on earnings below the income tax level, currently £3. Employees will pay 4d a week to the scheme, employers 3d and the State 2d. The unemployment insurance scheme, though, will only apply to the 2.4 million workers in engineering and building.

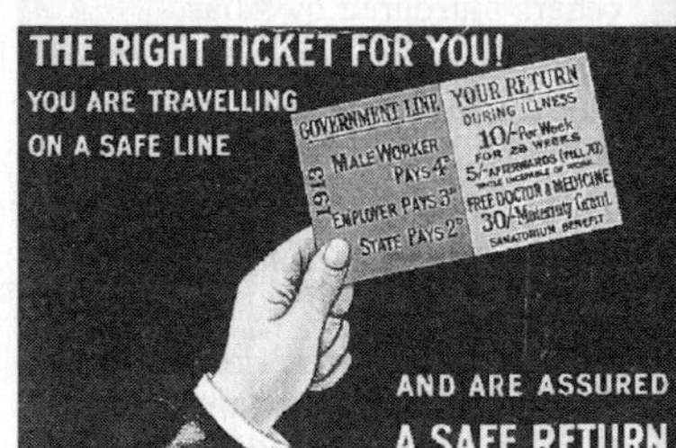

Liberal ticket to social security.

WS Gilbert drowns in rescue attempt

May 30. Sir W.S. Gilbert died suddenly and dramatically yesterday by drowning in his swimming pool at his home near Harrow, Grim's Dyke. Although he was 74, he was in the habit of taking a daily swim in the pool. He was accompanied by two schoolgirls, to whom he was giving a swimmimg lesson when one of them got into difficulties. Sir William swam to her very fast and when she placed her hand on his shoulder, he suddenly sank and failed to reappear. His body was recovered from the bottom of the eight-foot deep pond by two gardeners using a boat. A heart attack is suspected.

1911

JUNE

Su	Mo	Tu	We	Th	Fr	Sa
				1	2	3
4	5	6	7	8	9	10
11	12	13	14	15	16	17
18	19	20	21	22	23	24
25	26	27	28	29	30	

1. UK: First electric trolley buses go into service in Leeds and Bradford.

1. Rome: Huge monument is unveiled to late King Victor Emmanuel II.

4. France: Settlement of often rancorous argument over application of term "champagne".

7. Mexico: Over 100 are killed in an earthquake in Mexico City.

8. Berlin: Kaiser Wilhelm vetoes President Taft's choice of US ambassador to Germany.

9. Rome: Italian foreign minister says Italian interests in Africa are limited to Tripolitania and Cyrenaica.

13. Paris: First performance of the ballet "Petrushka" by Igor Stravinsky.

16. Morocco: The French army occupies the city of Fez (→2/7).

20. Wimbledon: The tennis meeting opens; for the first time there are more than 100 male contestants (→8/7).

21. Mexico: Former President Diaz departs for exile in Paris.

26. New York: Ziegfeld Follies open at the Jardin de Paris; songs include "Everybody's Doing It" by Irving Berlin.

26. Paris: Joseph Caillaux becomes premier after the resignation of Ernest Monis' government.

29. Reading: University College gets go-ahead to apply for charter as independent university.

30. London: King George V gives Coronation Fete at Crystal Palace for 100,000 London children.

BIRTH

24. Argentinian racing driver Juan Fangio.

DEATHS

9. US temperance advocate Carry Nation (*25/11/1846).

14. Norwegian composer Johann Svendsen (*30/9/1840).

Coronation of George V

King George and Queen Mary in procession down Fleet Street.

June 22. In ceremonies lasting no less than seven hours at Westminster Abbey, amid sumptuous church and state pageantry, King George V was today crowned "King of the United Kingdom of Great Britain and Ireland and of the British Dominions beyond the seas, Defender of the Faith, Emperor of India".

One of the more moving moments came when the new king's eldest son, the Prince of Wales, knelt to offer his allegiance: "I do become your liegeman of life and limb and of earthly worship, and faith and truth I will bear unto you, to live and die against all manner of folks, so help me God." When the prince rose to his feet, he touched his father's crown and then kissed him. The King drew his son close and they embraced.

The Abbey had been transformed for the coronation. Vivid new blue carpets highlighted banks of red tulips, white lilies and blue delphiniums. Rising tier upon tier above the often richly-robed guests were the choristers, faces scrubbed bright and with their red soutanes and white ruffles lit by an intermittent sun filtering through the stained glass windows. And at the centre of everybody's attention was the golden canopy, held aloft by four noblemen, where George V was consecrated and invested with the ancient regalia of kingship.

In the congregation were many reminders that George V headed the largest Empire in the world: from premiers and cabinet ministers of the dominions to Indian princes wearing jewelled turbans and clothes of gold. Among these princes were men whose families go back further than even the western monarchs who today were alongside them. Outside the Abbey, crowds stood in their tens of thousands. Throughout the country, the coronation was celebrated. Toasts were drunk, bonfires blazed.

US senators to be directly elected by voting public

June 12. The Americans have made a great change to the way that they elect their senators, which is intended to give more power to the ordinary voters. At present the senators, two from each state, are chosen by the state legislature for a four-year term. This system means that the senators reflect the political bent of local politicians.

Under the new proposals the senators would now be elected for six-year terms by the voters of each state. The above move, which requires an amendment to the constitution, has to be approved by the Senate and passed by the House of Representatives.

Tie-breaking win in golf come-back

June 30. Harry Vardon, perhaps the greatest name in golf, broke a lean spell of eight years in which he had failed to finish in the first three in any Open, to win the English championship at Sandwich today and equal, at the age of 41, the record of five Open victories set by his perennial rival James Braid.

A near-disastrous final round of 80 saw Vardon, the tall Channel Islander, tied for the lead with the Basque, Arnaud Massy, and it was not till the 35th hole of the play-off that he clinched victory.

Open champion Harry Vardon.

1911

JULY

Su	Mo	Tu	We	Th	Fr	Sa
						1
2	3	4	5	6	7	8
9	10	11	12	13	14	15
16	17	18	19	20	21	22
23	24	25	26	27	28	29
30	31					

1. London: Parliament passes the Shops Act, introducing a compulsory half day holiday for shop workers.

5. Balkans: Reported that 10,000 Montenegrin troops have been mobilised on the Albanian border.

5. Portugal: Revolt against the new republic is put down after street fighting in Lisbon.

7. Mexico: President Francisco Madero establishes a liberal regime.

8. Wimbledon: Anthony Wilding beats Herbert Barrett for the Men's Singles title; Dorothea Chambers beats Penelope Boothby for the Ladies' Singles championship.

9. US: 652 deaths in a week reported during heatwave.

9. Ireland: The King opens the Royal College of Science in Dublin.

11. Paris: 60,000 masons go on strike, paralysing the building industry.

13. Wales: Investiture of the Prince of Wales in Caernarvon Castle.

14. Wales: The King opens new buildings of University College of North Wales at Bangor.

15. Belfast: Police carry out baton charges to break up riots in Protestant West Belfast.

16. Egypt: Field Marshal Herbert Kitchener is appointed Consul-General at Cairo.

18. UK: King George V arrives in Edinburgh on a Coronation visit.

22. London: King guarantees creation of new peers to ensure unamended passage of Veto Bill through Lords.

28. France: Army chief General Michel resigns over the Dreyfus Affair; General Joseph Joffre succeeds.

30. France: Frenchman Victor Garrigou wins the Tour de France.

BIRTH

5. French statesman and President (1969-74) Georges Pompidou (†2/4/74).

Women in costume march for votes

June 17. Between about 40,000 and 60,000 supporters of the enfranchisement of women marched through the streets of London today in a five-mile long procession. The marchers had come from both Britain and overseas. Many were dressed as famous women such as Boadicea, Joan of Arc and Queen Victoria.

One of the most impressive groups was the 700 women who have been imprisoned for the cause, each proudly displaying a silver arrow as a mark of their suffering and carrying a banner which read "From prison to citizenship".

Marchers were drawn from all walks of life and all classes: factory-girls and aristocrats, actresses and university graduates. An enthusiastic meeting at the Albert Hall ended with the announcement that funds now stood at £103,000.

UK ports paralysed by shipping strike

June 14. Under banners proclaiming "War declared! Strike for liberty", the seamen's union in Liverpool and Southampton today called for a national strike and for its members to refuse to sign on for voyages unless its demands are met.

The seamen's leaders want a joint employer-union conciliation board for settling disputes and a minimum wage of £5 10s a month for seamen and firemen on cargo vessels, with higher rates for skilled hands and those on passenger ships (→20/7).

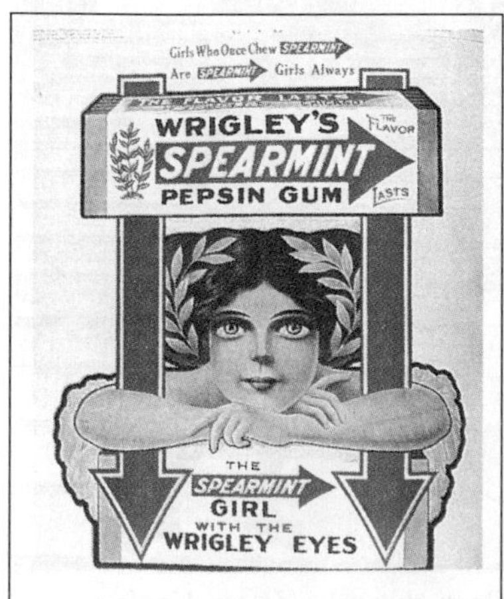

Gunboats stoke tension over Morocco

July 2. The sudden announcement yesterday that the Kaiser has despatched a German gunboat, the "Panther", to the Moroccan port of Agadir has caused surprise and dismay in Paris and concern in London as to Germany's motives.

The German note to France insists the sole purpose of the "Panther's" visit is to protect German firms at Agadir, "where considerable agitation exists". A German firm active in European financial circles, the Brothers Mannesmann, has claimed to have substantial interests in Agadir, but this is questioned in London.

Agadir is a closed port, not open to legitimate trade with Europeans; notoriously, it is used by Berbers for the smuggling of guns into the interior. British speculation is that Germany may be preparing to stake a claim to a naval base on the Atlantic coast. The dispatch of the "Panther" follows mounting discontent in Germany at France's growing influence in Morocco, emphasised by the occupation of Fez by an expeditionary force earlier this year (→15/9).

Kaiser Wilhelm: a French view.

Rioters killed by troops in Wales

July 20. Nine people were killed, three by soldiers' bullets, in a night of furious rioting at Llanelli, South Wales, last night. The disturbance, in which shops were looted and 80 railway wagons burned, came as a climax to a railway strike which is threatening to paralyse Britain.

Six of the victims were killed and 20 others injured when burning trucks, filled with railway detonators and bottled carbide, exploded in their midst.

Troops of the Worcester Regiment opened fire on a stone-throwing crowd, killing three and wounding another after a train had been boarded by strikers trying to force the driver and fireman from the footplate.

As the rioting increased in ferocity and the troops advanced on the crowd with fixed bayonets, the rioters turned on the two magistrates who had read the Riot Act, looting and burning their shops and homes.

Railwaymen are striking in support of their docker colleagues who have brought Britain's ports to a standstill and caused industrial unrest throughout the country. Dockers are seeking a minimum wage of thirty shillings a week and better working conditions (→8/8).

The new Prince of Wales rides to his investiture at Caernarvon Castle.

1911

AUGUST

Su	Mo	Tu	We	Th	Fr	Sa
		1	2	3	4	5
6	7	8	9	10	11	12
13	14	15	16	17	18	19
20	21	22	23	24	25	26
27	28	29	30	31		

1. Germany: The government decides to fortify Heligoland in the North Sea (→9/10).

3. North Africa: First military use of aeroplanes when Italians reconnoitre Turkish lines near Tripoli (→28/9).

7. London: The Government defeats a vote of censure over handling of Lords Veto Bill.→

9. London: Hottest day in the capital for 70 years: 97 degrees Fahrenheit in the shade (→26).

10. London: Commons sets MPs' new salaries at £400.

15. Brussels: 215,000 demonstrate in favour of universal suffrage (→24/11).

16. Manchester: Reported that the city is living on food reserves and that famine threatens (→18).

18. London: Parliament Bill and Official Secrets Bill receive Royal Assent.

18. London: 50,000 troops are on duty as 200,000 strike (→29).

23. UK: Violent anti-Semitic riots are reported in Wales.

24. US: Crowd of 3000 cheer as a black man is burnt alive.

24. Portugal: Arriaga is elected first constitutional president of the republic (→1/10).

26. UK: Ten die and 12 are injured at Consett in County Durham when a coach carrying a choir crashes.

26. London: Reported that 2,500 children have died in the recent heatwave.→

29. UK: Inquest on two strikers shot dead by troops at Llanelli returns verdicts of justifiable homicide (→5/9).

29. Plymouth: German officer Phil Max Schultz committed for trial for spying under new Official Secrets Act.

31. Paris: Director of the Louvre Homolle is sacked following theft of Mona Lisa (→12/12/13).

BIRTH

6. US comedienne and producer Lucille Ball (†26/4/89).

Riots rock Britain: troops called in

An "armoured motor" with troop escort for policemen engaged in strike duties in Liverpool.

Aug 8. Fifty thousand armed troops were preparing to join other forces in London last night while Liverpool was wracked by riots in which at least two men were shot dead.

A nationwide strike by stevedores, railwaymen, carters and other transport workers is bringing much of the country to a standstill. Manchester and other major cities are fearing widespread famine.

Three warships are anchored in the Mersey in which a queue of merchant ships and passenger liners is waiting to be unloaded. Naval detachments are preparing to join troops and hard-pressed police in the City where an estimated 200,000 people have taken to the streets.

Much of Liverpool is without electricity because coal is not reaching the power stations. In London, buses have been taken of the roads due to petrol shortages. Strike-breaking vans were stoned, and police leave cancelled.

Labour MP Keir Hardie told a strike meeting at London's Tower Hill: "The masters show you no mercy. They starve you, they sweat you, they oppress you. Pay them back in their own coin."

In Parliament, the Home Secretary, Winston Churchill, defended his tough line against strikers, saying they were endangering the country's industrial wealth and other men's jobs.

The House of Lords surrenders its veto

Aug 10. Just before eleven o'clock tonight, the House of Lords gave up the struggle of claiming it was born to rule. By a narrow majority it accepted the Liberal government's Parliament Bill asserting the supremacy of the Commons. It did so in the knowledge that the King has promised to side with the elected MPs in an ultimate showdown.

The Archbishops of Canterbury and York and 11 Bishops voted for the Bill limiting Lords' power to delay legislation and two Bishops against. The Tories saw the writing on the wall.

Leonardo's Lisa is lifted from Louvre

Aug 22. The unthinkable has happened. Someone has stolen the Mona Lisa, to the horror of Paris and the art world.

The thief slipped into the Louvre during the night and took off with Leonardo da Vinci's masterpiece. The acutely embarrassed curators of the Louvre claim only a madman would have pinched a picture so well known he could not hope to sell it, but this does not explain how the museum's most keenly-guarded attraction just vanished. This, like Mona Lisa's smile, remains an enigma (→12/12/13).

Thousands die in record heatwave

Aug 28. The recent record-breaking heat wave with temperatures of up to 97 degrees has set Britain's death rate soaring. With a mortality rate for all ages of 19 per 1,000, London is now the second most unhealthy city in the world.

It is children who are most at risk. During the last week of July, 382 children up to the age of two died in the city. In the week just ended, the figure rocketed to 855. Questions are now being asked as to whether the authorities have done all they could to counter the distressing loss of life.

1911

SEPTEMBER

Su	Mo	Tu	We	Th	Fr	Sa
					1	2
3	4	5	6	7	8	9
10	11	12	13	14	15	16
17	18	19	20	21	22	23
24	25	26	27	28	29	30

1. France: Women attack fruit and vegetable shops as part of riots against high price of food.

4. China: Reported that 100,000 have died in flooding along the Yangtse-kiang River.

5. UK: Trades Union Congress bitterly condemns use of troops in recent strikes.

6. Italy: 30,000 deaths from cholera reported this year.

7. Paris: Poet Guillaume Apollinaire is arrested, and later released, for theft of Mona Lisa (→ 12/12/13).

10. China: Floods are killing 300 people a day in Shanghai.

15. Berlin: French ambassador Paul Cambon and the German foreign minister discuss future policy towards Morocco (→ 23).

15. Ireland: General railway strike begins.

18. Spain: Martial law is proclaimed as general strike is declared in Valencia.

19. St. Petersburg: Czar Nicholas appoints Vladimir Kokovtsev premier in succession to Stolypin (→ 22).

22. St. Petersburg: Military tribunal condemns Stolypin's assassin Bogrov to be hanged.

22. Canada: R. L. Borden succeeds Wilfred Laurier as PM following election victory.

23. Belfast: Meeting of 50,000 Ulster Unionists addressed by Sir Edward Carson rejects any possibility of Home Rule.

23. Berlin: France and Germany settle Moroccan dispute (→ 3/11).

28. North Africa: Italy declares war on Turkey for possession of Tripolitania. →

BIRTHS

19. British writer and 1983 Nobel Prize winner William Golding (†19/6/93).

24. Soviet leader Konstantin Chernenko (†10/3/85).

DEATH

18. Russian politician Peter (Pyotr) Stolypin (*14/4/1862). →

Russian Premier dies after opera attack

Devastation caused by a bomb in an earlier attempt to kill Stolypin in 1906.

Sept 18. Russia's hard-line Premier, Peter Stolypin, died today, having been shot while at the Kiev opera last week. Known for his ruthless and uncompromising ways, Stolypin, who was 49, had made many enemies and had been a target before for assassination.

During an interval he had risen from his seat in the first row of the stalls and stood facing the audience. The assassin, Mordkha Bogrov, entered the hall wearing evening clothes, walked down the aisle and fired two shots at close range into Stolypin's liver and spine from a Browning revolver.

Police grabbed him and prevented him from being lynched by the crowd. The shooting was watched by Czar Nicholas II and two of his daughters who were sitting in a box overlooking the stage. Ironically Stolypin had been visiting Kiev with the Czar for the unveiling of a statute of Czar Alexander III, Nicholas' predecessor, whose reactionary policies have contributed to Russia's present turmoil.

Bogrov is both a socialist lawyer and a police informer. He gave information about an attempt on Stolypin's life to the police even before the premier arrived in Kiev, and was allowed in the opera house to point out the potential assassin. Bogrov is also a Jew and there is considerable unease about the possibility of a retaliatory pogrom.

Winged messenger: putting the finishing touches to the plane which on September 9 took the world's first airmail, from Hendon to Windsor.

Italy attacks Turks in Tripoli harbour

Sept 30. Brushing aside Turkey's reply to its 24-hour ultimatum, the Italian government yesterday, ordered its warships to mount an assault on Tripoli. One Turkish gunboat is reported sunk.

Messages from Tripoli make it clear that the Italians never intended to negotiate over their demand that Turkey consent to a military occupation of Tripolitania and Cyrenaica, the only territories in North Africa not under European rule.

Before the ultimatum had even been put to Constantinople on Thursday, Italian warships had been sighted off the port of Tripoli the previous evening. Yesterday morning, hours before the ultimatum expired at 2.30pm, an Italian destroyer entered the harbour and an officer came ashore to order Italian citizens to take refuge aboard an Italian steamer lying at anchor.

Italy's action sent shares tumbling on the Berlin Stock Exchange. Turkish loans lost up to twopence halfpenny on the day (→ 5/10).

First Channel swim for thirty-six years

Tom Burgess en route to France.

Sept 6. A full 36 years after Matthew Webb first swam the English Channel, his feat was emulated today. At his 13th attempt, after a swim of more than 22 hours 30 minutes from Dover (an hour longer than Webb), Thomas Burgess, a Yorkshireman from Rotherham, waded ashore at Cap Gris Nez.

1911

OCTOBER

Su	Mo	Tu	We	Th	Fr	Sa
1	2	3	4	5	6	7
8	9	10	11	12	13	14
15	16	17	18	19	20	21
22	23	24	25	26	27	28
29	30	31				

1. Portugal: Royalist peasants revolt in the north, demanding restoration of monarchy (→ 3).

2. Mexico: Francisco Madero is elected president (→ 24).

3. Portugal: Royalists beaten by Republican troops in battle at Oporto.

5. North Africa: Italians take Tripoli (→ 20).

6. UK: The Duke of Connaught leaves to become Governor-General of Canada.

7. Balkans: Many die in Italian bombardment of Albanian town of Point Medua.

9. Southampton: Launch of "HMS King George V", Royal Navy's biggest ship.→

9. China: Major cities in revolt against imperial rule (→ 12).

10. UK: Government sets up Industrial Council to settle future disputes between workers and employers.

11. US: 700 die in earthquake in southern California.

12. China: Provisional Government proclaimed in South China as revolt assumes civil war proportions; Sun Yat-Sen is president of provisional assembly.→

16. US: Discovery of plot to assassinate President Taft.

20. North Africa: Italians bombard Benghazi and land 4,000 troops.→

22. Spain: Martial law rescinded.

23. Manchester: First Ford Model T produced outside the US rolls off the production line.

23. Crete: Cretan parliament votes for unification with Greece.

23. North Africa: Italians complete their occupation of Benghazi (→ 1/11).

24. Mexico City: Rebel supporters of Emiliano Zapata carry out raids around the capital.

DEATH

29. US journalist and publisher Joseph Pulitzer (*10/4/1847).

Pu Yi surrenders power

Oct 30. In a desperate attempt to rally support against the victorious Republican rebel armies, Pu Yi, the five-year-old boy Emperor of China, today agreed to grant a constitution.

On the advice of Prince Chun, the Regent, he also ordered the formation of a new cabinet composed entirely of commoners, thereby finally surrendering the Manchu domination over China which has lasted for three centuries.

The chances of the imperial house surviving the civil war now seem slim. The rebellion, which began as a popular rising among a small group of revolutionary troops at Wuchang in central China only three weeks ago, has spread like wildfire through the cities.

Since the death of the Dowager Empress three years ago, the authority of the throne has greatly declined. The five-year-old emperor has, not surprisingly, proved unable to keep control in face of demands for change and reform. Revolutionary leaders like Dr Sun Yat-sen are openly hostile to the Manchu rule and their ideas have swept the country.

The government in Peking pinned its hopes on the well-trained Northern Army. But this force of 30,000 men has made no progress because its officers are in doubt about the loyalty of its soldiers.

Nor is the prospect more comforting as far as strong-man Yuan Shi-kai is concerned. He is a former provincial governor-general on whom the government relied to deal with the uprising. But at the moment there is no sign that he is prepared to suppress the revolutionaries.

Last week he excused himself on grounds that he had a bad foot. It is believed that he is calculating the revolution's chances before making a move (→ 2/11).

Italian flag flies over Turkish Tripoli

An Italian army doctor tends a wounded soldier during the campaign.

Oct 20. An Italian expeditionary force of some 9,000 rifles and two squadrons of cavalry completed landing operations at Tripoli today. Forts in the town were seized and the Italian flag raised. Further along the coast, Benghazi was taken after a naval bombardment.

The authorities have imposed a rigid system of censorship. All reports must go to Rome, where they are held up in the most arbitrary manner. The suspicion is that Italian losses are higher than admitted.

From Constantinople it is reported that the Italians, not anticipating having to operate in the interior, arrived with little transport. But the Turkish Governor of Tripoli requisitioned all available camels and retreated with his garrison into the desert (→ 23).

Sea Lord Churchill puts Navy on alert

At the helm: Winston Churchill.

Oct 23. Winston Churchill was named today as the new First Lord of the Admiralty. This switch from being Home Secretary pleases the Labour Party on which the Government relies for support in the present hung Parliament. In recent years Mr. Churchill has incensed Labour with his use of troops to quell several incidents of civil and industrial disorder. He inherits a policy of checking the rate of increase in naval expenditure and may try to change it (→ 9/11).

1911

NOVEMBER

Su	Mo	Tu	We	Th	Fr	Sa
			1	2	3	4
5	6	7	8	9	10	11
12	13	14	15	16	17	18
19	20	21	22	23	24	25
26	27	28	29	30		

1. North Africa: Italians carry out first aerial bombing, on Tanguira Oasis in Tripolitania (→8).

2. London: 6,000 cabbies go on strike.

2. China: Hankow is burnt by Imperial troops (→10).

2. Egypt: Martial law is proclaimed and 200 arrests made following widespread Moslem discontent.

3. North Africa: Morocco becomes a French protectorate under new Franco-German treaty.→

5. North Africa: Italy announces the annexation of Libya, Tripolitania and Cyrenaica.→

6. London: Imperial Cancer Research Fund says the disease may be hereditary.

6. US: Maine decides on prohibition of alcohol.

8. London: Arthur Balfour resigns as leader of the Conservative and Unionist Party.→

9. London: At Lord Mayor's Banquet Churchill says Royal Navy aims to maintain superiority over German fleet.

10. China: Imperial troops massacre republicans at Nanking (→2/12).

14. London: New London Opera House opens on Kingsway.

14. US: Announced that Joseph Pulitzer's will left endowment for journalism prizes.

15. Detroit: The Chevrolet Motor Company is incorporated.

16. France: King Peter of Serbia arrives on an official visit.

17. London: Lord Plymouth saves the Crystal Palace at Sydenham by buying it for the nation.

24. Liverpool: 21 die, 114 are injured in a mill explosion.

DEATH

25. French socialist theorist Paul Lafargue (*15/1/1842).

Suffragette rally after mass jailing

Nov 24. Lady Constance Lytton, sister of the Earl, was among those appearing at Bow Street Court today in the wake of the suffrage riots outside Parliament earlier this week. Lady Constance, who became one of the movement's heroines last year when, disguised as a working class woman, she was forcibly fed in Walton jail, was fined £2 for wilful damage. Altogether more than 200 women and a handful of men were arrested in Tuesday night's clashes.

In stormy scenes wave after wave of women attempted to rush the police cordons as others went on a rampage of destruction, smashing windows in government buildings and business premises throughout the area. The women had been angered by the government's proposed Manhood Suffrage bill which extends the male franchise, yet does nothing for women.

The movement claims it is a "slap in the face for women". The decision to demonstrate was taken when a direct appeal to the Prime Minister was rebuffed.

Last night a defiant Christabel Pankhurst told a packed rally at the Savoy Theatre: "When women are being knocked about, men do nothing. But when £5 of plate glass is broken, it's thought to be serious." To laughter, another supporter said it was the proudest moment of her life when she got a stone thrown through a window.

Suffragettes demonstrate outside the Foreign Office in Downing Street.

Mill explosion rocks Liverpool

Nov 24. Twenty-one people were killed and more than 100 injured this afternoon when an explosion rocked a Liverpool factory. The explosion blew off the roof and sent flames scorching through Bibby's Mill, one of the largest factories in the city where 1,300 people make oil cakes for cattle feeding.

Survivors spoke of "a terrific bang like an earthquake" and "a terrific wind throwing us violently off our feet". As the building crumbled, massive iron doors were hurled into the street. Some workers were rescued from window ledges by the fire brigade.

Trouble is brewing downstairs, m'lord

Nov 29. Some 20,000 women – maids and mistresses – packed and overflowed London's Albert Hall this evening in protest at Government plans to make householders pay National Insurance contributions for their servants.

To loud cheers from the huge audience, speaker after speaker roundly condemned the Chancellor, Lloyd George, over the Bill. Far from protecting the poor, they claimed, the Bill would force many employers to choose between cutting their servants' wages to pay the extra tax, and doing without servants at all (→16/12).

Bonar Law chosen to succeed Balfour as Tory leader

Bonar Law: in the driving seat.

Nov 13. Cigar-smoking Andrew Bonar Law, Canadian-born Glas gow businessman, became the Tory Party leader today. He succeeds Arthur James Balfour who has re signed for health reasons.

Mr Bonar Law was a compro mise choice. Neither of his stronger rivals – Austen Chamberlain and Walter Long – could muster maj ority support. In an acceptance speech at London's Carlton Club the Opposition's new leader said nothing about the party's future policy. Afterwards he reluctantly posed for photographs.

New weekly reading for women.

How Europe's empires carved up the map of Africa

Nov 4. A Franco-German treaty made public today disclosed that Germany has recognised the right of France to establish a protectorate in Morocco. In return, France has ceded to Germany about 96,525 square miles (and some one million people) in the northern French Congo bordering the German Cameroons. The agreement marks a further stage in the colonisation of Africa by the European powers.

European explorers first began to make inroads into "the dark continent" in the 18th century, but until 1870 their impact was limited. Only the northern and southern fringes betrayed much evidence of European settlement or cultures.

In the last 40 years, however, there has been a scramble for Africa as the European powers sought to assemble ever greater empires. Africa became the cockpit for colonial rivalries; in one generation the map of a continent has been redrawn with new boundaries, new names and new masters.

Today's agreement is another stage in this process, although it takes no account of Spanish claims to Morocco. Libya is also disputed between Italy and Turkey. And the colonisation has not been achieved without resistance. There have been wars or rebellions against European rule in South Africa, South-West Africa, Nigeria and the Sudan. Only Ethiopia and Liberia can now claim any independence.

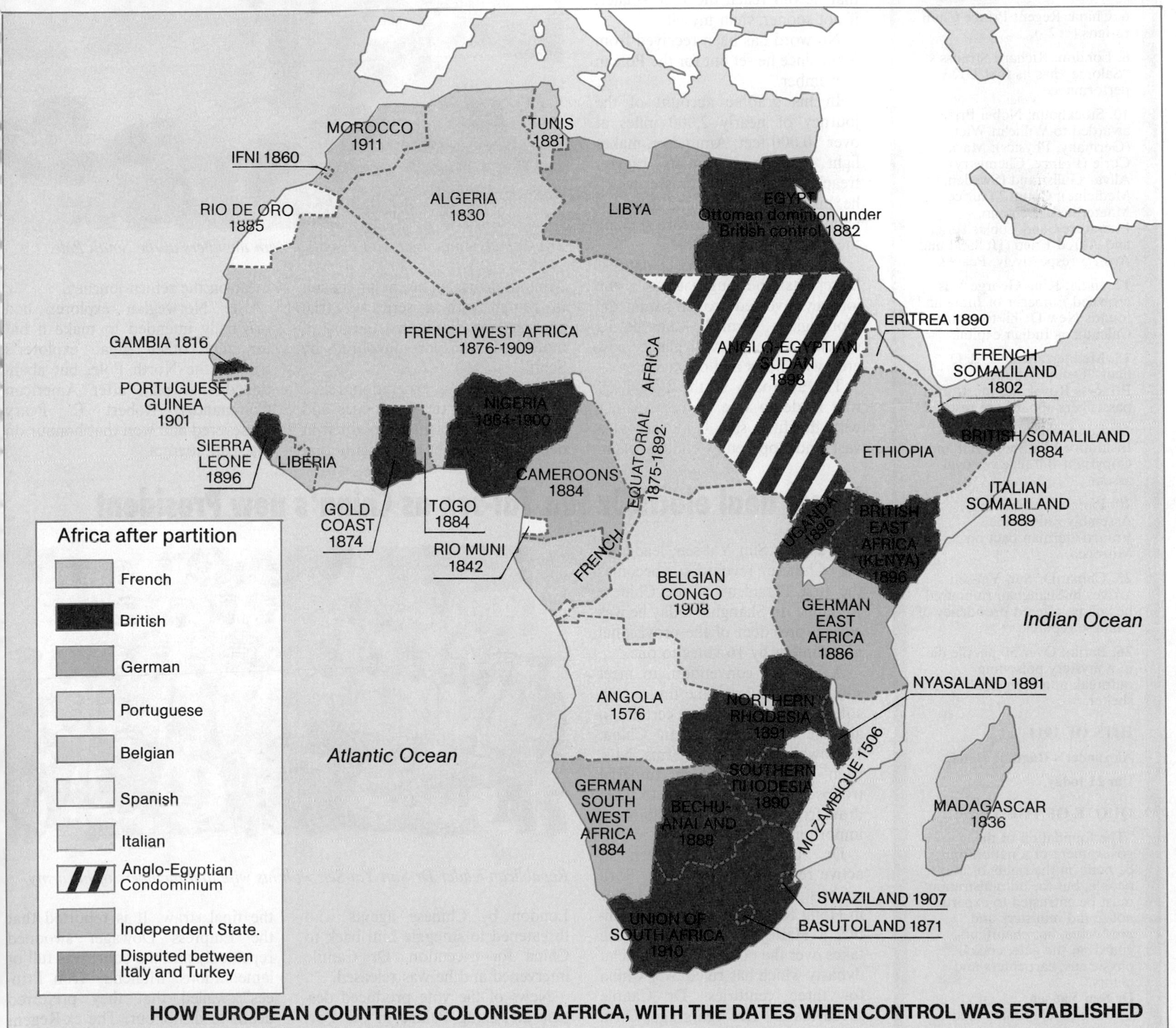

HOW EUROPEAN COUNTRIES COLONISED AFRICA, WITH THE DATES WHEN CONTROL WAS ESTABLISHED

1911

DECEMBER

Su	Mo	Tu	We	Th	Fr	Sa
					1	2
3	4	5	6	7	8	9
10	11	12	13	14	15	16
17	18	19	20	21	22	23
24	25	26	27	28	29	30
31						

2. China: Republicans recapture Nanking (→6).

6. Far East: Mongolia declared a Russian protectorate.

6. China: Regent Prince Chun resigns (→25).

8. London: Richard Strauss's "Salome" has its first UK performance.

10. Stockholm: Nobel Prizes awarded to Wilhelm Wien (Germany, Physics); Marie Curie (France, Chemistry); Allvar Gullstrand (Sweden, Medicine); Count Maurice Maeterlinck (Belgium, Literature); and Tobias Asser and Alfred Fried (Holland and Austria respectively, Peace).

12. India: King George V is crowned Emperor of India and founds New Delhi, to replace Calcutta as Indian capital.

13. Mediterranean: P & O liner "Delhi" founders; Princess Royal and most other passengers aboard are rescued.

16. London: National Insurance Bill, Shops Bill and Copyright Bill receive royal assent.

20. Paris: The National Assembly ratifies the Franco-German pact on Morocco.

25. China: Dr Sun Yat-sen arrives in Shanghai; rumoured he will be offered presidency of Chinese republic.→

26. Berlin: Over 50 people die in a mystery poisoning outbreak at a municipal shelter.

HITS OF 1911

Alexander's Ragtime Band.

I'm 21 today.

QUOTE OF THE YEAR

"The foundation of the government of a nation must be built on the rights of the people, but the administration must be entrusted to experts: not grand ministers and presidents, but chauffeurs, guards at the gate, cooks, physicians, carpenters and tailors."
Dr Sun Yat-sen,
Chinese revolutionary leader.

Amundsen beats Scott to South Pole

Dec 14. Norwegian explorer Roald Amundsen has won the race to the South Pole – a goal sought by Britons since the beginning of this century.

In a message from the Antarctic, Amundsen said that he had seen no sign of Captain Robert Scott and his party although he agreed that "it is exceedingly likely that he did reach the Pole – later, if not sooner, than myself".

No word has been received from Scott since he set out for the Pole in November.

In his graphic account of the journey of nearly 2,000 miles at over 10,000 feet, Amundsen makes light of the mountain ranges, treacherous ice and crevasses which he, his four comrades and their dog teams had to cross before making the final dash to the Pole.

"Everything went like a dance," he reports. The roughest part of the journey involved crossing what the Norwegians termed "the devil's dancing room", a vast glacier covered with holes and crevasses.

The approach to the Pole itself was made in fine, sunny weather with the final slog being across a vast and apparently endless plain.

Triumphant Amundsen with essential team members at the South Pole.

Amundsen began his polar assault in March with a series of trial marches and discounted the use of motorised transport favoured by Scott.

The successful expedition relied entirely on dog-drawn sledges and proposes to supplement food left in depots along the route with dog meat on the return journey.

The Norwegian explorer had originally intended to make a bid for that other great explorer's trophy, the North Pole, but abandoned that plan after American Commander Robert E. Peary persevered and won that honour on his sixth attempt.

Peace deal elects Dr Sun Yat-sen as China's new President

Dec 29. Dr Sun Yat-sen, leader of the Chinese revolution, becomes the first President of the Chinese Republic. In Shanghai today he was elected president of the provisional government by 16 votes to one.

A national convention, to meet soon, will decide on the future constitution and is almost certain to abolish the monarchy in China. Meanwhile, armistice terms have been agreed by which Imperial troops are given five days to withdraw from their present positions in important cities.

Dr Sun Yat-sen has been an active reformer for 30 years. Born a Christian, and trained as a doctor in Hong Kong with Dr James Cantile, a Harley Street specialist, he takes over the power of the Manchu dynasty which has ruled over China for three centuries. Dr Cantile saved his life five years ago. On a visit to London, Sun Yat-sen was lured into the Chinese legation in London by Chinese agents who threatened to smuggle him back to China for execution. Dr Cantile intervened and he was released.

Republican leader Dr Sun Yat-Sen with his wife and members of his army.

News of the vote produced despair at Peking Palace in the Forbidden City, still under Imperial control, where it was regarded as the final straw. It is reported that the Empress Dowager swooned repeatedly and the court was full of lamentations. Manchu "Iron Princes" wailed that they preferred death to dishonour. The ex-Regent left the Forbidden City in a closed carriage under escort.

Camden Town leads UK avant-garde

The **"Camden Town Group"** is the unappealing name for 16 painters of the English avant-garde who have held their first two shows this year. Founded by **Walter Sickert**, they include such figures as **Augustus John, Lucien Pissarro, Wyndham Lewis, Henry Lamb** and **Spencer Gore**.

Sickert, who was a pupil of Whistler, shows several paintings of nudes in dusky and dingy bedrooms in Camden Town as well as the audience in the gallery at music halls, of which Camden Town has many.

Some of these artists use light, flat areas of colour and seem to be under the influence of the "Post-Impressionists" **Cezanne, van Gogh** and **Gauguin** – whose work was shown for the first time in London last year by Roger Fry to general incomprehension.

Meanwhile, in Paris, the Salon d'Automne has devoted a room to the so-called "Cubists". Cubism was originated by **Picasso** and **Georges Braque**, who are now being joined by other painters such as **Juan Gris** and **Marcel Duchamp**. The critic **Guillaume Apollinaire** champions the objectives of this strange, fractured form of painting which is meaningless to most visitors to the Salon.

Germany, too, has a new movement in art. The "Blue Rider" group, led by **Kandinsky** and **Franz Marc** and named after an almanack which they are editing, this month opened its first show in Munich.

German music has suffered the loss of **Gustav Mahler**, for ten years the conductor of the Vienna State Opera, at the early age of 50. Besides his nine symphonies, he left sketches for a tenth and "Das Lied von der Erde" – The Song of the Earth – which was performed after his death last May.

Stravinsky's "Petrushka", costume by Alexandre Derois for Nijinsky.

The most successful opera to be launched for several years was given at Dresden, where **Richard Strauss's** "Der Rosenkavalier" had a rapturous reception, with 25 curtain calls lasting over ten minutes.

The hit of the Russian Ballet's Paris season was **Stravinsky's** new work, "Petrushka". In it, **Nijinsky** dances the role of a puppet tragically in love with a ballerina.

Madame Curie wins second Nobel Prize

Dec 31. This year has seen two developments which open up entirely new fields of scientific research and an unprecedented second Nobel prize for Marie Curie. Mme Curie won her award for her work on the intensely radioactive elements polonium and radium; the new breakthroughs have been the discovery of superconductivity by Dutch physicist Heike Kamerlingh Onnes, and of radiation from outer space by Victor Francis Hess in Austria.

Kamerlingh Onnes is the world's leading authority on very low temperatures. He was the first person, in 1908, to liquefy helium, at a temperature of -269 degrees centigrade. This is only 4 degrees above absolute zero, the lowest temperature of all. While studying the behaviour of materials at these very low temperatures Onnes found that some metals, like lead and mercury, lost all electrical resistance close to absolute zero.

In theory, an electric current will flow in such "superconductors" for ever, something very close to perpetual motion. There is no explanation yet of this remarkable phenomenon.

Hess made his discovery while investigating the ubiquitous back-

Curie: award-winning work.

ground radiation detectable even in shielded chambers and hitherto assumed to come from traces of radio-activity in soil, air and water. Some of Hess's experiments involved flying instruments in balloons.

He expected radiation to decrease with increasing altitude. He found, however, that it actually increased. At six miles it was eight times higher than on the earth's surface. Hess has suggested that the radiation comes from outer space, but its origin still remains a mystery.

Cotton lock-out renders 300,000 idle

Dec 27. About 300,000 workers in the cotton industry are today idle after employers closed down their mills across Lancashire in an attempt to thwart a campaign by unions to force all spinners and weavers to become members.

The lock-out, which meant 420,000 looms were halted, is the climax of a dispute over who has the right to decide which workers should be hired. Virtually every weaving mill in the north of the county was shut, although the row centres on three non-unionists at Accrington and Great Harwood, who refused to accept membership of the Weavers' Association.

When union officials ordered a strike at the two sites, employers belonging to the Cotton Spinners and Manufacturers' Association agreed at a series of crisis meetings to joint action.

George V, crowned Emperor of India, has a reputation as an excellent shot. Here the new King-Emperor shows off his prowess from the howdah of an elephant on a hunting expedition in Nepal.

1912

JANUARY

Su	Mo	Tu	We	Th	Fr	Sa
	1	2	3	4	5	6
7	8	9	10	11	12	13
14	15	16	17	18	19	20
21	22	23	24	25	26	27
28	29	30	31			

1. UK: The National Telephone Company is taken over by the Post Office.

3. London: The cabinet is reported to be split down the middle on women's suffrage (→ 1/3).

4. UK: The Boy Scouts are granted a Royal Charter of Incorporation.

6. US: New Mexico becomes the 47th state of the Union.

8. London: Announced that the Lord Chamberlain will issue licences for censored music hall plays.

10. Paris: The French cabinet resigns (→ 13).

11. Paris: Prof. Dastre of the Sorbonne describes a pioneering cornea graft operation by Dr Magitot, which restored a blind man's sight.

13. Paris: Raymond Poincare becomes premier of coalition.

16. Peking: Many are killed by bomb in attempt to kill the viceroy, Yuan Shi-kai (→ 6/2).

19. London: The London General Omnibus Co. and London Underground Electric Railways Co. provisionally agree to merge.

22. Germany: Socialists triumphant with 25 per cent of vote in general election (→ 16/2).

25. London: Home Secretary Reginald McKenna explains government plans for disestablishing Church of Wales (→ 23/4).

25. UK: Labour Party conference urges defiance of Osborne Judgement (→ 6/8).

29. UK: Churchill and Irish leader Redmond decide to meet in a marquee on Glasgow Celtic FC's pitch (→ 30).

30. London: House of Lords rejects the Home Rule Bill (→ 9/2).

BIRTHS

10. Czech statesman Gustav Husak, President of Czechoslovakia 1968-87 (†18/11/91).

28. US artist Jackson Pollock (†11/8/56).

Scott comes second in South Pole race

Captain Robert Falcon Scott, at the base camp in Antartica.

Jan 17. Captain Robert Scott and his party have finally reached the South Pole – only to discover the heartbreaking evidence that their Norwegian rivals had beaten them by a month.

After a journey hampered by unusually bad weather, the five Britons arrived at the bottom of the world to find a tent and other traces of the expedition led by Roald Amundsen.

Scott's party left their final depot, 150 miles from the Pole, on January 3 with a month's supply of provisions.

"The prospect of success seems good, provided that the weather holds and no unforeseen obstacles arise," wrote Scott in his last entry before setting out on the final stage.

To reach the last depot, the party were forced to struggle through the worst December storm ever recorded in the Antarctic region. Sledges sank to their crossbars in wet snow and Scott's ponies were slaughtered for dog meat. At one stage, the explorers were managing less than five miles a day.

Scott made a previous attempt in the 1900-04 expedition but was forced back by the weather with only a few miles to go.

Loyalists beat drum against Home Rule

Jan 26. Over 30,000 people today attended protest rallies in Ulster against British government proposals to give Ireland Home Rule. Preceded by drums playing in the rain, they came in farm carts, traps, and charabancs to Omagh to hear the Ulster MP Sir Edward Carson declare: "If we cannot remain as we are, we will take the matter into our own hands."

Feelings in Ulster against Home Rule are now running so high that Liberals have so far been unable to book a hall for a meeting planned next month, at which Winston Churchill, First Lord of the Admiralty, is due to present the government's case for reform (→ 29).

"Lassitude" by Paul Poiret, one of his latest designs for evening dinner wear, with tight waistline and an overall sensuousness frowned on by some people.

1912

FEBRUARY

Su	Mo	Tu	We	Th	Fr	Sa
				1	2	3
4	5	6	7	8	9	10
11	12	13	14	15	16	17
18	19	20	21	22	23	24
25	26	27	28	29		

2. UK: Crew of 14 of submarine A3 perish in collision with gunboat off Isle of Wight.

4. UK: King and Queen return from trip to India.

4. UK: Big freeze takes hold as temperatures drop to as low as -35 degrees F (→ 14).

4. Berlin: Government announces bill to increase navy by 15,000 men (→ 8).

6. Peking: Viceroy Yuan Shi-kai becomes effective dictator of China.→

8. Spain: Torrential rain brings widespread deaths and damage in severe floods.

8. Berlin: Government says it will build 15 more dreadnoughts in 6 years as UK War Secretary Haldane arrives on diplomatic mission (→ 9).

9. Glasgow: Churchill says naval expansion is luxury for Germany, necessity for UK (→ 18/3).

9. Belfast: Carson says Home Rule would mean using the army to maintain justice for the Protestant minority (→ 1/4).

14. US: Arizona becomes the 48th state of the union.

14. London: Reported that 2 per cent of the capital's population are dying weekly from cold.

16. Berlin: Chancellor attacks victorious socialists, says government does not intend to increase democracy or set up parliamentary system (→ 18).

18. Berlin: Kaiser Wilhelm refuses to give customary audience to socialist victors

26. UK: 2,000 Derbyshire coal miners go on strike (→ 1/3).

28. US: Albert Berry makes world's first parachute jump from an aeroplane, over Missouri.→

BIRTH

27. British poet and writer Lawrence Durrell (†7/11/90).

DEATH

10. British antiseptic pioneer Joseph, Lord Lister (*5/4/1827).

Shaky start to new Chinese republic

Viceroy Yuan Shi-kai.

Feb 15. At noon today the Chinese cruisers in Shanghai fired a 21-gun salute and hoisted the Revolutionary flag, formally recognising the new government.

Last month the Emperor resigned and China officially became a republic. But the situation is still very confused. Yuan Shi-kai, who is currently the dictator of the north, seems certain to become the first president. But how much real control he will have over the south is just a matter of intense speculation.

The position of the Emperor is also anomalous. He retains his title, as do the nobles, and he will live in Peking and receive £400,000 annually. The eunuch system however, will be abolished.

Franz Reichelt died when he jumped from the Eiffel Tower with a parachute. It didn't open.

1912

MARCH

Su	Mo	Tu	We	Th	Fr	Sa
					1	2
3	4	5	6	7	8	9
10	11	12	13	14	15	16
17	18	19	20	21	22	23
24	25	26	27	28	29	30
31						

1. UK: Negotiations to settle the coal strike fail.→

3. Peking: Martial law is declared (→10).

4. London: 96 arrested following suffragette raid on House of Commons (→5).

5. London: Police raid offices of Women's Social and Political Union and arrest Mr and Mrs Pethick Lawrence (→28).

5. N. Africa: Dirigible airships used for the first time for military purposes when two Italian craft reconnoitre Turkish lines near Tripoli (→4/5).

7. France-UK: Frenchman Henri Seimet becomes the first to fly non-stop from Paris to London in his monoplane, taking three hours.

9. London: King lays foundation stone of County Hall, new London County Council headquarters.

10. Peking: Yuan Shi-kai installed as provisional President of Republic of China (→13/4).

12. Paris: Sarah Bernhardt's second film, "La Dame aux camellias", is released.

12. London: Royal Commission says vivisection is morally justifiable.

15. London: Drapers' Company offers to erect a senate house and new buildings for the University of London in Bloomsbury.

18. London: Churchill states government's intention to maintain Royal Navy supremacy (→22/7).

21. UK: Sir C. Assheton-Smith's Jerry wins the Grand National at Aintree.

28. London: Women's Enfranchisement Bill is defeated by 14 votes on its second Commons reading (→13/6).

28. London: University boat race ordered to be re-rowed when both boats sink.

BIRTH

27. British statesman James Callaghan, Prime Minister 1976-9.

Window-smashing shocks West End

Clearing up in Piccadilly after the suffragettes' smashing spree.

March 1. Militant suffragettes, many of them with stones and hammers hidden in their muffs, caused thousands of pounds' worth of damage in a window smashing rampage throughout the West End of London today. More than 120 women were arrested, including their leader Emmeline Pankhurst. In one of the most daring raids, she and two supporters hurled stones at Number 10 Downing Street, shattering windows on both sides of the door.

Groups of women struck simultaneously without warning and within 20 minutes the trail of destruction stretched from Oxford Street to the Strand via Piccadilly and Whitehall. Hard-pressed officers appealed to the public for help, but most of the women made no attempt to escape after they had struck their blows.

The women claim they have been driven to such actions by a government that not only refuses their demands but taunts them with not expressing themselves forcibly enough. The suffragettes' anger has been fuelled by the readiness of the government to make concessions to the miners who recently took militant action (→4).

France takes over Morocco in Fez pact

March 30. In the ancient city of Fez, which gave its name to the brimless red hat worn by Moslems, the Sultan of Morocco today signed a treaty giving France the right to establish a protectorate over his country. The last obstacle to the French takeover was removed by the agreement in November with Germany, who had resisted French penetration in the region.

A French resident-general will be appointed; he will respect the Sultan's religious prerogatives, but France will take control of Morocco's finances in order to ensure the payment of foreign debts (→17/4).

Bill gives miners a minimum wage

March 27. Just before 2am the House of Commons passed the controversial Coal Miners Bill, establishing for the first time the principle of a minimum wage. When the Prime Minister, Mr Asquith, introduced the bill on March 19, he hoped that it would be supported by the miners, whose strike has paralysed the economy since the end of February. So far there are over one million workers who have been laid off as a direct result. Mr Asquith refused to accept the union's demand for a minimum of five shillings a day for men and two shillings for boys, so Labour voted against the Bill (→6/4).

1912

APRIL

Su	Mo	Tu	We	Th	Fr	Sa
	1	2	3	4	5	6
7	8	9	10	11	12	13
14	15	16	17	18	19	20
21	22	23	24	25	26	27
28	29	30				

1. Vienna: Emperor Franz Josef orders the drafting of an Abdication Bill in a bid to call the bluff of opponents to his army plans.

1. London: Asquith introduces third Irish Home Rule Bill (→9).

3. Italy: New discoveries are announced at Pompeii excavations.

3. London: Wellington monument unveiled at Hyde Park Corner.

4. New York: Marconi publishes details of wireless compass.

6. UK: National Conference of Miners votes four to one to return to work.

9. Belfast: 240,000 demonstrate against home rule in presence of Tory leader Bonar Law (→9/5).

10. Wigan: Troops called in to quell riots.

10. Southampton: White Star liner "Titanic" has near-miss with liner "New York" as she leaves on maiden voyage.→

11. Italy: Umberto Boccioni publishes the "Manifesto of Futurist Sculpture".

13. UK: The Royal Flying Corps is set up.

17. Morocco: Troops revolt against French rule (→1/7).

17. London: Total eclipse of the Sun is visible.

18. New York: "Carpathia" arrives with Titanic survivors (→24).

19. Paris: Cabbies return to work after 144-day strike.

20. US: House of Representatives decides to make presidential and vice-presidential candidates reveal election campaign expenses.

23. London: Church of Wales Disestablishment Bill introduced in Commons (→16/5).

24. New York: Two "Titanic" officers say hundreds were lost because of inadequate numbers of lifeboats (→1/5).

24. UK: Barnsley beat West Bromwich Albion 1-0 in the replay of the FA Cup Final.

Terrible loss of life as Titanic sinks

"SS Titanic" in Cherbourg harbour on the first night of her ill-fated voyage, only four days from disaster.

April 15. More than 1,500 of the 2,340 passengers and crew of the "Titanic" drowned in the icy waters of the North Atlantic early this morning in the worst-ever disaster at sea. This great ship, the pride of the White Star fleet, proclaimed unsinkable because of its 16 watertight compartments, sank within hours of hitting an iceberg.

The survivors watched helplessly as the giant ship slid beneath the waves with all her lights still blazing. One of them was wireless operator, Harold Bride, who had had to swim for his life. "The ship was tilting gradually onto her nose – just like a duck that goes for a dive. I had only one thing on my mind – to get away from the suction. The band was still playing," he went on, "I guess all of them went down."

Three millionaires got away in the first boat, but others acted heroically. Colonel John Jacob Astor helped his own new bride and many other women and children into the boats, but remained on board until the end. Some wives chose to die with their husbands, rather than to be saved alone.

One of the most fortunate of the survivors was Colonel Archibald Gracie, who actually went down with the ship clinging to a rail but miraculously lived to tell the tale. "When the ship plunged down I was swirled around for what seemed an interminable time. Eventually I came to the surface to find the sea a mass of tangled wreckage."

The ship, on her maiden voyage to New York, was speeding through an ice field, hoping to win the Blue Riband for the fastest Atlantic crossing (→18).

Survivors watch as the unthinkable happens to the unsinkable.

Survivors come alongside the first ship on the scene, the liner "Carpathia".

1912

MAY

Su	Mo	Tu	We	Th	Fr	Sa
			1	2	3	4
5	6	7	8	9	10	11
12	13	14	15	16	17	18
19	20	21	22	23	24	25
26	27	28	29	30	31	

1. Canada: Announced that "Titanic" dead are to be buried in Halifax, Nova Scotia.→

1. Turkey: 165 people missing after US ship "Texas" hits a mine off Smyrna.

4. Turkey: Italy occupies the island of Rhodes (→ 18).

5. Munich: Second exhibition of the "Blaue Reiter" group, including works by Macke, Nolde, Picasso, and Klee.

5. Russia: First issue of the Bolshevik newspaper "Pravda" ("Truth").

12. UK: Army Air Battalion joins the Royal Flying Corps.

16. London: MPs give second reading to Welsh Church Disestablishment Bill (→ 4/3/14).

17. US: John Gahring, a farmer at Waterford, Pennsylvania, is the first to instal petroleum gas for cooking.

18. Italy: Prof. Mallada of the Royal Observatory at Mount Vesuvius becomes the first to descend to the bottom of the volcano's crater.

18. Turkey: The Dardanelles are re-opened for first time since Italian bombardment a month ago (→ 12/6).

23. Hungary: Many die in street battles between workers and police.

27. Spain: 80 perish in cinema fire at Villareal, Valencia.

28. Washington: US inquiry into "Titanic" disaster returns verdict of negligence (→ 3/7).

29. London: 100,000 dockers are now on strike (→ 15/6).

29. Balkans: Greece signs an anti-Turkish alliance with Bulgaria (→ 1/6).

31. Cuba: US Marines land to protect US interests.

BIRTH

26. Hungarian leader Janos Kadar, president 1956-88 (†6/7/89).

DEATHS

14. Swedish author August Strindberg (*22/1/1849).

30. US aviator Wilbur Wright (*16/4/1867).

Transport strike brings UK to standstill

Strike breaking van-drivers get a police guard for their own safety.

May 26. A Sunday crowd of 40,000 jammed Trafalgar Square today to hear union leaders demand the intensification of the strike in the Port of London and on the Medway. The column of marchers from London's dockland entered the square at 3.40 pm, when the band leading the Lightermen's group raised a great cheer by striking up the "Marseillaise".

The main speakers were Ben Tillett, leader of the dockers, and Harry Gosling, president of the National Transport Workers' Federation, which comprises the 15 unions in the Port of London. The response of the car-men, who drive the vans from the docks, is clearly crucial to the effectiveness of the strike. Horatio Bottomley also spoke and a warm message of support was read from the Labour MP, George Lansbury.

The Federation's core demands are those put forward when the strike was first called three days ago: 1. acceptance by employers of the union closed shop; 2. uniform rates of pay for the same ship work; and 3. recognition of the National Federation itself.

The dispute was triggered by the refusal of James Thomas, aged 63, a man employed for the past two years by the Mercantile Lighterage Company, to join the Amalgamated Society of Lightermen (→ 29).

Inquiry into "Titanic" tragedy opens

Surviving crewmen at Liverpool.

May 2. The remarkable feature of the first day of the inquiry into the sinking of the "Titanic" was that it managed to be so dull. Instead the key questions were being asked elsewhere – in the Commons.

Why were there so few lifeboats? How come the managing director of the owners, White Star Line, got away in the first lifeboat, when only twenty of the 180 Irish passengers were saved? Who was responsible on the boats for pushing swimmers back into the icy seas? Why was the "Titanic" sailing at top speed when there had been several warnings of icebergs?

Some lessons have been learnt. Yesterday the Hamburg-American Line claimed its new liner had enough boats for all (→ 28).

Nijinsky's "Faun": bestial or brilliant?

May 1. The premiere of the new ballet, *L'Apres Midi d'un Faune*, to the impressionistic tone-poem of Claude Debussy, caused great controversy in Paris. It is the first ballet created by Nijinsky, who also plays the faun, who wakes in a glade to watch a group of nymphs dancing.

He has created a new stylised form of movement, in which the dancers move sideways across the stage like figures in a classical frieze and halt with heads in profile but bodies turned to face the audience.

The last sequence, in which the faun dances alone with the scarf of one of the nymphs, was made so erotic by Njinsky that some critics declared it bestial. All performances are sold out.

Nijinsky: controversial.

Home Rule Bill gets through Commons

May 9. The British government's bill to give Home Rule to Ireland, won a majority of 94 at its second reading in the House of Commons tonight. Ministers greeted the vote of 360 MPs in favour to 266 against with cheers – and relief. Herbert Asquith, the Prime Minister, had earlier attacked the opposition of Ulster Unionists. "The British people, just and generous by nature, are not going to be frightened out of doing a just thing by the language of intimidation," he said (→ 12/7).

1912

JUNE

Su	Mo	Tu	We	Th	Fr	Sa
						1
2	3	4	5	6	7	8
9	10	11	12	13	14	15
16	17	18	19	20	21	22
23	24	25	26	27	28	29
30						

1. Balkans: Greece and Montenegro mobilise troops (→ 2/7).

5. London: Tailors call off their strike.

5. UK: Walter Raphael's Tagalie wins the Derby at Epsom, only the fifth filly to win in 132 years.

8. Paris: The Ballets Russes dance at the first complete performance of Ravel's ballet "Daphnis et Chloe".

8. Los Angeles: Carl Laemmie funds Universal Studios.

9. France: French naval submarine "Vendemiaire" sinks, drowning 24.

10. London: Viscount Haldane becomes Lord Chancellor (→ 12).

12. London: Colonel Seely becomes War Secretary in succession to Viscount Haldane.

13. Austria: Frau Vik Kunetiska is elected Austria's first woman MP, but Prince Thun of Bohemia refuses to sanction her election.

17. London: Government introduces Franchise and Registration Bill, abolishing plural voting and property qualification and setting 21 as voting age for all men (→ 12/7).

18. London: Home Rule Bill amendment to exclude four Ulster counties cuts the government majority to 69 (→ 12/7).

23. US: Bridge over Niagara Falls collapses, killing 47 people.

25. London: Asquith bitterly attacked in Commons for "torture" of force-feeding suffragettes in prison (→ 28).

28. UK: Suffragettes start window-smashing campaign at post offices and labour exchanges (→ 29).

29. Stockholm: The grand opening of the 5th Olympic Games.

29. London: Male suffragists are expelled from suffrage meeting addressed by Lloyd George (→ 18/11).

Taft nominated: Roosevelt goes it alone

June 22. The Republican Party today nominated President William Howard Taft as its candidate for election to a second four-year term. The convention in Chicago was tense. Supporters of former President Theodore Roosevelt walked out and within hours they had nominated him as a rival independent candidate.

Saying he felt "as strong as a bull moose", Roosevelt called for a Progressive party to enforce the commandment "Thou shalt not steal".

The split comes as the climax to bitter factional divisions in the Republican party. During the primary elections, President Taft was challenged not only by former President Roosevelt but also by Senator La Follette (→ 2/7).

Theodore Roosevelt: undeterred.

Cocaine could produce "race of fiends"

June 30. Cocaine, chloroform and ether have been condemned by American surgeons meeting in New York this month as unnecessary and dangerous anaesthetics. Cocaine is said to be the worst of all – one doctor said it would produce "a race of fiends" – but it is hoped that soon none of these three forms of anaesthetics will be used.

Nitrous oxide gas is recommended instead, as it does not produce unpleasant after-effects and is not poisonous. A prize has been offered for the design of a machine to deliver such gas. Otherwise heart disease has dominated the medical journals published this month.

Thomas Lewis, a London specialist, has described how heart abnormalities can be revealed by an electrocardiographic machine. James Herrick, of Chicago, has argued that obstruction of the heart's coronary vessels is not always fatal, although Dr E. Libman of New York believes that such blockages are more likely to occur in heavy cigar smokers.

Anyone for tennis? The latest fashion for this popular sport.

Transport strike comes to a halt

June 15. The national dock strike, called five days ago, has effectively collapsed. The year-old National Transport Workers' Federation called the strike when attempts to settle the two month-long dispute in the London docks broke down. Its demand has been that employers recognise a union closed shop, but the Port of London Authority has insisted that it is not allowed to discriminate between employers who recognise unions and those who do not.

Outside London, the strike was always patchy, with the Sailors' Union, the largest members of the Federation, withholding support.

1912

JULY

Su	Mo	Tu	We	Th	Fr	Sa
	1	2	3	4	5	6
7	8	9	10	11	12	13
14	15	16	17	18	19	20
21	22	23	24	25	26	27
28	29	30	31			

1. N. Africa: Morocco is declared a French protectorate (→ 11/8).

1. UK: Many shows and markets are cancelled in Yorkshire because of foot-and-mouth outbreak (→ 3).

2. US: Woodrow Wilson wins Democratic nomination for presidency (→ 5/11).

2. Balkans: Serbia joins the Greek-Bulgarian alliance against Turkey (→ 3/8).

3. Ireland: Police establish a ring round four Irish counties to prevent movement of cattle as foot-and-mouth outbreak is reported (→ 6).

3. London: Board of Trade inquiry into "Titanic" disaster finds Captain Smith, who went down with the ship, guilty of negligence.

6. UK: Foot-and-mouth breaks out over wide area of Surrey.

8. Italy: 15-month trial of Neapolitan Camorra gangsters finds nine accused guilty of murder; one prisoner cuts throat in dock.

8. Wimbledon: Ethel Larcombe beats Charlotte Sterry for the ladies' Singles title; Anthony Wilding beats Arthur Gore for the men's Singles crown.

9. UK: Large naval review at Spithead.

9. Yorkshire: 87 miners are killed in a huge colliery explosion.

12. London: Commons gives second reading to Franchise Bill (→ 28/1/13).

18. Dublin: Irish Nationalist leader Redmond is wounded by a hatchet thrown at Prime Minister's carriage by suffragist (→ 11/11).

22. UK: Admiralty recalls Mediterranean warships to North Sea to counter growing German fleet.→

23. US: Modesty League declares war on tight dresses.

27. London: Dock strike ends after 10 weeks.

31. Mexico City: Rebels hang two Americans.

Royal Navy boosts North Sea fleet

July 22. Britain is withdrawing her battleships from the Mediterranean and placing them on patrol in the North Sea in response to the continuing German naval build-up. The action follows the breakdown of Anglo-German talks aimed at slowing down the rate of expansion of the two countries' navies, which is causing growing concern on both sides of the North Sea.

Germany asked for a mutual declaration of neutrality in case either side became involved in war with a third power, but Britain turned the proposal down, fearing this would endanger relations with France and Russia.

Last week Winston Churchill, First Lord of the Admiralty, asked the Commons to agree an expanded naval budget, boosting the sum to be spent on ships and men this year to a record £45 million. Recruiting is to be stepped up in response to German moves. The large shipbuilding programme, which already includes four dreadnoughts, eight cruisers, 20 destroyers and a number of submarines, this year has been brought forward to counter the German threat.

The latest German yearbook on naval forces, "Nauticus", shows a sharp increase in naval shipbuilding, claiming France is spending the most per head on arms followed by Germany, Britain and the United States (→14/9).

Winston Churchill with the Kaiser on manoeuvres in Germany.

Huge Unionist rally opposes Home Rule

July 12. They came to celebrate the anniversary of the Battle of the Boyne in 1688, but it was the battle over Home Rule for Ireland which roused the passions of a 120,000-strong rally of Ulster's Orange Order today. They heard F.E. Smith, the Tory spokesman on Ireland, predict that Home Rule would be defeated.

He said: "You are sometimes asked whether you will resist the English Army. I say that even if this government had the wickedness, it is wholly lacking in the nerve required, to give an order which would shatter the civilisation of these islands" (→14/9).

Wilson nominated after 46 ballots

July 2. Exhausted delegates at the Democratic convention in Baltimore finally nominated Governor Woodrow Wilson of New Jersey to run for president after five days and 46 ballots.

The thrice-defeated candidate, William Jennings Bryan, had great influence. On the tenth ballot, when the New York delegation threw its vote to the speaker of the House, Bryan transferred his votes to Wilson, the leader of the progressive wing of the party (→5/8).

Doctors outraged at National Insurance

July 23. The British Medical Association called on all doctors to withdraw from the bodies set up to effect the new National Insurance Act, at its annual meeting in Liverpool today. The Act plans to extend medical care to the poor, who receive only one third as many doctors' visits as those with medical insurance. The government was blamed for not meeting the doctors' minimum pay demands to work the Act, which Sir James Barr, the new President, described as the most gigantic fraud since the South Sea Bubble. Doctors are giving at least £20 each to a fund to fight the new scheme (→20/12).

American Indian is the man of the games at Stockholm Olympics

July 22. With the number of sports pared down to 14 after the rambling programmes of previous games, the Stockholm Olympics consistently produced the highest standards of performance of any Games to date.

One great new athletics power emerged – Finland. Despite still competing under the Russian flag, the Finns introduced the great Hannes Kolehmainen, who won the crosscountry, the 10,000 metres and – breaking the world record by nearly half a minute – the 5,000 metres.

But the sensation was Jim Thorpe, an American of Indian descent, who won the pentathlon, and took the decathlon by an astonishing 680 points (→27/1/13).

The Swedish team enter the stadium for the opening ceremony of the fifth Olympiad of modern times, held on their home territory in Stockholm.

1912  Stockholm

Men Athletics

100m
1. Ralph Cook Craig USA 10.8
2. Alvah Meyer USA 10.9
3. Donald Lippincott USA 10.9

200m
1. Ralph Cook Craig USA 21.7
2. Donald Lippincott USA 21.8
3. William Applegarth GBR 22.0

400m
1. Charles Reidpath USA *48.2
2. Hanns Braun GER 48.3
3. Edward Lindberg USA 48.4

800m
1. James Edwin Meredith USA **1:51.9
2. Melvin Sheppard USA 1:52.0
3. Ira Davenport USA 1:52.0

1500m
1. Arnold Jackson GBR *3:56.8
2. Abel Kiviat USA 3:56.9
2. Norman Taber USA 3:56.9

5000m
1. Johannes Kolehmainen FIN **14:36.6
2. Jean Bouin FRA 14:36.7
3. George Hutson GBR 15:07.6

10,000m
1. Johannes Kolehmainen FIN 31:20.8
2. Louis Tewanima USA 32:06.6
3. Albin Stenroos FIN 32:21.8

Marathon
1. Kenneth McArthur SAF 2:36:54.8
2. Christian Gitsham SAF 2:37:52.0
3. Gaston Strobino USA 2:38:42.4

110m Hurdles
1. Frederick Kelly USA 15.1
2. James Wendell USA 15.2
3. Martin Hawkins USA 15.3

4x100m Relay
1. GBR *42.4 (David Jacobs, Harold Macintosh, Victor D'Arcy, William Applegarth)
2. SWE 42.6 (Ivan Möller, Charles Luther, Ture Persson, Knut Lindberg)

4x400m Relay
1. USA **3:16.6 (Melvin Sheppard, Edward Lindberg, James Meredith, Charles Reidpath)
2. FRA 3:20.7 (Charles Lelong, Robert Schurrer, Pierre Failliot, Charles Poulenard)
3. GBR 3:23.2 (George Nicol, Ernest Henley, James Tindal Soutter, Cyril Seedhouse)

High Jump
1. Alma Richards USA *1.93
2. Hans Liesche GER 1.91
3. George Horine USA 1.89

Pole Vault
1. Harry Babcock USA *3.95
2. Frank Nelson USA 3.85
2. Marcus Wright USA 3.85
3. William Happenny CAN 3.80
3. Frank Murphy USA 3.80

Long Jump
1. Albert Gutterson USA *7.60
2. Calvin Bricker CAN 7.21
3. Georg Aberg SWE 7.18

Triple Jump
1. Gustaf Lindblom SWE 14.76
2. Georg Aberg SWE 14.51
3. Erik Almlöf SWE 14.17

Shotput
1. Patrick McDonald USA *15.34
2. Ralph Rose USA 15.25
3. Lawrence Whitney USA 13.93

Discus
1. Armas Taipale FIN *45.21
2. Richard Byrd USA 42.32
3. James Duncan USA 42.28

Hammer
1. Matthew McGrath USA *54.74
2. Duncan Gillis CAN 48.39
3. Clarence Childs USA 48.17

Javelin
1. Eric Lemming SWE **60.64
2. Juho Saaristo FIN 58.66
3. Mór Kóczán HUN 55.50

Decathlon
1. James Thorpe USA 8412
2. Hugo Wieslander SWE 7724
3. Charles Lomberg SWE 7414

3000m Team (approx. 12km)
1. USA
2. Sweden
3. Great Britain

Cross Country Individual
1. Johannes Kolehmainen FIN 45:11.6
2. Hjalmar Andersson SWE 45:44.8
3. John Eke SWE 46:37.6

Cross Country Team (approx. 12km)
1. Sweden
2. Finland
3. Great Britain

Pentathlon
1. James Thorpe USA
2. Ferdinand Bie NOR
3. James Donahue USA

Standing Long Jump
1. Konstantin Tsiklitiras GRE 3.37
2. Platt Adams USA 3.36
3. Benjamin Adams USA 3.28

Standing High Jump
1. Platt Adams USA 1.63
2. Benjamin Adams USA 1.60
3. Konstantin Tsiklitiras GRE 1.55

Shotput, Both Hands
1. Ralph Rose USA 27.70 (15.23+12.47)
2. Patrick McDonald USA 27.53 (15.08+12.45)
3. Elmer Niklander FIN 27.14 (14.71+12.43)

Discus Throw, Both Hands
1. Armas Taipale FIN 82.86 (44.68+38.18)
2. Elmer Niklander FIN 77.96 (40.28+37.68)
3. Emil Magnusson SWE 77.37 (40.58+36.79)

Javelin, Both Hands
1. Julius Saaristo FIN 109.42 (61.00+48.42)
2. Vaino Siikaniemi FIN 101.13 (54.09+47.04)
3. Urho Peltonen FIN 100.24 (53.58+46.66)

Tug-of-War
1. Sweden
2. Great Britain

10km Walk
1. George Goulding CAN 46:28.4
2. Ernest Webb GBR 46:50.4
3. Fernando Altimani ITA 47:37.6

Men Swimming

100m Freestyle
1. Duke Paoa Kahanamoku USA 1:03.4
2. Cecil Healy AUS 1:04.6
3. Kenneth Huszagh USA 1:05.6

400m Freestyle
1. George Ritchie Hodgson CAN 5:24.4
2. John Gatenby Hatfield GBR 5:25.8
3. Harold Hardwick AUS 5:31.2

1500m Freestyle
1. George Ritchie Hodgson CAN **22:00.0
2. John Gatenby Hatfield GBR 23:39.0
3. Harold Hardwick AUS 23:15.4

100m Backstroke
1. Harry Hebner USA 1:21.2
2. Otto Fahr GER 1:22.4
3. Paul Keliner GER 1:24.0

200m Breaststroke
1. Walter Bathe GER *3:01.8
2. Wilhelm Lützow GER 3:05.0
3. Kurt Mahlisch GER 3:08.0

400m Breaststroke
1. Walter Bathe GER *6:29.6
2. Thor Henning SWE 6:35.6
3. Percy Courtman GBR 6:36.4

4x200m Relay
1. AUS/NZ **10:11.6 (Cecil Healy, Malcolm Champion, Leslie Boardman, Harold Hardwick)
2. USA 10:20 (Kenneth Huszagh, Harry Hebner, Perry McGillivray, Duke Paoa Kahanamoku)
3. GBR 10:28.2 (William Foster, Thomas Battersby, John Hatfield, Henry Taylor)

Springboard Diving
1. Paul Günther GER 79.23
2. Hans Luber GER 76.78
3. Kurt Behrens GER 73.73

High Diving
1. Erik Adlerz SWE 73.94
2. Albert Zürner GER 72.60
3. Gustaf Blomgren SWE 69.56

Plain High Diving
1. Erik Adlerz SWE 40.0
2. Hjalmar Johansson SWE 39.3
3. John Janssen SWE 39.1

Water Polo

1. Great Britain – 2. Sweden – 3. Belgium

Ralph Rose of San Francisco, silver medal winner in the shot put.

Women Swimming

100m Freestyle
1. Fanny Durack AUS 1:22.2
2. Wilhelmina Wylie AUS 1:25.4
3. Jennie Fletcher GBR 1:27.0

4x100 m Relay
1. GBR **5:52.8 (Bella Moore, Jennie Fletcher, Annie Spiers, Irene Steer)
2. GER 6:04.6 (Wally Dressel, Louise Otto, Hermine Stindt, Margarete Rosenberg)
3. AUT 6:17.0 (Margarete Adler, Klara Milch, Josephine Sticker, Berta Zahourek)

Platform Diving
1. Greta Johansson SWE 39.9
2. Lisa Regnell SWE 36.0
3. Isabelle White GBR 34.0

Greco Roman Wrestling

Featherweight
1. Kaarlo Koskelo FIN
2. Georg Gerstäcker GER
3. Otto Lasanen FIN

Lightweight
1. Eemil Wäre FIN
2. Gustaf Malström SWE
3. Edvin Matiasson SWE

Middleweight
1. Claes Johanson SWE
2. Martin Klein RUS
3. Alfred Asikainen FIN

Light Heavyweight (no gold medallist)
2. Anders Ahlgren SWE
2. Ivar Böhling FIN
3. Béla Varga HUN

Heavyweight
1. Yrjö Saarela FIN
2. Johan Olin FIN
3. Soren Marius Jensen DEN

Men Fencing

Foil Individual
1. Nedo Nadi ITA 7
2. Pietro Speciale ITA 5
3. Richard Verderber AUT 4/10

Epée Individual
1. Paul Anspach BEL 6
2. Ivan Osiier DEN 5
3. Philippe le Hardy de Beaulieu BEL 4

Epée Team
1. Belgium
2. Great Britain
3. Holland

Sabre Individual
1. Dr. Jenö Fuchs HUN 6
2. Béla Békéssy HUN 5/5
3. Ervin Mészáros HUN 5/6

Sabre Team
1. Hungary
2. Austria
3. Netherlands

Modern Pentathlon

1. Gösta Lilliehöök SWE
2. Gösta Asbrink SWE
3. Georg de Laval SWE

Rowing

Single Sculls
1. William Kinnear GBR 7:47.6
2. Polydore Veirman BEL (1 length)
3. Everard B. Butler CAN
4. Mikhail Kusik RUS

Coxed Fours
1. Germany 6:59.4
2. Great Britain (2 lengths)
3. Denmark

Eights
1. Great Britain 6:15.0
2. Great Britain
3. Germany

Coxed Fours, Inriggers
1. Denmark 7:47.0
2. Sweden (1 length)
3. Norway

Yachting

6m Class
1. France
2. Denmark
3. Sweden

8m Class
1. Norway
2. Sweden
3. Finland

10m Class
1. Sweden
2. Finland
3. Russia

12m Class
1. Norway
2. Sweden
3. Finland

Cycling

Individual Road Race
1. Rudolph Lewis SAF 10:42:39.0
2. Frederick Grubb GBR 10:51:24.2
3. Carl Schutte USA 10:52:38.8

Team Time Trial
1. Sweden 44:35:33.6
2. Great Britain 44:44:39.2
3. USA 44:47:55.5

Equestrian Sports

Three Day Event, Individual
1. Axel Nordlander SWE
2. Frederick von Rochow GER
3. Jean Cariou FRA

Three Day Event, Team
1. Sweden 139.06
2. Germany 138.48
3. USA 137.33

Dressage Individual
1. Carl Bonde SWE 15
2. Gustaf Boltenstern SWE 21
3. Hans von Blixen Finecke SWE 32

Grand Prix Jumping Individual
1. Jean Cariou FRA 186
2. Rabod von Kröcher GER 186
3. Emanuel de Blommaert de Soye BEL 185

Grand Prix Jumping Team
1. Sweden
2. France
3. Germany

Shooting

Free Rifle 300m 3 positions
1. Paul Colas FRA 987
2. Lars Jörgen Madsen DEN 981
3. Niels Hansen Ditlev Larsen DEN 962

Free Rifle Team
1. Sweden 5655
2. Norway 5605
3. Denmark 5529

Small-Bore Rifle, Prone
1. Frederick Hird USA 194
2. William Milne GBR 193
3. Harry Burt GBR 192

Small-Bore Rifle, Individual disappearing target
1. Wilhel Carlberg SWE 242
2. Johan Hübner von Holst SWE 233
3. Gustaf Ericsson SWE 231

Miniature Rifle Team 25m
1. Sweden 925
2. Great Britain 917
3. USA 881

Miniature Rifle Team 50m
1. Great Britain 762
2. Sweden 748
3. USA 744

Rapid Fire Pistol
1. Alfred Lane USA 287
2. Paul Palén USA 286
3. Johan Hübner von Holst SWE 283

Free Pistol 50m
1. Alfred Lane USA 499
2. Peter Dolfen USA 474
3. Charles Edward Stewart GBR 470

Military Revolver Team 30m
1. Sweden 1145
2. Russia 1091-118
3. Great Britain 1107-117

Clay Pigeon Team
1. USA 532
2. Great Britain 511
3. Germany 510

Military Rifle Individual 3 Positions
1. Sándor Prokopp HUN 97
1. Carl Osburn USA 95
3. Embret Skogen NOR 95

Military Rifle Individual Any Position
1. Paul Colas FRA 94
2. Carl Osburn USA 94
3. John Jackson USA 93

Military Rifle Team
1. USA 1687
2. Great Britain 1602
3. Sweden 1570

Running Deer Shooting (Single Shot) Individual
1. Alfred Swahn SWE 41
2. Ake Lundeberg SWE 41
3. Nestori Toivonen FIN 41

Running Deer Shooting (Single Shot) Team
1. Sweden 151
2. USA 132
3. Finland 123

Running Deer Shooting (Double Shot) Individua
1. Ake Lundeberg SWE 79
2. Edvard Benedicks SWE 74
3. Oscar Swahn SWE 72

Military Revolver Team 50m
1. USA 1916
2. Sweden 1849
3. Great Britain 1804

Mixed Shooting

Clay Pigeon Individual
1. James Graham USA 96
2. Alfred Göldel GER 94
3. Harry Blau RUS 91

Men Gymnastics

Individual All-around Competition
1. Alberto Braglia ITA 135.0
2. Louis Ségura FRA 132.5
3. Adolfo Tunesi ITA 131.5

Team All-around Competition
1. Italy 265.75
2. Hungary 227.25
3. Great Britain 184.50

Team Swedish System Gymnastics
1. Sweden 937.46
2. Denmark 898.84
3. Norway 857.21

Free System Team
1. Norway 114.25
2. Finland 109.25
3. Denmark 106.25

Football

1. Great Britain
2. Denmark
3. Netherlands

Tennis

Men singles
1. Charles Winslow SAF
2. Harold Kitson SAF
3. Oscar Kreuzer GER

Men singles (indoors)
1. André Gobert FRA
2. Charles Dixon GBR
3. Anthony Wilding NZE

Men doubles
1. SAF
2. AUT
3. FRA

Men doubles (indoors)
1. FRA
2. SWE
3. GBR

Women singles
1. Marguerite Broquedis FRA
2. Dora Köring GER
3. Molla Bjurstedt NOR

Women singles (indoors)
1. Edith Hannam GBR
2. Thora Gerda Sophy Castenschiold DEN
3. Mabel Parton GBR

Mixed Doubles
1. GER
2. SWE
3. FRA

Mixed Doubles (indoors)
1. GBR
2. GBR
3. SWE

(Key to symbols and abbreviations p. 1456)

1912

AUGUST

Su	Mo	Tu	We	Th	Fr	Sa
				1	2	3
4	5	6	7	8	9	10
11	12	13	14	15	16	17
18	19	20	21	22	23	24
25	26	27	28	29	30	31

1. UK: Air mail service opens between London and Paris.

1. Turkey: New cabinet abolishes martial law and releases all political prisoners (→3).

3. Turkey: Albania is granted limited autonomy; Albanian becomes official language and will be taught in schools (→9).

6. UK: Commons gives second reading to Trades Unions Bill, overturning the Osborne Judgement on political funds.

7. Far East: Russia and Japan reach agreement on their spheres of influence in Mongolia and Manchuria.

8. Germany: Over 120 die in Westphalian pit disaster.

8. London: George Buckle retires after 28 years as editor of The Times.

9. St. Petersburg: French premier Poincare, on official visit, promises to back Russia's stand in the Balkans (→15).

11. N. Africa: Moroccan Sultan Mulai Hafid abdicates (→1/9).

13. Paris: Dr. Gaston Odin announces he has isolated and cultivated microbe of cancer.

15. Vienna: Austrian foreign minister Count Berchtold proposes a great power conference on the Balkans (→9/9).

15. Boston: Helen Keller, born blind, deaf and dumb, says she has learned to sing.

26. UK: Worst August rainfall on record – six inches in 12 hours – causes floods that cut off Norwich and other towns.

31. London: Four men are shot and 20 hurt in clashes between union and non-union members as dockers return to work.

BIRTH

25. East German leader Erich Honecker (†29/5/94).

DEATHS

14. French composer Jules Massenet (*12/5/1842).

20. British founder of the Salvation Army William Booth (*10/4/1829).

Bull Moose is new third party in US

Aug 5. The new Progressive Party made it official today by nominating the former Republican president, Theodore Roosevelt, as its presidential candidate.

Six weeks ago, at the Republican convention in Chicago, several hundred Roosevelt supporters bolted the party and applauded Roosevelt when he called for an independent progressive party. Because Roosevelt also said that he felt "as strong as a bull moose", the press has dubbed his breakaway Progressives "the Bull Moose party".

Besides policy differences, there have been personality clashes between Roosevelt and the official candidate, his protege and successor, William H. Taft (→14/10).

General Booth to meet his C-in-C

Aug 20. General William Booth, founder of the Salvation Army, died at his home near London today. He was 83. He started to preach at the age of 17 and was expelled from two Methodist churches because of his wish to preach in the streets rather than the pulpit. His main mission began in a tent in East London in 1865. The army name and uniforms were adopted in 1877 and there are now 4,000 corps and 13,000 officers spread throughout the world.

Russian advocate of revolution Vladimir Ulyanov, alias Lenin, confers with fellow socialist Josef Dzhugashvili, alias Stalin.

1912

SEPTEMBER

Su	Mo	Tu	We	Th	Fr	Sa
1	2	3	4	5	6	7
8	9	10	11	12	13	14
15	16	17	18	19	20	21
22	23	24	25	26	27	28
29	30					

1. Morocco: French troops put down native uprising.

2. UK: TUC president Will Thorne opens annual conference with demand for common ownership and an attack on the government for behaviour in recent strikes.

4. London: 22 injured in tube collision on Piccadilly Line, first ever such accident on London's underground.

9. Athens: Mass demonstrations demand liberation of all Greeks from Ottoman rule.→

11. UK: Barbour clothing manufacturers founded.

12. Balkans: Bulgaria demands Macedonian independence from Turkey (→22).

14. Glasgow: 86 are injured in sectarian clashes at Celtic football ground.

14. Birkenhead: Super-dreadnought "HMS Audacious" launched at Cammell Laird shipyard.

17. UK: 15 die and 50 are hurt when a train collides with a bridge in Lancashire.

22. Japan: Hundreds die as a typhoon sweeps the country.

22. Turkey: The government extends concessions made to Albania to all provinces within Ottoman Empire (→23).

23. US: Mack Sennett releases first "Keystone Cops" film.

23. Aegean: Turks fire on a Greek steamer at Samos (→26).

24. London: New £10 million Chinese loan is floated in the City as the formation of Anglo-Chinese Bank is announced.

26. Athens: Greece demands compensation from Turkey for Samos incident (→30).

30. Balkans: Russia mobilises 245,000 troops as tension mounts in the Balkans (→1/10).

BIRTH

5. US avant garde composer John Cage (†12/8/92).

DEATH

1. British composer Samuel Coleridge-Taylor (*15/8/1875).

Russia anxious as Balkan troubles near boiling point

Sept 9. War fever is once again gripping the Balkans. The Russians have become so alarmed by the situation, which needs only one incident to set the quarrelling countries at each other's throats, that they have mobilised seven army corps in Warsaw.

A large proportion of the Bulgarian army is massed at points from which it is poised to strike at Adrianople on the direct railway line to Constantinople. So the Turks, taking no chances, have ordered a partial mobilisation under the pretext of "autumn manoeuvres" and concentrated their forces to face this Bulgarian threat. Serbia has also mobilised and it is rumoured that a joint Bulgarian-Serbian note has just been sent to Turkey which demands the autonomy of Macedonia. If no satisfactory reply is received to this note, then it is feared that Serbia and Bulgaria will declare war on Turkey, thus provoking the Russians and the Austrians to intervene.

The reaction in Turkey to these moves is that her neighbours, seeing her weakened by her war with Italy, will seek to wrest yet more provinces away from the Ottoman empire. The Turks will certainly vigorously resist such moves (→12).

Tom Brown in a scene from "Tom Brown's Schooldays" ; he was modelled on Augustus Orlebar who died on Sept 30.

▷

Loyalists pledge to fight Home Rule

Sept 28. A week of speeches and rallies reached a climax in Ulster today with the signing of a "solemn covenant" to defeat Home Rule. It was signed by 471,414 people, virtually all of them in Ulster but including some from England and Scotland. They pledged that in the event of an Irish parliament "being forced upon us" they would refuse to recognise its authority.

Sir Edward Carson, the leader of the self-styled Ulster loyalists, hopes the massive public support for the covenant will make English MPs more concerned about the future of Ulster. But there was no attempt to disguise the determination of Unionists to resist Home Rule. F.E. Smith, the Tory spokesman on Ireland, was cheered at one rally when he called the current crisis "one of those supreme issues of conscience to which the ordinary landmarks of permissible resistance to technical law are submerged".

Religious services filled the early part of the day before the ceremonial signing of the covenant by three leading Unionists, Sir Edward Carson, Lord Londonderry and Sir James Craig, MP. All the churches – except those of the Roman Catholics – held special services with one hymn a particular favourite: "Oh God, our help in ages past".

Sir Edward Carson and his party were escorted to Belfast City Hall by 200 Orangemen wearing bowler hats and carrying walking sticks. Queues later stretched for nearly three-quarters of a mile as people waited to sign the covenant. Desks borrowed from local schools lined every corridor of City Hall for people to sign. Some enthusiasts brought a sharp pin or razor blade so they could sign with blood.

Symbolically, too, Sir Edward had the tattered personal standard of William of Orange behind him as he spoke to the crowds. His appearance on the balcony was greeted by a volley of welcoming shots. He claimed support for the covenant "has put our enemies in such difficulty that they are thinking what on earth to do with us". Before returning to England he said he would be back – "whether for peace, I prefer it or, if it to be to fight, I shall not shrink". Another burst of shots bade him farewell (→7/1/13).

Ready to fight: Ulster Unionist leader Sir Edward Carson inspects a guard of honour as loyalist volunteers line the streets of Belfast.

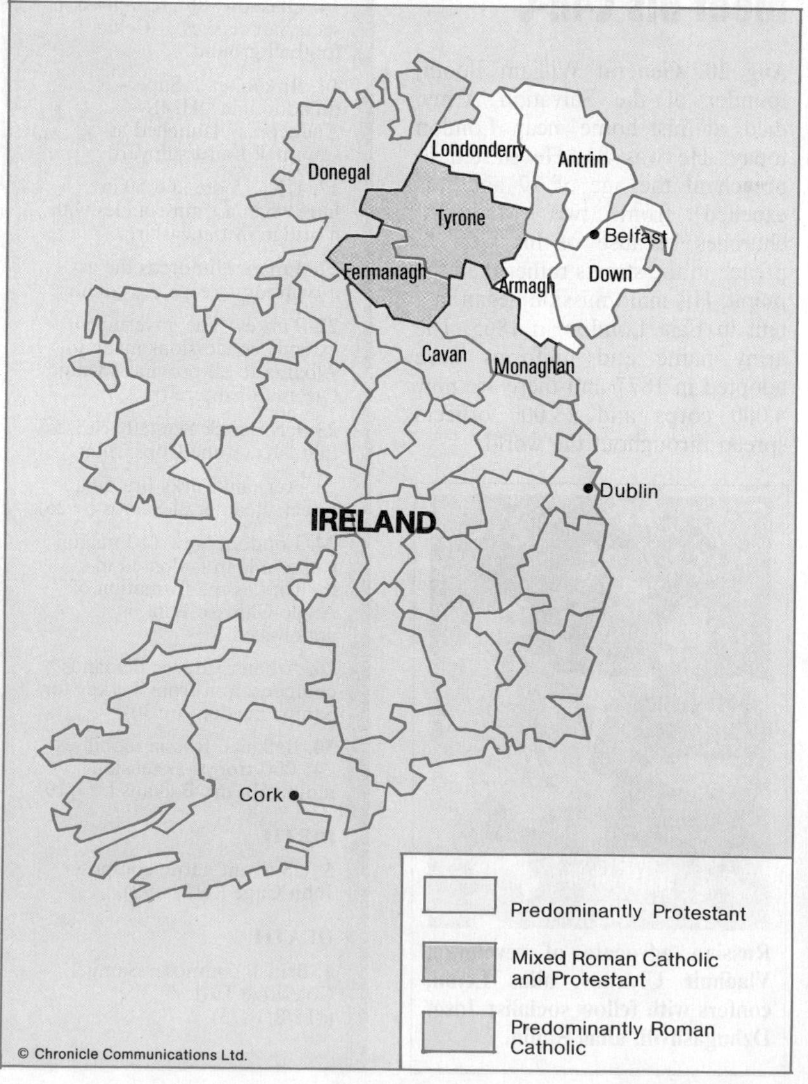

1912

OCTOBER

Su	Mo	Tu	We	Th	Fr	Sa
		1	2	3	4	5
6	7	8	9	10	11	12
13	14	15	16	17	18	19
20	21	22	23	24	25	26
27	28	29	30	31		

1. Balkans: Greece, Bulgaria and Serbia mobilise for war with Turkey.→

1. Berlin: The German foreign minister says that the great powers will not engage in a Balkan war (→3).

3. Balkans: Greece, Bulgaria and Serbia issue an ultimatum to Turkey (→6).

4. UK: 14 die when submarine B2 sinks after a collision with the German liner "Amerika".

5. Nicaragua: Revolutionaries are crushed, but four US troops are killed.

6. Balkans: Turkey offers reforms in disturbed provinces in a bid to avert war (→8).

8. Balkans: Montenegro declares war on the Ottoman Empire (→12).

9. Paris: Exhibition opens of Cubist "Gold Section", including Picabia and Leger.

11. Philadelphia: Leopold Stokowski conducts his first concert with the Philadelphia Orchestra.

12. UK: "HMS Iron Duke" is launched, the world's largest and most powerfully-armed battleship.

12. Balkans: Sultan orders mobilisation of Turkish army (→12).

14. Balkans: Turkey invades Serbia (→19).

14. US: Crazed gunman shoots Theodore Roosevelt in Milwaukee, but wound is not serious.

15. Greece: 62 Cretan deputies are acclaimed upon arrival at the Greek parliament.

19. Balkans: Allied armies invade Turkey (→23).

23. Balkans: Greece routs Turks at Sarandaporos (→31).

25. Germany: Premiere of Richard Strauss's opera "Ariadne auf Naxos".

26. London: Opening of new tunnel linking Woolwich and North Woolwich under the River Thames.

31. Balkans: Turkey seeks peace as allies threaten Constantinople.→

Turkey reels under Balkan offensive

Oct 31. The Turkish army is falling back in disorder beneath the hammer blows of the Bulgarians and their Serbian allies. Few could have expected when war was declared just two weeks ago that the once-feared Turkish army would be routed so swiftly.

When the Sultan ordered general mobilisation, he told his soldiers: "Your duty is not to allow your enemies to tread an inch of the sacred soil soaked with the blood of your ancestors." However, the latest despatches report the collapse of the Turkish defences along the Chatalja line, the last barrier protecting Constantinople from the depredations of advancing Bulgarian troops.

The Balkan League, comprising Serbia, Bulgaria, Montenegro and Greece, has turned fiercely on the nation which once ruled them, and seems determined to drive the Turks out of Europe.

Thousands of Turkish soldiers have perished in the Bulgarian advance – some 2,000 in Macedonia – and there are reports from Sofia that Nazim Pasha, the Turkish Minister of War and commander-in-chief in Thrace, has been shot or taken prisoner. This is, as yet, unconfirmed, but there is no doubt that the Turkish army has suffered a stunning blow and it is possible that Constantinople will fall with incalculable military and political consequences.

Bulgarian soldiers in formation moving up to the Serbian frontier.

This war became inevitable once Bulgaria had demanded autonomy for Macedonia, while Serbia, acting in collaboration with the Bulgarians, made its own equally harsh demands, which included complete demobilisation by Turkey.

The European powers, despite much diplomatic activity, proved unable to prevent the touch paper being lit and the Balkan powder keg exploded. Now, with the distant sound of the guns sending fear through the inhabitants of Constantinople, the Turks are wondering if the powers will intervene before they are forced to sue for peace.

It is this possibility which is causing the lights to burn late in the chancelleries of Europe. The fear is that the war will spread from the Balkans and engulf the rest of Europe (→ 1/11).

Eyes front! They're changing the facade at Buckingham Palace

The present frontage of Buckingham Palace which is to be transformed.

Oct 23. Buckingham Palace is to get a new look. From next summer the present lumpy, dull grey Mall frontage will give way to a grander design in Portland stone by distinguished architect Sir Aston Webb.

Most of the present Palace dates from 1825, when the great John Nash remodelled the existing house of 1703. In 1847 Blore, among other alterations to Nash's work, added the Mall front to enclose the original open courtyard. Webb will alter this facade to add greater dignity and unity to the Palace's public front. His changes include a massive frieze running the length of the facade and pilasters between the windows. The wings and portico will project further forward and be topped by dignified pediments.

Italian win leads to painful peace for Turks at Ouchy

Oct 18. Turkey lost another slice of its empire today when the Sultan ceded Libya to Italy in a peace treaty signed at Ouchy, Switzerland, after two months of negotiation. In return, Italy has agreed to remove its forces from Turkish islands in the Aegean Sea.

The treaty ends a war declared last September when Italy invaded Libya and inflicted decisive defeats on the Turks at Derna and Sidi Bilal. The affair has ended very much in Italy's favour but the Turks were keen to reach agreement in order to face the more pressing threat of their Balkan neighbours (→ 19).

Even in death they were not divided

Oct 17. Siamese twins, Millie and Christine, died today in Ohio within a few hours of each other. They were believed to be about 60 years old. The sisters attracted great curiosity, not all of it welcome: they were sold to be put on display as exhibits, danced in chorus lines and once in Philadelphia were even stolen, to be found later in London. Siamese twins are joined to each other's bodies and rarely survive for long. They take their name from two Siamese boys born in 1811, who not only survived, but together had 19 children.

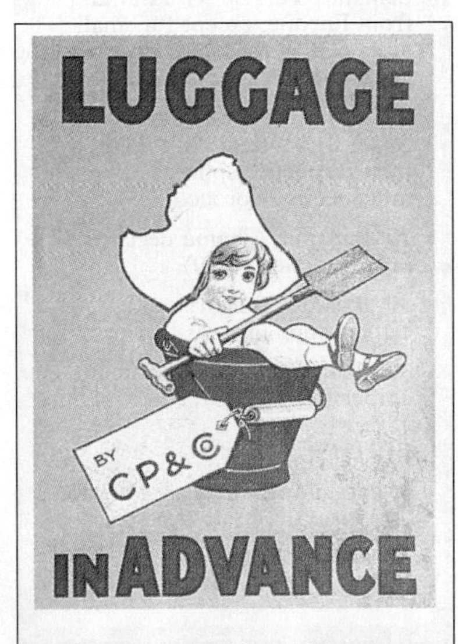

1912

NOVEMBER

Su	Mo	Tu	We	Th	Fr	Sa
					1	2
3	4	5	6	7	8	9
10	11	12	13	14	15	16
17	18	19	20	21	22	23
24	25	26	27	28	29	30

1. Balkans: Greece occupies Samothrace (→ 3).

1. UK: Vickers machine gun introduced into the British Army.→

3. France: Ponche and Prinard make the first flight in an all-metal aeroplane at Issy.

3. Balkans: Turkey asks the great powers to mediate in the war, allowing them one warship each through the Dardanelles (→ 5).

5. UK: British Censor of Films is appointed; he will classify films either "Universal" or "Not suitable for children".

5. Balkans: Bulgaria attacks Constantinople fortifications and cuts off the city's water supplies (→ 8).

6. Germany: Dr Friedman claims to have found a cure for tuberculosis involving the injection of a serum containing live tubercle bacilli.

8. Balkans: Greece captures Salonika (→ 18).

15. S. Africa: Imperial government decides to reduce British troops to 6,500.

15. US: On his 21st birthday, Vincent Astor inherits £15 million from his father, who went down on the "Titanic".

18. Balkans: Serbia takes Monastir (→ 19).

19. Balkans: Balkan alliance demands Turkish withdrawal from Europe, except for small area west of the Bosphorus, as condition of peace (→ 28).

27. N. Africa: France and Spain sign a treaty outlining their respective spheres of influence in Morocco.

28. Balkans: Albania declares independence (→ 30).

30. Balkans: Bulgaria and Turkey sign an armistice.

30. Balkans: Samos declares unification with Greece.→

BIRTHS

3. Paraguayan dictator Alfredo Stroessner.

26. French dramatist Eugene Ionesco (†28/3/94).

Democrat Wilson wins US presidency

President Woodrow Wilson waves to wellwishers on his election victory.

Nov 5. Woodrow Wilson, Governor of New Jersey, was today elected President of the United States. The first Democrat to be elected since Grover Cleveland in 1892, Mr Wilson won only 42 per cent of the vote. Theodore Roosevelt, as the Progressive candidate, won 27 per cent and the incumbent, President Taft, won a mere 23 per cent of the vote, winning only the two States of Utah and Vermont.

There was a surprisingly high vote for the socialist candidate, Eugene V. Debs. Some three-quarters of the votes went to candidates calling for change. The figures were Wilson, 6.3 million votes; Taft, 3.5 million; Roosevelt, 4.1 million; and Debs 897,000. A Virginian, Governor Woodrow Wilson was president of Princeton University, a political scientist whose books stressed the need for a strong executive government within the American system, and has proved a strong and progressive Governor of New Jersey where he successfully put his ideas into practice.

Treat sexes equally says divorce report

Nov 11. A call for men and women to be treated equally by the divorce laws comes today in the long-awaited report of the Royal Commission on Divorce. The recommendation is one of several which could have far-reaching implications for the state of marriage in this country.

The 200-page document also recommends putting divorce within the reach of the poor as well as widening the grounds for divorce to include desertion for three years, cruelty, habitual drunkenness, insanity and imprisonment under commuted death sentence, instead of only adultery (→ 28/1/13).

Turkey's enemies scent victory

Nov 30. After a war of just one month of almost unremitting defeat for the Turks, the opposing sides are holding talks between the front lines outside Constantinople.

It must not be thought, however, that the negotiators are exposed to the rough life of the common soldier. A seven-course lunch for 25 people is sent up by train every day from the best restaurant in Constantinople.

The indications are that the good food is having an ameliorating effect on the tempers of the combatants. The Balkan League, with the scent of good coffee as well as victory in its nostrils, is disposed to make peace.

The events of the past month have been dramatic. Albania has declared its independence from Turkey. The Serbians have occupied Durazzo. The Bulgarians are besieging Adrianople and are at the gates of Constantinople. Rarely has a defeat been more general than that of Turkey.

Perhaps the turning point in the war was the great battle of Lule Burgas in Thrace, which the Turkish government admitted was "a deadly blow", involving the loss of 40,000 men.

This battle, marked by the bloodiness of its hand-to-hand fighting, would seem to have ended Turkish power in Europe (→ 4/12).

Bulgarian reinforcements on top of a troop train at Mustapha Pasha on their way to join the Balkan war against the Turks at Adrianople.

1912

DECEMBER

Su	Mo	Tu	We	Th	Fr	Sa
1	2	3	4	5	6	7
8	9	10	11	12	13	14
15	16	17	18	19	20	21
22	23	24	25	26	27	28
29	30	31				

4. Balkans: Turkey concludes an armistice with all Balkan allies except Greece, which refuses to sign.

4. Balkans: Ismail Kemal forms first Albanian cabinet (→16).

5. Canada: Prime Minister Borden promises Britain £7 million for three new dreadnoughts.

5. Europe: Germany, Austria and Italy renew the Triple Alliance for six more years.

6. London: Prince Louis of Battenberg and Sir John Jellicoe become First and Second Sea Lords respectively.

10. Stockholm: Nobel Prizes awarded to Nils Dalen (Sweden, Physics); Francois Grignard and Paul Sabatier (France, Chemistry); Alexis Carrel (France, Medicine); Gerhart Hauptmann (Germany, Literature) and Elihu Root (US, Peace).

15. Paris: First performance of Alberic Magnard's "Berenice" at the Opera-Comique.

16. London: Balkan peace conference opens (→2/1/13).

18. Sussex: Discovery near Lewes of apparent human ancestor, nicknamed "Piltdown Man".

20. S. Africa: Premier Louis Botha forms a new cabinet.

20. UK: British Medical Association votes against providing service under new National Insurance law (→18/1/13).

25. Albania: Italy lands troops as revolt breaks out.

BIRTH

12. US boxer Henry Armstrong (†1988).

DEATH

30. German statesman Alfred von Kiderlen-Waechter (*10/7/52).

HITS OF 1912

Waiting for the Robert E. Lee.

It's a long way to Tipperary.

When I lost you.

Continents drifting says new theory

The neat fit between Africa and South America, so obvious on a map, may not be just coincidence, according to a theory proposed this year by German geologist **Alfred Wegener**. According to Wegener, there was once a single giant continent which broke up, the pieces drifting apart like rafts on a sea of molten rock; the map of the world today is the result of hundreds of millions of years of "continental drift". Patterns of glaciation, the distribution of related plants and animals, and apparent movements of the continents today support the idea, says Wegener.

The year also saw the publication of "The Theory of Psychoanalysis" by **Carl Gustav Jung**, a book likely to be significant and controversial.

Psychologist Carl Gustav Jung.

Viceroy survives assassination bid

Dec 23. A bomb was hurled at Lord Hardinge, the Governor-General of India, as he rode on the back of an elephant into Delhi today to take part in a Durbar arranged to celebrate the handing over of the new capital. The bomb exploded inside the howdah in which Lord and Lady Hardinge were riding. The Governor-General was seriously wounded and an attendant was killed. But Lady Hardinge was unharmed. Lord Hardinge's life, miraculously, is not in danger. A reward of 10,000 rupees has been offered for the capture of the bomber.

Arts: Music Hall on Royal Command

It has been a great year for the Music Hall. The variety artistes have been given the accolade of their first Royal Command Performance. On July 2 the Palace Theatre, decorated with three million roses, played host to the King and Queen. The stalls and dress circle were resplendent in tails while, in the upper tiers, the "regulars" all gave a vociferous welcome to their favourites.

The bill included **Harry Tate** in his celebrated motoring sketch, **Little Tich** in his big boots, **Vesta Tilley,** immaculate as a Piccadilly Johnnie, **George Robey** and, the King's special favourite, **Harry Lauder**, who went "Roamin' in the Gloamin'".

Anna Pavlova danced the celebrated "Dying Swan". There was much comment on the omission from the bill of **Marie Lloyd**, due to professional rivalries.

It has been a rich year for music hall songs. Miss Lloyd introduced "One of the ruins Cromwell knocked about a bit" (the Cromwell being a well-known public house) and the luscious "Lily of Laguna" was sung by **Eugene Stratton**.

But it was "Hullo Ragtime!" from America, which opened at the Hippodrome, that stormed the town. The hit from the show was "Alexander's Ragtime Band", delivered in a manner known as "coon shouting" by a lady with cropped hair, a hobble skirt and a huge ostrich feather on her head. **Irving Berlin** wrote it as well as an earlier hit "Everybody's Doing It, Doing It, Doing It".

The new age in musical entertainment was highlighted by the passing of a star from the old one, the Gilbert and Sullivan Savoyard **George Grossmith**, author with his brother, **Weedon**, of the little classic of English class humour, "The Diary of a Nobody".

London has seen its first Futurist exhibition from Italy. Artists like **Boccioni**, **Russolo** and **Balla** attempt to paint motion and noise.

"Ennui" by Walter Sickert: one of the year's notable new paintings.

1913

JANUARY

Su	Mo	Tu	We	Th	Fr	Sa
			1	2	3	4
5	6	7	8	9	10	11
12	13	14	15	16	17	18
19	20	21	22	23	24	25
26	27	28	29	30	31	

2. Balkans: At the London peace talks Turkey agrees to give up all its European territories except the area west of Constantinople (→ 8).

2. China: 300 Chinese troops are killed in a night raid by Tibetans.

7. London: Government introduces proportional representation into Home Rule proposals to safeguard interests of Protestant minority (→ 16).

8. Balkans: Peace talks almost founder as Turkey refuses to concede all allied demands (→ 9).

9. Balkans: Turkey breaches armistice by attacking Bulgarians at Lake Derkos (→ 17).

13. UK: First sick and maternity benefits under National Insurance Act.

13. Rome: Pope forbids films of a religious nature and bans films from church.

13. London: Two die as black fog descends on the city.

16. London: The Commons passes the Home Rule Bill which now goes to the House of Lords.→

16. China: President Yuan Shi-kai is defeated in elections.

17. France: Raymond Poincare is elected President of the Republic.

17. Balkans: Reported that Serbian troops are indulging in wholesale slaughter of non-combatant Moslems (→ 22).

18. London: British Medical Association drops its boycott of the National Insurance Act.

22. Balkans: Turkey accepts ultimatum from protecting powers, demanding withdrawal from Adrianople (→ 23).

23. Turkey: Young Turks revolt, angered by concessions in London peace treaty.→

BIRTHS

6. Polish leader Edward Gierek.

9. US politician Richard Milhous Nixon, 37th President 1968-74 (†22/4/94).

18. US comedian Danny Kaye (†3/3/87).

World's top athlete stripped of medals

Jan 27. Jim Thorpe, dubbed "the greatest athlete in the world" after his crushing victories at the Stockholm Olympics last year, was today stripped of his decathlon and pentathlon gold medals by the Olympic Committee.

Following newspaper revelations, Thorpe has admitted being paid $25 a week to play minor league baseball in North Carolina in 1909 and 1910, when he was already renowned as a top-class college footballer. The admission confirms Thorpe as a "professional" and so ineligible for the Olympics.

The US Amateur Athletic Union have stricken his name from all record books, though the runners-up in the two events have refused to accept the trophies in his place.

Jim Thorpe: unprofessional?

Young Turks coup threatens peace talks

Jan 31. The Young Turks have deposed the government of the Grand Vizier, Kiamil Pasha, and have thrown the whole process of the peace negotiations in the Balkans into jeopardy by refusing to accept the terms under which Turkey would hand over the historic fortress of Adrianople to Bulgaria.

In an interview after the coup, Talaat Bey, perhaps the most brilliant of the Young Turks, said: "We are going to save the national honour or perish in the attempt. We do not want a continuation of the war, but we are determined to keep Adrianople." There is no doubt that these strong words represent the feelings of many Turks, who are ashamed at their defeat at the hands of the Balkan League and are prepared to fight again rather than agree to the terms, which have been proposed by the league and supported by the European Powers.

The people have acclaimed the appointment of General Shefkat Pasha as Grand Vizier, and it is feared that if their mood is encouraged even more blood will soon be shed (→ 7/2).

In control: Young Turks patrolling the streets in an armoured car.

Home Rule falls at final fence

Jan 31. At one minute past midnight the House of Lords rejected Home Rule for Ireland. Voting was 326 against and only 96 for the bill proposed by the Liberal Government. But because of the limits placed on the power of the Lords by the 1911 Parliament Act, the blow may not prove fatal: their lordships can delay, but no longer veto.

The packed Lords chamber included many peers who attend only when Ireland is discussed. Some, like the Duke of Devonshire, who moved the rejection of the bill, have large Irish estates. One said Home Rule would make "the Irish a menace in war and a disturbing influence in peace" (→ 15/7).

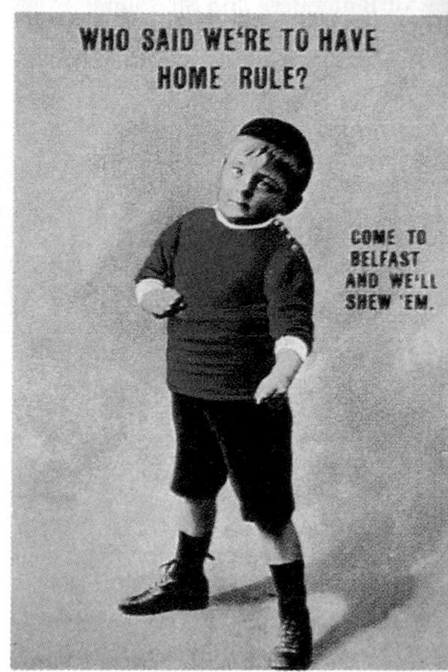

Ulster: getting the message across.

Speaker scraps Franchise Bill

Jan 28. The government has withdrawn its Franchise Bill and dashed any hopes of women winning the vote this session. The withdrawal came after the Speaker ruled that amendments changed its nature so radically that a new bill was needed. The move was immediately condemned by the suffragists. They denounced it as a betrayal and a trick to deprive them of their rights. In the immediate future, their only hope is a private member's bill. So they have now vowed to step up their militant strategy (→ 5/2).

1913

FEBRUARY

Su	Mo	Tu	We	Th	Fr	Sa
						1
2	3	4	5	6	7	8
9	10	11	12	13	14	15
16	17	18	19	20	21	22
23	24	25	26	27	28	

2. New York: Grand Central Station, world's largest railway station, opens.

3. London: First UK performance of Stravinsky's "Petrushka".

5. London: Sylvia Pankhurst is sent to prison and threatens to go on hunger strike (→19).

5. US: Michigan surgeon implants dog's brain in a man.

6. St. Petersburg: Government rejects Duma proposal to allow women to practise as lawyers.

7. Balkans: 5,000 Turks die in battle with Bulgarians at Gallipoli (→2/3).

7. Belgium: General strike threatened after parliament rejects universal suffrage.

8. UK: Suffragettes destroy London-Glasgow telephone line.

9. Mexico: Revolution erupts as Felix Diaz, nephew of former president, seizes capital; President Madero flees (→18).

13. London: UK premiere of Stravinsky's "Firebird".

14. London: Memorial service for Capt. Scott at St. Paul's.

17. New York: Opening of Armory Show, introducing "Modernists" to US, including Picasso and Matisse.

18. Mexico: Madero is formally deposed; Huerta seizes presidency.→

19. UK: Suffragette bomb devastates Lloyd George's new house at Walton Heath (→24).

19. St. Petersburg: Czar issues programme of celebrations of 300 years of Romanov dynasty.

24. London: Emmeline Pankhurst is arrested and charged in connection with Lloyd George bomb.→

25. US: Federal income tax is introduced.

25. London: Plans for tramway under St. Paul's are abandoned for fear of undermining cathedral.

26. Sardinia: Nelson's war stores for the Battle of Trafalgar are discovered.

Pankhurst trial opens

Mrs Pankhurst leaves court surrounded by admirers and policemen.

Feb 25. The trial of Emmeline Pankhurst on bomb charges opened at Epsom Court today. The suffragette leader sat pale-faced but calm as the charges were read out in the tiny crowded room. They relate to the attack a week ago when an explosion wrecked Lloyd George's new £2,000 golf villa at Walton Heath in Surrey.

No one was hurt in the outrage, but workmen had been due to start only 20 minutes after the bomb went off. The explosion was so strong that some local residents thought it was an earthquake.

Mrs Pankhurst described it as successful "guerrilla warfare" and said she accepted personal responsibility for all such acts, including arson at Kew Gardens and raids at Regent's Park (→2/3).

Deposed president shot down in street

Feb 23. Francisco Madero, the deposed president of Mexico, was shot to death in the streets of the capital last night. His vice-president was also gunned down and killed.

Like his brother, Gustavo, Madero was a victim of the ley fugo, or flight law, which in Mexico allows police to shoot anyone said to be fleeing arrest.

Madero was being transferred to prison late today when, according to his successor as provisional President of Mexico, General Victoriano Huerta, the two cars transferring him and other prisoners were attacked by armed men.

Both the former president and vice-president, the official statement said, had tried to escape and were then shot by their escorts. General Huerta promised "a strict investigation". Francisco Madero, sometimes known as "the apostle of democracy", was a journalist who led the opposition to the dictator, Porfirio Diaz, and was elected President. He had been arrested earlier this month while trying to flee the capital (→2/3).

Scott and companions found dead just 10 miles from safety

Feb 10. In a snow-covered tent in the desolation of the Antarctic wastes today, a relief party found the bodies of Captain Robert Falcon Scott and two of his companions, Dr Wilson and Lieutenant Bowers. A diary left by Scott confirmed the deaths of two more explorers, Petty Officer Evans and Captain Oates, on their attempted return from the South Pole in atrocious weather conditions.

Scott's diary tells of Evans's death from concussion after a fall on the Beardmore Glacier early on in the northward journey and of the heroic end chosen by Oates.

Oates, desperately ill and crippled by frostbite, had been begging the rest of the party to leave him in his sleeping bag. Finally, he walked from the tent into a blizzard, telling the others: "I am just going outside and may be some time." He was never seen again.

The three survivors were trapped with almost no fuel or food in their tent by a blizzard and died there just eleven miles away from a food depot.

Scott (centre) and his colleagues: a picture found with the bodies.

Scott's diary concludes: "I do not think we can hope for better things now. We shall stick it out to the end, but we are getting weaker, of course, and the end cannot be far. It seems a pity, but I do not think I can write more.

"For God's sake look after our people" (→14).

1913

MARCH

Su	Mo	Tu	We	Th	Fr	Sa
						1
2	3	4	5	6	7	8
9	10	11	12	13	14	15
16	17	18	19	20	21	22
23	24	25	26	27	28	29
30	31					

1. Europe: French and German socialists publish an anti-war manifesto.

2. London: Mobs attack suffragettes in Hyde Park and Wimbledon (→24).

2. US: Troops kill six of Mexican President Huerta's troops in a skirmish on the Arizona border.

2. Balkans: Allies order Turks to quit Adrianople, Gallipoli and the Aegean (→6).

4. London: Government introduces strict new air laws, imposing drastic restrictions on who may fly over UK.

4. Washington: Woodrow Wilson is inaugurated as 28th president of the US.

5. Paris: The government decides to introduce three-year national service.

6. Balkans: Greeks take Janina, capturing 32,000 Turks (→26).

12. Australia: Canberra becomes federal capital.

13. London: Royal Navy estimates are up by £16 million, and 146,000 more men are to be recruited.

18. Paris: Premier Aristide Briand resigns when the Senate rejects his proposals for electoral reform.

20. Greece: Duke of Sparta, eldest son of assassinated king, succeeds to throne as King Constantine I.

24. Manchester: Suffragettes lock Labour Party delegates into their conference hall.→

26. Balkans: Allies take Adrianople after 155-day siege (→31).

28. US: Revealed that prohibition is costing $2 million in decreased liquor revenues.

31. New York: A record 6,745 immigrants arrive at Ellis Island in one day (→9/5).

31. Balkans: 4,000 die in fierce fighting as Turks take Chatalja (→2/4).

DEATH

18. Greek King George I (*24/12/1845).

Cabinet ministers deny share charges

March 19. The political balloon of the so-called Marconi Scandal was deflated today by the High Court settlement of a sensational libel case. Two leading members of the government – Herbert Samuel, the Postmaster General, and Sir Rufus Isaacs, the Attorney-General – won a fulsome apology and costs from the French newspaper, "Le Matin". It withdrew unreservedly what the lawyers for the ministers called "imputations of the very grossest corruption".

The Court was told that "Le Matin" had reported rumours, rife in Britain, that the two men had bought, and subsequently sold at a good profit, shares in the Marconi company, which had won a contract for an Empire wireless telegraphy linkup. Both ministers denied on oath that they had ever dealt in British Marconi shares.

Sir Rufus, older brother of Marconi's managing director, said he had known nothing about the negotiations. Nor, he avowed, was there anything relevant or improper about his own past shareholding in an American company with an interest in the profits of Marconi.

The Attorney-General said that he had in the past sold some of those shares to David Lloyd George, the Chancellor of the Exchequer. There was laughter in Court when he explained that on account of market fluctuations Mr Lloyd George must by now have lost some hundreds of pounds on the transaction (→11/14).

George I of Greece is assassinated

The assassin, Alexander Schinas.

March 18. The King of Greece was assassinated in Salonika this afternoon. He was shot through the heart while taking his customary walk accompanied only by his aide into whose arms he fell.

King George had been staying in Salonika almost ever since the town was captured by his army from the Turks last November. His assassin was arrested, but apart from revealing his name, Alexander Schinas, would say no more.

King George, who was 68, was within a few days of completing his fiftieth year as sovereign. He will be succeeded by his son, Crown Prince Constantine.

The beloved brother of Queen Alexandra, he was the second son of King Christian of Denmark and was asked to be King of Greece only after the monarchy had been refused by Prince Alfred of Great Britain and by Duke Ernst of Saxe-Coburg (→20).

Asquith plays cat and mouse with women

March 31. A Bill aimed at dealing with the growing problem of hunger striking suffragettes has been introduced by the Home Secretary. Under the new system, if he feels their actions have endangered their health, they will be given a temporary discharge. The order will be for a fixed period and the prisoner subject to various conditions.

If she fails to return to complete her sentence or if she breaks the conditions, she can be re-arrested immediately. Concern has been mounting over the force-feeding of prisoners who adopt the hunger strike as a means of protest and the latest measures are seen as a cat-and-mouse strategy whereby the women will be released, but then re-imprisoned (→3/4).

A suffragist view of Asquith's bill.

On March 28 the first Morris Oxford left the converted military academy at Cowley. Seen here is the first factory built by William Morris under the city walls of the ancient university.

1913

APRIL

Su	Mo	Tu	We	Th	Fr	Sa
		1	2	3	4	5
6	7	8	9	10	11	12
13	14	15	16	17	18	19
20	21	22	23	24	25	26
27	28	29	30			

2. Washington: US Navy chief Admiral Fiske resigns, saying Navy is unprepared for war.

2. Balkans: 300 die as Montenegro troops take Mt. Tarabosh from the Turks (→22).

3. London: Emmeline Pankhurst found guilty of inciting arson and sentenced to three years in prison (→15).

4. UK: Covercoat wins Grand National at Aintree in which only two out of 20 horses finish.

8. Peking: Opening of China's first parliament.

11. London: Junior Minister Sir Stuart Samuel ordered to resign over Marconi shares scandal (→13/6).

11. English Channel: Aviator Gustav Hamel makes record double crossing in 90 minutes.

13. New York: £1 million war supplies loan arranged for UK.

13. Madrid: Anarchist attempts to assassinate King Alfonso XIII.

13. Belgium: 100,000 miners strike as a prelude to a general strike (→18).

14. New York: Dr Harry Plotz discovers a typhus vaccine.

15. London: Home Secretary bans public meetings by suffragettes (→5/5).

18. Berlin: Professor Behring makes new serum for diphtheria.

18. Belgium: 400,000 are now on strike.

19. London: Aston Villa beat Sunderland 1-0 in the FA Cup Final.

21. Scotland: Launch of Cunard's "Aquitania", world's largest liner.

22. Balkans: 8,000 die as Scutari falls to Montenegrins after six-month siege (→2/5).

24. Central Asia: Reported that Moslems are massacring Armenians (→20/4/15).

26. The Hague: International Women's Peace Conference opens.

Tragedy strikes triumphant Isadora

April 20. America's outspoken rebel against convention in life as well as in dance, Isadora Duncan, has cancelled all her packed performances indefinitely following the tragic deaths of her two children today.

Deirdre, aged seven, and Patrick, aged five, one fathered by Gordon Craig, the theatre designer and the other by Paris Singer, millionaire heir to a sewing machine fortune, were drowned. They were being driven home after lunching with her when the car stalled on an uphill gradient. The chauffeur got out to crank the engine when the car began to run backwards downhill and plunged into the Seine. Their nurse perished with them.

Tragic dancer Isadora Duncan.

Wilson reasserts presidential power

April 8. The American President, Woodrow Wilson, today appeared before a special joint session of the two houses of Congress to appeal for cuts in the tariff. He was the first President to appear before Congress in person since President Adams in 1801. His decision was a deliberate gesture, intended to assert presidential authority.

The House chamber galleries were packed to hear the nine-minute speech. Attacking high levels of tariff, President Wilson said: "We must abolish everything that bears even the semblance of privilege".

1913

MAY

Su	Mo	Tu	We	Th	Fr	Sa
				1	2	3
4	5	6	7	8	9	10
11	12	13	14	15	16	17
18	19	20	21	22	23	24
25	26	27	28	29	30	31

2. Balkans: Ottoman General Essad Pasha Toptani proclaims Albanian autonomy within the Ottoman Empire (→11).

5. London: Local unofficial referendum rejects women's suffrage (→6).

6. London: Commons rejects Franchise Bill by 266 votes to 219 (→7).

7. London: Suffragette bomb found in St. Paul's Cathedral (→14).

9. US: Report says that 900,000 immigrants have arrived in the US since July 1912.

11. Balkans: 150 troops die in a train crash at Drama.→

13. Oxford: The university decides to offer a Diploma in Business Studies.

14. London: Magistrate handling suffragettes receives a letter bomb (→4/6).

15. Paris: Nijinsky dances to Debussy's "Jeux".

19. Germany: Kaiser Wilhelm pardons three Britons convicted of spying.

20. France: The world's longest submarine, the 243ft "Gustave Zede", is launched at Cherbourg.

23. US: Thomas Edison invents a telephone recorder.

23. London: 10 mph speed limit is set at Hyde Park Corner, world's busiest car junction.

29. Paris: Uproar greets the premiere of the ballet "The Rite of Spring" by Igor Stravinsky.

29. Washington: Senator Tillman proposes a ban on smoking during executive sessions of the Senate.

30. Rome: Doctors claim they have discovered the cause of the disease pellagra.

31. US: 17th Amendment becomes effective; senators will henceforth be directly elected.

BIRTH

6. British film actor Stewart Granger, born James LaBlanche Stewart (†16/8/93).

Turks sign treaty ending Balkan war

May 30. The Balkan peace talks have at last been brought to a successful conclusion. Thanks largely to the efforts of Sir Edward Grey, principal agent in the negotiations, the peace treaty was signed at St James's Palace in London by Turkey and her erstwhile enemies of the Balkan League.

Dr S. Daneff, the Bulgarian delegate, expressed the view of the conference when he said: "I rejoice. This means peace not only for Bulgaria, but general peace."

However, even as he spoke, more storm clouds gathered over the Balkans as the allied countries of Serbia and Bulgaria failed to agree on the running of Macedonia – previously Turkish (→24/6).

Doctor diagnoses feminine fashions

May 17. Why do women enjoy dressing up? Dr C.T. Ewart, a distinguished London specialist, has identified two distinct types who experience an "emotional accompaniment of elation following the putting on of attractive garments".

In an address to psychiatrists, which attempted to analyse scientifically women's motives, Dr Ewart said that the first type loves pretty clothes for reasons of self-display even though she is careless of her appearence when alone. Type two received her impulses from a love for the beautiful and its relationship to her body.

All vanity? Modern evening wear.

1913

JUNE

Su	Mo	Tu	We	Th	Fr	Sa
1	2	3	4	5	6	7
8	9	10	11	12	13	14
15	16	17	18	19	20	21
22	23	24	25	26	27	28
29	30					

4. Epsom: Suffragette Emily Davison is seriously injured when she tries to stop the King's horse at the Derby (→ 8).

4. Budapest: Violence erupts in Hungarian parliament; premier resigns.

8. London: Emily Davison dies from her injuries without regaining consciousness (→ 10).

8. Berlin: Massive Olympic stadium is opened.

9. US: Government says Eastman Kodak violates Sherman monopoly law and should be broken up.

10. London: Emily Davison inquest returns verdict of death by misadventure (→ 11).

11. London: Male suffragist hurls bag of flour at Asquith in Commons chamber.→

11. Turkey: Grand Vizier assassinated.

13. London: Lloyd George and other ministers are exonerated over Marconi share dealing.

17. London: Seven suffragettes are found guilty of conspiracy at the Old Bailey.

24. London: President Raymond Poincare of France is warmly greeted when he arrives on official visit.

24. Balkans: Greece and Serbia break their alliance with Bulgaria over Macedonia and Thrace border dispute (→ 25).

25. Balkans: 616 deaths recorded as Bulgarian and Serbian troops clash, but war is not declared (→ 30).

26. UK: Emily Dawson is appointed the country's first woman magistrate (→ 29).

29. Norway: Parliament grants women equal electoral rights with men (→ 8/7).

30. Balkans: Bulgaria attacks Serbia and Greece (→ 1/7).

DEATHS

2. British poet Alfred Austin, Poet Laureate since 1906 (*30/5/1835).

8. British suffragette Emily Davison (*11/10/1872).→

Suffragettes mourn the Derby martyr

Emily Davison tried to seize the reins of the King's horse Anmer, but was fatally injured when it fell.

June 14. Thousands of suffragettes said a last, sad farewell today to the woman they regard as their martyred heroine – Emily Davison. Miss Davison, who died from injuries received when she fell under the King's horse at the Derby ten days ago, was laid to rest in the family vault in Morpeth, beneath a purple cloth inscribed by her mother "Welcome the Northumbrian hunger striker".

It marked the end of a day of mourning which, at its height, saw a vast procession move slowly across London watched by tens of thousands more. Flanked by a bodyguard of suffragettes dressed in white with black sashes, the coffin was drawn on an open carriage by four black horses and followed by four vehicles laden with hundreds of wreaths from across the world.

With ten bands playing funeral music and a dozen clergy at its head the procession moved slowly from Victoria to King's Cross station, uniting in grief women of all ages and all classes. Miss Davison, aged 40 and an English graduate, died six days ago in hospital.

Her rash and daring act of protest, when she dived under the rails and dashed into the path of the horses, was the last in a series which had led to her imprisonment and force-feeding on numerous occasions. Both rider and horse were brought down by her desperate act. The jockey is now recovering from his injuries. The horse appears unharmed (→ 17).

Germany boosts its peacetime army

June 6. The Reichstag has passed a bill authorising the German army to be increased from 653,000 to 863,000 men. In wartime, however, the new legislation allows for the creation of an army more than five million strong.

The reinforcement of German land forces is the brainchild of Chief of Staff General von Ludendorff, who is said to be increasingly concerned at the weakness of the Triple Alliance partners Austria and Italy. Austria has been under pressure in the Balkans while Italy is harassing the Turks in N. Africa. And with Britain, France and Russia growing ever friendlier, von Ludendorff fears for the security of the Reich's own frontiers.

Carpentier outguns Bombardier for title

June 1. The long-awaited match between two of Europe's most charismatic boxers ended in Ghent tonight in victory for the French prodigy, Georges Carpentier, who knocked out Britain's challenger for the heavyweight title of Europe, Bombardier Billy Wells.

Since he left the army to turn professional, Wells's elegant, upright style in the ring and his easy, charming manner outside it, have brought a new class of fight fan to the ringside in dinner jackets and evening-gowns.

But the 19-year-old Carpentier, who has had a similar effect on French boxing audiences, is already European welterweight, middleweight and light-heavyweight champion and his punching power felled Wells in the fourth round.

Wells floored by the new champ.

1913

JULY

Su	Mo	Tu	We	Th	Fr	Sa
		1	2	3	4	5
6	7	8	9	10	11	12
13	14	15	16	17	18	19
20	21	22	23	24	25	26
27	28	29	30	31		

1. Balkans: Greece and Serbia declare war on Bulgaria (→ 3).

3. Balkans: King of Rumania orders general mobilisation (→ 11).

3. S. Africa: Troops sent in as mine strike spreads to 40 pits (→ 5).

4. Wimbledon: Dorothea Chambers beats Slocock McNair for the Ladies' Singles title; Anthony Wilding beats Maurice McLoughlin for the Men's Singles crown.

5. S. Africa: Mine dispute settled after two days of rioting.

8. London: Sylvia Pankhurst is sentenced to three months in prison.→

8. Peking: Chinese parliament agrees to grant Mongolia independence (→ 16).

11. Balkans: Rumania declares war on Bulgaria and invades.→

15. London: House of Lords rejects Home Rule Bill a second time (→ 19).

15. London: Woman wearing a split skirt is seized in Richmond.

16. London: Robert Bridges is appointed new Poet Laureate following death of Alfred Austin on June 2.

16. China: Civil war reported to have broken out in Shanghai (→ 22).

19. Ulster: Carson says loyalists will never be beaten, in a speech in Antrim (→ 15/8).

21. France: Aviator Pegoud says parachutes are as safe as motor cars.

22. UK: 50 girls die in 20-minute factory fire.

22. Peking: Martial law is declared as unrest spreads (→ 18/8).

31. Wales: Lloyd George says Lords must be abolished.

BIRTHS

14. US politician Gerald Ford, 38th president, 1974-76.

29. British politician Jo Grimond, Liberal Party leader 1957-67 (†24/10/93).

Bulgaria rounds on former allies

A Montenegrin soldier takes a breather on the march through Albania.

July 31. The Treaty of London, which was signed only two months ago, has been torn up and war is raging through the Balkans again. Bulgaria has turned on her allies of the war against Turkey and marched against Serbia.

First reports of the fighting, which is very heavy, indicate that the Serbs are coping well with the Bulgarian attack.

The Greeks, also attacked by the Bulgarians, have allied themselves with the Serbs and it is expected that Rumanian and Montenegrin forces will also join the battle against the Bulgarians, who have been accused of appalling atrocities in the districts they have occupied.

This fresh outbreak of warfare might have been expected once the heavy hand of the Ottomans was removed, for the Balkan League allies are riven by jealousies dating from the Middle Ages.

Nowhere is the crisis in the Balkans felt more keenly than in St. Petersburg where the Czar had personally intervened in order to bring the quarrelling parties to arbitration.

The Czar's anger may be judged by his message to the Kings of Bulgaria and Serbia: "I wish to make it known that the state which begins this war will be responsible before the Slav cause and that I reserve to myself all liberty as to the attitude which Russia will adopt in regard to the results of such a criminal struggle."

Turkey has also become involved by sending a force to reoccupy the fortress town of Adrianople, lost to the Bulgarians under the terms of the London Treaty (→ 10/8).

SKEGNESS IS SO BRACING

Where is Sylvia? Pankhurst at large

July 21. Dozens of women, using hat pins and umbrellas, fought fiercely with police today as detectives struggled to re-arrest their leader. The violent scenes, which left both officers and suffragettes bruised and bloody, marked the end of an extraordinary week in which the police were repeatedly foiled.

It began on Tuesday when Sylvia Pankhurst made a dramatic surprise appearance at a public rally in defiance of her current licensed release from a three-year prison term. Angry women prevented the police from reaching her. Later a raid on her flat only caught a decoy. The police were more successful today and rushed Miss Pankhurst back to Holloway (→ 3/8).

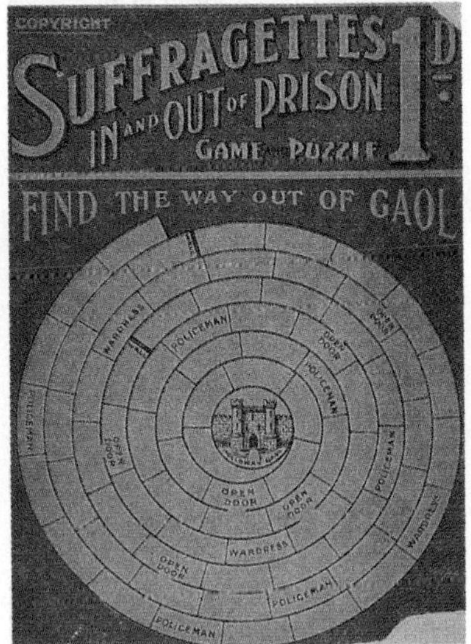

Cashing in on the suffragettes.

British fears on Baghdad railway calmed

July 28. Germany and Turkey have given way to British pressure and agreed to abandon plans for a rail link to the Persian Gulf. The deal should allay Britain's fears surrounding the construction of the Constantinople to Baghdad line.

The plan for the Ottoman railway dates back to 1899. It is being built with German money, expertise and manpower and was originally intended to link the Ottoman capital with major cities in Mesopotamia. The section from Constantinople to Aleppo is already open, while the Nisibin line should be completed by 1918.

What worried the British was the projected 80-mile extension from Basra to the Persian Gulf, which would have given Germany access to the sea and threatened British commercial and political interests in the Gulf region. Primarily, Britain believed that a German presence would undermine her sphere of influence in Persia and the security of the British protectorates of Kuwait and Bahrain.

However, there was also the fear of a German threat to India, so pressure was put on Germany and Turkey not to go ahead with the Basra spur.

1913

AUGUST

Su	Mo	Tu	We	Th	Fr	Sa
					1	2
3	4	5	6	7	8	9
10	11	12	13	14	15	16
17	18	19	20	21	22	23
24	25	26	27	28	29	30
31						

1. Belgium: Boxing effectively outlawed by new law requiring attendance of magistrates at bouts.

3. London: Suffragettes disrupt service with prayer for Sylvia Pankhurst (→5).

3. Russia: Police stop a football match in Kasimov, saying it is illegal assembly.

5. Devon: Suffragettes bomb several ministers' country homes (→28).

5. London: Delegation urges Asquith to reconsider a Channel Tunnel.

7. Farnborough: Aviator Samuel Cody is killed in an aeroplane crash (→8).

8. US: Aviator Wood sets new record by flying 277 miles non-stop in monoplane (→1/9).

14. London: Actor Herbert Wilson dies in hospital of injuries sustained when shot on stage as part of plot.

15. Ireland: Troops arrive to quell unrest after policeman shoots loyalist (→3/9).

18. China: Severe fighting is reported at Nanking, while 5,000 are said to have died in fighting at Canton (→7/9).

20. Vienna: Premier Istvan Tisza and Margrave Georg Pallaviani wound each other in a duel.

25. Washington: US announces arms boycott of Mexico after President Huerta orders expulsion of Americans (→10/9).

25. London: 10,000 painters and decorators strike for better pay.

28. UK: Suffragettes attack Asquith while he is playing golf at Elgin in Scotland (→1/10).

28. The Hague: Palace of Peace opens in the presence of US philanthropist Andrew Carnegie.

BIRTHS

13. Cypriot leader Archbishop Makarios, first president of Cyprus (†3/8/77).

16. Israeli statesman Menachem Begin (†9/3/92).

Bulgarians agree to a peace settlement

Aug 10. The Treaty of Bucharest was signed today bringing an end to the Second Balkan War. The result of this is that Bulgaria, which sought to impose its will by force on its allies of the Balkan League, has been made to give up most of the spoils it gained from Turkey in the previous encounter.

The treaty was made between: "His Majesty the King of Bulgaria on the one part, and their Majesties the King of the Hellenes, the King of Montenegro, the King of Rumania and the King of Serbia on the other part".

All got something out of it and even the Turks have profited from this second war because their forces remain in occupation of the strategic town of Adrianople (→21/9).

Report warns of motor-bus danger

Motor buses: a hazard?

Aug 14. Street deaths involving motor buses have risen five-fold since 1907, according to a House of Commons select committee report. Fatalities have increased at twice the rate of the rise in the number of buses. The committee recommends extra powers for the Board of Trade and local councils to regulate buses and suggests more attention to speed limits in busy areas. The present limit at Hyde Park Corner is 10 mph.

1913

SEPTEMBER

Su	Mo	Tu	We	Th	Fr	Sa
	1	2	3	4	5	6
7	8	9	10	11	12	13
14	15	16	17	18	19	20
21	22	23	24	25	26	27
28	29	30				

1. Paris: Bleriot performs first loop-the-loop (→9/10).

2. UK: 14 die when London express train crashes near Aisgill in the north of England.

3. Dublin: 50,000 attend funeral of a worker killed by police (→15).

6. New York: Noguchi isolates the virus of rabies.

7. Europe: German aviator Friedrich makes first Paris-Berlin passenger flight (→8).

7. China: Japan warns China it will intervene in the troubles after Chinese troops kill Japanese civilians (→10).

8. Germany: First flight of the biggest Zeppelin to date, L2, 160m long, 16m wide (→27).

10. Mexico: 350 US citizens are reported held captive since Wilson announced Mexican boycott.

10. China: 100 Japanese marines land at Nanking (→5/10).

11. Balkans: Cholera epidemic spreading; 1,500 Rumanian soldiers already dead (→21).

15. Ulster: Carson claims he has 150,000 volunteers ready to fight Home Rule.→

21. Balkans: Bulgaria and Turkey settle frontier dispute: Turkey keeps Adrianople (→24).

24. Balkans: Serbian troops mobilise after 3,000 Albanians occupy Dibra (→25/10).

27. France: Vedrines and Prevost set new air speed records at Rheims of nearly 118 mph (→29).

29. France: At Rheims, Prevost flies at 125 mph for the first time (→2/10).

BIRTHS

7. British actor Anthony Quayle (†20/10/89).

12. US athlete Jesse Owens (†31/3/80).

DEATH

29. German engineer Rudolf Diesel, inventor of the diesel engine (*18/3/1858).

Kaiser is worried by Italian role

Sept 7. In a resounding declaration of solidarity, Kaiser Wilhelm II of Germany, Count Franz von Hotzendorf of Austria-Hungary and General Alberto Pollio of Italy today reaffirmed their countries' support for the Triple Alliance. But doubts about Italy's reliability persist.

Italy and Austria have increasingly found themselves at odds in the Balkans; and after the pact was first signed in 1882, it was learned that Italy had insisted on a secret clause stating that it was not to be directed against Britain.

First Med crossing by French air ace

Sept 23. Four years after Bleriot flew across the English Channel, another Frenchman, Roland Garros, today became the first to fly the Mediterranean. He took off from Frejus in southern France at 6 am and landed at Bizerta, near Tunis, at 1.53 pm with only 1.3 gallons of fuel left. He had covered a distance of 558 miles – 437 of them over sea, making it the longest non-stop flight over the sea ever accomplished. And he succeeded despite strong headwinds which left him dangerously short of fuel (→27).

Even tobacco companies show their pride in the Royal Navy.

Ulster Unionists plan rebel "parliament"

Ulster fights back: anti-Home Rule leader Sir Edward Carson.

Sept 29. Ulster Unionists today decided to set up a provisional government on the day that a bill giving Home Rule to Ireland becomes law. The move was agreed at a meeting of the Ulster Unionist Council where Sir Edward Carson, newly elected as chairman, told his "parliament" : "We will scientifically, deliberately and carefully work out a plan which will make it impossible for a parliament in Dublin to govern this province."

Funds of £1 million are being set up to indemnify members of the Ulster Volunteer Force against loss or injury sustained when carrying out "the orders" of the provisional government. Committees are also being established for defence, finance, education, agriculture, trade and law and order. "We say to our enemies – we are ready, strike when you please," Lord Londonderry, one of Ulster's leaders, told delegates to the council today.

To show that Ulster's resistance is more than rhetoric some 15,000 men of the Ulster Volunteer Force (UVF) marched to Balmoral near Belfast for a military review. The salute was taken by General Sir George Richardson, formerly with the Indian Army, who took over command of the UVF in July.

The UVF claims to have 50,000 men, but is short of weapons. Some of its men at the Balmoral parade carried "guns" made out of wood and bought for a shilling and sixpence via newspaper advertisements. Nevertheless Irish leader John Redmond is taking Ulster's resistance seriously, confessing that he fears Ulster may yet be excluded from Home Rule (→8/10).

Berlin: inspection of cameramen lining the Kaiser's processional route.

1913

OCTOBER

Su	Mo	Tu	We	Th	Fr	Sa
			1	2	3	4
5	6	7	8	9	10	11
12	13	14	15	16	17	18
19	20	21	22	23	24	25
26	27	28	29	30	31	

1. London: Publication of Sir Almroth Wright's anti-women's suffrage book, claiming women are inferior to men (→13).

2. London: "Aero-bus" aeroplane sets new record by carrying ten people, including the pilot, at Hendon (→17).

6. China: Yuan Shi-kai is elected president of the republic (→5/11).

7. London: Government figures say paupers at record low as percentage of population.

8. Dundee: Churchill says Ulster's claims for exclusion from Home Rule cannot be ignored (→4/11).

9. Atlantic: 144 drown, 521 are saved when emigrant ship "Volturno" catches fire and sinks.

10. Mexico: President Huerta arrests 110 members of the Mexican Congress (→11).

11. Mexico: Huerta dissolves Mexican congress and declares himself dictator (→3/11).

13. London: Sylvia Pankhurst is arrested but escapes almost immediately (→15).

15. New York: Suffragettes hold baby shows to prove they are good mothers (→18).

16. Portsmouth: Launch of "HMS Queen Elizabeth", world's first oil-driven battleship (→15/12).

16. France: Five generals sacked in attempts to make the army more efficient.

17. Germany: World's biggest airship, "Zeppelin L2", explodes with the loss of all 28 on board.

18. New York: Emmeline Pankhurst arrives in the US but is ordered to be deported on grounds of "moral turpitude" (→20).

20. New York: President Wilson reverses deportation order on Emmeline Pankhurst and orders her immediate release (→1/11).

25. Balkans: Serbia withdraws from Albanian dispute under pressure from Austria.

418 miners trapped in a blazing pit

Oct 14. More than 400 men were trapped underground by an explosion and fire this morning in a coal mine at Sengenhydd in the Aber Valley. The explosion, which was audible in Cardiff 11 miles away, ripped through the pit just after 8am. All the shaft gearing at the entrance to the pit was reduced to matchwood, and a surface worker was decapitated by the blast.

Rescuers later recovered 21 bodies, and nearly 500 miners were lifted to safety from another part of the mine. But 418 men are still missing, sealed in the workings by walls of flame and deadly methane gas. Mining experts said there was no hope for them. An explosion at the same pit 13 years ago claimed 83 lives.

Armchair view of looping-the-loop

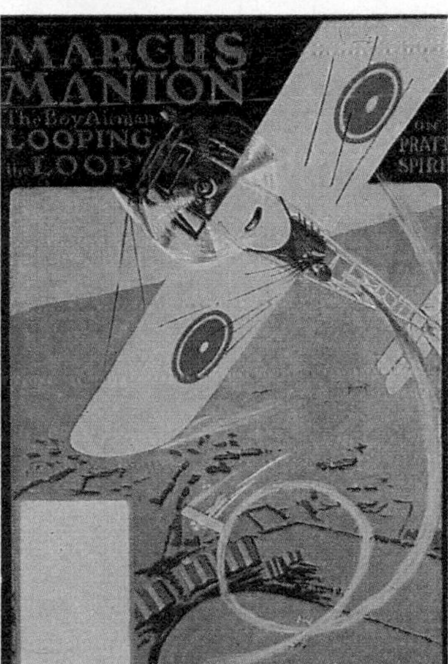

Defying the ground: flying feats.

Oct 9. Pilots are trying new stunts almost daily. One has just carried nine passengers on a biplane at Hendon, while others perform the near impossible and loop-the-loop. Thousands watched a French pilot, Adolphe Pegoud, loop-the-loop at Brooklands. He switched the engine off and turned his Bleriot monoplane onto its back for 30 seconds. He said afterwards that it was "as comfortable as sitting at home in an armchair".

Moving assembly line: a first for Ford

Cars can be assembled in under two hours on Ford's new production line.

Oct 7. Henry Ford today unveiled a moving assembly line for cars at his Highland Park, Michigan, plant. Since 1908, Ford's have operated a stationary assembly line using mass-produced precision parts, but the new 250-foot long moving line, where each worker performs a specialised function as the vehicle under assembly passes him, will result in a considerable increase in productivity.

It is estimated that the line will cut the labour required to assemble a chassis from 14 to under two man-hours. Each car can now be built in less than three hours and, using the new system, Ford hopes to manufacture as many as 250,000 Model Ts next year.

Dynamite blasts open Panama Canal

Oct 10. President Wilson today opened the Panama Canal from more than 4,000 miles away. At his desk in the White House, the President pressed a button, detonating 40 tons of dynamite to remove the last obstacle between the Atlantic and Pacific oceans. The canal has been called "the greatest liberty man has ever taken with nature". The hero today is Colonel George Goethals, the autocratic engineer who has been in charge of the project since 1907 (→17/11).

East meets West: the western lock fills to link the Atlantic and Pacific.

1913

NOVEMBER

Su	Mo	Tu	We	Th	Fr	Sa
						1
2	3	4	5	6	7	8
9	10	11	12	13	14	15
16	17	18	19	20	21	22
23	24	25	26	27	28	29
30						

1. Scotland: Suffragettes throw themselves in front of Asquith's car (→4/12).

3. US: Government orders prompt mobilisation of 500,000 men, for the first time in peacetime.

3. Mexico: President Wilson gives President Huerta an ultimatum to resign (→15).

4. Ulster: Businessmen refuse to pay tax until Home Rule is abandoned (→4/12).

5. China: Sino-Russian agreement that Mongolia will be independent under Chinese protection.

5. China: Yuan Shi-kai dismisses parliament and sets up a dictatorship.

6. Paris: Composer Camille Saint-Saens, aged 78, gives his farewell concert at the Salle Gaveau.

6. S. Africa: Mohandas K. Gandhi, leader of the Indian Passive Resistance Movement, is arrested (→11).

7. London: Music-hall artistes stage lightning strikes and win immediate pay rises.

8. Paris: Cubism is banned at the Salon d'Automne art exhibition.

11. S. Africa: Gandhi sentenced to nine months' imprisonment.→

15. Mexico: Rebel Pancho Villa takes Ciudad Juarez.→

16. Paris: Publication of vol. 1 of "A la recherche du temps perdu", by Marcel Proust.

17. Panama: The steamship "Louise" is the first vessel through the Panama Canal.

30. US: Charles S. Chaplin makes his film debut in Mack Sennett's "Making a living".

BIRTHS

2. US actor Burt Lancaster (†20/10/94).

5. British actress Vivien Leigh (†8/7/67).

7. French author Albert Camus (†4/1/60).

22. British composer Benjamin Britten, Lord Britten of Aldeburgh (†4/12/76).

Jailing of Gandhi sparks Natal riots

Nov 25. Two Indians were killed and 20 others injured in Natal today when police opened fire on a crowd demonstrating in protest at the jailing of Mohandas Gandhi, leader of the passive resistance movement in South Africa.

Widespread unrest broke out after Mr Gandhi refused to pay a fine for defying the new immigration law. He was sentenced to nine months. Mr Gandhi is a prominent lawyer who organised an ambulance corps during the Boer War.

Under the new law, Indians must not leave the province where they are resident. In practice, this means they must stay in Natal. Mr Gandhi set out to defy the law by leading a march of some 2,500 Indians into the Transvaal. When they were arrested and sent back to Natal, strikes and riots broke out and Indian shops closed.

Kaiser puts kibosh on tango for troops

The tango: banned from barracks.

Nov 17. The tango, currently the most popular dance in Berlin, has incurred imperial disfavour. The Kaiser has just issued an order to both the army and the navy "requesting" them not to dance either the tango or the two-step and to avoid families who do. Failure to observe the "request" would result in dismissal.

Mexican rebels close on capital

Mexican rebel Pancho Villa.

Nov 30. General Francisco Villa, "Pancho", claims that northern Mexico will be under his control within a fortnight and then it is "on to Mexico City".

Villa's men recently took Ciudad Juarez and are preparing to take Chihuahua. Then their plan is to move on Mexico City, where they will join up with forces commanded by General Carranza and together with others besiege the right-wing General Victoriano Huerta.

It was General Carranza who, last March, launched the "Guadelupe plan" calling for constitutional government. He has assembled a coalition of regional rebel leaders, including Villa and Alvaro Obregon in the north and Zapata in the south (→3/2/14).

Deal with Turkey gives UK Arab oil

Nov 30. Britain is to get the concession to exploit all the oil in Arabia, Mesopotamia and Syria. This new Anglo-Turkish Treaty will please Mr Winston Churchill, First Lord of the Admiralty, who wants the Royal Navy to have its secure supply of crude. A group headed by Lord Inchcape will also get 50 per cent of a company with the monopoly of the navigation on the Tigris and the Euphrates and there will be two British members on the board of Baghdad Railway.

1913

DECEMBER

Su	Mo	Tu	We	Th	Fr	Sa
	1	2	3	4	5	6
7	8	9	10	11	12	13
14	15	16	17	18	19	20
21	22	23	24	25	26	27
28	29	30	31			

2. Paris: Chamber of Deputies rejects Louis Barthou's finance bill; government resigns and Gaston Doumergue becomes premier (→16/3/14).

4. Plymouth: Emmeline Pankhurst is arrested on her return from the US (→3/1/14).

4. Ireland: Royal proclamation bans the import of arms into Ulster; ports will be watched (→15/1).

10. Stockholm: Nobel Prizes awarded to Heike Kamerlingh-Onnes (Holland, Physics); Alfred Werner (Switzerland, Chemistry); Charles Richet (France, Medicine); Rabindranath Tagore (India, Literature) and Henri Lafontaine (Belgium, Peace).

12. Florence: The Mona Lisa is recovered and Vincenzo Perugia arrested for its theft (→22).

15. Glasgow: Launch of "HMS Tiger", world's biggest battlecruiser (→1/1/14).

18. London: Lord Plymouth donates £35,000 to allow the Crystal Palace to be bought for the nation for £230,000.

22. Paris: Three arrested in connection with Mona Lisa theft (→31).

25. New York: Couple arrested for kissing in the street on Christmas Day; a judge fines them $15.

31. Paris: The Mona Lisa is returned to the Louvre (→5/6).

BIRTH

18. German statesman Willy Brandt, born Karl Frahm (†8/10/92).

HITS OF 1913

You made me love you.

Hello! Hello! Who's your lady friend?

He'd have to get under, get out and get under.

QUOTE OF THE YEAR

"Conscience is the internal perception of a particular wish operating within us."
Sigmund Freud
"Totem and Taboo", published 1913.

Arts: ballet sparks riot of the Spring

The Ballets Russes of **Diaghilev** have astounded the Paris public once again this year – this time by the music, if such it can be called, of **Igor Stravinsky** for the ballet, "The Rite of Spring". It consists almost entirely of pounding, reiterated rhythms and savage discords.

Soon after the curtain rose on the primeval Russian forest, where pagan rites were performed with "eurhythmic" movements, laughter and catcalling broke out and soon the Theatre des Champs-Elysees was a scene of pandemonium.

Half the audience was roused to derision and half to frenzy by the effect of the music. The choreographer, **Nijinsky**, had to stand on a chair shouting the beat to the dancers for the orchestra could hardly be heard above the demonstrations and counter-demonstrations, while some, like the composer **Debussy**, appealed for silence.

Also causing attention in Paris is an extraordinary new novel, published at his own expense by the author, **Marcel Proust**, an habitue of the salons of the aristocracy. His work, "A la Recherche du Temps Perdu" will run to many volumes. The narrator's buried memories of "lost time" are liberated by the taste of a madeleine cake dipped into a cup of tea.

Controversial Russian composer of "The Rite of Spring" Stravinsky.

A 28-year-old English writer, **D.H. Lawrence**, published "Sons and Lovers", about the sentimental education of a miner's son, like himself. He eloped last year with Frieda, daughter of Baron von Richthofen.

500,000 UK children ill-fed and diseased

Dec 16. One child in 12 at Britain's state elementary schools is suffering from disease or the effects of poor diet, according to a report out today by Sir George Newman, the chief schools' medical officer. Of six million schoolchildren, more than half need dental treatment and a third are unhygienically dirty. One child in ten has serious eye defects, nearly three in 100 have trouble hearing, two in 100 have heart disease, one in 100 has tuberculosis, one in 100 has ringworm and one in ten, he says, needs surgery for inflamed tonsils.

Hungry mouths to feed: a poor family in London's East End.

1914

JANUARY

Su	Mo	Tu	We	Th	Fr	Sa
				1	2	3
4	5	6	7	8	9	10
11	12	13	14	15	16	17
18	19	20	21	22	23	24
25	26	27	28	29	30	31

1. London: Lloyd George calls the build up of arms in Western Europe "organised insanity" (→26/2).

1. US: Opening of daily flights from Tampa, Florida, to St. Petersburg, Florida, first service of its kind (→2).

2. UK: Trehawke Davies is the first woman to loop-the-loop, at Hendon (→16).

3. London: Sylvia Pankhurst is rearrested under the "Cat and Mouse" Act (→4/2).

5. London: Grafton Group (Vanessa Bell, Roger Fry, Duncan Grant) opens an exhibition following break away from British Cubists.

5. Detroit: Henry Ford announces workers will share $10 million of company profits, and will be paid $5 for eight-hour day rather than $2.34 for nine-hour day.

7. Birmingham: Joseph Chamberlain decides to retire from Parliament (→2/7).

8. London: Doctors at the Middlesex Hospital claim to successfully treat cancer with radium (→4/3).

10. Japan: Nine million are reported starving in north-east Japan and on Hokkaido.

14. Paris: Actress Sarah Bernhardt receives Legion of Honour.

16. France: First French dirigible flies over Paris (→26/2).

18. UK: Submarine A7 is lost after diving near Whitesand Bay (→26/2).

21. London: Queen Victoria Memorial in front of Buckingham Palace is completed.

23. US: President Wilson asks Colonel George Goethals, Panama Canal builder, to be first governor of Canal Zone.

24. London: 20,000 builders go on strike (→2/4).

BIRTHS

5. French painter Nicholas de Stael (†16/3/55).

6. US actress Loretta Young.

Botha secretly deports top union leaders

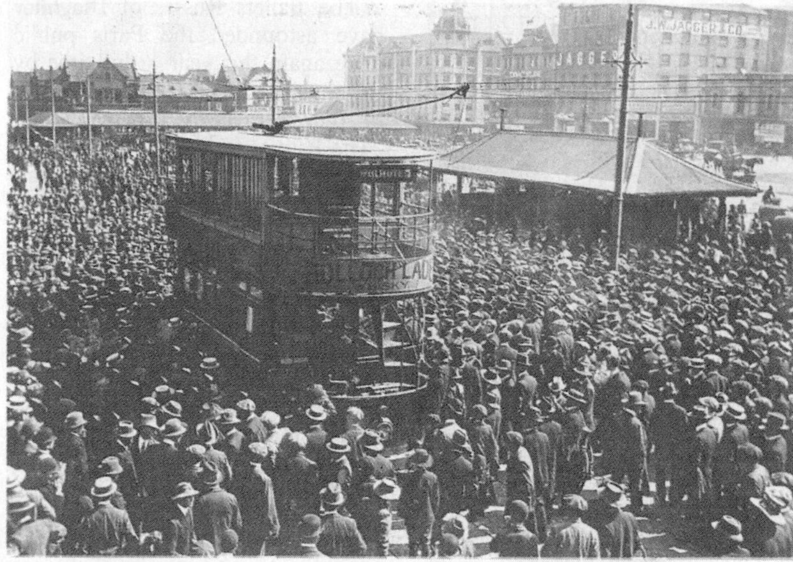

South African strikers surround a tram in central Johannesburg.

Jan 28. General Botha's South African government took its most drastic action yet today in an effort to break the two-week long general strike. Ten strike leaders were deported under conditions of great secrecy and the South African press were forbidden to report the event. Most South Africans do not know it has happened.

The men, several of whom had been arrested when the strike began, were taken in a shuttered and heavily guarded train from Transvaal to Durban. Surrounded by detectives and allowed only hand luggage, they were hurried aboard the Umgeni just before she sailed for England. The deported men include the most senior officials in the trade union movement.

The strike, over low wages and conditions of work, began in the gold and diamond mines and on the railways. The government declared martial law and a curfew and called up the Citizen Defence Army of about 60,000 men. Many have been killed and wounded in clashes between the strikers and the security forces.

In Glasgow, the Labour Party annual conference moved a special resolution condemning the deportation and the South African government. They also called for the recall of the Governor-General, Lord Gladstone (→24/3).

Playing on fears of invasion.

Cabinet troubles grow over Ulster

Jan 15. Andrew Bonar Law, Tory Opposition leader, warned tonight: "We are drifting inevitably to civil war". He told a party rally that there will be bloodshed if the government persists with Home Rule for Ireland and added: "We have given a pledge that if Ulster resists we will support her". He called for another general election soon.

This adds to the cabinet's cartload of trouble. A crisis is already looming over a threat by Winston Churchill, First Lord of the Admiralty, to resign in protest against Ministerial opposition to higher naval expenditure (→25/2).

1914

FEBRUARY

Su	Mo	Tu	We	Th	Fr	Sa
1	2	3	4	5	6	7
8	9	10	11	12	13	14
15	16	17	18	19	20	21
22	23	24	25	26	27	28

2. London: First UK performance of Richard Wagner's opera "Parsifal" at Covent Garden.

2. E. Africa: Inauguration of the 900-mile railway from Lake Tanganyika to Dar-es-Salaam.

3. Washington: President Wilson lifts the arms embargo on Mexico (→21/4).

4. UK: Suffragettes burn two Scottish mansions (→26).

6. Turkey: The government decides to admit women to Turkish universities.

9. London: Marconi announces he can light a lamp six miles away by wireless power.

10. UK: Novelist Thomas Hardy, 73, marries Eva Dugdale.

12. India: Rebel leader Govindgar sentenced to death for sedition.

15. Russia: Czar Nicholas II starts a campaign against excessive consumption of alcohol (→17/3/14).

19. London: Tory candidate Matthew Wilson wins Bethnal Green from Liberals in by-election on issue of National Insurance.

19. Paris: The new foot-high "Wigwam" hat is reported to be all the rage.

22. S. Africa: 600 blacks demonstrate against racial discrimination (→24/3).

26. Scotland: Suffragettes burn down Whitekirk parish church in East Lothian (→8/3).

26. Belfast: Launch of White Star liner "Britannic", UK's largest ship.

26. St. Petersburg: Polish aviator Igor Sikorsky carries 17 passengers in a twin-engined aeroplane.

26. London: Asquith rejects idea of a bill introducing compulsory military service (→17/3).

DEATH

25. British artist Sir John Tenniel, illustrator of Lewis Carroll's "Alice's Adventures in Wonderland" (*28/2/1820).

Ulster teeters on the brink of civil war

Loyalist members of the Ulster Volunteer Force show off their weaponry.

Feb 25. The paramilitary Ulster Volunteer Force (UVF) now has 100,000 armed men, it was claimed in Belfast today. With British ministers still silent about their next moves in the crisis over Ulster's opposition to Home Rule for Ireland as a whole, the increasing size and professionalism of the UVF has become a potent factor in stoking up the tension.

It is barely a year since the Ulster Unionist Council set up the UVF to help the provisional "government" for Ulster should the Home Rule bill ever become law. There are two main reasons for the UVF's swift growth.

First, there has been the failure of Sir Edward Carson's efforts to exclude Ulster from the scope of the bill, despite powerful backing from F.E. Smith and Bonar Law on the Tory front bench. Second, General Sir George Richardson, the UVF's commander, and his staff of English officers have greatly improved its organisation at county level, encouraging more men to join the ranks.

This sharpening of preparations was very evident yesterday when Sir George and his chief of staff, Colonel Hackett Pain, were in Co. Tyrone to watch an exercise involving six defending and six attacking companies. Afterwards the general called for more attacking practice. Among the men, the feeling is that civil war will come (→ 5/3).

British explorer finds Inca cities

Feb 18. Captain Campbell Besley, a British hunter and explorer, is the talk of New York. He arrived in the city today from the jungles of Peru to announce that his expedition had discovered the ruins of three Inca cities in forests near Cuzco. The largest city, called Plateryoyoc, contained buildings more impressive than London's Houses of Parliament, he says.

Two and a half years ago – on July 24, 1911 – a US historian, Dr Hiram Bingham, discovered near Cuzco the lost Inca capital of Machu Picchu.

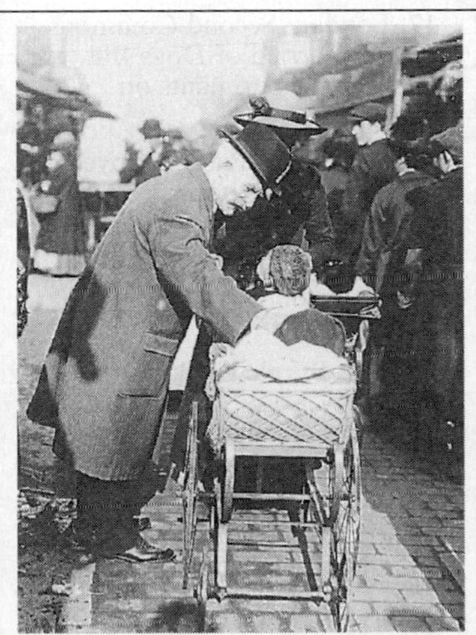

Catch them young: a candidate in the by-election for the East London seat of Poplar.

1914

MARCH

Su	Mo	Tu	We	Th	Fr	Sa
1	2	3	4	5	6	7
8	9	10	11	12	13	14
15	16	17	18	19	20	21
22	23	24	25	26	27	28
29	30	31				

4. UK: 15,000 sign petition protesting against disendowment provisions of Welsh Church Bill (→ 5).

4. Paris: Four-month-old Siamese twins are separated in successful operation (→ 19).

5. London: Welsh Church Disestablishment Bill reintroduced in the House of Commons (→ 21/4).

5. London: Irish Home Rule Bill introduced in the Commons (→ 6).

6. Ulster: Union Defence League issues 400,000 forms to be signed by anyone opposing home rule (→ 4/4).

8. London: Sylvia Pankhurst is arrested on her way to a demonstration in Trafalgar Square (→ 9).

9. Glasgow: Mrs Emmeline Pankhurst is arrested (→ 10).

12. London: Suffragette Mary Richardson is sentenced to six months in prison for damaging a Velazquez (→ 5/4).

17. Paris: Joseph Caillaux resigns as finance minister (→ 28/7).

17. Russia: The government announces an increase in the standing army from 460,000 to 1,700,000 (→ 1/4).

19. London: King George opens new headquarters of Royal National Institute for the Blind (→ 17/4).

21. US: French light-heavyweight champion Georges Carpentier is beaten by American Joe Jeanette.

24. S. Africa: British trade union leader Tom Mann arrives to meet local trade unionists.

26. London: Field Marshal Sir John French resigns as Chief of the General Staff.

27. UK: Mr T. Tyler's Sunloch wins the Grand National at Aintree.

30. Yorkshire: 100,000 miners strike for a minimum wage (→ 1/4).

BIRTH

26. US general William Westmorland.

Cabinet minister's wife shoots editor

March 16. Madame Caillaux, wife of the French finance minister, was invited to dine at the Italian embassy. Instead, she went to the offices of the Le Figaro newspaper, demanded to see the editor, Gaston Calmette, and shot him dead. She then coolly sent a message to the embassy saying she was held up.

The right-wing Le Figaro is attacking her husband, Joseph Caillaux, a radical, for planning to tax the rich. Calmette threatened to publish compromising letters written by Caillaux to his wife. It is thought that she asked the editor to hand them over, and when he refused, shot him dead (→ 17/3).

Artist's impression of the shooting.

Suffragette slashes picture with cleaver

March 10. One of the nation's most famous works of art, the Rokeby Venus, was slashed today in a savage act of vandalism. A militant suffragette, Mary Richardson, struck repeatedly at the Velazquez masterpiece with a foot-long meat chopper, almost under the noses of National Gallery attendants. Damage is estimated at £15,000 and experts says the £45,000 picture will never be the same again.

Miss Richardson, a 31-year-old journalist, said: "I have tried to destroy the picture of the most beautiful woman in mythological history in protest at the government's destruction of Miss Pankhurst, the most beautiful character in modern history" (→ 12).

European arms race fuels fears of war

War training: Kaiser Wilhelm II on manoeuvres with senior officers.

March 17. The grim prospect of war is looming larger in Europe with the arms race threatening to run out of control. In Britain the parties are divided on how to stop the race enveloping Europe in war.

The first Lord of the Admiralty, Winston Churchill, presented a new navy budget to the Commons today which he admitted was bigger than any before. He said: "It is our intention to put eight squadrons into service in the time it takes Germany to build five." This brought a challenge from Labour whose spokesman declared that: "Churchill's attitude represents a danger for the security of the country and for world peace."

Earlier this month Mr Churchill also had to ask for £2,500,000 more for the Royal Navy to boost oil reserves and speed up the battleship and aircraft programme. Meanwhile in Germany, Admiral Alfred von Tirpitz has admitted that his Navy is growing fast with 14 new major warships entering service this year.

In Austria-Hungary armaments are being given precedence in the budget and Russia has said it intends to quadruple the size of its army for a final show-down with Pan-Germanism.

However optimism is not dead. In Berlin a Frenchman told a pacifist group: "There is no innate hostility between our countries. We all want to live in peace."

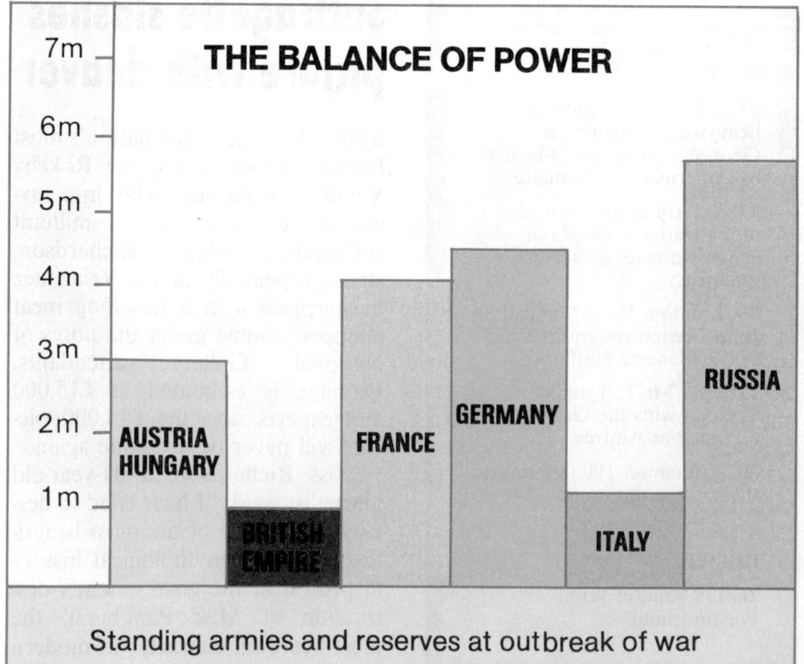

1914

APRIL

Su	Mo	Tu	We	Th	Fr	Sa
			1	2	3	4
5	6	7	8	9	10	11
12	13	14	15	16	17	18
19	20	21	22	23	24	25
26	27	28	29	30		

1. London: Electricians strike for shorter hours (→ 2).

1. Russia: 10,000 workmen strike in St. Petersburg (→ 7).

1. Australia: State premiers' conference approves Earl Grey's plan for a Dominion House on Aldwych.

2. Yorkshire: 140,000 miners are now on strike (→ 9).

4. Balkans: Albania mobilises and threatens war on Greece (→ 12/5).

5. London: Suffragettes throw bomb at a church (→ 9).

6. London: Home Rule Bill gets its first Commons reading (→ 25).

7. St. Petersburg: The Ministry of the Navy instructs shipyards to stop ordering from Germany (→ 3/5).

9. London: Reported that striking building workers' families are near starvation as £450,000 in wages has been lost (→ 27/5).

9. London: Suffragette smashes cabinets in the British Museum (→ 12).

12. London: Suffragette attacks Herkomer's portrait of the Duke of Wellington in the Royal Academy (→ 17).

14. London: Royal Commission recommends sweeping reforms in the Civil Service and an end to patronage.

17. London: Second Commons reading carried of Dogs Bill, outlawing experiments on dogs.

17. Yarmouth: Pier destroyed by a suffragette bomb (→ 4/5).

21. London: Welsh Church Disestablishment Bill given its second reading in the Commons (→ 15/9).

25. UK: Burnley beat Liverpool 1-0 in the FA Cup Final at Crystal Palace.

25. Ulster: Reported that the Ulster Volunteer Force has landed large quantities of ammunition (→ 25/5).

BIRTH

2. British actor Sir Alec Guinness.

Pygmalion is b**** likely to be a hit

April 13. Mrs Patrick Campbell scored a triumph last night in Mr Bernard Shaw's new play, "Pygmalion", as a Cockney flower-girl who is taught to speak like a lady by a professor of phonetics. Her tutor, Professor Higgins, played by Sir Herbert Tree, is so successful that she is accepted in society. Then, invited to walk home by a young swell, she replies in dulcet tones, "Walk? Not b**** likely!" This brought the house down.

The "sanguinary adjective" is now the latest in chic according to the play's own prediction.

Actress Mrs Patrick Campbell.

Cordial welcome for George V in Paris

April 21. The visit of King George and Queen Mary to Paris has been a popular success beyond all the expectations of courtiers and diplomats and has made the entente between Britain and France more cordial than ever.

More than 200,000 enthusiastic Parisians lined the route today as the royal couple drove along the Avenue des Champs Elysees to the Quai d'Orsay.

Improved relations between the two countries will be cemented in a round of ceremonies and banquets tomorrow and the next day.

US Marines intervene in Mexico crisis

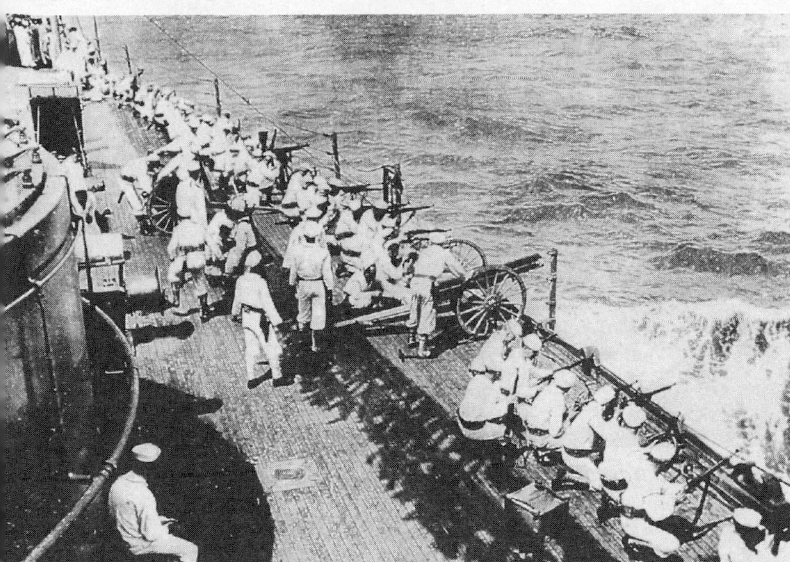

Field artillery and rifles brought to bear during the Vera Cruz landing.

April 21. A force of US Marines and bluejackets, 3,000 strong, today landed and seized the Mexican port of Vera Cruz. Fighting continues. So far the Americans have lost four men with 20 wounded, while the Mexican federal army garrison is reported to have lost 200 men.

The reason for the US landing is not known with certainty, but it is believed that President Wilson wanted to prevent German arms and munitions being shipped to General Huerta, the Mexican President who is under attack by revolutionary armies, because Wilson strongly disapproves of Huerta.

Now there are fears that the landing of US Marines could lead to war between the US and Mexico (→ 6/5).

Protests grow over forces' role in Ulster

April 4. A massive rally in London's Hyde Park today protested about the potential use of the British armed services in Ulster. Sir Edward Carson, the Ulster leader, denounced Winston Churchill, First Lord of the Admiralty, as "the butcher of Belfast" for putting the Third Battle Squadron on station off Ulster. But ministers are more concerned that around 70 Army officers have resigned over an order to move into Ulster. And Lord Hardinge, the Viceroy of India, has warned of serious consequences in India "unless the government makes peace with the army".

Cricket ball makers, on strike for higher wages, at Penshurst, Kent.

1914

MAY

Su	Mo	Tu	We	Th	Fr	Sa
					1	2
3	4	5	6	7	8	9
10	11	12	13	14	15	16
17	18	19	20	21	22	23
24	25	26	27	28	29	30
31						

3. St. Petersburg: Increase of 5 per cent in military budget is announced; Social Democrats are expelled from Duma after fighting in chamber (→ 13/6).

4. London: Suffragette attacks John Singer Sargent's portrait of Henry James in the Royal Academy (→ 13).

6. Mexico: President Huerta is said to be ready to resign on condition the US enters and pacifies Mexico (→ 3/7).

7. London: King George V opens the new King Edward VII Gallery of the British Museum.

9. Italy: 162 die in an earthquake in Catania.

12. Balkans: Reported that Serbians are inflicting terrible cruelties on Albanian Moslems (→ 19).

13. London: Suffragette Gertrude Mansell is sentenced to six months in jail for last month's attack on Herkomer's Wellington portrait (→ 22.).

15. London: Commons rejects idea of Scottish Home Rule Bill (→ 25).

19. Balkans: Essad Pasha is arrested for plotting against the Albanian government; rebel peasants in northern Albania threaten Durazzo (→ 20).

20. Balkans: Essad Pasha is deported from Albania (→ 3/6).

22. London: Government announces it will buy large share in Anglo-Persian oil company.

23. London: Amalgamation announced of the British India Steamship Co. and the Peninsular and Oriental Steamship Co. (→ 20/6).

25. London: Irish Home Rule Bill gets third Commons reading (→ 8/7).

26. Germany: Announced that the Bayreuth Wagner heritage will be presented to the German people in perpetuity.

27. UK: H. B. Duryea's Durbar II wins the Derby at Epsom.

BIRTH

5. US actor Tyrone Power (†15/11/58).

Women held after raid on Palace

May 22. Fifty-seven protesters were arrested today as they attempted to reach Buckingham Palace to present a "Votes for Women" petition to the King. Among them was Emmeline Pankhurst, looking frail and ill, whom police seized under the "Cat and Mouse" Act.

The demonstrators, some wielding Indian clubs, had tried to break through the 1,000 strong police cordon around the royal residence. The petition follows the defeat earlier this month of an enfranchisement Bill. So far more than 2,000 petitions, with over a million names, have been presented to Parliament (→ 1/6).

Police arrest a Palace protester.

Supertax increased

May 4. Higher direct taxation was the main feature of Mr Lloyd George's Budget today. The lower limit for paying supertax comes down from £5,000 to £3,000. It will start at 5d in the £, rising to a maximum of 1s 4d for those earning more than £7,000. Income tax itself now starts at 10 1/2d on a £1,000 income, rising to 1s 4d over £2,500.

1914

JUNE

Su	Mo	Tu	We	Th	Fr	Sa
	1	2	3	4	5	6
7	8	9	10	11	12	13
14	15	16	17	18	19	20
21	22	23	24	25	26	27
28	29	30				

1. UK: Suffragettes burn Wargrave Church, near Henley (→1).

1. UK: The General Post Office takes over the telephone system in Portsmouth, leaving Hull as the only UK city to control its own network.

3. Balkans: Albanian rebels demand replacement of the king by a Moslem (→4).

4. Balkans: Albanian city of Durazzo is in a state of siege; civil war threatens.

4. UK: Railway and mine workers join builders on strike: two million workers are now out (→11).

5. Florence: Mona Lisa thief Vincenzo Perugia is sentenced to one year 15 days in prison.

7. London: Suffragettes disrupt services at a number of churches in the capital (→9).

8. London: Alexander Borodin's opera "Prince Igor" is performed for the first time outside Russia, with the great bass Chaliapin.

9. London: Police raid offices of Women's Social and Political Union (→10).

10. London: Sylvia Pankhurst is arrested for the eighth time while on a march (→9/7).

11. London: Building workers have lost £1m in wages since they went on strike.

13. Russia: The monk Gregory Rasputin, confidant of the Czar and Czarina, is stabbed and wounded (→15/7).

14. London: Worst thunderstorm in memory causes several deaths as four inches of rain falls in three hours.

15. Europe: Denmark, Holland, Sweden and Switzerland form a defence league.

17. US: Finnish composer Jean Sibelius is awarded a Doctorate of Music by Yale University.

20. Hamburg: The Kaiser launches world's biggest ship, the liner "Bismarck".

20. London: Publication of "Blast" by Wyndham Lewis, launching anti-middle-class Vorticist movement.

Habsburg heir assassinated in Balkans

June 28. Two shots from a Browning automatic pistol, fired by a 19-year-old student, today killed the heir to the Austro-Hungarian throne, the Archduke Franz Ferdinand, and his morganatic wife, the Duchess of Hohenburg. It was the 14th anniversary of the marriage, for which Franz Ferdinand had taken an oath of renunciation to exclude from the throne any children they may have.

The assassin, Gavrilo Princip, darted out of the crowd as the car carrying the royal couple through the streets of Sarajevo, the capital of Bosnia, slowed to a stop to make a change of direction. The first bullet struck the Archduke in the neck, the second struck the Duchess, who had flung herself forward to protect her husband. She was hit in the stomach and died almost immediately, the Archduke some ten minutes later at 11 o'clock.

The outrage was evidently part of a carefully laid plot. Earlier, on their way to the town hall for an official reception, they had had a narrow escape when a bomb was flung at their car. It seems the Archduke picked it up and threw it into the road, where it injured the occupants of the car following.

At the town hall, the mayor, unaware of the incident, delivered a speech of welcome, which the Archduke interrupted: "We come to Sarajevo, Herr Burgermeister, and have a bomb thrown at us."

There are strong suspicions of Serbian complicity in the atrocity. The killer, who told police he wanted to take revenge for the oppression of the Serbian people, is believed to have been assisted, with weapons and forged papers, by a Serbian secret society of army officers known as the Black Hand. If this should prove to be the case, Austria can be expected to take the strongest action against Serbia.

But the Bosnian authorities are not without blame. No soldiers lined the streets, as is usual for a royal visitor, and there were few extra police on duty. Then, after the first abortive attempt, the royal route was changed, but the driver of the leading car forgot, or was not informed and caused great confusion by keeping to the original route (→30).

Countdown to tragedy: the couple at the start of their fatal journey.

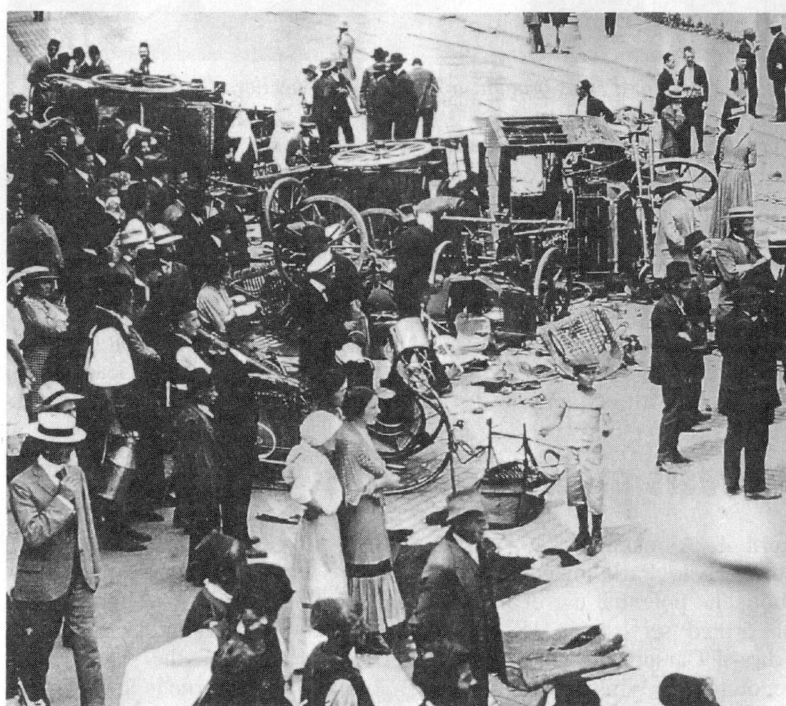

Stunned crowds surveying the scenes of chaos after the assassination.

One of the conspirators is bundled away by Bosnian police officers.

Death of Archduke sparks wave of revulsion in Europe

une 30. A tidal wave of horror and ndignation has swept over Europe n the wake of last Sunday's atro-ity in Sarajevo. The Times says it 'shakes the conscience of the vorld". The Daily Chronicle peaks of "a clap of thunder" over Europe. In Rome Pope Pius X, who s a sick man, fainted on hearing the news. In Vienna, it is reported that he Emperor, Franz Josef, broke lown and cried: "No sorrow is pared me".

Public feeling in the Austrian cap-tal is running high. Students have taged anti-Serbian demonstrat-ons, at which the Serbian flag has been burned. This feeling is said to be shared by the Foreign Minister, Count Leopold von Berchtold, who has been heard to express the view hat Austria must be prepared to go o the limit in pressing her demands on the "Serbian wasp's nest", even at the risk of provoking European complications.

In the Serbian capital, Belgrade, he conduct of the Press, which has nade little effort to conceal its satis-action at the crime of Sarajevo, nust bear a responsibility for the agitated state of public opinion. Nor has the government helped by ts failure to order a prompt and full nquiry into the allegations of complicity by the so-called Black Hand secret society (→25/7).

Pre-Biblical story of the Flood found

une 14. The original story of Noah and the Flood was written down on early Babylonian tablets, according o an Oxford University professor. Like the Book of Genesis the tablets name a gardener, "Nuhu", as the one who saved animal and human ife. They also blame Noah for the oss of eternal life. It was Noah, not Adam, who ate from the tree of life n the Garden of Eden in the Baby-onian story.

The professor has studied more han 50 of the tablets, which were unearthed at Nippur and are housed now in the University of Pennsylvania museum.

1914

JULY

Su	Mo	Tu	We	Th	Fr	Sa
			1	2	3	4
5	6	7	8	9	10	11
12	13	14	15	16	17	18
19	20	21	22	23	24	25
26	27	28	29	30	31	

5. Berlin: Kaiser Wilhelm II reaffirms Germany's alliance with Austria.→

6. Wimbledon: Norman Brookes beats Anthony Wilding in the Men's Singles Final; Dorothea Chambers beats Ethel Larcombe for the Ladies' Singles title.

8. London: Government says it might accept Lords amendment to Home Rule Bill excluding Ulster.→

9. London: Government report reveals harsh working conditions of women factory workers (→11).

13. London: The Performing Rights Society is formed.

15. St. Petersburg: French President Raymond Poincare arrives on a state visit to the Czar (→26).

24. London: Buckingham Palace conference fails to reach agreement on Ireland (→30).

25. Vienna: Austria breaks off diplomatic ties with Serbia after its rejection of the ultimatum of 23rd (→26).

26. Serbia: The army is ordered to mobilise.

26. St. Petersburg: Czar warns Germany he cannot remain indifferent if Serbian territory is invaded (→27).

27. Serbia: Austrian troops begin invasion (→28).

28. Paris: Mme Caillaux, wife of former finance minister, is acquitted of murdering the editor of "Le Figaro" (→31).

28. Vienna: Austria declares war on Serbia.

29. St. Petersburg: The Czar orders the mobilisation of 1,200,000 troops (→30).

30. Berlin: Kaiser Wilhelm II warns the Czar that Germany will mobilise unless Russia ceases to do so within 24 hours (→31).

30. London: Government agrees Irish Home Rule should be shelved in the face of the crisis in Europe (→7/9).

31. Berlin: The Kaiser issues a formal ultimatum to Russia and asks for assurances of French intentions (→1/8).

Amazement as King supports Loyalists

July 20. Against the background of threatened civil war in Ireland, the King today summoned party leaders – British and Irish – to a crisis conference at Buckingham Palace. According to Herbert Asquith, the Prime Minister, this highly-controversial move was made on cabinet advice. But immediately the King was accused of siding with the Ulster Unionists.

Surprised Liberal, Irish Nationalist and Labour MPs denounced the royal initiative as indefensibly partisan. From the Labour side, Keir Hardie said the King has precipitated the most serious constitutional crisis since Stuart times. He added: "King George is not a statesman. Born in the ranks of the working class, his most likely fate would have been that of a street-corner loafer. He is being made the tool of the reactionary classes to break the power of democracy."

The belief in the parliamentary lobbies is that with the European situation becoming more menacing, the Cabinet is banking desperately on the Palace conference to take heat out of the Irish question and allow the government to go slow over Home Rule. However, speaking for Ulster Unionists, Sir Edward Carson said: "The Cabinet is throwing upon the King the responsibility it should bear itself." The government replied by saying that everything must be done now to avert fighting in Ireland (→24).

Hostility to Home Rule seems likely to split the Emerald Isle.

Peace in Mexico as cease-fire signed

July 3. There are reports that President Huerta on July 1 authorised his delegates to sign a peace agreement with the United States. According to the telegram, General Huerta will resign and Vera Cruz will continue to be occupied by US troops. General Carranza, leader of the revolutionary forces, intends to send delegates to discuss with Gen. Huerta's representatives the question of whom should be the next President. President Wilson's personal representative, John Silliman, leaves Washington today for Mexico. He is expected to mediate between General Carranza and his rival General Pancho Villa.

Belgian bathing belles.

Austria issues ultimatum to Serbia

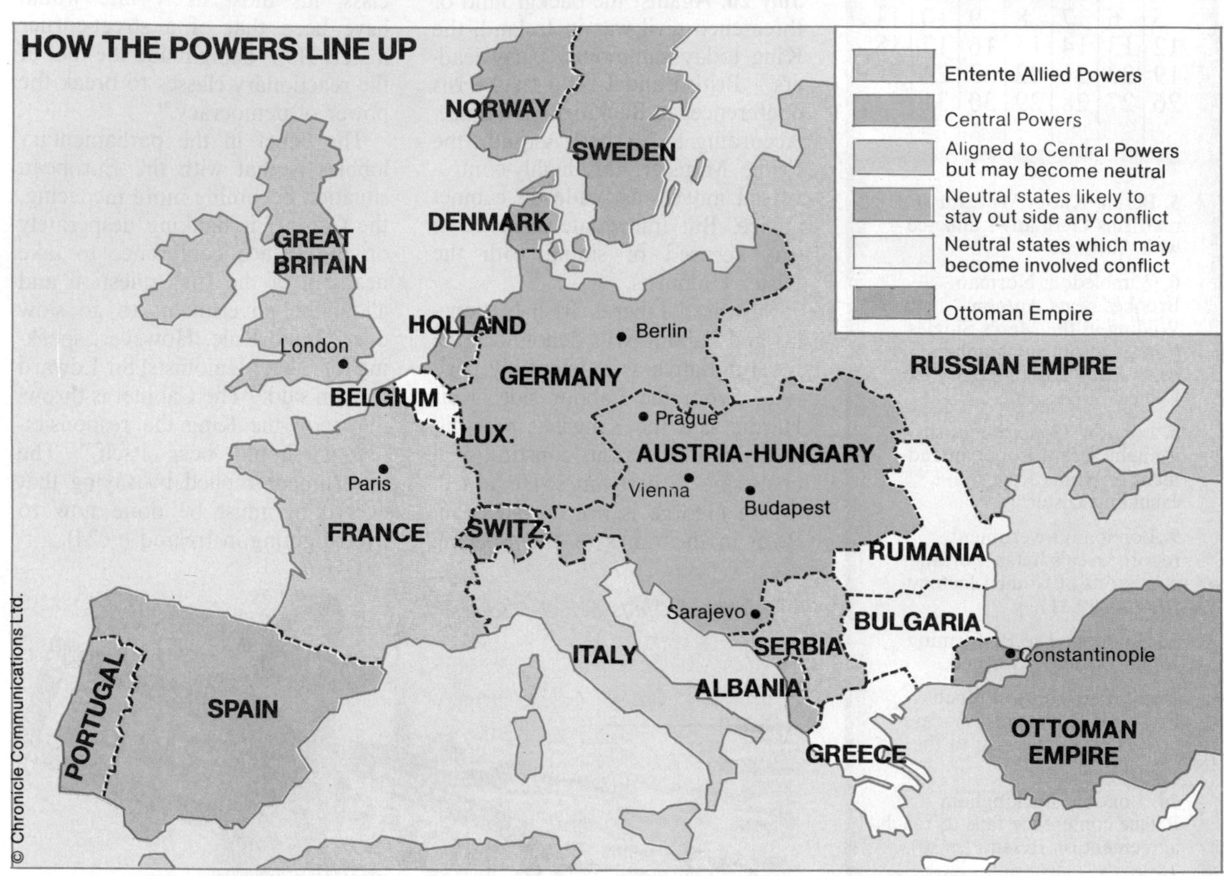

July 23. The Vienna government made war virtually inevitable today with a series of drastic and humiliating demands which Serbia cannot possibly accept without impairing her sovereignty.

Serbia has been told she must allow Austrian officials to take part in investigations, in Serbia, into Serbian complicity in the plot of June 28, and collaborate with Austrian representatives in suppressing subversive movements directed against Austria-Hungary. A reply must be given within 48 hours, that is, by 6pm Saturday.

The ultimatum by Vienna, almost a month after the Sarajevo crime, came like a thunderbolt to the chancelleries of Europe. It had been believed that, though relations with Belgrade were strained, Vienna would seek a settlement by negotiation, or arbitration.

The German Kaiser had talked of giving Austria full support, but he had then left for his usual yachting holiday in Norway. General von Moltke, head of the German army, was taking his cure in a foreign spa. The French President was on a state visit to Russia. The Serbian Prime Minister was away from Belgrade, preparing to launch his election campaign. The Russian ambassador to Vienna is absent on leave. Rarely can Europe have been so unprepared for a major international crisis (→25).

Britain's offer to mediate in Austrian crisis rejected as insolent

July 31. Events have unfolded with bewildering speed as British ministers have striven to avert the catastrophe of war in Europe. The Cabinet was wholly occupied with the Irish question until the moment last Friday when Sir Edward Grey, the Foreign Secretary, disclosed the contents of the Austrian ultimatum to Serbia.

Sir Edward's several proposals for mediation have repeatedly been overtaken by events. The Kaiser, at first conciliatory, suddenly took offence at what he saw as "British insolence" in making such suggestions. The Austrians, encouraged by the Kaiser's attitude, took the plunge and declared war. The Czar then ordered mobilisation of his army, followed by Germany and France. The question, still unanswered, is: Will Britain fight?

In Britain, the Royal Navy is being prepared for war although there are few other immediate signs of the crisis. However, tourists going abroad are advised to try Switzerland rather than Carlsbad or Marienbad (→6/8).

The Royal Navy: battle stations?

1914

AUGUST

Su	Mo	Tu	We	Th	Fr	Sa
						1
2	3	4	5	6	7	8
9	10	11	12	13	14	15
16	17	18	19	20	21	22
23	24	25	26	27	28	29
30	31					

1. Italy: The government proclaims neutrality.

1. Berlin: The Kaiser declares war on his cousin, the Czar; the first shots are fired (→2).

2. UK: Royal Navy is mobilised.

3. Paris: Germany declares war on France.

3. London: The Government tells Germany that the UK will stand by the 1839 Treaty of London guaranteeing Belgian neutrality, and will protect French coasts (→4).

4. Europe: Germany invades Belgium.

4. London: Sir John Jellicoe is appointed Supreme Admiral of the Home Fleets.→

6. New York: The cruiser Tennessee sails for Europe with gold for Americans stranded by the war.

6. Europe: Austria declares war on Russia; Serbia declares war on Germany (→9).

9. Europe: Germany and Austria threaten to attack Italy if it refuses to renounce its neutrality (→16).

16. Belgium: Liege falls to the Germans after unexpectedly fierce Belgian resistance and heavy German casualties (→17).

17. France: British Expeditionary Force lands (→20).

20. Belgium: German troops take Brussels (→23).

23. Japan: The Emperor declares war on Germany.

23. Europe: Germans are engaged along 150-mile Belgian front from Mons to Luxemburg as Russian troops penetrate 50 miles into Prussia (→26).

26. Paris: French premier Viviani forms a coalition government of national unity (→29).

29. E. Indies: New Zealanders occupy Samoa; the German governor surrenders (→31).

31. Russia: St. Petersburg is renamed Petrograd.→

DEATH

20. Pope Pius X (*2/6/1835).

War declared as Britons return from Bank Holiday

National spirit: cheering young men on the way to the recruiting office.

The euphoria: all over by Christmas

Aug 4. Britain's declaration of war against Germany sent cheering crowds surging through London, to gather in Downing Street and outside Buckingham Palace, singing the national anthem.

In the House of Commons, Herbert Asquith, the Prime Minister, was loudly cheered as he gave MPs details of the ultimatum calling on Germany to respect the neutrality of Belgium, guaranteed by Britain, Germany and France in the treaty of 1839. But the Kaiser has already dismissed this treaty as a mere "scrap of paper."

Three of Mr Asquith's ministers have resigned, including John Burns, the only Labour man in the Liberal government.

For most people, though, all doubts were resolved by Germany's invasion of Belgium this morning, thus putting into effect the notorious plan of Count von Schlieffen for fighting a two-front war by holding off Russia with minimal forces while overwhelming France with a massive flanking movement through Belgium.

Germany's rail system, built under the supervision of the General Staff, has been carrying hundreds of trains across the Rhine each day and some 1,500,000 men are believed to have been deployed already.

But Field Marshal Sir John French, who will command the British Expeditionary Force, has a high regard for the French army with its tradition of offensive élan and he has been heard to express the opinion that the war will be over by Christmas.

It is a view shared by many, though fiercely opposed by Lord Kitchener, the newly appointed Secretary for War, who believes the struggle will be a long one; he intends to mount a campaign for at least 100,000 volunteers for a new army. The Royal Navy, which had been on manoeuvres, has been put on a war footing with orders to be prepared to open fire at any moment.

On the Eastern Front, Russia has struck at East Prussia and Galicia; German and Austrian forces have answered with a drive into Poland.

In the City of London calm is returning after last Saturday when Bank rate rose to ten per cent, the Stock Exchange closed and long lines of people queued outside the Bank of England seeking to exchange banknotes for gold.

The Empire is rallying to the colours: Canada, Australia and New Zealand have already offered expeditionary forces. Chief Lewanika of the Barotse tribe of Northern Rhodesia has called on his people to make ready to help with the war effort (→10).

Life at the front: a Briton helps an injured comrade at Mons.

The reality: a bloodbath at Mons

Aug 31. British troops have been in action alongside their French and Belgian comrades in a bitter struggle for the town of Mons. The British Expeditionary Force of some 70,000 men crossed the Channel in a highly secret navy operation while the Germans still thought no troops had left England.

Despite the fighting skill of the BEF, the enemy proved too much, and on Sunday, August 23, the retreat began. Civilians in Mons, attending church, were caught in crossfire.

As the British forces, suffering heavy casualties, pulled back, some men of II Corps claimed to have been transfixed by the vision of a shining angel. Briefly, while it remained, the oncoming German cavalry was halted.

Bloody battles are being fought along an ever-shifting line from Belgium in the north to Alsace and Lorraine in the south, where the French opened their main thrust.

But the main danger is in the north. In under a month the Germans have swept over most of Belgium, crossed the Sambre and Meuse, forcing a French retreat to the Somme, the last barrier before Paris.

At home, it has been widely reported that a large force of Russian soldiers from Archangel has disembarked at Aberdeen and Leith and has started south, en route to France (→5/9).

Russians routed on Eastern front

Aug 31. The Russian army has suffered a terrible defeat on the Eastern Front in a battle at Tannenberg, which has raged for the past four days in the heavily wooded country along the borders of East Prussia.

Stragglers still making their way back through the lines tell of General Samsonov's Second Army being cut to pieces in a hail of German shellfire. The general himself is reported to have died in a mysterious fashion while retreating through the forest.

Something like 300,000 men are believed to have taken part in this titanic struggle. Cavalry swept through the villages under a blazing sun while white-bloused Russian infantrymen recklessly charged emplacements to use the bayonet against the grey-clad German machine-gunners.

Superior German artillery and a supply system built on the well-organised Prussian railway is believed to have ensured the victory of German organisational genius over Russian courage.

This setback has been acknowledged with commendable frankness by the authorities in Petrograd – the new name of the capital, St Petersburg being thought too Germanic.

The communique, which speaks of "severe losses", closes with the ringing assurance that "all measures necessary to counteract this deplorable event are being adopted with the utmost energy and determination".

Nevertheless, the defeat, coming after a chain of successes which saw the "Russian steamroller" moving surely, albeit slowly, into German territory, will change the shape of the campaign on the Eastern Front.

It is felt in Petrograd that the change in the Germans' fortunes was brought about by the arrival to lead the German army of General von Hindenburg, a professional soldier of the old school and General von Ludendorff, conqueror of the Belgian fort of Liege.

Until they arrived East Prussia trembled to the cry of: "The Cossacks are coming".

There is comfort for the Russians, however, in the news that their southern army has routed the Austrians at Lemberg (→ 3/10).

Many mere boys are among the Russian prisoners taken by the Germans.

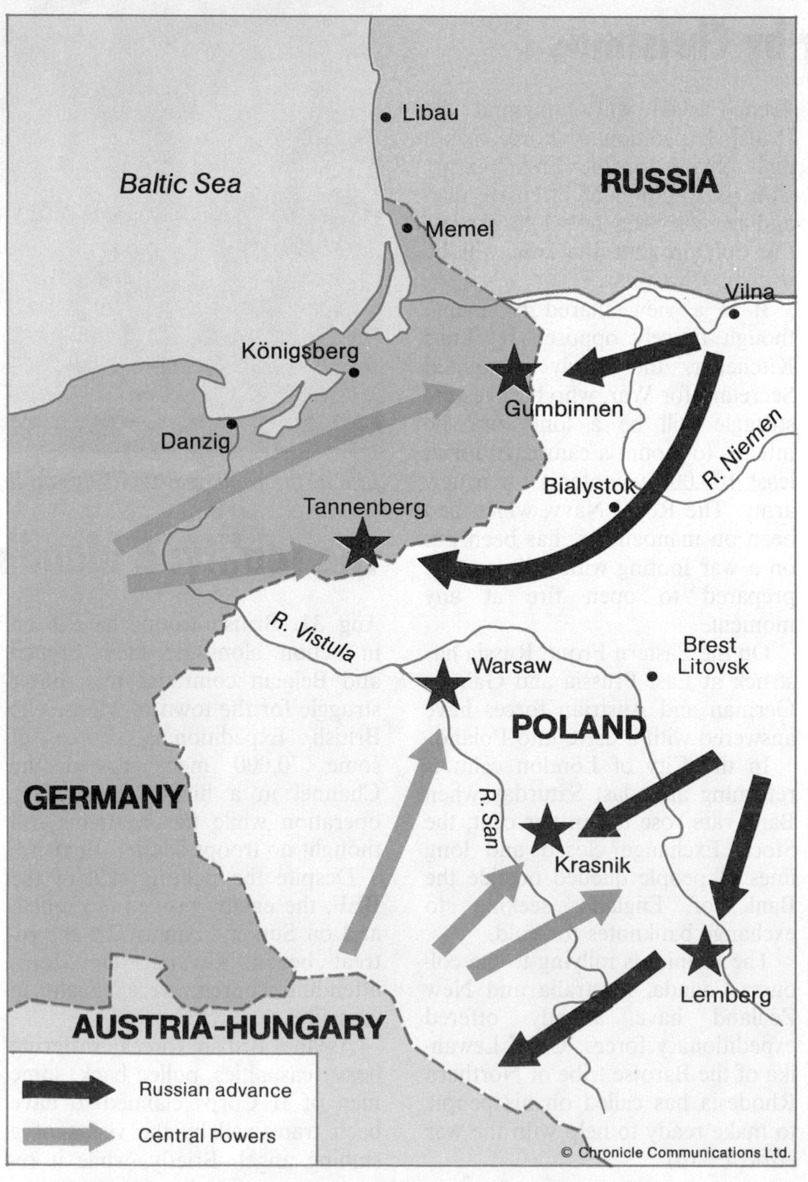

Olympia set up as concentration camp for German "spies"

Aug 10. The vast Olympia complex in Kensington has become a concentration camp. The Metropolitan Police have rounded up and detained 300 Germans there over the past few days. Many are suspected spies. Some are said to be "of good social position". There have also been wholesale arrests on espionage charges in different parts of the country and many hundreds of aliens' homes have been ransacked by the authorities.

These details were disclosed as parliament adjourned today for a fortnight after endorsing a massive programme of emergency legislation. The centrepiece is an all-embracing Defence of the Realm Act (DORA). This allows spies and saboteurs to be tried by court martial and ministers to rule by decree. With a party truce now in force Mr Asquith, the Prime Minister, is known to be working on a plan for putting the Irish problem on ice. It would involve acceptance of Home Rule but postponement of implementation until after the war.

Among the war measures so far announced are: restrictions on the movement of aliens, an inital £100 million parliamentary vote of credit, state control of Britain's main railway companies and some food price controls.

It was also announced that jailed suffragettes and strikers, recently convicted for assault, are to be released by King's Amnesty without conditions (→ 10/10).

Cowing Bull: a German view.

1914

SEPTEMBER

Su	Mo	Tu	We	Th	Fr	Sa
		1	2	3	4	5
6	7	8	9	10	11	12
13	14	15	16	17	18	19
20	21	22	23	24	25	26
27	28	29	30			

2. Turkey: The Sultan orders general mobilisation of Turkish forces (→28/10).

3. London: Queen Mary starts a "Work for Women" fund (→24/2/15).

3. Rome: Giacomo della Chiesa is elected Pope by the College of Cardinals with the name Benedict XV.

5. Europe: UK, France and Russia agree not to conclude separate peace treaties with Germany (→10).

5. France: Germans capture Rheims and take 12,000 prisoners (→14).

7. Ulster: Sir Edward Carson urges Ulster Volunteers to join the army (→15).

10. Far East: Japan agrees not to make separate peace with Germany.

10. S. Africa: Louis Botha proclaims loyalty to the UK in the war (→19).

15. London: Commons passes suspending bill to delay for one year operation of Irish Home Rule and Welsh Church Acts (→1/12).

19. S. Africa: The South African army takes Luderitzburg in German South West Africa (→23).

22. North Sea: British cruisers Cresy, Aboukir and Hogue are sunk with the loss of 1,500 lives.

23. S. Africa: Louis Botha takes personal command of South African troops in German South West Africa.

23. Germany: British aeroplanes bomb Zeppelin sheds at Dusseldorf.

26. Pacific: Australians take the port of Friedrich Wilhelmshafen in German New Guinea.

DEATHS

22. French writer Henri Alain-Fournier, killed in action (*3/10/1886).

26. German Expressionist painter August Macke, killed in action (*3/1/1887).

First shots are fired in war at sea

Royal Navy ships in rough seas, taken from battleship HMS Warspite.

Sept 23. German submarines have sunk three British cruisers off the Netherlands in the new war at sea. Hundreds have survived this first major set-back for the Royal Navy, but many faced a double ordeal. No sooner had they been picked from the water by a cruiser which had escaped destruction, than it too was sunk by a torpedo, throwing them into the sea again.

The naval war began three weeks ago with a successful British strike against the German fleet off Heligoland. Three German cruisers and two destroyers were sunk by a strong force of destroyers, cruisers and submarines.

Mines have been claiming their victims too. The light cruiser, HMS Amphion, was the first British warship to be hit, on August 6, but a number of fishing vessels and neutral ships have already been struck by mines in the North Sea.

The Admiralty claims Germany is laying them indiscriminately, using merchantmen rather than expensive warships to do so. Britain has refused to lay mines, claiming it is still possible to keep the sea lanes open to commerce. Earlier this month a torpedo gunboat, HMS Speedy, was hit by a mine 30 miles off the East Coast, only 15 minutes after she watched a drifter suffer the same fate.

Two days later the cruiser HMS Pathfinder was hit by a mine and the day after that the liner Runo was sunk off Hull with 300 Russian refugees on board. Most survived due to prompt rescue by a nearby fishing fleet (→17/10).

Naval strength of major European powers in 1914

	Britain	Germany	France	Italy	Russia	Austria-Hungary	Turkey
Dreadnoughts	24	13	14	1	4	3	1
Pre-Dreadnoughts	38	30	9	17	7	12	3
Battle cruisers	10	6	0	0	1	0	0
Cruisers	47	14	19	5	8	3	0
Light cruisers	61	35	6	6	5	4	2
Destroyers	228	152	81	33	106	18	8
Submarines	76	30	67	20	36	14	0

The Army calls for 500,000 more men

Sept 9. The Prime Minister, Herbert Asquith, today called for another 500,000 men to sign up for the army, promising that soldiers will be treated as never before.

The army has grown in size from just 386,000 men at the beginning of the war to 825,000 today and the aim is to place 1,200,000 men in the field soon. Mr Asquith said there was still an urgent need for more recruits, adding: "Let us get the men, that is the first necessity of the state".

Almost as many men are now joining the army in a day as are normally recruited in a year, and there have been many complaints by recruits about the poor state of training accommodation. The mood in the Commons is that in this war the soldier should be treated well and not have his needs ignored by those in authority.

Lord Kitchener has ordered officers to ensure the volunteers are given good accommodation, warning they will be held personally responsible if bad conditions are found. The number of training centres is being rapidly expanded, with local authorities providing accomodation in public buildings.

Many recruits will be allowed to live at home until they are required and those without rooms in barracks will receive two shillings a day board and lodging in addition to their one shilling pay.

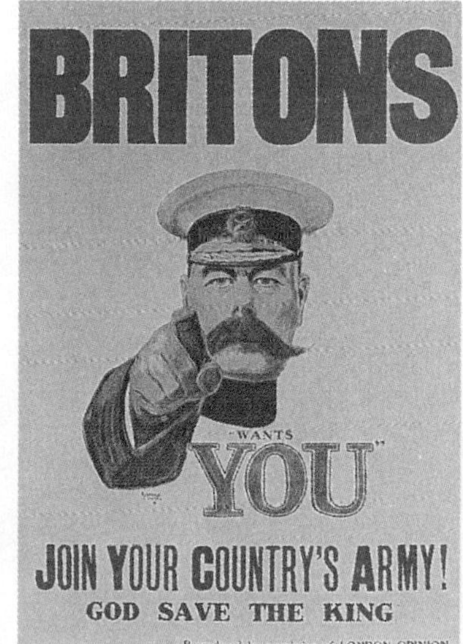

Gathering force: recruiting poster for the British Army.

Paris saved: Germans are in retreat

Sept 14. The first decisive battle on the Western Front has been fought along the banks of the Marne, with the Allies driving the Germans back to the Aisne and removing the threat to Paris. Hastily dug trenches have begun to appear in the German lines and these, when protected by barbed wire, virtually rule out a frontal assault.

Though the capital is now secure, the French cabinet has nevertheless departed for Bordeaux, after President Raymond Poincare issued a message to Parisians: "Frenchmen! Be worthy of these tragic circumstances. We will obtain victory in the end."

Right up to the beginning of the month the Germans had been pressing forward. But by September 6, General Joseph Joffre, reinforced with fresh troops, was opening his counter-offensive and forcing the Germans to swing back with their hinge on Verdun.

At a critical moment, when the offensive faltered, General Ferdinand Foch reported to GHQ: "My centre is giving ground; my right retiring. Situation excellent. I am attacking." He claimed his attack was decisive in thwarting the enemy, though the British believe their discovery of undefended bridges was the key to success.

General Joseph Gallieni in Paris also shares the honours. He commandeered 600 taxis to rush 6,000 troops to the front in relays. The whole campaign is reckoned to have cost the Germans and the Allies some 500,000 casualties. General French says British losses have been heavy, but added: "I do not think they have been excessive in view of the magnitude of the great fight."

At home, while Kitchener calls for 500,000 more volunteers, Queen Mary has appealed to women of the Empire to knit 300,000 pairs of socks for the troops.

On the Eastern Front, General Paul von Hindenburg took command when German forces were retreating; he all but annihilated the Russians at Tannenberg. But the Russians claim to be pushing back the Austrians in desperate fighting near Lvov. A Russian General Staff communique says: "We have taken many prisoners and ammunition columns. In one captured hospital we found 500 Austrians, all suffering from dysentery, which disease is depleting the enemy's ranks."

The first naval encounter of the war took place in the Bight of Heligoland when three new German cruisers were sunk, with the loss of 1,000 sailors, including a German admiral. No British ship was lost, but the cruiser Arethusa was holed in 30 places.

French soldiers open fire on the invaders in the Marne area.

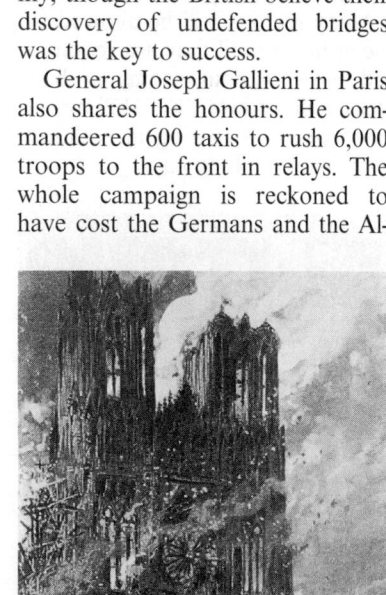

A shell hits Rheims cathedral during the German bombardment.

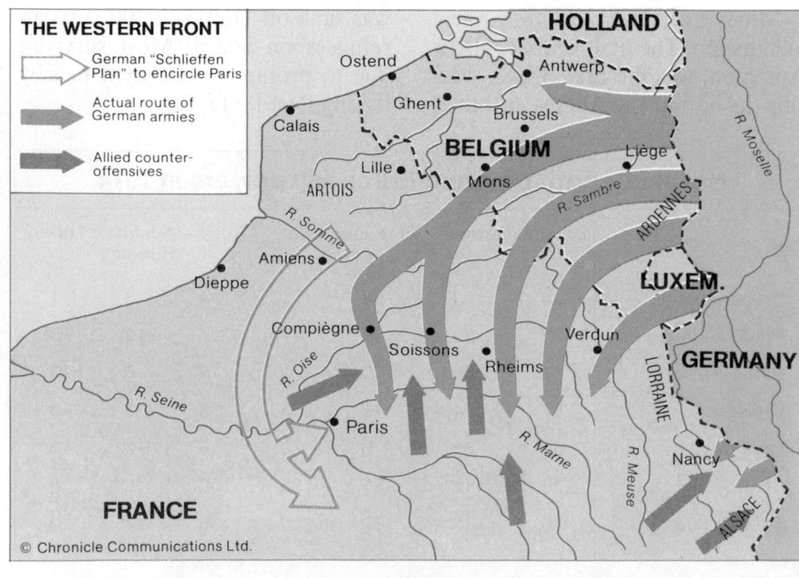

1914

OCTOBER

Su	Mo	Tu	We	Th	Fr	Sa
				1	2	3
4	5	6	7	8	9	10
11	12	13	14	15	16	17
18	19	20	21	22	23	24
25	26	27	28	29	30	31

3. Turkey: 2,500 are feared dead in an earthquake.

3. Russia: Czar Nicholas leaves for the front (→ 28).

4. London: The first bomb is dropped on the city (→ 7).

7. Belgium: Germans bombard Antwerp (→ 14).

11. France: Germans bomb Paris (→ 14).

13. US: Thomas Edison's miners' electric safety lantern is patented.

14. Belgium: French and British troops occupy Ypres.

14. Belgium: The government flees to France (→ 19).

17. North Sea: Royal Navy sinks four German destroyers off the Dutch coast (→ 22).

18. London: Hiram Maxim reveals invention of anti-Zeppelin incendiary bullet.

19. London: From today all licensed premises in the city must close at 10pm not 11pm.

22. Egypt: UK orders all foreign vessels out of the Suez Canal (→ 29).

26. Belgium: Reported that 7,000 Belgians face starvation (→ 2/12).

28. US: George Eastman announces invention of colour photographic process by Eastman Kodak Co.

28. Bosnia: Trial of conspirators to assassinate Austrian heir and his wife at Sarajevo ends; Gavrilo Princip escapes death penalty because he was under 21 when he shot the archduke and duchess (→ 4/2/15).

28. Black Sea: Turkey attacks Russian ports (→ 31).

30. London: Lord Fisher is appointed First Sea Lord in succession to Prince Louis of Battenberg (→ 3/11).

31. Black Sea: Turkey attacks Russian fleet (→ 1/11).

BIRTHS

6. Norwegian explorer Thor Heyerdahl.

27. Welsh poet and writer Dylan Thomas (†9/11/53).

Belgian cities fall to German troops

Oct 19. Since the great battles of the rivers last month, the front has shifted from France to Flanders as each side, recoiling from frontal attacks on entrenched positions, has sought to manoeuvre round the other's exposed wing. The response in every case has been more digging of trenches; and so the German and Anglo-French forces have steadily worked their way northwards to the Channel coast.

In the process the Germans set out to consolidate their position in Belgium; so Ghent, Bruges and Ostend have fallen, and the Belgian government has fled to France.

King Albert, with his Field Army and some British troops, was besieged in Antwerp and under bombardment. The port was finally taken on October 9; the Belgian force escaped after blowing up the forts, but about 1,000 British were forced to retreat into neutral Holland.

As the war of movement gave way to the quite new and unexpected trenches, a fierce struggle developed for key positions. On the British front in Flanders it was the town of Ypres, which the British Tommy was soon calling Wipers. Despite repeated and heavy German blows, the British held on, and the trench barrier from the Swiss border to the sea was completed.

With the appearance of a German aeroplane over Paris last week, another unanticipated dimension has been added to the war. The plane arrived soon after midday on Sunday, when the boulevards and the Champs Elysees were crowded. Field glasses were produced in an attempt to follow the hide-and-seek that ensued when a French biplane gave chase. There were several explosions from the bombs dropped by the German before he took cover in thick cloud.

It is still too soon to be sure that the other aerial menace, the Zeppelin, can be banished, but hopes have been raised by the news that Sir Hiram Maxim, the American-born inventor of the machine gun, who became a British citizen, has devised an incendiary bullet to ignite the Zeppelin's gases.

Reports reaching Amsterdam from Berlin say that the Socialist newspaper Vorwarts has incensed the authorities by publishing an article warning the bourgeois press against publishing misleading reports of Austrian victories.

Scene of panic in the port of Antwerp as the Germans advance.

Police round up thousands of aliens across the country

Oct 29. Anti-German feeling has forced the resignation of Prince Louis of Battenberg as First Sea Lord at the Admiralty. Prince Louis is German by birth and related to the Kaiser. Ironically, his son is serving with the Royal Navy.

The hostility to Germans has been fanned by a major round-up of aliens throughout Britain. Several concentration camps have been set up, one of which is housed in London's Olympia exhibition halls.

Four "suspect" foreigners had to be rescued by police from angry Welsh farmers last night after fleeing into the hills. One of them – a professor of languages – was studying the Welsh language.

An angry mob vents its anti-German feeling on a shopkeeper.

Allies explore new ways of raining death from the sky

Oct 7. The aeroplane is changing the grim face of war in Belgium and France into one where both sides now face an enemy hard to spot and even harder to hit. The British and the Germans are perfecting the skill of flying over each other's lines on reconnaissance flights.

Britain lost its first aircraft to enemy fire from the ground at the start of the war, but there was a new development earlier this week when a German aircraft was actually shot down by machine gun fire from another plane, and yesterday a pilot was forced to open fire on a German aircraft over Rheims with his revolver, for it was feared the enemy was about to drop one of his new hand-held bombs on the city.

The Royal Flying Corps is developing new weapons with mixed success. One is a steel dart known as the flechette. Thrown out of aircraft in their hundreds they are intended to cause mass casualties in the trenches below.

British troops fear devastating new German guns like the Black Maria, while the Germans believe the new fast firing of the British Lee-Enfield rifles is really from machine guns.

German casualty of the air war.

1914

NOVEMBER

Su	Mo	Tu	We	Th	Fr	Sa
1	2	3	4	5	6	7
8	9	10	11	12	13	14
15	16	17	18	19	20	21
22	23	24	25	26	27	28
29	30					

1. Europe: Russia, the UK and France break off diplomatic relations with Turkey (→3).

1. Germany: General Paul von Hindenburg becomes commander-in-chief on the Eastern Front (→15).

3. Turkey: Anglo-French ships bombard the Dardanelles (→4).

4. Turkey: Russia invades Armenia.

4. Constantinople: Turkey declares war on Russia, the UK, France and Serbia (→5).

5. Turkey: The UK annexes Cyprus (→5/1/15).

10. S. E. Asia: Australian cruiser Sydney sinks German cruiser Emden off Sumatra (→26).

15. E. Front: Russian troops reported to be advancing on Konigsberg in E. Prussia (→23).

16. W. Front: The Prince of Wales becomes aide-de-camp to Sir John French (→3/12).

19. Isle of Man: Austrian and German civilian internees riot at a detention camp.

20. Balkans: Bulgaria declares neutrality.

23. E. Front: Germans, advancing on 55-mile front, reported only 40 miles from Warsaw (→27).

26. UK: 700 die when HMS Bulwark blows up in the harbour at Sheerness, Kent (→8/12).

27. E. Front: Russians rout Germans on Polish front between Rivers Vistula and Warta (→6/12).

29. US: Ex-President Roosevelt criticises the US for its "tame and spiritless neutrality" in the war.

BIRTH

25. US baseball star Joe DiMaggio.

DEATHS

3. Austrian poet Georg Trakl (*3/2/1887).

14. British commander Field Marshal Earl Roberts of Khartoum (*30/9/1832).

European colonies sucked into conflict

African troops board a train for the journey to the front line.

Nov 13. The loyal South African forces of General Botha yesterday crushed the rebel commandos of General Christiaan de Wet at Mushroom Valley in the Orange Free State and so put an end to the opposition to the occupation of the German colony of South-West Africa.

It is now expected that the 40,000 men raised by General Botha and General Smuts will march against the Germans under the command of General von Heydebreck.

The situation in South Africa is typical of the way in which the European powers' colonies are being dragged into the continental war. In East Africa fighting is continuing to clear the German and native forces under Lieutenant Colonel Paul von Lettow Vorbeck out of German East Africa. An expeditionary force from the Indian army has been sent to reinforce the King's African Rifles in their fight against his forces in the open country of the foothills of Mount Kilimanjaro.

In the steaming malarial country of West Africa, commonly known as the "white man's grave", a combined British and French force has already defeated the Germans. On August 26, Lieutenant Colonel F.C. Bryant was able to signal triumphantly to the Colonial Office: "I have the honour to inform you that Togoland surrendered unconditionally to me today."

It was in this swift campaign that, on August 12, RSM Alhaji Grunshi became the first British or Empire soldier to fire at a German.

Women at war: Claridge's Hotel in London's Mayfair has opened its doors for sewing guilds to make clothes for servicemen and the poor.

War hits stalemate in muddy trenches

Nov 11. A continuous line of trenches, full of weary soldiers, now stretches from the North Sea to Switzerland, but with little movement since the Germans failed to reach Paris.

There is now a stalemate amid the mud and the barbed wire with reports from the front talking of little else but "alternate advances and retirements".

Nobody has yet developed a tactic to break the deadlock. In some areas men are playing football behind the lines. Elsewhere soldiers are said to be daring each other to go and attack enemy machine gun posts and return with their weapons to ease the monotony.

Soldiers entrenched on the front.

Income tax doubled to pay for the war

Nov 17. Income tax will be doubled next year. The new rates, set by David Lloyd George in his War Budget today, will be one shilling and sixpence in every pound on earned income and two shillings and sixpence on unearned. Beer and tea duties are also up.

The Chancellor announced a gigantic £350 million War Loan. He told MPs: "I am bound to assume the war will be long". It is now costing about £1,000,000 a day, and the Government accepts that it will have to borrow.

1914

DECEMBER

Su	Mo	Tu	We	Th	Fr	Sa
		1	2	3	4	5
6	7	8	9	10	11	12
13	14	15	16	17	18	19
20	21	22	23	24	25	26
27	28	29	30	31		

1. Ireland: Police seize newspapers accused of an anti-enlistment campaign (→ 1/5/15).

3. Belgium: The country is put under the control of the German Army (→ 4).

4. France: King George V meets King Albert of the Belgians during a visit to the British Expeditionary Force (→ 29).

6. E. Front: Germans capture the Polish city of Lodz (→ 15/1/15).

8. New York: Irving Berlin's musical "Watch Your Step" opens at the New Amsterdam Theatre.

9. Rome: Italy demands the South Tyrol from Austria as price of its neutrality (→ 13/1/15).

10. Stockholm: Nobel Prizes are awarded to Max von Laue (Germany, Physics), Theodore Richards (US, Chemistry), and Robert Barany (Hungary, Medicine); no Peace or Literature Prizes awarded.

16. Cairo: The UK declares Egypt a protectorate.

21. Berlin: Socialists issue manifesto explaining why they remain in the government; but they support Karl Liebknecht's refusal to vote more war funds (→ 23/6/15).

24. Europe: Germans have taken 578,000 Allied prisoners.

29. Belgium: Belgian newspapers halt printing in protest at German censorship; Cardinal Mercier calls for passive resistance (→ 19/10/16).

DEATH

8. German Vice-Admiral Count von Spee (*22/6/1861).

HITS OF 1914

Keep the home fires burning.

St Louis Blues.

QUOTE OF THE YEAR

"The lamps are going out all over Europe. We shall not see them lit again in our lifetime."
Sir Edward Grey
on the eve of Britain's declaration of war.

Bombardments bring war to UK civilians

Dec 16. Soon after dawn today, three German warships loomed out of the mist off the east coast and began shelling the British towns of Scarborough, Whitby, Hartlepool and West Hartlepool. Over 100 people, most of them civilians, were killed and 200 are known to have been injured.

Two British destroyers were hit, and four seamen killed, when they went to drive off the German force. Over 200 shells struck the four towns destroying homes and seriously damaging resort hotels and churches. West Hartlepool is in darkness tonight after a direct hit on the local gasworks.

The shellings add to the threat of possible Zeppelin bombardments, and, as one observer put it, will only "encourage recruitment".

Spotted: a deadly Zeppelin.

Truce in the trenches shocks generals

Dec 25. In one corner of the Western Front, where the British Tommy in his trench was only a few yards from the Boche in his, the war came to a halt, briefly, on this day of Christ's birth.

A Second Lieutenant of the Royal Field Artillery raised his head above the parapet and was astonished to see British and German soldiers standing in the open and making no attempt to shoot at each other.

The lieutenant met another officer and together they walked along the line as Germans waved and called out. Speaking in simple French, the Germans, holding out cigars, asked for English jam. The extraordinary incident has been much talked about, despite the authorities' stern disapproval.

Rudyard Kipling has written: "Who dies if England lives?" As the year closes, the magnitude of the sacrifices being demanded begins to emerge. British casualties are 100,000; at Ypres alone, the 7th Division of 12,300 men has been cut to 2,400.

Goodwill to men: rival troops put the war behind them – for now.

Germans badly hit in Falklands battle

Dec 11. The Royal Navy celebrated a magnificent victory off the Falklands today, in which four German cruisers – the Dresden, the Nurnberg, the Scharnhorst, and the Gneisenau – were sunk with no apparent British loss.

Details of the battle are still coming in as the Royal Navy continues to chase the remaining German light cruisers, but the King has already sent his congratulations. The battle, fought at night with just 12,000 yards between the fleets, practically eliminates German sea power except in the Baltic and North Sea.

The officially neutral American navy is said to be jubilant and Argentina, too, is rejoicing at the British success. Newspapers in Buenos Aires say it will make the Atlantic free again.

Arts: painterly blast for smug Britons

"Blast", the manifesto of the new Vorticist group of artists, was published by the painter and novelist, **Wyndham Lewis**, and made a stinging attack on the smugness of English culture. In their first group exhibition, painters like **William Roberts, David Bomberg** and the sculptor **Henri Gaudier-Brzeska**, attempt to combine elements of Cubism with the Futurists' love of modern machinery.

At Drury Lane, a brilliant season of Russian opera and ballet, new to London, was presented by **Sir Joseph Beecham**, introducing the great bass **Chaliapin** and the dancer **Karsavina**. Here **Thomas Beecham**, made his debut as conductor.

At the Old Vic the new manager, **Miss Lilian Baylis**, has founded the Old Vic Shakespeare Company and promises to perform the complete canon of our greatest playwright.

In the concert hall the year has seen first performances of two "mood pictures" by **Frederick Delius**, "On Hearing the First Cuckoo in Spring" and "Summer Night on the River". London has also heard **Ralph Vaughan Williams's** "London Symphony", and **Ravel's** "Daphnis and Chloe".

1915

JANUARY

Su	Mo	Tu	We	Th	Fr	Sa
					1	2
3	4	5	6	7	8	9
10	11	12	13	14	15	16
17	18	19	20	21	22	23
24	25	26	27	28	29	30
31						

1. UK: Military Cross introduced as decoration; first awards made.

1. Wimbledon: Announcement that the tennis championships will be suspended for the duration of the war.

1. North Sea: German submarine U-24 sinks HMS Formidable (→ 28).

1. London: British Army now stands at 720,000 men.

4. London: The Stock Exchange, closed since the start of the war, reopens for trading.

5. Central Asia: Turkish 9th Army Corps surrenders to Russians with loss of 50,000 Turks (→ 19/2).

7. Poland: Reported that Poles and Cossacks are slaughtering Jews or driving them from their homes.

9. Mexico: Pancho Villa signs treaty at Ciudad Juarez ending border conflict with US.

13. Central Italy: 29,000 die in a massive earthquake.

13. Vienna: Resignation of Austrian foreign minister Leopold Berchtold.

15. E. Front: New Russian army of 800,000 is advancing on West Prussia (→ 31).

25. US: Alexander Graham Bell sets new telephone call record of 4,750 miles between New York and San Francisco.

28. Atlantic: German warship sinks US ship William P. Frye (→ 30).

30. Irish Sea: Three UK merchant vessels are sunk by a German submarine (→ 4/2).

31. Paris: First performance of Maurice Ravel's Piano Trio at the Salle Gaveau.

31. Petrograd: Czar reveals he proposed arbitration at The Hague three days before Germany declared war.

31. E. Front: Tear gas is used for the first time, at Bolimov, against the Russians (→ 3/2).

BIRTH

30. British politician John Profumo.

Germans sunk in North Sea battle

The crew of the Blucher scrambles overboard as the pride of Germany's battle cruisers keels over.

Jan 24. British warships have scotched a German plan to bombard East Coast towns, and sunk the most powerful battle cruiser in the world, the Blucher. The Germans were spotted off Yarmouth this morning on the way to repeat last year's bombardment of Scarborough and Hartlepool.

Vice Admiral Sir David Beatty commanded the British squadron as the cruisers Lion, Tiger and Princess Royal kept up shell fire in a fast running fight across the North Sea. The Lion's 13.5 inch guns hammered into the Blucher until she fell out of line, rolled over and capsized on the Dogger Bank, the biggest ship destroyed so far.

Three other badly mauled German cruisers, the Derfflinger, the Seydlitz and the Moltke, ran back for the safety of their own minefields. One was hit so badly that many crew jumped into the sea as she fled.

British losses were light, the Lion suffering 11 wounded. The victory avenges the recent loss of the battleship Formidable.

Catholic outrage at Cardinal's arrest

Jan 4. Catholics throughout the world protested to the Germans today about the detention of Cardinal Mercier in his Malines Palace. The Germans moved in following the Cardinal's brave pastoral letter, "Patriotism and Endurance". In it he condemned the Germans for breaking their promise and violating Belgian neutrality. The Germans destroyed 15,000 copies of the letter and demanded that the Cardinal retract but he refused.

Windsor Castle is cut off by floods

Jan 7. The worst floods in the Upper Thames Valley since 1894 have driven over a thousand people into their upstairs rooms. Windsor Castle is now an island in a lake which has submerged the Eton playing fields. The milk and the post is being delivered by punt and even those wearing waders are getting their feet wet.

Zeppelins rain death from the sky

Jan 19. In a sinister new development of aerial warfare, a German Zeppelin crossed the Norfolk coast during the night to bomb unsuspecting British towns. Civilian deaths are numbered at more than 20 with 40 seriously injured.

Great Yarmouth and King's Lynn were the targets. Both towns were fully lit as the airship approached from the south, its engines "making a weird, peculiar burr", according to one local. Casualties include a small boy and his sister, killed when three cottages were completely destroyed at King's Lynn.

More bombs fell near Sandringham, which is the King's Norfolk home.

House in King's Lynn where a brother and sister met their deaths.

1915

FEBRUARY

Su	Mo	Tu	We	Th	Fr	Sa
	1	2	3	4	5	6
7	8	9	10	11	12	13
14	15	16	17	18	19	20
21	22	23	24	25	26	27
28						

3. E. Front: Russians cross Galician passes and pour into Hungary (→ 5).

3. Paris: Allied finance ministers gather for a conference (→ 12).

4. London: Announced that total UK casualties to date are 104,000 (→ 12).

4. Bosnia: Execution of conspirators to murder Archduke Franz Ferdinand and his wife, but not of Princip, who was under age when he shot the royal couple (→ 28/4/18).

5. E. Front: Russians kill 30,000 Germans in battle near Rivers Bzura and Rawka (→ 10).

10. E. Front: Germans surround Russians near River Nieman, taking 100,000 prisoners (→ 1/3).

10. Washington: Wilson warns Germany that attacks on US ships breach US neutrality; also protests to UK for allowing ships such as Lusitania to fly US flag to dupe Germans (→ 18).

12. W. Front: French begin offensive in Champagne (→ 10/3).

18. Berlin: The planned Berlin Olympic Games of 1916 are cancelled.

18. UK: The German sea blockade of Britain comes into force (→ 19).

19. UK: Norwegian ship "Belridge" is torpedoed off Folkestone; it is the first victim of German blockade (→ 1/3).

21. San Francisco: Opening of the "Universal Exposition" including exhibits from warring European states.

23. Bordeaux: Actress Sarah Bernhardt has her right leg amputated (→ 6/11).

24. France: 1,000 British suffragettes arrive to do war work (→ 1/3).

26. UK: Armaments workers on Clydeside go on strike for higher pay.

BIRTH

1. British footballer Sir Stanley Matthews.

All ships are fair game, say Germans

Feb 2. Germany's submarine blockade of the British Isles began today in a strategic gamble aimed at destroying the UK economy. The measure is an attempt to frighten neutral shipping away from Britain with the threat that any vessels moving in UK waters will be seen as fair game.

But in New York, where shipping companies are still smarting over the loss of two American vessels in the North Sea recently, one company spokesman described it as "a threat to the world".

The British Government has already ordered the Royal Navy to seize cargoes of grain and flour heading to Germany and treat them as contraband and the US has warned Germany against attacks on American vessels in the war zone.

British companies are taking a similar view and the cross-Channel ferries, including those to Holland, will continue to sail as usual. Whitehall experts believe the Germans still do not have sufficient submarines to be able fully to implement their threat even if they want to. The German Admiral von Pohl has claimed the move is to counter British merchant vessels flying the flags of neutral countries, a claim which has been fiercely denied in London. He threatened that every British merchant ship in the zone will be destroyed and that it will be impossible to avoid danger to the crews of neutral ships.

German U-Boat crewmen check the running of their deadly vessel.

UK moves to defend Suez against Turks

A Sikh machine-gun crew stationed on the Suez Canal awaiting the enemy.

Feb 2. Three columns of German-officered Turkish troops have been thrown back with heavy losses after a determined attempt to cross the Suez Canal from Sinai. The enemy completely failed in this attempt to cut the waterway, which is a vital link with India and the Empire in the East.

British patrols observed the Turkish force of 12 infantry companies moving westwards the night before the assault so defences were on the alert. Devastating British fire was put down, which practically annihilated the bridging parties as they tried to launch pontoons.

Imperial troops, mostly from the Indian Army, which engaged the invaders, reported that they fled in total disorder. The attacks were made 48 miles from Port Said south of Toussoum, where the Canal is at its narrowest, and near Neroche, the railway junction for lines linking the Suez with Cairo.

Battleships pound Turkish forts

Feb 19. The Royal Navy carried the war to the Turkish enemy today when a fleet of battleships and battle cruisers, supported by a French squadron, opened a day-long bombardment of the forts guarding the entrance to the Dardanelles.

Heavy shells from over a hundred guns pounded the earth forts, silencing the fire of all but one. The allied fleet under Vice-Admiral Sackville Carden suffered neither hit nor casualty.

A novel aspect of the battle was the presence of the aeroplane ship, Ark Royal, whose aircraft spotted for the big guns.

The forts were first bombarded from long range for over six hours. Admiral Carden then decided to send in the older ships to bring their smaller guns into action. They poured a murderous fire into the forts.

The bombardment has caused panic in Constantinople, which is expected to spread when action is resumed tomorrow.

1915

MARCH

Su	Mo	Tu	We	Th	Fr	Sa
	1	2	3	4	5	6
7	8	9	10	11	12	13
14	15	16	17	18	19	20
21	22	23	24	25	26	27
28	29	30	31			

1. E. Front: Reported that Russians have inflicted heavy defeat on Hindenburg's army at Prasnych (→ 4).

1. UK: Government creates a women's army battalion (→ 17).

4. Petrograd: Russian government claims rights to Dardanelles, backed up by France and the UK (→ 9).

9. London: Commons gives second reading to emergency bill passing control of all factories not already producing armaments to government for the duration (→ 30).

9. E. Front: Germans defeat Russians at Grodno (→ 20).

10. W. Front: British take Neuve Chapelle (→ 20).

11. UK: 200 perish when "HMS Bayano" is sunk off Scotland (→ 14).

14. Pacific: Royal Navy sinks battleship "Dresden" (→ 1/4).

16. UK: The Jockey Club decides not to suspend race meetings for the duration (→ 26).

16. US: 12,000 sign pledge of total abstinence from alcohol after Secretary of State condemns drink (→ 30).

20. E. Front: Russians capture Memel (→ 30/4).

20. W. Front: French offensive in Champagne fails (→ 26).

26. London: Lloyd George promises Sylvia Pankhurst that women will receive same pay as men for war work.

26. UK: Lady Nelson's Ally Sloper wins the Grand National (→ 24/4).

26. W. Front: British bomb Hoboken in Belgium, destroying two submarines (→ 5/4).

28. Switzerland: International Socialist Women's Conference in Berne calls for peace (→ 1/4).

30. London: King George V offers to abstain from alcohol as example to arms workers (→ 7/4).

BIRTHS

7. French statesman Jacques Chaban-Delmas.

20. Russian pianist Sviatoslav Richter.

Women urged to quit home for factory

March 18. The Government has issued an urgent appeal to the women of Britain to serve their country by signing on for war work. The aim is to get as many women as possible doing vital jobs so that men can be freed for fighting. Women are desperately needed in trade, industry, agriculture and above all in armaments, where thousands could be employed immediately making shells.

The Government is now setting up a Register of Women for War Service. Any women, trained or untrained, can sign on at her local Labour Exchange. The move has been warmly welcomed by leaders of the women's movement including Emmeline Pankhurst who said: "Women are only too anxious to be recruited".

During her recent visit to France she had seen many jobs previously done by men now being done by women, including bank telling and cab driving. Another official of the Women's Social and Political Union, Mrs Dacre Fox, said: "We believe women can be employed in almost any capacity of intellectual or physical work."

Mrs Fawcett, president of the National Union of Women's Suffrage Societies, said it would raise the standard for women in both work and wages. "This war has really had a good effect in bringing men and women together and making them rely upon mutual friendship and cooperation."

Mary Macarthur of the Central Committee on Women's Employment pointed out that 50,000 women were already employed in industry. In Birmingham women are making shrapnel shells, some as big as 12lbs, and the lighter parts of machine guns and rifles. They work from 8am to 5pm; the work is said not to be dangerous and the pay good (→ 26).

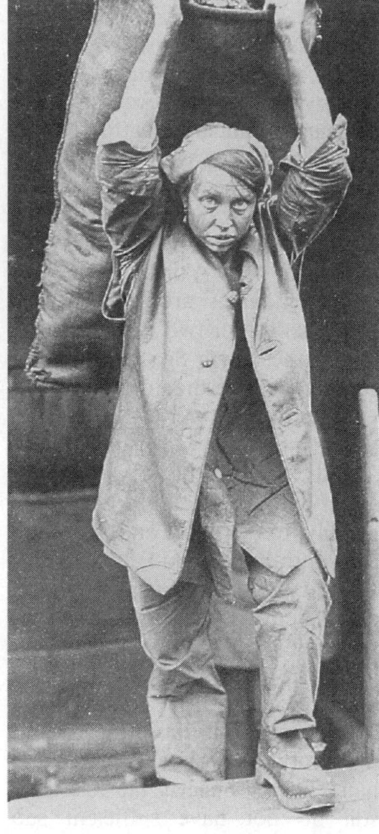

Home front: a coalwoman.

Navy's iron grip on German ports

March 1. The Royal Navy is striking back against submarine attacks on British shipping with a complete blockade of all German ports. Any ships now found carrying supplies to Germany will be taken into British or French ports and held there for the duration of the war.

A cheering House of Commons was told by Prime Minister Herbert Asquith today that Britain would take whatever steps were necessary to bring the the maximum economic pressure to bear on the enemy. He said Germany had adopted a policy of "torpedo at sight" any merchant vessel of any nation without regard to crew or passenger safety. Such attacks broke every law of the sea.

John Bull: ruling the waves.

Griffith's Ku Klux Klan movie epic faces ban for racism in US

Action: Griffith directing his new controversial motion picture.

March 31. The most impressive motion picture yet filmed, "The Birth of a Nation", opened in New York this month to heated contention. D. W. Griffith's epic shows the effect of the Civil War and its aftermath on a Southern family.

"Never before has such a combination of spectacle and tense drama been seen," says the New York Sun. Griffith, a Southerner, based his film on a play about the Ku Klux Klan, who ride to rescue Lillian Gish in white hoods holding fiery crosses. There have been furious protests against the picture's racialism and some cities are banning showings.

1915

APRIL

Su	Mo	Tu	We	Th	Fr	Sa
				1	2	3
4	5	6	7	8	9	10
11	12	13	14	15	16	17
18	19	20	21	22	23	24
25	26	27	28	29	30	

1. N. Sea: Germans sink three British trawlers (→ 27).

1. UK: Over 33,000 women have now signed up for war service (→ 17/7).

5. W. Front: French army begins broad offensive from Meuse to Moselle (→ 22).

6. Rome: Italy demands South Tyrol, Trieste and Istria from Austria as price of its neutrality (→ 15).

7. UK: Businessmen appeal for prohibition of alcohol.

8. Egypt: Attempted assassination of Sultan of Egypt.

15. London: Lloyd George is put in charge of munitions production (→ 20).

15. Vienna: Austria sets the age limit for recruits at 50 years (→ 18).

18. Italy: Neutrality talks with Austria break down (→ 26).

20. US: President Wilson urges strict neutrality in the war (→ 1/5).

20. London: Lloyd George urges the adoption of war economy (→ 29).

24. UK: Sheffield Wednesday beat Chelsea 3-0 in the FA Cup Final (→ 19/7).

27. Adriatic: Austrian submarine sinks French cruiser (→ 1/5).

29. London: Commons adopts Lloyd George's proposal for heavy increases in duties on alcohol (→ 3/5).

30. W. Front: Dunkirk in state of panic at bombardment from heavy German guns apparently 22 miles away (→ 3/5).

30. E. Front: Germans invade Russian Baltic provinces (→ 2/5).

BIRTH

7. US blues singer Billie Holliday (†17/7/59).

DEATHS

23. British poet Rupert Brooke, in Aegean campaign (*3/8/1887).

27. Russian composer Alexander Skryabin (*6/1/1871).

British launch spring offensive at Ypres

British soldiers go "over the top" under heavy German bombardment.

April 22. A desperate battle is being waged for a small hill on the right flank of the 30-mile front held by the British around the town of Ypres. The War Office communique speaks of "a successful action", but the situation on the ground appears rather more complicated.

The position known as Hill 60 is, in fact, the spoil from a nearby railway cutting. Last Saturday at 7pm five mines that had been run under the hill were detonated, the hill was stormed and the the German garrison overwhelmed.

Since then attack and counter attack have followed in quick succession, with neither side gaining a decisive hold on the vital hill. The fighting along the Ypres salient, with the heavy casualties and prodigious expenditure of material, is typical of what is happening elsewhere along the muddy Western Front.

After a much-trumpeted offensive along a 125-mile line, when Hindenburg was reported to have ordered a strategic retreat, the French losses are 69,000 men killed or taken prisoner and 164,000 wounded. They have captured a wood covering one quarter of a square mile.

Gas: the Germans' terrible new weapon

April 22. As dusk fell on the Western Front, both the Canadians and French Zouaves, holding the line north of Ypres, beheld an eerie spectacle. Drifting across from the German lines was a swirling greenish-yellow vapour.

Minutes later, the Zouaves were fleeing from their dugouts, coughing, half-blind and panic-stricken. Behind the cloud came Germans in gas-proof helmets. They tore a four-mile gap in the Allied front, but were checked by the Canadians, who had not been stricken.

There are, as yet, no gas masks for the Allies, and the British are preparing to go into battle holding wet cloths to their faces, hoping this will give some protection against the choking chlorine gas.

British victims of German gas.

King to put Royal drinking on ice

April 7. Buckingham Palace and other Royal Households will be "dry" from tomorrow. The King is leading a government campaign to cut down heavy drinking among armament workers which is slowing production.

"The continuance of such a state of things must inevitably result in the prolongation of the horrors and burdens of this terrible war," the King said in a letter.

He added that if it was: "deemed advisable, he would be prepared to set an example by giving up all alcoholic liquor himself.

Several cabinet ministers and judges are expected to follow the King's example. Meanwhile Lord Kitchener has already forsworn alcohol.

Willard weighs in as Big White Hope

Willard and Johnson battle it out.

April 5. Jess Willard, the 17-stone cowboy from Iowa, tonight reasserted white supremacy in the heavy weight boxing ring when, in a sun-drenched stadium in Havana, he defeated the black champion of seven years standing, Jack Johnson.

Johnson, who had fled vice charges in America, tired visibly half way through the 45-round contest, and fell to a knock-out blow in the 26th.

Allied troops storm ashore at Gallipoli

Gallipoli: the Allied camp at ANZAC Cove in the Dardanelles.

April 26. After a day of fierce fighting Allied forces have established themselves at six positions along the Gallipoli peninsula. The landings, which began before sunrise, were heavily opposed by well dug-in Turkish forces commanded by German officers.

British, ANZAC and French troops showed the utmost bravery in the face of machine-gun fire, as they stormed ashore under the protection of the battleship Albion.

The men unloaded from their transports on a calm sea and were carried into the beaches in cutters, towed by steam pinnaces.

At some beaches there was little opposition and as soon as the men got ashore they unloaded supplies and exercised the mules, cramped by their journey from the assembly point on the Greek island of Lemnos.

Reports from other beaches, however, tell of men, particularly of the Lancashire Fusiliers, who were mown down, caught on barbed wire, as they landed at "W" beach. There are similar reports from "V" beach where men of the Munsters, Hampshires and Dublin Fusiliers landed from the gangways of the steamer River Clyde. Many casualties were sustained on both sides.

Sad though these casualties are, much is expected of this enterprise, which Winston Churchill at the Admiralty hopes will knock the Turks out of the war. It is commanded by General Sir Hamilton and Vice Admiral de Robeck, who have their headquarters on the battleship Queen Elizabeth (→ 20/12).

Charles Chaplin stars this year in "The Tramp", in the role of a hapless, hilarious vagabond.

Secret treaty turns Italy against Kaiser

April 26. The worst fears of Germany and Austria about Italy, their Triple Alliance partner, have been realised. It is learned that Antonio Salandra, the Premier, has authorised the signing in London of a secret treaty with Britain, France and Russia; Italy will come in on the Allied side and her territorial claims against Austria will be satisfied. The Catholic Party wanted to stay neutral, Republicans were for the Allies and the Socialists split. A young radical, Benito Mussolini, started his own paper to campaign for the Allies.

1915

MAY

Su	Mo	Tu	We	Th	Fr	Sa
						1
2	3	4	5	6	7	8
9	10	11	12	13	14	15
16	17	18	19	20	21	22
23	24	25	26	27	28	29
30	31					

1. Ireland: Widespread resentment of new anti-alcohol measures reported.→

1. Atlantic: US steamer Gulflight is torpedoed off the Scilly Isles (→ 8).

2. E. Front: Austro-German troops launch offensive against Russia in Galicia (→ 4/6).

3. W. Front: French bombard the headquarters of the German Crown Prince (→ 9).

3. Rome: Italy leaves the Triple Alliance with Germany and Austria (→ 24).

3. London: Lloyd George's Budget statement says the war is costing the country £2.1 million a day (→ 7).

5. Far East: Japan issues an ultimatum to China (→ 8).

7. London: Lloyd George withdraws scheme to impose higher duties on alcohol.

8. Far East: Japan modifies its ultimatum, averting threat of war with China.

9. W. Front: Opening of second battle of Artois (→ 7/6).

10. London: Zeppelins carry out their first air raid on the capital (→ 29).

12. Washington: President Wilson demands explanation and compensation for Lusitania sinking.

13. London: King George strips his cousin the German Kaiser of the Order of the Garter.

22. UK: 122 die in UK's worst ever train crash, near Gretna Green in Scotland.

23. Rome: Italy declares war on Austria (→ 24).

27. UK: Around 270 are feared dead when HM Auxiliary Ship Irene explodes at Sheerness (→ 6/6).

29. London: Four people are killed in Zeppelin air raids (→ 6/6).

BIRTHS

6. US actor and director Orson Welles (†10/10/85).

20. Israeli soldier and politician Moshe Dayan (†16/10/81).

Party feuds laid aside to form a wartime coalition

May 25. A coalition government was formed today as "the best method for finishing the war successfully". This is the price Herbert Asquith has had to pay to avert a major political crisis over shortage of shells on the Western Front and failure in the Dardanelles.

He stays as Prime Minister, while 13 Liberals in the new Cabinet are joined by eight Tories and a Labour man. David Lloyd George takes a key new post of Minister of Munitions. Winston Churchill is demoted from the Admiralty to a junior place in the new team. There are rumours in the lobbies about differences betwen him and the admirals over operational matters.

Arms production slowed by drink

Drink ban for arms factories?

May 3. Allegations of heavy drinking by arms workers could lead to the government taking tough measures against alcohol abuse. David Lloyd George, the Chancellor of the Exchequer, has described Britain's three main enemies as "Germany, Austria and Drink" and a government advertisement asking for views on prohibition has brought 70,000 letters in favour. Lord Kitchener has complained of constantly slow deliveries of arms and supplies to troops on the Western Front (→ 7).

Americans fume over Lusitania sinking

The sinking of the Lusitania and the German medal celebrating the act.

Survivors of the outrage.

May 8. The huge Cunard liner Lusitania sank off the Irish coast yesterday after being torpedoed without warning by a German submarine. It is feared that 1,400 of the 1,978 men, women and children on board have drowned.

The famous ship was only eight miles off the Old Head of Kinsale on her return voyage from New York to Liverpool when she was hit by two torpedoes at 2.12pm. Within 21 minutes she had disappeared beneath the waves.

The casualties include 128 American citizens, among them many wealthy and prominent people such as Alfred Vanderbilt, the millionaire yachtsman. They are also said to include close friends of President Woodrow Wilson.

German-language newspapers in New York jubilantly recalled that the German ambassador, Count Bernstorff, took space in the newspapers there last Saturday to warn Americans not to sail on the Lusitania. But the American reaction to the sinking has been overwhelmingly pro-British.

In Washington the State Department said that it viewed the disaster "most seriously" and it is already being asked what effect the loss of American lives will have on public opinion and on President Wilson's neutrality policy. Former President Theodore Roosevelt has already condemned it as an "act of piracy".

Altogether there are thought to have been between 500 and 600 survivors, but some of those rescued were too exhausted to talk after hours in the water. Others told heart-rending stories of what they had seen. At least five of those drowned were women with babies in their arms.

One passenger, Ernest Cowper, a Toronto journalist, actually saw a torpedo heading for the ship. He was chatting to a friend just after two o'clock when he got a glimpse of a submarine's conning tower and then noticed the track of a torpedo. There was a loud explosion when the ship was hit forward and pieces of the hull flew into the air, Mr Cowper said. Shortly afterwards, she was hit again aft.

Another survivor was the library steward. He said passengers were at luncheon "chatting merrily" when "an awful explosion" shook them. Captain Turner and the other officers did their best to prevent panic, but at least one lifeboat fell into the sea.

The Lusitania, with her sister-ship the Mauretania, was one of the two finest liners afloat. She was capable of 25 knots, and it was thought that her speed made her safe against torpedo attack.

Police were called to the Cunard company's offices in Cockspur Street, which were besieged by well-dressed people seeking news. Confirmation of the loss caused a sharp fall in prices on Wall Street today (→ 13).

Londoners attack Germans in streets

May 13. A London mob pulled a German-born baker and his assistant from their Stepney shop today before setting it on fire. Police who tried to intervene were stoned and injured by the angry crowd.

This was just one of countless attacks on "suspect" aliens around the country as the Government prepared new laws of internment and deportation. Strong anti-German feeling has brought serious violence to the streets of British cities following the sinking of the Lusitania.

An elderly German-born chemist was covered with paint by another mob in the City of London while a group called "The Britishers Protection Committee" urged Londoners to take part in a demonstration on Tower Hill.

The crowd was to protest against "any kith or kin of German mutilators, poisoners and murderers of men, women and children being any longer allowed to be at large within the British Isles ... fearing riots, fires, the spread of disease, germs and poisoned water".

Many shops were forced to display a notice which declared: "This is not a German shop. God Save the King."

Venice bombed in Austrian air attack

May 25. The Austrians have responded immediately to Italy's declaration of war by bombing the city of Venice. The Austrian Taubers, flying at a great height, provided a spectacle for the Venetians as they circled overhead, easily visible in the light of early dawn. Then they dropped four bombs on the city and another seven in the bay and lagoon.

Guns of every description opened fire and, according to the Adriatico, "the sky of Venice was ablaze with war". The only casualties were four ladies injured by glass. The dangers of modern warfare seemed lost on the Venetians, who crowded on the bridges in a state of excitement.

Allied view of the enemy's aims.

German colony falls to Allies in Africa

May 13. At a cost of 1,769 casualties General Louis Botha, the South African Prime Minister who is leading his armies in the field, has captured German South West Africa, a territory of about 300,000 square miles, and taken 3,500 prisoners. General Botha's campaign against the Germans was delayed by the need to put down a rebellion at home mounted by hardline Boers, who consider the British to be the true enemy.

1915

JUNE

Su	Mo	Tu	We	Th	Fr	Sa
		1	2	3	4	5
6	7	8	9	10	11	12
13	14	15	16	17	18	19
20	21	22	23	24	25	26
27	28	29	30			

4. E. Front: Austro-German troops capture Przemysl in Poland as the Russian front begins to collapse.→

6. Balkans: 30,000 demonstrators call for Rumanian intervention in the war (→ 11).

6. UK: 24 die, 40 are injured in Zeppelin raids on the east coast (→ 12/12).

6. Berlin: The Kaiser says that in future passenger vessels will not be attacked by the German navy (→ 28).

8. Washington: William Bryan resigns as Secretary of State over war policy; Robert Lansing succeeds.

9. London: Bill creating Ministry of Munitions becomes law (→ 29).

11. Balkans: Serbian troops invade Albania and take Tirana.

15. UK: Mr S. Joel's Pommern wins the so-called "New Derby", run at Newmarket because the Army has requisitioned Epsom racecourse.

19. W. Front: Lieutenant Warneford VC is killed in a flying accident near Paris.

17. Turkey: German ambassador sends telegram to Berlin telling of Turkish systematic genocide of Armenians (→ 14/12).

18. W. Front: Artois offensive is halted (→ 20/7).

21. London: Government discloses terms of new war loan of £910 million.

23. Berlin: German industrialists outline new war aims: annexation of Poland, Ukraine and Baltic States (→ 26).

26. Berlin: The newspaper "Vorwarts" is censored for its publication of a Socialist peace manifesto.

28. UK: Liner Armenian is sunk by a German submarine off the Cornish coast (→ 2/7).

29. London: The Arundel Estate, between Shaftesbury Avenue and Coventry Street, is sold for a record £250,000.

29. London: Bill is introduced for creation of national register of all aged 15-65 (→ 5/7).

Russians lose Lemberg to Austrians

Advancing German reserves pour over the their front line parapet.

June 23. Fortunes change rapidly in the great campaign of the Eastern Front and the Austrians have retaken Lemberg, the capital of Galicia, which they lost to the Russians last year. According to a communique issued in Vienna, General Boehm-Ermolli entered the town yesterday afternoon with the troops of the Second Army.

The Russians' retreat was brought about by men of the Vienna Landwehr who, in some bloody fighting, captured the town of Rzezna and rendered Lemberg untenable. While the Russians are playing down the significance of this defeat, there can be no doubt that it will boost the morale of the Austro-Hungarians.

The loss of Lemberg follows swiftly on that of the ancient fortress town of Przemysl, which was captured by the Russians only ten weeks ago. It seems, however, that the Russians, faced by the breakthrough of the German army under General Falkenhayn, had made sure the fortress was untenable.

They completed the destruction begun by the Austrians, removing the great bronze cannon and methodically blowing up the forts and bridges and everything else that could be of service to the enemy.

Despite these reverses, the Russians are fighting well, the cavalry, in particular, routing whole companies of German troops with sudden sabre charges while the Russian infantrymen, armed with their long bayonets, are fighting with the obstinacy for which they are renowned.

VC for British flier who downed Zeppelin

June 8. A young British aviator has been awarded the Victoria Cross for bringing down a German Zeppelin with bombs.

In a single-handed operation, Flight Sub-Lieutenant Reginald Warneford succeeded in climbing his Morane aircraft to 6,000 feet above the airship which was preparing to land near Ghent in Belgium.

Six bombs fell on the German machine which burst into flames. The explosion turned Warneford's plane upside-down and the young naval pilot had to make a forced landing behind enemy lines before taking off again to safety.

Tragically, the burning Zeppelin crashed on to a Belgian convent, killing two children and two nurses in the wreckage (→ 19).

Warneford's deadly duel.

1915

JULY

Su	Mo	Tu	We	Th	Fr	Sa
				1	2	3
4	5	6	7	8	9	10
11	12	13	14	15	16	17
18	19	20	21	22	23	24
25	26	27	28	29	30	31

2. UK: Reported that 40,000 have so far enrolled for voluntary munitions work (→ 3).

2. UK: German submarines sink four British steamships off Cornwall and Ireland (→ 23).

3. E. Front: Germans continue advance into Poland (→ 7).

3. London: Government estimates war is now costing £3 million daily (→ 6).

6. Calais: British and French ministers hold the first Allied war conference (→ 25/8).

7. E. Front: Russians defeat Austro-German troops south of Lyublin, taking 11,000 prisoners (→ 20).

9. Africa: General Botha accepts surrender of all German forces in South West Africa (→ 11).

13. London: Royal Proclamation says all disputes must be reported to the Board of Trade before strike action is contemplated (→ 15).

15. UK: 200,000 South Wales miners strike for more pay (→ 20).

17. London: 40,000 women demonstrate for the right to help the war effort (→ 20/10).

19. London: The Football Association decides that no internationals or cup-ties will be played next season.

20. UK: Welsh coal dispute is provisionally settled (→ 25/8).

20. UK: Total UK casualties in the war: 330,995 (→ 21/8).

20. E. Front: Russians in retreat as Austro-Germans close on Warsaw (→ 6/8).

23. US: President Wilson tells Germany US stands for maritime freedom "without compromise, at any cost" (→ 25).

25. Atlantic: Germans sink two US merchant ships off Ireland (→ 16/8).

28. London: US novelist Henry James becomes a UK citizen.

DEATH

2. Mexican dictator Porfirio Diaz (*15/9/1830).

1915

AUGUST

Su	Mo	Tu	We	Th	Fr	Sa
1	2	3	4	5	6	7
8	9	10	11	12	13	14
15	16	17	18	19	20	21
22	23	24	25	26	27	28
29	30	31				

6. E. Front: The Austrian parliament demands the unification of Poland with Galicia as part of the Habsburg Empire (→9).

7. UK: First awards made of the new Naval General Service Medal.

9. E. Front: German and Austrian leaders propose separate peace with Russia, which Czar Nicholas rejects (→30).

14. UK: Nine die and 21 are hurt when Irish mail train from Euston is derailed.

16. Washington: Wilson and Lansing initiate an enquiry into German espionage activities in the US; involvement of senior officials suspected (→9/9).

19. Atlantic: German submarine sinks White Star liner "Arabic"; 26 Americans among 44 missing.

21. Rome: Italy declares war on Turkey (→2/9).

21. UK: Total UK casualties to date: 381,983.

23. W. Front: British squadron bombards German positions on Belgian coast (→25).

24. Paris: The newspaper "Le Figaro" launches a campaign denouncing press censorship.

25. UK: Welsh miners refuse to sign strike settlement (→31).

25. W. Front: French and British offensives in Artois and Champagne have reached stalemate (→4/9).

29. US: Gold shipment worth £55 million arrives to pay for war munitions (→9/9).

31. UK: Welsh miners agree to settlement of strike (→7/9).

31. E. Front: Germany and Austria partition Poland (→1/9).

BIRTH

29. Swedish actress Ingrid Bergman (†29/8/82).

DEATH

20. German doctor Paul Ehrlich, Nobel prizewinner and discoverer of diphtheria antitoxin (*14/3/1854).

Government denies call-up plans

July 5. Forced labour and military conscription "are not in the contemplation of the Government", Mr Asquith told Parliament today. The Prime Minister's statement failed to dispel suspicion that a compulsory call-up may be on the way, a feeling reinforced by the subsequent passing of a National Registration Bill.

A government spokesman said this was needed for census purposes and was without ulterior motive. However, the Whips were obviously nervous for many MPs, not seen in the House for months, turned up in uniform, having been given leave from their regiments at the government's request.

Brides in the Bath murderer to hang

July 1. Triple killer George Joseph Smith was convicted of murder and sentenced to death. The Old Bailey heard that Smith, a Bristol antique dealer, had bigamously married his three victims, using a series of aliases. Within months of each "wedding", he had insured his wife's life or persuaded her to make a will in his favour. Then he had taken each to a different lodging house and drowned her in the bath.

Woman dressed as Belgium on a patriotic march in London demanding the "right to serve".

Key Russian strongholds fall to Germans

Russian wounded in a temporary field hospital in an Orthodox church.

Aug 30. The great fortress of Brest-Litovsk has fallen to the Germans. This means that they have advanced 120 miles since the Russians abandoned Warsaw at the beginning of the month.

When Warsaw fell, it was said that the Russians retreated in good order "even taking the post boxes back to Petrograd", but since then their retreat has been swift and observers are beginning to talk of increasingly disloyal grumblings being heard in the Russian ranks.

Defeat followed defeat for the Russians throughout the month. First Warsaw, then the fortified positions at Ivangorod and then the important fortress of Kovno fell to the Germans.

The Kaiser sent a telegram to Field Marshal von Hindenburg claiming that "with Kovno, the first and strongest bulwark of the Russian defences has fallen into German hands".

Then Novo Georgievsk, the last Russian stronghold in Poland, was captured along with its garrison of six generals and 85,000 men and 700 guns.

Now Brest-Litovsk, famed as a hunting centre and reserve for the European bison, has fallen to von Mackensen's men. This is a grievous blow to the Russian army, which has been the anvil on which the German hammer blows have fallen. The Czar has, however, once again expressed his determination "to fight on until victory crowns our efforts".

Allies struggle to occupy Gallipoli

Aug 13. British and French forces launched another heavy attack yesterday against stubborn "Johnny Turk" and succeeded in occupying two strongly fortified lines of Turkish trenches.

The Turks refused to give up the struggle, however, and mounted a series of night attacks against the exhausted Allied troops in trenches filled with dead and wounded of both sides.

The men are worn out as much by the heat, and disease, and the flies feeding off corpses, as they are by the fighting.

1915

SEPTEMBER

Su	Mo	Tu	We	Th	Fr	Sa
			1	2	3	4
5	6	7	8	9	10	11
12	13	14	15	16	17	18
19	20	21	22	23	24	25
26	27	28	29	30		

1. Poland: Joseph Pilsudski launches movement for free Poland (→4).

2. Turkey: Royal Navy sinks four Turkish transport ships in Dardanelles (→14).

4. W. Front: War Office orders wearing of long boots rather than puttees.

4. E. Front: Germany takes Grodno (→5).

5. Petrograd: Czar Nicholas takes personal command of the Russian army (→19).

7. UK: The Trades Union Congress resolves to oppose conscription (→9).

9. UK: Lloyd George tells TUC: "We cannot win without you" (→18).

9. Washington: Wilson orders recall of the Austrian ambassador, implicated in plot to prevent manufacture of munitions for Allies (→15).

14. Balkans: Secret convention of Central Powers and Turkey guarantees Bulgaria Serbian and Greek parts of Macedonia if it enters the war against the Allies (→22).

18. London: Government reveals the war is costing £3.5 million daily.→

18. Berlin: Kaiser Wilhelm II gives new assurance that no neutral or passenger vessels will be attacked (→5/10).

19. E. Front: Germans take Vilna (→1/10).

19. Paris: First issue of satirical journal "Le Canard Enchaine" (→28/10).

22. Balkans: Bulgaria mobilises its army (→23).

23. Balkans: Greek King Constantine gives the order to mobilise (→24).

24. Balkans: Bulgaria moves against Serbia (→1/10).

27. London: 600 Austrians and Germans are taken for internment to Alexandra Palace (→4/1/17).

DEATH

26. British politician James Keir Hardie (*15/8/1856).

Allies smash through German lines

Sept 26. The great autumn offensive on the Western front has opened with two massive blows at the German lines – by the French in Champagne and the British in Flanders around Loos. Britain's New Army, recruited under Kitchener's scheme, has been proving itself in action.

Little more than 24 hours after the two attacks were launched, Marshal Joffre's communiques, expressing the "offensive a outrance" spirit, in which he firmly believes, were reporting successes: "After a new and very violent bombardment, our infantry rushed forward to assault the German lines ... The enemy has suffered very considerable losses from our fire and in the hand-to-hand fighting."

The British communiques also report advances, but are more cautious: "Hard fighting took place throughout the day with varying success ...". Some positions captured in the morning were "subsequently retaken by the enemy".

The combined French and British campaigns are intended to cut into the German salient, projecting into the heart of France. Once the breakthrough has been achieved, a general offensive will force the Germans into a retreat that could, in Joffre's view, "possibly end the war". But observers fear that the prolonged bombardment that preceded the attacks has removed the element of surprise and let the Germans bring up reinforcements.

French artist Georges Leroux's image of battle, called simply "Hell".

Rock-bottom price for Stonehenge

Sept 21. One of the world's most famous ancient monuments was knocked down at auction today for a mere £6,600. Stonehenge, along with 30 acres of surrounding downland, went under the hammer in Salisbury as Lot 15 of the Amesbury Abbey estate, formerly owned by Sir Edmund Antrobus. It was bought by a Mr C.H. Chubb.

Cost of war pushes taxes to record levels

Sept 21. Income tax is up by 40 per cent, there is a new War Profits Tax, customs duties are raised by 50 per cent on tea, tobacco and many other goods, and the halfpenny post is abolished. With these and other tough measures Reginald McKenna, Chancellor of the Exchequer in the new coalition government, today introduced the biggest-ever Budget in the nation's history. He told MPs: "These are unprecedented burdens but I know the taxpayer is determined to see the war through."

The standard rate of income tax was set at two shillings and elevenpence halfpenny in the pound for next year. People earning below £130 a year will be exempt. The tax bill for a man with £5,000 a year will be just over £1,000. Total revenue will be £387 million a year.

Russian troops are blessed by Czar Nicholas II, who this month took personal charge of the army.

1915

OCTOBER

Su	Mo	Tu	We	Th	Fr	Sa
					1	2
3	4	5	6	7	8	9
10	11	12	13	14	15	16
17	18	19	20	21	22	23
24	25	26	27	28	29	30
31						

1. Balkans: Reported that German and Austrian officers have been arriving to direct the Bulgarian army (→ 3).

3. Balkans: Russia tells Bulgaria to break with "enemies of Slavs" or face the consequences (→ 8).

5. London: Reported that recruiting authorities have cards with details of 150,000 men of military age in the capital (→ 1/11).

7. Washington: Thomas Edison is President of US Naval Consulting Board (→ 15).

8. Balkans: Russia opens hostilities against Bulgaria (→ 12).

12. Balkans: The UK breaks off relations with Bulgaria (→ 16).

15. Washington: President Wilson approves plans to expand the US Army (→ 4/11).

16. Balkans: Allies begin blockade of Bulgarian ports (→ 21).

20. London: Announced that women can apply for licences to be bus and tram conductors (→ 10/11).

28. Berlin: First performance of Richard Strauss's "Alpine Symphony".

28. France: King George V is severely bruised in a fall from his horse while inspecting troops.

29. London: 10,000 attend memorial service for Nurse Edith Cavell at St. Paul's Cathedral.

29. Paris: Socialist Aristide Briand becomes premier after resignation of Rene Viviani (→ 3/11).

31. Russia: 1.5 million Jews are reported starving (→ 10/2/17).

BIRTH

17. US playwright Arthur Miller.

DEATHS

12. British nurse Edith Cavell (*4/12/1865).→

23. British cricketer William Gilbert Grace (*18/7/1848).→

German war machine threatens Serbia

Oct 21. The situation in Serbia is grave. Belgrade has been occupied by the German-Austrian force under General von Mackensen, fresh from his victories in Poland; and the Bulgarians, eager to avenge their defeat in the Second Balkan War, are advancing from the east.

The railway line to Greece has been broken, effectively cutting off the Serbian army from the Allied force which recently landed at Salonika with the intention of reinforcing the Serbs.

Consequently it is feared that the gallant mountain men of Serbia, who routed the Austrians when they attempted their first invasion of Serbia last year, will be unable to resist the vastly superior forces massed against them.

The Serbian leader, King Peter, who joined his peasant subjects in the front line with a rifle and forty rounds when they repulsed the Austrians at Belgrade last year, stands little chance against the German war machine.

However, despite their efficiency and strength, it has been no walkover for the Germans. They had to fight for Belgrade street by street and are believed to have suffered 2,000 casualties.

Having been unable to come to Serbia's aid last year because the Western Front demanded every man and every shell, the Allied relief force, composed of British and French troops, was put together early this month in answer to King Peter's plea for help as the Germans and Bulgarians closed in.

The Allied force landed at Salonika in northern Greece, despite the opposition of King Constantine, the Kaiser's brother-in-law, who is known to be pro-German. The Allied cause is favoured, however, by the Prime Minister, Venizelos, who has resigned along with his cabinet. But there is no doubt where the Greek people's sympathies lie. Athens is currently full of crowds demonstrating in support of the Allies.

The troops are now entraining for the north from Salonika, but it is feared that with the Bulgarians sitting astride the railway line, and with much of the mountainous terrain impassable, they will have little effect on the outcome of the battle.

British soldiers in Salonika having a breather before heading for Bulgaria.

British nurse is shot on spy charge

Oct 12. Edith Cavell, a British nurse, was executed in Brussels today for treason by a German firing squad.

Miss Cavell had been running a school for nurses in Brussels since 1906. After war broke out she continued to treat the wounded of both sides, and her even-handed humanitarianism seemed to have won the respect of the occupying Germans.

It did not, however, save her life, despite an urgent campaign on her behalf by US diplomats in the Belgian capital. On August 5 she was arrested and charged with harbouring Belgians of military age, and with helping young English and French soldiers to escape to safety across the Dutch border.

An English clergyman, who visited her death-row cell two days ago, said she was admirably calm, well aware that she was guilty under German law, "but happy to die for her country" (→ 29).

Sister of mercy: Edith Cavell.

Death of cricket's first immortal

Oct 23. Dr William Gilbert Grace, cricket's greatest figurehead and the game's finest exponent to date, died today at his home in Kent at the age of 67. Arguably the most readily recognisable Englishman of the Victorian era, "W.G." dominated the first-class and Test game throughout its formative years, and his 126 first-class centuries, 54,896 runs and 2,876 wickets will provide targets for all aspiring players for years to come.

Law bans drinkers from buying rounds

Oct 13. Londoners who greet their friends with the traditional call of "What's Yours?" face a £100 fine or a six months' jail sentence, it was decreed today.

"Treating" is out in a new move to cut down excessive drinking. Ministers claim that ship-workers, many of them earning as much as £5 per week, are delaying essential ship refits, and that drinking is seriously affecting the level of arms production.

The Germans' best friend: Wolf the Alsatian messenger in action.

1915

NOVEMBER

Su	Mo	Tu	We	Th	Fr	Sa
	1	2	3	4	5	6
7	8	9	10	11	12	13
14	15	16	17	18	19	20
21	22	23	24	25	26	27
28	29	30				

1. London: The War Office announces that all men willing to serve in the forces will be issued with khaki armbands bearing the Crown.

1. London: Prime Minister Asquith says there are one million Britons on the Western Front (→ 9).

3. Paris: Premier Briand says France's only war goal is return of Alsace-Lorraine (→ 6).

4. Washington: President Wilson outlines US defence plans (→ 3/12).

6. Paris: Sarah Bernhardt returns to the stage.

6. Paris: Premier Briand meets with British War Secretary Lord Kitchener (→ 17).

8. Mediterranean: 208 die when Italian liner Ancona is torpedoed off Sardinia (→ 30/12).

9. London: British war casualties to date stand at 510,230 (→ 19).

17. Paris: Meeting of Franco-British ministerial council (→ 2/12).

18. London: New restrictions imposed on opening hours of London's clubs (→ 23/1/16).

19. London: Government says married men will not be called up until young unmarried men have been (→ 4/1/16).

19. Far East: Allies ask China to join the Entente.

21. Balkans: Austro-German troops reported to be in full control of Serbia (→ 29/12).

22. India: Mohandas Gandhi returns from South Africa.

25. US: Colonel William Simmons revives the Ku Klux Klan in Atlanta (→ 4/12).

29. London: Women first employed on permanent staff at Scotland Yard (→ 1/1/16).

BIRTH

9. US actress Hedy Lamarr, Austrian-born as Hedwig Kiesler.

DEATH

14. US black leader Booker T. Washington (*5/4/1856).

Czech nationalist calls for freedom

Nov 14. Tomas Masaryk, the most hard-headed and influential leader of the Czech nationalist movement, today issued a manifesto in Paris, calling for the establishment of a Czechslovak National Council and for the Czech legion to fight on the side of the Allies.

The war has intensified the Czechs' desire to be free of the Austro-Hungarian Empire, but Masaryk is only the latest in a line of freedom fighters stretching back to 1620. Born into a poor family, he first visited the US in 1878 where he married an American. Returning home he later became the first Professor of Philosophy at the new university of Prague. In 1914 he went into exile so he could better fight for his nation's independence.

Italians repulsed in fourth push to Alps

Nov 10. The Italian army has suffered heavy losses in their fourth attempt this year to gain a foothold on the Isonzo River.

The Austrians have consistently resisted the Italian bid to cross the Isonzo, and the wisdom of Italy's strategy in this tough terrain is questionable. Italians outnumber Austrians two to one, but have made no headway, despite Austrian losses which may be as high as the Italian toll of 250,000.

New war cabinet: Churchill dropped

Nov 11. Winston Churchill resigned from the government tonight and said he is going to France. He told the Prime Minister: "I am an officer and I place myself unreservedly at the disposal of the military authorities, observing that my regiment is in France. With much respect and unaltered friendship, I bid you goodbye."

The meteoric career of Mr Churchill, who has been an army colonel, was checked when he was sacked from the Admiralty six months ago. He feels that he has not had enough to do since then and his exclusion from the newly-formed war cabinet has been the last straw. It is now known that Mr Churchill quarrelled with Lord Fisher, who resigned as First Sea Lord this summer, and that he is bitter now about not having had clear guidance from the admirals before the naval attack on the Dardanelles.

However, there is considerable Tory hostility towards Mr Churchill and this must have been a factor in the Prime Minister's decision to exclude him from the top ministerial group, which needs harmony. Mr Churchill accepts that there are personality problems, but as for continuing criticism that he acted with reckless impetuosity while at the Admiralty in overriding the advice of the naval staff, he said: "I have a clear conscience".

Churchill with Lloyd George, the Minister of Munitions, in Whitehall.

The war cabinet will have six members – the Prime Minister, the First Lord of the Admiralty (Mr Balfour), the Secretary of State for War (Lord Kitchener), the Colonial Secretary (Mr Bonar Law), the Minister of Munitions (Mr Lloyd George) and the Chancellor of the Exchequer (Mr McKenna).

The military manpower shortage is high on this new group's agenda. It is understood that the Government has completed plans for compulsory call-up of medically fit single men and also those who got married recently.

The new women factory workers are twice as good as men

War means women in untraditional roles – reluctantly, men are impressed.

Nov 10. Women, who volunteered to help the war effort by taking over men's jobs, are proving immensely successful, according to the latest reports. One survey estimates that some factories are now two and a half times more productive. Foremen, who were reluctant originally, now praise the women's energy, punctuality and willingness.

The women's efforts are particularly vital in munitions production and many thousands of them, aged from 14 to middle-age, are now toiling 12 hours a day, seven days a week to meet the ever-increasing demand for arms and ammunition.

Some have come from domestic service; others have never worked at all before. The average wage is around 32 shillings a week for day shifts, £3 a week for nights. A further 100,000 women will soon be needed.

Raid on newspaper fuels row on "bad news" censorship

Nov 6. Ten Scotland Yard officers, led by Chief Inspector Fowler, raided the offices of "The Globe" newspaper in the Strand on Saturday afternoon and seized all copies of that day's issue, as well as Friday's.

Charles Palmer, the editor, says he was told the police acted on orders from General Sir Francis Lloyd, who was exercising his power under the Defence of the Realm Act. "I cannot say in what the Globe has offended," Mr Palmer said, "because no definite allegation has yet been made."

But political observers say the police swooped after the paper put out a billboard reading: "Lord Kitchener. The Globe Reasserts." For some time the paper has been insisting that the politicians find Lord Kitchener difficult to work with and would like to get rid of him as Secretary for War. But Kitchener is still a hero and reports that he may be sacked are thought to be bad for morale.

This is the first time the authorities have suppressed a well-established Conservative paper, though small radical papers have been closed down, including "The Labour Leader" – organ of the Independent Labour Party; "Forward" – the Glasgow socialist weekly, and "Tribunal", which campaigns against conscription.

Lord Kitchener: police acted to protect his name and army morale.

1915

DECEMBER

Su	Mo	Tu	We	Th	Fr	Sa
			1	2	3	4
5	6	7	8	9	10	11
12	13	14	15	16	17	18
19	20	21	22	23	24	25
26	27	28	29	30	31	

2. W. Front: General Joseph Joffre is appointed Commander-in-Chief of the French Army.

3. Washington: German attaches, including Franz von Papen, are dismissed (→ 7).

4. US: The state of Georgia recognises the Ku Klux Klan (→ 2/7/16).

7. Washington: Wilson asks for standing US Army of 142,000 with reserve of 400,000 (→ 5/1/16).

10. US: Ford makes its one millionth motor car (→ 3/1/16).

10. Stockholm: Nobel Prizes awarded to Sir William H. Bragg and his son Sir William L. Bragg (UK, Physics); Richard Willstatter (Germany, Chemistry), and Romain Rolland (France, Literature); no Peace or Medicine prizes awarded (→ 12/16).

12. Germany: Hugo Junkers builds the first all-metal aeroplane.

14. Central Asia: Reported that one million Armenians have been killed by Turks (→ 21/8/16).

17. UK: 14 die and 50 are hurt in a train crash near South Shields.

18. Washington: President Wilson marries.

30. Mediterranean: 400 die when a German submarine sinks the P & O liner "Persia" (→ 31/1/16).

BIRTHS

12. US singer and actor Frank Sinatra.

19. French singer Edith Piaf (†11/10/63).

HITS OF 1915

Pack Up Your Troubles In Your Old Kit Bag.

Back home in Tennessee.

QUOTE OF THE YEAR

"Patriotism is not enough. I must have no hatred or bitterness towards anyone".
Nurse Edith Cavell,
last words before her execution on 12/10/15.

Allies retreat from Gallipoli disaster

Gallipoli: troops from Down Under go over the top just three days before the campaign was called off.

Dec 20. In a laconic, single-sentence communique, this afternoon, the War Office in London revealed that the ill-fated Gallipoli expedition had been abandoned after ten months of bad luck, muddle, indecisiveness – and outstanding heroism by British, New Zealand and Australian troops.

The final act of evacuating some 90,000 men, with 4,500 animals, 1,700 vehicles and 200 guns was carried out with great skill and ingenuity, under the very noses of powerful Turkish forces. Not a single life was lost. Some 30,000 beds had been prepared for the wounded in Mediterranean hospitals, but these were not needed.

The evacuation was carried out at night-time. During the day, however, ships riding at anchor under Turkish observation could be seen disembarking troops and unloading guns and stores. The trick was that more men and materials were evacuated during the night than had been ostentatiously brought ashore during the day.

In the last stages, at Anzac Bay, when it seemed the Turks could not fail to hear what was going on, a destroyer trained its searchlight on the enemy's trenches. While the Turks concentrated their fire on the destroyer, the troops were lifted off the beaches.

As the last men were leaving, having set thousands of booby traps, a huge landmine in No-Man's-Land was exploded. The Turks, thinking the Australians were attacking, began a furious barrage of fire that lasted 40 minutes.

It was a better end than might have been expected to a sorry story that began when the Russians appealed to Britain and France for munitions. Ministers and military men in London agreed to let the Royal Navy try to get to Russia's Black Sea ports by forcing the passage of the Dardanelles; they also decided a back-up force of land troops would be needed.

At the last minute, however, Kitchener said he could not spare the men from the Western Front. Three weeks later he changed his mind and said he could send a division to join Royal Marines and troops from Egypt.

There were more changes of mind and conflicting views as to the value of the operation. Its proponents saw it as a chance to get round the deadlock on the Western Front by knocking out Germany's ally, Turkey, a development that would have a powerful impact on opinion in the Balkans.

But by the time the combined land and sea operation was mounted at the end of April, a full two months after the Navy had first bombarded the Dardanelles forts, all advantages of surprise had been lost and the Turks had heavily reinforced their positions.

When Bulgaria came into the war a clear route was opened for Germany to keep Turkey supplied. Britain decided to pull out and use the men, as today's announcement says, in "another sphere of operations" – in fact, to join the Anglo-French force at the Greek port of Salonika.

The House of Commons has been told the Dardanelles casualties were 25,000 dead, 76,000 wounded, 13,000 missing and 96,000 sick admitted to hospital.

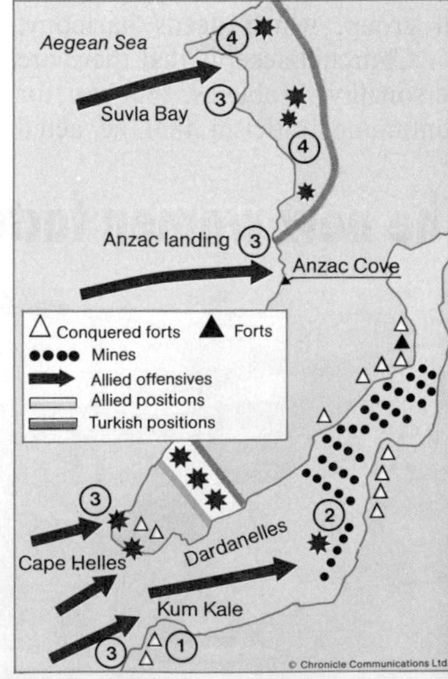

1. Feb 1915: The Royal Navy, eluding mines and machine gun fire, silences Turkish guns on the shores.
2. March 18: An Allied naval assault is halted as six ships are sunk in an undetected minefield.
3. April 25: Anzacs – soldiers from Australia and New Zealand – join British forces in principal landing.
4. August 6: Renewed assault with landings near Suvla Bay after three months of intensive fighting.

Allied command in top brass shake up

Joseph Joffre of France.

Sir Douglas Haig of Britain.

Dec 15. After just 16 months as commander of the British forces on the Western Front, Sir John French has been replaced by Sir Douglas Haig, First Army commander in Flanders. This announcement comes just two weeks after the appointment of General Joseph Joffre as commander-in-chief of the French army.

Though today's War Office announcement, issued shortly before midnight, speaks of gratitude for French's "conspicuous services," it has been known for some time that Haig has been critical of his superior and has voiced these criticisms to Kitchener at the War Office and to the King.

After the unsuccessful Battle of Loos last September, Haig accused French of falsely claiming to have provided reinforcements for Haig's forces at a critical moment.

The Western Front – running from Ostend across Flanders and then assuming a deep salient above Paris before swinging East to the fortress town of Verdun – has scarcely changed this year. On the Eastern Front, the Germans have pushed back the Russians deep into Poland, seizing Przemysl, Warsaw and Pinsk.

Arts: Tragic ends for literary heroes

The death of the poet **Rupert Brooke** on active service is mourned by all who saw him as the typical romantic hero of his generation. With a commission in the Royal Naval Division, Brooke was en route to the Dardanelles when he died of blood poisoning from a mosquito bite. He is buried on the island of Skyros. His collection, "1914 and Other Poems", was published after his tragic death at 28.

Another young poet, **Julian Grenfell**, died of wounds in France on the day that his stirring poem, "Into Battle", was printed in the Times, with the prophetic lines:

"If this be the last song you shall sing,
Sing well, for you may not sing another."

Otherwise, the literary year has been dominated by two best-sellers. **Joseph Conrad's** "Victory" is an adventure story set in South-East Asia. The life of his hero, Axel Heyst, is saved by the self-sacrifice of a girl who loves him but to whom he cannot respond emotionally. In despair he commits suicide. The novel has been praised for its tragic elemental force.

Somerset Maugham, best known till now for his plays, has brought out a long autobiographical novel, "Of Human Bondage". Like the author, its hero, Philip Carey, attends "Tercanbury" (Canterbury) school, Heidelberg University, and becomes a doctor. Handicapped by a club foot (whereas Mr Maugham suffers from a stammer) he becomes infatuated with a waitress, who comes to a bad end. "Mildred is a great creation, a sort of vampire of the teashop," wrote one critic, adding that her ugly world is depicted with unsparing realism.

The news of **Sarah Bernhardt** is that she was back on the Paris stage within months of the amputation of her right leg. She injured it jumping from the battlements as "La Tosca" and for years has been unable to stand unsupported.

Lieutenant Rupert Brooke: the poet who died a soldier's death.

Einstein challenges Newton over gravity

A new theory of gravity, which says it is a result of the curvature of space due to the presence of matter, was the major scientific event of 1915. It is proposed by Professor **Albert Einstein**, and is an extension of his 1905 Theory of Relativity, which dealt only with movement at steady speeds, making predictions about acceleration, and thereby gravity, too.

It is only on the macro and micro levels that Einstein's new theory differs from Newtonian ideas, but it has profound things to say about the universe as a whole. Einstein has suggested three ways to test it.

This year's Nobel Prize for Physics went to the father-son team of **W.H.** and **W.L. Bragg** for work on X-rays and crystals.

Professor Albert Einstein.

Forever England: One man's legacy

THE SOLDIER

If I should die think only this of me
That there's some corner of a foreign field
That is forever England. There shall be
In that rich earth a richer dust concealed;
A dust whom England bore, shaped, made aware,
Gave, once, her flowers to love, her ways to roam,
A body of England's, breathing English air.
Washed by the rivers, blest by suns of home.
And think, this heart, all evil shed away,
A pulse in the eternal mind, no less
Gives somewhere back the thoughts by England given;
Her sights and sounds; dreams happy as her day;
And laughter, learnt of friends; and gentleness,
In hearts at peace under an English heaven.

by
RUPERT BROOKE.

1916

JANUARY

Su	Mo	Tu	We	Th	Fr	Sa
						1
2	3	4	5	6	7	8
9	10	11	12	13	14	15
16	17	18	19	20	21	22
23	24	25	26	27	28	29
30	31					

1. UK: Two million more women are employed now than a year ago (→13/2).

3. New York: US industrialist Henry Ford returns from abortive peace mission to Europe.

4. London: Home Secretary Sir John Simon resigns over proposal to conscript single men.→

5. Washington: War debate starts in the Senate (→31).

9. Middle East: British defeat 60,000 Turks in Tigris battle (→17).

10. London: Herbert Samuel becomes Home Secretary, in succession to Sir John Simon (→12).

12. London: Commons gives second reading to Military Service Bill (→13).

13. UK: Miners unions vote overwhelmingly against conscription (→27).

14. Balkans: Montenegro capitulates to Austrian troops (→20).

14. Holland: Breach of Zuyder Zee dam at Katwoude in worst storms for 90 years causes widespread devastation.

17. Central Asia: Russia begins offensive against the Turks (→24).

20. Balkans: Montenegro rejects Austria's peace terms and resolves to continue fighting.

23. London: Announced that British Museum and Natural History Museum will close for the duration of war (→15).

24. Caucasia: Russians inflict heavy losses on Turks at Erzerum (→4/2).

27. UK: Labour Party conference votes heavily against conscription.

27. London: Royal assent given to the Military Service Bill, the Trading with the Enemy Bill, the Munitions Bill and the Parliament Bill (extending life of Parliament by one year) (→21/2).

31. US: President Wilson says the US Navy is ready for war if it comes (→6/2).

Commons go-ahead for Conscription Bill

New recruits from Bermondsey, south London, line up for inspection.

Jan 6. The House of Commons voted overwhelmingly tonight for military conscription. After two days of impassioned debate the die is now cast. Parliament's judgment is that voluntary effort is not enough to win the war and there must be compulsion on those deemed to be shirking their duty.

The decision follows publication of an analysis of the response to an intensive nationwide recruiting campaign. It suggested that upwards of half-a-million single men fit for service have not volunteered while about the same number of married ones are ready to join up, but have not yet been accepted. Government policy is to recruit single men first. The conscription decision is forcing the resignation of some ministers.

No more need of appeals like this.

Cameroon capital falls to the Allies

Jan 28. With the British in possession of the main port of Douala and the Navy blockading the coast, the Germans in the Cameroons, West Africa, have been hard pressed for the past year. Now French and Belgian forces, in a sweeping pincer movement, have captured the capital, Yaounde. The Germans, fighting a rearguard action, have retreated into the interior.

Togoland, the other German colony in West Africa, was occupied when war began by a British force from the Gold Coast (→18/2).

Mexican rebels kill Americans on train

Jan 16. Soldiers in the army of rebel General Pancho Villa have murdered 18 Americans. Most of the dead men worked for an American-owned mine. They were taken off a train 50 miles west of Chihuahua, stripped naked, lined up against the train and shot.

One passenger, Thomas Holmes, managed to escape by hiding in a lavatory. Troops under General Carranza have already captured and condemned to death the men responsible and one of Villa's generals has been shot (→9/3).

1916

FEBRUARY

Su	Mo	Tu	We	Th	Fr	Sa
		1	2	3	4	5
6	7	8	9	10	11	12
13	14	15	16	17	18	19
20	21	22	23	24	25	26
27	28	29				

2. Washington: The Senate votes to grant independence to the Philippines in 1921.

4. Turkey: The Crown Prince Yussuf Izzedin is assassinated (→2/3).

6. Washington: Germany accepts full liability for loss of US lives on the Lusitania and right of US to claim indemnity (→11).

8. Berlin: Food shortages cause riots (→20/3).

9. Africa: General Jan Smuts is appointed to command UK and South African troops in East Africa.

11. Berlin: Kaiser Wilhelm II orders intensification of submarine war (→15/3).

13. US: Figures show population is 101.2 million.

13. London: Government announces it will recruit 400,000 women to till fields (→22).

15. London: Royal Proclamation bans paper and tobacco imports (→17).

17. London: Government appeals against use of motor cars and motor cycles for pleasure.→

18. Africa: Allied occupation of German colony of the Cameroons is reported to be complete (→7/3).

21. London: Asquith asks Parliament to approve further war loan of £420 million (→22).

22. London: Government announces creation of Ministry of Blockade.

22. London: Government says women doing men's jobs will be paid the same if they are equally efficient (→10/3).

23. London: Prime Minister Asquith rebukes MPs who start a "Peace Debate" (→2/3).

25. W. Front: Gen. Joffre appoints Gen. Petain head of French 2nd Army (→8/3).

DEATHS

6. South American poet Ruben Dario (*11/18/1861).

28. US born author Henry James (*15/4/1843).

Major German assault on Verdun forts

French troops under German bombardment on the Verdun battlefield.

Feb 21. After a week of gales and rainstorms the sky cleared and, precisely at 7.15 this morning, a hurricane of shells began to rain down on Verdun, the key to French defences in the central sector of the Western Front.

Hour after hour the German bombardment continued, systematically demolishing the French positions line by line. The French, though uncertain whether the enemy is seeking a breakthrough or opening a battle of attrition, have kept the bulk of their troops out of the front lines in order to minimise their losses. The Germans, advancing behind their artillery, are being met with machine gun fire from widely scattered positions.

The French are at a disadvantage. In spite of intelligence reports suggesting that an attack on Verdun was imminent, Joffre stuck to his view that the Germans would strike in Champagne. Verdun's defences, which had been run down, were not restored.

Da da da . . . Dum dum dum . . .

Feb. Extraordinary goings-on are reported from the Cabaret Voltaire in Zurich, where artists in exile gather nightly to perform a new "art form" called simply Dada. A Rumanian poet, Tristan Tzara, claims to have named it by inserting a paperknife in a dictionary at random just as he composes poems at random by drawing words out of a hat. Several poems are declaimed simultaneously, and "noise concerts" for siren, rattle, and fire extinguisher are given. Dadaists, including Jean Arp, Max Ernst and Francis Picabia, claim to be using "anti-art" to reform art.

Upstairs told to cut back downstairs

Feb 23. Well-off families were asked today to give their servants their marching orders, for the sake of the war effort. The National Organising Committee for War Savings urged wealthy people to shut up part of their homes, close down labour-intensive and fuel-hungry garden greenhouses and have simpler meals so as to release servants, male and female, for "more useful purposes".

Last week the committee rapped the "selfish, thoughtless extravagance" of families who kept chauffeurs, and used cars and motor cycles for pleasure.

1916

MARCH

Su	Mo	Tu	We	Th	Fr	Sa
			1	2	3	4
5	6	7	8	9	10	11
12	13	14	15	16	17	18
19	20	21	22	23	24	25
26	27	28	29	30	31	

2. London: Military Service Act comes into force.

2. Turkey: Russians capture Bitlis in Kurdestan (→9).

5. UK: Zeppelin raids on eight counties kill 12 (→1/4).

6. London: Government says that from March 13 aliens may only enter "prohibited areas" with an identity book (→10).

7. Africa: Portuguese seize four German ships near South Africa (→9).

8. W. Front: French troops check Germans west of Verdun and retake Corbeaux.

9. Berlin: Germany declares war on Portugal.

9. US: Pancho Villa leads a raid into New Mexico, killing 17 Americans (→10).

10. UK: National Organising Committee for War Savings calls for less extravagance in women's dress (→18).

10. Mexico: US posse of 5,000 men are sent across the border to capture Pancho Villa (→15).

15. Mexico: 4,000 US soldiers under Brigadier-General John Pershing join hunt for Villa (→31).

15. Berlin: Admiral Alfred von Tirpitz resigns as Navy Minister; Admiral von Capelle succeeds (→18/4).

18. Liverpool: Women dockers withdraw when men refuse to work with them (→8/4).

20. Germany: Rationing begins as food shortages become acute (→1/5).

21. UK: Import of spirits, motors and pianos is banned for the duration of the war (→4/4).

21. Balkans: Austrian troops kill 9,000 Serbian civilians.

24. UK: Mr P. Heybourn's Vermouth wins the Grand National, run at Gatwick in Sussex.

27. Paris: Allied Powers conference opens (→20/5).

BIRTH

11. British statesman Harold Wilson, Labour Prime Minister (†24/5/95).

Allies agree on Ottoman carve-up

March 9. Britain and France have begun planning the division of the postwar remnants of Turkey's Near East empire into spheres of influence. Sir Mark Sykes and Georges Picot are the officials charged with the task of redrawing the map.

Britain will assume control over Palestine and Mesopotamia while the French will run Syria. Some areas will be allowed to pass directly into the hands of the Arab people, though this is unlikely to satisfy their ambitions, or to allay suspicion about the motives of the Europeans.

The main concern of the Foreign Office is to contain the threat from Egypt, while the French are concerned with Syria. Georges Leygues, a prominent French diplomat, remarked: "We shall only achieve control of the Mediterranean if Syria comes under our influence".

Russia, too, is closely involved in deciding the future of the Eastern Mediterranean. Sykes and Picot are apparently in agreement that Constantinople and the Straits are very important to Russia, a near neighbour of Turkey. The Petrograd government insists that Russian interests are taken into account in this post-war settlement.

Britain and France will insist on Constantinople being recognized as a free port and that the Straits, one of the world's great waterways, must remain open to merchant shipping of all nations.

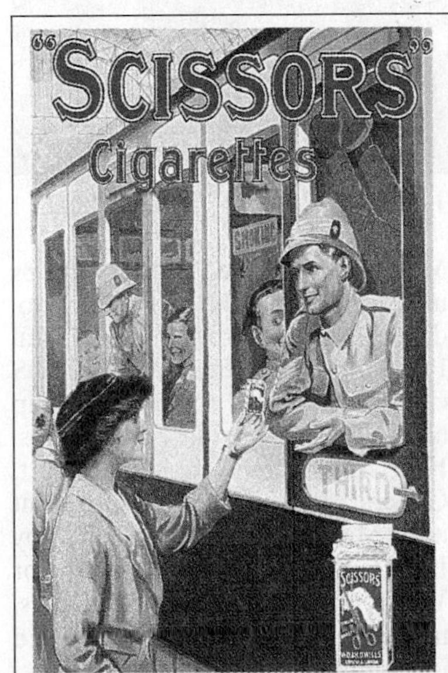

Police arrest strike leaders

March 28. Six of the ringleaders of the munitions strike on the Clyde have been arrested. Although the strike involves at most about 3,000 workers, the situation has become critical because the strikers have concentrated on a few key workshops. The production of certain kinds of heavy guns, urgently needed on the Western Front in France, has been brought to a halt by these tactics.

The strike is led by the Clyde Workers' Committee, which wants an end to conscription and any wartime restrictions on strikes and wages. The main trade union leadership has had nothing to do with the strike, but the committee has support amongst some of the most highly skilled men of the Amalgamated Society of Engineers. They are in vital jobs and have been able to disrupt output where it hurts the war effort most.

US cavalry routs Mexican rebels

Victorious Pershing (r.) with Villa.

March 31. United States troops under General John J. Pershing today routed the troops of General Pancho Villa. Four hundred US cavalry attacked the rebel camp and killed 30 of Villa's 500 troops. Four Americans were slightly hurt. General Pershing had been sent into Mexico with 6,000 men by President Wilson in retaliation for Villa's raid into the United States, in which 18 Americans were killed in Columbus, New Mexico.

1916

APRIL

Su	Mo	Tu	We	Th	Fr	Sa
						1
2	3	4	5	6	7	8
9	10	11	12	13	14	15
16	17	18	19	20	21	22
23	24	25	26	27	28	29
30						

4. London: Budget raises income tax and imposes wide range of taxes, especially on amusements (→ 12).

4. Rome: Prime Minister Asquith meets Pope Benedict XV.

5. London: The Military Medal is introduced as a decoration.

8. Norway: Women win the right to vote in national elections (→ 4/7).

10. Paris: The International Olympic Committee says the Games will not be held until the war is over.

12. London: Government drops its planned tax on rail tickets (→ 14).

14. France: The government imposes taxes on milk, sugar, coffee and other foodstuffs (→ 20/5).

14. London: Government pledges cash for diagnosis and treatment of venereal diseases (→ 13/7).

14. Turkey: Allies bomb Constantinople (→ 20).

18. Washington: President Wilson threatens to break off diplomatic relations with Germany if it continues total submarine warfare (→ 4/5).

19. London: Asquith says government could disintegrate unless differences on conscription are resolved (→ 25).

20. Petrograd: Russia refuses an armistice with Turkey (→ 20/5).

23. UK: Widespread commemoration of the tercentenary of Shakespeare's death.

24. Switzerland: Socialist pacifists attend the International Socialist Conference at Kienthal (→ 1/5).

25. British Empire: The first Anzac Day marks Gallipoli landings one year ago.

25. London: Secret session of Parliament decides to broaden the terms of conscription (→ 4/5).

BIRTH

22. US-born British violinist Sir Yehudi Menuhin.

British troops surrender to Turks at Kut

Rather than eat horsemeat Indian troops faced starvation during the siege.

April 29. After a siege which lasted 143 days, Major General Charles Townshend, commanding the 6th (Poona) Division, today surrendered to the Turkish general, Khalil Pasha, at Kut-el-Amara in Mesopotamia.

An announcement from the War Office in London blamed shortage of supplies and said resistance was conducted with "gallantry and fortitude". The German HQ in Turkey claimed that the surrender was unconditional and that 13,000 had been captured.

The news caused dismay. For a British force 9,000 strong to lay down its arms is without precedent in the war. The Indian Expeditionary Force, of which the division was a part, consisted of Indian and British army units. Last summer it advanced along the river Tigris towards Baghdad, 200 miles away.

Although the army was victorious at Ctesiphon, heavy losses forced a withdrawl. Townshend's division retreated to Kut, a small place in a loop of the river, and dug in there last December surrounded by the Turks. Townshend remained convinced that a relief force would come to the rescue and no serious attempt was made to break out.

General Gorringe's column was in fact only 20 miles away, but proved incapable of fighting a way through the Turkish cordon.

British and Indian troops suffered greatly from intense winter cold and lack of supplies. Moslem and Hindu soldiers of the Indian detachments starved rather than eat horsemeat. Royal Navy river steamers failed to break the blockade and one boat, the Junlar, fell into enemy hands.

For the first time an air drop was tried. British aeroplanes made desperate attempts to supply the besieged division but the 16,800 pounds of food that was delivered was not enough. Surrender talks began two days ago and finally, the white flag was hoisted.

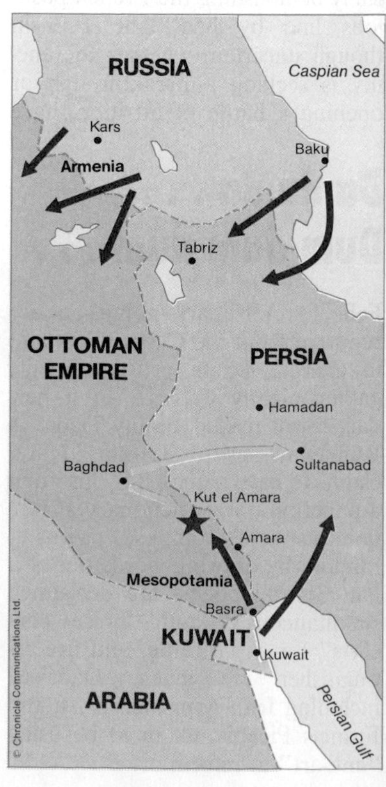

Irish rebels stage Dublin uprising

British troops hold a barricade in a Dublin street as rebels take control of key points in the city.

April 24. Eleven men were killed and 17 injured today when Dublin was plunged into full-scale rebellion against British rule. Rebels, proclaiming an "Irish Republic", have seized control of the post office in Sackville Street and are now under attack from British forces.

Bullets are peppering the stone building, but soldiers from the Royal Irish Rifles and the Dublin Fusiliers have been unable to break through its stout oak doors. Two flags now fly from the roof of the building: the traditional Irish one of green, with a harp of gold, plus one – which most people here have never seen before – coloured green, white and orange.

In what appears to be a concerted uprising, sentries were shot at Dublin Castle, headquarters of British rule in Ireland, and the courts building has been set at least partially on fire. "Four or five different parts of Dublin are in the hands of the rebels," admitted Augustine Birrell, Chief Secretary for Ireland.

He told MPs that mail boats between England and Ireland had been suspended and only one telephone line was still in operation. Troops are being moved to Dublin and a Royal Navy gunboat had entered the River Liffey to shell Liberty Hall, headquarters of the Irish Transport and General Workers Union. But Mr Birrell faced demands from Ulster Unionists for still tougher action. Rebels should be shot forthwith said one MP, while Irish Nationalist MPs sat in silence. Delays in granting home rule had led to their worst fears being realised. Padraic Pearse, a teacher who describes himself as Commandant-General, read a proclamation from the portico of the post office which declared that the Irish people wished to run their own country.

He continued: "The Republic guarantees religious and civil liberty, equal rights and equal opportunities to all its citizens, and declares its resolve to pursue the happiness of the whole nation" (→ 11/5).

The corner of Sackville Street and Eden Quay, showing the scars of the Royal Navy bombardment.

Britain's old enemy leads drive against Germans in Africa

April 17. The British have called on a once troublesome adversary, who became a staunch friend, to help them drive the Germans from their East African colony. The Boer leader General Jan Smuts, fresh from the victory he and General Louis Botha won in the South West Africa campaign, arrived in Kenya last February and has already turned the tide.

Smuts has avoided the fever-rampant coastal plain and driven south across Kilimanjaro's western foothills in order to advance along the railway to the coast.

At the start of the war the Royal Navy blockaded the colony, but on land the Germans, led by Colonel Paul von Lettow-Vorbeck, with a force of 3,000 Europeans and 11,000 Askari, heavily outnumbered the British East African Rifles and for a time threatened the Nairobi-Mombasa line in Kenya. Smuts, using South African, British, and Indian troops, now has Lettow-Vorbeck on the run.

Pilot in mid-air duel with Zeppelin

April 1. The Zeppelin that broke up while under tow by a patrol ship in the Thames Estuary last night is thought by the Admiralty to be the one hit by bombs dropped by a young New Zealand pilot who gained his wings only three weeks ago.

The first airships were spotted at about 9pm flying at 10,000 feet. More followed a few minutes later. Lieutenant Brandon, who sacrificed the security of his homeland to join the Royal Flying Corps, was flying around 6,000 feet when he saw an enemy airship high above him. He took his plane up to 9,000 feet and when he was above the Zeppelin, launched his attack.

Three of the first bombs he dropped hit their target but did not bring it down. Oblivious to the risk the pilot then swooped in for the kill. He took his plane to within machine-gun range and dropped more bombs on the Zeppelin, which then crashed.

1916

MAY

Su	Mo	Tu	We	Th	Fr	Sa
	1	2	3	4	5	6
7	8	9	10	11	12	13
14	15	16	17	18	19	20
21	22	23	24	25	26	27
28	29	30	31			

1. Germany: Socialist Karl Liebknecht is arrested following pacifist demonstrations (→ 2/8).

4. Berlin: The German government averts diplomatic breach with US by agreeing to scale down submarine war; but insists US oppose UK naval blockade (→ 31).

8. London: Commons gives backing to Daylight Saving plan to put clocks forward one hour in summer (→ 21).

8. W. Front: Germans begin fierce attacks along Meuse banks (→ 3/7).

9. UK: Government says Ireland will be excluded from conscription (→ 10).

10. UK: Lord Wimborne resigns as Lord-Lieutenant of Ireland (→ 11).

11. Ireland: Easter Rising casualties: 794 civilians, 521 police and troops killed and wounded (→ 12).

14. Ireland: Martial law eased in Dublin (→ 6/6).

15. Ireland: Former diplomat Sir Roger Casement goes on trial for high treason for taking part in Easter Rising (→ 29/6).

15. Italian Front: Austria launches an offensive against Italians in South Tyrol.

20. Turkey: Reported that British Empire troops have forced the Turks back from the River Tigris (→ 21/6).

20. London: The UK agrees to supply France with coal because most French mines are in war zone.

21. UK: British Summer Time starts.

23. London: Asquith asks for new war loan of £300 million, making total war credit of £2,382 million.

24. London: Air Board created.

30. UK: Sir Edward Hulton's Fifinella wins the wartime Derby, the "New Derby" at Newmarket

DEATH

11. German composer Max Reger (*19/3/1873).

Dreadnought fleets clash at Jutland

A Royal Navy warship opens fire during the North Sea battle.

May 31. The two most powerful navies in the world were limping home tonight from Jutland after what sailors are already calling "the greatest naval battle in history".

Just who won is not clear, with the Royal Navy claiming it has routed the German Fleet and driven it off the seas, while in Berlin they are talking about "the destruction of British naval power".

Certainly, the Germans ended up running back for the shelter of their coastal waters and the port of Wilhelmshafen but the Royal Navy appears to have lost more men and ships. Altogether Britain has lost one battleship, one battle cruiser and five destroyers along with 6,907 men. The Germans for their part lost a battleship, a cruiser and a destroyer and suffered 2,545 dead.

The two fleets opened fire yesterday after Vice Admiral Sir David Beatty had lured the Germans with a section of the fleet to a spot where the rest of the force, under the supreme command of Admiral Sir John Jellicoe, lay in wait.

The dreadnoughts hurled one-ton shells at each other through the drifting mist. Said one commentator: "All the theories of a century's peace were being put to the test amid the roar of battle and the flashes of the most powerful guns ever fired in anger at sea."

That sea tonight is reported to be awash with bodies; one steamer spotted 500 alone, but there are many tales of heroism. The leg of the commander of the destroyer "Shark" was shattered by a shell but when his last gunner died he dragged himself to the weapon and carried on firing.

On the battle cruiser "Queen Mary" a gunner told how his mates hung down from a ladder so he could grab their legs and be pulled to safety. "They were both worth a VC twice over," he said.

Now the Admiralty will be watching to see whether the Germans venture out into the North Sea again in force.

US President calls for peace league

May 27. President Wilson tonight called for a "league of nations" to keep peace in the world when the War is over. The United States, he said, would be willing to join an international organisation of that kind.

It would guarantee the freedom of the seas, protect small countries from aggression, and step in to stop wars which broke out in violation of treaties. The rule of force must be ended, Wilson said in Washington; the world had a right to live in peace.

Tighter call-up net snares married men

May 4. A tougher conscription plan is tonight on its way into law. MPs approved the call-up of all men between the ages of 18 and 41. This follows a statement by the Prime Minister that registration procedures and recruitment appeals have failed to produce enough volunteers for the Army.

The Government said that married men must be conscripted if there are fewer than 50,000 volunteers every month from now on. Such men will get help with rent, mortgages, hire purchase, rates, taxes and school fees. People rejected in the past as unfit for active service are to be re-examined.

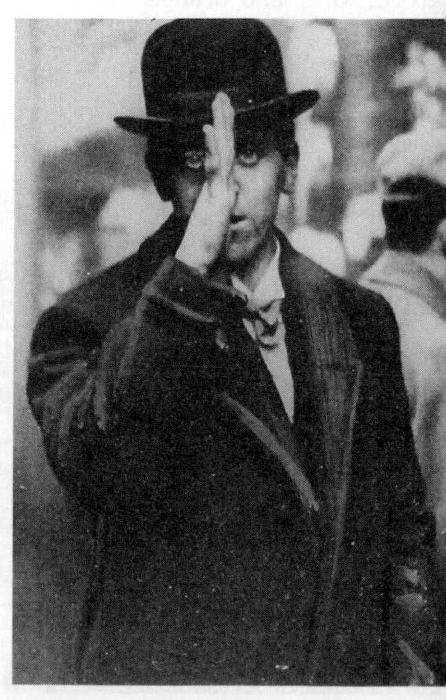

One man's view of conscription.

Rebels executed after Easter Rising

May 12. All seven rebels who signed the proclamation of an Irish Republic on Easter Monday are now dead. A brief announcement from the Irish command headquarters of General Sir John Maxwell today said that James Connolly had been executed. Injured in the fighting, he was the last to go.

Connolly was taken on a stretcher from Dublin Castle to an ambulance, which took him to Kilmainham Jail. There, he was placed in a chair, blindfolded, and executed by firing squad like the others.

A request for the body of Padraic Pearse, the rebel leader, for burial in consecrated ground has been refused. General Maxwell said that "given the sentimentality of the Irish" it would result in a martyr's grave.

Rebel leader James Connolly.

Summer days will be even longer

May 21. A brilliantly sunny day yesterday marked the start of what is popularly known as "summer time". Clocks throughout Britain were put forward by an hour at two o'clock to launch "daylight saving time", as it is known officially. Hundreds of thousands of tons of coal would be saved by the change, the Government told MPs earlier this month. Apart from objections by farmers, the prospect of lighter evenings has been welcomed. Clocks go back again in October.

1916

JUNE

Su	Mo	Tu	We	Th	Fr	Sa
				1	2	3
4	5	6	7	8	9	10
11	12	13	14	15	16	17
18	19	20	21	22	23	24
25	26	27	28	29	30	

1. Washington: National Defense Act comes into force, increasing National Guard to 450,000.

4. E. Front: Russian offensive against Austro-German forces begins under General Alexis Brusilov.→

6. Ireland: Ulster Unionist Council considers exclusion of Ulster from Home Rule (→23).

10. Chicago: Republicans nominate Charles Evans Hughes as Presidential candidate (→15).

13. London: Six-week opera season opens at Covent Garden under Sir Thomas Beecham.

15. St. Louis: Democrats renominate President Wilson as Presidential candidate (→11/11).

19. London: Tribich Lincoln, former MP for Darlington, is committed for trial for spying.

23. Ireland: Ulster Unionists vote in favour of partition (→12/7).

24. W. Front: Germans begin new Verdun offensive (→3/7).

26. Italian Front: Italians reported to have broken through Austrian lines in Trentino (→9/8).

27. London: King George says the Military Medal may be awarded to women.

28. London: Reported that the UK and France have abandoned London Declaration of 1914 not to make separate peace with Germany.

29. Dublin: Sir Roger Casement is found guilty of high treason and sentenced to death (→3/8).

BIRTH

9. US politician Robert MacNamara.

DEATHS

5. British army commander Field Marshal Earl Horatio Herbert Kitchener, Secretary of State for War from 1914 (*24/6/1850).→

6. Chinese politician and president Yuan Shi-kai (*16/9/1859).

Tide turns for Russia on Eastern Front

June 23. The Russian General, Alexei Brusilov, has scored a great victory. His offensive against the Austrians has resulted in the capture of most of Galicia, he has taken some 200,000 prisoners and the Austrians are fleeing towards the safety of the Carpathians.

It was the Russian cavalry that finally put the Austrians to flight at Sokal on the River Styr. The horsemen, their equipment muffled, crossed the river at night and fell on the Austrians' rear, causing the main force to panic.

They fled and are now being harried by the Cossacks and the Lancers while the infantry consolidate the captured territory.

The importance of Brusilov's splendid success is that not only will it hearten the Russian army and people who have suffered so much this year, but it will bring relief to the hard-pressed Allies on the Western Front.

The French, especially, will feel grateful for the sacrifices of their Russian allies if the Brusilov offensive relieves the pressure on them at Verdun.

Already it is reported that more than a hundred trains filled with German troops have been despatched from the western front to counter the Russian thrust.

Victory, but all is not well at home.

Arabs rise in revolt against the Turks

June 21. In the name of all Arabs, Hussein, Grand Sherif of Mecca and a descendant of the Prophet Mohammed, has proclaimed a revolt against the Ottoman Empire. Supported by the tribes of Arabia this powerful leader declared war on Turkey with the aim of realising Arab independence.

Already the Sherif's field forces in Arabia have scored notable victories. Mecca is firmly in his hands and so is Jeddah, the Red Sea port and gateway for Moslem pilgrims. There the Arab forces took 1,400 Turkish soldiers and 45 officers prisoner. Its capture means sea and trade links can now be reopened.

These victories have been achieved with British help, both military and financial, and when Hussein declared Arab independence he made it clear that this was what he had been promised. A military mission which is led by a brilliant 28-year-old Arabist, Captain T.E. Lawrence, is in Arabia advising Feisal, third son of the Sherif (→16/10).

Lord Kitchener is lost at sea

June 7. A pall of grief and dismay descended on the British people today after the Admiralty announced that Lord Kitchener was dead. He was 66 and travelling to Russia aboard the cruiser "Hampshire" when it struck a mine off the Orkneys; there were no survivors.

In 1914 Kitchener was almost alone in seeing the need to prepare for a long war. But he found politicians difficult to work with and his influence as Secretary for War had been waning. To the people he remained a true hero (→ 6/7).

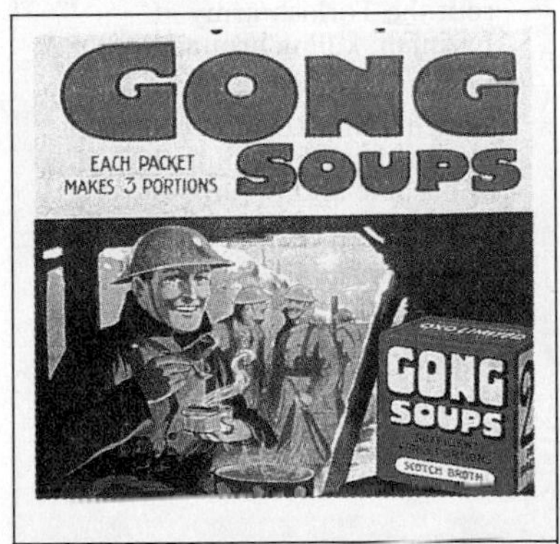

1916

JULY

Su	Mo	Tu	We	Th	Fr	Sa
						1
2	3	4	5	6	7	8
9	10	11	12	13	14	15
16	17	18	19	20	21	22
23	24	25	26	27	28	29
30	31					

1. US: Alcohol is prohibited in Michigan, Montana, Nebraska and South Dakota; 24 states are now dry (→ 21).

1. US: Coca-Cola Co. has introduced a new contoured bottle to make imitation difficult.

2. US: 39 die and hundreds are injured in race riots at East St. Louis, Illinois (→ 2/7/17).

4. London: Queen Mary opens the South London Hospital for Women in Clapham (→ 11).

6. London: Lloyd George becomes War Secretary in succession to Kitchener (→ 28/9).

6. Petrograd: Russia and Japan sign a peace treaty.

11. London: Queen Mary opens the Chelsea Hospital for Women (→ 8/9).

12. Ireland: The government prohibits carrying of arms without a permit (→ 23).

13. London: The Local Government Board issues rules for scheme to combat venereal diseases (→ 3/10).

15. US: The Pacific Aero Products Co. is founded by timberman's son William Edward Boeing.

17. E. Front: Russians drive Austro-Germans under Gen. Alexander von Linsingen across River Lipa (→ 14/8).

21. US: Prohibition Party holds its convention at St. Paul, Minnesota.

23. Dublin: Independent Irish Nationalists hold large meeting in Phoenix Park to protest at government's Irish partition proposals (→ 10/10).

27. Turkey: Russian troops rout the Turkish army at Erzinjan, killing around 34,000 (→ 5/8).

28. London: Royal Proclamation is issued banning import of cocaine and opium.

31. New York: 100 ammunition freight cars explode, killing 26.

DEATH

6. French painter Odilon Redon (*22/4/1840).

Carnage as Somme campaign opens

July 1. They came up to the front during the night, heavily laden with their packs, but marching at a smart, swinging pace, singing some music hall tune, accompanied here and there by a mouth-organ. They marched towards the points of flame stabbing the blackness, where the British shells were falling.

Officers in staff cars slid past, the motor cycles of despatch riders scooted across the market squares of small French towns and now and then a French sentry would raise an arm in a salute. One of them called out into the night: "Bonne chance, mes camarades".

The long-prepared British and French offensive on the Western Front, coordinated with Russian and Italian assaults, was about to begin, astride the River Somme in Picardy.

It was the biggest British army yet sent into battle, 26 divisions, every man a volunteer, on a 15-mile front. The French had promised 40 divisions, but in the event were able to produce only 18, their strength drained by the savage five month German attack on Verdun.

At 7.30am the artillery barrage was lifted and the British went over the top. Each man carried entrenching tools, two gas helmets, wire-cutters, 220 rounds of ammunition, two sandbags, two Mills bombs, groundsheet, haversack, water bottle and field dressing – almost 70 pounds of equipment each.

Burdened with this, the men moved into No Man's Land at little more than a slow walk, though the orders were to "push forward at a steady pace in successive lines". The aim was to seize, according to Field Marshal Haig's calculation, some 4,000 yards of enemy territory in the first day.

In the first five minutes of the battle thousands were cut down by relentless enemy fire. By nightfall, many battalions numbered barely a hundred men. The German defences were formidable and deep, so that the capture of first and second lines brought little advantage and no respite from the sweeping machine-gun fire. Nor had the bombardments of previous days destroyed more than part of the heavy barbed wire obstacles.

On every side there were dead and wounded. From midday, when the attack was suspended, until 4 pm, when the British artillery fire resumed, the Germans allowed stretcher-bearers to work in No Man's Land. The next morning saw another informal truce, but it was three days before all the wounded were collected.

A padre at the 21st clearing station behind the line described how the dying and the wounded were being brought in all day long, "but all cheerful, for they told us of a day of glorious success".

The success was limited to a few miles and 2,000 prisoners. The British had 60,000 casualties; the rate among officers was 60 per cent and 40 per cent among other ranks.

The French fared better, overrunning German positions, taking 4,000 prisoners and reporting light casualties.

Troops make their way through the muddy swamp that was once a forest.

All in it together: British soldiers support wounded German prisoners.

1916

AUGUST

Su	Mo	Tu	We	Th	Fr	Sa
		1	2	3	4	5
6	7	8	9	10	11	12
13	14	15	16	17	18	19
20	21	22	23	24	25	26
27	28	29	30	31		

2. Germany: Peace meetings are held in 35 cities (→ 25).

3. W. Front: French capture Fleury (→ 15/9).

4. Washington: The US pays $25 million for the Danish Virgin Islands.

5. Mediterranean: British beat Turks in a naval battle off Port Said.

5. France: American chewing-gum goes on sale.

7. Persia: The UK and Russia form an alliance with the Shah.

9. Italian Front: Italian troops take Gorizia (→ 15/9).

14. E. Front: Russians break new German line in E. Galicia (→ 22/9).

21. Turkey: British priest Rev. Harold Buxton reports Turkish massacre of 500,000 Armenians, deportation of one million (→ 22).

22. Washington: The US appeals to Turkey to end Armenian massacres (→ 24).

24. Turkey: Reports of another 12,000 Armenians massacred by Turks.

24. Germany: Socialist leader Karl Liebknecht is sentenced to four years' imprisonment for his part in peace protests in May.

24. Greece: Ex-premier Eleutherios Venizelos calls for Greeks to overthrow King Constantine and join the Allies in the war (→ 27/9).

27. London: Several thousand trade unionists protest in Hyde Park against high food prices (→ 29/9).

27. Balkans: Rumania declares war on Austria-Hungary; Germany declares war on Rumania (→ 1/9).

31. UK: British casualties for August alone are 127,000, one-fifth of total war deaths.

DEATHS

5. British composer George Butterworth (*12/7/1885).

16. Italian painter and sculptor Umberto Boccioni (*19/10/1882).

Hindenburg is new German supremo

The Kaiser with new army chief von Hindenburg and General Ludendorff.

Aug 27. The Kaiser has sacked General Erich von Falkenhayn as Chief of the General Staff and replaced him with Field Marshal Paul von Hindenburg, victor of the Battle of Tannenberg.

No reason has been given for this move but it is generally believed that the two men clashed over the disposition of forces, following Rumania's entry into the war on the side of the Allies.

Hindenburg wanted to rush men to face this new threat in the East but Falkenhayn refused, arguing that the war would be settled on the Western Front. The Kaiser stepped into the quarrel, retired Falkenhayn and gave Hindenburg command of the army.

This is a remarkable culmination of a career which stretches back to the Austro-Prussian war of 1866. He fought the French in 1870 and was appointed to the General Staff in 1878.

He helped build the modern German army, but when he retired in 1911 he thought his military career was over. However, when the Germans faced defeat in East Prussia in 1914, he was hurriedly recalled. Pausing only to be measured for a uniform in the new field grey, he went to war in the blue uniform of Prussia.

These marines at Salonika are from French Indochina, among the many thousands of colonial troops playing a vital role in the war.

New Ford set to roll horse into history

Aug 31. In a major marketing initiative, Ford has announced a cut price $250 touring car. And, to hold prices, it plans to do away with normal retail sales outlets by appointing garage owners as its selling agents. The move seems guaranteed to further increase Ford's already dominant share of the US car market.

Ford's only real rival now is General Motors, founded by William C. Durant in 1908 – the same year that Henry Ford brought out his amazingly successful Model T. Smaller companies, like Dodge Brothers, provide no real competition for Ford at the popular end of the market. Ford now plans to double its car production, which was over 508,000 in the last year. Its profits, at nearly $60 million, make it one of the most successful US companies.

The Ford-led "automobile revolution" has produced vast social change in the United States in the past eight years, above all in rural areas where the construction of hard-surfaced highways, garages and filling stations is doing almost as much to stimulate the economy as the war boom.

Some now even see the cheap car as reversing the recent flood of people off the farms and into the big northern cities. Said one car dealer: "An automobile beats a horse and buggy any day. It's quicker and it's cheaper."

Roger Casement is hanged in London

Aug 3. Sir Roger Casement, the former British diplomat who tried to smuggle a boatload of German arms into Ireland on the eve of the Easter Rising, was executed by hanging at Pentonville Prison in London today. He was convicted of high treason, under a 600-year-old law, for aiding the King's enemies in time of war. Casement had been a British Consul in Africa and South America until his retirement in 1913. At the outbreak of the war, he was in Germany and became active in raising support for Sinn Fein.

1916

SEPTEMBER

Su	Mo	Tu	We	Th	Fr	Sa
					1	2
3	4	5	6	7	8	9
10	11	12	13	14	15	16
17	18	19	20	21	22	23
24	25	26	27	28	29	30

1. Balkans: Rumanian troops beat the Austrians at Orsova.

1. Balkans: Bulgaria declares war on Rumania (→18).→

2. Washington: Senate passes bill introducing eight-hour working day.

3. UK: 13-Zeppelin raid causes two deaths and 13 injuries; one airship is shot down near London.

4. E. Africa: British forces occupy Dar-es-Salaam; 75 per cent of German East Africa is now under Allied control.

8. US: Wilson pledges to give women the vote at a suffrage convention (→2/10).

15. Italian Front: Italians begin a major new offensive at Trieste (→25/8/17).

16. Prague: Prime Minister Asquith and President Poincare of France recognise provisional government of "Czechoslovakia" (→6/12).

22. Balkans: Rumania and Russia defeat the Germans under Marshal August von Mackensen at Dobrudja (→5/1/17).

24. UK: Naturalist John Burroughs says moving pictures deprive people of their brain power.

25. Brussels: Anti-German demonstrations take place in front of the Royal Palace (→19/10).

27. Greece: King Constantine declares war on Bulgaria (→11/10).

28. London: Lloyd George gives UK war aims as "Germany's complete downfall".

29. London: Government proposes one meatless day among plans to cut food price rises (→10/10).

29. UK: Medical scientists announce the discovery of procedure by which internal organs can be photographed. The X-ray.

29. Berlin: Germany attacks the US, saying it is breaching its neutrality by allowing Americans to join Allied air forces (→5/10).

"Tanks" may change the face of warfare

Sept 15. The taste of victory, said a war correspondent at British HQ today, was like a strong drug to the men's hearts, so that "they laughed even while blood was streaming down their faces".

These were the infantrymen who went into battle on the Somme with a new weapon, conceived and built in strictest secrecy under the code name "Tank". This morning, tanks rolled over the German lines, scattering machine-gunners, crashing through strong points and on one occasion demolishing a sugar refinery the enemy had turned into a redoubt. Within two hours the British and Canadians had taken more than 2,000 prisoners and gained all their objectives.

A captured German officer was brought back in a tank as a terrified passenger. But only 32 of these deadly devices were deployed and some broke down. The tank's supporters had wanted to wait until large numbers had been built, but Haig, fighting a costly battle, refused. Had he waited, he might well have overwhelmed the enemy instead of gaining only seven miles on a 30-mile front.

These motor monsters, as the men call then, have transformed the whole character of the war and prisoners are saying: "Now Germany is kaput."

The Allies' latest weapon in action.

Village PC arrests Zeppelin crew in Essex

Sept 24. An Essex special constable was wakened last night by the humming of a German Zeppelin. While he was dressing, the droning stoped, and there was a loud explosion about a mile away. He set out to see what had happened, but before he arrived at the scene of the explosion, he met the crew of the Zeppelin coming towards him. Despite the fact that he was heavily outnumbered, the constable promptly arrested the Germans. It was not long before other officers reached the scene and a military escort had been summoned. The constable is quite unperturbed by the incident, for this afternoon he was back on duty directing traffic in his home town.

The wreck of the Zeppelin that crashed in the Essex countryside.

Rockefeller now worth $1 billion

Sept 29. The boom in share prices on the American stock market yesterday have created the world's first "billionaire". He is John D. Rockefeller, the founder of Standard Oil and benefactor to many educational and medical charities.

As long ago as 1907 he was known to own 247,692 shares of Standard Oil, more than three times as much as anyone else. Yesterday each of these shares was worth $2000. Even if he has not increased his stake in Standard Oil, Mr Rockefeller owns vast interests in various banks and railway companies as well as enormous blocks of national, state and municipal bonds. Rising share prices have almost certainly made him worth at least a billion dollars – or £250 million at $4 per £1.

Allies launch new Balkans offensive

Sept 18. The new offensive, launched by the allies from Salonika, is progressing well. The Serbs, rested after their epic march through Albania, are once more fighting on their native soil.

French troops carried the town of Florina by assault yesterday and the enemy is falling back in disorder. It appears that the Bulgarians, despite their many spies, were taken completely by surprise by the attack on Florina. The way is now open to Monastir.

Low necklines, high hemlines.

1916

OCTOBER

Su	Mo	Tu	We	Th	Fr	Sa
1	2	3	4	5	6	7
8	9	10	11	12	13	14
15	16	17	18	19	20	21
22	23	24	25	26	27	28
29	30	31				

1. UK: British Summer Time ends.

2. London: Queen Mary opens women's extensions of London School of Medicine (→ 16).

5. US: President Wilson says the US is prepared to fight for a "just cause" (→ 20).

7. W. Front: Allies break Somme front along ten miles (→ 24).

9. Greece: Spiridon Lambros takes over as premier (→ 11).

10. Ireland: Irish Nationalists resolve unanimously to resist conscription (→ 16/5/17).

10. London: The Government announces it will take control of wheat supplies.→

11. Greece: The French take charge of the Greek Navy (→ 16).

16. New York: Margaret Sanger and her sister Ethyl Byrne open the first birth control clinic in the US.

16. Greece: The Allies occupy Athens (→ 17).

17. Greece: The Allies recognise the pro-Allied rebel government of Eleutherios Venizelos opposed to Lambros administration (→ 2/11).

19. Belgium: Cardinal Mercier protests to the Germans about the deportation to Germany of Belgian workers (→ 7/11).

20. US: The US Army orders 375 new aeroplanes (→ 7/11).

24. W. Front: Second Battle of Verdun opens; French troops break German lines along four-mile front (→ 2/11).

31. UK: British casualties are more than 350,000 for last three months, or around 40 per cent of total war casualties.

BIRTH

26. French socialist Francois Mitterrand, President 1981- .

DEATHS

23. British pharmaceuticals manufacturer Sir Joseph Beecham (*1847).

31. US founder of Jehovah's Witnesses Charles Taze Russell (*16/2/1852).

War overshadows US election campaign

The President takes his mind off the election at a baseball game.

Oct 30. War in Europe has cast a long shadow over the 1916 American presidential election. President Wilson has done his best to paint himself as the peace candidate. He has openly called the Republican party the "war party". The Republican candidate, ex-US chief justice and currently Governor of New York, Charles Evans Hughes, found it difficult to make an impact at first. He has to keep the support of German-American conservatives who call for greater military "preparedness".

In the last few days, however, Hughes has chosen to appeal to traditional Republicans. He has concentrated his attacks on what he calls the President's "weak timidity" in not building up the armed forces.

Captain Lawrence backs Arab revolt

Oct 16. A fact-finding mission, led by Ronald Storrs of the Arab Bureau in Cairo, arrived today at the Red Sea port of Jeddah. The purpose of the visit to Arabia is to recommend ways of giving British support to the Arab Revolt against the Ottoman Empire.

With the mission is Captain T.E. Lawrence, a junior officer and orientalist, who has already created quite an impression in military intelligence. Lawrence, the 28-year-old son of an Anglo-Irish country gentleman, took a first-class honours degree at Jesus College, Oxford. Specialising in military history, he travelled in the Near East before the war.

His inclusion in the Storrs Mission is significant because of an influential paper he wrote earlier this year. It argued the strategic advantage of supporting the Arab revolt led by Sherif Hussein of Mecca. Two months ago Hejaz and the Taif garrison surrendered to his son, Abdullah. The task of the British mission will be to reinvigorate the campaign.

Action urged over 50,000 VD victims

Oct 3. Doctors are to be helped provide diagnostic tests and drugs to combat an increase in syphilis. Over 50,000 cases have now been reported amongst servicemen and a Royal Commission has been set up to examine the problem. But the Local Government Board today ruled out compulsory notification of the disease since patients who fear publicity might go instead to herbalists and quacks.

Dr Mary Scharlieb, a London specialist in women's diseases, has blamed prostitutes for the spread of venereal disease. What she calls undesirable and professional women, many of them foreign, "haunt the camps of the men in training" and "beset the arrival of our men at stations when they return on leave".

Many well-fed and strong young men, "overflowing with animal strength and spirits", are an easy prey, says Dr Scharlieb.

Price of a loaf reaches record levels

Oct 12. A loaf of bread will cost ten pence from next Monday, the highest ever price for the food which the poorest families in the nation rely on when they cannot afford anything else. The bakers blame the rise on the soaring cost of flour because of the disruption of wheat imports due to the war. The move comes hard on the heels of the Government's decision to set up a Royal Commission to control imports of wheat because of fears that excessive profits are being made. The bakers deny that they are just getting in their price rise before the Government brings in laws to peg prices.

War has made women a familiar sight behind the counter in British shops.

1916

NOVEMBER

Su	Mo	Tu	We	Th	Fr	Sa
			1	2	3	4
5	6	7	8	9	10	11
12	13	14	15	16	17	18
19	20	21	22	23	24	25
26	27	28	29	30		

2. W. Front: Germans abandon Verdun, quitting Vaux (→ 28).

2. Greece: King Constantine orders the army to intercept rebel pro-Allied troops of Eleutherios Venizelos (→ 1/12).

5. Berlin: Germany and Austria jointly proclaim Poland to be an independent kingdom (→ 15).

7. US: Jeannette Rankin of Montana becomes the first woman member of Congress (→ 14).

7. Belgium: Cardinal Mercier pleads for pressure to stop German deportations of Belgian forced labour (→ 15).

8. London: The Commons votes to sell Nigerian property owned by enemy citizens.

14. UK: Reported that 3.2 million women are employed outside the home (→ 30/1/17).

15. London: The Government announces the appointment of a Food Controller to regulate food consumption (→ 23).

15. Paris: Allies confer on ways to counter German mobilisation of Belgians and Poles (→ 7/12).

23. London: The Government puts money and securities on contraband list (→ 29).

23. Petrograd: Boris Sturmer, reactionary Rasputin protege, is replaced as premier by Alexander Trepov (→ 29/12).

28. France: Somme dead to date: Allies 650,000, Germans 500,000 (→ 3/12).

29. London: The Government announces it will take control of vacant agricultural land for food production (→ 1/12).

DEATHS

15. Polish Nobel prize-winning writer Henryk Sienkiewicz (*5/5/1846).

22. US author Jack London (*12/1/1876).

24. US-born inventor of the machine gun Sir Hiram Maxim (*15/2/1840).

21. Austro-Hungarian Emperor Franz Josef (*18/8/1830).→

Franz Josef dies, ruler for 68 years

Nov 21. Emperor Franz Josef, ruler of the Austro-Hungarian Empire since 1848, is dead. Beset by personal tragedy, he strove to hold his empire of 17 nationalities together throughout his long reign.

His wife, the Empress Elisabeth, was murdered by an anarchist in 1898. Nine years earlier, in 1889, his only son Rudolf apparently committed suicide with his lover Maria Vetsera at Mayerling, and the succession devolved on Franz Josef's great nephew, Franz Ferdinand. His murder at Sarajevo caused the war which threatens to destroy the empire Franz Josef fought so hard to preserve.

The late Emperor as a young man.

Wilson narrowly retains presidency

Nov 11. President Wilson has been re-elected in the closest presidential election since 1888. His Republican opponent, Charles Evans Hughes, ran well in the east – so well that on at one point on election day the electric sign in Times Square flashed news of a Hughes victory. Wilson was stronger in the west. He won States which are normally Republican such as Kansas as well as California. Wilson won 9.1 million popular votes while Hughes polled 8.6 million.

1916

DECEMBER

Su	Mo	Tu	We	Th	Fr	Sa
					1	2
3	4	5	6	7	8	9
10	11	12	13	14	15	16
17	18	19	20	21	22	23
24	25	26	27	28	29	30
31						

1. London: Government launches an inquiry into food prices, seeking to uncover cartel conspiracies.

1. Athens: King Constantine refuses to surrender to Allies, orders troops to resist occupation of Athens (→ 22/6/17).

2. London: The Government will sponsor more scientific research by British industry.

2. London: Government says no man under 26 will be exempted from military service on grounds of business or employment (→ 5/7).

3. W. Front: General Joffre is replaced by General Robert Nivelle as head of French forces on the Somme, following failure of offensive (→ 15).

6. Vienna: Czech nationalist Tomas Masaryk, a lecturer at London University, is sentenced in absence to death for treason.

7. Poland: Germans reported to have deported one million Poles for forced labour (→ 14/1/17).

10. Stockholm: Nobel Prize for Literature is awarded to Swedish poet Carl Gustav von Heidenstam; no other Prizes awarded (→ 10/12/17).

15. W. Front: Death toll of Verdun offensive stands at 364,000 Allies and 338,000 Germans (→ 31).

HITS OF 1916

If you were the only girl in the world.

Take me back to dear old Blighty.

Poor butterfly.

QUOTE OF THE YEAR

"Where all your rights become only an accumulated wrong; where men must beg with bated breath for leave to subsist in their own land ... then surely it is a braver, a saner and a truer thing to be a rebel than tamely to accept it as the natural lot of men."
Sir Roger Casement,
Irish nationalist, hanged for treason 3/8/16.

Rasputin murdered by Russian nobles

"Holy man" Gregory Rasputin.

Dec 30. Russia's infamous Siberian "seer" and "miracle worker", Gregory Rasputin, has been sensationally murdered by two relatives of Czar Nicholas II, concerned at the monk's pernicious influence on affairs of the state.

Rasputin, who came to St. Petersburg in 1905 as a "holy man", was lured to the home of Prince Yussupov where he was poisoned, shot, and bludgeoned before being dumped in the river Neva.

He became the confidant and confessor of the Czar's wife after using hypnotism to stop the bleeding of the haemophiliac heir to the throne.

US President puts out peace feelers

Dec 20. President Wilson has sent peace overtures to London. He proposes that all nations now at war should state what their peace terms are. The note came as a surprise, and an unwelcome one as far as London is concerned, because, following peace feelers from Berlin, it seems to endorse their initiative. The Germans are jubilant.

The US Secretary of State, Robert Lansing, has issued a statement denying any such intent. It added that the reason for the Note was that "we are drawing near to war ourselves", and the US therefore wanted to know the belligerents' terms.

Lloyd George is new Prime Minister

Dec 7. David Lloyd George – by some the most loved and by others the most distrusted politician in the land – is Britain's new Prime Minister tonight. The King has appointed him to succeed Herbert Asquith after three days of intensive plotting and high-level skulduggery inside the coalition government.

This began when Mr Asquith told the King that he could stand no more of the persistent, snide newspaper criticism of himself for dilatoriness, indecision and delay in conducting the war. He advised a reconstruction of the Government. Mr Asquith's friends believe that Mr Lloyd George has been masterminding a conspiracy against him with the help of Lord Northcliffe, owner of The Times.

The King first asked the Tory leader, Andrew Bonar Law, if he could form a new government. Mr Bonar Law declined and teamed up with Mr Lloyd George to oust Mr Asquith after a group of party bosses had quarrelled in the King's presence at Buckingham Palace.

Now Mr Lloyd George begins his premiership dedicated to more vigorous prosecution of the war. To that end he let it be known two days ago that he would favour a new-style cabinet of only four or five (instead of over 20).

He outraged Mr Asquith by privately suggesting this move to him some time ago – with Mr Asquith excluded from it. In advance of the Court Circular announcement about the premiership change, Britain's new leader talked with senior Labour MPs. He is understood to have offered them at least one place in his Cabinet and to have won their qualified support. Irish Nationalists now await a similar approach and they may be prepared to offer benevolent neutrality to the reshuffled Coalition. How much Mr Lloyd George and Mr Bonar Law were engaged in joint manoeuvres against Mr Asquith is the subject of excited lobby speculation.

It seems likely that they had agreed tactics before involving the King. It is widely agreed that the Asquith and Lloyd George factions are now irreconcilable.

Lloyd George with Allied commanders Douglas Haig and Joseph Joffre on a recent visit to the 14th Army Corps Headquarters at Meaulte.

The stalemate in the trenches makes for a bleak mid-winter

Dec 25. The third Christmas of the war has been the bleakest yet. Two years ago the men of Europe had gone to war cheerily confident of being "home by Christmas". Today there is no such optimism. Neither side achieved the great breakthroughs they sought during 1916 – and the cost in lives was immense. At Verdun, unofficial estimates of losses are 700,000 men. Further west, the great British offensive at the Somme proved even bloodier: 650,000 Allied soldiers perished, most of them British, along with 500,000 Germans. In places the front-lines were changed by a mile or two, but rarely for long, and never to achieve a significant strategic gain.

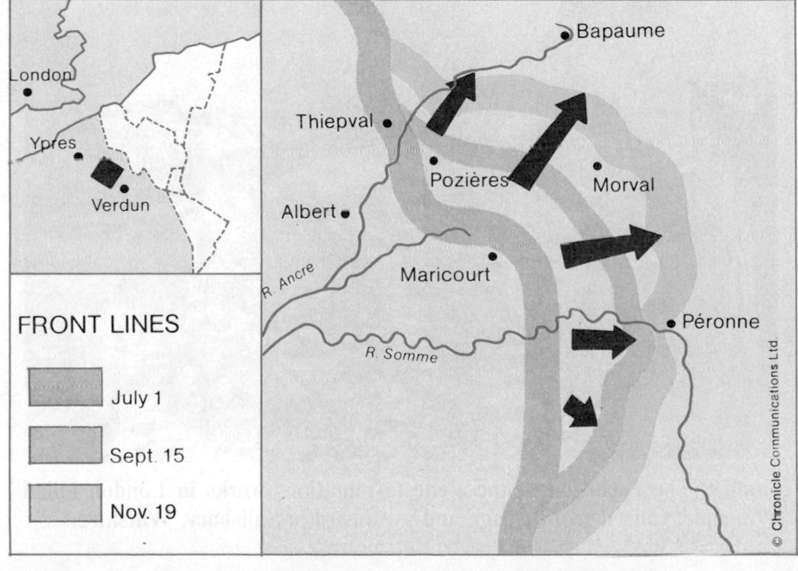

Arts: The American who out-Englished the English is dead

Two American writers who could not be more different died this year, **Henry James** and **Jack London**. The patrician Mr James seemed more English than American. He had lived in this country since 1876, become a British subject last year and received the honour of the Order of Merit only a short time before his death at 72.

He died, as he lived for the past 20 years, at Lamb House, Rye, Sussex, where he would write in the summerhouse of his walled garden. His output was prodigious – over 20 full-length novels, volumes of short stories, besides plays (unsuccessful) and essays.

His elder brother **William**, who died in 1910, was America's most famous psychologist and it was in psychology applied to his characters, especially his heroines, that Henry James was unsurpassed. Novels like "The Portrait of a Lady" deal with his favourite theme of American-European relations. The supernatural is called up unforgettably in "The Turn of the Screw".

US-born Englishman James.

Jack London, on the other hand, was by nature an adventurer, who made himself a powerful adventure story writer. His first-hand experiences as a seaman on a sealing ship or as a Klondike gold prospector went into such books as "The Call of the Wild" and "White Fang". He made over $1 million with his pen. An alcoholic, he died at 40.

1917

JANUARY

Su	Mo	Tu	We	Th	Fr	Sa
	1	2	3	4	5	6
7	8	9	10	11	12	13
14	15	16	17	18	19	20
21	22	23	24	25	26	27
28	29	30	31			

1. Mediterranean: Cunard liner "Ivernia" is sunk by a German submarine; 153 feared dead (→25).

4. London: Government agrees with Germany to an exchange of all internees over 45.

5. Balkans: Germans take Rumanian city of Braila as Russians retreat.

9. Petrograd: Czar Nicholas II appoints Prince Dmitri Golitzin as premier after resignation of Alexander Trepov.→

14. Poland: Provisional parliament is set up (→26).

16. Berlin: The Government proposes a military alliance with Mexico (→1/2).

17. New York: Dixieland Jazz Band opens at Reisenweber's Restaurant on 8th Avenue and 58th Street (→7/3).

25. Atlantic: 350 die when "HMS Laurentic" is sunk by a mine (→1/2).

26. Petrograd: The Czar endorses President Wilson's peace plans, calling for a free Poland with access to the sea (→31).

26. Germany: Total war expenditure to date estimated at £5,000 million.

29. Washington: Congress passes new immigration law requiring all immigrants over 16 to know 30 to 80 English words, and banning all Asians but Japanese.

30. London: Parliamentary Conference recommends giving the vote to married women over a certain age (→6/2).

31. Petrograd: Allied conference opens (→2/3).

31. Derby: Four are charged with conspiracy to murder Lloyd George.

31. Germany: Otto Hahn and Lise Meitner discover the radioactive element proactium.

DEATH

10. US Colonel William F. Cody, alias Buffalo Bill (*26/2/1846).→

Britain: victory loan to meet War debts

Jan 11. In a packed Guildhall and before the Lord Mayor of London, the Prime Minister David Lloyd George and the Chancellor of the Exchequer, Andrew Bonar Law, launched a patriotic appeal for the entire nation to subscribe to the new War Loan. The issue is to finance the staggering cost of the war, which is now running at £5.7 million a day.

The Prime Minister, fresh from the Allied conference in Rome, spoke movingly for 40 minutes. "At Rome", he said, "all had felt that, if victory was difficult, defeat was impossible." He called on men and women to subscribe to the loan "in order to shorten the war and save the lives of the brave young men at the Front".

War loan investment poster.

The terms of the twin loans were seen by the City as generous. The 5 per cent loan is for 30 years. If held until redemption in 1947, it would yield over 5.25 per cent a year. The 4 per cent loan is for 25 years and is income tax free. The Treasury will use part of the loans to buy them back, if necessary, to keep them above the price at which they were issued. The Prudential Assurance company has already said it will invest £20 million.

America: profits soar in peacetime boom

Jan 1. Last year was a boom year for the United States – the most prosperous in the country's history. As part of the war effort, the mass production methods that have proved so successful in the car industry have been applied to others, like shipbuilding, aircraft engine manufacture and the production of munitions. Their growth has created general prosperity. Prices are up, but wages have risen even faster – and so have profits.

Records are being set in all sectors of the economy: steel and iron output, foreign trade, consumer spending. Pessimists fear that the bubble may burst, but Frank A. Vanderlip, President of the National City Bank of New York, says that the business outlook for 1917 is excellent.

Jan 19. The explosion of the Venesta munitions works in London killed 69 people, caused vast damage and was heard in Salisbury, Wiltshire.

Wild West legend, Buffalo Bill, dies

Jan 10. One of the most colourful characters of the Wild West died today. William Cody was an army scout during the Sioux Wars and later won the contract to supply meat to workers building the Kansas City Railroad. In eighteen months he killed 4,820 buffalo – hence his soubriquet, Buffalo Bill. From 1883 he toured the US and Europe with his popular and thrilling Wild West Show. Among its many attractions were Chief Sitting Bull and "sharpshooting" Annie Oakley, but the show's biggest crowd-puller was always its owner, Buffalo Bill Cody.

Colonel "Buffalo Bill" Cody.

Strikes in Russia fuel war protest

Jan 9. While a new Russian offensive has got under way against German forces on the Baltic front, strikes are being called in munition factories in Petrograd.

There are widespread food shortages, and workers are protesting over the war and the terrible Russian losses. Ministers are continuing to come and go. Prime Minister Alexander Trepov, for example, resigned after only two months in office.

1917

FEBRUARY

Su	Mo	Tu	We	Th	Fr	Sa
				1	2	3
4	5	6	7	8	9	10
11	12	13	14	15	16	17
18	19	20	21	22	23	24
25	26	27	28			

1. Berlin: Germans step up submarine warfare, warning US and other neutrals that ships trading with the Allies will be torpedoed without warning (→ 3).

3. Washington: Wilson breaks off diplomatic relations with Germany after the US ship "Housatonic" is sunk off Sicily (→ 7).

3. Berlin: The Government introduces regulations on use of coal as shortages occur.

6. London: Neville Chamberlain announces scheme of non-military - national service for women (→ 13).

7. Germany: All US citizens in the country are held as government hostages (→ 17).

10. London: Zionist leader Chaim Weizmann meets with Government representatives to discuss a possible Jewish colony in Palestine (→ 7/5).

13. London: The Government allows women to become taxi-drivers (→ 29/3).

15. France: Government says restaurants can only serve two courses, only one of them meat, and that menus must be shown to the police.

17. Washington: Wilson and the Senate discuss the possibility of arming US ships against attack (→ 24).

22. UK: National Trust acquires 500-year lease on parts of Exmoor.

24. Washington: Publication of secret telegram from German foreign minister Arthur Zimmermann to Mexican government, asking Mexico to declare war on the US (→ 25).

25. Atlantic: 30 passengers, many of them Americans, die when the liner "Laconia" is torpedoed.→

26. London: The Government announces that five million people subscribed £1,000 million to the latest war loan (→ 24/4).

BIRTH

25. British writer Anthony Burgess (†22/11/93).

US arms ships to meet sub threat

Feb 26. US ships will soon be able to defend themselves against the German threat, following moves in Congress today aimed at allowing them to be fitted with weapons.

The US president, Woodrow Wilson, asked Congress for the means to maintain "an armed neutrality" to deal with unrestricted German submarine warfare. The moves are seen as a sequel to the breaking of relations with Germany and Austria on February 3, which itself followed Berlin's announcement that any vessel entering a proscribed area would be sunk without warning.

Ambassadors have been called home and the US Navy has seized two interned German cruisers. The New York State National Guard and the Navy militia have been ordered into service. The president told Congress that "arming US vessels would protect our ships and our people in their legitimate pursuits on the sea".

As he spoke, news of the sinking of the Cunard liner "Laconia" passed by word of mouth among the legislators. A total of 207 survivors from the ship have been landed in Ireland but at least 25 passengers have died. Even with this news many Congressmen still seem reluctant to grant the powers which bring the US a step nearer entering the war. Earlier this month the US ship "Housatonic" was sunk by the Germans, one of the 134 neutral vessels to be destroyed by them in the last three weeks (→ 21/3).

German navy propaganda poster.

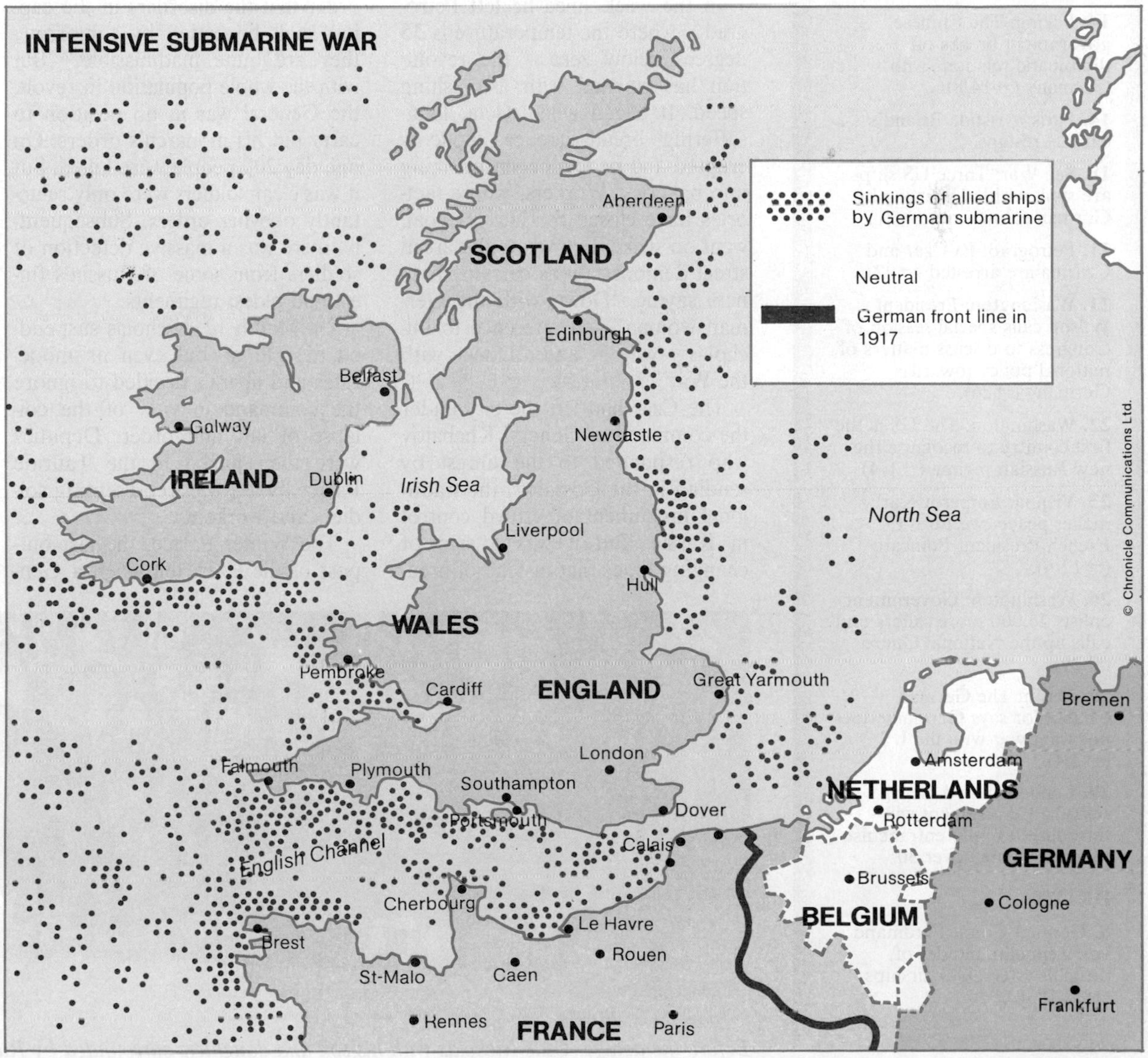

INTENSIVE SUBMARINE WAR

Sinkings of allied ships by German submarine

Neutral

German front line in 1917

© Chronicle Communications Ltd.

1917

MARCH

Su	Mo	Tu	We	Th	Fr	Sa
				1	2	3
4	5	6	7	8	9	10
11	12	13	14	15	16	17
18	19	20	21	22	23	24
25	26	27	28	29	30	31

2. Washington: Congress passes the Jones Act, under which Puerto Rico becomes US territory and its people US citizens.

2. Petrograd: The new session of the Duma begins (→ 10).

7. US: The Victor Co. issues world's first jazz recording, "The Dixieland Jazz Band One-Step".

8. London: Government Commission on the Dardanelles campaign lays part of the blame for its failure on Lord Kitchener.

10. Petrograd: Workers riot to protest against the war and famine.→

14. Peking: The Chinese government breaks off diplomatic relations with Germany (→ 14/8).

14. Paris: Aristide Briand's cabinet resigns.

18. Sea War: Three US ships are sunk without warning by German submarines (→ 21).

21. Petrograd: Ex-Czar and Czarina are arrested (→ 22).

21. Washington: President Wilson calls special session of Congress to discuss matters of national policy towards Germany (→ 26).

22. Washington: The US is the first country to recognise the new Russian regime (→ 1/4).

23. Vienna: Emperor Karl makes peace overtures to French President Poincare (→ 12/4).

26. Washington: Government enlists 26,000 more sailors and calls up the National Guard (→ 29).

29. Berlin: The German Chancellor says Germany does not want war with the US (→ 2/4).

29. London: Lloyd George says the Government will introduce a bill to enfranchise married women over 30.

DEATH

8. German Count Ferdinand von Zeppelin, builder of dirigible (steerable) airships (*8/7/1838).→

Czar abdicates: Russian revolt grows

March 16. Russia's monarchy fell at three o'clock this afternoon and power has passed, with practically no resistance and very little bloodshed, to a provisional government. Czar Nicholas II signed the form of abdication in the Imperial train and is going on to the military headquarters at Pskov to say goodbye to his armies.

The abdication caps months of turmoil. The Russian offensive on the German front has resulted in staggering casualties – two million in 1915 alone. The popular demand for peace has gone unheeded, instead the Czar showed his approval of the war by taking personal command a few months ago. Starvation gripped the nation and what little food there was was prevented from reaching the people by bureaucratic ineptitude.

In the week since he left Petrograd – where the temperature is 35 degrees below zero – the revolution has ripened with astonishing speed. It began when silent, long-suffering bread queues suddenly erupted and people began breaking into bakeries. Workers, whose factories have closed for lack of coal, went on strike. Crowds took part in street demonstrations carrying banners saying "Down with the German woman" – a reference to Nicholas's wife – and "Down with the War".

The Czar had left the city under the command of General Khabalov who responded to the unrest by sending in the Cossacks, the traditional instrument of crowd control in Russia. But it was a sign of changing times that instead of breaking heads they bantered good-humouredly with the crowds. Nicholas cabled Khabalov: "I order that the disorders in the capital shall be ended by tomorrow; they are quite inadmissible." But with the whole population in revolt, the General was in no position to carry out his monarch's orders. On one day 200 people were killed, but it was clear soldiers were only reluctantly obeying orders. Subsequently, there was a massive defection of soldiers from some of Russia's finest and oldest regiments.

To arms! Revolutionary soldiers and students on the streets of Petrograd.

On March 12, Nicholas suspended the Duma, but even its moderates and liberals decided to ignore the command in view of the collapse of law and order. Deputies were then joined in the Tauride Palace by a Soviet representing soldiers and workers.

The Winter Palace, the last outpost of the Czar, fell when a General commanding 1,500 loya[l] troops was given 20 minutes t[o] leave or face bombardment.

A central figure in the revolutio[n] is Alexander Kerensky, a 36-year old Duma member and socialis[t] revolutionary. So far the Bolshevik[s] have had little, if anything, to d[o] with it, or with the fall of the Cza[r] as their leaders are abroad or underground.

The first abdication form prepar[ed] by the generals passed the thron[e] to the Czar's son, aged 12. This wa[s] changed, at Nicholas's request, i[n] favour of his brother the Gran[d] Duke Michael. The final version o[f] the document concluded: "Ma[y] the Lord God help Russia".

There are many reasons for th[e] revolution, but a major one ha[s] been the shortage of such staples a[s] flour, coal and wood. People wer[e] cold and hungry, they had ha[d] enough.

Before the deluge: Czar Nicholas with his son and daughters surrounded by Russian army officers.

British win at Gaza: Turks demoralised

Victorious men of the Hampshire Regiment enter Baghdad on March 11.

March 27. On the borders of Palestine the British army, advancing from Sinai, today soundly defeated the Turks near Gaza. This victory, over a force 20,000 strong under the command of German Colonel Kress von Kressenstein, comes hard on the heels of news from Mesopotamia of the British capture of Baghdad.

From Sinai, General Sir Archibald Murray, GOC Egypt, signalled that his troops had advanced to Wadi Ghuzze, five miles south of Gaza. There they won an infantry and cavalry battle, inflicting heavy losses on the enemy. They took 900 prisoners, including the general and entire staff of the Turkish 53rd Division.

"All troops behaved splendidly", Murray reported. The way is clear for the advance into Palestine.

More details have been announced in the House of Commons of recent victories in Mesopotamia, which preceded the capture of Baghdad two weeks ago. After a series of brilliant operations along the river Tigris conducted by Lieutenant General Sir Stanley Maude, British and Indian troops outmanoeuvred the Turks and forced them to withdraw on Baghdad.

The British harried the retreating enemy, marching over 110 miles in fifteen days, a remarkable achievement in intense heat and through country denuded of supplies. They captured many prisoners and completely demoralised the Turks, who lost two-thirds of their artillery.

Outrage as sub hits UK hospital ship

March 20. A German submarine tonight torpedoed a British hospital ship, provoking the fury of the British Government and threats of retaliation against this "unspeakable crime against law and humanity".

Thirty one died and 12 are missing from the 12,000-ton "Asturias", hit without warning as she steamed with her Red Cross signs brightly illuminated. Fortunately there were no wounded on board when the attack happened. A German claim that British hospital ships carry munitions has been denied by the Government.

Count Ferdinand von Zeppelin, who died on the 8th, aged 78.

1917

APRIL

Su	Mo	Tu	We	Th	Fr	Sa
1	2	3	4	5	6	7
8	9	10	11	12	13	14
15	16	17	18	19	20	21
22	23	24	25	26	27	28
29	30					

1. Petrograd: Czar's assets confiscated by new regime (→ 6).

6. New York: 91 German ships are seized in New York harbour (→ 14).

6. Petrograd: Alexander Kerensky's regime introduces an eight-hour day for all workers and abolishes capital punishment.→

7. Cuba: Government declares war on Germany (→ 8).

8. Panama: Government declares war on Germany.

11. W. Front: Arras offensive opens; British pierce German lines to depth of three miles and take 11,000 prisoners (→ 16).

12. Switzerland: Austrian and Bulgarian diplomats approach Allied envoys to discuss peace terms.

14. Washington: Congress votes a $7,000-million war loan (→ 19).

17. Petrograd: On his return to Russia, Vladimir Lenin publishes his "April Thesis", demanding transfer of power to workers' Soviets (→ 7/5).

17. Sea War: Germans sink British hospital ships "Donegal" and "Lanfranc", killing 75 (→ 16/5).

18. US: Pacific Aero Products Co. changes name to Boeing Airplane Co.

19. Berlin: 250,000 workers end their strike when promised better rations and a say in running of food councils.

19. US: The ship "Mongolia" fires first US shots of the war, sinking a German submarine (→ 24).

24. Washington: Wilson signs War Finance Act, under which UK will be lent £200 million (→ 7/5).

28. W. Front: General Philippe Petain replaces General Robert Nivelle as French commander (→ 4/5).

DEATH

1. US ragtime composer and pianist Scott Joplin (*24/11/1868).

Easter offensive begins with prayer

April 16. In driving rain and chill mist, British, Canadians and Australian troops launched their spring offensive against Germans manning the famous Hindenburg Line opposite Arras. In the first hours all the main objectives were secured and over 2,000 prisoners taken.

The Canadians found the German defences had been completely wrecked by British bombardments, but rain had turned the trench systems into a vast morass. The eight tanks operating with the Canadians were all trapped in mud.

The men, who are now slogging their way through the enemy lines, were, only yesterday, to be seen in scores of village squares, with heads bowed, helmets removed, while the chaplains conducted the Easter Sunday service. Some of them are now coming back from the fighting, wounded but in good spirits. "We knocked hell out of old Fritz," they say. "Their dead were lying thick and the living put their hands up."

Further south, the French are doing less well. General Robert Nivelle's massive offensive, which the troops had been told would be "le dernier coup", has been smashed by powerful enemy counter blows. Now, after over 100,000 casualties, there are reports of indiscipline and even mutiny among the exhausted troops (→ 4/5).

A bomb-scarred church at Arras.

US enters war "to save democracy"

Glory, glory, Hallelujah! Boy scouts celebrate the US entry into the war on the side of the Allies.

April 6. America is at war. At 1.18 this afternoon President Woodrow Wilson, sitting in a tiny room in the White House, signed the declaration of war passed by Congress this week.

The war resolution went through the Senate by 90 votes to six, and the House passed the same measure by 373-50, following an emotional debate that lasted 17 hours. Opposing the motion, Jeannette Rankin, the only woman elected to Congress, said in tears: "I want to stand by my country but I cannot vote for war."

In his own speech on April 2 to a joint session of Congress, President Wilson had called for America to go to war, saying: "The world must be made safe for democracy".

The decision was greeted with lusty cheering in the public galleries of both houses, but it is reported that on his return to the White House the President remarked: "My message was one of death for young men. How odd it seems to applaud that." He then put his head in his hands and wept.

The decision represents a dramatic reversal, both for President Wilson personally and for the US as a whole, which, apart from a few foreign adventures, has for over a hundred years obeyed George Washington's final piece of advice to avoid "entangling alliances". Now, as the British Prime Minister, David Lloyd George, said at a press conference: "America has at one bound become a world power".

The story of America's entry into the war is one of a people determined to preserve their neutrality in the face of inexorable pressure from the belligerents, especially the sinking of US ships by German submarines.

For more than two years President Wilson has been doing his best to steer a middle course between the advocates of "preparedness", pushing for stronger armed forces, and several important groups who thought this policy likely to end in war.

Among the opposition were western radicals, socialists, Americans of German extraction, who did not want to go to war against Germany, and Irish-Americans, who did not want her to fight for Britain. After the sinking of the Lusitania in May 1915, it seemed that the advocates of preparedness were the stronger. But when Congress met a year ago the President found himself bitterly attacked by pacifist progressives, agrarian radicals and senators.

Although America's resources in terms of manpower and industrial production are potentially greater than those of any of the belligerents, with the possible exception of Germany, there are serious questions about how quickly this potential can be translated into effective fighting power.

While the US has the world's largest steel production, for example, and by far the world's biggest automobile industry, it manufactures no fighter aircraft whatever. The total strength of the US regular army is only 5,000 officers and 123,000 men, plus 8,500 part-time soldiers in the reserve National Guard.

It will necessarily be some time before new forces can be raised, and there is also some disagreement in the US about how easy it will be to transport an American expeditionary force to Europe, given the effectiveness of German submarine warfare.

"Doughboys" get their first taste of training for the trenches of Flanders.

Germans return Lenin to Russia in a sealed train

April 16. Vladimir Lenin, the Bolshevik leader, returned to Russia in blazing triumph today in a bizarre arrangement with the German general staff.

After ten years out of the country Lenin was welcomed like a returning prophet, and within hours he was calling for an end to the war, the overthrow of the provisional government, and the abolition of the police, army and bureaucracy.

The corrosive revolutionary left Zurich, where he had spent more than two years in exile, on April 9, with 17 other Bolsheviks. They were shipped across Germany in a sealed train as part of a secret deal reached with German ministers.

The German motive for helping Lenin reach Russia was purely military. He might, so the theory went, manage to provoke a new revolution in Russia, which, in turn, might reverse the Allied policy of the Provisional Government. Alternatively he might seek a separate peace and take Russia out of the war. Whatever happens, his presence inside Russia would be bound to create turmoil.

The party travelled through Sweden to Finland where Lenin resumed his political activity on Russian soil by convincing soldiers, that the war should end. He will soon meet his fellow exiles Leon Trotsky and Joseph Stalin to discuss tactics.

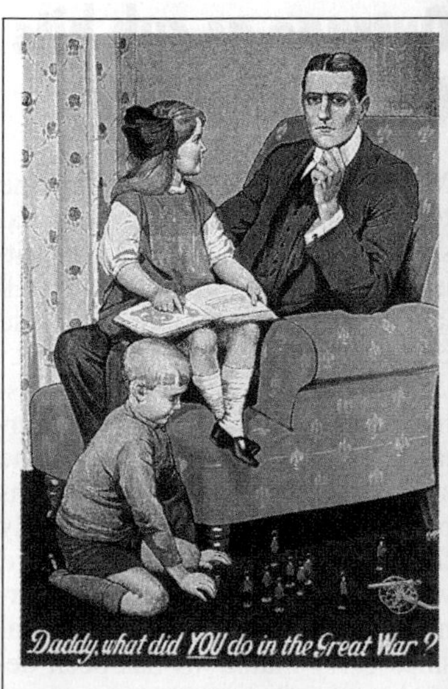

Daddy, what did YOU do in the Great War?

1917

MAY

Su	Mo	Tu	We	Th	Fr	Sa
		1	2	3	4	5
6	7	8	9	10	11	12
13	14	15	16	17	18	19
20	21	22	23	24	25	26
27	28	29	30	31		

1. Poland: Council of State demands German and Austrian agreement on creation of independent Poland (→ 2/7).

4. Mediterranean: British transport ship "Transylvania" is torpedoed and sunk, killing 413 (→ 16).

4. W. Front: Mutiny breaks out in sections of the French Army (→ 7/6).

7. Palestine: Reported that Jews are being terrorised by Moslems throughout the territory.

7. Washington: US War Department will send 10,000 army engineers to France (→ 15).

7. Petrograd: The city's soviet bans weekend street meetings (→ 10).

10. Petrograd: Duma president says Russia will not withdraw from the war against the Central Powers (→ 19).

12. Budapest: First performance of Bela Bartok's ballet "The Wooden Prince".

13. London: Bus drivers go on strike.

15. Washington: Selective Service Act is passed by Congress, calling for drafting of all men aged 21-30.

16. UK: First US naval flotilla arrives offshore (→ 5/6).

18. Paris: The Ballets Russes give the first performance of Erik Satie's ballet "Parade", based on a story by Jean Cocteau, with sets and costumes by Picasso.

19. Petrograd: The regime proposes peace without sanctions or territorial annexations (→ 28).

26. UK: German aeroplanes kill 76 civilians in bombing raids along the south-east coast of England.

28. Petrograd: Pan-Russian Peasants' Congress calls for democratic federal republic (→ 16/6).

BIRTH

29. US statesman John Fitzgerald Kennedy, 35th President 1961-1963 (†22/11/63).

King urges nation to tighten its belt

May 2. In a royal proclamation issued today from Buckingham Palace, the King calls for a national holding-back on bread consumption. At the same time it was revealed that the royal household has been on strict rations since February. The Master of the Household, Sir Derek Keppel, commented that the King would never ask, and has never asked, his people to make sacrifices in which he is unprepared to share.

The King exhorts heads of households to see that their families eat a quarter less bread than in peace time and avoid flour in pastry. The full text of the proclamation is to be read out in churches on four successive Sundays.

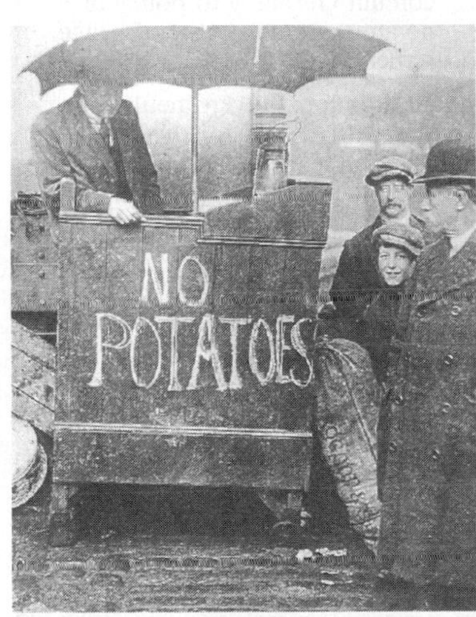

Shortages begin to bite in Britain.

Home Rule plans will exclude Ulster

May 16. The latest plans of the British government to give Home Rule to Ireland were today given to Irish party leaders at Westminster. If the Irish agree, a parliament will be set up in Dublin, but the six counties in Northern Ireland, which are believed to have a Unionist and Protestant majority, will continue under Westminster's jurisdiction.

A Council of Ireland, bringing together Westminster MPs from Ulster and MPs from the Dublin Parliament, is also proposed. But all the proposals are for the wartime only. A long-term settlement must await peace in Europe.

1917

JUNE

Su	Mo	Tu	We	Th	Fr	Sa
					1	2
3	4	5	6	7	8	9
10	11	12	13	14	15	16
17	18	19	20	21	22	23
24	25	26	27	28	29	30

3. Rome: Italy declares Albania a protectorate.

4. Brazil: The Government declares war on Germany and seizes all German ships in Brazilian ports.

5. US: Nearly 10 million men enrol for military service; Wilson warns of stiff penalties for draft dodgers (→ 27).

7. London: Winston Churchill returns to the government as chairman of the Air Board (→ 17/7).

7. W. Front: New Flanders offensive; British under Gen. Haig capture territory south of Ypres held by Germans since early 1915 (→ 27).

11. UK: Sailors refuse to take Labour delegates, including Ramsay MacDonald, to the Stockholm Peace Conference (→ 12/8).

14. Lancashire: 41 die in an explosion at an arms factory.

15. Ireland: Government announces the release of all prisoners held during the Easter Rising of 1916 (→ 11/7).

16. Germany: 200 die in smallpox epidemic in north of the country.

16. Petrograd: Pan-Russian Congress of Soviets opens; Lenin's declaration that Bolsheviks aim to rule Russia alone meets with general derision (→ 19).

17. US: Release of "The Immigrant" starring Charlie Chaplin.

19. London: Commons votes by 330 majority to give the vote to wives over the age of 30 (→ 11/9).

19. Russia: The first women's army battalion is formed (→ 23).

23. Petrograd: Soviet Congress votes to abolish the Duma (→ 16/7).

26. London: King George V orders members of the Royal Family to drop German titles: Saxe-Coburg-Gotha becomes Windsor and Battenberg becomes Mountbatten.

29. Kiev: Ukraine declares independence (→ 2/7).

Heroes' welcome for US troops in France

A US Marine recruiting poster.

June 27. The first American troopships reached the French coast at dawn this morning. The site of the landing had been a closely guarded secret but by the time the troops lined up for their first salute on French soil a huge crowd had gathered to cheer them enthusiastically. The crowd got bigger and the cheering got louder as each ship hove to and dropped anchor in the splendid summer sunshine.

Soon they will be off with thousands more of their countrymen to fight on the muddy battlefields. The troops are under the command of Major General "Black Jack" Pershing, a veteran of the Mexican and Philippine wars.

Convoy system to counter ship losses

June 1. Britain may at last have found the answer to the U-Boat menace in convoys of merchant vessels protected by warships. More than 100 British merchant ships were sunk by German submarines last month and fierce arguments have been raging in both the War Cabinet and the Admiralty as to how they can best be protected. Many in the navy believed there were not enough warships available for escort duty.

The first protected convoy has just arrived from Gibraltar without mishap and another from the US is expected within days. ▷

First aeroplane bombing hits London

A German aeroplane takes off from an airfield on the Western Front.

June 14. German aircraft have carried out the first bombing raid on London. More than 100 were killed and 400 injured in the 15-minute attack on the East End. The raid marks a sinister new role for the aeroplane which only three years ago was used solely for reconnaissance flights over enemy lines. Previous air raids over London were made by Zeppelins, which were easy targets to hit.

About 15 aircraft are thought to have been used in yesterday's raid, countered by anti-aircraft fire from the ground. One bomb fell on a school, killing ten children, and another crashed onto a railway station, hitting a train.

People climbed onto roofs to catch a glimpse of the aircraft, and although some MPs are pressing for air raid hooters or sirens to be installed, the Government feels they may lead to more chaos or people using the warnings as an excuse to take time off work.

Mobile early-warning system.

Pro-German Greek King forced to quit

June 22. King Constantine of the Hellenes, brother-in-law of the Kaiser, has been forced to abdicate by the Allies. His pro-German attitudes finally became too much for them, and they made it plain that if he did not step down they would recognise the provisional war government set up at the Allied base of Salonika.

The Allies, who claim the right by treaty to interfere in Greek affairs, accuse him of curtailing the liberty of his people by dismissing the Liberal, pro-Allied government of Mr Venizelos.

He will be succeeded by his second son, Prince Alexander. Mr Venizelos is expected to resume as Prime Minister.

1917

JULY

Su	Mo	Tu	We	Th	Fr	Sa
1	2	3	4	5	6	7
8	9	10	11	12	13	14
15	16	17	18	19	20	21
22	23	24	25	26	27	28
29	30	31				

2. US: Up to 75 blacks are murdered during race riots in East St. Louis, Illinois (→ 24/8).

2. E. Front: Alexander Kerensky leads a successful attack on Austro-Germans in Galicia (→ 13).

2. Poland: Joseph Pilsudski resigns from the Council of State (→ 15/9).

7. London: 37 die in German air raids (→ 10/8).

8. Washington: Government takes control of exports, food, fuel and war supplies (→ 4/8).

9. Berlin: Kaiser refuses to commit Germany to policy of no annexations as part of peace settlement (→ 14).

10. London: Government will test "war bread" for digestibility following complaints from the public.

11. Ireland: East Clare by-election is won by the Sinn Fein candidate Eamon de Valera (→ 23/10).

14. Berlin: Theobald von Bethmann-Hollweg resigns as Chancellor, succeeded by Dr Georg Michaelis, first non-aristocrat to hold the post.

14. Helsingfors: Finland proclaims independence from Russia (→ 18/11).

17. London: Winston Churchill is appointed Minister of Munitions (→ 23).

23. London: Prime Minister Lloyd George declares that "peace with Germany will only be achieved with the German people and not with its authoritarian regime" (→ 24).

24. London: MPs are alarmed by the revelation that the war is now costing the UK £7 million a day.

26. W. Front: German troops break through French lines along the River Aisne (→ 20/8).

31. UK: Mr A. Cox's Gay Crusader wins the postponed wartime "New Derby" at Newmarket.

DEATH

2. British actor-manager Sir Herbert Beerbohm Tree (*17/12/1853).

Pillow talk costs Mata Hari her life

July 25. Mata Hari, the glamorous Dutch dancer and adventuress (whose stage name meant "eye of the morning" in Malay) was sentenced to death today after being found guilty of spying by a French court-martial.

Born Margaretha Geertruida Zelle, she left her alcoholic Scots husband, called MacLeod, in Netherlands East Indies and came to Europe where she became as notorious for her military lovers as for her provocative Oriental dancing.

She was alleged to have passed on military secrets to German intelligence officers, and although she protested her innocence at the trial in Paris, her lurid lifestyle was used to damning effect (→ 15/10).

Mata Hari: provocative.

"We saw Virgin" claim in Fatima

July 17. Pilgrims are beginning to flock towards the small village of Fatima in Portugal where three shepherds' children claim to have seen visions of the Virgin Mary. Even some of the sceptics, who thought it was all childish fantasy, are now having second thoughts after the latest message. Lucia, 10, Francesco, 9, and Jacintha, 7, surely could not have made up such solemn sentiments or used such big words on their own.

Lenin is forced to flee

A soldier distributes revolutionary newspapers to eager Russian citizens.

July 16. Russia's provisional government has crushed a Bolshevik uprising, but has failed to capture its leader Vladimir Lenin. Reports say he escaped across the border to Finland aboard a train disguised as a fireman.

The uprising brought half a million people onto the streets of Petrograd carrying banners calling for an end to the war and the fall of the new provisional government. There was a great deal of shooting but most of it was wild and and went harmlessly into the air.

The authorities hit back by circulating a document "proving" that Lenin was a German agent, which was so effective that most regiments remained loyal. When Bolshevik strongholds in the capital, such as the Peter and Paul Fortress, were stormed, the uprising soon collapsed. Lenin's close colleague, Leon Trotsky, gave himself up to the police (→22).

Kerensky to head new reforming regime

July 22. Alexander Kerensky has been appointed Russian prime minister and has made it clear that Russia would continue the war with Germany. Kerensky, who retains the post of War Minister, replaces Prince Lvov and he will need all his brilliance, oratory, and energy to keep the country on the rails.

The provisional government's reshuffle comes at a critical time for the Russian armies on the Galician front. German reserves have checked an offensive and counter-attacked. Influenced by Bolshevik rhetoric, whole Russian divisions are refusing to fight (→13/8).

New premier Alexander Kerensky.

1917

AUGUST

Su	Mo	Tu	We	Th	Fr	Sa
			1	2	3	4
5	6	7	8	9	10	11
12	13	14	15	16	17	18
19	20	21	22	23	24	25
26	27	28	29	30	31	

4. Washington: The Administration says any man trying to avoid conscription may be executed.

13. London: Government withdraws passports of people wishing to attend Stockholm Peace Conference.

13. Petrograd: Kerensky sends a message to King George V pledging continued Russian role in the war (→4/9).

14. Peking: New Chinese President Feng Kua-Chang declares war on the Central Powers (→15/9).

15. Petrograd: The ex-Czar and his family are removed from Petrograd, possibly to Siberia (→30/9).

17. Berlin: The Kaiser backs Pope Benedict XV's peace plan (→28).

18. Washington: Food Administrator Herbert Hoover suggests each family should save 1lb of flour a week to help the war effort (→15/9).

20. Budapest: Owing to food shortages throughout Hungary, all prisoners serving less than two years in prison are released (→19/9).

20. W. Front: French break German lines at Verdun on an 11-mile front, taking 4,000 prisoners (→7/9).

24. Houston: 17 die when black soldiers riot after a white policeman strikes a black woman (→9/10).

25. Italian Front: Italians take Monte Santo, Austrian stronghold on Isonzo front (→24/10).

25. Germany: Court martial sentences five sailors to death following a naval mutiny at Wilhelmshafen.

25. London: New honours – Order of the British Empire and Companion of Honour – are presented for the first time.

28. Washington: President Wilson rejects Pope Benedict XV's peace proposals (→9/9).

BIRTHS

6. US actor Robert Mitchum.

18. US politician Caspar Willard Weinberger.

"Sale of honours" debated in Lords

Aug 7. Growing controversy about the sale of titles was reflected in a heated House of Lords debate today. The Prime Minister, David Lloyd George, was not mentioned by name, but the recent King's Birthday Honours List which he drew up was the focus of the debate. Some peers complained that the number of honours conferred as a reward for donations to party funds is now scandalous.

In opening the debate, the Earl of Selbourne said that Liberals and Tories "are tarred with the same brush". He called for a new rule that each honours proposal must be accompanied by a declaration that no payment or promise is associated with it. The debate ended inconclusively. The Commons has not yet taken up an invitation from the Lords three years ago to force an end to improprieties.

Lloyd George: title trouble?

Pontiff in peace plan proposal

Aug 14. Pope Benedict XV has made another major bid to bring the war to an end. His detailed peace plan is already on its way to the major powers. He suggests the return of the German overseas colonies in exchange for the restoration of the occupied parts of France, Belgium and Poland. His first peace bid in 1916 failed (→17). ▷

Britons bogged down in Flanders mud

Stretcher-bearers find it hard going in the Flanders quagmire.

Aug 20. As the Third Battle of Ypres unfolds to the accompaniment of ceaseless bombardments and remorseless rainstorms, it is becoming hard to decide whether it is the German machine-gunner or the Flanders mud that is to be feared most. At the British HQ, Field Marshal Haig speaks of "successful operations by our troops" and of "the capture of a series of strong points and fortified farms". But then it is conceded that the actual ground gained can be measured in "a few hundred yards."

For the first time in the war, aeroplanes have been employed in substantial numbers over the battlefield. Today's communique speaks of fierce fighting in the air, with twelve German machines brought down and five others "driven down out of control". Twelve British planes were lost.

The launching of the offensive was preceded by the firing of the heaviest load of shell yet unloosed in the war: over four million rounds from 3,000 British guns. The bombardment, coupled with double the average rainfall, wrecked the network of streams and dykes upon which the Flanders drainage system depends.

The fields around Passchendaele ridge have been turned into a quagmire, where a man can be sucked to his death if he should slip from the duckboards. The mounting toll of men reported missing offers telling evidence of this deadly hazard.

The French have contributed some of their best fighting troops to this battle. Operating on the British flanks, they have been capturing enemy positions with skill and dispatch, moving forward in loose order, in contrast to the attempted precision of the British.

In response to the merciless rain of British shellfire, Ludendorff has devised a defence system based on machine-gun positions in pillboxes unaffected by shelling. Even a direct hit fails to smash the concrete, though the gunners inside may die of concussion.

Inevitably, questions arise as to the reason such demands are being made on the heroism and stoicism of the troops in conditions that virtually rule out any substantial gains. Haig is believed to be seeking to keep the Germans off-balance so as to prevent them from making use of the troops just released from the Eastern Front.

A huge shell crater gapes among the ruins of the shattered town of Ypres.

1917

SEPTEMBER

Su	Mo	Tu	We	Th	Fr	Sa
						1
2	3	4	5	6	7	8
9	10	11	12	13	14	15
16	17	18	19	20	21	22
23	24	25	26	27	28	29
30						

3. UK: 108 die in German air raids on the Isles of Sheppey and Thanet.

4. Petrograd: Several grand dukes are arrested for allegedly plotting counter-revolution (→ 10).

7. W. Front: Germans bomb Allied hospitals, killing many Americans (→ 27/10).

9. London: Government rejects peace plans of Pope Benedict XV (→ 21).

10. Petrograd: Kerensky dismisses army chief Kornilov, who says he will march on Petrograd and overthrow regime (→ 15).

11. UK: 200,000 women now estimated to be working on the land (→ 25/10).

15. Washington: The US sugar industry is put under the control of Food Administrator Hoover (→ 18/10).

15. Petrograd: Kerensky proclaims Russia a republic (→ 23/10).

15. Peking: China offers 300,000 soldiers to aid the Allies on the W. Front (→ 29).

15. Poland: Central Powers hand over legislative and administrative power to a new provisional government.

17. Berlin: Government asks boys of 15 to volunteer for the army (→ 31/1/18).

19. Budapest: Count Mihaly Karoly, head of the Hungarian Independence Party, opens nationalist campaign for early peace (→ 21).

21. Vienna: Austria welcomes Papal peace plan, demanding peace with freedom of the seas, disarmament and arbitration (→ 4/12).

25. Buenos Aires: Chamber of Deputies votes to cut ties with Germany in the wake of a spying scandal (→ 5/10).

29. Peking: Government issues a warrant for the arrest of Sun Yat-sen.

DEATH

27. French impressionist painter Edgar Degas (*19/7/1834).→

Degas, great painter of the ballet, dies

An atmospheric "snapshot" of the Paris Opera orchestra painted in 1868-9.

Sept 26. Edgar Degas, too blind to paint for the past ten years, living alone and given to wandering the streets, an object of pity to passers-by, has died at 83. He was the greatest master of drawing among the Impressionist generation. He never painted in the open air and sought to capture effects, not of light, but of movement.

He found his subjects both on the racecourse and in the theatre, where his studies of ballet dancers, rehearsing or resting, conveyed physical strain as well as grace.

With unromantic precision his pastels depict women bathing, dressing or working as laundresses or acrobats. His interest in photography stimulated his "snapshot" style of apparently casual composition, but he maintained: "Nothing in art must be accidental, not even movement."

Shows among the shells boost spirits

Sept 18. Entertainers, from opera singers to jugglers, have joined the war effort to boost the spirits of British "tommies". "It takes a great deal of effort," said an officer, "but we might have lost this war if it had not been for the laughter."

Shows now take place regularly along the British front. One tonight near Verey included light opera, a Scottish comedian, a Charlie Chaplin impressionist and a trick cyclist. But a popular feature of most shows is the singalong.

Popular songs such as "These Hard Times" are roared out by men who know they could all be blown to bits tomorrow. Often, the same songs are heard again – in the trenches when the men return from the brief respite offered by these shows among the shells.

Russians routed at Riga

Jubilant German soldiers celebrate their victory over the Russians at Riga.

Sept 17. The Germans, pushing hard along the Baltic coast, have driven the Russians out of Riga, the strategic port on the Dvina, and are within striking distance of the Russian capital. A communique issued by the Germans says that the Russians were pounded by a heavy artillery barrage and were then attacked by the infantry.

Troops of the 12th Russian Army counter-attacked, but they were driven off, and tonight the War Ministry in Petrograd announced that Riga had been abandoned to the enemy. Reports of the fighting suggest that the malaise affecting the Russian troops, following the abdication of the Czar, still persists. The loyalty and clan, with which the Russians once went to war is sadly missing.

Petrograd, the Russian capital, is only 350 miles from Riga across open country and it is feared that, unless the Russians stiffen their resolve and begin fighting like an army again, the Germans will soon be marching in triumph past the Winter Palace.

Czar and his family are sent to Siberia

Sept 30. Russia's former Czar, Nicholas II, and his family have been moved to Tobolsk, a small town in Western Siberia, to protect them from the Bolsheviks.

The family's move from Petrograd in secret last month was personally directed by Alexander Kerensky, Prime Minister in the Provisional Government. He is said to have told the former Czar: "The Bolsheviks are after me and then they will be after you."

Although guarded by soldiers, the Czar is living in some comfort. Local inhabitants remove their caps and cross themselves when passing the mansion where the Imperial family is being held. Two civilian commissars have just arrived from Petrograd to take charge of the captives.

Ex-Czar and family at Tobolsk, hoping for safety from Bolsheviks.

1917

OCTOBER

Su	Mo	Tu	We	Th	Fr	Sa
	1	2	3	4	5	6
7	8	9	10	11	12	13
14	15	16	17	18	19	20
21	22	23	24	25	26	27
28	29	30	31			

2. London: Government declares trade embargo on Sweden, Norway, Denmark and Holland to stop supplies getting to the Germans.

5. Lima: Peruvian parliament votes to break off diplomatic relations with Germany (→ 7).

7. Montevideo: Uruguay breaks off diplomatic relations with Germany.

9. Washington: Government approves the creation of a black division of the US Army (→ 24/5/18).

12. Berlin: The head of the German navy, Admiral von Capelle, resigns.

15. Paris: Convicted spy Mata Hari is executed.

15. London: The Board of Trade calls on people to cut down unnecessary motoring for pleasure.

18. Washington: Food Administrator Hoover launches campaign for lower food prices (→ 16/1/18).

18. Belgium: German sailors at Ostend refuse to go on board submarines.

20. London: Eight Zeppelins kill 27 in an air raid; four are shot down over France on the homeward journey.

23. New York: Police foil a Sinn Fein plot to stage another Irish rebellion next Easter (→ 27/2/18).

23. Petrograd: Two days after Lenin's return to the city, the Bolshevik Central Committee votes to start an armed uprising against Kerensky's government (→ 7/11).

25. Washington: President Wilson makes a speech in favour of women's suffrage (→ 1/1/18).

27. W. Front: US troops fire their first shots of the war (→ 6/11).

31. Palestine: British troops capture Beersheba, taking 1,800 Turkish prisoners (→ 18/11).

BIRTH

21. US jazz trumpeter Dizzy Gillespie (†6/1/93).

Italian front folds: 293,000 captured

Italian soldiers haul a piece of heavy artillery into position on a hill during the disastrous campaign.

Oct 31. The Italian army has collapsed in a disastrous defeat in the mountainous country around Caporetto. German troops, advancing through the rain and snow, took the Italian Second Army by surprise, and routed it.

The Germans used gas, which was followed by a tremendous barrage from artillery batteries whose presence was not even suspected. The Italians broke and ran before the terrific German onslaught and the Italian Commander in Chief, General Cadorna, has been forced to withdraw to the Piave River, only 15 miles east of Venice, where he has been frantically establishing a new defence line against the Germans and Austrians, who are now streaming triumphantly down from the mountains.

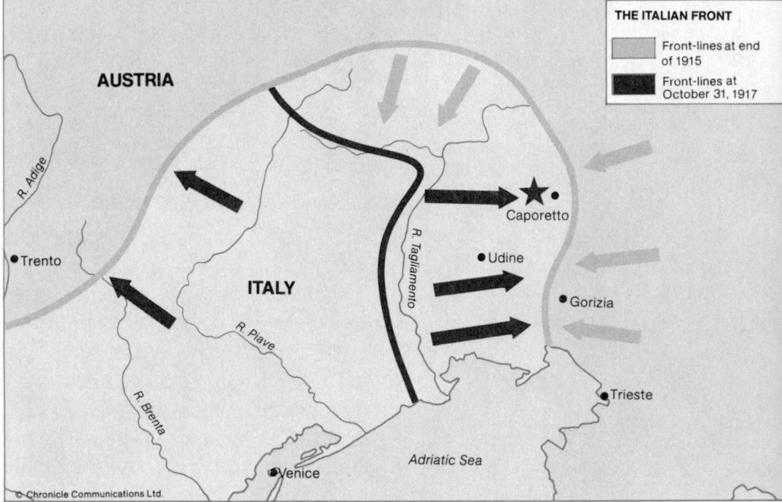

The Italian casualties have been very high. Some 10,000 have been killed and 30,000 wounded. The Austrians are claiming to have taken huge quantities of material. What is even more disturbing is that something like half a million Italian soldiers have thrown away their weapons and fled. The military police have set up road blocks to stop the deserters.

The extent of the trauma caused by this defeat may be judged by this communique just issued in Rome which says: "The bravery displayed by our soldiers in so many memorable battles fought and won in the past two and a half years gives our supreme command a pledge that this time too the army, to which the honour and safety of the country are entrusted, will know how to fulfill its duty."

The fact of the matter remains that the Italians have suffered a crushing defeat and their army is in disarray.

Labour Party plans serious bid for power

Oct 8. Labour will field at least 300 candidates in the first post-war General Election. The national executive stated today that it means to take full advantage of the Representation of the People Act, which will render millions of women eligible to vote for the first time. Labour expects a huge boost.

At the last election in 1910 the party collected 372,000 votes with 50 candidates standing and 42 elected. A high-powered party committee is to prepare a scheme of reorganisation and what will amount to a new party constitution for adoption next year. It is looking to the Co-operative Movement to provide much new finance.

An executive member said hopefully: "It will come as a great shock to the other parties". Labour has already embarked on an elaborate scheme for political organisation and education of women through the Unions and the Co-operative movement. This activity is expected to provoke equivalent action by their opponents so that the interparty truce may soon end.

Chequers to be new country seat for PM

Oct 5. The Chequers mansion and estate in the Chiltern Hills is to be used and maintained in perpetuity as the official country residence of Prime Ministers. This gift to the nation was announced today by the owner, Sir Arthur Lee.

Mr Lloyd George told him "Future generations of Prime Ministers will think of you with gratitude". Chequers is 35 miles from London near Great Missenden and there is a golf-course nearby.

1917

NOVEMBER

Su	Mo	Tu	We	Th	Fr	Sa
				1	2	3
4	5	6	7	8	9	10
11	12	13	14	15	16	17
18	19	20	21	22	23	24
25	26	27	28	29	30	

1. Norway: The Government protests to Germany over the sinking of neutral vessels.

5. London: The War Office agrees to supply British troops in France with Christmas puddings.

6. W. Front: Canadian troops capture the village of Passchendaele (→ 30).

13. London: Bankers and Chambers of Commerce call for the decimalisation of British currency.

15. London: Government announces it will censor all "pacifist" publications (→ 22/1).

16. Russia: Bolshevik troops take Moscow (→ 19).

18. Palestine: British troops capture Jaffa (→ 9/12).

18. Finland: Widespread violence accompanies socialist-led general strike (→ 9/12).

19. Petrograd: Revolutionary Diplomatic Committee is created, headed by foreign minister Leon Trotsky.→

23. Petrograd: The Bolshevik government begins publishing secret treaties between the Allies (→ 26).

24. New York: German violinist Fritz Kreisler announces retirement for the duration of the war.

26. Petrograd: Lenin offers an armistice to Germany and Austria (→ 29).

29. Paris: Great Allied Council meets to discuss future war strategy.

29. Petrograd: Peace talks with Germany open after the Kaiser agrees to a truce (→ 1/12).

30. W. Front: Arrival in France of the US "Rainbow Division", representing every state, under the command of Colonel Douglas MacArthur.

BIRTH

19. Indian prime minister Shrimata Indira Gandhi, nee Nehru (†31/10/84).

DEATH

17. French sculptor Auguste Rodin (*12/11/1840).

Kerensky ousted in Bolshevik coup

Nov 7. Russia's Bolsheviks overthrew the Provisional Government in Petrograd today in a sudden and virtually bloodless coup. The country's second revolution in eight months has brought Vladimir Lenin and Leon Trotsky to power and may easily be the end of any hopes for a liberal democratic Russia.

The Bolshevik takeover began when armed squads of revolutionaries occupied railway stations, post offices, telephone exchanges and banks as well as the cruiser Aurora, which flew the red flag and was anchored in the river Neva opposite the Winter Palace.

Several provisional government ministers – but not Alexander Kerensky, who had gone south to try and raise help from the army – were meeting in the building, protected by a women's battalion and a troop of cadets.

After the Aurora fired a single blank shell, and two shells fired from another battery struck the Winter Palace, the ministers gave up and Red Guards swarmed into the building.

The Bolsheviks are already presenting the event as an epic battle, but life in Petrograd has been largely undisturbed by the coup with shops, restaurants and theatres open and public transport continuing to run.

It remains to be seen whether the Bolsheviks, a minority led by emigres, will win the support of the rest of the country. But they have a popular slogan – "Peace, land, bread, and all power to the Soviets".

Soldiers in the courtyard of the Winter Palace in Petrograd

Jubilant crowds celebrate the Bolshevik seizure of power.

Allies concerned that Bolsheviks will pull Russia out of war

Nov 21. The "peace offensive", mounted by Lenin and his associates in Russia, is causing increasing concern, because of the adverse effect it could have on the military situation in France.

This week the Admiralty in London picked up a wireless message referring to a decision by the so-called Workers' and Peasants' government to begin demobilisation of the army, thus rendering Russia helpless before the Germans.

Now Leon Trotsky, Lenin's "Foreign Minister", or Commissar for Foreign Affairs as he describes himself, has delivered a note to foreign embassies in Petrograd, in which he calls for "a democratic peace" on the basis of no annexations, no indemnities and self-determination for all nations. He has proposed an immediate truce and the opening of peace negotiations.

Lord Robert Cecil, assistant Foreign Secretary, has responded in these terms: "I do not believe that the extremists in Petrograd really represent the views of the Russian people. I do not believe the Russian people will approve of the actions of those who arrest their generals and open peace negotiations with the enemy across the trenches."

The war-weariness of the Russian people is acknowledged in the West, but there is great anxiety at the prospect of the Germans being able to move large numbers of men from the East to mount an offensive in the West.

Balfour unveils plan for Jewish homeland

Nov 9. Britain is to give full support to the Jews in establishing a permanent national homeland in Palestine. A declaration of intent, drafted by Arthur Balfour, the Foreign Secretary and former Prime Minister, has been communicated to Baron Rothschild as the Zionists' representative.

The text declares: "His Majesty's Government view with favour the establishment in Palestine of a national home for the Jewish people, and will use their best endeavours to facilitate the achievement of this object, it being clearly understood that nothing shall be done which may prejudice the civil and religious rights of existing non-Jewish communities in Palestine, or the rights and political status enjoyed in any other country."

Zionist leader Chaim Weizmann.

The War Cabinet under Lloyd George believes that the declaration will encourage Zionists to throw their full weight behind the Allied effort. Until the recent dramatic events in Russia, it had been expected that Mr Balfour's declaration would be followed by the Zionists sending a mission of leading members of the Jewish community to Petrograd to urge more vigorous prosecution of the war.

Dr Chaim Weizmann and British Zionists will certainly be strengthened in their resolve to build up the existing community in Palestine. At present it consists of 50,000 Jews living in the Holy Land populated by half a million Arabs. Dr Weizmann earlier this year expressed the view that Britain would protect and support a Jewish Palestine.

Last spring Lord Robert Cecil, former assistant Foreign Secretary, informed Zionist leaders that the British Government would welcome a firm statement from World Jewry of their desire that this country should become their protecting power in Palestine.

As the collapse of the Ottoman Empire is heralded by the British advance towards Jerusalem, it is considered to be in the national interest to cooperate with the Zionists to secure Britain's position in the area.

An unscheduled stop for a tank that took part in the Cambrai offensive.

1917

DECEMBER

Su	Mo	Tu	We	Th	Fr	Sa
						1
2	3	4	5	6	7	8
9	10	11	12	13	14	15
16	17	18	19	20	21	22
23	24	25	26	27	28	29
30	31					

1. Washington: President Wilson protests against the Russian armistice plan (→7).

3. London: The Government refuses to recognise or communicate with the Bolshevik regime in Russia (→22).

5. Vienna: Emperor Karl says he is ready for any peace that guarantees the integrity of the Habsburg monarchy (→7).

7. Washington: President Wilson declares war on Austria with the almost unanimous approval of Congress (→15/1/18).

9. Helsingfors: The Finnish government demands the withdrawal of Russian troops (→6/1/18).

10. Stockholm: Nobel Prizes awarded to Charles Glover Barkla (UK, Chemistry); to Karl Adolph Gjellerup and Henrik Pontoppidan (Denmark, Literature), and to the International Red Cross Committee (Switzerland, Peace). No other prizes.

12. France: Ex-premier Joseph Caillaux is arrested for "intelligence with the enemy" because of advocacy of peace negotiations (→14/1/18).

18. Washington: The Senate votes in favour of prohibition.

23. Australia: Referendum opposes introduction of conscription.

30. Central America: Earthquakes wreck Guatemala City.

DEATH

17. First British woman doctor Elizabeth Garrett Anderson (*9/6/1836).

HITS OF 1917

For me and my gal.

Goodbye-ee.

QUOTE OF THE YEAR

"The world must be made safe for democracy."
President Wilson, addressing Congress two days before declaring war on Germany.

New Bolshevik Government begins peace negotiations

Dec 22. Peace talks opened today at Brest-Litovsk between Russia's new Bolshevik regime and delegates of the central powers led by the German Foreign Minister, Baron von Kuhlmann.

The Baron spoke of his great honour in presiding over a meeting to re-establish "a state of peace and friendship between Russia and the powers". But the Russians know the Germans intend to impose harsh conditions. Lenin has sworn to fulfil his pledge to make peace and his view may well prevail, but it does not meet with the approval of all his comrades.

Trotsky, for example, told a meeting in Petrograd yesterday that: "We did not overthrow the Czar and the bourgeoisie in order to fall on our knees before the German Kaiser and beg for peace ... We invoke all to a holy war against Imperialism in all countries."

It seems doubtful, however, that the demoralised Russian army could be made to fight again. After a week of armistice the war, which led to disaster in the field and revolution at home, would seem to be over for Russia.

It is a prospect which the Allies view with disgust and fear: disgust that the Bolsheviks should have betrayed Russia's allies, and fear that German divisions will be released to be thrown against the Allies on the Western Front.

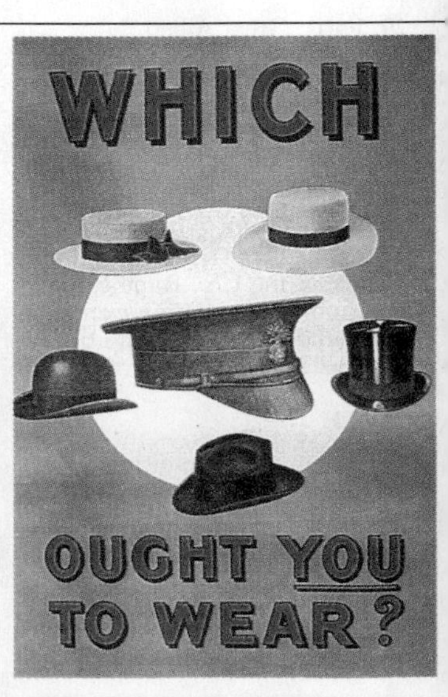

British take Jerusalem

The occupation of Jerusalem is proclaimed on the steps of the old citadel.

Dec 9. Jubilation in London greeted the announcement that Jerusalem had today surrendered to General Edmund Allenby. For the first time since the War began, church bells rang and Protestants and Roman Catholics celebrated with a "Te Deum" while Dr Hertz, the Chief Rabbi, declared: "Who knows that today's thrilling victory may form as glorious a landmark as any in the history of mankind".

In swift final moves General Allenby's Empire forces surrounded Jerusalem. First units into the city were Home Counties and Welsh regiments advancing from Bethlehem. London infantry and yeomanry completed the encirclement by an attack on enemy positions to the west.

The fall of Jerusalem marked the climax of a brilliant offensive against the Turks, which began last October with the capture of Beersheba. Martial law is to be declared and guards have been placed over Christian Holy Places; Indian army Moslems are watching over Moslem shrines.

Arts: Rodin dies, heaped with honours

A memorial service was held in Westminster Abbey for **Auguste Rodin**, the greatest sculptor of his time, who died aged 77 at his home outside Paris.

Rodin was elected to succeed **Whistler** as President of the Society of Painters, Sculptors and Engravers. In 1907 he came to Oxford to receive an honorary doctorate. He wore his velvet doctor's cap when Edward VII came to visit him at his studio at Meudon. In 1914 he presented 21 sculptures to the Victoria and Albert Museum.

He has left the contents of his studio to France to be shown in the Musee Rodin. His work was always controversial. Calais did not welcome his group, "The Burghers of Calais" and "The Kiss" was declared unfit for public exhibition at the Chicago World Fair.

His bust of Balzac in his gown was rejected and compared to "a toad in a sack". Rodin withdrew it and placed it in his garden. Bernard Shaw, who sat for him, said he was "the only man in whose presence I feel really humble". Last January Rodin married his companion for over 52 years, Rose Beuret, who died two weeks later.

Another riotous first night in Paris greeted "Parade", a circus ballet by **Jean Cocteau**, designed by **Picasso**. It is choreographed by **Leonide Massine** to music by the eccentric **Erik Satie**, who includes a typewriter in the score. In the programme the, poet **Apollinaire** has described the work as "sur-realisme".

In Holland a new art movement known as "De Stijl" has produced "constructive" painting by **Piet Mondrian**, in which arrangements of rectangular blocks of primary colour are said to penetrate the "inner structure of reality".

In the London theatre "The Maid of the Mountains" is challenging the popularity of "Chu Chin Chow". **J.M. Barrie's** new play is "Dear Brutus".

Mary Pickford, cinema sweetheart.

Pro-German coup succeeds in Portugal

Dec 12. Portugal's president, Bernardino Machado, is under arrest in Lisbon following a coup d'etat by pro-German army officers led by General Sidonio Paes.

The change of government in Portugal has serious implications for the Allied war effort. If Paes decided to switch sides and fight alongside Germany, a combined Portuguese-German effort in Africa would pose a serious threat to the security of British and captured German territories.

Closer to home, the Royal Navy would come under greater pressure from the Germans if their fleet were allowed to operate from Portuguese ports; bases in Gibraltar and Malta would be especially vulnerable.

Machado brought Portugal into the war as an ally of France and Britain in March 1916. This was ten months after a popular revolt overthrew the previous military dictatorship of General Pimenta de Castro, who had seized power in January 1915 after the Portuguese National Assembly voted to join the Allies. Castro was head of the same pro-German faction which has regained power under Paes.

Ex-premier Alfonso Costa has formed a provisional government, and Paes is shortly expected to take over as President. One of his first tasks will be to end the rioting in some cities against the high price of staple foods, such as bread and potatoes.

"We are making a new world", Paul Nash's 1917 vision of conflict.

1918

JANUARY

Su	Mo	Tu	We	Th	Fr	Sa
		1	2	3	4	5
6	7	8	9	10	11	12
13	14	15	16	17	18	19
20	21	22	23	24	25	26
27	28	29	30	31		

1. London: The US Women's Suffrage group sends a New Year goodwill message to Queen Mary (→ 10).

2. London: Lord Rothermere is appointed head of the Air Council.

6. Helsingfors: Two days after Russia, Germany recognises the independence of Finland (→ 12).

10. London: The House of Lords approves the Representation of the People Bill, giving married women over 30 the vote (→ 30).

10. Washington: The House of Representatives votes in favour of women's suffrage (→ 6/2).

12. Brest-Litovsk: Russia and Germany recognise the independence of the Ukrainian Republic (→ 5/2).

14. Paris: Ex-Premier Caillaux is jailed for "treason" – advocating a negotiated peace with Germany (→ 23/4/20).

15. Austrian Empire: General strikes take hold in Prague and Budapest as workers' peace movements gather pace.

16. Washington: President Wilson orders all except food industries to shut down for five days and then every Monday until 25 March to save coal (→ 4/2).

22. London: Government orders restaurants and eating houses not to serve meat on two days each week.→

30. London: Commons rejects Lords' amendment to Representation of the People Bill providing for proportional representation (→ 6/2).

31. UK: 103 sailors die and two submarines are lost in a series of collisions during a Royal Navy night exercise in the Firth of Forth.

31. Berlin: Martial law is declared following a series of strikes led by socialist Spartacists (→ 3/2).

BIRTHS

15. Egyptian leader Gamal Abdel Nasser (†28/9/70).

26. Rumanian leader Nicolae Ceausescu (†25/12/89).

Wilson's 14 points for post-war peace

Jan 9. In a speech to Congress yesterday President Wilson defined US war aims in 14 points. He spoke after an Inter-Allied conference failed to agree on their aims.

Among the points (see below) the President included open diplomacy, free trade and national self-determination – all long part of the agenda of British and American liberals. Many of his points had also been put forward by a secret policy group in New York, known as the Inquiry and led by a young journalist, Walter Lippmann.

The president's aim is to turn Germans against their government and to push Allied governments towards liberal peace terms.

Wilson with his 14 points for peace.

1. Open covenants of peace.
2. Absolute freedom of navigation upon the sea ... in peace and war.
3. Removal of trade barriers.
4. National armaments to be reduced to lowest point consistent with domestic safety.
5. Free, open-minded and impartial adjustment of colonial claims.
6. Evacuation of all Russian territory.
7. Evacuation of Belgium.
8. All French territory to be freed and Alsace-Lorraine to be returned.
9. Frontiers of Italy to be readjusted along lines of nationality.
10. Peoples of Austria-Hungary to be offered autonomous development.
11. Rumania, Serbia and Montenegro to be evacuated.
12. Turkish portions of Ottoman Empire to be assured of sovereignty.
13. Independent Polish state to be established with access to the sea.
14. An association of nations to be formed to guarantee independence and territorial integrity.

Red Army imposes people's diktat

Jan 28. Lenin has moved swiftly to consolidate the Bolshevik grip on Russia by creating both a Red Army and a security police force. Theoretically the army's task is to protect the country from external enemies, but Lenin is happy to use it internally. Nine days ago he used it to dissolve the Duma after it had rejected his motion to form a government of worker's councils.

He also established a body called the Cheka to "combat counter-revolution, speculation and sabotage". Following the dissolution of the Duma, the Cheka is arresting prominent public figures.

State forests to avert timber crisis

Jan 8. Two million acres of Britain are to be planted with trees under a state-sponsored forestry scheme. A report issued today proposes a Forestry Commission to ensure that in future Britain will have sufficient home timber for military and commercial needs. The war has exposed Britain's reliance on imported timber. Because of agricultural changes, only five per cent of Britain was wooded in 1914.

Meat's off two days a week as rationing begins to bite in UK

Jan 25. Meat will be off the menu today in all the best restaurants in town, for this is the start of the government's new two-meatless-days-a-week policy designed to deal with a grave food shortage.

London restaurants are facing up to this deprivation in a festive spirit. At the Piccadilly Hotel today's lunch menu is headed "Meatless Day" and offers a choice of four egg and six fish dishes. In the Ritz the emphasis is on fish, with whitebait, cod, grilled herring and, of course, lobster on offer. Many restaurants will be offering that new delicacy of the times – vegetable sausages.

The new regulations do not apply where a full meal costs 1s 2d or less. Those prepared to visit the cheaper establishments can have three ounces of beef or mutton and save money at the same time (→ 8/2).

Women workers handle some of the paperwork generated by rationing.

1918

FEBRUARY

Su	Mo	Tu	We	Th	Fr	Sa
					1	2
3	4	5	6	7	8	9
10	11	12	13	14	15	16
17	18	19	20	21	22	23
24	25	26	27	28		

1. Paris: 45 people are killed in a bombing raid by four squadrons of German Gotha aeroplanes.

3. Berlin: The local army chief orders strikers to return to work or be shot.

4. London: London County and Westminster Bank announces merger with Parr's Bank as Westminster Bank.

5. Petrograd: The government proclaims the separation of the Russian Church and state.

6. London: The Representation of the People Act receives the Royal Assent, giving vote to married women over 30.

8. London: Government announces London and Home Counties meat ration of 20oz per adult per week (→ 25).

11. Washington: Wilson tells Congress there can be no peace with Germany and Austria based on the fundamentals of Prussian autocracy.

11. London: Chaim Weizmann is appointed to head a commission investigating the Jewish colonies in Palestine (→ 7/3).

14. New York: Appearance of "Swanee", first successful song by 19-year-old George Gershwin, Russian-Jewish immigrants' son.

14. Warsaw: Demonstrations occur against the transfer of Polish territories to the Ukraine (→ 3/6).

15. Petrograd: Russia cuts loose from its former Entente Allies (→ 20).

24. Estonia: Independence from Russia is declared (→ 5/3).

25. London: Meat, butter and margarine rationing begins today (→ 7/3).

27. Ireland: Lawlessness is reported to be widespread (→ 9/3).

27. UK: British hospital ship "Glenart Castle" sunk by U-boat in the Bristol Channel.

DEATH

6. Austrian painter Gustav Klimt (*14/7/1862).

Trotsky blows hot and cold on peace plan

German troops on the burning streets of the Russian town Szawle.

Feb 20. The armistice on the Eastern Front ended at noon today and the Germans immediately attacked the demoralised Russian army to force the Bolsheviks to accept their humiliating terms.

First reports indicate that the Germans are marching virtually unopposed into Estonia and are threatening Petrograd. Their move comes as the climax to a chaotic series of moves by the Bolsheviks.

With the peace talks at Brest-Litovsk at an impasse because the Bolsheviks could not bring themselves to accept the German terms, Trotsky sent an amazing message by wireless to the Germans. In it he said: "We are not signing the peace of landlords and capitalists." But at the same time he asserted: "We cannot, and will not, and must not continue a war begun by Czars and capitalists."

This was followed by rumours that the Bolshevik regime had fallen, but reports from Petrograd say that Lenin, by casting his own vote, defeated Trotsky and is determined to have peace at any price.

Trotsky sent another wireless message yesterday, this time offering to accept the German terms. Meanwhile the Germans march on across the snow-covered land of northern Russia.

Advert for "Zog" cleaner.

Jericho falls to Australian cavalry

Feb 21. Australian cavalry took Jericho first thing this morning. It was pouring with rain and through the mist the mounted troops were disappointed to find that the city whose walls once crumbled at the blast of Joshua's trumpets is now a mere village.

But it is still a place of strategic importance only five miles from the river Jordan. The fall of Jericho deprives the Turks of their advance base for the defence of Palestine. It is the road centre by which their left flank received its supplies from the Hedfaz railway. General Allenby can now use the road parallel to the river as an axis of his advance north upon Syria.

Britain salutes her colonial heroes.

Labour plans state control of industries

Feb 26. For the first time the Labour Party today formally put itself on the side of Socialism. A special one-day party conference approved a new constitution, declaring common ownership and State control as objectives. It also set up a nationwide network of constituency organisations in readiness for the first elections after the war.

The constitution gives the trade unions the biggest say in running the party in return for dropping reservations about Socialism. Commented one delegate "It need only be a thing of the future".

The fourth clause in the constitution pledges Labour to secure "common ownership of the means of production and the best obtainable system of popular administration and control of each industry and service".

There were complaints by delegates from socialist societies that Arthur Henderson, the party secretary, had left the wording of this clause too ambiguous. However, Mr Henderson argued that organisation was more important, and that the vital task was to attract the millions of women over 30 shortly to get the vote for the first time. "Enormous opportunities open before us", he declared enthusiastically.

1918

MARCH

Su	Mo	Tu	We	Th	Fr	Sa
					1	2
3	4	5	6	7	8	9
10	11	12	13	14	15	16
17	18	19	20	21	22	23
24	25	26	27	28	29	30
31						

3. Turkey: The entire male population of the Armenian town of Samsun is massacred by Moslems.

5. Russia: Moscow is declared the new Russian capital in replacement for Petrograd (→7).

7. London: Andrew Bonar Law asks the Commons for another war loan of £600 million (→13).

7. Moscow: The Bolsheviks change their name to the Russian Communist Party (→5/4).

7. New York: The Palestine Restoration Fund completes plans for a new Jewish university in Jerusalem (→27/4).

9. London: New Military Service Bill raises maximum conscription age to 50 and introduces conscription for Ireland (→17).

17. Ireland: Police and Sinn Fein supporters clash in Belfast as Eamon de Valera attempts to hold a public meeting in defiance of a military proclamation (→23/4).

20. London: Government announces rationing of coal, gas and electricity; theatres are told to close at 10.30 pm, restaurants at 10.00 pm (→24/4).

21. UK: Mrs Hugh Peel's Poethlyn wins the Grand National.

25. US: The new Browning light machine gun with 1,000 yard range is tested successfully at Camp Dix, New Jersey.

26. W. Front: General Ferdinand Foch is appointed commander-in-chief of Allied forces in France (→31).

26. Turkey: British-led troops oust the Turks on the River Euphrates (→24/9).

29. Paris: 75 die and 90 are hurt when a German shell hits a church during a Good Friday service (→26/6).

DEATH

25. French composer Claude Debussy (*22/8/1862).→

Uneasy peace for Russia

March 3. The Bolshevik regime now governing Russia signed one of the most humiliating peace treaties in the history of warfare today when it capitulated to the Central Powers' terms at Brest-Litovsk.

Under these terms Russia surrenders Poland, Lithuania, Courland, Riga and part of Belorussia to Germany. In the Caucasus it cedes Kars, Batum and Ardahan to Turkey. It acknowledges the independence of the German-protected Ukraine. And the Bolsheviks also agreed to pay 3,000 million roubles in reparation.

The Germans are hailing this treaty as a great victory, but the peace promises to be uneasy. The Revolution and the overthrow of the 300-year-old Romanov dynasty has set primeval forces on the move in Russia, which will not be easily contained.

Russia is also faced with the anger of the Allies she has deserted. The Times, responding to delegates at the Soviet Congress who spoke of "the coming world revolution", argues that "the remedy for Bolshevism is bullets". And in the US the New York Times proclaims "Bolsheviki Yield Russia's Riches to Berlin".

The victory is not as complete as the Germans claim; they must still keep substantial forces in the east. But the troop trains have already started to roll to the west, which is exactly what the commanders of the Allied forces in France were hoping to avoid.

Debussy, one of the great innovators of music, has died

Debussy, by Marcel Baschat.

March 25. The French composer Claude Debussy died today of cancer. Born in 1862, Debussy's scanty formal education included piano lessons with the mother-in-law of poet Paul Verlaine. In Paris he befriended many Impressionist artists and Symbolist writers such as Mallarme; his music shows their influence and that of oriental music, which he heard at the 1889 Paris Exposition.

Conservative critics dislike Debussy's modal and whole-tone harmonies and his use of block chords; they panned his "Prelude a l'apres midi d'un Faune" (1894) as "formless". But there are countless admirers of his warm, delicate and lyrical style, and younger composers such as Stravinsky recognise him as one of music's great innovators.

School leaving age is raised to 14

March 13. British MPs tonight voted to raise the school-leaving age to 14 for all children. Mr H.A.L. Fisher, the Education Minister said in the Commons that young people had the right to an adequate education. The Education Bill which had its second reading today also proposes to institute compulsory part-time education in "continuation schools". Mr Fisher said the state had a duty to end the present wastage of "character ability and physique".

1918

APRIL

Su	Mo	Tu	We	Th	Fr	Sa
	1	2	3	4	5	6
7	8	9	10	11	12	13
14	15	16	17	18	19	20
21	22	23	24	25	26	27
28	29	30				

1. US: The first day of daylight saving is claimed as a success by US business.

2. Canada: Martial law is declared in Quebec as the leaders of the recent anti-conscription riots are arrested.

6. Far East: British and Japanese troops land at Vladivostock, one day after the arrival of US marines (→ 8).

8. Moscow: Lenin threatens to declare war on Japan because of the landings at Vladivostock (→ 26).

11. Vienna: Emperor Karl, in a peace offer to France, supports French claims on Alsace-Lorraine (→ 14/9).

14. US: The release of Charlie Chaplin's latest film "A Dog's Life".

18. London: New Military Service Bill receives the Royal Assent (→ 23).

19. Rome: Italy tells the Allies that it has sent troops to fight at the Western Front (→ 10/5).

21. Paris: The French Ministry of Provisions encourages people to eat horse meat (→ 11/9).

22. London: The Budget puts up taxes and abolishes the Penny Post (→ 8/5).

23. North Sea: British forces raid the Belgian seaports of Zeebrugge and Ostend, bottling up the two submarine bases (→ 10/5).

26. Moscow: The Soviet government establishes diplomatic relations with Germany (→ 27).

27. Petrograd: Grand Duke Alexis Nikolaievich is named ruler of Russia by the leaders of an aristocratic counter-revolution (→ 30).

27. Jerusalem: Chaim Weizmann explains the aims of the Jewish Zionist movement (→ 25/8).

30. Moscow: The Soviet government reinstitutes military service (→ 2/5).

BIRTH

25. US jazz singer Ella Fitzgerald.

‍erman troops hammer the Allies

‍ierman troops sweep all before them in their successful breakthrough.

‍Iarch 31. Joined by reinforce-ɪents from the now inactive East-rn Front and employing entirely ɪew tactics, Erich von Ludendorff ɪas delivered a smashing blow at ɪe Allied lines in France. Three ɪillion men are involved in the ffensive in the hope of achieving ictory before US troops arrive. In 40-mile advance, he has taken 0,000 prisoners.

The British line in the Arras sec-or has been shattered and Ludendorff seems about to realise his aim of rolling the British back to the Channel. At this critical moment, Ferdinand Foch, chief of the French General Staff, has taken over Allied operations.

The Germans struck after a short bombardment of high explosive, gas and smoke shells; then, instead of a massive infantry charge, they sent in shock troops to probe for weak spots to be exploited by infantry combat teams.

‍K "Tank Week" raises £138 million

‍Iarch 13. In a whirlwind "Tank Veek" to boost war savings, over 138 million has been raised, over alf of it in London. Bonar Law, ɔhancellor of the Exchequer, was heered when he announced the fig-res in the House of Commons.

Special "Tank Banks" were open-d in Trafalgar Square and other arts of the capital. At Marlbor-ugh House Queen Alexandra the ɔueen Mother received the sum of 387. 10s. 10d collected by child-en of the Queen Alexandra eague; she despatched her cheque or that sum by pigeon post to the ɔity "Tank Bank". Since last)ctober over £570 million has een raised in savings campaigns.

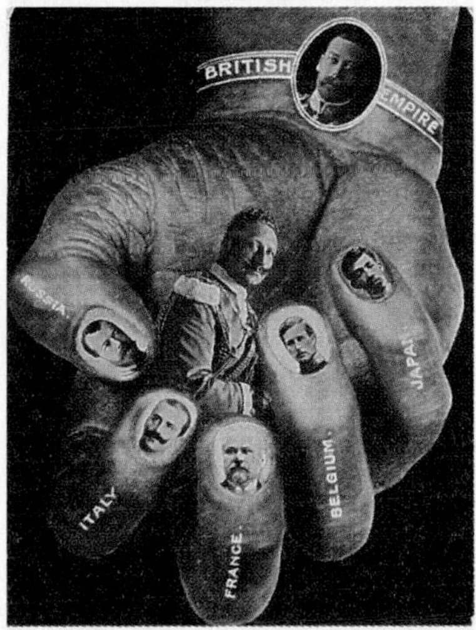

The Allies tighten their grip.

Red Baron shot down in flames

April 22. Germany's most feared pilot, the Red Baron Manfred von Richthofen, was shot from the skies and killed yesterday during the second Battle of the Somme.

German dignitaries granted him high military honours at the funeral held at the site of his death today. The Red Baron, named after his red Fokker triplane, destroyed a record 80 Allied aircraft in less than two years of fighting. He was hated by the British pilots. One said: "I hope he roasted all the way down."

His squadron, Richthofen's Circus, gained a reputation as deadly marksmen following his advice of waiting for the enemy to advance before firing.

Von Richthofen: the "Red Baron".

Irish protest at conscription plans

April 23. All work was suspended in Ireland yesterday as a protest against conscription. The trains did not run; the shops did not open. All the leading Irish nationalist politicians attended a Sinn Fein rally in Dublin where conscription was condemned as "declaring war on the Irish nation".

In Cork, 20,000 people signed an anti-conscription pledge after hearing Fr. Mathew, a Franciscan friar, lead the attack on plans to extend conscription to Ireland. "It would be in direct violation of the rights of small nations to self-determination, what the English say they're fighting for," he said. ▷

Royal Air Force formed to wreak revenge

No. 1 Squadron, Royal Air Force, with their S.E.5a aircraft.

April 1. The Royal Flying Corps and the Royal Naval Air Service were merged today into a new Royal Air Force, which seems to have been formed more out of a desire for revenge against the German raids on London than for any strategic or tactical reasons.

The new Chief of Air Staff, Lord Trenchard, has himself told army commanders in France that ministers are "quite off their heads as to the future possibilities of aeronautics for ending the war". He has warned the Cabinet not to be too optimistic about the capabilities of the new combined service.

Last year's air raids on London, which killed hundreds and dealt a blow to national pride, are behind the birth of the new RAF. They led to an inquiry by General Smuts into the lack of co-ordination by the RFC and RNAS. He pointed to rivalries and wastefulness, but also caught the mood of the time that, come what may, something had to be done.

Haig issues "Backs to the wall" call

April 13. As Ludendorff broadened his offensive and broke through the Allied lines at Ypres and further north, Sir Douglas Haig, the British C-in-C, this week delivered a personal message to all ranks: "Every position must be held to the last man: there must be no retirement. With our backs to the wall and believing in the justice of our cause, each one of us must fight on to the end."

In three weeks the Allies have lost 400,000 men, the Germans rather fewer, though most of their losses were elite shock troops who cannot readily be replaced.

The movement of Americans has been a closely kept secret and it was only revealed last night that substantial numbers have arrived in the British sector as much-needed reinforcements.

Portuguese troops, in action on the front opposite Neuve Chapelle, were subjected to a storm of gunfire that overwhelmed their defences.

Allied troops: the road to victory.

From the German HQ at Spa, the Kaiser has issued a rallying call to his army: "Everyone out here staking everything; everyone knows and trusts we shall win everything."

1918

MAY

Su	Mo	Tu	We	Th	Fr	Sa
			1	2	3	4
5	6	7	8	9	10	11
12	13	14	15	16	17	18
19	20	21	22	23	24	25
26	27	28	29	30	31	

2. Finland: Russian Red Guards in the south of the country are driven back by Finnish and German troops (→4).

4. Russia: Reported that "Nicholas Romanov and his wife" are now at Ekaterinburg (→13).

7. Managua: Nicaragua declares war on Germany and its allies.

8. London: Government takes control of the London Central Markets (→17).

9. Ireland: The British military commander-in-chief resigns.

10. W. Front: Reported that Amiens has been completely destroyed and that thousands have died from German mustard gas (→13).

13. Moscow: Reported that the government has ordered the trial of ex-Czar Nicholas (→30).

15. US: Airmail service is established between New York and Washington, cost 24c per ounce of mail.

17. London: Government abolishes compulsory meatless days (→18/6).

18. Ireland: 500 Sinn Fein members are arrested and imprisoned, including Eamon de Valera (→3/6).

24. New York: Reported that shortage of conscription age white men means hotels could take on black waiters.

25. Germany: Two troops of Bavarian cavalry are hanged for refusing to go to the Western Front.

26. Russia: Georgia and Armenia declare themselves independent (→26/6).

29. W. Front: German troops take Soissons and threaten Rheims as the Allied centre is forced back (→6/6).

30. Moscow: Martial law is declared (→13/6).

DEATH

14. US publisher and sports patron James Gordon Bennett (*10/5/1841).

A smokescreen of fireworks fails to save Navy raid

May 10. One of the most risky operations of the war ended in failure tonight. The navy planned to sink the cruiser "Vindictive", filled with concrete, at the mouth of Ostend Harbour to prevent the Germans using it, but the ship ran aground at the last minute.

The operation was a follow-up to last month's major raid on nearby Zeebrugge when several blockships were sunk across the mouth of the canal and harbour to prevent it being used by U-Boats, which leave the Belgian port every day to attack Allied shipping.

Plans for that attack had been under consideration since 1914, but all were rejected because of fears of the devastating power of the 26 German batteries, totalling 229 guns, along the coastline.

The first attack was led by the "Vindictive" and two specially-converted Mersey ferry boats with a draught so shallow they would avoid the unmarked sandbanks surrounding the harbour. At the same time an ageing submarine packed with explosives rammed the harbour wall to prevent German reinforcements arriving.

The operation was carefully rehearsed with a specially formed battalion of Royal Marines practising in Dover. Wing Commander F.A. Brock, of the firework firm, developed a new type of smokescreen to shield the fleet from gunfire as it approached the Belgian shore.

1918

JUNE

Su	Mo	Tu	We	Th	Fr	Sa
						1
2	3	4	5	6	7	8
9	10	11	12	13	14	15
16	17	18	19	20	21	22
23	24	25	26	27	28	29
30						

3. London: The Government calls for 50,000 Irish volunteers amid protests against planned Irish call-up (→20).

3. Helsinki: The Finnish parliament ratifies a peace treaty with Germany.

3. US: Nine ships are sunk by German submarines off the Atlantic coast (→9/10).

3. Paris: The UK, France and Italy agree to the declaration of an independent Polish state.

6. W. Front: US marines attack Germans near Chateau Thierry, taking 100 prisoners (→18).

13. Russia: The Soviet government and the Ukraine call a halt to hostilities (→17).

17. Berlin: Germany is reported to have offered the Russian Soviet government 40 million marks (→4/7).

18. London: The Government asks for a further war loan of £500 million (→19).

18. W. Front: Allied counterattack begins (→22).

19. London: The Government announces the introduction of general rationing.

20. London: The Government announces the postponement of Home Rule and the abandonment of Irish conscription.

22. W. Front: French General Charles Mangin stops the German advance 45 miles from Paris (→26).

24. Italian Front: Austrians reported to be fleeing across the River Piave pursued by Italians; 45,000 Austrian prisoners taken (→30/10).

26. UK: Former Russian leader Alexander Kerensky appears at the Labour Party Conference, denounces Brest-Litovsk as "treason".→

30. London: Reported that the British have shot down 4,102 German aeroplanes in the past year, against only 1,213 British losses.

DEATH

10. Italian composer Arrigo Boito (*24/2/1842).

Lloyd George fights off Asquith attack on conduct of war

Lloyd George in a quieter moment.

May 9. The most bitter confrontation of the war between Lloyd George and Asquith resulted in victory tonight for the Prime Minister. Mr Lloyd George won a decisive three-to-one Commons majority when he staked the government's life on rejection of what he chose to treat as a censure motion moved by his predecessor Mr Asquith.

This demanded an all-party investigation of allegations that Mr Lloyd George had lied about the strength of British forces on the Western front. These sensational allegations were made by Major-General Sir Frederick Maurice, formerly director of military operations at the War Office. He suggested that the Prime Minister quoted incorrect figures in a bid to lay blame for battle disasters on the generals and not the Government.

In an adroit performance, Mr Lloyd George claimed that figures he used had been supplied by the office Sir Frederick used to run. To MPs he cried: "I implore that there may be an end of this sniping." With that he won the vote, but the beginning of organised opposition to the government has now been seen.

Reds and Whites battle for soul of Russia

Close-cropped: Russian women warriors sacrifice hair to fight on front.

June 26. Lenin's Russia appears to be on the point of disintegration with the stage being set for a bitter civil war and more foreign intervention.

One of the most serious problems for Lenin and Trotsky's fledgling Red Army is the presence in Siberia of an independent Czech Legion of some 45,000 men, which is advancing westwards.

Former prisoners of war taken from the Austro-Hungarian army, the Czechs were reorganised by Alexander Kerensky to fight on the Russian front.

After Lenin made his humiliating peace with the Germans, these Czechs were to be allowed to leave Russia via Siberia and Vladivostock. This has not happened; instead the Czechs have been strengthened by anti-Bolshevik Russian officers and soldiers.

The Red Army is also having to fight on other fronts. In the Ukraine a White Volunteer Army, led by Czarist generals, has joined up with the fiercely independent Cossacks.

In the north, 130 Royal Marines have occupied Murmansk in order to prevent the port falling into German hands.

To attract recruits Trotsky has increased the pay of Red Army soldiers to 150 roubles, about £2, a month.

Big Bertha shells Paris from 65 miles

June 26. Paris is once again coming under the deadly fire of the gun they call "Big Bertha", a huge unwieldy howitzer, which has already claimed the lives of 800 of the city's inhabitants.

The horrific 420mm weapon is thought to be firing from around 65 miles away. Its targeting is crude and its 1,764-pound shells are falling indiscriminately around the capital. Experts believe its vast range means that if target estimates are just a fraction out, then the gun can miss them by miles.

The weapon, which is named after the wife of its manufacturer, Gustav Krupp, first bombarded the city on March 24, soon after the start of the second battle of the Somme. It was located and identified by aerial photography, no easy task as the giant gun is moved around at night on railway trucks or kept hidden under earth on the side of hills.

The gun now shelling Paris is thought to be the fourth. Its three predecessors were wrecked by aircraft or ground fire and one apparently blew itself up on its second day of use.

1918

JULY

Su	Mo	Tu	We	Th	Fr	Sa
	1	2	3	4	5	6
7	8	9	10	11	12	13
14	15	16	17	18	19	20
21	22	23	24	25	26	27
28	29	30	31			

1. UK: 100 are killed and 150 injured in an explosion at an armaments factory in the Midlands.

1. US: Charles Strite announces the invention of a new "pop-up" machine for toasting bread.

2. Washington: The administration recognises the Czech National Council as provisional government of Czechoslovakia (→ 13/8).

3. New York: Revealed that James Gordon Bennett (died 14/5) left money to endow a home for ageing journalists.

4. Moscow: The Pan-Russian Congress decides to adopt a socialist constitution for Russia (→ 6).

6. France: Spanish influenza is taking on epidemic proportions (→ 30/9).

6. Moscow: German ambassador Count Wilhelm von Mirbach-Harff is assassinated by socialist revolutionaries, opposed to Communists and Brest-Litovsk peace treaty (→ 10).

9. US: Henry Ford launches the first "Eagle" boat, new type of fast submarine-chaser.

10. Russia: New provisional government of Siberia is set up at Novonikolayevsk (→ 16).

11. London: Labour MP John Clynes is appointed Food Controller following the death of Lord Rhondda (→ 1/8).

19. Washington: Baseball is declared a "non-essential occupation" under "Work or Fight" law (→ 23).

23. Washington: Gen. Foch meets with Allied chiefs of staff Petain, Haig and Pershing to discuss a final offensive on the Germans (→ 31).

29. Berlin: Germany severs diplomatic relations with Turkey.

30. France: Frenchman Captain Sarret makes first ever parachute drop from an aeroplane, falling 800 feet.

BIRTH

14. Swedish film director Ingmar Bergman.

Czar and his family massacred in a cellar

The ex-Czar with his daughters.

July 16. Russia's Bolshevik rulers cold-bloodedly wiped out former Czar Nicholas II and his family today in revenge for the past and in fear for the future.

The Romanovs were shot and bayoneted to death in a cellar in Ekaterinburg, a fiercely pro-Bolshevik town in the Urals where the Imperial prisoners were taken on May 30. Also killed in the bloodbath were the family's doctor, valet, cook, parlourmaid and dog. The bodies were taken away to be dismembered and destroyed.

After his abdication last year the Czar had been living in fairly comfortable conditions in Tobolsk, a small town in northern Siberia. His move to Ekaterinburg has been a confusing tale of intrigue, cross-purposes and indecision, but the end result was that the family finished up in the wrong place at the wrong time.

With the Western Allies uninterested in his fate, it was decided by local Bolsheviks. They were aware of the advance of the Czechs and Whites towards Ekaterinburg, and so, alarmed that the town might become a major objective, asked Moscow what they should do about the family. They were told to take their own measures.

Factory-worker guards were replaced by Cheka executioners; the family were told they were going to be moved, and taken to the cellar. There the leader of the squad said: "Your relations have tried to save you. They have failed and we must now shoot you."

New Allied tactics get Germany on the run

July 31. Heavy fighting has resumed on the Western Front, following a month-long lull caused by a crippling influenza epidemic, and it begins to look as though the tide has turned for the Allies.

On July 15, von Ludendorff mounted his latest drive, optimistically called Friedensturm (peace offensive), across the Marne. After a four-mile advance, the enemy was halted. Three days later, the Allies counter-attacked and Ludendorff was forced to withdraw, leaving behind 25,000 prisoners.

French commander Foch.

The Germans have been knocked off balance by General Petain's new tactic of elastic defence. Mindful of the unrest in the army after the blood-letting of 1917, Petain and French commander General Foch went for defence in depth, allowing the first shock of an attack to be absorbed by a light front line, then striking back when the enemy's lines of communication were fully extended. Ludendorff's first early advantage in numbers has been massively eroded since last March.

He began with 208 divisions, of which 80 were in reserve. Now he is believed to have only 66 weakened divisions in reserve. And the Americans are beginning to arrive at the rate of 300,000 a month. "If we hold on until July," Petain said, "we can resume the offensive; after that victory will be ours."

Sex and marriage a[s] seen by Dr Stopes

Stopes: call for birth control.

July 1. Sex is not normally a topi[c] to be voiced in public, but a ne[w] book entitled "Married Love", b[y] Dr Marie Stopes, discusses wha[t] one reviewer called the sexua[l] responsibilities of marriage. Th[e] implication that sex has an importance beyond the procreation o[f] children reflects controversia[l] calls for contraceptive advice to b[e] made more available.

18,000 soldiers in formation as the Statue of Liberty.

1918

AUGUST

Su	Mo	Tu	We	Th	Fr	Sa
				1	2	3
4	5	6	7	8	9	10
11	12	13	14	15	16	17
18	19	20	21	22	23	24
25	26	27	28	29	30	31

1. London: The Government asks for a new war loan of £700 million (→ 12/11).

1. US: One million women are now reported to be working in factories (→ 24).

3. Washington: President Wilson decides to send a small force to aid the White Russians (→ 8).

5. Washington: War Industries Board tells newspapers to cut size of dailies by 15 per cent, of weeklies by 20 per cent (→ 25).

6. France: General Foch is promoted to Marshal; General Pershing is awarded the French Grand Cross (→ 8).

8. Russia: The Red Army under Trotsky captures Kazan from the Whites (→ 15).

13. London: The Government recognises the state of Czechoslovakia (→ 3/9).

15. Moscow: The US severs relations with Russia (→ 30).

17. Japan: The Government requisitions all rice stocks in a bid to put down food riots.

20. New York: Barbers raise price of haircut to 50 cents, shave to 25 cents.

24. UK: London underground workers strike for equal "war wages" for women doing men's jobs, one day after tram and bus conductresses ended a similar strike (→ 19/9).

25. Washington: War Industries Board says moving pictures are an "essential industry" and its employees can be exempted from the draft (→ 27).

25. Berlin: Rioters destroy pictures of Kaiser (→ 5/9).

25. Budapest: The Hungarian government expels Jews and confiscates their assets (→ 2/12).

27. Washington: Fuel Administration bans Sunday driving east of the Mississippi (→ 4/9).

30. Russia: Socialist revolutionary Fanya Dora-Kaplan badly wounds Lenin (→ 5/9).

BIRTH

25. US conductor and composer Leonard Bernstein (†14/10/90).

Final push: "black day for Germany"

A French machine-gun crew opens fire during the Allies' final, momentous, thrust on the German Army.

Aug 8. In Ludendorff's own words, it has been "the black day of the German army". When British, American, Canadian, Australian and French troops – 20 divisions in all – went into action near Amiens, the enemy collapsed.

The character of the war has changed. Tanks and planes are now being used in large numbers. More than 400 tanks spearheaded the initial attacks, and planes daily undertake low-flying, machine-gun strikes at German infantry columns. In one day of raids on the enemy's rear positions 26 tons of bombs were dropped, and in night raids 43 tons fell on rail junctions. The Germans are being pushed back to the old Hindenburg Line, the position they held before the spring offensive.

All along the ruptured front, pockets of Germans are being found hiding in shell holes and ruined buildings. They offer no resistance, but surrender at once, throwing down their helmets and equipment; everything, in fact, except a small sack in which are kept a few necessities such as bread, soap and razor.

Batches of prisoners are being brought back in a steady stream; many say they are fed up with the war and are glad to be taken. The toll of prisoners to date numbers 30,000. The battlefield is littered with abandoned weapons, including trench mortars and machine-guns but no field guns, which suggests that retreat had been anticipated, though for some reason the front-line infantry were left to fend for themselves.

On the French sector, south of the Somme, pressure on the enemy is being maintained after General Mangin's great victory in the Compiegne-Soissons area, where he retook territory the Germans held for only six weeks.

British land to aid the White Russians

Aug 2. A British-led force of 1,500 men has landed at Archangel, the north Russian port, to set up a base in the war against Germany. The expedition, which sailed from Murmansk, took the town without any opposition.

The landing has been long expected and coincided with a coup against the local Bolshevik Soviet. The Commander-in-Chief of the Allied forces, Major-General Frederick Poole, stated "The new government cordially invited our aid, and declared itself pro-Ally, anti-German, and determined not to recognise the Brest-Litovsk treaty."

General Poole's force also comprised a French battalion, some Poles, a detachment of US Marines, about 100 Royal Marines and a section of a machine-gun company.

The armada was fired on by Bolshevik shore batteries but there were only two casualties in the entire action.

General Poole has proclaimed martial law, introduced the death penalty for sedition, and abrogated various Bolshevik edicts giving power to the workers.

The Allied action appears to be designed to keep Archangel out of German hands and to link up with Czechs and Whites advancing from Siberia to form a new Eastern Front (→ 5/9).

Taxis for prisoners as policemen strike

Aug 31. London police went on strike for the first time yesterday. Prisoners were taken to court in taxis instead of Black Marias. Traffic chaos was avoided thanks to bus and taxi drivers, who did point duty during the rush hour. There was one fatal accident in the Brixton Road when a girl of 12 was knocked down by a van at a crossing normally controlled by a policeman. Over 2,000 policemen marched from Scotland Yard to Tower Hill for a mass meeting to press their demands for more pay and the reinstatement of a man dismissed for his political activities.

1918

SEPTEMBER

Su	Mo	Tu	We	Th	Fr	Sa
1	2	3	4	5	6	7
8	9	10	11	12	13	14
15	16	17	18	19	20	21
22	23	24	25	26	27	28
29	30					

2. UK: US labour leader Sam Gompers addresses the TUC's Golden Jubilee conference.

3. Washington: The US formally recognises the nation of Czechoslovakia (→15/10).

4. Washington: The War Department calls upon women to take men's jobs in munitions factories (→19).

5. Moscow: A British diplomat is killed when the UK consulate is attacked by Soviet government supporters.

5. London: Russian ambassador Maxim Litvinov is arrested and held in Brixton prison.

5. Germany: Berlin and the province of Brandenburg are declared to be in a state of siege (→27).

6. Peking: Hsu Shi-chang is elected President of the Chinese Republic.

11. France: War costs to date: F138 billion.

13. US: 14 million men register for conscription.

15. London, Washington: The US and UK governments reject an Austrian peace proposal (→27).

15. UK: C. H. E. Chubb presents Stonehenge to the nation.

19. UK: Women railway workers settle equal pay dispute; Government sets up commission to investigate equal pay for women (→23/10).

24. Palestine: British troops take Haifa, Acre and Es-Salt from the Turks (→1/10).

26. W. Front: Belgian King Albert leads Allied troops in Belgian operations (→30).

27. Washington: President Wilson says he will only negotiate with nations with parliamentary systems of government (→8/10).

27. Berlin: Count Georg von Hertling resigns as Chancellor, having succeeded Georg Michaelis only on 1/11/17 (→3/10).

28. Lausanne: First performance of Igor Stravinsky's ballet "A Soldier's Tale".

Allies break through the German lines

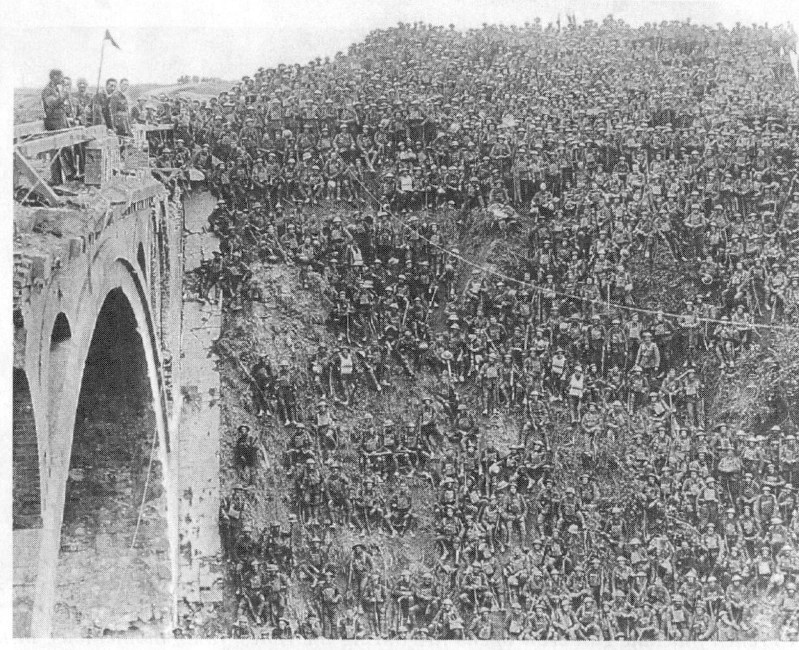

British troops pause for a breather on the advance through Belgium.

Sept 30. The Allies are sweeping all before them along the whole Western Front from the Scheldt in the north to Sedan at the southern end, after over 200 divisions attacked simultaneously. King Albert's 28 Belgian divisions, supported by British, American and French troops, have delivered crushing blows in Flanders, where the war began and the Germans quickly established themselves.

All along the line, the Germans are avoiding battle wherever possible, making a stand only in order to cover the retreat. As they pull back through Belgium, they are taking with them all men and boys from 16 to 60 to be used as forced labour, building emergency defences on the German frontier. Elsewhere, Germany's allies are collapsing.

In Palestine, General Edmund Allenby, with a fighting strength of 57,000 rifles, 12,000 sabres and 500 guns, has wiped out a Turkish force of about half that size, taken 75,000 prisoners and advanced 350 miles.

Emir Feisal's loyal Arabs helped to destroy the Turks' lines of communication, blowing up railways and other installations. Allenby then sent aircraft to bomb telegraph and telephone exchanges. The planes were also used to drop propaganda pamphlets on the ragged, half-starved enemy troops, showing, in pictures, how Turkish prisoners of war are living in comfort, well-fed and well-clothed, in British camps.

Advancing US troops rush to the aid of a comrade stricken by gas.

Spanish flu takes its toll in Britain

Sept 30. This month saw the first signs that the worldwide influenza epidemic had reached Britain. Absences from work rose; London's central telegraph office was crippled because 700 people were absent through illness. The situation seems certain to get worse.

Around the globe, this virulent strain of influenza has already caused millions of deaths. So far attempts to develop a vaccine to combat the disease have failed and some doctors are predicting that more people could die of influenza than were killed by the war.

The disease is known as Spanish flu, but it is by no means clear that it began in Spain. China and India have been the hardest hit to date, with millions reported dead. Now it is spreading through Europe and the United States amongst people weakened by wartime hardships. The US Federal Bureau of Health says that more US servicemen have died of influenza than of wounds suffered in battle (→23/10).

Bulgaria bows to final Allied thrust

Sept 30. Bulgaria has surrendered and is out of the war. Victorious Allied troops, advancing from northern Greece, took less than a fortnight to smash the Bulgarian army even with its stiffening of German troops.

The first hint that a great victory was in the making came with the news that the Franco-Serbian force in Macedonia had broken through to the River Vardar. Italian, Greek and British troops also scored significant victories over the Bulgarians who broke and, harried by aeroplanes, ran for the safety of the mountains.

By last Saturday they had had enough. A Bulgarian officer, carrying a white flag, walked into the British lines and asked for an armistice with a view to making peace. The armistice was then signed at Salonika at 11pm yesterday.

The Bulgarian surrender will do incalculable damage to the Germans. The Berlin stock exchange has already panicked.

1918

OCTOBER

Su	Mo	Tu	We	Th	Fr	Sa
		1	2	3	4	5
6	7	8	9	10	11	12
13	14	15	16	17	18	19
20	21	22	23	24	25	26
27	28	29	30	31		

3. Berlin: Prince Maximilian of Baden is appointed Imperial Chancellor in succession to Georg von Hertling (→9/11).

4. Bulgaria: King Ferdinand abdicates in favour of his son Boris.→

5. Vienna: Austria appeals to President Wilson for peace (→8).

6. UK: 430 die when two liners, one a US troop ship, collide off the Scottish coast.

7. Middle East: British troops take Beirut and Sidon.

8. Washington: President Wilson insists there can be no peace while the Central Powers occupy Allied territory.→

9. Irish Sea: 587 civilians die when a German submarine torpedoes the mailboat Leinster.

13. Washington: The Administration issues strict new regulations for saving food.

15. UK: The country's first oil well is inaugurated at Hardstoft in Derbyshire.

15. Prague: Czechoslovak republic is officially proclaimed (→30/11).

17. Budapest: Hungary declares independence from the Habsburg Empire (→30/11).

23. London: House of Commons votes by 274 to 25 to allow women to become MPs (→28/12).

23. UK: Many schools have been closed because of the current influenza epidemic (→26).

26. London: 2,225 deaths from influenza have been reported in the capital this week (→17/11).

30. Italy: The Austrian army has evacuated Italian territory.

31. Constantinople: Turkey surrenders; the Dardanelles are reopened to Allied shipping.→

DEATHS

24. French composer Alexandre Charles Lecocq (*3/6/1832).

31. Austrian painter Egon Schiele (*12/6/1890).

Lawrence leads Arabs into Damascus

Oct 1. Arab horsemen from distant Hejaz today galloped in triumph through the streets of Damascus. As the sun was rising over the mosques and spires, Major T.E. Lawrence, the young British officer whose tactical guidance has ensured the success of the Arab revolt, drove through the lanes in an armoured car. One Arab rider waved his head-dress and shouted, "Damascus salutes you!".

Led by the Emir Feisal, son of Sherif Hussein, now to be King of Syria, and his British friend Lawrence, who had fought the Turks all the way from Arabia, the Arabs were first into the capital.

At about the same time that they arrived, the first patrols of the Australian Mounted Division of General Allenby's army also converged on the great city, having fought their way from Egypt to Gaza, captured Jerusalem, and freed Palestine from Ottoman rule before finally entering Damascus.

The capture of the most famous city in the Arab world was an event filled with high emotion for Major Lawrence and for Feisal, the Arab prince who had led tribesmen on their long fighting, camel march from the barren wastes of Arabia. Multitudes of Syrians thronged the streets to celebrate liberation from the Ottoman Empire. The only Turkish soldiers remaining in Damascus today are the wounded, crammed in hospitals and abandoned by their doctors.

Major Lawrence on camelback.

There is a serious danger that law and order may break down in a place packed with an excitable mixture of desert and city Arabs. Notables who until the last minute worked with the Turks now proclaim their loyalty to the Allies. Already there are reports that some have been shot. General Allenby's first task will be to install a military government to keep order and restore the city's public services.

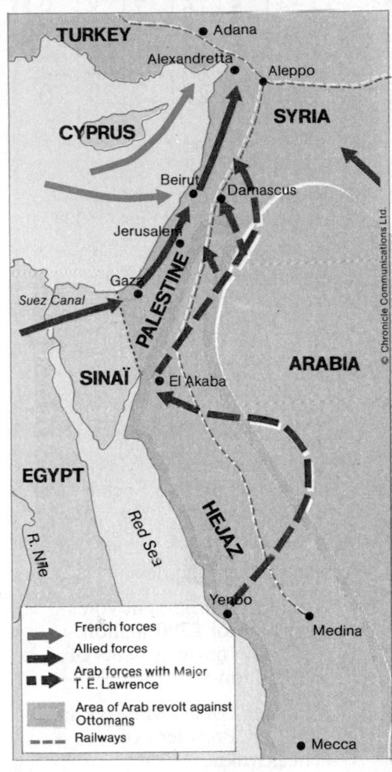

Conforming to arrangements agreed with Britain, the French will take control of Syria. General Allenby's army is preparing to move east to link up with French forces whose task is now to take the port of Beirut in Lebanon (→7).

Central Powers make peace overtures as Allies tighten noose

Oct 31. In the shadow of defeat, Germany appealed for an armistice. Though Berlin still keeps up the pretence that, should the Allied terms prove too hard, the people would be prepared to fight "a last national defensive battle", the evidence is all the other way. The retreating German forces on the Western Front show no sign of making a stand, and a discredited Ludendorff has been replaced by the realist, General Groener.

Germany's allies have already quit the field. Bulgaria was the first to go, followed by Turkey, and now the Austrian Emperor Karl, who succeeded Franz Josef two years ago, is desperately seeking an immediate armistice as his empire disintegrates.

German prisoners on the Italian front despondently await the war's end.

1918

NOVEMBER

Su	Mo	Tu	We	Th	Fr	Sa
					1	2
3	4	5	6	7	8	9
10	11	12	13	14	15	16
17	18	19	20	21	22	23
24	25	26	27	28	29	30

3. Vienna: Austria signs an armistice with the Allies (→11).

6. W. Front: German High Command orders withdrawal of troops across the Meuse.→

7. Germany: Socialists under Kurt Eisner declare a republic in Bavaria (→9).

9. Germany: Republic declared as Kaiser Wilhelm II abdicates; Chancellor Max von Baden hands over to Socialist Friedrich Ebert.→

11. Austria: Emperor Karl abdicates; republic declared.→

12. London: Parliament votes for war loan of £700 million; the UK now has war debts of £7,100 million (→25).

14. Prague: Tomas Masaryk is elected first President of Czechoslovakia.→

14. Warsaw: Josef Pilsudski becomes President of Poland with full dictatorial powers.

17. US: Report says deaths from influenza exceed US war dead of 53,000 (→18/3/1919).

19. London: Government says UK suffered over three million war casualties, including nearly a million dead.→

22. London: 100 women police patrols are appointed.

23. UK: League football resumes throughout the country.

25. London: Parliament is dissolved prior to General Election, after lifting many war restrictions (→28).

27. Germany: More than 1,500,000 Allied prisoners have been released.

28. Vienna: Government says it will try those responsible for starting the war.

BIRTH

11. Russian author Alexander Solzhenitsyn.

DEATHS

4. British poet Wilfred Owen (*18/3/1893).

19. French poet Guillaume Apollinaire, born Wilhelm Apollinaris de Kostrovitzky (*26/8/1880).

Victory! Germany signs the Armistice

Nov 11. Shortly before dawn today a party of Germans, including a Catholic politician and two army generals, entered a guarded railway carriage in the forest of Compiegne. Six hours later, at 11.00am, on the eleventh day of the eleventh month, after four and a quarter years of war, the guns fell silent on the battlefields of Europe. Germany had admitted defeat and signed an armistice.

The terms are hard, but it is not unconditional surrender. Germany has to hand over, in good condition, 5,000 heavy guns, 30,000 machine guns, 2,000 warplanes and all her U-boats; the surface fleet will be interned in British waters, with only caretaker crews. Five thousand locomotives, 150,000 wagons and 5,000 lorries are to be delivered. Allied troops will occupy the Rhineland, their upkeep to be paid for by Germany. Finally, the Allied blockade of Germany is to remain in force. These armistice terms were accepted, not by those who had started the war, but by men who had opposed it. The leader of the delegation received by Foch and the British Admiral Wemyss at Compiegne was Matthias Erzberger, who last year persuaded the normally docile Reichstag to pass a resolution calling for peace. The generals accompanying him had played no part in the senior councils of the war; they were there to concede defeat.

Marshal Foch accepts the German surrender on behalf of the Allies.

The end had come with unexpected speed. In the middle of October, Foch was still planning a new offensive for November 14, but in Germany Ludendorff was in a state of panic, begging the Kaiser to seek an immediate armistice before the front gave way. Wilhelm appointed as Chancellor Prince Max of Baden, who is regarded as a liberal, promised democratic reforms, and appealed to President Wilson for an armistice.

Wilson's terms, agreed with the British and French, required the immediate abandonment of submarine warfare. The Germans gave an undertaking, but the U-boats carried on anyhow, sinking the transport Leinster, with 600 civilians on board, and the cruiser Britannia, as late as November 9.

By now, though the High Command was desperate, it had no intention of getting involved in surrender negotiations. Hindenburg and Ludendorff faded into the background, and it was a civilian, accompanied by two minor army officers, who arrived at Compiegne with a white flag.

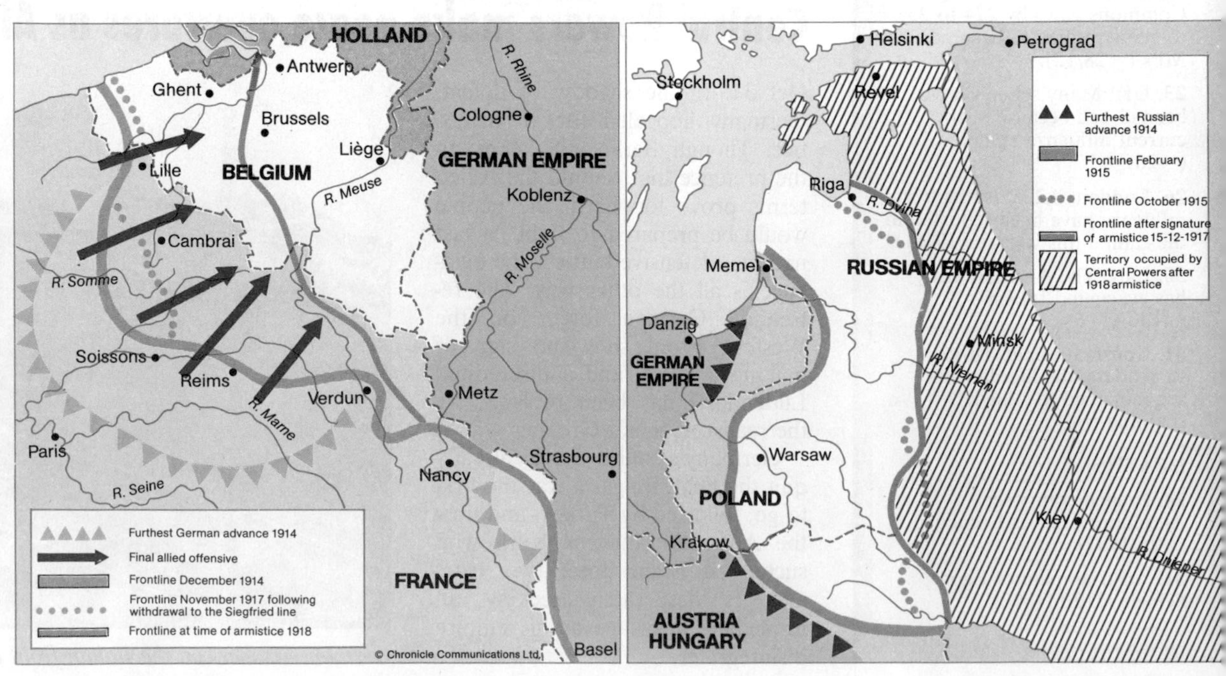

Jubilation marks the end of the war

Nov 15. Peace came to a war-weary Britain with unprecedented scenes of public revelry and rejoicing. The country, according to one observer, became "like a giant school let out".

Victory Day began quietly under sombre, granite skies. Then, at eleven o'clock precisely, as the armistice took effect, giant maroons – hitherto used as warnings of impending disaster – were fired throughout the country. Church bells began to ring. Boy Scouts cycled through cities and towns sounding the "all clear" for the last time on bugles and sirens.

Suddenly, the entire population, it seemed, rushed on to the streets, cheering, waving flags, hoisting every available serviceman shoulder-high, loosing off fireworks and dancing cakewalks in the squares until the early hours.

Factories closed at once. A staid Staff officer, resplendent with red tabs, was mobbed by whooping women munition workers who invaded his open car, while shop-girls in Knightsbridge cheered from the roofs of department stores.

By the time that Big Ben struck one o'clock – after four years of silence – London was a blaze of colour with flags of every Allied nation flying from hastily improvised flagpoles on thousands of rooftops.

Buses carrying signs declaring "To Berlin: Fare 1d" were heavily overloaded as they brought singing and shouting passengers to join the celebrations.

The King and Queen attracted huge crowds as they made an informal drive through the centre of London to Hyde Park. Thousands packed Downing Street and Whitehall to cheer Prime Minister Lloyd George and members of the coalition cabinet.

Street lights were unmasked. Blackout curtains were ripped down and shop windows were suddenly ablaze with light. Rigid wartime licensing laws were ignored and pubs were packed until they ran out of beer.

In Blackburn, the mayor – who is chairman of Blackburn Rovers Football Club – gave his 2,000 cotton workers £1 each and a two day holiday.

Hearts at peace: men of the 9th East Surrey cheer the news of armistice.

Send him victorious! British Empire servicemen and women cheer peace.

Exhausted soldiers snatch a break as the guns fall silent.

Four new nations arise from ashes of Habsburg Empire

Nov 30. The Empire, collected by the Habsburgs by war and marriage over a thousand years, is breaking up into its constituent parts whose inhabitants, despite being subject peoples for hundreds of years, have fiercely maintained their nationhood.

Four "new" nations whose roots go back into Europe's pre-history have already sprung from the smouldering ashes of the Austro-Hungarian oligarchy.

Austria, which has declared itself a republic and kicked out Karl, the last Habsburg Emperor, has an established civil service; with its history of universal suffrage, it should make the transition into the post-war world with comparatively little difficulty.

Czechoslovakia, with its troublesome mixture of Czechs and Slovaks, will face more difficulties but it has the advantage of being led by the popular Tomas Masaryk.

A man of lofty ideals, Masaryk served in the Austrian parliament and is married to an American. It is thought that an injection of New World freshness will do no harm to a statesman brought up in the atmosphere of an empire which had lived beyond its time. Masaryk is also fortunate in having the support of his pragmatic colleague, Eduard Benes.

There is no love lost between the Czechs and the Hungarians, the third of the "new" nations. The Hungarians regard the Czechs as traitors to the old Empire and the Czechs look on the Hungarians as oppressors. The Hungarians, or Magyars, are in fact an ancient and turbulent nation who, since 1867, enjoyed equality with the Austrians in the Empire.

Their new leader, the liberal aristocrat Michael Karolyi, faces a difficult task in controlling powerful factions within the country. It seems certain that Hungary is destined for a bitter struggle for power.

The fourth new country has no name yet. A confederation of the South Slavic peoples – Serbs, Slovenes, Croats, Montenegrins – it will be ruled by King Peter, who led Serbia to victory. ▷

Kaiser flees: revolt sweeps Germany

Nov 10. Kaiser Wilhelm II appeared at the Dutch frontier today with the Kaiserin, servants and possessions, in 12 motor cars driven by Prussian officers.

The German emperor has abdicated, leaving behind him a country gripped by revolutionary fervour. Socialist demonstrators fill the streets, sailors have mutinied and army troops are seizing their command posts. The Social Democrats seem to have the upper hand but they are being challenged by radicals such as Karl Liebknecht, whose Spartacus party has declared the birth of the "free socialist republic of Germany".

The Kaiser was later joined at the station by a train of 20 carriages from Germany, each filled with huge quantities of luggage, including motor spares. For an hour Wilhelm paced the platform at Eysden, ashen-faced, his hair completely white and then went to rest. When he reappeared he had discarded his Prussian General's uniform for mufti.

It was the mutiny of sailors at Kiel that sounded the alarm for the High Command. When the men refused orders, they realised that, realistically, the war was over.

All the same the Kaiser, who is still calling himself the King of Prussia, did not go easily. The new liberal Chancellor, Prince Max of Baden, politely suggested he should go "to save the country" at least a week ago. But it was not until General Groener, the new Chief of Staff, phoned him at Spa, in Belgium and said "If you won't abdicate, then the best thing for you to do is to shoot yourself" that he accepted that the end had come.

Yesterday, in a bid to fend off all-out revolution, Prince Max handed over to the President of the Social Democrats, Friedrich Ebert, a 47-year-old trade union leader and saddle-maker. Ebert stood up in the Reichstag, proclaimed a republic and announced that arms were being distributed to workers' and soldiers' councils. He then made Gustav Noske, the Mayor of Kiel and a socialist with unexpected qualities of military ruthlessness, Minister of Defence. Noske and General Groener immediately set about forming volunteer units of loyal anti-revolutionary soldiers. Over the length and breadth of Europe riot and revolution has taken hold. King Louis of Bavaria has fled. The Duke of Brunswick and five other German kings, princes and grand dukes have been chased out of their castles.

In Vienna, workers and students paraded the streets shouting "Down with the Habsburgs". Karl, Emperor since 1916, has abdicated. In Budapest, Count Michael Karolyi has proclaimed Hungary's independence from Austria. In Prague street fighting broke out as a Czechoslovak republic was proclaimed. Everywhere there are calls for social improvements in housing, food and the workplace.

The Kaiser virtually ignored social programmes while he ruled, being more interested in international affairs and military conquest. Occasionally he supported reform but he was just as likely to respond to calls for social improvements with repressive measures. Thus radicals flourished, taking their cue from the Bolsheviks.

As the war ends, internal fighting begins: soldiers and sailors man the guns.

Children swarm round a group of German soldiers home from the war.

German fleet surrenders to the Royal Navy

Nov 21. The German High Sea Fleet surrendered today in one o the most amazing sights ever witnessed in naval history. The surrender was one of the key conditions o the Armistice signed ten days ago.

Scores of German vessels, battleships, cruisers and destroyers are now lying at anchor in the Firth o Forth under the watchful eye of the navy. At the same time 39 U-boat sailed into Harwich to abandon the fight. Eye-witnesses say most of the German ships are in perfect condition. Said one: "It is the soul tha has faltered while the body is stil strong."

The Grand Fleet, commanded by Sir David Beatty, sailed early this morning to bring the German ships in and up to the last moment there was deep British suspicion that they might be the victims of a trick.

The British vessels sailed out o the Forth escorted by aircraft and with their guns ready to fire i necessary. They encircled the Germans, who were flying the white flag, and then all cruised back a just 10 knots, the maximum speed many of the defeated ships could manage.

There were so many warships a sea that nobody could see all of the two fleets at the same time. Said an observer on one warship: " It seemed as if the whole sea was full o circling battleships. Great masses of grey, silvered by the sunlight swinging round upon a foaming sea, tremendous, menacing and as symmetrically ordered as the figures in a dance."

Surrendered U-boats at Harwich.

Ten million dead: human cost of a war to end war

Nov 30. It was called the "Great War" and certainly there has never been anything like it in history. More countries were involved and more people perished – over ten million – than in any previous single conflict.

Three-quarters of a million men from Britain died, plus a further 200,000 from the Empire, of whom nearly a third were Indians. Yet the price of victory for other nations was even greater. France, with a population smaller than Britain's, had a death toll almost twice as high. Psychologically, too, France has suffered the scars of occupation, as have Belgium and Russia.

In addition to those who died directly from battle, gas, shell shock and, in the Middle East, malaria have all claimed victims. No class of society has been immune from the war's impact; casualties amongst junior officers were about three times higher than among ordinary soldiers and they included the eldest son of Herbert Asquith, the former British Prime Minister. No wonder people who now survive speak of "a lost generation".

Some corner of a foreign field: with peace comes time for relatives to mourn those who fell in battle.

SHIPPING LOSSES DURING THE WAR

	Tonnage	Warships*
Britain	9,055,000	1069
Germany	–	362
Norway	1,172,000	–
Italy	862,000	72
France	807,000	134
United States	531,000	14
Japan	270,00	11
Russia	–	50
Austria-Hungary	–	23

*including auxiliaries, eg minesweepers, colliers

THE COST OF THE WAR

Germany	37,775,000
Britain	35,334,012
France	24,265,583
United States	22,625,253
Russia	22,593,950
Austria-Hungary	20,622,960
Italy	12,413,998
Turkey	1,430,000
All Allied Powers	125,690,477
All Central Powers	60,643,160

Cost in thousands of dollars

MANPOWER AND CASUALTIES OF MAJOR POWERS 1914-1918

Millions of people

15 14 13 12 11 10 9 8 7 6 5 4 3 2 1

Total mobilised
Total military casualties (including PoWs)
Total Killed or died of wounds

AUSTRIA HUNGARY · BRITISH EMPIRE · FRANCE · GERMANY · ITALY · RUSSIA · TURKEY · USA

1918

DECEMBER

Su	Mo	Tu	We	Th	Fr	Sa
1	2	3	4	5	6	7
8	9	10	11	12	13	14
15	16	17	18	19	20	21
22	23	24	25	26	27	28
29	30	31				

1. Denmark: The Danish parliament passes an act to grant independence to Iceland (→17/6/44).

2. London: The War Cabinet decides to demand the Kaiser's extradition.

2. Poland: 3,200 Jews are reported murdered at Lvow (Lemberg).

5. Versailles: British representatives at the Peace Conference call for an end to conscription throughout Europe (→18/1/19).

6. London: The Government grants an eight-hour day to British railway workers.

7. Berlin: The Spartacist socialist movement calls for a revolution in Germany (→28/1/19).

10. Stockholm: Nobel Prizes awarded to Max Planck (Germany, Physics) and Fritz Haber (Germany, Chemistry). No other prizes awarded.

14. Paris: President Wilson arrives in Paris to a tumultuous welcome.→

18. UK: 11-day Lancashire cotton workers' strike ends.

24. London: The Local Government Committee on the Poor Law recommends the abolition of workhouses.

31. London: The coalition War Cabinet last meeting.

BIRTHS

21. Austrian diplomat and politician Kurt Waldheim, UN Secretary-General 1972-82.

25. Egyptian statesman Anwar El-Sadat, president 1970-81 (†6/10/81).

HITS OF 1918

If you could care for me.

After you've gone.

Till we meet again.

QUOTE OF THE YEAR

"I died in hell
(They called it
Passchendaele)."
Siegfried Sassoon,
Memorial Tablet
(Great War), November 1918.

Women vote for first time in UK election

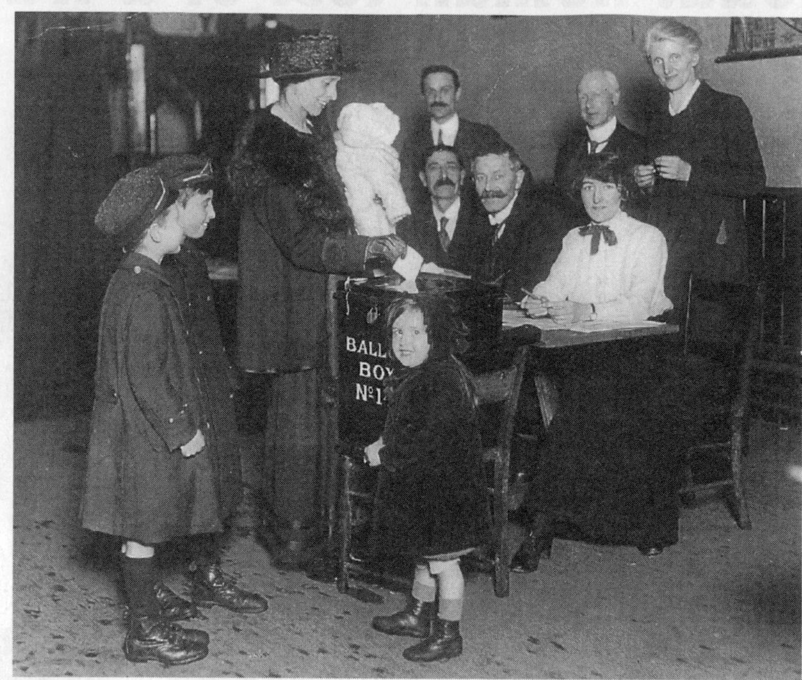

A woman casts her vote for the first time in a UK general election.

Dec 28. The Coalition Government led by David Lloyd George has triumphed in the momentous "Coupon Election" which he called immediately after the war was won. Results announced today show 478 MPs were elected "on the coupon" – a personal letter of endorsement which the Prime Minister sent to approved candidates. Opposition parties got 229 seats.

There are now 63 anti-Coalition Labour MPs and this makes their party the main Opposition one. Many eminent anti-Coalition Liberals are out, including ex-Premier Asquith, as are Labour stalwarts Henderson and MacDonald. Altogether nearly 11 million votes were cast in the election, twice as many as in the last one in 1910.

Party managers think that for the most part women over 30 voting for the first time have followed the allegiance of husbands or other close relatives.

Out of over 1,600 candidates 17 were women. The only one elected – Countess Markievicz for a Dublin seat as a Sinn Fein candidate – has said it is against her principles to take the oath of allegiance to the King and so she cannot attend Parliament.

Alsace-Lorraine welcomed back

Dec 8. The French government today paid an official visit to the newly-incorporated province of Alsace-Lorraine. France's occupation last month ended German rule dating back to 1871. But re-integration may not be that easy. German-speaking Alsace-Lorraine enjoyed autonomy within Germany; how it will take to direct rule from Paris is uncertain. Also, imposing France's anti-clerical laws on this largely Catholic region is likely to prove a headache to the new authorities.

Portuguese leader shot by assassin

Dec 15. Portuguese President Sidonio Paes died today, the victim of an assassin's bullet, only weeks after a previous unsuccessful attempt on his life. The popular President came to power just one year ago, on December 9 1917, following a bloody three-day revolution that ended in the overthrow of the regime of his predecessor, Bernardino Machado, in power since 1915. Under Paes, Portugal continued its role as a staunch ally of the Entente Powers in the Great War.

Europe welcomes US President

Dec 27. Today, for the first time, a British sovereign welcomed an American President to Britain. In a cordial ceremony at Charing Cross railway station, Their Majesties, King George V and Queen Mary met President and Mrs Wilson and then escorted them to Buckingham Palace where they are staying. The Mall was festooned with flags of the two countries.

Afterwards Mr Wilson lunched at Downing Street with the Prime Minister, David Lloyd George, Mr Asquith, Viscount Grey and Viscount Bryce, author of "The American Commonwealth".

When he arrived at Dover, Mr Wilson told an enthusiastic crowd that the war had "almost justified itself" because it "brought together great communities with a common object, the permanent maintenance of right".

Mr Wilson has already visited France. He arrived at Brest on December 13 on board the George Washington and visited Paris, where he met President Poincare and was presented with a golden key to the city. He reviewed a detachment of the American expeditionary force, telling them, "you have done what is was appointed to you to do. It had been a people's war", he went on, and its settlement must be a people's peace.

There will be a state banquet at Buckingham Palace tonight, and on Sunday Mr Wilson visits Carlisle, which was his mother's home.

Presidents Wilson and Poincare.

Beyond the trenches: how the arts saw the war

he late Wilfred Owen.

oetry: bitterness dims the patriotism

“Now God be thanked who has atched us with his hour,” wrote **upert Brooke** in anticipation of he war. And **Laurence Binyon** dded: “They went with songs to ne battle ... They shall not grow ld as we that are left grow old.” ut that was in September 1914, fter only one month of it.

By the time Brooke died – withut seeing the trenches – the solier-poets, who watched their comades annihilated in them, were inding bitterer words for the exerience of war.

Siegfried Sassoon, who was called “Mad Jack” because of his solitary expeditions in No Man’s Land, was the first to publish his disillusionment with the way the war was being run:

“Good morning, good morning, the
General said,
When we met him last week on our
way to the line,
Now the soldiers he smiled at are
most of them dead
And we’re cursing his staff for
incompetent swine.”

Sassoon wrote of “the unreturning army that was youth”. He told of “the simple soldier boy” who put a bullet through his own brain which was not what patriots at home were accustomed to hear.

Robert Graves was presumed killed in a shell-burst and read of his own obituary before his 21st birthday. He wrote coolly of an old sweat of a sergeant-major, who was bayoneted by his own men.

Sassoon declared he would not return to France – “I can no longer be a party to prolonging these sufferings”. But he felt obliged to, won the M.C. and survived. So did **Edmund Blunden** (another M.C.). Those killed included **Edward Thomas**, whose reaction to the horror was to remember the tiny English country station, Adlestrop, on a hot summer’s afternoon, **Isaac Rosenberg** and **Wilfred Owen**. “My subject is war and the pity of war,” he wrote in an introduction to his poems, still unpublished when he died. “The poetry is in the pity.”

“Troops Resting”, a portrayal of French soldiers by C. R. W. Nevinson.

Art: visions of gore and propaganda

The Imperial War Museum commissioned artists to record the war and bravely chose not only the established, like **Sir John Sargent** and **Sir George Clausen**, but young modernists like **Paul Nash** and his brother **John**, who produced calm, stylised pictures of the water-filled shell craters and shattered tree-stumps. One was titled “We Are Building a New World”.

John Nash produced “Over the Top”, in which men with fixed bayonets crawl like spiders into a snow-covered nothingness. The Futurist **C.R.W. Nevinson** and the Vorticist **William Roberts** found an angular modernity in the sharp, metallic shapes of shelldumps and tin helmets, in the boots, even in the blank expressions of exhausted soldiers.

Sargent painted a famous picture of blindfolded men holding on to the shoulder of the man ahead, called simply “Gassed”. Fashionable portrait painter **Sir William Orpen** painted the generals **Haig** and **French** but also, very realistically, “Dead Germans in a Trench”.

Chaplin in “Shoulder Arms”.

Songs: catching a train to oblivion

“Are We Down-Hearted? No!” That was the mood of the songwriters in 1914. “It’s a Long Way to Tipperary” but “Your King and Country Want You” so “Jolly Good Luck to the Girl Who Loves a Soldier”; she must, urged one, “Keep the Home Fires Burning.”

But by 1916 you were asking “What’s the use of worrying?” as you “Packed Up Your Troubles” and dreamed of gathering “Roses in Picardy.” By 1918 there was a bitter irony in carolling “Oh, Oh, Oh, it’s a Lovely War!” or a chirpy “Good Byeee!” as you left for the Front.

War’s terrible toll of artistic talent

So much promise was cut off so young. Besides its poets, England lost short story-writer **Saki** and composer **George Butterworth**. France lost sculptor **Henri Gaudier-Brezka**, the poet **Charles Peguy** and **Henri Alain-Fournier**, whose one magic novel “Le Grand Meaulnes” had appeared in 1913.

German Expressionists **Franz Marc**, painter of blue horses, and **August Macke** were killed and the Italian Futurist **Umberto Boccioni** died in a cavalry exercise. The Spanish composer **Enrique Granados** died in a U-boat sinking.

French poster on the horror of war.

1919

JANUARY

Su	Mo	Tu	We	Th	Fr	Sa
			1	2	3	4
5	6	7	8	9	10	11
12	13	14	15	16	17	18
19	20	21	22	23	24	25
26	27	28	29	30	31	

1. UK: Over 200 sailors on leave drown when the yacht Stornoway is wrecked off Scotland.

2. Turkey: 1.5 million Armenians alleged to have been massacred by Turks.

3. Europe: Announcement of new railway link, Paris-Athens the "Acropolis Express".

4. Rome: US President Wilson is received by the Pope while on official visit to Italy.

7. Washington: Thirty days official mourning ordered for ex-President Roosevelt.

10. London: Winston Churchill is appointed Secretary of State for War.→

13. London: Sir Satyendra Prassano Sinha becomes the first Indian peer.

14. Europe: Germany releases all Allied prisoners of war; the Allies release only sick German prisoners.

15. UK: Miners' Federation calls for a six-hour day and nationalisation of mines (→23).

16. Washington: 18th Amendment becomes law; Prohibition will take effect one year from now (→16/1/20).

18. Versailles: First formal session of Peace Conference; French premier Clemenceau is elected chairman (→1/2).

21. Dublin: First meeting of unofficial Irish "parliament" formed by 25 Westminster Sinn Fein MPs who refuse to attend the Commons (→28/4).

23. UK: 150,000 miners join nationwide strikes for shorter working week (→28).

28. UK: Over 200,000 strikers in many industries.→

BIRTH

1. US writer J. D. Salinger.

DEATHS

6. US statesman Theodore Roosevelt, president (1901-9) (*27/10/1858).

15. German socialist Rosa Luxemburg (*5/3/1871).→

15. German socialist Karl Liebknecht (*13/8/1871).→

Communist uprising crushed in Berlin

Jan 12. The Spartacists, who take their name from the last of the slaves' revolts against the Romans, have been defeated in their attempt to take over Berlin.

The revolutionaries, led by "Red Rosa" Luxemburg and the former Reichstag deputy, Karl Liebknecht, took to the streets against the government a week ago and seized a number of public buildings.

They failed in their attempt to occupy the War Office, however, because the Under-Secretary of State told the leader of the raiding party that he would need proper written authority to do so. The Spartacists demanded the formation of a true Socialist republic – the same sort of regime as the Bolsheviks have set up in Russia – but the government refused to bow to their demands.

Troops loyal to the government, along with units of the Socialist People's Militia and Freikorps soldiers, combined to suppress the revolt and four days ago started to reoccupy the public buildings.

There was much confused fighting in the streets with men on both sides manning barricades and fighting for individual buildings. Eyewitnesses speak of hundreds of bodies still lying in the streets where they had fallen.

The revolt collapsed when 3,000 Freikorps men marched into the city yesterday and the Spartacists, whose call to arms had been largely ignored by the workers, faded away (→16).

With old documents for sandbags, Spartacists fire on government troops.

Government troops and Spartacists in conference during a cease-fire.

Rutherford splits "the smallest particle"

Jan 3. Atoms have been "split" by artificial means for the first time by Professor Ernest Rutherford of the University of Manchester. In the process he transmuted atoms of one element, nitrogen, into those of oxygen, so partially realising the dreams of the alchemists.

Rutherford's method was to use the alpha particles, emitted by some radioactive materials, as projectiles to bombard nitrogen atoms. His experiments have finally proved that atoms are not the indivisible particles, the ultimate building blocks of matter, which once they were thought to be.

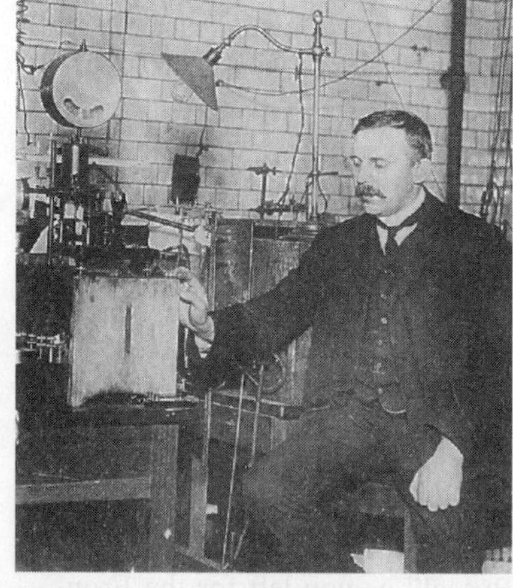

Rutherford in his laboratory.

Lloyd George's new cabinet line-up

Jan 10. In a cabinet reshuffle Mr Lloyd George today tacitly conceded his own weaker position within the coalition government. Most top posts go to Tories in the wake of their party's advance in the last month's election.

These include Andrew Bonar Law, who becomes Leader of the House, and Austen Chamberlain as Chancellor of the Exchequer. The former Prime Minister, Arthur Balfour, stays as Foreign Secretary while Sir F.E. Smith is made Lord Chancellor.

1919

FEBRUARY

Su	Mo	Tu	We	Th	Fr	Sa
						1
2	3	4	5	6	7	8
9	10	11	12	13	14	15
16	17	18	19	20	21	22
23	24	25	26	27	28	

1. Versailles: The UK, US, France and Italy agree on the basic principles of the League of Nations.→

3. London: The Tube is brought to a standstill by workers striking for shorter hours (→11).

4. Russia: US troops inflict heavy losses on Bolshevik forces (→3/3).

5. Germany: First public air service introduced, from Berlin to Weimar via Leipzig.→

7. Germany: Chancellor Friedrich Ebert denounces the terms of the Armistice at a cabinet convention in Weimar.

11. UK: Glasgow strike ends; unions postpone fight for a 40-hour week.

11. UK: The Government offers miners a pay rise and sets up a Commission to look into the coal industry (→12).

12. UK: Miners reject government terms (→21/3).

12. Rumania: King Ferdinand is reported wounded as a general insurrection spreads throughout the country.

17. Germany: The Government finally signs the Armistice, giving up territory to Poland.

19. France: French premier Clemenceau is shot by an anarchist (→14/3).

20. Budapest: A Communist revolt breaks out led by Bela Kun (→21/3).

22. Munich: Soldiers' and Workmen's Council declares Bavaria a soviet republic, a day after Premier Kurt Eisner is murdered (→22/4).

25. Versailles: France proposes setting the French frontier at the Rhine (→11/3).

26. London: MPs debate bills to create new ministries of Health and Transport.

27. London: National industrial conference opens, in which the Government is bringing together employers and workers.→

27. UK: Joe Beckett knocks out British heavyweight boxing champion Bombardier Wells.

Berlin revolutionary leaders murdered

Jan 16. "Red Rosa" Luxemburg and Karl Liebknecht, who were arrested after the failure of their Spartacist uprising in Berlin last week, were murdered yesterday.

The two Communist leaders were held by officers of the Garde Kallerie Schutzen Division, two of whom have been arrested. Reports from Berlin indicate that Luxemburg and Liebknecht were attacked by the officers who were supposed to escort them to prison.

Liebknecht died immediately, but "Red Rosa", who had spent most of the war in prison for trying to rouse the German working class against the war, lingered for some hours before dying. Their bodies are believed to have been thrown into a canal.

They are already being treated as martyrs in some circles. "Their blood is on the hands of the new government," said one socialist newspaper.

"Red Rosa" Luxemburg.

Riot Act is read to strikers in Glasgow

Jan 31. Glasgow's general strike took an ugly turn today. 20,000 demonstrators massed in George Square by the Municipal Buildings and Sheriff MacKenzie formally read the Riot Act, being hit by a bottle as he did so.

Foot and mounted police then broke up the demonstration; about 40 people were seriously injured. Elsewhere in Glasgow, strikers overturned a dozen tramcars while a tobacconist's shop and a jeweller's were looted.

Trouble was expected after the strike committee declared on Thursday that, unless the Government intervened, it would resort to "unconstitutional" action in support of the demand for a 40-hour week without loss of pay in order to create jobs for demobilised soldiers.

In the absence of the Prime Minister, Mr Bonar Law, the Leader of the House, telegraphed the Lord Provost to say that the 40-hour week was a matter to be resolved by the employers and the unions.

An officer lays into a striker during a police baton-charge.

President Wilson is proud midwife to League of Nations

Feb 14. President Wilson scored a major triumph at the Paris peace conference today, when delegates from 27 nations agreed to his proposal for a League of Nations to prevent war. The President had outlined his ideas for "a general association of nations" in a message to Congress last year.

In that speech he set out 14 proposals for the post-war settlement. Most of them covered such matters as the re-drawing of frontiers and self-determination for the former subject peoples of Austro-Hungary, but the President also wants to put an end to secret treaties.

Today's support for the idea of a League was only in general terms and the details have still to be filled in. But the President is optimistic. "I believe that the conscience of the world has long been prepared to express itself in some such way," he told delegates.

The agreement, or covenant, setting up the League will be incorporated in the peace treaty with Germany, now being discussed by the Paris conference. On this, delegates have found themselves deeply divided between those, like France, who want to see Germany made to pay, and the President, who wants a "just peace" (→25).

Fear of flu means strict hygiene measures for crowded public places. This man holds a spray used to disinfect London buses.

First air service links London-Paris

Feb 9. Passengers flew between London and Paris for the first time today. The flight in a Farman F60 Goliath aircraft took three hours 30 minutes to arrive at an airport near Versailles after it took off from Kenley, London, at 12.20pm. The twin-engined aircraft flew at a speed of 97 miles an hour.

Because of the continuing ban on civil flying, all the passengers were military. The French pilot of the biplane said very strong winds hit the aircraft during the flight but the passengers did not seem to mind, they were busy smoking and playing cards. Experts hope the historic flight will lead the way to a real passenger service once civil flying is resumed.

Unions want bigger slice of the cake

Feb 27. At the national industrial conference at Central Hall, Westminster, today the Prime Minister accepted a resolution from the Labour Party's Arthur Henderson setting up an employer/union committee to help solve the nation's industrial crisis. James Thomas MP, the leader of the National Union of Railwaymen, said that organised labour was determined to get a higher share of the post-war national cake.

Arthur Henderson: speaking for Labour at the industrial summit.

1919

MARCH

Su	Mo	Tu	We	Th	Fr	Sa
						1
2	3	4	5	6	7	8
9	10	11	12	13	14	15
16	17	18	19	20	21	22
23	24	25	26	27	28	29
30	31					

1. Spain: Martial law is declared following riots over food shortage.

3. Washington: Administration says the Great War cost the US $197,000 million.

4. Oxford: The University decides to drop Greek as a compulsory subject for entrance examinations.

5. UK: Trial flight of British 1,250 hp five-engined dirigible R-34, with enough fuel to fly to the US and back.

6. London: The Board of Trade reveals that women in paid occupations increased by 1.2 million during the War.

10. London: The Government is reported to be in favour of a Channel Tunnel.

11. Versailles: Allied supreme council orders German Navy cut to 15,000 men (→ 4/4).

12. Germany: The Government agrees to give up ships in Chilean ports in return for urgent food supplies.

14. Paris: Emile Cottin is sentenced to death for attempting to murder Premier Clemenceau.

16. UK: Invention of a wireless telephone enabling air pilots to talk in flight.

18. UK: Deaths in England and Wales exceeded births for the first time on record last quarter, due to influenza.

21. London: Government Commission on coal recommends giving miners a two shillings increase for a seven-hour day.

23. Venice: Italy takes charge of the Austrian naval fleet.

26. Budapest: Former Hungarian president Count Michael Karolyi is arrested by the communist regime.

28. UK: Mrs Peel's Poethlyn wins the Grand National.

29. S. America: UK scientists observing eclipse of the sun confirm Einstein's 1915 Theory of General Relativity.

29. Holland: Ex-Kaiser Wilhelm II says he would rather kill himself than submit to a trial by the Allies.

Lenin seeks to spark revolution in Europe

Leading the struggle: Red Army chief Trotsky with his troops.

March 3. Although Russia is still gripped by civil war, the Bolshevik leaders today established the Comintern, an official vehicle for world revolution.

The Comintern, the abbreviation for Communist International, was formed by Vladimir Lenin and other leading Bolsheviks, and it can be expected to be an important element of Soviet foreign policy in the future.

Lenin, who appears to have recovered fairly well from the attempt on his life by Fanya Dara-Kaplan, is arguing that the security of the regime depends on its being surrounded by friendly governments, so he advocates sparking revolutions throughout Europe. Predictably the Bolsheviks are claiming leadership of communism in the world Socialist movement. They believe that Europe is ready for revolution, and this is being held back by the timidity and cowardice of the Second, or Socialist, International.

The First International was established in London in 1864 with the aim of coordinating working class movements. This week's meeting of the Third International drew 45 voting delegates representing 19 groups. Because of the civil war only a handful of the delegates who attended the conference came from outside Russia.

Nationalist women wearing the traditional Moslem veil address a crowd in a street in the Egyptian capital of Cairo.

Germans go hungry as famine spreads

March 11. With famine sweeping Germany and much of Central Europe, the Allies have reached a compromise agreement to supply their former enemies with temporary food relief. Germany will pay $200 million from credits in neutral countries for the first shipment.

Before the war, German farmers could supply 95 per cent of the country's food. With fertiliser plants lacking such necessities as coal, transport and labour, the figure is now 45 per cent. Infant mortality is soaring. Some cities are on a potato ration of only two pounds a week.

With France insisting that Germans should work for their food, Britain and America are concerned that in the ensuing climate of resentment Bolshevik revolution could spread quickly in a weakened Germany already in the throes of a near-civil war.

Mussolini founds Fascist Party

Mussolini: armchair revolutionary.

March 23. Benito Mussolini, a socialist journalist who broke with the Italian Socialist Party at the beginning of the war, has formed his own party, the Fasci di Combattimento.

Appealing to veterans of the war, troubled by the malaise of post-war Italy, the party's policy is an emotive mixture of socialism and nationalism. Mussolini, son of a blacksmith and a schoolteacher, intends to fight both liberalism and communism (→ 19/11).

1919

APRIL

Su	Mo	Tu	We	Th	Fr	Sa
		1	2	3	4	5
6	7	8	9	10	11	12
13	14	15	16	17	18	19
20	21	22	23	24	25	26
27	28	29	30			

4. UK: Workers and employers agree to a truce at the industrial conference (→ 7).

4. Versailles: Allies and Germany sign agreement on Danzig, which is to become a Free City (→ 8).

5. Ireland: Eamon de Valera is elected president of Sinn Fein.→

7. UK: Delegates to the industrial conference agree to the idea of a National Industrial Council.

8. Versailles: Peace Conference decides to site headquarters of the League of Nations at Geneva in Switzerland (→ 14).

10. Mexico: Rebel leader Emiliano Zapata is killed by government troops.

11. Munich: Coup attempt aims to overthrow the soviet government of Bavaria.

13. UK: Petrol now costs around 3/6d a gallon.

14. Versailles: Germany's war reparations are provisionally set at £5,400 million (→ 30).

18. Russia: The Crimea is now entirely in the hands of the Bolshevik Red Army (→ 20).

19. London: The Government says it is sending more troops to Egypt to counter continuing nationalist unrest.

20. Ukraine: The Bolshevik First Army surrenders to the Ukrainians.

23. London: The coal commission begins to look at nationalisation (→ 29).

24. UK: Announced that the Prince of Wales is to become a freemason.

26. London: Chelsea beats Fulham 3-0 at Highbury for the London "Victory Cup".

29. UK: Socialist Sidney Webb suggests a scheme for nationalisation of the coal industry (→ 23/6).

29. Constantinople: 12 men, including ex-ministers, go on trial for committing atrocities and other crimes.

30. Versailles: Arrival of German Peace Conference delegates (→ 7/5).

Troops massacre protesters in Amritsar

April 13. Amritsar, holy city of the Sikhs in northern India, was the scene of riot and bloodbath today when troops, under the command of Brigadier-General Dyer, opened fire on an unlawful demonstration on a large piece of wasteland known as the Jallianwala Bagh, killing many women and children.

The shooting took place after several days of rioting following Gandhi's declaration of a hartal, a business strike, in protest against the passing of the new security laws proposed by the Rowlatt report, which are causing great indignation.

Serious rioting broke out across the sub-continent earlier this week and two days ago, when the notorious agitators, Dr Kichlu and Mr Satya Pal, were arrested at Amritsar, the mob destroyed the railway goods shed and marched in a great shouting horde on the European part of the city.

The rioters were repulsed by the civilian police, but rampaged through Amritsar killing at least three Europeans. The police then called for army reinforcements from Lahore.

Brigadier-General Dyer, a fiery Irishman educated in India, arrived to find thousands of demonstrators gathering and marched his small force of troops to disperse them.

Exactly what happened then is as yet unclear, but it is known that when the mob refused to leave, the troops opened fire. The huge crowd panicked, children were trampled and it is feared that there are many casualties.

Movie stars join to form United Artists

Griffith signs as (l. to r.) Fairbanks, Chaplin, lawyers and Pickford watch.

April 17. Four of the best-known names in pictures, Mary Pickford, Douglas Fairbanks, Charles Chaplin and D.W. Griffith, have teamed up to form their own film-distributing company, United Artists. Their object is to safeguard a share in the huge profits that are earned by their films. Although they are paid enormous salaries – Mary Pickford as "the world's sweetheart" is reputed to receive $100,000 a year – they want to be their own employers on films and share in distribution.

Miss Pickford and Mr Fairbanks plan to build a new studio in Hollywood to make pictures for United Artists release. Griffith is shooting "Broken Blossoms" this year with Lillian Gish. Chaplin, fresh from his greatest success as the most unmilitary of soldiers in "Shoulder Arms", is at work on "The Kid" with Jackie Coogan. He is still contracted to First National. ▷

De Valera seeks ticket to Paris peace talks

April 28. Eamon de Valera, the head of the Dail or Irish parliament, is now back in Ireland as a result of the amnesty for Sinn Fein activists. His return, after being imprisoned in Lincoln gaol last year and escaping earlier this year, has heightened speculation about future developments in Ireland.

"Dev", as he is known to his followers, is the political driving force behind Sinn Fein. He is likely to make the Paris peace conference his first target. In the Irish election, Sinn Fein fought to gain admission to the peace conference by the front door. So far, Britain's Prime Minister, David Lloyd George, has kept front and back doors firmly closed to Sean O'Kelly, Sinn Fein's "ambassador".

Lloyd George argues that the future of Ireland is an internal affair for the British parliament with Ireland's future to be resolved once the peace conference is over. However, Irish-born army officers, who served with the British forces in the war, have petitioned the King to give Sinn Fein a seat at the conference table. They have a special interest: given the mood in Ireland, their own safety could not be assured when they return home.

Dail leader de Valera.

British beat off Bolsheviks at Archangel

April 1. A Bolshevik offensive in northern Russia has been beaten off by Allied forces with the enemy suffering heavy losses.

A communique from the Front at Archangel said that British troops behaved with great gallantry and steadfastness and that losses, in consequence, were slight. Enemy dead and wounded were lying out in the forests surrounding the British posts. There is still some optimism that in the next few weeks it will be possible to send relief supplies to Admiral Kolchak's Siberian force.

Meanwhile the Murmansk and Archangel garrisons have both been troubled by Bolsheviks spreading propaganda among British and White soldiers. In Murmansk two British officers were murdered.

The situation in southern Russia looks very bleak for the the Allies, due largely to their extreme food shortages.

A British naval firing squad off Archangel ends one Bolshevik's struggle.

Central European soviets overthrown

April 22. Two fledgling socialist republics, modelled on Lenin's soviets in Russia, are in turmoil today, racked by internal feuding, while counter-revolutionary forces prepare to attack. The Bavarian Soviet Republic, proclaimed at the beginning of the year, barely survived a counter-coup mounted by Social Democrats; and troops loyal to Berlin are on the way.

Meanwhile, in Budapest, the Bolshevik Bela Kun, who was taken from gaol to lead a Soviet regime, is trying to raise a Red Army; but the men keep deserting him.

850,000 dogs face anti-rabies muzzle

April 23. An Irish terrier bit a "small white dog" in Surrey recently, and now Britain faces a rabies scare which has led to the muzzling of 850,000 dogs in London and the Home Counties.

London, Middlesex, Surrey and other Home Counties as well as Hampshire have been declared "controlled areas" and dogs leaving them without licences must be quarantined for six months unless they are "passing through".

1919

MAY

Su	Mo	Tu	We	Th	Fr	Sa
				1	2	3
4	5	6	7	8	9	10
11	12	13	14	15	16	17
18	19	20	21	22	23	24
25	26	27	28	29	30	31

1. Paris: 80 policemen are injured in May Day riots between police and workers.

1. UK: Aviation is once more open to civilians from today.

2. Bavaria: Berlin government troops enter Munich to overthrow the soviet regime.

3. Budapest: The Hungarian communist regime surrenders to Allied troops.

6. London: The Admiralty says helium is a non-inflammable substitute for hydrogen in airships.

7. Versailles: German delegates are presented with the Peace Treaty between 27 allies and associated powers (→20).

10. UK: Start of the country's first scheduled commercial air service, from Manchester to Southport, run by A. V. Roe (→30/9).

11. India: British troops defeat Afghan raiders (→24).

12. London: First post-war performance at Covent Garden: Beecham conducts Puccini's "La Boheme".

14. Germany: Two are sentenced to death for the murder of socialist leader Karl Liebknecht (→1/6).

15. Norwich: Nurse Edith Cavell, whose body has been brought back from Belgium, is re-interred.

20. Versailles: The Germans are given more time to sign the Peace Treaty (→31).

24. Afghanistan: British aircraft bomb Jellallabad and Kabul.

25. Atlantic: British airmen Harry Hawker and Lt. Grieve are rescued from the sea 850 miles off Ireland, after failing to fly the Atlantic non-stop.→

28. London: The Government launches an inquiry into London's traffic problem.

30. London: The Government refuses to recognise a police trade union, but offers a pay rise to police officers.

31. Versailles: German delegate Count Brockdorff-Rantzau resigns rather than sign the Peace Treaty (→17/6).

First plane crosses the Atlantic Ocean

May 27. A plane has flown across the Atlantic. This incredible feat was achieved by the United States Navy seaplane NC-4, which arrived today in Lisbon, having flown 3,150 nautical miles in a little less than 44 hours of flying time.

The plane, piloted by Lt. Commander A.C. Read and Lt. Stone, left Rockaway, New York, on May 8 and flew to Newfoundland. The actual Atlantic crossing was made in three stages. The biggest was 1,200 miles from Trespass Bay to the Azores. Then came a 150-mile hop along the Azores and a final 800 miles to Lisbon (→9/10).

British and Afghans in border clashes

May 11. Troops under General Barrett have inflicted a sharp reverse today on the invading Afghans at Bagh Springs. The whole of the frontier area is up in arms with tribesmen threatening Landi Kotal and martial law being proclaimed in Peshawar. It is expected however that General Barrett, well equipped with guns and aeroplanes, will soon control the situation.

Reports had been reaching London for some time about the possibility of an Afghan incursion following the murder of the pro-British Emir Habibullah. His third son, Amanullah Khan, who has taken over the throne, is known to be hostile towards the government of India.

1919

JUNE

Su	Mo	Tu	We	Th	Fr	Sa
1	2	3	4	5	6	7
8	9	10	11	12	13	14
15	16	17	18	19	20	21
22	23	24	25	26	27	28
29	30					

1. Berlin: The body of murdered socialist Rosa Luxemburg is discovered in a canal (→16/1).

1. Germany: A "Rhine Republic" is proclaimed in several Rhineland cities.

2. UK: Lady Diana Manners marries Conservative politician Duff Cooper.

3. US: 67 arrests follow suspected anarchist bomb attacks yesterday on the homes of seven US justice officials.

4. UK: Lord Glanely's Grand Parade wins the "Victory Derby", back at Epsom for the first time since 1914.

4. Washington: The Senate approves a Constitutional Amendment providing for women's suffrage.

6. Baltic: British warships sink two Bolshevik ships in Kronstadt harbour.

7. Germany: Artist Max Beckmann's first exhibition opens in Frankfurt.

9. Constantinople: The Turkish Sultan's palace is destroyed by fire.

10. Central America: The US warns Costa Rica not to pursue its expected invasion of Nicaragua.

12. Wales: Nationalists call for a Welsh regional parliament.

16. Vienna: Communist demonstration leads to eight deaths and many injured.

17. Versailles: The German delegates are stoned when they leave the Peace Conference for Berlin (→20).

20. Berlin: Philipp Scheidemann resigns as German Chancellor, rather than sign the Peace Treaty.→

22. US: 200 are feared dead after a tornado strikes Fergus Falls, Minnesota.

23. London: The Government's coal commission recommends nationalisation of the mines (→9/10).

27. UK: The Labour Party Conference votes in favour of going on strike for political purposes.

Germans pull the plug on captive fleet

The scuttled "Nurnberg" begins to settle at the stern as its crew surrenders.

June 21. German sailors today carried out a final act of defiance at their captors when they opened the sea cocks on the 70 vessels interned at Scapa Flow in the Orkneys and scuttled them.

The action took the British authorities totally by surprise. It began at noon when the skeleton crews, who have all been left completely unguarded on the vessels, were seen to raise the German Eagle flag. It was a signal for the sinking to begin and at 12.15 the first vessel was seen to start listing, turn turtle and then slide beneath the water. The rest soon followed.

The German sailors began jumping overboard onto rafts and several were killed when British troops opened fire when they refused orders to stop. Of the whole fleet, valued at around £50,000,000, only one battleship, a light cruiser, and a few destroyers remain afloat. The British fleet was at sea on exercise when the surprise action took place, but a few guardships and tugs managed to tow some cruisers and destroyers onto beaches.

The German Rear-Admiral, von Reuter, in command of the 1,800 strong skeleton crews, admitted ordering the ships' destruction, saying he understood the armistice had been terminated and that he was following instructions issued at the beginning of the war that no German warships should be surrendered.

Alcock and Brown fly Atlantic non-stop

June 15. A Vickers-Vimy biplane, flown by Captain John Alcock from Britain and navigated by Lt. Arthur Whitten Brown of the US, landed in a bog on the Irish coast at Clifden today, completing the first nonstop flight across the Atlantic. The Rolls-Royce powered bomber, fitted with long range fuel tanks, took off from Newfoundland yesterday and completed the 1,900 mile flight in 16 hours 12 minutes, averaging 120 miles per hour. It was a "terrible journey," declared Alcock. The aircraft flew through fog and sleet storms, with its crew sustained only by coffee and beer, sandwiches and chocolate.

Alcock and Brown come ashore.

▷

German fury at Versailles treatment

June 28. Outside the Palace of Versailles, at ten minutes to four this afternoon, the crash of gunfire told a wildly cheering crowd that the Germans had at last signed the peace treaty. The Great War, that cost almost ten million Allied and enemy lives, was officially ended, but to many of those who watched the grim-faced German delegates at the moment of signing it hardly felt like peace.

The Germans were accepting terms that had been imposed on them, virtually without negotiation. They had, for almost two months, been refusing to sign and had caved in only under the threat of military occupation.

The treaty – 200 pages, 75,000 words, 440 clauses – was drawn up over a period of five months at the Paris conference of the victorious Allies. They spent much of the time quarrelling over the extent of the punishment to be applied to Germany. Lloyd George, the British Prime Minister, fighting a general election at home, had promised to "squeeze the German lemon until the pips squeak". But even he is aghast at the French demands.

President Poincare wanted Germany to be partitioned and a separate peace made without Prussia. This has been rejected by America and Britain, but the terms finally agreed are, in Lloyd George's view, so harsh that "we shall have to fight another war all over again in 25 years at three times the cost".

Germany is called on to make a provisional compensation payment of 20 billion gold marks; the final reparations figure will be decided later. Territory totalling 87 square km, with a population of 7,000,000, must be surrendered to neighbouring states. The left bank of the Rhine will remain under Allied occupation for up to 15 years.

When the treaty was presented to the German Foreign Minister, Count Ulrich Brockdorff-Rantzau, he protested: "The demand is made that we shall acknowledge that we alone are guilty of having caused the war. Such a confession in my mouth would be a lie." The French Premier, Georges Clemenceau, curtly told him he had 15 days in which to make "observations", but there would be no negotiations. The German Cabinet resigned after Brockdorff-Rantzau showed them the treaty and even President Ebert wanted to quit. A week of public mourning was decreed.

In the Assembly deputies sang "Deutschland uber Alles" after delivering emotional speeches on the impossibility of signing the treaty. Thousands of copies of it are circulating, and crowds daily take to the streets to burn the French flag. Germans blame US President Wilson, because they say he has not kept to his promise to bring about peace on the basis of his Fourteen Points; and the League of Nations, which Wilson sees as a guardian of peace, is in the German view no more than a self-serving alliance of victors.

Reluctantly, the Germans have recognised that they have no choice, and last week the National Assembly, with some bitterness, finally accepted the treaty by a majority. Brockdorff-Rantzau was not present for the signing today; just two lower-ranking officials, Dr Muller and Dr Bell, stepped into the chamber when Georges Clemenceau said: "Faites entrer les Allemands".

Versailles Treaty authors Clemenceau, Wilson and Lloyd George.

Children settle down to celebrate the Versailles peace with a tea party.

1919

JULY

Su	Mo	Tu	We	Th	Fr	Sa
		1	2	3	4	5
6	7	8	9	10	11	12
13	14	15	16	17	18	19
20	21	22	23	24	25	26
27	28	29	30	31		

2. Edinburgh: Airship R-34 leaves on its Atlantic crossing.→

4. France: Demobilisation law comes into force.

6. London: Thanksgiving service for the Peace Treaty is held in St. Paul's Cathedral.

9. London: The Government decides to raise the price of coal by six shillings a ton.

12. Europe: The Allies lift their blockade of Germany.

15. London: US General Pershing arrives to lead the Peace Celebration Parade through the capital (→ 19).

16. Washington: Plans are announced for a National Guard of 440,000 men.

18. London: Sir Edwin Lutyens' new war memorial, the Cenotaph, is unveiled in Whitehall.

18. Berlin: The Reichstag votes against separation of Church and State.

19. Los Angeles: An aeroplane is used for the first time to arrest a speeding motorist.

19. UK: Peace parades take place throughout the country.

21. London: Committee of Inquiry recommends the creation of a London Traffic Board.

22. London: MPs approve at a single sitting a bill to ratify the Versailles Treaty.

25. UK: Four-day-old coal strike is settled as miners accept a 14.2 per cent increase in piece rates.

28. Chicago: 4,000 troops are called out to quell rioting by blacks that has left 14 dead and 76 injured.

31. London: 6,203 Metropolitan Police officers who answer today's strike call are summarily dismissed (→ 4/8).

BIRTH

15. Irish-born British writer Iris Murdoch.

DEATH

1. British physicist John Strutt, Lord Rayleigh (*11/12/1842).

Germany declared republic at Weimar

July 31. After the stormy debates on the peace treaty, deputies have returned to constitution-making. Parliament is to keep the old name Reichstag, election will be by proportional representation and seats will be allocated to names on party lists, which means that membership of the Reichstag will in effect be determined by a small number of party activists.

The constituent assembly, elected by universal suffrage, with women voting for the first time, moved to Weimar in order to escape the shadow of the unlamented Kaiser. But the upsurge of national feeling over the treaty brought the deputies hurrying back to Berlin and last Monday they voted by 262 to 75 to adopt what will still be known as the Weimar Constitution. Social Democrats and centre parties voted for it, and the extreme left and right were against.

The months of near anarchy in the country have persuaded the assembly to go for a presidency with far-reaching powers to govern in an emergency.

Game, set and style to Lenglen

Short dress, bare arms and sheer brilliance assure Lenglen of victory.

July 5. The astonishing 20-year-old prodigy Suzanne Lenglen today won the delayed women's final. Wimbledon, recovering from the rain which washed out play on Friday, hailed its first post-war singles champion and its first-ever from a non-English speaking nation.

It was a final so closely fought that even King George, watching the game with Queen Mary, confessed to feeling "quite ill" with tension during the final set. The tall, athletic French girl, playing in an unusually short, loose and sleeveless dress, saved two match points in the final set to beat the 40-year-old 1914 champion, Dorothea Chambers, 10-8, 4-6, 9-7. Gerald Patterson is new Men's champion.

Police trade union issues strike call

July 30. Policemen throughout the country were urged to join a lightning strike tomorrow against the Police Bill now going through the Commons. The Police Union is angry about the clause which will stop policemen taking part in normal trade union activities. Instead they will join a new body to be called the Police Federation.

Last year's strike, which left London policeless, fuelled the worries of those who feel that trade unionism in the police is the first step towards a communist revolution. The Government is determined to get the Bill through and has promised summary dismissal for those police who strike.

The strike call may only be answered by a few. Their mood has changed since last year when over 12,000 police came out in London alone. Most policemen have been mollified by the big pay increases promised in the Bill and the immediate payment of a lump sum of £10 to cover arrears. This is equal to at least ten weeks' pay for an experienced policeman.

British airship in first Atlantic round trip

July 13. The British airship R-34 landed in Norfolk today after the first two-way crossing of the North Atlantic by air. On board was the first transatlantic air stowaway, rigger William Ballantyne, who hid on board after he was dropped from the crew at the last moment. The R-34, with a crew of 30, left Edinburgh on July 2, arriving at Long Island, New York, on July 6, taking slightly longer than the liner Mauretania to make the crossing. One crew member had to parachute to the ground on arrival to help anchor the airship.

R-34 landing at Pulham in Norfolk after her transatlantic return trip.

Dempsey thrashes Willard in three rounds

July 4. Jack Dempsey, the 24-year-old copper miner from Colorado, tonight conducted his own Independence Day celebrations by pummelling his way to the world heavyweight championship in Toledo, Ohio. He overpowered the giant cowboy Jess Willard, champion for the last four years, in three merciless rounds.

Dempsey, who is nicknamed The Manassa Mauler and already both renowned and feared for his menacing style, his ungainly crouching stance and his relentless refusal to retreat, was giving away more than four stone in weight to the holder. But he unleashed a non-stop barrage from the first bell and knocked the astonished Willard down no fewer than seven times before the end of the first round.

By the end of the third many of the 45,000 spectators – the promotors are believed to have taken a record $1 million in gate money – were shouting "Stop it! Stop it!", and Willard's trainer capitulated by throwing two towels into the ring.

The battered Willard, whose wife had unfortunately chosen this occasion to watch her husband fight for the very first time, immediately announced that it was his intention to retire from professional boxing.

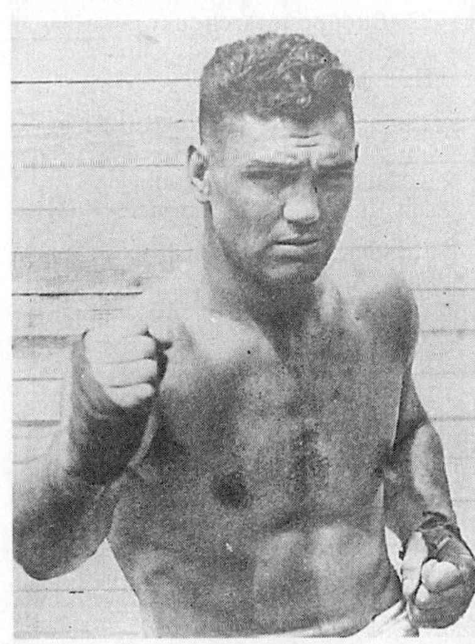

"Manassa Mauler" Dempsey.

1919

AUGUST

Su	Mo	Tu	We	Th	Fr	Sa
					1	2
3	4	5	6	7	8	9
10	11	12	13	14	15	16
17	18	19	20	21	22	23
24	25	26	27	28	29	30
31						

3. Liverpool: Riots break out as the police strike leads to widespread law-breaking (→4).

4. Liverpool: 300 rioters are arrested as the Army intervenes to tackle lawlessness during the police strike.

4. Budapest: Rumanian troops occupy the city, ending Bela Kun's 133-day-old communist republic (→9).

6. London: King George V awards PM David Lloyd George the Order of Merit for his services in wartime.

9. Budapest: Archduke Josef, leader of the new Hungarian regime, recognizes the Treaty of Versailles (→22).

9. Asia: The UK signs an agreement with Persia, promising a loan of £2 million and administrative advice.

10. London: Police discover a communist revolutionary plot in a raid in Acton, West London.

15. Paris: The Government says it lost 60 per cent of its air force in the War.

16. Ireland: Sinn Fein supporters are involved in serious rioting throughout the island (→11/9).

19. London: Bill disestablishing the Church of Wales, postponed by the War, receives Royal Assent.

21. Mexico: US cavalry kill four bandits believed to have kidnapped two US airmen.

22. Budapest: Archduke Josef resigns as head of the Hungarian regime.

25. London: Beginning of daily flights to Paris, the world's first international scheduled daily air service.

28. Germany: A Polish-backed uprising in Upper Silesia is crushed by German troops.

DEATHS

11. Scottish-born US millionaire philanthropist Andrew Carnegie (*25/11/1835).

27. South African leader General Louis Botha (*22/9/1862).→

Smuts takes over in South Africa

Lieutenant-General Jan C. Smuts.

Aug 31. General Jan Smuts has succeeded Louis Botha as South African Prime Minister. He is 49 years old and played a significant part in the conquest of Germany's colonies in East and South West Africa. After serving as state attorney in the Boer republic of Transvaal, he joined the Boer commandos when war broke out in 1899 and proved a troublesome adversary. But with the granting of self-government to South Africa he became a firm friend of Britain.

Botha, who died on August 27 after a short illness, and Smuts were familiar figures at the Paris peace conference; it is said that after reading the terms of the Versailles treaty Smuts was unable to sleep.

Rising hemlines and a lighter look are key features of this autumn's Paris fashions.

1919

SEPTEMBER

Su	Mo	Tu	We	Th	Fr	Sa
	1	2	3	4	5	6
7	8	9	10	11	12	13
14	15	16	17	18	19	20
21	22	23	24	25	26	27
28	29	30				

3. US: President Wilson leaves on a tour of the country to get support for the League of Nations (→5).

5. US: President Wilson says US faces the choice of "peace partnership or armed isolation" in a speech at St. Louis.→

6. Vienna: The Austrian National Assembly agrees to sign the Versailles Peace Treaty (→20).

9. Mexico: Nearly 500 are feared dead in the sinking of the Spanish liner Valbanera in the Gulf of Mexico.

10. UK: The Trades Union Congress votes in favour of nationalisation of the mines (→9/10).

12. Munich: German Workers' Party leader Adolf Hitler addresses a meeting of the party (→24/2/1920).

18. US: Roland Rohlfs sets a new flight altitude record of 34,610 feet in his Curtiss Wasp.

20. Vienna: The Austrian Government reveals that the German Kaiser urged Austria to begin the Great War.

21. Europe: The Paris to Constantinople Orient Express runs for the first time since the War.

22. UK: 50,000 iron foundry workers go on strike for higher wages (→11/10).

25. UK: Lord Leconfield gives Scafell Pike to the nation in memory of the Great War dead.

27. London: Prime Minister Lloyd George calls the rail strike an "anarchist conspiracy". →

28. US: Mobs, enraged at alleged black attacks on women, lynch a black and burn the courthouse in Omaha, Nebraska.

30. UK: End of the UK's first scheduled civil air service, after 194 flights from Manchester to Southport at four guineas one way (→10/5).

DEATH

26. Italian soprano Adelina Patti (*19/2/1843).

Rationing returns to beat rail strike

Sept 27. The national rail strike began today at midnight. A spokesman for the Government said that as the unions had declared a railway war, "it is going to be fought, so long as the Government has the fighting of it, with the full resources of the community".

Mr Roberts, Food Controller, has invoked emergency powers to reduce the size of rations of certain foodstuffs. The weekly sugar ration is halved to 6 oz and butcher's meat limited to 1s 8d.

The Government, which has been caught somewhat on the hop by this sudden strike, is also very concerned about the supply of milk and mail, but Field Marshal Sir Douglas Haig's presence in Downing Street yesterday indicates that the Prime Minister will, if needed, use the military (→5/10).

Londoners fight to get on a tram.

Italian poet seizes city from League

Sept 23. The swashbuckling Italian poet-aviator, Gabriele d'Annunzio, has occupied the Adriatic city of Fiume – once Austrian but now held by the League of Nations – with 2,600 men and claimed it for Italy. The Italian government has condemned this action as mutinous but today d'Annunzio is a hero to his countrymen who regard Fiume as one of the spoils of war.

President Wilson suffers breakdown

Troubled peacemaker Wilson.

Sept 22. President Wilson has been forced by illness to abandon his tour of the Mid-West and the West, where he has been appealing for support for his peace treaty.

In Pueblo, Colorado, last night he made a moving speech, invoking those American soldiers who had died during the war, "those dear ghosts, who still deploy upon the fields of France". For a moment Mr Wilson broke down in tears.

Every night the President has been tormented by headaches and insomnia. This morning, however, the left side of his face was paralysed and his doctor declared that he had suffered "a complete nervous breakdown". With blinds drawn, the Presidential train set off for Washington (→2/10).

Sinn Fein banned but Collins flees

Sept 11. Britain today declared the Dail Eireann, or "Irish Parliament", illegal. So the assembly, set up by Sinn Fein MPs elected to Westminster last December, comes to an end. Police and soldiers surrounded the Mansion House in Dublin yesterday, but Michael Collins, the provisional "Minister of Finance", escaped through a skylight.

1919

OCTOBER

Su	Mo	Tu	We	Th	Fr	Sa
			1	2	3	4
5	6	7	8	9	10	11
12	13	14	15	16	17	18
19	20	21	22	23	24	25
26	27	28	29	30	31	

2. Washington: White House doctors say President Wilson is "a very sick man".

2. Paris: French MPs ratify the Versailles Peace Treaty.

5. UK: The rail strike ends.

9. London: Prime Minister Lloyd George rejects nationalisation of the mines.

10. Vienna: Premiere of Richard Strauss's opera "Die Frau ohne Schatten".

10. UK: Teachers ask for a 100 per cent increase in their pre-war salaries.

11. UK: Settlement is reached in the iron founders' strike.

13. Paris: Premier Georges Clemenceau says he will retire from the French cabinet after November elections (→30/11).

16. London: Government Commission is set up to look into a system of federal devolution for the UK.

17. Tokyo: The Japanese government says it will spend around £30 million on aviation development.

23. London: Ex-Viceroy of India Lord Curzon takes over as Foreign Secretary from Tory leader Arthur Balfour.

24. Egypt: Two are killed and ten hurt when police fire on a nationalist demonstration (→6/11).

25. UK: Six Sinn Fein prisoners escape from Strangeways Prison.

27. London: Government figures show a national debt of £473,645,000.

29. Germany: Anti-Semitism is reported to be spreading through the country.

BIRTHS

8. Canadian statesman Pierre-Elliot Trudeau.

22. British writer Doris Lessing.

26. Iranian Shah Mohammed Reza Pahlevi (†27/7/80).

DEATH

18. British peer Viscount William Waldorf, Lord Astor (*31/3/1848).

Trotsky's Reds are bleeding the Whites

Oct 21. The tide in Russia has turned in favour of the Bolsheviks and Trotsky's Red Army. After nearly two years of civil war and foreign intervention, the Reds are poised to defeat the Whites.

Despite the inevitable flow of optimistic statements of success by White generals, it is clear the Red Army is proving successful on every front.

Early this month Cossack forces, commanded by General Anton Denikin, were 200 miles south of Moscow. A Royal Air Force unit attached to Denikin was poised to bomb Moscow with RE8 reconnaissance aircraft. The Bolsheviks seemed on the point of defeat but Denikin overstretched himself.

The Whites were also threatening Petrograd. The former Czarist General Nikolai Yudenich, whose forces included a British tank corps, reached the outskirts of the city, which seemed to be at his mercy. It was an illusion. When the Red Army counter-attacked the retreat began. The situation is not much better for Admiral Alexander Kolchak whose forces at one stage were some 450 miles east of Moscow.

Trotsky (l.) with a comrade.

The campaign has since gone disastrously wrong and Red forces under General Tukharchevsky have broken through the Urals and are pushing on to Omsk.

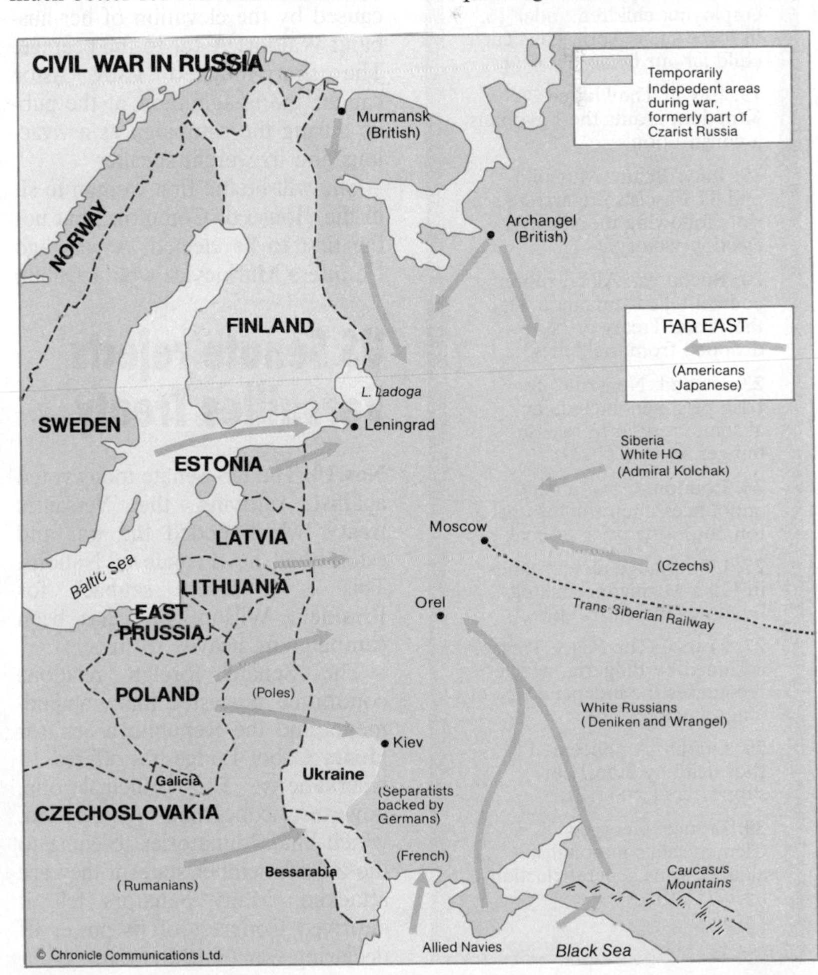

1919

NOVEMBER

Su	Mo	Tu	We	Th	Fr	Sa
						1
2	3	4	5	6	7	8
9	10	11	12	13	14	15
16	17	18	19	20	21	22
23	24	25	26	27	28	29
30						

1. US: Indian reservations in Arizona are opened to mineral prospectors.

1. Germany: The Government says it will shut down the country's railways for ten days to save coal.

2. US: 500,000 coal miners strike for a 60 per cent pay rise, a six-hour day and a five-day week (→ 10/12).

3. London: Labour win control of 14 out of 28 boroughs in the London municipal elections.

5. US: Republican Governor Calvin Coolidge is re-elected.

7. London: The Olympia Motor Show opens for the first time since 1913.

11. British Empire: The first anniversary of the Armistice is marked by two minutes' silence at 11 am.

15. US: Tax penalties on firms employing children under 16, in force since April, have cut child labour by 40 per cent.

19. Egypt: The United Kingdom grants the Egyptians a constitution.

19. Italy: Benito Mussolini and 37 Fascists are arrested in riots following the Socialist election victory.

20. Bucharest: Allied supreme council tells Rumania to sign the Peace Treaty or be dropped from the Allies.

23. Ireland: New rules for Irish prisoners include an absolute refusal to release hunger strikers (→ 29).

24. London: Government announces a ten shillings per ton cut in the price of coal.

27. US: A huge meteor lands in Lake Michigan, shaking buildings in nearby cities.

27. France: The Peace Treaty is signed by Bulgaria, which recognises the independence of Yugoslavia.

29. Dublin: A policeman is shot dead by Sinn Fein supporters (→ 11/12).

30. France: Georges Clemenceau's nationalist alliance wins general elections (→ 17/1/20).

Nancy Astor is elected as woman MP

Lady Astor (centre) listens as the returning officer announces her victory.

Nov 28. Viscountess (Nancy) Astor, who was born in America, became Britain's first woman MP today. She held a safe Plymouth seat for the Tories in a by-election caused by the elevation of her husband Waldorf Astor to the peerage. The sharp-tongued Lady Astor caught the imagination of the public during the campaign as a vivacious and irreverent speaker.

She will be the first woman to sit in the House of Commons, but not the first to be elected. A year ago Countess Markievicz won a Dublin consitituency for Sinn Fein, but made herself ineligible by refusing to take the oath of allegiance to the monarch.

Lady Astor told the voters: "Pray for me. Old Lloyd George with all his faults is the best we have got." At Westminster she intends to dress plainly. "I want to make it possible for the humblest woman who may be elected to follow the precedent I set", she said. The Parliamentary authorities say they have made "certain arrangements for lady members" (→ 1/12).

US Senate rejects Versailles Treaty

Nov 19. The US Senate today voted against ratifying the Versailles treaty, which ended the war and established the League of Nations. This is a severe set-back for President Wilson, who has been campaigning heavily for it.

The Senate foreign relations committee suggested many amendments and the Republican Senator Henry Cabot Lodge has offered 14 reservations. The principal one, however, concerned Article ten, which binds signatories to come to the aid of member states if they are attacked. Many Senators felt it deprived Congress of its power of declaring war (→ 19/3/1920).

Police open fire on Egyptian rioters

Nov 16. Nationalist demonstrators set fire to three police stations in Cairo today and the Egyptian police and infantry were forced to open fire on them.

Then, as the mobs gathered in the Abdin Square, British troops were summoned and, armed with rifles and heavy sticks, they chased the demonstrators through the streets and restored order.

The protest began quietly with students carrying the Egyptian flag marching in procession and chanting slogans, but then they started to attack the police. Sixty people have been treated for gunshot wounds and ten have died (→ 19).

1919

DECEMBER

Su	Mo	Tu	We	Th	Fr	Sa
	1	2	3	4	5	6
7	8	9	10	11	12	13
14	15	16	17	18	19	20
21	22	23	24	25	26	27
28	29	30	31			

1. London: Lady Astor takes her Commons seat.

3. Italy: Several cities are paralysed by a general strike.

4. London: This year's spending on the Royal Navy will be around £157 million.

6. London: An exhibition of modern French art includes works by Matisse and Derain.

10. Australia: The Smith brothers are the first to fly from the UK to Australia.

10. US: Striking coal miners accept President Wilson's offer pay offer and return to work.

10. Stockholm: Nobel Prizes go to Johannes Stark (Germany, Physics); Jules Bordet (Belgium, Medicine); Carl Spitteler (Switzerland, Literature) and Woodrow Wilson (US, Peace).

15. UK: RAF commander Sir Hugh Trenchard presents proposals for making the force permanent.

19. Dublin: Lord French, Lord-Lieutenant of Ireland, escapes an attempt on his life outside Phoenix Park.→

23. London: Royal Assent is given to the Sex Disqualification Removal Bill, opening professions to women (→ 30).

24. Washington: President Wilson says railways taken over in the War will return to the owners on March 1, 1920.

30. London: The first woman bar student is admitted to Lincoln's Inn.

DEATH

3. French artist Auguste Renoir (*25/2/1841).→

HITS OF 1919

Don't dilly-dally on the way.

I'm forever blowing bubbles.

Dardanella.

QUOTE OF THE YEAR

"There are a lot of hard-faced men who look as if they have done rather well out of the War."
John Maynard Keynes,
The Economic Consequences of the Peace, December 1919.

Irish partition is planned

Dec 22. Ireland will have self-government with two Parliaments – one for the north, one for the south; the whole island will remain part of the United Kingdom. This latest plan was announced by Mr Lloyd George in Parliament today. He acknowledged that the scheme is not generally acceptable.

Reflecting the mood of a generation of mainland politicians, the Prime Minister said: "No party in Ireland is prepared to accept anything except the impossible. But that is no excuse for British government inaction." Certain important powers – including foreign policy and defence – will be reserved to the Imperial Parliament under this proposed constitutional settlement. A Council of Ireland, with equal membership from north and south, is also to be set up as a forum and as a nucleus of a United Irish Parliament of the future. Nationalist MPs absented themselves from the Commons during the Prime Minister's statement. "We refuse to listen to any proposals about total partition," they said. Ulster Unionists – less hostile – doubt if the Government is really serious in its assertions about going ahead with the plan.

Eclipse test proves Einstein's theories

The revolutionary ideas embodied in **Albert Einstein's** Theory of Relativity have been confirmed by expeditions to West Africa and Brazil, organised by the Royal Astronomical Society. They found that the path of light from a star, passing close to the sun, was bent by its gravitational field in exactly the way Einstein predicted.

These new observations confirm his theory of General Relativity of 1915, which extended the earlier Special Theory to include gravity. According to Einstein the Newtonian theory of gravity is only true on the scale of the solar system, or of everyday life. On the atomic scale, and that of the universe as a whole, very different rules apply.

Keynes predicts economic disaster

Dec 31. A highly critical study of the Versailles Peace Treaty, published this month by the 36-year-old economist, John Maynard Keynes, is now the economics "book of the year". The author, a wartime Whitehall official, was the Treasury representative in Paris until June, when he resigned to write "The Economic Consequences of the Peace".

Keynes makes sharp comments about President Wilson and his other "Big Four" colleagues at Paris, but the bite of his analysis is that the Paris Treaty only settles political grudges and will create chaos by depressing German and other European economies to starvation point.

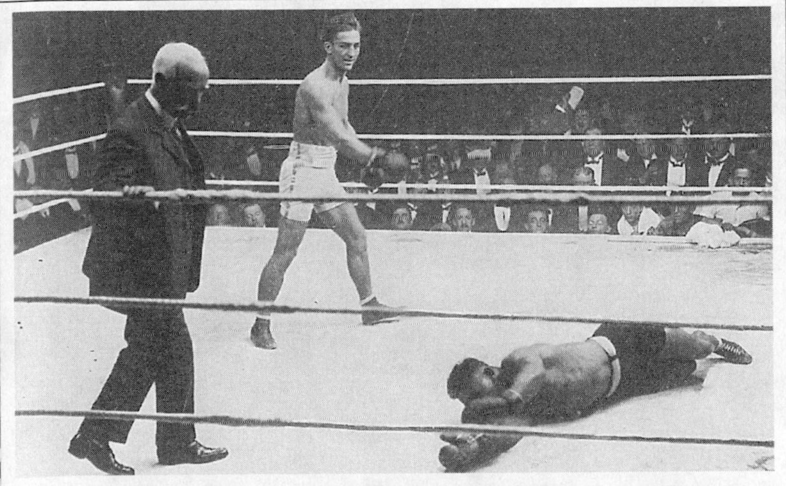

Heavyweight king Georges Carpentier KO'd Joe Beckett in 70 seconds.

Arts: Jazz is exported, Renoir is dead

The Original Dixieland Jazz Band was a roaring success on its UK tour.

The death of **Pierre Auguste Renoir** at 78 was announced this month from the villa he built outside Cannes on the French Riviera. He moved there in 1903 in the hope of improving the rheumatism which crippled him – without success. He continued to paint from a wheel-chair with a brush strapped between his fingers in a glass studio built in his garden. On the day he died, he finished work on a flower painting with the words, "I believe I am beginning to understand something about it".

Renoir, a tailor's son from Limoges, was apprenticed as a porcelain painter at 13 before entering an art studio. With his fellow-student, **Claude Monet**, he worked in the forest of Fontainebleau in the 1860s, where they developed the technique of Impressionism.

But Renoir's greatest successes were his portrait and figure studies, such as "La Loge", "Le Moulin de la Galette", "Les Parapluies" and the ample nudes to which he returned in his later years. He married one of his models, Aline, in 1882 and they had three sons.

The year heard the first performances of the Cello Concerto by **Elgar** and **Gustav Holst's** suite "The Planets", of which "Mars – the Bringer of War" was composed appropriately in the summer of 1914. Visiting London, the Ballets Russes premiered two new works: **Leonide Massine's** "La Boutique Fantasque", set to playful pieces by Rossini and designed by **Derain**, and an amusing Spanish "miller's tale", **Manuel de Falla's** "The Three-Cornered Hat", with decor by **Picasso**. Massine partnered **Mme Karsavina** as the miller and his wife with huge energy.

There was equally violent enthusiasm for the **Original Dixieland Jazz Band** from America, which played at the London Palladium and toured Britain. The five-piece band is led by **Nick La Rocca**, the trumpeter and composer of "Tiger Rag", which brings audiences to their feet shouting and clapping in a most unBritish manner.

In the theatre **Bernard Shaw** presented his "Heartbreak House", a parable many thought modelled on Chekhov's "The Cherry Orchard". **Somerset Maugham** clearly modelled the hero of his novel "The Moon and Sixpence" on the life of Paul Gauguin. He is shown as a monster of artist's egotism.

"Dance in Town", by Renoir.

1920–1929

1920

JANUARY

Su	Mo	Tu	We	Th	Fr	Sa
				1	2	3
4	5	6	7	8	9	10
11	12	13	14	15	16	17
18	19	20	21	22	23	24
25	26	27	28	29	30	31

2. US: 2,700 arrests are made in 33 cities in a "Red Scare" ordered by Attorney-General Palmer.

3. France: The last US troops leave.

5. US: Red Sox baseballer Babe Ruth is bought by the Yankees for a record $125,000.

9. London: The Government announces plans to build 100,000 new homes in the coming year.

10. English Channel: 35 drown when the steamer Treveal is wrecked.

12. Ukraine: 29,000 Jews are feared to have died in massacres.

14. Paris: Lloyd George receives the Grand Cross of the Legion of Honour, France's highest award.

15. Paris: The Allies frame their demand for the extradition from Holland of ex-Kaiser Wilhelm II (→23).

16. Europe: The Allies decide to lift their trade blockade of Soviet Russia.

17. France: Paul Deschanel defeats premier Clemenceau in elections for a successor to President Raymond Poincare (→19).

19. France: Andre Millerand succeeds the retiring Georges Clemenceau as premier.

21. Helsinki: The Baltic states decide to form a defensive alliance against Russia.

23. The Hague: The Dutch government refuses to extradite the ex-Kaiser.

27. Hungary: First elections under universal suffrage show monarchist support (→29/2).

30. Ireland: Cork and Limerick declare allegiance to Sinn Fein's illegal Irish parliament, the Dail Eireann.

BIRTH

20. Italian film director Federico Fellini (†31/10/93).

DEATH

24. Italian artist Amedeo Modigliani (*12/7/1884).→

Blood flows in Berlin after demo erupts

"Vote Spartacus": there is strong left-wing opposition to the government.

Jan 13. A massive but peaceful demonstration organised by the Independents against the Works Councils Bill turned into a bloody tragedy in Berlin today when agitators incited the crowd into storming the Reichstag.

The police guard retaliated with rifle fire and then machine guns were turned on the crowd. The firing went on for only a minute or two while the terror-stricken men and women ran in all directions. When it ended the ground before the Reichstag was dotted with dead and wounded, their blood mingling with the wind-driven rain.

It was a terrible scene, with the struggling crowd dammed up against the Brandenburg Gate, and cries of fear echoing over the rattle of the machine guns.

Time gentlemen please! US bans booze

Jan 16. The Eighteenth Amendment to the US Constitution, prohibiting the manufacture and sale of alcohol, went into force today.

This closes a long chapter in American history. Maine enacted prohibition in 1851; churches saw drinking as a sin and women saw saloons as a threat to the home. By the beginning of the Great War two-thirds of the States had prohibition. But a national law was needed to stop liquor being shipped into dry areas.

However, not everyone is confident of success. The Mayor of New York has said he will need 250,000 police to enforce it.

A group of regulars raise their glasses in a final toast before Prohibition.

US boycotts first meeting of League

Jan 16. The League of Nations was inaugurated today at a meeting in the Clock Room of the French Foreign Office – but in the absence of the country whose president had fought hardest for the world body during the Paris peace talks.

Leon Bourgeois, the French chairman, regretted the absence of President Wilson and said he hoped his difficulties with Congress would be overcome. "Then the work of the Council will assume that particular force that should be associated with our work," Bourgeois said. Lord Curzon, for Britain, declared that a seat would be kept vacant for America.

Modigliani: a short life but a full one

"Seated Nude" of 1912-23.

Jan 27. Amedeo Modigliani, Italian painter of controversial nudes, died in Paris last Saturday night, worn out at the age of 35 by excesses of drink and drug-taking. The following night his model and mistress, Jeanne Hebuterne, threw herself from a fifth-floor window. She was nine months pregnant.

"I want a short life but a full one", "Modi" used to say in the bars and cafes where he drank himself incapable nightly, paying his bills with five-franc sketches. His elongated portraits of women found favour in a London show last year.

1920

FEBRUARY

Su	Mo	Tu	We	Th	Fr	Sa
1	2	3	4	5	6	7
8	9	10	11	12	13	14
15	16	17	18	19	20	21
22	23	24	25	26	27	28
29						

2. Russia: The Soviet government recognises the independence of Estonia.

3. Germany: The Allies ask the Germans to hand over 890 political and military leaders for trial as war criminals (→5).

5. Berlin: The German government refuses to turn over alleged war criminals to the Allies (→10).

9. Washington: Democrats in the House of Representatives vote against compulsory military service or training (→23).

10. Berlin: Ex-Crown Prince Wilhelm offers himself for trial on behalf of the 890 on the Allies' wanted list.

12. Washington: The Senate again fails to compromise over membership of the League of Nations (→19/3).

15. London: The League says the Sultan can stay in Constantinople but that Turkey must have no army.

17. London: The police are told they will get cars instead of horses.

20. Russia: Archangel is captured by the Red Army.

22. Berlin: 21 arrests are made in anti-Semitic violence.

23. London: War Secretary Winston Churchill says conscription will give way to an army of 220,000 volunteers.

24. Poland: Thousands are feared dead in a typhus epidemic.

25. UK: Ex-PM Herbert Asquith, who lost his seat at the last election, is returned as MP for Paisley, near Glasgow.

26. Russia: Lenin promises to create a democratic parliament and pay off 60 per cent of Russian debts (→27).

27. Washington: The US says Russia's promises are a propaganda dodge to make peace with the Allies.

29. Budapest: The monarchy is restored, with Miklos Horthy as regent (→28/3).

DEATH

19. US explorer Rear Admiral Robert Peary (*6/5/1856).

Red Army drives out White Allies

Feb 22. The large Allied force, which landed in southern Russia last December to save the area from anarchy, is on the verge of defeat and withdrawal.

The force of some 90,000 men, including among their number French, Greek, Polish, and Rumanian troops, was intended to bolster the fortunes of General Anton Denikin in his struggle with the increasingly triumphant Red Army.

There has been chaos in the area with Nationalist, Anarchist and Bolshevik bands fighting one another in a free-for-all cut-throat war. From the outset the Allied force has been hit by fierce cavalry raids from all sides and even its Odessa base is under attack.

The Cossack armies commanded by Denikin, who has been declared de facto ruler of the Caucasus, are also disintegrating under pressure from General Semyon Budenny's Red calvalry. The British air force and tank detachment attached to Denikin is expected to be withdrawn in the next few weeks.

In Siberia the Red Army has advanced steadily along the line of the Trans-Siberian railway. Admiral Kolchak, who briefly became the "Supreme Ruler of Russia" and has since been deserted by allies and friends, was seized by the Bolsheviks in Irkutsk, and shot. His body was then pushed through a hole in the ice so it would disappear for ever. An eyewitness account said he died "like an Englishman".

The American force of several thousand men has begun to leave Vladivostock. Bolsheviks have entered the city, but they seem happy to let the Allies move out in their own time. The Japanese appear to be staying on.

In control: Lenin addresses a crowd as Red Army chief Trotsky looks on.

League of Nations launched in London

Feb 11. The Council of the new League of Nations, meeting at St James's Palace in London, got down to business today with an agreement to set up an International Court of Justice, as called for in the League Covenant.

The Council, which is made up of delegates from Britain, France, Japan, Belgium, Spain, Greece, Italy and Brazil, has also to appoint a High Commissioner for Danzig, now a "free city" detached from Germany.

League line-up: Arthur Balfour (standing) at the top table.

German Workers' Party slams Jews

Feb 24. An extremist political group, which appeared on the scene in the wake of the brief Bavarian Soviet Republic, today published a programme for creating a Third German Reich. According to its spokesman, Adolf Hitler, a former army corporal, the group is to call itself the National Socialist German Workers' Party and will campaign against the "Versailles Diktat" as well as Jewish and capitalist influence in German society.

Hitler, who was known by his mother's name of Schicklgruber until he joined the army in 1914, once earned a living painting picture postcards in his native Austria; he is now devising banners, posters and a swastika flag for his party. He is also said to be practising public speaking.

1920

MARCH

Su	Mo	Tu	We	Th	Fr	Sa
	1	2	3	4	5	6
7	8	9	10	11	12	13
14	15	16	17	18	19	20
21	22	23	24	25	26	27
28	29	30	31			

1. US: The railways, commandeered in the War, are returned to their 230 owners (→24/12/19).

1. Turkey: Moslems are reported to have slaughtered 14,000 Armenians in recent massacres (→11).

2. Turkey: The League says the state of Turkey will be restricted to the province of Anatolia (→8).

7. Russia: The Red Army is reported to have started a major offensive against Poland (→7/5).

8. Middle East: Syria proclaims its independence from Turkey, with Emir Feisal as king (→10/8).

10. Ireland: The Ulster Unionist Council accepts the Government's plan for an Ulster Parliament (→31).

11. London: Near East Relief Campaign requests aid for the 1.25 million out of five million Armenians believed left alive (→16).

16. Turkey: Allied troops occupy Constantinople in protest at the Turkish genocide of Armenians.

17. London: Queen Alexandra unveils a monument to Nurse Edith Cavell next to the National Gallery.

17. Holland: Following the attempted coup in Berlin, the Dutch make the ex-Kaiser promise to abandon politics.→

20. Ireland: The mayor of Cork, Sinn Feiner Tomas MacCurtain, is assassinated (→26).

26. Dublin: A magistrate is dragged from a tram and murdered by Sinn Feiners, this year's 29th political murder.→

27. UK: The Grand National is won by Major T. Gerrard's Troytown.

28. Budapest: The Hungarian parliament is dissolved; the regent Miklos Horthy becomes dictator.

31. London: MPs pass the Home Rule Bill, but Unionist leader Sir Edward Carson warns it will lead to disaster (→5/4).

Final attempt fails to get US into League

March 19. A final attempt to ratify the Versailles treaty and so make the United States a member of the League of Nations was defeated in the US Senate today, ending a long and bitter fight.

Last November, the treaty was defeated when a large number of reservations were made by the Republican Senator Henry Cabot Lodge. His objections centred on Article Ten, under which the US would have to go automatically to war if another member state was attacked. But they also reflected hostility to Britain, who would allegedly control six votes because the Dominions would vote.

The result today was a defeat for a compromise plan, which included some of Lodge's reservations, that had been worked out by a group of Republican and Democratic Senators and which had the support of Britain. A major reason for the defeat was that President Wilson, one of the architects of the treaty, who is incapacitated by a stroke, refused to vote for it

Senator Lodge mustered 49 votes for the treaty with his reservations. But 23 loyal Democrats followed the President, and they were joined by 12 "Irreconcilables" who were unwilling to vote aye with or without reservation. So the United States will not be a member of the League.

Monarchist coup attempt in Berlin fails

March 17. The attempted coup by reactionary forces in Germany has failed. The would-be Chancellor, Dr Wolfgang Kapp, has fled from Berlin, and the forces of his military ally, General Baron von Luttwitz, are pulling out of the city, which they seized without opposition last Friday.

They failed because they did not secure the full support of the army, because President Ebert stood firm against them as he had against the Spartacist revolt in January, and because Germany was paralysed by a strike "to destroy this return of bloody reaction". General Luttwitz threatened to "crush any strike", but on the orders of the Social Democratic government, that "not a hand must be moved", the workers responded by suspending the vital services. Even the waiters went on strike.

The coup was mounted, according to General Luttwitz, because "we want to oppose Bolshevism". It is generally believed, however, that the real purpose was to restore a Prussian-style monarchy.

More Irish shot as death toll mounts

March 26. The arrival of 800 "special constables" from England has heightened tension in Ireland, already running high after the assassination this month of Tomas MacCurtain, Lord Mayor of Cork.

Known as the "Black and Tans" because of their uniforms, the specials are jobless men demobbed from the army, paid ten shillings a day. Sensitivity in the powder keg of Ireland seems to be noticeably absent in their eagerness to get a job done. And the violence goes on.

Yesterday a policeman was shot when Sinn Fein captured a barracks in Co. Kilkenny and two people died when a mob attacked 120 British soldiers returning from a a theatre in Dublin (→3/4).

Mary Pickford married screen colleague Douglas Fairbanks in Los Angeles on March 29.

1920

APRIL

Su	Mo	Tu	We	Th	Fr	Sa
				1	2	3
4	5	6	7	8	9	10
11	12	13	14	15	16	17
18	19	20	21	22	23	24
25	26	27	28	29	30	

1. Germany: The German Workers' Party becomes the National Socialist German Workers' Party.

2. Washington: Women mount a picket on the British embassy, demanding freedom for Ireland (→3).

3. Ireland: Sinn Fein vows to make British government of Ireland impossible through an arson campaign (→5).

5. Ireland: The anniversary of the Easter Rising is marked by burning of 120 police stations and 22 tax offices (→13).

5. Jerusalem: The British declare martial law and troops intervene to restore order as Jews clash with Arabs (→25).

6. Germany: French troops occupy Frankfurt.→

9. Washington: Congressmen vote for peace with Germany, as the US has not ratified the Versailles Treaty (→19/11/19).

13. Ireland: 300,000 workers strike in protest at the British treatment of Sinn Fein prisoners (→14).

14. Ireland: 89 Sinn Fein hunger strikers are unexpectedly let out of Dublin prison, but 100 remain in jail (→10/5).

17. Sweden: Wolfgang von Kapp, leader of the recent German coup attempt, is arrested in Stockholm (→17/4).

19. San Remo: The League meets to discuss the British role in Palestine and other matters.→

21. US: 140 are killed and hundreds injured by a tornado that sweeps across the southern states.

23. Turkey: The Turkish parliament in Ankara ousts Sultan Mehmet VI; Mustafa Kemal heads new regime.

24. London: Aston Villa beat Huddersfield 1-0 in the first FA Cup Final since 1915, played at Stamford Bridge.

25. San Remo: The League proposes fixing Germany's war indemnity at 3,000,000,000 marks a year for 30 years.

26. Palestine: Arabs launch attacks on British troops.

French occupy the Ruhr

French troops marching through the industrial city of Essen.

April 7. French troops have marched into the major cities of the Ruhr and there have been skirmishes between their Moroccan soldiers and angry mobs of German nationalists in which a number of people have been killed. Student leaders are reported to have climbed onto motor cars to harangue the crowds.

The French move came in response to the arrival of German forces in the area who were attempting to thwart plans by armed communists to seize control of this industrial centre.

Under the terms of the Treaty of Versailles, Germany is allowed to keep 40,000 soldiers in the neutral zone. This figure has now been exceeded without the authorisation required by the treaty.

The Germans have sent a telegram to the Allies insisting that the situation has become so serious they could no longer wait for permission to enter the Ruhr on a temporary basis. The French, however, see this as an excuse to reoccupy the area and have reacted swiftly and decisively.

League gives Palestine mandate to UK

April 25. A three-hour session of the San Remo conference today confirmed the British mandate over Mesopotamia and Palestine. Syria is entrusted to France. These decisions practically wrap up the conference, which has been hammering out a peace treaty with Turkey. Business was concluded so rapidly that the British mission has ordered its special train to be ready the day after tomorrow.

Zionist and Jewish circles welcomed confirmation that Britain is to take over Palestine and the fact that the Balfour Declaration will be incorporated into the treaty. They said it meant that at last, after many centuries, the Jews could begin work to re-establish their ancient homeland under a stable and civilised government. The Jews had always desired to be under British trusteeship and the Holy Land is of interest to all peoples.

Zionist leaders in San Remo acclaimed the decision, which will allow Jewish energy and capital to flow towards Palestine to develop the country to the advantage of all its inhabitants. Dr Max Nordeau said: "With one foot already in the Holy Land, we shall now enter Palestine with firm steps, declaring: Here we are; here we remain."

After a three-hour meeting Lloyd George and the French Prime Minister, M. Millerand, reached agreement about enforcing the Treaty of Versailles.

1920

MAY

Su	Mo	Tu	We	Th	Fr	Sa
						1
2	3	4	5	6	7	8
9	10	11	12	13	14	15
16	17	18	19	20	21	22
23	24	25	26	27	28	29
30	31					

1. US: Nationwide demonstrations mark May Day.

4. Washington: 88 Congressmen appeal to Lloyd George to free Irish prisoners held without trial.→

6. London: France beats England 2-1 in a women's football international.

7. Ukraine: Polish troops seize Kiev from the Red Army (→28).

14. Ireland: There have been 94 attacks in recent days on police stations, according to the Government (→17).

16. Berne: Switzerland votes to join the League of Nations.

17. Ulster: Sinn Fein supporters engage in pitched street battles with Unionists in Londonderry.

18. Oxford: Women professors are given equal status to their male colleagues in the University.

19. Persia: The Red Army invades northern Persia from the Caspian Sea.

21. London: The Government proposes a car tax of £1 per horsepower.

22. Mexico: President Venustiano Carranza is murdered by troops under rebel General Rodolfo Herrera.

24. France: President Deschanel falls from a sleeper train; he is found wandering along the line in his pyjamas.

24. Belgium: The seventh modern Olympic Games are inaugurated at Antwerp.

27. Washington: The Senate rejects the League of Nations' offer of a US mandate in Armenia.

27. Czechoslovakia: Tomas Masaryk is elected president; Eduard Benes is foreign minister.

28. Poland: War is declared between Poland and Russia; Poland appeals to the Allies for help (→23/8).

30. UK: At least 20 drown in serious floods in Lincolnshire.

30. Rome: Pope Benedict XV canonises Joan of Arc, on the anniversary of her death in 1431.

Hunger strikers are set free by Britain

A "special" searches suspects.

May 10. Forty Irish prisoners, who have been on hunger strike at Wormwood Scrubs prison in London for up to a fortnight, were released today. The Government gave no explanation for the release, but it is believed ministers wanted to avoid creating martyrs.

Violence is already running high in Ireland itself. Four policemen were ambushed at Timoleague in Co. Cork today. Three fell dead and the condition of the fourth is critical. The deaths bring the total number of policemen killed in this county alone to 19 in less than three months. Two days ago 31 abandoned police stations in Co. Cork were set on fire. The Royal Irish Constabulary was last night commended for its bravery by the Lord Chancellor, Lord Birkenhead.

The latest wear for the tango.

1920

JUNE

Su	Mo	Tu	We	Th	Fr	Sa
		1	2	3	4	5
6	7	8	9	10	11	12
13	14	15	16	17	18	19
20	21	22	23	24	25	26
27	28	29	30			

1. Spain: Foundation of the Spanish Communist Party (PCE).

1. Mexico: Adolfo de la Huerta becomes president, following the assassination of Venustiano Carranza on May 20.

2. UK: The Derby at Epsom is won by Major Giles Loder's Spion Kop.

4. Paris: The Treaty of Trianon is signed, bringing peace between Hungary and the Allies.→

5. US: Census shows New York's population is 5.6 million; Los Angeles (0.57 million) is biggest city in western US (→25).

8. Italy: Riots follow the government's announcement of an increase in the price of bread.

9. London: The Government turns down League offer of Armenian mandate, already refused by US.

9. London: King George V opens the Imperial War Museum, housed at Crystal Palace.

13. Geneva: Opening of the International Feminist Congress.

15. US: Mob of 5,000 lynches three blacks at Duluth, Minnesota (→21).

16. The Hague: Opening of the League of Nations Permanent Court of Justice.

20. Ulster: Five die in fierce rioting.→

21. US: A black is riddled with bullets after a mob fails to lynch him in Georgia.

22. France: Allies fix German reparations for the Great War at £12,500 million (→27).

25. Washington: US Census Bureau says population of US is 105,000,000.

27. Berlin: New Socialist-dominated Reichstag is told the government must fulfil its Versailles Treaty obligations.

29. San Francisco: Disorder marks the Democratic Convention's debates on the issues of Ireland and Prohibition (→5/7).

Treaty redraws the map of Europe

June 4. The Treaty of Trianon, which cuts Hungary to a quarter of its old size, was signed today. This almost completes the drastic redrawing of the map of Europe which has been under way since the war ended.

The war destroyed four empires – German, Austrian, Russian and Turkish – and in sorting out the bits President Wilson's principle of self-determination has been followed as a way of easing the tensions that ignited the war. But there are fears that it may in fact replaces old tensions with new ones.

The treaty makers removed from the old empires territories with national minorities, but in doing so created "reverse" minorities. For example, Czechs and Slovaks, minorities under the Habsburgs, now form Czechoslovakia, which has a German minority.

Germany was dealt with by the Versailles Treaty, which gave territory to Poland and Lithuania, North Schleswig to Denmark and Alsace-Lorraine to France.

Several treaties broke up the Austro-Hungarian Empire: St Germain created Yugoslavia and Czechosolvakia, gave Galicia to Poland, Transylvania to Rumania, and Istria, Trentino and South Tirol to Italy, while Neuilly gave Greece and Yugoslavia bits of Bulgaria.

In August a meeting at Sevres will mainly deal with Turkey's Middle East territories (→10/8).

Reinforcements move into Londonderry

June 24. Troops are being sent from England to reinforce the garrison at Londonderry where 17 people have died and many more injured in riots this month. In parliament, ministers came under political fire about the escalating violence in Ireland with calls for an emergency debate.

Mr Bonar Law, speaking for the Government, said the Army commander in Londonderry had full powers "to deal with the situation and call for whatever force he considers necessary". Already ordered to the troubles in Ireland are the South Wales Borderers, the Northumberland Fusiliers and the Royal Scots Fusiliers amongst other regiments.

A newly-armed Dublin policeman.

Republican Party nominates Harding

June 12. The Republican convention today nominated Senator Warren G. Harding of Ohio as its candidate for President in a convention marked by late-night deals in Chicago's Blackstone Hotel.

The leading contender was General Leonard Wood, hero of the Cuban war, second was Illinois Governor Lowden, with Harding a poor third. However some 300 delegates were controlled by senators, and they wanted Harding who was nominated on the tenth ballot. The little-known Governor Coolidge of Massachusetts will be Harding's running-mate.

1920

JULY

Su	Mo	Tu	We	Th	Fr	Sa
				1	2	3
4	5	6	7	8	9	10
11	12	13	14	15	16	17
18	19	20	21	22	23	24
25	26	27	28	29	30	31

1. Germany: The German government surrenders her largest airship, L71, to the UK.

3. Wimbledon: Suzanne Lenglen beats Dorothea Chambers for the Ladies' Singles title; William Tilden is first American to win the Men's Singles final, beating Gerald Patterson.

4. Belgium: Allied premiers meet German leaders for the first time since the Versailles Treaty, at the resort of Spa.

5. UK: New airmail service starts to Amsterdam, costing threepence per ounce of mail.

8. Ireland : British troops set up roadblocks outside Dublin (→ 23).

12. US: British barber Charles Stephens dies when he goes over the Niagara Falls in a barrel.

13. London: The London County Council bans the employment of foreigners in almost all council jobs.

15. London: Fuel Research Board, looking into alternatives to petrol, says UK will have 0.75 million cars by 1921.

15. US: British challenger Shamrock IV beats US holder Resolute in first round of America's Cup yacht race.

16. London: Official end to the war with Austria is declared.

18. Germany: Ex-Kaiser Wilhelm's youngest son Joachim commits suicide at Potsdam outside Berlin.

23. Belfast: 14 die and 100 are hurt in fierce rioting.

24. London: Mr F. Courtney wins an "Aerial Derby" air race at average speed of 153.5 mph.

27. US: America's Cup is won by the US yacht Resolute.

28. Washington: David Lloyd George appeals for US to join the League in a speech at the Lincoln Memorial.

31. London: Foundation of the Communist Party of Great Britain, branch of the Moscow Third International (→ 1/8).

Cox and Roosevelt to run for Democrats

July 5. After 44 ballots James M. Cox, governor of Ohio, was today nominated by the Democrats as their presidential candidate. His running-mate is a surprise choice: Franklin D. Roosevelt of New York, only 38 years old and assistant secretary of the Navy.

This San Francisco convention began on June 28 in disarray. They were divided over such great issues as Prohibition and the ratification of the Versailles Treaty, negotiated by the Democrats' stricken leader, Woodrow Wilson, whose oil portrait was unveiled to cheers.

The party's choice was handicapped by uncertainty about who would have received the President's endorsement. But the leading candidate was Mr Wilson's Treasury Secretary and son-in-law, William G. McAdoo. Second was Attorney-General A. Mitchell Palmer, who is unpopular with labour for prosecuting union organizers.

Cox was the candidate of New York, Chicago and Ohio party machines. Vote by vote, Cox's total grew, while anti-McAdoo delegates sang, to the tune of the Battle Hymn of the Republic, "Every note is on the payroll".

The choice of young Mr Roosevelt, bearer of a great but not a Democratic name, was a gesture to the beaten Wilson wing of the party.

Cox and Roosevelt: pro-League.

Mexican rebel packs it in for a pension

July 8. The Mexican government of Adolfo de la Huerta has accepted the surrender of General Francisco Pancho Villa, perhaps the most celebrated guerrilla leader to come out of the last ten years of revolutionary war in Mexico.

Although Villa made himself unpopular in the US by his attacks on Americans in Mexico, and even more so by his daring 1915 raid into the US, which led to General Pershing's invasion, Villa has a Robin Hood reputation with the peasants of northern Mexico.

It is doubtless for this reason that President Huerta has granted Pancho Villa full citizenship and a pension for life. He plans to retire and become a rancher.

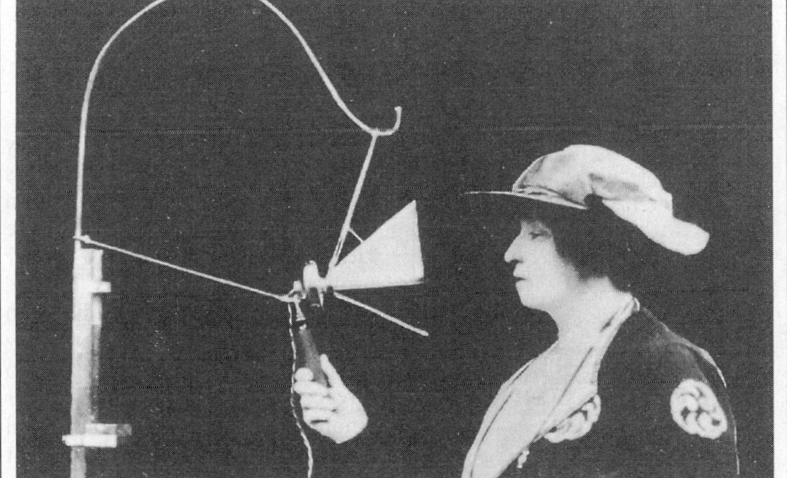
June 15. Nellie Melba makes the first advertised wireless broadcast.

Germany told to cut down her arms

July 9. After protesting against an Allied occupation threat, German ministers at Spa today finally signed a protocol promising to carry out the disarmament clauses of the Versailles treaty by the beginning of next year. One minister, Herr Gessler, who is responsible for the army, the Reichswehr, refused to sign.

The British Prime Minister, David Lloyd George, accused the Germans of deliberately evading the treaty's disarmament clauses. Germany should have reduced her army to 100,000; it is still over 150,000. Nor has she yet got rid of her air force, abolished conscription, or delivered to the Allies all weapons not allowed under the treaty. The Germans are protesting against having to disband the Security Police and the Home Guard; they say such action should take place only after the civilian population has been persuaded to surrender its weapons.

UK abandons its man in Damascus

July 24. The French Expeditionary Force has occupied Damascus and the port of Aleppo, following a sharp fight with Arab forces on the road to the Syrian capital.

General Henri Gouraud, the one-armed French commander, had reacted quickly when the Arabs, led by Emir Feisal, broke an agreement and attacked a French garrison. Feisal, who styled himself King of Syria, has now fled the capital.

The cause of the dispute is the San Remo agreement, which gave France a League of Nations' mandate over the former Ottoman lands of Syria and Lebanon. Feisal, leader of the Arab revolt against the Turks, was installed in Damascus only three months ago by the British General Allenby. He opposed the mandate and resisted French military occupation.

Feisal looked to the British for help, but Prime Minister Lloyd George agreed with the French that co-operation with Feisal had no chance of success. Britain therefore abandoned him.

1920

AUGUST

Su	Mo	Tu	We	Th	Fr	Sa
1	2	3	4	5	6	7
8	9	10	11	12	13	14
15	16	17	18	19	20	21
22	23	24	25	26	27	28
29	30	31				

1. London: Opening of the first congress of the British Communist Party.

2. London: The Government reveals new bill to restore order in Ireland, including suspension of jury trials (→3).

3. Belfast: Catholics riot in protest at the presence of British troops in Ireland.

6. US: Police open fire on striking tram drivers in Denver, Colorado, killing three and injuring 13.

9. UK: The Labour Party says it will call for a general strike if Britain declares war on Russia.

11. Geneva: First ecumenical conference is held, bringing together European, US and Eastern Churches.

13. Paris: Visiting Greek premier Eleutherios Venizelos is wounded in an assassination bid by two Greek soldiers.

14. Antwerp: King Albert of the Belgians opens the sixth Olympic Games of modern times.→

16. Poland: US warships are sent to Danzig as a precautionary measure, as Russian troops close on Warsaw.→

18. London: The first two night bus services are introduced.

22. Ireland: Seven policemen are murdered by the IRA (→25).

25. London: Lloyd George refuses to release Lord Mayor of Cork Tomas MacSwiney, on hunger strike in prison (→29).

26. Washington: The 19th Amendment is ratified, giving women the vote in federal elections.

29. Belfast: 11 die and 40 are hurt in street battles in the city.

31. London: A police report reveals that the growing number of motor cars has led to an increase in road deaths.

BIRTHS

22. US writer Ray Bradbury.

29. US jazz musician Charlie Parker (†12/3/55).

UK fliers aid Poles to turn the Red tide

Bolshevik troops at a German internment camp after fleeing the Poles.

Aug 23. The Polish Army, vowing to fight to the last man to defend Warsaw, has beaten the Bolsheviks back from the gates of the capital. Some reports say the Bolshevik forces operating against the Polish left wing are in danger of being cut off and are therefore menaced with a great disaster.

A communique from the Polish General Staff claims: "Our detachments continue to advance with great dash and bravery, pursuing the enemy, who are fleeing in disorder and panic." Another message indicates that the Poles have recaptured the fortress of Novominsk and started an offensive against Brest-Litovsk.

British airmen are playing an important role in the Polish defeat of Trotsky's new Red army. The Polish Commander-in-Chief has recorded "with gratitude the fruitful activities of the Third Flying Division, commanded by Major Fauntleroy".

There is now an atmosphere of victory in the Polish camp and much satisfaction among the French Mission, for it was General Weygand's plan, along with Polish courage, that saved Warsaw from General Budenny's Red Cossacks.

The Polish successes would seem to have foiled Russian plans to spread communism throughout Europe. Reports from Petrograd speak of Bolshevik plans to crush the Poles and then link up with the German communists to form a new front against the Allies.

FOX'S GLACIER MINTS
Look for the name FOX on every mint

New minty freshness from Fox.

Turkey loses 80% of Ottoman Empire

Aug 10. At Sevres today Turkey signed a peace treaty with the Allies which will cost that defeated nation 80 per cent of the land ruled by the Ottoman Empire. Among other provisions the treaty gives Thrace, the Aegean Islands and Smyrna to Greece.

This loss of land, especially to Greece, is causing much anger among the Turks. Mustafa Kemal has formed a resistance movement whose members have sworn never to give up those regions in which Turks form the majority.

Albert Hill wins two Olympic gold medals for Britain

Aug 30. The Olympic Games hosted by Antwerp achieved gloriously what many believed to be impossible – the revival of world sporting competition so soon after Belgium's cruel suffering in the Great War.

The organisation proved superb, and though the track in the 30,000 seat stadium was slow and heavy, and was not helped by weeks of intermittent rain, the athletics programme produced some outstanding performances. The remarkable Finnish onslaught continued: Hannes Kolehmainen, double champion eight years before, won the Marathon and a young compatriot, Paavo Nurmi, beaten into second place in the 5,000 metres, responded with victory in both 10,000 metres and cross-country.

Jubilant Hill after the 1,500 metres.

But the man of the track was surely a 31-year-old railway guard from England. Albert Hill, who runs with Herne Hill Harriers in South London, served the full four years of the War in the Army and the Royal Flying Corps.

Splendidly relaxed, he took three hours' sleep before each race, and so was able to manage five hard races in five days, winning the gold medal in both the 800 metres and the 1,500 metres.

1920  Antwerp

Men Athletics

100m
Charles Paddock USA 10.8
Morris Kirksey USA 10.8
Harry Edward GBR 11.0

200m
Allen Woodring USA 22.0
Charles Paddock USA 22.1
Harry Edward GBR 22.2

400m
Bevil Rudd SAF 49.6
Guy Butler GBR 49.9
Nils Engdahl SWE 50.0

800m
Albert Hill GBR 1:53.4
Earl Eby USA 1:53.6
Bevil Rudd SAF 1:54.0

1500m
Albert Hill GBR 4:01.8
Philip Baker GBR 4:02.4
Lawrence Shields USA 4:03.1

5000m
Joseph Guillemot FRA 14:55.6
Paavo Nurmi FIN 15:00.0
Erik Backman SWE 15:13.0

10,000m
Paavo Nurmi FIN 31:45.8
Joseph Guillemot FRA 31:47.2
James Wilson GBR 31:50.8

Marathon
Johannes Kolehmainen FIN 2:32:35.8
Jüri Lossmann EST 2:32:48.6
Valerio Arri ITA 2:36:32.8

110m Hurdles
Earl Thomson CAN ** 14.8
Harold Barron USA 15.1
Frederick Murray USA 15.2

400m Hurdles
Frank Loomis USA ** 54.0
John Norton USA 54.3
August Desch USA 54.5

3000m Steeplechase
Percy Hodge GBR *10:00.4
Patrick Flynn USA
Ernesto Ambrosini ITA

4x100m relay
USA ** 42.2
FRA 42.6
SWE 42.9

4x400m relay
GBR 3:22.2
SAF 3:24.2
FRA 3:24.8

High Jump
Richmond Landon *USA 1.935
Harold Muller USA 1.90
Bo Ekelund SWE 1.90

Pole Vault
Frank Foss USA ** 4.09
Henry Petersen DEN 3.70
Edwin Myers USA 3.60

Long Jump
William Petersson SWE 7.15
Carl Johnson USA 7.095
Erik Abrahamsson SWE 7.08

Triple Jump
Vilho Tuulos FIN 14.505
Folke Jansson SWE 14.48
Erik Almlöf SWE 14.27

Shotput
Ville Pörhölä FIN 14.81
Elmer Niklander FIN 14.155
Harry Liversedge USA 14.15

Discus
Elmer Niklander FIN 44.685
Armas Taipale FIN 44.19
Augustus Pope USA 42.13

Hammer
Patrick Ryan USA 52.875
Carl Johan Lind SWE 48.43
Basil Bennet USA 48.25

Javelin
Jonni Myyrä FIN 65.78
Urho Peltonen FIN 63.50
Paavo Johansson FIN 63.095

Decathlon
Helge Lövland NOR 6803.355
Brutus Hamilton USA 6771.085
Bertil Ohlson SWE 6580.030

3000m Team
USA
Great Britain
Sweden

Cross Country Individual (approx. 8,000m)
Paavo Nurmi FIN 27:15.0
Erik Backman SWE 27:17.6
Heikki Limatainen FIN 27:37.4

Cross Country Team (approx. 8,000m)
Finland
Great Britain
Sweden

Pentathlon
Eero Lehtonen FIN 14
Everett Bradley USA 24
Hugo Lahtinen FIN 26

56 lb. Weight Throw
Patrick McDonald USA *11.265
Patrick Ryan USA 10.965
Carl Johan Lind SWE 10.25

Tug-of-War
Great Britain
Netherlands
Belgium

3000m Walk
1. Ugo Frigerio ITA *13:14.2
2. George Parker AUS 13:20.6
3. Richard Frederick Remer USA 13:23.6

10,000m Walk
1. Ugo Frigerio ITA 48:06.2
2. Joseph Pearman USA 49:40.8
3. Charles Gunn GBR 49:44.4

Men Swimming

400m Breaststroke
1. Håkan Malmroth SWE 6:31.8
2. Thor Henning SWE 6:45.2
3. Arvo Aaltonen FIN 6:48.0

100m Freestyle
1. Duke Paoa Kahanamoku USA 1:01.4
2. Pua Kela Kealoha USA 1:02.2
3. William Harris USA 1:03.0

400m Freestyle
1. Norman Ross USA 5:26.8
2. Ludy Langer USA 5:29.0
3. George Vernot CAN 5:29.6

1500m Freestyle
1. Norman Ross USA 22:23.2
2. George Vernot CAN 22:36.4
3. Frank Beaurepaire AUS 23:04.4

100m Backstroke
1. Warren Paoa Kealoha USA 1:15.2
2. Ray Kegeris USA 1:16.2
3. Gérard Blitz BEL 1:19.0

200m Breaststroke
1. Hakan Malmroth SWE 3:04.4
2. Thor Henning SWE 3:09.2
3. Arvo Aaltonen FIN 3:12.2

4x200m Freestyle relay
1. USA ** 10:04.4
2. AUS 10:25.4
3. GBR 10:37.2

Springboard Diving
1. Louis Kuehn USA 675.4
2. Clarence Pinkston USA 655.3
3. Louis Balbach USA 649.5

High Diving
1. Clarence Pinkston USA 100.67
2. Erik Adlerz SWE 99.08
3. Harry Prieste USA 93.73

Plain High Dive
1. Arvid Wallman SWE 183.5
2. Nils Skoglund SWE 183.0
3. John Jansson SWE 175.0

Water Polo
1. Great Britain/Ireland
2. Belgium
3. Sweden

Women Swimming

100m Freestyle
1. Ethelda Bleibtrey USA *1:13.6
2. Irene Guest USA 1:17.0
3. Frances Schroth USA 1:17.2

400m Freestyle
1. Ethelda Bleibtrey USA *4:34.0
2. Margaret Woodbridge USA 4:42.8
3. Frances Schroth USA 4:52.0

4x100m Freestyle relay
1. USA *5:11.6
2. GBR 5:40.6
3. SWE 5:43.6

Springboard Diving
1. Aileen Riggin USA 539.9
2. Helen Wainwright USA 534.8
3. Thelma Payne USA 534.1

Platform Diving
1. Stefani Fryland-Clausen DEN 34.6
2. Eileen Armstrong GBR 33.3
3. Eva Ollivier SWE 33.3

Boxing

Flyweight
1. Frank Gennara USA
2. Anders Petersen DEN
3. William Cuthbertson GBR

Bantamweight
1. Clarence Walker SAF
2. Chris J. Graham CAN
3. James McKenzie GBR

Featherweight
1. Paul Fritsch FRA
2. Jean Gachet FRA
3. Edouardo Garzena ITA

Lightweight
1. Samuel Mosberg USA
2. Gotfred Johansen DEN
3. Clarence "Chris" Newton CAN

Welterweight
1. Albert "Bert" Schneider CAN
2. Alexander Ireland GBR
3. Frederick Colberg USA

Middleweight
1. Harry Mallin GBR
2. Georges Arthur Prud'Homme CAN
2. Moe H. Herscovitch CAN

Light Heavyweight
1. Edward Eagan USA
2. Sverre Sörsdal NOR
3. H. Franks GBR

Heavyweight
1. Ronald Rawson GBR
2. Sören Petersen DEN
3. Xavier Eluère FRA

Greco Roman Wrestling

Featherweight
1. Oskar Friman FIN
2. Heikki Kähkonen FIN
3. Fritiof Svensson SWE

Lightweight
1. Eemil Wäre FIN
2. Taavi Tamminen FIN
3. Frithjof Andersen NOR

Middleweight
1. Carl Westergren SWE
2. Artur Lindfors FIN
3. Matti Perttila FIN

Light Heavyweight
1. Claes Johanson SWE
2. Edil Rosenqvist FIN
3. Johannes Eriksen DEN

Heavyweight
1. Adolf Lindfors SWE
2. Poul Hansen DEN
3. Martti Nieminen FIN

Freestyle Wrestling

Featherweight
1. Charles Edwin Ackerly USA
2. Samuel Gerson USA
3. P.W. Bernard GBR

Lightweight
1. Kalle Anttila FIN
2. Gottfrid Svensson SWE
3. Peter Wright GBR

Middleweight
1. Eino Leino FIN
2. Väinö Penttala FIN
3. Charles Johnson USA

Light-Heavyweight
1. Anders Larsson SWE
2. Charles Courant SUI
3. Walter Maurer USA

Heavyweight
1. Robert Roth SUI
2. Nathan Pendleton USA
3. Ernst Nilsson SWE

Men Fencing

Foil Individual
1. Nedo Nadi ITA 10
2. Philippe Cattiau FRA 9/14
3. Roger Ducret FRA 9/19

Foil Team
1. Italy
2. France
3. USA

Epée Individual
1. Armand Massard FRA 9
2. Alexandre Lippman FRA 7
3. Gustave Buchard FRA 6

Epée Team
1. Italy
2. Belgium
3. France

Sabre Individual
1. Nedo Nadi ITA 11
2. Aldo Nadi ITA 9
3. Adrianus de Jong NETH 7

Sabre Team
1. ITA – 2. FRA – 3. NETH

Modern Pentathlon Individual

1. Gustav Dyrssen SWE
2. Erik de Laval SWE
3. Gösta Runö SWE

Rowing

Single Sculls
1. John Kelly sen. USA 7:35.0
2. Jack Beresford jun. GBR 7:36.0
3. D. Clarence Hadfield d'Arcy NZE 7:48.0

Double Sculls
1. USA 7:09.0
2. Italy 7:19.0
3. France 7:21.0

Coxed Pairs
1. Italy 7:56.0
2. France 7:57.0
3. Switzerland

Coxed Fours
1. Switzerland 6:54.0
2. USA 6:58.0
3. Norway 7:02.0

Eights
1. USA 6:02.6
2. Great Britain 6:05.0
3. Norway 6:36.0

Yachting

Finn Monotype Class 12 ft
1. Netherlands Beatrijs III
1. Netherlands Boreas

Finn Monotype Class 18 ft
1. Great Britain Brat

6m Class
1. Norway Jo
2. Belgium Tan-Fe-Pah

6m Class 1907 rating
1. Belgium Edelweis
2. Norway Mami
3. Norway Stella

6.5m Class
1. Netherlands Oranje
2. France Rose Pompon

7m Class
1. Great Britain Ancora

8m Class
1. Norway Sildra
2. Norway Lyn
3. Belgium Antwerpia

8m Class rating 1907
1. Norway Ierne
2. Norway Fornebo

10m Class 1919 rating
1. Norway Mosk II

10m Class 1907 rating
1. Norway Eleda

12m Class rating 1919
1 Norway Atlanta

12m Class rating 1907
1. Norway Keira II

30m²
1. Sweden Kublan

40m²
1. Sweden Sif
2. Sweden Elsie

Cycling

Individual Road Race
1. Harry Stenqvist SWE 4:40:01.8
2. Henry Kaltenbrun SAF 4:41:26.6
3. Fernand Canteloube FRA 4:42:54.4

Team Time Trial
1. France 19:16:43.2
2. Sweden 19:23:10.0
3. Belgium 19:28:44.4

1000m Sprint
1. Maurice Peeters NETH 1:38.3
2. Thomas Johnson GBR one wheel
3. Harry Ryan GBR

2000m Tandem
1. Great Britain 2:49.4
2. South Africa
3. Netherlands

Team Pursuit Race 4000m
1. Italy 5:20.0
2. Great Britain
3. South Africa

50km Track Race
1. Henry George BEL 1:16:43.2
2. Cyril Alden GBR
3. Piet Ikelaar NETH

Equestrian Sports

Three Day Event Individual
1. Helmer Mörner SWE 1775.00
2. Age Lundström SWE 1738.75
3. Ettore Caffaratti ITA 1733.75

Three Day Event Team
1. Sweden 5057.50
2. Italy 4735.00
3. Belgium 4560.00

Individual Dressage
1. Janne Lundblad SWE 27.937
2. Bertil Sandström SWE 26.312
3. Hans von Rosen SWE 25.125

Individual Grand Prix Jumping
1. Tommaso Lequio ITA -2
2. Alessandro Valerio ITA -3
3. C. Gustaf Lewenhaupt SWE -4

Grand Prix Jumping
1. Sweden -14
2. Belgium -16.25
3. Italy -18.75

Individual Figure Riding
1. Bouckaert BEL 30.5
2. Fiel FRA 29.5
3. Finet BEL 29.0

Team Figure Riding
1. BEL – 2. FRA – 3. SWE

Gymnastics

Individual All round Competition
1. Giorgio Zampori ITA 88.35
2. Marco Torrès FRA 87.62
3. Jean Gounot FRA 87.45

Team Combined Competition
1. Italy 359.855
2. Belgium 346.785
3. France 340.100

Football

1. BEL – 2. SPA – 3. NETH

Field Hockey

1. GBR – 2. DEN – 3. BEL

Shooting

Rapid Fire Pistol
1. Guilherme Paraense BRA 274
2. Raymond Bracken USA 272
3. Fritz Zulauf SUI 269

Free Pistol
1. Karl Frederick USA 496
2. Afranio da Costa BRA 489
3. Alfred Lane USA 481

Small Bore Rifle Prone
1. Lawrence Nuesslein USA 391
2. Arthur Rothrock USA 386
3. Dennis Fenton USA 385

Military Revolver Team (30m)
1. USA 1310
2. GRE 1285
3. SUI 1270

Military Revolver Team (50m)
1. USA 2372
2. SWE 2289
3. BRA 2264

Free Rifle Team
1. USA 4876
2. NOR 4741
3. SUI 4698

Free Rifle 3 Positions
1. Morris Fisher USA 997
2. Niels Larsen DEN 985
3. Östen Östensen NOR 980

Individual Military Rifle 300m Prone
1. Otto Olsen NOR 60
2. Léon Johnson FRA 59
3. Fritz Kuchen SUI 59

Individual Military Rifle 300m standing
1. Carl Osburn USA 56
2. Lars Jörgen Madsen DEN 55
3. Lawrence Nuesslein USA 54

Individual Military Rifle 600m Prone
1. Carl Hugo Johansson SWE 58
2. Mauritz Eriksson SWE 66/6
3. Lloyd Spooner USA 56/5

Military Rifle Team 300m standing
1. Denmark 266
2. USA 255
3. Sweden 255

Military Rifle Team 300m Prone
1. USA 289
2. France 283
3. Finland 281

Military Rifle Team 600m Prone
1. USA 287/283/284
2. South Africa 287/283/279
3. Sweden 287/275

Military Rifle Team 300 + 600m Prone
1. USA 573
2. Norway 565
3. Switzerland 563

Miniature Rifle Teams
1. USA 1899
2. Sweden 1873
3. Norway 1865

Running Deer, single shot
1. Otto Olsen NOR 43
2. Alred Swahn SWE 41
3. Harald Natvig NOR 41

Team Running Deer, single shot
1. Norway 178
2. Finland 159
3. USA 158

Running Deer, double shot
1. Ole Andreas Lilloe-Olsen NOR 82
2. Fredric Landelius SWE 77
3. Einar Liberg NOR 71

Team Running Deer, double shot
1. Norway 343
2. Sweden 336
3. Finland 284

Clay Pigeon Team
1. USA 547
2. Belgium 503
3. Sweden 500

Mixed: Clay Pigeon
1. Mark Arie USA 95
2. Frank Troeh USA 93
3. Frank Wright USA 87

Tennis

Men – singles
1. Louis Raymond SAF
2. Ichiya Kumagae JPN
3. Charles Winslow SAF

Men – doubles
1. GBR – 2. JPN – 3. FRA

Women – singles
1. Suzanne Lenglen FRA
2. E. Dorothy Holman GBR
3. Kathleen "Kitty" McKane GBR

Women – doubles
1. GBR – 2. GBR – 3. FRA

Mixed Doubles
1. France
2. Great Britain
3. BOH/Great Britain
3. USA/Great Britain

Mixed Doubles
1. FRA – 2. GBR – 3. CZE

Polo

1. GBR – 2. SPA – 3. USA

Rugby

1. USA – 2. FRA

Weightlifting

Featherweight
1. Frans de Haes BEL 220.0
2. Alfred Schmidt EST 212.5
3. Eugène Ryther SUI 210.0

Lightweight
1. Alfred Neuland EST 257.5
2. Louis Williquet BEL 240.0
3. Florimond Rooms BEL 230.0

Middleweight
1. Henri Gance FRA 245.0
2. Pietro Bianchi ITA 237.5
3. Albert Pettersson SWE 237.5

Light Heavyweight
1. Ernest Cadine FRA 290.0
2. Fritz Hünenberger SWE 275.0
3. Erik Pettersson SWE 272.5

Heavyweight
1. Filippo Bottino ITA 270.0
2. Joseph Alzin LUX 255.0
3. Louis Bernot FRA 250.0

(Key to symbols and abbreviations p. 1456)

1920

SEPTEMBER

Su	Mo	Tu	We	Th	Fr	Sa
			1	2	3	4
5	6	7	8	9	10	11
12	13	14	15	16	17	18
19	20	21	22	23	24	25
26	27	28	29	30		

1. Middle East: France proclaims the creation of the state of Lebanon, with the government at Beirut.

2. New York: 3,000 dock workers refuse to unload British vessels until the UK takes troops out of Ireland.

3. US: Harding says he will seek revision of the Treaty of Versailles so the US can join the League of Nations.

6. US: Start of a daily east-west airmail service between San Francisco and New York.

7. Norwich: The Library Association outlines its scheme to create a travelling library service.

9. Italy: 500 die in earthquakes that leave 20,000 homeless.

11. UK: A. Moorhouse sets a new motor cycling speed record of 100mph at Brooklands motor circuit.

16. Paris: French president Paul Deschanel resigns through ill health; an election is called (→23).

16. New York: A massive bomb explosion on Wall Street kills 30 people and injures 300 (→18).

18. New York: Russian Alexander Brailovsky arrested for the Wall Street bombing.

20. Belgium: The League approves the Belgian annexation of Eupen and Malmedy from Germany.

22. London: The "Flying Squad" of the Metropolitan Police is formed.

23. France: Premier Alexandre Millerand is elected president of France; new premier will be Georges Leygues.

27. Ireland: Police arrest Sinn Feiner Countess Markiewicz, elected first woman MP, but who did not take her seat (→30).

30. Ireland: Sinn Fein president de Valera demands complete Irish independence and British withdrawal.

30. Africa: The French take possession of Togo.

Gandhi's party opts for non-violence

Sept 10. The Indian National Congress today voted to adopt Mr Gandhi's programme of non-cooperation with the Indian Government. In a long statement he listed those measures which he assured his party would obtain a "complete responsible government" for India in a year.

Among these measures were the renunciation of titles and honorary offices, the boycott of foreign goods, the boycott of legislative councils, and the gradual withdrawal of children from government schools and lawyers from practice. Mr Gandhi said the only weapon in their hands was noncooperation and non-violence should be their creed.

Hollywood star on murder charge

Accused: "Fatty" Arbuckle.

Sept 5. Millions of fans of Roscoe "Fatty" Arbuckle, whom many thought the world's funniest comedian, stopped laughing today when their hero was charged with the rape and murder of Hollywood actress, Virginia Rappe.

Arbuckle's alleged assault took place during what was described as an orgy in a San Francisco hotel room.

Miss Rappe, whose picture adorns the sheet music of "Let me Call You Sweetheart" was looking for a part in an Arbuckle film. She told rescuers: "I'm dying. Roscoe did it." Arbuckle has denied the charges (→12/4/22).

1920

OCTOBER

Su	Mo	Tu	We	Th	Fr	Sa
					1	2
3	4	5	6	7	8	9
10	11	12	13	14	15	16
17	18	19	20	21	22	23
24	25	26	27	28	29	30
31						

1. Middle East: Figures show 416 British troops have died in the last three months fighting Mesopotamian rebels.

2. Poland: The Poles claim they have taken 42,000 Russian prisoners (→6).

5. Hamburg: The world's largest liner, the Bismarck, is destroyed by fire.

6. Latvia: Poland and Russia sign an armistice at Riga.

7. Oxford: The first 100 women are admitted to study for full degrees.

9. Ireland: Cork city hall is partly destroyed in a bomb attack (→12).

12. Ireland: The IRA murders two British Army officers and three policemen (→17).

14. Russia: The Soviet government recognises the independence of Finland.

16. UK: Coal miners' strike begins.→

17. Ireland: Sinn Feiner Michael Fitzgerald is the first imprisoned hunger striker to die, after 68 days' fast (→25).

19. New York: A judge rules that communist party membership is sufficient grounds for deportation from the US.

20. London: Sylvia Pankhurst is charged with sedition after calling upon workers to loot the docks (→28).

20. London: King George V approves burial of an unknown soldier in Westminster Abbey on Armistice Day.

22. Moscow: Lenin escapes an assassination attempt.

25. London: MPs give second reading to Emergency Powers Bill to counter miners' strike (→3/11).

25. London: Tomas MacSwiney, jailed Lord Mayor of Cork, dies after a 78-day hunger strike.→

28. London: Sylvia Pankhurst is sent to prison for six months for sedition.

31. Ireland: Seven policemen are killed as a Sinn Feiner is hanged in Dublin for murdering another (→2/11).

Hunger striker's death sparks riots across Ireland

Oct 27. The death of hunger striker Tomas MacSwiney, Lord Mayor of Cork, has led to new outbreaks of violence in Ireland. Two British Army officers died when they were fired upon while searching a Dublin house for IRA men and ammunition. The IRA men escaped over the rooftops. Two policemen have also been killed in an ambush on a main road in Co. Roscommon.

It is now impossible to obtain up-to-date and reliable figures for the numbers killed and injured, as official sources no longer provide them. It was announced last week that in future casualty figures would be given only once a month. Meanwhile, the Vatican has heard conflicting calls from Britain and Ireland, either to praise the hunger strikers as martyrs or to condemn their deaths as self-inflicted murder.

Nationalist Tomas MacSwiney.

Hands up all those who want to stop

Oct 10. As the Ministry of Transport prepares to bring in an annual tax of £1 per horse-power (which can be paid quarterly) on privately owned motor cars, it has been announced that two compulsory signals are about to be introduced for all drivers. To signal a turn or slowing up, the driver will project his arm horizontally from the right hand side of the vehicle. The raised arm from the same side will indicate "stop".

Miners' strike is biting

Policemen struggle to control a crowd of strikers in London's Whitehall.

Oct 18. From this morning every mine in Britain is idle. Over the weekend the Prime Minister issued a message that "the nation must and will resist such an attack with all its strength". Robert Smillie, president of the Miners' Federation, said in Lanarkshire on Sunday that it was not a fight against the community or the government, but against the coal owners defended by the government.

The Government's offer to submit to an impartial tribunal the miners' claim of two shillings more per shift for men, one shilling for youths and 9d for boys under 16, and to abide by the result, was rejected on Friday by the miners' delegate conference. So, too, was the Government's offer to accept the higher minimum wage, provided coal production was restored to its previous levels.

Critical now will be the attitude of railwaymen and transport workers – the miners' partners in the Triple Alliance. Their executives are watching the situation closely, but have taken no official action yet. London's 25,000 commercial road transport workers, however, voted on Saturday to join the strike.

Meanwhile, a "state of emergency" has been declared to preserve coal stocks. All advertisement and display lighting is totally forbidden. London last night looked as if wartime had returned. The public is urged to use as little water as possible to save coal used for pumping.

The Food Controller has cut the sugar ration from 12 to 8 oz, and issued an order banning food hoarding. Hyde Park in the West End and Woodford Green in East London will act as depots for lorries bringing in milk from the country and taking back food.

Once people have had time to get home, passenger train services will be severely cut, but not workmen's trains. The crisis has hit the pound, which fell last week from $3.50 to $3.465.

Miners' leader J.H. Thomas.

1920

NOVEMBER

Su	Mo	Tu	We	Th	Fr	Sa
	1	2	3	4	5	6
7	8	9	10	11	12	13
14	15	16	17	18	19	20
21	22	23	24	25	26	27
28	29	30				

1. Armenia: Turks are reported to have seized the town of Hadjin and butchered 10,000 Armenians (→22).

2. Ireland: Four more policemen and a soldier are murdered by the IRA in escalating violence.

3. UK: Coal miners vote by only a narrow majority to continue their strike, and decide to call it off.

4. China: Report that severe famine is leading some Chinese to sell their children to buy food.

5. Europe: Britain, France and Italy pledge mutual support in their spheres of influence in Turkey.

9. Rome: Pope Benedict XV bans the film "Holy Bible" for its naked portrayal of Adam and Eve.

10. London: The body of the unknown British soldier arrives from France for interment in Westminster Abbey (→11).

11. Paris: The unknown French soldier is buried under the Arc de Triomphe.

11. Ireland: Sinn Feiners chant through the two-minute silence on Armistice Day.→

13. Geneva: 5,000 representatives from 41 nations attend the opening of the first League of Nations full session.

14. US: Charlie Chaplin is divorced by his wife, who says the name Chaplin "gets on my nerves".

16. Greece: Premier Venizelos resigns following his defeat in national elections.

19. Constantinople: The city is swamped by the arrival of 100,000 White Russian refugees from the Crimea.

22. Geneva: The League decides to help Armenia.

25. London: The Government announces plans for a Severn Barrage, which will generate 500,000 hp of electricity.

27. Ireland: Sinn Fein founder Arthur Griffith is arrested (→29).

29. Ireland: The IRA kills 15 army cadets.

Last stand of White Brigade in Crimea

Nov 16. Russia's long, bloody and chaotic civil war is over and Bolshevism has triumphed. The final battle between the Red Army and the Whites has ended in the Crimea with a resounding defeat for Baron Wrangel.

Wrangel, who took over from Denikin in March, did a tremendous job and turned a defeated mob into a disciplined army. But once the Bolsheviks had settled their campaigns against the Ukrainians and the Poles, he was outnumbered, and out-supplied.

Wrangel's withdrawal was under French protection. Ships have evacuated 146,000 disarmed soldiers and refugees who are being taken to Tunisia.

The White Baron: Baron Wrangel.

France and UK set German war debts

Nov 14. After months of wrangling, Britain and France have agreed on rules for getting Germany to meet the war reparations bill. France has won her point that the bill must be backed up by the threat of sanctions if Germany fails to pay. The French have accepted Britain's view that an early date should be fixed for talking to the Germans about how much they can pay; the Germans are pleading poverty after losing territory and resources under the peace treaty. ▷

Bloody Sunday: IRA kills 14 soldiers

Nov 21. Fourteen British officers and officials were killed in their beds shortly after dawn today. It marked the start of a day of blood-letting remarkable even amid the recent violence of Ireland.

Later in the day, also in Dublin, soldiers and the special police known as the Black and Tans surrounded the Gaelic Athletic Association's headquarters at Croke Park, just as a football match was due to start. Shots were fired and 12 people were killed, either by the gunfire or because they were trampled to death by the fleeing crowd. And tonight two men were shot by the military at Dublin Castle.

Several of the British officers who died in the IRA's dawn raid were plain-clothes men. They had been living in rented homes or hotels. Terrified maids, responding to a knock on the door, were asked at gunpoint to identify the officers' bedrooms. Some officers were then dragged to adjoining rooms, so that they would not be shot in front of women and children.

All the officers had arrived in Ireland recently as part of the effort to boost Army intelligence, which so often has appeared to lag behind that of IRA commander Michael Collins. There is a firm belief amongst the military leaders that they can win by force. General Sir Neville Macready, the Army commander-in-chief, and Lord French, the Lieutenant-Governor of Ireland, regard the troubles as a minority revolt, despite the fact that the people behind the IRA violence are MPs who have been elected with huge majorities to Westminster.

So more reinforcements have been poured into Ireland by the British authorities. The Army now has 43,000 soldiers in Ireland and they have been joined by the special constabulary known as the Black and Tans.

With 300 police barracks abandoned or blown up, and Catholics quitting the Royal Irish Constabulary, the force has been given a tough ex-British Army commander, General Tudor, to give it a more military role.

Black and Tan auxiliaries hold up a Sinn Feiner during recent troubles.

Republican Warren Harding sweeps to victory in US elections

Nov 2. Warren Gamaliel Harding, the Republican candidate, was easily elected President of the United States today.

There was never much doubt about the eventual winner. Senator Harding started comfortably in the lead. The Democratic candidate, James Cox, governor of Ohio, was always fighting an uphill battle, hampered by support for the unpopular Versailles treaty and League of Nations. At first the Republicans planned to keep Senator Harding to a "front porch" campaign, but he proved an effective speaker, calling for a return to "normalcy".

The margin of victory, however, comes as a surprise. Harding won 16.1 million votes to 9.1 million and 404 electoral votes to 127.

Newly-elected President Warren Gamaliel Harding with his wife.

1920

DECEMBER

Su	Mo	Tu	We	Th	Fr	Sa
			1	2	3	4
5	6	7	8	9	10	11
12	13	14	15	16	17	18
19	20	21	22	23	24	25
26	27	28	29	30	31	

3. London: Rudyard Kipling wins £2 damages from a medical firm that used part of his poem "If" in an advert.

5. Greece: A referendum calls for the return of ex-King Constantine, ousted by the Allies in 1917 (→19).

7. Washington: President Wilson's last annual speech to Congress omits talk of League, but urges loan to Armenia.

10. Stockholm: Nobel Prizes awarded to Charles Guillaume (Switzerland, Physics); Walther Ernst (Germany, Chemistry); Schack Krogh (Denmark, Medicine) and Knut Hamsun (Norway, Literature). Peace prize awarded to Leon Bourgeois.→

15. Geneva: China and Austria are admitted to the League of Nations.

18. Middle East: Britain and France reach agreement on the frontiers of Syria and Palestine.

19. Greece: King Constantine returns, despite Anglo-French opposition.

23. London: Jewish leaders launch a £25 million appeal for Palestine.

23. London: King George V signs Irish partition bill.

26. South America: Thousands are feared dead in an earthquake that struck Chile, Bolivia and Argentina.

29. India: Mohandas Gandhi predicts a "sea of blood" under continued British rule.

31. Italy: Poet Gabriele d'Annunzio agrees to hand over Fiume to Italy rather than fight the Italian army.

HITS OF 1920

Wyoming Lullaby.

Avalon.

Margie.

QUOTE OF THE YEAR

"Puritanism: the haunting fear that someone, somewhere, may be happy."
H. L. Mencken,
on effect of Prohibition in US.

Martial law is finally declared in Ireland

Irish special constables at the funeral of a comrade murdered by the IRA.

Dec 11. Martial law was declared in large areas of Ireland yesterday in an attempt to curb the spiral of violence. In the south and west, whole villages and towns have been virtually destroyed by fire as the British army, supported by the Black and Tans, step up their campaign to catch the IRA gunmen.

The toughest resistance has been in the city and county of Cork; martial law now covers both. It has also been imposed in Kerry where IRA snipers have made it virtually impossible for the security forces to use the main roads. Tipperary and Limerick, too, are under martial law – and not surprisingly since, in the city of Limerick, gunmen are sandbagged into the tops of high tenements, while in Tipperary they have staged daring daytime raids and captured vast quantities of explosives.

Both sides in the struggle are now desperate and reprisals are getting more savage. This morning, the IRA wounded soldiers in Cork; tonight, the centre of the city of Cork is a ball of fire, as the security forces retaliate and seek to deny hide-outs to the gunmen.

Woodrow Wilson wins Nobel Peace Prize

Dec 10. The 1919 Nobel peace prize was presented tonight in Christiania, Norway, to President Woodrow Wilson for his work for peace and a lasting settlement of the issues which led to the Great War.

Mr Wilson played the leading part at the Paris peace talks, which virtually adopted as their agenda his "Fourteen Points" and the ideal that nations should be able to determine their own fate.

The award nevertheless comes at an ironic time. In September 1919 Mr Wilson suffered a stroke which left him paralysed; he was unable to collect the peace prize announced last December. In March the US Senate rejected the treaty; last month his party and his policies were firmly rejected when Harding was elected president.

Dram ban? No thank you man, say Scots

Dec 5. After a fiercely fought campaign between "wets" and "drys", Scotland has voted against prohibition. The fight was essentially between the nonconformist church on one hand and the whisky distillers and licensees on the other.

Voters were deluged with leaflets from both sides. The "wets" showered theirs from aircraft bearing the slogan "Vote No Change" on the wings. They appealed to voters on economic grounds; the "drys" on moral grounds.

In Aberdeen, sandwich-board men bearing the legend "Hell is the Well of Whisky" were quickly followed by others whose boards asked "Oh, death, where is thy sting?".

One aged voter waved his walking stick as he entered the Partick polling station, shouting vehemently "Down with the curse of Scotland!".

Arts: new voices as Europe goes Dada

Dada has been breaking out and causing confusion all over Europe. In Paris, **Marcel Duchamp** has scandalised the bourgeois with his version of the Mona Lisa – with moustache. At a Dada Festival of poetry and music, **Tristan Tzara**, the original Dadaist, was joined by poets **Andre Breton, Paul Eluard** and **Louis Aragon**. Tzara has the letters D A D A inscribed on his forehead, above his monocle.

In Berlin an International Dada Fair was held by **George Grosz**, whose savage pictures caricature militarism and male lust. The effigy of a German soldier with a pig's head hung from the ceiling. Grosz was fined for "insulting the army".

Cologne held a Dada exhibition of work by **Max Ernst** and **Jean Arp**, which was closed by the police. Spectators were invited to smash the paintings. Hanover's Dada leader is **Kurt Schwitters** who makes "pictures" out of rubbish.

The Dadaists adopt the anarchist slogan, "Destruction is also Creation!". Their aim to destroy all conventional ideas of art was demonstrated by **Francis Picabia** in a "Tableau Dada", a stuffed monkey, framed and inscribed "Portrait de Cezanne ... Renoir ... Rembrandt". But Dada is also chic. Picabia's vernissage was attended by smart society and the young composer **Francis Poulenc**, one of "Les Six", played jazz.

But the "succes fou" in Paris is **Colette's** novel "Cheri", the story of an ageing courtesan's love affair – her last – with the young son of a friend, a subtle study of feminine psychology from the inside.

Francis Scott Fitzgerald.

Shakespeare: ousted by movies?

Two new voices emerged in America where cinema continues to boom: **Sinclair Lewis** in "Main Street" satirises small-town America, while **F. Scott Fitzgerald** catches the spirit of fast-living youth in "This Side of Paradise".

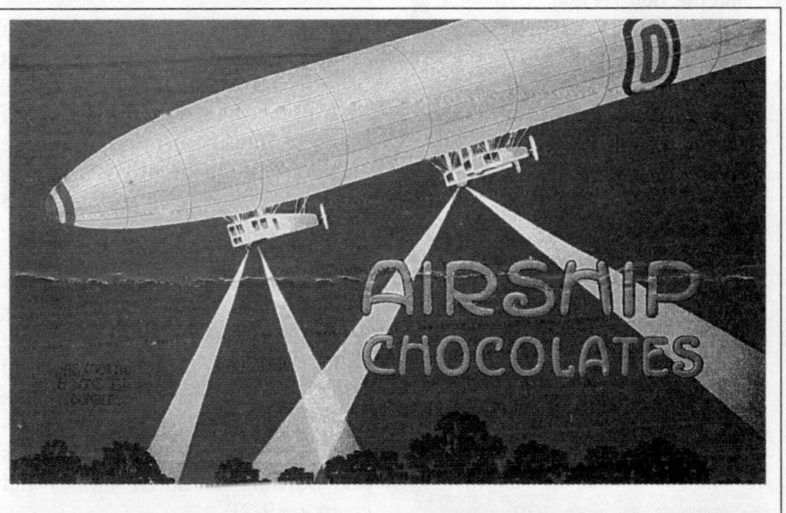

1921

JANUARY

Su	Mo	Tu	We	Th	Fr	Sa
						1
2	3	4	5	6	7	8
9	10	11	12	13	14	15
16	17	18	19	20	21	22
23	24	25	26	27	28	29
30	31					

1. US: Naval seaplane NC-5 flies 702 miles with five passengers in record nine hours 15 minutes.

2. Spain: 160 passengers and crew are feared drowned when the ship Santa Isabel sinks off Villa Garcia.

3. UK: Announcement of the completion of airships R-36 and R-37, capable of carrying 50 passengers.

6. Berlin: Statistics show that a quarter of the city's 485,000 children are diseased or malnourished.

10. Washington: President-elect Harding asks for a simple inauguration ceremony (→4/3).

12. Paris: The Leygues government falls after defeat in Chamber of Deputies (→16).

13. Germany: Plans are announced for a huge 1443-ton submarine with 35mm armour plate, capable of 17.5 knots.

14. UK: Unemployment stands at 927,000 (→15/2).

16. Paris: Aristide Briand is appointed premier by President Millerand.

20. Ireland: Six policemen are killed by the IRA.→

20. English Channel: The Royal Navy submarine K5 sinks with the loss of 56 crew members.

23. Dublin: Eight die in fighting between the British and the IRA (→1/2).

24. Berne: The Swiss government bars the import of foreign labour.

25. US: Unemployment stands at 3,473,000.

26. UK: Seventeen people are killed when two passenger trains collide in Montgomeryshire.

28. Berlin: Professor Albert Einstein causes a stir with his suggestion that the universe could be measured.

28. Paris: The Allies finally fix Germany's reparations at £10 billion over 42 years (→5/2).

British tanks ordered to roll into Dublin

British troops standing guard over their tank in a deserted Dublin street.

Jan 22. British tanks rolled over Dublin's cobbled streets yesterday and took up positions in the docks and market areas. As they came into position, there was firing from a timber store. Snipers had taken up positions behind a wall of planks. The troops are in full battle dress and heavily armed. The areas occupied are a zig-zag of old warehouses and faded red brick tenements. Dublin Castle is remaining tight-lipped about the reason for this sudden move. But tonight two areas of the city are sealed off with barbed wire and gates.

In the past few days martial law has been extended to embrace the counties of Clare, Limerick, Kilkenny, Waterford and Wexford. The aim is to catch gunmen on the run and those who have already left areas where martial law has been proclaimed. All the counties in the extreme south are now sealed off by the military with essential supplies being moved from Dublin by sea; the roads are not considered safe. Householders are stocking up for what they call "a long siege" with queues at breadshops and potatoes being bought by the sackfull.

General Strickland, who is in command of the Army in Cork, has ordered all 20,000 householders to paste a list of occupants on the back of their front doors. The list is to include age, sex and occupation; the information is to assist the search for weapons (→23).

Indian parliament opens to rioting

Jan 10. The Duke of Connaught landed at Madras today at the start of his visit to India, during which he will inaugurate the Chamber of Princes and the Council of State and Imperial Legislative Assembly in Delhi. Unfortunately the Duke's visit is taking place against a background of rioting.

Mr Gandhi, the nationalist leader who now controls the Congress party, has sworn not to co-operate with "this satanic government" and his campaign for independence is turning to violence with mobs looting bazaars, attacking road convoys and burning landlords' homes and crops (→9/2).

Divorce details may shock women jurors

Jan 25. Six women made legal history today when they were sworn in as the first female jurors ever to sit on a Divorce Court jury. Opponents have argued that women would be shocked by case details, but not one of the six took advantage of the clause which can grant exemption because of the nature of the evidence.

The only tricky moment came when some "abominable and beastly" letters and pictures had to be shown to the jury. It was feared that they would terrify an unmarried woman so the jury decided that only the men should see them. The women agreed not to look.

1921

FEBRUARY

Su	Mo	Tu	We	Th	Fr	Sa
		1	2	3	4	5
6	7	8	9	10	11	12
13	14	15	16	17	18	19
20	21	22	23	24	25	26
27	28					

1. Ireland: Troops burn down houses in Middleton in retaliation for the murder of three policemen (→11).

3. London: Lloyd George gives Germany four days to accept Allied reparations or produce an alternative.→

8. S. Africa: General Jan Smuts is elected Prime Minister of the Union.

9. India: The Duke of Connaught opens the new Indian Central Legislature in Delhi.

11. Ireland: A Cork labourer is murdered as an alleged police informer (→16).

12. London: Winston Churchill is appointed Colonial Secretary.

16. Ireland: Eight Sinn Fein supporters are shot dead in a gun battle with the army (→20)

17. US: Figures reveal there were nine million cars in the United States in 1920.

18. France: Aviator Etienne Oehmichen makes the first flight, as opposed to lift off, in a helicopter (→13/11/07).

19. Washington: The Senate limits immigration to 355,461 people a year.

19. Paris: France signs a military and economic co-operation agreement with Poland.

20. Ireland: An ex-soldier is dragged from hospital in Cork and killed by Sinn Feiners (→7/4).

23. Persia: Reported that General Reza Khan has staged a coup d'etat.

24. Washington: Herbert Hoover is appointed Secretary of Commerce.

26. Moscow: The Soviet government signs treaties respecting the territorial integrity of Persia and Afghanistan.

28. Armenia: Reported that Turks have carried out horrific massacres of Armenians near Kars and Alexandropol.

DEATH

8. Russian anarchist Peter Kropotkin (*9/12/1842).→

War debt demand causes German outcry

Feb 5. The Allied reparations bill has been received "with pain and indignation", a German government spokesman told the Reichstag on Wednesday. Reparations on the scale demanded by the Allies would lead to "the economic and political pauperisation of the German nation". Germany, it is claimed, would disappear from the world as a purchaser and a consumer, and her "powers of resistance against the danger of Bolshevism" would be seriously weakened.

The reparations bill, which was agreed at a meeting of experts in Paris last month, requires Germany to pay more than 200 billion gold marks (£10 billion) over the next 42 years up to 1963. In addition, an annual 12.5 per cent tax is to be levied on German exports.

German public opinion appears to be firmly behind the government. The national trade union federation says the Allies are trying to introduce slavery into the country. In Bavaria, extreme nationalists and communists are joining in demands for an alliance with Soviet Russia against the Western powers.

But Lloyd George, the British Prime Minister, speaking in Birmingham, said Germany must pay for the devastation she had caused in France. The reparations bill was well within Germany's capacity to pay, he said.

The first helicopter flight has lift off

A French helicopter demonstrates the flying potential of rotary wings.

Feb 18. A French engineer has managed to achieve true flight in a helicopter, and claims to have solved the problem of how to match power and weight in the machines.

Other pioneers have succeeded in getting their machines to hover a few inches off the ground using massive motors, but every time they tried to get higher the weight of the machine and its engine drove them back. Now Etienne Oehmichen has told the French Academy of Science that he has managed flight using just a 25 hp motor attached to a simple structure weighing a total of only 100 kilos.

He estimates rotors only need eight and a half horse power to lift 135 kilos. However, he has yet to discover the important trick of how to keep a helicopter stable.

Unemployment tops a million in Britain

Ex-servicemen reduced to a life of street hawking by the lack of jobs.

Feb 16. The Government is to increase unemployment benefit from 15 shillings to 18 shillings a week for men and from 12 shillings to 15 shillings for women as soon as a bill is passed amending the Unemployment Insurance Act. The benefit will in future be paid for 26 weeks in the year, instead of the present 15. This was announced today by Dr Macnamara, the Minister for Labour, in the debate on the King's Speech at yesterday's State Opening of Parliament.

Unemployment is now over one million. The latest official figures stand at 1,039,000, including 368,000 ex-servicemen. In addition, there are 600,000 working on short time.

The Government's concern over unemployment is evident from the passage written into the King's Speech which said: "The most pressing problem which confronts you is that of unemployment, consequent upon a world-wide restriction of trade".

The Minister said that the figures were "very large" and, although they have been higher in previous recessions, the explosion in prices since the Armistice has made them particularly grave.

Anti-Soviet sailors mutiny at Kronstadt

Feb 5. As Lenin's Bolsheviks arrive in Moscow for the party congress to debate how much freedom, if any, the Russian people should be allowed, sailors at the Kronstadt naval base outside Petrograd are in ferment, holding meetings and, to cries of "Down with Bolshevik tyranny!", passing resolutions demanding free elections. Bolshevik commissars on the spot have been imprisoned. A delegation of sailors sent to Petrograd has been arrested.

The insurrection has surprised and shocked Lenin and his colleagues, since the sailors of Kronstadt were among the Bolsheviks' most fervent supporters in 1917. Leon Trotsky, Commissar for War, called them "the pride and glory of the revolution".

Prince of anarchists dies in Moscow

Feb 8. Prince Kropotkin, a leading theorist of anarchism, who became disappointed by Bolshevik rule in Russia, has died in Moscow at the age of 78.

Kropotkin lived in England for 30 years until he returned to Russia after the February 1917 Revolution, believing that it would become the first stateless society. Although held in great esteem, he withdrew from public life.

Kropotkin began to foster revolutionary propaganda among Russian workers in 1872 and spent two years in prison. He opposed all state power and favoured abolition of private property.

Feb 3. US premiere of Charlie Chaplin's first full-length film, "The Kid", co-starring in the title role Jackie Coogan.

1921

MARCH

Su	Mo	Tu	We	Th	Fr	Sa
		1	2	3	4	5
6	7	8	9	10	11	12
13	14	15	16	17	18	19
20	21	22	23	24	25	26
27	28	29	30	31		

1. Australia: Australia wins the fifth test against England by nine wickets, setting a record by winning every match in the series.

3. South China Sea: 862 die when the steamer Hong Moh is shipwrecked.

4. Washington: Harding and Coolidge are sworn in as President and Vice-President.

6. US: Figures show cancer deaths were up six per cent in 1920 from 1919 to 5,361.

6. US: The police chief in Sunbury, Pennsylvania, orders skirts no shorter than four inches below the knee.

11. Oxford: Queen Mary is the first woman awarded a degree from the University when she receives an honorary degree.

15. Africa: Belgium cedes Ruanda to the UK.

16. Havana: Jose Capablanca and Emanuel Lasker draw for the World Chess Championship after only 50 moves.

17. London: Andrew Bonar Law resigns as Tory leader through ill-health (→21).

20. Germany: Upper Silesia votes by 65 per cent to remain part of Germany.

21. London: Austen Chamberlain becomes Tory leader in succession to Bonar Law (→19/10/22).

23. US: Arthur Hamilton makes a world record parachute jump from 24,400 ft over Illinois, landing safely.

24. Hamburg: At least 20 are killed in a communist-led attempt to seize control of the city.

26. US: Charles Paddock sets a world record for the 200 metres of 20.8 seconds (→23/4).

26. UK: Mr T. McAlpine's Shaun Spadah wins the Grand National at Aintree.

31. UK: State of emergency declared after a coal strike is called (→3/4).

31. UK: Churchill tells Jews the UK will abide by the Balfour Declaration and give them a homeland in Palestine.

Lenin's economy to allow enterprise

March 12. The Bolsheviks have been told by Lenin that state planning of the economy is to be ended. Forced requisitioning of crops is to stop and peasants will be encouraged to sell their produce on the open market. Private trading is to be restored and partnership deals with foreign capitalists will be made.

In his speech to the tenth congress of the Communist Party in Moscow, Lenin admitted he had made mistakes, but he did not say Communism was being abandoned; it was only being postponed until the economy had recovered. As he put it: "Two steps forward, one step back".

Even so, it is being seen as an embarrassing political somersault by a revolutionary leader who prided himself on his mastery of Karl Marx's economic theories. A year ago when Trotsky warned the party's Central Committee that the economy was collapsing and that a free market must be allowed for peasants and tradesmen, he was ridiculed by Lenin, who told him there was no going back from the planned economy.

Lenin absorbed by his copy of Pravda at his desk in the Kremlin.

Trotsky accepted the rebuke and threw himself with renewed energy into enforcing war communism, the system that had enabled them to fight the civil war and survive foreign intervention. He called for the militarisation of labour and said deserters should be sent to concentration camps.

Allies occupy Germany to collect debts

March 8. Germany's failure to give a satisfactory response to the Allies' demands for war reparations today led to British, French and Belgian troops crossing the Rhine and occupying Dusseldorf and other Ruhr towns.

Lloyd George told MPs of a plan to force the Germans to pay up. Every purchaser of German goods would be required to give a proportion, possibly 50 per cent, of the purchase money to the Treasury; the German exporter would then apply to his government for reimbursement. The procedure would be adopted by all countries claiming reparations.

But some businessmen are sceptical. They fear that the Germans could get round the arrangement by trading through neutral third countries, such as Sweden, Holland or Denmark. The principle of reparations has been accepted by the Germans, but they say they can pay only a quarter of the £10 billion demanded by the Allies.

French troops in Dusseldorf six days after the occupation began.

Kronstadt rebels crushed by Trotsky

March 17. Trotsky, acclaimed by the sailors of Kronstadt as their revolutionary leader in those heady months of 1917, today ordered a picked Red Army force to storm the naval base and crush an anti-Bolshevik insurrection by those same sailors.

After an artillery bombardment, the Bolshevik troops, with white sheets over their uniforms, advanced across the frozen bay, to be met by a storm of fire from the sailors. The ice broke and wave after wave of white-sheeted attackers perished in the freezing sea.

The sailors, most of whom are country boys, have been demanding better treatment for peasants and free elections to city soviets. But Trotsky called them "blinded" and acted before the spring thaw would have enabled the base to get supplies from friendly Baltic countries. The sailors were finally crushed after a night-long battle in a blizzard. Many fled to Finland, where the American Red Cross is feeding them.

First clinic for birth control in London

The clinic that caused the uproar.

March 17. The country's first birth control clinic opened in London today in the face of bitter opposition from clergymen and doctors, who fear it will encourage immorality. Its founder is Dr. Marie Stopes, the 41-year-old palaeobotanist whose book "Married Love" caused a sensation when it appeared in 1918. The Holloway clinic aims to give free consultations and cheap contraceptives, particularly the cervical cap, to poorer women overburdened by child-bearing.

"Red Seal" silk hosiery.

1921

APRIL

Su	Mo	Tu	We	Th	Fr	Sa
					1	2
3	4	5	6	7	8	9
10	11	12	13	14	15	16
17	18	19	20	21	22	23
24	25	26	27	28	29	30

1. Philippines: 15,000 are left homeless when a fire destroys 3,000 houses.

3. UK: Coal rationing starts.→

4. Turkey: Greek troops suffer 5,000 casualties in fighting with Turks at Eskiskehr.

5. Geneva: International Red Cross conference proposes new limitations on warfare.

7. Ireland: Sinn Feiners shoot dead a 60-year-old woman in Castlerea, the first woman to die in current violence (→14).

10. Peking: Sun Yat-sen is elected President of China (→5/5).

12. Detroit: Henry Ford is now making one million cars a year (→10/5).

13. UK: Lloyd's Bank takes over Fox, Fowler and Co., the last provincial English bank to issue its own banknotes.

14. Dublin: Sir Arthur Vickers, former keeper of Dublin Castle, is murdered (→4/5).

19. Germany: The funeral of the ex-Kaiserin Augusta Victoria turns into a monarchist demonstration.

20. Washington: General John Pershing is appointed Chief of Staff of the US Army.

23. UK: King George V watches Tottenham Hotspur beat Wolverhampton Wanderers 1-0 in the FA Cup Final at Stamford Bridge.

25. Moscow: The Soviet government makes all foreigners except diplomats eligible to be called up to work.

26. London: For the first time, police on motor cycles patrol the city.

30. London: A judge speaks of the "demoralisation caused by mass unemployment".

BIRTH

16. British actor Peter Ustinov.

DEATH

11. German ex-Kaiserin Augusta Victoria, wife of Kaiser Wilhelm II (*22/10/1858).

Trade union support for miners caves in

Wigan miners are urged by their union to continue the coal strike.

April 15. The national strike by the "Triple Alliance", due to begin at 10 o'clock tonight, has been called off. At the last minute the railway and transport unions decided not to come out in support of the Miners' Federation in its dispute with the coal owners.

By themselves, the miners are in a weak position to resist the employers' demands that, with wartime controls on coal due to be removed this month, and in the current economic slump, wages should be lowered and set locally, not by national negotiation. The other unions would not, however, go along with the further demands that all coal mining profits and losses should go into one national "pool" and that the Government should subsidise the industry.

The "Triple Alliance" has thus failed in its first serious test. The miners asked for support two weeks ago, when the Government declared a state of emergency and rationed coal, using for the first time the Emergency Powers Act brought in six months ago when the miners were last on strike.

Then a week ago, navy, army and air reserves were recalled to the colours and the Government appealed for all "loyal citizens capable of bearing arms", aged between 18 and 40, to volunteer for 90 days service in new units of the Regular Army which would be called "Defence Units".

Harding turns down League of Nations

April 12. President Warren Harding today told Congress that the United States will "have no part" in the League of Nations. His speech was loudly cheered, especially by fellow Republicans.

The League was the brainchild of the former President, Woodrow Wilson, but American membership was a victim of the Senate's refusal to ratify the Versailles Treaty, signed by Wilson.

While rejecting the League, Mr Harding said that his administration would nevertheless cooperate with foreign governments in non-political ways.

The world's fastest human gets faster

April 23. Charles Paddock, the USA's flamboyant blond Olympic champion sprinter, today proved himself "The World's Fastest Human", winning the 100 metres at Redlands, California, in an astonishing 10.4 seconds, a full fifth of a second better than the world record set by his fellow-American Donald Lippincott nine years ago.

Paddock's historic sprint – preceded, as always, by his ostentatiously touching wood for luck, and climaxed by his famous exaggerated leap for the tape – was also timed at 9.6 seconds at 100 yards, equalling that world record.

1921

MAY

Su	Mo	Tu	We	Th	Fr	Sa
1	2	3	4	5	6	7
8	9	10	11	12	13	14
15	16	17	18	19	20	21
22	23	24	25	26	27	28
29	30	31				

1. France: The French army mobilises for an advance into the Ruhr if Germany defaults on reparations payments (→2).

2. Germany: The government is given ten days' grace by the Allies to pay their reparations demand.→

4. Glasgow: Irish violence spreads to Britain as Sinn Feiners murder a Glaswegian police inspector (→13).

5. Peking: Dr Sun Yat-sen formally takes office as President of China.

7. UK: Japanese Crown Prince Hirohito arrives on an official visit.→

8. Sweden: Capital punishment is abolished.

10. Detroit: Ford turns out a record 4,072 cars in one day.

13. Ireland: Nominations close for elections to the Northern and Southern Ireland parliaments created by the 1920 Act (→14).

14. London: Sinn Feiners carry out a wave of attacks on relatives of Royal Irish Constabulary members (→24).

17. US: Figures out today show the US population stands at 105,710,620.

22. UK: The US thrashes Britain nine rounds to three in the first golf international between the two countries.

22. Chicago: The city says women with short skirts and bare arms will pay fines from $10 to $100.

24. Ireland: Sinn Fein wins 124 out of 128 Southern Irish seats; Ulster Unionists win 40 out of 52 seats in Northern Ireland (→26).

26. Ireland: Lloyd George invites Eamon de Valera and first Northern Irish Prime Minister Sir James Craig to talks.in London (→7/6).

31. US: The first Austrians and Germans are granted citizenship since the US entered the Great War.

BIRTH

21. Soviet scientist and dissident Andrei Sakharov (†16/12/89).

Concern as skirts rise and morals decline

May 15. There is mounting alarm over the latest fashions in women's dress, which critics claim are immodest and immoral. Skirts have been steadily rising since the war and now thousands of women are revealing the calves of their legs. In America, where there has been widespread condemnation of the trend towards "minimum clothes and maximum cosmetics", Utah is considering imprisoning inappropriately dressed women.

The fashionable young woman of today tries to emulate men. She has a flat chest, straight clothes and short hair. Almost everywhere the corset is in decline. Women, many of whom did men's jobs in the war, say they want styles that reflect their new freedom, and designers have been quick to catch on to the economic advantage in making shorter, simpler dresses which need less material.

Guardians of traditional values, however, are worried that the styles encourage loose behaviour, especially when combined with other disturbing new trends among women: smoking, drinking, wearing make-up and dancing the latest wild dances. New York State, shocked by such dances, has just passed a law giving the State Commissioner the power to censor them (→ 22).

Short frocks come into fashion.

British troops sent to keep order in Egypt

May 23. Serious rioting by nationalists broke out today in Cairo and Alexandria. Egyptian troops quickly dispersed the mobs in Cairo but in Alexandria British soldiers had to be called out to restore order. Snipers fired on the troops from rooftops but the British suffered only minor casualties.

Many houses were set on fire and the rampaging mobs smashed the windows of European shops. It is feared that two Europeans were seized by the rioters and burnt to death. First reports say that 23 people have been killed in Alexandria. The trouble rose out of the departure for London of a delegation to discuss the Milner report about the future of Anglo-Egyptian relations. The streets are now quiet and the shops open.

Japanese Crown Prince inspecting Grenadiers at the Tower of London.

Germans accept the Allies' debt terms

May 11. With only a few hours to go before the expiry of the Allied ultimatum, the German government has finally agreed to pay the war reparations. The issue had threatened to precipitate a crisis because of the vehement and well-known opposition by several ministers from right-wing parties and their resignation would have brought down the government. At the last minute their parties gave them special dispensation to stay.

It was a pragmatic fudge because although the reparations deal, which included disarmament and the trial of war criminals, was very unpopular, there was never any realistic hope of resisting it. Failure to agree would simply have meant an Allied occupation.

Immigration quotas set to save US jobs

May 19. The era of virtually free entry to the United States is over. New immigration laws announced today lay down quotas which will limit new immigrants each year to three per cent of each nationality which lived in America in 1910. In effect, this will favour immigrants from Britain, Ireland, Germany and Scandinavia at the expense of those from southern European countries such as Italy and Greece. Immigration from Japan will also be curbed. The moves follow fears of job losses and too many non-English-speaking immigrants.

Flying Finn sets new world record

May 22. Paavo Nurmi, inheritor of Finland's great distance-running tradition and double gold medallist at last year's Olympic Games, has now become a record breaker. His first world mark was set today as – with stopwatch in hand throughout the race to confirm his relentless even pace – he destroyed a strong field in Stockholm to finish in 30 minutes 40.2 seconds, trimming a full 18 seconds off Jean Bouin's ten-year-old 10,000 metres record.

1921

JUNE

Su	Mo	Tu	We	Th	Fr	Sa
			1	2	3	4
5	6	7	8	9	10	11
12	13	14	15	16	17	18
19	20	21	22	23	24	25
26	27	28	29	30		

1. US: 85 die in race riots after a black is arrested for assaulting a white woman in Tulsa, Oklahoma (→ 11/9).

1. UK: The Derby is won by J. B. Joel's Humourist; for the first time, the result is broadcast "live" by wireless.

4. US: 500 are feared dead as floods sweep eastern Colorado.

6. London: King George V opens Southwark Bridge.

7. Belfast: The new Northern Irish parliament assembles.→

10. UK: Unemployment has reached 2.2 million.

12. UK: Sunday postal delivery and collection ends.

15. UK: Two million workers involved in pay disputes.

20. Washington: The city imposes a fine on women smoking of $25, followed by $100 per cigarette.

20. Petrograd: The first food cargo ship in three years arrives in the port.

22. China: Civil war has broken out over Sun Yat-sen's election as president.

23. Belfast: First formal debates in the Northern Ireland parliament.

24. UK: The world's largest airship, the R-38, built in the UK for the US Navy, makes its maiden flight at Bedford.

25. UK: Rainfall ends a 100-day drought.

28. UK: The coal strike ends with a government agreement to subsidise the coal industry; miners to go back on July 4.

30. Washington: Harding nominates former President Taft as US Chief Justice.

BIRTH

10. Greek-born Prince Philip Mountbatten, Duke of Edinburgh, husband of Queen Elizabeth II.

DEATHS

5. French playwright Georges Feydeau (*8/12/1862).

29. US-born society beauty Lady Jennie Churchill, mother of Winston (*9/1/1854).

King opens first Ulster Parliament

June 22. King George V was in Belfast today to open the new Northern Ireland Parliament, the parliament that nobody wanted. Southern Irish leaders believe in a united Ireland, while Sir Edward Carson and other Unionists fear the new parliament means less influence for Ulster at Westminster.

After a carriage drive through Belfast streets gay with bunting, the King, speaking with a sad voice, said: "Everything that touches Ireland finds an echo in the remotest parts of the Empire". In a speech known to have been inspired by General Jan Smuts of South Africa, the King spoke to the whole of Ireland and pleaded for peace and reconciliation.

Communist Party formed in China

June 30. The revolution in Russia, the translation of Karl Marx's works and the rise of a student movement have led to the formation this month of a Chinese communist party. The inaugural meeting, held at a girls' school in Shanghai, called for the "overthrow of the capitalist class". Among those who attended this meeting was Mao Tse-tung, a library assistant and primary school teacher.

June 5. George Feydeau, French author who gave a Parisian flair to farces, died aged 59.

1921

JULY

Su	Mo	Tu	We	Th	Fr	Sa
					1	2
3	4	5	6	7	8	9
10	11	12	13	14	15	16
17	18	19	20	21	22	23
24	25	26	27	28	29	30
31						

1. China: Chen Tu-hsiu is elected president of the new Communist Party; Mao Tse-tung is a founder member.

2. Wimbledon: Suzanne Lenglen retains the ladies singles' championship; Bill Tilden retains the men's title.

2. US: President Harding signs a Peace Decree, ending war with Germany and Austria.

2. UK: 1,363,121 people are on poor relief, the highest number ever recorded.

5. Vienna: Scientists claim they have carried out successful eye transplants on fish, frogs and rats.

7. London: South African premier General Smuts meets King George V to discuss the Irish situation (→ 8).

8. Ireland: Eamon de Valera agrees to talks with Lloyd George on an Irish truce (→ 12).

10. China: Mongolia declares independence as a people's republic, the world's second communist state (→ 5/11).

11. Europe: Lloyd George and French premier Briand endorse President Harding's plan for a disarmament conference.

12. London: Eamon de Valera arrives for talks with Lloyd George and representatives from Ulster (→ 18).

18. London: Ulster negotiators leave the truce talks, saying they will take no further part in negotiations.→

18. France: Albert Calmette and Camille Guerin give a child the first BCG vaccination against tuberculosis.

19. US: Over 8,000,000 women are now in paid employment, 87 per cent as teachers or secretaries.

29. Germany: Adolf Hitler is voted president of the National Socialist German Workers' Party.

31. Brussels: A new law divides Belgium into French and Flemish provinces.

BIRTH

18. US astronaut and politician John Glenn.

Gandhi urges "Buy Indian" cloth drive

July 28. A meeting of the All-India Congress Party in Bombay yesterday voted to boycott the forthcoming visit of the Prince of Wales to India. A resolution was also adopted urging a complete boycott of foreign cloth on the lines suggested by Mr Gandhi. He said that he was determined to make the success or failure of the cloth boycott the acid test of the country's fitness for "civil disobedience".

It was also decided that dealers be permitted to retain existing stocks of foreign cloth for re-exportation only. There is no doubt that if this boycott is effective it will seriously harm Lancashire's cotton mills and Britain's long-established export trade to India.

Spanish humiliated by Moroccan rebels

July 26. Spain is reeling from a devastating military defeat inflicted on their forces in Morocco by a young Berber leader, Abdel Krim, son of a tribal chief, who once served with the Spanish. The Mellila garrison of some 2,000 men has been wiped out, and its C-in-C, General Fernandez Silvestre, committed suicide to avoid falling into the rebels' hands.

During the Great War the Germans gave Abdel Krim guns to fight the French; instead he has turned them on the Spanish and seems set to destabilise the whole Spanish position in Morocco. Silvestre was a friend of King Alfonso and his death in such circumstances is certain to have political repercussions at home.

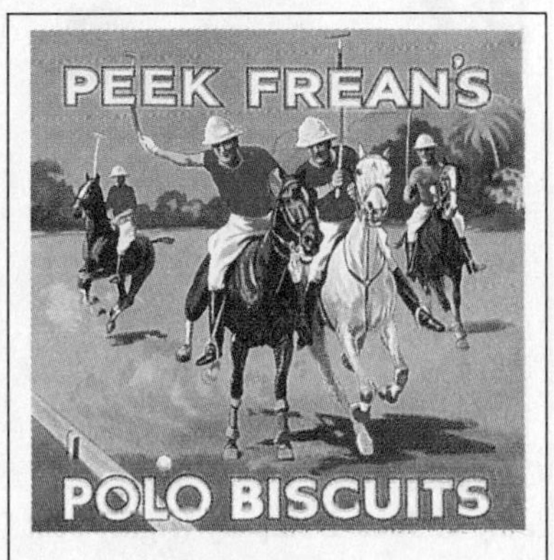

Irish truce is declared

July 22. Ireland now has a truce after months of the most savage fighting the country has ever known – and it looks like holding. Over the past few days events have moved with a dramatic swiftness. Even the peace move came so suddenly as to cause surprise.

A peace conference had been in progress in Dublin's Mansion House for days. Hopes were not high as it included a number of people who had not spoken a civil word to each other in months. Then on July 20 General Sir Neville Macready, the commander-in-chief, was invited to the talks.

He arrived wearing full military uniform, a revolver in his pocket, and apprehensive. As he had left for the talks, news came that the IRA were trying to blow up a patrol of Gordon Highlanders elsewhere in the city. The omens were not good.

At the Mansion House he saw Catholics kneeling on the footpath saying the rosary. He was surprised that they gave him a warm cheer. At the front door the nationalist Lord Mayor himself greeted the General and took him to the gilded conference room. He was shown Eamon de Valera's reply to the peace overture from the British Prime Minister, David Lloyd George. De Valera's letter reads: "The desire you express on the part of the British government to end centuries of conflict between the peoples of these two islands and to establish relations of neighbourly harmony is a genuine desire of the people of Ireland."

Seeking harmony: de Valera.

The General asked if they could get the cease-fire message through to their men in the hills. They assured him that there was no line of communication to beat their bush telephone. He said that he expected them to release people they had kidnapped such as the Earl of Bandon, whom he said was over 70 and perfectly harmless. General Macready has been ordered by Whitehall to give Michael Collins and other fighters free passage as "lawful belligerents".

July 1. Jack Dempsey (right) beat Georges Carpentier in four rounds.

Italian anarchists in US found guilty

July 14. After eight hours, a jury in Massachusetts today found two Italian anarchists guilty of murder. But the verdict seems unlikely to end the widespread controversy, which has surrounded Nicola Sacco and Bartolomeo Vanzetti ever since they were accused of murdering two men during a payroll robbery last year.

Both Sacco and Vanzetti have denied any involvement in the crime and none of the $16,000 stolen during the robbery has been traced to them. American liberals and unions have rallied to their defence, alleging they are victims of anti-bolshevik hysteria. Sentences have yet to be announced.

Sacco and Vanzetti.

Navy shocked as planes sink ships

July 21. American flyers have demonstrated another role for the destructive might of the aeroplane when, in a military test, they sank the former German battleship Ostfriesland with six 2,000 pound bombs in just 25 minutes.

Naval officers had claimed that only big guns would be able to sink an armoured ship. But Brigadier General William Mitchell and his men proved them wrong today.

They flew their six Martin bombers 100 miles off the Virginia coast to where the ship was moored and scored three direct hits with 1,000 pound bombs. They finally sunk her by dropping 2,000 pound bombs close by, splitting her open at the seams. Said an observer: "A bomb was fired that will be heard around the world".

1921

AUGUST

Su	Mo	Tu	We	Th	Fr	Sa
	1	2	3	4	5	6
7	8	9	10	11	12	13
14	15	16	17	18	19	20
21	22	23	24	25	26	27
28	29	30	31			

4. London: Poplar Council are given until the end of the month to set a rate (→ 1/9).

5. Naples: 50,000 mourners attend the funeral of Enrico Caruso, who died on August 2.

6. Dublin: All but one jailed Sinn Fein MPs are released (→ 14).

6. Berlin: Huge tax increases are proposed to pay for German reparations (→ 15).

7. New York: Organs replace orchestras in Broadway's biggest cinemas.

9. Moscow: Lenin appeals to the "international proletariat" for famine relief.

10. Paris: The Allied Supreme Council agrees on the partitioning of Silesia between Poland and Germany.

14. Ireland: De Valera rejects Lloyd George's offer of Dominion status for Ireland (→ 26).

15. Germany: Economic crisis grows as the value of the German mark declines; currently £1 equals 340M (→ 26).

16. Yugoslavia: Alexander becomes king on the death of Peter.

18. Russia: The US agrees to start an immediate famine aid programme.

19. UK: Unemployment is down to 1,640,600.

23. Baghdad: Emir Feisal is crowned King of Iraq.

24. UK: 27 Britons and 16 Americans die when the airship ZR II explodes during a trial flight at Hull.

25. India: Over 1,000 people die in riots on the Malabar coast.

26. Dublin: The Dail Eireann backs de Valera's refusal of Dominion status for Ireland within the British Empire (→ 15/9).

26. Germany: Finance minister Matthias Erzberger is murdered by extreme right-wingers (→ 29/9).

30. UK: In the final Test match of the season, England beat Australia for the first time this year.

Ielp us, pleads Lenin, as famine worsens

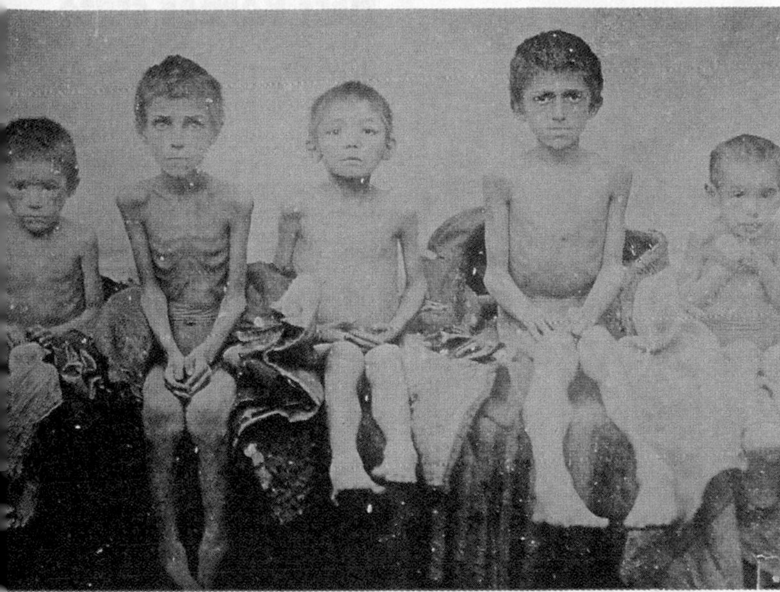

A few of the younger victims of the famine sweeping across Russia.

\ug 4. Russia is in the grip of a errible famine and its Bolshevik eaders are appealing to the world ommunity for help. Some 18 nillion are said to be starving, yphus and cholera are rampant, nd cannibalism has been reported.

The worst-hit area is the huge /olga region to the east of Moscow. Reports say peasants are mixing lay with their grain and have been triven to eating twigs. They have laughtered their starving cattle ind are fleeing the area in huge numbers, heading towards the owns, to find food.

The immediate cause of the famne is a drought which wiped out the harvest, but the area, as well as the whole of Russia, is devastated by the effects of the revolution and the civil war.

Following the mutiny of Soviet sailors at the Kronstadt naval base, Vladimir Lenin introduced the New Economic Policy, a strategic retreat from Marxism, in order to stay in power. But restoring private trade and ending the arbitrary seizure of food from the peasants has come too late to deal with the famine.

Lenin has now said Russia needs outside relief if it is to survive. Britain, America and other countries are responding.

Kemal tightens grip as Greeks advance

Aug 5. Mustafa Kemal has been appointed virtual ruler of Turkey, at least in the short term. The Grand National Assembly, meeting at Angora, has not only made him Supreme Commander of the army but also given him power to act in the name of the Assembly for three months.

His future prospects depend on his ability to halt the Greeks, who are continuing their advance from Smyrna in pursuit of their claims to the Aegean coast of Asia Minor. Kemal's men, fighting with their usual tenacity, had blocked the Greeks before the town of Eskishar but, late last month, the Greek army renewed its offensive and drove the Turks out of the town, capturing a great deal of military booty.

The pursuit of the defeated Turkish army continues, with cavalry, aeroplanes and tanks chasing the disorganised column across the plains. The Greeks are claiming that the Turkish army is restless and officers are demanding Kemal be removed as a traitor.

It is difficult to judge the extent of this discontent but there is little doubt that Kemal must conjure up a military success soon if he is to retain power.

It is said in Athens that Kemal has authorised the Porte to appeal to the Allied Powers to help negotiate peace with Greece.

Caruso dies, but records live on

Caruso, as seen on cigarette card.

Aug 3. All flags flew at halfmast in New York today at the news from Naples that Enrico Caruso has died at 48 of peritonitis.

Caruso began by singing in the cafes of Naples. He made his opera debut at 22. Strangely, both Verdi and Puccini doubted his ability in the early days, although he was to be incomparable in "Rigoletto", "Tosca" and "La Boheme".

He reigned at the Metropolitan Opera in New York, where he was paid nearly £700 a night. He was the first major singer to record, making 154 recordings and receiving almost £1 million in royalties.

Census reveals unequal sexes

\ug 23. First results of the census aken in June show an increase of lmost two million in the population of Great Britain since 1911, naking a grand total of 42,767,530. Of these some 7.4 million live in London. However, the population growth is lower than in any previous ten-year period.

With almost two million more vomen than men, it might seem hat the war is the key factor behind he slower rate of growth. But the atio of women to men has not changed that dramatically. Today here are 1096 women for every 1000 men as against 1068 in 1911.

Bank Holiday Britons break records as day tripping booms

Aug 1. Thousands of Britons risked the rain and packed excursion coaches and trains heading for the coast, rivers, race-courses and countryside – breaking all records on the fiftieth anniversary of the first Bank Holiday.

By noon, as holiday-makers thronged the seafronts at Brighton, Southend and other resorts, the cities were deserted. In the North, "town full" notices appeared on the roads into Blackpool where packed trains were arriving at ten-minute intervals.

Fifteen hundred people joined a mass rambling rally in Surrey. Five people died when a tram crashed at North Shields.

Seaside postcard shows how day-trippers enjoyed their Bank Holiday.

1921

SEPTEMBER

Su	Mo	Tu	We	Th	Fr	Sa
				1	2	3
4	5	6	7	8	9	10
11	12	13	14	15	16	17
18	19	20	21	22	23	24
25	26	27	28	29	30	

1. London: Nine Poplar councillors are arrested for refusing to set a rate, in defiance of a court order.→

3. US: 400 armed striking miners surrender to troops.

5. Liverpool: Price of bread is cut to 1s for a 4lb loaf.

7. London: Ministry of Health tells Islington Council that £3 13s 6d a week is too much to give a poor family on relief.

10. London: Crowds in Trafalgar Square demand the release of the arrested Poplar councillors (→12/10).

11. US: The Ku Klux Klan takes over Lanier University in Atlanta, Georgia, and says it will teach "Americanism".

15. London: Lloyd George cancels talks on Ireland when de Valera says he will only represent a "sovereign state" (→19).

19. Dublin: De Valera tells Lloyd George he will not set conditions for Anglo-Irish talks (→29).

21. Germany: An explosion at the BASF chemical works near Ludwigshafen kills 574 and injures over 1,000.

22. Europe: The Baltic States of Latvia, Lithuania and Estonia join the League of Nations.

23. UK: Independent Liberal Mrs Wintringham wins the Louth by-election, the second woman MP to take her seat.

26. France: French aviator Sadi Lecointe flies at a record 205 mph.

26. Prague: Eduard Benes becomes Czechoslovak premier.

29. London: Lloyd George invites de Valera to talks on an Irish treaty next month (→11/10).

29. Germany: The mark continues to decline so that £1 now equals about 500M (→4/10).

DEATH

27. German composer Engelbert Humperdinck (*1/9/1854).

World's most famous tramp comes home

Charlie Chaplin mobbed by admirers on his return to London.

Sept 9. The little tramp returned to the city of his birth today – to be mobbed by thousands of admirers in frantic scenes as the boat train pulled into Waterloo Station.

No baggy trousers, hat, false moustache or cane for Charlie Chaplin, however. He arrived at Southampton as a tourist and seemed bewildered at the strength of his boisterous reception.

Traffic was held up in Piccadilly when another crowd surrounded the Ritz Hotel – where a suite had been reserved for the film star. The crowd refused to move until Chaplin – born in Lambeth in 1889 – appeared on a balcony and threw carnations down to his fans.

Charlie Chaplin, Britain's number one box office draw, was signed up by the Keystone studios in 1913 when he went touring with Fred Karno.

London's cinemas have been quick to cash in on Chaplin's visit with re-runs of the films like "The Vagabond", "Easy Street", "The Rink" and "The Immigrant", films which many believe are destined to become screen classics.

His latest film, "The Kid", is one of the most expensive ever made with a budget of $500,000.

Rebels to set up first Berber state

Sept 19. The 39-year-old Berber leader, Abdel Krim, who annihilated the Spanish garrison in northern Morocco and captured vast quantities of arms, has announced that he is establishing an independent republic in the mountainous Rif territory he has conquered. If he succeeds, it will be the first Berber state in history, for the Berbers, though they call themselves "Imazighen" or free men, have always lived under foreign rule Carthaginian, Roman or Arab.

Abdel Krim's humiliation of the Spanish has caused a sensation among North African nationalists. In Algeria, the writer Messali Hadj says Abdel Krim has set an example to all the oppressed people of the Moslem world.

Berber leader Abdel Krim.

Evening dress made by Worth.

Women jailed in Poplar rates protest

Sept 6. A crowd of some 3,000 men and women massed around Poplar Town Hall in London yesterday to protest against the arrest of five women councillors. Their male colleagues, including George Lansbury, were arrested last week and are already in Brixton prison. They have been jailed for refusing to levy a rate. According to councillors, the central rate equalisation scheme would mean the poor people of Poplar have to pay a rate of 11s 10d in the pound, more than the average for London.

Two or three men wanted to stop the arrests, but the crowd cheered Miss Susan Lawrence when she said the women were determined to carry their protest to prison like the men. "You cannot rescue us. You can only make us look cowards" she said. She held up a copy of "The Future of Local Taxation" which she was taking to read in prison.

The crowd followed the arresting cars to the borough boundary with the local drum and fife band adding to the enthusiastic atmosphere. In their farewell messages the women stressed the need to deal with unemployment in London.

George Lansbury sent a message "We are starving inside the prison so that you may not starve outside." Apparently he has only had two tiny pieces of bread since his arrest last Saturday.

1921

OCTOBER

Su	Mo	Tu	We	Th	Fr	Sa
						1
2	3	4	5	6	7	8
9	10	11	12	13	14	15
16	17	18	19	20	21	22
23	24	25	26	27	28	29
30	31					

1. Washington: A US agenda for talks on the role of the four powers in the Pacific is accepted by the UK, France and Japan (→ 12/11).

3. Berlin: Waiters strike for higher pay, refusing tips.

4. Berlin: Owing to the fall of the mark the government puts a 100 per cent surcharge on all imports (→ 17).

6. Brussels: A conference of 16 countries meets to discuss famine aid for Russia (→ 5/12).

7. US: Ex-President Taft is elected head of the Unitarian Church.

7. Turin: The first International Sociology Conference opens.

8. UK: 36 people are killed when the steamer Rowan sinks off Scotland.

11. London: Irish Treaty conference opens (→ 31).

17. Germany: The mark continues to plummet; £1 is worth 720M (→ 22).

20. Lisbon: Portuguese premier Antonio Granjo is assassinated during an attempted military coup.

20. London: Labour rejects government unemployment relief plans, saying the benefit levels are too low.

21. Hungary: Ex-Habsburg Emperor Karl launches a bid to regain the throne of Hungary.→

22. Berlin: The German government resigns as the economic crisis deepens (→ 7/11).

26. Leipzig: The first German war criminal, Karl Heynen, is sentenced to nine months in jail for cruelty to POWs.

27. Hungary: Ex-Emperor Karl is held on a British warship in the Danube (→ 4/11).

31. London: MPs back Lloyd George's Irish policy as negotiations with de Valera's Sinn Fein continue (→ 6/12).

DEATH

23. British inventor of the pneumatic tyre John Boyd Dunlop (*5/2/1840).

Females quake at Valentino's Sheikh

Valentino in "The Sheikh".

Oct 31. The new sensation of the cinema is Rudolph Valentino of the flashing eyes. This glamorous Italian actor, born Rodolfo di Valentina d'Antonguella, is luring women back to see "The Sheikh" again and again. Earlier this year he made his name as a "Latin Lover" in "The Four Horsemen of the Apocalypse" and now, in Arab head-dress and flowing robes, he invites a willing slave-girl, played by Agnes Ayres, to "Fly with me – into another dawn". Men, it appears, do not like Valentino and critics describe "The Sheikh" as "a shocker to set flappers blushing". They show no reluctance to be shocked.

Emperor Karl's comeback fails

Oct 25. Undeterred by the utter failure of his theatrical coup last Easter, the ex-Emperor Karl has made a fresh attempt to regain the throne of Hungary. This time the attempt was more serious. He gathered a 12,000 strong army and, accompanied by ex-Empress Zita, slipped out of exile in Switzerland to march on Budapest.

However, he was defeated and captured yesterday by troops loyal to the Regent, Admiral Horthy, in a bloody battle outside the capital. His failure is welcomed by the Allies who would not countenance his return to the throne.

1921

NOVEMBER

Su	Mo	Tu	We	Th	Fr	Sa
		1	2	3	4	5
6	7	8	9	10	11	12
13	14	15	16	17	18	19
20	21	22	23	24	25	26
27	28	29	30			

1. London: Norman Hill forms a company to produce ring-bound personal organiser files.

4. Tokyo: Japanese premier Takashi Hara Kei is assassinated by a Korean.→

5. Mongolia: The new Soviet Republic signs a friendship treaty with Lenin's Russian government.

6. Budapest: The Hungarian parliament votes to depose the Habsburg dynasty following the failed monarchist coup.

7. Germany: The mark's collapse continues; £1 now buys 1,200M (→ 1/12).

9. US: The Unknown Soldier arrives in the US from France for reburial in Arlington Cemetery.

12. Washington: Opening of the Great Power conference on disarmament and the Pacific (→ 13/12).

15. India: 16 Gurkha troops killed by anti-British rebels.→

18. New York: The city police says cocaine, heroin and synthetic drugs are entering the US from Germany.

21. Belfast: Troops are sent in to restore order as rioting breaks out in East Belfast (→ 22).

22. Belfast: At least ten people die in widespread shootings throughout the city.

23. Washington: President Harding bans doctors from prescribing beer, closing a Prohibition loophole.

26. Washington: President Harding calls for more international conferences to settle world problems.

30. London: Sir Basil Thompson retires after 40 years as head of the Metropolitan Police Special Branch.

BIRTH

27. Czechoslovak statesman Alexander Dubcek, party leader 1968 (†7/11/92).

DEATH

22. British socialist pioneer Henry Mayers Hyndman (*7/3/1842).

Rioting as Gandhi burns foreign cloth

Nov 17. The streets of Bombay were today lined with vast crowds, all cheering the Prince of Wales as he drove to Government House. Elsewhere in the city, however, there was serious rioting as Mr Gandhi, using the occasion to draw attention to his campaign against the import of foreign cloth, arranged a bonfire of cloth and clothes.

The mob gathered at the bonfire, turned violent, and wrecked and burnt tramcars, looted shops and stoned Europeans. A common but mistaken belief that the Prince's presence would prevent the use of firearms undoubtedly increased the size and ferocity of the mob.

When several policemen had been killed and wounded, the police opened fire on the rioters and there were a number of wounded. Troops have now been transferred to the area of the disturbances and the Viceroy has postponed his departure to deal with the crisis.

Hirohito becomes Regent of Japan

Nov 5. At the age of 20, Crown Prince Hirohito has been named Regent of Japan and will take over from his father as effective head of state. An imperial announcement stated that the decision was taken because the mental condition of Emperor Yoshihito precluded him from "paying further attention to his state duties".

The Emperor's physical condition is unchanged, but it has been known for some time that he has been incapable of ruling.

The Regent assumes power at a difficult time after the assassination of Hara Kei, head of the first parliamentary government. An authoritarian reformer, he was elected in 1918.

Mussolini becomes "Il Duce" of Fascists

Mussolini, in his National Militia uniform, keeping an eagle eye on Italy.

Nov 7. Benito Mussolini, the blacksmith's son from poverty-stricken Romagna, has declared himself "Il Duce", the leader of the National Fascist Party. Formerly a Socialist and editor of the Milan Socialist Party's newspaper, Avanti, before the war, the square-jawed Mussolini is now violently opposed to Socialism.

He supported the poet-airman D'Annunzio's occupation of Fiume and has played the nationalist card with the Italian business community. The businessmen, frightened by the formation of the Italian Communist Party last year, and the wave of Communist-led strikes, have been generously funding the Fascists. Mussolini has responded by sending in his black-shirted "Squadristi" to beat up Bolsheviks, break strikes and terrorise Socialist workers' clubs.

The Fascists have become known in political circles as an expression of the "radicalism of the right" which subordinates individual liberty to the state.

Mussolini himself boasts "we allow ourselves the luxury of being aristocratic and democratic, reactionary and revolutionary". Thirty-five Fascists were elected to Parliament this year. It seems certain the power of "Il Duce" will grow.

Treaty seals Afghanistan's independence

Nov 22. After protracted negotiations, Sir Henry Dobbs, head of the British mission in Kabul, has today signed a treaty of friendship between Afghanistan and Great Britain which, it is hoped, will restore the old friendly relations between the two countries.

Under the treaty Britain recognises Afghanistan's independence and there is to be an interchange of Ministers in London and Kabul. On their part, the Afghans have promised that no Russian consulates will be permitted in the Ghazni, Jalalabad or Kandahar areas.

Both governments have promised to tell the other beforehand of any major operations they may find necessary to keep order along the frontier. It is understood that Sir Henry Dobbs' good work is to be suitably recognised by the award of the KCSI.

1921

DECEMBER

Su	Mo	Tu	We	Th	Fr	Sa
				1	2	3
4	5	6	7	8	9	10
11	12	13	14	15	16	17
18	19	20	21	22	23	24
25	26	27	28	29	30	31

1. Germany: The mark leaps suddenly to 750 to the pound, causing more panic than when it was falling (→ 2/1/22).

2. S. Africa: The British Army hands over to the Union's forces, ending 125 years of South African service.

5. Moscow: The Communist Party admits that 20 million Soviet citizens are facing starvation (→ 22).

7. London: King George V orders the release of all Sinn Fein prisoners following the signing of the Treaty (→ 16).

10. Stockholm: Nobel Prizes to Albert Einstein (Germany, Physics); Frederick Soddy (UK, Chemistry); Anatole France (France, Literature); Peace Prize awarded in Christiania to Karl Branting (Sweden) and Christian Lange (Norway).

12. India: Gandhi organises a complete boycott of the Prince of Wales' visit to the town of Allahabad (→ 25).

16. London: Parliament ratifies the Irish Treaty (→ 21/1/22).

20. Washington: A filibuster by Democrats blocks the Administration's anti-lynching bill.

22. Washington: Congress creates a $20 million fund to aid famine victims in Russia (→ 1/1/22).

25. India: A mass boycott greets the Prince of Wales when he arrives in Calcutta.

DEATH

16. French composer Charles Camille Saint-Saens (*9/10/1835).

HITS OF 1921

The fishermen of England.

Three o'clock in the morning.

Kitten on the keys.

QUOTE OF THE YEAR

"I am signing my own death warrant."
Michael Collins,
founder of the IRA, signing the Treaty creating the Irish Free State.

Four powers sign a naval agreement to control Pacific

Dec 13. The world became a safer place today when the Great Powers signed a new treaty in Washington aimed at controlling military build-up in the Pacific. They also agreed to continue talking to finalise a pact, aimed at preventing the kind of naval building race witnessed before the war.

The United States in particular has been concerned at Japanese expansion into the Pacific, her claims on China and the way she has led advances in naval design. That problem dates back to before the war when Japan ordered warships from British yards far more powerful than anything under construction for the UK itself.

Admiral Kato of Japan told the Washington Conference that his country was ready to make sweeping reductions in its navy as it did not require a fleet of the same size of those of Britain and America. But while Japan has made concessions over the Pacific, it wants the US to make reductions at its bases in the Philippines, Guam and the Hawaiian islands.

French Bluebeard sentenced to die

Dec 1. The guillotine awaits Henr "Bluebeard" Landru, found guilty by a Versailles jury of the murders of ten women and the son of one o them.

The jury took three hours to reach their verdict. Before they re tired, Landru sprang to his feet and pleaded his innocence, ending with the bombastic cry "Jurymen, do your duty".

Landru had been a notoriou swindler before he started placing advertisements in the lonely heart columns of newspapers for a potential wife, who so often turned into a victim.

When the police finally caught up with Landru, they found a diary in his flat in which each murder wa recorded in every detail. A furthe search in Landru's villa found a stove choked with ashes and human bone fragments (→ 25/2/22).

Irish offered Free State

Dec 7. Shortly after midnight yesterday, British and Irish negotiators finally signed an agreement giving independence to Ireland. Right to the last moment, it was uncertain whether the talks would succeed. At one stage the Prime Minister, David Lloyd George, threatened to put down the Irish "rebellion" by force if the treaty was not signed.

The peace treaty has three main provisions:

1. Twenty-six southern counties are to become independent and will be known as the "Irish Free State".
2. Six of the eight counties which form historic Ulster will remain part of the United Kingdom and continue to send MPs to Westminster.
3. A boundary commission will draw the dividing line between the north and south with a Council of Ireland to discuss the eventual reunification of the country.

In effect, the Irish Free State becomes an independent dominion like Canada. It will have its own parliament, raise its own taxes and have an army and navy, although Britain's Royal Navy will continue to maintain four bases in Ireland.

Points of contention are likely to be the oath of allegiance and the prospects for future reunification. The Irish resisted the idea of an oath of allegiance to the King after what they see as "700 years of repression". So this has been watered down to an oath of allegiance to Ireland plus a declaration that they will be faithful to the King.

On the question of the border,

Lloyd George at Chequers.

Michael Collins, one of the Irish leaders, returned to Downing Street today to seek reassurances that areas with large nationalist majorities near the border could opt to join the south. The Prime Minister assured him that this was so. Ministers, in fact, believe that ultimately Ireland would be best served by having one parliament in Dublin. The Irish, too, hope the division will not be permanent, but Ulster's leaders show no sign of bowing to Dublin rule.

Arts: Lawrence's nude wrestling offends

D. H. Lawrence has produced a sequel to his book which was condemned as obscene during the war. All copies of "The Rainbow" were withdrawn and destroyed in 1915, but so far no prosecution has been mounted against the new novel, "Women in Love".

It deals, like the previous book, with the erotic relationships of two couples. Ursula and Gudrun, the daughters of one of the couples in "The Rainbow", are in love with two friends who are almost blood-brothers.

Some readers see in Birkin and Ursula portraits of the author and his German wife, Frieda, formerly von Richthofen, cousin of the flying ace, with whom he eloped to Germany shortly before the war. The scene of Japanese wrestling between the two naked men is startling, as is the frankness of the language employed. The paper "John Bull" has called it "A Book the Police should Ban".

Lytton Strachey, having pilloried his "Eminent Victorians" brilliantly and mercilessly three years ago, has turned his sharpshooting on Queen Victoria herself. Like all the Bloomsbury Group, Strachey attacks Victorian humbug, which he ridiculed in his portraits of Florence Nightingale, Gen. Gordon, and Dr Arnold. He shows a grudging admiration for the Matriarch of Windsor. But Victorians will never seem the same.

Neither will detective fiction, after the appearance of a new and ingenious talent in **Miss Agatha Christie**. In "The Mysterious Affair at Styles" she introduces a solemn

Author David Herbert Lawrence.

yet sharp-witted Belgian detective, Hercule Poirot, of whom we may well hear more.

France has lost two famous names in the arts. **Georges Feydeau** was the master of farce and once said of his craft, "To write a good vaudeville you take the most tragic situation you can and reveal its burlesque side". His last works "A Flea in Her Ear" and "Look After Lulu" were his neatest.

Camille Saint-Saens, the 86-year-old composer, has died in Algiers. He won European fame with his opera "Samson and Delilah" but the rest of his huge output of operas and symphonies is largely forgotten, except "Danse Macabre" and "Le Cygne", employed by **Mme Pavlova** to accompany her dying swan solo. **Sibelius's** Fifth Symphony has been given its first performance in London.

Insulin discovery gives hope to diabetics

Medical history was made this year with the isolation of insulin, a natural chemical that may make it possible for diabetics to lead normal lives, instead of facing almost certain death. The work was done in Toronto, Canada, by **Frederick Banting** and **Charles Best**.

Insulin controls the level of the energy-giving sugar glucose in the blood. In diabetes insulin is lacking. For some time scientists have suspected that it comes from special cells in a digestive organ called the pancreas. Hitherto all attempts at isolating it have failed, as outside the body the pancreas digests its own insulin.

Banting and Best ingeniously overcame this difficulty and obtained an insulin extract from dogs that cured diabetes in other dogs. Their experiments are not yet complete, but there is every reason for hoping that insulin will cure human diabetics too.

This year's Physics Nobel Prize went to **Albert Einstein**, not for his relativity theories, but for successfully explaining the so-called photoelectric effect in terms of the quantum theory.

New statues recently uncovered at Angkor in French Cambodia.

1922

JANUARY

Su	Mo	Tu	We	Th	Fr	Sa
1	2	3	4	5	6	7
8	9	10	11	12	13	14
15	16	17	18	19	20	21
22	23	24	25	26	27	28
29	30	31				

1. Russia: An estimated 33 million people are now in danger of starvation.

2. Germany: The mark is plummeting out of control; £1 buys 32,000 marks (→ 6).

4. Belfast: Two die and six are wounded when the army fires on demonstrators.

5. Washington: The arms conference adopts a declaration outlawing submarine warfare against merchant ships.

6. Cannes: The Allies agree to a deferment of German war reparations (→ 31).

7. Washington: The arms conference agrees to outlaw the use of gas in warfare.

9. S. Africa: A strike begins in the Transvaal mines (→ 6/3).

12. London: The Government announces an amnesty for all Irish political prisoners.

13. UK: 804 deaths from influenza were reported last week in England and Wales.

14. London: Lloyd George and new French premier Poincare agree to end the Allied Supreme Council.

18. Rome: Pope Benedict XV is confined to bed.→

19. Paris: The Salon des Independants refuses to show works by Dadaist Francis Picabia.

20. London: The National Liberal Council is formed with Lloyd George as president and Churchill as vice-president.

25. France holds England to an 11-11 draw in a rugby international at Twickenham.

28. Washington: 107 people die when the roof of the Knickerbocker Theatre collapses under the weight of snow.

31. Germany: The cost of living has risen 73.7 per cent since January 1921.

DEATHS

5. British polar explorer Sir Ernest Shackleton (*15/2/1874).→

22. Pope Benedict XV, born Giacomo della Chiesa (*21/11/1854).→

Irish Parliament votes to accept treaty

The Irish Parliament discusses the proposed treaty with Britain.

Jan 21. After a debate of fiery words and high drama, the Dail Eireann, the provisional Irish parliament, has approved the treaty with Britain which sets up the Irish Free State. The voting was 64 in favour, and 57 against, and afterwards, Eamon de Valera refused the presidency of the Dail. So with the country's best-known politician not prepared to implement the treaty, Ireland's political future is still uncertain.

The debate on the treaty lasted nine days. Miss Mary MacSwiney, sister of the Lord Mayor of Cork, who died on hunger strike, spoke of "Ireland's grossest betrayal ever", and Cathal Brugha, the Defence Minister, savaged Michael Collins for accepting so much less than they had fought for together. De Valera made clear his opposition to the treaty, forecasting "internal strife".

Arthur Griffith, the leader of the delegation that signed the treaty last month, will replace Eamon de Valera as president, while the new head of the government is Michael Collins, the former London bank official who became finance minister in the first provisional government in 1918.

US churchmen slam jazz as jungle music

Jan 30. Until the war, jazz was largely confined to the American south. New Orleans had been its cradle, but today Chicago is hailed as the new capital of the jazz world. Here Joseph "King" Oliver is blowing up a storm with his Creole Jazz Band and leading an exodus of top jazz musicians to the cities of the north and west. New York, too, is succumbing to the insistent beat of jazz as gramophone records bring the new music to new audiences. By no means everybody approves. One group of American churchmen this week condemned jazz music as "a return to the jungle".

Dancing to Ben Travers' jazz.

Shackleton, polar explorer, dies

Jan 5. Sir Ernest Shackleton, regarded by many as the finest explorer of his age, died today of a heart attack while in South Georgia on his fourth expedition to the Antarctic.

Shackleton, then a lieutenant, accompanied Captain Robert Scott on the first polar expedition in 1901-04, and his own expedition in 1908-09 nearly reached the South Pole.

In his last expedition (1914-16), Shackleton and his party made an incredible trek to safety by small boat and sledge after his ship, Endurance, was marooned by ice. The journey involved an 800-mile hike over some of the roughest terrain in the world.

Sir Ernest Shackleton.

Peace-maker Pope, Benedict XV, dies

Jan 22. Pope Benedict XV died o[f] pneumonia early this morning. Made Pope in September 1914, h[e] spent much of the first four years o[f] his reign trying to bring the Grea[t] War to an end. He conceived tw[o] major peace plans and used hi[s] emissaries to put them before th[e] Great Powers. Both plans failed but Benedict continued to strive fo[r] an end to the carnage (→ 12/2).

1922

FEBRUARY

Su	Mo	Tu	We	Th	Fr	Sa
			1	2	3	4
5	6	7	8	9	10	11
12	13	14	15	16	17	18
19	20	21	22	23	24	25
26	27	28				

1. UK: An alarming 117 outbreaks of foot and mouth disease have been reported throughout the country (→ 7).

2. India: 22 policemen die in a riot at Chauri Chaura.

4. China: Japan agrees to restore Shantung to the Chinese government.

5. Detroit: Ford buys the Lincoln Motor Co. for $8,000,000 (£1,800,000).

6. Washington: The arms conference ends.

7. Paris: Marie Curie is elected to the Academie des Sciences.

7. UK: 8,500 cattle, 1,000 sheep and 2,500 pigs will be slaughtered as 477 foot and mouth outbreaks are reported.

9. US: Mexican rebels destroy railway lines and bridges in an attack on El Paso, Texas.

11. Northern Ireland: The IRA murders four policemen at Clones, County Monaghan.

13. India: The Indian National Congress suspends its civil disobedience campaign in the face of mounting violence (→ 18/3).

14. Geneva: German and Polish representatives meet to discuss the disputed border of Upper Silesia.

15. The Hague: The Permanent International Court of Justice opens.

17. London: MPs approve the Irish Free State Bill, which sets up a boundary commission for the two parts of Ireland.

18. Cairo: Three Englishmen are shot dead in the street.→

20. Lithuania: The city of Vilna votes to join Poland.

25. Boston: L. T. Brown jumps a record height of 6 feet 4.75 inches.

25. France: Murderer "Bluebeard" Landru is guillotined.

26. Paris: The UK and France agree on a 20-year alliance between the two countries.

28. London: Princess Mary, only daughter of George V and Queen Mary, marries Viscount Lascelles.

Archbishop of Milan elected as Pope

Feb 12. The new Pope is to be Cardinal Achille Ratti, the Archbishop of Milan, who is 65. He will be the 257th Pope and will take the name of Pius XI. Highly educated and widely travelled, he is a former legate and nuncio to Poland. He wants to improve links with all Catholics in the east. His first priority, however, is ending the quarrel between the Vatican and the Italian government.

Cardinal Ratti was born in a small town called Desio, which is near Milan. He comes from a prominent middle class family and like Pope Benedict XV, who died last month, thinks it vital for the Pope to take the role of international peacemaker.

The 257th Pope: Pius XI.

Report calls for savage spending cuts

Feb 25. The "Geddes Axe" will chop a massive £87 million off public spending programmes, if the Government accepts the advice of a Committee on National Expenditure. In a final report today the committee, under the chairmanship of Sir Eric Geddes, called for pay cuts for civil servants, the armed forces, the police and teachers. Their pay now totals £257 million a year, compared with £90 million for fewer people before 1914.

"The country cannot continue to support a burden of this magnitude," the Committee said. It was wrong, for example, for a country policeman to be paid £234 a year on top of boot and clothing allowance. As for school teachers with their short terms and long holidays, they had better also do with less: "Most of them have already spent two years in training college at public expense and this ought to be remembered".

In reviewing forces' pay, the committee noted that since the war it had risen much faster than factory pay and needed to be reduced, especially as industrial rates were likely to fall still further.

Norah Scott at Marconi's Chelmsford broadcasting station: singing with musical accompaniment provided the first wireless "entertainment".

Independence is attacked as fraud

Feb 28. Lord Allenby, British High Commissioner in Egypt, today proclaimed the country an independent state and Sultan Fuad became King Fuad. Egyptian nationalists, however, say the "independence" is a fraud, since Britain has insisted on retaining responsibility for the security of the Suez Canal, the military defence of Egypt and the Sudan, and the protection of foreign interests and minorities in the country.

Though Egypt was formally a dependency of Turkey until the last war, Britain has had advisers and a military presence in the country since 1882.

Reader's Digest is born under a bar

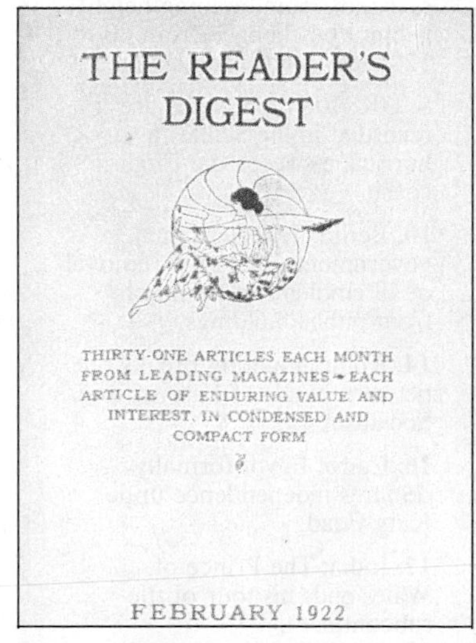

THE READER'S DIGEST
THIRTY-ONE ARTICLES EACH MONTH FROM LEADING MAGAZINES • EACH ARTICLE OF ENDURING VALUE AND INTEREST, IN CONDENSED AND COMPACT FORM
FEBRUARY 1922

Reader's Digest's first edition.

Feb 5. DeWitt Wallace, the son of a US Presbyterian minister, today put out the first issue of an interesting pocket-sized magazine. Called "The Reader's Digest", it aims to inform, entertain, inspire and guide people in their daily lives.

With Lila Acheson, his wife, 32-year-old Wallace founded the company last year with just $5,000 in capital – setting up shop below an illegal bar, or "speakeasy", in New York's Greenwich Village.

The first issue, being sent to 1,500 subscribers, opens with an article entitled: "How to Keep Young Mentally". The article's length: one and a half pages.

1922

MARCH

Su	Mo	Tu	We	Th	Fr	Sa
			1	2	3	4
5	6	7	8	9	10	11
12	13	14	15	16	17	18
19	20	21	22	23	24	25
26	27	28	29	30	31	

1. London: Establishment of the Civil Aviation Advisory Board.

3. Italy: Members of Mussolini's Fascist Party attempt to take over the city of Fiume (→ 5).

5. Italy: Fiume surrenders to the Fascists.

5. US: Annie Oakley shoots a record 98 out of a hundred clay targets from 16 yards.

6. S. Africa: A general strike breaks out in Johannesburg.→

6. London: Wealthy heiress Edwina Ashley announces her engagement to Lord Louis Mountbatten.

7. London: The Royal Institute of British Architects says maximum building height will not be changed from 80 to 120 feet, as has been claimed.

8. UK: 108 mph winds are recorded in the Scillies as a hurricane sweeps the English coast.

10. Berlin: The German government orders the removal of all emblems of monarchy from public buildings.

14. Rome: Fighting breaks out between bands of Fascists and Socialists.

16. Cairo: Egypt formally declares independence under King Fuad.

17. India: The Prince of Wales ends his tour of the subcontinent.

20. Moscow: A German doctor is called to attend Lenin.

21. London: Queen Mary opens Waterloo Station.

24. UK: H. Kershaw's Music Hall wins the Grand National at Aintree, one of only three of the 32 runners to finish.

25. Rome: Pope Pius XI urges a crusade against immodest women's fashions.

29. Washington: The US Census Bureau reports that 11 per cent of the population cannot speak English.

31. London: The Irish Free State (Agreement) Act gets Royal Assent.

Gandhi sentenced to jail

Dressed in his loin cloth Gandhi weaves as he awaits the court's sentence.

March 18. Mahatma Gandhi, the Indian nationalist leader, pleaded guilty to three charges of sedition at Ahmedabad today and was sentenced to six years "simple imprisonment" which means that he will not have to do hard labour. Dressed in his customary loin cloth and shawl as he stood in the dock, the scrawny lawyer was unrepentant.

In a long statement he said that preaching disaffection against the existing system of government in India had "become almost a passion with me". He took all the blame for the recent disturbances at Madras, Bombay, and Chauri Chaura, but said that if he was released he would still play with fire.

Non-violence was the first and last article of his faith, he said, and he was there "to submit cheerfully to the highest penalty that could be inflicted". The judge, addressing Gandhi, said it was impossible to ignore the fact that in the eyes of millions of his countrymen he was a great patriot and leader, but his duty was to judge him as a man who admitted that he had broken the law and committed an offence against the state.

Martial law to quell gold mine rioting

March 11. Martial law was proclaimed in Johannesburg and the Rand gold mining districts after a strike by white miners led to the sabotage of trains, attacks on natives and gunfights between strikers and police. In the town of Brakpan, strikers' commandos looted the homes of mining officials and burned furniture while singing the Red Flag.

The strike was called by the white miners' union, the South African Industrial Federation, after the employers proposed to open semi-skilled jobs to non-European workers.

"B Specials" are new target for IRA

March 22. The Belfast riots took a turn for the worse yesterday as the IRA singled out the "B Specials" for retaliation against a wave of Protestant attacks on Catholics in the city. Two members of the Specials Constabulary were gunned down in the city as shoppers watched, while in Co. Tyrone another Special was found dead beside his cattle.

The "B Specials" are a newly formed force of part-time policemen, highly motivated and armed. Nearly all are members of the Protestant Orange Order and are feared by many Catholics.

1922

APRIL

Su	Mo	Tu	We	Th	Fr	Sa
						1
2	3	4	5	6	7	8
9	10	11	12	13	14	15
16	17	18	19	20	21	22
23	24	25	26	27	28	29
30						

3. Moscow: At Lenin's suggestion, Joseph Stalin is given the minor post of Communist Party General Secretary.

4. Brussels: Armand Jeanns, the man who betrayed Nurse Edith Cavell, is sentenced to death.

6. London: Labour suffers heavy defeats in elections to the London Boards of Guardians.

7. France: Six die when two aircraft of the London to Paris air service collide over Poix on the Somme.

9. Dublin: Michael Collins says civil war is threatening in Ireland (→ 15).

10. Italy: International conference opens at Genoa.→

12. UK: Ex-Tory PM Sir Arthur Balfour is created Earl of Whittinghame.

13. US: Massachusetts opens all public offices to women.

14. UK: Sir Ross Smith, first to fly from England to Australia, dies in an air crash.

15. Ireland: The IRA seize Kilmainham jail (→ 25).

18. Genoa: Western leaders bar Germany from the talks on Russia as a protest against the Rapallo deal (→ 24/6).

20. London: The US Rockefeller Foundation says it has a site in Gower Street for a London School of Hygiene.

25. Ireland: An army Brigadier-General is murdered by gunmen (→ 23/5).

29. London: Huddersfield Town beat Preston North End 1-0 in the FA Cup Final at Stamford Bridge.

BIRTH

16. British author Kingsley Amis.

DEATHS

1. Former Austrian Emperor Karl (*17/8/1887).

8. German General Erich von Falkenhayn (*11/11/1861).

28. Former French President Paul Deschanel (*13/2/1855).

1922

MAY

Su	Mo	Tu	We	Th	Fr	Sa
	1	2	3	4	5	6
7	8	9	10	11	12	13
14	15	16	17	18	19	20
21	22	23	24	25	26	27
28	29	30	31			

1. London: The Budget cuts 1s. off income tax, 4d. off a pound of tea, and lowers post and telephone charges.

3. UK: A Wolseley 10 establishes 14 new motor speed records.

7. Cairo: King Fuad claims the Sudan for Egypt, forcing talks with the UK on sovereignty.

10. UK: The National Conference of Labour Women calls for the state to subsidise motherhood.

10. UK: Dr Ivy Williams of Oxford is the first Englishwoman called to the bar.

11. UK: George Duncan scores a record round of 68 at St. Andrew's.

15. London: Tory leader Austen Chamberlain asks Western powers to join an enquiry into Turkish massacres.

18. US: A black boy is tortured and burned at the stake for the alleged murder of a white woman.

19. Berlin: Reported that a US publisher has bought the ex-Kaiser's memoirs for $1,000 million.

20. France: 102 people die when the liner Egypt sinks off Ushant following a collision with another vessel.

22. Northern Ireland: MP William Twaddell is killed by a bomb in a Belfast street (→23).

22. London: The highest May temperatures for 50 years, 88 degrees F in the shade.

23. Irish Free State: Sinn Fein is declared illegal in six counties following a series of violent incidents (→16/6).

25. UK: Airmen Macmillan, Blake and Broome leave Croydon, Surrey, in an attempt to fly round the world.

26. Moscow: Lenin suffers a stroke.

31. UK: Lord Woolavington's Captain Cuttle wins the Derby at Epsom.

31. Paris: The Reparation Commission agrees to a partial moratorium on Germany's 1922 repayments.

Germans do secret deal with Russians

April 16. Western leaders attending the economic conference at Genoa were stunned today to learn that Russian and German officials had met secretly the night before at Rapallo, a few miles away, and signed a treaty re-establishing full diplomatic relations and promising cooperation in economic development.

The Genoa conference, called to discuss international aid for Russia, had been denounced by Moscow as a plot. The Germans seized the opportunity; there are reports that they will help Russia rebuild its arms industry and in return will be allowed to manufacture in Russia weapons banned by the Versailles treaty.

Fatty Arbuckle is acquitted by jury

April 12. Roscoe "Fatty" Arbuckle walked free from a San Francisco courthouse today, knowing that his career was in tatters.

Although the jury had cleared him of murder and rape charges, Arbuckle remains a fallen star after the revelations of an orgy in a San Francisco hotel, in which a young starlet Virginia Rappe was allegedly raped and crushed to death.

Arbuckle's films have been withdrawn by cinema chains throughout a shaken United States.

LNER GOLF
Illustrated Booklet free from Passenger Managers Liverpool Street Station, London E.C.2, LNER York, Waverley Station, Edinburgh; Traffic Superintendent LNER Aberdeen, or any LNER Enquiry Office

Vatican objects to UK rule in Palestine

May 27. In a surprise demarche today the Vatican intervened in the Palestine problem. In a note to the League of Nations, Papal diplomats objected to the Britain's proposed mandate over Palestine on the grounds that such an arrangement would threaten religious equality.

The unexpected Vatican argument is that the creation of a national home for the Jews in that country would give a privileged position to what the note describes as "the adherents of Zionism".

The British mandate, already approved by the French, is about to be confirmed by the League of Nations. An agreement has also been reached between Britain and the United States guaranteeing equal treatment in Palestine to all citizens of every member of the League.

As the US is not a member of the international organisation, a separate treaty to safeguard the rights and interests of American citizens in Palestine was considered necessary. Under the terms of the treaty, Americans will now be permitted to engage in commerce and industry on an equal footing with other nations.

South are victorious in Chinese civil war

May 5. The rebel Chinese army of Manchuria, commanded by General Chang Tso-lin, is today retreating in total disaster after being defeated by the rival army of General Wu Peifu. Fierce fighting, in which the rebel forces suffered 7,000 casualties, has left General Wu victorious and firmly in control of Peking. His success in the battle for the capital virtually ends the civil war between north and south China.

It broke out almost a year ago when the Kwangsi party took up arms against the nominal election in Canton of Sun Yat-sen as President of China. For a time China has had two Presidents. Sun Yat-sen still rules the south.

The Peking government has recognised General Wu so in turn he is expected to support President Hsu Shih-chang to the end of his term of office. A constitutional convention is planned to unite the north and south.

The problem of how to make Russia pay

May 19. The Allies, meeting in Genoa, took time off from wrangling over German reparations and moved to the even thornier question of Russia's debts. Lenin's Bolshevik regime has repudiated debts contracted under the Czar and refuses to pay compensation for property seized during the revolution. Though the Russians did agree to come to Genoa, it was not to negotiate, as the others had hoped, but simply to demonstrate their intransigence.

They have been told by the Allies that diplomatic recognition is out of the question until the debt issue has been settled. This evening the conference broke up without the Allies reaching agreement on a common front. The only thing they do agree on is that somehow Russia must be made to pay up. They plan on holding another meeting next month at The Hague.

Ridiculous? Maybe. Voluminous, certainly. The latest leggings for men are tent-like "Oxford Bags".

Liberal MP jailed on fraud charges

May 29. The Liberal MP, Horatio Bottomley, was today sentenced to seven years penal servitude for fraud. So ends the adventurous career of an extraordinary demagogic trickster. He cheated thousands of small savers into parting with about £150,000 for spurious Victory Bonds – a kind of sophisticated raffle. "Callous frauds", said the judge.

Bottomley, founder of the weekly popular journal John Bull, has already been through a series of libel actions and company flotation disasters. As usual he conducted his own defence.

Liberal MP Horatio Bottomley.

Divorced women to get better deal

May 26. A parliamentary bill aimed at easing some of the pain of unhappy marriages was given its second reading today. The Separation and Maintenance Orders Bill will permit magistrates to grant such orders without a woman having to leave her home as at present. Another aim is to stop a prison sentence cancelling a maintenance debt. At the moment 50 per cent of orders lapse after a few weeks and men often find it easier to go to jail than to pay, causing poor women considerable hardship.

1922

JUNE

Su	Mo	Tu	We	Th	Fr	Sa
				1	2	3
4	5	6	7	8	9	10
11	12	13	14	15	16	17
18	19	20	21	22	23	24
25	26	27	28	29	30	

1. Italy: Fascists have taken Bologna and the areas around Modena and Ferrara.

3. US: Norwegian explorer Roald Amundsen sets out from Seattle on an expedition to the North Pole.

4. Budapest: The first socialists are elected to the Hungarian parliament.

5. UK: Margaret Davies is elected the first woman president of the Co-operative Congress.

8. London: Plumes, veils and trains are reported to be back in fashion this year.

13. Vienna: Austria says it is bankrupt.

14. Moscow: A three-man council will govern Russia while Lenin recovers from his stroke.

15. Washington: Figures show a drop in alcohol-related deaths by 21 per cent since prohibition started.

16. Irish Free State: The first general election is held in the new state (→20).

18. US: Scientists at Columbia University claim the sun produces a vitamin "D" in the body which prevents rickets.

20. Irish Free State: The pro-Treaty party is victorious in elections; anti-Treaty Republicans heavily defeated.→

23. London: Police arrest 20 men in connection with Field Marshal Sir Henry Wilson's murder (→18/7).

26. Wimbledon: The King opens the tournament at its new site in Queen's Road.

28. Dublin: Free State troops fight the IRA for control of the law courts building (→30).

30. Dublin: The IRA surrenders the law courts to Free State troops (→5/7).

BIRTH

10. US actress and singer Judy Garland (†22/6/69).

DEATH

24. German politician Walter Rathenau (*29/9/1867).→

IRA shoot British army chief in London

June 22. Field Marshal Sir Henry Wilson, the former Chief of the Imperial General Staff, was gunned down yesterday as he walked to his home in London's Belgravia. His killers were two Irishmen who had served with the British Army in the war. After a chase both were captured by the police, the capture of one having been facilitated by a milkman. But there are fears today that the assassination could spark further trouble.

Nobody knows whether or not the killers were acting on orders from outside the country, but Arthur Griffith, president of the Irish Free State, denounced the murder in a statement last night. He said: "It is a principle of civilised government that the assassination of a political opponent cannot be justified or condoned."

Though born in what is now the Irish Free State, Field Marshal Wilson was an Ulsterman and he upset the Asquith government by a partisan attitude to Army officers who prefered resignation to fighting in Ulster (→23).

Field Marshal Sir Henry Wilson.

Climbers reach 26,000 feet up Everest

June 12. A British Everest expedition has climbed to within 3,200 feet of the summit of the world's highest mountain, according to reports reaching London today.

The British mountaineer and leader George Leigh Mallory and his two companions have succeeded in reaching 26,800 feet without the aid of oxygen – the highest altitude any climber has yet achieved.

The expedition is tackling the great peak via the north col. They have found their way towards the summit barred by a series of uncharted glaciers, which, together with appalling weather conditions, are causing delays and rendering any further progress up the mountain virtually impossible.

George Mallory climbing Everest.

Far right guns down moderate minister

June 24. Gunmen murdered German foreign minister Walter Rathenau outside his home in a Berlin suburb today. The identity of the killers of the 55-year-old minister is unknown, but the finger of suspicion points towards extreme right-wing German Nationalists, infuriated at Rathenau's negotiation in April of the Treaty of Rapallo with Lenin's Communist government. The Treaty provided for normal diplomatic relations between Germany and Russia and the abandonment by both countries of claims for reparations.

Rathenau, who directed the distribution of raw materials in the Great War, was a left-wing Jew. Quite apart from his role in the Rapallo negotiations, this made him a target of abuse from the fanatically anti-Communist and anti-Semitic German right (→17/7).

1922

JULY

Su	Mo	Tu	We	Th	Fr	Sa
						1
2	3	4	5	6	7	8
9	10	11	12	13	14	15
16	17	18	19	20	21	22
23	24	25	26	27	28	29
30	31					

1. US: The world's first shopping centre, the Country Club Plaza, opens.

3. Paris: Lloyd George proposes world disarmament to the League of Nations.

5. Dublin: The last anti-treaty rebel stronghold surrenders to Free State troops (→ 13).

9. Germany: Total financial collapse is feared following the spectacular drop in the mark's value (→ 24/8).

12. Wimbledon: Suzanne Lenglen beats Molla Mallory for the Ladies' Singles title; Gerald Patterson beats Randolph Lycett for the Men's title.

13. London: Bank lending rates are cut to three per cent, the lowest since 1914.

13. Dublin: The Irish Army Council is formed, with Michael Collins as commander-in-chief (→ 21).

14. Paris: President Millerand escapes an assassination attempt.

17. London: King George V opens County Hall, the new headquarters of the London County Council.

17. Germany: Police arrest two extreme Nationalists for the murder of foreign minister Walter Rathenau.

18. UK: Joseph O'Sullivan and Reginald Dunn are sentenced to death for the murder of Sir Henry Wilson.

18. UK: Lord Louis Mountbatten marries Edwina Ashley; the Prince of Wales is best man.

19. Rome: Fascist leader Benito Mussolini warns the Italian government against suppressing his supporters.

21. Irish Free State: Government troops capture Waterford and Limerick from the rebels (→ 27).

24. Paris: The League of Nations Council approves the British mandate in Palestine, the French in Syria.

27. Irish Free State: Republicans spring 105 prisoners from Dundalk jail (→ 6/8).

Germans seek to defer war debts

July 27. Germany has angered the French government with her note to the Allies saying that because of the financial crisis in the country the reparations payments cannot be continued. An urgent meeting of Allied ministers is being arranged.

In Paris, newspapers are saying that if Germany does not pay up, then France should at once cease payments on her war debts owed to Britain. But the British have already said this is not acceptable, because Britain is indebted to America for arms supplied during the war.

Weissmuller sets swimming record

Swimmer Johnny Weissmuller.

July 9. One of sport's classic time barriers was decisively broken today as Johnny Weissmuller, an 18-year-old Austrian-born American immigrant from Chicago, became the first man to swim 100 metres in less than a minute.

For more than a decade, and for two Olympic Games, the Hawaiian Americans Duke Kahanamoku and Pua Kela Kealoha, with their traditional island adaptation of the front crawl, have dominated the speed events, bringing the record down from 63 to 60.4 seconds. Now, with a remarkable performance of 58.6 seconds, Weissmuller has opened a new era in American sprint-swimming, and returned the record to the US mainland.

1922

AUGUST

Su	Mo	Tu	We	Th	Fr	Sa
		1	2	3	4	5
6	7	8	9	10	11	12
13	14	15	16	17	18	19
20	21	22	23	24	25	26
27	28	29	30	31		

1. France: 20 die and 32 are injured when a train carrying pilgrims to Lourdes crashes.

3. London: The government decides to provide 500 aeroplanes for home defence.

5. Germany: Einstein flees the country after he is threatened by the extremist group that murdered Walter Rathenau.

6. Irish Free State: A rebel attack on Dublin is defeated; 160 prisoners are taken (→ 7).

7. Irish Free State: The IRA blows up the telegraph cable station at Waterville, cutting US lines to Europe (→ 12).

10. The Hague: The International Court of Justice ends its sitting.

12. Dublin: Dail president Arthur Griffith dies of a heart attack.→

14. London: Publishers Cassell have paid £90,000 for UK and US rights to Lloyd George's memoirs.

17. US: Federal agents begin a crackdown on hip-flasks.

18. Paris: First congress of the International Federation of Feminine Athletes.

24. Germany: After its brief recovery the mark is on the way down again; £1 is worth around 8,000 marks.→

28. US: The first advertisement is broadcasted.

29. Turkey: The Turks have launched a major offensive against the Greeks to recover land lost after the Great War (→ 2/9).

31. Berlin: The German government is given a six-month respite by the Allies in reparations payments.

DEATHS

2. British-born inventor of the telephone Alexander Graham Bell (*3/3/1847).

12. Irish politician Arthur Griffith (*31/3/1872).→

14. British newspaper owner Alfred Harmsworth, Lord Northcliffe (*15/7/1865).→

22. Irish politician Michael Collins (*16/10/1890).→

Pioneer of popular newspapers dies

Newspaper owner Lord Northcliffe.

Aug 14. Lord Northcliffe, who died yesterday at the age of 57, was the pioneer of popular newspapers. He founded the Daily Mail in 1896 on the one-murder-a-day formula. Most stories were less than 250 words and had to fit his idea of news. "King Alfonso is always smiling. The smile is not news. If you get a picture of Alfonso weeping, that would be news," he said.

Altogether his newspapers reach one in six homes in Britain. He rescued The Times in 1908 and stamped it with his own image. "Most of the ordinary man's prejudices are my prejudices and are therefore the prejudices of my newspapers," he claimed. But Times readers were not so ordinary and many did not like it.

Value of German mark nosedives

Aug 24. The German mark went into free fall against the dollar today. It appears that the panic was triggered by rumours that French troops were marching into the Ruhr, following Germany's failure to pay a £2 million instalment of its war reparations, due a few weeks ago.

For months now the mark has regularly fallen by 30 or 40 points a day against the dollar. Today it was falling by over 100 points an hour. The mark has now halved in value in the last ten days. ▷

Irish leader Michael Collins is shot dead

Irish Nationalist leader Michael Collins addressing the masses.

Aug 22. Michael Collins, the Irish warrior politician who became a legend in his own lifetime in the fight for Irish independence, is dead. He was killed today by a ricochet bullet during an ambush at Eal-na-Blath in his native Cork. Collins was both chairman of the Irish Free State and commander-in-chief of its army.

With the death last week in hospital of Arthur Griffith, the Dail's president, after a short illness, Ireland has now lost the two staunchest supporters of last December's historic Treaty which created the Irish Free State. Indeed, only one of the members of the Irish delegation who signed the Treaty is still a member of the government: E. J. Duggan, a Dublin solicitor, who is Minister of Home Affairs.

General Richard Mulcahy, the chief of staff for the Free State army, is the key man in the immediate future. A slim, quietly-spoken former civil servant, he masterminded the capture last week of the city of Cork from anti-Treaty forces. Last night he issued a statement to the Irish Army: "Stand calmly by your posts. Bend bravely and undaunted to your work, let no cruel act of reprisal blemish your bright honour. You are each inheritors of Michael Collins' strength, bravery and unfinished work."

PICNICS.
TAKE THE MOTOR-BUS
FOR PICNICING.

Milan in the grip of Mussolini's fascists

Aug 4. Mussolini's Fascists have violently broken the Communist-led strike in Milan and today they are in control of the city. Sixteen trucks filled with black-shirted men drove at great speed to the Town Hall while battalions of Fascisti marched through Milan's famous Galleria area of restaurants and cafes and took the Municipal Council by storm from the rear.

One of the trucks then smashed down the front doors, overcoming the resistance of a small guard of Carabinieri and troops. The whole building was swiftly occupied and the Bolsheviks' red flags were thrown from the windows to be replaced by the national flag (→ 30/10).

1922

SEPTEMBER

Su	Mo	Tu	We	Th	Fr	Sa
					1	2
3	4	5	6	7	8	9
10	11	12	13	14	15	16
17	18	19	20	21	22	23
24	25	26	27	28	29	30

2. Turkey: Turkish troops capture the Greek commander-in-chief, General Tricoupis, and several other generals (→ 4).

4. Turkey: The Greeks ask for an armistice as Turkish troops advance on Smyrna (→ 9).

5. US: James Doolittle makes the first coast-to-coast flight in under 24 hours, taking 21 hours 19 minutes.

7. Managua: The Nicaraguans may leave the League because they cannot afford the financial demands of membership.

9. Turkey: The Greeks are ousted from Smyrna, ending their presence on the eastern Aegean seaboard (→ 14).

10. Italy: P. Bordino in a Fiat beats Felice Nazzaro in the first motor race at the Monza track near Milan.

14. Turkey: 1,000 die as Turkish troops burn Smyrna (→ 18).

15. Berlin: German Chancellor Joseph Wirth declares "Bread first, reparations second".

18. London: The government sends Lord Curzon for urgent talks with the French on the Aegean crisis (→ 19).

19. Turkey: Mustafa Kemal says he will not advance on the Allied neutral zone if Turkey is assured of eastern Thrace (→ 23).

21. Dublin: The Dail approves the constitution of the Irish Free State (→ 4/10).

22. Washington: A bill becomes law giving women the same citizenship and naturalisation rights as men.

23. Turkey: The Allies promise eastern Thrace to Turkey as Turkish troops enter the neutral zone.→

26. Greece: Following the Greek defeat in Turkey King Constantine abdicates; George II succeeds.→

30. London: A telephone toll exchange system is inaugurated in the capital.

30. London: Labour leaders denounce the government's policy in the Near East (→ 1/10).

British warn Turks to halt advance

Sept 29. The crushing defeat that Turkey has inflicted on Greece has brought the Turks right up to the barbed wire of the British positions at Chanak on the Asian side of the Dardanelles. This is a situation full of danger, for they have already established observation posts which can speedily be converted into gun positions threatening navigation in the Dardanelles.

The cabinet and the service chiefs, meeting today, have decided that this is intolerable and have despatched instructions to the British commander, General Sir Charles Harington, to insist on the immediate evacuation of the Neutral Zone by Kemal's troops. The Allies have been informed.

Kemalist officer with his troops.

Lyons forms a new sidecar company

Sept 4. William Lyons today celebrates the legal coming-of-age of the sidecar company he founded a few months ago with a coal merchant's son, William Walmsley, whom he met in Blackpool. Lyons, impressed by the sidecars his friend made, thought of several ways to produce them more cheaply. So, with guarantees of £500 each, they formed the Swallow Sidecar Company, a partnership that was not legally binding until today – Lyons' 21st birthday (→ 30/9/35).

1922

OCTOBER

Su	Mo	Tu	We	Th	Fr	Sa
1	2	3	4	5	6	7
8	9	10	11	12	13	14
15	16	17	18	19	20	21
22	23	24	25	26	27	28
29	30	31				

1. Turkey: Mustafa Kemal orders a halt to the Turkish advance on British positions in the Chanak neutral zone (→ 3).

3. Turkey: Talks open between the Turks and Greeks (→ 11).

4. Dublin: The Irish government offers amnesty to all who lay down their arms and surrender seized property (→ 5/12).

5. UK: Reported that six million National Savings Certificates have been sold.

7. Washington: Mrs W. H. Felton of Georgia is sworn in as the first woman US senator.

11. Turkey: The Treaty of Mudania is signed by Turkey and the Allies, recognising Turkish occupation of eastern Thrace (→ 15).

11. London: Britain signs a treaty of alliance with Iraq.

14. London: The last turf is laid on the playing field of the Imperial Stadium at Wembley, Middlesex.

15. Turkey: The Greeks sign the Mudania treaty and begin to evacuate Thrace.

17. London: Lloyd George opens the headquarters of the Port of London Authority on Tower Hill.

18. London: The British Broadcasting Company is formed (→ 15/11).

21. London: 95 acres of Ken Wood, Hampstead, is to be given to the London County Council as public open space.

23. London: Andrew Bonar Law is formally re-elected Conservative Party leader (→ 26).

26. London: Parliament is dissolved and an election called for November 15 (→ 15/11).

26. Rome: The cabinet of Luigi Facta resigns in the face of Fascist opposition.→

31. Washington: The US says it will join the International Court of Justice in The Hague.

DEATH

24. British chocolate manufacturer George Cadbury (*19/9/1839).→

Fascists march on Rome

Mussolini and his fellow Fascists after their unopposed march into Rome.

Oct 30. Benito Mussolini, the "Duce" of the Fascists, is today the dictator of Italy, a position won for him by 24,000 of his black-shirted men who marched on Rome from Naples. Their leader was not with them. He was waiting in Milan, prepared to flee to Switzerland if the march should fail.

There was little opposition, however; the blackshirts were met with cheering crowds and King Victor Emmanuel summoned Mussolini to Rome, sending a special train for him. Government troops blew up the tracks and he had to finish the journey in an open car.

He swaggered into the Quirinal Palace spattered with mud but triumphant. The King gave in to him because he was convinced that any opposition would mean all-out civil war and the fall of the Royal House. They appeared together three times on the palace balcony, to the cheers of the throng. The crowd's enthusiasm seemed to indicate that the Italians are delighted at the prospect of being ruled by a strong leader (→ 16/11).

Oct 6. Death of Marie Lloyd, the popular star of English music halls. She was 52.

Philanthropic cocoa king, Cadbury, dies

Oct 25. George Cadbury, who made a fortune from chocolate and then used much of it for the benefit of the workforce, died yesterday at the age of 83. In 1861 when George joined the family firm there were 15 workers. Today there are 9,000.

He moved the factory from Birmingham to a greenfield site in Bournville. He donated a 250-acre site for a model village for his workforce and sold the houses to them at cost price on cheap loans. He was a deeply committed Quaker and taught a workers' class every Sunday. He campaigned for social reform through the Daily News which he bought in 1891.

Tory rebellion ousts Lloyd George: new PM is Bonar Law

Oct 19. Today has been one of high political drama. Mr David Lloyd George is no longer the Prime Minister, the Tories have disowned Austen Chamberlain as party leader and the coalition government is dead. Tory peers and MPs met at the Carlton Club. Mr Chamberlain wanted their backing to prolong the life of the Coalition. Instead they voted by 187 to 87 to end it. Immediately Tory ministers resigned from the government. Thus isolated Mr Lloyd George went to the King and also resigned. It was the end of an era.

The King asked Andrew Bonar Law to form a new government. He agreed, but first wants to be re-elected to the Tory leadership, which he quit last November for health reasons. The most telling anti-Coalition speech at the Carlton Club was made by Stanley Baldwin, President of the Board of Trade. He warned that Mr Lloyd George is ruining the Tory Party, just as he previously wrecked the Liberals.

Tories and Liberals are now in disarray with serious personality clashes in the higher echelons of both parties, while Labour's strength is growing. It looks as though Britain may be moving towards a period of three-party politics (→ 23).

Prime Minister Andrew Bonar Law.

1922

NOVEMBER

Su	Mo	Tu	We	Th	Fr	Sa
			1	2	3	4
5	6	7	8	9	10	11
12	13	14	15	16	17	18
19	20	21	22	23	24	25
26	27	28	29	30		

1. Ankara: Kemal abolishes the monarchy; Sultan Abdul Mejid II remains Caliph, or Turkish spiritual leader (→ 24).

1. Germany: The mark continues to fall; £1 is worth around 20,000 marks (→ 14).

2. London: Labour loses heavily in borough council elections in the capital.

5. Egypt: Lord Carnarvon and Howard Carter discover the tomb of the Pharaoh Tutankhamun.→

9. London: Sir William Horwood, Metropolitan Police Commissioner, is poisoned by arsenic-filled chocolates.

11. Chile: 1,000 die in an earthquake.

14. Berlin: Joseph Wirth, Chancellor since 10/5/21, resigns over the economic crisis (→ 22).

16. Rome: Mussolini tells the Italian Chamber of Deputies to obey him or be dissolved (→ 25).

20. Switzerland: Opening in Lausanne of the conference to settle the Turkish dispute with Greece and the Allies (→ 4/2/23).

21. Paris: Ex-premier Clemenceau warns that militarists may destroy German democracy (→ 30).

22. Berlin: Wilhelm Cuno becomes Chancellor.

22. Paris: Russian exiles name Grand Duke Nicholas as Czar in the belief that the masses will restore the monarchy.

24. Ankara: Ex-Sultan Abdul Mejid is installed as Caliph.

25. Rome: The Italian Chamber of Deputies grants Mussolini absolute power for one year (→ 5/2/23).

28. Athens: Five ex-cabinet ministers and one army officer are executed for high treason for losing the Turkish war.

30. Munich: A crowd of 50,000 hears Adolf Hitler address a National Socialist Party rally (→ 27/1/23).

DEATH

18. French writer Marcel Proust (*10/7/1871).

Treasures of Tutankhamun unearthed

Nov 29. Three days ago, in Egypt's Valley of the Kings, two British archaeologists became the first humans to gaze on the sumptuously filled tomb of the Pharoah Tutankhamun for over 3,000 years.

One of the men, Howard Carter, has been searching for the tomb of Tutankhamun ever since he stumbled across a mention of him 30 years ago. So it was with great excitement that earlier this month a flight of sixteen steps, leading to a door marked with the Pharoah's seal, was uncovered at the site he was excavating near Luxor.

Immediately he sent for his sponsor, the Earl of Carnarvon, and they made a hole in the door and Carter held a candle into the chamber beyond. He surveyed the scene and when the earl asked what he saw, is reported to have said, "Many wonderful things".

It is now known that they include golden statues, beds inlaid with ivory and jewels, a golden throne studded with gems, gold sandals painted with hunting scenes and many other treasures, undisturbed since 1337 BC (→ 4/4/23).

Outside Tutankhamun's tomb.

Conservatives win overall majority

Nov 16. The Tories rule Britain on their own again tonight for the first time since they lost power in 1906. Andrew Bonar Law and party have swept into office with an overall majority of 75. If the 1918 election was a plebiscite for Lloyd George, this has been one against him.

His group in the fragmented Liberal Party has been massacred. This enormously helped Labour, which now has 142 MPs compared with 63 last time. Labour thus now becomes the main Opposition party.

In spite of recent party splits the Tories have won on a programme offering tranquillity while Labour has advanced on the social reform ticket.

Mr Churchill is one of the casualties. Most significant newcomers are a militant Labour group dubbed the Red Clydesiders.

Wireless programmes make the news

Nov 15. Yesterday evening at 6 o'clock the first regular news broadcast was made from a room in Marconi House in the Strand. The material was supplied by Reuters News Agency and read by Arthur Burrows.

Most listeners had to use headphones but for the fortunate few loudspeakers made it possible for whole families to listen. It is now over two years since wireless was proved possible with the broadcast of Dame Nellie Melba which was heard all over Europe. Now the British Broadcasting Company plans to bring us a daily diet of concerts, talks and news.

Two women taking a drive through the country in the latest model of the Austin Tourer; popular motoring has boomed since the Great War.

Macdonald chosen to lead Labour

James Ramsay MacDonald.

Nov 21. The Labour Party today elected James Ramsay MacDonald as their new leader. Veteran MPs complained about new ones having ganged up for him in advance. Cock-a-hoop Glasgow Socialists sent Mr MacDonald a congratulatory telegram. It read: "Labour can have no truck with tranquillity". The party is now trying to throw senior Liberals off their seats on the Opposition front bench.

1922

DECEMBER

Su	Mo	Tu	We	Th	Fr	Sa
					1	2
3	4	5	6	7	8	9
10	11	12	13	14	15	16
17	18	19	20	21	22	23
24	25	26	27	28	29	30
31						

1. Warsaw: Joseph Pilsudski resigns as president of Poland (→16).

5. London: The Irish Constitution Bill, creating the Irish Free State, becomes law (→6).

6. London: King George V proclaims the existence of the Free State of Ireland (→7).

7. Ireland: Dail member Sean Hales is murdered by anti-government "Irregulars" (→17).

10. Stockholm: Nobel Prizes awarded to Niels Bohr (Denmark, Physics), Frances Aston (UK, Chemistry), Sir Archibald Hill and Otto Meyerhof (UK and Germany respectively, Medicine), Jacinto Benavento (Spain, Literature) and Fridtjof Nansen (Norway, Peace).→

14. London: John Reith is appointed General Manager of the BBC.

16. Warsaw: President Gabriel Narutowicz is assassinated after only two days in office.

17. Dublin: The last British troops leave (→10/4/23).

24. Rome: Pope Pius XI's first encyclical calls for world peace.

26. Paris: The Allies' War Reparations Committee says Germany has deliberately defaulted on repayments (→2/1/23).

30. Moscow: Soviet Russia is renamed the Union of Soviet Socialist Republics.

31. US: Figures show there were 57 reported lynchings in 1922, 18 in Texas alone.

31. Paris: The French government rejects a German offer of a non-aggression pact.

HITS OF 1922

Limehouse Blues.

I wish I could shimmy like my sister Kate.

Chicago.

QUOTE OF THE YEAR

"The totality of thought is a picture of the world".
Ludwig Wittgenstein,
Tractatus Logico-Philosophicus, 1922.

Solar system model wins Bohr a Nobel

Nobel Prize winner Niels Bohr.

Danish physicist **Niels Bohr** was awarded the Nobel Prize for Physics this year for his work on the structure of the atom. His great triumph was to marry the quantum theory and the idea of an atom as a solar system in miniature: a packet of energy, the central concept of the quantum theory, corresponds to a planetary electron jumping from one orbit to another. Bohr's theory predicted the way particular atoms emit energy with great accuracy.

The Chemistry Prize was awarded to **F. W. Aston** of Britain. Together with **F. W. Soddy**, who won last year's prize, he developed the idea of isotopes: atoms with different weights but identical chemical properties. Aston also invented an instrument called the mass spectrograph to detect them.

Lovers found guilty of Ilford murder

Dec 11. Edith Thompson was today found guilty of murder after a trial which attracted unprecedented all-night queues to the Old Bailey. Her victim was her husband, Percy Thompson, and her accomplice was her lover, Frederick Bywaters. Letters written by Edith Thompson to Bywaters were cited by prosecution lawyers as proof of a plot to kill Mr Thompson, of Ilford, Essex, so the couple could marry. They pleaded not guilty, but today were both sentenced to death.

Arts: Ulysses lures intellectual smugglers

The publishing event of the year occurred in Paris where the owner of an obscure bookshop, **Sylvia Beach**, brought out a limited edition (1,000 copies) of a novel entitled "Ulysses", which has been banned from sale in the US and Britain on grounds of immorality.

The New York Society for the Prevention of Vice seized copies of the literary magazine which serialised it and obtained its conviction. Such is the reputation of its author, **James Joyce**, a Dubliner who has lived abroad since 1904, that the book has become a cult. Copies are smuggled in from Paris by the intelligentsia.

"Ulysses" is a very complex and detailed novel, in which the adventures of Homer's epic hero are paralleled by those of Leopold Bloom, in the doings of a single day in Dublin, June 16, 1904. Bloom, his wife Molly and Stephen Dedalus, representing the author's younger self (as he did in "Portrait of the Artist as a Young Man") are the primary characters. Their inner thoughts and desires are presented in a series of interior monologues such as Molly Bloom's 38-page soliloquy which closes the book.

The author of an equally ambitious attempt to order the experience of an individual human being over time, **Marcel Proust**, died in Paris in November aged 51 with his panoramic work, "A la Recherche du Temps Perdu" (Remembrance of Things Past) apparently unfinished. Six parts have now appeared (the second won the Prix Goncourt in 1919) but to the time of his death

Buster Keaton, star of "Cops".

Proust was revising and rewriting the remainder, which exceeds a million words in all.

An asthmatic, he withdrew from a brilliant social life in 1905 to a room sound-proofed with cork, writing only by night. "My instrument is not a microscope," he declared, "but a telescope directed at Time." With it he retrieved the social and sensual world of the Belle Epoque, its corruption and its disintegration with the coming of war. But he also took what he called "a diver's search" into the depths of human consciousness.

London has seen an experimental play by Italian **Luigi Pirandello**, "Six Characters in Search of an Author", in which they invade a rehearsal, strangely alive, and demand to be put into a play.

Tuning in the wireless on Christmas Day: 1922 painting by W.R. Scott.

1923

JANUARY

Su	Mo	Tu	We	Th	Fr	Sa
	1	2	3	4	5	6
7	8	9	10	11	12	13
14	15	16	17	18	19	20
21	22	23	24	25	26	27
28	29	30	31			

1. France: Sadi Lecointe sets a new air speed record of 217.5 mph.

2. Paris: The Allies agree to cut German reparations to £2,800 million (→ 9).

6. Washington: The Senate votes to withdraw US troops stationed in Germany.

7. Russia: Rumours are circulating that Lenin is close to death (→ 19/3).

9. France: French troops prepare to occupy Essen as Germany is again declared in default on reparations (→ 11).

11. Germany: Against UK and US advice, French and Belgian troops enter Essen unresisted (→ 18).

13. Washington: The Senate agrees to admit 25,000 Armenian orphans into the United States.

15. London: The engagement is announced of Prince Albert, Duke of York, to Lady Elizabeth Bowes-Lyon (→ 26/4).

18. Germany: There are now 112,000 marks to the pound as the economic crisis deepens (→ 1/2).

21. Germany: Ruhr miners announce a strike in protest at the French occupation (→ 24).

24. France: A court-martial sentences six German industrialists to heavy fines for disobeying the French.→

28. Brussels: 100,000 French-speaking Belgians demonstrate in protest at the use of Flemish at Ghent university.

29. Germany: 20 Germans die in the first outbreak of violence against the occupation of the Ruhr (→ 1/2).

BIRTH

31. US writer Norman Mailer.

DEATHS

3. Czech writer Jaroslav Hasek (*30/4/1883).

9. British writer Kathleen Murry, alias Katherine Mansfield (*14/10/1888).

11. Ex-Greek King Constantine I (*2/8/1868).

Germans defy the occupying French

Jan 25. The favourite tune in the industrial towns of the Ruhr these day is "Deutschland uber Alles." Crowds gather around statues of Bismarck and other German national heroes to shout insults at the French troops and sing, again and again:

Deutschland, Deutschland uber Alles, uber Alles in der Welt.
(Germany stands for me above all, above all the world!).

The French sent in 100,000 troops to collect the coal, timber and other war reparations Germany was being slow to deliver. The Germans responded with strikes, sabotage, and massive street demonstrations, which the French dispersed with cavalry charges and shots over the heads of the crowds. Commerce and industry have come to a halt. But Raymond Poincare, the French Premier, says: "France is here to stay until she gets complete satisfaction".

That may take some time. In Berlin, the Chancellor, Wilhelm Cuno, has called on the Ruhr workers to offer "passive resistance" to the occupation and he is, in effect, sending them strike pay. The money, however, is losing its value by the day.

The German mark stood at 7,000 to the US dollar at the beginning of this year; when the nine French divisions, with a Belgian detachment, arrived, the mark plunged to 18,000 overnight. And its collapse is accelerating.

Poincare, it is said, has become obsessed by the need to make Germany pay for the devastation suffered by France in the war. But collecting the debt has proved difficult. A French businessman had the idea of occupying the Ruhr. But that led to another difficulty: the British and Americans objected.

The British Prime Minister, Bonar Law, said occupation would not produce the results desired; the Ruhr, with a population of three million, is the jugular vein of German industry and foreign occupation would strangle the German economy. Already, Bonar Law argued, Germany was on the point of industrial collapse. A moratorium on reparations was needed.

Poincare, fervently supported by his Defence Minister, Andre Maginot, brushed aside such arguments. He said Germany's industrialists had speculated with the mark in order to evade reparations. Besides, Germany was secretly arming, as well as openly recruiting for paramilitary organisations.

The French have reacted to the campaign of strikes and sabotage with arrests, deportations and the death sentence; troops have been put into all industrial installations and both public transport and coal stocks taken over. Engineers have been brought from France. When Poincare announced the occupation in the French Chamber he was given a massive vote of confidence.

But Marshal Foch and Clemenceau, both in retirement, were apprehensive, fearing that the cost in manpower and in foreign goodwill, might in the end prove too high. The one certain consequence already visible to the foreign visitor is that France's paralysing blow to Germany's industrial power has given the German people a sense of unity they have not known since 1914.

French troops arriving in the Ruhr. The move accelerated Germany's inflation.

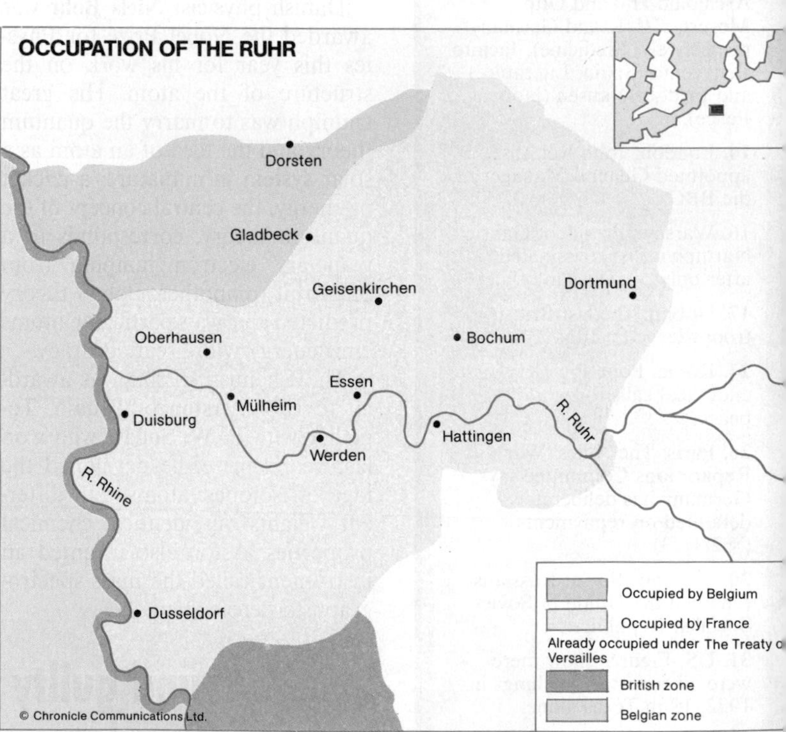

Nazi Party holds its first rally in Munich

Jan 27. The National Socialist Party, led by the former corporal Adolf Hitler, is holding its first public congress in Munich, a city where the Party enjoys much support, especially in the beer-halls where old soldiers gather. The streets are full of flags and banners carrying the crooked cross emblem of the swastika, an ancient Eastern device adopted by the party as its symbol.

There was much applause when Herr Hitler, a fiery orator, called for the repeal of the Treaty of Versailles. Most Germans consider the treaty too harsh and blame it for many of the country's problems. Herr Hitler has struck a sympathetic chord with them.

Stalin is too rude Lenin says in memo

Joseph Stalin: rude and unbearable.

Jan 4. Reports are circulating in Moscow of sensational and unprecedented criticism by Lenin of the Communist Party's General Secretary, Joseph Stalin. It had been thought that Stalin enjoyed the full confidence of the Party, but now Lenin, a sick man, has written: "Stalin's rudeness is becoming unbearable in the office of the General Secretary. Therefore, I propose the comrades should think about ways of removing him from that post." These comments appear as a postscript to an assessment of prominent party members, dictated to his secretary by Lenin as his political testament.

1923

FEBRUARY

Su	Mo	Tu	We	Th	Fr	Sa
				1	2	3
4	5	6	7	8	9	10
11	12	13	14	15	16	17
18	19	20	21	22	23	24
25	26	27	28			

1. Germany: French troops put a cordon round the Ruhr to prevent movements of coal to unoccupied Germany (→25).

1. Germany: Inflation worsens; £1 is now worth 220,000 marks (→10).

4. Switzerland: Turkey refuses to sign the Lausanne Treaty (→7).

5. Rome: Mussolini orders the arrest of several hundred socialists (→23/4).

5. London: Cox's Bank announces its merger with Lloyd's Bank.

7. Ankara: The Turks refuse an Allied demand to withdraw warships from Smyrna (→23/4).

10. Berlin: The Reichsbank, Germany's central bank, begins large sales of gold to bolster the mark.

13. Washington: President Harding calls a conference of state governors to discuss the enforcement of Prohibition.

16. US: Jazz singer Bessie Smith makes her first recording, "Down-hearted Blues".

18. France: 27 die when the Paris-Strasbourg express hits a freight train.

21. S. Africa: A. C. Russell hits a record century in both innings in England's test match win over South Africa.

24. Washington: President Harding urges the Senate to approve US memberhip of the International Court (→3/3).

25. Germany: The French occupy more territory along the Rhine and tighten their blockade (→1/3).

28. London: The Lords pass a bill saying husbands are no longer deemed to have coerced wives who commit offences in their presence.

BIRTH

12. Italian film director Franco Zeffirelli.

DEATH

10. German physicist Wilhelm Roentgen (*27/3/1845).→

Even sweaters can be chic, says Chanel

Feb 16. French fashion queen, Gabrielle "Coco" Chanel, the designer responsible for some of the most startling changes in women's appearance in the last couple of years, has now decreed that even sweaters can be chic. Such is her sway in the world of fashion that it's expected that the idea will be greeted enthusiastically.

Coco, as she is universally known, has been a leader in the trend towards a new freedom in clothes. Her straight, boyish lines in soft, light fabrics, along with short skirts, low heels and bobbed hair, create a look that greatly appeals to the new woman of the Twenties, determined to shake off the constrictions of whalebone and ruffles and lead a more active life.

Once an orphaned peasant girl, Coco doesn't only influence clothes but smell as well; her newly launched perfume, Chanel No. 5, is very successful.

Making it smart not to look rich.

Turks keep Greek refugees in squalor

Feb 13. There are 10,000 Ottoman Greeks huddled in desperate misery in the Selimie Barracks in Scutari, living in the most appalling conditions. These unfortunate people, all Turkish citizens of Greek origin, have been driven from their homes on the Black Sea coast and are being held in the barracks to await deportation to Greece.

Greece has already taken a million refugees and can take no more, so for three weeks these people have waited, wrenched from prosperity to a condition scarcely better than death. Smallpox has broken out. The Greek hospital nearby has 300 cases and is full. The only food is half a loaf a day from the American Near East Relief Association.

The Turks have been warned about their behaviour, but their only reply has been to send yet more people to Scutari.

Bessie Smith, one of America's greatest blues singers.

Roentgen, X-ray pioneer, dies

Feb 10. Wilhelm Roentgen, the discoverer of X-rays, died today in Munich at the age of 77. His great moment came in 1895 while studying "cathode" rays. He found that when cathode rays impinged on the end of the evacuated tube in which they were produced other rays were emitted. In a few weeks' intense experimentation he identified the main properties of these mysterious new "X"-rays, above all their extraordinary powers of penetration. Their use to see inside the human body has transformed some aspects of medicine.

1923

MARCH

Su	Mo	Tu	We	Th	Fr	Sa
				1	2	3
4	5	6	7	8	9	10
11	12	13	14	15	16	17
18	19	20	21	22	23	24
25	26	27	28	29	30	31

1. Germany: The Franco-Belgian authorities impose the death penalty on anyone sabotaging transport lines (→3).

3. Washington: The Senate rejects President Harding's proposal to join the International Court.

3. Germany: French troops occupy the Rhine ports of Mannheim and Karlsruhe.→

5. US: Montana and Nevada introduce the first US old age pensions of $25 a month.

5. UK: Minister of Health Sir Arthur Boscawen loses his seat of Mitcham, Surrey, to Labour (→7).

7. London: Bonar Law appoints Neville Chamberlain as Minister of Health.

9. New York: 30 city policemen are revealed as members of the Ku Klux Klan (→14).

14. US: Two judges in Baton Rouge, Louisiana, are barred from the state appeal court as Ku Klux Klan members.

17. Washington: President Harding says he will run for re-election.

21. Paris: Scientists claim smoking is beneficial as nicotine forms anti-bacterial chemicals.

23. UK: S. Sanford's Sergeant Murphy wins the Grand National at Aintree.

23. Dublin: The government imposes a 33.33 per cent tax on British goods, including motor cars.

26. UK: 15,000 Norfolk farm hands go on strike for higher wages (→21/4).

27. London: Telegraphic links are established between the UK and Afghanistan.

30. India: New financial measures come into force, including restoration of salt tax.

BIRTH

22. French mime artist Marcel Marceau.

DEATH

26. French actress Sarah Bernhardt (*22/10/1844).→

Lenin quits after stroke

March 9. The career of Vladimir Lenin, Soviet leader since the Bolsheviks seized power in Russia five years ago, came to an end today. Lenin suffered a massive stroke, which deprived him of the power of speech and completely paralysed him.

Lenin, 53, has suffered ill health since last May, when he had his first stroke. He had a second in December and has not spoken in public for nearly four months.

Nevertheless, despite his fragile state of health, he has been at the centre of affairs, engaged in plans for reorganising both the government and the party.

Lenin is known to be particularly concerned both about the growth of bureaucracy and the future behaviour of Joseph Stalin, a Georgian and the party's general secretary. There is growing evidence that Lenin fears a bitter struggle for power in Russia will take place within the party after he has gone. Front-runners to follow him are Stalin, Trotsky – in some respects Lenin's equal but with no great following in the tight Bolshevik circle – and the leader of the Comintern, Grigori Zinoviev.

Lenin relaxing in the country.

Rioting Germans shot in French-occupied Ruhr

March 31. The famous Krupp steel works at Essen in the Ruhr was the scene of an ugly clash between German workers and French troops this morning. Nine Germans were killed and 43 injured.

The dozen French troops had come to requisition trucks and were pelted with sticks, stones, lumps of coal and bolts of metal. The French escaped after opening fire; they returned later with armoured cars.

"I cannot understand why England and America stand by and permit French soldiers to shoot down our workmen," a Krupp spokesman said. The French, who occupied the Ruhr last January, have had difficulty in securing and transporting the coal and other materials they are claiming as war reparations (→1/4).

French troops at war in the Ruhr.

New tax rubs salt into Indian wounds

March 24. The salt tax is to be restored, it was agreed by the Council of State meeting in Allahabad yesterday in order to balance the budget, despite the appeal of Mr Sastri, who said that the Council did not realise the conditions under which many of the population lived. Many families were living below the bare margin of subsistence. To them an anna was an anna and a rupee a rupee. Mr Innes, the commercial member, replied that the submerged tenth was not peculiar to India. Indeed, when they considered the starving, ragged figures on the winter streets of London and compared them with the poorest of the poor in warm Madras, the balance swung in favour of India as far as the standard of living was concerned (→30).

Paris pays homage to Sarah Bernhardt

The last picture of a great actress.

March 29. All Paris came to a halt in mourning for Sarah Bernhardt, whose cortege was like a royal procession. She is equally mourned in London, where she often received greater homage than in Paris.

Her first visit was to play Racine's Phedre in 1879. She was so paralysed with fear that she fainted as the curtain fell. After a bitter parting from the Comedie Francaise, her many triumphant tours enabled her to buy her own theatre, which was named after her.

Her pathos moved audiences to tears. "Her voice was liquid gold," said a critic, "She spoke verse as the nightingale sings." She was 78.

Wives can divorce faithless husbands

March 2. There were enthusiastic cheers today when the Commons passed the second reading of the Matrimonial Causes Bill by 231 votes to 27. The Bill will put the sexes on an equal footing by allowing a wife to petition for a husband's adultery. At present only the reverse is possible. The House also agreed to a second reading for the Legitimacy Bill, enabling parents to legitimise a child by marrying after its birth (→18/7).

1923

APRIL

Su	Mo	Tu	We	Th	Fr	Sa
1	2	3	4	5	6	7
8	9	10	11	12	13	14
15	16	17	18	19	20	21
22	23	24	25	26	27	28
29	30					

1. Germany: Directors of Krupp's Works in Essen are arrested for the riots at the end of last month (→ 1/5).

4. Moscow: Lenin suffers another stroke.

4. Egypt: The Earl of Carnarvon dies from an insect bite.

8. India: 8,000 are feared dead from plague in the past week.

10. Dublin: Liam Lynch, head of the "Irregulars", dies in prison from wounds (→ 24/5).

13. Paris: Madame Alfred Mortier is the first woman admitted to the Academie Francaise.

13. India: Englishwoman Mrs Ellis is murdered at Kohat and her 17-year-old daughter kidnapped (→ 22).

15. New York: The first public showing takes place of a "sound on film" picture.

16. London: Chancellor Stanley Baldwin's budget cuts 6d off income tax and 1d off a pint of beer.

17. Moscow: The 12th Communist Party Congress opens with criticism of Stalin and other leaders.

19. Paris: General Maxime Weygand, second-in-command of French troops in the War, is made commissioner of Syria.

21. UK: The Norfolk farm hands strike ends.

21. Rome: Mussolini replaces the workers' May Day holiday with a holiday to mark the founding of Rome.

22. India: Kidnap victim Mollie Ellis is rescued.

23. UK: A £100,000 endowment plan is announced to make Stratford-upon-Avon a literary and dramatic centre.

23. Rome: The Catholic Party resigns from Mussolini's government.

26. UK: The Duke of York and Lady Elizabeth Bowes-Lyon are married.→

30. Washington: The Supreme Court says alcohol is only permitted on ships more than three miles offshore.

Man on white horse saves the day

PC Storey on his white horse clears the crowd from the pitch at Wembley.

April 28. The great Empire Stadium at Wembley staged its first sporting spectacular today, and narrowly escaped a mass disaster. The Football Association Cup Final between Bolton Wanderers and London's West Ham United was designed to show off Britain's splendid sports arena fully a year before it becomes the centrepiece of the Empire Exhibition. The stadium, which is designed to hold 100,000, attracted a huge crowd.

Unfortunately there was a serious miscalculation and as many as 126,000 football fans were allowed to pay at the turnstiles; and, by yet yet another more serious oversight, another 75,000 managed to scale the inadequate boundary walls to gain free admission to the terraces.

Naturally, the swollen crowd spilled onto the playing area. It was feared that a decision to cancel the match would spark off even worse trouble, but just when that decision seemed inevitable PC George Storey, mounted on a white horse, patiently coaxed the many thousands of frustrated fans to clear the pitch and allow the game to start.

Vast sections of the crowd can have seen nothing of the contest (which Bolton won 2-0), but early reports of mass injury were largely unfounded, and despite the crush the rival supporters remained calm, good natured and remarkably well behaved.

Lady Elizabeth Bowes-Lyon smiles a little nervously as she leaves her parents' home in Bruton Street. Her dress, the subject of great speculation, is revealed as she heads for Westminster Abbey and the Duke of York.

Dance till you drop craze sweeps US

April 14. The growing craze for marathon dancing in mid-America – with youngsters endangering life and limb for handsome prize money – is taxing legal minds in the United States.

One couple collapsed after dancing for 45 hours. A marathon in Baltimore was stopped by police after 53 hours. In Cleveland, a winning girl's ankles were swollen to twice their normal size after she had worn out five male partners, and a Houston couple are still dancing after 45 hours.

Record dancer Alma Cummings.

Commission urges sex education

April 19. Sex education should be taught in schools and homes, says a new report from the National Birthrate Commission. The report, presented today to the Minister of Education, claims this "difficult and delicate task" is vital to young people's moral safety and welfare.

It recommends answering children's questions as fully and frankly as is appropriate. It acknowledges that many parents find this impossible and calls for the training of specialised teachers. The report also urges a better diet, better recreation facilities and more sunshine – in many cities smoke cuts out half the light.

1923

MAY

Su	Mo	Tu	We	Th	Fr	Sa
		1	2	3	4	5
6	7	8	9	10	11	12
13	14	15	16	17	18	19
20	21	22	23	24	25	26
27	28	29	30	31		

1. Germany: Count Krupp von Bohlen, head of Krupps, is arrested in connection with the riots at the end of March (→ 8).

3. US: John MacReady and Oakley Kelley cross the US non-stop in a monoplane, flying 2,700 miles in 27 hours.

6. China: 150 passengers on the Tientsin-Pukow railway are kidnapped by bandits (→ 13).

8. Count Krupp von Bohlen is sentenced to 15 years in prison; other Krupp directors get heavy sentences (→ 5/6).

10. Lausanne: The USSR's envoy to the Turkish talks is slain by a Swiss who claims Bolsheviks killed his family.

13. China: The government accepts the ransom terms of the railway kidnappers.

16. Washington: President Harding reappoints a black rejected as collector of customs in New Orleans.

18. London: Prime Minister Andrew Bonar Law is reported to be ill.→

21. Paris: The International Congress of Dancing Masters condemns the foxtrot and the tango.

23. Belgium: The national airline Sabena is formed.

24. Ireland: De Valera orders the Irregulars to lay down their arms.

26. France: The first 24-hour Le Mans motor race is won by Frenchmen Lagache and Leonard.→

26. Lausanne: Turkey and Greece reach agreement at the peace talks (→ 8/7).

27. US: The Ku Klux Klan refuses to reveal the names of its members, in defiance of the law.

31. USSR: Petrograd Opera House is badly damaged by a fire; many die in the panic to leave the burning building.

BIRTHS

1. US author ("Catch 22") Joseph Heller.

27. US statesman Henry Kissinger.

Tories elect Baldwin PM

Tory Prime Minister Stanley Baldwin working at his desk at Chequers.

May 21. Stanley Baldwin became Prime Minister today following Andrew Bonar Law's resignation on being told that he has incurable cancer of the throat. Mr Baldwin will continue as Chancellor of the Exchequer for the time being. He announced a government team with few changes from the last one.

Mr Bonar Law made no recommendation to the King about a successor. Like many other politicians it appears that he expected the monarch to send for Lord Curzon, the Foreign Secretary. There is some mystery in the Parliamentary lobbies over how it turned out to be Mr Baldwin instead.

Beneath the facade of a simple country gentleman, the new Prime Minister is a skilful political operator. But even he has not yet managed to heal wounds left in the Tory Party by last year's Carlton Club decision, masterminded by Mr Baldwin, to kill the Lloyd George coalition government.

Austen Chamberlain and other leading ex-Coalition Tories said they do not wish to serve under Mr Baldwin. Mr Lloyd George called for unity in the Liberal ranks to help in getting rid of the government. Surprising his own Labour supporters, Mr Ramsay MacDonald said "Baldwin's outlook is very close to ours".

Meanwhile there is relief across party lines that the King did not ask a peer to form a government. That, said Labour, would have caused big trouble.

The latest in racing car technology lines up at Le Mans for the first 24-hour motor race. The winning team covers more than 2,200 kilometres.

Hobbs scores his hundredth century

May 8. Jack Hobbs, the Surrey and England opening batsman and the most prolific run-scorer the game has seen, today completed his 100th century in first-class cricket: he made a match-winning 116 not out in a low-scoring county championship game against Somerset at Bath.

Hobbs joins a select band of just two other "century centurions", the great Dr W.G. Grace (126 hundreds), and Surrey's Tom Hayward (104 hundreds), who, by coincidence, was instrumental in introducing the young Hobbs, a fellow Cambridgeshire man, to the Oval in 1905.

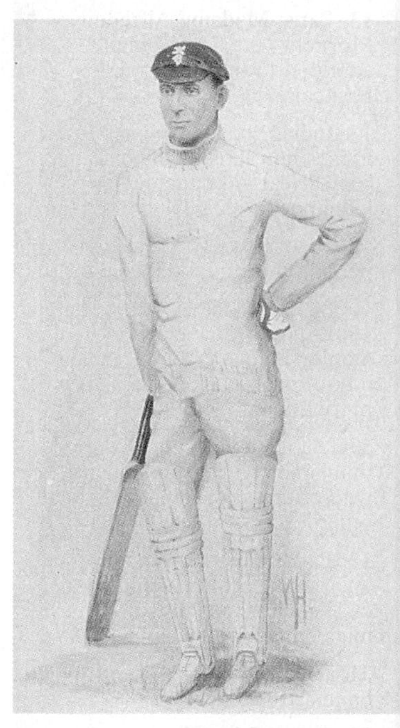

"Century centurion" Jack Hobbs.

BBC opens new London studios

May 2. New wireless studios were opened at Savoy Hill yesterday by the British Broadcasting Company. The walls are lined with six layers of sacking five miles long and there is heavy felt on the floor to reduce noise interference. A better sound is promised for the band of the Grenadier Guards and the evening dance music. Today a new programme, "Woman's Hour", will be launched by Princess Alice with a talk on adoption.

1923

JUNE

Su	Mo	Tu	We	Th	Fr	Sa
					1	2
3	4	5	6	7	8	9
10	11	12	13	14	15	16
17	18	19	20	21	22	23
24	25	26	27	28	29	30

1. UK: Actress Mrs Hilton Philipson becomes the third woman MP.

3. Rome: Mussolini approves a bill to give Italian women the vote in municipal elections.

4. Spain: The Archbishop of Saragossa, Cardinal Soldevila, is murdered.

5. Germany: French troops seize railways in the Ruhr.

6. UK: B. Irish's Papyrus wins the Derby at Epsom, jockey Steve Donoghue's third successive win.

7. London: King George V grants a charter of incorporation to the Federation of British Industries.

8. London: MPs pass the Matrimonial Causes Bill, allowing wives to divorce husbands for adultery (→ 18/7).

13. Paris: The Ballets Russes give the first performance of Stravinsky's ballet "Les Noces" (The Marriage).

14. China: President Li Yuan-hung is captured by troops while trying to flee from Peking.

15. Persia: Up to 20,000 are reported dead after an earthquake caused an avalanche that buried five villages.

15. Sofia: Reported that ousted premier Stambouliski has been shot dead while trying to flee the country.

18. Germany: £1 is now worth 600,000 marks.→

20. US: President Harding relinquishes control of his newspaper, the Marion Star.

22. London: MPs pass the Universities of Oxford and Cambridge Bill, granting them £100,000 annually.

26. London: The government says it will boost the UK's home air defences from 18 squadrons to 52.

27. Rome: Pope Pius XI condemns the Franco-Belgian military occupation of the Ruhr.

30. Germany: 10 Belgian troops are killed by a bomb planted on a train at Duisburg (→ 6/7).

German mark declining dangerously

June 22. The President of the German Reichsbank, Dr Rudolf Havenstein, today described Germany's financial situation as "most desperate". Since June 1 the mark has lost nearly half its remaining value and was trading today at 622,000 to the pound. On New Year's Day the rate was still under 85,000.

The collapse of the German currency began with the failure of the Allies at the London Conference last August to agree on a moratorium on German war reparations. The position has become catastrophic since the French and Belgian armies occupied the Ruhr earlier this year. Passive resistance by miners means that Germany is not even producing enough coal for itself.

Prices at Berlin market, June 9

1lb beef	7700 - 10900
1lb pork	8200 - 9600
1lb butter	11800 - 13600
1lb margarine	6900 - 8700
1lb potatoes	102 - 118
1lb tea	27250 - 43600
1lb coffee	23600 - 32750
1lb sugar	1270 - 1410
1lb flour	1730 - 2360
1 egg	800 - 810

All prices in marks

Children play with bundles of banknotes made worthless by inflation.

Klan claims a million members in US

June 30. The Ku Klux Klan, the US secret society which uses violence to defend white Protestant supremacy against Negroes, Jews, Catholics and foreigners, claims it now has one million members.

The Klan was founded after the Civil War and the emancipation of the slaves, and its strength was in the southern states. Originally a social club, it degenerated into anti-Negro terrorism and was disbanded by its head, General Nathan B. Forrest, in 1869.

In 1915 the Klan was revived by William Simmonds. Its new head, known as the Imperial Wizard, is a dentist called Hiram Evans. He says the Klan opposes President Harding's plans for a world court and is against any alliance with foreign nations.

Ku Klux Klan novices in Baltimore take the oath before cross and flag.

Army coup topples Bulgarian regime

June 9. The army has staged a bloodless coup in Bulgaria, toppling the Premier, M. Stambouliski, and replacing him with Professor Alexander Zankoff. It seems that the conspiracy was hatched by the League of ex-Army Officers and had the support of King Boris.

The new regime immediately proclaimed a state of siege, but traffic, which was held up by troop movements, has been resumed and the capital is quiet.

The fate of M. Stambouliski is not known but a proclamation has been issued saying: "Bulgarian liberty dawns again. The regime of deceit, violence and murder has collapsed under the weight of its crimes, and a new era has arrived."

1923

JULY

Su	Mo	Tu	We	Th	Fr	Sa
1	2	3	4	5	6	7
8	9	10	11	12	13	14
15	16	17	18	19	20	21
22	23	24	25	26	27	28
29	30	31				

4. US: Jack Dempsey beats Tom Gibbons after a full 15 rounds to keep his world heavyweight title.

5. US: President Harding leaves for a tour of Alaska (→ 28).

6. Germany: France and Belgium warn Berlin that relations will be severed unless it condemns Ruhr violence (→ 12).

7. Wimbledon: Suzanne Lenglen beats Kathleen McKane for the Ladies' Singles title; William Johnson beats Francis Hunter for the Men's Singles championship.

8. Lausanne: The Turks and the Allies agree a peace treaty restoring to Turkey Aegean areas and Armenia, lost after the War (→ 24).

10. Rome: Mussolini dissolves all opposition parties (→ 16).

12. London: Stanley Baldwin tells France and Belgium to leave the Ruhr for fear of starting a new world conflict (→ 20).

13. London: MPs pass Lady Astor's Liquor Bill, banning sale of alcohol to people under 18 (→ 31).

16. Rome: Mussolini bans gambling throughout Italy.

18. London: The Matrimonial Causes Bill receives Royal Assent.

20. London: Baldwin proposes a committee of experts to investigate Germany's ability to pay war reparations (→ 29).

24. Lausanne: The Treaty of Lausanne between Turkey, Greece and the Allies is signed.

25. Bulgaria: 103 are reported killed in a train crash.

28. US: President Harding falls ill with ptomaine poisoning at Grants Pass, Oregon (→ 2/8).

29. Paris: France and Belgium reject the UK plan for an expert reparations committee (→ 2/8).

31. London: Royal Assent given to several bills including Housing Bill, Liquor Bill, Oxford and Cambridge Bill.

Retired Mexican rebel murdered

July 20. Pancho Villa, the revolutionary turned rancher, today fell victim to vengeance. He and three of his bodyguards were shot dead by six gunmen believed to be linked to the Herrera family, four members of whom Villa had killed during the Mexican revolution.

Villa became a fugitive at 16 when he killed a man molesting his sister. As "bandit-general" he led a revolutionary army until seeking a quieter life in retirement as a rancher. He had recently been learning to read and to type, but the presence of bodyguards, unavailing though they were today, shows that violence was never far away.

Pasta ousts wurst as Tyrol Italianised

July 18. The Italian government has issued its timetable for the "Italianisation" of the South Tyrol, the former Austrian territory ceded to Italy after the Great War.

Henceforth Italian is to be the official language of this largely German-speaking area, and will be compulsory for all schoolchildren. Austro-German immigration into the region, renamed "Alto Adige", will initially be banned, and a three-month limit will be put on all visits by Austrians and Germans.

July 6. Suzanne Lenglen wins the Wimbledon Ladies' Singles for the fifth successive year.

1923

AUGUST

Su	Mo	Tu	We	Th	Fr	Sa
			1	2	3	4
5	6	7	8	9	10	11
12	13	14	15	16	17	18
19	20	21	22	23	24	25
26	27	28	29	30	31	

1. London: The government announces new schemes for unemployment relief.

3. Washington: Calvin Coolidge is sworn in as President (→ 10).

6. UK: American swimmer Henry Sullivan swims the English Channel in 28 hours (→ 12).

7. Germany: The pound is now worth 15 million marks, up from only nine million yesterday (→ 12).

10. US: A national day of mourning marks the funeral of President Harding in his home town of Marion, Ohio.

12. UK: Argentine swimmer Enrique Tirbocchi swims the Channel in a record 16 hours 33 minutes.

12. Berlin: Chancellor Cuno resigns as the German economy collapses; Gustav Stresemann takes over (→ 17).

17. Washington: President Coolidge offers to help solve the German reparations crisis (→ 22).

21. US: The city of Kalamazoo, Michigan, forbids dancers to stare into their partners' eyes.

21. London: Seven-week long dock strike ends.

22. Paris: France says it will neither cut its reparations demand nor let the matter go to the International Court (→ 6/9).

24. Turkey: British troops are evacuating Istanbul (formerly Constantinople).

27. London: Neville Chamberlain takes over from Stanley Baldwin as Chancellor of the Exchequer.

BIRTHS

16. Israeli statesman Shimon Peres.

29. British actor and film director Sir Richard Attenborough.

DEATH

2. US statesman Warren Gamaliel Harding, President 1921-3 (*2/11/1865).→

US President dies: Coolidge sworn in

The new President of the US.

Aug 2. US President Warren G. Harding died suddenly tonight, aged 57. Mr Harding, a former senator from Ohio, had been ill for a week after a tiring tour of Alaska. His administration has lately been plagued by scandal.

The Hardings were staying in San Francisco. While his wife was reading to him in their hotel suite, the President said "That's good! Read me some more!" Then he collapsed with a stroke.

Former Vice-President Calvin Coolidge succeeds to the presidency. Coolidge, known for his taciturnity, was governor of Massachusetts and won prominence for his handling of a Boston police strike (→ 3).

Looking up to the symbol of prosperity: the new Ford.

1923

SEPTEMBER

Su	Mo	Tu	We	Th	Fr	Sa
						1
2	3	4	5	6	7	8
9	10	11	12	13	14	15
16	17	18	19	20	21	22
23	24	25	26	27	28	29
30						

1. Japan: A huge earthquake devastates Tokyo and Yokohama (→ 3).

2. Germany: At the "German Congress" in Nuremberg Nazi leader Adolf Hitler fiercely attacks the Weimar Republic.→

2. Irish Free State: The government wins 63 out of 107 seats in the Free State's first general elections.

3. Washington: President Coolidge appeals for a US relief fund for the Tokyo earthquake victims.→

6. London: Opening of the Tivoli in the Strand, London's new "super-cinema".

6. Germany: £1 is now worth 200 million marks (→ 12).

9. US: 23 sailors die when seven US destroyers are wrecked off Santa Barbara, California.

10. Geneva: The Irish Free State is admitted to the League of Nations.

12. Africa: The Crown takes over Southern Rhodesia from the British South Africa Company (→ 1/10).

12. Germany: £1 is worth 600 million marks (→ 15).

15. US: Oklahoma is put under martial law by Governor Walton in a bid to suppress the Ku Klux Klan (→ 25/10).

15. Germany: The Reichsbank raises interest rates to 90 per cent to stem the demand for money (→ 22).

18. India: The Indian National Congress agrees to launch a civil disobedience campaign.

22. Germany: Chancellor Stresemann calls a conference of state premiers to discuss the Ruhr and economic crises (→ 26).

24. Germany: Doctors say that inhaling smokers absorb eight times more nicotine than those who do not.

26. Germany: President Friedrich Ebert declares a state of emergency throughout the country.→

29. Palestine: The British mandate officially takes effect from today.

Quake razes Tokyo: 300,000 dead

Tokyo lies devastated after Japan's biggest earthquake, leaving the homeless to build makeshift huts from the debris.

Sept 16. One million refugees, clutching fragments of homes destroyed by an earthquake last week, have joined a pitiful mass exodus from Tokyo, marching into the countryside in the face of such further disasters as typhoons, flooding and epidemics.

Those who have stayed behind wait in two-mile-long queues for a daily ration of one riceball each. Relief workers fear the death toll from Japan's greatest earthquake could rise above 300,000.

In all 2.5 million people were made homeless when Tokyo and Yokohama were levelled, and entire communities were hit by widespread flooding after the rivers Fukuro, Chiyo and Takimi burst their banks.

Cholera is now spreading as survivors resort to drinking from ditches; martial law has been declared in areas of civil unrest and many relief camps are overwhelmed.

But even as the dust settles, the huge task of rebuilding has begun, spurred on by the knowledge that much of Japan's industry has escaped the devastation.

Typical of the tragedies created by the earthquake was the ordeal suffered by a British lecturer. He had escaped injury but found his Japanese wife and her mother in the debris of their home, still sitting where they had been sewing. They survived but another relative burned before their eyes as they dug in vain to free him from the burning wreckage.

Dictator takes tough line in Bavaria

Sept 30. Dr von Kahr, the newly-appointed dictator of Bavaria, has moved swiftly and imposed martial law to quell the state's internal unrest, which has partly been brought about by the challenge of the Fascist movement led by Adolf Hitler.

Both right-wing leaders oppose the Berlin regime but von Kahr, regarded as the most dangerous opponent of the Weimar Republic, yesterday promised to put down "any resistance to my authority by every means at my disposal".

Specifically, the dictator, a former premier who wants an independent Bavaria, has taken a tough stance against the threat of Hitler's more militaristic Bavarian Fascists, using loyal troops to break up their mass rallies.

His takeover comes at a time of economic and political upheaval in Germany as the mark collapses and inflation spirals. On the streets, columns of spike-helmeted Fascist supporters in gold, red and blue tunics overran Nuremberg, replacing the Republican flag with the Kaiser's standard.

An estimated 400,000 Bavarian Fascists, many in goose-stepping formation, packed the streets in support of Hitler's growing anti-Semitic organisation.

The King of Spain connives at coup

Sept 13. The Army seized control of Spain today with the full approval of King Alphonso XIII. The man behind the coup is General Miguel Primo de Rivera, the brilliant soldier who has been Captain General of Valencia, Madrid and Catalonia.

His first action has been to suspend the Cortes, the Spanish parliament, and set up a military directorate. Many Spaniards look to him to restore the nation's honour with a successful campaign against the rebel Abdel Krim in Morocco and to provide firm government at home.

1923

OCTOBER

Su	Mo	Tu	We	Th	Fr	Sa
	1	2	3	4	5	6
7	8	9	10	11	12	13
14	15	16	17	18	19	20
21	22	23	24	25	26	27
28	29	30	31			

1. London: The Broadcasting Committee recommends a ten shillings wireless licence, 7/6d will go to the BBC.

1. Rhodesia: Britain agrees to the creation of an autonomous Southern Rhodesian government.

2. Turkey: The last Allied forces leave Istanbul.

4. UK: Five men are rescued from a flooded mine at Redding near Falkirk, after being trapped for ten days.

8. London: Sir Edward Hulton sells the Evening Standard, Daily Sketch, Sunday Herald and other titles to Lords Rothermere and Beaverbrook for £6,000,000.

12. Turkey: The national capital is moved from Istanbul to Ankara.→

13. Berlin: The government assumes dictatorial powers, with the approval of the Reichstag (→15).

13. UK: Lord Ripon leaves Fountains Abbey, Yorkshire, to the nation.

16. London: The government plans to spend £50 million on unemployment relief.

20. Germany: Bavaria breaks off relations with the Reich (→21).

21. Germany: A republic is declared in the Rhineland (→22).

21. UK: Czechoslovak President Tomas Masaryk arrives on an official visit.

22. Germany: £1 is worth 183,000,000,000 marks.→

25. US: Oklahoma legislature suspends Governor Walton pending trial for his bid to suppress the Ku Klux Klan.

28. Paris: Premier Poincare says France will not leave the Ruhr and Rhine or cut its reparations demands.

BIRTH

15. Italian author Italo Calvino (†19/9/85).

DEATH

30. British statesman Andrew Bonar Law, Prime Minister 1922-23 (*16/9/1858).

US oil scandal involves ex-minister

Oct 28. A pattern of possible wrongdoing has begun to emerge in a Senate committee investigating the leasing of the government's oil reserves at Teapot Dome and Elk Hills to private concerns. The two valuable reserves were transferred from the US Navy to the Department of the Interior in 1921.

Last year, Secretary of the Interior Albert B. Fall leased, without competitive bidding, the Teapot Dome fields in Wyoming to Harry F. Sinclair, the president of Mammoth Oil Co., and the Elk Hills reserves in California to Edward L. Doheny, a friend.

Fall, who resigned his cabinet post some months ago, was asked at the committee hearings why he had failed to seek competitive bids. "Business, purely," he replied. "I knew I could get a better price without calling for bids." Despite repeated questioning, Fall denied accepting money from either Sinclair or Doheny, apart from expenses for a business trip to Europe on behalf of Sinclair.

Other witnesses have suggested that Fall may have profited from the oil transfers.

Under fire: politician Albert Fall.

French invasion fuels German crisis

Oct 27. In a virtual act of war the French have occupied the Rhineland areas of Bonn and Wiesbaden, as retaliation for Germany's failure to fulfil promised timber shipments.

This can only serve to aggravate the severe political and economic crisis gripping the country, which is riven by separatist movements and attempted coups against the Berlin government. The occupied area, for example, is controlled by a Socialist-Communist coalition while a right-wing dictator runs Bavaria.

There have been riots in Berlin, as police with drawn swords clashed with marchers from working class districts protesting about unemployment. Looting has been widespread since the price of a 4lb loaf rose almost overnight from an astonishing 34,000,000 marks to an unbelievable 480,000,000 marks.

Using cardboard tubes to set new waves in ladies' hairstyles.

Kemal is first head of Turkish republic

Oct 29. Mustafa Kemal today proclaimed Turkey a Republic and himself its first President. He thus confirms his position as master of Turkey, a position won on the battlefield and in the council chamber. His crushing counter-attack against the Greeks, which drove them out of Turkey, marks him as a man of military genius.

He has also won political laurels, emerging triumphant from the Lausanne peace conference last year, with a guarantee of Turkey's frontiers and the abolition of the treaties giving special privileges to foreigners in Turkey.

Turkish President Mustafa Kemal.

Billboards blight the countryside

Oct 18. The motoring boom is opening up the British countryside not only to a new breed of visitors but also to new forms of commercial exploitation. "Unsightly hoardings and advertisements" along the sides of roads are today condemned by the Ministry of Transport.

In a letter to all county councils, the Ministry says that the recent increase in advertising billboards is "disfiguring" the countryside. It urges local authorities to take action in order "to safeguard the amenities of the public highways under their control". Pressure is also mounting on private companies to withdraw their advertisements.

1923

NOVEMBER

Su	Mo	Tu	We	Th	Fr	Sa
				1	2	3
4	5	6	7	8	9	10
11	12	13	14	15	16	17
18	19	20	21	22	23	24
25	26	27	28	29	30	

2. US: Navy airman H. Brow sets a new air speed record of 259 mph in a Curtiss racer.

2. Berlin: The Social Democrats resign from the government (→ 6).

6. Berlin: 1,000 shops are looted during a spate of anti-Semitic rioting.→

8. London: The Imperial Conference ends with Dominions gaining the right to make foreign treaties.

8. Munich: Adolf Hitler stages a coup attempt (→ 11).

11. Munich: Hitler is arrested at Essing, a village outside the city.→

13. Paris: The French government agrees to the creation of a committee of experts to examine the German economy (→ 29).

15. Berlin: To end inflation the government introduces a new unit of currency, worth 1,000,000,000 m (→ 16).

16. Paris: The UK and Italy refuse a proposal by France that it should occupy more of Germany (→ 17).

17. Berlin: The Reichsbank says its branches will not accept deposits after November 22 (→ 23).

19. London: The government gives details of a planned subsidy scheme for UK agriculture.

23. Berlin: After losing a vote of confidence, Stresemann resigns as Chancellor (→ 29).

25. UK: The first transatlantic wireless broadcast to the US is made.

28. Washington: President Coolidge appoints a commission to investigate the release of political prisoners.

29. Berlin: Dr Wilhelm Marx becomes Chancellor.

29. Germany: An international commission under US banker William Dawes is set up to examine Germany's economy.

BIRTH

18. US astronaut Alan Shepard, first American in space.

Hitler held after beer-hall putsch

Nov 12. An obscure ex-corporal and a famous field marshal are under arrest in Munich today after a farcical attempt to seize power ended in an exchange of gunfire outside the old Bavarian royal palace.

The affair began last Thursday evening in the city's biggest beer hall, the Burgerbraukeller, where Gustav von Kahr, the recently appointed dictatorial state commissioner of Bavaria, was due to deliver a lecture on the moral justification for political dictatorship. The audience included General von Lossow, the local army commander, and members of the Bavarian government.

Von Kahr had scarcely opened his mouth before a gang of men wearing brown shirts burst into the hall waving guns. One of them, a man with a toothbrush moustache, jumped on a chair, fired a shot at the ceiling and shouted: "The national revolution has begun".

The man, Adolf Hitler, leads the Nazis, a small, extreme Nationalist and virulently anti-Semitic party. Bavaria is already a dictatorship, in response to the violent discontent with which the French occupation of the Ruhr has been met. But Hitler believed the time had come to turn the Bavarian dictatorship into a national one and march on the socialist government in Berlin.

Hitler, claiming he had the backing of the war hero, Field Marshal Erich von Ludendorff, proceeded to appoint von Kahr and von Lossow as members of his "government".

Ludendorff, who had been fetched from his home outside the city, berated Hitler for attempting a putsch without first asking him, but then sent for his uniform and agreed to join, as did von Lossow and Colonel von Seisser, of the state police. By now the beer hall was cheering wildly.

It was a different story at army HQ and von Lossow quickly abandoned support for the putsch, as did von Seisser and von Kahr. Not that they disliked Hitler's views; they just did not believe he could win.

By next morning, Hitler, having made no plans to fight for power, and after vainly appealing to Kronprinz Rupprecht to help him out, was ready to quit. Ludendorff, however, believing his prestige would carry the day, insisted on a march through the city to try to win over the army.

Outside the royal palace they were confronted by a police cordon. Somebody fired a shot, killing a police officer. The police replied with a volley of rifle fire. A man with his arm linked to Hitler fell, mortally wounded. Hitler fled. He was picked up yesterday, hiding in a village outside Munich.

Ludendorff is under house arrest. Hitler, who threatened suicide but has changed his mind, looks like going to prison. A party comrade, Rudolf Hess, has suggested he could spend his time there writing a book.

Adolf Hitler with fellow conspirator Erich von Ludendorff (centre).

Hitler's brownshirts parade the swastika before Kronprinz Rupprecht (left).

Tutankhamun yields up more treasures

Nov 23. It is almost a year to the day since Howard Carter and his team made what is probably the most exciting archaeological find ever – the tomb of Tutankhamun. Since then Carter and his team have uncovered more treasures.

In January, they entered a shrine where many of the Pharoah's personal effects were unearthed. These were dramatic enough, but even more exciting discoveries lay in a second shrine entombed behind a sealed door.

There was a huge alabaster urn laced with gold and silver, on which were mounted two figures representing upper and lower Egypt. A gilded mace and sceptre lay near the urn. The walls of the inner shrine are etched with gold hieroglyphics, one of which Carter has identified as the figure of the Pharoah worshipping the goddess Isis. Dr Alan Gardiner, the noted philologist, has undertaken the task of deciphering the others.

The shrines have also yielded magnificent gold-covered statues of various deities worshipped by the Ancient Egyptians, exquisitely carved figures and breathtakingly beautiful wall-paintings as bright now as they were when they were done more than 3,000 years ago.

The shrine also contains a huge linen coffin cover under which it is hoped even more treasures will be found and, for the first time, the burial customs for a pharoah, dead for nearly 33 centuries, will be revealed.

Carter kneels before the shrine.

Sadly, Lord Carnarvon, the rich Egyptologist who funded Carter's work, is no longer alive to see what lies beneath the gigantic cover. In March of this year he was bitten by a mosquito. The bite turned septic and he returned to Cairo to recover. The infection was successfully treated, but he contracted pneumonia shortly afterwards and died on April 5.

Baldwin calls a snap election

Nov 6. Stanley Baldwin has called a snap election. Less than a year after leading the Tories back to power with a comfortable majority, the Prime Minister announced today that the Government needs a new mandate. His decision has upset some top Tories still irked over his part in ending the Lloyd George Coalition last year. But with the battle declared they are rallying behind his trade protection banner.

The Prime Minister explained: "The only reason for the election is that we promised to have one before any fundamental change in tariff policy." That change is the proposal of higher duties on foreign non-food imports and some preferential treatment for Empire goods. Labour is campaigning for a capital levy on "individual fortunes" over £5,000 and for nationalisation of the mines, railways and electric power stations. It also pledges "to restore to the people their lost rights in the land" without spelling out in much detail how this would be done. The Liberals under Mr Asquith are again urging free trade. Mr Lloyd George is playing second fiddle, but his friends are saying he has come-back plans involving Empire development.

A loaf of bread? That'll be 200,000,000,000 marks, please

Nov 15. A loaf of bread in Berlin now costs over 200 billion marks and a construction worker is paid three trillion marks a day. In effect the currency is valueless.

Externally, the mark now stands at 4 trillion to the dollar – if you can find anyone to sell a dollar. The rate at which inflation has galloped since June means that new value bank notes and postage stamps are no longer printed. Existing ones are just overstamped.

The trade unions, with a total membership now of some 12 million, have been demanding that the government should take direct action and confiscate all food, clothes and boots, ration them, and prohibit the production of all luxury items.

The Communists, naturally, are arguing that the inflation is a symptom of the collapse of the capitalist system. The inflation has been a complete disaster for anyone with liquid savings. Those who failed to transfer their wealth into bricks and mortar or other real assets, or get it out of the country, have been financially wiped out.

In an effort to restore financial order, the Reichsbank today issued a "new mark", each worth a trillion existing marks and pegged at the 1914 level of 4.2 to the dollar. It remains to be seen whether this move will end Germany's inflationary nightmare.

HOW THE MARK DECLINED IN VALUE

Date	Marks*
July 1914	20.4
January 1919	43.3
January 1920	314.9
January 1921	315.4
January 1922	932.1
January 1923	87,343.9
July 1923	1,717,582.9
August 1923	22,455,411
September 1923	480,459,000
October 1923	122,764,600,000
November 1923	20,142,000,000,000

*Number of marks per pound, based on exchange rate of £ = $ 4.86

HOW A LOAF OF BREAD SOARED IN PRICE

1918	0,63
January 1923	250
July 1923	3465
September 1923	1,512,000
November 1923	201,000,000,000

Prices in marks

1923

DECEMBER

Su	Mo	Tu	We	Th	Fr	Sa
						1
2	3	4	5	6	7	8
9	10	11	12	13	14	15
16	17	18	19	20	21	22
23	24	25	26	27	28	29
30	31					

2. Washington: President Coolidge launches his campaign for the 1924 Republican nomination.

3. UK: Seven die and 46 are injured in an accident at Nunnery Colliery, Sheffield.

6. UK: Winston Churchill is defeated in the seat of West Leicester (→ 7).

7. UK: The general election returns eight women MPs.→

10. Stockholm: Nobel Prizes awarded to Robert Millikan (US, Physics), Fritz Pregl (Austria, Chemistry), Sir Frederick Banting and John Macleod (Canada, Medicine), William Butler Yeats (Irish Free State, Literature). No Peace Prize awarded.→

13. London: Lord Alfred Douglas is sentenced to six months in prison for libelling Winston Churchill.

14. UK: 73,500 animals have been slaughtered as a result of the epidemic of foot and mouth disease.

17. UK: Agreement is reached on the formation of the Imperial Air Transport Co.

19. Paris: The Chamber of Deputies grants Marie Curie an annual pension of 40,000 francs (£530).

21. UK: Final state of the parties after the election: Tories 257, Labour 191, Liberals 158, others 8.

27. Tokyo: The regent Hirohito escapes an assassination attempt.

BIRTH

2. Greek-born US soprano Maria Callas, born Cecilia Kalogeropoulos (†16/9/77).

HITS OF 1923

Parisian Pierrot.

Who's sorry now.

Farewell Blues.

QUOTE OF THE YEAR

"The house ... a machine for living."
Le Corbusier,
"Towards a New Architecture", 1923.

British election ends in a stalemate

Campaigning for the Liberals in Plymouth before the General Election.

Dec 11. The Cabinet decided today to face the new hung parliament – and certain defeat – before resigning following its severe General Election rebuff. Mr Baldwin announced that this will be "at the earliest possible moment" – in just under a month. He hopes that in this tangled situation the nation will be relieved to get peace from politics at least over Christmas.

Six days after polling, the constituency results are now nearly all in and the final tally looks like being Tories 258, Labour 191 and Liberals 159. So the Tories have net losses of over 90 seats while Labour and Liberals have net gains of about 50 and 40 respectively.

Without going into coalition, Labour and Liberals intend to throw the Tories out of office. It is assumed that the King will then invite Ramsay MacDonald – as leader of the second largest party – to form Britain's first Labour Government, less than 24 years after the party was formed as a limited political experiment.

The new parliamentary arithmetic suggests that any new government will be brittle and that there will be yet another election before long. There are also Labour hints of policy changes to keep the Liberals sweet.

First Pip and Squeak annual.

Gustave Eiffel, the tower builder, dies

Dec 28. Gustave Eiffel, the celebrated French engineer, has died aged 91 after suffering a cerebral haemorrhage. Born in Dijon, he was behind some of the most impressive building projects in Europe, including the very famous Parisian tower which bears his name and has now become a symbol of France. Yet the structure, which in 1889 was daringly innovative, almost never left the drawing board three years earlier due to Eiffel's terrible struggles to convince financiers he was serious.

Arts: encounters in a Waste Land

Everyone interested in poetry is talking about "The Waste Land", **T. S. Eliot's** long poem published by Leonard and Virginia Woolf's Hogarth Press, after first being printed last year in Mr Eliot's new magazine, "The Criterion".

Many cannot recognise it as poetry. It is a collage of quotations and echoes of other writers, Shakespeare, Dante, Saint Augustine and the Buddha among them, as well as sexual episodes, jazz-like rhythms, and Cockney vulgarities in a public house at closing time. It calls up a desolate picture of spiritual emptiness and aridity.

It has outraged lovers of "Georgian" poetry as much as Joyce and Stravinsky have outraged traditionalists. Sir John Squire calls it "incomprehensible" and F.L.Lucas "one of the maggots that breed in the corruption of poetry".

Mr Eliot, an American with an English wife, works in a City bank (Lloyds Foreign and Colonial). He dedicates the poem to his fellow-American poet, **Ezra Pound**, who severely cut it before publication. Despite its difficulty it has become a cult among undergraduates.

A still stranger form of poetry is "Facade", an "entertainment" of rhythmical verses which were declaimed by the author **Edith Sitwell** through a megaphone from behind a curtain at the Aeolian Hall. There was a musical accompaniment written by **William Walton** for small ensemble. Critical reactions varied from bewilderment to derision.

Nobel prize-winner W.B. Yeats.

There were some titters from the audience which included **Osbert** and **Sacheverell Sitwell, Lytton Strachey, Mrs Woolf** and **Noel Coward**, who gave a parody of the occasion shortly afterwards in the revue "London Calling" as the poetess "Hernia Whittlebot".

The early death of **Katherine Mansfield** at 35 has removed a most promising and sensitive short story writer whose best work in the collection, "The Garden Party", appeared only last year.

This year's Nobel Prize went to **W.B. Yeats**, poet of the Celtic twilight, founder of the Irish National Theatre and now a senator.

Anna Pavlova performing her famous dance "The Dying Swan".

1924

JANUARY

Su	Mo	Tu	We	Th	Fr	Sa
		1	2	3	4	5
6	7	8	9	10	11	12
13	14	15	16	17	18	19
20	21	22	23	24	25	26
27	28	29	30	31		

2. Paris: The city's main railway stations are closed as the level of the Seine rises due to flooding.

3. Egypt: Tutankhamun's stone sarcophagus is discovered in his tomb at Luxor (→12/2).

6. Athens: Turkish President Mustafa Kemal escapes a bomb attempt on his life, but his wife is injured.

9. Germany: The leader of the "Rhineland Republic", Herr Heinz, is assassinated at Speyer.

10. UK: Submarine L-34 sinks off Weymouth; all 43 on board are feared dead.

16. Paris: The Pasteur Institute says it has isolated the bacillus causing rabies.

22. Moscow: A council is appointed to succeed Lenin: Grigori Zinoviev, Leon Kamenev and Joseph Stalin (→26).

25. Paris: French premier Poincare signs a treaty of alliance with premier Eduard Benes of Czechoslovakia.

26. USSR: Petrograd is renamed Leningrad in honour of the late leader (→28).

27. Rome: Mussolini signs a pact with Yugoslavia, under which Italy annexes the free city of Fiume.

27. Rome: Mussolini dissolves the Chamber of Deputies, saying parliamentary rule is causing a drift to anarchy.

28. Moscow: Announced that Lenin's body will be embalmed for permanent public display.

29. UK: Eight-day rail strike ends.

30. Washington: Ex-President Wilson is reported to be seriously ill (→3/2).

31. Germany: Prussian state executioner Paul Spaethe lights 45 candles for the 45 people he has killed, then kills himself.

DEATH

21. Russian statesman Vladimir Ilyich Lenin, born Ulyanov (*22/4/1870).→

Father of the Russian Revolution dies

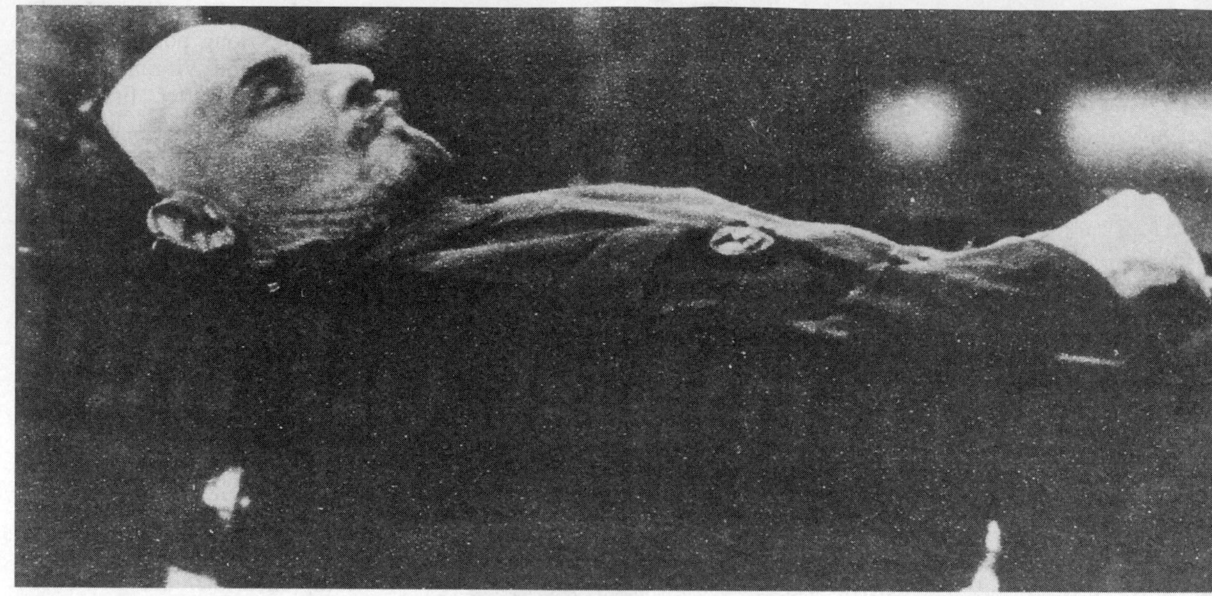

Man of Destiny: Vladimir Ilyich Lenin, founder of Soviet Russia, lies in state in Moscow.

Jan 21. The provincial lawyer turned political agitator, who made a revolution that shook the world, died today after a long illness. Vladimir Ilyich Ulyanov, who styled himself Lenin, was 54.

His death leaves a power vacuum in the Soviet state he created out of the chaos of civil war and famine that gripped Russia after 1917, and there are bitter rivalries inside the Politburo.

Lenin suffered three strokes between May 1922 and March 1923. Before his speech was affected, he spent much of his time dictating his "testament", which gave advice to the party and recorded his opinion of senior Politburo members. Stalin is believed to come out particularly badly.

In these last years as an invalid he spoke often of mistakes, of his Soviet state having taken a wrong turning, of corruption and incompetence in the party. It was not at all as he had imagined it as a young man when he had been converted to Socialism after the execution of his brother, Alexander, in 1887 for his part in the attempt on the life of Czar Alexander III.

The Ulyanovs were a respected middle-class family in the small town of Simbirsk on the Volga. Lenin, the third of five sons of a schools' director, was 25 when his political activities led to prison and exile in Siberia in 1895. Here he married Krupskaya, an idealistic young social worker he had met in St. Petersburg.

Lenin soon discarded his early notions of helping the workers to struggle for better pay and conditions. As set out in his most influential tract, "What is to Be Done?", he advocated the creation of an elite, tightly disciplined party of professional revolutionaries, who would act on behalf of the masses.

It was disagreement over this policy that led to the split between the Bolsheviks, who supported him, and the Mensheviks, who wanted a more democratic organisation.

In exile he began publishing a daily newspaper, Pravda, in 1912.

What of Russia's next five years?

At the outbreak of war he tried unsuccessfully to persuade members of the Socialist Congress of the Second International to forget their nationality and join together in overthrowing their governments.

As a man, Lenin was a paradoxical combination of an uncompromising ascetic, unwilling to consider reform instead of revolution, and a pragmatist willing to negotiate with capitalist powers when it was in his interest.

In 1917, for example, when the time came, as he put it, "to give history a push", he jumped at the chance offered by the Germans and with a score of other Bolsheviks travelled in the sealed train back to Russia and his destiny.

Having spent years laying the foundations, Lenin's Bolshevik Party was able to seize control with relatively little effort. On November 9 he formed the first Soviet government and became its chairman, a post he held until his death.

Lenin pursued his objectives with single-minded ruthlessness, unsparing with comrades and enemies alike. In office he met the challenges of civil war, famine and epidemic with the unhesitating use of repression. On the other hand his last major initiative was his New Economic Policy in March 21, giving peasants free use of their land.

As he lay dying, Stalin was asserting himself as never before at the party conference (→22).

Labour comes to power

Jan 22. The King today appointed James Ramsay MacDonald as Britain's first Labour Prime Minister. A list of the new cabinet was issued immediately. Eleven of its 20 members are of working-class origin. Two were Tories and one a Liberal until recruited because of acute shortage of talent within Labour's own ranks.

The new minority government – like the Tory one defeated on a vote of confidence last night – must depend on Liberal goodwill for its survival. It is not expected to last long.

Mr MacDonald told his party that he is in office but not in real power and the Government must therefore lower its socialist sights. Labour's left-wingers, including the so-called Red Clydesiders, are conceding that there cannot be a social revolution overnight. Some have withdrawn personal objections to taking ministerial posts. Mr MacDonald had no difficulty in brushing aside a call from a few party zealots for a cabinet salary cut.

Labour PM Ramsay MacDonald.

His one revolutionary gesture so far is an order to Foreign Office staff to start work an hour earlier than before – at ten o'clock as from tomorrow morning. Having decided to be his own Foreign Secretary, Mr MacDonald now needs to work overtime.

Reduction of unemployment and a bolder housing programme are named as the new Government's policy priorities. This is intended as re-assurance that no extreme measures will be attempted. However the financial world shivers. "Now is the time for unflinching courage," said the Lancashire and Yorkshire Bank chairman. "The enthronement of a Socialist government is a serious national misfortune", added Winston Churchill.

At 10 Downing Street the Prime Minister's daughter, Isabel, said of her new home: "It's awfully complicated, but very nice". That also sums up the thoughts of Britain's new rulers as they step hesitantly tonight at the end of a long march into the corridors of power.

First Olympic showcase for winter sports

Jan 31. After the controversy and strong opposition that accompanied proposals for an Olympic festival of winter sports, the first series of competitions sanctioned by the International Olympic Committee, who have not yet granted them the title of "Olympic Games", has ended after a week of top-class performance on snow and ice in the French Alps at Chamonix, in the shadow of Mont Blanc.

Competitors from 18 nations took part (almost all men – only figure skating included sections for women), and ironically it was the Scandinavian countries, who had most fiercely opposed the establishment of a rival to their own traditional Nordic Games, who dominated the medals table.

Most prominent were a 29-year-old Norwegian, Thorlief Haug, who won the 18km and 50km cross-country races and the Nordic combined title, as well as a bronze medal in the special ski-jumping and a Finn, Clas Thunberg, who won three gold medals, a silver and a bronze for speed skating.

1924

FEBRUARY

Su	Mo	Tu	We	Th	Fr	Sa
					1	2
3	4	5	6	7	8	9
10	11	12	13	14	15	16
17	18	19	20	21	22	23
24	25	26	27	28	29	

1. London: The Labour government recognises the USSR.

2. Moscow: Alexei Rykov succeeds Lenin as President of the Council of Commissars.

4. France: Norway wins first place in the medals table at the Winter Olympics.

4. India: Mahatma Gandhi is released from prison in Bombay.

6. Washington: Woodrow Wilson is buried in the crypt of the National Cathedral in a simple ceremony.

7. Rome: Italy recognises the USSR as both countries sign a commercial treaty.

7. London: Mrs Helena Normanton is the first woman barrister to practise at the Old Bailey.

8. US: The first execution by gas chamber takes place.

11. Athens: A new Greek government is sworn in, composed entirely of republicans (→ 13/4).

16. UK: A dock strike paralyses every port in the country (→ 17).

17. UK: A four-pound loaf of bread goes up a halfpenny to eightpence-halfpenny as a result of the dock strike (→ 26).

23. London: Britain agrees to accept five per cent of German produce in war reparations rather than 26 per cent.

24. London: Winston Churchill says the Labour government will follow reasonable actions with extremist ones.

26. UK: Transport and General Workers Union dockers agree to end the strike, but other workers stay out.

26. Munich: Adolf Hitler and Erich von Ludendorff go on trial for their part in the failed "beer-hall putsch" (→ 1/4).

28. UK: Home Secretary Arthur Henderson, hitherto a minister without a seat, is returned as MP for Burnley.

29. London: MPs give a second reading to a bill giving the vote to all women aged 21 and over.

Rhapsody over new Gershwin piece

Feb 12. "Rhapsody in Blue" for jazz band and piano was the hit of a concert in New York's Aeolian Hall. Described as "an experiment in modern music", it was given by Paul Whiteman and his band. Its composer, George Gershwin, is best known for his song "Swanee".

From the jazzy wail of the opening clarinet glissando, it transfixed an audience, which included Rachmaninov, Stokowski and Heifetz, with the brilliance of the 25-year-old composer's playing.

Gershwin says he wrote the piece in a month, mainly on a train to Boston, and had it orchestrated by the band's arranger, Ferde Grofe. He calls it "a musical kaleidoscope of America, our pep, our blues, our metropolitan madness".

Composer George Gershwin.

Petrol price rise sparks concern

Feb 4. A fourpence-halfpenny rise in pump prices is leading to fears of an end to the motoring boom. Petrol now costs around two shillings a gallon, and the Automobile Association's secretary said today this would deter many from buying the new "popularly-priced" generation of small cars. It is not the first time that the AA have complained about the rising cost of petrol; four years ago 1,250,000 motorists signed a petition calling for a law to control its price.

Tutankhamun's regal splendour revealed

Howard Carter examines the golden effigy of the ancient Egyptian king.

Feb 12. The news that the lid on Tutankhamun's sarcophagus was to be raised today attracted a large crowd to Luxor. Scientists, minor officials and tourists mingled in the stifling heat outside the tomb, hoping to be among the first to see what treasures it held.

It was cooler in the chamber below but the atmosphere was electric as Howard Carter, the man who discovered the tomb fifteen months ago, supervised the raising of the heavy lid which covered the sarcophagus.

The first thing to meet Carter's eye was a dull, drab linen shroud. This was carefully rolled back and when those present saw what it covered, gasps of amazement could be heard from all around the chamber. For almost 3,300 years the cloth has covered a breathtaking, golden effigy of the king that fills the entire stone coffin.

The gold body is guarded by magnificent gilded carvings of the goddesses Isis and Neith. The figure clutches the crook and flail, emblems of regal authority in ancient Egypt. Olive leaves, wilted with the passing of thousands of years, encircle the figure's brow: and on the forehead are emblazoned the cobra and vulture – the emblems of Upper and Lower Egypt. The face has eyes of argonite and obsidian with eyelids and eyebrows inlaid with shining lapis lazuli glass.

Lying among all the brilliant gold is a small wreath of flowers that, astonishingly, still retain their colours; possibly put there by Tutankhamun's wife in a touching farewell gesture.

Wilson dies: a broken piece of machinery

Feb 3. The Great War claimed its final casualty this morning with the death of the former US President Woodrow Wilson in Washington. Although as president he led the US to victory in the war and pioneered an impressive series of domestic reforms, Wilson left office in 1920 a sick and shattered man. "I am a broken piece of machinery", he told a friend a few days before his death.

Wilson's greatest ambition, the creation of the League of Nation, "to make the world safe for democracy", was shattered by the Senate's rejection of US membership in 1919. Already ill, he collapsed from nervous exhaustion on a 10,000 mile tour around the US to raise popular support for his policies and spent his last months in the White House severely ill and unable to take key decisions.

1924

MARCH

Su	Mo	Tu	We	Th	Fr	Sa
						1
2	3	4	5	6	7	8
9	10	11	12	13	14	15
16	17	18	19	20	21	22
23	24	25	26	27	28	29
30	31					

1. US: 20 are feared dead and 100 hurt in a huge explosion that wrecks 40 buildings at Nixon, New Jersey.

2. London: Milk is reduced to sevenpence a quart.

2. 2. London: Public vehicles are allowed into Hyde Park for the first time since 1636.

3. Ankara: Kemal abolishes the Caliphate, the spiritual leadership of Islam, and ends religious education.→

5. Washington: President Coolidge says the Philippines cannot expect independence in the near future.

6. Rome: Pope Pius XI has a wireless installed.

9. Paris: The French franc is falling; £1 is worth 117 francs.

10. New York: The federal Supreme Court upholds the state's laws banning late night working for women.

13. Berlin: The Reichstag is dissolved ahead of a general election at the end of next month (→5/5).

15. Rome: King Victor Emmanuel III gives soldier-poet Gabriele d'Annunzio the title Prince of Montenevoso.

15. Cairo: King Fuad opens the first Egyptian parliament.

16. Italy: King Victor Emmanuel III enters Fiume for its formal annexation by Italy.

18. US: The film "The Thief of Baghdad" opens, starring Douglas Fairbanks.

20. London: Winston Churchill loses the Abbey by-election to the Tories; Fenner Brockway is third.

24. Washington: The House of Representatives votes $10 million to buy food for German women and children.

28. Washington: Attorney-General Harry Daugherty resigns over the Teapot Dome oil scandal.→

DEATH

29. British composer Sir Charles Villiers Stanford (*30/9/1852).

Mosley applies to join Labour Party

March 31. Oswald Mosley, wealthy ex-Tory, upper-crust maverick MP, now sitting as an Independent, applied today for Labour Party membership. He wrote to Ramsay MacDonald, the Prime Minister: "You stand forth as the leader of the forces of progress in their assault upon the powers of reaction. I ask leave to range myself beneath your standard."

Mr Mosley – a forceful speaker – has been supporting Labour in the Commons and his move is no surprise. It is welcomed by Mr MacDonald as underlining his assertion that Labour is not a single-class movement. The new recruit is married to a daughter of Lord Curzon, Tory ex-Foreign Secretary and former Viceroy.

Maverick MP Oswald Mosley.

Imperial Airways is ready for take-off

March 31. Britain at last has its own national airline, Imperial Airways. The government is behind the formation of the new carrier, which it has promised to subsidise so it can develop quickly. Imperial Airways has been formed by the merger of four smaller companies, and has a fleet of 13 aircraft flying from Croydon.

Greek King is democratically deposed

March 25. The Greek parliament today voted to depose King George II. This can have come as no surprise to the unfortunate monarch, for hostility to the Glucksberg dynasty is so great that the king was forced to flee last year and go into exile in Rumania, homeland of his wife, Queen Elizabeth.

The next step on Greece's road to republicanism is to be a referendum, in which the people will decide if they wish to do away with the monarchical system. Given the present temper of the people, the republicans are confident that the title of King of the Hellenes will disappear for ever.

Crowds filled Athens in a holiday mood today. There was no trouble, the people waved small flags carrying the message "Republic and Reconciliation" and the Assembly chamber was overflowing with members anxious to savour this historic day.

Admiral Konduriotis stays in charge of the government, but he will now act as Regent until a new constitution is drawn up.

So probably the last chapter is ended in the bizarre history of the modern Greek monarchy, with King George I assassinated, the pro-German Constantine forced to abdicate, Alexander dead of a monkey bite and now George II deposed (→ 18/4).

Attorney-General resigns in oil scandal

March 28. President Coolidge today asked for the resignation of Harry M. Daugherty, the US Attorney-General. His fall is the latest twist in what is known as the Teapot Dome scandal, involving the leasing of Federal oil reserves to private interests.

The central figure in the scandal was not Daugherty but Interior Secretary Albert B. Fall. In January, he admitted to the Senate committee investigating the affair that, in return for leasing the Teapot Dome field to Harry F. Sinclair, he had received a large loan.

Daugherty, however, had angered the Senate committee by ordering federal agents to spy on them. He also refused to testify before them or to allow them to look at secret files.

Daugherty is also a highly controversial figure. A member of the so-called "Ohio gang", associated with the previous President, Harding, he managed his campaign in 1920. At the time there were allegations that he had misused money in the Veterans' Bureau and opened warehouses full of confiscated alcohol and sold it to bootleggers. In demanding his resignation, President Coolidge said Daugherty was a "source of increasing embarrassment".

Winds of change blowing in Turkey

March 3. Mustafa Kemal pushes on relentlessly with his campaign to westernise and modernise Turkey. Today a law was passed abolishing the Caliphate and expelling the Caliph and his family from the country. Kemal is also planning to ban many of Moslem Turkey's most cherished religious and cultural traditions.

His new laws, which include banning polygamy, are certain to to be resented by devout Moslems. But such is the fervour of Kemal's supporters that the newspaper Ilera carries the headline: "Farewell to the Orient".

Extravagant sash and ribbons set off matching suit and hat in the latest French fashions.

1924

APRIL

Su	Mo	Tu	We	Th	Fr	Sa
		1	2	3	4	5
6	7	8	9	10	11	12
13	14	15	16	17	18	19
20	21	22	23	24	25	26
27	28	29	30			

1. London: A strike halts work on the British Empire Exhibition at Wembley (→ 3).

3. London: The strike at Wembley ends; the Exhibition will open on time.→

4. UK: The BBC begins broadcasting for schools.

7. London: The Labour Government suffers its first defeat, on the Rent Restrictions Bill.

7. Japan: A broadcast from Newark, New Jersey is heard a record 9,000 miles away in Tokyo.

9. Paris: The Dawes Commission passes its findings on reparations to the relevant countries (→ 15).

12. Washington: Congress approves a bill to restrict Japanese immigration.

13. Washington: President Coolidge wins the Republican presidential nomination.

15. Paris: France and the UK accept the Dawes plan for German reparation payments.→

18. Greece: Referendum results show a majority of 433,420 in favour of abolishing the monarchy.

21. UK: Ramsay MacDonald tells the York Labour Party conference "it is easier to make a revolution than a cabinet".

23. France: The franc stabilises; £1 is worth 65 francs.

24. London: The government recognises the Greek Republic.

24. UK: The Harwich to Zeebrugge boat train is inaugurated.

26. Wembley: Newcastle United beat Aston Villa 2-0 in the FA Cup Final.

29. London: Labour's first budget cuts fourpence off a pound of tea and a penny-halfpenny off a pound of sugar.

30. UK: An air service between Liverpool and Belfast is inaugurated.

BIRTH

3. US actor Marlon Brando.

Hitler's sentence is "slap on the wrist"

Nazi leader Hitler behind bars.

April 1. A Munich court, packed with noisy sympathisers, cheered the derisory sentence passed on Adolf Hitler, the Nazi leader who gained notoriety for his abortive beer hall putsch last November. He was given five years in prison for high treason, but told he could be paroled in six months.

The sentence is seen as a timid slap on the wrist, administered, fittingly, on April Fools' Day, by judges who betrayed their sympathies by allowing Hitler to do pretty much as he wished, interrupting witnesses and making speeches about Wagner and Karl Marx. Hitler's co-conspirator, Erich von Ludendorff, was acquitted.

US movie moguls in major merger

April 16. MG joined with M today to form a new giant American film company with a roaring lion as its trademark. Initially known as the Metro-Goldwyn Corporation, the new company is an amalgamation of Metro Pictures, Goldwyn Pictures and the Louis B. Mayer Company, worth a total of $65 million on Wall Street. It brings together two large chains of American cinemas and will use the 40-acre Goldwyn Studios in California as its production centre. ▷

Italians give Mussolini vote of confidence

Fascists salute Benito Mussolini, their victorious leader.

April 17. Mussolini's Fascists have scored a sweeping victory in the Italian general election. An early assessment of the results shows that they have won nearly 400 out of 535 seats in the new Chamber. Among them are some Liberals, who do not approve of Il Duce's policies, but believe he provides the last defence against Communism.

The Fascists can thank their efficient organisation for much of the success. They established headquarters in every one of Italy's 8,000 towns and communes. Accusations are being made of intimidation by the Fascist "squadristi" and fraud at the ballot box.

However, one description of a polling station speaks of the voting being conducted in such silence even "the buzz of a mosquito might be heard". For Italy, supposedly the country of easy excitability, it was a day of quiet – another of the "Mussolini miracles".

The results reflect not only the Fascist efficiency but also Il Duce's personal prestige in a nation determined to end the factionalism which has done so much harm to the country since the war.

Germans agrees to US reparation plan

April 16. Germany has agreed to the latest plan for paying reparations to the Allies, drawn up by the American banker, Charles Dawes. Germany is to get a £45 million loan in order to stabilise the economy; the Reichsbank is to be reorganised to control inflation; all reparations payments are to be secured by a lien on Germany's internal taxes, the railways and industries. Dawes says that Germany must be allowed to earn an export surplus in order for her to be able to pay her debts in the long run.

25,000 Indians die as plague spreads

April 6. The plague, which has so far claimed 25,000 victims, is spreading throughout the Punjab where over 9,000 people have died in a week. The courts have been closed and houses deserted as those who are able to flee the ravages of the disease do so. An emergency grant of 50,000 rupees has been placed at the disposal of the Director of Public Health. Disinfection and inoculation programmes are under way, and more than 9,000 rats have been killed.

King opens Imperial exhibition by sending telegram to himself

April 23. The King sent a telegram to himself today – routed from London to London via the British Empire. The electric message passed through Canada, New Zealand, Australia, South Africa, India, Aden, Egypt and Gibraltar, taking an incredible one minute and 20 seconds to go round the world before being returned to the King "in good order" by a young telegram boy, Henry Annals, in front of 50,000 people in Wembley Stadium.

Over six million wireless owners all over the country joined the crowds in the Stadium to hear the King open the Exhibition. The British Broadcasting Company at Savoy Hill reported that radio reception had been "excellent" throughout the nation – even as far away as John O'Groats.

Queen Mary visits the Burma Pavilion at the British Empire Exhibition.

1924

MAY

Su	Mo	Tu	We	Th	Fr	Sa
				1	2	3
4	5	6	7	8	9	10
11	12	13	14	15	16	17
18	19	20	21	22	23	24
25	26	27	28	29	30	31

4. France: Etienne Oehmichen makes the first 1km circuit in a helicopter at Valentigney.

4. London: Sir Edward Elgar is appointed Master of the King's Musick.

5. Germany: Conservatives make big gains in the general election, but the Socialists remain the largest party (→26).

6. Belfast: The Northern Irish government refuses to join a boundary commission with the Free State.

8. Baltic: The League grants the port of Memel to Lithuania.

9. US: The Young Women's Christian Association says working women should dress strikingly to succeed.

11. France: Premier Poincare is beaten in elections that give the left control of the Chamber of Deputies (→1/6).

14. London: The Lords discusses the introduction of driving tests to curb the rise in the number of road accidents.

21. Chicago: Two wealthy 19-year-olds kidnap 14-year-old Bobby Franks.→

22. London: The Master Builders Association offers to build 50,000 houses at 9c 650 each.

22. London: The Lords discuss a proposal to build a bridge across the Thames by St. Paul's Cathedral (→14/8).

26. London: The Italian King and Queen arrive on a visit; black-shirted Fascists are among well-wishers.

26. Berlin: Wilhelm Marx resigns as Chancellor amid conservative opposition to the Dawes plan (→4/6).

30. Rome: Socialist deputy Giacomo Matteotti denounces the Fascists for election rigging (→10/6).

30. S. Rhodesia: Assembly meets for first time as country becomes self-governing colony.

DEATH

4. British children's story writer Edith Nesbit (*19/8/1858).

The "sick" rich kids who killed for thrills

Richard Loeb and Nathan Leopold: students who confessed to murder.

May 31. Two bored 19-year-old sons of Chicago millionaires have confessed to strangling a neighbour to show their own "intellectual superiority". Nathan Leopold and Richard Loeb, both successful students at the University of Michigan, kidnapped and killed 14-year-old Bobby Franks ten days ago, and then demanded $2,000 ransom from his parents. The egotistic pair told police they had wanted to "murder someone" for a long time to see how a victim reacted and thought they were too clever to be caught by detectives with "inferior minds". Their horrified parents said the sick duo murdered for "thrills," and will plead not guilty due to emotional illness.

Stalin emerges as Russian strongman

May 25. Joseph Stalin is emerging as the Soviet Union's strongman following the death in January of Vladimir Lenin. The short, pockmarked Georgian general secretary has achieved several tactical successes at the current Communist party congress, including preventing a debate on Lenin's posthumous "testament" known to be sharply critical of Stalin's character.

Stalin has banded with Grigori Zinoviev and Leon Kamenev, two magnetic revolutionaries, to oppose a third, Leon Trotsky, who has refrained from attacking him. Stalin's opponents give every sign of underrating him.

Death-ray inventor spurns UK funding

May 27. A British inventor has spurned a Government offer of £1,000 – as a down payment – if he can prove the effectiveness of his so-called "death-ray".

H. Grindell-Matthews claims that his secret beam, which allegedly carries electricity along wireless waves, can stop a motorcycle engine at 15 yards and could destroy aircraft. He has refused an impartial examination by the Air Ministry and taken his invention to France.

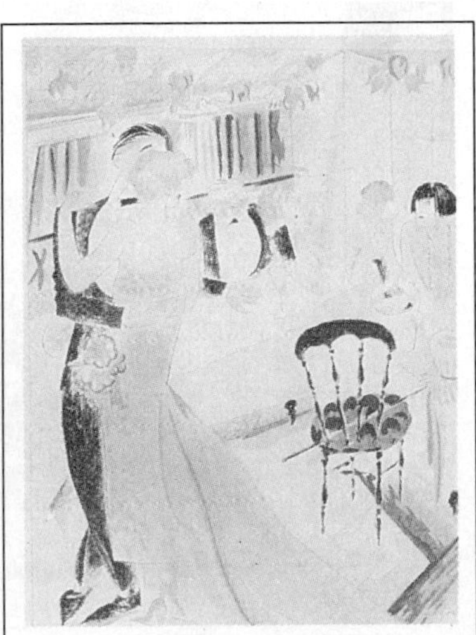

Nightclubbing is all the rage.

1924

JUNE

Su	Mo	Tu	We	Th	Fr	Sa
1	2	3	4	5	6	7
8	9	10	11	12	13	14
15	16	17	18	19	20	21
22	23	24	25	26	27	28
29	30					

1. Vienna: The Austrian Chancellor, Ignaz Seipel, is wounded in an assassination attempt by a Socialist.

1. Paris: Premier Poincare resigns; the left calls for the resignation of President Millerand (→ 10).

4. UK: Lord Derby's Sansovino wins the Derby at Epsom.

4. Berlin: Marx forms a new government and urges the Reichstag to approve the Dawes Plan (→ 6).

6. Berlin: The Reichstag votes 247 to 183 in favour of the Dawes Plan.

8. US: 10,000 American Indians gather at Sand Springs, Oklahoma, to discuss problems for Indians in the modern US.

10. Paris: President Alexandre Millerand resigns (→ 14).

13. London: Week-old London Tube strike collapses.

14. Paris: New President Gaston Doumergue asks Edouard Herriot to form a ministry.

17. S. Africa: General Jan Smuts loses his seat as nationalists win the general election.

19. Finland: Paavo Nurmi sets a new 1,500 metres world record of 3 minutes 52.6 seconds.

23. Wimbledon: The tennis tournament opens with, for the first time, a simple seeding system for competitors (→ 5/7).

26. Detroit: German Hugo Junkers and Henry Ford meet to discuss the building of all-metal aeroplanes.

28. US: 300 are reported dead after a tornado swept through Colorado.

29. London: The Prince of Wales announces he will start looking for a bride.

30. Washington: President Coolidge tells an annual budget meeting that taxes and expenditure should be cut.

DEATH

3. Czech author Franz Kafka (*3/7/1883).

Two climbers die within 1,000 feet of Everest summit

June 19. News finally reached London today of the tragic end to an expedition to conquer Mount Everest. Climbing with oxygen, George Leigh Mallory and Andrew Irvine were said to be less than 1,000 feet from the 29,028ft summit and "going strong" when the bad weather came down and the support team lost sight of them in a swirling snowstorm.

The expedition's photographer, Mr N. E. Odell, whistled and yodelled to locate them, but no trace of the two climbers has been found. Before he left for Nepal earlier in the year, Mallory was asked why he was so desperate to climb the world's highest peak. "Because it's there," he answered.

Pay to dockers on strike is illegal

June 5. The Government has won a legal battle with Poplar Council over the payment of outdoor relief to striking dockers. A number of local firms objected that the men were fit for work so weren't entitled to any money. The defence that the men would have been attacked if they had worked was rejected. "If they had really wanted work they could have obtained it had they shown more determination", said the judge, awarding costs against the Poplar Guardians.

Doumergue is new French President

June 13. Gaston Doumergue was yesterday elected president by France's parliament. He obtained 515 votes against his opponent Paul Painleve's 309.

His predecessor Millerand has been driven from office by the leftist Cartel, helped by radical leader Edouard Herriot's refusal to form a government under him.

The rightist Bloc National is taking comfort from the election of the moderate Doumergue instead of Cartel candidate Painleve. ▷

Fascists murder Socialist opponent

Matteotti (right): feared dead.

June 10. Giacomo Matteotti, one of the most respected of the Italian Socialist leaders, was abducted in broad daylight today by a gang of Fascists on a Rome street. He has not been seen since and it is feared that he has been murdered.

Ten days ago Signor Matteotti, a Deputy, made a forceful speech in the Chamber, denouncing the Fascists and the atmosphere of terror in which the elections were held. He gave details of the intimidation and fraud the Fascists used to obtain their huge majority and demanded that the elections be declared void. He ended his speech prophetically: "And now get ready for my funeral" (→ 5/1/25).

Wireless beams up to go down under

June 2. England spoke to Australia last night – by wireless. It is the first time a wireless conversation (as opposed to telegraphy) has been held between the two countries, or over so great a distance.

The wireless pioneer Guglielmo Marconi commented: "I am satisfied that it will be easy to conduct conversations in a practical way. There will be no distance in future over which we can't telephone."

The transmissions, by the Amalgamated Wireless Company, were between Poldhu in Cornwall and Vaucluse, Sydney.

1924

JULY

Su	Mo	Tu	We	Th	Fr	Sa
		1	2	3	4	5
6	7	8	9	10	11	12
13	14	15	16	17	18	19
20	21	22	23	24	25	26
27	28	29	30	31		

1. London: Police warn cyclists to avoid roads heavily used by cars, following a steep rise in fatal accidents.

2. London: The Government rejects the idea of a Channel Tunnel.

5. Paris: The Olympic Games open with 42 nations taking part, but not Germany.→

5. Wimbledon: Kathleen McKane beats Helen Wills for the Ladies' Singles title; Jean Borotra is the first French Men's Singles champion, beating Rene Lacoste.

6. Brazil: Government opponents take Sao Paulo; 250 are killed.

7. Washington: President Coolidge's 16-year-old son dies of blood poisoning.

7. Paris: The Prince of Wales unveils a memorial to British war dead in Notre Dame cathedral.

9. New York: The Democrats nominate John Davis for President and Charles Bryan for vice-president.

12. Cairo: Egyptian premier Zaghlol Pasha escapes an assassination attempt by a student.

15. Dublin: The Irish Free State releases Eamon de Valera and other political prisoners.

16. London: A ten-nation conference on the Dawes proposals begins (→ 2/8).

20. US: The National Council of Catholic Women starts a campaign for modesty in women's dress.

25. Athens: The Greek government says it is ordering the expulsion of 50,000 Armenians from Greece.

27. USSR: A severe sugar shortage threatens as it is learnt that the country's beet crop has failed.

28. India: Many deaths are reported in flooding in the south of the country which has destroyed many villages.

DEATH

27. Italian composer Ferruccio Busoni (*1/4/1866).

Liddell and Abrahams lead UK gold rush

The Dashing Scot, Eric Liddell.

The Flying Finn, Paavo Nurmi.

July 30. The eighth Olympic Games, held for the second time in their history in Paris, were memorable for the uncompromising weather – the temperature for the 10km cross-country was more than 40 degrees, and half the field failed to finish – for the British sprinters, for the incredible Flying Finn Paavo Nurmi, and for Johnny Weissmuller's three gold medals in the swimming pool.

On the track Britain's best fancied sprinter, the Scottish Rugby international Eric Liddell, forsook the 100 metres to avoid competing in heats on a Sunday, switched to the 400 metres, and with his all-out, arm-flailing attack at the finish, set a new record.

Harold Abrahams, a Cambridge law student, triumphed against all odds in the 100 metres. He broke America's domination of the event by beating both the world record holder, Charley Paddock, and the highly favoured American, Jackson Scholz, to become the first European to win the Olympic title.

For Nurmi it was gold all the way – five victories in all: the sweltering cross-country (by nearly a minute and a half); two team races; and, most astonishing of all, the finals of the 5,000 metres and the 1,500 metres, both in record time, within the space of an hour and forty minutes.

You're not properly dressed at the seaside without a matching hat.

1924 Paris

Men Athletics

100m
1. Harold Abrahams GBR ** 10.6
2. Jackson Scholz USA 10.7
3. Arthur Poritt NZE 10.8

200m
1. Jackson Scholz USA 21.6
2. Charles Paddock USA 21.7
3. Eric Liddell GBR 21.9

400m
1. Eric Liddell GBR *47.6
2. Horatio Fitch USA 48.4
3. Guy Butler GBR 48.6

800m
1. Douglas Lowe GBR 1:52.4
2. Paul Martin SUI 1:52.6
3. Schuyler Enck USA 1:53.0

1500m
1. Paavo Nurmi FIN *3:53.6
2. Willy Schärer SUI 3:55.0
3. Henry Stallard GBR 3:55.6

5000m
1. Paavo Nurmi FIN *14:31.2
2. Ville Ritola FIN 14:31.4
3. Edvin Wide SWE 15:01.8

10,000m
1. Ville Ritola FIN ** 30:23.2
2. Edvin Wide SWE 30:55.2
3. Eero Berg FIN 31:43.0

Marathon
1. Albin Stenroos FIN 2:41:22.6
2. Romeo Bertini ITA 2:47:19.6
3. Clarence Demar USA 2:48:14.0

110m Hurdles
1. Daniel Kinsey USA 15.0
2. Sydney Atkinson SAF 15.0
3. Sten Pettersson SWE 15.4

400m Hurdles
1. F. Morgan Taylor USA + 52.6
2. Erik Vilén FIN *53.8
3. Ivan Riley USA 54.2

3000m Steeplechase
1. Ville Ritola FIN *9:33.6
2. Elias Katz FIN 9:44.0
3. Paul Bontemps FRA 9.45.2

4x100m relay
1. USA *41.0 (Francis Hussey, Louis Clarke, Loren Murchison, Alfred Leconey)
2. GBR 41.2 (Harold Abrahams, Walter Rangeley, Lancelot Royle, William Nichol)
3. NETH 41.8 (Jacob Boot, Henricus Broos, Jan de Vries, Marinus van den Berge)

4x400m relay
1. USA *3:16.0 (Con Cochrane, Alan Helffrich, Olivier MacDonald, William Stevenson)
2. SWE 3:17.0 (Artur Svensson, Erik Byléhn, Gustaf Wejnarth, Nils Engdahl)
3. GBR 3:17.4 (Edward Toms, George Renwick, Richard Ripley, Guy Butler)

High Jump
1. Harold Osborn USA *1.98
2. Leroy Brown USA 1.95
3. Pierre Lewden FRA 1.92

Pole Vault
1. Lee Barnes USA 3.95
2. Glenn Graham USA 3.95
3. James Brooker USA 3.90

Long Jump
1. William De Hart Hubbard USA 7.445
2. Edward Gourdin USA 7.275
3. Sverre Hansen NOR 7.26

Triple Jump
1. Anthony Winter AUS ** 15.525
2. Luis Brunotto ARG 15.425
3. Vilho Tuulos FIN 15.37

Shotput
1. Clarence Houser USA 14.995
2. Glenn Hartranft USA 14.895
3. Ralph Hills USA 14.64

Discus
1. Clarence Houser USA *46.155
2. Vilho Nittymaa FIN 44.95
3. Thomas Lieb USA 44.83

Hammer
1. Frederick Tootell USA 53.295
2. Matthew McGrath USA 50.84
3. Malcolm Nokes GBR 48.875

Javelin
1. Jonni Myyra FIN 62.96
2. Gunna Lindstrom SWE 60.92
3. Eugene Oberst USA 58.35

Decathlon
1. Harold Osborn USA ** 7710.775
2. Emerson Norton USA 7350.895
3. Aleksander Klumberg EST 7329.360

3000m Team
1. Finland
2. Great Britain
3. USA

Cross Country Individual
1. Paavo Nurmi FIN 32:54.8
2. Ville Ritola FIN 34:19.4
3. Earl Johnson USA 35:21.0

Cross Country Team
1. Finland
2. USA
3. France

Pentathlon
1. Eero Lehtonen FIN
2. Elemér Somfay HUN
3. Robert Legendre USA

10,000m Walk
1. Ugo Frigerio ITA 47:49.0
2. George Goodwin GBR 48:37.9
3. Cecil Charles McMaster SAF 49:08.0

Men Swimming

100m Freestyle
1. Johnny Weissmuller USA *59.0
2. Duke Paoa Kahanamoku USA 1:01.4
3. Samuel Kahanamoku USA 1:01.8

400m Freestyle
1. Johnny Weissmuller USA *5:04.2
2. Arne Borg SWE 5:05.6
3. Andrew Charlton AUS 5:06.6

1500m Freestyle
1. Andrew Charlton AUS ** 20:06.6
2. Arne Borg SWE 20:41.4
3. Frank Beaurepaire AUS 21:48.4

100m Backstroke
1. Warren Paoa Keoloha USA *1:13.2
2. Paul Wyatt USA 1:15.4
3. Károly Bartha HUN 1:17.8

200m Breaststroke
1. Robert Skelton USA 2:56.6
2. Joseph de Combe BEL 2:59.2
3. William Kirschbaum USA 3:01.0

4x200m Freestyle Relay
1. USA ** 9:53.4 (Wallace O'Connor, Harry Glancy, Ralph Breyer, Johnny Weissmuller)
2. AUS 10:02.2 (Maurice Christie, Ernest Henry, Frank Beaurepaire, Andrew Charlton)
3. SWE 10:06.8 (Georg Werner, Orvar Trolle, Ake Borg, Arne Borg)

Springboard Diving
1. Albert White USA 696.4
2. Peter Desjardins USA 693.2
3. Clarence Pinkston USA 653.0

High Diving
1. Albert White USA 97.46
2. David Fall USA 97.30
3. Clarence Pinkston USA 94.60

Plain High Diving
1. Richmond Eve AUS 160.0
2. John Jansson SWE 157.0
3. Harold Clarke GBR 158.0

Water Polo

1. France
2. Belgium
3. USA

Women Swimming

100m Freestyle
1. Ethel Lackie USA 1:12.4
2. Mariechen Wehselau USA 1:12.8
3. Gertrude Ederle USA 1:14.2

400m Freestyle
1. Martha Norelius USA *6:02.2
2. Helen Wainwright USA 6:03.8
3. Gertrude Ederle USA 6:04.8

200m Breaststroke
1. Lucy Morton GBR *3:32.2
2. Agnes Geraghty USA 3:34.0
3. Gladys Helen Carson GBR 3:35.4

100m Backstroke
1. Sybil Bauer USA *1:23.2
2. Phyllis Harding GBR 1:27.4
3. Aileen Riggin USA 1:28.2

4x100m Freestyle Relay
1. USA ** 4:58.8 (Gertrude Ederle, Euphrasia Donnelly, Ethel Lackie, Mariechen Wehselau)
2. GBR 5:17.0 (Florence Barker, Grace McKenzie, Irene Vera Tannor, Constance Mabel Jeans)
3. SWE 5:35.6 (Aina Berg, Wivan Pettersson, Gulli Everlund, Hjördis Topel)

Springboard Diving
1. Elizabeth Becker USA 474.5
2. Aileen Riggin USA 460.4
3. Caroline Fletcher USA 436.4

High Diving
1. Caroline Smith USA 33.2
2. Elizabeth Becker USA 33.4
3. Hjordis Topel SWE 32.8

Boxing

Flyweight
1. Fidel Labarba USA
2. James McKenzie GBR
3. Raymond Fee USA

Bantamweight
1. William Smith SAF
2. Salvatore Tripoli USA
3. Jean Ces FRA

Featherweight
1. John Fields USA
2. Joseph Salas USA
3. Pedro Quartucci ARG

Lightweight
1. Hans Nielsen DEN
2. Alfredo Copello ARG
3. Frederick Boylstein USA

Welterweight
1. Jean Delage BEL
2. Héctor Méndez ARG
3. Douglas Lewis CAN

Middleweight
1. Harry Mallin GBR
2. John Elliott GBR
2. Joseph Beecken BEL

Light Heavyweight
1. Harry Mitchell GBR
2. Thyge Petersen DEN
3. Sverre Sörsdal NOR

Heavyweight
1. Otto von Porat NOR
2. Sören Petersen DEN
3. Alfredo Porzio ARG

Greco Roman Wrestling

Bantamweight
1. Eduard Pütsep EST
2. Anselm Ahlfors FIN
3. Vänö Ikonen FIN

Featherweight
1. Kalle Anttila FIN
2. Aleksanteri Toivola FIN
3. Erik Malmberg SWE

Lightweight
1. Oskar Friman FIN
2. Lajos Keresztes HUN
3. Kalle Westerlund FIN

Middleweight
1. Edvard Vesterlund FIN
2. Artur Lindfors FIN
3. Roman Steinberg EST

Light Heavyweight
1. Carl Westergren SWE
2. Rudolf Svensson SWE
3. Onni Pellinen FIN

Heavyweight
1. Henri Deglane FRA
2. Edil Rosenqvist FIN
3. Rajmund Baló HUN

Freestyle Wrestling

Bantamweight
1. Kustaa Pihlajamäki FIN
2. Kaarlo Mäkinen FIN
3. Bryant Hines USA

Featherweight
1. Robin Reed USA
2. Chester Newton USA
3. Katsutoshi Naito JAP

Lightweight
1. Russell Vis USA
2. Volmari Vikstrom FIN
3. Arvo Haavisto FIN

Welterweight
1. Hermann Gehri SUI
2. Eino Leino FIN
3. Otto Müller SUI

Middleweight
1. Fritz Hagmann SUI
2. Pierre Ollivier BEL
3. Viho Pekkala FIN

Light Heavyweight
1. John Spellman USA
2. Rudolf Svensson SWE
3. Charles Courant SUI

Heavyweight
1. Harry Steel USA
2. Henri Wernli SUI
3. Andrew McDonald GBR

Men Fencing

Foil Individual
1. Roger Ducret FRA 6
2. Philippe Cattiau FRA 5
3. Maurice van Damme BEL 4

Foil Team
1. France
2. Belgium
3. Hungary

Epée Individual
1. Charles Delporte BEL 8
2. Roger Ducret FRA 7
3. Nils Hellsten SWE 7

Epée Team
1. France
2. Belgium
3. Italy

Sabre Individual
1. Dr. Sándor Posta HUN 5
2. Roger Ducret FRA 5
3. János Garay HUN 5

Sabre Team
1. Italy
2. Hungary
3. Netherlands

Women Fencing

Foil Individual
1. Ellen Osiier DEN 5
2. Gladys Muriel Davis GBR 4
3. Grete Heckscher DEN 3

Modern Pentathlon Individual

1. Bo Lindman SWE
2. Gustaf Dyrssen SWE
3. Bertil Uggla SWE

Rowing

Single Sculls
1. Jack Beresford jun. GBR 7:49.2
2. W. Garrett Gilmore USA 7:54.0
3. Josef Schneider SUI 8:01.0

Double Sculls
1. USA 6:34.0
2. France 6:38.0
3. Switzerland 3 lengths

Coxless Pairs
1. Netherlands 8:19.1
2. France 8:21.6

Coxed Pairs
1. Switzerland 8:39.0
2. Italy 8:39.1
3. USA 3 lengths

Coxless Fours
1. Great Britain 7:08.6
2. Canada 7:18.0
3. Switzerland 2 lengths

Coxed Fours
1. Switzerland 7:18.4
2. France 7:21.6
3. USA 7:23.0

Eights
1. USA 6:33.4
2. Canada 6:49.0
3. Italy

Yachting

Finn
1. Léon Huybrechts BEL 2
2. Henrik Robert NOR 7
3. Hans Dittmar FIN 8

6m Class
1. Norway 2
2. Denmark 5
3. Netherlands 5

8m Class
1. Norway 2
2. Great Britain 5
3. France 5

Cycling

Road Race Individual
1. Armand Blanchonnet FRA 6:20:48.0
2. Henri Hoevenaers BEL 6:30:27.0
3. René Hamel FRA 6:30:51.6

Team Time Trial
1. France 19:30:14.0
2. Belgium 19:46:55.4
3. Sweden 19:59:41.6

1000m
1. Lucien Michard FRA 12.8 (last 200 m)
2. Jacob Meijer NETH
3. Jean Cugnot FRA

2000m Tandem
1. France 12.6 (last 200 m)
2. Denmark
3. Netherlands

Team Pursuit Race (4000m)
1. Italy 5:15.0
2. Poland
3. Belgium

50km track
1. Jacobus Willems NETH 1:18:24.0
2. Cyril Alden GBR one wheel
3. Frank H. Wyld GBR lm

Equestrian Sports

3 Day Event Individual
1. Adolf van der Voort van Zijp NETH
2. Frode Kirkebjerg DEN
3. Sloan Doak USA

3 Day Event Team
1. Netherlands
2. Sweden
3. Italy

Dressage Individual
1. Ernst Linder SWE
2. Bertil Sandström SWE
3. Xavier Lesage FRA

Grand Prix Jumping Individual
1. Alphonse Gemuseus SUI -6
2. Tommaso Lequio ITA -8.75
3. Adam Królikiewicz POL -10

Grand Prix Jumping Team
1. Sweden -42.25
2. Switzerland -50.0
3. Portugal -53.0

Men Gymnastics

All-around Individual Competition
1. Léon Stukelj YUG 110.340
2. Robert Prazak TCH 110.323
3. Bedrich Supcik TCH 106.930

Team Combined Exercises
1. Italy 839.058
2. France 820.528
3. Switzerland 816.661

Parallel Bars
1. August Güttinger SUI 21.63
2. Robert Prazak TCH 21.61
3. Giorgio Zampori ITA 21.45

Horse Vault
1. Frank Kriz USA 9.98
2. Jan Koutny TCH 9.97
3. Bohumil Morkovsky TCH 9.93

Sidehorse
1. Josef Wilhelm SUI 21.23
2. Jean Gutweniger SUI 21.13
3. Antoine Rebetez SUI 20.73

Sidehorse Vault
1. Albert Séguin FRA 10.00
2. Jean Gounot FRA 9.93
2. François Gangloff FRA 9.93

Horizontal Bar
1. Léon Stukelj YUG 19.730
2. Jean Gutweniger SUI 19.236
3. André Higelin FRA 19.163

Flying Rings
1. Franco Martino ITA 21.553
2. Robert Prazak TCH 21.483
3. Ladislav Vácha TCH 21.430

Rope Climbing
1. Bedrich Supcik TCH 7.2
2. Albert Séguin FRA 7.4
3. August Güttinger SUI 7.8
3. Ladislav Vácha TCH 7.8

Football

1. Uruguay
2. Switzerland
3. Sweden

Shooting

Rapid Fire Pistol
1. Henry Bailey USA 18
2. Wilhelm Carlberg SWE 18
3. Lennart Hannelius FIN 18

Small Bore Rifle
1. Pierre Coquelin de Lisle FRA 398
2. Marcus Dinwiddie USA 396
3. Josias Hartmann SUI 394

Free Rifle Team
1. Switzerland 4617
2. Norway 4534
3. France 4511

Free Rifle 3 Positions
1. Morris Fisher USA 95
2. Carl Osburn USA 95
3. Niels Larsen DEN 93

Running Deer Shooting, single shot
1. John Boles USA 40
2. Cyril Mackworth-Praed GBR 39
3. Otto Olsen NOR 39

Running Deer Shooting, single shot, team
1. Norway 160
2. Sweden 154
3. USA 148

Running Deer Shooting, double shot
1. Ole Andreas Lilloe-Olsen NOR 76
2. Cyril Mackworth-Praed GBR 72
3. Alfred Swahn SWE 72

Running Deer Shooting, double shot, team
1. Great Britain 263
2. Norway 262
3. Sweden 250

Clay Pigeon Shooting, team
1. USA 363
2. Canada 300
3. Finland 360

Shooting – mixed

Clay Pigeon Shooting
1. Gyula Halasy *HUN
2. Konrad Huber *FIN
3. Frank Hughes USA

Tennis

Men – singles
1. Vincent Richards USA
2. Henri Cochet FRA
3. Umberto Luigi de Morpurgo ITA

Men – doubles
1. USA
2. France
3. France

Women – singles
1. Helen Wills USA
2. Julie Vlasto FRA
3. Kathleen McKane GBR

Women – doubles
1. USA
2. France/Ireland
3. Bohemia/Great Britain

Mixed Doubles
1. USA
2. USA
3. Netherlands

Polo

1. Argentina
2. USA
3. Great Britain

Rugby

1. USA
2. France
3. Romania

Weightlifting

Featherweight
1. Pierino Gabetti ITA 402.5
2. Andreas Stadler AUT 385.0
2. Arthur Reimann SUI 382.5

Lightweight
1. Edmond Décottignies FRA 440.0
2. Anton Swerina AUT 427.5
3. Bohumil Durdis TCH 425.0

Middleweight
1. Carlo Galimberti ITA 492.5
2. Alfred Neuland EST 455.0
3. Jean Kikkas EST 450.0

Light Heavyweight
1. Charles Rigoulot FRA 502.5
2. Fritz Hünenberger SWE 490.0
3. Leopold Friedrich AUT 490.0

Heavyweight
1. Giuseppe Tonani ITA 517.5
2. Franz Aigner AUT 515.0
3. Harold Tammer EST 497.5

(Key to symbols and abbreviations p. 1456)

1924

AUGUST

Su	Mo	Tu	We	Th	Fr	Sa
					1	2
3	4	5	6	7	8	9
10	11	12	13	14	15	16
17	18	19	20	21	22	23
24	25	26	27	28	29	30
31						

2. London: The Allies agree to the Dawes Plan for German reparations and urge Germany to endorse it.→

2. London: The Prince of Wales attends a huge Boy Scouts jamboree at Wembley Stadium.

6. London: The Labour government concludes a trade agreement with the USSR.

10. Berlin: The black, red and yellow "Union banner" first appears at a celebration of the German constitution.

13. China: As many as 50,000 are feared dead and two million homeless after severe floods.

14. Paris: Scientists claim that clouds around Mars prove it has the same atmosphere as Earth.

14. London: The Royal Fine Arts Commission warns that a new St. Paul's bridge could damage the Cathedral.

17. Germany: French and Belgian troops have evacuated the towns of Offenburg and Appenweier (→ 29).

20. London: Agreement is reached to allow 3,000 UK families emigrate to Canada and live on farms.

21. Pacific: Scientists believe they have uncovered remains of an ancient civilisation in the Galapagos Islands.

25. London: The government begins to look at the possibility of generating electricity from the tides of the River Severn.

26. Montreal: Henry Ford defends the Ku Klux Klan as a body of patriots (→ 30).

29. Berlin: The Reichstag gives its overwhelming approval to the Dawes Plan.→

30. US: Six die in clashes with the Ku Klux Klan at Herrin, Illinois.

BIRTH

12. Pakistani soldier and politician Zia ul-Haq (†17/8/88).

DEATH

3. Polish-born British author Joseph Conrad (*3/12/1857).

New mark to end German currency crisis

Aug 8. Following the $200-million Dawes Loan to Germany earlier this year and the restructuring of German reparations payments to the Allies, the Berlin authorities have taken further steps to boost confidence in the German financial system.

The Reichsbank has been made constitutionally independent of the government, thus allaying fears that political pressure might be put on the central bank to print huge volumes of paper money as was the case during the three years before last summer's complete inflationary collapse. To symbolise the restoring of financial stability, the old mark has been replaced by the new Reichsmark.

Against a new inflation.

New record set for Atlantic crossing

Aug 25. The "Mauretania" has set a new record for crossing the Atlantic at the ripe old age of 17 years. The Cunard liner completed the official 3,198 miles crossing in five days one hour and 35 minutes at an average speed of about 30 miles an hour, beating her previous record made 14 years ago before her conversion to oil fired boilers. So confident was her master in her performance that his estimate of arrival time in Cherbourg was only three minutes out.

Germany accepts deal on war debts

Aug 15. The protocol on Germany's war debts and related problems, worked out at the London conference earlier this month, is due to be signed tomorrow by Germany and the Allies. The French and Belgians responded to Germany's acceptance of the Dawes Plan for resuming reparations payments by giving an undertaking to begin evacuating their troops from some Ruhr towns at once and to complete the operation within a year (→ 17).

The Prince of Wales inspects Scouts at Wembley with Baden-Powell.

1924

SEPTEMBER

Su	Mo	Tu	We	Th	Fr	Sa
	1	2	3	4	5	6
7	8	9	10	11	12	13
14	15	16	17	18	19	20
21	22	23	24	25	26	27
28	29	30				

1. West Indies: A hurricane ravages the Virgin Islands, leaving 80 people feared dead.

1. Berlin: Germany makes its first reparations payment under the Dawes Plan of 20 million marks (→ 7).

2. Moscow: Reports say a bomb has been found in Lenin's tomb.

3. USSR: A revolt breaks out in the southern soviet republic of Georgia (→ 16).

5. UK: The TUC Conference at Hull votes to take industrial action to prevent war if necessary.

7. Germany: 180,000 people who had been expelled from the Ruhr are allowed to return.

8. China: 360 British troops land in Shanghai as civil war rages (→ 13/10).

11. Berlin: The government rejects a claim by the former Kaiser's family to estates worth £300,000.

12. Rome: Fascist deputy Armando Casalini is shot dead on a tram by a communist.

16. USSR: After much alleged brutality the government quells a revolt in Georgia (→ 2/10).

20. Egypt: Excavations uncover the earliest surviving stone buildings on earth.

22. Geneva: The League of Nations receives the draft of a protocol aimed at outlawing war (→ 1/10).

23. Berlin: The government decides to seek entry to the League of Nations.

28. US: Three US Army aeroplanes land in Seattle, Washington, after a 27,000-mile round-the-world flight.

28. India: Gandhi says his fast will only be broken by his death if Hindu-Moslem riots do not cease.

BIRTHS

16. US actress Lauren Bacall.

28. Italian actor Marcello Mastroianni.

30. US author Truman Capote (†25/8/84).

1924

OCTOBER

Su	Mo	Tu	We	Th	Fr	Sa
			1	2	3	4
5	6	7	8	9	10	11
12	13	14	15	16	17	18
19	20	21	22	23	24	25
26	27	28	29	30	31	

2. Geneva: 47 League members sign the compulsory arbitration protocol.

2. USSR: Leon Trotsky arrives to command the Red Army in Georgia as renewed fighting breaks out.

4. Milan: Mussolini says the Fascist Party is "above Parliament".

7. UK: Labour bars communists from joining the party and rejects a Communist Party move to affiliate.

10. USSR: Seven million people are reported suffering from famine after the failure of this year's harvest.

13. Arabia: Wahabi forces under Ibn Saud enter Mecca (→20).

17. London: Everest mountaineers say Mallory and Irving probably reached the summit before their deaths.

20. Arabia: Ibn Saud pledges to protect all persons, property and holy places.

21. Istanbul: 3,500 arrests are made as the Turks begin the expulsion of Greeks.

22. London: The Ministry of Health bans preservatives in cream, butter, margarine and other foodstuffs.

24. London: The Foreign Office publishes "Zinoviev Letter", allegedly from Moscow, urging UK revolution (→26).

26. Moscow: The Soviet government denounces the Zinoviev Letter as a hoax.→

28. Paris: France recognises the USSR.

31. London: A cabinet committee is appointed to investigate the authenticity of the Zinoviev Letter (→4/11).

BIRTH

1. US statesman James Earl Carter, President 1976-1980.

DEATHS

12. French author Anatole France (*16/4/1844).

29. British author Frances Hodgson Burnett (*24/11/1849).

Gandhi on hunger strike as penance

Sept 18. Mahatma Gandhi is to fast for twenty-one days in despair at the recent riots between Moslems and Hindus. It will be an expression of his "unbearable hopelessness". "Nothing I say or write", he says, "can bring the two communities together". Even as he spoke there were reports of further riots at Kohat, in which 20 Hindus and 11 Moslems were killed.

Gandhi, speaking in Allahabad, reserved the right to drink water with or without salt. "It is both a penance and a prayer. As it is penance I need not have taken the public into my confidence but I publish it as, let me hope, an effective prayer to Hindus and Moslems, not to commit suicide".

PM claims car runs on biscuit shares

Britain's PM, as others see him.

Sept 12. Ramsay MacDonald confirmed today that on becoming Prime Minister, he reluctantly accepted a Daimler and £30,000 worth of shares in the biscuit firm McVitie and Price. The shares will provide income to run a car for the rest of his life. "I only technically own them," the Premier explained.

The benefactor was "a dear old friend", Sir Alexander Grant, who felt every Prime Minister ought to have a car. Sir Alexander has previously been awarded a baronetcy for public benefactions.

Row over sedition charge topples Labour

Oct 9. The shaky minority Labour Government died tonight when Tories and Liberals combined to carry a vote of censure. Mr MacDonald at once advised the King to order another general election. It will be on October 29 – only 11 months since the last one.

The Prime Minister was at the end of his tether after weeks of fierce "No money for Bolshevik murderers" opposition to government plans for a loan to Russia. But the government has fallen over a more trivial issue – its handling of the Campbell case.

J. R. Campbell, acting editor of the Communist paper, "Worker's Weekly", published an open letter to the Forces: "Don't allow yourselves to be used to break strikes", it said. With the approval of the Attorney-General – new to the Labour Party and to politics – Campbell was charged with incitement to mutiny. There was uproar in the Labour ranks. Campbell had been decorated for wartime bravery in the army.

Then, the Attorney-General changed his mind and dropped the prosecution. Nobody has impugned his professional integrity. It was just a muddle. But the Government was accused of putting improper political pressure on its law officer. That was its death warrant.

Campaigning Tory leader Baldwin.

Chinese leader flees on Japanese steamer

Oct 13. The bitter civil war in China, which has been raging for over three years, seemed to reach a decisive point today with the collapse of the Northern faction's HQ in Shanghai.

Lu Yungh-s'ang, the commander, surrendered this morning and fled with his staff aboard a Japanese steamer. Before leaving he issued a statement blaming his defeat on shortage of ammunition and men. The immediate cause of the surrender was the defection to the enemy of an entire division of Northern troops, leaving the road to Shanghai open and thousands of leaderless troops marauding near the city. British sailors and marines have been put on the alert.

Chekiang troops, whose leader has abandoned the struggle.

Zinoviev Red scare drives voters into Conservative camp

Oct 31. The Tories have romped to a huge General Election triumph – thanks to an eve-of-poll Red bogeyman appearance. They have 419 seats in the new Parliament compared with 258 in the last. Labour is down from 191 to 151 and the Liberals from 159 to a rump of 40. The Liberal leader, Mr Asquith, heads the election casualties.

The Zinoviev Letter is widely thought to have been a major factor in this political earthquake. The letter – allegedly from the Communist International to British Communists – gave instructions for starting a revolution. A copy was mysteriously obtained and published by the Tories just before polling day. Was the letter a forgery? Today the answer is awaited. But the vote-counting is over.

Zinoviev: did he write the letter?

League debates a plan to ban war

Oct 1. A plan to outlaw war by requiring all international disputes to be referred to arbitration was presented to the League of Nations Assembly today. Lord Parmoor, for Britain, said much would depend on the effectiveness of economic sanctions to enforce judgements. If they failed and force had to be used, the League would be limited to making recommendations.

1924

NOVEMBER

Su	Mo	Tu	We	Th	Fr	Sa
						1
2	3	4	5	6	7	8
9	10	11	12	13	14	15
16	17	18	19	20	21	22
23	24	25	26	27	28	29
30						

1. Belfast: Eamon de Valera is sentenced to a month in prison for entering Ulster illegally (→7).

3. Blackpool: 13 people die in a train crash.

4. London: The cabinet committee says it cannot determine whether the Zinoviev Letter is a hoax (→21).

4. US: Texas elects the first woman state governor, "Ma" Miriam Ferguson.

5. Peking: Ex-"Boy Emperor" Pu Yi is expelled from the Imperial Palace and all Manchu titles abolished.

7. Dublin: The Irish government declares an amnesty for all convicted in connection with the Civil War.

11. New York: Prices soar to record highs on Wall Street as 2,258,399 shares are traded.

12. Rome: Mussolini opens Italy's new one-chamber parliament (→13).

13. Rome: Mussolini introduces a bill to let women vote in national elections (→5/12).

19. London: A new cabinet committee set up by the Tory government says the Zinoviev Letter is genuine (→21).

19. Cairo: Sir Lee Stack, Governor-General of the Sudan, is shot dead by Egyptians.→

20. Paris: First performance of the ballet "The Creation of the World" by French composer Darius Milhaud.

21. London: Tory Foreign Secretary Austen Chamberlain repudiates the Anglo-Soviet treaty agreed by previous government.

26. Moscow: A special session of the Communist Party called by Stalin, Zinoviev and Kamenev denounces Trotsky (→16/1/25).

DEATHS

4. French composer Gabriel Faure (*12/5/1845).

29. Italian composer Giacomo Puccini (*22/12/1858).

Churchill back with Tories as Chancellor

Nov 6. Back in the Premiership after a massive Tory victory, Stanley Baldwin took a taxi to Buckingham Palace this evening and talked to the King. He then named Winston Churchill, who was returned this time as a Constitutionalist, Chancellor of the Exchequer.

The appointment is a big surprise because Mr Churchill has no experience in finance. Being now parted from the Liberals, he thought he might get a Government job – but not such a big one. It is expected that he will now start wielding an economy axe with his usual gusto, as it is no secret that he considers the outgoing Labour Government was overspending.

The size of their success at the polls has startled the Tories. The Duke of Sutherland warned the Primrose League today that millions of votes could go back to other parties next time. The Tory motto must be "Coats off and no armchairs". Labour's Ramsay MacDonald said candidly of his short run in office "It was longer than we thought it would be. But make no mistake, we will be back."

Churchill – a surprise Chancellor.

US President returned despite oil scandal

Nov 4. President Calvin Coolidge won a landslide victory in the presidential election today, in spite of the Teapot Dome corruption scandal, which he inherited from the Harding administration.

Republican Coolidge and his Vice-Presidential running mate, Charles G. Dawes, virtually swept the board in the electoral college, winning 382 votes to 136. All the votes won by his opponents, John W. Davis for the Democrats, and the Progressive, Senator Robert M. Lafollette of Wisconsin, came from the South.

Coolidge polled nearly 16 million votes, against eight million for Davis and under five million for Lafollette. The campaign was unusually apathetic, perhaps because the country is prosperous.

UK punishes Egypt for death of Briton

Nov 24. Zaghlol Pasha, the Egyptian Prime Minister, resigned today after refusing demands contained in the stiff British ultimatum, intended to punish Egypt for the assassination in Cairo last week of Major-General Sir Lee Stack, Governor-General of the Sudan.

Escorted by an entire regiment of Lancers, Field Marshal Lord Allenby, the High Commissioner, presented Britain's demands, which required Egypt to apologise, to punish the criminals, pay a fine of £500,000 and remove all Egyptian officers and units from the Sudan. A separate army is to be set up in Khartoum controlled by the Sudan government.

Ex-Egyptian PM Zaghlol Pasha.

1924

DECEMBER

Su	Mo	Tu	We	Th	Fr	Sa
	1	2	3	4	5	6
7	8	9	10	11	12	13
14	15	16	17	18	19	20
21	22	23	24	25	26	27
28	29	30	31			

1. London: The government signs a commerce treaty with Germany.

2. Mexico: It is revealed that Charlie Chaplin has married 16-year-old Lita Grey.

5. Rome: Mussolini introduces a bill enforcing widespread press censorship (→ 3/1/25).

6. London: The London County Council decides central heating is too expensive to instal in council houses.

8. Germany: General election shows deadlock, but Socialists make some gains (→ 11).

10. Stockholm: Nobel Prizes awarded to Karl Siegbahn (Sweden, Physics), Willem Einthoven (Holland, Medicine), and Wladyslaw Reymont (Poland, Literature). No Chemistry or Peace Prize.

11. Berlin: Dr Wilhelm Marx resigns as Chancellor (→ 15/1).

18. Rome: Pope Pius XI denounces the USSR.

22. London: Police sanction trials of covered-top buses.

24. Tirana: Albania is declared a republic.

25. China: 800 soldiers are shot for looting at Kalgan.

29. New York: John D. Rockefeller jr. gives $1,000,000 to the Metropolitan Museum of Art.

BIRTH

2. US politician and soldier General Alexander Haig.

DEATH

24. Russian artist Leon Bakst (*24/4/1866).

HITS OF 1924

All alone.

Fascinating rhythm.

It had to be you.

QUOTE OF THE YEAR

"The paradox of British politics: the moment one appropriates power one becomes impotent."
James Ramsay MacDonald, Britain's first Labour Prime Minister, 1924.

Hitler out on parole with dictated book

Hilter, who has plans to publish.

Dec 20. Paroled after serving just eight months for high treason, Adolf Hitler, leader of the Nazis, an extreme German Nationalist party whose members wear brown shirts, says he plans to publish a book he dictated to a colleague, Rudolf Hess, while in Landsberg fortress.

His gaolers treated him as an honoured guest and gave him a room of his own with a view overlooking the River Lech; visitors flocked to Landsberg to pay him homage and bring him gifts, in spite of the fact that his attempted putsch in a Munich beer hall last year was a complete fiasco.

He wants to call his book "Four and a Half Years of Struggle against Lies, Stupidity and Cowardice". Friends have told him to think of a shorter title.

Christmas tragedy: worst UK air crash

Dec 24. Eight people died today in Britain's worst air crash when an Imperial Airways aircraft plummeted to the ground, seconds after taking off from Croydon aerodrome.

Relatives and friends of the passengers on board the Paris-bound flight had just finished their Christmas greetings and watched the plane leave the runway, when black smoke was spotted coming from its tail. It dived into a housing estate nearby. The UK's previous worst disaster was in 1922 when six died in a mid-air collision.

Arts: voyage from adventure to pessimism

The death of **Joseph Conrad**, who was christened Korzcniowski, removes a major writer who did not begin writing until he was nearly 40, and then in a language foreign to him. After leaving Poland he joined the English merchant navy for several years, gaining a master's certificate and mastery of written English – he never spoke it well.

His early novels were of seafaring and adventure in the Far East, but later pessimism about the anarchy of the world darkened his books. He treats of "the loneliness that surrounds, envelops and clothes every human soul from the cradle to the grave and perhaps beyond".

This year's literary talking point is **E.M. Forster's** new novel, "A Passage to India" – his first for 14 years – which has already sold over 70,000 copies in Britain and America. Argument rages whether it is "fair" to the British Raj or maligns the attitudes which Anglo-Indians adopt to the natives.

After the Amritsar massacre five years ago, opinion in India is very sensitive. Mr Forster points out that his visits to India in 1912 and 1921 (as secretary to a Maharajah) brought him in contact "not only with the gorgeous East but with the real East".

The closing words of Dr Aziz to his English friend Fielding have caused most controversy: "Clear out, you fellows, double quick I say. We may hate one another but we hate you most. If it's fifty or five hundred years we shall get rid of you, yes, we shall drive every blasted Englishman into the sea. And then you and I shall be friends."

Master of the King's Musick.

The most popular living composer, **Giacomo Puccini**, died this month at 65, leaving his long-awaited opera "Turandot" still uncompleted. Puccini's close friend, **Arturo Toscanini**, who conducted his requiem in Milan cathedral, has entrusted **Franco Alfano** with the task of finishing it from his sketches. Three other composers, **Gabriel Faure, Ferrucio Busoni** and **Sir Charles Stanford** also died.

Sir Edward Elgar was made Master of the King's Musick and the King and Queen paid their first visit to a Promenade concert at the Queen's Hall, conducted as always since 1895 by **Sir Henry Wood**.

Indian epic author E.M. Forster.

Bernard Shaw's "Saint Joan".

1925

JANUARY

Su	Mo	Tu	We	Th	Fr	Sa
				1	2	3
4	5	6	7	8	9	10
11	12	13	14	15	16	17
18	19	20	21	22	23	24
25	26	27	28	29	30	31

1. Norway: The capital Christiania is renamed Oslo.

2. Australia: Australia score a record 600 runs in their first innings against England; Jack Hobbs gets his record 2,000th test run in England's first innings.

3. Rome: Mussolini assumes full dictatorial powers (→ 5).

5. Rome: Mussolini forms a new Fascist cabinet.→

7. Germany: Launch of the Emden, the first German warship built since the Great War.

11. Peking: The city is seized by Chi Hsieh-yuan and Sun Chuan-fang.

13. Germany: 25 die and 60 are injured in a train crash in Westphalia.

15. Berlin: Hans Luther, an Independent, becomes Chancellor; nationalists are in the cabinet for the first time.

17. Moscow: Mikhail Frunze succeeds Trotsky as War Commissar.

20. US: Miriam Ferguson is sworn in as Governor of Texas.

23. Chile: The government is overthrown in a military coup d'etat.

24. Washington: President Coolidge says he "wouldn't be seen dead" in the "Oxford Bags" worn by some students.

24. US: 25 million people see a total eclipse of the sun; in the UK it is obscured by cloudy skies.

28. Paris: Film star Gloria Swanson marries the Marquis de la Falaise de la Coudraie.

30. Turkey: The government expels the Greek Orthodox Patriarch of Constantinople, Constantine II, from Istanbul.

30. UK: Distillers Co., Buchanan Dewar and John Walker and Sons agree a merger (→ 30/4).

BIRTHS

14. Japanese author Yukio Mishima (†25/11/1970).

26. US actor Paul Newman.

Trotsky fired from Soviet War Council

Jan 16. Joseph Stalin has moved decisively against Leon Trotsky and ousted him from leadership in the Soviet Communist party. Trotsky, who played a leading role in organising and carrying out the 1917 October Revolution, is effectively under house arrest. He has been sacked as Commissar for War. Hundreds of his friends and supporters have been arrested by the Cheka security police and exiled to remote areas of Russia.

Trotsky is the first major victim of the power struggle which has followed Vladimir Lenin's death, and his position in the ruling Politburo has been steadily weakening for several months.

Too restless and individualistic to be a good politician, Trotsky has proved no match for Stalin, who has allied himself with the leading Bolsheviks Zinoviev and Kamenev. Many Bolsheviks distrust Trotsky because until 1917 he supported the Mensheviks and opposed Lenin.

Although there has been a personality clash, Trotsky and Stalin differ on some of the most pressing problems facing the new Soviet Union. Trotsky believes passionately in the doctrine of "permanent revolution", which means concentrating on fomenting international revolution, while Stalin has been arguing for "socialism in one country" – that the first task of the party was to build up Russia.

Leon Trotsky, before his downfall, takes the salute in Red Square.

Under Lenin, Stalin gathered enormous power in his own hands, and displacing Trotsky consolidates it. As chief of the armed forces Trotsky was a formidable opponent, but he has left office without apparently attempting to rally the army, which he has led for the last seven years, to his defence.

Rugby player sent off for foul play

Jan 3. An unprecedented incident marred the touring New Zealand All Blacks' fine 17-11 victory over England at Twickenham, when the New Zealander, Cyril Brownlie, was sent off the field for foul play. The opening minutes of the match had seen a succession of ill-tempered brawls, and both teams had been warned twice by the referee, Mr A.E. Freethy, who said after the match that when he subsequently saw Brownlie "deliberately kick an Englishman on the ground" he had no option but to send him off. It is the first time such a severe sanction has been applied in an international match.

The "All Blacks" demonstrate their Maori "war cry" before the match.

Mussolini begins drive on opponents

Jan 5. Benito Mussolini has today shown his iron fist, taking action against opponents of Fascism within and outside the government. All the Cabinet Ministers have resigned but it appears that only the Liberal ministers, Sarrochi and Casati, will actually relinquish their portfolios. Their places will be filled by loyal Fascists. Thus Mussolini is ridding himself of those moderate politicians who gave his government some respectability.

Police searched opposition members' homes, closed meeting halls and disbanded political clubs. Mussolini, a former journalist, has made newspapers a special target. Those accused of printing "false news" were seized and their journalists arrested. It is now feared that Il Duce will sweep away every vestige of democracy.

1925

FEBRUARY

Su	Mo	Tu	We	Th	Fr	Sa
1	2	3	4	5	6	7
8	9	10	11	12	13	14
15	16	17	18	19	20	21
22	23	24	25	26	27	28

1. Berlin: First meeting of the "Front of Red Fighters", the combat wing of the German Communist Party (KPD) (→ 1/9).

5. Paris: New summer fashions for women show higher waistlines and fuller skirts.

5. USSR: 10 people are arrested for alleged conspiracy to assassinate Gregory Zinoviev.

6. S. Africa: Scientists claim a fossilised skull they have discovered is that of a prehistoric ape-man.

11. Portugal: The government is overthrown.

14. Germany: The state of emergency and ban on the Nazi Party is lifted in Bavaria.→

15. London: The Zoo in Regent's Park announces it will instal lights to cheer the animals during London fogs.

16. London: A special committee says Waterloo Bridge should be rebuilt and a subway constructed under the Strand.

17. London: Ex-Liberal PM Herbert Asquith takes his seat in the Lords as the Earl of Oxford and Asquith.

18. Washington: President Coolidge suggests a new international conference on smaller naval vessels.

22. Paris: The Chamber of Deputies votes against keeping a French embassy in the Vatican.

25. Turkey: A Kurdish uprising breaks out against the government of Mustafa Kemal (→ 16/4).

26. Italy: Reports indicate the Leaning Tower of Pisa leans more every year and is in danger of collapse.

27. Munich: Adolf Hitler makes his first public appearance since his release from prison.→

DEATH

28. German statesman Friedrich Ebert, first president of the republic 1919-25 (*4/2/1871).

Hitler's Nazi Party will shun violence

Feb 27. Adolf Hitler today returned to the scene of his abortive putsch just over a year ago: in the Munich Burgerbraukeller he spoke at the first mass meeting of his resurrected Nazi party. Many old comrades were absent: some are dead, some, like Hermann Goering, are in exile, and some, like Ludendorff, have broken with Hitler.

Hitler persuaded the Bavarian authorities to lift the ban on his party and its newspaper by giving a promise of good behaviour, renouncing the use of force and promising to seek political power only through legal means. About 4,000 turned up for the beer hall meeting. Despite his promises, he rounded off his speech with the words: "To this struggle of ours there are only two possible issues. Either the enemy pass over our bodies or we pass over theirs."

England win Test in Australia at last

Feb 18. England's cricketers ended a drought of nearly 13 years in Melbourne, with victory in the fourth Test by an innings and 29 runs – their first win against Australia since August 1912. The splendid batting on the first day, and the fine bowling of Kilner, Hearne and Tate, mark the return to a quality of English cricket not seen since the Great War.

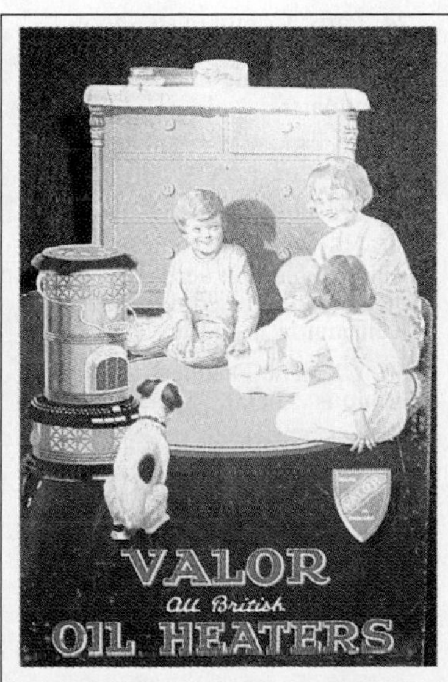

1925

MARCH

Su	Mo	Tu	We	Th	Fr	Sa
1	2	3	4	5	6	7
8	9	10	11	12	13	14
15	16	17	18	19	20	21
22	23	24	25	26	27	28
29	30	31				

2. Japan: A new law is proposed abolishing property qualification and establishing universal manhood suffrage.

2. Austria: A new currency is introduced, the schilling.

4. Washington: Calvin Coolidge is inaugurated as president.

9. US: Governor Miriam Ferguson bans the wearing of masks in public, an anti-Ku Klux Klan move.

11. London: Premiere of the show "No No Nanette".

13. London: MPs approve the Summer Time Bill, making daylight saving permanent.

17. US: 900 are reported killed and 3,000 injured when a tornado hits Illinois, Indiana and Missouri.

18. London: Fire destroys two floors of Madame Tussaud's waxworks museum.

19. France: The International Motor Racing Federation decides to institute a world motor racing championship.

27. London: Lord Burnham, reporting on teachers' pay, recommends fixing salaries for six years (→ 9/4).

27. UK: D. Goold's and Fred Archer's Double Chance wins the Grand National at Aintree.

28. UK: Cambridge wins the Boat Race after Oxford sinks; the second time that only one boat has finished.

31. UK: Hope is abandoned of rescuing 35 men trapped in a flooded mine at Scotswood-on-Tyne, Northumberland.

BIRTH

26. French composer and conductor Pierre Boulez.

DEATHS

12. Chinese Nationalist leader Dr. Sun Yat-sen (*12/11/1866).→

20. British statesman Lord George Nathaniel Curzon (*11/1/1859).→

30. Austrian founder of anthroposophy Rudolf Steiner (*27/2/1861).

Chiang follows Sun as Chinese leader

March 12. General Chiang Kai-shek, the remarkable Chinese banker who went to Japan to learn the art of war, is to become leader of the Kuomintang, the so-called people's party of the South. He succeeds Dr Sun Yat-sen, who died of cancer this morning in Peking. Known as the "Father of the Republic", Sun Yat-sen was a British-trained medical doctor, who overturned the Manchu dynasty.

General Chiang was one of his aides in the revolution of 1911 and in protracted battles to win military and political supremacy. He is a fervent nationalist, who visited the Soviet Union two years ago for help in building the Kuomintang army, which is now 40,000 strong.

Chiang Kai-shek and predecessor.

Crosswords provide clue to good health

March 8. Crosswords are good for you. That is the reassuring message today from the Chicago department of health. Two months ago W. R. Baker, president of the British Optical Association, voiced fears that the new crossword craze could cause headaches arising from eye-strain. But the Chicago verdict is that solving crossword puzzles gives us a mental kick, which is good for our health and happiness. A nursery game in Britain in the last century, crosswords returned here in their present form last year. ▷

US state bans the teaching of evolution

March 23. The State of Tennessee has made it a crime to teach the theory of evolution in its schools. Signing the bill into law today, Governor Austin Peay described the move as a "distinct protest against an irreligious tendency to exalt so-called science and deny the Bible".

Five other southern states are imposing similar laws – although opponents are almost certain to challenge them under the constitutional principle which separates the church from matters of state. No longer can any teacher in any Tennessee state-supported school propound Darwin's theories – or any theory, for that matter, that contradicts the Bible's account of the Creation.

Govenor Peay declared in ringing tones that "the very integrity of the Bible in its statement of man's divine creation is denied by any theory that man descended or has ascended from any lower order of animals".

Curzon, statesman and Viceroy, dies

March 20. The Marquess Curzon of Kedleston, most brilliant ex-future Prime Minister of them all, died today at 66. The prize which was his life's ambition finally eluded him two years ago when the King chose the humdrum Stanley Baldwin to form the government.

George Nathaniel Curzon was deemed too grand for these democratic days. Long ago he was dubbed "the very superior person", having been born with the advantages of affluence, noble descent and phenomenal brainpower. He was Viceroy of India at 40, served in Lloyd George's War Cabinet and as Foreign Secretary from 1919 until last year's election. A high Tory, he suffered for being too loyal to Lloyd George.

UK plans navy base for Singapore

March 19. Britain is bolstering its strategic links with the Empire by establishing a major naval base at Singapore. It will be used as a vital supply and maintenance centre for the Royal Navy in the Far East and will help to secure links with colonies like Hong Kong and other possessions in the Pacific.

A huge floating dock, seized from the Germans at the end of the war, will be sent out to boost facilities while other work, which will cost £400,000 in all, goes ahead.

Many MPs are concerned that the new base will be seen as a threat to Japan. The Labour Party leader Ramsey MacDonald spoke for them when he condemned the decision and described it as "absolutely deplorable".

All aboard for the Elephant: travellers at Leytonstone prepare to use the service of the London General Omnibus Company.

1925

APRIL

Su	Mo	Tu	We	Th	Fr	Sa
			1	2	3	4
5	6	7	8	9	10	11
12	13	14	15	16	17	18
19	20	21	22	23	24	25
26	27	28	29	30		

1. London: The government sets up an enquiry into the future of British broadcasting.

1. Palestine: Arabs protest against the opening of the Hebrew University of Jerusalem.

4. Berlin: Field Marshal Paul von Hindenburg announces his candidature for the German presidency.→

9. London: The government accepts Lord Burnham's recommendations on teachers' pay.

10. Paris: Radical Edouard Herriot resigns as premier (→17).

13. US: A gastronomic survey reveals that Americans are primarily "steak eaters".

14. Sofia: King Boris of Bulgaria escapes a Bolshevik assassination attempt when his car is ambushed and fired on (→17).

16. Turkey: The Kurdish uprising ends.

17. Paris: Paul Painleve becomes premier.

17. Sofia: 150 people are killed when a bomb explodes at a funeral.

19. S. Africa: Police fire on a group of blacks at Bloemfontein.

23. Morocco: Troops of rebel leader Abdel Krim enter French Morocco (→14/5).

24. Paris: Communists shoot dead three men at a municipal election meeting in Montmartre.

25. UK: Sheffield United beats Cardiff City 1-0 in the FA Cup Final at Wembley.

30. US: Orville Wright says he will give his first aeroplane to the Science Museum in South Kensington, London.

30. UK: The Distillers whisky group is officially formed.

BIRTH

14. US actor Rod Steiger.

DEATH

15. US artist John Singer Sargent (*12/1/1856).

Germany elects its first President

April 25. In a closely contested election, the revered 78-year-old wartime hero, Field Marshal Paul von Hindenburg, has become Germany's first directly elected president, the women's vote being crucial. With 14,700,000 votes, he was one million ahead of his rival, Wilhelm Marx, a former Chancellor, who had the support of the Socialist and Centre parties. Although Hindenburg wants to see the monarchy restored, and was backed by assorted right-wing parties, including the Bavarians and German Nationalists, he has nevertheless pledged himself to uphold the republican constitution.

Machines to make light of housework

April 27. Women could soon be freed from much of the drudgery of housework by new machines. Mass production methods, pioneered in engineering, are now being used on the home front; one example is the new electric washing and wringing machine.

Catering establishments already have machines for washing dishes and preparing food, and experts predict that smaller scale versions, able to do these tasks in an ordinary home, are just around the corner for many people.

Answering the cook's dreams.

Churchill returns to gold

April 28. Britain is back on the gold standard. There is sixpence off the standard rate of income tax and there is a great new national insurance scheme with State pension age reduced to 65. These were the highlights of today's exciting Budget introduced by Winston Churchill.

The Chancellor hailed the gold standard restoration as proof of Britain's post-war economic recovery. It means that the nation is again committed to exporting gold when there is no other way of meeting debts abroad. Within 15 minutes the pound was quoted in New York at four dollars 83 cents – its highest for ten years. It is now revealed that big new American bank credits for Britain have recently been negotiated.

With income tax down to four shillings in the pound, a person earning £1,000 a year will now have to pay just under £100 in tax while someone on £500 will pay about £19. The new contributory insurance scheme will embrace 15 million people, who, with dependents, represent 70 per cent of the population. Men and their employers will pay fourpence a week and for women the rates are half.

From 1928 all contributors over 65 will receive ten shillings a week; from 1926 that amount will be paid to widows for life.

The fall and rise of the pound

Year	$
1914	4.86
1919	4.43
1920	3.66
1921	3.85
1922	4.43
1923	4.57
1924	4.42
1925	4.86

What £1 has been worth in dollars (annual averages)

UK to help migrants to travel Down Under

Apr 8. Over the next ten years, almost half a million men and women will be encouraged to leave Britain and make their homes in Australia. The federal government there has promised low-interest loans of £34 million in total to the state governments. The money borrowed is to be used to buy land much of which will be earmarked for 450,000 British settlers.

Money will be made available to build roads, bridges and railways, and to help the settlers buy their stock, equipment and the materials they will need to build houses. Under the scheme announced today by the Australian Government and the Colonial Office in London, for every £750,000 lent to any of the state governments, a further £130,000 will be provided by Britain. The British contribution will fund the settlement of 450,000 British immigrants who will be taught the skills necessary to manage and develop their new farms. It is hoped that 34,000 British families will be encouraged to seek a new life "down under".

One of thousands of families heading for the promised land of Australia.

Art Deco: style for the post-war world

Latest evening modes demonstrate clean lines derived from Cubism, and the vibrant, exotic influence of Russian ballet designer Leon Bakst.

ART INDUSTRIE
EXPOSITION INTERNATIONALE
DES ARTS DÉCORATIFS
ET INDUSTRIELS
MODERNES
PARIS AVRIL-OCTOBRE 1925
Loi du 10 Avril 1923.

The new style permeates interior and exterior design as well as clothes.

April 30. The "post-war" style has found its identity and its name at the huge Paris Exposition des Arts Decoratifs which is spread along both banks of the Seine. It is drawing millions of visitors, both French and foreign, to admire the display of architecture, interior design and high fashion.

"Art Deco", the overall label for the style, is Cubism domesticated. All the clutter of Belle Epoque decoration has gone in favour of simple geometrical shapes defined by angles, curves and circles, elegantly combined in clean outlines. In fashion, the colour schemes are strong and barbaric, drawn from the orange, violet, emerald, gold and silver of Bakst's exotic designs for Russian ballets such as "Scheherezade". Paul Poiret's lavish gowns are shown on three barges on the Seine. "Le Pavillon d'Elegance" shows the gowns of Chanel, Patou and Lanvin.

On view are the brilliant textiles by painter Raoul Dufy, wallpapers by Marie Laurencin, furniture by Jacques-Emile Ruhlmann and streamlined crystal figurines by Rene Lalique.

1925

MAY

Su	Mo	Tu	We	Th	Fr	Sa
					1	2
3	4	5	6	7	8	9
10	11	12	13	14	15	16
17	18	19	20	21	22	23
24	25	26	27	28	29	30
31						

2. US: A US Navy seaplane sets a new record by remaining in the air for 28 and a half hours.

6. Germany: Republicans protest against the election of Field Marshal von Hindenburg as president (→ 12).

8. S. Africa: A bill is passed making Afrikaans the official language of the Union.

9. London: The King opens the second season of the British Empire Exhibition at Wembley.

12. Berlin: Hindenburg is sworn in as president.

13. London: The Gold Bullion Standard Act is passed, returning the UK to the Gold Standard.

14. Morocco: It is reported that the French have scored numerous successes against the Riff rebels under Abdel Krim.

18. UK: A report by the TUC declares that the "Zinoviev letter" was a forgery.

20. London: High Commissioners Lord Allenby of Egypt and Herbert Samuel of Palestine resign.

23. London: The King lays the foundation stone of the new Lloyd's Insurance building in Leadenhall Street.

27. UK: H. E. Morris's Manna wins the Derby.

28. London: The Home Secretary orders all known "subversives" to be barred from entering the country.

30. London: King George V opens the rebuilt Great West Road from Chiswick to East Bedfont.

BIRTH

19. US black militant leader Malcolm Little, "Malcolm X" (†21/2/1965).

DEATHS

14. British author H. Rider Haggard (*22/6/1856).

22. British commander Field Marshal John French, Earl of Ypres (*28/9/1852).

23. British publisher Sir Edward Hulton (*3/3/1869).→

Teacher of evolution is charged in US

May 25. The world's press descended on the small Tennessee town of Dayton today to watch the trial of a young teacher, John Scopes, on a charge of teaching Darwin's theory of evolution.

They found a carnival atmosphere surrounding the courtroom, with a hundred different religious sects holding revivalist meetings, and "Holy Rollers" twitching and kicking in ecstasy in the hot and dusty streets.

The case – already known as "The Monkey Trial" – is the first to be brought under a new law introduced by Bible fundamentalists, who are represented in court by William Jennings Bryan. He is a former Secretary of State and Presidential candidate, who believes that "the hand that writes the pay cheque rules the school". The defence is being conducted by Clarence Darrow, a noted civil rights lawyer, who sees the case as one of tolerance against bigotry. The judge has ruled against hearing scientific evidence.

John Scopes with his lawyers.

Britain gains a Mediterranean colony

May 1. Cyprus today became a British colony, thus recognising a situation which has existed since 1878 when the Ottoman Empire, in a separate agreement during the Congress of Berlin, was "persuaded" to place it under British administration. Then, in 1914, when Turkey joined in the war on the side of Germany, the British annexed it.

The new arrangement gives Cyprus the same status as any other British colony with the right to join the Commonwealth. It does not, however, promise to be a particularly happy addition to the "Club", for its mixed population of Turks and Greeks distrust each other, and look to their home countries for protection rather than to Britain.

This is not the first time Britain has owned Cyprus; it was captured by Richard the Lionheart from the Byzantines in 1191.

Jockey Steve Donoghue, who rode Mr H. E. Morris's Manna to victory in the Derby.

Hulton, the priestly press baron, dies

May 24. Sir Edward Hulton, who died yesterday, might have become a priest if his elder brother had not been killed in a fall from a penny farthing bicycle. He was then groomed for the family business and turned it into one of the great popular newspaper groups.

His printer father began with a racing tipsheet, which he transformed into one of the first mass circulation Sunday newspapers, the Sunday Chronicle, entirely devoted to sport and popular stories. Sir Edward added two more Sundays, four dailies and the London Evening Standard, before ill health forced him to sell out two years ago for a rumoured £6 million.

Modern girls put Pope in a flap

May 8. Influential Catholic bishops in north east Italy today decided to ban scantily dressed or bare-legged women from church. The move, said to have the approval of the Pope himself, comes as part of a stinging attack on women's "scandalous" fashions and their growing involvement in sport which, say the bishops, is "utterly incompatible" with a woman's dignity.

The attack comes on the heels of a recent announcement in Silesia that immodest women would be denied marriage rites. Outrage at women's changing dress and behaviour is not confirmed to the Catholic Church. Traditionalists everywhere are concerned that morals decline as hemlines rise.

Also today the Dean of Durham condemned the trend for "educated English women" to confess their immorality in the divorce court with "utter shamelessness".

As well as endangering women's moral welfare, some doctors claim current fashions may be bad for physical health, causing puffiness and chafing of the legs, rarely a problem with long skirts.

Elegance in fur and short skirts.

1925

JUNE

Su	Mo	Tu	We	Th	Fr	Sa
	1	2	3	4	5	6
7	8	9	10	11	12	13
14	15	16	17	18	19	20
21	22	23	24	25	26	27
28	29	30				

2. Ottawa: The Canadian government claims all land between Alaska and Greenland up to the North Pole.

2. UK: The report of the National Council of Public Morals withholds approval of contraceptives.

6. Detroit: Walter P. Chrysler founds the Chrysler Motor Company.

7. Cairo: Nine people are sentenced to death for the murder of Sudan Governor-General Sir Lee Stack (→23/8).

8. UK: Yorkshire's P. Holmes gets the highest individual score at Lords of 315 not out, breaking an 1820 record.

10. US: Tennessee issues a new biology textbook denying evolutionary origin of human life (→21/7).

11. London: The first reported aerial murder takes place when a London gem dealer is thrown out of an aeroplane.

14. Germany: "Neue Sachlichkeit" ("New Realism") exhibition opens in Mannheim, with works by Grosz, Beckmann and Dix.

15. Germany: Scientists report the discovery of two new elements, masurium and rhenium.

16. Paris: The government accepts Germany's offer of a security pact.

20. Germany: Herr Schaetzle demonstrates a new wireless telephone invention for cars.

22. Hong Kong: A general strike begins in the British colony.

24. Berlin: The Reichstag is invaded by people whose money became worthless during 1923 hyper-inflation.

25. Athens: General Theodoris Pangalos seizes power in a military coup d'etat.

29. US: Santa Barbara is severely damaged in an earthquake.

29. London: The King opens the Canadian government's new building in Trafalgar Square.

Civil war flares in China

Aukuochun prisoners contemplate the unburied corpses of their comrades.

June 23. There is increasing alarm among foreign residents in China that the present chaotic situation may produce another revolt comparable to the blood-letting of the Boxer Rebellion in the early years of the century.

A three-week strike by Chinese workers in Shanghai has paralysed the port. Constant rioting by students heightens the tension.

So once again the Chinese are in the grip of a strong anti-foreigner movement; after the "Shanghai incident", in which British police opened fire on the mob, anti-British feelings are running high. "Kill the English!" is a common war cry.

Things are made worse by the lack of authority of the central government in Peking as regional warlords compete for power. Feng Yuhsiang, the "Christian" General, has offered his troops to the government for a war against the British.

Meanwhile, the Yunnan army was driven from Canton by pro-Communist forces of the Kuomingtang, officered by Russians. China is once again in a state of civil war.

Coward's "Hay Fever" blows into town

Brief encounter: Noel Coward and Lillian Braithwaite, going places.

June 9. This is the year of Noel Coward, who has had no less than three plays open in the West End. First came "The Vortex", transferred from Hampstead. Despite being dubbed "Dustbin Drama" by Sir Gerald du Maurier, it was a great success and Mr Coward was widely acclaimed for his performance as a drug addict.

"Fallen Angels" was called "a degrading spectacle" because of the drinking scene in which Edna Best and Tallulah Bankhead become steadily more bitchily abusive.

Last night "Hay Fever" in which a theatrical family insult and humiliate their guests in a monstrously selfish manner opened. Mr Coward claimed that at least this play was "as clean as a whistle". He wrote it, we learn, in three days.

Blacks are banned from skilled jobs by law in S. Africa

June 29. The colour bar is to become legal in South Africa. MPs have passed a bill to exclude the black, coloured (mixed race) and Indian communities from skilled or semi-skilled work in industries throughout the country.

Until the white miners' strike in the Witwatersrand gold fields in 1922, most people had assumed the colour bar was legal – it was certainly widely practised – but the miners' bid to stop blacks being given semi-skilled jobs led to the discovery that an old Transvaal Republic regulation had never been adopted when the Union of South Africa was formed in 1910.

Now the government is not only regularising the situation in the mines, but extending it to all industries. The English-speaking South Africa Party, with its more liberal traditions in Natal and Cape Provinces, has tried to block the bill by using its majority in the Senate. But the government is invoking a constitutional device to call a joint sitting of both houses, when it will use its big Assembly majority to steamroller the bill through.

Another constitutional change has been passed by a joint sitting: the Dutch language, used by the Boers for 300 years, has been replaced by Afrikaans, a Dutch-based dialect.

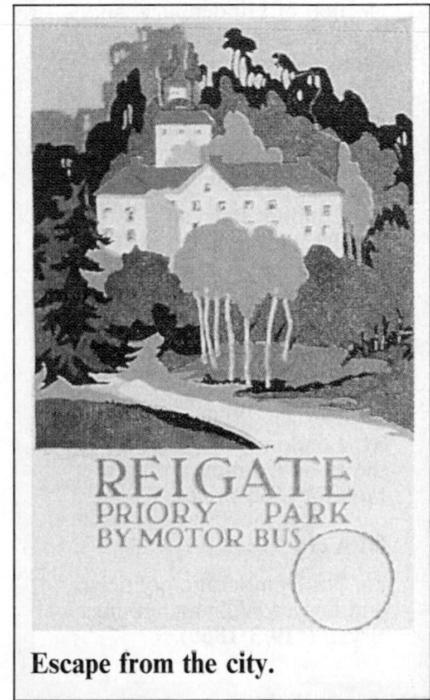

Escape from the city.

1925

JULY

Su	Mo	Tu	We	Th	Fr	Sa
			1	2	3	4
5	6	7	8	9	10	11
12	13	14	15	16	17	18
19	20	21	22	23	24	25
26	27	28	29	30	31	

1. UK: It is reported that the railway companies plan cuts of £6,000,000 annually.

1. UK: The first International Congress of Radiology opens.

2. New York: Two girls are arrested and fined $5 each for smoking on the subway.

4. UK: F. L. Barnard wins the King's Cup for an air race round Britain.

6. Wimbledon: Suzanne Lenglen beats June Fry for her sixth Singles title; Rene Lacoste is Men's Singles champion.

9. London: The government says it will not abandon British rights in China.

12. US: The pro-evolution pastor of Dayton, Tennessee, is forced to quit following threats against him.→

13. London: The King opens the British Medical Association's new headquarters in Tavistock Square.

14. Germany: French and Belgian troops begin their evacuation of the Ruhr.

16. UK: Scientists claim they have successfully innoculated animals against cancer.

18. UK: It is reported that ten million people listen to BBC wireless broadcasts.

22. Berlin: To mark the election of Hindenburg, an amnesty is granted to prisoners jailed before June 15 1915.

23. Vienna: Professor Sigmund Freud becomes chairman of the International Psychoanalytical Foundation.

24. London: Patricia Cheeseman, a patient at Guy's Hospital, has first successful treatment for diabetes.

25. The Bishop of Durham flees in a motorboat after facing abuse from a crowd during the Miners' Gala.

31. London: First meeting of the Food Council, set up to monitor food prices.

DEATH

26. US Democratic politician and lawyer William Jennings Bryan (*19/3/1860).→

Teacher fined $100 after "Monkey trial"

John Scopes: convicted for challenging the literal truth of the Bible.

July 21. Even though the principal witness was discredited under cross-examination, a Tennessee jury rejected Darwinism today. They found biology teacher John Scopes guilty of teaching evolution in a state school and fined him $100. An appeal is certain to go to the state's supreme court.

So many people tried to cram their way into the hearing that the courthouse was in danger of collapse before the judge moved the proceedings to the gardens outside.

Hundreds of religious fundamentalists cheered, sang hymns and prayed in the streets as the jury handed the verdict to the judge.

William Jennings Bryan, the key prosecution witness, had ridiculed many of Darwin's theories, particularly those involving man's descent from monkeys, before facing questioning by Clarence Darrow, the noted defence attorney.

"The creation might have been going on for a long time?" he asked. "It might have continued for millions of years," admitted Bryan.

Bryan made it clear in his evidence that he did not accept the Bible literally at all times; and demonstrated ignorance of other religions and civilisations. Public laughter forced the judge to adjourn the court at one point.

New bill to curb divorce reporting

July 16. A bill to restrict the salacious reporting of divorce cases was given its second reading in the Lords today. Such reporting, in all its disgusting detail, was largely responsible for the present deterioration in public morals, according to Lord Darline. The amount published had increased almost every day since the Divorce Court was set up 75 years ago.

Britain's licence to cover cases in "nauseous and intimate" detail was unparalleled elsewhere and gave us a bad reputation abroad. The Lord Chancellor, however, pointed out that for some purposes publicity was necessary to justice.

Government backs down over miners

July 31. The month-long crisis in the coal industry is over. Late last night the employers accepted Mr Baldwin's offer that they withdraw their demands for longer working hours and lower wages in return for the Treasury's subsidising consequent losses for the next nine months.

The owners gave notice on June 30 that from tomorrow the industry would no longer work the maximum 7-hour day, or pay the minimum wage rates agreed last year. Until yesterday the government had rejected the idea of a subsidy. Mr Churchill will now have to find the estimated extra £10 million in his next Budget.

"Mein Kampf" is Hitler's manifesto

July 18. Adolf Hitler, who gained notoriety with his abortive beer hall putsch, has finally published the book he dictated in prison. Described by detractors as Hitler's Book of Dreams, *Mein Kampf* (My Struggle) is a rambling mixture of self-pitying autobiography, diatribes against Jews, the glorification of man as a fighting animal and a call to the German people to join his Nazi party and spearhead a national revival.

Buttock-baring boys break byelaws trying to cool off this summer.

1925

AUGUST

Su	Mo	Tu	We	Th	Fr	Sa
						1
2	3	4	5	6	7	8
9	10	11	12	13	14	15
16	17	18	19	20	21	22
23	24	25	26	27	28	29
30	31					

3. US: A court in Indiana orders a motorist who killed a pedestrian to spend one hour alone with the victim's body.

4. Eastern Europe: Flooding is reported in Czechoslovakia and Upper Silesia after heavy rainfall during the summer.

5. Washington: 50,000 miles of roads are designated "US Highways" by the Interstate Highways Board.

8. Washington: The first National Congress of the Ku Klux Klan opens.→

8. French aviators Landry and Drouhin set new record non-stop, covering 2,732 miles.

12. China: Many deaths are reported during a riot of striking cotton workers in Tientsin.

14. Paris: Signature of a Franco-German customs and excise treaty.

16. US: Charlie Chaplin's film "Gold Rush" opens.

17. Vienna: Anti-Semitic rioting marks the opening of a Zionist conference.

19. UK: Mineworkers agree to participate in the government's inquiry into miners' pay.

19. China: The government of Canton bans British and Japanese ships from leaving or entering the region's ports.

20. India: Viceroy Lord Reading sets up a Royal Commission on Indian Currency and Finance.

20. Paris: Professor Cazzamali claims the human brain emits radio waves.

23. Cairo: Seven of the nine found guilty of murdering Sudan Governor-General Sir Lee Stack are hanged.

26. Morocco: Marshal Philippe Petain takes command of French troops fighting Abdel Krim.

31. Mediterranean: The Italian submarine Veniero is reported lost with its crew of 55.

31. Birmingham: Reported that General Motors is negotiating to buy the Austin Motor Co. (→ 13/9).

Big Klan parade is a wash-out

Aug 8. More than 40,000 members of the Ku Klux Klan marched through Washington today. A ceremony afterwards, however, was cancelled due to heavy rain.

The Klan is a secret society dedicated to preserving white supremacy in America, and to opposing foreign influences, especially that of the Roman Catholic Church.

After the Civil War, the Klan terrorised newly freed Negroes in the South. Disbanded in 1869, it was revived in 1915. Recently the Klan has been more political and has attracted many members from outside the former Confederacy, especially from small towns in the Middle West. Last year the Klan played an important part in denying the Democratic nomination to the Catholic, Al Smith.

Centurion Hobbs outscores Grace

Aug 18. In front of a tiny Tuesday crowd at Taunton, Jack Hobbs, Surrey's great opening batsman, scored his second hundred in two days against Somerset – the first to equal, the second to surpass, W. G. Grace's total of 126 career centuries – and, at the same time, to record his 14th century of the season, an unprecedented feat.

With Hobbs, even at 42, at the peak of his form, he seems certain to set even higher targets for aspiring future record-breakers.

Charlie Chaplin in a scene from "The Gold Rush", which has its world premiere this month.

1925

SEPTEMBER

Su	Mo	Tu	We	Th	Fr	Sa
		1	2	3	4	5
6	7	8	9	10	11	12
13	14	15	16	17	18	19
20	21	22	23	24	25	26
27	28	29	30			

1. Paris: Olympics founder Pierre de Coubertin retires as head of the International Olympic Committee.

1. Germany: Ernst Thalmann becomes leader of the German Communist Party (KPD).

2. Australia: The government announces new tariffs that include preferences for UK goods.

3. US: 14 die when the US Navy airship Shenandoah is wrecked in a storm over Caldwell, Ohio.

5. US: Water is sold by the gallon as drought grips the southern and south-western states.

9. UK: The TUC votes against the amalgamation of all British trade unions.

13. Birmingham: General Motors drops its planned purchase of the Austin Motor Company.

15. Berlin: The Germans are invited to attend the Locarno security conference in Switzerland (→ 5/10).

20. Rome: The city's first underground railway line is opened.

22. Washington: Navy Secretary Wilbur says the US Navy must have its own air force.

25. US: The US Naval submarine S-51 sinks after a collision with a steamship, with the loss of 37 lives.

27. Finland: Norwegian Charles Hoff sets a world pole vault record of 4.25 metres.

29. UK: The Labour Party conference rejects a proposal for a link up with the British Communist Party.

BIRTHS

16. US musician B. B. King.

8. British actor Peter Sellers (†24/7/1980).

DEATH

29. French statesman and Nobel Peace prizewinner Leon Bourgeois, first President of the League of Nations (*21/5/1851).

Everybody's doing the Charleston now

The dance that mothers detest.

Sept 1. The dance that scandalised America is now taking Britain by storm. The Charleston, which takes its name from the South Carolina town where it was born, is adored by flappers and just as fervently detested by their mothers.

The dance, performed at frenetic tempo by turning in your toes and kicking out your legs while syncopating your arm movements, is now being performed at the smartest night spots; a hit with both shop girls and debs.

Anti-British rioters shot in Shanghai

Sept 7. Shanghai police opened fire last night as a large rioting mob of 20,000, led by students, closed in on a police station in the settlements. Three Chinese were wounded, one badly. Demonstrators carried banners attacking "British Imperialism" to mark the anniversary of signature of "unequal treaties" granting concessions to foreigners. They stoned five British police constables barring their way. ▷

Traffic in Piccadilly gets the green light

Congestion caused by the motoring boom calls for stringent measures.

Sept 29. White traffic lines are to be painted on roads all over the country in an attempt to reduce accidents. The Ministry of Transport will set the standards and arrange grants to pay the bills. The idea is to separate traffic streams at intersections or on dangerous bends. Experiments are being made with various indelible materials.

In London another traffic experiment is under consideration to reduce congestion. Traffic lights are proposed in Piccadilly to give an uninterrupted flow past several intersections at a time.

Meanwhile the opening next week of the 1925 Motor Show at Olympia heralds a surge of new cars on to the roads. With no motor show in Paris this year, Olympia becomes the focus of an international industry. Its 500 stands will show the latest models from Belgium, France, Italy, Canada and the United States as well as from Britain. New designs will be more numerous than in any year since 1913 – a measure of public enthusiasm for the motor age.

Another sign of a thriving industry is the choice it offers at both ends of the price range. As little as £145 buys a three-seater Citroen or £150 a two-cylinder Jowett (with self-starter) while the cheapest Rolls-Royce goes for £1,891, a big Daimler £1,650 or a Minerva £1,350. The new cars are both cheaper and faster, with many makes claiming top speeds above 60 mph, plus four-wheel brakes.

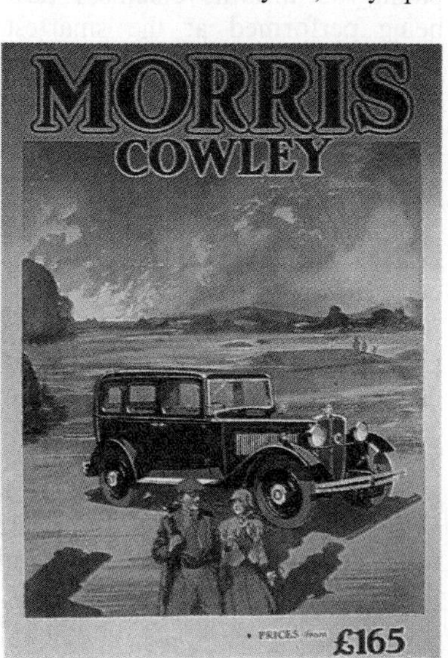

The new models are cheaper.

Traffic control in New York.

1925

OCTOBER

Su	Mo	Tu	We	Th	Fr	Sa
				1	2	3
4	5	6	7	8	9	10
11	12	13	14	15	16	17
18	19	20	21	22	23	24
25	26	27	28	29	30	31

1. New York: Woolworth heiress Mrs James Donahue is robbed of $750,000 in jewels while in her hotel bathroom.

5. Switzerland: The Locarno Conference opens.→

6. UK: The Archbishop of Canterbury blames poor preaching and outdated clergy for low church attendances.

8. UK: Opera singer Nellie Melba announces that she will retire.

9. Germany: A diver broadcasts to Hamburg from the North Sea bed, a distance of 100 miles.

13. UK: Six-week old seamen's strike ends.

14. London: Police raid the headquarters of the British Communist Party, arresting six and seizing documents.→

19. Algeria: A Franco-US expedition discovers ancient sea shells, proving the Sahara was once partly submerged.

19. UK: The "Autogiro", a Spanish helicopter-like invention, is tested at Farnborough in Hampshire.

22. Balkans: Greek troops enter Bulgaria over a border dispute (→24).

24. Balkans: Bulgaria and Greece agree to let the League decide on their border confrontation (→29).

28. US: A census shows the US Indian population stands at 349,595.

28. Paris: Painleve forms a new left-wing dominated cabinet; ex-premier Aristide Briand is foreign minister.

29. Balkans: Greece has withdrawn its troops from Bulgaria, as instructed by League of Nations.

31. London: The British Empire Exhibition at Wembley closes.

31. Persia: Reza Khan Pahlevi deposes Shah Ahmed Mirza, ending the Kajar dynasty.

BIRTH

13. British stateswoman Margaret Thatcher, first UK woman prime minister.

Germany will not fight France again

Oct 16. In the Swiss tourist resort of Locarno today, Germany was at last reconciled with her former enemies. Gustav Stresemann, the German Foreign Minister, joined colleagues from Britain, France, Belgium and Italy in signing a mutual security pact.

It also affirms the post-war frontiers set out in the Versailles Treaty and accepts the demilitarisation of the Rhineland. In a separate agreement, Germany, France and Belgium undertake not to go to war against each other.

The signing was announced to a waiting crowd outside. When delegates left the building there were loud cheers, especially for the Germans. Sir Austen Chamberlain, the British Foreign Secretary, held up a copy of the pact as he rode away. The signing of the pact on his 62nd birthday is seen as a very good omen.

Germany in a debtor's chains.

First three-engined plane starts flying

Oct 19. Air travellers will fly in greater safety from now on following the delivery of the first three-engined aircraft to Imperial Airways. The Handley Page Hampstead airliner is fitted with three 385hp Siddeley Jaguar engines, mounted on the wings and nose. Tests show that the plane can climb with only two of them running and it will descend only slowly with just one engine switched on. In trials each engine in succession has been switched off then turned on again by gently diving.

Baker's witty rear end wows all Paris

Baker, at the Folies Bergeres.

Oct 27. Josephine Baker, the sensational 19-year-old dancer of "Le Revue Negre", is the talk of Paris. Her Charleston, slapping her buttocks in tempo to "Yes, sir, that's my baby!" and her bare-breasted mating dance, wearing nothing but strategic circles of coloured feathers, arouses audiences to frenzy.

Colette calls her "a most beautiful panther", Picasso "the Nefertiti of today", and Anita Loos speaks of her "witty rear end".

Poiret and Schiaparelli are designing clothes for her, painters are begging her to sit for them and the Folies Bergeres are wooing her to join the show.

British Communists on sedition charges

Oct 21. Two more prominent British Communists were arrested and charged at Bow Street today with offences under the 1797 Incitement to Mutiny Act. This brings to 12 the number of party members rounded up after consultations between the Home Office and Scotland Yard. Police are examining documents seized in recent raids.

The party declared tonight "We cannot be smashed. Continue to fight against the coming capitalist offensive", prompting fears of an early insurrection attempt.

1925

NOVEMBER

Su	Mo	Tu	We	Th	Fr	Sa
1	2	3	4	5	6	7
8	9	10	11	12	13	14
15	16	17	18	19	20	21
22	23	24	25	26	27	28
29	30					

2. UK: 20 are feared dead when a dam bursts and floods the Dolgarrog power station in North Wales.

3. London: Labour makes big gains in elections to the London County Council.

4. Budapest: Arrests follow the discovery of an alleged Communist plot.

5. Rome: Mussolini bans all left-wing parties (→ 7).

6. Moscow: Peasant-born Kliment Voroshilov is chosen to succeed Trotsky as head of the Red Army.

7. Rome: The Liberal Party joins the Fascists (→ 20).

9. Germany: Foundation of the Nazi "Schutzstaffel" (Protection Squad), or SS.

12. UK: The submarine M-1 is lost in the Channel with all 68 on board feared dead.

13. S. Africa: Premier James Hertzog says the cabinet wants segregation of blacks and more areas for their own use.

14. Paris: Opening of the first surrealist exhibition.

17. Lebanon: Druze rebels are reported to be menacing Beirut.

19. Sandringham: Queen Alexandra suffers a heart attack.→

20. Rome: A law is passed banning Freemasons and other secret societies (→ 24/12).

23. Paris: Painleve resigns as premier (→ 28).

25. London: 12 Communists arrested last month are jailed for sedition (→ 1/12).

26. Berlin: The Reichstag approves the Locarno agreement.

28. Paris: Aristide Briand becomes premier and forms his eighth ministry.

BIRTH

20. US politician, Democratic Attorney-General Robert F. Kennedy (†6/6/68).

DEATH

20. Danish-born British Queen Alexandra (*1/12/1844).→

Tutankhamun found to be a 15-year-old

Nov 13. Three years of painstaking work by Howard Carter and his team of experts came to a dramatic climax at Luxor two days ago when the bandages that swathed Tutankhamun's mummified body were unwound.

First investigations indicate that he was about 15 when he died. As the bandages were removed, 143 gold and jewelled ornaments, including charms for the boy-king's protection in the underworld, were revealed.

The king's fingers and toes were protected by gold stalls. Most magnificent of all, his head lay under a gold mask which Carter believes is a perfect portrait of the king as he was just before his death.

When the mask was carefully removed and the bandages on the head were unwound, scientists found the king's long-lashed eyes were partly opened, staring up at them from a face of greyish skin, which was cracked and brittle: the top lip was turned upwards, revealing the front teeth.

It was hard for anyone there to realize that this was the face of a boy who had been dead for more than 3,000 years.

King Tutankhamun.

Jeeves shimmers into readers' affections

Nov 6. The further adventures of a gentleman and his valet, Bertie Wooster and Jeeves, are published today, creating another classic master-servant relationship in literature.

Jeeves, the creation of P.G. Wodehouse, first appeared in book form last year as "The Inimitable Jeeves". Now "Carry On, Jeeves" consolidates his character of suave, tactful omniscience, ever ready to solve a crisis accompanied with an apt quotation.

Bertie, Jeeves observes, "is prone to smile weakly and allow his eyeballs to protrude". He himself is prone to "shimmer" into the room and announce his presence with a sound "like a sheep clearing its throat on a distant hillside".

"Will there be anything further, sir?" Certainly. Please carry on, Jeeves.

Pelham Grenville Wodehouse, the creator of Jeeves.

▷

Generous Queen Alexandra is dead

Danish-born Alexandra in 1911.

Nov 20. Queen Alexandra, widow of King Edward VII, died today at Sandringham. Born one of two beautiful Danish princesses – the other became Empress of Russia – she was welcomed to Britain with a poem by Tennyson:

"Sea-Kings' daughter from over the sea, Alexandra! Saxon and Norman and Dane are we, but all of us Danes in our welcome of thee, Alexandra!"

The Queen, who liked to live amidst vases of roses, was renowned for her generosity. She would give away family heirlooms to friends and the King, her son, would send Lord Esher, most tactful of courtiers, to get them back.

Drunken drivers to get jail sentences

Nov 20. Up to four months in jail is the fate that awaits drunken drivers under a new law. MPs considering the Criminal Justice Bill yesterday voted down a prison penalty for reckless driving, but they kept it for drunkenness while in charge of a car. Critics complained about the difficulty of telling when a driver is drunk, but the Home Secretary stood firm and approved a £50 fine as an extra.

1925

DECEMBER

Su	Mo	Tu	We	Th	Fr	Sa
		1	2	3	4	5
6	7	8	9	10	11	12
13	14	15	16	17	18	19
20	21	22	23	24	25	26
27	28	29	30	31		

1. London: The government survives a vote of censure condemning the Communist trials as against free speech.

3. New York: Police smash the biggest liquor ring since prohibition started, making 20 arrests.

5. Berlin: Dr. Luther resigns as Chancellor.

5. Berlin: Rubens' "St. Theresa" is discovered after being hidden for 200 years.

9. UK: The National Opera Trust is formed.

10. Stockholm: Nobel Prizes go to James Franck and Gustav Hertz (Germany, Physics), Richard Zsigmondy (Germany, Chemistry), G. B. Shaw (UK, Literature); Peace Prize awarded in Oslo to Austen Chamberlain (UK) and Charles Dawes (US). No Medicine Prize.

12. US: The first "Motel" is opened by James Vail in San Luis Obispo, California.

16. Geneva: The League of Nations makes a provisional settlement of a border dispute between Turkey and Iraq.

18. Moscow: The Party Congress advocates a gradual "single country" growth of Communism.

21. USSR: Opening of the film "Battleship Potemkin" by Sergei Eisenstein.

24. Rome: Mussolini declares himself answerable only to the King of Italy.

28. London: Hendon aerodrome is bought by the government.

HITS OF 1925

Show me the way to go home.

Always.

Manhattan.

QUOTE OF THE YEAR

"I don't like the family Stein;
There is Gert, there is Ep,
there is Ein.
Gert's writings are punk,
Ep's statues are junk,
And nobody understands Ein."

Anonymous, 1925.

The British "renege" on border pledge

Dec 3. The border between the North and South of Ireland is to remain unchanged after all. Stanley Baldwin, the Prime Minister, told the Commons to-night that he had finally signed an agreement confirming the border as it existed before the 1921 Peace Treaty.

That treaty was only signed because Lloyd George assured the southern Irish that a Boundary Commission would allow enclaves of Nationalists and Unionists to move from one side to the other before the line was fixed. But last week the Commission admitted defeat and no report was published.

British Ministers, however, declared themselves pleased. The Chancellor, Winston Churchill, said: "The Border question which has always hung over us is absolutely settled." Leopold Amery, Dominions Secretary, predicted that "north and south should now live in peace for all time".

BBC reaches an audience of 10 million

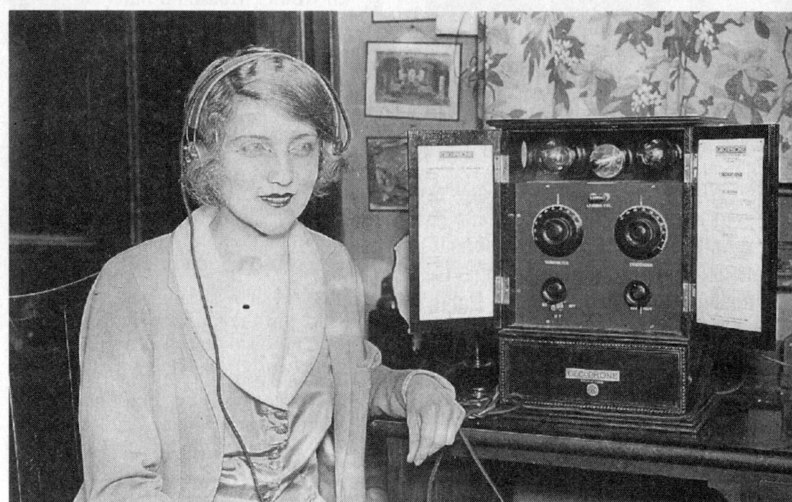

A wireless receiving set is fast becoming a must for British living-rooms.

Dec 3. John Reith, managing director of the British Broadcasting Company, yesterday called for the removal of the prohibition on news broadcasting before 7pm. He also told the House of Lords inquiry that it is now technically possible to broadcast parliamentary debates.

The BBC already puts out 10,000 talks a year and music to suit all tastes while its education programmes reach over 1,000 schools. The boom in wireless set sales has produced an audience of over ten million in three years. Mr Reith also stressed that announcers were all trained in "the right pronunciation of the English tongue".

Surgeon mends a girl's broken heart

Dec 31. Surgical operations which can take place inside the heart have been the highlight of the year in medicine. A London surgeon, Henry Souttar, succeeded in dilating or stretching a damaged heart valve of a young girl. The valve had been interrupting blood flow through the heart. After exposing the heart, and incising it, Mr Souttar stretched the valve with his finger to improve blood flow. The patient was well three months later.

It was the first attempt to reach the valve in this way. Mr Souttar claims that the heart is like any other organ, with the only problem being its rapid movement.

Also encouraging for the future has been the use of insulin as a treatment for diabetics. Out of 86 people treated at St Bartholomew's Hospital in London, only 18 have died, and 12 of these from other causes. Diabetics can inject themselves, but errors by one patient led to 15 leg ulcers and admission to hospital in a coma.

Joan of Arc wins Nobel Literature Prize for Shaw

Dec 10. Bernard Shaw's response to the award of the Nobel Prize was typical: "No doubt it is a token of gratitude for the sense of world relief that I have published nothing this year". It is, of course, in recognition of his greatest and most successful play, "St. Joan", which was first performed last year.

Shaw had been contemplating a play about Joan of Arc for years but did not begin it until he saw Sybil Thorndike performing and decided that he had found his ideal Joan.

"I have told the story exactly as it happened. All I have done is to put down the facts," he said. "The trial scene is merely a report of the actual trial. I have used Joan's very words". In fact he has added Joan's great final speech of defiance of the tribunal, among other things.

The play has proved his greatest success at the box office in Britain, America and Europe. Shaw, therefore, has declined the prize money, saying it was "a lifebelt thrown to a swimmer who has already reached the shore in safety".

G. Bernard Shaw: on dry land.

Arts: Woolf ventures into new waters

Two brilliantly original novels have been hailed this year, one English, one American. **Virginia Woolf** has taken fiction into new waters in "Mrs Dalloway", using an experimental technique of directly recording consciousness, that "semi-transparent envelope surrounding us", as she has called it.

The novel concerns the seemingly trivial events of one day in London in 1923, the day on which she is to give a smart party and a young man, unknown to her, is to kill himself. It is a dazzling montage of scenes in the capital unified by the strokes of Big Ben. At the same time interior sensations and memories interleave the past and the present.

From **F. Scott Fitzgerald**, the chronicler of the Jazz Age (his phrase) comes "The Great Gatsby" named after a bootlegger with unsavoury connections. Gatsby is seen by the world through the haze of glamour which surrounds the continual parties he gives at his Long Island mansion.

His tragedy is his unrequited obsession with the rich girl, Daisy, for whose sake he has made his fortune. The ironic theme of the book is America's love affair with riches in the booming, bootlegging Jazz Age, which "raced along under its own power, served by great filling stations full of money."

The Surrealists, a new movement in poetry and painting, held their first exhibition in Paris. As defined by the poet **Andre Breton**, Surrealism aims at "pure psychic automatism, free of all control by reason." Surrealists also believe in the "omnipotence of the dream."

It originated partly from the irrationality of Dada, partly from the theories of **Sigmund Freud**. The artists exhibiting included **Max Ernst, Paul Klee, Giorgio di Chirico, Joan Miro** and **Picasso**.

Surrealist pictures cannot be described – they have to be experienced. They are a far cry from the stylish portraits which **Sir John Sargent**, who has died, painted of rich Edwardians – until he got bored with being "the Van Dyck of our age", as **Rodin** called him.

Films of the year: "The Battleship Potemkin" (**Eisenstein**), with an amazing sequence of a massacre on the Odessa steps, and "The Gold Rush" (**Chaplin**). The British Broadcasting Company conducted an experiment by relaying to the listening nation the sound of the laughter from the Tivoli cinema in the Strand in the sequence where Charlie wakes to find his cabin perched on a precipice. It was billed as "Ten minutes of laughter with Charlie Chaplin".

The sculptor **Jacob Epstein** has the habit of causing outrage with whatever he does. His statue of the "Risen Christ" was denounced by a Jesuit priest as resembling "a degraded Asiatic-American or Hun-Jew" and this summer even his memorial to **W.H. Hudson** in Hyde Park, entitled "Rima", has been tarred and feathered and daubed with green paint. It consists of a bas relief of a naked female torso surrounded by birds. But his portrait busts are keenly sought: sitters include **Bernard Shaw** and **Albert Einstein**.

In Montmartre the eccentric composer **Erik Satie**, who lived as a recluse, was found dead in an apartment cluttered with music and newspapers and bundles of love letters which he had written to the painter **Suzanne Valadon** but never sent. His piano music with strange titles ("Piece in the form of a Pear") was far in advance of its time. His three dreamy "Gymnopedies" were written as long ago as 1888 and orchestrated by **Claude Debussy**.

A new farce, "A Cuckoo in the Nest" by **Ben Travers** is packing the Aldwych theatre.

Chronicler of the Jazz Age: author Scott Fitzgerald with his wife, Zelda.

Eisenstein's "Battleship Potemkin".

1926

JANUARY

Su	Mo	Tu	We	Th	Fr	Sa
					1	2
3	4	5	6	7	8	9
10	11	12	13	14	15	16
17	18	19	20	21	22	23
24	25	26	27	28	29	30
31						

1. US: America leads the world with 61 per cent of the telephones in existence; 27 per cent are in Europe.

2. Rome: Mussolini issues a decree creating the Royal Academy of Italy (→3).

3. Rome: Mussolini now holds the posts of foreign minister and war minister as well as prime minister (→20).

5. UK: The first widows' pensions are paid out at post offices.

6. Germany: The airline Lufthansa is founded.

7. Hungary: Prince von Windischgraetz, Fascist vice-president of Hungary, is arrested for forgery; the Fascist leader Archduke Albert resigns (→26/5).

10. Berlin: Fritz Lang's film "Metropolis" opens.

12. Paris: The Pasteur Institute announces the discovery of an anti-tetanus serum.

13. US: 65 are feared dead after a mine explosion in Wilburton, Oklahoma.

15. Ankara: The Turkish government adopts the Swiss civil code as the basis of its legal system.

20. France: The congress of the banned Italian Communist Party opens in Lyons (→31).

25. UK: Surgeon Sir Berkeley Moynihan says cancer of the tongue is caused partly by smoking.

27. Washington: The Senate votes in favour of the US joining the International Court of Justice.

28. Brussels: Funeral of Cardinal Mercier.

29. Moscow: All students are ordered to do compulsory military training.

31. Rome: Benito Mussolini assumes the power to rule by decree.

DEATH

24. Belgian Primate Cardinal Desire Mercier (*21/11/1854).

Device sends moving images by radio

Jan 27. Moving pictures transmitted by wireless were demonstrated at the Royal Institution in London today by inventor John Logie Baird.

In Baird's system a scene is converted to varying electrical signals with the help of a camera that is partly mechanical and partly electrical. The signal is then transmitted by wireless. At the receiving end the scene is recreated by wholly electrical methods using a device familiar to scientists called a cathode ray tube.

The pictures in today's demonstration were crude and flickering, their quality far below that of the moving pictures to be seen in any cinema. But the principle of "television" has been proved. Although it is an invention still in its infancy, Baird believes that it could one day turn every home into a moving picture theatre.

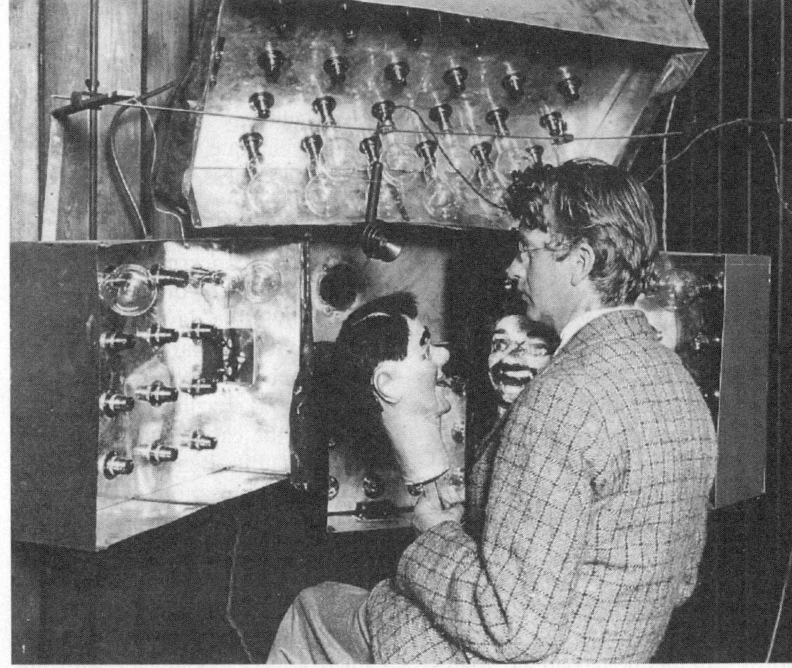

Baird with two ventriloquist dolls – the first image to be "televised".

British troops pull out of the Rhineland

Jan 30. The British flag was hauled down in a blaze of sunshine at three o'clock this afternoon and some thirty minutes later the last British troops, men of the King's Shropshire Light Infantry, left Cologne.

After seven years, the occupation of the Rhineland was at an end. In the final ceremony in the Cathedral square, the military band played a selection, not of British tunes, but of American ones, including Yankee Doodle and Swanee River.

In a midnight ceremony on the steps of the Cathedral, the Lord Mayor, Dr Konrad Adenauer, delivered a speech of thanksgiving and the crowd sang the German national anthem "Deutschland uber Alles".

New King names his country Saudi Arabia

Ibn Saud, flanked by advisors.

Jan 8. Abdul Aziz ibn Saud was today proclaimed king of the Hejaz at a special ceremony in the Grand Mosque at Mecca. He had summoned a gathering there of all the sheikhs, merchant princes and imams of the province. Just 24 years after this formidable Arab leader set out from exile in Kuwait to capture his natal desert city of Riyadh, he had in fact become king of what he intends to name Saudi Arabia. The final stage of Ibn Saud's triumphal march to power came last month when he arrived in Jeddah to accept its surrender. His traditional clan enemy, Hussein, Sheikh of Mecca, had already abdicated, and his son Ali then followed him into exile.

New authority to organise electricity

Jan 15. A new board is to coordinate electricity supplies, linking them in a national "grid". Outlining the plan today, Stanley Baldwin, the Prime Minister, said he expected doubled consumption in 15 years. Although 17 local frequencies cannot be interconnected, the power will be standardised at 50 cycles.

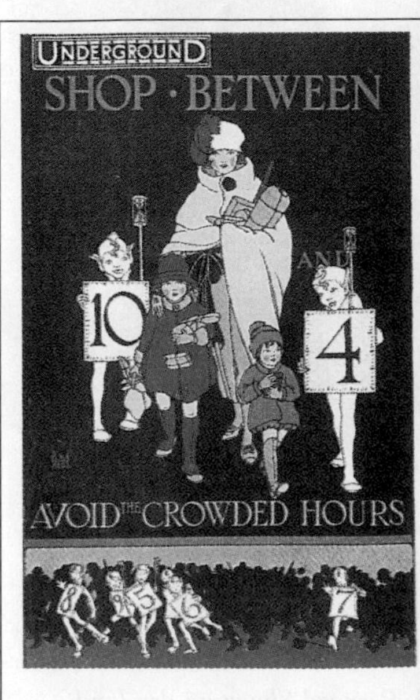

1926

FEBRUARY

Su	Mo	Tu	We	Th	Fr	Sa
	1	2	3	4	5	6
7	8	9	10	11	12	13
14	15	16	17	18	19	20
21	22	23	24	25	26	27
28						

3. Prague: Czech becomes the official language of Czechoslovakia, but rights of minority languages are guaranteed.

4. Monaco: Premiere of Maurice Ravel's opera "L'Enfant et les sortileges".

4. S. Africa: The Colour Bar Bill gets its third reading; Jan Smuts calls it "a firebrand flung into a haystack" (→17/3).

5. UK: The Food Council recommends the sale of food by standard measures (→20).

8. Berlin: The German government applies to join the League of Nations.

9. London: Flooding occurs in the suburbs after 18 days of continuous rain.

11. Mexico: The Calles government nationalises all church property (→7/8).

16. France: Suzanne Lenglen beats US champion Helen Wills in a match at Cannes.→

17. London: Government announces it is to give £2,000,000 for the development of Kent coalfields.

18. Teheran: Anglo-Persian treaty gives a further 25-year contract to the Anglo-Persian Oil Company (→21/3/51).

18. Mexico: The discovery is announced of five cities built by the Maya civilisation in the Yucatan.

19. Italy: 200 Mafia leaders are reported to have been arrested in Sicily.

20. London: The Food Council says it should be illegal to give short weight or measure (→6/7).

21. France: Suzanne Lenglen announces her retirement from singles play.

23. Washington: President Coolidge says a large air force would threaten world peace.

25. Warsaw: The Polish government asks to join the council of the League.

BIRTH

2. French statesman Valery Giscard d'Estaing, President 1974-81.

Beware drink and drugs, girls told

Hooked on the evil weed.

Feb 17. Modern young women are turning to drink and drugs in a desperate bid to cope with their hectic lives, a doctor warned today.

Dr J. S. Russell told the Institute of Hygiene that an abnormal lifestyle of nights of frivolity followed by days of excitement, coupled with the poisons of tobacco and alcohol, strained the nervous systems.

"Scarcely has the age of 20 been reached before the lines that belong to the face of a woman of middle age have become evident in such girls." His words follow a recent warning from another eminent doctor, who condemned the current craze for the willowy figure. Such women in trying to look like "weak and weedy men" could increase the risk of consumption.

A frivolous young lady showing off her "dangerously thin" figure.

1926

MARCH

Su	Mo	Tu	We	Th	Fr	Sa
	1	2	3	4	5	6
7	8	9	10	11	12	13
14	15	16	17	18	19	20
21	22	23	24	25	26	27
28	29	30	31			

1. London: The Government recognises Ibn Saud as King of Hejaz or "Saudi Arabia".

5. London: Four paintings by Constable are stolen from the Royal Academy.

9. Geneva: The League begins to consider Germany's admission (→13).

10. Egypt: The tomb of a parent of the Pharaoh Cheops, builder of the Great Pyramid, is discovered at Giza.

12. London: A Bill creating the Central Electricity Board is published.

12. Rome: The Senate passes new industrial relations laws, abolishing strikes.

13. Geneva: The League refuses Germany a permanent seat on the League council (→4/9).

15. Rome: Five Fascists go on trial for the murder of Socialist leader Giacomo Matteotti.→

17. New York: Richard Rodgers' musical "The Girl Friend" opens.

17. S. Africa: The English-speaking liberaldominated Senate rejects the Colour Bar Bill.

18. Peking: 17 are killed and 16 wounded when troops fire on demonstrating students.

18. London: The Post Office announces the introduction of cash-on-delivery parcel post (→29).

20. London: For the first time in the history of the competition, Scotland beats England for rugby's Calcutta Cup.

22. London: A one-way traffic system comes into operation at Hyde Park Corner.

24. London: The government says it will accept the report of the Coal Commission.→

24. US: Marion B. Skaggs starts the Safeways chain of general stores in Maryland.

26. UK: A. C. Schwartz's Jack Horner wins the Grand National at Aintree.

29. UK: Cash-on-delivery parcel post begins.

US model is not suitable for BBC

March 5. In a unanimous report, published last night, the radio committee of inquiry recommends that broadcasting should be run by a public corporation to be known as the British Broadcasting Commission. They say "the United States system of uncontrolled transmission is unsuited to this country".

The committee also wants to avoid government domination of the new body. It proposes that the executives shall be hired by commissioners of "judgment and independence". The commissioners will be appointed by the King and accountable to Parliament.

The committee praised the present BBC, a company owned by the wireless makers, for keeping a balance between different public tastes such as for jazz bands and classical music. They also suggest the wireless licence stays at ten shillings.

Pilot makes first return trip to Cape

Cobham – back from the Cape.

March 13. A cheering crowd welcomed the pilot Alan Cobham into Croydon aerodrome tonight as he completed his mammoth 16,000-mile flight from London to Cape Town and back. He was away nearly three months and braved sandstorms and waterlogged air strips on the trip. He believes it may lead to the setting up of a commercial air route across Africa. ▷

Miners angered by calls for pay cuts

March 24. The Miners' Federation of Great Britain will not accept the recommendations of the Royal Commission on the Coal Industry that the general level of wages must be cut and the 1924 minimum wage agreement abolished. The miners have adopted the slogan "Not a penny off the pay, not a minute on the day".

The Royal Commission under the chairmanship of Sir Herbert Samuel and with three other distinguished members, including Sir William Beveridge, was set up last summer. The government then averted a total lockout in the coal industry by agreeing to subsidise non-economic coal production for nine months while the Commission produced its report.

While proposing radical changes for the industry in future, including compulsory profit sharing for mine workers and paid annual holidays, the Samuel Commission declared that the coal subsidy was an indefensible burden on the rest of industry and that, since some 73 per cent of all coal was now being produced at a loss, wage cuts were inevitable if the industry was to survive and jobs were to be preserved.

The first liquid rocket is launched

March 6. The first-ever rocket to be powered by liquid fuels was launched today from a field in Massachusetts. Its inventor, Robert H. Goddard, hopes that, in future, more powerful versions will be able to carry scientific instruments high into the earth's atmosphere.

Goddard's rocket, about four feet long and six inches in diameter, was fuelled by gasoline and liquid oxygen and launched from a metal frame which held it upright.

Besides a lot of power for a given weight, liquid-fuelled rockets are much more controllable than ones that are merely scaled-up fireworks. If rocketry has a future it is likely to be along these pioneering lines. Because they carry their own oxygen, rockets could, in theory, operate in space.

£250,000 needed for Stratford theatre

Among the ruins of the burnt-out Shakespeare Memorial Theatre.

March 24. A national appeal to replace the Shakespeare Memorial Theatre, which burnt down at Stratford-on-Avon on March 6, is launched today.

The theatre opened in 1879 on a site beside the Avon given by Charles Flower of the Stratford brewery. The appeal, launched by the heads of the three political parties together with Thomas Hardy, the novelist, claims that at the old theatre it was possible for a visitor to see eight different Shakespeare plays in one week.

"The nation will call for the building of a new theatre worthy of Shakespeare's native town," they declared, appealing for £250,000. Sir Frank Benson, former director of Stratford Festivals, said that originally in 1885 "we were lucky if the receipts for a week amounted to a day's takings now".

Matteotti's killers will serve three months

March 24. Cheers ended the trial of the Fascist killers of the Socialist Deputy, Giacomo Matteotti, today when two of the accused were acquitted and the other three were found guilty of "unintentional murder". They were sent to prison for six years, but even these light sentences will be reduced because of the time the accused have spent waiting to be tried, and also because of the recently declared amnesty. It is not expected that any of these Fascist strong-arm men will serve more than 75 days.

Crimes against Members of Parliament normally require heavy sentences, but the jury found in this case that Matteotti was attacked, not because of his anti-Fascist stance in the Chamber, but because he was head of the Socialist Party.

1926

APRIL

Su	Mo	Tu	We	Th	Fr	Sa
				1	2	3
4	5	6	7	8	9	10
11	12	13	14	15	16	17
18	19	20	21	22	23	24
25	26	27	28	29	30	

1. Germany: Foreign minister Stresemann says Germany should little by little recover its status of great power.

2. India: The worst Hindu-Moslem riots for many years break out in Calcutta (→4).

4. India: Martial law is declared in Calcutta as rioting continues.→

7. Moscow: The government refuses to attend the coming international disarmament talks in Geneva.

10. Berlin: The ex-Imperial House of Hohenzollern owes 7,000,000 marks in taxes, according to the government.

16. Berlin: Measures are announced to give unemployed people an allowance for 39 weeks.

17. London: 20,000 members of the Women's Guild of the Empire demonstrate for an end to strikes and lockouts.

18. Morocco: The French and Spanish fail to agree with rebel leaders in talks to end the revolt led by Abdel Krim (→26/5).

24. London: Bolton Wanderers beat Manchester City 1-0 in the FA Cup Final.

24. Berlin: Germany signs a friendship treaty with the USSR.

25. Persia: Reza Khan Pahlavi is crowned Shah of Persia.→

25. Milan: Arturo Toscanini conducts the premiere of Puccini's last opera Turandot, completed by Franco Alfano.

25. US: The Association of University Professors says American football is a moral menace for students.

26. London: One-way traffic scheme is introduced in Trafalgar Square and is an instant success.

BIRTH

21. Queen Elizabeth II of Great Britain and Northern Ireland.→

DEATH

19. British actor Sir Squire Bancroft (*14/5/1841).

rish woman's shot misses Mussolini by a short nose

Aussolini, the survivor.

April 7. A most bizarre attempt was made on Benito Mussolini's life today when the Honourable Violet Gibson, daughter of an Irish peer, shot at him from close range. The bullet grazed the bridge of his nose, but although he bled copiously, he was not seriously hurt.

Miss Gibson was arrested, but there is considerable mystery about her motives for attempting to kill the Italian dictator. He was surprised by the fact his would-be assassin was female. "Fancy, a woman!" he said, and then went on to harangue his supporters: "If I go forward, follow me. If I go back, kill me. If I die, avenge me". This was the third attempt on his life. His followers now think he is under divine protection.

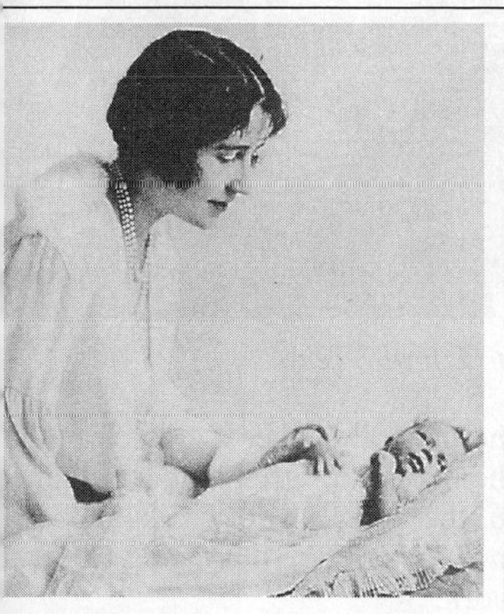
The Duchess of York with her first baby, Princess Elizabeth, who was born on April 21.

Savage riots rock India

April 24. The inter-communal riots between Hindus and Moslems in Calcutta have broken out again. The original riots were caused by Hindus playing their religious music outside a mosque. This time the fighting flared because of a rumour that Hindus had beaten two Moslems to death. The word ran like wildfire through the alleys and so Moslems, arming themselves with knives and clubs, took to the streets.

Tramcars and buses were stoned and stopped, passengers were dragged out and beaten. The tram and bus services were resumed after the rioters had been cleared away by armed police. A squad of policemen with a European sergeant is now guarding every vehicle.

This fresh outbreak follows the attacks made by militants of both communities on each other's places of worship. The bitterness of the rioting has been deepened by the attempts each side has made to burn down and defile mosques and temples. The rioting has also been used by gangs of hooligans as cover for organised looting. Many shops and houses have been cleaned out.

At one stage an armoured car had to be used to head off a mob of about 1,000 Moslems, who were heading for the Hindu quarter armed with all sorts of weapons. The armoured car commander was forced to open fire with his machine gun in order to disperse the crowd.

Some horrific killings have taken place. One Bengali woman was disembowelled and one terrible sight on the Esplanade, in the centre of the European city, was the arrival of a tramcar bearing, as its only passenger, a mutilated body. A gang had stopped the tram, beaten the passengers and ordered the driver, on pain of death, to drive the body to the Esplanade.

It is impossible to tell how many people have died so far because bodies are still being picked up in the back streets. A conservative estimate is over a hundred. There is an uneasy calm in the city tonight, with the army in control, but no-one knows when the killing and looting will start again.

Coal crisis looms as peace talks falter

April 30. A national coal stoppage has now begun. With the nine-month government coal subsidy ending at midnight and with most of Britain's miners under notice of lockout from the same moment, the employers' final offer today was a return to their 1921 minimum wage structure.

This would be equivalent to an average wage cut of about 13 per cent, and a "temporary" increase of the working day from seven to eight hours. It was flatly rejected. The miners will now appeal for support from the whole of the trade union movement. Mr J. H. Thomas, the railwaymen's leader, tonight said that the TUC would consider its position tomorrow and that it would be called upon to make "the most momentous decision any body of trade unionists had had to make up their minds upon".

Huddersfield score first League hat-trick

April 30. Huddersfield Town have clinched their third successive Football League title, a feat no other club has managed since professional football was officially established in England in 1888. Their unprecedented run of success can be attributed almost entirely to their authoritative manager, Herbert Chapman, who brought them from comparative obscurity at the end of the War to the FA Cup in 1922, and to their first two championships. Despite Chapman's much-publicised move to Arsenal, in North London, at the start of the 1925-6 season, Huddersfield were left with a balanced and well-integrated team fully qualified to exploit the new relaxation in the offside law (from three to two defenders required in front of an attacker), and their goal tally rose from 69 in the 1924-5 season to a record 92 in the triumphant hat-trick campaign.

One-time trooper crowns himself the Shah of Persia

The new Shah with his son.

April 25. A new dynasty was born in Persia today when Ali Reza Khan, a former Cossack cavalryman who became prime minister, had himself crowned Shah at the Royal Palace in Teheran. The ruling house is to be named Pahlavi.

With the title King Pahlavi, Reza Khan has in fact ruled the country as a dictator after an almost unanimous vote in the Majlis deposed the then Shah last autumn. There was talk of a republic being established but ambition and Moslem conservatism make that unlikely.

1926

MAY

Su	Mo	Tu	We	Th	Fr	Sa
						1
2	3	4	5	6	7	8
9	10	11	12	13	14	15
16	17	18	19	20	21	22
23	24	25	26	27	28	29
30	31					

1. UK: The miners go on strike; the TUC calls a General Strike of essential services in sympathy (→ 3).

2. India: Indian women are allowed to stand for election to public office.

3. UK: The General Strike begins at midnight.→

7. US: Official figures show that motor vehicles now account for one-third of US imports.

10. UK: Talks begin to end the General Strike (→ 12).

12. UK: The TUC calls off the General Strike.→

12. Warsaw: Polish Joseph Pilsudski leads a military coup (→ 13).

13. Warsaw: Pilsudski takes control; he puts President Wojciechowski under arrest (→ 1/6).

17. Berlin: Socialist Dr Wilhelm Marx becomes Chancellor again following Luther's resignation on May 12.

18. Geneva: Opening of the international conference on disarmament.

19. Syria: 600 are reported dead following French bombardment of Damascus during a rebellion.

24. Berlin: Finnish athlete Paavo Nurmi sets a new world record for the 3,000 metres race, of eight minutes 25 seconds.

26. Budapest: The Fascist vice-president Prince von Windischgraetz is found guilty of forging French banknotes.

28. Burma: 1,200 people are reported killed by a cyclone and tidal wave.

28. Lisbon: Portugese General Manuel Gomes da Costa seizes power in a coup d'Etat.

31. Washington: President Calvin Coolidge urges Europe to cut its arms spending in order to bring down taxes and avoid another world war.

BIRTH

25. US jazz musician Miles Davis (†28/9/91).

General Strike: TUC calls out workers

May 5. The first general strike in British history began at midnight yesterday after the general council of the Trades Union Congress voted to back the miners following the breakdown on Saturday night of their negotiations with coal-mine owners.

The critical talks with the TUC at Downing Street ended late on Sunday, after printers on the Daily Mail refused to print a leading article under a headline "For King and Country" written by the editor, Thomas Marlowe, which denounced the TUC's plans as a revolutionary act aimed at destroying the Government.

Mr Baldwin was persuaded, notably by Winston Churchill and Neville Chamberlain, to write immediately to the TUC denouncing this "gross interference with the freedom of the press" and insisting that the TUC repudiate the printers' action and withdraw its strike notices.

Until then, observers had hoped that the crisis might be averted by a "formula", drafted by Lord Birkenhead, under which the coal owners would withdraw their lock-out notices and the TUC would "urge" the miners to accept in principle the "temporary" reduction in wages recommended in March by the Samuels Commission.

A formal state of emergency was declared on Saturday in a special edition of the London Gazette. The country has been divided into areas, with emergency arrangements being run by Civil Commissioners. In calling the general strike of the nation's vital services, the TUC stressed that it would still distribute essential foodstuffs.

As a precaution against expected violence, troops have been deployed in South Wales, Yorkshire and Scotland. The unions have attacked this as evidence that "naked force will be used to smash the miners". On Saturday all British Broadcasting Company stations carried a message from the Prime Minister, read by the managing director, John Reith, calling on all to "Keep steady! Remember that peace on earth comes to all men of goodwill".

But so far there has in fact been very little violence. The only serious incidents have been in Glasgow, where mobs have tried to drive public vehicles off the road and have indulged in looting. But the police, using large numbers of special constables, have contained them without loss of life even there.

Indeed, after the second day of the general strike, it was clear tha the necessities are being maintaine in the towns and cities and tha most people are managing to get t work.

More trains ran today than o Tuesday and tramway and omnibu services, staffed by volunteers, ap peared in many towns (→ 10).

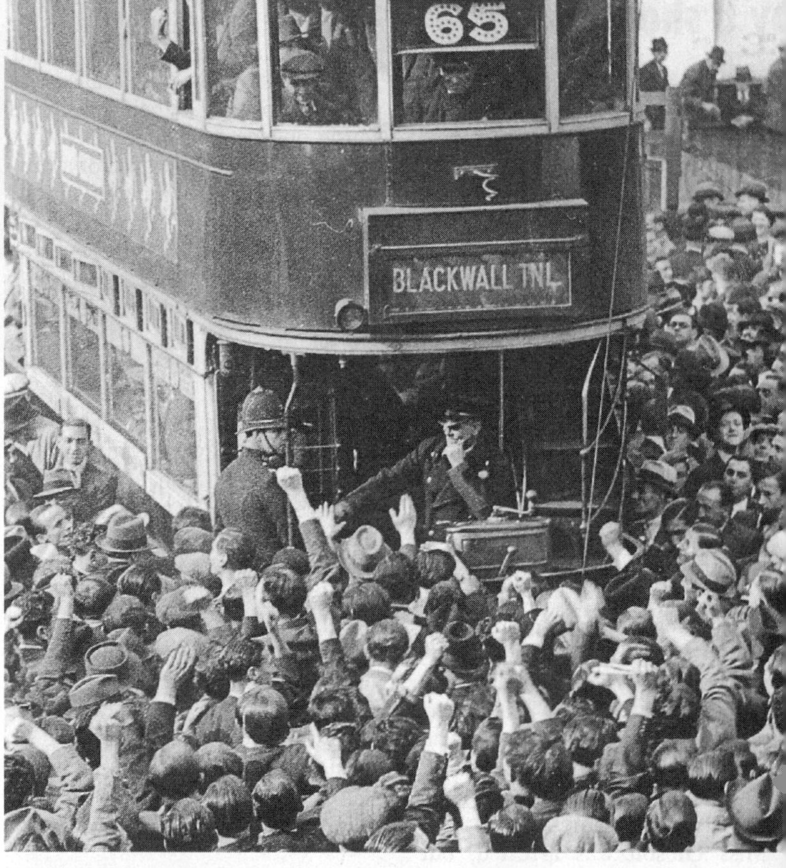

Crowds salute in triumph after immobilising a London tram.

An armoured car braves the journey down Oxford Street.

Showdown: class war splits Britain

Women volunteers help out with the mail at London's General Post Office.

Middle classes rally to beat the strike

May 10. Undergraduates, stockbrokers, barristers and other white-collar professionals realised boyhood fantasies today as they climbed on the footplates of strikebound trains and worked up steam.

More still were driving London's buses and lorries filled with essential food supplies. For many (the undergraduates in particular) it is a light-hearted break from routine.

But there is also a widespread determination on the part of the establishment that the strike should disrupt daily life as little as possible. As the secretary of the MCC remarked: "As far as we can see, we have no intention to allow cricket to be interrupted".

Over 6,000 men and women have lined up in the quadrangle of the Foreign Office to sign with the Organisation for the Maintenance of Supplies.

There are more serious undertones, however, as scores of suited city office workers continue to queue at London police stations to be sworn in as special constables.

The Commissioner of Police called for "capable citizens under 45 with the requisite health, strength and vigour" to be prepared for duty.

Churchill is robust editor-in-emergency

PLEASE PASS ON THIS COPY OR DISPLAY IT

The British Gazette

GENERAL STRIKE OFF

The Morning Post.

ON FRIDAY, MAY 14, THE MORNING POST will RESUME PUBLICATION

Price ONE Penny

The "Gazette" declares victory.

May 8. The first issue of the "British Gazette" appeared today under the ebullient editorship of Winston Churchill, Chancellor of the Exchequer. Printed on the commandeered presses of the Morning Post, it will provide daily and officially-approved news in the absence of ordinary newspapers.

Mr Churchill is demanding unconditional surrender by the strikers, whom he calls "the enemy". He has declined to publish a peace appeal from the Archbishop of Canterbury. His robust mood contrasts with most of the rest of the Cabinet, who hope for an early end to the strike.

Embattled miners to fight on alone

May 20. The miners have rejected the Prime Minister's terms for ending the three-week-old coal dispute. Despite the fact that the TUC called off the general strike over a week ago, the miners' delegate conference today passed a resolution to continue the fight.

Miners' leaders such as Arthur Cook and W.P. Richardson are bitter at the way the miners have been "deserted" by the trade union movement. But the TUC team, led by its chairman, Arthur Pugh, and its acting secretary, Walter Citrine, had little alternative when it went to No. 10 on May 12 but to call off the nine-day General Strike unconditionally, for it was crumbling.

On the first day of the strike only 849 trains ran in the entire country. By May 12 this was up to some 5,500. After May 8, when a detachment of Grenadier Guards with 20 armoured cars escorted a convoy of 100 food lorries from the docks to the Hyde Park depot, London's supplies were assured.

The TUC leaders rapidly saw that out of solidarity with the miners they had stumbled into declaring a general strike, which put them in an impossible direct challenge to the Government's authority. For this they had neither the will nor the means (→8/7).

W.P. Richardson, miners' official.

Big guns knock out Moroccan rebels

May 26. Abdel Krim, the rebel leader from the Riff mountains of Morocco who inflicted a crushing defeat on the Spanish five years ago, today surrendered unconditionally to an overwhelmingly superior French-led force. Marshal Philippe Petain, hero of Verdun during the Great War, directed the Franco-Spanish campaign against Abdel Krim, and recruited 40,000 native troops to bring his strength to 160,000, backed by artillery. The Spanish contributed another 90,000 men. The rebels, holed up in the supposedly impregnable Targuist, numbered 30,000. Krim is to be exiled to Reunion in the Indian Ocean.

Airship and plane fly over North Pole

American pioneer Richard Byrd.

May 13. An international team of pioneer flyers made history today, when they arrived safely at Nome in Alaska, having flown over the North Pole in an airship. Among those on board were the conqueror of the South Pole, Roald Amundsen of Norway, Lincoln Ellsworth of the United States and Umberto Nobile of Italy. They took off from Spitzbergen on the 11th, reached the North Pole early the next day and dropped flags before continuing on to Alaska.

This exploit comes only days after another polar flight by two Americans, Floyd Bennett and Navy Commander Richard Byrd, in a Fokker trimotor aircraft. They took off from Spitzbergen, north of Norway, on the morning of May 9, flew over the Pole and returned to base 16 hours later.

1926

JUNE

Su	Mo	Tu	We	Th	Fr	Sa
		1	2	3	4	5
6	7	8	9	10	11	12
13	14	15	16	17	18	19
20	21	22	23	24	25	26
27	28	29	30			

1. Warsaw: Ignac Moscicki takes over as President, but Pilsudski remains effective dictator.→

2. UK: Lord Woolavington's Coronach wins the Derby at Epsom.

5. London: Britain signs an accord with Turkey over disputed territory on the Turkish-Iraqi border.

8. London: Soprano Dame Nellie Melba gives her farewell performance at Covent Garden.

10. Geneva: Brazil leaves the League of Nations; Spain threatens to do so, but changes its mind.

14. India: Riots between Hindus and Moslems break out in Rawalpindi.

16. Naples: Fascist leader Aurelio Padovani is killed when a balcony collapses.

17. Germany: The rules of the road are unified.

19. London: 100,000 women go on a march for peace.

21. Wimbledon: The 50th tournament opens; Prince Albert, Duke of York, plays in the Doubles (→3/7).

24. London: Papers taken in 1925 raids on the Communist Party are published, including Russian ideas for strike chaos.

25. Africa: German archaeologist Dr Borchardt claims he has located the lost city of Atlantis in the Sahara Desert.

28. Ottawa: Liberal Prime Minister William Mackenzie King and his cabinet resign in the wake of a customs scandal (→15/9).

29. Rome: Mussolini's government increases the working day by one hour as part of an efficiency drive.

30. Paris: French police thwart a plot to kill Spanish King Alfonso XIII during his current visit to France.

BIRTHS

1. US actress Marilyn Monroe (†5/8/62).

3. US poet Allen Ginsberg.

Pilsudski seizes power in Poland

June 13. Marshal Josef Pilsudski, the Polish war leader, has staged a successful coup d'etat in Warsaw and now enjoys dictatorial power. The president and the cabinet have been forced to accept his demands, and have named him permanent commander of the army, and he cannot be overruled by the cabinet or by acts of parliament. In effect, this makes him dictator of Poland.

Pilsudski, while admired by the Poles, is also regarded with some trepidation. He hates the Russians – he was sent to Siberia for plotting to kill Czar Alexander III – and it is feared he may lead Poland into another war against Russia.

Amateur in record win of the Open

June 25. Bobby Jones, a 25-year-old lawyer from Atlanta, Georgia, who has twice won the Amateur Championship in Britain, today became the first amateur since 1897 to take golf's greatest prize, the Open. In the event's first visit to Lytham St Anne's, on the Lancashire coast, Jones's four-round total of 291 led a quartet of Americans (the others all professionals) to the top four places.

Bobby Jones drives out the pros.

1926

JULY

Su	Mo	Tu	We	Th	Fr	Sa
				1	2	3
4	5	6	7	8	9	10
11	12	13	14	15	16	17
18	19	20	21	22	23	24
25	26	27	28	29	30	31

2. London: The government is to import large quantities of food as the coal strike enters its third month.→

3. Wimbledon: Jean Borotra beats Howard Kinsey in the Men's Singles final; Kitty Godfree beats Lili de Alvarez for the Ladies' Singles title.

3. France: 19 are reported killed and 100 injured when the Paris-Le Havre train crashes.

4. Germany: The first congress of the reconstituted Nazi Party begins, called by Adolf Hitler.

6. London: The Sale of Food Bill is introduced to give effect to the recommendations of the Food Council.

7. London: Rudyard Kipling is awarded a gold medal by the Royal Society of Literature.

10. US: Lightning strikes a US Navy munitions dump, causing an explosion visible for 30 miles.

14. London: From next year broadcasting will be in the hands of a new British Broadcasting Corporation.

16. US: Rudolph Valentino's latest film "Son of the Sheikh" opens (→15/8).

23. Rome: Mussolini says Italy must expand or suffocate.

23. Paris: A coalition is formed under Raymond Poincare as the franc falls on foreign exchanges.

24. Manchester: The first greyhound racing track opens at Belle Vue.

26. US: Governor Miriam Ferguson resigns after losing in the primary elections for governor.

27. London: A circular traffic system comes into operation at Piccadilly Circus.

29. London: County Council medical officers praise the hygienic value of modern fashions.

30. Berlin: Professor Wolff Heide announces a colour film process that offsets the need for screens and filters.

Duke of York courts Wimbledon crowds

A right royal display.

July 3. Wimbledon has celebrated its Golden Jubilee in great style over the past fortnight, from the parade of past champions on the opening day to Kitty Godfree's British victory in the ladies' singles. The highlight of the tournament for the vast crowds, though, was the appearance of the Duke of York, second in line to the throne, competing with Louis Greig in the men's doubles on Centre Court. They went out in straight sets to the former champions A.W. Gore and Roper Barrett.

Labour MPs disrupt the House of Lords

July 8. The Coal Mines Bill was enacted tonight amid extraordinary scenes in the Lords, just as there were signs that the miners' strike is crumbling. The Bill allows longer working hours, but, according to government sources, only one miner in five will be paid less.

Militant Labour MPs visited the House of Lords and, as the King's assent to the new law was promulgated, they yelled "Murder Bill" at shocked peers, and "Four hours for you. Eight hours for miners". Back in the Commons, Tory MPs called for stiff action to check what sounded like revolution on their own doorstep.

1926

AUGUST

Su	Mo	Tu	We	Th	Fr	Sa
1	2	3	4	5	6	7
8	9	10	11	12	13	14
15	16	17	18	19	20	21
22	23	24	25	26	27	28
29	30	31				

1. Barcelona: Premier Miguel Primo de Rivera escapes an assassination attempt.

3. London: The capital's first traffic lights come into operation at Piccadilly Circus.

5. Paris: France and Germany sign a trade accord.

7. Mexico: President Calles rules out foreign mediation in the current battle between the government and the Church (→19).

11. New York: Eastman Kodak Co. says it is working on colour motion pictures.

13. UK: Three million tons of coal have been imported since the miners' strike started (→18).

15. New York: Rudolph Valentino undergoes emergency surgery for a ruptured appendix.→

18. UK: Miners reopen negotiations with the government to end their three-month old strike (→24).

19. Mexico: President Calles rejects a plea by Mexican bishops to suspend recent anti-clerical laws.

22. Greece: A coup led by Georgios Kondylis overthrows the regime of General Theodoros Pangalos.

24. UK: Riots break out among striking coal miners.

26. Turkey: Leaders of a plot to topple Mustafa Kemal are executed.

29. Germany: Nuremburg hosts a big National Socialist Party rally.

30. London: Jack Hobbs scores 316 at Lords, the ground's highest ever individual innings.

31. UK: Lancashire wins the county cricket championships for the first time since 1904.

31. S. Africa: 15,000 people are reported to be heading for a new diamond field in the Transvaal.

DEATH

23. Italian-born US film star Rudolph Valentino (*6/5/1895).→

Woman swims Channel in record time

"We didn't expect you so soon" - Gertrude cuts man's time by two hours.

Aug 6. Gertrude Ederle, bronze medallist in the 400 metres freestyle two years ago at the Paris Olympic Games, has become the first woman to swim the Channel - and in a time faster than any of the men who have done it since Captain Webb's pioneering swim 51 years ago.

The 19-year-old New Yorker overcame the cold, the strength-sapping tides and currents, and an unexpectedly sharp wind, to cross from Cap Gris Nez to the Kent coast in 14 hours 31 minutes, more than two hours quicker than the record set by the Argentinian Sebastian Tirabocchi three years ago.

England regain Ashes after 14 years

Aug 18. England have regained the Ashes after 14 years, with a victory by 289 runs in the fifth Test match at The Oval. With the first four three-day Tests of the series all ending in draws, this final match was to be played to a finish. With their new young captain, Percy Chapman, in full command, and the veteran Wilfred Rhodes recalled at the age of 48 to wrap up Australia's second innings, it was a triumph for the selectors.

The unquestioned cornerstone of England's victory was the fine second innings opening partnership by Hobbs (100) and Sutcliffe (161) on a damp pitch, which then saw Australia all out for a meagre 125 amid scenes of wild jubilation.

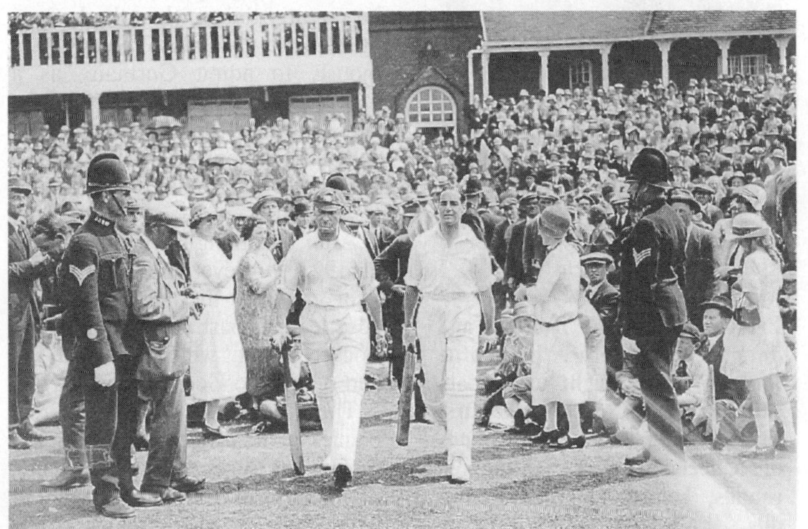

Hobbs and Sutcliffe - architects of today's triumph - seen earlier at Leeds.

Female fans mourn death of Valentino

Aug 23. His real name was Rodolfo Guglielmi di Valentina d'Antonguella, but to the fans who today queued to pay homage to their idol, he was simply Valentino: the glamorous star of films such as "The Sheikh", who has died in New York at the age of only 31.

He had been in hospital for only five days, suffering first from a ruptured appendix. Then a gastric ulcer caused complications from which he died, babbling a mixture of French and Italian. News of his death caused hysteria, with one fan reported to have shot herself. The actor, who arrived in the United States in 1913, achieved stardom in films such as "The Four Horsemen of the Apolcalypse" and "Blood and Sand".

Valentino savours Arabian scents.

Southern Railway opts for electric

Aug 9. Steam engines will disappear from the Southern Railway, it was announced yesterday. In their place will come engines using electricity supplied by a third rail. More than 230 miles of track will be converted to the new system, which will also replace the overhead electric system used in parts of south-east England. Although steam enthusiasts may be dismayed, the £3 million improvement scheme - due to be completed in 1928 - is said to promise a better service.

1926

SEPTEMBER

Su	Mo	Tu	We	Th	Fr	Sa
			1	2	3	4
5	6	7	8	9	10	11
12	13	14	15	16	17	18
19	20	21	22	23	24	25
26	27	28	29	30		

2. China: Chiang Kai-shek launches an offensive aimed at capturing Hankow.→

4. Geneva: The League rejects Spain's application for a permanent seat on the League council (→ 7).

5. Irish Free State: 50 people are reported killed and 20 hurt in a fire at a cinema in Drumcollegher, Limerick.

7. Madrid: The government decides to quit the League of Nations.

9. UK: The TUC conference is adjourned because of disorder after a motion to give financial aid to the miners (→ 5/10).

11. Berlin: German Otto Peltzer wins 1,500 metres race in a record three minutes 51 seconds.

11. Spain: A referendum gives overwhelming support to premier Primo de Rivera.

13. London: Northern Line extension from Clapham Common to Morden opens; the 17-mile Tube from Morden to East Finchley via Bank is the world's longest tunnel.

15. Chicago: Jelly Roll Morton and his band Red Hot Peppers hold their first recording session.

15. Canada: The Liberals under William Mackenzie King are returned to power in the general election.

19. US: 1,500 are reported dead and nearly 40,000 homeless after a hurricane sweeps Florida (→ 23).

20. Chicago: Al Capone's Hawthorne headquarters is sprayed with machine gun fire in broad daylight.

23. US: Florida drafts its unemployed to help clear up after the hurricane.

28. New York: "Gentlemen Prefer Blondes" opens.

28. UK: The 13th edition of the Encyclopaedia Britannica is completed.

BIRTH

23. US jazz musician John Coltrane (†17/7/67).

Chiang Kai-shek is winning the civil war

A cavalry patrol loyal to General Chiang Kai-shek rides through Canton.

Sept 8. Grave news from the Yangtse River front in the Chinese civil war reached London yesterday. The "Red" army of General Chiang Kai-shek's Kuomintang has captured Hankow, an important city and treaty port. The southern Reds also took Wuchang on the opposite bank and Hangyang, the greatest arsenal in China. There is now a danger that they may soon control the whole of China as far as Peking.

After their crushing defeat, Northern troops, commanded by Wu Pei-fu, are in full retreat along the Hankow-Peking railway. Wu's army was originally estimated to have a strength of 150,000. The fact that only 10,000 are left means that the rest have gone over to the enemy, or have simply "melted" as is common in Chinese warfare.

In a gallant action Royal Navy gunboats rescued five British merchant officers held by 600 Chinese soldiers on board a ship in the Yangtse. In the fight 13 British sailors died. One merchant officer is missing.

Philadelphia: Gene Tunney and Jack Dempsey before their battle for the heavyweight championship of the world. For the first time ever the title changed hands on a decision: after fighting ten rounds, Tunney emerged victorious.

League votes to admit Germany

Sept 8. Gustav Stresemann scored another foreign policy success for his country today, when the League of Nations Assembly voted unanimously to admit Germany as a member. Stresemann, leader of the conservative People's Party, was a vehement supporter of the war and in 1919 voted against the Versailles treaty.

After becoming Foreign Minister in 1923, however, he was conciliatory towards the Allies and played a leading part in promoting the Locarno pact, which signaled the end of Franco-German hostility.

The acceptance was not entirely painless. Brazil resigned and Spain threatened to because neither has a permanent seat. Russia and the US have no seats either, which weakens the League's authority.

1926

OCTOBER

Su	Mo	Tu	We	Th	Fr	Sa
					1	2
3	4	5	6	7	8	9
10	11	12	13	14	15	16
17	18	19	20	21	22	23
24	25	26	27	28	29	30
31						

1. Warsaw: Pilsudski officially becomes Polish premier.

2. UK: A French airliner bursts into flames over Kent, killing seven passengers.

5. UK: 250,000 striking miners have now returned to work (→ 15).

7. Paris: The 20th international motor show opens.

7. Rome: The Fascist Party is decreed the party of the State; Mussolini assumes total power and all opposition is banned (→ 23).

10. New York: Greta Garbo opens in "The Temptress".

14. London: Ex-PM Lord Oxford and Asquith resigns as leader of the Liberal Party.

15. UK: 47 are hurt when police clash with striking Welsh miners at Glencymmer Colliery, near Port Talbot.

16. India: Sectarian rioting breaks out during a Hindu festival.

19. London: Opening of the Imperial Conference (→ 20/11).

22. London: The motor show opens at Olympia.

23. Moscow: Leon Trotsky and Grigori Zinoviev are expelled from the Communist Party Central Committee.

23. Rome: A decree bans women from holding public office.

26. Brussels: Launch of a new currency unit, the Belga, worth five francs, aimed at stabilising the country's economy.

31. Rome: A 15-year-old boy is lynched after firing a shot at Mussolini, tearing the dictator's coat.

BIRTHS

18. German actor Klaus Kinski (†23/11/91).

18. US rock musician Chuck Berry.

DEATHS

20. US socialist leader Eugene Debs (*5/11/1855).

31. Hungarian-born US escape artist Ernst Weiss, alias Harry Houdini (*6/4/1874).→

Harry Houdini dies of burst appendix

Oct 31. Harry Houdini lost his life-ong game of dicing with death to-day. The world-famous escapolo-gist died in a Detroit hospital at the ige of 52.

Houdini's ability to escape, chained and handcuffed, from a water-filled milk churn gained him in international reputation. His most famous stunt involved him being suspended high in the air, upside down, manacled and trussed up in a straight-jacket.

The master-escaper even suc-ceeded in breaking free after being ocked naked in some of America's most closely guarded prisons.

He also claimed that his stomach muscles could withstand powerful punches. He had just boasted of this to a class of students in Montreal when one of them stepped up with-out warning and hit him twice just above the appendix.

On his arrival back in America, Houdini was in great pain. Doctors removed his appendix, but periton-itis had set in.

Houdini, who had a lifelong fas-cination with spiritualism, was not-ed for his exposures of fake med-iums.

Houdini – one brag too many.

Britain delighted by bear of little brain

Oct 14. Mr A. A. Milne's small son, Christopher Robin, is the most celebrated child in juvenile litera-ture since Alice Liddell – thanks to the vogue for his father's book of verse about him, "When We Were Very Young", which has run into 14 editions in two years.

Christopher Robin reappears to-day, aged six, with his teddy bear in "Winnie-the-Pooh". When he is told a male bear cannot be called Winnie, he replies "Don't you know what "the" means?" Pooh, a "bear of little brain" but enormous charm, is the favourite in these adventures of nursery animals wit-tily drawn by E. H. Shepard.

To Australia and back by air in 58 days

Oct 1. Aviation history was made today when the veteran long-distance pilot Alan Cobham landed his sea plane on the Thames at Westmins-ter to complete his record 28,000-mile round-trip to Australia.

Thousands packed both banks of the river to see the pilot, who earl-ier this year flew to Cape Town and back, return home in triumph. It took his De Havilland 50 biplane 29 days each way on the journey across Europe, the Middle East, India and the Dutch East Indies.

Mr Cobham believes sea planes will be the most suitable for the journey in future as they can put down in areas without air strips, although it will still be some time before ordinary travellers can cover all the route by air.

Cobham makes his final descent.

1926

NOVEMBER

Su	Mo	Tu	We	Th	Fr	Sa
	1	2	3	4	5	6
7	8	9	10	11	12	13
14	15	16	17	18	19	20
21	22	23	24	25	26	27
28	29	30				

1. Berlin: Philosophy professor Dr. Josef Goebbels is chosen to head the Berlin district Nazi Party.

2. UK: The formation of Imperial Chemical Industries is announced.

3. UK: Bookies strike at Windsor in protest at the new betting tax that came into force on November 1.

8. Philippines: A typhoon devastates the island of Luzon, claiming a reported 175 lives.

9. UK: 15.4 million tons of coal have been imported in the pit strike, which has lost the industry £300 million.→

12. Dutch East Indies: Nationalists in Java launch a rebellion against Dutch rule.

12. Nicaragua: President Adolfo Diaz calls for US aid to suppress a revolt by the Liberal Party.

13. Italy: Mario de Bernardi sets a world seaplane speed record of 246 mph.

17. USSR: Married couples are to get stamped identity cards, it is announced.

21. New York: Opening of "The Great Gatsby", based on Scott Fitzgerald's novel.

25. Rome: Mussolini restores the death penalty.

26. Bucharest: A cancer specialist is called in to attend King Ferdinand.

27. Italy: Mount Vesuvius erupts.

28. Washington: The Hoover Report reveals that the US is enjoying its highest ever standard of living.

30. China: The US sends warships to Hankow to prevent feared Communist attacks on foreigners.

30. New York: S. Romberg's operetta "The Desert Song" opens.

DEATHS

2. US sharpshooter Annie Oakley (*13/8/1860).

26. US arms inventor John Moses Browning (*21/1/1855).

We aren't losing an Empire but gaining a Commonwealth

Nov 20. The British Empire had an historic facelift today. An Imperial Conference in London announced that Canada, Australia, New Zea-land, South Africa and Newfound-land will be self-governing domin-ions. Under the Crown they will have equal status with Britain as members of the British Common-wealth of nations and be masters of their own destiny.

The King's title will be changed to acknowledge that, although the Irish Free State is also a Dominion, the King is no longer its sovereign. In deference to Irish nationalist senti-ment the words "United Kingdom" are therefore being dropped from the title. There will now be appro-priate legislation to implement these innovations. The unique non-independent status of India is un-changed. In Australia the acting premier said: "Even if we have a personality of our own, we all remain British".

The King's title is now "George V, by the Grace of God, of Great Britain, Ireland and the British Dominions beyond the Seas, King, Defender of the Faith, Emperor of India". In the presence of Empire leaders, the Prince of Wales unveiled a tablet in Westminster Abbey in honour of one million Empire men killed in the Great War.

Il Duce has divine protection says Pope

Nov 2. The notion that Benito Mussolini enjoys the protection of divine providence was given Papal blessing today. When the Duce escaped the fourth attempt on his life, this time by an 18-year-old boy, Pope Pius observed: "This is a new sign that Mussolini has God's full protection".

Divine protection or not, Il Duce's followers are making the most of his escape. He is being praised for his cool behaviour during the attack and thousands of sympathetic telegrams have been sent to him. What is also emerging is that the Fascists are using the attempt to strike at their enemies. Secretary General Turati, whipping up 50,000 Blackshirts in Rome, declared: "Nothing but death will satisfy us".

The Fascist leader in Rome.

Miners finally agree to end pit strike

Nov 12. At three o'clock this morning, miners' leaders and the Government reached agreement on the ending of the six-month-old coal dispute. In effect the miners have caved in to the employers' demand that working hours be increased from seven to eight.

The miners' executive also conceded the principle that agreements should be negotiated locally and not nationally. It agreed that the union would "do all in its power" to get an immediate return to work. In return, the owners have agreed "temporarily" not to cut wages below pre-April levels, except in Durham, Northumberland, Cumberland and North Wales.

As a concession to the miners, the Government has agreed to give an independent tribunal powers for six months to examine and vary district agreements. In the past five weeks there has been a steady drift of miners back to work. Over 300,000 were back yesterday.

Shaw's problem is giving money away

Nov 18. Nothing but embarrassment has resulted from Mr Bernard Shaw's refusal of the Nobel Prize money of £7,000, awarded to him a year ago. The Royal Swedish Academy cannot dispose of the money except to him and he has been deluged with begging letters.

Exasperated by the impasse, Shaw declared: "I can forgive Alfred Nobel for having invented dynamite, but only a fiend in human form could have invented the Nobel Prize!"

The solution is for him to receive the money and immediately give it away to the newly formed "Anglo-Swedish Literary Alliance".

At Waddon you can fly the latest biplanes, or just watch.

1926

DECEMBER

Su	Mo	Tu	We	Th	Fr	Sa
			1	2	3	4
5	6	7	8	9	10	11
12	13	14	15	16	17	18
19	20	21	22	23	24	25
26	27	28	29	30	31	

2. London: Stanley Baldwin ends emergency powers assumed during the General Strike (→9).

3. UK: Novelist Mrs Agatha Christie disappears from her Surrey home.→

6. Rome: Mussolini approves a tax on bachelors (→15).

9. UK: Coal restrictions in force during the miners' strike come to an end.

10. Stockholm: Nobel Prizes go to Jean Perrin (France, Physics), Theodor Svedberg (Sweden, Chemistry), Johannes Fibiger (Denmark, Medicine), Grazia Deledda (Italy, Literature); the Peace Prize is awarded in Oslo to Aristide Briand (France) and Gustav Stresemann (Germany).

15. Italy: The Roman fasces, symbol of authority and origin of the name "Fascist", is adopted as national emblem.

21. UK: Oswald Mosley wins the Smethwick by-election for Labour after a rowdy campaign.

25. Japan: Hirohito ascends the throne on the death of his father Emperor Yoshihito.

27. UK: Imperial Airways announces the first scheduled air service to India from the New Year (→8/1/27).

28. Melbourne: Victoria score a first-class record innings of 1,107 runs against New South Wales.

DEATHS

5. French artist Claude Monet (*14/11/1840).→

25. Japanese Emperor Yoshihito (*31/8/1879).

29. Austrian poet Rainer Maria Rilke (*4/12/1875).

HITS OF 1926

Black Bottom.

Bye Bye Blackbird.

QUOTE OF THE YEAR

"Not a penny off the pay, not a minute on the day."
Arthur James Cook,
Miners' Federation secretary, during the General Strike.

Strange case of the vanishing novelist

Agatha Christie: found in hotel.

Dec 14. A nation-wide police hunt for Agatha Christie, the novelist whose abandoned car was found in Surrey recently, ended last night when Colonel Archie Christie identified a guest at a Harrogate hotel as his wife.

Yorkshire police were told when a maid at the hotel spotted a marked similarity between a newspaper photograph of Mrs Christie and one of the hotel guests. Colonel Christie travelled north and reclaimed his missing wife, who has no recollection of how she came to be in Yorkshire. Until she regains her memory, the mystery is likely to remain as intriguing as the plots she so skilfully weaves for her books.

Sculpting dinosaur eggs in Mongolia

Dec 31. What could be traces of man's earliest ancestors have been found in Outer Mongolia by an expedition from the New York Museum of Natural History. Objects found so far, all of them thousands of years old, include tools of flint and jasper, fireplaces, and ornaments carved from, of all things, petrified dinosaur eggs.

Europe was once favoured as the site of man's origins, but older remains have turned up in Africa and India. Now East Asia is a possibility too, though the expedition leader, Chapman Andrews, thinks there may have been a migration there from Europe.

Monet, the purist, dies

Claude Monet in the garden of his home at Giverny, where he died.

Dec 6. The last Impressionist painter, who was also the first, has gone. Claude Monet has died at 86 at his lovely home, Giverny, in Normandy, where he had lived for more than 50 years, comforted by the beautiful garden he created.

The last 20 years of his life were among his most productive. He took the water garden he had made as his subject, painting ever larger and more delicate canvases, some of them 14 feet wide. In 1922 he presented 19 of them to France.

In a specially built studio in the garden he placed the canvases end to end in a curve to create a panorama of water-lilies without end.

Monet's picture, "Impression, Sunrise", shown in 1873 gave rise to the name Impressionist, applied in mockery at first. He remained the purest of the group, painting the same subject over and over again in differing conditions of light – as he did of the Thames at Westminster.

He once said that he would like to paint like a blind man whose sight has just been restored. When his near-blindness from cataract was cured three years ago he put his wish into practice.

One of Monet's Impressionist masterpieces, "The Beach at Trouville".

Arts: Bauhaus is affecting our house

The Bauhaus school of architecture and design has moved from Weimar, where it was founded in 1919 by architect **Walter Gropius**, to Dessau, where he has designed a severely functional building of steel and glass.

Bauhaus teaching stresses that every craft employed should contribute to a single work of art – the building and its contents. One product of Bauhaus design is the modern kitchen, with counters and cupboards placed around the walls. Another is stainless steel furniture.

Gropius has gathered round him such distinguished teachers as **Kandinsky, Klee, Marcel Breuer** and **Mies van der Rohe**.

Riots are nothing new at the Abbey Theatre, Dublin, but a free fight on the stage broke out in a performance of **Sean O'Casey's** new play about the Easter Rising, "The Plough and the Stars".

Women mounted the stage to remonstrate with the actors and a man, clinging to the curtain as it was lowered, was knocked into the orchestra pit. **Yeats**, founder of the theatre, addressed the audience – "You have disgraced yourselves" – and called the police.

In London the play and O'Casey were both given a warm welcome. Humorous even when portraying tragic events, as in his "Juno and the Paycock" seen here last year, O'Casey is yet another fine playwright to come out of Ireland.

Fred Astaire and his sister **Adele** have London at their nimble feet in **George Gershwin's** "Lady Be Good", which rises to new heights of syncopation in "Fascinating Rhythm".

Author T.E. Lawrence: thinking.

The reputation of **Franz Kafka** is growing in Germany after the publication of his novels "The Castle" and "The Trial". Kafka, an insurance official who died of tuberculosis two years ago, left instructions that they should be burnt, but his wishes were disregarded.

In "The Trial" Joseph K. wakes up one morning to be arrested, although he does not know what he has done wrong – a typical Kafka nightmare situation.

The death of **Rudolph Valentino** at 31 caused desperation and several suicides. But **Ramon Novarro's** Latin looks soon replaced him. His debut was in "Ben Hur".

Film star Greta Garbo.

Desk lamp by Christian Dell.

1927

JANUARY

Su	Mo	Tu	We	Th	Fr	Sa
						1
2	3	4	5	6	7	8
9	10	11	12	13	14	15
16	17	18	19	20	21	22
23	24	25	26	27	28	29
30	31					

1. UK: The British Broadcasting Corporation (formerly Company) broadcasts its first programmes.

1. London: The Bankers' Clearing House says cheques are becoming more popular as a means of payment.

2. Lisbon: Bubonic plague is reported to have broken out.

5. New York: Fox demonstrates the "Movietone", which synchronises sound with motion pictures.

8. India: The first scheduled London-Delhi flight arrives after 63 hours; Air Minister Sir Samuel Hoare is on board.

9. Montreal: 77 children die in ten minutes in the panic to escape a burning theatre.

10. Los Angeles: Charlie Chaplin's wife Lita Grey files for divorce (→22/8).

15. Rome: Winston Churchill meets Mussolini.

17. Mexico: 100 are killed when an archbishop leads a revolt of Catholics against the government.

21. UK: The number of telephones in use is now estimated to be 500,000.

25. Washington: President Coolidge says the US will seek to protect the lives of Americans in China.

26. Oxford: The student magazine "Isis" deplores the fashion for floppy "Oxford Bags" trousers.

28. Glasgow: Eight die and ten are injured when the city is hit by a hurricane.

29. London: Opening of the Park Lane Hotel, the country's first hotel with a private bathroom for each bedroom.

31. Germany: Allied military control of Germany ends; German rearmament will now be under League control.

31. Peking: The Chinese government protests to Britain about its decision to send troops to China.→

BIRTH

30. Swedish statesman Olof Palme (†28/2/86).

British troops to China as rioting flares

The "Execution Patrol" marches through Shanghai, bayonets at the ready.

Jan 31. A British army division of 12,000 men, commanded by Major-General John Duncan, is today under orders to sail for China. Its task is to defend British nationals in Shanghai. The 40,000 foreigners who reside there are increasingly under threat from an upsurge of xenophobia accentuated by the Chinese civil war. The strong Royal Navy presence in Chinese waters will also be reinforced.

Despite opposition from the Labour Party, the Government decided on strong action as the Nationalist army from Canton advanced to within striking distance of the great port. The last straw was when rioting mobs of Chinese in Hankow district caused a serious affray in the British riverside enclave.

Not only are there hostile mobs but there is the threat of the rampaging armies of the northern war lords. They are about to come under attack from General Chiang Kai-shek's Nationalists, who are currently concentrating for a decisive assault upon on the city. They were last reported some 100 miles south of the port and the final battle cannot be long delayed.

Both Chiang Kai-shek's administration in Canton and the Chinese government in Peking protested at the British military moves, describing them as unnecessary and provocative (→18/2).

Doctor warns of "cancer scourge"

Jan 24. The British Medical Association gave a special lecture today, dealing with the growing danger of cancer. The Minister of Health, Neville Chamberlain, began by stating that between 1850 and 1925 death from cancer had increased almost fivefold. Then Sir Berkeley Moynihan, the President of the Royal College of Surgeons, pointed out that in the past 20 years, while there had been a fall in the general death rate, deaths from cancer of the breast and tongue had risen by 28 and 39 per cent.

Sir Berkeley spoke of the two prongs of the attack on cancer. The first is to discover its cause and the second is to educate people. Doctors must teach the public and themselves to recognise cancers that respond to early treatment.

He warned of the dangers of delay in diagnosis or treatment, which occurs when patients are deceived by ignorant and pretentious quacks. Then, he said, a small local cancer may be allowed to enlarge and spread, at which point there is the certainty of death because "if we wait until we know, we wait until we cannot cure". By cancer education he hoped that the public would think of cancer rather than forget it, and so be frightened to life and not frightened to death.

Jobless fear used to cut postal wages

Jan 12. The Government hit bac at Post Office workers in the indus rial court yesterday. They ar claiming an average wage rise of 4 per cent which would cost the tax payer more than £7 million a year Provincial postmen now earn 1/3 an hour, twice as much as in 191 and about the same as builders labourers. The Government want to cut a halfpenny off the to hourly rates and a penny off thos of young postmen. With unemploy ment 200,000 up at 1.4 million, th Government believes it can affor to be tough. National spendin dropped 1.5 per cent last yea because of the coal strike. It is nov rising partly because of a bi increase in the use of cheques.

Lack of wood puts steel in golf swing

Jan 21. George Duncan, the forme Open champion, who has returne to Britain after a successful seaso on the American professional cir cuit, has prophesied a radica advance in the game – the replace ment of wood by steel in the shaf of the golf club. The shortage o hickory wood in the US will in crease the urgency to find an alte native, to satisfy the fast-growin popularity of the game.

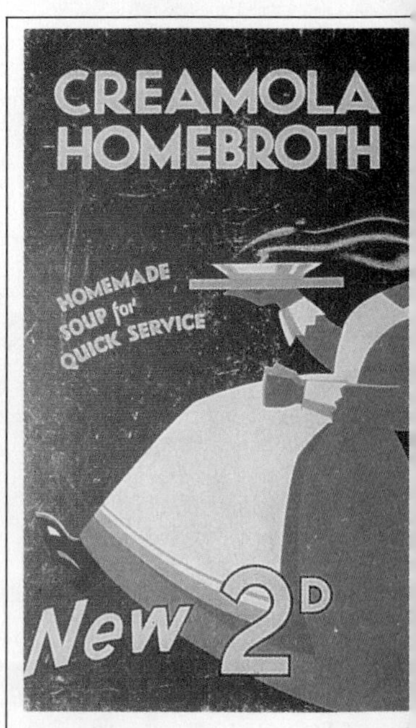

1927

FEBRUARY

Su	Mo	Tu	We	Th	Fr	Sa
		1	2	3	4	5
6	7	8	9	10	11	12
13	14	15	16	17	18	19
20	21	22	23	24	25	26
27	28					

1. London: Britain sends new offer to Canton, but goes ahead with defence of Shanghai.→

3. Berlin: Chancellor Wilhelm Marx says his government is dedicated to upholding the Weimar Constitution.

8. UK: Proposed revisions to the Book of Common Prayer are published, including sex equality in the wedding service (→30/3).

9. UK: Morris Motors buys Wolseley Motors for £730,000.

12. UK: Ten vessels collide and three sink in the fogbound English Channel.

14. Yugoslavia: 600 are feared dead when an earthquake hits the south of the country.

14. UK: 10 people die in a train crash at Hull.

16. UK: Coal merchants blame continuing shortages on the inefficiency of railways since the General Strike.

18. Shanghai: 65,000 workers go on strike in protest at the presence of foreign troops in the city.→

21. UK: British Industries Fair opens in London and Birmingham.

22. London: BBC chief John Reith says BBC news must be responsible, as three million homes now have wireless sets.

23. London: The government says it is sending a warship to protect British interest in Nicaragua as unrest continues.

25. Warsaw: Pilsudski's government approves freedom of movement between Poland and the Free City of Danzig.

26. UK: 1,000 people a week are currently dying from influenza.

28. UK: Floods and gales hit the country, causing havoc.

28. Budapest: 70 arrests follow the discovery of an alleged Communist plot to overthrow the government.

BIRTH

21. French fashion designer Hubert Taffin de Givenchy.

Briton sets world land speed record

Waterlogged sands slow Malcolm Campbell during a previous failed attempt on the world record.

Feb 4. Malcolm Campbell drove his car Bluebird through the world land speed record today at a speed of 174.224 mph along the Pendine Sands in Carmarthenshire, Wales.

It is the third time he has broken the record, but his three most recent attempts have all ended in failure; a similar fate almost befell him this time when Bluebird ground to a halt after just 100 yards. "My heart was quaking," said Campbell, but he was saved when the car started again and sped off.

He again avoided disaster in the middle of the record-breaking run when the wind tore off his goggles, temporarily blinding him. "It was a most terrifying moment and an experience I never wish to have again as long as I live," he said later.

Campbell's British-built car, Bluebird, is powered by a 500 hp Napier-Aero engine, which has also been used on several planes which have set new British aviation records in recent years (→29/3).

Portuguese government crushes coup

Feb 9. A revolution in Lisbon, involving heavy fighting and the loss of some 200 lives, has been put down by the government of General Antonio Carmona in its first trial of strength since he came to power in a coup himself last May. Heavy artillery fire and aerial bombing directed at the Naval Arsenal, centre of the revolt, crushed the rebels, who were composed of disaffected military enemies and democrats. Life is now returning to normal in the city.

Audiences amazed by child violinist

Feb 6. A boy violinist in short trousers caused a sensation in Paris tonight with his effortless playing. Yehudi Menuhin performed the "Symphonie Espagnole" written by Lalo for the Spanish virtuoso, Sarasate, in 1875. It was a fantastic technical feat for a boy of ten.

But little Yehudi has been astounding audiences since he was seven, when he played the Mendelssohn violin concerto accompanied on the piano by his teacher in Oakland, California. He played with the San Francisco symphony orchestra at nine.

Of Russian-Jewish parentage, he is now to be taught in Paris by George Enescu, the Rumanian virtuoso, who himself made his debut at seven (→7/12/30).

Boy wonder Yehudi Menuhin.

British troops in battle for Shanghai

Feb 25. Two thousand British troops today moved into defensive positions around the borders of the Shanghai international settlement. A ring of infantry with artillery support protects the area.

A critical stage has now been reached in the civil war, in which the Nationalists are battling it out with the Peking government for the control of China. Marshal Sun Chuang-fang's defeated Peking army is now retreating towards Shanghai, its last defences at Sunkiang, only 25 miles away, having been overrun by nationalist forces of General Chiang Kai-shek.

Major-General John Duncan arrives tomorrow with Colonel Viscount Gort. He will find the Gloucesters, the 3/14 Punjabis, and a company of the Durham Light Infantry already in the line. The remaining Durham companies and the Suffolks are in reserve. Alongside them are Italian units and 300 French. The Royal Navy has 12 cruisers, the aircraft carrier HMS Hermes, and a flotilla of nine destroyers in Chinese waters (→21/3).

1927

MARCH

Su	Mo	Tu	We	Th	Fr	Sa
		1	2	3	4	5
6	7	8	9	10	11	12
13	14	15	16	17	18	19
20	21	22	23	24	25	26
27	28	29	30	31		

1. UK: 53 miners are feared dead in a firedamp explosion in a pit at Ebbw Vale in Wales; 150 are trapped.

2. US: Russian ex-premier Alexander Kerensky arrives in the US; he predicts the downfall of the Soviet regime.

4. London: The price of a four-pound loaf drops to ninepence.

7. Washington: The Supreme Court declares unconstitutional a Texas law banning blacks from voting in primaries.

8. Iraq: Archaeologists find what they claim is a 5,000-year-old manicure set on the site of the ancient city of Ur.

10. Germany: The Bavarian government lifts its ban on Nazi leader Adolf Hitler speaking in public (→ 1/5).

11. London: A bill is introduced for a compulsory quota of UK films in the country's cinemas.→

15. UK: Petrol prices drop to one and fourpence-halfpenny a gallon.

18. Mexico: The country is reported close to revolution as hostility grows to anti-clerical government policies.

21. Shanghai: British troops repel an attempt by Nationalists to invade the foreign concession.→

23. Berlin: National Socialist supporters are involved in street clashes with Communists.

24. China: British and US warships shell Nanking as Britons and Americans die in attacks on the city (→ 7/4).

25. UK: The first Grand National broadcast by wireless is won by Mrs M. Partridge's Sprig.

30. London: The Convocation of the Church of England approves proposed changes to the Book of Common Prayer (→ 26/4).

BIRTH

27. Russian-born US cellist Mstislav Rostropovich.

Nationalist forces conquer Shanghai

British sailors march into Shanghai watched by curious Chinese onlookers.

March 21. The victorious Nationalist army of General Chiang Kai-shek entered the terrified and chaotic city of Shanghai today. Barely a shot was fired as the Peking army of northern warlords collapsed in mass desertions. Thousands of defeated soldiers fled into the city. They offered their rifles and pistols for sale at ten cents apiece. A British infantry platoon turned back 500 trying to enter the international settlement.

For General Chiang the capture of the richest port in China is a decisive event in his attempt to win the civil war and unite the nation. The northern commanders have abandoned their troops; the leader, Marshal Sun Chuang-fang, crossed the Yangtse to safety on the northern bank while another warlord, General Chang Tsung-kiang, described as an officer "incapable of organising a whelk stall", has retired towards Pengpu.

It is a time of great anxiety for foreigners here. Prolonged strikes were organised by Nationalists and their Bolshevik allies. These were countered by a reign of terror imposed by General Li Poa-chen, the defence commissioner, who executed dozens of students and agitators. Fifty were beheaded in one day. Their heads were then suspended from telegraph poles. Now that Nationalists occupy the city, foreigners fear they may be blamed for these outrages (→ 28/4).

Film-making that becomes an Empire

March 26. The founding today o the Gaumont-British Film Corpor ation, with capital of £2,500,000 is evidence that Britain intends t catch up with the lead in film making that the Great War gav to Hollywood. It follows th announcement ten days ago o British Incorporated Pictures which intends to make motio pictures on an Empire-wide scale.

The bill now before parliament t institute a "quota" of British film to be shown at all cinemas – 12.: per cent next year, rising to 25 pe cent in stages – is intended to res cue British film-makers from thei present frustration, the "block booking" of cinemas for months even a year, ahead by America distributors for films still unmade.

South Africa in grip of a diamond fever

March 4. Some 25,000 digger today joined in a rush to stake thei claims in new South African dia mond fields at Grasfontein. Minin syndicates hired 50 trained athletes who raced ahead of the crowd an grabbed the pieces of land that ha been identified beforehand. I recent years production of stone from alluvial deposits has rise sharply; in consequence, the aver age value per carat has fallen fron £8 to little more than £2.10s. Bu diggers are still succumbing t diamond fever.

Briton exceeds 200mph to smash Campbell's speed record

March 29. Major Henry Segrave set a new world land-speed record of 203.841 mph in his "Mystery" car on the Daytona Beach racetrack in Florida today. During a pit-stop to change the tyres on his 1,000 hp racing car, Segrave said the wind pressure at such a high speed was making steering all but impossible. Malcolm Campbell, the previous record holder with a speed of 174.883 mph, congratulated his fellow-countryman on an "excellent feat", but said he was already practising on a new faster car so he could regain the record (→ 19/2/28).

Major Segrave goes for a test spin before making his speed challenge.

1927

APRIL

Su	Mo	Tu	We	Th	Fr	Sa
					1	2
3	4	5	6	7	8	9
10	11	12	13	14	15	16
17	18	19	20	21	22	23
24	25	26	27	28	29	30

2. France: England is beaten by France for the first time at rugby, by three points to nil in front of 35,000 spectators.

4. London: The Trades Disputes Bill is introduced, outlawing sympathy strikes and compulsory political levies (→16/5).

5. US: Johnny Weissmuller sets three swimming records to hold every freestyle distance from 100 yards to the half-mile.

7. London: The Foreign Secretary, Sir Austen Chamberlain, says Britain refuses to be drawn into the Chinese civil war (→18).

7. Paris: Abel Gance's epic film "Napoleon", shown on three screens, is premiered at the Opera.

9. US: Death sentences are confirmed on anarchists Nicolas Sacco and Bartolomeo Vanzetti (→23/8).

11. London: Churchill says the pit strike cost £150 million; Budget puts up wine, film and tobacco duties.

13. London: Baldwin says the government will give the vote to all women from the age of 21 (→7/5/28).

16. US: Cecil B. De Mille's epic "King of Kings" opens.

18. China: A split between Nationalist and Radical elements of Chiang Kai-shek's Kuomintang is reported.→

19. UK: Teachers call for the school leaving age to be raised from 14 to 16.

21. Cardiff: King George V opens the National Museum of Wales.

23. London: Arsenal's goalkeeper scores an own goal to give Cardiff City a 1-0 victory in the FA Cup Final.

26. London: Archbishop of Canterbury Randall Davidson is slammed for his "popish" proposals on the Prayer Book (→6/7).

30. London: An International Tobacco Exhibition opens as a surgeon says there is "no risk of cancer from tobacco".

Left and right clash in Shanghai streets

April 28. Street fighting has broken out in Shanghai between Nationalist troops, now occupying the city, and Communist trade union officials. The conflict began as General Chiang Kai-shek, the Nationalist leader, began setting up a new government in the city. The immediate cause of the conflict was the call for a general strike – the second such call in less than a month.

In response Nationalist soldiers raided trade union strongholds, and shooting broke out in which 16 were killed. The fighting has strained relations between the Communist supporters of the General and his more moderate Nationalist allies. So, concerned that radical soldiers may support the Communists, General Chiang has invited Communist leaders to a conference in Nanking.

Indecent Sex lands Mae West in jail

Naughty actress Mae West.

April 19. Miss Mae West, actress of saucy repute and producer of such shows as "The Virgin Man", was today found guilty of indecent behaviour in her production of "Sex" on Broadway. Miss West, who incurred a ten-day jail sentence and a $500 fine, claimed police attending "Sex's" opening night had voiced no objections. In later shows, however, the diminutive actress was said to have introduced lewder material which caused offence.

1927

MAY

Su	Mo	Tu	We	Th	Fr	Sa
1	2	3	4	5	6	7
8	9	10	11	12	13	14
15	16	17	18	19	20	21
22	23	24	25	26	27	28
29	30	31				

1. Berlin: Adolf Hitler holds his first Nazi Party meeting in the German capital.

2. Washington: President Coolidge calls for doubled relief efforts for flood-stricken areas of the southern US (→5).

3. India: Riots between Sikhs and Moslems in Lahore leave 14 reported dead and 100 injured.

4. Geneva: International Economic Conference opens.

5. US: Floods in Mississippi now cover 23 square miles.

9. Canberra: Duke of York opens the new Australian Parliament House.

10. London: Plans unveiled to rebuild Waterloo and Lambeth Bridges and build a two-deck bridge at Charing Cross.

12. London: Police raid the offices of the USSR trade delegation, Argos.→

16. London: French President Gaston Doumergue arrives on a state visit.

18. US: 42 people, mainly children, die when a mentally ill man blows up a school in Bath, Michigan.

18. USSR: A provisional synod of the Russian Orthodox Church meets, headed by the Metropolitan Sergei (→19/8).

20. Saudi Arabia: The Treaty of Jeddah is signed, under which Britain recognises Saudi Arabian independence.

21. UK: Southern Railway introduces the first employee shareholding scheme.

25. Ottawa: Canada joins Britain in breaking off diplomatic and trade relations with the USSR.

26. Detroit: Henry Ford and his son Edsel drive the 15-millionth Model T off the production line.

27. Czechoslovakia: Tomas Masaryk is re-elected president.

30. Paris: Premiere of Igor Stravinsky's oratorio "Oedipus Rex", words by Jean Cocteau.

31. London: King George V decorates aviator Charles Lindbergh (→13/6).→

Russian diplomats ordered to quit UK

May 24. The Government today severed diplomatic relations with Russia after accusing the Soviet mission in London of espionage and organising subversion throughout the British Empire. Russia's diplomats and trade mission members were told to get out within ten days. British officials have also been recalled from Moscow.

Sir Austen Chamberlain, the Foreign Secretary, told the Russians: "The limits to our patience are now reached". The rupture follows a raid on the Soviet trade delegation (Argos) and disclosure in Parliament that seized documents proved Russian diplomats were engaged in illegal activities. One Soviet official was caught burning papers. Said Mr Baldwin: "systematically abused diplomatic relations endanger peace." (→3/6)

Girls getting that shingling feeling

May 19. The current rage for women to shingle their hair has led to an astonishing boom in the number of hairdressers. At the last census (before short hair was so widely popular) there were 32,000 hairdressers and barbers. Now their ranks have swelled by a further 11,000. The figures are contained in a report, released today, on shorter shop-opening hours (→19/3/28).

The new popular hairstyle.

Lindbergh is first to fly Atlantic solo

May 21. A 25-year-old pilot became a new international hero tonight when he touched down in front of a crowd of 100,000 people at Le Bourget airport, completing the first solo non-stop flight between New York and Paris.

Boyishly good-looking, Captain Charles Lindbergh also needed great courage to fly his Ryan NYP monoplane, the Spirit of St. Louis, across the Atlantic, sometimes dipping to within ten feet of the wave-tops, and staying alert by munching home made sandwiches.

His 3,600 mile flight was accomplished in 33 hours 39 minutes at an average speed of 107.5 mph. But until a few weeks ago Lindbergh was the dark horse in the race to win the $25,000 prize offered for the first non-stop flight from New York to Paris.

It seemed only his backers, a group of St. Louis businessmen, believed in him. But he made a daring one-stop flight from California to New York to gain a lead over his rivals before taking off on the record-breaking flight from Roosevelt Field on Long Island at dawn yesterday.

His departure was big news on both sides of the Atlantic as the Spirit of St. Louis, overloaded with fuel, staggered drunkenly into the sky, after barely clearing the trees at the end of the runway. Alerted by radio and newspapers, large crowds gathered along the American coast to watch for the young captain's aeroplane as it flew north.

It turned east towards the Atlantic at St. John's, Newfoundland at 7.15pm New York time. From then on Lindbergh flew by dead reckoning, sometimes climbing as high as 10,000 feet.

He reported seeing the lights of Paris at 10 o'clock tonight and touched down at Le Bourget at 10.24 to the roar of the crowd, who rushed forward to welcome the new hero, clearing two companies of French troops out of the way in the process. Lindbergh, born in Detroit and raised in Minnesota, is a quiet midwesterner, who appeared taken aback by the warmth of the reception. The race to be first across the Atlantic galvanised public interest so that the cause of aviation will also be boosted by this epic flight.

Charles Lindbergh in front of the plane he flew across the Atlantic.

Labour MPs' fury at Bill to curb unions

May 16. After a ferocious parliamentary battle, Labour MPs exploded in fury and frustration tonight. They all stormed out of the Commons in a desperate boycott when the Government used the guillotine rule to stop a filibuster against the legislation to clip trade union wings. The Opposition bitterly accepted that the Trades Disputes Bill will soon become law.

This measure is the Tory retribution for last year's General Strike and the Government's proof of victory over the unions. Sympathetic strikes are to be outlawed. So is industrial action calculated to coerce the government. Civil servants may no longer be in unions affiliated to the TUC.

Also, in future, trade unionists wanting to back Labour financially must contract into paying a levy for party funds instead of paying automatically or contracting out. Defiantly Labour said: "This means the battle of the century and serious conflict of class" (→23/6).

Empire tunes into voice of London

May 21. Wireless listeners around the world tuned into the latest news and cricket scores live from London for the first time today. Radio 2LO's programmes were rebroadcast on short wave by Philips' engineers in Holland, and heard in Australia, India, New Zealand and South Africa. The successful experiment has encouraged the BBC, which hopes to set up a world radio service soon.

1927

JUNE

Su	Mo	Tu	We	Th	Fr	Sa
			1	2	3	4
5	6	7	8	9	10	11
12	13	14	15	16	17	18
19	20	21	22	23	24	25
26	27	28	29	30		

1. UK: Mr F. Curzon's Call Boy wins the Derby.→

3. London: Soviet diplomats leave from Victoria as sympathisers, including Labour MPs, sing "The Red Flag".

4. Dutch East Indies: Ahmed Sukarno founds the Indonesian Nationalist Party.

6. China: Chiang Kai-shek's Nanking government breaks off relations with the USSR.

7. UK: The Co-Operative Congress votes to merge with the Labour Party.

9. London: The King and Queen attend a concert given by violinist Fritz Kreisler.

13. New York: Charles Lindbergh is given a ticker-tape welcome.

14. Managua: The US signs an aid pact with Nicaragua, allowing the US to intervene in political unrest.

17. China: Chang Tso-lin is made dictator in command of the three Northern armies fighting the Kuomintang.

18. Germany: Opening of the Nurburgring motor racing circuit.

19. London: 20,000 take part in a "Festival of Youth" at Crystal Palace.

21. S. Africa: Nationalists attack the proposed new Union flag, which includes the Union Jack (→25/10).

23. London: The Trades Disputes Bill is passed, amid Labour protests.

24. London: The University of London buys a large site in Bloomsbury for £525,000.

26. London: Communists and Fascists clash in Hyde Park.

27. UK: The Duke and Duchess of York return from a tour of Australasia.

29. Hawaii: US Navy airmen Maitland and Hegenberger land after a 2,400-mile flight from California, the world's longest flight over the sea.

DEATH

14. British writer Jerome K. Jerome (*2/5/1859).

Russians execute 20 as British spies

June 9. Anglo-Soviet relations took another turn for the worse today as the Russians executed 20 alleged spies and accused Britain of paying for their "subversive activities", including the assassination two days ago of the Soviet ambassador to Poland, Mr Voikoff.

A statement from Moscow said the Collegium of the State Political Department condemned the men to death and they were executed later that same day. There was no suggestion that the accused were tried before they were shot.

Among the unfortunate 20 were two former Russian Princes, an ex-Chamberlain of the Czar's court, and an official of the Russian state bank. According to the Soviets, most had been in touch with British intelligence who financed their activities. These included a near-fatal assassination attempt on Bukharin in 1922, a plot against Stalin's life and the planting of bombs in Moscow and Leningrad, as well as Voikoff's shooting.

Another of the condemned was a former cavalry captain accused of conspiring with the famous British spy, Sidney George Riley, to try to kill Soviet diplomats. Riley, who was arrested in Russia in 1925, claimed he was told by Churchill to carry out acts of terrorism.

New Ryder Cup is won by Americans

June 30. America's professional golfers have won the handsome new trophy, presented by the Hertfordshire seed merchant, Samuel Ryder, defeating their British counterparts by the decisive margin of 9.5 – 2.5 in the last 12 matches.

Britain's representatives, under the captaincy of the former winner of the US Open, Ted Ray, were anxious to avenge their amateur compatriots, who have yet to win the Walker Cup after four attempts, but the Americans, on their home ground in Worcester, Massachusetts, and captained by the great Walter Hagen, proved too consistent.

Sun's total eclipse seen by millions

June 29 For the first time in 200 years a total eclipse of the Sun was seen in Britain early today. Because of patchy cloud many watchers were disappointed, but others in northern England, including the Astronomer-Royal at Giggleswick in Yorkshire, were able to see the full eclipse.

Totality lasted for less than half a minute, but lucky observers got a good view of the glowing corona around the Sun when it was obscured by the Moon. They also saw a "prominence" of incandescent gas, like a reddish arch on the edge of the moon. Its height has been calculated at 50,000 miles.

"Call Boy" won the Derby – the race was broadcast live by the BBC.

1927

JULY

Su	Mo	Tu	We	Th	Fr	Sa
					1	2
3	4	5	6	7	8	9
10	11	12	13	14	15	16
17	18	19	20	21	22	23
24	25	26	27	28	29	30
31						

1. Berlin: Reichstag members are involved in scuffles on the floor of the chamber.

4. London: King Fuad of Egypt arrives on a state visit.

5. Wimbledon: Frenchman Henri Cochet beat Jean Borotra in the men's Singles final; Helen Wills of the US beat Lili de Alvarez for the ladies' Singles title.

6. London: The Church of England approves the proposed revision of the Book of Common Prayer (→15/12).

9. Geneva: US cruiser demands cause outrage at current international talks on naval reductions (→4/8).

11. Palestine: 26 people are reported killed in an earthquake.

15. UK: US amateur golfer Bobby Jones wins the British Open.

15. UK: 20 Player's Navy Cut cigarettes now cost elevenpence halfpenny.

17. Vienna: Order is finally restored after the recent rioting.

18. Edinburgh: The British Medical Association expresses concern at the "threat" of a possible state medical service.

21. Bucharest: Prince Mihai, aged five, succeeds to the throne after the death of King Ferdinand.

24. Belgium: 80,000 people attend the unveiling of the Menin Gate war memorial at Ypres.

27. Ukraine: 120 are reported shot dead in a Communist purge.

30. Canada: Stanley Baldwin and the Prince of Wales arrive for Canadian Diamond Jubilee celebrations.

BIRTH

4. Italian actress Gina Lollobrigida.

DEATHS

10. Irish statesman Kevin O'Higgins (*7/6/1892).→

20. Rumanian King Ferdinand (*24/8/1865).

Irish leader shot after church service

July 10. Kevin O'Higgins, vice-president of the Irish Free State, was gunned down today by men in a waiting car while he walked from church in a Dublin suburb. As he lay dying on the road, other men pushed through the crowd and pumped his body full of bullets.

His hopes of a united Ireland had been shattered by the 1921-23 civil war. In a recent speech he said: "We preferred to burn our homes, blow up our bridges, rob our banks and saddle ourselves with millions of debt ... and now we wonder why the Orangemen are not hopping over the border like fleas to come under our jurisdiction."

The murderers got away despite a police escort; there are fears tonight of renewed civil war (→16/8).

Garbo's love scene boosts box office

Greta Garbo and John Gilbert.

July 1. Audiences are flocking to see the new Swedish actress, Greta Garbo, who has suddenly eclipsed Mary Pickford and Clara Bow, opposite screen lover John Gilbert.

It is an open secret that he fell in love with her during the filming of "Flesh and the Devil", borne out by the passion of their scenes together. The fan mail and box office takings are so heavy that their next film, "Anna Karenina", has been retitled "Love" so that the billboards can now read: "Greta Garbo and John Gilbert in Love". ▷

Vienna rocked by revolutionary riots

July 15. Loyal troops, ferried to Vienna along the Danube, have put down the revolt that threatened to engulf Austria. The trouble started when three men of the anti-socialist front, Kaempfers, were acquitted of the murder of two communists, who were killed in a fracas last January.

The communist press was outraged and printed furious editorials calling for the killing of all the judges, juries and the middle-class. Workers took to the streets; fires were started, shops looted, and ten thousand stormed the Ministry of Justice and set it alight.

Police fired on the crowd with a machine gun and the rioters replied with rifles. An attempt was made to rush the parliament, but the police threw a strong cordon round the building.

Chancellor Ignaz Siegel was asked to declare a state of emergency. He refused, but when he did decide to call out the Volkswehr, the men mutinied and refused to leave their barracks. Labour leaders then declared a general strike and the opposition parties demanded Chancellor Siegel's resignation, but instead of accomodating them he sent messages to the provinces by aeroplane summoning reinforcements.

There are now 12,000 troops and police patrolling the debris-strewn streets of the city in which 89 people are thought to have died. One immediate result of the rioting is the renewal in Germany of demands for the annexation of Austria (→ 17).

The burning Ministry of Justice becomes an issue in Austria's elections.

Mysterious Fujitsuru not to be sniffed at

July 21. Drug dealers are becoming more ingenious in their smuggling, but were still unable to prevent British officials seizing a huge haul of heroin in Hong Kong, says a newly published government report.

Some smugglers are concealing their wares by mixing them with other chemicals, the report reveals, such as the shipment of a strange substance known as Lubrinol, seized in Southampton, which was found to contain morphine.

Another dealer caught selling cocaine on the streets of London had smuggled it into the country hidden inside his waterproof belt. When police began arresting his alleged accomplices on the continent one of them, an Austrian called Brancker, committed suicide before he could be charged.

The police's biggest success was the seizure in Hong Kong of 8,200 ounces of cocaine from a passenger arriving by steamer from Europe, but there have also been numerous seizures in Britain of bottles and tins of cocaine labelled "Fujitsuru" throughout the past year. So far police have been unable to trace the drugs syndicate behind these.

Joanna Southcott is no Pandora

July 11. One of Joanna Southcott's mysterious boxes – said to contain revelations "of a profound significance" – was opened today. The nineteenth-century religious fanatic had insisted that the box should only be opened with 24 bishops present. One attended the ceremony – "out of curiosity".

The significant revelations consisted of an ancient pistol (unloaded), pamphlets, trinkets, a night cap, a purse and a book called "The Surprises of Love".

1927

AUGUST

Su	Mo	Tu	We	Th	Fr	Sa
	1	2	3	4	5	6
7	8	9	10	11	12	13
14	15	16	17	18	19	20
21	22	23	24	25	26	27
28	29	30	31			

1. UK: The Bank Holiday is the wettest for many years.

2. US: President Coolidge says he will not run in 1928.

3. Berlin: The city is linked by wireless telephone to Buenos Aires, 7,000 miles away.

4. Geneva: Naval arms talks break up in disagreement.

5. New York: Many people injured by two subway blasts, protests at the Sacco-Vanzetti case (→ 6).

6. Baltimore: The mayor's house is bombed.→

7. Germany: Lina Radke-Bratchsauer runs 800 metres in a record 2 mins 23.8 seconds.

8. Paris: Vets say they have found a distemper vaccine.

10. US: Astronomers claim the universe is 192 quadrillion miles wide.

12. Bolivia: 80,000 Indians revolt against the government.

13. UK: Petrol is cut to 1/1d a gallon, cheapest since 1902.

14. China: Chiang Kai-shek resigns Nanking command.

15. UK: New regulations limit the length of cars to 27 feet six inches.

16. London: Wembley Stadium sold for greyhound racing.

17. USSR: 10,000 reported homeless as hurricane destroys 22 Siberian villages.

18. France: Forest fires sweep the South of France.

19. USSR: The Orthodox Church recognises the Soviet government.

22. Los Angeles: Lita Grey wins a divorce and $825,000 from Charlie Chaplin.

24. UK: 12 die in a train crash at Sevenoaks, Kent.

24. London: A seven-bedroom house in Holland Park costs £1,750.

29. S. Africa: The Labour Minister says he wants British miners rather than blacks.

BIRTH

13. Cuban leader Fidel Castro.

Irish leader saved in Dail by one vote

Aug 16. Irish Free State President William Cosgrave won a vote of confidence in the Dail today on the casting vote of the Speaker. Voting was 71-71, but even more significant was the presence in the chamber of Eamon de Valera and his Fianna Fail party. For six years they have won up to 30 per cent of the seats, but refused to take them because the peace treaty with Britain involves signing an oath of allegiance to King George V.

Following the violent death of Kevin O'Higgins last month, the Irish government passed legislation, which required those who won seats in the last election to take them or otherwise forfeit their rights.

De Valera felt he had no option but he has a party, now the main opposition, more divided than when it split with Sinn Fein. An angry response to the tough law and order methods used by the Government since the murder of O'Higgins dominated yesterday's proceedings. These include widespread searches of homes for men and weapons and taking people into custody for questioning, sometimes more than 100 a day. Some felt his death was the government's fault since the procedure for guarding O'Higgins, the Justice Minister, was obviously inadequate.

Tom Johnson, the Labour leader who moved the motion, spoke first and declared that the emergency measures would not serve the cause of peace or social well-being. President Cosgrave in reply said: "We stand for one army and no others in the state ... no matter what sacrifices might be entailed." (→20/9)

Anarchists go to the electric chair

Aug 23. The Italian-born anarchists Sacco and Vanzetti were executed in Massachusetts this morning, despite worldwide protests that they are innocent. The pair, convicted six years ago of murdering two people during an armed robbery, walked calmly to the electric chair. "Long live anarchy", shouted Sacco as he entered the death-chamber. In London, thousands of people gathered in Hyde Park to mourn the executions.

New signs aim to curb road deaths

Aug 4. Experimental signs to act as guides for pedestrians are soon to be erected on the crossings at Trafalgar Square and along Oxford Street between Marble Arch and Tottenham Court Road. The crossings will be marked with white lines painted on the carriageway and the words "look left" or "look right". These are part of a programme of precautions to improve the safety of pedestrians when crossing one-way streets in London (→ 29/11/28).

August. Londoners are grateful for the new covered-top buses, which are allowed to run past Buckingham Palace for the first time.

1927

SEPTEMBER

Su	Mo	Tu	We	Th	Fr	Sa
				1	2	3
4	5	6	7	8	9	10
11	12	13	14	15	16	17
18	19	20	21	22	23	24
25	26	27	28	29	30	

1. Poland: Floods in Galicia kill up to 200 people, leaving a reported 15,000 homeless.

6. India: 15 people die in Moslem-Hindu riots at Nagpur.

7. London: A six-wheeled bus goes on a trial run.

8. Edinburgh: The TUC votes to sever links with Soviet trades unions.

10. US: France wins the Davis Cup for the first time.

10. Geneva: Foreign Secretary Sir Austen Chamberlain says Britain must put the Empire before closer ties with Europe.

12. Leningrad: Nine alleged British spies are executed.

13. UK: The birthrate in 1926 was the lowest since 1860.

14. Japan: 3,000 are reported killed when a tidal wave hits Kiu-Siu Island.

15. Geneva: Canada is elected to the Council of the League of Nations.

16. Berlin: President von Hindenburg denies German responsibility for the Great War.

19. Nicaragua: Rebel leader Augusto Sandino launches an attack on government troops at Las Flores.

22. Rome: Pope Pius XI gives $100,000 for flood victims in the southern US.

23. The Hague: Germany is admitted to the International Court of Arbitration.

23. Chicago: Doctors claim 60 per cent of infant deaths are due to the mother smoking.

24. UK: This summer was the worst since 1879 with up to 80 per cent more rain than normal.

28. Lithuania: The government claims the Polish town of Vilna as capital of Lithuania.

29. US: A five-minute tornado in St. Louis kills 69 and injures 600.

30. New York: Baseballer Babe Ruth hits his record 60th home run of the season.

DEATH

14. US dancer Isadora Duncan (*27/5/1878) →.

Tangled shawl ends Isadora's tragic life

US dancer Isadora Duncan.

Sept 14. Isadora Duncan's troubled life came to a dramatic end tonight when she was strangled by her own shawl. As she set out for an evening drive in Nice in a red Bugatti sports car, the fringe of the shawl was, unknown to her, dangling in the spokes of the rear wheel beside her.

"Adieu mes amis. Je vais a la gloire!" she called to friends watching her go – and the first turn of the wheels broke her neck. At 49, it was the end of a tragic life. The poet she married in Russia hanged himself two years ago. Americans rejected her as a revolutionary on her last tour. Defiantly, she bared her breast on stage.

Clean shaven look wins over whiskers

Sept 10. Long hair for women and beards and moustaches for men are now out of date. That was the expert view today at the Hairdressing and Allied Trades exhibition in London. Women, encouraged by "scientific" assurances that they would not go bald through having their hair cut short, were being invited to shed their tresses for more "avant-garde" bobs. An Institute of Trichologists' official also claimed that baldness in Englishmen was likely to decrease as the fashion for shorter and healthier hair became more popular. ▷

"I was robbed" cries challenger Dempsey

Gene Tunney struggles back to his feet after 15 seconds on the floor.

Sept 22. The world heavyweight champion, Gene Tunney, survived the most punishing contest of his career, and his second million-dollar fight with former champion Jack Dempsey, to retain his title on a points decision in Chicago.

Tunney's upright style, contrasting vividly with Dempsey's uncompromising aggressive crouch, won him seven of the ten rounds, but it was the drama of the seventh round that led to furious protests by Dempsey and his supporters.

After a desperate all-out attack the challenger laid Tunney flat on the canvas, but inexplicably failed to retire to a neutral corner. It was five or six seconds before the referee ushered him across the ring and started the count.

A full 15 seconds after the blow, Tunney staggered to his feet to survive the rest of the round, steady himself, and then finish the fight. Dempsey said afterwards he would appeal: "I was robbed of the championship". It is certainly a fight whose outcome will be debated by fans for decades (→1/2/28).

Ashcroft and Olivier shine in Birmingham

Sept 3. Two young actors who have recently joined Sir Barry Jackson's Birmingham repertory company give good accounts of themselves as sweethearts up against strong parental opposition in John Drinkwater's play "Bird in Hand". Peggy Ashcroft plays the daughter of an innkeeper, who has been going for drives with the squire's son, Gerald. Her father suspects the young man's intentions are not honourable and declares: "People should stick to their own class!" Love finds a way. Gerald is played by Laurence Olivier.

Moderates return in Irish elections

Sept 20. President W.T. Cosgrave has won his second Irish Free State general election in three months with an effective majority of six. It was a rowdy, rough affair, with two people losing their lives in the closing stages of the campaign.

The face of Irish politics is rapidly changing with the two big parties now running almost level; Cosgrave's party won 61 seats and de Valera's Fianna Fail 57 (→11/10).

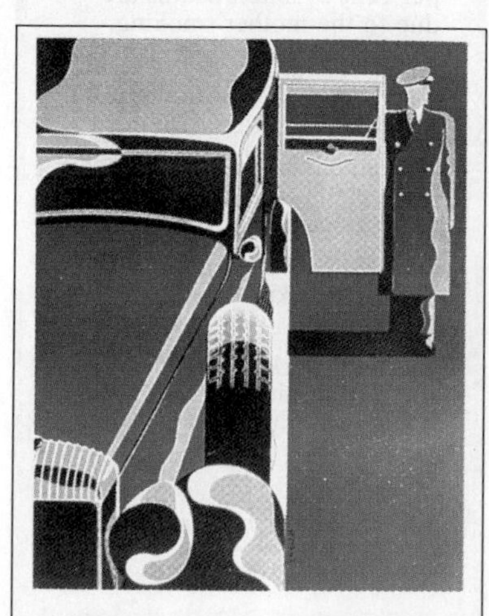

1927

OCTOBER

Su	Mo	Tu	We	Th	Fr	Sa
						1
2	3	4	5	6	7	8
9	10	11	12	13	14	15
16	17	18	19	20	21	22
23	24	25	26	27	28	29
30	31					

1. Moscow: The USSR signs a non-aggression pact with Persia.

4. Mexico City: 14 people are shot for a military coup bid.

5. Blackpool: The Labour Party conference votes to nationalise the mines.

6. New York: The Stock Exchange begins trading in foreign shares.

7. France: A memorial to Indian troops is unveiled at Neuve Chapelle.

10. US: The scandal-hit Teapot Dome oil fields are restored to the US government.

11. Ireland: W.T Cosgrave is re-elected President of Irish Free State.

13. UK: The first horse race solely for women jockeys takes place at Newmarket.

15. Iraq: The country's first oil strike is made at Kirkuk.

16. UK: Mona Maclennan, who claimed she swam the Channel in a record 13 hours 12 mins, admits it was a hoax.

17. Norway: The first Labour government is elected.

18. Berlin: The government bans dancing bears from the streets of the capital.

20. US: A Massachusetts professor says he has made a rapid-computation machine.

24. USSR: Three British "spies" are sentenced to die.

26. Yugoslavia: 260 die when a train falls into a ravine.

27. New York: The first sound news film, "Fox Movie-tone News", is released.

28. UK: 50 are reported dead and 400 left homeless when a storm hits Lancashire.

29. China: Russian archaeologist Peter Kozlov discovers the tomb of Genghis Khan.

30. Paris: France and Yugoslavia sign a treaty, boosting the "Little Entente" with the Czechs, Rumanians and Poles.

BIRTH

16. German author Günter Grass.

Blackfaced Jolson stars in first talkie

Jolson with co-star May McAvoy.

Oct 6. The first live dialogue ever heard in films brought the audience to its feet applauding. "The Jazz Singer" stars Al Jolson, who introduces four "talking segments" in which he also sings.

Warner Brothers, who produced "The Jazz Singer", have already used the Vitaphone system to provide synchronised music in "Don Juan", but this is the first time that dialogue has been added. "You ain't heard nothin' yet", came Jolson's voice rather indistinctly from the screen and the reaction was one of rapture.

Some, like Charles Chaplin, think sound is a passing novelty – he gives it three years. But the "Film Spectator" comments: "The Jazz Singer definitely establishes that talking pictures are imminent. If I were an actor with a squeaky voice I would worry" (→21/8/28).

Union Jack storm ends in compromise

Oct 25. A long and bitter dispute over South Africa's national flag was finally resolved today when the National Party Prime Minister, General J.B.M. Hertzog, agreed on a design which incorporates the Union Jack and the vierkleur flags of the old Boer republics. He has resisted this in the past because the Union Jack is widely seen as a hated symbol of English domination over Boers.

1927

NOVEMBER

Su	Mo	Tu	We	Th	Fr	Sa
		1	2	3	4	5
6	7	8	9	10	11	12
13	14	15	16	17	18	19
20	21	22	23	24	25	26
27	28	29	30			

1. London: The late Lord Iveagh has left Ken Wood House and his priceless art collection to the nation.

3. Sydney: 37 are feared dead when a liner rams a ferry.

4. Italy: Major de Bernardi sets an air speed record of 296 mph.

6. US: Flooding in New England has so far led to 150 reported deaths.

7. Moscow: Trotsky and Zinoviev head an opposition parade on the tenth anniversary of the Revolution.→

8. UK: A survey shows people drink more tea and coffee and less beer since the Great War.

10. New York: General Motors announces a dividend of $62 million, the largest in US history.

11. Washington: The International Radio Telegraph conference agrees to compulsory arbitration in radio disputes.

13. UK: Britain's first automatic telephone exchange is installed at Holborn in London (→ 17/1/28).

15. UK: The Public Morals Committee says easy access to contraceptives "produces poorer hereditary stock".

18. France: Jules Rimet, head of the International Football Association (FIFA), announces the creation of a "World Cup" (→30/7/30).

19. London: 200 unemployed Welsh miners arrive in London after marching 180 miles.→

22. New York: George Gershwin's show "Funny Face" opens.

23. Berlin: Germany and Poland sign a trade pact.

24. Edinburgh: Comedian Sir Harry Lauder is given the freedom of the city.

25. Algeria: 300 are feared dead in severe floods.

28. Warsaw: The Polish government denies it has plans to annex Lithuania.

29. Buenos Aires: Frenchman Alexandre Alekhine wins the World Chess Championship from Jose Capablanca.

Bus profits to pay for losses on Tube

Oct 24. London's buses, tubes and trams should be co-ordinated under one management, says a report submitted to the Ministry of Transport today. But the railway companies which serve the capital would be excluded from the centralised management structure backed by the London and Home Counties Traffic Advisory Committee.

The committee believes that reform is becoming urgent as traffic congestion worsens in London. Coordination would enable different forms of transport to help each other rather than compete against each other. Profits from buses or trams could be used to avert fare rises on the more costly underground railway services. They could also finance expansion of the London transport network.

Motor cars are now kings of the road

Oct 28. How the motor vehicle became king of the road is told today in the figures issued by the Road Fund. In the calendar year 1926 motor vehicle licences numbered about 1,729,000 and horse-drawn 127,248. The gross revenue from these came to £19,032,000. Compared with the previous year the revenue was 10.4 per cent up and the number of motor vehicles 11.8 per cent up. Horse-drawn vehicles, by contrast, were down by 17.1 per cent. The spread of motoring has been so great that there is now one vehicle to every 26 people.

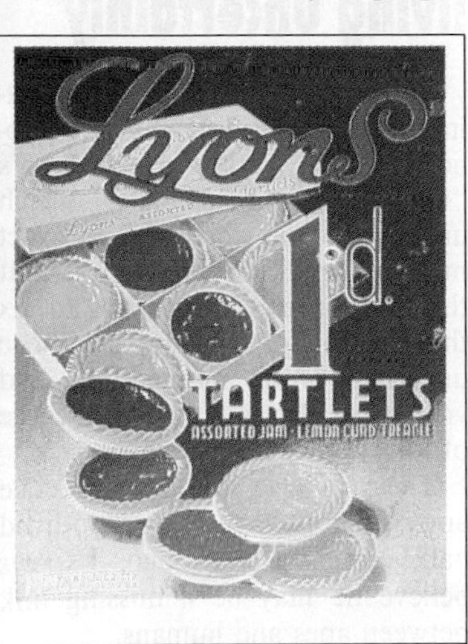

Miners march but PM goes to ground

Welsh miners arriving in London greeted by their leader, A.J. Cook.

Nov 23. The Prime Minister, Mr Stanley Baldwin, yesterday refused to meet the 200 unemployed Welsh miners who walked 180 miles from the Rhondda Valley to London.

The men marched into a rainy Trafalgar Square carrying lighted lamps, knapsacks and mugs and supported by brass and fife bands. They wore red ribbons in their caps and a few of them held aloft banners which sported the emblem of the Communist hammer and sickle.

Arthur Cook, secretary of the Miners' Federation, told them that unemployment in the mining industry was the country's most urgent problem. "Unless the Government faces the situation" he said "a revolutionary situation will be created in this country which no leader will be able to withstand." He told the Prime Minister: "The Government will be compelled, in the interests of the nation, to take over the mining industry."

In another protest last night dustmen sang "The Red Flag" in Hammersmith Town Hall. They were demonstrating against the council's decision to give the dust collection to a private contractor, who claims he would be able to save them £5,000 a year.

Nuremberg: Hitler gives the Nazi salute to party members. The crowd's chant of "Heil Hitler" is now common in Germany, where President von Hindenburg has retected his nation's responsibility for the Great War.

Stalin expels Trotsky

Trotsky's enemies draw their daggers following his expulsion by Stalin.

Nov 15. Joseph Stalin has routed his political opposition and expelled Leon Trotsky and Grigori Zinoviev from the Soviet Communist Party. Trotsky, a close colleague of Lenin during the Bolshevik revolution ten years ago, has already been expelled from the Party's ostensibly policy-making Central Committee.

His eclipse as leader of the "combined opposition" was widely predicted following his speech during the summer, charging Stalin and his allies with a lack of foresight, efficiency and determination. But it was his actions last week, during official celebrations to mark the anniversary, which made his expulsion from the party a virtual certainty.

Together with Zinoviev, Trotsky led their followers through Moscow streets in a peaceful demonstration, which only criticised the ruling group by implication. But it was enough to bring the power struggle to a head and Stalin acted with characteristic speed and ruthlessness in forcing through a decision to expel them (→16/1/28).

Commons sets up India commission

Nov 25. The House of Commons today approved the appointment of the Commission, led by Sir John Simon, to travel to India to study the working of the Constitution granted by Great Britain after the war. Despite objections couched in violent terms by Mr Saklatvala, the Parsee Communist who sits for North Battersea, the House was unanimous in wishing "Godspeed" to the Commission which sets out in January (→13/8/28).

"War in 20 years" says Army chief

Nov 3. A grim prediction, that there may only be 20 years' peace before there is another war with Germany, was made tonight. The Treaty of Versailles may prove to be a "constant source of trouble", warned Lieutenant-General Sir A. Montgomery-Massingberd. There would be 90 million Germans in 20 years with no space for expansion. "Defeat in the Great War no doubt rankles in the German mind and will continue to do so", he said.

1927

DECEMBER

Su	Mo	Tu	We	Th	Fr	Sa
				1	2	3
4	5	6	7	8	9	10
11	12	13	14	15	16	17
18	19	20	21	22	23	24
25	26	27	28	29	30	31

1. Washington: Commerce Secretary Hoover says the average US salary is $1,280 a year (£260).

2. Moscow: The 15th Party Congress opens; Trotsky's disgrace is confirmed.

2. New York: Ford's Model A, successor to the Model T, goes on show to the public.

5. Rumania: Anti-Hungarian riots take place at Nagyvarad, near the Hungarian border.

10. Stockholm: Nobel Prizes go to Arthur Compton (US) and Charles Wilson (UK, Physics); Heinrich Wieland (Germany, Chemistry); Julius Wagner-Jauregg (Austria, Medicine) and Henri Bergson (France, Literature); Peace Prize awarded in Oslo to Ferdinand Buisson (France) and Ludwig Quidde (Germany).

10. London: Greyhound racing begins at Wembley Stadium.→

12. Washington: President Coolidge approves a $1,000 million five-year naval building programme.

14. China: Chiang Kai-shek's forces crushs a Communist coup attempt in Canton.→

19. China: 600 alleged Communists are executed by the Nationalists.

25. UK: A white Christmas as Britain is swept by freezing blizzards.

27. New York: Florenz Ziegfeld's "Show Boat", music by Jerome Kern, opens.

31. UK: Food supplies are air-dropped into villages cut off by snow.

HITS OF 1927

Among my souvenirs.

Ain't she sweet.

Sometimes I'm happy.

QUOTE OF THE YEAR

"An expert is someone who knows some of the worst mistakes in his subject, and how to avoid them."

Werner Heisenberg, author of the "Uncertainty Principle".

Russians expelled from Shanghai

Dec 15. The Nationalist government today ordered immediate closure of the Soviet Consulate in Shanghai as General Chiang Kai-shek's troops began rounding up Communists in the city.

Mr Kozlovsky, the Consul-General, has been given his passport and ordered to leave by the first available boat. The Soviet Dal Bank is also to be shut down, as well as other Russian commercial agencies.

The expulsion follows the attempted communist coup in Canton. Mr C.C. Wu, the Foreign Minister, accused the Soviets of giving support to the plotters. In Peking, 13 Russians have been shot for revolutionary activities.

Searching for "Bolshevik" leaflets.

Physicists' year of living uncertainly

The year has been a disconcerting one for physicists with the publication of **Werner Heisenberg's** "Uncertainty Principle", which undermines the whole idea of exact measurement. The Principle is that the more precisely you try to fix the position of a body, the more uncertain is its momentum, and vice versa. Fortunately the degree of uncertainty is very small!

The year also saw new evidence emerge about Java Man, who lived half a million years ago. Experts believe he may be a missing link between apes and humans.

"Popish" prayer book is rejected

Dec 15. Hats and order papers were thrown into the air and wild cheering broke out when the House of Commons voted today to reject the new Book of Common Prayer. The decisive speech came from Sir Thomas Inskip, the Solicitor-General, who claimed it went too far towards Rome in permitting the reservation of the Blessed Sacrament for the Communion of the Sick.

This was the most controversial change in the new book which also alters the marriage service, so that the wife no longer promises to "obey" her husband. Supporters fear that today's vote might lead to the disestablishment of the Church of England, whose Assembly backed the new book (→ 19/3/28).

Betting Britain goes to the dogs

Dec 10. Greyhound racing, popular in America for nearly a decade, has taken Britain's cities by storm this year, providing the betting excitement traditionally associated with horse racing within the scope – and the spare evening time – of the working man. With the opening of a track at the Empire Stadium, Wembley, to match those at the White City and Harringay, London now has three venues barely a year after dogs first chased a mechanical hare round Britain's first track at Belle Vue, Manchester.

For films in the front room.

Arts: jungle sounds mark Jazz Age

Monti Ryan singing with Percival MacKey's jazz band on the roof of the London Palladium.

Jazz, a term loosely applied to any syncopated dance music until now, is finding its identity in America, although it still comes in two versions, black and white. The foremost black jazz composer, **Duke Ellington**, has taken up residence at the Cotton Club in Harlem with an 11-piece band this year and is becoming widely known through his broadcasts.

Ellington's trade mark is "jungle sound" created by "growling" brass, tom-toms and "wa-wa" mutes. With his trumpeter, **Bubber Miley**, the Duke composes much of the band's music – "Black and Tan Fantasy", "Creole Love Call" and "Cotton Club Stomp", for example.

An amazingly dexterous cornet-player, **Louis Armstrong**, made his name in Chicago after leaving New Orleans, displaced, like so many musicians, by the closing of the red-light district of Storyville in 1917. He played with King Oliver and his Creole Jazz Band and is now recording with his "Hot Five" such numbers as "Heebie Jeebies" and "St James's Infirmary Blues".

Also recording are the leading Blues singers, **Ma Rainey**, a rumbustious character known as "the Mother of the Blues", and **Bessie Smith**, of a searing emotional impact, sometimes accompanied by Louis Armstrong on cornet.

In New York **Fletcher Henderson's** band features the first major saxophone soloist, **Coleman Hawkins**. But the biggest band is white – **Paul Whiteman** and his Orchestra, playing what he calls "symphonic jazz" (Whiteman was a viola player in symphony orchestras). In his line-up are such top white musicians as the trumpeter, **Bix Beiderbecke**, trombonists **Jack Teagarden** and **Tommy Dorsey** and a vocal group, the Rhythm Boys (**Bing Crosby** among them).

Elsewhere in the arts this year **Marcel Proust's** epic has been completed at last and the sequence is being published in English under the title "Remembrance of Things Past" in Mr Scott-Moncrieff's translation. Notable novels include "To the Lighthouse", Virginia Woolf's symbolic story, in which she depicts her own father, and "Tarka the Otter", a remarkable evocation of an otter's world by **Henry Williamson**, who kept one at his home in Devon until it escaped.

Edward Kennedy "Duke" Ellington (centre) performing with his band.

1928

JANUARY

Su	Mo	Tu	We	Th	Fr	Sa
1	2	3	4	5	6	7
8	9	10	11	12	13	14
15	16	17	18	19	20	21
22	23	24	25	26	27	28
29	30	31				

1. Nicaragua: Five US Marines die and 23 are wounded in a clash with rebel followers of Sandino (→ 3).

2. US: From today Pan-American Airways are the first airline to use male stewards.

3. Nicaragua: 1,000 more US Marines are sent to fight the Sandinist rebels (→ 29/2).

5. UK: 466,000 people over 65 receive their first state pensions of ten shillings a week.

7. London: Telephone lines are cut off by the floodwaters of the Thames.

9. USSR: 30 opposition leaders, including Trotsky, are served with internal banishment orders.→

10. UK: Longer skirts are coming back into fashion, according to dressmakers.

12. Rome: The Italian press is banned from reporting suicides or sensational crimes.

14. Libya: 100 tribesmen are killed in clashes with Italian troops.

16. Rome: The government says it may abolish trial by jury because juries are too lenient.

16. Cuba: President Coolidge opens the Pan-American Conference in Havana.

18. London: Three Britons are sentenced for ten years for spying for the USSR.

19. UK: Figures show the birth rate in 1927 was the lowest on record.

23. US: Presidential candidate Herbert Hoover says he will keep Prohibition.

23. Palestine: A severe earthquake rocks Nazareth near Jerusalem.

29. Berlin: Germany signs a treaty with Lithuania for arbitration on the League-occupied city of Memel.

DEATHS

11. British author Thomas Hardy (*2/6/1840).→

29. British commander Field Marshal Earl Haig (*19/6/1861).

Stalin exiles all key opposition figures

Trotsky practising his shooting skills as his position becomes precarious.

Jan 16. In a dramatic move Joseph Stalin has further humiliated his defeated political rivals and sent many of them into exile far from Moscow. The security police, OGPU, have rounded up some 30 leading anti-Stalin Bolsheviks, including Leon Trotsky, who has been sent to Alma-Ata on the Russian-Chinese frontier.

The list of those purged includes two of Trotsky's most prominent allies, Grigori Zinoviev and Leon Kamenev, but there are reports they have been allowed to remain in European Russia at the price of renouncing their views. If this is so then Stalin's triumph over his ex-comrades is complete.

The opposition has been banished under a decree in the criminal code prescribing punishment for "counter-revolution". The Soviet press has not so far reported the crackdown, which comes at the time of a grave social crisis, predicted by Trotsky among others.

Several cities and towns are threatened with famine with the government's purchases of grain from the peasants falling far short of what is needed. Meanwhile there are no exports and almost no consumer goods (→ 25/11).

Hungry Chinese sell children for food

Jan 20. So desperate is the famine caused by the civil war that starving Chinese peasants are selling their children to get food. The China International Famine Relief Commission reports that in Shantung province four million people have been reduced to beggary. Young girls are sold as prostitutes for between £1 and £5 depending on their beauty. Boy children are sold to childless couples.

Thousands of famished people wander aimlessly in the countryside living off roots, tree bark and chaff. In the provincial capital of Tsinan-Fu 25,000 refugees are sleeping in the bitterly cold streets. Their only food is gruel from charity kitchens.

Phone use in UK is expanding fast

Jan 27. Extensive plans to broaden and update London's phone system were announced today. These include the building of 52 new exchanges and 73 exchanges converted to the automatic principle. The plans were described by the controller of the capital's telephone service as "the ultimate provision for over half a million subscribers" and a response to the widespread increase of telephone use (→ 1/1/29).

Londoners die and Tate threatened as Thames bursts banks

Jan 6. The Thames burst its banks today, flooding low-lying districts of London, drowning 14 people – including four young sisters – in their basement homes. Hundreds more have been made homeless along the length of the grey, swollen river.

The vaults of the Palace of Westminster were flooded. The usually dry moat of the Tower of London was water-filled once more. Damage to property was extensive.

Twelve Landseer paintings were badly damaged at the Tate Gallery, although the Turner collection was saved.

The cause of the disaster was the much-feared combination of a sudden thaw and a high tide.

Shopping for meat in a flooded street on the outskirts of London.

Hardy, chronicler of rural England, dies

Thomas Hardy looks at "Tess", his tragic tale of love.

Jan 16. Thomas Hardy was buried beside Dickens in Westminster Abbey today; leaders of contemporary letters – Kipling and Barrie, Galsworthy and Shaw, Gosse and Housman – were his pall-bearers.

As his ashes were lowered into the paving of Poets' Corner, watched by his widow, Florence, his heart was being buried in the grave of his first wife Emma in the little churchyard of Stinsford, in the heart of the Wessex he immortalised in so many novels.

He deliberately confined himself to Wessex and encouraged readers to identify the places he described, such as Casterbridge, with their originals, such as Dorchester, where he lived for the last 43 years.

"The description of these backgrounds has been done from the real," he wrote. "The domestic emotions have throbbed in Wessex nooks with as much intensity as in the palaces of Europe and there was quite enough human nature in Wessex for one man's literary purpose." He was also describing a way of life and speech which he knew intimately before it quite vanished.

After 30 years of prose, he turned to poetry, writing impassioned stanzas to his first wife after her death in 1912 and crowning his verse with "The Dynasts". He was 87.

1928

FEBRUARY

Su	Mo	Tu	We	Th	Fr	Sa
			1	2	3	4
5	6	7	8	9	10	11
12	13	14	15	16	17	18
19	20	21	22	23	24	25
26	27	28	29			

1. Egypt: The last discovery in Tutankhamun's tomb is of jars containing his vital organs.

1. Miami: Jack Dempsey announces his retirement from the boxing ring.

3. India: Serious rioting greets the arrival of the Simon Commission on the government of India.

4. Vienna: Austrian Nazis protest at the presence of black singer Josephine Baker.

5. London: The Medical Research Council says Vitamin D can be produced artificially.

7. London: The Church of England approves the amended revisions to the Prayer Book.

10. London: "The Chained Swan" pub, the first building built after the Great Fire of London, is demolished.

11. Switzerland: The second Winter Olympics open in St.Moritz (→19).

12. UK: 11 are killed as a gale sweeps across Britain.

15. UK: The Oxford English Dictionary is complete after 70 years work costing £300,000.

19. Switzerland: The St. Moritz Winter Olympics end.

19. US: Malcolm Campbell sets a land speed record of 206.35 mph at in his car "Bluebird" at Daytona (→22).

20. London: Britain recognises Transjordanian independence.

22. US: American Frank Lockhart is injured when he drives into the sea trying to beat Campbell's speed record.

25. US: A new device is demonstrated to stop the fluttering of television images.

26. Germany: The first large passenger aeroplane built by the firm of Messerschmitt crashes during a trial flight.

29. Nicaragua: Five US Marines die in an ambush by Sandinist rebels.

DEATH

15. British statesman Herbert Henry Asquith, Earl of Oxford and Asquith, Liberal Prime Minister 1908-1916 (*12/9/1852).→

US arrival claims to be Czar's daughter

The same woman? Anastasia aged ten (left) and Mrs Chaikovsky aged 25.

Feb 6. A very mysterious young woman, calling herself Anastasia Chaikovsky and claiming to be the youngest daughter of the murdered Russian Czar, reached the United States today. Mrs Chaikovsky arrived in New York on board the liner Berengaria and avoided a crowd of waiting reporters and photographers.

As Mrs Chaikovsky tells it, she managed to survive the bloody massacre of the Russian royal family by the Bolsheviks in 1918 and escaped from Russia with the help of a Russian soldier.

She says that one of the purposes of her visit to the United States is to have her jaw reset – it was broken by a bayonet thrust from a Bolshevik soldier.

Mrs Chaikovsky was met by the son of the Czar's doctor, who was killed in the cellar with the royal family. Mr Gleb Botkin greeted her as "Your Highness" and declared she was certainly the Grand Duchess with whom he played as a child. He denied the public were being hoaxed.

Rumours have persisted that some or all members of the Royal family are still alive, and that a lost fortune exists, so the riddle of Anastasia exerts the greatest public fascination.

King leads tributes at Asquith's death

Feb 15. Herbert Henry Asquith, first Earl of Oxford and Asquith, died today aged 75. The King led worldwide tributes to Britain's longest serving Prime Minister this century.

From 1908 to 1916 easy-going Asquith guided the nation through much of its most turbulent period. One of his greatest achievements was educating the monarchy into being relaxed about the emergence of the Labour Party.

Halfway through the Great War he was ousted from Downing Street by the dexterous artifice and more frenzied energy of Lloyd George. The feud between the two Liberal leaders is only now ended. Asquith drew a strict line between work and play and moved easily across it. He enjoyed life ardently and delighted in feminine company.

Asquith at the dispatch box.

1928

MARCH

Su	Mo	Tu	We	Th	Fr	Sa
				1	2	3
4	5	6	7	8	9	10
11	12	13	14	15	16	17
18	19	20	21	22	23	24
25	26	27	28	29	30	31

1. US: Dr Herbert Evans announces the discovery of a sixth vitamin, "Vitamin F".

4. UK: Revealed that the Daily Mail forced publication of the Zinoviev Letter, strongly suggesting it was a fake.

5. Germany: Elections show the National Socialists as most popular party in Bavaria.

6. Peking: A Communist raid leaves a reported 3,000 dead while 50,000 flee the city (→ 7/4).

11. UK: Blizzards sweep Britain; it is -9 degrees Celsius (16F) in London.

12. Mediterranean: The British colony of Malta becomes a Dominion.

13. US: 300 die and 700 are missing when a dam bursts near Los Angeles.

19. London: The Industrial Fatigue Research Board says a cup of tea aids efficiency and curbs industrial discontent.

19. UK: The final draft of the revised Book of Common Prayer is issued (→ 14/6).

21. London: Foreign Secretary Chamberlain says expediency, not prejudice, forbids women's recruitment as diplomats.

21. Washington: Charles Lindbergh is presented with the Congressional Medal of Honor by President Coolidge.

23. UK: Mr. H. S. Kenyon's Tipperary Tim wins the Grand National at Aintree.

23. Saudi Arabia: King ibn Saud orders the Wahabi tribes to stop fighting and return to their tribal areas.

26. New York: Nearly five million shares sold in record trading on Wall Street (→ 16/5).

28. France: Military service is reduced to one year.

30. Cairo: The Egyptian government protests to Britain over its interference in Egypt's internal affairs.

30. Rome: The Boy Scouts and other non-Fascist youth movements are ordered to be disbanded within 30 days.

BIRTH

4. British author Alan Sillitoe.

The caps fit and women are wearing them

March 19. Women's hair, which has been getting shorter and shorter over the past few years, will now disappear from view altogether, if a new fashion catches on. Skull caps of gold and silver tissue, unveiled at today's Women's Wear Exhibition in London, are designed to cover the ears as well as the hair.

Other new fashions at the show included coloured stockings, coats with bold geometric patterns, and many sporting styles, particularly jumpers with asymmetric necks. Skirts are barely to the knee.

The emphasis is still very much on the young, active, boyish look – what George Bernard Shaw has called dress for "real human beings" rather than "upholstery for Victorian angels". One of the reasons for the trend is said to be the increasing number of women entering the business world.

But not everyone is pleased. Last month the German Post Office banned skirts shorter than eight inches below the knee, while at the beginning of the year confectioners were complaining that the slimming craze was putting them out of business.

Modelling the new skull cap.

RAF strafes marauding Arab tribesmen

March 3. British forces are taking measures to counter a huge raid by 20,000 Wahabi religious tribesmen aimed at Kuwait and the Iraq frontier. These marauders, mounted on camels, are sweeping across the desert and King ibn Saud, their nominal sovereign, has little authority over them.

His threat to send a force to deal with them has never materialised, and the duty of protecting Southern Iraq and Kuwait against their aggression has fallen on the British.

The tribesmen have already lost a number of men from strafing attacks by the RAF, although they have shot down one aeroplane, killing the pilot. Two squadrons have now been sent to Kuwait, an armoured train is running between Shaibah and Ur of the Chaldees, and two sloops have joined the gunruiser Emerald.

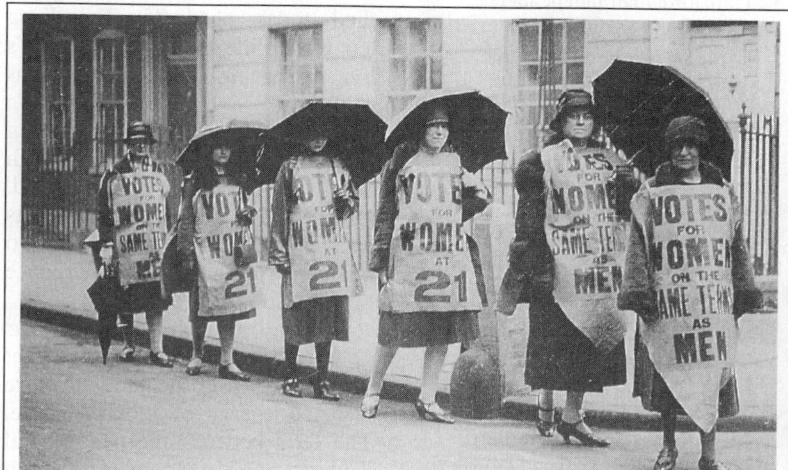

March 29. The Suffragettes' long campaign finally came to an end today as the House of Commons overwhelmingly passed the Equal Franchise Bill giving the vote to all women aged 21 or over (→ 7/5).

1928

APRIL

Su	Mo	Tu	We	Th	Fr	Sa
1	2	3	4	5	6	7
8	9	10	11	12	13	14
15	16	17	18	19	20	21
22	23	24	25	26	27	28
29	30					

1. Turkey: 60 are reported dead as an earthquake strikes the country (→ 14).

2. London: The BBC unveils plans for programmes debating politically controversial issues.

3. London: The manuscript of "Alice in Wonderland" is sold to a US buyer for £15,400.

6. Rome: Handshaking is banned as unhygienic.

9. Ankara: Islam is abolished as the Turkish state religion.→

11. Dublin: Announced that the Free State is to get its own coinage, with purer silver than Britain's.

12. Newfoundland: A Junkers aeroplane with a crew of three lands after the first non-stop East-West Atlantic flight.

13. London: The Zoo acquires a 100-year-old Chilean tortoise.

14. Bulgaria: An earthquake leaves 500 people feared dead and 80,000 homeless (→ 22).

14. Paris: French aviators Costes and Le Brix land after a record 42,625-mile round-the-world flight.

17. China: 470 are reported dead when a coal mine floods in Fushung.

21. London: Blackburn Rovers beats Huddersfield Town 1-0 in the FA Cup Final.

22. Greece: Corinth is devastated in an earthquake that leaves a reported 50,000 homeless.

23. Nicaragua: Sandinist rebels capture US-owned mines, taking five workers hostage.

28. Rome: Mussolini says that "degenerate and bewildering" elections must end (→ 12/5).

29. France: The moderate right under Raymond Poincare wins national elections.

BIRTH

23. US actress and diplomat Shirley Temple.

DEATH

25. "White" Russian leader Count Peter Wrangell (*27/8/1878).

Chinese Nationalists launch major attack

Chiang Kai-shek's Nationalist troops march on across the Yellow River.

April 7. Chinese Nationalist troops today launched their long expected offensive with the ultimate aim of capturing the capital Peking. General Chiang Kai-shek, the commander-in-chief, ordered his troops to attack across the Yellow river on a 400-mile front from the sea to Haichow. The line of advance is along the Lunghai railway westwards towards Changteho.

Nationalist authorities are keeping details of the assault secret, refusing to allow foreign observers to accompany their troops. In these circumstances it is difficult to tell how the attack is going. But in Shanghai today it became known that the offensive is three pronged, and its first objective is the town of Weihsien on the Tsingrao-Tsinan railway.

The Nationalist commander-in-chief has set up his headquarters in the railway town of Hsufowchu and is personally taking command of operations with a quarter of a million men at his disposal. Facing him is a force of 80,000 while, on his left flank, General Sun Chuang-fang threatens him with an army of 50,000 (→31/5).

Turkish children set to learn ABC

April 9. Premier Mustapha Kemal of Turkey has taken another revolutionary step in his efforts to drag his backward nation into the Western world. From now, Turkish schools will teach the A to Z of the Roman alphabet instead of the Alif-Yen of the Arabic.

A new dictionary is being prepared to teach the Roman alphabet in schools and newspapers will be printed in both Arabic and Latin script. It is expected that in 15 years time the Arabic script will disappear from public use.

The official reason given for this fundamental change is that Turkish illiteracy stems mainly from the difficulty of learning Arabic. But another important reason is that it will cut the links between Turkish and Arabic cultures (→10/1/29).

April 12. The King of Italy, Victor Emmanuel III, escaped unhurt after a bomb attempt on his life, but 14 were killed.

1928

MAY

Su	Mo	Tu	We	Th	Fr	Sa
		1	2	3	4	5
6	7	8	9	10	11	12
13	14	15	16	17	18	19
20	21	22	23	24	25	26
27	28	29	30	31		

2. US: A monument to the Wright brothers is unveiled at Kittyhawk, North Carolina, site of the first powered flight.

7. London: MPs give an unopposed third reading to the Equal Franchise Bill, giving the vote to all women aged 21.

11. US: Sir Joseph Duveen pays a record £175,000 for a Raphael "Madonna and Child".

12. Rome: The electorate is cut from 12 million to three million as the Senate replaces the Chamber of Deputies with an appointed Fascist Council (→21).

16. UK: The Prince of Wales opens Britain's longest road bridge, the Royal Tweed Bridge.

19. London: Britain backs the Kellogg-Briand plan to outlaw war, formulated by the US and France (→27/8).

21. Rome: The Papal Secretary tells Catholics to dissociate themselves from Fascism.

21. Germany: The National Socialist vote declines and the Socialist vote increases in national elections (→13/6).

23. Buenos Aires: A suspected anti-Fascist bomb at the Italian embassy kills 22 and hurts 41.

24. London: Piccadilly Circus Tube station is to get 11 escalators, the largest number at any station in the world (→10/12).

27. Arctic: Italian Umberto Nobile's airship Italia crashes onto the ice after flying over the North Pole (→20/6).

28. Nottingham: Jack Hobbs scores his 150th century, at Trent Bridge.

29. US: Motor firms Chrysler and Dodge merge as the third-biggest US car makers after Ford and General Motors.

31. China: Chiang Kai-shek's Nationalist forces advance to within 20 miles of Peking (→3/6).

BIRTH

30. French film director Agnes Varda.

Dixie Dean scores 60th goal of season

Record goal scorer Dixie Dean.

May 1. The end of the football season has witnessed a welter of goal scoring feats that would have seemed impossible before the relaxation of the offside laws three years ago. No fewer than seven English and two Scottish league clubs scored over a hundred goals. Jimmy Smith, of the Scottish second division champions Ayr United, scored 66 goals; and in the last match of the far more competitive English season, Dixie Dean, centre-forward for the champions Everton, drove home his record 60th league goal.

New notes planned by Bank of England

May 14. The Bill to allow the Bank of England to issue £1 and 10s. notes, as well as those for £5 and more, passed its Second Reading yesterday. The number issued will be restricted in line with the gold reserves. The Government claims the big rise in cheque use will finance expansion. Labour protested, however, that the restriction would hit cash dependent workers, and might cause a recession.

Japanese guns mow down the Chinese

The Japanese Emperor inspects sound detectors used to warn of air raids.

May 11. The Japanese garrison at Tsinan-Fu are today masters of the stricken provincial capital of Shantung, after three days of savage fighting, in which the besieged Japanese force of 5,000 scythed down human waves of Nationalist troops with machine gun and artillery fire. More than a thousand Chinese were killed while Japanese losses amounted to 14 soldiers and 16 civilians. General Chiang Kai-shek's disorganised men have now retreated 50 miles south.

The battle began when Nationalist forces advancing towards Peking occupied the city. The Japanese units, which were there to protect their nationals as the Northern Chinese army retreated, claimed that the ill-disciplined soldiers began an orgy of murder and looting. Japanese civilians were stripped and whipped through the streets.

General Fukada, the garrison commander, issued an ultimatum, demanding punishment of Chinese soldiers. This was rejected by General Chiang Kai-shek, who ordered his army to storm the city. With the help of reinforcements the Japanese in the old city were able to put the Chinese to flight.

'Ello, 'ello, 'ello! What do we 'ave 'ere then? Three policemen about to fight crime on their brand new Royal Enfield motorcycles.

Panic selling hits Wall Street stocks

May 16. Wall Street share prices plunged today as more shares changed hands than ever before in stock market history. Trading volume was 4,820,840 shares. Most of the selling took place in the last two hours with some leading shares falling by as much as 40 points.

The fall was triggered by massive selling of aircraft shares such as Curtiss Aero and Wright Aeronautical. Panic selling then spread to the market leaders including General Motors, General Electric, US Steel and Montgomery Ward.

No particularly bad economic or financial news was issued during the day and stock market experts were unable to provide any explanation of what had provoked the dramatic slump (→16/11).

Flying Scotsman sets new record

May 1. A new era of rail travel was ushered in yesterday with the "Flying Scotsman" service which now makes daily non-stop runs in each direction between Edinburgh and London. Speeds of over 70 miles per hour were achieved at times during the 392-mile journey, and both trains arrived ahead of schedule. Each had two drivers who received a silver plate (and tobacco pouch) as mementoes.

Flying doctor takes off in Australia

May 15. A flying doctor service has been started by the Australian Inland Mission covering 250,000 square miles of Queensland and Central Australia where there are only 10 local doctors. Dr. K. St. Vincent Welch has just offered his services and the Queensland and Northern Territory Aerial Service – QANTAS – will provide a pilot and a DH-50 based at Cloncurry. A low-power, pedal-drive Morse radio transmitter-receiver, with a range of 300 miles, will allow long distance consultations and will summon Dr Welch to fly to the site of an emergency.

1928

JUNE

Su	Mo	Tu	We	Th	Fr	Sa
					1	2
3	4	5	6	7	8	9
10	11	12	13	14	15	16
17	18	19	20	21	22	23
24	25	26	27	28	29	30

3. Peking: Marshal Chang Tso-lin evacuates the city as Chiang Kai-shek's army advances.→

6. UK: The Derby at Epsom is won by Sir Hugo Cunliffe-Owen's Felstead.

9. Australia: The "Southern Cross" lands in Brisbane after the longest flight over water, 7,000 miles from California.

13. Berlin: Dr. Wilhelm Marx resigns as Chancellor (→28).

13. London: Harrods buys the retailer D. H. Evans.

14. London: MPs reject the latest revision of the Book of Common Prayer (→27/7).

15. Edinburgh: The Flying Scotsman narrowly beats an aeroplane in a race from London to Edinburgh.

20. Belgrade: Two deputies are shot dead by a Radical deputy during a heated debate in the Yugoslav parliament.

23. Germany: A rocket-powered car built by Opel is wrecked in a test after reaching a speed of 156mph.

23. France: The franc is devalued at 124.21 to the pound.

25. US: Unemployment has reached two million.

25. Cairo: King Fuad dismisses Prime Minister Nahas Pasha (→19/7).

26. Houston: New York Governor Al Smith wins the Democratic nomination for presidential candidate.

27. Darlington: 23 people are killed in a train crash.

27. Warsaw: Marshal Pilsudski resigns (→25/8/30).

28. Berlin: Socialist Hermann Muller is sworn in as Chancellor.

BIRTH

14. Argentine revolutionary Ernesto "Che" Guevara Serna (†8/10/67).

DEATH

14. British women's rights campaigner Emmeline Pankhurst (*4/7/1858).

Earhart is first woman to fly Atlantic

June 18. An American woman brought her seaplane down in a South Wales estuary today and so became the first woman to fly the Atlantic. Miss Amelia Earhart, 29, left Newfoundland at 2.51pm yesterday and battled against terrible weather across the Atlantic to arrive near Llanelli at 12.40pm today. Her fuel supply was so low she had to throw out equipment to stay airborne, but she stepped out looking relaxed in a woollen coat and brightly hued bandeau.

Miss Earhart and her two male companions had no idea where they were when they came down; they had hoped to reach Southampton. Many thought the aircraft had crashed when it hit the water and several men threw themselves into the estuary fully clothed in a bid to reach the plane.

Miss Amelia Earhart (left).

Republican Peking surrenders peacefully

June 8. In tattered uniforms and bearing ancient weapons, the advance guard of the Nationalist army, which has fought its way to the capital from the Yellow River, entered Peking yesterday. Hundreds of shouting students welcomed them; Republican flags had been hastily removed and replaced with the colours of the Kuomintang.

Marshal Chang Tso-lin, head of the former government, whose army retreated from Peking five days ago, took ceremonial leave of the corps diplomatique before quitting the city. To maintain order until the arrival of the victorious Nationalists, he left behind the 47th Brigade. This move reasured the local population and the foreign community. The force was given an assurance of eventual safe conduct to Manchuria.

The fall of Peking crowns the efforts of General Chiang Kai-shek, the Nationalist commander, to unify China and end the civil war (→ 6/10).

Suffragists mourn Pankhurst's death

June 18. Emmeline Pankhurst, the First Lady of women's suffrage, was buried today in an emotional ceremony attended by hundreds of her old comrades, many wearing the colours of the Women's Social and Political Union.

Mrs Pankhurst was an outspoken advocate of militant tactics, which brought about some of the most shocking outrages of peacetime. Her later years, however, were spent more peaceably – firstly in Canada and then as a Conservative in Whitechapel. Today she was saluted as an "heroic leader and staunch friend".

Amundsen killed in rescue attempt

June 20. The Norwegian explorer Roald Amundsen died today when his seaplane crashed near Spitzbergen in an Arctic rescue attempt. Amundsen – the first man to reach the South Pole – had set off with a companion in search of an Italian airship flown by General Umberto Nobile, with whom he had flown over the North Pole. Nobile, together with five of his crew, are known to be safe after crashlanding on the Arctic tundra. Wireless messages from Amundsen's aircraft ceased after some hours and a search has confirmed his and his companion's fate (→ 12/7).

1928

JULY

Su	Mo	Tu	We	Th	Fr	Sa
1	2	3	4	5	6	7
8	9	10	11	12	13	14
15	16	17	18	19	20	21
22	23	24	25	26	27	28
29	30	31				

1. India: 15 die in a riot between Sikhs and Moslems at Khargpur.

1. Mexico: General Alvaro Obregon is elected president (→ 17).

3. US: The first commercially available television set, made by Daven Corporation, goes on sale for $75.

4. US: Jean Lussier goes over Niagara Falls in a rubber ball.

5. Brazil: Two Italians set a world record by flying 5,000 miles non-stop from Rome.

7. Wimbledon: Rene Lacoste beats Henri Cochet in the Men's Singles final; Helen Wills beats Lili de Alvarez for the Women's Singles title.

8. India: 18 die when an East Indian Railway train is derailed after saboteurs removed part of the track.

10. London: The Lords reject the Rabbits Bill, allowing their destruction, fearing it will mean a shortage for shooting.

12. Arctic: Umberto Nobile and the crew of the airship Italia are finally rescued, by a Soviet icebreaker.

17. Mexico City: President Obregon is assassinated at a lunch to celebrate his election earlier this month (→ 25/9).

22. Tokyo: Japan breaks off relations with China.

24. UK: Mourners at the funeral of actress Dame Ellen Terry wear summer dress at her request.

25. UK: Captain de Havilland sets a world record by flying his plane Gipsy Moth at 21,500 feet.

28. Amsterdam: The eighth Olympic Games open (→ 12/8).

31. London: A government committee says smallpox can be eradicated from the world by systematic vaccination.

BIRTH

26. US film director Stanley Kubrick.

DEATH

21. British actress Dame Ellen Terry (*27/2/1847).

Primate to resign over prayer book

July 27. Randall Davidson is to resign as Archbishop of Canterbury next November. He was bitterly disappointed last month when the House of Commons rejected the new prayer book for the second time and by a bigger majority.

His opponents, however, will not be pleased because he is to be succeeded by the Archbishop of York, Cosmo Lang, the chief advocate of the new book. Today one leading opponent, Sir William Joynson-Hicks, the Home Secretary, called for Lang to "devote himself to the real call of the church – the evangelisation of the people".

Archbishop Randall Davidson.

King Fuad is new Egyptian dictator

July 19. King Fuad, in a Royal decree issued today, ended parliamentary government in Egypt. With his ministers he now intends to rule by decree and has suspended parts of the constitution. Freedom of the press no longer exists; there will be no new elections for at least three years and public meetings of the opposition party are prohibited.

These harsh measures were taken to deal with a crisis which originated in the downfall of Nahas Pasha. This followed the revelations that the insane Prince Seifeddin had escaped from an asylum in Sussex.

1928

AUGUST

Su	Mo	Tu	We	Th	Fr	Sa
			1	2	3	4
5	6	7	8	9	10	11
12	13	14	15	16	17	18
19	20	21	22	23	24	25
26	27	28	29	30	31	

1. Yugoslavia: Croatian deputies set up a separatist parliament in Zagreb.

1. UK: Morris Motors launch their latest model, the Morris Minor.

2. US: Cecil B. De Mille joins Metro-Goldwyn-Meyer as a director.

5. Brussels: The International Socialist Congress opens.

9. Dutch East Indies: 1,000 are reported killed when a volcano erupts.

11. US: Commerce Secretary Herbert Hoover accepts the Republican nomination for presidential candidate (→ 6/11).

13. India: Nationalists issue a draft constitution calling for Dominion status and a two-chamber parliament.

16. USSR: Compulsory military service is introduced.

17. Aberdeen: Captain Wedgwood Benn, Liberal MP for 21 years, is elected Labour MP in a by-election.

20. Greece: Veteran statesman Eleutherios Venizelos wins 228 out of 250 seats in a general election.

21. US: Joseph Schenk, head of United Artists Corporation, says "talkies" are just a fad and will not remain popular.

25. Tirana: President Ahmed Zog declares Albania a kingdom and himself king (→ 1/9).

31. Berlin: First performance of Bertolt Brecht's "Threepenny Opera" with music by Kurt Weill.

BIRTH

22. German composer Karlheinz Stockhausen.

DEATHS

12. Czech composer Leos Janacek (*3/7/1854).

17. British Liberal statesman and historian Sir George Trevelyan (*20/7/1838).

19. British Liberal statesman Richard, Viscount Haldane (*30/7/1856).

Britain signs a treaty outlawing war

Aug 27. Another big step towards ensuring peace in Europe was taken today when delegates of 15 countries, meeting in the French Foreign Ministry in Paris, signed a Pact for the Renunciation of War. First to sign, using a large gold pen, was Gustav Stresemann, the German Foreign Minister, who was loudly cheered.

The pact is largely the work of Frank Kellogg, US Secretary of State, in collaboration with Aristide Briand, the French Foreign Minister. France is particularly gratified at having persuaded the Americans to take part, since their failure to join the League of Nations has seriously weakened that organisation's credibility (→ 6/9).

US President Coolidge signs the Kellogg-Briand pact renouncing war.

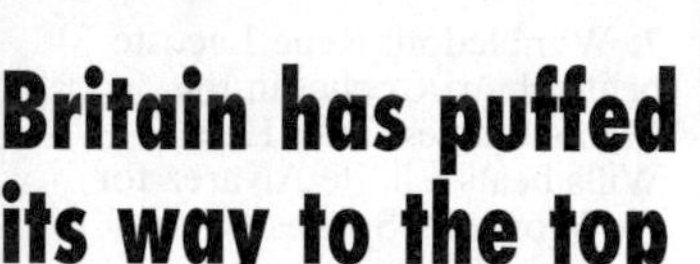

Britain has puffed its way to the top

Aug 10. The people of the United Kingdom are the greatest cigarette smokers in the world, consuming 77,458,000 pounds of tobacco in 1924 compared with 23,766,000 in 1907, according to a report of the Imperial Economical Committee.

The rise of tobacco consumption from 2.4 lbs per head in 1917 to 3.4 in 1927 is due to the growth of the cigarette habit, especially among women. The pipe is no longer so popular, taking only 35 per cent of the tobacco consumed, while cigar smoking has also declined.

The agricultural development of Southern Rhodesia, 75 per cent of whose tobacco exports to the UK are for cigarettes, is closely linked with tobacco production. In Nyasaland, tobacco represents 80 per cent of its exports in 1927. This pleasing growth of Empire production is now closely watched by USA interests.

Queen Mary cigarettes.

Olympics go international at Amsterdam

Percy Williams, winner of the 100 metres and 200 metres races.

Aug 12. The Olympic Games hosted by Amsterdam have fully realised Pierre de Coubertin's vision: the nations of the world in friendly competition. After a succession of Games dominated by North America and Western Europe, Amsterdam welcomed more than 3,000 competitors from 46 countries.

Familiar names still headed the roll of honour: Paavo Nurmi again won a gold in the 10,000 metres; so did Johnny Weissmuller in the pool. Britain's Douglas Lowe brilliantly recaptured the 800 metres title he won in Paris, and Lord Burghley, heir to the Marquess of Exeter, became the very first non-American to win the 400m hurdles.

But the base has now clearly broadened. The United States won only a single individual track race, the football competition went, for the second time, to Uruguay, with Argentina as runners-up; a Japanese athlete won his country's first Olympic gold, in the triple jump; a French-Algerian and a Chilean took the first two places in the marathon; and an amazing 50,000 crowd saw India beat the host nation to win the hockey gold medal. At last, it seems, the Olympic Games is truly a World Games.

1928  Amsterdam

Men Athletics

Event	Name	Nation	Result
100m			
1.	Percy Williams	CAN	10.8
2.	Jack London	GBR	10.8
3.	Georg Lammers	GER	10.9
200m			
1.	Percy Williams	CAN	21.8
2.	Walter Rangeley	GBR	21.9
3.	Helmut Körnig	GER	21.9
400m			
1.	Raymond Barbuti	USA	47.8
2.	James Ball	CAN	48.0
3.	Joachim Büchner	GER	48.2
800m			
1.	Douglas Lowe	GBR	*1:51.8
2.	Erik Byléhn	SWE	1:52.8
3.	Hermann Engelhard	GER	1:53.2
1500m			
1.	Harry Larva	FIN	*3:53.2
2.	Jules Ladoumégue	FRA	3:55.8
3.	Eino Purje	FIN	3:56.4
5000m			
1.	Ville Ritola	FIN	14:38.0
2.	Paavo Nurmi	FIN	14:40.0
3.	Edvin Wide	SWE	14:41.2
10,000m			
1.	Paavo Nurmi	FIN	*30:18.8
2.	Ville Ritola	FIN	30:19.4
3.	Edvin Wide	SWE	31:00.8
Marathon			
1.	Mohamed El Ouafi	FRA	2:32:57.0
2.	Miguel Plaza	CHI	2:33:23.0
3.	Martti Marttelin	FIN	2:35:02.0
110m Hurdles			
1.	Sydney Atkinson	SAF	14.8
2.	Stephen Anderson	USA	14.8
3.	John Collier	USA	14.9
400m Hurdles			
1.	David Burghley	GBR	*53.4
2.	Frank Cuhel	USA	53.6
3.	F. Morgan Taylor	USA	53.6
3000m Steeplechase			
1.	Toivo Loukola	FIN	*9:21.8
2.	Paavo Nurmi	FIN	9:31.2
3.	Ove Andersen	FIN	9:35.6
4x100m Relay			
1.	USA =* 41.0		(Frank Wykoff, James Quinn, Charles Borah, Henry Russell)
2.	GER 41.2		(Georg Lammers, Richard Corts, Hubert Houben, Helmuth Körnig)
3.	GBR 41.8		(Cyril Gill, Ellis Smouha, Walter Rangeley, Jack London)
4x400m Relay			
1.	USA ** 3:14.2		(George Baird, Emerson Spencer, Fred Alderman, Raymond Barbuti)
2.	GER 3:14.8		(Otto Neumann, Richard Krebs, Harry Storz, Hermann Engelhard)
3.	CAN 3:15.4		(Alexander Wilson, Philip Edwards, Stanley Glover, James Ball)
High Jump			
1.	Robert King	USA	1.94
2.	Benjamin Hedges	USA	1.91
3.	Claude Ménard	FRA	1.91
Pole Vault			
1.	Sabin Carr	USA	*4.20
2.	William Droegemuller	USA	4.10
3.	Charles McGinnis	USA	3.95
Long Jump			
1.	Edward Hamm	USA	*7.73
2.	Silvio Cator	HAI	7.58
3.	Alfred Bates	USA	7.40
Triple Jump			
1.	Mikio Oda	JAP	15.21
2.	Levi Casey	USA	15.17
3.	Vilho Tuulos	FIN	15.11
Shotput			
1.	John Kuck	USA	** 15.87
2.	Hermann Brix	USA	15.75
3.	Emil Hirschfeld	GER	15.72
Discus			
1.	Clarence Houser	USA	*47.32
2.	Antero Kivi	FIN	47.23
3.	James Corson	USA	47.10
Hammer			
1.	Patrick O'Callaghan	IRL	51.39
2.	Ossian Skiöld	SWE	51.29
3.	Edmund Black	USA	49.03
Javelin			
1.	Erik Lundkvist	SWE	*66.60
2.	Béla Szepes	HUN	65.26
3.	Olav Sunde	NOR	63.97
Decathlon			
1.	Paavo Yrjölä	FIN	** 8053
2.	Akilles Järvinen	FIN	7932
3.	John Kenneth Doherty	USA	7707

Women Athletics

Event	Name	Nation	Result
100m			
1.	Elizabeth Robinson	USA	=* 12.2
2.	Fanny Rosenfeld	CAN	12.3
3.	Ethel Smith	CAN	12.3
800m			
1.	Lina Radke	GER	** 2:16.8
2.	Kinue Hitomi	JAP	2:17.6
3.	Inga Gentzel	SWE	2:17.8
4x100m Relay			
1.	CAN ** 48.4		(Fanny Rosenfeld, Ethel Smith, Florence Bell, Myrtle Cook)
2.	USA 48.8		(Mary Washburn, Jessie Cross, Loretta McNeil, Elizabeth Robinson)
3.	GER 49.0		(Rosa Kellner, Leni Schmidt, Anni Holdmann, Leni Junker)
High Jump			
1.	Ethel Catherwood	CAN	1.59
2.	Carolina Gisolf	NETH	1.56
3.	Mildred Wiley	USA	1.56
Discus			
1.	Halina Konopacka	POL	*39.62
2.	Lillian Copeland	USA	37.08
3.	Ruth Svedberg	SWE	35.92

Men Swimming

Event	Name	Nation	Result
100m Freestyle			
1.	Johnny Weissmuller	USA	*58.6
2.	István Bárány	HUN	59.8
3.	Katsuo Takaishi	JAP	1:00.0
400m Freestyle			
1.	Alberto Zorilla	ARG	*5:01.6
2.	Andrew Charlton	AUS	5:03.6
3.	Arne Borg	SWE	5:04.6
1500m Freestyle			
1.	Arne Borg	SWE	*19:51.8
2.	Andrew Charlton	AUS	20:02.6
3.	Clarence Crabbe	USA	20:28.8
100m Backstroke			
1.	George Kojac	USA	** 1:08.2
2.	Walter Laufer	USA	1:10.0
3.	Paul Wyatt	USA	1:12.0
200m Breaststroke			
1.	Yoshiyuki Tsuruta	JAP	*2:48.8
2.	Erich Rademacher	GER	2:50.6
3.	Teofilo Yldefonzo	PHI	2:56.4
4x200m Freestyle Relay			
1.	USA ** 0:36.2		(Austin Clapp, Walter Laufer, George Kojac, Johnny Weissmuller)
2.	JAP 9:41.4		(Hiroshi Yoneyama, Nobuo Arai, Tokuhei Sada, Katsuo Takaishi)
3.	CAN 9:47.8		(F. Munro Borne, James Thompson, Garnet Ault, Walter Spence)
Springboard Diving			
1.	Peter Desjardins	USA	185.04
2.	Michael Galitzen	USA	174.06
3.	Farid Simaika	EGY	172.46
Platform Diving			
1.	Peter Desjardins	USA	98.74/6
2.	Farid Simaika	EGY	99.58/9
3.	Michael Galitzen	USA	92.34/15

Water Polo

1. Germany
2. Hungary
3. France

Women Swimming

Event	Name	Nation	Result
100m Freestyle			
1.	Albina Osipowich	USA	*1:10.0
2.	Eleonor Garatti	USA	1:11.4
3.	Margaret Joyce Cooper	GBR	1:13.6
400m Freestyle			
1.	Martha Norelius	USA	** 5:42.8
2.	Maria Johanna Braun	NETH	5:57.8
3.	Josephine McKim	USA	6:00.2
200m Breaststroke			
1.	Hilde Schrader	GER	3:12.6
2.	Mietje Baron	NETH	3:15.2
3.	Lotte Mühe	GER	3:17.6
100m Backstroke			
1.	Maria Johanna Braun	NETH	1:22.0
2.	Ellen Elisabeth King	GBR	1:22.2
3.	Margaret Joyce Cooper	GBR	1:22.8
4x100m Freestyle Relay			
1.	USA ** 4:47.6		(Adelaide Lambert, Eleonor Garatti, Albina Osipowich, Martha Norelius)
2.	GBR 5:02.8		(Margaret Joyce Cooper, Sarah Stewart, Irène Vera Tanner, Ellen E. King)
3.	SAF 5:13.4		(Kathleen Russell, Rhoda Rennie, Marie Bedford, Frederica J. van der Goes)
Springboard Diving			
1.	Helen Meany	USA	78.62
2.	Dorothy Poynton	USA	75.62
3.	Georgia Coleman	USA	73.38
Platform Diving			
1.	Elizabeth Pinkston-Becker	USA	31.60
2.	Georgia Coleman	USA	30.60
3.	Lala Sjoqvist	SWE	29.20

Boxing

Flyweight		
1.	Antal Kocsis	HUN
2.	Armand Appel	FRA
3.	Carlo Cavagnoli	ITA
Bantamweight		
1.	Vittorio Tamagnini	ITA
2.	John Daley	USA
3.	Harry Isaacs	SAF
Featherweight		
1.	Lambertus van Klaveren	NETH
2.	Victor Peralta	ARG
3.	Harold Devine	USA
Lightweight		
1.	Carlo Orlandi	ITA
2.	Stephen Michael Halaiko	USA
3.	Gunnar Berggren	SWE
Welterweight		
1.	Edward Morgan	NZL
2.	Raúl Landini	ARG
3.	Raymond Smillie	CAN
Middleweight		
1.	Piero Toscani	ITA
2.	Jan Hermánek	TCH
3.	Leonard Steyaert	BEL
Light Heavyweight		
1.	Victor Avendano	ARG
2.	Ernst Pistulla	GER
3.	Karl Leendert Miljon	NETH
Heavyweight		
1.	Arturo Rodriguez Jurado	ARG
2.	Nils Ramm	SWE
3.	M. Jacob Michaelsen	DEN

Greco Roman Wrestling

Bantamweight		
1.	Kurt Leucht	GER
2.	Jindrich Maudr	TCH
3.	Giovanni Gozzi	ITA
Featherweight		
1.	Voldemar Väli	EST
2.	Erik Malmberg	SWE
3.	Giacomo Quaglia	ITA
Lightweight		
1.	Lajos Keresztes	HUN
2.	Eduard Sperling	GER
3.	Edvard Westerlund	FIN
Middleweight		
1.	Väinö Kokkinen	FIN
2.	László Papp	HUN
3.	Albert Kusnets	EST
Light Heavyweight		
1.	Ibrahim Moustafa	EGY
2.	Adolf Rieger	GER
3.	Onni Pellinen	FIN
Heavyweight		
1.	Rudolf Svensson	SWE
2.	Hjalmar Eemil Nyström	FIN
3.	Georg Gehring	GER

Freestyle Wrestling

Bantamweight		
1.	Kaarlo Mäkinen	FIN
2.	Edmond Spapen	BEL
3.	James Trifunov	CAN
Featherweight		
1.	Allie Morrison	USA
2.	Kustaa Pihlajamäki	FIN
3.	Hans Minder	SUI
Lightweight		
1.	Osvald Käpp	EST
2.	Charles Pacome	FRA
3.	Eino Leino	FIN
Welterweight		
1.	Arvo Haavisto	FIN
2.	Lloyd Appleton	USA
3.	Maurice Letchford	CAN
Middleweight		
1.	Ernst Kyburz	SUI
2.	Donald Parker Stockton	CAN
3.	Samuel Rabin	GBR
Light Heavyweight		
1.	Thure Sjostedt	SWE
2.	Arnold Bogli	SUI
3.	Henri Lefevre	FRA
Heavyweight		
1.	Johan Richthoff	SWE
2.	Aukusti Sihvola	FIN
3.	Edmond Dame	FRA

Men Fencing

Foil Individual		
1.	Lucien Gaudin	FRA
2.	Erwin Casmir	GER
3.	Giulio Gaudini	ITA
Foil Team		
1.	Italy	
2.	France	
3.	Argentina	
Epée Individual		
1.	Lucien Gaudin	FRA
2.	Georges Buchard	FRA
3.	George Calman	USA
	Léon Tom	BEL
Epée Team		
1.	Italy	
2.	France	
3.	Portugal	
Sabre Individual		
1.	Odon Tersztyánszky	HUN
2.	Attila Petschauer	HUN
3.	Bino Bini	ITA
Sabre Team		
1.	Hungary	
2.	Italy	
3.	Poland	

Women Fencing

Foil Individual		
1.	Hélène Mayer	GER
2.	Muriel B. Freeman	GBR
3.	Olga Oelkers	GER

Modern Pentathlon

1.	Sven Thofelt	SWE
2.	Bo Lindman	SWE
3.	Helmuth Kahl	GER

Rowing

Event	Name	Nation	Result
Single Sculls			
1.	Henry Pearce	AUS	7:11.0
2.	Kenneth Myers	USA	7:20.8
3.	Theodore Collet	GBR	7:29.8
Double Sculls			
1.	USA		6:41.4
2.	Canada		6:51.0
3.	Austria		
Coxless Pairs			
1.	Germany		7:06.4
2.	Great Britain		7:08.6
3.	USA		7:20.4
Coxed Pairs			
1.	Switzerland		7:42.6
2.	France		7:48.4
3.	Belgium		7:59.4
Coxless Fours			
1.	Great Britain		6:36.0
2.	USA		6:37.0
3.	Italy		
Coxed Fours			
1.	Italy		6:47.8
2.	Switzerland		7:03.4
3.	Poland		
Eights			
1.	USA		6:03.2
2.	Great Britain		6:05.6
3.	Canada		6:03.8

Yachting

Finn		
1.	Sven Thorell	SWE
2.	Henrik Robert	NOR
3.	Bertil Broman	FIN
6m Class		
1.	Norway	
2.	Denmark	
3.	Estonia	
8m Class		
1.	France	
2.	Netherlands	
3.	Sweden	

Cycling

Event	Name	Nation	Result
Road Race Individual (168km)			
1.	Henry Hansen	DEN	4:47:18
2.	Frank W. Southall	GBR	4:55:06
3.	Gosta Carlsson	SWE	5:00:17
Team Time Trial			
1.	Denmark		
2.	Great Britain		
3.	Sweden		
1,000m Time Trial			
1.	Willy Falck Hansen	DEN	1:14.4
2.	Gerard Bosch van Drakestein	NETH	1:15.2
3.	Edgar Gray	AUS	1:15.6
Sprint (1000m)			
1.	Roger Beaufrand	FRA	13.2
2.	Antoine Mazairac	NETH	
3.	Willy Falck-Hansen	DEN	
Tandem (2000m)			
1.	Holland		11.8
2.	Great Britain		
3.	Germany		
Pursuit Race Team (4000m)			
1.	Italy		5:01.8
2.	Netherlands		5:06.2
3.	Great Britain		

Equestrian Sports

Event	Name	Nation	Result
3 Day Event Individual			
1.	Charles F. Pahud de Mortanges	NETH	1969.82
2.	Gérard Pieter de Kruyff	NETH	1967.26
3.	Bruno Neumann	GER	1944.42
3 Day Event Team			
1.	Netherlands		5865.68
2.	Norway		5395.68
3.	Poland		5067.92
Dressage Individual			
1.	Carl Friedrich Frhr. V. Langen	GER	237.42
2.	Charles Marion	FRA	231.00
3.	Ragnar Ohlson	SWE	229.78
Dressage Team			
1.	Germany		669.72
2.	Sweden		650.86
3.	Netherlands		642.96
Grand Prix Jumping Individual			
1.	Frantisek Ventura	TCH	0/0/0
2.	Pierre Bertran de Balanda	FRA	0/0/2
3.	Charley Kuhn	SUI	0/0/4
Grand Prix Jumping Team			
1.	Spain		0/2/1:33.0
2.	Poland		0/2/1:36.0
3.	Sweden		0/2/1:39.0

Men Gymnastics

Event	Name	Nation	Result
All-around Individual			
1.	Georges Miez	SUI	247.500
2.	Hermann Hänggi	SUI	246.625
3.	Léon Stukelj	YUG	244.875
Combined Exercises Team			
1.	Switzerland		1718.625
2.	Czechoslovakia		1712.250
3.	Yugoslavia		1648.750
Parallel Bars			
1.	Ladislav Vacha	TCH	18.83
2.	Josip Primozic	YUG	18.50
3.	Hermann Hänggi	SUI	18.08
Long Horse Vault			
1.	Eugen Mack	SUI	9.58
2.	Emanuel Löffler	TCH	9.50
3.	Stane Derganc	YUG	9.46
Sidehorse			
1.	Hermann Hänggi	SUI	19.75
2.	Georges Miez	SUI	19.25
3.	Heikki Savolainen	FIN	18.83
Horizontal Bar			
1.	Georges Miez	SUI	19.17
2.	Romeo Neri	ITA	19.00
3.	Eugen Mack	SUI	18.92
Rings			
1.	Léon Stukelj	YUG	19.25
2.	Ladislav Vácha	TCH	19.17
3.	Emanuel Löffler	TCH	18.83

Women Gymnastics

Event	Name	Result
Combined Exercises Team		
1.	Netherlands	316.75
2.	Italy	289.00
3.	Great Britain	258.25

Football

1. Uruguay
2. Argentina
3. Italy

Field Hockey

1. India
2. Netherlands
3. Germany

(Key to symbols and abbreviations p. 1456)

CHART

Weightlifting

Event	Name	Nation	2 Arm Press	Snatch 2 Arm	Clean and Jerk 2 Arm	Total
Featherweight						
1.	Franz Andrysek	AUT	77.5	*90.0	*120.0	*287.5
2.	Pierino Gabetti	ITA	80.0	*90.0	112.5	282.5
3.	Hans Wölpert	GER	** 92.5	82.5	107.5	282.5
Lightweight						
1.	Kurt Helbig	AUT	85.0	97.5	*135.0	322.5
2.	Hans Haas	GER	*90.0	*102.5	*135.0	322.5
3.	Fernand Arnout	FRA	85.0	97.5	120.0	302.5
Middleweight						
1.	Roger François	FRA	102.5	102.5	130.0	** 335.0
2.	Carlo Galimberti	ITA	** 105.0	97.5	130.0	332.5
3.	August Scheffer	NETH	97.5	*105.0	125.0	327.5
Light Heavyweight						
1.	Sayed Nosseir	EGY	=* 100.0	*112.5	** 142.5	** 355.0
2.	Louis Hostin	FRA	=* 100.0	110.0	** 142.5	352.5
3.	Johannes Verheijen	NETH	95.0	105.0	137.5	337.5
Super Heavyweight						
1.	Josef Strassberger	GER	*122.5	107.5	142.5	** 372.5
2.	Arnold Luhaar	EST	100.0	*110.0	*150.0	360.0
3.	Jaroslav Skobla	TCH	100.0	107.5	*150.0	357.5

1928

SEPTEMBER

Su	Mo	Tu	We	Th	Fr	Sa
						1
2	3	4	5	6	7	8
9	10	11	12	13	14	15
16	17	18	19	20	21	22
23	24	25	26	27	28	29
30						

1. Tirana: Ahmed Zog is crowned King Zog I of Albania.

5. London: Figures show that an average of three people a day died on London's roads from April to June this year.

6. Moscow: The USSR signs the Kellogg-Briand Pact (→26).

9. Milan: 22 die when a car taking part in the Grand Prix d'Europe overturns at 125 mph and ploughs into spectators.

11. UK: Professor Hill of Glasgow University claims scientists will soon be able to produce cells artificially.

15. Caribbean: A hurricane sweeping through the West Indies kills a reported 300 on the island of Guadeloupe (→18).

16. Glasgow: Launch of the P & O liner Viceroy of India, first liner to have oil-fired electric turbines.

18. US: Between 200 and 400 are reported killed when the hurricane strikes Florida.

19. New York: The "Vitaphone" talkie "The Singing Fool" opens, starring Al Jolson.

20. Rome: The Grand Fascist Council becomes Italy's supreme legislative body, replacing the Chamber of Deputies.

23. Madrid: 200 are feared dead when the Novadades Theatre is destroyed by fire.

24. India: Nationalists throw out a government-backed bill to expel all Communists.

24. UK: Labour MP Sir Oswald Mosley says his title "doesn't mean anything" and is not worth giving up.

25. Mexico: Emilio Gil is elected president to succeed the assassinated Obregon.

26. Geneva: 23 nations sign an act of the League assembly embodying the Kellogg-Briand anti-war pact (→16/8/29).

28. Germany: The state of Prussia lifts the ban on Adolf Hitler speaking in public.

28. Washington: The US recognises the Chinese government of Chiang Kai-shek.

Germ-killing mould is found by accident

Professor Alexander Fleming at his desk in St Mary's Hospital.

Sept 30. A mould which attacks many different kinds of harmful bacteria has been discovered by Professor Alexander Fleming of St Mary's Hospital in London. He hopes it will be possible to isolate a substance from the mould which can be used in the fight against human disease.

Chance played a big part in Fleming's discovery. He left a plate of Staphylococcus bacteria, which are responsible for many human infections, out in his laboratory for a few days. When he inspected it he noticed that it had become contaminated with mould, and that around the mould patches were rings that were clear of bacteria. It looked as though the mould was producing a chemical that killed the bacteria, or at any rate stopped them growing.

Fleming has identified the mould as Penicillium Notatum, which often grows on stale bread. It kills many kinds of bacteria besides Staphylococci, and does not harm human white blood cells, a preliminary indication that it may be safe to use in humans.

However, isolating the active chemical from the mould is likely to be difficult, so penicillium extracts are unlikely to be available for medical use for some time, even if they prove to be safe.

Clutchless car on 25,000-mile trial

Sept 7. An invention that automatically changes a car's gears will be exhibited at the Motor Show next month. It has just passed a road test of 25,000 miles. The device eliminates the clutch pedal.

It is the brainchild of Mr J.H. Robertson, an engineer who developed the mechanism as a hobby, spending some £20,000 of his own money on it. For the test it was fitted to an 8 hp. car and driven in differing traffic around the country. Several manufacturers are showing an interest because they believe that simplified driving could enlarge the British market, which lags behind that of America.

Sept 19. Walt Disney with his new cartoon star Mickey Mouse, who made his first appearance in a sound film today with the release of "Steamboat Willie".

1928

OCTOBER

Su	Mo	Tu	We	Th	Fr	Sa
	1	2	3	4	5	6
7	8	9	10	11	12	13
14	15	16	17	18	19	20
21	22	23	24	25	26	27
28	29	30	31			

1. UK: "Elastoplast" sticking plaster dressings are first manufactured in Hull.

3. Spain: 43 sailors die when the French submarine Ondine collides with a Greek steamer off the Spanish coast.

6. Peking: A new Chinese constitution is promulgated; Chiang Kai-shek becomes President of the republic.

9. UK: Motor-traders say Britons on £400 a year or more can afford a car.

9. London: After a series of tests the BBC rejects the idea of a trial television service.

10. Newcastle: The King opens the £100,000 Tyne Bridge, containing Britain's largest steel arch.

12. London: The City of London Corporation throws out a scheme for a new bridge over the Thames at St. Paul's.

12. US: An "iron lung" is used for the first time, on a young polio victim at Boston's Children's Hospital.

13. UK: Ten days of official mourning are declared on the death of the Dowager Empress Marie of Russia, Queen Alexandra's sister.

15. US: The world's largest airship, Graf Zeppelin, lands in New Jersey after a 111-hour flight from Germany (→1/11).

20. China: Chiang Kai-shek invites Henry Ford and four other Americans to become honorary economic advisors (→22).

20. Washington: Inventor Thomas Edison receives a special Congressional medal for his life's work.

22. China: Chiang Kai-shek expels Soviet military and governmental advisors.

25. London: First showing of the first all-talking film, Edgar Wallace's "The Terror".

26. Rumania: At least 30 are reported killed when the Paris-Bucharest train crashes.

27. India: Inauguration of the world's biggest dam, containing 14 square miles of water, near Poona.

Stalin issues a five-year economic plan

Rykov, Stalin, and Red Army commander Voroshilov (left to right).

Oct 1. Joseph Stalin's first Five-Year plan went into operation today. It is a grandiose scheme for catapulting the Soviet Union into the forefront of European nations. Designed to industrialise and utterly transform the country, it sets targets for every basic industry and for every factory and workshop. Stalin is endeavouring to lay the foundations of a modern industrial society very quickly.

The plan goes hand in hand with a revolution in the countryside, prompted by the chronic danger of famine. Stalin is planning to merge small-holdings into "collective" farms, which would belong to villages as a whole and be cultivated by modern methods.

The intention is that this will free more men and women for work in the towns where the Five-Year plan needs them. But whether Russia's peasants will put their backs into making the new "collectivisation" system work remains to be seen (→ 5/1/30).

Liquor deaths fuel drive on speakeasies

Oct 10. New York "Speakeasy" owners face murder charges if their illegal "hooch" is found to be poisonous, declared Mayor Jimmy Walker today. This move follows a series of raids on illicit drinking houses across the city in which 21 barmen were arrested.

Bootlegged whisky, contaminated with wood alcohol, has claimed 518 lives already this year. Last year the death toll was 719, and 33 people have died in the city in the last week. Samples of liquor seized by police have been sent to the City's public analyst and charges may follow.

It is nine years since the introduction of Prohibition, the "noble experiment", and politicians are becoming concerned at the growing lawlessness and gangsterism that it generates (→ 28/1/30).

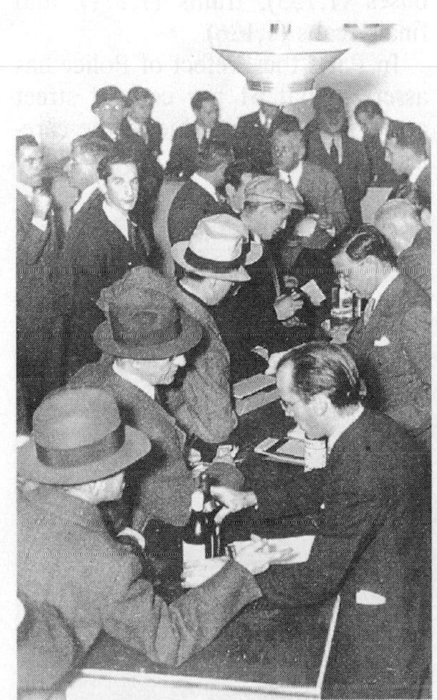

Queueing up for illegal booze.

1928

NOVEMBER

Su	Mo	Tu	We	Th	Fr	Sa
				1	2	3
4	5	6	7	8	9	10
11	12	13	14	15	16	17
18	19	20	21	22	23	24
25	26	27	28	29	30	

1. Germany: The airship Graf Zeppelin arrives back after its return flight from the US.

4. France: The Radical Party decides to split from the government of Raymond Poincare.→

5. Sicily: Mount Etna erupts (→ 11).

7. US: Franklin Delano Roosevelt is elected governor of New York State.

11. Sicily: Lava from Etna threatens Catania, having destroyed a large area including villages and railways.

12. Atlantic: The liner Vestris sinks off Virginia, with the reported loss of one-third of its 339 passengers.

15. London: The Director General of Roads says Hyde Park Corner is the world's busiest traffic junction.→

16. New York: A record 6.6 million shares are bought and sold in hectic trading on the New York Stock Exchange (→ 24).

19. Berlin: Foreign Minister Gustav Stresemann says Germany will not barter the Rhineland for lower reparations.

22. London: The King is confined to bed with a congested lung; Queen Mary assumes his duties.→

22. UK: The first pound and ten-shilling notes come into circulation.

23. New York: The Stock Exchange shuts for one day to clear backlogs from record trading of 6.9 million shares.

25. USSR: Trotsky's secretary dies on hunger strike in protest at the alleged torture of Trotskyists.

27. Nicaragua: President-elect Hoover arrives for talks with President Moncada on the Sandinist rebel threat.

27. London: The BBC unveils plans for a new £500,000 building in Portland Place.

30. Mexico City: Emilio Portes Gil is sworn in as president.

Hirohito crowned Emperor of Japan

Nov 10. The Regent Hirohito was today crowned emperor of Japan, a throne occupied since before written records began by his "heavenly and imperial ancestors". The new emperor confidently declared that the spiritual union between sovereign and people was the essence of the Japanese personality. At an elaborate ceremony, Hirohito pledged himself to work for the moral and material improvement of his "beloved subjects". Crown Prince at the age of 20, he was then named Regent seven years ago when he took over from his sick father and effectively became head of state.

Japan's new 27-year-old Emperor.

Radicals shut out of French cabinet

Nov 11. Raymond Poincare has formed a new French government. Although nine of its members, including the prime minister, were in his previous cabinet, the four Radical Socialists are out, so the new cabinet marks a sharp break with the left.

M. Poincare made big concessions to keep the four in, but not big enough. "Very well, then" he said, "I will do without them."

For the first time for 30 years the Interior Ministry has not gone to a Radical Socialist. ▷

Hoover sweeps to victory in US poll

Nov 6. Herbert C. Hoover was today easily elected President of the United States. He defeated the Democratic candidate, Governor Alfred E. Smith of New York, by 444 votes to 87 in the electoral college.

Although "Al" Smith, the first Roman Catholic candidate, carried only eight states – six of them in the solidly Democratic South – he received 15 million votes, against the 21.4 million cast for Hoover, the most votes ever polled by a Democrat. The Happy Warrior, as he was called, did far better in big cities than any other Democrat could have done.

Although Smith campaigned jovially in a brown bowler hat and his campaign song was titled "From the Sidewalks of New York", Smith was the best-financed Democrat ever. Millions were raised for him by John J. Raskob of General Motors.

The new President, once a Californian engineer, was the Secretary of Commerce under Coolidge. He first came into national prominence by organizing relief to Belgium and as head of the Food Administration in the War.

A conservative Republican, Hoover spoke much of individualism and of the coming abolition of poverty. The campaign has been unusually dirty. A Republican whisper predicted that Smith's victory would bring the Pope to America.

Mr Hoover's Vice-President will be Senator Charles Curtis of Kansas, who won the nomination by a single vote after attacking Hoover personally.

Herbert Hoover (third from left) on the eve of the Presidential election.

Traffic boom causes deaths to soar on Britain's roads

Nov 29. Deaths in street accidents in London during the three months of July, August and September came to 309. This brings this year's total to 872, two more every week than last year.

A White Paper issued earlier in the year showed that in Great Britain as a whole there were 133,943 road accidents in 1927 and 5,329 deaths. Both figures were increases, as they have been every year since 1921. The fatalities average out at over 14 people killed every day and 148,575 a year injured.

Analysis of accidents according to the type of vehicle shows that by far the commonest offender is the private car. The latest London figures show 10,878 private cars involved in accidents resulting in injury. Trade and commercial vehicles came next with 6,048. Then came motor cycles (4,706), buses (1,753), trams (1,271), and finally cabs (1,126).

In Paris the Prefect of Police has asserted that 61 per cent of street accidents there are due to the carelessness of the victims (→ 12/12).

Another addition to the accident statistics: a three car pile-up on Finchley Road in North London.

Stalin is purging Trotsky supporters

Nov 25. Hundreds of supporters of Leon Trotsky have been arrested and exiled in the Soviet Union as Joseph Stalin tightens his grip on the country. The moves came after the Trotskyists held rallies in Moscow and other cities to mark the anniversary of the 1917 revolution.

In Kiev there were more than 100 arrests and in Leningrad some 80. The arrests are being carried out by the OGPU secret police. Trotsky's secretary is said to have died in prison after going on a hunger strike in protest over the treatment of Stalin's opponents. Trotsky is by no means the only target of Stalin's wrath. Nikolai Bukharin, head of the Communist International, is another Communist leader under increasing pressure (→ 16/1/29).

Bukharin, persecuted by Stalin.

Doctors in midnight rush to the Palace

Nov 23. The Royal doctors last night rushed to Buckingham Palace as the King's condition worsened. He has been suffering from a fever and congestion of the lungs. This morning a large unmarked truck drove through the Palace gates, bringing one of the new X-ray machines. A bulletin says there is no cause for concern; however, the Prince of Wales has cut short his visit to Africa (→ 2/12).

1928

DECEMBER

Su	Mo	Tu	We	Th	Fr	Sa
						1
2	3	4	5	6	7	8
9	10	11	12	13	14	15
16	17	18	19	20	21	22
23	24	25	26	27	28	29
30	31					

2. London: The King grows worse; he was reportedly on oxygen during the night (→4).

4. London: A Council of State is appointed to act in the King's place as his condition deteriorates further (→12).

5. Australia: England wins the first test against Australia by a record 675 runs.→

6. S. Africa: General Smuts says his party will fight the coming elections on a platform of votes for women.

10. Stockholm: Nobel Prizes go to Sir Owen Richardson (UK, Physics); Adolf Windaus (Germany, Chemistry); Charles Nicolle (France, Medicine) and Sigrid Undstet (Norway, Literature). No Peace Prize awarded.

10. London: Piccadilly Circus Tube station opens.

12. London: The King is said to be greatly improved after an operation on his lung.

12. London: The Lords approve a bill to make driving tests compulsory.

13. New York: George Gershwin's "An American in Paris" is first performed.

15. South America: The League makes a plea for peace as fighting breaks out on the Bolivia-Uruguay border.

20. China: Britain signs a tariff agreement with the government, formally recognising Chiang Kai-shek.

24. Rome: A law is passed for the draining of the Pontin Marshes in north Italy.

28. US: Figures reveal nine blacks were lynched in 1928, the fewest in 40 years.

HITS OF 1928

A room with a view.

I can't give you anything but love, baby.

Ol' Man River.

QUOTE OF THE YEAR

"How does a man live? By completely forgetting he is a human being."

Bertolt Brecht, The Threepenny Opera, 1928.

Hammond stars as England triumph

Record scorer Walter Hammond.

Dec 20. England's triumphant tour of Australia continued with victory by eight wickets in Sydney to follow their crushing win by 675 runs at Brisbane. An utterly commanding innings of 251 – the second highest in Test match history – by Walter Hammond, in only his second match against Australia, set up an England total of 636 – a record for any Test innings.

Afghans revolt as the veil is lifted

Dec 17. King Amanullah's army has mutinied and he has taken refuge with Queen Suriya in a fort held by loyal troops just outside Kabul. The rebels have attacked Kabul and there is serious fighting afoot in the Afghan capital. Fighting is also reported in Jellalabad.

It is clear that this is no normal tribal uprising but a full-scale revolution occasioned by the drastic reforms introduced by the King and the Queen, including abolishing the veil worn by Afghan women.

The King's Turkish and Russian advisors are felt to be in some danger as they are blamed for the introduction of the reforms designed to modernise Afghanistan (→7/1/29).

Arts: strange literary blooms offend

It has been a year for the weirder and wilder fruits in the garden of literature and they have caused, predictably, a good deal of offence to conservative tastes. "The Well of Loneliness", a novel by **Radclyffe Hall**, which treats of intimate relationships between women, was withdrawn on the advice of the Home Secretary, to whom the publishers submitted it for an opinion. But this was not before it had been condemned by the editor of the Sunday Express, who declared he "would sooner give a healthy boy or girl a dose of prussic acid than acopy of it".

Following this, the Home Secretary was asked by the Daily Herald why he did not take action against **Compton Mackenzie's** novel "Extraordinary Women", which treated the same subject with, it alleged, "cynical flippancy". No action was forthcoming and the novel speedily sold out.

Then came "Decline and Fall", a work of extraordinary self-assurance by **Evelyn Waugh**, who is a mere 25 years old. Mr Waugh spent some years after leaving Oxford as a schoolmaster, as his barbed and witty novel bears witness. His amoral characters and sharp-tongued brilliance have won the praise of no less a critic than **Arnold Bennett**.

Another cynical voice in fiction is that of **Aldous Huxley**, who this year has published "Point Counter Point". His "Antic Hay" was condemned by the Sunday Express as "ordure and blasphemy".

The late actress Dame Ellen Terry.

The death of **Ellen Terry** at 81 ended a career that began at the age of eight. She continued to give recitals of Shakespeare throughout the war and seemed ever young.

"Bolero", composed by **Maurice Ravel** for the dancer **Ida Rubinstein**, has been given at the Paris Opera. It consists of one theme repeated to an unvarying rhythm for 15 minutes, growing ever louder. It was, surprisingly, a triumph. In London "Show Boat", by the late **Jerome Kern**, was also a triumph for **Paul Robeson**, especially "Ol' Man River".

Playwright George Bernard Shaw takes a dip in the sea at Antibes.

1929

JANUARY

Su	Mo	Tu	We	Th	Fr	Sa
		1	2	3	4	5
6	7	8	9	10	11	12
13	14	15	16	17	18	19
20	21	22	23	24	25	26
27	28	29	30	31		

1. UK: Figures released show 1.6 million telephones in Britain, 3.6 for every 100 people.

3. London: Conductor Sir Thomas Beecham and the BBC agree to form a permanent symphony orchestra.

5. Melbourne: England win the third test against Australia by 332 runs, including a record second innings of 332 (→ 8/2).

7. Afghanistan: King Amanullah restores the veil for women and abandons European dress (→ 14).

10. Belgium: Tintin a new cartoon character by Herge appears for the first time in the paper "Vingtieme Siecle".

10. Turkey: Latest reforms include adoption of the metric system and of the Western weekly "day off".

11. USSR: The working day is reduced to seven hours (→ 24/9).

14. New York: Premiere of George Gershwin's musical "Strike Up The Band".

14. Afghanistan: King Amanullah abdicates in favour of his brother Inayatullah (→ 17).

16. Moscow: Nikolai Bukharin resigns as head of the Communist International after disagreements with Stalin (→ 30).

17. Afghanistan: King Inayatullah abdicates in favour of rebel chief Bacha-i-Sachao, who leads a coup.

23. USSR: The secret police OGPU arrests a reported 400 Trotskyists for an alleged plot to start a civil war.

29. Germany: US motor manufacturers General Motors buys the German firm Opel.

30. USSR: Leon Trotsky is ordered out of the country (→ 13/2).

BIRTH

15. US civil rights leader and Nobel Peace prize-winner Dr Martin Luther King (†4/4/68).

DEATH

13. US marshal Wyatt Earp (*19/3/1848).→

Yugoslav King declares himself a dictator

Jan 6. King Alexander has today established a royal and military dictatorship in Yugoslavia. He has appointed General Peter Jivkovich, commander of the Royal Bodyguard, as Prime Minister, and has suspended the constitution. He has also dissolved Parliament and ordered that while it is suspended, laws will be enacted solely by Royal Decree. Alexander has no designs to be dictator for life, but felt he had no other choice but to seize power.

This is the latest move in the King's attempts to unify his country, torn by the rival nationalistic ambitions of the Serbs, Croats and Slovenes. It follows demands made by the Croats for a federal form of government giving autonomy to Croatia.

These demands were rejected by the other parties and the King, in the words of a Royal Proclamation issued this morning, "arrived at the conclusion that the way we have hitherto followed can no longer be pursued".

The new dictator: King Alexander.

In his proclamation the King, who led the Serbian forces in the war, argued: "Parliamentary life has always been my ideal, but blind political passions have so abused it that it has become an obstacle to all profitable work in the State ... I am determined to fulfil my duty without flinching until the end."

US army plane flies 150 hours non-stop

Jan 7. All records for distance flying were shattered today by a US army aircraft, the Question Mark, which landed at Los Angeles airport after a flight of 150 hours and 40 minutes. The aircraft had flown more than 11,000 miles around a closed course after taking off on New Year's Day at 7.46am.

During the flight it took on fuel from a sister aircraft several times. The Fokker trimotor would have stayed airborne longer but it was forced to land when an engine fault developed which could not be repaired in flight.

Army Air Force officials say the demonstration that an aircraft can be successively refuelled in flight will be of enormous significance for the future of commercial and military aviation.

Jan 30. The Prince of Wales tours mining districts in northern England expressing sympathy for their low wages and poor living conditions.

Wyatt Earp dies with his boots off

Jan 13. With his Colt .45 Buntline Special hanging from the brass bedpost, Wyatt Earp, the legendary former Marshal of Dodge City, died with his boots off last night. His end came peacefully while he was asleep, at the age of 80.

Earp rode into the lawless Kansas cattle township and assumed the role of law-enforcer at the behest of the town meeting. As a sideline, Earp ran a successful brothel and cabaret.

When he became marshal, Earp, a former gunfighter, said: "I was hired to do the killing".

Wyatt Earp, "hired to kill."

General puts down Sally Army mutiny

Jan 18. From his Surrey sickbed, General Bramwell Booth managed today to put down an insurrection in the ranks of his Salvation Army. Lawyers acting for the 72-year-old son of the Army's founder secured a High Court injunction overturning an Army Council vote to declare him unfit to command.

General Booth, who is suffering from a nervous disease, challenged his dismissal on the basis of a deed executed by his late father in 1904. The council had voted him out by 55 to 8.

After the vote, councillors, including American and European leaders, sang:

"When we cannot see our way,
Let us trust and still obey."

1929

FEBRUARY

Su	Mo	Tu	We	Th	Fr	Sa
					1	2
3	4	5	6	7	8	9
10	11	12	13	14	15	16
17	18	19	20	21	22	23
24	25	26	27	28		

1. USSR: Zinoviev and Kamenev are put under house arrest as 1,600 Trotskyists are exiled to Siberia.

4. London: The first area of "green belt" is approved, a five-mile long stretch near Hendon.

5. Belfast: Eamon de Valera is arrested for entering Northern Ireland (→ 8).

6. Bombay: At least 30 people are reported to have died in Hindu-Moslem riots over the last few days.→

8. Belfast: Eamon de Valera is sentenced to one month in prison for illegal entry into Northern Ireland (→ 6/3).

8. Adelaide: England win the fourth test against Australia by 12 runs (→ 16/3).

10. Mexico: Gil escapes an assassination attempt when his train is bombed.

13. Washington: In one of his last acts as president, Coolidge signs a bill to build 15 cruisers and an aircraft carrier.

13. London: The Salvation Army High Council elects Commander Higgins to take over from General Booth.

14. Munich: Singer Josephine Baker is banned from the stage for "indecent behaviour".

15. Germany: 3.2 million people are now out of work.

17. US: The first in-flight movie is shown on a Universal Air Line flight from St. Paul to Chicago.

21. Washington: Charles Lindbergh is appointed Federal Aviation Adviser to the US Department of Commerce.

21. Paris: Trotsky is refused political asylum (→ 11/4).

25. S. Africa: A bill giving the votes to "coloureds", but not to blacks, is defeated.

27. US: Charles Lindbergh and his fiancee escape almost unhurt when their plane overturns on landing.

DEATH

12. British courtesan and actress Lillie Langtry (*13/10/1853) →

Gangsters massacred on Valentine's day

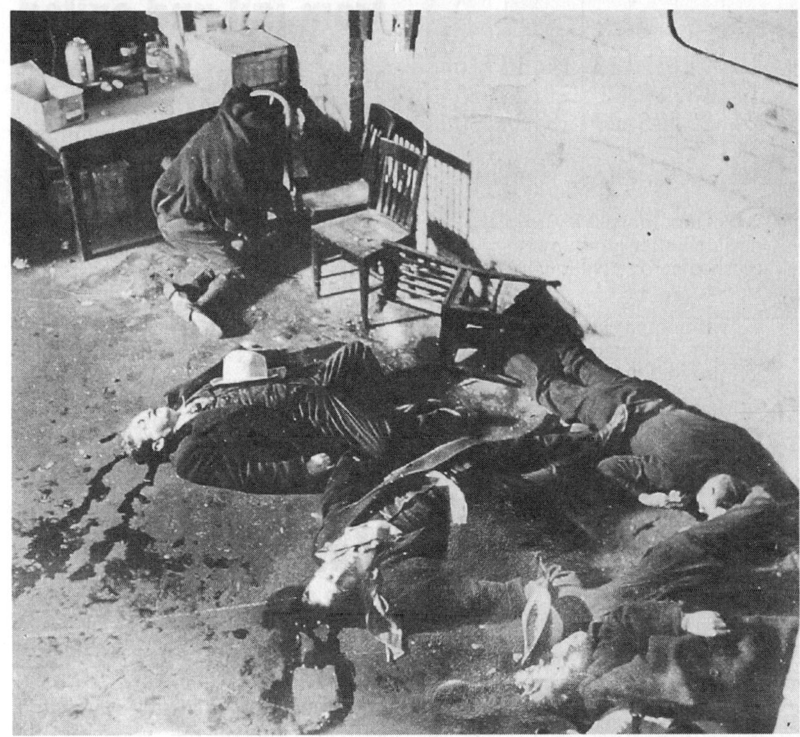

The victims of the most brutal gangland killing ever seen in Chicago.

Feb 14. Seven men were lined up today, their backs to a beerhouse wall in a Chicago side street, and mown down by sub-machine guns.

The killers were gangsters, members of the Al Capone-led mob, which is defending its monopoly of bootlegged liquor, extortion and prostitution in the city. Some of them were wearing police uniforms to create the impression that this was a normal raid. The dead men were said by police to be remnants of a mob led by George "Bugsy" Malone.

Police Commissioner William F. Russell was livid at the impersonation of the police officers and described the shooting as "a war to finish. I've never known a challenge like this". Greater, perhaps, than the current investigation of more than half the Chicago force for alleged corruption.

Mussolini makes pact with Pope

Feb 11. The Vatican State came into being at noon today when the Italian leader, Benito Mussolini, and Cardinal Gaspari, the Pope's Secretary of State, signed a treaty in the Lateran Palace designed to end six decades of ill-feeling between Church and State in Italy.

The signing of the treaty, with a golden pen given by Pope Pius XI and afterwards presented to Il Duce, guaranteed the sovereignty of the Vatican.

One of its 27 articles set out the services which the Italian government will supply to the Vatican, while another specifies the immunities to be enjoyed by inhabitants of the Vatican City. Special emphasis is placed on the sanctity of marriage and the State also agrees that Roman Catholicism is the state religion and Catholic education is obligatory in schools.

Under a special financial convention, the Holy See, in a definitive settlement of all its financial relations with Italy, accepts 750 million lire in cash and 1,000 million in Italian State bonds bearing interest at five per cent.

The Pope later reassured parish priests: "Some say my territory is too little, but, instead, I wished for little, even the least possible, for good reasons ... criticisms leave us calm, because the responsibility is entirely ours." (→ 25/7)

Exiled Trotsky arrives in Constantinople under heavy guard

Feb 13. The Soviet Union's power struggle with Leon Trotsky is at an end now that he has reached Turkey, after being expelled from his homeland for alleged "anti-Soviet activities". Trotsky's expulsion was proposed to the Politburo by Joseph Stalin and passed on a split vote. Trotsky was the Soviet leader's most dangerous opponent, even in exile near Alma-Ata, but Stalin has shrunk from imprisoning him.

Having removed Trotsky from the Russian scene, Stalin is already turning his attention to "right-wing" leaders. Nikolai Bukharin has lost his post as head of the Communist International, while Alexei Rykov has been removed from the post of premier (→ 11/4).

Trotsky in exile, fearful of assassination and guarded by two soldiers.

Actress and beauty Lillie Langtry dies

Feb 12. When Lillie Langtry died today at her Riviera home aged 74, few remembered the sensation her beauty created when, at 18, she arrived in London from Jersey and was dubbed "the Jersey Lily".

It was an age of beauties and also of photography. Soon her hourglass figure was on the postcards, in the newspapers and shop windows. But only those who saw her in the flesh could appreciate her flawless complexion and deep violet eyes.

The interest that the Prince of Wales took in her was well-known, but she attracted far more eager crowds than royalty did. Her slightest doings were recorded. After an untalented career as an actress, she married Sir Hugo de Bathe.

The late Lillie Langtry.

One hundred die in Indian religious riot

Feb 8. About a hundred people have died in the most horrible fashion in the course of the continuing riots between Hindus and Moslems in Bombay. A truce was arranged between the warring parties this afternoon and Hindus and Moslems were seen talking together as the shops opened. But trouble began again when the slashed body of a Hindu was found. British troops had to open fire.

1929

MARCH

Su	Mo	Tu	We	Th	Fr	Sa
					1	2
3	4	5	6	7	8	9
10	11	12	13	14	15	16
17	18	19	20	21	22	23
24	25	26	27	28	29	30
31						

2. Peking: Martial law is declared after a mutiny is crushed among Nationalist troops.

4. Washington: Herbert Hoover is inaugurated as US president.

6. Madeira: 100 people are reported killed in an earthquake.

8. Mexico: Catholic rebel troops take the town of Juarez after a three-hour battle in which 24 are killed.

10. Cairo: Women are granted limited rights of divorce by the government.

13. Rome: Aviator Umberto Nobile resigns from the army after being officially blamed for the "Italia" airship crash.

14. London: The Food Council says milk should cost 7d a quart in winter and 6d a quart in summer.

15. Istanbul: In an interview with the "Daily Telegraph", Trotsky says he will give up politics.

16. Melbourne: Australia wins the last test of the current series, won 4-1 by England to keep the Ashes.

17. London: The King walks outdoors for the first time since his illness began last November.

21. Pittsburgh: 21 miners are killed in a pit explosion.

22. UK: Mrs M Gemmell's Gregalach, a 100-1 outsider, wins the Grand National at Aintree.

23. London: Cambridge win the centenary Boat Race; of the 80 races each university has now won the race 40 times.

26. Paris: Marshal Foch is laid to rest near Napoleon in the Invalides.

30. London: A 5,000-mile airmail service opens serving India, Egypt, Palestine and Iraq.

DEATH

20. French commander Marshal Ferdinand Foch (*2/10/1851).

De Valera released from jail and exiled

March 6. Eamon de Valera was released today from a Belfast jail. His speeches in the North, drumming up support for his Fianna Fail party, had alarmed the authorities, but fearing a demonstration by sympathisers they released him a day early. He was driven in a car with the blinds drawn to the little used station of Adavoyle, close to the border, where he was put on the Belfast-Dublin express. In Dublin the President has promised "to crush" attacks on jurors hearing political trials.

Mussolini claims 99% vote Fascist

March 25. Mussolini's Fascist regime today claimed to have won 99 per cent of the votes in the Italian general election. The official line is that the mere 136,198 votes cast against the government show that opposition to Il Duce has dwindled almost to nothing.

Actually the fact that the entire election was under the direction and control of the government, that the whole campaign was conducted by government orators, and that public meetings or speeches by the opposition were outlawed, largely accounts for its success (→ 19/4).

March 11. Major Henry Segrave sets a new land speed record of 231 mph in "Golden Arrow" at Daytona Beach (→ 13/6/30).

1929

APRIL

Su	Mo	Tu	We	Th	Fr	Sa
	1	2	3	4	5	6
7	8	9	10	11	12	13
14	15	16	17	18	19	20
21	22	23	24	25	26	27
28	29	30				

2. Florence: Foreign Secretary Sir Austen Chamberlain has a friendly meeting with Mussolini.

7. New York: A bomb addressed to Governor Roosevelt is discovered by the New York post office.

10. UK: Figures show that Britain's birth rate in 1927 was only 85 per cent of the death rate, the lowest ever on record.

11. Berlin: Trotsky is refused political asylum in Germany (→ 8/6).

14. Monte Carlo: The first Monaco Grand Prix is won by Williams of Great Britain in a Bugatti.

14. London: The first delivery of airmail from India, 15,000 letters, arrives two minutes early at Croydon aerodrome.

15. London: Sir James Barrie donates copyright fee of the story "Peter Pan" to the Great Ormond Street Hospital for Sick Children.

15. London: Churchill's Budget abolishes the 325-year-old tea duty, cutting fourpence off a pound of tea.

19. Rome: The Roman "fasces", the Fascist emblem, is incorporated into Italy's national coat of arms.

20. Rome: King Victor Emmanuel III and Mussolini open the first all-Fascist parliament.

22. Manchester: Services start from Chat Moss, Britain's first municipal airport.

27. London: Bolton Wanderers beat Portsmouth 2-0 in the FA Cup Final.

30. London: Britain agrees to ratify the 1925 League of Nations protocol banning the use of all poison gases in warfare.

BIRTH

8. Belgian singer Jacques Brel (†9/10/78).

DEATH

4. German engineer Carl Benz, the builder of the first internal combustion motor car (*25/11/1844).

JS planes to bomb ebels in Mexico

pril 6. President Hoover has sent merican warplanes down to the rizona border after an incident in he Mexican town of Naco which is lose to the frontier. Eighteen US rmy air force aircraft are now lying south, armed with bombs nd machine guns.

The immediate cause was the vounding of four American who vere caught in the cross-fire when ebels in the Mexican civil war ried, without success, to storm a overnment fort in the town. Later here was a clash between a US atrol and the rebels.

Mexico remains convulsed by ivil war between the government f President Emilio Portes Gil and he rebels, many of whom are nown as "cristeros" – peasant ollowers of Christ the King, backd by the Church.

RAF flies non-stop from UK to India

pril 26. Links with India received boost yesterday when the RAF nade the first non-stop flight from Britain. A Fairey long-range monolane, piloted by Squadron Leader .G. Jones, landed in Karachi, 50 ours 37 minutes after taking off rom Cranwell, Lincolnshire. Fuel hortage prevented it going on to Bangalore and gaining a new world istance record.

The flight is a second major deveopment in links with India in a nonth. The Empire air service bean carrying letters there at the end f March.

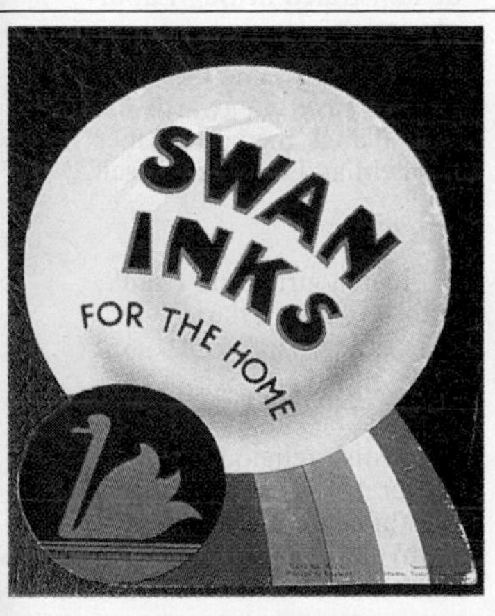

1929

MAY

Su	Mo	Tu	We	Th	Fr	Sa
			1	2	3	4
5	6	7	8	9	10	11
12	13	14	15	16	17	18
19	20	21	22	23	24	25
26	27	28	29	30	31	

1. Berlin: Eight people die in May Day clashes between Communists and police (→3).

2. US: The film "Bulldog Drummond" is released, starring Ronald Colman.

3. Berlin: The city is declared under a state of siege as nine more people die in riots.→

5. Bombay: A curfew is imposed in a bid by authorities to quell new Hindu-Moslem riots that have left 21 dead.

9. Philippines: A total eclipse of the sun is visible for three and a half minutes.

10. London: The King dissolves parliament; the general election campaigns begin (→31).

13. Persia: 3,000 are reported killed in an earthquake in Khorassan province in the last fortnight.

19. Barcelona: The Universal Exhibition opens; the modernist German Pavilion by Mies van der Rohe causes a stir.

22. Rome: Mussolini bans beauty shows and contests, calling them immoral.

24. New York: "The Cocoanuts" opens, first film with former Vaudeville stars, the Marx Brothers.

27. India: Nationalist Pandit Nehru calls for rebellion if India does not get Dominion status by the year's end.

28. Moscow: Maxim Gorky is elected to the central executive of the Congress of Soviets, although not a candidate.

29. London: An experiment in Oxford Street using traffic lights, the US method of traffic control, is approved (→13/9).

31. UK: 13 women MPs are elected in the General Election, including Lloyd George's daughter Megan.→

BIRTH

4. US actress Audrey Hepburn (†20/1/93).

DEATH

21. British statesman Archibald Primrose, 5th Earl of Rosebery, PM 1894-96 (*7/5/1847).→

Labour and Tories suitors for Liberal hand

Road workers waiting to vote outside a polling station in East London.

May 31. Britain's general election has ended in stalemate. The Tories have most votes but Labour most seats. The Liberals have failed to make any substantial recovery but will hold the balance of power in the new parliament. Tonight it appears that the final three-party tally of seats will be: Labour 288, Tories 260 and Liberals 59.

Mr Baldwin was back at No. 10 Downing Street today. It was hinted that he will reshuffle his Tory government team and then face Parliament. If this happens it will be up to the Liberals to decide whether to keep the Tories in office or put Labour in.

On arrival at Euston from Caernarvon, Mr Lloyd George was coy. "Holding the balance is a very responsible position," he said. At King's Cross Mr Ramsay MacDonald's words were drowned by a welcoming brass band and cheering socialist crowds. With the voting age for women now reduced from 30 to 21, six million more votes were cast in this election than in 1924. The "flapper vote" is thought to have helped Labour slightly.

While awaiting results, displayed as usual outside newspaper offices, some high-spirited young ladies decorated the Trafalgar Square lions in party colours. A good-humoured constabulary advised them to calm down (→7/6).

One of the posters used in the victorious Labour Party election campaign.

First Academy Awards

The first Academy Award winners: Frank Borzage and Janet Gaynor.

May 16. The Academy of Motion Picture Arts and Sciences, to give it its full title, founded recently at the suggestion of Louis B. Meyer of MGM to help the industry attain more dignity, has hit on a way of attracting world attention to its products – or so it hopes.

Last night the Academy's first awards for outstanding achievements by actors, directors, writers, technicians and producers were presented by its president, Douglas Fairbanks. They take the form of gold-plated statuettes, just over a foot tall, of a naked man plunging a sword into a reel of film. The awards are to be annual.

Among the winners were actress Janet Gaynor, German actor Emil Jannings, directors Frank Borzage and Lewis Milestone and writer Ben Hecht.

Charles Chaplin only managed runner-up, while Al Jolson, who received nothing, said: "I can't see what Jack Warner can do with his. It can't say yes."

Al Capone is jailed for carrying a gun

May 17. Chicago's underworld King, Al Capone, was behind bars for the first time in his life today, but said he was looking forward to a relaxing stay in Philadelphia Prison. Al Capone and his trusty bodyguard, "Slippery Frank" Cline, both received one-year jail sentences after being caught "carrying concealed deadly weapons". Prison authorities say Capone will not be allowed to live a "high life" in prison but may be allowed the odd luxury, such as a beer and a day off to see a baseball match (→ 17/3/30).

Rosebery, a man of fulfilment, dies

May 21. Archibald Philip Primrose, fifth Earl of Rosebery, had three ambitions: to win the Derby, to marry the richest heiress in England and to become prime minister. He died today, aged 82, having fulfilled them all.

He won the Derby not once, but thrice. In 1878 he married Hannah, the only child of Baron Amschel de Rothschild. And in 1894, when Mr Gladstone retired, Queen Victoria called on him to form a government. He stayed prime minister 15 months and then turned to literature, writing several biographies.

Communists are fighting running battles with police in Berlin

May 3. The mass attacks on police in Berlin, launched by Communist demonstrators on May Day last Wednesday, have now lasted three days and show no sign of abating. Nine people were killed yesterday, bringing the total of known dead to fifteen. A curfew is in force and police have been ordered to shoot on sight anyone seen on the streets after dark.

Whether or not the Communists are acting under orders from Moscow, as is popularly assumed, they may well feel they can exploit the present situation in the country. The world slump has hit Germany hard; unemployment is soaring, and the government is without a stable majority in the Reichstag (→ 22/9).

May Day demonstrators under attack from Berlin policemen.

1929

JUNE

Su	Mo	Tu	We	Th	Fr	Sa
						1
2	3	4	5	6	7	8
9	10	11	12	13	14	15
16	17	18	19	20	21	22
23	24	25	26	27	28	29
30						

2. London: 18 countries, including Britain, sign a new international shipping safety convention.

3. New York: Actor Douglas Fairbanks Junior, 19, marries actress Joan Crawford, 23.→

5. UK: Mr W. Barnett's Trigo wins the Derby at Epsom.

7. Rome: The Vatican becomes a sovereign state as the Lateran Treaty comes into effect (→ 25/7).

8. London: Prime Minister Ramsay MacDonald makes his first wireless broadcast on the need to cut unemployment.

8. Istanbul: Trotsky asks for asylum in Britain (→ 11/7).

13. China: Soviet troops cross the Chinese border in retaliation for raids on USSR consulates (→ 18/7).

14. S. Africa: General Hertzog's Nationalists win the general election.

17. UK: Seven passengers die when an Imperial Airways aeroplane bound for Zurich crashes into the Channel.

17. Berlin: Opening of the world congress on women's work.

21. Mexico: The government signs an accord with the Church, modifying anti-clerical policies.

26. Tokyo: The government ratifies the Kellogg-Briand Pact banning war, the last of the signatories to do so.

27. New York: The first, tiny, colour television image is demonstrated at Bell Laboratories.→

28. Germany: The German Physics Institute awards its Max Planck medal to Albert Einstein and Planck himself.

BIRTH

12. Dutch girl Anne Frank, author of the "Diary" (†12/3/45).

DEATH

16. British religious leader General William Bramwell Booth, head of the Salvation Army (*8/3/1856).

MacDonald forms new Labour cabinet

June 7. Ramsay MacDonald today announced the composition of Britain's second Labour Government. For the first time there is a woman in the Cabinet – Margaret Bondfield as Minister of Labour – but otherwise the Prime Minister has generally played safe with his appointments. Senior posts go to the right wing of his party.

This may ease his difficult position, for like its 1924 predecessor the new Government has no overall Commons majority and will be depending on Liberal goodwill for survival. In a novel publicity stunt Mr MacDonald named his team in front of talkie cameras admitted to the Downing Street garden.

The incoming premier's preparations for taking over were well advanced when Mr Baldwin tendered his resignation to the King three days ago. Contrary to its initial inclination, the outgoing Cabinet decided it would be frivolous to court parliamentary defeat and more dignified to quit without parleying with Mr Lloyd George and his Liberals in the hope of keeping office precariously.

Reducing unemployment will be Mr MacDonald's top priority. J.H. Thomas, the former railway union leader, has been made Lord Privy Seal with a special mission to shorten the dole queues quickly. There will be no extremist socialist measures; respectability is the premier's order of the day. In foreign affairs there will be a resumption of diplomatic relations with Russia and vigorous pursuit of disarmament.

Britain's first Labour Cabinet in the garden of 10 Downing Street.

There is greater hostility among Tories in the new Parliament to the vote-splitting Liberals than to Labour. During the election the campaign trails of Messrs Baldwin and MacDonald crossed at Crewe. They agreed that whatever happened at the polls it was desirable "to keep the Welshman (Lloyd George) out" (→2/7).

Allies work out a new deal to rejig German war debts

June 8. Germany can now expect to finish paying off her war debts to the Allies by the year 1988. Under the Young Plan, named after the American banker, Owen Young, and agreed by the Allies this week in Paris, Germany will pay a total of $7.8 billion between now and 1966 in annual instalments. Subsequent payments will be negotiated later, but Germany can expect to pay many millions of dollars fewer than was originally intended.

The payments, which will be made to a new international compensation bank, will cover the debts incurred by the Allies during the war, chiefly in America; but Germany is no longer being asked to pay the cost of reconstruction in France. The Young Plan also removes Allied controls over the German economy.

In spite of the concessions made by the Allies, the plan is being attacked by extreme nationalists in Germany. The Nazis and the ex-soldiers' private army, the Stahlhelm, are staging demonstrations to pressure the Reichstag into rejecting it (→13/11).

Roses show way to colour television

June 27. Full colour television pictures were shown today by Bell Laboratories in New York. The quality of the pictures – flags and a bunch of roses – was reported to be good, but the screen was tiny and the engineering so complex that a practical system is still far off.

The process works by having a separate system for each of the three primary colours, with three cathode ray tubes at the receiving end. The pictures are combined with a system of mirrors to produce the image, on a screen no larger than a postage stamp.

Le Mans records fall to the big Bentleys

June 16. The British successes at the Le Mans 24-hour endurance sports car race, which have blossomed so dramatically in the decade since the Great War, reached a triumphant climax this year with the giant Bentleys taking the first four places.

The Grand Prix d'Endurance was won by a six-cylinder Bentley, driven by Captain Woolf Barnato and H.R.S. Birkin, who covered a record 1,765 miles in the 24 hours, some 70 miles further than the second Bentley and a full 200 miles more than the first non-British car to finish, a French-entered Stutz. Of the 25 starters, only ten managed to complete the full 24 hours. Having been led off the start by George Eyston in another Stutz, the Barnato/Birkin Bentley had captured the initiative by the end of the first of the ten-mile laps, and was never headed thereafter. It established a new record for the circuit of 81.12 miles per hour.

The race, run in the most gruelling of conditions – strong sun, high temperatures and constant swirling dust – during the daylight hours, was watched by a huge crowd in holiday mood, vast numbers of whom set up makeshift camps in the centre of the circuit and stayed throughout the night.

Film and cigarette card star Joan Crawford, 23, married 19-year-old actor Douglas Fairbanks Jr. this month in New York.

1929

JULY

Su	Mo	Tu	We	Th	Fr	Sa
	1	2	3	4	5	6
7	8	9	10	11	12	13
14	15	16	17	18	19	20
21	22	23	24	25	26	27
28	29	30	31			

1. Nanking: Britain and China sign an agreement under which Britain will help build up the Chinese navy.

2. London: The King opens parliament; the King's Speech is the first for a Labour government.

4. London: The government announces plans to increase unemployment benefit.

6. Wimbledon: Helen Wills beat Helen Jacobs in the Ladies' Singles final; Henri Cochet beat Jean Borotra for the Men's Singles title.

11. UK: The government refuses Trotsky asylum (→26/6/30).

12. Germany: The giant six-engined Dornier Do X flying boat makes its maiden flight.

15. London: Britain invites the USSR to discuss the resumption of diplomatic relations (→29).

17. Moscow: The USSR breaks off relations with China and begins to mobilize along the Chinese border.→

21. US: The German liner Bremen crosses the Atlantic from east to west in a record four days and 18 hours (→31).

26. Greece: 12 sailors are killed in a shooting accident aboard HMS Devonshire.

26. Paris: Veteran statesman Raymond Poincare resigns as premier because of ill health; Aristide Briand succeeds.

28. Geneva: 48 countries sign a convention on the treatment of prisoners of war.

29. London: A Soviet representative meets the Foreign Secretary for talks on restoring Anglo-USSR ties.

31. UK: Attorney-General Sir William Jowitt, a former Liberal MP, is returned as Labour MP for Preston.

31. UK: The liner Bremen makes the eastbound Atlantic crossing in a record four days, 14 hours and 30 minutes.

DEATH

15. Austrian writer Hugo von Hoffmansthal (*1/2/1874).

Tension mounts on Sino-Soviet border

Chinese troops rush to the frontier amid growing fears of a Soviet invasion.

July 27. Border clashes between Soviet and Chinese troops, following the rupture of diplomatic and trade relations between the two countries, have brought fresh fears of war. Russian troops began concentrating on the Amur river frontier because of a quarrel over the jointly-run Eastern railway.

Moscow delivered an ultimatum, accusing the Chinese of seizing control of a section of the line, and withdrew all Soviet officials. Last week Soviet troops were reported to have captured Pogranichnaya, near Vladivostock, where the railway joins the Trans-Siberian line.

In London the Foreign Office described the situation as "serious, but not grave". General Chiang Kai-shek ordered his army to stand united against the Soviet menace, but China is ill-prepared for war and has made no moves. In Washington Mr Stimson, the US Secretary of State, reminded Chinese and Russian diplomats that both countries had adhered to the anti-war provisions of the Kellogg Peace Pact (→22/12).

Pope Pius ventures beyond the Vatican

July 25. Pius XI today became the first Pope to leave the Vatican since 1870. He blessed a crowd of some 300,000 from a specially erected altar on the Basilica steps. He then moved out of St. Peter's Square in a magnificent procession led by the Swiss Guards.

Since he came to office seven years ago, Pius XI has worked to end the quarrel with the Italian government. Yesterday's historic occasion was supported by the Italian Court and the aristocracy. The government arranged for full sovereign honours, so the Italian army was lined up on the Basilica steps and all along the limits of the Piazza Rusticucci.

Submarines crash: 24 are feared dead

July 9. Twenty-four seamen died today when two submarines collided in the Irish Sea while returning home on the surface from an exercise. One submarine, the H47, sank immediately in about 50 fathoms of water while the other, the L 12, was able to limp into Milford Haven.

Most of the dead were from the sunken H47 but, by a miracle, three men in its conning tower were thrown clear of the doomed vessel by the impact of the collision and survived. Tonight another submarine was in position near the sunken H47 ringing out morse messages on a bell, but there seems little chance that anyone is still alive inside the hull.

Lawrence's nudes are seized in police raid on art gallery

July 5. Scotland Yard detectives last night seized twelve paintings by D.H. Lawrence, the novelist, after receiving complaints about the exhibition of them at a Mayfair gallery. The paintings were all of nudes with such titles as "Spring" and "Fight with an Amazon".

They have been on show for a fortnight and were referred to under the heading "A Disgraceful Exhibition" by the Daily Telegraph with the suggestion that action should be taken.

Lawrence, who lives near Florence, published his latest novel there last year with the title "Lady Chatterley's Lover". It deals with the love affair between a woman, whose husband is impotent from war disablement, and the gamekeeper on their estate. There are passages of unprecedented frankness using common swear-words, which have never been employed in a work of literature. Lawrence claims that he wishes to "cleanse" them of dirt: "I put forth this novel as an honest, healthy book."

There has been a spate of accusations against "obscene" literature. Joyce's "Ulysses" was described even in the Sporting Times (The Pink 'Un) as "enough to make a Hottentot sick". Aldous Huxley's "Antic Hay" was attacked and "The Vortex", by Noel Coward, described as "the ordure of an unprincipled smart set" by the Sunday Express.

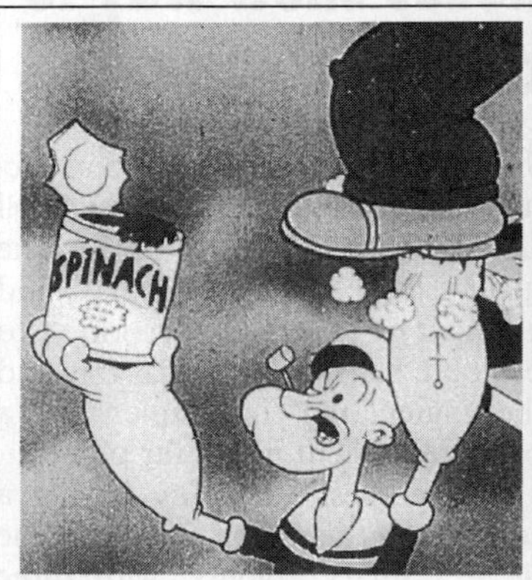

July 1. American cartoonist Elzie Segar created Popeye, the spinach-eating and pipe-smoking sailor.

1929

AUGUST

Su	Mo	Tu	We	Th	Fr	Sa
				1	2	3
4	5	6	7	8	9	10
11	12	13	14	15	16	17
18	19	20	21	22	23	24
25	26	27	28	29	30	31

1. Paris: The world's first congress on radiotherapy opens.

1. London: Dairy producers put up the price of milk to sevenpence a quart.

4. Jerusalem: The Wailing Wall is the scene of Arab-Jewish unrest as Jews demand its undisputed possession (→ 25).

6. London: Britain and Egypt agree a draft treaty for the evacuation of British troops, except from the Suez Canal.

7. US: The German airship Graf Zeppelin takes off for a round the world flight from Lakehurst, New Jersey.→

11. Zurich: Zionist leader Dr Chaim Weizmann founds the Jewish Agency.

16. China: Chinese troops clash with Soviet forces in Manchuria; first breach of the Kellogg-Briand Pact (→ 9/9).

18. Vienna: The Austrian Army bans the hugely successful novel "All Quiet on the Western Front" by Erich Remarque (→ 12/1929).

21. UK: Flying Officer Waghorn reaches a record 350 mph in the new Supermarine Rolls-Royce S.6 seaplane (→ 7/9).

21. India: Mahatma Gandhi is elected president of the Indian National Congress, but refuses to accept the post (→ 21/12).

25. Jerusalem: The British declare martial law as Arabs and Jews continue fighting; 57 deaths are reported so far.→

26. UK: The Ministry of Health says two-thirds of the population will be middle-aged and elderly by 1950.

28. The Hague: The war reparations conference agrees Britain should get two-thirds of its claim.

DEATHS

3. German scientist Emil Berliner, inventor of the gramophone disk (*20/5/1851).

19. Russian impresario Sergei Diaghilev, founder of the Ballets Russes (*31/3/1872).→

British troops restore order in Palestine

Aug 31. Palestine, baking in the summer heat, is sullenly quiet this weekend. British bullets have stopped the rioters for the moment but there are ominous reports that a considerable force of Arabs has crossed the Syrian border and is marching on Jerusalem. Aircraft have been sent to keep watch on them.

It is still not known what caused the outbreak of violence between the Jews and the Arabs, but it is possible that it stems from Arab hostility to Jewish access to the Wailing Wall in that part of Jerusalem which is Holy to both Jew and Moslem.

Tempers are so frayed in the heat that the smallest incident can spark ancient animosities. Some of the worst rioting took place at Safed on Thursday when armed Arabs attacked the Jewish population. Eight Jews were killed and whole streets of houses set ablaze, leaving 3,000 homeless. Subsequent looting was only checked when a Jewish group of the Defence Corps arrived.

One of the heroes of the troubles is Superintendent Cafferata, the only Englishman in Hebron, burial place of Abraham, sacred to both Jew and Moslem, when the rioting started. Revolver in hand, he stopped the slaughter inside the ghetto and forced a crowd 80-strong to lay down their arms. The Arabs, who respect bravery, have named him "The Man of Lead".

Graf Zeppelin girdles earth in 21 days

Aug 29. The airship Graf Zeppelin completed an historic trip around the world today when she returned to Lakehurst, New Jersey, 21 days seven hours and 26 minutes after she took off.

The giant rigid dirigible left Lakehurst, along with her crew of 37 and 16 passengers, in the early hours of August 7 and made only three stops on her 19,500-mile round-the-world trip.

The airship, captained by Dr Hugo Eckener, first flew to her home base of Friedrichshafen in Germany. From there she travelled over Siberia to Japan, where she stopped at Tokyo. She then flew westwards over the Pacific Ocean to Los Angeles, where she stopped again before returning to the east coast at Lakehurst where she landed at 8.47 am (→ 14/10).

The airship stops off in Tokyo.

Crack London policemen to get radio cars

Aug 10. Linked by the latest mobile radios and driving a new fleet of high-performance cars, leading Scotland Yard detectives are from today being turned into the best equipped force in Britain to tackle increasing professionalism amongst criminals. Metropolitan Police Commissioner Viscount Byng has pledged that underworld gangs would in future need more than speedy getaways to evade capture by his elite Flying Squad. The Yard was proud to have a new formidable weapon against lawlessness, he said. Ever since the squad was set up nine years ago, its members have protested, with considerable public support, that they have lacked manpower and technical back-up. So even before they take charge of their new radio cars in two weeks' time, the squad's strength will be doubled.

Diaghilev, genius of the ballet, dies

Ballet master Serge Diaghilev.

Aug 19. The great impresario, Serge Diaghilev, died suddenly in Venice today, during his annual holiday on the Lido, following his ballet season at Covent Garden.

Diaghilev will be remembered for the great talents which he continually attracted to make the Russian Ballet supreme. After his rupture with Nijinsky, he found Massine; after Massine, George Balanchine as choreographer and Serge Lifar as principal dancer.

Composers from Stravinsky and Serge Prokoviev (whose "L'Enfant Prodigue" was premiered this year) onwards and every modern artist of note from Picasso downwards were eager to serve Diaghilev.

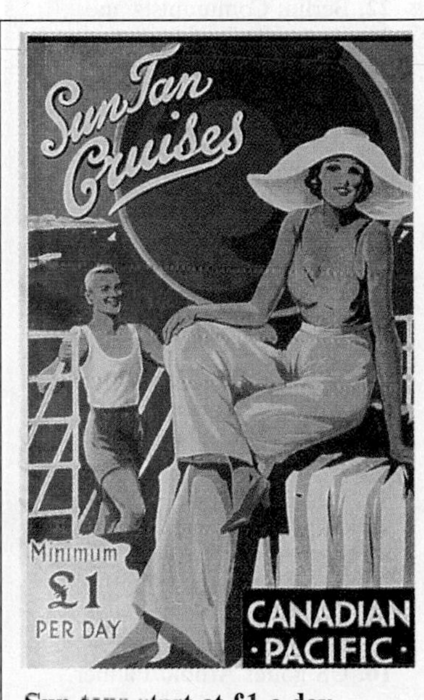

Sun tans start at £1 a day.

1929

SEPTEMBER

Su	Mo	Tu	We	Th	Fr	Sa
1	2	3	4	5	6	7
8	9	10	11	12	13	14
15	16	17	18	19	20	21
22	23	24	25	26	27	28
29	30					

1. Berlin: A bomb explodes outside the Reichstag, causing damage but no injuries.

4. London: The Baird Co. agrees to make experimental television broadcasts using BBC transmitters.

5. Palestine: The first British casualties occur during clashes with Bedouins at Gaza.

9. China: Heavy fighting between Chinese and Soviet troops is reported along the Manchurian border (→11).

11. China: The Chinese army is reported in retreat from a heavy Soviet attack (→22/12).

12. Rome: Mussolini relinquishes seven cabinet posts.

13. London: G. B. Shaw tells the Congress for Sexual Reform: "As a playwright I am an expert on sex appeal."

14. The Hague: The US finally joins the International Court of Justice.

16. South America: Bolivia and Paraguay sign a peace treaty to end their 10-month old border dispute.

17. Lithuania: The dictator Voldemaras is overthrown.

19. London: The Home Office says Britons drink 60 per cent less than in 1914 and the number of drunks is decreasing.

22. Berlin: Communists and Nazis are involved in armed street confrontations.

24. USSR: Workers are granted two days off a week.

25. Vienna: The government of Chancellor Steeruwitz resigns under pressure from the Right.

26. Vienna: Johann Schober becomes Chancellor with support of Christian Socialists and Nationalists.

27. London: Britain agrees to the restoration of relations with the USSR.

30. Germany: The first rocket-powered aeroplane, invented by Fritz von Opel, makes its maiden flight.

BIRTH

10. US golfer Arnold Palmer.

Briton sets air speed record to win trophy

Sept 7. Britain proved itself the leading force in aircraft design today, winning the important Schneider Trophy race with speeds never before attained in the air.

A crowd of two million watched the race around a circuit over the Solent as daring British and Italian pilots flew at speeds in excess of 300 mph. The winner was Flying Officer Waghorn in a Supermarine Rolls-Royce S.6, flying so fast it would have flown from London to Brighton in just eight minutes.

Experts believe there was a 1,080 -pound force on his body as he banked the seaplane powered by an advanced engine, which was first conceived by Sir Henry Royce, who immediately scratched his ideas out with a stick on a beach.

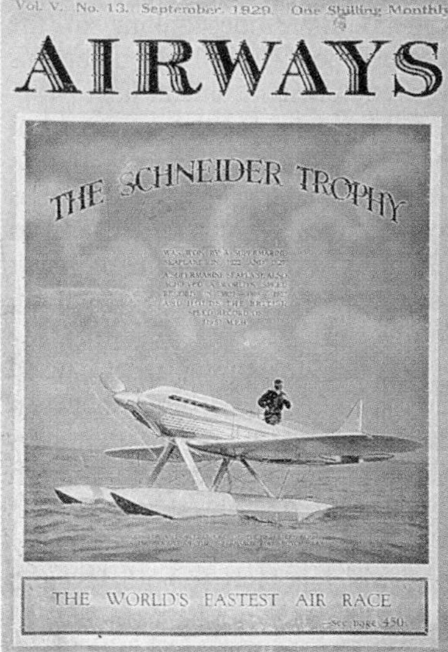

The victorious Rolls-Royce S6.

French premier proposes United Europe

Sept 5. Aristide Briand, the French premier, pursued his ideal of a United States of Europe today at a meeting of the League of Nations at Geneva. He declared that a "federal tie must exist between peoples grouped geographically like the peoples of Europe".

His speech was not greeted with much enthusiasm by the assembled ministers; at the lunch, which followed the meeting, the proposal was discussed with a diplomatic politeness. Eduard Benes, head of the Czech delegation, later described the occasion as a "first-class funeral". M. Briand, chief architect of the Locarno Pact and winner of the Nobel Prize, is unlikely to be put off by the polite rebuffs of his colleagues. He understands full well the difficulties facing his proposal, principally the problem of distrust between France and Germany.

Berlin would insist on retrieving the territory taken from Germany after the war before considering such a proposal, while Britain, with its Empire reponsibilities, would also be unwilling to commit itself to Europe.

Red to stop, green to go, says report

Sept 13. Traffic lights, which are now in use in 21 British provincial towns, are to be standardised. As on the railways, red will signal stop and green go, but amber will warn of a coming change. The Minister of Transport has consulted police chiefs in most of the towns using the lights, and has also drawn on American experience. Earlier this year he arranged a trial of the American system in Oxford Street, enabling traffic to keep up an average speed of 10 mph along it. The Minister notes that lights may be unsuitable where horse-drawn traffic abounds.

1929

OCTOBER

Su	Mo	Tu	We	Th	Fr	Sa
		1	2	3	4	5
6	7	8	9	10	11	12
13	14	15	16	17	18	19
20	21	22	23	24	25	26
27	28	29	30	31		

1. London: Coal goes up by 1/2d a ton; the best coal now costs 53 shillings a ton.

2. London: A government committee is set up to consider establishing National Parks in Britain.

3. Belgrade: The informal term Yugoslavia is declared official name of the Kingdom of Serbs, Croats and Slovenes.

3. Berlin: Julius Curtius is appointed foreign minister on Gustav Stresemann's death.

4. Washington: Ramsay MacDonald arrives for talks on naval reductions (→9).

9. Washington: Hoover and Ramsay MacDonald declare that war between Britain and the US is "unthinkable" (→15/1/30).

13. Australia: James Scullin's Labour Party wins the general election.

16. London: The government says another half million people, mainly widows, will get pensions.

17. Kabul: The Afghan national assembly elects rebel leader Nadir Khan King of Afghanistan.

18. China: 12,000 troops mutiny, looting the city of Wuhu.

19. New York: "Black Saturday" as record share sales hit the stock market.→

22. Paris: Veteran statesman Aristide Briand's 11th government resigns (→31).

24. Brussels: The visiting Italian crown prince Umberto and his fiancee escape an assassination attempt.

26. London: It is announced that all buses will be red, as trials with yellow-and-red buses have been unpopular.

28. London: The Stock Exchange feels the first shock waves from Wall Street; shares fall sharply (→23/11).

31. Paris: Andre Tardieu forms a government.

DEATH

3. German statesman Gustav Stresemann (*10/5/1878).

Black Thursday: Wall Street crashes

)ct 24. In an unprecedented ⁄ave of fear, confusion and panic, ıearly 13 million shares changed ıands on the New York Stock Exhange today. Dazed brokers wadd through a sea of paper clutching rightened investors' orders to "sell t any price".

At the peak of the panic selling his morning, the market ceased to unction as such and turned into a nad clamour of salesmen looking or non-existent buyers. Stocks vere being dumped overboard for vhatever they could bring, and rices plummeted as much as ten oints between sales. Radio Corp, or example, which had been rading at 114 earlier this year was vorth only 45 this morning.

The crisis started early, when the heer volume of selling caused rices to drop sharply. The ticker ape started to lag behind, and as rices fell faster and further, spot uotations began to show shocking ollapses in value. Orders to sell ame in from worried punters and oardrooms across the US. The botom truly dropped out at around 1.30.

At midday New York's leading ankers held an emergency meeting t the office of J.P. Morgan & Co. 'his merest hint of intervention pread through the rumour-hungry tock Exchange like wildfire, sending prices back up again.

Police riot squads were called to ry to disperse the hysterical rowds gathering in Wall Street waiting the news. When the baners emerged from their hour-long iscussion, the mob surrounded nem, eager to hear the bland assurnces of Thomas W. Lamont, J.P. Morgan's senior partner: "There as been a little distress selling on ne Stock Exchange," he said, addng that the situation was "technial rather than fundamental". The narket was essentially sound, simp- undergoing a period of readjustnent after four years of a strong ull market.

The afternoon saw prices recover trongly, largely thanks to the big ankers' reassuring statements and renzied efforts to prop up the market. In some cases, the late support as so strong that there was actual- an improvement on the day.

Most experts claim that there is nothing in the general conditions to warrant pessimism. The deluge of selling today is said merely to have pumped water from a number of highly saturated overvalued securities. But the fact is that today's crash affected good issues as much as bad ones. New York bankers were tonight blaming the panic on the technical inadequacy of the ticker-tape system in processing such massive volume trading.

Whatever the reasons, the spree of easy money and over-confidence is now over. The bear market has returned with a vengeance, crushing the dreams of an army of small investors some of whom lost everything; 11 speculators are said to have committed suicide (→28).

Anxious speculators throng downtown New York as stocks crash.

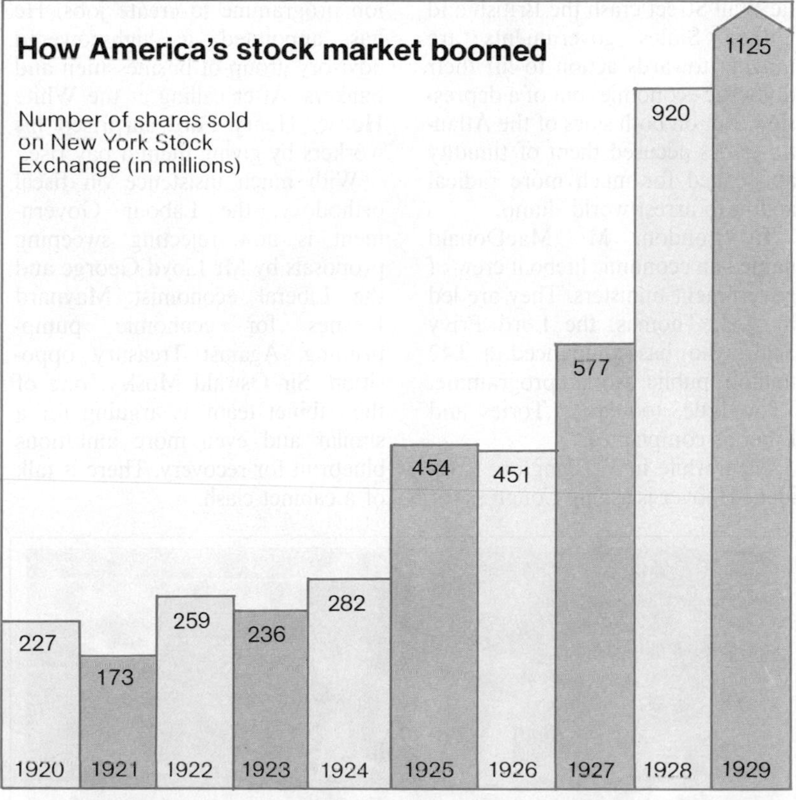

New UK airship, the R.101, makes maiden voyage

Oct 14. London's traffic stopped and crowds everywhere looked skyward as the R.101, the world's biggest airship, made her maiden voyage yesterday over the capital.

There were 52 people on board the huge airship as she took off from Cardington near Bedford for her five-hour, 300-mile flight over the South East. She first flew up to a height of 2,000 feet to test her valves, then headed south, while passengers, enjoying a four-course lunch in her dining saloon, marvelled at her quietness; they could hear the sound of car horns and trains on the ground below.

Her crew are provided with parachutes and knives for the canvas in case of emergency (→28/7/30).

Britain's new airship, the R.101.

Union funds to face fresh curbs

Oct 25. The Cabinet gave the go-ahead today for a bid to undo the last Tory Government's union curbing legislation enacted after the General Strike. The proposed new law will abolish the "contracting in" proviso for payment by union members of the political levy, which helps to finance the Labour Party. "Contracting out" will be substituted. "We can have our revenge, too", a Labour spokesman said.

1929

NOVEMBER

Su	Mo	Tu	We	Th	Fr	Sa
					1	2
3	4	5	6	7	8	9
10	11	12	13	14	15	16
17	18	19	20	21	22	23
24	25	26	27	28	29	30

1. UK: Petrol has fallen to 1/7d a gallon.

3. Italy: Mussolini tells Italian war-wounded "There is too much talk of peace".

5. India: The longest electrified railway in the Empire opens, running 116 miles from Bombay to Poona.

7. London: The government warns it will ban any new coaches capable of 60 mph.

8. Paris: Albert Einstein receives an honorary degree from the Sorbonne.

10. New York: A record 16 parachutists jump together for 2,000 feet.

13. Basle: The Bank for International Settlements is created to collect reparations under the Young Plan (→3/1/30).

15. China: Britain returns Chingkiang to the Chinese, although it was ceded in perpetuity in 1861.

17. Moscow: Nikolai Bukharin is expelled from the Politburo.

18. China: Japan begins the invasion of Manchuria.

20. Paris: The first exhibition opens of paintings by Salvador Dali.

21. Detroit: Henry Ford announces a wage rise for all his workers (→23).

26. Brussels: The government of Henri Jaspar resigns over a proposal to make Ghent university entirely Flemish.

29. Antarctica: US pilot Richard Byrd flies over the South Pole.

30. London: The Road Traffic Bill is published; it will raise the speed limit, but establish a fitness test for drivers.

BIRTH

12. US actress and Princess of Monaco Grace Patricia Kelly (*14/9/82).

DEATHS

6. German statesman Prince Max of Baden, last Imperial Chancellor (*10/7/1867).

24. French statesman Georges Clemenceau (*28/9/1841).

Economists clash after Wall Street crash

A victim of the crash trying to raise some money by selling his car.

Nov 23. One month after the horrific Wall Street crash the British and United States governments are moving towards action to lift their domestic economies out of a depression. But on both sides of the Atlantic critics accused them of timidity and called for much more radical action to arrest world slump.

In London, Mr MacDonald named an economic lifeboat crew of government ministers. They are led by J.H. Thomas, the Lord Privy Seal, who has announced a £42 million public works programme. "Too little, too late," Tories and Liberals complained.

Meanwhile in Washington, President Hoover is asking Congress for extra funds for a federal construction programme to create jobs. He has appointed a high-powered advisory group of businessmen and bankers. After calling at the White House, Henry Ford surprised his workers by giving them a pay rise.

With much insistence on fiscal orthodoxy, the Labour Government is now rejecting sweeping proposals by Mr Lloyd George and the Liberal economist Maynard Keynes for economic pump-priming. Against Treasury opposition, Sir Oswald Mosley, one of the cabinet team, is arguing for a similar and even more ambitious blueprint for recovery. There is talk of a cabinet clash.

One penny buys a bottle of warm milk, complete with a hygienic straw for making slurping noises, for these London schoolchildren.

1929

DECEMBER

Su	Mo	Tu	We	Th	Fr	Sa
1	2	3	4	5	6	7
8	9	10	11	12	13	14
15	16	17	18	19	20	21
22	23	24	25	26	27	28
29	30	31				

2. London: Britain's first 22 public telephone boxes come into service.

5. UK: 19 people drown at sea and seven are killed on land as a 94 mph hurricane sweeps across Britain.

6. Turkey: Women get the vote for the first time.

7. UK: English turkeys are twopence a pound cheaper this Christmas than last, at 2/- for an eight-pound bird.

8. Germany: The Nazis are victorious in Bavarian municipal elections.

10. Stockholm: Nobel Prizes go to Louis de Broglie (France, Physics), Sir Arthur Harden (UK) and Hans von Euler-Chelpin (Sweden, Chemistry); Christiaan Eijkman (Holland) and Sir Frederick Hopkins (UK, Medicine); and Thomas Mann (Germany, Literature). Peace Prize awarded in Oslo to Frank Kellogg (US).

12. Germany: The last British troops on the Rhine leave their base at Wiesbaden.

14. Athens: The Greek parliament elects Alexander Zaimis president.

21. India: The All-India National Congress opens in Lahore (→23).

22. Egypt: The extreme nationalist Wafd Party wins the general election (→11/1/30).

23. India: The Viceroy escapes unharmed when a bomb goes off aboard his train (→27).

27. Lahore: The All-India National Congress demands independence and threatens civil disobedience (→2/1/30).

BIRTH

12. British playwright John Osborne (†24/12/94).

HITS OF 1929

Tip-toe through the tulips.

Stardust.

QUOTE OF THE YEAR

"Wall Street Lays An Egg".

Variety magazine, headline after the Wall Street Crash.

69 children die in fire

Dec 31. Sixty-nine children, including babes in arms, died tonight when panic swept through a packed cinema in Paisley, Scotland, after a fire broke out as 2,000 were watching a special Hogmanay film show.

Most of the dead were trampled or suffocated under the weight of other children who tripped and fell during the rush to escape. A further 47 youngsters, aged between five and 14, were badly injured, and rescue teams fear the death toll, from what is Britain's worst cinema fire, could rise to 80.

When firemen were able to break into the Glen Cinema they found a stairway just ten steps from safety choked by dead and dying. On top of the breast-high mass of bodies was an 18-month-old child and the position of others revealed a terrifying picture of what happened when the children rushed from their seats to escape the fumes.

Some were huddled together, like the two friends located behind a curtain in the orchestra pit. Others, in blind panic, tried to find an escape route by trying to climb the screen. More were found in each others' arms beneath seats. Gas light fittings were broken during the chaos and some victims may have been poisoned. On the street, tramcars and volunteers helped to get casualties to hospital.

Tragically, what the children had not known was that the source of the fumes, a burning reel of film, was located early in the emergency and had been thrown out of the building. They also ignored open fire doors (→ 2/1/30).

Sino-Russian truce settles rail clash

Dec 22. The Sino-Soviet border dispute over the Eastern Railway, ended today, after border skirmishes and the Russian invasion of Manchuria which almost led to war.

It started when the Chinese arrested some Russians, expelled others and seized the railway, following raids on Russian consulates in Manchuria which had produced evidence that Soviet railway officials were using their offices as communist propaganda centres. Today both sides agreed to withdraw troops and China has agreed to disband the anti-Bolshevik White Guards.

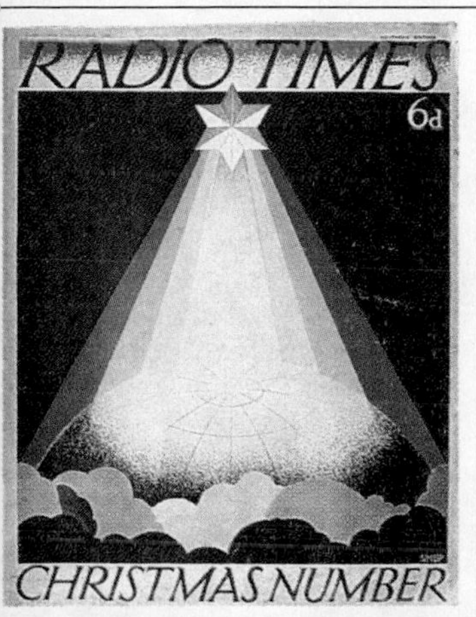

It all began with a bang, say scientists

The theory that our universe started with a gigantic explosion thousands of millions of years ago, and has been expanding ever since, came to maturity this year. Bold theoretical speculation has been borne out by painstaking observations with the world's biggest telescopes.

On the theoretical side extensions of **Einstein's** relativity theory pointed to the possibility of an expanding universe. Observations of distant galaxies showed that their light is shifted to the red end of the spectrum, a sign that they are moving away from us at great speed, the pattern to be expected in an expanding universe.

Calculations suggest that the expansion began some two billion years ago, presumably with the gigantic explosion which provided the momentum to drive the expansion which has been continuing ever since.

On a more mundane level, one of the more important medical advances of 1929 was made by **Charles Best**, the co-discoverer of insulin. He found that a natural substance, called heparin, was able to stop the blood from clotting. This has now been used to prevent thrombosis in the veins of a human patient.

Arts: unquiet echoes of trench warfare

For ten years after it ended, no-one wanted to read about the Great War; now, suddenly, it is the subject most in demand. Today's war books and plays are deliberately anti-heroic compared with the war-fever of 1914.

The runaway best-seller is **Colonel T.E. Lawrence's** "Revolt in the Desert", his shortened account of the guerrilla war he waged on the Turks in the Hedjaz desert at the head of his beloved Arab tribesmen. The full text, entitled "The Seven Pillars of Wisdom", some 350,000 words long, has been privately circulated. Colonel Lawrence, now serving in the RAF in India as Aircraftman Shaw, has forbidden that it be published in his lifetime.

The trench warfare of most serving men's memory has been evoked this year by books written from both sides of No Man's Land: "All Quiet on the Western Front" by the German **Erich Maria Remarque** and "Goodbye to All That" by **Robert Graves** are equally sombre and disillusioned.

German author Erich Remarque.

The waste and horror are vividlly realised on stage in "Journey's End", set in an officers' dug-out in 1918. The nerves of every man are at breaking point and they are shown to be aware of the pointlessness of their fate before the final shell-burst wipes out the post. This first play by an insurance agent, **R.C. Sherriff**, is breaking box office records in many countries.

Not a shot is fired in "The Silver Tassie", but **Sean O'Casey's** play spells out the same message of war's futility just as powerfully. The war-paralysed hero, played by **Charles Laughton**, once led the football team to win the silver tassie; now in his wheelchair he is an uncomfortable reminder of an event they would rather forget. The rejection of this play by **W.B. Yeats** led to O'Casey leaving Dublin.

American participation in the war has produced a fine novel from **Ernest Hemingway**, who volunteered for ambulance service on the Italian front. "A Farewell to Arms" combines his bruising experience with a tragic love affair, conveyed in spare, unemotional prose.

The Nobel Prize has gone to **Thomas Mann**, whose masterpiece, "The Magic Mountain", is set symbolically in a sanatorium.

Thomas Mann, winner of the 1929 Nobel Prize for Literature.

1930–1939

1930

JANUARY

Su	Mo	Tu	We	Th	Fr	Sa
			1	2	3	4
5	6	7	8	9	10	11
12	13	14	15	16	17	18
19	20	21	22	23	24	25
26	27	28	29	30	31	

1. Palestine: It is reported that the site of the biblical city of Sodom has been found, five miles north of the Dead Sea.

2. Glasgow: Police arrest the manager of the Glen Cinema, Paisley, where 69 children died on New Year's Eve.

3. The Hague: The second conference on reparations opens (→20).

6. Germany: Ex-Chief of Staff Max von Hoffmann is implicated in a plot to overthrow the Soviet regime.

8. France: Five Italian Socialists are arrested for plotting anti-Fascist outrages on the Riviera.

11. Cairo: A new Egyptian parliament opens after 18 months of dictatorship.

12. Atlantic: 23 die when the Royal Navy tug St. Genny sinks in a gale off Ushant.

13. China: Two million are reported to have died of starvation; famine threatens millions more.

15. London: Ramsay MacDonald urges abolition of the battleship by world powers.→

20. Philippines: 14 towns are devastated in a typhoon.

20. The Hague: End of the second reparations conference.

22. London: The government announces plans to create an economic advisory council.

24. London: MPs approve a bill abolishing the offences of blasphemy, blasphemous libel, atheism, schism and heresy (→25/2).

26. India: A mock "Independence Day" is celebrated peacefully (→14/2).

27. London: Women civil servants vote in favour of compulsory retirement of women on marriage.

28. US: Figures show a 600 per cent rise in deaths from alcohol since the beginning of prohibition in 1920.

BIRTH

20. US astronaut Edwin "Buzz" Aldrin.

Stalin declares all farms are collectives

Stalinist peasants, collectively making clear their hatred of "kulaks".

Jan 5. Joseph Stalin has turned over the vast Soviet Union to collective farms and agricultural co-operatives. Having been encouraged by the initial success of the venture, he has given orders for collectivisation to be extended. Tens of thousands of agents have been dispatched to the countryside to deal with the "kulaks", or rich peasants, and to drive the reluctant, less wealthy ones into the collective farms.

Stalin's measures are the result of the threat of famine, which has been threatening the country for the past two years. He is offering poor farmers rewards for embracing collectivisation: each family will be allowed to own a house, garden, stable and one car. They will also be able to keep any income from the sale of their garden vegetables.

The revolution in the countryside to some extent surpasses all previous revolutions. From Stalin's viewpoint, it is a deliberate way of strengthening party control over the traditionally highly undisciplined Russian peasant (→24/2).

Viceroy bombing is deplored by Gandhi

Jan 2. The All-India National Congress, meeting in Lahore, has overwhelmingly passed Mr Gandhi's resolution demanding "complete independence" from Britain. Mr Gandhi did not, however, meet with similar success when he proposed a resolution deploring the bomb attack on the Viceroy's train and "congratulating the Viceroy and Lady Irwin and their party, including the poor servants, on their fortunate and narrow escape".

It had been hoped that the reference to the "poor servants" would ensure an easy passage for the resolution, but the great marquee was filled with indignant cries when it was announced that the resolution had been carried on a show of hands (→26).

Major naval powers seek to cut fleets

Jan 31. The eyes of the world, in the form of hundreds of journalists, are on London this week where the great Five Power Naval Conference began today. Its aim is to control the arms race, which threatens to become just as destabilising as that which led to the Great War.

King George summed up the feelings of many when, in his opening speech broadcast to the world, he condemned the fierce naval rivalry which "has led to a feeling of insecurity between nations and even to the risk of war".

The conference between Britain, the US, France, Italy and Japan is designed to add to the controls set out by the Washington Treaty of 1922, but there are many differences to be resolved (→21/4).

Riots follow fall of a Spanish dictator

Jan 29. The resignation today of General Primo de Rivera, the Spanish dictator, for "health and personal" reasons, has been followed by fierce battles between the police and boisterous throngs of students in Madrid. Shouts of "Long live the King" were answered with cries of "Long live the Republic". All is turmoil here and although General Berenguer, that brave old soldier, has been appointed Premier, he appears to have problems in filling his cabinet (→6/2).

Bradman's score of 452 sets a record

Jan 6. Donald Bradman, the Australian prodigy who scored two centuries in his first series against the England touring team last year, has broken all first-class records in amassing 452 not out in a single innings. Batting for New South Wales against Queensland in a Sheffield Shield match at Sydney, he scored at the rate of some 65 runs per hour and hit 49 fours. His unbeaten total eclipsed the record of his Test colleague from Victoria, Bill Ponsford, whose 437 has now stood for just two seasons (→31/5).

Top cricketer Don Bradman.

1930

FEBRUARY

Su	Mo	Tu	We	Th	Fr	Sa
						1
2	3	4	5	6	7	8
9	10	11	12	13	14	15
16	17	18	19	20	21	22
23	24	25	26	27	28	

1. London: A bomb, believed planted by Indian nationalists, is found at the British Museum.

3. Washington: Ex-President William Taft resigns as US Chief Justice through ill health (→ 8/3).

3. India: The first "Untouchable" to be elected wins a seat on Bengal local council.

4. London: At the naval reduction talks, Britain and the US agree to scrap eight battleships (→ 11).

6. Madrid: The Spanish government announces an amnesty for all political prisoners (→ 14).

8. Rome: Pope Pius XI denounces the USSR for its persecution of Christians.→

11. London: France and Japan block a move at the naval talks to abolish submarines (→ 21).

14. Madrid: The government of Damaso Berenguer resigns.

14. India: National Congress decides on a campaign of civil disobedience, starting with a boycott of the salt tax (→ 12/3).

17. Paris: Andre Tardieu resigns as premier following a narrow five-vote defeat in the Chamber of Deputies (→ 21).

21. London: MPs give a second reading to the Rural Amenities Bill, which aims to preserve the countryside.

21. Paris: Leftist Camille Chautemps forms a cabinet, which is promptly defeated; Tardieu returns as premier.

22. Mansfield: The first cup tie under artificial light is played.

24. USSR: Reports claim that an average of 40 "kulaks" – rich peasants – are being murdered every day by Stalin's agents (→ 1/3).

25. London: The bill to abolish blasphemy as an offence is dropped.

26. UK: The TUC approves the idea of child benefit payments.

27. UK: X-rays reveal a portrait by Hans Holbein the Younger under a later painting.

Beaverbrook founds an Empire Party

Feb 22. Lord Beaverbrook, the dynamic Canadian-born millionaire newspaper owner, today launched the United Empire Party. He is in collaboration with his fellow Press baron, Lord Rothermere, and people in the Tory Party increasingly critical of Mr Baldwin over last year's Tory election debacle and the current feeble resistance to Labour in office.

The new party was at once ridiculed by the Tory hierarchy as another frivolity in Lord Beaverbrook's erratic career. It stands for creation of an Empire free trade area, with the Dominions providing all Britain's food, while British industry provides the rest of the Empire with all its manufactured goods. Mr Baldwin dismissed this as utterly impracticable.

Lord Beaverbrook plans to fund election candidates against official Tory ones. Outraged Tories suggest his motive is anti-Baldwin spite and it could open the floodgates to socialism.

Beaverbrook: Empire champion.

Anglicans blast Soviet persecution

Feb 12. Soviet religious persecution was denounced today by the convocations of Canterbury and York. In a strong speech Dr Lang, the Archbishop of Canterbury, vehemently attacked the Soviets for "the long and shocking tale of the imprisonment, the exile, the deliberate putting to death of prelates and parish priests, of monks and nuns, and of the humblest folk". In a speech in Oxford last week Alexander Kerensky, the head of the Russian provisional government in 1917, claimed that 2,000 churches had been closed in the past year. Some had been turned into "Clubs of the Godless" and in many towns the ringing of all church bells is forbidden.

Another church is closed and its priceless ikons piled onto a lorry.

A new and distant planet is sighted

Feb 18. A new planet, orbiting beyond Neptune, has been discovered by American astronomer Clyde Tombaugh. It has been named Pluto. Astronomers have searched for such a planet for many years, as it could explain peculiarities in the orbit of Uranus. Hitherto, however, they have been unsuccessful.

Tombaugh started work a year ago comparing pictures of the same part of the sky taken at different times, in the hope of detecting an object moving against the fixed background of the stars. He compared thousands of pictures, each showing tens or hundreds of thousands of stars, before he was eventually successful. Pluto is so distant that the change in its position was only just detectable (→ 24/5).

Lutyens quits over new Thames bridge

Architect Sir Edwin Lutyens.

Feb 23. Sir Edwin Lutyens, the world-famous designer of The Cenotaph, has resigned from the Royal Institute of British Architects because of the growing opposition to government plans to build a bridge across the Thames at Charing Cross. His resignation followed a warning that his "reputation was suffering" from his endorsement of the project, which has been widely criticised on architectural grounds, as well as its cost. it faces fierce opposition in the Commons.

1930

MARCH

Su	Mo	Tu	We	Th	Fr	Sa
						1
2	3	4	5	6	7	8
9	10	11	12	13	14	15
16	17	18	19	20	21	22
23	24	25	26	27	28	29
30	31					

1. USSR: Thousands of Russian peasants are reported to be fleeing to Poland to avoid collectivisation.→

3. France: 200 people are feared dead as floods strike the south-west of the country.

6. New York: Two die when police clash with demonstrators protesting at US unemployment.

10. New York: The police chief issues employers with a blacklist of "Communists".

12. Berlin: The Reichstag approves the Young Plan on reparations.

14. London: The Channel Tunnel Committee approves building a tunnel from England to France (→5/6).

17. Philadelphia: Al Capone is to leaves prison, after serving ten months of his year's term for carrying a gun (→17/3).

21. London: The French walk out of the naval talks (→3/4).

22. London: Former Prime Minister Arthur Balfour is buried in Westminster Abbey.

23. Uganda: The Prince of Wales narrowly escapes a charging elephant.

28. UK: W. Midwood's Shaun Goilin wins the Grand National at Aintree.

30. New York: Governor Roosevelt appoints a special board to tackle unemployment.

BIRTH

22. US composer Stephen Sondheim.

DEATHS

2. British writer David Herbert Lawrence (*11/9/1885).

6. German naval commander and statesman Admiral Alfred von Tirpitz (*19/3/1849).

8. US statesman and lawyer William Howard Taft, President 1909-13 (*15/9/1857).

16. Spanish statesman Miguel Primo de Rivera, Prime Minister 1923-30 (*8/1/1870).

19. British statesman Arthur James Balfour, Prime Minister 1902-05 (*25/7/1848).→

Gandhi ready to die defying salt tax

March 12. Mahatma Gandhi today began his march to the sea, 300 miles away. His purpose is to defy the British law establishing a government monopoly on producing salt. In a final message before he set out Gandhi said: "I repudiate this law and regard it as my sacred duty to break the mournful monotony of compulsory peace that is choking the heart of the nation for want of a free vent."

His intention, when he arrives at the sea on the Gulf of Cambay near Jalalpur, is to make a symbolic amount of salt from sea water and thus court arrest. He and his followers also intend to seize existing stocks of salt - if they are allowed to do so.

He started out soon after dawn from his ashram near Ahmedabad where an enormous crowd had gathered, all in a festive mood. As Gandhi took his first steps he looked so old and cold it seemed doubtful that he would prove equal to the rigours of the march. He was accompanied by 79 followers from all parts of India and behind the procession came a lorry containing masses of hand-woven cloth, presumably for distribution to poor people on the march. The party reached the village of Aslaji some ten miles out before noon and they prepared to spend the rest of the day and night there. Gandhi then made a speech calling on his followers to be prepared "for the worst, even death, for defiance of the salt tax" (→6/4).

Gandhi in Ahmedabad at the start of his 100-mile march to the sea.

Unemployment in the UK tops 1.5 million

March 10. Unemployment's upward spiral reached a new peak today when the Government announced the latest figure of more than 1.5 million, a rise of about 500,000 since Labour came to power. Since the election nine months ago, the Ministry of Labour has reported a steady increase, and the latest jobless figure was presented with no indication that the trend will change in the coming months. Leading trade unionists denounced the total, compiled from statistics gathered at Employment Exchanges, as showing the "sickening effects of promises belied and hopes deferred". However, the problem of lengthening dole queues as the world economy slumps after last year's Wall Street crash is besetting all countries, not just Britain.

Police fighting with unemployed demonstrators in East London.

Rich farmers are Stalin's new target

March 16. Joseph Stalin's colossal collectivisation plan is turning into a cruel civil war with his latest campaign to wipe out the kulaks, or rich farmers. Stalin has given orders for the two million or so kulaks - who with their families may number ten million people - to be "liquidated as a class".

It is believed that kulaks are already being deported to Siberia and their houses and barns turned over to collective farms. Rather than co-operate with the government, the fiercely independent kulaks are slaughtering their cattle, smashing their farm machinery and burning their crops.

During Lenin's New Economic Policy the kulaks had helped greatly in feeding the towns, but now they are out of business. One report said that collectivisation has already annihilated 35 per cent of the total cattle stock and the Government is bracing itself for a serious famine later this year. Stalin is said to be actively seeking aid from abroad (→26/6).

Balfour, Tory statesman and PM, dies

March 19. The Earl of Balfour, Tory Prime Minister nearly 30 years ago, died today at the age of 81. He was the King's friend and adviser for half a century. Arthur James Balfour succeeded his uncle, Lord Salisbury, in the premiership in 1902. He held many high posts before and since and was still a cabinet member until a year ago.

His career was tranquil and Olympian. Born to wealth, the political hurly-burly was not for him. He was a self-contained bachelor with an austere life-style, except for staying in bed till lunchtime.

He will be remembered for the Balfour Declaration, committing Britain to fostering a national home for the Jews in Palestine. Winston Churchill described him tonight as being "the greatest member of the House of Commons since Mr Gladstone".

Ex-Tory premier Lord Balfour.

Princes and rich villains rile the censors

March 17. Sordid themes have upset the British Board of Film Censors in the last year. No fewer than 300 films were either sent back for changes or rejected altogether, according to the board's annual report issued today.

The report lists some of the factors which upset the censors. These include coarse speech, women in a state of intoxication, ministers of religion in "equivocal situations", marital infidelity, criminals shown to be either affluent or apparently successful and references to the Prince of Wales.

"Unwarranted references to well-known characters" generally is a problem, says the board. So is what it calls "backstage dramas". Immoral characters and "atmosphere of riotous luxury" invests a life of irregularity with a spurious glamour, says the report. Although the talkies are still a minority, they make matters worse.

March 17. Al Capone relaxing after his release from prison today.

1930

APRIL

Su	Mo	Tu	We	Th	Fr	Sa
		1	2	3	4	5
6	7	8	9	10	11	12
13	14	15	16	17	18	19
20	21	22	23	24	25	26
27	28	29	30			

1. UK: Poor Law Guardians are abolished.

1. Germany: Josef von Sternberg's film "The Blue Angel" opens, starring Marlene Dietrich.

3. London: Italy refuses to sign a naval reductions pact unless France does.→

3. UK: The car firms of Rover, Lanchester and Standard announce they will merge.

4. London: The Archbishop of Canterbury approves the free discussion of sex.

7. UK: The Automobile Association issues its one millionth badge.

10. Bombay: Police raid the headquarters of the Indian National Congress (→20).

11. New York: Scientists predict that man will land on the moon by the year 2050.

12. London: Cambridge wins its 41st Boat Race, taking the lead over Oxford for the first time since 1863.

14. London: The Budget puts sixpence on income tax and increases surtax and death duties.

16. London: Labour Minister Margaret Bondfield introduces a bill for a 48-hour week in industry.

18. Rumania: Over 100 are reported killed when a church burns down in Costesti.

20. India: The Viceroy imposes an ordinance for the suppression of terrorism, following a series of attacks.

23. UK: Britain's first all-electric Totalisator comes into operation at Newmarket.

26. London: Arsenal win the FA Cup for the first time, beating Huddersfield Town 2-0 at Wembley.

28. London: Hamlet plays at the Old Vic, with John Gielgud starring in the title role.

DEATH

21. British poet Robert Bridges, Poet Laureate from 1913 (*23/10/1844).

Chiang Kai-shek is challenged by Reds and warlords

April 23. The long battle of General Chiang Kai-shek, the Chinese Nationalist commander-in-chief, to establish control over all China, is being challenged again this week. Two powerful forces threaten his government, which is, despite internal rivalries, now securely established in Nanking.

At the beginning of this month General Yen Hsi-chan, the aggressive northern warlord, mounted a surprise "punitive expedition", which drove General Chiang's troops back to the southern bank of the Yellow river. But the Nationalists fought back successfully and Chiang Kai-shek is now preparing a counter-offensive.

Fortunes change quickly in these local internal wars. On both sides huge forces of ill-equipped peasant soldiers, led by bullying officers, are easily persuaded either to desert or change sides.

A more serious long-term threat to the regime than warlords is the growing power of the Kremlin-controlled communists. After General Chiang purged communist elements from his Kuomintang forces, a Red Army of 10,000 men established their base in the Kuangsi province in central China. They then moved out of Chingkanshan, the capital, to the rural areas to drum up support among the peasants. At the same time it is believed that they are under Soviet orders to infiltrate the governments of the large cities, to take them over.

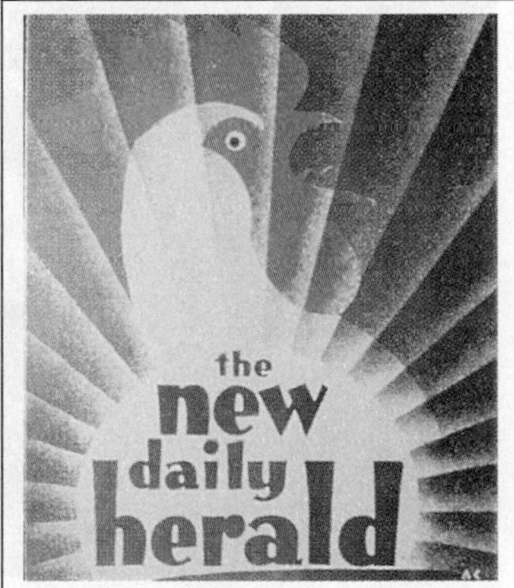

The Daily Herald is launched, Britain's Labour newspaper.

Gandhi risks arrest by breaking salt law

Gandhi in Dandi being congratulated on his 300-mile march across India.

April 6. Mahatma Gandhi reached the coast at Dandi yesterday at the end of his 300-mile march in protest against the salt law. He looked thin and strained, but was obviously elated. All through the night his followers arrived on foot and in buses and prayed at the house where he is staying.

At 5.30 this morning, clad only in his loin-cloth, he walked into the sea for a ceremonial bath of purification. Then, to cries of "Hail Deliverer," he bent down to pick up a small piece of natural salt. He thus broke the salt law imposing taxes on the production of salt. It had been his intention to break the law by working on the deposits of salt left on the mud flats by the high tides. But the police forestalled him, destroying the deposits by stirring them into mud – much to the fury of the activists who marched with Gandhi. Nevertheless, he has broken the law, if only symbolically, and is courting arrest. Gandhi has warned his followers to be prepared "for the worst," and has defied the British to arrest him. It remains to be seen if the authorities will oblige. His son, Ram Das, was arrested today for selling salt illegally and Gandhi broke that law too by auctioning a piece of salt for 1,600 rupees (→31/5).

April 1. The King meets the Arsenal team at Wembley Stadium where they won the FA Cup today, beating Huddersfield Town 2-0.

First woman flies down to Australia

April 24. Amy Johnson, the 27-year-old daughter of a Hull fish merchant, arrived today in Darwin, the first woman to fly from Britain to Australia solo.

Johnson began her 10,000-mile flight in the second-hand Gipsy Moth, Jason, 19 days ago. The aircraft cost just £600 and she had only 100 hours flying experience. She left Croydon almost unnoticed, but the world became fascinated with reports of flying blind through sandstorms, forced landings in Java where she patched up her wings with sticking plaster, and her ju jitsu training to fight off Arab sheikhs. Dressed in khaki shorts and sun helmet for most of the route, she is the new heroine.

Amy Johnson waves to the crowd.

Powers put brake on naval rivalry

April 21. The London Naval Treaty, limiting the size and number of warships and submarines possessed by the great powers, was signed in a ceremony at St. James's Palace today. The pact is the result of 14 weeks of talks by the five great powers, Britain, the US, Japan, France and Italy. The latter two are refusing to agree to the specific terms of the treaty and the naval limitations will apply only to Britain, the US and Japan (→24/7).

1930

MAY

Su	Mo	Tu	We	Th	Fr	Sa
				1	2	3
4	5	6	7	8	9	10
11	12	13	14	15	16	17
18	19	20	21	22	23	24
25	26	27	28	29	30	31

1. UK: Australian cricketer Don Bradman scores 236 in his first match in England (→31).

5. Burma: 6,000 are reported killed in a massive earthquake that devastates Pegu.

9. London: John Masefield is appointed Poet Laureate to succeed Robert Bridges, who died last month.

10. UK: British cars take the first four places in the "Double Twelve Hours" race at Brooklands.

16. UK: The Americans win the Walker Cup golf trophy.

19. London: Othello opens starring Paul Robeson, Peggy Ashcroft, Sybil Thorndike and Ralph Richardson.

19. S. Africa: White women are given the vote for the first time.

20. Oxford: Gloucester declare at a record score of 627 for two wickets against Oxford University.

22. Damascus: France gives Syria its own constitution.

23. Malta: The prime minister, Lord Strickland, escapes an assassination attempt.

24. US: The name "Pluto" given to the planet discovered in February is officially recognised.

26. Paris: The International Olympic Committee recommends Berlin as host for the 1936 Games.

29. London: The BBC forms its own permanent symphony orchestra under the directorship of Adrian Boult.

31. UK: Don Bradman is the first Australian to score 1,000 runs in England by the end of May (→12/7).

BIRTH

31. US actor Clint Eastwood.

DEATHS

13. Norwegian Arctic explorer Fridtjof Nansen (*10/10/1861).

25. British churchman Randall Davidson, Archbishop of Canterbury 1903-28 (*7/4/1848).

Get-tough policy to deal with Gandhi

May 31. Sweeping new measures to deal with Mr Gandhi's campaign of disobedience were announced today by the Viceroy, Lord Irwin. Picketing has been made illegal and so has instigating the refusal to pay taxes and attempts to suborn civil servants and soldiers.

These measures are the consequence of the unrest which has swept India following the arrest of Gandhi on May 5, when he was woken at his camp in Karadi, allowed to brush his teeth, say his farewells and was put on the Gujarat Mail bound for Bombay.

Taken off the train before it reached Bombay and driven to jail in a large yellow Studebaker, he behaved, and was treated, with great civility. The arresting officers raised their hats to him and he shook their hands.

He told a reporter, who was present when he was taken from the train, that he hoped there would be no troubles: "I have done my best to prevent them."

But he had no control over the police. There were brutal scenes when 2,500 of his followers, protesting at the government-owned saltworks at Dharasana, shuffled unresistingly towards the police lines in the blazing sun. They were beaten to the ground with steel-tipped staves; hundreds suffered broken heads and bones. Abbas Tyabji, Gandhi's Moslem successor as leader of the raid, was arrested, and leadership of the campaign is now in the hands of Mrs Sarojini Naidu who was educated at King's College, London and Girton, Cambridge.

A protest in Bombay by Gandhi's supporters erupts into violence.

Gandhi's arrest and imprisonment, under a law which enables the authorities to hold him "during the pleasure of the government", have sparked strikes, riots and the burning of liquor shops throughout India. Armoured cars are patrolling the streets of important cities. Martial law has been declared at Sholapur where there was a bloody attempt by Gandhi's supporters to take over the town. Two Moslem policemen were burnt to death and the District Collector with only 100 armed police and 30 volunteers faced a mob of 10,000.

By its new measures the government means to make it plain it will not give in to the civil disobedience campaign. But Mr Gandhi is proving to be as much trouble inside jail as he was outside (→23/6).

Labour and Liberals fall out over issue of electoral reform

May 22. The minority Labour Government's life hangs on a thinner thread than ever tonight. That is the meaning of the breakdown of negotiations between Labour and Liberal leaders over electoral reform. Mr MacDonald has told Mr Lloyd George that he cannot definitely pledge the Government to change the voting system before the next General Election. The Liberal leader has retorted that the Prime Minister had better not rely on the Liberals to bail out the Government any longer. An informal Lib-Lab pact is thus ended.

However, Lloyd George is no keener on forcing an early election than turkeys are to volunteer for Christmas. The Liberals have no stomach for the hustings at present and may abstain in crucial Commons votes for a while. This will allow the lame-duck Government to limp along, although it can expect neither to run a full term nor to implement much socialism.

One crumb of comfort for Mr MacDonald was the huge defeat for Sir Oswald Mosley today when, following his resignation from the Government, he moved a censure motion against it at a private meeting of Labour MPs. He only got 29 backers so it now looks as though Sir Oswald, although a magnetic orator, won't be able to mount any serious challenge for the party leadership.

Attlee steps into Oswald Mosley's shoes

May 20. Sir Oswald Mosley stormed sensationally out of the Government today in protest over unemployment. The Prime Minister Ramsay MacDonald had made him Chancellor of the Duchy of Lancaster specifically to deal with that problem. His defection follows bitter cabinet in-fighting and there is some feeling at Westminster that it could destabilise the government.

Sir Oswald is furious at the rejection of his radical blueprint for direction of industry and huge borrowing to promote expansion. His post now goes to Major Clement Richard Attlee, ex-public school and former Mayor of Stepney, who is well thought of in moderate Labour circles. Recently he was an impressive member of the Simon Commission on India (→22).

Sir Oswald Mosley changes sides.

Petticoat's decline hits cotton trade

May 1. Cotton industry bosses today lamented the "almost total eclipse" of the petticoat – and the rise of the short skirt. They claim these trends have led to a drop in sales of more than two hundred million yards a year. One commented: "Where our daughters wear three or four yards of cotton cloth, our mothers used to wear ten."

Moreover the modern woman is tempted to spend her money on all kinds of other goods, rather than just fabrics as her grandmother did. Over the next few days, during National Cotton Week, more than 10,000 shops around the country will be promoting cotton goods in an energetic bid to boost the ailing industry.

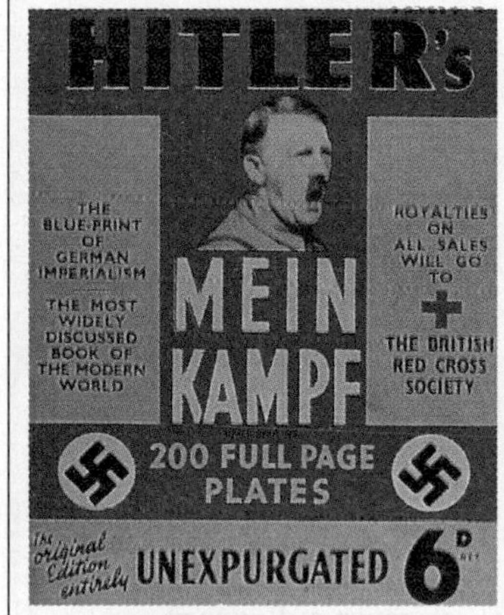

A new edition of Hitler's book "Mein Kampf" is issued, with all profits going to the Red Cross.

1930

JUNE

Su	Mo	Tu	We	Th	Fr	Sa
1	2	3	4	5	6	7
8	9	10	11	12	13	14
15	16	17	18	19	20	21
22	23	24	25	26	27	28
29	30					

1. London: Italian conductor Arturo Toscanini makes a triumphant British debut at the Royal Albert Hall.

2. UK: The "Daily Chronicle" and "Daily News" merge to form the "Daily News and Chronicle".

4. UK: The Aga Khan wins his first Derby with the horse Blenheim.

5. London: In a government reshuffle Emmanuel Shinwell is made Secretary for Mines.

5. London: The government rejects a plan for a Channel Tunnel between England and France.

8. Bucharest: The Rumanian parliament votes to oust King Ferdinand and elects as king the exiled Crown Prince Carol.

10. UK: Trades unionists protest at the "invasion" of industry by women.

12. Germany: German Max Schmeling beats American Jack Sharkey for the world heavyweight boxing title.

13. UK: Sir Henry Segrave is killed when his speedboat capsizes on Lake Windermere at a record speed of 98 mph.

13. Miami: Al Capone is arrested on a perjury charge.

19. London: The government rejects a Tory demand for a cut in unemployment benefit payments.

20. New York: The revue "Hot Chocolates" opens with Fats Waller and Louis Armstrong; songs include "Ain't Misbehavin'".

20. UK: Bobby Jones wins his third British Open Golf Championship.

22. France: British cars take the first four places in the Le Mans Grand Prix.

23. London: Neville Chamberlain becomes chairman of the Conservative Party.

23. London: The Simon Commission recommends a federal India and the separation of Burma.→

30. Baghdad: Britain recognises Iraqi independence.

Purges cleansing Russia, says Stalin

Stalin (front row standing, second from right) at the 16th Party Congress.

June 26. Purges are good for the country, Joseph Stalin, the Soviet leader, told the 16th Communist Party Congress in Moscow today. Stalin, who has pushed through rapid industrialisation and collectivisation, justified his purges of supporters of Leon Trotsky, his most vociferous critic, who has been sent into exile in Europe.

He boasted that in the last three years more than 6,000 Trotskyists had been sent into exiled, banished or imprisoned; 5,800 party members had abandoned Trotskyism altogether and another 34,000 people considered too "right wing" had had their party membership withdrawn.

The congress was surprised by his triumphant statement: "We are on the eve of our transformation from an agrarian into an industrial country", and his prediction that the Five-Year plan would be fulfilled in three.

India should be federation says report

June 23. The Simon Commission, which was greeted with black flags and a boycott when it went to India over two years ago, has presented the last volume of its painstaking report on the way India is governed and given its recommendations for the future.

It draws a graphic picture of the extraordinary diversity of race, religion, language and caste among India's 319 million people and suggests that this whole vast mass of land and peoples should one day be ruled as a federation, uniting the independent princely states with the British Indian provinces.

The Commission found itself "unanimous on all fundamental matters". It has not, however, had the benefit of talking to the Indian leaders who are now in jail. Mr Gandhi and his followers still insist on absolute independence.

America gets chilly Birdseye view of peas

June 6. A group of Massachusetts grocers put a labour saving device on sale today – frozen peas. American housewives have been buying frozen meat and fish for several years, but it is the first time vegetables have been available. This is thanks to the "quick-freeze" technique pioneered by Clarence Birdseye, founder of the eponymous giant frozen food company. The problem with all other food-freezing methods is that, when thawed, the product tends to be tasteless and soggy. His breakthrough was to notice, on a trip to northern Canada, that when food is frozen very quickly it stays fresh.

Last French troops leave Rhineland

June 30. The French government today pulled its last troops out of the Rhineland – five years before the date set for evacuation in the Versailles Treaty.

Under the terms of Versailles, Germany must not place any armed forces on the left bank of the Rhine and must also respect a demilitarised zone extending for 30 miles east of the river. The presence of French troops in Germany ensured that the treaty terms were observed.

But skilful negotiation by Gustav Stresemann, the late German Foreign Minister, persuaded the French that Germany has put militarism behind her. Stresemann shared the Nobel Peace Prize for his part in negotiating the 1925 Locarno Pact that reconciled the wartime enemies.

Ladies take plunge in rainbow colours

"The pearl of the plage" in the sea.

June 30. Women wearing brightly coloured bathing costumes leapt into the Serpentine today at the opening of the Hyde Park Lido for mixed bathing. One had queued for 11 hours to be the first in the water.

The dazzling hues of the swimsuits are a daring contrast to the discreet black of yesteryear and may bring accusations of immodesty. Fashion conservatives can be comforted by other trends though: dresses are showing a softer, more feminine line and skirts are back below the knee.

1930

JULY

Su	Mo	Tu	We	Th	Fr	Sa
		1	2	3	4	5
6	7	8	9	10	11	12
13	14	15	16	17	18	19
20	21	22	23	24	25	26
27	28	29	30	31		

1. US: Northland Transport Co. starts a nationwide bus service as the Greyhound Co.

4. UK: 13 die and many are hurt in an explosion at a chemical factory in Yorkshire.

7. Wimbledon: Helen Moody beats Elizabeth Ryan in the Women's Singles final; Bill Tilden beats unseeded Wilmer Allison for the Men's Singles title.

8. London: The King opens India House in the Aldwych, appealing for peace in India.

10. China: Communist armies unite to attack Hankow.

11. Chicago: 72 people die in a heat wave.

13. Uruguay: The first World Cup begins in Montevideo.→

14. London: The government says it will borrow £10 million for the unemployed.

16. Berlin: President Hindenburg authorises the German budget by decree after the Reichstag refused to pass it.

17. London: A Labour MP seizes the Commons mace, causing the biggest uproar in the House for years.

20. UK: M. E. Foster is the first woman to win the King's Prize for shooting at Bisley.

20. Moscow: Maxim Litvinov becomes foreign minister in succession to Georgy Chicherin.

22. Italy: An earthquake in the Naples area leaves up to 3,000 dead and 6,000 injured.

24. London: MPs approve the London Naval Treaty.

28. UK: The airship R.100 begins its maiden flight across the Atlantic (→ 1/8).

29. UK: An X-ray uncovers a portrait by Holbein of Henry VIII's brother-in-law the Duke of Suffolk.

30. China: The skull of a man who lived a million years ago has been found at Chou Kou Tien, it is announced.

DEATH

7. British writer Sir Arthur Conan Doyle (*22/5/1859). ›

Navy is sent to quell Egyptian riots

July 22. The battleships "Queen Elizabeth" and "Ramillies", each with eight 15-inch guns, are sailing for Alexandria to deal with the riots erupting in Egypt. The Egyptian premier, Sidky Pasha, has been told that Britain will hold him responsible for the protection of foreign lives and property.

The disturbances, arising from the dismissal of the nationalist premier, Nahas Pasha, are anti-monarchical and anti-British.

Cairo was quiet after yesterday's riots in which six people were killed, but there were further outbreaks at Port Said, where a mob attacked the municipal stables and set fire to them, after freeing the horses and mules. The mob dispersed when police opened fire.

Police battling with rioters in the Egyptian city of Mansurah.

The first World Cup is won by Uruguay

July 30. Uruguay, the host and by far the smallest nation in the competition, won Football's first World Cup in Montevideo, recovering from 2-1 down at halftime to beat Argentina 4-2 in front of 90,000 spectators, many of whom had sailed across the River Plate estuary the night before from Buenos Aires.

It was hardly a genuine world competition. All four British football associations left FIFA, the world body, in 1926 in a dispute over payments to players in the amateur game, and were not invited to participate. The four European nations who had bid against Uruguay to stage the competition – Italy, Holland, Spain and Sweden – stayed away, as did the talented Hungarians, Austrians and Germans. Indeed, only Belgium, Rumania, Yugoslavia and France defended Europe's football reputation, and of these only Yugoslavia survived the high-scoring qualifying groups.

Uruguay beat them 6-1 in the first semi-final; Argentina, whose Guillermo Stabile was the tournament's highest goal-scorer, beat the United States 6-1 in the other, to set up the dramatic all-South American final.

Conan Doyle has to solve final mystery

July 7. Sir Arthur Conan Doyle, who died of a heart attack today, was the creator of an immortal, Sherlock Holmes, but he set far more value on preaching immortality through spiritualism. He spent £250,000 of his earnings on doing so around the world.

What would Holmes have said of such beliefs? But Doyle was a great all-rounder: a doctor, reporter (of both Boer and Great Wars), cricketer (who played for the MCC), divorce reformer, and campaigner against miscarriages of justice.

Bradman's triple ton sets record for individual Test innings

July 12. Test match statistics have been rewritten at Leeds where Australia's Donald Bradman, scoring almost at will against the England bowlers, set a new record score of 334, comprehensively beating the 287 made by R.E.Foster at Sydney 27 years ago. In the course of his non-stop punishment, Bradman also set a record for the number of runs scored in a single day of a Test match (309 – and he didn't come in to bat until the first wicket had fallen on the first morning), bringing his total for the series to 728, an Australian record – with two Tests still to play.

Donald Bradman at the wicket during Australia's tour of England.

1930

AUGUST

Su	Mo	Tu	We	Th	Fr	Sa
					1	2
3	4	5	6	7	8	9
10	11	12	13	14	15	16
17	18	19	20	21	22	23
24	25	26	27	28	29	30
31						

1. Montreal: The airship R.100 arrives from Britain after a flight of 77h 35 mins (→ 5/10).

2. Rome: The Italian government authorises the Vatican to issue currency up to one million liras a year.

5. Washington: Douglas MacArthur is appointed Chief of Staff of the US Army.

6. London: Britain signs a commerce treaty with Rumania.

9. UK: Jack Hobbs scores his 54,921st run, beating W. G. Grace's record aggregate of 54,896.

12. Central Asia: The Turkish and Persian armies launch an offensive on Kurdish rebels.

15. India: Martial law is declared in Peshawar.

18. Sydney: The two halves of the new Harbour Bridge are joined.

21. London: The Duchess of York gives birth to her second daughter.

22. UK: Australia wins the Ashes.

25. Poland: Marshal Pilsudski is appointed Prime Minister and Minister of War.

25. Peru: President Augusto Leguia resigns following a coup.

28. UK: 24 people have died in a heatwave; temperatures in London soar to 94 degrees F (34 degrees C).

30. UK: Morris announce their new 14.9 hp Morris Major, which costs £215.→

BIRTHS

5. US astronaut Neil Armstrong.

17. British poet Ted Hughes, Poet Laureate from 1984.

25. British actor Sean Connery.

DEATHS

26. US actor Lon Chaney (*1/4/1883).

29. Irish academic, known for linguistic confusion, the Rev. Dr. William Spooner (*22/7/1844).

Unemployment breaks two million barrier

Aug 7. Within 14 months the ranks of Britain's unemployed have nearly doubled, with a figure of two million being announced today by the Ministry of Labour. The Labour Government is under intense pressure to reverse the trend by introducing policies to boost the economy. It is the highest total since 1921 and includes nearly 39,000 who joined the queue for work in one recent week.

The latest figure of 2,011,467 comprises 1,431,505 men, 56,024 boys, 476,041 women and 47,897 girls. Economists say this represents a new phase of industrial depression. They point out that the rise has continued unchecked by normal seasonal improvements. Yet employment over the same period has improved in Germany, Sweden, Denmark and Italy.

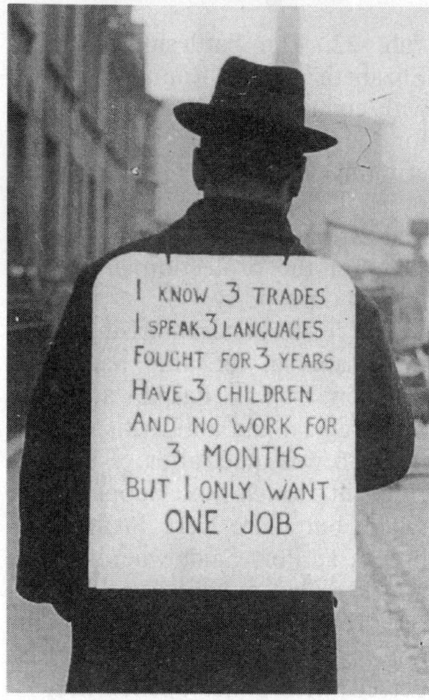

A protest by one of the 2m jobless.

Bishops give backing to birth control

Aug 14. The Church of England today gave a cautious go-ahead for the use of birth control. This momentous decision, announced in an Encyclical Letter from the Archbishop of Canterbury, follows weeks of debate by the bishops.

The letter emphasises motives rather than methods. The use of contraceptives for selfishness, luxury and mere convenience is strongly condemned. But it adds that when conception would be wrong, "if there is good moral reason why the way of abstinence should not be followed, we cannot condemn the use of scientific methods, which are thoughtfully and conscientiously adopted".

The letter also calls for strict controls over the sale and advertising of contraceptives. It urges sex instruction for children, condemns trial marriages and calls for the rescue of sex from "degradation in thought and conversation" and the preservation of the "beauty of family life".

At work on the shop-floor of Cowley car works in Oxford, where the new 14.9 hp Morris Major is being produced – it will sell for £215.

1930

SEPTEMBER

Su	Mo	Tu	We	Th	Fr	Sa
	1	2	3	4	5	6
7	8	9	10	11	12	13
14	15	16	17	18	19	20
21	22	23	24	25	26	27
28	29	30				

1. London: The Prince of Wales is promoted to Vice Admiral, Lieutenant-General and Air Marshal.

2. China: General Yen Hsi-chan forms a rebel government in Peking.

4. London: Opening of the Cambridge Theatre.

5. Germany: Ex-Kaiser Wilhelm II wins a libel action against the newspaper "Morgenpost".

6. Argentina: Radical President Hipolito Irigoyen is overthrown by army officers led by General Uriburu.

10. Geneva: The League of Nations 60th session opens with a debate on the question of the Saarland.

15. Germany: Nazi leader Adolf Hitler is barred from taking his Reichstag seat for being an Austrian citizen.→

18. US: The Americans win the America's Cup yacht race off Rhode Island.

20. London: First performance of Sir Edward Elgar's fifth Pomp and Circumstance March.

24. London: Premiere of Noel Coward's play "Private Lives".

25. Germany: Hitler denounces the peace treaties, saying he wants to build a huge conscript German army.

29. New York: The state Democrats under Governor Roosevelt adopt the abolition of prohibition as a policy (→ 30).

29. London: George Bernard Shaw declines the offer of a peerage.

30. New York: Franklin D. Roosevelt wins the Democratic nomination for re-election as governor (→ 4/11).

BIRTH

7. Belgian King Baudouin acceded 1951 (†31/7/93).

DEATH

30. British Conservative statesman Frederick Edwin Smith, Lord Birkenhead (*12/7/1872).

Nazis come second in German election

Hitler is presented with a bouquet after the National Socialists' triumph.

Sept 15. In a stunning election triumph Adolf Hitler's National Socialists have increased their representation in the Reichstag ninefold from 12 deputies to 107 and become the second largest party after the Socialists. The Nazi vote has gone up from 800,000 in 1928 to 6,409,000, only 2,000,000 behind the Socialists.

The mounting economic crisis played a part in swinging voters towards the extremes – the Communists are in third place but blame must also be put on the more moderate parties, who refused to back the Catholic Centre Party Chancellor, Heinrich Bruening, and obliged him to rule by Presidential decree.

The election result sent shock waves through the Berlin Bourse, with shares falling by as much as 20 points. One suggestion being aired is that Hitler should be made Chancellor. His inexperience would cause him to make such a mess, so the theory goes, that he would be out of office in no time and the German people would be cured of any fondness for extremist fascist-style politics (→ 13/10).

London spreading as building booms

Sept 15. London is enjoying an unprecedented building boom. Figures released today show that since 1920, 250,000 new buildings have sprung up, transforming the city's appearance. Old slum areas, offices, and shops have gone to make way for bigger, better and more modern structures.

Many familiar landmarks have disappeared; Regent Street, in the West End, is now completely rebuilt and the last private houses in Oxford Street have been replaced by the new Gamage's store. Elsewhere, streets have been widened and remodelled. In central London alone, new housing has been provided for 200,000 people.

Sept 27. Golfer Bobby Jones completes the supposedly "impossible" Grand Slam and wins the US national amateur golf championship.

1930

OCTOBER

Su	Mo	Tu	We	Th	Fr	Sa
			1	2	3	4
5	6	7	8	9	10	11
12	13	14	15	16	17	18
19	20	21	22	23	24	25
26	27	28	29	30	31	

1. London: The Imperial Conference opens (→ 14/11).

1. UK: 14 miners die in an explosion at Grove Colliery near Walsall.

2. London: The government unveils plans to bring London Transport into public ownership under one authority.

5. Athens: The first Balkan Congress opens.

6. Berlin: Chancellor Heinrich Bruning meets with Adolf Hitler.

9. UK: Secretary for the Dominions J. H. Thomas loses his seat on the Labour Party executive to Oswald Mosley.

10. US: Three airlines merge to form Transcontinental and Western Airlines, TWA.

13. Berlin: There is uproar at the opening of the Reichstag when Nazi deputies turn up in uniform, illegal for civilians.→

14. New York: George Gershwin's musical "Girl Crazy" opens, it includes the song "I got rhythm".

16. France: A line of defences known as the Maginot Line is to be built along France's frontier with Germany.

18. UK: A slump in sales of the revised Book of Common Prayer is reported; the 1662 version is still preferred.

20. UK: Chaim Weizmann resigns as president of the Jewish Agency and of the Zionist Organisation.→

21. Germany: 240 are reported killed in a colliery explosion at Alsdorf in Prussia.

22. London: Richard Stafford Cripps is appointed Solicitor-General.

24. China: Chiang Kai-shek converts to Christianity.

27. London: Russian-born pianist Vladimir Horowitz makes his London debut.

30. Ankara: Turkey and Greece sign a treaty of friendship.

BIRTH

10. British playwright Harold Pinter.

Jews are furious at new Palestine plan

Oct 20. Dr Weizmann, president of the Jewish Agency, today accused the British government of planning to restrict Jewish immigration to Palestine. He said he intended to resign his presidency in protest against Mandate policy declared in the White Paper.

Describing the proposal yesterday, Ramsay MacDonald said it was a plan to give more self-government to the people of Palestine, both Jews and Arabs. In accordance with the terms of the Mandate, he said, the administration would favour neither Arab nor Jew at the expense of the other.

Zionists claim that this is a reversal of policy expressed in the Balfour Declaration of 1917, which offered a national home to the Jews. They are also offended by the Prime Minister's demand for concessions over their secessionist ideals. "It is no more a question of the Jewish people as a whole," said Dr Weizmann. "The Jewish people shrinks to such individual Jews as are now resident in Palestine."

Army officers seize power in Brazil

Oct 26. The revolutionary junta, which seized power in Brazil during a three-week popular uprising, today appointed Dr Getulio Vargas their provisional president.

The army officers took power following growing disenchantment with President Luis and his elected successor Dr Julio Prestes, both part of a clique that has dominated Brazil for the last 40 years. The US was taken by suprise by the uprising, having firmly supported the Luis government, and now fears her trade will suffer as a result.

After restoring law and order, the new government says its immediate aims will be the "reconciliation of the Brazilian family, the maintenance of all national pledges abroad and the pacification of all minds within the country".

Although the uprising was largely bloodless, it did claim 27 victims when the rebels opened fire on a German liner as she left Rio de Janeiro harbour (→ 1/11).

R.101 airship explodes in a ball of flame

The remains of the R.101 after a fireball killed 44 of its passengers.

Oct 5. Disaster struck the world's biggest airship last night when the R.101 exploded in a fireball as she hit a French hillside not long after setting out on her first journey to India.

A total of 44 people, including Air Secretary Lord Thomson, are known to have died in the crash near Beauvais, with just eight surviving. The King has expressed his "horror" at the tragedy, and although a full investigation into what caused it has yet to begin, it seems likely that the disaster will set the cause of airships back years.

Indications are that heavy rain may have been to blame, forcing the 777-foot-long airship to lose height. Engineer H.J. Leech said: "The rain suddenly came down, and so wetted the ship that she answered badly to the helm. Twice she dipped dangerously and then on the third occasion she ran nose first into a hill and burst into flames with a tremendous explosion."

The officer in command became aware that the £600,000 airship was dangerously near the ground and he sent an urgent message "slow down" to the engine car but it was too late.

The five and a half million cubic feet of hydrogen on board exploded. Within seconds she was reduced to nothing but a skeleton of twisted steel. Eye witnesses, woken from their beds by the roar of the crash, told of "a great yellow glare shot with tongues of flame". Another engineer, A.V. Bell, explained how a water tank burst above his head on impact and saved his life. "The water came drenching down on us. This was our salvation."

Nazi thugs attack Jewish traders

Oct 13. Today's meeting of the new Reichstag, in which the Nazis have 107 deputies, was marked by rowdy scenes in the chamber and violent anti-Jewish demonstrations in the streets of Berlin. The mobs, evidently Nazi supporters, chanted "Down with the Jews", and smashed windows of Jewish-owned stores. In the Reichstag Nazi speakers were shouted down by Communists.

1930

NOVEMBER

Su	Mo	Tu	We	Th	Fr	Sa
						1
2	3	4	5	6	7	8
9	10	11	12	13	14	15
16	17	18	19	20	21	22
23	24	25	26	27	28	29
30						

1. Brazil: President Vargas announces the dissolution of the Brazilian congress.

4. US: Roosevelt is re-elected Governor of New York as the Democrats win control of the House of Representatives (→ 7).

5. Italy: Prominent Italians are seized for plotting to overthrow Mussolini.

7. US: New York Governor Franklin Roosevelt denies he is seeking the presidency.

9. Austria: The Socialists are victorious in elections to the Austrian parliament; Nazis and Communists win no seats.

10. London: Over 30 people are injured when four elephants stampede during the Lord Mayor's Show.

11. Helsinki: The Finnish government introduces anti-Communist repressive measures.

12. London: The King opens a round-table conference on the future of India (→ 20).

13. France: 40 people are killed in a landslide in the city of Lyons.

14. Japan: Prime Minister Hamagushi is shot dead by an extreme right-wing militant.

17. US: Champion golfer Bobby Jones announces his retirement.

20. London: Indian delegates to the round-table conference pledge full equality for the "Untouchables" (→ 19/1/31).

20. London: The government announces it is to give opera its first state subsidy.

24. London: The London School of Economics survey says London has better education, less larceny, but lower morals and more fraud than in 1890.

25. Japan: 300 reported dead after an earthquake destroys the town of Mishioma.

28. Geneva: International Economic Conference to discuss the depression ends after ten days.

30. Germany: The Nazis are victorious in municipal elections in Bremen.

Ras Tafari crowned ruler of Abyssinia

Nov 2. Amid scenes of barbaric splendour, Ras Tafari was today crowned King of Kings and Emperor Haile Selassie of Abyssinia. The capital, Addis Ababa, was thronged by thousands of tribesmen, whose spears, shields and lionskin cloaks offered a striking contrast to the brilliant uniforms of foreign dignitaries. King George was represented by the Duke of Gloucester.

Haile Selassie, aged 41, robed in crimson velvet trimmed with gold, rode to church in the ex-Kaiser's coronation coach for a ceremony conducted by an archbishop of the Coptic church. Abyssinia and Liberia are the only states in Africa with black rulers.

Abyssinian ruler Haile Selassie.

Inconclusive end to Imperial conference

Nov 14. The Imperial Conference ended in London today without agreement on measures to encourage Empire trade. An offer of reciprocal tariff preferences made by Canada and other Dominions was rejected by the British because of determined opposition to tariffs in any form by the free traders in the Cabinet.

Another attempt is to be made at a meeting in Ottawa within 12 months. By then, many observers predict that the minority Labour government will have fallen.

1930

DECEMBER

Su	Mo	Tu	We	Th	Fr	Sa
	1	2	3	4	5	6
7	8	9	10	11	12	13
14	15	16	17	18	19	20
21	22	23	24	25	26	27
28	29	30	31			

2. Washington: President Hoover asks Congress for $150 million for the unemployed.

3. London: Opening of the Adelphi Theatre.

4. London: MacDonald promises electoral reform, a concession to the Liberals (→16/1/31).

7. UK: Publication of Oswald Mosley's manifesto advocating a public works programme to meet the economic crisis.

7. London: 13-year-old Yehudi Menuhin plays to over 5,000 at the Albert Hall.

10. Stockholm: Nobel Prizes go to Sir Chandrasekhara Raman (India, Physics); Hans Fischer (Germany, Chemistry); Karl Landsteiner (Austria, Medicine); and Sinclair Lewis (US, Literature). Peace Prize awarded in Oslo to Lars Soderblom (Sweden).

12. Spain: Republican rebels take a border town in the north of the country.→

15. London: A draft Highway Code is issued.

15. London: A Commons Select Committee recommends an end to the death penalty.

19. US: Stravinsky's "Symphony of Psalms" is first performed in Boston.

19. London: A bill is introduced to relax curbs on picketing (→28/1/31).

20. Moscow: Ex-premier Rykov is reported among recent victims of a purge.

23. India: The British governor of the Punjab is wounded in an assassination attempt.

30. US: The first photograph of the earth's curvature is exhibited in Cleveland, Ohio.

HITS OF 1930

The King's Horses.

On the sunny side of the street.

QUOTE OF THE YEAR

"Victory gained by violence is tantamount to a defeat".

Mahatma Gandhi, launching Indian civil disobedience.

Republican coup fails in Spain

Captured Spanish rebels.

Dec 16. Major Ramon Franco, the swashbuckling transatlantic airman, has been revealed as one of the leaders of the failed Republican coup in Madrid. More fortunate than Captain Galan and Lieutenant Hernandez, who were executed, Major Franco made a thrilling escape from Madrid airport with shells crashing round his plane. He landed on the proprty of Mr Cyril Charles, an Englishman, in Portugal, and has been interned. His brother, the highly respected General Francisco Franco, played no part in the plot.

New fibre, Nylon, is stronger than silk

What could become an important new synthetic fibre material was discovered this year by **Wallace Carrothers** of the Du Pont company in America. It has chemical linkages similar to those in silk, but after stretching is even stronger than the natural material. It has been named Nylon, and one of its first uses is likely to be for ladies' stockings.

The year also saw a startling new development in the world of physics. The British physicist **Paul Dirac** has suggested that subatomic particles, like the electron and the proton, have counterparts dubbed antiparticles. When a particle and its antiparticle collide, they both vanish in a burst of energy.

Arts: Garbo talks and calls for "vhisky"

This year talking pictures began to talk properly. "Garbo talks!" proclaimed the billboards for "Anna Christie". Her voice – deep and smoky – went perfectly with her looks when she uttered her first smouldering line: "Gimme a vhisky with ginger ale on the side – and don't be stingy, baby!"

Not so rosy is the outlook for her frequent co-star, **John Gilbert**, who came an inglorious cropper in "His Glorious Night"; when he opened his mouth to say "I love you, I love you, I love you", as he kissed a girl all the way up the arm, audiences giggled at his "pear-shaped" tones.

Swedish **Garbo** has a German challenger in **Marlene Dietrich**, who plays a cabaret singer who is the ruin of a pathetically obssessed **Emil Jannings** in "The Blue Angel" directed by **Josef von Sternberg**.

From France comes a **Rene Clair** film, "Sous les Toits de Paris", held together by its catchy title-song played on a street-singer's accordion. In "The Love Parade" the debonair **Maurice Chevalier** from France makes his mark opposite **Jeanette Macdonald**; it is directed with his usual elegance by the German, **Ernst Lubitsch**.

Alfred Hitchcock's first sound film, "Blackmail", uses the repeated sound of the word "knife" to play on the heroine's nerves. And **Lewis Milestone's** direction of "All Quiet on the Western Front" has won an Academy Award.

It has been a vintage year for performances in the theatre. **John Gielgud's** Hamlet at the Old Vic was hailed by critic **James Agate** as "subtle, brilliant, vigorous, imaginative ... the high water mark of English Shakespearean acting in our time". The play, uncut, lasts for four hours and the cast includes **Donald Wolfit** and **Martita Hunt** as Claudius and his queen.

The new star: Marlene Dietrich.

Paul Robeson, with his sonorous voice and presence, proved the superiority of a black actor's Othello opposite a simple and sincere Desdemona from **Peggy Ashcroft**.

The feuding couple of "Private Lives" were played by the author, **Noel Coward**, and **Gertrude Lawrence** with such relish that the Daily Telegraph critic wrote: "They smash gramophone records over each other's heads and roll on the floor still thumping, kicking, possibly biting. Do people of apparent breeding really do these things?" Very rude, Coward.

John Gielgud as Hamlet.

Dracula appears for the first time.

1931

JANUARY

Su	Mo	Tu	We	Th	Fr	Sa
				1	2	3
4	5	6	7	8	9	10
11	12	13	14	15	16	17
18	19	20	21	22	23	24
25	26	27	28	29	30	31

1. UK: The Road Traffic Act comes into force, introducing traffic policemen and compulsory third party insurance.

4. Vienna: Thousands of Nazis demonstrate outside a cinema showing the film "All Quiet on the Western Front".

6. Iraq: A royal palace dating from 550 BC has been discovered at the site of the ancient city of Ur.

8. London: The Royal Commission on Transport recommends faster trains and cheaper fares (→ 13/3).

10. Moscow: Vyacheslav Molotov, head of the Council of Commissars, says half of the USSR's agriculture will be collectivised by 1932 (→ 11/2).

15. Germany: Unemployment reaches 4.76 million (→ 24/2).

16. London: The Electoral Reform Bill ends plural voting (→ 3/2).

19. London: The Round Table Conference on India ends.→

21. London: MPs defeat the Education Bill, which would have raised the school-leaving age from 14 to 15 (→ 2/3).

22. London: Doctors claim to have discovered a method of immunisation against polio (→ 28/4/32).

26. India: Gandhi is released from prison (→ 1/2).

27. Paris: Pierre Laval forms a government.

28. London: MPs give the Trades Disputes Bill a second reading (→ 3/3).

29. Geneva: The League condemns Poland for mistreatment of the German minority in Polish Upper Silesia (→ 28/5/33).

30. UK: 26 feared dead in Whitehaven pit explosion.

30. Helsinki: A report claims that there are 662,200 prisoners in Soviet penal camps.

DEATHS

3. French commander Marshal Joseph Joffre (*12/1/1852).

23. Russian ballerina Anna Pavlova (*12/2/1881).→

Churchill quits over federal India plans

Jan 26. Winston Churchill resigned from Mr Baldwin's shadow cabinet tonight, after speaking openly in the Commons against his leader's India policy. He is backing the Indian princes and becoming increasingly isolated within the Tory Party in opposing the conciliation of Indian nationalism.

Mr Churchill denounced a preliminary report from the India Round Table Conference on the country's future constitution. This envisages ultimate Dominion status with a federal scheme of limited self-government in the meantime.

"The scheme offers no prospect of salvation," said Mr Churchill. However, Ramsay MacDonald, the Prime Minister, and Mr Baldwin both say it gives the best hope, and parliament is behind them. Gandhi has said civil disobedience will continue until full independence is granted (→ 1/2).

Pope Pius opposes sexual freedoms

Jan 8. Pope Pius XI today called on all Catholics to stem the tide of sexual liberation. In a 16,000-word encyclical he reinforced the prohibition of divorce and trial marriages and any form of birth control even within marriage. He hit out against abortion – "the legalisation of killing of innocent creatures before they are born". He also attacked films, newspapers and novels for not showing proper respect for the sanctity of marriage (→ 31/5).

Pavlova, mistress of the ballet, dies

Anna Pavlova as the Dying Swan.

Jan 23. Anna Pavlova, the dancer who inspired generations of ballet students, has died at her home, Ivy House on Hampstead Heath, at the age of 49. She had made her home in London since 1912, when she left St. Petersburg never to return.

She had been prima ballerina of the Imperial Ballet since 1906 – the year after Fokine created the Dying Swan solo for her. In 1909 Diaghilev brought her to Paris with his Ballets Russes as co-star with Nijinsky. His seemingly superhuman powers of soaring aloft overshadowed her and she left to found her own company and tour the world with it.

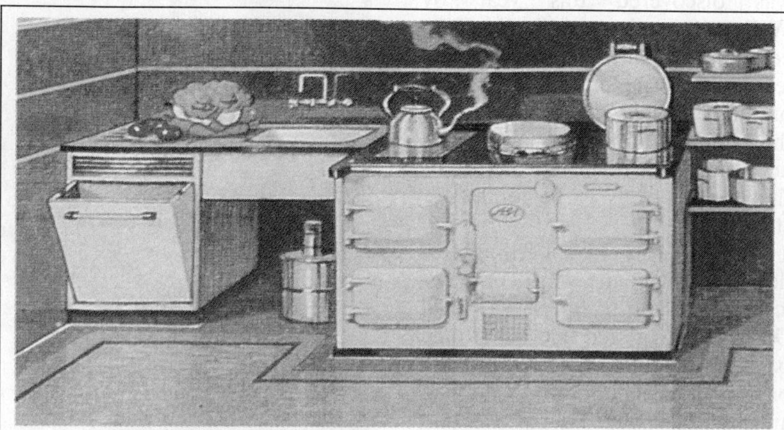

The Aga cooker is now the centrepiece of thousands of rural kitchens.

1931

FEBRUARY

Su	Mo	Tu	We	Th	Fr	Sa
1	2	3	4	5	6	7
8	9	10	11	12	13	14
15	16	17	18	19	20	21
22	23	24	25	26	27	28

1. India: Gandhi and his colleagues order civil disobedience to continue (→ 17).

2. Berlin: Nazi deputies in the Reichstag demand Germany's withdrawal from the League of Nations.

3. London: MPs give a second reading to the Electoral Reform Bill (→ 16/3).

4. Plymouth: Nine airmen die and two are hurt when an RAF flying-boat sinks.

6. Washington: The Senate agrees to $20 million aid for drought victims in the South and Mid-West.

8. France: Briton Joyce Cooper sets a European swimming record for the 100 metres of 1 minute 10 seconds.

11. Moscow: The government orders agriculture specialists to work on collective farms for two months without pay.

12. Japan: The first television broadcast is made of a baseball match.

15. Madrid: Police clash with Republicans following yesterday's resignation of premier Damaso Berenguer.→

17. India: Mahatma Gandhi has his first meeting with the Viceroy, Lord Irving (→ 4/3).

18. Madrid: Admiral Aznar forms a Royalist cabinet.→

19. UK: Charlie Chaplin gets a rapturous reception when he arrives on a visit.

21. Moscow: Leon Trotsky is stripped of his Soviet citizenship (→ 25/7/33).

23. Chicago: Judge Frank Patten orders the arrest of Al Capone (→ 12/6).

24. Germany: Unemployment now stands at 4.99 million.

28. UK: Imperial Airways start a new route connecting London with central Africa.

BIRTH

8. US actor James Dean (†30/9/55).

DEATH

23. Australian soprano Dame Nellie Melba (*19/5/1861).

Mosley's party of "vitality and manhood"

Feb 28. Sir Oswald Mosley today formed his own party after losing patience with Labour for rejecting his radical ideas for economic regeneration. He is calling it the New Party. It is dedicated to "complete revision of parliament to change it from a talk-shop to a workshop". It rejects both Liberal free trade dogma and Tory love of tariff protection.

"We will harness modern machinery and ask for a mobilisation of energy, vitality and manhood to save the nation," said Sir Oswald. The New Party – "a party of action" – favours greater state intervention in industry. It plans to fight at least 400 seats at the next election. Westminster's reaction was: 'perfectly absurd". Labour will boot Sir Oswald out (→ 10/3).

The founder of the New Party.

Bluebird flies into the record books

Feb 5. Proclaiming British supremacy in design, engineering and workmanship, Captain Malcolm Campbell today stepped elated from his specially-built Bluebird car after setting a new world land speed record on the flat sands at Daytona Beach in America. The 245mph feat, achieved in poor visibility, establishes the popular speed hero as the only living driver to have exceeded 200mph (→ 24/2/32).

Spanish King foils coup attempt

Feb 18. Martial law and press censorship, which were abolished only last week, were re-imposed in Spain today, as King Alfonso struggles to retain his Royal Prerogatives. No government has yet been formed, following the resignation of General Berenguer, and there is talk tonight of a "Cabinet of Monarchical Concentration". Meanwhile the carnival festivities in Madrid are continuing (→ 12/4).

Traffic "rationalisation" in Oxford St will ban horses and slow vehicles, prohibit turning round or waiting, and introduce automatic signals.

1931

MARCH

Su	Mo	Tu	We	Th	Fr	Sa
1	2	3	4	5	6	7
8	9	10	11	12	13	14
15	16	17	18	19	20	21
22	23	24	25	26	27	28
29	30	31				

2. London: Sir Charles Trevelyan resigns as Minister for Education.

3. Washington: "The Star-Spangled Banner" becomes the official US anthem.

3. London: The Trades Disputes Bill is dropped after Liberal amendments.→

4. India: The Viceroy agrees to end the government's salt monopoly in return for an end to civil disobedience (→ 9).

6. London: The government joins the US, France, Belgium and Canada in taking steps to stop Soviet grain dumping.

9. London: The Tories decide not to attend future Round Table talks on India.→

10. UK: The Labour Party expels Sir Oswald Mosley (→ 7/4).

13. London: The London Transport Bill will merge the capital's transport services under one body (→ 1/7).

19. London: Tory Duff Cooper wins the St. George's, Westminster, by-election.

21. Berlin: Germany and Austria sign a customs pact (→ 25).

22. UK: Six die when the Royal Scot derails near Leighton Buzzard.

25. Geneva: Britain urges the League to review the Austro-German trade pact (→ 5/4).

27. UK: Lord Beaverbrook ends his Empire Crusade movement.

27. UK: Cecil Taylor's Grakle wins the Grand National.

31. Nicaragua: 1,100 people die in Managuan earthquake.

31. London: A Court of Inquiry claims a gas leak caused the 1930 R.101 disaster.

BIRTHS

2. Soviet leader Mikhail Gorbachev.

11. Australian-born media magnate Rupert Murdoch.

DEATH

27. British writer Enoch Arnold Bennett (*27/5/1867).

Hundreds die as "peaceful protest" engulfs India

March 25. A most appalling orgy of bloodshed is raging through Cawnpore in India today, following the outbreak of communal rioting. The riots started when Moslem shopkeepers refused to obey the Hindu demand for a "hartal", a cessation of all work, in memory of the three agitators who were hanged in Lahore yesterday for murder.

After the first onslaught it was the Moslems who were the most bloodthirsty. Gangs of them paraded the streets and pounced on Hindu wayfarers, bludgeoning them to death. Shocked eyewitnesses speak of women and children having their throats cut and being thrown into drains. It is believed that over 200 people have died.

Hindu temples and Moslem mosques have been looted and set alight while houses of both communities are burning furiously all over the city. A detachment of Highland Light Infantry is now keeping order and a curfew order has been issued, forbidding people to leave their houses at night.

Orders have also been issued forbidding the carrying of lathis and the assembly of more than five persons. Meanwhile, Moslems are fleeing the city (→ 29/8).

Riot-stricken Cawnpore in ruins.

The Lib-Lab pact is heading for divorce

March 16. The minority Labour Government was narrowly outvoted again in the Commons tonight. This was its sixth defeat in the past year. It happened because the fragmented Liberals are no longer all acquiescing in keeping the government alive.

Its latest rebuff was the rejection of the clause in the Electoral Reform Bill abolishing university representation. The main part of the legislation provides for a limited forum of proportional representation, included to buy Liberal support. But Mr Lloyd George cannot now guarantee that backing, and the feeling at Westminster is that the Government will soon die.

Skirts see-saw in battle of hemlines

Fashion leaders like it long.

March 13. The return of the long skirt was condemned by women today as an infringement of their liberty and comfort. One speaker told a meeting of the National Union of Societies for Equal Citizenship that it was no coincidence that women had gained freedom in dress and freedom in politics at the same time. "When our clothes get long again and our legs are tied up, our minds will suffer," she said.

Though fashion leaders have pushed longer skirts for the past couple of seasons, a style favoured by the Queen, many women still go for shorter hemlines.

1931

APRIL

Su	Mo	Tu	We	Th	Fr	Sa
			1	2	3	4
5	6	7	8	9	10	11
12	13	14	15	16	17	18
19	20	21	22	23	24	25
26	27	28	29	30		

1. Mediterranean: 30 die when the French liner Florida is hit by a British aircraft carrier.

4. Nicaragua: Martial law is declared in Managua; an American is shot (→15).

5. Berlin: Germany confirms its customs deal with Austria (→17/5).

7. UK: The Labour Party bans all supporters of Oswald Mosley (→30).

10. London: Publication of a bill that would legalise Sunday opening of cinemas.→

12. Spain: Election results show that Republicans have swept the polls in most Spanish cities.→

15. Nicaragua: Sandinist rebels capture Puerto Cabezas after a brief campaign in which four US Marines died (→16).

16. Nicaragua: The US announces it will withdraw troops by the end of June (→26/9/32).

19. US: Unemployment stands at seven million.

20. Turkey: The Republican People's Party of Mustafa Kemal wins a landslide in national elections (→4/5).

21. London: Ex-King Alfonso XIII arrives in exile (→25).

22. Cairo: The government signs a friendship treaty with Iraq, Egypt's first treaty with another Arab state (→14/5).

25. Wembley: Second Division champions West Bromwich Albion beat Birmingham 2-1 in the FA Cup Final.→

25. Madrid: Ex-premier General Damaso Berenguer is jailed for alleged embezzlement (→11/5).

27. London: The Budget puts twopence on a gallon of petrol, which now costs one and fourpence halfpenny (→14/5).

30. UK: Mosley's New Party splits the Labour vote and lets in the Tory in the Ashton-under-Lyne by-election (→20/9).

30. China: Rebels under General Chan Chai-tong split with Chiang Kai-shek and take control of Canton.

Spain declared a republic as King flees

April 14. King Alfonso has abdicated and Spain has been declared a Republic. His downfall has been expected since the collapse of the military dictatorship of his friend, Primo de Rivera, last year and it became inevitable last week when the Republicans won an overwhelming majority in the Cortes, the Spanish parliament.

It was then made clear to him that the only alternative to leaving voluntarily was civil war. His abdication today came in a dramatic scene at his palace when he signed the document of renunciation.

With the ink still wet on the paper he stood up and, facing the statesmen who had forced him to abdicate, said: "I believe I have conscientiously served my country. Such has been my intention. At this moment I feel more a Spaniard than ever." Tonight, while Madrid celebrates, the Royal Family are on their way to London.

Republicans celebrate victory.

Bill allows movies to be shown on Sunday

April 20. The Sunday opening of cinemas is expected to become legal after MPs tonight gave a Second Reading to the Sunday Performances, Regulation, Bill, despite strong opposition. It was introduced by the government following a recent High Court decision that Sunday cinemas were illegal, and in the light of a "conservative" estimate that around 500,000 people were currently attending cinemas on the Sabbath. Supporters now intend to push for a relaxation of restrictions on other activities currently banned on Sundays such as concerts, exhibitions – of animals or inanimate objects – and public debates. Profits from such entertainments would go to charity. However, opponents of the Bill have vowed to continue their fight to prevent anything ruffling the calm of the Sabbath.

The triumphant West Bromwich Albion team after their 2-1 defeat of Birmingham City in the FA Cup Final at Wembley on April 25.

1931

MAY

Su	Mo	Tu	We	Th	Fr	Sa
					1	2
3	4	5	6	7	8	9
10	11	12	13	14	15	16
17	18	19	20	21	22	23
24	25	26	27	28	29	30
31						

1. New York: President Hoover officially opens the 1,245-foot, 102-floor Empire State Building.

4. Ankara: Mustafa Kemal is re-elected president of the republic by the Turkish National Assembly.

6. France: The French International Colonial Exhibition opens at Vincennes near Paris.

7. UK: Flight-Lieut. Waghorn dies from injuries in a plane crash on the 5th, the 42nd RAF airman killed this year.

9. UK: British cars take the first 12 places in the second "Double Twelve-Hours" race at Brooklands.

11. Spain: Riots and anti-clerical demonstrations break out in several cities (→8/6).

14. London: The Bank of England's lending rate of interest is cut to 2.5 per cent, the lowest for 22 years (→31/7).

14. Bologna: The conductor Arturo Toscanini is punched for refusing to play the Fascist anthem "Giovanezza" (→21).

14. Cairo: 23 die and 180 are killed in riots that mar voting in the Egyptian general election.

15. Rome: Pope Pius XI condemns Communism.→

17. The Hague: The International Court is to look into the legality of the Austro-German customs pact (→29/8).

19. Moscow: Stalin announces the second five-year plan for the Soviet economy.

21. Milan: Arturo Toscanini's passport is withdrawn (→10/6).

25. UK: 28,000 people visit Whipsnade Zoo, which opened on the 23rd, causing chaos.

26. France: Auguste Piccard and Charles Kipfer take off in a balloon in an attempt to reach the stratosphere.→

30. Rome: Mussolini suspends the organisation, Catholic Action.→

DEATH

12. Belgian violinist Eugene Ysaye (*16/7/1858).

Fascists are anti-Christian says Pope

May 31. In a tough Papal letter, "Non abbiamo bisogno", Pope Pius XI today distanced himself from Mussolini's Fascists. It is only two years since the Pope successfully healed the split between church and state in Italy. Now he has been forced to reopen it due to attacks on priests and church property and the closing by the Government of hundreds of Catholic organisations.

Fascism is "entirely given over to hate, to irreverence and to violence", said the Pope. Earlier this year he denounced both atheistic communism and laissez-faire capitalism (→11/2/32).

Swiss professor floats to 52,000 ft

May 28. A balloon flight to a height of 52,462 feet ended successfully last night, on an Austrian glacier. On board were the Swiss professor Auguste Piccard and fellow scientist Charles Kipfer, who became the first men to reach the stratosphere. An enclosed aluminium gondola, designed by Piccard, enabled them to survive the intense cold and rarified air at that height.

May 1. Opening of the Empire State Building – world's tallest.

1931

JUNE

Su	Mo	Tu	We	Th	Fr	Sa
	1	2	3	4	5	6
7	8	9	10	11	12	13
14	15	16	17	18	19	20
21	22	23	24	25	26	27
28	29	30				

1. Rome: Mussolini bans Catholic youth organisations.

2. London: Unusually, the King creates no new peers in his Birthday Honours List.

3. UK: Mr. J. A. Dewar's Cameronian wins the Derby at Epsom.

7. UK: Britain's most violent earthquake on record is felt from the English Channel to the Scottish Highlands.

8. Madrid: A mob lynches the city's Royalist ex-mayor (→28).

10. Hong Kong: Six of the 20-man crew of the sub HMS Poseidon are saved after it sank yesterday.

11. London: The government says it will not cut unemployment benefit (→29/6).

12. Chicago: Al Capone and 68 henchmen are charged with breach of Prohibition laws.→

14. France: 350 are reported killed when a pleasure boat capsizes on the River Loire.

15. Warsaw: Poland signs a trade and friendship treaty with the USSR (→24/8).

16. UK: An electric "tote" is used at Ascot for the first time.

17. Shanghai: The British arrest Nguyen Ai Quoc, also known as Ho Chi Minh, founder of the Indochinese Communist Party.

19. UK: Farmers are forbidden to move any livestock in an attempt to check an epidemic of foot-and-mouth.

22. Rome: The Fascist clampdown on secret societies continues as 124 Mafia members are jailed for life.

24. Moscow: The USSR signs a treaty of neutrality with Afghanistan.

28. Spain: Socialists win the general election (→14/7).

29. UK: Unemployment now stands at 2.66 million (→27/7).

DEATH

13. British businessman and philanthropist Jesse Boot, first Lord Trent, founder of Boots the Chemist (*2/6/1850).

Commission urges reductions in dole

June 4. To avert national financial disaster, unemployment pay should be cut by two shillings to 15/- a week for men and 13/- for women. The dole should be paid for not more than 26 weeks in any one year and unemployment insurance contributions must be increased.

These key proposals by a Royal Commission created panic today in government circles; since a substantial number of Labour MPs are implacably opposed to them, they are unlikely to be implemented. Mr MacDonald hopes to delay big economy moves until the autumn when another and more wide-ranging report on expenditure will be available. The cabinet is seriously divided over dole cuts and the TUC is up in arms (→11).

Feds tighten net on top liquor barons

"Scarface" Al Capone (centre).

June 23. American lawmen are closing in on "Scarface" Al Capone and another liquor baron, Arthur "Dutch Schultz" Flegenheimer. Beer-runner Flegenheimer, freed on $75,000 bail, is soon to face charges of tax evasion. This morning, federal agents found a dummy bank account in which he has deposited $856,000 over the past six months. Capone and 68 members of an alleged beer syndicate were charged on June 12 for 5,000 offences against the prohibition law. Capone is accused of conspiracy dating back to 1922. ▷

Maestro refuses to play Duce's anthem

June 10. Maestro Arturo Toscanini was today given permission to leave his homeland after nearly a month of virtual house arrest which saw his life and property threatened.

Last month Bologna decided to hold a Fascist festival for high officials, hoping to force Toscanini to play the Fascist anthem "Giovanezza", which he had earlier refused to do. When the maestro would not comply, Fascist thugs outside the theatre beat him and his wife with canes. They were not seriously hurt but Toscanini's passport was taken.

Though the Italian press was silent, many Italians were outraged. Days later, a student demonstration was broken up by police amid shouts of "Evviva Toscanini!" and "Abbasso il Fascismo" (→ 5/6/33).

Delay German debt payments says US

June 22. In a dramatic bid to get the world economy moving out of the slump, President Herbert Hoover has proposed that all war debt payments should be suspended for one year, from next month.

He says there is no question of cancelling any of the debts owed to the United States, but that the "abnormal movement of gold" into the US is causing international trade to stagnate. Mr Hoover's action came in response to an appeal from President von Hindenburg, who says Germany's gold reserves are running out (→ 13/7).

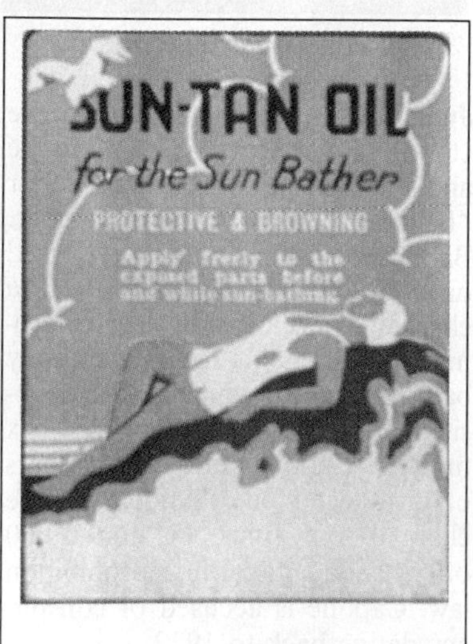

1931

JULY

Su	Mo	Tu	We	Th	Fr	Sa
			1	2	3	4
5	6	7	8	9	10	11
12	13	14	15	16	17	18
19	20	21	22	23	24	25
26	27	28	29	30	31	

1. Wimbledon: 21-year-old hopeful Fred Perry loses in the semi-final; the men's final will be all-American like last year (→ 4).

2. London: Labour MP John McGovern is forcibly expelled from the Commons.

3. London: The Coal Bill is introduced, fixing miners' pay and hours for a year (→ 7).

4. Wimbledon: Cilly Aussem beats Hilde Krahwinkel for the Women's Singles title; Sydney Wood is awarded the Men's Singles crown after Frank Shields withdrew before the final.

6. UK: Census results show the lowest rate of increase in the population since 1801; at 44.8 million it is almost at a standstill.→

8. London: After a rapid passage, the Coal Bill receives the Royal Assent.

9. Italy: Kaye Don sets a speedboat record of 110 mph in his boat Miss England II.

10. UK: Bentley Motors calls in a receiver.

13. Germany: All banks close until August 5 following the collapse of the Danatbank.→

14. Madrid: The first Republican Cortes, or Spanish parliament, opens (→ 3/8).

17. China: Rebels launch a drive on Tientsin (→ 18/9).

19. India: Three die and 50 are injured when police fire on a mob in Bangalore (→ 22).

22. India: Sir Ernest Hotson, acting Governor of Bombay, is wounded in an assassination attempt.

23. London: The Civil Service Royal Commission recommends opening almost all the service to women.

27. UK: Unemployment now stands at a record 2.71 million (→ 30/3/32).

29. Moscow: George Bernard Shaw meets Stalin.

BIRTH

1. French actress Leslie Caron.

Spending cuts call shocks Government

July 31. The most far-reaching reductions in state expenditure in the nation's history were proposed today to check a plunge to financial disaster. The Economy Committee, headed by Sir George May, former secretary of Prudential Assurance, recommended salary cuts for police, teachers and the armed forces, lower unemployment pay and many other drastic across-the-board economies. Altogether there would be a £96 million saving in a full year. Substantial tax increases are also advised.

The cabinet was shocked by the May report. Labour MPs were enraged. Parliament begins its summer recess tomorrow and, before leaving for his Scottish holiday, Mr MacDonald has appointed a cabinet commitee to consider the report with a view to action in the autumn.

Philip Snowden, the Chancellor of the Exchequer, tonight called on the Tory and Liberal Parties to share responsibility for this vast attack on public spending. Replying for the Tories, Mr Baldwin said: "Let us first know the Government's intentions."

In the parliamentary lobbies it was said that Sir Montague Norman, Governor of the Bank of England, has warned the Government that Britain's gold reserves are dwindling dangerously (→ 2/8).

First trolley buses to run in London

July 1. Twenty years after they made their debut in Yorkshire, trolley buses begin regular services in the London area for the first time this month. Sixty vehicles are being introduced in the Kingston and Twickenham suburbs – and these are expected to foreshadow a large-scale switch from trams to trolleys.

These "trackless trams" have become increasingly popular in many British cities. They are powered by electricity drawn from an overhead cable drawn to the bus by roof-mounted poles. As tramlines become due for renewal, many operators are switching to trolleys since overhead wires are cheaper and don't interfere with other traffic (→ 1/7/33).

The "trackless tram" in London.

Britain starts to drift southwards

July 6. The latest census returns, published today, show that Britain's population has reached a new high of 44,790,485 – packed 685 to the square mile. The 1920s saw 30 per cent fewer deaths than the 1900s.

The statistics reveal a steady drift to the south; northern counties report a drop of nearly half a million. Cities, especially London and in the Home Counties are growing at an unprecedented rate. In the last ten years, 14 towns have doubled their populations.

Credit for Germans as mark collapses

July 22. After a three-hour emergency meeting of finance ministers in London yesterday, Britain, the US and France agreed to renew the recent credits for Germany for three months, instead of three weeks. This, it is hoped, will tide Germany over her present difficulties until a more comprehensive settlement, possibly including further credits, can be worked out. German banks have been shutting their doors to halt a run on funds as confidence in the mark, at home and abroad, collapsed (→ 5/8).

1931

AUGUST

Su	Mo	Tu	We	Th	Fr	Sa
						1
2	3	4	5	6	7	8
9	10	11	12	13	14	15
16	17	18	19	20	21	22
23	24	25	26	27	28	29
30	31					

2. London: The Bank of France and New York Federal Reserve each lend the Bank of England £25,000,000.→

3. China: Hundreds die when a dam on the River Yangtse-Kiang near Hankow bursts during a typhoon (→31).

3. Spain: Catalonia votes overwhelmingly in favour of self-government.

5. Germany: Banks re-open for normal trading for the first time since July 13 (→7/1/32).

6. UK: J.A. Mollison completes a flight from Australia in a record 214 hours.

10. Cuba: President Machado declares martial law to quell a rebellion (→20).

12. New York: Gangster "Legs" Diamond is sentenced to four years for liquor offences (→18/12).

17. UK: 14 die as gales and floods hit the country.

20. Cuba: Fighting breaks out in Havana (→8/8/33).

24. Moscow: The USSR and France sign a non-aggression pact.

26. UK: The Labour Party national executive, Labour MPs and the TUC decide to oppose the government (→28).

27. New York: Bankers agree to give Britain £60 million in short-term credit.

28. UK: Ramsay MacDonald is ousted as Labour leader; he is succeeded by Arthur Henderson (→29/2/32).

29. London: Mahatma Gandhi arrives in Britain to attend the second Round Table conference on India (→15/9).

29. Vienna: Austria pulls out of the customs pact with Germany before the International Court judgement (→5/9).

31. China: Thousands are now reported dead and homeless after the damburst on the rain-swollen River Yangtse-Kiang.

DEATH

7. US jazz musician Bix Beiderbecke (*3/10/1903).

Coalition takes over as Labour falls

Aug 24. The Labour Government is dead and the nation is suffering its worst financial crisis. An all-party "Government of Co-operation" has been formed to cope with the emergency. Led by the outgoing Prime Minister Ramsay MacDonald, it will take "whatever steps may be deemed necessary" to restore confidence in sterling "on which the well-being of a large part of the civilised world rests".

This was the climax to the political crisis of the past fortnight as the British economy lurched towards the precipice. A run on the pound reached desperate proportions in the last few days, as the cabinet wrangled endlessly and finally split over remedial action.

Mr MacDonald resigned when a majority of the cabinet, backed by the TUC, shrank from endorsing draconian spending cuts. He advised the King to invite other party leaders to join in forming the new Government which will embark on full-blooded retrenchment policies. The King agreed.

Tory and Liberal chiefs had been in emergency sessions at Buckingham Palace while the cabinet writhed in its agony of conscience. It is stressed in Whitehall that this National Government is unlike past coalitions. Indefinite party collaboration is out. There will be another General Election when the economy is on the mend.

The new and smaller MacDonald Cabinet has ten members – four Labour, four Tory and two Liberal. With most Labour MPs already denouncing the Prime Minister as a traitor to his party, it is clear that Mr Baldwin will be the Government's strong man. Mr MacDonald and the few Labour MPs staying loyal to him are certain to be expelled from the party ranks within a few days.

In modern times there has never been such a party convulsion. Mr MacDonald said in a broadcast: "I have changed none of my ideals. I have a national duty."

The crisis became uncontrollable when Sir Montague Norman, Governor of the Bank of England, warned the Prime Minister that national bankruptcy was near. With Central Europe also in financial collapse, other countries are demanding gold from Britain in large quantities instead of holding sterling, in which they have no confidence.

This called for tough action but the cabinet was impotent. As number two man now, Stanley Baldwin becomes Lord President of the Council, while the leading Liberal, Sir Herbert Samuel, is Home Secretary. They are backing Mr MacDonald's denial of a bankers' ramp against Britain (→27).

Heads of the National Government: Baldwin (l.) and Ramsay MacDonald.

Waiting for the latest news outside the locked gates of Downing Street.

1931

SEPTEMBER

Su	Mo	Tu	We	Th	Fr	Sa
		1	2	3	4	5
6	7	8	9	10	11	12
13	14	15	16	17	18	19
20	21	22	23	24	25	26
27	28	29	30			

1. London: MacDonald decides to give domestic problems priority over any international conferences (→ 7).

1. London: The first night of trial floodlighting of important buildings causes traffic chaos as sightseers pour into town.

2. Belgrade: King Alexander ends his dictatorship.

5. The Hague: The International Court says the Austro-German customs pact was unacceptable.

7. London: The King decides to take a pay cut of £50,000 a year while the economic crisis lasts (→ 8).

8. London: Police arrest 17 demonstrators in Whitehall protesting at the government's emergency measures (→ 15).

11. British Honduras: Over 700 deaths are reported when the colony is lashed by 100 mph winds.

13. UK: George Stainforth achieves a record 404 mph in a Supermarine with a Rolls-Royce "R" engine (→ 29).

13. Austria: A coup d'etat by the Heimwehr (national guard), led by the extreme right-wing General Walter Pfrimer, fails (→ 20/5/32).

15. UK: 12,000 Royal Navy sailors strike at Invergordon in protest at cuts in servicemen's pay.→

20. Glasgow: Sir Oswald Mosley is chased and stoned by a crowd of Socialists and Communists (→ 23/4/33).

23. London: The Stock Exchange re-opens after being closed for two days because of the economic crisis (→ 28).

24. India: 19 people are killed by police during anti-Hindu rioting in Kashmir.

28. Copenhagen: Denmark abandons the gold standard; Norway, Sweden and Egypt did so yesterday (→ 11/12).

29. UK: Stainforth breaks his own air speed record by flying at 408.8mph.

DEATH

29. British artist Sir William Orpen (*27/11/1878).

Crisis: Britain devalues the pound

Sept 20. Britain has been forced off the gold standard. In a dramatic Sunday night anouncement, the Government said this had been decreed to prevent further withdrawals of gold, and to stop foreign speculation against the pound. Emergency legislation will be rushed through Parliament tomorow.

It is expected that this epoch-making move will lead to a 30 per cent devaluation of sterling, from $4.86 to around $3.40 to the pound. The move follows exhaustion of foreign credits and failure of the fierce emergency Budget ten days ago to check the run on sterling. Foreign bankers were shaken when sailors at Invergordon mutinied against the ten per cent budget cut in pay for all State employees.

Panic erupts outside the Bank of England after the announcement.

Philip Snowden, the Chancellor of the Exchequer, who stayed at the Treasury when the National Government was formed, said that he is now taking powers to introduce exchange controls, but does not expect these will have to be used. He considers that British citizens will patriotically decline to send funk money abroad. Lobby correspondents were invited to write that there is no excuse for panic.

With the new Government having won comfortable votes of confidence, the party leaders – MacDonald, Baldwin and Samuel – are beginning to settle into their novel partnership. "The typhoon is passing," said the Prime Minister. But there is still widely-strewn wreckage and no guarantee of quiet weather (→ 23/8).

Crisis: the unemployed protest and the Royal Navy mutinies

Sept 30. Throughout yesterday and last night there were clashes between police and demonstrators in London as a month of strikes and even a mutiny, protesting at the Government's austerity programme, grew to a close. Despite allegations that those involved were Communists, most were simply unemployed workers.

There was a riot near Battersea Town Hall tonight as 5,000 demanded the restoration of full unemployment pay, while in the West End postal workers, protesting at pay cuts, brought traffic to a halt.

Sterling has been devalued by 30 per cent, the gold standard has been abandoned to stop the run on the pound, and all servicemen have found their pay cut by as much as 25 per cent to stop the country "living beyond its means".

Police and demonstrators in London fight for possession of the Red Flag.

One of the most disturbing protests came at Invergordon, on the Cromarty Firth, when 12,000 ratings on 15 ships in the Atlantic Fleet staged what has been described as a mutiny in protest at the new pay rates, which leave many men with only 25 shillings a week. They were angry that news of the cuts was only passed on when they had left their home ports for the isolated base, so avoiding trouble in navy towns like Portsmouth.

The men, led by Able Seaman Len Wincott, occupied a shore canteen, had meetings on a recreation ground and prevented the ships from sailing for two days. But, although they had access to firearms, violence was limited to a beer glass, which hit an officer's head, and a few broken windows. The men finally returned to the ships singing "The more we are together the merrier we will be" (→ 2/10).

Japan makes move into Manchuria

Sept 18. Japanese troops guarding the South Manchurian railway today launched a surprise attack on the Chinese garrison at Mukden. An official report states that between 70 and 80 Chinese soldiers were killed.

"Firing began at 10 pm, shells continuing to fall every ten minutes," it stated. The Governor of Manchuria ordered his garrison not to retaliate because he believes the attack is designed to provoke an incident to provide a pretext for a Japanese occupation (→28/10).

Gandhi makes plea for Indian freedom

Sept 15. In courteous but unequivocal language, Mr Gandhi today demanded that India be given its independence. Putting his proposals to the Round Table Conference at St James's Palace, he argued that if any settlement was reached it could only be on the basis of a partnership such as existed between two absolute peoples.

He spoke of India being held, not by force, but by a "silken cord of love". He still aspired to be a citizen, "not in the Empire, but in a Commonwealth" (→4/11).

Sept 6. Adolf Hitler is greeted by a sea of brown shirts at Gera. The Nazis have just won power in the government of Thuringia.

1931

OCTOBER

Su	Mo	Tu	We	Th	Fr	Sa
				1	2	3
4	5	6	7	8	9	10
11	12	13	14	15	16	17
18	19	20	21	22	23	24
25	26	27	28	29	30	31

1. London: Oxford Street's new traffic lights are reported to speed up evening rush hour traffic by 90 per cent.

2. Glasgow: 49 arrests follow two nights of riots in protest at the government's emergency measures (→30/3/32).

6. London: A general election is called for October 27.→

9. Leeds: William Walton's cantata "Belshazzar's Feast" is first performed, conducted by Malcolm Sargent.

11. Berlin: Hitler and the Nationalist leader Alfred Hugenberg agree a pact to defeat Chancellor Bruning (→17).

13. UK: Premiere of Noel Coward's show "Cavalcade".

14. Madrid: Manuel Azana becomes president on the resignation of Alcala Zamora (→10/12).

16. Madrid: The government legalises divorce (→24/1/32).

17. Germany: 100 people are hurt in clashes between Nazis and Communists in the city of Brunswick (→15/11).

20. Dublin: 12 groups, including the IRA, are banned, and a tribunal is set up for "treasonable activities".

22. Chicago: Al Capone is jailed for 11 years for tax dodging, the longest term ever given in the US for the offence.

23. Cyprus: 150 British troops arrive after riots in which the Limassol commissioner's house was burnt down (→25).

25. Cyprus: The Bishop of Kyrenia is arrested after further rioting.

26. New York: First performance of Eugene O'Neill's play "Mourning Becomes Electra".

31. Geneva: 21 nations agree to a year's moratorium on arms production.

DEATHS

18. US scientist and inventor Thomas Alva Edison (*11/2/1847).→

21. Austrian playwright Arthur Schnitzler (*15/5/1862).

Election rout for Labour

Ramsay MacDonald is returned as PM in National Government landslide.

Oct 28. The National Government stays in power after the largest election landslide in history. Labour is completely routed. With the General Election results nearly all declared, it is known tonight that the final score will be 554 seats for the Government and only 56 against.

Ramsay MacDonald carries on as titular Prime Minister. But supporting him there are now 473 Tory MPs and just 13 from his own National Labour party, along with 68 assorted Liberals. Two years ago 288 MPs were elected on the straight Labour ticket and there were 260 Tories. Now, in the astonishing upheaval, there are just 52 Labour. The voters have overwhelmingly given all-party government the "doctor's mandate" blank cheque it sought for continuing the economic recovery treatment.

There were no signs during the campaign that the leaders, who teamed up on a temporary basis this summer, yet want to revert to normal party politics, despite their differences. Except for George Lansbury, every member of the former Labour Cabinet has lost his seat. Sir Oswald Mosley's New Party is destroyed and Mr Lloyd George has lost his influence. "A response beyond our dreams," said Mr MacDonald (→3/11).

End comes for inventor Thomas Edison

Oct 18. Thomas Alva Edison, probably the most prolific inventor of all time, died early this morning at his home in New Jersey. He was 84.

Almost without formal education, Edison began as a newsboy on a train at 12. When he was 15 the father of a small boy he rescued from the railway track taught him telegraphy, which led indirectly to his first successful invention: a stock ticker machine, which he sold for $40,000. With the proceeds he started his amazing career. He was responsible for, or made major contributions to, the telephone, the gramophone, electric light and moving pictures. In all he patented 1,100 inventions.

Edison in his laboratory.

1931

NOVEMBER

Su	Mo	Tu	We	Th	Fr	Sa
1	2	3	4	5	6	7
8	9	10	11	12	13	14
15	16	17	18	19	20	21
22	23	24	25	26	27	28
29	30					

3. London: Labour does badly in local elections, winning only three out of 28 London boroughs.

4. London: Herbert Samuel is appointed leader of the Liberal Party in succession to David Lloyd George.

5. London: The new cabinet has Baldwin as Lord President of the Council and Neville Chamberlain as Chancellor.

6. Rome: The government awards prizes to Italy's biggest families (→ 11/2).

7. London: The BBC announces a new Empire-wide radio service from a new station to be built at Daventry.

8. US: Scientist Frederick Allison announces the discovery of a new element, halogen.

10. UK: Publication of "Rumour and Nightfall", a novel by a promising new author, Graham Greene.

15. Germany: The Nazi Party wins elections in the state of Hesse (→ 7/12).

16. London: The government introduces the Abnormal Importations Bill to put a 100 per cent duty on all imports (→ 20).

17. UK: Gandhi demands complete control for India over her own foreign and military affairs (→ 1/12).

19. Belfast: The luxury liner Bermuda is gutted by fire while in dock.

20. London: The Abnormal Importations Bill gets Royal Assent after a rushed passage through Parliament.

20. UK: 42 die in an explosion at Bentley Colliery, Yorkshire.

20. UK: Rolls-Royce buys Bentley Motors.

25. Australia: The Labour government is defeated.

30. India: The government takes drastic new powers to suppress terrorism in Bengal (→ 6/12).

30. UK: His Master's Voice and Columbia have merged as Electrical and Musical Industries (EMI).

Gandhi goes native to meet his Emperor

Nov 4. Mahatma Gandhi took tea with King George V and Queen Mary, the Emperor and Empress of India, at Buckingham Palace today. The King was formally dressed in a frock coat, but Mr Gandhi wore his simple loin-cloth and his torn woollen shawl, which had been mended with "khadi" cloth. It had been somewhat soiled by the London weather so he wore it inside out.

The leader of India's nationalist movement bowed to the Emperor and the two men shook hands warmly. They then withdrew from the other guests and spoke together for five minutes.

Mr Gandhi later refused to reveal what passed between them, but when asked if the King had given him any encouragement, he replied: "Encouragement is given not by kings but by God."

It is understood, however, that all was not as friendly as it seemed on the surface. The King is much displeased by the way the Indians boycotted the visit of the Prince of Wales, and expressed that displeasure in his usual forthright manner. It does not seem to have been a constructive meeting (→ 17).

Gandhi sets example of economy.

US peace call halts Japanese in Manchuria

28 Oct. American diplomacy has scored a temporary success by arranging a truce in the three week old Manchurian war, provoked by Japan's capture of Mukden. Henry Stimson, the US Secretary of State, has negotiated a truce while the League of Nations studies the dangerous situation.

The Manchurian incident began with a surprise attack on Mukden launched by plotting officers of the elite Kwantung army, stationed in the Liaotung Peninsula and along the South Manchurian Railway.

Sino-Japanese relations had already been embittered by two other incidents. Japan claims that the Chinese had tried to sabotage a bridge on the Japanese owned railway. Then came the arrest and execution of a Japanese officer spy. But the real purpose of the Mukden attack was to satisfy Japanese militarists and to seize power throughout Manchuria (→ 28/1/32).

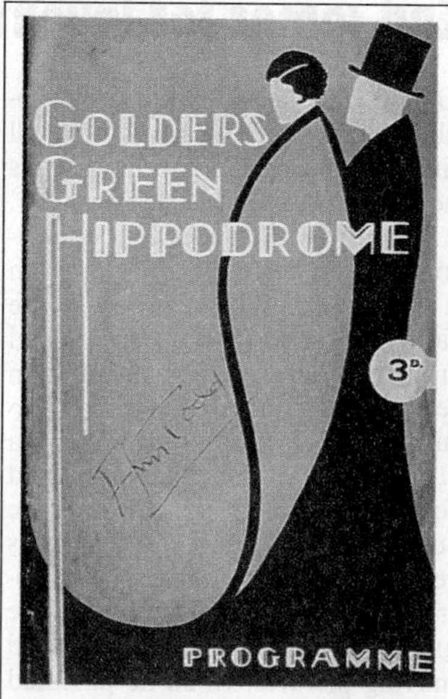

Prince of Wales in "Buy British" drive

Nov 16. The Government is bringing in the ever-popular Prince of Wales in an effort to give its "Buy British" campaign a boost. He is to broadcast tonight from the Birmingham radio studio at 7.10 pm. The campaign also aims to promote British goods overseas, so that later in the evening a Government talk on the theme will be broadcast to Australia.

Meanwhile the Government will rush a law through next week to curb the dumping of goods which have been flooding in from Europe and Russia.

1931

DECEMBER

Su	Mo	Tu	We	Th	Fr	Sa
		1	2	3	4	5
6	7	8	9	10	11	12
13	14	15	16	17	18	19
20	21	22	23	24	25	26
27	28	29	30	31		

1. London: The Round Table conference on India ends in failure (→ 6).

6. India: The Bengal Congress will boycott British goods.→

7. Germany: Reported that the Nazis would sterilise some races to ensure "Nordic" dominance (→ 12).

10. Stockholm: Nobel Prizes go to Carl Bosch and Friedrich Bergius (Germany, Chemistry); Otto Warburg (Germany, Medicine); and Erik Karlfeldt (Sweden, Literature). Peace Prize awarded in Oslo to Jane Addams and Nicholas Murray (US). No Physics Prize.

10. US: The Chrysler motor company is to open a factory in Britain.

11. Tokyo: The Japanese government abandons the gold standard (→ 11/7/32).

12. Germany: Hitler tells British and American journalists he is a democrat (→ 22/2/32).

15. UK: Following London experiments, traffic lights are to be used all over Britain, it is announced (→ 16/5/33).

18. New York: Gangster Jack "Legs" Diamond is shot dead as he sleeps in the state capital of Albany.

22. Rome: A falling roof wrecks the Vatican Library.

25. London: Britain and France call for new reparations talks (→ 7/1/32).

30. Holland: Adalbert Smit forms a Dutch Nazi party.

31. Moscow: Sergei Rachmaninov's music is banned as decadent.

HITS OF 1931

Goodbye.

The Peanut Vendor.

Just one more chance.

QUOTE OF THE YEAR

"The only methods we shall use will be English ones. We shall rely on the good old English fist."

Sir Oswald Mosley, founder of the New Party, 1931.

Zamora wins in Spain

Alcala Zamora acknowledges the cheers after his election.

Dec 10. Senor Niceto Alcala Zamora was elected to be Spain's first constitutional President today by the National Assembly. A lawyer of great reputation and a noted orator, he first entered the Chamber of Deputies in 1905.

At first a monarchist, he became a republican under the regime of the military dictator Primo de Rivera. Declaring that he had lost all faith in the existing monarchy, he led his liberal group into the republican camp. It was this action, more than any other, which led to King Alfonso's abdication last April.

Senor Zamora is a man of some wit and the people of Madrid gleefully passed on his comment on the elections planned by his predecessor. "They would not be brutally sincere," he said, "but sincerely brutal." (→8/7/33)

British crack down as India talks fail

Dec 30. A firm and clear warning was issued to Mr Gandhi and the Congress leaders today by the Viceroy, Viscount Willingdon, that the Government of India will no longer tolerate subversive activities. The Viceroy referred to the "determined efforts of a most unconstitutional and seditious character" and said he would not allow non-co-operation to impede the work of constitutional reform.

This is the latest step in the turmoil following the failure of the London Round Table talks. Since then, Mr Gandhi has returned to India, threatening further disobedience; a British magistrate has been killed by two girl students; Jawaharlal Nehru and Abdul Gaffar Khan, the "Frontier Gandhi", have been arrested, and troops have fired on rioters (→1/1/32).

The definition of television changes

The development of television continued apace during 1931. HMV demonstrated a system with much higher definition than the 30 lines per picture of current BBC transmissions. Rival systems are under development in the United States and elsewhere.

The world's first atom-smashing machine was tested in Cambridge. Built by **John Cockcroft** and **Ernest Walton**, it accelerates the subatomic particles called protons with a high electric voltage. These are then used as projectiles to bombard and smash target atoms.

Nobel winners included the German chemists **Carl Bosch** and **Friedrich Bergius** for their work on high pressure reactions – used for making ammonia from atmospheric nitrogen – and **Otto Warburg** for work on respiration.

Arts: ballet finds home at Sadler's Wells

British ballet took a big step forward with the transfer of **Ninette de Valois's** company from the Old Vic to Sadler's Wells, where they now perform regularly when the opera is not there. Miss de Valois, born in Ireland as Edris Stannus, was a soloist with Diaghilev's company and has choreographed several ballets, including, this year, "Job" to the music of **Ralph Vaughan Williams**.

Constant Lambert, her musical director, is the composer of "The Rio Grande", set this year as a ballet by **Frederick Ashton**, who dances with the company founded by **Marie Rambert** at the Mercury Theatre. For the Camargo Society he devised "Facade" to a suite of **William Walton's** music with great success. **Alicia Markova**, an English-born ballerina formerly with Diaghilev's Ballets Russes, is joining de Valois.

The musical event with the greatest impact was the premiere of "Belshazzar's Feast" at the Leeds Festival, conducted by **Dr Malcolm Sargent.** The words of the Book of Daniel have been set by **William Walton** for baritone, chorus and massive orchestral forces. The story goes that **Sir Thomas Beecham** said jokingly to the composer: "Why not throw in a brass band as well?" Walton added two brass bands.

The "wonder child", **Yehudi Menuhin**, gave his first London performance in the Beethoven violin concerto under Beecham, while **Dame Nellie Melba**, who gave her last performance at Covent Garden in 1926 before the King and Queen, has died in Sydney aged 69.

Mary Clare in "Calvalcade".

Death also removed **Arnold Bennett**, whose industry in producing a daily stint of several thousand words never failed him. His Five Towns novels were full of characters fighting to better their lot in a grim environment and usually succeeding by their wits, like Denry in "The Card". Last year Bennett returned to his best form in "Imperial Palace", the world of a luxury hotel laid bare in all its backstairs detail. Bennett loved good living, but it was typical of him to know all about the army behind the scenes.

The two smash hits of 1931 are "City Lights", **Chaplin's** silent challenge to sound films, and **Noel Coward's** "Cavalcade" of English life since 1899.

Charlie Chaplin in "City Lights".

Novelist Arnold Bennett.

1932

JANUARY

Su	Mo	Tu	We	Th	Fr	Sa
					1	2
3	4	5	6	7	8	9
10	11	12	13	14	15	16
17	18	19	20	21	22	23
24	25	26	27	28	29	30
31						

1. India: The Congress Party decides to resume its campaign of civil disobedience (→4).

2. USSR: 68 die in a rail crash outside Moscow.

4. India: Gandhi and fellow Nationalist leader Vallabhai Patel are arrested.→

7. Berlin: Chancellor Bruning says Germany is unable to meet her reparations repayments (→9/7).

8. Japan: Emperor Hirohito escapes an assassination attempt.

9. Paris: Veteran statesman Aristide Briand resigns through ill health (→16/2).

13. India: Opening of the Lloyd Barrage or Sukkur Dam, the world's largest irrigation project.

14. US: Figures show unemployment stands at 8.2 million (→5/8).

18. France: 18 die in bus accident between Abbeville and Paris.

19. London: The US Hoover Electric Cleaner Co. has decided to build a factory at Perivale in Middlesex.

21. New York: The Automobile Club of America is to be dissolved, a victim of the Depression.

23. New York: State Governor Franklin Delano Roosevelt says he will run for president for the Democrats (→2/7).

24. Spain: The Jesuits are expelled and their property confiscated.

25. Moscow: The USSR and Poland sign a non-aggression pact.

27. UK: 50 crew members are feared dead when the Royal Navy submarine M.2 sinks.

28. China: The Japanese occupy Shanghai.→

30. Finland: The government lifts prohibition of alcohol.

DEATH

7. French politician Andre Maginot, builder of the military fortifications known as the Maginot Line (*17/2/1877).

Advancing Japanese capture Shanghai

The Japanese launch their successful attack on the city of Shanghai.

Jan 31. The capture of Shanghai by Japanese forces confirms the belief that the Manchurian Incident was planned as a preliminary to what amounts to a full-scale invasion of China. As bitter fighting continues on the northern front in Manchuria, the Japanese troops are now encamped in key positions in other parts of China.

Chinese troops are still fighting back in the north. They report the successful ambush of a supply train, but an assault upon enemy positions north of Harbin was driven off after sharp hand-to-hand fighting, with the loss of hundreds of lives. No notice has been taken of cautious attempts by the League of Nations to persuade Japan to halt its military actions in Manchuria.

Ill-fated attempts by the United States to end the war, including the diplomatic initiatives of Henry Stimson at the State Department, have proved a miserable failure in deterring the aggression of the Japanese military forces.

President Herbert Hoover has dispatched the 31st Infantry Regiment to join British, Italian and French reinforcements to protect the large foreign population of Shanghai. Two Royal Navy cruisers, with a battalion of infantry and artillery, are also heading for China (→1/2).

Dartmoor governor nearly killed in riot

Jan 25. Months of brooding discontent erupted into violence last night as convicts went on the rampage in Dartmoor Prison. Seventy inmates and six warders were injured when truncheon-wielding police charged the rioters. The prison governor and a Home Office Commissioner owed their lives to lifer George Donovan, who had previously been reprieved an hour before he was due to be hanged, when he rushed between them and the mutiny's leaders. Troops with machine guns surround the prison tonight to foil escape attempts.

Scott, editor of the Guardian, dies

Jan 1. Mr C.P. Scott, the man who made the Manchester Guardian one of the country's most respected newspapers, died early this morning, aged 85. He was one of the last great owner-editors. The paper was founded by his uncle, John Taylor, as a sevenpenny weekly in 1821 and Scott succeeded Taylor's son as editor in 1872.

In his 57 years in the editor's chair he stamped his personality and his liberal and pacifist views on the paper. His concern for elegant prose was legendary and he brought in young men from the universities to write it.

Congress leaders arrested in crackdown on Gandhi "cabinet"

Jan 6. The round-up of Congress leaders started in the early hours of this morning, following the Government's declaration that the party's Working Committee, often called "Gandhi's Cabinet", was illegal.

Mr Gandhi himself was arrested two days ago. He was prepared for gaol, taking a pair of sandals, a mattress, warm clothing and a portable spinning wheel with him. It is expected that about 100 of his colleagues will now join him.

Meanwhile, business is at a standstill in Bombay, and shops selling foreign cloth are being picketed by women dressed in orange-coloured saris. So far, however, there has been no trouble in the city (→20/9).

Government forces pursue Gandhi supporters after their leader's arrest.

1932

FEBRUARY

Su	Mo	Tu	We	Th	Fr	Sa
	1	2	3	4	5	6
7	8	9	10	11	12	13
14	15	16	17	18	19	20
21	22	23	24	25	26	27
28	29					

1. China: Japanese troops land in Nanking.→

2. Geneva: Disarmament talks begin, attended by representatives of 60 nations (→ 5).

4. London: The Chancellor announces a 10 per cent tariff on imports, with concessions for the Empire (→ 29).

5. Geneva: France proposes the creation of an international police force.

7. Oslo: The Scandinavian countries, Belgium and Holland sign a convention for economic co-operation.

12. London: A bill is introduced to improve youth courts, raise the age of juveniles and ban whipping of under 14s.→

15. Berlin: Hindenburg agrees to seek re-election as German president (→ 22).

16. Paris: Laval's government resigns after the French senate rejects votes for women (→ 19).

18. London: A study says nurses should get £30 more for the first year, £35 for the second and work no more than 13 hours a day.

19. Paris: Paul Painleve forms a left-leaning government (→ 10/5).

22. Berlin: Hitler says he will run for president against Hindenburg (→ 25).

24. US: Malcolm Campbell beats his own land speed record at Daytona, reaching 253.4 mph (→ 22/3/33).

25. Berlin: Hitler is granted German citizenship (→ 13/3).

29. London: Britain abandons free trade as the Import Duties Bill gets the Royal Assent (→ 25/4).

BIRTHS

6. French film director Francois Truffaut (†21/10/84).

18. Czech film director Milos Forman.

27. British-born US actress Elizabeth Taylor.

DEATH

10. British author Edgar Wallace (*4/12/1875).→

Japan sets up Manchurian puppet state

Feb 19. The Japanese government has established a puppet regime in occupied Manchuria. Since last autumn a successful campaign has left the Japanese army in control of the whole of Manchuria. The rich north eastern industrial province is to be re-named Manchukuo -' a further extension of Tokyo's pretence that it acted in self-defence.

The Japanese claim that the population is not Chinese and that anyway the Nationalist government does not exercise sovereignty. General Chiang Kai-shek's regime, weakened by civil war and undermined by communist plotting, has been unable to put up much resistance to the invaders (→ 1/3).

Proclamation of the new state.

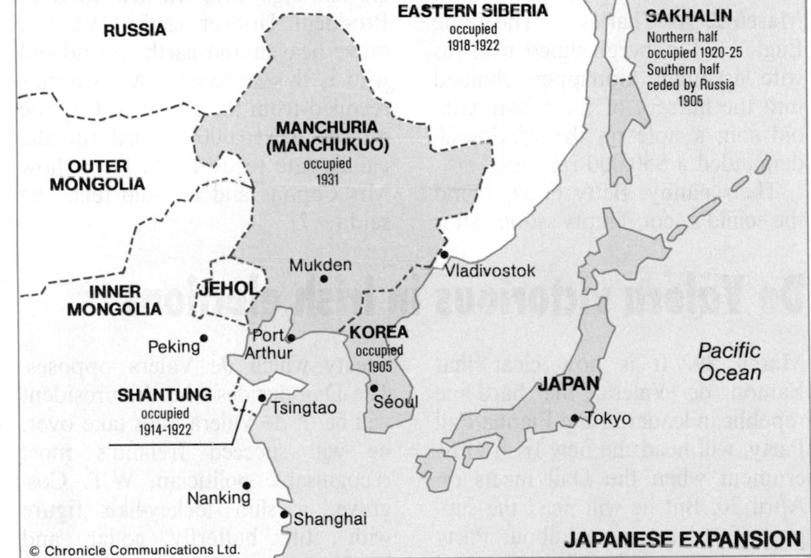

Edgar Wallace dies 170 books later

Feb 10. The death occurred today in Hollywood of Britain's most prolific author, Edgar Wallace, who has 170 books and plays to his name and sales of five million a year, most of them "shockers".

Wallace made himself into a journalist by writing letters to the newspapers. He was a foundling, who was adopted by a Billingsgate fish porter, and at 11 was selling papers in Ludgate Circus. He joined the army, then reported the Boer War.

No one would take his first book, "The Four Just Men", so he published it himself. It sold 3,250,000 copies but he had sold the rights for £75. He was 56.

Pope Pius XI meets Italian dictator

Feb 11. The Italian dictator, Benito Mussolini, met Pope Pius XI for the first time today and promptly threw himself upon his knees and kissed the Pope's hand. Pius then invited Il Duce into his library where they talked for an hour.

The meeting was organised to mark Lateran Treaty Day, a holiday created three years ago to celebrate the settling of the differences between the Holy See and the government. Today's meeting also celebrated the tenth anniversary of the Pope's coronation and signals the mending of relations between Fascism and Catholicism (→ 9/7/33).

Poor children to be spared the whip

Feb 12. The House of Commons gave the first reading today to a Bill, which will abolish the whipping of children under the age of 14, and make major changes in juvenile court procedure.

Despite overall approval of Mr Oliver Stanley's proposals, some MPs argued that they would introduce a level of class discrimination into legalised corporal punishment. As one member put it: "Why abolish for the children of the poor what was good for the children of the rich in public schools?"

Feb 23. One of the many casualties of riots which followed a demonstration in Bristol city centre, protesting about high unemployment.

1932

MARCH

Su	Mo	Tu	We	Th	Fr	Sa
		1	2	3	4	5
6	7	8	9	10	11	12
13	14	15	16	17	18	19
20	21	22	23	24	25	26
27	28	29	30	31		

1. China: 2,000 deaths are reported in clashes between Chinese and Japanese troops at Shanghai (→5).

2. US: 100,000 join in the manhunt for the Lindbergh baby's kidnappers.→

3. US: States begin study of 20th Amendment to shorten "lame duck" period between election and inauguration (→6/2/33).

7. US: The Lindberghs receive two notes from the kidnappers of their baby (→12/5).

9. Manchuria: Pu Yi, the last Emperor of China, is installed as head of the Japanese puppet state of Manchukuo (→5/5).

13. Germany: Hindenburg fails to secure a majority in the presidential election; the result will be decided in a run-off (→10/4).

15. London: The industrialist Samuel Courtauld gives Home House, Portman Square, to his new art institute.

15. London: The BBC makes its first broadcast from the new Broadcasting House (→20/5).

18. Sydney: Opening of the Sydney Harbour Bridge, the world's longest single-arch span.

18. UK: W. Parsonage's Forbra wins the Grand National at Aintree.

22. Dublin: De Valera tells Britain he intends to abolish the Loyal Oath to the King (→27).

27. Dublin: The IRA warns de Valera it will not cease its activities until a republic is secured.→

31. UK: A new shell can pierce 12 inch armour plate from a distance of ten miles.

DEATHS

5. US musician and "March King" John Philip Sousa (*6/11/1854).

7. French statesman Aristide Briand (*28/3/1862).

14. US industrialist George Eastman, founder of Kodak (*12/7/1854).

Air hero Lindbergh's baby is kidnapped

Lindbergh's wife and baby son.

March 2. As Charles – "The Lone Eagle" – Lindbergh dined with his wife last night, kidnappers climbed into the nursery of their 20-month-old son; a note on the windowsill demanded a $50,000 ransom.

Their nanny, Betty Gow, found the child's cot empty soon after 10pm. She and Colonel Lindbergh made a frantic search of the New Jersey mansion before he announced to his wife: "Anne, they have stolen our baby".

The kidnappers left few clues. Apart from the illiterate ransom note, which read: "We warn you for making anyding public ... the child is in gut care", police found a home-made ladder and muddy footprints.

The kidnapping of Charles A. Lindbergh Jr. has started the most intensive man-hunt in history, with 100,000 officers and civilian volunteers searching along the entire Eastern seaboard.

Within hours, the small town of Hopewell was packed with reporters and sightseers. In Washington, President Hoover said: "We will move heaven and earth to find out who is this criminal." As America recoiled from the news, Al Capone offered a $10,000 reward for the child's safe recovery. "I know how Mrs Capone and I would feel," he said (→7).

De Valera victorious in Irish elections

March 29. It is now clear that Eamon de Valera, the hard-line republican leader of the Fianna Fail Party, will head the new Irish Government when the Dail meets on April 20. But he will need the support of at least some Labour Party members to put him in office and keep him there. It looks an uneasy alliance. Labour supports the Fianna Fail policy on domestic issues, but it is pro the Anglo-Irish Treaty which de Valera opposes. The Dail decides who the president will be; if de Valera does take over, he will succeed Ireland's most recognisable politician, W.T. Cosgrave, a slim jockey-like figure with stiff butterfly collar and bowler hat at a slight angle.

De Valera won't have it easy. His old comrades in the IRA warned him last night: "The Treaty must go lock stock and barrel." (→30/4)

Joblessness blamed for rise in crime

March 30. Mass unemployment is a major factor in the growing number of crimes recorded in Britain, the Home Office claimed today.

Figures for 1930 revealed an increase of 12,450 to 147,031 – with larceny the most prevalent. The greatest increase was in the industrial north and Wales, where unemployment was at its highest. The absence of parental supervision during the war was said to be another factor (→30/10).

Sexy rector in West London love nest

The rector who may be defrocked.

March 31. Frequent visits to London by a Norfolk clergyman, and his association with teenage girls, brought him before a Consistory Court today. The Rev. Harold Francis Davidson, rector of Stiffkey, faces defrocking if the charges against him are proved.

The prosecution alleged that Davidson, aged 60, spent Sundays in his parish and weekdays in a rented bed-sitter in Shepherd's Bush. Waitresses in Lyons and ABC teashops had complained of his pestering them and a model told the court that he had set her up in lodgings.

Two girls complained that Davidson had taken them to the rectory to work as servants – but left them destitute, forced to sleep in fields (→12/6).

Chief witness Barbara Harris.

1932

APRIL

Su	Mo	Tu	We	Th	Fr	Sa
					1	2
3	4	5	6	7	8	9
10	11	12	13	14	15	16
17	18	19	20	21	22	23
24	25	26	27	28	29	30

2. London: The brilliant young Tory MP Edward Marjoribanks, stepson of Lord Hailsham, shoots himself.

4. Pittsburgh: Scientists isolate Vitamin C.

7. London: Sir Austen Chamberlain is elected chairman of the London School of Hygiene and Tropical Medicine.

7. France: 49 are reported killed when the French submarine Promethee sinks off Cherbourg.

11. South America: Nine volcanoes along 400 miles of the Andes and Patagonia begin erupting.

13. Berlin: The government bans the Nazi paramilitary groups the SS and the SA (→24).

14. New Zealand: Civil service pay cuts cause the country's worst-ever riots; 23 police and hundreds of rioters are hurt.

16. Bucharest: The palace of King Carol of Rumania is destroyed by fire.

17. Ethiopia: Emperor Haile Selassie abolishes slavery.

19. London: The Budget imposes only one new tax, fourpence on tea.

23. London: Newcastle United beat Arsenal 2-1 in the FA Cup Final at Wembley.

24. Berlin: The Nazis lead in four state elections; in the Prussian state parliament their seats rise from six to 162 (→25/5).

25. UK: New import tariffs come into force; 30 per cent on manufactured goods and 33.3 per cent on steel (→28/9).

26. London: Peers approve the Motor Traffic Bill, making drivers who kill guilty of manslaughter.

27. UK: Imperial Airways begins a regular service between London and Cape Town.

28. US: Scientists announce the development of the first vaccine against yellow fever.

BIRTH

27. French actress Anouk Aimee, born Francoise Dreyfus.

Hindenburg beats Hitler for presidency

President Paul von Hindenburg: the victor after a humiliating run-off.

April 10. After contemptuously brushing aside his challenger in Germany's presidential election as "that Bavarian corporal", Paul von Hindenburg then found himself forced into a humiliating run-off ballot in order to secure the necessary absolute majority. He has received over 19 million votes, an increase of 800,000 on the first-round figures and enough to give him 53 per cent of votes cast. But Adolf Hitler, the fanatical Nazi leader, increased his share of the vote, by 2,000,000, to over 13 million – a rise of almost 37 per cent. Hindenburg, 85, legendary victor of Tannenberg in the Great War, had the support of Social Democrats and centre parties and his victory should have been a walk-over. But Hitler, aided by his propaganda chief Josef Goebbels, mounted a massive campaign with funds donated by Ruhr industrialists, addressing mass meetings and distributing films and records of his speeches. Though he lost, Hitler sees the result as a victory for National Socialism.

FIRST BALLOT: March 13 1932
Total votes: 37.65 million

V. Hindenburg (Centre parties SPD) 49.6%
Other Candidates
Winter
Duesterberg DNVP 6.8%
Thälmann (Communist party)
Hitler (National Socialism Nazi party) 30.1%

SECOND BALLOT: April 10 1932
Total votes: 36.49 million

V. Hindenburg (Centre parties SPD) 53% ELECTED BY AN ABSOLUTE MAJORITY
Other Candidates
Thälmann (Communist party)
Hitler (Nazi party and DNVP) 36.8%

Shakespeare to play in a "jam factory"

April 23. The new Shakespeare Memorial Theatre beside the Avon at Stratford was opened on Shakespeare's birthday by the Prince of Wales, just six years after its Victorian Gothic predecessor was burnt to the ground.

Considerable criticism has been provoked by the building's appearance. It was designed by an unknown woman architect, Elizabeth Scott, who won the competition. She stated that it was designed purely to meet the practical requirements of presenting plays, with no thought for the exterior, which has been compared to a "jam factory".

Today's inaugural production was "Henry IV" – Parts I and II both being given.

Pennine hikers risk prison for pleasure

April 24. Five men were arrested today after a "mass trespass" in which thousands of hikers went for a walk on Kinder Scout, near Edale in the Peak District. The men were arrested after clashes with gamekeepers who were seeking to keep the ramblers off private land. It was the most dramatic day yet in the increasingly bitter battle over the right for public access to mountains and moors. The Peak District, close to Sheffield and Manchester, is in the forefront of the campaign. Out of 150,000 acres, only 1,212 are open to the public. Most moors are privately owned and used for grouse shooting.

Countryside access is in dispute.

Dail drops loyalty oath to British King

April 30. It was after midnight when the Dail voted 77 to 71 to abolish the oath Irish MPs take promising to be faithful to the British monarch. The President, Eamon de Valera, said: "Unlike the British Dominions, we have never freely admitted that our right to sovereign independence derives from a British statute."

In reply Frank McDermot said: "We're an ancient nation behaving like guttersnipes", adding that "we could always remove ourselves from the Commonwealth" (→19/5).

1932

MAY

Su	Mo	Tu	We	Th	Fr	Sa
1	2	3	4	5	6	7
8	9	10	11	12	13	14
15	16	17	18	19	20	21
22	23	24	25	26	27	28
29	30	31				

1. Moscow: A million people take part in the annual May Day parade.

3. Palestine: An Anglo-American expedition reports the discovery of three Neanderthal skeletons.

5. China: Japanese troops withdraw from Shanghai after an armistice is signed (→ 1/10).

8. France: The parties of the Left win a majority in national elections (→ 3/6).

11. London: Britain warns the Irish Free State it will lose tariff preference if it abolishes the Loyal Oath (→ 19).

13. UK: 23 Dartmoor convicts are sentenced to between six months and 12 years for the prison revolt in January (→ 25/1).

15. Tokyo: Militarists assassinate premier Ki Inukai.

19. Dublin: The bill abolishing the Loyal Oath becomes law (→ 6/7).

21. Athens: Eleutherios Venizelos resigns as premier (→ 25).

21. Ireland: Amelia Earhart lands after flying the Atlantic in record time.

23. UK: Premiere of Ivor Novello's new play "Party".

25. Athens: A new government is formed under premier Andreas Papanastasiou.

25. Berlin: The Prussian state parliament chamber is wrecked in a fight between Nazis and Communists (→ 30).

30. Dublin: The biggest ever sweepstake opens on the Epsom Derby with £4 million in prize money.

30. Berlin: Heinrich Bruning resigns as Chancellor (→ 31).

31. Berlin: Hindenburg invites Franz von Papen to form a government (→ 1/6).

BIRTH

24. British playwright Arnold Wesker.

DEATH

7. French statesman Paul Doumer (*22/3/1857).→

French President is slain

President Doumer is rushed to hospital, mortally wounded by gunshots.

May10. France remains in a state of national shock following the assassination of President Paul Doumer. Details of his murder are now emerging. He went from the Elysee Palace to attend a charity event at the Rothschild Foundation, where books were being sold for the benefit of ex-servicemen authors.

He was talking to one of these writers, the novelist Claude Farrere, when a large man pushed through the crowd, pulled out a revolver and started firing, crying, "This is only the beginning". He was eventually disarmed and the President was rushed to hospital, but his wounds were fatal and he died 14 hours later. The assassin claimed that his name was Paul Brede, but it has been established that his real name is Gorguloff, a White Russian emigre with a hatred for Communism. The Doctors have pronounced him insane.

Today the National Assembly met to appoint M. Doumer's successor. The Deputies chose, by an overwhelming majority, the moderate, Albert Lebrun (→ 13/9).

A three-piece pyjama suit and a cocktail outfit on show at this year's British Industries Fair.

Body of Lindbergh baby found in wood

May 12. A truck driver found the body of Charles A. Lindbergh's kidnapped baby today in a wood just five miles from the American hero's home. The child had been bludgeoned to death. It is 73 days since 20-month-old Charles Jr. was taken from his nursery while his parents dined downstairs.

Every bank in America has been alerted to look for the serial numbers of the $50,000 ransom paid to the kidnapper. They are beginning to appear in northern New York City. A police "profile" of the kidnapper suggests he is a carpenter of German extraction, probably living in the Bronx (→ 16/8).

Moderate Dollfuss in power in Austria

May 20. Engelbert Dollfuss, the Christian Socialist leader who rose to prominence as head of the Austrian Farmers' League, has been appointed Chancellor of Austria to succeed Herr Karl Buresch, who failed to form a government.

Herr Dollfuss's position is not particularly secure. He has a majority of only one vote in the Austrian Parliament, and it took him two attempts to get that. His first one failed when he tried to ignore the other parties, so he has been forced to form a coalition with the so-called Patriotic Bloc (→ 10/5/33).

BBC opens its new London headquarters

May 20. The new headquarters of the BBC in Portland Place stands at the top end of Regent Street, looming like a liner under its radio masts. It was officially opened today although the first programme was broadcast from the building two months ago – Henry Hall and the BBC Dance Orchestra.

The elliptical building, designed by Val Myers and Watson Hart, is of ferro-concrete faced with Portland stone. The relief over the entrance representing Prospero and his airy spirit, Ariel, is by Eric Gill. A plaque in the entrance hall bears the motto "Nation Shall Speak Peace Unto Nation".

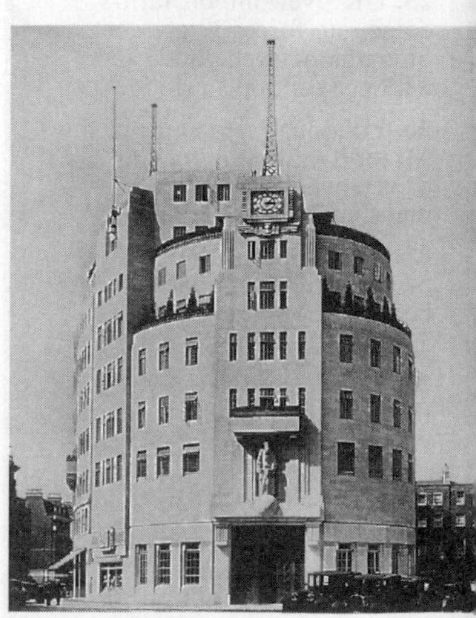

The south front of the BBC's HQ.

1932

JUNE

Su	Mo	Tu	We	Th	Fr	Sa
			1	2	3	4
5	6	7	8	9	10	11
12	13	14	15	16	17	18
19	20	21	22	23	24	25
26	27	28	29	30		

1. UK: Mr. Tom Walls' April the Fifth wins the Derby at Epsom.

1. Berlin: Franz von Papen forms a cabinet that excludes the Nazis (→4).

3. Paris: Edouard Herriot becomes premier following the election defeat of the Right under Andre Tardieu (→14/12).

4. Berlin: The Reichstag is dissolved in advance of elections next month (→14).

5. Rome: Police foil a conspiracy to assassinate Mussolini (→18).

6. UK: The world's fastest train, the Cheltenham Flyer, reaches a record average speed of 81.6 mph over 77 miles.

7. The Hague: The International Court settles a Franco-Swiss border row in favour of Switzerland.

10. UK: Gene Sarazen wins the golf Open Championship, the ninth US victory in succession.

12. UK: The Rector of Stiffkey struggles to grab the Bible from a stand-in clergyman during a service (→8/7).

14. Berlin: Hitler undertakes not to oppose Chancellor von Papen (→16).

16. Berlin: Von Papen lifts the government's ban on the Nazi paramilitary groups, the SA and SS (→17/7).

16. US: Herbert Hoover is renominated as Republican presidential candidate (→2/7).

18. Rome: Two men are executed for plotting to assassinate Mussolini.

20. Brussels: The governments of Belgium, the Netherlands and Luxembourg are studying the idea of a customs union.

21. New York: American Jack Sharkey wins the world heavyweight boxing title off German Max Schmeling.

25. London: India's cricketers begin their first test match at Lord's against Douglas Jardine's England side.→

29. Bangkok: The military coup leaders announce a new liberal constitution.→

Siamese army ends absolute monarchy

June 29. The Siamese army tonight seized power in Bangkok in a coup d'etat against the absolute monarchy which has ruled for 60 years. Senior officers described their action as a "peaceful revolution". The only casualty so far is the Royal chief of staff, killed as the ruling family was hunted down.

King Prajadhipok was absent from the capital. For several months he had attempted to quell open protest and rising discontent in Siam brought on by the economic crisis. Many government employees lost their jobs and joined those hostile to dictatorial Royal rule.

No leader of the revolutionaries has yet been named, but the military declared it was their aim to restrict the King's power by imposing constitutional rule. The cabinet will be made to resign and the Princes are to be forced out.

India takes first steps on Test stage

June 28. India took a major step in international cricket at Lord's today, completing their first-ever Test match. Despite losing to England, they made the host team work hard, dismissing Sutcliffe, Holmes and Woolley for a mere 19 runs on the first morning, thanks to the hostile pace bowling of Mohamed Nissar. However, they succumbed in turn to the unaccustomed pace of Bill Voce and the young Yorkshireman Bill Bowes, playing in his first Test.

ROYAL AIR FORCE
DISPLAY
HENDON SAT 25TH JUNE

1932

JULY

Su	Mo	Tu	We	Th	Fr	Sa
					1	2
3	4	5	6	7	8	9
10	11	12	13	14	15	16
17	18	19	20	21	22	23
24	25	26	27	28	29	30
31						

2. Wimbledon: Helen Moody (nee Wills) wins her fifth Women's Singles title, beating Helen Jacobs; H. Ellesworth Vines beats "Bunny" Austin for the Men's Singles crown.→

5. UK: The first main-line electric express train runs from London Bridge station to Three Bridges in Sussex.

5. Lisbon: Antonio de Oliveira Salazar is appointed premier at the head of a Fascist regime.

6. London: MPs approve a bill putting duties on imports from the Irish Free State (→18).

8. UK: The Rector of Stiffkey is found guilty of disreputable association with women (→21/10).

11. Basle: The World Bank calls for a return to the gold standard (→19/4/33).

13. London: Britain and France agree to confer on the debts they owe to the US.

17. Berlin: 15 die in clashes between Communists and Nazis (→20).

18. Geneva: Turkey becomes the 56th member of the League of Nations.

18. Dublin: The Irish senate approves a bill authorising tit-for-tat tariff reprisals against Britain (→2/1/33).

19. London: King George V opens Lambeth Bridge.

20. Berlin: Von Papen removes the Socialist premier of the state of Prussia (→26).

21. UK: Doctors say young people slim, smoke and drink too much and have too little sleep, clothes or food.

25. Paris: The trial opens of President Doumer's alleged assassin, Paul Gorguloff (→27).

26. Berlin: War minister Kurt von Schleicher says Germany is ready to rearm.→

27. Paris: Gorguloff is sentenced to death (→13/9).

30. Los Angeles: The Olympic Games are opened (→14/8).

DEATH

23. Brazilian aviator Alberto Santos-Dumont (*20/7/1873).

Nazis double seats in the Reichstag

Nazis shout "Heil Hitler".

July 31. German voters today handed Adolf Hitler's brownshirts a resounding election victory: with 230 seats the National Socialists now form the biggest party in the Reichstag, though they are still short of a majority in the 608-seat chamber.

In four years since the 1928 elections, the Nazis have won some 13 million new votes, most of them at the expense of the middle-class centre parties. The Social Democrats, with 133 seats, lost many working-class votes to the Communists, the third largest party, with 89 seats (→4/8).

Lausanne deal ends German war debts

July 9. After three weeks of negotiations in Lausanne, Switzerland, the Allies today acted to ease Germany's economic crisis by suspending all reparations payments. Edouard Herriot, the French Premier, spoke of a new era of goodwill, and of violence giving way to reason; but Franz von Papen, the new German Chancellor, made a long speech about the sufferings of Germany (→22/12).

Roosevelt to run on Democrat ticket

July 2. Franklin Delano Roosevelt has won the Democratic nomination for US President. Although he failed to win his home state of New York – which went to the popular Catholic, Alfred Smith – he got enough votes on the fourth ballot for a convincing victory.

A cousin of former President Teddy Roosevelt, he lives in Hyde Park, an English-style estate in the Hudson Valley. He was stricken by polio in 1921, but fought back to become Governor of New York in 1928. He championed the "forgotten men" of the Depression. Today he said: "I pledge you, I pledge myself to a new deal for the American people" (→31/10).

"Four Musketeers" win sixth Davis Cup

July 31. The "Four Musketeers" of French tennis – Jean Borotra, Rene Lacoste, Jacques Brugnon and Henri Cochet – reached another milestone in their remarkable partnership, by defeating the US 3-2 in Paris: their sixth consecutive Davis Cup win.

Borotra, aged 34 and known as the "Bounding Basque", had to draw on all his reserves to beat the brilliant Wimbledon champion, Ellsworth Vines, 13 years his junior, in the singles.

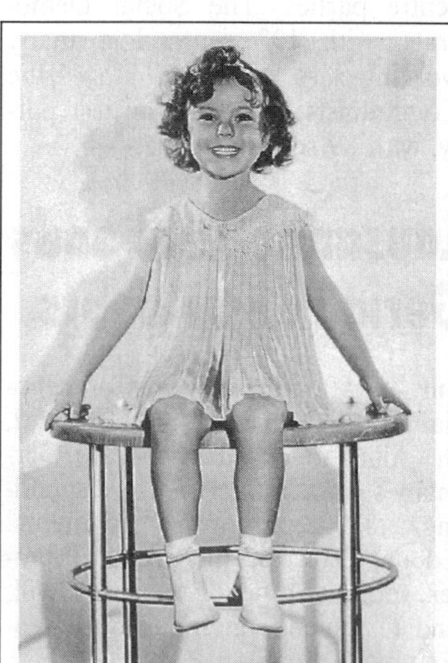

Four-year-old Shirley Temple is well on her way to screen fame.

1932

AUGUST

Su	Mo	Tu	We	Th	Fr	Sa
	1	2	3	4	5	6
7	8	9	10	11	12	13
14	15	16	17	18	19	20
21	22	23	24	25	26	27
28	29	30	31			

2. Los Angeles: Britain's Tommy Hampson wins the 800 metres Olympic gold medal in a world record time of 1 minute 49.8 seconds.→

4. Berlin: The government threatens to impose stiff measures to counter street rioting (→9).

5. US: Figures show unemployment now stands at around 11.6 million.

6. Italy: The first Venice Film Festival opens.

9. Berlin: The government issues a decree imposing the death penalty for political terrorism (→13).

11. US: President Hoover admits that Prohibition has failed and should be abolished (→22/3/33).

11. Spain: General Jose Sanjurjo is arrested after the failure of a monarchist revolt in Seville (→6/9).

13. Berlin: Hitler refuses to serve as vice-chancellor under Von Papen (→22).

14. Rome: Marconi completes work on the first short-wave radio.

16. US: A second son is born to Anne and Charles Lindbergh.

20. London: At the Oval, Jack Hobbs protests at the head-high bowling of Yorkshire's Bill Bowes (→23/1/33).

22. Berlin: Nazis riot in court after five other Nazis are convicted of murdering a Communist.→

25. Manchester: Premiere of Noel Coward's play "Words and Music".

27. UK: Three-letter car number plates appear; the first in London is AMY 1.

30. Berlin: Nazi Hermann Goering is elected president of the Reichstag (→1/9).

BIRTH

17. Trinidadian writer Vidiadhar Surajprasad Naipaul (→1986).

DEATH

14. US dog and film star Rin Tin Tin.

German Chancellor bars Nazis from power

Aug 29. A depressed Adolf Hitler is today reported to be under heavy pressure to mount a putsch after his attempts to become German Chancellor have been frustrated by the present Chancellor, Franz von Papen, and President von Hindenburg, who gave Hitler a lecture on the street violence of his Nazi Storm Troopers. Von Papen, scion of an impoverished Westphalian aristocratic family, wants to see an authoritarian state, but not one run by the Nazis.

Hitler, whose 1923 putsch fiasco landed him in gaol, insists he will seek power only by legal means. With 230 seats making them the largest party in the Reichstag, the Nazis are talking of voting with the Communists to bring down von Papen (→30).

Will Hitler try another putsch?

Texan typist is star of Los Angeles Games

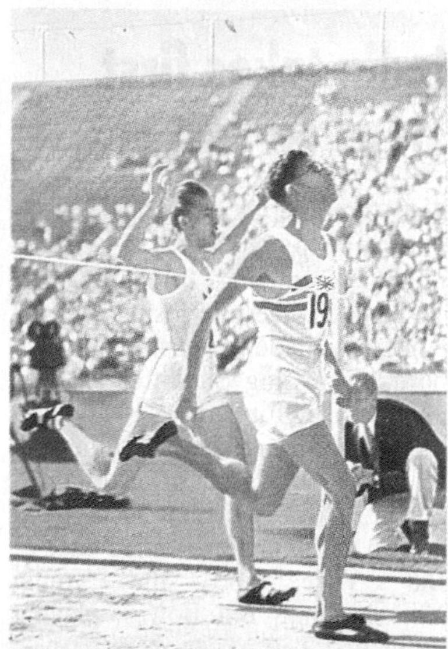

Briton Hampson wins 800m gold.

Aug 14. Los Angeles successfully countered fears that entries to their Olympic Games would drastically fall because it was so far away. They subsidised athletes' travel, built an "Olympic village" and drew vast crowds to the Coliseum.

Tommy Hampson won one of four golds for Britain, but the US topped the medals' table and provided the most remarkable athlete of the Games: Mildred "Babe" Didrikson. Much to her disgust, this 18-year-old Texan typist was only allowed to enter three events. Even so she set a world record for the 80 metres hurdles, won the javelin, and took silver in the high jump – the only Olympic athlete ever to have won medals for running, jumping and throwing.

Eddie Tolan of the USA (extreme left) on his way to victory in 100m final.

1932  Los Angeles

Men Athletics

100m
Eddie Tolan USA *10.3
Ralph Metcalfe USA 10.3
Arthur Jonath GER 10.4

200m
Eddie Tolan USA *21.2
George Simpson USA 21.4
Ralph Metcalfe USA 21.5

400m
William Carr USA ** 46.2
Benjamin Eastman USA 46.4
Alexander Wilson CAN 47.4

800m
Thomas Hampson GBR ** 1:49.7
Alexander Wilson CAN 1:49.9
Philip Edwards CAN 1:51.5

1500m
Luigi Beccali ITA *3:51.2
John Cornes GBR 3:52.6
Philip Edwards CAN 3:52.8

5000m
Lauri Lehtinen FIN *14:30.4
Ralph Hill USA 14:30.0
Lauri Virtanen FIN 14:44.0

10,000m
Janusz Kusocinski POL *30:11.4
Volmari Isohollo FIN 30:12.6
Lauri Virtanen FIN 30:35.0

Marathon
Juan Carlos Zabala ARG *2:31:36.0
Samuel Ferris GBR 2:31:55.0
Armas Toivonen FIN 2:32:12.0

110m Hurdles
George Saling USA 14.6
Percy Beard USA 14.7
Donald Finlay GBR 14.8

400m Hurdles
Robert Tisdall IRL 51.7
Glenn Hardin USA ** 51.9
F. Morgan Taylor USA 52.0

3000m Steeplechase
Volmari Isohollo FIN 10:33.4
Thomas Evenson GBR 10:46.0
Joseph McCluskey USA 10:46.2

4x100m Relay
USA ** 40.0 (Robert Kiesel, Emmett Toppino, Hector Dyer, Frank Wykoff)
2. GER 40.9 (Helmut Körnig, Friedrich Hendrix, Erich Borchmeyer, Arthur Jonath)
3. ITA 41.2 (Giuseppe Castelli, Ruggero Maregatti, Gabrielle Salviati, Edgardo Toetti)

4x400m Relay
USA *3:08.2 (Ivan Fuqua, Edgar Ablowich, Karl Warner, William Carr)
2. GBR 3:11.2 (Crew Stoneley, Thomas Hampson, David Burghley, Godfrey Rampling)
3. CAN 3:12.8 (Raymond Lewis, James Ball, Philip Edwards, Alexander Wilson)

50km Walk
Thomas Green GBR 4:50.10
Jānis Dalinsch LIT 4:57.20
Ugo Frigerio ITA 4:59.06

High Jump
Duncan McNaughton CAN 1.97
Robert Van Osdel USA 1.97
Simeon Toribio PHI 1.97

Pole Vault
William Miller USA *4.315
Shuhei Nishida JAP 4.30
George Jefferson USA 4.20

Long Jump
Edward Gordon USA 7.64
Charles Lambert Redd USA 7.60
Chuhei Nambu JAP 7.45

Triple Jump
Chuhei Nambu JAP ** 15.72
Erik Svensson SWE 15.32
Kenkichi Oshima JAP 15.12

Shotput
Leo Sexton USA *16.005
Harlow Rothert USA 15.675
Frantisek Douda TCH 15.61

Discus
John Anderson USA *49.49
Henri Jean Laborde USA 40.47
Paul Winter FRA 47.85

Hammer
Patrick O'Callaghan IRL 53.92
Ville Porhola FIN 52.27
Peter Zaremba USA 50.33

Javelin
Matti Järvinen FIN *72.71
Matti Sippala FIN 69.80
Eino Penttila FIN 68.70

Decathlon
James Aloysius Bausch USA ** 8462.23
Akilles Järvinen FIN 8292.48
Wolrad Eberle GER 8030.80

Women Athletics

100m
Stanislawa Walasiewicz POL ** 11.9
2. Hilde Strike CAN 11.9
3. Wilhelmina von Bremen USA 12.0

800m Hurdles
1. Mildred Didrikson USA ** 11.7
2. Evelyne Hall USA 11.7
3. Marjorie Clark SAF 11.8

4x100m Relay
1. USA ** 46.9 (Mary Carew, Evelyn Furtsch, Annette Rogers, Wilhelmina von Bremen)
2. CAN 47.0 (Mildred Frizzel, Lilian Palmer, Mary Frizzel, Hilda Strike)
3. GBR 47.6 (Eileen Hiscock, Gwendoline Porter, Violet Webb, Nellie Halstead)

High Jump
1. Jean Shiley USA ** 1.657
2. Mildred Didriksen USA ** 1.657
3. Eva Dawes CAN 1.60

Discus
1. Lillian Copeland USA *40.58
2. Ruth Osburn USA 40.12
3. Jadwiga Wajsowna POL 38.74

Javelin
1. Mildred Didriksen USA *43.68
2. Ellen Braumüller GER 43.49
3. Tilly Fleischer GER 43.00

Men Swimming

100m Freestyle
1. Yasuji Miyazaki JAP 58.2
2. Tatsugo Kawaishi JAP 58.6
3. Albert Schwartz USA 58.8

400m Freestyle
1. Clarence Crabbe USA *4:48.4
2. Jean Taris FRA 4:48.5
3. Tsutomu Oyokota JAP 4:52.3

1500m Freestyle
1. Kusuo Kitamura JAP *19:12.4
2. Shozo Makino JAP 19:14.1
3. James Cristy USA 19:39.5

100m Backstroke
1. Masaji Kiyokawa JAP 1:08.6
2. Toshio Irie JAP 1:09.8
3. Kentaro Kawatsu JAP 1:10.0

200m Breaststroke
1. Yoshiyuki Tsuruta JAP 2:45.4
2. Reizo Koike JAP 2:46.6
3. Teofilo Yldefonzo PHI 2:47.1

4x200m Relay
1. JAP ** 8:58.4 (Yasuji Miyazaki, Masonori Yusasa, Takashi Yokoyama, Hisakichi Toyoda)
2. USA 9:10.5 (Frank Booth, George Fissler, Marola Kalili, Manuella Kalili)
3. HUN 9:31.4 (András Wanié, László Szabados, András Székely, István Bárány)

Springboard Diving
1. Michael Galitzen USA 161.38
2. Harold Smith USA 158.54
3. Richard Degener USA 151.82

High Diving
1. Harold Smith USA 124.80
2. Michael Galitzen USA 124.28
3. Frank Kurtz USA 121.98

Water Polo

1. Hungary
2. Germany
3. USA

Women Swimming

100m Freestyle
1. Helene Madison USA *1:06.8
2. Willemijntje den Ouden NETH 1:07.8
3. Eleonor Saville USA 1:08.2

400m Freestyle
1. Helene Madison USA ** 5:28.5
2. Lenore Kight USA 5:28.6
3. Jennie Maakal SAF 5:47.3

200m Breaststroke
1. Clare Dennis AUS *3:06.3
2. Hideko Maehata JAP 3:06.4
3. Else Jacobsen DEN 3:07.1

100m Backstroke
1. Eleanor Holm USA 1:19.4
2. Philomena Mealing AUS 1:21.3
3. Elizabeth Valerie Davies GBR 1:22.5

4x100m Freestyle Relay
1. USA ** 4:38.0 (Josephine McKim, Helen Johns, Eleanor Saville, Helene Madison)
2. NETH 4:47.5 (Marie Vierdag, Maria Oversloot, Cornelia Laddé, Willemijntje den Ouden)
3. GBR 4:52.4 (Elizabeth Valerie Davies, Helen Varcoe, Margaret Joyce Cooper, Edna Hughes)

Springboard Diving
1. Georgia Coleman USA 87.52
2. Katherine Rawls USA 82.56
3. Jane Fauntz USA 82.12

Platform Diving
1. Dorothy Poynton USA 40.26
2. Georgia Coleman USA 35.56
3. Marion Roper USA 35.22

Men Gymnastics

All-around Individual Competition
1. Romeo Neri ITA 140.625
2. István Pelle HUN 134.925
3. Heikki Savolainen FIN 134.575

All-around Team Competition
1. Italy 541.850
2. USA 522.275
3. Finland 509.995

Parallel Bars
1. Romeo Neri ITA 18.97
2. István Pelle HUN 18.60
3. Heikki Savolainen FIN 18.27

Floor Exercises
1. István Pelle HUN 9.60
2. Georges Miez SUI 9.47
3. Mario Lertora ITA 9.23

Long Horse Vault
1. Savino Guglielmetti ITA 18.03
2. Alfred Jochim USA 17.77
3. Edward Carmichael USA 17.53

Sidehorse
1. István Pelle HUN 19.07
2. Omero Bonoli ITA 18.87
3. Frank Haubold USA 18.57

Horizontal Bar
1. Dallas Bixler USA 18.33
2. Heikki Savolainen FIN 18.07
3. Einari Terasvirta FIN 18.07

Rings
1. Georges Gulack USA 18.97
2. William Denton USA 18.60
3. Giovanni Lattuada ITA 18.50

Rope Climbing
1. Raymond Bass USA 6.7
2. William Galbraith USA 6.8
3. Thomas Connelly USA 7.0

Club Swinging
1. George Roth USA 8.97
2. Philip Erenberg USA 8.90
3. William Kuhlmeier USA 8.63

Tumbling
1. Rowland Wolfe USA 18.90
2. Edward Gross USA 18.67
3. William Hermann USA 18.37

Field Hockey

1. India
2. Japan
3. USA

Boxing

Flyweight
1. István Enekes HUN
2. Francisco Cabañas MEX
3. Louis Salica USA

Bantamweight
1. Horace Gwynne CAN
2. Hans Ziglarski GER
3. José Villanueva PHI

Featherweight
1. Carmelo Robledo ARG
2. Josef Schleinkofer GER
3. Carl Carlsson SWE

Lightweight
1. Lawrence Stevens SAF
2. Thure Ahlqvist SWE
3. Nathan Bor USA

Welterweight
1. Edward Flynn USA
2. Erich Campe GER
3. Bruno Ahlberg FIN

Middleweight
1. Carmen Barth USA
2. Amado Azar ARG
3. Ernest Pierce SAF

Light Heavyweight
1. David Carstens SAF
2. Gino Rossi ITA
3. Peter Jorgensen DEN

Heavyweight
1. Santiago Lovell ARG
2. Luigi Rovati ITA
3. Frederick Feary USA

Greco Roman Wrestling

Bantamweight
1. Jakob Brendel GER
2. Marcello Nizzola ITA
3. Louis Francois FRA

Featherweight
1. Giovanni Gozzi ITA
2. Wolfgang Ehrl GER
3. Lauri Koskela FIN

Lightweight
1. Erik Malmberg SWE
2. Abraham Kurland DEN
3. Eduard Sperling GER

Welterweight
1. Ivar Johansson SWE
2. Vaino Kajander FIN
3. Ercole Gallegati ITA

Middleweight
1. Välnö Kokkinen FIN
2. Jean Földeak GER
3. Axel Cadier SWE

Light Heavyweight
1. Rudolf Svensson SWE
2. Onni Pellinen FIN
3. Mario Gruppioni ITA

Heavyweight
1. Carl Westergren SWE
2. Josef Urban TCH
3. Nikolaus Hirschl AUT

Freestyle Wrestling

Bantamweight
1. Robert Pearce USA
2. Odon Zombori HUN
3. Aatos Jaskari FIN

Featherweight
1. Hermanni Pihlajamäki FIN
2. Edgar Nemir USA
3. Einar Karlsson SWE

Lightweight
1. Charles Pacome FRA
2. Károly Kárpáti HUN
3. Gustaf Klarén SWE

Welterweight
1. Jack Van Bebber USA
2. Daniel MacDonald CAN
3. Eino Leino FIN

Middleweight
1. Ivar Johansson SWE
2. Kyösti Luukko FIN
3. Jozsef Tunyogi HUN

Light Heavyweight
1. Peter Mehringer USA
2. Thure Sjostedt SWE
3. Eddie Scarf AUS

Heavyweight
1. Johan Richthoff SWE
2. John Riley USA
3. Nikolaus Hirschl AUT

Men Fencing

Foil Individual
1. Gustavo Marzi ITA
2. Joseph Levis USA
3. Giulio Gaudini ITA

Foil Team
1. France
2. Italy
3. USA

Epée Individual
1. Giancarlo Cornaggia-Medici ITA
2. Georges Buchard FRA
3. Carlo Agostini ITA

Epée Team
1. France
2. Italy
3. USA

Sabre Individual
1. Gyorgy Piller HUN
2. Giulio Gaudini ITA
3. Endré Kabos HUN

Sabre Team
1. Hungary
2. Italy
3. Poland

Women Fencing

Foil Individual
1. Ellen Preis AUT
2. Judy Heather Guinness GBR
3. Erna Bogen HUN

Modern Pentathlon

1. Johan Oxenstierna SWE
2. Bo Lindman SWE
3. Richard Mayo USA

Rowing

Single Sculls
1. Henry Pearce AUS 7:44.4
2. William Miller USA 7:45.2
3. Guillermo Douglas URU 8:13.6

Double Sculls
1. USA 7:17.4
2. Germany 7:22.8
3. Canada 7:27.6

Coxless Pairs
1. Great Britain 8:00.0
2. New Zealand 8:02.4
3. Poland 8:08.2

Coxed Pairs
1. USA 8:25.8
2. Poland 8:31.2
3. France 8:41.2

Coxless Fours
1. Great Britain 6:58.2
2. Germany 7:03.0
3. Italy 7:04.0

Coxed Fours
1. Germany 7:19.0
2. Italy 7:19.2
3. Poland 7:26.8

Eights
1. USA 6:37.6
2. Italy 6:37.8
3. Canada 6:40.4

Yachting

Finn Monotype Class
1. Jacques Lebrun FRA
2. Andriaan Mass NETH
3. Santiago Amat Cansino ESP

Star Class
1. USA
2. Great Britain
3. Sweden

6m Class
1. Sweden
2. USA
3. Canada

8m Class
1. USA
2. Canada

Cycling

Road Racing Individual (100km)
1. Attilio Pavesi ITA 2:28:05.6
2. Guglielmo Segato ITA 2:29:21.4
3. Bernhard Britz SWE 2:29:45.2

Team Time Trial
1. Italy 7:27:15.2
2. Denmark 7:38:50.2
3. Sweden 7:39:12.6

1000m Time Trial
1. Edgar Gray AUS *1:13.0
2. Jacobus Van Egmond NETH 1:13.3
3. Charles Rampelberg FRA 1:13.4

Sprint 1000m
1. Jacobus Van Egmond NETH 12.6
2. Louis Chaillot FRA
3. Bruno Pellizzari ITA

2000m Tandem
1. France 12.0
2. Great Britain
3. Denmark

Team Pursuit (4000m)
1. Italy 4:53.0
2. France 4:55.7
3. Great Britain 4:56.0

Equestrian Sports

3 Day Event Individual
1. Charles F. Pahud de Mortanges NETH 1813.83
2. Earl Thomson USA 1811.00
3. Clarence von Rosen Jr. SWE 1809.42

3 Day Event Team
1. USA 5038.083
2. Netherlands 4689.083

Dressage Individual
1. Xavier Lesage FRA 343.75
2. Charles Marion FRA 305.42
3. Hiram Tuttle USA 300.50

Dressage Team
1. France 2818.75
2. Sweden 2678.00
3. USA 2576.75

Grand Prix Jumping Individual
1. Takeichi Nishi JAP -8
2. Harry Chamberlin USA -12
3. Clarence von Rosen Jr. SWE -16

Grand Prix Jumping Team (No winner, all of the participating nations disqualified.)

Men Shooting

Rapid Fire Pistol
1. Renzo Morigi ITA 36
2. Heinz Hax GER 36
3. Domenico Matteucci ITA 36

Small Bore Rifle, Prone
1. Bertil Rönnmark SWE 294/296
2. Gustavo Huet MEX 294/290
3. Zoltán Hradetzky-Soós HUN 293

(Key to symbols and abbreviations p. 1456)

Weightlifting

		2 Arm Press	2 Arm Snatch	2 Arm Clean and Jerk	Total
Featherweight					
1. Raymond Suvigny	FRA	82.5	87.5	117.5	=* 287.5
2. Hans Wölpert	GER	85.0	87.5	110.0	282.5
3. Anthony Terlazzo	USA	82.5	85.0	112.5	280.0
Lightweight					
1. René Duverger	FRA	*97.5	102.5	=*125.0	=* 325.0
2. Hans Haas	AUT	82.5	100.0	=*125.0	307.5
3. Gastone Pierini	ITA	92.5	90.0	120.0	302.5
Middleweight					
1. Rudolf Ismayr	GER	102.5	*110.0	132.5	** 345.0
2. Carlo Galimberti	ITA	102.5	105.0	132.5	340.0
3. Karl Hipfinger	AUT	90.0	107.5	*140.0	337.5
Light Heavyweight					
1. Louis Hostin	FRA	*102.5	=*112.5	*150.0	=* 365.0
2. Svend Olsen	DEN	*102.5	107.5	*150.0	360.0
3. Henry Duey	USA	92.5	105.0	132.5	330.0
Heavyweight					
1. Jaroslav Skobla	TCH	112.5	115.0	*152.5	*380.0
2. Václav Psenicka	TCH	112.5	*117.5	147.5	377.5
3. Josef Strassberger	GER	*125.0	110.0	142.5	377.5

1932

SEPTEMBER

Su	Mo	Tu	We	Th	Fr	Sa
				1	2	3
4	5	6	7	8	9	10
11	12	13	14	15	16	17
18	19	20	21	22	23	24
25	26	27	28	29	30	

1. Berlin: Five Nazis condemned to die for murdering a communist have their sentences commuted to life (→8).

2. UK: The International Rugby Board condemns modern scrummage methods.

4. Vienna: Opening of the World Peace Conference.

5. Los Angeles: Film director Paul Bern, husband of Jean Harlow, commits suicide.

6. Madrid: The government abolishes the death penalty (→9).

7. UK: The Aga Khan's horses take four of the first five places in the St. Leger.

8. Berlin: Hitler declares that providence has chosen him for a great mission (→12).

9. Madrid: The government acknowledges the autonomy of the region of Catalonia (→10/1/33).

12. Berlin: Von Papen threatens to dissolve the Reichstag by decree if it tries to make him resign (→14/10).

13. Paris: Paul Gorguloff, assassin of President Doumer, is guillotined.

20. UK: The three Methodist Churches unite to form the largest Free Church body in Britain.

20. India: Gandhi begins a fast in Poona jail to protest at limited franchise and representation of Untouchables (→24).

24. India: The Poona Pact is signed extending the voting rights of Untouchables; Gandhi ends his fast (→24/12).

26. Nicaragua: Sandinist rebels engage in heavy fighting with government troops at Lindo Lugar and Jinotega (→24/12).

28. London: Sir John Simon replaces Herbert Samuel as leader of Liberals supporting MacDonald's government.→

29. London: Among other new appointments Richard A. Butler becomes Under-Secretary for India.

30. Rome: Pope Pius XI condemns Mexican anti-clericalism but tells Catholics to abide by Mexican laws.

MacDonald isolated as Liberals quit

Sept 28. The National Government had a serious internal upheaval today when four cabinet ministers – all Free Traders – resigned. They walked out in protest over new Empire agreements, making lower tariff deals with foreign countries more difficult. Three were Liberals and the other was Lord Snowden, former Labour Party stalwart and ex-Chancellor.

Ramsay MacDonald pleaded in vain with them not to abandon him. He said that with them gone he would be a prisoner of the Tories, and that his position would be humiliating and likely to become untenable (→29).

Mersey tunnel longest underwater

Sept 4. A £7-million tunnel, running beneath the River Mersey from Liverpool to Birkenhead, which has taken seven years to dig, moved closer to carrying traffic today when engineers agreed on a ventilation system to extract the carbon monoxide exhaust fumes. From next year an estimated 3,000 vehicles every hour will use the roadway, the world's longest underwater tunnel.

The Austin Car Co. introduces their new model, the "Ten": will it be as successful as their hugely popular "Baby" Seven?

1932

OCTOBER

Su	Mo	Tu	We	Th	Fr	Sa
						1
2	3	4	5	6	7	8
9	10	11	12	13	14	15
16	17	18	19	20	21	22
23	24	25	26	27	28	29
30	31					

1. Geneva: The League slams Japan for violating treaties in its war with China (→19/2/33).

3. Baghdad: Iraq becomes independent as Britain's mandate ends and joins the League.

3. Mexico City: The Mexican parliament votes to expel the Papal Legate.

6. Oxford: John Turner, 17, is the first Briton to be treated with an "iron lung", at the Wingfield Morris Hospital.

8. London: The London Philharmonic Orchestra gives its first concert, under creator and director Sir Thomas Beecham.

10. UK: 19 drown when a pit cage crashes into water at the bottom of Plank Lane Colliery, Lancashire.

11. Belfast: A curfew and cordon is imposed following clashes between police and unemployed workers (→30).

14. Berlin: The government unveils plans for direct presidential rule in the state of Prussia (→20).

16. Berlin: Albert Einstein puts the Earth's age at ten billion years.

18. London: Britain ends its trade treaty with the USSR (→22).

20. Berlin: A decree orders schools to teach Article 231 of the Versailles Treaty, saying Germany caused the War.

22. Moscow: Stalin threatens trade reprisals against Britain for ending the Anglo-USSR trade agreement (→19/4/33).

25. London: Police pay is to be cut by another five per cent, making ten per cent in all.

25. UK: George Lansbury is elected leader of the Labour Party (→8/10/35).

27. UK: "Greek Memories" by Compton Mackenzie is withdrawn for revealing who headed the Secret Service in the Great War (→12/1/33).

31. Boston: Franklin Roosevelt says he would introduce a five-day week and federal aid for the unemployed if elected president (→8/11).

Lenin's colleagues purged by Stalin

Oct 9. Joseph Stalin demonstrated again today that he will not tolerate criticism, and expelled two of the leading Bolsheviks from the Communist Party. For the second time in a few years Grigori Zinoviev and Leon Kamenev, who shared power with Stalin after Lenin's death, lost their party cards and were sent to Siberia. Nearly 20 other prominent Communists have so far shared their fate.

They were charged with attempting to restore capitalism and receiving "documents from a counter-revolutionary group". This could refer to a journal written by exiled Leon Trotsky, which is known to be reaching Russia with bitter criticisms of Stalin's increasingly harsh rule.

Discontent is rife in the party and Stalin is in a tough mood (→22/10).

Russia's loyal youth.

Sex case rector is defrocked by court

Oct 21. A Norfolk clergyman, the Reverend Harold Davidson, became plain "Mr" today after he had been found guilty of "grave scandal to the Church" and defrocked.

The Consistory Court had heard how the former Rector of Stiffkey associated with women of loose character, accosted young women for immoral purposes and made improper suggestions to a waitress in a Chinese restaurant. Davidson denied the charge (→28/7/37).

Police clash with jobless

Police in Bristol mount baton charges against unemployment protesters.

Oct 30. Pitched street battles broke out in London again today between police and supporters of the hunger marches, which have become flash-points for violent anti-government protests across Britain in the past two weeks. A 15,000-strong rally in Trafalgar Square against means tests and mass unemployment was marred by youths who wrecked cars, smashed windows and tried to break through police lines.

It was the fourth day of rioting which began when 2,000 marchers from the provinces joined thousands of supporters at Hyde Park. Nearly 5,000 police fought with youths for two hours. Fifty people were injured and 14 arrested. Later, Scotland Yard seized dozens of spiked staves, sticks and cudgels. Their discovery strengthened belief in some quarters that the marches, led by the Communist-run National Unemployed Workers' Movement, were funded and orchestrated from Moscow. Other sympathy protests in London have led to disorder and arrests.

During an East End visit, Prince George was met with shouts of "down with the means tests. We want bread". In Belfast, one man was shot dead during a protest and armoured police vehicles enforced a curfew.

The Prime Minister, Ramsay MacDonald, has ordered an urgent review of the Government's policies on unemployment (→1/11).

Lancashire hunger marchers on the long road to London.

1932

NOVEMBER

Su	Mo	Tu	We	Th	Fr	Sa
		1	2	3	4	5
6	7	8	9	10	11	12
13	14	15	16	17	18	19
20	21	22	23	24	25	26
27	28	29	30			

1. London: Police clash with marchers trying to present a petition against the Means Test to the Prime Minister (→4/2/33).

2. Hamburg: 12 people are shot when Communists attack Nazis.

5. UK: A five-day old strike of 200,000 Lancashire cotton workers ends after the strikers agree to a wage cut.

6. Germany: The Nazis lose 34 seats in Reichstag elections as the Nationalists gain ground (→17).

9. Moscow: Stalin's wife Nadya Alliluieva dies suddenly at the age of 30; suicide is suspected.

12. UK: 25 are feared dead after a pit explosion at Edge Green, Ashton-in-Makerfield.

16. Belfast: The Prince of Wales opens Stormont, Northern Ireland's new parliament building.

17. London: The third Round Table conference on India opens (→24/12).

17. Berlin: Von Papen resigns after failing to form a government (→21).

18. Cape Town: Amy Johnson lands after cutting 10.5 hours off the previous fastest flight time from London.

21. Berlin: Hitler refuses the Chancellorship if it means combining with other parties, as Hindenburg wants.→

25. UK: The actors' union Equity votes to operate a closed shop from the beginning of 1933.

28. Teheran: The Persian government ends the 1901 oil concession operated by the Anglo-Persian Oil Company.

30. London: The BBC begins a series of broadcasts to mark the 75th birthday of Sir Edward Elgar.

30. Moscow: The government says it will allow people to emigrate in return for a large fee in foreign currency.

BIRTH

29. French politician Jacques Chirac.

Briton Galsworthy gets Nobel Prize

Nov 11. The Nobel Prize has gone to John Galsworthy, the fourth writer from Britain to win it. It is for the Forsytes that he will be remembered. He has been labouring on their story since 1906 when Soames Forsyte first appeared as "A Man of Property". The first trilogy was published as "The Forsyte Saga" in 1922, but there have been many additions since, including "Flowering Wilderness", out today.

Besides this saga of the English bourgeoisie, Galsworthy has written 31 plays. Of these, "Justice" led to a reform of prison conditions.

Galsworthy: Nobel for Literature.

Election setback for Hitler's Nazi Party

Nov 24. Suddenly things are not looking so good for Hitler's Nazis. With 196 seats they remain the largest party in the Reichstag, but in this month's election they lost 2,000,000 votes and 34 seats. They went into the campaign short of funds after big business, alarmed by Nazi cooperation with Communists in the Reichstag and in the Berlin transport strike, switched their money to the Nationalist Party, which backs the Chancellor, Franz von Papen. The Nationalists took votes from the Nazis and now have 52 seats. The tide that was going to sweep the Nazis to power appears to be ebbing (→2/12).

Landslide for Roosevelt

The 32nd President of the United States promises a "new deal".

Nov 8. In one of the most massive victories ever, Franklin Delano Roosevelt today defeated the sitting Republican President, Herbert Hoover. He won all but six of the 48 states in the presidential election and a majority of more than seven million in the popular vote. In the electoral college he won overwhelming support to end up with a score of 472 against Hoover's 59.

His victory is the nation's verdict on an administration which has failed to deal with depression, farming bankruptcies, bank closures and soaring unemployment. It is also a personal triumph for a man who has convinced the people that he can revive their flagging fortunes. Roosevelt himself succeeded early, becoming a state senator at 28 and winning the Democratic nomination for vice-president at only 38. His career seemed doomed when polio paralysed his legs ten years ago. But he triumphed over his illness to become a hugely energetic Governor of New York. His presidential campaign, in which he travelled over 12,500 miles by train, put healthier men to shame.

"The country needs, the country demands, bold, persistent experimentation," Roosevelt said. He has promised them a "new deal". He plans to boost public spending on the railways, the roads, electric power and the farms. He intends to bring in laws to regulate the banks and the stock markets. He wants unemployment insurance for all. Above all he has promised that as President he will see to it that "no American will starve" (→22/12).

Waiting to register at the emergency unemployment relief office.

Capes for evening bareback hiding

Nov 19. Backless gowns, once considered so shocking, are still at the fore-front of fashion for evening wear, even if they no longer have the same power to scandalise. Many are being worn with little capes but it's a style dictated more by climate than modesty.

Day and night, ready-to-wear clothes, which have made enormous strides recently, are proving increasingly popular. Modern techniques and growing skill in getting the sizing right mean that more and more fashions can be produced at a reasonable price. Also recent import duties on cloth have encouraged Britain to develop its own expertise in the field.

As seen from behind.

Richards rides into the racing records

Nov 22. Gordon Richards, champion jockey five times in the last seven years, and already assured of retaining his title this year, rode his 188th winner of the season today at Warwick, beating Frank Wootton's twentieth-century record for a season's total with several days left before the end of the Flat.

Since the retirement of Steve Donoghue, and despite missing the 1926 season to have treatment for tuberculosis, the Shropshire-born Richards has reigned supreme as a flat-race jockey. Only the legendary Victorian Fred Archer is able to claim a rate of success which is comparable.

1932

DECEMBER

Su	Mo	Tu	We	Th	Fr	Sa
				1	2	3
4	5	6	7	8	9	10
11	12	13	14	15	16	17
18	19	20	21	22	23	24
25	26	27	28	29	30	31

2. Berlin: Kurt von Schleicher is appointed Chancellor (→7).

5. London: The government suggests issuing bonds to cover its debt to the US (→15).

7. Berlin: Communists and Nazis engage in fierce hand-to-hand fighting in the Reichstag (→22/1/33).

10. Stockholm: Nobel Prizes go to Werner Heisenberg (Germany, Physics); Irving Langmuir (US, Chemistry); Sir Charles Sherrington and Lord Edgar Adrian (UK, Medicine); John Galsworthy (UK, Literature). No Peace Prize.

12. Moscow: The USSR restores relations with Japan.

14. France: Herriot resigns as premier following his government's defeat in the Chamber of Deputies (→19).

15. London: Britain pays the US $95,500,000 (£27,000,000) in gold.

19. Paris: Paul-Boncour forms a government (→30/1/33).

19. UK: The BBC makes its first Empire broadcast via its new Daventry transmitter (→25).

22. Glasgow: 15 are injured when jobless workers clash with police; one policeman is thrown into the Clyde.

24. London: The Round Table conference on India ends.

25. London: King George V makes the first royal Christmas Day broadcast to the Empire.

28. India: Britain says it is to release 28,000 prisoners, including Gandhi (→29/3/33).

HITS OF 1932

Love is the sweetest thing.

Forty-second Street.

The sun has got his hat on.

QUOTE OF THE YEAR

"I am waging a war in this campaign ... against the Four Horsemen of the present Republican leadership: The Horsemen of Destruction, Delay, Deceit and Despair."

Franklin Delano Roosevelt, elected US President 1932.

Future perfect in a Brave New World

Aldous Huxley's "Brave New World" has been the talking point of the literary year. His chilly vision of the future seemed to many readers too far-fetched for words. Babes fertilised in laboratory bottles? "Sleep-learning" through whispering microphones to condition the young to be obedient citizens?

With sterilisation, sexual promiscuity is practically a duty, to discourage that unruly emotion, love. The talkies have become a sensual experience – "The Feelies" – and people have discovered a mildly exhilarating drug without after-effects, Soma, which is much in use at parties. Whatever next?

The more this painless, trouble-free world is described, the more repellent it sounds, since it suppresses all man's capacity for independent thought and feeling. It is a sombre warning – "one of the half-dozen most important books published since the war", comments **Rebecca West**.

One book has been suppressed this year for political reasons. It is **Compton Mackenzie's** "Greek Memories" which revealed the name of "C", the head of the British Secret Service, in which Mackenzie served during the war. He was summoned under the Official Secrets Act.

Lytton Strachey, of the unkempt moustache and bushy red beard, of effete voice and waspish pen, scourge of eminent Victorians but romantic chronicler of the love between Elizabeth and Essex, has died. Among the new authors,

Visionary writer Huxley.

Evelyn Waugh has added to his satirical reputation with "Black Mischief". A fast-moving thriller of unusual quality, set on the Orient Express and entitled "Stamboul Train", has come from a new name in fiction, **Graham Greene**.

A high-spirited and bracingly "modern" piano concerto came from **Maurice Ravel**, who uses the piano like a percussion instrument as in jazz. Nevertheless he manages to build up a sea of dissonance into a most soothing slow movement.

With the founding of the London Philharmonic Orchestra by **Sir Thomas Beecham**, English music has acquired two first-class ensembles in two years. In 1930 the BBC formed its symphony orchestra which has set new standards under **Dr Adrian Boult**.

Mackenzie: revelations banned.

In Hollywood Rin Tin Tin has at last turned up his paws but the American public instead has taken to its heart a precocious four-year-old, **Shirley Temple**, star of her own picture, "Red-Haired Alibi". Two time-honoured characters have found new incarnations: lord of the jungle Tarzan in the well-developed shape of the recent Olympic swimming champion, **Johnny Weissmuller**, and the monster Frankenstein, hauntingly portrayed by **Boris Karloff**.

A warm welcome was given to **Stan Laurel** and **Oliver Hardy** on their visit to Britain, as the screen's most popular two-man comedy team. The **Marx Brothers** (this year seen in "Horse Feathers") have proved themselves as the most anarchic screen threesome.

Atom smashing at Cambridge gets to the heart of matter

This was a vintage year for atomic physics at Cambridge. **John Cockcroft** and **Ernest Walton** used their new atom-smashing machine to transmute lithium atoms into those of helium, the first such transformation by artificial means. And **James Chadwick** discovered a new subatomic particle: the neutron. Along with protons, neutrons are building blocks of the atomic nucleus.

In the United States, **Karl Jansky** of Bell Laboratories has reported an intriguing discovery: radio waves are reaching earth from the direction of the constellation Sagittarius. No messages are involved – the signals are like static – but if stars produce radio waves these could provide new insights and give rise to a new science: radio astronomy.

An exciting medical development of 1932 was the discovery by a German doctor, **Gerhard Domagk**, that injections of a dye called Prontosil protect mice against infections of streptococci in the living body.

If it is safe for humans, it could be the first of a family of potent new drugs.

Development of television continued with the demonstration by RCA in the United States of an all electronic system. Hitherto television cameras have scanned scenes mechanically. An all-electronic system is regarded as an important advance.

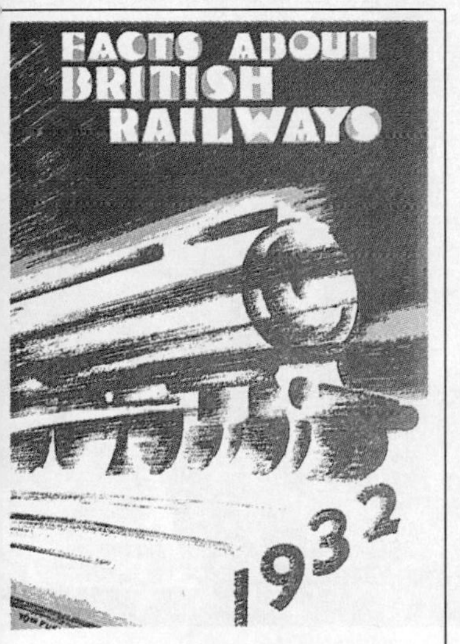

Allies plagued by war debt repayments

Dec 22. The outgoing US President, Herbert Hoover, has been rebuffed by his successor, Franklin D. Roosevelt, who refused to cooperate in setting up a commission to examine the thorny question of war debts. Roosevelt, a Democrat, evidently believes he can do better than Hoover, the Republican, but political observers are doubtful.

The problem is that, essentially, all the money is owed to the US, and the constant flow of funds across the Atlantic leaves European countries impoverished, destabilises exchange rates and blocks world trade. Hoover says the best way to restore stable currencies would be to re-examine the debts of countries that have maintained their payments.

This month four countries, France, Belgium, Poland and Hungary, defaulted on their payments; six, Britain, Italy, Finland, Czechoslovakia, Lithuania and Latvia, paid up. Britain, which met her payment by taking just over £27 million from her gold reserves, hopes Hoover's idea for suspending or even writing off the debts, will be adopted (→ 15/2).

Physicist James Chadwick.

1933

JANUARY

Su	Mo	Tu	We	Th	Fr	Sa
1	2	3	4	5	6	7
8	9	10	11	12	13	14
15	16	17	18	19	20	21
22	23	24	25	26	27	28
29	30	31				

1. Tokyo: Japan rejects the non-aggression pact with the USSR signed last July.

2. Dublin: The Dail is dissolved; de Valera calls an election for the 24th.→

4. London: A study says hospital out-patient departments should be improved to cut queues and overcrowding.

9. London: A report says betting on greyhounds should be banned.

9. UK: New army uniforms are worn for the first time.

10. Spain: Martial law is imposed as a Communist revolt spreads in the southern provinces.→

12. London: Author Compton Mackenzie is fined for breach of the Official Secrets Act in his book "Greek Memories" (→27/10/32).

13. Washington: President Hoover vetoes a bill to give the Philippines independence in ten years (→17).

17. Washington: Congress overrides Hoover's veto of the bill for Filipino independence.

22. Berlin: Nazi paramilitaries scuffle with Communists at a Nazi rally (→25).

24. S. Africa: General Smuts calls for a national cabinet of the main parties (→17/5).

25. Dresden: Police kill nine Communists at a Nazi rally (→28).

27. Europe: A flu epidemic is getting worse and spreading throughout the Continent.

28. Berlin: Von Schleicher resigns as Chancellor.→

30. Paris: Edouard Daladier becomes premier (→23/10).

BIRTH

29. French singer Sacha Distel.

DEATHS

5. US Republican statesman Calvin Coolidge, president 1923-29 (*4/7/1872).

31. British author and Nobel prize-winner John Galsworthy (*14/8/1867).

Martial law in Spain as revolution grows

Jan 10. The New Year has begun in Spain as violently as the old one ended. The Anarchists, joined by Anarcho-Syndicalists and Communists, have fomented uprisings in Catalonia, Levante and Andalusia.

The combined forces of revolution have threatened to call a general strike tomorrow and, in retaliation, the government has authorised premier Manuel Azana to declare martial law if the situation gets out of hand.

In many places undeclared martial law is already in operation. In Seville a number of people have been wounded in exchanges of gunfire. Several bombs have gone off in the city and the Garde Civile have set up road blocks where people are searched for bombs and firearms.

Learning from the experiences of last autumn, when a wave of strikes swept across the country and assassins used their guns to settle political rivalries, the Governor of Seville has ordered troops to guard workers, while heavily armed bodyguards are being hired to protect politicians.

The revolutionary dance of death.

In Barcelona, where bombs have killed five people in the last few days, a joint Syndicalist-Anarchist manifesto has been issued. It calls on opponents of the government to disrupt telephone, telegraph and railway lines and to "burn all old fashioned archives". Spain does indeed seem to be descending into violent anarchy.

One Dail seat gives power to de Valera

Jan 28. President Eamon de Valera has a majority of one in the Irish Dail, with the vote finally in. It is not the large majority for which he campaigned, and it will make him dependent on Labour.

He will be under heavy pressure from hard-line republicans within his party, such as Sean McEntee, Oscar Traynor and Frank Aitken, to make the ending of partition between north and south Ireland a top priority. These are men who will not be dismissed lightly. The President's campaign speeches, however, would indicate that he intends to chip away at the 1922 Anglo-Irish Treaty rather than try for a major change.

Nationalist MPs who have boycotted the Northern Ireland parliament since being elected are considering if they can sit in the Dail instead. They regard the Dail as the all-Ireland parliament envisaged in Article One of the Treaty (→30/8).

MCC bodyline tour is "just not cricket", protest Australians

Jan 23. In cricket's most serious crisis since England first played against Australia 56 years ago, the MCC agreed to bring its players home should the Australian board decide to cancel the current tour.

The future of the tour has been in doubt since the "bodyline" controversy reached a climax during England's victory in the third Test at Adelaide. There the Australian wicket-keeper was struck a severe blow on the head when batting against Harold Larwood and their captain, Bill Woodfull, after being twice hit by bouncers, accused England of "not playing cricket".

The point of contention has been England's bowling strategy, devised to counter the prodigious run-scoring abilities of Australia's batsmen – principally the incomparable Donald Bradman. This involves using their fast bowlers, led by Larwood and Bill Voce, to bowl on the line of the batsmen's legs and body, and restrict their strokeplaying options with cordons of fielders on the leg side. "Leg theory" has worked well for England's captain Douglas Jardine, but it has placed the future of the game in jeopardy.

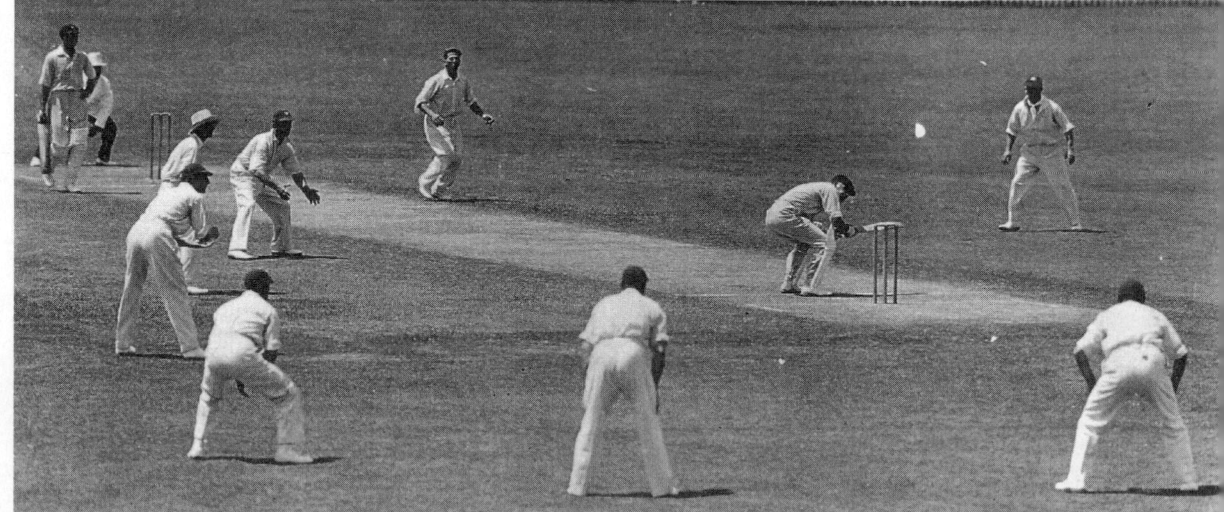

Bill Woodfull of Australia ducks to a rising ball from England's Harold Larwood during the fourth Test.

Hitler takes over as Chancellor of German Reich

Jan 30. At noon today, and after weeks of back door intrigues involving bankers, army officers and right-wing politicians, Adolf Hitler, the flamboyant Nazi leader, became Chancellor of Germany. He was appointed by President von Hindenburg, the man who only last November rejected him out of hand because he believed a Hitler cabinet would be "bound to develop into a party dictatorship".

The abrupt change in the attitude of the 85-year-old President has been brought about by the virtual collapse of parliamentary government, as the country seems poised on the brink of civil war with daily, bloody street battles between Hitler's National Socialists and the Communists. It was former Chancellor Franz von Papen who assembled the new package.

Apart from Hitler there are only two other Nazis in the eleven-man Cabinet: Wilhelm Frick, a former police officer, is Minister of the Interior; and Hermann Goering, wartime aviator and, until recently, a drug addict, is Minister without Portfolio (but also minister in charge of police in Prussia).

The rest of the Cabinet, all right-wing Nationalists, believe, along with von Papen, that they will soon tame Hitler and his wild men in brown uniforms with swastika armbands.

Hitler, 44 in April, high school drop-out, house painter and wartime army corporal, is seen by many as a rabble-rouser and nothing more. His speeches, delivered in a hoarse shouting, rising to a crescendo, bring his audiences to their feet, stabbing the air with Fascist salutes and chanting "Sieg Heil!" He denounces "the criminals of 1918" and the Versailles peace treaty; he vilifies Jews and extols the Aryan race.

News of Hitler's appointment brought Communist demonstrators on to the streets of Berlin, calling for a general strike. But tonight it is the brownshirts, marching in torchlight parades, who are being hailed by the crowds.

Less than a month ago, Hitler and his comrades were becoming demoralised as popular support began to wane. It was then that von Papen, plotting his own return to power, arranged for Hitler to meet the Cologne banker Kurt von Schroeder; this was followed by a meeting with Paul von Hindenburg.

Within a week the old President gave way, and not only agreed to accept Hitler but also fell in with the plot to install a Nazi sympathiser, General Werner von Blomberg, as Defence Minister in order to win the support of the army for the new government.

Hitler has always refused to accept anything less than the Chancellorship. The failure of Schleicher and von Papen to secure parliamentary rule has put it in his lap.

Hitlerism was born of the middle classes' longing for order, the fear of Bolshevism by bankers and industrialists, and the militaristic Junkers' nostalgia for German *Machtpolitik*.

It might be here to stay. "Once we decide to go to Berlin we shall never leave it. My aim is a complete victory for the movement," said Hitler last month (→2/2).

Adolf Hitler, flamboyant leader of the National Socialists, receiving congratulations on his appointment.

Out with the old order, in with the new. Aged President Paul von Hindenburg greets Germany's sober-looking, smart young Chancellor.

1933

FEBRUARY

Su	Mo	Tu	We	Th	Fr	Sa
			1	2	3	4
5	6	7	8	9	10	11
12	13	14	15	16	17	18
19	20	21	22	23	24	25
26	27	28				

1. London: Premiere of the piano concerto by Ralph Vaughan Williams.

2. Berlin: Hitler imposes curbs on left-wing parties and the press, but says: "No-one wants peace more than I do" (→ 10).

4. London: 50,000 demonstrators gather in Hyde Park protesting against unemployment (→ 10/7).

6. Washington: The 20th Amendment is passed, bringing the presidential inauguration forward to January 20.

6. London: A report says milk marketing in Britain should be centralised.

7. Ankara: Mustafa Kemal bans Arabic prayers and "Allah", the Arabic word for God.

8. UK: Hoover carpet cleaners are now selling at £4/19/6d.

10. Berlin: Hitler declares war on parliamentary democracy at a Nazi rally (→ 16).

14. Oxford: Quintin Hogg and Randolph Churchill are among those who try to reverse the "King and Country" debate.→

16. Berlin: The writer Heinrich Mann quits the Prussian Academy of Arts in protest against the Nazis (→ 23).

16. Australia: England win the Ashes at the end of their controversial "Bodyline" tour.

19. Tokyo: Japan says it will quit the League of Nations if it is condemned for its actions in China.→

20. US: Giuseppe Zingara, failed assassin of President-elect Roosevelt, is sent to jail for 80 years (→ 6/3).

23. Germany: Bavaria overturns Hitler's ban on opposition newspapers (→ 24).

24. Germany: Hitler authorises Nazi paramilitaries to act as police in the state of Prussia (→ 28).

28. Germany: Communist playwright Bertolt Brecht goes into voluntary exile in protest against the Nazis.→

28. London: The King sees his first talkies, a Disney cartoon and "Good Companions".

Mystery fire guts German Reichstag

Feb 28. The Reichstag went up in flames last night, and today in the streets of Berlin, where the acrid odour of incineration still hangs in the air, people can be heard saying that the gutted, smoke-blackened building represents the funeral pyre of German democracy.

It was coming up to ten o'clock in the evening when a police officer sounded the alarm; by the time firemen arrived the building was ablaze in several different places. A young Dutchman, said to have been found on the premises, has been charged with arson.

Cabinet ministers were quickly on the scene. Among the first was Hermann Goering. As he got out of his car he shouted: "The Communist Party is the culprit. This is a Communist crime against the new government. We will show no mercy. Every Communist must be shot on the spot."

Adolf Hitler, the Chancellor, agreed. "This is a God-given signal," he said. "There is nothing that shall stop us now crushing out this murder pest with an iron fist." It was no idle threat. Today, he prevailed upon the aged President von Hindenburg to sign a decree "for the protection of the People and the State".

The decree suspends all legal guarantees for personal liberty, freedom of speech and the Press and the right of assembly. Hitler has at last got the dictatorial powers he has been demanding from the moment he took office at the beginning of the year.

Though he claims to be faced with a Communist terrorist plot, his Nazi Storm Troopers, now enrolled as special military police, are also cracking down on Socialists and others. Socialist and Communist newspapers have been suppressed and the parties' posters for next Sunday's elections have been torn down. One liberal paper was suspended for saying that some actions of the government were having a depressing effect on the Bourse. No public figure or newspaper in any way critical of the regime seems likely to survive.

Long before last night's fire, Nazi leaders were expressing their contempt for democratic institutions and proclaiming their determination to crush all opposition. A series of decrees earlier this month severely curbed the activities of the Press and put restrictions on foreign publications. The radio has been virtually taken over by Dr Goebbels, Hitler's propaganda chief. Prominent pacifists have had their passports confiscated.

In case any doubts remained as to the Nazis' intentions, Wilhelm Frick, the Interior Minister, said last Friday that, whatever the results of the general election, Hitler intended to remain in power. In words that anticipated today's Presidential decree, supposedly triggered by the Reichstag fire, Frick said that by election day "a state of emergency will exist which will authorise the government to remain in office".

As it happened, these remarks were made on the same day as Goering, exercising his powers as police minister for Prussia, which controls two-thirds of Germany, ordered a raid on Karl Liebknecht Haus, the Communist Party HQ. The party had abandoned it weeks ago, but Goering, exploiting the public's apprehensions over the country's political instability, claimed to have found evidence of a revolutionary plot.

That evidence, if it exists, has not been published, but more has become known today about the young man who was arrested in the Reichstag. He is Marinus van der Lubbe, described by acquaintances as a simple-minded Communist hanger-on. Goering wanted him executed on the spot, but it now seems he will be put on trial.

Whatever emerges then, it is certain that, as Hitler said, the fire has come as a godsend to the Nazis. An election campaign that has already seen 50 anti-Nazis and 18 Nazis killed is going to become even more violent (→ 29/9).

Flames lick the glass dome of the Reichstag: are the Communists to blame?

Gunman shoots at President Roosevelt

Feb 15. Franklin D. Roosevelt, US President-elect, narrowly escaped assassination tonight after giving a speech in Bay Front Park, Miami. As he sat in his car near the bandstand five shots rang out, wounding Anton Cermak, the Mayor of Chicago, who was standing on the running board of the car, and four other people. Mayor Cermak is not expected to live.

The would-be assassin, Giuseppe Zingara from Hackensack in New Jersey, was knocked to the ground by a policeman and arrested. Police quoted the gunman as saying: "I'd kill every president." Found in his clothing was a newspaper clipping about the assassination of President McKinley by an anarchist in 1901.

Mr Roosevelt, who won a landslide victory three months ago, had spent the day on a fishing cruise aboard Vincent Astor's yacht before going to Bay Front Park.

When he arrived at the park, he stood in the car, microphone in hand, and spoke to a crowd of over 10,000. He had just finished the speech and was posing for photographs when the first shot rang out, followed by four more. Mayor Cermak slumped to his knees and rolled to the pavement, a bullet in his chest. A woman standing nearby grabbed the gunman's wrist and the final shot was deflected before a policeman knocked Zingara to the ground (→20).

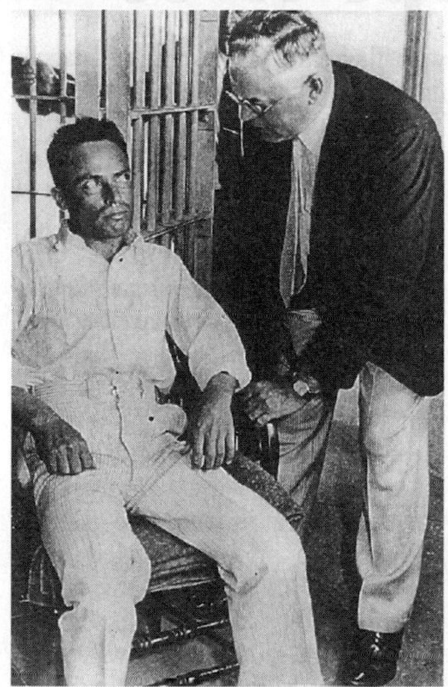

Giuseppe Zingara in custody.

Japan storms out of League of Nations

Feb 25. The long-threatened breach between Japan and the League of Nations came this afternoon after the Special Assembly condemned the Japanese for causing the war in Manchuria. "Japan has left the League of Nations with a heavy heart," said Mr Matsuoka, the chief delegate. He claimed that China was not a truly sovereign country because the Nanking government controlled only four of her 18 provinces. Mr Matsuoka was the only delegate of the 42 to vote against the Assembly's resolution. Siam abstained, and the vote was deemed to be unanimous because the voice of an interested party does not count.

The League condemned Japan, saying she should leave Manchuria and an autonomous government be set up. Dr Yen, the Chinese delegate, speaking in impeccable English, acclaimed the League's "courageous verdict".

Dreaming spires fired by peace debate

Feb 16. Uproar at Oxford University tonight. A party of invaders stormed the university's Union Society debating hall and – before stupefied onlookers – ripped a page recording last week's debate out of the Union minute-book. The earlier debate had carried a motion by 275 votes to 153: that this House will in no circumstances fight for its King and Country. This decision infuriated the Union's invaders – members of various colleges and also some Fascist party supporters.

Once the raiding party had left, Mr F. M. Hardie, the Union President, vowed that the motion would be reinstated. However, Prince Leonid Lieven, a former Union official, told Hardie: "Sir, even if you are not prepared to defend your King and country, might you not have defended the Minute book?"

1933

MARCH

Su	Mo	Tu	We	Th	Fr	Sa
			1	2	3	4
5	6	7	8	9	10	11
12	13	14	15	16	17	18
19	20	21	22	23	24	25
26	27	28	29	30	31	

1. Germany: Hundreds are arrested as the Nazis round up their political opponents (→9).

3. New York: Premiere of the film "King Kong".→

6. US: Banks are ordered to close for a four-day bank holiday in 47 states (→10).

6. Miami: Mayor Anton Cernak, wounded in the attempt on Roosevelt's life, dies of his wounds.

8. UK: Sainsbury's shops sell butter at one shilling a pound, eggs at one shilling a dozen and tea at ten pence a pound.

9. Munich: Nazis occupy the Bavarian state parliament and expel deputies (12).

10. Washington: Congress passes the Emergency Banking Act, ordering banks to stay shut while they are examined (→12).

12. US: Many banks given a clean bill of health are re-opened (→7/4).

12. Berlin: Hindenburg bans the flag of the republic and orders the Imperial and Nazi flags to fly side by side (→13).

13. Germany: Jews are reported to be leaving in great numbers for neighbouring countries (→14).

14. Germany: The Nazis ban kosher meat and extend the ban on left-wing papers (→15).

15. Berlin: Hitler proclaims the Third Reich (→20).

20. Germany: The Nazis open the first concentration camp, at Dachau near Munich.→

22. Washington: Roosevelt approves a 21st Amendment to the Constitution, which would effectively repeal Prohibition (→5/12).

24. UK: Mrs. Ambrose Clarke's Kellsboro' Jack wins the Grand National at Aintree in record time.

26. Germany: Air minister Hermann Goering denies that Germany's Jews are in danger (→28).

28. Berlin: Hitler orders a boycott of Jews and Jewish shops (→1/4).

MacDonald talks peace with Il Duce

March 23. The Prime Minister went to the House of Commons today to justify his meeting with Signor Mussolini in Rome and his new disarmament proposals. Mr MacDonald told the packed House that his plan was to remove the causes of war in Europe.

His explanation did not, however, please Mr Churchill, who delivered a bitter attack on the Premier's foreign policy which, he declared, had "brought us nearer to war and made us weaker, poorer and more defenceless".

This outburst provoked a spirited reply from Captain Eden, Under-Secretary for Foreign Affairs, who called Mr Churchill's criticism "mischievous absurdity" (→21/5/33).

Benito Mussolini greets the British Prime Minister in Rome.

Commons approves new plan for India

March 29. The Government today received an emphatic endorsement in the House of Commons for its new plans for a Federal Constitution to govern India. The House voted 449 to 43 to set up its Select Committee on the proposals. Mr Churchill's grand attack on the Bill had been eagerly awaited but it failed miserably. It was not even repulsed, it just faded away; there was no weight or power in it and it lacked his usual fighting spirit. ▷

Roosevelt offers ray of hope to US

Roosevelt (r.) drives through Washington with ex-President Hoover.

March 4. Franklin D. Roosevelt was sworn in as President today in one of the most extraordinary days in US history. In the morning the depth of the financial crisis was revealed when the banks closed in the main financial centres of New York and Chicago. In Washington half a million cheering people lined the streets, despite a biting cold wind, as the President drove from the Capitol to the White House.

Roosevelt was smiling and waving. The streets were decorated with flags and the music of marching bands echoed through the city. The inaugural speech was heard by 100,000 people on the east plaza of the Capitol and millions gathered around their radio sets.

Roosevelt told them "the only thing we have to fear is fear itself ... The money changers have fled from their high seats in the temple of our civilisation. We may now restore that temple to the ancient truths." He won his biggest applause when he said he would ask Congress for powers as great as would be granted if "we were in fact invaded by a foreign foe" to deal with the crisis.

Immediately after the ceremony the new President met with key advisers to draw up plans for banking relief and new work initiatives. He has called Congress to an emergency session next week. Today his message was directed at the 13 million Americans who have no jobs. He told them: "This nation asks for action, and action now. Our greatest primary task is to put people to work" (→16/6).

Jews and liberals fear for their lives as Hitler's terror takes hold

March 23. The German parliament committed suicide today and put Chancellor Hitler and his Nazis above the law.

It was done quite legally, though in an atmosphere of terror, both inside Berlin's Kroll Opera House, where the deputies were meeting (within sight of the burned-out Reichstag), and in the streets outside, where Storm Troopers stamped and roared: "Full powers, or else ..." Thus the so-called Enabling Bill, which allows Hitler rather than the President to rule by decree, was passed.

The vote was taken against a background of mounting lawlessness throughout the country. The persecution of Jews is being stepped up and thousands of them are making arrangements to get out of the country while it is still possible. Dr Goebbels, who now has the title of Minister of Public Enlightenment, has denounced "Jewish vampires", who are said to have heaped up millions by "blackmail, trickery and swindling".

It has become commonplace to see groups of Storm Troopers, armed with revolvers and pieces of piping, roaming the streets looking for Jews to beat up. They leave their victims lying on the pavement and nobody comes to help. In some instances Jews have been forced to flog one another, sometimes into unconsciousness. Nazi thugs burst into the Dresden Opera House and ejected the musical director, Fritz Busch. The Berlin home of Leon Feuchtwanger, author of "Jew Suss", was broken into by Nazis, who tore up papers and stole the manuscript of his new novel, "Josephus". Nazis sent from Berlin have also ejected the elected government of Bavaria and replaced it with one of their commissioners.

Hitler Youth: image of the future.

In spite of the violence and intimidation practised by the Nazis during the election campaign, they failed to get a majority of votes. They did come out top of the poll, with 17,277,180 votes. But that represented only 44 per cent of the total. Social Democrats held their position as the second largest party, with 7,181,629 votes; the Centre Party actually increased its vote by 200,000 to 4,424,900.

The result meant Hitler had to depend on Centre Party and Nationalist deputies for the two-thirds majority for his Enabling Bill. Communists and some Social Democrats were noticeably absent, having been arrested (→26).

Campbell sets land speed record in US

Campbell – fastest man on earth.

March 22. Sir Malcolm Campbell, the speed fanatic, set a new world land-speed record of 272 mph in his car, Bluebird, at Daytona Beach in Florida today. The 47-year-old admitted he thought he was going to die during the run when the massive car, powered by an aero-engine, hit a bad bump on the 20-mile long beach, and flew through the air for 30 feet. "It was a terrible tussle to get her straight again," he said.

Sir Malcolm, who learned how to drive while still at school, is a keen big-game hunter, but spends most of his time preparing for record attempts. Friends say he is gloomy before each event and consults fortune tellers.

The film "King Kong" (in which the central character, a giant gorilla, falls in love with a human) brings to the screen the latest in special-effects technology.

1933

APRIL

Su	Mo	Tu	We	Th	Fr	Sa
						1
2	3	4	5	6	7	8
9	10	11	12	13	14	15
16	17	18	19	20	21	22
23	24	25	26	27	28	29
30						

1. UK: Cambridge win the Boat Race for the tenth time in succession.

1. Berlin: Einstein is among the thousands of Jews whose bank accounts are seized by the Nazis.→

3. Nepal: Four Britons make the first flight over Mount Everest.

4. Berlin: Foreigners are ordered to obtain a police permit before they can leave Germany (→ 8).

5. The Hague: The International Court says Greenland is Danish, not Norwegian as claimed by Norway.

7. Washington: Roosevelt introduces a bill to create a $2,000 million fund to insure bank deposits (→ 17).

8. Berlin: All "non-Aryan" officials are ordered to retire (→ 13).

10. Italy: Francesco Agello sets an air speed record of 423.7 mph.

12. Moscow: The trial begins of six British engineers accused of spying.→

13. Germany: All Jewish teachers in the state of Prussia are dismissed (→ 2/5).

17. Washington: Roosevelt agrees to a $144 million cut in US military spending (→ 19).

19. Washington: The US comes off the gold standard to prevent a drain on gold stocks (→ 21).

19. London: A bill banning Soviet imports becomes law.

21. Washington: MacDonald and Roosevelt meet to discuss economic recovery (→ 27).

23. Rome: Sir Oswald Mosley meets Mussolini.→

27. Washington: The Senate approves Roosevelt's new Agricultural Adjustment Bill to aid US farmers (→ 12/5).

30. Peru: President Luis Sanchez Cerro is assassinated.

DEATH

22. British motor car builder Sir Frederick Henry Royce (*27/3/1863).

Nazis hound terrified Jews from office

April 1. The boycott of Jewish businesses in Germany, ordered by the Nazi government, has started with acts of violence against Jews. In many parts of the country, Jewish-owned stores have been forced to close.

Some of them have had their windows smashed, and those windows that remain intact are plastered with posters reading: "Germans, defend yourselves against Jewish atrocity propaganda. Buy only at German shops!"

Big, uniformed SA guards stand threateningly outside shops to enforce the boycott. The stores in Stettin have sent their employees on holiday. Jewish professors have been prevented from entering the University at Munster, while lawyers and bankers have been barred from their offices.

The German press has denied that the boycott has been violent, but an announcement today reveals the truth: "During the past few days there have been repeated excesses, in the course of which the shop windows of many Jewish establishments have been smashed. It is pointed out that the real sufferers from these actions are not the Jewish firms, but the German insurance companies, and that, in the last resort, it is national property that is being destroyed" (→ 4).

Nazis harass a Jew in Berlin.

Popular revulsion grows at Nazi excesses

April 30. Seven young Fascists, dressed in black and peddling anti-Semitic literature, were surrounded by an angry 6,000-strong crowd in London's Piccadilly Circus tonight.

It was the latest violent, popular backlash against the emergence of Sir Oswald Mosley's Fascists and the repression of Jews in Germany. Only two days ago Mosleyites broke up meetings of rival Fascists who had given only lukewarm support to the boycott in Berlin of Jewish traders.

In response, Jews in London's East End displayed anti-German posters until police insisted they be removed (→ 7/5).

April 3. Westland Wallace biplane makes the first flight over Everest.

Britons sentenced for spying in USSR

April 18. At the end of an unusual trial in Moscow, a Soviet court today sent to prison two British engineers out of six charged with spying, wrecking and bribery. Three of the Britons, all of whom worked for the firm of Metropolitan-Vickers, were deported and one was acquitted.

One of the British defendants "confessed" to the charges after being held for a month in the Lubyanka prison. But another told the court that the case was a "frame-up, staged on evidence of terrorised Russians". Ten Russians were given sentences ranging from 18 months to ten years.

The Foreign Office deplored the sentences and Britain is expected to retaliate by banning all Russian imports except those brought in under licence.

Engineer Leslie Thornton on trial.

Everton win FA Cup playing by numbers

April 29. Everton continued their run of success today, adding a 3-0 Cup Final victory over Manchester City to their second division title in 1931 and their League Championship in 1932. An undistinguished match, it was only notable for being the first in which players wore numbered shirts – Everton from 1 to 11, Manchester City "backwards" from 22 (goal) to 12.

1933

MAY

Su	Mo	Tu	We	Th	Fr	Sa
	1	2	3	4	5	6
7	8	9	10	11	12	13
14	15	16	17	18	19	20
21	22	23	24	25	26	27
28	29	30	31			

1. London: MPs approve an Anglo-German trade pact.

2. Berlin: Hitler bans trade unions (→5).

5. Berlin: Hitler proposes "eugenic" laws to ban mixed Jewish and "Aryan" marriages and to begin sterilisation.→

7. London: Fascists and Jews clash in the West End (→15/10).

8. US: The first execution by gas chamber is carried out, in the state of Nevada.

9. Spain: Bombings and shooting mark a general strike (→9/12).

10. Vienna: Chancellor Engelbert Dollfuss bans Nazi meetings (→14).

12. Washington: The Agricultural Adjustment Act becomes law (→18).

14. Vienna: Riots mark the visit of an envoy of Hitler's Nazi regime (→7/6).

15. Amsterdam: Scientists achieve a record low temperature of 0.27 degrees above absolute zero.

16. London: Traffic lights are now being installed in the capital at the rate of one set a day.

18. Washington: The Tennessee Valley Authority is created to develop the area's resources (→6/6).

18. S. Africa: A coalition between Generals Hertzog and Smuts wins the first elections in which women have voted.

21. Rome: Britain agrees to a ten-year non-aggression pact with Italy, Germany and France.

24. UK: The TUC calls for a boycott of Germany to protest against Hitler.

28. Germany: The Nazis seize all property of the German Communist Party (KPD) (→28).

28. Danzig: The Nazis are victorious in elections in the free city (→5/8).

31. UK: Lord Derby's Hyperion wins the Derby at Epsom.

Nazis burn books and harass unions

"Un-German" books from a long blacklist meet their end on the pyre.

May 10. A huge bonfire of books judged by the Nazis to be "un-German" is burning tonight in the square in front of Berlin University. A similar bonfire burnt in Munich where thousands of school-children watched as "Marxist" books were thrown onto the pyre. "As you watch the fire burn these un-German books," the children were told, "let it also burn into your hearts love of the Fatherland."

The books come from the long blacklist published last month of books to be removed from all public libraries. It includes works by authors such as Heinrich Mann, Upton Sinclair and Erich Maria Remarque, who wrote "All Quiet on the Western Front".

Any books that depict war in unpleasant colours are destined for the flames. Their places on the shelves are being filled with the works of Herr Hitler, whose "Mein Kampf" is to be stocked in large numbers, and other leading Nazis. New books ordered by the libraries are to be by writers unknown abroad and, from their titles, seem to be novels written to glorify war.

One of the new plays reflects the spirit of the times. Called "Rothschild Wins At Waterloo", it elaborates the theory that the fortunes of the banking house were based on early news of Napoleon's defeat.

Alongside the book-burning, the Nazis are continuing their purge of the trade union movement. Storm Troopers swept through union offices last week, arresting labour leaders and seizing their files.

The Nazis say they are hunting Marxists, but their real targets are the Socialists, whose strong opposition to the Nazis is rooted in the union movement (→28).

SUPER 1933 HOMES

BARNEHURST PARK ESTATE
BARNEHURST, KENT

9/6 WEEKLY

£395 FREEHOLD

The dream of suburban bliss.

Marlene starts a mode for menswear

May 21. Thousands of women are following the trend set by film star Marlene Dietrich and wearing men's clothes. Grey flannel trousers are particularly popular and commentators have already nicknamed the style "Dietrickery".

The glamorous German actress caused a sensation in Paris on Friday when she arrived from America dressed in a man's brown suit, coat and beret. The colour of her red necktie exactly matched her lips and nails. As her husband struggled with 17 pieces of luggage, Miss Dietrich was almost mobbed by the excited crowd. There is actually a law in Paris against a woman attracting "undue attention" by walking the streets in male attire.

Dietrich en route to Europe.

Mexican Rivera in Marxist mural row

May 13. Communist aspirations collided head-on with capitalist principles on the walls of the Rockefeller Center on New York's Fifth Avenue where Nelson Rockefeller has invited Diego Rivera, the Mexican painter, to decorate a wall of the RCA building. Rivera is known for his massive murals and his Communist sympathies (he is a personal friend of Trotsky).

Rivera's mural showing man's advance through technology to a workers' Utopia included a prominent portrait of Lenin, which caused a storm in the New York papers. As a result, Rockefeller asked him to remove it, which he refused to do.

Rivera was paid off and his mural destroyed. Last night Rivera declared in a speech at the town hall that his work was intended to further the proletarian cause. It has not prevented him from painting the Ford automobile plant for the Detroit Art Institute.

1933

JUNE

Su	Mo	Tu	We	Th	Fr	Sa
				1	2	3
4	5	6	7	8	9	10
11	12	13	14	15	16	17
18	19	20	21	22	23	24
25	26	27	28	29	30	

1. Los Angeles: Charlie Chaplin secretly marries Paulette Goddard.

5. Italy: Conductor Arturo Toscanini refuses to conduct at the Bayreuth Wagner festival in protest at the Nazis.

6. Washington: Congress approves the National Industry Recovery Act.→

6. Berlin: The Nazis set up a Race Council to encourage "Aryan" births and check mixed marriages (→7).

7. Berlin: Hitler orders the border with Austria closed to non-Nazis (→19).

8. Madrid: Manuel Azana is dismissed as premier.

12. London: The King opens the World Economic Conference (→15).

13. Vienna: Hundreds of Nazis are arrested; Chancellor Dollfuss will fly back from the London economic talks (→19).

14. Berlin: German Jews are banned from the 1936 Berlin Olympics.

15. London: The economic conference draws up a plan to stabilise currencies (→23/7).

19. Vienna: Dollfuss bans all Nazi organisations (→14/8).

20. London: Iraq's King Feisal arrives on an official visit.

21. US: The American Federation of Labor says 1.7 million new jobs have been created in the last two months (→30/9).

22. US: The Illinois Waterway opens, linking the Great Lakes of the northern US with the Gulf of Mexico.

26. London: The King lays the foundation stone of the University of London's new Bloomsbury site.

27. UK: Britain wins the Ryder Cup, beating the US by one point.→

29. New York: Italian Primo Carnera beats Jack Sharkey to become world heavyweight boxing champion.

30. Berlin: Hindenburg bars the appointment of a Nazi to head the Lutheran Church (→15/7).

Roosevelt signs New Deal legislation

June 16. President Roosevelt today signed the National Industry Recovery Act. It marks the climax to the whirlwind of legislation that has blown through Congress in the 99 days of emergency sittings since his inauguration. The new law, which he has called the most important ever passed by Congress, gives the Government wide powers to control industry.

The Act will be administered by a new agency, the National Recovery Administration, which will bring management and unions together to fix wages, shorten working hours and regulate production in an effort to beat the Depression. A further $3 billion is to be allocated to public works and to boost the economy.

Americans on a work programme put their backs into street-widening.

Today's measure confirms the astonishing change in the American mood since Roosevelt took over. He has taken huge new powers for the Federal Government in a nation devoted to decentralised state rule. He has brought in controls over finance and industry in a country where free enterprise is gospel. He has gone over the heads of the nation's leaders to ordinary Americans through his hugely popular radio fireside chats. And he has enhanced his popularity by repealing the Prohibition laws. "I think this would be a good time for a beer," he said at the time.

Altogether 13 major measures have been passed by the Congress. They have provided money to bail out the banks and the farmers and to help home-owners behind with their mortgages. The Civilian Conservation Corps has been established to provide tree-planting work for the young unemployed. The Tennessee Valley Authority is to be set up to rehabilitate one rural area with hydro-electric power and forests. So far over a million jobs have been created (→21).

Hitler bans all opposition parties

Sweeping out the red pests.

June 23. Germany has become a one-party state, in fact if not yet in name, though that will soon be remedied. The last Social Democrats have been thrown out of the Reichstag as "subversive and inimical to the state", the National Party is to be absorbed by the Nazis, and the few remaining non-Nazi deputies do as they are told. Changing the constitution, however, will be a mere formality. All institutions are already being taken over by the Nazi Party. Officials of trade unions and employers' organisations have been sacked and replaced by Nazis on the orders of Dr Robert Ley, an alcoholic chemist from Cologne, who has become head of the new German Work Front. Ley has withdrawn Germany from the International Labour Office, which, he says, is run by "blackguards, Jews, Communists and Roman Catholics".

The Boy Scouts have been dissolved and young Germans are to join a Hitler Youth organisation under the anti-Semitic Baldur von Schirach. Meanwhile Bernhard Rust, an unemployed provincial schoolmaster and the new Minister of Science, Education and Popular Culture, is rewriting school textbooks to include such subjects as "racial science" (→26/7).

British golfer Henry Cotton. After Britain's victory in this month's Ryder Cup, there is great optimism that he might take the Blue Riband at the Open Golf Championship at St Andrew's.

1933

JULY

Su	Mo	Tu	We	Th	Fr	Sa
						1
2	3	4	5	6	7	8
9	10	11	12	13	14	15
16	17	18	19	20	21	22
23	24	25	26	27	28	29
30	31					

1. US: Roscoe Turner flies from New York to Los Angeles in a record time of 11 hours 30 minutes.

1. Germany: Premiere of Richard Strauss's opera "Arabella".

3. London: Opening of Richmond, Chiswick and Hampton Court Bridges.

4. India: Gandhi is sentenced to one year's imprisonment (→ 20/8).

7. UK: British doctors isolate the virus of influenza.

8. Wimbledon: John Crawford beat Ellesworth Vines in the Men's Singles Final; Helen Moody beat Dorothy Round for her sixth Singles title.

10. UK: Unemployment is down to 2.44 million.

14. Berlin: The Nazis ban all opposition activity (→ 18).

15. Germany: All the Protestant Churches merge as the German Evangelical Church (→ 16/1/34).

17. UK: Cricketer Jack Hobbs scores his 194th century.

18. Berlin: German citizenship is declared conditional on Nazi membership (→ 20).

20. London: 30,000 Jews march on Hyde Park to protest against Nazi anti-Semitism (→ 21).

21. Geneva: World Jewish organisations appeal for League aid in curbing Nazi excesses (→ 23).

23. Germany: Importing banned books is decreed punishable by death.→

25. Marseilles: Leon Trotsky and his wife arrive to continue their exile in France, which has granted them asylum.

27. London: The government says it is setting up a "Sterling Group" to maintain economic stability in the Empire.

28. London: A detached house at Mill Hill, just north of London, now costs £800.

30. France: A British team that includes Fred Perry wins the Davis Cup, ending France's seven-year supremacy (→ 10/9).

Nazis to sterilise "imperfect" Germans

Eager young Nazis hear Hitler's plans for a strong and pure Aryan race.

July 26. In the wake of a stream of official decrees directed at strengthening and purifying the German race, Hitler's cabinet yesterday announced plans for the compulsory sterilisation of people suffering from blindness, deafness, physical deformity, hereditary imbecility, epilepsy and St Vitus' dance. The sterilisations will be carried out without the consent of the victims; force can be used if necessary.

Last month a committee of experts on population questions was appointed to consider measures to increase the size of German families and to recommend ways of putting an end to the "mixture of races and degeneration of German families". Another decree, which provides for the granting of cheap loans to newly-married couples, specifically forbids the spending of the money in Jewish shops.

Other recent measures against the Jews include a ruling from the Nazi-controlled Medical Association that Jewish doctors can issue medical certificates only to people of their own blood (→ 29/8).

Hitler signs a pact with the Vatican

July 9. The new concordat between the Holy See and the German Reich was initialled today by Cardinal Pacelli, the Papal Secretary of State, and Herr von Papen, the German Vice-Chancellor. Within an hour of the signing, Herr Hitler rescinded his orders dissolving Roman Catholic organisations.

Later, addressing 70,000 Storm Troopers, he said the treaty and the disappearance of the Catholic party signified the end of the fight for political power. "Stronghold after stronghold we have taken", he said. "There are gigantic tasks before us, but we shall master them. No one can resist us."

Economic summit ends in failure

July 23. The World Monetary and Economic Conference ended today in total failure. Delegates from 66 nations had gathered in London to discuss trade barriers, most-favoured-nation status and the gold standard. No consensus was reached on any issue. In his closing speech, the British Prime Minister Ramsay MacDonald could say only that the situation delegates faced – unemployment, bankruptcies, unbalanced budgets, undeveloped resources – was "a challenge to the wisdom of man".

New board for all London transport

July 1. What is thought to be the world's largest transport company began life today with the creation of the London Passenger Transport Board. It brings together under one publicly-owned organisation all the underground, bus, trolley and tram services that serve the capital – everything, in fact, except the main-line railway services. Nor is the new empire confined to city streets; it stretches deep into the home counties as far as Luton, Reigate and Wycombe. In all, 4,000 million journeys are made on the new network each year and the service employs 71,000 people.

Helen Moody seizes sixth Wimbledon title

July 8. The Wimbledon Championships ended with the most competitive ladies' singles final since the War. It was won, for the sixth time in the last seven years, by the American Helen Wills Moody, 6-4, 6-8, 6-3, over the British challenger from Dudley, Dorothy Round.

The first two sets were so close that the Centre Court crowd became almost hysterical with the tension of the hot afternoon, especially when Miss Round took the second after a long and heated argument between the two line judges and the umpire when she was leading 7-6. The incident unsettled both women and the experienced American won only by making fewer errors.

Mrs Wills Moody (r.) wins again.

1933

AUGUST

Su	Mo	Tu	We	Th	Fr	Sa
		1	2	3	4	5
6	7	8	9	10	11	12
13	14	15	16	17	18	19
20	21	22	23	24	25	26
27	28	29	30	31		

2. Nicaragua: Martial law is declared throughout the country.

5. Danzig: Poland signs a treaty with the Free City for greater use of its port.

7. London: The government publishes an outline of its plans for the future constitution of Burma.

8. Cuba: President Gerardo Machado declares a state of war as rioting against his dictatorship grips the island (→12).

12. Cuba: The army, under Sgt. Fulgencio Batista, ousts Machado, installing Dr Carlos de Cespedes as president.

14. Austria: A newspaper reveals an alleged plan by the Nazis to invade Austria (→19).

17. Berlin: An American surgeon is attacked for failing to salute Hitler (→18/9).

18. Iraq: 600 Kurds and Syrians are reported killed in clashes on the Iraq-Syria border.

19. Italy: Mussolini meets Austrian Chancellor Dollfuss at Rimini (→24).

20. India: Gandhi is rushed to hospital on the fourth day of his latest fast.→

24. Italy: Pope Pius XI visits the Papal summer retreat at Castelgandolfo, the first Pope to do so since 1870.

24. Italy: Mussolini pledges aid to Austria (→11/9).

25. Rome: Italy signs a non-aggression treaty with the USSR.

28. UK: Drought threatens as the temperature touches 90 degrees F (32 degrees C).

30. France: The airline Air France is created.

BIRTHS

18. Polish film director Roman Polanski.

21. British mezzo-soprano Dame Janet Baker.

DEATH

23. Austrian architect Adolf Loos (10/12/1870).

De Valera strikes at IRA and Blue Shirts

Aug 30. The Irish Free State Government has acted swiftly to defend itself from two groups of armed men roaming the country, the "Blue Shirt" national guard and the IRA. Two armed policemen have been put on permanent guard outside President de Valera's office, and the doors of government buildings are firmly closed all day.

The soldiers, on guard with fixed bayonets, have been reinforced by a new force of 360 armed police, drawn from those who took part in the Anglo-Irish war of independence. All the Army's armoured vehicles have been put in two barracks north and south of Dublin's river Liffey.

In recent days the Government has banned a mass meeting of the 40,000 strong "Blue Shirts", led by General Eoin O'Duffy, who was sacked as chief of police, and raided an IRA camp in the Dublin mountains (→9/10).

Irish President de Valera.

Gandhi leaves jail weighing 90 pounds

Aug 23. Mahatma Gandhi, weighing only 90 pounds, has been released today from Sassoon hospital in Poona because, after five days of his latest "fast unto death", the doctors feared that his emaciated body could no longer stand the strain of fasting. He too thought he was dying; he refused even to sip water, and shared out his few personal belongings among the nurses.

He was taken to the hospital from Yeravda jail, which he had described as his "permanent address", when he started his fast in protest against a refusal to allow him to continue his work with the Untouchables while in prison.

He had deliberately courted arrest, rejecting an order permitting him to reside only within the limits of Poona, and had been sentenced to a year's imprisonment. He is completely unrepentant.

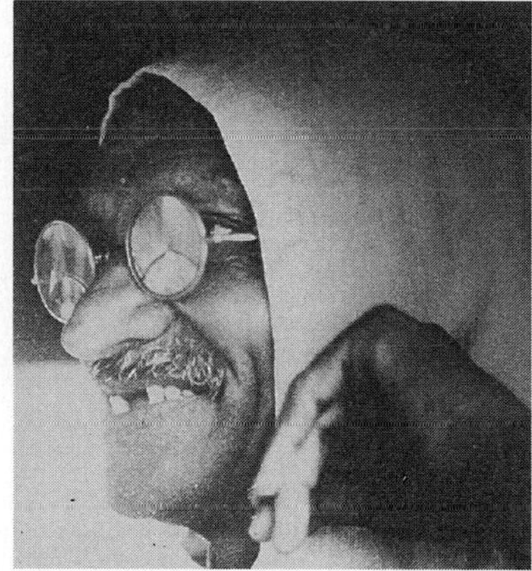

Mahatma Gandhi: unrepentant.

Nazis herd Jews into concentration camps

Aug 29. It has been officially confirmed that the Nazis are rounding up large numbers of Jews and sending them to concentration camps. Some have been arrested on charges of "fighting Storm Troopers" and others for "consorting with German girls". But the Jews are not the only ones. The outlawed Socialist Party says that 45,000 prisoners are being held in 65 camps, the largest being Dachau.

Some foreign correspondents have been allowed into Dachau, and report that the camp consists of concrete huts used by munition workers until 1918 and now surrounded by electrified barbed wire.

The space between the double fence is patrolled by armed sentries who shoot anyone attempting to escape without challenge. Herr Wekerle, the Prison Commandant, said: "Four men made a dash for it last week. They got a hundred yards before the bullets hit them."

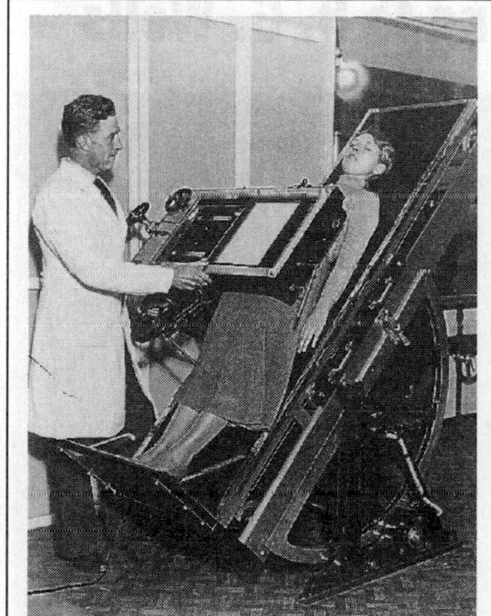

Demonstration of the latest in radiology: an X-ray couch.

How absolutely, definitely frightful

Aug 14. It's definitely not a joking matter, so far as Richard Hardy of Bayswater, London, is concerned. He gets frightfully annoyed, as he told readers of the Daily Telegraph this month, about what he called a "plague of catchwords – worse than the blare of motor horns".

His claim that these words were polluting and devaluing the English language has drawn attention to the words most in fashion this summer. Top of Mr Hardy's hate list is the word "definitely" – a tired adverb to which, he says, his children are now slaves. He says: "With them, everybody or everything is either "definitely this" or "definitely that" or "definitely something else."

Other words whose use irritates Mr Hardy and others who have joined the debate are: "frightfully", "absolutely", "too awfully" and "priceless". What drives these linguistic critics to despair is both the frequency of the catchwords and their imprecision. "Day by day," moans Mr Hardy, "our ears are pestered by the repetition of commonplace terms that soon grow threadbare and should never have been forced out of their obscurity." Absolutely. I mean, it's definitely too awful.

1933

SEPTEMBER

Su	Mo	Tu	We	Th	Fr	Sa
					1	2
3	4	5	6	7	8	9
10	11	12	13	14	15	16
17	18	19	20	21	22	23
24	25	26	27	28	29	30

1. London: Kenneth Clark, aged 30, is appointed director of the National Gallery.

4. UK: Forest fires rage through Dorset and Hampshire following recent dry weather.→

7. Warsaw: Poland has talks with the USSR and Rumania on a possible united front against Germany.

11. Vienna: Dollfuss says democracy is dead in Austria (→20).

12. UK: Rainfall ends the recent drought and puts out the forest fires.

15. UK: A report says Britain is healthier than ever, but still has slums, bad diet, and polluted milk and water (→5/10).

18. Baghdad: King Ghazi is crowned following the death of his father King Feisal in Switzerland on the 8th.

18. Berlin: A decree says all doctors must be Nazis (→23).

20. Vienna: Dollfuss assumes dictatorial powers when the cabinet resigns (→3/10).

21. Washington: Roosevelt orders $75 million to be spent on clothing and feeding the unemployed this winter.

23. Germany: Field Marshal von Ludendorff, Hitler's old comrade, is outlawed as a Communist.

25. Turin: The Turin Shroud is shown to a crowd of 25,000 people.

28. London: Anti-Nazi uproar breaks out when German actor Werner Kraus appears at the Shaftesbury Theatre.

30. Germany: Unemployment stands at 3.85 million.

BIRTH

22. British writer Fay Weldon.

DEATHS

7. British Liberal statesman Edward Grey, Viscount Grey of Falloden (*25/4/1862).

8. Iraqi King Feisal (*1855).

8. US industrialist Robert Chesebrough, inventor of Vaseline in 1870 (*1837).

Nazi show trial for Reichstag accused

Sept 29. A yellow-faced and apathetic Dutchman, Marinus van der Lubbe, today admitted to a Leipzig court that he had set fire to the Berlin Reichstag, the German parliament building, last February.

With the help of a map of the huge building – and reading a confession said to have been made by van der Lubbe in prison – the court's president then described how the Dutchman had, in a mere 20 minutes, set light to woodwork, furniture and curtains in dozens of rooms using only firelighters and his own shirt.

The map had one omission: no sign of the tunnel which links the building to the home of Hermann Goering, the Reichstag's president and chief minister to the Nazi leader Adolf Hitler (→22/12).

Marinus van der Lubbe in court.

FDR to spend millions on poor this winter

Sept 30. In another radical measure to help the 3.5 million US families on relief, President Roosevelt today announced a $700 million programme. The money will come from federal, state and local funds, but, whereas before today federal funds were only available if matched by local funds, from now on federal money will be doled out in any case to the needy areas.

Harry Hopkins, administrator of federal relief, denied that the new programme would mean dishing out "salt pork and beans" to the poor. "We will give them a balanced diet," he said. Much of the food will come from the huge farm surpluses which the Government holds in storage.

Today's move follows a cascade of measures to help the poor. Just over a week ago Roosevelt gave over $75 million of surplus food and clothing to them. New jobs have been provided, including some novel ones like painting murals in post offices and recording folk songs. Bank deposits below $5,000 have been guaranteed, protecting the savings of the poor against bank collapse.

Things to come, according to H. G. Wells

Sept 1. After Aldous Huxley's discomfiting vision of a Brave New World, H.G.Wells gives us his vision of "The Shape of Things to Come" today (Hutchinson, 10s 6d). Immediate outlook: decline and fall of civilisation as we know it.

The Soviet experiment will become hidebound in dogma, while the capitalist US Treasury will soon be unable to afford its armed forces. There will be war between Germany and Poland by 1940. Later a great pestilence will leave New York a deserted ruin.

Forced at last to co-operate, man will create the world state and live happily. When? In AD 2059.

Wells, as seen by Max Beerbohm.

Fred Perry wins US Open tennis title

Sept 10. Fred Perry, the former world table tennis champion and now the mainstay of Britain's Davis Cup challenge, today became the first Briton to win the United States Open tennis championships since H.L.Doherty took the title in 1903, six years before Perry was born.

Though a Briton was facing an Australian (the Wimbledon champion Jack Crawford), Forest Hills was packed. The match fluctuated dramatically for the first three sets, with Perry taking the first, Crawford winning the second (an epic 13-11) and third; but then, exhausted and demoralised by his opponent's relentless drive, the Australian collapsed 6-0, 6-1, to leave Perry a decisive winner.

Perry hits his way to victory.

Forest fires follow summer heatwave

Sept 10. More fires raged across southern England and Wales today. Four square miles of the New Forest and hundreds of acres of Epping Forest blazed out of control as firemen, soldiers and Sunday picnickers tried to beat back the flames with branches torn from trees. Near Monmouth last night 100-feet flames lit up vast areas of burning Crown woodland. Two cars were burnt out in the New Forest, but, astonishingly, there are no reports of deaths. The fires follow a month-long heatwave, with temperatures of up to 90 degrees Fahrenheit (→12).

1933

OCTOBER

Su	Mo	Tu	We	Th	Fr	Sa
1	2	3	4	5	6	7
8	9	10	11	12	13	14
15	16	17	18	19	20	21
22	23	24	25	26	27	28
29	30	31				

1. Germany: The German Post Office establishes the first "telex" operation, between Berlin and Hamburg.

3. Vienna: Chancellor Dollfuss is shot and injured by an Austrian Nazi, but vows to continue in office (→10).

4. Geneva: Britain and Italy attack Nazism during a League session (→10).

5. London: Health Minister Sir Hilton Young announces a slum clearance scheme.→

9. Dublin: De Valera introduces three bills to reduce even further the jurisdiction of the British Crown.

10. Geneva: The League appoints a commissioner for political refugees, especially those now fleeing Germany.→

12. Washington: Plans are unveiled to turn the island of Alcatraz, in San Francisco Bay, into a prison.

15. Manchester: Sir Oswald Mosley and Fascist sympathisers are stoned by a crowd.

18. US: A mob of 2,000 lynches a black man accused of attacking a white woman (→15/12).

19. Australia: Charles Ulm flies from Britain to Australia in a record six days 18 hours.

20. Washington: Roosevelt invites Soviet foreign minister Litvinov to discuss a possible US recognition of the USSR (→17/11).

20. Rome: Mussolini denounces President Roosevelt as a dictator.

23. Paris: Edouard Daladier resigns as premier (→26).

24. France: 37 die and 87 are hurt when the Cherbourg to Paris express is derailed and plummits over a precipice.

26. Paris: Sarraut forms a new leftist government (→26/11).

31. US: The research ship Atlantis returns to port with evidence of life in the deepest parts of the oceans.

DEATH

29. French statesman Paul Painleve (*5/12/1863).

Hitler quits the League

Herr Hitler arrives at a meeting of Berlin Nazis to explain his decision.

Oct 14. A dramatic announcement by the Nazi government in Berlin today says that because of the "humiliating and dishonouring demands of the other Powers", Germany will take no further part in the Geneva Disarmament Conference and, in addition, will withdraw from the League of Nations.

Herr Hitler fiercely condemned the attitude of the other powers towards Germany: "The German people and their government are deeply humiliated by the deliberate refusal of a real, moral and actual equality to Germany."

Tonight he gave a long speech over the radio, in which he reiterated Germany's peaceful intentions. Equality, not arms, was his aim, he said. The news dropped like a bombshell on Geneva, arriving just as Sir John Simon was assuring journalists of the prospects of success for an agreement on disarmament.

So great is the consternation caused by Herr Hitler's announcement that it is considered likely that the conference will have to be postponed indefinitely.

A referendum is to be held next month to give the German people the opportunity to give their approval to Herr Hitler's policies. It is pointed out, however, that as all the other parties have been outlawed, only the name of the Nazi Party will be on the ballot paper. The result of the poll could be a foregone conclusion (→12/11).

Government speeds up slum clearance

Oct 5. Health Minister Sir Hilton Young opened the Conservative Party conference at Birmingham today with news of heartening progress in Britain's slum clearance programme.

The next five years, he said, will see over a million people rehoused and 210,000 slum dwellings demolished in a £95 million scheme. Local authorities which do not meet their targets will find the Ministry's compulsory powers applied in full, he warned.

Feeding the masses

Oct 23. The Lyons organisation proudly announced the opening of a new London "Corner House" today and the operation of a revolutionary concept in mass catering.

Behind the scenes at the vast cafe, which offers food and music to 2,000 people at a time, waitresses will fill their orders along a "one way" system, signposted with notices like "fried fish" or "soups", to speed customer service.

The Corner House, which has moved from its former Oxford Street site, will employ more than 1,000 staff.

Arab rioters oppose Jewish immigration

Oct 27. A state of emergency has been declared in Jaffa and other coastal towns in Palestine after ugly clashes between Arab rioters and police. More than 9,000 demonstrators gathered to show their anger at continued Jewish immigration, and over 20 were killed and 130 wounded. Clashes also affected the ports of Haifa and Nablus, where Arabs attacked police stations. In Jaffa tonight, Arab rioters failed to disperse after an official warning. When the Palestine Police charged, Arabs in the crowd began shooting, and they returned fire.

By-election shock for MacDonald

Oct 25. Labour has won a significant fight against the National Government in capturing East Fulham today. A Tory majority of 14,521 there in 1931 is now a Labour one of 4,840. The 29 per cent swing is by far the biggest of its several recent by-election rebuffs.

The campaign was fought on both unemployment and disarmament. But in victory John Wilmot, the Labour candidate, stressed the peace theme. He said: "The message is that the British people demand that the Government give a lead to the world by initiating immediately a policy of general disarmament." Government Ministers saw the result as proof of growing pacifist feeling (→1/11).

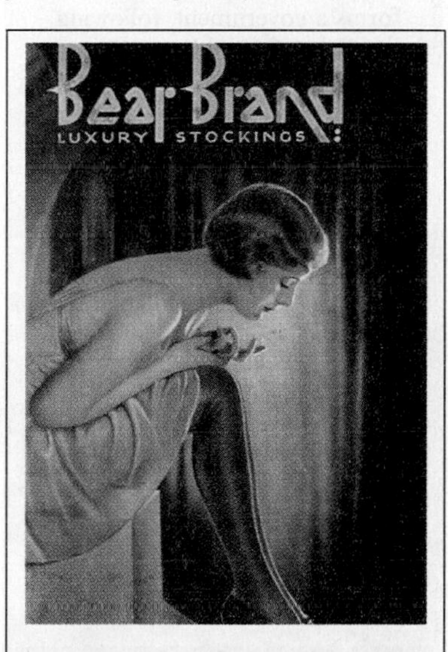

1933

NOVEMBER

Su	Mo	Tu	We	Th	Fr	Sa
			1	2	3	4
5	6	7	8	9	10	11
12	13	14	15	16	17	18
19	20	21	22	23	24	25
26	27	28	29	30		

1. UK: The Labour Party makes big gains in local elections.

2. Munich: Noel Panter, a British journalist accused of treason, is released.

3. Spain: Right-wing parties make big gains in national elections (→ 12).

5. France: Marcel Deat founds a new Socialist Party (→ 26).

8. Kabul: King Nadir Shah is assassinated; his 18-year-old son Zahir Shah succeeds.

10. Austria: Martial law is declared and the death penalty extended (→ 4/12).

11. Berlin: President Hindenburg urges Germans to vote for Hitler.→

12. Spain: One person is killed in a bid to kill the Fascist leader Jose Primo de Rivera, son of the ex-premier (→ 9/12).

14. Berlin: The new Reichstag is opened; all the members are Nazis, there are no women and no Jews (→ 23).

17. US: Claude Rains makes his screen debut in "The Invisible Man".

17. Washington: The US establishes diplomatic and trade relations with the USSR.

23. Germany: Hitler suppresses two monarchist groups, fearing a plot to restore the ex-Kaiser (→ 29).

26. Paris: Camille Chautemps forms a government, following the resignation of premier Albert Sarraut.

28. London: New grounds for divorce are proposed, including cruelty, drunkenness and insanity.

29. Berlin: An appeal court rules that being Jewish is insufficient grounds for sacking an employee (→ 2/12).

30. London: Examination of the skeletons of the alleged "Princes in the Tower" indicates they died in the reign of Richard III.

BIRTH

23. Polish composer Krzysztof Penderecki.

Britain announces boost for defences

Nov 29. The Government today admitted its policy of cutting arms spending in the hope other nations will follow had failed. Now the forces will receive a boost aimed at bringing Britain up to match the strength of the other great powers.

Lord Londonderry, the Air Minister, told the Lords: "We cannot continue in our present inferiority. Our air force must be as strong as that of any other nation."

In the Commons, Stanley Baldwin said the defence of the country would, from now on, be treated as one, so that spending on the three services can be tailored to meet the potential threat. Britain could not continue to stand alone half disarmed. Britain now has just 850 military aircraft compared to 1,650 in France and 1,000 each in the US and Italy. Mr Baldwin, the Lord President, still hopes international controls can be set on arms spending. He warned that a "sudden and quick" increase in air force spending would lead to bad feeling with Germany.

The Government's action follows fears that arms cuts have left the nation vulnerable. Earlier this month the First Lord of the Admiralty announced a new naval building programme, admitting that the policy of building small ships, in the hope other countries would follow the example, had failed.

Nazis win 95% vote in German plebiscite

Nov 12. Chancellor Hitler was given massive popular support today for his decision to walk out of the Geneva disarmament conference. In the plebiscite on the issue, 95 per cent of voters said Yes. And in the voting for the one-party Reichstag, the Nazis received 92 per cent of the votes. Spoiled papers accounted for the rest.

Throughout the afternoon Nazi Storm Troopers went from door to door, sending off to the polling station anyone unable to produce the metal disk stamped with the word "Ja" handed out when a ballot is cast. In the Dachau concentration camp outside Munich, 2,154 out of 2,242 inmates voted for the regime that imprisoned them (→ 14).

Germany flocks to the Nazi flag.

Dancer Fred Astaire is a bright new cinema star: what style!

Slimming and tank, new words for 1933

Nov 21. Are we speaking English or American these days? Purists must wonder as they read the supplementary volume of the Oxford English Dictionary reflecting changes over the past 50 years.

Americanisms include graft, once-over, dope, and step-on-the-gas while from Australia comes the phrase "no flies on me". Other words in common usage today – and presumably saying something about modern times – are robot, tank, ga-ga, slimming, profiteer and photostat.

1933

DECEMBER

Su	Mo	Tu	We	Th	Fr	Sa
					1	2
3	4	5	6	7	8	9
10	11	12	13	14	15	16
17	18	19	20	21	22	23
24	25	26	27	28	29	30
31						

2. Berlin: Hitler tells Hindenburg to remain president as long as he wants (→ 6).

4. Austria: Nazi leader Alfred Frauenfeld is arrested.

6. Berlin: The Nazis say they plan to abolish women's suffrage (→ 12).

8. Los Angeles: Actress Mary Pickford files for divorce from Douglas Fairbanks Sr.

10. Stockholm: Nobel Prizes go to Erwin Schrodinger (Austria) and Paul Dirac (UK, Physics), Thomas Morgan (US, Medicine) and Ivan Bunin (France, Literature). No Chemistry or Peace Prizes.

12. Berlin: The new Reichstag meets for 12 minutes and adjourns indefinitely.

15. US: A black man freed by a court in Tennessee is lynched by a mob.

18. Newfoundland: The Dominion reverts to Crown Colony status and direct British rule to avert financial collapse.

22. Leipzig: Dutchman Marinus van der Lubbe is sentenced to death for burning the Reichstag (→ 10/1/34).

23. France: 190 people are killed when the Nancy express train hits the Strasbourg express near Meaux.

29. Bucharest: Liberal premier Ion Duca is murdered by a Fascist.

31. New York: Republican Fiorello La Guardia is sworn in as mayor.

DEATH

4. German writer Stefan George (*12/7/1868).

HITS OF 1933

Smoke gets in your eyes.

Who's afraid of the Big Bad Wolf?

Stormy weather.

QUOTE OF THE YEAR

"Proposed: That this House will in no way fight for King and Country."

Oxford Union Society, motion for debate, February 9, 1933.

Red uprising in Spain

Armed Communist insurgents run riot in the streets of Madrid.

Dec 9. Communist rebels are still active in many parts of Spain following their weekend attempt to seize power. More than 100 people have died, 27 of them in the destruction of the Barcelona-Seville express. A mine was placed on the line where it crosses a ravine near Valencia; when the express detonated it, several carriages crashed onto the rocks below. It seems that the communists were infuriated by the success of the conservative parties in the recent election and made a desperate bid for power; in the process they have done some terrible things. There is fighting everywhere and tonight Granada is lit by the glare of its burning churches.

The bottle is back as US prohibition ends

Dec 5. America toasted farewell to prohibition today after 14 dry years when Utah became the last state to ratify the 21st Amendment. Introduced after the war, prohibition was evaded on a large scale: "bootlegging" fell under the control of major criminals, leading to gang warfare, especially in Chicago.

Repeal of prohibition was a plank in the Democratic platform in 1928 and 1932, and a proposal to enact it was put before Congress three weeks after President Roosevelt's inauguration. The president today called on the nation to practise moderation and prevent a return to the "repugnant conditions" that had brought about prohibition in 1920.

America makes up for lost time at the end of 14 dry years.

Arts: Jewish artists flee from Germany

The Nazi rise to power has left the intellectual and artistic elite of Germany, many of whom are Jews, dismissed from their posts and scattered into exile. Among musicians who have fled the country are the pioneer of atonal music, **Arnold Schoenberg**, dismissed from the Prussian Academy of Arts, conductors **Erich Kleiber** and **Otto Klemperer**, of the Berlin State Opera, and **Fritz Busch**, conductor of the Dresden Opera.

The music of **Paul Hindemith**, who is not Jewish, has been banned from the radio. Only **Richard Strauss** among leading composers seems unaffected. His new opera "Arabella" has been well received. **Arturo Toscanini** refused to conduct at the Bayreuth festival in protest at the Nazi treatment of artists.

Bertolt Brecht and **Kurt Weill**, whose musical play "The Threepenny Opera" had run since 1928 in Berlin, have left, as have film director **Fritz Lang** and playwright **Ernst Toller**.

The greatest name in German letters, **Thomas Mann**, is in Switzerland. His novelist brother **Heinrich** and **Arnold and Stefan Zweig** are on the list of banned authors whose works were removed from public libraries and burnt. So was **Erich Maria Remarque** for his anti-war "All Quiet on the Western Front".

In July the world-famous Bauhaus, by now in Berlin, was closed and its building occupied by the Gestapo. Its new director, **Ludwig Mies van der Rohe**, like his predecessor **Walter Gropius**, is in exile along with the Bauhaus painters **Vassily Kandinsky** and **Paul Klee**.

Otto Dix's "Seven Deadly Sins".

An unmissable arrival on the London skyline is Battersea power station, the largest yet built in England. Its three fluted chimneys (a fourth is to be added) rise for 337 feet, like upturned table legs, above massive brick plinths styled by **Sir Giles Gilbert Scott**, better known for his cathedral at Liverpool. This so-called "cathedral of power" has been accepted by a public at first horrified by the smoke threat.

Writing about the Depression is in vogue. "Love on the Dole" by **Walter Greenwood** is a stage hit from Manchester starring **Wendy Hiller**, while **George Orwell** worked as a scullery-hand and disguised himself as a tramp to bring us the grim reportage of "Down and Out in Paris and London".

Sir Thomas Beecham conducts the London Philharmonic Orchestra.

1934

JANUARY

Su	Mo	Tu	We	Th	Fr	Sa
	1	2	3	4	5	6
7	8	9	10	11	12	13
14	15	16	17	18	19	20
21	22	23	24	25	26	27
28	29	30	31			

1. Germany: The law for sterilisation of "inferior" citizens comes into effect (→24/5/35).

3. UK: Road signs are to be standardised, including a sign for "main road ahead", but no "stop" sign (→28/3).

6. Berlin: Nazi Ludwig Muller takes over as head of the German Evangelical Church (→7).

7. Paris: Pierre Laval and Mussolini settle disputed frontiers between French and Italian colonies.

7. Germany: Nazi control of the Protestant Church is denounced from the pulpit by 6,000 pastors (→11).

9. UK: Butter costs tenpence a pound, the cheapest in living memory; it costs 3/- a pound in France (→14/3).

10. Germany: Alleged Reichstag arsonist Marinus van der Lubbe is guillotined.

11. Germany: Police raid the homes of clergy who oppose the Nazis (→29/10/35).

12. Austria: The first death sentence is imposed since the foundation of the republic.

16. London: Winston Churchill says: "We have never been so defenceless as we are now," in a radio broadcast.

16. Berlin: Goering orders the dissolution of all Freemasons' lodges (→2/2).

17. S. Africa: A poor prospector finds the world's third-largest diamond, 726 carats.

19. Washington: Roosevelt orders $21 million to be spent on US war veterans (→2/6).

22. Paris: 750 are arrested as Communists and Royalists battle with police (→6/2).

26. Berlin: Germany signs a ten-year non-aggression pact with Poland (→20/2).

27. Paris: Chautemps resigns in the wake of the Stavisky affair; Edouard Daladier forms a new government (→7/2).

31. Washington: The dollar is devalued to 59.6 cents to protect US trade.

Mosley calls for a modern dictatorship

Blackshirt leader Sir Oswald Mosley harangues the Fascist faithful.

Jan 21. Sir Oswald Mosley spoke tonight in Birmingham at the biggest rally which the British Union of Fascists (BUF) has held since its formation two years ago. An estimated 10,000 people attended. They included about 3,000 of his dedicated supporters who gave him the Fascist salute in the style accorded to the continental dictators.

Sir Oswald said he will ask the nation to return a Fascist majority at the next election. He described his aim as a "modern dictatorship" – one with complete powers to act as it wants for the benefit of the people. Then he added: "The Fascist government will be armed with powers to overcome the problems the people want overcome." Many of the BUF members wore black shirts and leather belts – uniform copied from Mussolini.

As usual now at BUF meetings, some roughneck stewards were involved in scuffles with hecklers. They snatched hats from people who refused to take them off during singing of the national anthem.

Some Tory supporters, who had sympathised with Sir Oswald, are now repulsed by his strong-arm tactics, and there seems no likelihood of his winning any parliamentary seats. In the parliamentary lobbies there is frequent talk about a need for tougher public order laws to curb BUF activities (→9/6).

Mystery surrounds a swindler's suicide

Jan 8. The notorious swindler Alexander Stavisky has committed suicide in a ski-chalet at Chamonix in France. He shot himself through the head as policemen entered through an open window. They found him comatose, with blood streaming from his head. Rushed to hospital, he died a few hours later.

Three policemen had tracked him down to the villa where he was hiding under a false name. It appears he anticipated their arrival and preferred death to arrest.

His death, however, will only serve to increase the scandal surrounding his life. Already, it is whispered that the suicide was faked with allegations that the police killed Stavisky because he knew too much and was about to confess, compromising his many highly-placed protectors.

The affair has already claimed its first political casualty. The Colonial Secretary, M. Dalimier, resigned today after admitting his role in recommending Stavisky's fraudulent Municipal Credit Bonds. Premier Chautemps has promised an inquiry. The opposition will no doubt allege he is trying to cover up his party's embarrassing connections with Stavisky (→27).

Flying circus aids in Indian earthquake

Jan 17. It is now feared that some 2,000 people died in last Monday's earthquake in Bihar and that £1 million worth of damage has been caused to property. The whole area of Monghyr is said to be flooded by sulphur-impregnated water and mud, flowing from the huge fissures which have opened in the earth.

Doctors, nurses and supplies are being rushed to the affected areas by aeroplanes and motor cars. In an imaginative move the Bihar government is also trying to arrange for Captain Barnard's flying circus to tour the province to ascertain the extent of the damage.

Further slight shocks were recorded in Calcutta today, but there has been no damage and the city is quiet.

More phones in British homes

Jan 1. Last year, London's telephone exchanges handled almost 800 million calls, more than half of which went through automatic exchanges. Statistics issued today show that the number of telephone users nationally is also on the increase. There were 274,000 new installations in 1933, almost double the figure for the previous year. More countries now have telephone links with Britain and last year in London alone, 637,000 overseas calls were made (→21/6/35).

Magazines for modern enthusiasms appear on the newstands.

1934

FEBRUARY

Su	Mo	Tu	We	Th	Fr	Sa
				1	2	3
4	5	6	7	8	9	10
11	12	13	14	15	16	17
18	19	20	21	22	23	24
25	26	27	28			

1. Austria: A socialist uprising begins against the "Fatherland Front" of Chancellor Dollfuss.→

2. Berlin: The Nazis are rewriting the Psalms to remove all reference to Jews (→22/6).

6. Paris: Right-wing groups take to the streets, calling for the resignation of the government.→

9. Balkans: A Balkan Pact is signed by Rumania, Greece, Yugoslavia and Turkey (→17/3).

12. France: Rioting accompanies a one-day general strike called by left-wing parties and the trades unions (→5/3).

16. London: Premiere of Noel Coward's play "Conversation piece" at His Majesty's Theatre.

17. Belgium: King Albert dies in a climbing accident near Namur; his son succeeds as Leopold III (→22).

20. Berlin: Anthony Eden meets Hitler in an atmosphere of "general cordiality" (→31/3/35).

22. Brussels: Thousands turn out for the funeral of King Albert.

23. London: MacDonald refuses to see 500 "hunger marchers" after their month-long march from Glasgow.

24. Germany: Millions swear allegiance to Hitler at ceremonies in Munich and Berlin.

25. US: 23 are reported dead after tornadoes sweep through southern states (→7/4/35).

28. Manchuria: Ex-Chinese Emperor Pu Yi accepts the throne of Japanese-occupied Manchuria, or "Manchukuo" (→1/3).

BIRTH

27. US consumer advocate Ralph Nader.

DEATHS

23. Nicaraguan rebel General Augusto Sandino (*1893).→

23. British composer Sir Edward William Elgar, Master of the King's Musick from 1924 (*2/6/1857).→

Elgar, England's greatest composer, dies

Feb 24. Sir Edward Elgar died yesterday as he preferred to live, within sight of the Malvern Hills. Tributes to his genius poured in from Strauss, Sibelius, Paderewski – as well as from nearer home; Lord Berners called him "the greatest English composer since Purcell".

Elgar had no formal musical training except from his father, whom he succeeded as a church organist in Worcester. He gained early experience as bandmaster at Worcester county lunatic asylum. He later became conductor of the London Symphony Orchestra.

The "Enigma Variations", followed by "The Dream of Gerontius", brought him worldwide recognition at the age of 42. His First Symphony received over 100 performances worldwide within a year. Only recently Elgar came out of his long retreat to conduct and record his violin concerto with the young virtuoso, Yehudi Menuhin. He was working on a Third Symphony, for the BBC, when he died.

Enigmatic Sir Edward Elgar.

Socialist uprising is crushed in Austria

Feb 17. There is fear for the future of Austria tonight, following the ruthless crushing of the uprising by the Social Democrats. Hundreds of demonstrators were killed and wounded in Vienna when the army used machine guns and field guns to clear the streets.

The government has declared a State of Emergency. The Socialist Mayor of Vienna, Karl Seitz, has been arrested along with a number of other leading members of the Social Democrats and it is expected that the party will be proscribed.

The government's handling of the situation is causing much unease. Some foreign newspapers have been confiscated and reports are circulating that Adolf Hitler may annex Austria. Many Jews are fleeing the country (→28/3).

Vienna's arrested Social Democrats are carted off in a butcher's truck.

French premier has to resign after riots

Feb 7. Edouard Daladier resigned as premier of France today, following two days of bloody rioting in the streets of Paris. It is difficult to discern a theme behind the rioting, except to note that the stench of scandal surrounding the affair of the swindler Stavisky has fouled political life in France, and there is discontent with a number of measures taken by the Daladier government.

The ex-servicemen, in particular, have been demanding his resignation and it was their threat to mount a parade, armed with grenades and other "souvenirs" from the war, which eventually caused him to telephone President Lebrun in the middle of a Cabinet meeting and offer his resignation.

The previous president, Gaston Doumergue, has agreed to take over the Premiership, on condition that he gets the wholehearted support of all former premiers still taking an active part in political life.

The news that M. Daladier had resigned was received at the Bourse with immense relief and the "Marseillaise" was sung with fervour. A few minutes later, French Rentes rose by one point (→12).

Somoza's Guards gun down opponent

Feb 22. Nicaraguan National Guardsmen last night shot dead General Augusto Sandino and three others in a bloodbath at Managua airfield. Sandino had denounced the guardsmen's leader, General Anastasio Somoza.

After dining with President Juan Sacasa, the killers seized Sandino, his brother and two aides, and took them by truck to the airfield.

Sandino had worked peacefully with the Sacasa government for a year, since the withdrawal of the US Marines, who were aligned with former President Mocada and the feared National Guard.

Dr Pedro Zepeda, a friend of the President, expressed the nation's grief at Sandino's death and warned that Somoza was likely to attempt a coup.

1934

MARCH

Su	Mo	Tu	We	Th	Fr	Sa
				1	2	3
4	5	6	7	8	9	10
11	12	13	14	15	16	17
18	19	20	21	22	23	24
25	26	27	28	29	30	31

1. London: The Prince of Wales says: "I see no reason why women should not wear shorts" (→16/5).

3. US: Gangster John Dillinger escapes from jail in Indiana using a wooden fake pistol.→

5. Paris: An anti-Fascist manifesto is signed by French intellectuals including Andre Gide (→14/7/35).

8. Berlin: A new German car costing only £61 is centre of attraction at a motor show opened by Hitler (→26/2/36).

9. Germany: The British film "Catherine the Great" is banned because its star and director are Jewish.

12. Japan: The new torpedo boat Tomozuru capsizes with the loss of more than 100 lives (→21).

13. London: The government says its slum clearance plans already involved rehousing for 1.24 million people (→9/8).

14. El Salvador: 250 die and 1,000 are hurt in an explosion on a train in the capital San Salvador.

14. UK: Farmers appeal to the government as eggs drop to the lowest price since 1914, between 6d and 9d a dozen.

17. Rome: Italy, Austria and Hungary sign a co-operation pact (→4/4).

17. London: Cambridge wins the Boat Race in a record time of 18 minutes 3 seconds.

18. Rome: Mussolini urges German rearmament (→6/4/35).

21. Japan: 1,500 are reported killed when fire sweeps through the city of Hakodate.

23. Mrs Dorothy Paget's Golden Miller wins the Grand National at Aintree.

24. Washington: An act grants independence to the Philippines in 1945 (→15/9/35).

28. Vienna: The diminutive Chancellor Dollfuss bans jokes about his size (→30/4).

BIRTH

9. Soviet cosmonaut Yuri Gagarin (†27/3/68).

Japan appoints Pu Yi puppet Emperor

March 1. Wild scenes of high nostalgia broke out in Hsinking today as Pu Yi, once known as the boy Emperor of China, was enthroned by the Japanese masters as puppet Emperor of conquered Manchuria, now known as Manchukuo. The streets were thronged with bemedalled soldiers, Mongol cavalry, painted geishas and Lama priests. Delegations of Chinese nobles appeared in ornate and splendid clothes, hidden in boxes since the days when the Empress held magnificent court before the revolution.

At his first court Pu Yi, now using the title Kangte, exclaimed: "The Empire of Japan, in the name of righteousness and justice, assisted the establishment of this state. Armed hostilities have ceased. The country is bathed in the radiance of the sun and moon." (→24/4)

Pu Yi, Emperor of Manchukuo.

Dillinger shoots his way out of trouble

March 31. John Dillinger – wanted in several states on charges of bank robbery and murder – has blasted his way out of a police trap in St. Paul, Minnesota. Firing a machine gun into a ring of officers, he leapt into a green sedan and sped off with two accomplices. Blood was found on the ground near the shoot-out.

Dillinger has twice before been seized and escaped imprisonment. He usually leads a gang of five or more thugs and a retinue of female companions. The US Department of Justice seeks any information on him. He is 5'7" tall, weighs about 153 pounds and claims to drink and smoke very little. He has a scar on the back of his left hand and a mole between the eyebrows (→30/6).

Dillinger with some of his toys.

Labour in control of London council

March 8. Labour rules the capital of the Empire. Tonight, for the first time, the party has a clear majority on the London County Council, having defeated the Tory Municipal Reform group 69 to 55 in the local elections; the Liberals were wiped out. Herbert Morrison, who has led Labour to power at County Hall, promises to bring new humanity into running London. This up and coming politician was the metropolitan party's secretary 15 years ago. He was an efficient Minister of Transport in the Labour Government from 1929 to 1931, and now claims to have built up a team which will eventually make the LCC a model for good local government.

Testing time for British motorists

March 28. A comprehensive programme of measures to improve road safety is contained in the Government's Road Traffic Bill, out today. Tests will have to be taken by all new drivers. For the first time too, pedestrians may be penalised for walking dangerously. A speed limit will be imposed in towns and experiments with pedestrian crossings will be made in London.

When similar crossing schemes were introduced in Paris, deaths in its streets dropped from 292 to 237, despite a large increase in traffic. Another matter for experiment is the use of horns. Here too the findings will be applied to the rest of the country later, assuming a successful outcome (→12/4).

Slimming blamed for potato sales slump

March 21. The slimming craze among women has led to a dramatic slump in the potato market, traders heard today. Now the Potato Marketing Board is to launch a major campaign to "convince the fair sex that they are on the wrong lines when they cut out potatoes to get slim". The chairman of the Fruit and Potato Trades Association told the annual conference: "Consumption seems to have been contracting, like the ladies." The slender figure has been all the rage since designers launched short skirts, bobbed hair and a generally boyish look. The style, however, has been widely criticised, notably by men who like their women more curvaceous and by doctors who fear women may be endangering their health (→8/10/35).

1934

APRIL

Su	Mo	Tu	We	Th	Fr	Sa
1	2	3	4	5	6	7
8	9	10	11	12	13	14
15	16	17	18	19	20	21
22	23	24	25	26	27	28
29	30					

1. Berlin: Hitler bans the work of the Carnegie Endowment for International Peace (→16).

4. Moscow: Latvia, Estonia and Lithuania renew their pacts of friendship with the USSR until 1945 (→5/5).

7. Norway: 57 are feared dead when a cliff crumbles, plunging two towns into the sea.

8. Bucharest: The Rumanians foil a plot to kill King Carol.

11. Spain: Saragossa is put under a state of emergency following a strike call by anarchists (→25).

12. UK: 126 have died in road accidents since April 7, but traffic lights have cut the number of accidents in London (→18/6).

14. Rome: Mussolini cuts all salaries and increases the tax on bachelors by half.

16. Greece: Ten die in an Italian bombing raid on the island of Rhodes (→29).

16. Berlin: The Nazis announce plans to forbid the divorce of parents (→20).

17. London: Neville Chamberlain's Budget takes 6d off income tax and raises unemployment benefit.

20. Berlin: Goering denies French claims that Germany is secretly rearming (→27).

25. Madrid: Martial law is declared as the government resigns (→11/6).

27. London: Britain and France warn Germany against defaulting on reparations payments (→14/6).

28. London: Manchester City beat Portsmouth 2-1 in the FA Cup Final at Wembley.

29. Rome: The Italian parliament votes to remove its last remaining powers (→10/6).

30. London: The government sets up a committee to study the feasibility of a public television service (→1/2/35).

DEATH

11. British actor-manager Sir Gerald du Maurier (*26/3/1873).

Bayonets back Austria's new dictator

Austria's "saviour", Dr Dollfuss, acknowledges the applause in Vienna.

April 30. Chancellor Engelbert Dollfuss was made dictator of Austria today by a rump parliament, which then proceeded to vote itself out of existence.

There was no effective opposition because the seats normally occupied by the Social Democrats were empty and their names deleted from their desks. Most of them are in prison or concentration camps, following their revolt against the government two months ago.

It was left to two Pan-German representatives, Dr Kaempel and Dr Foppa, to protest. They said: "Before the world we protest against this regime, which has no majority behind it and which, for over a year, has ruled unconstitutionally, supported by bayonets."

"We protest against the restriction of liberty, against the mass persecution of innocent men, women and children, against the system of hostages, concentration camps and of spies and informers, who are undermining the morality of the nation."

Dr Dollfuss showed signs of nervousness at the beginning of this unexpectedly outspoken attack, but, surrounded by his supporters wearing their Heimwehr (Austrian Fascist) uniforms, he soon relaxed. Dr Kaempel and Dr Foppa were jeered out of the House and parliament rose (→25/7).

Japan warns West: "Hands off China"

April 24. Japan's "Hands off China" warning to the Western powers was reinforced today. A statement from Tokyo asserted that, although Japan still favoured an open door policy in China, it could not let the importation of military planes and arms into that country go without protest.

For Britain, Sir John Simon, in a "friendly communication", has asked for clarification of the Japanese attitude. It is believed that the Tokyo statement is linked to demands for naval parity to be made at the forthcoming naval conference. Japan plans to increase the size of her air force (→18/6/35).

House building is booming in Britain

April 6. Official figures just released show that in the last ten years 1,900,000 houses have been built in England and that many of them are being bought with the help of building societies. Last year the societies advanced a record £100 million to house-buyers.

Plans have now been announced to build 285,000 local authority houses by 1938, giving jobs to 110,000 men; so the boom in the building industry looks set to continue (→9/8).

A large mailbag betrays Mr Sodoroff's plans for revolution

April 17. Leon Trotsky, the exiled Russian revolutionary, is homeless again today after the French cancelled his political asylum. He had been living secretly in a villa near Paris for six months when he should have been in Corsica.

Trotsky's whereabouts came to light when the police entered the house of man called Sodoroff on orders from the local Mayor, who had became curious about the large volume of mail the address was receiving. The police, having climbed through the barbed wire fence surrounding the house, found Trotsky with plans for an organisation called the Fourth International, which urged the overthrow of existing governments.

Mr and Mrs Leon Trotsky in France: now they will have to move on.

1934

MAY

Su	Mo	Tu	We	Th	Fr	Sa
		1	2	3	4	5
6	7	8	9	10	11	12
13	14	15	16	17	18	19
20	21	22	23	24	25	26
27	28	29	30	31		

1. UK: The Orient Line is offering return sea passage to Australia for £124 first class and £57 third class.

3. New York: British author H. G. Wells stands by his prediction of another major war by 1940.

5. Moscow: The USSR extends its non-aggression pact with Poland until 1945 (→8/6).

6. Middle East: Saudi Arabian forces capture the Yemeni city of Hodeida (→13).

9. Moscow: Pravda attacks Lenin's widow for underrating Stalin in her book "Memories of Lenin".

13. Jeddah: Saudi Arabia signs a truce with Yemen (→27/6).

15. Latvia: Karlis Ulmanis becomes dictator.

16. Wimbledon: Women will be allowed to wear shorts this year, despite the misgivings of officials (→7/7).

17. Belgium: 42 miners are feared dead after an explosion at a mine near Mons; a second blast kills 17 rescuers.

19. Bulgaria: Fascists seize power in a coup aided by King Boris.

21. UK: Barker's grade one lounge suits are on sale for four guineas.

24. Czechoslovakia: Tomas Masaryk is elected president for the fourth time.

25. Dublin: The Dail votes to abolish the Irish Senate.

28. Moscow: The party newspaper Izvestia says the USSR is ready to join the League of Nations (→10/9).

30. Berlin: The trial begins of 111 alleged Communists.

BIRTH

9. British playwright Alan Bennett.

DEATHS

23. US criminal Bonnie Parker (*1/10/1910).→

23. US criminal Clyde Barrow (*24/3/1909).→

25. British composer Gustav Holst (*21/9/1874).

New Nazi legal system has no appeal

Herr Hitler and Goebbels: dining out on the death of justice.

May 2. Angered by a lingering attachment to the rule of law among Germany's judges, Hitler has decided to create a separate People's Court which will have the sole right to try cases of treason. Hearings will normally be held "in camera" and there will be no right of appeal against the court's judgments.

The new court will consist of two professional judges and five laymen from the Nazi Party, security police and the armed forces; all will be directly appointed by Hitler. There already exists a Special Court of three judges who must be party members. Created by Hitler last year, this court tries cases of political crime or, as the official decree puts it, "insidious attacks on the government" (→30).

Bonnie and Clyde shot in police trap

May 23. The law finally caught up with Bonnie and Clyde today. After a four-year partnership, in which they killed at least twelve people, Clyde Barrow and Bonnie Parker drove at speed into an ambush in Louisiana.

Minutes later, Texas Rangers found their bodies – a revolver and shotgun clutched in their lifeless hands – riddled with over 50 bullets. A half-eaten sandwich and a saxophone were found in the car.

Bonnie and Clyde had carved a lethal trail of murder and menace throughout the south-western states of America, robbing banks, petrol stations and diners. Both were in their mid-20s when they were finally killed.

Clyde wields a machine gun ...

... while Bonnie settles for a revolver.

1934

JUNE

Su	Mo	Tu	We	Th	Fr	Sa
					1	2
3	4	5	6	7	8	9
10	11	12	13	14	15	16
17	18	19	20	21	22	23
24	25	26	27	28	29	30

1. UK: Ex-PM Lloyd George helps troops fight a 1,000 acre heath fire near his home in Surrey.

2. Washington: $6,000 million aid is voted for farmers in drought-stricken areas.

4. London: Britain stalls payment of war debts to the US pending their revision.

6. UK: The Maharajah of Rajpipla's Windsor Lad wins the Derby at Epsom.

8. Eastern Europe: Poland, Rumania and the USSR sign a pact guaranteeing their present frontiers (→4/8).

11. Spain: The southern provinces are paralysed by striking peasants (→5/10).

13. Berlin: Hitler rejects a mutual aid pact with the USSR (→15).

14. New York: American Max Baer beats Italian Primo Carnera for the world heavyweight boxing title.

14. Berlin: The Reichsbank, Germany's central bank, puts a six-month moratorium on German loan repayments (→25).

18. London: Reports indicate people are getting used to pedestrian crossings.→

20. London: Dismantling of old Waterloo Bridge begins; it will be offered for sale.

22. Munich: Wagner's operas have been adapted to have Nazi settings and to glorify National Socialism (→29).

25. London: A 20 per cent duty is put on German goods in retaliation for Germany's debt moratorium (→4/7).

27. Saudi Arabia: King Ibn Saud and the Imam of Yemen sign a peace treaty to end their "Desert War".

29. Germany: Flags are flown at half-mast on the anniversary of the Versailles Treaty.→

30. US: Escaped gangster John Dillinger kills a policeman in a bank raid in Indiana (→22/7).

DEATH

10. British composer Frederick Delius (*29/1/1862).

Hitler buries the knife in Brownshirts

June 30. Flying into Munich in the early hours of today, Adolf Hitler, Chancellor of Germany, drove out to a fashionable lakeside hotel. There, Ernst Roehm, one of Hitler's closest comrades from the earliest days of the Nazi party, was dragged from his bed and shot. Several hundred others – some say many thousands – in Munich and Berlin have been executed in what is being spoken of as the Night of the Long Knives.

According to Josef Goebbels, Hitler's propaganda chief, Roehm and other leaders of the 2,000,000-strong SA, the Storm Troopers' organisation, were plotting to overthrow Hitler. Goebbels described in a radio broadcast how Hitler confronted the plotters: "He throws his anger into their pale faces and tears off their identification lapels."

In the wake of the killings, lurid stories of debauchery and perversion among senior Storm Troopers are being put about. In the hotel room next to Roehm's was Obergruppenfuehrer Edmund Heines. According to one report: "A shameless sight presented itself to the eyes of those who entered. Heines lay in bed with a homosexual youth. The disgusting scene which took place on the arrest of Heines and his companion is not to be described."

Before the Long Knives: head Brownshirt Ernst Roehm follows Hitler.

Whether or not there was a plot such as Hitler has claimed, Berlin has been rife with rumours for weeks. One account has the army generals, backed by the dying President Hindenburg, telling Hitler they will take over if he does not get rid of the SA thugs and stop all talk of the socialist-style revolution Roehm and his friends have been pressing for.

That Hitler has almost certainly done. The SA leadership has been wiped out and the rank and file, having been sent on leave and told not to wear the uniform, effectively dismissed. But the purge has extended beyond the SA. A former Chancellor, General Kurt von Schleicher, and his wife Elisabeth were shot at their home outside Berlin. They were among scores of non-Nazis and ex-Nazis who died. It looks as though the purge was also used as an opportunity to pay off some old scores (→ 13/7).

Fist fighting and stink bombs mark Fascists' rallies

June 9. The fierce fighting which regularly breaks out in London and other centres between Sir Oswald Mosley's black-shirted Fascists and their opponents is causing grave disquiet in Westminster.

Public concern was highlighted by a Mosleyite "rally" at the Olympia stadium last night. The Fascist leader's speech was punctuated by constant shouts and fierce fist fighting between his stewards and hecklers. The air was foul with the smell of stink bombs. Opponents were manhandled and thrown bodily out of the building. One woman was subdued by ju-jitsu trained women blackshirts. Casualties were described as "numerous"; at least one man was critically injured.

Outside the hall, flag-waving Communists carried on a running battle with Mosley's club-wielding guards. Inside, Mosley, speaking in a blaze of light, blamed "red agitators from the ghettos" and said the violence showed the need for his "disciplined" force.

Government ministers expressed their disgust, however. Sir Kingsley Wood said: "Certain movements in the country might very well shake parliamentary government in the future". (→ 9/9)

New crossings will cut road death toll

June 12. In a bid to reduce deaths from road accidents, now running at 22 a day in Great Britain, some 60 official crossings have been set up in central London for pedestrians. The crossings, which are experimental, are all sited at places where traffic is controlled by lights or police. The Ministry of Transport's official notice explains:

"Pedestrians must not obstruct a vehicle proceeding in the general line of traffic movement, i.e. straight ahead, but vehicle traffic turning at right angles must give way to pedestrians using the marked crossings."

Pedestrians in breach of the rules are liable to incur fines of five shillings (→ 18/3/35).

Mussolini watches as Italy wins first World Cup in Europe

June 10. In front of a beaming Benito Mussolini in the Stadio Torino in Rome, Italy pulled back from a goal down to take Czechoslovakia into extra time, and then to clinch the second World Cup 2-1 with a goal by Sciavio, which made him the tournament's joint top scorer.

The British nations, still out of FIFA, were not invited to play, and Uruguay, the holders, crippled by a players' strike, did not come to what turned out to be a full-blown Fascist jamboree, supported with a fervour which almost demanded victory from the host nation.

The co-favourites, the stylish Austrians, fell by a single goal to the super-fit Italians in the Milan semi-final, while the Czechs easily disposed of Germany 3-0 to set up the feverish climax in Rome (→ 15).

The Italian football team gives the Fascist salute before beating Czechoslovakia 2-1 in Rome to win soccer's second World Cup final.

Next to Mussolini Hitler looks shabby

June 15. Italy's Fascist dictator, Benito Mussolini, was very much in charge today when he welcomed Adolf Hitler to Venice. In the grey Fascist militia uniform, with flashing medals and tassels, he made the German dictator look quite shabby in his belted raincoat and felt hat. It was the two dictators' first meeting. They said afterwards they favoured "frequent personal contact". There was just a hint of possible friction in the communique's reference to Austria. Germany, it said, recognised that Austria's independence should be maintained, but on the other hand was not able to guarantee it (→27/7).

Venice: Duce greets Chancellor.

Briton wins Golf Open after 11 years

June 29. Henry Cotton, the 27-year-old professional at the Waterloo Club in Brussels, fought off a stomach upset on the final afternoon which almost forced him to abandon the round, to win the Open Championship at Royal George's, Sandwich, today. His victory brought the title back to Britain after an 11-year gap.

Cotton's last round of 79 – a poor showing after his record-breaking 65 on the second day – still left him five strokes clear of the South African Sid Brews and Alf Padgham of Sundridge Park.

1934

JULY

Su	Mo	Tu	We	Th	Fr	Sa
1	2	3	4	5	6	7
8	9	10	11	12	13	14
15	16	17	18	19	20	21
22	23	24	25	26	27	28
29	30	31				

1. New York: Joseph Kennedy is made head of the Securities and Exchange Commission, the new US financial watchdog.

3. Berlin: Vice-Chancellor von Papen resigns.

4. London: Britain reaches agreement with Germany over its loan repayments.

7. Wimbledon: Fred Perry is the first British men's champion for 25 years, beating Jack Crawford in the Men's Singles final; Briton Dorothy Round beats Helen Jacobs in the Women's Singles final.→

10. Moscow: The secret service OGPU is abolished and replaced by the Commissariat for Internal Affairs (→1/11).

13. Berlin: Hitler justifies "the Night of the Long Knives", claiming the SA were plotting to overthrow him (→2/8).

18. Liverpool: The King opens the Mersey Tunnel, the longest underwater tunnel.

21. US: A heat wave in the Mid-West kills 206 people in three days.

26. Vienna: The government orders a round up of Austrian Nazis following the murder of Dollfuss (→27).

27. Rome: Mussolini orders more than 40,000 troops to the Austrian border (→16/8).

29. Vienna: Dr Kurt von Schuschnigg is appointed chancellor (→31).

30. London: Stanley Baldwin says: "The frontier of England is not now the chalk cliffs of Dover but the Rhine."

31. Vienna: Dollfuss's murderers shout "Heil Hitler" before they are hanged (→16/8).

BIRTH

21. British director, writer and satirist Dr Jonathan Miller.

DEATHS

4. Polish-born French physicist and Nobel Prize winner Marie Curie (*7/11/1867).

25. Austrian statesman Engelbert Dollfuss (*4/10/1892).→

England wins double Wimbledon victory

July 7. Britain crowned Wimbledon with a rare double – winning both men's and women's singles championships for the first time since 1909. Fred Perry, already the United States and Australian Open champion, crushed Jack Crawford, the reigning Wimbledon champion, 6-3, 6-0, 7-5 to recapture the title for Britain after a long gap of 25 years.

Earlier in the day in a long, three-set battle, Dorothy Round, the disappointed runner-up last year to Helen Moody, had overcome American Helen Jacobs 6-2, 6-8, 6-3. She then ended the day on a perfect note by winning the mixed doubles with her Japanese partner Ryuki Miki (→12/9).

Miss Round and Miss Jacobs.

Fred Perry, on his way to victory, grimaces with concentration.

Himmler to head concentration camps

July 13. A mild-mannered former chicken farmer with a streak of sadism has been appointed overlord of Nazi Germany's notorious concentration camps. He is Heinrich Himmler, 33-year-old chief of Hitler's black-uniformed praetorian guard, the SS; he played a key role in last month's "blood purge" in which many leading Storm Troopers were summarily put to death. Until now the camps, which sprang into existence within weeks of the Nazis taking power, have been run by Storm Troopers.

Himmler has put the day-to-day running of the camps in the hands of Theodor Eicke, commandant of Dachau, outside Munich. The camps are to be reorganised to improve efficiency, and the elite Death's Head units of the SS, the "Totenkopfverbaende", will take-over guard duties. A women's camp at Ravensbrueck is planned.

The Nazis claim the camps are mild reform centres for Germans who have not yet seen the light. Eicke's rules for Dachau offer a less cosy picture. Anyone refusing to obey an order, or shouting or talking at work or on parade, can be shot on the spot or hanged. The Eicke regulations are now to be applied in all the concentration camps (→15/8/35).

Austrian leader allowed to bleed to death

Dollfuss's coffin is guarded by members of his old army regiment.

July 25. A gang of Nazis, wearing army and police uniforms, burst into the office of Austria's Chancellor Engelbert Dollfuss in Vienna towards noon today and opened fire at close range. He was wounded in the throat and left for over four hours to bleed to death while the assassins, holding other ministers hostage, tried to negotiate safe conduct to the German border for themselves. After Dr Kurt Rieth, the German envoy, had intervened, a promise was given, then retracted when it was found that Dollfuss was dead. Over 150 Nazis were arrested.

A few blocks away other Nazis seized the radio station and forced an announcer, with a pistol at his head, to broadcast a statement saying the Dollfuss cabinet had resigned. In a three-hour battle for the station, three police and two Nazis were killed.

In Germany, Hitler was given news of the events in Vienna while he was listening to Wagner's "Das Rheingold" at the Bayreuth festival. He became very excited, but when it became clear the putsch had failed he issued a statement disowning the Austrian Nazis. But Mussolini, the Italian leader, seems to have no doubt that Germany had a hand in the plot. On hearing of Dollfuss's murder, Mussolini ordered four divisions, 40,000 men, and a squadron of warplanes to the Austrian border (→27).

Dillinger shot down outside the cinema

July 22. John Dillinger was shot dead tonight in front of a Chicago cinema. He was wanted for daring bank hold-ups, 16 murders and some spectacular prison breaks. Dillinger eluded the law through invention and disguise. He grew a moustache and had a facelift. He poured acid on his fingertips to eradicate fingerprints. While in an Indiana prison, he smeared a piece of wood with shoe polish and waved the instant revolver at guards. Tonight, Dillinger saw a Clark Gable gangster film. When he came out, the show was over.

Plans for massive expansion of RAF

July 19. The RAF is being boosted by 41 new squadrons to try to bring it up to strength compared to Britain's European neighbours. The aim is to have about 1,310 aircraft by 1938, Stanley Baldwin told the Commons today. Although MPs are pleased that at last the Government is taking steps to boost the UK's air defences, many still say they the moves are "insufficient" to meet the potential threat. France already possesses 1,650 aircraft, Italy and Russia have 1,500 each, and the numbers are growing (→28/11).

1934

AUGUST

Su	Mo	Tu	We	Th	Fr	Sa
			1	2	3	4
5	6	7	8	9	10	11
12	13	14	15	16	17	18
19	20	21	22	23	24	25
26	27	28	29	30	31	

2. Berlin: Hitler assumes the title "Fuehrer" on the death of Hindenburg(→6).

4. Moscow: The USSR assumes diplomatic relations with Bulgaria (→10/9).

5. Algeria: 100 Jews and Arab are reported dead after a day of religious rioting.

6. Germany: A 65-mile line of torches marks the route of Hindenburg's funeral procession.→

9. UK: Figures show that 1,246,000 people have been rehoused and 2,328,000 houses built since 1918 (→16/1/35).

11. London: Germany wins nine of 11 events in the fourth Women's World Games.

13. Birmingham: Austin launches its two-seater "Opal" model of the Austin Seven.

16. Rome: Mussolini recalls the troops he sent to the Austrian border after the death of Dollfuss (→27/9).

19. US: Al Capone is taken on a prison train to the top security Alcatraz jail.

20. Geneva: The US joins the International Labour Organisation.

22. London: Australia wins the fifth Test of the current series by 562 runs to win the Ashes.

24. Berlin: Hitler issues "Ten Commandments" for "bodily purity" when choosing a spouse (→31).

26. Irish Free State: Ex-IRA leaders begin recruiting a "Citizens' Army" with the aim of setting up a workers' state.

28. London: Prince George of Kent is to marry Princess Marina of Greece, the first foreign bride for a British prince this century (→29/11).

31. Berlin: Hitler introduces a job scheme that will favour unemployed fathers before bachelors (→4/9).

DEATH

2. German commander and statesman Field Marshal Paul von Hindenburg (*2/10/1847).→

Hindenburg dies: Hitler is supreme

Soldier-statesman Hindenburg.

Aug 19. Adolf Hitler cleared the last remaining hurdle to total power today when 38 million Germans gave him a remarkable 90 per cent vote of approval for his decision to become head of state as well as Chancellor. Just over four million voted No.

President Hindenburg, 87, died at nine in the morning of August 2; three hours later, at noon, Hitler announced that the title of President was being abolished and that he was to be known as Fuehrer and Reich Chancellor. And, after styling himself Supreme Commander of the Armed Forces, he has exacted from all officers and men a "sacred oath of unconditional obedience," not to Germany, but to himself personally (→16/10).

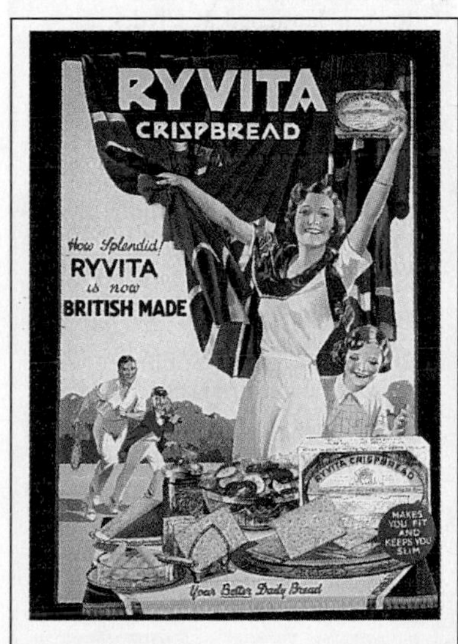

1934

SEPTEMBER

Su	Mo	Tu	We	Th	Fr	Sa
						1
2	3	4	5	6	7	8
9	10	11	12	13	14	15
16	17	18	19	20	21	22
23	24	25	26	27	28	29
30						

1. US: 400,000 textile workers come out on strike (→22).

3. London: Evangeline Booth becomes the Salvation Army's first woman general.

4. Nuremberg: 750,000 attend the opening of the Nazi Party conference.→

7. US: Senator Huey Long orders 2,000 troops into Louisiana to back his month-old "dictatorship" (→6/11).

9. London: 18 are arrested as police separate Fascist and anti-Fascist marchers.

10. Geneva: The League Council votes unanimously to admit the USSR.

12. New York: Fred Perry retains the US tennis championship.

16. Munich: Lutherans march to anti-Nazi songs in a demonstration against Hitler (→29/10/35).

18. Rome: Mussolini decrees that Italians aged eight to 55 must have military training (→30/10).

21. Japan: Up to 1,500 people are reported dead after a typhoon strikes the centre of the country.

22. US: The textile workers' strike ends following intervention by President Roosevelt.

25. US: The American yacht Rainbow wins America's Cup.

26. UK: The Queen Mary, the first ship over 75,000 tons, is launched at Clydebank (→24/3/36)

27. London: Britain, France and Italy reaffirm their support for an independent Austria.

29. Poland: Conscription is introduced for men and women (→3/1/36).

BIRTHS

20. Italian actress Sophia Loren, born Sophia Scicoloni.

28. French actress Brigitte Bardot, born Camille Javal.

DEATH

9. British artist and critic Roger Fry (*14/12/1866).

262 miners are killed in pit disaster

Sept 22. The death toll from a mine explosion rose to 262 early today when three members of the rescue team were killed after fighting for hours to locate fellow pitmen entombed below ground. Pit wives received in silence news that there was little hope of survivors being found; they joined a pathetic trail away from the scene at Gresford Mine, near Wrexham, to mourn their loss in the worst pit disaster for 21 years.

Rescue teams called in at 2am have been able to bring out only 16 bodies. Fresh outbreaks of fire underground have hampered their work and tons of boulders have been taken down in the pit cage to form a barrier. Between rescuers and the helpless casualties lay a path of red hot coal and poisonous fumes; each could only work for three minutes before collapsing. One said: "It is a living hell down there."

However, amid the despair came the account of one miner who inched his way to safety up a 200-feet vertical shaft just two feet wide.

The Chief Inspector of Mines, Sir Henry Walker, said it might be necessary to abandon efforts and seal the entire mine with the loss of 2,000 jobs. A relief fund has already raised over £7,000 (→27/3/37).

Hitler's Reich will "last 1,000 years"

Sept 5. Striding triumphantly in to the Leopold Hall for the Nazi Party's Nuremberg rally today, Hitler was greeted by thunderous cheers and massive drum rolls.

On a stage backed by a giant swastika, and with the cameras of film director Leni Riefenstahl on him, he sat with arms folded and jaw set, as Adolf Wagner, Gauleiter of Bavaria, declaimed: "By the National Socialist revolution, the German form of life has been definitely settled for the next thousand years."

Lindbergh baby case: man held

Sept 28. A man has been arrested for the murder, in March 1933, of the Lindbergh baby.

Bruno Hauptmann, an illegal German immigrant, is being held in the Bronx County jail, New York. He was found in possession of some of the ransom money that Colonel Charles Lindbergh paid for the return of his child. Hauptmann is known to have escaped from a German prison years ago.

Today a spoon, bent into a knife-like implement, was found hidden in the accused man's cell (→8/10).

Sept 26. The Queen launches the Cunard-White Star liner Queen Mary, the biggest, safest and most powerful ship in the world today.

1934

OCTOBER

Su	Mo	Tu	We	Th	Fr	Sa
	1	2	3	4	5	6
7	8	9	10	11	12	13
14	15	16	17	18	19	20
21	22	23	24	25	26	27
28	29	30	31			

1. UK: Long-distance phone rates are cut to a maximun of threepence for unlimited time at night.

5. Spain: An uprising begins in Catalonia.→

5. Moscow: Churchwardens, choristers and bellringers are given the vote, but not priests.

8. New York: Charles Lindbergh identifies Bruno Hauptmann (→29/1/35).

10. Rome: Italy renews an offer of a pact with Yugoslavia (→11).

11. Yugoslavia: Anti-Italian and anti-Hungarian riots follow the assassination of King Alexander.→

16. Berlin: Hitler is to retain his titles of Fuehrer and Reich Chancellor for life (→17).

17. Belgrade: Ten-year-old King Peter takes the salute at the funeral of his father King Alexander (→22/11).

17. Berlin: Hitler cuts income tax for large families; the bigger the family, the less income tax has to be paid (→19).

19. Germany: The German army is reported to be 300,000 strong, three times the size allowed by the Treaty of Versailles (→28/11).

23. India: Gandhi resigns as leader of the All-India Congress (→19/11).

26. London: An 18-month-old baby is kept alive in a hospital "oxygen bed" (→21/6/35).

27. Siam: King Prajadhipok says he will abdicate (→2/3/35).

30. Rome: Mussolini orders all six to eight-year-olds to join a special corps for pre-military training (→13/11).

BIRTH

13. Greek singer Nana Mouskouri.

DEATHS

9. Yugoslav King Alexander I (*16/12/1888).→

15. French statesman Raymond Poincare (*20/8/1860).

Catalonia independence bid crushed

Oct 8. Fierce fighting continued in many parts of Spain yesterday, following an attempt to declare Catalonia an independent state, which coincided with a violent nationwide strike called by the Socialist and Syndicalist trade unions. The unions are protesting against the inclusion of three Catholic Popular Actionist ministers in the new, rightist government.

However the situation was rapidly brought under control by the arrival of a warship carrying a battalion of the Spanish Foreign Legion from Morocco. As midnight was striking the troops, with flags flying, marched from the harbour to the sound of bugles and drums.

Martial law has been pronounced throughout Spain and 8,000 Monarchist officers, placed on the retired list at the time of King Alfonso's abdication, have been invited over the wireless to resume service with the colours.

Fighting is still continuing in Madrid, where a fierce struggle is raging for possession of the northern railway station. Sounds of intense rifle and machine-gun fire can be heard from many other parts of the city. The capital's garrison has been mobilised to relieve the exhausted civil guard. Shots were fired at the home of the premier, Senor Lerroux, last night, but noone was hit. International traffic was still being delayed last night, but a number of British holiday makers arrived at Hendaye in the first train to cross the frontier since the outbreak of violence. They said they were very thankful to be in France after their trying experiences (→ 21/2/36).

The Spanish Civil Guard rounds up leftist agitators in Asturias.

King of Yugoslavia arrives in Marseilles and is assassinated

Oct 9. King Alexander of Yugoslavia and Louis Barthou, the French Foreign Minister, were assassinated in Marseilles this afternoon, as they were driving from the harbour, a few minutes after the King had landed from the cruiser Dubrovnik.

A man, later identified as Petrus Keleman, a Croatian nationalist, ran from the crowd lining the pavement, jumped on the running board of their car and opened fire with a Mauser pistol at point-blank range. Despite his own wounds M. Barthou tried to shield King Alexander. But the King was already beyond help. He died on the floor of the car.

The unfortunate Foreign Minister might have been saved if a tourniquet had been applied to the wound in his arm, but he was neglected in the confusion and bled to death.

General Alphonse Georges, who was travelling in the royal car, grappled with the assassin and was shot four times, his life being saved by a medal, which deflected one bullet from his heart. Keleman, whose Mauser carried a 20-round magazine, then shot a policeman who grabbed him by the shoulder. It was only then that the crowd realised what was happening. Lieutenant Colonel Piollet, riding escort to the royal car, drew his sabre and slashed at Keleman, but wounded the chauffeur who was clinging to the assassin's arm. Keleman was then wounded in the head by a policeman and was stamped on by the mob. He has since died (→ 17).

Lt. Col. Piollet (l.) draws his sword on Keleman, too late to save the King.

Mao begins a long march to save his shattered troops

Oct 21. Chinese rebel Communist forces, besieged and defeated by the Nationalist armies of General Chiang Kai-shek, are attempting to break out of encirclement. It will not be an easy task, for the Nationalist commander with 700,000 troops has sealed off their Kiangsi stronghold with a network of barbed wire and concrete blockhouses.

The Communists, led by a Hunan peasant named Mao Tse-tung and estimated to be 100,000 strong, have begun a desperate attempt to fight their way out on what will be a long hard march through hostile territory to Yenan, 6,000 miles north (→ 20/10/35).

Communist leader Mao Tse-tung.

Little Gloria says she prefers auntie

Oct 24. Gloria Vanderbilt does not want to live with her mother. Mrs Vanderbilt is seeking custody of her ten-year-old daughter, who has a $2.8 million trust fund. But Gloria prefers to remain with her aunt, Mrs Harry P. Whitney, with whom she has lived for years.

Mrs Vanderbilt's own mother testified in court that her daughter had neglected Gloria virtually from birth.

1934

NOVEMBER

Su	Mo	Tu	We	Th	Fr	Sa
				1	2	3
4	5	6	7	8	9	10
11	12	13	14	15	16	17
18	19	20	21	22	23	24
25	26	27	28	29	30	

1. USSR: 12,000 are exiled to Siberia as enemies of the state (→1/12).

2. Munich: Two Americans are seized as spies.

6. US: Senator Huey Long calls for the secession of the state of Louisiana from the US (→10/9/35).

7. US: Premiere of Rachmaninov's "Rhapsody on a Theme of Paganini" in Baltimore under Leopold Stokowski.

8. Paris: Doumergue resigns as premier; Flandin succeeds.

12. UK: Film distributors warn that Britain has an excess of cinemas and that many of them will close.

13. Rome: The government orders all teachers to wear the Fascist uniform during school hours (→24/1/35).

15. London: Britain proposes a new naval treaty with equality for the Japanese Navy (→19/12).

19. India: The Congress Party wins almost half the seats in elections to the Indian legislative assembly (→11/2/35).

21. New York: Premiere of Cole Porter's musical "Anything Goes".

22. Geneva: Yugoslavia sends the League a note accusing Hungary of being behind the death of King Alexander.

25. Ankara: Mustafa Kemal tells Turks to adopt a surname by January 1, 1935; his will be "Ataturk", "Father of Turks" (→26).

26. Ankara: All inherited titles are abolished (→14/12).

26. Bonn: Theologian Dr Karl Barth is dismissed for refusing to swear loyalty to Hitler (→7/1/35).

29. London: Prince George, Duke of Kent, marries Princess Marina of Greece.

30. Egypt: A royal decree annuls the constitution and dissolves the Egyptian parliament.

30. UK: The Flying Scotsman reaches a record speed of 97.5 mph between London and Leeds (→5/3/35).

Churchill warns of weak UK defences

Nov 28. Winston Churchill today warned that Britain's weak defences could lead to Britain being "tortured into absolute subjection" in a war with Germany, with no chance of ever recovering.

In a major speech to the Commons calling on the Government to step up defence spending, he told MPs that Germany's munitions factories were already working "under practically war conditions"; by 1937 her air force would be double the strength of Britain's.

Churchill said that while there was no reason to think Germany would attack, it was not pleasant to feel that she could: "The time has come when the mists surrounding German armaments should be cleared away." (→4/3/35)

New GPO plan for posting by numbers

Nov 20. In an attempt to speed up mail deliveries, the Post Office is to introduce numbered postal districts in every provincial town in Britain.

Each house and business will receive leaflets and maps explaining the new system and giving numbers to be included in addresses.

The GPO believes that the system will be especially helpful at Christmas-time when thousands of temporary staff are employed on sorting mail.

London and some other major cities already have numbered postal areas.

Ice hockey is catching on with the smart set; these fashionable players discuss the day's sport.

1934

DECEMBER

Su	Mo	Tu	We	Th	Fr	Sa
						1
2	3	4	5	6	7	8
9	10	11	12	13	14	15
16	17	18	19	20	21	22
23	24	25	26	27	28	29
30	31					

1. Leningrad: Stalin's aide Sergei Kirov is murdered at his desk (→20).

2. US: Olympic swimming champion Johnny Weissmuller star for the first time of a new film "Tarzan of the Apes".

4. UK: Return rail fares are to be cut to a penny a mile.

5. Africa: Abyssinian and Italian troops clash on the Somali frontier (→16).

7. New York: Scientists produce anderosterone, the first hormone to be made artificially.

10. Stockholm: Nobel Prizes go to Harold Urey (US, Chemistry); George Whipple, George Minot and William Murphy (US, Medicine); and Luigi Pirandello (Italy, Literature). Peace Prize awarded in Oslo to Arthur Henderson and Sir Norman Angell (1933) (UK).→

12. Liverpool: 200 schoolchildren and parents are injured when a schoolroom floor collapses.

14. Turkey: Women get the vote (→1/1/35).

16. Rome: Mussolini rejects League arbitration in its dispute with Abyssinia.→

18. Switzerland: The Fascist Congress opens at Montreux, attended by 16 nations.

19. Tokyo: Japan renounces the 1922 Washington Naval Treaty (→1/4/35).

20. Moscow: Kamenev and Zinoviev are arrested (→29).

27. Tehran: The government decrees that Persia will now be known as Iran.

29. Leningrad: After a brief trial, Nikolayev and 13 others are shot for Kirov's murder.→

HITS OF 1934

Isle of Capri.

I only have eyes for you.

You're the top.

QUOTE OF THE YEAR

"How to Win Friends and Influence People".

Dale Carnegie, book title.

Secret trials and purges after death of Stalin's aide

Dec 29. The revolver shot which killed Sergei Kirov, a close associate of Joseph Stalin, earlier this month has set in motion a machinery of terror in the Soviet Union. More than 100 people have been summarily tried and executed and there is no reason to think the blood lust has been slaked.

The assassin is said to be Leonid Nikolayev, a young dissident Communist, who has been sent for trial with 13 others. Stalin has gone to Leningrad, where Kirov was the Communist Party boss, to interrogate him personally. The shooting, said the Central Committee had

Stalin (r.) helps bear Kirov's ashes.

been "at the treacherous hand of an enemy of the working class".

Kirov was a genuinely popular party leader who, although close to Stalin, had been critical of his personal rule. His death is now clearly the occasion for another severe crackdown by Stalin on real and imaginary opposition.

Within a week of the killing, 66 people in Moscow and Leningrad, described as "White Guard terrorists", were convicted and shot. It has come as no surprise that two leading Old Bolsheviks, Grigori Zinoviev and Leon Kamenev, have been linked with Nikolayev, arrested and once again sent into internal exile (→17/1/35).

Italy and Abyssinia in border clashes

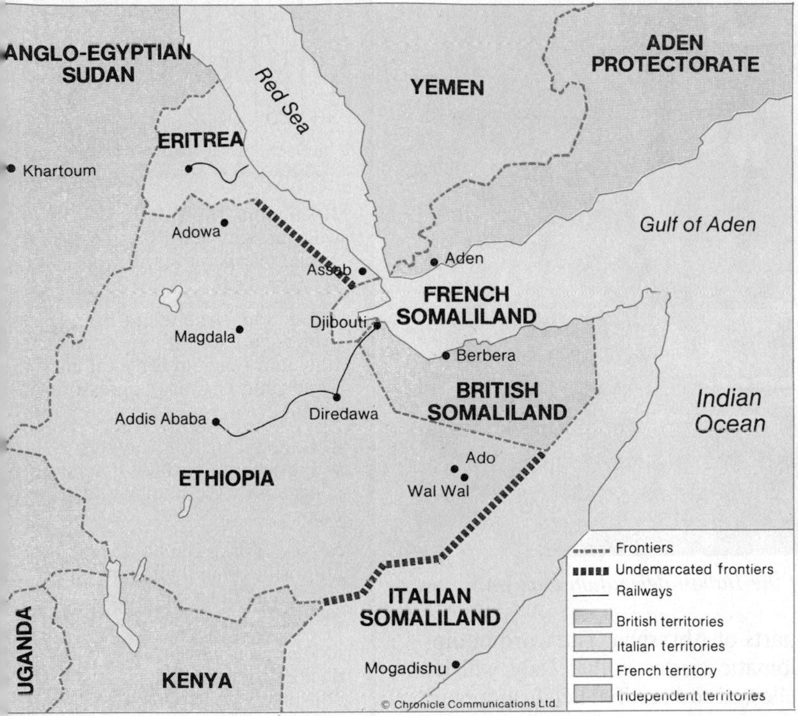

Dec 16. War clouds are gathering over the Horn of Africa after an incident involving Italian and Abyssinian troops at Wal Wal, a desert oasis near the border with Italian Somaliland. In a telegram to the League of Nations in Geneva, the Abyssinian Government has drawn attention to "the gravity of the situation". The Italians have rejected an Abyssinian call for arbitration and instead are demanding compensation.

The incident took place towards the end of last month, when a joint Anglo-Abyssinian commission which was seeking to settle the boundary line in the area arrived at Wal Wal to find the Italians in occupation. The Italians apparently suddenly opened fire on the commission's Abyssinian escort. The Italians, however, claim that it was the Abyssinians who started the shooting. Then last week, according to the Abyssinians, Italian planes bombed two villages.

In Rome, foreign observers are recalling a previous occasion when Italy, seeking to expand her African possessions, attacked Abyssinia at Adowa in 1896. Then the Italians were roundly defeated. The speculation is that Benito Mussolini, the Italian dictator, may be seeking a return match (→3/1/35).

One author finds he's won a Nobel Prize

Dec 10. People have been baffled by, and shouted abuse at, the plays of Luigi Pirandello, who received the year's Nobel Prize for Literature. But such incomprehension hardly surprises him; as one of the characters in his "Six Characters in search of an Author" says: "Each of us has his own private world. We think we understand each other: but we never do."

Despite causing an uproar in Rome, the play had great success in London in 1922. The same year saw the opening of his play "Henry IV", whose hero believes he is the Emperor – or rather keeps up this pretence with those around him because it is preferable to "reality".

Pirandello lost his family fortune in Sicily when he was 36 and had to live by teaching. His wife went mad – slowly. Watching her do so, he wrote, "enabled me to convey the psychology of the alienated". In 1924 he became a member of the Fascist Party and in 1928 left Italy for Berlin. "For me ... emptiness," he wrote. "I am a traveller without luggage." His latest work, an opera, opened in Germany last year with Hitler present.

Arts: talented trio lost to English music

Besides **Elgar**, death robbed English music , within four months, of **Gustav Holst** and **Frederick Delius.** Holst began his career as a trombonist and the dazzle of brass is characteristic of his best-loved works, "The Planets" and "The Perfect Fool". Delius is more controversial.

Stricken with paralysis in 1923, and developing blindness while he was composing his poignant music for "Hassan", Delius only continued composing thanks to his devoted amanuensis, **Eric Fenby**. His music was more popular in Germany than in England – he was the son of an immigrant Bradford wool merchant – until **Sir Thomas Beecham** championed his melting harmonies.

Mr and Mrs Frederick Delius.

To set against the losses was the gain of Glyndebourne, where **John Christie** has built a small opera house on to his beautifully situated country house in Sussex. The first Mozart opera festival opened with "The Marriage of Figaro" and "Cosi Fan Tutte" sung in the original Italian. The standard of performance, under two refugees from Nazi Germany, conductor **Fritz Busch** and producer **Carl Ebert**, opened all eyes.

The London Underground has a new look. The stations now being built are designed by **Charles Holden** with clean, streamlined looks, like the drum-shaped Arnos Grove. They are built in brick with wide rectangular window panes and concrete lids. Holden was commissioned by **Frank Pick**, who also commissioned the Underground logo and distinctive sans-serif type from **Edward Johnston**, the diagrammatic map of the tube lines from **Harry Bech** and the famous London Transport posters by **E. McKnight Kauffer**.

Holden also designed the bus stops, litter bins and the headquarters of the new London Passenger Transport Board at 55 Broadway, in Westminster. Its entrances are surmounted by massive brooding figures of "Night" and "Day" by **Jacob Epstein**, which provoked a storm of abuse. Holden's most popular work to date is the underground concourse at Piccadilly Circus.

New duo Fred Astaire and Ginger Rogers sparkle in "The Gay Divorcee".

1935

JANUARY

Su	Mo	Tu	We	Th	Fr	Sa
		1	2	3	4	5
6	7	8	9	10	11	12
13	14	15	16	17	18	19
20	21	22	23	24	25	26
27	28	29	30	31		

1. Africa: The Italian colonies of Cyrenaica, Tripoli and Fezzan are merged under the name of Libya (→ 15).

1. Turkey: Western-style surnames become obligatory (→ 6/2).

2. London: Britain agrees to buy more Irish cattle in return for selling more coal to the Irish Free State.

3. Geneva: Abyssinia appeals to the League for action against Italy.→

7. Berlin: The government announces the abolition of the powers of the German states.

10. Los Angeles: Mary Pickford wins a divorce from Douglas Fairbanks Sr.

11. US: A handwriting expert at Bruno Hauptmann's trial claims he wrote all the kidnap notes to the Lindberghs (→ 29).

13. Germany: The inhabitants of the Saar go to the polls to vote on a return to the Reich.→

15. Africa: Mussolini unites Eritrea and Somaliland as Italian East Africa (→ 21).

16. London: The government announces a Housing Bill that will make it illegal to exceed overcrowding limits.

17. Moscow: Kamenev and Zinoviev are among 21 jailed for "moral guilt" of Kirov's murder (→ 22/8).

17. Geneva: The League decides to return the Saar to Germany on March 1 (→ 19/2).

19. Washington: Roosevelt calls for a tax on inheritances.

21. Africa: Abyssinians kill 107 in French Somaliland (→ 15/2).

24. Rome: Mussolini dismisses the entire Italian cabinet.

29. US: On the last day of his cross-examination Bruno Hauptmann admits he has lied since his arrest (→ 13/2).

30. Moscow: The Kremlin says the Red Army is 940,000 strong, not 562,000 as the West believed.

BIRTH

8. US rock and roll singer Elvis Presley (†16/8/77).

France and Italy do a deal over Africa

Laval signs as Mussolini and members of the Italian delegation look on.

Jan 7. The Italian dictator, Benito Mussolini, and Pierre Laval, the French Foreign Minister, tonight hailed their two days of talks in Rome as a major contribution to world peace. The official communique is vague about what was actually agreed, referring only to the signing of "agreements relating to the interests of the two countries in Africa and documents registering their community of views on European subjects".

Behind this bland diplomatic language, it is understood, lies a hard-nosed deal in which France will get Italy's support to stop Hitler intervening in Austria in return for giving Italy a free hand to annex parts of Abyssinia. The word in diplomatic circles is that Italy will be allowed to "rectify" her frontiers to the extent of adding to her Eritrean colony, a piece of territory larger than Greece.

The Abyssinians have no doubts at all about Italy's intentions. In an appeal to the League of Nations they say the Italians are massing troops and tanks on the border and reconnaissance planes are regularly violating Abyssinian airspace. The Abyssinians have asked for a meeting of the League Council to consider the threat to peace. The Council has power to take any action "deemed wise and effectual" to safeguard peace (→ 15).

LEXICON
THE WONDER GAME
WADDINGTON'S
LEXICON CARD GAME
THE GAME OF SKILL · EXCITEMENT · AND INTEREST
Suitable for all ages
2/6 PER PACK
EXCITING · EDUCATING · FASCINATING

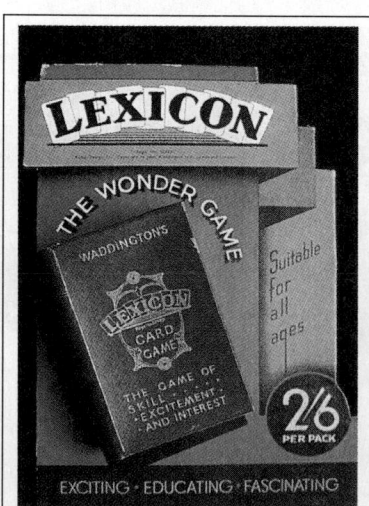

Brush up your vocabulary with the latest craze: "Lexicon" is loads of fun for half a crown.

Disputed territory votes for Hitler

Jan 15. Wild rejoicing throughout Germany has greeted the result of Sunday's plebiscite on the return of the coal-rich Saar territory. A record 99 per cent of Saarlanders went to the poll and 477,000 (90 per cent) voted to be reunited with Germany; 46,500 (9 per cent) voted to remain under League of Nations administration; 2,124 (.04 per cent) voted for union with France. Under the terms of the Versailles Treaty, France has had the right to exploit Saar coal mines for 15 years as compensation for the wartime destruction of French mines (→ 17).

1935

FEBRUARY

Su	Mo	Tu	We	Th	Fr	Sa
					1	2
3	4	5	6	7	8	9
10	11	12	13	14	15	16
17	18	19	20	21	22	23
24	25	26	27	28		

1. London: The BBC says it will start the world's first public television service this year (→ 22/3).

3. London: Britain and France propose a pact with Germany, Italy and Belgium for joint air force action against aggressors (→ 14).

4. London: British heavyweight champion Jack Petersen is beaten by German Walter Neusel.

5. New York: The boxing authorities rule that championship bouts must be a maximum of 15 rounds.

6. Washington: The US decides to close its Moscow consulate.

6. Turkey: Elections are held for the Turkish parliament, with women voting for the first time.

11. Geneva: The League begins a debate on the border dispute between Abyssinia and Italy (→ 15).

14. Berlin: Hitler says he supports the Anglo-French proposal for a mutual air defence pact.

15. Addis Ababa: Emperor Haile Selassie says Abyssinia only wants peace with its neighbours.→

17. Germany: An eight-hour working day is introduced.

18. Berlin: Two women are beheaded for spying (→ 10/4).

19. Germany: The first British troops leave the Saar territory (→ 1/3).

22. UK: Actor Sir Cedric Hardwicke says Hollywood's experiments with colour film will revolutionise the industry.

23. Geneva: Paraguay quits the League (→ 17/4).

25. Paris: Louis Lumiere shows an experimental three-dimensional film at the Academie des Sciences.

28. Rome: Italy claims Abyssinia is massing troops on the Somali border (→ 30/3).

DEATH

8. German painter Max Liebermann (*20/7/1847).

Guilty verdict in Lindbergh case

Hauptmann, flanked by New Jersey officials, awaits verdict and sentence.

Feb 13. The eyes of the world focussed on the small courtroom at Flemington, New Jersey, today as Bruno Hauptmann, a 33-year-old unemployed carpenter and illegal immigrant, was sentenced to death for the kidnapping and murder of aviator Charles Lindbergh's 20-month-old baby.

The evidence against Hauptmann was circumstantial, but damning. Scientific testimony claimed that the ladder used to reach the Lindberghs' nursery had been made by the defendant. Hauptmann was arrested after he had paid for petrol with a ten dollar note known to be paid as part of the $50,000 ransom. The ransom note contained spelling errors often made by Hauptmann in the past; and $13,750 of ransom money was found in a cellar at his New York home.

The German-born Hauptmann strongly denied the charge but could not explain a big change in his life style dating from the abduction. He was impassive as he was led, manacled, from the court to face the electric chair (→20/6).

Italians sail for Africa

Feb 23. Italian troops in tropical uniforms and khaki sun helmets boarded the Vulcania, a commandeered cruise liner, at Messina, Sicily, today, as Benito Mussolini, the Italian dictator, abandoned all pretence of seeking a peaceful solution to the border dispute with Abyssinia.

General Rodolfo Graziani, who is C-in-C Italian forces in East Africa, supervised the boarding. Before the troops arrived, ammunition, tanks, horses, mules and donkeys had already been taken on board. A second commandeered liner, the Leonardo da Vinci, will sail with more troops on Tuesday.

Italy is reckoned to have about 25,000 men in the two colonies of Eritrea and Italian Somaliland, well equipped with tanks. Over 200 aircraft, for the most part bombers, are known to have been sent out in recent weeks. At home, the call-up of conscripts continues.

Abyssinia is said to be capable of putting upwards of 80,000 men in the field, armed with rifles and some machine-guns. The air force consists of twelve planes.

Since the first border clashes at the desert oasis of Wal Wal were reported at the turn of the year, the Italians have made repeated allegations of further Abyssinian attacks. After Emperor Haile Selassie took the dispute to the League of Nations, Mussolini promised to negotiate and to observe a neutral zone in the Wal Wal region.

But then the Italians accused the Abyssinians of delaying tactics while the Abyssinians accused the Italians of not replying to their notes. At the Abyssinian legation in Rome, the charge d'affaires said he was preparing to leave at a moment's notice (→28).

Italian troops embark for Eritrea.

Bill gives Indian states more say

Feb 11. The historic Government of India Bill, providing for limited home rule, was approved in principle in the House of Commons tonight. An emotional clash between the Government and a massive group of Tory dissidents, led by Mr Churchill, ended in a 404-133 voting triumph for Stanley Baldwin.

The Tory leader, who is expected soon to take over from the ailing Ramsay MacDonald as Prime Minister, said India can now march towards full partnership within the Empire. It was a sell-out of Britain's imperial heritage, his critics retorted. In personal terms Mr Churchill has had a set-back and stays in the wilderness (→19/3).

Gracie Fields lands record film contract

Feb 10. The latest astronomical film offer has gone to Gracie Fields, the throstle of Rochdale. She has signed a two-year contract with Associated Talking Pictures to make three films, for which she will receive the unprecedented sum, for a British artist, of £150,000.

The company claimed yesterday that it was as much, if not more, than Garbo receives. "Our Gracie", as she is known in Lancashire, said: "I don't really like it. There's too much responsibility. Give me a cottage and ten shillings!"

She made her name singing "Sally" in revue as the Great War ended and followed it with comedy songs such as "The Biggest Aspidistra in the World". Filming starts next month at Ealing.

Lancashire lass Gracie Fields.

Sad day for cricket when Hobbs retires

Feb 25. Jack Hobbs, Surrey's and England's greatest batsman, has announced his retirement from the first-class game. In his 54th year, with his health uncertain, he has decided not to pursue further the quest for his 200th century that has been his principal aim since he bowed out of Test cricket in 1930.

He bequeathes a formidable set of batting records, some of which, even though his career included four blank seasons (1915-1918), seem almost impregnable: his 16 centuries in a season (1925), his 168 three-figure opening partnerships and, most notably, the 61,237 runs in his career and his 197 first-class centuries.

1935

MARCH

Su	Mo	Tu	We	Th	Fr	Sa
					1	2
3	4	5	6	7	8	9
10	11	12	13	14	15	16
17	18	19	20	21	22	23
24	25	26	27	28	29	30
31						

1. Athens: Ex-premier Eleutherios Venizelos launches a coup attempt.→

1. Germany: The Saar returns to Germany (→6).

2. Bangkok: King Prajadhipok abdicates because his government rejected plans for more democracy in Siam (→7).

5. UK: An LNER steam train travels from London to Newcastle, at a record maximum speed of 108 mph (→27/9).

6. Berlin: Goering says a German army of 400,000 is insufficient (→11).

7. US: Malcolm Campbell sets a record land speed of 276.8 mph (→3/9).

7. Switzerland: Nine-year-old Prince Ananda, now in Europe, is crowned King of Siam.

9. USSR: Nikita Khrushchev is elected chief of the Moscow Communist Party.

11. Berlin: The German air force or Luftwaffe is officially created in a proclamation by Hermann Goering (→18).

13. Jerusalem: A 3,000-year-old archive is found that supports parts of the Bible.

15. Paris: The government doubles military service to two years (→3/4).

18. London: Britain protests at Germany's introduction of conscription (→23).

19. India: British troops open fire on a huge crowd of Moslems rioting against Hindus; 27 are killed (→21/7).

22. Berlin: The world's first high-definition television service is inaugurated (→8/8).

23. Paris: France, Britain and Italy agree to a united front against German rearmament (→28).

27. UK: Major N. Furlong's Reynoldstown wins the Grand National at Aintree.

28. Moscow: Lord Privy Seal Anthony Eden arrives for talks with Soviet foreign minister Maxim Litvinov.→

30. Abyssinia: The government refuses to negotiate further with Italy (→7/5).

Europe begins to beat drums of war

Hitler marches into Saarbrucken to take possession of the Saar; the world is hoping this concession will pacify Germany.

March 31. Germany's massive rearmament programme was at the head of the agenda in the Moscow talks between Anthony Eden, the Lord Privy Seal, and Maxim Litvinov, the Soviet Foreign Minister. The communique, issued today as Mr Eden was preparing to leave the Soviet capital, reflected the shared anxieties by referring to the need "in the present international situation" to promote collective security through the League of Nations. The two sides also expressed the hope that Germany might be persuaded to join an East European security pact.

In the light of the sweeping demands made by Hitler only last week, it must seem a forlorn hope. Mr Eden's Moscow visit followed a visit to Berlin with the Foreign Secretary, Sir John Simon, when the German Fuehrer presented them with a series of demands that included: air force parity with Britain and France; a navy of 400,000 tons (almost as large as Britain's); and a 500,000-strong conscript army, five times the size which is permitted under the Treaty of Versailles.

Hitler is also seeking reunion with East Prussia by getting rid of the Polish Corridor, annexation of parts of Czechoslovakia to take in 3,500,000 Sudeten Germans, and an Anschluss with Austria.

Germany's introduction of conscription, announced on March 16, was explained by Nazi leaders as a response to British rearmament. Yet Britain's plans (see below) had themselves been proclaimed as a response to German militarism. Until this month, ministers had hesitated to endorse military pleas for rearmament, fearing that any action would annoy Hitler. But now, with spending on defence last year barely changed from that of ten years ago, the Government has agreed to back its belief in collective security with stronger armed forces (→17/4).

Britain increases defence spending to counter German threat

March 4. New expansion plans for the Army, Navy and Air Force were unveiled by the Government today in a white paper on defence that marks a major shift in British policy and which is intended to show Germany that Britain does not view her rearmament lightly.

The proposals were contained in a memorandum which calls for an increase in the size of the Fleet, along with a boost in warships' defence against air attack, more aircraft for the RAF and new coastal and anti-aircraft defences.

"Our attempt to lead the world towards disarmament by unilateral example has failed," said Mr Baldwin for the Government. He said Germany's rearmament threatened to put peace at peril. While the German leaders said they desired peace, Britain could not ignore the way Germany's forces were being mobilised, he added.

The warning comes on the eve of an important Anglo-German meeting in Berlin, and leading members of the Government are insistent that Herr Hitler himself should be told of Britain's strong views.

Much of the emphasis is on defence against air attack, following fears that a vast area of Britain could be hit by air raids from bases bordering the Channel (→31).

Burying the ghost of Versailles.

Revolt in Greece firmly suppressed

March 12. The attempt by the former Greek president, Eleutherios Venizelos, to return to power, by stealing a fleet and inciting an Army Corps to mutiny, has ended in utter defeat. Venizelos and his allies, who are opposed to the growing support for the restoration of the monarchy, have fled after 11 days of uncertain dominance on the island of Crete, and are now refugees on the Italian island of Kassos in the Dodecanese.

In Athens General Kondylis, who put down the revolution, was greeted with laurel wreaths and cheering crowds holding up his portrait. Great glee is being caused by Venizelos' remark that: "I have definitely retired from politics for ever." (→ 10/9)

Police bang gong at speeding drivers

March 18. A 30-mile-an-hour speed limit in built-up areas came into force at midnight; it will be reviewed at the end of 1939. The affected areas are streets with lighting, except some exempted streets where the lamp-posts have been painted with black and white stripes.

Police cars with gongs will halt offenders. Mr Leslie Hore-Belisha, the Transport Minister, has called on religious leaders to support the measure (→ 4/7).

MP tells House of early plumbing job

March 14. No new working class flat should be complete without a bath, a Labour MP pleaded today. Introducing his amendment to the Government's Housing Bill, Tom Smith told the House that his first house had a bath but no bathroom.

"I had to make a syphon from a piece of hosepipe from the copper to the bath, and then fix another for the cold water," he said. "It was not a pleasant job." Mr Smith hoped that the Commons would dismiss the "old argument" that the working class would keep coal in their bathrooms.

1935

APRIL

Su	Mo	Tu	We	Th	Fr	Sa
	1	2	3	4	5	6
7	8	9	10	11	12	13
14	15	16	17	18	19	20
21	22	23	24	25	26	27
28	29	30				

1. Tokyo: Japan rejects an alliance with Germany (→ 6).

3. Vienna: The government announces plans to boost its army and introduce two years conscription.

6. Rome: Mussolini says he favours curbs on German rearmament (→ 17).

7. US: Tornadoes kill 26 and injure 150 in the state of Mississippi.→

7. Danzig: The Nazis win 60 per cent of the vote in elections in the free city.

10. Germany: The sale of English newspapers is restricted (→ 12).

12. Berlin: All "non-Aryans" are expelled from the German Chamber of Writers and banned from literary work (→ 13).

13. Berlin: The Nazis say they will go to war against their enemies in the Church (→ 26).

15. London: Chamberlain claims that Britain has "80 per cent recovered" from the Depression.

17. Geneva: The Council of the League of Nations slams Hitler's reintroduction of conscription.→

21. China: Over 2,000 die in an earthquake on the island of Formosa.

23. Moscow: Stalin opens the 50-mile long Moscow underground railway (→ 9/7).

26. Berlin: 15,000 Nazis take part in an anti-Church rally in support of paganism (→ 24/5).

27. London: Sheffield Wednesday beat West Bromwich Albion 4-2 in the FA Cup Final at Wembley.

28. Berlin: Hitler orders 12 submarines in defiance of the Treaty of Versailles (→ 21/5).

29. UK: Glass reflectors or "Cat's Eyes", invented by Percy Shaw, are first used on British roads.

30. UK: Petrol costs 1/6d a gallon.

BIRTH

19. British comedian and musician Dudley Moore.

US is hit by dust storms

Oklahoma: a farmer and his sons seek shelter from the dust storm.

April 11. The dust storm that swept across the USA's "breadbasket" today created a staggering trail of destruction. Kansas, Colorado, Wyoming, Oklahoma, Texas and New Mexico were all affected.

Increasingly severe dust storms are hanging like a black scourge over half the country, wiping out millions of dollars' worth of crops, forcing thousands to flee their homes and paralysing all activity in some districts. While humans can protect themselves with masks during a storm, livestock suffer miserably.

The incidence of dust pneumonia among children is growing. Little relief is in sight, as dust piles up inside houses; schools and businesses are closed; traffic is stopped and bereaved families cannot bury their dead. In Texas, even the birds are afraid to fly.

Warlike Germany condemned by League

April 17. Nazi Germany's unilateral repudiation of the Versailles Treaty's limitations on the size of her armed forces was roundly condemned today in a resolution endorsed by 13 out of the 14 members of the Council of the League of Nations. Only Denmark, who was unwilling to offend her powerful neighbour, abstained. The voting was over in three minutes.

Hitler made strenuous last-minute efforts to get all reference to Germany removed from the resolution. In a phone call to Geneva, the German Foreign Office said that if the resolution went through unchanged Hitler would refuse to take part in any further international negotiations. The Council ignored the threat.

Maxim Litvinov, the Soviet Foreign Minister, said Germany had embarked on a policy of revenge and conquest. Mr Litvinov then caused some concern by suggesting the terms of the resolution should be extended to apply to countries outside Europe. This was taken to refer to the current Japanese aggression against China. After an appeal from Sir John Simon, the British Foreign Secretary, and the French and Italian delegates, Mr Litvinov said he would not press his amendment (→ 28).

1935

MAY

Su	Mo	Tu	We	Th	Fr	Sa
			1	2	3	4
5	6	7	8	9	10	11
12	13	14	15	16	17	18
19	20	21	22	23	24	25
26	27	28	29	30	31	

1. Washington: The Senate votes to extend the National Industrial Relief Act (NRA) by another 10 months (→27).

2. Paris: France and the USSR sign a mutual assistance pact in case of attack.

4. London: Leicester Square tube station opens, with the world's longest escalator.

7. Italy: 200,000 more troops are mobilised for the conflict in East Africa (→10).

10. Paris: France asks Britain to help curb Mussolini's designs on Abyssinia (→20).

13. UK: T. E. Lawrence is seriously ill after a motor cycle accident in Dorset.→

17. London: 19-year-old Vivien Leigh, who recently shot to fame on stage, signs a record £50,000 film contract.

20. Addis Ababa: Abyssinia calls for a special meeting of the League of Nations to defend her against Italian aggression (→13/7).

21. Berlin: Hitler broadcasts to the world that Germany wants peace but will not reduce armaments (→18/6).

24. Rome: Pope Pius XI condemns the Nazi sterilisation of 56,244 "inferior" German citizens.

26. Czechoslovakia: The Nazis make important gains in local elections.

27. Washington: The US Supreme Court rules the NRA unconstitutional (→3/8).

28. UK: 29,000 have applied to join the RAF since the government announced plans to boost the force (→11/1/36).

29. France: The liner Normandie leaves for the US on her maiden voyage (→3/6).

DEATHS

13. Polish commander and statesman Marshal Joseph Pilsudski (*5/12/1867).

17. French composer Paul Dukas (*1/10/1865).

19. British soldier and writer Colonel Thomas Edward Lawrence, "Lawrence of Arabia" (*15/8/1888).→

Celebrations for King's Silver Jubilee

May 6. It was a day of triumph and pageantry in London today, as King George and Queen Mary celebrated their Silver Jubilee. It is 25 years since he became King, following the death of his father, Edward VII. The occasions brought the biggest crowds on to the streets since Armistice Day in 1918.

Their majesties looked a little surprised by the warmth of the welcome as they drove to St Paul's. At Nelson's column, tiers of youngsters cheered their heads off in between licks of ice cream cones; passing St. Clement Dane's, there was a wonderfully light and merry peal of bells.

At St. Paul's, all eyes were on Queen Mary, resplendent in white with a necklace of five rows of pearls and brilliant stones. On her head was a toque, also in white. The King was in the scarlet uniform of a Field Marshal.

Four generations of the royal family were in the Cathedral. They included the King's granddaughters, Princess Elizabeth, following the order of service very carefully, and her small sister, Princess Margaret Rose, who tried to get the guard of honour of Boy Scouts to chat.

The most discussed feature of the day was the mongrel that trotted in front of the royal carriage and then hid beneath it. Soldiers tried to corner him with their swords, the police fared no better with truncheons. The crowds called him the Jubilee Dog (→28/1/36).

London crowds celebrate their Majesties' 25 glorious years of rule.

Britain hangs out the flags at Silver Jubilee street parties.

The RAF will be trebled in two years

May 22. The RAF will be trebled in size over the next two years to ensure Britain does not lag behind Germany in air power. A total of 920 new aircraft will be built bringing the total strength of the RAF by 1937 to 1,500 aircraft, the same number as Herr Hitler has said he intends for Germany.

At the same time a new type of heavy bomber, superior to any yet flying, will be brought into service along with new fighters, much faster than Germany's.

This announcement was made in the Commons today on the behalf of the Government by Stanley Baldwin, the Tory leader, who admitted to MPs that Britain now faced a "time of emergency", although he stressed that there was no need for panic. One fear is that the German dictatorship will be able to concentrate more resources on building up its air forces than Britain, although Mr Baldwin said British manufacturers will be given a free hand to bring new aircraft into service in half the normal time.

The expansion means 2,500 more pilots and nearly 20,000 additional personnel. A total of 31 new air bases will be built, along with five new training schools (→28).

Owens breaks five records in a day

May 25. Jesse Owens, a 21-year-old Alabama student, has broken five world records and equalled a sixth in a single afternoon. At the Big Ten championships at Ann Arbor, Michigan, Owens began by equalling the 9.4 seconds record for 100 yards, then set world records for the long jump (8.13 metres), 220 yards and the rarely run 220 yards hurdles, establishing en route the records for the shorter 200 metres and 200 metres hurdles. From first to last, the record-breaking took just 45 minutes (→3/8/36).

Lawrence of Arabia dies after bike crash

May 19. Colonel T. E. Lawrence, or "Lawrence of Arabia", now plain Mr T. E. Shaw, died today, after lying unconscious for five days with his skull fractured by a motor cycle accident. He was riding from Bovington army camp in Dorset, where he once served in the Tank Corps, to his nearby cottage, Clouds Hill, and swerved to avoid two boy cyclists.

His story of his exploits with the Arab rebels was told in his best-seller "Revolt in the Desert", but far more fully in "The Seven Pillars of Wisdom", which he refused to publish in his lifetime.

This version describes how he was briefly captured by the Turks and submitted to assault and humiliation. Those who have seen the edition printed privately for 120 subscribers say it is a literary masterpiece; it will now be published.

One mystery is the dedication "To S. A.", for whom "I gathered these tides of men into my hands and wrote my will across the sky in stars". The other is why he became an anonymous ranker for 14 years; he only left the RAF two months ago. He told a friend that it was "a happy penance for too rich and full a youth" (→29/7).

Lawrence of Arabia, in RAF guise.

Indian quake destroys famous hill station

May 30. A great earthquake, which shook British Baluchistan today, wrecked the famous hill station of Quetta and killed 20,000 people. Among the dead are 53 Britons, most of them officers and airmen of the RAF, whose headquarters in the military and railway capital were devasted by the shock. Many aircraft were destroyed. At this time of the year Quetta, 5,500 feet above sea level, is crowded with Britons escaping the Indian heat. The only information comes from the military wireless station and details are still vague, but it is known that whole towns have been totally obliterated.

The King has sent a telegram of sympathy and relief trains with medical supplies are on the way. The police force was wiped out when its barracks collapsed, so British troops are on patrol.

Britain rushes for the sun: "the shortest cut to the sea, is good enough for me!" cries the charabanc party in this Donald McGill postcard.

1935

JUNE

Su	Mo	Tu	We	Th	Fr	Sa
						1
2	3	4	5	6	7	8
9	10	11	12	13	14	15
16	17	18	19	20	21	22
23	24	25	26	27	28	29
30						

1. Paris: Pierre Flandin resigns as premier (→4).

2. Paris: Briton Fred Perry beats German Gottfried von Cramm in the French international tennis championship (→6/7).

3. New York: The French liner Normandie arrives after a record Atlantic crossing of four days three hours.

4. Paris: Pierre Laval becomes premier (→7).

5. UK: The Aga Khan's Bahram wins the Derby at Epsom.

7. Paris: Pierre Laval is given emergency powers to save the falling French franc (→6/8).

10. New York: Scientists claim that vitamin B-1 will cure neuritis (→20/8).

12. Argentina: Bolivia and Paraguay sign an armistice to end their three-year-old war over the disputed Chaco area.

15. UK: 14 die in a railway crash at Welwyn Garden City.

18. London: Britain signs a naval pact with Germany.→

20. US: Hauptmann appeals against his death sentence for kidnap and murder of the Lindbergh baby (→14/10).

21. London: A Croydon telephonist wins a GPO competition to find a voice for the Speaking Clock (→24/7/36).

24. Dresden: Premiere of Richard Strauss's opera "Die Schweigsame Frau" ("The Silent Woman").

27. US: Scientists succeed in crystallising a disease virus for the first time.

28. UK: Alfred Perny wins the British Open golf championship.

28. Washington: Roosevelt orders a federal gold vault to be built at Fort Knox, Kentucky.

30. Munich: Reported that Hitler uses a double to foil potential assassins.

BIRTH

21. French writer Francoise Sagan, born Francoise Quoirez.

Japan imposes her will on China after victory in the north

June 18. The Nationalist government of China today caved in to a Japanese ultimatum, following Japan's bloodless victory in Manchuria, now Manchukuo. It agreed to the removal of a division of their troops from the north and the replacement of government officials by ones chosen by the Japanese. Furthermore, General Sung Cheh-yuan, Governor of Chahar and one of the few Chinese commanders who successfully resisted the Japanese in 1933, is to be dismissed.

The ultimatum was provoked by the arrest of three Japanese secret service agents, described by Tokyo as "civilian officials". Japan used this incident as a pretext to instal "friendly" administrators in Peking and Tientsin, claiming that native Chinese civil servants were hostile. The changes demanded in the north use the same technique, which was successful in establishing the puppet empire of Manchukuo.

Young Chinese peasant volunteers.

By submitting to the new Japanese demands, China's leader Chiang Kai-shek stands to lose much of his political and military influence in northern China, but with his government already at war with Chinese Communist rebels he had little choice (→26/11).

Baldwin becomes PM

June 7. Stanley Baldwin is Prime Minister again today, following the resignation of Ramsay MacDonald for health reasons. The all-party National Government continues, with Tories holding 16 of the 22 places in a reconstructed cabinet. Four National Liberals and two National Labour MPs are included.

Mr MacDonald stays in the team as Lord President and nominally No. 2 man; he is joined by his son Malcolm as Colonial Secretary. This is the first time for 70 years that father and son have been in the same cabinet. The new premier promised high priority for tackling unemployment and said that there will be no reversion to normal party politics at the next election.

The National Government, originally formed as a temporary expedient in 1931, hopes to ride on indefinitely and there are rumours that Mr Baldwin may not wait long before seeking a new mandate.

A cabinet novelty this time is double-banking at the Foreign Office: Sir Samuel Hoare is the new Foreign Secretary and Anthony Eden becomes the first Minister for League of Nations Affairs. This reflects the Government's declared support for collective security, including, in the last resort, war against an aggressor. Mr Eden is expected to support a more robust foreign policy and faster rearmament. In a farewell message, Mr MacDonald called for a continuation of the National government. A piper played "Will ye no come back again?" and there was a big crowd at Euston when the exhausted man, who led Labour to power and then deserted the party, left for his native Lossiemouth. He said he would be back after a rest. But he knew he travelled north into his own political twilight.

New PM Stanley Baldwin.

Anger mounts over German naval deal

June 19. The French Government is fuming over the Anglo-German naval accord, signed yesterday, which allows Berlin to build up her naval power once again.

The accord has caused a major rift in the normally very close relationship between London and Paris. The French feel that the British Government was duped into signing the deal, which effectively removes the controls on German naval rearmament included in the Treaty of Versailles.

Britain signed the accord after Ambassador von Ribbentrop asked Britain to agree to relax the agreements on naval strength. The accord supposedly limits the size of the German fleet to 35 per cent of that of the Royal Navy.

At present the German fleet consists of three pocket battleships, six light cruisers and 12 torpedo boats. The treaty gives Herr Hitler British approval to massively increase this; Germany can build five battleships, two aircraft carriers, five heavy cruisers, 11 light cruisers and 65 destroyers. The thinking of the War Office is that Britain will always be able to maintain her lead. But a Paris newspaper said: "Does London imagine that Hitler has renounced any of the projects indicated in his book 'Mein Kampf'? If so, the illusion of our friends across the Channel is complete" (→ 8/7).

Lindbergh's pump keeps organs alive

June 21. The Rockfeller Institute in New York reported today that, in April, Alexis Carrel succeeded in keeping internal organs of an animal alive outside the body for the first time. This was made possible by the invention of a pump-oxygenator by flyer Charles Lindbergh. The device controls temperature, pressure and oxygen, and prevents infection or bloodclotting.

During a series of 26 experiments a cat's thyroid gland lived in the organ chamber for over 20 days and an ovary enlarged from 90 to 284 mg in five days. Suprarenal gland, spleen, heart, and kidney were also studied in the 26 experiments.

June 1. A major civil defence exercise brings this eerie sight as thousands of women throughout England don skull-like gas-masks.

1935

JULY

Su	Mo	Tu	We	Th	Fr	Sa
	1	2	3	4	5	6
7	8	9	10	11	12	13
14	15	16	17	18	19	20
21	22	23	24	25	26	27
28	29	30	31			

1. Japan: 227 die in floods.

1. Cuba: Tne army foils an alleged Communist plot to overthrow the government.

4. London: The Ministry of Transport says dipped car headlights will be compulsory (→ 2/11).

5. Washington: The National Labor Relation Act comes into force, guaranteeing the freedom of trade unions (→ 3/8).

6. Wimbledon: In a repeat of June's French international, Fred Perry beats Gottfried von Cramm for the Men's Singles title; Helen Moody beats Helen Jacobs for her seventh Women's Singles crown.

8. Berlin: A naval programme is announced to build 28 submarines, 16 destroyers and two giant cruisers.

9. Moscow: Tunnel engineers on the new underground railway discover Ivan the Terrible's torture chamber.

13. Addis Ababa: Haile Selassie rejects the idea of an Italian sphere of influence in Abyssinia.→

15. Berlin: Nazis beat Jews along the Kurfurstendamm (→ 19).

19. Berlin: Anti-Semite Wolf von Helldorf is made chief of the Berlin police, to purge the city of Jews and Communists (→ 15/8).

21. India: 10 die when troops open fire on rioting Moslems (→ 8/2/36).

25. London: The government bans arms sales to either Italy or Abyssinia (→ 28).

28. Italian East Africa: Abyssinians kill 40 Italian troops in a surprise night attack (→ 2/8).

29. UK: T. E. Lawrence's "Seven Pillars of Wisdom" is published.

DEATHS

3. French engineer and motor manufacturer Andre Citroen (*5/2/1878).

13. French soldier Major Alfred Dreyfus, centre of the notorious "Dreyfus Affair" (*19/10/1859).

Abyssinia vows to fight to last man

July 18. Faced with the prospect of an imminent Italian attack on his country, Emperor Haile Selassie of Abyssinia today made a fighting speech to parliament in the capital Addis Ababa. Declaring that it is better to die for freedom than to live as a slave, he said he would lay down his own life for his country.

"For forty years, Italy has desired to conquer our country," the Emperor said to a solemn and silent parliament, "but Abyssinia knows how to fight to the last man to preserve the country's independence. Italians, fortified though they may be by all modern weapons, will yet see how a poor but united people will defend their country and their Emperor." (→25)

French front pledge to oppose Fascism

July 14. Bastille Day passed peacefully today with a splendid military parade and much dancing in the streets, despite the rival gatherings of Fascists and anti-Fascists. It was the left-wing which gathered the most support, with a crowd of some 250,000 listening to speeches in the Bois de Vincennes. The Popular Front – the alliance of Radical Socialists and Communists – met on the bicycle track in an "assize of peace and liberty" and pledged to fight Fascism.

The
OFFICIAL RULE BOOK of
The League of Ovaltineys
This Certifies that
WARNING:

The Ovaltineys sing the praises of hot, milky bedtime drinks.

1935

AUGUST

Su	Mo	Tu	We	Th	Fr	Sa
				1	2	3
4	5	6	7	8	9	10
11	12	13	14	15	16	17
18	19	20	21	22	23	24
25	26	27	28	29	30	31

1. UK: Hull City Council is asked by the government to look into the feasibility of a new bridge over the Humber.

2. Geneva: The great powers call a new conference to try to settle the Italy-Abyssinia conflict (→16).

3. Washington: 18,000 musicians are to get jobs in a federal "arts relief" programme (→14).

6. France: Serious unrest breaks out in Paris, Le Havre and Brest in protest at government economies (→5/11).

8. Berlin: Goering takes control of the new German television service (→15).

10. Mexico: A plot to kill President Lazaro Cardenas is foiled (→1/9).

13. Italy: 1,000 are reported killed when a dam bursts at Oveda.

14. Washington: Roosevelt signs the Social Security Bill, introducing welfare for the old, sick and unemployed (→31).

15. Berlin: On Hitler's orders, the Nazi swastika becomes the German national flag.→

16. Paris: Haile Selassie offers new concessions to Italy as diplomatic moves to halt an Italian invasion continue (→18).

18. Paris: Mussolini rejects Anglo-French plans for a negotiated settlement of the Ethiopian conflict (→25).

20. US: Scientists at the University of California announce the isolation of vitamin E.

22. Moscow: Georgi Dimitrov is to succeed Zinoviev as head of the Communist International (→25/9).

25. Addis Ababa: Abyssinia is put on a war footing in anticipation of an Italian invasion (→28).

28. Italy: Mussolini says the Abyssinian dispute must be settled by force of arms, not negotiations (→6/9).

31. Washington: Roosevelt signs the Neutrality Bill, banning arms sales to countries at war (→5/10).

Hitler bans German-Jewish marriages

Aug 15. As the Nazis prepare for this year's Nuremberg rally next month, it is becoming clearer than ever that the persecution of Germany's Jews is to be stepped up. Julius Streicher, a former school teacher who is the party boss in Nuremberg, has ordered that "race defilers" are to be arrested on the spot. In effect, marriage between Jews and non-Jews is banned; and Jewish boys and Aryan girls who have been seen merely walking together have been carted off to concentration camps.

It is also plain that a determined effort is being made to exclude Jews from public places. The signs are everywhere, outside shops, hotels, restaurants and places of entertainment: "Juden unerwuenscht" (Jews Not Wanted).

In the Nazi vocabulary, Jews are "Untermenschen" (sub-humans) and, as such, cannot expect to be treated as equals. For what it's worth, a Jew is anyone with one Jewish grandparent. Streicher, a notorious pornographer and editor of "Die Stuermer", which thrives on obscene tales of Jewish sexual crimes, has a fancy for going around cracking a whip and boasting of the countless thrashings he has meted out to Jews (→19/9).

The preacher of race hatred grasps the swastika, emblem of Nazism.

Sun (and prosperity) lures holiday crowds

Wish you were here? Eastbourne's esplanade on Bank Holiday Monday.

Aug 5. Brilliant sunshine today lured more Britons to the coast and countryside than on any previous Bank Holiday. So many people poured into Brighton – police estimated there were 500,000 day visitors – that in places the shingle was invisible beneath the bodies. Special trains and motor coaches were packed, as the nation celebrated signs of increasing prosperity. Unemployment has fallen from a high of 3.1 million to just below two million over the last three years. Another feature of this year's Bank Holiday (other than the sunny weather) was the increasing numbers of people using aeroplanes to reach their destination. Sports fixtures also reported record crowds.

1935

SEPTEMBER

Su	Mo	Tu	We	Th	Fr	Sa
1	2	3	4	5	6	7
8	9	10	11	12	13	14
15	16	17	18	19	20	21
22	23	24	25	26	27	28
29	30					

1. Mexico: It is announced that women workers are to be given the vote.

3. US: Over 200 are reported dead when a hurricane hits Florida.

6. Geneva: The League appoints a five-power committee to arbitrate in the Abyssinian crisis (→7).

7. Rome: Mussolini pledges a truce in Abyssinia while the League confers (→18).

7. UK: The Aga Khan's Bahram wins the St. Leger, completing the treble of St. Leger, 2,000 Guineas and Derby.

8. USSR: Coal miner Alexis Stakhanov wins a prize for digging 175 tons, starting the "Stakhanovite" award system.

10. Athens: Fierce street fighting takes place as the Greek parliament debates the restoration of the monarchy (→10/10).

12. UK: 16 miners die in a pit accident at Mapplewell in Yorkshire.

15. US: Millionaire aviator Howard Hughes reaches a record air speed of 347.5 mph.

15. Philippines: Quezon is elected president in the first elections since the US granted a new constitution (→18).

18. Philippines: US General Douglas MacArthur is appointed to organise the new Philippine army.

18. Geneva: The League sends Italy and Abyssinia a peace plan; Italy would gain privileges and some land (→20).

20. Addis Ababa: Haile Selassie refuses to concede privileges for Italy (→22).

22. Rome: Mussolini rejects the League's peace plan and demands the disarmament of the Abyssinian army (→4/10).

25. Moscow: Stalin ends food rationing in the USSR.

27. UK: LNER's new Silver Jubilee sets a record rail speed of 112 mph (→19/2/36).

30. Boston: Premiere of George Gershwin's opera "Porgy and Bess".

Jews banned from German public life

Hitler (bottom centre) at a rally in Tannenberg: today's Nuremberg decrees are the harshest anti-Jew laws yet.

Sept 19. When Hitler announced his new decrees at Nuremberg last Sunday, he claimed they were intended to create a "tolerable relationship" between Jews and Aryans. In fact, the effect has been to make life even less tolerable for Germany's Jews.

They have been deprived of their German citizenship and are now merely "subjects" without rights. Most shopkeepers are afraid to be seen serving a Jew for fear of being beaten up or getting their windows smashed.

Jews are now excluded from employment in public services and are having their pension rights taken away. They are barred from teaching, journalism, farming, radio, the theatre and films. Though they are not yet legally barred from law or medicine, they are, in practice, being excluded.

The already-existing veto on marriage or extra-marital relations between Jews and Aryans has become law under the Nuremberg decrees. A Jew is forbidden to employ an Aryan maidservant under 35 years. In Frankfurt this week maidservants have been dragged from their beds by Nazi thugs and told not to return to their Jewish employers.

Finally, the Nuremberg decrees forbid a Jew to raise the German flag – if he should think of doing such a thing (→12/10).

Malcolm Campbell in Bluebird smashes 300-mph barrier

Sept 3. Sir Malcolm Campbell set a new world record today when his car, Bluebird, made two astonishing runs along the Bonneville Salt Flats in Utah at an average speed of 301.337 mph. He broke his own record of 276.816 mph set at Daytona beach last March.

He narrowly escaped disaster when a front tyre burst at 290 mph as he slowed down, an incident the modest Sir Malcolm described as a "ticklish moment". For a while a stream of salt whipped up by the wind forced him to drive blind.

He was born in 1885 and has always been a keen racer, setting speed records for motorcycles, aircraft, cars and boats (→2/9/37).

Record breaker Sir Malcolm Campbell is not shy to give his endorsement.

1935

US Senator shot by political opponent

Sept 10. US Senator Huey Long died today after doctors conducted a third blood transfusion in a last-ditch effort to save his life.

The Louisiana politician was gunned down two days ago by Dr Carl Weiss, leader of a faction opposed to Long, and son-in-law of a judge called B.H. Pavy. Immediately afterwards Weiss was killed by the senator's bodyguards.

Weiss shot Long in the stomach just outside the chambers of the Louisiana House of Representatives on Sunday night. Among the legislation being enacted in the House was a gerrymandering of Judge Pavy's judicial district which would have virtually prevented his re-election.

Many Louisiana residents are grief-stricken at the loss of their leader and recall that last month Long predicted there would be an attempt on his life (→ 31/1/36).

Assassinated Senator Huey Long.

Jaguar is king of the new car jungle

Sept 30. Among the most interesting British cars already announced for next month's Motor Show is the new SS Jaguar, a stylish touring saloon with a 90-mph top speed. William Lyons, the head of SS Cars, asked dealers to put a price on it. Their replies averaged £632. He then revealed the price was £385. Other new models range from Ford's V-8 at £225 to the £1,850 V-12 from Rolls. Independent front springs are featured in several new cars (→ 2/10).

OCTOBER

Su	Mo	Tu	We	Th	Fr	Sa
		1	2	3	4	5
6	7	8	9	10	11	12
13	14	15	16	17	18	19
20	21	22	23	24	25	26
27	28	29	30	31		

1. Germany: Sport becomes compulsory in schools (→ 12).

2. UK: Rolls-Royce announce their new 50 hp, 12-cylinder Phantom III, costing £1,850.

5. Washington: Under the Neutrality Act, the US declares an arms embargo on Italy and Abyssinia (→ 11).

6. Abyssinia: The Italians take Adowa and Adigrat (→ 9).

9. Geneva: Austria and Hungary refuse to impose sanctions on Italy (→ 10).

10. Athens: The national assembly votes to restore the monarchy (→ 25/11).

10. Geneva: 50 nations agree to impose sanctions on Italy (→ 11).

11. Geneva: The League puts an arms embargo on Italy, but not on Abyssinia.→

12. Berlin: Jewish and black American jazz is banned from German radio (→ 21/12).

14. US: Lindbergh baby killer Bruno Hauptmann gets 30 days' grace to appeal to the US Supreme Court (→ 5/12).

15. Berlin: Hitler creates the Reich's General Staff (→ 21).

20. UK: 11 people die in a 92 mph gale.

21. Geneva: Germany officially quits the League (→ 2/1/36).

23. Ottawa: Mackenzie King forms a Liberal government after his party's record majority in the general election.

25. London: Baldwin calls a general election for the middle of November (→ 16/11).

29. Berlin: Hitler declares an amnesty for Lutherans and rebukes Nazi paganists.

31. London: The government says it will raise the school-leaving age from 14 to 15 (→ 13/2/36).

DEATHS

20. British Labour leader Arthur Henderson (*13/9/1863).

22. Ulster Unionist leader Edward Carson, Lord Carson (*9/2/1854).

Mao's long march ends: a legend begins

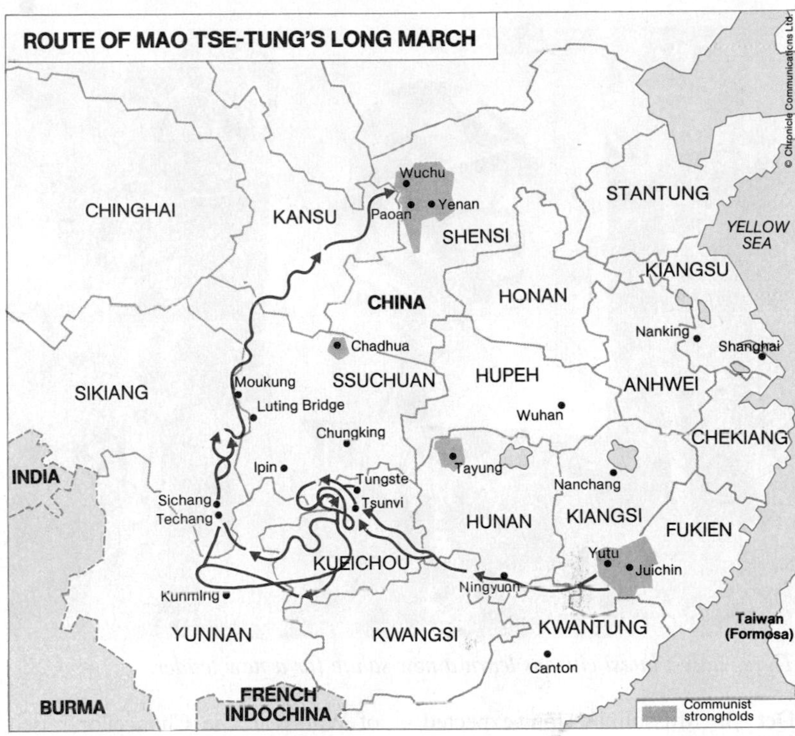

Oct 20. After twelve months of marching, fighting and suffering, the battered remnants of the Communists' First Front army, commanded by Mao Tse-tung, has finally reached comparative safety in Yenan. There, in the wilds of Shensi province in north-west China, they hope to set up a Soviet state, reinforced by converts they have made on the journey.

The long march has established Mao Tse-tung as undisputed leader of the hard-core Communists and a permanent threat to the Nationalist government.

The march began when the Communists broke out of the Kiangsi province where the Nationalists had encircled them. They then took a circuitous route of 6,000 miles to safety, harassed both by the Nationalists and by warlords and bandits, finally crossing the high Yangtse at Chou P'ing Fort. Only 30,000 arrived; more than 100,000 perished along the way. There are hopes that the Second Front army, which took another route, may eventually join them.

Desperately short of supplies and ammunition, Mao's army frequently had to disperse. The most notable battle was at an iron chain bridge at Luting on the river Tatu where, although planks had been removed, 22 volunteers managed to cross (→ 23/2/37).

Mao Tse-tung, under the Red Flag, exhorts his followers to keep marching.

Mussolini's Fascist troops march into Abyssinia

Tigre: Italy's latest citizens learn a new salute for a new leader.

Emperor Haile Selassie takes the salute from his patriotic troops.

Oct 3. Mussolini's long-expected invasion of Abyssinia began at dawn yesterday, with thousands of young Italian infantrymen cheering as they crossed the border from Eritrea and began the heavy slog up the valleys.

Italian bombing planes roared overhead, striking first at the border town of Adowa, scene of Italy's humiliating defeat at the hands of Abyssinians in 1896. Two of the bombers were reported to be piloted by Mussolini's sons, Vittorio, aged 19, and Bruno, aged 18, while a third had his son-in-law, Count Galeazzo Ciano, as pilot.

Tonight the Italian force, under General Emilio de Bono and numbering 100,000 men, including Eritrean askaris, is reported to be advancing on a 40-mile front and to be within 12 miles of Adowa. Another army, commanded by General Graziani, is mounting a drive north from Italian Somaliland, but is reported to be held up by rainsoaked tracks.

When news of the attack reached the Emperor Haile Selassie in the capital, Addis Ababa, the order for general mobilisation was read by the Imperial Chancellor to an assembly of tribal chiefs and troops gathered in the courtyard of the royal palace.

After briefly recounting the history of the dispute, beginning with the Italian attack at the desert oasis of Wal Wal, the Chancellor raised his voice and cried: "The hour is grave. Arise, each of you, take up arms and rush to the defence of your Emperor and your country." With that, the war drums began. They thundered out the mobilisation orders from Addis Ababa to chiefs and governors across the length and breadth of Abyssinia.

The Abyssinian Ministry of Foreign Affairs has telegraphed the League of Nations in Geneva, denouncing the Italian aggression as a breach of the League Covenant. The Abyssinians claim that the first bombs on Adowa struck a hospital bearing the Red Cross. Mussolini raised the curtain on his African adventure with a speech on Wednesday afternoon from the balcony of his office in the Palazzo Venezia in Rome. "A solemn hour is about to break in the history of our fatherland," he said. The wheel of fate had begun to turn and could not be stopped.

Italy's 40 million men, women and children had been ordered to gather in town and village squares to hear wireless relays of the speech. Il Duce, as Mussolini styles himself, showed defiance when he referred to the threat of economic sanctions by the League of Nations. "We will answer with our discipline and our abstemiousness and our spirit of sacrifice," he said. The speech lasted 18 minutes and was wildly cheered.

In London, the British cabinet held a two-hour meeting on the crisis in the morning, and in the afternoon key ministers and service chiefs were called to Downing Street. It is being stressed that any action by Britain must be coordinated with France. But the French are saying they will not do anything to upset the accord they recently reached with Italy (→ 6).

Invasion is stiffest test League of Nations has yet faced

Oct 22. Sir Samuel Hoare, the Foreign Secretary, told the House of Commons today that Britain was trying to uphold the League of Nations in its greatest test over the Italian invasion of Abyssinia. If the League failed, he said, "the world will be faced with a period of danger and gloom".

He gave an encouraging assessment of the likely effectiveness of economic sanctions "if they are collectively applied", but at times he sounded less than enthusiastic about operating them. He said there was still a breathing space before economic pressure could be applied to Italy. Could that not be used to make it "unnecessary to proceed further along the unattractive road of economic action against a fellow League member, an old friend and a former ally?"

In a passage that suggested the Foreign Secretary believed Italy was justified in looking for colonies in Africa, Sir Samuel reminded MPs that he had been the first public figure in Britain to admit that Italy had a case for territorial expansion and economic development.

As for any kind of military action to stop Italy, Sir Samuel ruled it out completely. "The pre-condition for military sanctions, namely collective agreement at Geneva, has never existed," he said. He also ruled out suggestions for closing the Suez Canal to Italy as "dangerous and provocative talk".

While the European powers debate sanctions, the Italians are claiming victories. They say 10,000 Abyssinians have surrendered near Adowa. In Addis Adaba nothing is known of the fighting there, since the government's only telephone line to the north has been cut. Italy's first casualty list, published in Rome, included 30 dead and 70 wounded. Five of the dead are Italians; the rest are auxiliaries from Eritrea (→ 8/11).

Attlee is new leader of the Labour Party

Oct 8. Clement Richard Attlee, a mouse-like, middle-class Fabian, was today elected stop-gap leader of the Labour Party. There will be a contested election for the job in the next Parliamentary session. Mr Attlee had been deputy leader.

The previous leader, George Lansbury, resigned after being outvoted at last week's party conference. As a Christian pacifist he could not stomach support for economic sanctions and possible use of force against Italy over Abyssinia. He was denounced by Ernest Bevin, leader of the biggest union, for "hawking his conscience" around the country.

Labour is now firmly committed to supporting the League of Nations and the principle of collective security, but under its new management it will still vote against British defence spending (→26/11).

Clement Attlee - now in charge.

Keep-fit fad finds favour in Britain

Oct 8. The slogan "use your vigour to keep your figure" is drawing thousands of women into keep-fit classes across the country, a new report reveals today. The Central Council of Recreative Physical Training, set up only a few months ago to promote such activity, says that the demand for gymnasia is already outstripping supply. Classes are no sooner opened than filled.

An official said: "A survey we have just completed shows that there are thousands of adolescents, men and women anxious to form keep-fit classes." Some of the most enthusiastic members are turning out to be older women, some even in their sixties, who love slimming exercises done gently to music.

So fast-growing is this novelty that later this week over 130 organisations devoted to various forms of physical activity will be holding a special conference in London.

Elsewhere today, the new-found enthusiasm for keeping active was echoed in shoe fashions on show at the annual Shoe and Leather Fair. This featured shoes with the lowest heels for more than a decade; fashion experts believe the trend has been inspired by new styles of ballroom dancing. Like the Charleston, these are not done well in high heels.

Gatwick soon to be site of new airport

Oct 31. Britain will soon have the most advanced airport in Europe when Gatwick aerodrome opens in two months' time to relieve congestion at Croydon. The airport will have its own station on the main London to Brighton line, to which it will be linked by an underground subway, complete with shops and air conditioning. Air traffic control will be capable of handling six aircraft at a time (→6/3/36).

1935

NOVEMBER

Su	Mo	Tu	We	Th	Fr	Sa
					1	2
3	4	5	6	7	8	9
10	11	12	13	14	15	16
17	18	19	20	21	22	23
24	25	26	27	28	29	30

1. Rome: Anti-British protests mark the decision to impose sanctions on Italy from November 18th (→8).

2. London: Chamberlain announces plans to spend £100 million on British roads in the next five years (→1/2/36).

5. Paris: 20 people go on trial in connection with the activities of the swindler Alexandre Stavisky (→17/1/36).

6. UK: The prototype of the Hawker Hurricane fighter makes its maiden flight.

8. Abyssinia: The Italians complete their occupation of Tigre province when they seize the capital Makale.→

11. US: Orvil Anderson and Andrew Stevens set an altitude record of 74,000 ft in a balloon.

12. US: A Texas mob of 700 lynches two blacks accused of murder (→11/4/36).

13. Cairo: Two are reported dead and 88 hurt after anti-British riots (→26/8/36).

14. Manila: Manuel Quezon is sworn in as first president of the US "Commonwealth of the Philippines".

15. UK: General election casualties include Ramsay MacDonald, who loses to Labour's Emmanuel Shinwell.→

20. Abyssinia: Many Italians are killed in an Abyssinian attack on Sasa Baneh (→23).

23. Rome: Mussolini threatens to quit the League if sanctions continue (→5/1/36).

25. Athens: King George II returns from exile to a rapturous reception.

26. London: Clement Attlee is re-elected Labour leader.

28. Berlin: Hitler declares all men from 18 to 45 army reservists (→30).

30. Berlin: "Non-belief in Nazism" becomes legal grounds for divorce (→21/12).

DEATH

20. British commander John Rushworth Jellicoe, Earl Jellicoe Admiral of the Fleet in the Great War (*5/12/1859).

League states start applying economic sanctions to Italy

Nov 18. The economic sanctions imposed on Italy by the League of Nations, and agreed to by 50 states, take effect from today. The next step the League has to consider is the imposition of an oil embargo, which could cripple Italy's capacity to fight the war in Abyssinia.

Sanction-fighting regulations are now in force in Italy. Friday is to be a meatless day in restaurants and butchers' shops will close. Registered letters are being opened to ensure that not more 50 lire is sent out of the country.

But the sanctions-busters are at work. Last week an arms consignment of 29 wagons from Czechoslovakia arrived in Vienna and was sent on to Italy (→23).

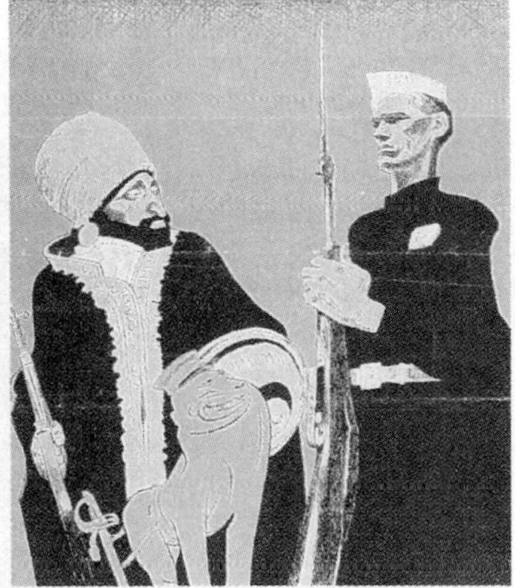

Might is right in Abyssinia.

Greece votes to restore monarchy

Nov 25. King George II of Greece returned to his country today after 12 years in exile, restored to his throne by a referendum. He received a welcome from his people which was friendly, even if it was not exactly exuberant.

General Kondylis, who put down the anti-monarchist revolt led by the former Premier Venizelos last March, seems set to be the power behind the throne. "The presence of the King as supreme arbiter", he says, "will bring an end to internal dissensions. A new era starts from today." (→1/12)

Japan backs breakaway Chinese state

Nov 26. Japanese troops today marched into Peking, the ancient capital of China, in support of a coup organised by Tokyo with the help of some Chinese, setting up a so-called autonomous state in Hopei province in the north.

The head of the breakaway state is Yin Ju-kang, who was originally installed as commissioner of the province when it was set up as a demilitarised zone after the withdrawal of Chinese troops this year. He has announced that the newly created state, with its capital at Tungchow, only 12 miles from Peking, would be known as the Autonomous Federation for Joint Defence against Communism.

Mr Yin declared that the new state would recognise Chinese sovereignty but intended to work with Japan "for the rescue of China". To signal their support further, the Japanese have also moved a force of 12,000 Manchukuo troops, under Japanese officers, to the Great Wall which marks the boundary between China and Manchukuo.

The Japanese presence in Peking was particularly domineering. Some 500 Japanese soldiers of the Tientsin Garrison caused great alarm when they marched into the foreign legation area on their "manoeuvres". Simultaneously, troops occupied the international racecourse in the city of Tientsin.

Colonel Takahishi, a Japanese army spokesman, claimed that another breakaway movement was growing rapidly outside the demilitarised zone, led by the governor of the Chahar province (→25/2/36).

Japanese soldiers telephone at an advanced artillery observation post.

General election sweeps Tories to power

Nov 16. The National Government – now Tory in all but name – is back in power with a huge majority. The final score in the general election is likely to be Tories 432, Labour 154, Liberals 20 and Others 9. Tory leader Stanley Baldwin said: "Trust us to continue working for national restoration."

The National Labour remnants on the Government side are obliterated. Both Ramsay MacDonald and his son Malcolm lost their seats. The Liberals, who were only able to contest one seat in every four, are now finally relegated to the status of a minor party. After its 1931 debacle Labour has managed to treble its number of MPs, in spite of acute differençes between its pacifist and rearmament wings.

Tory leaders say that they now have a mandate for big increases in defence spending. During the campaign they spoke guardedly about that, and voters showed more interest in housing and unemployment.

A 71 per cent turn-out at the polls reflected greater apathy than there was in the three previous elections (→26).

1935

DECEMBER

Su	Mo	Tu	We	Th	Fr	Sa
1	2	3	4	5	6	7
8	9	10	11	12	13	14
15	16	17	18	19	20	21
22	23	24	25	26	27	28
29	30	31				

1. Middle East: Turkey, Iraq, Iran and Afghanistan sign a non-aggression pact.

1. Athens: King George II declares an amnesty for all involved in the failed Republican coup in March.

5. US: Bruno Hauptmann is granted an interview by the US Board of Pardons.→

7. London: The Naval Conference opens; Japan demands parity with Britain (→25/3/36).

10. Stockholm: Nobel Prizes go to Sir James Chadwick (UK, Physics); Jean Curie and Irene Joliot-Curie (France, Chemistry); Hans Spemann (Germany, Medicine). Peace Prize awarded in Oslo to Carl von Ossietzky (Germany). No Literature Prize.

12. Cairo: King Fuad restores Egypt's 1923 parliamentary constitution (→28/4/36).

14. Prague: 86-year-old Masaryk resigns as president through old age (→18).

17. US: The Douglas DC-3 makes its maiden flight (→25/6/36).

18. Czechoslovakia: Eduard Benes, Masaryk's chosen successor, is elected president (→14/9/37).

21. Germany: Jewish doctors are forced to resign from private hospitals (→1/1/36).

22. London: Anthony Eden is appointed Foreign Secretary.→

24. Moscow: The Kremlin claims the Soviet navy is five times bigger than it was five years ago (→29/11/36).

27. Berlin: Hitler offers Britain air force limitations (→25/1/36).

HITS OF 1935

Blue Moon.

Red sails in the sunset.

Cheek to cheek.

QUOTE OF THE YEAR

"There will be peace if Britain is strong and known to be; there will be war if she is weak and thought to be."

James Louis Garvin, Editor of The Observer from 1928.

New British device can spot airplanes from a distance

A method of detecting aeroplanes by reflecting radio waves off them was patented this year by **Mr Robert Watson-Watt**. The principle is to send out a very short pulse of radio waves and to measure the time the reflection takes to return, from which the aeroplane's distance can be calculated.

Radio detection clearly has enormous military implications. It could be used to detect ships at sea too, for both military and civil purposes such as avoiding collisions.

The year also saw a startling development concerning the nature of viruses, the infectious agents responsible for many human diseases. Viruses are known to be far smaller than bacteria, because they can pass through very fine filters, but so far they have never been isolated in pure form. Now American scientist **Oliver Wendell Stanley** has managed to produce a virus, one that causes a disease of tobacco plants, in the form of crystals. The question naturally arises: are entities which can be crystallised alive? If not alive how do they multiply, as viruses certainly do when they infect something?

This year an elusive substance called vitamin E was at last obtained in pure form. Vitamin E is important in animal reproduction and might be used to treat some forms of human sterility. It is a member of the growing family of vitamins whose absence from our diet causes diseases.

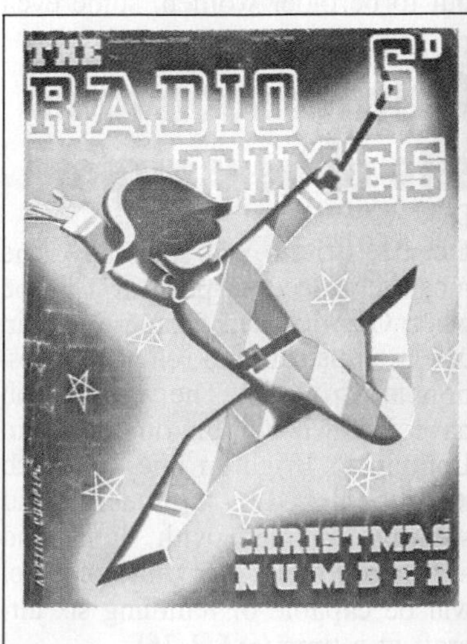

Row forces Hoare to quit

Laval (right) made a deal with Hoare. Eden (left) violently dissented.

Dec 18. Sir Samuel Hoare, the Foreign Secretary, resigned today in sensational circumstances. The official announcement came after Mr Baldwin had given him an unprecedented "Apologise or quit" ultimatum. This is how the Prime Minister has responded to the public outcry, and anger inside the cabinet, over the deal which Sir Samuel had made with France's premier, Pierre Laval, for appeasing Signor Mussolini over Abyssinia.

Under the Hoare-Laval pact, which will now be dead, Italy's right to keep the most fertile parts of Abyssinia which it has conquered would be recognised. Anthony Eden, Minister for League of Nations Affairs, threatened to quit unless Mr Baldwin disowned the Foreign Secretary forthwith. With a critical Commons debate looming, the Prime Minister decided he must move against Sir Samuel or risk wrecking the Government.

So he has brought the crisis to a brutal climax. The Foreign Secretary flatly refused to apologise and withdraw from his deal with Premier Laval: his friends are complaining that he has been double-crossed by cabinet colleagues, who had originally backed him.

Church leaders are now joining politicians of all parties in denouncing the Hoare-Laval pact as a cynical betrayal of a small nation. However, it is gloomily recognised that the League has proved to be impotent in a crisis, and that the Italian dictator will get away with his aggression unless other nations are prepared to go to war (→22).

Lindbergh comes to live in England

Dec 23. Charles Lindbergh is today making a slower crossing of the Atlantic than the one which made him famous in 1927, when he was the first man to it alone and became a hero. He is travelling by ship – to start a new life in England. With him are his wife Anne and two-year-old son, Jon. After the kidnapping and death of their first child, the couple have been plagued by threats promising the same fate for Jon (→3/4/36).

Drake scores seven goals against Villa

Dec 14. As Arsenal overwhelmed Aston Villa 7-1 in their First Division clash today, Villa's hard-pressed defence allowed Arsenal's centre-forward Ted Drake just eight shots at goal. He scored with seven of them, monopolising Arsenal's score-sheet and equalling one record in top-flight football that seemed impregnable – the seven goals scored in the first League season of 1888-89 by James Ross in his first game for Preston.

Arts: Gielgud and Olivier share Romeo

T. S. Eliot revived verse drama with emphatic success in his play "Murder in the Cathedral", about the killing of Thomas a Becket, which was produced in the chapter house of Canterbury Cathedral, where the murder took place. It was later played in London, with **Robert Speaight** as Becket.

John Gielgud's production of "Romeo and Juliet" was a must, following his phenomenal success in his second "Hamlet". He and **Laurence Olivier** alternated in the roles of Romeo and Mercutio, with **Peggy Ashcroft** as Juliet.

Olivier's gauche, impulsive and adolescent Romeo did not find favour with the critics but did with the public. The other "Romeo and Juliet" this year was the ballet to highly dramatic music by **Sergei Prokoviev**.

New York went wild over the opening of **George Gershwin's** Negro folk opera, "Porgy and Bess", which contains one of his ripest melodies in "Summertime". In London, **Cole Porter's** "Anything Goes" was the hit musical after a similar triumph on Broadway.

Fred Astaire and **Ginger Rogers**, whose tap-dancing film partnership blossomed last year in Porter's "The Gay Divorcee" ("Night and Day"), consolidated it this year in **Jerome Kern's** "Roberta" ("Smoke Gets in your Eyes") and hit the high spot with "Top Hat", for which **Irving Berlin** wrote them such numbers as "Cheek to Cheek" as well as the title song, a dance display of the utmost elegance.

Big-band jazz has taken a new turn with the formation of the **Benny Goodman** orchestra. Goodman's brilliant clarinet playing and the musical arrangements by **Fletcher Henderson** have earned him the title "King of Swing".

A new, cheap form of book with paper covers priced at only sixpence has been brought out by **Allen Lane** and named Penguin. Will such a flimsy object catch on with the reading public?

Academy award winner Shirley Temple is now a seasoned performer, starring in "Curly Top".

The aloof Greta Garbo stars with Fredric March in "Anna Karenina".

1936

JANUARY

Su	Mo	Tu	We	Th	Fr	Sa
			1	2	3	4
5	6	7	8	9	10	11
12	13	14	15	16	17	18
19	20	21	22	23	24	25
26	27	28	29	30	31	

1. Germany: The law banning Jews from employing women under 35 comes into force; 10,000 women lose jobs (→ 2).

2. Berlin: Hitler tells the League to mind its own business on Germany's treatment of Jews.

3. Warsaw: The Polish government frees 27,000 prisoners under a general amnesty.

4. New York: The first "hit-parade" appears in the magazine "Billboard".

5. Abyssinia: Italian bombers raze Daggha Bur (→ 2/3).

9. Washington: The National Democratic Committee endorses Roosevelt for president in the 1936 election (→ 26/6).

11. London: The RAF is reported set to expand at the rate of a squadron a week (→ 14/8).

13. London: Rudyard Kipling is gravely ill.→

17. Paris: The Stavisky corruption trial ends with nine convictions and 11 acquittals.

19. India: The Aga Khan is weighed in gold; at 16 stone he is worth £25,000 (→ 27/5).

20. London: Figures show pay rose by an average 1.5 per cent in 1935, highest since 1924.

21. London: Edward VIII is proclaimed King.

22. Paris: Pierre Laval resigns as premier (→ 24).

24. Paris: Albert Sarraut forms a government (→ 8/6).

25. Berlin: Interviewed by French paper "Paris-Soir", Hitler says he wants to recover Germany's lost colonies (→ 7/3).

30. UK: Premiere of the play "The Dog Beneath the Skin" by Wystan H. Auden and Christopher Isherwood.

31. US: Huey Long's widow is appointed to serve out his term.

DEATHS

18. British poet and writer Rudyard Kipling (*30/12/1865).→

20. British King George V (*3/6/1865).→

Nation mourns George V

Rest in peace: His Majesty lies in State at Westminster Hall.

Jan 28. King George V was laid to rest today at Windsor amidst the tombs of his ancestors. Some 124 naval ratings pulled the gun carriage, carrying the body of the sailor King, through the silent and crowded streets from Westminster Hall to Paddington station.

King Edward VIII, looking sad and forlorn, walked immediately behind them, but when the procession reached Hyde Park he fell back in line with his brothers, the Dukes of York, Gloucester and Kent. Queen Mary, in black and heavily veiled, followed in a carriage.

As the procession passed 145 Piccadilly, home of the Duke and Duchess of York, a small figure in a window dropped a deep curtsy. It was Princess Margaret Rose's farewell to her grandfather. At the same time Princess Elizabeth was leaving from the garden entrance by car for Paddington to take the train to Windsor with Queen Mary. Visiting kings, princes and leading politicians from 47 nations followed the King's body to the tomb.

The splendour today was in striking contrast to the first of the processions that preceded the King's burial. After his death at Sandringham, his coffin had been taken at dusk across the fields on a farm trolley to Sandringham church.

A lone piper strode before it playing the "Skye Boat Song". Behind came the beloved Jock, the King's grey cob, with an empty saddle. Friends and estate workers followed, scarcely a dozen in all, for this very private occasion.

The King was first of all a countryman, who came to the throne because of the death of an elder brother. But the advent of wireless made him the best known monarch in history. His gruff voice lent weight to his thoughts. Most famous of his sayings was: "I don't like abroad, I've been there." (→ 28/5)

Obolensky leads England to victory

Jan 4. England have beaten New Zealand in a Rugby Union international for the first time, thanks to two splendid tries by 19-year-old Alexander Obolensky, the Russian prince who came to England as a baby and is now at Oxford.

His first was an orthodox right wing's try. The second, which set up England's 13-0 victory, brought the crowd to its feet. Obolensky took a pass on the right inside his own half and, as the All Black cover raced across to intercept, he veered diagonally across the field leaving the entire defence wrong-footed to score an historic try far out on the left wing.

Kipling, unofficial poet laureate, dies

Jan 19. Rudyard Kipling knew fame and extraordinary success all his writing life, from the age of 21 up till his death yesterday at 70. Although it was India that formed him and was the subject of his best stories, one of them revealed the misery of his boyhood alone in England, while "Stalky and Co" described his rough schooling.

It is ironic that Kipling was never made Poet Laureate – he also refused all honours, including even the Order of Merit – but he was the nation's unofficial laureate, who produced the warning "Recessional" ("Lest We Forget") on the day of the Diamond Jubilee.

The late Rudyard Kipling.

1936

FEBRUARY

Su	Mo	Tu	We	Th	Fr	Sa
						1
2	3	4	5	6	7	8
9	10	11	12	13	14	15
16	17	18	19	20	21	22
23	24	25	26	27	28	29

1. London: Figures show there were 2,581,027 registered cars on the road, a rise of 17.5 per cent on 1934.

3. London: A strike at Smithfield meat market cuts off the capital's meat supply.

5. US: Opening of Charlie Chaplin's film "Modern Times".→

6. Germany: Hitler opens the fourth Winter Olympic Games at Garmisch-Partenkirchen.→

8. India: Jawaharlal Nehru is elected president of the Indian National Congress, making him effectively heir apparent to Gandhi (→19/10).

11. London: Artist Dame Laura Knight is the first woman appointed to the Royal Academy.

13. London: MPs give a second reading to the Education Bill, which would raise the school-leaving age to 15 (→31/7).

17. Paraguay: Military rebels seize the capital Asuncion (→18).

18. Paraguay: President Eusebio Ayala resigns (→11/3).

19. Germany: A rail speed record of 124.2 mph is achieved by a passenger train.

20. Berne: The Swiss government bars entry to Nazi Party members.

21. Madrid: Premier Azana declares an amnesty for 30,000 political and other prisoners.→

24. London: In his first major speech as Foreign Secretary, Anthony Eden advocates peace through strength (→27/11).

25. Tokyo: Two cabinet ministers, die in an attempted coup by militarists (→28).

28. Tokyo: The militarist rebels surrender.→

29. Washington: President Roosevelt signs the second Neutrality Bill, banning loans to countries at war.

DEATH

27. Russian physiologist Ivan Pavlov, 1904 Nobel Prize winner (*26/9/1849).

The Left comes to power in Spain

The first political prisoners leave Barcelona jail after the new amnesty.

Feb 21. Spain's new left-wing government has ordered an amnesty for 30,000 political prisoners. Formal releases are taking place this evening throughout the country. Meanwhile martial law is in force in four provinces as sporadic violence erupts like brush fires.

However, yesterday's broadcast by the Premier, Senor Azana, in which he promised "liberty, prosperity and justice", was well received. The newspaper, A.B.C., says that the Premier's words might have been spoken on behalf of a government of any complexion.

The new government is composed mainly of personal friends of the premier. They are mostly unknown as politicians, which gives them the advantage of not having to face a prejudiced public.

Several of them once formed the "pandilla del Ateneo" the school of students who would gather to listen to Senor Azana in the Ateneo, the literary club of Madrid. Governing a country as turbulent as Spain, however, will be a sterner task than literary criticism.

Already the Communists, furious at being excluded from the Cabinet, are seeking to undermine the new government (→15/3).

Charlie Chaplin cocks a snook the talkie revolution with "Modern Times", a silent parable (with music) about today's machine age.

Britain wins first ice hockey gold

Feb 16. Great Britain has broken Canada's stranglehold on Olympic ice hockey to win the Winter Olympic gold medal at the German resort of Garmisch-Partenkirchen, clinging on to the single point they needed by drawing a nail-biting match with the United States, which remained goalless despite three periods of extra time.

Britain's team, composed largely of players of British parentage brought up in Canada (two of them, indeed, were banned from the tournament on grounds of doubtful eligibility, only to be reinstated shortly before the first match) beat the favourites, Canada, 2-1 in the penultimate round, to end the Canadians' sequence of gold medals stretching back to 1920.

Coup fails, but Japan swings right

Feb 29. Fears were expressed today that, although the army coup d'etat in Tokyo has collapsed with the surrender of its leader, Captain Teruzo Ando, it may still result in greater say in the government by the very right-wing military. The three-day revolt was fuelled by a National Socialist-type hatred of big business and a push for Imperial glory. A thousand young officers seized government buildings and intended to kill the Prime Minister. However, the Imperial Guard surrounded them (→8/7/37).

Hitler launches his "People's Car"

Feb 26. The first factory for the manufacture of Germany's "people's car", the Volkswagen, has been opened in Saxony by Adolf Hitler. Designed by Ferdinand Porsche of Auto-Union fame, the car is intended for mass-production at popular prices. Its features include a streamlined body, an air-cooled engine mounted at the rear, and torsion bar springs. The idea is to put the nation on wheels, doing for Germany what Henry Ford did for the United States.

1936

MARCH

Su	Mo	Tu	We	Th	Fr	Sa
1	2	3	4	5	6	7
8	9	10	11	12	13	14
15	16	17	18	19	20	21
22	23	24	25	26	27	28
29	30	31				

1. UK: Golden Miller wins the Cheltenham Gold Cup for the fifth time in succession.

2. Geneva: The League threatens to put an oil embargo on Italy (→8/4).

3. Rome: Mussolini nationalises the Italian banks (→23).

5. UK: The new Spitfire fighter aeroplane makes its maiden flight.→

8. Paris: The government calls a meeting of the signatories of the Locarno Pact (→11).

11. Paraguay: The army sets up America's first Fascist regime.

12. London: The Locarno signatories condemn Hitler's occupation of the Rhineland.

13. London: Sir Thomas Inskip is appointed to the new post of Minister for the Co-ordination of Defence.

15. Madrid: The army says it will act if premier Azana fails to curb violence (→10/5).

19. London: The text is issued of the Midwives Bill, which proposes a national service of salaried midwives (→30/4).

23. Rome: Mussolini says he will nationalise key industries.

24. UK: The liner Queen Mary runs aground twice at Clydebank (→27/5).

25. London: Britain, the US and France sign a Naval Treaty; Japan walked out of the talks on January 15.

27. UK: Major Furlong's Reynoldstown wins the Grand National for the second year running.

29. Germany: Results of a plebiscite show 99 per cent approval of Hitler (→5/4).

BIRTH

3. Swiss actress Ursula Andress.

DEATHS

11. British commander Admiral of the Fleet Earl David Beatty, (*17/1/1871).

21. Russian composer Alexander Glazunov (*10/8/1865).

Nazis enter Rhineland

The crowds salute Hitler's troops goose-stepping into the Rhineland.

March 7. The stomp of the jackboot sounded again in the cities of the Rhineland today – and the people rejoiced. Goose-stepping German troops began arriving at dawn, seven hours before Hitler told the Reichstag he had ordered them in, and defied the treaties of Versailles and Locarno.

The French have been thrown into confusion, with the politicians urging military action, and the generals pleading for restraint. The British are unlikely to be any help. They are begging the French to do nothing until Hitler's action has been given "full consideration". Yet the German High Command was apparently against the adventure and General von Blomberg, the War Minister, gave orders that, should the Western Powers show signs of a firm response, the troops were to pull back at once.

Hitler has proposed a new treaty to guarantee peace for 25 years, which the British see as evidence of his pacific intentions. After all, one newspaper comments, he has merely re-occupied his own backyard. True enough, but it's also a 100 miles nearer France (→12).

Vickers' "Supermarine Spitfire I" goes on show for the first time at Eastleigh Aerodrome in Southampton. The new fighter is fitted with a 12-cylinder liquid-cooled Rolls-Royce "Merlin" engine, the exact horsepower of which cannot be revealed for defence reasons, but there is no doubt that this is the Royal Air Force's most powerful weapon.

1936

APRIL

Su	Mo	Tu	We	Th	Fr	Sa
			1	2	3	4
5	6	7	8	9	10	11
12	13	14	15	16	17	18
19	20	21	22	23	24	25
26	27	28	29	30		

1. Vienna: The government re-introduces military service, in violation of peace treaties (→29).

3. US: Lindbergh baby killer Bruno Hauptmann is executed.

5. Germany: People who did not vote in last month's plebiscite lose their jobs (→27).

7. S. Africa: Native Representation Act bans blacks from office but lets them elect three whites to represent them.

9. Rome: Mussolini admits aiming to set up a puppet state in Abyssinia (→15).

11. US: The Georgia national guard saves a black man from a lynch mob.

13. UK: Joe Payne scores 10 goals for Luton Town in its 12-0 defeat of Bristol Rovers.

15. Abyssinia: The Italians occupy Dessye, advancing 125 miles in five days (→30).

17. Madrid: Parliament dismisses President Niceto Alcala Zamora for trying to dissolve it unconstitutionally (→10/5).

19. Palestine: 11 die and 50 are hurt in rioting between Arabs and Jews in Tel Aviv (→25/5).

21. London: The Budget puts 3d in the pound on income tax (→22/5).

25. London: Arsenal beat Sheffield United 1-0 in the FA Cup Final at Wembley.

27. Berlin: Hermann Goering is put in charge of German economic affairs (→26/5).

29. Vienna: The government sends troops to the border with Germany, fearing invasion (→15/5).

30. London: MPs give a second reading to the Midwives Bill (→31/7).

30. Abyssinia: Resistance crumbles as the Italians prepare to take Addis Ababa (→2/5).

DEATHS

28. Egyptian King Fuad (*16/3/1868).→

30. British poet and classical scholar Alfred Edward Housman (*26/3/1859).

Horror grows over use of poison gas

April 8. The Italian use of mustard gas on the Abyssinians has aroused widespread horror, the British Foreign Secretary, Anthony Eden, told the League of Nations today. The action violated the Geneva Convention of 1925 and allegations of barbarous practices by the enemy offered no excuse. Italian aircraft are reported to be dropping canisters of gas on civilians as well as troops. Even Red Cross units have been attacked.

Mr Eden hinted that if the war is not ended soon further measures might have to be taken against Italy. But nobody now believes oil sanctions will be imposed. It is six months since Mussolini sent his forces into Abyssinia and, though it has taken them a lot longer than expected to defeat their ill-armed foe, they appear to be on the point of doing so. They are expected in the capital, Addis Ababa, in the next few days (→9).

Teenage student is Egypt's new King

April 28. The 16-year-old Crown Prince Farouk was today proclaimed King of Egypt. The Prince, who is completing his education in Britain, was telephoned last night by Queen Nazli with news that his father King Fuad had died unexpectedly. The new King, due back in Egypt later this week, will rule with a Regent (→26/8).

King Fuad's successor, Farouk.

1936

MAY

Su	Mo	Tu	We	Th	Fr	Sa
					1	2
3	4	5	6	7	8	9
10	11	12	13	14	15	16
17	18	19	20	21	22	23
24	25	26	27	28	29	30
31						

2. Abyssinia: Emperor Haile Selassie and his family flee to Jibuti, French Somaliland (→5).

5. Abyssinia: Addis Ababa falls to Italian troops (→8).

8. Palestine: Haile Selassie arrives in exile (→9).

9. US: The German airship Hindenburg arrives at Lakehurst, after a 62-hour flight from Frankfurt (→6/7).

9. Rome: Mussolini announces the annexation of Abyssinia with Marshal Badoglio as viceroy.→

10. Spain: The Cortes elects Manuel Azana president of Spain in succession to the ousted Zamora (→13/7).

15. Vienna: Chancellor Kurt Schuschnigg becomes head of the Fatherland Front, ousting Ernst von Starhemberg (→10/10).

15. London: Amy Johnson arrives back after a return flight to Cape Town in a record 12 days and 15 hours.

17. Bolivia: President Tejada Sorzano is ousted in a coup.

18. London: Jasmine Bligh and Elizabeth Cowell join the BBC as its first women announcers (→11/6).

22. London: Colonial Secretary James H. Thomas resigns for allegedly leaking advance details of the Budget (→2/6).

22. US: Opening of the film "A Night at the Opera" starring the Marx Brothers.

24. Geneva: A League report claims there are 30,000 drug addicts in Britain.

24. Belgium: The Rexists, Belgian Fascists, win 21 seats in the general election.

26. Berlin: 276 monks go on trial for "immorality" (→17/6).

27. UK: The Aga Khan wins the Derby for the second year running with Mahmoud; one of his horses comes second.

28. London: King Edward VIII's coronation is set for May 12, 1937.

30. Moscow: The Kremlin lifts the ban on employing former Czarists.

Queen Mary sails on her maiden voyage

The Queen Mary (left) belches white smoke as she gets ready to sail.

May 27. Amid great excitement, the Queen Mary, Britain's 80,733-ton super-liner, left Southampton on her maiden voyage today, making a four-and-a-half hour journey to Cherbourg before steaming on to New York – a journey she is expecting to complete in around four days at a record average speed of approximately 31 knots.

Some 1,840 privileged passengers on the new Cunard liner – dubbed "Britain's Masterpiece" by its owners – were given a frenzied send-off from Southampton Docks, as crowds cheered, a band played and a host of admiring spectators surrounded the giant ship in escort vessels.

A goodwill radio message was also sent to the Queen Mary's commander, Sir Edgar Britten, by the King. On both sides of the Atlantic, enormous media interest surrounds the progress of this vast, yet speedy, liner as she begins the 3,000-mile trip to New York.

Two American companies have arranged for daily broadcasts to be made from the ship during her journey, while the British press enticingly promises that "scenes on board will be described from every conceivable angle".

Cunard expect the ship to sail with a full complement of pasengers in the coming months, lured by her speed, prestige and luxury. The price of a trans-Atlantic trip on the Queen Mary is advertised as being "from £37 5s" – including meals and accomodation (→1/6).

Arabs and Jews clashing in Palestine

May 25. Six weeks of rioting between Arabs and Jews have brought Palestine to a state of lawlessness bordering on open rebellion. Eleven people have died, and 50 were wounded in intercommunity clashes. Britain is blamed by both sides. Arabs in Nablus have ordered a general strike, with the demand that Britain stops Jewish immigration and land buying. A curfew has been declared in many places.

Fierce fighting broke out last night near the Jewish colony of Mesha, close to Mount Tabor, when a force of 300 Arabs converged on it from all directions. A small police patrol, which engaged them, was forced back towards Mesha. There they joined another handful of police equipped with a Lewis gun. They were rescued by the arrival of a patrol of the Loyal Regiment stationed at Nazareth, who put the Arabs to flight.

A serious situation has also developed at Gaza where Arabs cut power and telegraph lines. Troops with armoured cars were called in. English families took shelter in police barracks (→21/6). ▷

Italy has its Empire now

Mussolini proclaims his Fascist empire from the Palazzo Venezia in Rome.

May 9. The Italian dictator has won his war. "Italy at last has her empire," Mussolini proclaimed from the Palazzo Venezia balcony tonight. "It is a Fascist empire because it bears the indestructible sign of the will and power of Rome." He announced to a wildly enthusiastic crowd that the King would now be known as Victor Emmanuel, King of Italy and Emperor of Abyssinia (not Ethiopia as Haile Selassie and his people know their country).

It was the second time in a week that Mussolini appeared on the balcony to boast of victory. On Tuesday the occasion was the entry into Addis Ababa of Italian troops under Marshal Pietro Badoglio, the general Mussolini appointed after sacking General de Bono for allowing the war to drag on and encourage League of Nations critics.

The Emperor Haile Selassie's feudal chiefs fought one set-piece battle, at Mount Aradam, and were scattered. Badoglio followed up with a succession of blows that gave the enemy no chance to recover. Even so, the Italians, better armed and better organised, should have overrun the country in weeks rather than months; but it hardly matters now (→3/6).

Smart set flock to have ears pierced

May 9. A close look at fashionable lobes in Mayfair would reveal tiny holes, as a new fashion craze for pierced ears sweeps the smart set. Until now it was unusual before middle age or later, but this season debutantes and young married hostesses are flocking to have their ears pierced.

One specialist, who estimates that he is piercing a hundred ears a month, said: "Women want to wear large pearl ear-rings. They are afraid of losing them if they are screwed on or clipped on." Trendsetters like the Duchess of Kent, the Duchess of Gloucester and the new Vicereine, Lady Linlithgow, have all adopted the style.

Women in the Royal Family, who need to wear certain jewels for State occasions, must have pierced ears. Queen Mary had hers done as a little girl by her maid.

1936

JUNE

Su	Mo	Tu	We	Th	Fr	Sa
	1	2	3	4	5	6
7	8	9	10	11	12	13
14	15	16	17	18	19	20
21	22	23	24	25	26	27
28	29	30				

1. New York: The Queen Mary arrives to a tumultuous welcome (→30/8).

2. London: A tribunal finds ex-Colonial Secretary James Thomas guilty of leaking Budget details (→11).

3. London: Haile Selassie arrives in exile (→15).

4. Paris: Socialist Leon Blum becomes premier after election gains of the Popular Front alliance of left-wing parties.→

5. US: Governor Alfred Landon of Kansas is chosen as Republican presidential candidate (→26).

6. UK: Gatwick airport opens.

10. US: Herbert Hoover calls the New Deal "Fascism" (→26).

11. London: James Thomas announces his resignation from the Commons.

11. London: The BBC names Leslie Mitchell as its first television announcer (→21/8).

15. London: Britain abandons sanctions against Italy (→19).

15. UK: The Wellington bomber makes its maiden flight.

17. Berlin: Heinrich Himmler is appointed head of the Reich's police force (→1/8/37).

19. Paris: The government decides to lift sanctions against Italy (→26).

20. London: Formation of the Building Societies Association.

25. US: The first commercial flight of the Douglas DC-3 is made by American Airlines.

26. US: The Democrats choose President Roosevelt to run for a second term (→3/11).

26. Geneva: Haile Selassie is welcomed on his arrival to address the League (→30).

30. Geneva: Italian delegates are outraged when Haile Selassie addresses the League (→4/7).

DEATHS

14. British writer Gilbert Keith Chesterton (*29/5/1874).

14. Russian writer Maxim Gorky (*16/3/1868).

RAF wages war on Arabs from the air

June 21. Four RAF planes went into action today machine-gunning a group of 70 Palestinian Arabs who had ambushed British troops. They made sorties at low level against the marauders. Three were hit by Arab ground fire but returned safely to base. Last week RAF planes were also used to ward off an Arab attack on a Jewish colony on Mount Gilead.

In today's fighting, the first serious clash between Arabs and the British army in the Palestine troubles, an army convoy from Jaffa to Haifa was attacked near Tulkarm, 20 miles north west of Nablus.

The planes intervened after a call for reinforcements brought troops with tanks and armoured cars racing to the spot. In an engagement lasting seven hours the marauders lost ten dead. Two British soldiers were killed (→15/9).

The British lion in Palestine.

Socialists come to power in France

June 8. Within five days of sweeping to power as Prime Minister in a Socialist Popular Front coalition Leon Blum has ended the strikes which have crippled France by granting pay rises of 12 per cent, a 40-hour working week, an annual two weeks' paid holiday and collective bargaining. The union leader Leon Jouhaux exulted: "For the first time in history an entire class has won improved conditions." Employers are less keen (→19).

1936

JULY

Su	Mo	Tu	We	Th	Fr	Sa
			1	2	3	4
5	6	7	8	9	10	11
12	13	14	15	16	17	18
19	20	21	22	23	24	25
26	27	28	29	30	31	

4. Wimbledon: Helen Jacobs beat Hilda Sperling in the Women's Singles finals.→

4. Geneva: The League drops Abyssinia (→15).

6. US: The Hindenburg crosses the Atlantic in under 46 hours (→6/5/37).

9. London: Prime Minister Baldwin plans to add £750,000 to the dole budget.

11. New York: Athlete Jesse Owens wins a place in the US team for the Berlin Olympics (→3/8).

11. Berlin: Hitler recognises Austrian independence (→25).

13. Spain: Monarchist leader Jose Calvo Sotelo is murdered (→17).

14. UK: Mass production of gas masks begins; the target is one for every citizen (→16/11/37).

15. Geneva: The League repeals sanctions against Italy (→25).

17. Spanish Morocco: General Francisco Franco heads an uprising against the government at Melilla (→19).

19. Spain: General Franco arrives in Cadiz at the head of rebel Spanish foreign legionaries (→24).

20. Switzerland: The Montreux Conference recognises Turkish sovereignty of the Dardanelles.

24. Madrid: The government appeals for foreign help in the civil war.→

24. UK: The GPO's Speaking Clock service begins (→30).

25. Berlin: Hitler recognises Italy's occupation of Abyssinia (→27/8).

26. France: The King unveils the Canadian Great War memorial on Vimy Ridge.

28. UK: Britain wins the Davis Cup tennis trophy for the fourth successive year.

30. UK: 248,828 calls were made to the Speaking Clock in its first week.

31. London: Royal assent is given to the Education Bill and the Midwives Bill (→9/8).

Fascist rebels spark civil war in Spain

July 31. The Civil War that erupted in Spain when the army rose against the Republican government two weeks ago is being fought with the utmost ferocity. Atrocities are being carried out by both sides as they struggle for the advantage all over Spain.

General Franco, one of the leaders of the insurgent forces, has warned the government in a telegram from his headquarters in Morocco that: "The Spanish Restoration Movement will triumph very shortly and we will demand explanations of your conduct."

"The energy which we will employ will be in proportion to the resistance which you may put up. We urge you especially to avoid useless shedding of blood."

The success of the insurgents is not, however, guaranteed. General Sanjurjo, who was due to be the Supreme Commander of the rising, was killed in an aircrash eleven days ago, and now command is split between General Franco, General Quipo del Llano in Seville and General Mola Vidal in Pamplona.

The insurgents, moreover, will find it difficult to ferry Franco's men across the Straits of Gibraltar from Morocco, for almost every ship in the Spanish navy has declared itself for the government, with the crews arresting and often murdering their officers.

Both sides in this increasingly bloody conflict have appealed for help from outside. The Popular Front government has asked its counterpart in France for assistance, while the Nationalists have turned to Italy and Germany.

The government seems unlikely to get any help from France, which is opposed to any intervention in Spain's internal affairs. It remains to be seen what the Nationalist emissaries will bring back from Rome and Berlin.

In the meantime, warships of Britain, France, Italy, Germany and the United States are standing off the Spanish coast, ready to evacuate any of their own countrymen. At Barcelona, Rear Admiral Max Horton, commander of the cruiser London, saved the city from being shelled by an Italian cruiser, after communists had sacked the Italian consulate (→8/8).

Hundreds of government volunteers leave Madrid to fight the rebels.

Fascist chief General Franco (centre), flanked by Cavalcanti and Mola.

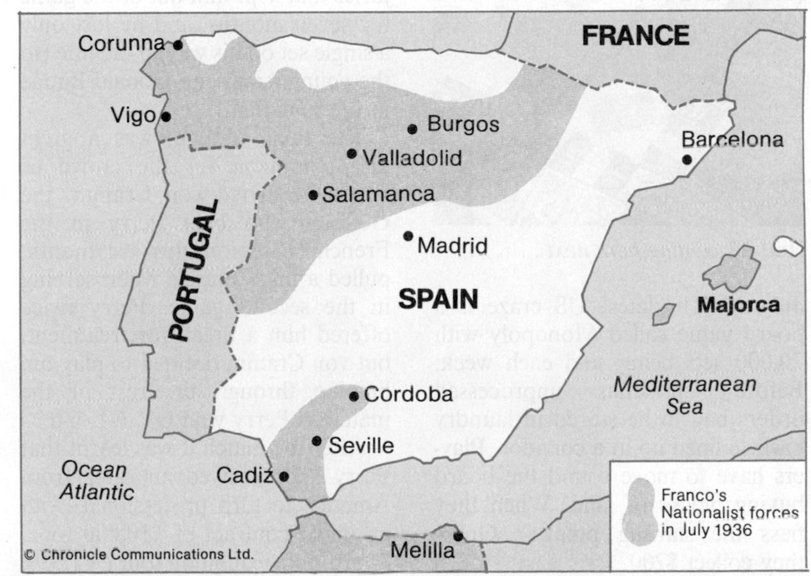

Scottish journalist tries to kill the King

July 16. A few hours after an apparent assassination attempt as he rode among the Guards, King Edward donned plus-fours and calmly played a round of golf today.

The King was returning to Buckingham Palace after presenting new colours to six Guards battalions. As the procession reached Constitution Hill, a woman in the crowd saw a man produce a revolver.

Seconds later, Special Constable Anthony Dick seized the man and knocked the revolver away. It fell in the roadway close to the King's horse. The King went on to the Palace where Queen Mary congratulated him on his escape.

Late yesterday George Andrew McMahon, described as a journalist, was charged at Bow Street with "being in possession of a revolver with intent to endanger life".

The Home Secretary, Sir John Simon, told a hushed House of Commons that the revolver was found loaded in four of its chambers. "The whole House will be profoundly thankful that the risk to which His Majesty was exposed was so promptly averted," he said.

Failed killer McMahon is arrested.

At Bow Street, McMahon was alleged to have said: "The King was not hurt in any way, was he? It is all the fault of Sir John Simon. I wrote to him last night and phoned him this morning". (→14/9)

A new board game has just passed Go

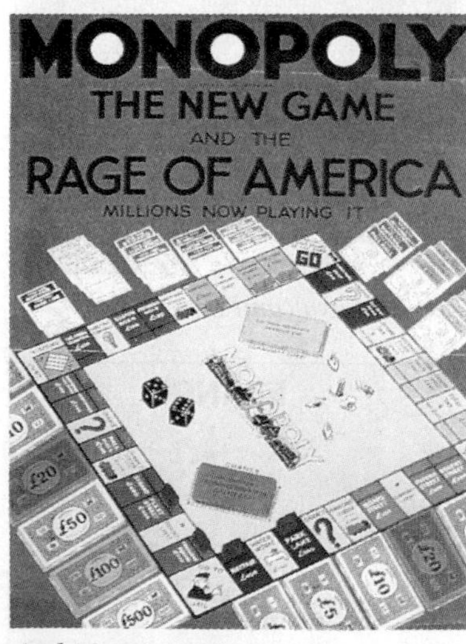

And it's coming here next ...

July 30. The latest US craze is a board game called Monopoly with 20,000 sets being sold each week. Before Christmas unprocessed orders had to be stored in laundry baskets lined up in a corridor. Players have to move round the board buying blocks of land. When they pass the starting point – Go – they collect $200.

Perry pulls off hat trick at Wimbledon

July 3. Fred Perry has won the Wimbledon singles title for the third year in succession, a feat no man has achieved since the old Challenge Round was abandoned after the Great War and the defending champion has been obliged to play right through the tournament.

Perry showed no signs of the injuries that kept him out of the game for seven months, and he lost only a single set on his way to the title (to the young American Donald Budge in the semi-final).

The final, though, was a great disappointment for the crowd as Baron Gottfried von Cramm, the German who beat Perry in the French championships last month, pulled a thigh muscle when serving in the second game. Perry twice offered him a break for treatment, but von Cramm decided to play on, limping through the rest of the match as Perry won 6-1, 6-1, 6-0.

After the match it was learnt that Perry had received an offer from America to turn professional, with an initial contract of £10,000 for a four-month exhibition tour (→12/9).

1936

AUGUST

Su	Mo	Tu	We	Th	Fr	Sa
						1
2	3	4	5	6	7	8
9	10	11	12	13	14	15
16	17	18	19	20	21	22
23	24	25	26	27	28	29
30	31					

1. Berlin: Adolf Hitler opens the Berlin Olympics.→

3. Berlin: Jesse Owens wins the 100 metres gold (→4).

4. Berlin: Jesse Owens wins a gold in the long jump (→5).

5. Berlin: Jesse Owens wins the 200 metres gold.→

6. UK: 57 die in a pit blast at Wharncliffe Woodmoor, Yorkshire.

8. Spain: The rebels close the frontier with Gibraltar (→13).

10. Yugoslavia: The King leaves Sibenik on an Adriatic cruise; Mrs Wallis Simpson is among his guests (→16/10).

11. Berlin: Joachim von Ribbentrop is appointed ambassador to Britain (→4/2/37).

12. Paris: France agrees to loan arms to Poland.

13. Spain: Rebels bomb San Sebastian.→

14. London: The Air Ministry says it plans an RAF reserve (→2/1/37).

17. UK: A four pound loaf goes up a halfpenny to eight pence halfpenny, the dearest for six years (→11/9).

19. Moscow: The "Trial of the 16" opens (→24).

21. London: The BBC makes its first television broadcast from Alexandra Palace (→26).

24. Moscow: "The Sixteen" are sentenced to death.→

26. London: The BBC broadcasts its first full television programme.→

27. Rome: Italy plans to issue bonds to fund Abyssinian development (→23/9).

28. UK: Derbyshire win the county cricket championship for the first time in 62 years.

BIRTH

1. French fashion designer Yves Saint-Laurent.

DEATHS

2. French aviator Louis Bleriot (*1/7/1872).

19. Spanish writer Federico Garcia Lorca (*5/6/1899).

Former allies of Stalin executed after show trials

Aug 25. After an extraordinary five-day show trial in Moscow, a firing squad today executed 16 of Stalin's opponents including two of his former allies – Grigori Zinoviev and Leon Kamenev. The executions were carried out in the Lubyanka prison where the accused had been held for many months.

During the trial Zinoviev and Kamenev "confessed" to their involvement in the assassination of Sergei Kirov, the Leningrad party boss; to plotting with exiled Leon Trotsky to bring down Stalin, and to collaborating with foreign powers to overthrow the State.

Andrei Vishinsky, the State Prosecutor, denounced the accused, several of whom had been close colleagues of Lenin for many years, as: "contemptible, base, vile, despicable murderous scoundrels, not tigers or lions but merely mad Fascist police dogs, humanity's dregs, the scum of the underworld, traitors and bandits".

As some of the accused wept in the dock he ended the unedifying spectacle with the vengeful cry: "Shoot these mad curs, every one of them."

The accused were not allowed defence lawyers, but 200 spectators, including foreign diplomats, were permitted to watch the proceedings. The Soviet spectators applauded the death sentences. The confessions of the accused have been the only basis for the proceedings and verdicts (→29/1/37).

Stalin, a Trinity, leads the State, the Party, and the Comintern.

Massacre in the bullring

Badajoz: a government plane lands in the street after bombing the town.

Aug 29. Nowhere can the cruelty of this civil war be seen more clearly, unless one's eyes are blinded by tears, than in the bullring of Badajoz. There, in that place of ritual death, the Moors and Legionaires of Colonel Yague's victorious column slaughtered many hundreds of disarmed militiamen, after they took the city in a fierce battle on August 14.

The capture of the city, the scene of a famous victory by Wellington over the French, is of great strategic importance to the Nationalists, for it opens up the whole of the Portuguese border to their forces and will enable them to establish their lines of communication to General Mola's forces in the north.

Spain is now divided in half. The Nationalists hold the south-west and the north while the government controls Madrid, the north-east and part of the north-west. Both sides also hold isolated pockets which are almost all under siege.

It is becoming increasingly obvious that the key to the fighting is the disciplined force that General Franco did so much to create in Africa. It was these soldiers that dealt with Badajoz so effectively, and since Franco controls this weapon it seems likely that he will become Supreme Commander of the Nationalists.

At the same time a new influence is being felt on the battlefield. General Mola has faced stiffening resistance in his drive on Irun, as the result of the appearance of foreign volunteers fighting for the Republican cause (→4/9).

Egypt independent, Britain keeps rights

Aug 26. The Anglo-Egyptian treaty signed today by Anthony Eden and Nahas Pasha, the Prime Minister, ends the British protectorate over Egypt and secures for Britain control over the Suez Canal for 20 years. The alliance will continue after that in perpetuity and Britain will retain the right to keep 10,000 troops in the canal zone. The RAF remains free to fly anywhere over Egyptian territory, but Egypt now becomes an independent state after 50 years of occupation (→14/11).

Queen Mary wins the Blue Riband

Aug 30. Britain's super-liner, the Queen Mary, having crossed the Atlantic in record time, today regained the Blue Riband for Britain. Her time of three days, 23 hours and 57 minutes to the Bishop Rock, Scilly Isles, from the Ambrose Light, New York, was three hours and 31 minutes faster than the previous record set by the French liner, Normandie, last June. Tonight also marks a double crossing by the Queen Mary in 11 days, having left Southampton for the record voyage on the 19th (→5/3/37).

BBC adds sound to television pictures

Aug 26. Nearly 7,000 people queued at Olympia today to see the first-ever talking pictures on television. They were transmitted from the BBC's new studios ten miles away at Alexandra Palace. Hitherto the BBC has only been able to produce silent pictures. Today's transmission was for the several new sets at the Radio Exhibition.

Leslie Mitchell, the BBC's only male announcer, made his television debut. Although he is a confident broadcaster, he seemed ill at ease in head and shoulder view. He was staring into space and the perspiration on his face from the heat of the studio was all too evident. The make-up artist had done her best but to the viewer he appeared to have a black eye.

Excerpts from new films were shown. There was a superb rendering by Paul Robeson of "Ol' Man River" from "Showboat", and a moving scene from "Rembrandt" starring Charles Laughton and Gertrude Lawrence, but it was not all entertainment and viewers saw a new documentary in which A.P. Herbert and Julian Huxley traced the history of writing from cave drawing to newspapers.

Several of the new sets, which are expected to cost about 100 guineas, were on view in all shapes and sizes. The biggest was 22 by 18 inches but most were ten by eight inches. Most depend on a cathode ray tube, shaped like a flask, which faces the viewer. In one HMV model the tube is vertical and the image is projected through a mirror. Ekco is showing a set which works on an optical and mechanical system.

The pictures from today's transmission on the Baird system came over very well. Tomorrow their rivals, Marconi-EMI, will be trying to do even better (→1/10).

Dorothea Lange, working for Roosevelt's Farm Security Administration, took this photograph in poverty-stricken California. This migrant fed her children on stolen frozen vegetables and trapped birds.

Jesse Owens is star of Nazi Games

Aug 16. The Berlin Olympic Games closed with a host of records by the 53 competing nations and 5,000 athletes and must be considered a sporting success, despite the Germans making it clear that their spectacular and highly efficient organisation ultimately had one aim; to glorify the Nazi regime of Adolf Hitler.

The games were awarded to Berlin before Hitler came to full power, and once his dictatorial and racial policies became clear there were moves, particularly in the US with its influential Jewish population, to organise a boycott.

This failed but the Germans, to ward off some of the criticism, selected a few token Jewish competitors in their team. However, in the event it was not the Jews but a Negro, who caused the gravest embarrassment to the Nazis and dogma of Aryan supremacy.

For the undisputed star of the Games was very much non-Aryan and very black. The boyish, ever-smiling, ever-modest Jesse Owens destroyed two world-class sprint fields to win the 100 metres and 200 metres; he won the long jump, in one of the greatest field event contests in Olympic history, over the (equally modest and likeable) German Lutz Long; and he took his fourth gold medal leading the United States to a world record in the 400-metre relay.

These victories presented the Nazi regime with a problem. When Hans Woelke won the shotput on the first day Hitler had the champion paraded before him but after Owens' first win Hitler faced the dilemma of recognising him too, or flouting world opinion, and the admiring German crowd, by ignoring him. Propaganda minister Josef Goebbels dubbed Owens and the other American blacks "black mercenaries" but in the end Hitler was persuaded not to appear publicly with the winners.

Even so, when Lutz Long finished second to Owens, Hitler congratulated him privately and ignored Owens. Then after Owens' final 200 metre triumph, while the crowd rose to salute him, Hitler left the stadium.

Owens apart, other notable performances included: the Korean Kitei Son, running reluctantly in the colours of the Japanese Empire, who won the marathon from Britain's Ernie Harper; the British 4 x 400-metre relay squad who brilliantly stole a gold medal from the USA; and, in what many consider to have been the best track race in the 40 years of the modern Olympic Games, New Zealander Jack Lovelock's record win over world record holder Glenn Cunningham (USA) and the reigning Olympic champion Luigi Beccali (Italy) in the 1500 metres.

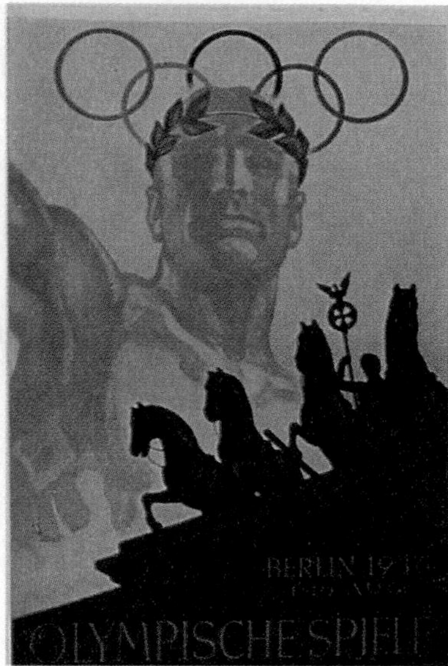

The poster depicts an Aryan hero.

Jesse Owens runs for another gold at the Games. Hitler refused to even shake his hand, because he was black.

Men Athletics

100m
1. Jesse Owens USA 10
2. Ralph Metcalfe USA 10
3. Martinus Osendarp NETH 10

200m
1. Jesse Owens USA *20
2. Matthew Robinson USA 21
3. Martinus Osendarp NETH 21

400m
1. Archie Williams USA 46
2. Arthur Godfrey Brown GBR 46
3. James Lu Valle USA 46

800m
1. John Woodruff USA 1:52
2. Mario Lanzi ITA 1:53
3. Philip Edwards CAN 1:53

1500m
1. John Lovelock NZL ** 3:47
2. Glenn Cunningham USA 3:48
3. Luigi Beccali ITA 3:49

5000m
1. Gunnar Hockert FIN *14:22
2. Lauri Lehtinen FIN 14:25
3. Henry Jonsson SWE 14:29

10,000m
1. Kussosiniski POL 30:15
2. Arvo Askola FIN 30:15
3. Volmari Iso-Hollo FIN 30:20

Marathon
1. Kitei Son JAP *2:29:19
2. Ernest Harper GBR 2:31:23
3. Shoryu Nan JAP 2:31:42

110m Hurdles
1. Forrest Towns USA 14
2. Donald Finlay GBR 14
3. Frederick Pollard USA 14

400m Hurdles
1. Glenn Hardin USA 52
2. John Loaring CAN 52
3. Miguel White PHI 52

3000m Steeplechase
1. Volmari Iso-Hollo FIN ** 9:03
2. Kaarlo Tuominen FIN 9:06
3. Alfred Dompert GER 9:07

4x100m Relay
1. USA ** 39.8 (Jesse Owens, Ralph Metcalfe, Foy Draper, Frank Wykoff)
2. ITA 41.1 (Orazio Mariani, Gianni Caldana, Elio Ragni, Tullio Gonnelli)
3. GER 41.2 (Wilhem Leichum, Erich Borchmeyer, Erwin Gilmeister, Gerd Hornberger)

4x400m Relay
1. GBR 3:09.0 (Frederick Wolff, Godfrey Rampling, William Roberts, Arthur Godfrey Brown)
2. USA 3:11.0 (Harold Cagle, Robert Young, Edward O'Brien, Alfred Fitch)
3. GER 3:11.8 (Helmut Hamann, Friedrich von Stülpnagel, Harry Voigt, Rudolf Harbig)

50km Walk
1. Harold Whitlock GBR *4:30:41
2. Arthur T. Schwab SUI 4:32:09
3. Adalberts Bubenko LAT 4:32:42

High Jump
1. Cornelius Johnson USA *2.0
2. David Albritton USA 2.
3. Delos Thurber USA 2.0

Pole Vault
1. Earle Meadows USA *4.
2. Shuhei Nishida JAP 4.2
3. Sueo Oe JAP 4.2

Long Jump
1. Jesse Owens USA *8.
2. Luz Long GER 7.8
3. Naoto Tajima JAP 7.7

Triple Jump
1. Naoto Tajima JAP *16.0
2. Masao Harada JAP 15.6
3. John Patrick Metcalfe AUS 15.5

Shotput
1. Hans Woellke GER ** 16.2
2. Sulo Bàrlund FIN 16.
3. Gerhard Stöck GER 15.6

Discus
1. Kenneth Carpenter USA *50.
2. Gordon Dunn USA 49.
3. Giorgio Oberweger ITA 49.2

Hammer
1. Karl Hein GER *56.
2. Erwin Blask GER 55.0
3. Fred Warngärd SWE 54.8

Javelin
1. Gerhard Stöck GER 71.8
2. Yrjö Nikkanen FIN 70.7
3. Kalervo Toivonen FIN 70.7

Decathlon
1. Glenn Morris USA ** 790
2. Robert Clark USA 760
3. Jack Parker USA 72

Women Athletics

100m
1. Helen Stephens USA *11 (wind assisted World Record)
2. Stanislawa Walasiewicz POL 11
3. Käthe Krauss GER 11

1936 Berlin

80m Hurdles
. Trebisonda Valla ITA 11.7
2. Anni Steuer GER 11.7
3. Elizabeth Taylor CAN 11.7

4x100m Relay
. USA 46.9 (Harriet Bland, Annette Rogers, Elizabeth Robinson, Helen Stephens)
2. GBR 47.6 (Eileen Hiscock, Violet Olney, Audrey Brown, Barbara Burke)
3. CAN 47.8 (Dorothy Brookshaw, Mildred Dolson, Hilda Cameron, Aileen Meagher)

High Jump
. Ibolya Csák HUN 1.60
2. Dorothy Odam GBR 1.60
3. Elfriede Kaun GER 1.60

Discus
. Gisela Mauermayer GER *47.63
2. Jadwiga Wajsowna POL 46.22
3. Paula Mollenhauer GER 39.80

Javelin
. Tilly Fleischer GER *45.18
2. Luise Krüger GER 43.29
3. Maria Kwaśniewska POL 41.80

Men Swimming

100m Freestyle
. Ferenc Csik HUN 57.6
2. Masanori Yusa JAP 57.9
3. Shigeo Arai JAP 58.0

400m Freestyle
. Jack Medica USA *4:44.5
2. Shumpei Uto JAP 4:45.6
3. Shozo Makino JAP 4:48.1

1500m Freestyle
. Noboru Terada JAP 19:13.7
2. Jack Medica USA 19:34.0
3. Shumpei Uto JAP 19:34.5

100m Backstroke
. Adolf Kiefer USA *1:05.9
2. Albert Vandeweghe USA 1:07.7
3. Masaji Kiyokawa JAP 1:08.4

200m Breaststroke
. Tetsuo Hamuro JAP *2:41.5
2. Erwin Sietas GER 2:42.9
3. Reizo Koike JAP 2:44.2

4x200m Freestyle Relay
. JAP ** 8:15.5 (Masanori Yusa, Shigeo Sugiura, Masaharu Taguchi, Shigeo Arai)
2. USA 9:03.0 (Ralph Flanagan, John Macionis, Paul Wolf, Jack Medica)
3. HUN 9:12.3 (Árpád Lengyel, Oszkár Abay-Nemes, Odön Gróf, Ferenc Csik)

Springboard Diving
. Richard Degener USA 163.57
2. Marshall Wayne USA 159.56
3. Al Greene USA 146.29

Platform Diving
. Marshall Wayne USA 113.58
2. Elbert Root USA 110.60
3. Hermann Stork GER 110.31

Water Polo

. Hungary
2. Germany
3. Belgium

Women Swimming

100m Freestyle
. Hendrika Mastenbroek NETH *1:05.9
2. Jeannette Campbell ARG 1:06.4
3. Gisela Arendt GER 1:06.6

400m Freestyle
. Hendrika Mastenbroek NETH *5:26.4
2. Ragnhild Hveger DEN 5:27.5
3. Lenore Wingard USA 5:29.0

200m Breaststroke
. Hideko Maehata JAP 3:03.6
2. Martha Geneger GER 3:04.2
3. Inge Sörensen DEN 3:07.8

100m Backstroke
. Dina Senff NETH 1:18.9
2. Hendrika Mastenbroek NETH 1:19.2
3. Alice Bridges USA 1:19.4

4x100m Freestyle Relay
. NETH *4:36.0 (Johanna Selback, Catherina Wagner, Willemijntje den Ouden, Hendrika Mastenbroek)
2. GER 4:36.8 (Ruth Halbsguth, Leni Lohmar, Ingeborg Schmitz, Gisela Arendt)
3. USA 4:40.2 (Katherine Rawis, Bernice Lapp, Mavis Freeman, Olive McKean)

Springboard Diving
. Marjorie Gestring USA 89.27
2. Katherine Rawis USA 88.35
3. Dorothy Poynton Hill USA 82.36

Platform Diving
. Dorothy Poynton Hill USA 33.93
2. Velma Dunn USA 33.63
3. Käthe Köhler GER 33.43

Boxing

Flyweight
. Willi Kaiser GER
2. Gavino Matta ITA
3. Louis Daniel Laurie USA

Bantamweight
1. Ulderico Sergo ITA
2. Jack Wilson USA
3. Fidel Ortiz MEX

Featherweight
1. Oscar Casanovas ARG
2. Charles Catterall SAF
3. Josef Miner GER

Lightweight
1. Imre Harangi HUN
2. Nikolai Stepulov EST
3. Erik Agren SWE

Welterweight
1. Sten Suvio FIN
2. Michael Murach GER
3. Gerhard Petersen DEN

Middleweight
1. Jean Despeaux FRA
2. Henry Tiller NOR
2. Raúl Villareal ARG

Light Heavyweight
1. Roger Michelot FRA
2. Richard Vogt GER
3. Francisco Risiglione ARG

Heavyweight
1. Herbert Runge GER
2. Guillermo Lovell ARG
3. Erling Nilsen NOR

Greco Roman Wrestling

Bantamweight
1. Márton Lörincz HUN
2. Egon Svensson SWE
3. Jakob Brendel GER

Featherweight
1. Yasar Erkan TUR
2. Aarne Reini FIN
3. Einar Karlsson SWE

Lightweight
1. Lauri Koskela FIN
2. Josef Herda TCH
3. Voldemar Väli EST

Welterweight
1. Rudolf Svedberg SWE
2. Fritz Schäfer GER
3. Eino Virtanen FIN

Middleweight
1. Ivar Johansson SWE
2. Ludwig Schweikert GER
3. József Palotás HUN

Light Heavyweight
1. Axel Cardier SWE
2. Edwins Bietags LAT
3. August Neo EST

Heavyweight
1. Kristjan Palusalu EST
2. John Nyman SWE
3. Kurt Hornfischer GER

Freestyle Wrestling

Bantamweight
1. Odön Zombori HUN
2. Ross Flood USA
3. Johannes Herbert GER

Featherweight
1. Kustaa Pihlajamäki FIN
2. Francis Millard USA
3. Gosta Jonsson SWE

Lightweight
1. Károly Kárpáti HUN
2. Wolfgang Ehrl GER
3. Hermanni Pihlajamäki FIN

Welterweight
1. Frank Lewis USA
2. Ture Andersson SWE
3. Joseph Schleimer CAN

Middleweight
1. Emile Poilvé FRA
2. Richard Voliva USA
3. Ahmet Kirecci TUR

Light Heavyweight
1. Knut Fridell SWE
2. August Neo EST
3. Erich Siebert GER

Heavyweight
1. Kristjan Palusalu EST
2. Josef Klapuch TCH
3. Hjalmar Nyström FIN

Men Fencing

Foil Individual
1. Giulio Gaudini ITA
2. Edward Gardère FRA
3. Giorgio Bocchino ITA

Foil Team
1. Italy
2. France
3. Germany

Epée Individual
1. Franco Riccardi ITA
2. Saverio Ragno ITA
3. Giancarlo Cornaggia Medici ITA

Epée Team
1. Italy
2. Sweden
3. France

Sabre Individual
1. Endre Kabos HUN
2. Gustavo Marzi ITA
3. Aladár Gerevich HUN

Sabre Team
1. Hungary
2. Italy
3. Germany

Women Fencing

Foil Individual
1. Ilona Elek HUN
2. Helene Mayer GER
3. Ellen Preis AUT

Modern Pentathlon

1. Gotthard Handrick GER
2. Charles Leonard USA
3. Silvano Abba ITA

Men Canoeing

Kayak-1 1000m
1. Gregor Hradetzky AUT 4:22.9
2. Helmut Cämmerer GER 4:25.6
3. Jacob Kraaier NETH 4:35.1

Kayak-2 1000m
1. Austria 4:03.8
2. Germany 4:08.9
3. Netherlands 4:12.2

Canadian-1 1000m
1. Francis Amyot CAN 5:32.1
2. Bohuslav Karlik TCH 5:36.9
3. Erich Koschik GER 5:39.0

Canadian-2 1000m
1. Czechoslovakia 4:50.1
2. Austria 4:53.8
3. Canada 4:56.7

Kayak-1 10,000m
1. Ernst Krebs GER 46:01.6
2. Fritz Landertinger AUT 46:17.7
3. Ernest Riedl USA 47:23.9

Kayak-2 10,000m
1. Germany 41:45.0
2. Austria 42:05.4
3. Sweden 43:06.1

Jack Lovelock of New Zealand during final dash to tape to win 1936 Olympic 1500 metre event in record time of 3:47.8. Glenn Cunningham, behind Lovelock, was second. His time was 3:48.4, which also bettered previous world record.

Canadian-2 10,000m
1. Czechoslovakia 50:35.5
2. Canada 51:15.8
3. Austria 51:28.0

Folding Kayak-1 10,000m
1. Gregor Hradetzky AUT 50:01.2
2. Henri Eberhardt FRA 50:04.2
3. Xavier Hörmann GER 50:06.5

Folding Kayak-2 10,000m
1. Sweden 45:48.9
2. Germany 45:49.2
3. Netherlands 46:12.4

Rowing

Single Sculls
1. Gustav Schäfer GER 8:21.5
2. Josef Hasenöhrl AUT 8:25.8
3. Daniel Barrow USA 8:28.0

Double Sculls
1. Great Britain 7:20.8
2. Germany 7:26.2
3. Poland 7:36.2

Coxless Pairs
1. Germany 8:16.1
2. Denmark 8:19.2
3. Argentina 8:23.0

Coxed Pairs
1. Germany 8:36.9
2. Italy 8:49.7
3. France 8:54.0

Coxless Fours
1. Germany 7:01.8
2. Great Britain 7:06.5
3. Switzerland 7:10.6

Coxed Fours
1. Germany 7:16.2
2. Switzerland 7:24.3
3. France 7:33.3

Eights
1. USA 6:25.4
2. Italy 6:26.0
3. Germany 6:26.4

Yachting

Finn Monotype Class
1. Daniel Kagchelland NETH 163
2. Werner Krogmann GER 150
3. Peter Scott GBR 131

Star Class
1. Germany 80
2. Sweden 64
3. Netherlands 63

6m Class
1. Great Britain 67
2. Norway 66
3. Sweden 62

8m Class
1. Italy 55
2. Norway 53
3. Germany 53

Cycling

Road Race Individual (100km)
1. Robert Charpentier FRA 2:33:05.0
2. Guy Lapébie FRA 2:33:05.2
3. Ernst Nievergelt SUI 2:33:05.8

Team Time Trial
1. France 7:39:16.2
2. Switzerland 7:39:20.4
3. Belgium 7:39:21.0

1000m Time Trial
1. Arie van Vliet NETH *1:12.0
2. Pierre Georget FRA 1:12.8
3. Rudolf Karsch GER 1:13.2

1000m Sprint
1. Toni Merkens GER 11.8
2. Arie van Vliet NETH
3. Louis Chaillot FRA

Tandem 2000m
1. Germany 11.0
2. Netherlands
3. France

Team Pursuit (4000m)
1. France 4:45.0
2. Italy 4:51.0
3. Great Britain 4:53.6

Equestrian Sports

Three-Day Event Individual
1. Ludwig Stubbendorf GER 37.70
2. Earl Thomson USA 99.90
3. Hans Mathiesen-Lunding DEN 102.20

Three-Day Event Team
1. Germany -676.65
2. Poland -991.70
3. Great Britain -9195.50

Dressage Individual
1. Heinz Pollay GER 1760.0
2. Friedrich Gerhard GER 1745.5
3. Alois Podhajsky AUT 1721.5

Dressage Team
1. Germany 5074.0
2. France 4846.0
3. Sweden 4660.5

Grand Prix Jumping Individual
1. Kurt Hasse GER 59.2
2. Henri Rang ROM 1:12.8
3. József von Platthy HUN 1:02.6

Grand Prix Jumping Team
1. Germany -44.00
2. Netherlands -51.50
3. Portugal -56.00

Weightlifting

		2 Arm Press	2 Arm Snatch	2 Arm Clean and Jerk	Total
Featherweight					
1. Anthony Terlazzo	USA	=*92.5	*97.5	122.5	** 312.5
2. Saleh Mohammed Soliman	EGY	85.0	95.0	*125.0	305.0
3. Ibrahim Hassan Shams	EGY	80.0	95.0	*125.0	300.0
Lightweight					
1. Anwar Mohammed Mesbah	EGY	92.5	*105.0	*145.0	** 342.5
1. Robert Fein	AUT	*105.0	100.0	137.5	** 342.5
3. Karl Jansen	GER	95.0	100.0	132.5	327.5
Middleweight					
1. Khadr Sayed el Touni	EGY	** 117.5	** 120.0	*150.0	** 387.5
2. Rudolf Ismayr	GER	107.5	102.5	142.5	352.5
3. Adolf Wagner	GER	97.5	112.5	142.5	352.5
Light Heavyweight					
1. Louis Hostin	FRA	*110.0	*117.5	145.0	*372.5
2. Eugen Deutsch	GER	105.0	110.0	*150.0	365.0
3. Ibrahim Wasif	EGY	100.0	110.0	*150.0	360.0
Heavyweight					
1. Josef Manger	GER	*132.6	122.5	155.0	** 410.0
2. Václav Psenicka	TCH	122.5	125.0	155.0	402.5
3. Arnold Luhäär	EST	115.0	120.0	*165.0	400.0

Shooting

Small-Bore Rifle (prone)
1. Willy Rögeberg NOR ** 300
2. Ralph Berzsenyi HUN 296
3. Wladyslaw Karas POL 296

Rapid-Fire Pistol (25m)
1. Cornelius van Oynn GER 36
2. Heinz Hax GER 35
3. Torsten Ullman SWE 34

Free Pistol (50m)
1. Torsten Ullman SWE ** 559
2. Erich Krempel GER 544
3. Charles des Jammonières FRA 540

Gymnastics

All-around Individual
1. Alfred Schwarzmann GER 113.100
2. Eugen Mack SUI 112.334
3. Konrad Frey GER 111.532

Combined Exercises Team
1. Germany 657.430
2. Switzerland 654.802
3. Finland 638.468

Parallel Bars
1. Konrad Frey GER 19.067
2. Michael Reusch SUI 19.034
3. Alfred Schwarzmann GER 18.967

Floor Exercises
1. Georges Miez SUI 18.666
2. Josef Walter SUI 18.500
3. Eugen Mack SUI 18.466
3. Konrad Frey GER 18.466

Long Horse Vault
1. Alfred Schwarzmann GER 19.200
2. Eugen Mack SUI 18.967
3. Matthias Volz GER 18.467

Side Horse
1. Konrad Frey GER 19.333
2. Eugen Mack SUI 19.167
3. Albert Bachmann SUI 19.067

Horizontal Bar
1. Aleksanteri Saarvala FIN 19.367
2. Konrad Frey GER 19.267
3. Alfred Schwarzmann GER 19.233

Rings
1. Alois Hudoo TCH 19.433
2. Léon Stukelj YUG 18.867
3. Matthias Volz GER 18.667

Women Gymnastics

Combined Exercises Team
1. Germany 506.50
2. Czechoslovakia 503.60
3. Hungary 499.00

Basketball

1. USA
2. Canada
3. Mexico

Football

1. Italy
2. Austria
3. Norway

Handball

1. Germany
2. Austria
3. Switzerland

Hockey

1. India
2. Germany
3. Netherlands

Polo

1. Argentina
2. Great Britain
3. Mexico

(Key to symbols and abbreviations p. 1456)

1936

SEPTEMBER

Su	Mo	Tu	We	Th	Fr	Sa
		1	2	3	4	5
6	7	8	9	10	11	12
13	14	15	16	17	18	19
20	21	22	23	24	25	26
27	28	29	30			

2. UK: Results of the 1935 Road Traffic Census show a 95 per cent rise in the number of bicycles in four years.

4. Spain: Irun, in the north, falls to the rebels (→ 9).

7. UK: The new King Edward VIII stamps are the most popular ever; 130,000,000 sold in the first five days.

9. London: Opening of the international conference for non-intervention in the Spanish Civil War (→ 17).

10. India: A massive landslide destroys seven Himalayan villages, reportedly leaving hundreds dead.

11. UK: Sirloin costs 1/7d and salmon 3/3d a pound; apples cost 3d and tomatoes 6d a pound (→ 18).

12. US: Fred Perry beats Donald Budge to become the first foreigner to win the US tennis championship outright (→ 6/1/37).

14. London: George MacMahon is sentenced to 12 months hard labour for "intent to alarm the King".

15. Palestine: The British authorities ban a planned Arab congress called to consider a strike in the territory (→ 7/7/37).

17. Spain: Franco's troops take Maqueda, between Toledo and Madrid (→ 22).

18. London: An economic study says the average family needs £6 a week to keep it above the "poverty line".

21. Germany: The German army begins its largest manoeuvres since 1914 (→ 23/10).

22. Madrid: The food shortage in the city worsens (→ 28).

23. Geneva: The League reverses its bar on Abyssinia, granting the country a seat (→ 28/11).

28. Spain: General Franco is appointed head of the rebel forces.→

DEATH

21. British engineer Frank Hornby (*1863).→

Franco's rebels poised to attack Madrid

Government militia defending the Alcazar fortress against Franco's rebels.

Sept 30. The two-month long siege of the Alacazar palace fortress was raised today when General Franco captured Toledo. The 1,200 cadets and officers, together with their women and children, who have been holding out in the ruins of the once elegant palace since the war began, welcomed their rescuers after bitter hand-to-hand fighting between Franco's Moorish troops and the militiamen.

They were in rags, their faces, yellow and gaunt, plainly showing the suffering they had undergone. Cadets looked like old men. The women, who had shared their hardships, embraced the soldiers and kissed the rifles and the medallions on the tunics of the Fascists. Eighty cadets were killed during the siege and two children were born. The relief of Toledo is, however, much more than a morale-boosting victory for the insurgents. It opens up the way to the capital. Madrid is only 40 miles away to the north-east and Franco, now commander-in-chief of the insurgent forces, is already preparing his advance.

He issued a statement today saying: "Now there is no time to waste. Madrid's plans of resistance make me smile. We shall get there as fast as we can march, crushing whatever ridiculous resistance is attempted."

Meanwhile, great activity is taking place in Madrid as the Republicans prepare to meet Franco's assault. Large forces of militia have been mobilised and armed from a secret stock. Tonight they are marching to the Front (→ 3/10).

Big new film studios open at Pinewood

Sept 30. England's country-house version of a Hollywood studio was inaugurated today at Pinewood, near Iver, Buckinghamshire, at a lunch chaired by J. Arthur Rank, whose chain of Odeon cinemas has been growing for two years.

Several production companies – British National, Paramount and Herbert Wilcox – have moved in. They will have the use of eight sound stages, covering seven acres.

Pinewood will be the main rival to the nearby Denham Studios of Alexander Korda, which produced the famous "Private Life of Henry VIII" recently. British films are fighting for a larger share of screen time. Over £1,000,000-worth of them are locked up "in the can", awaiting distribution. These include Hitchcock's "Sabotage" and Korda's "Rembrandt", which gives Charles Laughton his finest role since Henry VIII. Korda and Laughton are now working on the film of Robert Graves's novel of the Roman Empire, "I, Claudius".

It was revealed that British cinema-goers spend £40 million a year on 950 million tickets, at an average price of less than one shilling.

Meccano inventor, Frank Hornby, dies

Sept 21. Few men can have given so much pleasure to children – albeit almost exclusively to young boys – as Frank Hornby, who died today at the age of 73.

It is 36 years since Liverpool-born Frank Hornby devised a simple system of interchangeable metal parts, from which a child could build models. He called it Meccano, and sets of what he called "an educational toy" became a world bestseller.

His train sets, superbly accurate clockwork and electric-powered models of great British locomotives and rolling stock, have always been in demand. So, too, are his famous "Dinky" toys.

British lady flyer first across Atlantic

Sept 6. More than 5,000 people turned out in New York today to welcome the first woman to fly across the Atlantic alone, Beryl Markham, aged 33. She arrived in America yesterday when she crashed her aircraft on landing at Cape Breton Island, Nova Scotia, and was flown south in a special aircraft to Floyd Bennett Airport, New York, today. The only sign of the accident was a sticking plaster over one eye, and now Mrs Markham says she is thinking of flying back to Europe alone as well.

1936

OCTOBER

Su	Mo	Tu	We	Th	Fr	Sa
				1	2	3
4	5	6	7	8	9	10
11	12	13	14	15	16	17
18	19	20	21	22	23	24
25	26	27	28	29	30	31

1. London: The BBC begins regular television broadcasts from Alexandra Palace (→9/2/37).

3. Spain: A cabinet reshuffle brings anarchists into the government for the first time; four become ministers (→4).

4. Spain: Government troops recapture Maqueda, south of Madrid (→5).

5. UK: The Labour Party conference votes to remain neutral in Spain (→7).

7. Spain: The government sets up an autonomous Basque government in Guernica (→15).

10. Vienna: Schuschnigg absorbs the Fascist Heimwehr into his Fatherland Front, becoming dictator of Austria.

11. Philippines: 109 deaths are reported when a typhoon strikes the islands.

12. UK: Two trains are ferried between Dover and Dunkirk, beginning the London to Paris through service.→

15. Spain: Franco's forces clash with government troops only 25 miles from Madrid (→22).

16. London: Lord Beaverbrook calls on the King and agrees to arrange press silence on his relationship with Mrs Wallis Simpson (→27).

18. Venice: 23 are reported killed in an earthquake.

22. Spain: The government will move to Barcelona (→23).

23. Berlin: Hitler orders the "Condor" legion to Spain to fight alongside Franco (→29).

24. Berlin: Hitler officially recognises Italy's King Victor Emmanuel III as Emperor of Abyssinia (→25).

25. Berlin: Hitler and Italian foreign minister Count Nobile Ciano draft a pact (→1/11).

26. Spain: Franco begins a drive towards Catalonia.→

27. Ipswich: Mrs Wallis Simpson wins a divorce from her husband Ernest (→12/12).

29. Baghdad: Pro-Western Iraqi Kemalists come to power in an army coup.

Jarrow jobless begin march to London

Oct 5. Thousands of people gathered in the streets of Jarrow today, and many businesses stopped work, as 200 unemployed men began their long march to London.

They are carrying with them an oak casket, containing a petitition with 11,572 signatures, which they hope to present to the Government on November 4. The leaders of the march sported three big banners proclaiming it the "Jarrow Protest March".

Locals call it the Jarrow Crusade; an appeal raised £800 to support it. The money has been used to buy leather and nails so that the men can mend their boots. £1 per head is being saved for the return journey by train.

The marchers are hoping to focus attention on the 68 per cent unemployment level in the town, which was dependent on the shipbuilding and heavy iron and steel trades.

The strength of local support was evident from the attendance at the service at Christ Church before the march. The Bishop of Jarrow, the Right Rev. J.G. Gordon, conducted the service. In the congregation were the Mayor, the town clerk and many councillors, as well as the young Labour MP, Miss Ellen Wilkinson. The brass band accompanied the marchers to the town boundary. They are spending their first night in the Church Institute at Chester-le-Street in County Durham (→11/11).

From Albert Road to Downing Street: the marchers set off from Jarrow.

Moslem and Hindu rioters are flogged

Oct 19. Rioting has broken out again between Hindus and Moslems in Bombay. This time it began when Moslems objected to the erection of a Hindu temple near one of their mosques. The casualties in five days of violence now amount to 60 dead and 500 injured.

A number of arrests were made this evening and 60 of the rioters were sentenced to be flogged. Six were punished straight away and then released from gaol to show their backs as examples to discourage others.

Fresh meat, which has been unobtainable, will be available tomorrow, much to the relief of European residents who have been living on fish, vegetables and tinned meat.

Animals in the zoo, which had no meat at all one day and only one-third rations on others, have been roaring all day and night, and the people living in the surrounding district have been unable to get any sleep (→1/4/37).

First train drives onto Channel ferry

Oct 12. The launch today of a train ferry service between Dover and Dunkirk was celebrated on both sides of the Channel. The service, which cost about £1,000,000 to introduce, will enable passengers to travel from London to Paris by the same sleeping-car and not change on to different transport at each end of the Channel crossing, as had been required up until now. The new service will officially start operating tomorrow; a train will leave Victoria station at 10pm and arrive in Paris at 8.55 the following morning. French Ambassador, M. Corbin, declared that the development was "a link which would strengthen the bond between two great nations".

The cross-channel train ferry is an amazing feat of modern engineering.

100,000 clash with Fascists in East End

Mosleyites and their opponents clash at the "Battle of Cable Street".

Oct 11. One hundred thousand people built barricades and thronged the streets today in an attempt to prevent a march by 7,000 blackshirted supporters of Fascist leader Sir Oswald Mosley through London's East End. London had been anticipating this day of violence for weeks, but the fury of opposition to the Fascists surprised even the police, who were forced to stop the march through working class districts. Even before Mosley – wearing a black, military-cut uniform with riding breeches and jackboots – addressed his supporters, his limousine's windscreen was shattered.

Cable Street saw the worst of the rioting with lorries overturned, bricks hurled at police and the roads strewn with broken glass to prevent charges by mounted police. A Jewish tailor and his son were thrown through plate glass windows by blackshirts. Eighty people, including 15 police, were injured and 84 arrests were made (→ 10/11).

Franco's rebels driven back from Madrid

Oct 29. General Franco's relentless drive on Madrid has been held up by the Republicans south of the capital. Fierce infantry attacks, with air and artillery support, stopped the over-confident insurgents in their tracks outside the Escorial, the ancient palace of the Spanish Kings, and the last natural bulwark before the city's defences.

The Nationalists have, however, succeeded in cutting the Aranjuez-Madrid road today, and this means that all the capital's communications, except those to the east, are in Franco's hands.

General Mola, commanding the insurgent attack, says he has four columns converging on Madrid and a "fifth column" of supporters inside the city, which would rise in support of the attackers when the time came (→ 7/11).

Relishing the fight against Franco.

1936

NOVEMBER

Su	Mo	Tu	We	Th	Fr	Sa
1	2	3	4	5	6	7
8	9	10	11	12	13	14
15	16	17	18	19	20	21
22	23	24	25	26	27	28
29	30					

1. Rome: Mussolini announces the anti-Communist Axis with Germany; he urges Britain and France to join.

2. UK: Labour loses 81 seats in local elections (→ 5/3/37).

3. London: King Edward opens his first parliament (→ 12).

4. London: The city's tramways will be converted to trolley buses over the next five years.

7. Spain: The government flees to Valencia (→ 18).

8. Berlin: The Nazis are reported to be dropping foreign words from German language.

9. Berlin: Germany admits it is building aircraft carriers.

10. London: Publication of the Public Order Bill (→ 1/1/37).

11. London: Publication of the Marriage Bill.→

12. Southampton: The King begins a two-day visit to inspect the Fleet.→

14. Cairo: Egypt ratifies the Anglo-Egyptian treaty concluded in August (→ 26/5).

16. France: 40 die in a blast at a gunpowder factory near Marseilles.

18. Spain: Hitler and Mussolini recognise Franco's provisional government in Burgos (→ 20).

20. Spain: One of the rebel leaders, Antonio Primo de Rivera, is executed by Republicans at Alicante (→ 26).

24. Oxford: Industrialist Lord Nuffield gives £2,000,000 to the University for a medical research school.

26. Spain: The US moves its embassy to Valencia from Madrid (→ 1/12).

27. London: Foreign Secretary Anthony Eden warns Germany Britain will fight to protect Belgium (→ 19/12).

28. Tokyo: Japan recognises the Italian occupation of Abyssinia (→ 25/2/37).

29. Moscow: The Kremlin claims that the USSR has the world's biggest air force of 7,000 planes.

"Something must be done" declares King on Welsh visit

Nov 18. King Edward VIII got a tremendous reception in South Wales today from the unemployed and the employed, including miners rushing up from the pit, their faces still black with coal dust. His tour has been a great personal triumph. He altered his route to take in the devastated site of Dowlais Steel Works, which once made some of the finest steel in the Empire.

At Dowlais the King saw several thousand unemployed men clearing the site for the building of an occupational centre. Afterwards he was clearly moved by what he had seen, for he declared firmly that "something must be done" (→ 3/12).

The King sees for himself.

Baldwin snub for Jarrow marchers

Nov 11. In a tough speech today Stanley Baldwin, the Prime Minister, said it would be cowardice for him to receive the Jarrow marchers. "This is the way in which civil strife begins, and civil strife may not end until it is civil war," he said. Even Labour Party leaders have been nervous about showing too much support, and the marchers' Hyde Park rally was organised by the Communist Party.

Crystal Palace fire best show in town

Nov 30. No fireworks display in history could ever match this one. Millions turned out from as far away as Margate and Brighton to watch the fiery, spectacular end of the Crystal Palace in South London last night.

It was soon after 8pm that flames were first noticed in the huge glass structure. By 8.30 the entire centre transept was fully ablaze and had come crashing to the ground while thousands of Londoners packed buses, trains and taxis to see it.

Many forced their way through police barricades and risked death from collapsing towers as they fought to get close. Five hundred firemen fought the blaze, but such was the heat that many had to be relieved after short periods.

By 9.15pm, as three great explosions added to the confusion, special trains were being laid on from main London stations and mile-long queues of traffic were holding up additional fire engines.

The pilot of an Imperial Airways air-liner returning from Paris reported that he could see the blaze from mid-Channel, and others were warned to avoid the numerous aircraft – some chartered by private parties – flying over the area.

As the palace – designed by Sir Joseph Paxton for the Great Exhibition of 1851 in Hyde Park, and later re-erected at Sydenham – continued to burn, thousands of birds were released from the aviary to rise in flocks, only to be overcome by smoke and crash back into the flames.

The skeleton of the gutted pavilion rises above a mass of twisted girders.

Fascist powers in formal alliance

Nov 25. An agreement, designed to "protect European culture and civilisation and world peace from the Bolshevik menace", was signed by Germany and Japan today. This complements a similar pact – or "Axis" – reached earlier this month between Germany and Italy.

Both parties deny that there are any secret military or economic clauses, but say that they will take stern measures against persons who act "in the service of the Communist International or give assistance to its subversive work".

It would appear, then, to be an arrangement between the secret police forces of both countries, similar to that made between the German and Italian secret police when Herr Himmler and Herr Heydrich visited Rome last month.

Sir Eric Phipps, the British Ambassador in Berlin, and Francois Poncet, the French Ambassador, were among those who witnessed the ceremony. The Soviet Ambassador was not invited.

Radio talks contribute to Roosevelt's impressive re-election

Nov 3. President Roosevelt today routed his Republican opponent, Governor Landon of Kansas, in nearly every state of the Union. Despite blizzards and torrential rain in different parts of the country, there was a massive turnout of the newly enlarged 55 million electorate. In most states, Roosevelt was ahead by two to one; in the electoral college Landon won only eight of the 531 votes. Even Pennsylvania, which had been Republican for 20 years, went to the Democrats.

Roosevelt is the first president to win a second four-year term since Woodrow Wilson did in 1916. His resounding victory underlines his success at building a coalition between many different elements in the country for his New Deal policies. His support comes from trade unions, the blacks and other ethnic groups and many intellectuals.

It was a popular victory. In Times Square, New York, traffic was totally blocked by people waving flags and motorists sounding their horns in jubilation. His popularity arises from his style as much as from his ambitious legislation to combat the Depression. In his now famous radio talks, he explains his policies in a way no President has done before. As comedian Will Rogers said: "Everybody understands him – even the bankers." Landon's one bright moment came just after midnight when the first return from a New Hampshire village showed a win for him by five votes to two (→20/1/37).

Roosevelt wins again: his formidable wife Eleanor takes a back seat.

Grounds for divorce may be widened

Nov 20. The Marriage Bill, which will reform divorce law in Britain by permitting wider grounds, was given its second reading today. Mr A.P. Herbert, the writer and Independent MP, said current law encouraged immorality: "People are forced to choose between two abominations – adultery or perjury."

The new grounds are desertion, cruelty, incurable insanity, drunkenness and imprisonment under a death sentence; no divorce would be allowed in the first five years of marriage. Opponents of the Bill argue that easier divorce would "sacrifice the children", but in reply Mrs Tate told them that denying divorce was not in children's best interests: "Mutual hatred between parents cannot be hidden."

The reforms, said to have widespread public support and the approval of the Archbishop of Canterbury, also aim to bring divorce more within the reach of the poor as originally suggested by the Divorce Commission (→7/7/37).

1936

DECEMBER

Su	Mo	Tu	We	Th	Fr	Sa
		1	2	3	4	5
6	7	8	9	10	11	12
13	14	15	16	17	18	19
20	21	22	23	24	25	26
27	28	29	30	31		

1. Spain: 5,000 Germans land at Cadiz to join Franco's rebels (→ 19).

3. London: The Duke and Duchess of York arrive from Scotland as urgent talks take place on the Royal crisis (→ 11).

6. Mexico City: Mexico grants asylum to Trotsky (→ 22).

8. Nicaragua: Anastasio Somoza is elected president.

9. UK: An air crash kills 14 people, including autogiro inventor Juan de la Cierva.

10. Stockholm: Nobel Prizes go to Victor Hess (Austria, Physics); Peter Debye (Holland, Chemistry); Sir Henry Dale (UK) and Otto Loewi (Austria, Medicine); and Eugene O'Neill (US, Literature). Peace Prize awarded in Oslo to Carlos Lamas (Argentina) (→ 30/1/37).

11. Windsor: Edward VIII ceases to be King during a lunch with Churchill.→

16. Buenos Aires: The Pan-American Peace Conference adopts pacts to maintain peace in the Americas.

19. London: Eden urges Germany to stop sending troops to Spain (→ 29).

20. El Salvador: 200 people are reported dead in an earthquake.

22. Norway: Trotsky leaves for Mexico (→ 9/1/37).

29. Spain: Government troops release a German freighter, following protests from Berlin (→ 7/1/37).

DEATH

10. Italian playwright Luigi Pirandello (*28/6/1867).

HITS OF 1936

The way you look tonight.

When I'm cleaning windows.

QUOTE OF THE YEAR

"No earthly power can check our triumphant movement. Spain is saved!"

General Francisco Franco, Commander in Chief of rebel Phalangist forces in Spain.

Edward VIII renounces crown for love

Dec 12. Britain and the Empire have lost their King. Edward VIII sailed into exile in the early hours of this morning. He chose abdication as the price of freedom to marry the woman he loves.

It was an agonising climax to the protracted constitutional crisis, which has gripped world attention for many months, but about which the British people are only now officially aware. Stanley Baldwin, the Prime Minister, gave his account to parliament as soon as King Edward signed the Instrument of Abdication and had been succeeded by his younger brother, now King George VI, 48 hours ago. The Prime Minister told MPs how the ex-King insisted on marrying Mrs Wallis Simpson, the American who had recently divorced her second husband. The cabinet and the Dominion Premiers pleaded with him not to do so. They told him that the people would not regard Mrs Simpson as a suitable person to be Queen.

The King suggested a morganatic marriage, which would neither give any children the right to succession nor make her Queen. The cabinet ruled this out as unconstitutional and the Archbishop of Canterbury, Cosmo Lang, urged Mr Baldwin to protect public morality by standing firm. Mr Baldwin went to the King, took a strong drink and told him that his choice must be between a marriage of which the cabinet approved and abdication.

All this happened in furtive negotiations involving all the Royal Family, kept secret in Britain by voluntary press censorship organised by Lord Beaverbrook, newspaper tycoon and friend of Edward.

After a poignant farewell broadcast tonight, the ex-King boarded a destroyer at Portsmouth and left for France to join Mrs Simpson. The pillars of British society were shaken but they still stood.→

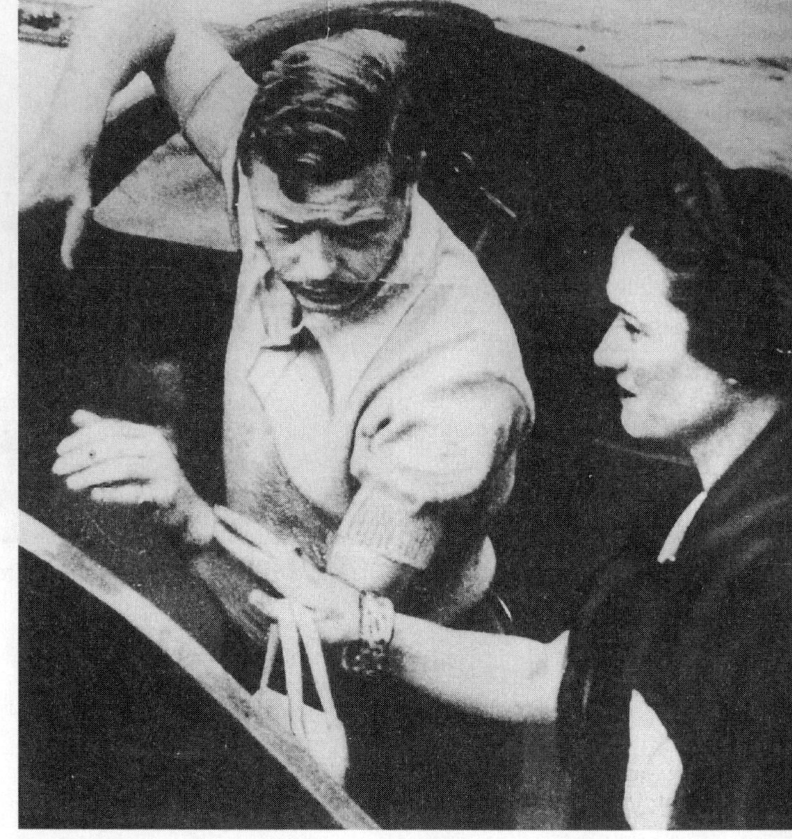

A touch of love: the King with Mrs Simpson this summer in Yugoslavia.

The King speaks: "Why I need the help of the woman I love"

Dec 11. Seated alone in Windsor Castle, King Edward VIII tonight spoke by radio to his subjects at home and abroad. This is part of what he said:

"At long last, I am able to say a few words of my own ... I want you to understand that in making up my mind I did not forget the country or the Empire which as Prince of Wales, and lately as King, I have for 25 years tried to serve. But you must believe me when I tell you that I have found it impossible to carry the heavy burden of responsibility and to discharge my duties as King as I would wish to do without the help and support of the woman I love ... God bless you all. God Save the King."→

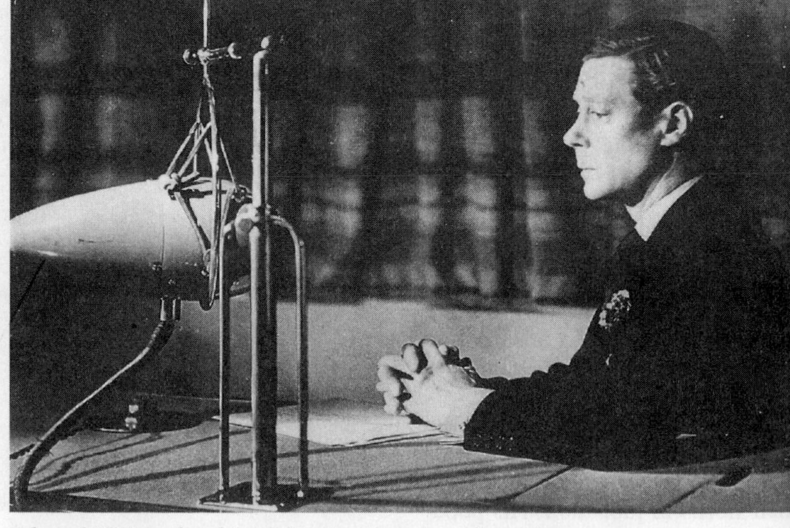

Edward VIII makes his abdication speech to the nation.

Secret love story that split Britain

How Fleet Street broke the silence

Dec 3. British newspapers broke their silence today and the nation learned of the constitutional drama being played out in Royal circles. For weeks, Fleet Street has seethed with frustration as newsmen read of the King's romance in American and European newspapers while their own stayed silent.

The "conspiracy of silence" was inspired by Lord Beaverbrook, owner of the Daily Express, after a plea from the King to spare Mrs Simpson from notoriety.

Unaware of the King's intention to marry the divorcee, Beaverbrook agreed and persuaded Esmond Harmsworth, owner of the Daily Mail and chairman of the Newspaper Proprietors' Association, to refrain from publishing what was clearly a sensational story. Other national newspapers fell into line. There was no stopping the sale of foreign newspapers in Britain, however, and rumour was rife throughout the country.

The Yorkshire Post opened the floodgates for Fleet Street. Reporting an address guardedly critical of the King – "some of us wish that he gave more positive signs of awareness" – by the Bishop of Bradford, the Post referred to foreign press reports and said: "They plainly have a foundation in fact."→

The shattered ex-King drives off for France, and Mrs Simpson.

Shy Bertie succeeds as King George VI

Dec 12. The shy, diffident Prince Albert was proclaimed King today, with the nation still shocked by his brother's abdication – something that had not happened in England since 1399.

The new King addressed his Accession Council at St. James's Palace nine hours after Edward had left for exile. Speaking in a low, slightly halting, nervous voice he pledged himself "to work above else for the welfare of the British Commonwealth of Nations". The King is known to friends and family as "Bertie". He's a crack shot, and has played in the Wimbledon championships. After inferior schooling with a tutor, he went to the Royal Naval College, Osborne, as a cadet, where he came 86th in his finals. In the War he saw action at the Battle of Jutland and then served with the RAF. He and the new Queen have two children, the Princesses Elizabeth and Margaret. Unless they have a son, ten-year-old Elizabeth is the new heir.→

Arts: diving suit nearly kills Dali

The Surrealists have surfaced from their subconscious depths with an International Exhibition in London. **Salvador Dali**, the group's master publicist, was there wearing a diving suit. He gave a lecture, unfortunately inaudible through his helmet. What he had been saying was "Let me out!" – the helmet had stuck and he nearly suffocated.

His pictures include "The Persistence of Memory", which shows watches in process of melting into a barren dream landscape. The idea apparently came to him when he was eating ripe Camembert cheese – "the clocks are merely the soft, crazy Camembert of time and space," he explained.

In Russia the doctrine of "Socialist Realism" is inexorable. Two years of popular success ended for **Shostakovich's** opera "Lady Macbeth of Mtsensk" when Stalin saw it, resulting in its condemnation in Pravda as "petty-bourgeois sensationalism". **Rachmaninov** has been banned as decadent while **Sergei Prokoviev**, who returned to Russia in 1933, has taken no risks by setting a popular folk tale, "Peter and the Wolf", to music.

Denounced are the poet **Osip Mandelstam**, exiled for a poem criticising Stalin, the stage director **Meyerhold** and the short story writer **Isaac Babel**. **Maxim Gorky**, lately the sponsor of Socialist Realism and associate of Stalin, has died in mysterious circumstances.

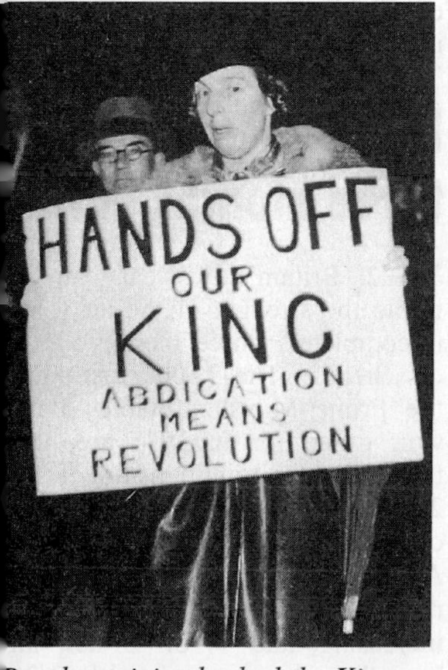

Popular opinion backed the King.

How a Prince met a girl from Baltimore

Dec 3. It was at a party given by Thelma, Lady Furness – with whom the then Prince of Wales was having a love affair – that Mrs Simpson came face to face with the future King.

It was six months, however, before they met again in January 1932, and Mrs Simpson began the first of many visits to Fort Belvedere, the Prince's grace-and-favour castellated home near Windsor. In June the following year the Prince gave a birthday party for her at Quaglino's and later dined with the Simpsons at their flat in Bryanston Court.

In 1934 Lady Furness went to America, leaving her close friend, Mrs Simpson, to "look after" the Prince. It was during this time that the two became inseparable.

The woman whose romance with the future King was to shake a nation was born Wallis Warfield in Baltimore in 1896 – two years after the birth of Edward. In 1916 she married a young naval aviator, Earl Winfield Spencer, who turned out to be neurotic and obsessional; they were divorced in 1927.

In the following year she married Ernest Simpson, a naturalised Englishman and a soldier, who was described as a "quiet man with scholarly tastes" (→3/6/37).

Spending the way to cure depression

Dec 31. How to tackle – and prevent – another economic depression is the theme of this year's "The General Theory of Employment, Interest and Money" from the pen of the British economist, John Maynard Keynes. He says a depression is caused by demand being insufficient to buy all the goods society can produce. Keynes says the money supply should be increased by lowering interest rates and stimulating investment, including spending on public works, and tolerating an unbalanced budget to increase consumer demand.

1937

JANUARY

Su	Mo	Tu	We	Th	Fr	Sa
					1	2
3	4	5	6	7	8	9
10	11	12	13	14	15	16
17	18	19	20	21	22	23
24	25	26	27	28	29	30
31						

1. Spain: Germans seize a government ship at Bilbao in retaliation for the seizure last month of a German vessel (→3).

3. London: Britain protests to Franco about the shelling of the steamer Blackhill off northern Spain (→7).

5. Ankara: The government plans to conscript women from 16 to 60 in time of war.

6. New York: Fred Perry makes his debut as a professional tennis player.

7. Berlin: Hitler agrees to support a non-intervention pact on Spain if all other powers do likewise (→10).

9. Rome: The government bans inter-racial marriages in the Italian colonies in Africa.

9. Mexico: Trotsky arrives (→18/4).

10. London: Britain bans volunteers from fighting in Spain, imposing a two-year jail sentence for offenders (→13).

12. UK: 30 are feared dead when the Finnish ship Johanna Thorden sinks off Scotland.

13. Washington: The US puts a ban on joining either side in the Spanish Civil War (→17).

17. Moscow: The USSR refuses to halt aid to the Republicans in Spain (→8/2).

18. London: Horse-drawn traffic is banned from a wide area of the West End.

20. Washington: Roosevelt is sworn in for a second term in the first inauguration ceremony held in January.→

22. US: 150,000 are reported homeless when the Ohio River floods, killing 16 (→26).

26. US: Cincinnati is paralysed as the Ohio flood death toll mounts to 135; 750,000 are now reported homeless.

30. Berlin: Hitler guarantees the neutrality of Belgium and the Netherlands (→13/10).

30. Berlin: Hitler bans Germans from accepting Nobel Prizes (→5/3/37).

BIRTH

30. British actress Vanessa Redgrave.

Stalin's court purges 17 "Trotskyites"

Accused by Trotsky, and others, of engineering show trials.

Jan 29. The so-called "trial of the 17" has ended in Moscow with expected death sentences for 13 accused, but prison sentences for four others. Karl Radek, probably the best-known Soviet propagandist, and the former Soviet ambassador to London, Gregori Sokolnikov, were each sentenced to ten years' imprisonment.

The Stalin show trials were otherwise running true to form, with many of the accused readily confessing to high treason, collusion with foreign powers and conspiracy with Leon Trotsky to overthrow Stalin. Sentences were then quickly carried out, despite the restoration of the right of appeal. All of them have been described as "Trotskyites" but Trotsky, now in exile in Mexico, has strongly denied links with them and insisted Stalin had engineered the trials to maintain power.

One of the those sentenced to death, Grigori Piatakov, who had responsibilities for the munitions industry, was the chief defendant. He pleaded for clemency, having lost "my party, my friends, my family and myself".

Another formidable Old Bolshevik, Nikolai Bukharin, has been removed from the editorship of the leading newspaper Izvestia (→12/6).

Faultless Fonteyn has London at her feet

Jan 19. The 18-year-old English dancer Margot Fonteyn scored a triumph at her debut in "Giselle" at Sadler's Wells. When Alicia Markova left the Wells two years ago, the company was without a prima ballerina. It is so no longer.

Giselle is the ballet equivalent of the part of Hamlet. The heroine is required, like Ophelia, to go mad and to rise from the grave as an ethereal spirit. Fonteyn, partnered by Robert Helpmann as the Prince, drew an expectant house. "Never has there been a more joyous, engaging Giselle," said a critic.

Margot Fonteyn studied at the Sadler's Wells school, run by Ninette de Valois. Her real name is Peggy Hookham.

Fonteyn, in the role of Giselle.

One-third of the US badly off, says FDR

Jan 20. Despite his landslide victory last November, President Roosevelt today showed he was under no illusions about the difficulties ahead. In his inauguration speech he told the crowd standing in the rain at the Capitol: "I see one-third of a nation ill-housed, ill-clad, ill-nourished."

He said he was speaking not out of despair but out of hope: "If I know aught of the spirit and purpose of our nation, we will not listen to comfort, opportunism and timidity. We will carry on."

In the past a new President has had to wait until March 4 to be inaugurated, but after the financial chaos of the last months of the Hoover presidency, the constitution was changed to bring the date forward two months (→5/2).

Public Order Act comes into force

Jan 1. The death-knell sounded today for Sir Oswald Mosley's British Union of Fascists (BUF) when the Public Order Act came into force. The new law bans political uniforms and empowers the police to stop political processions when there is risk of disorder. The Government is acting on the assumption that this will effectively end provocative marches – especially through inner-city Jewish areas – which have frequently led to violence in the past few years. The BUF is not itself proscribed (→2/8).

RAF hits target three months early

Jan 2. Britain's two-year plan to treble the strength of the air force is complete – three months ahead of schedule. The 2,500 extra pilots the Prime Minister, Stanley Baldwin, called for in 1935 are now trained or in training, and of the 2,000 extra personnel required, only 1,000 more are now wanted. At the same time the rate at which new aircraft are being delivered is increasing, and 40 of 49 new air bases have been completed (→2/2).

1937

FEBRUARY

Su	Mo	Tu	We	Th	Fr	Sa
	1	2	3	4	5	6
7	8	9	10	11	12	13
14	15	16	17	18	19	20
21	22	23	24	25	26	27
28						

1. Moscow: The 13 "Trotskyists" are executed.

2. Paris: The Chamber of Deputies votes a 19 million defence budget to match German military spending (→21/6).

4. London: German ambassador von Ribbentrop gives a Nazi salute to King George.

8. Spain: Malaga falls to Franco, aided by 15,000 Italians (→16).

9. UK: The cheapest television receiver is cut from 95 guineas to 60 guineas (→12/5).

12. UK: Petrol goes up a halfpenny to 1/7d.

14. Rome: Pope Pius XI, who has been seriously ill, walks for the first time in two months.

16. London: Britain, Italy, Germany, the USSR and 23 other powers agree to halt military aid to Spain.→

16. US: The artificial fibre "Nylon" is patented.→

18. Cairo: An Imperial Airways flying boat arrives from England after a non-stop flight of 13 hours 30 minutes.

20. Spain: The international ban on aiding Republican forces comes into effect (→22).

21. Abyssinia: 3,000 Abyssinians, planning an attack on Addis Ababa, are annihilated by the Italians (→23).

22. Spain: Britain, France, Germany, Italy, Portugal and the USSR agree to a cordon around Spain to enforce their arms ban (→26).

23. London: Italy protests to Britain for inviting Haile Selassie to send an envoy to the King's coronation (→25).

25. Abyssinia: The Italians execute Haile Selassie's son-in-law Ras Desta Demtu.

26. Spain: Portugal and the USSR withdraw from the Spanish cordon pact (→28).

28. Spain: Franco begins a big offensive in Aragon (→1/3).

BIRTH

26. Spanish artist Eduardo Arroyo.

Idealists flock to Spain

International Brigade comrades greet each other along the Aragon front.

Feb 16. Idealists from all over the world are making their way to Spain to fight in the civil war. Most of them are joining the International Brigade, heavily engaged in the defence of Madrid. This brigade, although organised and led by Communists, is not entirely Communist; its ranks include many young men, from all walks of life, who are opposed to Fascism.

At the same time other young men, from the same towns and the same schools, are fighting on behalf of General Franco's Nationalists, convinced that that they must prevent the spread of Communism.

One of the most surprising aspects of this rush to arms is the number of intellectuals who have put aside their pens and taken up the rifle. Peter Kemp, one of the brightest of the young graduates from Cambridge, is fighting with the Carlist forces in Franco's army, while George Orwell, author of "Down and Out in Paris and London", has put his principles into practice and joined the International Brigade. Many of these young men, some of them totally unprepared for war, have perished, especially in the recent fighting south-east of Madrid. Sixteen English prisoners, taken by the Nationalists at Arganda, have now been put to work with picks and shovels on roads and bridges blown up by Madrid's defenders.

There are an estimated 59,000 foreign volunteers fighting for the government: 28,000 Frenchmen, 14,000 Belgians, 11,000 Czech, British, Italian and German anti-Fascists, along with 6,000 Russian army "volunteers".

Franco's army has 25,000 German and 30,000 Italian army "volunteers" and some 5,000 real volunteers from many countries. The British government has warned that Britons who enlist on either side are liable to two years in prison. Britain has also urged all other states to prevent the despatch of volunteers and troops, but many of them are already too deeply involved (→20).

Spending on Navy will be highest since Great War

Feb 2. The Chancellor, Neville Chamberlain, warned today that the £1,500 million the Government plans to spend on arms over the next five years may not be enough. The Government already plans to borrow £220 million a year in future and it seems likely that taxes will have to rise to fuel the increase in defence spending.

Socialist MPs are still angry over the enormous cost of building up Britain's arms stocks, although Mr Chamberlain warned that the country could not expect to take on powerful new enemy fleets with old warships.

The naval building programme this year will come to £50 million, the highest since the Great War, and over the next four years the bill for naval construction wages alone should come to £100 million. A total of 500,000 tons of ships are on order for this and next year.

By the end of the year every shipyard in the country qualified to build warships will be working to almost full capacity, despite a labour shortage (→13/4).

British liner holed by mine off Spain

Feb 25. A British liner with 100 passengers on board was last night holed by a mine off the coast of Spain. The mine ripped a large hole in the side of the 10,600-ton Llandovery Castle. With water entering two holds, Captain C.A. Aylen limped 20 miles to the nearest harbour – Port Vendres in France.

Pumps worked at full pressure to clear water from the holds, but by the time the ship arrived off Port Vendres early this morning she was listing heavily. Tugs are standing by and lifeboats have been slung out over the ship's sides, ready to evacuate the passengers who were sailing from Marseilles to South Africa. Although nobody appears to have been injured by the blast, the mining of the Mediterranean will intensify concern about the threat to neutral shipping posed by the Spanish Civil War.

Chiang refuses alliance offer from Mao

Feb 23. Generalissimo Chiang Kai-shek, head of the Chinese government, has firmly rejected proposals by the Communists that they and the Nationalists should join forces to fight against the Japanese invaders.

This apparently patriotic invitation came from Mao Tse-tung, who is the undisputed master of Red forces now mustered in Yenan. He was the leader of the so-called long march which saved the Communist forces from annihilation by the Nationalists. In December General Chiang was even taken hostage by a warlord trying to unite him with Communists in a campaign against Japan, so strong is the hatred of the invader.

But although he is all too aware of the threat to China from Japanese troops currently occupying parts of the country, General Chiang still considers that the threat of a Communist takeover is even more dangerous. He does not trust Mao, who calls his troops "the national revolutionary guard", which gives a clue to the future arrangement he has in mind. Under the cloak of fighting a patriotic war Mao and his Reds, the General believes, would attempt to impose a Communist government upon China (→ 29/9).

Going it alone: Chiang Kai-shek.

Roosevelt takes on US Supreme Court

Feb 5. President Roosevelt today brought forward his controversial new plan to bring fresh blood to the Supreme Court which has been blocking some of his most crucial New Deal legislation. The court, which is predominantly conservative in membership, has provided some of the only effective opposition to Roosevelt's radical measures.

The new plan would allow the President to nominate up to six additional justices, if those aged 70 or more refuse to retire. Roosevelt said that too often judges stay on "beyond their physical and mental capacity".

In the Congress, former President Herbert Hoover accused Roosevelt of "court packing". He said the measure was merely designed to secure approval of questionable New Deal programmes. The court has ruled the National Recovery Act as unconstitutional. The President can appoint the justices but he is powerless if none retires or dies (→ 14/9).

Plan for national fitness campaign

Feb 4. A massive £2 million campaign to make Britons fitter and healthier was unveiled today. Key features of the Government's wide-ranging plans include: more gymnasia, playing fields, swimming baths, campsites and community centres plus the creation of a national college of physical training.

Oliver Stanley, the Education Board President, said: "We are not out to compel but to attract. We want people to be fit all through their lives because being fit will make their lives happier, their work easier, their leisure more enjoyable. There is something for every age and every taste."

Advances have already been made in the physical conditions of school children and the new scheme, along with a compaign for better nutrition, aims to reach young people and adults, particularly those stuck in offices and factories. The initial £2 million outlay will be followed after three years by £150,000 a year.

1937

MARCH

Su	Mo	Tu	We	Th	Fr	Sa
	1	2	3	4	5	6
7	8	9	10	11	12	13
14	15	16	17	18	19	20
21	22	23	24	25	26	27
28	29	30	31			

1. Spain: The rebels are defeated at Toledo (→ 4).

3. Australia: The Australians win the fifth Test against England to retain the Ashes.

4. Madrid: Riots have broken out because of food shortage (→ 3/14).

5. London: Labour increases its majority from 12 to 26 in London County Council elections.

9. Germany: The police deport 2,000 alleged to be "dangerous criminals" or "offensive to public morals" (→ 30).

12. UK: Figures show that 824 people earned over £30,000 in 1936.→

16. Paris: Conductor Sir Thomas Beecham is presented with the Legion of Honour.

18. US: 500 die as a suspected gas blast ignites a huge fire at a school in New London, Texas.

19. UK: Mr Lloyd Thomas's Royal Mail wins the centenary Grand National.

20. UK: England beat Scotland at Murrayfield for the first time for rugby's Calcutta Cup, International Championship and Triple Crown.

20. London: George VI's coinage will include a new 12-sided threepenny piece (→ 14/4).

24. London: The new Ministers Bill would raise the PM's salary to £10,000 and give the cabinet official status.

24. London: Oxford wins the Boat Race after 13 successive Cambridge victories.

27. UK: Police serve 40 summonses in connection with the September 1934 Gresford pit tragedy, when 262 died.

30. Germany: Hitler is reported to have patched up his feud with Ludendorff dating from the 1923 Munich putsch (→ 20/12).

DEATHS

16. British statesman Sir Austen Chamberlain (*16/10/1863).

20. British golfer Harry Vardon (*9/5/1870).

Survey shows UK's 800 millionaires

March 3. The wealth bracket in Britain is expanding, according to Inland Revenue statistics released this week. Up goes the number of millionaires from 775 last year to 824.

Some 69 people are now also on annual incomes exceeding the £100,000 mark and 85,449 people are on £2,000 and upwards a year. The general rise in wealth means that 50,000 more people are paying income tax, joining a grand total of 3,350,000. Some do escape – the introduction of new allowances by the Revenue has freed 250,000 people from tax – but not the dead; death duties produced a record haul of £88 million (→ 12).

Orwell takes Road to Wigan Pier

March 9. George Orwell took a journey into the heart of depressed Britain last year and the result is "The Road to Wigan Pier" – an unsparing report of the life of the unemployed with descriptions of the squalor in the lodgings where he stayed over a tripe shop and a long polemical essay about the need of the "lower upper-middle class", as he describes himself, to embrace the working man and socialism.

His problem in doing so is other socialists, whom he sees as "vegetarian cranks in sandals".

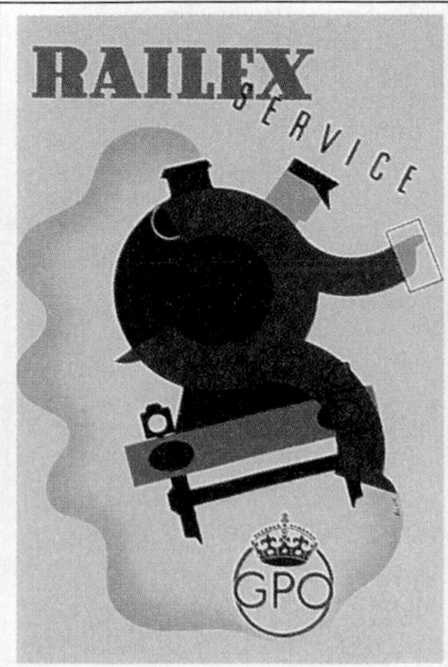

The Post Office gets it there.

1937

APRIL

Su	Mo	Tu	We	Th	Fr	Sa
				1	2	3
4	5	6	7	8	9	10
11	12	13	14	15	16	17
18	19	20	21	22	23	24
25	26	27	28	29	30	

1. India: The Indian constitution comes into being under the Government of India Act; Burma is separated (→11).

3. Spain: 15 Soviet bombers raid Cordoba (→9).

5. France: The French liner Normandie wins the Blue Riband off the Queen Mary.

9. Madrid: Loyalists launch a fresh bid to raise the siege of the city by Franco's forces (→20).

11. India: 29 die in clashes on the north-west frontier.

13. UK: The aircraft carrier HMS Ark Royal is launched.→

14. New York: Rodgers and Hart's musical "Babes in Arms" opens.

14. UK: The new threepenny bit comes into circulation.

16. US: A new Boeing bomber called the "Flying Fortress" is shown for the first time.

19. Berlin: Hitler says Germany is willing to talk on arms reductions.

20. London: The Budget puts 3d on income tax and a new "National Defence Contribution" tax on profits.

20. Spain: Franco declares his Phalangist movement to be the only permitted Spanish party (→21).

21. Spain: Franco's forces shell Madrid in the heaviest bombardment of the war so far (→26).

23. UK: The King unveils a memorial to King George V at Windsor.

26. Spain: Franco occupies Durango, a key town on the way to Bilbao.→

27. San Francisco: Opening of the world's longest suspension bridge, the Golden Gate Bridge, 4,200 ft long.

27. London: The King opens the National Maritime Museum at Greenwich.

30. London: 30,000 bus workers go on strike (→26/5).

30. Dublin: The new constitution is published, dropping allegiance to the Crown and renaming Eire (→21/7).

Hitler's hand in horrors of Guernica

April 27. Guernica, the cultural and spiritual home of the Basques, was destroyed yesterday by the bombers of the German air force sent to help Franco by Adolf Hitler. It was market day and the square was crowded when the bombers, Heinkel 1-11s and Junker 52s, escorted by fighters, appeared and pounded Guernica with high explosives; they then set it alight with incendiary bombs and strafed it with machine-gun fire.

Eyewitnesses told correspondents of the death that rained down on them. "They bombed and bombed and bombed," said the mayor. One reporter, who arrived in the city soon after the planes had left, said: "As we drew nearer, on both sides of the road, men, women and children were sitting, dazed.

"I saw a priest in one group. I stopped the car and went up to him. His face was blackened, his clothes in tatters. He couldn't talk, and pointed to the flames about four miles away, then whispered: "Aviones ... bombas ... mucho, mucho."

In the city soldiers were collecting charred bodies. They were sobbing like children. There were flames and smoke and grit, and the smell of burning human flesh was nauseating. Houses were collapsing into the inferno.

"It was impossible to go down many of the streets, because they were walls of flame. Debris was piled high. The shocked survivors all had the same story to tell: aeroplanes, bullets, bombs, fire."

Today, those who can are leaving Guernica, their possessions loaded into farm wagons, pulled by oxen, victims of a calculated act of terror. There were military targets in Guernica – it is a communications centre and it has a munitions factory – but there is no evidence that the German bombers aimed for them. They simply unloaded their bombs indiscriminately on this undefended town (→6/5).

A survivor of the bombing looks out on a landscape of horror and pain.

Ark Royal launched

The Ark Royal is launched.

April 20. Thousands lined the docks at Birkenhead to see the launch of the Ark Royal, Britain's aircraft carrier. The ship cost £3 million.

Green belt planned to stop city sprawl

April 1. A "green belt" around London is proposed today by the London County Council. It plans to spend £2 million buying open spaces in the home counties, partly to provide recreation and partly to curb the suburban sprawl which has characterised the 1930s. New tube lines north and west of London, plus new roads, have been followed by builders offering semi-detached houses for between £600 and £800. With the capital now housing no fewer than one in four of the total population of England and Wales, the London County Council has decided to join other local authorities in the south-east in backing a green belt to limit further growth.

Trotsky calls for the overthrow of Stalin

April 18. Leon Trotsky, the inspirer of international communism, now living in Mexico, today called for a new revolution to get rid of Joseph Stalin. Trotsky told a committee convened in Mexico, and headed by Professor John Dewey, to investigate Moscow's charges that he was conspiring with Germany and Japan to form an "anti-Soviet alliance", that Stalin and his Soviet bureaucracy had to be overthrown.

Trotsky, who has been the chief defendent in absentia in the Soviet Union's recent series of show trials, went on to say that if war came, and Russia found itself allied with Britain and France, it might emerge as capitalist, because it now teeters between socialism and capitalism. Stalin is unlikely to ignore this latest outburst (→23/5).

1937

MAY

Su	Mo	Tu	We	Th	Fr	Sa
						1
2	3	4	5	6	7	8
9	10	11	12	13	14	15
16	17	18	19	20	21	22
23	24	25	26	27	28	29
30	31					

1. London: Sunderland beat Preston North End 3-1 in the FA Cup Final.

3. New York: Margaret Mitchell wins a Pulitzer Prize for her novel "Gone with the Wind".

6. Spain: 5,000 women and children begin to be evacuated from Bilbao (→9).

7. Washington: An inquiry begins into the Hindenburg disaster (→11).

9. Spain: The rebels reach the last line of the Bilbao defences (→13).

11. Berlin: Hitler bans all flights by hydrogen-filled airships.

12. London: The BBC makes its first television outside broadcast, of King George's coronation procession (→24/8).

13. Spain: Eight crew die and 24 injured when an explosion holes the Royal Navy destroyer HMS Hunter (→16).

16. Spain: Premier Largo Caballero resigns (→18).

18. Spain: Franco is defeated at Guadalajara (→31).

20. Moscow: 44 people are executed as Japanese spies.

23. Mexico: Trotsky outlines the "Fourth International", a loose network of opponents of Stalin.

25. Rome: Mussolini tells Italy's Jews to "uphold Fascism or leave".

26. London: The bus strike ends.

26. Geneva: Egypt joins the League as its 59th member.

27. London: Stanley Baldwin bids farewell to the House of Commons.→

31. Spain: German warships bombard Almeria in retaliation for the attack on the Deutschland (→31).

31. Spain: Germany and Italy decide to withdraw from the non-intervention cordon around Spain (→3/6).

DEATH

23. US tycoon John D. Rockefeller (*8/7/1839).

Giant airship explodes

The Hindenburg: going up in smoke, dropping down to earth.

May 6. The giant airship Hindenburg exploded in a ball of fire as she came in to land in New Jersey tonight, killing at least 33 of her passengers and crew. The cause of the fire is unknown, but it is believed it may have been caused by static electricity igniting her hydrogen gas as she approached the mooring mast after a thunderstorm.

One eye witness said: "I can only compare the explosion to a set scene on the talkies. She just went in the air in bits and pieces." Within minutes the airship, which had crossed the Atlantic from Frankfurt, was reduced to a burnt-out tangle of white hot metal, as detachments of sailors from the nearby Lakehurst naval base fought to rescue passengers.

The £380,000 airship had been delayed for 12 hours by headwinds over Newfoundland. She circled the airfield waiting for a lull in the thunderstorm, and had just dropped her mooring lines from a height of about 300 feet when the disaster struck, and a flash was seen to come from her rear gondola.

In Germany Herr Hitler and Dr Goebbels have both been informed of the disaster, which came after the Hindenburg had made ten perfectly safe trips back and forward across the Atlantic (→7).

Spanish bombers hit German battleship

May 29. The German "pocket battleship" Deutschland was bombed by Spanish government planes in the harbour at Ibiza in the Balearics today. Two bombs struck the warship. One hit the side of the deck and did little damage, but the other penetrated the crew's quarters in the bow and killed 23 men. Another 83 have been wounded, 19 of them seriously.

On hearing the news Herr Hitler flew from Munich to Berlin, where he held a conference attended by Admiral Raeder, General Goering and Field Marshal von Blomberg. A statement was later issued which declared: "This criminal attack compels the German government to take measures which it will at once communicate to the Non-Intervention Committee."

The Deutschland is steaming towards Gibraltar tonight with her dead on board and her flag at half-mast (→31).

Chamberlain takes over from Baldwin as Prime Minister

May 28. Neville Chamberlair became Prime Minister today wher – as expected – Stanley Baldwir resigned in the warm afterglow o the Coronation. He is making very few cabinet changes and promise brisk and business-like conduct o the nation's affairs.

Mr Chamberlain's style of leadership may be less relaxed than tha of his phlegmatic predecessor. He i a more austere figure, keen on administrative efficiency.

On retirement Mr Baldwin ha been awarded the customary earldom. It is already widely recognised that he has been a political genius. He often appeared as a gauche operator, but somehow "Hones Stan" managed to see Britain through its two great peace-time crises of the General Strike and the Abdication. Across party lines it i agreed he has earned a rest.

Mr Chamberlain outside No. 10.

Coronation of George VI, the unlikely monarch

May 12. With all the pomp and ceremony of time-honoured tradition, King George VI and Queen Elizabeth were crowned at Westminster Abbey today, watched by people who had travelled from the farthest parts of the Empire.

It was 26 years since the Coronation of the King's father, and London has had a tremendous air of excitement for days. At 10.30am the golden coach, drawn by eight greys, left Buckingham Palace for the Abbey. It was a splendid sight with four postilions and six footmen, plus eight grooms and four Yeomen of the Guard walking along side. The King was in robes of deep red and snow-white ermine, with the oddly named Cap of Maintenance on his head.

As the carriage pulled up at the Abbey, the young Duke of Norfolk who, as Earl Marshal of England, was in charge of the arrangements, looked at his watch. Big Ben struck 11am. The Duke smiled. Everything was on time. Then came the first hitch. As the Queen's procession was about to set off up the nave it was delayed. An elderly cleric had fainted and there was delay in getting him moved.

The Queen's procession was led by Maltravers Herald Extraordinary, his uniform a dazzle of red and gold in keeping with his name. The Queen, flanked by two bishops, was smiling and relaxed in a gown of ivory satin, embroidered in pure gold thread with the emblems of the British Isles and the Dominions. Her 18ft train of purple velvet was carried by six maids-of-honour, under the observant eye of the Mistress of the Robes, the Dowager Duchess of Northumberland.

As Queen Elizabeth passed the royal box where Queen Mary stood, the older Queen curtsied. She had broken with tradition by attending; previously, Queens' dowagers did not attend the coronation of their successors.

Many saw her coming as a gesture of support for her shy son, who had succeeded in such sad circumstances. Indeed, she visited the Abbey several times in the preceding weeks offering advice from her own coronation in 1911.

The King, with a retinue of 36, was preceeded by courtiers carrying his regalia, including the Sceptre with the Cross containing the 530-carat diamond known as the Star of Africa, and flanked by the Bishops of Durham and Bath and Wells.

Looking on were his two daughters, Princess Elizabeth and Princess Margaret Rose, who sat in a box between Queen Mary and her daughter, the Princess Royal.

Then came the first words of the long service spoken by Dr Cosmo Lang, Archbishop of Canterbury: "Sirs, I here present to you King George, your undoubted King ..." The huge congregation responded, shouting in unison: "God Save King George."

As the King knelt at the altar to take the Oath there was a quiet shuffle among the bishops. The Bishop of Durham and the Bishop of Bath and Wells were to hold the words in front of the King. But neither could find them. So the Archbishop lowered his Order of Service for the King to read.

After the crowning, the King, in keeping with tradition, lowered his head and all the peers put on their coronets. The Queen was crowned with a circlet of diamonds including the legendary Koh-i-noor diamond, once said to have belonged to Queen Mumtaz Mahal in whose memory the Taj Mahal was built.

As the crown was placed on the Queen's head, all the royal ladies and the peeresses, wearing elbow-length gloves, raised their coronets to their own heads. Princess Elizabeth commented to her aunt that they all looked like swans!

The trumpets sounded. The processions reformed. Rain, which had threatened all day, held off until their Majesties had reached Buckingham Palace (→28/7).

On Buckingham Palace balcony, the newly-crowned King's solemnity contrasts with his daughters' cheerful smiles.

The King passes through Trafalgar Square on his way to the Abbey.

1937

JUNE

Su	Mo	Tu	We	Th	Fr	Sa
		1	2	3	4	5
6	7	8	9	10	11	12
13	14	15	16	17	18	19
20	21	22	23	24	25	26
27	28	29	30			

1. London: Neville Chamberlain withdraws the defence tax on profits proposed in the Budget (→16).

2. UK: Mrs G. B. Miller is the first woman owner to win the Derby at Epsom with her horse Midday Sun.

3. Spain: Rebel commander General Emilio Mola dies in a plane crash (→19).

6. Munich: Catholic youths clash with Nazis (→20).

9. Jerusalem: A Royal Commission is looking into the possibility of a divided Palestine (→7/7).

12. Moscow: Eight generals are shot as spies.→

16. London: Chancellor Sir John Simon outlines a new Defence Contribution Scheme for a five per cent profits tax.

17. UK: The play "The Great Romancer" about Dumas is causing a stir because of its lead actor, Robert Morley.

19. Spain: Bilbao falls to Franco's rebels (→26).

20. Germany: The Nazis close all Catholic schools in Bavaria (→19/7).

21. Paris: Leon Blum's Popular Front ministry resigns (→22).

22. Paris: Camille Chautemps forms a government.

26. Rome: Mussolini says Italy will back Franco in the Spanish Civil War (→27).

27. Berlin: Hitler says he is finished with collective action on the Spanish conflict (→29).

28. New York: The Guggenheim fund for art is set up.

28. Moscow: 36 more alleged "spies" are executed (→21/10).

29. London: Germany and Italy oppose Anglo-French patrols around Spain (→17/7).

DEATHS

7. US actress Jean Harlow (*3/3/11).→

18. French statesman Gaston Doumergue (*1/8/1863).

19. British author Sir James Barrie (*9/5/1860).

Eight Soviet generals face a firing squad

June 12. Joseph Stalin's Purge has reached out to the Red Army and swept away Marshal Tukhachevsky and eight other top generals and admirals. After a secret trial the military leaders were found guilty of plotting a coup d'etat and passing secrets to the Germans.

Tukhachevsky was a man of military genius and the real moderniser of the Red Army. He stood with Stalin atop the Lenin Mausoleum at the May Day parade, but was demoted 11 days later. The announcement about him and his colleagues has come as bombshell. It is believed that they showed no remorse and there were no "confessions". The Soviet press is describing them as "poisonous pygmies." Pravda declared: "The reptile of Fascist espionage has many heads but we will cut off every head and paralyse and sever every tentacle."

Tukhachevsky was wounded when he was arrested and brought to Stalin on a stretcher. After a row he was taken back to the Lubyanka prison where four other Marshals signed his death warrant (→28).

Duke of Windsor weds his beloved Wallis

The Duke and Duchess with Herman Rogers and Major Edward Metcalfe.

June 3. In the romantic setting of a chateau in a valley near Tours, Wallis Simpson married the former King today and became the Duchess of Windsor. Although hundreds of French sightseers had arrived in Tours, the ceremonies themselves were simple with few witnesses.

The first, conducted by the Mayor of Monts, was to comply with French civil law. The salon at the Chateau de Cande was decorated with two large vases of pink carnations and red peonies; the bride and groom sat in armchairs before a table covered with fawn coloured velvet embroidered in gold. The Mayor said that he represented a nation "which has always been sensitive to the charm of chivalrous unselfishness and bold gestures prompted by the dictates of the heart".

Fifteen minutes later, in the music room of the chateau, the couple were married under the rites of the Church of England by the vicar of St. Bride's, Doncaster. The room had been hastily converted into a chapel and the Duke and Duchess knelt in front of an old oak chest which served as an altar.

Later, after a buffet wedding breakfast, the newly-married couple left for their honeymoon in Austria. The Duke issued a statement which said: "After the trying times we have been through we now look forward to a happy and useful private life ..." (→22/10)

Hollywood's Harlow dies, aged only 26

Blonde bombshell Jean Harlow.

June 7. Hollywood's first "sex-goddess", Jean Harlow, has died of a kidney disease in a Los Angeles hospital at the age of 26. Actor William Powell – one of her frequent co-stars – was at her bedside. Born Harlean Carpentier in Kansas City, she first came to Hollywood with the businessman husband she had eloped with at 16; her first film part was in the war saga "Hell's Angels" (1930).

In subsequent films, like "The Public Enemy" and "Redheaded Woman", she played tough-but-alluring femmes fatales. More recently she starred in screwball comedies such as "Riffraff", but her offscreen life never matched the fun of her reel life, and she had been ill for a year.

Joe Louis captures heavyweight crown

June 22. Joe Louis, the 23-year-old "Brown Bomber" from Detroit, has become the first black world heavyweight champion since Jack Johnson lost his crown in 1915.

Though Louis found himself dumped on the canvas early in the contest, he battered the champion of two years' standing, James J. Braddock, for seven punishing rounds before knocking him out a minute into the eighth. The 31-year-old loser was so badly hurt that he had to be carried from the blood-splattered ring (→30/8).

1937

JULY

Su	Mo	Tu	We	Th	Fr	Sa
				1	2	3
4	5	6	7	8	9	10
11	12	13	14	15	16	17
18	19	20	21	22	23	24
25	26	27	28	29	30	31

2. Pacific: Aviator Amelia Earhart disappears on the last half of a round-the-world flight from California.

3. Wimbledon: American Donald Budge beats Gottfried von Cramm for the Men's Singles title; Dorothy Round beats Jadwiga Jedrzejowska for the Women's Singles title.

5. UK: The train Coronation Scot reaches Edinburgh in a record six hours from London.

7. London: Debating the Marriage Bill, the Lords cut the minimum marriage time from five to three years (→23).

8. China: Japan attacks China from the puppet empire of Manchukuo (→13).

9. UK: Henry Cotton wins the British Open Golf Championship for the second time.

10. US: Composer George Gershwin is reported to be seriously ill in Hollywood.→

13. China: Chinese and Japanese troops clash outside Peking (→8/8).

17. Spain: 600 native Moroccan rebel troops die in a Republican ambush (→3/8).

19. Munich: Opening of the "Degenerate Art" exhibition of works mainly by Germany's best modern artists (→6/8).

21. Eire: Eamon de Valera is re-elected president (→29/12).

23. London: MPs pass the Marriage Bill.

28. Belfast: A bomb explodes close to the King and Queen on their Coronation visit.

28. UK: Harold Davidson, ex-Rector of Stiffkey, is mauled by a lion at a Skegness amusement ground (→30).

30. UK: The ex-Rector of Stiffkey dies.

BIRTH

9. British artist David Hockney.

DEATHS

11. US composer George Gershwin (*26/9/1898).→

20. Italian engineer Guglielmo Marconi (*25/4/1874).

UK plans state for Jews in Palestine

July 7. To end the "irreconcilable conflict" between Jews and Arabs, the British Government today announced proposals to partition Palestine. The plan, put forward in a White Paper, is to divide the mandated territory into three parts. Two-thirds of the country would be an Arab state, and one-third would provide a national home for the Jews. The Holy cities of Jerusalem (which also contains Moslem holy places), Bethlehem and Nazareth are to be placed under permanent mandate to Great Britain.

There would be a grant of £2 million for Trans-Jordan and Arabs would be compensated. Jews reacted unfavourably (→11/8).

George Gershwin's summertime ends

The composer of "Porgy & Bess".

July 11. George Gershwin died today in Hollywood from a brain tumour, at the age of 38. He was to music what F. Scott Fitzgerald was to fiction: between them they made the Twenties the Jazz Age.

The Twenties' shows he created with George S. Kaufman, to lyrics by his brother Ira, seemed to equal Gilbert and Sullivan for the 20th Century. His latest show, "Shall We Dance?", has just been filmed with Astaire and Rogers. Songs like "The Man I Love", "Summertime" and "I Got Rhythm" may prove a more enduring legacy than his Rhapsody in Blue and "An American in Paris".

1937

AUGUST

Su	Mo	Tu	We	Th	Fr	Sa
1	2	3	4	5	6	7
8	9	10	11	12	13	14
15	16	17	18	19	20	21
22	23	24	25	26	27	28
29	30	31				

2. London: The ban on political marches in the East End imposed on June 21 is extended for six weeks (→10/10).

3. Rome: The Vatican accepts an envoy from General Franco (→25/8).

6. London: The government expels three German journalists from Britain (→9).

8. China: The Japanese occupy Peking (→14).

9. Berlin: The Nazis expel The Times' correspondent in retaliation for the expulsion of three Germans from Britain.

11. Zurich: The World Zionist Congress says it opposes Britain's plans for a partitioned Palestine (→27/9).

12. Baghdad: General Bakr Sidki Pasha, Iraq's dictator, is assassinated.

14. Shanghai: Hundreds are reported dead in a Japanese bombing raid on the city (→17).

17. Shanghai: The evacuation of British and other foreign residents begins (→19).

17. Australia: Protests take place against an alleged flood of immigrants "of the wrong type" from southern Europe.

19. London: Britain offers to mediate in the Sino-Japanese War (→26).

24. UK: The company GEC announces a new television receiver for under £50.

25. Spain: Franco's troops capture the port of Santander (→21/10).

26. China: The British ambassador to China is wounded by Japanese planes.→

29. China: The government signs a non-aggression pact with the USSR.

30. New York: Joe Louis beats Britain's Tommy Farr in his first heavyweight title defence at Madison Square Garden.

31. Paris: A government decree creates the Societe Nationale des Chemins de Fer Francais, French Railways.

BIRTH

8. US actor Dustin Hoffman.

Runner Wooderson sets mile record

Wooderson does it again.

Aug 28. Sydney Wooderson, the thin, short, bespectacled Blackheath Harrier, today set a new world record for the mile handicap race at Motspur Park, lowering the American Glenn Cunningham's three-year-old mark by 0.4 seconds to 4 minutes 06.4 seconds.

Ever since he ran the mile under 4 minutes 30 seconds as an 18-year-old, the studious-looking athlete has stirred the imagination of his many British fans, and the serious leg injury that prevented him competing in the Olympic Games last year undoubtedly robbed the Berlin 1,500 metres of even greater drama.

Sunbathing gets more popular.

Japanese bombers batter Shanghai

A Chinese baby screams for his dead mother on the tracks of Shanghai's bombed South railway station.

Aug 29. Shanghai is today experiencing all the horrors of modern war. A pall of smoke hangs over the great port, set afire by waves of Japanese aircraft dropping incendiary bombs. Air power is being used with naked ferocity to clear the way for their advancing army. In the north, Japanese troops have seized Peking.

A great battle began as Nationalist forces counter-attacked outside the city. As fires spread to the Shanghai international settlement, 2,000 British women and children were evacuated aboard the P & O liner Rajputana. A British battalion has arrived to reinforce the Settlement garrison which is in a highly exposed position.

Great damage has also been caused by Chinese planes raiding enemy positions and warships in the river. The greatest slaughter of the campaign so far came when bombs from Chinese planes attacking Japanese warships fell on an amusement park, killing over 1,000. Total civilian casualties now number more than 2,000.

Last week, as the big new Japanese offensive developed, the Chinese air force bombed one of their destroyers while the Izumo, the 9,000 ton Japanese flagship lying in the river, was torpedoed. In air battles the Chinese claim to have shot down 12 Japanese bombers raiding Shanghai and Nanking.

Today the British Government protested strongly after Sir Hugh Knatchbull-Hugessen, the British ambassador to China, was seriously wounded in a Japanese air raid. The planes machine-gunned his car, as he drove from Nanking to Shanghai, although it flew a large Union Jack. The Foreign Office has demanded a formal apology and punishment for those officers responsible (→ 6/9).

Buchenwald concentration camp opens

Aug 1. Heinrich Himmler, who was last year appointed Reichsfuhrer of the SS (Schutzstaffel) and chief of German police, has reported to Chancellor Adolf Hitler, the German Fuehrer, on his reorganisation of concentration camps.

A new establishment has been opened at Buchenwald to house prisoners considered to be enemies of the state. Changes have been made in the administration of other camps already in existence. They are located at Dachau, Sachsenhausen and Lichtenburg, which takes women prisoners. Each of these camps is under the control of Himmler and is guarded by 1,500 troopers, serving in the elite SS security force. SS Colonel Karl Koch is to take command at the new and very large camp established at Buchenwald.

It has been constructed, in the words of the official report, to achieve "functional unity and capacity". The Nazi regime has been using concentration camps for the last four years for the confinement in primitive conditions of Jews, Communists and other political suspects (→ 30/10).

Cricket's promising younger generation

Aug 30. Yorkshire today clinched cricket's county championship with a thrilling victory over Hampshire in their final match of the season. Runners-up are Middlesex for whom Patsy Hendren, in his final first-class match, scored his 170th century. Hendren was applauded all the way to the crease, but it is the new generation of cricketers who have caught the eye this season. Len Hutton of Yorkshire and Denis Compton of Middlesex promise great things for the future.

1937

SEPTEMBER

Su	Mo	Tu	We	Th	Fr	Sa
			1	2	3	4
5	6	7	8	9	10	11
12	13	14	15	16	17	18
19	20	21	22	23	24	25
26	27	28	29	30		

1. Spain: A British warship is attacked by an unidentified submarine (→ 2).

2. London: Britain calls for a conference on "piracy" in the Mediterranean (→ 8).

3. Hong Kong: 300 are reported dead after a typhoon strikes the colony.

5. Germany: The biggest ever Nazi rally marks the opening of the Nazi congress in Nuremberg.→

6. London: Japan refuses to apologise for wounding Britain's envoy to China (→ 13).

8. Rome: Mussolini rejects Britain's call for a piracy conference (→ 14).

10. UK: The TUC votes for rearmament.

13. Geneva: China appeal for League aid against the Japanese (→ 25).

14. Washington: Roosevelt admits surprise that his liberal Supreme Court nominee was once a Klansman (→ 4/10).

14. Switzerland: Italy refuses to take part in the Anti-Piracy Patrol adopted today by nine-power talks at Nyon (→ 21).

16. London: Opening of the film "Victoria the Great" starring Anna Neagle.

21. Rome: Mussolini relents and agrees to join the Piracy Conference.

25. China: The Japanese bomb the Chinese Nationalist capital Nanking, leaving a reported 200 dead (→ 28).

27. Palestine: More than 100 Arabs have been arrested following the murder yesterday of two British officials (→ 1/10).

28. Geneva: The League condemns the Japanese invasion of China.→

DEATHS

2. French founder of the modern Olympics Baron Pierre de Coubertin (*1/1/1863).

14. Czech statesman and philosopher Tomas Masaryk (*7/3/1850).

26. US singer Bessie Smith (*15/4/1894).→

Hitler calls for more "living space"

The fascist conquerors, Benito Mussolini and Adolf Hitler, look forward to ever greater victories for their respective empires.

Sept 28. The German and Italian dictators staged a massive floodlit demonstration in Berlin tonight – to announce that they believed in peace. Almost a million Germans were assembled in the Field of May, the setting for last year's Olympics. When the massive Olympic bell began to toll, searchlights swept the field before settling on the balcony where Hitler and Mussolini were standing.

"We are spinning no plans that will further split an already divided Europe," Mussolini said. "The Rome-Berlin axis is not directed against other peoples." The Duce went on to talk about "the criminal economic sanctions" imposed by the League of Nations in an attempt to cripple Italy's war effort. In spite of that, Fascist Italy had won and the "resurrected Roman Empire" was a fact.

Mussolini's Abyssinian conquest seems to have given his fellow dictator something to think about. At the Nazi party's annual Nuremberg rally earlier this month, Hitler made Germany's demand for colonies one of the main points in his speech. "Without colonies Germany's space is too small to guarantee that our people can be fed safely and continuously. The attitude of other Powers to our demand is simply incomprehensible." He called on those "other Powers" to read the signs of the times.

Hitler has often spoken of Germany's need for more territory: "Lebensraum" (living space), as he calls it. He discusses it at length in "Mein Kampf", where he criticises the Kaiser for seeking colonies in Africa. Germany, Hitler wrote, must expand in the East, largely at the expense of Russia. His Nuremberg speech suggests Italy's conquest of Abyssinia may have made him think again (→13/10).

Campbell shatters water speed record

Sept 2. The British speed ace Sir Malcolm Campbell today set a new world water speed record of 129 mph, on a run he only intended as a trial. Sir Malcolm told onlookers he was making a test run following repairs to the cooling system on Bluebird, when he took her out on to Lake Maggiore, Switzerland, but he still beat his own record time of 126.32 mph set yesterday by 3.1 mph. That speed itself was 4.64 mph better than the best time of his rival, Commodore Wood.

A large crowd cheered him as he stepped ashore. Last night at a celebration dinner a toast had been drunk to "a great English sportsman" (→28/10).

Bessie will sing the blues no more

Sept 26. Blues singer Bessie Smith has died in a car crash in Mississippi. Surrounding her death were rumours that local hospital treatment, which might have saved her, was denied because she was a Negro. Born in Chattanooga, Tennessee, around 1894 or 1898, she began to developed a rich blues voice in her late teens, together with a noted on-stage charisma. Her first songs were recorded in 1923 – including "Downhearted Blues" – and sold millions. More lately a victim of alcoholism and fickle musical tastes, she had returned to playing in the "honky tonk" bars where she began.

Chiang joins forces with Mao to oppose the Japanese threat

Sept 29. In face of the full-scale assault on China by the Japanese, General Chiang Kai-shek has been forced to come to an arrangement with his hated Communist rival Mao Tse-tung. At a meeting in Nanking the two leaders agreed that their mutually hostile armies must now unite. Only a few months ago, before full-scale war began, General Chiang rejected such co-operation. Despite the formal agreement and Mao's undertaking to dissolve his Red army and reorganise his militia, General Chiang remains suspicious. A committee will control joint military operations (→9/10).

Chinese troops at Pootung take precautions against the use of poison gas.

New arrival at the newsagents.

1937

OCTOBER

Su	Mo	Tu	We	Th	Fr	Sa
					1	2
3	4	5	6	7	8	9
10	11	12	13	14	15	16
17	18	19	20	21	22	23
24	25	26	27	28	29	30
31						

1. Palestine: Britain deports several Arab leaders.→

4. Washington: Despite his former membership of the Ku Klux Klan, Judge Hugo Black joins the Supreme Court.

6. Washington: Roosevelt condemns Japanese aggression in China (→9).

9. China: Japan launches a major offensive (→27).

12. Oxford: Lord Nuffield gives £1,000,000 to the University for a new college.

13. Berlin: Hitler pledges to defend Belgium.

14. London: The first London Motor Show opens at Earl's Court.

15. Germany: Krupp conceals arms during a visit to its factory by the Duke of Windsor.→

17. France: Rheims Cathedral is reopened and reconsecrated following its restoration after Great War damage.

18. Rome: Italy admits 40,000 Italians are aiding Franco (→6/11).

21. Moscow: 62 are executed in Stalin's latest purge.

24. UK: Jean Batten lands after a record flight from Australia of five days, 18 hours and 18 minutes.

26. London: King George opens the first Parliament of his reign.

27. Tokyo: Japan rejects a proposed conference in Brussels to settle the Sino-Japanese War.

28. US: Briton George Eyston sets a and speed record of 309 mph on the Great Salt Lake (→19/11).

30. US: Dr Joachim Prinz of Princeton University says German Jewry will be extinct within ten years (→29/11).

31. Liverpool: The first mass is sung at the city's new Roman Catholic cathedral.

DEATH

19. British scientist Lord Ernest Rutherford, 1908 Nobel Prize winner (*30/8/1871).→

Mosley struck by stone at Fascist rally

Sir Oswald Mosley leads another British Union of Fascists march.

Oct 10. A stone hit Sir Oswald Mosley on the head today, knocking the Fascist leader unconscious, as he prepared to address a crowd of 8,000 in Liverpool. Blood streaming from his temple, he was rushed to hospital.

His loudspeaker van had driven on to waste ground under a hail of bricks and bottles from a hostile crowd. Mosley was standing on the van's roof when he was hit. As supporters rushed to his aid, mounted police charged to disperse the crowd and made 15 arrests.

The meeting concluded with Fascists and Communists singing "God Save the King" – both sides giving their respective salutes of upraised palms and clenched fists.

This was the second serious incident involving Mosley and his supporters in a week. Four days ago, as Mosley led 2,700 blackshirts – 500 of them women – through South London, 111 opponents were arrested as they tried to bar the route with costers' barrows, barbed wire and overturned vehicles.

The Government has refused appeals from the Labour Party to ban "provocative" marches and rallies by the extreme right-wing, anti-Semitic party.

Jewish immigration to Palestine curbed

Oct 20. The British authorities in Palestine have published an ordinance limiting Jewish immigration. This is because of the violent reaction by the Arabs to the increasing Jewish population.

Recently, for example, there was the Arab attack on the Jewish colony at Rosh Pinah when a bus crowded with Jews was ambushed five miles outside Jerusalem. Then, after widespread outrages, the border with Syria has been closed, while in Jerusalem, patrolled by armed troops, a curfew is in force and a declaration of martial law can be expected soon; five members of the Arab Higher Committee have been arrested and deported.

Last week Arab terrorists used a landmine to destroy the Haifa-Lydda railway line, derailing a train. They also blew up a bridge. Others opened fire on a train taking the Royal Sussex Regiment to Egypt, even though it was preceded by an armoured trolley car with machine-gunners and searchlights.

Despite these incidents there is great resentment in the Jewish community at the ordinance. Its leaders insist that, as agreed, numbers ought to depend upon the country's economic capacity to absorb settlers, and, further, that the ordinance violates the mandate by discriminating against immigrants on the basis of religion (→14/11).

Duke and Duchess of Windsor in cordial meeting with Nazis

Oct 22. Flowers and cries of "Hail Edward" greeted the Duke and Duchess of Windsor as they arrived in Berlin today. Large crowds thronged the station to watch Dr Robert Ley, leader of Hitler's Labour Front, hand the Duchess a bouquet of pink and yellow roses.

Other Nazi leaders, including Hitler's adjutant, were among the party who waited on the platform to meet the couple who later met the Fuehrer himself. The Duke and Duchess are in Berlin ostensibly to "study social conditions and housing problems". Today they visited the first "National Socialist model factory", lunching with the workers before attending a concert given by the Nazi district orchestra (→5/11).

The Windsors are charmed by Hitler and delighted by Nazi Germany.

Franco tightens his grip on northern Spain

Nationalist soldiers round up Republican fighters at Somosierra.

Oct 21. Gijon, the last stronghold of the Republican forces in North Spain, surrendered to General Franco's army today, with 6,000 soldiers laying down their arms and whole battalions of the Republican army changing sides, amidst scenes of high emotion.

When the first Nationalist troops marched in, they found the inhabitants had beflagged their houses as if for a festival, every balcony displaying the red and gold Carlist colours, while some also took the precaution of flying the white flag of surrender.

Political prisoners, who had been held as hostages in floating prisons in the harbour and in a number of buildings in the town, were set free, and were at once appointed to maintain order in place of the Republican officials who had fled.

Nationalist warships captured 12 ships carrying fugitives from Gijon and a number of Republicans were taken prisoner. Among the captured ships were the destroyers Ciscar and Jose Luis Diez and some armed trawlers.

The seizure of these ships means that the Government fleet has been reduced to impotence. Franco now has complete command of the sea in Spanish waters. His troops continue to tighten their grip on the north, pushing west towards Aviles and advancing on Oviedo (→28/11).

Ernest Rutherford, atomic genius, dies

Oct 19. Lord Rutherford, one of the greatest physicists of the twentieth century, died today in London at the age of 66. Born in New Zealand, he had been professor of physics at Cambridge since 1919.

Rutherford's great discoveries were all connected with the atom. He helped to elucidate the nature of radioactivity; he discovered that atoms are mostly empty space, with nearly all their mass concentrated in a tiny dense nucleus; and he was the first to transmute atoms artificially, by bombarding them with radioactive particles.

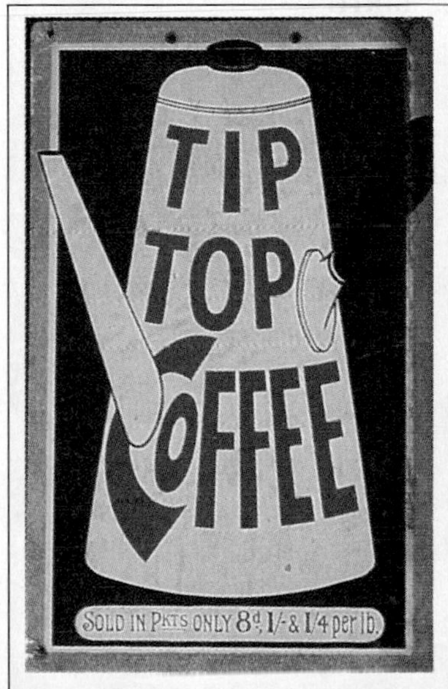

1937

NOVEMBER

Su	Mo	Tu	We	Th	Fr	Sa
	1	2	3	4	5	6
7	8	9	10	11	12	13
14	15	16	17	18	19	20
21	22	23	24	25	26	27
28	29	30				

1. London: The government says the BBC is to begin broadcasting in Spanish, Portuguese and Arabic.

3. Danzig: The police seize Jewish bank deposits.

5. France: The Duke of Windsor cancels a US trip for fear of hostility.

6. Rome: Italy signs the anti-Communist pact between Germany and Japan.

7. Moscow: 1,000,000 people parade on the 20th anniversary of the Revolution.

9. China: The Japanese take Shanghai (→6/12).

11. London: A Coal Commission is envisaged under the Coal Bill, published today.

12. UK: "Out of Africa", by Danish writer Karen Blixen, is published.

14. Jerusalem: Six Arabs and a Jew die in religious clashes.

17. Berlin: Lord Halifax, Lord President of the Council, arrives for talks with Hitler on Sudetenland Germans (→21).

19. US: George Eyston breaks his own month-old land speed record on the Great Salt Lake, achieving 311.42 mph.

19. London: Typhoid breaks out in the suburbs.

21. Berlin: Lord Halifax leaves after "frank and comprehensive" talks.

23. New York: Opening of John Steinbeck's play "Of Mice and Men".

27. UK: Steve Donoghue, many times champion jockey, rides in his last race.

28. Spain: Franco tells the government to surrender by December 12 or face a massive offensive (→21/12).

29. London: 999 is Scotland Yard's emergency number from 8 am today.

DEATHS

6. British actor Sir Johnston Forbes-Robertson (*16/1/1853).

9. British statesman James Ramsay MacDonald, first Labour PM 1924, PM again 1929-35 (*12/10/1866).→

Ramsay MacDonald dies, despised by the party he led

Mr MacDonald after he resigned.

Nov 10. The House of Commons paid moving tributes today to Ramsay MacDonald, who died at sea yesterday. The life of Britain's first Labour Prime Minister – now reviled and rejected by the party he nurtured and then betrayed – ended on a voyage to America.

The illegitimate son of a Highland farm worker, he died on his way to the West. Before embarking, he said that he was leaving in search of rest. He spoke of Tir nan Og, the Valhalla land of harmony and eternal youth, which, according to an ancient Celtic legend he heard from his grandmother, lies to the West.

Neville Chamberlain, the Prime Minister, eulogised Mr MacDonald's achievements in international affairs. Speaking for Labour, Mr Attlee skated round the controversial final phase of his old leader's career. He spoke instead of how, in the earlier fullness of his powers, he had fought against heavy odds for socialism.

The House was engulfed in a wave of emotion, forbearance and sympathy. Ramsay MacDonald is gone, but the Labour Party is still his monument. His career will rank as one of the great political tragedies of the century. A few of his former party comrades intend to go to his funeral – but only a few.

Non-Nazi parents will lose their children

Nov 29. German parents risk having their children taken from them if they are not sufficiently rigorous in drilling Nazism into them. Hitler insists there is no room for independence in the rearing of children. "Your child belongs to us already," he told a critic soon after becoming Chancellor. In future, every child would grow up knowing only Nazi values, he said.

Now a judge has laid it down as a matter of law. A Christian pacifist family at Waldenberg in Silesia refused to teach their children the Nazi ideology and were taken to court. The judge said: "The law as a racial and national instrument entrusts German parents with the education of their children only on condition that they educate them in the fashion that the nation and the state expect."

The judge ruled that the parents were creating an environment in which the children would grow up "enemies of the state". He ordered the children to be made wards of the state.

In his first few years of power, Hitler avoided confrontation with the churches, and in July 1933 signed a concordat with the Vatican, which specifically safeguarded the Catholic Youth Association. Three years later he outlawed it and ordered that all German youth must be reared "physically, intellectually and morally in the spirit of National Socialism".

Commons go-ahead for air raid shelters

Nov 16. MPs today voted in favour of a plan for air raid shelters to be erected in most of Britain's towns and cities, although Labour were against it, fearing it would mean big rises in the rates. Winston Churchill, a supporter of shelters for three years, told the Commons that they were "indispensable". Well-organised precautions would mean air attacks on Britain would not be worthwhile, he said.

Trials on different types of shelters are already going ahead, following experiments at Shoeburyness. A full scale model of a London street, complete with electric mains, gas and water supplies, was built at the Essex site, and semi-armour-piercing bombs dropped on it to see what the effect was.

The Under-Secretary for Home Affairs, Geoffrey Lloyd, told MPs it would generally be better for people to stay in their homes, although shelters would be constructed in built-up areas, and two million free sand bags were being provided to local authorities. He revealed that the Government had already drawn up plans for the evacuation of London if necessary.

This Chinese family was caught in the crossfire near Shanghai: the man is dying in his wife's arms. Their child does not understand.

1937

DECEMBER

Su	Mo	Tu	We	Th	Fr	Sa
			1	2	3	4
5	6	7	8	9	10	11
12	13	14	15	16	17	18
19	20	21	22	23	24	25
26	27	28	29	30	31	

1. Tokyo: Japan recognises Franco's regime (→21).

2. London: General Viscount Gort is made Chief of the Imperial General Staff.

6. China: The Japanese reach the outskirts of Nanking (→13).

8. London: Joseph Kennedy is made US ambassador.

10. Glasgow: 34 die and and 92 are injured when an express train crashes in a blizzard.

10. Stockholm: Nobel Prizes go to Clinton Davisson (US) and Sir George Thomson (UK, Physics); Sir Walter Haworth (UK) and Paul Karrer (Switzerland, Chemistry); Albert von Szent-Gyorgi (Hungary, Medicine); and Roger Martin du Gard (France, Literature). Peace Prize awarded in Oslo to Viscount Edgar Cecil (UK).→

11. Geneva: Italy leaves the League.

13. China: The Japanese army occupies Nanking.→

17. London: Publication of "Spanish Testament" by Arthur Koestler.→

21. Spain: Republicans capture Franco's stronghold of Teruel.

25. New York: Toscanini conducts his first radio broadcast.

29. Dublin: The new constitution comes into force; the republic is called Eire.

BIRTH

21. US actress Jane Fonda.

DEATHS

20. German commander Erich von Ludendorff (*9/4/1865).

28. French composer Maurice Ravel (*7/3/1875).→

HITS OF 1937

A nice cup of tea.

September in the Rain.

The folks who live on the hill.

QUOTE OF THE YEAR

"Holiday with pay! Holiday with play! A week's holiday for a week's wage."

Billy Butlin, slogan for his holiday camps, 1937.

Britain furious with Japan for sinking Royal Navy ships

Dec 22. The British Government is demanding the punishment of Japanese commanders responsible for recent attacks on British ships on the Yangtse river. In a note of protest to Tokyo, it insisted that "adequate punishment of those responsible is the only method by which further outrages can be prevented". Japan had offered "profound apologies" but that was not considered enough, as earlier promises of preventive measures had obviously not been effective.

Ten days ago at Wuhu, Japanese planes and ground forces attacked a tug, HMS Ladybird, with British diplomats and naval officers on board. A rating was killed and another badly wounded. Field artillery then opened up on merchant ships nearby, hitting one. A Royal Navy officer who protested was told by the apologetic Japanese commander that he had orders to fire on any ship moving in the river.

In another incident above Nanking, where British merchant ships were concentrated in a designated safety zone, attacks were made upon them and on two accompanying warships. Tokyo also admitted sinking the US navy gunboat Panay and two tankers. Five Americans were killed and others wounded. The spokesman blandly explained they were mistaken for Chinese vessels.

Viscount Cecil wins Nobel Peace Prize

Dec 10. This year's winner of the Nobel Peace Prize is Viscount Cecil of Chelwood, president of the League of Nations Council. In 1919, as Under-Secretary for Foreign Affairs, Lord Cecil helped to draft the League of Nations Covenant and was the British representative at various disarmament conferences. The Prize is the latest of many honours that have been bestowed on the former cabinet minister. A recipient of the Woodrow Wilson Peace Prize, he was recently made an honorary Doctor of Law from Columbia University.

Death of Ravel, grand old man of French composers

Dec 27. The French composer Maurice Ravel – a major figure of 20th-century European music – has died in Paris at the age of 62. Earlier this month Ravel, who suffered from aphasia, underwent brain surgery.

Ravel began to study piano at the age of seven and harmony at 11. In 1889, when he was 14, he entered the Paris Conservatoire, where he remained until 1905. During this period he composed some of his most famous works, including "Miroirs" and "Sonatine".

Of Ravel's purely orchestral works, the "Rapsodie espagnole" (1907) and "Bolero" are the best known and reveal his mastery of instrumentation. His most famous opera, "L'Enfant et les Sortileges", appeared in 1925. Throughout his life Ravel strived for perfection of form and style.

Human ancestor is unearthed in Java

Dec 10. Parts of the skull of one of man's ancestors, who lived a million years ago, have been discovered on the island of Java. The remains are twice as old as those of Pithecanthropus erectus, also from Java, previously the earliest known "missing link" between the apes and Homo Sapiens – the holy grail of all palaeontologists.

The remains of Java man consist of a lower jaw, a few teeth and a badly cracked top to a skull. The teeth are very like those from primitive humans, but the lack of a fully developed mastoid process near the ear is a feature more ape-like than human.

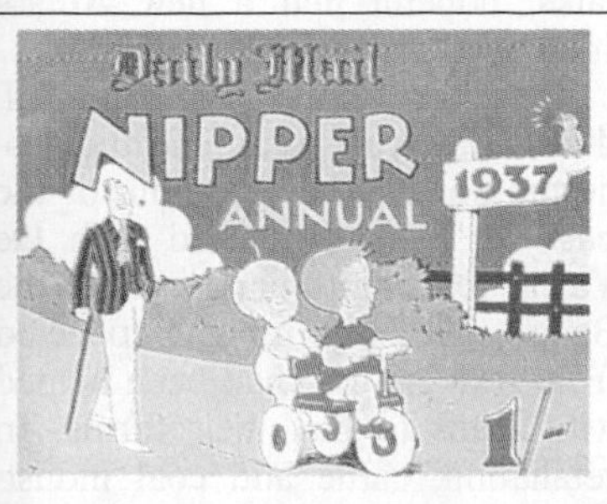

Arts: Nazis exhibit "Degenerate Art"

Picasso portrays Hitler's bombardment of the Basque capital of Guernica in all its violence and terror.

A full-scale attack on modern art – "a decadent by-product of Bolshevik Jewish corruption" – was launched by Hitler when he opened a new art gallery, the Haus der Kunst, in Munich. A crowd of 30,000 heard him blame the decadence of German art before the Nazis on Jewish art dealers and critics, who promoted "something new at any price".

He added: "We had Futurism, Expressionism, Realism, Cubism, even Dadaism. Could insanity go further? There were pictures with green skies and purple seas. There were paintings which could only be due to abnormal eyesight."

Herr Hitler, himself a one-time painter of conventional street scenes, went on to threaten that people who see things in such ways should be dealt with under the programme for sterilising the insane.

To demonstrate just what the Fuehrer disapproves of so strongly, the Haus der Kunst next day showed an exhibition of "Degenerate Art". It included the work of the Expressionists **Emil Nolde**, all of whose paintings have been removed from German galleries, and **Ernst Ludwig Kirchner**, now in exile.

Also condemned are **Franz Marc**, of the Blue Rider group, famous for his blue and red horses, **Max Beckmann**, stripped of his Frankfurt professorship, and the sculptor **Ernst Barlach**, over 300 of whose statues have been removed.

The centre-piece of the exhibition is the anti-war horror picture, "The Trench", by **Otto Dix**, also a satirical painter of pre-Nazi nightlife, who has been sacked from Dresden academy. Others under the Nazi ban are **Oskar Kokoschka** and the brilliant caricaturist of militarism and Nazism, **George Grosz**, who escaped to America.

Art has struck back at Fascism in Spain with the showing of **Picasso's** "Guernica", the sensation of a Paris exhibition. Within weeks of the German bombing, Picasso had produced his immense nightmare image of the atrocity.

The first artist to die for his views in Spain was the non-combatant playwright **Federico Garcia Lorca**. He was arrested in Granada after it fell to the Falangists and executed in secret. The revered philosopher **Miguel de Unamuno**, denounced them to their faces for their slogan, "Viva la Muerte" (Long live Death) before he died at Salamanca.

The Civil War has attracted many writers to Spain, some to fight, like **Andre Malraux**, who raised a force of Great War pilots and machines, or to act as observers. **Ernest Hemingway**, aficionado of the bullfight, is sending vivid despatches from Madrid under shellfire to an American news agency, while **George Orwell** has joined an anarchist brigade. Before he left he reviewed "Spanish Testament" by **Arthur Koestler**, correspondent for the News Chronicle, who stayed on in Malaga after it fell to Franco, was jailed under sentence of death and only saved from execution by pressure from Britain.

The war inspired Joan Miro...

and a host of lesser poster artists.

1938

JANUARY

Su	Mo	Tu	We	Th	Fr	Sa
						1
2	3	4	5	6	7	8
9	10	11	12	13	14	15
16	17	18	19	20	21	22
23	24	25	26	27	28	29
30	31					

1. London: Gracie Fields gets a CBE in the New Year's Honours; Lord Nuffield is made a viscount.

3. London: The government says all schoolchildren are to be issued with gas masks.→

3. London: The BBC starts its first foreign language service, in Arabic.

4. Bucharest: All Jews in Rumania are banned from employing women under the age of 40 (→16).

5. Madrid: Civilians are told to leave within 30 days (→12).

9. Germany: Opening of the first "Ahnenhalle" "churches" dedicated to Germany, the Germans and Hitler.

12. Spain: Franco's provisional regime is recognised by Austria and Hungary (→19).

14. Paris: Premier Chautemps resigns; Leon Blum is asked to form a government (→18).

16. Bucharest: Rumania wants to expel 500,000 Jews (→10/2).

17. Moscow: Mikhail Kalinin is elected president of the USSR's Supreme Praesidium.

17. London: Eamon de Valera arrives for talks with Neville Chamberlain (→19).

18. Paris: Blum fails to form a government; Chautemps becomes premier again (→13/3).

19. Barcelona: 200 people are reported killed in an air raid by Franco's forces (→30).

24. London: The BBC broadcasts television's first opera, Wagner's "Tristan und Isolde" (→31/5).

26. Australia: The Dominion celebrates the 150th anniversary of European settlement (→25/10).

27. Leicester: The city carries out a mock wartime "black-out" exercise.

30. Barcelona: Many civilians are reported to be dying in air raids by Franco's Nationalists (→15/2).

BIRTH

31. Dutch Queen Beatrix of Orange-Nassau.

Hi-ho, hi-ho it's off to a film we go

Film-maker Walt Disney contemplates models of the lovable seven dwarfs.

Jan 14. People said that cartoon films would never be more than short fillers between pictures, but Walt Disney has proved them all wrong with his first, feature-length cartoon, "Snow White and the Seven Dwarfs". The film was a big gamble, requiring two million drawings and three years' work, but the world seems captivated by the result. The seven dwarfs – Happy, Sleepy, Bashful, Sneezy, Grumpy, Dopey and Doc – have been taken to everyone's hearts, especially for their choruses "Whistle While You Work" and "Hi-Ho, Hi-Ho, It's Off To Work We Go".

Snow White herself has two poignant ballads in the Frank Churchill score, "I'm Wishing" and "Some Day My Prince Will Come". There is hardly a dry eye in the cinema when he does – waking her from death-like sleep in the glass coffin with a kiss – even though the audience is watching no more than an animated drawing.

Disney has never found room for sentiment before in the comic mayhem of his Silly Symphonies, which began with Mickey Mouse in 1928, and went on to introduce the ingenious Pluto, the dumb Goofy and the irascible Donald Duck. Now he plans to follow up Snow White and the lucrative by-products – nursery books and toys – with more full-length fairy stories (→7/2).

Children at a council residential school near Windsor practise gas-mask drill, as is compulsory for all children under a new law.

Freud consciously arrives in London

Jan 6. Sigmund Freud, founder of psychoanalysis, arrived in London early this morning. The ferry train was switched to another platform so that the frail 82-year-old could avoid the press. Special permission has been given for Freud, his family and some of his students to live and work in London, which will now replace Vienna as the home of the psychoanalytical group.

The Nazis have been persecuting Freud for some months now, both because he is a Jew and because of his ideas. He was several times visited by the Gestapo and his exit visa was only obtained after the intervention of the American President Franklin Roosevelt (→23/9/39).

Psychoanalyst Sigmund Freud.

Optimistic end to Anglo-Irish talks

Jan 19. Eamon de Valera, now styled "Taoiseach" under the new Irish Constitution, left London last night for Dublin after two days of talks, hopeful that a new Anglo-Irish agreement will be signed.

There are hopes in Whitehall that it will bring to an end the economic war that has gone on for the past six years. It started with De Valera refusing to hand over to the British Treasury money collected from farmers who had been helped with loans to buy their farms. In retaliation, cattle and coal industries were hit by high tariffs (→25/4).

1938

FEBRUARY

Su	Mo	Tu	We	Th	Fr	Sa
		1	2	3	4	5
6	7	8	9	10	11	12
13	14	15	16	17	18	19
20	21	22	23	24	25	26
27	28					

1. London: The BBC's television service will be one and a half hours on weekday evenings, one hour on Sundays (→ 17).

1. Italy: Italian troops adopt the German-style goose-step.

4. Berlin: Hitler sacks or moves 40 senior army officers.→

4. Berlin: Joachim von Ribbentrop becomes Foreign Minister.

7. London: British film censors give "Snow White and the Seven Dwarfs" an "A" certificate.

10. Rumania: King Carol ousts anti-Semitic premier Octavian Goga and becomes dictator (→ 18/4).

14. Germany: Hitler tells Austrian Chancellor Schuschnigg to free all Nazis and appoint a pro-Nazi minister (→ 16).

15. Spain: Franco recaptures Teruel and advances towards the coast (→ 23/3).

16. Austria: Goering is to visit Vienna to consolidate the pact with Germany (→ 16).

16. New York: Toscanini withdraws from the Salzburg Festival in protest at Austria's deal with Hitler (→ 20).

17. London: John Baird demonstrates a large-screen prototype colour television.

19. Vienna: Schuschnigg tells Austrian Jews they have nothing to fear (→ 20).

20. Berlin: Hitler demands the right of self-determination for Germans in Austria and Czechoslovakia (→ 24).

24. US: The first nylon-based products go on sale in New Jersey: toothbrushes (→ 20/2/39).

24. Vienna: Schuschnigg vows to defend Austria's independence (→ 27).

25. Oxford: Philip Toynbee is elected Oxford Union president; Balliol student Edward Heath is Union librarian.

27. Austria: Troops surround Graz to prevent a march by Austrian Nazis (→ 1/3).

Eden quits over appeasing Il Duce

Eden (l.) with Lord Halifax.

Feb 21. Anthony Eden resigned tonight from the post of Foreign Secretary. He told Mr Chamberlain: "I have become increasingly conscious of differences between us."

The Foreign Secretary has resented the Prime Minister's action in talking personally to the Italian Ambassador Signor Grandi, instead of leaving that to the Foreign Office. Mr Chamberlain is ready to recognise Italian annexation of Abyssinia in return for an unwritten agreement on withdrawal of Italian volunteers from Spain.

Mr Eden considers that the Prime Minister is too anxious to please both Hitler and Mussolini, and that this is dangerous (→ 2/5).

Sexual smear on fired Nazi generals

Feb 10. Adolf Hitler has crushed opposition among the officer corps of the German army by sacking two leading generals and appointing himself Supreme Commander of the armed forces. The two army chiefs have each been smeared by sexual innuendoes; it is said that the Field Marshal Werner von Blomberg married a former prostitute and that General Werner von Fritsch is a homosexual.

1938

MARCH

Su	Mo	Tu	We	Th	Fr	Sa
		1	2	3	4	5
6	7	8	9	10	11	12
13	14	15	16	17	18	19
20	21	22	23	24	25	26
27	28	29	30	31		

1. Austria: 20,000 Nazis defy the government and march in the city of Graz (→ 9).

3. London: The government will spend £106.5 million on defence this year, as against £82 million in 1937 (→ 7).

4. Prague: Czech premier Milan Hodza says Czechoslovakia will defend itself.→

7. London: Chamberlain defends Britain's rapid rearmament programme.→

9. Vienna: Schuschnigg calls for a plebiscite on Austrian independence (→ 11).

11. Vienna: Schuschnigg resigns; pro-Nazi Arthur Seyss-Inquart succeeds (→ 11).

11. Austria: German troops invade on Seyss-Inquart's invitation (→ 13).

13. Paris: Leon Blum becomes premier following Chautemps' resignation on the 10th (→ 8/4).

13. Vienna: A "Reunification Act" is decreed, recognising the "Anschluss" Germany's annexation of Austria.→

17. London: Flogging should be abolished, a committee recommends (→ 26/6/39).

18. Vienna: The murderer of Dollfuss is to be reburied with full Nazi honours (→ 26).

23. Spain: Franco advances towards Catalonia as bombing of Barcelona continues (→ 3/4).

25. UK: Mrs Marion Scott's Battleship wins the Grand National at Aintree (→ 1/6).

26. Berlin: Goering warns Jews to quit Austria (→ 6/4).

30. UK: £11 million is to be spent on new RAF aero dromes (→ 30/1/39).

31. London: Plans for a National Theatre in South Kensington, designed by Lutyens, are unveiled.

BIRTH

17. Soviet-born ballet dancer Rudolf Nureyev (†6/1/93).

DEATH

1. Italian poet and soldier Gabriele d'Annunzio (*12/3/1863).

Superior equipment winning for Franco

March 23. General Franco's troops attacked all along the eastern front today, relentlessly pushing the battered government forces back towards Catalonia. The Nationalists claim to have captured thousands of prisoners as well as large quantities of war material.

They used smoke screens for the first time in this war to win control of Tardienta and Sangarrene on the Aragon front. Large numbers of new tanks and field guns were used by the Nationalists with little reply from the government guns, while in the air Franco's planes were obviously superior (→ 19/4).

The Fascists' angel of peace!

Passenger aircraft are nobody's baby

March 8. A big shake-up in British aviation was ordered by the Government today, following fears that the poor record of Imperial Airways was endangering Britain's preeminent place in passenger flight.

The state-subsidised airline has been ordered to reorganise the way it is run and share out some of its routes with British Airways. It has been told to concentrate on routes to the Empire rather than Europe. A Government report says there is "extreme disquiet" over civil aviation, with the supply of passenger aircraft "nobody's baby" and all efforts going into the production of warplanes (→ 20/10).

Austrians cheer as Hitler marches in

Exultant crowds greet the German Nazis as they march through Vienna, capital of Hitler's native land.

March 14. Adolf Hitler drove into Vienna today amid scenes of tumultuous enthusiasm. The church bells pealed in welcome to the German dictator, who has made the once independent Austria just another province of Germany.

Wearing the brown uniform of his Storm Troopers, Hitler stood upright in his open car, giving the Fascist salute to the wildly cheering crowd, which watched from every possible vantage point.

Young Nazis attempted to break through the police cordon shouting: "We want to see our Fuehrer. Hitler. Hitler." Young girls in national dress threw flowers into his car. Older people wept with joy. The crowds here, as along most of the route, were composed mainly of lower-middle-class people. Passing slowly between the masses of cheering people, the procession, headed by tanks and followed by field guns, arrived at the Hotel Imperial at 5.45pm. The hotel had been requisitioned for Hitler's party and emptied of its guests.

He entered the hotel to appear shortly afterwards on the balcony, where he took the salute while German and Austrian troops marched past. Then he withdrew, but the crowd in the square cheered so frenziedly that he came out on the balcony again before retiring to talk with Austrian officials.

Still the crowd yelled for him until he reappeared with the aged Austrian General Krauss to promise that "the German nation will never again be rent apart". Thus Hitler returned to the capital of his native land, where he had so long lived in poverty and obscurity, a capital which, until today, had rejected his political theories. Now he is the absolute ruler of an empire of 74 million people including the six million whom he added at the stroke of a pen last night.

Tonight he was given a welcome from his supporters such as few Habsburg Emperors ever had. It was an impressive demonstration of enthusiasm. It was also an impressive demonstration of German organisational ability.

Nazi supporters were brought into Vienna from as far away as Czechoslovakia to cheer and salute and cry "Heil Hitler" (→10/4).

Soviet show trials end in the death of 18 top commissars

March 15. One of the most sensat ional of the Moscow show trials ha ended with the execution of some o the highest-ranking Soviet figures including Nikolai Bukharin, whon Lenin once called the "darling" o the Bolshevik Party. Eighteen o the 21 confessed to incredibl crimes of treason and were shot i the Lubyanka prison.

Among those standing trial charged with collaborating wit foreign powers to dismember th USSR and overthrow socialism were Alexei Rykov, former prem ier, and Genrikh Yagoda, onetim head of the secret police and in stigator of the purges which hav swept away thousands in the pas three years.

Stalin puts the past behind him.

"Spring cleaning" of Austrian Jews

March 18. A pogrom, called "the great spring cleaning" by the Nazi newspapers, is being carried out at great speed in Austria. Jews are being excluded from their professions, Jewish judges have been dismissed, shops have been forced to put up placards saying "Jewish concern". Theatres and music-halls have been "spring cleaned" and among the artists Vienna will know no more are Richard Tauber and Max Reinhardt (→19/6).

Chamberlain pledges to defend France

March 24. Britain is ready to go to war to defend France and Belgium against unprovoked aggression, but is not guaranteeing automatically to fight to protect Czechoslovakia. Mr Chamberlain made this momentous policy statement in the House of Commons today.

The Prime Minister added, however, that if Czechoslovakia is attacked "it is well within the bounds of probability that other countries would almost immediately be involved". Although tortuously worded this is his second strong statement this month. He has already spoken about "the almost terrifying power" which Britain is building with the rearmament programme.

In Berlin there was guarded reaction to the speech and the German news agency delayed issue of the text. Officials expressed annoyance that Britain intends to keep a close watch on the development of relations between Germany and Czechoslovakia. Nazi leaders say outsiders have no right to interfere. They insist that the problem of German minorities is private.

Rebel pastor sent to Nazi death camp

March 4. Pastor Niemoeller, the German Confessional Church leader, was today sent to the Sachsenhausen concentration camp for "re-education". There he will join 3,000 inmates under the "Death's Head" battalion of the SS. The pastor, a former U-boat commander, has become a focus of resistance to Nazi ideas. The German court released him with a fine of only £180, but he was immediately rearrested, on leaving the court (→30/10/39).

1938

APRIL

Su	Mo	Tu	We	Th	Fr	Sa
					1	2
3	4	5	6	7	8	9
10	11	12	13	14	15	16
17	18	19	20	21	22	23
24	25	26	27	28	29	30

1. London: Britain and the US abandon the London naval treaty to allow the building of battleships.

3. Spain: Franco takes Lerida, one of the principal towns in Catalonia (→ 14).

4. London: All Britons will be measured for gas masks, the government announces.

6. Vienna: Key Jewish figures in the community are sent to Dachau concentration camp (→ 7).

7. Vienna: The Nazis seize Rothschild's Bank; Baron Rothschild is arrested.

7. UK: The police recommend that all bicycles should be fitted with rear lights (→ 9/5).

8. Paris: Blum resigns as premier following the defeat of his radical budget; Edouard Daladier takes over (→ 12).

10. London: Unity Mitford causes a disturbance by wearing a swastika at a socialist rally in Hyde Park (→ 1/5).

12. Paris: Daladier gets sweeping powers to build up French defences (→ 24/11).

16. Rome: An Anglo-Italian Pact is signed (→ 2/5).

18. Bucharest: King Carol arrests 2,000 Nazis for plotting a coup (→ 22/9/39).

21. Dublin: Douglas Hyde is elected Eire's first president.

26. India: 26 people die in riots at Mysore.

26. London: The Budget raises income tax; the top rate is 5/6d in the pound (→ 27/9/39).

28. London: A committee says workers should get a week's paid holiday.

30. London: Preston North End beat Huddersfield Town 1-0 in the FA Cup Final.

BIRTH

15. Italian actress Claudia Cardinale.

DEATHS

8. US jazz musician Joe "King" Oliver (*11/5/1885).

12. Russian bass Feodor Chaliapin (*13/2/1873).

Franco's forces divide Republicans in two

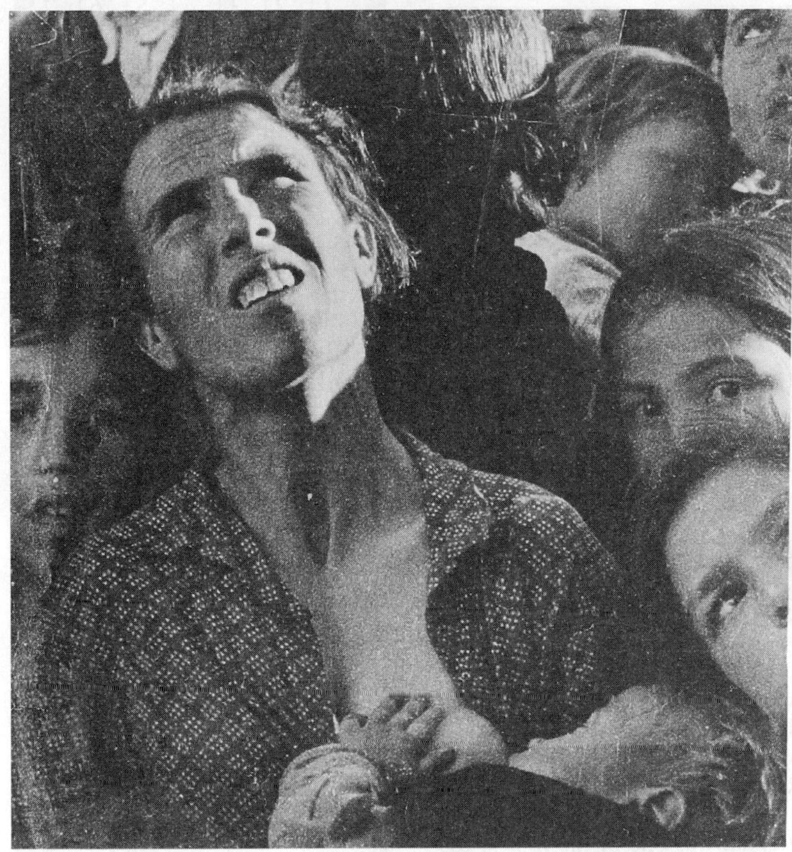

Even as a Spanish mother's frightened eyes scan the skies, new life grows.

April 19. General Franco's troops have won a stunning victory in Catalonia, capturing Vinaroz and other towns along the coast between Valencia and Barcelona, cutting Republican Spain in two. Franco believes that the war is effectively over and in a broadcast urged the Republicans to surrender.

He said he had beaten "the Reds" but bore "no hostile sentiments towards other nations. We are fighting purely for our civilisation. We do not believe in a democratic liberal regime for the damage it has done to Spain is very great."

Desperate efforts were made by the Republican forces to prevent Franco's advance to the sea. Batches of unarmed recruits were sent to the front with orders to take over the rifles of the troops they relieved.

The American contingent of the International Brigade, fighting as the Lincoln-Washington Battalion, performed heroically in the battle before Tortosa where they held up the Nationalist forces, forcing them to divert their attack further south. But they suffered terribly in the fighting in which they faced tanks, guns and bombers (→ 3/7).

Football pools condemned as a menace

April 25. Britain's football pools came under fire as tradesmen joined with Baptists and Post Office workers to condemn the country's biggest gambling industry.

A Worthing butcher complained to the National Chamber of Trade's conference that his women customers were buying cheap foreign meat "to save money for the pools". The Baptist Union condemned the "phenomenal growth" of the pools industry which is "injurious to moral sense and healthy sport".

Sub-postmasters were asking for extra payments for handling football coupons, with some sub-offices handling up to 7,000 coupons weekly. One sub-postmaster said that the Government should run the pools themselves – and then they could spend the profits on giving a better standard of living to post office workers (→ 5/5).

Navy bases ceded in Irish treaty

April 25. Eire wins big defence and financial concessions under the Anglo-Irish Agreement, the Prime Minister told the Commons today.

Eire is to get the naval bases denied her in the 1921 Treaty; tariffs imposed by Britain since 1932 are to be eased, or abolished; the Irish are to remove their duty on British coal; and they will make one final payment of £10 million to Britain for moneys advanced to Irish farmers to buy out their landlords. This all amounts to a saving for Ireland of about £140 million.

The naval bases at Cobh and Berehaven in Co. Cork and Lough Swilly in Co. Donegal are being handed over with all their buildings, ammunition and armaments.

There is no agreement about Royal Navy access to them in time of war, as it is understood in Whitehall that this must come from the Irish. Ironically, Home Rule faltered in 1914 over the need for the ports to be fully available to Britain in time of war, and when the independence treaty was finally signed the ports were excluded.

The British have long found de Valera difficult, but this time he and the PM got on well and Mrs Chamberlain's lunch party overran the allotted time by over an hour. On returning to his hotel, de Valera was congratulated by a waiting visitor, Joseph P. Kennedy, the US ambassador.

GERMANY
the Land of Music

The refined view of herself that Germany wishes to project.

Referendum says 99% support Anschluss

"One People. One Reich. One Fuehrer" : Austria agrees with Hitler.

April 10. Herr Hitler has scored a sweeping triumph in the plebiscite on the annexation of Austria, which was held throughout Germany and Austria today. Late tonight it was officially announced that 99.75 per cent of the votes cast in Austria were in favour of the union with Germany.

Hitler recorded his vote in a second-class waiting room at Berlin station on his return from Vienna, where he had made his final election speech on Saturday. It was probably unnecessary, judging by the scenes in the polling booths.

It would have taken a courageous man or woman to vote "No" in a room hung with Swastika flags and filled with Storm Troopers. After making their cross, voters were decorated with a gilt badge showing Hitler's head surrounded by the words: "One People. One Reich. One Fuehrer."

Cardinal Innitzer, Archbishop of Vienna, was one of the first to cast his vote. He gave the Hitler salute as he entered and left the polling booth and proudly wore his "One Fuehrer" badge.

Even before the final result was known, torchlight processions were formed in Vienna. The streets were filled with excited crowds who gathered round the loud-speakers, greeting the "Yes" total with cheers and the figure for the "No" vote with derisive laughter.

Jews were forbidden to vote and threatened with severe penalties if they tried to do so (→ 17/8).

Anglo-French pact to defend Czechs

April 29. Top-level Anglo-French talks ended in London tonight with a vague new promise to defend Czechoslovakia. A communique said that Britain, already pledged to preservation of French integrity, is bound to give support if France fights to resist German aggression against the Czechs.

The British and French prime ministers agreed on an early joint approach to Herr Hitler. They want the German leader to understand that invasion of Czechoslovakia – ostensibly in defence of that country's German-speaking minority – must lead to war.

The French Premier, M. Daladier, said: "Our countries have never been closer." The communique stated that improvement in relations with Italy is important. This is interpreted in Whitehall as meaning that Anglo-French diplomacy will now be aimed at discouraging Signor Mussolini from making any far-reaching military cooperation agreement with Germany. It is thought that the Italian leader is undecided about that (→ 12/6).

1938

MAY

Su	Mo	Tu	We	Th	Fr	Sa
1	2	3	4	5	6	7
8	9	10	11	12	13	14
15	16	17	18	19	20	21
22	23	24	25	26	27	28
29	30	31				

1. London: Fascists are attacked after a Mosleyite meeting.

3. Rome: Hitler meets Mussolini amid great ceremony (→ 7).

4. Rome: The Vatican acknowledges Franco as leader of Spain (→ 16).

5. London: MPs approve the Anglo-Irish agreement.

7. Rome: Hitler and Mussolini pledge lasting friendship.

9. London: Scotland Yard says it is to start using police dogs.

10. UK: Thomas Cook is offering eight days on the French Riviera this summer for £8/17/6d.

11. UK: Refrigerators are reduced in price, to £22.

12. London: MPs call for an enquiry into the nation's air defences (→ 30/1/39).

14. Berlin: England footballers give the Nazi salute before their match with Germany, which they win 6-3.

16. Rome: The Pope and Franco exchange envoys.

17. London: Six die and 60 are hurt in a tube crash at Charing Cross station.

18. Vienna: The Nazis introduce compulsory physical exercise (→ 25).

20. Prague: The government orders 400,000 troops to the Austro-German border (→ 30).

22. Italy: The volcano Stromboli erupts.

24. Jerusalem: A curfew is imposed following riots (→ 25/7).

25. Austria: Hitler makes the small town of Braunau, his birthplace, a city (→ 7/6).

27. Dublin: De Valera calls a general election (→ 19/6).

30. Prague: All Czechs from six to 60 are ordered to have defence training (→ 12/6).

31. London: The BBC broadcasts its first game show called "Spelling Bee" (→ 12/9).

31. Hungary: The mummified hand of St. Stephen, Hungary's patron, leaves Budapest; it has not been moved since 1038.

Mussolini praised as UK signs pact

May 2. A "new era" in Britain's relations with Italy was promised by Mr Chamberlain tonight when he won House of Commons approval for the recently-negotiated Anglo-Italian Agreement. He spoke warmly about Italy's new vigour and efficiency under the stimulus of Signor Mussolini's personality.

The Prime Minister said that the pact removes a danger spot in Europe and paves the way for future co-operation in peacekeeping. "The clouds of mistrust and suspicion have been cleared away," he told MPs.

The deal, which includes British recognition of Italy's annexation of Abyssinia and an Italian promise to withdraw troops from Spain, was fiercely attacked by Labour as "A sell-out to Fascism" (→ 11/1/39).

Hitler and Mussolini during their negotiations in Italy.

Marquess sells off half of Cardiff

May 17. Half the city of Cardiff was sold for £20 million today in the biggest property deal in British history. The property comes from the estate of the Marquess of Bute and includes 20,000 houses, 1,000 shops and 250 public houses as well as theatres, farmland and villages. Lord Bute, who is descended from Robert III, King of Scotland in the fourteenth century, has held on to two castles. In the Great War he joined the army as a private on 2s.9d a day under the family name of Crichton-Stuart (→ 16/6/39).

King and Queen open Scottish exhibition

Their Majesties at the Empire Exhibition, Bellahouston Park, Glasgow.

May 3. The pipes skirled, the flags flapped and it looked as if half the population of Scotland had come to see the King open the Empire Exhibition in Glasgow today.

The King and Queen ascended the Tower of Empire in a lift that moved at 500 feet a minute. Then it was on to the United Kingdom Pavilion to see the "Fitter Britain" exhibit. They stood fascinated by a stream of ping-pong balls illustrating the circulation of the blood.

At lunch Lord Elgin, the exhibition president, presented the Queen with the Badge of the Order of the Thistle, Scotland's highest order of chivalry, set in precious stones.

The final stop during the five-hour visit was the highland village An Clachan. On the flagged pavement outside a thatched cottage, Mary Morrison from Barra was spinning wool and singing an old lament "Leaving Barra". She told their Majesties that it was the first time she had left Barra and that she had come to the Exhibition "riding all the way in an aeroplane".

They went on to visit the North Hillingdon Trading Estate, where farmland is being turned into an industrial estate by 1,400 men to help the growing unemployment on the Clyde. At dusk the Royal train stopped at the remote moorland station of Drumclog to give them a quiet night (→19/7).

May 10. Miners' children anxiously await news at Markham Colliery, near Chesterfield, where at least 15 men have died in an explosion; hope is fading for over 60 who remain trapped a mile underground.

1938

JUNE

Su	Mo	Tu	We	Th	Fr	Sa
			1	2	3	4
5	6	7	8	9	10	11
12	13	14	15	16	17	18
19	20	21	22	23	24	25
26	27	28	29	30		

1. UK: Mr Peter Beatty's Bois Roussel wins the Derby at Epsom (→24/3/39).

1. UK: The Bren gun enters service; the name comes from Brno, the Czech town where it was first made, and Enfield, where it is made in Britain.

3. Berlin: A law is passed for the confiscation of "degenerate art" (→11/7).

7. Austria: The Nazis says that all Austrians who want to marry must prove their "Aryan" ancestry (→10).

9. London: The government signs a contract to buy 400 planes from US makers (→24).

12. Czechoslovakia: The Sudeten German party makes big gains in national elections (→6/9).

14. UK: England draws the first Test against Australia, but Denis Compton scores his first test century (→21).

14. London: Sir John Reith is to leave the BBC to become head of Imperial Airways.

15. China: The Yellow River bursts its banks in the worst flooding since 1855, threatening the Japanese Army (→21/10).

19. Eire: Early election returns indicate a victory for de Valera's Fianna Fail Party.

21. Manchester: Australia's Don Bradman scores 100 in 73 minutes at Old Trafford (→25/7).

24. UK: The RAF launches a new recruitment campaign; it receives 1,000 enquiries on the first day (→28).

27. Vienna: All Jews are given 14 days' notice by their employers (→30).

28. London: The government says it will double Britain's anti-aircraft defence forces (→15/7).

30. Vienna: Kurt Schuschnigg, last chancellor of pre-Nazi Austria, is to be tried for treason (→1/7).

30. US: A new comic strip has appeared this month; it is called "Superman".

Joe Louis floors Max in round one

June 22. In the sweetest victory of his awesome career the world heavyweight champion, Joe Louis, clinically and mercilessly disposed of the only man ever to have beaten him, the 33-year-old former title holder from Germany, Max Schmeling.

Schmeling was already an ex-champion two years ago when he caught the aspiring young 22-year-old unawares and knocked him out. Tonight in New York there was no question of a repeat. In the fourth and, so far, the easiest defence of his title, Louis's punching power demolished the challenger; he knocked him down three times, and then finished him off after only two minutes and four seconds of the first round.

Max Schmeling: defeated.

No German children to speak to Jews

June 19. German children have been recruited for the Nazis' anti-Jewish campaign. Boys of 13 and younger, armed with brushes and buckets of white paint, marched along the Frankfurterallee in a Jewish neighbourhood of east Berlin today and daubed the Star of David on shops pointed out to them by adults.

In schools, children are asked where their parents buy school clothing, and those who admit that it comes from a Jewish shop are made to stand in a corner; playing with or even speaking to Jewish children is forbidden (→7/10).

Japanese bomb Canton mercilessly

June 8. Tonight the Chinese city of Canton is a terror-stricken, defenceless shambles and the authorities no longer have time to count the dead. For the past ten days the constant drone of planes has heralded a merciless rain of Japanese bombs.

The death toll must run into five figures. Sirens no longer sound; when the first sound of a fresh swarm of bombers is heard, soldiers and police run through the streets shouting the chilling phrase "They are coming". Bell ringers, too, make pathetic attempts to sound a warning. Often, however, there are false alarms and the city is kept in a state of unbearable suspense.

The Japanese are determined to bomb Canton into submission. However, although most anti-aircraft guns have been silenced and General Chiang Kai-shek has no fighters to spare for its defence, the city refuses to surrender.

Great areas are blazing ruins, illumination provided only by the flames of blazing oil installations. The power stations have been wrecked and there is often no electricity even for the hospitals. Scarcely is the current restored by hours of heroic labour, than the power stations are again destroyed by yet another devastating raid. Three bombs fell on the American Lingnan University. Engineers employed by a British company escaped through blazing debris after the waterworks they were repairing were again hit (→24/8).

Victims of Japanese raids which have terrorised Canton and Shanghai.

Italy wins its second World Cup

June 19. The Italian football team, again under the inspirational management of Vittorio Pozzo, beat the fancied Hungarians 4-2 in a half-empty Stade Colombes in Paris, to retain the World Cup they had won at home four years earlier.

With the British teams still not participating, and with both Argentina and Uruguay sulking at home, only Brazil presented a threat to the European nations. They provided the highest scorer of the tournament – Leonidas, with eight goals – and beat Sweden 4-2 in the third-place match; but the Italians contained them with ease in the first semi-final; the Swedes, who had come to prominence after their 8-0 drubbing of Cuba in the second round, were humbled 5-1 by Hungary in the other.

JAEGER
The new shooting Floor opens July 20th

Suburban blues

June 8. The loneliness of suburban wives is proving a grave social problem, a coroner's court heard today. At the inquest of a Barnet housewife, who gassed herself, a doctor said: "She was one of the thousands of women who are suffering suburban neurosis. Out-patients departments are full of them". Experts believe the problems arise because women are left at home all day with not enough to do and too much time to think and worry about their troubles (→31/7/39).

Spanish volunteers set to return home

June 21. A plan to enable foreign volunteers to withdraw from Spain has been agreed by the London non-intervention committee. After months of delicate discussions, the governments of Britain, France, Italy, Germany and Russia have given their approval.

The next step is to secure the approval of both sides in Spain, after which commissions will be sent to arrange for the safe withdrawal of the volunteers.

Those most affected will be the men and women of the International Brigade, who arrived in Spain from all over the world to fight for the Republican government against General Franco's Nationalist rebels. Franco also has his volunteers, but most of his foreign support comes from the regular forces of Germany and Italy.

The Brigade, while predominantly Communist, has also attracted many intellectuals committed to opposing Fascism (→10/10).

1938

JULY

Su	Mo	Tu	We	Th	Fr	Sa
					1	2
3	4	5	6	7	8	9
10	11	12	13	14	15	16
17	18	19	20	21	22	23
24	25	26	27	28	29	30
31						

1. Rome: Mussolini puts curbs on books by Jews (→5).

1. Berlin: Hitler says the Reich will assume responsibility for Austria's debts (→3).

2. Wimbledon: Americans win all five titles; Don Budge beat "Bunny" Austin in the Men's Singles final, Helen Moody beat unseeded Helen Jacobs for her record eighth Women's Singles title (→8/7/39).

3. Spain: Franco gains four miles in a new drive on Valencia (→3/9).

5. Vienna: Many Jews are reported to have killed themselves in recent days (→14).

6. Palestine: 20 die in a bomb attack on an Arab cafe (→25).

7. London: Augustus John opens a show of art banned in Germany, by Bechmann, Kandinsky and others.→

10. New York: Howard Hughes sets off on a round-the-world flight.→

11. Canada: Eskimos in the Arctic complain of a heatwave: it is 67 degrees F (19C).

14. Rome: Italy officially adopts Nazi-style anti-Semitism (→8/8).

15. London: The government orders 1,000 Spitfire fighters (→15/2/38).

18. Dublin: US pilot Douglas Corrigan lands, but says he meant to fly to California (→5/8).

19. Paris: King George VI and Queen Elizabeth arrive to a tumultuous welcome (→17/5/39).

20. UK: Summer wear for men includes slacks for 30 shillings and shorts for 17/6d.

22. Germany: Jews are ordered to carry special identity cards (→3/8).

22. UK: Peaches cost one penny each, oranges are two for a penny.

25. UK: Australia win the fourth Test against England to keep the Ashes.

29. Denmark: Dane Jenny Kammersgaad is the first to swim the Baltic, 37 miles in 40 hours nine minutes.

Modernists suffer from "defective sight"

Artist Magnus Zeller's view of "Der Hitlerstaat" ("The Nazi State").

July 11. Hitler today made a savage attack on a London exhibition of the work of artists who have been branded as "degenerate" in Germany: "They have had to hasten this exhibition because if they wait a year or two they will have to admit our achievements in the cultural sphere also. Health, vigour and beauty are the symbols of National Socialist Germany. For the Modernists, we have no place.

"In the name of the German race, I wish to forbid such lamentable unfortunates who plainly suffer from defective sight. They can live and work where they choose but not in Germany."

Herr Hitler was speaking at the opening of the Munich House of Art where the pictures in the exhibition are mainly modelled on the romantic 19th-century style which he favours. The London exhibition features internationally-known German Expressionists such as Beckmann, Marc, Liebermann, Kokoschka and Kandinsky. All are in exile and one, Ernst Kirchner, shot himself in Paris last month.

Hughes sets record flying round world

July 15. More than two million New Yorkers gave the tycoon aviator, Howard Hughes, a ticker-tape welcome after he had set a new record for round-the-world flight.

Hughes and his four-man crew landed in Brooklyn yesterday just three days, 19 hours and 17 minutes after taking off on their trip to publicise the World's Fair. Their twin-engined, Lockheed aircraft averaged 208mph on the 14,824-mile flight via Paris, Moscow, Omsk and Yakutsk in Siberia, Fairbanks, Alaska, and Minneapolis.

Hughes cut in half the previous round-the-world record of seven days and 18 hours set up by Wiley Post five years ago.

Helen Moody wins her 8th Wimbledon

July 2. Playing with single-mindedness, ruthless efficiency and great self-confidence, Helen Wills Moody, at 32, captured for a record eighth time the Wimbledon singles title she first won 11 years ago.

After her surprisingly difficult semi-final (12-10, 6-4) against the German Hilde Sperling, it seemed that at last her great rival and compatriot, Helen Jacobs, might have a chance of avenging the defeats she had suffered in the finals of 1929, 1932 and 1935. But, yet again, it was Helen Jacobs who wilted. Handicapped by an ankle injury sustained in practice before the final, she went down 6-4, 6-0 to the ice-cool veteran.

Bomb blast in Palestine

July 25. A bomb hidden in a basket today detonated in the market place at Haifa, the chief port of Palestine. The explosion, close to the place of an earlier bomb outrage, killed 43 people and wounded 42 others.

A shore party of ratings from HMS Repulse rapidly cordoned off the area to prevent fresh trouble, finding time to put the wounded market donkeys and mules out of their misery. At the railway station Arabs stoned Jews, killing two, and Jewish shops were set ablaze. A mechanised Hussar regiment is on the way from Egypt to join two infantry battalions already on their way. By the autumn three brigades will be stationed there.

In three weeks 123 people have been killed in terror attacks by Arabs and by Jews. In Jerusalem a curfew was declared after a terrorist bomb exploded near the Mosque of Omar, killing ten Arabs. Staff officers sitting on the terrace at the King David Hotel pursued and captured three Arabs, who threw a bomb at a nearby Jewish house. Major H. W. Mirehouse, who is attached to the General Staff, led the chase (→ 6/10).

Destruction and carnage in Haifa.

Mallard steams into railway record books

July 3. A British locomotive today set a new world record speed for steam engines of 126 miles per hour. Mallard, a streamlined Gresley A4 Pacific, achieved the new record for just over 300 yards near Peterborough on the London and North Eastern Railway line between Newcastle and London.

On the footplate were Driver Duddington and Fireman Bray from Doncaster while the engine's designer, Nigel Gresley, was on board to record the speed.

Mallard maintained a speed of over 120mph for over five miles, beating the previous British record of 114mph set by Coronation Scot on the Euston line last year. A speed of 127mph has been claimed by an American steam engine, but this has not been proven.

A later photograph of Mallard, the fastest steam locomotive in the world. It set a new world record speed for steam engines of 126 miles per hour.

1938

AUGUST

Su	Mo	Tu	We	Th	Fr	Sa
	1	2	3	4	5	6
7	8	9	10	11	12	13
14	15	16	17	18	19	20
21	22	23	24	25	26	27
28	29	30	31			

3. Rome: Mussolini bans foreign Jews from attending Italian higher education institutions (→ 8).

4. UK: Bryn Jones transfers from Wolves to Arsenal for a record £13,000 fee.

5. New York: Douglas "Wrong-Way" Corrigan is given a ticker-tape welcome home and an "error-proof" compass.

7. New York: The Queen Mary sets a record for the westward Atlantic crossing of 3 days, 23 hours, 48 minutes (→ 15).

8. Italy: There are now five anti-Smitic periodicals (→ 1/9).

10. Moscow: The USSR and Japan agree a truce following weeks of border clashes.

13. Germany: 16 die when a Czech airliner crashes.

15. Vienna: The Nazis say they will name a suburb and a street after the murderers of Chancellor Dollfuss (→ 17).

15. UK: The Queen Mary sets a record for the east-bound Atlantic crossing, three days 20 hours (27/9).

17. Germany: Austria's former leaders, including Schuschnigg, are being held in Dachau concentration camp (→ 28/11).

20. London: Sydney Wooderson runs the half-mile in a world record one minute 49.2 seconds.

22. Cambridge: A gearless, clutchless car is tested.

24. China: Japanese troops shoot down a Chinese airliner and machine-gun 19 passengers trying to flee (→ 21/10).

28. Prague: The Sudeten German party begins talks with president Benes (→ 5/9).

30. Egypt: Cairo is surrounded by water as the Nile overflows.

BIRTH

15. British author Frederick Forsyth.

DEATH

7. Russian stage director Constantin Stanislavsky (*17/1/1863).

Hutton and England set record Test scores

Record-breaker Len Hutton out at last – after 364 runs in 13 hours.

Aug 24. England's cricketers re-wrote the books in the final Test match at the Oval, beating Australia by the unprecedented margin of an innings and 579 runs to level the series.

The steady annihilation of the Australian bowling was led, for a full 13 hours and 17 minutes, by the Yorkshire batsman Len Hutton, whose innings of 364 beat Donald Bradman's Test record by 30 runs.

England declared their innings closed at a massive 903 for seven only after the Australians' biggest run scoring threat had been eliminated when Bradman fell and broke a shin bone. Australia then crumbled twice in a day and a half to give England victory.

Envoy recalled for Czech crisis talks

Aug 31. The German threat to Czechoslovakia is being viewed with the utmost gravity in Whitehall. Sir Neville Henderson, British Ambassador in Berlin, has been recalled for consultation and the Cabinet met yesterday to discuss his report.

Meanwhile, Britain's position in the event of an attack on Czechoslovakia was the subject of a statement by Sir John Simon, the Chancellor of the Exchequer. He restated Mr Chamberlain's warning of March 24.

The Prime Minister said then that Britain could give no guarantee to go automatically to the assistance of Czechoslovakia if she were attacked, but went on to declare: "Where peace and war are concerned legal obligations are not alone involved and, if war broke out, it would be unlikely to be confined to those who have assumed such obligations.

"This is especially true," he went on, "in the case of two countries like Great Britain and France, devoted to the ideals of democratic liberty and determined to uphold them."

"That declaration," said Sir John, "holds good today" (→ 30/9).

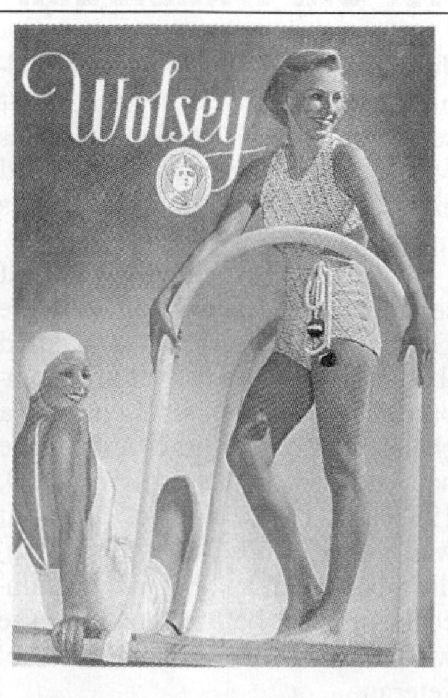

1938

SEPTEMBER

Su	Mo	Tu	We	Th	Fr	Sa
				1	2	3
4	5	6	7	8	9	10
11	12	13	14	15	16	17
18	19	20	21	22	23	24
25	26	27	28	29	30	

1. Rome: Mussolini expels all Jews who entered Italy after 1918 (→ 16/10).

3. Spain: Franco launches a heavy drive along the River Ebro in Catalonia (→ 16/12).

4. Berne: The Olympic Committee decides to hold the 1944 Games in Helsinki.

5. France: Troops are sent to the Maginot Line and leave is cancelled as tension grows over Czechoslovakia (→ 6).

6. Prague: Benes offers self-government to the Sudetenland (→ 8).

8. Czechoslovakia: Sudeten Germans hold mass rallies to call for union with Germany (→ 13).

12. London: The BBC shows its first film on television, "Man of the Moment".

13. Prague: Konrad Henlein's Sudeten party breaks off talks with Benes (→ 14).

14. Czechoslovakia: Martial law is extended in the Sudetenland to quell German agitation (→ 18).

16. US: George Eyston beats the 350.2 mph land speed record set just two days ago by John Cobb, reaching 357mph.

18. Prague: Czech premier Milan Hodza appeals for calm among Czechs hostile to Germany (→ 21).

21. Prague: The government agrees to Anglo-French plans to cede the Sudetenland to Germany; Czechs protest (→ 22).

23. Prague: General mobilisation follows premier Hodza's resignation and replacement by General Jan Syrovy (→ 28).

25. London: There is a rush among Londoners for new gas-masks as international tension escalates.

26. Barcelona: 68 die in a high-speed train crash.

28. Berlin: Hitler calls a four-power conference to discuss the Czech crisis.→

BIRTH

23. Austrian actress Romy Schneider (†29/5/82).

Czechoslovakia deal is agreed in Munich

Sept 30. There will be no war over Czechoslovakia. It was officially announced in Munich at 1.45 this morning that agreement on a peaceful solution of the crisis had been reached following a conference lasting nearly twelve hours between Mr Chamberlain, Monsieur Daladier, Herr Hitler and Signor Mussolini.

It is not a solution that will please everyone, and certainly not the Czechs, who were not present at the conference, for it grants almost all Herr Hitler's demands. Under the agreement the Sudeten region of Czechoslovakia, which is inhabited by a German-speaking minority, will be handed over to Germany.

Munich: Mussolini shakes Neville Chamberlain's hand as Hitler, Daladier, Goering and Ciano look on.

The terms of the pact stipulate that "the evacuation of the region shall be completed by Oct 10, without destruction of any of the existing installations" and "the occupation by stages of the predominantly German territories by German troops will begin on Oct 1." Thus Herr Hitler has won again by subversion and the threat of war.

Disorders in the German areas instigated by Herr Henlein, leader of the Sudeten Nazis, led to Hitler declaring a fortnight ago: "I can only tell the representatives of the democracies that, if these tormented creatures cannot by their own exertions come to their rights, they will demand both their rights and assistance from us." He went on to threaten: "I stated in my speech of February 22 that Germany would not allow the illtreatment of these three and a half million Germans to continue. I now request foreign statesmen to allow themselves to be convinced that this was not a mere phrase."

The German dictator built up the war tension by revealing that 462,000 men were working on fortifications in the Rhineland, 30 miles deep and "the most gigantic of all time". He added: "The great new fortresses in the West will be ready by the winter. Behind them stands armed Germany."

In face of this sabre-rattling Britain mobilised the Fleet four days ago while France manned the Maginot line and called up the Reserves.

Announcing the mobilisation of the Fleet, the Prime Minister said: "I am a man of peace to the depths of my soul. Armed conflict between nations is a nightmare to me, but if I were convinced that any nation had made up its mind to dominate the world by fear of its force I should feel it should be resisted. Under such a domination the life of people who believe in liberty would not be worth living."

He flew twice to Germany in his attempts to secure peace while the world prepared for war. In Munich he has succeeded at the very last moment at the price of truncating Czechoslovakia and appeasing Herr Hitler.

The Czechs get nothing out of this pact except a guarantee that the remains of their country will be protected against aggression (→5/10).

Chamberlain flies home and promises "Peace for our time"

Sept 30. Mr Chamberlain had a tumultuous welcome home tonight on his return from Munich. "I believe it is peace for our time", he said about the agreement he signed there with Herr Hitler.

The Prime Minister was greeted by a huge, cheering throng at Heston aerodrome. Then he appeared on the Buckingham Palace balcony with the King and Queen before more rejoicing crowds. Back at 10 Downing Street, Mr Chamberlain waved a copy of the new Anglo-German accord and said that his mission had brought peace with honour.

Under the agreement German troops will enter ceded Czechoslovakian territory tomorrow. However, many MPs of all parties said: "It's a sell-out to Hitler." (→27/10)

Back in London Mr Chamberlain shows off the new peace accord.

Launch of largest liner ever built

Sept 27. The largest liner the world has ever seen was launched today – and very nearly entered the water unnamed.

The Queen Elizabeth, which will weigh 80,000 tons when complete, took the crowds of onlookers and workers at John Brown's yard on the Clyde by surprise when timbers restraining her broke and she started to slide towards the water.

The Queen and the two princesses were chatting to the assembled dignitaries from the yard and the Cunard White Star Line, but the Queen quick-wittedly leaned forward to release the champagne which just managed to crash onto the tip of the ship's bows as she gathered speed down the slipway.

1938

OCTOBER

Su	Mo	Tu	We	Th	Fr	Sa
						1
2	3	4	5	6	7	8
9	10	11	12	13	14	15
16	17	18	19	20	21	22
23	24	25	26	27	28	29
30	31					

1. Czechoslovakia: German troops march into the Sudetenland as Teschen, Czech Silesia, is annexed by Poland (→3).

3. London: Duff Cooper resigns as First Lord of the Admiralty over Chamberlain's appeasement of Hitler (→5).

5. Prague: President Benes resigns.→

6. Palestine: 60 Arabs die after a six-hour gun battle with British troops (→19/10).

7. Berlin: Jews are ordered to hand in their passports within a fortnight (→28).

9. New York: A new device for aircraft safety, called an "altimeter", is demonstrated.

13. Budapest: Tension is mounting amid calls for the annexation of southern parts of Czechoslovakia (→23).

16. Italy: Many Jews are rounded up and charged with plotting against the government (→28).

19. Berlin: Hitler decorates American aviator Charles Lindbergh with the Service Cross (→15/11).

20. UK: Imperial Airways' 42-passenger Ensign plane makes its maiden flight (→9/9/39).

21. Tokyo: 226 people are reported killed in a typhoon.

23. Budapest: Hungary rejects Czech proposals for ceding Czechoslovak areas (→2/11).

25. London: The Duke of Kent is appointed Governor-General of Australia (→24/4/39).

28. Marseilles: A huge fire kills 74 and destroys a large area of the city.

28. Germany: Many Jews are rounded up and expelled to Poland (→9/11).

31. US: Orson Welles' vivid radio production of "War of the Worlds" causes widespread panic because of its realism (→12/38).

BIRTH

3. US rock and roll singer Eddie Cochran (†17/4/60).

Germans march into Czechoslovakia

Oct 5. Adolf Hitler walked over the border into his latest conquest yesterday as head of the German army occupying the once-Czech Sudetenland.

Konrad Henlein, whose carefully organised riots precipitated the Czech crisis, and who has now been made Commissioner for the Sudeten, walked at his side, while a company of "Free Corps" wearing German steel helmets formed the guard of honour.

Hitler was greeted with tremendous enthusiasm. When he arrived at Eger, capital of the area, the main square was packed with cheering people. The church bells pealed and loud-speakers announced: "Here comes our Fuehrer, the liberator of the Sudetenland."

Hitler spoke to them from the town hall. It was an uncompromising piece of oratory: "I am able to greet you for the first time as my people, and I bear you the greetings of the whole German nation ... This greeting is at the same time a vow. Never again shall this land be torn from the Reich".

"Over the great German Reich lie as protection the German shield and the German sword. You are part of this protection and will have from now on, like all other Germans, to do your share ..."

"Thus we begin our march into the great German future, and in this hour we wish to thank the Almighty for giving us His blessing on our way in the past and ask Him to accompany our way in the future."

Meanwhile, Polish troops have also marched into Czechoslovakia, claiming territory in Teschen-Silesia. But even more dismemberment threatens. The Czech government, following a Note from Hungary, has agreed to establish a mixed Commission to arrange for the satisfaction of Hungarian claims.

The mood in Czechoslovakia is becoming increasingly desperate. The feeling is that the rump of the country is left with no possibility of independent existence or of pursuing a foreign policy of her own.

Entirely abandoned by her former allies, many people feel their only course is to seek accommodation with Germany. France and Britain are held responsible for the country's ruin (→14/3/39).

Cheering crowds welcome Hitler as his troops invade Czechoslovakia.

Munich deal causes revolt in Tory ranks

Oct 27. The Government today won the Oxford by-election with its majority halved from the 1935 General Election figure. It has been a remarkable contest. Quintin Hogg, the triumphant Tory candidate, hailed the result as Mr Chamberlain's victory and a vindication of the Munich Agreement.

His straight-fight opponent was A.D. Lindsay, Master of Balliol College, standing as an Independent Progressive and backed by Labour, Liberals and dissident anti-Chamberlain Tories, including Winston Churchill, Anthony Eden and Harold Macmillan. Student Tories led by Edward Heath campaigned on the slogan "A vote for Hogg is a vote for Hitler."

An anti-Chamberlain bandwagon is now rolling; Duff Cooper, the First Lord of the Admiralty, has resigned from the Cabinet and, simultaneously, several senior Tories have been voting against the Prime Minister.

However, in pleading for the vote of confidence which he won, Mr Chamberlain told MPs: "I have nothing to be ashamed of." He paid tribute to Czechoslovakia for its sacrifices to Germany and said that the Bank of England is giving the Prague Government a £10 million loan.

The Prime Minister added: "The path to appeasement bristles with obstacles. We must remain on guard" (→17/3/39).

1938

NOVEMBER

Su	Mo	Tu	We	Th	Fr	Sa
		1	2	3	4	5
6	7	8	9	10	11	12
13	14	15	16	17	18	19
20	21	22	23	24	25	26
27	28	29	30			

2. Czechoslovakia: Following "arbitration" by Hitler, Hungary annexes the southern parts of Slovakia and Ruthenia (→ 30).

4. UK: 14 die when a British airliner crashes on Jersey.

7. Paris: A Polish Jew shoots dead German diplomat Ernst von Rath in protest at the Nazi expulsions of Jews.→

8. US: Roosevelt's Democrats lose 72 seats in the House of Representatives in congressional elections.

9. London: The government calls a round-table conference on the future of Palestine (→ 27/2/39).

10. Vienna: 18 synagogues are destroyed in a wave of fire-bomb attacks (→ 10).

10. Munich: Jews are given to 48 hours to quit the city or face a concentration camp (→ 12).

11. Ankara: Ismet Onu succeeds Kemal Ataturk as president of Turkey (→ 18).

12. Berlin: Hitler fines the Jewish community one billion marks for the death of von Rath in Paris (→ 14).

14. Berlin: Jews are expelled from colleges (→ 15).

15. Washington: Roosevelt condemns Nazi anti-Semitism (→ 23).

15. Berlin: Charles Lindbergh says he plans to settle in Germany (→ 15/1/39).

18. Ankara: 20 are trampled to death at Ataturk's lying-in-state.

23. Berlin: Hitler puts a 20 per cent tax on property of Jews with over 5,000 marks (→ 12/12).

24. Paris: Chamberlain and Daladier visit the Duke and Duchess of Windsor (→ 18/3/39).

28. Vienna: Widespread purges of Nazis are reported to have led to 135 deaths (→ 4/7/39).

DEATH

10. Turkish statesman Mustafa Kemal Ataturk (*12/3/1881).

Plan to partition Palestine dropped

Oct 19. The Cabinet today approved new proposals for Palestine, which involve abandoning the scheme for partition recommended last year. Dividing the country into an Arab and a Jewish state is no longer considered to be either equitable or even practicable.

Malcolm MacDonald, the Colonial Secretary, proposes instead a complete change in policy. Palestine will now remain under British rule and ultimately become a unified state under British control. Swift measures were taken in Jerusalem to establish martial law. But it will be some time before the country is completely pacified (→ 9/11).

Canton is occupied by the Japanese

Oct 21. The Rising Sun, flag of Japan, tonight flies over Canton, the biggest city in South China. A Japanese mechanised column of 3,000 men, led by tanks, stormed into the city, after spearheading a drive through 100 miles of enemy territory in nine days.

As the vanguard reached the eastern suburbs, a gigantic explosion shook the city as the Chinese blew up the great £500,000 Pearl River bridge. Generalissimo Chiang Kai-shek fled Canton to seek refuge inland. This is Japan's greatest military success since the fall of Shanghai (→ 10/2/39).

A new magazine was launched this month called Picture Post.

Women cheer as Jews beaten senseless

Laughing Berliners enjoy the results of a night of anti-Jewish attacks.

Nov 9. The whole of Germany's Jewish community was tonight subjected to a reign of terror without precedent in modern times in a civilised country. Dr Josef Goebbels, the Minister of Public Enlightenment and Propaganda, claims the orgy of violence and arson was a spontaneous reaction to the assassination of a German diplomat in Paris by a young Polish Jew, but the events bear all the hallmarks of an officially organised pogrom.

The attacks began simultaneously throughout the country, followed a clear pattern and, in marked contrast to past anti-Jewish outbreaks, in which loutish Storm Troopers were prominent, were joined by respectable-looking middle-class folk. In Berlin, fashionably dressed women clapped and screamed with laughter and some held up their babies to watch Jews being beaten senseless by youths with lead piping. It is being called Kristallnacht (Crystal Night). More than 7,000 Jewish shops were looted. Hundreds of synagogues were burned down. An unknown number of Jews died. To save insurance companies from bankruptcy, the Nazis say they will confiscate any money the Jews may receive and give it back to the insurers.

Broken glass alone accounts for millions of marks-worth of damage. It is said Goering was not pleased when he heard most of the replacement glass will have to be imported and paid for in scarce foreign currency. "They should have killed more Jews and broken less glass," he fumed (→ 10).

African home offer to Jewish refugees

Nov 21. Britain is offering to settle Jewish refugees from Germany in different parts of the colonial empire. Tanganyika has earmarked 30,000 acres of land, and smaller areas in Kenya, Northern Rhodesia and Nyasaland may be available. Announcing this in the Commons, Mr Chamberlain said the number of refugees Britain can accept is limited. Eleven thousand of them have come from Central Europe since 1933 (→ 2/12).

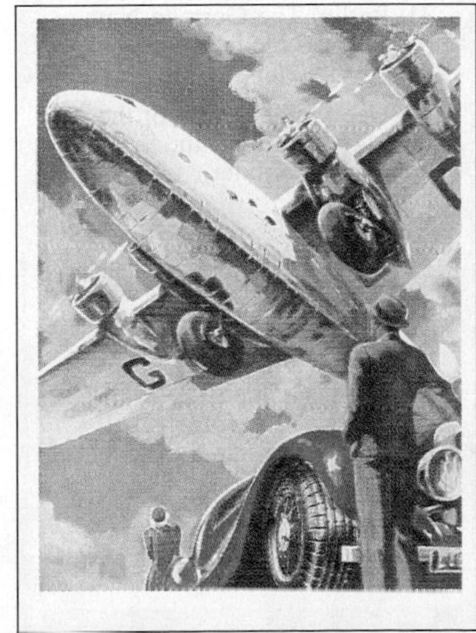

1938

DECEMBER

Su	Mo	Tu	We	Th	Fr	Sa
				1	2	3
4	5	6	7	8	9	10
11	12	13	14	15	16	17
18	19	20	21	22	23	24
25	26	27	28	29	30	31

1. London: The government unveils plans for a "National Register", stating what everyone will do in time of war (→2/2/39).

2. UK: 206 German Jewish refugee schoolchildren arrive (→24/6/39).

6. Paris: France and Germany sign a pact on the inviolability of their present frontiers.

8. Germany: Launch of Germany's first aircraft carrier, the Graf Zeppelin (→31).

9. Lithuania: Memel Germans demand to join the Reich (→21/3/39).

10. Stockholm: Nobel Prizes go to Enrico Fermi (Italy, Physics); Richard Kuhn (Germany, Chemistry); Corneille Heymans (Belgium, Medicine); and Pearl Buck (US, Literature). Peace Prize awarded in Oslo to the Nansen International Office for Refugees.

11. London: Sir Edwin Lutyens is elected president of the Royal Academy.→

16. Spain: Franco restores ex-King Alfonso's citizenship (→26).

21. London: The government plans to spend £200,000 on air raid shelters (→9/2/39).

24. Rome: Pope Pius XI attacks Italian anti-Semitism (→10/2/39).

26. Spain: Franco is reported to have advanced 20 miles in two days (→2/1/39).

31. Berlin: The German Navy plans to double her U-boat fleet (→14/2/39).

31. US: Maiden flight of the Boeing Stratoliner, the first pressurised airliner.

DEATH

25. Czech writer Karel Capek (*9/1/1890).

QUOTE OF THE YEAR

"There has come back from Germany to Downing Street peace with honour. I believe it is peace for our time."

Neville Chamberlain, September 30, 1938.

Germans confiscate all Jewish property

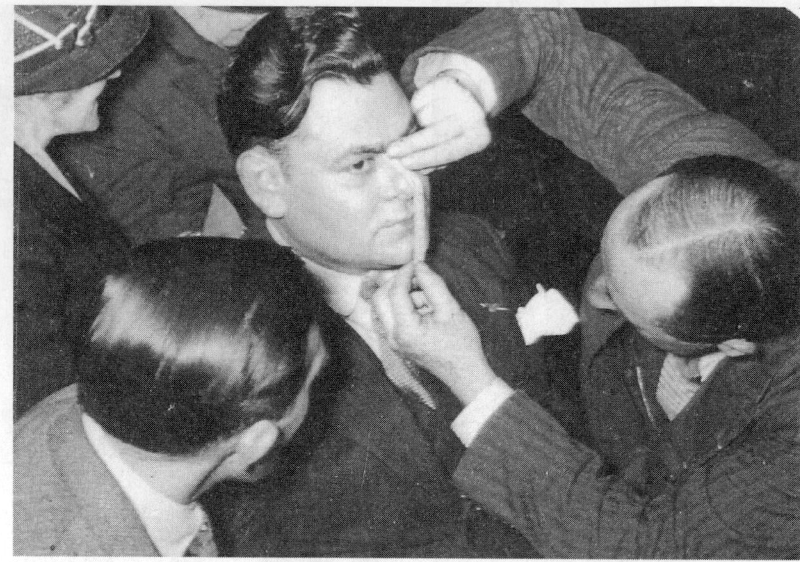

Is he Jewish? Nazi authorities measure up a suspect's "Semitic" nose.

Dec 12. Walther Funk, a one-time financial journalist and now Economics Minister, has found a way to ban Jews from any kind of business activity while avoiding disrupting of the German economy. Jews are forbidden to deal in property, jewellery or precious metals, or freely operate bank accounts. Any securities they own will be disposed of as the Minister judges to be in the national interest. Jewish businesses will be closed down by specially appointed executors. Germany's Jews have thus been robbed of everything, apart from minor objects and the money they actually carry in their purses (→17/1/39).

New chemical may ease menopause

A development, which may well change the lives of women in health and sickness, has been reported by Professor **E.C. Dodds** from London's Middlesex Hospital. He has created a chemical called diethylstilboestrol which is three times as powerful as the naturally-occuring female hormone oestrone. It should prove to be of great value in the treatment of menstrual disorders and also in relieving the symptoms of the menopause. It is now being tested on the uterus, vagina and mating habits of rats.

In another significant medical development, routine police testing for the alcohol in driver's breath has begun in Indiana, USA. This could soon be applied to motorists in other countries. A "Drunkometer" designed by **R.N. Harger** tested 1,000 cc of breath from 1,750 drivers over a week-end in April. Around one in 250 were under the influence of alcohol. The law in Indiana now states that those with an alcohol level of 0.15 per cent and above are drunk.

Arts: Martians on the air cause real-life drama in the streets

"Ladies and gentlemen, I have a grave announcement to make. Incredible as it may seem, strange beings who landed in New Jersey tonight are the vanguard of an invading army from Mars."

It was Hallowe'en and the voice on the radio was that of a 23-year-old actor, **Orson Welles**. He was broadcasting a dramatisation of **H. G.Wells'** famous novel "The War of the Worlds" on the American CBS network. But as voices went on to describe Martians "as high as skyscrapers" felling crowds with deadly gas, thousands of radio listeners took it for a real newscast, fled into the streets in panic or drove wildly for the open spaces.

Police switchboards, roads and churches were jammed; people claimed that they had actually seen the Martians, although four warnings were given that the broadcast was science fiction. Welles claimed he had feared the show "might bore people". It certainly maddened them – afterwards.

Real wars have given birth to two

Orson Welles: space invader.

totally different kinds of books. "Homage to Catalonia" is **George Orwell's** report of what he saw in Spain, not only at the front, where he was wounded by a bullet in the throat, but also in Barcelona as the revolution collapsed in warring factions and he became a hunted man.

Evelyn Waugh saw the war in Abyssinia as a Daily Express correspondent. His novel "Scoop" is an hilarious satire on the fatuity of the Press, the deceits of its reporters and the vanity of its proprietors.

It was another bad year for German musicians. **Bruno Walter**, conductor of the Vienna opera, has fled to France where the violinist **Fritz Kreisler** is exiled too; pianist **Artur Schnabel** has found refuge in Switzerland, as has composer **Paul Hindemith**.

In Venice the film of the Berlin Olympics by **Leni Riefenstahl**, who also glorified Hitler's Nuremberg rallies, has been shown in two parts, for it is five hours long. For all its brilliant photography it is tiring.

In Paris **Suzanne Valadon**, the first working-class woman painter to achieve equal respect with men, has died. Her funeral was attended by **Picasso, Braque** and **Derain**. Her son is **Maurice Utrillo**. She was an artist's model for **Renoir** before she began painting herself.

Architecture's public face is modern and decorated

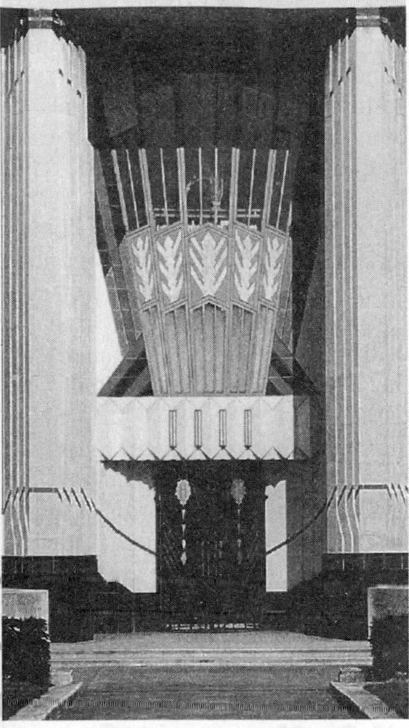
Doorway of the Hoover factory.

The Viceroy's House, New Delhi. Sir Edwin Lutyens' masterpiece is the Empire's finest new public building.

Dec. The completion this month of Norwich City Hall (designed by **C. H. James** and **R. Pierce**) marks one of the highpoints of public architecture in the 1930s. A triumphant mix of traditional Neoclassical and Dutch-influenced Modern architecture, the new City Hall is one of the most attractive large-scale buildings designed this decade.

On a smaller scale, a similar approach has been successfully adopted on the London Underground. Commissioned by Frank Pick, the chief executive of the London Passenger Transport Board, **Charles Holden** has designed a distinguished group of buildings for LPTB's rapidly expanding network that welds the British Georgian tradition to modern ideas imported fresh from Holland, Sweden and Denmark.

But, for the most part, adventurous new public buildings have been designed in the Paris and Hollywood-inspired Art Deco style. The Daily Express building (**Sir Owen Williams** with Ellis & Clarke, 1932) has brought fresh glamour to Grub Street. Fleet Street is still reeling from this startling building clad in glossy black glass and featuring a cinema-style foyer.

Of the hundreds of new cinemas built this decade, London's New Victoria Theatre (**W.E. Trent** and **E. Warmsley Lewis**, 1930) is one of the most dignified. A bold, sculptural facade hides a colourful Art Deco interior bringing Hollywood glamour to the West End.

Motorists heading west out of London on the new dual-carriageway Western Avenue are unlikely to miss the most glamorous factory of the decade. The Hoover Factory (**Wallis Gilbert and Partners**, 1932) has been designed by a team of New York architects. The Manhattan Art Deco style is not to everyone's taste, but the Hoover factory has certainly brightened up the production-line look.

Homely Bexhill-on-Sea is the unlikely beneficiary of the first continental Modern-style public building of significant scale (**Erich Mendelssohn** and **Serge Chermayeff**, 1936). Built according to Bauhaus principles, the De La Warr Pavilion is built of light-weight steel, like an airship, and clad in concrete. Like nearly all buildings in the Bauhaus style, Bexhill Pavilion is the work of refugees, in this case from Germany and the Soviet Union. Paradoxically, the grandest British public building of all completed this decade is not in Britain at all.

The Viceroy's House, New Delhi (**Sir Edwin Lutyens**, completed 1931) is a palace on a monumental scale. Designed in a way that fuses the Indian Moghul tradition with British Neoclassicism, the building flies in the face of the fashionable Modern style of Europe's leading avant-garde practioners, **Le Corbusier, Mies van der Rohe** and **Walter Gropius**.

New Victoria Cinema, London.

Bournemouth's Palace Court Hotel celebrates the Art Deco style.

1939

JANUARY

Su	Mo	Tu	We	Th	Fr	Sa
1	2	3	4	5	6	7
8	9	10	11	12	13	14
15	16	17	18	19	20	21
22	23	24	25	26	27	28
29	30	31				

1. Berlin: All women under 25 are ordered to do one year's civilian service for the Reich.

2. Spain: Nationalists arrest Ernest Golding, British consul in San Sebastian, for alleged spying (→23).

3. London: The Navy is planning a huge reorganisation to boost its firepower (→1/6).

4. Tokyo: Fascist Baron Hiranuma becomes premier (→3/8).

7. US: Al Capone is moved from Alcatraz to San Pedro's Terminal Island prison.

8. Berlin: Church leaders are punished for condemning anti-Semitic excesses (→17).

9. Berlin: Hitler opens the Reichstag building, refurbished after the fire of 1933.

11. Rome: Neville Chamberlain and Foreign Secretary Lord Halifax visit Mussolini.

15. Moscow: Charles Lindbergh is attacked as "Hitler's Lackey".

17. Berlin: Jews are banned from being dentists, vets, and pharmacists, also banned from driving, going to cinemas, theatres, or concerts (→23/2).

20. Cairo: King Farouk is declared the Caliph, spiritual leader, of Islam.

23. Barcelona: The city is put under martial law as Franco's troops close in (→26).

24. Chile: 30,000 are reported killed when a massive earthquake destroys the cities Chillan and Concepcion.

25. London: Sir Stafford Cripps is expelled from the Labour Party.

28. London: The Committee on Nursing Services reports that nurses are overworked and underpaid.

BIRTH

29. Australian writer Germaine Greer.

DEATH

28. Irish poet and playwright William Butler Yeats, 1923 Nobel Prize winner (*13/6/1865).→

Victorious Franco sweeps into Barcelona

Fearful Loyalist refugees flee from Barcelona, General Franco's latest prize.

Jan 26. General Franco's victorious troops entered Barcelona today against only sporadic resistance. General Yague's greatly feared Moors approached from the west, while Nationalist troops went in from the north in a classic pincer movement.

They were greeted by throngs of people who emerged from the underground stations where they had sheltered from Franco's bombers. Many of them gave the Fascist salute and some carried portraits of the Nationalist leader.

Conditions in the city are very bad. The blockade has reduced the people to the point of starvation and many lives were lost both in the bombing raids, carried out by the Italian air force, and in the internecine struggle for power between rival Republican factions.

Anticipating the fall of the city, thousands of people have fled in the past few days. Many have been killed by strafing attacks and the survivors are waiting at the border for permission to enter France.

The Government has fled to Figueras where it has established itself in the villa belonging to Senor Matteo – the newly-appointed Nationalist Mayor of Barcelona (→9/2).

RAF takes 400 new planes a month

Jan 30. The RAF is now taking delivery of more than 400 aircraft a month, four times as many as were being produced a year ago. While it is still behind the 600 a month being produced by Germany, experts say Britain is not far from achieving that goal. The aim is to have a total of 2,840 aircraft by March next year, even though Germany is already thought to possess up to 4,500 front line machines.

The RAF now has 5,800 pilots and an urgent appeal is being made to employers to release reserve and volunteer flyers for six months' full-time training (→15/2).

Awesome power as the atom is split

Jan 28. It may be possible to exploit the energy in the atom, following the discovery of a new radioactive process: nuclear fission. This could be used to produce weapons of unprecedented power, or as a virtually inexhaustible source of energy.

In fission, uranium atoms, bombarded with neutrons, split into two halves, releasing energy and more neutrons, which can split more uranium atoms, and so on.

The process was discovered by the German physicist Otto Hahn. His results have just been reported by his former colleague, Lise Meitner, now a refugee in Sweden.

IRA bombs blast mainland cities

Jan 17. Police began a round-up of hundreds of suspected IRA sympathisers tonight after a series of bomb outrages in London, Manchester, Birmingham, and Alnwick, Northumberland.

In London, a home-made bomb shattered the Southwark control room of the Central Electricity Board; another damaged a cable bridge at Harlesden. In Manchester the banks of the Ship Canal were damaged.

At Southwark, police found an IRA "proclamation" demanding the removal of all British forces from Ireland and calling for all Irishmen to assist in the cause. Additional guards have been placed on key installations and Cabinet Ministers (→3/2).

W.B. Yeats, voice of Ireland, is dead

The late W.B. Yeats: Irish voice.

Jan 28. William Butler Yeats, the voice of Ireland whom many regard as the finest poet now writing in English, has died aged 73. Yeats first found fame as a lanky aesthete of the "Celtic Twilight", writing poems of Irish legend and love lyrics to Maud Gonne, who twice refused to marry him. With Lady Gregory he founded the Irish National Theatre, but, in 1916, "all changed, changed utterly: a terrible beauty is born". His later poems, such as "Byzantium", are full of terrible beauty.

1939

FEBRUARY

Su	Mo	Tu	We	Th	Fr	Sa
			1	2	3	4
5	6	7	8	9	10	11
12	13	14	15	16	17	18
19	20	21	22	23	24	25
26	27	28				

2. London: The government announces plans to appoint 12 Civil Defence Commissioners in case of war (→9).

2. London: MPs vote in favour of contributory pensions for needy members.

3. London: A hunt for IRA terrorists follows bomb blasts at Tottenham Court Road and Leicester Square tube stations (→5).

5. Coventry: Four fires break out, believed to have been started by the IRA (→10/3).

7. London: Round table talks on Palestine open (→27).

8. London: Peers pass the Bastardy Bill, making blood tests compulsory in paternity suits.

9. Spain: Nationalist troops occupy Minorca (→26).

10. China: The Japanese occupy Hainan Island off the Chinese coast (→21/6).

14. Germany: The launch of the 35,000-ton battleship Bismarck.

15. London: The government plans to spend £580 million on defence in 1939, £175 million more than in 1938 (→29/3).

16. Rome: The German envoy to the Vatican asks the College of Cardinals to elect a Pope sympathetic to Fascism (→2/3).

20. London: The British Industries Fair opens; on show is a tub that does its own washing.

20. US: Nylon stockings go on sale for the first time at $1.15 a pair (about five shillings).

23. Berlin: Jews are ordered to give up all precious stones and metals (→25).

25. Berlin: A decree says at least 100 Jews a day must quit the Reich (→5/3).

26. Paris: President Manuel Azana abandons all claim to the presidency of Spain.→

27. Palestine: 31 Arabs die in clashes with Jews (→17/3).

DEATH

10. Pope Pius XI, born Achille Ratti (*31/5/1857).→

MPs cry "Shame" as Franco is recognised

Pro-Franco troops, besieged for two months in Toledo, cheer his victory.

Feb 28. The British Government's recognition of General Franco caused furious scenes in the House of Commons today. The Opposition greeted the Prime Minister with shouts of "Heil Chamberlain" and "Now the Vulture", but their vote of censure was defeated by 344 votes to 137.

Mr Chamberlain responded to the taunts by justifying the granting of recognition on the grounds that General Franco had gained possession of the greater part of Spain, and that nobody could say how much of the Republican government remained or where it could be found.

Labour's leader Clement Attlee was unusually ferocious in his attack on the PM who, he said, would always recognise a government which outraged every law, human and divine, but any government which obeyed the rules of civilisation was "bound to be done down by the Prime Minister". All this fury was probably made unnecessary by the news that Senor Azana, President of Republican Spain, has resigned (→2/3).

New constitution plan for Palestine

Feb 27. Winston Churchill has accused the Government of breaking faith over Palestine in the hope of a quiet life. The new constitution states that, despite the 1917 Balfour Declaration's promise of a national home for the Jews, Palestine should not become a Jewish state.

Immigration is fixed at 75,000 over five years with the Jewish population to be held at one-third of the total. An independent Arab-Jewish state will be set up in 1949, with members of both communities serving in government. The League of Nation's mandate will then end.

Malcolm MacDonald, the Colonial Secretary, said there was no ideal scheme for the Palestine problem. It was "a conflict between right and right".

Pope who attacked the Nazis is dead

Feb 10. Pope Pius XI died early this morning at the age of 81. His 17-year-reign was marked by his efforts to heal the rift between Church and state in Italy and to build world peace, but he was overtaken by events. Priests were persecuted in Italy and Germany and Pius then spoke out against the evils of Nazism (→16).

Free air raid shelters are to be distributed to London homes

Feb 9. The Home Office announced plans today to provide shelters to thousands of homes in districts most likely to be bombed. The steel-built, tunnel-shaped shelters are made in sections and can be erected by two people without skill or experience.

Families earning less than £250 a year will receive their shelters free. Priority will be given to householders in London's 28 metropolitan boroughs and other potential target cities around the rest of the country. To be effective, the shelters, which can be stored pending an emergency, need to be partly sunk into the ground. Measuring 6 feet 6 inches by 4 feet 6 inches, they can be extended for larger families (→5/4).

In case of bombs – Londoners receive their free air-raid shelters.

1939

MARCH

Su	Mo	Tu	We	Th	Fr	Sa
			1	2	3	4
5	6	7	8	9	10	11
12	13	14	15	16	17	18
19	20	21	22	23	24	25
26	27	28	29	30	31	

1. Washington: The US recognises Franco's government (→2).

2. Paris: Great War hero Marshal Philippe Petain is named as French ambassador to Spain (→28).

3. US: Opening of John Ford's western "Stagecoach", starring John Wayne.

5. Germany: Jews are drafted to work for the Reich (→7/6).

10. UK: 20 IRA terrorists are jailed for 20 years for conspiring to cause explosions; two others get shorter terms (→9/6).

10. Prague: Joseph Tiso, premier of Slovakia, is sacked to preserve Czechoslovak unity (→13).

12. Rome: Coronation of Pope Pius XII (→9/4).

13. Berlin: Hitler tells the Czech government to grant Slovakia and Ruthenia independence (→14).

14. Czechoslovakia: The Germans march into Bohemia as the Hungarians occupy Ruthenia (→15).

15. Czechoslovakia: Hitler declares Bohemia-Moravia a German protectorate.→

17. London: The round table talks on Palestine end in failure (→22/5).

17. London: Chamberlain denounces Hitler and recalls the British ambassador from Berlin (→29).

18. Paris: The Chamber of Deputies gives premier Daladier full powers in the face of the growing crisis.

21. Lithuania: Memel is ceded to the Germans (→11/10).

24. UK: Sir Alexander Maguire's Workman wins the Grand National at Aintree (→24/5).

26. UK: The first commercial oil find in Britain is made at Eakring in Nottinghamshire.

29. London: Chamberlain unveils plans to double the size of the Territorial Army.→

30. New York: Hitler's nephew William Hitler calls his uncle "a menace".

Jeers greet Hitler's entry into Prague

March 15. Herr Hitler entered Prague as a conqueror last night and raised his standard on the Hradzin Castle, ancient palace of the Bohemian kings and residence of the presidents of the now vanished republic of Czechoslovakia. It is less than six months since the Nazi dictator declared that Germany had no more territorial claims in Europe.

The German invasion followed only two days after Hitler presented Prague with an ultimatum which included the following demands:

Complete independence for Slovakia and Ruthenia.

Formation of a new Czech government without M. Beran, the Premier, and General Sirovy, the Defence Minister.

Payment to Germany of gold and foreign exchange.

The crisis followed the same pattern as that which led to the occupation of the Sudetenland and brought the world to the brink of war last September. Riots were fermented and German newspapers carried screaming headlines such as "Bloody Terror of the Czechs against Germans and Slovaks creates an Intolerable Situation."

The reception the German army has received is, however, in striking contrast to the tumultuous welcome given to it in the Sudetenland and, previously, in Austria.

The jack-booted troops marching into Prague today have been received with storms of hooting and hissing. Even when the Fuehrer himself appeared, riding proudly in a powerful car decked with swastikas and surrounded by Nazi leaders, the clamour continued.

The demonstrators appeared to be regardless of their own safety. Many courageously sang the national anthem. Others wept unashamedly.

In the face of this opposition General Blaskowitz, Commander-in-Chief of the Army of Occupation, has imposed a curfew on Prague. All cafes, restaurants, theatres and cinemas have been closed. Pitiful scenes were witnessed at the railway stations as crowds of Jews and opponents of the Nazis, knowing what is in store for them, sought to escape.

In the House of Commons, the Prime Minister said that Herr Hitler's coup was a shock to confidence. He emphasised that, for the first time, the Fuehrer had occupied territory not inhabited by people of German race (→17/11).

Forced to salute the invading Nazis, Prague's populace can only weep.

Commons cheer as Chamberlain pledges to defend Poland

March 31. Britain and France are now pledged whole-heartedly to defend Poland against attack. MPs on all sides cheered Mr Chamberlain when he gave this solemn undertaking today. An Anglo-French-Polish military alliance will be sealed next week.

"The Prime Minister's statement may prove as momentous as any made in this House for a quarter of a century," said Labour deputy leader Arthur Greenwood. Leslie Hore-Belisha, the Secretary for War, declared that the Army has a field force of 19 divisions and that "if we are involved in war our contribution will not be half-hearted nor based on any theory of limited liability" (→6/4).

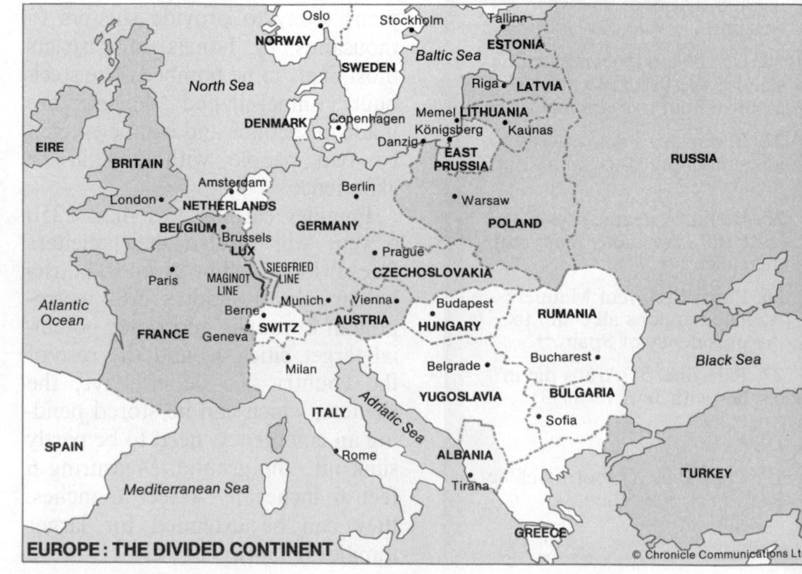

Civil war ends as Franco takes Madrid

March 28. The white flag has been hoisted over Madrid; Franco is firmly in control of the capital and the Spanish Civil War has ended in victory for the Nationalist forces. There was no resistance and no disorder. All classes fraternised during the day, and tonight there is wild rejoicing that the battle for Madrid, which has lasted almost three years, is at last over.

As soon as the white flags were hoisted over the principal buildings, the Republican leaders fled to Valencia and Franco's "Fifth Column" took over. As the first Nationalist troops entered the city at 10 o'clock this morning, a solitary Republican gun fired six shots as a last gesture of defiance.

Soon after, the first priest to be seen publicly in Madrid for nearly three years appeared in the Calle Alcala. He was given a rapturous reception, men and women kneeling about him asking to be blessed. The cry tonight in Madrid is "Viva Franco" (→ 1/4).

Madrid was a Loyalist stronghold, now its people salute Franco's troops.

Habemus Papam: Pius XII is Pope

March 2. After the shortest conclave in papal history, Cardinal Eugenio Pacelli was elected Pope today on his 63rd birthday. The tradional "Habemus Papam" – "We have a Pope" – was heard by 100,000 people in St. Peter's Square. Millions more heard the news at the same time from the Vatican wireless station. Unusually for a Pope, Cardinal Pacelli is a career Vatican official. He was Secretary of State to Pius XI and is to take the name of Pius XII.

German Government officials attacked the breach with tradition, but they really fear him for his anti-Nazi views. Vatican sources, however, stress his diplomatic qualities. Recently he held back an address by Pius XI attacking the Nazi ban on mixed marriages (→ 12/3).

Territorial Army is to be doubled

March 29. Preparations for a war with Germany are going full ahead with the announcement today that the Territorial Army is being doubled in strength to a total of 340,000 men. The Government has ordered the building of more weapons factories, more camps and vast supplies of boots and uniforms.

This move has come with the recognition by Forces' chiefs that the French army alone would not be able to withstand an attack by Hitler, and that once again Britain may be forced to send men to fight a land war on the Continent.

The measures will bring the army up to a total strength of 32 divisions. A rush of volunteers is expected and local authorities have been ordered to build new drill halls as rapidly as possible (→ 27/4).

1939

APRIL

Su	Mo	Tu	We	Th	Fr	Sa
						1
2	3	4	5	6	7	8
9	10	11	12	13	14	15
16	17	18	19	20	21	22
23	24	25	26	27	28	29
30						

1. Spain: The Nationalists declare the Spanish Civil War officially at an end (→ 7/5).

4. Iraq: The King is killed in an accident; four-year-old Emir Faisal succeeds.

5. UK: Britain's largest aircraft carrier, HMS Illustrious, is launched at Barrow (→ 25).

6. London: Britain, France and Poland sign a mutual assistance pact in case of attack (→ 28).

7. Albania: Mussolini's troops invade (→ 8).

8. Albania: Italian troops seize the capital Tirane; King Zog flees (→ 9).

9. London: Britain warns Italy not to go beyond Albania.→

9. Rome: Pope Pius XII denounces violations of international treaties (→ 8/5).

10. Holland: Dutch troops are sent to the German border (→ 18).

11. Glasgow: The city bans darts in pubs because they are "too dangerous".

15. Washington: Roosevelt asks Hitler for a pledge that he will not invade 31 named states (→ 5/9).

18. London: Chamberlain vows to go to the aid of Holland, Denmark or Switzerland if they are attacked (→ 20).

20. London: The government says it will set up a Ministry of Supply (→ 25).

25. London: The Budget includes £1,322 million to be spent on defence (→ 12/6).

26. Germany: Fritz Wendel sets a new air speed record of 484.4 mph in a Messerschmitt fighter.

28. Berlin: Hitler tears up the 1934 naval treaty with Britain and denounces the mutual assistance pact with Poland (→ 11/5).

29. London: Portsmouth beat Wolverhampton Wanderers 4-1 in the FA Cup Final.

30. Moscow: Russia proposes a mutual aid alliance with Britain and France (→ 3/5).

Bill to provide air raid shelters and evacuate children

April 5. Britain braced itself for war today as the Government announced plans for the immediate evacuation of 2,500,000 children should hostilities begin.

The Commons gave the Civil Defence Bill a second reading without a division, despite Opposition fears about the lack of deep shelters in London and other heavily-populated centres.

The Health Minister, Mr Walter Elliot, said that the timetable for evacuation within the space of a few days – "a colossal task" – was being worked out with the transport authorities.

People proposing to evacuate themselves should observe the rule "women and children first". Others should stay at work. The minister revealed that 279,435 shelters – providing cover for 1,500,000 people – had been delivered and 80,000 were being made weekly.

Megan Lloyd George, the Liberal, said that the Government had "resolutely refused to make up their minds about deep shelters". She wanted sound-proof shelters to avoid the equivalent of shell-shock.

Plans were also unveiled for the appointment of 12 commissioners – "men of national standing ... capable of undertaking great responsibilities" – with plenary powers to organise civil defence in London and the provinces should their regions be cut off (→ 16/8).

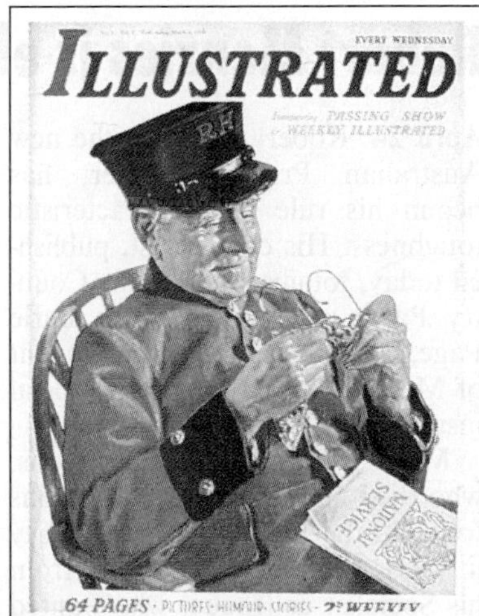

Never too old to fight – the Pensioners go on parade.

Britain plans to introduce conscription

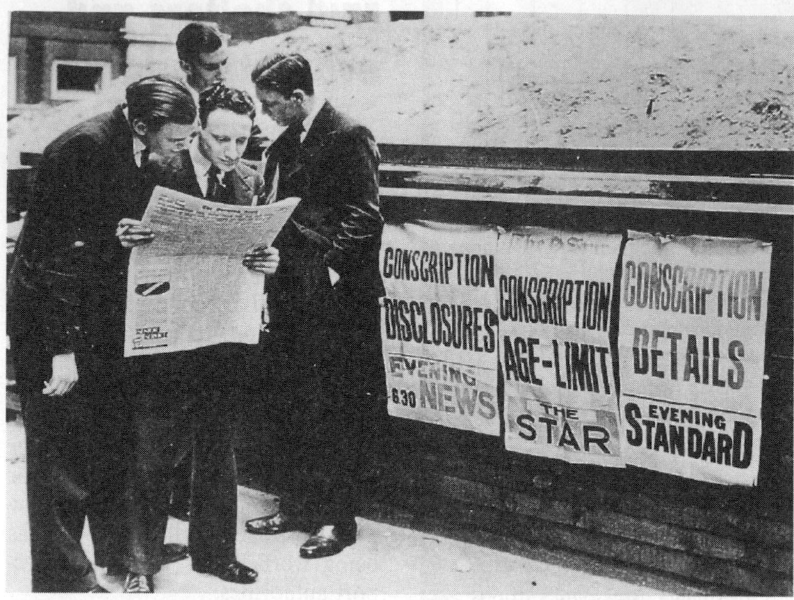

Young men who'll be in the firing line read about the call-up regulations.

April 27. A grave and subdued House of Commons endorsed the Government's decision to conscript men of 20 for military service last night. Labour voted against the Government, although many believe that they had done so after much heart-searching. In a rare and emotional appeal to the Opposition, the Prime Minister said that the decision was of national importance. "A very little weight one way or the other might decide whether war is going to come or not," he told the House.

"Conscription", said Mr Chamberlain, "is a departure from our cherished traditions" – although the Government's proposals had given comfort, relief and encouragement to Britain's friends. Labour's Aneurin Bevan opposed the measure. "We have lost and Hitler has won," he declared. Although Mr Attlee, the Opposition leader, was more moderate, he warned the House: "It is very dangerous to give generals all they want."

The Opposition claimed lack of consultation by the Government. Mr Chamberlain said that a decision was vital before a major speech by Herr Hitler in the Reichstag tomorrow.

A compulsory national register of youths under 21 is being compiled and conscripts will face six months of intensive training before being transferred to the Territorials or special reserve (→ 1/5).

Crisis as Mussolini occupies Albania

April 13. The consequences of Mussolini's occupation of Albania deepened today when, at an emergency meeting of the House of Commons, the Prime Minister pledged that Britain would go to the aid of Greece and Rumania in resisting any threat to their independence. An identical pledge was given simultaneously by the French.

Meanwhile, there are many reports of troop movements in Europe. Spain has concentrated forces near Gibraltar. The German government informed the British Admiralty that it was sending a fleet to exercise off Spain and crews of the British Mediterranean Fleet were ordered back to their ships.

In Rome an excited crowd cheered Mussolini when he appeared on the balcony of the Palazzo Venezia to announce that the Fascist Grand Council had approved the King of Italy's acceptance of the Albanian crown. The rightful wearer of that crown, King Zog, has fled his country to seek exile in Greece.

Il Duce used the tactics of his ally Hitler to subjugate his tiny neighbour. He first complained that Italian residents in Albania were being oppressed by "roving armed bands" and then, ignoring all attempts by the Albanians to negotiate, he sent in his troops.

His action was approved today by the Fascist Grand Council, which "expressed the gratitude of the Italian people to the Duce, founder of the Empire".

Robert Menzies is elected Australian PM

April 24. Robert Menzies, the new Australian Prime Minister, has begun his rule with characteristic toughness. His cabinet list, published today, totally excludes the Country Party whose leader, Sir Earle Page, has been a vigorous opponent of Menzies' plans to bring in social insurance.

Menzies succeeds Joseph Lyons, who died earlier this month. Lyons founded the United Australia Party in 1931, after he broke away from his Socialist colleagues who wanted to deal with the depression by defaulting on British loans.

The previous Government was a two-party coalition, but Menzies clearly feels strong enough to go it alone. He hopes to win popular support both for his social insurance policies and for strengthening Australia's defences in the face of the Japanese threat. Two new ministries will now be formed in these areas.

The new Prime Minister, who is only 44, has risen rapidly to political power. After practising as a barrister, he entered the state parliament in Victoria in 1928. By 1934 he was Attorney-General in the Lyons cabinet, a role in which he quickly made his mark.

Merle Oberon and Laurence Olivier star in William Wyler's film of "Wuthering Heights".

1939

MAY

Su	Mo	Tu	We	Th	Fr	Sa
	1	2	3	4	5	6
7	8	9	10	11	12	13
14	15	16	17	18	19	20
21	22	23	24	25	26	27
28	29	30	31			

1. London: The Military Training (Conscription) Bill is introduced (→ 19).

2. Berlin: Hitler offers the Danish government a non-aggression pact (→ 31).

3. Moscow: "Pro-Western" foreign minister Litvinov is dismissed and replaced by Vyacheslav Molotov (→ 19).

7. Geneva: Spain leaves the League of Nations (→ 5/8).

8. Rome: Pope Pius XII asks Germany, Italy, France, Britain and Poland to attend peace talks in the Vatican (→ 27/10).

11. London: Chamberlain warns Hitler that the use of force in Danzig means war (→ 30/7).

14. Los Angeles: Sam Goldwyn controls United Artists after buying out Charlie Chaplin, Mary Pickford and Douglas Fairbanks.

15. UK: Theatre managers approve a minimum weekly wage of £2 10/- for Equity members.

17. Quebec: The King and Queen arrive at the start of their North American tour (→ 7/6).

19. UK: The TUC decides not to oppose the government's conscription plans (→ 26).

19. London: MPs debate the Soviet offer of a treaty with Britain and France (→ 26).

20. US: Pan-American Airways begins scheduled transatlantic services to Europe.

25. London: The bill creating a Ministry of Supply is introduced (→ 9/10).

26. London: The Military Training Bill receives Royal Assent (→ 3/6).

26. Moscow: Britain and France propose talks with Stalin on a mutual aid pact.→

30. Oxford: The first woman fellow at a male college is Miss A. Bradbury, appointed bursar at Balliol College.

31. Berlin: Germany signs a non-aggression pact with Denmark (→ 1/6).

Italy and Germany sign Pact of Steel

As Italy and Germany forge their Fascist alliance, Mussolini demonstrates his home-grown goose-step.

May 22. After more than a year of vacillation, Mussolini has finally joined up with Hitler. In the Reich Chancellery in Berlin at 11.06 this morning, the foreign ministers of Germany and Italy, Joachim von Ribbentrop and Count Galeazzo Ciano, signed the "Pact of Steel" – a political and military alliance, committing the countries to supporting each other in time of war with "all military forces".

A special clause, insisted on by Hitler, said the two nations "are resolved to act side by side and with united forces to secure their living space". Although Hitler and Mussolini might seem to have much in common ideologically, Italy has always been wary of Germany's territorial ambitions: witness Mussolini's response in July 1934 when he sent troops to the Austrian border after Nazis staged a putsch in Vienna and murdered Chancellor Dollfuss.

Some diplomatic observers suggest that the reason he has not looked to the Western powers for support against Hitler was because they opposed his attack on Abyssinia. The reality, though, is that their failure to act when Hitler began rearming Germany, and again when he occupied the Rhineland, persuaded Mussolini that they could not be relied upon.

After the signing ceremony, Ciano invested Ribbentrop with the Order of the Annunziata, the highest Italian order of knighthood. Afterwards, Field Marshal Goering complained that he should have had the award, since the alliance was really his work (→ 1/9).

Stalin cautious on British proposals to join new pact

May 27. Britain's overtures to Russia for an agreement to prevent aggression in Europe are being digested in Moscow, as Soviet foreign policy undergoes a major revision, but there is growing evidence that Joseph Stalin may be preparing to abandon the quest for collective security or any rapprochement with the West.

Stalin's diplomacy last month made two moves in opposite directions. He proposed the conclusion of an alliance and military convention between Britain, France and Russia, but it is also believed that Soviet diplomats in Berlin have been cautiously broaching the subject of closer Russo-German co-operation.

Stalin's manoeuvres have clearly continued in the past few weeks with the replacement of Maxim Litvinov as Foreign Minister by Vyacheslav Molotov, a powerful Old Bolshevik. Since the end of the show trials Molotov has emerged as Stalin's principal lieutenant. Who could be better for negotiating with the Nazis?

In the recent House of Commons foreign affairs debate, there was support for an alliance with Russia from Lloyd George, Churchill and Eden, but Stalin may well feel that while the British Government wishes to be able to call on Russia as an ally, it may not want a formal coalition, and would try to deny him any real influence on its policies (→ 31/7).

UK farmers urged to dig for victory

May 3. Britain's farmers were today urged to plough up grazing pastures in a new Government drive to increase the proportion of food produced at home. At present less than a third of the British diet is produced at home. But ministers fear that food imports would be imperilled by an outbreak of war. So farmers will be paid £2 an acre to plough up and re-seed pastures. The Government hopes that one million acres will be converted to food or arable production (→ 25).

10,000 women protest at Palestine plan

May 22. Led by Mrs Herzog, wife of the Chief Rabbi, 10,000 Jewish women marched through Jerusalem today. Their aim was to publicise Jewish hostility to the British White Paper on Palestine, describing it as "a fatal error". The procession, which included doctors, teachers and nurses as well as numbers of farm workers, headed for the British military and civil headquarters in the King David Hotel.

There they presented a petition that had been "written in the blood and tears of Jewish womanhood throughout the world in whose name we speak". It continued: "We can never acquiesce in this British breach of faith. We pray that the British fatal error will be rectified at this eleventh hour, thus averting a very grave injustice contemplated by Britain, which is the greatest catastrophe which the Jewish people have faced."

The Jews are particularly alarmed at proposals to reduce immigration, fearing that Arabs will predominate under the new plan. Professor Yellin of the Hebrew University today returned his OBE in protest against the "betrayal" (→ 20/7).

Stalin and new minister Molotov.

1939

JUNE

Su	Mo	Tu	We	Th	Fr	Sa
				1	2	3
4	5	6	7	8	9	10
11	12	13	14	15	16	17
18	19	20	21	22	23	24
25	26	27	28	29	30	

1. UK: The Royal Navy's latest submarine, HMS Thetis, sinks during trials; 79 men are trapped aboard.→

1. Berlin: Hitler guarantees the frontiers of Yugoslavia.

3. UK: Britain's first military conscripts are enrolled (→1/10).

7. US: The King and Queen arrive on the first visit by a reigning British monarch to the US.→

7. Germany: Several hundred Polish Jews are deported to Poland (→21).

9. UK: More than 30 bombs go off in post boxes in cities around Britain (→25).

12. UK: 750 planes a month are reported to be under construction for the RAF (→13/7).

15. London: The government announces plans for a new Ministry of Information (→3/10).

16. French Indochina: The French submarine Phenix sinks with the loss of 69 crewmen.

17. Liverpool: The 34,000-ton liner Mauretania leaves on her maiden voyage.

21. Berlin: The Nazis order curbs on the business activities of Czech Jews (→24).

21. China: The Japanese capture the international treaty port of Swatow.

22. UK: The King and Queen return from their successful tour of North America.

24. Brazil: President Getulio Vargas allows 3,000 German Jews to enter Brazil (→6/7).

25. UK: Police raids follow more IRA bomb blasts in the West End of London which left 19 people injured.→

26. Paris: Public executions are abolished (→25/10).

27. London: The whole of New Zealand Avenue in the City is destroyed by fire.

30. London: Five IRA men are sentenced to 20 years in jail (→28/7).

BIRTH

11. British motor racing driver Jackie Stewart.

71 die in three-day agony of stricken sub

Rescuers drag lucky survivors from a hole cut in the stricken Thetis.

June 4. More than 70 men have died in the tragic sinking of the submarine Thetis, after three days of suspense-filled attempts at rescue.

The new submarine sank during trials in Liverpool Bay, but was soon spotted with her stern sticking up above the surface. The Navy instantly sent 21 warships to the spot as plans were made to cut a hole in her hull so the crew, and a civilian trials team, could escape.

The drama continued as small boats from the warships tapped out morse messages on the side of the stricken submarine and anxious onlookers listened to the desperate replies of the trapped crew. Four men managed to escape through a hatch, but it appears the crew could not close it again, and the vessel slowly filled with water.

Yesterday salvage vessels passed hawsers underneath the Thetis and hauled her bows to the surface. Six men jumped out from her hatches, but three soon died. The cables then snapped and the submarine slipped back beneath the surface (→22/7).

King and Queen at the NY World Fair

June 12. King George VI and Queen Elizabeth made a memorable visit to New York yesterday to visit the World Fair. Arriving from Washington, the royal couple were taken along the Hudson River to the Fair. Ships in the harbour sounded welcoming whistles and "Flying Fortresses" flew overhead as republican New Yorkers turned out in force to cheer the reigning monarch in their midst. Later their majesties were driven to the family home of President Roosevelt. New York's mayor sent a message: "The King and Queen are having a swell time; tell Mrs Roosevelt they'll be late for dinner."

Irish government outlaws the IRA

June 23. The government of Eire today suppressed the Irish Republican Army. Tomorrow's parade to the grave of Wolfe Tone, an annual Republican pilgrimage, has also been banned. The Irish Army has surrounded Bodenstown cemetery, with instructions to use force if necessary.

In Dublin some were surprised that Eamon de Valera should ban old comrades in arms. Others felt he had no option given their bombing campaign against the British. Wolfe Tone was a barrister, the most celebrated figure of the failed revolution of 1798 (→30).

Seaside town is up for sale in Sussex

June 16. The entire Sussex seaside town of Littlehampton has been sold for development by its owner, the Duke of Norfolk, it was revealed today.

Littlehampton, at the mouth of the River Adur, has been in the possession of the Norfolk family for centuries and includes 1,100 acres of open land.

Hundreds of leaseholds and general house properties are included in the deal, and 850 acres of land have been allocated for possible new building.

Going through a programme of physical jerks in the gym of their London headquarters, members of the Women's League of Health and Beauty show admirers that exercise can be fun and fashionable too.

1939

JULY

Su	Mo	Tu	We	Th	Fr	Sa
						1
2	3	4	5	6	7	8
9	10	11	12	13	14	15
16	17	18	19	20	21	22
23	24	25	26	27	28	29
30	31					

1. London: The curtain falls for the last time on the Lyceum Theatre, at the end of John Gielgud's "Hamlet" run.

2. London: The King has approved the formation of the Women's Auxiliary Air Force.

4. Vienna: Nazi thugs beat up the Archbishop of Vienna, Cardinal Theodor Innitzer.

6. Berlin: All Jews in the Reich are ordered to join a new Reich "Union of Jews".

8. Wimbledon: Bobby Riggs beats Elwood Cooke in the Men's Singles final; Alice Marble beats Kay Stammers in the Women's Singles final.

10. UK: Len Harvey beats Jock McAvoy for the world, British and Empire light-heavyweight boxing crown.

13. London: Chancellor Sir John Simon announces new defence borrowings of £500 million.

14. London: The government says all infants and nursing mothers will get fresh milk free or at no more than 2 pence a pint.

19. London: General Sir Archibald Wavell is appointed Commander-in-Chief of British forces in the Middle East (→ 9/8).

20. Danzig: 2,000 Nazi guards arrive from Germany.→

20. Tibet: A five-year-old boy is reported to have been chosen as the new Dalai Lama (→ 22/2/40).

22. UK: The submarine HMS Thetis is lifted from the sea bed, seven weeks after the tragedy in which 71 died.

26. London: One person dies and 18 are hurt in a suspected IRA bomb blast (→ 27).

27. London: 40 houses in North London are raided in a hunt for IRA bombers.→

27. Moscow: An Anglo-French delegation arrives to discuss a three-power defence pact (→ 31).

31. London: Chamberlain says that three power military talks will begin in Moscow immediately (→ 11/8).

Hitler's designs on Danzig spark crisis

Hitler Youth and Maidens turn out in Berlin to hail their conquering hero.

July 30. It begins to look as though the Baltic port of Danzig could provide the spark to set off the explosion of a European war. The Germans are smuggling arms and military instructors into the Free City, and local Nazis are increasingly acting as though it has been returned to Germany. Attacks on Poles have become a regular occurrence, and Poles employed in the shipyards are being arrested and deported to concentration camps in Germany.

Poland, however, has no intention of allowing Hitler to get his way. The city, sitting at the mouth of the Vistula river, occupies a vital strategic position; at the Treaty of Versailles a Polish corridor was established along the river, giving the country access to the Baltic. Losing the city would mean losing access to the sea. Though it is a predominantly German city, in the Polish view it cannot revert to Germany, but must remain a Free City under League of Nations mandate.

The Polish stand is backed by the British Government. In the House of Commons earlier this month, Mr Chamberlain, the Prime Minister, said that if Poland felt obliged to use force to maintain the status quo in Danzig then Britain would go to her aid (→ 31/8).

Illegal Palestine immigrants face curbs

July 20. Malcolm MacDonald, the Colonial Secretary, last night warned that the illegal entry of thousands of Jews into Palestine was fanning the flames of Arab revolt. Suspicious Arabs thought that Britain was condoning it so as to get round declared policy, and this was perpetuating dangerous bitterness.

He told the Commons of organised attempts to smash the Government's policy by breaking Palestine law. The immigration quota for October to March next year has been suspended because of the large numbers of illegal Jewish arrivals; that total will now be deducted from future quotas. Steps are being taken in countries of embarkation to check illegal immigration and to detain the ships being used.

Denying that the Government was indifferent to the plight of refugees, he said that 75,000 were allowed to enter over a five-year period, but Palestine could not solve the whole refugee problem, though special provision was made for people from Central Europe. What the Colonial Secretary condemned was the organised traffic in immigrants. In two months 8,000 had tried to smuggle themselves in. Of those entering now, 40 per cent were Polish and Rumanian, not from "Greater Germany".

Drastic measures taken against IRA

July 29. A big round-up of suspected IRA terrorists began tonight as soon as new anti-terrorism legislation came into force. The Home Office drew up 19 expulsion orders and many arrests were made. There were unprecedented scenes at Euston Station when the Irish Mail train had to run in three parts to cope with an exodus of Irishmen returning home.

Special security precautions were ordered in London and other cities. The public will be banned from the Houses of Parliament this weekend, and bus conductors are not allowing passengers to carry suitcases. The draft new law, which has been rushed through Parliament, allows arrests without warrants. Many more can be expected (→ 25/8).

From dream semis to suburban sprawl

An Englishman's suburban castle.

July 31. Four million new houses have now been built in Britain in the years since the Great War. This building boom has been concentrated in – but not confined to – the south-east of England, but the dream of a "home of your own" "semi" has turned once rural areas into little more than suburbs. Overall some 60,000 acres a year have been used for building, prompting some local authorities to buy up land outside cities as "green belt" and others to call for controls on "ribbon development" along the new highways.

1939

AUGUST

Su	Mo	Tu	We	Th	Fr	Sa
		1	2	3	4	5
6	7	8	9	10	11	12
13	14	15	16	17	18	19
20	21	22	23	24	25	26
27	28	29	30	31		

1. US: Band leader Glenn Miller records the song "In the mood" (→12/1943).

5. Madrid: Franco executes 53 following the murder of the police chief.

9. UK: The King inspects the 133 ships of Britain's newly mobilised Auxiliary Fleet at Weymouth (→31).

11. Moscow: Britain's envoy to military talks, Admiral Sir Reginald Ranfurly-Plunkett-Ernle-Erle-Drax, arrives (→31/10).

14. S. Africa: President Antonio Carmona of Portugal is the first foreign head of state to visit the Union.

16. London: The Registrar-General says everyone will have an identity card and number in the event of war (→24).

17. Germany: Hitler closes the border with Poland in Upper Silesia (→20).

20. Poland: Troops are rushed to the border as tension continues to mount (→22).

22. London: Britain and France reaffirm their pledge to assist Poland (→26).

23. Brussels: Belgium restates its neutrality in the coming conflict (→6/10).

24. London: Chamberlain is granted wide-ranging war powers (→3/9).

25. London: All movable treasures are taken to safety from the major museums, galleries and Westminster Abbey (→31).

26. London: Hitler demands Danzig, the Polish Corridor, and the end of the Anglo-French pledge to Poland (→29).

28. London: The Admiralty closes the Baltic and Mediterranean to British merchant shipping (→31).

29. Berlin: Hitler sends Poland an ultimatum on Danzig and the Corridor.→

30. Paris: 16,000 children are evacuated.→

31. London: The Army and RAF reserves are called up; the Royal Navy is mobilised.→

Hitler and Stalin vow not to go to war

Aug 23. In a move that surprised and shocked the Western Powers, Germany and the Soviet Union today signed a Non-Aggression Pact, making the outbreak of a European war virtually inevitable. The signing took place in the Kremlin; Joachim von Ribbentrop signed for Germany and Vyacheslav Molotov for the Soviet Union. After the ceremony Joseph Stalin, the Soviet leader, proposed a toast. "I know how much the German people love their Fuehrer," he said. "I should therefore like to drink to his health."

It is now apparent that, even as the British military mission was arriving in Moscow for talks on a pact directed at discouraging German aggression against Poland, the Soviet Union was already in secret negotiation with Hitler. It is not known which side made the first move, but it is clear that, for Hitler, an immediate understanding with Moscow was of prime importance.

The final article in the treaty says it "comes into force immediately after it has been signed" and will be ratified "in the shortest possible time". The two sides bind themselves to refrain from every use of force against each other and pledge themselves not to join with other powers in a hostile alliance.

For Hitler and Stalin, the two dictators who for the past six years, at least, have been engaged in mutual vilification, it is quite a turnabout.

The pact makes German militar[y] action much more likely. Everywhere in Germany today heav[y] transport, motor cycles and civilia[n] aircraft are being commandeered. General Walther von Brauchitsch, army C-in-C, is to broadcast a message to all soldiers nex[t] Saturday evening.

Ribbentrop and Molotov, watched by Stalin, confirm the pact.

First jet takes to German skies

Aug 27. An aeroplane powered by an entirely new type of engine flew for the first time today. Technically the engine is a gas turbine, but to initiates it is known as the "jet" engine, as it works by expelling a jet of hot gas at very high speed.

The aircraft is the German Heinkel He-178. Though it is the first to fly powered by a jet engine, a gas turbine was first operated successfully on the ground in Britain, by Air Commodore Frank Whittle, in April 1937.

Jet engines work by taking in air at the front, compressing it, feeding fuel into the stream and burning it. The resulting jet of hot gases emerging from the rear of the engine propels the aircraft.

In time jet engines will dramatically increase the speed of aircraft, and in theory they should use less fuel than propeller-driven aircraft, too (→13/11).

New Yorkers go off to see the Wizard

Judy Garland: on the road to Oz.

Aug 18. "The Wizard of Oz", a Technicolor film of Frank Baum's children's classic, made a star of 17-year-old Judy Garland tonight. She plays Dorothy, who sings Harold Arlen's "Over the Rainbow" and goes off to see the Wizard with a Scarecrow (Ray Bolger), Tin Man (Jack Haley) and Cowardly Lion (Bert Lahr).

IRA bombers kill five in Coventry

Aug 25. Five people were killed an[d] nearly 50 injured today in the wors[t] bomb explosion since the IR[A] began its campaign eight month[s] ago. Police believe the bomb wa[s] planted in a tradesman's bo[x] tricycle left standing in Broadgate the main street of Coventry.

The bomb exploded just befor[e] 2.30pm, shattering more than 2[…] shopfronts and blasting holes in th[e] road. Cars were overturned; glass handbags and children's toys wer[e] scattered everywhere. The centre o[f] the town, crowded with weeken[d] shoppers a few minutes earlie[r] looked like a battlefield.

One of the dead, Laura Ansell o[f] Earlsdon near Coventry, was due t[o] be married in a fortnight. Workme[n] saw a young man run away fro[m] the scene of the explosion toward[s] the railway station. He had alread[y] left on a Birmingham train befor[e] police reached the station.

Europe walks in the shadow of impending war

On the march: men and armour of the German army parade in Berlin.

Together, but far from home: Britain's young evacuees go to the country.

Forces on alert as Polish crisis deepens

ug 31. Europe's mobilisation for var is almost complete. Throughout Poland posters have gone up ordering all reservists and retired roops, as well as men up to the age of 40 with call-up papers, to report o barracks. France has been calling-up reservists for the past ten lays, and today the railways were equisitioned. Belgium announced hat its frontier and anti-aircraft lefences are fully manned. Full nobilisation for defence of the fronters is under way in Switzerland.

In Britain the call up continues o disrupt daily life; West Ham ootball club lost most of its players esterday when their papers for the Essex Regiment searchlight section rrived.

In London, the Admiralty issued orders closing the Mediterranean nd the Baltic to British merchant hipping. Insurance rates have been doubled. The King yesterday visited the War Office and the Air Ministry to inspect deep bomb and gas proof shelters.

In Berlin, though Hitler is set on having his war with Poland, he is reported to be still hoping he can somehow manoeuvre the British Government into reneging on its pledge to go to Poland's aid. Through a Swedish intermediary, the German dictator sent a message to London offering Britain a pact to defend the British Empire. In return, Britain should help Germany obtain Danzig and the Polish Corridor. Germany must also have her colonies returned to her.

The British, apparently, have declined Hitler's offer to defend the Empire. As for Poland, Britain pointed out that she was bound by treaty to defend the Poles if they were attacked (→ 1/9).

Children lead the evacuation from cities

Aug 31. Britain's cities and towns are strangely quiet today. The children are leaving. Labelled and clutching their few personal possessions and gas-masks, over 1.5 million of them are being evacuated to safe areas in the country. The great exodus began at 5.30am yesterday and will continue for the rest of the week.

Parents wishing to evacuate their children were told to send them to school with no more than spare clothing, toothbrush, comb and a handkerchief – and a bag of food for the day.

Schools have become reception centres with fleets of buses – taken off their usual routes – conveying the evacuees to the main-line stations. Seventy-two London underground stations have been partly closed to the public to speed the long-planned operation. Few parents know where their children will end up tonight – although the Government says they will be told "as soon as possible".

Throughout the country, billeting officers are preparing to receive "townie" children and introduce them to their temporary hosts. Already, reports are coming in of country folk shocked by the verminous condition of some children from city slums; and equal horror expressed by city-bred children at their strange surroundings. For many, it was their first sight of cows and other farm animals.

Meanwhile, Britain's historic treasures are being moved to safety. The Coronation Chair has been taken by train to an unknown destination, as have art objects from galleries and the British Museum. Historic records are being put on film before leaving (→ 3/9).

1939

SEPTEMBER

Su	Mo	Tu	We	Th	Fr	Sa
					1	2
3	4	5	6	7	8	9
10	11	12	13	14	15	16
17	18	19	20	21	22	23
24	25	26	27	28	29	30

1. Poland: German troops invade at 5.45 am.→

1. Rome: Mussolini announces Italy's neutrality.

2. Warsaw: 21 die in a German air raid.→

3. London and Paris: War is declared on Germany.

4. Germany: French troops cross the German frontier into the Saarland.

5. Washington: Roosevelt declares US neutrality (→30).

6. Poland: The government flees from Warsaw to Lublin (→17).

7. Germany: Troops are despatched to meet the French.

9. UK: Imperial Airways suspends passenger bookings (→24/11).

12. France: Chamberlain flies in for talks with the Allied Supreme Council (→19).

12. London: The Forces' entertainment organisation ENSA is formed.

17. Poland: Soviet troops invade.→

18. Atlantic: The aircraft carrier HMS Courageous is sunk with the loss of 500 men (→30).

19. London: Chamberlain says the war will not end until Hitlerism is destroyed (→30).

20. London: Reports tell of an anti-German revolt in Bohemia, Moravia and Slovakia.

22. Rumania: Scores of executions follow the murder by Fascist Iron Guards of premier Armand Calinescu.

26. Paris: The French Communist Party is dissolved by the government.

27. London: The War Budget raises income tax to its highest ever figure of 7/6d. in the pound.

29. Warsaw: Polish troops evacuate as the city surrenders to the Wehrmacht.→

DEATH

23. Austrian psychoanalyst Sigmund Freud (*6/5/1856).

Germany and Russia invade Poland

Sept 30. Poland lies shattered, partitioned yet again by her more powerful neighbours, and the English language has acquired a terrifying new word: "blitzkrieg", meaning lightning war.

Shortly before 6am on Friday, September 1, German forces crossed the Polish frontier in the wake of heavy aerial bombardments. They went on to prove conclusively that fast-moving armoured forces operating in combination with warplanes could overcome the stalemate of trench warfare.

The Wehrmacht force of 1.25 million men that swept into Poland included six armoured divisions and eight motorised divisions with armoured units. The Luftwaffe knocked out the Polish railway system and shot the Polish air force out of the sky.

A few days before the invasion Hitler delivered a long speech on the radio, complaining that the Polish government had rebuffed all his efforts to reach a peaceful solution to the problem of Danzig and the Polish Corridor. Then a few inmates of Germany's concentration camps were drugged and photographed at frontier posts as "casualties" of a Polish "attack". The early German communiques spoke of its operations as counter-attacks.

The German forces, striking south from East Prussia and east from Germany proper, had cut the Corridor by September 3 – the day Britain and France declared war – and by September 8 had covered over 140 miles to reach the gates of Warsaw, subsequently devastated by two weeks of nightmarish bombing. On the 17th Russia invaded, and two days ago the partition of Poland was agreed in Moscow. The Soviets get 76,000 square miles of the eastern region with its population of 12.8 million, while Germany takes most of the west, including Warsaw.

The invasion has been condemned by almost every sovereign state and Russia has been expelled from the League of Nations. An estimated 60,000 Poles have been killed, 200,000 have been wounded and 700,000 are now prisoners. The Polish government has fled to Rumania and Poland as a state has ceased to exist (→2/10).

The Polish cavalry. Magnificent but no match for the German blitzkrieg.

Victorious German troops round up dispirited civilians on the streets of Warsaw. The capture of the city, after two weeks of nightmarish bombing, came as the climax to Hitler's lightning invasion of the country.

In a mood of grim satisfaction Britain is at war

Sep 3. "This country is now at war with Germany. We are ready." The fateful words came at last from the Prime Minister's lips in the House of Commons at noon today. There was profound silence but also a sense of immense relief and grim satisfaction. The shilly-shallying is over. The die is cast.

Outside in the Sunday sunshine the crowds shared those feelings. Whatever the future holds, Britain's national honour is upheld. Tonight the King broadcast to the Commonwealth. He told his subjects: "We can only do the right as we see the right, and reverently commit our cause to God."

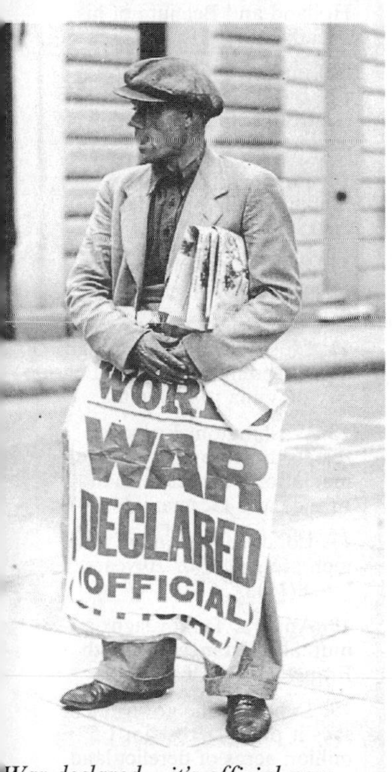

War declared – it's official now.

The formal declaration of war was at 11am when Britain's ultimatum to Germany expired. The Germans had not suspended their attack on Poland so Britain was at war with Hitler's Reich. Mr Chamberlain's statement in Parliament took just two minutes. Winning the war will take longer.

Half-an-hour after its declaration, air raid sirens sounded in London. It was a false alarm. An unidentified aircraft – subsequently proved to be friendly – had been seen approaching the south coast.

The Prime Minister spoke decisively today. It was different last night. MPs in emergency session expected him to announce an ultimatum and he held back. When Arthur Greenwood, Labour's acting leader, rose to speak, there was a cry from the Tory benches of "Speak for England". He demanded no more delay.

Behind the scenes cabinet ministers were divided and dithering. Eventually Mr Chamberlain agreed to send the ultimatum and it was delivered in Berlin at 9am today. With no reply received two hours later, the German Embassy in London was formally notified that a state of war exists.

The French Government sent a similar ultimatum to Berlin today, and its declaration of war came from Paris at 5pm. A joint Anglo-French statement said that the two governments will avoid bombing of civilians and do not intend to use poison gas or germ warfare. It asked the Germans to do likewise. Otherwise, the Allies must revise their positions (→12).

Prime Minister Chamberlain drives to the House, ready to declare war.

In a Paris cafe British and French troops drink a toast to victory.

Allied ships fall victim to German subs

Sept 30. French guns are pounding the German lines near Saarbrucken on the Western Front and some units have managed to push over the frontier into Germany, but at sea it is the U-boats of the Reich which have taken the lead in these first three weeks of war.

A U-boat sank the Glasgow liner Athenia with the loss of 112 lives on the day war was declared, prompting an immediate Allied blockade of German ports. On September 4, the RAF bombed a German fleet at the North Sea entrance to the Kiel Canal, but almost as much British effort has gone into dropping six million leaflets on Germany calling for surrender. They implore the Germans to "insist upon peace", but their effect is pitiful: so far 20 Allied ships have become the victims of U-boats.

Some still cannot believe it is war. The Air Minister, Kingsley Wood, rejected a plan to bomb the Black Forest on the grounds it is private property (→16/10).

Nations take sides as war is declared

Sept 30. The world's nations have rapidly taken up their positions with regard to the outbreak of war in Europe. The Commonwealth has, as expected, joined Great Britain in the fight against Nazism. The United States has also taken up its expected stance, that of neutralism.

President Roosevelt has made a proclamation of neutrality similar to that made by President Wilson at the outbreak of war in 1914, three years before America entered the war. In one proclamation the President has denied US territory to the belligerents, and in another he has embargoed the shipment of arms to all those countries in which, he said, "a state of war unhappily exists".

Meanwhile European nations not so far involved in the war are taking military precautions: Yugoslavia has issued orders for general mobilisation and Sweden and Norway, while determined to remain neutral, have put their armed forces on the highest alert (→4/11).

Britain responds to war with regulations

Sept 30. After a month of anxiety, false alarms and uncertainty, Britain is settling down for a war-time winter. The Government had expected 100,000 casualties during the first few weeks of the war. Hospitals had been cleared, mortuaries stacked with piles of cardboard coffins, and lime-pits dug to cope with the dead. Every home has a hand-operated stirrup-pump and long-handled shovel to deal with incendiary bombs. Memories of the Spanish Civil War and Guernica were still fresh.

But the blitzkrieg did not happen. Instead, Britain is being bombarded by regulations, exhortations and petty officialdom. Public Information Leaflet No. 1 urges everyone to carry a luggage label with their name and address. A national register is being completed and identity cards will be issued by the end of the month.

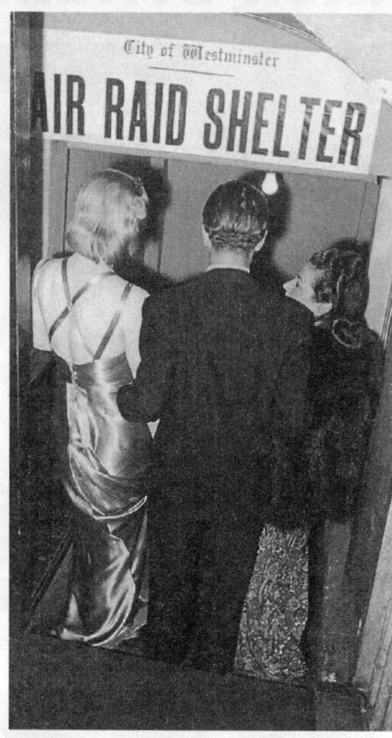

Precautions at the Paradise Club.

As they stumble home through blacked-out streets, avoiding vehicles with dimmed-out headlights, Britons are fast becoming used to the air-raid wardens' cries of "Put that light out!". Giant posters have appeared urging the populace to save, dig, work, buy war bonds, not travel, not waste nor spread rumours – all for victory.

The blackout is total with the shops long since sold out of black curtain material. Householders are urged (Leaflet No.2) to paint the edges of their windows black. Even the slightest chink of light can lead to heavy fines. Road deaths have doubled, forcing the Government to ease vehicle lighting restrictions – headlamps had to be covered with cardboard with two-inch wide holes – and allow one headlight to be lit.

Commuters glow an eerie blue in dimmed railway compartments, while unlit buses cause chaos to drivers and passengers alike. Since crime has been minimal this month, the CID have interned 6,000 suspect aliens (→ 9/10).

Polish refugees hope for sanctuary as they arrive in London by ship.

Churchill back as Cabinet reshuffled

Sept 4. The excited signal was flashed to the Fleet "Winnie's back". Winston Churchill is First Lord of the Admiralty again – the post he held 25 years ago at the outbreak of the last war. He now joins a small "war cabinet".

Mr Chamberlain has also recalled Anthony Eden to be Dominions Secretary, outside the cabinet but with special access to it. So the two leading Tories most closely associated with resistance to Hitler are promptly out of the political wilderness and back into action.

Alongside the cabinet reshuffle, it was announced that the King has made General Viscount Gort VC, who has been Chief of the Imperial General Staff, the new commander of British Field Forces. There will be new government departments of Food, National Service, Information and Economic Warfare.

Mr. Churchill with 615 squadron.

Labour and Liberal leaders have declined to join Mr Chamberlain's reconstructed team, but they have stated that they will fully support the war effort. In a formal statement the Labour Party pledged: "all the energy and devotion of the Labour Movement to secure the aggressor's defeat".

There is all-round satisfaction that self-governing Australia, New Zealand and Canada have instantly supported the Mother Country by also declaring war. The old Empire has come up trumps.

1939

OCTOBER

Su	Mo	Tu	We	Th	Fr	Sa
1	2	3	4	5	6	7
8	9	10	11	12	13	14
15	16	17	18	19	20	21
22	23	24	25	26	27	28
29	30	31				

1. UK: 250,000 more conscripts are called up (→ 12/10).

2. Washington: The US recognises the Polish government in exile set up in Paris (→ 13).

3. London: Chamberlain says a new Whitehall department to handle censorship and control of news is to be set up.

5. Riga: Latvia signs a mutual aid pact with the USSR.

6. Berlin: Hitler reassures Holland and Belgium of his friendship (→ 11).

9. London: The Prices of Food Bill is introduced to control profiteering, following a series of complaints (→ 19).

10. Finland: The Finns mobilise their Baltic fleet (→ 25/11).

11. Paris: Premier Daladier rejects Hitler's peace overtures.→

11. Moscow: The USSR signs a pact ceding the former Polish city of Vilna to Lithuania.

13. Washington: Roosevelt rejects a plea by Hitler for mediation between Britain, France and Germany (→ 24).

17. London: Four more IRA men are jailed for 20 years (→ 18/11).

19. Ankara: Turkey signs a mutual assistance pact with France and the UK.

19. London: The government says it plans to reclaim 1.5 million acres of derelict land for agriculture (→ 25).

24. France: The first casualty clearing station is set up by the British Expeditionary Force.

25. London: The government is to drop unfinished pre-war legislation (→ 1/11).

28. Germany: The SS proposes that all Jews should be made to wear a yellow Star of David (→ 30).

28. UK: 35 die in a pit explosion near Dunfermline in Scotland.

31. Moscow: Soviet foreign minister Molotov says the USSR will remain neutral (→ 14/12).

Royal Oak is sunk in its home base

Oct 16. More than 800 are believed to have died aboard the battleship Royal Oak after she was hit by a German torpedo in her home base of Scapa Flow two days ago. The sinking has come as a shock because most thought it impossible for a U-boat to penetrate the anchorage's defences, and that the battleship's armour would repel a torpedo. Only 396 crew survived.

Today, in a separate development, German aircraft carried out an air raid on the Firth of Forth, the first time in the present war that enemy planes have reached Britain. The raid, on the naval base at Rosyth, took the defenders by surprise. No air-raid warnings were sounded but four bombers were shot down.

The U-boat war is intensifying and around 156,000 tons of British shipping has fallen victim to German submarines. One French steamer, the Louisiane, was shelled and sunk in the Atlantic because she refused food supplies to a U-boat which stopped her. Many servicemen's wives and their children lost their lives in another attack on the steamship Yorkshire.

By contrast, estimates are that around one-third of the 60 German U-boats thought to be ready for action at the beginning of the war have now been sunk. Meanwhile, the blockade of Germany is tightening, with more than 100 ships a week passing through the North Sea being searched and some German ships captured (→20/11).

A British sub going off on patrol.

Report tells of Nazi cruelty toward Jews

Oct 30. The horrors of the Nazis' dreaded concentration camps were documented in a massive Government White Paper published today. It is a collection of reports, said to be of unimpeachable authority, painstakingly collected by British diplomats in Germany over the past few years.

"The treatment (of inmates) is reminiscent of the darkest ages in the history of man," says the White Paper. The Government explains that it was forced to make the revelations because of "shameless and unscrupulous German propaganda" accusing Britain of atrocities in South Africa 40 years ago.

Hitler is said personally to have ordered the flogging of Jews. There are terrifying and detailed descriptions of barbarous and systematic tortures inflicted mainly by guards aged 17 to 20 in the Dachau and Buchenwald camps. Some prisoners go mad. Others feign escape attempts in order to get shot and be released from the agony of living.

One British official suggests that mass sexual perversion in Germany can be the only explanation for the otherwise inexplicable sadistic cruelty of SS camp guards, who appear to revel and vie with each other in the authorised regime of brutality and terror (→10/12).

The British land 158,000 men in France

Oct 12. British troops are now in France in strength. So far 158,000 men of the British Expeditionary Force, together with 25,000 vehicles, have been taken across the Channel to bolster the French defence under General Gamelin, the French Supreme Commander.

The troop movements are being heralded as a great achievement. A small team of War Office planners worked out every detail of the programme, helped by just seven clerks and typists. Devious routes were taken across Britain to avoid air attacks on convoys. The men moved in small groups, concealed by day and only travelling at night, and there was not a single casualty. The RAF has been over France for some weeks carrying out reconnaissance flights on the Siegfried line. The War Secretary, Leslie Hore-Belisha, told the Commons that troops were also being sent to the Middle East to reinforce British interests there.

At the same time a general call-up has started, drawing 250,000 men over 20 into the armed forces. At present there are no plans to conscript younger men.

Few of those eligible will be exempt from the call-up, except those in reserved occupations and the clergy. Men who can show their families would suffer exceptional hardship may apply for a postponement and those who do not want to fight can ask to have their names entered on a register of conscientious objectors (→24).

An excited crowd gathers round a bullet-riddled Nazi warplane that has crash-landed on a Scottish moor.

Hitler furious at Allies for turning down peace offer

Oct 24. An end to Hitler's month-long peace offensive was signalled tonight by Joachim von Ribbentrop, the German Foreign Minister. In a speech in Danzig, he accused Britain of "secretly and relentlessly preparing for war against Germany for years", but victory in the war was "guaranteed by Hitler". The German people, Ribbentrop said, would fight to the bitter end.

Hitler is reported to be angry that his peace overtures have been rebuffed by Britain and France. After his blitzkrieg conquest of Poland, Hitler told the Reichstag that he wanted only peacc and friendship with Great Britain and France; there was absolutely no reason for a war to be fought in the West.

He proposed a conference of leading European nations to determine the future of the continent. This was followed by big headlines in the Nazi party newspaper, the Voelkisher Beobachter: "Germany's will for peace – No war aims against France and England."

Hitler got his answer in a House of Commons statement by Neville Chamberlain, who described the Hitler proposals as "vague and uncertain" containing "no suggestions for righting the wrongs done to Czechoslovakia and Poland." The British Prime Minister, who a year ago had returned from Munich with Hitler's signature on a piece of paper promising peace, now said no reliance could be put on "the promises of the present German government".

1939

NOVEMBER

Su	Mo	Tu	We	Th	Fr	Sa
			1	2	3	4
5	6	7	8	9	10	11
12	13	14	15	16	17	18
19	20	21	22	23	24	25
26	27	28	29	30		

1. London: The government says butter and bacon will be rationed from mid-December (→ 14).

4. Washington: Congress approves the "Cash and Carry" Bill, which ends the arms embargo.→

7. Washington: An Anglo-French purchase commission is set up to buy US defence materials.

10. Switzerland: General mobilisation is ordered.

13. UK: The first bombs are dropped on British soil, on the Shetlands (→ 23).

14. UK: Petrol is increased by a penny halfpenny a gallon to 1/9d. halfpenny a gallon.

14. London: The government announces bigger family allowances for servicemen (→ 22/12).

17. Prague: Nine Czech students are executed by the Nazis for leading anti-German demonstrations (→ 24).

18. London: Three IRA bombs go off in Piccadilly Circus (→ 26).

21. Berlin: Two Britons are arrested for involvement in the failed bomb attempt on Hitler's life.

23. UK: German planes drop mines in the Thames estuary.

24. Czechoslovakia: 120 students are shot by the Gestapo.

24. London: Imperial Airways and British Airways merge to form the British Overseas Airways Corporation.

25. Finland: The USSR tells Finnish troops to pull back 16 miles from the Russian border (→ 26).

26. London: One person is killed and 22 injured when IRA bombs go off at Victoria and King's Cross stations.

26. Helsinki: The Finns ignore Soviet demands for the withdrawal of Finnish troops; border clashes occur (→ 28).

28. Moscow: Stalin renounces the Finno-Soviet non-aggression pact (→ 30).

30. Finland: Soviet planes bomb Helsinki and Viipuri.→

Munich bomb blast fails to catch Hitler

Hitler comforts the relatives of those killed by a bomb meant for him.

Nov 8. Seven people were killed and over 60 injured when a bomb exploded in the Buergerbraukeller, in Munich tonight soon after Hitler had delivered his traditional speech on the anniversary of his abortive 1923 putsch.

The speech was shorter than usual and the Fuehrer, instead of staying to talk of old times with party comrades, as he has done in past years, took his leave at once. Almost immediately the bomb, which had been hidden behind the speaker's platform, went off.

For several hours after the explosion, the Ministry of Propaganda in Berlin was insisting that it knew nothing of the incident. But then Nazi journalists employed on the party newspaper, the Voelkischer Beobachter, said they had been told the bomb had been planted by British agents. According to one source Heinrich Himmler, chief of the SS, arranged for the bomb to be planted by a concentration camp prisoner, who can later be arrested and make a "confession" implicating the British.

Himmler's purpose is said to be to gain more support for the war by stirring up feeling against the British. German morale is thought to be poor. Recently, a rumour went round Berlin saying the British government had resigned and the war would end. People when they heard it rushed into the streets cheering and dancing (→ 21).

US ends embargo on selling arms

Nov 4. At a press conference this afternoon President Roosevelt said that tomorrow he would sign the Neutrality Bill. This will allow Britain and France to buy arms and munitions in the United States.

This ends a fierce debate in Congress over neutrality which has been going on since Congress met in a special session on September 21. It also ends the conflict between FDR and the isolationists which began when Congress passed the first Neutrality Act in 1935.

One immediate effect will be to make 800 planes available to Britain and France. Allied war orders are expected to total £250 million over the next few weeks (→ 7).

Magnetic mines intensify sea war

Nov 20. A new type of magnetic mine is taking its toll in the North Sea. So although U-boats are finding it harder to mount surface attacks, the sea war is getting worse.

The Admiralty believes five British ships and several foreign vessels have been sunk by the new mines, including the neutral Dutch ship, the Simon Bolivar, sunk with the loss of 140 lives. They are laid by specially-designed U-boats.

The German newspapers are boasting about the mines which go off even before they touch the hull of a vessel. While minesweepers are at work clearing shipping routes, many of the mines are adrift and difficult to find.

Helsinki in flames as Russia invades

Nov 30. The Soviet Union invaded tiny Finland today; Red aircraft savagely bombed Helsinki, leaving areas in flames. Heavy fighting was reported along the 50-mile Karelian isthmus front where the Red Army was hoping to punch holes in the Mannerheim Line.

The attack came after the Finns ignored an ultimatum to surrender part of Karelia, which Stalin says is needed for the defence of Leningrad. The Finns have also made it clear they do not regard themselves as part of the Russian sphere of influence.

Early reports of the fighting suggest the Red Army will not find the Finns a push-over. They are known to have well-organised defences along the Mannerheim Line, with pillboxes and artillery batteries, and they have units of very mobile ski troops. At the same time the Russian command has been weakened by the recent purges.

In an appeal for international aid, Radio Finland claimed that the Russian offensive had been largely repulsed, but the populations of Abo, Viborg and other towns are being evacuated and in the far north people have fled over the border into Norway.

In Washington President Roosevelt appealed to both sides not to bomb civilians (→ 6/12).

Margarine, clogs, patches and despair. The Depression is still real on this Wigan street corner.

1939

DECEMBER

Su	Mo	Tu	We	Th	Fr	Sa
					1	2
3	4	5	6	7	8	9
10	11	12	13	14	15	16
17	18	19	20	21	22	23
24	25	26	27	28	29	30
31						

1. Germany: Mass deportations of Jews from occupied lands begin under the direction of Adolf Eichmann.

4. France: King George VI visits British troops.

6. London: Britain agrees to send arms to Finland (→ 23).

10. Stockholm: Nobel Prizes go to Ernest Lawrence (US, Physics); Adolf Butenandt (Germany) and Leopold Ruzicka (Switzerland, Chemistry); Gerhard Domagk (Germany, Medicine); and Frans Sillanpaa (Finland, Literature). No Peace Prize awarded.

13. Uruguay: The German battleship Graf Spee reaches Montevideo harbour (→ 17).

14. Geneva: The League expels the USSR.

19. UK: The first Canadian troops have arrived.

22. UK: Women arms workers demand the same pay as male counterparts (→ 28).

23. Moscow: Stalin sacks General Meretzkov, in charge of the war against Finland, as Finnish successes continue (→ 31).

24. Germany: Hitler spends Christmas with his troops on the Western Front.

28. UK: Food rationing is to be extended to sugar and meat.

31. Finland: The Finns claim they have pushed the Russians back beyond the border on a 150-mile front (→ 2/1/40).

DEATH

12. US actor Douglas Fairbanks (*23/5/1883).

HITS OF 1939

Washing on the Siegfried Line.

Over the rainbow.

QUOTE OF THE YEAR

"This is the people's war. It is our war. We are the fighters. Fight it then. Fight it with all that is in us. And may God defend the right."

Jan Struther, "Mrs Miniver".

Germans scuttle pride of their fleet

Dec 17. The Graf Spee went down in flames tonight, scuttled by her crew after she was trapped in the River Plate by British warships.

Her captain, Hans Lansdorf, shot himself through the head as one of the most amazing chapters in naval history ended. The 10,000-ton pocket battleship, pride of the German fleet, blew herself up and settled in the middle of the river off Montevideo, after the Uruguayan authorities denied her time to make repairs and put to sea again for the inevitable battle that would have followed.

The £3.75-million battleship had been plaguing merchantmen in the South Atlantic and Indian Ocean for weeks. However, the Royal Navy managed to trace her movements by picking up the radio signals from her victims.

Finally three cruisers – the Exeter, Ajax and Achilles – attacked and, after a day-long battle, she limped into Montevideo harbour with 36 crew members dead and 60 injured. Despite protests from the German Ambassador, the Uruguayan Government threatened to intern the ship if she did not put to sea. Finally the order came through from Hitler himself that she should be scuttled. Thousands thronged the waterfront expecting to see her sail to battle, but instead they witnessed a huge explosion which sent her to the bottom. Her ending was a bitter blow to a party of US businessmen too. They had chartered a plane at £1,250 a head and were due to fly to Uruguay to see the battle.

Battered by the British and scuttled by her captain, the Graf Spee sinks.

Arts: despite the black-out, the West End is far from dark

War has stripped the National Gallery of its treasures, gone to safe storage "somewhere in Wales", but their place has been taken by music. **Myra Hess**, the distinguished pianist, immediately organised a series of daily lunch-time chamber concerts. They are drawing crowds of listeners.

After the initial black-out, the West End theatre's long-running successes have reopened: **Emlyn Williams'** "The Corn is Green", **Dodie Smith's** "Dear Octopus", and the Lambeth Walk musical "Me and My Girl". **Ivor Novello** and his "The Dancing Years" have had to give way at Drury Lane to the Forces' entertainers, ENSA. The Royal Opera House is being used as a dance hall.

It was an historic night when the Lyceum, sacred to Henry Irving's memory, dropped its final curtain on a week of sell-out performances of "Hamlet" by **John Gielgud**, a great-nephew of Irving's partner Ellen Terry.

An Academy Award went to **Bernard Shaw** for his screenplay of "Pygmalion". "Ridiculous," was his comment, "I have already received the credit for the play." But he has changed some scenes, including the last-minute return by **Wendy Hiller's** spirited Eliza to Professor Higgins, played with huge charm by **Leslie Howard.**

Other British triumphs are "Goodbye Mr Chips", directed by **Michael Balcon** with **Robert Donat**, and **Charles Laughton's** moving portrayal of "The Hunchback of Notre Dame".

The outstanding book of the year is **John Steinbeck's** "The Grapes of Wrath", an epic of the "Okies", the migrant underdogs of America.

Against the background of Hitler's rise to power, **Christopher Isherwood's** "Goodbye to Berlin" tells of the unforgettable Sally Bowles, the good-time girl at large in its sleazy cabarets.

Oxford made **P.G.Wodehouse** dress up in a mortar-board and gown to become an honorary doctor of letters, praising the purity of his style – in Latin.

Clark Gable and Vivien Leigh.

Ivor Novello: the Dancing Years.

1940–1949

1940

JANUARY

Su	Mo	Tu	We	Th	Fr	Sa
	1	2	3	4	5	6
7	8	9	10	11	12	13
14	15	16	17	18	19	20
21	22	23	24	25	26	27
28	29	30	31			

1. London: Two million 19 to 27-year-olds are called up.

2. Finland: 200,000 Soviet troops launch a new offensive (→ 7).

3. Canberra: Australia pledges aeroplanes and 3,000 airmen for the Allies.

5. London: Oliver Stanley replaces Leslie Hore-Belisha as Secretary of State for War.

6. France: The Germans gain ground in a fierce onslaught along a 120-mile front north of Paris (→ 17).

7. Finland: 50,000 Soviet troops are reported to have died since the war with the USSR began (→ 11).

9. UK: 152 are feared dead when the Union Castle liner is sunk by a mine off the south-east coast (→ 20/2).

10. UK: 35 die when German planes attack 12 ships, sinking three in a flare up of the sea war.

11. Stockholm: Sweden pledges all possible aid to Finland.→

13. London: An Indian murders Sir Michael O'Dwyer, ex-governor of the Punjab.

17. Belgium: Captured German documents apparently reveal plans for an attack on Belgium and Holland (→ 8/3).

17. UK: The Thames freezes for the first time since 1888 as a cold wave strikes Europe.

18. Scandinavia: Sweden, Norway and Denmark reaffirm their neutrality (→ 29/2).

24. UK: The Jockey Club cancels this year's Derby.

26. Berlin: The Nazis warn that listening to foreign radio is an offence punishable by death.

27. UK: The worst storm of the century sweeps the country.

29. London: Laurence Olivier's wife Jill Esmond wins a divorce.

BIRTH

21. US golfer Jack Nicklaus.

Fierce Finnish stand frustrates Russia

Finnish soldiers prepare to bury some of their Russian enemies, their bodies frozen solid by the icy cold.

Jan 19. Six weeks into the Russo-Finnish Winter War, Finland's gallant little army continues to block the advance of seven Soviet divisions and is inflicting terrible casualties; in some places the Russians have been driven back almost to their own frontier.

The intense cold – in Karelia it is 57 degrees below zero – has stopped all action on some fronts, and an appalling number of troops on both sides have been frozen to death. An attempt to bypass the Karelian isthmus and attack from Lake Ladoga to the north, where there were no fortifications, has failed. Besides the cold, aid has come from Swedish and Norwegian volunteers.

The Finns have humiliated the Red Army, and dropped three million leaflets on Leningrad to rub it in. The Russians are untrained for guerrilla war in forests against ski patrols of snipers armed with automatic rifles. In one attack across the ice the Russians were suddenly caught in dazzling beams of Finnish searchlights and mown down by machine-gun and artillery fire.

Reports say that the Russians are so angry and frustrated by their failure that they are brawling in their camps, and pilots are fighting each other in the air. However, Moscow denies that scores of Red Army officers have been recalled to be punished (→ 1/2).

Unity Mitford comes home on a stretcher

Jan 3. Unity Mitford, fourth of the six "hons and rebels" daughters of Lord Redesdale, and a devoted admirer of Hitler, came home from Germany today, carried on a stretcher down the gangplank of the cross-Channel ferry at Folkestone. She was pale and her hair came forward over her right temple where the bullet had entered.

Unity, now 24, used to sit in the Osteria Bavaria restaurant in Munich waiting for Hitler to come in. Eventually he noticed her and invited her to his table. She became known as the Storm Troop Maiden. When war broke out she went into the Englischer Garten and put the gun to her head. Hitler gave special permission for her to return home via Switzerland.

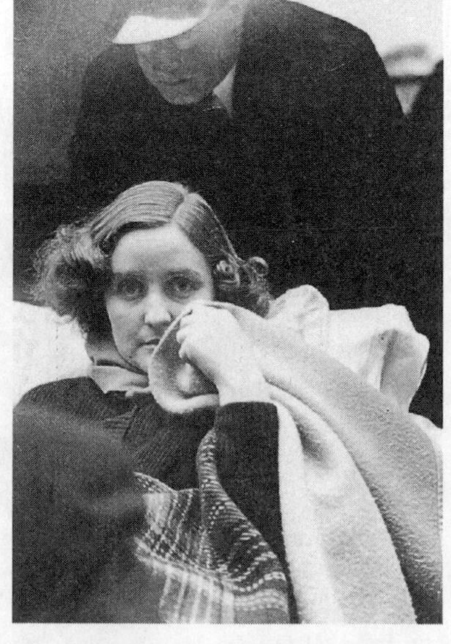

The Storm Troop Maiden returns.

Equal pay for war work, say women

Jan 26. The Government was today urged to give women war workers the same pay and conditions as men. The call came at a special meeting in London of leading women's groups which condemned current practices. Speaker after speaker told of wage cuts and worsening conditions as employers tried to use the high level of unemployment among women to get skilled labour at unskilled wages.

The meeting also called for the training of women as factory supervisors, ready for the influx of women into war industries. The debate follows recent allegations of prejudice against women among trade unions.

1940

FEBRUARY

Su	Mo	Tu	We	Th	Fr	Sa
				1	2	3
4	5	6	7	8	9	10
11	12	13	14	15	16	17
18	19	20	21	22	23	24
25	26	27	28	29		

1. 1 Finland: The Soviet Army launches an attack in Karelia.→

5. Paris: Chamberlain and Churchill visit the Supreme Allied War Council.→

7. Birmingham: Two IRA men are hanged (→ 23/3).

10. Prague: Czech Jews are ordered to close their shops and cease economic activity.

15. Berlin: Senior Wehrmacht officers are reported to have protested at the brutal behaviour of the SS in Poland (→ 27/3).

16. Finland: Soviet troops pierce the Mannerheim Line of Finnish defence (→ 18).

17. Norway: Sailors from HMS Cossack rescue 300 British prisoners from the German ship Altmark.→

18. Finland: The Soviet Army claims it has captured four Finnish towns (→ 23).

19. UK: The destroyer HMS Daring is sunk.

22. Tibet: The new five-year-old Dalai Lama is enthroned.

23. Finland: The USSR presents the Finns with its peace terms (→ 27).

23. London: The crews of Graf Spee victors HMS Exeter and HMS Ajax are cheered by huge crowds.

25. UK: The first squadron of the Royal Canadian Air Force arrives in Britain (→ 20/6).

27. UK: The first British volunteers leave for Finland (→ 13/3).

28. UK: The liner Queen Elizabeth sails secretly on her first journey, to the US to await the end of the war (→ 7/3).

28. London: The government authorises the High Commissioner for Palestine to transfer land from Arabs to Jews (→ 6/3).

29. Scandinavia: Norway, Sweden and Denmark protest to Germany against the sinking of neutral ships by U-boats (→ 9/4).

DEATH

11. British author and politician John Buchan, Lord Tweedsmuir (*26/8/1875).

War puts the British onto short rations

Shoppers are less than impressed by the first food rationing since 1918.

Jan 8. For the first time since 1918, Britain faces food-rationing today. Butter, sugar, bacon and ham can be bought only on production of ration books. The ration allows:

*Butter ... four ounces

*Sugar ... 12 ounces

*Bacon or ham, uncooked ... four ounces

*Bacon or ham, cooked ... three and a half ounces.

Coupons are not needed in restaurants or canteens for bacon and ham consumed on the premises, but hotel guests are required to hand over their ration books to the proprietors. The rigid rationing laws demand the compulsory registration of every household with their local shops.

Meat rationing is likely to be introduced next month, and all slaughtering in Britain will stop while the Government prepares a livestock control scheme. Meat will be rationed on the basis of value. Offal, rabbit, poultry, game and fish will not require coupons for the time being; nor will brawn, sausages, pies or paste (→ 11/3).

Six million hear Haw Haw's jaw jaw

Jan 1. A former factotum of the British Fascist leader, Sir Oswald Mosley, has become a popular wartime broadcaster. Dubbed Lord Haw Haw because of his nasal drawl, William Joyce broadcasts from Germany and seeks to undermine public confidence in the BBC and the British Press. A recent survey put his audience at an estimated six million people, one sixth of the listening public.

A widespread rumour has him announcing that a certain clock in a certain town in England had stopped – and so it had, some minutes before the broadcast! Some people have been prosecuted for passing on such rumours. But his scripts are surely written for him by Germans who believe that such terms as "old chap" and "honest Injun" are commonly used by the British working man (→ 6/2).

Joyce rehearses before the war.

All shipping fair game for U-boats declares Hitler

Feb 20. German U-boat commanders have been ordered to attack all neutral shipping as well as Allied vessels, according to information received from Berlin.

At present many neutral ships passing through the Channel call in at British ports, to have their cargo checked and be granted a certificate stating that they are free of contraband bound for Germany. Berlin now says that act makes all neutrals suspect, and U-boat commanders have been ordered to open fire without question. Merely sailing a zigzag course is said to be grounds for immediate torpedoing.

The order will affect small neutrals like Holland worst of all, as all her shipping now passes through British ports for clearance, but Norway, Sweden and Denmark are all preparing protests to Berlin. The Norwegian Foreign Minister told Parliament in Oslo that 50 Norwegian ships had been sunk since the beginning of the war – all victims of Nazi U-boats or aircraft strikes.

Hitler hopes to force all neutrals to divert their exports from Britain and other overseas markets to Germany, and where the Reich is not itself the purchaser of the cargo, Germany would be used as a clearing house (→ 29).

The actress Greta Garbo, far from alone with Melvyn Douglas in "Ninotchka", a film by Ernst Lubitsch.

Careless words cost lives, Britons told

Feb 6. The Government today launched a nationwide anti-gossip campaign to warn people of the danger of careless talk during the war. About 2,500,000 posters will be distributed for display in offices, barbers' shops, banks, docks, hotels and pubs. Well-known artists have helped with their production.

The worry is that information about the positions of ships, troops and munitions may too easily be reaching German ears. One poster shows Hitler crouching under a bus seat, another with his elbow on a bar counter and a third lying on a luggage rack. A picture of a torpedoed ship has the caption "A few careless words may end in this". Others read "Walls have ears" and "Keep it dark".

And be like Dad – keep Mum.

Daring raid liberates 300 British POWs

Rescued from the Altmark, some of the 300 sailors safe on HMS Cossack.

Feb 26. More than 300 British prisoners-of-war have been rescued in a daring raid on a German tanker hiding in a Norwegian fjord.

The men, who were all taken from ships sunk by the Graf Spee, had been locked away in atrocious conditions on board the tanker Altmark. The German ship was spotted by the destroyer Cossack off the Norwegian coast, but ran for shelter in a narrow fjord. As darkness fell the Cossack inched her way towards the vessel and then a boarding party attacked.

The 12,000-ton tanker tried to ram the destroyer but ran onto rocks, and while some of the German crew died in the fight, others escaped ashore across the ice. The British were all found locked below decks and told harrowing stories of their captivity at the hands of the dedicated Nazi captain.

What has particularly angered the Government is that neutral Norway appears to have attempted to help the Germans keep their prisoners aboard. Two Norwegian gunboats were with the Altmark when the raid took place. Earlier, when the tanker called at Bergen, a "search" by the Norwegian authorities failed to discover the men.

Britain has protested, saying: "The record of this ship must have been well-known to the Norwegian Government", and complaining that Norway has failed in its duty as a neutral state. One prisoner described the search: "We tried to attract their attention by making a terrific noise. It was incredible the Norwegians did not hear us."

Buchan, a Scot of sound views, dies

Feb 11. Few men have combine popular authorship with public af airs as notably as John Buchar alias Lord Tweedsmuir, Governo General of Canada, who died toda aged 64. To most people he will b remembered as the creator c Richard Hannay, gentleman adver turer, hero of "The Thirty-Nin Steps", "Greenmantle" and "Th Three Hostages" – especiall those who read them as boys.

Buchan's full life included bein a Scottish MP, head of Reuters an Lord High Commissioner of th Church of Scotland. A son of th Manse, he wrote manly stories i which wrongdoing is defeated b Scotsmen of sound views.

Buchan: author and administrator.

Russian casualties soar in Finland

Feb 13. The biggest battle of the Winter War is raging today along the Mannerheim Line, with the Russians flinging six divisions, about 100,000 men, supported by several hundred tanks, into the attack. For the first time since the offensive began, the hard-pressed Finns are not claiming that the enemy has been repulsed. In fact, the Finns are being forced to abandon some of their positions along the Mannerheim Line.

Soviet losses in the frontal assault, which began with a tremendous artillery barrage, are enormous – perhaps as high as 40,000 men – but there is a constant stream of replacements.

Much of the Russian success is due to their tactical skill in the use of large numbers of tanks. Soviet bombing raids have also been stepped up, bringing the number of civilians killed in the last three months to nearly 400. The Finns are appealing to the world for help as they make their last stand (→16).

Churchill in Paris to strengthen alliance

Feb 6. The Supreme War Council met in Paris yesterday and for the first time that indomitable warrior, Mr Winston Churchill, took part in its deliberations. Mr Chamberlain, the Prime Minister, and the French premier, M. Daladier, led their delegations, and it is understood they conducted most of the discussion with only minor interventions from their ministers.

The subject which most closely concerned them was how Britain and France could best send aid to Finland in order to enable tha country to sustain its gallant resis ance to the Russian invaders.

On the journey back from Franc by destroyer today, a loose min was seen floating in the Channel Mr Churchill immediately sugges ed it should be blown up by gunfire The guns were accurate and, to M Churchill's delight, the mine explc ded with a satisfactory bang. A large piece of the mine casing land ed on the destroyer, but no one wa hurt (→28/3).

1940

MARCH

Su	Mo	Tu	We	Th	Fr	Sa
					1	2
3	4	5	6	7	8	9
10	11	12	13	14	15	16
17	18	19	20	21	22	23
24	25	26	27	28	29	30
31						

1. Berlin: Roosevelt's special peace envoy to Europe, Sumner Welles, meets Hitler and Ribbentrop.→

2. UK: Cambridge wins the unofficial Boat Race at Henley.

5. UK: The Navy seizes seven Italian ships laden with coal for Germany in the English Channel; Italy protests (→ 9).

6. London: MPs attack the policy of giving Palestinian land to Jews, but a censure motion is defeated.

8. The Hague: Martial law is declared throughout the Netherlands (→ 2/4).

9. UK: Britain releases Italian coal ships on the eve of Ribbentrop's visit to Rome.

11. UK: Meat rationing begins (→ 19).

13. Moscow: Finland signs a peace treaty with the USSR.→

14. Finland: Up to 500,000 Finns begin the evacuation of areas ceded to the USSR.

15. Birmingham: The year's first football matches are played as the wartime ban is lifted.

16. UK: The first British civilian dies in an air raid in Scotland (→ 25/8).

18. Italy: Mussolini meets Hitler at the Brenner Pass in the South Tyrol.

19. London: A woman is fined £75 for buying sugar for 140 weeks' rations; she took it home in a Rolls-Royce (→ 26/11).

20. Paris: Edouard Daladier resigns as premier (→ 22).

22. Paris: Paul Reynaud becomes premier.

23. UK: IRA prisoners riot in Dartmoor prison.

25. UK: The two-seater fighter-bomber Mosquito makes its maiden flight.

27. Berlin: Himmler orders the construction of a concentration camp at Auschwitz near Krakow in Poland.

28. London: The Supreme War Council meets; Britain and France agree not to negotiate separate armistices.

Red Army finally overwhelms the Finns

These Russians are prisoners, but the Finns were defeated in a bitter war.

March 13. The vicious 14-week Russo-Finnish Winter War is over, with defeated Finland surrendering a large part of its territory. The evacuation of half a million people living in the Karelian isthmus, scene of the war's bloodiest fighting, is expected.

The Finnish-Soviet peace treaty, signed in Moscow today, also gave the Soviet Union a base on the Hango peninsula. The terms were harder than those originally proposed by the Russians, but Russia could have easily occupied Helsinki.

The war has been deeply humiliating for Joseph Stalin because, for much of it, the Red Army took a drubbing from the Finns. Having brilliantly organised their defences along the Mannerheim Line, the Finns thwarted all Soviet attempts to break through the strategically important passage.

Soviet casualties have been terrible - perhaps as high as a million dead - but the end came for the Finns when Marshal Klementi Voroshilov was replaced as commander by Marshal Semyon Timoshenko; he brought the whole vast weight of the Red Army to bear, and they were overwhelmed by sheer weight of numbers.

It has been a traumatic experience for the Russians and exposed the Red Army's very serious weaknesses for the world, and especially for Hitler, to see. Russia's prestige and bargaining power has sharply declined.

Vivien Leigh wins an Academy Award

March 1. Vivien Leigh, the controversial choice to play Scarlett O'Hara in "Gone With the Wind" - the most coveted role in pictures - won an Academy Award for her performance last night. The picture earned five awards, including those for its director, Victor Fleming, and producer, David O.Selznick, who cast the unknown Miss Leigh over the heads of every leading actress in Hollywood. The award for best actor also went to an English player, Robert Donat in the title role of "Goodbye Mr Chips".

"Gone with the Wind", all three hours 45 minutes and £1 million-worth of it, is breaking box office records in America. Advance bookings for its London showing next month are unprecedented (→ 18/4).

Vivien Leigh: academic points.

Queen Elizabeth on maiden voyage

March 7. The liner Queen Elizabeth ended her secret maiden voyage today as she slid into an anchorage off New York's Staten Island, to stay there in safety until the war is over. The 85,000-ton ship was painted in drab grey as camouflage, but saw no enemy submarines as she sprinted across the Atlantic at 24 knots. The liner is not completed and, although she carries no guns or other forms of defence, she is fitted with an anti-mine device.

US peace envoy makes fruitless visit

March 16. The mission of President Roosevelt's envoy, Sumner Welles, to see if peace negotiations in Europe are possible, has failed. Only in Rome did the US Under-Secretary of State receive any encouragement. There Mussolini and the Italian Foreign Minister, Count Ciano, said that peace talks were possible, though in vague terms.

In Berlin Hitler issued a secret order against showing any interest in negotiations, and his Foreign Minister, Ribbentrop, met Welles with a two-hour harangue, his eyes closed throughout, in the manner of "the Delphic oracle".

Welles's visits to Paris and London also failed to furnish any grounds for believing peace talks are possible. French officials expressed a willingness to talk, but did not believe that Germany would be interested. British officials were even more emphatic; they told the President's emissary that there could be no lasting peace until Nazism had been destroyed and the Germans had been taught that "war does not pay" (→ 13/4).

1940

APRIL

Su	Mo	Tu	We	Th	Fr	Sa
	1	2	3	4	5	6
7	8	9	10	11	12	13
14	15	16	17	18	19	20
21	22	23	24	25	26	27
28	29	30				

1. Berlin: A law is passed completing the annexation of Austria, or "Ostmark" as it is now to be called.

2. Rome: Mussolini orders the mobilisation of all Italians over 14 years old (→ 11/6).

2. Holland: Dutch troops are put on full alert along the German frontier (→ 10/5).

4. Paris: 36 out of 44 Communist deputies are sentenced to five years in jail.

5. UK: Lord Stalbridge's Bogskar wins the Grand National at Aintree.

8. Oslo: Norway protests as the Royal Navy begins mining of its waters to hinder ore exports to Germany.→

10. Stockholm: Sweden insists on its neutrality.

13. Washington: Roosevelt condemns the invasion of Norway and Denmark (→ 29).

14. Norway: The Allies recapture Narvik (→ 30).

18. London: Advance ticket sales for the British premiere of "Gone with the Wind" have reached a record £10,000.

19. Berne: The Swiss government issues instructions for mobilisation in the event of invasion by Germany.

23. London: The War Budget introduces a purchase tax; cigarettes now cost 8d. halfpenny a packet (→ 23/7).

25. Dublin: Six people are killed by an IRA land mine at Dublin Castle.

29. Washington: Roosevelt appeals to Mussolini to help halt the war in Europe (→ 10/6).

30. Norway: The Germans claim they have advanced and taken the towns of Dombaas and Stoeren.→

DEATHS

9. British actress Beatrice Tanner, Mrs Patrick Campbell (*9/2/1865).

18. British historian and Liberal statesman Herbert A. L. Fisher (*21/3/1865).

28. Italian soprano Luisa Tetrazzini (*29/6/1871).

Hitler invades Denmark and Norway

April 9. The British had a plan to lay mines in Norwegian territorial waters and stop the Germans shipping iron ore from the ice-free port of Narvik. Yesterday, however, as the Royal Navy set about its task, it received an unpleasant surprise. Sailing up from the south and heading for the fjords were flotillas of German warships escorting troopships. A full-scale invasion of Norway was beginning, Denmark having already been overrun with only a few shots from the Royal Guard.

Apart from the vital supplies of iron ore, the Germans have another reason for wishing to lay hands on Norway's ports. In the last war Britain, with a barrage of mines supported by warships patrolling the North Sea, kept the Kaiser's Navy bottled up. This time, Germany intends to have bases in Norway from which she can sweep down on British shipping in the North Atlantic.

Last night German warships appeared off the Norwegian capital, Oslo, and came under fire from shore batteries, armed with 28cm guns made by Krupps in 1892. The newest German cruiser, Bluecher, was hit and sank with the loss of 1,000 men. The pocket battleship Lutzow was damaged. The capital eventually fell to airborne troops who landed at the city airport.

Germans man a heavy gun during intense fighting on the Norwegian front.

King Haakon and his government have escaped to a village 70 miles inland, and from a low-powered local radio have broadcast the order for mobilisation. Though the Norwegians put up a determined resistance, the Germans succeeded in getting ashore seven divisions within 48 hours and have now seized the main ports. In Oslo, a radio broadcast of a very different kind has been made. A Nazi sympathiser, Major Vidkun Quisling, whose name has instantly become a synonym for traitor, went into the national radio station, proclaimed himself head of the government, and ordered all resistance to Germany to cease. It didn't, but the phoney war is over (→ 14).

British troops join battle for Norway

April 30. The British and French are hitting back in the battle for Norway. Troops have been landed at half a dozen key points and are reported to be pushing back the Germans near Trondheim.

The biggest successes for the Allies have been in the far north, at Narvik. Ten German destroyers have been sunk for the loss of two British. The 2,000-strong German garrison in the port is commanded by Brigadier General Eduard Dietl, who has known Hitler since the days of the Beer Hall putsch. When he saw the destroyers being sunk, he retreated into the mountains with his men.

Snow has been falling heavily in the region, and this has delayed the landing of British troops, who are not equipped for arctic operations. There is also a pressing need for air support. German planes regularly carry out reconnaissance flights; sooner or later they will attack.

Yesterday, at Andalsnes in central Norway, King Haakon and his cabinet were taken aboard the British cruiser Glasgow and moved to Tromsos, far above the Arctic Circle, where a provisional capital will be proclaimed tomorrow.

Though the Germans have established a firm hold on the southern half of Norway, which includes all the main population centres, the price for the German Navy has been high. The most reliable Allied estimates say Germany has only three cruisers and four destroyers left. The losses in merchant shipping have also been heavy and it is hard to believe they can be made up. If Hitler were to be called on to mount another seaborne invasion he would be hard pressed to find the ships (→ 2/5).

Hitler has missed the bus claims PM

April 2. In reviewing the progress of the war Mr Chamberlain confidently told Parliament today: "Hitler has missed the bus". The Prime Minister assured MPs that Allied strategy is strangling Germany's economic life. War trade agreements have been made with Norway, Sweden, Iceland, Belgium, Holland and Denmark, to guarantee limitation of their future trade with the Reich.

Mr Chamberlain also said that British naval action has stopped the passage of Nazi cargo ships from Scandinavia: that means that vital Swedish ore supplies should no longer reach Germany through Norway. There are also steps to prevent war materials from getting through by land routes not previously used (→ 7/5).

1940

MAY

Su	Mo	Tu	We	Th	Fr	Sa
			1	2	3	4
5	6	7	8	9	10	11
12	13	14	15	16	17	18
19	20	21	22	23	24	25
26	27	28	29	30	31	

1. UK: Postage goes up a penny to twopence halfpenny.

2. Norway: The Allies will withdraw their forces south of Trondheim (→6/6).

6. New York: John Steinbeck wins a Pulitzer Prize for his novel "The Grapes of Wrath".

6. UK: Unemployment falls below one million for the first time in 20 years.

7. London: Admiral Sir Roger Keyes leads a Commons attack on Chamberlain during a heated debate on Norway.→

9. Denmark: Britain occupies the Danish possessions of Iceland and the Faroe Islands.

9. London: A bill is introduced to impose the death penalty for sabotage.

10. UK: Internment begins for all German and Austrian men aged 16 to 50.→

13. London: Dutch Queen Wilhelmina arrives in exile (→14).

14. London: Lord Beaverbrook becomes Minister for Aircraft Production; Ernest Bevin is Minister of Labour (→2/8).

14. Holland: Dutch forces are ordered to stop fighting (→15).

15. Holland: The Germans occupy The Hague (→18).

19. Paris: General Maxime Weygand replaces General Maurice Gamelin as Allied Commander-in-Chief (→21).

21. France: German troops reach the Aisne River and Amiens on the Somme, 60 miles from Paris (→25).

22. UK: Petrol goes up by a penny halfpenny to 1/11d. halfpenny.

24. Mexico City: Trotsky is injured in an attack on his home (→21/8).

25. France: The Germans take Vimy; Ghent in Belgium also falls (→27).

27. France: The Germans take Boulogne, cutting off British and French troops (→30).

30. UK: The first evacuated British troops arrive from Dunkirk.→

Dutch and Belgians fall to blitzkrieg

Nazis troops storm a railway station in the Netherlands, another stop on their trans-Europe advance.

May 10. In Berlin it meant an early start to the day for the conceited and humourless former champagne salesman who is Hitler's Foreign Minister. Seated behind his desk in the Wilhelmstrasse, and well rehearsed for the piece of Nazi hypocrisy that was about to be acted out, von Ribbentrop called in the Belgian and Dutch envoys.

He told them that Germany's armed forces had crossed the borders of their countries in order, as he put it with a straight face, to protect their neutrality in view of an attack the British and French were planning. So the Belgians and Dutch forces had no need to fight against the Germans.

In fact, the German attacks began several hours before the envoys were treated to the Nazi's charade. There has been widespread bombing of airfields, communications and military strong-points during the night, and airborne troops began taking off before dawn. Along a front of 150 miles well-armed troops, accompanied by light artillery, sprang forward out of the darkness. Vital bridges and airfields were seized before the defenders could go into action. Thus blitzkrieg came to the Low Countries.

In spite of numerous warnings, and of intelligence reports of the presence of at least 28 German divisions assembled across the frontiers, the Belgians and Dutch were caught unprepared – for the usual reason that they had refused to undertake resolute defence measures, coordinated with the Allies, for fear of offending the Germans.

Army leave was cancelled, then restored; there was some work on roadblocks; and the Dutch had plans for opening the dykes, hoping the flooding would keep the Germans at bay, but the Germans had made plans to deal with such trifles.

As the Germans began their attack, Queen Wilhelmina addressed the populace: "After our country, with scrupulous conscientiousness, had observed strict neutrality ... Germany made a sudden attack on our territory without warning." She then asked the people to take up arms. Both she and the anti-British King Leopold are trusting the Allies to come to their aid.

The Allied contingency plan calls for an Anglo-French force to advance into Belgium and take up positions in support of, or with, the Belgian army. The Allied right flank will be only lightly covered, since the Ardennes in southern Belgium are taken to constitute an impassable barrier.

Lord Gort, the British C-in-C in France, received the alert at 5.30 this morning; at 6.45 he was ordered into action. The Allied plan requires his forces to be in position in two days. That may well be too late. The massive Eban Emael fortress on the Liege front has fallen, and tonight the Belgian army is beginning to disintegrate.

The Dutch have repulsed a German force that attempted to capture The Hague and seize the royal family, but the great port of Rotterdam is about to fall after being pulverised by an aerial bombardment, in which at least 800 people died. The lessons of Poland, it seems, have gone unlearned (→13).

Chamberlain hands over to Churchill

May 10. Winston Churchill is now Prime Minister, but is it too late? He is forming an all-party Coalition Government. Neville Chamberlain, totally discredited, resigned tonight after three days of desperate political manoeuvre and turmoil, against the background of mounting military catastrophe.

Mr Churchill intends to tell the nation the stark truth about its peril. He has prepared his words for Parliament: "I have nothing to offer but blood, toil, tears and sweat." But there is also his determination about ultimate victory.

Events have moved swiftly since Mr Chamberlain asked for a vote of confidence two days ago in a debate on the British debacle in Norway. In that debate the veteran Tory Leo Amery sensed the mood and used the words of Cromwell. He almost spat at the Prime Minister: "Depart, I say, and let us have done with you. In the name of God, go!" Nothing could have been more savage. On top of that another Tory old-stager, Sir Roger Keyes, making a startling appearance in his uniform of Admiral of the Fleet, joined in the emotional denunciation of operational bungling in Norway.

Government spokesmen pleaded that at any moment the greatest storm might burst on the Western Front and this was no time for rocking the boat. Mr Churchill, still at the Admiralty, said the Norway fiasco was his fault, too. Finally, the battered Prime Minister appealed to "my friends" for Tory loyalty. A vote was taken 281 for and 200 against – but 41 Tories voted against Mr Chamberlain and some 60 abstained.

Mr Churchill is Prime Minister, and offers "blood, toil, tears and sweat".

Then the rebels refused future co-operation with the Government unless Labour and Liberals were brought into it.

Labour refused unless Mr Chamberlain quit. The Prime Minister decided to do so in favour of Lord Halifax, the Foreign Secretary. Labour declined to serve under him. It had to be Churchill.

Labour leaders discussed the shape of the coalition with the new premier tonight. Their party will be fully represented in it and they pledged preservation of national unity. Mr Chamberlain will stay in the War Cabinet. Labour's leader, Clement Attlee, will be deputy Prime Minister and Lord Halifax is Foreign Secretary.

Powerful outsiders, like the newspaper owner Lord Beaverbrook and the trade union leader Ernest Bevin, have also been recruited. As at a similar terrible moment in the Great War, stronger men have been brought into government to rescue Britain (→ 14).

Oswald Mosley is interned as British Fascists are held

May 31. Sir Oswald Mosley, leader of the British Union of Fascists returned from a drive today to find Special Branch detectives with a warrant for his arrest. He is spending tonight in Brixton prison.

At the same time, 33 other Fascist sympathisers were detained under a regulation which allows for the detention of members of organisations which "have had associations with the enemy".

Among those arrested was Captain A.M. Ramsay, president of the Right Club and Conservative MP for Peebles since 1931. A Government spokesman said that Captain Ramsay was not a member of the Fascist party, nor was John Beckett, a former Labour MP and secretary of the British People's Party who was also arrested.

Some new restrictions have led to an increasing series of arrests of aliens and "suspected persons" along the east coast of the United Kingdom. About 3,000 German born citizens have been banned from 39 "vulnerable" counties, and 11,000 other aliens are affected.

All 16 to 45-year-old male aliens of whatever nationality, in the coastal district between the Isle of Wight and the Moray Firth, have to report to the police daily and observe an 8pm to 6am curfew. "It is intended that the rigour of these measures should be mitigated as soon as circumstances permit," said the Home Office (→ 20/7).

Oswald Mosley: failed Fuehrer.

Bill gives government powers over all persons and property

Ernest Bevin: Labour overlord.

May 22. It took Parliament under three hours today to rush into law the most drastic constitutional measure known in British history. The Emergency Powers Act gives the Government practically unlimited authority over every person and all property in the land.

Banks, the munitions industry, wages, profits and conditions of work are all now under State control in this unprecedented mobilisation of manpower and wealth. In his first speech for the new Government Clement Attlee, the Labour Party leader, urged calm and said: "Everybody should continue at their jobs until ordered to do otherwise." As Minister of Labour, Ernest Bevin has dictatorial power to direct anybody to do anything required in the nation's fight for survival and freedom.

A Production Council and a Munitions Board have been swiftly set up tonight under ministerial control. Men in aircraft factories are to work ten hours a day, seven days a week, and there is power to impose a 100 per cent tax on profits. Further dire measures are in the pipeline.

The Government explained that it now has sufficient powers, even if the country is invaded or parliament is unable to meet. Plans exist, of course, for MPs to work outside London if necessary (→ 5/6).

British troops are encircled on the French coast

May 31. British troops are fighting a desperate rearguard action on the French coast around Dunkirk as German troops finally move in and surround them.

Yesterday the first men of the British Expeditionary Force arrived home after being picked off the beaches. They told how they had been bombed and machine-gunned from the air as they waded out to the ships. But despatches from the French coast say the Allied troops are "still fighting incessantly and in good order" and covering the embarkation of their comrades.

The British and the French have been driven back to the coast by a large German force of 750,000 men; thousands of both soldiers and refugees have been killed trying to escape along the packed roads. The key to the German advance was the surrender of Belgium three days ago, leaving a vast gap beween the French and British front lines through which they poured.

Fortunately the BEF commander General Gort had foreseen such an emergency and, though many Belgian troops have ignored their King and kept on fighting, he ordered a retreat towards Dunkirk to begin on May 19. The British Government was not hopeful of getting more than 45,000 troops out of the country at first, but many more now look like being saved because the German heavy armour and tanks have now halted their advance on Hitler's orders; he believes they will get bogged down in the marshes near the coast.

One private told how he had marched with a machine gun bullet in his foot more than 30 miles a day for several days to the coast. Another described how British artillery put up a barrage a mile long in one sector. "The Germans just advanced right into it," he said. "Their casualties must have been tremendous. More and more men were thrown into the fight and they came on relentlessly."

One infantryman, who had not eaten for days, said: "Fleeing refugees hampered our movements all the time. The Germans spared neither man, woman nor child. They were mown down by the great German war machines which came on wave after wave. They stopped for no one. It was mass murder at its worst."

The Allies have fought over every inch of territory, only giving up towns like Calais and Boulogne after terrific fights, aided by shelling from British warships offshore.

For days crowds have gathered along the south-east coast of Britain to catch a sight of the bombing, smoke and fires, which can easily be seen and heard from across the Channel (→4/6).

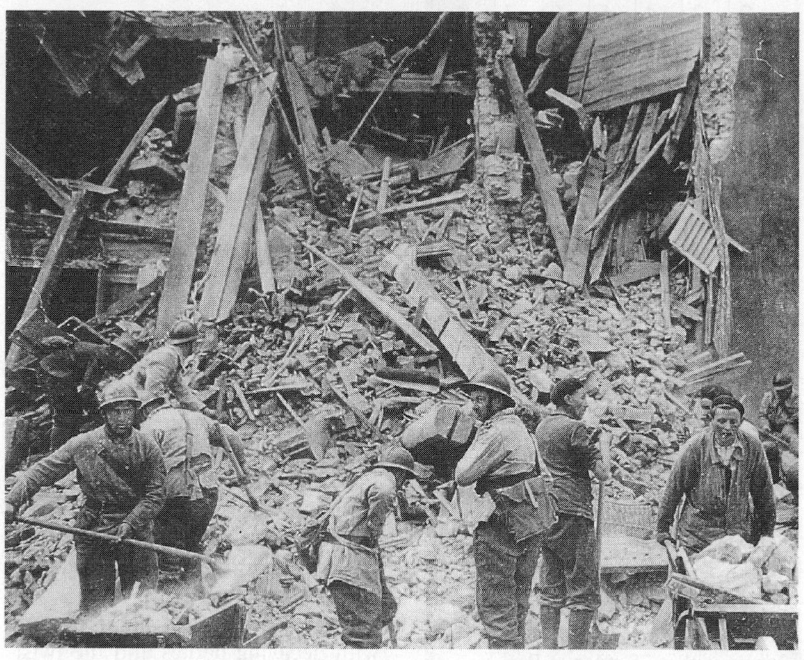

French troops and rescue workers search for victims of a blitzkrieg raid.

Belgium and Holland surrender to Nazis

May 28. In the early hours of this morning the Belgian armed forces, acting on the orders of their King, surrendered to the Germans. By this action they opened a gap in the front, through which Germany's armoured divisions are pouring to threaten the Anglo-French troops already in danger of being rolled up from the rear by the German thrust in the Ardennes.

Leopold's action was taken against the advice of his government. Last Saturday, ministers called on him at his HQ and begged him not to surrender and become a prisoner of the Germans, but Leopold was obdurate. Belgian troops had fought bravely, but, he added, betraying his defeatism, the Allied cause was lost. The Belgian monarch's conduct was in marked contrast to that of Queen Wilhelmina when the Dutch sought an armistice two weeks ago.

She ordered the Dutch merchant fleet to be placed at the disposal of the British and ensured that the gold reserves and the vast diamond treasure at Amsterdam were taken aboard British warships before she and her family took ship to England, to continue the fight.

The rapidity with which the Low Countries were brought to submission has, inevitably perhaps, led to talk of Fifth Columnists and Quislings betraying their countries by acts of sabotage. Maybe such things happened; but in the end it was the panzers and bombers that were decisive (→4/6).

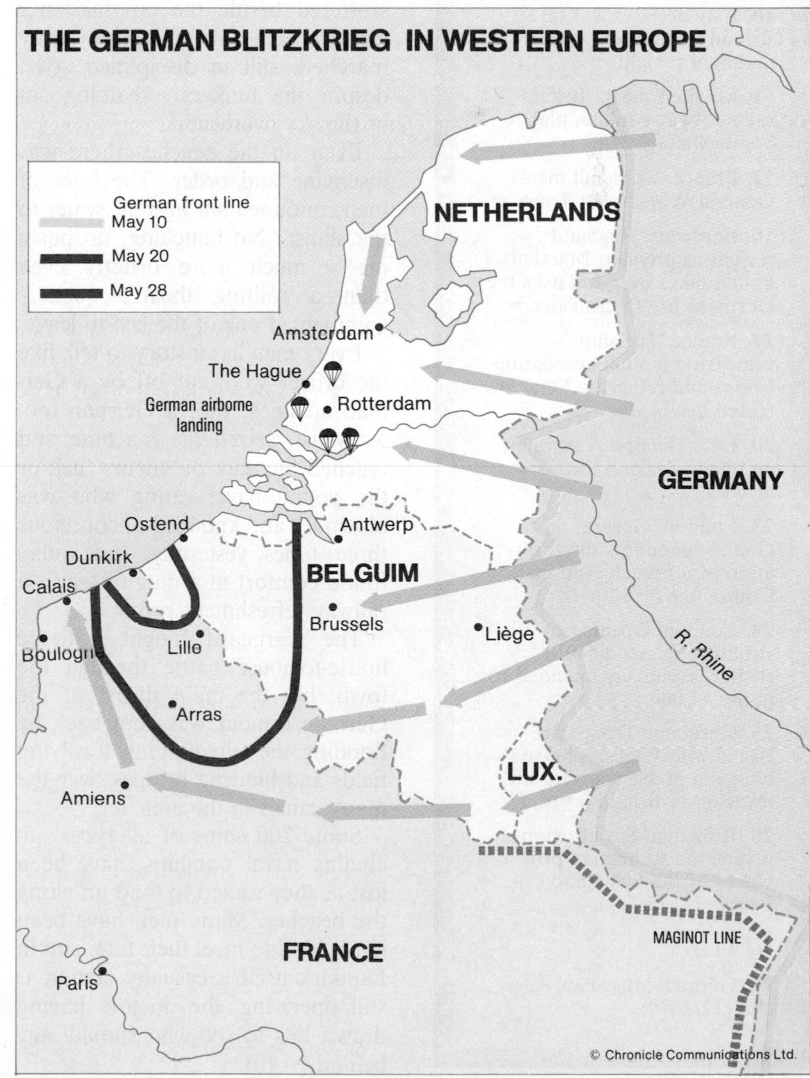

1940

JUNE

Su	Mo	Tu	We	Th	Fr	Sa
						1
2	3	4	5	6	7	8
9	10	11	12	13	14	15
16	17	18	19	20	21	22
23	24	25	26	27	28	29
30						

1. France: The Germans bomb the Rhone valley and Marseilles (→ 3).

3. Paris: German aerial bombing kills 45 (→ 5).

4. Berlin: The Germans admit they lost over 10,000 men in the invasion of the Low Countries.

5. London: The government bans all strikes.

5. Paris: Brigadier-General Charles de Gaulle is appointed Under Secretary of War (→ 18).

6. Norway: The evacuation of Narvik is completed.

10. France: The Germans are now within 35 miles of Paris; the French government moves to Tours (→ 12).

10. Italy declares war on Britain and France from midnight tonight.→

11. Mediterranean: Britain raids Libya as Italian planes bomb Malta (→ 4/8).

12. France: Churchill meets General Weygand at Tours.→

16. Bordeaux: Reynaud resigns as premier; Marshal Petain takes over and asks the Germans for an armistice.→

17. France: The ship Lancastria is sunk evacuating troops and refugees; 2,800 are feared dead.

20. UK: The first Australian and New Zealand troops arrive.

23. London: General de Gaulle announces the formation of a French National Committee (→ 8/8).

24. London: Opening of Britain's biggest air raid shelter, eventually intended to house 11,000.

25. Germany: Troops are issued with English phrase books in preparation for an invasion of Britain (→ 16/7).

28. Rumania: Soviet troops invade the Rumanian provinces of Bukovina and Bessarabia (→ 6/9).

DEATH

29. German artist Paul Klee (*18/12/1879).

Allied forces evacuated from Dunkirk

June 4. Operation Dynamo, the great evacuation of Dunkirk, is complete. Tonight men were still coming ashore from the huge fleet of destroyers, ferries, fishing vessels, and even river cruisers, which have delivered the British Expeditionary force, along with vast numbers of French and Belgian troops, from the prospect of total annihilation.

Crowds, waving Union Jacks and yelling "Well done, boys", were waiting on the shore of the south coast ports as the 338,226 troops who have been rescued were put aboard trains for barracks or home. For days they have been sheltering from the incessant waves of German bombs and machine-gun bullets, raking the Dunkirk beaches and harbour.

The beaches are littered now with decaying bodies and the twisted shapes of hundreds of battered vehicles. Weapons of all kinds are scattered beside the coastal lanes along which the retreating army marched, still in disciplined style, despite the Junkers screaming out of the sky overhead.

Even on the beaches there was discipline and order. The lines of men continued out into the water to the ships: "No bunching, no pushing – much more orderly even than a waiting theatre queue," commented one of the last to leave.

Every man has a story to tell, like the officer who, cut off by a German advance, shot a German motorcyclist, seized his machine and reached Dunkirk on enemy fuel; or the young naval rating who was blown up and knocked unconscious three times yesterday, but today found comfort in a mug of tea in a railway refreshment room.

The rearguard fought a fierce house-to-house battle through the town, but the main thrust of the German armour was kept back by flooding the surrounding low-lying fields and blowing bridges over the many canals in the area.

Some 200 ships of all types, including naval warships, have been lost as they waited to load up along the beaches. Many men have been left behind to meet their fate, and in Dunkirk itself a casualty station is still operating, the doctors having drawn lots to see who should stay behind (→ 10).

British soldiers struggle to reach the "little boats" off Dunkirk beach.

Survivors climb a ladder to safety.

Invaders burn a French town.

German troops parade up the Champs Elysees

June 14. The Nazi swastika flies from the Eiffel Tower and the Arc de Triomphe today, and Parisians with grim expressions stand on the pavements to watch Germans marching up the Champs Elysees for the first time since 1871. It is a day of mourning, for Paris and for France.

According to the Germans, they offered to treat Paris as a non-belligerent zone if the city surrendered at once. French delegates went out to meet the Germans and proposed that only the city proper and not its environs should surrender. The Germans responded by threatening instant bombardment if the French tried to haggle.

With that, the French signed, and soon after 7am the first German motor-cyclists rode into the capital. They were followed by cameramen, radio technicians and announcers, who are now in the Place de la Concorde recording the march past of German troops. The Paris sun shines for Hitler as the cameras roll.

The French High Command says Paris was given up because there was no military reason why it should be defended, but the Germans claim that the Armee de Paris, which was to defend the capital, has been scattered. The French government, which fled the city four days ago for Tours, has now moved on to Bordeaux, where demoralised cabinet ministers are talking about giving up the fight.

Some two million Parisians are reckoned to have fled the city; roads to the south are blocked with women, old folk and children, pushing carts loaded with their possessions. From time to time, German dive-bombers come tearing out of the sky to rake the columns with gunfire. Civilians who remain in the city have to watch signs going up on cinemas, restaurants, and even brothels, reserving them for German soldiers. A sign on the Chamber of Deputies reads: "Deutschland siegt auf allen Fronten" – Germany conquers on all fronts (→16).

As the victors parade beneath the Arc de Triomphe, Parisians either flee or face a future under occupation.

Churchill proposes union with France

June 16. In the final hours before the apparently inevitable French government surrender to Germany, Mr Churchill tonight made the supreme gesture. He proposed that Britain and France should no longer be two nations but a single Franco-British Union with common citizenship.

The Prime Minister invited the French leaders to join in a declaration of indissoluble union. There was no response, but he hopes it will encourage French resistance 'to a system which reduces mankind to a life of robots and slaves". He then appealed to the US to 'bring her powerful material aid to the common cause. And thus we shall conquer" (→22).

French sign armistice in coach used for 1918 German surrender

June 22. Today the French came to the forest of Compiegne, and to the historic railway coach in which General Foch handed the Germans the armistice terms in November 1918, only this time it was to surrender themselves.

Hitler was on hand to relish the humiliation of the French. He took his seat in the chair used by Foch in 1918. The head of the French delegation, General Charles Huntziger, protested that the German terms were "merciless" and much more harsh than those imposed on Germany by France in 1918.

The French were forced to sign this evening, and the cease-fire will take effect next Tuesday, after the Italians have added their signature to a document that puts half of France under occupation (→1/7).

Hitler might well dance for joy, as he celebrates the French surrender.

Red Army rolls into Baltic: Lithuania is first to fall

June 17. The Soviet army is marching, unopposed, into Lithuania following the government's acceptance of an ultimatum which accused Lithuania and the other Baltic states of a military conspiracy against the Soviet Union and demanded immediate access to the country for Stalin's army.

The Soviet troops crossed the frontier yesterday. Two hundred tanks led the march on the capital, Kaunas. Troops took up positions at all public buildings and Soviet administrators arrived by air.

As they flew in, Dr Smetona, the President of Lithuania, flew out with his family and other leading officials. It is believed that they will seek sanctuary in Germany or Sweden.

Troops continue to pour across the border today, and countless tanks and armoured cars bearing the Red Star of Communism are rolling along Lithuanian roads. Reports reaching Stockholm suggest that up to half a million Russian soldiers are on the move.

The country is quiet. There has been no resistance. The radio has warned the population to maintain discipline. However, the 35,000 Germans living in Lithuania are making their preparations to leave. Their Legation was besieged today by Germans wanting to return to the Reich.

The question that is preoccupying the Baltic countries is whether the Russians will be satisfied with their occupation of Lithuania, or whether they will also march into Latvia and Estonia which, like Lithuania, were part of the Russian empire before the Revolution.

Given the terms of the ultimatum, in which all the Baltic states were accused of "conspiring" against the Soviet Union, the outlook is bleak for both countries

Two reasons for Stalin's move are being considered. Either he wants to strengthen his already dominant position in the Baltic as a barrier against Germany, or the occupation, like that of the eastern part of Poland, was part of a covert deal arranged with Hitler's approval and connivance (→21/7).

Britain fights on alone

Churchill: "their finest hour".

June 18. With France suing for peace and collapsing into the arms of the German army, Mr Churchill reported to Parliament today on future prospects. Britain now fights on alone. In stirring words he told MPs: "Let us brace ourselves to our duty and so bear ourselves that if the British Commonwealth and Empire lasts a thousand years men will still say, 'This was their finest hour'."

The Prime Minister asserted that there are reasonable hopes of final victory and said that Britain will fight on for years if necessary.

In the grounds of Buckingham Palace, the King is practising revolver-shooting. He has said that, if need be, he will die there fighting. The Queen is refusing to leave him and flee to Canada with her daughters, as an estimated 13,000 well-off women and children have done already.

In general the public is remarkably unruffled and is accepting Mr Churchill's assurances that, with a million and a quarter men under arms, the country can successfully repulse German invasion. However, it has been grimly accepted in Whitehall for some time now that France cannot be saved, and that bloody battle on British soil may well be the next phase of the war.

Mr Churchill explained to MPs how most of Britain's best-trained troops are now safely back from France and that the Navy is well-placed to block the huge supplies needed by a German invading force for continuous battle (→25/6).

"Flame of French resistance must not go out" – de Gaulle

De Gaulle: the French fight on.

June 18. General de Gaulle, a little-known French armoured warfare expert, is emerging as the centre of resistance to his country's capitulation to the Germans. Speaking to his countrymen over the BBC last night, he urged them to fight on.

"I, General de Gaulle," he said, "invite French officers and soldiers who are on British territory or who are coming here, with or without arms, to join me. I also invite engineers and workers who are experts in the arms industry to join me".

"Whatever happens," he urged his listeners, "the flame of the French resistance must not go out and it will not go out."

General de Gaulle, an immensely tall and imperious officer, served with honour in the last war, in which he was taken prisoner. Earlier this year, he was made Brigadier General and appointed Under-Secretary of War (→23).

Mussolini has declared war on the Allies

June 11. Mussolini has declared war on the Allies. Britain and France were formally notified by the Italian Foreign Minister, Count Ciano, that hostilities would begin at midnight. At the same time the Italians warned Switzerland, Yugoslavia, Turkey, Egypt and Greece that, while they did not intend to drag "other peoples" into the conflict, it would "depend entirely on their own attitude".

This news was greeted grimly in London where an official statement said that the Allies' preparations were complete and we "know how to meet the sword with the sword".

In Paris, facing the advancing German army, M. Reynaud, the premier, commented bitterly: "It is at this moment, when France, wounded but valiant and undaunted, is fighting against German hegemony for her own independence as well as for that of the whole of the rest of the world, that Mussolini has chosen to declare war on us."

M. Reynaud's words were reflected in the United States where President Roosevelt said that Italy had 'scorned the rights of security of other nations".

The New York Times is even more forthright: "With the courage of a jackal at the heels of a bolder beast of prey, Mussolini has now left his ambush. His motives in taking Italy into the war are as clear as day. He wants to share in the spoils which he believes will fall to Hitler, and he has chosen to enter the war when he thinks he can accomplish this at the least cost to himself". (→11)

1940

JULY

Su	Mo	Tu	We	Th	Fr	Sa
	1	2	3	4	5	6
7	8	9	10	11	12	13
14	15	16	17	18	19	20
21	22	23	24	25	26	27
28	29	30	31			

1. France: Petain's government moves to Vichy (→4).

1. London: The government advises women to conserve wood by having flatter heels (→10).

2. UK: German bombers carry out their first daylight raid (→10).

4. Vichy: Petain breaks ties with Britain following the attack on the French fleet at Mers-el-Kebir.→

9. London: The Duke of Windsor is appointed Governor of the Bahamas.

10. London: The British Union of Fascists is banned (→20).

10. English Channel: The Luftwaffe attacks British convoys.→

12. Vichy: Laval is appointed Petain's successor (→16).

16. Vichy: The regime strips naturalised Jews of their citizenship (→31).

16. Berlin: Hitler is reported to have postponed his attack on Britain until the full moon.

17. Chicago: The Democrats choose Roosevelt to run for a third term as president (→23/10).

19. UK: General Sir Alan Brooke becomes commander-in-chief of British home forces.

20. London: The government bans the buying or selling of new cars (→23).

21. Baltic: Lithuania, Latvia and Estonia vote to become part of the USSR.

23. London: The government imposes a 24 per cent tax on luxuries.

25. English Channel: 400 are feared dead when the Germans torpedo a French ship carrying French sailors to Britain.

30. London: The government says all of Europe and North Africa are to be blockaded (→9/12).

31. Vichy: The regime imposes the death sentence on all French servicemen who join a foreign army (→8/8).

Luftwaffe attacks ships in Channel

July 10. Reichsmarschall Hermann Goering has been given the task of destroying British air power; until that has been achieved the German High Command refuses to contemplate any attempt to invade Britain.

Goering's immediate tactics have become clear in recent days, as the aerial attacks on shipping in the Channel have increased. Yesterday, a Latvian-registered steamer off the south coast was attacked by German planes and sank within two hours. Twelve of the crew were rescued by fishermen who put out to sea. A Dutch ship, which was machine-gunned in the same attack, reached port flying the "medical assistance wanted" signal.

But Goering's purpose is not simply to sink ships. Intelligence reports say that the latest German assessment of British strength gives the RAF 1,500 machines; the Germans reckon the British are short of trained pilots.

Goering's tactics are to lure the planes of Fighter Command into battles over the English Channel where he counts on his Luftwaffe pilots, operating their Messerschmitts at short range, winning the dog fights. A plane lost over the sea will be a pilot lost, Goering believes. He is not having things all his own way, though.

In yesterday's attacks on shipping the Luftwaffe lost 37 planes, according to the Air Ministry in London.

Besides, there are reports that the shipping convoys are to be withdrawn, so the RAF can husband its resources for other tasks.

One of these is to attack German shipping which is being assembled in support of the projected invasion. British calculations say the Germans would need at least 250 vessels to transport a force of about 100,000 men across the Channel. The most likely landing places would appear to be in the Dover to Hastings sector of the coast – where William of Normandy landed in 1066 (→10/8).

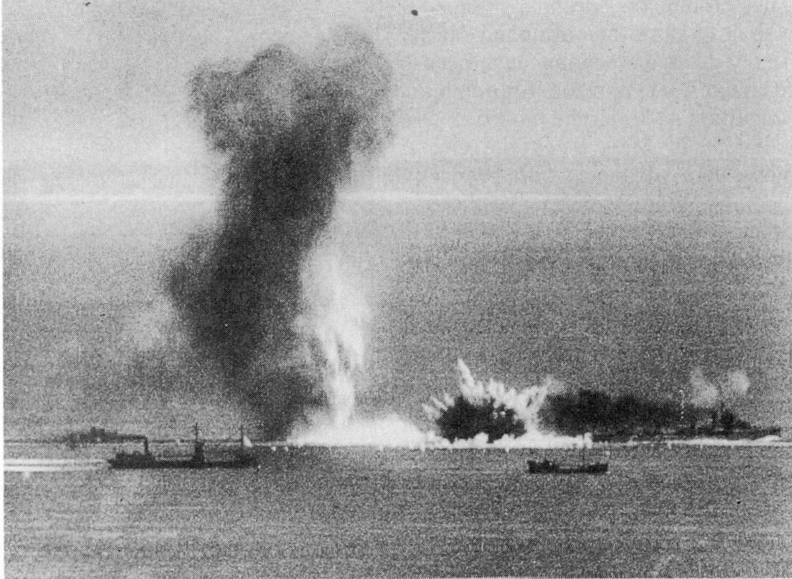

All too vulnerable to Luftwaffe air power, a convoy suffers in the Channel.

1,000 die as Britain sinks French fleet

July 3. The Royal Navy removed the threat of the French fleet falling into German hands today by destroying a large part of it at anchor in Algeria – killing a thousand French sailors in the process.

Both the Prime Minister, Winston Churchill, and Admiral Sir James Somerville, who led the raid, deeply regret the loss of life and are concerned at its effect on Anglo-French relations. However, the raid is also seen as restoring British confidence, battered by Dunkirk.

The attack began after a six-hour ultimatum to the French commander – to surrender his ships and sail for Britain or America – ran out. Force H, consisting of the battle-cruiser Hood (the biggest warship in the world), two battleships, an aircraft carrier and support craft, moved in.

First, flying boats blocked off the exit to the port at Mers-el-Kebir near Oran, and then a ten-minute aerial and naval bombardment destroyed the vessels without any damage to the British Fleet.

At the same time, more than 200 French vessels have been seized in British ports with only one incident, when an officer on the submarine Surcouf was shot as he tried to prevent the take-over. Then, in the Mediterranean, a French battleship, cruisers and smaller vessels moored with the British Fleet at Alexandria have been told they will not be allowed to leave port.

Mr Churchill told the Commons tonight of the grim decision of the War Cabinet, but it was generally accepted that the action was necessary, and certainly President Roosevelt is known to be in favour. General de Gaulle, the French officer trying to raise a "Free French" force in Britain, has not commented on the attack.

Petain turns France into a Fascist state

July 11. Marshal Henri Petain, the former hero of Verdun, has assumed supreme power in France. Following the dissolution of the Third Republic, decrees have been issued giving Petain powers as President and Prime Minister with the title of Chief of the French State.

There will be a parliament but its role will be purely advisory. The Senate and the Chamber will meet only when he summons them. Defeated France took on further aspects of a Fascist state with the replacement of the traditional cry of "Liberty, Equality, Fraternity" by "Work, Family and Fatherland", as the new regime called for a return to "traditional values".

"The French Government", said Petain last night, "will request permission from Germany to transfer to Paris" (→12).

Home Guard is ready to repel invaders

July 23. Today the new Local Defence Volunteers, originally armed with little more than armbands and hastily devised weapons, have been renamed – at Winston Churchill's suggestion – the Home Guard.

It was in May, when the Germans were advancing into France, that the War Minister, Anthony Eden, called for men "not presently engaged in military service between the ages of 17 and 65 to come forward and offer their services to make assurance doubly sure ..."

Within a week, 250,000 men had enrolled. Many of them were veterans of the Great War, keen to "do their bit". Their initial antics – with aged rifles, shotguns, cutlasses borrowed from museums and broomsticks converted into pikes with carving knives – were greeted with tolerant smiles. It was the first citizens' army since Napoleon threatened invasion in 1803.

One platoon used 48 Lee Enfield rifles, formerly used in a Drury Lane patriotic tableau; another, in Lancashire, was armed with six-foot spears. Ingenious weapons were devised, such as catapults to throw "petrol bombs", and piano wire stretched across lanes to decapitate motorcyclists.

The first LDV units were very democratic, electing their leaders: senior officers stood shoulder to shoulder with former privates, and two bishops were among the first to enrol, but with the introduction of uniforms and real weapons, military discipline became the norm.

Today the Home Guard is proving itself daily to be more and more effective – guarding key installations, releasing regular units for more essential duties and showing the value of "local knowledge" in manoeuvres.

Veterans: proud to "do their bit".

German invasion of the Channel Islands

July 1. German forces landed on the Channel Islands last night without opposition. The islands were demilitarised last week after a decision was taken that they would be too difficult to defend. At the same time it was disclosed that a considerable number of the islanders had already been removed to mainland Britain. Crops and cattle have also been brought over.

A brief announcement from the Ministry of Information added: "Telegraphic and telephonic communications have been cut and no further information is at present available." However, it is understood, that many of the population have chosen to stay behind for the duration of the war. Some policemen have also remained, along with a number of those involved in civil administration.

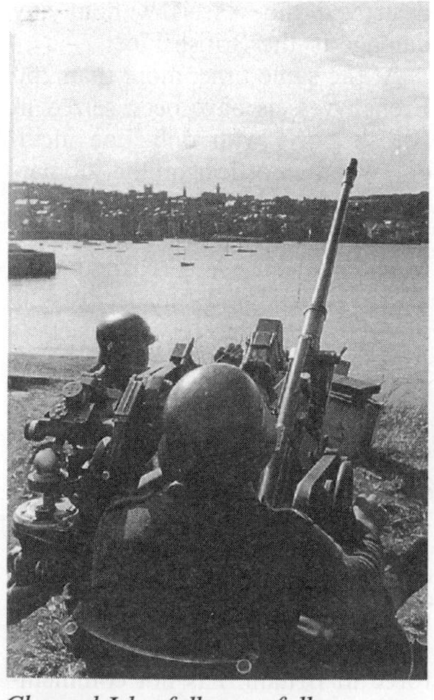

Channel Isles fall peacefully.

1940

AUGUST

Su	Mo	Tu	We	Th	Fr	Sa
				1	2	3
4	5	6	7	8	9	10
11	12	13	14	15	16	17
18	19	20	21	22	23	24
25	26	27	28	29	30	31

1. Moscow: Molotov reaffirms Soviet neutrality but says it is hard to foresee good relations with Britain (→12/11).

2. London: Lord Beaverbrook is appointed to the War Cabinet (→22/12).

4. East Africa: The Italians attack British Somaliland from bases in Abyssinia.→

7. Europe: Alsace-Lorraine and Luxembourg become part of Germany.

8. London: Churchill signs an alliance with de Gaulle's Free France movement (→31).

10. Germany: Today is "Eagle Day", the date by which the Luftwaffe planned to win air superiority from the RAF (→15).

12. Albania: A revolt begins against the Italian occupation (→28/10).

15. UK: The RAF is reported to have shot down 144 out of 1,000 raiding planes, losing only 27 of its own aircraft.→

18. UK: The first German plane is brought down over London (→25).

19. East Africa: British Somaliland falls to the Italians (→20/9).

23. France: The RAF bombs German gun installations on the French coast which have bombarded Dover.

24. Egypt: The Italians continue their recent series of air raids from Libya (→29).

25. London: The Luftwaffe carries out its first bombing raid on London (→27).

27. UK: The Luftwaffe carries out night raids on 21 British towns and cities (→4/9).

29. Egypt: Italian aircraft bomb the Suez Canal (→12/9).

31. London: French colonies of Chad, Cameroons, Equatorial Africa and Tahiti have joined Free France since 26th.

DEATHS

18. US motor tycoon Walter Chrysler (*2/4/1875).

21. Soviet statesman and socialist theoretician Leon Trotsky (*7/11/1879).→

Revenge is sweet as the RAF rains bombs on Berlin

Aug 26. Berlin was shaken this morning by a British bombing raid as the RAF struck back swiftly for the attack on London at the weekend.

British planes flew over the city for nearly three hours dropping bombs and propaganda leaflets. The Prime Minister, Winston Churchill, personally ordered the raid as a morale-boosting physical and psychological revenge for the first Luftwaffe bomb attack on London. The aircraft went over in two waves and all returned safely.

Hitler was reported to be away from the city at the time, but he is known to be furious with Marshal Goering, who had assured him that the British bombers could never reach Berlin (→1/9).

Ack-ack over Berlin for a change.

Petain rounds up his chief opponents

Aug 8. The Vichy government has started a purge against its opponents. Four prominent men – the former premiers Leon Blum and Edouard Daladier, ex-Minister of the Interior Georges Mandel, and General Gamelin, the former army commander – have all been arrested and charged with "causing the defeat of France". General de Gaulle, leading the French Resistance from London, has been sentenced to death in absentia (→7/10).

uftwaffe hits at Britain's airfields

'ighter pilots rush to "scramble" their Hurricanes as the Battle of Britain rages above southern England.

ug 18. The Luftwaffe has switch-d its attacks to targets in southern ingland, and the Battle of Britain as begun in earnest. The Air Min-stry in London reckons that more han 1,000 German planes are be-ng sent over Britain daily.

In the ten days since mass raids egan, the RAF claims to have des-royed 694 German planes, for the ss of 150 of its own. The RAF aved 57 of its pilots. Since pilots are harder to replace than mach-ines, the Luftwaffe has also begun rescue attempts for pilots downed over the Channel, using Red Cross-marked transport planes, which the RAF attack. Now when a plane crashes there is a race on between the British patrol boats and the German planes to find the pilot and either rescue him or take him prisoner.

Newspaper reports in neutral capitals suggest that the success of the RAF in blunting the effect of the Luftwaffe's offensive rests very largely on a still-secret radio de-vice, which is capable of detecting the presence of enemy aircraft at a distance of 75 miles. This allows the RAF Spitfires and Hurricanes to remain on the ground, instead of using up petrol in lengthy patrols. The fighters can still get into the air before the Luftwaffe appears.

talin's agent assassinates Trotsky with ice pick in Mexico

ug 21. Leon Trotsky, the exiled olshevik leader, was assassinated oday in Mexico City by an obscure ndividual posing as a supporter. 'he assassin, almost certainly act-ng on orders from Joseph Stalin nd his secret police, smashed 'rotsky's head with an ice pick. 'rotsky, who was working on an ccusatory biography of Stalin, had een sentenced to death by one of ne Moscow treason tribunals.

Before losing consciousness in ne ambulance taking him to hos-ital, Trotsky whispered: "I am ure of victory of the Fourth Inter-ational. Go forward."

He is said to have told his guards ot to kill his assassin, Ramon Aercader.

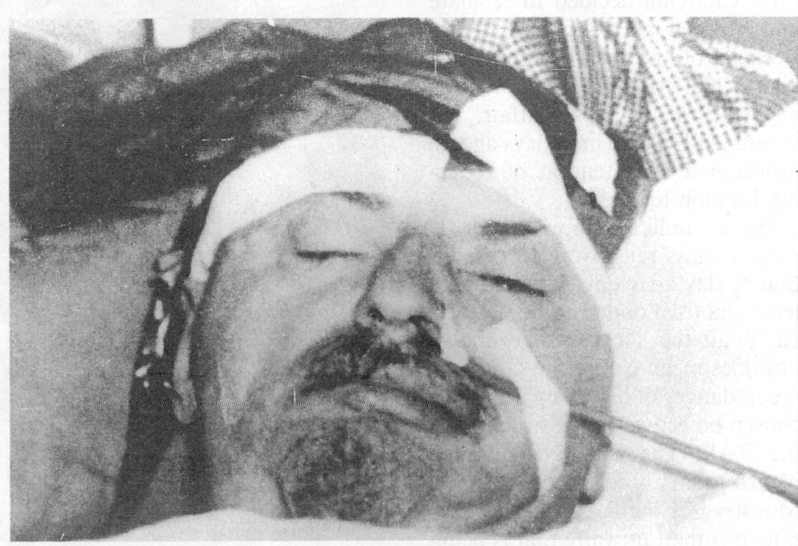

Leon Trotsky, once Stalin's rival, lies dying of irreparable brain damage.

Churchill's stirring speech on debt of many to "the Few"

Aug 20. Mr Churchill scaled new oratorical heights tonight when he delivered another pep talk to the nation. In an exuberant, confident report to Parliament on the state of the war, he paid tribute to the RAF pilots in the Battle of Britain.

"Never in the field of human con-flict", he declared, "was so much owed by so many to so few."

Mr Churchill disclosed that Brit-ain will give the United States 99-year leases of naval and air bases in Newfoundland and the West In-dies. This transaction, he said, means that these two great English-speaking democracies will be en-twined to mutual advantage for a hundred years. And he went on: "No one can stop it. Like the Miss-issippi it keeps rolling along. Let it roll on in full flood, inexorable, irresistible, to broader lands and better days."

MPs cheered throughout the speech. Britain now bristles with two million soldiers, he went on, "rifles and bayonets in their hands" ready to resist invasion (→ 7/9).

British Somaliland attacked by Italy

Aug 7. The Italians continued their advance into British Somaliland from Abyssinia yesterday. They are moving in three columns, and a communique issued in Cairo last night said: "On Monday an Italian column occupied Zeila without op-position. On the same day Hargeisa was captured by a strong force, which included tanks, artillery, machine guns and aircraft.

"Our delaying force fell back after inflicting severe casualties, including three tanks, on the enemy. A small motorised force of the Somaliland Camel Corps haras-sed the enemy without themselves suffering any loss."

The British forces have so far been using skirmishing tactics against the Italians' lengthening lines of communication. It is expect-ed that the real British resistance will begin in the mountains between Hargeisa and Oadweina (→ 19).

1940

SEPTEMBER

Su	Mo	Tu	We	Th	Fr	Sa
1	2	3	4	5	6	7
8	9	10	11	12	13	14
15	16	17	18	19	20	21
22	23	24	25	26	27	28
29	30					

1. Munich: The RAF bombs the city for the first time (→9).

2. Berlin: The Germans order France to pay 400 million francs (£2.3 million) to maintain occupying troops.

4. Berlin: The Battle of Britain begins as Hitler threatens to raze British cities in reprisal for RAF bombings.→

5. Baltic: 4,000 German troops are reported drowned when a Royal Navy sub torpedoes the ship Marion.

6. Bucharest: King Carol abdicates in favour of his son Michael after his pro-German premier resigned (→7/10).

9. London: 400 deaths are reported in renewed Luftwaffe bombing (→15).

9. Hamburg: The RAF carries out a three-hour raid on the city (→21/10).

12. Egypt: Italian troops advance across the frontier from Libya.→

15. London: The BBC says 185 German planes have been shot down over the city in a single day.→

16. US: Registration for military service becomes obligatory for men aged 21 to 35.

20. Rome: Mussolini meets German foreign minister Ribbentrop to discuss the division of African colonies.

22. Indochina: The Japanese invade Tonkin, northern French Indochina (→27).

23. West Africa: The Royal Navy lands de Gaulle with a force of Free French troops at Dakar in Senegal (→25).

24. London: The King introduces the George Cross and George Medal "for valour and outstanding gallantry".

25. Senegal: De Gaulle abandons his Free French attack on Dakar.

26. Atlantic: 46 survivors are found from the evacuee ship City of Benares, sunk on 22nd with the reported loss of 306.

29. New York: Premiere of "Strike up the Band" starring Mickey Rooney and Judy Garland.

Air forces wage "Battle of Britain"

Sept 7. Shortly after five o'clock this afternoon the drone of aircraft grew louder over the East End of London. Over 300 German bombers, escorted by double that number of fighters, were coming up the Thames. They bombed Woolwich Arsenal, a power station, a gas works, the docks and the City.

Two hours later another 250 bombers appeared. More came in during the night, the last attack taking place shortly after 4am. Luftwaffe pilots, returning to their bases in northern France, spoke of London being "an ocean of flames".

These mass attacks represent yet another switch in tactics, suggesting that, for all his boasts, Goering does not really know how he can bring Britain to its knees. After confidently telling Hitler he would destroy the RAF in time for a German invasion this year, he sent the Luftwaffe after British shipping in the Channel. Then he switched to attacks on airfields and radio installations.

To launch his latest offensive, Goering turned up in northern France. "This is the historic hour when our air force for the first time delivers its blows right into the enemy's heart," he said. He described how he watched waves of planes leaving for England.

It is by no means certain, though, that the decision to abandon military targets for attacks on population centres was taken by Goering. During the raids on airfields a few loose bombs fell on London suburbs. Churchill decided to retaliate and ordered an attack on Berlin. Because of the distance the RAF planes had to travel the raid was inevitably a small-scale affair, but it enraged Hitler. Three days ago he proclaimed his intention of reducing London to rubble.

He is unlikely to succeed. If today's mass raids were to be continued, day after day, it would take ten years for London to be destroyed. What the latest change of tactics does mean is that the Germans are in danger of losing sight of their chosen objective, the destruction of the RAF. The Luftwaffe lost 99 planes today, according to the Air Ministry, for the RAF's 22. At that rate, it is the Luftwaffe that is being destroyed (→9).

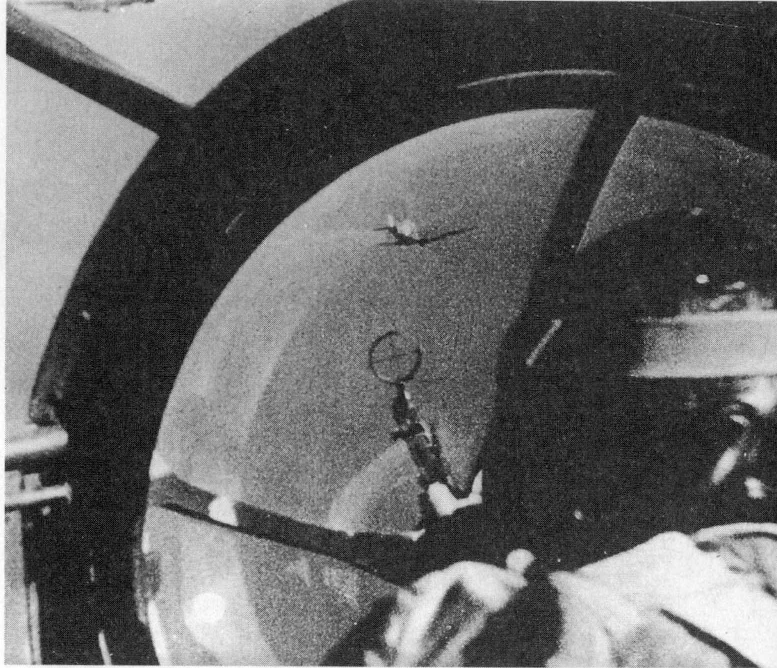

A Spitfire dives through a bomber formation, watched by a hostile gunner.

Later in the Blitz: children look up from a shelter as the fighters duel.

Blitz puts Londoners in the Front Line

Sept 30. Hitler's long-awaited Blitz on London has started. Every evening, wave after wave of Luftwaffe bombers drone over the capital; suddenly Londoners are in the front line.

It was late afternoon on September 7 when 300 bombers began an attack on London's East End. Within minutes, the Docks were ablaze. More than 400 people were killed in that savage overture to the Blitz, and 1,600 badly injured; thousands were made homeless. Since that first attack 7,000 people have been killed and 9,000 injured.

London has adapted to its ordeal with a stoicism which has impressed foreign observers, particularly the American correspondents. For thousands of people, the Blitz means safe, but uncomfortable, nights spent on crowded underground station platforms, emerging in the mornings not knowing whether they have homes to go to.

For those – the vast majority – who choose to remain on the surface, nights are spent in shelters or basements, sleep often made impossible by the sound of bombs, anti-aircraft guns and the shrill bells of fire engines and ambulances.

Yet, despite the chaos, London continues to function as a commercial centre. Each morning, the city's red buses pick their way past bomb craters and wreckage to get Londoners to work. "Business as Usual" is a familiar sign.

Overstretched rescue services are performing prodigious feats daily, burrowing deep into wrecked buildings to pull victims to safety; and yet, despite the chaos, there has been no sign of wholesale looting, and crime is minimal. Heroism by police and firemen is the norm.

The bombs fall impartially on rich and poor alike. The King and Queen were in Buckingham Palace when it was hit. The British Museum and 10 Downing Street have been damaged, and St. Paul's was in grave danger from an unexploded bomb. Radio listeners heard a bomb hit Broadcasting House during the news.

Londoners have not lost their traditional cockney humour. A police station, its windows shattered, bears a sign saying "Be good, we're still open" (→10/10).

Luftwaffe over London: two Dornier 217 bombers above the East End.

At the height of the Blitz Londoners use the Underground for shelter.

Japan forges an alliance with the European Axis

Sept 27. Japan today signed a ten-year pact with Germany and Italy, thereby converting the Berlin-Rome axis into a triangle for aggression. Although the ceremony in Berlin marks an undoubted success for Adolf Hitler, in practical terms the alliance simply recognises an existing arrangement.

The three countries have to their own satisfaction divided Europe and Asia into spheres of influence. They promise mutual military and economic aid. In the threatening words of the Nazi Foreign Minister, Ribbentrop: "The pact is a military alliance between the three mightiest states of the world, comprising over 250 million people."

One of the objects of the treaty is to warn the United States not to enter the war against Germany. The Japanese threat, if it came to war in the Pacific, might ensure that America devoted most of its resources to campaigns in the East. The three powers were careful to insert a clause to reassure Russia, but the Kremlin must be uneasy at this new development (→7/11).

RAF bombs Italians as Egypt is invaded

Sept 15. British armoured units today inflicted heavy losses on Italian troops advancing across the Libyan border to invade Egypt, while RAF planes bombed troop concentrations.

A communique from Cairo HQ reported that the enemy had occupied Sollum and the frontier customs post at Musaid, evacuated by the Egyptian Frontier Force last summer. Two Italian divisions, supported by corps troops and divisional artillery, are establishing a loose front between the coastal road and a desert escarpment to the south east.

One enemy column descending the coastal plain at Halfaya, south of Salum, suffered heavily when it was pounded by British artillery fire. On the other hand, the Italians claim to have shot down two Blenheims (→12/9).

1940

OCTOBER

Su	Mo	Tu	We	Th	Fr	Sa
		1	2	3	4	5
6	7	8	9	10	11	12
13	14	15	16	17	18	19
20	21	22	23	24	25	26
27	28	29	30	31		

1. Helsinki: Finland signs a military and economic treaty with Germany.

3. London: Neville Chamberlain resigns "for health reasons" from the government (→ 9/11).

4. Italy: Hitler and Mussolini have a three-hour meeting at the Brenner Pass.→

7. Vichy: Petain repeals an 1870 decree giving Algerian Jews French citizenship (→ 18).

7. Rumania: German and Italian troops invade (→ 12).

9. London: Churchill is elected as leader of the Tory Party unanimously, following Chamberlain's resignation (→ 22/12).

10. London: A bomb destroys the high altar of St. Paul's Cathedral (→ 14/11).

12. Bucharest: The city is occupied by Axis troops.

13. UK: 14-year-old Princess Elizabeth makes her radio debut in a broadcast to child evacuees.

14. Vichy: Married women are banned from working in public services (→ 18).

18. Vichy: Petain bans Jews from the public service, and from high positions in industry and the press (→ 9/11).

21. New York: Ernest Hemingway's novel "For Whom the Bell Tolls" is published.

21. Berlin: The most intensive RAF bombing raid yet lasts four hours and is claimed to cause severe damage (→ 25).

23. London: The Air Ministry gives the first details of alleged German invasion plans.

25. Germany: High casualties and huge fires are reported after further RAF raids on Berlin and Hamburg (→ 16/11).

30. Vichy: Petain calls on the French to collaborate, to "maintain French unity within the new European order" (→ 15/12).

BIRTH

23. Brazilian footballer Edson Arantes do Nascimento, alias Pele.

Battle begins for control of Atlantic

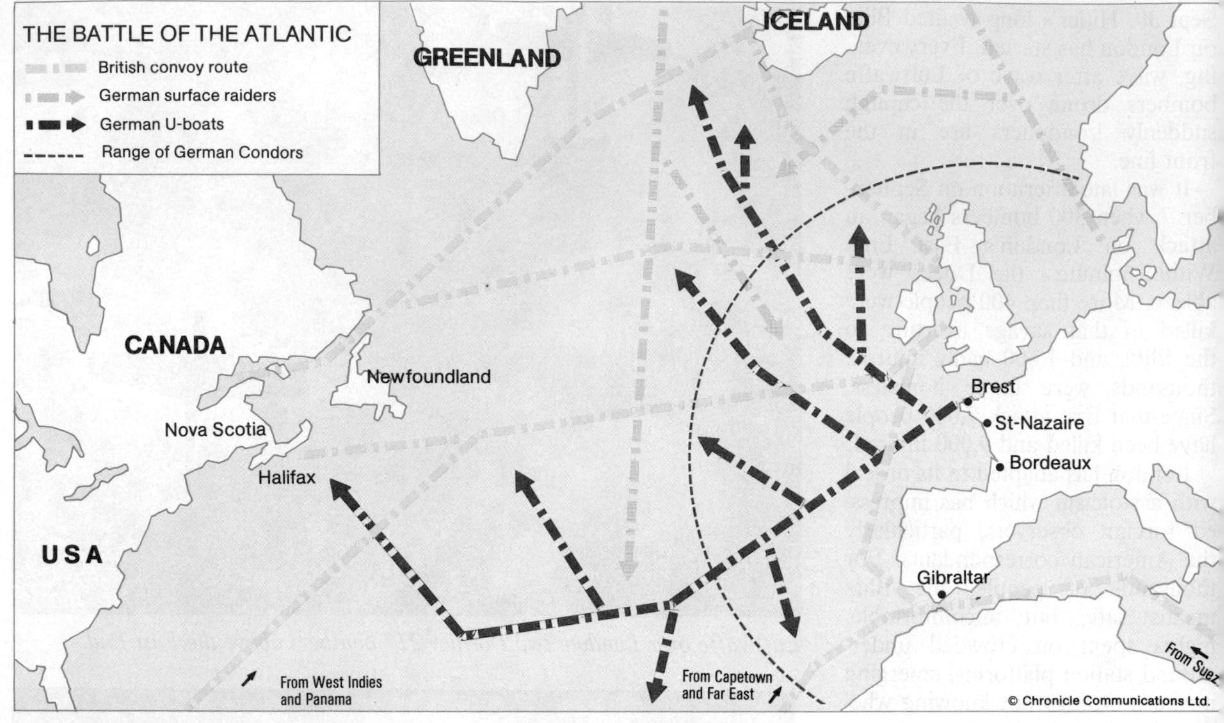

Oct 30. A new German menace has cast its shadow across the field of battle. It is now known that Grand Admiral Erich Raeder has fitted out merchant ships as armed raiders and that five of these, evading Royal Navy patrols, are in the Atlantic. They are more powerfully armed and generally faster than the British armed merchant cruisers. They have already sunk or captured 36 ships, amounting to 235,000 tons.

The German success with these raiders will, for the time being, act as compensation for Hitler's shortsightedness in giving a low priority to the construction of U-boats. The Germans started the war with 26 U-boats, and about as many again have been built, but 30 have been destroyed and of the remainder only one-third are operational at the same time.

Their effectiveness, however, will be greatly increased when the Germans begin using France's Atlantic ports: the journey from bases to operation areas will be cut by 450 miles.

The German threat to Britain's Atlantic lifeline will continue to grow. In the next few weeks two of Germany's famous pocket battleships, the Hipper and the Scheer, will come into service.

Though Hitler has not yet admitted as much, the long-promised invasion of Britain has almost certainly been shelved for this year at least. With the Luftwaffe having lost the Battle of Britain, Hitler has decided to try to beat his only fighting foe by starving her out.

In the Battle of the Atlantic, the front line will be manned by sailors of the Royal Navy and seamen of the Merchant Navy. The merchant seamen are all volunteers and their pay is £9. a month, plus 2s. 6d. a day danger money (→ 10/4/41).

Greece is attacked by Italian troops

Oct 28. Italy launched an unprovoked invasion of Greece today, following a three-hour ultimatum demanding right of passage for Italian troops across Greece. Ten divisions moved across the border from Albania, and Italian aircraft bombed Athens. British warships immediately went to the help of the Greeks, and Britain's determination to give full aid to Greece in resisting the aggressor was expressed in messages from the King and the Prime Minister (→ 22/11).

Roosevelt denies he plans to go to war

Oct 23. President Roosevelt, in a speech in Philadelphia today, attacked what he called "the fantastic mis-statement" that his Administration "has secretly entered into agreements with foreign nations".

The President is sensitive to such charges as next month's presidential election looms. In particular, Republican speakers are insinuating that he has contracted a secret commitment with Britain to go to war, a charge which is all the more plausible because last month he did reveal a previously secret agreement made with Mr Winston Churchill, by which Britain is giving the US bases in the Atlantic and the Caribbean, in return for 50 overage destroyers.

After the German conquest of the coastline of Western Europe in June, the Prime Minister sent a message asking, as "a matter of life or death", for some of America's Great War destroyers. The President, facing opposition from isolationists in the "America First" movement, hesitated, but finally agreed to the exchange by "executive agreement", which does not require Congress approval (→ 5/11).

Hitler has little luck looking for allies

After meeting Franco and Petain, Hitler stops to greet Mussolini in Italy.

Oct 24. Hitler crossed Europe in an armoured train to meet Francisco Franco yesterday on the Franco-Spanish frontier; he tried to pressure the Spanish dictator into coming into the war against England.

Hitler turned Franco down last summer when, with France beaten and England expected to collapse, he offered to join up and share the spoils. Now that Hitler does need him, the wily Spaniard has changed his tune. He told Hitler that Spain would come in, but only if it was given the French territories in North Africa, military and economic aid, and after Germany invaded England.

Returning home, Hitler stopped his train at Montoire, near Tours, to try to persuade Marshal Petain, head of the Vichy regime, to come into the war against England. Petain expressed sympathy but said French opinion was not ready for such a gesture (→2/12).

Like father like daughter: Princess Elizabeth, with her sister Margaret, making her first broadcast to the people of Britain.

1940

NOVEMBER

Su	Mo	Tu	We	Th	Fr	Sa
					1	2
3	4	5	6	7	8	9
10	11	12	13	14	15	16
17	18	19	20	21	22	23
24	25	26	27	28	29	30

1. France: Prehistoric cave paintings are discovered at Lascaux in the Dordogne.

4. Greece: Greek troops push back advancing Italians.→

7. London: Britain, Australia and the US agree on defence co-operation in the Pacific.

9. Vichy: Petain dissolves all trade unions and employers organisations.

11. US: Willys launches its light car for the US Army, called "Jeep" from the initials G. P. for "General Purpose".

12. Berlin: Soviet foreign minister Molotov arrives for talks with Hitler.

13. New York: Opening of Walt Disney's "Fantasia".

14. Coventry: The mediaeval city is devastated by the worst air raid of the war; 1,000 civilians are killed (→20).

15. Warsaw: 350,000 Jews are now confined to a ghetto.

16. Hamburg: The RAF drops 2,000 bombs in the heaviest attack yet on the city (→20).

18. London: Churchill confirms deal to lease bases in the West Indies to the US, in exchange for destroyers.

20. Midlands: The Luftwaffe pounds Birmingham and other towns all night (→29).

20. Budapest: Hungary joins the Axis (→24).

24. Bratislava: Slovakia joins the Axis.

28. Sardinia: The Fleet Air Arm torpedoes seven Italian warships.

29. Liverpool: The city is bombed by an intensive Luftwaffe raid (→30).

30. Southampton: A seven-hour air raid causes severe damage.→

DEATHS

9. British Conservative statesman Neville Chamberlain, prime minister 1937-40 (*18/3/1869).→

26. British newspaper baron Harold Harmsworth, Lord Rothermere (*26/4/1868).

Roosevelt wins a record third term

Nov 5. President Franklin D. Roosevelt was today re-elected by an overwhelming margin over the Republican candidate, Wendell Wilkie. He will be the first President in American history to serve a third four-year term.

The President did better than expected, winning 449 votes in the electoral college to Willkie's 82, and more than 27 million votes to Willkie's 22 million. On the other hand, Roosevelt's share of the vote at 54.7 per cent was lower than in 1936 (60.8 per cent) and 1932 (57.4 per cent). The Republicans chose Wilkie, a lawyer and "amateur", over the Ohio Senator Robert Taft. Conservative Democrats broke with Roosevelt, as did the labour leader John L. Lewis, but attempts to call Roosevelt a "dictator" backfired (→29/12).

Roosevelt: America's favourite.

Chamberlain will be haunted by Munich

Nov 9. Neville Chamberlain died of cancer today, aged 71. The former Prime Minister knew before resigning from the War Cabinet last month that he could never resume state duties.

Controversy will rage for years over his Munich agreement with Hitler, but tonight there are worldwide tributes to a great patriot and devoted servant of the nation for having struggled to preserve world peace and freedom.

Goering strikes at provincial cities

Nov 30. Something very odd happened in London on a certain night this month. For the first time in almost two months the air raid sirens were not sounded. People asked themselves what could have gone wrong. On the next night, matters became clearer. The German bombers were attacking cities and towns in the provinces. Once again Goering had changed his tactics.

The Germans are now making a major effort to knock out British industry with special squadrons, equipped with new navigational devices, and trained to attack specific targets. The new tactics began with a blitz on Coventry, when 600 tons of high explosives and thousands of incendiaries were dropped.

Birmingham, Sheffield, Manchester and Glasgow were next. After these, the ports came under attack from the 400 bombers sent over Britain each night. The Luftwaffe has also returned to London, though on a reduced scale on most nights.

Deaths from the air raids have been coming down, Churchill has told the House of Commons. In the first week of intense raids 6,000 people were killed. The weekly figure now is around 3,000. In the London raids, the Prime Minister said, it is taking a ton of bombs to "kill three-quarters of a person".

The King and Queen have regularly stayed at Buckingham Palace. They were there one Friday a few weeks ago when six bombs fell on the Palace, one of which wrecked the Chapel (→29/12).

The ruins of Coventry Cathedral, devastated by a night of bombs.

Their Majesties tour the East End, though the Palace has suffered too.

A sad case of: Yes we have no bananas

Nov 26. A bleak Christmas lies ahead for a besieged Britain. With vital shipping space needed for war supplies, the country is becoming accustomed to food shortages. Carrots will take the place of dried fruit in millions of Christmas puddings; from Christmas Eve, no more bananas will be imported; and a price haggle with Spanish growers threatens a serious shortage of marmalade oranges, lemons and onions.

Lord Woolton, the Minister of Food (who has given his name to the austerity "Woolton Pudding") has hinted at extra tea and sugar for the festivities, but has asked for people to use less milk because of a current shortage. He has asked the population to make "small sacrifices" during Christmas, but he was not prepared to place controls on luxuries like turkeys, confectionery – even caviar.

It could be a cold Christmas, too, for Blitz-worn Londoners. Most of London's coal was imported by sea. Now it relies on the congested railway services. The Army has been asked to help (→3/12).

Greeks put Italian invaders to flight

Nov 22. The Greeks have defeated the Italian invaders in a great victory at Koritza, the Italian headquarters in Albania. The Italians, whose retreat has developed into a rout, have abandoned large quantities of stores and munitions. The Greeks have not merely driven the aggressors from their territory; they are seriously threatening the Italian position in Albania itself. Tonight, RAF planes are attacking the fleeing Italians (→6/12).

1940

DECEMBER

Su	Mo	Tu	We	Th	Fr	Sa
1	2	3	4	5	6	7
8	9	10	11	12	13	14
15	16	17	18	19	20	21
22	23	24	25	26	27	28
29	30	31				

1. London: Joseph Kennedy resigns as US ambassador to Britain.

2. Madrid: An Anglo-Spanish finance pact is signed; Franco vows to keep out of the war.

3. London: The Food Minister announces extra Christmas rations of four ounces of sugar and two ounces of tea.

6. Rome: Marshal Pietro Badoglio is sacked as Italian chief of staff following the setbacks in Albania (→23).

10. Stockholm: No Nobel Prizes are awarded this year.

12. Egypt: 30,000 Italians are reported captured by British and Commonwealth troops.

15. Paris: The ashes of Napoleon II are returned from Vienna; the German publicity gesture is ill-attended.

15. Vichy: Laval is arrested for planning to remove Petain as Vichy leader and move closer to Germany (→17).

17. Vichy: Laval is released on Hitler's orders.

22. London: Anthony Eden becomes Foreign Secretary; Lord Halifax is appointed ambassador to the US.

23. Albania: The Greeks capture Chimera and take over 800 Italians prisoner.

26. New York: Opening of "The Philadelphia Story" starring Katharine Hepburn.

DEATH

21. US novelist Francis Scott Fitzgerald (*24/9/1896).

HITS OF 1940

A nightingale sang in Berkeley Square.

Whispering Grass.

QUOTE OF THE YEAR

"We shall defend our island, whatever the cost may be, we shall fight on the beaches, we shall fight on the landing grounds, we shall fight in the fields and in the streets, we shall fight in the hills: we shall never surrender."

Winston Churchill, speech of June 4, 1940.

The City is an inferno

A building burns near St. Paul's, another victim of 10,000 fire bombs.

Dec 29. The Germans chose to-
ight, a Sunday, to try to set fire to
he City of London. The raid had
clearly been planned with typical
German thoroughness. It was timed to coincide with the tidal low-
point in the Thames, and the water
mains were severed at the outset by
high explosive parachute mines.
Then at least 10,000 fire bombs
were unloaded.

For a time the fires raged out of control, as firemen were unable to use the mains supply or pump water from the Thames. When the water came on again, pumped from more distant mains, the exhaust pipes of fire engines became red hot through the continued high pressure pumping by 20,000 firemen.

They were later reinforced by soldiers and civilians. In a dramatic incident, an unknown soldier lost his life. He was an old soldier; no stripes, just many ribbons. He and a fireman were playing a hose on a 60-feet high wall engulfed in flames when it crashed down, burying them both beneath tons of bricks.

Luckily for the City the raid was broken off just when the Luftwaffe seemed to be winning. The Air Ministry believes this was due to the weather unexpectedly deteriorating over low-lying German airfields.

As a result of the raid, firewatching duties will be tightened up; they were made compulsory for employees at large premises last September, but some firms have been lax in enforcing them. The new penalty will be a £100 fine and/or three months in prison (→21/3/41).

US is "the arsenal of democracy"

Dec 29. In one of his "fireside chat" radio broadcasts last night, President Roosevelt called the United States "the arsenal of democracy". The President said his purpose was "to keep you now, and your children later, out of a last-ditch war for the preservation of American independence", and he called on the US to send "more of everything" to those "in the front lines of democracy's battle".

American sales of munitions to Britain have been hampered by the Neutrality Acts passed by Congress. Last summer the President made the sale of 500,000 rifles possible by declaring them surplus to American requirements. More recently he was able to hand over 50 over-age destroyers. Britain will also be able to buy US military aircraft.

But in general, US industry is not ready for war production, and it will take time as well as money before Britain will receive much material from the US. However, the President has now clearly signalled that he wants such help to grow; before the election he was reluctant to do so for fear of provoking Congress (→11/3/41).

Britain launches North Africa attack

Dec 9. The first major British land offensive against the Italians in the Western Desert today took enemy forces completely by surpise. Within hours our troops had taken 1,000 prisoners, captured an Italian camp near Sidi Barani, killed an Italian General and captured his second-in-command.

General Sir Archibald Wavell, the C-in-C, himself gave first news of the attack. Cross-legged and hands in pockets, he said: "Our forces began to carry out an engagement against the Italian armies in the Western Desert at dawn this morning."

During the chill desert night British columns moved up to their start lines. In the starlit sky they could see waves of RAF bombers flying westwards to attack bases and airfields.

The Great Dictator marches in too late

Chaplin: spot the difference.

Chaplin's long-awaited film, "The Great Dictator", hailed as "withering political satire", arrived too late to be satirical in Blitz-torn London.

Chaplin's dictator, Adenoid Hynkel, raving gibberish into the microphone, is a brilliant parody. The scene where fellow-dictator Benzino Napoloni's train fails to stop at the red carpet – so both train and carpet are shunted to and fro – is pure Chaplin.

Also pure Chaplin, unfortunately, is the naive long-winded address to the audience that ends the film, exhorting nations to brotherhood instead of hatred. Like the film as a whole, it comes two years too late.

The year also brought us **Garbo** in her first comedy role in **Ernst Lubitsch's** "Ninotchka". Arriving in Paris as a dour Russian emissary, she thaws out delightfully under the influence of champagne.

Walt Disney has followed "Snow White" with the creation of "Pinocchio", a puppet that comes to life, supported by such lovable Disney-folk as Jiminy Cricket. **Hitchcock** has given us "Rebecca" and the brooding atmosphere of Manderley, where the second Mrs de Winter (**Joan Fontaine**) faces her predecessor's implacable housekeeper Mrs Danvers (**Judith Anderson**).

Ernest Hemingway published his novel of the Spanish Civil War, "For Whom the Bell Tolls", and **Graham Greene**, his powerful story of the persecutions of a priest in Mexico under dictatorship, "The Power and the Glory."

1941

JANUARY

Su	Mo	Tu	We	Th	Fr	Sa
			1	2	3	4
5	6	7	8	9	10	11
12	13	14	15	16	17	18
19	20	21	22	23	24	25
26	27	28	29	30	31	

1. Italy: The RAF bombs Taranto and Naples as well as Italian bases in Libya (→3).

3. Libya: Australian troops launch a major assault on the Italians at Bardia, taking 5,000 prisoners (→5).

4. US: German actress Marlene Dietrich becomes a US citizen.

5. Libya: Bardia falls; 25,000 men and six generals are captured (→7).

7. Libya: British and Commonwealth troops capture Tobruk airport.→

9. Abyssinia: The RAF bombs Italian positions as tribesmen attack on the ground (→15).

10. Malta: British bases on the Island are bombed by Italian and Luftwaffe planes (→30/11).

15. Abyssinia: Emperor Haile Selassie is reported to have returned to help anti-Italian rebels (→27).

17. Glasgow: Churchill says: "We will not fail mankind at this turning point in our fortunes" (→14/8).

20. Washington: Roosevelt is inaugurated for his third term as president (→11/3).

21. Rumania: An attempted coup by the Fascist "Iron Guard" fails amid bloody riots and massacres (→8/12).

23. North Africa: 100,000 Italian prisoners have been taken so far in the North African campaign (→30).

27. Eritrea: British and Commonwealth troops advance 100 miles into Italian-occupied territory (→6/3).

30. Libya: Derna falls to General Wavell's troops after a fierce three-day battle (→1/2).

DEATHS

4. French philosopher Henri Bergson (*18/10/1859).

5. British airwoman Amy Johnson (*1/7/1903).→

8. British commander and Boy Scouts founder Lord Robert Baden-Powell (*22/2/1857).

13. Irish author James Joyce (*2/2/1882).→

Commonwealth troops capture Tobruk

Italian troops surrender as Anzacs take Mussolini's Fascist stronghold.

Jan 22. An Anzac bush hat run up a flagpole marked the British and Australian victory at Tobruk this morning. An Australian cavalry regiment took this North African port a few hours ago from the Italians with an uphill charge, but when they arrived in the main square there was no Union Jack available to replace Mussolini's flag, so they hoisted one of their own hats.

It was a suitable climax to a spirited campaign which, within a few weeks, has brought General Wavell's Army of the Nile right into Libya. The Italians, who took a heavy battering from land, sea and air, surrendered in droves as the infantry, supported by tanks and Bren gun carriers, stormed the port, losing only 500 men.

In the campaign so far 100,000 Italian prisoners have been taken. Among them in Tobruk was the corps commander and a number of senior officers. The Italian force is shattered and General Wavell will now be tempted to push on towards Benghazi (→23).

Neutral Eire hit by surprise air raids

Jan 2. German bombs fell on neutral Southern Ireland tonight and, although nobody was killed, several people were injured. The raids were along a 100-mile line down the eastern side of the country, and some fell near The Curragh where both British and German airmen are interned.

Only a partial black-out is in force in Eire, and there seems little doubt that the German pilots would have known where they were dropping their bombs. The Eire Government issued a brief statement, but has so far refused to condemn the attack. Many feel the intention behind the raids is to warn Eire that she will feel the full force of German arms if she dares to abandon her neutrality and grant Britain the naval bases she needs in the south (→26/1/42).

Daily Worker closed for being defeatist

Jan 8. The Government's decision to suppress the Communist Daily Worker was overwhelmingly endorsed by MPs today as the Minister for Home Security, Herbert Morrison, used his sweeping powers to ban further publication of the newspaper. He said that it was constantly agitating against the war and, if allowed to continue, might begin to undermine public morale.

Mr Morrison said that Communist politicians behind the Daily Worker have been behaving contemptibly. After every air raid they gave out leaflets telling people whose homes were damaged that the war was just a plot to make profits for the capitalists.

Eleven left-wing MPs voted against the ban. "You're showing snivelling hypocrisy," Mr Morrison told them (→26/4/42).

Dubliner dies in Swiss exile

Jan 13. From Zurich comes news c the death of James Joyce. Althoug he left his native Dublin in 190 and last saw it in 1912, no man ha written more obsessively about th city – in "Dubliners", in "Portrai of the Artist as a Young Man" and of course, in "Ulysses", which wa banned in America and Britain, bu declared not obscene by an Amer can court in 1933.

Joyce's next "work in progress was published in excerpts over th next 17 years and finally complete as "Finnegan's Wake" in 1939. I describes the dream of an Irish pub lican in language of such multipl punning and layers of symbolism a to be pronounced "the obscures book ever written by a genius".

In 1931 Joyce married Nor Barnacle, who left Dublin with hin and who inspired Molly Bloom.

James Joyce: the final portrait.

Amy Johnson is feared drowned

Jan 5. Amy Johnson, the femal flyer who made history by flying solo to Australia, is missing, fearec drowned, after an aircraft she wa flying ditched in the Thame Estuary. Miss Johnson, aged 38 has been flying aircraft from fact ories to RAF bases for the past six months. Eyewitnesses said her air craft's engine appeared to have cu out before it plunged into the sea Small boats soon found the wreck age, but no sign of Amy.

Fingers will burn in food price freeze

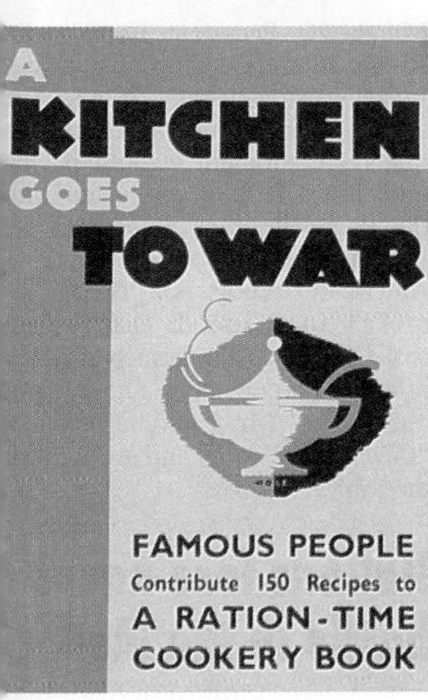

Cooking on Home Front rations.

Jan 14. Sweeping new price controls to counter food profiteering were announced today. Wholesalers and retailers have been ordered not to sell certain foods – ranging from dead poultry to pickles – at prices higher than those charged at the beginning of last month. More than 20 food items, including coffee, cocoa, rice, spaghetti, biscuits, custard and jelly, are effectively frozen in price.

Announcing the controls the Food Minister, Lord Woolton, revealed that growing numbers of speculators had appeared in the food industry. "These people are trying to render a bad service to the nation," he said. "They will have their fingers burned as a result of the stabilising order." More price controls are likely in the near future.

The average working-class family in Britain lives on a weekly budget of less than £5 a week, a Ministry survey revealed. The Government review of the cost of living index began in 1937, although no decisions are likely until the end of the war.

Nine thousand homes of industrial and clerical workers earning less than £250 a year also came under scrutiny. The Ministry of Labour figures show average weekly spending as: Food ..£1. 14s 1d; Rent, etc ....10s 10d; Clothes ...9s 4d; Fuel, light ...6s 5d; Other ...£1.5s 7d (→ 6/2).

1941

FEBRUARY

Su	Mo	Tu	We	Th	Fr	Sa
						1
2	3	4	5	6	7	8
9	10	11	12	13	14	15
16	17	18	19	20	21	22
23	24	25	26	27	28	

1. Libya: The RAF carries out a heavy raid on Tripoli (→ 7).

3. Rome: Mussolini declares southern Italy a war zone and puts it under martial law (→ 5/2/43).

5. UK: The war is now costing Britain £11 million a day (→ 7/4).

6. London: The government issues an official recipe for "Blitz Broth" (→ 17/3).

7. Libya: British and Commonwealth troops take Benghazi.→

10. Iceland: The island is bombed by the Luftwaffe (→ 7/5).

12. Oxford: A policeman with septicaemia is first to be successfully treated with penicillin (→ 24/10/43).

12. Balkans: 400,000 German troops are believed to have arrived as steady troop movements continue (→ 14).

14. Sofia: Bulgaria accepts German occupation (→ 17).

16. East Africa: The last Italian troops are expelled from the Sudan (→ 26).

17. Sofia: Bulgaria and Turkey sign a non-aggression pact, under German pressure (→ 1/3).

18. Singapore: Australian troops arrive to reinforce the British garrison (→ 21).

19. Berlin: Hitler warns Greece to end the war with Italy or face Germany fighting with the Italians (→ 23/4).

21. Tokyo: Japan warns Britain against military movements in south-east Asia (→ 24/4).

24. Berlin: Hitler threatens a new U-boat war of unprecedented fury.

28. Vichy: Petain accepts a Japanese ultimatum to settle the disputed border of French Indochina (→ 29/3).

DEATHS

19. British conductor and composer Sir Herbert Hamilton Harty (*4/12/1879).

28. Spanish ex-King Alfonso XIII (*17/5/1886).

Rommel's Afrika Korps arrives in Tripoli

The Afrika Korps' advance guard takes up position in North Africa.

Feb 14. The advance guard of a German force to be known as the Afrika Korps landed in Tripoli, in North Africa, today. It is a panzer division that has been specially trained for desert warfare, commanded by General Erwin Rommel.

He has orders from Adolf Hitler to rescue Mussolini's forces, which have suffered a series of humiliating defeats by Field Marshal Wavell's British army.

Meanwhile, the British are continuing their advance across Libya; last week they took Benghazi after a dash from Tobruk which they captured last month. Mussolini is reported to be furious at the poor showing of his army of Africa and has shown his temper by dismissing Generals held responsible for the fiasco. So far nothing has been able to stop the headlong flight of the army commanded by Marshal Rodolfo Graziani. It remains to be seen whether the newly-arrived German divisions can stiffen Italian resolve.

So far the British have enjoyed air supremacy. This may now be challenged by the arrival of Luftwaffe squadrons (→ 15/3).

Italian Somaliland falls to pincer assault

Feb 26. "Hit them hard and hit them again" was the order of the day issued by Lieutenant-General A.G. Cunningham, the East African army commander, launching the pincer assault which led to the fall yesterday of Italian-held Mogadishu, the main port of Somaliland.

Among the Empire troops which stormed across 300 miles of hard country in a month to cut Mogadishu off from the main enemy forces, were South Africans, the Gold Coast Regiment and the King's African Rifles.

The Italian Empire is collapsing and even Mussolini has admitted the capitulation of 200,000 troops in Libya, a tenth of his entire army. He also revealed the loss of 1,000 aircraft, so he is now entirely dependent on German support (→ 16/3).

1941

MARCH

Su	Mo	Tu	We	Th	Fr	Sa
						1
2	3	4	5	6	7	8
9	10	11	12	13	14	15
16	17	18	19	20	21	22
23	24	25	26	27	28	29
30	31					

1. Sofia: Bulgaria joins the Axis; the Germans complete their military occupation (→ 3).

2. Turkey: The Dardanelles are closed to all ships without Turkish permits and pilots (→ 4).

3. Bulgaria: German troops advance towards the Greek border; Turkish troops are on alert (→ 5).

4. Ankara: Turkey refuses to join the Axis, saying "it is better to die".

5. London: Britain breaks off relations with Bulgaria (→ 13).

6. Abyssinia: Haile Selassie's troops capture the Italian stronghold of Burye (→ 27).

10. Belgrade: Hitler gives Yugoslavia an ultimatum to join the Axis (→ 25).

13. Albania: A fresh Italian offensive, personally directed by Mussolini, is crushed (→ 28/12/42).

15. North Africa: Rommel's Afrika Korps launches an attack on British and Commonwealth forces (→ 21).

16. East Africa: British and Commonwealth troops recapture Berbera, capital of British Somaliland (→ 27).

19. UK: Rissoles (vegetable sausages) are to be mass-produced at 8d. a pound (→ 2/6).

20. London: The BBC lifts its ban on employing conscientious objectors.

21. Libya: The British take Italy's last stronghold in eastern Libya (→ 28).

25. Belgrade: Prince Paul, the Yugoslav Regent, signs a pact with Germany Axis.→

27. East Africa: Keren in Eritrea and Harar in Abyssinia fall to British-led forces (→ 1/4).

29. Vichy: Petain creates a General Commissariat for Jewish Affairs (→ 12/5).

DEATHS

13. British trade unionist Tom Mann (*15/4/1856).

28. British author Virginia Woolf (*25/1/1882).→

Call for 100,000 women to do war work

Out of the kitchen and into the factories for Britain's women at war.

March 17. Womanpower for the war effort – that was the call today from the Minister of Labour, Ernest Bevin, as he announced the first steps in a massive mobilisation plan. Registration of 20- and 21-year-old women will begin next month, with the aim of filling vital jobs in industry and the auxiliary services.

One of the prime targets will be to get shell-filling factories working round the clock. Only a few days ago Mr Bevin urged 100,000 women to step forward and volunteer, with the words: "I cannot offer them a delightful life. I want them to come forward in the spirit that they are going to suffer some inconvenience but with a determination to help us through."

Women are also desperately needed to take over all kinds of other jobs to free men for active service. First preference will be given to experienced women, but Mr Bevin is also looking to those who have never worked before to join the women's auxiliaries.

As yet, married women with young children are exempt, but those who can do war work locally will be backed up by a huge expansion in day and night nurseries, and child minding-systems. Special welfare arrangements are to be made for women who have to leave home.

"Transfer of women from their home is one of the biggest industrial problems of the war," said Mr Bevin. "I am putting pressure on management to give greater attention to the reception of women and facilities for their comfort. The first month in a new job will be the worst."

The drive for young women coincides with one for men of 41 and 42. Male trainees will earn £3.0s.6d, female £1.18s a week (→ 19).

FDR signs lease-lend pact with UK

March 11. President Franklin D. Roosevelt today signed the Lease-Lend agreement with Britain. The idea of letting Britain use American military equipment without paying until after the war originated with the President. Last November the British Ambassador confessed to American reporters "Britain is broke". In a "fireside chat" broadcast FDR used the homely analogy of lending a neighbour a hose to put out a fire. Mr Churchill replied: "Give us the tools and we'll finish the job" (→ 10/4).

Italians lose naval battle in the Med

March 28. British warships today destroyed a large part of the Italian fleet in battle off Crete without suffering a single casualty themselves. Seven warships were sunk, and 4,000 Italian lives lost, when the cruiser Orion acted as a decoy to draw the unthinking Italians towards the main British force, dodging their shells until they were within range. The first Italian to be attacked, the cruiser Fiume, did not even have time to swing her eight-inch guns into action before she received a British broadside (→ 3/4).

Raid on Norway sinks 11 ships

March 4. British troops today sank 11 German ships, and destroyed fish-oil factories used to produce glycerine for explosives, in a daring dawn raid on the Lofoten Islands off Norway.

A power station was also destroyed, and oil storage tanks set on fire, in the attack which took the Germans completely by surprise. Ten Norwegian Quisling traitors collaborating with the Nazi occupying force were brought back to Britain, along with 300 Norwegian volunteers who want to fight the Germans. Many Norwegians took part in the raid, the first time they have played a role in Allied operations since their country was occupied last year (→ 10/9).

Coup ousts pro-Nazi leader in Yugoslavia

March 27. Ominous reports of German troop movements towards the Yugoslav border came from Sofia last night, following the overthrow of the pro-Axis Tsvetkovitch government

The coup d'etat, organised by General Simovitch, is regarded as a serious setback to German military and political plans for the Balkans. Berlin reacted by asking if the new government intended to endorse the existing Axis Pact.

It is out of the question. Last night the people took to the streets shouting "Down with the traitors". British and Russian flags were carried side-by-side by demonstrators crying: "Down with Hitler".

Immediately the coup was known to have succeeded the Council of Regency resigned and King Peter, who is 17, assumed full powers as sovereign. Shortly afterwards the pro-German Prince Paul fled from the capital.

The first announcement of the revolt was made in London by Mr Churchill. He declared that Britain would give full support if the Germans attack Yugoslavia. Tonight the Yugoslav army is taking up its battle positions (→ 17/4).

South-East is hit by new spring Blitz

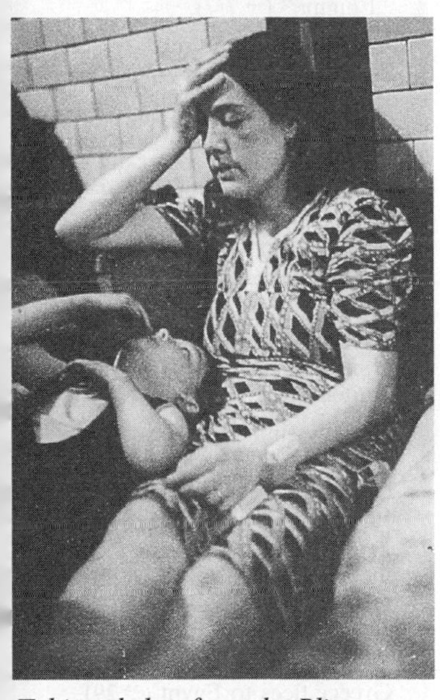

Taking shelter from the Blitz.

March 21. London and south-east England have been the main target in the Luftwaffe's spring night raids. One 500-pound bomb hit a crowded suburban dance hall. Of 150 dancers – munition workers, soldiers on leave and girl typists in party frocks – four, including three girls, were killed. It was disclosed yesterday that the Germans made a deliberate attempt to destroy Buckingham Palace last week. The attack began with the dropping of flares, which lit up the Palace; showers of incendiary bombs followed. The Germans then began to make low-level bombing runs. The Palace escaped a direct hit (→ 16/4).

Death by drowning for Virginia Woolf

March 30. Hope has been abandoned for Virginia Woolf, the novelist, who disappeared two days ago on a walk along the River Ouse near her home, Monk's House, Rodmell, Sussex. She is believed to have drowned herself in the river.

She is understood to have left letters for her husband, Leonard Woolf, and her sister, the painter Vanessa Bell. Mrs Woolf had recently completed another novel, always a time of mental strain for her. She had had several breakdowns in the past.

The house in Bloomsbury where she and her husband ran the avant-garde Hogarth Press, which published her, was recently bombed. It was the meeting-place for the "Bloomsbury Group".

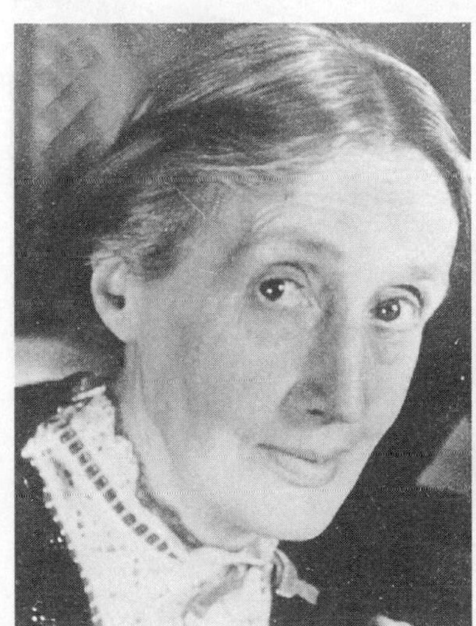

Virginia Woolf: an enigmatic end.

1941

APRIL

Su	Mo	Tu	We	Th	Fr	Sa
		1	2	3	4	5
6	7	8	9	10	11	12
13	14	15	16	17	18	19
20	21	22	23	24	25	26
27	28	29	30			

1. London: MPs reject a government proposal for Sunday opening of theatres.

1. East Africa: British and Empire troops take Asmara, capital of Eritrea (→ 28).

3. Libya: British-led troops evacuate Benghazi in the face of Rommel's advance (→ 10).

3. Budapest: Hungarian premier Count Paul Teleki commits suicide rather than join the war as a German ally.

4. Iraq: Ex-premier Rashid Ali, an Axis supporter, seizes power (→ 17).

6. Yugoslavia: Axis troops invade.→

6. Abyssinia: South African troops occupy the capital Addis Ababa (→ 5/5).

7. London: The War Budget raises income tax to a record 50 per cent.

9. New York: Opening of the film "The Road to Zanzibar" with Bob Hope, Bing Crosby and Dorothy Lamour.

10. Libya: British and Australian troops are besieged at Tobruk (→ 13).

13. Libya: The Germans occupy Bardia; there is now fighting along the Egyptian frontier (→ 26).

13. Moscow: Stalin signs a neutrality pact with Japan, recognising Manchukuo.

16. London: 500 planes drop around 100,000 bombs in an all-night attack, among the heaviest of the war (→ 10/5).

17. Iraq: British troops cross the border (→ 2/5).

19. Zurich: Premiere of Bertolt Brecht's play "Mother Courage".

23. Greece: King George and the Greek government abandon Athens for Crete.→

24. Singapore: More reinforcements land to boost the British and Commonwealth garrison.

26. Egypt: Three columns of Afrika Korps troops cross from Libya (→ 26/7).

28. East Africa: Free French troops advance into pro-Vichy French Somaliland (→ 19/11).

US, fearing German threat to convoys, occupies Greenland

April 10. President Roosevelt announced today that the United States has reached an agreement with the government of Denmark to send forces to Greenland, a Danish possession.

The President stressed that the US would protect Greenland and ensure that it remained a Danish colony after the war. The immediate cause of the US move was concern in Washington about German reconnaissance flights in the North Atlantic, endangering the vital convoys bringing war supplies from American factories to Britain.

More generally, it fits into the way President Roosevelt has been allowing the US to take over responsibility for a bigger share of the job of protecting the convoys, leaving the RAF and the Royal Navy to concentrate on fighting the war in Europe and the Middle East.

The President has to take care not to annoy the isolationists who are still powerful inside – and outside – the US Congress.

Using the new "wolfpack" tactic, in which several U-boats operate together, the German navy, under Admiral Doenitz, has stepped up its attacks on British shipping.

The US Navy has formed an "Atlantic Fleet Support Group" of destroyers and flying boats, which will now be able to patrol further from new bases they intend to build on Greenland (→ 31/5).

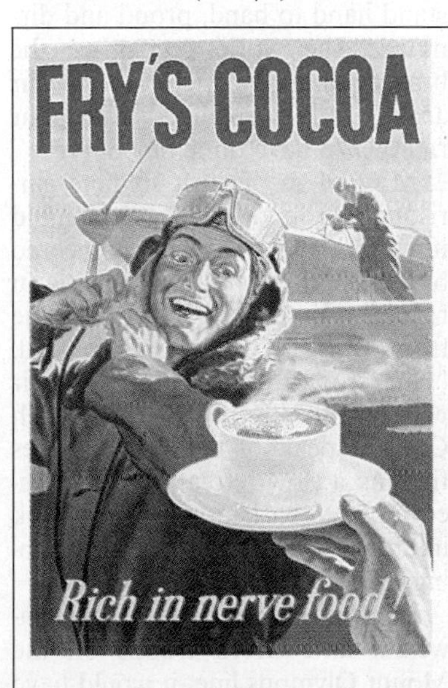

Yugoslavia falls to Balkan Blitzkrieg

April 17. The brave resistance of the Yugoslav armed forces has been crushed by German armour striking from Hungary, Rumania, Bulgaria and Germany itself.

Shortly before midnight the German High Command stated: "All the Yugoslav armed forces which had not been disarmed before, laid down their arms unconditionally at nine o'clock tonight. The capitulation comes into force at noon tomorrow."

Meanwhile German troops, freed by the collapse of the Yugoslavs, have pushed on into Greece, striking across from Salonika to put in peril one of the most vital roads in the Balkan war strategy. It leads from Albania to the heart of Greece and forms the line of retreat for the Greek army.

At British headquarters in Cairo it was pointed out that this might have repercussions on the British and Commonwealth troops fighting alongside the Greeks. There was no attempt to minimise the gravity of the situation.

It was emphasised, however, that the whole British line was intact at all points. The Australians, said the spokesman, were holding their positions against the heaviest attacks yet made on the Balkan front, launched by the Germans regardless of the heavy casualties they had suffered.

Observers from the front say that the Nazis are using at least ten divisions south of Servia alone, and throwing their entire weight into the attack, to force a quick decision regardless of cost.

Hundreds of Stukas and Messerschmitts are supporting the attack, but the defenders are standing up well against the rain of bombs. RAF bombers are pounding the enemy's supply lines (→ 5/10).

Just captured – a young partisan.

British pushed out of Greece as Athens falls to the Germans

April 27. The Germans marched into Athens yesterday and the swastika is flying over the Acropolis. Advance units of motor-cyclists entered the city in the morning and were followed by heavy mechanised detachments, which had overcome the British rearguard on the road from Thebes.

The Greek newspapers carried one last message of independence before the Nazis arrived: "Greeks! Be worthy of your history and stand hand to hand, proud and dignified. The world recognises the bravery and the victories of our army and recognises also our rights. We have done our duty."

Most of the British soldiers garrisoned around Athens left amid moving scenes. They were cheered by large crowds bidding them "au revoir". Yesterday's communique from British GHQ in Cairo said: "Our troops are continuing their withdrawal." Reports from south Greece speak of the Allied forces fighting a slow retreat to the southernmost embarkation point. Greek infantry, with no chance of escaping, had covered the British flank.

But for the feats by the Commonwealth and Greek troops on the Mount Olympus line, it would have been impossible to have saved more than a small fraction of the force. As it is, a large amount of guns, mechanised equipment and munitions has still been lost.

The Greeks will not forget the fight for Mount Olympus. A bulletin issued just before the fall of Athens said: "The heroic exploits of our Allies, the Australians and New Zealanders, are weaving new legends around the slopes of Mount Olympus, and the brilliant action of a party of Australians who had been surrounded, and hacked their way through the Germans, killing 300 and taking 150 prisoners, has won them universal admiration."

The conduct of the RAF has also won much praise. Its pilots fought desperately against German superiority in the air to protect the troops from the Stukas, and to stem the Nazi advance (→ 20/5).

As Greece falls British troops are rounded up by German paratroopers.

1941

MAY

Su	Mo	Tu	We	Th	Fr	Sa
				1	2	3
4	5	6	7	8	9	10
11	12	13	14	15	16	17
18	19	20	21	22	23	24
25	26	27	28	29	30	31

1. New York: Premiere of the film "Citizen Kane" directed by, and starring, Orson Welles.

2. Iraq: British and Iraqi troops clash for the first time at Habbaniyah (→ 4).

4. Iraq: British troops occupy the airport and docks of Basra.→

5. Addis Ababa: Haile Selassie enters the city to great acclaim, exactly five years after the Italians marched in (→ 20).

7. Iceland: A German weather ship is seized, yielding documents on the German master coding machine "Enigma" (→ 7/7).

12. London: MPs meet for the first time in their temporary home, the House of Lords.

12. France: Hitler and Ribbentrop have secret talks with Vichy leaders (→ 14).

14. Paris: French police arrest around 1,000 Jews and hand them over to the Germans (→ 21).

16. Berlin: Professor Karl Hausofer, a close friend of Rudolf Hess, is arrested.

20. Abyssinia: The Duke d'Aosta, viceroy of Italian East Africa, formally surrenders to British Empire forces (→ 16/6).

21. Paris: The Germans order the US to withdraw their representatives in the city by June 10 (→ 2/6).

23. Crete: King George II of Greece flees to Egypt (→ 29).

24. S. Africa: Premier Smuts is made a field-marshal of the British Empire (→ 21/10/42).

24. Atlantic: HMS Hood is sunk by the Bismarck; it is feared that only a handful of her 1,421 crew survived.→

28. Egypt: German ex-world heavyweight champion Max Schmeling is reported captured trying to flee British troops.

29. Crete: The Germans seize the capital Canea (→ 1/6).

31. London: The first US food ship arrives in Britain (→ 14/6).

BIRTH

24. US singer Bob Dylan, born Robert Zimmerman.

A night that nearly took the heart out of London

Churchill at the bombed Commons.

Undaunted amidst the ruins: St. Paul's Cathedral (seen here during a raid last December) has survived again.

May 11. Even Londoners, hardened by the horrors of nine months of the Blitz, were shaken by last night's terrible raid. In brilliant moonlight, 550 German planes indiscriminately dropped hundreds of high explosive bombs and 100,000 incendiaries in a few hours.

The Nazi High Command described it as "a reprisal for the methodical bombing of the residential quarters of German towns, including Berlin".

Civilian casualties were 1,400 dead – the most for a single raid – and included the mayors of Westminster and Bermondsey.

Much of historic London suffered. The chamber of the House of Commons was reduced to a heap of rubble. Big Ben was scarred – although the clock continues to maintain perfect time. The Lords' chamber was also hit, but it is usable by the Commons: the Lords will meet in their Robing Room.

The roof of the 12th-century Westminster Hall was set ablaze, and the square tower of Westminster Abbey has fallen in. The British Museum was damaged by fire, and St. Paul's Cathedral – which has survived several bombs in previous raids – was hit once again. Not one of the capital's four largest railway stations emerged unscathed. Inevitably, there were stories of miraculous escapes. A firewatcher at one hospital that was hit told of being blasted through the building and landing on top of a telephone kiosk. Hundreds more were less lucky, and remained buried for hours under tons of rubble before rescuers reached them.

Other British cities, ports in particular – Liverpool, Belfast, Clydebank, Southampton, Portsmouth and Plymouth – have been heavily "blitzed" in recent months, with massive damage and loss of life. Hull, on the East coast, has taken a particularly cruel battering.

However, London has bravely taken the lion's share, with 20,000 killed and 25,000 badly injured, but such was the ferocity of last night's attack that at times it seemed that the spirit of "London can take it" might be weakening. For the first time people have been seen weeping in the streets in despair at such destruction.

The moonlight may have helped the Germans, but British fighters also took advantage of the clear bright night. According to Whitehall sources, RAF planes downed 29 bombers, while the city's anti-aircraft guns accounted for a further four (→ 17/6).

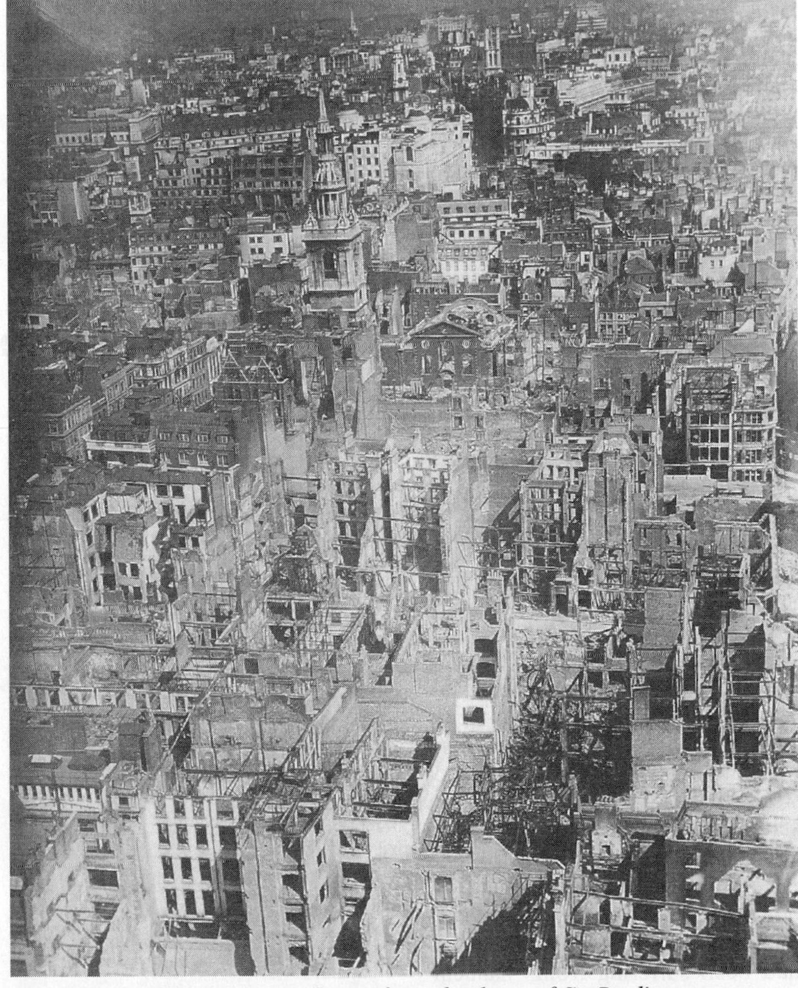

The shattered City – an aerial view from the dome of St. Paul's.

▷

Sweet revenge as Bismarck is sunk

The "unsinkable" Bismarck, pride of the German fleet, receives a devastating hit from a British warship.

May 27. Germany's newest and fastest battleship, the 45,000-ton Bismarck, claimed to be unsinkable, was lying at the bottom of the Atlantic tonight after a three-day hunt to the death by the Royal Navy. Around 100 British vessels are thought to have taken part in the biggest naval chase ever.

The pursuit was fuelled by a desire to avenge the sinking of the British fleet's pride, the 42,000-ton HMS Hood, by the Bismarck a few days ago. That attack took place in the North Atlantic, between Norway and Iceland, and around 1,300 men are thought to have died as the great warship seemed to tear herself apart when her munitions magazine was hit. The new battleship Prince of Wales was damaged too – she had put to sea so fast, there are still civilian dockyard workers on board.

When the news came through every naval commitment in the western Mediterranean and north Atlantic was abandoned to aid the chase; the aircraft carrier Ark Royal steamed north from Gibraltar to take part. The Royal Navy vowed to "pursue and destroy" the battleship, chasing her for 1,750 miles, from Greenland to 550 miles west of Land's End, as she tried to head to the safety of the port of Brest.

Most of the Bismarck's 1,000-plus crew are thought to have died in the relentless bombing by aircraft from the Ark Royal, which ended as the battleships Rodney and King George V finished her off today, aided by a final torpedo strike from HMS Victorious (→11/10/43).

Hitler's deputy lands in Scotland to see the Duke of Hamilton

May 10. The man who parachuted from a crashing Messerschmitt fighter plane near Glasgow last Saturday night probably brought a peace offer from Hitler – or he may be just a mental case. He is Rudolf Hess, Hitler's trusted deputy. Found with a broken ankle in a field by a local ploughman, the Nazi was taken home and offered a cup of tea. Hess said he never drank tea late at night.

Hess said he had an important message for the Duke of Hamilton, whom he had met once. A British statement rejected talk of peace overtures, saying there could be no negotiations with Nazis. After a 24-hour silence, German radio stations put out a statement that Hess had been suffering from "hallucinations" (→16).

Rudolf Hess as Hitler's deputy.

Inspecting the crashed aircraft.

Germans launch an invasion of Crete

May 20. The Germans today launched an airborne invasion of Crete. Preceded by heavy dive-bomber raids on the island's airfields, German paratroopers landed just before dawn and were immediately counter-attacked by British, New Zealand and Greek forces.

The paratroopers were followed by landings from troop carriers and gliders. By 6.30am, Nazi planes were attacking continuously in support of the landed troops, but heavy casualties were inflicted on the paratroopers as they floated down.

Announcing the attack in the House of Commons, Mr Churchill said many of the German soldiers were wearing New Zealand army uniforms (→23).

Successful flight of the first British jet

May 15. Britain's top secret new aircraft powered by a jet engine made its first flight at RAF Cranwell today. Frank Whittle, an engineer, has been working on the concept of gas turbine propulsion for years. The Gloster E28/39 is fitted with his revolutionary 850-pound thrust engine, which promises much greater speed than a propeller-driven plane. Now the race is on to get the jet into war service before German engineers can do so.

Coup keeps Iraq out of Nazi hands

May 31. The Nazi-sponsored attempt to win control of Iraq through an Arab revolt has been foiled. With British troops surrounding Baghdad, the pro-German prime minister of Iraq, Rashid Ali, was today compelled to surrender. He is replaced by Emir Abdullah, who is already setting up a new government.

Under the terms of the new agreement, Britain will have access to all road and rail communications in the country, while guaranteeing to preserve Iraqi independence. This secures a strategically important region.

1941

JUNE

Su	Mo	Tu	We	Th	Fr	Sa
1	2	3	4	5	6	7
8	9	10	11	12	13	14
15	16	17	18	19	20	21
22	23	24	25	26	27	28
29	30					

1. Crete: British and New Zealand troops are evacuated to Egypt, admitting heavy losses.

2. Vichy: Petain imposes further restrictions on the rights of Jews (→ 13).

5. Transjordan: Vichy planes bomb the capital Amman.

8. Syria: British Empire and Free French forces launch an invasion of the pro-Vichy territory (→ 13).

11. Poland: Reports show German troop movements on the Soviet border (→ 22).

13. Vichy: Petain announces the arrest of 12,000 Jews for "plotting to hinder Franco-German co-operation" (→ 30).

13. Syria: Allied troops encircle Damascus.→

14. Washington: Roosevelt orders the freezing of all German and Italian assets (→ 19).

17. UK: The RAF reveals that "radio-location" has been Britain's key weapon against German bombers (→ 18/9).

19. Berlin: Germany expels US consuls; Italy does the same (→ 20).

20. Washington: Roosevelt calls the Nazis "international outlaws" engaged in "piracy" for world conquest (→ 28/8).

22. USSR: Germany invades along a 1,800-mile front with Finnish and Rumanian allies.→

24. Washington: Roosevelt says the US will help the USSR however it can (→ 27).

26. UK: The Army stages a huge mock invasion in Northern Ireland.

27. Moscow: A British military mission arrives (→ 30).

30. Vichy: Petain severs relations with the USSR.→

DEATHS

4. German ex-Kaiser Wilhelm II (*27/1/1859).

6. US motor engineer Louis Chevrolet (*25/12/1859).

29. Polish statesman and pianist Ignacy Paderewski (*6/11/1860).

Nazis break pact and invade Russia

Last year it was France; now it is Russia. A German gun crew takes up position for a fresh assault.

June 30. German panzer divisions are smashing into Russia. Minsk, over halfway to Moscow, has fallen, and desperate tank battles are taking place near Kiev in the Ukraine. The Germans claim that two Russian armies have been encircled and would "in a few days be forced to capitulate or be annihilated".

The Russian army, numbering over seven million, was obviously caught unprepared by the German onslaught at dawn on June 22, despite obvious indications that Hitler was about to break his non-agression pact with Stalin.

The Germans had massed 100 army divisions and, together with their Finnish and Rumanian allies, rolled over the 1,800-mile border from the Arctic Circle to the Black Sea.

Mr Molotov, the Commissar for Foreign Affairs, broke the news to the Russian people in a broadcast in which he described the German action as "this unheard-of attack on our country which is without example in the history of civilised nations".

Mr Churchill responded to the invasion by promising Russia "whatever help we can; we have offered any technical or economic assistance in our power." He went on to say: "We are resolved to destroy Hitler and every vestige of the Nazi regime. From this nothing will turn us. We will never parley, never. I gave clear and precise warnings to Stalin of what was coming. I can only hope these warnings did not fall unheeded."

In Moscow, military music is being played over the radio, interspersed with news of the fighting and programmes featuring the heroic deeds of the Russian forces. Bulletins report meetings at factories all over the country vowing to "smash to smithereens the hordes of the bloodthirsty Fascist German dogs."

On the battlefield it is obvious that the Germans have made huge gains in territory, but observers point out that Russia is a vast country and that, as Napoleon found to his cost, the mere possession of territory does not ensure victory.

It is apparent that the Germans are attempting to score another blitzkrieg victory, designed to knock the Russians out of the war before an ever-lengthening chain of supply becomes a major problem. It is felt in military circles that, if the Russian army can hold on until the snows come, then the German panzers, unsuited to the intense cold of the Russian winter, will run into great difficulties.

Meanwhile, the Russians are striking back with their air force, bombing targets in Finland, East Prussia and Constanza, the Danube oil port (→ 1/7).

Hard-pressed, the Red Army fights on with troops, tanks and courage.

▷

Margarine coupons needed to buy clothes

Very natty, sir – and for you just 26 precious clothing coupons.

June 2. From today every shop-window tailor's dummy will have a sign saying how many coupons, in addition to the cost, are required to buy an article of clothing – 16 for a raincoat, seven for boots, two for gloves and so on. Until the new coupons are printed, margarine coupons in ration-books will serve to buy clothing.

A special scale is being introduced for growing, or extra-large, children; people losing their clothing through enemy action will be allowed roughly two years' supply of coupons.

A Board of Trade spokesman said that low-paid families will not be affected, although "families on £4 to £5 a week will have to reduce clothing purchases by about a quarter and above that income the reduction will get considerably higher".

Three women – a business-woman, a housewife and a buyer – advised the Board in deciding on the minimum clothing requirements for a woman for a year.

Despite the new law, a reporter who visited Petticoat Lane – the traditional street market in London's East End – watched 400 articles of rationed clothing being sold with not one coupon being exchanged (→4).

Pro-Nazi French lose Damascus

June 21. After two weeks of sharp fighting, British Imperial troops, including Australians and Indians, are today in control of Damascus. Vichy-French troops evacuated the Syrian capital in disarray to avoid further casualties, after clashes with Free French units operating with the Allies.

Britain had accused Vichy of allowing the Axis powers to use air bases in French mandated territory. General de Gaulle's troops announced: "We come to wash out the shame of Vichy capitulation." The next objective of the Allies is Beirut (→13/7).

Surrender of Italian troops in Abyssinia

June 16. The remnants of an Italian division, shattered in the Battle of the Lakes in Abyssinia, has surrendered to British forces. A communique from GHQ, Cairo, today announced that its commander General Pralermo had capitulated.

The General is the fourth Italian divisional commander to be captured in the region of the Lakes. His defeated division took to the hills, where it was being harried by Abyssinians, and ran out of supplies. During the advance on Soddu four Italian colonial divisions were effectively destroyed through casualties and desertion (→4/7).

1941

JULY

Su	Mo	Tu	We	Th	Fr	Sa
		1	2	3	4	5
6	7	8	9	10	11	12
13	14	15	16	17	18	19
20	21	22	23	24	25	26
27	28	29	30	31		

1. Moscow: Stalin sets up a Committee of Defence to run the Soviet war effort (→8).

2. London: Premiere of Noel Coward's play "Blithe Spirit".

4. Abyssinia: Italy's General Gazzera surrenders.

4. UK: Coal rationing begins (→17/9).

6. London: 15 hours 48 minutes of sunshine make this the capital's sunniest day of the century.

8. London: The Soviet military mission is cheered on its arrival (→13).

13. London: Britain and the USSR conclude a mutual assistance pact (→16).

13. Syria: British and Vichy forces sign an armistice.

16. USSR: German troops are reported to be advancing on Leningrad; Smolensk, south-west of Moscow, falls (→20).

20. Moscow: Stalin takes over as Soviet defence commissar.→

23. Vichy: Petain agrees to let Japan use French military bases in Indochina (→27).

24. Vichy: All Britons are ordered to leave Vichy France (→27/8).

25. London: The government freezes Japanese assets throughout the Empire; the US follows suit (→26).

26. Washington: General Douglas MacArthur is appointed to command US forces in the Far East (→26).

26. Tokyo: Japan freezes all British and US assets in retaliation for similar moves against the Japanese (→3/11).

27. Indochina: Japanese troops advance into Cambodia and Thailand; Saigon is occupied.→

30. London: Stalin restores relations with the Polish government in exile; they both sign a friendship pact (→8/8).

DEATHS

10. US jazz pianist "Jelly Roll" Morton (*20/9/1885).

11. British archaeologist Sir Arthur Evans, excavator of Knossos (*8/7/1851).

Wodehouse faces jail for broadcast

July 8. A statement was made in Parliament about the possible prosecution after the war of author P.G. Wodehouse for "assisting the enemy" by broadcasting from Germany to America.

Wodehouse was interned when the invading Germans reached Le Touquet where he lived. He spent a year in camps and a lunatic asylum in Upper Silesia. On his release, he broadcast five talks from Berlin entitled "How to be an Internee without Previous Training".

He was promptly denounced as a traitor in the Press. "Cassandra" of the Daily Mirror accused him of "pawning his honour for the price of a soft bed". Nobody knows what he actually said.

BBC promotes V for Victory campaign

July 20. At midnight – zero hour for Britain's new V for Victory campaign – the BBC started to get occupied Europe familiar with its rhythm. The opening notes of Beethoven's Fifth Symphony are the same as the Morse code for V and these were repeatedly broadcast on all overseas services.

Mr Churchill explained: "The V sign is the symbol of the unconquerable will of the occupied territories and a portent of the fate awaiting the Nazi tyranny." At the same time the BBC urged listeners in Europe to go during darkness and chalk the V sign on doors, walls and pavements in order to rattle the Germans.

V signs will now also be appearing all over Britain. There is a feeling this will catch on.

Giving the V-sign to the Fuehrer.

German panzers power into Russia

July 21. German panzer forces, often operating far in advance of their supporting infantry, have driven a great wedge between the armies defending Moscow; last night Berlin claimed that the Russians were retreating along the whole front from the Baltic to the Black Sea. As a mark of how serious the danger to Moscow is, Stalin has taken over the post of Commissar for Defence and is now in command of Russia's defences.

Reports from the front suggest that the Germans are also making progress in their advance towards Leningrad, but there are indications that a Russian counter-attack has retaken Smolensk.

The Russians are increasingly using guerrilla tactics against the German shock-troops, which often push on without securing their rear. After a major battle, the Russians withdraw their main forces but leave behind suicide groups to harass the advancing enemy.

The Russian newspapers are full of stories of their heroism. Typical is that of Lieutenant Sobachnikov, leader of a group of guerrillas who attacked an airfield held by the Germans. He attacked at night, killing 20 Germans, then, learning from a prisoner that Nazi bombers were expected to arrive in the morning, he welcomed them in and captured nine aircraft without firing a shot.

Reports from the Ukrainian front speak of desperate Russian resistance in the outskirts of Kiev with anti-tank and machine-gun fire meeting the advancing enemy from every window and alley. The Russians have also thrown their latest heavy tanks into the battle.

In the north, Tallin, the capital of Estonia, is in flames. This city of 150,000 people has been transformed into a raging inferno of fire and destruction, in accordance with Stalin's "scorched earth" policy of denying anything of use to the invader.

He has decreed that every item of property, food and machinery must be burned. One German correspondent flying over Tallin said that observation was practically impossible because of the clouds of black smoke rising from the destroyed city. Other cities will no doubt suffer the same fate (→30).

A Russian mother protects her baby against a backdrop of devastation.

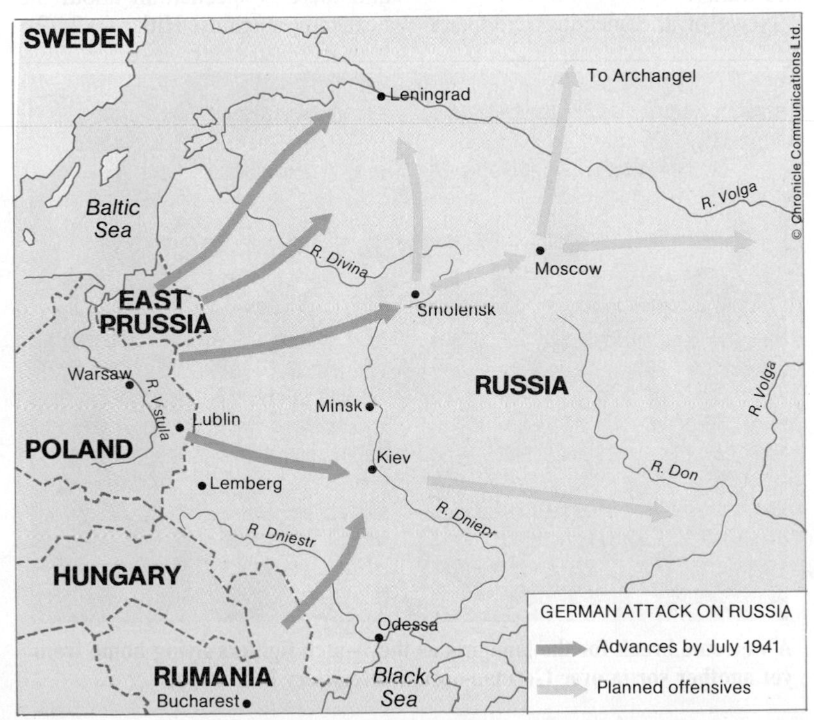

Japanese invasion threatens Thailand and Cambodia

July 27. Thousands of Japanese troops today moved into Saigon, capital of French Indochina. Major-General Sumita arrived here two days ago to set up headquarters and organise the seizure of military and naval bases.

Japanese troops have also begun disembarking in Cambodia, where 8,000 men are to be garrisoned in the capital Phnom Penh within striking range of Thailand, which she intends to force to join the Japanese "new order" in East Asia. The Chinese are convinced that Japan wants the Thai naval and air bases in turn for use in attacks on Burma and Singapore.

Japan's moves came soon after an announcement by the French Vichy regime that Tokyo had been given a free hand in Indochina on the pretext that it was threatened by British and Gaullist plots.

As Japan began large-scale mobilisation and dispatched strong naval forces south, America and Britain denounced her as an aggressor. Even isolationists approved President Roosevelt's action. This was combined with moves to freeze all Japanese assets abroad (→6/8).

American troops take over Iceland

July 7. President Roosevelt has informed Congress that US forces have landed in Iceland to prevent it being occupied by the Germans.

Iceland, an independent country before the war, was occupied by Britain early in 1940 to forestall Germany turning it into a base for harassing the vital seaborne trade between Britain and the US. In April, reports that the Nazis were planning an attack helped the President to make up his mind. In June he ordered a Marine brigade of 4,000 men to sail in two weeks.

This will release British troops from the 20,000-man garrison and free British shipping. Mr Roosevelt said that the Marines will "eventually" replace British troops. The British government welcomed the American move.

1941

AUGUST

Su	Mo	Tu	We	Th	Fr	Sa
					1	2
3	4	5	6	7	8	9
10	11	12	13	14	15	16
17	18	19	20	21	22	23
24	25	26	27	28	29	30
31						

1. Washington: Roosevelt bans US aviation fuel exports outside the western hemisphere and British Empire.→

6. Tokyo: Japan proposes concessions to the US in south-east Asia in return for unfreezing Japanese assets (→ 7).

7. Australia: The government says it will not stand by and watch Japanese expansion in the Pacific (→ 8/9).

8. Berlin: The Soviet air force carries out its first raid on the German capital (→ 12).

12. USSR: Odessa is reported to be surrounded as German troops push to the Black Sea (→ 17).

16. Moscow: Stalin agrees to talks in Moscow between the USSR, Britain and the US (→ 28).

17. USSR: German troops occupy the Soviet naval base of Nikolaev on the Black Sea.→

20. France: 50,000 people are arrested in occupied and Vichy France as a hunt goes on for railway saboteurs (→ 21).

21. Paris: 5,000 Jews are rounded up and interned at Drancy, the holding camp for deportation (→ 27).

25. USSR: The Red Army evacuates Novgorod, 100 miles south of Leningrad (→ 29).

27. Vichy: Laval is wounded in an assassination attempt by a young Frenchman (→ 16/10).

28. Washington: Roosevelt creates a board to send US arms shipments to countries fighting the Axis (→ 1/9).

29. Estonia: The Germans capture the capital, Tallin, devastated as part of Soviet scorched earth policy (→ 31).

31. USSR: The Finns push the Russians back to the old Finnish frontier before the 1940-41 Winter War (→ 31).

31. USSR: The Red Army launches a counter-offensive on the River Dnieper (→ 2/9).

DEATH

7. Indian author Rabindranath Tagore, 1913 Nobel Prize winner (*7/5/1861).

Atlantic Charter agreed

The President and the Prime Minister confirm the Western alliance.

Aug 14. In the utmost secrecy Mr Churchill and President Roosevelt have had a momentous meeting at sea. In a round of conferences over three days they have drawn up a declaration of the joint war and peace aims of their two nations.

Tonight they proclaimed in their Atlantic Charter that Britain and the United States have no territorial claims to make, that aggressor nations must be disarmed, and that after the war "all men shall be enabled to live in freedom from fear and want".

News of the meeting had been kept from the British public, but America was agog because Mr Roosevelt was reported to have left mysteriously in his yacht "on a fishing trip". It is believed that the two leaders have been on a British battleship and an American cruiser off the New England coast.

The President suggested the meeting and it can be assumed that practical American help for Britain was discussed as well as lofty post-war aims. The Big Two were accompanied by their Service chiefs and there is speculation about the next moves against Hitler (→ 24/9).

A welcome break for the landgirls as they watch fighters flying home from yet another sortie over German-occupied territory in Europe.

UK and Russia attack Iran to expel Germans

Aug 25. British and Soviet troops marched into Iran today, encountering only token opposition. The jointly-agreed operations were planned to dislodge the Nazi German Fifth Column established there and to forestall an attempted coup by the Axis powers.

British and Gurkha troops advanced across the Iraq border from Khanikin; another force landed at Abadan while Indian troops secured Bandar Shapur, seizing seven Axis merchant ships. Airborne troops were dropped on the oilfields to protect Britons and prevent sabotage. Reports state that, although bursts of machine-gun fire were heard, the attitude of most Iranians was one of "benevolent interest".

Soviet troops invaded from the north between the Caspian Sea and the Turkish frontier, capturing Tabriz. The occupation will secure the oilfields and provide a convenient route for the supply of war material to Russia (→ 16/9).

Russians blow up dam to halt Nazis

Aug 25. Stalin has made a supreme sacrifice in pursuit of his "scorched earth" policy. In a telephone call to his old comrade Marshal Budenny, the Soviet C-in-C in the Ukraine, he ordered the destruction of one of the Soviet Union's greatest industrial achievements, the gigantic Lenin-Dnjeproges dam.

Budenny's engineers, operating under cover of darkness in face of the advancing Germans, set their dynamite and utterly destroyed the dam, on which the whole of the industrial district of the central Ukraine depends for its power.

Completed in 1932, it was a showpiece of Soviet engineering, although much of it was built by American engineers. The decision to destroy it is typical of the Russians' readiness to sacrifice everything to hold up the invader.

The military effect of this action has been to turn the flat land into a morass, bogging down Hitler's panzers (→ 12/9).

1941

SEPTEMBER

Su	Mo	Tu	We	Th	Fr	Sa
	1	2	3	4	5	6
7	8	9	10	11	12	13
14	15	16	17	18	19	20
21	22	23	24	25	26	27
28	29	30				

1. New York: Roosevelt vows to do "everything in our power to crush Hitler and his Nazi forces" (→30/10).

2. USSR: The Germans and Russians are reported to be fighting just 30 miles from Leningrad.→

4. US: An unidentified submarine attacks the US destroyer Greer.

8. Indochina: Vietnamese nationalist leader Ho Chi Minh forms the Vietnam Independence League, the Viet-Minh (→27/3/43)

10. Oslo: The German commissioner for Norway declares martial law in the city (→4/10).

14. USSR: An RAF unit arrives to aid the Soviet air force (→18).

16. Tehran: The Shah of Iran abdicates.→

17. London: The government orders potatoes to be sold at 1d. so people will eat more of them (→2/12).

18. London: Britain says it will reveal the secrets of "radio-location" to the USSR (→23).

19. Tehran: British and Soviet troops enter the city.

19. USSR: Kiev falls to the Germans (→21).

21. USSR: The Germans cut off the Crimean peninsula from the rest of the USSR.

23. Germany: Preparations for the Russian winter are under way, including taking blankets from troops in France (→24).

24. USSR: The Germans claim to be fighting in the suburbs of Leningrad (→26).

24. London: Adherence to the Atlantic Charter is pledged by nine exiled governments (→22/12).

25. London: General de Gaulle announces the creation of a French provisional government in exile (→26/10).

26. Leningrad: The RAF has its first engagement in Russia, flying to aid the city (→30).

30. Leningrad: The Soviet army claims it has retaken the outskirts of the city (→2/10).

Nazi noose tightens round Leningrad

Nazi storm-troopers fight their way through a burning Russian village.

Sept 12. The most intense fighting is taking place round Leningrad where Field Marshal von Leeb has thrown the entire weight of his forces against the city's embattled defenders. The fighting is taking place in driving rain, which is turning the dirt roads into quagmires, holding up the panzers as they charge the Russian defences.

Despite the rain, great air battles are taking place over the city, with British-built Hurricanes and Spitfires, flown by crack Russian pilots, taking great toll of the Stukas trying to knock out Soviet strong-points and airfields. The Germans are throwing all their best men and material into the Battle of Leningrad, desperate to take the city before the winter sets in, but Marshal Voroshilov's armies remain the stubborn masters of the whole mighty outer ring of Leningrad's fortress defences.

M. Lozovsky, Vice-Commissar for Foreign Affairs, has denied German claims that the city had almost been taken. These claims are pure fantasy, he said: "It was Goebbels, not the German army, who almost entered the city" (→14).

Allies destroy coal stocks on Spitzbergen

Sept 9. Allied troops today seized the Arctic island of Spitzbergen in a pre-emptive strike designed to stop its enormous coal stocks falling into German hands. Seven hundred Norwegians miners are all being brought back to Britain to join the fight against the Nazis.

Canadian forces led the strike, backed up by British and Free Norwegian troops, not knowing if they would meet German resistance as they went ashore. There was considerable secrecy and the Canadian troops were only told of their destination when their ships had entered the Arctic Circle.

They were given a warm welcome by the Norwegians there, who do not like supplying coal for the German war effort. Spitzbergen could also be of vital importance, being near the supply route between Britain and North Russia.

Jews ordered to wear Star of David

Sept 6. Today the German secret police published an order which will forbid all Jews over the age of six to appear in public without a yellow Star of David. "This star, made from yellow cloth with a black edge, has six points and bears the words 'Jews'," it says.

The order, which comes into effect on 19 September, requires Jews to obtain police permission before leaving the area in which they live.

The penalty for violating the new regulation is a fine of 150 marks or six weeks in jail. It seems likely to apply eventually throughout the areas occupied by the Germans (→1/10).

German Jews made marked men.

New Shah promises fair government

Sept 17. The new Shah of Iran, the 21-year-old Mohammed Reza Pahlevi, swore the oath of office before parliament today with occupying British and Soviet troops encamped on the outskirts of Tehran. He promised to rule as a "completely constitutional monarch".

The Shah's father was so unpopular he was forced to abdicate. Ministers resented his bullying; he once beat one of them with the flat of a sword and threw him in prison for daring to argue (→19).

1941

OCTOBER

Su	Mo	Tu	We	Th	Fr	Sa
			1	2	3	4
5	6	7	8	9	10	11
12	13	14	15	16	17	18
19	20	21	22	23	24	25
26	27	28	29	30	31	

1. Berlin: 163,696 Jews are estimated to be still living in Germany (→ 1/1/42).

2. Leningrad: The Soviet army launches a counter-attack as the winter's first snows begin to fall (→ 8).

3. New York: Premiere of "The Maltese Falcon", John Huston's directing debut, starring Humphrey Bogart.

4. Norway: The Germans warn Norwegians they face starvation if anti-Nazi unrest continues (→ 30).

5. Yugoslavia: Soviet bombers arrive to aid partisan insurgents led by Josip Broz Tito (→ 3/5/42).

8. USSR: German troops take the town of Orel, strategically important in the advance on Moscow (→ 12).

10. Luxembourg: A referendum on annexation by Germany ends in failure when 97 per cent of voters abstain.

12. USSR: Bryansk, another key town on the way to Moscow, falls to the Germans (→ 19).

16. Vichy: Daladier and Blum are jailed for life for "causing France's defeat" (→ 21).

20. USSR: The government has removed to Kuibyshev, 500 miles east of Moscow.→

21. France: 50 French hostages are shot by the Germans for the killing of a German officer in Nantes (→ 24).

23. New York: Premiere of Walt Disney's "Dumbo".

24. France: 150 more hostages are ordered to be shot following the death of a senior German officer in Bordeaux.→

25. USSR: The Germans take the Ukrainian city of Kharkhov (→ 26).

26. USSR: The town of Stalino is evacuated (→ 2/11).

30. Norway: The RAF carries out a devastating raid on the German naval supply base at Aalesund (→ 12/12).

BIRTH

8. US politician and black civil rights leader Jesse Jackson.

Jubilant Hitler nears gates of Moscow

Oct 20. Stalin declared a state of siege in Moscow today as four panzer armies, each consisting of 5,000 tanks, massed along the 300-mile front from Kalinin to Orel under four of Germany's leading tank generals – Guderian, Hoth, Hoeppner and Reinhardt.

The capital's defiance in the face of this threat was expressed by Stalin in an order of the day. "Moscow will be defended to the last," he declared. "The population is keeping calm and ready to give the Soviet army defending Moscow every possible help."

The German drive against Moscow has now lasted 18 days, longer than any other thrust in the Russian campaign. Hitler is so eager to take the capital that he has withdrawn two panzer armies from his northern and southern groups, considerably weakening them.

The German army is not only fighting the Russians in the battle for Moscow. It is also fighting the bitter Russian winter which defeated Napoleon. Yesterday, incidentally, was the day on which Napoleon began his disastrous retreat from Moscow in 1812.

Russian war correspondents report that the battlefield is already covered with a thick carpet of snow: "On the roads a hard coating of ice glistens. We know what the Russian winter is like. It is terrible for those who are not accustomed to it."

The bad weather, however, has not prevented the battle continuing with unabated violence. Berlin radio last night broadcast accounts of how eight armies, under Marshal Timoshenko's command, were smashed on the road to Moscow.

However, it has since had to admit that fierce Russian counterattacks have been launched in the very areas where gloating reports described how the Soviet army had been annihilated.

"Grit your teeth!" is the cry in Moscow tonight. "Squeeze the enemy's throat" (→ 25).

Hitler meets his youngest SA man.

Sub war claims the first US destroyer

Oct 30. More than 70 American sailors died tonight in the first U-boat attack on a US destroyer in the Atlantic. Congressmen are fuming at the attack on the USS Reuben James, on convoy duty west of Iceland. Forty-four members of her crew were rescued.

America has now moved a long way from her original position of absolute neutrality, and there have already been talks in Washington between senior naval staff from America, Britain and Canada. These led to the US escorting Atlantic convoys, which is greatly relieving the Allied war effort.

This is the third attack on American warships in a month, but although President Roosevelt maintained the disasters will not mean a break in relations with Germany, it appears they will mean a strengthening of ties with Britain.

HELP SCOTLAND'S
HARVEST

The pro-US faction resigns in Japan

Oct 17. The resignation last night of Fumimaro Konoye, the Japanese Prime Minister, and all the cabinet, has precipitated a political crisis with international implications.

Konoye represented a school of thought which argued that Japan could reach agreement with the United States. Emperor Hirohito has appointed General Tojo, a war minister more closely identified with the Axis powers' alliance, to succeed him.

De Gaulle calls for the French to strike

Oct 26. General de Gaulle, leader of the Free French, today called for a national five-minute strike in protest at the German occupation which has carried out scores of civilian executions recently.

In a broadcast seen as a direct challenge to Berlin, he said: "The enemy thought he could frighten France. But France is going to show the world that she belongs to nobody but herself." He urged the nation to stop work in fields, factories, offices and schools later this week "to show the invader that our country is not cowed by savagery".

His call comes a week after German military leaders ordered the shooting of about 200 Frenchmen, held hostage in revenge for the assassination of Colonel Holts, Field Commander in Nantes, and a top Nazi officer in Bordeaux. Both areas tonight were being ringed by troops as the Gestapo carried out house-to-house searches. The Vichy government, trying to halt the executions, has blamed British secret agents (→ 25/12).

1941

NOVEMBER

Su	Mo	Tu	We	Th	Fr	Sa
						1
2	3	4	5	6	7	8
9	10	11	12	13	14	15
16	17	18	19	20	21	22
23	24	25	26	27	28	29
30						

2. USSR: Simferopol, the Crimean capital, falls after a three-week battle (→ 13).

3. Tokyo: The US ambassador cables a warning to Roosevelt of possible plans for a Japanese attack on the US (→ 10).

4. S. Africa: South African forces capture five Vichy French ships before they can be scuttled.

6. Moscow: Ex-foreign minister Maxim Litvinov is appointed Soviet ambassador to the US.

7. UK: In a speech at Hull, Churchill says "Britain's resolve is unconquerable" .

8. Mediterranean: The Royal Navy wipes out two Italian convoys (→ 13).

10. London: Churchill pledges to join the US "within the hour" if it went to war with Japan (→ 16).

12. France: Vichy war minister General Charles Huntziger dies in an air crash.

13. USSR: Sevastopol in the Crimea falls to German and Rumanian troops (→ 21).

16. Tokyo: The foreign minister says there are limits to Japan's "conciliatory attitude" towards the US (→ 17).

17. Washington: Kichisaburo Nomura, Japan's ambassador, opens talks aimed at improving relations with the US (→ 26).

18. London: General Sir Alan Brooke takes over as Chief of the Imperial General Staff.

19. North Africa: British and Commonwealth troops begin a major offensive on the Germans and Italians (→ 23).

23. North Africa: New Zealand troops occupy Bardia.→

26. Washington: Japan asks the US to lift trade restrictions; Roosevelt will, if Japan pulls out of south-east Asia.→

27. Copenhagen: Riots greet Denmark's decision, under German pressure, to join the Axis.

30. Malta: The island suffers' its 1,000th air raid (→ 25/3/42).

Ark Royal falls to Italian torpedo

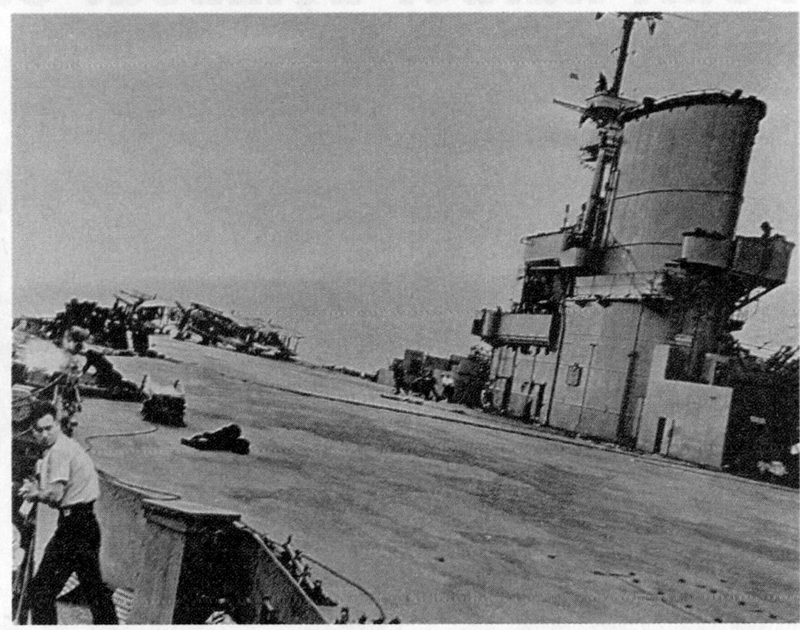

Disaster for HMS Ark Royal, victim of an Italian submarine's torpedo.

Nov 13. HMS Ark Royal, the ship the Axis powers claim to have sunk many times, finally fell victim to an Italian U-boat's torpedo today. The aircraft carrier was just preparing for the final run into the shelter of Gibraltar when she was hit. Eighteen sailors are believed to be missing, although some may have been picked up by other vessels not yet in port.

The Ark Royal immediately started listing after the torpedo struck, so much so that some crewmen slid down ropes onto the deck of a destroyer alongside. For a while the list was checked; then she sank while under tow. One eye witness said: "It was as though an athlete at the prime of his powers with a score of laurels to his credit had been knifed in the back in a dark alley."

Ark Royal's aircraft have destroyed more than 100 German and Italian planes since 1938, and both countries claim to have sunk her in the past. Her eventual loss is a big blow because it will probably make it easier for the Axis to deliver arms and men to Libya (→ 12/9/42).

Desert Rats gnaw at Nazi supply lines

Nov 30. In a long-range sweep through the Western Desert, southwest of the main battlefield round Tobruk, a British column has penetrated 80 miles into Cyrenaica. Today it is at Augila on the right flank of Rommel's Afrika Korps. From there it can harass his communications, already under attack from RAF bombing on the main coast road to Tripoli.

Recently re-styled as the Eighth Army, British Commonwealth forces under the command of General Sir Claude Auchinleck have scored significant successes against the German and Italian troops. Since they launched a new drive ten days ago, the "Desert Rats" have advanced 50 miles westwards from their start-line near the Egyptian border. After hard fighting they broke through to make contact at Sidi Rezegh with the garrison of Tobruk, which had been under siege for 33 weeks. To achieve this the New Zealanders, supported by British tanks, made a remarkable march of nearly 100 miles.

It is difficult to form an overall picture of these very fluid operations which are being fought across barren deserts; there is certainly nothing like a continuous line.

Rommel has reorganised his battered Afrika Korps panzers and mounted a counter-attack. Its columns were broken into small units and hunted by the British armour, but they are still raiding the Eighth Army's communications (→ 26/1/42).

US-Japan relations are deteriorating

Nov 30. General Hideki Tojo, the new Japanese Prime Minister, has failed to reply to America's proposals for improving relations. Instead, in violent language he recently threatened to "purge" Anglo-American influence in the Far East.

This means that a climax is fast approaching in the conflict which began when the Japanese seized control of French Indochina. America riposted by joining Britain in severing trade with Japan and freezing her assets abroad.

Earlier this month, Winston Churchill warned Japan that if she went to war with the US, a British declaration of war would follow within the hour. A powerful naval force is ready to serve in the Pacific and Indian Oceans (→ 1/12).

Bitter cold slows German advance

The Nazis meet "General Winter".

Nov 21. "Take Moscow or perish" is the slogan in Berlin today, where it is admitted that the latest drive against the capital is dictated by the German army's urgent need to secure permanent winter quarters in the Soviet capital. With the prevailing temperature 27 degress below freezing point, the unprepared Germans are seizing the warm winter clothing of the Russian people in the occupied territory (→ 12/12).

1941

DECEMBER

Su	Mo	Tu	We	Th	Fr	Sa
	1	2	3	4	5	6
7	8	9	10	11	12	13
14	15	16	17	18	19	20
21	22	23	24	25	26	27
28	29	30	31			

1. Tokyo: Tojo rejects US proposals for better relations as "fantastic and unrealistic" (→6).

3. Paris: The Germans threaten reprisals after the attempted murder of a German officer and a cafe bombing.

6. Washington: Roosevelt appeals personally to Japan's Emperor Hirohito to avoid a war with the US.→

8. London: Britain declares war on Japan (→10).

8. Pacific: The US islands of Wake and Guam are reported to have fallen to the Japanese.

10. South-East Asia: The Japanese invade Malaya and land in the Philippines.

10. South-East Asia: The battleship Prince of Wales and battle cruiser Repulse are sunk by the Japanese.→

11. Berlin and Rome: Hitler and Mussolini declare war on the US.

15. London: The government says that scrap-metal collections must be quadrupled (→2/2/42).

19. Berlin: Hitler becomes Commander-in-Chief of the army when Field Marshal von Brauchitsch resigns.

22. Washington: Churchill arrives for talks with Roosevelt.→

25. Canada: Free French forces take the pro-Vichy islands of St. Pierre and Miquelon off Canada (→19/2/42).

30. Ottawa: Churchill tells Canada's parliament: "The tide is turning."

HITS OF 1941

Boogie-Woogie Bugle Boy.

White Cliffs of Dover.

Blues in the Night.

QUOTE OF THE YEAR

"Our enemies have performed a brilliant feat of deception, perfectly timed and executed with great skill."

President Roosevelt, on the assault on Pearl Harbor.

Pearl Harbor bombed: US is at war

The USS Virginia and USS Tennessee, just two of the ships destroyed in Japan's attack on Pearl Harbor.

Dec 7. "White House says, Japanese attack Pearl Harbor": this fateful message, tapped out by the Associated Press teleprinters at 2.22pm New York time today, shattered a peaceful Sunday afternoon and ended a long struggle on the part of isolationist forces in the US to stay out of the war.

Imperial headquarters in Tokyo announced tonight that Japan was at war with the United States and Britain. Several hours earlier 360 Japanese warplanes had made a massive surprise attack on the US Pacific Fleet in its home base at Pearl Harbor in Hawaii. Japanese planes also attacked American bases in the Philippines and on Guam and Wake islands in the middle of the Pacific.

Twelve days ago, with assurances from Premier Hideki Tojo that "there is nothing to fear in this war", six aircraft carriers, with support from submarines and battleships, secretly left the Kurile islands for Honolulu and war. Today the planes caught the US Navy completely unawares and in two hours sank or seriously damaged five battleships, 14 smaller ships and 200 aircraft, and killed over 2,400 people. Luckily for America, two aircraft carriers, appear to have been out of the harbour at the time.

While the air attacks were actually in progress, the Japanese ambassador in Washington, Admiral Nomura, and a special envoy from Tokyo, Mr Kurusu, were meeting the American Secretary of State, Mr Cordell Hull. When the Japanese diplomats handed a note from Japan to Mr Hull, he replied that he had "never seen a document that was more crowded with infamous falsehoods and distortions".

This evening, President Roosevelt met with his top war ministers as well as the full cabinet and leaders of Congress. He has begun to dictate a message which he will deliver to a special session of Congress tomorrow afternoon, when it will be officially informed that a state of war exists.

"There is no doubt," said Andrew May, the chairman of the House of Representatives military affairs committee, "that within a few hours Congress will give him whatever authority he needs to prosecute the war all-out."

Army and navy officers, rounded up from their homes and weekend golf clubs, were tonight streaming into the War and Navy Department building (→8).

Britain declares war on Axis puppets

Dec 8. Britain declared war today on Finland, Rumania and Hungary. This follows the failure of the three Axis satellites to respond to ultimata demanding that they stop military operations in support of the German armies. The British move is a diplomatic formality and it will not change the shape of the fighting. It has been made to please Russia, and could help to improve uneasy relations between London and Moscow.

Not long ago Mr Churchill suggested to Marshal Stalin that it would be better not to make a declaration of war on Hitler's puppets. He argued that this would create a false impression that they were all in a grand alliance solidly against the Allies, when in fact they may change sides.

The Soviet leader's reaction was frosty. He insisted on the declaration as proof of British good faith. Mr Churchill is now in personal correspondence with Marshal Stalin to boost mutual trust (→13/6).

Japan's lightning advance in SE Asia

Japanese troops celebrate their successful attack on the Chinese enemy.

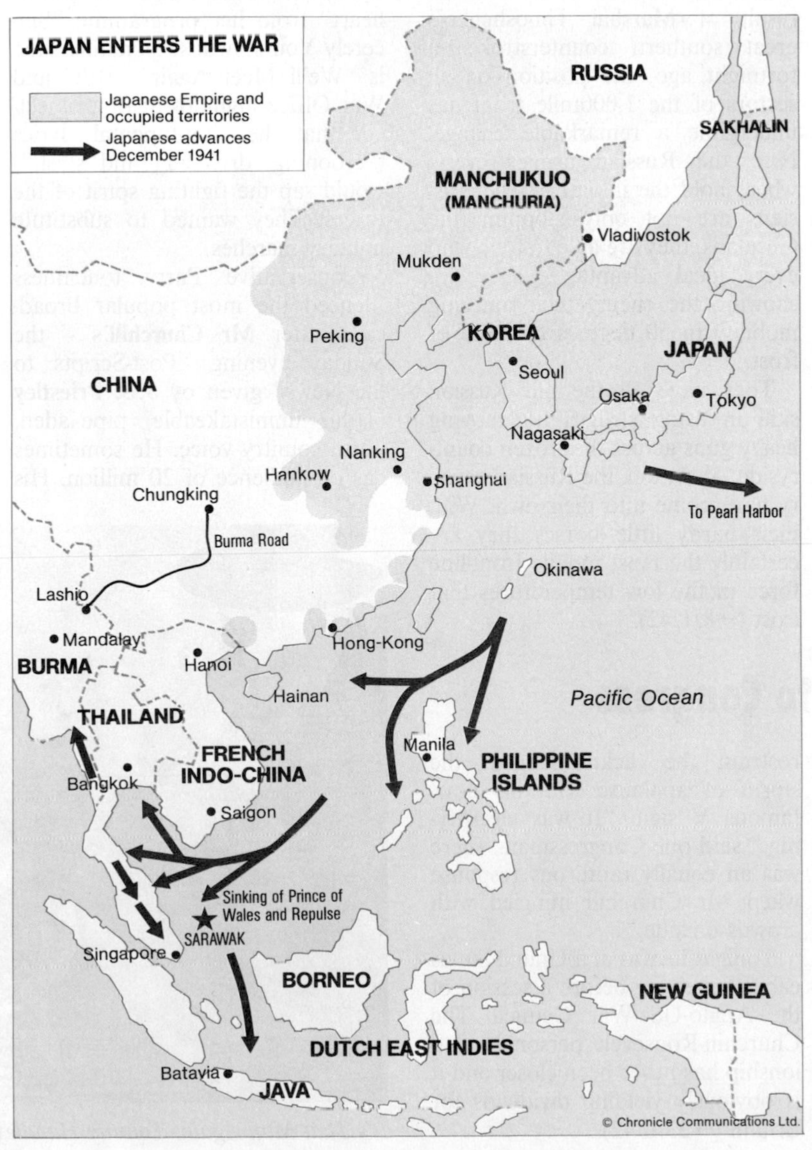

Dec 25. Hong Kong fell to the Japanese today. After a seven-day battle on the island, the hopelessly outnumbered defenders, 6,000 strong, were compelled to surrender unconditionally.

A communique from London on this new disaster in the Far East, only three weeks after the start of the lightning Japanese onslaught, stated that the Governor had decided that no further resistance was possible: "So ends a great fight against overwhelming odds."

This evening Sir Mark Young, the Governor, after talks with the Japanese commanders at the Peninsular Hotel in Kowloon, finally gave in. The garrison of British and Commonwealth troops must disarm by noon tomorrow.

In the final stages of the battle, the infantry battalions were facing two entire Japanese divisions, a force estimated at 40,000 men. Finally, with the colony's reservoirs in enemy hands, the garrison was down to 24 hours' supply of water.

The Japanese assault on Hong Kong is just part of a massive offensive in the Pacific and South-East Asia which began with the infamous surprise raid on Pearl Harbor on December 7, which killed 3,000 US servicemen and badly damaged the US Pacific fleet.

On December 10, Japanese divisions invaded British-held Malaya and the northern Philippines as well. In the middle of the month, the loss of the battleship HMS Prince of Wales and the battle cruiser Repulse off the Malayan coast badly reduced British naval strength in the area.

In Malaya some Japanese troops landed at Kuantan, while other units pressed down from Thailand. British forces are fighting hard to hold the offensive, but Penang is in danger. There have been air raids on Singapore, where British defences are being strengthened.

The Japanese have already taken the islands of Guam and Wake to the east, and they are advancing on Luzon, the largest of the Philippine islands. US and Filipino ground forces, led by General Douglas MacArthur, total about 130,000 men, and are falling back towards the Corregidor fortress to the south-west (→2/1/42).

Unmarried women between 20 and 30 will be called up

Dec 2. All single women between 20 and 30 are to be called up. Some will soon be in anti-aircraft crews along with men. Others will take over desk jobs now done by medically-fit men. Up to 1,700,000 women are involved in the Government's new conscription plans.

The call-up age for men is lowered to eighteen-and-a-half and, at the other end of the age scale, men up to 50 will be liable for military service. Mr Churchill told MPs today: "Here is another instalment of toil and sweat. We must call upon the nation for further sacrifice and exertion."

The manpower situation is now acute in both the Forces and the factories. Some conscripted women may also be put into the police and the fire services and, to meet future needs, the registration of women up to 40 – both single and married – will now begin.

Boys and girls between 16 and 18 must also register. Mr Churchill said: "We must be careful particularly that our boys do not run loose." The idea is that these youngsters should be encouraged into suitable pre-military training after interviews with the school authorities. There will be deferment of call-up for university students and others with approved places in higher education (→15).

Forces combine to raid Norway

Dec 12. The Navy, Army and Air Force have carried out the first combined services' raid on Norway, sinking eight enemy ships and leaving a trail of havoc ashore.

The entire German garrison on the island of Vaagso in northern Norway was either captured or killed in the raid, in which Free Norwegian troops joined British commandos as they stormed ashore.

At the same time RAF bombers attacked German heavy gun positions and wrecked a Nazi air base, thought to be part of the German supply line, just down the coast (→1/2/42).

▷

Russia repels panzers

The icy weather is the real conqueror of Germans on the Eastern Front.

Dec 12. The Russians have turned on the German invaders and have inflicted a series of smashing defeats on Hitler's panzers. Following the recapture of Rostov in the south, General Zhukov has counter-attacked the German forces besieging Moscow and routed them.

Solechnaya Gora, 40 miles north-west of Moscow, the nearest the Nazi spearhead has come to the capital, has been recaptured. According to last night's communique, more than 400 towns and villages have been retaken in five days' fighting. Some 30,000 Germans have been killed, and nearly 700 tanks captured or destroyed.

The Russians claim that "German plans for surrounding and capturing Moscow have ended in a fiasco". Jubilant Russians are now pursuing their erstwhile besiegers. Since the recapture of Rostov as a result of Marshal Timoshenko's great southern counterstroke, a fortnight ago, the position on all sectors of the 1,000mile front has undergone a remarkable change. Now the Russian armies everywhere hold the initiative. The Russians are not only stopping the Germans, they are able to follow up every local advantage. They are showing the enemy their amazing mobility in 50 degrees or more of frost.

They have all the old Russian skill in using sledges for moving heavy guns across the frozen countryside. Now, too, the Russian cavalry have come into their own. With their hardy little horses they are certainly the most mobile front-line force in the low temperatures that exist (→8/1/42).

Churchill gives V sign to Congress

Dec 26. Winston Churchill was wildly cheered when he delivered a fighting speech to both Houses of the US Congress today. His Christmas visit to Washington appears to be rousing American opinion to a new level of enthusiasm in supporting Britain's war effort.

The Prime Minister made full use of his oratorical powers. He struck all the right notes, including copious quotations from Abraham Lincoln and mentioning his own American mother. As he left the rostrum he acknowledged the storm of applause with his now-famous V sign. "It was electrifying," said one Congressman. There was an equally rapturous response when Mr Churchill mingled with crowds outside.

Tonight he was at a United States cabinet meeting before a session of the Anglo-US War Council. The Churchill-Roosevelt personal relationship has never been closer and it is obviously yielding dividends for Britain (→23/6/42).

Arts: radio entertains as the bombs fall

The radio has become the main source of entertainment of a nation kept in at night by the raids. If the invasion were to start between 8.30 and 9pm on a Thursday, runs the joke, there would be no opposition because everyone would be listening to **Tommy Handley** in ITMA ("It's That Man Again").

In a breathless half-hour, a kaleidoscope of motley and improbable characters are whirled in and out of the ITMA door (an essential sound effect). Their lines have become national catch-phrases, such as the charwoman Mrs Mopp's "Can I do yer now, sir?" or the well-lubricated tones of Colonel Chinstrap replying "I don't mind if I do" to anything that could be taken for the name of a drink.

Instantly recognisable in every barrack-room is the voice of **Vera Lynn**, known as "the Forces' Sweetheart" from her programme "Sincerely Yours" whose signature tune is "We'll Meet Again". BBC and War Office high-ups at first objected that her sentimental lyrics ("crooning, drivelling and slush") would sap the fighting spirit of the forces. They wanted to substitute military marches.

Conservative Party touchiness silenced the most popular broadcasts after **Mr Churchill's** – the Sunday evening "Post-Scripts to the News" given by **J.B. Priestley** in his unmistakeable, pipe-laden, north country voice. He sometimes has an audience of 20 million. His post-war aims for Britain sounded too Socialist for some politicians' taste and he was confined to the North American network.

Orson Welles as "Citizen Kane".

The popularity of the "Brains Trust" has taken the BBC by surprise. Its three thoughtful pundits, philosopher **Dr Joad**, biologist **Julian Huxley**, and old sea-salt **Commander Campbell**, who argue on matters serious and trivial, receive 5,000 letters a week.

Crime novelist **Dorothy Sayers** has written a radio classic in "The Man Born to be King", a dramatisation of the life of Jesus treated as a human story. It was only broadcast after violent protests by the Lord's Day Observance Society.

It's That Man Again: Tommy Handley and Co. are invaluable for morale.

1942

JANUARY

Su	Mo	Tu	We	Th	Fr	Sa
				1	2	3
4	5	6	7	8	9	10
11	12	13	14	15	16	17
18	19	20	21	22	23	24
25	26	27	28	29	30	31

1. Washington: 26 countries affirm their opposition to the Axis in the "Declaration of the United Nations" (→15).

1. Germany: 131,823 Jews are still estimated to be living in Germany.→

2. Philippines: Japanese troops take Manila (→3).

3. London: General Sir Archibald Wavell is named head of Allied forces in the south-west Pacific (→11).

7. Washington: Roosevelt presents Congress with the property biggest-ever US budget estimate of $58,927 million (→1/2).

8. USSR: Soviet troops push back the Germans in the Crimea (→31/3).

11. South-East Asia: Japanese troops land on Borneo and other islands (→20).

13. London: Exiled governments discuss the issue of trials for war crimes.

15. Rio de Janeiro: 21 American countries agree to break ties with the Axis.

15. India: Gandhi names Nehru as his successor (→23/3).

17. Las Vegas: Actress Carole Lombard and her mother are among 22 found dead in the wreck of a TWA airliner.

20. Singapore: The Japanese carry out daylight bombing raids (→23).

23. Pacific: Japanese troops land on New Guinea and the Solomon Islands.→

29. Libya: German and Italian troops take Benghazi (→27/5).

29. London: Churchill wins a 462 majority in a confidence vote, the biggest government majority since war began (→4/2).

30. Dublin: The government claims US troop landings in Northern Ireland violate Eire's neutrality (→25/6/43).

31. Singapore: The Japanese lay siege to the island (→9/2).

BIRTH

17. US boxer Muhammad Ali, born Cassius Clay.

Allies fail to halt Japan in Malaya

Jan 28. "You can get shot at from six sides at once. The Japanese buzz around you like bees," said a British infantryman in the force resisting the Japanese in Malaya.

On the west coast, enemy troops have penetrated to within 50 miles of the island fortress of Singapore. They are advancing in three columns against fierce opposition from Allied troops. RAF reconnaissance reported that, in the north, Japanese reinforcements were swarming in like ants.

More landings are reported at Muar. The enemy is using special landing boats which have been brought overland to Malaya. They are equipped with heavy machine-guns. The invaders are using all forms of transport and, at one point, the Australians ambushed and killed an entire patrol of 30 bicycle troops.

After seven weeks' fighting our forces are still in retreat. The gravity of the situation is demonstrated by an order to evacuate all civilians from a mile-wide strip on the northern shore of Singapore island.

Last week Japanese troops opened another front, landing on the Solomon Islands and New Guinea and threatening Australia, only 800 miles away. "For the first time in history Australian territory has been attacked," declared Mr Curtin, the Prime Minister. "The enemy's next stroke may well be an attempt on the mainland itself. We are ready" (→31).

A British soldier patrols in Burma.

Nazis agree on the "Final Solution"

Jan 20. When Josef Goebbels, the Nazis' propaganda boss, was heard to let drop the remark that such-and-such was the final solution, ears pricked up. Although Goebbels was apparently only suggesting the provision of brothels for foreign workers, the fact is that the words "final solution" are also being used by Nazi leaders in references to a secret meeting called by Reinhard Heydrich, right-hand man to the Gestapo chief, Himmler.

Heydrich, speaking to officials of government departments, is said to have been obliged to admit that the final solution refers to "the Jewish problem" and involves plans for the total extermination of the estimated 11,000,000 Jews in Europe.

Many thousands of Jews are believed to have been killed already, somewhat haphazardly, by shooting or beating. Under Heydrich's plan the task will be carried out more systematically in special camps with facilities for mass extermination. Heydrich's violent anti-Semitism is said to be fuelled by persistent rumours that his mother was half-Jewish (→26/3).

First US troops land in Europe

Jan 26. Several thousand infantry troops of the United States Army landed in Northern Ireland this morning. They are the first US troops to set foot in Europe – other than Iceland – since the Great War when the American Expeditionary Force arrived in France to reinforce the Allies.

Today's landing was a carefully kept secret. Even the band of Royal Ulster Rifles were not told where they were going, or why. Nevertheless, they managed a creditable version of "The Star-Spangled Banner" as the first ship docked.

The Americans were warmly welcomed by Sir Archibald Sinclair, the Secretary for Air, who had flown over from London. He told the troops: "Your safe arrival here marks a new stage in the world war. It is a gloomy portent for Mr Hitler; nor will its significance be lost on General Tojo" (→30).

Germany is pushing back the 8th Army

Jan 26. Panzers are today racing forward against British positions in the Western Desert. From their start line at El Agheila, General Erwin Rommel's tanks have penetrated 150 miles eastwards towards Egypt. Tonight they were reported at Msus, a desert junction of tracks through the sand.

This implies that the important town of Benghazi is again under threat and that the tank battle, which has been going on for four days, is going against us. Rommel's heavy tanks are beating our lighter armoured vehicles and a greatly reinforced Afrika Korps has achieved tactical surprise.

The trouble is that the Eighth Army has been overstretched, which has meant poor communications and loss of momentum. It took Jedabya two weeks ago while pushing mobile patrols right up to the Axis line between El Agheila and Marad. A further problem was the pocket of 7,000 cut-off Axis troops holding out in the British rear in strong positions at Halfaya.

As Lieutenant-General Ritchie set about re-forming his army and re-supplying it for another move forward, the Germans struck (→29).

Rommel's gunners at Benghazi.

1942

FEBRUARY

Su	Mo	Tu	We	Th	Fr	Sa
1	2	3	4	5	6	7
8	9	10	11	12	13	14
15	16	17	18	19	20	21
22	23	24	25	26	27	28

1. Pacific: The US Navy attacks Japanese bases in the Gilbert and Marshall Islands (→ 9).

2. UK: Rose-hip syrup goes on sale nationwide; 2,000,000 more children get free cod liver oil (→ 3).

3. London: Maximum clothes prices are laid down by the government; a suit must cost no more than £4 18s 8d (→ 18).

4. London: Lord Beaverbrook becomes Minister of War Production (→ 19).

9. Singapore: Japanese forces land on the island.→

11. London: Epstein's huge new sculpture "Jacob and the Angel" goes on show.

14. South-East Asia: The Japanese invade Sumatra (→ 15).

19. London: Sir Stafford Cripps joins the War Cabinet; Beaverbrook leaves through ill-health (→ 2/7).

19. France: Ex-premiers Daladier, Reynaud and Blum face a second trial for "causing the defeat of France" (→ 27).

22. Burma: Civilians are evacuated from Rangoon as fighting takes place 80 miles north-east of the city (→ 28).

22. UK: Dr William Temple becomes Archbishop of Canterbury

23. UK: Sir Arthur Harris takes over as head of RAF Bomber Command (→ 26/3).

23. Brazil: Austrian author Stefan Zweig and his wife kill themselves, in apparent despair over conditions in Austria.

24. Ankara: The German ambassador, ex-Chancellor Franz von Papen, escapes an assassination bid.

27. Vichy: Petain tells the US that the Germans will not take over the French fleet (→ 14/4).

28. South-East Asia: 13 Allied warships are reported to have been sunk in the Java Sea (→ 8/3).

DEATH

23. Austrian author Stefan Zweig (*28/11/1881).

Japan takes Singapore

Some of the thousands of prisoners, taken after the fall of Singapore.

Feb 15. Singapore, the great naval base and a fortress considered to be impregnable, today surrendered to the Japanese. No details are yet known in London, but Tokyo claims that the capitulation was negotiated this morning when Lieutenant-General Percival, under a flag of truce, met the Japanese commander-in-chief in the Ford works on Bukit Timah Hill.

In a broadcast to the nation last night, Winston Churchill described the loss of the fortress, which cost £50 million, as "a heavy and far-reaching military defeat". He concluded: "Here is the moment to display that calm and poise, combined with grim determination, which not so long ago brought us out of the very jaws of death."

The consequences for the Allies are grave. The fall of Singapore deprives the Allies of their only major dry-dock between Durban and Pearl Harbor. Simultaneously, Japan has acquired this valuable naval asset for future operations in the Indian Ocean.

Japanese troops massed for the assault at the beginning of the month, as British troops withdrew and blew up the Johore Causeway. After days of heavy bombardment they landed by night on the island six days ago (→ 22).

'A BIT OF HOME'
RED CROSS & St JOHN
needs your help for
Prisoners of War

Quisling dances to Nazi tune in Oslo

Feb 1. Vidkun Quisling today got his reward for collaborating with the Nazis when they invaded Norway two years ago. His German masters have installed him as puppet Prime Minister, replacing Governor Terboven.

Under the new constitution, the state of war between Germany and Quislingite Norway is ended. Quisling's inaugural speech made his position perfectly clear.

"This is not only Germany's but Norway's war, the Germanic people's and Europe's war against England, America, Russia and international Jewry," he said.

Oslo has not received its new premier enthusiastically. Most citizens stayed indoors to avoid the armed contingents of Hird Guard storm-troopers (→ 7/4).

Quisling: adding to the language.

Beetroots put the bloom on ladies' lips

Feb 18. "Plimsoll lines" are beginning to appear on hotel and public baths as a fuel shortage hits Britain. Even the King, it is reported, has had such lines painted on baths in Buckingham Palace. The population is urged to take fewer baths, and to use no more than five inches of hot water when they do so. Shared baths are also encouraged.

The situation is not being helped by a soap ration of one tablet allowed every month. The Government has refused extra rations for districts like London where water is exceptionally hard – although miners are able to obtain ration-free soap at their pithead baths.

Shaving soap is unrationed but difficult to obtain; razor blades are in equally short supply. Users are encouraged to re-sharpen their blades by running them around the insides of glass tumblers – which are also virtually unobtainable.

With an equal shortage of cosmetics, women are driven to use cooked beetroot juice for lipstick and soot for eye makeup. Gravy browning "paint" is substituting for silk stockings, with pencilled-in seams (→ 3/3).

1942

MARCH

Su	Mo	Tu	We	Th	Fr	Sa
1	2	3	4	5	6	7
8	9	10	11	12	13	14
15	16	17	18	19	20	21
22	23	24	25	26	27	28
29	30	31				

1. France: British troops raid and destroy a German radio-location centre at Bruneval near Le Havre.→

3. US: 100,000 Japanese Americans are to be evacuated from a huge area of the West Coast, now a "military zone".

4. London: Sir William Jowitt is appointed head of planning for reconstruction after the war.

5. London: Civil servants' pencil sharpeners are withdrawn to conserve pencils (→11).

8. South-East Asia: Java capitulates to the Japanese (→12).

10. London: Figures show Britain's war spending has topped £9,050 million, more than for the entire Great War.

11. London: The government says it will ban the baking of white bread (→17).

12. Philippines: MacArthur leaves for Australia in the face of Allied defeat, but says: "I shall return" (→17).

17. London: The government announces the introduction of fuel rationing (→15/4).

17. Australia: MacArthur is appointed to succeed Wavell as chief of Allied forces in the Pacific region (→5/4).

22. London: The BBC broadcasts its first daily morse code news bulletin to the French Resistance (→30/4/43).

23. UK: Sir Stafford Cripps leaves for talks with Indian leaders on the future of the sub-continent.→

26. Germany: The Nazis begin the deportation of Jews to the concentration camp at Auschwitz in Poland (→1/4).

26. Germany: 200 RAF planes carry out a heavy raid on the towns of the Ruhr valley.→

31. USSR: An Allied convoy reaches Murmansk safely despite fierce German attacks (→3/8)

BIRTH

25. US singer Aretha Franklin.

RAF begins terror bombing campaign

March 28. Over 200 aircraft of RAF Bomber Command tonight launched a shattering raid on the Baltic port of Lubeck, a shipbuilding and industrial centre. Hundreds of tons of incendiaries and high explosives were dropped, and about half the built-up area has been destroyed by fire.

It is believed that the RAF is using a new device which enables the maximum number of aircraft to be concentrated over the target in a short space of time. All the thousands of fire bombs were dropped within half an hour, overwhelming the German fire-fighters.

The RAF has begun a round-the-clock offensive against German arms factories, German-controlled industries in France and German gun emplacements in the Calais area. On Sunday night the Krupp works at Essen were pounded by the big new 4,000-pound bomb carried by the RAF's new four-engined bombers. Yesterday afternoon, Spitfires escorted the bombers to industrial plants near Bethune. Spitfires shot down eight German fighters when they escorted bombers in an attack on Le Havre (→29/4).

Bombs are loaded into an RAF Wellington before another night's work.

Skirts go up and turn-ups turn down

March 3. Hemlines are set to rise again – and that's official. This time, however, the trend will be dictated not by designers in Paris but by the Board of Trade in London. The Board's new utility cloth, plus the limit on the number of styles, will mean fashion is strictly a no-frills affair.

Likely changes in menswear include no double-breasted coats, no sleeve buttons and no turn-ups on trousers. Utility suits made by authorised tailors will be a standard price, but wealthy dandies will still be able to buy the cloth and have it made up into 30-guinea suits by their Savile Row tailors (→5).

The first team may be at war, but the ladies' reserve plays on with boys.

Vital convoy fights through to Malta

March 25. A British convoy carrying vital supplies has got through to the island of Malta, escorted by a Royal Navy force that was outnumbered and outgunned by attacking Italian warships.

Two days after leaving Alexandria the British escort and flotilla of four light cruisers came under air attack, and Italian warships approached: a 35,000-ton battleship and six cruisers. Admiral Sir Philip Vian, C-in-C Mediterranean, at once gave orders to attack.

For over two hours Vian's ships fought off the superior force, inflicting heavy damage on the battleship, while the convoy took cover behind a smokescreen and headed for Malta. Two ships were sunk within sight of the island; the other two reached Valletta, only to be sunk while the cargo was being unloaded (→10/5).

Commandos raid Nazi submarine base

British Marine prisoners under guard following the St. Nazaire raid.

March 27. The big Nazi U-boat base at St. Nazaire was left a raging inferno of fires and explosions tonight as British commandos stormed ashore from the destroyer Campbeltown.

The ship rammed the main dock gates at 20 knots. Five tons of explosives on board then put out of action the only dry dock on the Atlantic coast of France capable of taking the huge battleship Tirpitz.

But this most important of all combined operations so far in the war was not without cost; many commandos were taken prisoner. The War Office decided on the daring action after two German battle-cruisers slipped through the Allied blockade and made it to Norway.

The Campbeltown was specially prepared for her task with strengthened bows and delayed action explosive. She defied heavy fire up the Loire estuary before she hit home. The French Resistance played a major part in the plan.

After destroying dock equipment, the commandos made their escape down-river in fast launches. A German ship in the estuary tried to stop the troops departing, but she was mistakenly destroyed by the Nazis' own guns (→ 19/8).

India is promised Dominion status

March 29. Sir Stafford Cripps, special envoy from the Cabinet, unfolded British plans for full independence for India when he met Mr Gandhi in New Delhi today. He produced a draft declaration which, if accepted by an Indian constituent assembly, would mean Indian self-government after the war. The sub-continent could be either one Dominion, or two, if the Moslems preferred that. There would be special arrangements for territories ruled by the Indian princes.

As a left-wing Socialist, Sir Stafford is on friendly terms with many Indian leaders, but his mission already seems doomed. Initial Hindu reaction is that there must be self-government at once. This is bad news for the cabinet, which desperately wants to stabilise conditions in India now that the threat of Japanese invasion is growing.

Mr Gandhi has lost no time in advising his followers to reject the plan. He says that, if India is invaded, there should be no resistance to the Japanese and that, in the meantime, the campaign of civil disobedience must continue. Mr Churchill is worried that this campaign is fanning American suspicions and dislike of remaining traces of British imperialism (→ 26/8).

Mirror is threatened with suppression for shipwreck cartoon

ZEC
"The price of petrol has been increased by one penny."—Official.

Philip Zec's controversial cartoon: the Government may ban the Mirror.

March 26. The Government today warned the Daily Mirror that it will be suppressed unless it behaves. Herbert Morrison, the Home Secretary, told MPs that the newspaper has repeatedly published scurrilous misrepresentations with reckless indifference to the national interest.

He had reminded the Mirror that it could be shut down under wartime Defence Regulations. Its latest offences are calling army chiefs boneheads and publishing a cartoon showing a distressed seaman on a raft over the words "The price of petrol has been increased by one penny". Most MPs considered that this caption was intended to suggest that seamen are having to risk their lives to boost oil company profits. Mr Churchill resents such criticism of the war effort (→ 7/4).

1942

APRIL

Su	Mo	Tu	We	Th	Fr	Sa
			1	2	3	4
5	6	7	8	9	10	11
12	13	14	15	16	17	18
19	20	21	22	23	24	25
26	27	28	29	30		

1. Germany: The number of Jews in Germany is now put at 51,257 (28/6).

3. USSR: The Germans retreat from Kharkhov as Soviet troops break through (→ 22/5).

7. India: The Indian National Congress Working Committee rejects British plans for the future of India (→ 12).

7. Norway: All the clergy hand in their resignations to the government (8/10).

9. Pacific: The Japanese take Bataan, capturing 36,000 Allied prisoners (→ 17).

12. New Delhi: Nehru pledges "no surrender" to the Axis despite the rejection of Britain's plans (→ 9/8).

14. Vichy: Petain bows to German pressure and reappoints Laval as premier (→ 15).

15. London: The government bans embroidery on women's underwear and nightwear (→ 13/5).

15. France: The trial of pre-war statesmen is abandoned as increasing discredit is brought on Vichy leaders (→ 19).

17. Burma: The main oilfields are destroyed to prevent them falling into Japanese hands (→ 18).

18. South-East Asia: Lord Louis Mountbatten is put in overall command of combined Allied operations (→ 2/5).

19. Vichy: Laval is sworn in as premier and foreign, interior and information ministers (→ 22/6).

22. Germany: Captive French General Henri Giraud escapes from the fortress of Konigstein.

25. London: 16-year-old Princess Elizabeth registers for war service (→ 25/8).

28. Washington: President Roosevelt orders a price freeze on all major domestic items (→ 3/10).

30. Salzburg: Hitler meets Mussolini.

BIRTH

24. US actress and singer Barbra Streisand.

ɜeorge Cross goes o people of Malta

ɩpril 16. After four months of lmost daily air battles over Malta, ɕing George has announced the ward of the George Cross – the ivilian VC – to the island fortress ı the Mediterranean. The King aid in his message to the Govrnor, Lieutenant-General Sir Wilam Dobbie, that the "heroism and levotion" of a brave people "will ɔng be famous in history".

Another message to the people of ɅAalta, from Viscount Cranborne, ne Colonial Secretary, spoke of the nemy's massed bombers and fightrs being thrown against the island.

Malta presents a constant threat ɔ the Axis lines of communication ɹith Rommel's forces in North ɅAfrica, and in recent months the ɜermans have made a determined ffort to bomb the island into subɹission. Several attempts have been nade by the Royal Navy to get upplies through, and virtually all avc cithcr failed or been crippled.

There are believed to be about 00 German and 200 Italian warɩlanes based on Sicily, and these are sed for day and night bombing aids on Malta's airfields and the ɩockyards. Reliable figures for ꞦAF strength are not available but, ince reinforcements cannot for the resent be sent by sea, it is likely hat any available Spitfires are flyɪg in from aircraft carriers kept ɩut of the range of German bombrs.

Malta has had over 2,000 raids nd alerts; half of these have taken ɩlace in the first four months of this ear (→14/8).

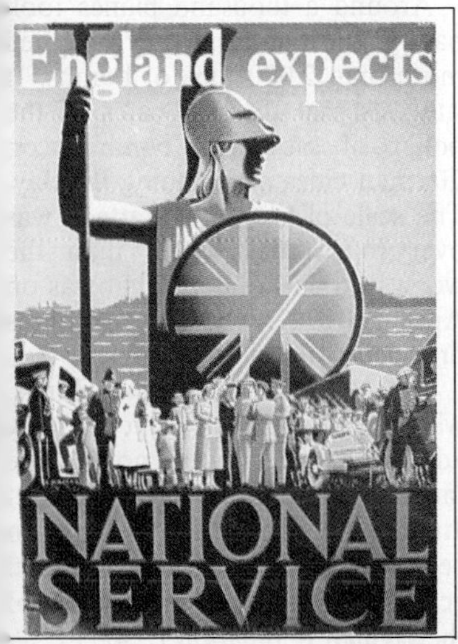

Nazis begin raids on "Baedeker towns"

Only the walls of the English shrine remain after a raid on Coventry.

April 29. Enraged by the RAF's devastation of the Baltic port of Lubeck a month ago, Hitler issued a directive to the Luftwaffe to step up its attacks on British targets with raids that would have severe consequences for the civilian population. The first raid came a week ago, when about fifty bombers hit Exeter. The next target was Bath, on two successive nights, and then Norwich, and York where bombs destroyed the 15th-century Guildhall.

But the RAF is hitting back with a vengeance. The Baltic port of Rostock has been wrecked by a series of fire-bombings spread over four nights. Told of the devastation, Hitler is said to have heaped abuse on his air chiefs and demanded that every British city in the Baedeker guide book be razed to the ground.

The Luftwaffe attacks have been highly damaging, if only because the so-called Baedeker towns have lacked strong defences. This is now being remedied and the German losses of planes – and pilots – are steadily mounting. With the Russian front still making heavy demands, it is questionable whether the Luftwaffe can keep up its militarily pointless raids much longer just to satisfy the Fuehrer's wounded pride (→31/5).

Surprise bombing of Ceylon by Japan

April 5. Japanese naval aircraft were beaten off today with heavy losses when they tried to repeat their Pearl Harbor surprise tactics on Ceylon. They struck at Colombo, the British air and naval base guarding the western approaches to the Bay of Bengal, but this time the defences were on the alert and the Japanese failed to destroy ships or installations.

Of the 75 attacking aircraft, 25 were shot down by RAF fighters and two more by ground fire. Five more were claimed probably shot down, while 25 others damaged by fire were unlikely to have made it back to the fleet.

British naval intelligence believes that the number of aircraft used indicated that a Japanese naval force of at least one, and probably two, aircraft carriers is operating in the Indian Ocean. Each of the carriers in service has a complement of 60 aircraft. Efforts are under way to locate the Japanese fleet.

The raid began at 8am and developed into a concentrated assault on the harbour and the suburb of Ratmalana and its airfield, eight miles from the city. Low cloud made it impossible to see the raiders, but the sounds of dog-fights were soon heard high in the sky.

"It is a great piece of work," said Admiral Sir Geoffrey Layton, Ceylon's C-in-C. "It is entirely due to the manner in which we have prepared ourselves." He offered rewards for the capture of Japanese pilots who had baled out (→9/4).

Japan shocked as US bombs Tokyo

April 18. The realities of war were brought home to the ordinary people of Tokyo and other Japanese cities today when American B-25s made a lightning raid. Little damage is thought to have been inflicted by the bombers, but the US military is hoping that the raid will have a big psychological impact.

The element of surprise was crucial. Most Japanese had no idea that there were any American planes within flying distance. The bombers are believed to have come from the aircraft carrier Hornet, which is about 600 miles away from the Japanese coast. It was not as big a shock as the bombing of Pearl Harbor was for the Americans, but there is no doubt that it will bring home to the Japanese the growing strength of the American presence in the Pacific. The carrier is protected by a large navy task force commanded by Admiral Halsey.

General James Doolittle, who led the raid, took the planes in so low that one of the flyers is said to have been able to watch a ball game in progress (→2/5).

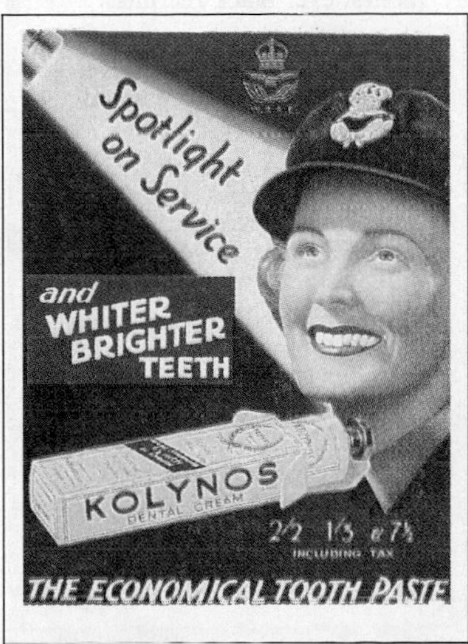

1942

MAY

Su	Mo	Tu	We	Th	Fr	Sa
					1	2
3	4	5	6	7	8	9
10	11	12	13	14	15	16
17	18	19	20	21	22	23
24	25	26	27	28	29	30
31						

1. Moscow: Stalin says the USSR has no territorial ambitions in foreign countries.

2. Burma: The Japanese take Mandalay (→6).

3. Yugoslavia: German reinforcements arrive to fight Tito's partisans (→14/7).

4. Indian Ocean: British troops land on the pro-Vichy French colony of Madagascar (→7).

6. Philippines: 10,000 US and Filipino troops surrender to the Japanese on Corregidor (→8).

7. Madagascar: The northern naval base of Diego Suarez surrenders to the British.

10. Malta: The German-Italian offensive ends after 11,000 missions (→16).

12. US: A US merchant ship is sunk by a submarine in the mouth of the Mississippi River; 27 die.

13. London: The government postpones plans for fuel rationing after widespread opposition (→14).

14. UK: Women's war fashions now include "bare legs for patriotism" (→3/6).

17. Bristol: Cripps says the government is anxious to open a second front in Europe (→18).

18. UK: The biggest contingent of US troops yet to arrive lands in Northern Ireland (→25/6).

20. US: The US Navy signs up its first ever black recruits.

22. USSR: The Germans admit that a Soviet offensive around Kharkov has pierced the city's defences.→

27. Prague: A state of emergency follows the wounding of Reinhard Heydrich, Nazi governor of Bohemia (→4/6).

31. Australia: Three Japanese midget submarines raid Sydney Harbour (→7/6).

DEATHS

7. Austrian conductor Felix Weingartner (*2/6/1863).

29. US actor John Barrymore (*15/2/1882).

Russians foil Nazi summer offensive

May 31. A tremendous battle is raging in Russia for the Donetz river-crossings south of Kharkov, with the Germans pressing to capture Izyum while the Russians attempt to retake Kharkov which has been in German hands for the last eight months.

The armies of General von Bock and Marshal Timoshenko are joined in fierce hand-to-hand fighting, with both sides pouring in men and materiel. An official Russian despatch from the Kharkov front claims that 14 waves of massed German tanks were hurled back, including their most modern ones, 500 of which were lost.

This is part of Hitler's much-publicised spring offensive, which opened on May 12 with a smashing onslaught by tanks and dive-bombers on the Soviet lines on the Kerch peninsula in the Crimea.

Two panzer divisions thundered across broken country through fields which, although scarred by last autumn's battles, are now covered with wild flowers and fresh green spring grass.

Squadrons of Stukas droned overhead to bomb concrete blockhouses where Soviet anti-tank gunners waited behind their guns, while heavier bombers attacked the lines of supply.

However, the Russians forestalled the development of the main German offensive, by striking towards Kharkov and inflicting severe casualties on the Germans, who were still holed up in the winter "hedgehog" positions. The outcome remains in the balance as the battle rages on (→7/6).

A Russian mother bids her son farewell as he leaves to join the partisans.

Rommel's offensive drives the Allies back

Rommel considers his next attack.

May 27. Across the sparsest desert in the whole of Libya, and by the light of an almost full moon, German panzer divisions early this morning launched their long-expected offensive.

In a spectacular manoeuvre, General Rommel switched a number of tanks from north to south in an attempt to turn the British southern flank. Since dawn, a great tank battle has been raging around Bir Hakeim, with the British Eighth Army engaged all the way to Gazala on the Mediterranean.

Both sides are depending on air support, with the German dive-bombers attacking our forward positions and the RAF continually raiding airfields and supply columns between Benghazi and the battle zone.

The reinforced German forces engaged in this offensive are the 25th panzer under General Bismarck, the 15th panzer, led by General von Nehring, and the 19th armoured division (→21/6).

Thousand bombers devastate Cologne

May 31. Royal Air Force chiefs today claimed to have destroyed more than 200 factories in last night's raid on Cologne. They said they had done more damage in one night than in the previous 1,300 RAF raids on the city.

Around a thousand planes took part in the raid, and they dropped more than 2,000 tons of bombs. It suggests that the advocates of the policy of saturation bombing on German cities are winning the day. The scale of last night's attack was over four times bigger than the worst raid on London. That was on April 16, 1941, when the Germans dropped 440 tons of bombs.

Air Marshal Sir Arthur Harris, who led last night's attack, freely admits that there were no specific targets. He claims that such blanket attacks on the main population centres will disrupt the German economy and destroy the morale of the civilian population (→4/7).

Japan and US wage Battle of Coral Sea

May 8. The American and Japanese navies were tonight both claiming victory in one of the most unusual sea battles ever. Not one shot was fired at an enemy vessel by any of the ships taking part.

Instead, they just acted as huge launch pads for the carrier-borne aircraft which roared off to do the fighting.

The ships never faced each other directly, or even saw each other, and it is now becoming clear that, in the war in the Pacific and Far East, it is aircraft which will decide sea battles.

The effect of the encounter is that the Americans have stopped the Japanese from landing at Tulagi in the Solomons and Port Moresby in New Guinea, but not without considerable cost to themselves.

The aircraft carrier Lexington was sunk and the Yorktown was damaged. In addition the United States lost a destroyer, a tanker and more than 60 planes. Most members of the Lexington's crew were rescued.

In the five days of fighting the Japanese lost an aircraft carrier and several cruisers and destroyers, but even more importantly they were dealt their first serious setback since the attack on Pearl Harbor. Japanese expansion across the Pacific Ocean may have been checked by the use of better intelligence and carrier tactics borrowed from the enemy's own book (→31).

Britain signs 20-year pact with Russia

May 26. Britain and Russia tonight signed a 20-year treaty of alliance and mutual assistance. The two nations are now pledged to full collaboration in war and peace. A similar pact between the United States and Russia is in preparation. There will now be a speed-up in military supplies to the Soviet Union and it is stated that "full understanding" exists about the urgency of opening a second front in Europe as soon as possible.

In a cordial message to the Kremlin Mr Churchill declared: "From now on the three Great Powers will march step by step together." Mr Stalin replied: "The close collaboration of our countries after the war is ensured."

The treaty was negotiated during a six-day visit to London by Mr Molotov, the Soviet Foreign Minister. He stayed at Chequers, the Prime Minister's country residence. He was given the codename "Mr Brown" and motored daily to Downing Street for talks (→31).

Wearing their labels, evacuee children wait for the train to safety.

1942

JUNE

Su	Mo	Tu	We	Th	Fr	Sa
	1	2	3	4	5	6
7	8	9	10	11	12	13
14	15	16	17	18	19	20
21	22	23	24	25	26	27
28	29	30				

1. Mexico City: Mexico declares war on the Axis.

3. London: The government announces it will take over Britain's coal mines (→31/7).

4. Prague: Heydrich, "The Butcher of Moravia", dies from wounds sustained when his car was blown up.→

7. USSR: The Red Army launches a new offensive on Sevastopol (→29).

8. Australia: The Japanese shell Sydney and Newcastle (→7/8).

10. London: Economist John Maynard Keynes is made a peer.

13. Rumania: US bombers strike at the Rumanian oilfields (→13/9).

14. US: Premiere of the ballet "Rodeo" by Aaron Copland.

16. Mediterranean: British forces sink one Italian cruiser and two destroyers in the "Battle of the Convoys".

18. Washington: Churchill arrives for talks with Roosevelt.→

21. Libya: Tobruk falls to Rommel's troops; 25,000 Allied soldiers are believed taken prisoner (→25).

22. Vichy: Laval broadcasts to France and says: "I wish victory for Germany!" (→1/7).

25. Egypt: General Claude Auchinleck takes over command of the Eighth Army.→

27. Egypt: The Eighth Army abandons Mersa Matruh; the Germans claim they have taken 6,000 prisoners (→6/7).

28. France: All Jews over six years old in occupied France are told to wear the Star of David (→29).

29. USSR: The Germans launch an offensive at Kursk, south of Moscow (→19/7).

30. Germany: All remaining Jewish schools are closed (→2/9).

DEATH

4. German Nazi official Reinhard Heydrich, architect of the Final Solution (*7/3/1904).

Churchill and FDR talk in Washington

June 23. After weekend strategy talks in Washington Mr Churchill and President Roosevelt announced dramatically at 2am "our aim is the earliest maximum concentration of Allied war power upon the enemy". As usual the Prime Minister's hazardous journey to the United States was shrouded in secrecy.

Harry Hopkins, the President's closest adviser, said "If necessary, second, third and fourth fronts will be opened. America is not training three million troops to play tiddlywinks with Germany. We will pen the German army in a ring of steel."

Churchill: broadcasting defiance.

Eisenhower to lead US forces in Europe

June 25. Major-General Dwight Eisenhower has been given the command of all United States forces in Europe. His headquarters will be in London. Last night he said that the creation of the command was "a logical step in coordinating the efforts of Great Britain and the United States".

The move has given rise to speculation that an Allied landing in Europe will be attempted soon, despite the recent losses in Libya and Egypt (→22/7).

US routs Japan in Battle of Midway

June 7. The Japanese navy was forced to withdraw tonight after four days of savage fighting on the sea and in the air around Midway Island in the Pacific.

The US Admiral Chester Nimitz claimed to have sunk two or three Japanese aircraft carriers and damaged a dozen other warships, including three battleships, in one of the biggest naval encounters in history.

US chiefs hope the battle may mark the turning-point in the war in the Pacific as US dive-bombers, screaming down on the Japanese carriers, wrought death and destruction.

One Japanese sailor told how his carrier was taken by surprise by the American bombers, which made their task that much easier because the aircraft were still crowded together on the deck. Their torpedoes then wreaked havoc and tore more holes along the water-line. "Explosions of fuel and munitions devastated whole sections of the ship," he said.

The Commander-in-Chief of the US fleet, Admiral Ernest King, said American losses were "inconsiderable". He has said he believes the battle will alter the course of the war. However, the American destroyer Hammon was sunk by an enemy submarine, and there are reports still coming in that the aircraft carrier Yorktown had to be abandoned after it was hit. The Japanese attack began on June 3, the same day as their aircraft raided Dutch Harbour in the Aleutian Islands.

A destroyer stands by a stricken and listing carrier off Midway.

Fears in Egypt as advancing Germans close in on Cairo

June 25. With the Eighth Army routed by General Rommel's whirlwind armoured breakthrough, Axis forces are once again across the border into Egypt. Demoralised by the loss of Tobruk after a fierce land and air assault, our forces have retreated into Egypt back to the old defence lines at Sidi Barani. The naval base at Alexandria, and Cairo itself, are now threatened.

The loss of Tobruk four days ago was a bitter blow, coming hard on the heels of a disastrous defeat in the Western Desert. Panzer tanks crashed through the lines in the El Duda sector, completely outgunning British armour, which was just too weak to hold them off. Infantry followed up and the defences were completely swamped.

The enemy claims to have taken 25,000 prisoners and to have captured quantities of material, which he is now pressing into service against the Allies (→27).

Nazis have killed one million Jews

June 29. According to a report from a Polish underground group, which has just reached Jewish leaders in London, over 700,000 Jews have been murdered by the Nazis in Poland alone. In Rumania the death toll is 125,000, and in Holland, Belgium and France, Jews are being executed in large numbers daily. In all, over a million Jews have been killed, making this one of the worst massacres ever.

In Poland the Nazis have been using a special van fitted as a poison gas chamber. Up to ninety men, women and children are herded into such vans. In many villages all the Jewish men have been forced to dig their own graves, and have then been machine-gunned in a public square.

The Warsaw ghetto is effectively a concentration camp with 600,000 Jews living 19 to a room. Deaths from starvation and disease occur daily, and medical supplies have been denied to children under five and adults over 50 (→30).

Nazis slaughter Czech village in reprisal for Heydrich murder

June 10. Decked out in his Obergruppenfuehrer's uniform, Reinhard Heydrich, the Hangman of Europe and architect of the Final Solution, regularly rode around Prague in a sports car without a police motor-cycle escort. He believed the Czech people admired their Nazi Protector of Bohemia.

One morning last month, driving to his offices in the ancient Hradcin Castle, he slowed his car at the approach to a bridge. The next moment the car was blown to pieces by a bomb and Heydrich was lying in the road with a broken spine.

A few hours later Himmler flew in with a team of doctors, but Heydrich's wounds turned gangrenous. As death approached, Himmler plotted retribution.

Yesterday morning, trucks of the German security police surrounded a small village outside Prague. All the males, 173 men and boys, were shot, 198 women were taken to Ravensbruck concentration camp, and 98 children were sent to another concentration camp. The village of Lidice was then razed to the ground. Himmler is threatening to kill a few thousand more Czechs.

Heydrich's assassins were two members of the Free Czech forces who had parachuted from an RAF plane. They escaped after throwing their bombs and were given sanctuary in a church, but died later in a gun battle (→12/7).

Surrounded by 199 corpses, German soldiers survey their bloody revenge on the Czech village of Lidice.

1942

JULY

Su	Mo	Tu	We	Th	Fr	Sa
			1	2	3	4
5	6	7	8	9	10	11
12	13	14	15	16	17	18
19	20	21	22	23	24	25
26	27	28	29	30	31	

1. Vichy: Laval lets Germans enter unoccupied France to hunt for Resistance radio transmitters (→14).

4. Holland: German air bases are bombed by the US Air Force from British bases (→11).

7. Rome: The Vatican says women without stockings are now allowed into St. Peter's.

8. US: British-born actor Cary Grant marries Woolworth heiress Barbara Hutton a week after becoming a US citizen.

10. North Africa: Mussolini returns to Rome, having joined his troops for an expected triumphal entry into Cairo.

11. Danzig: Lancasters, the RAF's newest bombers, bomb U-boat yards in the city (→15).

12. US: A Mid-West town is officially named after the Czech town of Lidice, scene of last month's Nazi atrocity (→12/12/43).

14. London: De Gaulle's Free France forces are renamed "Fighting France" (→11/8).

14. Yugoslavia: The Germans slaughter 700 in reprisal for the killing of the Zagreb Gestapo chief (→16).

15. Germany: The RAF carries out its first daylight raid on the Ruhr industrial area.→

16. Yugoslavia: A new revolt against Nazi rule is reported (→14/9/43).

19. USSR: The Germans take Voroshilovgrad (→28).

22. London: Churchill rejects the US idea of a second front before the end of 1942 (17/8).

27. UK: Sweet rationing begins (→31).

28. USSR: The Russians begin the evacuation of Rostov.→

30. Ottawa: Canada's parliament votes for full conscription.

31. UK: Driving for pleasure is banned (→25/10).

BIRTH

16. Australian tennis player Margaret Court, nee Smith.

German advance is halted at El Alamein

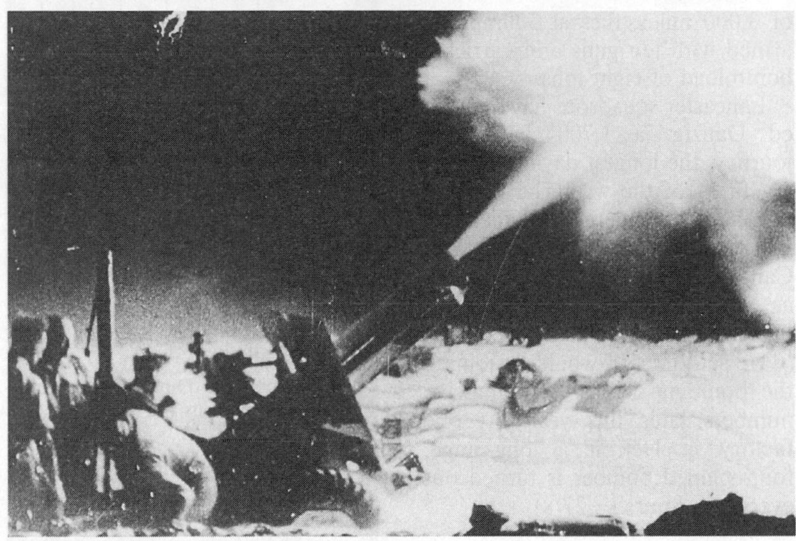

A British gun crew firing at the height of the night-long artillery barrage.

July 6. After a run of defeats, the Eighth Army has beaten back the great German desert offensive. For three days both sides threw everything they had into the battle, but today the British line at El Alamein has held.

For the first time, General Claude Auchinleck's forces have seized the initiative and struck back hard on the Axis flank; German troops are moving back westwards and attempting to regroup.

General Rommel's offensive, in which he used the massed armour of three divisions like a meat cleaver to hack a route into Egypt, rapidly advancing over 300 miles, seems to have been decisively halted. For three days it was touch and go, but then the familiar rhythm of a desert campaign began to assert itself; as the attacker outruns his supplies, the defender falls back on his reserves and grows stronger.

At El Alamein the pendulum began to swing back for the Allied forces. With fresh troops and new equipment they dominated the battlefield, their massed artillery wreaking havoc along the narrow front between El Alamein and the Qattara depression (→6/8).

Russian stronghold falls to Germans

July 1. Russia's great Black Sea fortress of Sevastopol has fallen to the Germans after a nine-month siege and the past few days of bitter street fighting. Following the loss of Kerch and Kharkov, it is the third great defeat for the Russians this summer.

The loss of Sevastopol was officially conceded in a Soviet communique, which then praised the "iron steadfastness" of the defenders and claimed the German army had suffered more than 300,000 killed or wounded. While this figure is impossible to confirm, it is clear that the defenders have rendered a great service to the hard-pressed Russian forces, holding up the German spring offensive by tying down General von Mannstein's 11th Army.

The final German-Rumanian offensive against the naval base was launched in early June, and the city was the daily target of hundreds of bombers. The Germans also used a giant siege gun. There has been terrible destruction, and high Russian casualties. Some 26,000 Russian wounded fell into German hands out of a force of about 100,000. During the last-ditch resistance, defenders fought wearing gas masks because of the appalling stench of unburied bodies in the July heat (→1/8).

Mistaken orders by Admiralty dooms Arctic convoy PQ-17

July 10. Four merchant ships sheltered in Archangel harbour, northern Russia, tonight – the battered remains of convoy PQ-17, originally 33 vessels strong, now destroyed by days of German attacks compounded by Admiralty stupidity.

The convoy sailed despite intelligence reports of a massive German fleet off northern Norway. Contrary to normal practice, orders on its movements came direct from London rather than the local commander. Confusion over reports of enemy movements led the First Sea Lord to believe that the Germans were about to attack. So, contrary to normal practice, he ordered the convoy to scatter. The enemy, which had been deterred by the navy, moved in to pick off the defenceless merchant ships.

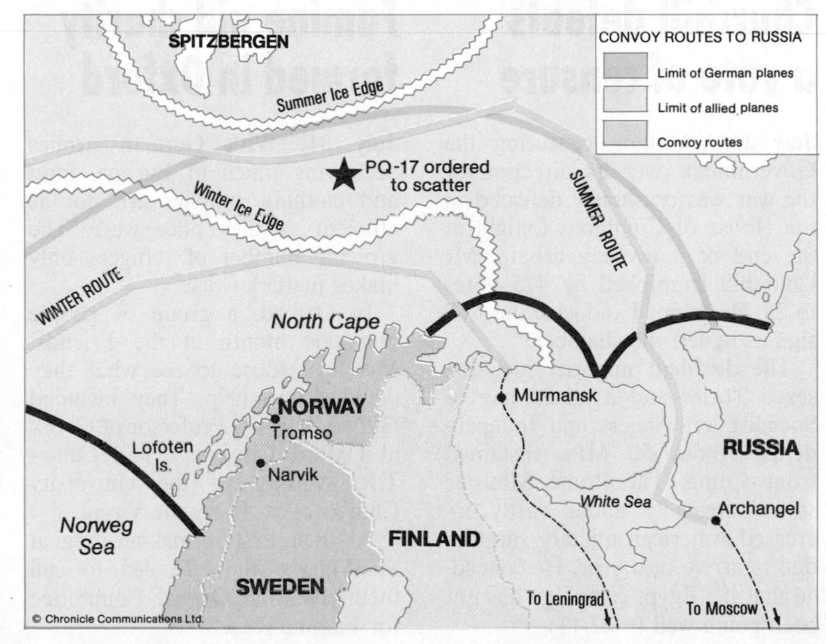

"Bomber" Harris will "scourge" Nazis

July 31. The German people have been told to expect devastating air raids "every night and every day, rain, blow or snow" by the RAF and the United States Air Force. The man who gave them this message, in a broadcast in German, is Air Marshal Sir Arthur Harris, who took over as chief of Bomber Command last February. He promised to "scourge the Third Reich from end to end".

Sir Arthur's grim warning comes in the wake of a succession of attacks on German industrial cities delivered by a type of heavy bomber newly taken off the secret list: the Avro Lancaster, which has a range of 3,000 miles, flies at 300mph, is armed with ten guns and carries a bomb load of eight tons.

Lancaster squadrons have attacked Danzig, a 1,700-mile return journey, the longest daylight bombing flight of the war. The plane is produced at underground factories in Britain, and also at factories in Canada, safe from the Luftwaffe – as Sir Arthur reminded the Germans.

He said the US would be joining the bombing offensive in massive numbers later this year. At one factory in Detroit a long-range, four-engined bomber is turned out every two hours (→27/8).

Bomber crews with a sample of the weapons destined for German cities.

Churchill defeats a vote of censure

July 2. A motion censuring the Government over its direction of the war was crushingly defeated in the House of Commons tonight at the end of a two-day debate. Mr Churchill triumphed by 475 votes to 25. He grinned and gave the "V" sign as he left the chamber.

The dissident minority included seven Tories and a mixed bag of Socialist left-wingers and Independents. About 30 MPs abstained from voting. The Prime Minister spoke doggedly about vastly increased American military supplies due to arrive next year. He conceded that the Egypt campaign has not been going well (→22/11).

Famine aid charity formed in Oxford

July 31. With German armies occupying much of Europe, food and clothing supplies are not as efficient as they once were. The growing number of refugees only makes matters worse.

In Oxford, a group of people met this month at the Friends' Meeting House to see what they could do to help. They included Gilbert Murray, Professor of Greek at Oxford University, and Canon T.R. Milford of the University Church of St. Mary the Virgin.

At their first formal meeting at St. Mary's, they decided to call themselves the Oxford Committee for Famine Relief.

1942

AUGUST

Su	Mo	Tu	We	Th	Fr	Sa
						1
2	3	4	5	6	7	8
9	10	11	12	13	14	15
16	17	18	19	20	21	22
23	24	25	26	27	28	29
30	31					

1. USSR: The Germans cut the railway line from Stalingrad to Krasnodar (→6).

4. London: The Duke of Kent names Roosevelt as his second son's godfather (→25).

5. Washington: Dutch Queen Wilhelmina visits the White House.

6. USSR: The Germans advance on Stalingrad from the south (→23).

7. Pacific: US Marines land on Guadalcanal in the Solomon Islands.→

11. London: The new Waterloo Bridge, built through the Blitz, is opened.

11. Vichy: Laval agrees that 150,000 workers will go to Germany in exchange for 50,000 French POWs (→15).

14. Malta: An Allied convoy arrives safely after surviving fierce attacks by Axis forces (→10/12/43).

15. Vichy: 5,000 Jews are arrested in unoccupied France (→26).

18. London: The government reveals that Churchill visited the Eighth Army in Egypt en route to Moscow (→30).

21. Pacific: US forces raid the Japanese-occupied Gilbert Islands (→23/9).

22. Rio de Janeiro: Brazil declares war on Germany and Italy after the sinking of several Brazilian ships.

23. USSR: The Germans cross the River Don, the last obstacle to an all-out assault on Stalingrad (→2/9).

25. France: Military service in the German Army becomes compulsory for men in the annexed province of Alsace.

26. France: A round-up of Jews begins in occupied France (→20/9).

26. London: The government lifts its ban on the Daily Worker.

27. Holland: British and US bombers attack Rotterdam (→10/9).

30. Egypt: Rommel launches a new offensive in Africa (→30/9).

Montgomery takes over the 8th Army

Aug 6. After the severe mauling administered to them by Rommel and his Afrika Korps, the British and Commonwealth forces in the Western Desert have been given new commanders. General Sir Harold Alexander becomes C-in-C Middle East and General Bernard Montgomery becomes commander of the Eighth Army.

Alexander and Montgomery both distinguished themselves in the Dunkirk evacuation. Montgomery, the aggressive type of soldier, is known to believe in spartan methods of training. Last June, as GOC South-East Command, he organised a ten-day endurance test, in which men marched and carried out battle exercises while living on iron rations only (→18).

Duke of Kent dies in a plane crash

The Duke of Kent: a Royal death.

Aug 25. The Duke of Kent, youngest brother of King George VI, was killed yesterday when a flying-boat crashed during a trip to Iceland. A pilot who had risked his life during visits to many bomb-hit British towns, the 39-year-old duke was the first Royal to die on active duty, although Buckingham Palace sources say his death was not due to enemy action. Only seven weeks ago he celebrated the birth of his third child (→3/3/43).

eavy Allied casualties in Dieppe raid

ug 19. The biggest Allied assault n Hitler's Fortress Europe was ompleted this afternoon after sev-ral thousand British, Canadian, merican and Free French troops ad been ashore at Dieppe for nine ours.

An ammunition dump, a six-gun attery, anti-aircraft battery and a adio-location station were destroy-d, but the communique issued to-ight by Admiral Lord Louis Iountbatten's Combined Operat-ons HQ admits that casualties are kely to have been heavy because of e "very fierce" fighting which apidly developed.

Furious air battles took place as e enemy attempted to break up e Allied aerial umbrella over the nd and sea forces. German air osses are put at 82 planes certainly estroyed, and another 100 probab-. The Allies lost 95 planes.

The Germans are claiming that e operation was an attempted full-cale invasion, which was repulsed ith heavy Allied losses. Accord-ng to a communique from the uehrer's HQ, over 300 invasion arges and 28 tanks were destroyed, and three destroyers, two motor torpedo boats and two transports were sunk. Over 1,500 prisoners, including 60 Canadian officers, were taken.

Statements issued by Mountbatten's HQ insist that the operation was not an invasion, but a planned reconnaissance in force intended to gain vital experience in mounting an amphibious attack against coastal positions, using large numbers of troops with heavy equipment (→10/10).

The faces of Dieppe survivors show just how fierce the fighting has been.

hurchill has surprise summit in Moscow

ug 17. Mr Churchill has been in Ioscow for four days. This drama-c secret was disclosed to a startled ation tonight. The Prime Minister as met Mr Stalin for the first time nd it is the first-ever visit by any ritish Prime Minister to Russia hile in office.

A British official said that the Kremlin talks, which senior American envoys also attended, will mark a turning-point in the war "for the complete destruction of Hitlerism". No details were given, but the opening of a second front in Europe was obviously discussed. Mr Churchill arrived in Moscow in a United States bomber (→7/4/43).

hurchill and Stalin, plus onlookers, in their secret Moscow talks.

Americans attack Solomon Islands

Aug 7. Fighting their way through what remained of Japanese opposition, elements of the US Marine Corps have today made a successful landing on the Solomon Islands. The Marine First Division landed on Florida Island at 8.00am, then moved on to establish a bridgehead on Guadalcanal within two hours. By nightfall they had moved inland about one mile.

Despite some counter-attacks from the Japanese defenders, the Marines encountered only light resistance. The speed and efficiency of their attacks were backed up by support from planes based on three US aircraft-carriers, the Wasp, the Saratoga and the Enterprise, all commanded by Rear-Admiral Frank Fletcher.

Once the Marines have consolidated their position they hope to reach and take over the airport that the Japanese have been building on Guadalcanal (→21).

Gandhi heads 50 Indians arrested in dawn raids

Aug 9. In a carefully planned dawn raid today, Bombay police arrested Mahatma Gandhi and fifty other leaders of the All-India Congress. The move came less than 12 hours after the Congress had passed by a 20-1 majority a "Quit India" resolution, and a few hours before a massive civil disobedience campaign was due to begin.

This morning's move followed consultations with the India Office and the War Cabinet in London. The British Government was worried about the effect the campaign might have on war production and the defence of India.

Later in the day the police were forced to fire on jeering, stone-throwing crowds in six different parts of Bombay. Five people were killed and around 20 wounded. Others, including 15 police, were hurt by stone-throwing. The biggest crowd, of 20,000, was at Shiva-Ji Park, where Gandhi was to have addressed a meeting.

Gandhi was in the bath when the police called. They allowed him to take his spinning-wheel with him to the place of detention, a large bungalow known as the Aga Khan Palace (→10/2/43).

Jane, the soldier's favourite strip, helped spot bombers for the Allies, even if her dog was born in Germany and she always seemed to have problems keeping her uniform in order.

1942

SEPTEMBER

Su	Mo	Tu	We	Th	Fr	Sa
		1	2	3	4	5
6	7	8	9	10	11	12
13	14	15	16	17	18	19
20	21	22	23	24	25	26
27	28	29	30			

1. Tokyo: Japanese foreign minister Shigenori Togo resigns "for personal reasons".

2. USSR: The Germans reach the Volga, north of Stalingrad (→6).

3. Madrid: Franco sacks the head of the Falangists and assumes full control of the government.

4. Belfast: Police clash with IRA sympathisers following the execution of a 19-year-old Republican (→6).

6. USSR: The Germans take the major Black Sea naval base of Novorossiisk (→8).

6. Belfast: Two policemen are shot dead by the IRA (→15/1/43).

8. Stalingrad: The Germans attack Soviet Army positions in the west of the city (→11).

10. Germany: The RAF drops 100,000 bombs on Dusseldorf in under an hour (→13).

11. Stalingrad: The Germans drive a wedge through the Soviet positions, threatening the city centre.→

13. Germany: The RAF carries out its 100th raid on Bremen (→23/10).

13. Rumania: The RAF and Soviet Air Force cause severe damage to Ploesti, centre of the country's oil industry (→1/8/43).

16. Madagascar: The British present the island's pro-Vichy Governor-General with armistice terms.→

20. Paris: The Germans murder 116 people in retaliation for increasing attacks on German officers (→2/10).

23. New Guinea: Australian and US forces under General MacArthur begin an offensive against the Japanese (→27).

23. Madagascar: The British capture the island's capital of Antananarivo.

27. New Guinea: The Japanese pull back in the face of the advancing Allies (→20/10).

30. Egypt: The Eighth Army seizes key German positions near El Alamein in a dawn raid (→23/10).

SS slaughter Jews in Warsaw ghetto

Sept 2. German SS troops have mounted a major operation in Warsaw and "cleared" its Jewish ghetto, killing some 50,000 people. The destruction of the walled enclave with grenades and flame throwers took place over several weeks. Jews removed from the ghetto were either executed by gassing or sent to concentration camps.

The operation met with some resistance, while other Jews committed suicide by staying in their burning homes or jumping from roofs. Heinrich Himmler last week ordered the liquidation of all Jewish ghettos by special groups of the SS. At the outbreak of the war there were more than eight million Jews in Europe, including two and a half million in Poland (→23/11).

Survivors of the ghetto penned ready for the concentration camps.

Record death toll as sub sinks POW ship

Sept 12. In an ironic twist to the submarine war 1,800 Italian prisoners of war were torpedoed by their German allies. The German U-boat number 156 scored a direct hit on the British transport ship Laconia, but it was only as the ship was going down that the Commander realised that most of the 3,000 people on board were Italians.

He immediately put out a distress call. By the time the German rescue ships had reached the scene the Americans had arrived as well. While the battle between them was going on the Laconia sank. Only 1,000 people of those on board are believed to have been saved.

This mistake, however, only underlines how successful the U-boat offensive has been. The Allies have lost five million tons of shipping so far this year, and in June alone a ship was going down every four hours. Worse still, there will be soon 400 new U-boats in service.

At least 1,800 prisoners of war are feared to have died on the Laconia.

Madagascar falls to British advance

Sept 18. British troops today occupied the chief port of Madagascar and are less than 75 miles away from the capital, Antananarivo. Vichy-French resistance seems to be crumbling. French troops retired from the port of Tamatave during the night after 20 British warships appeared off the coast. It took only a few shells from the navy to cause the town to surrender.

Yesterday Madagascar's Vichy Governor-General, M. Annet, refused the British armistice terms. The British attack on Madagascar began in May with the occupation of the naval base of Diego Suarez. Just over a week ago, 18 ships landed new forces at several points on the island.

The strategic importance of the island lies in the control of the 200 mile-wide Mozambique Channel. British convoys pass through it on the Cape route to the Middle East, Russia and India. The Allies have admitted to the sinking of three ships carrying vital war supplies there recently, and the Germans claim to have sunk many more.

In addition, Japanese submarines have been using the island as a refuelling base. British intelligence believes Japan was planning to seize the island to launch an attack on Africa (→23).

Stalingrad is defended house-by-house

A German soldier uses a flame-thrower in an attack.

Sept 18. Hitler's offensive against Stalingrad, "the city of Stalin" and a main centre of Soviet industrial strength, has developed into the greatest war of attrition the world has ever seen. The German offensive using 22 divisions, which opened so brilliantly has stuck fast, and a tremendous battle is being fought in the "Verdun on the Volga".

The German 6th Army under General von Paulus has driven the Russians back into the city, where they are holding on to nine miles of the river bank. With the river behind them, the Russians are clinging to every house and defending the ruins of every factory in the face of relentless dive-bombing attacks. German and Russian soldiers jeer at and curse each other across the street. They can hear each other breathing in the next room as they reload. Hand-to-hand fighting goes on among the rubble with knives and twisted steel.

The Soviet General Chuikov's tactics are to get as close to the enemy as possible. Although heavily outnumbered, the Russians are managing to regain at night the territory the Germans capture during the day with their superior firepower. Stalingrad is no longer a city, but an enormous cloud of burning, blinding smoke (→ 15).

1942

OCTOBER

Su	Mo	Tu	We	Th	Fr	Sa
				1	2	3
4	5	6	7	8	9	10
11	12	13	14	15	16	17
18	19	20	21	22	23	24
25	26	27	28	29	30	31

2. France: Ex-premier Edouard Herriot is arrested.→

3. Washington: President Roosevelt orders a freeze on wages, rents and farm prices (→29/11).

4. Berlin: Hitler says that occupied countries must make up the food shortage caused by the Allied blockade.

6. London: 16-year-old galley boy John Conroy wins the British Empire Medal for bravery on Russian convoys.

8. Norway: The state of emergency is extended and arrests and executions follow recent anti-German activity.

11. US: Boxer Joe Louis tells pressmen: "My fighting days are over."

15. Stalingrad: The Germans start a new offensive on Soviet positions (→29).

16. London: The Allies take the first steps towards setting up a commission to investigate war crimes.

20. Pacific: Two US destroyers are lost during fighting in the Solomon Islands (→1/1/43).

21. London: Field Marshal Jan Smuts of South Africa addresses both Houses of Parliament.

23. Genoa: Severe damage is caused in the RAF's biggest raid of the war on Italy (→25).

23. North Africa: The Eighth Army under Montgomery begins a big offensive along the coast at El Alamein.→

24. UK: A giant task force led by General Eisenhower leaves for North Africa (→24/12/43).

25. UK: The milk ration is cut to two and a half pints a week.→

25. Italy: The RAF conducts round-the-clock raids on the Milan-Genoa-Turin triangle (→31).

26. Berlin: Himmler becomes interior minister in a major purge of the Nazi Party and army high command.

29. Stalingrad: 60,000 Germans launch a fresh assault on Soviet positions, but advance only 50 yards (→26/11).

British chain POWs in tit-for-tat move against Germans

Oct 10. Britain and Germany have become embroiled in a vicious tit-for-tat reprisals race, with prisoners on both sides now being locked in chains.

The moves began when the Nazis chained up 2,500 Allied prisoners captured after the Dieppe raids, claiming it was a reprisal for the British Commandos chaining up the German prisoners, an action the War Office has fiercely denied ever happened. That move was then followed by both Britain and Canada chaining up German prisoners.

The German action has angered the Prime Minister, Winston Churchill. "In his fear and spite, Hitler turns upon the prisoners of war, who are in his camps and in his power. To show weakness of any kind to such a man is only to encourage further atrocities," he said.

Urgent talks are now going on with the Swiss Red Cross authorities in an effort to calm the situation and there does at least appear to be hope that the Germans will step down. Berlin Radio said tonight: "It is to be hoped that the High Command will once again be satisfied with the British explanation, however peculiar it may sound, as it is naturally extremely regrettable that innocent people should suffer for the barbarous and clumsy methods employed by the British military authorities."

Boosting the wartime economy.

Canterbury bombed in "reprisal" raid

Oct 31. Canterbury tonight became the latest of Britain's cathedral cities to suffer a fierce German "reprisal raid" – one week after the RAF had bombed the industrial city of Milan. The Luftwaffe attacked in two waves: a short but intensive attack at dusk followed by another raid at night. In all, 52 tons of bombs were dropped, causing extensive casualties. Although the cathedral grounds were ringed with fire, firemen managed to save the building itself by hurling incendiary bombs from the roof.

Earlier in the year the cathedral cities of Norwich, Exeter and York, as well as Georgian Bath, all suffered bombing attacks in what the Germans then termed the "Baedeker Raids" (→6/12).

Confectioners rent cardboard cakes

Oct 25. Cardboard "wedding cakes" with "icing" made from chalk are being offered for rent by confectioners in lieu of the real thing. "No person shall put sugar on the exterior of a cake after the same has been baked," says a Ministry of Food regulation.

Shop-bought cakes will not normally include more than 20 per cent of oils and no more than 30 per cent sugar, and confectioners are forbidden to add more than one covering of jam or chocolate (→6/11).

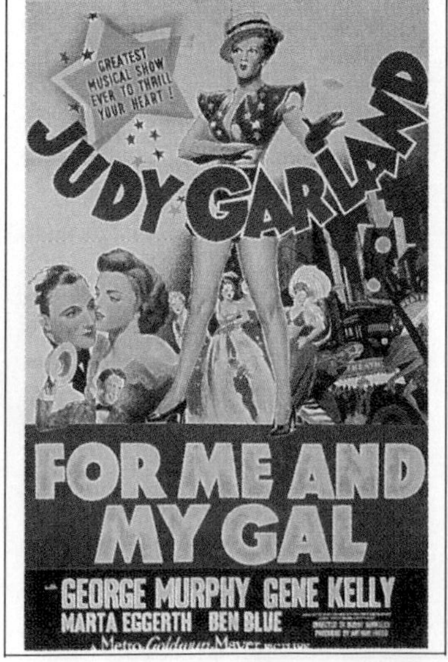

Monty scores triumph at El Alamein

An official photograph of the North African campaign: surrender in the desert as a sandstorm clouds the battlefield.

In command: General Montgomery poses before the battle commences.

Oct 30. The pale gold of a full moon cast a sheen over the desert as General Bernard Montgomery gave the fateful command; within the instant one thousand guns thundered into action. The battle of El Alamein had begun.

Under the shelter of the bombardment, and backed up by aerial bombing, the Eighth Army infantry attacked on two fronts. Line after line of steel-helmeted men with rifles at the ready, bayonets fixed, moved steadily forward. Behind them came the engineers, clearing the minefields, and the heavy armour ready to exploit any break in the enemy lines.

By dawn the infantry had punched deep into the Afrika Korps positions, but had not broken through. The German minefields and anti-tank batteries were five miles in depth.

The best estimates of the relative strengths of the opposing armies give Montgomery a two-to-one superiority in men and machines. Half the 100,000 Axis troops are Italians, for whom the Germans have so little respect that every Italian formation must be corseted with a German one. Montgomery's 200,000 men include Britons, Australians, New Zealanders, Indians, Frenchmen and Greeks.

Most of the Axis tanks are obsolete Italian machines, known as self-propelled coffins. The Eighth Army's tank force includes new American Shermans and self-propelled guns. In the air, the Axis has over 600 aircraft, but fewer than 300 are German. Montgomery can count on about 800 planes.

Because of Malta, now mightily reinforced with planes, upwards of 40 per cent of Axis shipping between Italy and North Africa is being sunk. The Afrika Korps is desperately short of supplies, petrol in particular.

When Montgomery struck, a week ago, Rommel was in a sanatorium in Germany. His place had been taken by a General Stumme, who came under fire when the battle opened and died of a heart attack. Rommel has rushed back from Germany to find the Eighth Army clawing into his defences, taking prisoners, and smashing his remaining panzers.

He threw in his reserves in a bid to retake his lost positions, but he has been stopped in his tracks by a storm of gunfire and bombing from the air. It is reckoned Rommel has only 90 tanks left, while the Eighth Army has almost 800. When he took over, Monty told the Eighth Army they would hit the Afrika Korps for six. They are doing just that (→3/11).

1942

NOVEMBER

Su	Mo	Tu	We	Th	Fr	Sa
1	2	3	4	5	6	7
8	9	10	11	12	13	14
15	16	17	18	19	20	21
22	23	24	25	26	27	28
29	30					

1. France: Strikes break out in Haute-Savoie in protest at Vichy's forced recruitment of labour for Germany (→8).

3. El Alamein: Montgomery breaks through Rommel's front line (→4).

3. Yugoslavia: The Bosnian capital of Bihacs falls to Tito's partisans.

4. El Alamein: Rommel is reported in full retreat; 9,000 Axis prisoners have been taken and 300 tanks destroyed (→8).

6. UK: The Church of England ends its rule forcing women to wear hats in church (→19).

8. Vichy: Pierre Laval severs diplomatic relations with the US (→9).

8. North Africa: Rommel retreats back into Libya.→

9. Vichy: Canada and Mexico break ties with the Laval regime.

9. Tunisia: The Germans land forces in Tunis.→

10. Algiers: Admiral Darlan, Vichy military chief in Algeria, orders an end to resistance to the Allies (→11).

11. France: The Germans and Italians begin the occupation of Vichy France.→

13. Libya: Tobruk is recaptured by the Allies (→15).

19. London: The government says it will boost house-building before the end of the war (→22/12).

22. London: Sir Stafford Cripps leaves the war cabinet, to be replaced by Herbert Morrison (→20/9/43).

23. West Africa: Darlan says pro-Vichy French West Africa is joining the Allies (→27).

23. Geneva: It is reported widely that the Nazis are systematically murdering Jews throughout Europe (→13/12).

29. US: Coffee rationing begins (→1/12).

BIRTH

15. Israeli pianist and conductor Daniel Barenboim.

Germans are routed near Stalingrad

At last the tide turns as Soviet troops drive back the German invaders.

Nov 26. The Soviet counterblow at Stalingrad has begun, with Russian troops smashing through German and Rumanian lines and threatening to destroy General von Paulus's 6th Army. Two Russian relief columns have reached the Don and joined up near Kalach, 40 miles west of Stalingrad, effectively tightening a noose around a quarter of a million German troops.

The Russians, who are advancing so fast that many of the Germans have been shot in the back trying to retreat, claim to have killed or taken prisoner 77,000 enemy soldiers. Many others, cut off from their supplies, are freezing to death on the steppes near the Don river.

The news of the counteroffensive has been received with immense joy and relief by General Chuikov's battered troops, hanging on grimly to a narrow strip of ruins in the city whose capture has obsessed Hitler. For all that, their position continues to be uncomfortable since ice-floes on the Volga now make it impossible to supply reinforcements of men and equipment.

Stalin forecast in his November 7 anniversary speech that "there would soon be a holiday in our streets". Russia's victory may mark a shift in the balance between the two forces (→20/12).

French scuttle fleet in Toulon harbour

Nov 27. The French fleet was scuttled by its crews six hours after German tanks rumbled into the great naval base of Toulon before dawn this morning. Munition dumps, oil tanks and all stores of value in the naval arsenal were blown up, along with the coastal batteries.

Some of the warships fired on the Germans to gain time for the ships to be sunk, and the captains of all the vessels stayed on their bridges till their ships went down. Many of these brave officers lost their lives.

Among the ships that were sunk was the battleship Provence and the two modern battle-cruisers, Dunkerque and Strasbourg. Two submarines escaped by slipping out to sea to join the Free French forces, but a third was lost when it struck a mine.

The destruction of the fleet has brought an end to the fear that it might fall into Axis hands and thus sway the balance of naval power.

General de Gaulle, broadcasting to his countrymen, spoke with pride of the sailors who "saw through the odious veil of lies which, since June 1940, hung before their eyes. In one brief instant they understood to what terrible end they had been led.

"France heard the guns of Toulon, the explosions, the desperate shots fired in a last stand. A tremor of pain, of pity, of rage shook the whole country. On to victory. There is no other road" (→24/12).

Church bells ring for El Alamein victory

Nov 15. Suddenly, the bells of victory were ringing out along the length and breadth of the land. From the towers of great cathedrals they sounded the nation's joy at the news from Egypt.

It was the first time that church bells had been sounded since the threat of German invasion in 1940. The whole world heard the sound of Britain's rejoicing through the BBC's overseas services.

After a peal rang out from bomb-shattered Coventry Cathedral – where the spire and bell-tower are still standing – an announcer asked: "Did you hear them in Occupied Europe? Did you hear them in Germany¿' In London the bells of St. Paul's Cathedral led the chorus of celebration by the few remaining City churches.

Many of the bellringers were volunteers from the services. A soldier and sailor joined the team in the belfry of St. Martin-in-the-Fields.

At St. Paul's the King and Queen watched a march-past of 1,000 civil defence workers from all parts of Britain, celebrating Civil Defence Day, while Dr Temple, the Archbishop of Canterbury, paid tribute to the courage of the country's firemen, anti-aircraft command, police and wardens (→8/12).

US troops lead landings in North Africa

Allied troops begin their campaign against the Vichy French in Africa.

Nov 7. The greatest armada of ships and aircraft ever assembled for a single operation today landed American troops in Vichy-French North Africa. As Rangers, Marines and infantry landed from the sea, paratroopers dropped on key airports in Morocco and Algeria. They had taken all their objectives by nightfall.

An Allied communique from London stated that lack of resistance at most points indicated that the French had no desire to oppose American entry. The only resistance came from naval and coastal defence guns; two small ships were lost in Oran harbour, and a torpedo attack disabled a transport ship.

The invasion was diplomatically delicate, but the American commander, Lieutenant-General Dwight Eisenhower, made it clear that France was not the enemy: "We come amongst you to repulse the cruel invaders who would remove for ever your rights ... to live your own lives in peace and security."

The surprise operation, which brought 140,000 American troops from the US, marks the beginning of a great Allied offensive that is intended to trap the Axis forces in a giant pincer movement. Fresh British divisions will soon join the Americans and move eastwards against the German Afrika Korps, already being driven west by the victorious British Eighth Army led by General Montgomery.

Rommel's army was last week decisively outfought and broken at the battle of El Alamein. General Ritter von Thoma, a senior commander, was among the 9,000 prisoners taken. In the battle, which began with a massive artillery barrage, more than 260 German and Italian tanks were destroyed. The Axis lost 300 aircraft in combat, and a similar number were destroyed on the ground (→ 10).

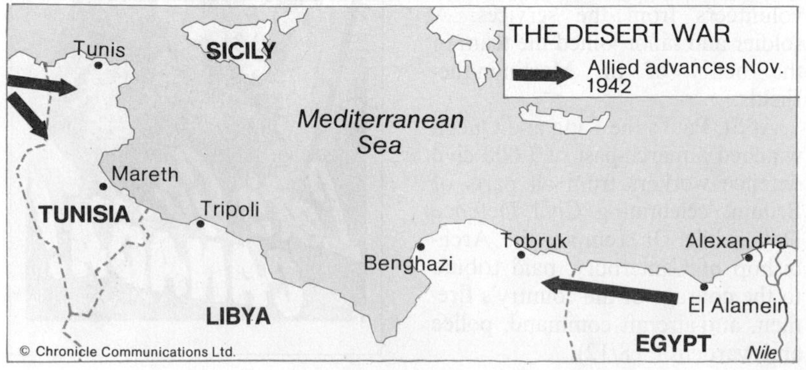

1942

DECEMBER

Su	Mo	Tu	We	Th	Fr	Sa
		1	2	3	4	5
6	7	8	9	10	11	12
13	14	15	16	17	18	19
20	21	22	23	24	25	26
27	28	29	30	31		

1. US: Petrol rationing begins (→ 7/2/43).

2. London: Foreign Secretary Anthony Eden says the United Nations hold the key to the new post-war world.

5. US: Two pilots power-dive the new Thunderbolt fighter at a record 725 mph.

6. Europe: The Allies' biggest daylight raid hits a number of targets in Holland (→ 20/1/43).

8. Tunisia: Axis troops withdraw almost to Tunis.

13. UK: British Jews hold a day of mourning for the victims of Nazi genocide (→ 17).

16. London: The TUC backs the Beveridge Report (→ 30).

20. USSR: The Soviet Army attacks German forces on the Don (→ 4/1/43).

22. London: The government says caterers may not raise charges for Christmas (12/4).

26. Algiers: Giraud takes over as French high-commissioner for North Africa (→ 30).

28. London: The Board of Education says the government plans to make school meals permanent.

28. Albania: 600 Italians are reported to have died in clashes with Albanian rebels (→ 7/6/43).

30. UK: British insurance companies attack the Beveridge Report (→ 18/2/43).

30. Algiers: Giraud arrests 12 prominent Vichy officials to prevent further assassinations (→ 7/1/43).

HITS OF 1942

This is the Army, Mr Jones.

White Christmas.

We'll meet again.

QUOTE OF THE YEAR

"It is not the end. It is not even the beginning of the end. But it is perhaps the end of the beginning."

Winston Churchill, Commons speech on the El Alamein victory, November 10, 1942.

Allies condemn the Nazis' atrocities

Dec 17. Nazi slaughter of the Jews was condemned today in a declaration read at the same time by governments in Moscow, Washington and London. The statement accused the Germans of "now carrying into effect Hitler's oft-repeated intention to exterminate the Jewish people in Europe". It warned that "those responsible for these crimes shall not escape retribution".

The statement was read to a hushed House of Commons by Anthony Eden, the Foreign Secretary. He read it in reply to a question by the Labour member for Nelson and Colne, Sydney Silverman, who is himself a Jew, about German plans to deport all Jews to Eastern Europe and to put them to death there (→ 28/1/43).

US breakthrough in atomic bomb test

Dec 2. Atomic energy became a reality today. At 3.45pm American physicists, led by Enrico Fermi, withdrew control rods from an atomic "pile" of uranium rods and graphite blocks in a disused squash court in Chicago University, allowing neutrons from the splitting of uranium atoms to split other uranium atoms in a sustained and controlled chain reaction.

The pile could make electricity; it will actually produce the atomic explosive, plutonium, for the top secret Manhattan project.

Vichy leader shot for backing Allies

Dec 24. Admiral Jean Francois Darlan, High Commissioner for French North Africa, was shot today in Algiers. He died on the way to hospital. General Henri Honore Giraud was named immediately to succeed him.

Darlan, once a supporter of Vichy's collaboration with Germany, changed sides after the Allied landings in North Africa. His assassin was a young Frenchman who considered he had betrayed Marshal Petain (→ 26).

Welfare state proposed

Dec 1. Britain's blueprint for post-war social security – what is already being referred to as the Welfare State – was revealed today in the Beveridge Report. The plan, designed by Sir William Beveridge and now being examined by the Government, is aimed at bringing the entire adult population into a comprehensive, compulsory insurance scheme, giving protection against sickness, unemployment, old age and support for families.

It is hailed as a charter for social security from the cradle to the grave, and is based on the principle of universal flat-rate contributions and benefits. From dawn the BBC has been telling Nazi-occupied Europe that here is the proof that, even in the midst of war, Britain is grappling with social problems. The Beveridge proposals envisage full and free medical and hospital treatment for everyone. There will be retirement pensions for all – rising to £2-a-week for husband and wife. Family allowances of eight shillings a week will be paid for children of school age after the first child.

There will be a single weekly contribution of four shillings and threepence a week for men workers, with an employer's contribution of half-a-crown. Rates for women will be lower. The means test for dole payments will generally be abolished.

The report acknowledges that a completely new structure of administration will be needed and it recommends the Government establish a Ministry of social Security to handle it (→16).

British push Japanese back in Burma

Allied troops search the Japanese dead during their advance in Burma.

Dec 19. Troops of the 14th Indian Division, commanded by Major General W.L. Lloyd, are today advancing down the Mayu Peninsula on the Bay of Bengal, pushing the Japanese back into Burma. First reports suggest that the combined British and Indian force is meeting little opposition as it thrusts down both sides of the Mayu Range.

The little port of Maungdaw has already been captured, while a patrol of the 1/15th Punjabis has made contact with the enemy at Buthdaung on the other side of the range. Progress remains slow because of the inhospitable terrain – mountains and jungle, criss-crossed by fast streams.

The object of this attack, which is the first real offensive undertaken by British forces since the Japanese conquest of Burma, would seem to be the occupation of the peninsula, followed by an assault on the strategically important Akyab Island. With Akyab and its port as a base, the whole of the Upper Arakan could be retaken, the first step to the freeing of Burma (→24/4).

Arts: Hollywood beaten at its own game as true war stories invade the reel world

War has taken over the cinema and, so far, British war films have put Hollywood's in the shade. The most popular, "In Which We Serve", written by **Noel Coward** with the help of **Lord Louis Mountbatten**, concerns the sinking of a destroyer, like Mountbatten's ship HMS Kelly, and the emotions of its crew struggling to survive. Coward plays the patrician Captain and the lower decks are represented by petty officer **Bernard Miles**, a cockney **John Mills** and a scared **Richard Attenborough**. It rouses audiences to cheering.

So, too, does "Desert Victory", a documentary shot during the ten-day battle of El Alamein by 20 cameramen of the Army Film Unit, five of whom were killed or badly hurt. The long crescendo of the artillery barrage before battle begins is the most awesome in cinema history. **Roy Boulting** edited over a million feet of film.

Other war documentaries are **Humphrey Jennings'** "Fires Were Started", a portrait of the Blitz with real firemen, and "Target For Tonight", a Wellington bomber's sortie over Germany, using its real crew. "The First of the Few" is the story of **R.J. Mitchell** (played and directed by **Leslie Howard**), the designer of the Spitfire on which Britain's survival depends.

By contrast, Hollywood's idea of Britain under fire seems rose-tinted in "Mrs Miniver", in which **Greer Garson** plays an undaunted English middle-class mother who rallies the loyal villagers. It collected six Oscars, and America gave Miss Garson a heroine's reception. **Mr Churchill** said the film was worth 100 warships as propaganda. Meanwhile Hollywood showed in "Casablanca" and "The Maltese Falcon" that at fiction it has no rivals.

The Proms, displaced by bombing to the Royal Albert Hall, heard Shostakovitch's Seventh Symphony, written in Leningrad under siege, whose score was sent out on microfilm in the diplomatic bag.

Noel Coward: playing at sailors.

Bogart and Bergman in Casablanca: "Here's looking at you, kid".

1943

JANUARY

Su	Mo	Tu	We	Th	Fr	Sa
					1	2
3	4	5	6	7	8	9
10	11	12	13	14	15	16
17	18	19	20	21	22	23
24	25	26	27	28	29	30
31						

1. Pacific: The Japanese begin to withdraw from Guadalcanal in the Solomon Islands (→ 10).

4. USSR: The Soviet Army claims it has captured the important German air and rail base of Chernyevskaya (→ 18).

7. Libya: General Philippe Leclerc's Free French troops take Oum-el-Araneb, main Axis base in south Libya (→ 13).

10. Pacific: A major US offensive begins on Guadalcanal (→ 2/2).

13. Libya: General Leclerc's Free French troops merge with the Eighth Army under Montgomery (→ 23).

13. London: The government says only standard grey or blue school uniforms will be allowed, to save on dye.

14. Morocco: Churchill, Roosevelt and de Gaulle open talks in Casablanca.→

15. Belfast: Four IRA prisoners escape from the Crumlin Road prison.

17. UK: Lloyd George receives hundreds of congratulatory telegrams on his 80th birthday.

18. Leningrad: The Soviet Army breaks the 16-month siege of the city (→ 21).

21. USSR: The Russians take Voroshilovsk (→ 31).

24. North Africa: The Eighth Army crosses the border into Tunisia in pursuit of the retreating Germans (→ 18/2).

27. Germany: The US Air Force bombs the German cities of Wilhelmshaven and Emden (→ 30).

28. Berlin: Hitler orders the mobilisation of the whole population from 16 to 65.

28. London: A document has come to light, allegedly from the German Army, blaming the SS for Nazi atrocities (→ 16/2).

30. Germany: Berlin is bombed twice today in the RAF's first daylight raid on the city (→ 31).

DEATH

24. British trade union leader John Burns (*20/10/1858).

Germans surrender in Stalingrad

The war's greatest battle comes to an end as the German siege of Stalingrad collapses into abject defeat.

Jan 31. After a week of heavy fighting in Stalingrad, Field Marshal von Paulus surrendered today to a Red Army lieutenant. A small pocket is still holding out in the northern part of the totally devastated city on the Volga, but what is arguably the greatest battle of the war so far is at an end.

Von Paulus was captured at his headquarters in the basement of what had been Stalingrad's biggest store. A young lieutenant who negotiated the surrender told him: "Well, that finishes it." Von Paulus replied with a "miserable look". Fifteen other generals surrendered at the same time.

It is thought that some 100,000 German troops have been killed, or have died from starvation and the cold, since Stalingrad was surrounded three weeks ago, and twice that number since the Germans were encircled in November.

The Field Marshal twice rejected a surrender ultimatum by the Russians, although his position was hopeless. German promises to fly 500 tons of food, fuel and ammunition a day to Stalingrad proved empty. Since December his troops have been eating what was left of the Rumanian cavalry division's horses, and rations were reduced to a few ounces of bread.

Finally, when he was on the point of surrendering, Hitler forbade it, and promoted him to Field Marshal because no German Marshal had yet surrendered. "Sixth Army will hold their positions to the last man," he instructed. Today the Field Marshal refused to obey orders any longer (→ 8/2).

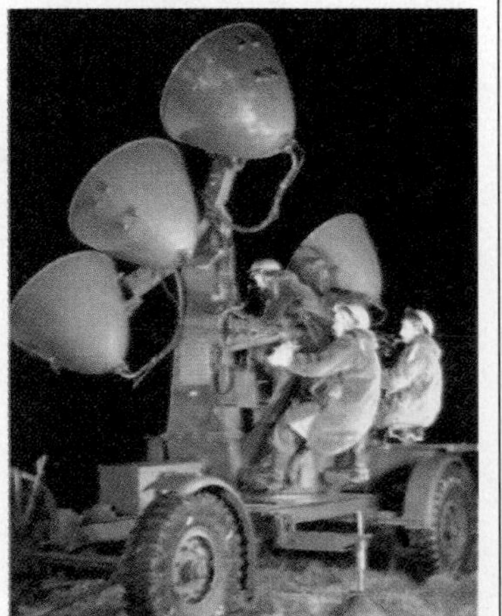

Women of the ATS setting their sights on German night-flyers on raid over southern England.

Conference of Allied powers in Casablanca

Jan 24. Churchill and Roosevelt called a press conference today to explain what they and their military chiefs have been talking about for the past ten days. It looks as though Italy will be the next to receive Allied attention after North Africa has been cleared of Axis forces in the next few weeks.

The American President said they were pledged to continue the war relentlessly until they had brought about the "unconditional surrender" of Germany, Italy and Japan. Mention of Italy caused some surprise, since word had gone round that the Italians, never very enthusiastic about the war anyway, might be encouraged to change sides if they were not expected to surrender unconditionally.

There was the usual trouble with the Free French leader, General de Gaulle, who still has not forgiven Churchill and Roosevelt for invading French North Africa without telling him in advance. He sees himself as the true representative of France, and objected to being asked to meet the French North African leader, General Henri Giraud, on French territory under Anglo-American auspices. Churchill says the heaviest cross he has to bear in this war is de Gaulle's Cross of Lorraine (→ 28/11).

Children killed when bomb hits school

Jan 21. Thirty-eight schoolgirls were killed in a raid yesterday as they waited to watch a performance of "A Midsummer Night's Dream". Six teachers at the Catford Central School for Girls also perished. The German planes were attacking south-east England in daylight, and experts believe they were testing British defences. The RAF are claiming 14 enemy planes destroyed.

Most of the dead children were aged between five and seven. One hundred and fifty children had stayed behind after school dinner to watch the play when German bombers swooped low, scoring a direct hit. Frantic parents joined Civil Defence workers in a rescue operation throughout the night. Gunner Charles Alford, aged 35, was on leave when he heard the bomb fall. He arrived at the school to see the body of his four-year-old daughter, Brenda, carried from the wreckage. He was still digging with others last night for his other daughter, Lorinda, aged seven.

One of the first Civil Defence workers to reach the scene said: "There were no balloons up and the air raid warning had not gone ... there was a terrific explosion and the school just fell to pieces. It seemed a never ending job passing the dead and injured children out from the wreckage."

Civil Defence workers and civilians search in vain among the rubble.

Allies take Tripoli as Germans retreat

Jan 23. Allied troops have captured Tripoli, the last remaining Italian-held city of Mussolini's African empire. It is exactly three months to the day from the start of the El Alamein offensive by the Eighth Army, supported by Free French troops from Chad.

The armoured cars of the 11th Hussars entered the town before dawn. By midday the Union Jack was flying in the main square, the Piazza Italia. General Montgomery, in his familiar Tank Corps beret and battledress, received the formal surrender (→ 24).

Berlin hit by first daytime bombing

Jan 31. RAF Mosquito fighter-bombers launched two daring daylight raids on Berlin just as the Reich Marshal, Hermann Goering, was to deliver a broadcast celebrating ten years of the Nazi regime.

The German defences were taken completely by surprise by the first daylight raid, for hardly any flak was encountered. One pilot said: "I imagine all the gunners were tuned in to Goering and that they had left their posts." A second attack was made in the afternoon, just as Propaganda Minister, Josef Goebbels, was broadcasting (→ 2/3).

1943

FEBRUARY

Su	Mo	Tu	We	Th	Fr	Sa
	1	2	3	4	5	6
7	8	9	10	11	12	13
14	15	16	17	18	19	20
21	22	23	24	25	26	27
28						

2. Stalingrad: The last pockets of German resistance surrender to the Russians.

2. Pacific: The Japanese launch a last-ditch effort to regain control of the Solomon Islands.→

4. Morocco: 24 Communist ex-deputies imprisoned by Vichy are released on the orders of Giraud (→ 31/5).

5. Rome: Mussolini sacks his son-in-law Count Nobile Ciano as foreign minister and assumes the post himself.

7. US: Shoes are to be rationed at three pairs a year to save shoe leather (→ 29/4).

8. USSR: The Soviet Army recaptures Kursk from the Germans (→ 14).

10. India: Gandhi begins a 21-day fast to protest at his imprisonment in Poona (→ 21).

12. UK: Lord Nuffield creates the Nuffield Foundation, Britain's biggest charitable trust, with a gift of £10 million.

14. USSR: Rostov and Voroshilovgrad fall to advancing Soviet troops.→

16. Berlin: Himmler decides to eliminate the Jewish ghetto in Warsaw (→ 19/4).

17. Washington: Madame Chiang Kai-shek arrives to address Congress (→ 22/11).

18. Tunisia: The Germans under Rommel start a new thrust, taking three towns in central Tunisia (→ 25).

19. Holland: The Germans seize Dutch works of art for Hitler's gallery in Linz, Austria.

21. India: Nationwide prayers are said for Gandhi, whose life is now in danger (→ 1/3).

23. London: Labour and the TUC decide to drop demands for the immediate implementation of the Beveridge Report for national unity (→ 9/4).

23. London: A Commons committee recommends equal war compensation payments for men and women.

25. Tunisia: Rommel is again in retreat as the Allies reverse his offensive.→

Japan abandons Solomon Islands

Feb 9. The hard-fought six-month battle for Guadalcanal in the Solomon Islands has been won by America. Frank Knox, the US Navy Secretary, said today that all enemy resistance on the island "has apparently ceased". This followed a surprise announcement from Tokyo that some Japanese forces were being withdrawn from both Guadalcanal and New Guinea.

Possession of the airstrip and harbour at Guadalcanal will provide first-rate facilities for US forces within range of Japan's base at Rabaul (→ 14/5).

Errol Flynn cleared of rape charges

Feb 6. A Los Angeles court today acquitted Errol Flynn, the film actor, of three rape charges. The jury of nine women and three men deliberated for 13 hours before giving their verdict.

Swashbuckling Flynn, 33, was accused of molesting 17-year-old Betty Hansen at a Bel Air dinner party last October. A week later, a night club entertainer, Peggy La Rue Satterlee, claimed Flynn had attacked her on board his yacht, Sirocco.

Flynn consistently denied having relations with either girl. His acquittal today received wild enthusiasm in the courtroom.

Doing a man's job in America.

Russians liberate cities held by the Nazis

Feb 16. The Red Army has made a start to driving the Germans from the Soviet Union, and in the space of ten days has liberated four key cities. Harried by bold and rapid Russian thrusts, the Germans are retreating in some confusion to the line from which they had started last summer. The front has moved over 200 miles west in less than three months.

Three cities recaptured by the Russians are Kursk, one of the bastions of last winter's German line, Rostov, the base for drive on the Caucasus, and Voroshilovgrad, another chief "hedgehog" position. Today it was the turn of Kharkov, a chief enemy base, to fall to the advancing Red Army.

Yet the picture is not all bleak for the Germans now that Hitler has been persuaded, after the lesson of Stalingrad, that he has to allow retreat. The 1st Panzer Army has withdrawn from the Caucasus through Rostov, and there are signs that some of the Russian armies are exhausted.

Field Marshal von Mannstein may be looking to catch the Russians on the hop, shorten his line and counter-attack, but the mood in Russia is exuberant; the press is using phrases like "Stalin's military genius" (→14/3).

Freed from her hiding place a Ukrainian girl is helped by the Red Army.

US drives back the Nazis in Tunisia

Feb 26. American troops are driving Rommel's Afrika Korps out of yet another North African stronghold, the Kasserine Pass in the mountains of central Tunisia. Only ten days ago they were crushed by German armour and dive-bombers. Today these are nowhere to be seen and the Nazis are in retreat.

Rommel is pulling back to establish new lines of defence to the south and east. He is nearly surrounded; the Eighth Army is advancing with its powerful Churchill tanks from the east, and another American force is ready to move in from Algeria in the west (→7/4).

Labour rebels want welfare state now

Feb 18. The Government today announced acceptance of the Beveridge Plan in principle. But it made many important reservations – particularly about cost and keeping private medical practice alongside a national health service. It gave no date for post-war implementation of the reforms.

There was an immediate explosion of rage from Labour MPs led by Aneurin Bevan and Emmanuel Shinwell. In the biggest revolt yet against the coalition leadership, 119 Labour backbenchers voted for early and full implementation of the new social security scheme (→23).

1943

MARCH

Su	Mo	Tu	We	Th	Fr	Sa
	1	2	3	4	5	6
7	8	9	10	11	12	13
14	15	16	17	18	19	20
21	22	23	24	25	26	27
28	29	30	31			

1. India: Gandhi ends his fast (→18/6).

2. Berlin: The RAF drops 900 tons of bombs on the city centre in half an hour (→6).

3. London: The King is reported to have a part-time war job in a munitions factory (→12/6).

6. Germany: The RAF pounds the Ruhr city of Essen.→

7. UK: The "Wings for Victory" savings campaign begins today.

9. Poland: Seven villages are reported razed and their males massacred in reprisal for attacks on Germans (→13/4).

10. France: Unrest breaks out over forced labour conscription for Germany; there are Resistance attacks in Brest (→30).

14. USSR: The Germans re-occupy Kharkhov in a counter-offensive against the Russians (→13/7).

18. South America: Pro-Vichy French Guyana joins the Free French (→18).

18. Algiers: Giraud abolishes Vichy's anti-Semitic laws (→26).

20. UK: In a poll held by Equity, British actors vote three to one in favour of opening theatres on Sundays.

24. London: Cabinet secretary Lord Maurice Hankey calls the anti-U-boat campaign "our greatest failure" (→24/6).

26. France: The Germans arrest all Britons in Vichy France, fearing an Allied invasion (→5/4).

27. Washington: Roosevelt proposes putting Indochina under Allied control rather than returning it to France.

27. Germany: Saboteurs blow up key bridges on the River Oder in the eastern city of Frankfurt.

30. France: The RAF drop French Resistance leader Jean Moulin into German-occupied territory (→21/6).

DEATH

28. Russian composer Sergei Rachmaninov (*1/4/1873).→

Bombing raids aim to smash heart out of German industry

March 12. A picture of fearful devastation in Germany's industrial heartland, the Ruhr, was presented to the House of Commons yesterday by Sir Archibald Sinclair, the Air Minister. He said some 2,000 factories have been destroyed or badly damaged, a million tons of steel have been lost, coal output is down by 20 per cent, and almost 400 acres of Dusseldorf have been laid waste.

In what is being spoken of as the Battle of the Ruhr, Essen has been hit by a 1,000-ton raid that smashed over 30 engineering shops. One bomb produced an explosion that sent a sheet of yellow-orange flame shooting 1,000 feet into the air.

Berlin has also come in for a pounding. Incendiaries as well as high explosives were dropped, and RAF pilots said the fires were visible 200 miles away.

Goebbels has given the German papers orders to admit the severity of the bombings, and the destruction of dwellings, while insisting that damage to factories is not affecting war production. According to reports from Berlin by neutral correspondents, the authorities now acknowledge that considerable self-control is necessary for the population, both during and after bombing raids (→1/4).

Victory may be in sight, but there's no time to relax yet and there's plenty of digging to do.

178 die in air raid ;helter accident

Iarch 3. A middle-aged woman, :arrying her baby, tripped and fell ıs she went down a flight of steps o the safety of a tube shelter. An :lderly man fell over her. Within econds, 178 people were crushed o death in one of the war's worst :ivilian disasters.

It happened at the large Bethnal Green shelter soon after the alert or a daylight raid. A Ministry statement said: "Those coming in from he street could not see exactly vhat had taken place and continu:d to press down the steps. There vere hundreds of people crushed ogether on top of one another, cov:ring the lower steps and landing, :ompletely blocking the stairvays." The woman survived. Her ɔaby died.

Rachmaninov, the great virtuoso, dies

Sergei Rachmaninov, russian pianist, conductor and composer: a romantic musician.

Iarch 28. Sergei Rachmaninov lied at his home in Beverly Hills oday, aged 69. Already a worldamous virtuoso, he left Russia for good in 1917, but most of his bestoved music was written there, including his two great piano con:ertos, Nos. Two and Three, and ıis Preludes. In America, he proluced a fourth concerto and the 'Rhapsody on a Theme of Paganini". His last work was his 'Symphonic Dances" (1940).

1943

APRIL

Su	Mo	Tu	We	Th	Fr	Sa
				1	2	3
4	5	6	7	8	9	10
11	12	13	14	15	16	17
18	19	20	21	22	23	24
25	26	27	28	29	30	

1. London: The RAF presents Churchill with wings on its 25th Anniversary; he says "you carry doom to tyrants." (→15).

5. France: The Vichy regime hands Daladier, Blum, Reynaud and Mandel over to the Germans.

7. Salzburg: Hitler and Mussolini conclude four days of talks on North Africa (→14).

7. Holland: The Germans are reported to be reinforcing Dutch coastal defences, anticipating an invasion in May (→9/5).

9. London: The government says it will introduce a unified "national health service" (→24/6).

12. London: The budget raises the price of drinks and puts a 100 per cent tax on luxuries (→3/5).

14. Tunis: Rommel evacuates his troops as the Allies launch their final thrust (→28).

15. Germany: The RAF drop 8,000lb. "Blockbuster" and 4,000lb. "Factory-smasher" bombs on Stuttgart (→21).

16. Mexico City: Jacques Monard gets 20 years for killing Trotsky, including six months for carrying a pick.

21. Germany: The RAF bombs Berlin and three other cities to mark Hitler's 54th birthday (→29).

28. Tunisia: The Allies are now reported to be within 20 miles of Tunis (→7/5).

29. Washington: Roosevelt orders miners to continue working as a coal strike threatens (→1/5).

29. Baltic: The RAF carries out its largest-scale minelaying operation of the war (→17/5).

30. London: The Polish government withdraws its request for a Red Cross investigation into Katyn (→7/12).

DEATH

30. British Socialist and author Beatrice Webb, Lady Passfield (*22/1/1858).

Mass grave of 4,000 Polish officers found

April 26. The Germans have accidentally uncovered a mass grave of 4,000 Polish officers in a forest at Katyn, near the Soviet city of Smolensk, and are insisting they were murdered by the Russians. The macabre discovery is giving rise to intense friction between the Soviet Union and the Polish Government-in-exile in London, as well as between Stalin and the Allies.

The Poles were among some 15,000 officers who were taken prisoner or deported by the Russians after Germany and Russia "partitioned" Poland in 1939. The Poles in London have been uneasy ever since about the fate of the officers and had raised the issue with the Russians several times without being given a satisfactory answer.

A German inquiry has claimed that the Polish officers were shot by the Russian NKVD security police in 1940 – before the offensive against Russia. They claim the Russians tried to cover up their crime by using captured German ammunition. The London Poles are giving some credence to the German version by asking for a neutral investigation of the Katyn graves.

What can be seen as an obscure incident has produced a furious reaction from the Russians and a first-class diplomatic row. Stalin has severed relations with the Polish Government-in-exile, and is preparing to set up a Polish administration friendly to Russia (→30).

Plan for a world economy published

April 7. The Keynes Plan for postwar financial disarmament and an international bank to nurture economic co-operation was published by the government today. It is intended for discussion by the proposed United Nations organisation.

The highly technical scheme drawn up by John Maynard Keynes, inventor of most modern economics and adviser to successive British governments, has already been informally discussed and cautiously welcomed by United States experts. Its central proposal is for a currency union based on international bank-money. There would be an international monetary fund capable of helping any nation out of temporary difficulties when its currency is under strain.

In return, that nation would have to adopt policies aimed at restoring equilibrium. Mr Keynes sees such arrangements as a means of avoiding world economic slumps. The government is not yet committed to backing them. President Roosevelt has said he wants a new international monetary deal so long as it is not philanthropy at American expense.

Let the bells ring out, says Churchill

April 20. With the threat of invasion long since lifted, the country's church bells can be rung regularly once again, the Prime Minister told a delighted House of Commons yesterday. "We have reached the conclusion that existing orders can now be relaxed and the church bells can be rung on Sundays and other special days in the ordinary way to summon worshippers to church."

The Archbishop of York, among others, has been campaigning for the restoration of church bells – for so long the warning of impending invasion. And so the bells of his York Minster will be broadcast to the nation on Easter Sunday.

Utility design, ration-book fabric but fashion won't give in no matter how little is in the shops.

Jews chased through Warsaw sewers

A Jewish child stands bewildered as Hitler's SS go about their systematic massacre of the Warsaw ghetto.

April 19. An SS officer with a fancy for shooting Greeks has been transferred from Athens to Warsaw and given the task of crushing an unprecedented uprising of Jews in the city ghetto.

General Juergen Stroop has recruited some 2,000 troops from local garrisons and sent them into the ghetto as though into battle, wearing steel helmets, riding armoured cars, and armed with machine guns, grenade launchers, mortars and flame-throwers.

A pall of black smoke hangs over Warsaw. When the gates of the ghetto are opened to allow more troops in, you can get a glimpse of Germans and Polish police standing guard, while somewhere beyond the fire-blackened houses the rattle of machine-gun fire is punctuated by single heavier explosions. Then comes the crash of dynamite going off, followed by a rush of smoke and dust and the grinding rumble of a collapsing building.

More soldiers appear, in trucks and wearing dark goggles. Unlike the SS men, they are wearing drab brown uniforms and they are armed only with rifles and bayonets. Most of them are Ukrainians who once served in the Soviet army.

Himmler has promised Stroop that, if the massacre is carried out with speed and efficiency, campaign honours will be awarded to those taking part. Stroop is sending daily reports to Himmler, and has told him the whole business should be cleared up in three or four days.

When the Nazis set up the Warsaw ghetto in 1940, it held more than 300,000 Jews. Two years later most of them had either died of starvation or disease, or been "resettled", the SS term for being carted off to an extermination camp.

Not even the methodical Germans, with their appetite for detail, can be sure how many Jews remain. People have been dying every day, dropping in their tracks. Bodies are wrapped in sheets of newspaper and tossed in heaps on to a truck. Probably 50,000 to 60,000 Jews remain. They have been seized with a desperate courage. Somehow they have got hold of a few guns, and they are standing up to the massive firepower of Stroop's squads.

This morning Poles were running to and fro, pointing to the high ghetto wall topped with broken glass and barbed wire and calling out to one another: "It's happened. The Jews have started fighting." Everybody had taken it for granted that these last few Jews would go quietly, as the millions of others had done. But no, not these Jews. "Listen to the shooting and the bombs. Look at the fires."

As the German troops advance relentlessly through the warren of dilapidated buildings, killing and dynamiting, the Jews, men and women, have retreated into the sewers, still fighting.

Stroop's task is proving a good deal tougher than he reckoned. How can it have happened that these "sub-humans and natural cowards", as he calls them, are able to cause so much trouble for the Master Race? It seems that Stroop has not yet found the answer.

In Berlin, Goebbels has been told of what he calls "a truly grotesque situation" in Warsaw. He says the Jews tried to escape through underground passages, whereupon the passages were flooded. "It is high time all the Jews were evacuated," he sniffs (→ 19/6).

1943

MAY

Su	Mo	Tu	We	Th	Fr	Sa
						1
2	3	4	5	6	7	8
9	10	11	12	13	14	15
16	17	18	19	20	21	22
23	24	25	26	27	28	29
30	31					

1. US: Miners begin a strike in protest at wage freezes (→ 2).

2. Washington: The coal strike is called off minutes before Roosevelt signs an order to seize mines.

4. London: Polish leader General Sikorski tells Poles in a broadcast that they must remain friendly to the USSR (→ 5).

5. Moscow: Stalin states his desire for a strong, free Poland after the war (→ 4/7).

5. Rome: Mussolini says: "many millions of Italians are suffering from the African sickness" (→ 10).

7. Tunis: The Allies enter the Tunisian capital to wild acclaim from the population.→

9. Holland: The Germans declare martial law in anticipation of an Allied invasion.

10. Italy: The Allies bomb Sicily (→ 13).

11. Washington: Churchill arrives for talks with Roosevelt.→

13. Italy: A state of emergency is declared in the south of the country amid fears of Allied invasion (→ 20).

14. Australia: 299 are feared dead when a Japanese submarine torpedoes a hospital ship without warning (→ 17/7).

15. UK: Ascot holds its first wartime race meeting.

18. Germany: A state of emergency is declared in the Ruhr area following the RAF's "Dambuster" raid (→ 24).

20. Italy: Allied planes attack Italian airfields, destroying over 100 aircraft (→ 25).

24. Germany: 2,000 tons of bombs are dropped on Dortmund in the RAF's heaviest air raid to date (→ 24/7).

25. Washington: Churchill and Roosevelt end their talks (→ 10/8).

25. Italy: The US Air Force bombs Sardinia (→ 9/6).

31. Algiers: Generals de Gaulle and Giraud set up a seven-member French "provisional government" (→ 1/6).

Ruhr is devastated by "dambusters"

May 17. Tonight walls of water swept down the Ruhr and Eder valleys in Germany, destroying everything before them, after the RAF had attacked and breached two huge dams.

The raids, by specially fitted Lancaster bombers using new "bouncing" bombs, designed to penetrate the dams at their most vital point, were planned to cripple Germany's vital industrial heartland.

The bombers of 617 Squadron, led by Wing-Commander Guy Gibson, flew in low and dropped their specially designed bombs, which skimmed over the surface of the water and then sank before exploding at the foot of the dam.

A 100-yard breach was opened up in the Mohne Dam. The Eder Dam, the largest in Europe, which normally holds back a 17-mile reservoir, was also destroyed and its 18,000 hp power station was wrecked.

Reports say 1,500 people have been killed so far. A flood tide swept through the town of Mulheim on the Ruhr, swamping coal mines and ironworks and forcing most inhabitants to flee to higher ground.

The banks of the river Ruhr were broken, and one flood reached five miles from the river's normal course. It crashed through the huge industrial city of Dortmund, filling its air raid shelters and causing incalculable damage. More than 40 per cent of the city's 543,000 inhabitants were driven from their homes.

The Germans admit the raids caused massive damage: "Severe damage was done and very serious casualties suffered by the civilian population." (→ 18)

A massive breach gapes in the Mohne Dam as tons of water pour through.

Churchill makes historic address to joint session of Congress

May 19. Speaking with easy familiarity and bubbling confidence, Mr Churchill delivered another historic speech at a joint session of the United States Congress in Washington tonight. While he spoke bells pealed at St. Paul's in London as the King led national thanksgiving there for the Allied victory in Tunisia.

The Prime Minister, introduced by Sam Rayburn, Speaker of the House, as "one of the outstanding figures on all the earth", told the Americans: "We will wage war at your side against Japan while there is breath in our bodies and while blood flows in our veins." He pledged RAF help to reduce Japanese cities to ashes.

Mr Churchill reviewed the progress of the war with enthusiasm and was frequently cheered. His speech came over the wireless to this country with remarkable clarity. He has been staying with President Roosevelt at the White House for a week now. It is their fifth meeting since they drafted the Atlantic Charter in 1941. Their heart-to-heart exchanges are the mainspring of Allied strategy planning. There is talk about the two statesmen meeting Mr Stalin later this year. In the meantime the White House discussions, which were attended by the top British and American military chiefs, have been about division of effort between Europe and the Far East.

It has not been disclosed how Mr Churchill travelled to Washington this time. The President rebuked journalists for indulging in risky speculation about this (→ 25).

Mr Churchill meets American sailors during his talks with the President.

Victorious Allies capture 110,000 Germans in Africa

May 12. All organised resistance by German and Italian troops in North Africa ceased tonight. General Sixt von Arnim, the German C-in-C, was captured in Cap Bon, together with his entire staff, by a reconnaisance patrol of the British First Army. He promptly issued orders for surrender.

The only unit to hold out a little longer was the 90th Light Division, which continued fighting in the mountains. They refused one demand for surrender by General Freyberg, commander of the New Zealand division with which they had often clashed, but then finally agreed to give in.

The Allied forces have taken 110,000 Germans prisoner, more than the Russians captured at Stalingrad, and 40,000 Italians. Deprived of air support, though with ample supplies, they simply crumbled in the Cap Bon peninsula. So tight was the blockade of Tunisia that only 1,000 men escaped by sea (→ 13).

All women must do part-time war work

May 3. A new government order is to make part-time war work compulsory for women of 18 to 45. The latest call-up move by the Labour Minister, Ernest Bevin, is aimed at those who have no domestic responsibilities but so far have been slow to "do their bit".

The number of part-time workers (defined as up to 30 hours a week) under the present voluntary system is 600,000, most of them women, but thousands more are needed in shops and factories as the demand for fighting men grows.

Each order will last from a minimum of three weeks to a maximum of around six months. During the specified period, bosses may not sack workers and workers may not leave, other than in exceptional circumstances. Absenteeism will be an offence, but government officials will not direct anyone to work where wages and conditions are below standard (→ 17/5).

Tide begins to turn in the U-boat war

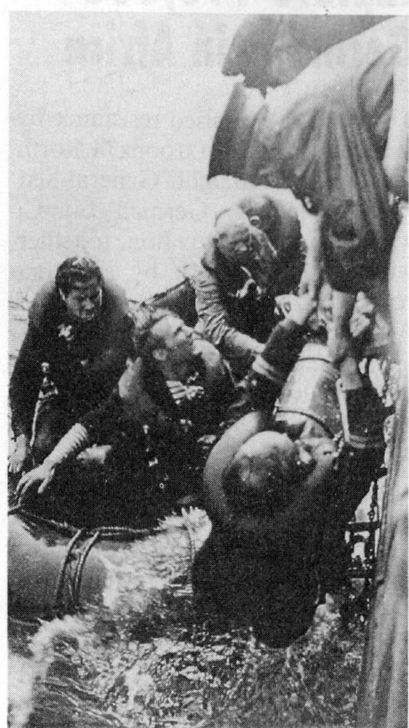

U-boat sailors saved from death.

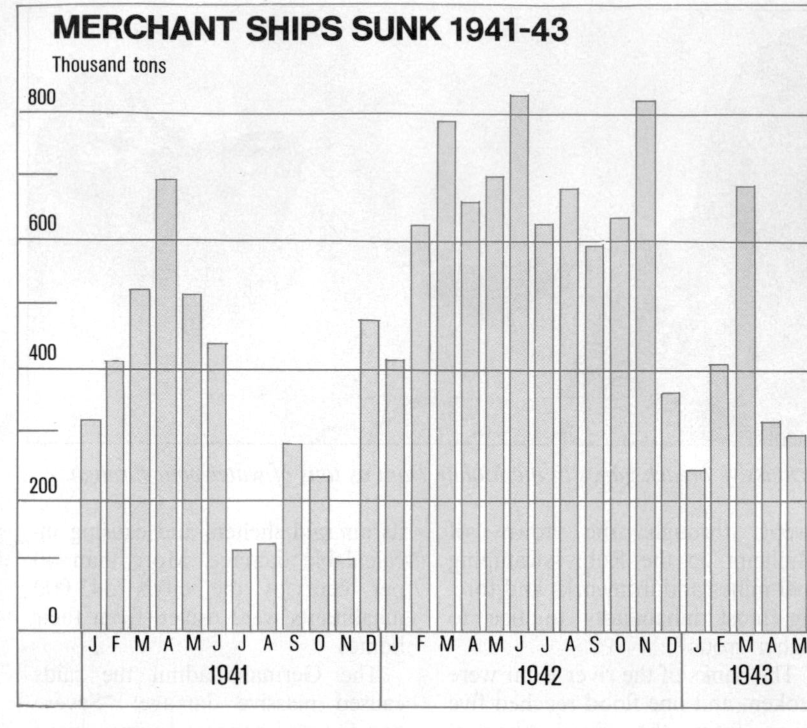

May 24. New techniques are dramatically turning the tide in the Allies' favour in the Atlantic war. At last the U-boats are on the run.

The German High Command calculated some time ago that, if 800,000 tons of Allied shipping could be sunk each month, then the war against the Axis would be doomed. Throughout all last year they maintained a crippling series of attacks on Allied ships, claiming nearly 650,000 tons a month.

In March this year U-boats sank 627,000 tons of Allied shipping in the Atlantic, but it was the last month of success. In April they sank 245,000 tons, but this month only 18,000 tons have been lost, with 17 U-boats sunk. For the first time the balance favours the Allies.

The key to this turn-around appears to have been the release of Allied escort ships and aircraft carriers from North Africa. When these were brought into the Atlantic, it was the first time that the Allies had aircraft on the scene capable of hunting U-boats to the end. Before, the subs had managed to reap their grim harvest out of range of air cover.

Scientific developments have also helped to spot more U-boats than previously. A new radar system is capable of detecting much smaller objects than before, and Asdic sets, which find submarines under water with sound waves, have also helped. In addition, there are depth charges, which explode at shallow depths, and a mortar system which fires 24 bombs around a U-boat at once.

Last month eight U-boats were lost in one attack on a convoy off Greenland, an area previously treacherous for Allied shipping.

Intelligence gathering has improved, too. The Navy can pick up U-boat radio signals and divert convoys away from the killer packs. The change in fortune is thought to be hitting U-boat crews' morale. There are signs that fewer of the craft dare venture out into the Atlantic now (→ 29).

Comintern dropped to soothe the Allies

May 15. Joseph Stalin has dissolved the Comintern, the international Communist organisation, as a gesture to impress Britain and America. A statement said the organisation, set up in 1919 to promote communism and conquer the world for international socialism, was out of date. The move follows Stalin's May Day speech, which was full of friendly words for the Western Allies.

Clothes rationing puts money in pockets

May 17. Clothes rationing has saved the country £600 million so far, according to a Board of Trade survey out today. The average family of four now spends around £30 a year on clothing – £7.10s a head – compared to £20 a head prewar. Rationing, which will have been in force for two years in June, has saved 500,000 tons of shipping and released thousands of workers for war factories, the report adds. Rationing is expected to be further reduced in September (→ 30/6).

Do-it-yourself haute couture.

1943

JUNE

Su	Mo	Tu	We	Th	Fr	Sa
		1	2	3	4	5
6	7	8	9	10	11	12
13	14	15	16	17	18	19
20	21	22	23	24	25	26
27	28	29	30			

1. Algiers: De Gaulle insists on the dismissal of all officials who collaborated with the Vichy regime (→ 4).

3. US: A United Nations Food Conference ends with a call for fairer distribution of food in the post-war world.

4. Buenos Aires: A military coup ousts President Ramon Castillo (→ 5).

4. Algiers: General Giraud is appointed commander-in-chief of Free French forces (→ 6).

5. Buenos Aires: A military junta is formed under President Arturo Rawson; new labour minister is Juan Peron.

7. Albania: Italian troops start to withdraw (→ 28/8).

9. Mediterranean: The Allies begin an assault on the Italian island of Pantelleria.→

12. Mediterranean: The Italian island of Lampedusa falls to the Allies (→ 10/7).

12. Algiers: King George VI arrives to meet the Allies (→ 25).

18. India: General Wavell is appointed Viceroy of India, with General Auchinleck as commander-in-chief.

19. Berlin: Goebbels declares the city "free of Jews" (→ 16/8).

21. France: Resistance leader Jean Moulin is arrested (→ 8/7).

24. UK: The Engineering Union calls for the introduction of "pay-as-you-earn" taxation (→ 7/7).

25. Eire: De Valera loses his majority but remains head of largest single party after a general election.

25. London: The King returns from his visit to Allied forces in North Africa.

29. Atlantic: U-boats are reported to have been withdrawn to counter an Allied invasion of Europe (→ 1/10).

30. London: The government says signposts can be re-erected in most rural areas (→ 2/7).

DEATH

1. British actor and director Leslie Howard (*3/4/1893).→

Leslie Howard on board missing plane

June 1. Leslie Howard, the film actor and director, is one of the 13 passengers missing on a civil airliner shot down by the Germans in the Bay of Biscay on its way from Lisbon to Southern Ireland. It signalled "Enemy aircraft attacking."

He had been giving lectures in Spain, as a result of which 900 Spanish cinemas agreed to show British war films. He will be mourned as the cinema's foremost English gentleman-romantic.

He gave memorable performances as Ashley Wilkes in "Gone With The Wind", as Professor Higgins in "Pygmalion", and in his own films, "Pimpernel Smith" and "The First of the Few". He was 50.

Leslie Howard: one among many.

Assault begins on Europe's underbelly

June 11. Allied shock troops today occupied the Axis stronghold on the Mediterranean island of Pantelleria – and introduced a new tactic to modern warfare. It is the first time that a major fortress has been conquered from the air without the help of land forces.

The island, between Tunisia and Sicily, had been battered by Allied bombers continuously for 13 days. British troops and tanks did not land until noon today, 20 minutes after the garrison commander surrendered (→12).

De Gaulle pledges to restore freedom

June 6. In a broadcast on Algiers Radio tonight the new French Committee of Liberation pledged itself to restore "all French liberties, the laws of the Republic and the Republican regime". It promised to destroy completely "the arbitrary powers" imposed by the Vichy government. The Committee, with Generals de Gaulle and Giraud as joint Presidents, declared itself last Thursday as supreme power over all French territory not held by the enemy and over all the Free French forces (→26/8).

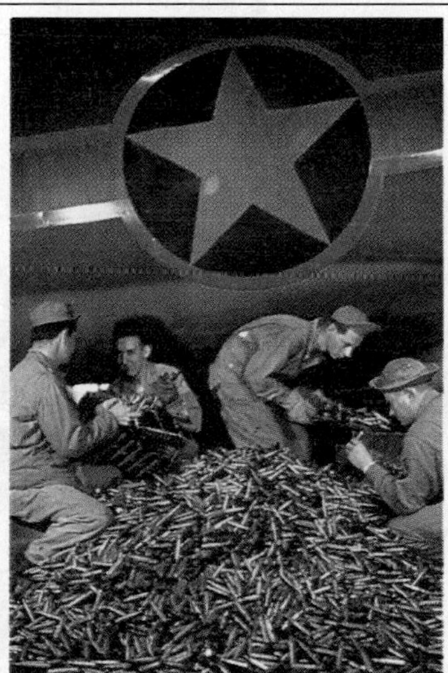

Staff Sergeant F.T. Lusic, his bomber, the "Meat Hound", and the ground crew who service her are all part of the many ways in which America is helping the Allies win the war.

1943

JULY

Su	Mo	Tu	We	Th	Fr	Sa
				1	2	3
4	5	6	7	8	9	10
11	12	13	14	15	16	17
18	19	20	21	22	23	24
25	26	27	28	29	30	31

2. UK: Figures show that women's pay has risen by 80 per cent since 1938.

5. USSR: The Germans launch a full-scale offensive along a 170-mile front in the Kursk area.→

7. London: The government says it will consider the introduction of "pay-as-you-earn" taxation.

10. Italy: The first Allied troops go ashore on Sicily along a 100-mile front (→13).

12. London: The LCC unveils plans for London that include a ring road around the city.

13. Sicily: The Allies capture Augusta and Ragusa and land new forces near Catania (→19).

14. New York: Gary Cooper and Ingrid Bergman open in the film "For Whom the Bell Tolls".

16. London: A white paper on post-war education advocates free schooling for all up to the age of 16.

17. Pacific: The US and Japanese navies clash near the island of Bougainville.

19. Italy: Hitler and Mussolini meet in northern Italy to discuss the worsening military situation.→

24. Hamburg: The city is bombed twice in 24 hours; 2,300 tons are dropped in the heaviest RAF raid yet (→3/8).

26. Rome: Badoglio declares martial law to prevent civil war (→27).

27. Rome: Badoglio asks the Allies for peace terms as demonstrations celebrate Mussolini's downfall (→28).

28. Rome: The Fascist Party is abolished (→29).

29. Italy: Political prisoners are released; Eisenhower offers "peace with honour" if Italy ends aid to Germany (→2/8).

DEATHS

4. Polish statesman and commander General Wladislaw Sikorski (*20/5/1881).→

8. French Resistance leader Jean Moulin (*20/6/1899).→

Spy wormed secrets from female clerk

July 28. A British Communist Party organiser was alleged, at an Old Bailey trial today, to have "wormed vital secrets" from an Air Ministry woman clerk. Douglas Springhall was sentenced to seven years' imprisonment for obtaining information about munitions – "calculated to be useful to the enemy" – from Olive Sheehan, who had access to documents on secret experiments. He had told her she would be helping the Soviet Union; she has already been sentenced to three months.

Mr Justice Oliver told Springhall: "I do not think, on your record, it is likely that your purpose was to communicate these things to Germany, but to communicate them to someone I have no doubt whatever."

Polish PM is killed in an air crash

July 4. Poland's Prime Minister in London, General Wladislaw Sikorski, was killed today in an air crash shortly after taking off from Gibraltar. General Sikorski, who was also Commander-in-Chief of the Polish Army, was flying to the Middle East to inspect Polish forces. The only survivor of the 17 passengers and crew was the pilot, a Czech.

Spanish eye-witnesses said all four engines of the Liberator aircraft cut out within seconds of it leaving the ground, and then described how it plunged into the sea. Among other passengers were General Sikorski's Chief of Staff, and his daughter.

General Sikorski's death comes at a time of lingering Soviet-Polish enmity, arising both from his calls for an eventual return of Poland's pre-war boundaries and from the discovery in a Russian forest of the mass grave of Polish officers. General Sikorski's conviction that the Russians were responsible for the murders has not made him popular with the other Allies, either.

German broadcasts said that General Sikorski had fallen a victim to the dirty tricks of the "Allied Secret Service".

Germans routed in massive Kursk tank battle

July 13. The greatest tank battle in history, fought on the flat cornlands around Kursk, south of Moscow, has ended in a smashing defeat for the German army.

The battle started nine days ago when Hitler threw the finest divisions of the Wehrmacht and the Waffen SS, equipped with the latest Tiger and Panther tanks, into a pincer attack, aimed at biting off a bulge in the Russian line, east of Orel and Kharkov, at Kursk.

Hitler, desperately needing a victory following his disaster at Stalingrad, attached enormous importance to this offensive. He announced that it "would shine like a beacon around the world".

The Russians have captured copies of his order of the day: "This ... (is) ... an offensive of such importance that the whole future of the war may depend on its outcome. More than anything else, your victory will show the whole world that resistance to the German army is hopeless."

However, the Germans ran into trouble immediately. The Russians were fully prepared for the attack with fresh men and fresh equipment from the Siberian factories. Among their surprises for the panzers has been the 50-ton assault gun, nicknamed the "Conquering Beast" by the Red Army. The nine-mile range of its 152mm howitzer has proved too much for the German tanks.

The fighting has been ferocious; the summer sky was stained by columns of smoke rising from literally hundreds of burning tanks and aircraft. Villages have been torn apart by the storm of shellfire.

Russian tanks firing a barrage against SS and Wehrmacht opposition during the nine-day battle for Kursk.

Specialised tank-busting aircraft from both sides have been roaming the battlefield. One Russian commentator radioed this description: "Here come the Stormovik bombers. Now there are bright tongues of flame dancing all along the line of German tanks. They have been set on fire. The planes are away and our artillery begins to talk. Hundreds of shells are pouring over our heads smashing into the enemy positions."

The Germans were forced to admit that "the enemy's resistance is not shaken to such a degree that it would be justifiable to foresee an early operative German success".

Yesterday the Russians counter-attacked on a front north and east of Orel under orders to "bleed the enemy white": it quickly became a bloodbath. Today Hitler ordered a cease-fire (→4/8).

A German soldier, his gun smashed, awaits life as a Russian prisoner.

The changing technology of tanks

July 31. This month's tank battles in Russia illustrate the way in which the "motor monsters" of 1916 have changed. Throughout the inter-war period every nation has improved two vital aspects of tank technology: firepower and protection. Heavier armour, larger guns and more penetrative shells have appeared, although all the major producers – Britain, Russia, Germany, and America – have all been forced to tailor military needs to economic realities. Since the German invasion began in 1941, tank development has raced ahead. Sloping frontal armour 80-160mm thick is nearly universal while gun barrels have expanded in length and breadth, making their effective range up to 2000 yards. The only drawback to such technical gains has been logistic. The larger, heavier vehicles, equipped with greater firepower are now far harder to maintain and supply.

Allies take Palermo in Sicily landing

July 23. The Sicilian capital, Palermo, has fallen to the Americans without a struggle. In a rapid thrust to the north from the Allied-held southern part of the island, US troops overwhelmed the city yesterday, trapping an estimated 45,000 Axis troops who must now either surrender or be annihilated.

General Eisenhower, the Allied C-in-C, described the success as "the first page in the story of the liberation of the European continent". Axis troops are now on the run right across the island.

Further south, the Axis-held port of Catania is besieged. It is being softened up with a fierce bombardment from sea and air while the British Eighth Army, under General Montgomery, advances on it from the south, and Canadian troops drive east, against fierce resistance from German panzers, to cut off the city from behind.

Meanwhile, the American Seventh Army is today advancing along the island's northern coast road, pursuing Italian troops towards the volcanic massif of Mount Etna. It is here that Axis forces plan to fight a final rearguard action, to allow the evacuation that has just begun from the port of Messina to be completed.

The attack on Palermo – the result of a 60-mile advance in just 58 hours – was so swift that the defenders had no time to demolish dock and railhead facilities which had escaped Allied bombs.

The victory also deprives the Axis of one of its chief Mediterranean submarine bases, and has given the Allies access to a new airfield, from which planes can strike at German and Italian positions far behind the battle lines. US Warhawks, for instance, today shot down 17 enemy fighters in a raid over the island of Sardinia, and Flying Fortress bombers plastered the railway marshalling yards at Foggia, on the eastern side of southern Italy (→25).

The first American troops hit the shores of Sicily on the way to Palermo.

Allied bombing raid on Rome avoids antiquities but kills 1,400

July 19. Five hundred US bombers rained 1,000 tons of high explosive onto the Italian capital today in a massive daylight raid. For two and a half hours Rome shuddered under its first air-raid, as 4,000-pound bombs devastated the city's railyards, airfields, factories and government offices, but pilots were under strict orders to avoid Rome's famous historical buildings and the Vatican.

A Swedish newsman who toured the city immediately afterwards reported: "All the well-known streets and squares, beloved by the world's tourists, look as peaceful as ever." But around the US targets, he said, "fires were still raging, and the dead were being dragged from under the ruins, for the loss of life was extremely high" (→23).

As Allied bombs fall on the suburbs of Rome, the Pope urges patience.

Mussolini deposed as Allies invade; Badoglio succeeds

July 25. Mussolini, Fascist dictator of Italy for 21 years, has fallen from power. King Victor Emmanuel has assumed command of the Italian armed forces, and the anti-Fascist Marshal Badoglio has been appointed Prime Minister and Chief of Government.

This dramatic news, broadcast by Rome radio tonight, comes at a time when Italian soldiers in Sicily are surrendering in their thousands, and it is obvious that the Allied invasion of Italy itself will not be long delayed.

Both the King and the Marshal appealed to the Italian people for loyalty and said that the war would continue, but it is expected that the Duce's downfall will soon be followed by Italy's surrender.

Mussolini has made no public appearances for weeks; none of the recent events has brought him into the open. He neither visited bombed cities nor rallied his followers when the Allied invasion of Sicily rendered all his pledges worthless.

The news of his resignation did not come as a surprise in London, in view of the obvious difficulties of his regime and the vain appeals for help which the Fascist leaders have recently made to Germany.

At the same time it is being received with the greatest satisfaction as the first sign of the inevitable collapse of Fascism and, after it, of Nazism (→26).

French Resistance chief is executed

July 8. Jean Moulin ("Max"), the French underground leader, is dead after being tortured by the Gestapo. He was 44.

He was captured on June 21, when a traitor told the Gestapo of a meeting of Resistance chiefs at Caluire, on the river Saone.

Moulin was President of the National Resistance Council. He had been imprisoned once before, in November 1940, for refusing to sign a statement blaming Senegalese soldiers for murders committed by Germans (→21/10).

1943

AUGUST

Su	Mo	Tu	We	Th	Fr	Sa
1	2	3	4	5	6	7
8	9	10	11	12	13	14
15	16	17	18	19	20	21
22	23	24	25	26	27	28
29	30	31				

1. Rumania: The US Air Force bombs Axis oil installations at Ploesti.

2. Sicily: The Allies break through the final Axis defence lines on the island (→ 13).

4. USSR: The Soviet Army captures the key town of Orel from the Germans (→ 19).

6. UK: The British Medical Association expresses opposition to the Beveridge Plan (→ 22/9).

8. Pacific: John F. Kennedy, son of the ex-US envoy to Britain, saves the crew of his stricken torpedo boat (→ 24/11).

8. Berlin: One million citizens are being evacuated on Goebbels' orders (→ 17).

10. Quebec: Churchill arrives for talks with Roosevelt and Canadian premier Mackenzie King (→ 24).

13. Italy: The Allies bomb Rome, Turin and Milan (→ 14).

14. Rome: Badoglio declares Rome an open city (→ 15).

15. Sicily: The Allies launch an assault on Messina.→

16. Poland: An uprising breaks out in the Jewish ghetto in the city of Bialystok (→ 2/9).

19. USSR: The Soviet Army advances into the Ukraine (→ 22).

22. Washington: The Soviet ambassador to the US, Maxim Litvinov, is replaced by Andrei Gromyko.

22. USSR: The Germans quit Kharkhov, their chief base in the southern USSR (→ 8/9).

25. Quebec: The Allies name Lord Louis Mountbatten as Supreme Allied Commander, South-East Asia.

26. London: The Allies recognise de Gaulle's Algiers-based French Committee of National Liberation (CFLN) (→ 17/9).

28. Bulgaria: King Boris dies from an assassin's bullet (→ 8/11).

DEATH

28. Bulgarian King Boris III (*30/1/1894).

Hamburg "wiped off the map" by air raid

Aug 3. RAF night bombers and the US Air Force attacking by day have poured more than 10,000 tons of bombs on Hamburg in the past eight days. Seven square miles of Germany's second city have been wiped out, the Air Ministry claimed today, and the city's shipyards and factories are being systematically reduced to rubble. A greater weight of bombs has fallen on Hamburg in this period than during the whole of the 1940-41 Blitz.

After a two-day lull, bombers attacked the city again last night, flying through violent electric storms to reach their target. Thirty bombers failed to return. Aircrews reported seeing fires spreading throughout the Hamburg docks area. New waves of bombers were guided by the fires.

Many U-boats are believed to have been destroyed on their slipways. The Elbe tunnel – comparable to the Mersey tunnel in importance – has been demolished.

Civilian casualties are known to be exceptionally heavy, particularly with the introduction of new phosphorus incendiary bombs creating such intense heat that "burning asphalt makes the streets look like rivers of fire". Before yesterday's raid, 6,000 people were known to have been killed, with 25,000 injured. A Danish consular official in the city has now claimed that the figure is 200,000 deaths, including 2,000 Danish workers (→ 8).

Churchill and FDR in Quebec summit

Aug 24. A war strategy conference between Mr Churchill, President Roosevelt and Canada's Prime Minister Mackenzie King ended in Quebec tonight with a buoyant "forward now to victory" communique. It said that Allied leaders are planning to meet more frequently in the future as the reach of military action "spreads and deepens in several quarters of the globe". Such meetings will include one or more with Mr Stalin.

The reference to action on several fronts is taken to mean that British and American forces are being prepared for imminent new operations.

Allies win Sicily as Messina is captured

A tank pushes through the ruins during the Allied attack on Sicily.

Aug 17. The last Axis defences on Sicily crumbled today as British and American troops met up in Messina, opposite the toe of Italy. The whole of Sicily is now in Allied hands. Long-range guns are already pounding coastal batteries on the mainland, Allied warships are shelling the coast roads out of Reggio, and bombers are harrying targets along the length of Italy.

John Daly, an American broadcaster, was with the first platoon to reach Messina city hall at 8.25am – 50 minutes ahead of the British. "We did not arrive in style," he reported. "In fact we walked the last seven miles practically on tiptoe, fearing to touch abandoned equipment lest it contained booby-traps. We watched the ground for mines until our eyes ached."

Then, at 9.15am, a lieutenant colonel of the Eighth Army drove up to the advancing Americans. All he said was: "Hello, Yanks. Congratulations." Daly added: "The city is a complete ruin. Bombs and craters take the place of streets and buildings. The few people were listless and haggard with the horror of what they had been through" (→ 3/9).

RAF bombs secret Nazi weapon base

Aug 17. RAF bombers attacked a top-secret Nazi weapons base on Peenemunde Island in the Baltic Sea tonight. The base is believed to be a centre for the production of rockets and 'flying bombs'.

Air Chief Marshal Sir Arthur Harris chose a moonlit night for the raid by Lancaster bombers, to make sure they could see their targets – a factory used to produce the weapons, and a special test runway – and drop 1,500 tons of explosives and incendiaries (→ 24/10).

Lord Louis Mountbatten – a Royal sailor goes to war with his fellow countrymen.

1943

SEPTEMBER

Su	Mo	Tu	We	Th	Fr	Sa
			1	2	3	4
5	6	7	8	9	10	11
12	13	14	15	16	17	18
19	20	21	22	23	24	25
26	27	28	29	30		

2. Poland: It is reported that concentration camp inmates are being used for medical experiments.

3. Italy: The Allies land on the mainland opposite Messina (→4).

3. Rome: Badoglio signs a secret armistice with the Allies (→4).

4. Italy: The Allies capture Reggio di Calabria, a vital centre on the "toe" of Italy.→

8. USSR: The Russians take Stalino, in the River Donets basin (→25).

9. Italy: The Allies land at Salerno, near Naples, meeting stiff German resistance (→10).

10. Rome: German troops occupy the city (→12).

12. Italy: The Allies take Brindisi on the "heel" of Italy (→17).

14. Yugoslavia: Partisans are advancing along the Dalmatian coast; Allied officers have reached Tito (→19/10).

17. Algiers: De Gaulle sets up a Consultative Assembly as part of the French Committee of National Liberation (→12/11).

17. Italy: The Germans are retreating from Salerno as the Allies join in a continuous line across southern Italy (→19).

19. Italy: Italian troops seize control of Sardinia (→20).

20. London: Chancellor of the Exchequer Sir Kingsley Wood dies after a cabinet meeting (→24).

20. Italy: The Allies begin an attack on Naples (→30).

24. London: Sir John Anderson is appointed Chancellor of the Exchequer.

26. USSR: The Soviet Army enters the suburbs of the Ukrainian capital Kiev (→7/10).

30. Italy: The Allies enter Naples as the Germans pull back (→6/10).

BIRTH

29. Polish trade union leader Lech Walesa.

Italy signs an armistice

An American corpsman gives a plasma transfusion to a wounded comrade.

Sept 8. Italy has surrendered to the Allies unconditionally. In a broadcast this evening, General Eisenhower announced that a representative of Marshal Pietro Badoglio, Prime Minister of Italy since the fall of Mussolini in July, had signed a military armistice with the Allies several days earlier.

Hostilities between the armed forces of the Allies and those of Italy terminated at once, Eisenhower declared. Then, in a clear invitation to Italy to turn on its former ally, he added: "All Italians who now act to help eject the German aggressor from Italian soil will have the assistance and support of the Allies." In the wake of the broadcast, which followed a secret meeting four days ago between Eisenhower and Badoglio, the Italian government halted all ships, trains and vehicles carrying German troops, and the Italian garrison on Corsica was reported to have overpowered German forces on the island.

The sudden capitulation took the Nazis by surprise. Less than an hour before the broadcast, Berlin radio was reporting "solid resistance" by Italian and German troops to the British invasion of southern Italy (→9).

Mussolini is spirited away by Germans

Sept 12. The Germans claimed tonight to have rescued Mussolini from his prison somewhere in Italy. A special announcement from Hitler's HQ in Berlin said: "German parachutists, and men of the security service and the armed SS, today carried out an operation for the liberation of Mussolini, who had been imprisoned by the clique of traitors. The coup succeeded. The Duce is at liberty."

This is the first definite news of Mussolini since he resigned seven weeks ago. There are no details yet of how his rescue was carried out, but the involvement of parachutists suggests a daring behind-the-lines operation.

Mussolini is escorted to freedom.

East front bastion is recaptured by Red Army advance

Sept 25. The Red Army's spectacular advance over the last month was crowned today with the capture of Smolensk, where the German Blitzkrieg of 1941 first met trouble. A spectacular amount of territory has been liberated since the world's biggest tank battle took place in July around Kursk.

The series of bold fast attacks on German lines has led to the recapture of a whole string of Russian cities: Kharkov; Taganrog, which the Germans had held ever since the autumn of 1941; the whole of the Donbas; Novorossiysk; and Kremenchug, the important rail junction on the east bank of the River Dnieper (→26).

"PAYE" plans for British taxpayers

Sept 22. Soon income taxpayers will have tax deducted on pay day, instead of reporting earnings to the Inland Revenue afterwards and being told how much they owe. The scheme is called PAYE – Pay As You Earn.

It is attractively presented as taxation without pain. Roll up, the Government said today, and buy for twopence a guide to it all and you will get your very own personal tax code number, too. Tax evasion will obviously be more difficult in future (→2/11).

Churchill proposes "Anglo-US Union"

Sept 9. The Prime Minister today called for Anglo-American cooperation to continue long after the war is over, and even envisaged common citizenship in the future.

Mr Churchill was speaking at Harvard University in Cambridge, Massachusetts, at a ceremony conferring on him the degree of doctor of law. "Our common tongue," he said, "is a priceless inheritance and it may well some day become the foundation of a common citizenship."

1943

OCTOBER

Su	Mo	Tu	We	Th	Fr	Sa
					1	2
3	4	5	6	7	8	9
10	11	12	13	14	15	16
17	18	19	20	21	22	23
24	25	26	27	28	29	30
31						

1. Atlantic: U-boats have returned in the last ten days, sinking several ships (→ 11).

4. Corsica: The island falls to the French Resistance; it is the first department of France to be liberated.

6. Rome: The Germans are reported to be looting the city of art treasures ahead of the Allied advance (→ 13).

7. USSR: The Soviet Army mounts a new thrust on German positions along the River Dnieper (→ 13).

11. Arctic: The Allies torpedo the battleship Tirpitz in the first reported use of a midget submarine (→ 9/11).

12. Atlantic: The Allies land on the Azores; Portugal grants them permission to maintain a garrison.

13. USSR: The town of Melitopol falls to the Russians, cutting off rail links to Germans in the Crimea.→

14. Italy: The Allies break through German defence lines along the River Volturno (→ 31).

19. Sweden: 4,200 British PoWs are exchanged for Germans in the first major exchange of the war.

20. London: The Allies reach final agreement on the creation of a United Nations war crimes commission.

21. France: A Resistance attack releases 14 Resistance prisoners in Lyons.

24. Austria: The Allies carry out their first air raid on the Reich from Italian soil (→ 15/11).

28. London: The Court of Appeal rules that savings from housekeeping money belong to the husband.

29. London: Troops take over from striking dockers (→ 2/12).

BIRTH

22. French actress Catherine Deneuve, born Catherine Dorleac.

DEATH

31. Austrian stage director Max Reinhardt (*9/9/1873).

German looting as Italy declares war

Oct 13. Italy completed her military about-face today by declaring war on Germany, her ally until little more than five weeks ago. The Prime Minister, Marshal Badoglio, urged Italian soldiers to fight against the Germans "to their last man" because of Germany's "repeated and intensified acts of war".

The declaration follows a wave of atrocities and looting since the Italian surrender last month. In Rome, German troops have been stealing Old Masters, priceless manuscripts and art treasures.

Naples, now under Allied control, was subjected to a five-day reign of terror as retreating soldiers took revenge on their Italian "betrayers". In one case, the Germans planted land mines under a room, herded more than 100 civilians into it – then detonated them.

Soldiers roamed the city almost at random, looting and blowing up buildings. Hospitals were attacked to destroy their stocks of food. Water mains and sewers were dynamited to foul water supplies. Thousands of civilians have died. Resistance has been savagely put down. In the village of Aversa, near Naples, 80 Italian policemen and 20 civilians were shot in reprisal for the death of a single German.

Meanwhile, tens of thousands of disarmed Italian soldiers are being crammed into sealed trains under guard and taken to Germany as slave labour (→ 14).

Neapolitan mothers mourn for their sons, killed during guerrilla battles.

Night river crossing cracks German line

Oct 29. The Red Army has crossed the River Dnieper and broken the Germans' 1,300-mile defence front in many places. Vital German positions at Zaporozhie and Dnepropetrovsk in the south have been captured. The German "Dnieper Line" is cracking from top to bottom.

The Russians performed an astonishing feat. Obviously none of the Dnieper bridges was usable, so at night many thousands of men rowed or paddled across in small craft or, more often, on improvised rafts, planks, garden benches or a few barrels strung together. The Germans were taken by surprise; furthermore, the Russians were amazed and delighted to find that their allegedly powerful fortifications along the river had not even been built. After the bridgeheads were established, the Russians laid pontoons across the river. German air strikes at these were repelled by Russian fighters.

The Germans still hold the Crimea – probably because Hitler is determined the Allies should not have the opportunity to use airfields there to bomb Rumanian oilfields.

Penicillin is saving many Allied lives

Oct 24. Penicillin is now being used to treat the infected wounds of those fighting in the Mediterranean, it was announced today. This is just over three years since E. Chain, H. Florey and their Oxford colleagues stated that penicillium-notatum mould cured certain infections in mice, rats and cats.

The effectiveness of this powerful new drug is demonstrated by the case of a soldier who was delirious with grave blood poisoning from wound sepsis. He was flown from Italy to Algiers where he was treated by a specially formed penicillin. Within a few days he had completely recovered.

Archbishops warn of "moral laxity"

Oct 19. Promiscuity and moral laxity were strongly condemned today by the Archbishops of Canterbury and York, following a frightening rise in venereal disease rates since the start of the war.

The churchmen gave their backing to practical measures to combat the menace, which they say is bringing ruin and unhappiness to thousands and posing "a grave danger to the health of the nation", but they added: "Moral self-control is essential if the spread of this evil is to be checked."

Off with the old, on with the new.

Italian troops join Yugoslav partisans

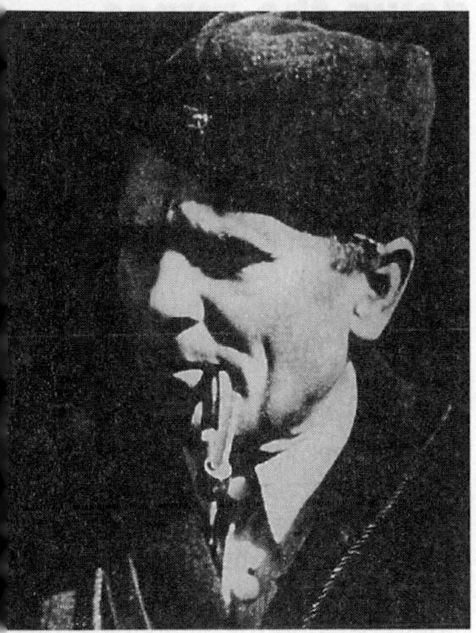

Marshall Tito: Yugoslav leader.

Oct 19. Italian units, which only a few days ago were helping the Germans in their attempts to crush Tito's partisans in Yugoslavia, have now joined up with them. A communique from the Yugoslav National Army of Liberation says the whole of the Italian Venezia division is now fighting alongside Tito's men.

The activities of the partisans were described by a German commentator last night as: "a festering sore. For two weeks now operations have been carried out against them. The fighting is not over yet. Booty captured shows that the partisans are armed to the teeth. Fiume has been attacked twice" (→5/12).

Allies held up at Monte Cassino

Oct 31. Allied armies trying to inch their way up the boot of Italy – "like a bug on one leg," as Winston Churchill put it – have run into stiff resistance north of the Volturno River. The Nazis have transformed the Benedictine monastery at Monte Cassino into an almost impenetrable fortress.

The Allies are short of men, and geography is against them: the Appennines make ideal shelter for Nazi machine-gun nests; there are few roads; the land is marshy. The weather is against them, too: fog hampers Allied planes, and winter is close (→4/11).

1943

NOVEMBER

Su	Mo	Tu	We	Th	Fr	Sa
	1	2	3	4	5	6
7	8	9	10	11	12	13
14	15	16	17	18	19	20
21	22	23	24	25	26	27
28	29	30				

1. Moscow: After a fortnight's talks, Allied foreign ministers agree on closer military ties and Austrian independence.

2. London: The Chancellor says that PAYE will apply to all wage earners.

4. Italy: The Allies seize Isernia, a key German position on the way to Rome (→30).

6. USSR: Kiev falls to the Russians.

8. Bulgaria: 400 are reported killed in an uprising in the south-east of the country (→18).

9. London: Churchill tells MPs that 60 U-boats have been destroyed in the last three months (→26/12).

11. Beirut: French troops arrest the Lebanese government after it declares Lebanon independent (→21).

12. Algiers: De Gaulle, head of the CNLF since Giraud became army chief, opens the Consultative Assembly (→19).

15. Italy: RAF Wellington bombers are reported to be using new techniques to allow night-time precision bombing (→25/11).

18. Bulgaria: The Germans evacuate Sofia.

19. France: Petain is reported to be a prisoner of the Germans.

21. Beirut: The French release the Lebanese government and reinstate the president.

22. London: The Labour Party protests at Sir Oswald Mosley's release from prison.

24. Pacific: The Gilbert Islands fall to the Allies (→16/12).

30. Rome: Badoglio strips King Victor Emmanuel III of his official titles (→2/12).

BIRTH

22. US tennis player Billie Jean King (nee Moffit).

DEATH

22. US lyricist Lorenz Hart (*2/5/1895).

Churchill, FDR and Stalin meet in Tehran

With peace in mind – the Big Three sort out plans for the post-war world.

Nov 28. The three Allied leaders – Prime Minister Churchill, President Roosevelt and Marshal Stalin – have arrived in Tehran for their first meeting together. The Big Three hope to agree on their grand design for smashing Germany. They also intend to sign a lofty declaration about ensuring a post-war world free from tyranny.

The Prime Minister and President began the momentous conference today with personal assurances to the Soviet leader that the Anglo-US invasion of France is definitely on for next year. Service chiefs with them at this momentous meeting are discussing broad strategy with their Russian opposite numbers. The aim is co-ordinated action to squeeze the German armies from east, west and south.

During preparations for the summit, Marshal Stalin gave notice that he wants it accepted now that not only will Germany have to be carved up, but also that, after victory, there must be frontier adjustments favourable to Russia. Mr Churchill and the President are not digging in against this.

The Western leaders hope that a few relaxed dinner parties in the next few days will help to establish better personal relations with the Soviet leadership. Marshal Stalin has arrived in a prickly, suspicious mood and surrounded by a huge secret police bodyguard bristling with machine-guns.

During pre-summit small talk the President teasingly accused Mr Churchill of being a dictator. When the Prime Minister feigned indignation, the Marshal just managed a faint smile.

Western Allies meet Chiang Kai-shek

Nov 25. Winston Churchill, President Franklin Delano Roosevelt and Marshal Chiang Kai-shek met today in secrecy in Cairo for an historic conference – the first time that the British and American leaders have been joined by the Chinese. His presence means that the main items on the agenda are the war against Japan and the postwar aims of the Allies.

Because the conference was mainly concerned with the Far East, and because the Soviet Union is not at war with Japan, Marshal Stalin was not invited on this occasion. He may attend a later meeting.

It is expected that the Big Three will re-assert their determination to ensure the unconditional surrender of Japan. There is a plan for a Pacific Charter on the lines of the 1941 Atlantic Charter. Marshal Chiang will insist on securing the return to China of Formosa and Manchuria, seized by the Japanese. The three are also united on the need to punish the Japanese, and to strip from them all territories taken by force. ▷

RAF promises to bomb Berlin to nothing

Nov 25. Berlin will be bombed "until the heart of Nazi Germany ceases to beat" declared Sir Arthur Harris, chief of RAF Bomber Command, today, following three night raids which have reduced much of the capital to burning rubble.

His words were translated into deeds later tonight, when squadrons were heard crossing the coast to deliver what the Air Ministry called another "crushing assault" on the Nazi war industry's centre.

Even senior German officials admit that up to 10,000 people may now have been killed by RAF raids over the last 11 months, during which 12,000 tons of bombs were dropped.

Renewed attacks on Berlin began a week ago, when 1,000 bombers pounded factories with more than 2,500 tons of high explosives.

Since then Berlin, the largest Reich city and a major manufacturing centre, has been in ruins. Overground railways have been hit, field kitchens have been set up in devastated streets, and German army engineers have been brought in to help fire-fighters. Buildings are being dynamited by troops to stop flames spreading. Scores of suburban factories have been badly damaged. Sir Arthur said: "The Battle of Berlin progresses. It will continue as opportunity serves and circumstances dictate, until the heart of Nazi Germany ceases to beat."

But as Berlin prepares plans for a mass evacuation, the German propaganda machine threatens retaliation against Britain through a secret weapon.

Berlin comes under the bombers.

Ailing Mosley is released from jail

Nov 20. Sir Oswald Mosley, the upper-class ex-Labour MP and leader of the British Union of Fascists who wanted a deal with Hitler, has been released from jail. He will stay under house arrest. Herbert Morrison announced the controversial decision today after consulting the cabinet. He told MPs that it has been taken on medical grounds – Mosley has phlebitis – also, he is no longer a big security risk.

Britain's Number One Fascist has been imprisoned for the past two-and-a-half years. One early reaction to his release came from Will Lawther, leader of the miners' union, who said that it could have a serious effect on peace in the coalfields. Some Labour MPs also voiced resentment.

Mr Morrison, looking like someone carrying someone else's can, protested that there had been a cabinet decision and nobody need doubt his own mixed feelings and aversion to Fascism (→22).

Oswald Mosley: a sick man freed.

1943

DECEMBER

Su	Mo	Tu	We	Th	Fr	Sa
			1	2	3	4
5	6	7	8	9	10	11
12	13	14	15	16	17	18
19	20	21	22	23	24	25
26	27	28	29	30	31	

2. Italy: The Germans make a surprise attack on the town of Bari, on the eastern coast (→29).

4. Cairo: Churchill and Roosevelt meet president Ismet Inonu of Turkey and agree on closer ties.

5. Yugoslavia: Tito announces the creation of a provisional government.

7. London: The government says the list of war criminals and collaborators is "scores of thousands" long (→19).

10. Malta: Roosevelt visits the island and pays tribute to its inhabitants.

12. Moscow: Exiled Czech leader Eduard Benes signs an agreement for post-war co-operation with the USSR.

16. Pacific: The Allies invade the island of New Britain off New Guinea.

19. USSR: After the first war crimes trial, three Germans are found guilty of atrocities and hanged at Kharkhov.

22. London: The government says there are only enough turkeys for one family in ten this Christmas.

29. Italy: Canadian troops seize the Adriatic port of Ortona.

DEATHS

15. US jazz pianist and composer Thomas "Fats" Waller (*21/5/1904).→

22. British author and illustrator Beatrix Potter (*28/7/1866).

HITS OF 1943

You'll never know.

Brazil.

My heart and I.

QUOTE OF THE YEAR

"We are the loyal, obedient, steadfast and unconquerable fighting men of the Germanic people and of the Fuehrer: the SS of the German Reich."

Heinrich Himmler, speech to the SS at the time of the destruction of the Warsaw Ghetto, April 1943.

"Bevin Boys" are called up to work down the mines

Dec 2. One out of every ten men called up between the ages of 18 and 25 will now be ordered to work in the coal mines, instead of going into the forces. The scheme, announced today by Ernest Bevin, the Minister of Labour, has been introduced on account of acute manpower shortage. Many young miners have eagerly volunteered for the forces to get away from the pits.

The conscript miners – to be chosen by ballot – are already dubbed the Bevin Boys. This mixing of the classes in the coalfields should be good for democracy, says the government. Miners' leaders are hostile, but conscripts may still get a welcome in the valleys.

The original Bevin Boy himself.

Germany loses her last great warship

Dec 26. The last major ship in the German navy, the great battleship Scharnhorst, was sunk by the Royal Navy tonight, after an attack on an Allied convoy bound for Russia went wrong. With the Bismarck gone and the Tirpitz sunk, Britain's heavier ships may now be released to fight in other seas.

Details are still coming in of the engagement in the Arctic Sea off northern Norway. It appears the German attacked several times but, in the dim light of this time of year, she may not have seen a British battleship coming within range until it was too late to escape her 14-inch guns.

Ike to be invasion chief

General Eisenhower and one of his tank crews prepare to conquer Europe.

Dec 24. A Texas-born West Point graduate, who had never heard a shot fired in anger and never held a field command, until he led the invasion of French North Africa last year, is to be supreme commander of the Allies' biggest operation, the invasion of Western Europe. The appointment of General Dwight D. Eisenhower was announced today by President Roosevelt, who praised Eisenhower's performance in North Africa and Italy.

Eisenhower's field commander will be the victor of El Alamein, General Montgomery, now universally known as Monty. Monty's cocky self-assurance as a military strategist and tactician may not go down too well with the American, though in North Africa Eisenhower is said to have demonstrated a gift for getting senior Allied officers to work together with little friction.

Both Eisenhower, or Ike, as he is known, and Monty have been recalled to Britain to begin planning work with RAF Air Chief Marshal Sir Arthur Tedder, who will be Ike's deputy.

A cigarette in his mouth, one German rests during the struggle for Kiev as what remains of this major Russian town collapses into fiery ruin.

Arts: sentimental songs comfort troops

Glenn Miller and his American Air Force Band keep the music swinging.

The songs of the Second World War are not written to march to, like those of the First, but to get sentimental over. After a few early barrackroom choruses ("Kiss Me Goodnight, Sergeant-Major") the mood changed. Even the White Cliffs of Dover were a place to see Blue Birds Over and men back from leave wanted to say Thanks for that Lovely Weekend.

The more sophisticated remembered the Last Time they Saw Paris and believed that a Nightingale Sang in Berkeley Square.

A Lancashire lass and lad are the two singers most in demand for troop concerts – **Gracie Fields** and **George Formby**. "Our Gracie" was under a temporary cloud of disapproval in 1940 for marrying an Italian, her producer Monty Banks, just as Italy declared war. Now she is singing to the troops in North Africa and newly-liberated Sicily, giving them her mixture of comedy ("Walter, Lead me to the Altar") with the sudden tearjerking contrast of Gounod's "Ave Maria" in a voice of startling purity. But the homely, innocent ukulele-playing style of "Our George" never alters.

Then the American forces arrived and, with them, the American Forces Network, with a different kind of patriotic sentiment: "Ma, I Miss Your Apple Pie" they sang and "Praise the Lord and Pass the Ammunition". "This Is the Army, Mr Jones" warned **Irving Berlin** in a morale-boosting film, but he hit them – and us – right on the button with the White Christmas that **Bing Crosby** kept dreaming of.

"In the Mood" had been every schoolboy's piano piece since 1939, but it was an eye-opener to hear it played by **Glenn Miller's** American Air Force Band, together with his moody "Moonlight Serenade". Also from 1939 came "Lilli Marlene", which was beamed nightly to the Afrika Korps and overheard by the Eighth Army, who provided their own lyrics. Now an English version has been recorded by another Marlene – Dietrich.

The world of song-writing lost two talents it could ill spare – **Lorenz Hart** and **Fats Waller** both ain't misbehavin' no more.

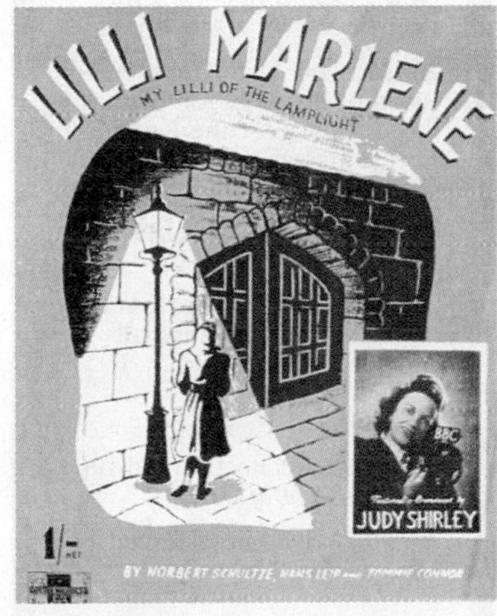

Lilli Marlene – both sides' girl.

1944

JANUARY

Su	Mo	Tu	We	Th	Fr	Sa
						1
2	3	4	5	6	7	8
9	10	11	12	13	14	15
16	17	18	19	20	21	22
23	24	25	26	27	28	29
30	31					

3. Berlin: An RAF raid hits Hitler's Chancellery.→

4. USSR: Soviet troops cross the pre-war Polish border (→ 5).

4. Berlin: Hitler orders the mobilisation of all children over the age of ten.→

5. London: Exiled Polish leaders insist on recognition by the USSR before the Polish Resistance aids the Russians (→ 17).

10. Rome: Mussolini's son-in-law and ex-foreign minister Count Ciano is among 18 sentenced to die for treason (→ 11).

11. UK: "Midget" cigar-box sized radios will go on sale after the war at £6 each.

11. Rome: Count Ciano and four others found guilty of treason against Mussolini are shot.

15. London: The "European Advisory Commission" decides to divide Germany into occupation zones after the war (→ 3/7/45).

16. UK: General Eisenhower takes over as Supreme Commander of Allied invasion forces in Europe (→ 18/2).

17. Moscow: The USSR rejects a Polish proposal for negotiation over the Polish frontier (→ 26/2).

19. Leningrad: The Soviet Army breaks through the German siege lines.→

21. Canberra: Australia and New Zealand sign a Pacific Pact (→ 30).

26. Moscow: A Soviet commission of investigation blames the Germans for the Katyn Forest massacre.

29. US: Launch of the world's biggest warship, the USS Missouri.

30. Pacific: The Allies launch an assault on the Marshall Islands (→ 4/2).

DEATHS

1. British architect Sir Edwin Lutyens (*29/3/1869).

23. Norwegian artist Edvard Munch (*12/12/1863).

Surprise American landing at Anzio

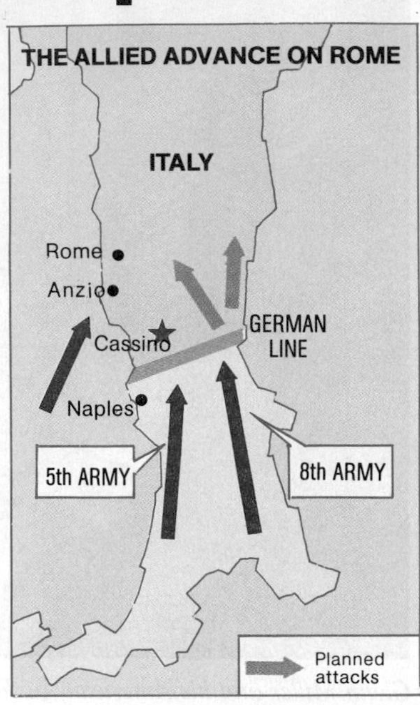

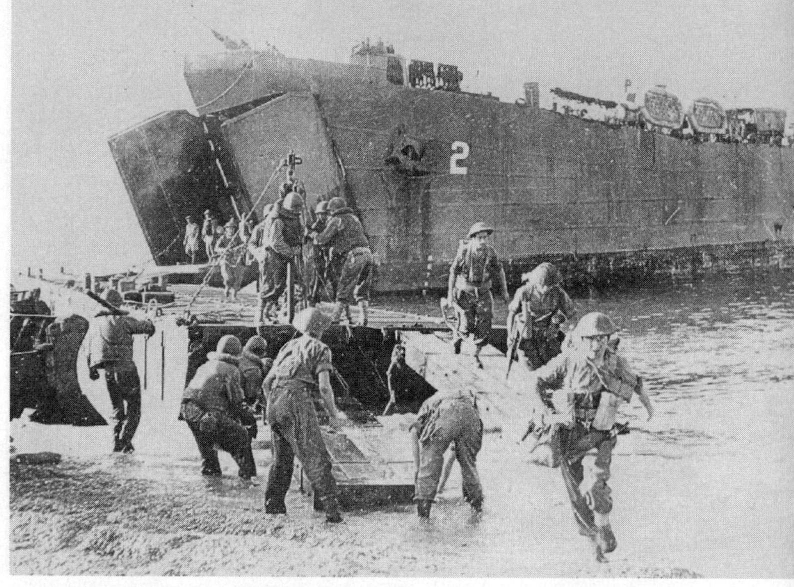

Troops come ashore in Southern Italy during the Allied landings.

Jan 22. Thousands of British and American troops stormed ashore at Anzio just 30 miles south of Rome today and are thrusting swiftly eastwards to cut the supply lines of the 100,000 German troops on the Garigliano front.

The invading force met hardly any opposition, having achieved complete surprise. Reinforcements in men and material continue to pour ashore as an armada of landing craft, with powerful naval and air cover, shuttle to and from the beachhead.

The sea is calm and a majestic fleet of warships and transports rides at anchor, protected by an umbrella of fighters. Occasionally the big guns of a battleship fire at targets miles inland, as the Germans react to the invasion.

Forward patrols, who have already achieved their first day's objectives, are beginning to meet German patrols and increased artillery opposition, but so far there is no sign of a counter-attack.

One of the main objectives of the forces now striking inland will be Littoria, 11 miles east of here, the site of the pre-war international airport for Rome. Its capture will provide an excellent base for the Allied air forces. After that the next stop is Rome (→ 16/2).

US troops tortured on death march

Jan 28. A wave of anger swept Britain and America today after joint statements denounced Japanese brutality towards Allied POW's. The Foreign Secretary Anthony Eden told MPs of the torture of British and Indian troops. He said that 1,800 men aboard a torpedoed Japanese ship were left to drown beneath battened-down hatches: "Let the Japanese reflect that their war record will not be forgotten."

It was also claimed that thousands of American POWs have died on marches to prison camps in the Philippines. Captured at the fall of Bataan and Corregidor, the men were allegedly tortured, starved to death and murdered. Three escaped American officers have made sworn statements detailing acts of appalling brutality.

Allies rain 2,300 tons of bombs on Berlin

Jan 20. RAF Bomber Command's onslaught against Berlin, which began last November, continued last night with the biggest-ever bomb load dropped on the Nazi capital. In just over half an hour 600 Lancasters and Halifaxes released more than 2,300 tons of bombs, starting at least 30 big fires.

A Swedish correspondent reports from the city that the sirens sounded at 7pm and within minutes the first bombs were falling. Some of the RAF's big four-engined planes dived through a 3,000-ft thick blanket of cloud to unload their bombs from a couple of hundred feet. Upwards of 17,000 tons of bombs have now fallen on Berlin in two months (→ 3/4).

DNA is solution to big biological mystery

Jan 1. One of the great mysteries of biology has been solved. Genes, those hereditary units which determine the characteristics of all living things, are made from a chemical called deoxyribonucleic acid, DNA for short. This breakthrough is the work of Oswald T. Avery and his colleagues at the Rockefeller Institute in New York. It depended on the finding that an extract of DNA can change non-infectious pneumonia germs to an infectious form.

Although the mystery of the nature of the genetic material has been solved two even bigger ones remain: how are hereditary instructions encoded in DNA and how does it pass them on from parent to offspring.

Russians smash siege line at Leningrad

Jan 19. In a special Order of the Day issued tonight, Joseph Stalin has broken the news that the Russian army has scored a spectacular victory over the German forces which have besieged Leningrad for the last two years.

Attacking south of the battered, hungry city, Russian armoured forrces have torn a 25-mile wide hole in the German siege lines, smashing seven enemy divisions and capturing 37 of the long-range siege guns which have been systematically bombarding the city. In five days of fighting on this front more than 20,000 Germans have been killed and 1,000 taken prisoner. Among the booty captured are 195 guns of all calibres.

Messages from Moscow say the Russian onslaught was launched after the German positions had been pounded by the greatest concentration of artillery yet seen in this war.

Tonight Moscow's own guns are thundering out a 20-salvo salute to celebrate the victory and the end to Leningrad's long ordeal (→ 17/2).

A liberated civilian embraces a member of the victorious Red Army.

RAF boosted by new jet fighters

Jan 7. Brief details of a new fighter aircraft, powered not by a propellor, but by a jet engine were revealed last night by Britain and the US. The revolutionary engine for the new Gloster jet fighter was developed by 36-year-old Group Captain Frank Whittle and the first test flight was made over two and a half years ago in May 1941.

Most details of the new aircraft remain secret, but it is said to outstrip all others in performance, notably in speed and climb rate. If the war lasts it could be a great boost for the RAF. The Germans are thought to have been working on a similar aircraft capable of speeds of 500 mph (→ 9/6/45).

Nazis planning to breed Aryan elite

Jan 29. The Nazis are now planning to accelerate the "purification" of the German race. The idea comes from Martin Bormann, Hitler's personal secretary, for whom human perfection is an SS officer.

Bormann is turning moral convention on its head by encouraging chosen unmarried women to bear the children of the Nordic elite. The Lebensborn ("Fountain of Life") society will look after the pregnant women, and bring up the children. Soon he plans to have 10,000 children in 22 homes.

Already 200,000 suitably Aryan children have been torn from their mothers in occupied countries to be raised as Germans.

1944

FEBRUARY

Su	Mo	Tu	We	Th	Fr	Sa
		1	2	3	4	5
6	7	8	9	10	11	12
13	14	15	16	17	18	19
20	21	22	23	24	25	26
27	28	29				

1. France: The Forces Francaises de l'Interieur (FFI) is created, unifying all Resistance movements (→ 13).

2. France: Forced labour in Germany is extended to all Frenchmen from 16 to 60.

4. Pacific: US warships shell the Japanese home island of Paramishu (→ 25).

7. Helsinki: The city is bombed twice by the Soviet Air Force (→ 24).

9. UK: The King and Queen eat a one shilling lunch with miners and say: "It is a long time since we had a better meal."

13. France: The Allies drop weapons for the Resistance in Haute-Savoie, south-eastern France.

14. Washington: The US declares neutrality in the frontier dispute between the USSR and Poland (→ 26).

16. London: The BBC says it will develop schools radio to accompany the new education system being planned.→

18. Moscow: Stalin awards Eisenhower the USSR's highest military honour, the Order of Suvorov First Class (→ 27/4).

21. Tokyo: Hideki Tojo becomes chief of staff of the Japanese Army (→ 8/9/45).

22. UK: Lemons will be available for Shrove Tuesday this year at sixpence-halfpenny a pound.

24. Helsinki: The Finnish premier announces that his country is ready to make peace (→ 11/6).

25. Pacific: The US Air Force attacks Japanese bases on Guam and in the Marianas.→

26. UK: Oxford wins the third wartime Boat Race on the River Ouse.

26. London: The Polish government rejects the Curzon Line, reached by the USSR and Germany in 1939, as its eastern frontier (→ 24/7).

DEATH

1. Dutch artist Pieter (Piet) Mondrian (*7/3/1872).

Cabinet shapes post-war plans for schools and health

Feb 17. Post-war conditions in Britain are now getting increased attention from the Coalition Cabinet. Today it announced plans for a national health service and at the same time it continued to make progress with its legislation for radical education reform.

A Government White Paper pledged that "the country's full resources will be brought to bear in promoting good health in all its citizens". This means a free and comprehensive medical service for everybody as soon as possible after the war. It could cost £148 million a year to run.

The Education Bill, introduced by R.A. Butler, will become law later this year. It raises the school-leaving age first to 15 and then, after some years, to 16. There will be three types of free secondary education without a means test – grammar, secondary modern and technical.

At the beginning of each school day there will be a compulsory act of non-denominational collective worship. Local authorities will be under an obligation to provide school playing fields, gymnasia and swimming baths (→ 21/3).

This boy soldier, just 15 years old, is in Germany's front line.

American forces launch Pacific assault

Feb 29. American troops today stormed ashore at Los Negros in the Admiralty Islands. This new assault on the Japanese positions in the Pacific came as the climax of a month of Allied successes.

The assault, codenamed "Operation Brewer", rushed troops towards the beaches in fast destroyers instead of the customary slow landing craft. The beachhead will be held at all costs and although the enemy has already suffered heavy losses in counter-attacks fresh Japanese assaults are expected tonight.

Japanese commanders are well aware of the importance of Los Negros, which will provide a base for the next phase of the island-hopping advance of the American forces commanded by General Douglas MacArthur.

The General, who watched the landings from a warship off-shore, announced that the conquest of the island will isolate 50,000 enemy troops on the Bismarck Archipelago and so open the way for the next jump towards the Philippines.

The Allied offensive has made good progress during the last few weeks. American bombers began by raiding Guam for the first time since the Japanese captured this US base shortly after the attack on Pearl Harbor. Admiral Chester Nimitz reported that the assault destroyed 135 Japanese planes and sank 11 ships. Only six US aircraft were lost.

Ten days ago US soldiers, sailors and marines successfully invaded Eniwetok Atoll in the Marshall Islands. Their commander, Rear Admiral Turner, reported a well-executed attack, which began with a diversionary onslaught upon Truk Island. "Troops went ashore under the cover of battleship gunfire and with close support of low-flying naval aircraft," he said. The Marshalls will serve as a useful base for the next advance (→24/4).

Wounded Americans rest in a captured Japanese bivouac on New Georgia.

End of cloth ban allows tailors to line their pockets

Feb 1. Clothing restrictions were lifted today, to the jubilation of tailors, MPs and the public. Men can now look forward to turn-ups, lined pockets and double-breasted jackets, women to pleats and plenty of buttons. The lifting of the ban after two years follows a decision to make unrestricted demob suits.

A Tailors' Guild spokesman said: "Popular opinion has killed the austerity suit. Everybody hated sacrificing coupons for it." Twenty-six coupons will be needed for non-austerity suits, 24 for ones still made of utility cloth. Unsold austerity suits will be distributed in Europe to refugees.

Fibreglass beats austerity rations.

Red Army traps ten German divisions

Feb 17. In a battle that lasted without respite for 14 days, General Koniev's troops on the Ukrainian front have destroyed ten divisions of the German Eighth Army which were trapped south-east of Kiev.

In one of Stalin's increasingly frequent Orders of the Day announcing sweeping victories, the Russian leader says : "The Germans abandoned 52,000 killed on the battlefield. All the German equipment and arms were captured and 11,000 prisoners were taken."

This victory is the biggest of its kind since the destruction of the German Sixth Army at Stalingrad. Many Germans surrendered, despite an order from Hitler instructing them to commit suicide if their position became hopeless. Tonight Moscow's guns are again firing a victory salute (→22/3).

Allies defend air raid on Monte Cassino

Feb 16. Allied leaders today defended bombing the Benedictine monastery on Monte Cassino, the rock fortress which blocks the road to Rome and which has cost the lives of so many Allied soldiers.

Speaking in the House of Lords, Viscount Simon, the Lord Chancellor, explained the British government's attitude. He said that, subject to military necessity, every effort would be made to avoid damage to monuments which were part of our Christian heritage.

However, the necessities of war must be put far in front of any consideration of special historical or cultural values. Referring specifically to the bombing of Monte Cassino, he said that the buildings themselves were of small importance. Most of them dated from the 19th century. They were decorated with frescoes by German artists. In Washington, Mr Roosevelt declared that the bombing was justified because the Germans had been using it for military purposes. He referred to an order issued by General Eisenhower which said that historical monuments were bound to be respected "so far as war allows".

The order added: "If we have to choose between destroying a famous building and sacrificing our own men, then our men's lives count infinitely more and the buildings must go. Nothing can stand against military necessity."

Those who saw the bombing, by a massed formation of Flying Fortresses, speak of it with awe: "There was a flash as might be expected from a giant striking titanic matches on the hillside. Then a pillar of smoke, 500 feet high, hid the hill and hid the monastery from view. It was curiously beautiful, curiously sinister." (→17/3)

Stalingrad honour

Feb 2. The Mayor of Stalingrad was today presented with a gift from King George VI – a Sword of Honour intended to symbolise His Majesty's admiration for the heroes of Stalingrad.

The ceremony in Moscow, attended by Marshal Budyenny and the British Ambassador, Sir Archibald Clark Kerr, marked the anniversary of the German army's surrender there.

1944

MARCH

Su	Mo	Tu	We	Th	Fr	Sa
			1	2	3	4
5	6	7	8	9	10	11
12	13	14	15	16	17	18
19	20	21	22	23	24	25
26	27	28	29	30	31	

2. London: The government narrowly avoids defeat in a vote on pay for the armed forces.

2. Italy: The Allies claim they have regained areas around the Anzio beachhead lost in a German offensive (→17).

3. UK: The RAF admits it is dropping new 12,000 pound bombs in its latest raids on German cities (→10/4).

4. UK: Tests in Bath on 3,361 children allegedly prove that babies conceived in winter become more intelligent.

8. London: The government announces plans to build 300,000 houses after the war.

8. UK: The Spitfire is being fitted with a bigger engine.

10. London: Education Minister Butler says the ban on women teachers marrying will be lifted because of their "great war effort" (→28).

13. Moscow: The USSR restores diplomatic relations with Italy.

17. Italy: The Allies launch a heavy assault on Monte Cassino, which has been nearly razed by Allied bombing (→11/5).

18. Hungary: The Germans begin to occupy the country.→

21. London: Peers approve, after some criticism, plans for a National Health Service.

22. Eastern Europe: The Germans continue their march into Hungary; German troops cross into Slovakia (→23).

24. London: The government agrees a four-year pact with the miners.

26. London: Churchill says "the hour of our greatest effort is approaching."

28. London: MPs vote to give women teachers the same pay as men (→20/1/45).

31. London: Three women and a man are found guilty under the 1735 Witchcraft Act of pretending to be mediums.

DEATH

24. British commander Major General Orde Charles Wingate (*26/2/1903).→

British glide into Burma

British jungle fighters dropped from gliders to attack the Japanese.

March 19. The most spectacular and daring operation of the Burma campaign, carried out with the utmost secrecy, was revealed today with the announcement that a large Allied force had been landed by glider 200 miles behind the Japanese lines.

Men, mules and all the equipment for a large, self-contained force, including a bulldozer, were flown in bright moonlight without opposition over the 7,000-foot Chin Hills and planted securely in a strategic position.

While men of a north country regiment secured the perimeter of the landing ground, American engineers put the bulldozer to work clearing the ground for the main force to land.

Within 12 hours the Allied forces had carved an airstrip out of the jungle for a fully-equipped fighter squadron.

There is another story behind this coup. It was made possible by an air supremacy so complete that not a single Japanese plane crossed the sky. During previous four days Allied aircraft made a series of devastating raids on any enemy airfield from which detection or opposition might come.

It was a truly Allied operation. The British framed the tactics and planned the mission while the Americans gathered the pilots to tow in the gliders. The Allies' ability to maintain supplies by air is turning the tide in Burma (→31).

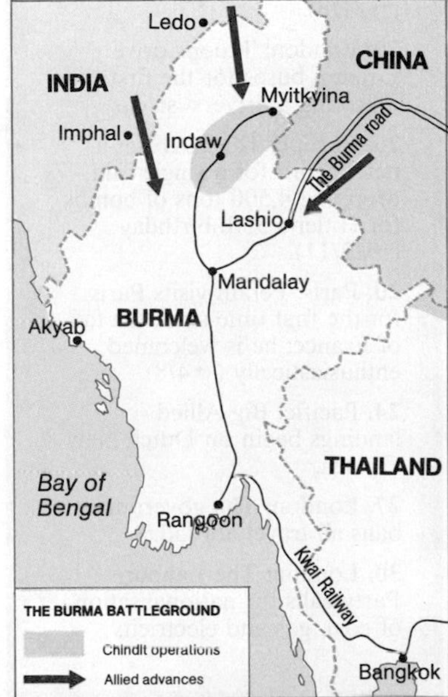

Britain blockades Eire as invasion fever intensifies

March 12. From tonight all travel between Britain and Ireland – both Ulster and the South – is banned. This is decreed "for paramount military reasons and the coming supreme effort of the war". Ireland is now sealed off from Britain in a bid to stop details of Allied invasion preparations from reaching Dublin where spies would tell Berlin.

About 250,000 Irish people working in this country are affected by the ban. Applications for exemption on compassionate grounds will be considered by the Home Office. The dramatic move follows President de Valera's refusal of President Roosevelt's request that Eire should expel enemy diplomatic and consular envoys.

The Irish leader said that such action would breach his country's neutrality. He has been assured by the Americans that there is no Anglo-US intention of invading the South, but he is still not for kicking out the Germans (→1/4).

Striking UK miners paralyse industry

March 8. At least 87,000 of the 100,000 Welsh miners came out on strike today, leaving 156 of the 200 pits in South Wales idle. Each day the strike lasts means a loss of 70,000 tons of coal. The pits affected include those producing the best steam coal in the world, which is vital for the munitions factories, railways and ships' bunkers.

In a desperate attempt to end the strike, the Minister of Fuel and Power, Major Lloyd George, met with miners' leaders and the coal owners at Imperial Chemical Industries House in Westminster. After a four-hour meeting they hammered out a peace formula which they hope will be accepted.

The strike arose because of the recent Porter award designed to secure more uniform mining wages across the country. Welsh miners believe it does not allow sufficiently for the more difficult Welsh seams nor for their traditional right to cheap coal (→24).

Hungarian Jews face new threat

March 23. The German coup overthrowing the Hungarian government has brought fear to the Jewish population. Until now Hungary's 800,000 Jews have lived in comparative safety. Some 50,000 of them are forced to do back-breaking work in labour camps, but they have not suffered the brutalities inflicted on the Jewish populations of the other European countries under Nazi domination.

So far they have escaped the shadow of the concentration camps, but reports from Hungary today say that one of the first of the new Nazi masters to arrive in Budapest is the notorious Adolf Eichmann, the man responsible for sending Europe's Jews to the Auschwitz concentration camp (→5/4).

Orde Wingate, hero of Burma, is killed

March 24. General Orde Wingate, leader of the Chindits wreaking havoc behind the Japanese lines, has been killed in an aircraft crash in Burma. Wingate, often likened to Lawrence of Arabia, first worked out his principles of unorthodox warfare while fighting with the Jewish "Night Squads" against Arab raiders in Palestine. He then applied them to fighting the Italians in the Ethiopian campaign, before turning his fierce attention to the Japanese (→9/4).

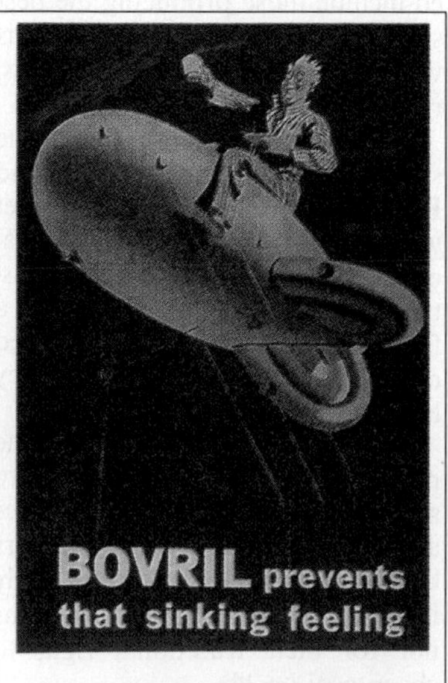
BOVRIL prevents
that sinking feeling

1944

APRIL

Su	Mo	Tu	We	Th	Fr	Sa
						1
2	3	4	5	6	7	8
9	10	11	12	13	14	15
16	17	18	19	20	21	22
23	24	25	26	27	28	29
30						

1. Switzerland: 50 Swiss die when the US Air Force bombs Schaffhausen by mistake.

1. London: The government bans visitors from going within ten miles of the coast from the Wash to Land's End (→27).

2. Rumania: The Russians cross the Rumanian border (→16).

5. Hungary: The Germans begin deporting Jews (→1/5).

6. UK: Today is the first day of PAYE taxation.

7. Berlin: Hitler suspends all laws in the German capital and makes Goebbels dictator of the city (→25/7).

9. Burma: Allied forces make a second glider landing behind Japanese lines (28/1/45).

10. Europe: The RAF drop a record 3,600 tons of bombs in a single raid on Germany, France and Belgium (→20).

10. US: Robert Woodward and William van Eggers synthesise quinine, an anti-malaria agent.

11. London: The BBC says its first post-war aim is television for all.

13. USSR: The Soviet Army captures the Crimean capital of Simferopol.→

16. Eastern Europe: The RAF makes its first raid on Rumania, from bases in Italy (→31/8).

20. London: Troops drive London buses for the first time following a drivers' strike.

20. Europe: The RAF set a new record for a single raid, dropping 4,500 tons of bombs for Hitler's 55th birthday (→12/11).

20. Paris: Petain visits Paris for the first time since the fall of France; he is welcomed enthusiastically (→4/8).

24. Pacific: Big Allied landings begin on Dutch New Guinea.→

27. London: The government bans all travel abroad.→

30. London: The Labour Party calls for nationalisation of coal, gas and electricity.

Invasion plans turn UK into armed camp

General Eisenhower quizzes a GI during pre-invasion manoeuvres.

April 27. Britain has become one gigantic armed camp as General Dwight D. Eisenhower completes his plans for the Allied invasion of Hitler's Fortress Europe. All coastal areas have been banned to visitors, and all overseas travel by foreign diplomats in London has been forbidden, as has the privilege of sending diplomatic dispatches without inspection.

Large-scale military exercises are taking place in different parts of southern England, with fake concentrations of troops and dummy ships to keep the enemy guessing as to where and when the Allied assault will be mounted.

Railway timetables are being reorganised to enable hundreds of thousands of British, American and Commonwealth troops to be moved to the invasion assembly points.

Airborne landings by parachutists and glider troops are being rehearsed. Amphibious operations are being practised, with special equipment for landing tanks, heavy guns and supplies.

Hundreds of minesweepers have been assembled to clear channels through the enemy's mine barrier. Constant air reconnaissance is maintained over enemy positions across the Channel. The enemy's rear areas are being softened up by day and night air attacks on railway marshalling yards, airfields and military positions in France and Germany (→15/5).

De Gaulle appointed head of French forces

April 9. General Charles de Gaulle became Commander-in-Chief of the Free French forces today. The move ends the battle for power between de Gaulle and General Giraud, co-presidents of the Committee of National Liberation since it was set up last June.

Giraud, a veteran of the First World War, has been commander since 1942. He claims today's move is illegal, and he is not content with his new title of Inspector-General. De Gaulle has the support of the younger officers both for his ideas for fighting the war and for planning for peace-time France. Allied leaders, who are mostly concerned to secure the effective organisation of French forces for the invasion of Western Europe, are nervous about today's move.

De Gaulle is a powerful and prickly personality, and his bold plans to organise and arm the French Resistance are suspect because of the virtually autonomous Communist Resistance cells. Churchill asked recently how de Gaulle could guarantee that "the arms they receive will not be turned against each other?" (→15/5)

Victorious Red Army powers through the Crimea

April 16. The Red Army is sweeping the Germans out of the Crimea. Today, the remnants of nine German and Rumanian divisions, once more than 100,000 strong, were being harried through the streets of Sebastopol and in the open country around those other ancient battlefields, Inkerman and Balaclava.

It is only five days since the Russians opened their campaign to recapture the Crimea with three armoured thrusts smashing into the German defences across the neck of the peninsula. The Black Sea port of Odessa fell almost immediately, and was followed by Kerch, the easternmost town in the Crimea, as well as the vital railway junction of Dzankhoi. The capture of Odessa came as the climax of a 13-mile thrust which left 5,500 Germans dead, and a mass of equipment destroyed.

Now Yalta on the south coast has been taken, and the Germans are desperately trying to organise a "Dunkirk" to save their troops pinned against the sea by the Russian tanks. In an all-out drive to isolate the Crimea, the Soviets are using their air and naval supremacy to back up their land forces' inexorable advance. As the options for evacuation narrow by the hour, the Germans are sending relief convoys to those Crimean ports they still hold in a last-ditch attempt to rescue at least a remnant of their troops. Russian Stormovik bombers are taking a dreadful toll of these ships and, in fact, only a few civilians and high-ranking officers have managed to escape.

The harbour at Sevastopol is choked with wrecked ships, and thousands of enemy troops have been drowned. The Red Air Force raided the harbour again last night, and sank a 3,000-ton transport laden with soldiers as it was trying to steam to safety in the dark.

The Crimean victories are being celebrated across Russia with salvoes of victorious gunfire. Marshal Stalin has issued an Order of the Day urging the Russian forces not to allow any of the Germans to escape: "The arrogant invaders run like rats, the ground hot beneath their feet. Destroy their ships. Shoot down their planes. Don't allow a single enemy to escape retribution." As the Soviets gather for the last push to Sevastopol, some 118,000 "rats" are already dead (→ 9/5).

Burning buildings surround German soldiers as Wiebsk is caught in the middle of the battle.

US troops set to occupy New Guinea

April 24. Japanese troops left positions in New Guinea so fast that when the Americans landed today they found enemy breakfasts ready, but un-eaten, on the beach. General MacArthur's troops had bypassed enemy strongholds at Hanse and Wewak to strike hard and unexpectedly 500 miles further along the coast, taking the enemy completely by surprise.

Advance forces, which seized the town of Hollandia, are now within striking distance of the next objective – an airstrip garrisoned by 1,000 Japanese. Its capture would give the Americans surer air control over all New Guinea (→ 27/5).

First pre-fabricated house is ready: 500,000 more promised

April 30. The first of 500,000 prefabricated homes for Britain went on show in London today. Designed for demobilised servicemen and bombed-out families, the steel-built, single-storey dwelling received universal praise.

Covering 616 square feet, the "prefab" has two bedrooms and a living room, bathroom, lavatory and a kitchen – a single unit comprising washbasin, washing copper, cooking stove, sink and draining boards and refrigerator. The kitchen table folds neatly away into the wall.

"Prefabs" will be built by the motor industry and experts say they can be erected in a few hours by a small number of workmen (→ 17/7).

After the bombs, many homeless people will find shelter in prefabs.

1944

MAY

Su	Mo	Tu	We	Th	Fr	Sa
	1	2	3	4	5	6
7	8	9	10	11	12	13
14	15	16	17	18	19	20
21	22	23	24	25	26	27
28	29	30	31			

1. Moscow: Stalin tells Bulgaria, Rumania and Hungary to declare war on Germany.

2. London: Eden says General Franco has agreed to reduce Spanish links with Germany.

3. The Hague: RAF Mosquitoes successfully pinpoint and bomb a single target, the air ministry.

5. Yugoslavia: Tito's partisans raid German positions in the city of Zagreb (→25).

8. London: The exiled Czech government signs a convention allowing the Soviet army to liberate Czechoslovakia (→18/10).

9. US: The Manhattan Ear, Nose and Throat and New York hospitals open the first eye bank.

9. USSR: The Soviet army captures Sevastopol, winning control of the whole Crimea.

11. Italy: The Allies launch a new assault on Cassino (→18).

15. Algiers: The Consultative Assembly declares itself the provisional government of France (→3/6).

17. London: The Dominion prime ministers' meeting endorses Allied war plans.

18. Italy: British and Polish troops capture Cassino (→23).

23. London: Lord Keynes says new world monetary plans are the beginning of international economic co-operation.

23. Italy: The Allies begin an offensive from Anzio.→

25. Yugoslavia: Tito escapes to the hills as the Germans capture his Bosnian HQ (→14/6).

26. France: The Allies carry out extensive air raids on French cities (→4/6).

27. Pacific: The Allies land on Biak Island, 900 miles from the Philippines (→21/7).

DEATHS

9. British composer Ethel Smyth (*23/4/1858).

12. British author and critic Sir Arthur Quiller-Couch (*21/11/1863).

German spine broken at Monte Cassino

A wastland of war: Monte Cassino after suffering a four-month siege.

May 25. Allied forces breaking out of the Anzio bridgehead have linked with troops of the main Fifth Army, and a single Allied front now stretches right across Italy, reaching to within 25 miles of Rome at its nearest point.

Practically the whole of the Appian Way up to that distance is in Allied hands, with the exception of Cisterna where today Allied tanks and infantry were wiping out the last German resistance in the centre of the town.

The Allies broke through the defences in the outskirts early in the day. Since then a house-to-house battle has raged among the crumbled ruins of buildings, routing out snipers, machine-gunners and a few anti-tank guns. Now the troops are marching on Rome.

The foundations of this great victory were laid a week ago when British and Polish troops finally took the ruins of Monte Cassino, captured 1,500 men of the Germans' crack 4th Parachute Regiment and broke the spine of the "Gustav Line" defences.

Then, two days ago, British and American troops in the Anzio beachhead launched their breakout offensive. Today both Allied armies are shaking hands and the Germans are on the run (→4/6).

Stone Age fossils found in Africa

May 5. Fossils and tools used by men of the Old Stone Age 250,000 years ago have been discovered in the Great Rift Valley in Kenya, 40 miles from Nairobi, in an excavation led by Dr L.S.B. Leakey of the Coryndon Museum.

They show the importance of Africa in human evolution, and include hand axes, cleavers and other tools, associated with the bones of many different kinds of animal: extinct species of elephant, hippopotamus and giraffe, and a pig as big as a rhinocerous.

47 POWs shot in mass escape bid

May 28. Forty-seven British and Allied airmen have been shot by the Gestapo after escaping from their prison camp, a shocked House of Commons heard today. A total of 96 airmen had tunnelled their way from the "escape proof" Stalag Luft III in Silesia. Fourteen are still at large.

The Germans are claiming that the 47 dead were shot while "resisting arrest or attempting to escape a second time". The British Government is urgently seeking details from the Swiss (→16/4/45).

Rommel prepares to counter Allied plans to invade Europe

May 15. In the latest anti-invasion move in France all passenger trains have been cancelled, on the orders of Field Marshal Erwin Rommel, the anti-invasion C-in-C recently appointed by Hitler. All communications between Vichy France and neutral countries have been banned, in an attempt to prevent military and political information reaching the Allies through the Free French in Algiers.

Armed militiamen recently searched the Hotel Thermal, offices of the Vichy War Ministry, and seized the diplomatic pouches for Madrid, Lisbon and Berne. It is said that messages from Resistance groups in France to the Free French abroad were discovered. Several War Ministry officers were arrested, and others are being questioned.

Marshal Petain, the Vichy leader, is coming under heavy pressure to move to Versailles. At least twice his bags have been packed, but at the last minute the old man has changed his mind. If he continues to resist, the Germans may decide to remove him by force when the invasion comes (→26).

Rommel takes charge in Europe.

1944

JUNE

Su	Mo	Tu	We	Th	Fr	Sa
				1	2	3
4	5	6	7	8	9	10
11	12	13	14	15	16	17
18	19	20	21	22	23	24
25	26	27	28	29	30	

1. Eire: De Valera's Fianna Fail wins an overall majority in the general election.

4. France: The Allies drop 8,000 tons of bombs in a raid on German coastal positions centred on Boulogne.→

5. Rome: King Victor Emmanuel abdicates in favour of Crown Prince Umberto (→ 9).

7. Belgium: King Leopold III is arrested.

8. Italy: Allied troops capture the port of Civitavecchia (→ 19).

9. Rome: Ex-premier Ivanoe Bonomi is chosen to head a provisional government.

11. USSR: The Russians open a new offensive against the Finns in Karelia (→ 20).

13. UK: The first V-1 bomb lands in England.→

14. France: General de Gaulle visits liberated areas (→ 16).

14. Yugoslavia: Tito and royalist leaders agree on a united front to fight the Germans (→ 20/10).

16. France: King George VI visits the invasion forces fewer than six miles from the battlefront.→

17. Reykjavik: Iceland becomes an independent republic.

19. Italy: The Allies take Perugia as Elba surrenders to French troops (→ 19/7).

20. Finland: The Russians take the key Karelian port of Viipuri (→ 29).

22. France: The Allies seize two V-1 launch sites on the Cherbourg peninsula (→ 9/7).

23. London: The government says it will purchase and rebuild land in bombed areas.

25. USSR: The Soviet Army breaks through the German "Fatherland Line" of defence in White Russia (→ 3/7).

29. Helsinki: Under heavy German pressure, President Risto Ryti agrees to continue fighting the USSR (→ 19/9).

30. US: Opening of the Bretton Woods economic conference in New Hampshire (→ 22/7).

Rome liberated by Allies

June 4. Rome fell to the Allies today with the American General, Mark Clark, leading the rush to be first into the Eternal City. Rome itself is of little strategic importance, but of great psychological value. When he was told the news President Roosevelt said: "The first Axis capital is in our hands. One up and two to go."

There was little fighting in the city itself as US tanks rolled along the Appian Way. A rearguard fought a brief, useless skirmish at the Forum, and snipers are still active, falling silent one-by-one as they are winkled out.

Overhead, the sky is full of Allied aircraft, patrolling above the advancing armies. Every now and again one swoops down on the retreating Germans with cannon blazing as its pilot spots a target, but little damage has been done to the city either by bombing or in the final flurry of fighting.

The Germans ignored Hitler's order to blow up the Tiber bridges; the city's historic sites are intact; the Vatican City is untouched, and only the railway yards seem to have suffered heavy damage from pinpoint bombing attacks.

Soldiers, rolling into the city in their jeeps, are being met by crowds of Italian civilians, who are wild with excitement. Women are throwing flowers to the troops, men are handing round bottles of wine and shouting "Inglese Viva ... Americano Viva". There is no doubt about their pleasure at being occupied by the Allies.

For the troops, however, it is a bitter-sweet pleasure, coming after months of harsh and bloody fighting against crack German troops at Anzio and Monte Cassino. While Rome itself fell easily, as the Allies advanced 15 miles in 24 hours, few will forget the battles which led up to this victory.

At the start of the offensive three weeks ago, General Alexander, Allied C-in-C, Italy, told his men: "Throughout the past winter you have fought hard and valiantly ... tomorrow we can see Victory ahead ... We are going to destroy the German armies in Italy."

Since then his men and the American forces at Anzio have fully justified his confidence (→ 8).

General Mark Clark visits Rome.

De Gaulle plans to set up provisional French government

June 3. General Charles de Gaulle, who only two months ago was made Commander-in-Chief of the Free French forces, today showed his determination to stamp his ideas on the peace as well as the war. The Committee of National Liberation in Algiers announced that it is the new provisional government of France. It plans to take over from the Vichy just as soon as the Allies liberate France.

Meanwhile it wants to assume some Government powers. De Gaulle said today that the only legitimate French currency is that which has been approved by the Committee. At present French francs are printed by the Vichy Government, and the Allied command also distribute their own.

Over the next few days, however, the knottiest bone of contention will be the role of the French Resistance. De Gaulle wants to arm and organise them. Allied leaders are unsure about meshing Resistance cells with professional armies, and fearful that there might be dissension between the right-wing and left-wing cells (→ 16/8).

De Gaulle stands up for France.

US bombers reach Japanese mainland

June 15. The long-prepared air offensive against the heartland of Japanese imperialism has finally begun in earnest. American Super-Fortress B-29s, the big brothers of the Flying Fortress, have today bombed Japan.

Their targets were industrial installations in Kyushu, most southerly of the Japanese islands. The raid was announced in a special communique from the War Department. It gave no details about damage inflicted, and there was no mention of any aircraft being lost. However, General George C. Marshall, the American Chief of Staff, described the attack as "a new type of offensive against our enemy".

The strategy of heavy bombing, used so effectively against Nazi Germany, is now being adapted to destroy the Japanese war industry and weaken morale in preparation for the invasion.

The point has been expressed by Henry Stimson, the American Secretary of War, who said: "These pioneers have shortened our road to Tokyo." (→ 11)

D-Day: Allied troops storm ashore in Normandy

June 6. A terse, low-key announcement from General Eisenhower's HQ told the world that the long-awaited invasion of Europe had at last begun: "Allied naval forces, supported by strong air forces, began landing Allied armies this morning on the northern coast of France." No place names were given, nothing that would help the enemy.

The Germans say the landings were made in Normandy at about twelve points along more than a hundred miles of coast from west of Cherbourg to Le Havre. Heavy fighting is raging and the town of Caen is under attack.

It is the biggest combined land, sea and air operation of all time, and it began yesterday evening when airborne troops took off from airfields in southern England. Between midnight and the June dawn at 5.30, they landed by parachute or glider at key points behind enemy lines.

Throughout the night RAF bombers have pounded German batteries along the French coast. At daybreak more than 1,300 heavy bombers of the US Eighth Air Force took over the attack, with fighter escorts of Mustangs, Lightnings and Thunderbolts. Fighters have been in the air continuously since just before dawn – bombing, strafing and patrolling. Substantial naval forces swept enemy mines from the invasion route.

A seaborne force of several thousand ships, brought together from widely scattered ports in Britain, converged on the invasion coast soon after 5am. While battleships stationed far out to sea, and destroyers closer inland, pounded the German defences, engineers demolished beach obstacles and troops came up behind them with tanks and self-propelled artillery.

The weather is not as good as General Eisenhower had hoped. There is a strong north-westerly blowing off shore, and high seas are causing handling problems for the landing craft.

The Germans appear to believe that the Normandy operations may be a feint to distract attention from the real invasion point. British and American air reconnaissance has shown that the strongest German defences are in the Pas de Calais, and a powerful armoured force in the area has not been moved.

One of the thousands of Allied troops who hit the beaches of Normandy in the historic D-Day landings.

The question commanders on both sides will be asking is whether the Allies can bring in reinforcements faster by sea than the Germans can by land. In ordinary circumstances the land-based forces should have the advantage, but the RAF and the Americans have been attacking railways, bridges, radar stations and supply columns. Allied air superiority means the only time the German forces can make large-scale movements will be during the hours of darkness.

Tonight, in the House of Commons, Mr Churchill told MPs that the operation "is proceeding in a thoroughly satisfactory manner. Many dangers and difficulties which appeared extremely formidable are now behind us."

The losses at sea have been less than feared, and the resistance of enemy batteries has been greatly weakened by bombings from warplanes and ships. By nightfall, the Prime Minister revealed that Allied forces had penetrated several miles inland on a broad front.

The King and the Prime Minister, with General Smuts, the South African Prime Minister, visited the invasion's Supreme Commander General Eisenhower at his HQ yesterday afternoon (→ 14).

Troops consolidate their position on Sword beach before moving inland.

A drink on the road to victory.

Joy as the Tricolour flutters over Cherbourg

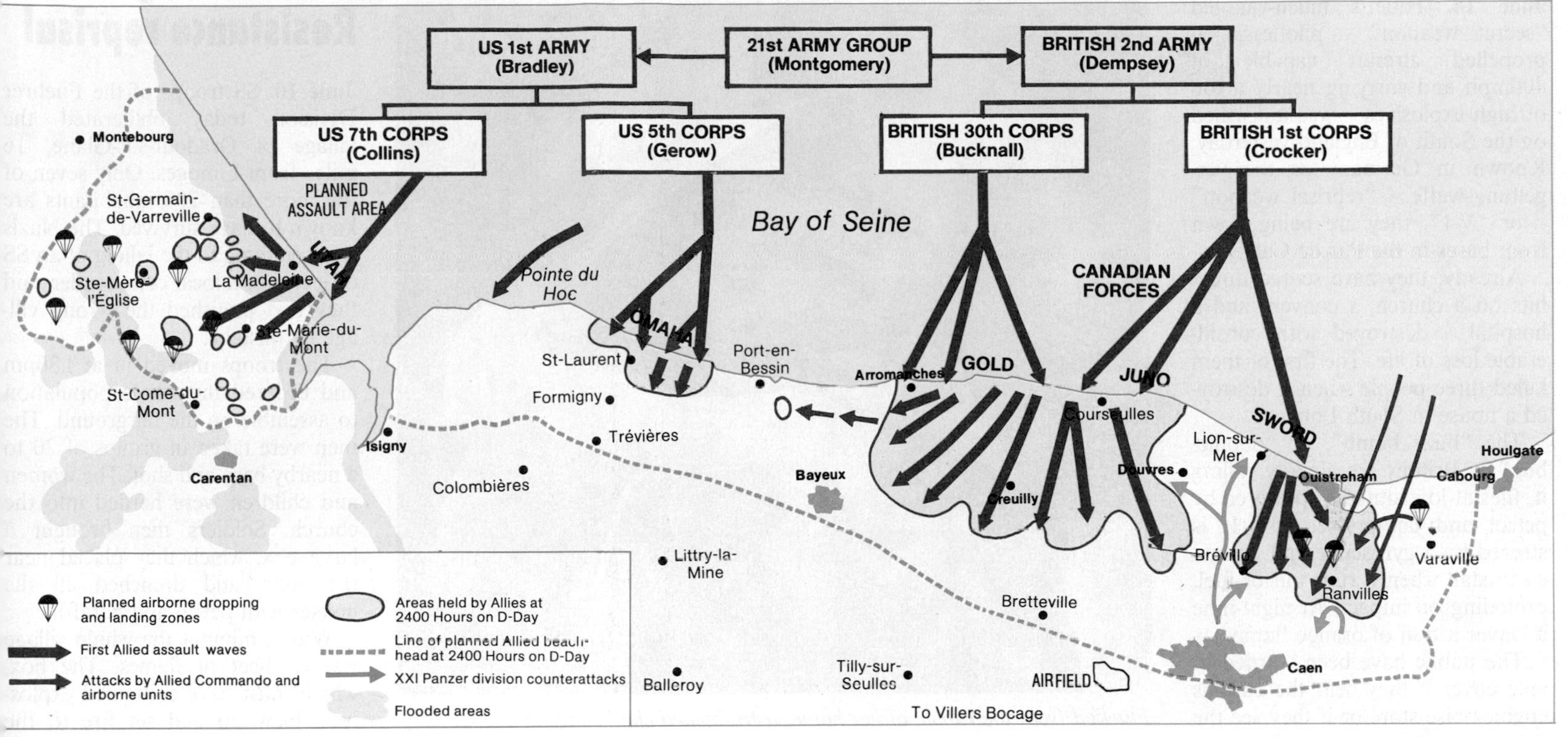

June 27. The Americans have seized the biggest prize yet in the Normandy campaign. Yesterday the garrison commander of the great port of Cherbourg, General Karl von Schlieben, surrendered, and today the naval forts and arsenal were captured. Over 20,000 prisoners have been taken, and the Tricolour once again flies from the Hotel de Ville.

Cherbourg was a formidable fortress, and the American assault was carried out with skill and audacity. By D-Day plus 6 the Allies had linked up their beachheads to form a continuous front. The Americans then thrust westwards across the Cotentin peninsula, and by D-Day plus 11 they had cut off von Schlieben's forces in the port.

But the enemy hung on. For almost two weeks, while the defenders, established in heavy concrete fortifications, kept the Americans at bay, the thunder of explosions and the rising clouds of smoke told that the port facilities were being systematically destroyed.

The Americans reduced the pillboxes by attacking them from the rear, blasting in the steel doors and throwing in phosphorous grenades to flush out the defenders.

Elsewhere in the Allied bridgehead, progress has been less spectacular. On the central sector the ancient Norman town of Bayeux has been captured, and Allied forces under Field Marshal Montgomery are thrusting south-east in an attempt to swing round behind the heavily defended town of Caen.

Monty appears deliberately to have drawn the main weight of the German armour on to the Caen sector in order to lighten the enemy resistance to the American force heading for Cherbourg.

The Germans are beginning to show signs of being short of materials. In addition to the regular Tiger and Panther panzers, they have been using obsolete French tanks which are defenceless against the latest Allied guns. Supplies to the German forces continue to be disrupted by Allied air attacks. All the Seine bridges below Paris and most of the bridges across the Loire have been destroyed.

General de Gaulle, the Free French leader, visited liberated France after the capture of Bayeux. News of his arrival was announced by loudspeaker in the streets; he was loudly cheered. Climbing on a cafe table, he said: "I am happy to be back on the soil of France and to find myself in this patriotic Norman town." He led the crowd in singing the Marseillaise.

The King visited the beachhead to hold an open-air investiture for officers. Montgomery, in battle-dress and wearing his two-badge black beret, was waiting on the beach to greet the King.

Allied casualties in the first 15 days of battle totalled 40,549, according to figures issued by Supreme Headquarters. The British lost 1,842 killed, 8,599 wounded, and 3,131 missing. The Americans lost 3,082 killed, 13,121 wounded, and 7,959 missing. The Canadians lost 363 killed, 1,359 wounded, and 1,093 missing (→31/7).

Some resisted – others did not; this collaborator is driven out of town.

"Miracle weapon" threatens London

June 14. Hitler's much-vaunted "secret weapon" – pilotless, jet-propelled aircraft capable of 400mph and carrying nearly a ton of high explosives – was unleashed on the South of England yesterday. Known in Germany as the vergeltungswaffe – "reprisal weapon" – or "V-1", they are being flown from bases in the Pas de Calais.

Already, they have scored direct hits on a church, a convent and a hospital – destroyed with considerable loss of life. The first of them killed three people when it destroyed a house in South London.

The "buzz bomb", or "doodlebug" as Britons are already calling it, flies at low altitudes, powered by petrol and compressed air. It is steered by a gyroscope and designed to stall when it runs out of fuel, exploding on impact. At night-time it leaves a trail of orange flame.

The public have been warned to take cover if they hear the curious engine-noise stop, or if they see the flame disappear. It can take up to fifteen seconds for the V-1 to explode. The popular belief is that as long as you can hear the rocket engine, you're still safe.

Anti-aircraft guns are proving initially to be ineffective against the new weapon, although hundreds of "ack ack" units are being rushed to the south coast. RAF fighter pilots are desperately seeking new techniques to counter the high-speed menace in what has become known as "bomb alley" over Kent and Sussex.

A blanket of secrecy has been imposed on "hits" by V-1s to avoid the enemy tracking their successes and calibrating the machines more effectively. However, the Germans are claiming heavy damage at Bromley, Kingston, Sevenoaks and Southampton. "For nearly 30 hours, Southern England has been shaking as if in the grip of an earthquake," one German newspaper claimed. "Thick, unbroken layers of smoke still lie over large areas."

In the Commons Herbert Morrison, the Minister of Home Security, said that the Government had known for some time that the Germans were preparing this latest onslaught. "There is no reason to think that raids by this weapon will be as heavy as the raids with which the people of this country are already familiar," he said.

"Counter-measures have already been and will continue to be applied with full vigour." Already, bombers are attacking the launch sites across the Channel.

As Londoners braced themselves for another blitz, with "doodlebugs" often falling in broad daylight on crowded shopping streets, the real terror was quickly recognised. "As they fly overhead, we pray that the engine will not stop," said one air raid warden. "Then we feel guilty because we've wished it on someone else. The silence is terrifying."

The German description of the pilotless aircraft as a "miracle weapon" is causing less concern than Dr Goebbels' use of the phrase "V-1", hinting that this is the first of several such secret weapons to be faced as the war turns in Britain's favour (→11/7).

Plucked from the rubble of her home, a frightened child clings to safety.

Hitler's "miracle weapon", the V-1 flying bomb, moving towards London.

Nazis kill entire French village in Resistance reprisal

June 10. SS troops of the Fuehrer Division today obliterated the village of Oradour-sur-Glane, 16 miles from Limoges. Only seven of the more than 700 inhabitants are known to have survived. The Nazis were reacting to the killing of an SS officer, but a local commander said they had punished the wrong village by mistake.

The troops moved in at 1.30pm and ordered the whole population to assemble on the fairground. The men were taken in groups of 20 to a nearby barn and shot. The women and children were herded into the church. Soldiers then brought a large box, which they placed near the altar, and drenched all the houses with petrol and paraffin.

Within minutes the whole village was a sheet of flames. The box, which must have contained explosives, blew up and set fire to the church. Women were shot as they tried to climb out of the windows. One woman fainted as she fell and was left for dead. She escaped to a nearby village at nightfall.

The village is now only charred ruins. In the church even the bells melted, and what was left of the bodies of some of the children were visible in upright position near the confessional.

US bomb Japanese bulwark in Pacific

June 11. Carrier-borne aircraft from the American Pacific Fleet yesterday carried out effective attacks upon the heavily-defended Japanese strongholds in the Marianas islands, striking at bases on Saipan, Tinian and Guam. This action was part of a general offensive against Japanese strong points guarding the way to the Philippines and to Japan itself.

Three weeks ago carrier-based planes launched the series of new attacks by raiding Wake Island. Since then Liberators have caused great destruction at Saipan. They reported that on their last sortie they saw only 12 enemy fighters, of which two were shot down (→15).

1944

JULY

Su	Mo	Tu	We	Th	Fr	Sa
						1
2	3	4	5	6	7	8
9	10	11	12	13	14	15
16	17	18	19	20	21	22
23	24	25	26	27	28	29
30	31					

3. USSR: Minsk, the last big German base on Soviet soil, falls to the Russians (→13).

3. London: The evacuation begins of children from the capital because of the V-1 bombings.→

6. Berlin: Field Marshal von Rundstedt is sacked as supreme commander of the German army in the west (→9).

9. France: Caen falls to the Allies.→

11. Washington: Roosevelt agrees to run for a fourth term (→20).

13. Lithuania: The capital Vilna is captured by the Soviet army on its advance through the Baltic states (→22/8).

17. London: The government unveils plans for new houses costing 13/1d. a week to rent.→

19. Italy: the Allies take Livorno and Ancona (→11/8).

20. Chicago: Roosevelt wins nomination for a fourth term.→

21. Berlin: Troops pour into the city following the attempt on Hitler's life (→23).

21. Pacific: US troops land on Guam (→27).

22. US: End of the Bretton Woods economic conference (→27/12/45).

23. Germany: Himmler launches a manhunt to catch the generals implicated in the plot against Hitler (→6/8).

24. Poland: The Soviet Army captures Lublin (→28).

25. Berlin: Hitler names Goebbels "Reich Plenipotentiary for the Total War Effort" (→11/11).

27. Pacific: Guam is taken (→8/12).

28. Poland: The Soviet Army storms key German strongholds, including Bialystok, Lvov and Brest-Litovsk (→30).

30. Poland: the Soviets bombard Warsaw.→

DEATH

31. French author and aviator Antoine de Saint-Exupery (*29/6/1900).

Allies drive Germans from Normandy

July 31. In their first major tank operation, the American First Army have smashed through the German lines in the St. Lo sector and captured the enemy's rear artillery positions. The American Third Army have swung westwards to overrun Brittany. On the eastern sector the British and Canadians have captured Caen and are racing for the heights to the south-east. At last the Allied forces are free of the thick hedges of the bocage and are heading for open country. The Battle of Normandy has become the Battle of France.

It took the American First Army less than 36 hours to break through the German defences around the communications centre of St. Lo. Before they went in, over 2,000 Allied bombers dropped 4,000 tons of bombs on enemy positions. The Germans put up a tough fight, but their infantry was operating without coordinated artillery support, suggesting that communications have been disrupted.

Some German units have been ready to surrender at the first sight of an Allied plane. When a fighter-bomber on reconnaissance came upon a convoy of tanks, the crews jumped out and fled, leaving white flags on the vehicles. The heaviest weight of German armour remains opposite the British-Canadian sector around Caen.

At least seven panzer divisions and four armoured battalions are believed to be in position there, while no more than three panzer divisions are facing the Americans. The Germans have evidently decided that a British-Canadian breakthrough south-east of Caen would leave the road to Paris wide open.

The Germans put up stubborn resistance in an attempt to hold on to Caen, the hub of 12 major roads. It was finally taken in a pincer movement, with the British driving from the north and the Canadians thrusting from the west.

The whole town appears to have been obliterated by bombing and shellfire. It is impossible to discern the layout of streets. Here and there a few sticks of furniture stand out from the rubble. Many of the enemy troops captured are not Germans. They include Hungarians, Rumanians, and one Iranian (→9/8).

American infantrymen advance on what remains of a Normandy chateau.

No shoes, and no transport either, for this group of German prisoners, who only surrendered to the Allied advance after hours of hard fighting.

Mass evacuation as V-1s fall on London

July 11. The second mass wartime exodus of children from London is under way as the Germans intensify their "buzz bomb" attacks on the the south-east.

More than 41,000 mothers and children left London yesterday; others are being evacuated from "bomb alley" – the route used by the doodlebugs across Sussex, Surrey and Kent. Over a million children in all are being moved, many of them returning to their former billets in the country.

In the Commons yesterday, Mr Churchill said that between 100 and 150 flying bombs were being launched against Britain every day. A total of 2,754 bombs had caused 2,752 deaths and 8,000 casualties.

The Prime Minister revealed that "an unseen battle" against the new weapon had been under way for more than a year, with 50,000 tons of bombs dropped on launching sites and other targets. "London will never be conquered and will never fall," he said.

Eight new purpose-built deep shelters are being opened in London. Air-conditioned, with private cubicles for families, and canteen facilities, the new shelters are for the use of ticket-holders only. Most Londoners prefer to sleep in steel built "Morrison shelters" which have replaced dining-tables in many households.

Hitler escapes bomb assassination bid

The one that got away: Hitler shows Mussolini his wrecked headquarters.

July 20. At his Wolf's Lair HQ in East Prussia, the Fuehrer was today listening to a report on the deteriorating military situation on the Russian front when a violent explosion shattered the conference room, killing at least three officers – but not Hitler.

Soon afterwards, he made a radio broadcast to the German people, saying: "A very small clique of ambitious, unscrupulous and at the same time criminally stupid officers laid a plot to remove me." He accused a crippled war hero, Colonel Graf Klaus von Stauffenberg, of planting a suitcase bomb under the conference table. Saying he had only minor burns and cuts, the Fuehrer took his escape as a sign that Providence was preserving him to continue his life's work.

The plot appears to have involved many more than a "very small clique". During the hour or so when it was believed Hitler had died, prominent serving and retired senior officers committed themselves to the coup. For a time orders were being issued in Berlin on behalf of a "new Reich government", but tonight the capital is back under Nazi rule; von Stauffenberg and others have been hanged (→21).

Truman to be FDR's running mate in US

July 21. In a dramatic turnaround at the Democratic convention in Chicago tonight, President Roosevelt got a new running-mate for the election next November. The Vice-President, Henry A. Wallace, won the first ballot, but on the second Senator Harry S. Truman crushingly defeated him by 1,100 votes to 66. The third candidate, Justice William O. Douglas, polled only four votes.

President Roosevelt had let it be known that he wanted a change, and on the second vote the Douglas supporters switched their votes, having seen he could not win.

Unlike the President, Truman comes from humble origins. He is the son of a small-town Missouri farmer who could not afford to send him to college. His first job was with a railway construction gang at $35 a month. After fighting in France in the First World War, he opened a men's haberdashery shop in Independence, Missouri. That venture collapsed and he went into politics as a county judge.

He proved to have a better head for politics than for business, but he is still little-known nationally. He was eating a sandwich when the result was announced. Not surprisingly, he seemed stunned. He came to Chicago intending to vote for a fellow senator and was drafted at the last minute (→7/11).

Germans retreat as Russian war machine advances on Warsaw

July 31. The 400-mile-long German line between Riga in Latvia and Warsaw, the Polish capital, appears to be breaking down tonight and, according to both Moscow and Berlin, the Red Army has opened the battle for Warsaw itself.

A German military spokesman said that fighting was taking place along an arc only six miles from the city, following the linking of the Russian forces south, east and north-east of the city.

Warsaw's capture will open the German heartland of East Prussia to the avenging Russian army, and for the first time in this war the Germans will experience what it is like to be occupied by an enemy army (→20/8).

A German tank, disabled in retreat, smoulders next to a member of its crew.

Homes to be fit for housewives

July 17. The Government today revealed plans to build between three and four million houses in the first decade after the War. The shape of the house to come was revealed in a Ministry of Health document, "Design of Dwellings".

Houses will be bigger, with three bedrooms, well-equipped kitchens, better heating arrangements, constant hot water, efficient plumbing, larger windows and storage space. The report recommends "what has been the long-felt want of the average family, a clean, cheerful room where meals can be taken with the maximum of convenience to the housewife".

1944

AUGUST

Su	Mo	Tu	We	Th	Fr	Sa
		1	2	3	4	5
6	7	8	9	10	11	12
13	14	15	16	17	18	19
20	21	22	23	24	25	26
27	28	29	30	31		

1. UK: Scientists say that DDT has been found to act as an anti-malarial insecticide.

2. Berlin: Germany breaks off relations with Turkey.

4. Vichy: The Germans order Petain to leave; he refuses (→ 19).

6. Berlin: The trial opens of alleged anti-Hitler bomb plotters.→

9. France: British and Canadian forces begin a new offensive south of Caen (→ 12).

11. Italy: Churchill arrives on a visit to Allied headquarters.

12. Channel: The first PLUTO (Pipe Line Under The Ocean) begins to send fuel from the Isle of Wight to Cherbourg.

12. Vichy: Laval orders the release of ex-premier Edouard Herriot.

13. Berlin: The Germans say the new V-2 flying bomb is ready for use (→ 9/9).

15. France: A massive Allied force lands on a 100-mile coastal strip from Nice to Marseilles.→

17. Germany: The Russians reach the East Prussian frontier (→ 13/10).

19. Vichy: The SS arrests Petain and takes him to Belfort (→ 15/9).

22. Italy: The Allies take Florence.

23. France: Marseilles and Grenoble fall to the Allies.→

25. Bucharest: Following King Michael's armistice with the USSR on August 23, Rumania declares war on Germany.→

26. Sofia: Bulgaria says it will quit the war and disarm Germans on its soil (→ 6/9).

29. France: Nine Frenchmen are shot outside a Roman amphitheatre in the south as Gestapo collaborators (→ 1/9).

31. London: The King makes Montgomery a field marshal (→ 5/1/45).

DEATH

19. British conductor Sir Henry Wood (*3/3/1869).

French tanks lead Allies into Paris

After four years of brutal Nazi occupation, the population of Paris celebrates the return of freedom.

Aug 25. The Nazi swastika has gone from the Eiffel Tower. Today, after four grim years, the Tricolour flies once again for Parisians.

First of the Allied forces into the city was the French Second Armoured Division, under General Jacques Leclerc. This evening General de Gaulle entered the capital. He said: "I wish simply and from the bottom of my heart to say, 'Vive Paris'."

The Allied armies advanced fast after the Normandy breakout. General George Patton's American Third Army swept through Orleans, Chartres and Dreux to link up with the British advancing on Rouen. The Germans are now pulling back across the Seine.

General Eisenhower, anxious to avoid a battle for Paris, encircled the city and contacted the French Resistance. The police went on strike and seized the Ile de la Cite on the Seine. Street fighting broke out, and the Prefecture was taken over by Resistance forces. Paris Radio broadcast a proclamation by the German authorities, saying: "Irresponsible elements have taken up arms against the occupation authorities. This revolt will be rigorously suppressed."

At this point, Eisenhower sent orders to Leclerc to go in. The first infantry patrols, supported by tanks, entered the city last night. General Leclerc arrived this morning just before ten, while sporadic fighting was still going on. On the Boulevard Raspail, grenades were thrown from an upstairs window, and German snipers are still active.

At the Police Prefecture, Leclerc received the German commander, General Dietrich von Choltitz, who signed the surrender document and then ordered the cease-fire: "Arms will be stacked. Personnel will assemble without arms at places to be indicated and will wait for orders there." Von Choltitz defied an order from Hitler to destroy Paris before surrendering.

Tonight most – but not all – Parisians are celebrating. There have been ugly scenes as collaborators have been dragged through the streets and beaten. Police have had to protect captured German officers from lynchings. Tomorrow de Gaulle will proclaim the Fourth Republic (→ 29).

German troops, ordered to defend until death, surrender to the Allies.

▷

Russia captures Bucharest and its oil

Aug 31. The Russians, fighting alongside their new allies, the Rumanians, have swept into the Ploesti oilfields, which have been supplying Germany with a third of her military oil.

Rumanian troops are now fighting under Soviet command, following Marshal Ion Antonescu's decision to change sides last week.

The loss of the oilfields will strike a serious blow at Germany. Ploesti produced five and a half million tons of crude oil a year, all of which was refined on the spot. Allied bombers have mounted a series of attacks on the refineries which have cut their capacity from ten million to two million tons a year.

Now even this will be denied to Hitler's tanks and aircraft. There are already signs of an increasing oil shortage, with most of the remaining units of the German navy laid up, unable to put to sea because they have no fuel oil. The Germans must now rely on their synthetic oil plants in Silesia, and there is little doubt that they will come under heavy attack from the air.

Meanwhile, having taken the oilfields, the Russians have pushed on into the capital, Bucharest. The first Red Army soldiers to enter the city belonged to a scouting unit of tanks and motorised infantry.

The further this vanguard of General Malinovsky's army progressed towards the centre of the city, the more crowded the streets became. The pavements were packed with people shouting greetings and showering the Russians with bouquets.

The entry of the Soviet troops into Bucharest marks the conclusion of one of the swiftest campaigns carried out by the Red Army since going over to the offensive at Stalingrad.

The campaign has lasted only 12 days, but during that time the Russians have smashed through powerful fortifications, routed strong enemy forces, and covered 250 miles.

Behind the advancing troops, special squads are hunting down German saboteurs. The Rumanian people are joining in the chase. Anti-German feeling among the Rumanians is such that Red Army soldiers have difficulty in guarding their prisoners (→ 10/10).

Joy and relief are plain to see as these Rumanians greet liberation.

Officers in plot to kill Hitler strangled with piano wire

Aug 8. After a two-day trial by the notorious People's Court, a field marshal, four generals and three other officers were today sentenced to death for their part in the July plot against Hitler. The Judge told them: "You are nothing but Schweinhunde."

The executions were carried out within two hours of the Court's passing sentence. They are believed to have died in the most painful manner possible, suffering strangulation by piano wire strung from meathooks.

More trials are on the way. Five more senior officers have been named, and an £80,000 reward has been offered for information as to the whereabouts of the Mayor of Leipzig, Dr Karl Goerdler, who disappeared on July 20, when it turned out that Hitler had not, after all, died in the explosion at his HQ. Diplomats, senior police officers, professors and clergymen are among the several thousand on the Gestapo lists (→ 11/9).

Nazi death camps found in Poland

Aug 27. The first proofs of what has been only a terrible rumour have come to light in Poland today. Revealing what appears to be the supreme Nazi atrocity, Polish and Soviet officials have shown the press the Maidenek concentration camp. Here an estimated 1.5 million people, of every race and creed, have been systematically murdered under conditions of clinical efficiency.

Inside an electrified barbed-wire fence, interspaced with 14 machine-gun posts, the 670-acre camp contains rows of neat green barrack huts. Next to them stand the gas chambers and crematoria. Each new batch of prisoners, arriving by cattle-truck from all over Europe, were methodically gassed to death. Their bodies, stripped of all possessions, were then burnt to ashes. Clothing and valuables went to Germany, and the ashes used as fertiliser (→ 27/1/45).

Nazi tanks raze Warsaw

The last survivors of the Polish Home Army defeated by German tanks.

Aug 20. The Germans, attempting to crush the Polish uprising in Warsaw, are using Tiger tanks to shell the Old City which has been seized by the Polish Home Army under the commmand of General Bor-Komorowski.

The tanks are reducing the fine old buildings of Warsaw to rubble, but their supporting infantry are finding the house-to-house fighting extremely costly as the Poles battle grimly for each one.

A communique from General Bor received in London today claimed the destruction of three Tigers and three of the even heavier Goliaths at the barricades. "German units, isolated in the University building and in the former residence of the Prime Minister, are being supplied by the Luftwaffe. We are holding our positions in Lazienki Park."

However, while the Poles are fighting most gallantly, they have limited supplies, and if help does not arrive soon they will inevitably be crushed. Supplies could be dropped to them by British and American heavy bombers, but they would need the Russians' permission to operate on this front. The Red Army is very close to Warsaw, but for the moment it seems to have come to a halt (→ 15/12).

Allies open second front in France

Aug 16. For the first time the Free French Army is participating in the invasion. Today a contingent under General de Tassigny landed with a massive Allied force on the French coast between Nice and Marseilles. Several small towns were taken in the attack, and by nightfall troops of the US Seventh Army were fighting in the streets of Cannes.

The Resistance also played an important role, wresting control of several Savoy villages from the Germans and fighting them on the streets of Marseilles. In Paris tonight the Marseillaise was sung on the streets when the news came through (→ 23).

Channel Islanders to have meat again

Aug 3. German troops were last night reported to be leaving Jersey and Guernsey now the American advance into Brittany has removed any of their strategic value for the Nazis. The Channel Islands were occupied in 1940, but it may still be some time before any of the 30,000 evacuees are allowed to return to their homes. Lord Portsea, who acted as spokesman for the islanders throughout the war, commented: "The most urgent thing will be to send the people food. They used to obtain all their meat from England, but during the German occupation they have been forced to become a nation of vegetarians."

1944

SEPTEMBER

Su	Mo	Tu	We	Th	Fr	Sa
					1	2
3	4	5	6	7	8	9
10	11	12	13	14	15	16
17	18	19	20	21	22	23
24	25	26	27	28	29	30

1. France: Allied troops capture Dieppe and Arras and reach the Belgian frontier (→ 4).

4. Belgium: The Allies capture Brussels and Antwerp and cross into Holland (→ 8).

5. London: Belgium, Holland and Luxembourg sign a treaty of customs union.

5. Stockholm: Sweden says it will bar entry to Nazis attempting to flee.

6. Sofia: Bulgaria declares war on Germany (→ 20/10).

7. London: Evacuations are suspended (→ 9).

8. Brussels: The Belgian government under Hubert Pierlot returns from exile in London.→

9. London: The first V-2 bomb lands, killing three.→

10. Quebec: Churchill and Roosevelt open talks.→

10. Belgium: Canadian troops capture Zeebrugge (→ 30).

11. Germany: The US First Army under General Omar Bradley leads the Allies onto German soil (→ 10/10).

11. Berlin: Seven more generals die for plotting to kill Hitler.

15. Paris: The provisional government says it will try Vichy war criminals (→ 11/4/45).

19. Helsinki: Finland signs an armistice with the USSR.

20. France: The Allies capture Boulogne (→ 30).

21. Philippines: MacArthur's forces launch an assault on the Japanese near Manila (→ 20/10).

22. Estonia: The Russians capture the capital, Tallinn (→ 13/10).

27. Albania: Soviet troops and Yugoslav partisans cross the border (→ 10/11).

30. France: Calais falls to Canadian troops (→ 23/10).

DEATHS

13. British humorist Heath Robinson (*31/5/1872).

27. French sculptor Aristide Maillol (*8/12/1861).

Allies free Belgian cities as retreating Nazis breach dykes

Sept 9. Allied troops have swept across Belgium and are now just 20 miles from the German border, ready to take on the heavily fortified Siegfried line.

British troops liberated Brussels to scenes of near-delirium on the streets, having maintained an advance of around 25 miles a day as the enemy retreated. Just before dawn today columns of American tanks swept into Liege, wildly cheered by thousands of Belgians.

The retreating Germans have tried to buy time by flooding low-lying land in both Belgium and Holland, but the Allied advance is moving so swiftly that on some roads the Allied armour is running right into the back of the retreating German columns, leading to wheel-to-wheel battles which are fought so closely that air attack is impossible.

What has been described as "the biggest traffic jam in history" took place on the Mons-Brussels road on Sunday, when the Allies wrecked more than 900 German trucks and 750 horse-drawn vehicles.

Many German units are simply coming out of the woods, unshaven and dishevelled, to surrender, saying they do not want to fight under the fanatical SS.

Surrendering Germans have to be treated with caution, however; some open fire after they have given themselves up and then fight on to the last bullet (→ 10).

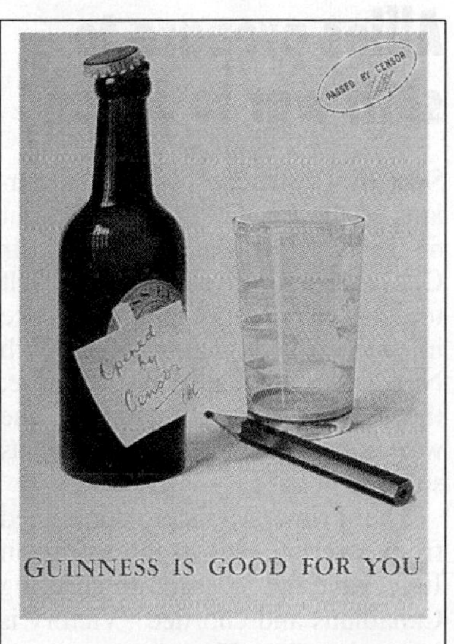

Paras cut off at Arnhem

With far too few stretchers, Arnhem's wounded have to help each other.

Sept 25. An audacious airborne operation that promised to shorten the war by several months has ended in bloody failure. General Eisenhower had tried to use his First Airborne Army to seize three bridges which would give the Allies control of the lower Rhine.

A US airborne division was to seize the bridges at Nijmegen and Grave, while the First British Airborne Division had to capture the farthest bridge over the Rhine at Arnhem. Another US airborne division would protect the other landings, while the British Guards Armoured Division would force their way through the German lines to relieve the airborne forces.

British paratroopers captured the northern end of the Arnhem bridge, but the enemy held on to the town, and bad weather prevented the flying in of reinforcements and supplies. The Guards' armour got through to the Americans at Nijmegen and Grave, but was unable to break through to Arnhem. After eight days battling against overwhelming odds, the British pulled back across the Rhine; of the original 10,000, 2,400 returned.

Silent rockets bring terror to London

Sept 9. A second Battle of London is being fought with a new and terrible weapon. V-2s, long-range rockets, 15 tons in weight and carrying one-ton warheads, are being launched on the city from Holland and Germany, adding to the havoc caused by flying bombs.

The rockets give no warning except for a "tearing sound, like an express train" as they land vertically from heights of 50 miles at faster than the speed of sound. The first, which hit Chiswick in West London, caused a blast wave which could be felt for miles.

The Government is maintaining a veil of secrecy over the new weapons. Frequent explosions heard in London are being put down to "gaswork explosions" in an attempt to confuse the Germans.

Attempts to bomb launch sites are made difficult by the mobility of the new weapon, which can be fired from a simple concrete base.

Another German rocket – the V-2.

Germans on the run throughout Europe

Sept 15. German troops were on the run across Europe last night, as Allied soldiers broke through the main German defence of the Siegfried line and finally liberated the town of Nancy, the key bastion of eastern France, which Hitler decreed should be held at all costs.

Leading elements of an American combat unit drove into the town through streets lined with cheering people. Although there are still many Nazi snipers attempting to disrupt the advance, the way is now open to move into Germany. Already there are reports that civilians are fleeing the Rhineland in their scores of thousands.

Soldiers involved in the panic-stricken retreat are clinging to every available vehicle to get home, but when they do cross the borders into Germany many are said to be spending their time trying to find their families rather than reporting for more duty (→10/10).

Allies prepare to shift war to Japan

Sept 16. Destruction of "the barbarians of the Pacific" – the knockout of Japan – is the next job. Mr Churchill and President Roosevelt tonight ended another conference in Quebec with that resolve. With Nazi Germany nearing collapse, they settled plans for shifting the war effort to the Far East theatre as soon as possible.

The Prime Minister, suntanned from a recent visit to the troops in Italy, gave the "V" sign to cheering Canadians and chortled "Victory is everywhere" (→21).

Bright lights return as black-out lifted

Sept 17. In Nottingham parents took their children to the market square to see street-lights for the first time in their lives, and throughout most of Britain the lights had come on again. After five years of darkness, the Government has relaxed stringent black-out regulations and allowed modified street-lighting. Only certain coastal areas will remain in darkness. Railway stations are to be lit once again; and passengers in trains, buses and trams will be able to read again at night (→20/11).

British troops sprint through a town left destroyed by fleeing Germans.

1944

OCTOBER

Su	Mo	Tu	We	Th	Fr	Sa
1	2	3	4	5	6	7
8	9	10	11	12	13	14
15	16	17	18	19	20	21
22	23	24	25	26	27	28
29	30	31				

2. Mediterranean: British troops land on Crete (→17).

5. Berlin: Goebbels announces that food rations will be cut (→16).

8. London: Sir William Jowitt is appointed Britain's first Minister of Social Insurance.

9. Moscow: Churchill arrives for talks with Stalin.

10. Germany: The Allies surround Aachen and order the Germans to surrender.→

13. Latvia: The Soviet Army enters the capital Riga (→18).

15. Budapest: The government of Miklos Horthy asks for an armistice, but is ousted by pro-Nazis (→29/11).

16. Germany: The weekly bread ration is cut by 200g (3oz) to 2.2kg (1lb).

17. Athens: Rival partisans begin to fight each other; a bomb goes off during a victory parade (→1/11).

18. Czechoslovakia: The Russians sweep across the border along a 170-mile front.

20. Philippines: General MacArthur lands on the central Philippine island of Leyte.→

23. France: The Allies recognise de Gaulle's provisional government (→28).

26. London: The Archbishop of Canterbury, William Temple, dies after two years in office (→4/1/45).

27. Holland: British troops capture Tilberg as Canadians take Bergen (→2/11).

28. Paris: De Gaulle orders the Resistance to disarm (→7/11).

30. Washington: Premiere of Aaron Copland's one-act ballet "Appalachian Spring".

DEATHS

26. British prelate William Temple, Archbishop of Canterbury from 1942 (*15/10/1881).

26. British Princess Beatrice Mary Victoria Feodore, youngest child of Queen Victoria (*14/4/1857).

MacArthur returns to the Philippines

Oct 21. General Douglas MacArthur today fulfilled his promise to return to the Philippines. Wearing his famous sunglasses and battered service cap, he strode up the beach at Leyte. A few days before, spearhead troops of his 250,000-strong invasion force fought their way ashore on this central island of the Philippines.

It was thinly defended because the Japanese wrongly expected the assault to begin upon the outlying Mindanao. Their navy began bringing reinforcements back to Leyte, but it was severely depleted after five days of bruising naval engagements with the US Seventh Fleet, under Vice-Admiral Thomas Kinkaid. Two divisions of the Japanese fleet had been destroyed, including a carrier and numerous cruisers and destroyers. This evening American warships are pursuing the battered survivors.

"In the Battle of Leyte Gulf the Japanese navy has suffered its most crushing defeat of the War," declared General MacArthur. The most serious US loss was the carrier USS Princeton, so badly damaged that she had to be finished off with US torpedoes.

Recently Japan has been employing a new and alarming weapon – human suicide bombs. Naval pilots deliberately dive their aircraft into the decks of American ships to ensure greater accuracy. The Japanese call this tactic a kamikaze, or "divine wind", mission. The pilots wear ceremonial uniforms, and fly aircraft fitted with impact bombs (→9/1/45).

General Douglas MacArthur keeps his promise as he comes ashore again.

Fighting their way across the island of Leyte, troops dodge incoming fire.

United Nations plan for post-war peace

Oct 9. A new world-wide organisation for preserving peace will be set up after the war. It will be called the United Nations. From their respective capitals Britain, China, the United States and Russia today simultaneously announced proposals for future world security, agreed at their recent four-power meeting at Dumbarton Oaks, Washington, DC.

These proposals will be the basis of a United Nations Charter to be negotiated at a later conference. All peace-loving nations will be invited to join. The organisation will have a Security Council. The Big Four, with France joining them later, will have permanent seats, and another six seats will be filled by smaller countries.

All nations will promise to make armed forces available, when the Council demands them, for combined military action to confront potential warmakers. President Roosevelt commented: "No would-be aggressor should ever get started." That is the great hope still to be made reality (→25/4/45).

Rommel chooses an honourable death

Oct 14. Erwin Rommel, who was made a Field Marshal by Hitler for his victories in North Africa, is dead. The Nazis say he died from injuries received when his car was attacked by RAF planes. The truth is, Rommel knew of the July plot to get rid of Hitler. When this came out, Hitler said that if Rommel committed suicide he would have a hero's funeral. Otherwise, he faced the People's Court. Rommel took poison.

▷

Allies take first city in the Fatherland

Oct 20. The first German city fell to the Allies today after eight days of street fighting and bombing. Aachen had been offered a choice – "surrender or die" – and chose the latter. The Nazis threatened to punish those who did not resist, which led to mayhem. A Czech reporter described the scene: "Gestapo and soldiers were looting the town, grabbing in mad lust the property of their own people although they had no hope to carry it away. I found its people crushed to desperation by a double misery, by our onslaught and by the cruelties of their Nazi masters" (→ 24/11).

Red Army and Tito capture Belgrade

Oct 20. The Red Army, linking up with Tito's ragged but hard-fighting partisans, today liberated Belgrade, the capital of Yugoslavia. The German garrison, by-passed on both banks of the Danube, was annihilated.

The Russians were supported by their new-found allies, Bulgaria and Rumania, who have both cut their ties with Hitler and declared war on Germany. All three armies are now sweeping up from the south-east in a great upper-cut aimed at Budapest. Meanwhile, Tito is continuing to harry the Germans in their fighting retreat from the Balkans.

Hitler forms Home Guard for Germany

Oct 18. In a desperate preparation for the coming Allied invasion of Germany, Hitler tonight ordered the call-up of all able-bodied males from 16 to 60 for a new force named the Volksturm, or People's Guard. The Fuehrer complained of "the defection of all our European allies" and said Germany now stood alone against "our Jewish international enemies". The Volksturm HQ will be in the mountain caves at Salzkammergut, suggesting that Hitler is thinking of making a last stand in Bavaria.

British land in Greece

Oct 14. British troops returned to Athens today, three and a half years after being driven out by the Germans. Colonel Earl Jellicoe, the renowned guerrilla fighter, led a small group of soldiers, accompanied by an ever-growing band of Greek partisans, into the city. They had made their way along 28 miles of blown-up roads from the little airfield at Megara, captured a few days ago.

The city went mad with joy when they arrived, and an RAF plane, which flew over the city a few hours later, reported that all the streets were bedecked with flags and flowers, while long, cheering columns, waving banners, wound through them.

This great day has come only ten days after British seaborne and airborne forces captured Patra on the Gulf of Corinth and, finding little opposition, started to push towards the Greek capital.

The plight of the people is urgent. The Germans and Italians have robbed them of virtually everything. A packet of cigarettes costs one English gold sovereign and there is little food to be had.

A child rescued by the Red Cross.

However, the first relief ships are already steaming towards Greek ports, and the Dakotas which only a few days ago were delivering paratroops are now being used to deliver bread.

Meanwhile, higher up the Adriatic, a furious battle is being fought for Corfu with British troops, supported by Albanian patriots, attacking the German garrison (→ 17).

In scenes of utter devastation the Polish Home Army refused to give in, continuing to fight against overwhelming odds and protected by little but the rubble of their own homes, until superior German firepower left them with no alternative but to flee or, for many, accept surrender.

1944

NOVEMBER

Su	Mo	Tu	We	Th	Fr	Sa
			1	2	3	4
5	6	7	8	9	10	11
12	13	14	15	16	17	18
19	20	21	22	23	24	25
26	27	28	29	30		

1. Greece: British troops capture Salonika (→ 18/12).

2. Holland: British troops seize Flushing (→ 16).

5. Hungary: Soviet tanks enter Budapest (→ 29).

6. Cairo: Lord Moyne, British Minister-Resident in the Middle East, is murdered (→ 8).

7. Paris: De Gaulle calls for a French occupation zone in Germany (→ 23).

8. Cairo: Two members of the Stern Gang, a Zionist terrorist group, confess to the murder of Lord Moyne (→ 17).

10. Albania: The Allies recognise the government of partisan leader Enver Hoxha.

11. Berlin: Himmler is given control of the German Army, which is incorporated into the Nazi Party (→ 24/5/45).

12. Paris: Churchill is given the freedom of the city (→ 30).

16. Holland: The Germans are reported to have blown up the town hall at Heusden with 200 people inside, killing 135.

17. London: Churchill says all terrorist groups in Palestine must be eradicated.

20. London: The lights are switched on in Piccadilly, the Strand and Fleet Street after five years of blackout.

20. Paris: P. G. Wodehouse is arrested.

23. France: French troops under General Leclerc enter Strasbourg.→

26. London: General Alexander is promoted to Supreme Allied Commander in the Mediterranean (→ 1/12).

27. UK: 90 die in an explosion at an RAF bomb dump near Burton-on-Trent.

29. Hungary: The Russians cross the Danube and pierce German defences in the south of the country (→ 13/1/45).

30. London: Churchill celebrates his 70th birthday (→ 25/1/44).

DEATH

22. French statesman Joseph Caillaux (*30/3/1863).

RAF bombers sink German ship Tirpitz

Nov 12. Three RAF 12,000-pound bombs today finally put paid to Germany's last major warship, the Tirpitz. The ship, which always threatened more than she delivered, is tonight lying on her side on the bottom of Tromso Fjord in northern Norway after the attack by Lancaster bombers.

The Lancasters were armed with special armour-piercing bombs designed by Barnes Wallis, the engineer who created the bombs used to blast the German dams in the Ruhr. One bomb hit her amidships, another on the bows and a third on her stern.

The Tirpitz, which was only completed in 1941, has been attacked eight times in all during the war, usually as she sheltered in Alten Fjord. There were long periods when she was damaged too badly to fight after the attacks by the Fleet Air Arm and midget submarines of the Royal Navy. She made brief sorties to little effect, but while she still existed she remained a threat to Allied convoys to Russia.

The Germans believed that the ship, and her sister vessel the Bismarck, were unsinkable but Mr Wallis's earthquake bomb is said to be able to penetrate several feet of concrete without losing any of its explosive force.

Churchill warns Zionist gangsters

Nov 17. In an official statement on the assassination in Cairo on November 6 of Lord Moyne, Minister-Resident in the Middle East, Mr Churchill has condemned the killers, presumed to be members of the extreme Zionist Stern Gang. Comparing them to "gangsters worthy of Nazi Germany" he warned that many of Zionism's staunchest supporters might well change their minds if such attacks persisted.

He called upon members of the Jewish comunity to police such incidents, and promised determined governmental action. In Palestine, a spokesman for the Jewish agency called on law-abiding members of the Jewish community to reject any calls for more terrorist attacks.

FDR is US president for the fourth time

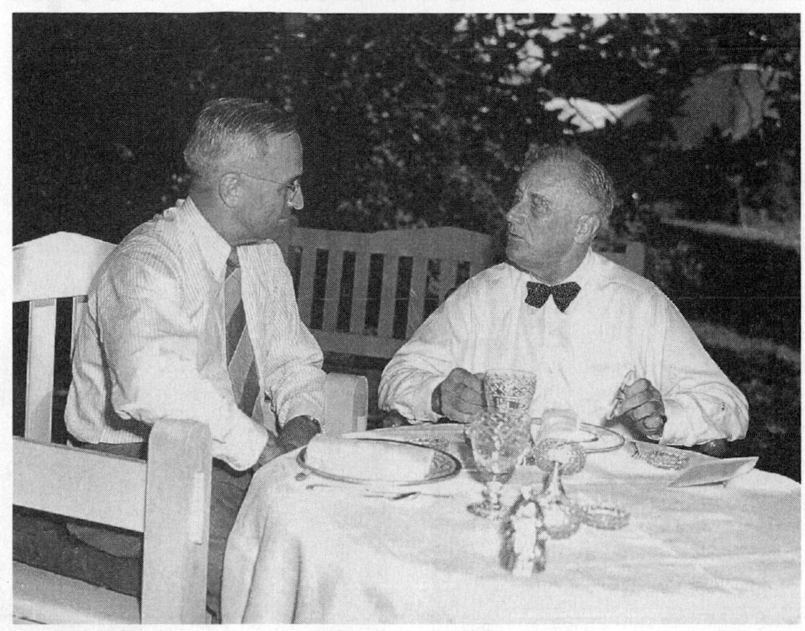

Lunching with Vice-President Truman, FDR looks towards a fourth term.

Nov 7. President Franklin Delano Roosevelt today won an unprecedented fourth term of office as US President. He was already the longest-serving US President. No other President has served more than two terms. The last to do so was Woodrow Wilson, who also had to fight an election while leading the US in a world war.

Roosevelt's majority was only three million compared with the nine million landslide he won in 1936. This time, however, Roosevelt was unable to carry through the barnstorming countrywide campaigning that characterised his earlier triumphs. He was pronounced fit by his doctors, but it is evident that the strain of war leadership has taken its toll, along with the polio that keeps him confined to a wheelchair. His Republican opponent, Thomas E. Dewey, the Governor of New York state, fought a better campaign than either of the president's earlier opponents (→20/1/45).

In a fight for freedom, there's no difference between the sexes: men and women alike have joined Italy's partisans to drive out the occupiers.

Antwerp is opened to Allied convoys

Nov 28. The first Allied convoy sailed into the Belgian port of Antwerp today, signalling a dramatic shortening of the supply lines to the battlefront. Men and material which had to be unloaded at ports in France and hauled overland will now be able to be sent directly from English ports.

Antwerp was actually captured undamaged at the beginning of September, but the Germans held on to strong defensive positions, many behind water barriers, in the Scheldt estuary. One stronghold, Walcheren Island, was taken by British commandos after the RAF blew a 400-yard gap in a dyke. The sea poured in, drowning the German defenders (→19/12).

The war is over for Home Guard

Nov 11. Britain's Home Guardsmen hung up their guns today after four and a half years' service. The auxiliary army, created in 1940 when invasion appeared imminent, has been "stood down", although members will retain their weapons and uniforms. Many members have been engaged on anti-aircraft duties.

At its peak, the Home Guard numbered 1,084 battalions – 1,701,208 men and 31,824 women. Every member will be given a certificate of service and officers will have honorary ranks.

Patton's tanks roll into the Saarland

Nov 24. The tanks of General George Patton's forces have burst into one of Germany's most strategically vital regions, the Saar Basin.

At the same time British troops are advancing around Cologne, while the French invade past Strasbourg. The German retreat in this mining region is looking disorganised and panic-stricken, with ammunition dumps left behind, in contrast with the careful mining of streets to delay the advance in other places (→9/12).

1944

DECEMBER

Su	Mo	Tu	We	Th	Fr	Sa
					1	2
3	4	5	6	7	8	9
10	11	12	13	14	15	16
17	18	19	20	21	22	23
24	25	26	27	28	29	30
31						

1. Washington: The rank of five-star general is created and awarded to Eisenhower.

5. Germany: General Patton's troops reach the Siegfried line (→ 4/2/45).

6. Germany: 20 million people are reported to be homeless after Allied bombing (→ 30/1/45).

8. Pacific: Iwo Jima suffers the heaviest US air raid of the Pacific War (→ 19/2).

10. Stockholm: Nobel Prizes go to Isidor Rabi (US, Physics); Otto Hahn (Germany, Chemistry); Joseph Erlanger and Herbert Gasser (US, Medicine); Johannes Jensen (Denmark, Literature); and International Committee of the Red Cross (Peace).

10. Moscow: De Gaulle and Stalin sign a treaty of alliance (→ 16/1/45).

15. London: Churchill backs Stalin's planned Polish border (→ 1/1/45).

22. Indochina: Vo Nguyen Giap forms the Vietnamese People's Army (→ 10/3/45).

25. Athens: Churchill arrives to try to end the civil war (→ 1/9/46).

27. London: Lloyd George announces his retirement from Parliament (→ 1/1/45).

DEATHS

13. Russian artist Wassily Kandinsky (*4/12/1866).→

16. US bandleader Glenn Miller (*1/3/1904).→

HITS OF 1944

There goes that song again.

Mairzy Doats.

QUOTE OF THE YEAR

" A weapon of unparalleled power is being created. Unless some international agreement about the control or the use of the new active materials can be obtained, any temporary advantage, however great, may be outweighed by a perpetual menace to human society."

Niels Bohr, scientist, in letter to Churchill and Roosevelt.

Ardennes breakout surprises Allies

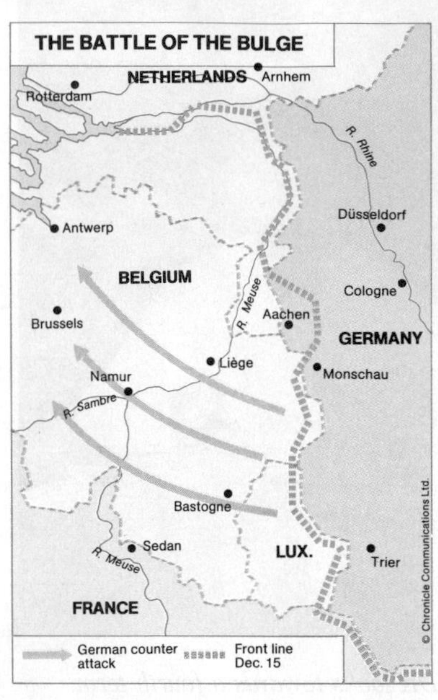

Germans troops during their surprise attack through the Ardennes forest.

Dec 19. On a day of fog and cloud when Allied planes were grounded, the Germans made their move. Mustering 24 divisions, ten of them armoured, Field Marshal von Rundstedt lunged at the Allied front in Belgium, following the same line of advance through the Ardennes forest as the conquering German armies of 1940. German paratroops in Allied uniforms dropped behind the American lines. The Allies, as Monty has put it, have been caught on the hop.

Eisenhower had left this central sector weakly defended while he used Montgomery's 21st Army Group in the Low Countries and Patton's Third Army in the south to spearhead Allied thrusts into Germany. Von Rundstedt has driven between the two, severing the front and making an effective overall command impossible.

The offensive began at dawn last Saturday, with von Rundstedt calling on his troops to "give your all in one last effort". By today, Tuesday, the Germans have penetrated more than 30 miles into Belgium in a drive towards the River Meuse. Von Rundstedt's objective is to cross the Meuse, then sweep north, past Liege and Brussels, and recapture Antwerp to cut the vital supply route for the Allied armies in the north.

Many of the German divisions are under-strength and need re-equipping, but Sepp Dietrich's Sixth SS Panzer Army is well-trained and at full strength. This force had been observed by RAF reconnaissance in a rear area near Aachen. Early this month it vanished. Now it is hammering the US First Army near Malmedy and Stavelot on the road to Liege.

A spokesman at Shaef, the Allied HQ in Paris, said today that the offensive had undoubtedly been planned by Hitler in the belief that even a partial success on the battlefield would delay the final onslaught against Germany by up to three months. The Allies, for their part, argue that the fighting could hasten the end of the war, since the Germans have no further reserves to call on. When the weather clears and the Allies can exploit their air superiority, von Rundstedt's days may be numbered (→ 9/1/45).

Glenn Miller goes missing over Channel

Dec 16. Glenn Miller, the man who gave the world "In the Mood" and "Moonlight Serenade", is missing. Colonel Miller and two companions were passengers on a routine flight to France where his band was due to play. No distress call was heard and no wreckage sighted.

Miller's distinctive arrangements, a strong saxophone element in his orchestra combined with muted brass, have dominated the broadcasting of swing music during the latter part of the war. A trombonist himself, Glenn Miller took his place among Duke Ellington, Benny Goodman, the Dorsey brothers, Artie Shaw, Count Basie and other masters of jazz and big band swing in America during the thirties.

Miller volunteered for active service in 1941, but was persuaded that his music would be more valuable boosting morale. So for much of the war the Miller Orchestra has played in war zones in the Pacific, the UK and Europe.

Ring roads planned for a new London

Dec 13. Express highways, satellite "new towns" and an encircling "green belt" of countryside form part of a master plan for the future of London published today. Over one million people would move out of the capital, if the plan proposed by Professor Patrick Abercrombie is accepted. It also proposes four ring roads around London and the development of a "transocean" airport at Feltham.

Civil war grips Greece

Dec 18. The attempt by the left-wing National Liberation Front, EAM, to seize power in Greece would seem to have been thwarted today by British forces in Athens. Major General Scobie, the British commander, turned to the offensive against the rebels in the early hours of the morning, after remaining on the defensive for a fortnight.

It was a noisy night, with five separate engagements going on. Three of them were mounted by the British, and two by EAM's military wing. In one of these the rebels overran the Averoff prison, but by the end of the night British forces were in control of the main road from Athens to Piraeus.

The Parthenon, towering over the scene of the night battles, was illuminated by flares, while the sounds of modern warfare echoed round Mount Hymettus, normally famous for its honey.

This sad situation in Greece, with civil war breaking out so soon after the nation's liberation, is causing much heart-searching in Westminster. The use of British troops in what appears to be a purely Greek quarrel is not looked on with favour in the Labour party.

Mr Churchill has promised to arrange an early debate, in which Mr Eden and possibly the Prime Minister himself will speak. Two Labour backbenchers have already proposed an amendment objecting to the use of British troops in suppressing "those popular movements which have valorously assisted in the defeat of the enemy and upon whose success we must rely for future friendly cooperation with this country" (→25).

Right-wing troops positioned outside a police station during the uprising.

Queen thanks women for their war work

Dec 6. The war could not have been won without the "magnificent" efforts of the women of Britain, the Queen said today. Praising all those who worked for Civil Defence, the fire, ambulance and police services, and the WVS., Her Majesty said they had made her hopeful as well as proud. "It may well be that all which we women have endured in this war may indirectly save our children and grandchildren from another," she said. The Queen was speaking at Westminster's County Hall to a large gathering of women's representatives from all parts of the country. Princess Elizabeth was at her side.

The Queen paid special tribute to the three million women of the Civil Defence: "You have inscribed your names indelibly on the national role of honour."

Among those presented to the Queen was 83-year-old Miss Caroline Howell, a London rest centre assistant who has not had a day off sick in four years.

Arts: golden age dawns on London stage

The Old Vic company, bombed out of its home in Waterloo Road, has been reborn in glory at the New Theatre in London's West End. **Ralph Richardson** and **Laurence Olivier** are setting new standards of acting and production in "Peer Gynt" and "Richard III".

In Old Vic company tradition, each plays a small part to support the other's leading role. One leading critic, **James Agate**, wrote that Olivier's Richard had "a great deal of Irving in the bite and devilry, the sardonic impudence, the sheer malignity of it".

Almost simultaneously Olivier unveiled his matchless "Henry V", a film which he directed as well as playing the king. It was shot in Ireland in colour at a record cost of £475,000, and the destruction of the French knights at Agincourt by the English archers, to **William Walton's** music, has the audiences cheering. This is a scene which Shakespeare, of course, did not include.

At the same time **John Gielgud** is giving his fourth Hamlet, which Agate rates his best, while he calls **Donald Wolfit's** King Lear "the greatest I have seen". A golden age of acting has dawned.

Sir Henry Wood, who founded the Promenade Concerts and conducted every season since 1894, had a stroke on the podium and died soon after making a token appearance at the Jubilee Prom.

Death also removed Britain's premier architect, **Sir Edwin Lutyens**, the last to design whimsical English country houses on the grand scale. His Viceroy's House and capitol buildings in New Delhi were the last word in imperial pomp, but the Cenotaph in Whitehall avoided grandiosity.

Olivier in the film of "Henry V".

Four leading modern artists are dead: in Norway **Edvard Munch**, in New York **Piet Mondrian**, the austere Dutch abstract painter, in Paris **Wassily Kandinsky**, who invented abstraction, and the neo-classical sculptor, **Aristide Maillol**.

The French aviator-novelist, **Antoine de Saint-Exupery**, was shot down on a flight from North Africa, having just published "The Little Prince", a fable for adults.

T.S. Eliot has completed "Four Quartets", long meditative poems named after remote places. Their themes, such as time and mortality, are interwoven like chamber music.

Vera Lynn, "the Forces' Sweetheart", and Stainless Stephen in Calcutta.

1945

JANUARY

Su	Mo	Tu	We	Th	Fr	Sa
	1	2	3	4	5	6
7	8	9	10	11	12	13
14	15	16	17	18	19	20
21	22	23	24	25	26	27
28	29	30	31			

1. London: Lloyd George becomes Earl Lloyd George of Dwyfor (→ 26/3).

1. London: Britain refuses to recognise a Soviet-backed provisional Polish government in Lublin (→ 28/2).

4. London: Geoffrey Fisher is appointed Archbishop of Canterbury to succeed William Temple, who died last year.

5. Germany: Montgomery is appointed Supreme Allied Commander north of the Ardennes (→ 3/12/46).

9. Philippines: US troops land on Luzon Island, 107 miles from Manila (→ 1/2).

13. Budapest: The entire city is now in the hands of the Russians (→ 21).

15. London: The first boat-train in five years leaves for the Continent.

16. Paris: De Gaulle nationalises the Renault factories (→ 9/4).

17. Warsaw: The city falls to Soviet and Polish troops (→ 29).

19. London: A report says that British anti-aircraft rockets caused the panic at Bethnal Green tube station in 1943 that left 173 dead.

20. London: Butler says the state will pay 55 per cent of the cost of the new education system.

20. Washington: Roosevelt is inaugurated for his record fourth term (→ 12/4).

21. Budapest: Hungary declares war on Germany (→ 6/3).

23. Germany: The Allies take St. Vith, last German stronghold in the Ardennes "Bulge" (→ 22/3).

28. China: The first supply convoy reaches China from Burma, via the reopened Ledo Road.

29. Poland: The Russians advance across the German border, 95 miles from Berlin (→ 6/2).

31. Germany: Soviet troops cross the River Oder north of Frankfurt, 40 miles from Berlin (→ 2/2).

Allies roll back the Ardennes offensive

Allies score a mid-winter victory at Bastogne in the Battle of the Bulge.

Jan 9. The Battle of the Bulge is almost over. Despite snowstorms, with drifts four feet high, the Germans are being squeezed out of their Ardennes salient, with heavy losses. Speaking at his battle HQ in North-West Europe, Monty said German forces in the Bulge were in the process of being "written off".

The turning-point in the battle came when the weather cleared towards the end of last month. German armour, having driven 60 miles into the Allied lines, was then within a few miles of the Meuse. Allied heavy bombers went into action, pulverising troops and supply lines and causing fuel and ammunition to run low.

General Hasso von Manteuffel tried to lay hands on the huge American supply dumps in Bastogne by inviting the garrison to surrender. In their initial advance the Germans by-passed the town, hoping it would fall into their lap later. Now, with their offensive broken, they have returned with five divisions. The answer to von Manteuffel's surrender call came from the Bastogne garrison commander, Brigadier General Anthony McAuliffe, in one word: "Nuts!" (→ 23)

Russians discover horror of Auschwitz

Jan 27. The concentration camp at Auschwitz was captured today by Marshal Zhukov's men as the Red Army continued its sweeping advance through Poland and into Germany. The camp has long been notorious as a "death factory" where Jews from all over Europe were sent to be slaughtered or worked to death.

By the time the Russian tanks battered through the gates, most of the surviving inmates had been marched off in the direction of Germany. The Russians have found only 5,000 prisoners alive at the camp, all of them near to death from starvation and disease, and mounds of skeletal corpses (→ 29).

Worst ever sinking claims 7,000 lives

Jan 31. As many as 7,000 people are feared dead after the sinking last night of the German liner *Wilhelm Gustloff*, by a Soviet submarine off the Hela Peninsula in the Baltic. It is the greatest loss of life at sea ever recorded.

The ship was packed with refugees from East Prussia. She sank swiftly when torpedoed by S.13, a submarine based in the Finnish port of Turku.

Food riots break out in Berlin as civilians dig trenches

Jan 30. Berlin is a city of bombed-out buildings and cold, hungry people. During the distribution of food in the working-class district of Neukollen, police opened fire after a crowd tried to seize the supplies. Several women were killed when they overturned a wagonload of potatoes. People are feverishly digging trenches for the defence of the city. For the past week columns of lorries, laden with government documents, have been leaving the city for Bavaria. In his broadcast tonight on the 13th anniversary of his coming to power, Hitler railed against the Treaty of Versailles and said the achievements of the Nazis in restoring German strength had "aroused the envy of our impotent democratic onlookers" (→ 31).

A military field kitchen doles out meagre rations to hungry Berliners.

1945

FEBRUARY

Su	Mo	Tu	We	Th	Fr	Sa
				1	2	3
4	5	6	7	8	9	10
11	12	13	14	15	16	17
18	19	20	21	22	23	24
25	26	27	28			

1. Philippines: US troops advance 25 miles into Japanese-held territory and free over 500 prisoners of war (→6).

2. Germany: The Russians take Stettin (→11).

4. Germany: US troops break through the Siegfried line (→8).

4. USSR: The Big Three meet at Yalta in the Crimea.→

6. Philippines: MacArthur announces the capture of Manila and the liberation of 5,000 prisoners (→16).

6. Berlin: Himmler says German commanders in Poland have been shot for "cowardice and dereliction".

8. Germany: The Allies launch a big offensive in the north-west (→9).

9. Germany: British and Canadian troops advance four miles from Cleves (→27).

11. Germany: The Russians cut a 100-mile gap in German defences on the Oder (→14).

14. Germany: The Russians seize seven main German strongholds and 200 villages in Silesia (→27).

16. Philippines: US troops attacks the stronghold of Corregidor on Luzon (→19).

19. Pacific: US troops under Admiral Spruance land on the island of Iwo Jima.→

20. Cairo: Churchill and Roosevelt meet to discuss the war against Japan (→5/3).

22. Germany: 6,000 Allied bombers pound German transport lines (→11/3).

23. Ankara: Turkey says it will declare war on Germany.

24. Cairo: Premier Ahmed Maher Pasha is shot dead after reading out royal decree declaring war on Germany and Japan.

27. Germany: The Allies enter Monchengladbach (→1/3).

28. Paris: The US signs a lend-lease deal with France.

28. London: The government defeats a motion regretting that Poland could not decide its own fate at Yalta (→21/6).

Dresden devastated; 130,000 killed

Piles of rubble are all that remains of Dresden, once a showplace city, devastated by a night of bombing.

Feb 14. In a night and a day of relentless bombardment, RAF and US Air Force heavy bombers have reduced Dresden to a smoking ruin. The city's peacetime population of 600,000 is believed to have been raised to almost a million because it was thought to be safe. It is impossible to be certain how many people died; estimates vary between 60,000 and 130,000. Total casualties have been put as high as 400,000.

Towards midnight last night, 800 four-engined Lancaster bombers deluged the city with tons of incendiaries and high explosives. Today, at noon, over 400 American B-17s appeared over the still-smoking ruins and resumed the destruction. German fighters and anti-aircraft guns appear to have put up very little resistance.

Dresden, famed for its 17th and 18th-century baroque and rococo art and architecture, and Dutch and Flemish paintings, has been compared to Florence. But the city is also an industrial centre and is said to be an important communications network for the German armies on the Eastern Front. Even so, the devastating raids have provoked widespread criticism. Some observers have accused the Chief of RAF Bomber Command, Air Chief Marshal Sir Arthur Harris, of clinging to the his increasingly controversial theory that terror bombing can by itself destroy the enemy's will to fight.

Senior Allied military officers are said to be none too pleased about the raids. They would have preferred to see the bombers used to step up attacks on German communications and oil installations. They claim to have evidence that the air attacks mounted by the Allies during the Ardennes offensive last December reduced German production of aviation fuel to a few thousand tons a month. The controversy continues (→22).

Senior members of Bomber Command plan new raids on Germany's cities.

▷

Marines raise the flag on strategic island of Iwo Jima

Feb 23. A platoon of marines today hoisted the Stars and Stripes on the peak of Mount Surabachi, highest point on the island of Iwo Jima, after four days of savage fighting. This heavily fortified island, only 750 miles south of Tokyo, is strategically vital; its fall will provide a base for fighters escorting B-29 bombing raids on Japan.

But the battle is not over yet. The Americans, led by the Fifth Marine Division, are fighting one of their most bloody campaigns. The 21,000-strong Japanese garrison is grimly determined. They have tunnelled deep into the island's volcanic rock and set up concealed pillboxes to cover the landing beaches. The preliminary bombing left these defences undamaged, and beaches of soft volcanic ash impeded the use of vehicles to bring up supplies from the beach. Both sides are reported to have suffered heavy casualties.

In the Philippines, American troops have liberated Manila, the capital. Airborne troops also recaptured Corregidor, the island fortress where the US Army suffered a humiliating defeat nearly three years ago. In Manila, isolated groups of enemy troops desperately held out in strongholds in Fort McKinley and Intramuros. While the fighting continued, General MacArthur launched the move to regain Corregidor whence he fled in 1942.

Old Glory flies high on Iwo Jima.

Allies carve up post-war world at Yalta

Churchill, Roosevelt and Stalin work out the future of a free world.

Feb 12. The Big Three – Churchill, Roosevelt and Stalin – tonight announced decisions of far-reaching importance to the future of the world. They have agreed on how Germany will be finally smashed, divided and punished. They have planned the invasion of mainland Japan. And they have carved out their own post-war zones of influence across the globe.

All this was done at Yalta in the Crimea, where the leaders have conferred secretly for the past eight days. Their communique about enforcing unconditional surrender on Germany stated that Britain, France, America and Russia will each occupy a separate zone when the fighting is over. A Central Control Commission will have headquarters in Berlin.

Following the recent spectacular Soviet military successes, Marshal Stalin arrived at Yalta in a strong bargaining position. This is reflected in decisions about proposed frontier changes in Russia's favour at Poland's expense, and in tacit Anglo-US acceptance of Soviet supremacy over Eastern Europe.

President Roosevelt is giving more attention now to victory over Japan than to the European settlement, and there is some British uneasiness about that (→28).

The Allied forces are closing in on Berlin

Feb 28. Berlin, battered night and day from the air, can feel the talons of the Allied armies closing round it. Four nights ago, by moonlight so clear a smokescreen had to be laid to conceal their operations, the American Ninth and First Armies stormed across the Roer River to break into the plain of Cologne.

A few days earlier Marshal Koniev's troops crossed the Oder river and are now well on the way to Dresden and threatening to outflank the German capital to the south. Meanwhile, Marshal Rokossovsky has advanced 45 miles in four days in the north, threatening to cut off the Germans in the port of Danzig and at the same time protecting the right flank of Marshal Zhukov's direct thrust towards Berlin.

Yet the question that must be asked is: what will be left of Berlin for them to capture? Last night's devastating raid by the RAF started enormous fires and as the people tried to flee they were trapped by the tank barriers, trenches and barbed wire already put up as defences against the forthcoming assault by the Red Army (→6/3).

1945

MARCH

Su	Mo	Tu	We	Th	Fr	Sa
				1	2	3
4	5	6	7	8	9	10
11	12	13	14	15	16	17
18	19	20	21	22	23	24
25	26	27	28	29	30	31

1. Germany: Monchengladbach falls to the Allies (→6).

5. Washington: The US invites 39 nations to security talks at San Francisco next month (→25/4).

5. Burma: The British capture the Japanese base of Meiktila, cutting Burma in two (→3/5).

6. Germany: Cologne falls to the Allies (→22).

7. Germany: The Germans are reported to be evacuating the rocket base at Peenemunde as the Russians advance (→30).

10. Indochina: Tran Kim declares the independence of Vietnam (→11).

10. Tokyo: The centre of the city is devastated by fire bombing (→18).

11. Indochina: Cambodia declares its independence (→2/10).

11. Germany: 1,000 bombers carry out the biggest ever daylight raid, destroying the Krupps factory.

15. Bahamas: The Duke of Windsor resigns as governor of the islands.

18. Tokyo: All schools and universities are closed and everyone over six is ordered to do war work (→7/4).

20. Paris: France signs an economic pact with Belgium, the Netherlands and Luxembourg.

22. Berlin: Albert Kesselring replaces von Rundstedt as German commander in the west (→1/5).

25. Germany: Montgomery bans British troops from fraternising with locals (→14/7).

30. Germany: The Russians capture Danzig and cross from Hungary into Austria (→25/4).

DEATHS

Dutch Jewish girl Anne Frank, author of the "Diary", at Bergen-Belsen. (*12/6/29)

26. British Liberal statesman David Lloyd George, Earl Lloyd George of Dwyfor, Prime Minister 1916-22 (*17/1/1863).→

Allies cross Rhine as booby trap fails

March 25. The Allied armies are today poised to thrust deep into the Ruhr, the industrial heart of Germany, after their stunningly successful crossing of the Rhine and the capture, within days, of the cathedral city of Cologne.

At one vital point, an alert American sergeant spotted a railway bridge at Remagen which the Germans had failed to demolish. He raced across it with his platoon, dodging German fire. A couple of booby traps went off but failed to damage the structure. The sergeant and his men hid in bomb craters to await reinforcements.

To the north, Montgomery prepared his crossing in characteristic fashion with careful attention to detail. Massive quantities of stores and ammunition, amphibious craft and bridging equipment were assembled behind a heavy smoke-screen. In the weeks and days before the assault, constant aerial attacks were made on the enemy positions, and especially on the airfields where reconnaissance had identified a new and dangerous threat, jet-propelled fighter planes.

The crossing took place at night after a 2,000-gun bombardment. Commandos were given the task of seizing the town of Wesel, while Canadians and Americans established bridgeheads on the flanks. Then, yesterday morning, two airborne divisions were dropped behind the enemy positions by 1,500 planes and 1,300 gliders. It was an operation on a scale almost equal to that of D-Day (→4/4).

Infantrymen of the US Seventh Army cross the Rhine in assault boats.

Last-ditch defenders wiped out this US tank as it entered Cologne.

Declarations of war on Germany

February 2: Ecuador
February 8: Paraguay
February 13: Peru
February 14: Chile
February 16: Venezuela
February 23: Turkey
February 23: Uruguay
February 24: Egypt
February 26: Syria
February 27: Lebanon
March 1: Saudi Arabia
March 2: Finland
March 27: Argentina

"Werewolves" kill German collaborators

March 25. A band of German youths calling themselves the "Werewolves" have claimed responsibility for today's assassination of Karl Oppenhoff, the Mayor of Aachen. He had just been installed in office by the Americans.

These Nazi fanatics seek to prevent collaboration between Germany and her "invaders", concentrating so far on simple acts of sabotage. They have been most active in Germany's western territories where the Allies are gaining ground.

The killing of the Mayor is a natural progression. Aachen, called Aix-la-Chapelle by the French, lies within a disputed region on the Belgian border.

The Werewolves work underground; this is the first time details about them have emerged. The Allies will reinforce security measures, and intend to try any captured members as adults.

The spellbinding Lloyd George dies

March 26. Daughter Megan held one hand and new wife Frances the other as David, first Earl Lloyd George, died today. He was 82. Thus ended the tempestuous journey of a political genius and social reformer of restless energy, courage and intense passion. He laid the foundations of the Welfare State. He led the nation through the Great War. He wrecked the Liberal Party.

With his Celtic fire he was the century's most spellbinding orator, mixing words with magic. "Lloyd George", said Winston Churchill, "was the greatest Welshman since the Tudor Kings."

The former Prime Minister at 72.

Communists take over in Balkans

March 6. The Soviet Union is wasting no time in making political capital out of the Red Army's sweeping victories in the Balkans. Marshal Tito, a dedicated Communist, has today been confirmed as the undisputed leader of Yugoslavia, while left-wing governments have taken over Bulgaria and Rumania and appear to be falling under the control of the Kremlin.

1945

APRIL

Su	Mo	Tu	We	Th	Fr	Sa
1	2	3	4	5	6	7
8	9	10	11	12	13	14
15	16	17	18	19	20	21
22	23	24	25	26	27	28
29	30					

1. Japan: US troops land on Okinawa (→ 1/6).

4. Germany: The Allies take Osnabruck (→ 15).

7. Pacific: The US Navy sinks Japan's biggest battleship, the Yamamoto (→ 17/5).

9. Paris: De Gaulle nationalises Air France (→ 21/11).

11. Paris: Vichy police chief Lucien Rottee is sentenced to death (→ 26).

15. Germany: Allied troops liberate the concentration camp at Bergen-Belsen (→ 17).

16. Germany: The Allies enter Nuremberg, surround Leipzig and advance on Hamburg (→ 20).

16. Baltic: The RAF sinks Germany's last pocket battleship, the Lutzow.

17. Germany: US troops liberate Buchenwald (→ 19).

19. London: Churchill says of the concentration camps: "No words can express our horror" (→ 30).

20. Nuremberg: The city, scene of huge Nazi rallies, falls to the Allies on Hitler's 56th birthday (→ 25).

23. London: The partial blackout ends (→ 15/7).

25. Germany: US and Soviet troops meet on the River Elbe at Torgau.

25. Vienna: Karl Renner, Austrian chancellor in 1919, becomes chancellor to head provisional government (→ 5/5).

26. France: Petain is arrested on the Swiss border (→ 23/7).

28. Italy: Mussolini is executed as the Allies take Milan and Venice.→

30. Germany: US troops liberate Dachau.→

DEATHS

12. US Democratic statesman Franklin Delano Roosevelt, president four times 1933-45 (*30/1/1882).→

28. Italian dictator Benito Mussolini (*29/7/1883).→

30. German dictator Adolf Hitler (*20/4/1889).→

Reich's final days: Allies in Berlin

As Berlin burns around them and the Fuehrer cowers in the depths of his bunker, Russian troops fight on.

April 30. Hitler's Berlin is being crushed in a storm of blood and fire. Russsian T-52 tanks have plunged into the heart of the Reich capital, and last night the Russians were in control of about a third of the city, with their troops approaching the road and rail junction of Spandau in the west.

The city is in a state of panic. Soldiers are throwing away their weapons and deserting. Some have been rounded up by fanatical SS guards, who shoot them on sight. Low-flying Russian planes are machine-gunning people in the streets. Everywhere, bodies are left where they have fallen.

Hitler is said to be in a subterranean fortress beneath the Chancellery, and directing the "defence" of the city, though in the present state of chaos the word is scarcely appropriate. In his Order of the Day two weeks ago, he seemed completely detached from reality. After the usual tirade against "the Jewish-Bolshevik arch-enemy", he claimed: "The enemy is being met with formidable artillery and infantry, replenished with numerous fresh formations." Elsewhere, the Western Allies and the Russians are swarming over Germany. Americans and Russians met at Torgau on the Elbe, and Montgomery, pushing his men across the Elbe further north, plans a rendezvous with Americans and Russians on the Baltic.

In the corridor between the Allied and Russian armies, towns and cities are flying white flags from church steeples. Allied soldiers are being taken off combat duties to organise the movement of refugees. In the past three weeks, the Western Allies have taken over a million prisoners, bringing the number captured since D-Day to over 2,250,000 (→ 1/5).

In the heart of Hitler's devastated capital Russians and Americans link up.

The Fuehrer kills himself

Hitler with his bride, Eva Braun.

April 30. It was not his fault. It was the English and Americans, serving the Jewish-Bolshevik conspiracy, who were to blame – but not only the enemy. The generals were incompetent and his closest party comrades had deserted him. In language that echoed the lugubrious title he had wanted to bestow on his book twenty years before, Hitler spent his last days in the Berlin bunker ranting about the betrayals, cowardice and lies all around him.

The end came this afternoon. According to survivors, who escaped while the Russians were virtually hammering on the Chancellery doors above ground, the Fuehrer slipped away to his room. Minutes later a shot was heard. Members of his staff found him on a sofa, dead from a gunshot wound in his mouth. A revolver lay on the floor.

Beside him was the body of Eva Braun, whom he had married the day before; she had taken poison. It was ten days after Hitler had celebrated his 56th birthday.

Much has to be learned about the last days of the man whose maniacal spirit hypnotised millions of ordinary Germans and many not-so-ordinary industrialists, army generals and Junker landowners, who put him in power, but it seems that long after Goering, Himmler and others who prospered in the Third Reich had seen the war was lost, and had got out of Berlin, Hitler retreated into fantasy and went on issuing orders for counter-attacks by non-existent armies.

But the delusions of his last days were no more deranged than the words and deeds of his years of triumph, when he extolled the German "master race", murdered his party comrades, and set out to exterminate the Jewish people.

The Austrian boy who earned a few shillings painting picture postcards and went on to cause the death of some 30 million people in Europe, millions of them Germans, still calls for an epitaph. Churchill has it. "Hitler", he said in that year of Britain's lonely defiance, 1940, "is a bloodthirsty guttersnipe" (→6/6).

One of the last pictures: the Fuehrer greets the Hitler Youth last month.

Duce is shot then strung up by his heels

Flanked by his mistress and an aide, Mussolini hangs head down in Milan.

April 28. Mussolini and his mistress, Clara Petacci, were shot by Italian partisans today, and strung up by their heels from the facade of a petrol station in Milan's Piazza Loretto. According to reports from Milan, the former dictator was arrested by a partisan leader known only as "Bill".

Mussolini, wearing a German cap, was found hiding under a pile of coats when the partisans stopped a convoy of eight cars. He immediately raised his hands, vainly begging for mercy.

After a brief trial presided over by Cino Moscatelli, a Communist partisan leader, Il Duce and those with him were condemned to death and shot with a burst of machine gun fire. According to Silvio Baridon, a leader of the Green Flame partisans, Mussolini appeared dazed and indulged in no heroics.

Others in the party, which included the Fascist bosses, Carlo Scorza and Alessandro Pavolini, are said to have cried "Long live Italy" as they died. There was little heroic about the scene in the Piazza Loretto. Mussolini's body hung among a ghastly retinue of corpses, his mistress obscenely strung up by his side (→29).

Germans in Italy surrender to the Allies

April 29. The war in Italy is over. The remnants of 22 German divisions and six Italian Fascist ones, totalling nearly a million men, have today surrendered unconditionally to Field Marshal Alexander, the Allied commander.

Secret negotiations for the surrender were begun three weeks ago, the initiative coming from General Wolff, SS commander in Italy. He sent a message through Cardinal Schuster, Archbishop of Milan, offering his capitulation to the Italian Committee of National Liberation. The actual surrender should have taken place three days ago, but was delayed by orders from Germany.

It was finally signed at Allied headquarters at Caserta this afternoon (→4/5).

A glimpse into Hell as Nazi death camps fall

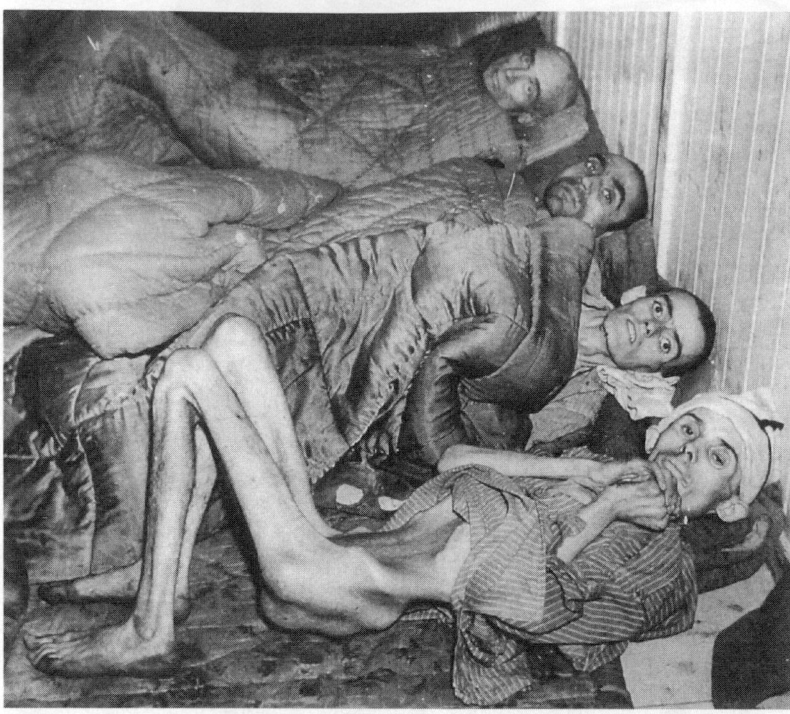

These survivors of the "Final Solution" await transfer from Buchenwald.

SS women at Belsen unload corpses and toss them into a communal grave.

April 30. The Allies had known of the existence of concentration camps for years, but no one could have guessed at the extent of the horror being unfolded today, as more and more camps are liberated by shocked soldiers. What is emerging is the awful truth about a cold-blooded and systematic attempt by the Nazis to destroy an entire section of the human race.

For millions of Jews, Poles and other victims, rescue has come too late. In one camp alone, near a village called Belsen, British soldiers found 40,000 prisoners, many of them beyond human help, suffering from starvation, typhus, typhoid and tuberculosis. Great heaps of naked rotting corpses testify to the callousness of the SS guards. One such heap of unclothed women prisoners measured 80 yards in length, 30 yards in width and four feet in height. Children played near this pile and close to gutters filled with dead.

Almost all the living and the dead are grossly emaciated, stick-like figures, their skin pulled so tight to their skulls that they are hardly recognisable as human beings. Despite every effort, more than 600 are being buried daily.

A senior medical officer described Belsen as "the most horrible, frightful place I have ever seen. I am told that 30,000 prisoners died in the last few months. I can well believe the figure".

As British troops entered the camp, the German guards were shooting prisoners trying to take potatoes from a pit in the camp. Several guards, including women, have been shot trying to escape; others have committed suicide.

At the Buchenwald concentration camp, American forces are fighting to save the lives of 20,000 prisoners, although 2,500 of these are so close to death that there is little hope for them. They include 900 boys under 14, their parents either dead or among the millions of homeless refugees wandering Europe today. American doctors are feeding them with every drop of milk available until they can begin to digest solid foods.

It will be months, possibly years, before the dreadful balance sheet of death is completed, but already proven stories of unbelievable cruelty are emerging. At Buchenwald, the victorious army preserved the portable scaffold from which prisoners were hanged publicly, a lampshade made from tattooed human skin for the camp commandant's wife, brass-studded leather lashes, even shrunken heads.

Many prisoners have even been used as medical "guinea pigs" and subjected to operations without anaesthetics (→ 21/5).

"United Nations" is born in San Francisco

April 25. Delegates from 46 states gathered in the San Francisco Opera House today to plan the United Nations organisation to replace the League of Nations. Harry Truman, who has just succeeded the late Franklin Roosevelt as president, told them by telephone from the White House: "We must make certain by your work here that another war will be impossible." Ironically the 47th place, reserved for Poland, the first nation to suffer from the Germans, was vacant. The US and Soviet Russia have not been able to agree that the new Polish government is independent.

The conference arose from the discussions last autumn between the US, Soviet Russia and Britain. The Chinese foreign minister has joined with the foreign ministers of these three to set the agenda for the present meeting. Tributes were paid to Roosevelt, who personally put so much energy into it (→ 26/6).

Looted Nazi art hoard found in iron mine

April 15. Priceless art treasures looted by the Nazis, along with Hitler's library and 20 cases of his letters, were discovered today in a mine on the Loser Plateau in Austria. There are pictures by Rembrandt, Rubens, Leonardo da Vinci, Titian, van Dyck, Raphael, Goya, Breughel and Michelangelo and the famous Ghent Altarpiece.

Much of the loot was stolen by Goering from Monte Cassino, and the cases were still labelled with his name. In February the Nazis ordered Dr Wilhelm, a director of the Vienna Museum, to live in the mine and receive the pictures. They had wired up the mine with eight 1,000-pound bombs so that the hoard could be destroyed if necessary.

SS troops were given the order to detonate, but before they could do so Dr Wilhelm, with the help of the Free Austria workers, had cut the fuse wires and blown up the entrance to the shaft (→ 13/5).

Allied prisoners reveal horrors of the German camps

April 16. Liberated Allied prisoners are telling horrific stories of life in German POW camps with frequent beatings and starvation rations.

So far about 30 of the 70 camps for Allied prisoners have been liberated. This morning a camp near Hamburg, containing 700 men who had been captured at Arnhem, was reached by the tanks of the the Seventh Armoured Division.

The officer in charge was a regimental sergeant-major who told how he hid in a tunnel for five days to avoid being marched further east. Those present said the cheering of the freed men drowned out the noise of battles still going on nearby.

Many of the men are still suffering from malnutrition, following forced marches from East Prussia last year. There are reports that eight men had only one loaf between them a day in some camps.

Elsewhere the Germans are only making half-hearted attempts to move men away from the Allied fronts. A POW in Stalag IIID near Berlin told how, as the gates were flung open, local women were waiting outside imploring the British troops to take them away to save them from falling into the hands of the advancing Russians (→6/9/46).

Hungry and sick, but free at last.

Roosevelt dies on the eve of victory

April 12. President Franklin Delano Roosevelt died suddenly at 3.35pm central time today at the age of 63. He died when victory for the Allies can be only weeks away. German resistance is collapsing, and the US and Soviet armies are within range of Berlin. In the Pacific the Japanese are on the run; the US Air Force is daily battering their major cities.

He died just two weeks before the Conference on International Organisations is due to start in San Francisco. This ambitious effort to create a supranational body to outlaw war owes much to Roosevelt's personal initiative.

Roosevelt died in his bedroom in a small bungalow on Pine Mountain in Warm Springs, where he had gone regularly over the past twenty years for treatment for his polio. He was having his portrait painted when he complained of a severe headache and fainted. He died two hours later, of a cerebral haemorrhage, without recovering consciousness.

Only his two doctors were present when he died. Mrs Eleanor Roosevelt was told the news by telephone in New York where she was attending a charity function. Standing by her was Mrs Woodrow Wilson, widow of the last US President to die after the strain of running a major war.

Mrs Roosevelt said that the President had not been feeling well for some time, and for the last few days he had taken only gruel, having no taste for other food. She sent a message to their four sons serving in the armed forces: "He slept away this afternoon. He did his job to the end as he would have wanted."

The Vice-President, Harry S. Truman, aged 61, was sworn in as 33rd President at the White House at 7.09pm. The son of a Missouri farmer, he was virtually unknown when he became vice-president. The verdict on him in Washington is that he has done much of value to the war effort.

Despite worries about his lack of experience, many are confident in his ability to carry on where Roosevelt left off. Truman chaired a congressional investigating committee which has worked to eliminate waste in the war effort.

The late Franklin Roosevelt, seen here meeting with Churchill at Yalta.

Admiral Doenitz is Hitler's successor

April 30. A former U-boat commander, once certified insane and sent to Manchester Lunatic Asylum, was today chosen by Hitler to succeed him before the Fuehrer killed himself. Grand Admiral Karl Doenitz said on Hamburg radio that he will continue the war, but almost nobody believes this. Himmler has already tried to surrender to the Western Allies.

Hitler chose Doenitz because all his old cronies were telling him the war was lost. Only Goebbels, the propaganda chief who said a big lie was more likely to be believed than a small one, remained loyal; he died with Hitler in the bunker.

As for Doenitz, he was taken prisoner in the last days of the First World War; he spent a year in Manchester Asylum.

Vienna is liberated with buildings intact

April 13. Vienna, occupied by the Nazis seven years ago, was liberated by Marshal Tolbhukin today after several days of vicious hand-to-hand street fighting. The Germans, who lost 130,000 prisoners in the battle for the city, made their last stand in the old Jewish quarter and in two business areas but, while their casualties were heavy, little damage was done to the city.

Moscow radio said last night that "the population of Vienna and other parts of Austria have helped the Red Army and prevented the Germans from making a stand. Having thus assisted in the liberation of the city, they have earned immortal merit by saving cultural monuments and vital installations, and have saved the honour of the Austrian nation." The Red Flag and the Austrian tonight fly side-by-side over Vienna.

Vienna, another victim of the war.

1945

MAY

Su	Mo	Tu	We	Th	Fr	Sa
		1	2	3	4	5
6	7	8	9	10	11	12
13	14	15	16	17	18	19
20	21	22	23	24	25	26
27	28	29	30	31		

1. Germany: Field Marshal von Rundstedt is captured.

1. Berlin: Doenitz declares himself the new Fuehrer.→

2. Europe: All 1,000,000 German troops in Italy and Austria surrender (→4).

3. Burma: The British 14th Army takes Rangoon.→

4. Europe: The Germans surrender in Holland, north Germany and Denmark (→5).

5. Austria: Daladier, Reynaud, Blum, Gamelin, anti-Nazi Pastor Niemoller and Kurt von Schuschnigg are released.

5. Norway: The Germans surrender.→

8. Berlin: Field Marshal Keitel signs Germany's final act of capitulation.→

9. Germany: Goering gives himself up to the Americans (→23).

10. Prague: The last European capital to be liberated cheers as Soviet troops enter the city.

13. Austria: £2,000,000 worth of looted French art treasures is found.→

16. London: The government says 750,000 troops will be demobbed this year (→17/8).

17. Malaya: The Royal Navy battles with the Japanese in the Malacca Straits (→1/6).

21. Germany: Belsen concentration camp is razed to the ground (→17/9).

23. Germany: Himmler kills himself in British custody.→

29. London: The convoy system is ended for ships in non-combat zones.

29. Germany: William Joyce, "Lord Haw-Haw", is arrested (→25/6).

31. Syria: A cease-fire is ordered after fighting between French and Syrian forces.

DEATHS

1. German Nazi Josef Goebbels, Hitler's propaganda chief (*29/10/1897).

23. German Nazi Heinrich Himmler, head of the SS (*7/10/1900).

Germans surrender in Rheims school

The Red Flag flies over the Reichstag building in Berlin on V-Day.

May 7. Peace came to a battered Europe at 2.41am today in a small red schoolhouse in Rheims where General Eisenhower, the Allied Supreme Commander, has his HQ.

After General Alfred Jodl, Army Chief of Staff, the German emissary, had signed the instrument of unconditional surrender, he said: "With this signature, the German people and the German armed forces are, for better or worse, delivered into the victors' hands." General Bedell Smith, Eisenhower's Chief of Staff, signed for the Western Allies, and General Ivan Suslapatov was witness for Russia.

First news of the German acceptance of total defeat came in a broadcast over Flensburg radio by Count Schwerin von Krosigk, the German Foreign Minister, who said that to continue the war would "only mean senseless bloodshed and futile disintegration".

The Germans delayed signing in order to allow as many soldiers and refugees as possible to give themselves up to the Western Allies rather than to the Russians. But the end had really come three days earlier in Field Marshal Montgomery's tent on the desolate Luneburg Heath, south of Hamburg. Monty received the surrender of all German forces in north-west Germany, Holland and Denmark.

Over a week ago, on April 29, the Germans in Italy, almost a million men, surrendered to Field Marshal Sir Harold Alexander. Five days ago the Russians announced the capitulation of the Berlin garrison. The German forces in Norway surrendered last night after the German C-in-C in Norway, General Hans Boehme, had issued a blustering Order of the Day about being undefeated.

German generals are being rounded up by the hundred. Field Marshals Gerd von Rundstedt, Heinrich Brauchitsch and Erich von Manstein, and over 150 other officers, are being brought to Britain. They will be put to work on farms near Bridgend in Wales (→8).

Generals Montgomery and Bedell Smith accept Germany's final surrender.

Battle-weary Europe faces victory and defeat

US servicemen and Englishwomen celebrate the end of European fighting.

A German soldier, his battles all fought, feels the bitterness of defeat.

Britain resounds to victory celebrations

May 8. Suddenly it was all over, and Britain took to the streets to celebrate the victory. All at once the drabness and privation of five wartime years were forgotten, temporarily at least, in a blaze of multi-coloured flags, fireworks and flood-lights.

By mid-day, Whitehall and the Mall were packed with a crowd that set up a huge roar as Winston Churchill drove past to lunch at the Palace. Even so, nothing had been said officially.

As Big Ben chimed out 3pm, the vast congregation of excited Londoners fell silent, listening to the Prime Minister's broadcast over loudspeakers. Although Japan remained to be subdued, he said, the war in Europe would end at midnight. "Advance Britannia!" he proclaimed. "Long live the cause of freedom! God Save the King!"

It was the signal for the release of years of pent-up feelings. Fifty thousand people went wild with joy, shaking hands at first then kissing and hugging strangers, dancing, blowing whistles, throwing confetti and forming impromptu parades. A massive "hokey-cokey" snaked around Queen Victoria's statue; crowds at the Palace railings shouted: "We want the King!"

Almost shyly, the Royal Family stepped into the sunlight on the Palace balcony, the King, Queen and Princesses holding hands. It was the first of eight appearances that they would make that day, each time to wave to an ever-swelling throng of jubilant citizens.

As darkness fell, the two princesses, Elizabeth and Margaret, escorted by Guards officers, slipped out of the Palace by a side door and joined in the crowd's shouts of: "We want the King!"

In Whitehall, an equally jubilant crowd cheered themselves hoarse as Winston Churchill, wearing his famous siren suit and homburg hat, appeared on the Ministry of Health balcony. The Guards' Band struck up "For He's a Jolly Good Fellow", and the crowd cheered again. The Prime Minister sang and conducted the crowd in "Land of Hope and Glory".

The celebrations were not to stop there. After the Royal Family and Mr Churchill had made their final appearances, Londoners streamed to Piccadilly where licensing laws had been suspended for the night. Uniformed servicemen were carried shoulder-high through the mass of revellers. In the rest of the country there were similar scenes of unrestrained joy, but this was London's night (→ 16).

Germans are weary, hungry and crushed

May 23. When they are not looking for food, Germans are to be seen attempting to clear the rubble, brick by brick, often working with bare hands, in the hope of having a shelter before next winter.

Other Germans have a more disagreeable task. They have been assigned to the concentration camps, to clear the skeleton-like corpses of the Nazis' victims. In some camps, heaps of charred bodies are lodged against the perimeter wire, where they were set on fire by Nazi guards before fleeing. The Allies are arranging for civilians, who say they knew nothing about the camps, to be taken on educational visits.

German soldiers will be sent to France, Holland and Belgium to spend the next few years repairing the damage they caused in the early years of the war. The fanatics of Hitler's Death's Head Waffen SS are being sent to an island off the German coast until it is decided what to do with them.

Most of the best-known Nazi leaders have been rounded up. Himmler was spotted near Hamburg and taken to a British camp. When a medical officer tried to inspect his mouth he crunched a cyanide pill and died within minutes.

The rest of the gang – Goering, Ribbentrop, Field Marshal Wilhelm Keitel, Hitler's army toady, Julius Streicher, the Jew-baiter, and Dr Hjalmar Schacht, the financial wizard who made Nazi economics work, but ended up a prisoner for being too close to an anti-Hitler cabal – are expected to stand trial for war crimes (→ 7/6).

Nations jockey to win post-war spoils

May 31. Royal Navy ships have put in at Copenhagen to round up the last remnants of the German fleet and to support the Danish government. In the last days of fighting British army units were ordered to get to Denmark quickly, after the Allies received reports of Russian paratroopers being dropped. Two are said to have been found.

Elsewhere politicians are also jockeying for position in the new post-war world. The Czech leader, Dr Eduard Benes, is back in Prague, but very much in the shadow of the Red Army occupying forces.

General de Gaulle is trying to reassert French power in Syria and Lebanon, despite a joint promise with Britain in 1941 to recognise their independence.

In Greece, as the German forces withdrew, well-armed Communist guerrillas attempted to seize power. British forces are seeking to put down the revolt.

There are signs that Stalin intends to keep Britain and America out of Eastern Europe. Churchill gave a veiled warning of this in his broadcast earlier this month. "There would be little use in punishing the Hitlerites", he said, "if totalitarian or police governments were to take the place of the German invaders."

British troops recapture Rangoon

One of many Japanese prisoners taken as the Allies recapture Rangoon.

May 3. Today, just three years after the capital of Burma fell to the Japanese, the British 14th Army marched into Rangoon. They arrived there only 24 hours after a SEAC communique announced the landing of British troops at the mouth of the Rangoon River in support of the spearhead driving on the city from the north.

The fall of the capital marks the end of the main campaign in Burma leaving only mopping-up operations against enemy forces still fighting in a pocket west of the Rangoon-Mandalay road. Other Japanese are retreating eastwards into Siam.

In its rapid march on the capital, the 14th Army advanced at a record rate of 300 miles in 25 days. This was made possible by a highly-organised system of air supply on a scale unprecedented in modern warfare. Its speed completely disorganised the Japanese defences, which had been softened by an air attack by 100 Liberator and Mitchell bombers (→ 17).

Coalition government resigns as party politics are set to return

May 23. The coalition government is dead and there will be a general election – the first since 1935 – on July 5. In preparation for it Mr Churchill resigned today, and was immediately asked by the King to form a new caretaker government. As Prime Minister again, his first act was to advise the King to dissolve parliament next month.

So the decks are now cleared for a return to party politics. Mr Churchill's interim team will be a Tory one. Labour has rejected his plea to keep the coalition going until the end of the Japanese war in return for a promise to enact Welfare State legislation. It saw this as a Tory ploy to buy time to improve party organisation. Labour's one is in better shape (→ 4/6).

Churchill gives the famous V-sign, but will he lead Britain in peacetime?

1945

JUNE

Su	Mo	Tu	We	Th	Fr	Sa
					1	2
3	4	5	6	7	8	9
10	11	12	13	14	15	16
17	18	19	20	21	22	23
24	25	26	27	28	29	30

1. Japan: Japanese troops retreat on Okinawa.→

4. Germany: The first German troops are demobbed and sent to work on the land to aid food production.

5. Berlin: Allied supreme commanders sign pact for the occupation of Germany.→

6. Berlin: The Russians find a body, believed to be Hitler's, under the Chancellery (→ 1/11).

7. London: Churchill and Truman say the Allies sank 700 U-boats during the war.

7. Channel Islands: The King visits the islands, paying tribute to their bravery under German occupation.

9. UK: The RAF announces the new Vampire jet fighter, capable of 500 mph.

11. Borneo: Allied troops establish four beachheads in British North Borneo.

11. Canada: Mackenzie King's Liberal Party are returned to power in a general election.

12. London: Eisenhower receives the freedom of the City and is awarded the Order of Merit.

14. India: Nehru and seven other leading Indians are released by the British (→ 19/9).

15. London: A Royal Proclamation officially ends a parliament that has lasted nine and a half years (→ 25/7).

15. Hamburg: Hitler's foreign minister, von Ribbentrop, is captured by the British.

19. Brussels: King Leopold III refuses to abdicate (→ 20/7).

21. Moscow: 12 members of the former Polish government-in-exile are jailed for acting against the Soviet Army (→ 28).

26. London: Bow Street court decides that William Joyce will be tried for treason.→

28. Warsaw: A government of national unity is to include members of the London government-in-exile (→ 5/7).

29. Prague: Czechoslovakia cedes Carpathian-Ruthenia to the USSR (→ 3/8).

Russia will occupy half of Germany

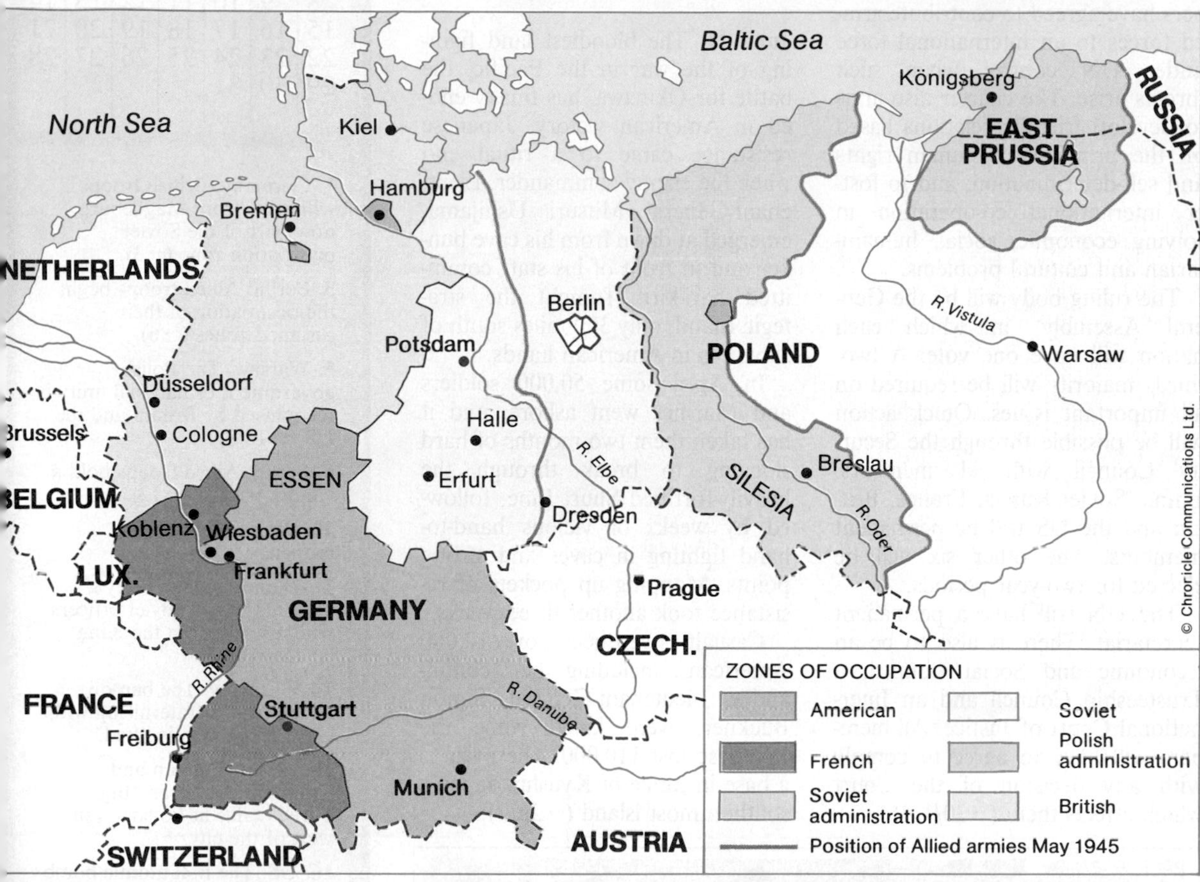

June 6. Russia is to take over control of about half of the total territory of Germany, according to details published in Moscow papers today. The stories obviously have official sanction, despite the rule of secrecy adopted by the European Advisory Council responsible for defining the zones of occupation.

The council's decisions will not be to everyone's liking. A map issued to the Soviet press shows that the Red Army's zone extends in some places far to the west of the present line of demarcation between the Russians and the Western Allies. It includes the whole of the German states of Thuringia, Saxony, Mecklenburg and Anhalt.

This means that the American troops, now in some parts of Thuringia and Saxony, will have to withdraw over 150 miles to the west, abandoning the towns of Leipzig, Chemnitz, Weimar and many others to the Russians.

British forces will not be so heavily affected. They will have to withdraw only from a small area around Wismar, where the Second Army made contact with the Russians. Lubeck, Hamburg and the Kiel Canal are to remain under British control.

The situation with regard to Berlin is that it will be divided into four zones, to be occupied individually by Russia, America, France and Britain, with a joint Control Commission. However, the German capital will be within the Russian area of control, so the Western Allies' zones will be completely surrounded by the Red Army.

Official circles in London refused to make any comment, but it is pointed out that it has always been recognised that the positions reached by the various Allied forces in their pursuit of the Germans before they surrendered would not necessarily be those they would occupy after the war.

Crossing from the American to the Soviet zone in occupied Germany.

Labour will need a sort of Gestapo to rule, says Churchill

June 4. In a radio broadcast tonight Mr Churchill opened the General Election campaign on a note of extraordinary stridency. The Prime Minister warned the nation that, if elected, a Labour Government could not afford free expression of public opinion. "They would have to fall back on some form of Gestapo," he said.

Labour's policy was abhorrent to the British people, he went on, because that party "finds a free Parliament odious". The extravagance of this attack on people who were his coalition colleagues for so long startled many Tories. Mr Attlee will reply tomorrow.

Fury in the Labour hierarchy is tempered by a feeling that Mr Churchill has made a major error of judgment and insulted the intelligence of the electorate which, it hopes, will conclude that he has changed from inspired national leader to grubby party politician, ready to demean himself to win votes at any price (→ 15/6).

Lord Haw Haw will be tried for treason

June 26. The voice of the well-dressed man was familiar, only too familiar, to the two British officers gathering wood on the Danish border. "Surely, you are William Joyce," said one. The man reached for his pocket and was shot at once in the thigh. Lord Haw Haw, whose wartime propaganda broadcasts from Germany had amused and infuriated millions, was in British hands.

Despite his contention that he is not a British subject – he claims to have been born in New York – a court decided today that Joyce will face trial for treason. The prosecution claims that Joyce had three times declared himself to be British, and his German naturalisation certificate stated "German, formerly English".

Joyce told his captors: "I was motivated not by a desire for personal gain, but solely from political conviction" (→ 17/9). ▷

United Nations formed

June 26. Delegates from 50 states today signed the World Security Charter to establish an international peace-keeping body to be called the United Nations. General Smuts, Prime Minster of South Africa and elder statesman of the delegates, summed up its purpose: "It provides for a peace with teeth; for the unity of peace-loving peoples against future aggressors; for a united front amongst the greatest powers, backed by the forces of the smaller powers as well."

First to sign – and with a bamboo brush – was Dr Wellington Koo for China. The US Secretary of State, Edward Stettinius, signed last for the US as host nation. President Truman said: "If we had had this charter a few years ago – and above all, the will to use it – millions now dead would be alive. If we should falter in the future in our will to use it, millions now living will surely die."

The key provision in the charter is that for collective measures to remove threats to peace. All members have agreed to contribute armed forces to an international force under UN control when such threats arise. The charter also aims to develop friendly relations based on the principle of human rights and self-determination, and to foster international co-operation in solving economic, social, humanitarian and cultural problems.

The ruling body will be the General Assembly, in which each nation will have one vote. A two-thirds majority will be required on all important issues. Quick action will be possible through the Security Council with 11 members. China, Soviet Russia, France, Britain and the US will be permanent members. The other six will be elected for two-year periods.

The UN will have a permanent secretariat. There is also to be an Economic and Social Council, a Trusteeship Council and an International Court of Justice. All members will have to agree to comply with any decision of the Court which affects them (→ 30/1/46).

Germans forced to view camp cruelties

June 7. German civilians are being taken on forced visits to the Nazi death camps, to view for themselves the hideous evidence of mass extermination which many have refused to accept ever took place.

Coachloads are being taken daily to the former camps to see the gas chambers, which SS guards, with cruel euphemism, called "bathhouses", and ovens, in which hundreds of thousands of victims were cremated, many of them while still alive.

Grim-faced Allied soldiers act as "guides", pointing out the piles of human ashes, unburned bones, hair shorn from newly-dead women, toys taken from children before they were herded into the gas chambers, and torture equipment used by sadistic SS guards. One exhibit is a "sound machine" built to hide the noise of human screams.

Many of the witnesses leave the camp in tears. Others appear indifferent and claim they are being subjected to Allied propaganda.

83 bloody days for US to take Okinawa

June 21. The bloodiest land fighting of the war in the Pacific, the battle for Okinawa, has finally ended in American victory. Japanese resistance came to a ritual end when the enemy commander, Lieutenant-General Mitsuri Ushijama, emerged at dawn from his cave bunker and in front of his staff committed hari-kiri. Tonight the strategic island, only 300 miles south of Japan, is in American hands.

In April some 50,000 soldiers and Marines went ashore, and it has taken them two months of hard slogging to break through the heavily-fortified Shuri Line, followed by weeks of vicious hand-to-hand fighting in caves and strong points. Mopping up pockets of resistance took another three weeks.

Casualties were heavy; over 12,000 Americans, including their commander Lieutenant-General Simon Buckner, were killed while the Japanese lost 110,000. The prize is a base in range of Kyushu, Japan's southernmost island (→ 26/7).

As peace breaks out all over Europe these war-weary Americans arrive home in New York City, courtesy of the SS Queen Elizabeth.

1945

JULY

Su	Mo	Tu	We	Th	Fr	Sa
1	2	3	4	5	6	7
8	9	10	11	12	13	14
15	16	17	18	19	20	21
22	23	24	25	26	27	28
29	30	31				

1. Germany: British troops withdraw from Magdeburg, now part of the Soviet occupation zone (→ 3).

3. Berlin: Allied troops begin the occupation of their assigned zones (→ 6).

5. Warsaw: The Polish government of national unity is recognised by Britain and the US (→ 16/8).

6. Berlin: Allied troops hold a victory parade (→ 12).

10. Paris: The Louvre reopens.

12. Berlin: Montgomery presents senior Soviet officers with awards from the King (→ 15).

14. Germany: The ban on Allied troops fraternising with German women is lifted.

15. Berlin: Truman and Churchill arrive for "Big Three" talks at Potsdam, just west of the city.→

16. US: The first atomic bomb tests take place in the New Mexico desert (→ 6/8).

20. London: The government gives local authorities the power to requisition empty houses.

20. Brussels: Belgium's premier asks Leopold III to abdicate for his "grave and unpardonable mistakes" (→ 19/1/46).

21. Germany: The Allies decide on Nuremberg for war crimes trials (→ 29/8).

23. Paris: The trial of Petain opens.→

24. Potsdam: Churchill, Attlee and Eden fly home for the general election results.→

26. Potsdam: The Allies tell Japan to surrender or face "prompt and utter destruction" (→ 6/8).

28. New York: A US Army B-25 bomber lost in fog hits the Empire State Building; 13 die and 26 are hurt.

29. London: The BBC introduce the Light Programme and resume regional services.

31. London: Field Marshal Alexander is appointed Governor-General of Canada.

Labour landslide in general election

Surrounded by his colleagues, Britain's new Prime Minister Clement Attlee, sits for the official photograph.

July 26. Labour is in power with an absolute and overwhelming majority for the first time in Britain's history. The party has had a sensational landslide victory in the general election. Results of the July 5 voting – all declared today – show Labour with 393 seats, Tories with 213, Liberals 12 and Independents 22.

So the nation which reveres Winston Churchill as its wartime saviour rejects him for its peacetime good.

Shaken as the results stacked up against him, he went to the King and resigned. Then – magnanimous, as he advised with the Germans – he said: "The decision has been recorded. I have therefore laid down the charge which was placed upon me in darker times. It only remains for me to express my profound gratitude for the unflinching support they have given their servant through these perilous years."

The new Prime Minister, Clement Attlee, is a man of fewer words. He said: "We are facing a new era. Labour can deliver the goods." The forces' vote went overwhelmingly against the Tories, and Labour has won many seats in once "true-blue" English shire counties and suburbia. The Liberals have been crushed, and 13 Tories of cabinet rank were defeated.

The new Government has been elected on Labour's "Let Us Face The Future" manifesto. Its programme of public ownership and social reform is the most detailed ever presented by any party. Herbert Morrison, main architect of the election victory, is Number Two man in the new Government and will have overall responsibility on the home front. Ernest Bevin is Foreign Secretary. With Mr Attlee this triumvirate leads a motley crew of Labour MPs, who include old trade union warhorses, university dons, Services officers, lawyers, company directors and a few Old Etonians. Between puffs on his pipe Mr Attlee said in an expansive moment: "Fine lot". Tomorrow he will lead the new delegation back to the Potsdam conference. Stalin will be surprised. He thought the Tories would win by 80 seats. So did the Tories (→20/8).

"Iron Curtain" slams down as the Allies fall out at Potsdam

July 31. The conference of the victorious powers has become a meeting of mistrust. Two weeks ago Churchill, Truman and Stalin travelled to Potsdam, historic residence of German emperors, to chart a course for post-war Europe. They disagreed about where Germany's frontiers should be drawn; the Western powers objected to Poland, with Russian encouragement, seizing huge areas of Germany and expelling millions of Germans.

Stalin brushed aside calls for free elections in East European countries, and ignored complaints about difficulties raised for Western officials in those countries. Churchill complained that an Iron Curtain was being slammed down against the West (→5/3/46).

Two new faces – Attlee and Truman – and the end of Big Three unity.

Vichy leader Pierre Laval is handed to the French forces

July 31. Pierre Laval, the Vichy chief for most of the German occupation, was handed over to the French today. Marshal Petain, the first leader of Vichy, is currently on trial for treason in the High Court in Paris. Laval is certain to be tried too. After 1942 Petain was a figurehead, and Laval became the executive head and a willing Nazi tool. Laval was flown by a German pilot from his temporary refuge in Spain to an airport near Linz, in the American zone of Austria. He hoped the Americans would treat him more leniently, but they passed him straight on to the French (→1/8).

Allies step up attack on Tokyo

July 16. A powerful Royal Navy task force, including the carrier Formidable and the battleship King George V, today joined with the US Third Fleet, commanded by Admiral William Halsey, in dawn raids on the Tokyo area. This is the most powerful fleet ever assembled in the Pacific. In addition to the raid on Tokyo, Murorau was shelled and bombers attacked four other Japanese cities (→26).

The lights go on all over Britain

July 15. After more than 2,000 nights of blackout and dim-out, Britain was ablaze with light once again last night. In London, thousands flocked into the West End to see the switch-on. Hundreds gathered on the boarded-up statue of Eros to see Piccadilly Circus return to its pre-war brilliance.

The switch-on, coinciding with the end of double summer-time, brought a near-carnival atmosphere in many parts of the country. In heavily-bombed Croydon the streets were packed as 7,000 street-lamps came back on once again, and civic ceremonies were held at resorts on the previously heavily-darkened south coast. ▷

1945

AUGUST

Su	Mo	Tu	We	Th	Fr	Sa
			1	2	3	4
5	6	7	8	9	10	11
12	13	14	15	16	17	18
19	20	21	22	23	24	25
26	27	28	29	30	31	

1. Paris: Laval is returned to the city for trial (→ 15/10).

3. Prague: All Germans and Hungarians in Czechoslovakia are deprived of citizenship (→ 26/5/46).

6. Hiroshima: The city is destroyed by an atomic bomb.→

7. Belgrade: Tito refuses to allow King Peter II to return (→ 29/11).

8. Moscow: Stalin declares war on Japan (→ 10).

10. Manchuria: Soviet troops have advanced 120 miles in two days (→ 19).

11. Japan: MacArthur is named as Allied Supreme Commander to accept the Japanese surrender.→

14. London: The secret of "Radar", radio-location and ranging, is disclosed.→

15. US: Rationing of petrol, fuel oil and oil stoves ends.

15. Paris: Petain, aged 89, is sentenced to death for treason, but reprieved by de Gaulle on account of his age (→ 9/10).

16. Moscow: The USSR and Poland sign a treaty fixing their mutual border.

19. Manchuria: The Russians occupy Harbin and Mukden, accepting the surrender of 100,000 Japanese.→

20. London: Ernest Bevin slams East European elections as "one kind of totalitarianism replaced by another".

20. Oslo: Nazi premier Vidkun Quisling goes on trial (→ 10/9).

22. London: Attlee says the Bomb means "a naked choice between world cooperation and world destruction" (→ 22/11).

26. London: Sir Arthur "Bomber" Harris to retire.

28. China: Mao Tse-tung arrives at Chungking for talks with Chiang Kai-shek to try to avert a civil war (→ 5/4/46).

29. Japan: The Allied occupation begins (→ 2/9).

29. Nuremberg: Goering and Hess head the list of the first 24 Nazis to be tried for war crimes (→ 20/11).

A-bomb vaporises Japanese cities

All that remains of the once thriving Japanese city of Hiroshima, test-bed for the world's mightiest weapon.

Aug 9. For the second time an atomic bomb fell upon Japan today, obliterating Nagasaki, the shipbuilding centre on the Japanese island of Kyushu. Smoke and dust clouds completely covered the town and rose five miles high in a giant mushroom-shaped cloud. Japan claims that 70,000 perished and more are dying daily.

The world's first atomic bomb, with 2,000 times the blast power of the "Grand Slam" British bomb yet only a tenth of the size, destroyed Hiroshima three days ago. Both raids were carried out by the US Army Air Corps' Super-Fortress aircraft.

President Truman delivered a fresh warning: "If Japan does not surrender, atomic bombs will be dropped on her war industries." He had already threatened "a rain of ruin from the air, the like of which has never been seen on this earth".

The plane that carried the Hiroshima bomb was named "Enola Gay" after the mother of the pilot, Colonel Paul W. Tibbets. Also on board was Captain William Parsons, US Navy, who described the flash of the explosion as being as brilliant as the sun. Concussion from the burst struck the plane ten miles away with the force of a near-miss by flak. Reconnaissance planes have reported that, four hours after the explosion, nothing could be seen of the city but a pall of smoke and fires round the outskirts.

The wonder weapon, created by British and American scientists, is described as the greatest scientific discovery in history. They worked round the clock to have it ready for action.

Mr Churchill said: "By God's mercy British and American science outpaced all German efforts. The possession of these powers by the Germans at any time might have altered the result of the war and profound anxiety was felt by those who were informed". (→ 11)

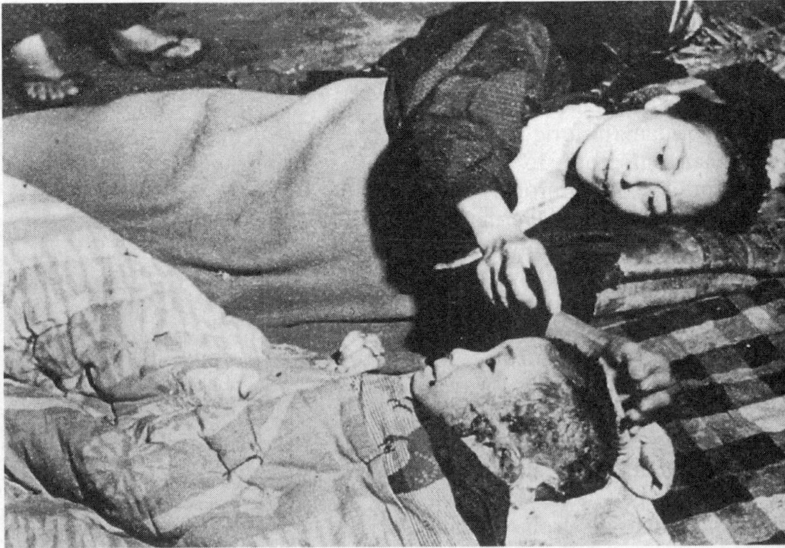

Victims of the A-bomb, a mother and her child lie in a burnt-out bank.

How the first atomic bomb was made

A mushroom cloud, trademark of the atomic bomb, rises over Hiroshima.

Aug 10. A secret project, which involved a 100,000 workers and took years to bring to completion, lay behind the atomic bomb dropped on Hiroshima in Japan. Three new cities, and factories covering several square miles, were built from scratch, yet the vast majority of the workers did not even know what they were making.

These are some of the newly-revealed secrets of the "Manhattan Project", which created, for better or for worse, the most devastating weapon of all time. The project was directed by Major General Leslie L. Groves and cost two billion dollars. Central to the Project was the new city of Los Alamos in the New Mexico desert, which grew until it had 70,000 inhabitants.

Here an international team of scientists, under the direction of Dr Robert Oppenheimer of the University of California, carried out the basic research for the bomb, and designed and built it. Two gigantic factories, one at Oak Ridge in Tennessee, the other at Hanford, Washington, produced materials for the bomb. Their exact nature has not been revealed, but is known that uranium is involved.

Shortly before the war the German scientist Otto Hahn discovered that atoms of a form of uranium called uranium-235 would undergo fission – that is, splitting into two roughly equal halves, with the release of energy in a chain reaction, which could provide the basis of an atomic bomb.

However, uranium-235 forms less than one per cent of natural uranium and, as it has identical chemical properties to the other 99 per cent, separating it is a very formidable task. This is presumably one of the tasks undertaken at the big Manhattan Project factories.

According to a statement by Mr Winston Churchill, British scientists played a major part in the early days of the research, before the US came into the war. However, when the vast scale of the enterprise became clear all work was transferred to the United States (→6/11).

Hirohito: we surrender

Aug 14. Japan has surrendered unconditionally to the Allies. The announcement was made simultaneously tonight by Mr Attlee and President Truman. Emperor Hirohito of Japan will order all his military, naval and air commanders to cease active resistance and surrender their arms.

So ends the war which, for Britain, has lasted only a few days short of six years. The return of peace is to be celebrated in this country by two days of public holiday and a broadcast by King George. Mr Attlee spoke to the nation by radio at midnight, declaring: "Japan has today surrendered. The last of our enemies is laid low."

In America, President Truman addressed the crowds from the portico of the White House, saying: "This is the day we have been waiting for since Pearl Harbor."

The moment of peace came during a brief ceremony on board the USS Missouri. Representatives of the Japanese government read a brief statement from Emperor Hirohito recognising the American victory and acknowledging that US forces, under General Douglas MacArthur, will occupy Japan.

Afterwards General MacArthur, reporters: "It is my earnest hope, and indeed the hope of all mankind that from this solemn occasion a better world shall emerge out of the blood and carnage of the past." He was proud of the Allied achievements, but looked forward to a time when both sides would "rise to that higher dignity that alone benefits the sacred purposes we are about to serve".

American celebrations were marred by an announcement from the Navy Department that the heavy cruiser USS Indianapolis had been sunk with the loss of almost all hands by enemy action in Philippine waters. Her last mission was to carry material for the atomic bomb to the American base at Guam.

The formal surrender of Japan will be received by General MacArthur, appointed Supreme Allied Commander today. After the signing of the documents of capitulation, the official Victory Day of celebration will be announced.

Britain and China are to be represented at the ceremony, as will Russia, even though the Soviet Union did not declare war on Japan until after the atomic bomb had been dropped. Russian armies then invaded Japanese Manchuria.

In Tokyo, a weeping crowd gathered before the Imperial Palace wailing and prostrating themselves before the monarch, still worshipped as a god. "Forgive us, O Emperor," they said. Tokyo radio declared: "We are moved to tears by His Majesty's infinite solicitude." Then transmission went silent.

Final parade: diconsolate Japanese troops in Burma hear the war is lost.

▷

Japanese lay down arms to the Red Army

Aug 19. A Soviet communique announced tonight that the Kwangtung Army, a crack Japanese formation in Manchuria, has surrendered to them. During the day 100,000 prisoners were taken, and more are pouring in as the half a million strong army crumbles and gives up all resistance.

Russian airborne troops had taken the four main cities in Manchukuo, the puppet state the Japanese set up after their invasion of China. Now the Japanese garrisons in Mukden, Harbin, Kirin and Hsinking, the capital, are waiting to lay down their arms. Two Russian armies known as the First and Second Far Eastern Front are active in this theatre of operations.

At Manila, in the Philippines, 16 Japanese envoys arrived and began peace discussions, not attended by General MacArthur. Staff officers questioned them about facilities for the Allied entry into Japan (→ 29).

Labour song is Red Flag to a bulldog

Aug 20. There were extraordinary scenes when the new House of Commons met for the first time today to elect its new Speaker. The solid phalanx of unknown faces on the Government side signalled Labour's first real electoral victory.

The defiant shrunken Tory ranks cheered vociferously when Mr Churchill arrived. They burst into singing "For He's a Jolly Good Fellow", and Labour at once staged its counter-demonstration. The great new choir of the Left roared the Red Flag battle hymn. The new Speaker, Colonel Clifton Brown, said: "I wondered whether I was going to be Speaker or director of a musical show."

Mr Attlee will name his full cabinet team within the next few days. He has spoken already of his determination that it will guide Parliament and the nation through the greatest social revolution in their history. The journey into peace will be on a bumpy road (→ 24).

Britain toasts V-J Day

This time it's really finished – children celebrate VJ-Day.

Aug 14. It was not until midnight last night that Britain learnt of the total surrender of Japan in a broadcast by the Prime Minister, Clement Attlee. "The last of our enemies is laid low," he said.

With much of the population sleeping, celebrations were muted at first; but the constant sounding of ships' sirens and railway train whistles were already heralding two days of national rejoicing.

Over the Thames from London, bonfires long since prepared for this occasion blazed from Orpington to Ramsgate; and the crowds began to gather in London, as they had for VE-Day, long before dawn.

By two o'clock this morning, Piccadilly was in full party mood. American servicemen, wearing carnival hats carrying their national flag, were leading impromptu processions, beating drums, blowing whistles and throwing fireworks. A fire engine had to fight its way through a crowded Coventry Street, although it could hardly be recognised because the number of blue RAF uniforms on board.

The Government has declared a two-day holiday, and tonight the BBC is broadcasting through the night to advise commuters to stay at home. Announcements about the holiday are also being made at railway stations.

Tomorrow the crowds are expected to equal those of the last celebration, but already London's churches are filling with worshippers for specially-arranged services of thanksgiving.

In most parts of London and every provincial city and town, street parties have already been prepared, and a mass of bonfires will burn from every vantage point on the land this evening (→ 16/9).

Broke Britain will have to tighten her belt, warns Attlee

Aug 24. With peace comes greater austerity instead of plenty. This was Mr Attlee's grim message to Parliament today. He told MPs that Britain is in serious financial trouble as a result of the abrupt ending of Lend-Lease by the United States Government. Mr Churchill backed the Prime Minister. There will now have to be major cuts in imports of food, cotton, tobacco and petrol. Goods produced for home consumption will have to be exported instead, and food stocks held for consumption by American forces will be eaten by Britons. Whitehall will seek a new credit deal with the US (→ 13/12).

One million to be demobbed by 1946

Aug 17. Britain is raising the rate at which servicemen are demobilised from 115,000 to 171,000 a month. It is planned to release over a million men and women by December. A million workers are also to be released from munitions work. Emmanuel Shinwell, the Minister of Fuel and Power, has announced a drive to increase coal production by 18 million tons annually, and made a plea to miners and their managers to "contribute the utmost effort" (→ 27/1/46).

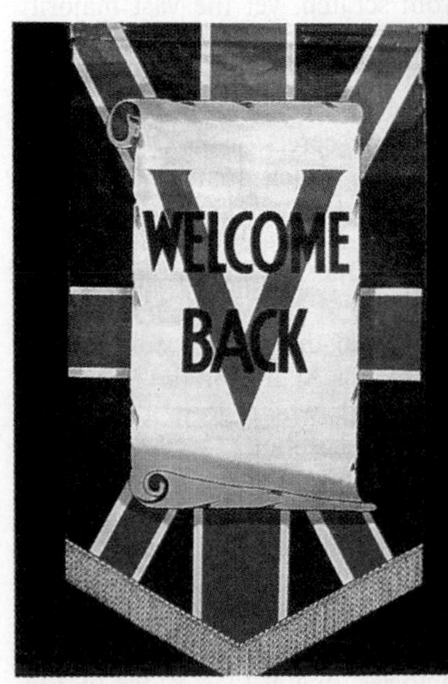

Welcome back to British troops.

The price of victory and defeat: 55 million dead

The nuclear bombs that fell on Hiroshima and Nagasaki ended the Second World War, and began an era in which any new global confrontation could imperil the survival of mankind itself. The war which has just ended was deadly enough: over 55 million people were killed.

Unlike what we now have to call the First World War – at the time, the "Great War" was supposed to be "the war which ends wars" – the last six years wrought great destruction upon civilians as well as upon combatants. Russia, Poland and – in fighting little-reported in the West – China bore the brunt of these human casualties (see below).

Europe faces years of rebuilding; Greece and Poland have lost one-fifth of their dwellings, Russia and Germany probably more but no reliable figures are available. Britain was relatively lucky, with a mere 6.5 per cent of her houses destroyed. Political turmoil seems inevitable, but lives lost can never be recaptured, while those who grieve will never forget.

Russia, 1941: winners or losers have all to pay the price of a war, and this one has cost the lives of 55 million people.

HOW GERMAN PRODUCTION DEFIED THE BOMBERS

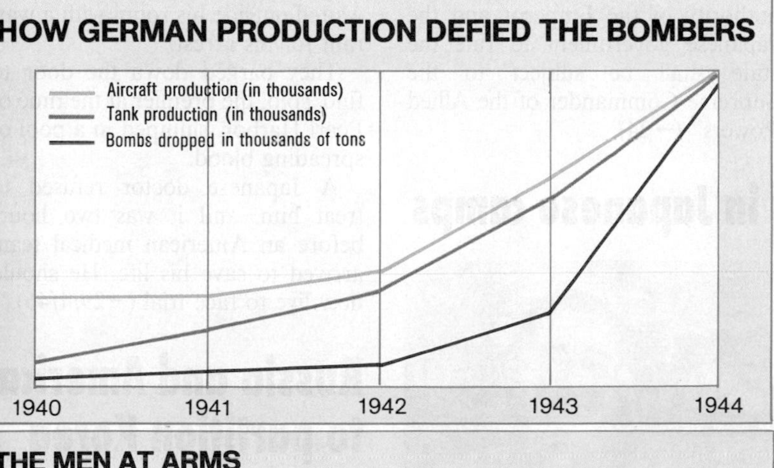

THE MEN AT ARMS

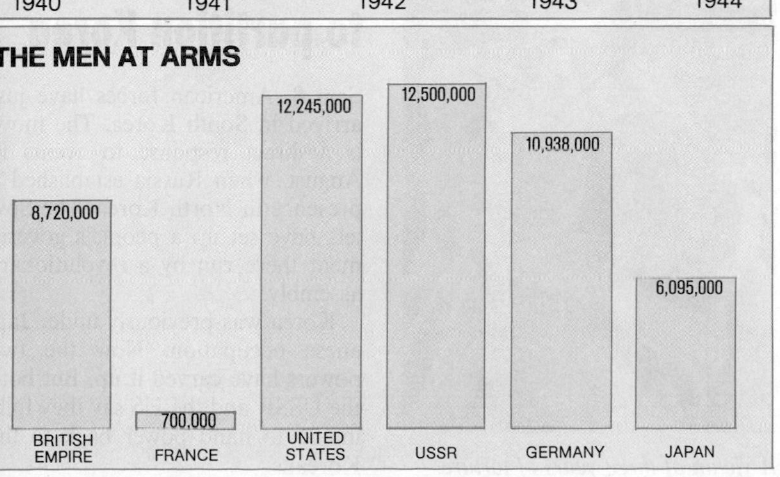

THE HUMAN CASUALTIES OF WAR

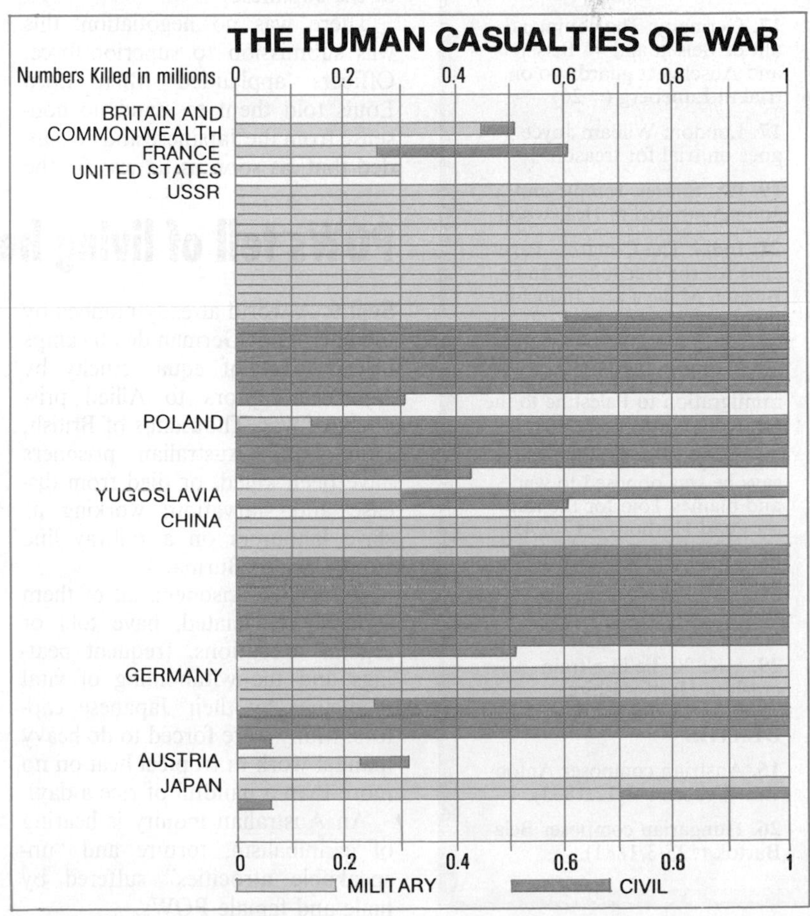

1945

SEPTEMBER

Su	Mo	Tu	We	Th	Fr	Sa
						1
2	3	4	5	6	7	8
9	10	11	12	13	14	15
16	17	18	19	20	21	22
23	24	25	26	27	28	29
30						

1. Hong Kong: British troops take over control of the colony.

2. UK: Press censorship ends.

2. Tokyo: MacArthur formally accepts the surrender of the Japanese on the aircraft carrier Missouri in Tokyo Bay.→

5. Singapore: British troops land and take control without any opposition.→

8. Japan: The US-born propaganda broadcaster known as "Tokyo Rose", Iva Togori, is arrested (→10).

10. Oslo: Quisling is sentenced to death for treason (→24/10).

10. Tokyo: MacArthur orders the arrest of Tojo.→

15. Austria: The composer Webern is shot dead by a US sentry after failing to understand an order to stop.

16. London: A Victory Thanksgiving service is held in Westminster Abbey.

17. Germany: The commandant of Belsen and 44 Belsen and Auschwitz guards go on trial at Luneberg (→26).

17. London: William Joyce goes on trial for treason.

19. US: Shirley Temple and John Agar wed in Hollywood.

21. India: The Congress Party calls for the freedom of India, Burma, Malaya and Indochina from colonial rule (→12/2/46).

23. London: The government refers the issue of Jewish immigration to Palestine to the United Nations (→2/10).

24. Tokyo: Emperor Hirohito says he was opposed to war and blames Tojo for the raid on Pearl Harbor (→17/6/45).

26. Luneberg: A Polish Jew breaks down in the witness box when describing his ordeal in Auschwitz (→17/11).

29. UK: 30 die in a train crash in Hertfordshire.

DEATHS

15. Austrian composer Anton von Webern (*3/12/1883).

26. Hungarian composer Bela Bartok (*25/3/1881).

Japanese bow before their conquerors

The guards of Changi Jail, scene of many cruelties, bow to the British.

Sept 12. Defeated Japanese generals, swordless and disconsolate, shuffled forward in the Singapore Council Hall today to sign the formal surrender. The Allied Commander, Lord Louis Mountbatten, warned in an order of the day: "I shall tolerate no evasion on the part of the Japanese."

There was no negotiation; this was submission to superior force. Officers applauded when Lord Louis told them to stand no nonsense from the Japanese and demanded that, as soon as he was fit, the absent Field Marshal Terauchi, the Japanese commander, must sign and pay homage.

Last week the Japanese Foreign Minister, in morning dress, signed the total surrender document in the presence of General Douglas MacArthur on board the battleship USS Missouri in Tokyo Bay. Its final article lays down that: "The authority of the Emperor and the Japanese government to rule the state shall be subject to the Supreme Commander of the Allied Powers" (→24).

POWs tell of living hell in Japanese camps

Sept 9. A world already numbed by the horrors of German death camps heard today of equal cruelty by Japanese captors to Allied prisoners of war. Thousands of British, Dutch and Australian prisoners have been killed, or died from disease and starvation, working as slave labourers on a railway line from Siam to Burma.

Returning prisoners, all of them seriously emaciated, have told of regular executions, frequent beatings and the withholding of vital medicines by their Japanese captors. Many were forced to do heavy manual work in tropical heat on no more than a handful of rice a day.

An Australian inquiry is hearing of cannibalism, torture and "unspeakable atrocities" suffered by male and female POWs.

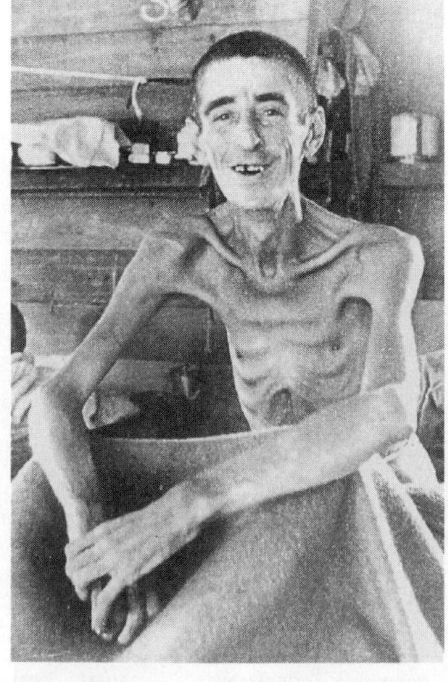

A victim of three years of torture.

Home Rule is promised for India

Sept 19. India will have independence "at the earliest possible date". Over the years this promise has been heard from London before, but tonight it sounded more definite. In a worldwide broadcast Mr Attlee said it is time for Indians to reconcile differences and decide their own destiny.

The Government announced that it will soon convene a constitutional conference, as pledged in wartime declarations. Its aim will be self-rule in whatever form India wants. Regardless of hazards, Mr Attlee seems determined to hasten the sunset on this part of the British Empire. Labour has the parliamentary majority to do it (→21).

Ex-premier of Japan fails to kill himself

Sept 8. Crying "Let MacArthur have my corpse ... I would not be judged by a conqueror's court", General Hideki Tojo today shot himself in the heart. The suicide attempt came as US Army officers waited outside his room with a warrant for his arrest.

They barged down the door to find Tojo, the premier at the time of Pearl Harbor, slumped in a pool of spreading blood.

A Japanese doctor refused to treat him, and it was two hours before an American medical team arrived to save his life. He should now live to face trial (→29/4/46).

Russia and America to partition Korea

Sept 8. American forces have just arrived in South Korea. The move is a direct response to events in August, when Russia established a presence in North Korea. The Soviets have set up a people's government there run by a revolutionary assembly.

Korea was previously under Japanese occupation. Now the two powers have carved it up. But both the USSR and the US say they fully intend to hand power back to the Koreans.

1945

OCTOBER

Su	Mo	Tu	We	Th	Fr	Sa
	1	2	3	4	5	6
7	8	9	10	11	12	13
14	15	16	17	18	19	20
21	22	23	24	25	26	27
28	29	30	31			

2. Germany: Eisenhower relieves Patton of his command after his comments to press on uprooting Nazis (→9/12).

2. Indochina: A cease-fire is agreed after fighting between Vietnamese insurgents and French troops.

4. UK: 17,000 dockers are now out on strike over pay.→

5. Rome: Pope Pius XII names Cardinal Jozsef Mindszenty as Primate of Hungary.

5. Tokyo: Baron Kijuro Shidehara is appointed Japan's new premier (→10/5/46).

7. Southampton: The first Far East prisoners of war return on the liner Corfu.

9. Paris. Laval is sentenced to death, without right of appeal, for treason (→10).

10. France: The head of the pro-Nazi French Militia, Joseph Darnand, is executed.

14. South-East Asia: Nationalists declare war on the Dutch in the Dutch East Indies (→31).

19. Budapest: Martial law is declared throughout Hungary because of unrest (→30/1/46).

20. Vienna: The Allies recognise the provisional Austrian government of Dr. Karl Renner (→20/11).

23. London: Hugh Dalton's budget cuts income tax from ten to nine shillings in the pound.

23. France: Communists win 142 seats, Socialists 140 and Popular Republicans 133 in elections for a new Assembly.

28. UK: RAF jet fighter flies at a record 540 mph (→7/11).

31. Java: Allied troops mobilise after a British brigadier is murdered while negotiating with Nationalist rebels (→8/11).

DEATHS

15. French statesman and Nazi collaborator Pierre Laval, three times pre-war premier, twice head of government under Vichy (*28/6/1883).→

24. Norwegian Nazi Vidkun Quisling, premier of occupied Norway (*18/7/1887).→

"Shirtless ones" put Juan Peron in power

Colonel Juan Peron, the people's choice as new leader of Argentina.

Oct 17. Colonel Juan Peron was asked to take over the government of Argentina today, only eight days after he had been ousted and imprisoned by his army colleagues. He threatened them with civil war, and thousands of workers took to the streets of Buenos Aires demanding his release and reinstatement.

The workers, called "shirtless ones", are members of unions Peron created while Secretary of Labor and Social Welfare. Yesterday, after several days of processions and rioting, the military leadership gave in to the clamour for his release. They announced he had not been arrested, but was merely being protected from possible attack.

In fact Peron is in the military hospital with pleurisy. He refused President Farrell's invitation to take over the Government, but this is seen as a tactical manoeuvre. He demanded and got the immediate resignation from the Government of the two generals who overthrew him.

Clearly Peron has routed the divided military leadership. Those left in the cabinet are mainly his friends. The Argentine General Confederation of Labour has called a 24-hour strike on behalf of Peron. He is on the verge of achieving his dream, which is to be President of a populist government based on the support of workers, army officers and the police.

Not everyone in Argentina will be pleased. A week ago it was the students and teachers who were marching on the streets. Their hatred of Peron is such that the bolder spirits were shouting "Death to Peron" (→4/6/46).

Allies execute two key collaborators

Oct 24. Two leading Nazi collaborators have been executed this month. Pierre Laval, the Vichy leader, was shot by a French firing squad on October 15; he tried to poison himself first, and died shouting "Vive la France". And today Vidkun Abraham Quisling, the Norwegian premier during the German occupation, was also shot. Both men had been convicted of high treason. Quisling was also found guilty of causing the deaths of thousands of Norwegians.

Dock strike: troops are unloading ships

Oct 14. Over 6,000 troops will be unloading food ships in British ports today as the the dock strike deepens. Some 43,000 dockers have now stopped work, and there are queues of ships waiting to unload, particularly in London and Hull, and on Merseyside. The dockers are hoping to secure a national minimum wage of 25 shillings a day.

The strike is unofficial, but it is supported at most of the country's ports, with a few exceptions. In South Wales, for example, dockers are still working; yesterday they unloaded oranges at Cardiff. In Middlesbrough 900 dockers came back to work this morning and will be moving vital iron ore supplies. In Glasgow, however, 4,600 strikers voted to stay out (→5/11).

Troops unload a supply ship.

Stalin orders drive for Soviet A-bomb

Oct 29. Stalin has ordered a crash programme to develop an atomic bomb for Russia. The day after the US bomb destroyed Hiroshima, he summoned five leading scientists to the Kremlin, and told them to catch up with the US in the minimum time, regardless of cost. Leonid Beria, the secret police chief, has been put in charge of all the laboratories and industries which will produce the bomb. Captured German specialists are also working on the project.

1945

NOVEMBER

Su	Mo	Tu	We	Th	Fr	Sa
				1	2	3
4	5	6	7	8	9	10
11	12	13	14	15	16	17
18	19	20	21	22	23	24
25	26	27	28	29	30	

1. Berlin: A British intelligence report ends speculation that Hitler is alive (→ 30/12).

3. London: The government announces that all civil aviation will be state-owned and controlled (→ 11/2/46).

5. UK: 43,000 dockers end their seven-week unofficial strike.

6. Moscow: Molotov says the USSR will build its own atomic bomb (→ 22).

7. UK: An RAF Gloster Meteor jet flies at a record 606 mph at Herne Bay in Kent.

8. Java: The British order Indonesians at the Surabaya naval base to surrender (→ 17).

12. Yugoslavia: Marshal Tito's National Front secures an overwhelming majority in a general election (→ 29).

13. London: Bevin says the UK and US will co-operate in trying to devise a plan for Palestine's future (→ 27/12).

16. Paris: The United Nations Educational, Scientific and Cultural Organisation (UNESCO) is founded.

17. Dutch East Indies: Ahmed Sukarno declares the rebel Republic of Indonesia (→ 29/6/46).

17. Germany: Josef Kramer, the "Butcher of Belsen", is sentenced to death.→

18. Bulgaria: The Communist-led Fatherland Front wins elections; opposition parties refused to take part (→ 8/9/46).

20. Vienna: Karl Renner becomes Austrian president (→ 25).

21. Paris: De Gaulle announces his new cabinet, which includes Communists (→ 5/12).

22. London: Attlee tells MPs that the A-bomb has made the world a more dangerous place.

25. Austria: The moderate People's Party wins a general election with 84 seats; Communists have three (→ 30/10/46).

29. Belgrade: The newly-elected Constituent Assembly declares a federal republic, ousting King Peter (→ 22/12).

German leaders on trial at Nuremberg

Defendants listen from the dock as the Nazis go on trial for the war.

Nov 20. Their faces are familiar from a thousand photographs and newsreels; but these men, who spread terror and ruin in Europe, are now just grey, nervous and nondescript.

Hitler's old associates were today brought to the Palace of Justice at Nuremberg, scene of the Fuehrer's rallies, to answer for their crimes before a tribunal formed by Britain, America, Russia and France.

In the dock are Goering, Hess, Ribbentrop, Keitel, Doenitz, Streicher, von Papen, who helped to put Hitler in power, Fritz Sauckel, the slave labour overlord, and a dozen others. The charges are: waging a war of aggression, violating the laws and customs of warfare, and crimes against humanity.

"The privilege of opening the first trial in history for crimes against the peace of the world imposes a grave responsibility," Justice Jackson, the chief US prosecutor, said. "The wrongs we seek to condemn and punish have been so calculated, so malignant and so devastating that civilisation cannot tolerate their being ignored."

All the evidence of "greed, duplicity and torture" would be from "books and records which the defendants kept with their Teutonic passion for thoroughness" (→ 1/12).

Riots flare in both Palestine and Cairo

Nov 2. Rioting broke out in Egypt today as Arabs throughout the Middle East joined mass demonstrations on the 28th anniversary of the Balfour Declaration on the establishment of a Jewish homeland in Palestine. Jerusalem itself was deserted as Arabs began a general strike. Sympathy protests extended as far as Tunis and Morocco. In Egypt 200 people were injured in Cairo while at least six people died in Alexandria. A total of more than 300 arrests were made as demonstators looted synagogues in Palestine (→ 13).

De Gaulle is elected President of France

Nov 13. General Charles de Gaulle was today elected President of the French Provisional Government by the unanimous vote of the 555 deputies. He opposed the armistice of 1940 after the German invasion, and fled to London where he formed the Free French forces. He started the Committee of National Liberation in Algiers in 1943, and led the triumphant return of French troops to Paris last year. He was condemned to death by the Petain Vichy regime of 1940, but spared Petain's life after he was convicted of treason last August (→ 21).

1945

DECEMBER

Su	Mo	Tu	We	Th	Fr	Sa
						1
2	3	4	5	6	7	8
9	10	11	12	13	14	15
16	17	18	19	20	21	22
23	24	25	26	27	28	29
30	31					

1. Nuremberg: Hess, who admitted he faked amnesia, is ordered to stand trial with his fellow Nazis (→ 8/1/46).

5. Paris: The French government nationalises five banks (→ 4/1/46).

6. Washington: An Anglo-US loan agreement is signed.→

9. Frankfurt: General Patton suffers chest injuries and is paralysed from the neck down when his car hits a truck.→

10. Stockholm: Nobel Prizes go to Wolfgang Pauli (Austria, Physics); Ilmari Virtanen (Finland, Chemistry); Sir Alexander Fleming, Sir Ernst Chain and Lord Howard Florey (UK, Medicine); Gabriela Mistral (Chile, Literature); and Peace Prize awarded in Oslo to Cordell Hull (US).

16. Moscow: "Big Three" foreign ministers Molotov, Bevin and James Byrne open talks (→ 26).

20. Rome: Mussolini's daughter, Edda Mussolini Ciano, is jailed for two years for aiding Fascism.

22. Washington: The US recognises Tito's government in Yugoslavia.

26. Moscow: Allied foreign ministers end their talks with agreement on UN control of atomic weapons (→ 21/1/46).

27. Palestine: Terrorists bomb four cities (→ 16/1/46).

30. Berlin: Hitler's will confirms his intention to commit suicide (→ 2/1/46).

DEATH

21. US commander George Smith Patton (*11/11/1885).→

HITS OF 1945

Cruising down the river.

We'll gather lilacs in the spring.

My guy's come back.

QUOTE OF THE YEAR

"All animals are equal, but some are more equal than others."

George Orwell, "Animal Farm", published 1945.

Syria, Lebanon to be free

Dec 13. In the House of Commons today the Foreign Secretary, Ernest Bevin, said that agreement has been reached with the French government on the joint withdrawal of forces from Syria and Lebanon. The pact is the end result of negotiations which began in September, when Bevin met Georges Bidault, his French counterpart.

With hostilities in the Middle East and Mediterranean over, the Allies are now in a position to implement the full independence which France gave to the Levant States in 1941. A further meeting to thrash out the final details will be held in Beirut next week.

It is generally agreed that Bevin deserves the congratulations he got from the opposition spokesman, Anthony Eden, this evening. Observers are hoping that withdrawal will remove a number of misunderstandings which should never have happened in the first place.

British intervention in Syria stemmed from the policy of the Vichy government, aiming only at restoring order in an unstable area of the Middle East. Ministers say French fears that Britain wanted to supplant them in a traditional sphere of influence are unjustified.

With both countries now in the United Nations, there is every reason to believe they will settle down to ordered self-government.

Crash kills "blood-and-guts" Patton

The gungo-ho general in Tunisia.

Dec 21. "Old Blood and Guts", General George S. Patton, died today in hospital in Heidelberg, Germany, from chest wounds suffered in a car accident earlier this month. The self-righteous 60-year-old war hero was responsible for victories in both North Africa and the Western Front. His Seventh Army, together with the British Eighth Army, conquered Sicily in 38 days, but he was not popular with the British top brass, especially his arch-rival Montgomery, and his outspokenness resulted in two demotions. He even urged children to study nursing and warfare to prepare for the next war.

Commons votes to accept a US loan

Dec 13. The House of Commons voted overwhelmingly tonight both for acceptance of a massive £1,100 million loan from the United States and for setting up an International Monetary Fund and International Bank to regulate the world economy.

Most Tories, guided by Mr Churchill, abstained from voting, but a sizeable minority, egged on by the maverick newspaper owner Lord Beaverbrook, voted against both propositions. The vote was widely seen as a parting of the ways between nostalgic, last-ditch defenders of Imperialism and a majority accepting that this country can no longer go it alone (→ 13/7/46).

IMF and the World Bank established

Dec 27. Two new bodies were created today to help avoid another world depression like that of the 1930s. The International Monetary Fund will maintain stable exchange rates through a world currency pool. The Bank for Reconstruction and Development will channel loans from the rich to the poorer countries for reconstruction and development projects. The idea came from the UN Bretton Woods meeting last July.

Arts: patronage records war for posterity

Despite state patronage for war art, this War has produced less memorable painting, poetry or even popular song than the Great War. Some 30 war artists were employed to record it. Far the best-known results were the drawings by **Henry Moore** of people sheltering from raids on the London Underground platforms, wrapped in their blankets like rows of mummified corpses.

Paul Nash produced evocative paintings of the vapour-trailed skies of the Battle of Britain, and of the wreckage of German warplanes in a moon-cratered landscape that he called "Totes Meer" (Dead Sea). The scars of the Blitz in urban streets became romantic scenery for artists like **John Piper** and **Graham Sutherland**. None recorded the civilian war effort better than **Stanley Spencer** in a series of huge close-up canvases of "Shipbuilders on the Clyde". **Dame Laura Knight**, the first woman Royal Academician, painted women at war, hauling barrage balloons or turning shells.

Evelyn Waugh, who served in the Royal Marines, wrote the funniest novel of the phoney war, "Put Out More Flags". Then, in contrast with wartime austerity, he gave vent to an unashamed nostalgia for pre-war, upper-class life at Oxford or in country houses in "Brideshead Revisited", now in huge demand.

Celia Johnson and Trevor Howard in "Brief Encounter".

George Orwell found a publisher, after many rejections, for his fable of how Stalin perverted the ideals of the Russian revolution. "Animal Farm", so short, simple and moving, is perhaps the most effective satire written in English since Swift.

Escape from the war is the reason for the cult of two films made by **David Lean** from **Noel Coward** plays – "Brief Encounter", a tale of love heroically suppressed, and "Blithe Spirit", reproducing the play which has run since 1941, with **Margaret Rutherford** as its unforgettable medium, Madame Arcati.

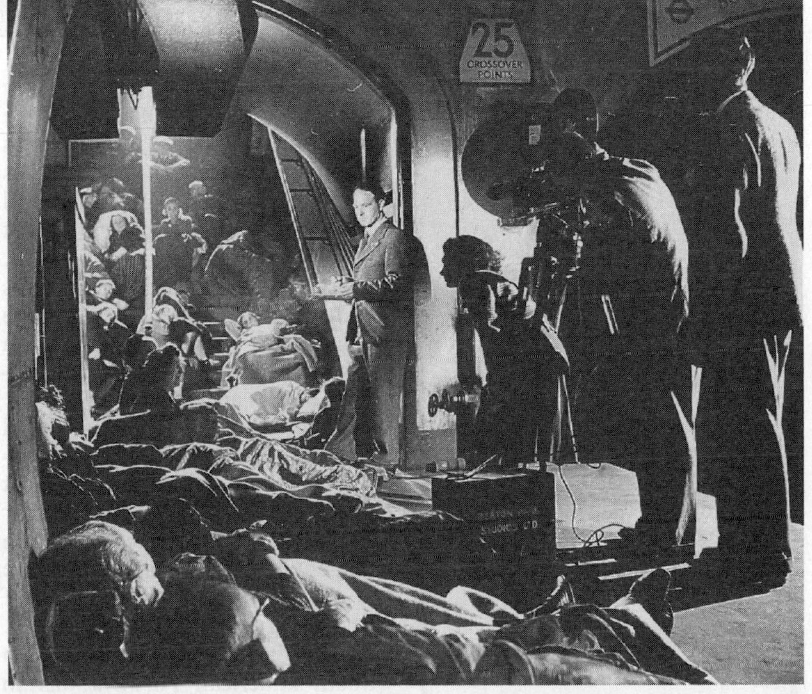

Henry Moore goes back underground to recapture the worst of the Blitz.

1946

JANUARY

Su	Mo	Tu	We	Th	Fr	Sa
		1	2	3	4	5
6	7	8	9	10	11	12
13	14	15	16	17	18	19
20	21	22	23	24	25	26
27	28	29	30	31		

1. London: Churchill gets the Order of Merit.

1. UK: 15 die in a rail crash at Lichfield, Staffordshire.

2. Germany: A third copy of Hitler's will is found at Dortmund.

4. France: Riots over a bread shortage break out in Paris and Rouen (→ 20).

6. North Vietnam: Ho Chi Minh wins elections (→ 6/3).

7. Berlin: 2,000 Polish Jews leave the Soviet sector.

8. Nuremberg: The trial of Goering and von Ribbentrop opens (→ 23).

9. London: Churchill leaves for a holiday in Florida, saying: "I've earned it."

10. UK: A British "GI Bride" marries her fiance by transatlantic telephone.→

11. Tirana: King Zog is dethroned; Albania declared a people's republic (→ 28/8).

16. Middle East: The Kings of Egypt and Saudi Arabia insist Palestine is Arab land (→ 25/4).

19. Brussels: The Belgian government rejects Leopold III's call for a referendum on his remaining king (→ 17/2).

20. Paris: De Gaulle resigns, declaring he is retiring from politics (→ 17/5).

21. London: The United Nations sets up an Atomic Energy Commission (→ 29).

22. UK: British pit owners protest at Labour's plan to nationalise the coal mines.

23. Nuremberg: Hess asks to conduct his own defence; Streicher suffers a mild heart attack (→ 7/2).

25. Guernsey: The island decides to drop its feudal system of government.

28. UK: The first post-war bananas arrive in Britain (→ 25/2).

29. London: The United Nations Council picks Norwegian diplomat Trygve Lie as its first Secretary-General.

30. Budapest: Hungary is declared a republic.

UN holds first session

Jan 30. The King made a speech of welcome and the Prime Minister spoke as a proud host at the inaugural session of the United Nations General Assembly today.

Post-war weakness or not, Britain counts, and this was history in the making. It is 26 years to the day since the ill-fated League of Nations was formed, and there is determination that this new organisation must not also fail.

Mr Attlee told the assembly of delegates from 51 nations, meeting in a spruced-up Central Hall, Westminster: "It is for the peoples of the world to make their choice between life and death. Our aim is the negation of war and the creation of social justice and security."

The Archbishop of Canterbury was an early arrival in the hall, where a gold map of the world, encircled by olive branches, hung from a lofty ceiling above the platform. He prayed that the world's tomorrows will always be peaceful.

Down to business, the Assembly had its first skirmish. Russia and her satellites were outvoted in the election of UN's first president. They wanted Norway's Foreign Minister, Trygve Lie, in the job, but by a small majority Paul Spaak of Belgium got it. Lie is now in line to become Secretary-General.

Brave hopes for a peaceful world.

Outside the hall there was great public excitement in the watching crowd. The vicious gale that blew up overnight had subsided and the sun shone. Mr Attlee seemed to sense the mood. The outlook was brighter now, he said, than when the League of Nations was formed without the presence of the United States and Russia. Now, with them involved, the world is more united. American and Russian delegates fingered their papers as he spoke. Euphoria is premature (→ 18/4).

Councils seek aid to rebuild cities

Jan 17. "New Towns" may be built in Britain to ease the housing shortage and rehouse victims of German bombing, the Housing Minister, Lewis Silkin, hinted today. An entirely new approach to post-war "development areas" was also under consideration, with the emphasis on diversified employment instead of domination by a single employer, he said.

In the meantime the worst hit cities, Hull and Coventry in particular, are pleading for state aid in replacing houses, shops, schools and the other essentials of a community. Hull, where 7,444 houses were destroyed and 86,722 damaged, has lost rateable value of 15 per cent. "We need 30,000 houses," said the city's spokesman. "We could get along much quicker if we had priority with materials and labour." Hull lost 25 of its schools by bombing and 85 were partially damaged. "The result," said the education committee chairman, "is that we have as many as 50 children in a class."

The Minister said that it was for local authorities to prepare the plans and submit them to the Government. He hoped that they would not be deterred by fears of the financial outcome (→ 8/5).

The first civilian flights take off from the airfield at Heathrow

Jan 1. Test flights started today from a new major airport to the west of London, to be known as Heathrow. This future terminus for all long-distance flights to and from the capital is at present a great plain of earth with few facilities, apart from a row of huts and tents and some telephone boxes, but the plan is to spend £20 million on development of what will be Britain's largest airport.

Building work is going ahead rapidly; already a 3,000-yard runway has been built. The plan is that the airport will open to regular traffic in June, and it is expected to be popular with pilots, for there are no apparent obstructions to takeoff or landing.

Today's test flight by British South American Airways was to Montevideo (→ 16/12).

Lord Winster officially opens Heathrow, Britain's newest civil airport.

GI brides trained in American ways

Jan 22. The first of 50,000 GI brides arrived at their special transit camp today en route to rejoin their soldier husbands in America. Two "brides' expresses" brought 344 women, the youngest only 16, and their 116 children from Waterloo in first-class style to Tidworth, Hampshire. Army staff looked after their luggage and coaches conveyed them to the camp.

Mothers are sleeping three to a room with their babies beside them. Rules at the camp, where they will stay until sailing for New York on the Queen Mary and the Argentina, include one which says "Brides are requested to keep out of the kitchen". It is expected to take until July to transport them all (→ 10/2).

Slow demob sparks strikes by RAF

Jan 27. More than 2,000 angry airmen are on strike in India, Ceylon, and Singapore, in protest at the slow rate of demobilisation. The Air Ministry today warned that their action will only delay their return home. Men could not be released all at once, it said, due to a shortage of ships, but the airmen are still angry, and have described the warning as "high-handed". Indian troops have had to be drafted in to replace the strikers guarding Japanese POWs building Singapore airfield (→ 21/2).

TB and VD are top targets of new NHS

Jan 3. Speaking to 2,000 children, Aneurin Bevan, the Health Minister, said that illness and death rates were lower than they had been in 1944, but that tubercolosis and venereal disease remained problem areas. He claimed he would transform the uncoordinated and unrelated current system into a single comprehensive national health service, providing all health care for every citizen without regard to the depth of his purse. Doctors would remain independent, but be expected to cooperate (→ 7/3).

1946

FEBRUARY

Su	Mo	Tu	We	Th	Fr	Sa
					1	2
3	4	5	6	7	8	9
10	11	12	13	14	15	16
17	18	19	20	21	22	23
24	25	26	27	28		

1. London: The planned British European Airways will offer fares of £7 10/- to Paris and £8 10/- to Amsterdam (→ 1/8).

4. Moscow: The USSR says it has found 190,000 bodies of Russian, Polish, French and British prisoners in Silesia.

7. Nuremberg: The trial of Hess opens (→ 21/3).

8. US: Scholars appointed complete the "Revised Standard Version" of the Bible.

9. Moscow: Stalin announces a new five-year economic plan.

9. London: The UN condemns Franco regime in Spain (→ 4/3).

10. New York: The first GI Brides arrive from Britain.

12. Washington: The US reports that Argentina is still giving refuge to Nazis.

14. Moscow: Averill Harriman resigns as US ambassador to the USSR (→ 22/9).

14. Paris: The International Olympic Committee announces that the 1948 Games will be held in London.

17. Belgium: Communists make significant gains in national elections.

18. Canada: 15 alleged Soviet spies are arrested, making 37 arrests in four days (→ 20).

20. Moscow: The USSR admits it has been spying in Canada (→ 1/5).

21. London: The government says 1.1 million will still be in military service by 1947, from a wartime peak of 5.1 million.

25. London: The government appeals to 4,000 firms to save coal, saying London only has a week's supply left.

25. China: Mao Tse-tung and Chiang Kai-shek agree to establish a National Army, in which Communists and Nationalists will join.

27. New York: The film "Road to Utopia" opens starring Bob Hope, Bing Crosby and Dorothy Lamour.

28. Washington: The US Army says it will use German V-2 bombs to test radar's anti-rocket capabilities.

Civil war looms in India as violence flares

Royal Indian Navy ratings parade through Bombay to support Congress.

Feb 12. The mood in India is becoming very dark, with the various communities digging further into their entrenched positions. The tension is almost palpable; it is as though men know a great storm is coming. The mutiny by the Indian Navy at Bombay earlier this month was indicative of the turmoil.

That was put down by British reinforcements, and only one man was killed, but if such a highly disciplined force can mutiny, the prospects for peace among India's turbulent peoples are slight. Already there has been bloody rioting in a number of cities. Sixty people died in Bombay when demonstrators, demanding freedom from British rule, set fire to grain warehouses, banks and shops, and overturned buses and cars. Police opened fire and the riot was quelled by armoured cars (→ 4/4).

IBM introduces fast electronic calculator

Feb 14. An "electronic brain", capable of doing in seconds calculations which could take a human mathematician hours, is operating at the University of Pennsylvania. Known as ENIAC (Electronic Numerical Integrator and Computer) the machine has 18,000 electronic valves but no moving parts.

ENIAC is more than an electronic adding machine. It has a memory, and can be "programmed" to do many different kinds of calculation. In fact machines like ENIAC are bound to become major assets for scientists and engineers with complex and repetitive calculations to perform. They could find a role in commerce, too, for processing things like pay rolls.

Professor Douglas Hartree of Cambridge University, who played a part in the machine's evolution, commented: "The idea originated to assist gunnery in the war." It is still in its infancy. The multiplicity of the problems which it can handle has not yet been defined.

Riots erupt in Cairo

Feb 21. British troops in Cairo today opened fire on angry crowds demanding an end to foreign influence. Twelve people are reported to have been killed and over 100 wounded. Egyptians also went on strike to drive home their demands for unification with Sudan. The new premier Sidky Pasha has banned further demonstrations (→ 7/5).

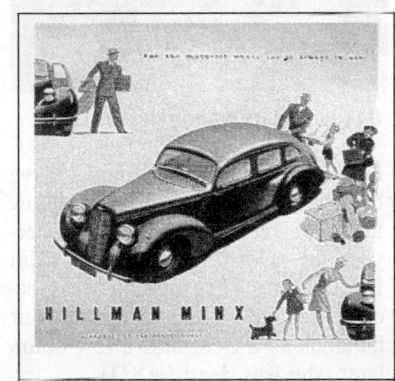

Britons return to war-time rations

Feb 7. A world food shortage has brought about the return of rationing on a near-wartime basis, the Minister of Food, Sir Ben Smith, told the Commons today. Bread's wheat content is to be reduced to its 1942 level, and bread will be darker. The butter, margarine and cooking fat ration is to be cut from eight to seven ounces weekly.

Rice will no longer be imported. The supply of cereals for animal and poultry consumption is to be reduced; and the Government hold out no hope for an increase in meat, bacon, poultry or eggs.

The biggest single factor was the need to feed 30,000,000 Germans, for whom famine loomed after their agricultural industry had been destroyed (→ 6/3).

Three-year-old dies of banana overdose

Banana boats come back at last.

Feb 25. For years bananas have been nothing but a memory. Now they are returning, but for three-year-old Dorothy Shippey from Bridlington, Yorkshire, a treat became a tragedy. She was given four bananas as a treat and a few hours later, she was dead (→ 8/3).

1946

MARCH

Su	Mo	Tu	We	Th	Fr	Sa
					1	2
3	4	5	6	7	8	9
10	11	12	13	14	15	16
17	18	19	20	21	22	23
24	25	26	27	28	29	30
31						

1. London: The Royal Navy reveals it planned to use icebergs as wartime bases.

2. North Vietnam: Ho Chi Minh is elected president.→

4. Washington: The Big Three pledge to aid Spain if Franco goes (→ 24/6).

5. London: Figures show that British wages are 80 per cent higher than in 1938 (→ 1/6).

6. London: The Food Ministry issues a recipe for squirrel pie.

8. London: Bananas arrive at Covent Garden Market for the first time since 1939.

11. Moscow: Churchill is denounced in Pravda as an anti-Soviet warmonger (→ 24).

13. Yugoslavia: Soldiers seize Tito's Nationalist opponent, General Draja Mihailovich, found hiding in a cave (→ 15/7).

14. Nuremberg: Goering takes responsibility for his actions during the war (→ 21).

18. London: A select committee recommends MPs salaries of £1,000 a year.

19. Paris: The colonies of Martinique, Guadeloupe, Guyana and Reunion become departments of France (→ 29).

20. London: The government says women may be diplomats but only if they do not marry.

21. London: Aneurin Bevan presents his full NHS proposals to parliament.

21. Nuremberg: Goering denies that he or Hitler knew of the Final Solution (→ 25).

24. Moscow: Stalin announces the immediate withdrawal of Russian troops from Iran (→ 14).

24. London: The BBC begins broadcasts in Russian (→ 29/9).

25. Nuremberg: Hess refuses to take the witness stand (→ 13/4).

28. London: The government promises free school milk and dinners.

29. Africa: The Gold Coast becomes the first British colony with a majority of Africans in its parliament.

31. Greece: Monarchists win the first elections since 1936.

Churchill warns of Europe's Iron Curtain

Churchill and Truman talk to America from the rear of a special train.

March 5. "From Stettin in the Baltic to Trieste in the Adriatic an Iron Curtain has descended across the Continent." In sombre voice Winston Churchill delivered this warning tonight. He spoke to an audience in the mid-West town of Fulton, Missouri, but his message about a growing Soviet menace was aimed at the whole free world.

He continued: "The dark ages may return on the gleaming wings of science. Beware, I say. Time may be short." Behind the curtain across Europe, Russia might even now be preparing for spreading Communist tyranny, added Mr Churchill.

Against this background, Britain's wartime Prime Minister appealed for an Anglo-American "fraternal association" to preserve peace. This pact would involve joint use of all the naval and air bases of either country all over the world. Mr Churchill also predicted eventual common citizenship for the two nations (→ 11).

Barriers collapse at FA Cup tie: 33 die

March 9. Thirty-three football fans were killed, and 500 others were badly hurt today, when steel barriers collapsed at the Bolton Wanderers' ground, Burden Park, after thousands of supporters broke down fencing to get into a packed enclosure to watch the FA Cup-tie with Stoke City. The Home Secretary, Chuter Ede, is expected to order an inquiry.

Police, who had closed entrance gates nearly an hour before the trouble, had been overwhelmed by the surging crowd who broke down perimeter fencing to get in. Several fans were crushed to death, but further casualites were avoided when officers let fans escape by pulling down more fencing around the pitch.

BMA sets up fund to fight the NHS

March 7. Doctors today launched a £1 million fighting fund to oppose plans for a national health service, and warned that they might refuse to cooperate. The British Medical Association said that it had a duty to its 50,000 members to back any individual doctors who might suffer financially, and to defend the profession.

It has already received about £100,000 in donations towards the campaign costs. A BMA statement said: "Should the Government prove obdurate and refuse to modify proposals in the Bill, which the profession might consider to strike at the essential freedoms of medicine, the doctors of this country might have to decide not to work in the new service" (→ 21).

Police swoop on blackmarketeers

March 27. Police and Ministry of Food enforcement officers are co-operating in a nationwide sweep on food blackmarketeers, it was revealed today. There are road-blocks around London and other major cities. Lorries, vans and private cars are being searched for eggs, meat and poultry which are fetching more than double their fixed price when sold "under the counter". Several food shops and restaurants have also been raided and their books examined.

Enforcement officers have also been busy checking market stalls throughout London, where a trade in "coupon free" clothing is said to flourish (→25/8).

France recognises Ho's Vietnam state

Vietnam leader Ho Chi Minh.

March 6. France has bowed to reality and recognised the Communist Democratic Republic of Vietnam. It is to be an autonomous state within French Indochina. Ho Chi Minh, elected President four days ago, helped start the French Communist Party in 1920. He later worked in China as a Comintern agent and then went on to found the Indochinese Communist Party in 1930. He led resistance to the Japanese invasion, and last year proclaimed independence (→28/12).

1946

APRIL

Su	Mo	Tu	We	Th	Fr	Sa
	1	2	3	4	5	6
7	8	9	10	11	12	13
14	15	16	17	18	19	20
21	22	23	24	25	26	27
28	29	30				

1. US: Tidal waves in the Pacific kill 300 in Hawaii, and hit Alaska and the West Coast.

3. UK: A committee recommends mounting a big international exhibition in London in 1951.

4. Paris: Dr. Petiot is sentenced to death for 27 murders.

5. UK: The first Grand National since 1940 is won by Mr J. Morant's Lovely Cottage (→5/6).

7. Teheran: Iran reveals that the USSR is to get 51 per cent control of Iranian oil for 25 years (→21/5).

10. Japan: Shigeru Yoshiba's Liberal Party wins the first Japanese general election in which women voted.

13. Germany: 58 Matthausen concentration camp guards are sentenced to death (→15).

15. Nuremberg: Nazi racial theorist Alfred Rosenberg explains why Jews must be destroyed (→23/5).

17. London: The government plans to nationalise the iron and steel industries (→5/9).

18. Geneva: The League of Nations is dissolved (→3/8).

19. Washington: Truman promises a million tons of wheat a month for Europe and Asia (→25).

23. London: Commonwealth premiers meet.

25. Palestine: Jewish terrorists kill seven in a British Army car park (→1/5).

25. UK: Loaves are cut by four ounces and brewing by 15 per cent to save grain (→30/5).

26. London: A bomb is detonated in St. James's Park.

28. China: The Communists seize Tsitsihar, capital of Nunkiang province (→5/5).

29. Tokyo: Tojo's trial begins.

30. Paris: The Big Four rule out a return of the South Tyrol to Austria (→10/5).

DEATH

21. British economist John Maynard Keynes, Lord Keynes (*5/6/1883).

Gandhi endorses Britain's "good faith"

Mr Nehru ponders his new responsibilities as India's leader designate.

April 4. The British cabinet delegation to India, led by Sir Stafford Cripps, talked for several hours yesterday with the Hindu leaders, Mr Gandhi and Dr Azad, the president of the Congress Party. The discussion centred on Mr Gandhi's demand for the establishment of an interim government for India as soon as possible.

Dr Azad said tonight: "Our talks were as between friends trying to find a solution to a problem. There is no reason why we should not be in a position within a short time to see the results of our labours mature." Later, Mr Gandhi told a crowd of followers: "The mission has come in good faith. It will not betray us."

Today the delegation will meet the Moslem leader, Mr Jinnah, for equally important talks in which the Moslem League will present its case in equally persuasive fashion. It seems that the line along which Hindu opinion is crystallising is a Federation of States. So far there is no sign of the Moslems accepting such an arrangement (→16/5).

Big Four try to iron out treaty details

April 25. The Big Four talks opened in Paris today with a surprising concession from Soviet Russia. Mr Molotov, the foreign minister, reversed the stand taken at the London conference last autumn, and agreed to France taking part in the talks on the Balkan treaties.

The foreign ministers of France, the US, Britain and Soviet Russia will rotate the chairmanship each day. There are three official languages so that each minister can speak in his own tongue. The spring sunshine seems to have affected the mood, but there are clashes ahead. The West is pushing for an independent Trieste, while the Russians are demanding heavy reparations from Italy (→30).

US recognises Tito's Yugoslav regime

April 18. The United States has finally recognised the People's Republic of Yugoslavia led by Marshal Tito, albeit reluctantly. The statement specifically dissociates the US from Tito's policies, his methods of achieving power and his "failure to implement the guarantees of personal freedom promised its people".

Tito, the son of a blacksmith, became the most effective partisan leader against the Nazis. His rival, General Mihailovich, however, had the support of the US, Britain and the USSR. After the war Tito's Communists won the election, and he had King Peter II deposed. The US questions whether the election was really free.

1946

MAY

Su	Mo	Tu	We	Th	Fr	Sa
			1	2	3	4
5	6	7	8	9	10	11
12	13	14	15	16	17	18
19	20	21	22	23	24	25
26	27	28	29	30	31	

1. London: It is announced that penicillin will soon be freely available.

1. London: Alan Numm May is jailed for ten years for passing nuclear secrets to the USSR.

3. Jerusalem: British troops are stoned by Arabs protesting at the Anglo-US plan for Palestine (→24).

5. China: Civil war erupts between Communists and Nationalists on the Yangtse River (→19/8).

9. Rome: King Victor Emmanuel III abdicates (→3/6).

10. Paris: The Big Four agree to placing Italy's former colonies in North Africa under UN control (→27/11).

16. London: Attlee announces plans for an independent, united India (→16/6).

17. Paris: The coal mines are nationalised (→13/10).

20. London: The government proposes free scholarships to universities.

21. US: David Niven's wife dies after an accident at a Hollywood party given by Tyrone Power.

21. Teheran: Iran confirms that Soviet troops have left.

23. Nuremberg: Hitler Youth leader Baldur von Schirach opens his defence (→28).

24. London: Churchill warns that the Suez Canal will be in danger if Britain pulls out of Egypt (→17/7).

24. Palestine: The Arabs refuse to discuss the Anglo-US plan (→18/6).

25. Amman: Transjordan becomes an independent kingdom called Jordan with Emir Abdullah its King.

26. Czechoslovakia: The Communists win the general election.

28. Germany: Himmler's deputy Oswald Pohl is arrested at Bremen; Rudolf Hoess, ex-commandant at Auschwitz, is sent for trial (→19/6).

29. UK: Rail fares rise; a return from London to Edinburgh now costs £6 18/9d.

Anglo-US partition plan for Palestinians

May 1. Fresh unrest is expected in the Holy Land, following publication of a joint Anglo-American report on Palestine, which offends both Arabs and Jews. It recommends that the present British mandate should continue "until Arab-Jewish hostility disappears", the goal being UN trusteeship.

The report is in favour of some kind of partition. It recognises Palestine as a Jewish national home, but adds that it can never be a purely Jewish land because it lies at the crossroads of the Arab world. The Arab population also looks upon Palestine as its homeland.

The committee recommends that 100,000 Jewish victims of Nazi and Fascist persecution should be admitted to Palestine this year. This figure compares with the present rate of 1,500 a month, and will cause great indignation among the Arabs without satisfying the Jews (→3).

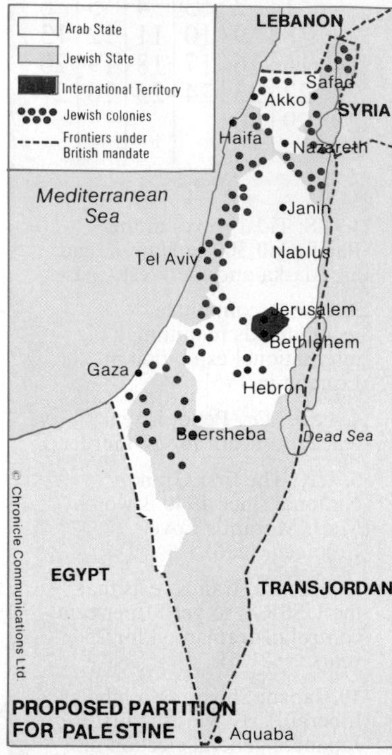

Each missing, presumed dead, but now this husband and wife are reunited.

Uproar at Attlee plan to get out of Egypt

May 7. There was uproar in the Commons today following the announcement by Mr Attlee that all British forces are to be withdrawn from Egypt. The Prime Minister's statement provoked an immediate demand from Mr Churchill that the sitting be adjourned to discuss the issue.

Following an admission from Mr Attlee that the British withdrawal depended on effective arrangements being made for the defence of the Suez Canal, Mr Churchill drew loud cheers from his side when he said that the only way of keeping the Canal open was to have British troops garrisoned there. Despite attacks, the Government intends to proceed with the plan (→24).

Britons tighten belts as rationing bites

May 30. As the Western nations mobilise against the growing threat of world famine, the British Government is preparing to ration bread for the first time today. The new food minister, John Strachey, told the Commons that a decision to ration would be an assurance of "security for our daily bread". Supplies of butter and other fats were also threatened.

The peacetime loaf, already darker than the wartime "victory bread", will be rationed on the basis of energy consumed. Workers in heavy industry will have more than clerical workers and others using less physical effort.

Bread rationing is certain to lead to a major political row. Winston Churchill described it as "an example of the public privations which arise from Socialist incapacity" (→25/11).

"New towns" to house one million

May 8. The Government plans to spend £380,000,000 on creating 20 new towns which, it is hoped, will house one million people. The plan was outlined in the House of Commons today by the Minister of Town and Country Planning, who told MPs that houses will be built for all income groups, not just the working classes. He said that he intends to create environments which will encourage a sense of culture and civic pride in those who will live in them (→4/11).

Freddie Mills falls to US contender

May 14. After ten savage rounds at London's Harringay Arena, the world light-heavyweight title, vacant since 1942, has been won. Freddie Mills, the British claimant, fought with courage and determination, after going down four times in a traumatic second round under the attack of the American claimant Gus Lesnevich. Mills fought back, but four more knock-downs in the tenth finished him.

Servicemen queue up for a divorce

May 11. With nearly 50,000 service divorces still outstanding in the courts, the Attorney-General, Sir Hartley Shawcross, has announced the immediate appointment of 35 legal teams to deal with this major social problem. The cases involve around 80,000 men and women, as well as many of their children, all of whom are waiting for three years to have their lives sorted out.

Quoting statistics derived from the Marriage Guidance Council, Mr Skeffington-Lodge, MP, claimed that 40 per cent of girls under twenty were pregnant on their wedding day, and a quarter of all births were illegitimate. "It is as easy today", he suggested, "to obtain a marriage licence as to buy a dog licence."

The Attorney-General refused to accept Mr Skeffington-Lodge's statistics, which he felt must have been taken from an atypical group, but agreed that the situation was deplorable. It was intolerable that so many people, often fresh from fighting the war, should be stopped from rebuilding their lives. The cost to the children, both in regard to their security and their education was equally high. These new measures should help (→ 28/11).

New grants to aid the poor scholars

May 20. Students who have won places at universities but have been unable to take them up due to economic pressure, will be cheered by a statement issued today by the Ministry of Education. As of this autumn any student who has won an award other than a state scholarship or local authority major award will be eligible for a grant to cover maintenance during their course.

Families earning less than £600 p.a. will receive a full grant. Higher earners will pay a small sum, while those on £1,500 or above will not be eligible.

Double or quits for British scientists

May 27. Plans to double the output of Britain's scientists were revealed today by the Committee on Scientific Manpower. Warning that any further delay would leave the country bereft of its world status, unable to restore its standard of living and without the means to expand the Empire, a White Paper called for the building of at least one new university and the immediate injection of government cash.

If this is not done at once, current statistics project a shortfall by 1955 of 26,000 scientists, a disaster for Britain's growth.

No slow, just quick, quick, quick for these fans of the jitterbug, the new American dance craze that's taking over Britain's ballrooms too.

1946

JUNE

Su	Mo	Tu	We	Th	Fr	Sa
						1
2	3	4	5	6	7	8
9	10	11	12	13	14	15
16	17	18	19	20	21	22
23	24	25	26	27	28	29
30						

1. London: Milkmen strike for a minimum weekly wage of £5/4/6d.

3. Italy: A referendum calls for the abolition of the monarchy (→ 7).

5. UK: The Derby, back at Epsom after six years, is won by Mr. Ferguson's Airborne.

7. Italy: Royalist riots occur in Rome, Naples and Pisa (→ 10).

8. London: Britain and the US agree in principle to an 11-state German Federation (→ 10/7).

9. Thailand: King Ananda Mahidol is shot dead; he is succeeded by Bhumibol Adulyadej (→ 13/8).

10. Rome: The Republic of Italy is declared, but King Umberto II refuses to go, alleging poll irregularities (→ 12)

12. Rome: Premier Alcide de Gasperi assumes the functions of head of state (→ 28).

16. London: Britain invites Indian leaders to set up an interim government (→ 24).

17. Japan: The Allies decide not to try Hirohito as a war criminal (→ 3/11).

18. Palestine: A curfew is in force after Jewish terrorists kill two British officers and kidnap three others.→

19. Nuremberg: Hitler's architect Albert Speer begins his defence (→ 26/8).

24. New York: The UN Security Council votes 7-4 against cutting ties with Franco's Spain.

24. UK: Morris raise car prices; two-door saloons cost £270, four-door £290.

24. India: The Congress Party rejects Britain's independence plan (→ 29/7).

28. Rome: Enrico de Nicola is elected provisional president of the Italian Republic.→

DEATHS

8. German author Gerhart Hauptmann (*15/11/1862).

14. British scientist and pioneer of television John Logie Baird (*13/8/1888).→

King quits after 35 days on throne

June 13. King Umberto II of Italy today conceded the seeming end of the monarchy in his country, following last week's referendum result in favour of a republic.

After just 35 days on the throne, he symbolically gave in to the constitutional change by flying to Spain, seen off only by a handful of airport workers.

His sudden departure led to rioting in Rome, where monarchists had expected King Umberto to pursue allegations of vote-rigging through the courts. As late as yesterday he had indicated he would stay and fight.

But in the end the Italian cabinet issued a statement supporting the establishment of a republic under Premier de Gasperi.

TV pioneer John Baird dies at 58

Logie Baird: small screen star.

June 14. John Logie Baird, the television pioneer, died today in Bexhill-on-Sea. He was 58. In 1926, at the Royal Institution in London, he was the first person to show television pictures of objects in motion, and his system was used for experimental public transmissions in Germany as well as Britain. However, when the BBC started its new television service in 1936, it chose a Marconi-EMI system in preference to Baird's. ▷

Peron installed as Argentinian President

Juan Peron receives the news of his election victory over Jose Tamborini.

June 4. General Juan Peron was today installed as President of Argentina. In his inaugural address to the Senate and Chamber, he pledged to maintain Argentina's sovereignty and to uphold its international commitments.

Argentina respected other countries, he said, "but I demand that this respect be reciprocated. We cannot permit anyone, great or small, to intervene in matters affecting our sovereignty."

Ecstatic crowds greeted Peron as he drove through Buenos Aires to Government House.

Jewish terrorists are condemned to death

June 27. Leaders of Irgun Zvai Leumi, the Jewish terrorist organisation, have promised that the three Britons that they hold as hostages will be killed, if death sentences passed on two of their number are carried out.

Two months ago, two terrorists were found guilty of firing at British troops, laying a bomb and taking a machine-gun from an armoured car. The British fear that a commutation of the sentence will be seen as a sign of weakness, and that it could spark off a new round of terrorist activities.

Meanwhile, there were emotional scenes in the Jerusalem court today when 30 Jewish terrorists received 15-year jail sentences. Hysterical relatives wailed in the public galleries while in the dock the prisoners sang Resistance songs (→ 2/7).

Indonesian leader calls for war on Dutch

June 29. President Ahmed Sukarno of Indonesia has launched a national appeal for all to join in fighting for freedom against the Dutch. Limited autonomy has recently been granted to some of the islands in this great archipelago, but there is widespread dissatisfaction.

On the main island, Java, there is discontent with the amount of independence so far granted, and in Sumatra there is pressure for the island to break away, while in the rest of the Dutch East Indies, the Nationalists are demanding that elections should be held within three years.

President Sukarno was himself recently ousted as prime minister of Java by Mr Sjahrir who is considered to be a moderate, willing to work with the Dutch and the British. Sukarno has now mounted a counter-coup and kidnapped his old enemy. Then he declared martial law.

1946

JULY

Su	Mo	Tu	We	Th	Fr	Sa
	1	2	3	4	5	6
7	8	9	10	11	12	13
14	15	16	17	18	19	20
21	22	23	24	25	26	27
28	29	30	31			

1. Pacific: An atomic bomb is exploded, sinking three ships and damaging 31 out of 73 (→ 25).

2. Palestine: A massive cache of arms belonging to the illegal Jewish army Haganah is discovered.→

3. UK: The Jockey Club says it is going to install photo-finish cameras on all racecourses.

6. Wimbledon: Yvon Petra beats Geoff Brown for the Men's Singles title; Pauline Betz beats Louise Brough for the Women's Singles crown.

8. Oxford: Margaret Roberts, a Somerville undergraduate, is elected president of Oxford University Conservatives.

10. Paris: Foreign Secretary Bevin says the Big Four must unite to govern Germany (→ 20/10).

13. Washington: A £937 million loan to Britain is approved.

15. Belgrade: General Mihailovich is found guilty of treason and sentenced to death.→

17. Egypt: 25 are injured when five bombs blast the British Services Club at Alexandria.

20. Washington: A congressional committee exonerates Roosevelt of any blame for the Pearl Harbor attack.

24. London: Fuel Minister Emmanuel Shinwell warns there is not enough coal to get through the winter (→ 23/12).

25. Pacific: The first sub-surface atomic explosion is detonated at Bikini Atoll (→ 18/8).

26. Jerusalem: 376 alleged terrorists are arrested as an Anglo-US panel recommends the partition of Palestine (→ 7/8).

30. London: From today a decree absolute will be granted six weeks after a decree nisi, not six months as previously (→ 28/11).

DEATH

29. US author Gertrude Stein (*3/2/1874).

Moslems ready for civil war in India

July 29. Dangerous decisions were taken by the All-India Moslem League in Bombay today. Delegates voted unanimously to withdraw the League's acceptance of the British cabinet mission's long-term plans for India's constitution; to revert to the demand for a fully sovereign Moslem state of Pakistan; and to resort to "Direct Action" to achieve their aims.

The League's Council called on all Moslems in India to be ready for every sacrifice, and to prepare for the "coming struggle".

The Council accused the British of having broken solemn pledges, and the Congress Party of being bent upon setting up a caste-Hindu "Raj" in India with the connivance of the British.

The League's leader, Mr Jinnah, later said: "Bloodshed and civil war must be avoided if possible. But now there is no more room left. Now let us march on ... If you want war we accept it." (→ 19/8)

Tito executes his old partisan ally

July 17. Early this morning, General Draja Mihailovich, the former Yugoslav guerrilla leader who, in the early stages of the war, led his Chetnik partisans against occupying German and Italian troops, was executed by a firing squad. He had been found guilty of treason and collaboration by a Belgrade court two days ago.

When Yugoslavia was occupied in 1941, Marshal Tito, the Communist leader, led his men into the hills to organize the resistance. There he met up with Mihailovich and his bearded soldiers. For a while the two leaders joined forces, but when Tito won full Allied support for his tactics, Mihailovich switched to supporting the Germans and Italians in a bid to defeat the Communists.

With the Allied victory in Eastern Europe, and Tito established as Yugoslavia's first Communist prime minister, many collaborators have now been executed along with Mihailovich or sentenced to death in absentia.

Zionist guerrillas bomb British HQ

Sightseers inspect the wreckage of the King David Hotel, blown up today.

July 22. A time-bomb planted by Jewish terrorists today destroyed one wing of the King David Hotel in Jerusalem, the HQ of the British Palestine Army Command. The official statement lists 42 dead, 52 missing and 53 injured.

Within minutes an army cordon was thrown round the area. Total curfew has been imposed in the centre of Jerusalem. In a statement tonight the Jewish Agency expressed horror at the outrage.

The bomb plot had been well planned. Just after noon a lorry, guarded by two armed men, drew up at the hotel's basement entrance. Two others unloaded several milk churns packed with explosives, which they took to the kitchens of the Regency Restaurant under the offices of the Secretariat. On their return they wounded a British army officer who challenged them. Guards fired back, wounding one, but all escaped in a waiting taxi.

A second group fired at the hotel to cover the escape. Two diversionary bombs, timed to go off before the main explosion, had also been planted. Two minutes earlier a woman rang a local newspaper, saying: "This is a movement of Jewish Resistance. We are about to blow up the government offices. We have warned them."

This seems to have been a crude attempt to blame Haganah, an illegal Jewish army, but one rarely associated with terrorism. Deputy Superintendant Catling of the Palestine Police CID, who had a narrow escape in the hotel, was probably correct when he said: "This has all the earmarks of the Stern Gang" (→26).

An explosion off Bikini Atoll in the Pacfic shows the A-bomb's awesome power; somewhere beneath the mushroom cloud is a US warship.

1946

AUGUST

Su	Mo	Tu	We	Th	Fr	Sa
				1	2	3
4	5	6	7	8	9	10
11	12	13	14	15	16	17
18	19	20	21	22	23	24
25	26	27	28	29	30	31

1. London: British European Airways is created.

3. New York: Ireland and Portugal join the list of applicants for membership of the UN (→13).

7. London: Britain tells the US it will not allow further illegal entry into Palestine.→

9. Algeria: Nationalist leader Ferhat Abbas proposes an independent Algerian Republic within the French Union.

12. US: Rex Harrison makes his Hollywood debut in "Anna and the King of Siam".

13. New York: The USSR vetoes Thai and Portuguese entry to the UN (→28).

18. US: Einstein deplores the use of the atomic bomb and says Roosevelt would never have allowed it.

19. UK: Footballers threaten to strike for a minimum weekly wage of £7.

20. Nuremberg: The prosecutors reject Hess's plea of insanity (→26).

22. Oslo: Opening of the European Games.

24. New Delhi: Wavell appoints Nehru head of a provisional government (→2/9).

25. UK: The black market in nylons, chocolates, perfume and other scarce goods is reported to be flourishing.

26. Nuremberg: Schreiber reveals that the Nazis were poised to begin germ warfare and experimented at Dachau (→31).

28. New York: The US says it will veto Albanian and Mongolian UN entry if the USSR vetoes Western countries (→29).

29. New York: The UN Security Council votes to admit Sweden, Iceland and Afghanistan (→17/11).

31. Nuremberg: The War Crimes trial ends; only Hans Frank, Nazi governor of Poland, pleaded guilty (→30/9).

DEATH

13. British author H.G. (Herbert George) Wells (*21/9/1866).

Thousands die as Hindu-Moslem riots break out in India

Aug 19. Calcutta is in a state of bloody turmoil today, after three days of fighting between Moslems and Hindus over a British plan for India's constitution. More than three thousand people have been killed, and their bodies are still heaped in streets.

The area has been virtually cut off; telegraph, postal and telephone services are still suspended. Armoured cars and tanks are the only vehicles allowed in. Food supplies have reached dangerously low levels, and starvation threatens to add to the crisis faced by hospitals, which have been overwhelmed by 10,000 casualties.

Two battalions of British troops in Calcutta have opened fire on gangs which refused to obey a curfew, but today the Bengal government said violence was now "definitely under control".

Hindus have suffered the heaviest casualties from the rioting, which broke out during a day of action organised by the Moslem League in protest at British proposals for the formation of an interim all-India government.

The Moslem minority, pledged to create its own state of Pakistan, insists on a split into two countries and looks set to refuse seats on any interim executive council (→24).

Moslems surround a dead Hindu.

Full-scale civil war breaks out in China

Starving Chinese civilians beg for food as the civil war rages unabated.

Aug 19. Only months after the Japanese surrender, the Communist leader Mao Tse-tung is ready to resume fighting the Chinese civil war, temporarily suspended during the world war. Indeed, clashes began as Russian troops pulled out of Manchuria in the spring.

In a national broadcast today he declared open war on the KMT (Kuomintang) nationalist regime of the war leader Marshal Chiang Kai-shek. He has more than a million men in uniform in his Red Army, and claims to control twice as many guerrillas in the countryside.

Although the KMT and the Chinese Communist party have battled for twenty years, this is the first time that there has been a formal declaration of war. The fact that Mao feels able to make such a strong gesture reveals his confidence that his long and bitter struggle to establish a Communist regime is nearing success.

Both sides in China were caught off guard by the sudden collapse of the Japanese. Marshal Chiang ruled in his wartime capital of Chungking, while Mao held sway in the north-west from his headquarters in Yenan. American efforts to reconcile the two, so as to reconstruct China, have failed (→ 14/10).

British ban Jews from Palestine

Aug 11. Today two more ships are expected to join the flotilla of misery outside the port of Haifa. The ships, carrying 1,500 Jewish refugees from Europe to Palestine, are stranded there by a blockade of British warships and have become floating slums. The new arrivals will be intercepted by a destroyer.

Barbed-wire has been strung along the harbour wall to prevent escape, and onshore camps are holding a further 3,000 Jews as Britain decides whether to risk heightening the month-long crisis by shipping them to Cyprus (→ 15/9).

RATION
DINNERS
Homely Savoury Dishes
adapted to war conditions
for Families & Canteens
2D

The war may be over, but the kitchen is still on short rations.

1946

SEPTEMBER

Su	Mo	Tu	We	Th	Fr	Sa
1	2	3	4	5	6	7
8	9	10	11	12	13	14
15	16	17	18	19	20	21
22	23	24	25	26	27	28
29	30					

1. Greece: A referendum approves overwhelmingly the restoration of the monarchy (→ 10).

2. India: Nehru's cabinet is sworn in (→ 22/11).

4. Paris: An airliner bound for London crashes, killing 21.

5. London: Archibald Forbes is named as head of the Iron and Steel Board.

6. London: Nine RAF men who escaped from Stalag Luft III in a glider receive MBEs.

8. Bulgaria: A referendum rejects the monarchy under nine-year-old King Simeon.

10. Greece: Communist republicans close the road from Athens to Salonika (→ 25).

14. London: Downing Street security is to be tightened after the theft of the Chancellor's cigarette case from No. 11.

15. Palestine: The Jewish Agency orders an end to Jewish terrorism (→ 4/10).

19. Newfoundland: The wreckage is found of an airliner which went missing yesterday with 49 passengers.

20. France: Opening of the first Cannes Film Festival, originally scheduled for September 1939 (→ 7/10).

22. Washington: Averill Harriman is appointed Commerce Secretary.

25. Greece: Civil war is reported to be looming as republican unrest continues (→ 27).

27. Athens: King George II returns from exile (→ 16/11).

27. London: The government announces that cupro-nickel will replace silver in British coins from 1947.

29. London: The BBC's new "Third Programme" starts broadcasting.

30. Nuremberg: The war crimes tribunal begins to deliver its judgement (→ 1/10).

DEATH

16. British composer Granville Bantock (*7/8/1868).

Churchill issues call for a united Europe

Sept 19. A "United States of Europe" to ensure future peace was urged by Winston Churchill today. In a speech broadcast world-wide from Zurich, he said that reconciliation and partnership betwen France and Germany must be the first step in its creation.

But the ex-premier pictured "millions of free Europeans, now scanning dark horizons for the approach of a new form of tyranny and terror. They needed a regional mutual protection pact."

He continued: "Time may be short. At present there is a breathing space, but if we are to form a united states of Europe – or whatever name it may take – then we must begin now. I say to you: Let it arise."

Fans fill terraces as soccer is reborn

Sept 1. League football returned to post-war England yesterday, with record crowds braving the rain to see the first Saturday league programme since 1939. In all some 950,000 fans packed the terraces, with six clubs attracting over 50,000: Chelsea (who beat Bolton 4-3), Everton, Sunderland, Tottenham, Aston Villa and Wolverhampton, whose 6-1 win over Arsenal provided Division One's most dramatic scoreline.

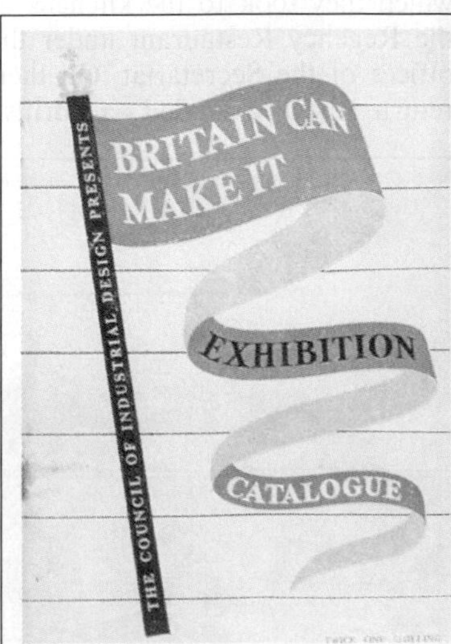

THE COUNCIL OF INDUSTRIAL DESIGN PRESENTS
BRITAIN CAN MAKE IT
EXHIBITION
CATALOGUE

Flying an optimistic flag at the Britain Can Make It Exhibition.

1946

OCTOBER

Su	Mo	Tu	We	Th	Fr	Sa
		1	2	3	4	5
6	7	8	9	10	11	12
13	14	15	16	17	18	19
20	21	22	23	24	25	26
27	28	29	30	31		

1. Nuremberg: 12 Nazis are sentenced to death and Hess gets life; five are jailed and three acquitted (→ 10).

3. UK: The air fare from London to New York is now £146 13/6d.

7. France: "Brief Encounter" wins the prize for the best British film at the Cannes Film Festival.

10. Nuremberg: The war crimes tribunal rejects pleas for clemency from 11 Nazis sentenced to death (→ 16).

11. China: Nationalist troops capture Kalgan, a Communist base in the north (→ 16).

11. London: MPs approve a memorial to Roosevelt in Grosvenor Square.

13. Paris: A referendum approves the constitution of the new Fourth Republic, with less power for the president.

16. Nuremberg: Goering commits suicide shortly before he is due to be executed.→

16. China: Chiang Kai-shek offers the Communists a peace plan.

18. New York: The city offers the UN a 350-acre site at Flushing Meadow for its permanent home (→ 11/12).

20. Berlin: Voters go to the polls in the city's first free election in 14 years.

24. London: Ralph Richardson opens in Edmond Rostand's "Cyrano".

25. Germany: The Soviets are reported to be dismantling German arms factories and taking them to the USSR.

30. Vienna: Austria's parliament calls for an end to the Allied occupation.

31. Rome: Britain's embassy is wrecked by two explosions; Jewish terrorists are suspected (→ 8/11).

DEATHS

15. German Nazi Hermann Goering (*12/1/1893).→

16. German Nazi Joachim von Ribbentrop (*30/4/1893).→

Top Nazis are executed at Nuremberg

Oct 16. Ten Nazi war criminals mounted the gallows erected in the prison gymnasium at Nuremberg early today. Two were missing: Hitler's deputy, Martin Bormann, believed dead, tried "in absentia"; and Hermann Goering, who had committed suicide a few hours earlier with a cyanide pill.

There were three black-painted wooden scaffolds in the long, wide room. Two were used alternately, the third being kept in reserve.

First to enter the execution chamber was Joachim von Ribbentrop, Foreign Minister in the regime that was to last a thousand years. The time was 1.11am. His arms were seized by two army sergeants as he walked through the door. Handcuffs were replaced by a leather strap. He climbed the 13 steps to the platform without hesitation, gave his name in a loud voice and, as the black hood was placed on his head, said "I wish peace to the world". The trap was sprung and he fell from view, hidden behind a dark curtain.

Field Marshal Wilhelm Keitel, who had told the Tribunal he had just obeyed orders, was next. His last words were: "More than two million German soldiers went to their death for their fatherland. I follow now my sons – all for Germany."

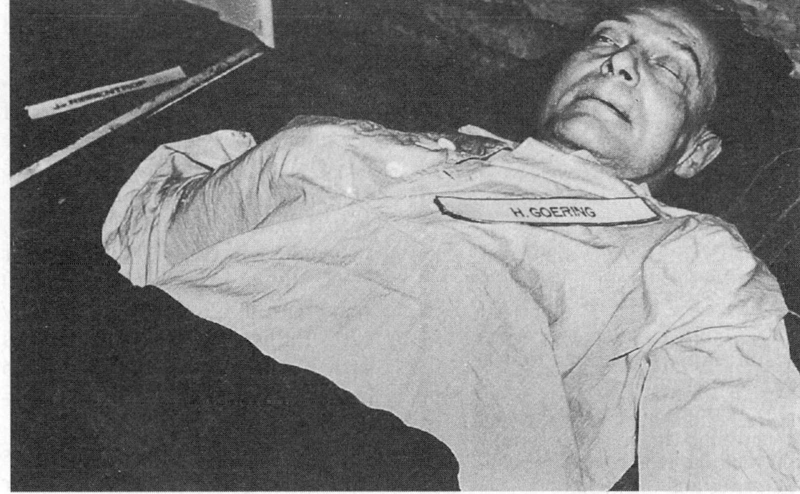

Goering cheated the hangman, taking cyanide hours before his execution.

Ernst Kaltenbrunner, successor to Heydrich, the Butcher of Prague, licked his lips and glanced around him; Alfred Rosenberg, chief exponent of the master race theory, had nothing to say; Hans Frank, governor of occupied Poland and a recent convert to Roman Catholicism, came in smiling; Wilhelm Frick, "Protector" of Bohemia, stumbled as he mounted the steps; Julius Streicher screamed "Heil Hitler!" and could be heard groaning after he fell through the trap; Fritz Sauckel, the slave labour boss, limped on his left clubfoot up the steps; General Alfred Jodl, in his Wehrmacht uniform, was haggard and nervous; last to die was Arthur Seyss-Inquart, Hitler's governor in Austria, who called for peace and understanding between peoples. Between executions, hangmen and guards were allowed to light up cigarettes.

New research links smoking to cancer

Oct 2. Could smoking be a cause of lung cancer? This was the question reviewed today at a medical symposium at the University of Buffalo in the United States. At present men are six times more liable to develop lung cancer than women, according to Dr. William Reinkoff.

Now that more women are smoking, however, he wondered whether this ratio would be reduced as more women get the disease as a result of the habit. In his own opinion, the trend would mean that more women will suffer lung cancer.

The doctors at the meeting knew that the discussions might cause unnecessary alarm, since the link between smoking and cancer could not be proved for years. However, most believed that the risk of causing phobias was a lesser evil than indifference or inertia.

Let more Jews into Palestine, urges US

Oct 4. On Yom Kippur – the Jewish Day of Atonement – President Truman has renewed a diplomatic war with Britain over the future of Palestine. He backed the Jewish Agency plan for creation of a viable Jewish state in an "adequate" area of Palestine. Also, he reiterated an earlier demand for Britain to admit 100,000 Jewish displaced persons in Europe to Palestine immediately.

Mr Attlee reacted sharply. A few days ago he asked the President to keep quiet. Tonight a Foreign Office statement accused the President of sabotaging delicate British negotiations with Jews and Arabs. These are now at a critical stage.

It was freely said in Whitehall that his concern is Jewish votes in New York. Arab leaders warned that aggressive American policy over Jewish immigration could mean revocation of all Middle East oil concessions and severance of diplomatic relations (→ 31).

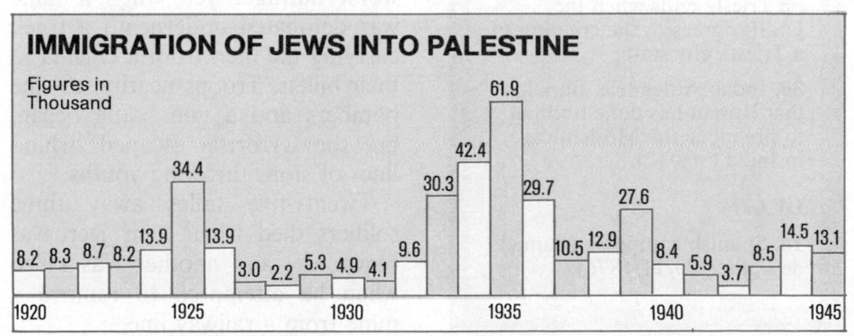

1946

NOVEMBER

Su	Mo	Tu	We	Th	Fr	Sa
					1	2
3	4	5	6	7	8	9
10	11	12	13	14	15	16
17	18	19	20	21	22	23
24	25	26	27	28	29	30

1. UK: Labour make gains at the expense of independents in municipal elections.

3. Tokyo: Hirohito announces a new constitution, denying his divinity as emperor.

4. London: An enquiry opens into a proposed new town at Crawley in Sussex.

6. US: Congressional elections give the Republicans control of both the House of Representatives and the Senate.

7. UK: The Ford Prefect is on sale at £275, the Ford Anglia at £229.

8. Palestine: Jews boycott British goods (→ 2/12).

9. US: The Lockheed Constellation, capable of carrying a record 168 passengers, makes its maiden flight in California.

10. London: The King unveils an addition to the Cenotaph at the Remembrance parade: MCMXXXIX - MCMXLV.

13. New York: Albania protests to the UN about Britain's mine-sweeping in the Corfu Channel.

16. Greece: Fierce fighting is reported between Greek troops and Macedonian rebels.

17. Bangkok: To secure UN membership, Thailand returns areas of Cambodia and Laos annexed in 1941.

21. UK: Widespread flooding occurs after the eighth successive day of rain.

22. Oxford: Anthony Wedgwood Benn is elected treasurer of the Oxford Union Society.

25. London: The government says food controls are to be relaxed, but bread will still be rationed.

27. Paris: Big Four deadlock on Trieste ends when the USSR agrees to the creation of a Trieste city state.

30. India: Attlee tells Jinnah that Britain has done nothing to prejudice the Moslem case in India (→ 6/12).

DEATH

14. Spanish composer Manuel de Falla (*23/11/1876).

Lords debate the "tidal wave of divorce"

Nov 28. A "tidal wave" of divorce is sweeping the country, the House of Lords heard today. The Lord Chancellor said that 38,000 petitions were due this year and a further 50,000 next. "When we think of the unhappiness that means we are faced with an immensely serious problem," he said.

In 1945 there were 25,000 cases, two and a half times the number for 1938 and a huge increase on 40 years ago: in 1905 there were only 670. Earlier this year there was such a back-log of cases waiting to be heard that judges had to sit during the summer recess.

Many of the broken marriages are between servicemen and their wives; victims, matrimonial experts believe, of too-lengthy separations or too-hasty marriages in wartime. Many couples found themselves virtual strangers afterwards. Others met new partners during the enforced absences of the past seven years: about 70 per cent of last year's divorces were for adultery.

Today's debate on the need for revision in proceedings brought an attack on the civil ceremony by the Archbishop of Canterbury, who condemned its "startling brevity" of three minutes and two concluding sentences. Such conditions failed to convey the serious, life-long obligation of marriage, he said.

The six months between a decree nisi and a decree absolute was cut in August to six weeks.

Jewish terrorists kill eight British troops

Jewish suspects are lined up after an explosion hit Jerusalem's station.

Nov 17. Eight British servicemen were killed in Jerusalem today, as Jewish terrorists launched a wave of bombings and shootings. Eleven other members of the security forces were badly hurt.

Four died in what was one of the worst outrages yet, when a mine was detonated underneath a truck carrying the men from a cinema to their billets. Troops nearby saw the bombers and a gun battle began, but the terrorists escaped behind lines of stone-throwing youths.

Twenty-five miles away three soldiers died when their jeep was blown up, and another was killed when he attempted to remove a mine from a railway line.

The latest attacks coincide with the arrival this week of Moshe Sneh, leader of Haganah, the self-styled Jewish defence group, and reports that the British military strength is soon to be increased.

Haganah has been involved in an underground war against the other Jewish terror groups, the Stern Gang and Irgun Zvai Leumi, by blowing up their arsenals.

Scotland Yard have stepped up government protection of senior political figures, following threats of Jewish extremists to extend their campaign to Britain. Armed guards have been assigned to homes of ministers and Westminister staff have been warned about parcel bombs.

All dislike the new Indian assembly

Nov 22. India's Constituent Assembly, which is due to hold its first meeting on December 9, was attacked by both Hindus and Moslems today. Mr Jinnah, the Moslem League leader, said he would boycott the Assembly and described it as "one more blunder".

"It is quite obvious," he said, "that the Viceroy is blind to the present serious situation and is playing into the hands of Congress." At the same time the Congress leader, Pandit Nehru, was telling his followers that the only good thing about the Assembly was that "Britain will not be directly represented on it" (→ 30).

Biro's ball gives new point to pens

Nov 22. A revolutionary new pen which writes 200,000 words without refilling, blotting or smudging has gone on sale. The Biro, which costs 55s, is the creation of Hungarian journalist Ladislao Biro, who became fascinated by printers' quick-drying ink when he was an editor in Budapest.

His invention combines a rotating ball point with a tiny capillary tube to hold the ink. Biro, who fled to Argentina to escape the Nazis, sold out two years ago to his English backer, H.G.Martin, who is now marketing the pens.

Television production, halted for the war, is now back on line.

1946

DECEMBER

Su	Mo	Tu	We	Th	Fr	Sa
1	2	3	4	5	6	7
8	9	10	11	12	13	14
15	16	17	18	19	20	21
22	23	24	25	26	27	28
29	30	31				

2. Palestine: Five British troops die in a bomb attack.

3. London: Field Marshal Montgomery and Lord Mountbatten are made Knights of the Garter.

6. London: Anglo-Indian talks end in failure after three days.

7. US: A hotel fire in Atlanta, Georgia, kills 137.

10. London: The government is to set up a Tourist Board.

10. Stockholm: Nobel Prizes go to: Percy Bridgman (US, Physics); James Sumner, John Northrop and Wendell Stanley (US, Chemistry); Hermann Muller (US, Medicine); and Hermann Hesse (Switzerland, Literature). Peace Prize awarded in Oslo to Emily Balch and John Mott (US).

11. New York: John Rockefeller offers the UN a site for a skyscraper on the East River.

14. New York: The UN rejects South Africa's proposal to annex South West Africa.

16. London: Details are unveiled of expansion plans for Heathrow airport.

20. S. Africa: Smuts says race equality "does not work".

23. London: The cotton industry warns of imminent stoppages because of fuel shortages (→27).

27. UK: 12 cotton mills close and a four-day week is planned in the Midlands because of a lack of coal.

DEATHS

10. US author Damon Runyon (*4/10/1884).

25. US actor W. C. Fields, born William Claude Dukenfield (*29/1/1879).

HITS OF 1946

A gal in calico.

It's a pity to say good night.

QUOTE OF THE YEAR

" You can keep the things of bronze and stone and give me one woman to remember me just once a year."

Damon Runyon, author of "Guys and Dolls", died 1946.

Vietnamese under French martial law

Dec 28. The French Government proclaimed martial law throughout Indochina tonight, as the country was threatened by civil war. French loudspeaker trucks toured the streets of Hanoi, the capital, ordering rebels to surrender their arms. Anyone found carrying arms will be shot on sight.

The situation has deteriorated since Hanoi was bombarded last week in an attempt to restore French authority. President Ho Chi Minh fled the capital, together with a number of leading officials. He advised his supporters to take up armed resistance. "If you have no sword," he said, "arm yourselves with axes and sticks."

As head of a friendly state, Ho was received in Paris recently to settle details of independence within the French Union. During his stay the colonial High Commissioner proclaimed an independent republic in French Indochina, demonstrating the extent of the conflict between Paris and the local colonial administrators. The Socialist Prime Minister, Leon Blum, said things were "not alarming".

Plan to nationalise railways and ports

Dec 18. The House of Commons voted tonight to nationalise the railways, road haulage and the ports. Labour MPs triumphantly sang the Red Flag as they queued up in the division lobby to endorse this latest instalment of the Government's sweeping public ownership programme.

The vote came at the end of an intemperate three-day debate. Tory leaders warned vehemently that the legislation threatens to do immense damage to the economy. A giant state monopoly would be a racket at the expense of the consumer. Government Ministers retorted that the railways are a national disgrace and must be revived without having to face cut-throat competition.

For the Tories, Anthony Eden said: "It's a disaster." Herbert Morrison, the Home Secretary, replied: "The people voted for it."

Arts: public funds to boost post-war art

The arts are coming out of wartime hibernation. The Arts Council of Great Britain has been founded at the suggestion of **Lord Keynes**, who was appointed its first chairman, with a budget of £230,000 to support the fine arts.

BBC radio has begun a Third Programme, offering serious music, poetry and drama on an unprecedented scale. At Stratford-on-Avon the Memorial Theatre has reopened under **Sir Barry Jackson**. A revolutionary production of "Love's Labours Lost" has set the theatrical world talking about its 21-year-old director, **Peter Brook**.

Meanwhile an actor with an almost blank face on which to project expression has made his mysterious quality felt. **Alec Guinness** first caught attention in **Jean-Paul Sartre's** claustrophobic play "Huis Clos" (Vicious Circle), and then as the charming, good-hearted Herbert Pocket, in **David Lean's** film of "Great Expectations". At the Old Vic he played the Fool in "King Lear" and stole the notices even from **Olivier's** King. He shone recently in the tiny part of Abel Drugger in "The Alchemist".

Ralph Richardson added the grotesque Cyrano de Bergerac to his Old Vic repertoire, folowing his acclaimed Falstaff in "Henry IV". He also starred in "An Inspector Calls" by **J.B.Priestley**, in whose plays he had appeared so often before the war.

When the Old Vic company visited New York in May, tickets changed hands unofficially for $50. In London, under Old Vic policy of being a theatre of the poor, half the seats cost less than two packets of cigarettes.

Ralph Richardson plays Falstaff.

The death of **H.G. Wells** on the eve of his 80th birthday followed his despairing book out last year, "Mind at the End of its Tether". After so many Utopian visions of man's future, he reverted to the pessimism about human nature of his early masterpiece "The Time Machine".

Death also claimed **Gertrude Stein**, keeper of a Paris salon which **Picasso, Matisse, Braque** and many other artists attended.

Ingrid Bergman and Cary Grant in Alfred Hitchcock's film "Notorious".

1947

JANUARY

Su	Mo	Tu	We	Th	Fr	Sa
			1	2	3	4
5	6	7	8	9	10	11
12	13	14	15	16	17	18
19	20	21	22	23	24	25
26	27	28	29	30	31	

1. London: Ralph Richardson gets a knighthood in the New Year's Honours.

3. Washington: Congress is broadcast on television for the first time.

7. US: George Marshall becomes Secretary of State as James Byrnes retires on health grounds (→27/6).

8. UK: Steel works close down through a lack of coal.

9. Vietnam: General Leclerc leaves after breaking with Ho Chi Minh.

10. London: The Electricity Bill is published, revealing that the government will pay £370 million for 190 firms (→14/2).

12. Palestine: Terrorists end a truce by blowing up a police station in Haifa (→15).

13. London: The government moves to end the hauliers strike (→16).

13. UK: The most popular radio shows are "Radio Forfeits", "Dick Barton" and "Woman's Hour".

15. Palestine: Irgun rejects a plea by David Ben-Gurion and Golda Meir to end terrorist attacks.→

16. London: Hauliers vote for a return to work (→22).

16. Paris: Vincent Auriol is elected first president of the Fourth Republic (→17).

17. Paris: Veteran statesman Leon Blum resigns as caretaker premier (→22).

19. Greece: 300 die when a ship hits a mine (→9/7).

22. Paris: Socialist Paul Ramadier forms a new cabinet (→4/5).

25. Miami: Al Capone dies of a massive brain haemorrhage, aged 48 (→23/12).

29. UK: Chaos and power cuts spread as freezing weather grips Britain; the temperature today fell to -16 degrees F.

DEATHS

23. French artist Pierre Bonnard (*13/10/1867).

25. Italian-born US criminal Al Capone (*17/1/1899).

British families evacuated from Palestine

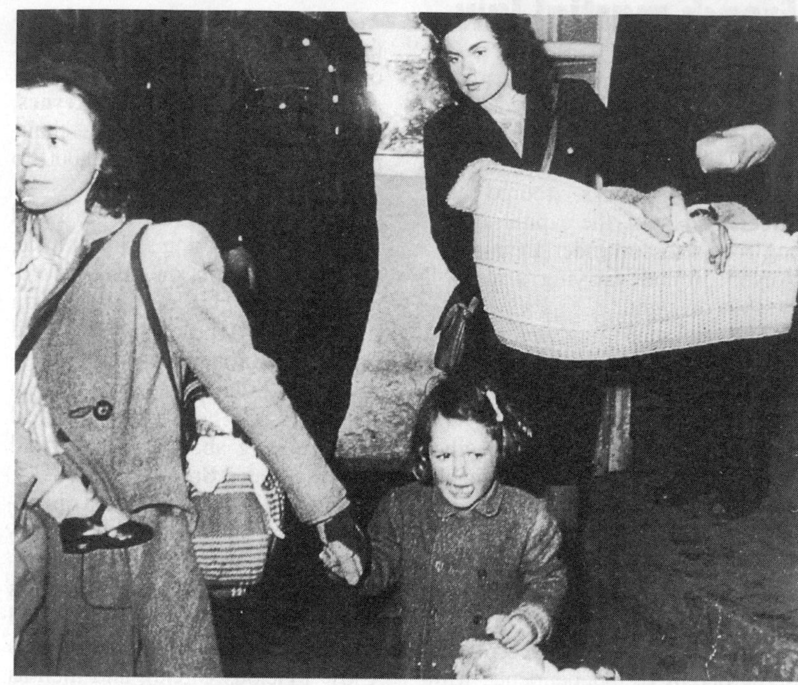

British families queue to leave Palestine as the situation deteriorates fast.

Jan 31. Faced with a deteriorating security situation in the UN mandated territory of Palestine, the High Commissioner, General Sir Alan Cunningham, has ordered the evacuation of all British women and children, and others described as "non-essential civilians".

The move comes in the wake of attacks on British citizens by Jewish terrorists, who threaten to kill two Britons kidnapped this week, if the death sentence on a convicted terrorist is carried out.

Britain, which wants to satisfy Jewish aspirations without provoking the Arabs, favours partition. The one million Arabs are determined that the 600,000 Jews shall remain a minority in a united Palestine. Jews everywhere, nursing the scars of the Nazi holocaust, are fired by the Zionist vision of a Jewish national home (→2/2).

Polish elections rigged, says US

Jan 19. The leader of the Polish Peasant party, Stanislaw Mikolajczyk, said tonight that he was going to demand that his country's general election be declared null and void because it was not "free and unfettered", as the Yalta Agreement required.

There had been no secrecy at the polls, he said, and his party's observers had been banned. He also complained about a novel method used to weaken his party: a telegram sent to his supporters, supposedly by his party, announcing his death in an air-crash.

One official British observer reports that almost total cynicism prevails about the election. Everyone, he says, knows that its conduct has been marked by repression, intimidation and falsification at every stage, and that the result will bear no relation to the actual wishes of the people. There is little doubt that the result of the election will be the formation of a government dominated by the Communist Party.

The United States has already condemned the elections as "fraudulent" and says this may have serious internal and international consequences. Britain also views the elections as being neither free nor unfettered, and is likely to protest to the United Nations (→4/2).

Troops used to move food as transport strike begins to bite

Jan 8. Servicemen have been called in to maintain essential supplies as much of Britain faces a meatless weekend and growing shortages of other foodstuffs. A strike by road haulage workers has left thousands of tons of meat likely to rot in warehouses, said Food Minister John Strachey.

With an unofficial dockers "defence committee" calling for the blacking of goods carried by road, lengthy queues have formed at food shops. Nearly all London butchers were sold out last night; for later customers it was corned beef only. Some shops have rationed potatoes to no more than two pounds a head.

The London County Council will open 35 civic restaurants to ease the problems that people are having feeding at home (→12/2).

Grateful Clapham housewives queue up as the army delivers their meat.

Labour nationalises Britain's coal mines

Emmanuel Shinwell (l), Minister of Fuel, opens a newly-nationalised pit.

Jan 1. As New Year dawned, flags were hoisted at Britain's 1,500 collieries. They heralded today's change of ownership: the pits now belong to the nation. This part of the Government's nationalisation programme ought to have quickened socialist heartbeats most, but not so.

After generations of struggling for improved conditions, miners' leaders are unconvinced about a promised new deal. Hated capitalist pit owners have been bought out, yet many miners are suspicious of their new bosses – the National Coal Board – which put up the flags this morning, and are now the landlords in their villages. At Coal Board headquarters in London the cabinet mustered for a handing-over ceremony. Cricket-loving Mr Attlee said: "The NCB is going in to bat on a distinctly sticky wicket". Emmanuel Shinwell, the Minister of Fuel, warned: "The promised five-day week for miners is difficult. Coal exports are down to vanishing point."

As he spoke, reports arrived of continuing massive absenteeism from the pits – and not just on account of the New Year holiday. A fuel crisis looms. In the coalfields there is more lingering resentment than rejoicing. The New Jerusalem may still be some time coming (→ 2/2).

New rations slice meat even thinner

Jan 22. Once again, Britons tightened their belts today as the fresh meat ration was reduced from 1s 2d to one shilling's worth weekly. The only compensation was an increase in the allowance of corned beef – and other tinned meat – by 2d to 4d. In a gloomy review, the Government predicted a cut in bread rationing, no increases in supplies of bacon, eggs or fish, and a small increase in the butter and sugar rations. Wheat stocks were "uncomfortably low," said a government spokesman. One result is an immediate cut in beer production by up to 50 per cent (→ 30/6).

His first pair of leather shoes, thanks to Red Cross generosity.

1947

FEBRUARY

Su	Mo	Tu	We	Th	Fr	Sa
						1
2	3	4	5	6	7	8
9	10	11	12	13	14	15
16	17	18	19	20	21	22
23	24	25	26	27	28	

1. Portugal: 16 die when a DC-3 Dakota from Paris crashes near Lisbon.

1. Rome: Alcide de Gaspari forms a cabinet of Christian Democrats, Communists and Socialists (→ 10).

2. Palestine: The RAF begins evacuating Britons (→ 6).

4. Washington: Truman meets the new Polish ambassador and tells him Poland broke a pledge to hold free elections (→ 3/11).

6. London: The first evacuees from Palestine arrive (→ 10).

7. US: Max Gardner, new US ambassador to Britain, dies of coronary thrombosis on his way to take up his post.

10. UK: A British doctor says some of the Nazis' medical experiments were of value to science.

10. Palestine: Three members of the Irgun terrorist group are sentenced to death (→ 2/3).

14. UK: Welsh miners agree to work on Sunday for the first time (→ 21).

15. China: Chiang Kai-shek blames the continuing war in China on US refusal to supply the Nationalists with arms.

20. London: The government announces Britain will quit India by June 1948.→

21. London: The government calls for more sweat from the workers (→ 13/3).

22. UK: The weather has led to the cancellation of 59 football matches so far this month (→ 26).

23. Germany: British and US agents have rounded up hundreds of hidden Nazis in the last two days (→ 24).

24. Nuremberg: Ex-chancellor Franz von Papen is jailed by the Allies for eight years as a major Nazi (→ 10/3).

25. Oxford: Undergraduate Kenneth Tynan of Magdalen College is well reviewed for his role in a play by Ibsen.

26. UK: Domestic fuel rationing seems likely as the freezing weather continues (→ 2/4).

Lord Mountbatten appointed last Viceroy of India

Feb 20. Lord Mountbatten has been appointed Viceroy of India, in order to preside over the transfer of responsibility for that huge dominion to the Indian people. He replaces Field Marshal Lord Wavell, who is compensated by the award of an Earldom.

Announcing these developments to a packed House of Commons today, the Prime Minister, Mr Attlee, said that it had seemed that the opening of the new and final phase in India was the appropriate time for the termination of Lord Wavell's "wartime appointment".

There was a dramatic scene in the House when Mr Attlee refused repeated demands by Mr Churchill, the Leader of the Opposition, that he should disclose "the differences, divergencies or disagreements" between the Viceroy and the Government, which had led to Lord Wavell's "dismissal".

Mr Churchill, conspicuously dressed in a heavy black overcoat, was at his most pugnacious. "In all the history of Parliament," he growled, "such a matter has never been denied discussion". But Mr Attlee would not be drawn (→ 7/3).

Lord Mountbatten: India's final British supremo is enrobed.

Frozen Britain works by candlelight

Prisoners are recruited to help Britons struggling in the grip of one of the worst winters ever recorded.

Feb 12. Heavy snowstorms and sub-zero temperatures are combining with a serious fuel shortage to bring Britain to its economic knees. Over four million workers have been made idle by power cuts – and with hundreds of coal trains unable to battle their way through 20-feet high snowdrifts, thousands of homes are without heat or light for long periods of the day.

In Norfolk, Lincolnshire and Yorkshire the RAF is dropping food for stranded villagers and their animals. Isolated farms display sheets as a distress signal. The towns of Buxton and Bridlington have been cut off. Sheffield is without milk. A hamlet near Widdlecombe-in-the-Moor, Devon, has sent a telegram saying: "No bread since Jan. 27. Starving."

Hundreds of rail passengers have been stranded by drifts. Three coachloads of women passengers, returning from a pantomime, were trapped on the Yorkshire moors and kept warm by singing, as nearby villagers dug their way through deep drifts to rescue them. Doctors and nurses have been doing their rounds in the Fells on horseback.

Non-stop blizzards have stopped all shipping in the Channel, creating a new threat to food supplies. Fishing fleets have been kept in port, and air travel is in chaos with only three aircraft – instead of the usual 42 – landing at London's three main airports today. Troops have been called in throughout the country. In Dorset the army is experimenting with flame-throwers to clear drifts. Five hundred prisoners have been enlisted for snow clearance in Yorkshire.

The weather has seriously dislocated road and rail transport throughout the country. The Great North Road, Britain's north-south artery, is blocked for 22 miles by ten-foot drifts. Coal stocks are piling up at the pits, while electricity and gas industries struggle to maintain minimal supplies of power. 60 main-line trains a day are being cancelled to make room for urgently needed coal.

Emergency regulations are creating confusion, with industry struggling to continue during "off-peak" hours, and domestic consumers without power during the mornings and afternoons. A team of government inspectors is seeking out "pirates" using power illicitly.

Buckingham Palace is candlelit; so are Ministry offices, banks the law-courts and department stores. But although no lifts are working in the big shops, and no "shopping special" trains are running, they are all very busy (→ 22).

The public learn to drink by candlelight as they discuss the fuel crisis.

US fears Russia has atomic secrets

Feb 3. Russia has discovered the secrets of the US A-bomb, but is unsure how to use them, the Senate Atomic Committee was told today. Bernard Baruch, the former US representative to the United Nations Atomic Energy Commission, testified that questions asked by Soviet delegates at the UN showed they had seen highly classified US information on the atomic bomb, but did not understand its significance. He said Soviet spies must have infiltrated US atomic plants in Canada, a charge denied in Ottawa, and called for tighter security at all atomic installations (→ 29/8).

Treaty takes land from German allies

Feb 10. Italy was today called on to pay the price of Mussolini's 1939 "Pact of Steel" with Hitler. Under the peace treaty signed at the French Foreign Ministry today, the Italians will have to pay reparations to the Western Allies and give up their African colonies. Rhodes and the rest of the Dodecanese Islands, seized by Italy from the Turks in 1912, and formally ceded to Italy when she joined the Allies in the First World War, are now to be given to Greece. Other treaties oblige Finland, Hungary and Rumania to cede territory to the Soviet Union (→ 15/11).

Berlin dance hall blaze kills Britons

Feb 8. Nine British soldiers were among 80 people burned to death tonight, when they were trapped inside a Berlin dance hall destroyed by fire. A party of Royal Engineers had gone to the Loebel cafe, in the British sector, for a fancy dress ball. One private led his German partner to safety but lost his life when he returned to the blazing building to rescue another girl as the roof collapsed.

Survivors said first floor windows were barred and exits had become blocked by bodies of dancers unable to escape.

1947

MARCH

Su	Mo	Tu	We	Th	Fr	Sa
						1
2	3	4	5	6	7	8
9	10	11	12	13	14	15
16	17	18	19	20	21	22
23	24	25	26	27	28	29
30	31					

1. Jerusalem: A bomb goes off at the British officers' club.→

3. UK: 800,000 return to work as some power is restored (→ 6).

4. France: Britain and France sign a 50-year alliance.

5. New York: Andrei Gromyko accuses the US of seeking a monopoly of nuclear energy.

6. London: MPs approve the government's plan to quit India (→ 7).

6. UK: 300 roads are blocked and 15 towns cut off by the snow as the appalling weather continues.

7. India: Violence has left 293 dead in the Punjab; troops are sent to Amritsar.→

10. Moscow: The Big Four meet to discuss the future of Germany (→ 14).

13. London: The government announces a ban on mid-week sport to try and boost productivity (→ 1/6).

14. Manila: The US signs an agreement for a 99-year lease of air and naval bases in the Philippines.

14. Moscow: The USSR says it holds 890,532 German prisoners of war (→ 24).

18. UK: Prince Philip of Greece becomes a naturalised Briton (→ 11/6).

19. Palestine: Menachem Begin, leader of the Irgun terror group, is top of the British wanted list (→ 24/4).

24. Moscow: Marshall proposes a cut in the armies policing Germany (→ 31).

29. UK: Mr J. McDowell's Caughoo, a 100-1 outsider, wins the Grand National.

31. Moscow: Marshall rejects a Soviet demand for reparations as the price of German economic unity (→ 24/4).

31. Madrid: A Regency Council is created to name a new Spanish monarch, after Franco's death (→ 5/2/48).

31. London: The Bishop of London blames Hollywood for Britain's high divorce rate (→ 1/4).

More violence as Mountbatten arrives

Injured Indian policemen receive treatment after violence in Lahore.

March 31. The arrival of Lord Louis Mountbatten in India as Viceroy has been marred by violence with Hindus and Moslems killing each other in communal riots as the country lurches bloodily towards independence.

In Bombay the death toll has reached 147, while in the country the dead lie uncounted. Villages have been razed and vultures feed off the bodies of men, women and children strewn in the bamboo thickets.

Areas of Amritsar, holy city of the Sikhs, have been burnt to the ground. Police have been forced to open fire on fighting mobs of Hindus and Sikhs on the one side, and Moslems on the other.

There has also been trouble in Bihar, in the shadow of the Himalayas. The Biharis are normally mild and gentle people, and the violence among them is a measure of the task facing Lord Mountbatten.

However, he may take heart from the welcome he has been given by India's leaders. Last night he met Mr Gandhi for the first time. Their talks were probably the most cordial of any between a Viceroy and a nationalist leader (→ 6/4).

US crusade against Communism begins

March 12. US President Truman told Congress today that America must abandon her traditional policy of isolationism and intervene throughout the world to oppose Communism. "I would not recommend it except that the alternative is much more serious. The foreign policy and national security of this country are involved," he said in a speech calling for an immediate $400 million in aid to the Greek and Turkish governments, who are opposed by Communist rebels. Truman's speech is seen as the start of a more vigorous US foreign policy which may make global conflict with Russia inevitable (→ 20/10).

Martial law for the Jews in Palestine

March 2. After a series of terrorist attacks throughout Palestine, in which 20 British soldiers and civilians were killed, martial law has been imposed on five Jewish areas, including the Jewish city of Tel Aviv. The attacks have divided the Jewish community. Haganah, the main Jewish defence organisation, opposes terrorism, but supports attacks on railways and other links, and is involved in smuggling Jewish refugees into Palestine. But there are two small underground Jewish groups who believe terrorism will make Britain quit (→ 19).

Government acts to stem divorce flood

March 27. Bodies like the Marriage Guidance Council are to get government aid in a bid to stem the flood of divorces, now running at a record 50,000 a year, the Lord Chancellor announced today. There are already "marriage menders" in over 100 towns and cities across the country. However, reconciliation was not always desirable, he said. "Sometimes the sooner the girl is rid of the man the better."

In the House of Lords, the Archbishop of Canterbury claimed that divorce reforms had created a Frankenstein monster (→ 31).

Like a great deal of the country, the town of Shrewsbury has suffered in the floods after the big freeze. Here people make their way along duckboards that should alleviate some of the problems of getting around.

1947

APRIL

Su	Mo	Tu	We	Th	Fr	Sa
		1	2	3	4	5
6	7	8	9	10	11	12
13	14	15	16	17	18	19
20	21	22	23	24	25	26
27	28	29	30			

1. UK: The Public Morality Council slams artificial insemination as illegal and adulterous (→ 11/6).

2. UK: Recent flooding has killed two million sheep (a week's meat ration) and damaged 500,000 acres of wheat (a month's bread) (→ 21).

3. UK: The private medical company BUPA is founded.

6. India: Troops are sent in to quell riots which have left 1,000 dead (→ 15).

9. Moscow: Secretary of State Marshall proposes the revision of Poland's borders (→ 16).

11. UK: James Mason and Margaret Lockwood are voted Britain's favourite film stars.

14. Southampton: The luxury liner Queen Elizabeth runs aground.

15. London: The Budget puts a packet of 20 cigarettes up from 2/4d. to 3/4d (→ 17/6).

15. India: The new Indian parliament appeals for non-violence (→ 23/5).

15. Southampton: The Queen Elizabeth is refloated.

18. Moscow: The four-power talks on Germany are reported to be in disarray.→

21. London: The Food Ministry says retailers must replace bad eggs issued in rations (→ 30/6).

22. UK: A photo-finish camera is used for the first time, at Epsom.

24. London: The government bans the use of coal and gas fires until September (→ 27).

26. London: Charlton Athletic beat Burnley 1-0 to win the FA Cup.

27. London: Fuel Minister Shinwell says gas will be nationalised by the end of 1947 (→ 7/5).

DEATHS

1. Greek King George II (*20/7/1890).

7. US car maker Henry Ford (*30/7/1863).→

20. Danish King Christian X (*26/9/1870).

Barracks blown up by Jews in Tel Aviv

British soldiers clear up the mess after the latest Stern Gang bombing.

April 24. Four British policemen were killed and six others injured in a massive explosion at the police barracks at Sarona, east of Tel Aviv, today. Hundreds of windows in the town were shattered by the blast, which was heard 30 miles away in Rehovoth. There were two bombs of a new type, more powerful than anything used previously in Palestine.

The bombs are thought to have been planted by the Jewish Stern Gang. Two men arrived at the barracks in a Palestine Post Office van, claiming to have come to repair a faulty telephone line. They produced identity cards but the duty corporal was suspicious and searched the van. The bombs, however, were hidden under the chassis.

The attack is only the latest in a series by the Stern Gang. On Tuesday they blew up a troop train near Rehovoth, killing eight soldiers and civilians and injuring another 41, six seriously. Yesterday, a British businessman, Morris Collins, was kidnapped in the corridor of a Tel Aviv hotel. He was released later after he had convinced his captors he was Jewish (→ 4/5).

714 die as inferno engulfs Texas City

April 19. Two days of enormous explosions and uncontrollable fires have devastated 90 per cent of Texas City, in the United States and killed at least 714. The disaster began yesterday morning, when a fire aboard a French ship in the harbour spread to a nearby chemical plant, and then, as if attached to a fuse, triggered explosions in a chain of oil refineries. Early this morning came the biggest blast of all, when the inferno engulfed High Flyer, a ship packed with explosive nitrate. "It just rained steel out there," said a nurse who watched the vessel explode, and Red Cross workers said the disaster resembled the worst of the Blitz in London.

Allies in Moscow agree to disagree

April 24. The foreign ministers of the wartime alliance ended a 46-day meeting in Moscow today, having agreed only to set up a commission to examine their disagreements on the post-war settlement. For the US, George Marshall accused the Russians of wanting to bleed Germany dry by excessive reparations demands. Mr Molotov rejected a call from Ernest Bevin, for Britain, that Austrian POWs should be returned, even though the Allies had not agreed on a peace treaty. Mr Bidault, for France, joined Mr Molotov in opposing the administration of Germany as a single economic unit under a central German government (→ 9/5).

Henry Ford, motor car mogul, is dead

April 7. The most successful of the car industry's pioneers, Henry Ford, died today, aged 83. The man who revolutionised modern transport with his mass-produced Model T cars, died by candlelight during a power-cut caused by floods in Detroit. His factories built 31 million vehicles, and made fortunes for investors. He also paid high wages to his workers, viewing them as customers-to-be.

He had recently handed the business over to his grandson, Henry Ford II, who is 29.

British challenger's title hopes floored

April 15. All hopes of a British challenge to Joe Louis's world heavyweight title – the first for ten years – evaporated at Harringay, when Bruce Woodcock crumbled under the onslaught of another American hopeful, the powerful and merciless Joe Baksi.

Woodcock, a tall Yorkshireman who still holds the British and European heavyweight titles, was sent sprawling in the first round by three crashing left hooks from Baksi, and never recovered. He hung on until the seventh, when the fight was stopped.

Happy and glorious – the Royal Family are touring South Africa to an enthusiastic welcome from all of the country's many races.

1947

MAY

Su	Mo	Tu	We	Th	Fr	Sa
				1	2	3
4	5	6	7	8	9	10
11	12	13	14	15	16	17
18	19	20	21	22	23	24
25	26	27	28	29	30	31

1. US: The skeletons of a herd of mammoths are unearthed at Tucson, Arizona.

2. Tokyo: The Allies grant Japan the right to continue flying its "Rising Sun" flag (→ 12/11/48).

4. Paris: President Auriol sacks Communist cabinet members for voting against the government (→ 27/10).

7. UK: Nine miners die in a pit explosion at Barnsley (→ 19).

9. Hamburg: 150,000 march through the city to protest at food shortages (→ 15).

11. London: The Tory Party issues its "Industrial Charter".

12. UK: Derby County are about to sign Liverpool's Billy Steel for a record £15,000 transfer fee.

12. New York: Arabs appeal to the UN for an independent Palestine (→ 5/6).

14. London: Churchill leads a United Europe rally (→ 11/6).

15. London: Bevin says Britain and the US have agreed to merge their German occupation zones (→ 29).

19. London: The House of Lords attacks a plan for a power station on Bankside, opposite St. Paul's Cathedral (→ 24/7).

21. London: The City proposes demolishing the Mansion House as part of massive rebuilding plans.

25. Helsinki: Finland says it is to experiment with Soviet-style collective farming (→ 6/4/48).

29. New York: 38 die and ten escape when a United Airlines DC-4 crashes on take off at LaGuardia airfield (→ 15/6).

29. Germany: Wives of top Nazis are arrested, including Frau Goering (→ 25/11).

31. Cairo: Moroccan rebel Abdel Krim, escaped from Reunion Island after 11 years, tells France to quit Morocco.

DEATH

8. US born department store founder Henry Gordon Selfridge (*1864).

Cabinet agrees to partition of India

May 23. The cabinet today took the historic step of agreeing to Lord Mountbatten's proposal for the partition of India into two states, one Moslem and the other Hindu. The Viceroy is to have a series of talks with Lord Listowel, the Secretary for India, on matters of detail, and will then fly back to New Delhi for the discussions with Indian leaders.

The cabinet meeting was imbued with the knowledge of the urgency of the situation. Any thoughts that India could remain one nation were dissolved by the reports of Lord Ismay, chief of the Viceroy's personal staff, who made it plain that the British administration must break down unless urgent measures were taken.

What has to be decided now is the form that the two new nations will take. The Hindu Congress Party, while resigned to partition, still favours a joint administrative capital, but the Moslem League insists on the formation of Moslem "Pakistan" states in the North-West and North-East. Mr Jinnah, President of the Moslem League, said in New Delhi yesterday that the League would demand a corridor, linking the two proposed Moslem areas.

He said that he was in favour of an alliance between "Pakistan" and "Hindustan", the suggested name for the Hindu group of provinces. But, he said, Moslems would "fight every inch" against the separation of Bengal and the Punjab.

One of the most delicate matters to resolve is the division of the Indian Army between the two new states. It will cause much heartache when the army, with all its tradition and its renowned loyalty to Britain, is torn apart.

It is estimated that from the present army, 54 Hindu, 19 Moslem, 12 Sikh and 37 Gurkha units could be detached as individual formations. But then the heavy equipment must be divided, along with the Air Force's planes and the Navy's ships. As one saddened officer said last night: "Even Solomon would find this task beyond him."

It is understood that this tricky and emotional problem will not be dealt with until a final decision on partition has been reached by the Indian leaders themselves.

The leaders must also decide whether their new states will become members of the Commonwealth. It is expected in Whitehall that they will choose to do so, but it is emphasised that it will be their choice.

It is to be hoped that today's decision will be welcomed by all the peoples of India; it is feared, however, that there is much blood yet to be spilt (→ 13/6).

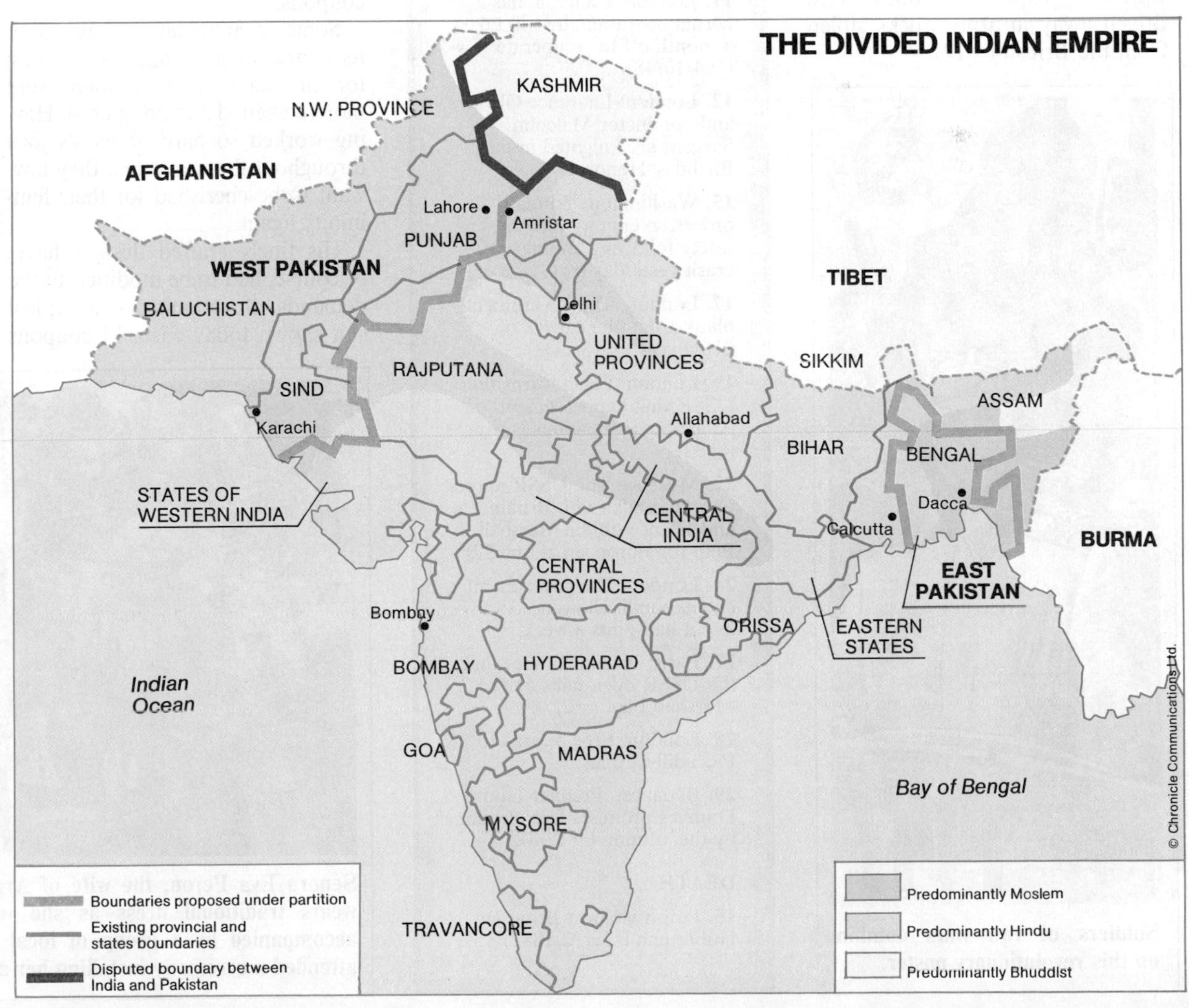

Zionists blast open prison: 251 freed

May 4. Zionist guerrillas blasted their way into a prison in Acre, Palestine, today in broad daylight. They released 251 prisoners, who were a mixture of Jews and Arabs, from the prison in which four alleged terrorists were hanged only three weeks ago.

The attack was cleverly planned by the Irgun group, which blew up the King David Hotel in Jerusalem ten months ago. Irgun commandos set off several explosions in the two streets to divert attention, while 100 guerrillas, many wearing stolen British uniforms, stormed the prison.

The guard towers were strafed by heavy gunfire from jeeps, while explosives were planted under the walls. Smoke bombs covered the escape. Fourteen Jews were killed in the attack and several British soldiers were injured. Many of the prisoners, who had apparently been warned to expect the attack, were driven away in army trucks stolen from the British (→12).

Soldiers of two wars combine on this revolutionary poster.

1947

JUNE

Su	Mo	Tu	We	Th	Fr	Sa
1	2	3	4	5	6	7
8	9	10	11	12	13	14
15	16	17	18	19	20	21
22	23	24	25	26	27	28
29	30					

1. London: Labour Minister George Isaacs makes a plea for more women in work.

2. London: A fire at a rubber dump in Mitcham blots out the sun in the area.

5. London: Bevin and Eden are among public figures who receive letter bombs; Jewish terrorists are suspected (→12/7).

7. London: The musical "Annie Get Your Gun" opens to enthusiastic reviews.

7. UK: Baron de Waldner's Pearl Diver wins the Derby.

10. Ottawa: Truman arrives on the first state visit to Canada by a US president.

11. London: Princess Elizabeth is made a Freeman of the City (→9/7).

11. London: Churchill has a hernia operation; he will take a month off to recuperate (→4/10/48).

12. London: Laurence Olivier and conductor Malcolm Sargent are knighted in the Birthday Honours.

15. Washington: Truman orders an enquiry into air safety following another DC-4 crash yesterday (→6/1/48).

17. London: The government plans a flat-rate car tax of £10 a year (→13/11).

19. London: Bevin warns the USSR that "appeasement" in Anglo-Soviet relations is over (→22).

22. Moscow: The USSR agrees to attend talks with Britain and France on the Marshall Plan for European aid (→27).

24. London: The government cuts the milk allowance to two and a half pints a week.→

27. Paris: Britain, France and the USSR open talks on the Marshall Plan (→2/7).

28. London: Eros returns to Piccadilly Circus.

29. Budapest: Premier Lajos Dinnyes promises free elections by the autumn (→12/8).

DEATH

15. Polish violinist Bronislaw Huberman (*19/12/1882).

Dior's hour-glass is new look for women

June 3. Christian Dior's sensational New Look is sweeping British women off their feet. With its hour-glass shape and use of yards of material, the Look has been the centre of controversy, ever since its launch in Paris this Spring.

Critics, including a junior trade minister, Harold Wilson, have condemned it as irresponsibly frivolous and wasteful, but women, tired of years of drab utility clothing, appear to adore it. Mid-summer lines, unveiled today, confirm that the ultra-feminine figure-of-eight shape is in, and the utility look with its square shoulders is firmly on the way out.

The essence of the New Look is romance: soft shoulders, handspan waists and full billowing skirts well below the calf. Dior, who startled the fashion world with his very first show this year, said he wanted it to liberate all women from a poverty-stricken, parsimonious era, obsessed with ration books and clothing coupons.

Some commentators have seen its appeal as a nostalgic hankering for the days when women were more cossetted and pampered. Having worked so hard at men's jobs throughout the war years, they now want to be cherished for their femininity again.

His finely crafted designs have, of course, had to be modified to the demands of rationing – a typical suit shown today costs 14 coupons

Dior's smart farewell to austerity.

– and the needs of the growing ready-to-wear market.

Despite the limits on production of non-utility clothing, manufacturers have nonetheless plunged into maximum production to meet the demand: one store sold 700 suits in two weeks. New materials include rayon, corduroy and other man-made fibres (→24/8).

Senora Eva Peron, the wife of Argentina's leader Colonel Juan Peron, wears traditional dress as she walks through the streets of Seville accompanied by a group of local girls. "Evita" as she is known, had attended a ceremony installing her as "Chamber Maid of Honour".

Food rations are cut as crisis deepens

Two years after the war but rations are still being cut: over a thousand people in a London potato queue.

June 30. The Government ordered a dire new economy drive today. It puts Britain back to wartime austerity – or worse. "Export or die" and "Work or Want" are among new official slogans.

Hugh Dalton, the Chancellor of the Exchequer, warned Parliament that food rations may have to be cut again, but denied there will be greater public hardship. He announced substantial reductions in tobacco and petrol imports, and said that newspapers will revert to wartime size – four pages. Mr Dalton revealed that more than half of last year's huge American loan has already been spent and that the economic crisis is now desperate. "A severe shortage of dollars is making itself felt in almost every part of the world," he said. The Opposition accused the Government of underplaying the gravity of the situation while the nation slides towards a precipice.

The tinned meat ration was cut today to twopence-worth a week. But the sweets ration is up from four to five ounces, and extra sugar is promised for jam-making.

There are again reports of serious divisions within the cabinet as it wrestles with the dollar crisis. But a plot to oust Mr Attlee and make the Foreign Secretary, Ernest Bevin, the Prime Minister in his place appears to have fizzled out. However there are signs that the strain is telling and several of the more senior cabinet members have been away ill recently (→ 1/8).

Truman condemns coup in Hungary

June 21. President Truman today accused the Russian army of helping the Communist minority in Hungary to force changes in the Hungarian government. At a press conference in Washington, the President, who is renowned for his plain speaking, denounced the Communist coup as an outrage.

He approved a sharply worded note of protest to be sent to the Soviet commander in Budapest. State Department officials, however, pointed out that the note was couched in somewhat milder terms than those Mr Truman used at his conference.

It says that the United States does not want to engage in recriminations, but at the same time accuses the Soviets of being responsible for the resignation and exile of Premier Nagy. It also accuses the Russians of breaking the Yalta agreement, and asks for a joint investigation of the situation.

The note goes on to suggest that the US might put the whole affair before the United Nations. As proof of its intentions the US is suspending a $15 million credit to Hungary "pending clarification of developments".

Warning on sexual temptation at work

June 11. Workplaces can be moral minefields for young people, a Church of England report claims today. The Youth Council report warns of sexual temptation and degrading initiation rites, which, it says, are "exceptionally prevalent in offices, shops and factories". The council's chairman, the Bishop of Willesden, commented that churchgoers seem unaware of the "strains and temptations to which young people who have left school are daily subjected".

The report, which also attacks the "fantastic growth of gambling" and the low standard of honesty in factory life, adds that couples preparing for married life "are up against the false romanticism" of the cinema and radio. It calls for the Church to press ahead with its vital youth work (→ 7/7).

India's Moslem and Hindu leaders agree to partition plans

June 15. The Congress Party today endorsed the acceptance by their leader, Pandit Nehru, of the British plan for the partition of India. Following the acceptance of the plan by the Moslem leader, Mr Jinnah, who has broadcast an explanation to his followers on the North West Frontier, Congress's endorsement clears the last political hurdle to partition.

There is a problem, however, with some of the Maharajahs, who are planning to declare their independence and have built up their armies to lend weight to their argument. British intervention is expected to improve this situation.

The Viceroy, Lord Mountbatten, held talks today with the leaders of Congress and the Moslem League and broad agreement was reached on plans for the actual procedure of partition. Lord and Lady Mountbatten have now left for a short holiday at Simla (→ 4/7).

Lord and Lady Mountbatten meet the Mahatma to discuss India's future.

Marshall offers aid plan

Secretary of State Marshall (c.), telling Britain about his plans for Europe.

June 5. The United States must now save Western Europe again – this time from the ravages of post-war slump and the threat of Communism. In a speech at Harvard today, George Marshall, the American Secretary of State, said that the US must be ready to do this with substantial additional help for the nations outside the Russian orbit. He warned that the aid can only be effective if these nations draw together economically.

The speech coincided with a denunciation by President Truman of Soviet moves to tighten Moscow's grip on Hungary, Rumania and Bulgaria. Even so, Mr Marshall vaguely held out the prospect of including Russia in an expanded aid programme to get Europe on its feet again.

While avoiding details, he also made it clear that the next moves are up to European Governments. From London Mr Bevin was quick off the mark with a "thank you" telegram. The Foreign Secretary started on preparations for a concerted response. "This could be the last chance. It must not be lost," he told Foreign Office aides (→ 24).

Anglo-US talks on Marshall aid plan

June 24. Clement Attlee and other cabinet ministers today met senior US officials, invited to London for the first joint talks about implementing the Marshall Plan for massive aid to Europe.

Mr Bevin, the Foreign Secretary, reported on his progress in organising a collective response to the US call for closer European integration. He is going to Paris next week for a meeting with French and Soviet leaders. There is already Russian hostility to "dollar enslavement" and little prospect of East-West co-operation.

However, Mr Bevin is hustling and enthusiastic. He told MPs: "When the Marshall proposals were announced I grabbed them with both hands. Europe can wait no longer" (→ 27).

Mr Bevin lights up before leaving for Paris to discuss Marshall's plans.

1947

JULY

Su	Mo	Tu	We	Th	Fr	Sa
		1	2	3	4	5
6	7	8	9	10	11	12
13	14	15	16	17	18	19
20	21	22	23	24	25	26
27	28	29	30	31		

1. China: Chiang Kai-shek orders the general mobilisation of Nationalist troops against the Communists (→ 20/5/48).

2. Paris: The USSR rejects the Marshall aid plan, which Britain and France accept.→

4. London: The Indian Independence Bill is published.→

5. Wimbledon: Jack Kramer beats Tom Brown in the Men's Singles final; Margaret Osborne wins the Women's Singles title.

7. UK: There have been 50,000 divorces so far this year, compared with 10,000 a year before the war.

9. Athens: 2,500 alleged Communist plotters are arrested (→ 20/8/48).

10. London: The government says Princess Elizabeth will get extra ration coupons for her wedding dress (→ 18/8).

12. Prague: Czechoslovakia rejects the Marshall plan as 16 European nations open talks in Paris.→

12. Palestine: Two British Army sergeants are kidnapped.→

18. London: The National Parks Committee proposes a coastal path around the English and Welsh coasts.

19. Rangoon: The Burmese premier is assassinated.→

21. East Indies: Dutch troops launch a drive against Indonesian nationalists in eastern Java (→ 3/8).

24. London: Britain's first atomic power station will soon start up at Harwell, Berkshire; another is planned at Sellafield (→ 15/8).

25. London: Overseas Trade Minister Harold Wilson and other trade envoys to Moscow are hurt in an air accident.

29. New York: Soviet UN delegate Gromyko vetoes a US resolution for a Balkan frontier commission.

31. London: The Transport Ministry approves plans for the world's biggest suspension bridge over the River Severn.

First non-white head of a British dominion chosen

July 10. Mohammed Ali Jinnah, the Moslem leader, is to be Governor General of Pakistan when India is partitioned into the two new states. This is an historic appointment, for Mr Jinnah will be the first coloured man to be governor-general of a British dominion.

The news came as a complete surprise to the people of India when it was announced over All-India radio tonight. Mr Jinnah was told the news of the announcement by his sister, and, while refusing to comment, received the congratulations of his many friends at his home in New Delhi.

At the same time the leaders of Congress have done Lord Mountbatten a great honour by choosing him to be Governor-General of their new state, which will be called India, and not Hindustan, as was first suggested.

The appointments were announced amid cheers in the House of Commons today by Mr Attlee. He also announced that the Moslem League had agreed that Lord Mountbatten should be chairman of the Joint Defence Council until India and Pakistan were able to administer the armed forces themselves (→ 15/8).

Mr Jinnah with Mr Nehru: the two leaders of the newly-divided land.

Princess Elizabeth to wed Greek prince

July 9. The long-expected engagement of Princess Elizabeth to Lieutenant Philip Mountbatten was announced today. All around Buckingham Palace there were crowds, thousands strong, standing under umbrellas and cheering the young couple at each appearance on the Palace balcony.

There had been an air of expectancy all day. The Princess looked particularly happy when she arrived with her parents at the Royal International Horse Show at White City in a heavy downpour. As she climbed the steps to the royal box she positively beamed.

Princess Elizabeth, who is 21, first met her fiance, aged 26, at her parents' coronation. Lieutenant Mountbatten was born in Corfu, the son of the late Prince Andrew of Greece and his wife, who is a sister of Lord Mountbatten (→ 10).

The royal couple in a formal pose.

British keep out Exodus

British officials inspect the damage to the refugee ship "Exodus 47".

July 18. Some 5,000 would-be Jewish immigrants on the Haganah Ship, Exodus, reached Haifa today. They used tear-gas, smoke bombs, steam jets, iron bars and tins of food in an effort to fight off a boarding party of British naval ratings.

The fight lasted an hour and a half, and then the Jews were transferred to three waiting ships. Twenty-five Jews were taken to hospital where three died later. The rest will be taken to Cyprus, bringing the number of Jews detained there to 20,000. The Exodus is an old troopship, previously called the President Garfield. It left Baltimore last February, captained by an American Jew, and with many young Jews amongst the ship's crew.

The 5,000 Jews were picked up on July 10 at the small French port of Sete, near Marseilles.

The clamour for a Jewish state in Palestine is rising. Last week Dr Weizmann, the Zionist leader, gave a major speech in which he called upon the British to remove immigration restrictions (→ 31).

Marshall aid plan splits Europeans

July 13. After a meeting in Paris of only two days, foreign ministers of all European countries, with the exception of the Soviet bloc and Finland, agreed on a European recovery programme to be put to the United States. "It was the quickest conference I have ever presided over," Ernest Bevin, British Foreign Secretary, said last night.

The recovery programme, drawn up at the invitation of George C. Marshall, US Secretary of State, will be funded by the US. Last month, Marshall warned that Europe must have help or "face economic, social, and political deterioration of a very grave character."

The Paris conference decided to keep open an invitation to the Soviet bloc to join the programme later, but that will certainly not happen.

The Czech government originally accepted an invitation, only to have to make an about-turn, after Stalin had summoned Klement Gottwald, the Communist Prime Minister, to Moscow; Poland hesitated then turned down an invitation, and Finland, though not in the Soviet bloc, must take care not to offend her powerful neighbour.

The Marshall Plan, as the recovery programme is being called, aims to give Europe the food, the raw materials and the machinery that will enable the people to rebuild their war-torn lands (→ 10/9).

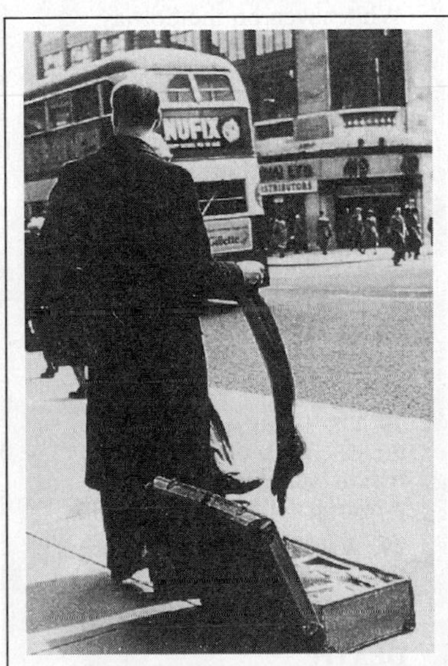

A spiv touts his suitcase of illegal nylon stockings to customers on an Oxford Street pavement.

Burmese premier is assassinated

July 19. U Aung San and six other Ministers of the Burma Executive Council were assassinated today by a gang of six men, who burst into the Council Chamber and sprayed it with Stengun fire. The Governor, Sir Hubert Rance, called in armed police and troops, and a number of men have been arrested. Among them is U Saw, a former Prime Minister and one of U Aung San's chief opponents (→ 17/10).

Zionists hang kidnapped British soldiers

July 31. The bodies of two British soldiers were discovered hanging from two eucalyptus trees at 6.30 this morning in Bnel Zion, a suburb of Nathanya, near Haifa. Pinned to their shirts were notices saying they had been executed as spies.

The soldiers, Sergeant Mervyn Paice, aged 43, and Sergeant Clifford Martin, aged 20, were kidnapped two weeks ago. Five thousand British troops were searching for them, but the bodies were found by a Jewish police patrol. In Tel Aviv tonight there were several clashes between British troops and Jews. According to Jewish reports, police armoured cars fired on a bus carrying civilians and a bomb was thrown from an armoured car into a busy cafe, killing five Jews and injuring 16.

Jewish leaders were summoned to Government House tonight. Unless they can guarantee to curb the Irgun guerrillas the Government intends to introduce martial law in Jewish Palestine (→ 5/8).

1947

AUGUST

Su	Mo	Tu	We	Th	Fr	Sa
					1	2
3	4	5	6	7	8	9
10	11	12	13	14	15	16
17	18	19	20	21	22	23
24	25	26	27	28	29	30
31						

1. London: The cabinet meets the TUC for urgent talks on the economic crisis (→ 6).

3. Belgrade: Yugoslavia signs an alliance treaty with Bulgaria.

5. Switzerland: Eva Peron arrives to a welcome of tomatoes and stones (→ 7/2/48).

5. Palestine: 35 Zionist leaders are detained for terrorist activities (→ 22).

6. London: Attlee outlines a crisis plan for the British economy in the Supplies and Services Bill (→ 10).

9. UK: 18 die and 74 are hurt in a train crash at Balby in Yorkshire.

10. Karachi: The Pakistani parliament meets for the first time.→

10. London: In a radio broadcast, Attlee appeals for a wartime-style national effort to tackle the economic crisis (→ 27).

12. Hungary: Reports claim that election committees are disenfranchising opposition voters in the general election (→ 1/9).

15. UK: Britain's first atomic reactor starts up at Harwell.

15. UK: 111 miners are trapped after a pit blast at Whitehaven on the Solway Firth.

18. London: Princess Elizabeth will go on honeymoon without a trousseau owing to the cloth shortage (→ 20/11).

22. France: The refugee ship Exodus heads for Hamburg after 4,400 Jews on board are refused entry to France (→ 8/9).

24. India: 10,000 are believed to have died in border clashes in the Punjab (→ 24/9).

29. US: Scientists announce the discovery of plutonium fission, suitable for nuclear power generation (→ 11/11).

29. Washington: The US urges the USSR to take part in four-power talks on Korea.

DEATH

21. Italian car designer Ettore Bugatti (*15/9/1881).

Crisis austerity plan for Britain unveiled

Aug 27. The full horror and gravity of the mounting financial crisis hit the nation tonight when the Government announced the first instalment of new austerity cuts. The cabinet made it known that there is worse to come. It admitted that the situation had worsened since Mr Attlee warned parliament three weeks ago of "peril and anxiety" over Britain's inability to pay for imports.

Among other food cuts, the total meat ration is reduced by twopence to one shilling's worth a week. Ration books will be needed in hotels after two nights. Pleasure motoring is stopped. Foreign holidays are banned after next month, and businessmen going to Europe will be allowed no more than £8 a day in foreign currency.

Cuts will be needed in British Army occupation costs in Germany and talks are proceeding about the terms of last year's Anglo-US loan agreement. In Washington the immediate reaction was cool. Officials said they had expected bigger rationing cuts and they accused Mr Attlee of timidity in his efforts to get Britain out of pauper status.

There was also American criticism of Mr Dalton, the Chancellor, for having allowed part of the American loan to be diverted, to allow "Egyptian pashas to spend dollars on mink coats for girl friends".

The dictatorial powers taken by the Government under the recent Supplies and Services Act – the Tories call it the SS Act – may soon be used to direct labour into essential jobs and restrict materials for non-essential industries. Miners are to get bigger meat rations, while fishermen and farmers will have extra bread and cheese.

All this should save about £228 millions a year, but the dollar shortage has never been more frightening. Mr Attlee called again for sacrifice akin to wartime and said: "I have no easy words for the nation. I cannot say when we shall emerge into easier times" (→ 15/9).

Mr Attlee outside Number 10.

UN arranges truce in Indonesian crisis

Aug 3. The Dutch and Indonesian Governments today complied with a UN Security Council resolution and agreed to a cease-fire after a fortnight of fighting between their armies in the Dutch East Indies. It is the first time the newly-formed United Nations has succeeded in halting a military conflict.

Indonesia was granted independence by the occupying Japanese shortly before their defeat, but the Dutch refuse to recognise this and last month advanced against republican forces in the tobacco and rubber-rich region of Sumatra. They then began an offensive in Java, capturing all the main ports on the island and cutting off Indonesian forces in Central Java before today's ceasefire came into force.

The Dutch Government has accepted a US offer to mediate in the conflict, but the Indonesians say the UN should enforce the ceasefire and are demanding that the Dutch troops withdraw to their previous positions (→ 19/9/48).

Edinburgh to hold an arts festival

Aug 24. In a gesture of defiance a[t] Britain's climate of austerity, th[e] city of Edinburgh today launche[d] an International Festival of Musi[c] and Drama which is to be an annua[l] event. The city, its noble architec[-]ture unscarred by the war, is bedeck[-]ed with flowers and flags. Unde[r] the festival director, Rudolf Bing, i[t] is playing host to 800 performers o[f] 20 nationalities.

They include the Louis Jouve[t] and Jean-Louis Barrault compan[-]ies from Paris, and the Vienna Phil[-]harmonic Orchestra, reunited wit[h] their pre-war conductor, Brun[o] Walter. The singing of Kathlee[n] Ferrier, the playing of Schnabe[l] Szigeti, Fournier and Primros[e] are the musical highlights.

Autumn styles are entering Dior era

Aug 4. Autumn fashions will be les[s] dramatic than Spring's controver[-]sial New Look, experts predict. But Dior, who burst on the scen[e] with a fashion revolution earlie[r] this year, will still be very influ[-]ential. Well-defined waists an[d] mid-calf soft skirts remain th[e] dominant lines. Popular fabric[s] include velvet, now easier to find.

Dior's New Look, autumn version.

Sun sets on British Raj

The citizens of Calcutta take to the streets to welcome Independence Day.

Aug 15. British rule in India, which lasted for a momentous 163 years, came to an end on the stroke of midnight last night and two new dominions, Pakistan and India, were born out of Britain's Indian Empire.

A conch shell was blown in the Constituent Assembly in New Delhi amid cheers from the members, as the hands of the clock ticked away the seconds to the independence for which the Indians have striven for so long.

Then every member of the Assembly took a pledge, promising that: "At this solemn moment, when the people of India, through suffering and sacrifice, have secured freedom, I, as a member of the Constituent Assembly of India, dedicate myself in all humility to the service of India and her people to the end that this ancient land attain her rightful place in the world."

Lord Mountbatten, who relinquished the panoply of empire as Britain's last Viceroy, and immediately became governor-general of the new Dominion of India, has been rewarded by a grateful Government in London with an Earldom for his part in expertly managing Britain's retreat.

One of his last acts as Viceroy was to deliver a moving message of congratulation from King George VI to the people of Pakistan saying: "I send you my greeting and warmest wishes on this great occasion when the new Dominion of Pakistan is about to take its place in the British Commonwealth of Nations. In thus achieving your independence by agreement you have set an example to the freedom-loving peoples throughout the world."

The celebrations were marred by violence. Even independence cannot end racial hatred (→ 24).

Lord Mountbatten, still Britain's representative, salutes in Pakistan.

1947

SEPTEMBER

Su	Mo	Tu	We	Th	Fr	Sa
	1	2	3	4	5	6
7	8	9	10	11	12	13
14	15	16	17	18	19	20
21	22	23	24	25	26	27
28	29	30				

1. Hungary: The Communists win the election (→ 30/7/48).

5. Washington: The US and Britain agree to joint control of the Ruhr mines.

7. Sheffield: Steelworks close because of a coal shortage during the strike of 45,000 south Yorkshire miners (→ 31/1/48).

7. Paris: French police say they have foiled a plot by the Zionist Stern Gang to bomb London from the air.

8. Hamburg: Jewish refugees aboard the ship Exodus disembark (→ 26).

10. Washington: Marshall announces an interim aid plan for Europe (→ 5/10).

11. Belfast: 20 are feared dead in an explosion aboard a liner.

12. London: President of the Board of Trade, Cripps, launches export drive under junior minister Harold Wilson.→

15. London: The government begins to spend Britain's gold reserves to pay for imports (→ 16).

16. US: Briton John Cobb sets a land speed record: 394 mph.

16. London: The government suspends its programme of nationalisation because of the economic crisis (→ 29).

18. Czechoslovakia: 142 are arrested for plotting to murder Eduard Benes (→ 23/1/48).

18. New York: The USSR envoy accuses the US of war-mongering in an address to the UN General Assembly (→ 3/1/48).

23. Sofia: Nikola Petkov, leader of the opposition Agrarian Party, is executed.

29. UK: To cut fuel costs, the Midlands will have no power one day a week (→ 30).

30. London: The government asks women to avoid the trend for longer skirts and save cloth in the national interest (→ 7/10).

DEATH

20. US politician Fiorello La Guardia, ex-mayor of New York (*11/12/1882).

Britain ready to leave Palestine

Sept 26. Britain has decided to get out of Palestine in the near future, irrespective of whether Arabs and Jews reach agreement on the future of the territory. Addressing the UN General Assembly in New York, Arthur Creech-Jones, the Colonial Secretary, said Britain was not prepared to try to impose a solution in Palestine by force of arms. The decision to turn in the mandate amounts to a rebuke for the UN and the United States, both of whom have made proposals for reconciling Arab and Jewish interests, but have refused to take responsibility for their implementation. In Palestine, both sides welcomed Britain's decision (→ 11/10).

Harold Wilson joins the Cabinet at 31

The youngest cabinet minister yet.

Sept 29. Sir Stafford Cripps was promoted to Minister for Economic Affairs, equal in status to Mr Dalton, the Chancellor of the Exchequer, in a ministerial reshuffle tonight. His post as President of the Board of Trade goes to Harold Wilson, who now joins the cabinet as its youngest member, at the age of 31. Mr Attlee regards Mr Wilson as a possible high-flyer (→ 3/7/48).

Moslems massacred on Punjab border

Sept 24. A train full of Moslem refugees, bound from Delhi to the safety of Pakistani territory, has been ambushed at Amritsar, the Sikh holy city in the East Punjab, and 1,200 people have been massacred in the worst single incident of slaughter since the partition of India last month.

About 600 survivors, most of them wounded, reached Lahore by road today. They had saved themselves by hiding under the piled-up bodies of their fellow-passengers, emerging when their attackers grew tired of killing.

They told harrowing stories. When their train reached Amritsar and stopped a short distance beyond the platform, Sikh troops and a mob of armed Sikh civilians opened fire on the crowded train from both sides of the track; then they charged it, hacking and stabbing with spears and swords.

They swore that the escorting Hindu troops fired over the heads of the attackers, and that the only man who tried to save them was the British officer commanding the escort, who machine-gunned the mob until his ammunition ran out and he was killed. The slaughter continued for three hours.

But this was not the only incident. Another Moslem refugee train reached Lahore yesterday carrying the bodies of 72 children after it had been ambushed by a Sikh band. It is also reported that a Moslem refugee convoy, passing through Amritsar on foot, lost 200 dead.

As a result of these incidents the governments of India and Pakistan have stopped all refugee traffic through the Punjab. Movement will only be resumed when "a reasonable margin of safety" can be assured for the convoys.

There have also been military moves. Pakistan has sent reinforcements, over a brigade strong, to the Lahore area, near the border of the two Dominions, to help the civil authorities cope with the flood of refugees (→27/10).

A grim scene follows the massacre of Moslems during sectarian clashes.

Cavalier Compton sweeps to summer glory and record books

Sept 20. After a summer during which his batting matched the brilliant sunshine, Denis Compton has ended the season with a total of 3,816 runs and 18 centuries. Both figures are records. Compton beat the previous record of 3,518 set by T. Hayward of Surrey in 1906 and the 16 centuries scored by Jack Hobbs in 1925. Close behind him was his Middlesex team-mate, Bill Edrich, with 3,539 runs and 12 centuries.

But it was Compton's cavalier style – typified by his unorthodox sweep stroke – which brought the crowds flocking. He made his test debut in 1937, at the age of 19, but is also a gifted soccer player, playing left-wing for Arsenal and winning several wartime international caps. The hope is that he retains his spectacular form against Australia next year (→14/8/48).

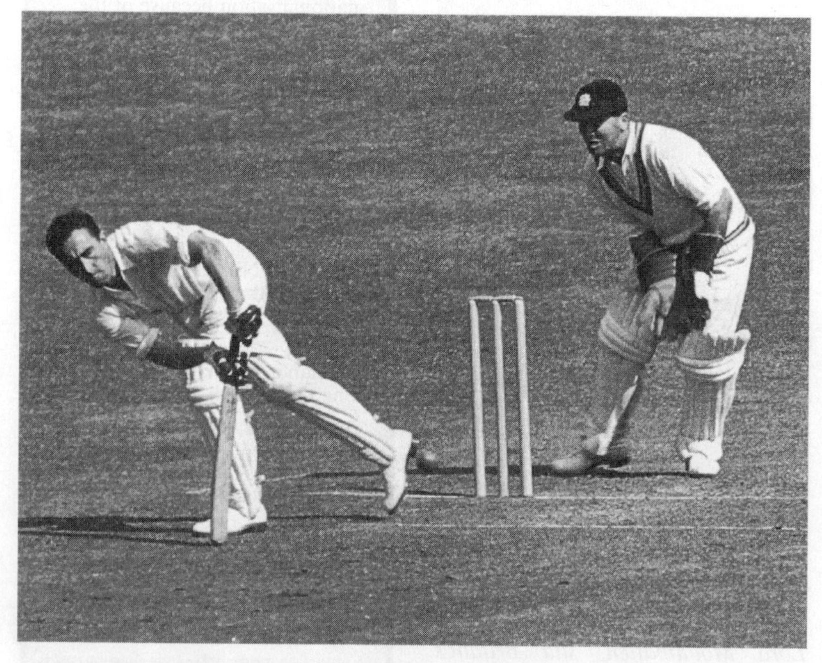

Denis Compton at the Canterbury Festival – making it look so simple.

1947

OCTOBER

Su	Mo	Tu	We	Th	Fr	Sa
			1	2	3	4
5	6	7	8	9	10	11
12	13	14	15	16	17	18
19	20	21	22	23	24	25
26	27	28	29	30	31	

1. US: Rita Hayworth files for divorce from Orson Welles.

1. UK: Austin unveils the "A40" to replace the "8" and "10" models (→7).

3. Amsterdam: Queen Wilhelmina says she will abdicate in favour of her daughter Juliana.

5. Washington: Truman appeals for a meatless Tuesday and a Thursday without poultry and eggs to aid Europe (→22/11).

7. London: The government proposes regular compulsory inspections for cars (→9).

9. London: The government cuts the bacon ration to one ounce a week (→8/11).

11. Palestine: Syrian troops are reported to be massing on the border as the US agrees to partition (→10/11).

15. UK: Archbishop Fisher rebukes the Bishop of Birmingham for unorthodoxy in his book "Rise of Christianity".

17. Rangoon: Britain grants Burmese independence from January next year (→4/1/48).

20. Washington: An investigation begins into communism in Hollywood.→

23. London: 12-year-old Julie Andrews steals the show in the revue "Starlight Roof".

24. London: 31 die in a train crash at Croydon (→26).

26. UK: 21 die in an express train crash near Berwick-upon-Tweed (→6/11).

27. France: De Gaulle calls for a general election and a new constitution (→20/11).

27. India: The Hindu Maharajah of Kashmir, a mixed Hindu and Moslem state, agrees to join India (→30).

30. Pakistan: The government rejects Kashmir's decision to join India (→2/11).

DEATHS

4. German physicist and 1918 Nobel Prize winner Max Planck (*23/4/1858).

13. British Socialist and author Sidney Webb, Lord Passfield (*13/7/1859).

1947

NOVEMBER

Su	Mo	Tu	We	Th	Fr	Sa
						1
2	3	4	5	6	7	8
9	10	11	12	13	14	15
16	17	18	19	20	21	22
23	24	25	26	27	28	29
30						

1. Europe: The "Benelux" customs union comes into effect after ratification by its three member states (→ 12/3/48).

3. London: Polish opposition leader Mikolajczyk, under a death sentence in Warsaw, arrives in Britain (→ 3/9/48).

6. London: Five die in three train crashes as thick fog envelops the city (→ 18/4/48).

8. UK: Potatoes are now rationed to three pounds per person per week (→ 11).

10. Palestine: The US agrees to Britain ending its mandate on May 31 1948 (→ 16).

11. London: The government says that vegetarians will not receive extra potato rations.

14. UK: Three, including a German V-2 expert, are reported killed during secret rocket tests in Buckinghamshire.

16. Palestine: The first British troops leave.→

19. Vienna: Communists are dismissed from the government (→ 25).

20. Paris: Veteran statesman Leon Blum takes over as premier from Paul Ramadier (→ 24).

22. Oxford: US Secretary of State George Marshall receives an honorary Doctorate of Civil Law (→ 8/1/48).

24. Paris: Robert Schuman becomes premier following Blum's failure to form a cabinet (→ 4/1/48).

25. London: The Big Four meet for a second time to discuss the future of Germany and Austria (→ 16/12).

26. London: The government outlines its plans for nationalisation of the railways (→ 1/1/48).

28. London: The Food Ministry promises more meat, sugar and sweets this Christmas (→ 27/3/48).

DEATH

28. French commander General Philippe de Hauteclocque, alias Leclerc (*22/11/1902).

Ronald Reagan warns against witch-hunt

Walt Disney promises that his cartoon characters are real Americans.

Oct 23. Film star Ronald Reagan appeared before a Congressional committee investigating Communism in America today, and warned of the dangers of a witch-hunt in Hollywood. "I hope that we are never prompted by fear or resentment of Communism into compromising any of our democratic principles in order to fight them," he told the House Committee on Un-American Activities.

There was a long drawn-out "Ooh" from the mainly female audience in the committee room as Mr Reagan, the President of the Screen Actors Guild, began testifying. The atmosphere was in marked contrast to the hysteria at yesterday's hearing, when the committee chairman claimed to have evidence of at least 79 Hollywood "subversives", but refused to name them.

Actor Robert Taylor then testified that the film industry was "packed with evidence of Communist activities", but was unable to name any party members, although he said several were "disruptive influences" including screen writer Lester Cole. Concern at the committee's activities today led a group of actors to form the Committee for the First Amendment, and several stars, including Humphrey Bogart, Gene Kelly, Danny Kaye, and Jane Wyatt plan to protest outside the committee (→ 25/11).

US plane breaks the sound barrier

Oct 14. American test pilot, Chuck Yeager, today became the first man to travel faster than sound. Flying from a base in California in his Bell X1 rocket plane, he broke through the sound barrier with a noise like a clap of thunder, at over 600mph.

The barrier exists because the pressure wave, which travels in front of slower planes, pushes air out of the way but it cannot travel faster than sound. Thus at these speeds it becomes like the wake behind a ship, and the plane hits the still air directly.

No petrol, and no need to work either as rationing continues.

Chancellor resigns over Budget leaks

Nov 13. Hugh Dalton, the Chancellor of the Exchequer, resigned in sensational circumstances tonight. He confessed that he had personally disclosed his tax proposals to a journalist a few minutes before delivering yesterday's Budget speech. He apologised to MPs for this "great indiscretion". In accepting his resignation, Mr Attlee said nothing detrimental to the state had happened. The leak was simply a human error.

The Prime Minister hinted that Mr Dalton will be back in the cabinet. The leak enabled The Star, one of London's three evening newspapers, to publish a brief and accurate "Stop Press" column forecast of the tax changes. Mr Attlee told a colleague: "Pity. Dalton never could keep his mouth shut" (→ 1/12).

Hugh Dalton, before the disaster.

Referendum to fix Kashmir's border

Nov 2. With troops of the Indian army holding their positions in Kashmir against the pro-Pakistan "Free Kashmir" army, Pandit Nehru, Prime Minister of India, has pledged that a referendum will be held when "the invaders are driven out" and law and order are established. "The fate of Kashmir," he said, "will be left in the hands of the people of Kashmir" (→ 23/12).

Arab fury as UN divides Palestine

Nov 30. The UN General Assembly set the stage for an Arab-Jewish war yesterday when it voted to partition Palestine and set up a Jewish state, an Arab state and a separate regime for the city of Jerusalem. No provision is made for enforcing the UN decision. Palestine's Jewish leaders are jubilant, though they have no intention of observing the strict limits on immigration called for by the UN.

The Arabs are enraged, and their spokesman, Dr Hussein Khalidi, has called for "a crusade against the Jews." In Jerusalem, Arabs went on the rampage, overturning buses and killing six Jews. But Star of David flags are flying in the city and Jews are dancing in the streets (→ 7/12).

Blacklist for ten Hollywood "Reds"

Nov 25. Leaders of the US film industry today blacked ten Hollywood writers and producers, who were cited for contempt of Congress, after allegations that they were Communist sympathisers. They said none of the ten, who include screen writers Lester Cole and Ring Lardner Jr., would be re-employed until "he is acquitted or has purged himself of contempt and declares under oath he is not a Communist". Lawyers for the ten accused Hollywood of acting like ignorant cattle "stampeded into surrendering" their integrity, and predicted the courts would rule the action unconstitutional (→ 2/8/48).

Reports that Russia has tested A-bomb

Nov 11. Reports reaching the West indicate Russia has exploded her first atomic bomb at a secret site in Siberia. The Russians say the 12-pound device "functioned perfectly", and that the explosion was felt over a radius of about 19 miles. Around 280 scientists witnessed the explosion. Western experts say they may understand the theory of the bomb, but they cannot yet mass produce it (→ 19/4/48).

Bells ring out for Royal wedding

Princess Elizabeth and the Duke of Edinburgh on their way back home.

Nov 20. Princess Elizabeth, the heir-presumptive to the throne, was married today to Prince Philip, the Duke of Edinburgh, at Westminster Abbey, in a glittering ceremony such as the nation has not seen for a decade.

The bridegroom was listed as Lieutenant Philip Mountbatten on the order of service, but he had been given the title Prince Philip, Duke of Edinburgh, by the King earlier in the day at a private ceremony.

The crowds, many of whom had slept out overnight, were 50 deep along the Mall and down Whitehall. They cheered wildly as the King and his daughter drove to Westminster Abbey in the Irish state coach, escorted by the Household Cavalry, resplendent in scarlet tunics, on black horses.

The bride's beautiful ivory dress was embroidered with flowers of beads and pearls. Her tulle veil hung from a circlet of diamonds. It was designed by Norman Hartnell, who took it to the Palace himself last night, in a six foot long white box.

The congregation of 2,500 had striking contrasts. There were Heralds, Gentlemen-at-Arms and others in uniforms vivid as playing cards, and all around in the pews people in their daytime grey suits.

The ceremony itself was simple; as one of the presiding prelates said, the same as for "any cottager getting married in her village church in the Dales this afternoon".

The wedding breakfast was at Buckingham Palace, where the 500-pound wedding cake was cut with the sword of the bridegroom's grandfather, Prince Louis of Battenberg. As the carriage of the newlyweds drove away to Waterloo station, the royal family ran across the Palace quadrangle showering the couple with pink rose petals.

They are honeymooning at Broadlands in Hampshire, and will live at Clarence House, for which Parliament has just voted £50,000 for re-decorating (→ 26/4/48).

1947

DECEMBER

Su	Mo	Tu	We	Th	Fr	Sa
	1	2	3	4	5	6
7	8	9	10	11	12	13
14	15	16	17	18	19	20
21	22	23	24	25	26	27
28	29	30	31			

1. London: A government white paper lists planned cuts in capital expenditure (→ 3).

3. London: The government pushes through an Order to defeat "spivs and drones" (→ 6/4/48).

4. New York: Premiere of Tennessee Williams' play "A Streetcar Named Desire".→

7. Palestine: Jews and Arabs "call up" young men to fight (→ 1/1/48).

10. Stockholm: Nobel Prizes go to Sir Edward Appleton (UK, Physics); Sir Robert Robinson (UK, Chemistry); Carl and Gerty Cori (US) and Bernardo Houssay (Argentina, Medicine); Andre Gide (France, Literature); and Peace Prize awarded in Oslo to The Friends Service Council (UK) and The American Friends Service Committee (US).

16. London: Bevin accuses the USSR of duplicity over Germany after the breakdown of Big Four talks (→ 31/3/48).

19. Belgrade: Yugoslavia signs a friendship treaty with Rumania (→ 22/3/48)).

23. UK: 220 Dartmoor inmates stage a protest against prison food (→ 14/4/48).

28. Kashmir: Moslem guerrillas clash with Indian troops (→ 16/1/48).

30. Bucharest: King Michael is forced to abdicate by the pro-Soviet government (→ 4/3/48).

DEATH

14. British statesman Stanley Baldwin, Earl of Bewdley, PM 1923-24, 1924-29, 1935-37 (*3/8/1867).→

HITS OF 1947

They say it's wonderful.

Maybe it's because I'm a Londoner.

QUOTE OF THE YEAR

"So long as there are tears and suffering, so long our work will not be over."

Pandit Jawaharlal Nehru, first Prime Minister of India.

Greatest migration ends

Terrified Moslems flock to the traditional sanctuary of Fort Purana Quilla.

Dec 23. The last Moslem refugees from India crossed into Pakistan during the week-end. They completed their journey without incident and were taken into the overflowing refugee camps.

They were lucky, for it is estimated that 400,000 people, both Moslems and Hindus, have been slaughtered since the partition of the old India, while a further 100,000 have suffered cruelly from starvation and exposure.

Official figures announced today show that more than 8,500,000 refugees, almost equally divided between Hindu and Moslem, have crossed the Indo-Pakistan border in the last four months in "the largest migration in history".

Refugee trains moved 2,300,000 but the majority had to fight their way through hostile country in bullock cart convoys. They were frequently attacked and often marooned by floods with all their cattle and possessions.

The settling of these refugees is posing huge problems for the new states. They must be housed, given land and found jobs and helped to rebuild their lives (→28).

Baldwin, three times Prime Minister, dies

Dec 14. Earl Baldwin of Bewdley has died at the age of 80. In three separate spells of office he was Prime Minister for more than seven years between the wars.

At different times Stanley Baldwin was seen as the nation's saviour and as a national disaster. He shrewdly saw the country through the traumas of the General Strike and the Abdication. Later execration was heaped upon him for complacently neglecting rearmament.

An emollient Tory, Baldwin had not the temperament to rouse the nation, yet with his pipesmoking, country-squire image, he established a remarkable ascendency over parliament and the public. This sprang from trust in his integrity and acceptance, even by opponents, that he meant well.

Arts: Britten wins immense acclaim

England has found an opera composer of the first rank in **Benjamin Britten**. His opera "Peter Grimes", the tragic story of a mad Suffolk fisherman, repeated at Covent Garden the immense acclaim it won at Sadlers Wells in 1945. The title role was again sung by Britten's close friend, the tenor **Peter Pears**. There are orchestral interludes which magically evoke the North Sea.

French painting mourned **Pierre Bonnard**, who died aged 79 at Le Cannet on the Cote d'Azur. He had lived there since 1925 and made his own domestic life the subject of his paintings – interiors, tables laid for meals, and his wife Marthe, who was extremely neurotic, in the bath, where she spent a disproportionate amount of her time.

The most accomplished art forger of the century was exposed when **Hans van Meegeren**, a Dutch painter of 57, was accused of having sold art treasures to the Germans during the war. His defence was that he had painted them himself. He admitted to forging five Vermeers, some of which were now hanging in Dutch museums, notably "The Supper At Emmaus", which was hailed as a newly discovered masterpiece by the experts. Van Meegeren died in prison.

Before leaving Hollywood, where he was under suspicion as a Communist, the German playwright **Bertolt Brecht** saw his play "Galileo" performed by **Charles Laughton**, who had worked with him on the text. On Broadway, **Tennessee Williams'** play, "A Streetcar Named Desire", caused a sensation, mainly because of the brutal, half-incoherent portrayal of a Polish immigrant, played by **Marlon Brando**, who rapes the heroine. Brando is a product of the new Actors' Studio, which teaches its pupils the "Method", based on the work of Stanislavsky.

Stratford's new man, Peter Brook.

In London, the smash hits are two American musicals, **Irving Berlin's** "Annie Get Your Gun", and another breezy, open-air show by **Richard Rodgers** and **Oscar Hammerstein**, called "Oklahoma!".

Benjamin Britten at the keyboard in his home at Aldeburgh, Suffolk.

1948

JANUARY

Su	Mo	Tu	We	Th	Fr	Sa
				1	2	3
4	5	6	7	8	9	10
11	12	13	14	15	16	17
18	19	20	21	22	23	24
25	26	27	28	29	30	31

1. UK: The railways are nationalised from midnight tonight (→ 1/4).

1. Mediterranean: The Royal Navy boards two Panamanian ships of illegal Jewish immigrants (→ 16).

3. London: Attlee blasts the USSR's "new imperialism".→

4. France: The Saar is granted self-rule (→ 25).

6. Paris: 15 die when a DC-4 airliner crashes on a flight from Brussels (→ 1/2).

8. Washington: Marshall tells the Senate that US failure to help rebuild Europe will put it into the hands of police states (→ 20/3).

12. Washington: The US Supreme Court orders the state of Oklahoma to admit a black girl to law school.

15. London: Britain signs an alliance with Iraq, renewing a pact of 1930.

16. Karachi: Pakistan accuses India of armed aggression and systematic annihilation of Moslems (→ 19).

19. New York: India and Pakistan accept UN mediation in their dispute.→

20. Germany: The Russians are reported to hold art worth £42 million from Dresden.

23. Czechoslovakia: Communists take over in Slovakia, alleging their opponents plan a revolt (→ 21/2).

25. Paris: The franc is devalued from 480 to 864 to the pound (→ 24/7).

31. London: the Coal Board lost £5.44 million in the last quarter of 1947 (→ 13).

BIRTH

27. Soviet ballet dancer Mikhail Baryshnikov.

DEATHS

8. German poet and sculptor Kurt Schwitters (*20/6/1887).

30. Indian leader Mohandas Karamchand "Mahatma" Gandhi (2/10/1869).→

30. US aviation pioneer Orville Wright (*19/8/1871).

Mahatma Gandhi is shot by assassin

Jan 30. Mahatma Gandhi, the man who, more than any other, secured India's freedom from British rule, was assassinated by one of his own countrymen in New Delhi today.

Mr Gandhi, still weak from his recent fast for Hindu-Moslem unity, which brought him close to death, was being helped across the gardens of Birla House by his grand-nieces, Manu and Ava, to attend a prayer meeting, when a young man stepped from the crowd and shot him three times.

Mr Gandhi, dressed as usual in his home-spun cloth, fell to the ground mortally wounded, but raised his hands in front of his face in the Hindu gesture of greeting, seemingly to his assassin. He cried out "Ram; Ram" (Oh God; Oh God) and died about 25 minutes later.

The killer, who has been named as Nathuram Godse, a fanatical Hindu, was seized by Sergeant Devraj Singh of the Indian Air Force and hustled away as the weeping, hysterical crowd, shouting "Kill him, Kill him" tried to lynch him.

Mr Gandhi's body, draped in a white cotton sheet, with the face uncovered, was carried on to the terrace of Birla House tonight. The lights were switched off, except for one spotlight focussed on the body.

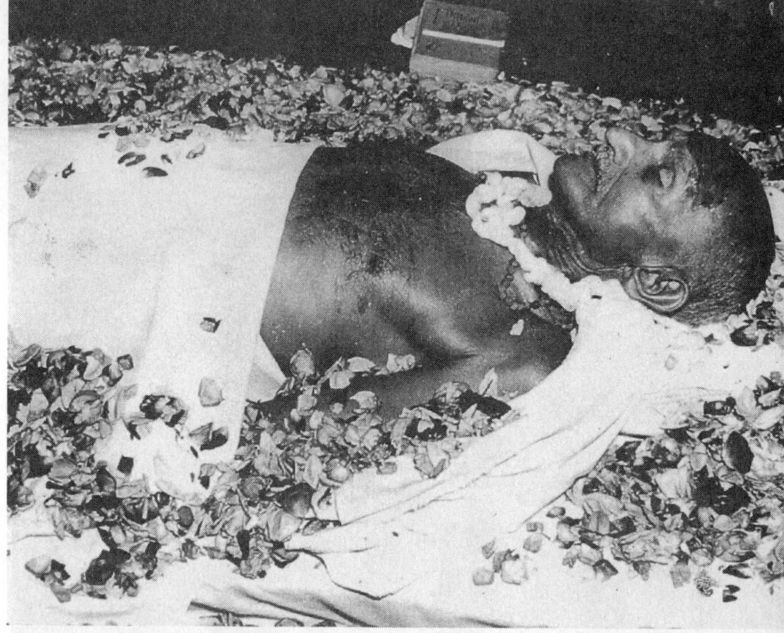

Gandhi, the lifelong apostle of peace, now victim of an assassin's bullet.

Tomorrow will bring poignant and unforgettable scenes on the banks of the Jumna River, where thousands will gather to mourn Mr Gandhi as his body is cremated and his ashes cast into the river.

Pandit Nehru, India's Prime Minister, is moving among the grieving crowds tonight, telling them the tragic story of the day's events, and urging them to refrain from giving violent expression to their sense of loss. Broadcasting to the nation, he said: "I do not know how to tell you and how to say it. Our beloved leader is no more."

Nobody yet knows why Gandhi was killed, but there is great fear of the consequences which this wild deed may heap upon a nation which has already suffered so much bloodshed and terror (→ 31).

Riots erupt as Indians mourn the loss of Gandhi

Jan 31. Mass mourning for the death of Mr Gandhi has turned to violence, with arson and riots erupting in many areas. Trouble broke out in Bombay as soon as the news of the assassination reached the city, and police had to fire on rioters in the Null Bazaar, a notorious centre of communal strife.

The inter-communal tension has been made worse by the news that Nathuram Godse, the killer, belonged to an extreme Hindu group opposed to Mr Gandhi's message of communal and religious tolerance. It was for this cause that the "Mahatma" fasted for six days just before he was killed.

Fear of the consequences has spread to Pakistan, where it is felt that Mr Gandhi's death will release the brake on forces determined to crush Pakistan (→ 2/2).

Police wear gas masks as they disperse protestors after Gandhi's funeral.

Doctors threatening boycott of new NHS

Jan 27. Medical consultants and specialists in the London area voted by 766 to 11 last night to reject service under the National Health Act in its present form. The boycott threat was led by Lord Horder, chairman of the British Medical Association, who claimed that doctors would be "selling our heritage and things will get worse".

Leading surgeon, John Dickson Wright, complained that doctors would become paid servants without a say in an administration run by an army of civil servants.

The Minister of Health, Aneurin Bevan, has insisted that doctors will not be full-time salaried employees when the National Health Service is introduced in July, and that doctors not in a practice will be fully protected (→ 18/2).

Soviet imperialism attacked by Labour

Jan 22. Moves towards consolidation of the free nations of Western Europe, in face of provocative Soviet expansionism, were announced by Mr Bevin, the Foreign Secretary, in Parliament tonight. He robustly denounced Russia's intervention in the affairs of East European states and said: "We are at a critical moment in the organisation of the postwar world. The Communist process goes ruthlessly on."

Britain is now working for ever-closer ties with France, and talks have begun about a treaty with Belgium, Holland and Luxembourg for economic co-operation.

Dick is kept on a tight rein by Auntie

Jan 16. Writers and producers of the BBC's popular radio serial "Dick Barton, Special Agent" have been issued 12 rules designed to protect Dick's upright character. Typical is rule 5, which lays it down that his violence "is restricted to clean socks on the jaws". Other rules: "Sex plays no part in his adventures", "He never lies", and no swearing.

Death toll rises as Jews and Arabs clash

Royal Irish Fusiliers arrest members of Haganah suspected of terrorism.

Jan 16. A massive explosion on the roof of a food store near the Wailing Wall shook Jerusalem just after midnight. There was extensive damage, and a pall of smoke over Zion Gate. Casualties are not yet known but later in the day, in Haifa, seven Arab children were killed when a house was blown up by Haganah, the Jewish defence force. Today's incidents, reprisals by the Jews for recent Arab attacks, reflect the escalation of the fighting between Arabs and Jews since the United Nations decided on the partition of Palestine to allow for the establishment of a homeland for the Jews. Over 2,000 people have been killed in the last six weeks. United Nations officials put the figures at 1,069 Arabs, 769 Jews, 123 British and 23 others.

Two refugees looking for a home.

Just a week ago an Arab force of about 600 crossed the border from Syria, where they had been training, and attacked three Jewish settlements. On this occasion the Haganah joined with the British to repulse the attacks. The Jews dug trenches for the soldiers while Spitfires flew over the marshes and low-lying hills, forcing the Arabs to take cover.

Two weeks ago the Semiramis Hotel in Jaffa was blown up, burying around 30 people in the ruins. This was the work of the militant group of Jewish guerrillas, the Stern Gang, who alleged that the hotel was the headquarters of two Arab National Youth organisations which had been responsible for attacks on Jews.

British forces are trying to work with moderate elements on both sides to contain the carnage, but with little success. It is no longer safe to walk the streets of Haifa, since rival groups are raking each other with rifle fire (→ 29/2).

Burma independent when stars say so

Jan 4. At 4.20 this morning, an hour chosen by Burmese astrologers as the most auspicious for the birth of a new republic, the guns of the cruiser HMS Birmingham crashed out a celebration of the independence of the Union of Burma.

While the guns were sounding their message, a large group of statesmen and diplomats gathered somewhat sleepily at the Secretariat, Burma's Houses of Parliament, for the ceremony of lowering the Union Jack and hoisting the national flag of Burma.

As the Union Jack was slowly lowered, star shells burst overhead, church bells rang throughout Rangoon and rifle volleys were fired by jubilant Burmese soldiers. The city is to give itself over to celebration for the next five days.

Bill abolishes right to a double vote

Jan 30. In future general elections nobody will be allowed more than one vote. Plural voting is outlawed by the Government's Representation of the People Bill, published today. Until now a university graduate could vote both at his university and in his home town. A businessman has had two or more votes – one at home and others at business addresses.

The Bill abolishes the 12 university seats in the Commons. This, and boundary adjustments, reduce its number of seats from 640 to 608. The historic City of London constituency is amalgamated with Finsbury and Shoreditch. "The whole thing's a damned shame," said a university MP (→ 17/2).

Straight as an arrow to Paris.

1948

FEBRUARY

Su	Mo	Tu	We	Th	Fr	Sa
1	2	3	4	5	6	7
8	9	10	11	12	13	14
15	16	17	18	19	20	21
22	23	24	25	26	27	28
29						

1. Atlantic: 31 are feared dead in a British South American Airways Tudor IV crash (→ 2/3).

2. New Delhi: India bans private armies (→ 28).

3. UK: Elsie Beyer becomes the first woman general manager of the Shakespeare Memorial Theatre, Stratford.

5. Madrid: Franco re-opens the frontier with France.

6. London: MPs pass the Women's Service Bill, making the ATS and WAAF permanent (→ 13).

7. Washington: General Omar Bradley succeeds Eisenhower as US Army supremo.

8. Switzerland: The Winter Olympics at St. Moritz ends with Sweden leading the Swiss and the US in gold medals.

10. Colombo: Ceylon becomes an independent dominion.

12. London: The War Office says eight of the 19 Gurkha battalions in India will join the British Army (→ 28).

13. London: The ATS and WAAF become the Women's Royal Army Corps and Women's Royal Air Force.

16. North Korea: A people's republic is proclaimed with Soviet backing (→ 1/5).

17. London: MPs pass the Representation of the People Bill.

18. London: In a British Medical Association poll, 86 per cent of doctors vote against joining the NHS (→ 15/4).

21. Prague: President Benes says there can be no totalitarian Communist regime in Czechoslovakia.→

27. Prague: Gottwald slams Western condemnation of his takeover (→ 10/3).

28. India: The last British troops leave (→ 20/6).

29. Palestine: 28 British soldiers die and 33 are injured when a train hits a Stern Gang mine (→ 11/3).

DEATH

11. Soviet film director Sergei Eisenstein (*23/1/1898).→

Communists stage Czechoslovak coup

Feb 27. The Communists have seized power in Czechoslovakia. While a mob, hastily bused from factories on the outskirts of Prague, demonstrated noisily this afternoon, Klement Gottwald, the Communist Prime Minister, announced that President Benes had accepted the resignation of the 12 Centre and right-wing ministers.

Gottwald stated that his new list of Ministers had then been accepted by President Benes. In the new government the Communists and their allies, the left-wing Social Democrats, hold almost every important post. The premier is a Communist; so are two of the three deputy premiers.

Noone knows what Benes thinks of these developments. He was to have addressed the nation by radio tonight, but did not do so. This was the second postponement of his broadcast, and the fear is that he has fallen under some kind of restraint by the Communists.

Certainly their tactics over the past few days have been most menacing. The use of mass rallies has been one of the features of the crisis. This morning, for example, a mass meeting of Communists and trade unionists from the factories was summoned to demonstrate confidence in the new Government, although the names of its members had not been published. A counter-demonstration was mounted by Prague students, who still retain the liberal tradition of the earlier years of the republic.

They attempted to get through to the President's palace, the Hradcany Castle, in the old city. They were turned back by the police and members of the works militia – trades union police – all fervent communists, who wear armbands and carry guns.

Concern over the situation in Czechhoslovakia was expressed today by M. Bidault, the French Foreign Minister. He recalled that at the time of the Nazi takeover of Czechoslovakia he said: "The peril is upon us." Today, he said: "It may be useful to consider this after, alas, scarcely nine years."

The hopes of those who oppose the Communist takeover must now rest with Jan Masaryk, son of the late, revered President Masaryk, who retains his position as Foreign Minister.

Communist leader Gottwald addresses a rally outside the Kinsky Palace.

As the situation in Palestine continues to deteriorate, another bomb sends Arabs and Jews into the streets, fleeing the destruction of their homes while their rival representatives escalate the bloodshed and anarchy.

De Valera's 16-year premiership ends

Feb 18. Having been returned in the Irish general election with the largest party, Eamon de Valera has just been voted out of office by the Dail. The vote brought to an end a 16-year premiership. John A. Costello, aged 56, a brilliant lawyer, is the new Prime Minister.

Angry farmers, economic decline, poor health services and strikes, including one by school teachers, contributed to De Valera's downfall. When the vote rejecting him was announced, he took off his reading glasses and left the chamber, without even a nod to the stunned benches behind him, or the exuberant ones opposite.

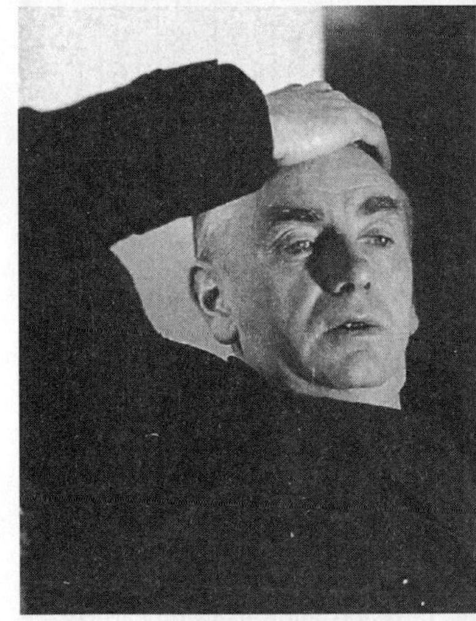

Costello: tie-breaking politician.

Costello leads Ireland's first coalition government. He's a compromise leader; the obvious choice was General Richard Mulcahy, leader of Fine Gael, the second largest party, but he was unacceptable to minor party leaders.

A national hero when he accepted the keys of Dublin Castle from the departing British Army, Mulcahy afterwards supported the execution of gunmen in the civil war, believing it to be necessary if the infant state was to survive.

The first aim of the new government is economic expansion. Declared Agriculture Minister, James Dillon: "We will submerge England in eggs and bury her in bacon" (→17/11).

Visionary Soviet director, Eisenstein, dies

Feb 11. Sergei Eisenstein, the Soviet film director who won world-wide fame with "The Battleship Potemkin", has died of a heart attack at 50, with his great epic trilogy, "Ivan the Terrible" still incomplete.

In 1941, with the Germans at the outskirts of Moscow, Eisenstein and his crew were despatched to Kazakhstan on Stalin's orders to shoot the picture about the Czar who first unified Russia. Part One was awarded a Stalin prize, but Part Two, showing Ivan's brutal police rule, was banned by the Central Committee. Part Three was still to come.

Eisenstein made preliminary drawings of every sequence of a film and worked very closely with the composer, Sergei Prokofiev, who wrote the music for Ivan and for "Alexander Nevsky". This culminated in a battle on the ice, in which the invading Teutonic knights were thrown into the waters of Lake Peipus.

UK warns Argentina over the Falklands

Feb 16. A Royal Navy cruiser set sail for the Falkland Islands tonight as Britain warned Argentina it would not overlook the challenge created by her own naval operations in the area.

Both Argentina and Chile are believed to have put men ashore in the South Shetland Islands, part of the Falkland Islands Dependencies just north of Antarctica, and vessels from both countries are operating in waters there. The stated aim is to enforce their claims to sovereignty but the belief is that they are merely sabre-rattling and testing the UK's willingness to hold on to the islands.

The Government wants the international court to decide the issue. A statement said: "The Government considers the British title to the Falkland Islands Dependencies to be well-founded, and has been willing that it should stand the test of international arbitration."

1948

MARCH

Su	Mo	Tu	We	Th	Fr	Sa
	1	2	3	4	5	6
7	8	9	10	11	12	13
14	15	16	17	18	19	20
21	22	23	24	25	26	27
28	29	30	31			

1. London: MPs approve a defence pact to back an association of Western powers.

2. London: 19 die when a DC-3 from Brussels crashes (→15/4).

4. London: Ex-King Michael of Rumania breaks silence and says he was made to abdicate by the Communists.

5. Falkland Islands: Governor Miles Clifford protests to the Argentine Navy for its presence at Deception Island.→

7. Argentina: The Peronists win a general election.

7. London: All political marches in the city are banned for three months to thwart a Mosleyite march on May 1 (→15).

11. Jerusalem: The offices of the Jewish Agency are blown up (→22).

12. Brussels: Britain and France conclude a draft treaty of alliance with the Benelux countries.→

12. Prague: Thousands file past the open coffin of Jan Masaryk (→7/5).

20. Mr J. Proctor's Sheila's Cottage wins the Grand National at Aintree.

22. Belgrade: Tito says they will allow Italy to have Trieste in return for the town of Gorizia (→25).

23. London: Rinty Monaghan of Belfast knocks out Jackie Paterson to become world flyweight boxing champion.

25. Rome: Italy rejects Tito's deal to swap Trieste for Gorizia (→4/7).

27. London: The government announces a cut in the cheese ration from two to one and a half ounces a week (→8/4).

27. Egypt: King Farouk lays the foundation stone of the Aswan Dam.

31. Germany: The Russians begin controlling Western military trains travelling to Berlin (→1/4).

DEATH

10. Czech statesman Jan Masaryk (*14/9/1886).→

Soviets walk out of Berlin talks in fury

March 20. Relations between the four Allied powers, jointly occupying Berlin, worsened today when Soviet delegates walked out of a meeting of the Allied Control Council, the body officially charged with governing Germany, saying it "in practice no longer exists". The Russians claim the Western powers snubbed the council by holding a secret meeting in London to discuss Germany's future. The Soviet action, coupled with reports of Red Army troop movements, and the comments of a Communist politician in Berlin, has increased fears that a Russian move against Berlin is imminent (→13/5).

Ban on radicals in the Civil Service

March 15. The Prime Minister was loudly cheered when he told MPs today that known or suspected Communist and Fascist party members or associates in the Civil Service will be removed immediately from posts vital to state security. They will be offered other work. The BBC governors are left to decide whether to order similar action. The numbers likely to be involved are small.

Mr Attlee said that the Government is taking the only prudent course. Some Whitehall union leaders have been calling for this purge for some time (→20/5).

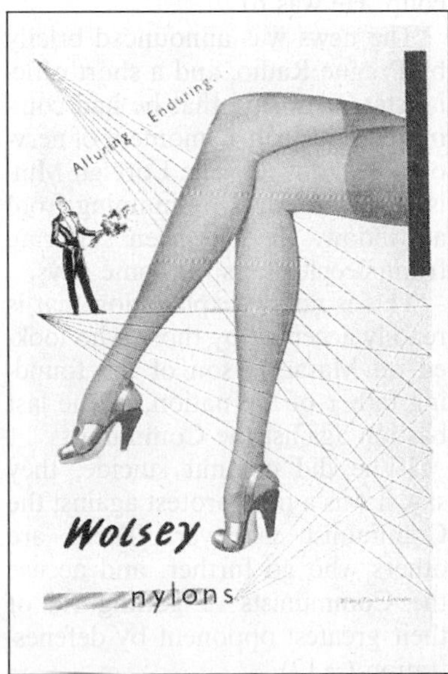

Jews blow up the Arab quarter in Haifa

March 22. Palestine today had one of its ugliest days of violence. In Haifa, Jews blew up two areas in the Arab quarter, killing 17 and injuring at least another 150. The Arabs responded with mortar attacks on the Jewish business quarter. Four mortar bombs fell on a British police station, killing one constable and injuring another seriously. Fierce fighting was still going on in Haifa last night.

At Har Tuv, 20 miles west of Jerusalem, British troops had to use their biggest 25-pounder guns to shell Arab positions in the hills. There were more than 100 casualties, including 60 killed. This afternoon the bodies of two men, believed to be British soldiers, were found near Har Tuv. They had been severely beaten and stripped of all identification marks. The latest escalation was sparked off by the bombing of the Jewish Agency headquarters in Jerusalem two weeks ago. Twelve people were killed, including Leib Yaffe, the head of the Jewish National Fund, which finances new settlers.

The Agency building is one of the most heavily guarded in Jerusalem, but the bomb was planted in a stolen American Consulate car with several American flags painted on it. The Arab driver wore a consulate uniform which deceived the guards (→29/4).

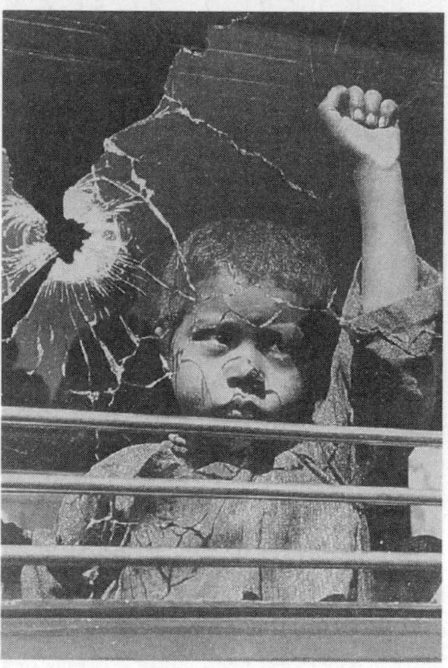

An Arab child stares sadly from the window of his school bus, after it had been fired on by Jewish terrorists.

Did Masaryk jump or was he pushed?

March 10. Jan Masaryk, Foreign Minister of Czechoslovakia, was found lying dead in the courtyard beneath his flat at the Foreign Office in Prague this morning, just two weeks after the Communist coup. He was 61.

The news was announced briefly by Prague Radio, and a short official statement said that he had committed suicide in a "moment of nervous breakdown". The Foreign Minister, it said, died by jumping from a window. He had been suffering from sleeplessness for some days.

This is not an explanation that is readily accepted by those who looked on Masaryk, son of the founding father of the nation, as the last bastion against the Communists.

If he did commit suicide, they say, it was a final protest against the Communist takeover. There are others who go further, and accuse the Communists of getting rid of their greatest opponent by defenestration (→12).

Western Europeans create defence pact

March 17. Britain, France and the Benelux countries signed a 50-year treaty of alliance today, pledging to defend one another against attack, and to co-operate on cultural, social and economic matters.

Although the defence pact does not mention the Soviet Union by name, it applies to any threat of aggression on the continent, unlike previous European treaties which only covered mutual aid against Germany. The Five Power Pact was endorsed as "a notable step" by US President Harry Truman, who came as close as constitutionally possible to guaranteeing US military intervention in the event of Soviet aggression in Europe.

After the signing ceremony at the Palais des Academies in Brussels, Britain's Foreign Secretary, Ernest Bevin, described the treaty as a new beginning. "I am convinced the fate of Europe and the world will be decided by the work done here," he said.

1948

APRIL

Su	Mo	Tu	We	Th	Fr	Sa
				1	2	3
4	5	6	7	8	9	10
11	12	13	14	15	16	17
18	19	20	21	22	23	24
25	26	27	28	29	30	

1. UK: The electricity industry is nationalised.

5. Berlin: 15 die in a mid-air collision between a BEA airliner and a Soviet fighter (→30/6).

5. Egypt: 25 die in riots in Alexandria following a police strike.

6. London: The Budget puts a tax on investment income but raises tax allowances on earned income (→8).

6. Helsinki: Finland signs a ten-year mutual defence pact with the USSR.

8. London: Fuel Minister Hugh Gaitskell says motorists will be rationed to 90 miles a month from June 1 (→25).

9. Palestine: The Arab village of Deir Yassin is massacred by Irgun and Stern Gang terrorists (→14).

12. London: A memorial to President Roosevelt is unveiled in Grosvenor Square.

14. London: MPs vote 245-222 to suspend the death penalty for a five-year trial period (→2/6).

15. London: Aneurin Bevan offers doctors freedom of partnership, practice and criticism under the NHS (→7/6).

15. Eire: 38 die when a Pan-American Constellation crashes at Shannon (→4/7).

18. UK: 24 die in a rail crash at Winsford, Cheshire.

19. Pacific: The US has tested a new atomic weapon at Eniwetock Atoll in the Marshall Islands.

21. London: Premiere of Vaughan Williams' Sixth Symphony by Adrian Boult.

24. London: Manchester United beat Blackpool 4-2 in the FA Cup Final.

25. UK: The weekly milk ration goes up a pint to three and a half pints (→26/5).

26. London: A new General Certificate of Education is unveiled, to replace School and Higher School Certificates.

26. London: The King and Queen celebrate their Silver Wedding (→4/6).

Russia stops the traffic to Berlin

April 1. The Cold War took a turn for the worse today as the Russians began imposing rigid checks on all road and rail traffic between Berlin and the Western Zones. The fear is that this initial act could turn into a full scale blockade of the four-power city, in an effort to squeeze out the West or to at least protest at the way Marshall Aid is affecting Soviet influence throughout the country. Britain said it will resist any attempts to stop its trains to Berlin, but today cars on the road to the capital were all being delayed by Soviet checks (→18/6).

Jewish forces agree to truce in Jaffa

April 29. Jewish leaders agreed to a truce today in the Arab seaport of Jaffa, which they have been attacking for five days. The Palestine Government had told them that if they did not agree to a cease-fire the British army would drive them out. Only a week ago the Jews took Haifa, the only deep sea port, in an all-day battle which left 400 dead. The Arabs surrendered and agreed to evacuate the city, which had a population of 80,000 Jews and 60,000 Arabs (→9/5).

One of Haganah's commandos.

1948

MAY

Su	Mo	Tu	We	Th	Fr	Sa
						1
2	3	4	5	6	7	8
9	10	11	12	13	14	15
16	17	18	19	20	21	22
23	24	25	26	27	28	29
30	31					

1. North Korea: The Soviet-backed government adopts a constitution claiming jurisdiction over all Korea (→ 31).

3. New York: Tennessee Williams wins the Pulitzer Prize for best US play for "A Streetcar Named Desire".

5. Tel Aviv: David Ben-Gurion chairs a meeting of a provisional Jewish government of Palestine.→

6. US: Publication of Norman Mailer's first novel "The Naked and the Dead".

7. Prague: The government adopts a new Soviet-style constitution (→ 19).

11. Rome: Liberal Luigi Einaudi is elected president.

13. New York: Andrei Gromyko resigns as Soviet envoy to the UN.

13. UK: Figures show that the birth rate in 1947 was the highest for 26 years.→

15. Palestine: British troops withdraw.

16. Tel Aviv: Dr Chaim Weizmann is named first President of Israel (→ 1/6).

19. UK: Eight Czech exiles land at Manston, Kent in a "borrowed" Czech airliner (→ 7/6).

20. UK: twenty civil servants have so far been suspended for Communist or Fascist views.

20. China: Chiang Kai-shek is re-elected President (→ 1/9).

26. UK: 12 extra clothing coupons each are be available from today until the end of September (→ 28/7).

27. London: MPs vote against an enquiry into the "Nenni" goodwill telegram from Labour MPs to Italian Communists.

28. S. Africa: Smuts resigns as premier; Nationalist leader Douglas Malan takes over (→ 10/6).

31. London: Hugh Dalton returns to the cabinet as Chancellor of the Duchy of Lancaster.

31. South Korea: President Syngman Rhee claims jurisdiction over all Korea, asking US troops to remain (→ 12/8).

Arab forces muster as Israel is born

May 14. At 4pm today, eight hours before the British mandate in Palestine was due to end, the Jews proclaimed the new state of Israel. David Ben-Gurion, the Jewish Agency leader, is to be Prime Minister of a provisional government until a general election is held in October. Most vehicles in Tel-Aviv are now sporting the new blue-and-white Israeli flag: two horizontal bars and a Star of David.

The proclamation said: "We members of the National Council, representing the Jewish people in Palestine and the Zionist movement of the world, met together in solemn assembly on the day of the termination of the British mandate for Palestine, and by virtue of the natural and historic right of the Jewish people, and by resolution of the General Assembly of the United Nations, hereby proclaim the establishment of a Jewish state in Palestine to be called "Israel". "

Israel is to open its doors to all Jewish immigrants, revoking immediately the 1939 British law limiting immigration. There is a pledge of social and political equality for all, full freedom of education and culture, and equal rights for Arab inhabitants. The state appealed to the United Nations for help, and said it would be applying for UN membership.

President Truman, in a shock announcement from the White House a few seconds after the proclamation, recognised the Provisional Government. The news stunned delegates to the UN. Even the US and British delegations had no prior warning of the President's intentions.

Arab reaction has been predictable. Egyptian troops are massing on the southern border, and Nokrashy Pasha, the Prime Minister, is expected to broadcast at midnight, ordering them to move into Palestine. In Amman, King Abdullah of Transjordan said: "The Balfour Declaration (of a Jewish national home) has disappeared." He is expected to order the Arab Legion to go in to help the Arab forces already mustering. The Jews are braced to defend themselves, with the 30,000-strong Haganah fully mobilised as the official army of the new state.

British forces are now moving out. The High Commissioner, General Sir Alan Cunningham, sails from Haifa at midnight. This morning he left Government House in Jerusalem to the sound of a piper's lament. The Union Jack was hauled down and the International Red Cross took over the big square building on Hill South.

Sir Alan, in his last broadcast, appealed for moderation and peace in the wake of the British withdrawal. His appeal is unlikely to be heeded. Jewish forces today were taking over all key buildings in the cities, including Jaffa. Arab forces were consolidating their hold on several villages south of Bethlehem and there was sporadic fighting in many parts of the country.

No boundaries were proclaimed for the new state. The only hope for peace rests with whether Jews and Arabs can agree to some variant of the partition proposals put to the UN last November (→ 15/5).

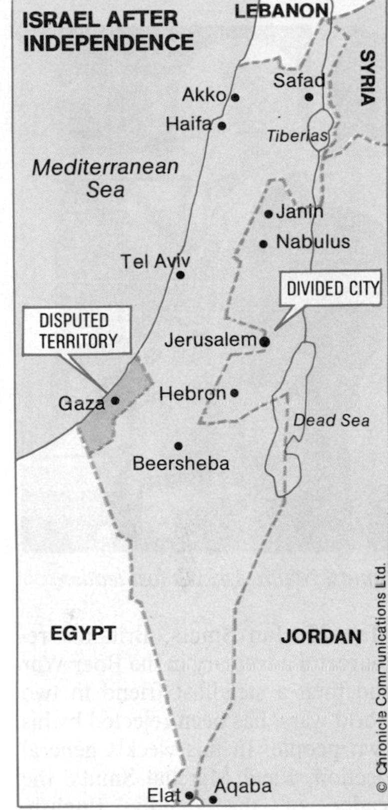

President Chaim Weizmann.

Israelis clamber over an Egyptian Spitfire, forced down near Tel Aviv. ▷

Jan Smuts loses seat after 24 years

Smuts, South Africa's lost leader.

May 27. Jan Smuts, Britain's resourceful adversary in the Boer War and then a steadfast friend in two world wars, has been rejected by his own people. In this week's general election, Field Marshal Smuts, the leader of the mainly English-speaking United Party and South African Prime Minister since 1939, lost his seat to a candidate of the race segregationist Nationalist Party, which represents Afrikaans-speaking whites. In the all-white election, the Nationalists, many of whom supported Hitler during the war, are winning seats right across the country, and seem certain to form the next government (→28).

Birthrate soars in bonnie baby boom

May 13. There is a boom in babies, says today's Registrar General's report, which shows that the birth-rate last year was 21 per cent greater than the rate needed to maintain the population – the highest for 26 years. There were 193,865 babies born in the last quarter alone.

The abnormally high rate is attributed to the fact that many couples are "catching up" on the lost war years. The figures also show record new lows for infant mortality – 41 per 1,000 – and still births – 24 per 1,000. Illegitimate births made up five per cent of the total, a slight drop on 1946.

1948

JUNE

Su	Mo	Tu	We	Th	Fr	Sa
		1	2	3	4	5
6	7	8	9	10	11	12
13	14	15	16	17	18	19
20	21	22	23	24	25	26
27	28	29	30			

1. New York: Israel and the seven states of the Arab League agree to a UN request for a month's truce (→30).

2. London: Peers throw out the bill suspending the death penalty for five years (→9).

4. London: It is announced that Princess Elizabeth is expecting a baby in the autumn (→21/7).

5. UK: The Aga Khan's My Love wins the Derby.

7. UK: Over 10,000 doctors, more than half the total, have joined the NHS after government reassurances (→20).

7. Prague: President Benes resigns (→14).

8. Germany: 83-year-old composer Richard Strauss is cleared by a Frankfurt "denazification" court.

9. London: The government proposes to keep hanging for certain types of crime (→15/7).

10. Cambridge: Field Marshal Smuts is installed as chancellor of the university.

11. Denmark: 150 die when the liner Kjobenhavn hits a mine and sinks.

14. Prague: Premier Klement Gottwald becomes president.

18. Germany: The Western Allies unveil the Deutschemark, to replace the Reichsmark in western Germany (→26).

20. UK: The British Dental Association tells dentists not to join the NHS (→5/7).

20. New Delhi: Lord Mountbatten leaves, handing over to Mr Rajagopalachari as governor general (→17/9).

24. London: Lillian Penson becomes vice-chancellor of London University, Britain's first woman vice-chancellor.

25. New York: World heavyweight champ Joe Louis knocks out Jersey Joe Walcott to retain his title.

26. Berlin: The Soviet army chief in Germany is arrested for speeding in the US sector (→1/8).

30. Israel: The last British troops leave (→9/7).

RAF flies into Berlin to beat blockade

Berliners watch an Allied transport coming in to land during the airlift.

June 30. The Western Allies are carrying out a round-the-clock airlift to beat the Russian blockade of Berlin. Every day now 200 Dakota aircraft are landing at RAF Gatow in the British zone of the city to bring in supplies to stop the population starving as the Russians put on the squeeze.

At present there is just enough food to last one month, and the Allies estimate they will have to airlift 2,500 tons of food a day to meet the requirements in the Western Zones. The shuttle of flights between the German capital and an airbase near Hanover is now so fast that an aircraft lands every four minutes. As bags of flour and oatmeal are unloaded by German labourers, the pilots flying in Operation Carter Paterson barely have time for half a cigarette before they are off again.

Mr Bevin has said that Britain will use all possible resources to keep the city alive, and George Marshall, the US Secretary of State, said: "We are in Berlin to stay." The Americans' feeling is that the Russians won't blunder into a war, but the crack-down on the city is tight. The Russians have banned movement of food from the Soviet areas into Berlin, and all surface transport is blocked (→6/7).

Rubber planters attacked in Malaya

June 22. Police are raiding the homes of communists and other left-wingers in Malaya in a bid to try and stop the rebel violence which has already claimed the lives of several British rubber planters.

In one day alone, 800 Communists and trade unionists were rounded up and a newspaper closed down by police operating under wide emergency powers. The mostly-Chinese rebels are armed with sten guns and pistols. Today one rubber planter was shot dead by two men who drove up to his bungalow on bicycles, while two others were shot at their office desks (→30/7).

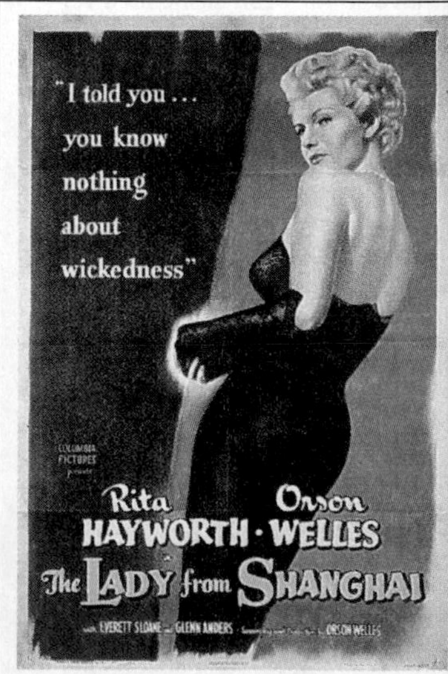

Orson Welles stars with Rita Hayworth in Columbia Pictures' "The Lady from Shanghai".

State of emergency to tackle dock strike

Their services no longer needed, strike-breaking soldiers leave the docks.

June 28. Draconian action was taken last night by the Government to deal with the dock strike. The King, who is on tour in Fife, called a Privy Council meeting in the Palace of Holyroodhouse, Edinburgh, and signed an Order-in-Council which gives the Government emergency powers under the 1920 Act. This means not only bringing in the troops to unload ships, but gives powers of arrest.

In a broadcast just before the BBC 9 o'clock news last night, Mr Attlee, the Prime Minister, said: "We must see the people are fed". Last week the ration was reduced to 6d worth of fresh meat and 6d worth of canned meat. He rebuked the strikers: "This strike is not against capitalists and employers. It is a strike against your mates."

No less than 232 ships are held up by the 19,000 unofficial strikers, who have been disowned by their union.

Surgeon does first operation inside heart

June 10. Three females who had been life-long invalids, barely able to walk, were given a new lease of life today by a surgeon, Mr R.C. Brock of Guy's Hospital, who, for the first time, operated on their hearts and cleared a blocked valve.

The females, aged between 11 and 23, had all been born "blue babies", that is, they were literally blue due to their blood getting insufficient oxygen. After the operation their colour was pink, two stopped squatting when they walked – characteristic of blue babies – and one was able to run. Two suffered complications of a stroke and a clot in one leg.

US Air Force Colonel "Chuck" Yeager flies the amazing Bell X-1 airplane to a new altitude record of 64,000 feet.

1948

JULY

Su	Mo	Tu	We	Th	Fr	Sa
				1	2	3
4	5	6	7	8	9	10
11	12	13	14	15	16	17
18	19	20	21	22	23	24
25	26	27	28	29	30	31

1. New York: Commercial flights begin at New York's Idlewild International Airport.

1. Oxford: The first Oxfam Shop opens.

2. UK: Henry Cotton wins the British Open Golf Championship for the third time.

3. Birmingham: Harold Wilson says in a speech that half his class went barefoot when he was at school.

3. Wimbledon: Robert Falkenburg beats John Bromwich for the Men's Singles title; Louise Brough beats Doris Hart for the Women's Singles crown.

6. Washington: Secretary of State Marshall protests to the Soviet ambassador about the blockade of Berlin (→2/8).

9. Israel: Egypt and Iraq attack Jewish positions as the month-long truce ends (→15/8).

13. UK: Figures reveal that the Coal Board lost over £23 million in the first year of nationalisation (→29/10).

15. London: MPs approve the government's compromise on the death penalty (→20).

16. UK: The world's first turbine-propellor aircraft, the Vickers Viscount, makes its maiden flight.

20. London: Peers reject the hanging compromise (→20/1/49).

21. London: The Duke of Edinburgh takes his seat in the House of Lords (→26/10).

24. Paris: Andre Marie takes over as French premier (→31/8).

28. London: The government says rationing of footwear and furnishing fabrics will end on September 9 (→13/9).

29. London: The King opens the Olympic Games (→14/8).

30. Budapest: President Zoltan Tildy resigns in protest at farm collectivisation (→3/8).

DEATHS

15. US commander General John Pershing (*13/9/1860).

23. US film director David Wark Griffith (*23/1/1875).

Russians urge the overthrow of Tito

July 4. The quarrel between Marshal Tito of Yugoslavia and the Russians, whom he accuses of trying to undermine him, has broken into the open with the announcement by the Cominform that it has expelled the Yugoslav party and severely censured Tito.

The Cominform, the international organisation of Communist parties, does not mince words. It accuses the Yugoslav leaders of "anti-Sovietism, Trotskyism, leanings towards capitalist states, inordinate ambition and grandeeism". It urges "healthy elements" to overthrow Tito (→18/8).

Marshal Tito and a favourite dog.

Shocking mid-air crash near London

July 4. Thirty-nine people died today in Britain's worst air disaster in decades, as two passenger aircraft collided over a hospital in Middlesex.

Both aircraft, an RAF Transport Command York and a Scandinavian Air Line Cloudmaster, were circling, hoping for a break in the weather, to land at RAF Northolt, when they collided over nearby Mount Vernon Hospital. Nobody survived the impact. The air disaster is the worst in Britain since 1921, when the R.38 crashed over the Humber, killing 45 (→21/10). ▷

NHS begins care from cradle to grave

July 5. The National Health Service – regarded as the most sweeping reform so far introduced by the Government – came into being today, together with a national insurance scheme and other welfare systems dealing with the unemployed and old people.

The Health Service offers free medical treatment for the entire population, with free prescriptions. Dental care, including providing dentures, is included in the revolutionary new scheme. It will also provide free glasses, and even wigs, under prescription.

As 992 local offices of the Ministry of National Insurance opened for operation today, 2,751 hospitals came under the control of new regional health boards. The Ministry of Health estimates that 19,000 doctors will have accepted service by the end of the week.

In a broadcast last night, the Prime Minister, Clement Attlee, welcomed the new service and said: "There are bound to be early difficulties with staff, accommodation, and so on. In a great plan like this, there must be some rough edges, but these will be overcome with patience and goodwill."

The Service represents a personal triumph for Aneurin Bevan, the Health Minister, who faced powerful opposition from the British Medical Association and many doctors when he began negotiations a year ago.

Health Minister Aneurin Bevan meets an early beneficiary of the NHS.

British wipe out Malayan rebels

July 30. Malayan Communist insurgents suffered their heaviest setback so far today, when a powerful force of British troops and police wiped out a network of hide-outs near Kuala Lumpur.

At least 22 rebels were killed and 47 captured with no military or police casualties reported. The raid took the rebels by surprise. An army officer said: "The rebels started pelting like rabbits in all directions and made no attempt to shoot it out." Any rebel who did not immediately surrender was shot.

This latest victory for the security forces comes just days after the Communist Party was banned in Malaya after Mr Creech Jones, the Colonial Secretary, revealed in the Commons that it had been the mainspring of a plot to set up a Communist state.

In another major operation this week, four columns of British troops, Gurkhas and rocket-firing Spitfires combed an area of the jungle south of the city and captured 100 rebels (→ 1/8).

Mills is world light-heavyweight champ

The two boxers shake hands before getting down to the day's real work.

July 26. Freddie Mills, the unpredictable light-heavyweight from London, shook off all memories of his humiliating defeat by Gus Lesnevich two years ago, modified his wild and reckless style, and, to the cheers of 46,000 excited fans at the White City stadium, narrowly beat Lesnevich on points to become undisputed world champion.

Apart from launching a powerful flurry in the tenth round, which had Lesnevich down twice, Mills fought an unusually disciplined and cautious fight, and left Lesnevich no room for manoeuvre.

1948

AUGUST

Su	Mo	Tu	We	Th	Fr	Sa
1	2	3	4	5	6	7
8	9	10	11	12	13	14
15	16	17	18	19	20	21
22	23	24	25	26	27	28
29	30	31				

1. Germany: The French zone is economically merged with the Anglo-US zone.

1. Malaya: The RAF is now leading the attack against Communist rebels.

3. Budapest: Pro-Soviet Socialist Arpad Szakasits is sworn in as Hungary's new president.

6. Moscow: British, US and French envoys have talks with Molotov to try and end the Berlin crisis.

8. UK: At least 12 die when a 70 mph gale hits Britain.

12. Washington: Truman recognises the South Korean Republic based in Seoul (→ 9/9).

13. US: Pan-American Airways cuts its transatlantic return fare by a quarter to £118 2/6d.

16. London: Several Eastern European Olympic athletes, including four Czechs, have decided not to return home.

18. Belgrade: The Danube states vote to exclude Britain, the US, France and Austria from a new Danube authority.

18. New York: The USSR vetoes Ceylon's entry to the UN.

19. Berlin: Soviet troops open fire on Germans demonstrating against Soviet occupation of the city.

20. Greece: Government troops defeat Communist rebels under General Markos Vafiades.

21. London: Britain warns that it will veto Israel's entry to the UN (→ 29).

25. Washington: Alger Hiss and Whittaker Chambers clash at the Un-American Activities Committee (→ 15/12).

29. London: Special Branch and MI5 uncover an explosives cache, believed to belong to the Jewish Irgun terrorist group (→ 17/9).

31. Paris: Robert Schuman returns as premier.

DEATH

16. US baseballer George Herman "Babe" Ruth (*6/2/1895).

Don Bradman bows out with a duck

Aug 14. On a day of virtually unrelieved Australian domination in the final Test at The Oval, the great Donald Bradman provided the biggest surprise of all. Coming in to bat in his last Test match to a standing ovation, with a humiliated England team at his mercy, he was bowled second ball for a duck by a crafty googly from Eric Hollies.

A mere four runs would have given Bradman, the most prolific batsman the world has seen, a Test average of over 100 per innings. However, he has the satisfaction of ending his career with yet another triumph over the old enemy, who collapsed to 52 all out to the fast bowling of Ray Lindwall (→10/9).

Bradman – an emotional farewell.

Optimism after envoys meet Stalin

Aug 2. Senior Western envoys met Stalin at the Kremlin tonight, amid optimism that the Soviets are at last ready to begin talks over the blockade of Berlin.

Hopes are that the meeting may lead to a four-Power conference to discuss not just the Berlin crisis, but the whole question of Germany. But, while Stalin was anxious not to be seen to be climbing down, the Western envoys, from Britain, America and France, were equally adamant that they will not negotiate under duress (→6).

US spy mania branded a "red herring"

Alger Hiss, branded a Communist, is unbowed as he faces his accusers.

Aug 2. Two US Congressional committees today began inquiring into allegations that over 30 US officials belong to a Communist spy ring, in what promises to be one of the biggest "witch hunts" of all times. President Truman denounced it as a "red herring", designed to divert attention from his efforts to push anti-inflation laws through the Republican-controlled Congress.

In the House Un-American Activities Committee, Whittaker Chambers, a self-confessed former spy and now an editor of Time Magazine, will be accusing a State Department official, Alger Hiss, of having given him secret government papers in the 1930s. Today Louis Budenz, a former editor of the Daily Worker, told the Senate Investigating Committee that the US Communist Party is "the fifth column of Russia" committed to the destruction of the American republic. He has renounced Communism for Roman Catholicism.

The investigations follow allegations made by Miss Elizabeth Bentley, another self-confessed Communist agent. The allegations have shocked America. Many think them improbable. But Mr Karl Mundt in the House, and Senator Joe McCarthy, the Wisconsin Republican, claim they have independent evidence to support the allegations.

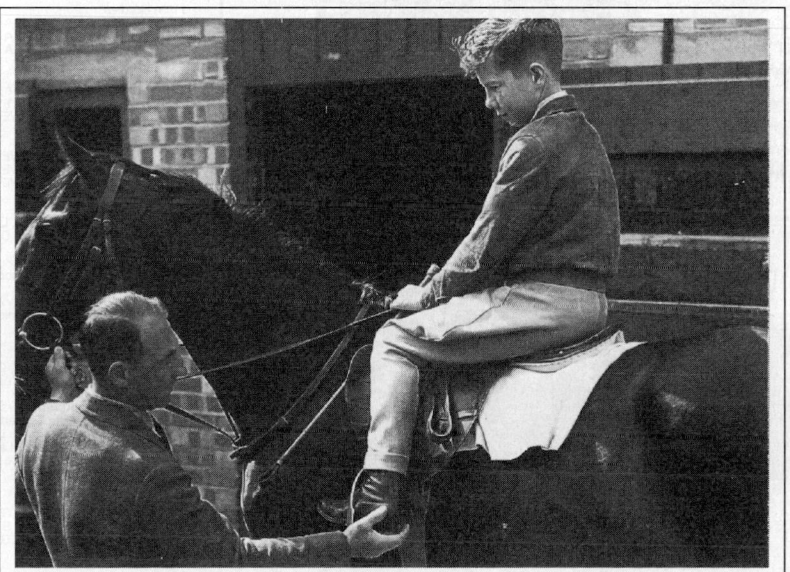

Twelve-year-old Lester Piggott is Britain's youngest race-winner.

Jerusalem attack breaches truce

Aug 15. Two Jewish soldiers were killed and three wounded in the worst fighting in Jerusalem since the truce was agreed on July 17. Cannon and machine-guns were used in the dawn attack which Israel Army HQ said was a "general assault" by Arab troops.

The Arabs claimed there had been a heavy Jewish attack on their outposts in the Bab el Wad area on the Jerusalem-Tel Aviv highway. However it started, the battle raged for about an hour from a point on the Bethlehem highway, south of the city to Beith Israel in the northern sector.

Only three days ago Count Bernadotte, the United Nations mediator, warned both sides that unless the shooting in the Holy City stopped he would invoke Security Council action. United Nations observers, one of whom was injured today, are investigating the origins of, and responsibility for, the start of the battle (→21).

"Comprehensive" school is planned

Aug 23. A new type of school called a "comprehensive" was announced today by Middlesex County Council. Three of the new schools, modelled on American high schools, will take pupils next month in Hillingdon and Potters Bar.

Unlike the schools established under the 1944 Education Act – the grammar, secondary modern and technical schools – entry to these comprehensive schools will not be based on examinations at the age of 11. A spokesman for Middlesex County Council said: "At 11 a child may not have an examination temperament, and may fail dismally. That failure may penalise him for a long time, not only in denying him grammar school and university education but in shattering his confidence."

Other councils are also planning comprehensive schools, notably London, and the Ministry of Education has asked for a report on the experiment. One disadvantage may be the size – up to 2,000 pupils – being planned. ▷

1948 London

The austerity Olympics

Aug 14. Twelve years and two abandoned Olympic Games after Hitler's 1936 Nazi propaganda spectacular in Berlin, the London Olympics, held amid the strictures of post-war austerity, have proved inexpensive, unpretentious and successful, despite the absence of three major sporting powers – Germany, the Soviet Union and Japan.

Without the resources to build new stadiums, the organisers used traditional venues: rowing was contested at Henley, shooting at Bisley, yachting at Cowes. But Wembley, with a new cinder track in the Stadium and the Empire Pool nearby, provided the main focus.

The war had clearly upset the balance of power in the major men's competitions. The Americans, with a total of 38 golds, dominated the track and field (none more so than the astonishingly mature Bob Mathias, who won the gruelling decathlon at the age of only 17). Britain failed to win an athletics gold medal for the first time since 1904 – her three golds came in rowing (two) and yachting. And for the first time for 40 years, no Finn won a track race.

The greatest impact came from countries new to any real Olympic tradition. Czechoslovakia provided the ungainly, agonised gait of the outsider, Emil Zatopek, who won the 10,000 metres by almost a full lap, setting a new record, and came within a whisker of taking the 5,000 metres as well; Jamaica supplied the superb long-striding grace of Arthur Wint in the 400 metres.

But most memorable of all, was Fanny Blankers-Koen, a 30-year-old Dutch housewife and mother, who arrived in London as world-record holder in the high jump and the long jump. She competed in neither; instead she won four track events – 100 metres, 200 metres, 80 metres hurdles and the 4x100 metres relay – to emerge as the personality of the Games (→16).

THE IMPORTANT THING IN
THE OLYMPIC GAMES IS NOT
WINNING BUT TAKING PART.
THE ESSENTIAL THING IN
LIFE IS NOT CONQUERING
BUT FIGHTING WELL.
BARON de COUBERTIN

The torch-bearer waits to light the Olympic flame and launch the Games.

Finish of the final of the men's 400 metres: Arthur Wint (Jamaica) is the winner.

Men Athletics

Event / Place	Name	Country	Result
100m			
1.	Harrison Dillard	USA	=*10.3
2.	Norwood Ewell	USA	10.4
3.	Lloyd LaBeach	PAN	10.4
200m			
1.	Melvin Patton	USA	21.1
2.	Norwood Ewell	USA	21.1
3.	Lloyd LaBeach	PAN	21.2
400m			
1.	Arthur Wint	JAM	46.2
2.	Herbert McKenley	JAM	46.4
3.	Malvin Whitfield	USA	46.9
800m			
1.	Malvin Whitfield	USA	*1:49.2
2.	Arthur Wint	JAM	1:49.5
3.	Marcel Hansenne	FRA	1:49.8
1500m			
1.	Henry Eriksson	SWE	3:49.8
2.	Lennart Strand	SWE	3:50.4
3.	Willem Slijkhuis	NETH	3:50.4
5000m			
1.	Gaston Reiff	BEL	*14:17.6
2.	Emil Zátopek	TCH	14:17.8
3.	Willem Slijkhuis	NETH	14:26.8
10,000m			
1.	Emil Zátopek	TCH	*29:59.6
2.	Alain Mimoun	FRA	30:47.4
3.	Bertil Albertsson	SWE	30:53.6
Marathon			
1.	Delfo Cabrera	ARG	2:34:51.6
2.	Thomas Richards	GBR	2:35:07.6
3.	Etienne Gailly	BEL	2:35:33.6
110m Hurdles			
1.	William Porter	USA	*13.9
2.	Clyde Scott	USA	14.1
3.	Graig Dixon	USA	14.1
400m Hurdles			
1.	Roy Cochran	USA	*51.1
2.	Duncan White	CEY	51.8
3.	Rune Larsson	SWE	52.2
3000m Steeplechase			
1.	Thore Sjöstrand	SWE	9:04.6
2.	Erik Elmsäter	SWE	9:08.2
3.	Gote Hagstrom	SWE	9:11.3

4x100m Relay
1. USA 40.6 (Norwood Ewell, Lorenzo Wright, Harrison Dillard, Melvin Patton)
2. GBR 41.3 (John Archer, John Gregory, Alistair McCorquodale, Ken Jones)
3. ITA 41.5 (Michele Tito, Enrico Perucconi, Antonio Siddi, Carlo Monti)

4x400m Relay
1. USA 3:10.4 (Arthur Harnden, Clifford Bourland, Roy Cochran, Malvin Whitfield)
2. FRA 3:14.8 (Jean Kerebel, Francis Schewetta, Robert Chef d'Hôtel, Jacques Lunis)
3. SWE 3:16.0 (Kurt Lundkvist, Lars Wolfbrandt, Folke Alnevik, Rune Larsson)

Event / Place	Name	Country	Result
50km Walk			
1.	John Ljunggren	SWE	4:41.52
2.	Godel Gaston	SUI	4:48.17
3.	Tebbs Lloyd-Johnson	GBR	4:48.31
10km Walk			
1.	John Mikaelsson	SWE	45:13.2
2.	Ingemar Johansson	SWE	45:43.8
3.	Fritz Schwab	SUI	46:00.2
High Jump			
1.	John Winter	AUS	1.
2.	Björn Paulson	NOR	1.
3.	George Stanich	USA	1.
Pole Vault			
1.	Guinn Smith	USA	4.
2.	Erkki Kataja	FIN	4.
3.	Robert Richards	USA	4.
Long Jump			
1.	Willie Steele	USA	7.8
2.	Thomas Bruce	AUS	7.5
3.	Herbert Douglas	USA	7.5
Triple Jump			
1.	Ame Ahman	SWE	15.
2.	George Avery	AUS	15.3
3.	Ruhi Sarialp	TUR	15.0
Shotput			
1.	Wilbur Thompson	USA	*17.
2.	Francis James Delaney	USA	16.
3.	James Fuchs	USA	16.
Discus Throw			
1.	Adolfo Consolini	ITA	*52.
2.	Giuseppe Tosi	ITA	51.
3.	Fortune Gordien	USA	50
Hammer Throw			
1.	Imre Németh	HUN	56
2.	Ivan Gubijan	YUG	54
3.	Robert Bennett	USA	53
Javelin			
1.	Tapio Rautavaara	FIN	69
2.	Steve Seymour	USA	67
3.	József Várszegi	HUN	67
Decathlon			
1.	Robert Mathias	USA	71
2.	Ignace Heinrich	FRA	69
3.	Floyd Simmons	USA	69

Women Athletics

Event / Place	Name	Country	Result
100m			
1.	Francina Blankers-Koen	NETH	1
2.	Dorothy Manley	GBR	1
3.	Shirley Strickland	AUS	1
200m			
1.	Francina Blankers-Koen	NETH	2
2.	Audrey Williamson	GBR	2
3.	Audrey Patterson	USA	2
80m Hurdles			
1.	Francina Blankers-Koen	NETH	*1
2.	Maureen Gardner	GBR	1
3.	Shirley Strickland	AUS	1

4x100m Relay
1. NETH 47.5 (Xenia Stad de Jong, Jeannette Witziers-Timmer, Gerda van der Kade-Koudijs, Francina Blankers-Koen)
2. AUS 47.6 (Shirley Strickland, June Maston, Betty McKinnon, Joyce King)
3. CAN 47.8 (Viola Myers, Nancy MacKay, Diane Foster, Patricia Jones)

Event / Place	Name	Country	Result
High Jump			
1.	Alice Coachman	USA	*1
2.	Dorothy Tyler	GBR	*1
3.	Micheline Ostermeyer	FRA	1
Long Jump			
1.	Olga Gyarmati	HUN	5.
2.	Noëmi Simonetto De Portela	ARG	5
3.	Ann-Britt Leyman	SWE	5.
Shotput			
1.	Micheline Ostermeyer	FRA	13
2.	Amelia Piccinini	ITA	13.
3.	Ine Schäffer	AUT	13
Discus			
1.	Micheline Ostermeyer	FRA	41
2.	Edera Cordiale-Gentile	ITA	41
3.	Jacqueline Mazeas	FRA	40
Javelin			
1.	Herma Bauma	AUT	45
2.	Kaisa Parviainen	FIN	43
3.	Lily Carlstedt	DEN	42

Men Swimming

Event / Place	Name	Country	Result
100m Freestyle			
1.	Walter Ris	USA	*5
2.	Alan Ford	USA	5
3.	Géza Kádas	HUN	5
400m Freestyle			
1.	William Smith	USA	*4:4
2.	James McLane	USA	4:4
3.	John Marshall	AUS	4:4
1500m Freestyle			
1.	James McLane	USA	19:1
2.	John Marshall	AUS	19:3
3.	Gyorgy Mitró	HUN	19:4
100m Backstroke			
1.	Allen Stack	USA	1:
2.	Robert Cowell	USA	1:
3.	George Vallerey	FRA	1:07
200m Breaststroke			
1.	Joseph Verdeur	USA	*2:3
2.	Keith Carter	USA	2:4
3.	Robert Sohl	USA	2:4

4x200m Freestyle Relay
1. USA ** 8:46.0 (Walter Ris, James McLane, Wallace Wolf, William Smith)
2. HUN 8:48.4 (Elemér Szathmáry, György Mitró, Irme Nyéki, Géza Kádas)
3. FRA 9:08.0 (Joseph Bernardo, Henri Padou, René Cornu, Alexandre Jany)

1948 London

Springboard Diving
Bruce Harlan USA 163.64
Miller Anderson USA 157.29
Samuel Lee USA 145.52

Platform Diving
Samuel Lee USA 130.05
Bruce Harlan USA 122.30
Joaquin Capilla Perez MEX 113.52

Water Polo

Italy
Hungary
Netherlands

Women Swimming

100m Freestyle
Greta Andersen DEN 1:06.3
Ann Curtis USA 1:06.5
Marie-Louise Vaessen NETH 1:07.6

400m Freestyle
Ann Curtis USA *5:17.8
Karen-Margrete Harup DEN 5:21.2
Catherine Gibson GBR 5:22.5

200m Breaststroke
Petronella van Vliet NETH 2:57.2
Beatrice Lyons AUS 2:57.7
Eva Novák HUN 3:00.2

100m Backstroke
Karen-Margrete Harup DEN *1:14.4
Suzanne Zimmerman USA 1:16.0
Judy Davies AUS 1:16.7

4x100m Freestyle Relay
USA *4:29.2 (Marie Corridon, Thelma Kalama, Brenda Helser, Ann Curtis)
DEN 4:29.6 (Eva Riise, Karen-Margrete Harup, Greta Andersen, Fritze Carstensen)
NETH 4:31.6 (Irma Schumacher, Margot Marsman, Marie-Louise Vaessen, Johanna Termeulen)

Springboard Diving
Victoria Draves USA 108.74
Zoe Ann Olsen USA 108.23
Patricia Elsener USA 101.30

Platform Diving
Victoria Draves USA 68.87
Patricia Elsener USA 66.28
Birte Christoffersen DEN 66.04

Boxing

Flyweight
Pascual Perez ARG
Spartaco Bandinelli ITA
Soo-Ann Han KOR

Bantamweight
Tibor Csik HUN
Giovanni Battista Zuddas ITA
Juan Venegas PUR

Featherweight
Ernesto Formenti ITA
Dennis Shephard SAF
Aleksy Antkiewicz POL

Lightweight
Gerald Dreyer SAF
Joseph Vissers BEL
Svend Wad DEN

Welterweight
Julius Torma TCH
Horace Herring USA
Alessandro D'Ottavio ITA

Middleweight
László Papp HUN
John Wright GBR
Ivano Fontana ITA

Light Heavyweight
George Hunter HUN
Donald Scott GBR
Maurio Cia ARG

Heavyweight
Rafael Iglesias ARG
Gunnar Nilsson SWE
John Arthur SAF

Greco Roman Wrestling

Flyweight
Pietro Lombardi ITA
Kenan Olcay TUR
Reino Kangasmaki FIN

Bantamweight
Kurt Pettersén SWE
Ali Mahmoud Hassan EGY
Halil Kaya TUR

Featherweight
Mehmet Oktav TUR
Olle Anderberg SWE
Ferene Tóth HUN

Lightweight
Gustaf Freij SWE
Aage Eriksen NOR
Károly Ferencz HUN

Welterweight
Gosta Andersson SWE
Miklós Szilvási HUN
Henrik Hansen DEN

Middleweight
Axel Gronberg SWE
Muhlis Tayfur TUR
Ercole Gallegati ITA

Light Heavyweight
1. Karl-Erik Nilsson SWE
2. Kaelpo Grondahl FIN
3. Ibrahim Orabi EGY

Heavyweight
1. Ahmet Kirecci TUR
2. Tor Nilsson SWE
3. Guido Fantoni ITA

Freestyle Wrestling

Flyweight
1. Lennart Viitala FIN
2. Halit Balamir TUR
3. Thure Johansson SWE

Bantamweight
1. Nasuh Akar TUR
2. Gerald Leeman USA
3. Charles Kouyos FRA

Featherweight
1. Gazanfer Bilge TUR
2. Ivan Sjolun SWE
3. Adolf Müller SUI

Lightweight
1. Celal Atik TUR
2. Gosta Frändfors SWE
3. Hermann Baumann SUI

Welterweight
1. Yasar Dogu TUR
2. Richard Garrard AUS
3. Leland Merrill USA

Middleweight
1. Glen Brand USA
2. Adil Candemir TUR
3. Erik Lindén SWE

Light Heavyweight
1. Henri Wittenberg USA
2. Fritz Stöckli SUI
3. Bengt Fahlkvist SWE

Heavyweight
1. Gyula Bóbis HUN
2. Bertil Antonsson SWE
3. Joseph Armstrong AUS

Men Fencing

Foil Individual
1. Jehan Buhan FRA
2. Christian d'Oriola FRA
3. Lajos Maszlay HUN

Foil Team
1. France
2. Italy
3. Belgium

Epée Individual
1. Luigi Cantone ITA
2. Oswald Zappelli SUI
3. Edoardo Mangiarotti ITA

Epée Team
1. France
2. Italy
3. Sweden

Sabre Individual
1. Aladár Gerevich HUN
2. Vincenzo Pinton ITA
3. Pál Kovács HUN

Sabre Team
1. Hungary
2. Italy
3. USA

Women Fencing

Foil Individual
1. Ilona Elek HUN
2. Karen Lachmann DEN
3. Ellen Muller-Preis AUT

Modern Pentathlon

1. William Grut SWE
2. George Moore USA
3. Gosta Gardin SWE

Men Canoeing

Kayak-1 1000m
1. Gert Fredriksson SWE 4:33.2
2. Johan Frederik Kobberup DEN 4:39.9
3. Henri Eberhardt FRA 4:41.4

Kayak-2 1000m
1. Sweden 4:07.3
2. Denmark 4:07.5
3. Finland 4:08.7

Kayak-1 10,000m
1. Gert Fredriksson SWE 50:47.7
2. Kurt Wires FIN 51:18.2
3. Eivind Skabo NOR 51:35.4

Kayak-2 10,000m
1. Sweden 46:09.4
2. Norway 46:44.8
3. Finland 46:48.2

Canadian-1 1000m
1. Josef Holecek TCH 5:42.0
2. Douglas Bennet CAN 5:53.3
3. Robert Boutigny FRA 5:55.9

Canadian-2 1000m
1. Czechoslovakia 5:07.1
2. USA 5:08.2
3. France 5:15.2

Canadian-1 10,000m
1. Frantisek Capek TCH 1:02:05.2
2. Frank Havens USA 1:02:40.4
3. Norman Lane CAN 1:04:35.3

Canadian-2 10,000m
1. USA 55:55.4
2. Czechoslovakia 57:38.5
3. France 58:00.8

Women Canoeing

Kayak-1 500m
1. Karen Hoff DEN 2:31.9
2. Alida v. d. Anker Doedans NETH 2:32.8
3. Fritzi Schwingl AUT 2:32.9

Rowing

Single Sculls
1. Mervyn Wood AUS 7:24.4
2. Eduardo Risso URU 7:38.2
3. Romolo Catasta ITA 7:51.4

Double Sculls
1. Great Britain 6:51.3
2. Denmark 6:55.3
3. Uruguay 7:12.4

Coxless Pairs
1. Great Britain 7:21.1
2. Switzerland 7:23.0
3. Italy 7:31.5

Coxed Pairs
1. Denmark 8:00.5
2. Italy 8:12.2
3. Hungary 8:25.2

Coxless Fours
1. Italy 6:39.0
2. Denmark 6:43.5
3. USA 6:47.7

Coxed Fours
1. USA 6:50.3
2. Switzerland 6:53.3
3. Denmark 6:58.6

Eights
1. USA 5:56.7
2. Great Britain 6:06.9
3. Norway 6:10.3

Yachting

Finn Class
1. Paul Elvstrom DEN 5543
2. Ralph Evans USA 5408
3. Jacobus Hermanus de Jong NETH 5204

Star Class
1. USA 5828
2. Cuba 4949
3. Netherlands 4731

Dragon Class
1. Norway 4746
2. Sweden 4621
3. Denmark 4223

6m Class
1. USA 5472
2. Argentina 5120
3. Sweden 4033

Swallow
1. Great Britain 5625
2. Portugal 5579
3. USA 4352

Cycling

Road Race Individual
1. José Beyaert FRA 5:18:12.6
2. Gerardus Petrus Voorting NETH 5:18:16.2
3. Lode Wouters BEL 5:18:16.2

Team Time Trial
1. Belgium 15:58:17.4
2. Great Britain 16:03:31.6
3. France 16:08:19.4

1000m Time Trial
1. Jacques Dupont FRA 1:13.5
2. Pierre Nihant BEL 1:14.5
3. Thomas Godwin GBR 1:15.0

Sprint 1000m
1. Mario Ghella ITA 12.0
2. Reginald Harris GBR
3. Axel Schandorff DEN

Tandem 2000m
1. Italy 11.6
2. Great Britain
3. France

Team Pursuit 4000m
1. France 4:57.8
2. Italy 5:36.7
3. Great Britain 5:55.8

Equestrian Sports

Three-Day Event Individual
1. Bernard Chevallier FRA +4
2. Frank Henry USA -21
3. Robert Selfelt SWE -25

Three-Day Event Team
1. USA -161.50
2. Sweden -165.00
3. Mexico -305.25

Dressage Individual
1. Hans Moser SUI 492.5
2. André Jousscaume FRA 480.0
3. Gustaf-Adolf Bolternstern Jr SWE 477.5

Dressage Team
1. France 1269.0
2. USA 1256.0
3. Portugal 1182.0

Grand Prix Jumping Individual
1. Humberto Mariles Cortés MEX -6.25
2. Rubén Uriza MEX -8
3. Jean-François D'Orgeix FRA -8

Grand Prix Jumping Team
1. Mexico -34.25
2. Spain -56.50
3. Great Britain -67.00

Shooting

Free Rifle, 3 Positions
1. Emil Grünig SUI 1120
2. Pauli Janhonen FIN 1114
3. Willy Rogeberg NOR 1112

Small Bore Rifle Prone
1. Arthur Cook USA ** 599/43
2. Walter Tomsen USA ** 599/42
3. Jonas Jonsson SWE 597/44

Rapid Fire Pistol
1. Károly Takács HUN ** 580
2. Carlos Enrique Diaz Sáenz Valiente ARG 571
3. Sven Lundqvist SWE 569

Free Pistol, 50m
1. Edwin Vasquez Cam PER 545
2. Rudolf Schnyder SUI 539/60/21
3. Torsten Ullman SWE 539/60/16

Men Gymnastics

All-around Individual
1. Veikko Huhtanen FIN 229.70
2. Walter Lehmann SUI 229.00
3. Paavo Aaltonen FIN 228.80

Combined Exercises Team
1. Finland 1358.30
2. Switzerland 1356.70
3. Hungary 1330.85

Parallel Bars
1. Michael Reusch SUI 19.75
2. Veikko Huhtanen FIN 19.65
3. Josef Stalder SUI 19.55
3. Christian Kipfer SUI 19.55

Floor Exercises
1. Ferenc Pataki HUN 19.35
2. János Mogyorósi-Klencs HUN 19.20
3. Zdenek Ruzicka TCH 19.05

Long Horse Vault
1. Paavo Aaltonen FIN 19.55
2. Olavi Rovo FIN 19.50
3. János Mogyorósi-Klencs HUN 19.25
3. Ferenc Pataki HUN 19.25
3. Leo Sotornik TCH 19.25

Side Horse
1. Veikko Huhtanen FIN 19.35
1. Paavo Aaltonen FIN 19.35
1. Heikki Savolainen FIN 19.35

Horizontal Bar
1. Josef Stalder SUI 19.85
2. Walter Lehmann SUI 19.70
3. Veikko Huhtanen FIN 19.60

Rings
1. Karl Frei SUI 19.80
2. Michael Reusch SUI 19.55
3. Zdenek Ruzicka TCH 19.25

Women Gymnastics

Combined Exercises Team
1. Czechoslovakia 445.45
2. Hungary 440.55
3. USA 422.63

Basketball

1. USA
2. France
3. Brazil

Football

1. Sweden
2. Yugoslavia
3. Denmark

Hockey

1. India
2. Great Britain
3. Netherlands

(Key to symbols and abbreviations p. 1456)

The Dutch Francina Blankers-Koen wins the 80m Hurdles.

Weightlifting

		2 Arm Press	2 Arm Snatch	2 Arm Clean and Jerk	Total
Bantamweight					
1. Joseph di Pietro	USA	*105.0	90.0	112.5	** 307.5
2. Julian Creus	GBR	82.5	*95.0	120.0	297.5
3. Richard Tom	USA	87.5	90.0	117.5	295.0
Featherweight					
1. Mahmoud Fayad	EGY	02.5	** 105.0	** 135.0	** 332.5
2. Rodney Wilkes	TRI	97.5	97.5	122.5	317.5
3. Jaffar Salmasi	IRN	*100.0	97.5	115.0	312.5
Lightweight					
1. Ibrahim Hassan Shams	EGY	97.5	*115.0	*147.5	*360.0
2. Appia Hamouda	EGY	105.0	110.0	145.0	*360.0
3. James Halliday	GBR	90.0	110.0	140.0	340.0
Middleweight					
1. Frank Spellman	USA	117.5	120.0	152.5	*390.0
2. Peter George	USA	105.0	*122.5	*155.0	382.5
3. Sung-Jip Kim	KOR	*122.5	112.5	145.0	380.0
Light Heavyweight					
1. Stanley Stanczyk	USA	*130.0	*130.0	*157.5	*417.5
2. Harold Sakata	USA	110.0	117.5	152.5	380.0
3. Gosta Magnusson	SWE	110.0	120.0	145.0	375.0
Heavyweight					
1. John Davis	USA	*137.5	*137.5	** 177.5	** 452.5
2. Norbert Schemansky	USA	122.5	132.5	170.0	425.0
3. Abraham Charité	NETH	127.5	125.0	160.0	412.5

1948

SEPTEMBER

Su	Mo	Tu	We	Th	Fr	Sa
			1	2	3	4
5	6	7	8	9	10	11
12	13	14	15	16	17	18
19	20	21	22	23	24	25
26	27	28	29	30		

1. China: Communist radio announces the creation of a North China People's Government (→30/10).

3. Warsaw: Communist leader Wladyslaw Gomulka is dismissed for advocating independence from Moscow.

4. Amsterdam: Queen Wilhelmina abdicates in favour of her daughter Juliana.

8. Oxford: An anonymous French shipowner has offered £1.5 million to found St. Anthony's College.

10. UK: Don Bradman winds up his first-class cricket career, having made centuries in his last three innings.

11. Karachi: Governor-General Jinnah dies of heart failure.

13. London: The government announces pay rises for student nurses; starting pay will rise from £145 to £200 (→1/11).

14. Washington: Scientists warn that the world is outgrowing its food supply.

17. Jerusalem: UN mediator Count Folke Bernadotte dies in a gun attack on his car by Jewish terrorists (→18).

18. Israel: 200 terrorist suspects are rounded up in the wake of Bernadotte's murder (→20).

19. Indonesia: Sukarno declares martial law after a Communist revolt in Madiun.

20. Israel: The Stern Gang terror group is outlawed (→21).

21. Israel: Irgun agrees to disband after an Israeli government ultimatum (→15/10).

23. London: For the second session running, peers reject the Parliament Bill, aimed at cutting their delaying powers.

27. Brussels: Western defence ministers agree to create a defence alliance (→26/10).

DEATHS

3. Czech statesman Eduard Benes, president 1935-38, 1940-48 (*28/5/1884).

11. Pakistani statesman Mohammed Ali Jinnah, first Governor-General of Pakistan (*25/12/1876).

Allies fly 895 planes a day into Berlin

Cargo planes deliver more of the vital supplies upon which Berlin depends.

Sept 18. The Allied airlift into Berlin set up a new record today, by flying in 7,000 tons of supplies in defiance of the three-month old Russian blockade.

British and American aircraft flew through fog, high winds and rain and made 895 flights into the city over a 24-hour period, carrying both food and fuel to the Allied sectors of the city. US pilots put on a special effort to celebrate Air Forces Day, flying in 651 times and carrying 5,572 tons of coal.

The record-breaking flights by Dakotas, Globemasters and York aircraft show the Allied determination to keep the city alive. Enough supplies are getting through to keep Berlin going, and it is thought likely the Russians will have to admit defeat soon (→18/10).

Effects of A-bomb worse than thought

Sept 29. Contamination from the Bikini atom bomb tests was far more difficult to eradicate than anyone anticipated, according to a book just published by Dr David Bradley, a scientist who took part. It was, says Bradley, the second underwater test on July 25, 1946, that caused most trouble.

These were some of its effects: ships were so heavily contaminated that they had to remain in the test area instead of returning to base; the thin coating of radioactive debris on external surfaces was almost impossible to remove; the highly dangerous element plutonium, produced in the blast, though present in the contamination, was undetectable by normal methods.

"I can think of no fact demonstrated by the Bikini tests which is more important in its widest implications than this difficulty of ridding habitable surfaces of our world of contaminating fission products", warns Bradley (→1/10).

India crushes rebel kingdom

Sept 17. The Nizam of Hyderabad surrendered today, after his forces had stoutly resisted an overwhelming assault by the Indian army for five days. The Army, supported by tanks and Spitfire fighter-bombers, made a three-pronged attack, seeking to occupy Hyderabad city and the nearby military cantonment of Secunderabad.

The crisis developed when the Moslem ruler of this largely Hindu state resisted India's warning that its troops would march in if the Nizam, who has not complied with demands that he should accede to India, failed to allow Indian troops to occupy Secunderabad.

Another Indian demand was the disbanding of the Razakars, the Moslem defence volunteers. The Nizam has now complied and in doing so he has signalled the end of Moslem dominance of his state.

The Indian troops, now on the outskirts of Hyderabad, are expected to make a formal entry into the capital tomorrow. The future of the Nizam is uncertain.

North Korea proclaims itself a republic

Sept 9. North Korea proclaimed its independence today with its leader, President Kim Il Sung, committed to reuniting the Korean peninsula, whether through force of arms or by negotiations. The new Communist state, formally known as the Democratic People's Republic of Korea, comprises the area occupied by Red Army troops in the final days of World War II, with its capital in Pyongyang. The American-occupied southern half of the peninsula has become the Republic of Korea led by Syngman Rhee. Both Presidents claim to be the rightful rulers of all of Korea, but have yet to hold free elections (→21/10).

It's playtime for all the family at every Butlin's Holiday Camp.

1948

OCTOBER

Su	Mo	Tu	We	Th	Fr	Sa
					1	2
3	4	5	6	7	8	9
10	11	12	13	14	15	16
17	18	19	20	21	22	23
24	25	26	27	28	29	30
31						

1. Chicago: The US Atomic Energy Commission says plutonium production is now on a "factory-size scale" (→2).

2. Moscow: The USSR drops its demand for a ban on atomic weapons (→15/12).

4. London: Publication of "The Gathering Storm", first volume of Churchill's history of the Second World War.

7. New York: The US vetoes Spain's entry to the UN (→8).

8. London: John Belcher MP is named in connection with alleged bribery at the Board of Trade (→9/12).

8. New York: Norway and Cuba are elected to the UN Security Council (→10/12).

11. London: The BBC broadcasts from Downing Street for the first time.

15. Israel: Israeli troops begin fighting again.→

18. Berlin: The Russians arm the East Berlin "Volkspolizei" (People's Police) as unrest grows against Soviet occupation (→16/11).

21. UK: 34 out of 40 aboard a KLM airliner die when it crashes in Ayrshire.

21. Seoul: General MacArthur arrives in Korea.

22. London: The communique ending Commonwealth premiers' talks omits "British" before "Commonwealth".

23. Rome: Pope Pius XII urges international control of Jerusalem.→

26. London: The King leads the first State Opening of Parliament since 1938 (→14/11).

26. Paris: Major Western powers agree the principles of a North Atlantic defence pact.

29. London: The Iron and Steel Bill is published, which would nationalise 107 iron and steel firms.

30. China: Chiang Kai-shek recognises the loss of Manchuria to the Communists.→

DEATH

24. Austrian composer Franz Lehar (*30/4/1870).

Chiang on the run despite massive US aid

Soldiers of Chiang's 4th army remain loyal despite his many defeats.

Oct 30. After his shattering defeat in Manchuria, the Chinese leader, Marshal Chiang Kai-shek, told his war council in Nanking today that the entire civil war with the Communists will be decided in the next three months.

Chiang's Nationalist armies are retreating south and hoping to make a stand below the Great Wall. They have been badly mauled in two weeks of fighting, with the loss of some 250,000 men, all trained and equipped by the United States.

Street-fighting is now going on in the provincial capital, Mukden, where the radio has been appealing for airliners to be sent to the city to evacuate officials and their families. Soon after this broadcast, the transmission suddenly broke off with the word: "Good-bye."

When the war with Japan ended three years ago, the Communists emerged from their remote hideouts in Yenan with a million-strong army, led by a little-known, former school teacher, Mao Tse-tung. In spite of massive aid from the US, Chiang has steadily lost ground to Mao's forces. If the Communists were to win, Chiang says, "it would be the beginning of another world catastrophe" (→9/11).

Sanctions called for by UN in Palestine

Oct 28. The United Nations Security Council was today asked for the first time to consider sanctions if Jewish and Arab forces do not withdraw to the agreed lines in the Negeb. The latest move is an effort to stop the fierce fighting which has continued, despite the pleas of the UN acting mediator to both sides to pull back to their positions before the fighting.

Dr Ralph Bunche, the acting mediator, reported that although the Negeb was now calm, the positions of the opposing forces threatened an outbreak of further fighting unless the truce lines were quickly re-established.

Egypt has begun to withdraw her troops from Southern Palestine, but as the Egyptians have moved out the Israelis have moved in. Today they occupied Isdud, a coastal town 20 miles south of Tel Aviv. According to the Israeli statement the local inhabitants came out carrying white flags and asking the Israeli forces to enter and take them under their protection.

Sanctions would be applied under Article 41 of the UN Charter which covers economic measures, the partial interruption of communications and the severing of diplomatic links, but not the use of armed forces.

Motor show models look good, but buyers may have to wait

Oct 27. The Motor Show that opens today at Earls Court is the first since the war to match the scale of pre-war exhibitions. It brings together American, French and Italian models, although with 32 stands, British car firms are the most numerous. However the export drive makes early delivery to British customers unlikely.

Morris and Austin will both have new models, though these will not reflect the two companies' recent pooling of ideas and resources to cut costs. Morris has a neat new Minor and two new Wolseleys.

Progress in styling is general this year. Besides the Minor there is a new Allard saloon with striking looks. Other eye-catching designs are to be found among the Daimlers and Rolls-Royces (→4/12).

The Motor Show displays plenty of new models, but most are for export.

1948

NOVEMBER

Su	Mo	Tu	We	Th	Fr	Sa
	1	2	3	4	5	6
7	8	9	10	11	12	13
14	15	16	17	18	19	20
21	22	23	24	25	26	27
28	29	30				

1. London: The government says jam rationing will end on December 5 (→4).

2. London: Publication of the Special Roads Bill, which plans 1,000 miles of "motorways".

3. US: The state of Kansas ends prohibition after 68 years.

5. US: The new M-46 tank is to be called the "Patton" after the famous wartime general.

9. China: The Communists cross the Great Wall (→17).

12. Tokyo: Tojo and 24 co-defendants are convicted of war crimes (→23/12).

14. London: Princess Elizabeth gives birth to a son (→23).

16. US: Truman refuses four-power talks on Berlin until the USSR lifts its blockade (→30).

17. Washington: The US agrees to boost its Marine force at Tsingtao, as requested by Chiang Kai-shek.

17. Dublin: The Dail gives a first reading to the Republic of Ireland Bill, under which Eire will leave the Commonwealth (→14/4/49).

23. London: The King cancels an Australian tour; he is suffering from a blood clot (→29).

26. London: Britain proposes a "Council of Europe".

28. Hungary: 1,000 political refugees are reported to be fleeing the country each month (→26/12).

29. London: The King's condition improves; he needs rest, not surgery (→15/12).

30. Berlin: The German Communist Party instals a city government in the Soviet Sector.

30. London: The worst fog in years leaves four dead in three train crashes; buses and police cars are taken off the road.

BIRTH

14. British Prince Charles Philip Arthur George, Prince of Wales.

Truman beats US polls

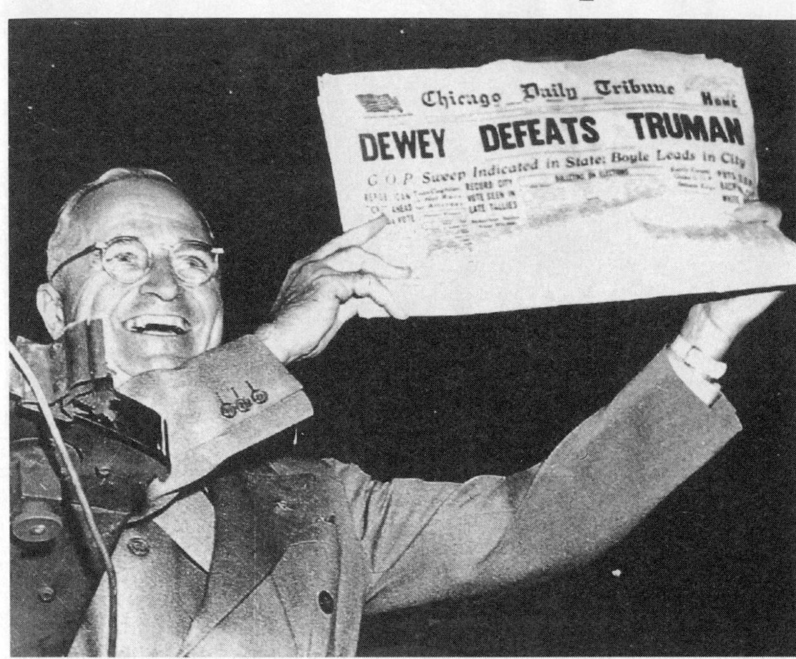

Never believe all you read in the papers: Truman is the next President.

Nov 3. The most astonishing 16 hours in American electoral history ended just after eleven o'clock this morning when the Republican favourite, Thomas E. Dewey conceded the election to President Harry S. Truman. Not only was the Presidency won with a very respectable two million majority of the popular vote, but the Democrats have been returned with majorities in both Houses of Congress.

All the pollsters and all the pundits had been forecasting a massive win for Dewey. Dr Gallup was on the radio last night, tying himself up in knots trying to explain why his poll was so wrong. The Washington Post, whose early edition screamed "Mounting Dewey vote indicates victory", has invited all the pundits and the President to dinner with humble pie on the menu. The Chicago Tribune headlined one edition "Dewey defeats Truman" and four hours later had to admit he had even been beaten in their own state of Michigan.

Government eases industrial red tape

Nov 4. The Government has begun to lift controls which have become increasingly unpopular with British industry. Harold Wilson, the President of the Board of Trade, announced the reduction of restrictions on the manufacture of a variety of articles including cutlery, fertilisers, fountain pens, jewellery, textile machinery, printing and soap-making equipment.

Meanwhile, the Ministry of Supply has relaxed their controls on 75 separate items, including machinery for bottling and capping, cocoa and confectionery, feed for livestock, abattoirs and bacon factories.

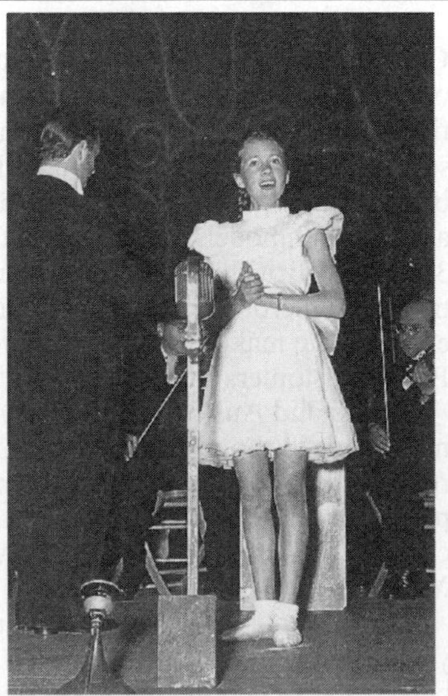

Young Julie Andrews sings for the Queen – a new star is born.

1948

DECEMBER

Su	Mo	Tu	We	Th	Fr	Sa
			1	2	3	4
5	6	7	8	9	10	11
12	13	14	15	16	17	18
19	20	21	22	23	24	25
26	27	28	29	30	31	

1. London: MPs approve a bill increasing National Service from 12 to 18 months.

4. UK: Leading car makers Austin, Morris, Ford, Rootes, Standard and Vauxhall agree to standardise motor parts.

6. Washington: Chambers tells the Un-American Committee Alger Hiss passed secrets to him for the USSR (→15).

9. London: John Belcher, MP, parliamentary secretary at the Board of Trade, will resign as a bribery probe continues.

10. New York: The UN Assembly adopts a declaration of human rights.

10. Stockholm: Nobel Prizes go to Lord Patrick Blackett (UK, Physics); Arne Tiselius (Sweden, Chemistry); Paul Muller (Switzerland, Medicine) and T. S. Eliot (UK, Literature). No Peace Prize.

15. Washington: Hiss is indicted for perjury.

15. France: The first French atomic reactor begins operation at Fort de Chatillon.

16. Indochina: France grants Cambodia independence.

19. Indonesia: Dutch airborne troops seize Jogjakarta and hold leading members of Sukarno's regime (→25).

25. Indonesia: The Dutch take Madiun (→1/1/49).

26. Budapest: Catholic primate Jozsef Mindszenty is held for "plotting against the government" (→9/2/49).

BIRTH

27. French actor Gerard Depardieu.

HITS OF 1948

It's Magic.

On a slow boat to China.

QUOTE OF THE YEAR

"I know of no other man in our time, or indeed in recent history, who so convincingly demonstrated the power of the spirit over material things."

Sir Stafford Cripps, of Gandhi, assassinated in 1948.

Princess Elizabeth christens her first son

Dec 15. The first-born child of Princess Elizabeth and the Duke of Edinburgh was christened today. He was named Charles Phillip Arthur George, and he will be known as Prince Charles. For his christening he wore a beautiful silk and lace robe, a family heirloom which had also been worn by his mother.

The ceremony was followed by a family lunch, and then, led by Queen Mary, they looked through Queen Victoria's photograph albums to decide whom the new Prince most resembles. Queen Mary herself was quite sure that the closest resemblance was to Prince Albert, husband of Queen Victoria, who carved a niche in English life with his support for education and industry.

Princess Elizabeth and heir.

Transistor cuts the valve down to size

A new device called the transistor made 1948 a memorable year for electronics. Transistors are capable of performing the same jobs as the thermionic valves used in most electronic devices, but they are no bigger than fingernails and consume hardly any power. As a result, tiny electronic devices will become possible. The transistor was invented at Bell Labs in the United States by **William Shockley**, **John Bardeen** and **Walter Brattain**.

Sex report probes bedroom secrets

Dec 31. Fifty-six per cent of American men have been unfaithful to their wives. This is just one of the findings of a survey published this year entitled "Sexual Behaviour of the Human Male", by Professor Alfred Kinsey, of Indiana University, who based it on interviews with 5,300 men about their sex life. Other surprising findings, perhaps, are that 90 per cent masturbate and 37 per cent have achieved orgasm with another man.

Japan's ex-leader hanged for war crimes

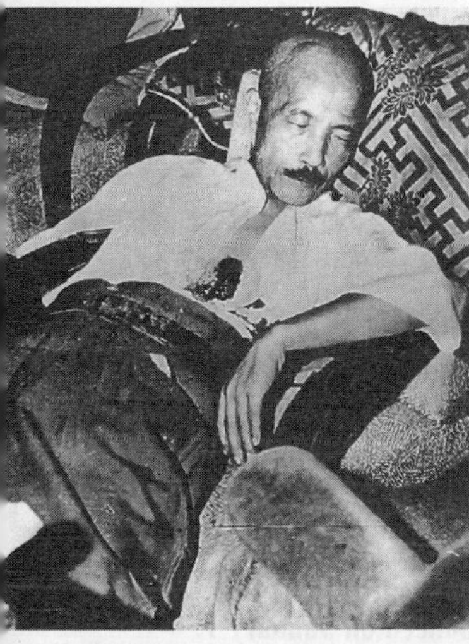

General Tojo failed to kill himself.

Dec 23. General Tojo, Japan's Prime Minister during the war, and six other war-time leaders, were hanged by the American Army at Sugamo Prison in Tokyo early this morning. Accused of whipping up a militaristic mood in Japan and inciting attacks on her Asian neighbours as well as America, they were convicted of "crimes against peace and responsibility for atrocities" by an international tribunal last month, along with 16 others who were sentenced to life imprisonment. Some of the condemned men, who included several generals and Japan's war-time Foreign Minister, recited Buddhist prayers as they walked to the gallows.

Arts: action painters steal the show

A painter who took his canvas off the easel, laid it on the floor and rushed at it, dripping and spattering paint at random, caused a sensation when his work was shown for the first time in New York.

Jackson Pollock, born on a Wyoming ranch, claims to have begun a new technique called Action Painting. The act the artist performs on his canvas is more important than subject matter. This way, he explains, he feels more a part of the painting. Magazines have dubbed him Jack the Dripper.

T.S. Eliot, who renounced his American citizenship to become British in 1927, has reached the summit of the orthodox literary establishment by being awarded both the Nobel Prize and the Order of Merit. He pronounced himself a classicist in literature, a royalist in politics and an Anglo-Catholic in religion. Yet he once provoked outrage with "The Waste Land".

The first major books to come out of the war have appeared. **Winston Churchill's** projected six-volume history begins with "The Gathering Storm", tracing the path to war in the Thirties. It is also a self-portrait of one of the main protagonists of the drama.

A world away from it is "The Naked and the Dead" by a 25-year-old US veteran, **Norman Mailer**. His novel describes, with realistic profanity, the lives of an assortment of GIs on reconnaissance patrol on a Japanese-held Pacific island. There are no heroics. Instead, a revulsion against the futility of war.

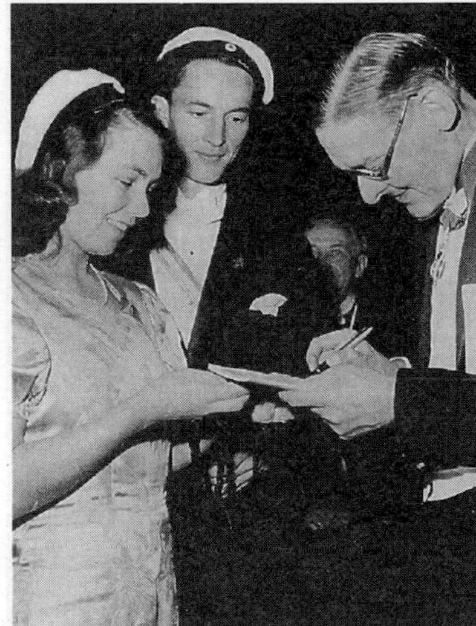

T.S. Eliot signs for fans in Sweden.

A powerful novel from South Africa, "Cry the Beloved Country" by **Alan Paton**, sounds the alarm at what is happening to blacks in the slums that surround the prosperous white cities, from which they are excluded by the colour bar, with ominous future implications.

Another artistic purge in Russia has been launched on Soviet composers. **Dmitri Shostakovich, Sergei Prokofiev** and **Aram Khachaturian** have been charged with writing anti-popular "formalist" music by culture commissar **Andrei Zhdanov.** Many of their scores and recordings have been destroyed.

Alec Guinness is transformed into Fagin for David Lean's latest film.

1949

JANUARY

Su	Mo	Tu	We	Th	Fr	Sa
						1
2	3	4	5	6	7	8
9	10	11	12	13	14	15
16	17	18	19	20	21	22
23	24	25	26	27	28	29
30	31					

1. Indonesia: The whole of Java is now reported to be under Dutch control (→ 11).

3. US: Tornadoes sweep Arkansas, leaving 41 dead.

5. Chicago: The Symphony Orchestra ends Furtwangler's contract as conductor because of his past position in Nazi Germany.

7. Washington: Dean Acheson becomes Secretary of State.

7. Israel: Five RAF reconnaissance planes are shot down by the Israelis (→ 25).

11. Washington: The US tells the Dutch to pull their troops out of Indonesia (→ 28).

12. Manchester: Margaret Allen is hanged for murder, the first woman to be executed in Britain for 12 years (→ 20).

13. China: Mao Tse-tung rejects a Nationalist peace bid as Communists shell Peking.→

17. West Indies: A British Tudor IV airliner disappears between Bermuda and Jamaica with 20 on board (→ 20).

17. Germany: The three Western Allies set up a Military Security Board for West Germany (→ 15/3).

19. Washington: Truman is inaugurated as president (→ 15/12).

20. UK: All Tudor IV airliners are withdrawn (→ 1/3).

20. London: Attlee sets up a Royal Commission on capital punishment (→ 3/5).

22. Eastern Europe: Stalin is reported to be seeking more control over Soviet satellites.

25. Israel: Ben-Gurion's Mapai (Labour) Party wins the first Israeli elections (→ 29).

28. New York: The UN demands immediate Dutch withdrawal from Indonesia (→ 29/6).

29. London: Britain recognises Israel (→ 24/2).

DEATHS

9. British comedian Tommy Handley (*17/1/1892).

21. British trade unionist and Labour politician James Henry Thomas (*3/10/1874).

Race riots flare in Durban: 106 dead

Black policemen surround a dead rioter, shot in the Durban disturbances.

Jan 15. After three days of the worst race riots in South Africa's history, the east coast port of Durban is quiet. But tension remains high and 2,000 troops and armed police are on guard.

The death toll has been given as 105 Africans and Indians, in approximately equal numbers, and one European, who was apparently shot by accident. The riots began on Thursday, after a rumour spread through the African locations that an African boy had been killed by an Indian. Gangs of Africans, armed with clubs, attacked Indian shops. Many Indians were clubbed or burned to death trying to defend their property. The boy was found later, unharmed. No European, Arab or Chinese shops were attacked, nor were the big Indian stores in town. Small traders were exclusively the targets (→ 3/6).

War nears its end as Mao takes Peking

Jan 22. As victorious Communist troops marched into Peking today, Chiang Kai-shek, China's leader for 22 years, announced his retirement. He was going home, he said, "to sweep the graves of his ancestors". In a farewell message to the Chinese people, the President called for an immediate cease-fire and peace talks.

Chiang's bitter opponent, Communist leader Mao Tse-tung, has rejected the appeal as "utterly unreasonable and hypocritical". Observers doubt that Chiang's retirement signals the end of the civil war, which began after Mao's "Long March" of 1935. The fall of Peking became inevitable after the Nationalists lost 600,000 men – 327,000 of them prisoners – in the key battle of Huai Hai on plains north of the capital.

Although the Nationalists fought well at first, they were badly led. In the final stage of the battle, when the Communists stormed the fortress city of Yungcheng, the defenders were reported to be starving and completely demoralised. Mao's forces have now begun to strike south towards Shanghai (→ 20/4).

UN cease-fire stills fighting in Kashmir

Jan 1. The war which India and Pakistan have been fighting over the beautiful mountain state of Kashmir, ends at midnight tonight. Cease-fire orders have been given by the C-in-Cs of India and Pakistan, General Sir Roy Bucher and Lt. General Sir Douglas Gracey.

The fighting started with the partition of India in 1947, when the Hindu ruler of Kashmir – 75 per cent of whose people are Moslem – opted to join India. His Moslem subjects rose against him, and war ensued between India and Pakistan. A plebiscite is now being arranged by the UN for the people to decide whether their future lies with India or Pakistan (→ 6/2).

Seven-inch record puts US in a spin

Jan 10. The new "micro-groove" seven-inch records – made of unbreakable vinylite – have just become available in America from two competing manufacturers, Columbia Records and RCA Victor. They promise extended play and much public confusion.

For the two rivals' new discs may both be the same size, but they play at different turntable speeds (RCA's at 45 rpm and Columbia's at 33.3 rpm). Conventional shellac records, however, run at 78 rpm, so much to their disgust, buyers of new records will also have to buy new equipment to play them on.

British speed king Malcom Campbell – pictured at Daytona, the site of many triumphs – whose death was announced on January 1.

1949

FEBRUARY

Su	Mo	Tu	We	Th	Fr	Sa
		1	2	3	4	5
6	7	8	9	10	11	12
13	14	15	16	17	18	19
20	21	22	23	24	25	26
27	28					

1. Budapest: Hungary is declared a people's republic (→ 2).

1. UK: The WRAF and WRAC, the women's services, are incorporated into Britain's armed forces.

2. Vienna: Istvan Barankovics, Hungary's opposition leader, arrives in exile (→ 14).

4. Tehran: The Shah is wounded in an assassination attempt (→ 29/1/50).

6. India: The vast estate of the Nizam of Hyderabad is to be nationalised (→ 27/4).

8. Dublin: The Irish government says it cannot join the North Atlantic alliance while Ireland is divided (→ 20).

8. US: An XB-47 jet bomber flies from Washington state to Maryland in a record three and three-quarter hours.

9. Los Angeles: Actor Robert Mitchum is jailed for two months for smoking marijuana (→ 28/8/51).

9. Washington: Secretary of State Acheson condemns the forthcoming trial of Cardinal Mindszenty.→

13. Ecuador: A mob burns the radio station in Quito after a dramatisation of "The War of the Worlds" causes panic.

17. Sofia: The Bulgarian government introduces a bill to cut Church ties with foreign governments.

18. Berlin: The millionth ton of airlifted supplies arrives in the Western sector (→ 16/4).

19. Washington: Ezra Pound, in a mental hospital and indicted for treason, wins the first Bollingen Poetry Prize.

20. Oslo: Norway votes to join the North Atlantic pact (→ 18/3).

25. London: The entire Tate Gallery is opened again for the first time since 1939.

28. Moscow: Stalin decrees sweeping cuts in the price of food, clothes and consumer goods (→ 4/3).

28. Vietnam: Seven French officers are killed by a Vietminh mine near Saigon (→ 8/3).

Truce is signed between Israel and Egypt

Feb 24. After 42 days of often acrimonious talks, Israel and Egypt signed an armistice on the island of Rhodes today. Dr Ralph J. Bunche, the United Nations mediator, has finally managed to bring the two sides together by omitting some of the more contentious issues from the agreement.

There is no mention, for instance, of Beersheba, the strategic crossroads town in the Negev Desert. Under the original UN partition plan it was Arab, but the Israelis have since captured it.

The Egyptians began the negotiations hoping to secure the territory between Hebron and the Dead Sea. Instead, the Israelis are being allowed to keep their forces much further east, including most of the Negev. The demarcation line goes right through Beersheba, and apparently Israeli troops are to be allowed to remain there.

West of the line, Israel has freedom of civilian movement and settlement, but must keep her troops out. Arrangements are being made by the United Nations to evacuate the pockets of Egyptian forces trapped in Israeli-controlled areas.

Today's armistice falls a long way short of a lasting peace. Egypt has still not agreed to recognise the state of Israel. The other Arab nations have yet to agree to the armistice. Israel's freedom of action, east of the armistice line, depends on the agreement of Transjordan which borders it. It is still not certain this will be forthcoming (→ 11/3).

Outrage at jailing of Hungarian priest

Feb 14. Determined to break the Catholic Church in Hungary, the Communist regime has staged a show trial of the country's primate, Cardinal Mindszenty. A Budapest court has sentenced him to life imprisonment after finding him guilty of treason, conspiracy to overthrow the government and black market currency deals. The cardinal confessed to most of the charges, but Western observers believe he was either drugged or tortured. Pope Pius XII says the Hungarians used a "secret influence" on him. The case has caused worldwide outrage; in the United States, President Truman described the verdict as "infamous" (→ 17/2/50).

Generals give Evita her marching orders

Eva Peron listens as General Franco addresses the crowds in Madrid.

Feb 18. Army leaders in the Argentine are trying to force President Peron's wife out of public life. They want her to retire and, preferably, go and live in Europe. Peron has countered by threatening to resign himself and the situation is now deadlocked because the Army does not want to risk a coup.

Evita, as she is known to the people, was a small-part actress on radio and in films when she met Peron in 1943. She now wields enormous power through her personality and energy. She effectively runs both the Health and Labour ministries. She controls a leading newspaper, La Razon. She heads the feminine branch of the Peronista party. She runs the Eva Peron Social Aid Foundation which channels state funds to the poor.

The Army have good reason to fear her. She organised the union demonstrations which forced them to release Peron from prison in 1945. She married Peron the following week. Her personal popularity with the labourers, helped him to then make his successful bid for the Presidency. He can still rely on her to organise popular demonstrations to support him when he needs to counter Army power (→ 3/11/51).

Fury at Fagin leads to Oliver Twist ban

Feb 23. Accusations of anti-Semitism, and a furious protest by up to 60 Jews, brought the showing of the British film, "Oliver Twist" to a halt at a Berlin cinema today. Offended by how Dickens' Jewish arch villain, Fagin, is portrayed, the protesters scuffled with German police outside the cinema and shouted: "Hitler has come to Berlin." The furore died down after an hour and a half, following a speech by "Victims of Facism" secretary, Herr Borchardt, claiming the Jews had won their point. It was the second time their protests had stopped the film (→ 6/8).

1949

MARCH

Su	Mo	Tu	We	Th	Fr	Sa
		1	2	3	4	5
6	7	8	9	10	11	12
13	14	15	16	17	18	19
20	21	22	23	24	25	26
27	28	29	30	31		

1. UK: Tudor IV airliners are banned from passenger flights after a series of accidents (→ 7/6).

5. Moscow: Stalin appoints Andrei Gromyko first deputy foreign minister (→ 24).

6. London: The UK has succeeded in manufacturing plutonium for the first time, at Harwell (→ 6/4).

7. Cairo: The Suez Canal Company agrees to allow five Egyptian directors onto its board (→ 19/5).

8. Vietnam: France recognises Bao Dai as head of a non-Communist Vietnam based in Saigon (→ 19/1/50).

11. Rhodes: Israel and Jordan sign a cease-fire (→ 15/4).

12. London: The King has an operation on his right foot (→ 30/12).

15. Germany: Britain drops its restrictions on German engineering industry's output (→ 8/4).

15. London: British South American Airways is to merge with BOAC.

17. London: The government issues the National Parks Bill, which would set up a National Parks Commission (→ 1/4).

18. Warsaw: The government asks the US to recall its ambassador for calling Poland a Soviet satellite (→ 31/11/51).

21. London: Marches are banned in London for three months after clashes between Communists and Mosleyites (→ 22/6).

24. Moscow: Alexander Vasilevsky replaces Nikolai Bulganin as head of the Soviet armed forces.

25. Copenhagen: Denmark agrees to join NATO (→ 4/4).

26. UK: Mr W. Williamson's Russian Hero wins the Grand National at Aintree.

31. Greece: Communist rebels begin an offensive in Thrace and Macedonia (→ 20/5).

DEATH

11. French commander General Henri Giraud (*18/1/1879).

Plans for NATO unveiled

March 18. Eight Western countries, including Britain, today reached agreement on a new alliance to be known as the North Atlantic Treaty Organisation, or NATO.

The alliance is intended to act as a deterrent against aggression, because each of the member states, due to ratify the treaty soon, has agreed that an attack on any one of them will be construed as an attack on all.

There has been much concern that the new alliance may only be seen as provoking the Soviet Union, but the Allies – Britain, the US, Canada, France and the Benelux countries – insist they are only seeking the "preservation of peace and security". Earlier this month Belgian Communists adopted a resolution opposing any "war of aggression against the Soviet Union"; strong opposition to the alliance has also been voiced by the left in Britain and France.

Ernest Bevin, Britain's Foreign Minister, has attempted to defuse the critics, saying the treaty was one of the greatest steps towards world peace and security since the end of the First World War. It was "purely defensive," he said. There were no secret clauses and no peaceful nation need have any fear of it. The alliance would be a "roof stretching over the Atlantic Ocean" (→ 1/12).

Molotov is out as USSR Foreign Minister

Foreign Minister Molotov (c) before he was ousted from Stalin's side.

March 4. Vyacheslav Molotov, whose "nyet" became a standing joke and a potent symbol of Soviet intransigence in negotiating with the West, stepped down today as Foreign Minister. Molotov is widely seen as Stalin's most faithful lieutenant, and there is no official explanation for the change. He is replaced by Andrei Vishinsky, prosecutor at the pre-war "show" trials, so a relaxation in hardline Soviet policies is unlikely.

Molotov is the only Soviet political leader to have shaken Hitler's hand. His name has been given to the "Molotov cocktail," the petrol bomb (→ 5).

Clothes rationing is abandoned in Britain

March 15. Clothes rationing – imposed in 1941 – ended in Britain today. Clothing coupons can be consigned to the "appropriate salvage channel," Harold Wilson, the President of the Board of Trade, told the Commons.

The utility scheme – in which ready-to-wear clothes are made under a cloth quota system – will continue. Price controls on clothing however, will stay with the Government ready to freeze prices if traders start to increase them.

The end of rationing will involve a direct saving of 10,000 workers, said Mr Wilson, as department stores made hurried overnight preparations for "celebratory sales" tomorrow (→ 2/4).

Five Oscars for Olivier's Hamlet

Olivier's Hamlet meets the ghost.

March 25. "Hamlet" today became the first British film to win an Academy Award for Best Picture. Sir Laurence Olivier also won an Oscar for his performance in the title role. He also directed the film, which is in black and white.

It had a mixed reception at its royal premiere last year. Many critics severely disapproved of the drastic cutting and rearrangement of the play to a length of two and a half hours. Some thought Olivier too old at 40 to play Hamlet, despite dyeing his hair blond. But the duel and his final leap from a high platform to kill the king were breath-taking. As his Ophelia, he chose 18-year-old Jean Simmons.

The Brown Bomber hangs up his gloves

March 1. After 25 successful defences of his world heavyweight title, a record approached by no other fighter, Joe Louis has announced his retirement.

The Brown Bomber is now nearly 35 years old, and even his greatest fans will applaud his decision to renounce the title while he remains at the top. Since the war, he has slowed appreciably, and his last two defences against Jersey Joe Walcott hinted strongly at a decline from the crisp, powerful athleticism of 12 years ago, when he faced and narrowly defeated his first title challenger, the brave Welshman Tommy Farr.

1949

APRIL

Su	Mo	Tu	We	Th	Fr	Sa
					1	2
3	4	5	6	7	8	9
10	11	12	13	14	15	16
17	18	19	20	21	22	23
24	25	26	27	28	29	30

1. London: MPs approve the National Parks Bill.→

2. UK: Coloured lights, floodlighting and neon signs are switched on as a 10-year-old ban is lifted (→ 6).

4. Washington: 12 nations sign the North Atlantic Treaty.→

6. London: The budget pegs food subsidies, meaning dearer cheese, butter, margarine and meat; beer is one penny cheaper (→ 24).

6. Washington: Truman says he would not hesitate to use the atomic bomb again if necessary (→ 23/9).

8. New York: The USSR vetoes South Korea's entry to the UN (→ 28/6).

8. Washington: The US, Britain and France reach agreement on the establishment of West Germany (→ 24).

11. UK: Labour lose 255 seats in local council elections, tying with the Tories in London with 64 seats (→ 23/11).

12. UK: Harry Gordon Selfridge, the store owner who died two years ago, left estate valued at only £1,544 13/6d.

15. Rome: Pope Pius XII calls for the internationalisation of the Holy Places in Jerusalem (→ 11/5).

16. Berlin: A record 12,941 tons of goods are airlifted into the city (→ 26).

18. Dublin: Eire is proclaimed the Republic of Ireland.→

20. China: Communists shell two British warships on the Yangtse, killing at least 26.→

24. UK: Chocolate and sweet rationing ends (→ 14/7).

24. Germany: A constitution is agreed for the western part of Germany (→ 6/5).

26. Moscow: The USSR calls for four-Power talks to end the Berlin blockade (→ 4/5).

30. London: Crowds flock to the Royal Academy to see the "moderns" panned by retiring RA president Munnings.→

30. London: Wolverhampton Wanderers beat Leicester City 3-1 in the FA Cup Final.

Communist forces advance on Shanghai

A Shanghai policeman about to shoot his prisoner, allegedly a Communist.

April 24. The Chinese Communist armies are advancing almost unopposed, on the city of Shanghai today in full pursuit of the fleeing Nationalist forces. Advance columns are reported to be within 24 miles of the huge city.

Thousands are fleeing Shanghai by sea and air, and British residents are being advised to prepare for evacuation. The city has been closed to streams of refugees from the north, although the atmosphere in Shanghai is reported "calm – but expectant". The city is preparing for a siege, with lengthy queues for rice and tinned foods. Prime Minister Ho Ying-chin has reiterated his intention of making a stand at Shanghai, although he himself has left for Canton with other members of the Government. Leading residents are appealing to the garrison commander not to carry out his intention of fighting "to the last man".

The British Embassy has failed to arrange a rescue, under ceasefire, of the frigate, HMS Amethyst, trapped in the Yangtse River after being shelled and damaged by Communist forces, with the loss of 43 men. Four other British ships have been shelled (→ 26/5).

New Bill will create National Parks

April 1. Britain is to have its first national parks, it was announced today – 77 years after Yellowstone, in the United States, became the world's first, and nearly 150 years after Wordsworth urged that the Lakes should be "a national property in which every man has a right and interest who has an eye to perceive and a heart to enjoy". The Lake District is one of 12 areas in England and Wales proposed as potential national parks to conserve natural beauty. None are proposed for Scotland.

India and Ireland become republics

April 27. India stays in the Commonwealth as its first republic and accepts the King as the unifying symbol of a free association of independent nations. The Republic of Ireland is born and refuses to be in the Commonwealth, but offers cooperation if partition of the Emerald Isle is ended.

With those two historic developments this month, Britain has formally recognised the march of time. The Mother Country has accepted parting with her two most turbulent children.

But, although India and Ireland, whose problems have overhung Westminster politics for a century, now go their own ways, they are not finished with Britain. In Delhi politicians spoke about the need for development aid. In Dublin they just spoke about Ulster (→ 3/5).

RA president in row over modernist art

April 30. The first Royal Academy dinner since 1939 made lively radio last night. The retiring president, Sir Alfred Munnings, a painter of racing scenes, made an out-and-out attack on modern art as "silly daubs" and "violent blows at nothing". As Picasso, Matisse and Henry Moore came in for ridicule, Academicians heckled him noisily. Listeners complained of how often the word "damned" was used.

Londoners queue for the first sweets to come off rations in seven years.

1949

MAY

Su	Mo	Tu	We	Th	Fr	Sa
1	2	3	4	5	6	7
8	9	10	11	12	13	14
15	16	17	18	19	20	21
22	23	24	25	26	27	28
29	30	31				

1. UK: The gas industry is nationalised (→ 16/8).

2. New York: Arthur Miller wins a Pulitzer Prize for his play "Death of a Salesman".

3. London: Introduction of the Ireland Bill, which would formally recognise the new Republic of Ireland.→

3. London: High Court judges are to get their first pay rises since 1872 (→ 4/8).

4. Turin: Italy's national football team are killed in an air crash.

4. New York: The USSR agrees to lift the Berlin blockade on May 12.→

5. London: The government says it will reinforce the Hong Kong garrison (→ 18/7).

6. Bonn: A parliamentary council approves the West German constitution by 47 votes to two.→

9. London: Britain's first "launderette" opens for a six-month trial at 184 Queensway, Bayswater.

11. New York: Israel is voted into the UN (→ 9/12).

13. UK: The first British jet bomber, the A1, makes its maiden flight (→ 30).

19. London: Egypt agrees to Britain's plans for a White Nile dam in Uganda.

20. Washington: The Western Allies reject talks with the USSR aimed at ending the Greek war (→ 14/8).

25. Paris: At Big Four talks, Secretary of State Acheson rejects the Soviet claim for reparations from Germany (→ 30/7).

30. UK: A test pilot makes the first British escape by ejector seat, from a prototype "Flying Wing" (→ 7/8).

31. UK: Work has begun on Europe's largest oil refinery at Fawley, near Southampton, due to cost £37.5 million (→ 7/8/50).

DEATH

6. Belgian author and philosopher Maurice Maeterlinck (*29/8/1862).

End of Berlin blockade

As the Berlin Blockade ends, crowds greet the first lorry-load of food.

May 12. Cheers broke out in Berlin this morning as cars drove into the city along the autobahn from the British sector of Germany, ending the Russian blockade.

Lights burned past midnight for the first time, and there were sighs of relief among the workers at the airport, who have handled a constant shuttle of aircraft bringing in supplies since last June at a cost to the Allies of $200 million.

Berliners feel they have beaten the Russians at their own game. The Soviet Union blocked off the city last year to protest at what they called intransigence by the Western Allies on the future of the city and Germany. The blockade ended today after negotiations in New York under the auspices of the UN.

The Russians also agreed to attend a new meeting of the Big Four foreign ministers, to drop their opposition to the creation of an independent West Germany and to give up their plans for a single currency for all of Berlin. Both sides agreed to give more autonomy to the city, while still retaining tight control over security, the constitution and foreign relations (→ 25).

Western sector of divided Germany is a Federal Republic

May 23. Four years after the shattering defeat of the Nazis, a new, democratic Germany is born. It is a good deal smaller than the old Germany, not least because it will not include the Soviet-occupied East Zone; only the British, US and French zones have come together to form the Federal Republic of Germany. In the Rhineland city of Bonn, birthplace of Beethoven and now to be the federal capital, crowds thronged the streets, waving the red, black and gold flag of the Weimar Republic, the Germans' previous attempt to establish a democratic political system.

In the building of the Pedagogical Institute in Bonn, Dr Konrad Adenauer, who was sacked as Mayor of Cologne and arrested by the Nazis, presided over a meeting of the West German Parliamentary Council, for the proclamation of the new republic. He said he hoped the democratic constitution would lead to the re-unification of Germany.

That seems unlikely. The Western Allies are not willing to agree to the Russians' terms, which would impose an Austrian-style neutrality on a disarmed Germany, and that would, in the Western judgment, be vulnerable to Soviet subversion (→ 25).

Shanghai falls to Mao's troops after a month-long siege

May 26. White flags are flying tonight in Shanghai, China's largest city, which fell suddenly with few shots being fired, after a month-long siege. Soldiers of Mao Tse-tung's Peoples' Liberation Army are now patrolling the streets.

Although a fierce battle continues to the east of the city, where Nationalist troops fight to keep open the one remaining escape corridor, defending troops are waiting at barricades to surrender their weapons to the green-uniformed Communist soldiers and be marched to prison camps.

The victors are putting up posters urging the population to stay calm – and assuring them that they have nothing to fear (→ 30/6).

Troops of Mao Tse-tung's Peoples' Liberation Army patrol in Shanghai.

Britain recognises new republic of Eire

May 11. The Ireland Bill, which recognises Eire as a republic, passed its second reading yesterday, nearly unanimously by 317-14. It was opposed by 12 Labour members and two Ulster MP's.

The Bill ends the Irish Republic's dominion status, but it will not be a foreign country; instead it will occupy a curious intermediate position, making Eire's constitution unique.

The southern Irish, for instance, will continue to be able to vote in British elections. The Prime Minister, Clement Attlee, told the House that the Bill was a practical solution, if not a very logical one, to Ireland being a republic.

British court frees "Marxist agitator"

May 22. A British court angered American justice officials today by refusing to extradite a Communist to the US to face a perjury charge. German-born Gerhart Eisler, seen as a dangerous Marxist agitator by Washington, was set free by senior magistrate, Sir Lawrence Dunne, in London. Seven days ago he was arrested on board a Polish ship and held in a cell.

The court ruled there was a lack of evidence against Eisler, who once said being beaten up and leading a strike were all in a day's work for an active Communist (→ 11/7).

Posing on their wedding-day – Rita Hayworth and Aly Khan look forward to married bliss.

1949

JUNE

Su	Mo	Tu	We	Th	Fr	Sa
			1	2	3	4
5	6	7	8	9	10	11
12	13	14	15	16	17	18
19	20	21	22	23	24	25
26	27	28	29	30		

1. Paris: The French government appeals for foreign wheat (→ 23/10).

2. Amman: Transjordan is renamed the Hashemite Kingdom of Jordan (→ 24/5/50).

3. S. Africa: The country's richest gold find yet is reported at Farm Erfdeel, Orange Free State (→ 15).

4. UK: Nimbus, ridden by E.C. Elliott, wins the Derby at Epsom.

5. Paris: Impresario Leon Volterra dies of a heart attack.

7. Puerto Rico: 54 die in a plane crash (→ 19/8).

8. UK: Lord Jersey gives Osterley Park to the nation.

13. Tokyo: General MacArthur accuses the USSR of inciting disorder in Japan (→ 29/9).

15. S. Africa: MPs approve the Citizenship Bill: Britons must wait five years for their papers (→ 16/12).

20. Wimbledon: A record 25,000 spectators attend the tournament's opening day.→

25. New York: Scientists say the anti-tuberculosis drug, Neomycin, has been fully tested on animals (→ 21/4/50).

26. Prague: Czech bishops openly accuse the government of persecution (→ 13/7).

27. London: Publication of Churchill's "Their Finest Hour".

28. Korea: The last US combat troops leave (→ 26/6/50).

28. UK: Harrow is Britain's most expensive public school, with annual fees of £315.

29. London: A study finds Britain's press incorrupt, uninfluenced by outside interests and unmonopolistic.

29. Indonesia: Dutch troops withdraw from Jakarta (→ 2/11).

30. China: Mao says that the USSR is China's true ally (→ 30/9).

BIRTH

22. US actress Meryl Streep.

Truman tries to calm "Red" hysteria in US

June 30. America is not going to hell, President Truman said today, as he tried to calm the wave of anti-Communist hysteria sweeping the nation. Answering questions at his weekly press conference in the White House, Truman said public hysteria frequently followed after periods of stress, such as war, but always eventually subsided.

He compared current events to those after the War of Independence when Congress passed the Alien and Sedition Acts, allowing for the deportation of aliens in war time and the imprisonment of anyone attacking the Federal Government. Both laws were later repealed and Truman used this as an analogy, saying that the nation didn't go to hell then, and it won't do so today. He also noted that the First World War was followed by the emergence of the Ku Klux Klan.

The current wave of hysteria has been fuelled by the "loyalty" investigations of the House Committee on Un-American Activities, whose most recent proposal, the screening of all books used in schools and colleges, was today dismissed by Truman as ridiculous.

Also contributing to the growing wave of intolerance is the exposure of Soviet agents, the latest being the conviction of Justice Department employee, Judith Coplon, for spying. Another under suspicion is Alger Hiss, who this month testified that he was never a Communist and did not pass on secret State Department documents (→ 8/7).

Wimbledon shocked by Gorgeous Gussie

June 30. Wimbledon's staid courts have taken many changes of fashion in their stride, and this year's sensation, the lace-trimmed panties peeping from beneath the white dress of the American, Gussie Moran, will doubtless lose their notoriety as fast as May Sutton's knee-length skirt in 1905, Suzanne Lenglen's bare arms and Helen Jacobs' shorts.

"Gorgeous Gussie's" lace trim stirred up a near riot among courtside press photographers during her early singles matches, and caused something of a rift between the upright members of the All-England Club and the outfit's flamboyant designer and Wimbledon perennial, Teddy Tinling.

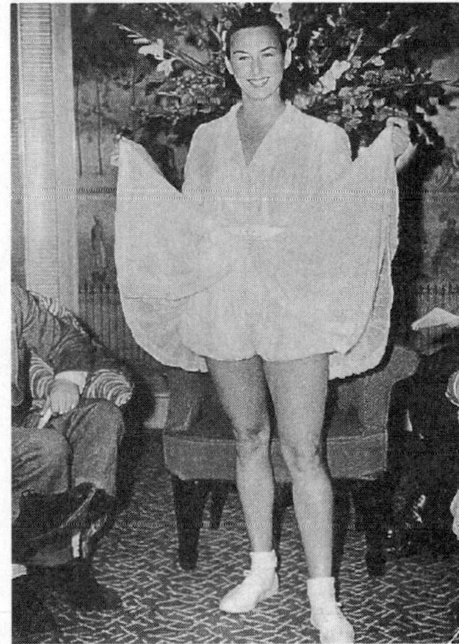

Gorgeous Gussie shows her form.

Percy Huxter, a popular clown.

1984 is a warning and not a prophecy

June 10. "Nineteen Eighty-Four", George Orwell's nightmare novel about a future world ruled through thought control by "Big Brother" is, he explains, not so much a precise prediction of what sort of society will arrive, as a warning of what could happen if totalitarian ideas develop to their logical conclusions. He added that it was not an attack on socialism or the Labour Party, which he supported. The book is selling out fast (→ 21/1/50).

1949

JULY

Su	Mo	Tu	We	Th	Fr	Sa
					1	2
3	4	5	6	7	8	9
10	11	12	13	14	15	16
17	18	19	20	21	22	23
24	25	26	27	28	29	30
31						

1. London: Work on more than half the ships in port halts as London dockers come out on strike (→ 3).

2. Wimbledon: Fred Schroeder beats Jaroslav Drobny in the men's singles final; Louise Brough beats Mrs Du Pont in the women's singles final (→ 15).

3. London: Attlee condemns the dock strike (→ 12).

5. China: Chiang Kai-shek appeals to the US for aid (→ 7/10).

8. New York: The jury at Alger Hiss's perjury trial is dismissed for failing to agree on a verdict (→ 25/1/50).

9. UK: South African Bobby Locke wins the Open Golf Championship after a replay against Harry Bradshaw.

11. UK: The Transport and General Workers Union bans Communists and Fascists from office.

12. London: 13,000 dockers are now out on strike (→ 22).

13. Rome: The Pope says that any Catholic aiding Communism faces excommunication.→

15. Geneva: Wimbledon finalist Jaroslav Drobny and Vladimir Cernik defect to the West.

18. Hong Kong: 3,800 British troops arrive, boosting the garrison by 50 per cent.

19. Indochina: Laos becomes independent.

22. London: The dock strike ends.

24. West Germany: Author Thomas Mann returns from exile.

27. London: Peers vote to admit peeresses in their own right to the House of Lords.

28. London: The government admits that the NHS costs 2/6d. a head per week, 1/4d. more than first thought.

30. Berlin: The mayor of the western sector asks for Marshall aid (→ 14/8).

BIRTH

19. Rumanian tennis player Ilie Nastase.

British frigate makes dash for freedom

Cheers as HMS Amethyst sails into Hong Kong after her Chinese torture.

July 30. In a daring 140-mile dash under cover of darkness along the flooded Yangtse River, the British frigate, Amethyst, reached safety today – four months after she was shelled and trapped by advancing Communist armies.

The frigate was shelled several times by Chinese batteries and returned fire as she steamed at speed, at one point breaking through a boom across the river. Her commander, Lieut-Cdr J.S. Kerans – who had replaced her dead captain – signalled the Admiralty: "Have rejoined the Fleet south of Woosung. No damage or casualties. God Save the King."

Kerans was forced to slip Amethyst's cable when his ship's fuel supplies were running low, and the crew were on half rations (→ 1/8).

Comet jet airliner flies at 500 mph

July 27. Years of secret development work came to fruition today as the world's first jet airliner, the De Havilland Comet, made its first flight.

The revolutionary aircraft has been kept firmly under wraps until recently to prevent the US aircraft industry stealing the British lead. The flight was made during ground handling tests at Hatfield. On his third taxi down the runway, pilot Group Captain John Cunningham allowed the aircraft to take off. The British Overseas Airways Corporation has ordered 16 of the aircraft, which it is hoped will be in service by 1952.

The De Havilland Comet: the revolutionary jet is unveiled at long last.

More rationing as UK crisis deepens

July 14. More belt-tightening measures for coping with Britain's alarming dollar shortage were announced today. The sugar ration is down to eight ounces a week. Sweet rationing is back at four ounces a head, and there is another cut in tobacco supplies.

Sir Stafford Cripps, Chancellor of the Exchequer, disclosed that the nation's deficit with America and Canada is running at the rate of £600 million a year – "one and a half times the total of our gold reserves, and that condition of affairs must be altered". However, he added, there is no suggestion that sterling should be devalued. "And that, I hope, is that," he said with some fervour (→ 1/9).

The Chancellor with Harold Wilson.

Vatican declares war on communism

July 13. Millions of Roman Catholics throughout the world are being asked to choose between their faith and the Communist Party. This evening the Vatican issued the Apostolic Acta, prepared under the personal direction of Pope Pius XII, which effectively excommunicates those who "knowingly and freely" join or support the Communist Party (→ 23/12/50).

1949

AUGUST

Su	Mo	Tu	We	Th	Fr	Sa
	1	2	3	4	5	6
7	8	9	10	11	12	13
14	15	16	17	18	19	20
21	22	23	24	25	26	27
28	29	30	31			

1. London: The King awards the DSO to the commander of HMS Amethyst (→ 1/11).

4. Prague: A Catholic priest is jailed for refusing the last rites to a Catholic woman (→ 12/11).

4. London: Figures show that juvenile crime rose by 16.7 per cent in 1948.

5. US: Ingrid Bergman announces intention to marry film director Roberto Rossellini.

6. Damascus: 12 are reported dead after a bomb blast at a synagogue (→ 29/11/50).

7. UK: A Gloster Meteor completes a flight lasting 12 hours three minutes, the longest jet flight yet made.→

8. France: The Council of Europe meets for the first time at Strasbourg; Turkey, Greece and Iceland join (→ 7/11).

11. US: "Gone With The Wind" author Margaret Mitchell is knocked down and seriously hurt by a car.

12. London: Starlings on the minute hand make Big Ben lose four and a half minutes, its slowest for 90 years.

14. Greece: Communist rebels under General Markos are defeated in the Vitsi mountains.

19. 24 people are killed in the crash of a BEA DC-3 in Yorkshire (→ 28/10).

24. UK: Essex and England pace bowler Trevor Bailey takes all ten Lancashire first-innings wickets at Clacton (→ 30).

25. New York: A system for broadcasting colour television is announced by RCA (→ 4/11).

27. Yugoslavia: Three Soviet armoured divisions are reported to be mobilised near the Yugoslav frontier (→ 30).

29. Belgrade: Tito asks the US for a loan to help beat the blockade imposed on it by the USSR (→ 30).

30. Moscow: The USSR denounces Tito's regime as "renegade" (→ 2/9).

DEATH

16. US author Margaret Mitchell (*8/11/1900).

Konrad Adenauer wins German elections

Dr Adenauer, seen surrounded by his friends, as the result comes through.

Aug 14. A tough-minded opponent of the Nazis, who was twice thrown into prison by them, has become Chancellor of the new Federal Republic. Dr Konrad Adenauer, at the age of 73, is leader of the Christian Democrats, who will form the government after yesterday's Bundestag elections, in which over 70 per cent of voters went to the polls.

When the Allies entered Germany, Dr Adenauer was reinstated as Lord Mayor of Cologne, then briefly sacked again by the British, who thought him an awkward customer. Close behind Adenauer's Christian Democrats come the Social Democrats, led by the fiery concentration camp survivor, Kurt Schumacher. The Communists failed to win a seat in the direct voting, although they may scrape home when votes are allocated for the block of seats filled by proportional representation. In some cities men and women voted separately, the women favouring the Christian Democrats, the men the Social Democrats (→ 16/1/50).

Mr Cube says no to nationalisation

Aug 16. The sugar refiners, Tate and Lyle, today announced all-out war against nationalisation of their industry, which is proposed in Labour's programme for the coming General Election. The firm also angrily rejected a Ministry of Food request for removal of anti-nationalisation slogans from its sugar cartons.

Tate and Lyle plan to popularise a small figure, called "Mr Cube" who will be depicted on bags of sugar, valiantly resisting state interference. Lord Lyle, veteran head of the company, blamed the nationalisation scheme on "long-haired boys from Bloomsbury" (→ 15/11).

Two tie for title of Champion County

Aug 30. For the first time this century, two teams will share the title of Champion County. After Middlesex had set the target in a remarkable late-season run by winning their last five matches, they had to wait, as Yorkshire played their final game at Newport, against last year's champions, Glamorgan, in the last three days of their reign, and hope that defeat would push them into second place.

However, Yorkshire never looked like faltering, as Coxon and Wardle dismissed the Glamorgan batsmen for 116 and a meagre 69 to win by 278 runs and claim their share of the title.

Sound of new speed records fills the air in Britain and USA

Aug 23. Britain and the United States are both vying to keep ahead in aviation, with new military and civil aircraft pushing for heights and speeds never before dreamt of.

The Handley Page Hermes made its first flight at Radlett, Herts today with its makers boasting it will be the fastest turbo-prop passenger plane yet, capable of 353 mph fully laden with 63 passengers and more than two and a half tons of baggage. But even that will not compare with the 500mph expected of the Comet passenger jet when it enters service.

British scientists are now working on a new delta-winged, research aircraft, the Avro 707, while at the same time, the Americans are pushing higher into the skies. Their new hero, the appropriately named pilot, Frank Everest, has just taken an experimental Bell X-1 plane to the atonishing height of over 64,000 feet, a new record, almost on the edge of space.

The plane, financed by a government fund for experimental aircraft, had its first flight in January 1946, but as its engines have become more sophisticated, so scientists found themselves facing a new problem: they had to develop a heat shield to protect the plane in supersonic flight (→ 27/9).

Richard Murdoch and Kenneth Horne – stars of radio's "Much Binding in the Marsh".

1949

SEPTEMBER

Su	Mo	Tu	We	Th	Fr	Sa
				1	2	3
4	5	6	7	8	9	10
11	12	13	14	15	16	17
18	19	20	21	22	23	24
25	26	27	28	29	30	

2. France: The Cannes Film Festival opens.

2. Belgrade: Tito ends Yugoslavia's air and naval pact with the USSR (→ 8).

8. Washington: The US lends $20 million to Yugoslavia (→ 28).

11. UK: The milk ration is cut from three to two and a half pints per week (→ 18).

13. New York: The USSR vetoes the entry of Austria, Italy, Finland and Nepal to the UN (→ 5/12).

17. Toronto: 207 die as fire sweeps the liner Noronic at its mooring.

18. UK: The milk ration is cut again to two pints (→ 25/10).

20. Paris: The government proposes a Western European monetary union.

22. Washington: George Marshall becomes head of the US Red Cross.

27. London: Chancellor Cripps raises the tax on company profits from 25 per cent to 30 per cent.

27. UK: 12 die when two Lincoln bombers collide over Nottinghamshire during an exercise (→ 12/1/50).

28. Moscow: The USSR rescinds its mutual assistance treaty with Yugoslavia (→ 30).

29. San Francisco: Wartime propaganda broadcaster "Tokyo Rose" is found guilty of treason (→ 6/12/50).

30. Peking: Mao Tse-tung is elected Chairman of the People's Republic of China (→ 1/10).

30. Belgrade: Poland and Hungary tell Tito they are renouncing their friendship pacts with Yugoslavia (→ 1/10).

BIRTH

4. US golfer Tom Watson.

DEATHS

7. Mexican painter Jose Clemente Orozco (*23/11/1883).

8. German composer Richard Strauss (*11/6/1864).

The pound is devalued by 30 per cent

Sept 18. Britain has devalued the pound sterling from four dollars three cents to two dollars eighty – a stunning 30.5 per cent reduction. The Treasury announced the dramatic decision tonight. The size of the devaluation shook world financiers who had not expected the once-proud pound to fall nearly so low against the now mighty dollar.

Sir Stafford Cripps, Chancellor of the Exchequer, explained that growing world distrust of Britain's currency made it essential to show that any further devaluation can be firmly ruled out. It was immediately recalled, however, that he had denied nine times since last January that devaluation would happen.

Some rise in the cost of living – perhaps five per cent – now seems inevitable. But the Chancellor said ferociously, that there is a paramount need to "put a stop" to wage increases. He also warned that the fourpence-ha'penny loaf will cost sixpence and there will be no increase in food subsidies.

In a broadcast, Sir Stafford promised that devaluation will boost British exports. He went on: "We thus start upon another stage in the magnificent struggle of our people to overcome the crushing difficulties imposed upon them by their sacrifices in the world war."

Britain's action has been echoed by the devaluation of nine other currencies – those of Australia, South Africa, New Zealand, India, the Irish Republic, Denmark, Norway, Egypt and Israel.

It was a Sunday of high drama in Whitehall. In advance of the announcement, Opposition leaders, trade union leaders and lobby correspondents were summoned by the Treasury for secret briefings. They were told to go first to other Government buildings, and from there, they were escorted through underground passages to see Sir Stafford. Some were locked in for hours after being told the new exchange rate.

It is now known that the devaluation decision was taken by the cabinet about three weeks ago, before Sir Stafford and Mr Bevin, the Foreign Secretary, left for a fortnight of financial talks in Washington. They ordered their officials to continue denying the devaluation possibility. Whitehall has never lied more eloquently. Tonight the Chancellor apologised for "necessary deception in a wicked world".

By Royal Proclamation, banks and stock exchanges will be closed tomorrow while the financial world tries to recover equilibrium after the huge shock (→ 27).

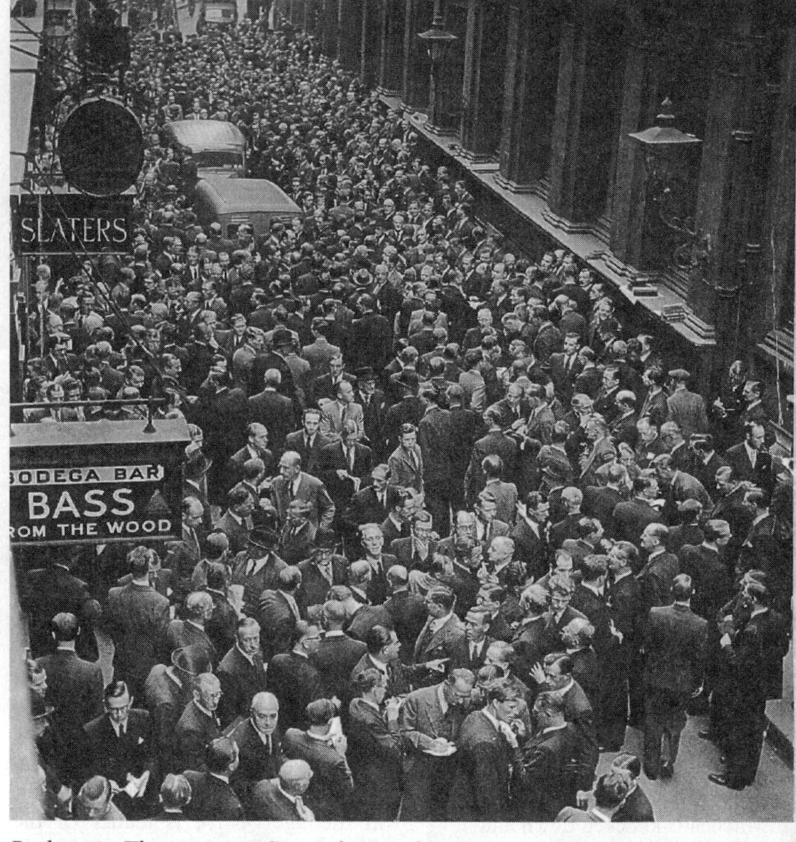

Brokers in Throgmorton Street discuss the economy as banks are closed.

The changing life of Mr and Mrs Britain

Sept 1. Striking changes in the social life of Britons have been revealed by a recently-published survey of the last ten years. As a nation, Britain is spending more on alcoholic drinks, but less likely to get drunk; spending less money on food, but more likely to eat out; and far more likely to end a rocky marriage through divorce.

Ten times more divorces are being granted now than in 1937, according to the Annual Abstract of Statistics. And more petitions are being filed for divorce by husbands than by wives – exactly the reverse of the pre-war situation.

Rationing has influenced eating habits; average sugar consumption fell from 103.9 pounds to 79.8 pounds, meat declined from 91.4 pounds to 67.3 pounds; but more coffee and cocoa were drunk, presumably as alternatives to rationed tea. Crime is rising, but convictions for drunkenness are less than half pre-war levels, and less than one-eighth of those in 1913 (→ 11).

Strauss, master of orchestration, dies

Sept 8. The death at 85 of Richard Strauss, whom Wagner's widow invited to conduct at Bayreuth, removes German music's last link with the 19th century. He was the only composer Hitler did not dare to touch. His first opera "Salome", with its dance of the seven veils, caused uproar in 1905. "Der Rosenkavalier", followed in 1911. His tone poems demonstrated his mastery of orchestration.

1949

OCTOBER

Su	Mo	Tu	We	Th	Fr	Sa
						1
2	3	4	5	6	7	8
9	10	11	12	13	14	15
16	17	18	19	20	21	22
23	24	25	26	27	28	29
30	31					

Western alarm as Russia tests A-bomb

Sept 23. The news that the Soviet Union has become a nuclear power and carried out an atomic explosion, sent the needle off the diplomatic Richter scale tonight, as the shock waves raced through Western capitals. Simultaneous announcements in London and Washington said the explosion took place within recent weeks. There has been no confirmation from Moscow, but at the United Nations General Assembly, the Soviet Foreign Minister, Andrei Vishinsky, called for a ban on atomic weapons.

Soviet work on the A-bomb has been going on since Hiroshima and possibly even before, but Western governments have doubted Stalin's ability to catch up with the United States, which has been stockpiling bombs since 1945. It was thought the Russians had neither the knowledge of nuclear physics nor the fissionable materials to produce their bomb for many years.

However, it would appear that uranium ore was obtained from mines in Czechoslovakia and East Germany, while German scientists have been persuaded or forced to help the Soviet effort. Furthermore to speed up production, Soviet agents have engaged in massive industrial espionage in the United States and Canada. Slave labour is believed to have been used to build several large complexes.

The explosion is believed to have taken place more than three weeks ago at a site in Kazakhstan, central Asia, and it may have been interpreted at first as an accident. The truth was revealed after rainwater samples were taken from contaminated clouds (→4/1/50).

Maiden flight of world's largest airliner

Sept 4. Britain's giant new airliner, the Brabazon, took to the air for her maiden flight today, representing the hope that the UK stays right at the forefront of aircraft development.

The 130-ton plane is thought to be the largest in the world. The prototype, which flew for 25 minutes today, has eight Rolls-Royce Centaurus engines and will carry 100 passengers.

Britain has been concerned for some time to make sure it maintains its share of the growing post-war world civil aviation market, and the new aircraft, specially built for the British Overseas Airways Corporation, is intended to fly the 3,500 miles between London and New York non-stop.

The Government's fear is that the Americans, with their ability to produce vast numbers of large bombers and transports, will become over-dominant, and the new aircraft is the result of a study by a government committee.

Britain's Bristol Brabazon, the largest passenger aircraft in the world.

1. Belgrade: Rumania and Bulgaria renounce their friendship pacts with Yugoslavia (→4).

2. Moscow: The USSR denounces West Germany as a breach of Potsdam and other Big Four agreements.→

4. Prague: The Czechs end their friendship pact with Tito (→20).

5. New York: The UN flag is hoisted over the new UN building.

6. San Francisco: "Tokyo Rose" is jailed for ten years and fined $10,000.

7. China: Nationalist defences are reported to be crumbling in South China (→13).

9. Geneva: 31 nations announce cuts in tariffs to encourage international trade.

13. China: The Communists begin to occupy Canton (→18).

14. Moscow: Stalin sends a congratulatory note to the leaders of the German Democratic Republic.

16. Greece: Communist rebels stop fighting, ending the civil war.

18. China: Communist troops seize the port of Amoy (→26).

20. New York: Yugoslavia is elected to the UN Security Council (→26).

23. Paris: Georges Bidault becomes premier (→8/2/50).

25. UK: A gallon of petrol goes up twopence halfpenny to 2/3d (→21/3/50).

26. Moscow: Stalin tells Tito to recall his ambassador, whom he claims is "a spy" (→14/11/51).

28. Azores: Violinist Ginette Neveu is among 48 killed when an Air France airliner crashes en route to New York (→1/11).

31. London: The Parliament Bill, cutting the Lords' delaying power from two years to one, is given a second reading for the third time (→29/11).

DEATH

28. French violinist Ginette Neveu (*11/8/19)

Nobel Peace Prize is won by Briton

Boyd-Orr: feeding the hungry.

Oct 12. Lord Boyd-Orr, a leading architect of Western food policies aimed at helping starving nations, has been awarded the Nobel Peace Prize, it was announced today.

Formerly Sir John Boyd-Orr, from 1945 to 1947 he was director of the United Nations Food and Agricultural Organisation.

He was informed of the decision of the Nobel Committee of the Norwegian Parliament in a telephone call. The 69-year-old peer said: "My first reaction was one of great surprise."

In line with tradition, no reason was given for his nomination. But he added: "I think the award has to be associated with my plans for the drawing up of a world food plan by governments."

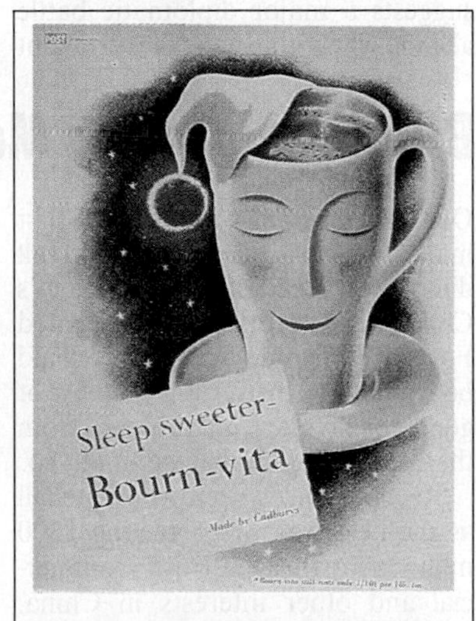
Sleep sweeter-
Bourn-vita

People's state in China

Revolutionary justice: a landowner, thus an enemy of the people, is shot.

Oct 1. Before milling, cheering crowds by the Gate of Heavenly Peace, in Peking, Mao Tse-tung proclaimed China a Communist Republic today, and looked to the rest of the world for recognition.

"This Government is willing to observe the principles of equality, mutual respect and territorial sovereignty," he declared.

The USSR was the first to recognise the new regime, declaring that the Communist victory "dealt a cruel blow to the aggressive plans of Imperialists in the Pacific region". The lukewarm reception given by the United States, which had backed the former Nationalist regime, suggests a major diplomatic battle ahead, when the new Government seeks recognition of their delegate by the United Nations as the legitimate spokesman for China. Chou En-lai has been appointed Premier and Foreign Minister of the new republic.

In the two-and-a-half years since large-scale civil war was resumed in China, a relatively small guerrilla army, occupying only country districts, has become a vast, well-equipped army and succeeded in conquering one of the largest countries in the world. The Nationalists were poorly led by corrupt generals, who made repeated strategic errors, and ill-treated a conscript army which originally heavily outnumbered the Communists (→ 7).

Britain recognises Mao's regime in China

Oct 26. Britain will be the first major Western power to grant full diplomatic recognition to Mao's China. The cabinet has accepted Foreign Office advice that it would be fruitless to insist on a long list of good behaviour guarantees from the Peking regime before doing so.

Recognition is seen in Whitehall as the best way of protecting £300 millions-worth of British commercial and other interests in China. The move will come after the current session of the UN Assembly is over, thereby deferring the thorny problem of which Chinese regime should have a UN seat – the Communists or the Nationalists, now fleeing Mao's army.

The United States, Canada and Australia are refusing to go along with Britain. Dean Acheson, the American Secretary of State, explained: "Communism is a very emotional subject in our country right now" (→ 6/1/50).

Stalin sets up Communist German state

Oct 12. Joseph Stalin has put the seal on Germany's division, and established the German Democratic Republic in the eastern half, controlled by Soviet troops. The decision was taken last week at a joint meeting of the praesidium of the Popular Council and the so-called anti-Fascist bloc. It was promptly denounced by the West as "illegal and unconstitutional".

Stalin's move follows the failure of his attempt to strangle West Berlin by preventing access to it. The year-long blockade ended in the summer and was broken by the extraordinary airlift of Allied supplies to the city. While West Berlin was besieged, the Federal German Republic has come into being, and this is one reason behind Stalin's creation of the "rival" GDR.

The Soviet occupation of East Germany has seen the systematic pillage of the economy in the form of war reparations, dismantling of factories, compulsory deliveries and the forming of "mixed companies".

By comparison with West German standards, the country is drab, scruffy, neglected and listless. The sense of defeat and humiliation in East Germany is even more depressing than the decay of its buildings. Not surprisingly, hundreds of thousands of East Germans have made their way to the West.

The first president is Wilhelm Pieck, one of the two joint chairmen of the Socialist Unity Party. Otto Grotewohl was named prime minister. But the country will continue to be controlled by large numbers of Soviet troops, backed up by the Soviet secret police, and all major decisions, seem likely to be taken in Moscow (→ 31/12).

1949

NOVEMBER

Su	Mo	Tu	We	Th	Fr	Sa
		1	2	3	4	5
6	7	8	9	10	11	12
13	14	15	16	17	18	19
20	21	22	23	24	25	26
27	28	29	30			

1. Washington: 55 die when a fighter hits an airliner, the worst US air disaster (→ 16).

1. UK: HMS Amethyst receives a tumultuous welcome on her return from China.

2. The Hague: A round table conference ends with recognition of the United States of Indonesia (→ 16/12).

3. London: The BBC reveals it is to buy the Shepherd's Bush studios of Rank Films for television (→ 4).

4. London: Rank Films sacks 150 staff, making 1,500 redundancies this year in Britain's film industry.→

7. Strasbourg: The Council of Europe holds its first session, chaired by Belgium's Paul Spaak (→ 9/5/50).

12. Prague: The government says church marriages will not be recognised from the end of the year (→ 12/5/50).

15. London: The government decides to postpone iron and steel nationalisation until January 1, 1951 (→ 30/6/50).

15. India: Nathuram Vinayak Godse is hanged for the murder of Gandhi (→ 26).

16. Atlantic: Twenty crew are missing after a USAF B-29 crashes off Bermuda (→ 17).

17. US: 18 crew die when two USAF B-29s collide in flight (→ 18).

18. US: Five die when a B-29 crashes off Florida (→ 20).

19. Monaco: Rainier III is sworn in as 30th ruling Prince of Monaco.

20. Norway: A plane carrying 35 passengers, mainly children, is missing.→

21. New York: The UN grants independence to all former Italian colonies (→ 2/5/50).

26. New Delhi: Indian MPs approve India's new constitution as a "sovereign democratic republic" (→ 26/1/50).

29. London: Peers reject the Parliament Bill a third time, but it becomes law as MPs have passed it three times.

Labour is soft-pedalling on socialism

Nov 23. Significant dilution of the Socialist content in Labour's programme for the next general election was announced today. After stormy argument, the party's national executive dropped nationalisation of the industrial assurance companies from its "shopping list" for extending State ownership.

This decision is part of a fierce ideological battle now raging for the soul of the party. It is between the left-wing zealots, led by Aneurin Bevan (with the weekly Tribune edited by Michael Foot, as his mouthpiece) and a right-wing orchestra consisting of the bulk of the cabinet and TUC hierarchy, conducted by Herbert Morrison. Mr Attlee is still keeping quiet, but is increasingly irked by what he sees as Bevanite disruption.

After the trauma of devaluation, the cabinet majority is lukewarm about all the nationalisation items in the party's latest policy document, "Labour Believes In Britain". They will still be included in the election manifesto, but, just as it is proposed insurance companies will be mutualised rather than state controlled, so other commitments will be watered down.

Attlee – Labour's balancing actor.

The Labour leadership considers that now is the time for digestion, after four years of social revolution, rather than embarking on yet more bruising changes. It may be difficult to sell the idea to the party faithful, but for a while it wants to sing the Red Flag only when absolutely necessary (→ 10/1/50).

Television taking over from cinema

Nov 4. An ominous picture of television's empire, expanding at the expense of a now faltering British film industry, emerges today as the BBC announce the purchase of the Rank film studios at Lime Grove, West London, for television use while Rank serves 120 of its workers with redundancy notices.

This brings the total number of film workers dismissed this year to 1,500, in contrast with the BBC's further plans to open a new television centre at White City. An urgent request for a £20 million loan to the ailing film industry has been made by MP Tom O'Brien, who is also general secretary of the National Association of Theatrical and Cinematograph Employees.

He explained that already, a substantial part of the £5 million given to film producers by the government-sponsored Finance Corporation – a sum meant to cover five years – has been spent. The only other source of money is the box-office (→ 25/7/50).

Plane crashes kill a record 142 this month

Nov 29. Planes fell from the sky with horrible frequency this month, as a whole series of air crashes claimed 142 lives across the world.

On the first day of the month, a fighter plane collided with an Eastern Airlines passenger airliner, cutting it in half, 100 feet above Washington's National Airport, and killing 55 men, women and children. The only survivor was the pilot of the fighter jet.

Later in the month, three disasters in three days, all involving B-29 Superfortresses, claimed a further 25 lives. A total of 18 crew members died in a 27,000 feet collision. In Bermuda, the downing of a B-29 launched the biggest peacetime air-sea rescue yet, which found 18 of the 20 crew alive but delirious, after 75 hours floating on the sea. Another B-29 crashed off Florida, claiming another five lives and now all Superfortresses have been grounded. Last week, a crash near Oslo killed 34 people, 27 of them orphan children, on their way to a rehabilitation centre. Finally, today, 28 people perished as a passenger jet exploded at Dallas airport (→ 12/3/50).

Tories say Nuts to a worthy scheme

Nov 21. By Tory special request, the controversial groundnuts scheme was on the House of Commons menu this evening. The Government's Overseas Food Corporation is in deep trouble again over the financial arrangements for its groundnut crops yielding vegetable oils in East African colonial territories.

Government ministers complained that the Opposition is trying to turn a worthy development project into a music-hall joke (→ 9/1/51).

British launch drive on Malayan rebels

Nov 11. British forces in Malaya have begun their biggest drive yet against concentrations of about 600 rebels hiding in dense jungle. Military chiefs now believe the end of operations may be in sight.

Units from four regiments have moved into deep jungle, intending to flush them out into wild country in the south-west of Malaya. After that, the British police, who have secured a special agreement with the Thai Government, are expected to go on and root out 1,000 more Communist rebels known to have assembled just over the border. That task will be undertaken by specially trained police squads, who have already killed 264 bandits in one area alone (→ 15/11/51).

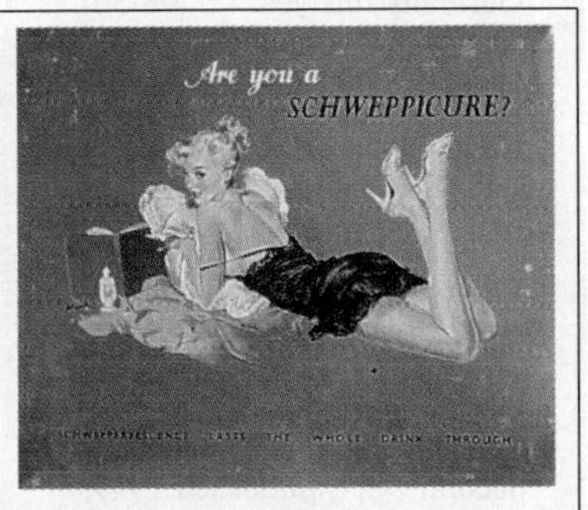

Glamour sells despite hard times.

1949

DECEMBER

Su	Mo	Tu	We	Th	Fr	Sa
				1	2	3
4	5	6	7	8	9	10
11	12	13	14	15	16	17
18	19	20	21	22	23	24
25	26	27	28	29	30	31

1. Paris: The NATO Defence Committee agrees to a general defence plan for its members (→27/1/50).

4. Singapore: Duncan Stewart, British governor of Sarawak, is stabbed by a youth opposed to British rule (→11/12/50).

5. New York: The UN votes to require member states to submit information on their military capability (→3/8/50).

9. New York: The UN approves the internationalisation of Jerusalem (→13).

10. Stockholm: Nobel Prizes go to Hideki Yukawa (Japan, Physics); William Giauque (US, Chemistry); Walter Hess (Switzerland) and Antonio Moniz (Portugal, Medicine); William Faulkner (US, Literature); and in Oslo to Lord Boyd-Orr (UK, Peace).

13. Israel: The government moves the capital from Tel Aviv to Jerusalem (→1/4).

15. US: Eisenhower says he will not be talked into running for president (→30/3/50).

16. Indonesia: Sukarno is elected first president.→

16. S. Africa: The Voortrekker Memorial to Boer pioneers is unveiled in Pretoria.

20. US: Clark Gable marries the former Lady Ashley.

21. Moscow: The USSR establishes a Soviet Peace Prize, awarded annually to citizens of any country.

26. US: Einstein publishes his new "Generalised Theory of Gravitation".→

31. Germany: 124,245 Germans are reported to have crossed from East to West Germany this year (→7/6/50).

HITS OF 1949

Buttons and Bows.

Riders in the Sky.

Baby, it's cold outside.

QUOTE OF THE YEAR

"One is not born a woman, one becomes one."

Simone de Beauvoir, "The Second Sex", published 1949.

Chinese Nationalists move to Formosa

Dec 8. With the Chinese Civil War confined to little more than sporadic resistance on the mainland, and the Communists firmly in control in Peking, the Nationalist Government has shifted its capital to Taipei, on the off-shore island of Formosa.

Nationalist Prime Minister Yen Hsi-shan has insisted that his government-in-exile is the true government of China. Despite Yen's claim, many world governments have already formally recognised Mao Tse-tung's regime.

For some time Formosa has been the favoured "retirement spot" for deposed Chinese Nationalist leaders – among them the brutal Sheng Shih-tsai – who had negotiated a possible Chinese alliance with Nazi Germany.

Generalissimo Chiang Kai-shek, the former president, is expected to arrive soon with other members of his Nationalist staff (→5/1/50).

Chiang Kai-shek leaving China.

Royal governess reveals Palace secrets

Dec 30. The memoirs of "Crawfie", governess to Princess Elizabeth and Princess Margaret, begin publication tomorrow. In the American magazine, "Ladies' Home Journal" she reveals that, as small children, her charges were mad about horses. Crawfie (Marion Crawford) was often "harnessed" and required to prance. The children had a "stable" of 30 toy horses, which were unsaddled at night.

Crawfie commented on this obsession to their father, then Duke of York, now King. He replied: "Think nothing of it. It's a family idiosyncrasy. My sister Mary was a horse till she "came out"." The King often visited the nursery to play "Snap" (→17/4/50).

Led by their governess, Miss Crawford, the two princesses visit a YWCA.

Pauling pinpoints protein deficiency

The discovery, by the American scientist **Linus Pauling**, that the debilitating disease sickle cell anaemia is caused by a tiny molecular error in the haemoglobin of the blood, was one of the most striking scientific events of 1949. Haemoglobin is one of the thousands of proteins in the body. All are built up from twenty or so standard subunits called amino acids. A single incorrect amino acid among the hundreds in haemoglobin causes sickle cell anaemia.

The year also saw a new theory of gravity from **Albert Einstein**, who has searched for 30 years for a theory unifying the four forces of nature: gravity, electromagnetism, and two sub-atomic ones. The theory is untested.

At Harwell a new cyclotron – an atom smashing machine – started work. It is the most powerful in Europe, powerful enough, it is hoped, to produce the recently discovered sub-atomic particles called mesons.

An important new theory of the workings of the immune system in man and animals, and how it leads to the rejection of grafts of tissues like skin from other individuals, came from Australian biologist **Frank Macfarlane Burnet**. His ideas could be a step towards an understanding of how to transplant organs successfully.

Sukarno will lead Indonesian state

Dec 28. Ahmed Sukarno arrived in triumph in the Indonesian capital of Jakarta today, after being elected as the first president of the newly independent republic by its constituent assembly. His return came a day after Queen Juliana of the Netherlands signed a treaty ending colonial rule over the former East Indies Empire, and agreeing to withdraw all Dutch troops there, except those in New Guinea, within seven months. In return, Sukarno's new government has promised not to nationalise Dutch economic interests in Indonesia against which his rebel army has waged a guerrilla war for the last 20 years.

Arts: British films dance off with Academy Awards

The Oscars carried off by "Hamlet" and "The Red Shoes" this year are recognition of the present high quality of British films. "The Red Shoes" ambitiously includes a full ballet in its story of backstage brouhaha in the dancing world. The choreography is by **Robert Helpmann**, who dances it with **Leonide Massine** and the young red-haired dancer of Sadler's Wells, **Moira Shearer**. The award-winning music by **Brian Easdale** was recorded by the Royal Philharmonic Orchestra under its founder, **Sir Thomas Beecham**, 70 this year.

A National Film Finance Corporation has been set up by **Harold Wilson**, the President of the Board of Trade, under the chairmanship of **Lord Reith**. It has £5 million of taxpayers' money, enough to finance 20 good films, it is estimated. The quota of British films to be shown in cinemas has been increased from 20 to 45 per cent.

British studios are dominated by two directors, **Carol Reed** and **David Lean**. Reed followed "Odd Man Out", which made the name of **James Mason** as an IRA gunman on the run, by obtaining a remarkable performance from seven-year-old **Bobby Henrey** as a boy who hero-worships a butler, in "The Fallen Idol". His latest, "The Third Man", written by **Graham Greene**, is an international hit. It gives **Orson Welles** his best part since "Citizen Kane", and the suspense generated against the seedy background of post-war Vienna, haunted by the zither music of **Anton Karas**, rivals anything that **Alfred Hitchcock** has done.

David Lean showed with "Great Expectations" how well he can translate the menace and humour of Dickens to the screen. Next he did it with "Oliver Twist", in which **Alec Guinness**, in a remarkable make-up, created a larger-than-life Fagin. So powerful was his villainy and his Jewishness that the film was banned in Berlin because of the protests of Polish Jews.

Fagin made Guinness an international name. He now follows it with a virtuoso set of character sketches as the eight members of the D'Ascoyne family who are murdered in "Kind Hearts and Coronets". With its wit, eccentricity and Englishness, this is a typical example of one of **Michael Balcon's** "Ealing comedies", named after the studios.

Other Ealing favourites are "Whisky Galore", written by **Compton Mackenzie**, about a real bonanza on a Hebridean island when a ship loaded with whisky ran aground there, and "Passport to Pimlico". This is a pleasing fantasy in which Pimlico discovers that it rightly belongs to Burgundy, not Britain, and promptly opts out of British post-war austerity.

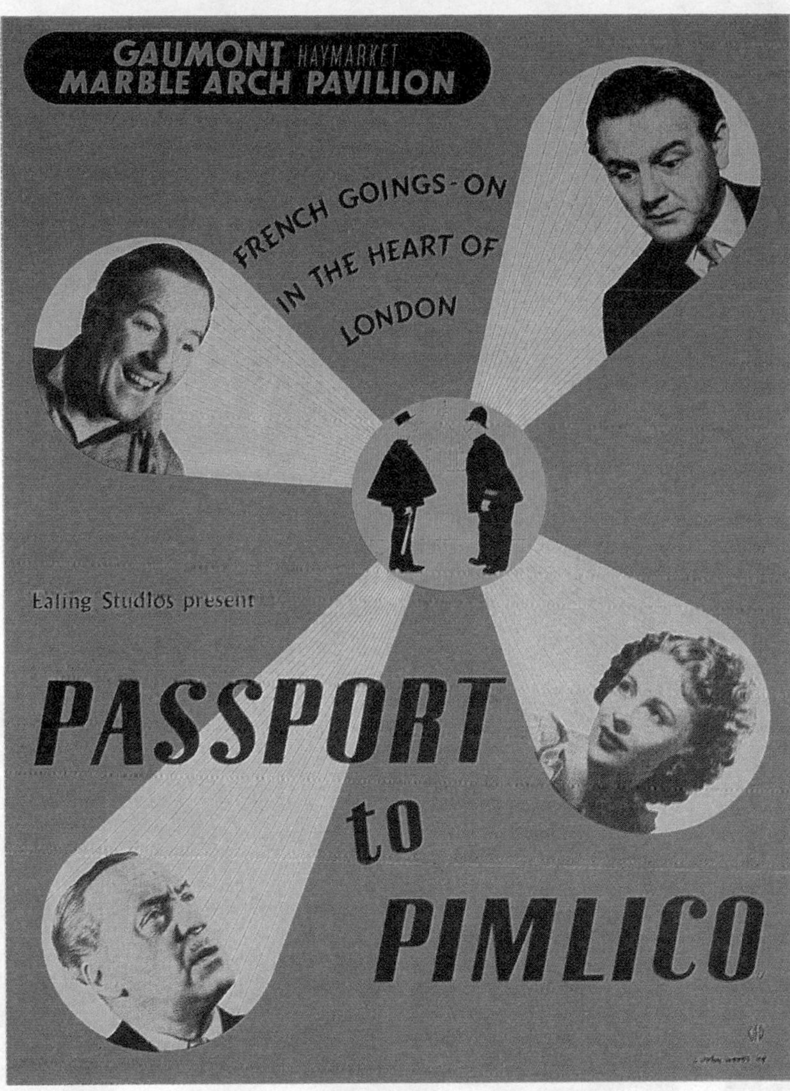

A London borough declares its independence in "Passport to Pimlico".

Backstage brouhaha and an Oscar for ballet's tribute "The Red Shoes".

Orson Welles and Joseph Cotten in Graham Greene's "The Third Man".

1950–1959

1950

JANUARY

Su	Mo	Tu	We	Th	Fr	Sa
1	2	3	4	5	6	7
8	9	10	11	12	13	14
15	16	17	18	19	20	21
22	23	24	25	26	27	28
29	30	31				

1. London: Sir Adrian Boult is appointed principal conductor of the London Philharmonic Orchestra.

4. London: Britain asks the US for a stockpile of atomic bombs (→31).

5. Washington: Truman rules out military aid to the Nationalist Chinese (→6).

6. London: Britain formally recognises Maoist China. (→10).

10. London: Attlee calls an election for February 23 (→13/2).

10. New York: Soviet envoy Malik walks out of the Security Council over the continued presence of Nationalist China.→

13. London: Premiere of Carol Reed's film, "The Third Man".

14. Washington: Acheson orders US consular staff out of mainland China (→22).

16. Bonn: Government to end rationing of all foods except sugar on March 1 (→2/2).

19. Peking: Mao recognises the North Vietnamese regime of Ho Chi Minh (→31).

21. US: Scientists at Berkeley announce the discovery of berkelium, the 93rd element.

22. Moscow: Chinese premier Chou En-lai arrives for talks with Stalin (→15/2).

24. UK: Joey Maxim of the US knocks out Britain's Freddie Mills for the world light-heavyweight boxing title.

26. New Delhi: India is proclaimed a republic (→8/4).

27. Washington: Eight nations sign the NATO defence plan (→18/5).

29. Iran: 1,500 reported dead in three earthquakes (→8/3/51).

31. Moscow: Stalin recognises Ho Chi Minh's regime; France protests (→7/2).

BIRTH

29. South African racing driver Jody Scheckter.

DEATH

21. British author George Orwell, born Eric Blair (*25/6/03).→

Russia walks out of UN in row over China

An empty seat at the UN symbolises the Soviet Union's withdrawal.

Jan 10. When the UN Security Council met, it was the turn of the Nationalist China delegate, Dr T.F. Tsiang, to take the chair. Promptly, the Soviet delegate, Jacob Malik, objected that Dr Tsiang was "a person who represents nobody," now the Koumingtang Nationalists have fled the mainland. But a resolution to bar Dr Tsiang was voted down.

The British delegate, Sir Alexander Cadogan, has found himself in a bizarre predicament. In London, the Foreign Office has recognised China's new Communist regime and withdrawn recognition from the Nationalists. Yet the FO told Sir Alexander to vote for Dr Tsiang in the Security Council.

British recognition for the Communists has upset the Americans, who point out that the civil war is continuing, with the Nationalists fighting from their new base on Formosa. The British answer is that the Communist leader, Mao Tse-tung, has the support of the Chinese people. Three Commonwealth countries, India, Pakistan and Ceylon, have followed Britain in recognising Mao (→14).

Hiss no spy but is guilty of perjury

Jan 25. Former State Department official, Alger Hiss, became the latest victim of the wave of anti-Communism sweeping America today, receiving a harsh five-year prison sentence for perjury, although no evidence was presented to show he was a Communist spy.

Hiss denied on oath meeting or passing secret government documents to Whittaker Chambers, a former Russian agent, and now a prosecution witness, but admitted the typewriter used to copy them had once belonged to him. A jury at an earlier trial were unable to decide if he was guilty, but he was convicted four days ago after a new trial and now plans to appeal, if necessary to the Supreme Court, to quash the verdict (→9/2).

British sub rammed in Thames estuary

Jan 12. A British submarine sank in the Thames estuary today, and 60 seamen on board are feared dead after it was accidentally rammed. The 1,575-ton HMS Truculent was later lying in 54 feet of water, as Navy divers began a major rescue operation for any survivors. She had been struck in a torpedo room by a Swedish ship weighing just 643 tons, but strengthened for ice-breaking.

Sixteen of the 76 men on board the sub were picked up by lifeboat soon after a special "subsmash" alert had gone out. Some survivors had been standing on the conning tower. Later a salvage tug was at the scene with air-compressors to try to raise the sub which had been on diving trials (→4/2).

Orwell did not enjoy the profits of gloom

Jan 21. George Orwell, who died today, was too ill with tuberculosis to enjoy the fame and fortune that came to him with his inspired allegory, "Animal Farm", in 1945. He retreated to the remote Scottish island of Jura, with his adopted baby son (his wife had just died) and had only just enough strength to write "Nineteen Eighty-Four" in between stays in a sanatorium.

His real name was Eric Blair, and in his early years was an Etonian and an officer of police in Burma. He reacted by turning dish-washer, tramp and down-and-out. He was shot through the throat fighting in Spain. He was married again in hospital a few weeks ago.

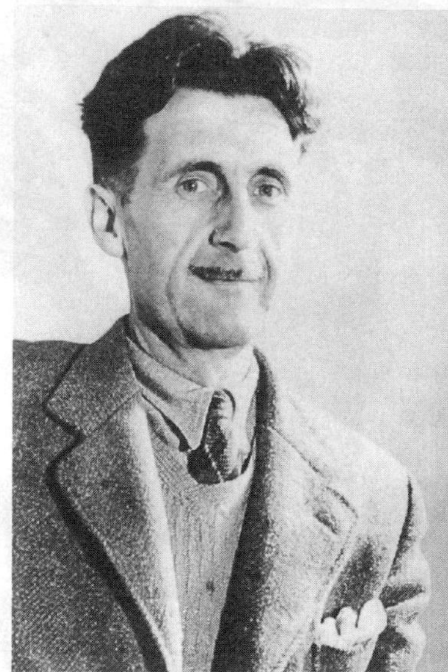

George Orwell: the nation's critic.

America plans to build an H-bomb

Jan 31. President Truman today gave the go-ahead to the American Atomic Energy Commission to research and produce the hydrogen bomb, expected to be 100 to 1,000 times more powerful than the atomic bombs dropped on Hiroshima and Nagasaki. Research is already under way into the new weapon, which will generate additional energy by fusing, instead of splitting atoms, fuelled by fears of Soviet intentions after she successfully tested an atomic bomb of her own, four months ago (→4/4).

1950

FEBRUARY

Su	Mo	Tu	We	Th	Fr	Sa
			1	2	3	4
5	6	7	8	9	10	11
12	13	14	15	16	17	18
19	20	21	22	23	24	25
26	27	28				

1. Moscow: The USSR calls for Japanese Emperor Hirohito to be tried as a war criminal (→3/9).

2. Berlin: The US says it will renew the airlift, if the Russians fail to end restrictions on land access to the city (→17/8).

4. UK: The final death toll from the HMS Truculent disaster last month is 64 (→9).

7. Brussels: The exiled King Leopold III rejects new calls for his abdication (→12/3).

8. Paris: The National Assembly approves a bill to legalise strikes and reintroduce collective bargaining (→28).

9. UK: A court martial finds the commander of the Truculent guilty of hazarding the ship and sentences him to a severe reprimand (→8/3).

10. London: Alleged spy Dr Klaus Fuchs claims he quit as a Soviet agent a year ago (→6/3).

13. UK: There are a record 1,866 candidates standing in the general election (→24).

14. S. Africa: Three townships around Johannesburg are the scene of racial violence between blacks and the police (→29/5).

17. Budapest: British businessman Edgar Sanders and American Robert Vogeler go on trial for spying (→21).

20. London: The government freezes all civil service wages.

21. Budapest: Sanders and Vogeler are both jailed for 13 years (→24).

24. UK: The Liberals lose a record 314 election deposits; 20 out of a record 126 women candidates are returned.→

24. Austria: Eugene Karp, US naval attache in Rumania and friend of Vogeler, is murdered on the Orient Express (→21/4/51).

28. Paris: The Assembly passes a bill curbing the sale of Coca-Cola (→5/4).

DEATH

26. British comedian Sir Harry Lauder (*4/8/1870).→

Labour wins election but majority is cut

Feb 24. Labour stays in office, but the general election has produced the closest result for 100 years. The final seats tally will be Labour 315, Tories 298, Liberals 9, Others 3. Party leaders are exhausted tonight after nearly 24 hours of nerve-twisting suspense while the votes were counted.

Back at 10 Downing Street, Mr Attlee made no immediate statement about the Government's future. Speaking for a frustrated Opposition, Mr Churchill said: "Parliament will be in an unstable condition now". It is virtually stalemate. The Government's single-figure overall majority indicates another election very soon. In a second, lame-duck term, the Government will be forced to shelve much of its programme for further nationalisation – such as the cement, sugar, water and shipping industries. Tories are already saying: "One more heave and socialism is dead."

The result confirms the big switch in public mood, apparent even before last year's devaluation crisis. No election has cast its shadow so far before it. The nation's verdict is that it wants the Welfare State, created after 1945, but is dissatisfied with economic management and prefers a period of consolidation to further Socialist experiment right now (→9/3).

Mr A.E. Stubbs, Labour hopeful, talking to Cambridgeshire farm workers.

East and West split over two Vietnams

Feb 7. Vietnam effectively became two separate nations today, when Britain and the US recognised Emperor Bao Dai as its ruler, only a week after Russia and her allies officially endorsed the rival regime, led by Ho Chi Minh.

Bao Dai's Saigon-based regime was also recognised as an associate state within the French Union, along with the Royalist regimes in Cambodia and Laos, by the French National Assembly last week. In contrast, Ho Chi Minh leads the nationalist guerrilla fighters against the French Army, and, although originally pro-American, is now armed and supported by the Communist bloc. The Anglo-American announcement, which also recognised the governments in Cambodia and Laos, is expected to be followed by similar declarations from other Western nations.

Nine Communist nations, including Yugoslavia and Albania as well as Russia, already recognise Ho Chi Minh as the legitimate leader of Vietnam.

The US has also paved the way for a more active role in Vietnam, with a statement warning she would take any necessary action to ensure "Indochina would not be hindered by internal dissension fostered from abroad," a thinly-disguised reference to the Soviet Union (→8/5).

FBI tip off leads to jailing of spy Fuchs

Feb 3. The top nuclear scientist Dr Klaus Fuchs, was today charged with giving Russian agents secret information about how to build atomic bombs. If convicted, he faces up to 14 years in prison.

Fuchs, aged 38, a German-born Communist, had been given full access to British and American research bases for seven years. It was only shortly before his arrest that the FBI in America discovered his betrayal and tipped off MI5.

The prosecution allege that Fuchs is guilty of the "grossest treachery" and saved the Russians years of research (→10).

Will ye no come back again Harry?

Feb 26. The little man with a stumpy walk, a broad Scots accent and a lovable personality, who turned himself from a miner into a worldwide favourite as a comedian and singer, has died at 79. Sir Harry Lauder was the most famous Scotsman of his age, being paid £2,500 a week at his peak. George V's favourite comedian, he was knighted for his war efforts in 1919.

It was his baritone voice that got him on to the stage. He wrote his own songs, among them "I Love a Lassie", "Stop Yer Ticklin' Jock" and "Roamin' in the Gloamin".

Scotland's comic favourite is dead.

Communist giants sign friendship pact

Mao and Stalin, with Bulganin: a treaty for Communism's superpowers.

Feb 15. Russia and China, the two great Communist nations, today announced they had formed a common, united front against the world. After three months of negotiations Stalin and Mao Tse-tung concluded a formal alliance, including a mutual defence treaty.

Stalin undertook to return his "war booty", seized by the Red Army in Manchuria, and to give up the Manchurian railway before the end of 1952. He yielded Port Arthur as well, but apparently will still maintain control over the strategically important port of Dairen. Stalin also committed himself to assisting China generously in economic development and pledged $300 million in aid.

Following the proclamation of the Chinese People's Republic last October, Stalin lost little time in inviting Mao to Moscow and received him with every sign of friendship and respect. The talks between the two leaders – who are both men of inexhaustible cunning – began in December. They lasted so long that rumours began to circulate that Mao had been taken hostage.

Thus, at the height of the Cold War, Stalin has suddenly acquired a great ally. It is clear that China will now have the role of protecting the Soviet Union's immense frontier with Asia, leaving Stalin to concentrate his military resources in Europe. Mao could benefit from Soviet economic, military and diplomatic aid and protection, while he establishes the control of central government throughout the country (→ 23/4).

Chief who married typist won't resign

Feb 14. Seretse Khama, chief designate of the Bamangato tribe of Bechuanaland, arrived in London today to discuss the furore created by his recent marriage to 24-year-old London typist, Miss Ruth Williams. He will meet Patrick Gordon-Walker, the Secretary for Commonwealth Relations, who is expected to ask him to give up his claim to the chieftainship because it may lead to "disturbances". Khama has said he will refuse, saying his tribe backs him (→ 16).

Anti-Red crusade is launched in the US

Feb 9. Senator Joseph McCarthy shot to national prominence in the US for the first time today when he launched a crusade against alleged Communist infiltration of Federal government. "I have here in my hand a list of 205 members of the Communist party still working and shaping the policy of the State Department," he told a meeting of the Ohio County Women's Republican Club. McCarthy offered no proof and refused to reveal any of the names on the list (→ 12/3/51).

1950

MARCH

Su	Mo	Tu	We	Th	Fr	Sa
			1	2	3	4
5	6	7	8	9	10	11
12	13	14	15	16	17	18
19	20	21	22	23	24	25
26	27	28	29	30	31	

3. Washington: The House of Representatives votes to admit Alaska as the 49th state.

6. London: Commonwealth Secretary Gordon-Walker tells Seretse Khama not to return to Bechuanaland (→ 16).

8. UK: Rover produces the first gas-turbine car.

8. UK: The RAF retires the last Lancaster bomber (→ 3/5).

9. UK: With the final declaration of Liverpool Moss Side, a Tory win, Labour's majority is only six (→ 29).

12. Brussels: A referendum votes 57.68 per cent for the return of King Leopold III, who refuses to abdicate (→ 18).

14. UK: "The Grass is Singing", a first novel by Doris Lessing, is published to great acclaim.

16. London: Following protests from his tribe, Seretse Khama is allowed to return to Bechuanaland.

18. UK: Roger Bannister runs the mile in a record four minutes 1.48 seconds.

18. Brussels: The government of Gaston Eyskens resigns rather than allow Leopold III to return (→ 20/7).

21. UK: A study says only 46 per cent of British households have a bathroom (→ 22).

22. London: The government unveils plans for a new town at Corby, Northamptonshire.

25. UK: Mrs L. Brotherton's Freebooter wins the Grand National.

29. London: Attlee suffers his first Commons defeat, in a vote on coal and petrol (→ 18/4).

30. US: Truman denounces Joseph McCarthy and two other senators as saboteurs of US foreign policy (→ 1/1).

DEATHS

12. German author Heinrich Mann (*27/3/1871).

19. US author Edgar Rice Burroughs (*1/9/1875).

30. French statesman Leon Blum (*9/4/1872).

Hunt is on for spy Fuchs's accomplices

March 6. Western intelligence services are hunting two Russian agents described by jailed atomic secrets spy, Klaus Fuchs. Since being sent to prison for 14 years, the former scientist at the Harwell weapons research centre in Berkshire has told how he met Soviet controllers in America and Britain. One, who had identified himself by wearing a red carnation, is thought to be the same man who obtained bomb research details four years ago from another jailed British scientist, Nunn May. In London, MI5 are also hunting a mystery woman who spent weekends with Fuchs (→ 23/10).

Atom spy Klaus Fuchs is jailed.

Heyerdahl tells of Kon-Tiki expedition

March 31. How a Norwegian anthropologist made a 5,000-mile journey across the Pacific on a raft to settle an argument, is told in Thor Heyerdahl's book, "The Kon-Tiki Expedition", published today. His theory was that Polynesian islanders must have originally sailed from South America. Experts said such a journey was impossible for primitives, so he decided to prove it. With a raft of balsa logs roped together, and a crew of five, all Scandinavians, he set off on a journey that lasted 101 days. This feat of seamanship proved at least the practicality of the theory – not to mention his courage. The raft is in a museum in Oslo.

Eighty killed in world's worst air crash

The wreckage of the Avro Tudor V, tomb of 80 Welsh rugby supporters.

March 12. Eighty people died today when a charter aircraft, previously flown on the Berlin airlift, crashed not far from Cardiff. The aircraft was carrying rugby fans home from the Wales v. Ireland International and the death toll is thought to be higher than any previous civil aircraft disaster anywhere in the world.

Eye-witnesses said they saw the Tudor V airliner come in low towards the airport in fine, clear weather. Then it started to climb, and its engines cut out. The aircraft immediately nose-dived into a field and broke into pieces.

Three survivors were taken to a farm a few hundred yards away. Two of them, who had travelled in the tail of the plane, escaped unhurt. Sixty ambulances were called to the scene to carry the bodies of the dead to the nearby RAF Station at St. Athan.

Tonight, Air Vice-Marshal D.C.T. Bennett, chairman of the plane's owners, Fairflight, said: "As far as we can see everything was in correct order on the aircraft." He said it had flown for over 1,400 hours and had been used extensively on the Berlin airlift.

He added: "In fact, it holds the record for the best achievement of any aircraft on the Berlin airlift. It flew more hours than any other British or US machine" (→17/10).

Members of the Burmese Special Police escort three prisoners during this week's countrywide round-up of suspected Communist agitators.

1950

APRIL

Su	Mo	Tu	We	Th	Fr	Sa
						1
2	3	4	5	6	7	8
9	10	11	12	13	14	15
16	17	18	19	20	21	22
23	24	25	26	27	28	29
30						

1. New York: The UN adopts a plan to divide Jerusalem (→14/2/51).

4. London: The government reveals plans for Britain's sixth atomic centre at Aldermaston in Berkshire (→22/6).

5. Paris: Police clash with more than 3,000 Communist demonstrators in Paris (→11/7).

7. Bechuanaland: Seretse Khama is refused permission to see his wife Ruth (→16).

8. New Delhi: Nehru and Khan sign the Indo-Pakistani pact on minorities agreed on April 5 (→16/0/51).

10. UK: The head of the National Hairdressers Federation says many men have longer hair than their wives (→26).

11. Moscow: The USSR says it has shot down a US bomber over Soviet-occupied Latvia (→21).

16. Bechuanaland: Seretse Khama is finally reunited with his wife (→13/11).

17. London: Princess Elizabeth is expecting another baby in August (→15/8).

18. London: The budget puts another 9d. on petrol tax, taking the price of a gallon to around three shillings (→26/5).

21. Moscow: The USSR refuses to apologise to the US for shooting down a US plane.

23. China: Chiang orders the evacuation of Hainan island, the last Nationalist territory outside Formosa (→1/5).

26. Birmingham: A survey of the city's teenagers reveals they spend free time at the cinema, reading comics and dancing.

27. Canberra: Prime Minister Menzies introduces a bill to ban the Communist Party and seize its assets (→6/6).

29. London: Arsenal beat Liverpool 2-0 in the FA Cup Final at Wembley.

DEATHS

3. German composer Kurt Weill (*2/3/1900).

8. Russian ballet dancer Vaslav Nijinsky (*12/3/1890).

India and Pakistan minorities pledge

Nehru: "We want to be friends."

April 5. The continuing communal violence between Hindus and Moslems in India and Pakistan has brought the two countries together to agree on a "bill of rights for minorities". It will apply especially to those pockets of minorities left behind in the bloody migrations after partition.

Surrounded by hostile people of a different faith, these minorities fall victim to sudden, murderous attacks and live constantly in fear. Today's agreement between India's Prime Minister, Pandit Nehru, and his Pakistani counterpart, Liaquat Ali Khan, is aimed at removing this fear, thus enabling the different communities to live in peace.

The agreement has teeth: "drumhead justice" will be imposed on people convicted of violating minority rights (→8).

Liner is found to be stuffed with nylons

April 4. Customs men raiding a transatlantic liner have seized smuggled nylon stockings, with a black market value estimated at more than £80,000, it was disclosed today. Soon after the 20,000 ton Franconia docked at Liverpool, special customs investigators boarded the ship, and found that she was "stuffed with nylons" – tucked in first class cabins and behind the ship's inner hull.

New kingdom of Jordan is created

April 24. King Abdullah of Jordan today annexed Arab Palestine, to create an expanded Kingdom of Jordan. Although widely expected, his move was greeted with fury by the other Arab states, who see the West Bank territory as a Palestinian homeland. However, Britain has endorsed the annexation, which allows her to extend the existing Anglo-Jordanian military alliance to the West Bank. The annexed territory, which includes East Jerusalem and Hebron, was captured by the Arab Legion in the war with Israel, and doubles Jordan's existing population (→ 20/7/51).

US man dies twice and returns home

April 21. A 65-year-old New Yorker will be leaving hospital today having been pronounced dead twice on the operating table. During the course of an abdominal operation his heart stopped beating on two occasions, but each time the normal rhythm was restored by manual massage of his heart. On both occasions the surgeon had to make an incision in his chest.

It happened at St John's Episcopal Hospital in Brooklyn, New York, where officials state that the patient has made a complete recovery. Although heart massage has saved others, it has never been used twice on the same patient (→ 17/6).

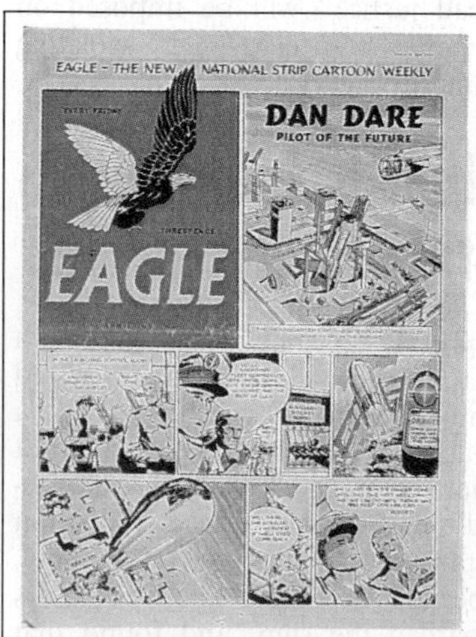

Ripping yarns from space as the newest boy's comic is launched.

1950

MAY

Su	Mo	Tu	We	Th	Fr	Sa
	1	2	3	4	5	6
7	8	9	10	11	12	13
14	15	16	17	18	19	20
21	22	23	24	25	26	27
28	29	30	31			

1. New York: The musical "South Pacific" wins the 1950 Pulitzer Prize for best original American play.

1. China: A new law bans polygamy, infanticide and the marriage of children (→ 22).

2. Rome: Wartime army chief Rodolfo Graziani is jailed for collaboration with Germany.

3. Birkenhead: The new 36,800-ton HMS Ark Royal is launched (→ 5/8).

4. London: Sir Malcolm Sargent succeeds Sir Adrian Boult as conductor of the BBC Symphony Orchestra.

7. India: 81 die in a rail crash at Patna; sabotage suspected.

8. Saigon: French intelligence says Ho Chi Minh has made a secret military agreement with Mao Tse-tung (→ 25).

9. West Germany: Chancellor Adenauer says his cabinet has accepted an invitation to join the Council of Europe (→ 15/6).

12. Prague: Czechoslovakia renounces its 1947 cultural agreement with Britain (→ 11/9/51).

18. London: 12 NATO foreign ministers adopt a six-point programme for strengthening ties between Western states (→ 26/9).

22. Peking: Mao offers Tibet regional autonomy, if it joins China (→ 28/6).

23. London: The BBC and sports representatives agree to the televising of 100 sporting events a year.

25. Vietnam: French troops are attacked by Viet Minh in Dong Khe (→ 18/9).

26. UK: Petrol rationing ends.→

27. UK: Mr M. Boussac's Galcador wins the Derby.

29. Cape Town: "Non-whites" plan a "Day of Mourning" to protest against the government's racial legislation (→ 14/6).

DEATH

24. British commander Field Marshal Lord Archibald Wavell (*5/5/1883).

Motoring booms as petrol rationing ends

Petrol rationing ends tomorow, but queues for petrol have begun today.

May 30. The first Whitsun holiday since petrol rationing ended brought out traffic, described by an AA official as an all-time record.

"From as far as ten miles out," he said, "cars were coming into London at 11pm in a solid mass." There were more than ten hours of sunshine from Kent to Lincolnshire.

"The end of rationing will be a great boon to holiday resorts," said the mayor of Buxton, who let off rockets and balloons. Shares of hotels rose in expectation of the announcement. At some garages drivers tore up coupons and danced round their cars. Petrol had been rationed for ten years (→ 1/6).

French plan for a federation of Europe

May 9. Robert Schuman, the French Foreign Minister, today took a first step towards creating a European Federation, by proposing a combined "High Authority", to control the coal and steel production of France and Germany.

The organisation, which would also be open to other European states including Russia, would modernise the industries, unify the trade tariffs of its members and control the export of the products. Schuman said his plan would create a "basis for solidarity" and serve as a foundation for a united Europe. The proposals were immediately welcomed by the German Government, which said it would contribute towards ensuring that another war with France became "unthinkable" (→ 19/3/51).

HMS Ark Royal, the fourth ship to bear the name, leaves the slipway.

1950

JUNE

Su	Mo	Tu	We	Th	Fr	Sa
				1	2	3
4	5	6	7	8	9	10
11	12	13	14	15	16	17
18	19	20	21	22	23	24
25	26	27	28	29	30	

1. UK: Petrol goes up to around 3/- a gallon, its highest price since 1920 (→ 10/7).

3. Nepal: A French expedition reaches the top of Annapurna.

6. Canberra: Menzies agrees to compromise on his bill to ban the Communist Party (→ 1/8).

7. Warsaw: East Germany signs a treaty recognising the Oder-Neisse Line as its frontier with Poland (→ 23).

9. London: A report into a riot at Enugu Colliery, Nigeria, when police killed 21 miners, blames the police chief.

14. S. Africa: Smuts resigns as leader of the United Party from ill health (→ 12/10).

15. Bonn: The West German Bundestag votes 220 to 152 to join the Council of Europe (→ 11/8).

18. Cairo: Egypt signs a security pact with Syria, Lebanon, Yemen and Saudi Arabia (→ 16/11).

22. UK: The head of Harwell atomic station says there could be nuclear-powered ships and submarines within ten years (→ 8/12).

22. Eastern Europe: Penal codes based on the USSR are being introduced in Hungary and Czechoslovakia.

23. Berlin: East Germany signs a treaty renouncing the rights of Sudeten Germans to live in Czechoslovakia (→ 12/8/51).

28. Formosa: The Nationalists order a halt to air and naval attacks on mainland China, as requested by the US (→ 18/7).

28. Korea: General MacArthur arrives at the war front from Japan (→ 29).

29. Moscow: Stalin turns down a US request to use its influence to halt the North Korean invasion (→ 3/7).

30. UK: Figures show that the National Coal Board made a £9.5 million profit in 1949 (→ 11/9).

30. Hungary: University theology departments are shut by the government (→ 6/8).

North Korea marches into the South

June 25. Communist North Korea invaded the independent southern half of this divided nation at dawn today. The invasion came without warning. Troops and tanks stormed over the frontier, while landing craft sailed down the east coast to land troops behind South Korean lines, and planes attacked the airfield at Seoul, the southern capital.

Within a few hours the Northern army had crossed the 38th Parallel, the agreed border between the two states, and had occupied all the territory north of the Imjin River. Reports say that their Russian-supplied tanks are already only 12 miles from the capital.

South Korea is hurriedly mobilising its army, and sending its troops into battle by train, lorry, bus and commandeered private cars, to meet the invaders. Early reports speak of four beachheads being established on the east coast.

The shock of this attack is ringing round the world. It seems certain to bring the Western Allies and the Communist bloc into conflict. The first political moves were made last night when the UN Security Council was urgently summoned at Lake Success, New York.

Russia was not there, as the Soviets are continuing their boycott in protest against Nationalist China's presence on the Council. This may prove a mistake, for the Council adopted a United States resolution condemning the North Korean attack as an "act of aggression", and calling for their withdrawal to the 38th Parallel.

The Americans will certainly push this advantage in the UN. Mr Truman flew back to Washington from his holiday weekend in Missouri, and it was reported that America has decided to give South Korea as much aid as possible, with supplies already being rushed from US bases in Japan.

Mr Truman told reporters on his arrival in Washington: "It could be a dangerous situation." He immediately went into conference with his senior military and diplomatic advisors. Meanwhile, in London, Mr Attlee has been carrying out similar consultations and will make a statement on the invasion in the House of Commons tomorrow.

Korea was occupied by American and Russian troops in 1945. Russia refused in 1947 to admit a UN commission and set up a Communist People's Republic. Elections were held in the American zone and the Republic of Korea established (→ 26).

Two wounded South Koreans are helped by friends to escape the fighting.

US offers military aid to South Korea

June 26. President Truman today ordered American air and naval forces to go to the aid of South Korea in its fight against the North Korean invaders. He also ordered the 7th Fleet to forestall any attack on Formosa. American forces in the Philippines are to be strengthened and military aid to the Philippines and Indochina speeded up.

In the House of Commons, Mr Attlee endorsed Mr Truman's actions, describing the invasion as "naked aggression" which "must be checked". Meanwhile, US aircraft and ships are already attacking the invading forces (→ 27).

UN backs opposition to the Communists

MacArthur returns to Korea.

June 27. The United Nations Security Council reacted to the North Korean invasion of South Korea today by recommending that all members of the UN "furnish such assistance to the Republic of Korea as may be necessary to meet the armed attack".

The Council took this decision in the absence of the Soviet Union, which is still boycotting meetings. It could not, therefore, challenge the US accusation that the Communists were carrying out "a well-planned, concerted and full-scale attack", or argue against the Council's decision which opens the way for America to intervene in Korea under the UN banner (→ 28). ▷

Royal Navy to aid Americans in Korea

June 28. British ships in the Far East are being placed under the command of US General Douglas MacArthur, to aid the United Nations in South Korea, following the crossing of the 38th parallel by North Korean forces two days ago.

The move, announced today by the Prime Minister, Mr Attlee, has been welcomed warmly by all sides in the House of Commons. Winston Churchill said: "Once again, America and Britain find themselves associated in a noble cause. When bad men combine, good must associate."

Meanwhile, the fall of the South Korean capital, Seoul, was confirmed today. The North Koreans, supported by 100 Russian-made tanks, are driving south with little resistance, although American fighters and light bombers continue to attack enemy troops north of the capital.

Britain currently has 22 ships in the Far East, including two aircraft carriers, the Triumph and the Unicorn and the cruiser Belfast. Combined with the US Fleet, they make up a force much larger than anything they are likely to face in those waters.

It will be the first time the two countries will have had the chance to join forces since the formation of the new NATO alliance. Fortunately, the move comes at a time when most of the Far East Fleet, based in Hong Kong, were already on their summer cruise in Japanese waters anyway (→29).

England's footballers lose 1-0 to the US

June 28. Shock results are the lifeblood of football, but no international result has so amazed sport as today's World Cup first round score of England 0, USA 1. Editors telephoned the agencies to check that it was not a mistake.

It was all too true. England came to the fourth World Cup in Brazil joint favourites with the dazzling Brazilians to win the Cup. In their opening match against Chile, England were able to leave out Stanley Matthews, yet win 2-0 with comfort. The team then travelled upcountry to Belo Horizonte, with its tiny stadium and bumpy pitch, to take on the ill-assorted team of multi-national immigrants that made up the American squad, who had already lost 3-1 to Spain.

The Americans, and their Scottish manager, Bill Jeffrey, were certain they had no chance. Not even when their centre-forward, Larry Gaetjens, headed home a stray shot just before half-time. But despite the wizardry of Tom Finney and constant driving of their captain Billy Wright, England could not force a goal. With the final whistle they could look forward only to an ignominious exit from their first World Cup (→ 16/7).

US surgeon first to transplant kidney

June 17. A dead patient's kidney was today transplanted into a living patient by R.H. Lawler, a Chicago surgeon. The patient is a woman of 44 with a distinctive kidney disorder, from which her mother, sister and uncle have died, whilst a first cousin survives. The donor, who had the same blood group, had died from liver disease and bleeding from the gut. After the removal of the patient's kidney, the blood vessels and ducts of the donor's kidney were successfully joined up, and its colour changed from bluish brown to reddish brown.

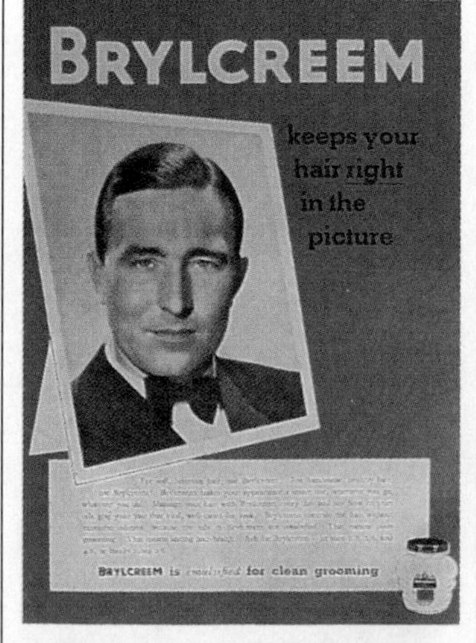

BRYLCREEM
keeps your hair right in the picture

Denis Compton stars for hair.

1950

JULY

Su	Mo	Tu	We	Th	Fr	Sa
						1
2	3	4	5	6	7	8
9	10	11	12	13	14	15
16	17	18	19	20	21	22
23	24	25	26	27	28	29
30	31					

1. UK: Ford launches its Consul and Zephyr range.

3. New York: North Korea accuses the US of "bare-faced aggression" (→31).

6. Wimbledon: The tournament's longest-ever set, in the men's doubles fourth round, ends 31 games to 29 (→8).

7. UK: Bobby Locke wins his second British Open Golf Championship in a row with a record aggregate of 279.

8. Wimbledon: John "Budge" Patty beats Frank Sedgman in the Men's Singles final; Louise Brough beats Margaret Dupont for her third successive Women's Singles title.

10. London: The government ends soap rationing (→16/2/51).

11. Paris: Rene Pleven forms a cabinet including socialists (→8/9).

15. UK: Churchill warns of a Third World War.

18. London: Britain bans the sale of oil to China (→21/10).

20. Brussels: Amid strikes and protests, Belgium's parliament authorises King Leopold III's return from exile (→22).

22. Brussels: Leopold III arrives after six years in exile; the Socialist government resigns in protest (→27).

25. UK: Figures show that production of television sets has jumped by 250 per cent this year (→31/10/51).

27. Brussels: Police clash with crowds protesting at the return of Leopold III (→31).

31. Formosa: MacArthur arrives for talks with Chiang Kai-shek on his possible role in the Korean conflict (→1/8).

31. Brussels: Leopold III abdicates in favour of his son Baudouin, 19 (→1/8).

31. London: J. Sainsbury's first self-service store has opened in Croydon.

DEATH

22. Canadian statesman William Mackenzie King, PM 1921-26, 1926-30, 1935-48 (*17/12/1874).

Sinatra's London debut is a sell-out

July 11. Frank Sinatra made his London debut last night to an ovation at a London Palladium that was besieged by fans. He has just ousted Bing Crosby as the highest paid singer in the US, by signing a radio contract worth £1 million.

Sinatra, whose career began ten years ago with the Tommy Dorsey band, has only been seen here in films, currently in "On The Town", as one of three sailors on leave.

London critics were somewhat tart about his concert. "You can hear every word he sings – which is sometimes a pity, considering his material," wrote one. "It is like being force-fed with treacle."

Crooner Sinatra signs for a fan.

Second World Cup win for Uruguay

July 16. Uruguay blunted Brazil's brilliant individualism, countered a one-goal deficit with two fine goals of their own, and won the final match in Rio to take the World Cup for the second time.

With England dismissed in the early rounds, Spain and Chile were no threat to the two South American giants. But in the end, despite Brazil's scoring power (Ademir's seven goals topped the list) and a crowd of 200,000 roaring them on, it was Uruguay who produced the discipline and character when it mattered.

Korean conflict begins to suck in world powers

A captured Communist surrenders to a member of the US 6th Cavalry.

Americans badly mauled in first battle

July 5. American troops fought their first major engagement in Korea today and were badly mauled when 40 North Korean tanks overran their forward positions south of Suwon. The Communist tanks were backed up by infantry, outnumbering the Americans two to one.

American artillery, firing at close quarters, knocked out five of the Russian-built T34 tanks, and the infantry destroyed two more. But they could not cope with them all and when their ammunition ran out they were forced to abandon their wounded and equipment.

The first news of the fierce struggle was given when survivors began to straggle back to HQ. "The infantry took a terrific pounding," said Lt.Col. Miller Terry, "as the tanks came down the road they swung their turrets on our positions."

The Americans are now fighting a series of desperate delaying actions, holding up the invaders while more troops are flown in. In Washington, it was announced that seven commercial airlines have been engaged by the US Defense Department for the task. For the moment, the United Nations forces engaged in Korea must look to the air for relief. General MacArthur's HQ announced tonight that bombers and fighters from the 27,000 ton carrier, Valley Forge, and the 13,350 ton British carrier, HMS Triumph, have made a series of highly successful strikes against military targets in Pyongyang, the North Korean capital.

Large fires were started at the port of Chinnampo. Two Yak aircraft were shot down and other aircraft were hit by straffing Seafire fighters on the ground (→14).

Beleaguered US wonder where Allies are

July 14. The Communist invaders have flung a fresh division in to spearhead their advance against tired American troops, fighting desperate rearguard actions to stem the North Korean march to the south. As each day goes past, so the Americans lose more and more ground. Today the North Koreans crossed the Kum river and tightened their grip on Taejon, provisional capital of South Korea, from which President Rhee has already fled.

The Americans are suffering severely from a shortage of specialised anti-tank guns and are having to use their divisional artillery to try to stop the advance of the T34s.

The infantry have lost many men trying to kill the tanks and the Americans are grumbling that they seem to be fighting all on their own: "When are we going to see some of those Aussies and Brits up here?" they ask as they wait in their slit trenches to fight off the next attack.

The situation is certainly very serious. A military spokesman admitted this today when he insisted that there is "no Dunkirk in sight in Korea. There is no doubt that we are going to hold these people."

"There is no question in my mind but that we are going to come out on top of the heap. We have got the means to handle the situation. Reinforcements are moving in and channels of communication and transportation are being kept open. Give us time and we will take the ball away and start going up the field."

More reinforcements steamed out of San Diego yesterday on two transports loaded with Marines, renowned for their expertise in amphibious operations (→26).

Britain decides to send troops to Korea

July 26. British troops are being sent to Korea to operate under the orders of the United Nations, the Defence Minister Emmanuel Shinwell told the Commons today.

The move was immediately welcomed in the United States, whose troops are assisting the South Koreans to stave off the rapid North Korean advance, which has now taken all but the south-western corner of the country. Mr Kee, the chairman of the House Foreign Affairs Committee said: "If there ever was a time when we should stand shoulder-to-shoulder it is now."

The Royal Navy in the Far East has already gone on a war footing and some reserves are being called up. Mr Shinwell said the troops now being sent to join them would be made up of infantry, armour, artillery and engineers (→31).

1950

AUGUST

Su	Mo	Tu	We	Th	Fr	Sa
		1	2	3	4	5
6	7	8	9	10	11	12
13	14	15	16	17	18	19
20	21	22	23	24	25	26
27	28	29	30	31		

1. Canberra: Prime Minister Menzies says a 3,000-strong Australian force will soon be sent to Korea (→ 7).

1. Brussels: Prince Baudouin is sworn in as Prince Regent; he will become King on his majority in September 1951 (→ 11/6/51).

3. New York: The UN Security Council rejects Mao's entry to the UN (→ 1/11).

5. London: The government announces a new programme to double arms production (→ 14/9).

6. Hungary: Several hundred non-Communists have been dismissed or arrested in the latest purge (→ 28/6/51).

7. Korea: The US launches its biggest attack on the North Koreans so far, at Chinju (→ 12).

11. Strasbourg: The Council of Europe approves a motion by Churchill urging the creation of a European army.

12. Korea: A division of North Korean troops crosses the Naktong River in a fresh assault on Taegu (→ 12).

15. London: Princess Elizabeth gives birth to her second child, a daughter.

17. Bonn: Adenauer calls for a West German army (→ 8/1/51).

20. London: Britain says a force of British infantry will leave Hong Kong to join the UN forces in Korea.→

24. Peking: Mao asks the UN to order the US Navy to quit the waters around Formosa (→ 31).

27. Belgium: Britain wins eight gold medals, more than any other country, in the European Games.

31. Washington: Truman says the US Navy will leave Formosan waters when the Korean War is settled (→ 1/9).

BIRTH

15. British Princess Anne Elizabeth Alice Louise.

DEATH

27. Italian author Cesare Pavese (*9/9/1908).

British troops disembark in South Korea

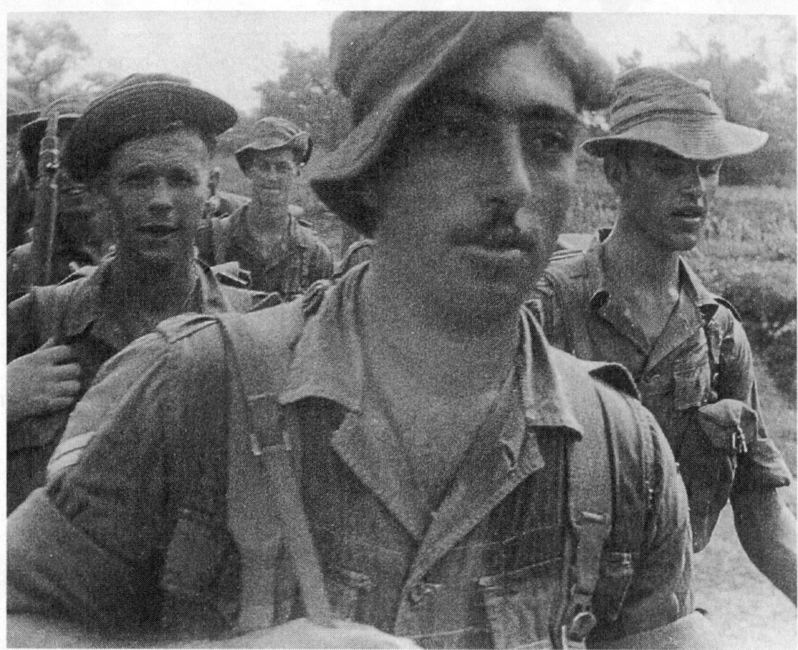

Some of the British troops who have joined the West's offensive in Korea.

Aug 29. British troops arrived in Korea today to bolster the US presence there after sailing from Hong Kong aboard the aircraft carrier Unicorn. The men from the 1st Battalion, Argyll and Sutherland Highlanders and the 1st Battalion the Middlesex Regiment, made an unopposed landing on the south-eastern coast, at a spot whose precise location is still secret.

While no numbers have been given, it appears likely the British will put around 4,000 men ashore over the next few weeks. Their presence will at last give some credence to what is supposed to be a United Nations force, but which up to now has been an exclusively American operation; they have so far committed two divisions and a brigade of Marines, with more on the way. However, despite air supremacy, the US and its South Korean allies have been forced back into the heavily defended south-eastern coastal tip.

As the British left Hong Kong a few days ago, they were told by the Commander-in-Chief, Far East Land Forces, Lt. General Sir John Harding: "Shoot quickly, shoot straight and shoot to kill."

Four days ago British naval forces made a commando raid on a small island in the port of Inchon, near Seoul, the now occupied capital. They destroyed a North Korean radio installation and a supply dump before withdrawing (→ 31).

First overseas TV broadcast by BBC

Aug 27. The BBC transmitted TV pictures live across the Channel from France for the first time this evening. The two-hour programme was transmitted in Calais by BBC presenters, Richard Dimbleby and Alan Adair, before an audience of 30,000, then beamed by microwave to Dover and relayed on to London. There was only a single, two-second break during the show and reception was reported to be as good as for other programmes (→ 1/2/51).

Channel record set by lady swimmer

Aug 5. The woman's Channel swim record was broken today by an American woman, who cut an hour off the time set 24 years ago. Florence Chadwick came ashore at Dover, after plunging into the waves 22 miles away at Cap Gris Nez, France and crossing the Channel in 13 hours and 23 minutes. But fellow American, Shirley France, was pulled hysterical and blue with cold from the sea eight miles from the English coastline.

1950

SEPTEMBER

Su	Mo	Tu	We	Th	Fr	Sa
					1	2
3	4	5	6	7	8	9
10	11	12	13	14	15	16
17	18	19	20	21	22	23
24	25	26	27	28	29	30

1. Korea: The North Koreans launch an offensive on UN troops along a 50-mile front (→ 4).

3. Japan: A typhoon sweeps Hokkaido, leaving 250 reported dead and 300,000 injured (→ 8/9/51).

4. Washington: The US says it downed a Soviet bomber "threatening" UN ships off Korea (→ 6).

6. New York: The USSR vetoes a Security Council motion condemning North Korea.→

7. London: Attlee has rejected a request from Quintin Hogg, just succeeded as Lord Hailsham, to sit as an MP.

8. France: The deportation begins of 268 foreign Communists seized yesterday.

11. UK: 115 trapped miners have been saved from a pit at Knochshinnnoch in Ayrshire; 13 are still missing (→ 28).

14. London: Admiral Guy Russell is appointed British commander-in-chief in the Far East (→ 29/1/51).

18. Vietnam: The Viet Minh occupy Dong Khe (→ 10/10).

22. Korea: The Allies capture Suwon, south of Seoul (→ 25).

25. Korea: UN forces recapture Seoul (→ 28).

26. London: NATO adopts the idea of an integrated European defence force, including West Germany (→ 19/12).

26. UK: A blue moon is visible from south-east England.

28. Korea: South Korean President Syngman Rhee returns to Seoul (→ 28).

28. Peking: Chou En-lai says China will intervene if North Korea is invaded (→ 29).

29. Korea: UN troops reach the 38th Parallel (→ 1/10).

DEATH

11. South African commander, statesman and philosopher Field Marshal Jan Christian Smuts, PM 1919-24, 1939-48 (*24/5/1870).→

Daring UN landing at Inchon surprises Communists

Sept 16. United Nations troops, tanks and guns are pouring ashore at the port of Inchon, on the west coast of Korea, from an armada of 260 ships. Yesterday's landings, codenamed "Operation Chromite", took the North Koreans completely by surprise, and the landing force is now pressing on inland. Its immediate objective is the capture of the Inchon area, and then to drive the Communists out of Seoul, the South Korean capital.

The fleet makes a brave sight, stretching for miles, as landing craft scurry backwards and forwards, building up the mass of material on the beaches.

General MacArthur, the UN commander, is here on board the flagship Mt McKinley. He is an expert in amphibious operations and it is understood that the idea for this sweeping left hook was his, and he pursued it despite opposition from high-ranking officers who feared the landing force would be cut to pieces.

In fact, the invasion fleet suffered more from natural hazards than from the enemy. It had to ride out a typhoon on its voyage from Japan and very precise calculations had to be made to land at high tide because Inchon has a 30ft tide – one of the largest in the world – and there was grave danger that the landing craft would be stuck on the mudbanks.

As it was, some of the US 5th Marines were forced to wade ashore in deep mud as they assaulted the island of Wolmi-do, which guards the approaches to Inchon. If there had been determined resistance they would have suffered massive casualties, but they took the island without losing a man.

Other forces landed on the mainland after a heavy preparatory bombardment by the fleet's heavy guns and supporting aircraft. But they did not have such an easy passage. There was a fierce battle for a point known as Cemetery Hill, in Inchon, and a North Korean machine gun bunker held up the Marines below a sea wall. But within six hours UN forces had entered the centre of Inchon.

Early this morning, men of the US 7th Infantry Division, new to the Korean conflict, started to land as the Marines continued to fight their way inland. Reports are coming in of the capture of Seoul's airfield at Kimpo. If this airfield has indeed been captured, it will provide the UN forces with a base for continuing the advance.

While this brilliant operation was being carried out with all of General MacArthur's old flair, the troops under General Walton Walker, bottled up for so long in the Pusan perimeter in the southeast, under constant North Korean attack, have gone onto the offensive.

It is hard slogging as they attempt to break through the North Korean lines. The roads are mined and are taking heavy toll of tanks and men, but new weapons – multiple 90mm guns and huge eight-inch howitzers – are pounding the North Korean positions.

"It is unbelievable that men can live through it," said Major General Hobart Gay, of the 1st Cavalry. However, enough do to cause heavy casualties among the Americans. One comfort for the troops is that General MacArthur has turned down an order from Washington cancelling their issue of one can of beer a day (→22).

Under cover of a massive sea bombardment, American Marines launch the United Nations attack at Inchon.

Old and young face the miseries of war on the roads near Inchon.

Eighty miners are killed in a colliery fire

Relatives wait at the pithead of the Cresswell Colliery after the disaster.

Sept 28. A huge underground fire today killed eighty miners whose escape was sealed off by a wall of flame. Many were trapped in suffocating fumes when they stopped to retrieve clothes. Rescuers found the men lying down as though they had tried to crawl along the miles of tunnels. They located 52 bodies.

About 240 men had been in the Cresswell colliery, in Derbyshire, as a coal conveyor belt began burning and set fire to electric cabling. The roof collapsed and survivors said flames and fumes spread faster than they could run. One miner died after returning below ground to try to find his workmates.

About 2,000 relatives gathered for a pit-head service. Virtually every street in the tiny community was mourning a loss (→ 20/11).

Smuts, guerrilla turned statesman, dies

Sept 11. The man who found a new name for the British Empire has died in South Africa. Jan Christian Smuts, the Boer farmer's son who became guerrilla leader, statesman and British Field Marshal, was 80. He took a Double First in Law at Cambridge, went back to fight against the British in the Boer War, afterwards becoming a staunch friend when Britain gave independence to South Africa. In 1917 at a dinner given for him by both Houses of Parliament, he spoke of the British Dominions as "this community of nations, which I prefer to call the British Commonwealth of Nations" (→ 14/5/51).

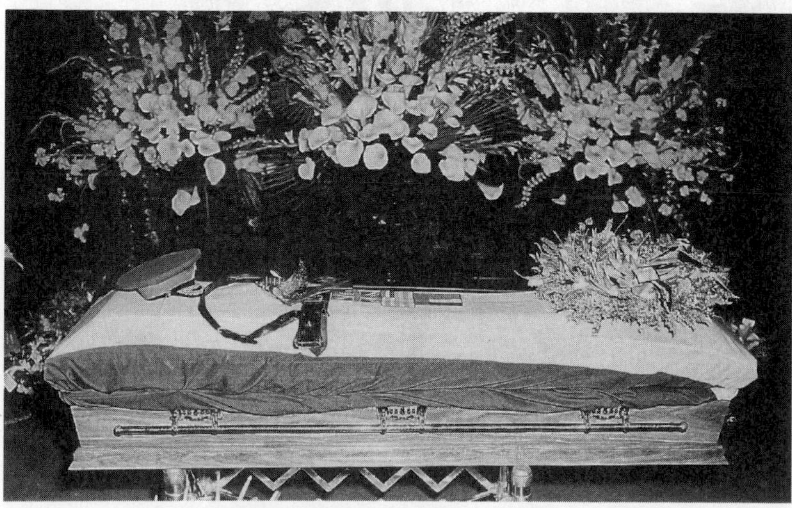

The coffin, with its single wreath from Jan Smuts' wife, lies in state.

1950

OCTOBER

Su	Mo	Tu	We	Th	Fr	Sa
1	2	3	4	5	6	7
8	9	10	11	12	13	14
15	16	17	18	19	20	21
22	23	24	25	26	27	28
29	30	31				

1. Korea: MacArthur tells North Korea to cease hostilities as South Korean troops cross the 38th Parallel (→ 13).

4. London: Three generations of the Bowler family attend a celebration to mark the centenary of the bowler hat.

6. Lebanon: The world's longest pipeline is completed, running 1,068 miles from US oil fields in the Gulf to Sidon (→ 6/9/51).

7. Washington: The US warns it will not tolerate interference in the government of Austria.

10. Vietnam: French troops are overwhelmed by the Viet Minh at Kaobang (→ 16).

13. Korea: UN forces push the North Koreans back almost as far as the capital, Pyongyang.→

16. Vietnam: The French abandon 250 miles of the Chinese frontier zone to the Viet Minh (→ 22/11).

17. London: 28 die when a BEA DC-3 Dakota crashes at Mill Hill, North London (→ 31).

21. London: Princess Elizabeth's daughter is christened Anne Elizabeth Alice Louise (→ 26).

21. Tibet: Chinese troops invade.→

23. London: An enquiry begins into Bruno Pontecorvo, the Harwell atomic scientist now reported to be in Leningrad (→ 23/2/51).

26. London: The King opens the restored House of Commons, destroyed in an air raid in 1941 (→ 8/2/51).

31. London: New teachers' salaries are announced from April 1 next year: £630 for men, £504 for women.

31. London: 28 die when a BEA Viking crashes at Heathrow Airport in fog (→ 14/11).

DEATHS

23. US singer and actor Al Jolson, born Asa Yoelson (*26/5/1886).

29. Swedish King Gustav V (*16/6/1858).

Cripps retires and Gaitskell takes over

Oct 19. Sir Stafford Cripps, Iron Chancellor and vegetarian, chief apostle of hair-shirt austerity, was forced by prolonged ill-health to resign from the cabinet tonight. After ten weeks' medical attention abroad, he has now been ordered a year's complete rest.

Mr Attlee announced that his successor is Hugh Gaitskell, up-and-coming Minister of Economic Affairs, who has been an MP for only five years. Some Labour veterans are certain to resent such quick advancement.

Mr Gaitskell is a passionate Labour right-winger.

Mao's troops march into Tibetan capital

Oct 30. Chinese Communist troops are encountering little resistance as they advance towards the Tibetan capital of Lhasa and have captured two frontier towns from the retreating Tibetan army, it was reported today. The Tibet government has appealed to India for "diplomatic help" to stop the invasion but fears the worst, and is preparing to send their spiritual leader, the Dalai Lama, into exile. It is believed the Chinese plan to instal the 13-year-old Panchen Lama as an alternative religious figurehead (→ 25/12).

Princess Elizabeth and the Duke of Edinburgh with their second child, a daughter Anne.

UN troops push through to Chinese border

A Marine calls for aid for when a comrade is badly wounded by a mortar.

Oct 27. North Korean resistance is crumbling in face of the advance of the United Nations' forces. The South Koreans, who are leading the advance, are reported to be only 50 miles from the Manchurian border, while the Commonwealth Brigade has reached Pakchon, 60 miles down the coast from the border.

The change in the situation in Korea since the Inchon landings and the hard-fought battle for Seoul, is astonishing. From defending a small perimeter around Pusan, the UN forces have occupied virtually the whole of Korea in only six weeks.

The North Korean army has disintegrated. Pyongyang, the Communists' capital, has fallen, and the North Korean people are welcoming the UN soldiers. Pyongyang is already in the backwaters of the war, evacuated so hastily, champagne bottles still stand on the bar of the Russian commissar's building, beneath the customary portrait of Stalin (→ 30).

Truman starts to rein in MacArthur

Oct 15. President Truman met General MacArthur on Wake Island today to discuss the political situation which has arisen following MacArthur's sweeping victory in Korea. With his forces pushing on to the border with China, the General is known to be keen to put an end to the threat posed by the Chinese Communist regime to American interests in the Far East.

Mr Truman, on the other hand, favours a far more cautious policy towards China. He wants Korea to be a "limited war" against a specific Communist aggression, rather than an anti-communist crusade. Apparently there was some direct talking between the two men (→ 27).

Truman meets with MacArthur.

1950

NOVEMBER

Su	Mo	Tu	We	Th	Fr	Sa
			1	2	3	4
5	6	7	8	9	10	11
12	13	14	15	16	17	18
19	20	21	22	23	24	25
26	27	28	29	30		

1. New York: Trygve Lie is elected to serve a second term as UN Secretary-General by the UN Assembly (→ 17).

4. Washington: Truman attends the funeral of the guard killed in the attempt on his life (→ 26/2/51).

6. Korea: MacArthur reports that Chinese forces have attacked UN forces near the Manchurian border (→ 7).

7. Korea: A US F.86 shoots down a MiG 15 in the first ever combat between jet fighters (→ 15).

9. London: ICI announces it will build a new factory at Redcar, Yorkshire, to produce a new fabric, "terylene".

13. London: Seretse Khama confirms reports he has renounced his chieftaincy of the Bamangwato tribe.

14. UK: Jack Gardner beats Bruce Woodcock to become British and Empire heavyweight boxing champion.

14. France: 58 die when a Canadian plane crashes in the Alps (→ 24).

17. New York: The UN grants independence to Libya.

20. London: The National Coal Board has been told to buy coal abroad (→ 1/2/51).

22. New York: 75 die when two trains collide on Long Island.

22. Indochina: Vietnamese, Cambodian and Laotian rebels meet for the first time (→ 11/1/51).

24. UK: A report into the Tudor V air disaster in March says overloading probably led to the crash, which killed 80 (→ 24/8/51).

27. Korea: A massive force of Chinese troops eject UN troops from the Manchurian border.→

30. New York: The USSR vetoes a UN resolution calling for the withdrawal of Chinese troops from Korea (→ 3/12).

DEATH

2. Irish author, playwright, critic and politician George Bernard Shaw (*26/7/1856).→

Shaw, scandalous genius, dead at 94

Shaw, seen on his 90th birthday.

Nov 2. George Bernard Shaw died at his home at Ayot St. Lawrence, Hertfordshire, today aged 94, long after most people have forgotten the rage and dislike that he took such pains to provoke when he was younger. He once described "G.B.S." as "my most successful creation". For many people GBS was the wrong-headed Irishman with a red beard and scandalously subversive opinions, who wore queer clothes, lived on vegetables, wrote plays that were not proper plays and claimed to be better than Shakespeare. But none would dispute that he was a genius. He left part of his fortune for establishing a new phonetic alphabet.

Farouk tells UK to quit Suez Canal

Nov 16. In a speech at the opening of the Egyptian Parliament in Cairo today, King Farouk demanded the "total and immediate" evacuation of British troops from the Suez Canal Zone, the revision of the 1936 treaty with Britain and the unity of Egypt and Sudan under the Egyptian Crown. The demands received a cool reception in London. A Foreign Office spokesman said the Suez issue had to be viewed in the context of the defence of the Middle East generally, and that involved many countries besides Britain and Egypt. Britain says the US supports this view (→ 5/4/51).

Chinese enter the war

Relatives weep as they identify the 300 victims of a political massacre.

Nov 28. United Nations forces in Korea are tumbling back in disarray, under the impact of a massive assault launched by Chinese forces across the Yalu two days ago. The UN soldiers, engaged in their own "end the war" campaign right up to the Chinese border, were caught completely by surprise.

The situation now is that there is some danger of the 8th Army being outflanked, while the US Marines, trapped at the frozen Changjin reservoir south of the Yalu, are fighting their way to the Sea of Japan.

The situation in the north-west is so serious that the 8th Army has called for all Marine aircraft, normally assigned to the north-east front, to be diverted to help stem the Chinese tide. MacArthur's headquarters says that over 200,000 Chinese soldiers are swarming over the border.

This attack caught the politicians by surprise as well as the soldiers, although the Chinese Foreign Minister, Chou En-lai, publicly warned the US that China would resist if US force entered North Korea. At the UN yesterday, the American delegate accused Communist China of "open and notorious aggression" (→30).

Puerto Ricans attempt to kill Truman

Nov 1. President Truman survived an assassination attempt today by two Puerto Rican nationalists. They tried to shoot their way into Blair House, in Washington, where the President is staying during repairs to the White House. In a fierce gun battle on the steps one assassin was killed and the other captured. One guard was killed and two others wounded.

Hearing the gunfire the President went to the window, but was told by the guards to keep back. He was unhurt and kept all his appointments this afternoon.

Puerto Rico was ceded by Spain to the US in 1898 after the Spanish-American War. It has had its own elected governor since 1948, but is still a US colony. Truman is puzzled by the attack because he is sympathetic towards demands for further self-determination (→4).

1950

DECEMBER

Su	Mo	Tu	We	Th	Fr	Sa
					1	2
3	4	5	6	7	8	9
10	11	12	13	14	15	16
17	18	19	20	21	22	23
24	25	26	27	28	29	30
31						

1. US: Drive-in cinemas have doubled to 2,200 in a year.

5. Korea: UN troops withdraw from Pyongyang.→

10. Stockholm: Nobel Prizes go to Cecil Powell (UK, Physics); Otto Diels and Kurt Alder (Germany, Chemistry); Edward Kendall (US), Tadeus Reichstein (Switzerland) and Philip Hench (US, both Medicine); Bertrand Russell (UK, Literature); and in Oslo to Ralph Bunche (US, Peace).

11. Singapore: Thousands of Malays riot against the return of "Jungle Girl", Bertha Hertogh, tc her Dutch parents.

12. Singapore: 19 die in clashes between troops and rioting Malays (→6/10/51).

16. Washington: Truman declares a national state of emergency as UN forces suffer further setbacks in Korea (→1/1/51).

19. US: Eisenhower is appointed head of NATO forces (→20/3/51).

23. Rome: Pope Pius XII says St. Peter's tomb has been discovered under the Vatican.

25. Tibet: The Dalai Lama has reportedly fled (→29/4/51).

29. Glasgow: A newspaper receives a petition to the King pledging to return the Stone of Scone if it stays in Scotland (→11/4).

DEATHS

27. German painter Max Beckmann (*12/2/1884).

31. Austrian statesman Karl Renner, chancellor 1919 and 1945 (*14/12/1870).

HITS OF 1950

I've got a lovely bunch of coconuts.

Music! Music! Music!

Mona Lisa.

QUOTE OF THE YEAR

" Are you sitting comfortably? ... then we'll begin."

Julia Lang, first presenter of the BBC's "Listen With Mother", launched in 1951.

Attlee worried that Truman plans to drop bomb in Korea

Dec 8. Talks over the past five days between Mr Attlee and President Truman ended tonight in Washington with a bland communique about resisting the Communist challenge with resolution and unity.

The real meat, however, lay in an assurance by Truman that he hopes never to use the atomic bomb in Korea. It was to get this assurance – amounting almost to a guarantee – that Mr Attlee made the trip. He had taken seriously recent unofficial American military talk about atomic intentions. The British delegation said unattributably: "If they ever meant it, they don't now."

The only Anglo-US differences at this summit meeting have been over the proposed admission of Communist China to the United Nations. Britain is in favour and America still opposed.

As Great War veterans (Major Attlee and Captain Truman) the two leaders are reported to have got on well, swopping 1914-18 yarns and breaking the early-to-bed rule they both normally follow (→28/1/51).

Scots Nats steal Coronation Stone

Dec 25. The Coronation Stone was stolen today from Westminster Abbey, where it has rested safely for 650 years. Scottish Nationalists said they were responsible, and claimed they had returned the hefty sandstone slab to the country it came from.

Detectives north of the border have been alerted and are on the look-out for a man and a woman, both with Scottish accents, who were seen in a car near to the Abbey during the night by a policeman.

The stone weighs 458 pounds and was wrested from underneath the Coronation Chair behind the High Altar and then dragged through a small door.

Historians say the stone was taken from Scone, in Scotland, by Edward I in 1296 and England had promised to return it (→29).

UN forces are in retreat

Dec 6. The Chinese are continuing their pell-mell drive south against the disorganised UN forces in Korea. Pyongyang, the North Korean capital, captured only six weeks ago, has already fallen to them and tonight a new defensive line is being established by UN troops "somewhere south of Pyongyang".

The depth of the penetration of the Chinese forces behind the Allies is not known, because the situation is confused by the bands of guerrillas who were left behind during the UN advance. They posed as farmers, but have now taken up their weapons again, and are attacking UN units making their way to safety.

Dumps of petrol and stores set on fire by the retreating Americans were still burning in Pyongyang as the Chinese entered the city yesterday in the wake of the rearguard, the British 29th Brigade.

The Communist forces were attacked by planes firing machine-guns, rockets and napalm. Many were killed crossing the Taedong River. One pilot described them as coming over "just like a crowd at a football match." A communique speaks of the "bottomless well of Chinese manpower" (→16).

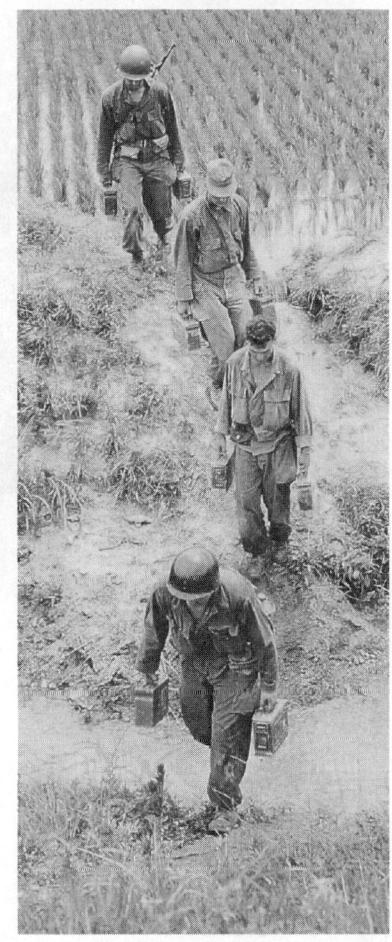

An ammunition run in the fields.

One of many allegedly political prisoners, humiliated by North Korea, crouches warily among lines of his fellows, at a camp near Pusan.

Arts: respectability and prizes for Russell

Bertrand Russell, always at the hub of controversy for his unpopular opinions, finds himself at the height of public respectability, with the award of the Nobel Prize, closely following upon the Order of Merit. Last year he delivered the first Reith lectures for the BBC.

Russell spoke on "Authority and the Individual", pointing out how individual freedom had been progressively reduced during his lifetime. He himself was deprived of his fellowship at Cambridge, and later imprisoned for writing against conscription in the First World War. During the Second, which he supported, he was judged unfit to lecture at a New York college as "an enemy of religion and morality" – a reference to his three marriages and to the radical reforms he suggested in "Marriage and Morals", a book for which he has now been awarded the Nobel Prize.

Russell has abandoned philosophy to campaign against nuclear arms. In 1948 he went so far as to advocate that the US, then the sole atomic power, should threaten Russia with the atom bomb in order to force it to disarm. He was much criticised for this.

An eye-witness report from the 18th Century has been selling as if it was today's news. It is the diary of **James Boswell**, Dr Johnson's friend, on his rake's progress through Georgian London. It was discovered at Malahide Castle, in Ireland, in 1927 and is only now published as "Boswell's London Journal".

The Old Vic theatre in Waterloo Road, which lost its roof in the bombing of 1941, reopened with an enchanting "Twelfth Night". The outstanding Viola was **Peggy Ashcroft**, who earlier had played a highly-praised Beatrice in **John Gielgud's** "Much Ado About Nothing" at Stratford-upon-Avon. **Sir Laurence Olivier** and **Sir Ralph Richardson** were dismissed by the Old Vic governors last year after their triumphs. The Old Vic will now be managed by **Tyrone Guthrie**.

The playwright of the moment is **Christopher Fry**, whose verse play "The Lady's not for Burning" was followed by his version of a **Jean Anouilh** play, "Ring Round the Moon", in which the fast-rising actor **Paul Scofield** plays twins, again directed by **Peter Brook**.

Russell gains yet another honour.

The poet **Ezra Pound**, who has been confined in a mental hospital in Washington since he was found unfit to stand trial for treason in 1945, has published "Seventy Cantos", including those he wrote when the American army put him into a steel punishment cage at Pisa in 1945, where he lost his reason. He had espoused Fascism and had broadcast on behalf of the regime from Rome throughout the war.

Epstein showed his statue "Lazarus" in a London art gallery.

1951

JANUARY

Su	Mo	Tu	We	Th	Fr	Sa
	1	2	3	4	5	6
7	8	9	10	11	12	13
14	15	16	17	18	19	20
21	22	23	24	25	26	27
28	29	30	31			

1. Korea: The Chinese launch a heavy assault north of Seoul, crossing the 38th Parallel (→4).

2. Saudi Arabia: The Arabian American Oil Company agrees to share its profits with the Saudi government.

4. Korea: Seoul is captured by Communist troops (→9).

8. Bonn: Adenauer accepts an East German invitation to talks on the reunification of Germany (→27/9).

9. Korea: The UN retreat continues as Wonju falls to the Chinese and North Koreans (→10).

9. London: The government drops its East African groundnut scheme; debts of £36.5 million will be written off.

10. Korea: UN troops fight back at Communist positions in Wonju (→25).

11. Vietnam: The Viet Minh launch an offensive against the French in the north of Tonkin.→

15. Washington: Truman asks Congress for $60 billion to prepare US forces for combat.

17. London: Aneurin Bevan becomes Minister of Labour (→9/3).

21. The Alps: The recent avalanche death toll rises to 108 as more occur in Italy, Austria and Switzerland.

23. Washington: Truman creates a Commission on Internal Security and Individual Rights.

25. Korea: UN ships bombard Inchon.→

29. London: Attlee announces plans to spend £4,700 million over three years and recall 255,100 reservists (→21/2).

30. New York: The UN names China as an aggressor in Korea (→5/2).

DEATHS

10. US author Sinclair Lewis, 1930 Nobel Prize winner (*7/2/1885).

30. German motor car engineer Ferdinand Porsche (*3/9/1875).

North Korean offensive halted by UN

Jan 26. United Nations forces have slowed down the joint Chinese and North Korean offensive, which was launched on a broad front near the 38th Parallel, the old frontier, on New Year's Day.

The offensive achieved considerable success. The Communist forces broke through the UN lines in several places and four days after they opened the offensive they took Seoul, capital of South Korea, for the second time.

These setbacks have led to rumours that General MacArthur would like to withdraw from Korea for purely military reasons and carry on the war against China by other means.

These rumours were scotched in the middle of the month when General Collins, the US Army Chief of Staff, and Gen. Vandenberg, the Air Force Chief of Staff, flew to MacArthur's Tokyo headquarters and then to Korea, bearing the message from President Truman that there was to be no retreat from Korea.

Collins told a press conference at 8th Army HQ: "Certainly we are going to stay in Korea. We are going to stand here and fight."

He admitted that "we have not been able to send as many reinforcements here as we should like," but promised that the first of the recruits mobilised under the selective training scheme in the US would soon be arriving.

"We must be sure we have enough weapons to equip them and sufficient facilities to train them," he said. He believed the 8th Army could "take care of itself" in the current situation. Major-General C.L. Ruffner, the 2nd Division's new commander, said after his first day: "I have no fear of the enemy, north, east or west of us. The 2nd Division will give a magnificent account of itself."

Events in the latter half of the month have borne out the commanders' confidence. While the Communists are still pressing forward, they are running into supply problems as their lines of communication lengthen, and are pounded incessantly from the air. The latest news is of limited offensives by the allies, taking them once again within striking distance of Seoul (→30).

South Korean civilians take the refugee trail away from the front line.

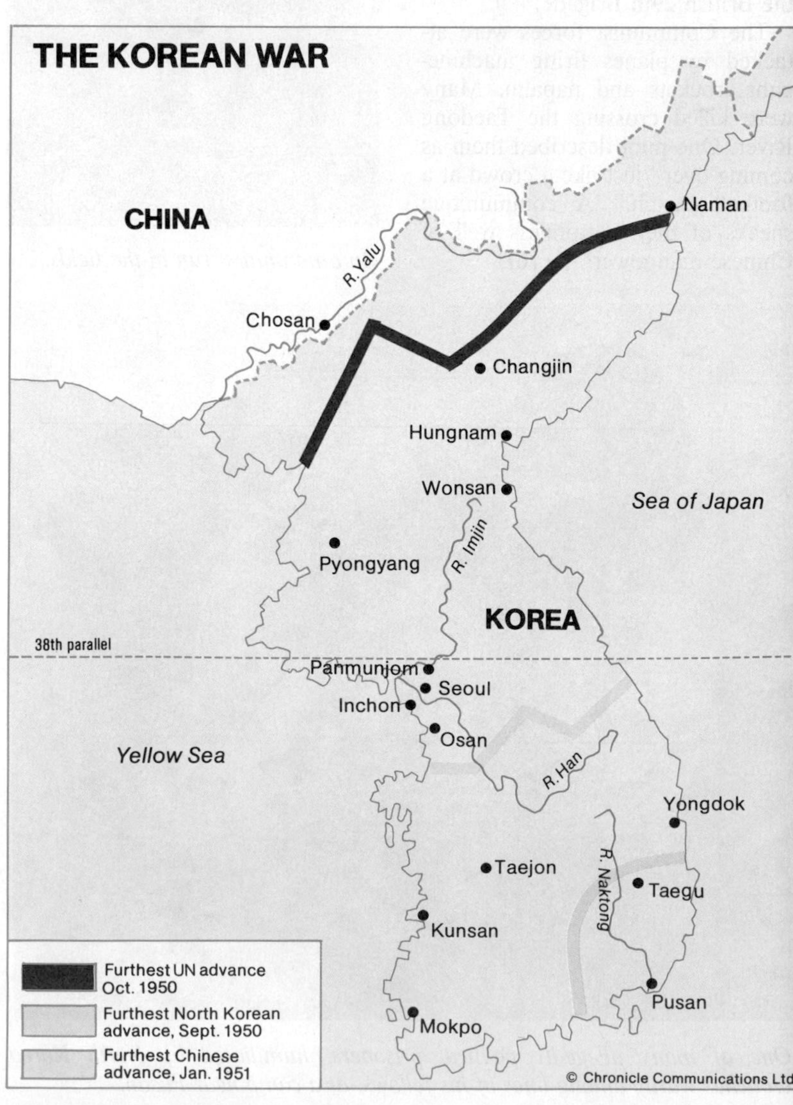

US tests nuclear bomb in Nevada desert

Jan 28. A large part of the sky across the south-west of the United States was lit up by the flash of a nuclear explosion today, as the second bomb test in two days went ahead in the Nevada desert.

In Las Vegas, 45 miles from the the boundary of the test grounds, observers saw a five-second flash, and felt a wind blowing through the streets of the city. In Boulder City, more than 100 miles from the explosion site, residents said the flash lit up whole rooms. The US Atomic Energy Commission issued a statement saying that patrols have found "no indication of any radiological hazards" from the explosion, but it asked for all civil aircraft flights to be grounded within a 150-mile radius of the test (→ 12/5).

Soldiers observe the A-bomb test.

Another sliver off UK's meat ration

Jan 27. The Government sliced twopence from Britain's weekly meat ration today – as negotiations with Argentina reached deadlock. With rump steak selling at 2s 8d per pound, the ration represents no more than four ounces per person, or five ounces of imported lamb chops.

Butchers, who are being compensated for their losses, have estimated that three ration books would be needed to buy a pound of meat, and 13 for a leg of lamb. The ration, a further reduction on a tiny 1s 6d worth, is the lowest that it has ever been. The meat shortage has created a growing blackmarket (→ 16).

At BBC, dialects 'ardly ever' appen

Jan 23. Radio news bulletins are to be read by only eight people instead of 19. The BBC, reverting to a wartime system, wants its Home and Light programme announcers to become easily recognized. The purpose is to have consistency of pronunciation and performance.

No men with "dialect voices" and no women will be among the chosen eight. "People do not like momentous events such as war and disaster to be read by the female voice," says the BBC. However, there will still be regional announcers. Overseeing the change is Mr John Snagge, head of home presentation (→ 1/2).

French counter-attack and save Hanoi

Jan 18. All is quiet today in Hanoi. After the fierce fighting of the last four days, the Viet Minh guerrillas have been forced to retreat, leaving behind them 500 prisoners and 6,000 dead. It is a major victory for the French, and reverses a string of defeats for them in Tonkin.

Much of the credit rests with the new High Commissioner and Commander-in-Chief, General Jean de Lattre de Tassigny. The General, called "King Jean" by his men because of his elegance and courtly manner, has put a new spirit into the troops. He flew into one besieged outpost and cabled his men to come and rescue him. They came in force and inflicted the first major defeat on General Giap's Communist guerrillas.

General Brink, head of the United States military mission to Indochina, is in Hanoi at present, observing the state of the war. He is due to report to Washington by the end of the month when Rene Pleven, the French Prime Minister, goes there to discuss the situation with President Truman (→ 14/11).

1951

FEBRUARY

Su	Mo	Tu	We	Th	Fr	Sa
				1	2	3
4	5	6	7	8	9	10
11	12	13	14	15	16	17
18	19	20	21	22	23	24
25	26	27	28			

1. UK: Coal and coke prices rise as a winter fuel shortage grows more acute (→ 29/5).

1. London: The BBC names eight radio news readers, including Alvar Liddell and Robert Dougall (→ 6).

5. Ivory Coast: The port of Abidjan is opened by a French junior minister, Francois Mitterrand.

5. Korea: UN forces push back to within five miles of Seoul (→ 10).

6. London: The BBC says its tests of Very High Frequency (VHF) transmission have been a success.

8. Oxford: Cecil Day-Lewis is elected Professor of Poetry at the University.

8. London: The King gets a ten per cent pay rise, the first of his reign (→ 13/4).

9. US: Swedish-born actress Greta Garbo becomes a US citizen.

10. Korea: UN forces capture the towns of Anyang and Yongdungpo (→ 17).

14. Tel Aviv: Ben-Gurion resigns (→ 2/5).

16. UK: A standard bottle of whisky goes up 1/8d. to £1 15/- (→ 19/5).

16. UK: Miss M. J. Ahern is appointed managing director of the John Lewis Partnership.

20. Gold Coast: The colony's first parliament is opened in Accra by the governor.

20. UK: This month has proved the wettest February since 1870.

21. Canada: The Canberra, Britain's first jet bomber, crosses the Atlantic in a record four hours 40 minutes (→ 16/4).

23. London: Convicted spy Klaus Fuchs loses his UK citizenship (→ 30/3).

28. Australia: England wins the fifth and final Test of this series, the first English victory in Australia since 1936.

DEATH

19. French author Andre Gide, 1948 Nobel Prize winner (*22/11/1869).

Sugar Ray avenges defeat by La Motta

Feb 14. Sugar Ray Robinson, by common consent the finest welterweight the world has seen, moved up to middleweight with such authority that, in his first division, he outfought the acknowledged hard man of New York, the Bronx Bull, Jake La Motta, and stopped him in the 13th round.

It was a poignant victory. Eight years ago La Motta became the first, and so far the only, man to beat Robinson, who had already fought 85 amateur and 39 professional contests without defeat.

Now, in a night the American papers are calling the St Valentine's Day Massacre, Robinson has had his revenge.

Two-term limit for Presidents of US

Feb 26. American presidents are to be limited to a maximum term of eight years in office, following the passage of the 22nd Amendment, which has been ratified by 36 of the US states, the required number for an amendment to the Constitution. Opponents argued the limit would turn a re-elected president into an unaccountable lame-duck during his final four years of office, but Congress decided the change would help curb presidential power.

Franklin Delano Roosevelt is the only past president who would have been restricted by the 22nd Amendment, he was elected four times and died after serving 12 years in the White House.

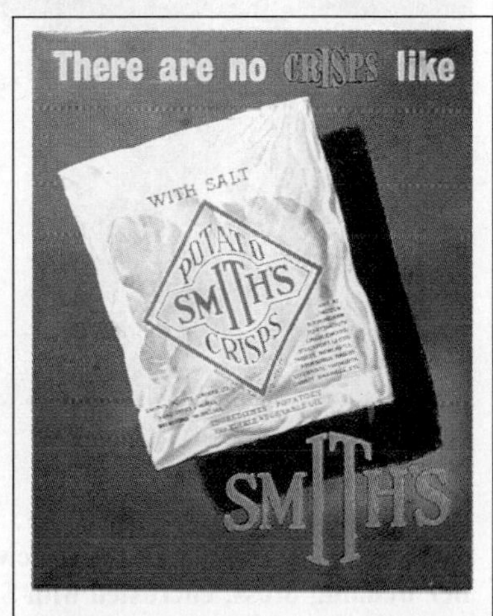

UN forces push back to the 38th parallel

North Korean prisoners under Marine guns during the Yalu river fighting.

Feb 17. Three separate offensives are being waged in Korea today. On the east coast, South Koreans, supported by naval bombardment, have driven up the coastal highway to the 38th parallel. In the West US and British troops have recaptured the port of Inchon and are shelling the Communists in Seoul. But in the centre, the Chinese have pushed back United Nations forces for more than eight miles.

The Communist thrust appears to be following the same lines as their attack last November. But there is one significant difference. Then the Allied forecs on either flank fell back; this time they are maintaining their ground and are threatening to strike the Chinese from the flank.

Communist resistance is also stiffening outside Seoul, where Allied forces have taken up positions in a 25-mile arc south of the city, separated from it only by the frozen Han river. The fourth battle for the city is about to begin (→27).

The Shah of Persia and his new wife Soraya Esfandayiari show off her wedding dress, encrusted with $1.5 million worth of diamonds.

1951

MARCH

Su	Mo	Tu	We	Th	Fr	Sa
				1	2	3
4	5	6	7	8	9	10
11	12	13	14	15	16	17
18	19	20	21	22	23	24
25	26	27	28	29	30	31

2. London: The government is defeated by four votes after a Commons debate on the shortage of raw materials.

4. New Delhi: The first Asian Games open.

8. Teheran: The Iranian parliament votes to nationalise the oil industry.→

9. London: Herbert Morrison replaces Ernest Bevin as Foreign Secretary; Bevin becomes Lord Privy Seal (→14/4).

9. London: MPs approve a bill making separation for not less than seven years grounds for divorce (→17/4).

12. Washington: Alleged spy Alger Hiss loses his Supreme Court appeal against his conviction for perjury (→9/7).

15. Teheran: Martial law is declared (→8).

16. Doncaster: Fourteen die when an express coach hits the mouth of a tunnel.

19. Paris: France, West Germany, Italy and the Benelux states sign a treaty to create a European Coal and Steel Community (→10/8/52).

20. London: Montgomery is appointed Eisenhower's deputy at Supreme Headquarters, Allied Powers Europe (→2/4).

24. London: The University Boat Race is called off after the Oxford boat sinks (→26).

26. London: Cambridge win the re-run Boat Race by 12 lengths.

27. Korea: UN and South Korean forces have crossed the 38th Parallel (→30).

29. US: Carol Reed's film, "The Third Man", wins an Oscar for best black and white photography.

31. New Delhi: Nehru offers India's help in trying to bring about a truce in the Korean War (→11/4).

DEATHS

6. British actor and composer Ivor Novello, born David Ivor Davies (*15/1/1893).

22. Dutch conductor Willem Mengelberg (*28/3/1871).

Rosenbergs found guilty of espionage

March 30. New Yorkers Julius and Ethel Rosenberg have been found guilty of wartime espionage in America's first atomic bomb spy trial. They were accused of stealing atomic secrets and passing them to Russia. Rosenberg, aged 32, an Army Signal Corps electrical engineer, and his wife, who is 35 continue to protest their innocence.

The key government witness in the three week trial in the Federal Court in New York City was David Greenglass, Mrs Rosenberg's brother. He confessed to his own role in the plot. Another witness who has confessed, Harry Gold has already been sentenced to 30 years in prison. The Rosenbergs will be sentenced soon (→5/4).

America's alleged spies face trial.

Iran's premier is shot by carpenter

March 7. The Iranian Premier, General Ali Razmara, was shot dead today in Teheran by a member of the extremist religious sect, the Crusaders of Islam. Asked why he had done it, the assassin, a 26-year old carpenter, said: "Why do they give the country to foreigners, so that I must do this deed?" Razmara recently began a campaign against corruption in government; he also planned to boost the economy by raising oil production under a new agreement signed with the Anglo Iranian Oil Company (→15).

MacArthur threatens invasion of China

US Superfortresses rain bombs on a chemical plant in Konan, North Korea.

March 30. General MacArthur, the United States' pro-consul in Japan and commander of the UN forces in Korea, is once again risking President Truman's wrath by demanding he be allowed to carry the war to China by attacking the "privileged sanctuary" of Manchuria.

The General has increasingly been making political statements, urging that restrictions imposed on his freedom of action should be removed. In this he has considerable support among Republicans in Washington, many of whom want him let off the leash to destroy the Chinese Communist regime.

Paradoxically, the political tensions have been heightened by the success of the UN forces in South Korea. Seoul has unexpectedly fallen without a shot being fired by its Communist defenders, and American troops have again crossed into North Korea. The frontier has also been crossed in strength by the South Koreans on the east coast.

At a time when the UN and Mr Truman are looking for a political settlement, any threat to North Korean or Chinese territory is regarded as unhelpful (→ 11/4).

Shooting after Iran votes to control its oil

March 15. Troops and tanks were patrolling the streets of Teheran yesterday after martial law was proclaimed to deal with "gangster elements" threatening the security of the Iranian capital. The move came after an attempt to assassinate Dr Zanganeh, Minister of Education in the cabinet of General Razmara, shot dead himself by a religious fanatic eight days ago. Dr Zanganeh was shot in the back, but survived.

Teheran political life has been in turmoil since the lower house of Parliament, the Majlis, unanimously voted to nationalise the oil industry, run by the Anglo-Iranian Oil Co. The upper house, the Senate, approved the nationalisation bill yesterday, but only 27 out of 60 Senators were present. Parliament has also voted to invite foreign oil experts to come and run the industry when the British leave.

The bid to seize the oilfields, which Britain has been developing since 1909, is seen in London as a surrender to extreme nationalists and Islamic fundamentalists, who regularly bring out the street mobs to put pressure on more moderate politicians. The Shah has apppointed Hussein Ala, former ambassador to the US, to replace General Razmara; in the present climate he is unlikely to last (→ 20).

1951

APRIL

Su	Mo	Tu	We	Th	Fr	Sa
1	2	3	4	5	6	7
8	9	10	11	12	13	14
15	16	17	18	19	20	21
22	23	24	25	26	27	28
29	30					

2. Paris: Eisenhower takes over as Supreme Allied Commander in Europe (→ 20/9).

5. US: Convicted spies Julius and Ethel Rosenberg are sentenced to death.→

5. London: The government approves, in principle, the withdrawal of British troops from the Suez Canal Zone (→ 10/9).

7. UK: Mr J. Royle's Nickel Coin wins the Grand National; only three out of 36 runners finish.

8. Teheran: Iran rejects British protests against the nationalisation of Iranian oil.→

11. Washington: Lieutenant General Matthew Ridgway is chosen to replace MacArthur in Korea (→ 19).

11. UK: The Stone of Scone is recovered at Forfar in Angus, after a 107-day hunt (→ 13).

15. Iran: The Abadan oil refinery closes.

17. London: The government withdraws its bill to make seven-year separation grounds for divorce.

19. US: General MacArthur calls Truman's Korean policy "blind to reality" (→ 23).

21. Budapest: Hungary says it will release convicted US spy Robert Vogeler.

23. Korea: The Chinese launch an attack on a 50-mile front in western and central Korea (→ 25).

25. Korea: UN forces retreat as the Chinese pour in reinforcements (→ 17/5).

28. London: Newcastle United beat Blackpool 2-0 in the FA Cup Final.

29. Peking: Chou En-lai orders the seizure of the assets of the British Asiatic Petroleum Company (→ 27/5).

DEATHS

14. British trade unionist and statesman Ernest Bevin (*9/3/1881).→

29. Austrian philosopher Ludwig Wittgenstein (*26/4/1889).

Bevan resigns over planned charges on teeth and glasses

April 22. Aneurin Bevan, Minister of Labour and stormy petrel of the socialist left, resigned in fury from the cabinet today. His acolyte Harold Wilson, the President of the Board of Trade, intends to quit tomorrow. They will be joined on the Commons backbenches by John Freeman, a like-minded junior War Office minister.

In the wake of these dramatic resignations the Labour Party is now in flames. The outgoing Ministers are the champions of the Left, in open revolt against the Government, both over the level of defence spending and the imposition of Health Service charges for false teeth and spectacles. These charges have just been included in the Budget by Hugh Gaitskell, the Chancellor, who is detested as a "dessicated calculating machine" by Messrs Bevan and Wilson.

Mr Attlee, at present in hospital recovering from a minor illness, had bedside visits from both men. Mr Bevan told him: "The policies are repugnant." The Prime Minister replied: "Thank you for your good work."

A period of splenetic Labour civil war has begun (→ 10/5).

Bevan at the Labour Conference.

Britons killed in Persian oil riots

April 12. Eight Britons, including two women and a child, are reported tonight to have been killed by rioters in the oil regions of Abadan and Bandur Mashur on the Gulf. The rioters charged through police lines, pushing women and children in front of them as a shield. Police opened fire and several people were killed.

A spokesman for the Anglo-Iranian Oil Co. said agitators moved in after strikes broke out in the port and oil installations. Abadan, which has the world's largest oil refinery and is the centre of Iranian industry, has been put under martial law. In the Iranian Parliament, Dr Mohammed Mossadegh, leader of the opposition National Front, is pressing for the immediate seizure of the Anglo-Iranian assets in the country (→ 15).

Rosenbergs are condemned to die

April 5. Judge Irving R. Kaufman today condemned Julius and Ethel Rosenberg to the electric chair and told them their crime was "worse than murder". They protest their innocence and blame the anti-Communist hysteria. The death penalty is reserved for wartime spying but in this case the atom secrets were passed to the Soviet Union – then American allies (→ 11/6).

Truman fires MacArthur

General MacArthur embraces Lt. Gen. Ridgway "somewhere in Korea".

April 11. President Truman today shocked America by dismissing General Douglas MacArthur from all his posts, including that of commander of the United Nations forces in Korea.

Soon after the announcement, at one o'clock in the morning, the White House published a series of documents showing that MacArthur had ignored repeated warnings by the President against making political statements.

In a broadcast explaining his reasons for dismissing the immensely popular General, the President said that US policy in the Far East was designed to prevent conflict spreading. "So far it has been successful. So far we have prevented World War Three," said the President.

It would be tragically wrong, he added, for the United States to take the initiative in extending the war.

"A number of events have made it evident that General MacArthur did not agree with that policy. I have therefore considered it essential to relieve him so that there would be no doubt or confusion as to the real purpose of our policy" (→ 19).

Unknown thieves took the famous Stone of Scone from one abbey, in Westminster; the police found it abandoned in another, at Arbroath.

Sub has vanished: 75 are feared dead

April 16. The entire 75-strong crew of a British submarine was feared dead tonight after the vessel went missing off the English south coast. Contact with the 1,600-ton Affray ceased after her last known dive. Experts at the Admiralty say air supplies will soon run out, even if the sub is undamaged.

One theory is that she was widely off course when battery failure led to lethal gases escaping. The disappearance is baffling naval officials. Their latest echo-sounding gear so far has only located a number of German U-boats (→ 18/5).

Ernie Bevin, famed as the dreadnought of Labour, is dead

April 14. Ernest Bevin died today, aged 70. The nation has lost a sturdy patriot whose wartime cabinet role probably contributed more to victory than anyone else's, except Churchill. The Labour movement has lost its dreadnought.

Friends were relieved when he was at last persuaded to resign as Foreign Secretary on his birthday last month. He was a spent force. But he will be differently remembered. From childhood drudgery he rose to become Britain's most powerful trade union leader. Mixed in his personality were brutality, humanity and shrewdness.

As Minister of Labour, his wartime mobilisation of 22 million troops and workers must rank among his greatest achievements.

He was a great internationalist. The Foreign Office was startled when he said: "My policy is to go to Victoria Station without a passport and buy a ticket to go where the hell I like" (→ 22).

Bevin speaks at the 1950 election.

1951

MAY

Su	Mo	Tu	We	Th	Fr	Sa
		1	2	3	4	5
6	7	8	9	10	11	12
13	14	15	16	17	18	19
20	21	22	23	24	25	26
27	28	29	30	31		

1. Munich: Radio Free Europe begins broadcasting to countries behind the Iron Curtain.

2. Israel: Syrian troops cross the demilitarised zone and occupy two Israeli villages (→4).

3. London: The King inaugurates the Festival of Britain and opens the Royal Festival Hall on the South Bank.→

4. Israel: Syria and Israel agree to ceasefire as called for by the UN; it lasts only three hours (→19/11).

9. London: The government agrees to pay new OAP rates at 65 (men) and 60 (women), not 70 and 65 as first planned (→7/11).

10. UK: The Tories gain in English and Welsh local elections; Labour loses Leeds, Bradford and Bristol (→19/9).

11. Moscow: Mikhail Botvinnik retains his world chess crown, as the 24th championship game is drawn.

18. UK: Britain's first four-engined jet bomber, the Vickers Valiant, makes its maiden flight (→5/7).

19. London: Britain warns Iran against trying to seize British oil properties (→20).

20. Teheran: Iran serves formal notice on the Anglo-Iranian Oil Co. that it is taking over its oil installations (→22).

22. Iran: 50,000 Iranians demonstrate in favour of the government's nationalisation plans (→1/6).

25. London: Foreign Office officials Guy Burgess and Donald MacLean disappear without leave (→7/6).

28. London: The Festival of Britain Pleasure Gardens open at Battersea.→

29. UK: 83 miners are feared dead after an explosion at Easington Colliery, Durham.

30. UK: Mr J. McGrath's Arctic Prince wins the Derby at Epsom.

BIRTH

23. Soviet chess player Anatoly Karpov.

First H-bomb is tested

May 12. The hydrogen bomb has come a step nearer with the successful test today of an atomic weapon on Eniwetok atoll in the mid-Pacific. The US Atomic Energy Commission and the Department of Defence claims that the test exceeded expectations, though their statement gives no details.

The hydrogen bomb, which taps the same source of energy as the sun and other stars, will be hundreds of times more powerful than the atomic bombs that destroyed Hiroshima and Nagasaki. It works by fusing together the nuclei of hydrogen atoms in a thermonuclear reaction, a process which only occurs at astronomically high temperatures, so that an H-bomb requires an atomic bomb as a trigger.

"Much useful information" on thermonuclear reactions was gained in this latest test, according to Alvin C. Graves, of the Los Alamos Scientific Laboratory (→3/9).

A Geiger-counter check for participants in the Eniwetok H-bomb test.

Two fellow generals attack MacArthur

May 23. Two of America's top generals have strongly criticised General MacArthur before a Senate committee inquiring into President Truman's decision to sack him from his Far Eastern command. Both General Omar Bradley, the chairman of the Joint Chiefs of Staff, and General George C. Marshall, who is Secretary of Defense, supported the President's decision. Bradley told the committee that MacArthur's strategy would have been dangerous.

It would, he said, have led to the "wrong war, at the wrong place, at the wrong time, and with the wrong enemy". General Marshall insisted that US operations in Korea were only part of a foreign policy designed to check aggression "in different fashions in different areas".

British and Anzacs repel Communists

May 17. British and Australasian troops have thrown back a mass attack on their lines by bugle blowing Chinese infantry, south of Chunchon. After being battered by tanks and artillery, the Chinese withdrew, leaving 400 dead on the moonlit battlefield.

This attack was part of a general offensive which is still in its earliest stages. So far the Chinese have not shown the "win all, lose all" determination of their attacks last month, in which the Gloucesters, under Lieutenant-Colonel Carne behaved with such gallantry.

Details are still emerging of their stand at the Imjin River against overwhelming odds. One man, "Big Bill" Speakman, running out of ammunition, threw rocks and beer cans at the Chinese.

South Africa ends "coloured" vote

May 14. The Afrikaner Nationalist majority in the South African Parliament today voted to remove the Coloured (mixed race) people from the electoral register. Coloureds have shared the vote with whites since the Cape became self-governing under the British in the last century. But Dr Theophilus Donges, the Minister of the Interior, said the government's action was necessary to avoid "the collapse of white civilisation in the whole of Africa". After an angry debate, the predominantly English-speaking United Party opposition rejected the minister's appeal for support, and voted 64 against to the government's 74.

Deal on religion offered to Tibet

May 27. The mountain state of Tibet, which surrendered to the Chinese army last year, is to be allowed religious freedom – "providing it severs all pro-imperialist ties". A delegation sent to Peking by the 16-year-old Dali Lama, Tibet's temporal and spiritual leader, has surrendered control of the army and foreign affairs to the Chinese Government in a 17-point agreement.

Behind the enforced "pact" is the need for Tibet's mineral wealth. Mining has not been allowed in the country until now because of religious proscription (→9/9).

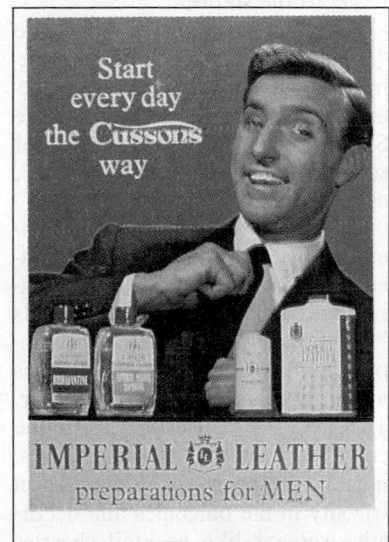

A lavish Festival gives Britons a pat on the back

Illuminations glitter across the South Bank arts complex, high-lighting the Skylon, symbol of the Festival.

Their Majesties visit the Festival.

May 4. A hundred years after the Victorians' Great Exhibition, crowds congregated on the South Bank of the Thames yesterday for the opening by the King and Queen of the long-awaited Festival of Britain. It is a government-sponsored event, described by Herbert Morrison as "the people giving themselves a pat on the back".

What for, he did not specify. Not for the end of austerity, which is still omnipresent. But as a gesture of faith in a brighter future, 27 acres of derelict, bomb-damaged London, near Waterloo, have been transformed into the exhibition site, tempting North Londoners across the river for another purpose than to get to the station.

Over much of the area curves the "Dome of Discovery" while floating floodlit above all, like an exclamation mark in aluminium, is the Skylon, with no visible means of support – "symbolising Britain", as someone commented dryly.

A team of architects and designers, led by Hugh Casson, have created an environment of what the festival director, Sir Gerald Barry, calls "fun, fantasy and colour" in complete contrast to the grim pillboxes and utilitarian Nissen huts of war. The stress is on spaciousness, gentle curves, strong colours and textures, notably natural wood, and a certain frivolity in the balconies and decorative screens like cocktail cherries on sticks. The style is best exemplified by the Royal Festival Hall, designed by Robert Matthew of the LCC architects' department, the only permanent building and London's long-awaited new concert hall. Some people are referring to this style as "contemporary".

The Festival Hall is causing much discussion. Its auditorium with projecting boxes all along its upper sides has excellent acoustics. People are visiting it to gaze at the interior decoration, chairs of bent laminated ply-wood and jungles of indoor greenery, which is likely to set a fashion. Down-river at Battersea Park, an exhibition of open-air sculpture and "mobiles" is soon to be joined by the Festival Pleasure Gardens.

A large fun-fair, treewalks, a railway designed by the cartoonist, Roland Emett, are promised, with girl orange-sellers dressed Nell Gwynn-style to recall the era of Charles II's Vauxhall Gardens.

The cost, now over £8 million, has been criticised by Conservatives and newspapers, which have dubbed it "Morrison's Folly". But the chief complaint of the public is that a cup of coffee costs ninepence (→ 30/9).

Fireworks at Battersea Gardens.

Crowds watch the King and Queen arrive at the Dome of Discovery.

1951

JUNE

Su	Mo	Tu	We	Th	Fr	Sa
					1	2
3	4	5	6	7	8	9
10	11	12	13	14	15	16
17	18	19	20	21	22	23
24	25	26	27	28	29	30

1. Washington: Truman warns Britain and Iran of the potentially explosive nature of their dispute (→ 19).

4. London: Tyrone Guthrie is appointed manager of the Old Vic theatre.

7. London: Princess Elizabeth stands in for her sick father at the traditional Trooping the Colour ceremony (→ 18/9).

8. London: A telegram from Burgess and MacLean says they are taking a "long Mediterranean holiday" (→ 11).

9. Nuremberg: The last group of Nazis convicted of war crimes by the Allied tribunal are hanged.

11. Brussels: King Leopold III announces that he will abdicate on July 16 (→ 16/7).

11. London: Herbert Morrison admits the "security aspects" of Burgess and MacLean "are under investigation".

13. Korea: UN troops take Pyongyang.→

14. Channel: The missing submarine 'HMS Affray' is located in 258 feet of water (→ 5/7).

18. UK: Britain gives the US Air Force permission for an air base at Greenham Common in Berkshire.

19. Teheran: The Iranian government breaks off talks with the Anglo-Iranian Oil Company (→ 25).

24. France: Peter Walker in a Jaguar is the first Briton in 16 years to win the Le Mans Grand Prix.

25. Teheran: Mossadegh introduces a bill imposing severe penalties on anyone trying to sabotage the oil industry.→

25. London: The first cadets start training at the Metropolitan Police college at Hendon, North London.

28. Budapest: Hungarian Archbishop Jozsef Groesz is jailed for 15 years for allegedly plotting the government's fall.

30. Korea: UN chief General Ridgway says he is ready to negotiate a cease-fire with Communist forces (→ 2/7).

Two diplomats missing; were they spies?

Burgess: one missing diplomat...

...and Donald MacLean, the other.

June 7. Two British diplomats, who served in sensitive posts in the Washington embassy, have vanished in circumstances suggesting they may have been undercover Soviet spies.

Donald MacLean, aged 38, was first secretary in Washington before becoming head of the American Department of the Foreign Office. Guy Burgess, aged 40, was for eight months second secretary in Washington. They disappeared from London two weeks ago.

Police in Britain, France, Germany and Austria have been asked to search for them, and inquiries have been made in Finland and other countries bordering on the Soviet bloc. A particular check has been made on the border between the British and Soviet occupation zones in Austria.

In London, a Foreign Office spokesman refused to speculate on whether the two men might have gone to the Soviet Union. He would only say that they had been suspended for being absent without leave, and that Burgess had a breakdown a year ago. But American newspapers make no bones about the Soviet connection. The "Journal-American" says the diplomats' disappearance is certain to cause a furore over Communist sympathisers in the Government, and the US Secretary of State, Dean Acheson, said it would be "quite a serious matter" if Burgess and MacLean turned out to be Soviet sympathisers (→ 8).

Korean cease-fire plan by Russians

June 26. The Soviet Union today surprisingly called for a cease-fire in the year-old Korean war, and talks to achieve a peaceful settlement. The proposal by Jacob Malik, the chief Soviet delegate to the United Nations, set off a flurry of diplomatic activity, with the Western Allies reacting cautiously, although positively.

What was a local war between North and South Korea has grown into an international conflagration with the United Nations intervention. Stalin, who is thought to have inspired the North Korean attack, has given Kim Il Sung arms, but not Russian personnel (→ 30).

Britons say "No" to Iranian oil plan

June 27. The 2,500 British employees of the Anglo-Iranian Oil Company today told the Iranian authorities they will not work for the projected nationalised corporation. Plans have been completed for the evacuation of all Britons in the oilfields, and the 8,000-ton cruiser, Mauritius, is at anchor in the Shattel-Arab waterway, ready to move up to the Abadan refinery. Iran has become markedly more intransigent with the oil company since Dr Mohammed Mossadegh, a fiery nationalist, became Prime Minister two months ago (→ 15/7).

De Valera is back as Irish premier

June 13. Eamon de Valera is back in power after the defeat of the Irish coalition government of John A. Costello. One reason for his victory, which decimated the Republican Party of Sean MacBride, was the vigorous opposition of the Roman Catholic Church to the coalition's health policies.

The coalition made southern Ireland a republic and accepted the British Ireland Act, a move bitterly opposed by de Valera because it accepted Ulster's status. Lowering inflation and increasing benefits will be top of his agenda.

Teenagers take their cars to America's newest form of entertainment – the drive-in movie: why queue for seats when you can sit in your car?

1951

JULY

Su	Mo	Tu	We	Th	Fr	Sa
1	2	3	4	5	6	7
8	9	10	11	12	13	14
15	16	17	18	19	20	21
22	23	24	25	26	27	28
29	30	31				

1. France: Argentinian Juan Fangio wins the European Grand Prix.

2. Korea: Ridgway agrees to meet Communist representatives at Kaesong to discuss a cease-fire (→ 8).

5. London: The Admiralty bans "Snort" breathing tubes on subs after that on HMS Affray was found to be faulty (→ 30/8).

7. Wimbledon: Richard Savitt beats Ken McGregor in the Men's Singles final; Doris Hart beats S. Fry in the Women's Singles final.

8. Korea: UN and Communist delegates meet for preliminary cease-fire talks at Kaesong.→

9. US: Writer Dashiell Hammett and Alphaeus Hunton are jailed for six months for contempt of court.

11. UK: Early census results show the English and Welsh population up 3.8 million to 43,744,924 in 20 years.

13. London: The Queen lays the foundation stone of the National Theatre.

15. Iran: Nine die in anti-British riots (→ 30).

16. UK: Len Hutton scores his 100th century.

16. Brussels: King Leopold III abdicates; his son swears the oath as King Baudouin I.

20. UK: The Hawker Hunter jet makes its maiden flight.

26. UK: Australian golfer Peter Thomson plays a British record round of 62.

30. London: Britain agrees to reopen talks with Iran (→ 6/8).

BIRTH

31. Australian tennis player Evonne Fay Goolagong.

DEATHS

13. Austrian-born US composer Arnold Schoenberg (*13/9/1874).

20. Jordanian King Abdullah ibn Hussein (*1881).→

23. French commander and Vichy leader Marshal Philippe Petain (*24/4/1856).

Turpin shocks world champion to win

July 10. Randolph Turpin, the British and European middleweight champion, caused one of boxing's greatest upsets at London's Earl's Court tonight, by battering the great Sugar Ray Robinson to a points defeat to take the world crown. He is the first British fighter to hold the title since the legendary Bob Fitzsimmons last century.

All the predictions were against a victory for the 23-year-old Midlander. Robinson had already fought eight men, six of them Europeans, since he won his title six months ago, and disposed of them all with ease. Despite the 41 professional victories to his credit, bookmakers were offering 3-1 against Turpin, and as much as 20-1 against his winning on points.

But Turpin proved the pundits wrong. His punch has always been dangerous, and early in the second round a short left hook from Turpin left Robinson hanging on in a clinch. From then on the challenger never relinquished the initiative. He kept on the attack, won at least nine of the 15 rounds, and cut the champion so badly over the eye that he needed 14 stitches.

Turpin sways from a vicious right.

Talks to begin on Korean cease-fire

July 26. Admiral Joy of the US Navy and General Nam Il of the North Korean army today led their delegations to the first substantive talks on a cease-fire for Korea. The talks are being held in a tea-house in the neutral zone set up at the town of Kaesong.

The first subjects on the agenda were the arrangements for a demarcation line, along with a demilitarised zone separating the two sides. The way in which the truce will be supervised and arrangements relating to the return of prisoners of war are also high on the list.

The atmosphere at the talks cannot be described as cordial. They opened with mutual distrust being expressed on both sides. It is feared that the discussions will be long, drawn out and acrimonious. And while they talk peace at Kaesong, the war goes on and soldiers continue to die (→ 5/8).

King of Jordan shot entering a mosque

July 20. King Abdullah of Jordan was shot dead in Jerusalem today outside the Mosque of Omar, one of Islam's holiest shrines. His assassin was a local tailor called Mustafa Shakir, a member of the Sanctuary of Struggle, an organisation long opposed to the King.

Shakir sprang from behind a gate as Abdullah walked towards the mosque and shot him in the back at close range, killing him instantly. The assassin was then shot dead by the King's bodyguards. A state of emergency was declared throughout Jordan following the assassination, and Abdullah's younger son, Emir Naif, proclaimed Regent. His heir, Emir Talal, is currently in Beirut being treated for a nervous breakdown.

Abdullah had ruled for the past 30 years, first as Emir of Transjordan and later as King of Jordan, but many felt he had betrayed the Palestinians by diverting his Arab Legion to occupy East Jerusalem during the war against Israel and then annexing it. Ironically, almost his last act was to condemn publicly assassinations.

Average housewife works a 15-hour day

July 10. The average housewife works an astonishing 75 hour week – and still has to put in overtime on Saturdays and Sundays. This picture has been built up by a Mass Observation pilot study which looked at 700 working-class homes in the London region.

It reports that "Mrs Average Housewife" has a normal working day of 15 hours. Her freedom is constricted by the tyranny of meals and by the children demanding attention. About a quarter of her day is spent in the kitchen.

Most women do their shopping on Fridays, spending between ten shillings and £2. When she does get some time to herself, the housewife spends it reading, listening to the radio, watching television or going to the cinema.

Max Faulkner, winner of this year's British Open golf championship.

1951

AUGUST

Su	Mo	Tu	We	Th	Fr	Sa
			1	2	3	4
5	6	7	8	9	10	11
12	13	14	15	16	17	18
19	20	21	22	23	24	25
26	27	28	29	30	31	

1. Washington: Truman ends tariff privileges for all Communist countries.

1. UK: Austin raise their car prices; the A40 goes up £31 to £685.

5. Korea: Communist representatives apologise for an incident when their troops entered the truce zone.→

6. Teheran: Britain and Iran open talks on the oil dispute.→

10. London: Britain signs a trade pact with Cuba.

12. East Berlin: Over a million young people take part in anti-US demonstrations.

15. UK: Basil Spence wins a competition to design a new Coventry Cathedral.

15. UK: Dartmoor is designated a National Park.

18. US: Figures show that the average US income in 1950 was $1,436 (£472).

21. Jamaica: 132 people are reported to have died in the hurricane that struck the island three days ago.

24. US: 50 die when a new DC-6 airliner crashes into a hill in California.

25. Belgrade: Emmanuel MacDonald Bailey sets a world record for the 100 metres of 10.2 seconds.

27. UK: The first 25 US Air Force F-86 Sabre jets arrive.

28. UK: Young girls are reported to be smoking Indian hemp in reefer cigarettes.

30. UK: 75 Welshmen and women protest at Trawsfynydd at the War Office's purchase of land in the area (→ 11/10).

31. West Germany: Deutsche Grammophon launches the first 33 rpm "Long-Playing" record.

DEATHS

14. US press magnate William Randolph Hearst (*29/4/1863).→

15. Austrian pianist Artur Schnabel (*17/4/1882).

21. British composer and critic Constant Lambert (*23/8/1905).

Oil workers quitting Persia as talks fail

A demonstrator brandishes his banner: slogans and the dove of peace.

Aug 23. It looks like the end of the road for British oil operations in Iran. With the failure of the British mission to Teheran, the Anglo-Iranian Oil Company has ordered all British, Indian and Pakistani employees to leave. Staff at the Abadan refinery will remain for the time being to show, in the words of Clement Attlee, the Prime Minister, "that the British oil industry is not deserting Iran". But there is virtually no prospect of resolving the crisis so long as Dr Mossadegh remains Prime Minister.

The head of the British mission, Richard Stokes, the Lord Privy Seal, spent three weeks talking with Dr Mossadegh, without making progress. Britain proposed that a joint Anglo-Iranian agency should operate the oilfields and the Abadan refinery on behalf of a National Iranian Oil Corporation and British firms should be allowed to sell the oil abroad.

Dr Mossadegh rejected these proposals and went to the Majlis for a vote of confidence. In a now familiar scene, he faltered and collapsed soon after opening his speech, and then resumed to loud applause. The Majlis gave him his vote, but some deputies openly admit they have been terrorised into voting for the Government by threats from extremist Islamic fundamentalist groups (→ 27/9).

Kenyan police fear growth of Mau Mau

Aug 24. Secret meetings are being held in the forest outside Nairobi, at which Africans take an oath to drive the white man from Kenya. The meetings, which seem to have begun last year, are organised by a society called Mau Mau, about which almost nothing is known.

The oath is said to have a powerful effect, and some Africans of the Kikuyu tribe, which is the only tribe affected so far, have gone to witch-doctors for help. Police have arrested a large number of oath-takers, but they admit that the power of the sinister Mau Mau is continuing to spread. Its influence is being linked to a big increase in burglaries in the white suburbs in Nairobi.

Hearst, colourful news tycoon, dies

Aug 14. William Randolph Hearst, who built a US newspaper empire on a diet of lurid crime, sex and scandal, died today in Beverley Hills at 88. Hearst refused to join his father's business and asked instead for a present of the San Francisco Examiner, then a staid local paper. From that he built his chain of 18 papers and nine magazines.

His private life was no less flamboyant. He owned two castles and funded his mistress, Marion Davies, in several films.

Both sides are cautiously optimistic about Korean peace talks

Aug 27. Some little progress was made at the Korean cease-fire talks today. General Nam Il, the chief Communist delegate, was described in a UN communique as being "more temperate in tone". After the meeting Brig-General Nuckols, the UN Press Officer, called the talks "encouraging" and said the Communists had "relaxed their dogmatic position". It seems the delegates have found sufficient common ground to be able to begin discussions on a cease-fire.

Meanwhile, men of the 1st Commonwealth Division have been killed, not by the enemy, but by lightning and floods (→ 23/11).

Commanders of the North Korean army pose after the cease-fire is signed.

1951

SEPTEMBER

Su	Mo	Tu	We	Th	Fr	Sa
						1
2	3	4	5	6	7	8
9	10	11	12	13	14	15
16	17	18	19	20	21	22
23	24	25	26	27	28	29
30						

1. San Francisco: The US signs a mutual defence treaty with Australia and New Zealand.

3. Washington: The US reveals that the USSR has exploded a second atomic bomb (→3/10).

5. US: Maureen "Little Mo" Connolly, at 16, is the youngest ever winner of the US Tennis Championships.

6. UK: Twelve million gallons of petrol blaze at Avonmouth Dock in Britain's biggest peacetime oil fire (→14).

9. Tibet: Chinese troops occupy Lhasa.

10. Venice: Vivien Leigh wins best actress prize at the Film Festival for her part in "A Streetcar Named Desire".

10. Egypt: Anti-British riots sweep the country following Egypt's decision to rescind its 1936 alliance with Britain (→14/10).

12. US: Briton Randolph Turpin loses his world middle-weight boxing title in a return fight with Sugar Ray Robinson.

14. UK: Attlee opens Europe's largest oil refinery at Fawley near Southampton.

18. London: Nine doctors diagnose that the King has a lung disease.→

19. London: Attlee calls a general election for October 25 (→21).

20. Ottawa: The NATO countries invite Greece and Turkey to join the alliance.

21. UK: The "Bevan Group" of Labour left-wingers publish a tract attacking trade union leaders and Gaitskell (→24/10).

27. Bonn: The Bundestag votes unanimously to make restitution for "unspeakable crimes" against the Jews.

27. Iran: Iranian troops seize control of the Anglo-Iranian Oil Company's refinery at Abadan (→28).

28. New York: Britain appeals for UN intervention in the Iran oil dispute (→3/10).

30. London: The Festival of Britain ends.

George VI has a major lung operation

Sept 23. An operation for the removal of the King's left lung was performed successfully at Buckingham Palace yesterday. A bulletin, signed by his eight doctors late last night, stated that his condition continued to be as satisfactory as could be expected. The two-hour operation, was carried out in the morning. The bulletin was delayed because doctors wanted to be sure of the King's condition.

Crowds surged towards the railings of Buckingham Palace when an official, accompanied by two policemen, brought the bulletin across the forecourt. It was set out in black crayon letters an inch and a half high, and encased in a picture frame. Photographers from all over the world pressed forward to take a picture as the official held it high.

A private service for the King's recovery was held in the Chapel at Lambeth Palace and conducted by Dr Geoffrey Fisher, the Archbishop of Canterbury. The Prime Minister, Clement Attlee, has cut short his holiday at North Berwick and returned to London (→8/10).

Czechs on express train to freedom

Sept 11. Twenty-five refugees from Communism escaped to the West yesterday aboard the "Freedom Express". The train roared through the last stop in Czechoslovakia, where accomplices had switched to a freight track and cut the brake lines, and on to West Germany.

Engineer Frazek Jarda, who fled with his wife and two children, said: "We did it because it was no longer bearable to live in an East European state." Their dramatic flight is the latest escape bid from behind the Iron Curtain. Other refugees have climbed, tunnelled and flown (→27/11).

Peace treaty finally signed with Japan

Sept 8. Japan put an official end to World War II today by signing a peace treaty with 48 other nations and then, using her newly-acquired status as a sovereign nation, immediately concluded a treaty allowing the US to station her military forces in the country. The terms of the peace treaty mean Japan will lose most of her empire and be barred from rearming, but Soviet Foreign Minister Andrei Gromyko said this was too light a punishment and attacked the treaty with the US as "a preparation for a new war". The US already has two divisions of troops in Japan.

In an epoch-making helicopter-borne assault, US Marines became the first troops to use the new machines under battle conditions in Korea.

1951

OCTOBER

Su	Mo	Tu	We	Th	Fr	Sa
	1	2	3	4	5	6
7	8	9	10	11	12	13
14	15	16	17	18	19	20
21	22	23	24	25	26	27
28	29	30	31			

2. UK: Manny Shinwell is ousted from Labour's national executive committee by Barbara Castle (→25).

3. Iran: Britons leave the refinery of Abadan (→7).

3. Indian Ocean: Britain's first atomic bomb is tested (→29/12).

6. Singapore: Sir Henry Gurney, High Commissioner for Malaya, is killed in a Communist ambush.

7. Teheran: The Shah says he approves his government's nationalisation of the Iranian oil industry (→6/12).

8. Montreal: Princess Elizabeth and Prince Philip arrive on a Canadian tour in place of the King.

11. London: Lord Mountbatten is appointed commander-inchief of British forces in the Mediterranean (→27/10/54).

11. UK: Richards rides his 200th winner of the season for the sixth season in a row.

14. London: Britain offers Egypt a new defence pact under which Britain would give up its Suez Canal rights (→15).

15. Cairo: Egypt rejects a defence pact with Britain.→

16. New Delhi: Pakistani premier Liaquat Ali Khan is assassinated by a Moslem.

21. Egypt: Four British warships are now in Port Said; more troops are heading for the Suez Canal Zone (→22).

22. UK: The government halts arms exports to Egypt (→2/11).

25. UK: The youngest Tory candidate in today's general election is Margaret Roberts, 26, standing in Dartford.→

30. London: The cabinet has Butler as Chancellor, Eden as Foreign Secretary, David Maxwell-Fyfe as Home Secretary.

31. Warsaw: Former Communist leader Wladyslaw Gomulka is arrested.

DEATH

6. US breakfast cereal tycoon and statesman William Kellogg (*7/4/1860).

Churchill arrives back at Number Ten

Oct 26. Winston Churchill is Prime Minister again. At 77, he is tonight forming his first peacetime government after the Tories' narrow general election victory. His chin jutted out as he drove from Buckingham Palace, having accepted the King's commission. It was as if he had also accepted British democracy's apology for having rejected him decisively in 1945. Or so some people thought.

Mr Churchill says he savours the challenge of a new beginning in the bid to revive the nation's post-war fortunes. There was excited talk in his camp about freeing his native land from the shackles of socialism and muddled mismanagement.

With nearly all results now declared the final score in yesterday's polling looks like Tories 321 seats, Labour 295, Liberals 6 and Others 3. The collapse of the Liberals, who fielded candidates in only one constituency in six and collected nearly two million fewer votes than in last year's stalemate election, was the main factor.

Liberal defectors sided overwhelmingly with the Tories. Acknowledging this, Mr Churchill has already offered them representation in the new cabinet. Their leader, Clement Davies, has rejected the invitation.

Polling stations were hardly closed before bitter Labour Party recrimination began. Mr Attlee, said angry left-wingers, had lost because he betrayed Socialism. This gives the Tories breathing-space as they begin trying to implement their campaign promise to make Britain "strong and free" (→ 30).

Mr Churchill returns to Downing Street, with a Tory majority of only 17.

British troops seize Suez Canal zone in a swift dawn raid

Oct 19. At dawn today the British forces were in control of all the key points on the Suez Canal. It was a near bloodless victory with no serious British casualties and only two dead and five wounded Egyptians.

The British troops, including paratroopers, landed here two nights ago, under the command of General Erskine. The operation began at dusk last night and men reached the tents of the Egyptian guards before they realised what was happening.

The prompt action reflects the rapidly deteriorating situation in the Canal Zone. The week began with a major British concession to Egypt, which has been asking for the withdrawal of British troops.

They offered a Middle East pact backed by France, Turkey and the US, which would include Egypt in a five nation defence organisation. Britain would then hand over her Egyptian base to it. Egypt rejected the olive branch and rioting broke out in the Zone (→ 21).

Joe Louis fails in US come-back bid

Oct 27. Joe Louis's attempt to clamber back to the top of the heavyweight tree has failed, and none of the fans who held the Brown Bomber in such awe during his great years will be sorry to hear that he has decided, for the second time in two-and-a-half years, to retire.

Debts, bad tax advice and the usual greed of hangers-on, all led to Louis coming out of his first retirement, and there was enough skill left to gain him applause and, last year, a chance to regain his title against the new champion Ezzard Charles. When that failed, the old sparkle seemed to have gone, yet still he fought on.

Tonight the end came in only the third defeat of his career, as the tough and so far unbeaten 28-year-old Rocky Marciano, himself making a strong bid for title-fight recognition, knocked the once great master through the ropes in the eighth round.

Britain is rapidly going down the tube

Oct 31. Manufacturers of television sets are predicting that the numbers of British homes with televisions will double within two years. Last year the figure was 344,000, but this year alone manufacturers plan to produce 250,000 sets. Although the BBC began the world's first regular TV service in 1936, early growth was slow, with fewer than 100,000 viewers ten years later – all in the London area. Then, in December 1949, came a new transmitter for the Midlands, to be followed by one in the Manchester area this year with Scotland's first due next year. Four in five of the population will then be within reach of television.

The box in the corner – one of 250,000 due to be taken home this year.

90mph Porsche is hit of Motor Show

Oct 17. Among all the new and exciting cars that have brought visitors flocking to the Motor Show today, two have stood out: one British and one, perhaps surprisingly, German.

The Porsche is the first German-made car to be exhibited here since the war and it is already making a real impression. Experts are united in their praise, and see this streamlined saloon, with its top speed of 90mph as not just one of the fastest but one of the safest modern cars.

At the other end of the market, aimed right at the family buyer, is the revamped version of the best-selling Austin 7. Styled like bigger models in the Austin range, and featuring more leg-room and a larger boot, the Austin is bound to do well. With an engine of just 800cc the new 7 is among the smallest cars available, and its price, as yet under wraps, is certain to make it one of the cheapest, too.

1951

NOVEMBER

Su	Mo	Tu	We	Th	Fr	Sa
				1	2	3
4	5	6	7	8	9	10
11	12	13	14	15	16	17
18	19	20	21	22	23	24
25	26	27	28	29	30	

2. Egypt: More British troops are flown into the Suez Canal Zone in the biggest troop airlift since the War (→6).

3. Buenos Aires: Eva Peron enters hospital for surgery; she has already had several blood transfusions (→11).

6. Cairo: The Egyptian government declares a state of emergency.→

7. Washington: Truman offers to sponsor Eisenhower as Democratic presidential candidate in 1952.

7. London: Chancellor Rab Butler announces a rise in the bank lending rate from two per cent to 2.5 per cent (→29).

11. Argentina: Juan Peron is re-elected president.

14. Belgrade: Yugoslavia signs a security pact with the US.

14. Vietnam: French paratroops capture the town of Hao Binh in less than 24 hours (→11/12).

15. Malaya: Terrorist threats have halted work on 16 rubber plantations.

16. Cairo: The Egyptian government offers to let a UN-supervised plebiscite decide the future of Sudan.

19. Tel Aviv: The Knesset elects Dr Chaim Weizmann for a second term as Israeli president.

23. Korea: UN and Communist negotiators agree "in principle" to a truce line.→

25. Egypt: The Egyptians take control of the town of Ismailia (→28).

27. Prague: Czech vice-premier Rudolf Slansky is arrested on a charge of espionage.

29. Damascus: Colonel Adeeb Shishekly overthrows the Syrian government.

28. Egypt: The British agree to withdraw from three towns, if the Egyptians promise to quell terrorism (→4/12).

29. London: The government announces plans to boost farming subsidies by £26 million.

British families are evacuated from Egypt

Local workers are searched by British troops stationed in the Canal Zone.

Nov 20. Mass evacuation of the families of British servicemen from Ismailia in the Canal Zone began today. Over 2,000 women and children have been trapped in their houses since the shooting war began between British troops and Egyptian police. Five Britons and nine Egyptians were killed. Apparently the Egyptian police had orders from Cairo to fire on army vehicles.

General Erskine, the British commander, has now secured the agreement of the Egyptian Governor of the Canal Zone that the police will not carry guns. But the situation is still tense. Cairo blames the British for the fighting. The minister of the Interior, Serag-el-Din Pasha, said it was "wanton, barbaric aggression against innocent civilians and police".

Large crowds watched the evacuation, glowering and jeering at the Bren gun carriers. They saw it as a victory in the struggle to get British troops out (→25).

Korea quiet under informal cease-fire

Nov 28. An eerie calm settled over the slit trenches and gun pits in the Korean front lines today, following the signing of an agreement establishing a truce line roughly along the line of the 38th parallel, the old frontier dividing North and South Korea. No one issued orders for the shooting to stop. It just happened.

General James Van Fleet, commander of the 8th Army, insisted that no cease-fire orders had been issued but it appeared that officers had been ordered not to undertake any offensive actions while the negotiators attempt to reach agreement on a full armistice. A major obstacle to be overcome is the repatriation of POWs (→18/12).

Austin and Morris agree merger terms

Nov 24. Austin and Morris plan to merge, making the combined business the biggest in the British motor trade and fourth internationally after the US "Big Three" of General Motors, Chrysler and Ford.

Lord Nuffield will be chairman, and Leonard Lord, curently chief executive of Austin, deputy chairman and managing director. The merger depends on a share offer. Ninety per cent of holders of Ordinary shares in each firm must accept an exchange.

This is the second time Morris and Austin have tried to get together. In October 1948 they tried sharing information and standardising, but the deal fell through within a year (→18/12).

1951

DECEMBER

Su	Mo	Tu	We	Th	Fr	Sa
						1
2	3	4	5	6	7	8
9	10	11	12	13	14	15
16	17	18	19	20	21	22
23	24	25	26	27	28	29
30	31					

1. UK: Premiere of Benjamin Britten's opera "Billy Budd".

3. East Berlin: East Germany turns down an invitation to both German states to take part in the 1952 Olympics.

4. UK: 23 die when a bus ploughs into a company of Marine cadets at Chatham.

6. Teheran: 10,000 police and students clash.

10. Stockholm: Nobel Prizes go to Sir John Cockcroft (UK) and Ernest Walton (Ireland, Physics); Edwin McMillan and Glenn Seaborg (US, Chemistry); Max Theiler (S. Africa, Medicine); Per Lagerkvist (Sweden, Literature); and in Oslo to Leon Jouhaux (France, Peace).

11. Vietnam: The Viet Minh launch an offensive in Tonkin.

15. The Hague: Britain and France ask the World Court to settle an ancient row over uninhabited Channel islands.

18. Korea: The Communists hand the UN a list of 3,100 UN prisoners of war (→21).

21. Korea: General Ridgway calls for the Red Cross to be allowed into Communist prisoner of war camps.→

27. US: Film critics vote "A Streetcar Named Desire" the best film of 1951.→

29. US: The US Atomic Energy Commission says it can produce useful electric power from nuclear energy.

DEATH

31. Soviet statesman Maxim Litvinov (*17/7/1876).

HITS OF 1951

Shall we dance?

If.

QUOTE OF THE YEAR

"I fired him because he wouldn't respect the authority of the President. I didn't fire him because he was a dumb son-of-a-bitch, although he was, but that's not against the law for generals."

President Truman, explaining why he dismissed MacArthur.

Row over missing POWs

Some of the 1100 British prisoners of war held incommunicado in Korea.

Dec 23. The UN cease-fire delegation today accused the Communists of failing to account for more than 50,000 prisoners. The reply was that most of them had been released at the front and that others had been killed in Allied air raids or died of sickness.

With only four days left to settle differences on the basis of the temporary truce line, the talks had made "absolutely no progress", said the UN spokesman. The Communists, he went on, "to all intents and purposes" rejected the Allied proposal for an immediate exchange of sick and wounded.

Then Rear Admiral Libby, the chief Allied delegate on the sub-committee dealing with the prisoners, questioned the accuracy of the Communist list of about 11,000 POWs.

He said to the Communists: "We are looking for the tens of thousands of men who must still be in your hands." He pointed out that they had previously claimed to hold 65,363 Allied prisoners.

Meanwhile, the Allied forces are taking no chances. Major-General Cassels, Commander of the Commonwealth Division, warns in his Christmas message: "The enemy may well think that he may catch us unprepared during Christmas. I know I can rely on you to prove him wrong."

Arts: operetta gives way to lusty sailors

The death of **Ivor Novello**, in the year that both "Kiss Me Kate" and "South Pacific" opened in London, points the contrast between the pre-war style of musical comedy and the gritty modern musical.

Novello's Ruritanian romances in never-never land were derived from operetta, but his gift for melody and theatricality filled the vast spaces of the Theatre Royal, Drury Lane, with them from "Glamorous Night" in 1935 to "King's Rhapsody", in which he was appearing until recently. They were from a different planet from the lusty sailors and their "broads" of "South Pacific".

When he was 21, Novello wrote his first hit, "Keep the Home Fires Burning", and he showed the same flair for timing as the Second World War ended by producing "We'll Gather Lilacs in the Spring Again". His last show opened in December this year with **Cicely Courtneidge**. Its title: "Gay's the Word".

Vivien Leigh, who won an Oscar for her performance in the film of "A Streetcar Named Desire", has been drawing the town to see her in the double role of Shaw's Cleopatra followed by Shakespeare's, opposite her husband, **Laurence Olivier**, as Caesar and Antony. It is their festival production at the St James's. Shaw's playful sex kitten was reckoned well within her powers, but **Kenneth Tynan** said she played Shakespeare's queen "with her little finger crooked" and Sir Laurence as Antony "climbed down so that she could pat him on the head".

Ivor Novello backstage in 1949.

The year's best-sellers are sea stories. "The Cruel Sea", by **Nicholas Montsarrat**, is a gruesomely detailed story of the men who did battle with the U-boats on Atlantic convoys. Naval manners under stress are the subject of "The Caine Mutiny", by **Herman Wouk**, in which a crazed captain is relieved of his command by his officers. But "The Catcher in the Rye", by **J.D. Salinger**, with its drop-out narrator, Holden Caulfield, shows every sign of becoming a cult. It is a book in which the generation gap yawns.

The icepick marks the spot: this footprint is allegedly that of the "Yeti", the "Abominable Snowman" of Himalayan folk-tales.

Anti-British riots flare up in Canal zone

Dec 4. British troops of the Royal Sussex Regiment came under Sten and rifle fire from a band of 40 Egyptians today in the second day of fierce fighting near the town of Suez. Thirty-three people have been killed (including three British and six Mauritanian soldiers) and well over 60 have been injured.

This new flare-up takes place less than a week after General Erskine, the British commander, agreed with the civil authorities that the Egyptian police should once more maintain law and order in the Canal Zone. The police are now fully armed again and showed yesterday that they are prepared to open fire on British troops immediately they return the fire of Egyptian civilian guerrillas.

The guerrillas are clearly getting a lot of support from the Egyptian Government. The police are also being encouraged to support them. Earlier this week the Egyptian Government gave decorations and promotions to the Ismailia policemen who fired on the British army in the riots there last month.

Egyptian newspapers today gave massive coverage to yesterday's fighting, accusing British troops of using artillery and firing on a hospital. Today the army has effectively sealed off the town of Suez. Trains and all other traffic in and out of the town have been stopped, except for those bringing in essential supplies.

Libya independent with UN assistance

Dec 24. King Idris el Senussi proclaimed the independence of Libya today in a broadcast from the capital, Benghazi. He paid tribute to all his countrymen who had taken part in the struggle for freedom in the former Italian colony. Italy immediately recognised the new Kingdom of Libya.

The path to independence was paved by the United Nations resolution of November, 21 1949. There have been delicate negotiations to safeguard Italian interests in Libya and to secure the future for the more than 40,000 Italians who still live there. Libya is applying for UN membership.

1952

JANUARY

Su	Mo	Tu	We	Th	Fr	Sa
		1	2	3	4	5
6	7	8	9	10	11	12
13	14	15	16	17	18	19
20	21	22	23	24	25	26
27	28	29	30	31		

1. UK: British headmasters criticise the new GCE exams, claiming the standard is too high for some pupils.

2. East Berlin: The East German government rejects a UN request to supervise free national elections (→ 30/8).

5. Washington: Churchill arrives for talks with Truman on world problems (→ 9).

9. Washington: Churchill consents to the US using British bases for "common defence" of the two countries (→ 17).

10. Washington: Truman, who offered to back Ike for president, admits to thinking him a Democrat (→ 29/3).

12. UK: The prototype Vickers Valiant, Britain's only long-range jet for carrying the atomic bomb, crashes (→ 5/3).

13. Teheran: The Iranian government orders British consulates to close (→ 20).

14. London: Sir Robert Watson-Watt wins a £50,000 government prize for his "initiation of radar" (→ 2/9/53).

15. London: Sir Gerald Templar becomes high commissioner for Malaya, succeeding the murdered Henry Gurney (→ 17/2).

17. Washington: Churchill addresses a joint session of Congress.

20. Teheran: Prime Minister Mossadegh denounces Iran's 1857 friendship treaty with Britain (→ 17/7).

22. UK: The driver of the bus which killed 23 military cadets in December 1951 is fined £20 and loses his licence for three years.

25. Egypt: 46 Egyptians die when British troops capture the police headquarters in Ismailia.→

29. London: Butler announces new austerity measures, including more NHS charges (→ 4/2).

31. UK: Princess Elizabeth and the Duke of Edinburgh leave for a tour of Kenya and other Commonwealth nations (→ 8/2).

A lone captain's 12 days on stricken ship

Captain Carlsen clings to rails of the freighter "Flying Enterprise".

Jan 10. A ship's captain's 12-day sea ordeal, trying to save his freighter from sinking, ended today when he swam to safety off the south coast of England. Henrik Carlsen jumped clear only 40 minutes before the Flying Enterprise slipped beneath the hurricane-driven seas, a final hiss of steam signalling the end of his remarkable drama.

It began on Christmas Day, when the American-owned vessel started to break up in mountainous waves shortly after leaving Hamburg. A day later Captain Carlsen ordered passengers and crew off the ship, which soon was listing at an angle of 85 degrees. Its smokestack was able to clip the tops of waves.

Alone but for a young ship's mate, and hoping for the weather to break, he secured a line from a British tug, but storms worsened off Falmouth and the exhausted pair were forced to abandon ship by leaping from the funnel.

"Ike" throws hat into Presidential ring

Jan 7. General Dwight D. Eisenhower, Supreme Allied Commander in Europe and America's most popular war leader, is prepared to run for President. In a long and carefully worded statement from his Paris headquarters today he said he would stick to his job of resisting the Communist threat in Europe, and not take any part in the primary election run up to the election. He gave his blessing, however, to the "Eisenhower for President" campaign that has started.

He confirmed that, although he has never been an active politician, he has always voted Republican. Senator Lodge, one of the most distinguished Republican leaders, has already entered his name in the New Hampshire primary (→ 10).

Cairo rocked by rampaging mobs

Jan 27. This morning, as dawn broke over the city, the full horror of yesterday's riots in Cairo, in which 17 British people were murdered or burnt to death, was revealed. The Turf Club, to which all the British elite in Cairo belonged, was almost totally destroyed, along with paintings of its historic members like Kitchener, Cromer and Allenby. Shepheard's Hotel, founded before the Suez Canal was built and one of the most famous hotels in the world, was very seriously damaged.

Many other buildings were burnt and looted, including Barclays Bank in Rue Kasr-en-Nil, the largest British bank in Cairo. The looting-lust and fanaticism of the crowd got so out of control that they even destroyed the consulate of a sister Arab country, Lebanon.

King Farouk has acted promptly to try to bring the situation under control. Tonight he dismissed the Wafdist government of Nahas Pasha, and imposed a dawn-to-dusk curfew with orders to the police to shoot at sight. British troops in the Canal Zone are on full alert, ready to move into Cairo at a moment's notice. Today men of the Scots Guards and a squadron of Vampire jets arrived in the Canal Zone from Cyprus, in case a move on Cairo is necessary (→ 2/3).

King George and Queen Elizabeth on the tarmac at London Airport after Princess Elizabeth had left for Australia.

1952

FEBRUARY

Su	Mo	Tu	We	Th	Fr	Sa
					1	2
3	4	5	6	7	8	9
10	11	12	13	14	15	16
17	18	19	20	21	22	23
24	25	26	27	28	29	

2. South Atlantic: Armed Argentinians force a British landing party on Graham Land to return to ship (→26/7).

3. Korea: The Communists agree that all freed prisoners should not fight again (→1/4).

4. London: The government offers farmers £5 an acre to plough up grassland for crops (→11/3).

6. Sandringham: The King dies peacefully in his sleep.

8. London: Elizabeth is proclaimed Queen on her return from Kenya.→

11. London: Queens Elizabeth, Elizabeth and Mary pay their respects to the late King, lying in state in Westminster Hall (→13).

13. London: The Duke of Windsor arrives to attend his brother's funeral (→14).

14. London: Crowds pay homage to the King in a continuous file past that lasts until 3.25 am.→

14. Oslo: The Winter Olympics open (→20).

17. Paris: Britain, the US and France put off W. Germany's full NATO membership (→10/4).

17. Malaya: Seven Gordon Highlanders are killed by insurgents (→22).

20. Oslo: Briton Jeanette Altwegg wins the Olympic gold medal for figure skating.

21. UK: Identity cards are abolished.

21. London: Actress Elizabeth Taylor weds Michael Wilding.

22. Malaya: 22 insurgents were killed by British troops in the last 48 hours (→27/12).

27. New York: The UN holds its first session in its new headquarters (→25/10).

29. Paris: Paul Reynaud becomes premier, when Edgar Faure quits after 40 days in office (→25/2/53).

DEATH

6. King George VI (*14/12/1895).

Nation mourns death of George VI

Feb 15. King George VI was laid to rest in the vault of his ancestors at St. George's Chapel, Windsor, today. A day of pageantry and ceremony began when the simple oak casket containing the King's body was moved from Westminster Hall.

While it lay there, some 305,806 people filed past to pay their last respects to the diffident man who had lived with them through the troubles of both war and peace and who had never aspired to be King.

As the coffin left Westminster on a gun carriage, Big Ben rang out, one beat a minute to mark the 56 years of the King's life. Men of the Household Cavalry in ceremonial dress walked in slow time to Paddington station, where the royal train was waiting.

As the solemn cortege passed Marlborough House, there was a poignant moment. Queen Mary, the King's mother, appeared at a window across which a blind was half drawn, and bowed her head. The King was the third of her sons to die.

On the train were Kings and Queens, Princes and Princesses, the great and near-great from the political world. In a statement, the Queen Mother said: "My only wish is to continue the work we sought to do together" (→9/4).

Three queens in mourning: Elizabeth II, her grandmother and mother.

Elizabeth, the princess who became a Queen while on safari

Feb 8. It was the Duke of Edinburgh who told his wife that she had become Queen. As they walked outside the Treetops Hotel in Kenya, the new Queen asked one of her staff if it would be possible to arrange a ride on a horse as it was such a lovely day.

Commander Michael Parker, the Duke's Equerry, took some time to get the Duke's attention and beckon him indoors. There he was told that a journalist in the royal tour press party had recently heard on the telephone from London that King George VI had died in his sleep.

The Duke was visibly shocked by the news. The Queen took it calmly. It was little over a week since she had said goodbye to her father at London airport. Though he survived a serious operation, he seemed in good heart. The official news came almost immediately after de-coding at the British High Commission in Nairobi.

The new Queen's immediate concern was to let people in Australia and New Zealand know that she would not be able to continue the royal tour, which it had been originally intended that her father would make.

Meanwhile, in London, the Accession Council was busy doing its job without the presence of the new monarch.

It was already dusk when the Queen arrived back at London Airport. She came down the steps a slim, pale figure in mourning black. The Prime Minister, Winston Churchill, and the Opposition Leader, Clement Attlee, both greeted her on arrival.

Her Majesty's servants – Churchill and Attlee await the new Queen.

Churchill reveals atomic bomb secret

Feb 26. Britain has developed an atomic bomb and has a plant capable of producing the weapon, the Prime Minister, Winston Churchill, told the Commons today.

The bomb will be tested this year in Australia, he went on, adding that the weapon had been developed by Clement Attlee's Labour administration, but kept secret from him until he was re-elected prime minister. He accused the Labour government of practising "Machiavellian art" by developing the bomb while denouncing atomic weapons.

The British development has been praised by the chairman of the US Senate's Atomic Energy Committee, Senator McMahon of Connecticut, who said its development would contribute to world peace "because it will add to the free world's total deterring power".

The test will be conducted in conditions which will ensure that there will be no danger from radioactivity to people or animals, a statement from Downing Street said. The device will probably be exploded from the top of a pylon, using the same method as that adopted by the Americans. New high-speed film cameras will record every stage of the explosion (→1/4).

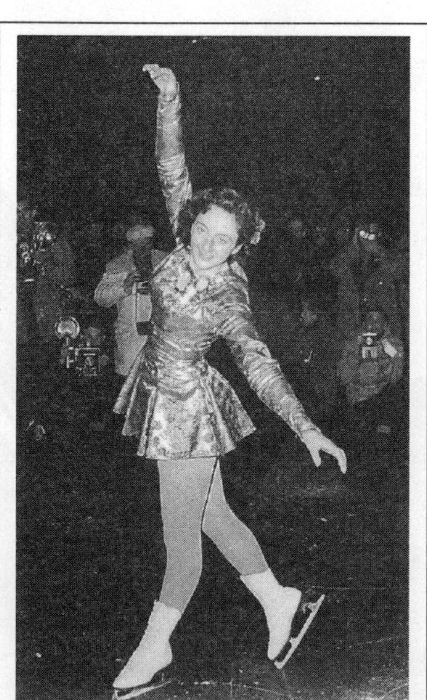

Ice-skater Jeanette Altwegg gave Britain her first gold medal for figure-skating at the Winter Olympics in Oslo.

1952

MARCH

Su	Mo	Tu	We	Th	Fr	Sa
						1
2	3	4	5	6	7	8
9	10	11	12	13	14	15
16	17	18	19	20	21	22
23	24	25	26	27	28	29
30	31					

2. Cairo: King Farouk suspends the Egyptian parliament for a month (→1/7).

5. London: 57 Bevanite Labour MPs defy a three-line whip on a defence vote (→4/4).

7. Peking: China claims the US is using germ warfare in Manchuria (→1/1/53).

10. Cuba: General Fulgencio Batista, Cuba's strong man from 1933 to 1944, ousts President Carlos Socarras (→26/7/53).

11. London: The Budget raises tax allowances and profits tax, cuts food subsidies and raises the bank rate to four per cent (→27).

14. UK: The British Standards Institution "Kite Mark" will replace the utility sign when the utility scheme ends (→17).

14. Washington: The US says it is doubling defence aid to Britain to £214 million.

17. UK: The government-sponsored utility scheme ends.

21. US: Vivien Leigh wins an Oscar for best actress for "A Streetcar Named Desire"; Humphrey Bogart is best actor in "The African Queen".

22. Frankfurt: 44 die when a KLM plane crashes while landing in rain and fog (→20/12).

22. US: Over 200 are reported killed and 2,500 hurt as a tornado sweeps six mid-west states.

25. UK: 20,000 NHS doctors are to get a pay rise of £500 a year, backdated to 1948 (→30/4).

25. Tunisia: French authorities arrest premier Hamed Shenik after a series of countrywide disturbances (→31/7/54).

27. UK: The cheese ration is to be cut to an ounce a week from April 20 (→7/4).

27. London: The government bars Seretse Khama as chief of the Bamangwato tribe.

29. London: Oxford wins the Boat Race, in blizzard conditions.

29. US: Truman pulls out of presidential race (→12/4).

Nkrumah is elected the first African PM

March 21. Dr Kwame Nkrumah, who was serving a prison sentence for sedition when his party won the Gold Coast's first general election, today became the first African Prime Minister south of the Sahara.

He adopted the name Kwame, the local word for Saturday, because his mother told him he was born on that day. He was about three years old when a British cargo ship ran aground near his home in a remote coastal village; the year was 1913, so he believes he is now 42. After many years in Britain and the US, he returned to the Gold Coast four years ago to campaign for an end to colonial rule. He was soon in trouble for publishing inflammatory articles in a paper he started, The Daily Mail.

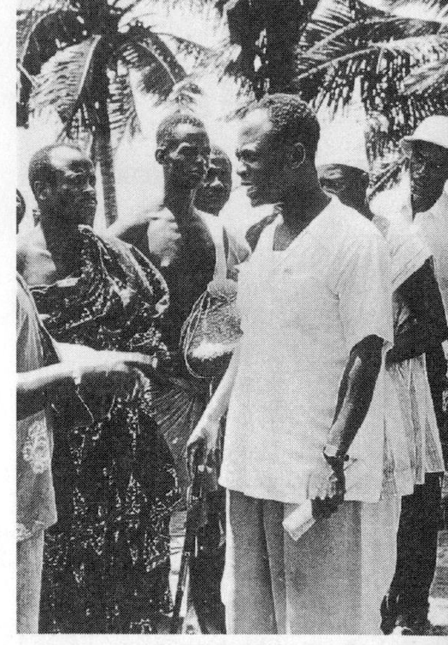

Dr Nkrumah tours the Gold Coast.

Legal clash sparks South Africa crisis

March 20. South Africa's hardline Prime Minister, Dr D.F. Malan, plunged the country into a constitutional crisis today when he told Parliament he would not accept a Supreme Court judgment invalidating a new law to remove the Coloured (mixed race) voters from the electoral register. The Court ruled that such a law needed a two-thirds majority in Parliament, because voters' rights were "entrenched" in the constitution (→29/5).

Artificial heart is used for first time

March 8. Officials of Pennsylvania Hospital in Philadelphia announced today that a mechanical heart has been successfully applied to a patient for the first time. Peter During was a 41-year-old steel worker, who later died of causes unrelated to the use of the equipment.

The device supported him for 80 minutes while nine doctors, five nurses and two technicians tried to find what was blocking the blood flow from his heart (→26/3/53).

Wet Mr Kelly has something to sing about

March 27. Hollywood has come up with its funniest spoof of itself in "Singin' in the Rain", more of a comic musical than a musical comedy. The sequence in which Gene Kelly sings the title number while tap-dancing his debonair way through a downpour deserves to be remembered as a classic example of Hollywood production at its best.

It has absolutely nothing to do with the story, which tells how the coming of sound upset the stars of the silent sheikh-and-flapper era. Jean Hagen lampoons a queen of the silent screen with a terrible voice undergoing the horror of filming with a microphone. Mr Kelly dances a Broadway ballet on electrified feet.

Gene Kelly's singing in the rain.

1952

APRIL

Su	Mo	Tu	We	Th	Fr	Sa
		1	2	3	4	5
6	7	8	9	10	11	12
13	14	15	16	17	18	19
20	21	22	23	24	25	26
27	28	29	30			

1. US: The US Atomic Energy Commission begins a new series of test blasts in Nevada (→22).

1. Korea: UN planes shoot down 10 Communist MiG-15s (→8/5).

2. London: Britain offers the Sudan a form of limited self-rule (→29/11/53).

4. London: Labour wins a majority of 55 in elections to the London County Council (→7/5).

5. UK: Mr H. Lane's Teal wins the Grand National.

5. US: The USAF unveils its latest jet bomber, the giant eight-engined YB-60 (→14/6).

7. London: The government says it will place £20 million orders in textile manufacturers worst hit by recession (→15/5).

9. London: The Queen says the Royal Family will retain the surname Windsor (→27/5).

10. Paris: Eisenhower asks Truman to relieve him as NATO chief from June 1 (→16).

12. Paris: Eisenhower says he will resign from the army if nominated as Republican presidential candidate (→11/7).

16. Paris: NATO's new headquarters opens at the Palais de Chaillot (→28).

22. US: 35 million TV viewers watch the most powerful atomic explosion yet in the Nevada desert (→3/10).

23. Bonn: Franco-German talks on the future of the Saar break down (→5/5).

24. West Germany: The Nuremberg tribunal begins hearings on the Katyn Forest massacre of 1940 (→15/6).

28. Paris: General Matthew Ridgway is appointed Eisenhower's successor as NATO chief (→30/5).

30. UK: The British pharmaceutical industry decides to sell its products in metric weights and measures (→15/9/55).

DEATH

21. British Labour statesman Sir Stafford Cripps (*24/4/1889).

French launch big push in Vietnam

April 26. French forces yesterday moved decisively to smash the Viet Minh resistance base 75 miles to the north-west of Saigon. Six thousand men were involved in a two-pronged attack deep into heavily forested hill country north of Tay Ninh, where the Viet Minh's political and military headquarters for the area is situated.

Jean le Tourneau, the French Minister Resident in Indochina, said today that France would ask the United Nations to intervene if Communist China actively entered the war. He warned that should the Communists win Indochina, the whole of southern Asia would be ripe for conquest (→11/10).

French paras attack at Tay Ninh.

US finally ends the Pacific war

April 15. In a brief ceremony at the White House this morning, President Truman marked the official end of World War II in the Pacific. He signed the peace treaty, and 49 states joined in recognising Japanese sovereignty. The Soviet Union has yet to sign. Truman also signed security treaties with Australia, New Zealand and Japan, and a mutual defence pact with the Philippines. Japan will start to govern itself again, as from April 28 next year.

1952

MAY

Su	Mo	Tu	We	Th	Fr	Sa
				1	2	3
4	5	6	7	8	9	10
11	12	13	14	15	16	17
18	19	20	21	22	23	24
25	26	27	28	29	30	31

1. US: TWA introduce a "Tourist Class"; nine other airlines are expected to follow suit shortly (→2).

3. London: Newcastle United become the first team since 1891 to win the FA Cup for two years running, beating Arsenal 1-0.

5. Bonn: West Germany adopts the third verse of "Deutschland Uber Alles" as its national anthem.

5. London: The federation of Northern Rhodesia, Southern Rhodesia and Nyasaland is agreed in principle (→5/2/53).

7. London: Iain Macleod is appointed Minister of Health (→9).

9. UK: Labour gains 609 seats in borough elections, taking control of 21 councils (→30/9).

10. France: Orson Welles's film of "Othello" wins a Grand Prix at the Cannes Film Festival.

15. London: The government announces an increase in the meat ration to 1/7d. a week (→28/8).

20. London: The Nature Conservancy Council declares eight areas of England and Scotland as nature reserves.

21. London: Thieves attack three postmen and steal a van carrying registered mail worth over £200,000 (→26/8).

27. London: The Queen gives permission for Britten to write a Coronation opera about Queen Elizabeth I and Essex (→4/11).

28. UK: The Aga Khan's Tulyar wins the Derby; Mrs J. Rank's Gay Time is second, ridden by Lester Piggott, 16.

29. S. Africa: MPs empower the government to reject a High Court ruling against its racist legislation (→1/6).

30. Paris: Eisenhower hands over to Ridgway as NATO chief; General Mark Clark succeeds Ridgway in Korea (→2/8).

DEATH

6. Italian educationalist Maria Montessori (*31/8/1870).→

Allies launch huge air strike in Korea

May 8. Allied fighter-bombers hammered the ancient Korean city of Suan today in raids which lasted from dawn to dusk. Bombs and napalm rained down on this supply centre, which was then raked with cannon and machine-gun fire from strafing fighters.

The attack served a political as well as a military purpose, coming just a day after General Ridgway, the UN commander, showed his exasperation with the Communists' delaying tactics by serving them with a "final" armistice proposal. The raids are believed to have seriously affected the enemy's ability to mount a large-scale offensive, and results are expected at the conference table (→3/6).

Maria Montessori, school pioneer, dies

May 6. The nursery education pioneer, Dr Maria Montessori, has died in the Netherlands, aged 81. Italy's first woman physician, Dr Montessori worked initially with brain-damaged children before applying her methods, which are based on self-discovery and spontaneity, to ordinary children. In 1907 she opened a school in Rome. After decades of neglect her work, emphasising early reading and writing, is now back in vogue.

Captains Mercer of Arsenal and Harvey of Newcastle shake hands at the start of this year's Cup Final at Wembley Stadium.

▷

Comet makes first scheduled jet flight

May 2. The jet era for passenger flight began today when the first scheduled Comet airliner left London airport for Johannesburg with 36 passengers on board.

Hundreds of spectators waved from office windows and the public enclosure as the British Overseas Airways Corporation aircraft took off and climbed steeply on the first stage of its 6,724-mile journey to Jonannesburg, which it was expected to reach in 18 hours 40 minutes.

The route was complex with stops at Rome, Beirut, Khartoum, Entebbe and Livingstone, Northern Rhodesia (→ 7/7).

Commons vote for women's equal pay

May 16. The principle of equal pay for women doing the same jobs as men was given all-party support in the House of Commons today. John Boyd-Carpenter, Financial Secretary to the Treasury, said that the Government would introduce such pay structures in stages. The first examples are expected to be in the Civil Service. Today Labour pressed for a definite date, claiming that "women are not going to wait much longer" (→ 25/1/55).

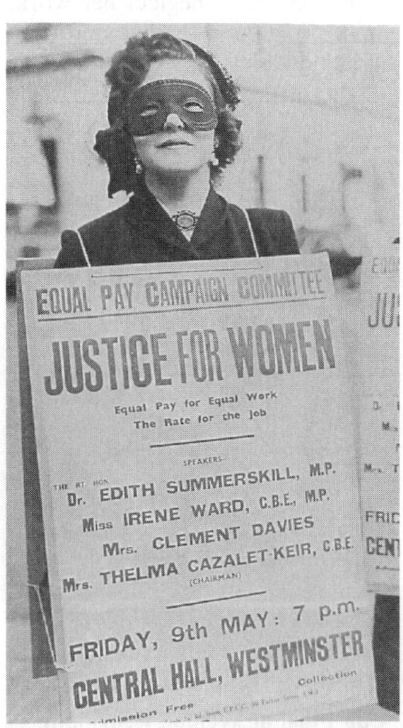

Banners demand equal pay-rates.

1952

JUNE

Su	Mo	Tu	We	Th	Fr	Sa
1	2	3	4	5	6	7
8	9	10	11	12	13	14
15	16	17	18	19	20	21
22	23	24	25	26	27	28
29	30					

1. S. Africa: Blacks, Coloureds and Indians launch a campaign of "defiance of unjust laws".→

3. Korea: US troops storm rebellious Communist POWs in camps on Koje Island, killing 30 (→ 8).

4. US: Eisenhower makes the opening speech of his presidential campaign, attacking one-party states.

8. Korea: Reports claim 100,000 Chinese reinforcements are on their way to the battle front (→ 23).

8. London: William Dickson is appointed to succeed Sir John Slessor as Chief of the Air Staff from next January (→ 29).

11. UK: Denis Compton hits his 100th century.

12. UK: Chris Chataway runs two miles in a record eight minutes 55.6 seconds.

14. US: Truman attends a ceremony to launch the USS Nautilus, the world's first atomic-powered submarine.

14. Moscow: Andrei Gromyko is appointed Soviet ambassador to Britain (→ 28/7).

16. Europe: The Schuman Plan, creating a coal and steel community, is ratified by member states (→ 10/8).

20. London: The government announces that "zebra" crossings will be marked by blinking orange beacons.

23. Korea: UN planes bomb North Korean hydro-electric plants (→ 29/8).

25. Washington: Truman vetoes the McCarran-Walter bill on immigration quotas as discriminatory (→ 27).

26. Washington: Congress overrides Truman's veto and passes the controversial immigration bill.

27. London: Foreign ministers of Britain, France and the US meet to discuss Western foreign policy.

29. UK: The prototype of the RAF's latest jet fighter, the delta-wing Gloster GA-5, crashes and explodes (→ 26/8).

Anne Frank's moving diary is published

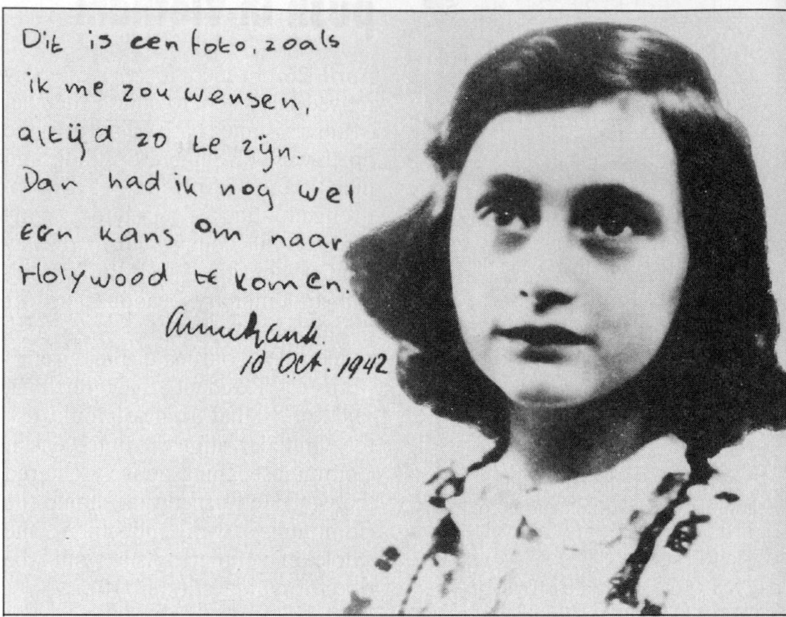

Anne Frank, the way "I would wish myself to look all the time".

June 15. Anne Frank was 13 when she began keeping her diary in 1942. She and her family, German Jewish refugees in Amsterdam, were living in a "secret annexe" to her father's place of business while the Germans rounded up all Jews.

For two years, eight people lived in claustrophobic confinement and fear of discovery, never going out of doors. Anne described the friction, her dreams, analysing herself with total honesty.

"I have now reached the stage where I don't care whether I live or die. What is going to happen will happen," she wrote. In July 1944 it did happen and they were sent to the camps. Only her father – and her diary – survived (→ 10/9).

South Africans protest at "unjust laws"

June 26. Singing "God Save Africa", Blacks, Coloureds and Indians today began a non-violent campaign against South Africa's apartheid laws. After crossing race segregation barriers and openly defying the law requiring them to carry official passes, they gave themselves up to police and refused to ask for bail. About 150 people were taken to prison; most of them were wearing gold, green and black armbands, the colours of the African National Congress (→ 29/8).

Soviets in move to cut off West Berlin

June 1. Today saw the lowering of the "iron curtain" between West Berlin and the surrounding Soviet Zone. As from midnight last night, all West Germans need special permits to enter the Eastern Zone. The ban does not apply to Berlin's road and rail lifelines to the West.

A three-mile security belt has been set up to reinforce existing restrictions on frontier crossings. This includes a 10-yard deep "shoot on sight" strip (→ 4/8/55).

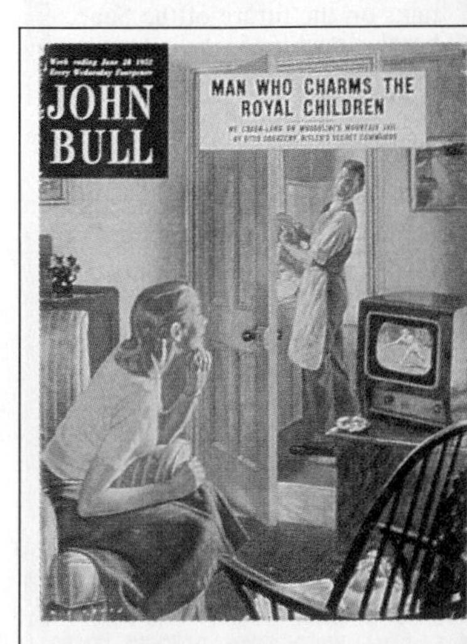

1952

JULY

Su	Mo	Tu	We	Th	Fr	Sa
		1	2	3	4	5
6	7	8	9	10	11	12
13	14	15	16	17	18	19
20	21	22	23	24	25	26
27	28	29	30	31		

1. Cairo: Hussein Sirry Pasha is appointed premier (→4).

4. Wimbledon: Australian Frank Sedgman beats Jaroslav Drobny, the Czech defector, for the Men's Singles title.→

4. Cairo: The government proclaims a state of alert in the capital (→23).

5. London: Thousands of Londoners bid farewell to the city's last tram, which runs from Woolwich to New Cross.

7. UK: The US liner "United States" crosses the Atlantic in a record three days, ten hours and 40 minutes (→16/8).

11. Chicago: Eisenhower wins the Republican nomination, with Senator Richard Nixon, as running mate (→12).

11. UK: South African Bobby Locke wins his third British Golf Open in four years.

12. US: Eisenhower resigns from the US Army (→26).

14. Jamaica: 700 arrests have been made in a new crackdown on marijuana trafficking.

17. Teheran: Mossadegh is replaced as prime minister by Ahmad Ghavam (→22).

19. Helsinki: Finnish President Juho Paasikivi opens the 15th Olympic Games (→3/8).

22. Teheran: Mossadegh is reappointed prime minister following riots in protest at Ghavam's appointment (→31).

23. Cairo: General Mohammed Neguib seizes power in a military coup.→

26. Chicago: Governor Adlai Stevenson of Illinois is chosen to run as Democratic presidential candidate (→5/9).

28. London: The new Soviet ambassador, Andrei Gromyko, takes up his post (→13/1/53).

30. Cairo: The titles of Bey and Pasha are abolished (→7/9).

31. Teheran: Mossadegh assumes emergency powers from the Shah (→11/9).

DEATH

26. Argentine politician Eva Peron, born Maria Eva Ibarguren (*7/5/1919).→

Evita, heroine of the shirtless ones, dies

Eva Peron, the controversial first lady of Argentina, lies in state.

July 26. At 9.42 tonight, Argentina learnt that Eva Peron was dead. "Our spiritual leader has gone!" cried the radio announcer. The First Lady had succumbed to ovarian cancer at the age of only 33.

Maria Eva Ibarguren was born at Los Toldos in 1919, the illegitimate daughter of a cook. At 15, singing in a Buenos Aires nightclub, she met Labour Minister Juan Peron. Less than 12 months later, he married her.

Her charisma and popularity exceeded that of her husband. In October 1945, Peron was arrested on a treason charge. Eva – or Evita, as she was also known – took to the airwaves, inciting the workers to rise up and free him. The ruling junta took fright and let him go. She championed many worthy causes, getting women the vote and legalising divorce. Argentina's "descamisados", or shirtless poor, loved her dearly. Evita's other side was not so admirable. Corruption, torture and "disappearances" were frequent under the Perons. But now she lies in state, wearing the stunning white evening dress in which she will be buried (→15/4/53).

17-year-old "Little Mo" wins Wimbledon

Little Mo playing to win, as ever.

July 5. Maureen Connolly, "Little Mo" to all her American fans, has won the Wimbledon singles title at her first attempt at the age of just 17 – the youngest All-England champion since the 15-year-old prodigy Lottie Dod last century.

The solid, unruffled strength and consistency of her ground strokes, her backhand in particular, have been well known to Americans for the past year. But Louise Brough, three times champion since the War and playing her fifth Wimbledon final, might have been expected to make her experience tell. She led 5-4 in the first set, and three deuces were called before the young Californian took the tenth game. Thereafter she gradually wore down the older player, and in the end won comfortably 7-5, 6-3.

Army coup boots out playboy king

July 26. King Farouk of Egypt sailed out of Alexandria this evening in his luxury yacht. He has abdicated in favour of his nine-month-old son, leaving all effective power in the hands of General Neguib, who led last Wednesday's army coup.

Farouk's fall follows a series of arms scandals in which his favourites were accused of supplying defective weapons at vast profits to themselves. It was his stubborn refusal to dismiss such favourites which led to Neguib's coup. There was some dancing on the streets and smiling faces everywhere as the "Playboy King" fled (→30).

Britons are older and more solitary

July 11. Britons are living longer, marrying earlier, divorcing more frequently and drifting away from the traditional manufacturing industries. These are among the findings of a preliminary report from the 1951 national census.

Twice as many people – 1.5 million – now live alone as in 1931. For the first time the census covered living conditions: one household in three still lacks a bath, while one in 20 has no piped water.

Travellers cluster for a place in history, as Central London's last tram prepares to leave.

Helsinki Olympic glories go to Zatopek and wife

Aug 3. Helsinki's Olympic Games, held in the Finns' magnificent new stadium and opened with their greatest Olympian, Paavo Nurmi, lighting the flame, will long be remembered by the British as the one in which they very nearly failed to win a single gold medal. It was not until a quarter of an hour before the closing ceremony, in the centre of the great stadium, that Colonel Harry Llewellyn and Foxhunter jumped a clear round to give Britain's show-jumping team the Prix des Nations title.

One man, though, dominated the Games: Emil Zatopek. The 29-year-old Czech not only regained his 1948 title by winning the 10,000 metres, but also sprinted round four men on the final bend to win the 5,000 metres and then, three days later, attempted the first marathon of his life, and won it by a minute and a half. Asked what it was like, he said it was boring.

It was an unprecedented treble, with all three performances setting new Olympic records. And if that wasn't enough, his wife Dana set an Oylmpic record for the javelin by 15 feet.

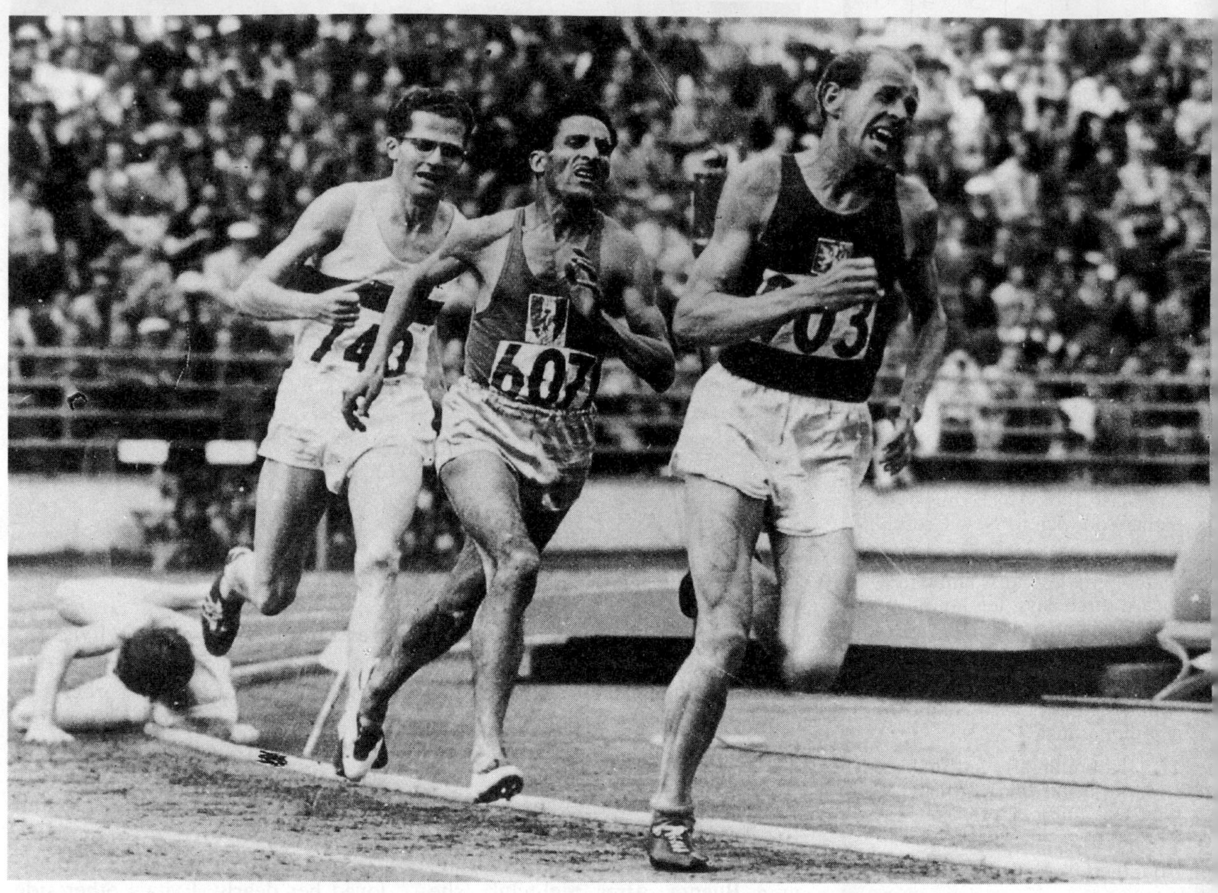

On the final bend of the 5,000 metres final: Zatopek leads from Mimoun and Schade, but Chataway falls.

Men Athletics

100m
1. Lindy Remigino USA 10.4
2. Herbert McKenley JAM 10.4
3. Emmanuel McDonald Bailey GBR 10.4

200m
1. Andrew Stanfield USA 20.7
2. W. Thane Baker USA 20.8
3. James Gathers USA 20.8

400m
1. Georges Rhoden JAM *45.9
2. Herbert McKenley JAM 45.9
3. Ollie Matson USA 46.8

800m
1. Malvin Whitfield USA =*1:49.2
2. Arthur Wint JAM 1:49.4
3. Heinz Ulzheimer GER 1:49.7

1500m
1. Josef Barthel LUX *3:45.1
2. Robert McMillen USA 3:45.2
3. Werner Lueg GER 3:45.4

5000m
1. Emil Zátopek TCH *14:06.6
2. Alain Mimoun FRA 14:07.4
3. Herbert Schade GER 14:08.6

10,000m
1. Emil Zátopek TCH *29:17.0
2. Alain Mimoun FRA 29:28.2
3. Aleksandr Anufriev URS 29:32.8

Marathon
1. Emil Zátopek TCH *2:23:03.2
2. Reinaldo Gorno ARG 2:25:35.0
3. Gustaf Jansson SWE 2:26:07.0

110m Hurdles
1. Harrison Dillard USA *13.7
2. Jack Davis USA 13.7
3. Arthur Barnard USA 14.1

400m Hurdles
1. Charles Moore USA *50.8
2. Yuri Lituyev URS 51.3
3. John Holland NZL 52.2

3000m Steeplechase
1. Horace Ashenfelter USA ** 8:45.4
2. Vladimir Kazantsev URS 8:51.6
3. John Disley GBR 8:51.8

4x100m Relay
1. USA 40.1 (Dean Smith, Harrison Dillard,Lindy Remigino, Andrew Stanfield)
2. URS 40.3 (Boris Tokaryev, Levan Kalyayev, Levan Sanadze, Vladimir Sukharyev)
3. HUN 40.5 (László Zarándi, Géza Varasdi, György Csányi, Bela Goldoványi)

4x400m Relay
1. JAM ** 3:03.9 (Arthur Wint, Leslie Laing, Herbert McKenley, George Rhoden)
2. USA 3:04.0 (Ollie Matson, Gerald Cole, Charles Moore, Malvin Whitfield)
3. GER 3:06.6 (Hans Geister, Günther Steines, Heinz Ulzheimer, Karl-Friedrich Haas)

50km Walk
1. Giuseppe Dordoni ITA *4:28:07.8
2. Josef Dolezal TCH 4:30:17.8
3. Antal Róka HUN 4:31:27.2

10km Walk
1. John Mikaelsson SWE 45:02.8
2. Fritz Schwab SUI 45:41.0
3. Bruno Yunk URS 45:41.0

High Jump
1. Walter Davis USA *2.04
2. Kenneth Wiesner USA 2.01
3. José Telles da Conceicáo BRA 1.98

Pole Vault
1. Robert Richards USA *4.55
2. Donald Laz USA 4.50
3. Ragnar Lundberg SWE 4.40

Long Jump
1. Jerome Biffle USA 7.57
2. Meredith Gourdine USA 7.53
3. Odön Földessy HUN 7.30

Triple Jump
1. Adhemar Ferreira Da Silva BRA ** 16.22
2. Leonid Sherbakov URS 15.98
3. Arnoldo Devonish VEN 15.52

Shotput
1. Parry O'Brien USA *17.41
2. Darrow Hooper USA 17.39
3. James Fuchs USA 17.06

Discus
1. Sim Iness USA *55.03
2. Adolfo Consolini ITA 53.78
3. James Dillion USA 53.28

Hammer
1. József Csérmák HUN 60.34
2. Karl Storch GER 58.86
3. Imre Németh HUN 57.74

Javelin
1. Cyrus Young USA *73.78
2. William Miller USA 72.46
3. Toivo Hyytiäinen FIN 71.89

Decathlon
1. Robert Mathias USA ** 7887
2. Milton Campbell USA 6975
3. Floyd Simmons USA 6788

Women Athletics

100m
1. Marjorie Jackson AUS =*11.5
2. Daphne Hasenjager-Robb SAF 11.8
3. Shirley Strickland AUS 11.9

200m
1. Marjorie Jackson AUS 23.7
2. Bertha Brouwer NETH 24.2
3. Nadezhda Khnykina URS 24.2

80m Hurdles
1. Shirley Strickland AUS ** 10.9
2. Maria Golubnitchaya URS 11.1
3. Maria Sander GER 11.1

4x100m Relay
1. USA ** 45.9 (Mae Faggs, Barbara Jones, Janet Moreau, Catherine Hardy)
2. GER ** 45.9 (Ursula Knab, Marga Petersen, Maria Sander, Helga Klein)
3. GBR 46.2 (Sylvia Cheeseman, June Foulds, Jean Desforges, Heather Armitage)

High Jump
1. Esther Brand SAF 1.67
2. Sheila Lerwill GBR 1.65
3. Aleksandra Chudina URS 1.63

Long Jump
1. Yvette Williams NZL *6.24
2. Aleksandra Chudina URS 6.14
3. Shirley Cawley GBR 5.92

Shotput
1. Galina Zybina URS ** 15.28
2. Marianne Werner GER 14.57
3. Klaudia Tochenova URS 14.50

Discus
1. Nina Romaschkova URS *51.42
2. Yelisaveta Bagryantseva URS 47.08
3. Nina Dumbadze URS 46.29

Javelin
1. Dana Zátopková TCH 50.47
2. Aleksandra Chudina URS 50.01
3. Yelena Gorchakova URS 49.76

Men Swimming

100m Freestyle
1. Clarke Scholes USA 57.4
2. Hiroshi Suzuki JAP 57.4
3. Göran Larsson SWE 58.2

400m Freestyle
1. Jean Boiteux FRA *4:30.7
2. Ford Konno USA 4:31.3
3. Per-Olof Ostrand SWE 4:35.2

1500m Freestyle
1. Ford Konno USA *18:30.3
2. Shiro Hashizume JAP 18:41.4
3. Tetsuo Okamoto BRA 18:51.3

100m Backstroke
1. Yoshinobu Oyakawa USA *1:05.4
2. Gilbert Bozon FRA 1:06.2
3. Jack Taylor USA 1:06.4

200m Breaststroke
1. John Davies AUS *2:34.4
2. Bowen Stassforth USA 2:34.7
3. Herbert Klein GER 2:35.9

4x200m Freestyle Relay
1. USA *8:31.1 (Wayne Moore, William Woolsey, Ford Konno, James McLane)
2. JAP 8:33.5 (Hiroshi Suzuki, Yoshihiro Hamaguchi, Toru Goto, Teijiro Tanikawa)
3. FRA 8:45.9 (Joseph Bernardo, Aldo Eminente, Alexandre Jany, Jean Boiteux)

Springboard Diving
1. David Browning USA 205.29
2. Miller Anderson USA 199.84
3. Robert Clotworthy USA 184.92

Platform Diving
1. Samuel Lee USA 156.
2. Joaquin Capilla Pérez MEX 145.
3. Günther Haase GER 141.

Water Polo

1. Hungary
2. Yugoslavia
3. Italy

Women Swimming

100m Freestyle
1. Katalin Szöke HUN 1:06
2. Johanna Termeulen NETH 1:07
3. Judit Temes HUN 1:07

400m Freestyle
1. Valéria Gyenge HUN *5:12
2. Eva Novák HUN 5:13
3. Evelyne Kawamoto USA 5:14

200m Breaststroke
1. Eva Székely HUN *2:51
2. Eva Novák HUN 2:54
3. Elenor Gordon GBR 2:57

100m Backstroke
1. Joan Harrison SAF 1:14
2. Geertje Wielema NETH 1:14
3. Jean Stewart NZL 1:15

4x100m Freestyle Relay
1. HUN ** 4:24.4 (Ilona Novák, Judit Temes, Eva Novák, Katalin Szöke)
2. NETH 4:29.0 (Marie-Louise Linssen, Koosje van Voorn, Johanna Termeulen, Irma Heijting-Schuhmacher)
3. USA 4:30.1 (Jacqueline La Vine, Marilee Stepan, Joan Alderson, Evelyn Kawamoto)

Springboard Diving
1. Patricia McCormick USA 147.
2. Mady Moreau FRA 139.
3. Zoe-Ann Jensen-Olsen USA 127.

Platform Diving
1. Patricia McCormick USA 79.
2. Paula Jean Myers USA 71.
3. Juno Irwin USA 70.

1952  Helsinki

Boxing

Flyweight
Nathan Brooks USA
Edgar Basel GER
Anatoly Bulakov URS
William Toweel SAF

Bantamweight
Pentti Hämäläinen FIN
John McNally IRL
Gennady Garbuzov URS
Joon-Ho Kang KOR

Featherweight
Jan Zachara TCH
Sergio Caprari ITA
Joseph Ventaja FRA
Leonard Leisching SAF

Lightweight
Aureliano Bolognesi ITA
Aleksy Ankiewiez POL
Erkki Pakkanen FIN
Gheorghe Fiat ROM

Light Welterweight
Charles Adkins USA
Viktor Mednov URS
Erkki Mallenius FIN
Bruno Visintin ITA

Welterweight
Zygmunt Chychla POL
Sergei Scherbakov URS
Victor Jörgensen DEN
Günther Heidemann GER

Light Middleweight
László Papp HUN
Theunis van Schalkwyk SAF
Eladio Herrera ARG

Middleweight
Floyd Patterson USA
Vasile Tita ROM
Stig Sjölin SWE
Boris Georgiev BUL

Light Heavyweight
Norvel Lee USA
Antonio Pacenza ARG
Anatoly Porov URS
Harri Siljander FIN

Heavyweight
Edward Sanders USA
No Silver Medal awarded
Andries Nieman SAF
Ilkka Koski FIN

(Ingemar Johansson (Sweden) was disqualified for "passivity" during the 2nd Round and therefore did not win the Silver Medal.)

Greco Roman Wrestling

Flyweight
Boris Gurevitch URS
Ignazio Fabra ITA
Leo Honkala FIN

Bantamweight
Imre Hódos HUN
Zakaria Chihab LIB
Artem Teryan URS

Featherweight
Yakov Punkin URS
Imre Polyák HUN
Abdel Rashed EGY

Lightweight
Schazam Safin URS
Gustaf Freij SWE
Mikulás Athanasov TCH

Welterweight
Miklós Szilvási HUN
Gösta Andersson SWE
Khalil Taha LIB

Middleweight
Axel Grönberg SWE
Kalervo Rauhala NOR
Nikolai Byelov URS

Light Heavyweight
1. Kaelpo Gröndahl FIN
2. Schalva Chikhladze URS
3. Karl-Erik Nilsson SWE

Heavyweight
1. Johannes Kotkas URS
2. Josef Ruzicka TCH
3. Tauno Kovanen FIN

Freestyle Wrestling

Flyweight
1. Hasan Gemici TUR
2. Yushu Kitano JAP
3. Mahmoud Mollaghasemi IRN

Bantamweight
1. Shohachi Ishii JAP
2. Rashid Mamedbekov URS
3. Kha-Shaba Jadav IND

Featherweight
1. Bayram Sit TUR
2. Nasser Givechi IRN
3. Josiah Henson USA

Lightweight
1. Olle Anderberg SWE
2. Jay Thomas Evans USA
3. Jahanbakte Towfigh IRN

Welterweight
1. William Smith USA
2. Per Berlin SWE
3. Abdullah Modjtabavi IRN

Middleweight
1. David Tsimakuridze URS
2. Gholam Reza Takhti IRN
3. György Gurics HUN

Light Heavyweight
1. Wiking Palm SWE
2. Henry Wittenberg USA
3. Adil Atan TUR

Heavyweight
1. Arsen Mekokishvili URS
2. Bertil Antonsson SWE
3. Kenneth Richmond GBR

Men Fencing

Foil Individual
1. Christian d'Oriola FRA
2. Edoardo Mangiarotti ITA
3. Manlio Di Rosa ITA

Foil Team
1. France
2. Italy
3. Hungary

Epée Individual
1. Edoardo Mangiarotti ITA
2. Dario Mangiarotti ITA
3. Oswald Zappelli SUI

Epée Team
1. Italy
2. Sweden
3. Switzerland

Sabre Individual
1. Pál Kovács HUN
2. Aladár Gerevich HUN
3. Tibor Berczelly HUN

Sabre Team
1. Hungary
2. Italy
3. France

Women Fencing

Foil Individual
1. Irene Camber ITA
2. Ilona Elek HUN
3. Karen Lachmann DEN

Weightlifting

		2 Arm Press	2 Arm Snatch	2 Arm Clean and Jerk	Total
Bantamweight					
Ivan Udodov	URS	90.0	*97.5	*127.5	*315.0
Mahmoud Namjou	IRN	90.0	95.0	122.5	307.5
Ali Mirzal	IRN	95.0	92.5	112.5	300.0
Featherweight					
Rafael Chimishkyan	URS	97.5	=*105.0	=*135.0	** 337.5
Nikolai Saksonov	URS	95.0	=*105.0	132.5	332.5
Rodney Wilkes	TRI	100.0	100.0	122.5	322.5
Lightweight					
Thomas Kono	USA	105.0	** 117.5	140.0	*362.5
Yevgeny Lopatin	URS	100.0	107.5	142.5	350.0
Verne Barberis	AUS	105.0	105.0	140.0	350.0
Middleweight					
Peter George	USA	115.0	*127.5	*157.5	*400.0
Gérard Gratton	CAN	=*122.5	112.5	155.0	390.0
Sung-Jip Kim	KOR	=*122.5	112.5	147.5	382.5
Light Heavyweight					
Trofim Lomakin	URS	125.0	127.5	*165.0	=*417.5
Stanley Stanczyk	USA	127.5	127.5	160.0	415.0
Arkady Vorobyev	URS	120.0	127.5	160.0	407.5
Middle Heavyweight					
Norbert Schemansky	USA	127.5	** 140.0	** 177.5	** 445.0
Grigory Novak	URS	*140.0	125.0	145.0	410.0
Lennox Kilgour	TRI	125.0	120.0	157.5	402.5
Heavyweight					
John Davis	USA	*150.0	*145.0	165.0	*460.0
James Bradford	USA	140.0	132.5	165.0	437.5
Humberto Selvetti	ARG	*150.0	120.0	162.5	432.5

Modern Pentathlon

Individual
1. Lars Hall SWE
2. Gábor Benedek HUN
3. István Szondy HUN

Team
1. Hungary 166
2. Sweden 182
3. Finland 213

Men Canoeing

Kayak-1 1000m
1. Gert Fredriksson SWE 4:07.9
2. Thorvald Strömberg FIN 4:09.7
3. Louis Gantois FRA 4:20.1

Kayak-2 1000m
1. Finland 3:51.1
2. Sweden 3:51.1
3. Austria 3:51.4

Kayak-1 10,000m
1. Thorvald Strömberg FIN 47:22.8
2. Gert Fredriksson SWE 47:34.1
3. Michael Scheuer GER 47:54.4

Kayak-2 10,000m
1. Finland 44:21.3
2. Sweden 44:21.7
3. Hungary 44:26.6

Canadian-1 1000m
1. Josef Holecek TCH 4:56.3
2. János Parti HUN 5:03.6
3. Olavi Ojanperä FIN 5:08.5

Canadian-2 1000m
1. Denmark 4:38.3
2. Czechoslovakia 4:42.9
3. Germany 4:48.3

Canadian-1 10,000m
1. Frank Havens USA 57:41.1
2. Gábor Novák HUN 57:49.2
3. Alfred Jindra TCH 57:53.1

Canadian-2 10,000m
1. France 54:08.3
2. Canada 54:09.9
3. Germany 54:28.1

Women Canoeing

Kayak-1 500m
1. Sylvi Saimo FIN 2:18.4
2. Gertrude Liebhart AUT 2:18.8
3. Nina Savina URS 2:21.6

Rowing

Single Sculls
1. Yuri Tyukalov URS 8:12.8
2. Mervyn Wood AUS 8:14.5
3. Theodor Kocerka POL 8:19.4

Double Sculls
1. Argentina 7:32.2
2. Soviet Union 7:38.3
3. Uruguay 7:43.7

Coxless Pairs
1. USA 8:20.7
2. Belgium 8:23.5
3. Switzerland 8:32.7

Coxed Pairs
1. France 8:28.6
2. Germany 8:32.1
3. Denmark 8:34.9

Coxless Fours
1. Yugoslavia 7:16.0
2. France 7:18.9
3. Finland 7:23.3

Coxed Fours
1. Czechoslovakia 7:33.4
2. Switzerland 7:36.5
3. USA 7:37.0

Eights
1. USA 6:25.9
2. Soviet Union 6:31.2
3. Australia 6:33.1

Yachting

Finn Class
1. Paul Elvström DEN 8209
2. Charles Currey GBR 5449
3. Richard Sarby SWE 5051

Star Class
1. Italy 7635
2. USA 7216
3. Portugal 4903

Dragon Class
1. Norway 6130
2. Sweden 5556
3. Germany 5352

5.5m Class
1. USA 5751
2. Norway 5325
3. Sweden 4554

6m Class
1. USA 4870
2. Norway 4648
3. Finland 3944

Cycling

Road Race Individual
1. André Noyelle BEL 5:06:03.4
2. Robert Grondelaers BEL 5:06:51.2
3. Edi Ziegler GER 5:07:47.5

Team Road Race
1. Belgium 15:20:46.6
2. Italy 15:33:27.3
3. France 15:38:58.1

1000m Time Trial
1. Russell Mockridge AUS *1:11.1
2. Marino Morettini ITA 1:12.7
3. Raymond Robinson SAF 1:13.0

1000m Sprint
1. Enzo Sacchi ITA 12.0
2. Lionel Cox AUS
3. Werner Potzernheim GER

Tandem 2000m
1. Australia 11.0
2. South Africa
3. Italy

Team Pursuit (4000m)
1. Italy 4:46.1
2. South Africa 4:53.6
3. Great Britain 4:51.5

Equestrian Sports

Three-day Event Individual
1. Hans von Blixen-Finecke SWE -28.33
2. Guy Lefrant FRA -54.50
3. Wilhem Büsing GER -55.50

Three-day Event Team
1. Sweden -221.94
2. Germany -235.49
3. USA 587.16

Dressage Individual
1. Henry Saint-Cyr SWE 561.0
2. Lis Hartel DEN 541.5
3. André Jousseaume FRA 541.0

Dressage Team
1. Sweden 1597.5
2. Switzerland 1579.0
3. Germany 1501.0

Grand Prix Jumping Individual
1. Pierre Jonquères d'Oriola FRA -8/0
2. Oscar Cristi CHI -8/4
3. Fritz Thiedemann GER 8/8/38.5

Grand Prix Jumping Team
1. Great Britain -40.75
2. Chile -45.75
3. USA -52.25

Men Shooting

Free Rifle 3 positions
1 Anatoly Bogdanov URS *1123
2. Robert Bürchler SUI 1120
3. Lev Vainshtein URS 1109

Small Bore Rifle Prone
1. Josif Sarbu ROM =*400/33
2. Boris Andreyev URS =*400/28
3. Arthur Jackson USA 399/28

Small Bore Rifle 3 positions
1. Erling Kongshaug NOR 1164
2. Vilho Ylönen FIN 1164
3. Boris Andreyev URS 1163

Rapid Fire Pistol
1. Károly Takács HUN 579
2. Szilárd Kun HUN 578
3. Gheorghe Lichiardopol ROM 578

Free Pistol 50m
1. Huelet Benner USA *553
2. Angel Léon de Gozalo ESP 550
3. Ambrus Balogh HUN 549

Running Deer Shooting, Single and Double Shot
1. John Larsen NOR ** 413
2. Per Olof Sköldberg SWE 409
3. Tauno Mäki FIN 407

Mixed Shooting Clay Pigeon Individual
1. George Généreux CAN 192
2. Knut Holmqvist SWE 191
3. Hans Liljedahl SWE 190

Men Gymnastics

All-around Individual
1. Viktor Chukarin URS 115.70
2. Grant Schaginyan URS 114.95
3. Josef Stalder SUI 114.75

Combined Exercises Team
1. Soviet Union 574.40
2. Switzerland 567.50
3. Finland 564.20

Parallel Bars
1. Hans Eugster SUI 19.65
2. Viktor Chukarin URS 19.60
3. Josef Stalder SUI 19.50

Floor Exercises
1. William Thoresson SWE 19.25
2. Tadao Uesako JAP 19.15
2. Jerzy Jokiel POL 19.15

Long Horse Vault
1. Viktor Chukarin URS 19.20
2. Masao Takemoto JAP 19.15
3. Takashi Ono JAP 19.10
3. Tadao Uesako JAP 19.10

Side Horse
1. Viktor Chukarin URS 19.50
2. Evgeny Korolkov URS 19.40
2. Grant Schaginyan URS 19.40

Horizontal Bar
1. Jack Günthard SUI 19.55
2. Josef Stalder SUI 19.50
2. Alfred Schwarzmann GER 19.50

Rings
1. Grant Schaginyan URS 19.75
2. Viktor Chukarin URS 19.55
3. Hans Eugster SUI 19.40
3. Dmitri Leonkin URS 19.40

Women Gymnastics

All-around Individual
1. Maria Gorokhovskaya URS 76.78
2. Nina Boscharova URS 75.94
3. Margit Korondi HUN 75.82

Combined Exercises Team
1. Soviet Union 527.03
2. Hungary 520.96
3. Czechoslvakia 503.32

Asymmetrical Bars
1. Margit Korondi HUN 19.40
2. Maria Gorokhovskaya URS 19.26
3. Agnes Keleti HUN 19.16

Floor Exercises
1. Agnes Keleti HUN 19.36
2. Maria Gorokhovskaya URS 19.20
3. Margit Korondi HUN 19.00

Side Horse Vault
1. Yekaterina Kalinchuk URS 19.20
2. Maria Gorokhovskaya URS 19.19
3. Galina Minaicheva URS 19.16

Balance Beam
1. Nina Bocharova URS 19.22
2. Maria Gorokhovskaya URS 19.13
3. Margit Korondi HUN 19.02

Team Exercise with Portable Apparatus
1. Sweden 74.20
2. Soviet Union 73.00
3. Hungary 71.60

Basketball

1. USA
2. Soviet Union
3. Uruguay

Football

1. Hungary
2. Yugoslavia
3. Sweden

Hockey

1. India
2. Netherlands
3. Great Britain

(Key to symbols and abbreviations p. 1456)

Arthur S. Wint, a tall runner from Jamaica who is a champion in the 400m and 800m races, has an exceptionally long stide.

1952

AUGUST

Su	Mo	Tu	We	Th	Fr	Sa
					1	2
3	4	5	6	7	8	9
10	11	12	13	14	15	16
17	18	19	20	21	22	23
24	25	26	27	28	29	30
31						

2. Washington: Truman signs a protocol to the NATO pact incorporating the European Defence Community (→16/12).

5. Tokyo: Japan resumes diplomatic relations with Nationalist China.

6. Middle East: The Arab League denounces Israeli and West German moves to set up diplomatic relations (→9/11).

10. Luxembourg: The European Coal and Steel Community is inaugurated.

14. Budapest: Matyas Rakosi is appointed premier of Hungary (→28/2/53).

14. UK: Foreign Secretary Anthony Eden marries the Prime Minister's niece, Clarissa.

16. UK: The Bristol Britannia airliner makes its maiden flight (→10/11).

19. UK: Housing minister Harold Macmillan says flood-stricken Lynmouth looks like "the road to Ypres" (→22).

22. UK: Surrey wins the county cricket championship outright for the first time since 1914.

22. UK: 22 people have died in the Lynmouth disaster; 11 are still missing (→18/9).

26. UK: The first "short, sharp shock" juvenile detention centre opens in Oxfordshire (→9/10).

28. London: Macmillan consents to council tenants buying their houses (→3/10).

29. Korea: UN planes attack Pyongyang (→1/9).

29. S. Africa: The High Court says that the bill to overrule its judgement against racist laws is null and void (→8/11).

30. UK: The Avro "Vulcan", the first four-engined delta-wing jet bomber, makes its maiden flight (→6/9).

30. Berlin: 16,000 people have fled East Germany in the past month (→2/3/53).

DEATH

20. German statesman Kurt Schumacher (*13/10/1895).

Freak flood roars through Devon village

What remains of the village of Lynmouth, after the flood rolled through.

Aug 16. Without warning, a large part of north Devon was hit by a disastrous flood early today. Thirty-six people are feared dead and thousands have been made homeless in the resort of Lynmouth, which was devastated when rivers burst their banks and swept down surrounding hills. The torrent swamped the area so quickly that the victims had no time to flee as their houses were buried beneath the unremitting flow of mud, rocks and debris.

As relief workers joined with troops to help survivors, one civic leader, surveying the scene, said: "In the darkness of a single night a part of Lynmouth has vanished for ever." About 250 square miles were flooded by freak storms. Nine inches of rain fell yesterday.

Three boy scouts were among the first to drown when their camp was hit by a mud river. A postman on his rounds also died. The list of missing includes two girl hikers.

The Red Cross has already begun sending in food supplies and fresh water. A disaster fund is soon to be launched nationwide to help rebuild the area (→19).

Public schoolboy is new king of Jordan

Aug 11. A Harrow schoolboy today became King of Jordan. Crown Prince Hussein was named by the Jordan parliament to succeed his father, King Talal, who is thought to be suffering from an incurable schizophrenia. King Talal has only recently returned from a Swiss clinic, but two Egyptian doctors called in by the Government pronounced him unfit.

The new King was on holiday in Switzerland with his mother, Queen Zain, when he heard the news. He is hoping to go to Sandhurst after Harrow, and a Regency Council of three will rule on his behalf. The same three people have already been ruling while King Talal has been ill (→2/5/53).

Across the Atlantic and back in 8 hours

Aug 26. A British Canberra bomber today broke all records when it made the first transatlantic round trip in a single day, flying from Northern Ireland to Gander, Newfoundland and back in seven hours 59 minutes. The twin-jet averaged 531 mph. It left Aldergrove with its three-man crew at 6.35am, landed at Gander at 11.09am local time and was back at 4.35pm (→30).

Curfew for Kenyans to fight Mau Mau

Aug 24. Speaking of "growing unrest and disregard for law and order", the Kenya Government today imposed a curfew in three districts outside Nairobi where gangs of arsonists belonging to the Mau Mau secret society have been setting fire to the huts of natives who refuse to take the Mau Mau oath to drive white people from the colony.

The oath, often administered at knife point, leaves the victim in such a state of superstitious fear that he dare not go to the police. Mau Mau is spreading rapidly among Kikuyu tribesmen, whose villages are in the "white highlands", where thousands of European farmers have settled (→7/10).

One of the new Vulcan bombers, central to Britain's air defences.

1952

SEPTEMBER

Su	Mo	Tu	We	Th	Fr	Sa
	1	2	3	4	5	6
7	8	9	10	11	12	13
14	15	16	17	18	19	20
21	22	23	24	25	26	27
28	29	30				

2. London: Field Marshal Sir William Slim is appointed Governor-General of Australia.

5. Chicago: Eisenhower says that, if elected, he will have a black in his cabinet (→20).

7. Cairo: General Neguib forces premier Aly Maher out of office and assumes control himself (→18).

10. Bonn: West Germany agrees to pay Israel £293 million in restitution for Nazi atrocities (→23/10).

11. Teheran: Britain and Iran begin fresh talks to try and settle the oil dispute (→16/10).

12. UK: Premiere of Noel Coward's play "Quadrille".

15. East Africa: Britain leaves the former Italian colony of Eritrea, which becomes federated with Ethiopia.

18. UK: The final death toll from the Lynmouth disaster stands at 31.

18. Cairo: The government is reported to be considering the nationalisation of the Suez Canal (→14/1/53).

19. Washington: Charlie Chaplin is investigated as a suspected "subversive" (→23).

20. US: Adlai Stevenson pledges to ensure equal employment rights for blacks and whites if elected (→24).

23. London: Charlie Chaplin visits the city for the first time in 23 years (→16/10).

23. UK: Yorkshire fast bowler Freddie Trueman, 21, wins the Cricket Writers' Club trophy as best young cricketer of 1952.

29. US: Truman blasts Eisenhower as the inept tool of the "unholy crew" that runs the Republican Party (→4/10).

30. UK: Bevanites win six out of seven constituency seats on Labour's NEC, ousting Hugh Dalton and Herbert Morrison (→11/10).

DEATH

26. Spanish philosopher and author George Santayana (*16/12/1863).

Nixon defends illegal fund charge on TV

Ike and Mamie watching Dick: the vice-president broadcasts for his life.

Sept 24. Senator Richard Nixon turned the tables on his opponents last night with a brilliant television performance. Any lingering suggestions that even at this late stage General Eisenhower might drop him as vice-presidential candidate were vanquished. Speaking in West Virginia today, Eisenhower said that Nixon was "not only completely vindicated as a man of honor but, as far as I am concerned, he stands higher than ever before".

Nixon was accused of misusing an $18,000 political fund provided by Californian businessmen and receiving gifts from them. He claimed he had spent everything on legitimate political expenses. He said his wife Pat did not own a mink but "a respectable Republican cloth coat". His voice throbbing with emotion he told viewers he would never return the cocker spaniel dog, "Checkers", given to his six-year-old daughter, Tricia.

Only those who recalled Nixon's ruthless use of the McCarthy witch-hunt in his own rise remained unconvinced (→29).

Huge US air raid near USSR border

Sept 1. Carrier-based aircraft mounted their greatest raid of the Korean War today when 160 warplanes struck at targets only 12 miles from the Russian border. Aircraft from the American carriers Boxer, Essex and Princeton hammered the oil refinery at Aoji and an iron foundry at Musan.

A large force of Sabre jet fighters patrolled "MiG Alley" to protect the attackers, and the raid took the enemy completely by surprise. Tonight the targets are reported to be burning fiercely, with smoke billowing up to 20,000 feet.

Vice Admiral J.J. Clark, Commander of the 7th Fleet, commented: "This is a sign that we mean business and that we intend fighting hard for our way of life" (→1/10).

Speed ace Cobb is killed on Loch Ness

Sept 29. Speed ace John Cobb, the 52-year-old holder of the world land-speed record, died today when his jet-engined speed boat Crusader disintegrated on Loch Ness. The boat hit three pressure waves which had built up in front of her at a speed of 240mph, plunging her nose into the water and smashing her apart.

Twenty-six die as jet fighter ploughs into crowd at air show

Seconds earlier, John Derry's plane was breaking the sound barrier.

Sept 6. Twenty-six spectators died today as a prototype jet aircraft fell apart over the Farnborough Air Show and plummeted into the crowd. The de Havilland 110 fighter had just broken the sound barrier, and the casualties were mostly caused by one of the engines falling among the crowd of 150,000 watching the display.

A total of 65 other people were injured as debris fell into spectators' stands and a car park. The Queen and Queen Mary have both expressed the sympathy for the families of those killed in the tragedy, which also claimed the lives of John Derry, the 30-year-old test pilot, and his observer Anthony Richards, aged 24. An official inquiry has begun (→1/1/53).

1952

OCTOBER

Su	Mo	Tu	We	Th	Fr	Sa
			1	2	3	4
5	6	7	8	9	10	11
12	13	14	15	16	17	18
19	20	21	22	23	24	25
26	27	28	29	30	31	

3. London: The government announces the end of tea rationing (→ 5/2/53).

4. Washington: Truman blames Eisenhower for the precarious position of US forces in Berlin (→ 5/11).

7. Kenya: A senior chief, Waruhui is murdered outside Nairobi; he recently denounced the Mau Mau (→ 19).

9. UK: A servant runs wild at the Earl of Derby's home, shooting dead two butlers and wounding the Countess (→ 11/12.)

11. Vietnam: Viet Minh forces under General Giap launch an offensive in the Thai highlands (→ 11/12).

16. UK: World premiere of Charlie Chaplin's film "Limelight" (→ 17/4/53).

16. London: The enquiry into the Harrow train disaster blames the dead train driver for the tragedy.

16. Teheran: Mossadegh breaks off relations with Britain, saying it refused to accept a settlement of the oil row (→ 16/8/53).

19. London: The government is to send troops to Kenya to help fight the Mau Mau.→

21. Kenya: Jomo Kenyatta, president of the Kenya African Union, is arrested (→ 30).

23. London: Labour MPs approve Attlee's motion ending unofficial groups within the Labour Party (→ 28).

23. West Germany: Field Marshal Kesselring, who has cancer, is released from his 21-year war crime jail term (→ 12/1/53).

25. New York: Communist China is refused UN entry for the third year running (→ 10/11).

28. London: Bevanite Labour MPs decide to suspend their operations (→ 11/11).

29. Kenya: Colonial Secretary Lyttelton arrives for an eight-day tour (→ 30).

30. Kenya: Troops round up 500 Mau Mau suspects (→ 14/11).

UK gets tough with Kenyan Mau Mau

Oct 21. British troops were flying into Nairobi last night as the Kenya Government, faced with a rapidly deteriorating security situation, declared a state of emergency and began rounding up suspected Mau Mau terrorists. In the past few weeks over 40 people have been murdered, including one of the colony's most respected figures, Senior Chief Waruhui, speared to death in broad daylight on a main road. The arrests continued into the early hours today.

The troops, including men of the Lancashire Fusiliers, arrived from the Suez Canal Zone in RAF transports. A battalion of the King's African Rifles is coming from Tanganyika. The 8,000-ton cruiser Kenya is due at Mombasa today.

The terrorists, who at first operated only at night, using pangas, now move about in daylight and have somehow acquired firearms. One of Mau Mau's favourite oaths goes: "When the reed-buck horn is blown, if I leave a European farm before killing the European owner, may this oath kill me."

Dinner parties and socialising have virtually ceased in Nairobi, and a European Home Guard has been formed. Armed with revolvers and rifles, the men patrol residential areas at night, leaving wives at home, each with a loaded revolver beside her bed (→ 21).

A British soldier checks his knife.

112 dead in three train pile up; smoking debris 50 feet high

Oct 8. A railway disaster left 112 people dead this morning, when a high-speed locomotive crashed into two trains that had collided in front of it moments earlier. Among 200 passengers hurt were commuters who had just stepped onto a station platform, as tons of twisted tracks and shattered carriages hurtled into the air.

Tonight, as a top-level investigation was under way, rescue teams were still using cutting gear to get to the bottom of the 50-foot pile of debris. Of those dug out hurt, 46 are on the critical list.

The accident, the second worst so far in British train history, occurred as the 7.31am commuter train to London was about to leave from the suburban Harrow and Wealdstone station. It was struck from behind by an express train from Perth travelling at nearly 60 mph. Wreckage, including the locomotive of the express, spilled onto other lines. A shocked signalman threw all the signals to danger, but he was too late; seconds later, a third train, travelling north from Euston, ploughed into the wreckage, rearing up and demolishing the footbridge and compressing the coaches still further. Emergency services, drawn from all over the capital, found a scene of grim devastation with carriages lying across six tracks under a pall of smoke.

It was by far the worst rail crash in Britain since 1915, when 227 people died in a five-train pile-up at Quintinshill in Scotland (→ 16).

Amid twisted rails, upended coaches and shattered locomotives the emergency services battle to save lives.

US guards kill 52 rioting Chinese POWs

Defeated Communist prisoners are herded back into jail by US troops.

Oct 1. Fifty-two Chinese prisoners of war were killed, and 140 wounded, when US guards opened fire in an attempt to end a demonstration in a POW compound on Cheju Island off south-west Korea. The demonstration was apparently organised by political leaders among the POWs to celebrate the third anniversary of the Communist takeover of China.

Anticipating trouble, the camp commander had issued specific orders forbidding any demonstration, but this morning, instead of forming work parties, the prisoners flew Communist flags and milled around shouting slogans. Some who did not want to join the demonstration were beaten.

The commander then issued orders over the loudspeaker for them to disperse. They refused, and so two companies of infantry were sent into the compound.

The prisoners, sheltering behind the stone walls of their partially-built winter barracks, met the infantry with showers of rocks and attacked them with clubs, tentpoles and barbed wire. The soldiers retaliated by opening fire (→5/12).

First atomic bomb tested by Britain

Oct 3. Britain's first atomic weapon has been successfully exploded in a secret test in the Monte Bello islands, off the north-west coast of Australia. The cloud from the blast had a ragged shape – unlike the familiar mushroom form of the American explosions.

The bomb was attached to a tower on one of the islands for the blast, which was observed by scientists and servicemen on both British and Australian warships nearby. Observers on a hilltop on the mainland 100 miles away also saw it.

One said: "We felt no ground shock wave but a heavy air pressure pulse smacked the mainland four minutes and 15 seconds after the flash" (→30/11).

Attlee hits out at leftist "wreckers"

Oct 11. Clement Attlee, sickened by the escalation of Labour's internal strife and personal vendettas, today branded Aneurin Bevan and his left-wing supporters as wreckers. He condemned them for running a party within a party. "Quite intolerable," he snapped.

The Labour leader's outburst came after right-wingers accused him of "dithering and doodling" while the party tears itself apart. The Bevanites have strengthened their position on Labour's national executive by getting two more members of their group – Harold Wilson and Richard Crossman – elected. The Tories are relishing Labour's discomfort as the civil war hots up (→23).

1952

NOVEMBER

Su	Mo	Tu	We	Th	Fr	Sa
						1
2	3	4	5	6	7	8
9	10	11	12	13	14	15
16	17	18	19	20	21	22
23	24	25	26	27	28	29
30						

4. London: The Queen opens her first Parliament (→8/12).

5. Washington: Truman invites Eisenhower to the White House to discuss issues of national importance.→

8. S. Africa: Police open fire on rioters, killing 14 blacks and wounding 39.→

10. Copenhagen: An SAS plane from Los Angeles is the first airliner to fly over the North Pole (→22/1/53).

10. New York: Trygve Lie resigns as UN Secretary General (→31/3/53).

11. London: Herbert Morrison beats Nye Bevan for Labour's deputy leadership by 194 votes to 82 (→27).

12. Teheran: Mossadegh makes a new offer to Britain for the settlement of the Anglo-Iranian oil dispute.

14. Kenya: The British governor closes 34 schools of the Kikuyu tribe, suspected of Mau Mau involvement.→

19. Vietnam: The French are facing an all-out offensive by the Viet Minh (→24).

20. Washington: Eisenhower chooses John Foster Dulles as Secretary of State (→20/1/53).

23. Iraq: Ten people die in two days of anti-Western riots.

24. Washington: The State Department accuses USSR of arming the Viet Minh (→28/4/53).

25. Kenya: 2,000 Kikuyu are rounded up as the Mau Mau begins open rebellion against British rule (→18/1/53).

27. London: The only left-wing Bevanite elected to the shadow cabinet is Nye Bevan himself (→8/5/53).

30. Europe: The Saarland votes against becoming part of West Germany (→1/12).

DEATHS

9. Russian-born Israeli statesman, chemist and humanitarian Dr Chaim Weizmann (*27/11/1874).→

18. French poet Paul Eluard (*14/12/1895).

Callas stuns with Bellini bel canto

Nov 9. The Royal Opera House at Covent Garden buzzed last night with the excitement that the discovery of a new soprano produces. Bellini's "Norma" is rarely staged because of the difficulty of the title role, but Maria Callas, the new Greek singer, showed herself more than equal to it.

She won warm ovations for brilliant, if wayward singing, and for her vivid dramatic powers. "No one will forget her fury when she rounded on her two-faced lover," wrote a critic. However, he thought her singing of the aria "Casta Diva" was flawed by a shrillness on the high notes.

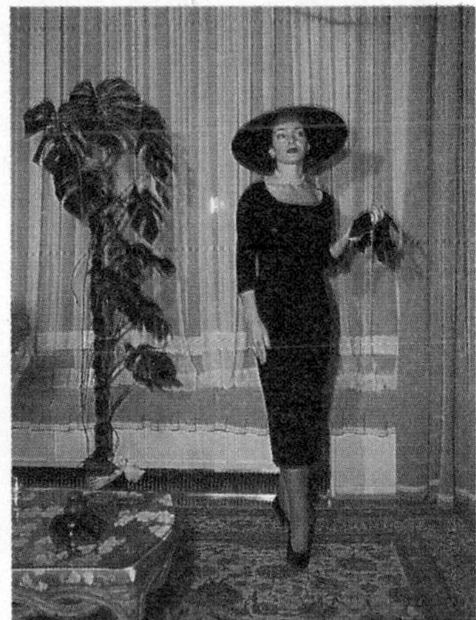

Maria Callas – a dramatic diva.

South African police open fire on rioters

Nov 9. An Irish nun who worked in a mission clinic in an African township was one of two Europeans killed in riots in South Africa during the weekend. Seventeen Africans died when police opened fire after they were charged by stone-throwing mobs in East London and Kimberley. Sister Aiden, formerly Elsie Quinlan from Cork, was stoned as she was driving near East London. Her car was overturned and set on fire. The East London riots started after meetings were banned because of a strike. In Kimberley, a beer-hall brawl led to the rampage. The other European killed was an insurance agent (→12/10/54).

"Ike" buries opponents in US election

Nov 5. Dwight D. Eisenhower swept to victory tonight over his Democratic opponent, Adlai E. Stevenson, in the US presidential election. He won the largest-ever popular vote of over 33 million, but his majority of 6,500,000 was short of President Roosevelt's landslide win by eight million in 1936.

It was an astonishing personal triumph. The outstanding feature of the results is the way Eisenhower won far more support than the Republican Party. They will have a majority of only one in the Senate and little more than ten in the House of Representatives.

This feature clearly confused the pollsters. Still smarting with memories of 1948, when they forecast a landslide for Governor Dewey over President Truman, every pollster suggested the race would be so close that the outcome was in doubt.

The result indicates the nation's wish for a father figure to calm worries over the war against the Communists in Korea. Although the new President does not assume power until next January, he flies to Korea, with the support of President Truman, in two weeks' time.

The result is no disgrace to Governor Stevenson, who polled more votes than any other Democratic candidate ever except President Roosevelt in 1936 and 1940. His campaign was largely run by devoted amateurs, who wept openly when he conceded defeat at his Springfield, Illinois, headquarters.

The election brings two young politicians into national prominence. Senator Richard M. Nixon, aged 39, will be the youngest-ever US Vice-President. He is best known for his support for Senator McCarthy's anti-Communist campaign. On the Democratic side John F. Kennedy, at 35, produced the major upset. He won the Senate seat in Massachusetts against the upper-drawer Republican, Henry Cabot Lodge. It was Lodge who first won Republican support for Eisenhower's nomination (→ 20).

A triumphant Eisenhower accepts the cheers of Republican supporters.

Island disappears as America tests the first hydrogen bomb

Nov 30. A device believed to be a hydrogen bomb was exploded by the United States on Eniwetok Atoll in the Pacific this month. According to one eye-witness account, a complete island disappeared in the blast.

In an official announcement, the US Atomic Energy Commission said that the test concluded a series which included "experiments contributing to thermo-nuclear weapons research".

Thermo-nuclear weapons is a technical term for hydrogen bombs, in which light atoms like hydrogen fuse together in a thermo-nuclear reaction. This liberates hundreds of times as much energy, since the fission at astronomically high temperatures needed to start the fusion reaction is produced by an atomic bomb acting as a trigger (→ 8/5/53).

A cloud marks the spot: all that remains of Eniwetok, a nuclear test site.

Jomo Kenyatta is charged with being head of Mau Mau

Nov 18. Jomo Kenyatta, Kenya's black nationalist leader, was today flown secretly to the remote country station of Kapenguria, a place with no telephone, railway or hotel. There, in the office of the District Commissioner, he was charged with managing the Mau Mau terrorist society.

Kenyatta was among the several hundred Kikuyu Africans rounded up as Mau Mau suspects in recent weeks. He spent the war years in Britain, married an Englishwoman and worked on a Sussex farm. Back in Kenya, he aroused the ire of white settlers by organising independent schools for Africans and involving himself in land rights agitation through a Kikuyu tribal pressure group (→ 25).

The first President of Israel is dead

Nov 9. Israel's president, Chaim Weizmann, died this morning at his home in Tel Aviv, aged 77. Born of humble parents near Pinsk in Russia, he lived to preside over a modern state forged by the courage of persecuted, abandoned and homeless Jews.

An early Zionist, world-famous chemist, intellectual and humanitarian, he was the natural choice to be Israel's first ruler (→ 8/12).

Audiences caught in Christie Mousetrap

Nov 25. Agatha Christie's latest play opened at the Ambassador's Theatre last night with "a fair degree of success". "The Mousetrap" begins with eight characters cut off in a snowbound house. One of them is known to be a killer, and soon proves it during a power-cut.

Miss Christie provides a wealth of suspicious characters with enough guilty pasts and false names to keep the audience guessing. "She maintains her form," runs one notice. Richard Attenborough plays the detective.

1952

DECEMBER

Su	Mo	Tu	We	Th	Fr	Sa
	1	2	3	4	5	6
7	8	9	10	11	12	13
14	15	16	17	18	19	20
21	22	23	24	25	26	27
28	29	30	31			

1. Bonn: Adenauer rejects the the Saar referendum on returning to Germany (→ 10/3/53).

5. Korea: President-elect Eisenhower visits the front.→

8. London: The Queen gives permission to have the Coronation televised (→ 25).

8. Israel: Itzhak Ben-Zvi becomes the president (→ 14/10/53).

10. Stockholm: Nobel Prizes go to Felix Bloch and Edward Purcell (US, Physics); Archer Martin and Richard Synge (UK, Chemistry); Selman Waksman (US, Medicine); Francois Mauriac (France, Literature); and in Oslo to Albert Schweitzer (France, Peace).

11. London: Lord Kemsley sells The Daily Graphic to Associated Newspapers.

16. Paris: NATO approves the appointment of Lord Mountbatten as chief of Allied forces in the Mediterranean (→ 10/2/54).

17. UK: Lord Nuffield, 75, resigns his directorships of the British Motor Company and Morris Motors.

18. US: Sugar Ray Robinson retires as world middleweight boxing champion.

20. US: 84 die in the world's worst air tragedy when a USAF transport crashes in Washington State (→ 5/1/53).

25. London: The Queen makes her first Christmas broadcast (→ 25/3/53).

27. Singapore: Ten Moslems die when their car is mined by Malay terrorists, the worst outrage in the colony yet.

HITS OF 1952

I'm singing in the rain.

I saw Mummy kissing Santa Claus.

QUOTE OF THE YEAR

"There will soon be only five kings left: the Kings of England, Diamonds, Hearts, Spades and Clubs."

King Farouk of Egypt, abdicated 1952.

Bentley will hang for his partner's crime

Craig (l.) and Bentley: both have been found guilty, but only one will hang.

Dec 11. Nineteen-year-old Derek William Bentley is to hang for the murder of a policeman, although his accomplice, who fired the shots, has escaped the death penalty because of his youth. Christopher Craig, aged 16, described by Lord Goddard, the Lord Chief Justice, as "one of the most dangerous criminals ever to stand in the dock" was sentenced to be detained at Her Majesty's pleasure.

Bentley and Craig were found guilty of the murder of PC Sidney Miles on the roof of a Croydon warehouse after a bungled robbery. Craig was carrying a .45 revolver and Bentley was armed with a knuckle-duster and a sheath knife. A police witness told the court that Bentley was heard to shout "Let him have it Chris" before Craig opened fire with nine shots. Lord Goddard said that this was the most serious piece of evidence against Bentley, although the defence claimed that the defendant had meant the gun itself.

The verdict recommended mercy for Bentley. His tearful father told reporters that he would petition the Queen, if necessary. The Home Secretary is planning to strengthen the laws on carrying firearms. Craig was said to be a member of a gang which obtained weapons from people who kept them as war souvenirs (→ 27/1/53).

The short cut from George to Christine

Dec 15. The tall blond who landed in New York last week is called Christine Jorgenson, but at one time her Christian name was George. As a male he had served in the American Army for two years, but feeling "in affections like a woman", he flew to Copenhagen where, after 2,000 hormone injections and six operations, both his sex and his name were changed.

She is not the first transsexual, but she is the first to make her sex change public. Today, "American Weekly" comes out telling her life story for which she was paid $30,000.

MacArthur in Korea peace talks with Ike

Dec 17. President-elect Eisenhower and General MacArthur, who was sacked by President Truman as Supreme Commander, Far East, met in New York today to discuss the general's plan for ending the war in Korea.

After lunch at the home of Mr John Foster Dulles, they issued a brief statement saying: "We discussed the problems of peace in Korea and in the world in general." Eisenhower has recently returned from a visit to Korea and his consultation with the sacked MacArthur will not be viewed favourably by Mr Truman's supporters (→ 6/4/53).

Arts: a run-down comedian grabs all the Limelight

Opinions differ sharply about "Limelight", which some call **Chaplin's** greatest film, others his most over-written and sentimental. The brilliant clown of silent film here plays a sad, run-down comedian in decline, being spurned by the music-hall audience that used to love him. Pathos was always Chaplin's forte and, as director as well as screenwriter, composer (of a theme that is being played everywhere) and star, he is free to indulge it as much as he likes. He does share his limelight with **Claire Bloom** as a young ballet dancer, and invites his old rival, **Buster Keaton**, to join him in a hilarious sketch – as pianist and violinist unable to get in tune together.

A new cinematic experience is "Rashomon", a Japanese story of murder and rape seen through four different pairs of eyes, directed by **Akira Kurosawa**. Another is the arrival of busty blonde bombshell **Marilyn Monroe**, ravishing in Technicolor in "Niagara".

In the theatre **Peggy Ashcroft** appears in "The Deep Blue Sea" by **Terence Rattigan** as a frustrated older woman infatuated by a young ex-war pilot. The eternal adolescent who breaks her heart is well played by a nonchalant newcomer, **Kenneth More**.

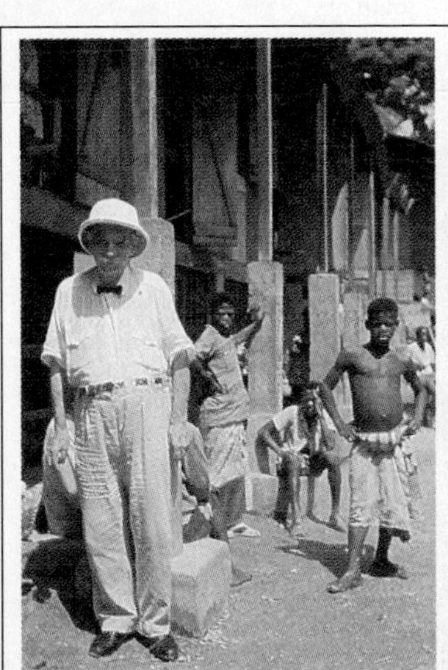

Albert Schweitzer, seen with patients at Lambarene, has received the Nobel Peace Prize.

1953

JANUARY

Su	Mo	Tu	We	Th	Fr	Sa
				1	2	3
4	5	6	7	8	9	10
11	12	13	14	15	16	17
18	19	20	21	22	23	24
25	26	27	28	29	30	31

1. UK: Arthur "Bomber" Harris, ex-head of RAF Bomber Command, is knighted in the New Year Honours (→2).

1. China: The first five-year plan comes into force (→30).

2. UK: The RAF's first supersonic fighters, 400 US-designed Sabres, arrive at RAF Abingdon (→16/2).

3. Paris: Premiere of Samuel Beckett's play "Waiting for Godot".

8. Belgrade: Tito agrees to meet seven Catholic bishops to discuss relations between the Church and state (→18/6).

10. Washington: Convicted spies Ethel and Julius Rosenberg appeal to Eisenhower for clemency (→11/2).

12. France: The trial opens in Bordeaux of 25 ex-SS men and 11 Frenchmen accused of the 1944 Oradour massacre (→13/2).

13. US: Lesser unveils a three-dimensional film technique called "Stereocinema" (→1/2).

14. Cairo: 25 army officers suspected of plotting a coup are arrested (→27/4).

18. Kenya: Governor Baring imposes the death penalty for administering the Mau Mau oath.→

20. Washington: Eisenhower is inaugurated as president (→30/6).

22. UK: BOAC grounds all its Stratocruiser airliners after finding an engine defect (→31).

25. Liverpool: The Canadian liner "Empress of Canada" is gutted by fire at her moorings.

27. London: A plea from 200 MPs for Derek Bentley to be reprieved is rejected (→28).

28. London: Bentley is hanged at Wandsworth Prison (→12/2).

30. Washington: Eisenhower withdraws the US Seventh Fleet from Formosa, so the Nationalists can attack China (→23/2).

DEATH

1. US country singer Hank Williams (*17/9/23).

Whites panic as Mau Mau uprising grows

Some of the 1,500 angry white settlers who marched against terrorism.

Jan 26. Enraged by the weekend murder of a European farmer, his wife and son, over a thousand white settlers marched through Nairobi to Government House today and demanded to see the Governor of Kenya, Sir Evelyn Baring, to put their case for a bigger say in running the colony and for tougher action against the anti-white Mau Mau terrorist society.

They claim that whole districts of the Kikuyu tribal reserve, in the white highlands, are under Mau Mau control. Sir Evelyn refused to see them, but he did announce that Major-General William R.N. Hinde, formerly deputy military governor in Berlin, is to take over the anti-Mau Mau campaign. The mood of the settlers is bitter.

Despite regular sweeps in the Aberdare Mountains, where many young Mau Mau are believed to be hiding, and the rounding up of hundreds of Kikuyu youths, gangs continue to attack white farms. Settler Commando Units, with Samburu tribal trackers, are being set up to hunt terrorists.

At a settler meeting in Nakuru, outside Nairobi, a speaker demanded the shooting of 50,000 Kikuyu. Elspeth Huxley, the author, who was born in Kenya, has written an article, reprinted in a local paper, in which she compares Jomo Kenyatta with Hitler (→1/4).

Jewish doctors on terrorism charges

Jan 13. Soviet security police have arrested nine distinguished Soviet doctors and accused them of plotting to kill Soviet political and military leaders. Six of the nine are Jewish, giving rise to fears that Joseph Stalin is poised to unleash a purge to end all purges. The doctors, all connected with the Kremlin hospital, were accused of killing party leaders and attempting to assassinate several marshals, so as to weaken the country's defences. The prosecution alleged that the doctors took their orders from Zionist groups and Western intelligence agencies (→6/2).

Tito is elected as Yugoslav president

Jan 14. Josip Tito, the Yugoslav-Communist and partisan leader, who broke with Soviet supremo Joseph Stalin in 1948, today became the country's president. He promised to continue his policy of "nonalignment" with either the Soviet or the Western bloc. In a colourful career Tito has fought in the Austro-Hungarian army, been an organiser for the Comintern, pinned down 12 German divisions in World War Two, and weathered the terrible tyranny of Stalin. He likes women, dogs, fishing, resplendent uniforms, diamond rings, good food and drink (→1/3).

Car ferry sinks off the coast of Ireland

Jan 31. A total of 128 people were feared dead tonight after the cargo doors burst open on an Irish Sea car ferry, the Princess Victoria.

The 2,694-ton British Rail ferry had just entered the open sea off Stranraer when the mountainous waves, caused by the weekend storms, smashed in through the cargo doors, and the ship soon developed a list to starboard.

Of the 44 survivors, 10 are members of the crew, although her master, Captain James Ferguson, went down with the vessel, saluting as she went under. An inquiry will be launched soon, and it seems certain that it will investigate just why the doors burst open. There has been some criticism that they were badly designed.

It appears the death toll might have been lower had rescue services been able to find her more quickly, but she had drifted from the position of her SOS message by the time a destroyer, HMS Rothesay, got there. Apparently she only had a ship-to-shore link, rather than a radio capable of sending out a general SOS call to ships in the area.

Questions are also being asked about her own safety equipment. Most of the corpses recovered were wearing life jackets, but men, women and children had been forced to jump into the sea and swim to liferafts rather than go over the side in lifeboats (→25/2).

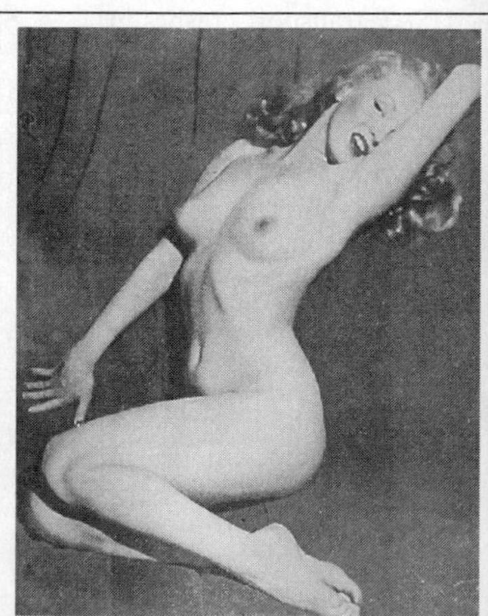

Some call it cheesecake, others just plain filth; but Marilyn Monroe, a photographic model with her eyes on the movies, is America's favourite pin-up.

1953

FEBRUARY

Su	Mo	Tu	We	Th	Fr	Sa
1	2	3	4	5	6	7
8	9	10	11	12	13	14
15	16	17	18	19	20	21
22	23	24	25	26	27	28

1. US: 20th Century Fox says its films will all now be produced by a new system called "Cinemascope".→

3. Holland: Over 1,000 deaths are reported after dykes burst, causing widespread flooding.

5. UK: Sweet rationing ends (→14/4).

5. Ireland: An Irish stud buys the Aga Khan's Derby winner "Tulyar" for a record price of £250,000.

6. USSR: A new Soviet encyclopaedia says the Jews are not a nation, and calls Zionists imperialist agents (→5/3).

9. UK: 283 are known to have died in the East Coast floods; 50 are still missing (→19).

11. Washington: Eisenhower turns down the Rosenbergs' request for clemency (→19/6).

12. UK: Magistrates vote to restore corporal punishment (→25/3).

13. Bordeaux: The Oradour trial ends; the defendants are sentenced to death or long jail terms (→18).

16. UK: The navy's latest aircraft carrier, HMS Hermes, is launched at Barrow (→29/8).

18. Paris: The National Assembly pardons 11 Frenchmen found guilty of complicity in the Oradour massacre.

19. London: Home Secretary Maxwell-Fyfe puts flood damage at £40 million.

23. Taipei: Chiang Kai-shek repudiates the 1945 alliance between Nationalist China and the USSR (→24/7/54).

25. Paris: De Gaulle attacks the European Defence Community (→18/6/54).

27. London: MPs give a second reading to a private member's bill to simplify English spelling.

28. Budapest: Hungary offers Britain an exchange of Cold War prisoners jailed for espionage (→4/7).

DEATH

24. German commander Gerd von Rundstedt (*12/12/1875).

East coast is devastated by flooding

Checking for castaways after the floods isolate houses on Canvey Island.

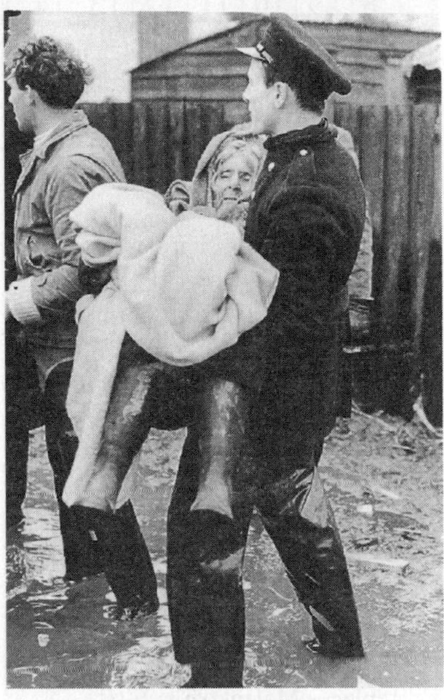

This octogenarian is safe at last.

Feb. Hurricane winds combined with high tides today to bring disaster to Britain's east coast. As sea defences collapsed from Lincolnshire in the north to Kent in the south, at least 280 people are known to have been drowned and thousands more made homeless.

A major rescue operation is under way to save hundreds of people trapped on rooftops by an eight foot wall of water, some in villages more than five miles inland. Damage is estimated in hundreds of millions of pounds.

In Essex, Canvey Island is said to be devastated, with 125 people drowned and 500 missing. Thirteen thousand inhabitants have been evacuated and 150 taken to hospital. Near Clacton, holiday chalets were under 12 feet of water and people were falling from rooftops into the floods from exhaustion.

Heavy casualties are reported from Norfolk where the death toll is known to number 60, including 12 American servicemen drowned near Hunstanton.

Mablethorpe and Sutton-on-Sea have been evacuated, with hundreds still awaiting rescue; in Suffolk, boats were rowed into church to rescue 40 trapped children.

The disaster came hard on the heels of the loss of the motor vessel Princess Victoria which foundered in a storm in the Irish Sea with the loss of 128 lives (→9).

Sunken car ferry sailed with doors open

Feb 25. The cargo doors on the ferry Princess Victoria were open when she left port on the day she sank last month, one of her crew told an astonished inquest today.

The car ferry sank off Belfast Lough with the loss of 128 lives, but today one of her crew, 44-year-old cargo man Thomas McQuiston, said the guillotine doors above the stern gates were never closed. A heavy wave hit the ship and burst them open. Said Mr McQuiston: "The water swept into the car deck and swept the cargo onto the starboard side, causing the ship to list. No attempt was or could be made to pump the water out" (→2/5).

Fox plan wide-angled view of the Bible

Feb 1. Cinema-goers are promised more spectacular viewing today, as the Twentieth-Century Fox Film Corporation announces plans to convert its entire movie-making operation to the wide-screen system, Cinemascope.

Comparing the move to "the transfer from silent pictures to sound in 1927", Fox will invest $25 million in 11 major Cinemascope productions, beginning with a Biblical epic, "The Robe".

It is hoped that the new system, which uses a special lens to project pictures onto a 145-degree curved screen, will attract more film goers in this television age. The switch will be backed up, Fox says, by stereophonic sound (→16/9).

Plan for federal Rhodesia unveiled

Feb 5. A master plan for the creation of a new British state, with a population of over seven million, in central Africa was published in London today.

The Federation of Rhodesia and Nyasaland will join the self-governing colony of Southern Rhodesia, with its overwhelmingly white electorate, to the two protectorates of Northern Rhodesia and Nyasaland, where Britain has declared the interests of the African people to be paramount.

Southern Rhodesia is the commercial centre, with a rich white farming community, to balance the mining and labour resources of the other two areas. British ministers have dismissed African critics as unrepresentative (→6/5).

1953

MARCH

Su	Mo	Tu	We	Th	Fr	Sa
1	2	3	4	5	6	7
8	9	10	11	12	13	14
15	16	17	18	19	20	21
22	23	24	25	26	27	28
29	30	31				

1. Ankara: Turkey, Greece and Yugoslavia sign a treaty of friendship (→ 15).

2. Berlin: 5,000 East Germans seek asylum in the West (→ 4/5).

5. Cambodia: King Norodom Sihanouk proclaims independence (→ 14/6).

6. Moscow: Georgi Malenkov is named premier and Party First Secretary (→ 14).

10. Bonn: The government bans the neo-Nazi Freikorps Deutschland (→ 6/9).

14. Moscow: Khrushchev replaces Malenkov as First Secretary of the Communist Party.→

15. UK: Tito's visit to Britain is the first by a Communist head of state (→ 17/1/54).

20. UK: Actress Vivien Leigh returns from the US with an acute nervous breakdown.

26. London: Police reveal that one of the corpses found at 10, Rillington Place was that of Christie's wife Ethel (→ 31).

28. UK: Mr J.H. Griffin's Early Mist wins the Grand National.

31. London: Queen Mary's funeral.

31. New York: Swede Dag Hammarskjold is chosen to succeed Trygve Lie as UN Secretary General (→ 10/4).

31. London: Christie is arrested and charged with murdering his wife on or about December 12 last year (→ 15/4).

DEATHS

5. Soviet leader Joseph Stalin, born Josef Vissarionovich Dzhugashvili (*21/12/1879).→

5. Soviet composer Sergei Prokofiev (*23/4/1891).

14. Czech leader Klement Gottwald, president 1948-53 (*23/11/1896).

23. French artist Raoul Dufy (*3/6/1877).

24. British Queen Mary, born Princess Mary of Teck, wife of King George V (*26/5/1867).→

28. US athlete Jim Thorpe (*28/5/1888).

Stalin dies of cerebral haemorrhage

Crowds throng Red Square to remember Stalin, a leader who was both Russia's saviour and her oppressor.

March 5. Joseph Stalin, who has ruled Russia with an iron fist for nearly 30 years, died tonight, aged 73. Four days ago Stalin suffered a brain haemorrhage. He lost speech and consciousness. His illness gave his successors just enough time to agree on the redistribution of top Communist Party and state offices, and on how they should face the country.

Pravda, the Party newspaper Stalin founded 40 years ago, has appeared with black borders surrounding the front page, and called for calm and "vigilance" in the "struggle against internal and external enemies", but already the country is reacting with the contradictory moods which Stalin's complex personality has inspired.

Some are weeping in anguish. Others, especially those in the labour camps and prisons the length and breadth of the country, are sighing with relief, but most people are clearly stunned, and afraid to think of the future.

No successor to Stalin has yet been named, but there are indications that his likely heir is Georgi Malenkov, a member of the Politburo. Nikita Khrushchev will organise the funeral arrangements.

Ironically, Stalin's body will lie in state for several days in the Hall of Columns, the old Noblemen's Club, where he put the old Bolsheviks on trial, strictly for show, before sending them to the Lubyanka Jail, where they were shot.

Stalin has been largely responsible for transforming Russia into the USSR, and was a brilliant military commander during World War Two, but, in his obsession with eliminating internal opposition, he may have been responsible for more deaths than any man in history, excepting possibly Genghis Khan and Hitler (→ 6).

Khrushchev emerges as key Soviet figure after bitter infighting

Stalin, with Nikita Khrushchev.

March 14. A major power struggle in the Kremlin, following the death of Joseph Stalin, has thrown the spotlight on Nikita Khrushchev and his grip on the Communist Party machine. Khrushchev, aged 59, has emerged as the head of the powerful party secretariat, and is now the only man to have a seat both on that body, where he can pack the party at will, and the ruling Politburo.

This internal feuding comes less than ten days after the death of Stalin and the succession of Georgi Malenkov to the twin posts of Prime Minister and First Secretary of the party. Malenkov today gave up the party post.

Infighting at the Kremlin began the moment Lavrenti Beria, the secret police chief, used his MVD troops, armed with tanks and flame-throwers, to seal off Moscow for Stalin's funeral. Then Stalin's personal aide, General Poskrebychev, disappeared. Now the 36-man Politburo has been brought down to 14, and five members of the Secretariat sacked.

Khrushchev is an interesting figure, combining a humble background and little formal education with great ambition. He joined the Party in 1918, and was elected a full member of the Politburo in 1939, the first of those Communists who entered the party after the Revolution to do so. He is therefore a total product of the Soviet era. After World War Two he superintended purges that wiped the Ukraine clear of opposition to the Stalinist regime (→ 4/4).

1953

APRIL

Su	Mo	Tu	We	Th	Fr	Sa
			1	2	3	4
5	6	7	8	9	10	11
12	13	14	15	16	17	18
19	20	21	22	23	24	25
26	27	28	29	30		

1. Kenya: Troops kill 24 Mau Mau and capture 36.→

3. UK: Air travel this Easter is up 20 per cent on last year.

4. Turkey: 97 are feared dead when a Turkish submarine collides with a Swedish freighter in the Dardanelles.

6. Washington: Adenauer begins talks with Eisenhower.

6. Korea: UN and Communist delegations meet at Panmunjon to discuss the exchange of sick prisoners of war.→

8. London: Eight people are killed in a crash on the Underground's Central Line near Stratford.

10. New York: Dag Hammarskjold is sworn in as UN Secretary General (→5/6).

14. London: The budget cuts income tax by sixpence in the pound (→23/10).

15. Buenos Aires: Six die in a bomb blast at a rally addressed by President Peron (→25/4/54).

15. London: Christie is charged with the murders of three more women (→29).

16. UK: The Queen launches the new royal yacht, Britannia (→4/5).

17. Kenya: One thousand Mau Mau suspects are rounded up near Nairobi (→29/5).

21. Korea: A second exchange of Allied and Communist prisoners takes place (→1/5).

24. UK: Churchill is invested as a Knight Companion of the Order of the Garter.

27. Cairo: Egypt and Britain open talks on the future of the Suez Canal Zone (→24/5).

28. Indochina: The French announce that Pakseng, the royal capital of Laos, has fallen to the Viet Minh (→13/5).

29. London: The police say Christie kept a cutting about the 1949 murders for which Timothy Evans died (→18/5).

DEATH

4. Rumanian ex-King Carol II, ruled 1930-40 (*15/10/1893).

Police launch a murder hunt for Christie

March 25. John Christie, once the key prosecution witness in a murder trial, is today himself the target of one of the biggest man-hunts for years after the remains of three women were found walled-up in his recently vacated London house in Rillington Place. A new tenant discovered the bodies as he prepared to build a bathroom.

The terraced house in a Notting Hill cul-de-sac became infamous three years ago as the scene of the murder of Mrs Beryl Evans and her 14-month-old daughter Geraldine. Timothy John Evans was convicted of their murders and hanged after evidence had been given by John Christie, who also lived in the house with his wife.

Evans protested his innocence throughout his trial, despite a claim by the police that he had confessed to them (→26).

Christie – wanted man on the run.

Successful tests of vaccine for polio

March 26. A vaccine against polio has been successfully tested on 161 adults and children, the man who developed the vaccine, Dr. Jonas E. Salk, announced today. He said that the level of antibodies in the subjects against the disease has remained steady for four and a half months, but that, although this was encouraging, a practical vaccine was not yet available (→25/4).

Death takes Queen Mary in her sleep

March 25. Queen Mary, the widow of King George V and grandmother of the Queen, died in her sleep last night at Marlborough House. A tall, regal figure, she became a legend in her own lifetime. For 50 years her dress never changed. Her jewelled toques sat on top of tightly-packed curls, and there was always the same style of coat and the silver-topped cane (→16/4).

Former President Harry S. Truman is welcomed to the new United Nations building in New York by Secretary-General Hammarskjold.

UN and Korean POWs are swapped

April 20. Allied and Communist sick and wounded prisoners were swapped at Panmunjon, Korea, today, while just a mile away the war continued unabated.

A total of 100 Allied prisoners were handed over, many wearing simple padded blue-style Chinese uniforms. They were immediately taken to a new "Freedom Village" at nearby Munsan, where they were handed cigarettes and toiletries by the Red Cross. There are fears that a number of the men have been indoctrinated or brain-washed by the Chinese while in prison, and specially-trained officers have arrived to re-educate them (→1/5).

Battle fatigue overwhelms this GI.

US regards Chaplin as dangerous alien

April 17. Charlie Chaplin announced today that he will never return to America, his home for 40 years. Under threat of proceedings to bar him if he went back, he has surrendered his "re-entry permit".

He was banned after he left for Europe last autumn to promote his film "Limelight". He said then: "I am not a Communist and I never have been." Chaplin, now 64, and his wife Oona recently settled at Vevey, Switzerland, with their four children. "I have been the object of vicious propaganda," he said.

Mau Mau leader Kenyatta is jailed

"Burning Spear" and his followers begin their jail sentences in Kenya.

April 8. In a darkening courtroom, dimly lit by a pair of paraffin lamps, with bolts of lightning piercing the evening sky outside, Jomo "Burning Spear" Kenyatta was sentenced to seven years' hard labour for managing the Mau Mau terrorist society. Five others who were tried with him at the remote Kapenguria station were also each given seven years for helping to run the Mau Mau. Kenyatta, speaking for all the accused, said they were not guilty, and he claimed the prosecution had been brought in order to crush the fight for the rights of the African people. He denied that they were anti-white (→ 17).

Structure for molecule of life suggested

April 25. One of the great mysteries of biology – how living things reproduce themselves – is solved by a structure proposed by two Cambridge scientists for a chemical called deoxyribonucleic acid (DNA). DNA is the material of the genes, via which hereditary characteristics are passed on from parent to offspring.

James D. Watson and Francis Crick have proposed two strands, made of complementary elements that fit together like lock and key, coiled up in a double helix. When the strands uncoil keys match with other locks, and locks with other keys, to produce two copies of the original double helix. Watson and Crick's structure, based on X-ray evidence and models, is published in the journal Nature (→ 23/2/54).

"Terrorist" doctors freed in the USSR

April 4. In a rare admission of error, the nine leading Moscow doctors accused of plotting to murder prominent Soviet figures have been freed. A minister said the doctors, most of them Jewish, had been "falsely accused and arrested". Pravda indicated they had all been tortured into confessing on Stalin's orders. The announcement of the "Doctors' Plot" raised fears of a renewal of state terror (→ 10/7).

1953

MAY

Su	Mo	Tu	We	Th	Fr	Sa
					1	2
3	4	5	6	7	8	9
10	11	12	13	14	15	16
17	18	19	20	21	22	23
24	25	26	27	28	29	30
31						

1. UK: Arsenal win the League Championship for a record seventh time.

2. Middle East: King Hussein of Jordan and King Feisal II of Syria are crowned.

4. UK: The Duke of Edinburgh is awarded his wings by the RAF (→ 2/6).

4. New York: Ernest Hemingway wins a Pulitzer Prize for "The Old Man and the Sea".

6. London: MPs give a second reading to the bill creating the Central African Federation of the Rhodesias and Nyasaland (→ 22/9).

8. US: An atomic bomb, nearly twice as powerful as the two dropped on Japan in 1945, is exploded in Nevada (→ 4/6).

8. UK: Gloucestershire wicket-keeper Arthur Wilson takes a record ten catches against Hampshire.

8. UK: Labour makes big gains in municipal elections.

13. Indochina: The Viet Minh are reported to have set up a base on the Thai-Laotian border (→ 31).

15. US: Rocky Marciano retains his world heavyweight boxing title by knocking out Jersey Joe Walcott.

18. London: The police exhume the bodies of Beryl Evans and her baby (→ 22/6).

21. London: MPs give a second reading to a bill aimed at removing rating anomalies.

24. Egypt: The first British families leave on the advice of the Foreign Office (→ 18/6).

24. Nepal: A British assault on the south face of Mount Everest fails (→ 1/6).

25. UK: Chris Chataway sets a new two-mile record of eight minutes 49.6 seconds.

29. Kenya: Kikuyu territory is sealed off from the rest of the colony.

DEATH

16. Gypsy jazz guitarist Jean-Baptiste "Django" Reinhardt (*23/1/10).

British POWs arrive home from Korea

Tears and cheers greet the POWs.

May 1. Twenty-two British prisoners of war flew into RAF Lyneham, Wiltshire, today after a 10,000-mile, seven-day flight home.

A large cheering crowd gathered to greet the men, four of whom were still on stretchers, as the aircraft landed. Some of the men, heroes of the Gloucestershire Regiment's historic stand at the Imjin River in April 1951, had been in prison for more than two years. All wore the blue flash of the American Presidential Citation, just awarded to them (→ 15/6).

Mystery surrounds BOAC Comet crash

May 2. All 43 on board were killed when a British Overseas Airways Corporation Comet jet airliner crashed in a storm about 25 miles north of Calcutta today. The cause of the disaster was not clear, but one eyewitness, a 14-year-old villager, said that he saw a bright red flash and what appeared to be a wingless plane flying low over trees in a storm. There were several explosions and the plane dived into the bed of a dry stream.

Experts believe the aircraft may have been hit by an extremely high velocity squall, but investigators will want to find out why the wings appear to have come off, whatever the weather (→ 11/6).

US warns of "domino effect" in Far-East

May 31. The United States is becoming increasingly concerned about the situation in Indochina, where France has appointed General Henri Navarre to replace General Raoul Salan as leader of the fight against the Communist Viet Minh forces.

John Foster Dulles, US Secretary of State, has emphasised how crucial the area is to the West. He maintains that, if the Viet Minh drive out the French and set up a Communist system, then the whole of south-east Asia will fall under Soviet domination" just like a row of dominoes". Meanwhile, the news from Indochina is of increased Viet Minh activity. They have established control of a small area in Siam opposite Paksane.

Several thousand young men are known to have crossed the Mekong river at this point, and the indications are that the Viet Minh are establishing a base in this inaccessible area from which they will launch a guerrilla campaign (→24/7).

Stanley Matthews wins his first FA Cup

"The wizard of dribble" powers his skilful way to FA Cup victory.

May 2. In the most exciting Cup Final yet staged at Wembley, Blackpool and their 38-year-old right-wing hero Stanley Matthews have at last won the FA Cup.

With less than half an hour of the game left to play, Blackpool, after two dreadful mistakes by their goalkeeper, were trailing their Lancashire rivals, Bolton Wanderers, 3-1. Then the veteran Matthews, passed for Mortenson to score; Mortenson got another with a rasping free-kick; finally, with a only a minute left, Matthews again beat his full-back, crossed into the goalmouth, and saw Perry put it in the net for a 4-3 win.

Hungry refugees flood into West Berlin

May 4. The refugee march from the Russian sector of Germany to West Berlin trebled in size today with the sudden, unexpected withdrawal of ration cards from two million people on the east of the border.

Food shortages in the Communist zone have become so dire that the refugees are still prepared to risk being shot dead. As 2,200 fled today Russian troops fired automatic weapons at a man driving a lorry heading for the American frontier patrol. He was unhurt, but his vehicle was dragged back across the dividing line. So far the Communists have turned down Western offers to send relief supplies worth £4 million to ease the famine (→17/6).

1953

JUNE

Su	Mo	Tu	We	Th	Fr	Sa
	1	2	3	4	5	6
7	8	9	10	11	12	13
14	15	16	17	18	19	20
21	22	23	24	25	26	27
28	29	30				

1. UK: Gordon Richards is the first jockey to be knighted.

4. US: The greatest atomic explosion yet, twice the power of the Hiroshima bomb, is detonated in Nevada.

5. Washington: The Senate votes to bar China's entry to the UN (→14/12/55).

7. London: Edmund Hillary and Colonel John Hunt are knighted.

8. London: Premiere at Covent Garden of Britten's Coronation opera, "Gloriana".

11. London: Len Hutton is the first professional cricketer to captain England.

11. UK: The Princess Victoria disaster report censures the ferry's owners, the British Transport Commission.

13. UK: Jim Peters is the first person to run a marathon in under two hours 20 minutes.

14. France: Jaguar cars finish first, second, fourth and ninth in the Le Mans 24-hour Grand Prix d'Endurance.

14. Cambodia: King Sihanouk flees to Thailand (→2/3/55).

15. Korea: 30,000 Chinese troops attack UN forces along a 30-mile front.→

18. Japan: 129 US servicemen die in the world's worst air tragedy when a Globemaster transport crashes near Tokyo (→5/9/54).

22. London: Christie's trial opens at the Old Bailey; he pleads insanity (→25).

24. US: Jacqueline Bouvier announces her engagement to Senator John F. Kennedy (→12/9).

25. Wimbledon: Jaroslav Drobny beats Budge Patty in the longest-ever singles match 8-6, 16-18, 3-6, 8-6, 12-10.

30. Washington: Eisenhower asks Congress to let him offer some of the US food surplus to poorer allies. (→8/1/54).

DEATH

16. British Labour politician Margaret Bondfield, first woman cabinet minister, 1929 (*17/3/1873).

Rosenbergs go to the electric chair

June 19. With a quiet dignity that impressed all observers, Julius and Ethel Rosenberg walked to the electric chair in Sing Sing Prison just after 8 o'clock tonight. Just before she received the 2,000-volt shock Ethel grasped the hand of the matron attending her and kissed her lightly on the cheek.

They are the first married couple to suffer the death penalty in the US, and the first to die for spying. They were convicted at the height of McCarthy's witch-hunt in 1951 and have been appealing ever since.

In Union Square, New York, a crowd of over 5,000 held a vigil last night to protest and to denounce President Eisenhower for refusing them a pardon (→16/9).

Sir Gordon Richards wins his first Derby

Sir Gordon Richards riding Pinza.

June 6. Proving that Coronation Year is a year for the veterans, the recently knighted Gordon Richards capped Stanley Matthews' Cup-winner's triumph by winning his first Derby at the 28th attempt.

His mount, the 5-1 favourite Pinza, dictated the race from Tattenham Corner, taking the lead a quarter of a mile from home, and winning by four lengths from the only horse whose victory could have drawn greater cheers from the crowd, the Queen's colt Aureole. ▷

Crowning glory as British expedition conquers Everest

Conquering the roof of the world.

June 1. Everest has been conquered at last. Signals from Kathmandu today confirmed that the New Zealander Edmund Hillary, and Tensing, the Sherpa who accompanied him on the final assault, had reached the 29,002-foot summit of the world's highest mountain.

It was at 11.30am on May 29 that the two men stepped on to the top of the world, a "symmetrical, beautiful snow-cone summit", said Hillary, very different from the harsh rocky ridge seen from below.

They spent 15 minutes taking photographs and eating mint cake before leaving the Union Jack, the Nepal national flag and the United Nations flag, together with some sweets and biscuits, a Buddhist offering from Tensing.

The conquest of Everest followed an unsuccessful attempt earlier in the month from camp seven on the South Col, which was beaten by fierce winds. The weather was fine and settled for Hillary and Tensing.

Their success is a triumph of "scientific" planning by the expedition's leader, Colonel John Hunt, who closely studied every previous attempt and the prevailing weather. Improved high-altitude nylon weatherproof clothing was also a major factor, together with lightweight oxygen equipment for use on the final stage (→7).

Vivat Regina! Elizabeth II is crowned

June 2. Queen Elizabeth, who in the Second World War drove military trucks and mended them, rode to her Coronation today in a golden coach pulled by eight grey horses. The ceremony at Westminster Abbey was one of solemn pomp and pageantry. Princes, peers, prime ministers and commoners heard the Queen take the Coronation Oath in a clear and light voice, binding her to the service of her people in Britain and in the Commonwealth.

The Duke of Edinburgh was by her side. He was the first after the Archbishop of Canterbury, Dr Fisher, to place his hands between those of the Queen in an act of homage.

This was the first Coronation ever to be seen by millions of people all over the world because of television. In their own homes they saw the unique ceremony, and heard the words that have been part of it for over one thousand years.

The gold coach was a memorable sight as it was pulled through the streets of London at walking pace. Despite the cold and the wet, few people minded the discomfort of standing for hours on the footpaths. Queen Salote of Tonga, a huge and beaming figure, waved vigorously to the crowds as her open carriage filled with rainwater.

As usual each Commonwealth Prime Minister had his own carriage, but, for the first time ever at a Coronation, there was a shortage of professional coachmen. Millionaire businessmen and country squires offered to dress up as Buckingham Palace servants and drive the British and other Prime Ministers. Their generous offer was accepted.

The sixth and final appearance of the Queen and the Duke of Edinburgh on the balcony of Buckingham Palace was at midnight. They waved to a huge cheering crowd which was still going wild with excitement. Bowler hats were waved high on umbrellas, balloons were released, and gaily coloured streamers careered into the Palace railings in the breeze.

Finally, hundreds of thousands on Victoria Embankment watched fireworks whooshing into the sky and being reflected on a moonlit Thames (→25/12).

Flanked by all the panoply of Church and State, and holding the ceremonial mace and sceptre, Queen Elizabeth II sits enthroned.

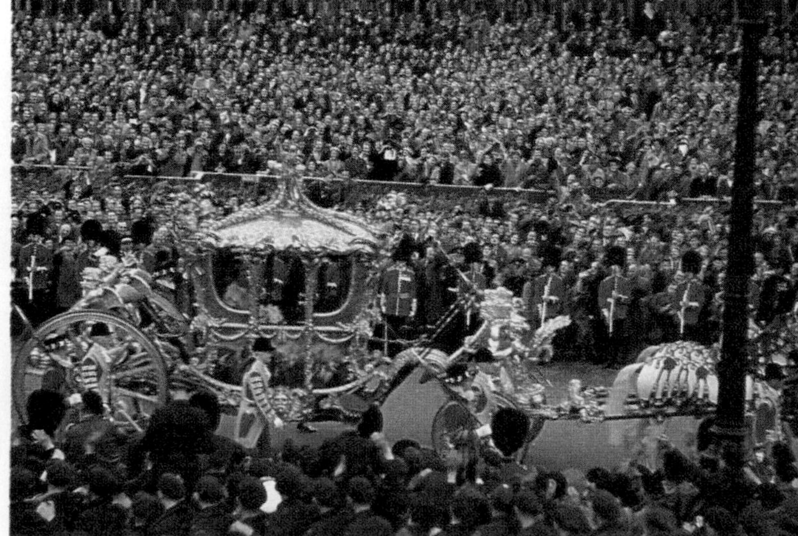

The crowds flock to welcome the Golden Coach, and its royal passenger as the Queen is driven from Westminster Abbey to Buckingham Palace.

Winston Churchill partly paralysed by a severe stroke

June 27. Mr Churchill has suffered a severe stroke. His left side is partially paralysed and he can hardly speak. He is now 79 and there is grave concern. A medical bulletin said today only that the Prime Minister needs complete rest and must lighten his duties for at least a month.

Mr Churchill collapsed four days ago and his doctors were seen arriving at 10 Downing Street. Only a few cabinet ministers have so far been told the full truth about his illness. Some newspapers know the facts. These have been suppressed on the initiative of Lord Beaverbrook, the newspaper owner.

18-month-old king is ousted in coup

June 18. Egypt's army leaders tonight deposed the infant King Fuad, and proclaimed a republic. The two strong men of the coup which ousted his father, King Farouk, last July have assumed the key posts. General Mohammed Neguib, aged 52, is President and Prime Minister, while Colonel Gamal Abdel Nasser, aged 35, is deputy premier and Minister of the Interior.

Announcing the end of the 148-year-old dynasty, the General described Farouk as a "pillar of imperialism". Fuad was asleep at his father's Italian villa when the news broke (→ 13/1/54).

Chinese launch new Korean offensive

June 15. Nearly 30,000 Chinese troops launched a surprise attack on Allied positions today, apparently in an effort to gain a propaganda victory before the Korean armistice is finally signed.

Latest reports say that the Chinese have been stopped by the American Third Infantry Division, but that two South Korean divisions were giving ground before mass assaults by Chinese urged on by bugles and cymbals.

Workers' uprising shakes East Berlin

Protesting East German workers brandish the western tricolour as they march past the Brandenburg Gate.

June 17. Scores of Soviet tanks and hundreds of troop-carriers poured into East Berlin last night to crush a two-day old anti-Soviet uprising by German workers, during which an undisclosed number of people were killed, hundreds injured, and buildings occupied by Soviet officials set on fire.

The man who climbed up the Brandenburg Gate to tear down the Red Flag was showered with cigarettes when he reached the ground. As Soviet tanks rumbled past, the crowd chanted "Ivan, go home".

The Soviet commandant in East Berlin, Major-General P.T. Dibrowa, has proclaimed martial law and ordered a 9pm to 5am curfew. The Soviet Zone has been sealed off from the West. Otto Grotewohl, Premier of the East German Government, blamed "provocateurs and Fascist agents of foreign powers" for the uprising. In fact, it was set off by a government order to workers on the Stalin Allee construction project for party officials to increase output by ten per cent.

The workers, women and men, downed tools and set off towards government buildings in the Wilhelmstrasse. Within a couple of hours a crowd of over 100,000 had gathered. A panicky Grotewohl cancelled the higher output decree, but by then it was too late. A workers' revolt in a workers' state had broken out (→ 12/7).

Christie sentenced to death for murder

June 25. John Reginald Halliday Christie was sentenced to death today for the murder of four women, one of them his wife, Ethel, at 10 Rillington Place, Notting Hill, London. All four had been strangled. Three of the bodies had been hidden behind a false wall and the fourth, his wife, was under the floorboards. He had attempted intercourse with three of them, all prostitutes, after making them unconscious with coal gas.

The balding, bespectacled transport clerk's plea of insanity was dismissed by the jury. The judge described the case as "a horrible one and a horrifying one".

Christie, a special constable, confessed to the four murders and told the police of three other killings, including that of Mrs Beryl Evans and her baby daughter. In 1950 Christie had been the principal Crown witness at the trial of Timothy John Evans, who was hanged for his wife's murder. The Evans family are now asking that the case be reviewed (→ 15/7).

Turpin wins back middleweight title

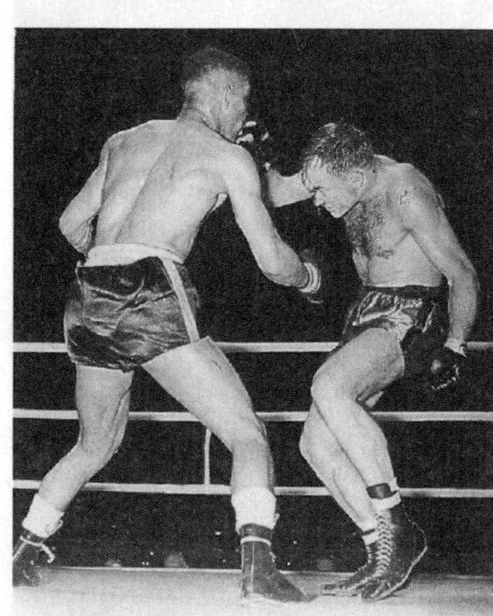

Champion Turpin stays on top.

June 9. Randolph Turpin has won back the world middleweight championship, in British eyes at least, by beating Charles Humez of France on points at the White City. He must now fight the winner of an American eliminator for his title to be recognised worldwide.

1953

JULY

Su	Mo	Tu	We	Th	Fr	Sa
			1	2	3	4
5	6	7	8	9	10	11
12	13	14	15	16	17	18
19	20	21	22	23	24	25
26	27	28	29	30	31	

1. UK: Conservative Airey Neave wins a by-election for Abingdon, Berkshire (→ 3/9).

1. London: MPs throw out a bill to suspend the death penalty for five years (→ 6).

4. Wimbledon: Victor Seixas beats Kurt Nielsen to win the Men's Singles final; Maureen Connolly beats Doris Hart to win her second Women's Singles final.

5. Kenya: 99 Mau Mau are killed in the latest British drive on terrorist strongholds.

6. London: The Home Secretary orders an enquiry into the conviction of Timothy Evans in 1949.→

10. UK: Ben Hogan of the US wins the British Open Golf Championship.

11. Washington: The State Department says South Korean leader Syngman Rhee has agreed to an armistice.→

12. East Berlin: Martial law is lifted (→ 24).

15. New York: Premiere of the film musical, "Gentlemen prefer Blondes", with Marilyn Monroe and Jane Russell.

15. US: Production is under way of Boeing's new B-52 eight-engined jet bomber.

15. London: Christie is hanged.

16. London: Hillary and Hunt receive their knighthoods; Tensing is awarded the George Medal (→ 31/12).

22. London: The government says it wants to cut London's airports from seven to three and to expand Gatwick.

24. Indochina: French paratroopers are dropped into Lang-Son (→ 29/11).

24. East Berlin: The East German minister for state security is dismissed following the recent riots (→ 4/8).

30. London: MPs debate a treaty with Libya giving Britain military bases for 20 years in exchange for aid.

DEATH

16. British author Hilaire Pierre Belloc (*27/7/1870).

Guns fall silent in Korea

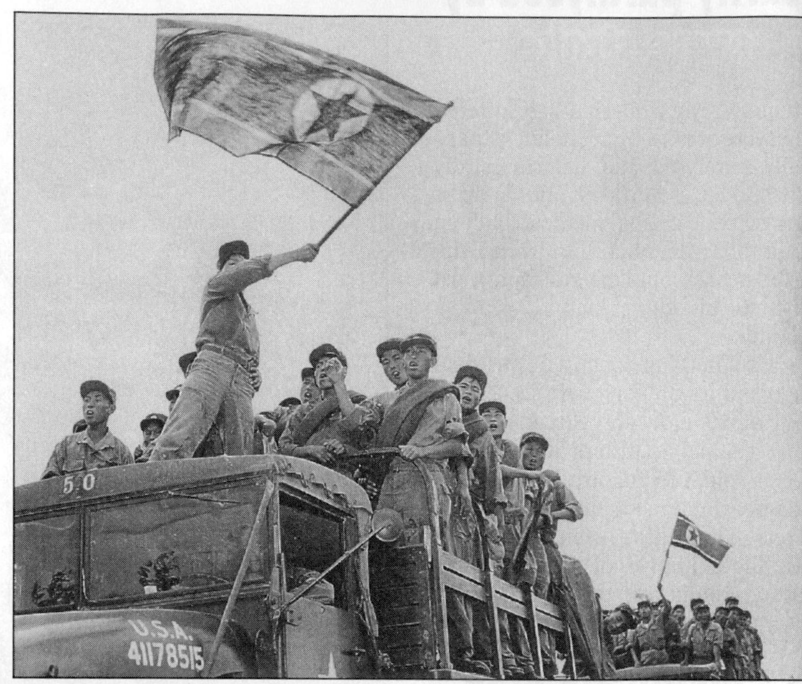

Truckloads of Communist POWs celebrate their return to the North.

July 27. The war in Korea is over after three years of bloody fighting which has cost over two million lives. The armistice was signed at Panmunjon at 10.01am today, and the guns will all fall silent at ten o'clock tonight.

The terms of the truce, which has taken two years of bitter wrangling to settle, stipulate that both sides will destroy their front line positions and withdraw for two kilometres. Allied troops will withdraw from the islands they occupy off North Korea, and the naval and air blockades will be lifted. Another important agreement is that no reinforcements of men or material will be brought in which will increase existing numbers and supplies. A special committee will be set up to supervise the exchange of prisoners of war.

The Allied Commander, General Mark Clark, said this evening: "It is good to have the bloodshed end. But a long and difficult road lies ahead. There are no short cuts. We must continue our efforts to seek and defend peace" (→ 20/9).

Soviet secret police chief on spy charge

July 10. Lavrenti Beria, the Soviet secret police chief, has been arrested at a Politburo meeting and charged with being a "Western agent" and plotting to seize power. Beria, who had been second in the Soviet hierarchy after Georgi Malenkov, was arrested at gunpoint last month at a meeting which called for his resignation.

Soviet marshals carried out the arrest on a pre-arranged signal from Malenkov. A purge is taking place in Beria's secret police. He has been in charge of security since 1941 (→ 12/9).

Rebel leader Castro is jailed in Cuba

July 26. Armed Cuban activists attacked two army barracks at Moncada, near Santiago, today. Troops loyal to President Batista repelled the attackers, described as Communists. An estimated 55 of the rebels were killed; the rest have been imprisoned, including their leader, Fidel Castro.

Castro, the son of a rich planter, was brought up by Jesuits and is now a lawyer. In his student days, he was allegedly involved with a Communist terrorist group; more recently he was implicated in an attempted coup in Dominica.

1953

AUGUST

Su	Mo	Tu	We	Th	Fr	Sa
						1
2	3	4	5	6	7	8
9	10	11	12	13	14	15
16	17	18	19	20	21	22
23	24	25	26	27	28	29
30	31					

1. UK: Bannister and Chataway are in the team that sets a mile relay record of 16 minutes 41 seconds.

4. West Berlin: 6,000 Communists from the East raid two food distribution centres in the western sector (→ 22).

4. UK: Dilys Cadwaladr is the first woman to win the Bardic Crown at the Welsh National Eisteddfod.

5. Korea: Doctors say that many returned POWs are sufffering from lung diseases.

5. US: Opening of the film, "From Here to Eternity".

8. Paris: Two million people stage a walk out in protest at planned cuts in the civil service and public services (→ 13).

13. Greece: Over 1,000 are reported to have died after earthquakes and tidal waves hit the Ionian Islands (→ 14).

13. France: A general strike paralyses the country.

14. Greece: Around 100,000 people are believed homeless after the disaster (→4/10/55).

16. Teheran: The Shah and Queen Soraya flee the country after a failed attempt to oust premier Mossadegh.→

17. Budapest: Nagy's government frees Briton Edgar Sanders, jailed for 13 years in 1949 for spying (→ 18/4/55).

17. London: Tractor makers Ferguson are to merge with Canadian firm Massey-Harris.

20. Morocco: Sultan Sidi Mohammed Ben Youssef is deposed by the French (→ 17/7/55).

22. East Berlin: The East Germans announce they will cease reparations to the USSR from January 1, 1954. (→ 1/1/54).

23. Teheran: The Shah appeals to the world for financial assistance (→ 5/9).

27. UK: The De Havilland Comet II makes its first test flight (→ 11/1/54).

29. UK: The latest British tank, the Carnarvon, is about to begin trials (→ 25/9).

Evans did kill his wife, says inquiry

July 14. On the eve of the execution of John Christie, the Rillington Place murderer, a government tribunal has failed to find a miscarriage of justice in the case of Timothy John Evans. The Welsh lorrydriver was hanged three years ago for the murder of his wife and daughter in the house in which Christie confessed to killing four women, including his own wife.

Labour MPs and the Howard League for Penal Reform have refused to accept the report by John Scott Henderson, QC, who has concluded that a confession by Christie of Mrs Evans' murder was unreliable and untrue and only made to "help his defence".

Christie, who gave evidence to the tribunal in his death cell, has refused to meet Labour MPs who want a full debate (→ 15).

Timothy Evans: hanged correctly?

Hungarian leader promises new deal

July 4. The incoming Hungarian Prime Minister, Imre Nagy, has unveiled to his restive people a plan which, if executed, would transform the country. Enforced collectivisation of agriculture is to end; individual trade and freedom of travel and worship will return; and internment camps could be abolished immediately. Nagy's Russian masters might not, however, approve of his intention to trade with capitalist as well as communist countries (→ 17).

Russia catches up in nuclear arms race

Aug 14. The Soviet Union has broken the American monopoly of the hydrogen bomb, according to Georgi Malenkov, the Soviet Prime Minister. Malenkov made his disclosure to the Supreme Soviet, Russia's Parliament, after a bitter attack on United States foreign policy. He then made a very brief reference to the fact that the Soviet Union is now the world's latest possessor of this most powerful of weapons.

The claim was greeted with both shock and scepticism in the West, where it was pointed out that no nuclear explosion has been detected at the Soviet Union's Kazakhstan test site since 1951. Only the United States is known to have so far produced a thermo-nuclear "device", but Western scientists said that a Soviet breakthrough was predictable in what has been a race to develop the H-bomb.

Soviet nuclear weapon development has been under the control of Lavrenti Beria, the Soviet secret police chief, who was recently arrested for spying (→ 21/1/54).

Shah returns to Iran after military coup

Aug 22. The Shah of Iran, restored to power after a military coup toppled the nationalist Mohammed Mossadegh, today returned from his Rome exile to Teheran to find the State Treasury empty. "The financial situation is desperate," he said. "It is not a matter of months or even weeks, but of days." General Fazollah Zahedi, who led the coup, said Dr Mossadegh faced two separate trials: one for misdeeds committed while he was prime minister, and a second for high treason, because he tried to usurp the Shah's power (→ 23).

England win back Ashes after 20 years

Aug 19. For the first time since winning the notorious Bodyline Tour of 1932-33, England have regained the Ashes.

After four drawn Test matches – including one saved from almost certain defeat by a heroic rearguard action by Trevor Bailey and Willie Watson – England combined the bowling of Fred Truman on the first day, important innings by the captain, Len Hutton, and Bailey, and the match-winning spin of Jim Laker and Tony Lock, to set the scene for the final afternoon as Bill Edrich and Denis Compton patiently steered the side to an eight-wicket victory.

Len Hutton plays a captain's innings as England take back the Ashes.

1953

SEPTEMBER

Su	Mo	Tu	We	Th	Fr	Sa
		1	2	3	4	5
6	7	8	9	10	11	12
13	14	15	16	17	18	19
20	21	22	23	24	25	26
27	28	29	30			

1. UK: Surrey win the county cricket championship for the second successive year.

2. London: The Radio show at Olympia includes a 27-inch television set – 15 inches larger than most existing sets (→23/2/54).

3. London: Florence Horsbrugh becomes Minister of Education, the first Tory woman cabinet minister (→14/4/54).

5. Washington: Eisenhower gives Iran a $45-million grant (→2/10).

6. West Germany: Konrad Adenauer is re-elected chancellor (→25/1/54).

8. Moscow: The USSR recognises the Austrian Republic.

10. Cyprus: At least 40 die in the island's worst recorded earthquake (→20/8/54).

12. Moscow: Nikita Khrushchev is elected first secretary of the Communist Party (→16/12).

16. New York: 20th Century Fox demonstrates "Cinemascope" with the film "The Robe".

16. Geneva: The wife and three children of missing diplomat Donald MacLean have disappeared (→21/3/54).

20. Korea: A Communist fighter pilot lands his MiG-15 near Seoul and surrenders to the Americans (→14/10).

23. London: The Royal Commission on capital punishment says juries should decide, whether to impose the death penalty (→1/10).

24. US: Rocky Marciano knocks out Roland LaStarza to keep his world heavywieght boxing title.

25. Libya: Briton Michael Lithgow reaches a record 737.3 mph in a Vickers Supermarine Swift F.4 jet (→4/8/54).

28. Warsaw: Catholic primate Cardinal Stefan Wyszynski is arrested (→18/10).

28. UK: Ford unveils its new Anglia and Prefect models (→20/10).

John Kennedy marries Jacqueline Bouvier

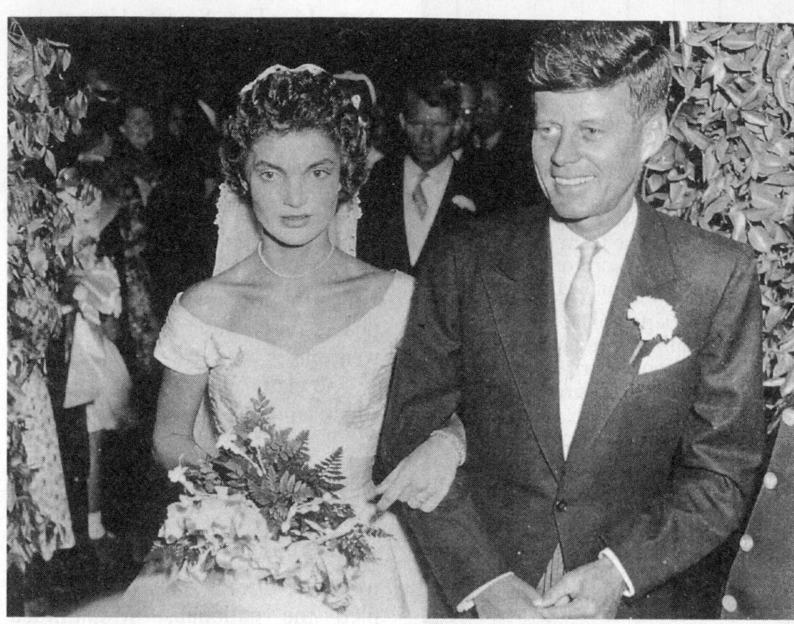

Jacqueline Bouvier and Jack Kennedy, with his brother Bobby in the rear.

Sept 12. John Fitzgerald Kennedy wed Miss Jacqueline Lee Bouvier this afternoon in Newport, Rhode Island. Nearly 3,000 people are reported to have tried to crash the high-society party to celebrate the marriage.

The new Mrs Kennedy was until recently the inquiring photographer for the Washington Times-Herald; she looked lovely, but a little bewildered, in her ivory silk gown.

The 36-year-old bridegroom is the eldest son of the prominent financier, and former US ambassador to London, Joseph P. Kennedy. After graduating from Harvard, he published his thesis "Why England Slept", which became a best-selling study of the rise of Fascism in Europe. In the war he served as a PT boat commander in the Pacific; his craft was sunk in 1943, but the crew was rescued.

He entered politics in 1946, winning a seat in the House of Representatives. Last year he defeated Henry Cabot Lodge for a Senate post in Massachusetts (→23/5/55).

Whites hang on to Northern Rhodesia

Sept 22. The government today announced several changes to the Northern Rhodesia constitution, after the London conference held to agree on amendments failed to reach a decision.

While the number of Africans on the Legislative Council has been boosted from two to four, white domination is to stay; there will also be two more Europeans on the Council – making their total 14.

The African delegates say that they cannot accept the changes, complaining that they "represent a further extension of political power to the settlers". They had hoped to achieve equal numbers of Africans and Europeans (→3/2/54).

Fashion's drawbacks: Nobody ever said that high fashion was supposed to be comfortable, but wearers of the new, ultra-high "stiletto" heels are wondering whether the latest in footwear is actually dangerous, too.

1953

OCTOBER

Su	Mo	Tu	We	Th	Fr	Sa
				1	2	3
4	5	6	7	8	9	10
11	12	13	14	15	16	17
18	19	20	21	22	23	24
25	26	27	28	29	30	31

1. UK: Scotland Yard uses TV for the first time in its hunt for murder suspect William Pettit (→10/2/55).

2. Teheran: The new government has launched an intensive drive on the Tudeh, Iran's Communist party (→30/11).

6. British Guiana: Britain orders troops and warships to the colony to forestall a feared Communist coup attempt (→9).

9. London: The government is to set up a commercial television service (→13/11).

9. British Guiana: The constitution is suspended (→27).

14. Southampton: 147 men of the Gloucestershire Regiment return from North Korean captivity (→12/8/54).

14. Jordan: Israeli troops attack three Jordanian villages, killing 56 (→16).

16. London: Britain protests to Israel over its raids into Jordan (→16/11).

18. Poland: Catholics take to the streets in protest at the arrest of the Polish primate Cardinal Wyszynski.

21. US: American Carl Olsen beats Britain's Randy Turpin to win the world middleweight boxing title.

23. London: Troops are called in to operate petrol tankers in replacement of striking tanker drivers (→5/11).

23. Italy: Heavy flooding wrecks at least 12 villages in the south of the country.

27. British Guiana: The British intern five members of the left-wing People's Progressive Party (→12/4/54).

31. UK: A record 30,031 new homes have been completed this month (→1/12).

31. US: The British team wins seven out of eleven trophies at the Pennsylvania National Horse Show.

DEATHS

3. British composer Sir Arnold Bax (*8/11/1883).

8. British contralto Katleen Ferrier (*22/4/12).→

Car prices plummet in under-cutting war

The new Ford Popular, the cheapest of Britain's small family cars.

Oct 20. Who builds the cheapest car on the British market? Claims have been made for Austin, Standard and Ford. Austin's contender is the two-door version of the A30, costing £475 including purchase tax. This is £6 less than Standard's four-door Standard Eight.

Last year's cheapest model, the Anglia, was no longer a contender, having been superseded by an 11 hp car selling at £511. Ford was said to have abandoned austerity motoring.

Now Ford have sprung a surprise – a cut-price revival of the old Anglia, re-named the Popular. At £390 (including tax), this gives Ford the world's cheapest four-cylinder car.

Ferrier, the unique contralto, is dead

Oct 8. Kathleen Ferrier's death from cancer has cut short, at 41, the career of a greatly loved singer with a uniquely rich and moving contralto voice. Her opera career only began in 1946 – she had been a switchboard operator.

Kathleen Ferrier: an early death.

Italy gets Trieste: Yugoslavia furious

Oct 8. Britain and the United States announced today that they are to withdraw their troops from Zone A of the Free Territory of Trieste. They are handing over control to the Italians, who already police the Zone with a British-trained force. The Italians lay claim to the whole territory and intend to press for a plebiscite on the issue.

The Yugoslavs, who occupy Zone B with 10,000 troops, were furious. President Tito "resolutely condemned" the action and said he would appeal to the UN. Crowds of demonstrators smashed windows at the British and American embassies and the Italian legation in Belgrade. They shouted: "We shall give our lives but not Trieste."

According to the Italian peace treaty, Trieste was to become independent under UN auspices. But the West and the Communists have not been able to agree the terms for the new state (→21/11).

1953

NOVEMBER

Su	Mo	Tu	We	Th	Fr	Sa
1	2	3	4	5	6	7
8	9	10	11	12	13	14
15	16	17	18	19	20	21
22	23	24	25	26	27	28
29	30					

2. Karachi: Pakistan's parliament decides that Pakistan will become an Islamic republic within the Commonwealth (→30/5/54).

5. London: All rationing is to end next year (→2/12).

5. Tel Aviv: Ben-Gurion resigns as prime minister; Moshe Sharett takes over.

11. US: The polio virus is identified and photographed for the first time.

11. London: MPs approve a bill allowing Prince Philip to become Regent, if necessary.

16. New York: The US joins Britain and France in a UN resolution condemning the Israeli raid on Jordan (→17/3/54).

17. London: Sir Arthur Bliss becomes Master of the Queen's Musick, in succession to the late Sir Arnold Bax.

21. Rome: Italy agrees to five-power talks on the future of Trieste (→29/4/55).

21. UK: Experiments on the skull of "Piltdown Man" reveal it is a 40-year-old hoax.

24. US: Senator McCarthy accuses ex-president Harry Truman of aiding many suspected Communists (→2/2/54).

26. London: Peers approve the government's plans for commercial television.

29. Vietnam: French paratroopers take Dien Bien Phu.→

29. Sudan: The pro-Egyptian National Unionist Party wins the first Sudanese general election (→6/1/54).

30. Teheran: Iran restores diplomatic relations with Britain (→19/12).

DEATHS

9. British poet Dylan Thomas (*27/10/1914).→

9. Saudi Arabian King Abd el-Aziz III ibn Saud (*1880).

27. US playwright Eugene O'Neill (*16/10/1888).

30. French artist Francis Picabia (*22/1/1879).

TV with adverts gets the go-ahead

Nov 13. Government plans for commercial television in competition with the BBC were announced today. Subject to parliament's approval, there will be a new public corporation which will license companies to provide programmes.

The companies will draw their revenue from advertisements. Not more than six minutes of advertising will be allowed in each hour's broadcasting; sometimes it will be less. A Government White Paper said that the new TV output – under strict controls – will start from stations in London and then Birmingham. To face the competition the BBC will get a £3 licence fee – up from £2 (→26).

King of Buganda is exiled with pension

Nov 30. King Freddie, the 29-year-old Kabaka of Buganda, was dispatched into exile today by Sir Andrew Cohen, Governor of the East African Protectorate of Uganda. Buganda is one of Uganda's four provinces and, with a million people, has a quarter of the population. King Freddie, Cambridge-educated and a Grenadier Guards officer, wants Buganda to be given independence separately from the other provinces, but the British believe a unified Uganda will be more viable. The deposed Kabaka will be given a pension to live in London (→17/10/55).

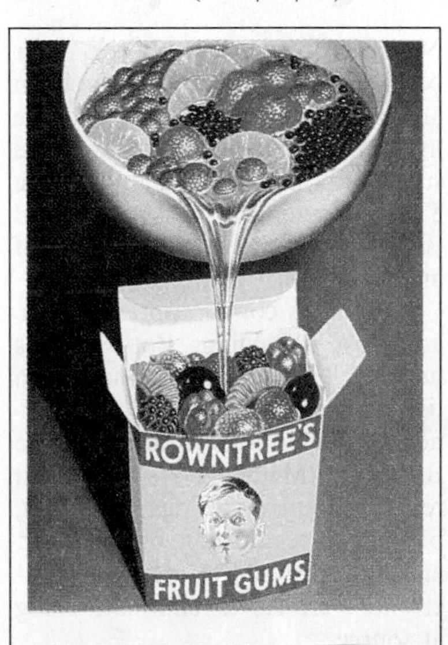

Dylan Thomas, raging Welsh bard, dies

Dylan Marlais Thomas – still raging until the end.

Nov 9. Dylan Thomas, the nearest thing our age has produced to a raging bard out of Celtic Wales, died today, only 39, at the Chelsea Hotel, New York, where he was on a lecture tour.

In an age of precise, sober-suited poets, he was renowned for heavy drinking and wild living. His public loved him for it.

His first poem was published because it won a newspaper competition – "And Death Shall Have No Dominion" was its title. He took up the same theme in his epitaph for his father: "Do not go gentle into that good night ... rage, rage against the dying of the light." His collected poems came out last year to much acclaim (→28/2).

French paratroops take Dien Bien Phu

Nov 29. Tough French paratroops and Foreign Legionnaires took the Communist Viet Minh forces by surprise today and captured the strategic plateau of Dien Bien Phu from the air. They fell out of the sky from Dakota transports and armoured helicopters.

General Navarre will replace his shock troops with infantry, then repair a nearby airfield built by the Japanese and use Dien Bien Phu as an offensive base. The French lost 14 men in "Operation Castor" and killed 60 Communists (→29/2).

England loses to Hungary at home

Nov 25. A dazzling display of football, utterly controlled in midfield and brilliantly inventive in attack, fully earned Hungary the honour of becoming the first overseas national team to defeat England at Wembley.

The margin of their victory, 6-3, hardly did justice to their all round superiority, and notwithstanding the hat-trick from their centre-forward Hidekguti, a 25-yard drive by Bozsik and two gems from their captain Ferenc Puskas, they could easily have scored ten.

Smog masks prescribed for pea-soupers

Nov 14. Starting next week, your NHS doctor can prescribe you an anti-smog mask. That is, if you live in a smoky industrial area and are subject to heart or lung diseases. There is a choice of two masks, and your doctor will decide which, if any, you need.

The masks come on prescription, and cost a shilling. Both designs have refill pads of gauze and cotton tissue. Research into the effectiveness of the masks continues. The British Medical Association regards them as stopgaps at best, pending a restoration of clean air, and look forward to increased government efforts to eliminate smog at source.

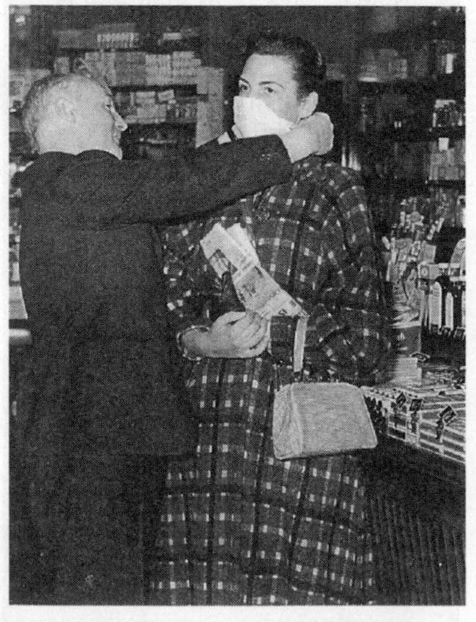

Getting a fitting for a smog mask.

1953

DECEMBER

Su	Mo	Tu	We	Th	Fr	Sa
		1	2	3	4	5
6	7	8	9	10	11	12
13	14	15	16	17	18	19
20	21	22	23	24	25	26
27	28	29	30	31		

1. London: Britain offers Malta a new constitution.

2. UK: Two million engineering workers stage a 24-hour strike for more pay (→17/2/54).

4. Australia: A large oilfield is struck in North-Western Australia (→12/1/54).

7. Washington: The US Supreme Court considers banning racial segregation in US schools (→17/5/54).

9. London: The government unveils a £10 million aid plan for Kenya (→15/1/54).

10. Stockholm: Nobel Prizes go to Frits Zernike (Holland, Physics); Hermann Staudinger (W. Germany, Chemistry); Sir Hans Krebs (UK) and Fritz Lipman (US, Medicine); Sir Winston Churchill (UK, Literature); and in Oslo to George Marshall (US, Peace).→

16. Moscow: Ex-secret police chief Beria confesses to "state crimes" and is committed for trial for treason.→

19. Teheran: The Shah calls a general election (→5/8/54).

25. London: In her Christmas speech the Queen vows to devote her life to the Commonwealth ideal (→12/1/54).

29. Laos: Viet Minh troops reach the Mekong River along the Thai border (→10/2/54).

31. UK: Jack Hawkins heads an opinion poll as Britain's most popular film star.

31. New Delhi: A British-led expedition to search for the "Abominable Snowman" arrives on its way to Nepal (→2/6/55).

DEATH

19. Robert Millikan, American physicist (*22/3/1868).

HITS OF 1953

Rags to Riches.

I love Paris.

Diamonds are a girl's best friend.

QUOTE OF THE YEAR

"We done the bugger!"

Sherpa Tensing, on the conquest of Everest, June 1953.

Chemistry of life is yielding to the probing of science

This has been an annus mirabilis for the study of the chemistry of life. Besides the **Watson-Crick** structure for the genetic material DNA, the year saw the completion of the first full chemical analysis of a protein. The protein in question is insulin, the hormone controlling the level of sugar in the blood that diabetics lack, and the project took the Cambridge biochemist, **Dr Frederick Sanger**, eight years.

Proteins are key chemicals in life, with innumerable roles in all living organisms from bacteria to man. All proteins consist of different combinations of about 20 standard sub-units, called amino acids, joined together in long chains. The structure of a protein is the key to its function. Insulin is a fairly simple protein, containing about 50 amino acids. Others contain hundreds of these sub-units.

Sanger worked out the structure of insulin by painstakingly breaking it down into smaller and smaller fragments, until he could identify the pieces. He could then work out the order in which they fitted together.

Another striking development was the impregnation of a woman with deep frozen sperm, by **Dr R.G. Bunge** and **Dr J.K.Sherman** of the University of Iowa Medical School. Experience with cattle shows that, in the deep freeze, sperm can be preserved for many years, so a man could father a child long after his death.

Churchill's history wins a Nobel Prize

Dec 10. Lady Churchill went to Stockholm today to receive the Nobel Prize awarded to her husband, who is at a conference in Bermuda, for his historical works.

He was referred to as "a Caesar who wields the stylus of a Cicero". Sir Winston's literary output is enormous. His history of the First World War and his biography of his ancestor, Marlborough, both took four volumes. His history of the Second World War will take six. His most popular book, "My Early Life", says of his only attempt at a novel – "Savrola" – "I have consistently urged my friends to abstain from reading it".

Soviet security boss is shot for treason

Dec 23. Russia's former security police boss, Lavrenti Beria, has been executed, following a secret trial on charges of plotting to seize power and of being a Western agent. Six other senior officers in Beria's secret police were also shot. Beria, who has been portrayed as Stalin's evil genius and a traitor, was arrested in June. It cannot be ruled out that he was planning to oust Georgi Malenkov, the Prime Minister, and assume power. Beria has thus joined Yagoda and Yezhov in the remarkable community of Soviet police chiefs who have not died a natural death (→17/1/54).

New housing tops 300,000 in a year

Dec 1. Harold Macmillan, the Housing Minister, told Parliament tonight that 301,000 new houses were built in the Government's second year in office. So, he said, the Tories' election pledge to reduce controls and get 300,000 extra homes a year has been amply fulfilled, with housing having priority second only to defence.

The Government is now allowing landlords to put up rents, in order to pay for repairs. Mr Macmillan called it "a triumph for private enterprise".

Arts: golden age of radio comedy

A radio show unlike any other is winning a cult following and becoming an unmissable weekly date for huge numbers of the young. "The Goon Show" does not make sense to anyone coming fresh to it – indeed it does not make sense at all, but the kind of anarchic nonsense it excels at has a wild streak of punning logic running through it reminiscent of Lewis Carroll.

The Goons are a trio who began their comic careers after war service, two of them, **Harry Secombe** and **Peter Sellers**, as graduates of the Windmill Theatre. The third is script-writer as well as performer, **Spike Milligan**. With the help of creative noises off, they create a cast of incredible but keenly relished characters – lunatics such as Major Bloodnok or Hercules Grytpype Thynne, a pair of extremely frail and elderly lovers, Henry Crun and Minnie Bannister, and two complete imbeciles, Eccles, a human Goofy, and the manic boy-scout, Bluebottle.

As in the days of ITMA, it seems as though half the population is conducting conversations in deliberately infantile, all-too-imitable Goonese. Despite several attempts by BBC high-ups to take the Goon Show off, radio comedy is enjoying a golden period. It began in 1948 when "Take It From Here" replaced ITMA. Its writers, **Frank Muir** and **Denis Norden**, introduced topical sketches, burlesques of cliche film dramas, and a situation comedy (tragedy?) called "The Glums", hilariously rendered by the resident threesome, **Dick Bentley**, **June Whitfield** and **Jimmy Edwards**, the bombastic anchor of the show.

A programme about, of all things, a ventriloquist's schoolboy dummy, named Archie Andrews, has caught on in no uncertain manner. "Educating Archie" has made the name not only of Archie (**Peter Brough**) but of his tutor, another graduate of the Windmill, **Tony Hancock**. Hancock portrays himself as an opinionated nobody, bristling with social pretensions, snobbery and prejudice against the ignorance of all around him. There are plans for him to be given his own half-hour comedy show.

The favourite film of Coronation year is a light-hearted romp with a vintage car named "Genevieve". France produced a blissful eccentric, **Jacques Tati**. His "Monsieur Hulot's Holiday" is a delight.

Death has taken America's senior playwright, **Eugene O'Neill**, with his last play – "A Long Day's Journey into Night" – about his actor-father still unperformed, although written back in 1941.

It has been a busy year for Shakespeare. **Richard Burton's** Hamlet began the complete canon at the Old Vic. **Alec Guinness** launched the Stratford, Ontario, festival with his Richard III. And Hollywood did justice to "Julius Caesar" with heavyweight acting from **John Gielgud** and **James Mason** as the conspirators while **Marlon Brando** made an unusual Mark Antony.

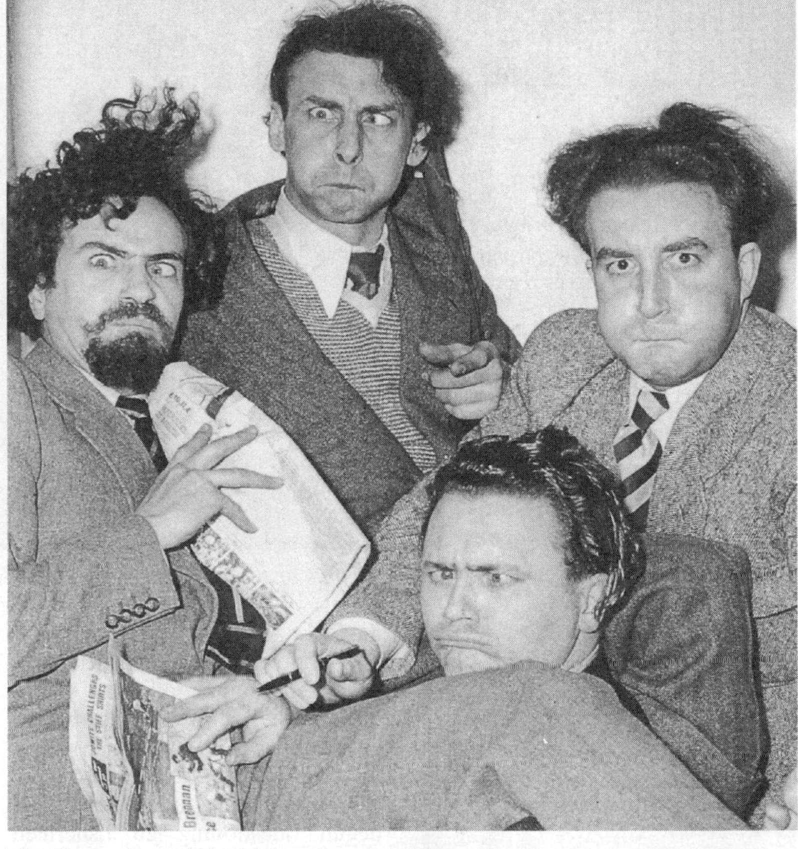

The Goons: From left, M. Bentine, S. Milligan, H. Secombe and P. Sellers.

"Professor" Jimmy Edwards.

Tony "Flippin' Kids" Hancock.

1954

JANUARY

Su	Mo	Tu	We	Th	Fr	Sa
					1	2
3	4	5	6	7	8	9
10	11	12	13	14	15	16
17	18	19	20	21	22	23
24	25	26	27	28	29	30
31						

1. UK: Flashing direction indicator lights become legal on motor vehicles in Britain.

1. West Berlin: Over 300,000 East German refugees registered last year, 1.7 per cent of the East German population (→ 26/9/55).

2. Rome: Pope Pius XII warns that television is a potential threat to family life (→ 6/6).

6. Sudan: Ismail Azhari is elected the first prime minister of the Sudan (→ 3/12/55).

8. Washington: Eisenhower proposes giving the vote to 18-year-olds.

12. Wellington: The Queen becomes the first reigning monarch to open the New Zealand parliament (→ 3/2).

12. Rangoon: The Burmese government and three oil companies agree on the creation of Burmah Oil (→ 17/12).

13. Egypt: 570 members of the fundamentalist Muslim Brotherhood are arrested (→ 28/2).

14. San Francisco: Marilyn Monroe marries ex-baseballer Joe DiMaggio.

15. Kenya: "General China", second most important military figure in the Mau Mau, is wounded and captured (→ 7/3).

17. USSR: The Kremlin warns the Ukraine against nationalist feelings as a purge continues in the republic of Georgia (→ 8/2/55).

21. US: The US Navy launches the Nautilus, the first nuclear-powered submarine (→ 22/3).

25. Berlin: Foreign ministers from the Big Four powers arrive to discuss East-West issues, particularly Germany.→

26. Yugoslavia: Tito is re-elected president (→ 5/10).

31. UK: 23 people are reported to have died in accidents on frozen ice as wintry weather grips Britain.

DEATH

11. British statesman John Simon, first Viscount Simon (*28/2/1873).

Comets grounded after a second crash

Victims of the Comet crash are carried to their burial place on Elba.

Jan 11. All British Overseas Airways Corporation Comet jets were grounded tonight following yesterday's mystery crash into the Mediterranean off Elba, with the loss of 35 lives. Anglo-Italian investigators have arrived at the scene and begun questioning 20 fishermen who saw the disaster. All agree that the aircraft suddenly burst into flames and plummeted into the sea.

The new crash follows the tragedy near Calcutta last year, when another Comet fell out of the sky for no apparent reason, and all BOAC's seven Comets around the world are being flown home now without passengers. They will then stay on the ground until the cause of the mystery crashes is discovered.

There are still few clues to the cause of the latest crash, which has destroyed any confidence in the world's first jet airliner. Experts believe some kind of structural failure may be behind the problem, caused by a high-speed plane running unexpectedly into turbulence in apparently fine weather (→ 4/2).

Re-united Germany divides the Powers

Jan 31. The Four-Power Foreign Ministers' conference in Berlin produced a direct East-West clash today over the issue of free elections in a re-united Germany. Anthony Eden, for Britain, proposed that an electoral law be prepared guaranteeing free elections in East and West Germany for an all-German Assembly, which would lead to an all-German Government.

Mr Molotov, for the Soviet Union, would have none of this. He wants an all-German Government to be formed before elections. The US and France backed Britain in rejecting this outright, since it gives legimitacy to the unelected East German regime, which is not recognised by the West (→ 18/2).

Tito dismisses his possible successor

Jan 17. Marshal Tito may be creating his own independent brand of Communism in Yugoslavia, but he made it dramatically clear today that he was not prepared to oversee a drift towards Western-style democracy. He removed his vice-president, Milovan Djilas, from the Communist Party Central Committee, and warned that any other "enemies" would be purged.

Djilas was Tito's second-in-command and was widely considered his probable successor, but he was by no means a yes-man. Djilas says that hard-line Communism is not the only route to socialism; he has also charged Tito with protecting bureaucracies of dubious value, and called for reforms (→ 26).

1954

FEBRUARY

Su	Mo	Tu	We	Th	Fr	Sa
	1	2	3	4	5	6
7	8	9	10	11	12	13
14	15	16	17	18	19	20
21	22	23	24	25	26	27
28						

2. Washington: The Senate votes $214,000 for McCarthy's committee; only William Fulbright opposes the fund (→ 18).

3. Southern Rhodesia: The first Central African Federation parliament opens.

4. London: BOAC announces that after making 50 modifications, its Comet fleet can now fly again (→ 9/4).

5. UK: Publication of Kingsley Amis's novel, "Lucky Jim" (→ 12/1954).

10. Washington: Eisenhower says he can think of no greater tragedy than for the US to get involved in Indochina (→ 19).

10. Berlin: The Western Allies reject a Soviet plan for a Pan-European security pact, to replace NATO (→ 2/10).

12. London: The government publishes a bill setting up an Atomic Energy Authority (→ 1/3).

15. UK: The 800th episode of BBC radio's "The Archers" is broadcast; it now has a record audience of ten million.

17. London: The government says meat rationing will end in July after 14 years (→ 4/5).

18. Washington: McCarthy's anti-Communist committee begins investigations of US Army personnel.→

18. Berlin: Four-Power talks accelerate peace in Asia but reach no accord on Germany and Austria (→ 5/5/55).

22. New Delhi: Prime Minister Nehru urges a truce between the French and the Viet Minh in Indochina (→ 14/3).

23. US: Jonas Salk's new polio vaccine is first used on children in Pittsburgh (→ 26/4).

23. New York: IBM says it has developed a "Transceiver" which transmits information in down telephone lines (→ 24/5).

24. London: American evangelist Billy Graham arrives on a three-month tour of Britain (→ 22/5).

28. London: First reading of Dylan Thomas's radio play "Under Milk Wood" at the Old Vic (→ 12/1954).

Study finds cancer linked to smoking

Feb 12. A relationship between smoking and lung cancer must be regarded as established, the British Standing Advisory Committee on cancer and chemotherapy said today. But the agent involved is unknown; atmospheric pollution or work risks may be causes. The Minister of Health warned against uninformed and alarmist conclusions.

Tobacco manufacturers which have done research replied that there was no proof smoking caused lung cancer. They pointed out that it occurs in those who never smoke, and in only a small proportion of those who do, and that it is more common in town than country, despite similar smoking rates (→21/6).

Australians warmly welcome the Queen

Feb 3. The Queen and the Duke of Edinburgh arrived in sun-drenched Sydney this morning for the first visit to Australia by a reigning monarch. Their liner, the Gothic, edged into the harbour through a lane of some 500 small craft.

The Queen was clearly excited by the warmth of the welcome as she stood on the bridge waving to port and starboard. As Gothic dropped anchor at Athol Bight, the headlands were covered with cheering people (→15/5).

A happy Queen meets Australia.

Egypt's leaders caught in revolving door

Egypt's leader General Neguib (l.) with coming man Lieut. Col. Nasser.

Feb 28. After months of infighting and a weekend of revolving-door leadership, General Mohammed Neguib, aged 53, has come out on top in the Cairo power struggle.

Last week the young officers' Revolutionary Council, which deposed King Farouk in 1952, accused Neguib of wanting to be a dictator, sacked him as Egyptian President and put him under house arrest. Colonel Gamal Abdel Nasser, aged 36, took over.

By Saturday pro-Neguib demonstrations were spreading throughout the country. In Cairo universities were closed after police and troops opened fire on students, killing at least ten. Pro-Neguib cavalry officers threatened to mutiny.

As suddenly as he had vanished, Neguib reappeared. "Just a summer storm which, thank Allah, is now over," he told a crowd from the balcony of the Revolution Palace, but foreign observers believe Nasser is still the man to watch (→29/3).

Senator McCarthy has gone too far

Feb 25. Senator Joseph McCarthy, who has recently been turning his investigation of alleged Communists in the government from the State Department to the army, today came into direct conflict with the White House, and may have gone too far.

The row began when the Senator, carrying out a one-man interrogation, told a much-decorated Brigadier General that he was "a disgrace to the uniform". He had been pressing him for information on an Army dentist who is accused of being a Communist. Afterwards the Secretary for the Army, Robert Stevens, told McCarthy that he would never allow army officers to be treated that way.

Two days ago both men met for a fried chicken lunch to resolve their differences, but it made matters worse. McCarthy put out a statement afterwards which all the morning newspapers interpreted as a complete surrender by the Army Secretary. Stevens sobbed on the telephone to senators last night and threatened to resign.

Today President Eisenhower intervened, and gave his full backing to Stevens. It was a clear warning to McCarthy that this time he had gone too far (→12/3).

French braced for showdown with guerrillas at Dien Bien Phu

Feb 19. The French forces dug in at Dien Bien Phu in Vietnam seem likely to get the decisive battle for which their commander, General Navarre, has been waiting. Reports indicate that the Viet Minh commander, General Giap, is gathering his guerrillas into large units to lay siege to the French fort.

It will be a hard nut for Giap to crack, for Dien Bien Phu is manned by some of France's best soldiers, paratroopers and Foreign Legionnaires who have prepared an extensive system of fortifications.

The French also have an airfield from which they can mount attacks on besieging forces. However, their strength in the air may also be their weakness, for if the airfield is knocked out the fortress will be cut off from reinforcements, except by parachute (→22).

French parachutists after over-running a Viet Minh machine-gun post.

1954

MARCH

Su	Mo	Tu	We	Th	Fr	Sa
	1	2	3	4	5	6
7	8	9	10	11	12	13
14	15	16	17	18	19	20
21	22	23	24	25	26	27
28	29	30	31			

1. London: MPs approve the bill creating the Atomic Energy Authority (→ 1/8).

1. Pacific: The US explodes its second hydrogen bomb at Bikini Atoll.→

1. London: It is announced that a television licence will go up from £2 to £3 from June 1 (→ 5).

5. London: The government introduces its Television Bill, which would set up an Independent Television Authority (→ 25).

7. Bonn: Adenauer urges the United States to return German private property seized during the War.

7. Kenya: Mau Mau leader "General Katanga" is captured; another leader, "General Tanganyika", surrenders.→

10. Washington: Eisenhower pledges not to involve the US in a war without a declaration of war by Congress (→ 20).

12. Washington: McCarthy claims the US Army tried to blackmail him to halt his attacks on Communists (→ 2/6).

17. Israel: 17 Israelis die in a terrorist attack on a bus near Beersheba (→ 28/3/55).

20. Washington: Eisenhower discusses Indochina with diplomatic and defence advisers and the French chief of staff (→ 31).

22. London: The London Gold Market opens for the first time since 1939; gold is priced at $35 an ounce.

25. US: William Holden and Audrey Hepburn win best acting Oscars; "From Here To Eternity" is best film.

25. London: MPs approve the establishment of commercial television (→ 22/9/56).

27. UK: Mr J.H. Griffin's Royal Tan wins the Grand National, after a race in which four horses died.

29. Cairo: General Neguib drops plans to hand power to an elected parliament (→ 18/4).

31. Washington: Eisenhower commits the US to united action to prevent a Communist takeover of South-East Asia.

Japanese fishermen burnt by H-bomb

The crew of the "Lucky Dragon" are inspected at Tokyo University.

March 22. The hydrogen bomb has claimed its first victims. The crew of a Japanese fishing boat, ironically called the Lucky Dragon, have returned to port suffering from serious radiation sickness caused by fallout from the American H-bomb test at Bikini Atoll at the beginning of the month.

The Lucky Dragon was fishing some 70 miles from Bikini, outside the prohibited zone, when the bomb exploded on March 1. To the crew it seemed as though the sun was rising in the west. A few hours later a fine white ash started to drift down. Soon two of the crew were vomiting and suffering from dizziness. Within the next day or two all members showed similar symptoms, including itchiness on the skin like sunburn. They realised something was wrong and headed for home. All the crew are now in hospital, some of them seriously ill. Tests have shown that the Lucky Dragon is heavily contaminated with radioactivity.

According to US government sources, the Bikini test was some 600 times as powerful as the bomb that destroyed Hiroshima, making it equivalent to 12 million tons of TNT. The explosion was so violent that it overwhelmed the measuring instruments, suggesting that the blast was considerably more powerful than expected (→ 2/4).

Mass surrender of Mau Mau is sought

March 9. The Kenya Government's attempt to organise the mass surrender of Mau Mau terrorists has come under fire from Europeans on the colony's Legislative Council. "Even if this unholy plan succeeds and some terrorists do surrender, the price we shall have paid will have been too high," one member said.

The security forces are using a captured Mau Mau leader, General China, to write to other terrorist leaders in the forest telling them: "Nothing further is to be gained from terrorism" (→ 11/4).

French under siege at Dien Bien Phu

March 14. The Communist Viet Minh today attacked the heavily defended French positions at Dien Bien Phu in the largest offensive yet mounted in the eight-year-old war in Indochina.

The importance of this attack cannot be exaggerated. It is clear from the strength of the initial infantry assaults that the Communists are prepared to risk the destruction of the major part of their army to defeat the French in this battle.

It is equally dangerous for the besieged French. There is no way out for them except through victory; no hope of air evacuation should they falter, and no way of marching out (→ 20).

"Third man" theory in UK spy scandal

March 21. Were missing diplomats Guy Burgess and Donald MacLean warned of their impending arrests by a third man? Rumours that they were "tipped off" before their flight by a senior diplomat colleague are rife in the corridors of Whitehall and bars of Fleet Street.

Suspicion is aimed at Harold "Kim" Philby, First Secretary at the British Embassy in Washington, a friend of Burgess. Mr Philby has been recalled to London for interrogation by MI6 (→ 14/4).

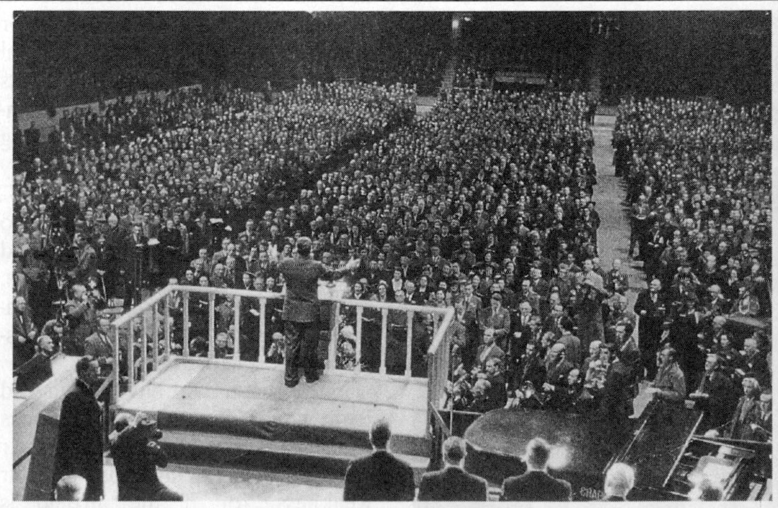

American-style "hot gospel" religion came to England when US evangelist Billy Graham drew monster crowds to Harringay arena.

1954

APRIL

Su	Mo	Tu	We	Th	Fr	Sa
				1	2	3
4	5	6	7	8	9	10
11	12	13	14	15	16	17
18	19	20	21	22	23	24
25	26	27	28	29	30	

2. New Delhi: Nehru calls for a halt to the build up of nuclear weapons (→ 5).

3. London: Oxford wins the 100th Boat Race.

5. London: Churchill says he and Roosevelt agreed in 1943 only to use an atomic bomb by mutual consent (→ 7).

7. Washington: It is announced that Eisenhower has ordered "greatly increased" production of weapons (→ 29).

11. Kenya: The authorities admit that the "General China" operation against the Mau Mau has failed.→

12. British Guiana: Dr Jagan, leader of the People's Progressive Party and ex-premier, is jailed for six months.

13. London: Britain and the US agree to study a NATO equivalent for South-East Asia and the western Pacific (→ 8/9).

14. London: Bevan resigns from the shadow cabinet over Labour's defence policy (→ 28).

14. Canberra: Soviet diplomat Vladimir Petrov asks for asylum and exposes a Soviet spy ring in Australia (→ 27).

18. Reading: At least nine babies die in a fire at a maternity home.

22. UK: The RSPCA sets out proposals for a safer Grand National, after the deaths of four horses this year.

25. Buenos Aires: Peron is re-elected and arrests four opposition leaders for "talking disrespectfully" about him (→ 14/12).

27. Canberra: Soviet defector Petrov suggests that missing diplomats Burgess and MacLean went to Moscow (→ 1/7).

28. London: Harold Wilson replaces Bevan in the Labour shadow cabinet (→ 24/6).

29. British Honduras: The anti-British People's United Party are victorious in a general election.

DEATH

10. French cinema pioneer Auguste Lumiere (*19/10/1862).

Big drive on Mau Mau

Mau Mau suspects are held under the gun as they await official screening.

April 24. After the failure of the "General China" operation to secure the mass surrender of the Mau Mau, security forces in Kenya today mounted the biggest round-up of the 18-month-old emergency.

An hour before dawn, 5,000 British and African troops, 1,000 armed police and thousands of loyal Kikuyu Home Guards moved in on Nairobi's squalid African locations. About 40,000 men will be arrested and half of them will be taken to camps for questioning.

The General China operation, named after the captured terrorist who appealed to other Mau Mau supporters to surrender, was abandoned after security forces waited 11 days for terrorist negotiators to turn up at the agreed rendezvous in the forest at the foothills of the Aberdare mountains.

A letter purporting to be from one of the negotiators was found in a cleft stick. It said other terrorists were threatening to kill them and asked for "sky-shouting aircraft" – planes fitted with loudspeakers – to fly over the forest, warning that nobody should be killed for wanting to negotiate.

Today planes are indeed flying over the forest, but they are RAF Lincoln bombers and rocket-firing Vampire jets (→ 9/5).

Father of the Bomb called a security risk

April 29. There is now a "blank wall" between atom scientist J. Robert Oppenheimer, father of the atom bomb, and nuclear secrets, President Eisenhower said today. The President added that, although he admired and respected Oppenheimer for his scientific leadership of the wartime Manhattan Project that produced the atom bomb, he had absolutely no regrets about suspending his security clearance on December 23. Oppenheimer's clearance was withdrawn after allegations that he had associated with Communists and delayed the development of the H-bomb.

Oppenheimer, who now heads the Institute for Advanced Study in Princeton, New Jersey, admits the former but denies the latter charge. President Eisenhower has appointed a three-man board to consider Oppenheimer's request for the restoration of his security clearance (→ 1/6).

Government orders Comets grounded after another crash

April 9. The Government stepped in tonight to ground all Comet jets, withdrawing their Certificates of Airworthiness until the cause of the latest crash in the Mediterranean yesterday is found.

All 14 passengers and seven crew died when an aircraft flying from Rome to Johannesburg fell into the sea 35 miles north of the island of Stromboli. The last heard of the aircraft was a message radioed half an hour after leaving Rome: "Over Naples; still climbing". It is thought the jet was flying through a storm at the time of the crash.

Yesterday's tragedy follows the disaster off Elba in January and last year's accident near Calcutta.

The chairman of the British Overseas Airways Corporation, Sir Miles Thomas, said: "We have had three inexplicable tragedies. They all follow a certain pattern on reaching or approaching maximum altitude at full power."

The aircraft will now go through full-scale tests of destruction at the Royal Aircraft Establishment, Farnborough. Meanwhile, the search for bodies and wreckage continues in the Mediterranean. The aircraft carrier Eagle has recovered five bodies, and others have been retrieved by fishing boats. Many ships are still searching, with the sea's surface lit up by flares dropped from aircraft at night (→ 14/5).

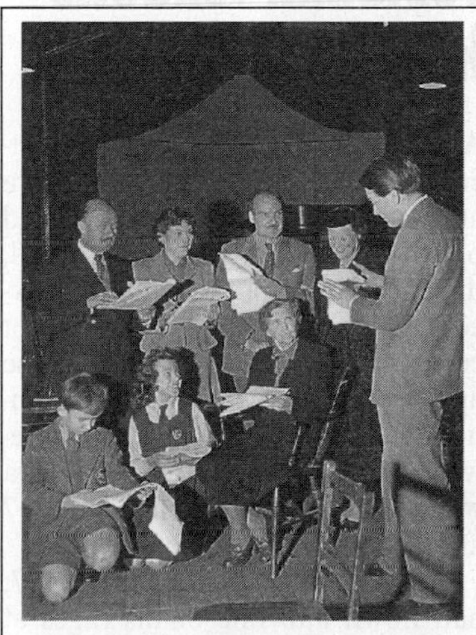

The Groves, billed as "Television's answer to the Archers", rehearse their first episode.

Independent trials of polio vaccine begin

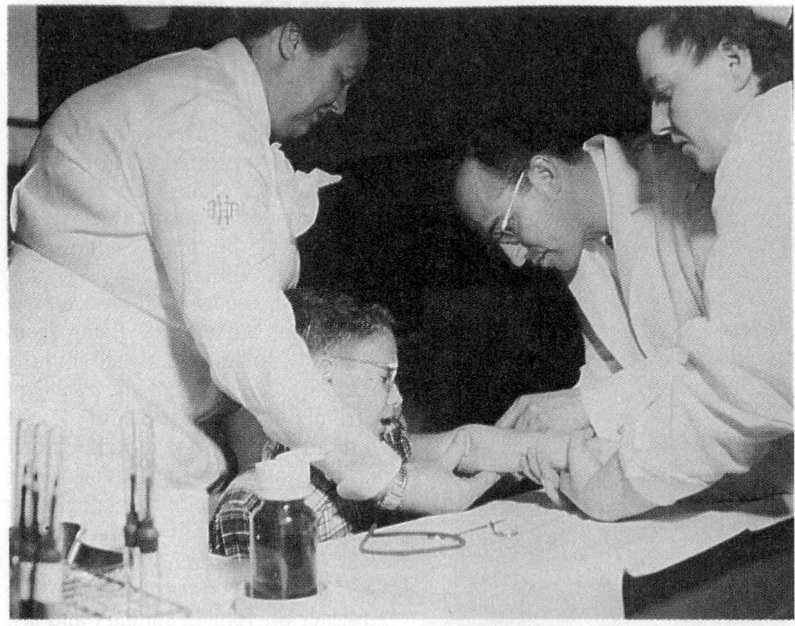

Dr Jonas Salk, discoverer of the polio vaccine, injects a small boy.

April 26. The National Foundation for Infantile Paralysis, New York, has announced that new trials of the polio vaccine already produced and tested by Dr Jonas E. Salk are to be independently organised and evaluated by Dr Thomas Francis, Jr, Chairman of the Department of Epidemiology, University of Michigan School of Public Health.

Research funds are to be controlled by the University. The findings will only be known to him and his staff and, as vaccine and dummy injections will be given under a secret coding system, they will not learn the final figures or be able to assess the efficacy of the vaccine until the very end of the trial.

In February the president of the National Foundation explained that there had been delays in producing enough of the vaccine for national trials. Most of the virus is grown at the University of Toronto and some of the vaccine manufacturers had had difficulty in killing it. New and more stringent processing controls have now been laid down and these have satisfied the National Institute of Health, he said (→12/4/55).

Toscanini conducts his final concert

April 4. Arturo Toscanini conducted the NBC Symphony Orchestra at Carnegie Hall last night, stepped off the podium on the last chord, dropped his baton and slowly walked off the platform. He did not come back to acknowledge the applause. Afterwards, it was announced that it had been his farewell concert with the orchestra which was created for him in 1937 after he had left Mussolini's Italy.

Maestro Toscanini, who is 87, had flown into one of his rages at the rehearsal and locked himself in his dressing room. He feared he could no longer trust his memory of the score.

Nasser now on top after seven weeks

April 18. Colonel Nasser is back in power as Egypt's Prime Minister, after outwitting President Neguib in a seven-week battle of wits. Neguib, sacked in February, made a come-back on a tidal wave of public support, but while Neguib was making a goodwill visit to Sudan, Nasser arrested the President's supporters at the cavalry barracks and organised demonstrations against him. Yesterday Neguib capitulated. He keeps the title of President, a figurehead without power, as he was intended to be when the young officers used him as a respectable front for their coup against Farouk (→27/7).

US warns China not to aid Vietnamese

April 8. In a typically opaque statement the US Secretary of State, John Foster Dulles, today warned China against aiding the Viet Minh in its war with France. Speaking in Washington, he said that the loss of Indochina to Communism would be a "terrific disaster" and called for a demonstration of solidarity.

He went on to say that "with a united will created, it will diminish, I hope, the need for united action. But there should be a willingness to have united action if events should be such as to require that."

Mr Dulles's statement was the result of intelligence reports which showed that China was actively helping General Giap in his assault on the beleagured French garrison at Dien Bien Phu.

Bill Haley rocks around the clock

April 12. Bill Haley and the Comets, billed as "The Nation's Rockingest Rhythm Group", look set to rocket up the charts with their latest record, "We're Gonna Rock Around the Clock" recorded today. Their special new sound, comprising a driving rhythm-and-blues dance beat, has already found success for Haley, a 29-year-old former country and western singer. The band's last release "Crazy, Man, Crazy" reached Number 14 in the charts (→19/7).

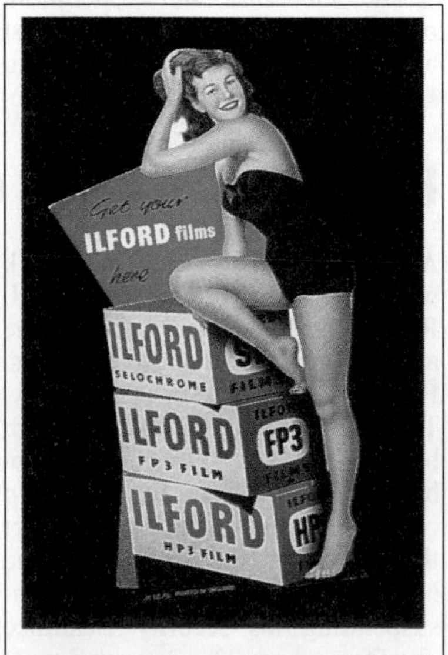

1954

MAY

Su	Mo	Tu	We	Th	Fr	Sa
						1
2	3	4	5	6	7	8
9	10	11	12	13	14	15
16	17	18	19	20	21	22
23	24	25	26	27	28	29
30	31					

1. London: West Bromwich Albion beat Preston North End 3-2 in the FA Cup Final.

3. Geneva: An international Vietnam conference opens (→8).

4.London: Housing minister Macmillan unveils plans to make house buying easier by lowering deposits (→4/7).

6. London: The Home Secretary says that the problem of "Edwardians" (Teddy Boys) is not widespread.

8. Geneva: France proposes a truce in Vietnam (→10).

9. Kenya: 25,000 Kikuyu tribesmen are reported to have been detained in a round-up in the capital Nairobi (→26).

10. Geneva: The Viet Minh reject France's call for a truce and demand freedom for Vietnam, Laos and Cambodia (→11).

11. Bangkok: The Thai government offers bases to the Western states from which to fight Communism (→21/7).

14. US: Boeing unveils the prototype 707 airliner (→20/7).

14. Athens: Communist China is granted entry to the 1956 Olympics; Nationalist China withdraws immediately.

15. UK: The Queen returns from her Commonwealth tour (→14/8/55).

22. London: 180,000 pack Wembley Stadium for the last rally of Billy Graham's tour (→30/4/5).

24. London: MPs vote themselves a pay rise from £1,000 to £1,500 a year.

26. Kenya: Mau Mau burn down the famous Treetops Hotel (→18/1/55).

29. UK: Stirling Moss and Reg Parnell win races during the first motor-racing event at the new Aintree track.

30. Karachi: East Pakistan's chief minister is sacked and charged with treason after calling for independence (→4/2/55).

DEATH

19. US composer Charles Ives (*20/10/1874).

Dien Bien Phu has fallen

French soldiers scuttle between positions at beleaguered Dien Bien Phu.

May 8. Dien Bien Phu, the French fortress in Indochina, fell to the Viet Minh today after a bloody 55-day siege. One strongpost, "Isabelle", some three miles from the main fortifications, is still holding out, but the rest has been lost in a stunning blow to French pride.

The Communists overran the last defences this morning, following an all-night battle. Just before the final wave of Viet Minh charged over the muddy battlefield, Brigadier General de Castries reported by radio telephone to Hanoi that he could hold out no longer.

In his dramatic message he said: "I have just ordered all able-bodied men to go to Isabelle by all means in their power. We can no longer do anything. We will not surrender. They're a few yards away ... now they're everywhere."

One of his last orders was to his gunners at Isabelle. He told them to open fire with their heavy artillery on his command post if the enemy broke through. Since then there has been no news of the General or of Mlle de Galard Terraube, the only woman in the fortress, who has been tending the wounded.

It was stated in Paris tonight that the garrison, now all captured or killed, numbered 16,000, including 3,000 parachuted in during the siege. French radio programmes played solemn music. All theatres have closed as a mark of mourning. It seems likely that this defeat will mark the end of French efforts to retain Indochina (→ 10).

Bannister breaks 4-minute-mile barrier

May 6. A barrier some experts once considered insurmountable, and which in recent years has become an elusive obsession for all middle-distance athletes, has at last been broken by a Briton.

Roger Bannister, a 25-year-old medical student, became the first man to run a mile in under four minutes at the university track at Iffley Road, Oxford, during a match between the University and the Amateur Athletic Association.

A chill wind threatened to hamper the world record attempt, but it dropped in time for the race; after the pace had been set in the early laps by Bannister's fellow-graduates Chris Chataway and Chris Brasher, he ran the last lap in 59 seconds to break the tape in 3 minutes 59.4 seconds, almost two seconds inside Gunder Haegg's nine-yearold record, and just three-fifths of a second inside the magic four minutes.

PATH TO FOUR-MINUTE MILE

Date	Name	Time
1 Apr 1861	J. Heaviside (Ire)	4:55-0
27 May 1861	J. Heaviside (Ire)	4:49-0
27 May 1861	N. Greene (Ire)	4:46-0
23 May 1862	George Farran (Ire)	4:33-0
10 Mar 1868	Walter Chinnery (GB)	4:29-6
3 Apr 1868	Walter Gibbs (GB)	4:28-8
31 Mar 1873	Charles Gunton (GB)	4:28-6
30 May 1874	Walter Slade (GB)	4:26-0
19 June 1875	Walter Slade (GB)	4:24-5
16 Aug 1880	Walter George (GB)	4:23-2
3 June 1882	Walter George (GB)	4:19-4
21 June 1884	Walter George (GB)	4:18-4
26 Aug 1893	Thomas Conneff (Ire/USA)	4:17-8
6 July 1895	Fred Bacon (GB)	4:17-0
30 Aug 1895	Thomas Conneff (Ire/USA)	4:15-6
27 May 1911	John Paul Jones (USA)	4:15-4
31 May 1913	John Paul Jones (USA)	4:14-4
16 July 1915	Norman Taber (USA)	4:12-6
23 Aug 1923	Paavo Nurmi (Fin)	4:10-4
4 Oct 1931	Jules Ladoumegue (Fra)	4:09-2
15 July 1933	Jack Lovelock (NZ)	4:07-6
16 June 1934	Glenn Cunningham (USA)	4:06-7
28 Aug 1937	Sydney Wooderson (GB)	4:06-4
1 July 1942	Gunder Hägg (Swe)	4:06-1
10 July 1942	Arne Andersson (Swe)	4:06-2
4 Sept 1942	Gunder Hägg (Swe)	4:04-6
1 July 1943	Arne Andersson (Swe)	4:02-6
18 July 1944	Arne Andersson (Swe)	4:01-6
17 July 1945	Gunder Hägg (Swe)	4:01-3
6 May 1954	Roger Bannister (GB)	3:59-4

Roger Bannister breasts the tape as he finishes his record mile.

Court outlaws racially separate schools

May 17. Racial segegation in the US state school system has been outlawed in a landmark decision by the Supreme Court today. The court overturned the 1896 ruling that education could be "separate but equal". Chief Justice Earl Warren wrote in his judgment: "Separated educational facilities are inherently unequal."

The decision affects about 8.5 million white children and 2.5 million Negroes attending segregated schools in the southern states. But integration will not happen without a fight. Senator Eastland of Mississippi said: "The South will not abide by nor obey this legislative decision by a political court." Mr Linder, Commissioner for Agriculture and a candidate for Governor of Georgia, said: "We are going to have segregation regardless of what the court rules" (→ 31/5/55).

IBM reveals calculating electronic brain

May 24. The electronic brain, hitherto confined to scientific laboratories, is moving into the office. The International Business Machines Corporation (IBM) has announced the development of a model specifically for business use.

The machine will consist of a central arithmetic and logic unit that will process information from a bank of cathode-ray memory tubes and from data stored on reels of magnetic tape, each able to hold as much information as a large city telephone directory. At ten million arithmetical operations an hour, the machine will raise existing calculating speeds a thousandfold.

Thirty of the brains have already been ordered, though delivery will not start until next year. IBM plans to rent the machines rather than sell them. A typical installation will cost $25,000 a month.

1954

JUNE

Su	Mo	Tu	We	Th	Fr	Sa
		1	2	3	4	5
6	7	8	9	10	11	12
13	14	15	16	17	18	19
20	21	22	23	24	25	26
27	28	29	30			

1. Washington: Atomic scientist Dr Robert Oppenheimer is found loyal and discreet, but is denied security clearance (→ 15).

2. Dublin: John Costello's Fine Gael party forms a government.

2. Washington: McCarthy alleges serious Communist infiltration of the CIA and nuclear weapons plants (→ 6).

4. S. Rhodesia: The government declares a state of emergency, as a rail strike causes coal shortages.

6. Washington: Eisenhower says he will prevent McCarthy investigating the CIA (→ 30/7).

10. UK: Edith Sitwell becomes a Dame; Somerset Maugham is made Companion of Honour.

11. UK: Publication of "Under the Net", a first novel by Iris Murdoch.

15. Washington: Dr Edward Teller claims Oppenheimer's lack of moral support delayed development of the H-bomb (→ 16).

16. Washington: Oppenheimer's successor says the H-bomb could not have been developed earlier (→ 17/2/55).

18. Paris: Pierre Mendes-France is voted premier by French MPs on a policy of making peace in Vietnam (→ 23/2/55).

21. US: The American Cancer Society says smokers aged 50 to 75 have a 75 per cent higher death rate than non-smokers (→ 29/11).

21. Finland: Australian John Landy runs the mile in three minutes 58 seconds, beating Roger Bannister's record.

24. London: The government drops a bill giving MPs a pay rise; Labour MPs protest (→ 8/7).

25. London: MPs give a second reading to the Television Bill (→ 31/7).

25. London: Doctors urge stricter drink tests on drivers than tongue-twisters and walking in a straight line (→ 8/11).

30. UK: An eclipse of the sun is visible throughout Britain.

Pope launches new Eurovision network

June 6. Pope Pius XII in Rome appeared on British TV screens tonight, and simultaneously on the screens of seven other European nations (France, West Germany, Switzerland, Italy, Belgium, Holland and Denmark) as part of a new exchange experiment between international television companies.

The feat, involving the linking-up of a complex 4000-mile long chain of relays, brings Britain not only the Pope, 900 miles away in Rome, but also pictures of a Swiss flower festival in Montreux.

Next the BBC plans to transmit their British contribution, including Glasgow police sports and the Queen at Horse Guards Parade, to the other countries involved in the link-up. In his TV address, the Pope hoped the new technology might "let the nations learn to know each other better" (→ 4/8).

Piggott is youngest Derby winner at 18

June 2. Eighteen-year-old Lester Piggott today became the youngest jockey ever to win the Derby when he rode the American-bred Never Say Die to victory at Epsom. The colt, a 33-1 outsider, won by two lengths from Arabian Night, with Darius, the 2,000 Guineas winner, a further neck away in third place.

Piggott took his mount into the lead with a furlong to go, although he had been prominent throughout. Rowston Manor, the favourite, was in the lead at Tattenham Corner, but faded to finish seventh.

It was an historic victory. Not only is Piggott believed to be the youngest-ever successful jockey, but Never Say Die was the first American-bred horse to win Britain's premier flat race since Iroquois in 1881. But Piggott's success is no surprise: he finished second two years ago.

US and UK agree on lofty peace ideals

June 29. Sir Winston Churchill and President Eisenhower tonight signed what they are calling the Potomac Agreement at the end of weekend talks in Washington. It referred in lofty generalities to their "intimate comradeship" in pursuit of world peace and justice.

In public the Prime Minister spoke about "the unbroken and unbreakable unity of the Anglo-American world". He wished the President good luck and Mr Eisenhower replied: "The same to you, Sir".

Privately there was uneasy talk between the US Secretary of State, Mr Dulles, and the Foreign Secretary, Mr Eden, about French Indo-china. Both accepted that Vietnam will have to be partitioned and the non-Communist part protected.

Sir Winston Churchill during his investment with the Order of the Garter, the highest level of knighthood that can be conferred as a British honour.

1954

JULY

Su	Mo	Tu	We	Th	Fr	Sa
				1	2	3
4	5	6	7	8	9	10
11	12	13	14	15	16	17
18	19	20	21	22	23	24
25	26	27	28	29	30	31

1. Canberra: Soviet defector Petrov tells an espionage commission that Soviet TASS pressmen are all spies (→ 23).

3. Wimbledon: Maureen Connolly beats Louise Brough for her third successive Women's Singles title.→

5. London: The government publishes plans for civil defence in the event of an H-bomb attack (→ 1/1/55).

8. London: Labour MPs accept the government's proposal for a £2 daily allowance rather than a pay rise (→ 28/9).

8. UK: Plans are unveiled for a new Scottish steel plant near Motherwell (→ 2/11).

9. UK: Australian golfer Peter Thomson, at 24, becomes the youngest winner of the British Open championship.

12. Vienna: Reports say at least 27 people have died in the worst floods in central Europe for over 100 years.

19. US: Recording of "That's All Right Mama", the first "single" by Mississippi-born singer Elvis Presley (→ 31/1/55).

20. UK: A public enquiry approves the expansion of Gatwick Airport (→ 27/9).

22. New York: Premiere of the musical film, "Seven Brides for Seven Brothers".

23. East Berlin: East German radio broadcasts a message from missing West Berlin security boss Otto John (→ 28/2/55).

24. Peking: The Chinese government apologises for the "accidental" shooting down of a British airliner yesterday (→ 9/8).

27. London: The government presents a bill to introduce a new Highway Code.

30. Washington: The Senate begins debating the possible censure of Senator McCarthy (→ 24/8).

31. London: The Television Bill gets Royal Assent (→ 4/8).

31. Paris: Mendes-France offers Tunisia autonomy (→ 27/8).

Sino-French pact ends Indo-China war

July 21. Agreement was reached in Geneva in the early hours of this morning to bring peace to Indochina. The main provision of the treaty calls for the division of Vietnam along the 17th Parallel, with the Communist Viet Minh controlling the north and Emperor Bao Dai controlling the south with French support.

The last major disagreements in these long-drawn-out negotiations were smoothed out during intricate discussions at La Bocage, the villa of the French delegation. The agreement is still far from perfect, but it is considered the best that could be arrived at inside the time limit – "midnight or never", set by the French Prime Minister, Pierre Mendes-France.

One weakness is that there will be no joint guarantee actually signed by all the Geneva Conference powers. The US is to make a unilateral declaration that it will not upset an agreement it can respect, while the other eight powers are expected to make verbal statements supporting the settlement. The formal record of the plenary session at which these statements are made will constitute the "guarantee".

Both sides in the Vietnam struggle meet in Trung Gia for a cease-fire.

M. Mendes-France obviously believes that he has achieved his objective of reaching "an honourable settlement"; others are less convinced. Senator Knowland, the Republican leader in the US Senate, said last night that the results of Geneva "will be considered throughout the Far East as a considerable victory for Communism in that area".

He prophesied: "We may regret that such an agreement has been forced upon the French" (→ 8/10).

British troops to pull out of Suez

July 27. The 65,000 British troops and airmen, and 18,000 men of the King's African Rifles, are to be pulled out of the Suez Canal base, under an agreement reached today with the Egyptian leader, Colonel Nasser. The evacuation of "Imperialist British forces" from the Canal Zone has been a prime policy aim of Nasser and the young officers from the moment they seized power two years ago.

British arms and equipment will be mothballed and the base will be maintained by Egyptian civilians. Britain retains the right to reactivate the base in the event of an attack on Turkey or an Arab state. The last British troops should leave the Canal Zone towards the end of 1956.

British forces have been in Egypt for almost 75 years, having been sent there in 1881 to suppress a revolution led by an earlier Egyptian army colonel, Ahmed Ali, who objected to Europeans being brought in to rescue the country's finances (→ 19/10).

Czech wins longest final at Wimbledon

July 2. Jaroslav Drobny, the 32-year-old Czech with Egyptian nationality, today won the singles title after the longest-ever final at Wimbledon, beating Australia's Ken Rosewall 13-11, 4-6, 6-2, 9-7.

Drobney wins, despite a bad knee.

Books are burned as rationing lifted

July 3. Housewives ceremonially tore up their ration books in Trafalgar Square last night as the Government announced the end of all rationing after 14 years. Meat was the last item to go, and already butchers were predicting price rises.

For the first time since the beginning of the war, Smithfield Market was open at midnight, instead of 6am, for the delivery of meat. Porters at the market were handling huge sides of beef, some weighing as much as 400 pounds. "We haven't seen the like since 1939," said a market spokesman. "It's extraordinarily good quality meat, too."

Members of the National Federation of Housewives were patrolling butchers' shops with notebooks today to check prices. "If we find that prices are not falling, we will hold protest meetings," said their Chairman.

Ration books were burned at several Conservative Association meetings (→ 8/7).

Germans beat Wunderteam for the Cup

July 4. Once again the "best" team has lost the World Cup in its final stages. The Hungarians provided the highest class of football in the early rounds in Switzerland and, in Koscis, gave the tournament a decisive top scorer with 11 goals. In the semi-final they scored four goals against the champions Uruguay (who had, in turn, beaten England 4-2 in the previous round and humiliated Scotland 7-0).

In the Berne final they faced Germany, who had beaten Austria 6-1 in the other semi-final. Hungary built up an early 2-0 lead, then lost their momentum. Germany drew level before half-time and, with six minutes left, Rahn scored Germany's winner.

West Germany's Rahn drives home his team's second, and equalising goal.

1954

AUGUST

Su	Mo	Tu	We	Th	Fr	Sa
1	2	3	4	5	6	7
8	9	10	11	12	13	14
15	16	17	18	19	20	21
22	23	24	25	26	27	28
29	30	31				

1. London: The UK Atomic Energy Authority is established (→20/1/55).

4. UK: Maiden flight of Britain's first supersonic fighter, the English Electric P-1 "Lightning" (→6/9).

4. London: The Independent Television Authority is set up under chairman Sir Kenneth Clark (→22/9/55).

5. Teheran: Britain and Iran sign a deal to give Anglo-Iranian Oil up to £238 million for nationalisation of its oil.

9. Taipei: Chinese Nationalists sink eight Communist Chinese gunboats off Formosa (→14).

10. UK: Sir Gordon Richards retires from the saddle.

10. The Hague: Indonesia and Holland sever their last remaining political ties.

14. Peking: A Labour Party delegation led by Clement Attlee arrives for talks (→17).

17. Washington: Eisenhower commits the US 7th Fleet to stop China invading Formosa (→6/9).

20. Athens: 78 are hurt in a march on the British Embassy by supporters of Enosis, the union of Cyprus with Greece (→18/12).

22. Switzerland: Juan Fangio of the Argentine wins the Swiss Grand Prix to become world motor racing champion.

24. US: Eisenhower outlaws the Communist Party (→27/11).

24. Rio de Janeiro: Brazilian president Getulio Vargas resigns amid corruption allegations and commits suicide.

26. UK: Publication of "The Fellowship of the Ring" by Oxford English professor John R.R. Tolkien.

28. Detroit: The US Amateur Golf Championship is won by Arnold Palmer.

29. Switzerland: Roger Bannister wins a gold medal in the 1,500 metres at the European Games.

31. UK: Surrey are County Cricket Champions for the third successive year.

Maiden flight for the new Boeing 707

July 15. America entered the era of jet air transport today when the four-engined Boeing 707 made its maiden flight from Seattle. The new aircraft uses many of the developments of Boeing's massive jet bomber programmes, but with its engines hung individually in pods beneath the wings so that a failure or fire in one would not affect another.

William E. Boeing's aircraft is much larger than the world's first passenger jet, the Comet, having a wing span of 130 feet and a length of 128 feet. It will be able to carry 219 passengers at a top speed over 600 mph.

Much of the cash for the development of the new jet comes from the US Air Force, which wants to buy it in a tanker form to refuel other aircraft in the air (→20).

Rabbits on the run from myxomatosis

July 1. Britain's rabbit population is close to being wiped out in some counties by the virus myxomatosis. In Kent, where last year the disease first caught hold, Sussex, and the south-west, farmers believe 90 per cent of burrows are affected.

But now environmentalists fear the rabbit may become a rare sight, and ecologists say the balance of nature will be disturbed badly if the epidemic continues. Farmers say the virus is necessary to stop rabbits damaging crops worth £50 million every year.

French colonies to get self-government

Aug 27. The French premier, Pierre Mendes-France, is desperately trying to steer a middle course between African nationalists, demanding independence, and French conservatives, afraid he will give away valuable colonial interests. His solution is to offer Morocco and Tunisia autonomy, but not yet independence.

M. Mendes-France had flown to Tunis to recognise Tunisia's "internal autonomy". Tonight he was back in Paris to see the National Assembly approve his policy of giving Morocco a system of regional assemblies.

The battle is not over yet, however. In Morocco, rioters are calling for the return of the exiled former Sultan, Sidi Mohammed Ben Youssef, who was deposed by France last year (→3/6/55).

Mendes-France flies in for talks.

Morning calm returns as UN quits Korea

Aug 12. The United Nations Command officially withdrew from Korea today, a year after the ceasefire was signed at Panmunjon, marking the end to three years of a bloody war over which the nuclear threat always loomed.

The "land of the morning calm" now reverts to what it was before the war – a land divided between the bitterly hostile regimes of the Communists in the North and the Republic in the South.

However, while the war appears to have had little effect on the political structure of Korea, it has played a major role in world affairs, with the UN taking to the battlefield for the first time to resist aggression.

Triumph and disaster mark Empire Games

Aug 8. Triumph and near-tragedy for British athletes marked the end of the Empire and Commonwealth Games in Vancouver.

First, in the much-heralded "Mile of the Century", Roger Bannister tracked, outmanoeuvred and finally outpaced the only other man to have run a four-minute mile, John Landy of Australia.

Then, with the crowd still buzzing with excitement, 35-year-old Jim Peters entered the stadium fully a quarter of an hour ahead of the marathon field – but exhausted in the 80-degree heat.

He swayed from side to side, staggered and fell to the cinder track and, with many of the hushed crowd in tears, collapsed half a lap from the finish. He was given oxygen on the track and rushed to hospital for treatment.

Peters falls after leading the race.

1954

SEPTEMBER

Su	Mo	Tu	We	Th	Fr	Sa
			1	2	3	4
5	6	7	8	9	10	11
12	13	14	15	16	17	18
19	20	21	22	23	24	25
26	27	28	29	30		

3. UK: The National Trust buys Fair Isle.

5. Dublin: 28 die when a Dutch KLM airliner crashes into the River Shannon.

6. UK: Rolls-Royce reveals it has developed a jet that takes off vertically, nicknamed the "Flying Bedstead" (→27/10).

8. Manila: Eight nations sign a defence pact for south-east Asia and the south-west Pacific region (→25/2/55).

10. Algeria: 1,000 are now believed to have died from yesterday's earthquake (→1/11).

14. London: Opening of Kidbrooke School, the LCC's first new comprehensive.

17. New York: World heavyweight champ Rocky Marciano beats Ezzard Charles for his 47th consecutive victory.

19. UK: The Federation of British Sun Clubs, a nudist organisation, holds its first annual meeting.

22. London: Premiere of Lennox Berkeley's opera, "Nelson".

24. London: A temple to the Roman god "Mithras" is discovered near the Mansion House.

27. Japan: 1,700 people are reported to have drowned after a ferry capsized (→15/11).

27. Peking: The People's Congress re-elects Mao as party chairman and names General Chu-teh his deputy (→9/2/55).

28. UK: The Labour Party votes by a narrow majority in favour of German rearmament (→29).

28. UK: The British Motor Company unveils its latest model, the Austin Cambridge.

28. Washington: Defector and former Polish security boss, Josef Swiatlo, is granted political asylum.

29. UK: Bevan attacks Labour's political and trade union leaders (→23/11).

DEATH

8. French painter Andre Derain (*10/6/1880).

Quake hits Algeria: 1,000 feared dead

This tiny victim is left homeless.

Sept 9. In just 12 seconds, a large Algerian town today was levelled by an earthquake which left 800 dead. Its destruction was so widespread that rescue workers believe most of Orleansville will have to be abandoned. Huge, gaping cracks formed in the streets, and those blocks of flats which did not collapse after the first major tremor were in ruins by the third. Of 70 shocks in the area in 24 hours, 16 were violent. An estimated 36,000 people have been made homeless.

Troops have been sent from all over the North African territory to help dig out the dead and injured. The death toll could exceed 1,000, say relief agencies (→10).

Red Chinese bomb Nationalist islands

Sept 6. Chinese Communist forces are still bombarding Nationalist targets on the island of Quemoy today, after an attack yesterday which lasted five hours and killed two US Army officers. Quemoy, the site of the first major Nationalist victory over the Communists in 1949, is only a few miles off the mainland. In reply the Formosa-based Nationalist president, Chiang Kai-shek, has attacked Communist-held Tateng Island (→27).

1954

OCTOBER

Su	Mo	Tu	We	Th	Fr	Sa
					1	2
3	4	5	6	7	8	9
10	11	12	13	14	15	16
17	18	19	20	21	22	23
24	25	26	27	28	29	30
31						

1. Nigeria: A federal constitution comes into effect.

2. London: A nine-power conference admits West Germany to NATO, but without its own nuclear arms (→30/12).

5. US: Marilyn Monroe sues DiMaggio for divorce citing conflicting career demands.

5. London: Italy, Yugoslavia, Britain and the US sign a treaty to end the Allied occupation of Trieste (→25).

6. UK: British premiere of Britten's opera, "The Turn of the Screw", first performed in Venice earlier this year.

8. Vietnam: Viet Minh troops begin to occupy Hanoi; US ships help move thousands of refugees to South Vietnam.→

12. S. Africa: the Prime Minister Daniel Malan, chief architect of apartheid, will retire at the end of next month (→2/12).

14. UK: Emperor Haile Selassie of Ethiopia begins a state visit (→4/11/55).

15. UK: Publication of William Golding's novel, "Lord of the Flies".

16. North America: 118 are reported dead after Hurricane Hazel ravaged eight US states.

19. Cairo: Britain and Egypt sign the Suez Canal agreement; British troops are to withdraw within 20 months.→

25. Trieste: British and US troops leave; all but a narrow strip of the city passes to Italy, the remainder to Yugoslavia.

27. London: Mountbatten is appointed First Sea Lord (→22/4/55).

27. Cairo: A mob burns the headquarters of the extreme Moslem Brotherhood (→29).

29. Egypt: Several Moslem Brotherhood leaders are rounded up following the attempt to kill Nasser (→13/11).

29. UK: Dockworkers' leaders end the month-old strike (→1/11).

30. Stockholm: The Swedish parliament approves the introduction of a national health care system.

Dock strike cuts UK sea trade in half

Oct 20. An estimated 51,000 port workers were on strike today in a national dispute which has halted half Britain's sea trade. The figure was reached when dockers at Hull, Southampton and Rochester voted today to join London dockers whose action began three weeks ago. Strikers, representing about two-thirds of the total work-force, claim they face compulsory overtime under changes to the Dock Labour Scheme. Sir Walter Monckton, the Minister of Labour, is expected to intervene to try and end the deadlock (→29).

Metal fatigue key to jet crash riddle

Oct 19. Metal fatigue has been blamed as the cause of the crash of the Comet jet off Elba earlier this year. Experts at the Royal Aircraft Establishment in Farnborough have discovered that part of the cabin roof containing the radio direction-finding aerial for the aircraft is quite likely to break up as a result of fatigue in an aircraft of an age of that involved in the Elba disaster.

The results of this scientific detective work have now been presented to the inquiry into that crash and the disaster involving another Comet which crashed mysteriously near Naples in April (→18/12).

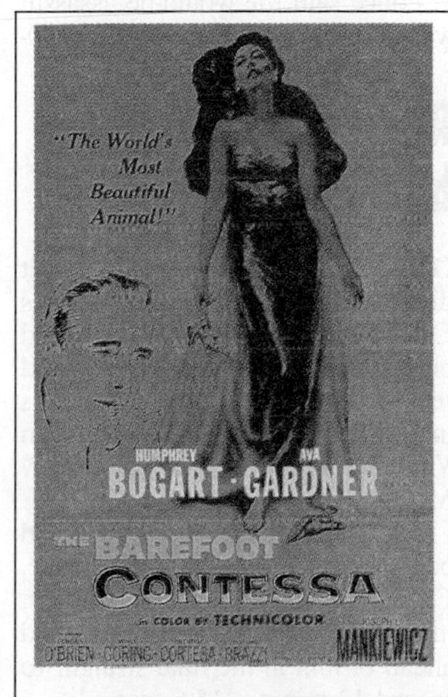

Nasser survives assassination attempt

Besieged in a train, Colonel Nasser acknowledges his fervent supporters.

Oct 26. Egypt's strongman, Colonel Gamal Abdel Nasser, escaped an assassination attempt tonight in Alexandria, where he was addressing a mass rally to celebrate the signing of the Anglo-Egyptian agreement for the withdrawal of British troops from the Canal Zone.

A man in the crowd fired several shots, all of which missed Nasser, and hit an electric light bulb above his head. "Catch that man," Nasser cried. "Gamal Abdel Nasser is safe. My blood is for you."

Police said the would-be assassin was Mahmoud Abdel Latif, a 20-year-old tinsmith from Cairo. He was found to be carrying a membership card of the fanatical Moslem Brotherhood. Within hours, police were rounding up Brotherhood members in Cairo and Alexandra.

The incident will almost certainly help Nasser in his drive for absolute power. He has already defeated the old politicians and the cautious moderates among the other young officers on the Revolutionary Command Council. Now the Brotherhood has exposed itself, and Nasser will not hesitate to strike hard (→ 27).

Record 5,000m run by Chris Chataway

Oct 13. In one of the greatest distance races ever seen Chris Chataway, the 23-year-old Oxford blue, broke the 5,000 metres world record by a remarkable five seconds in beating the European champion Vladimir Kuts in the London v Moscow match at the White City.

In front of an ecstatic crowd, and before a live TV audience, Chataway tracked the relentless, machine-like Kuts and inched ahead of him in the final straight to record 13 minutes 15.6 seconds.

Uncle Ho returns to a red Hanoi

Oct 10. Ho Chi Minh, the Communist leader who has been in hiding for eight years, has returned to Hanoi with little fanfare. The only announcement he made was a request for residents to keep the peace and go back to work.

Ho left the limelight to the military. Hanoi was awash with red as General Giap led thousands of soldiers through sectors that France evacuated yesterday under the terms of the armistice. The Tricouleur will fly no more (→ 29/4/55).

1954

NOVEMBER

Su	Mo	Tu	We	Th	Fr	Sa
	1	2	3	4	5	6
7	8	9	10	11	12	13
14	15	16	17	18	19	20
21	22	23	24	25	26	27
28	29	30				

1. UK: The dock strike officially ends.

2. Washington: Texan Lyndon B. Johnson will head the Senate in the new Democrat-controlled Congress.

2. London: The government ends the wartime system of issuing licences to builders (→ 1/12).

5. UK: Broadcaster Richard Dimbleby turns down a £10,000 a year offer to work for ITV.

8. London: MPs approve the new Highway Code (→ 8/12).

12. Paris: Interior Minister Francois Mitterrand says France will send troop reinforcements to Algeria (→ 5/1/55).

13. Cairo: Nasser ousts President Neguib and puts him under house arrest (→ 17).

15. Scandinavia: SAS begins the first scheduled flights to the western US over the North Pole, saving 500 miles (→ 23/1/55).

17. Cairo: Nasser assumes the powers, but not the title, of ousted President Neguib (→ 24/8/55).

23. London: The Labour Whip is withdrawn from seven MPs who voted against German rearmament (→ 16/3/55).

27. US: Ex-State Department employee Alger Hiss is released from prison after 44 months (→ 2/12).

29. Washington: The US National Cancer Institute claims a definite link between cancer and cigarette smoking.

DEATHS

3. French artist Henri Matisse (*31/12/1869).

15. British actor Lionel Barrymore (*28/4/1878).

28. Italian physicist Enrico Fermi (*29/9/01).

29. British comedian Sir George Robey, born George Wade (*20/9/1869).

30. German conductor Wilhelm Furtwangler (*25/1/1886).

Churchill's portrait less than pleasing

Churchill: force and candour?

Nov 30. Sir Winston Churchill celebrated his 80th birthday today by receiving a portrait from his fellow MPs, at a televised ceremony at Westminster Hall. Mr Attlee presented the painting by Graham Sutherland, who is noted for being pitilessly unflattering towards his sitters, such as Somerset Maugham and Helena Rubinstein. The artist shows Churchill seated, from below, gripping the arms of his chair. There is no sign of an impish Churchillian grin or cigar.

In his speech Sir Winston referred to it with marked lack of enthusiasm as "a remarkable example of modern art". To laughter he added: "It certainly combines force and candour." It is not known where it will hang.

Nationalist riots flare in Algeria

Nov 1. The trail of terror makes grisly reading: seven dead, 14 wounded, farmsteads destroyed, military and police targets hit. An orchestrated wave of partisan violence, centred on the Aures district, broke out in Algeria last night. The atrocities are said to be the work of nationalist terrorists, led by Ahmed Ben Bella and based in Cairo. The French were warned of the attack last week, but could do nothing – they have just seven gendarmes in Aures (→ 12).

1954

DECEMBER

Su	Mo	Tu	We	Th	Fr	Sa
			1	2	3	4
5	6	7	8	9	10	11
12	13	14	15	16	17	18
19	20	21	22	23	24	25
26	27	28	29	30	31	

1. UK: Old Age Pensions go up 7/6d. a week to £2 (→ 7).

2. Pretoria: Johannes Strijdom succeeds Malan as prime minister (→ 10/1/55).

7. London: The government announces plans to expand technical training (→ 14/1/55).

8. London: Publication of the Road Traffic Bill, which would bring in roadworthiness tests and parking meters.

9. London: Dr Roger Bannister retires from athletics to devote himself to his medical practice.

10. Stockholm: Nobel Prizes go to Max Born (UK) and Walther Bothe (Germany, Physics); Linus Pauling (US, Chemistry); John Enders, Thomas Weller and Frederick Robbins (US, Medicine); Ernest Hemingway (US, Literature); and in Oslo to the Office of the UN High Commissioner for Refugees.

14. Argentina: Divorce is legalised (→ 20/5/55).

17. London: The British Petroleum Co. is formed, owning 40 per cent of the new National Iranian Oil Company.

18. New York: 26 die when an Italian Airways airliner crashes at Idlewild Airport (→ 25).

19. London: Labour MP Anthony Wedgwood Benn wants to renounce his title of Viscount Stansgate (→ 18/2/55).

25. UK: 28 die and eight are rescued when a BOAC Stratocruiser crashes at Prestwick Airport.

30. Paris: The French parliament approves West German re-armament and NATO membership.

HITS OF 1954

Fly me to the moon.

Rock Around the Clock.

QUOTE OF THE YEAR

"What you said hurt me very much. I cried all the way to the bank."

Wladziu Valentino Liberace, entertainer, rebutting adverse criticism, 1954.

McCarthy is condemned by Congress

Red-baiting McCarthy takes on the US Army, and finally goes too far.

Dec 2. Senator Joseph McCarthy was condemned today by the US Senate for conduct unbecoming to a Senator. The vote was 67 to 22, with all the Democrats and about half the Republicans voting against the Wisconsin Senator.

Although McCarthy said he was determined to go on to investigate Communists in defence establishments, today's decision is clearly the beginning of the end of his influence. Next January the chairmanship of the Senate investigating committee passes to a Democrat.

He still has his supporters, however. Senator Jenner charged today that Democrats had allowed the Communists into government and that there was even evidence that they had penetrated the Republican Party.

British bars stoned by rioters in Cyprus

Dec 18. The Greek flag flew briefly outside the police station in Limassol today when a gang of youths, demanding union with Greece, tore down the Union Jack and raised the Greek flag in its place. Two of the rioters were subsequently shot when British troops were ordered to fire on the crowd.

In other parts of the town, which is situated on the south of the island, British-owned bars were stoned by mobs of chanting Cypriots. A British van was overturned and set alight, and fire brigade hoses were cut by the demonstrators.

It took police in Nicosia until late in the evening to control the disturbances and, when the Greek demonstrators had dispersed, a small group of Turks using sticks broke the windows of Greek-owned shops.

Forty-two Cypriots were arrested in the riots, which were sparked off when the United Nations announced that they had shelved a demand by the Greek Government that Cyprus be given the right of self-determination (→ 30/6/55).

Arts: radio dives into the sloe-black, slow sea of Llaregub

The radio play that **Dylan Thomas** had been promising the BBC for ten years was finished just before he left for New York, never to return. "Under Milk Wood" went out on the air with the voice of **Richard Burton** narrating Thomas's rich description of the little Welsh town of Llaregub (named for its meaning spelt backwards) beside "the sloe-black, slow, black, crow-black, fishing-boat-bobbing sea". The play's word-music and Rabelaisian humour won it instant success.

"Lord of the Flies" by **William Golding** gave its readers a frisson of horror when they realised that the schoolboys wrecked on a desert island, reverting to brute selfishness when bereft of adult supervision, were meant to be an allegory of us all when in extremis.

Ernest Hemingway's allegory, "The Old Man of the Sea", which won him this year's Nobel Prize, is more hopeful of human nature. It describes the fight to the death between an old Cuban fisherman and a giant marlin, which he tows home triumphantly only to have its carcase demolished by sharks. The old man is uplifted, not defeated.

James Stewart and Grace Kelly in Hitchcock's film "Rear Window".

A new voice, **Kingsley Amis** portrays a new comic hero in "Lucky Jim". Jim Dixon is an ex-grammar school ex-corporal, lecturing at a provincial university (like Amis). Exasperated by his professor and environment, he gets his own way by being rude, crude and subversive. If he weren't so funny, he would be insufferable.

1955

JANUARY

Su	Mo	Tu	We	Th	Fr	Sa
						1
2	3	4	5	6	7	8
9	10	11	12	13	14	15
16	17	18	19	20	21	22
23	24	25	26	27	28	29
30	31					

1. UK: The Vickers Valiant enters service with the RAF; it is the first British aircraft able to carry atomic bombs.

2. Panama: President Jose Remon is assassinated (→20/8).

5. Paris: Interior Minister Francois Mitterrand proposes integrating Algeria with France.

9. London: 400 Jamaicans arrive to find work.→

10. New York: Marian Anderson becomes the first black singer to sing at the Metropolitan Opera House.

10. S. Africa: The African National Congress plans protests at the planned eviction of blacks from Johannesburg (→10/2).

13. New York: Chase National Bank and Bank of Manhattan announce their merger.

14. UK: Petrol goes up 5d. a gallon to 4/6d. a gallon (→3/2).

18. Nairobi: Kenya's governor Sir Evelyn Baring offers an amnesty to Mau Mau.→

20. Switzerland: The World Health Organisation says in a report that atomic waste can be a serious health risk (→15/2).

21. UK: Archaeologists confirm suspicions that "Piltdown Man" was a complete hoax.

22. UK: Joe Davis achieves snooker's first official highest break of 147.

23. UK: 17 die and 43 are hurt when the York to Bristol express is derailed at Sutton Coldfield (→25).

23. Madrid: Franco implies that Prince Juan Carlos, grandson of Alfonso XIII, might be a future Spanish king (→1/11).

25. London: The government announces a scheme to give most women civil servants the same pay as men by 1961.

25. London: The government unveils details of a £1,240 million plan to electrify the railways (→1/4).

27. UK: Premiere of Michael Tippett's opera "The Midsummer Marriage".

31. New York: RCA demonstrates a music "synthesiser".

Immigration increases from West Indies

Some of Britain's West Indian immigrants on a night out in Birmingham.

Jan 23. Three hundred and eighty Jamaican immigrants were played ashore by a ship's band today when they landed at Plymouth. One described their feelings as a mixture of hope and anxiety. The group is the latest in a growing number of West Indians seeking homes and jobs in Britain. Two weeks ago 400, half of them women, arrived in London after a 20-day journey which cost each of them over £80.

There has already been concern about the numbers arriving, often with little or no money, and a government decision on controls is expected shortly.

Many of the immigrants are joining friends and families already here. Some have trades, others are willing to learn new skills or take whatever is available.

Today's group travelled on the liner, Fairsea, specially fitted for the migration traffic with 60-berth dormitories. Captain George Gladioli said: "They were among the cleanest, most respectable and intelligent passengers I have ever carried." The special boat train to London was met by several hundred Jamaicans. One man did claim that his countrymen were being given a false picture of life in Britain. "I cannot save anything of my wages," he said (→7/2).

Mau Mau amnesty infuriates whites

Jan 19. Mau Mau terrorists in Kenya were offered an amnesty today. They were told that, if they surrendered immediately, they would not be hanged, though they may be held in detention. The news brought a bitter reaction from the colony's Europeans. Humphrey Slade, leader of the moderate group on the Legislative Council, said: "This means that men who have killed inoffensive civilians by panga slashing, men who have disembowelled babies before their mothers' eyes, men who have eaten the brains of their human victims, will not even be prosecuted" (→21/4).

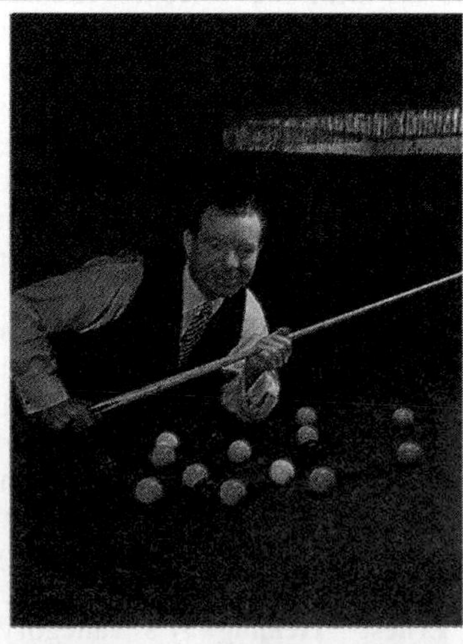

Joe Davis, Britain's snooker champion, who made the first-ever maximum break of 147 to be captured on television.

1955

FEBRUARY

Su	Mo	Tu	We	Th	Fr	Sa
		1	2	3	4	5
6	7	8	9	10	11	12
13	14	15	16	17	18	19
20	21	22	23	24	25	26
27	28					

1. US: Tornadoes kill 29 in the state of Mississippi.

3. UK: Figures show a record 347,605 new homes were built in Britain last year (→3/3).

4. London: Commonwealth leaders of government agree that Pakistan can be a republic within the Commonwealth (→7/8).

7. UK: An increase is reported in firms refusing to employ non-white workers (→8/3).

8. London: London Transport announces plans for a new tube line from Victoria to Walthamstow.

9. China: Compulsory military service is introduced (→4/4).

10. London: MPs vote by a majority of 31 to keep the death penalty (→28/4).

14. London: The National and Tate Gallery Act comes into force, making the Tate an independent institution.

15. London: The government unveils plans for 12 nuclear power stations in the next decade, costing £300 million.

17. London: A defence white paper says Britain is making hydrogen bombs (→1/3).

18. London: The Lords rejects Anthony Wedgwood Benn's bid to renounce the Stansgate title (→26/4).

22. US: Maureen "Little Mo" Connolly announces her retirement from competitive tennis; she plans to get married.

23. Paris: Edgar Faure takes over as premier after Mendes-France's is defeated on his North African policy.

25. Bangkok: The South-East Asia Treaty Organisation (SEATO) holds its first meeting.

25. UK: 70 main roads are impassable because of snow and ice.

28. Moscow: Missing British atomic scientist Bruno Pontecorvo says he is now working in the USSR (→4/3).

BIRTH

24. French racing driver Alain Prost.

Soviet premier quits, confessing failure

Marshal Bulganin, the new Soviet leader, visits Russian miners.

Feb 8. Nikita Khrushchev emerged today as undisputed master of the Soviet Union when his rival, Georgi Malenkov, was ousted after nearly two years in office. Khrushchev, who as First Secretary of the Communist Party has been laying down the law on every aspect of Soviet policy, forced Malenkov's resignation at a meeting of the Supreme Soviet.

In a letter of resignation which surprised delegates, Malenkov said that his "lack of experience" held back Soviet economic and agricultural progress. He was replaced by Marshal Nikolai Bulganin, the Defence Minister.

Khrushchev has been building up his power bases within the Soviet system, and at the same time launching himself as an international figure. He may not be the actual leader, but there are already signs he is moving the Soviet leadership towards a new strategy by modifying some of the more repressive elements of Stalinism (→31/5).

60,000 blacks to be evicted in S. Africa

Feb 10. In a military-style operation, 3,000 South African police, armed with Sten guns, swept into Sophiatown to begin removing some 60,000 Africans from the township and razing the homes.

Under the white Nationalist Government's new legislation Sophiatown, west of Johannesburg, has been designated a white residential area. It is, in fact, next to an existing white suburb. The displaced Africans were taken to Meadowlands, a new township 11 miles distant; most were freeholders in Sophiatown, but in Meadowlands they will be just tenants.

The African National Congress, forbidden to hold public meetings or call strikes, says it will protest by holding "Days of Prayer" to keep people from work (→26/6).

Motorway network planned for Britain

Feb 2. In a four-year plan to modernise Britain's road system, £212 million will be spent on new motorways and traffic black spots. New routes are planned from London to Yorkshire and from Birmingham to Preston. Nine or more towns will be unclogged by by-passes, including Doncaster, Grantham, and Maidenhead.

Coming only a fortnight after a 15-year plan to transform the railways and bring the steam era to an end, this adds up to a massive investment, but MPs have been quick to point out notable omissions. No Severn bridge is planned, nor a motorway to the Channel ports. The British Roads Federation goes so far as to call the scheme as "falling far short of the nation's urgent need".

1955

MARCH

Su	Mo	Tu	We	Th	Fr	Sa
		1	2	3	4	5
6	7	8	9	10	11	12
13	14	15	16	17	18	19
20	21	22	23	24	25	26
27	28	29	30	31		

1. London: Churchill reaffirms his belief in a nuclear deterrent (→8/5).

2. Australia: 200 die in flooding which leaves 44,000 homeless; 300,000 sheep die in New South Wales.

2. Cambodia: King Norodom Sihanouk abdicates in favour of his father Prince Norodom Suramarit.

3. London: The City is to become a "smokeless zone" from the beginning of October, it is announced (→4).

4. London: The Burnham committee recommends equal pay for women teachers, to be achieved in stages (→19/4).

4. Moscow: British defector Pontecorvo denies he is working on Soviet nuclear projects (→18/9).

8. UK: Bus crews in West Bromwich re-impose a colour bar which has already led to strikes.

11. London: Poet Stephen Spender walks out of a literary lunch after a speech criticising "obscure" modern verse.

13. S. Africa: The first production model of the new turbo-prop Bristol Britannia arrives from Britain.

16. London: Labour MPs vote to withdraw the Labour whip from Aneurin Bevan (→5/4).

20. New York: Premiere of the film "Blackboard Jungle" with Sidney Poitier.

22. UK: A new Highway Code is published.

24. New York: Premiere of Tennessee Williams' play "Cat on a Hot Tin Roof".

26. UK: Mrs W. Welman's Quare Times wins the Grand National.

30. US: Marlon Brando and Grace Kelly win best acting Oscars; "On the Waterfront" is best film.

DEATHS

11. British biologist Sir Alexander Fleming, 1945 Nobel Prize winner (*6/8/1881).

12. US jazz musician Charlie Parker (*29/8/20).

Israeli reprisal raid on the Gaza Strip

Feb 28. Israeli forces killed 36 soldiers and six civilians in a lightning raid on the Egyptian-held Gaza strip today. It was the first major violation of the armistice which ended full-scale fighting in Palestine in 1949. Egypt immediately protested to the United Nations about this "act of aggression".

Israeli supporters saw it as a reprisal for the hanging in Egypt last month of two Jews alleged to be spies. The attack is a blow to Egyptian military prestige at a time they are seeking leadership of the Arab nations. They are working for a united front against Anglo-American defence diplomacy and particularly the treaty between Turkey and Iraq (→18/4).

Dior's fashion ABC takes a leap back

Dior look, but made in England.

March 1. Fashion king Christian Dior has dropped his aitches this Spring. Last season's flat-chested "H" line has given way to the new "A" line – still flattish, but with an easier waist, pyramid-shaped skirt and a "wandering" belt that can be placed anywhere between mid-hip and just under the bust. Skirts are still just below the knee (→4/8).

▷

New row flares over the secrets of Yalta

March 16. Who fooled whom and at what price? Recrimination over the 1945 Yalta Agreement reshaping the post-war world flared again today. Hitherto secret documents about the Churchill-Roosevelt-Stalin deal, published in Washington, revived old controversy.

In London Sir Winston Churchill was angry over an accusation by some American politicians that he did not fight hard enough to get democracy restored in Poland.

The British line – more freely expressed now – is that President Roosevelt, by then in poor health, was too eager to give in to Stalin's demands because above all he wanted Soviet help in finishing the war with Japan.

Headlines missing due to strike action

March 26. No national newspapers appeared this morning because of a strike by 700 electricians and maintenance engineers. The Amalgamated Engineering Union and the Electrical Trades Union have rejected arbitration on their demand for a pay increase of £2 18s 6d a week. It is not known how long the stoppage will last (→ 21/4).

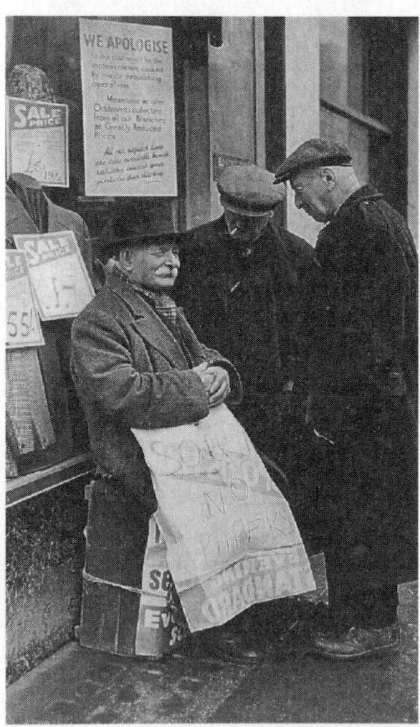

There's news, but the strike means no papers for people to read it.

1955

APRIL

Su	Mo	Tu	We	Th	Fr	Sa
					1	2
3	4	5	6	7	8	9
10	11	12	13	14	15	16
17	18	19	20	21	22	23
24	25	26	27	28	29	30

1. Hamburg: The airline Lufthansa is revived (→ 14/6).

3. Mexico: Over 300 die when a train plunges into a canyon near the city of Guadalajara.

3. Paris: Football representatives from eight countries set up a "European Cup" contest.

4. China: Manchurian party leader Kao-kang is dismissed and charged with seeking to topple Mao Tse-tung (→ 30/7).

7. London: Eden's first cabinet has Harold Macmillan as Foreign Secretary and R.A. Butler as Chancellor.→

12. US: Tests show that the Salk polio vaccine is effective; it will be introduced on a large scale soon (→ 8/5).

16. Strasbourg: Austria is admitted to the Council of Europe (→ 15/5).

18. Jerusalem: Israel and Jordan establish a neutral zone in the city (→ 24/8).

18. Budapest: Hungarian premier Ferenc Nagy is dismissed for "deviation"; Andras Hegedus takes over (→ 16/7).

19. London: The budget takes sixpence in the pound off income tax and increases tax allowances (→ 3/5).

21. UK: National newspapers reappear at the end of nearly a month-long strike.

21. Kenya: Two English schoolboys are found murdered by Mau Mau terrorists (→ 10/6).

22. London: Sir Gerald Templar is appointed Chief of the Imperial General Staff (→ 16/6).

26. London: Peers reject the Wedgwood Benn (Renunciation) Bill, Wedgwood Benn's second bid to lose his title.

29. Rome: Christian Democrat Giovanni Gronchi succeeds Luigi Einaudi as Italian president.

30. UK: US evangelist Billy Graham ends a six-week crusade in Scotland; nearly three million have heard him.

DEATH

18. German-born US physicist Albert Einstein (*14/3/1879).→

Churchill resigns as PM

Sir Winston holds the door as the Queen leaves dinner at Downing Street.

April 5. Now 80, and frail but indomitable, Sir Winston Churchill today resigned from the premiership. He is succeeded by Sir Anthony Eden, whom he first privately named as Crown Prince way back in 1942. Having decided the timing of the hand-over, Sir Winston told his relieved family: "No two men will ever change guard more smoothly." So it has worked out.

He accepted that he could not carry on any longer, although his recent major Parliamentary speech was one of his greatest. Britain's possession of the H-Bomb, he said in memorable words, may compel peace so that "safety will be the sturdy child of terror".

The old warrior stays in the Commons as a backbencher. He intends to stand again and is relishing the prospect of electioneering (→ 7).

Eden is ready for general election

April 22. Sir Anthony Eden has finally cleared the decks tonight for the general election, which he has called for May 26, only sixteen days after becoming Prime Minister. Almost as an afterthought, he has been formally elected Tory Party leader in succession to Sir Winston Churchill.

In his acceptance speech, Sir Anthony continued dressing the Tory shop-window – a process already begun with a tax-cutting Budget. He wants a property-owning democracy. More people will be encouraged to buy their homes and become company shareholders.

Labour leaders considered their election manifesto this afternoon. They plan to attack the Tories over the cost of living and renew calls for international talks about the H-Bomb. Opinion polls suggest that the new Premier is striking while his iron is hot (→ 17/5).

Eden: political window-dressing.

Ex-model charged with lover's murder

April 28. Ex-model Ruth Ellis was today sent for trial at the Old Bailey, accused of the murder of her lover. The 28-year-old platinum blonde is alleged to have shot racing driver David Blakely outside a pub in Hampstead, North London, on Easter Sunday.

His death – from two bullet wounds in the back – marked the violent end to a stormy relationship which began two years ago when twice-married Ellis was manageress of a Knightsbridge drinking club. Since then, the court heard, they had lived together on and off, and on the day of his death Ellis had been begging Blakely not to go, but to stay with her (→21/6).

Ruth Ellis: a crime of passion.

Afro-Asian summit blasts colonialism

April 24. Delegates from 29 "non-aligned" African and Asian countries have met at Bandung in Java. Many of them did not even exist ten years ago, but now they represent half the population of the world. "Peoples of the world who were silent have found their voices again," said Indonesian President Ahmed Sukarno in his opening address.

The conference closed today with a communique calling for an end to colonialism and racialism. France was attacked for its North African policy, and South Africa for apartheid.

Rival factions wage civil war in Saigon

A Binh Xuyen suspect is arrested during the fighting in and around Saigon.

April 29. Civil war has broken out in Saigon, capital of South Vietnam, between the government of Emperor Bao Dai and the quasi-religious Binh Xuyen faction. The affair is complicated by the fact that the Emperor insists on trying to rule his country from a villa in Cannes while the French support Binh Xuyen and the Americans support the Emperor.

Today's fighting, in which government paratroops and tanks were used against entrenched Binh Xuyen shock-troops, brought the number of dead to 160 and left the Chinese suburb of Cholon ablaze.

The trouble seems to have started when Premier Ngo Dinh Diem sacked the Saigon police chief, who is the leader of Binh Xuyen. The sect's fanatical and well-armed members then attacked the premier's palace with mortar fire, and he ordered out the troops.

There is more than a whiff of corruption in this affair. The Binh Xuyen are former river pirates and "General" Le Van Vien, the sacked police chief, was actually in prison when the Japanese invaded Indochina.

He is reported to have made a fortune by controlling the monopoly of the brothels and gaming houses in Cholon (→2/5).

Sporting their special red and green glasses, film fans enjoy the cinema's latest gimmick in the war against television – 3-D movies.

World's best known scientist is dead

April 18. Albert Einstein, probably the most famous scientist of all time, died today in Princeton, New Jersey, at the age of 76. Einstein was best known for his relativity theories, though his Nobel Prize in 1921 was awarded for work on the photo-electric effect.

Einstein was born in Ulm in Germany, and educated in Germany and Switzerland. He had great difficulty in finding work after graduation, but eventually got a job in the Swiss patent office. In parallel with his humdrum work there, he carried out some of his most important research, publishing three major papers, including the Theory of Special Relativity, one of the foundations of modern physics, in 1905. The reputation these won for him brought him a professorship in Zurich, and in 1913, one in Berlin.

Albert Einstein: pictured in 1932.

In 1930 Einstein went to California to lecture and he was still there when Hitler came to power in 1933. As a Jew there was little future for him in Germany, and he moved to the Institute of Advanced Study in Princeton, where he remained until his death.

In later life Einstein became a political figure of some influence. A letter he wrote to President Roosevelt about the implications of uranium fission was important in initiating the wartime atomic bomb project. Later Einstein strove to prevent the use of the bomb, and for nuclear disarmament.

1955

MAY

Su	Mo	Tu	We	Th	Fr	Sa
1	2	3	4	5	6	7
8	9	10	11	12	13	14
15	16	17	18	19	20	21
22	23	24	25	26	27	28
29	30	31				

1. UK: TGWU general secretary Arthur Deakin collapses and dies while making a May Day speech.

2. Saigon: Premier Ngo Dinh Diem foils a coup bid by General Nguyen Van Vy (→26/10).

3. London: The government ends purchase tax on non-woollen cloth following tariff cuts by India (→11/7).

4. London: Len Hutton is made an honorary member of the MCC, the first professional still playing to be elected.

7. London: Newcastle United appear in a record tenth FA Cup Final, beating Manchester City 3-1.

8. US: 25 Hiroshima victims arrive in California for plastic surgery (→10).

8. US: Use of the Salk polio vaccine is temporarily halted, after 41 inoculated people are reported to have the disease.

10. Moscow: The Kremlin proposes cuts in nuclear weapons (→20/6).

16. UK: Opening of the film, "The Dam Busters".

17. London: Eden and four ministers hold the biggest television press conference yet seen in Britain (→27).

20. Buenos Aires: The Roman Catholic Church is disestablished (→15/6).

23. Washington: Senator John F. Kennedy returns to the Senate after back surgery and seven months recuperation.

25. UK: Mme Leon Volterra's Phil Drake wins the Derby.

28. Bath: 16 Teddy Boys are arrested after a disturbance at the city's dance hall.

29. UK: 65,000 railmen go on strike in a dispute over pay differentials.

31. Washington: The US Supreme Court tells southern states to end racial segregation soon, but sets no date (→4/12).

DEATH

1. British trade union leader Arthur Deakin (*11/11/1890).

Warsaw Pact is signed

May 14. The Warsaw Pact, forming all the Eastern Bloc nations into a new military alliance, was signed today by the Soviet Prime Minister, Marshal Bulganin, and his counterparts in Europe's other Communist countries.

The treaty resembles the non-communist North Atlantic Treaty Organisation, and includes the Soviet Union, Poland, Czechoslovakia, Hungary, Rumania, Bulgaria, Albania and East Germany. It will be under the command of Marshal Koniev, aged 58, the head of the Russian ground forces, whose headquarters will be in Moscow. General Staffs from all the member states will also be based in the Russian capital, and units of the new combined army will be moved about "in accordance with the needs of joint defence", said a communique.

All the signatories have agreed to abstain from the use of force to resolve international issues, and vowed to collaborate for disarmament and peace under the 20-year treaty.

The new arrangements will have distinct advantages for Soviet policy, as Russia will now be able to station troops in any of her satellite states, so any incident which the Soviet Union chose to see as "aggression" would serve as an pretext to send in troops. The one European Communist country not in the Pact is Yugoslavia, which was expelled from the Cominform in 1948. The Soviets are making efforts to bring her back into the fold.

Tito and Khrushchev kiss and make up

Marshal Tito and Secretary Khrushchev talk, and bury Stalin's errors.

May 31. Nikita Khrushchev and President Tito have brought to an end the bitter antagonisms that arose between their two countries during the Stalin era. A communique issued at the end of the Soviet leader's week-long visit to Yugoslavia concedes that there are "different roads to Socialism".

During the visit Khrushchev made an effort to atone for past mistakes, and offered what he took to be a most handsome apology for past Soviet policy towards Yugoslavia, notably Stalin's excommunication of Tito from the true communist brotherhood, but the wounds were too recent to be healed so easily, and his Yugoslav hosts were not wholly impressed.

The visit was remarkable for Khrushchev's uninhibited public behaviour. He made no attempt to restrict his enjoyment of the official banquets, and was regularly seen less than wholly sober (→2/6).

First Briton wins Italian road race

Moss beats Italy in a German car.

May 1. Stirling Moss, the Grand Prix driver, has become the first Briton – and only the second non-Italian – to win the most formidable road-race in Europe, the Mille Miglia of Italy.

In his first continental race since signing for the Mercedes-Benz team, Moss crossed the finishing line in Brescia more than half an hour ahead of the runner-up, Juan Fangio, to complete the fearsome "Thousand Miles" (in fact, 992 miles) in ten hours seven minutes and 48 seconds, at a record average speed of 97.8 mph.

West Germany is a sovereign state

May 5. The Allied High Commissioners met today in Berlin for the last time in order to abolish themselves, thus giving Germany back the sovereignty she lost almost exactly ten years ago.

Dr Konrad Adenauer, the Federal Chancellor, promised the West "our foremost task will be to work for peace".

Liberated Germany, he said, still recalls "the millions of Germans who are forced to live separated from us ... Our cry to them is: You belong to us." He solemnly pledged to regain eastern Germany: "Our aim is a free united Germany in a free united Europe" (→12/6).

1955

JUNE

Su	Mo	Tu	We	Th	Fr	Sa
			1	2	3	4
5	6	7	8	9	10	11
12	13	14	15	16	17	18
19	20	21	22	23	24	25
26	27	28	29	30		

2. Belgrade: Tito and Khrushchev sign a declaration normalising relations and agreeing to expand economic ties (→ 7).

2. India: A British team under Charles Evans has conquered the highest unclimbed peak, Kanchenjunga (28,146 ft).

3. Tunisia: Nationalist leader Habib Bourguiba returns from exile as France grants Tunisia internal autonomy.

3. New York: Premiere of the film "The Seven Year Itch", starring Marilyn Monroe.

7. Moscow: The Kremlin invites West German Chancellor Adenauer to Moscow to establish relations (→ 8/9).

10. Kenya: The amnesty terms offered to the Mau Mau in January by the British governor are withdrawn (→ 24).

12. Washington: Adenauer arrives for talks with Eisenhower (→ 25/7).

14. UK: The rail strike is called off (→ 30).

14. London: The Association of British Travel Agents (ABTA) is founded (→ 17/10).

15. Buenos Aires: Peron exiles two prominent leaders of the Catholic Church (→ 17).

16. UK: 13 die when the submarine HMS Sidon sinks in Portland Harbour after an explosion (→ 4/7).

17. Buenos Aires: 202 are reported to have died in an armed uprising against President Juan Peron (→ 1/9).

20. London: Eden says that Britain has signed agreements with the US on the exchange of nuclear information (→ 15/7).

23. London: Labour's right wing retains its dominance after elections to the shadow cabinet (→ 7/12).

24. Kenya: Nine Mau Mau activists are sentenced to death for the murder of two English schoolboys in April (→ 19/10).

28. London: The Cambridge Footlights revue "Between the Lines", starring Jonathan Miller, opens in the capital.

30. UK: The dock strike is now in its sixth week (→ 31).

Anthony Eden wins the general election

May 27. The political deadlock created by the 1950 and 1951 general election stalemate results is broken at last. For the first time since 1865, a party in office has appealed for a fresh mandate and got it with a substantially increased majority.

Sir Anthony Eden appears to have got his election timing brilliantly right. He has won his vote of confidence before the economic clouds get any darker and industrial disruption increases. He has also strengthened his hand for East-West diplomatic negotiations looming up for this summer.

The Tories are back in power with an overall majority of 58. The party scoreboard will finally read Tories 344, Labour 277, Liberals 6, Others 3.

The election campaign has been enlivened by 80-year-old Sir Winston Churchill's boyish enjoyment in fighting and successfully defending his Woodford (outer London) constituency. He tossed colourful abuse at Labour's leading national figures and they responded gently.

When Tory victory was assured tonight, Sir Anthony went to his party headquarters and paid tribute to Britain's younger generation for having become active in politics. "We are the old party rejuvenated," he said. For Labour Hugh Gaitskell, the party treasurer, predicted policy changes to improve prospects for next time. He will be fighting now to reduce the influence of the Labour left.

In an eve-of-poll scare, the Tories produced an alleged plot within the Labour ranks to make Aneurin Bevan Prime Minister if Labour won the election. Mr Attlee fiercely attacked this as nonsense, but Labour looks like having problems (→ 23/6).

A dejected Mr Attlee receives the latest election news at 4.00am.

Austrians will be perpetually neutral

May 15. A treaty ending a decade of military occupation of Austria, and restoring the sovereignty lost by the Austrians when the Nazis took over 17 years ago, was signed in Vienna today by the Foreign Ministers of Britain, the United States, France and Russia.

The ceremony took place in the Belvedere Palace. Despite driving rain, thousands of cheering people crowded the Palace lawns. After the signing the government pledged that Austria would maintain and defend her "perpetual neutrality" and would join no military alliances and allow no foreign military bases on her soil.

State of emergency to deal with strike

May 31. The Government has declared a state of emergency as the crisis of the national dock strike deepens. The Queen signed the proclamation at a meeting of the Privy Council at Balmoral, as the stoppage by about 60,000 men entered its ninth day. The new regulations, under the Emergency Powers Act, can be used against anyone who threatens to deprive the community of the "essentials of life".

Last night Major Lloyd George, the Home Secretary, said the regulations were not aimed at strike-breaking. They will enable the Government to direct food supplies and maintain public order (→ 1/7).

Arms seized in raid on headquarters of Cypriot nationalists

June 30. Arms, ammunition, grenades and explosives were seized by Cypriot police tonight in a series of raids on terrorists' hide-outs. Ten members of EOKA, the terrorist organisation fighting for union with Greece, were arrested.

The raids come at the end of a month during which there have been bomb attacks on British troops in Famagusta and Nicosia and riots in Larnaca, sparked off when six Cypriots received sentences ranging from six to nine years' jail for having explosives with intent to overthrow the island's government.

British troops are co-operating with Cypriot police in setting up road blocks; RAF planes are patrolling the shores and a British frigate is anchored in Morphou Bay in the north of the island.

News that the British government has invited Greece and Turkey to a tripartite conference to discuss the deepening crisis was warmly welcomed by leaders of the island's Turkish community, but Greek leaders were adamant that formal recognition by the British of the principal of self-determination was an essential pre-requisite of the conference (→ 6/9).

Marilyn Monroe may have left her pin-up days behind, but all her fans will enjoy her new film "The Seven Year Itch".

Horrific crash at Le Mans kills eighty

Nightmarish scenes followed Europe's worst-ever motor racing disaster.

June 11. Eighty people died tonight when three cars crashed at 150mph on the Le Mans race-track, west of Paris, and ploughed into the spectators' grandstand. Some 100 people were also hurt, but despite the toll the event's organisers decided the race should continue.

This, the most disastrous accident in the history of motor racing, has badly damaged the image of the sport. The director of the course said: "I did not judge, in spite of the horror of the situation, that the race should be interrupted."

However, the winning Mercedes drivers gave up their titles after finding that one of their team cars was at the centre of the accident, which caused sickening scenes.

The vehicle had somersaulted a barrier and cut a swathe through the crowd, leaving children decapitated and other spectators dismembered. For 60 yards the sandy ground on one side of the eightmile track was drenched in blood. Witnesses spoke of a battlefield.

A record 250,000 crowd attended the 24-hour race and saw the mass start turn to tragedy as cars collided on a bend.

Guilty blonde model sentenced to hang

June 21. Femme fatale Ruth Ellis was today found guilty of the murder of the man she adored – and immediately sentenced to hang. Her trial had lasted only two days. The jury of ten men and two women took just 25 minutes to reach their verdict, after hearing that jealousy was no defence in English law, even if the man was having an affair with another woman.

Ellis shot David Blakely with a Smith and Wesson, which she claimed had been given to her three years ago as security for a debt at one of her bars. The ex-model and mother of two showed no emotion as Mr Justice Havers passed sentence. She will appeal (→ 13/7).

Police break up Congress protest

June 26. Police, armed with Sten guns and rifles with bayonets fixed, today broke up a self-styled Congress of the People in a non-white suburb of Johannesburg.

The Congress, called to protest about South Africa's apartheid laws and to demand the vote for all, was attended by 3,000 people. They were mostly Africans, Indians and mixed-race Coloureds, but about 50 whites also turned up.

Before the police raid, a special badge was presented to outstanding "Fighters for Freedom". The one non-South African to receive this special badge was the British Anglican missionary, Father Trevor Huddleston (→ 24/10).

1955

JULY

Su	Mo	Tu	We	Th	Fr	Sa
					1	2
3	4	5	6	7	8	9
10	11	12	13	14	15	16
17	18	19	20	21	22	23
24	25	26	27	28	29	30
31						

1. UK: Dockers' leaders order a return to work.

2. Wimbledon: Tony Trabert beats Kurt Nielsen in the Men's Singles final; Louise Brough beats Beverly Fleitz for her fourth Women's Singles championship.

4. London: Britain will transfer the Simonstown naval base to South Africa by April 1957 as part of a naval pact (→ 7).

6. Strasbourg: Britain and France outline a plan to include East Bloc states in the Council of Europe.

7. UK: A new supersonic Hawker Hunter crashes at the Farnborough Air Show, killing the pilot (→ 11/11).

10. London: Opening of Soho Fair, a festival aimed at ridding Soho of its seedy underworld associations.

11. UK: Coal prices rise by 18 per cent, their biggest ever rise (→ 3/8).

13. London: Ruth Ellis is hanged at Holloway Prison.

16. Budapest: Catholic primate Cardinal Mindszenty is released from jail and placed under house arrest.

17. UK: Stirling Moss wins his first grand prix, beating world champion Fangio in the British Grand Prix.

18. Geneva: The Big Four conference opens.→

18. US: "Disneyland" opens at Anaheim, California.→

22. London: The government permits the Kabaka of Buganda to return home to Uganda.

22. Lisbon: Oil magnate Calouste Gulbenkian (who died on July 20) left £300 million for art, education and charity.

25. Bonn: The Bundestag authorises the new West German Army of 6,000 volunteers, called "Bundeswehr" (→ 12/11).

27. London: The Clean Air Bill is published, which would create "smoke control areas".

30. Peking: Chinese premier Chou En-lai calls for an Asian-Pacific peace pact (→ 11/10).

Campbell breaks water-speed record

July 23. Donald Campbell brok the world water-speed record o Ullswater today, when he made tw runs over the lake in his turbo-je hydroplane Bluebird at an averag speed of 202.32mph.

Large crowds lined the side o the lake to see the 34-year-old so of the late Sir Malcolm Campbe make his record-breaking runs, a though afterwards Mr Campbe described the venture as "primaril scientific". He added: "We ar much more concerned with re search and the general behaviou and design of craft at these speed than we are with merely breakin the world's record."

Campbell, fastest over the water.

French troops act against Moroccans

July 17. After yesterday's proclam ation of martial law, French troop and armoured cars tonight too action against a Moroccan mob i the Medina, the old walled city c Casablanca.

When troops forced their way i after three hours of gunfightin they found the body of a Spanis teenager, stoned to death by th mob. Unconfirmed reports say a other three whites have bee murdered.

Tension remains high after ye terday's incident, when Moroccar surrounded the Resident-Gener calling for his death (→ 12/8).

Summit a success, yet nothing agreed

uly 23. The first East-West heads of government meeting since 1945 nded in Geneva today. With normal diplomatic humbug, Sir Anthony Eden, President Eisenhower, he French Premier, Edgar Faure, nd the Soviet Premier, Nikolai Bulganin, declared it a success. In ruth, they agreed about nothing – xcept that their Foreign Ministers vill meet again in the autumn for nother bid to solve the problem of Germany's future.

The Western leaders found the Russian delegation less sinister, but ot less unyielding, than in the days of Stalin. On the question of European security, Mr Bulganin totally rejected a British plan for free all-German elections followed by a peace treaty with a reunified Germany. He said that German reunification is unthinkable without the abolition of NATO.

Neither late-night conference sessions, apparently cordial banquets, nor anything else budged Mr Bulganin from that position. However, he said that the Big Four meeting was "a beginning", although it would have been better if Asia, Formosa and Communist China had been discussed. A thaw in the Cold War seems distant (→28/10).

Steel and glass Never-Never Land opens

Valt Disney's dream comes true for children at a park in California.

uly 18. The film-maker Walt Disney, the man who brought the vorld Mickey Mouse, saw his ream of a "Never-Never Land" or children and adults alike come o life today with the opening of Disneyland: a 160 acre steel and oncrete super amusement park at naheim, 22 miles outside Los ngeles.

The Disney "fantasy land", which cost $17 million to build, features such attractions as a drive in the car of the future, a ride on a Mississippi stern-wheeler and "Peter Pan Fly-Through" rocket trips to the moon. Ambitious constructions of a medieval castle and Main Street, USA, are also included at this Californian wonderland, which expects to attract crowds of around five million a year.

Nobel Prize winners oppose the Bomb

uly 15. A declaration urging nations to renounce war was published oday, signed by some of the orld's most eminent scientists cluding seven Nobel Prize inners, one of them the late Albert instein. Organised by the philosopher Bertrand Russell, it calls on governments to settle disputes peacefully, "in view of the fact that in any future war nuclear weapons will certainly be employed and that such weapons threaten the continued existence of mankind" (→8/8).

1955

AUGUST

Su	Mo	Tu	We	Th	Fr	Sa
	1	2	3	4	5	6
7	8	9	10	11	12	13
14	15	16	17	18	19	20
21	22	23	24	25	26	27
28	29	30	31			

3. London: Housing minister Duncan Sandys tells 140 local authorities to set up "green belts" similar to London's (→26/10).

3. London: Eamonn Andrews will compere a TV series called "This Is Your Life", starting this autumn.

4. Moscow: Bulganin rejects Eisenhower's proposal for mutual inspection of military establishments.

7. Karachi: Mohammed Ali resigns as prime minister of Pakistan.

8. Geneva: Opening of a conference on atomic energy attended by 3,000 scientists from 62 countries (→26/11).

12. Paris: The French government agrees on a programme of reform for Morocco.→

15. UK: Five armed IRA men are arrested trying to steal arms from an Army barracks at Arborfield, Berkshire.

17. London: England win the Oval test match, and the series, against South Africa.

20. New Delhi: Nehru breaks off relations with Portugal following the Goa massacre.

22. Morocco: The French open peace talks as the death toll reaches 1,000.

24. Cairo: Egypt breaks off talks with Israel aimed at lessening tension in the Gaza border area (→29).

24. UK: A US airman runs amok in Broadstairs, Kent, shooting three people dead and wounding nine.

26. UK: Surrey are County Cricket Champions for the fourth successive year.

29. Israel: Egyptian and Israeli fighters clash over Gaza for the first time since 1948 (→31).

31. Cairo: Egypt accepts a UN cease-fire in the border dispute with Israel; Israel is expected to follow (→3/9).

DEATHS

12. German author Thomas Mann (*6/6/1875).→

17. French artist Fernand Leger (*4/2/1881).

Queen's portrait is major RA attraction

The Queen, painted by Annigoni.

Aug 14. The Royal Academy Summer Exhibition has broken all attendance records since the First World War thanks to one portrait – that of the Queen by Italy's "modern old master", Pietro Annigoni. Over 250,000 have visited the exhibition, forming a crowd in front of the picture every day.

Annigoni, whose studio is in Florence, was given sittings by the Queen last year. He has depicted her in a romantic setting in a dashing pose in the cloak of the Order of the Garter. There are those who dismiss Annigoni as being all technique, but no vision (→13/10).

Audience unwilling to wait for Godot

Aug 10. The sound of seats tipping up, and about half the audience leaving the theatre, have become the standard background to "Waiting for Godot", the play by Samuel Beckett which was ridiculed by the London critics this week.

Two years ago it was welcomed in Paris as a perfect example of "Theatre of the Absurd". "As far as I am concerned the Paris intelligentsia can have it back" ..... "It tries to lift superficiality to significance through obscurity" ran typical notices. It is directed at the little Arts Theatre Club by a newcomer of 24, Peter Hall. ▷

Non-violent marchers shot entering Goa

Indian police keep a wary eye on the crowds demonstrating over Goa.

Aug 15. Twelve of the Indian passive resisters demanding that Portugal cede its enclave of Goa to India were shot dead today when they attempted to cross the border. Others who evaded the police were rounded up by Goan villagers armed with staves.

News of the shootings spread a pall of gloom over the camp from which the protesters had set out, adding to the despondency induced by the monsoon. V.D. Chitale, the Communist leader of the incursion, is among the wounded. The killings shattered the hopes of some optimists, who thought the Portuguese would not dare to deal drastically with the demonstrators. The incident, on India's Independence Day, is bound to worsen the already strained relations between India and Portugal. In New Delhi Mr Nehru, the Prime Minister, insisted that Goa was an integral part of India, but he said he would not use the army to seize the enclave from the Portuguese.

In reply Portugal made an official protest tonight at "grave acts of violation of sovereignty". According to the Portuguese, the responsibility for the bloodshed belonged "entirely to those who have excited, consented to and favoured the invasion" (→20).

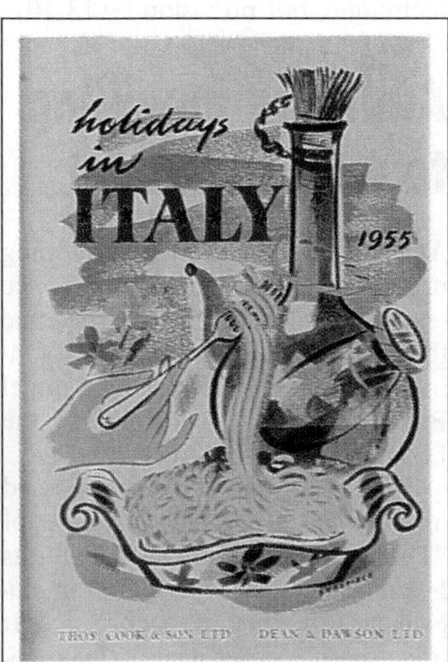

As Europe has settled down, and Britons become richer, the latest trend is taking holidays abroad.

Blue jeans hugging British buttocks

Aug 4. Figure-hugging jeans have become the number one bestselling style for women this summer. The craze which has already swept the United States, France and Canada is taking over Britain, and many shops have sold out their stocks. One buyer said: "We couldn't sell them fast enough."

Fashion pundits have warned "only wear them if you're young, slim-hipped and long-legged", but their advice is obviously being ignored. Women of every variety appear determined to squeeze themselves into skin-tight denim without so much as a backward glance.

Algerian death toll soars as riots flare

Aug 20. At midday today thousands of armed rebels staged a simultaneous attack on 25 French targets in Algeria's Constantine district. Official figures indicate that over 500 people were killed, and 226 injured, in the fighting.

The insurrection marked the second anniversary of the deposition of former Sultan of Morocco, Sidi Mohammed Ben Youssef, and was timed to coincide with a severe outbreak of Nationalist rioting in Morocco.

Philippeville, a coastal town with 6,000 inhabitants, was one target invaded by a crowd armed with knives, axes, guns and automatic weapons. The police and militia counter-attacked, killing over 100 and taking 300 prisoner.

Algeria's Governor-General, Jacques Soustelle, flew to Constantine to help restore order. An uneasy peace reigns tonight.

Mann, Germany's great novelist, dies

Aug 12. Germany's greatest novelist, Thomas Mann, died today in Zurich, where he made his home after the Nazis burned his books. His novels, from "Buddenbrooks" (1901) , through "Death In Venice" and "The Magic Mountain", to "The Confessions of Felix Krull" (1953) span German life and society through the traumas of two defeats and the sickness of Nazism.

Thomas Mann: Nobel prize winner.

1955

SEPTEMBER

Su	Mo	Tu	We	Th	Fr	Sa
				1	2	3
4	5	6	7	8	9	10
11	12	13	14	15	16	17
18	19	20	21	22	23	24
25	26	27	28	29	30	

1. Buenos Aires: Peron puts the city under a state of siege as students riot (→16).

3. Tel Aviv: Israel accepts the UN cease-fire in Gaza (→16/10).

6. UK: A force of British commandos is sent to Cyprus amid mounting tension (→7).

7. London: Talks between Britain, Greece and Turkey on the future of Cyprus break up without result (→15).

8. Moscow: Adenauer arrives for talks on establishing relations with the USSR (→13).

11. Cambodia: Ex-King Sihanouk's party wins the general election.

13. Moscow: The USSR establishes relations with West Germany.

15. London: The government anounces it will gradually introduce equal pay for women into the NHS.

15. Cyprus: EOKA, the guerrilla group fighting for union with Greece, is outlawed by the British (→18).

16. Buenos Aires: A revolt breaks out against Peron amongst the Argentine army and navy (→19).

18. Cyprus: A mob sacks the British Institute in Nicosia (→29).

18. USSR: Vladimir Kuts sets a world record for the 5,000 metres of 14 minutes, 46.8 seconds.

19. Buenos Aires: Peron is overthrown (→23).

22. UK: MG Cars unveils a new sports model, the MG-A.

23. Buenos Aires: General Eduardo Lonardi is sworn in as provisional president.→

26. East Germany: Conscription comes into force.

26. UK: Hughie Green's show, "Double Your Money", starts on ITV.

29. Cyprus: A general strike is called.→

DEATH

30. US actor James Dean (*8/2/1931).

General strike in Cyprus

Sept 30. Violent demonstrations against British rule in Cyprus continued here today – a day when the general strike, called by EOKA supporters as part of the continuing campaign for union with Greece, crippled communications throughout the island.

Cypriot police, backed by British troops whose presence has been increased since the tripartite talks between Britain, Turkey and Greece were suspended earlier this month, were stoned by gangs of youths when they tried to break up illegal processions and demonstrations.

Troops were ordered to shoot to kill if necessary, but although hundreds of arrests have been made no serious casualties have so far been reported. However, at Paphos, in the west of the island, the Union Jack and a portrait of the Queen were torn down from a public building during a demonstration which was later quelled by men from the Royal Scots.

At the other end of the island, in Lysi, soldiers from the Royal Inniskillings used bayonets to disperse a huge mob, and to force them to take down the barrier they had built to block the road to Nicosia, where police used tear gas to disperse demonstrators.

British troops, worried about the ever-present risk of violence flaring up between the Greek and Turkish communities, have taken over the police station in the city's Turkish quarter, where the cafes are filled with groups of Turkish Cypriots bent on retaliation (→22/11).

ITV begins new era of British television

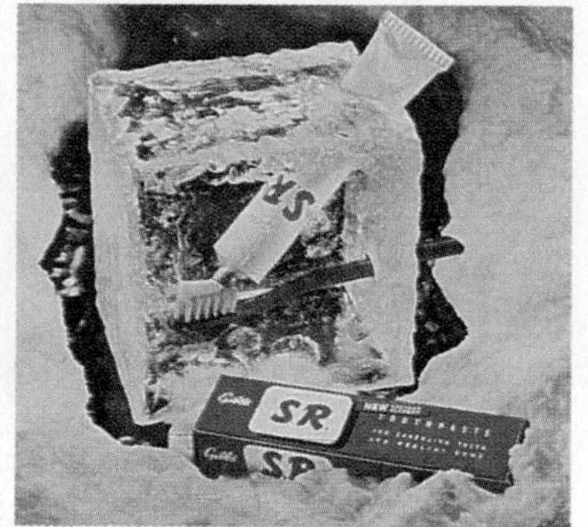

Toothpaste – first ad on screen.

Sept 22. Amid much speechifying and trumpeting commercial television opened up tonight, to give London viewers an alternative to BBC television for the first time.

Offerings from the two London commercial contractors, Associated Rediffusion and the Associated Broadcasting Company, included a variety show and drama excerpts linked by actor Robert Morley, plus a boxing match from Shoreditch. And although many had voiced concern about the advent of advertising on TV, the six minutes of advertisements screened during the 70-minute variety show proved tasteful, if anticlimactic. The first advertisement was for toothpaste.

The BBC went on the air half an hour earlier and countered commercial television's opening speeches from the Guildhall with "The Donald Duck Story". What really stole its rival's thunder, though, was a drama on steam radio – the death in a fire of Grace Archer, a leading character in "The Archers". The timing, the BBC would have you believe, was sheer coincidence.

James Dean dies in car smash at 24

Dean: lived fast and died young.

Sept 30. The actor and teen hero James Dean was killed instantly this evening when his Porsche Spider careered off a road outside Los Angeles. On-screen he was compared to Marlon Brando, but 24-year-old Dean only ever made three films: "East of Eden" and "Rebel Without a Cause", plus the yet-to-be-released "Giant". But "East of Eden" proved enough to gain him worldwide fame (→26/6).

Juan Peron flees to Paraguay after coup

Sept 24. Rather than turn former President Juan Peron into a martyr through trial and punishment, the new military junta in Argentina has recognised the "right of asylum" and packed him off to exile in Paraguay.

Peron has been hiding out on a Paraguayan gunboat in the harbour at Buenos Aires since Monday, when a revolution threw him from high office.

The power base for his ten-year-old regime started to crumble when he courted business interests over labour, stepped up his attacks on the Catholic church, and agreed to let Standard Oil of California develop Argentina's natural resources. Rebel forces seized control of the army and navy, and threatened to bombard the capital. The beleaguered government was quickly brought to its knees.

At the news of Peron's downfall wildly-cheering crowds rushed out into the rain on Monday. Statues of Eva Peron, the dictator's late wife, were dragged through the streets of Buenos Aires. The junta now has most of the country within its grasp, but isolated pockets of Peron's supporters continue to fight on (→2/10).

Burgess and MacLean were spies – official

Sept 18. After a four-year silence, the Foreign Office admitted today that Guy Burgess and Donald MacLean, the diplomats who fled Britain in May 1951, were believed to have been long-term Soviet agents. MacLean, aged 42, had been under investigation.

The disclosure confirmed the belief that Burgess, 44, and MacLean knew they were being watched and reported the fact to Moscow, which arranged their escape. The Foreign Office was prompted to make its statement by a newspaper article by Vladimir Petrov, a Soviet diplomat who defected in Australia. It refused to comment on his claim that the missing diplomats had been recruited for intelligence work while they were still undergraduates at Cambridge.

MacLean had been under "active" investigation, the FO said. Burgess had been withdrawn from Washington, where he was Second Secretary at the British Embassy, and his suitability for further foreign service was under review.

The two men are believed to have left the country on a ferry from Southampton to St. Malo (→11/11).

"Ike" in hospital: mild heart attack

The President when fighting fit.

Sept 24. Early this morning, President Eisenhower had what his doctors describe as a "moderate attack of coronary thrombosis" in his sleep. His condition is said to be satisfactory, although he has been placed in an oxygen tent at the Fitzsimons Army Hospital, Denver.

His wife, Mamie, is at his side, and Vice-President Richard Nixon flies in tomorrow. Political observers are now certain that "Ike" will not seek a second term (→11/11). ▷

1955

OCTOBER

Su	Mo	Tu	We	Th	Fr	Sa
						1
2	3	4	5	6	7	8
9	10	11	12	13	14	15
16	17	18	19	20	21	22
23	24	25	26	27	28	29
30	31					

2. Paraguay: Ex-President Peron arrives in exile (→13/11).

4. Athens: Field Marshal Papagos, the Greek premier, dies (→6).

6. Athens: Constantine Karamanlis becomes premier.

8. West Germany: Hitler's pilot, Hans Bauer, just released by the USSR, confirms Hitler's and Eva Braun's suicides.

11. China: The USSR leaves Port Arthur, which it is handing over to China.

12. English Channel: Florence Chadwick swims the Channel in 13 hours 55 minutes.

13. London: Group Captain Peter Townsend visits Princess Margaret and the Queen Mother at Clarence House (→27).

16. Sinai: Egyptian and Israeli troops clash near the El Auja demilitarised zone (→2/11).

17. Uganda: The Kabaka of Buganda returns (→18).

17. UK: BEA is to order a fleet of Vickers-Armstrong's new big turbo-prop airliners, the Vanguard.

18. Uganda: The Kabaka of Buganda transfers his powers to popularly elected ministers, the price of his return.

19. Kenya: It is reported that 13,000 have died and more than 70,000 jailed in three years of Mau Mau activity.

19. London: The BBC has bought Ealing Film Studios.

20. London: The BBC demonstrates colour TV at Alexandra Palace.

26. London: Purchase tax, post and phone charges go up in an autumn budget; housing subsidies and building are cut.

26. US: Opening of "Rebel Without A Cause", last film starring the late James Dean.

26. Saigon: South Vietnam is declared a republic with premier Ngo Dinh Diem as first president (→12/12).

27. London: Princess Margaret visits the Archbishop of Canterbury.→

Princess Margaret's wedding is off

The target of the world's press, Group Captain Townsend leaves his house.

Margaret: a lady not in waiting.

Oct 31. Princess Margaret has decided against marrying Captain Peter Townsend, who was equerry to her late father, after all. In a statement last night she declared: "I would like it to be known that I have decided not to marry Group Captain Peter Townsend. I have been aware that subject to renouncing my rights of succession it might have been possible for me to contract a civil marriage, but mindful of the Church's teaching that Christian marriage is indissoluble and conscious of my duty to the Commonwealth, I have resolved to put these considerations above all others."

The Princess came to the decision herself, so ending two weeks of intense press speculation, but there was known to be concern within the royal family, supported by a body of public opinion, that the Princess should marry a divorcee, suitable as he might be in every other way.

It was only if the Princess had made the decision to marry the Group Captain that the marriage would have been a matter for the Government. As the Princess is 25, she is free to marry without the Queen's consent under the Royal Marriage Act of 1772, but would have to wait a year. She would also, on marrying, lose her payments from the Civil List and her place as third in line to the throne.

Townsend came into the service of the royal family when King George VI said he would like his equerries to include men who had shown bravery in war. With a good manner, and outstanding as an organiser, Townsend, a much-decorated fighter pilot, was nominated by the Royal Air Force.

The first the public knew of a romance was in July 1953, when it was announced at the last minute that Townsend would not accompany the Queen Mother and the Princess on their visit to Africa. During the African tour he was posted to Brussels as Air Attache. The Princess was ill for the three following days, and did not carry out engagements. They were not to meet again until a fortnight ago, two years and three months later.

Group Captain Townsend was last night at Uckfield House, Sussex. At 9pm the butler told the waiting press: "He is not in a position to make a statement ... he is very distressed."

The princess and the Group Captain seen touring South Africa in 1947.

1955

NOVEMBER

Su	Mo	Tu	We	Th	Fr	Sa
		1	2	3	4	5
6	7	8	9	10	11	12
13	14	15	16	17	18	19
20	21	22	23	24	25	26
27	28	29	30			

1. Madrid: US Secretary of State Dulles and Franco hold talks to forge closer ties between the US and Spain.

2. Tel Aviv: Ben-Gurion forms a government (→7).

3. London: MPs give a second reading to the Clean Air Bill aimed at cutting smog in Britain's cities.

4. Addis Ababa: Emperor Haile Selassie grants a more liberal constitution on his silver jubilee.

7. Washington: The administration says it will sell arms to Israel.

10. London: The BBC is given the exclusive right to televise cricket Test matches.

11. UK: The first vertical take-off plane, the PD11, is reported to have been built.

11. Washington: Eisenhower arrives back in the capital after his heart attack seven weeks ago.

13. Buenos Aires: Provisional President Lonardi is ousted by Major General Pedro Aramburu.

16. US: Donald Campbell sets a new water speed record of 216.2 mph in his Bluebird speedboat.

20. UK: Ten die and 99 are hurt in a train crash near Didcot in Oxfordshire.

20. Washington: Talks open with Egypt on the financing of the planned dam on the River Nile at Aswan (→28/12).

22. Cyprus: Police use tear gas and baton charges to quell riots in Nicosia and Larnaca (→26).

26. Cyprus: British troops and terrorists fight running battles in the so-called "Murder Mile" of Famagusta.→

30. London: The first floodlit international football match is played at Wembley, between England and Spain.

DEATHS

5. French painter Maurice Utrillo (*26/12/1883).

27. Swiss composer Arthur Honegger (*10/3/1892).

South Africa walks out of UN Assembly

Oct 24. Today's United Nations debate on "the racial conflict in South Africa resulting from the policies of apartheid" was interrupted when the South African delegate, W.C. du Plessis, staged a walk-out protest. He complained that the UN was intervening in his country's internal affairs, thereby infringing its own charter.

South Africa has repeatedly ignored the UN's human rights committee, which has called apartheid a "seriously disturbing factor in international relations".

Big Four again in Geneva deadlock

Oct 28. Foreign Ministers of the Big Four quickly reached deadlock when they met in Geneva today in another bid for East-West accord on European security.

Mr Molotov again ruled out German reunification proposed by the West. He called for dissolution of both NATO and the Warsaw Pact. Harold Macmillan said that the West cannot accept that giving security to Russia must involve abandoning its own defences.

John Foster Dulles vainly pleaded with Mr Molotov to see the historic importance of the US offer to underwrite European non-aggression treaties.

All dressed up and nowhere to go – so these London Teddy Boys hang around the corner.

State of alert in Cyprus

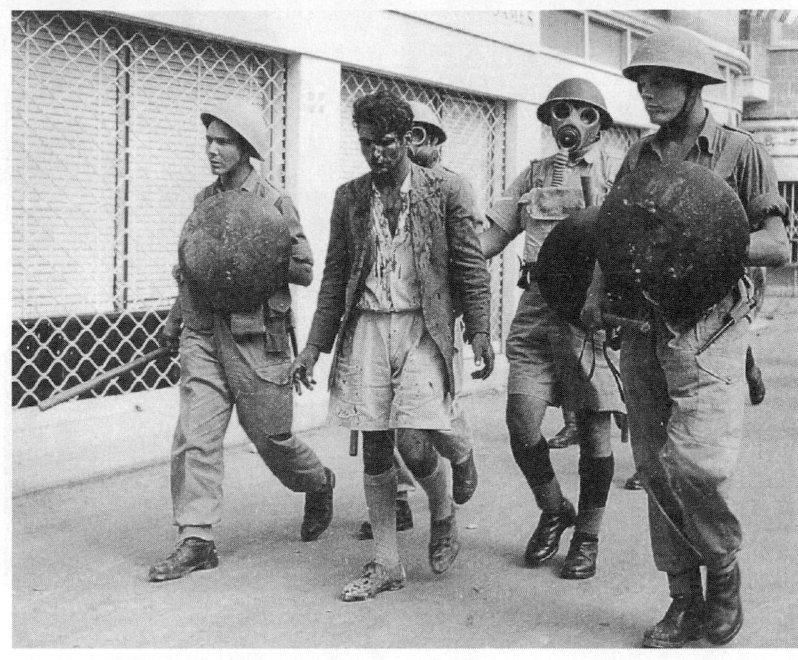

A Greek rioter, his face bloodied, is taken away by British soldiers.

Nov 28. Two days after another two British soldiers died in terrorist attacks in Cyprus, a state of emergency has been declared throughout the island. Sir John Harding, Governor of Cyprus, will assume wide powers to counter the terrorism that has seen five soldiers killed in the last month. It is expected that British troops on the island will be put on a war footing.

Archbishop Makarios, popular leader of the Greek Cypriots, said that the British Government had decided to use extraordinary measures to bend the national resistance of the Cypriot people. The state of emergency would make the crisis more acute.

The declaration grants the Governor draconian powers, authorising him to make any regulation he sees fit to maintain public order. He is given the power to detain or deport suspected terrorists, to impose curfews and censorship, and to requisition property. Discharging firearms at any person becomes an offence punishable by death, as do bomb throwing or laying, and carrying guns, ammunition or other explosive substances.

The state of emergency was declared on a day when Sir John was almost the victim of a terrorist attack. Because of the deepening crisis he decided not to attend the Caledonian Society's ball in Nicosia's Ledra Palace hotel, where a bomb attack injured four guests. When the ballroom was cleared, an unexploded grenade was found under the table reserved for Sir John and his party (→22/12).

West German army begins in a garage

Nov 12. In a short, casual ceremony at the Ministry garage the Defence Minister, Theodor Blank, today ended ten years of demilitarisation by commissioning West Germany's first soldiers. Of the 101 invested, only 12 wore uniforms.

The army is to be led by Hitler's Operations Chief, Lieutenant-General Heusinger, and one of Rommel's henchmen, now Bonn's NATO representative, General Speidel. Herr Blank said Germany now intended to take equal responsibility and have equal rights with its partners in the Western community.

Russia and France – who have suffered the most from German aggression in the past – are perhaps understandably suspicious of the move. But the rearmament of West Germany is definitely an essential part of the West's defence policy in Eastern Europe (→19/12). ▷

MP retracts charge Philby was Third Man

Kim Philby, the supposed "third man", denies the allegations to the press.

Nov 11. A Labour MP has withdrawn allegations that a former senior diplomat was involved in the disappearance of his colleagues Guy Burgess and Donald MacLean. In a Commons speech, Colonel Marcus Lipton had accused Mr Harold "Kim" Philby, until recently First Secretary at the British Embassy in Washington, of "dubious third man activities".

Philby immediately challenged the MP to repeat the statement outside Parliament, although he admitted an "imprudent friendship" with Burgess since they were at Cambridge, for which he had been asked to resign. He had met MacLean in the Thirties but he was "only a shadow in his memory".

Burgess had lived with him in Washington before his return to London in May 1951. "I more or less sponsored him in that rather hectic society," said Philby.

At a crowded press conference in a Kensington flat, Philby said: "I have never been a Communist, although I knew people who were Communists at Cambridge and for a year afterwards. The last time I spoke to a Communist, knowing he was one, was in 1934."

Mr Lipton told the Commons that, following Philby's statement and a speech by the Foreign Secretary, he was satisfied that his allegations were unjustified.

Philby told the press: "I think Colonel Lipton has done the right thing. So far as I am concerned the incident is now closed" (→13/12).

Russia explodes more potent bomb

Nov 26. The Soviet Union has confirmed reports that it recently exploded its "most powerful" hydrogen bomb – said by Khrushchev to be the equivalent of one million tons (a megaton) of TNT. The Russian statement said the tests were being carried out in the interests of national security, and set out once again proposals for the prohibition of nuclear weapons "with establishment of effective international control" (→29/12).

British mopeds see off the invaders

Nov 12. Battle is joined at Earls Court today, where British mopeds and scooters are resisting a foreign invasion. Mopeds are baby motor cycles (up to 50cc engine capacity) with pedal assistance. Nine British makes confront seven Continentals at prices from £40 to £80.

British scooters at the Cycle Show include the handsome Dayton Albatross, which cruises at 50mph, using fuel at 84 miles to the gallon.

1955

DECEMBER

Su	Mo	Tu	We	Th	Fr	Sa
				1	2	3
4	5	6	7	8	9	10
11	12	13	14	15	16	17
18	19	20	21	22	23	24
25	26	27	28	29	30	31

1. London: Britain protests to Moscow at attacks by Khrushchev in India and Burma on British colonial policy.

2. London: Twelve die and 40 are hurt in a train fire in Barnes.

2. UK: Rootes Motors takes over Singer Motors.

3. Cairo: Britain and Egypt sign an agreement granting independence to the Sudan.

9. US: Sugar Ray Robinson knocks out Carl Olson to regain the world middleweight boxing championship.

10. Stockholm: Nobel Prizes go to Willis Lamb and Polykarp Kusch (US, Physics); Vincent de Vigneaud (US, Chemistry); Axel Theorell (Sweden, Medicine); Halldor Laxness (Iceland, Literature); no Peace Prize.

12. North Vietnam: The US evacuates its Hanoi consulate.

13. West Berlin: Ex-West Berlin security boss Otto John flees back to the west from East Germany.

14. New York: The UN admits 16 new members, but bars Mongolia and Japan.

19. Saarland: The pro-German party wins elections.

20. UK: Cardiff becomes the capital of Wales.

28. UK: Britain is reported to be sending arms to both Egypt and Israel.

29. Moscow: Bulganin claims the USSR has developed a rocket which can carry an H-bomb 4,000 miles.

HITS OF 1955

Give me your word.

Cherry Pink and Apple Blossom White.

Rosemarie.

QUOTE OF THE YEAR

"The personality conveyed by the utterances which are put into her mouth is that of a priggish schoolgirl captain of the hockey team."

John Grigg, Lord Altrincham, writing on the Queen in "The National Review".

Britons in Cyprus form Home Guard

Dec 22. As indiscriminate bombing attacks continue in Cyprus, many British members of the business community in Nicosia have formed a Home Guard to protect their families from night attack by terrorists. The civilians, who are allowed to carry guns, have split the city into command areas which they patrol in pairs, keeping an ever-watchful eye out for anyone who might be a terrorist.

This comes at a time when tension in the city is running high. A week ago two off-duty soldiers window-shopping for Christmas presents on Ledra Street, were gunned down in retaliation for an island-wide clampdown on the Communist Party, during which 150 were arrested. Four days later three bombs were thrown into a popular bar in the city, leaving fifteen people injured and several more suffering from shock. An eyewitness said that the bar looked like a slaughterhouse. New orders to British servicemen place all hotels, bars and restaurants out of bounds unless all windows are protected with wire mesh.

Blacks begin bus boycott in Alabama

Dec 4. Last Thursday Rosa Parks ignored a driver's order to move to the back of the bus, as required by local race laws in Montgomery, Alabama. Today she was fined $1 as thousands of blacks boycotted the bus company in protest. Spokesmen said the boycott, which is very well organised, would continue until people who rode buses were no longer "intimidated, embarrassed and coerced". The boycotters say they are ready to help City Lines Buses and the local authorities to develop a more equitable and satisfactory transport system.

Mrs Parks, a black 42-year-old seamstress, has appealed against the fine, but her lawyers have not said whether they intend to attack the constitutionality of segregation itself. The Supreme Court already has one test case on the issue before it, relating to buses in South Carolina.

Clem goes to the Lords

Dec 7. Clement Richard Attlee, the most self-effacing man who ever became Prime Minister, resigned as the leader of the Labour Party today. Within hours the Queen made him an earl.

Mr Attlee told Labour MPs: "Before you turn to important business I have a personal statement. I want to end uncertainty over future leadership. I am resigning." Having presided over the 1945 Government's massive social reform programme, and then endured years of internal party wrangling, he had had enough.

At 72 he has timed his retirement to give the Shadow Chancellor, Hugh Gaitskell, the best chance of getting the job, and to dish his own deputy, Herbert Morrison. Clem is not as simple as he looks (→ 14).

Attlee steps down, by tube.

Gaitskell wins race for Labour leadership

Labour's new leader, Mr Hugh Gaitskell, arriving at Transport House.

Dec 14. By a clear majority Hugh Gaitskell, aged 49, was tonight elected leader by Labour MPs and peers. He got 157 votes, against 70 for Aneurin Bevan and 30 for Herbert Morrison.

The veteran Morrison, 68 next month and chief architect of Labour's famous 1945 election victory, at once resigned as deputy leader. He was in tears over his overwhelming rejection as successor to Earl Attlee. A manoeuvre by Mr Bevan, who suggested that both he and Mr Gaitskell should withdraw in Mr Morrison's favour, rebounded against both defeated candidates.

The result is a great success for Labour's right-wing and its trade union backers, but it probably presages more strife between left-wing Bevanites and Mr Gaitskell, whom they detest. The new leader appealed for party unity and Mr Bevan pledged loyalty. Tongues in cheeks were the order of the day.

Arts: enter Nabokov's shocking Lolita

"Lolita", a book that introduces the concept of a "nymphet" - a pubescent girl of 12 who proves far more likely to take sexual advantage than to have advantage taken of her – is a succes de scandale in America. It purports to be middle-aged Humbert Humbert's confession of his tormented desire for his seductive step-daughter.

The fact that he is not repulsed has caused outrage in some quarters, but it was partly disarmed by the distinction of **Vladimir Nabokov's** literary style. There is not an obscene term in the book, which marvellously describes the odyssey of the ill-matched couple across America from motel to motel. To some it is a heartless shocker, to others a tender, if perverted, love story.

Francoise Sagan, too, deals with hard-hearted adolescent girlhood in "Bonjour Tristesse", a novel which seized attention in France last year, now translated into English. Cecile, a precocious, sunbathing flirt, takes on her widowed father's mistress with tragic results. There is a typically French clarity and emotional toughness about this natural writer. She won the critics' grand prix at the age of only 18.

A bolder mixture of ruthlessness and sex is served up by **Ian Fleming** in a novel which continues the adventures of James Bond, known as Agent 007, which began in "Casino Royale" in 1953. This tale is entitled "Moonraker", with a well-drawn villain, Hugo Drax, and a climactic card game. Fleming's exotic travels and inside knowledge of intelligence (gained during the war) convey authenticity, enlivened by luxury living and glamorous, complaisant girls.

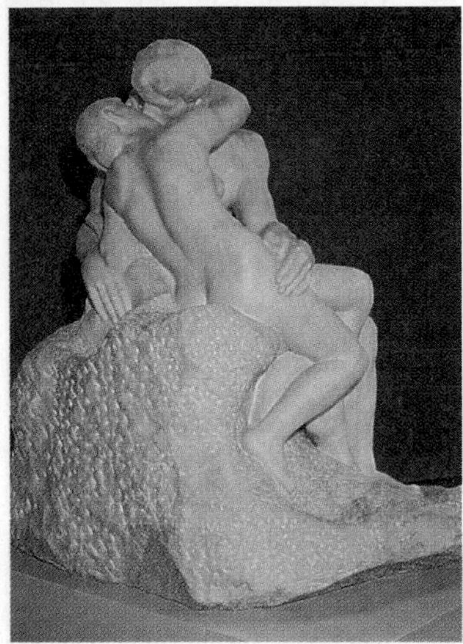

The Tate bought Rodin's "The Kiss" for Great Britain.

The deaths of **Maurice Utrillo** and **Fernand Leger**, following those of **Henri Matisse** and **Raoul Dufy**, have robbed French painting of its greatest colourists. Utrillo, an alcoholic, painted his views of old Montmartre from postcards, producing empty townscapes in subtle shades of white that always commanded high prices. Matisse's last arthritic years were spent creating pictures of exquisite expressiveness with cut-out shapes of brilliantly coloured paper which he manipulated.

Matisse spent his old age making cut-outs such as "The Snail" and "Jazz".

1956

JANUARY

Su	Mo	Tu	We	Th	Fr	Sa
1	2	3	4	5	6	7
8	9	10	11	12	13	14
15	16	17	18	19	20	21
22	23	24	25	26	27	28
29	30	31				

1. Khartoum: The Sudan is declared an independent republic.

1. South Vietnam: Pro-Western Ngo Dinh Diem wins the republic's first general election.

2. UK: The Astronomer Royal says the idea of space travel is "bilge".

3. UK: The headmaster of Eton says comprehensives are a real threat to education.

4. UK: Dr Arthur Michael Ramsey is named Archbishop of York.

5. Monaco: Prince Rainier III announces his engagement to actress Grace Kelly (→19/4).

9. Algeria: 26 die in attacks by Algerian rebels (→7/2).

11. Bath: A Home Guard unit ordered to disband by the Home Office refuses, saying: "We'll carry on in mufti."

13. Jordan: Anti-US rioters burn down an American hospital (→1/3).

15. Moscow: A new five-year plan is announced, calling for more heavy industry (→18/3).

16. Italy: The Winter Olympics open in Cortina d'Ampezzo (→6/2).

16. Cairo: Nasser assumes full executive powers (→16/6).

17. London: An enquiry opens into a proposed £55 million development of the Barbican area of the City (→25/5).

19. London: BEA now flies from London to Paris for £10, to Milan for £27 and to Zurich for £20 10/-.

25. London: Attlee takes his seat in the Lords (→18/6).

26. London: The import and export of heroin is banned.

30. Washington: Eden and Eisenhower meet for talks (→29/2).

DEATHS

23. Hungarian-born British film director Sir Alexander Korda (*16/9/1893).→

31. British author Alan Alexander Milne (*18/1/1882).

More British troops sent to Cyprus

British paratroopers unload their equipment after arriving at Nicosia.

Jan 12. Newly-arrived British paratroopers were patrolling the streets of Nicosia and Limassol today as tension mounted in Cyprus. The British Government has rushed in reinforcements following the murder of a Turkish policeman outside his home in Paphos, awakening the threat of serious inter-communal trouble.

The murder – the first of a Turkish-Cypriot by EOKA terrorists – brought thousands of Turks onto the streets threatening to take "five Greek lives for every Turk". Dr Kutchuk, leader of the "Cyprus is Turkish" party, condemned the killing and demanded strong measures by the Governor, Field Marshal Sir John Harding.

British troops captured eight EOKA men in a big sweep of the Troodos mountains, and seized a "formidable" haul of weapons. Three terrorists face the death penalty for carrying weapons.

Governor Harding has been holding secret meetings with Archbishop Makarios, the Greek-Cypriot leader, but there is little hope of meeting his demands for self-determination (→26/2).

Korda, father of the British cinema, dies

Jan 23. Sir Alexander Korda, the daring Hungarian producer, who more than any man saved the British film industry, died today, aged 67. He came to London in 1931, formed London Films, and began a run of success with "The Private Life of Henry VIII", starring Charles Laughton.

During the Thirties he built Denham Studios while producing such pictures as "The Ghost Goes West", "The Scarlet Pimpernel", with Leslie Howard, and "Fire Over England", Vivien Leigh's first film. After the war he made "The Fallen Idol", "The Third Man" and "Richard III" at Shepperton. Witty in six languages, he made £2 million and put most of it back into films.

Korda – Britain's movie czar.

Queen gets a warm welcome in Nigeria

Jan 29. Wildly-excited crowds running alongside the royal motorcade raised billowing clouds of red dust when the Queen and the Duke of Edinburgh made the 13-mile drive from the airport into Lagos at the start of their visit to Nigeria yesterday. At the entrance to the city the Queen left her car to be greeted by Chief Adele, president of the city council, and to receive a bouquet from a five-year-old Nigerian boy. "We are glad to be among the people of the capital who, for nearly a century, have belonged to the large family of the British Commonwealth," she said.

When the Queen and the Duke attended morning service today in the Cathedral Church of Christ, the pressures of the huge crowd outside snapped timber posts and bent steel barriers. A British police superintendent climbed on the barrier and then jumped on the shoulders of the crowd, hurling people back. A couple from the Gold Coast and their son, aged six, were extricated from the crush.

Time to get cows in with Bomb warning

Jan 17. Britain is to get a new air raid warning system to help protect people from radioactive fall-out in the event of nuclear attack. The advice is to stay indoors if there is an attack, because experts currently believe people in the area of the blast might be ill for as much as three months – or even die – if they are exposed to radiation.

The national warning system, which will cost £240,000, will be based on messages sent in by members of the Royal Observer Corps from around the country. The Corps already has observation posts at 15-mile intervals around the country, with telephone wires dug into the ground.

Priority will be to estimate which direction clouds of radiation from a blast will take. This will give farmers a chance to move their livestock indoors, and allow others to stock up with food, said General Sir Sidney Kirkman, the chief of Civil Defence (→25/10/57).

1956

FEBRUARY

Su	Mo	Tu	We	Th	Fr	Sa
			1	2	3	4
5	6	7	8	9	10	11
12	13	14	15	16	17	18
19	20	21	22	23	24	25
26	27	28	29			

1. Paris: Socialist leader Guy Mollet becomes premier.→

1. Washington: President Eisenhower and Eden sign declaration warning Third World countries against accepting Soviet aid.

3. London: Harold Macmillan, who succeeded R.A. Butler as Chancellor last December, pleads for wage restraint.→

6. Italy: The Winter Olympics end at Cortina d'Ampezzo.

6. UK: An opinion poll shows 49 per cent of Britons still favour the death penalty (→16).

7. Algiers: Mollet promises that France will not abandon Algeria (→2/3).

8. London: Britain signs an agreement aimed at granting Malaya independence by August 1957 (→3/8/57).

9. Oxford: W.H. Auden is elected Professor of Poetry.

14. Washington: Eisenhower's doctors say he is healthy enough to seek another term at the White House (→29).

14. Moscow: The 20th Communist Party Congress opens (→18/3).

15. Helsinki: Premier Urho Kekkonen is elected president of Finland.

16. London: MPs vote in favour of abolishing the death penalty (→16/6).

18. UK: The first provincial ITV station starts broadcasting.

21. London: The Duke of Edinburgh announces an award scheme for enterprising young people.

22. Portsmouth: Newcastle United beat Portsmouth 2-0 in the first league match played under floodlights.

23. West Germany: The army bans the goose-step (→9/7).

26. Cyprus: Colonial Secretary Lennox-Boyd arrives for talks with Makarios.→

29. Washington: Eisenhower says he will seek re-election as president (→26/4).

29. UK: Ex-BBC TV star Muffin the Mule makes his debut on ITV.

We ain't gonna ride in the back no more

Mrs Rosa Parks seated in the whites-only section of a Montgomery bus.

Feb 29. Alabama is in turmoil again today as black civil rights activists fight to desegregate American schools and bus services. Diehard whites are preparing further demonstrations after today's federal court ruling that the University of Alabama must readmit Autherine Lucy, its first black student.

Riots erupted when she was first admitted. Angry crowds threw eggs and rocks at her, and she was lucky to escape serious injury. The college suspended her, acting, they claimed, to save her from "great bodily harm", but the civil rights movement accused the college of giving in to mob rule. The federal court has now supported that view and ordered the college to provide adequate protection on her return.

The situation on the buses is even more explosive. Huge crowds have been protesting in Montgomery against the arrest of 115 blacks on charges of boycotting the city's buses. The trouble began two months ago when Rosa Parks, a Montgomery woman, refused to move from the front, whites-only, section of a city bus to the rear, in protest against bus segregation. She was arrested, fined and jailed. Blacks boycotted the buses in protest, and they were arrested for "organised boycott" (→1/3).

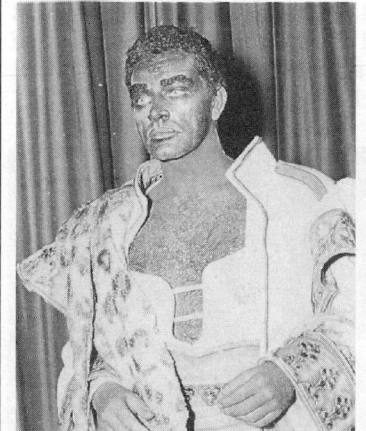

In the Old Vic's latest production of Othello, the role of Othello is to be taken by two actors: Burton and Neville. Here, Burton is offering his portrayal, which he acts every other night.

Tear gas greeting for French premier

Feb 6. The French Premier, Guy Mollet, was hissed, booed, pelted with tomatoes, stoned, and attacked with tear gas by mobs of French settlers when he arrived in Algeria today for talks with the settlers and Arab leaders. The talks take place against a background of 15 months of guerrilla warfare mounted by revolutionary Arab nationalists in the FLN, the National Liberation Front. The settlers, fearing Mollet will make concessions to the FLN, chanted "To the gallows, Mollet", as he retreated into Government House surrounded by 3,000 Republican Guards specially flown in from Paris (→7).

Bombings mark new Cyprus impasse

Feb 29. This morning Archbishop Makarios, the leader of Cyprus' Greek community, sent a message of goodwill to Turkish Cypriot spokesman Mufti Mehmed Dana. This was perhaps the only encouraging sign in a day of renewed EOKA bombings and inconclusive talks between Makarios and Colonial Secretary Alan Lennox-Boyd.

Britain is offering Cyprus a draft constitution which would allow eventual self-determination but lays down power-sharing by the Greek and Turkish communities.

The Archbishop is understood to have maintained his demands for self-determination, including a complete amnesty for all political offenders and a guarantee of a Greek Cypriot majority under any new constitution (→5/3).

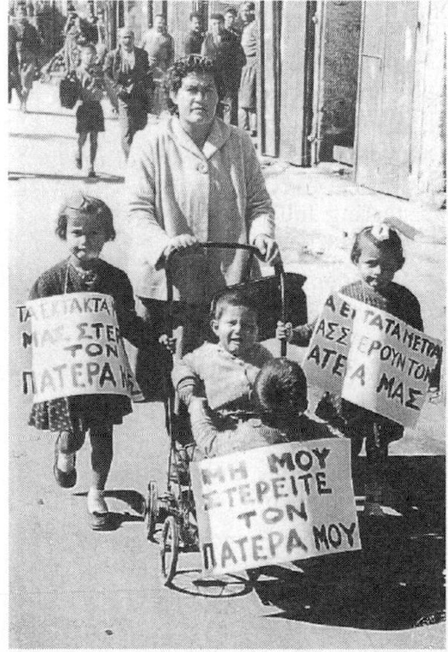

A Cypriot family march in protest.

Credit squeezed as the bank rate soars

Feb 17. Harold Macmillan, the Chancellor of the Exchequer, today announced a tighter credit squeeze, and cuts in milk and bread subsidies. The Bank Rate is hoisted to five and a half per cent – its highest level since the financial crisis of 1931.

Mr Macmillan said: "The nation must pause in its pursuit of a higher living standard. Inflation is obstinate and serious" (→22/3).

1956

MARCH

Su	Mo	Tu	We	Th	Fr	Sa
				1	2	3
4	5	6	7	8	9	10
11	12	13	14	15	16	17
18	19	20	21	22	23	24
25	26	27	28	29	30	31

1. US: Alabama University expels its first black student, Autherine Lucy, claiming she made false charges against it (→ 5).

2. Pakistan: The MCC apologises for insulting a local umpire during the current tour.

2. Paris: French Morocco is granted independence (→ 18).

4. UK: Footballers demand extra fees for televised matches.

5. Cyprus: Britain begins jamming radio broadcasts from Greece to the island (→ 10).

5. Washington: The Supreme Court upholds a lower court's ban on racial segregation in public colleges.→

10. Cyprus: Riots break out in protest at the deportation of Makarios (→ 20).

15. New York: Opening of the musical "My Fair Lady", starring Julie Andrews and Rex Harrison.

16. Aden: Anti-British strikes break out (→ 22/4).

18. France: A massive airlift of French troops to Algeria begins (→ 11/4).

20. Cyprus: Turks take to the streets, rioting and looting Greek shops.→

20. Tunisia: France recognises Tunisian independence, with Habib Bourguiba as first president (→ 11/4).

22. London: Macmillan reveals that Britain had a balance of payments deficit in 1955 of £103 million (→ 26/6).

23. Karachi: Pakistan is declared an Islamic Republic.

24. UK: Mrs L. Carver's E.S.B. wins the Grand National.

26. Saigon: The last French troops leave.

27. London: Promising students at the Royal Academy of Dramatic Arts include Albert Finney and Richard Briers.

28. Reykjavik: The Icelandic parliament calls for the withdrawal of US troops from the island.

Khrushchev slams Stalin

March 18. Joseph Stalin has been denounced as brutal, despotic and a criminal murderer in a sensational and explicit speech by his successor, Nikita Khrushchev, to the Soviet Communist Party elite, meeting in Moscow.

Details emerged today of a six-hour speech by Khrushchev at a closed session of the 20th Party Congress last month; they have already had the effect of a bombshell both in the Soviet Union and beyond its borders. It appears that the Soviet leader is attempting to end Stalinism once and for all, as well as to consolidate his own position.

Laying bare the worst of Stalin's iniquities, Khrushchev spoke of the late dictator's paranoia which led to the pre-war purges, his secret plots to murder critics and friends, and his erroneous military decisions which cost thousands of lives. He said Stalin showed cowardice and panic during the war. "Here we see no wisdom, but only a demonstration of ... brutal force", and he spoke of Stalin's "odious falsifications and criminal violations of legality".

When Khrushchev reached the later phase of Stalin's 30-year rule he seemed overcome by bitter hatred, and at one point delegates interrupted him. After he said Moscow had become a city ridden by plots and intrigue in which no one knew who might be the next victim, there were shouts of: "How did you stand it? Why didn't you kill him?" Khrushchev replied: "What could we do? There was a reign of terror. You just had to look at him wrongly and the next day you lost your head." There was indignation in the hall when Khrushchev said that, of 139 members of the Central Committee elected in 1934, 70 per cent were arrested and shot on charges of anti-revolutionary crimes.

Stalin would personally approve long lists of those to be arrested, beaten and tortured, sent to him by successive police chiefs.

Khrushchev debunked Stalin's image as a "military genius" in scathing language. He said he had ignored warnings that Hitler was about to attack Russia, and his other mistakes in 1941 had brought the country to the verge of disaster. Stalin had visited the front only once during the war, and never went to any liberated city.

Khrushchev also painted a shocking picture of Stalin's all-consuming vanity and the "glorification of his own person". He had been presented as an infallible sage, said the party secretary, and the greatest leader and sublime strategist of all times and nations, but he was often ignorant of what was happening in the Soviet Union.

Turning to the Soviet Union's foreign policy, Khrushchev insisted that Stalin had played a "shameful role" over relations with Yugoslavia, and had boasted that he had only to shake his little finger for Tito to fall.

The speech has already touched off violent rioting in Georgia, Stalin's homeland, but it is an event of world consequence which could lead to an improvement in Soviet relations with the West (→ 10/4).

Khrushchev, flanked by Zhukov (l.) and Bulganin, waves to the crowds.

Hussein dismisses British commander of Jordanian army

King Hussein with Glubb Pasha.

March 2. Lieutenant General John Glubb, commander of the Arab Legion, was summarily dismissed by King Hussein at 2pm today and given just two hours to leave the country with his family.

Best known as Glubb Pasha, he has served three Jordanian kings. Since 1939 he has turned the legion into the most efficient Arab fighting force, with 35,000 Bedouin soldiers and 450 British-trained officers.

Arab feeling has been inflamed by the recent use of the Legion to quell demonstrations against the Baghdad Pact between the Allies and Iraq. In addition, recent magazine articles had suggested that Glubb, not the 20-year-old King, was running the country. Hussein has bowed to popular opinion which backs the Arab nationalist movement led by Egypt (→ 14/9).

Steam is doomed as trains go electric

March 6. The days of steam trains on British railways are numbered. Today, in what he called a "bold" decision, the chairman of the British Transport Commission, Sir Brian Robertson, announced that electrified services would be introduced, taking power from overhead wires, continental-style. The first line to be converted is expected to be between Euston, Liverpool and Manchester, with 1959 the target for completion.

King plans to use "the weapon of love"

Dr King holds his press conference on the steps of the courthouse.

March 22. The Rev. Dr Martin Luther King vowed today to continue the fight for black rights, using "passive resistance and the weapon of love". He had just been convicted of organising the bus boycotts in Montgomery, Alabama, in which 115 blacks were arrested. The civil rights leaders responded with mass demonstrations, pilgrimages and days of prayer.

One of the arrested leaders, the Rev. Ralph Abernathy, called on the people "to pray to Almighty God and get into the hearts of Montgomery's people so that justice may be done".

At the secular level, justice is having a difficult time. The University of Alabama has defied the federal court order to readmit their first black student. Autherine Lucy has been "permanently expelled" on the grounds that she made "outrageous, false and baseless accusations" against college officials.

The tide of legislation is flowing, however. On March 5, the Supreme Court ruled that its 1954 Brown v Board of Education decision, which outlawed segregation in state schools, extends to tax-supported colleges. This follows the refusal of the University of North Carolina to admit three blacks on the basis of their race.

Yesterday President Eisenhower responded at last to pressure from civil rights leaders for support. He said: "It is incumbent on all the South to show some progress toward racial integration" (→10/4).

British deport Makarios

March 9. Archbishop Makarios, the leader of the Greek-Cypriot community, drove to Nicosia airport today bound for Athens – only to find himself deported and heading for the Seychelles and exile. His colleague and secretary, Bishop Kyprianos of Kyrenia, was with him on the flight.

As news of the deportation spread through Cyprus, bringing riots and threats of a massive bombing campaign by EOKA terrorists, the Governor, Sir John Harding, claimed that Makarios had been removed as "a major obstacle to a return to peaceful conditions" and that the archbishop had "actively fostered terrorism".

While troops and Special Branch officers searched the homes of the two men, the Governor issued a statement which alleged that Makarios had inspired Colonel Grivas, a former Greek army officer, to form EOKA, the terror organisation which has conducted a campaign of murder and bombing in Cyprus since 1953. It also accused the archbishop of organising funds to buy arms and explosives, and allowing his palace to be used for producing terrorist leaflets. In the Commons, Labour leader Hugh Gaitskell said the deportation was an "act of folly" (→10).

Makarios offers a final blessing.

Cyprus Governor spends night on a bomb

March 25. An island-wide curfew brought peace to Cyprus today, but earlier this week Field Marshal Sir John Harding literally spent the night sleeping on a time bomb. The bomb had been planted by a servant – an EOKA sympathiser – in Government House, but the timer proved faulty and it was exploded harmlessly in the grounds.

Afterwards Sir John drove through the empty streets of the capital, where thousands of troops were deployed for the one-day curfew imposed to avoid demonstrations on Greek Independence Day. All air services to the island were cancelled and trunk telephone calls banned.

Despite the restrictions, bombs were thrown at army patrols in Paphos in Western Cyprus (→1/4).

The Queen Mother's Devon Loch seems to be running well ...

... but there's a disaster at ground level and her feet start to slip ...

... and even though she rights herself and her jockey stays in the saddle ...

... ESB moves on through and wins this year's Grand National.

APRIL

Su	Mo	Tu	We	Th	Fr	Sa
1	2	3	4	5	6	7
8	9	10	11	12	13	14
15	16	17	18	19	20	21
22	23	24	25	26	27	28
29	30					

1. Cyprus: The first British civilian is murdered by EOKA terrorists (→2).

1. UK: The first US U-2 spy planes arrive at RAF Lakenheath.

2. Athens: King Paul of Greece declares his support for Archbishop Makarios (→21/5).

6. Warsaw: Former Communist leader Wladyslaw Gomulka is released from jail.→

7. Madrid: Spanish Morocco is granted independence (→11/6).

10. US: White men drag Nat King Cole off the stage as he sings to a white audience in Birmingham, Alabama (→23).

11. Algiers: The French government dissolves the Algerian parliament (→18/5).

14. Chicago: A device is demonstrated which records TV programmes on magnetic tape and plays them back.

16. Sofia: Bulgarian premier Vulko Chervenkov is forced to resign in an anti-Stalinist purge (→18/7).

18. London: Khrushchev and Bulganin arrive on an official visit.→

19. Gold Coast: African leaders propose independence for the colony, which would be renamed Ghana (→11/5).

22. Aden: British border guards clash with Yemeni troops (→16/1/57).

23. US: City Bus Lines in Montgomery, Alabama, order an end to segregated seating on their buses (→8/9).

26. Washington: Richard Nixon says he will seek renomination as candidate for vice-president (→25/6).

26. UK: The Archbishop of Canterbury says Premium Bonds "debase the nation's spiritual currency" (→26/7).

29. US: A report claims the US is capable of making intercontinental ballistic missiles.

DEATH

15. German artist Emil Nolde (*7/8/1867).

"I'd vote Tory" says visiting Khrushchev

An unlikely supporter – Khrushchev promises his vote to Sir Anthony.

April 26. Talks between the British Government and the Soviet leaders Bulganin and Khrushchev during their eight-day visit to Britain have ended "in a spirit of candour and realism", according to an official communique tonight.

But officials on both sides did not try to hide that there has been no new agreement about European security. The Premier, Mr Bulganin, has been urbane and bland, while Mr Khrushchev has sometimes been truculent in off-the-cuff statements during their tour of Britain. However, his official hosts did not quarrel with his summing up: "You do not like Communism. We do not like capitalism. There is only one way out – peaceful co-existence."

Embarrassed Labour Party chiefs admitted today that George Brown, a shadow cabinet minister, and Mr Khrushchev exchanged angry words during a boisterous and lengthy dinner party. Mr Khrushchev reportedly said afterwards that if he was a Briton he would vote Tory.

Rocky Marciano to retire undefeated

April 25. Rocky Marciano, never defeated as a professional boxer, and world heavyweight champion since 1952, has announced his retirement from the ring.

The 33-year-old son of a New England shoe-maker, Marciano will be remembered for his comparatively short (5ft 11in) stature, his uncompromising punching power, his termination, in 1951, of Joe Louis's comeback hopes, his defeat of Jersey Joe Walcott for the title, his six defences and his perfect record: 49 fights, 49 wins, in which only five opponents survived to hear the final bell.

Soviet thaw frees Polish prisoners

April 10. As part of the new Soviet de-Stalinisation campaign, the government has ordered the release of many leading Polish Communists imprisoned on Stalin's orders. One of those completely rehabilitated is Wladyslaw Gomulka, who was the Polish Party Leader until his arrest in 1949, when he was accused of Titoism and imprisoned. Gomulka was lucky not to have been shot; in his "secret speech" to the Twentieth Party Congress, Nikita Khrushchev confirmed that Stalin had ordered the murder of the entire pre-war Polish Communist leadership (→16).

Bonds give Britons chance of a flutter

April 17. A new £1 premium bond offering tax-free prizes of up to £1,000 was introduced by Harold Macmillan, the Chancellor of the Exchequer, today. Anticipating criticism on moral grounds, he said: "This is not a pool or lottery where you spend your money. The investor is saving his money." There will be a limit on individual holdings – perhaps £250.

The scheme was mocked by the Opposition as a squalid raffle, and denounced by some churchmen as an encouragement to gambling. It is part of a "Savings Budget" package to coax more money out of the public. Another innovation which was announced today is tax relief on annuity payments made on some pension schemes (→26).

Prince and his show girl wed in Monaco

The Prince and the showgirl wed.

April 19. In fairytales, a beautiful girl dreams that one day her prince will come. Today, in the suitably glamorous setting of the French Riviera, the fairytale came true for the American actress, Grace Kelly when she married Prince Rainier III, monarch of the miniature Principality of Monaco. The Catholic marriage ceremony was attended by over 1,200 guests, including dignitaries from 25 nations. Appropriately for a Hollywood star, the service was televised (→23/1/57).

1956

MAY

Su	Mo	Tu	We	Th	Fr	Sa
		1	2	3	4	5
6	7	8	9	10	11	12
13	14	15	16	17	18	19
20	21	22	23	24	25	26
27	28	29	30	31		

1. Berlin: 100,000 Germans demonstrate in favour of German re-unification (→ 21/6).

2. Kathmandu: Coronation of King Mahendra of Nepal.

2. London: Ex-RA president Sir Alfred Munnings calls the RA's Summer Show "bits of nonsense" hung on the wall.

4. Colombo: The Ceylon government tells Britain it wants British air and sea bases removed (→ 30/6/58).

7. London: The Health Minister refuses a campaign against smoking, saying he is not convinced it does harm (→ 26/6/57).

10. UK: Labour makes gains in municipal elections.

11. London: The Colonial Secretary approves Gold Coast independence (→ 18/9).

13. Monaco: Stirling Moss wins his second Grand Prix (→ 20/7/57).

15. London: Talks on the terms of independence for Singapore end in failure (→ 25/10).

16. London: Surrey's Jim Laker takes all ten Australian wickets for 88 in 46 overs runs at the Oval.

21. Pacific: The US drops the first H-bomb from a plane over Bikini Atoll (→ 13/2/57).

21. Cyprus: One person dies and 12 are hurt in renewed clashes in Nicosia (→ 23).

23. Cyprus: The government says everyone over 12 is to get an identity card.→

24. New York: Egypt and Israel agree to allow UN observation posts in the Gaza Strip (→ 20/12).

25. London: Redevelopment plans for the Barbican area aim to create a residential and cultural "oasis".

31. UK: Cricketer Len Hutton is knighted in the Queen's Birthday Honours (→ 27/7).

DEATH

20. British author, cartoonist and critic Sir Max Beerbohm (*24/8/1872).

Spy link in the missing frogman mystery

May 14. The Government admitted today that a frogman was carrying out "underwater tests" near the cruiser carrying the visiting Soviet leaders Nikita Khrushchev and Nikolai Bulganin.

Earlier it had denied any underwater activity near the Ordzhonikdze and two escorting destroyers, but now it is agreed that a frogman, Commander "Buster" Crabb, was carrying out trials of "certain equipment" in Portsmouth Harbour.

Soviet papers have accused Britain of "shameful underwater espionage" and "dirty work by enemies of international co-operation".

Commander Crabb disappeared during the operation and is presumed drowned (→ 26/6/57).

Commander Crabb ready to dive.

Osborne's ranting misfit looks back

May 10. A ranting young misfit called Jimmy Porter upset the conventions of middle-class English drama last night in "Look Back in Anger", a new play which is largely one long tirade by him against the English Establishment, focused on his middle-class wife.

John Osborne is the first new writer to have a play presented by the English Stage Company at the Royal Court Theatre. The critics summed up his hero as a "young pup" and "rotten with self-pity", but Kenneth Tynan said he represented post-war youth "as it really is" in "the best young play of its decade".

Algerians hack 19 French soldiers to bits

May 18. A search party sent out to look for a 19-strong French patrol, missing in the mountains between Algiers and Constantine, came upon a pool of blood near the tents of Arab nomads. In a silo close by, the searchers found the soldiers' bodies, decapitated and hacked to pieces. This is just the latest in a series of atrocities perpetrated in the increasingly savage uprising of Arab nationalists.

Last week 20 French settlers were massacred, and their farms burned down, some 20 miles west of Oran. In the Tlemcen region, near the Moroccan border, 16 French soldiers have been killed and 20 taken prisoner. When the insurrection began, in 1954, the rebels in the FLN numbered only a few hundred. Now they count their supporters in thousands, and they have killed over 100 civilian Europeans and over a thousand Arabs loyal to France. The French are paying a high price for their early scorn for Arabs as fighters (→ 26/5/57).

Self-service shops get mixed reception

May 23. Women have been warned against being "lured into overspending" by the new self-service shops now springing up across the country. The latest trend has doubled, even quadrupled, sales in many cases. Retailers claim the new system keeps prices down, but critics say it encourages pilfering, removes the personal touch, and threatens the livelihood of small shopkeepers, who cannot compete.

Large reward offered for capture of Greek-Cypriot terrorist

May 25. Posters appeared throughout Cyprus today offering a £10,000 reward for the capture of Colonel George Grivas, the Greek-born leader of the EOKA terrorist movement. Informants are promised protective custody and a passage to "anywhere in the world".

Grivas, whose orders are signed "Dighenis" – meaning "two peoples" – was the leader of the resistance units during the German occupation of Greece. A fierce nationalist, he achieved notoriety for his savagery against many Communist prisoners during the Greek civil war.

He has declared that EOKA's aim is Enosis – the union of Cyprus with Greece – and nothing but Enosis (→ 16/6).

Suspected Cypriot terrorists behind the wire at Camp Kokkinotrimithia.

1956

JUNE

Su	Mo	Tu	We	Th	Fr	Sa
					1	2
3	4	5	6	7	8	9
10	11	12	13	14	15	16
17	18	19	20	21	22	23
24	25	26	27	28	29	30

1. Moscow: Molotov resigns as Soviet foreign minister.

1. UK: A report by British doctors urges an 1nquiry into child abuse.

3. UK: British Rail abolishes Third Class coaches on trains.

6. UK: Mr M.P. Wertheimer's Lavandin wins the Derby.

8. Stockholm: The Queen arrives for a three-day visit.

9. Washington: Eisenhower undergoes emergency surgery for an intestinal obstruction.

11. Morocco: Emigration to Israel is prohibited.

13. Vienna: Herbert von Karajan is made artistic director of the Vienna State Opera.

13. Paris: Real Madrid win the first European Cup, beating Stade de Reims 4-3.

16. Cyprus: A terrorist bomb explodes in a restaurant, killing the US vice-consul (→ 12/7).

16. Cairo: New Soviet foreign minister Dmitri Shepilov opens talks with Nasser (→ 23).

18. UK: The Queen invests Sir Anthony Eden and Earl Attlee with the Order of the Garter.

21. East Berlin: The East German government claims it has released 19,000 people from jail in the last week.

23. Cairo: Nasser is elected President of Egypt unopposed.

24. Nigeria: 26 die in the crash of a BOAC airliner.

25. US: Senator John F. Kennedy launches a campaign to win the Democratic vice-presidential nomination (→ 29/7).

26. London: Chancellor Macmillan announces spending cuts of £76 million (→ 24/7).

29. London: Playwright Arthur Miller marries Marilyn Monroe.→

BIRTH

6. Swedish tennis player Bjorn Borg.

DEATH

11. British artist Sir Frank Brangwyn (*13/5/1867).

Polish workers riot against Communists

As tanks move down a Poznan street, rioting workers flee from the troops.

June 29. Martial law has been imposed on the Polish city of Poznan after riots which have left 38 people dead. Some of the dead were Communist officials caught by angry demonstrators after the police had opened fire. At one stage the rioters, led by rail workers, were in control of the secret police headquarters and the town hall.

Tanks were brought in to put down the demonstration, and machine-guns were used against the crowds in the streets near the Exhibition Hall where an international fair is being held.

Bernard Buckman, a British exporter, said that on the way to the hall he saw hundreds of workers marching down the main street, shoulder to shoulder. "They were quite good humoured, chanting slogans about "Cheaper Bread" and "Higher Wages". When they saw my car was flying the Union Jack, they cheered and clapped," he said.

"But within minutes of the police opening fire, the mood changed. When they heard a child was one of those shot down the demonstrators, roaring with rage, converged on the secret police headquarters. It soon became a regular battle. Ferocious street-fighting broke out" (→ 19/8).

Death penalty isn't quite dead yet

June 16. Progress in the abolition of Britain's death penalty suffered a set-back today when, by four votes, the House of Commons voted to retain hanging for murders committed by prisoners already serving life sentences. The amendment gives greater protection to prison officers. Two other amendments – to keep capital punishment as the penalty for killing in the course of an armed robbery and for killing a policeman – were defeated by comfortable majorities. Today's surprise defeat, however, has disturbed the complacency of the abolitionists and will strengthen the hand of the House of Lords to add more amendments of their own (→ 10/7).

British troops quit Suez Canal Zone

June 13. At 6.30 this morning a British brigadier shook hands with an Egyptian colonel and stepped aboard a transport for Cyprus. The last British troops were quitting the Canal Zone base, five days ahead of the deadline set in the 1954 Anglo-Egyptian agreement. British civilian technicians will remain in the Zone to help Egyptians maintain the base. A British Army spokesman said the departure was made "quietly and with dignity" – though not entirely amicably. The Egyptian strongman, Colonel Nasser, refused military honours to the departing British, but turned up later for his own parade (→ 21/7).

World record for 5,000m set by Pirie

June 19. Gordon Pirie, the tall, outspoken South London Harrier, predicted five years ago that one day he would run 5,000 metres in under 13 minutes 40 seconds. As the world record then stood at 13:58.2, his boast was dismissed as bombast.

In the clear air of Bergen, in Norway, Pirie has made good that boast, defeating the European champion Vladimir Kuts in a record 13 minutes 36.8 seconds.

The egghead and the hourglass – Arthur Miller and Marilyn Monroe.

1956

JULY

Su	Mo	Tu	We	Th	Fr	Sa
1	2	3	4	5	6	7
8	9	10	11	12	13	14
15	16	17	18	19	20	21
22	23	24	25	26	27	28
29	30	31				

1. US: The wreckage of two missing airliners is found in the Grand Canyon.

3. London: Pandit Nehru and New Zealand prime minister Sir Sidney Holland are given the freedom of the City.

5. London: The Clean Air Bill is passed.

7. Wimbledon: Lew Hoad beats Ken Rosewall in the Men's Singles final; Shirley Fry beats Angela Buxton for the Women's Singles title.

9. West Germany: Military service starts (→25/5/56).

10. London: The Lords overwhelmingly votes against the abolition of capital punishment.

10. Washington: Eisenhower confirms he will run for a second term (→29).

13. West Germany: Seven Hungarian students ask for asylum after arriving in a hijacked Hungarian airliner.

18. Budapest: Pro-Stalinist premier Matyas Rakosi resigns (→23/10).

21. Cairo: The World Bank follows Britain and the US in refusing to help fund the Aswan Dam.→

24. London: Eden tells British banks to keep up their credit squeeze (→10/12).

26. London: ERNIE (Electronic Random Number Indicator Equipment), to pick Premium Bond winners, is unveiled (→1/11).

28. London: The government freezes all Egyptian assets held in Britain (→30).

29. Washington: Democratic Senator Hubert Humphrey of Minnesota says he will seek the vice-presidency (→16/8).

29. France: The British Jaguar team wins the Le Mans 24-Hour race.

30. Ankara: Turkish prime minister Adnan Menderes says he wants Britain to stay in Cyprus (→28/9).

30. London: Eden tells Nasser he cannot have the Suez Canal, and imposes an arms embargo on Egypt (→1/8).

UK fury as Nasser seizes Suez Canal

July 26. Egyptians are dancing in the streets tonight after hearing their President, Colonel Nasser, announce that he has nationalised the Anglo-French-controlled Suez Canal Company. He was speaking, charged with emotion, at Alexandria on the fourth anniversary of his overthrow of King Farouk. Switching from classical Arabic into the Egyptian vernacular, Nasser said if the imperialist powers did not like what he had done they could "choke to death on their fury". He threatened to imprison any Canal employees, many of whom are British, if they tried to quit their jobs.

Neither Britain nor France have sought to hide their anger at the Egyptian dictator's arbitrary action in laying hands on the vital lifeline for oil supplies to Europe. The French, as builders of the 103-mile waterway through the desert from Port Said to Suez, are particularly outraged.

Nasser's sudden decision to seize the Canal comes in the wake of the refusal by Britain and the US to finance the building of the Aswan High Dam. The Egyptians were told their economy is too weak to sustain such a project, even with Western help. Most observers believe the decisive factor in influencing the Anglo-US decision was the secret purchase of $200 million worth of arms from the Communist bloc, for which Nasser has mortgaged Egypt's cotton crop for several years.

Ecstatic Egyptians assure Nasser that they approve his Canal seizure.

In his speech tonight, Nasser said he would use the revenues from the Canal to finance the building of the High Dam which, he claimed, would increase Egypt's cultivable land by more than half, and provide massive supplies of hydro-electric power. "We shall industrialise Egypt and compete with the West," Nasser cried. "We are marching from strength to strength."

As Nasser was speaking, steel-helmeted Egyptian police were cordoning off the Cairo administrative offices of the Canal Company. The main entrance was sealed with red wax. Police also moved in on the company's buildings in Ismailia.

Although Nasser has promised to pay compensation to the shareholders and not to interfere with Canal traffic, Sir Anthony Eden, the British Prime Minister, is insistent that "a man with Colonel Nasser's record" cannot be allowed "to have his thumb on our windpipe". The British and French are clearly determined to take action against Nasser (→28).

New constitution is planned for Cyprus

July 12. The British colony of Cyprus is to be given a new, liberal constitution and will be guided towards independence, but progress on these lines depends on the ending of terrorism on the island, Sir Anthony Eden told MPs tonight. Lord Radcliffe, an Appeal Court judge, is going to Cyprus for consultations before drawing up the new constitution. He is not expected to visit the Seychelles to see the exiled Archbishop Makarios, who is pushing for union with Greece, a prospect opposed by the island's Turkish minority, but pursued with violence by the Greek-speaking EOKA terrorists (→30).

Laker takes 19 wickets in a Test Match

July 27. Jim Laker, the Yorkshire-born Surrey off-spinner, produced the best bowling figures ever returned in any first-class match to rout the Australians in the fourth Test match at Manchester.

His nine for 37 in Australia's disastrous first innings had been quite remarkable. To follow that with all ten wickets for 53 runs, in a spell interrupted by rain and bad light, was well-nigh unbelievable, particularly as his Surrey colleague, Tony Lock, toiled for 55 overs at the other end without gaining any reward at all.

Yet this was Laker's second such feat this season. In May he took ten for 88 for Surrey against the Australians.

Howzat! 19-wicket Jim Laker.

1956

AUGUST

Su	Mo	Tu	We	Th	Fr	Sa
			1	2	3	4
5	6	7	8	9	10	11
12	13	14	15	16	17	18
19	20	21	22	23	24	25
26	27	28	29	30	31	

1. London: Britain, France and the US hold urgent talks on the Suez Canal crisis (→2).

2. London: The Suez talks end with a call for an international conference on the 16th (→4).

4. Portsmouth: Paratroopers sail for Cyprus aboard the aircraft carrier, HMS Theseus (→8).

6. China: Reports say 2,000 people are believed dead after a typhoon struck Chekiang province last week.

8. London: Eden broadcasts on the Suez crisis, saying Nasser cannot be trusted (→12).

11. US: Abstract artist Jackson Pollock dies when his speeding car hits a tree.

12. Cairo: Nasser turns down an invitation to the London conference on Suez (→16).

16. Chicago: Adlai Stevenson is chosen as Democratic candidate for president (→17).

16. London: The Suez conference opens.→

17. Chicago: Senator Estes Kefauver is picked to run for Democratic vice-president, beating John Kennedy (→22).

19. Warsaw: Rehabilitated ex-premier Gomulka returns to the Communist Party Central Committee (→20/10).

22. San Francisco: Eisenhower and Nixon are renominated by the Republicans to run for the White House (→6/11).

27. London: Michael Croft founds the National Youth Theatre.

28. Cairo: Nasser expels two British envoys for "spying".

30. London: Two Egyptian diplomats are expelled in a tit-for-tat move.

DEATHS

11. US artist Jackson Pollock (*28/1/12).

14. German playwright Bertolt Brecht (*10/2/1898).→

16. Hungarian-born US actor Bela Lugosi (*20/10/1884).

25. US sociologist Alfred Kinsey (*23/6/1894).

Users' new plan for control of Suez Canal

Sir Anthony Eden tells Britain that Suez is "a matter of life and death".

Aug 23. Robert Menzies, the Australian Prime Minister, is off to Cairo as head of a five-nation team charged with putting to Colonel Nasser a plan for international control of the Suez Canal. With him will be diplomats from the US, Sweden, Iran and Ethiopia. The plan was agreed at the 22-nation conference which ended yesterday. Four countries – India, Ceylon, Indonesia and the Soviet Union – refused to join in; the remaining 18 account for 95 per cent of shipping passing through the Canal.

The US Secretary of State, John Foster Dulles, arrived in London a week ago with the draft plan, which is aimed at persuading Nasser to abandon operational control of the Canal in favour of an international board associated with the United Nations. Dulles, though firm in condemning Nasser's seizure of the Canal last month, has been rather more conciliatory towards Egypt than the British and the French.

Sir Anthony Eden, the British Prime Minister, gave a strong hint in his broadcast speech earlier this month that, if Nasser did not accept a reasonable settlement, the use of force could not be ruled out. A Royal Proclamation calling up some reservists has been issued, and holiday charter firms are standing by with 100 planes to airlift troops to the Mediterranean (→29).

British and French troops sail for Suez

Aug 29. A massive build-up of British and French forces is taking place in the Eastern Mediterranean, foreshadowing the possibility of military operations against Egypt.

It was announced in London tonight that "in view of developments in Egypt and the Canal Zone", French troops were to be stationed in Cyprus. At the French Mediterranean port of Marseilles, troops have been boarding ships requisitioned by the Defence Ministry.

British forces have been leaving for Cyprus since the beginning of the month. The 13,350-ton aircraft carrier, Theseus, left Portsmouth three weeks ago with troops and equipment of the 16th Parachute Brigade. Colonel Lindsay Fawkes, their CO, said about half were National Servicemen.

Plans for a joint Anglo-French command in the Eastern Mediterranean are well advanced. General Andre Beaufre, an expert on airborne operations, has been recalled from Algeria to command the French units of the new command. Though defence spokesmen in London and Paris remain tight-lipped, the emphasis on airborne forces leaves little doubt as to what is in prospect (→2/9).

Brecht, playwright of the people, dies

Aug 14. Bertolt Brecht, famous in Germany as the author of "The Threepenny Opera", a Victorian version of "The Beggars' Opera", died today in East Berlin, where his work is regularly produced by the state-subsidised Berliner Ensemble which he founded. The Nazis suppressed his work, and he wrote many anti-Nazi plays in exile in Los Angeles.

In 1947 Brecht denied being a Communist, but left the US the next day. The East German government offered him a theatre to work in where his plays, including "Mother Courage", could at last be performed. Last year he was awarded a Stalin prize. He gave no support to the East German workers uprising in 1953.

A corps of traffic wardens proposed

Aug 30. When parking meters are introduced they will be supervised by a new body of part-time traffic wardens. These will have no powers of arrest, but in due course will probably relieve the police of some of their traffic duties.

Harold Watkinson, the Minister of Transport, is keen on the idea which has been found to work well in America. Ex-Servicemen and retired policemen are considered likely recruits. Meter revenues may pay for them (→16/4/57).

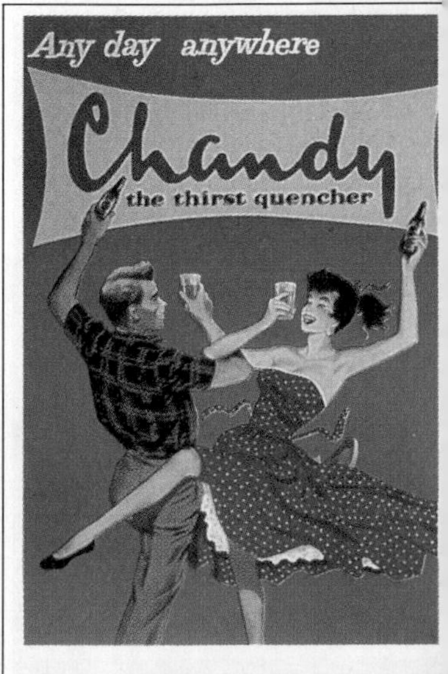

1956

SEPTEMBER

Su	Mo	Tu	We	Th	Fr	Sa
						1
2	3	4	5	6	7	8
9	10	11	12	13	14	15
16	17	18	19	20	21	22
23	24	25	26	27	28	29
30						

2. Cairo: Nasser says he will accept any solution to the Suez question "that does not affect sovereignty" (→5).

5. Tel Aviv: Israel breaks diplomatic silence and condemns Egypt over Suez (→9).

8. US: Clinton, Tennessee, is under a state of emergency as violence grows towards blacks trying to go to school (→11).

9. Cairo: Nasser rejects the US plan for international control of the Suez Canal (→12).

11. Washington: Eisenhower tells southern states to end schools segregation (→13/11).

12. London: Eden unveils a three-power plan for a Suez Users' Association; Nasser calls it "provocation" (→19).

14. Jordan: Ten Jordanians die in an Israeli raid (→13/2).

18. London: The Gold Coast will become Britain's first independent black African colony on March 6, 1957 (→2/3/57).

19. London: An 18-nation Suez Canal conference opens (→21).

21. London: The Suez talks end with agreement on setting up a Canal Users' Association.→

22. Panama: President Anastasio Somoza of Nicaragua is shot and gravely hurt visiting the Panama Canal Zone (→29).

26. London: Seretse Khama is to return to Bechuanaland after his six-year exile.

28. Moscow: The USSR and Japan agree a formula to end their state of war and restore full diplomatic relations.

29. Panama: Nicaraguan President Somoza dies; his son, vice-president Luis Somoza, takes over (→4/2/57).

BIRTH

29. British athlete Sebastian Coe.

DEATHS

7. British sportsman Charles Burgess Fry (*25/4/1872).

28. US air pioneer William E. Boeing (*1/10/1881).

Elvis' pelvis wins massive TV audience

Don't knock the rock, squares, 'cos the kids know that Elvis is the King.

Sept 10. Elvis Presley performed on American TV's Ed Sullivan Show last night and was viewed by 82 per cent of a potential audience of 54 million. With his best-selling record, "Heartbreak Hotel", in the charts since January, he is already a millionaire at the age of 21. Three years ago he was a truckdriver in his home-town of Memphis, where he was taken up by the local Sun Records company.

Last night he sang "Hound Dog" and "Love Me Tender", moving his hips, wrote a critic, "as if he was sneering with his legs". The New York Times dismissed his singing as "singularly distasteful." Not so to the teenagers, who made up the hysterical audience. Elvis's provocative gyrations and animal grunts sent them wild. It is being suggested that in future he should only be shown on TV from the waist upwards. Official disapproval only increases his appeal (→11).

British Cyprus troops in toffee tin blast

Sept 27. A "toffee tin bomb" planted in an army restroom wounded seven newly-arrived British soldiers today as they attended a "settling in" lecture. Ambulance men had to fight their way through dense clouds of dust and fumes to rescue the men, three of whom were in a critical condition. Several hundred civilian employees at the army camp were immediately rounded up for questioning.

The bombing follows the fatal shooting yesterday of a British army doctor as he drove his car through Nicosia.

A Royal Horse Guards' patrol in a mountainous district arrested three men burying a glass jar. It was found to contain a 250,000-word "war diary" allegedly written by the EOKA leader, George Grivas. It purports to describe activities which would convict Grivas of murderous conspiracy and implicate Archbishop Makarios in EOKA campaigns (→19/12).

Six captured members of EOKA.

Anglo-French talks on Suez solidarity

Sept 29. The pace of events in the Suez crisis is quickening. After a month of fruitless endeavours to get the agreement of Colonel Nasser to the international operation of the Canal, Sir Anthony Eden flew to Paris with Selwyn Lloyd, the Foreign Secretary, for talks with Guy Mollet, the French Premier, and Christian Pineau, his Foreign Minister. A communique says Anglo-French solidarity has been strengthened "in every respect".

A Suez resolution is to be put to the UN Security Council. There is an enigmatic reference to "further studies" being arranged to remove "minor points outstanding between the two countries". Observers in Paris suspect the communique disguises rather than discloses what was actually discussed.

The Paris meeting comes just over two weeks after midnight talks at 10 Downing Street between the British and French. Two days later the Suez Canal Company, meeting in Paris, gave permission to its 160 non-Egyptian pilots to quit their jobs. They walked out at the weekend, leaving the Egyptians with 65 pilots to handle the movement of shipping.

When Colonel Nasser rejected the 18-nation plan for operating the Canal, Mr Dulles produced another for the Users, but that, too, was rejected (→1/10).

Rioting Teddy Boys rock around clock

Sept 11. Showings of the film "Rock Around the Clock", featuring Bill Haley and his rock and roll band, the Comets, have been causing riots in cinemas all round the country. Police have been called to cinema after cinema to eject youths who "jive" in the aisles, clapping and chanting to the music.

After being ejected they continue dancing in the streets outside. The dialogue of the film is inaudible for cries of "We Want Bill" or "Rock, rock, rock". Some youths in "Teddy Boy" clothing have let off fireworks in cinemas. Many have been charged and fined for "insulting behaviour" (→7/2/57).

1956

OCTOBER

Su	Mo	Tu	We	Th	Fr	Sa
	1	2	3	4	5	6
7	8	9	10	11	12	13
14	15	16	17	18	19	20
21	22	23	24	25	26	27
28	29	30	31			

1. London: The Suez Canal Users' Association is formally inaugurated with 15 nations as members (→ 7).

1. UK: A Catholic report proposes legalising homosexual acts in private between consenting adults.

2. London: Bevan is elected Labour Party Treasurer.

7. New York: Foreign Secretary Selwyn Lloyd and US Secretary of State Dulles meet for talks on Suez (→ 13).

10. Hong Kong: Mobs attack Europeans as anti-British riots break out in mainland Kowloon (→ 25).

13. New York: The USSR vetoes UN approval of the Anglo-French proposal for control of the Suez Canal.→

15. UK: The RAF withdraws from service its last Lancaster bomber, used for training.

17. UK: The Queen opens Britain's first full-scale nuclear power station at Calder Hall

19. London: Railwaymen protest at the influx of black drivers.

20. Warsaw: Khrushchev flies in for urgent talks as anti-Soviet feeling grows (→ 21).

21. Warsaw: Rehabilitated "moderate" Gomulka is elected premier.→

23. Hungary: Demonstrators throughout the country call for independence and the withdrawal of the USSR.→

25. Singapore: 15 die in anti-British riots (→ 11/4/57).

28. Poland: Catholic primate Cardinal Stefan Wyszynski is set free (→ 18/11).

30. Cairo: Britain and France tell Israel and Egypt to withdraw from the Suez Canal within 12 hours.→

BIRTH

18. Czech-born US tennis player Martina Navratilova.

DEATH

7. US frozen food pioneer Clarence Birdseye (*9/12/1886).

Hungarians rise against Soviet rule

Oct 26. Hungary has risen in revolt against Soviet domination. For three days the ordinary people have been fighting Soviet tanks and the hated security police, the AVH, and demanding freedom from Moscow. They have put out the Red Star on the Parliament buildings and replaced it with the Hungarian national flag.

Casualties are already heavy; some estimates put the dead at 3,000 as the people attack the tanks with their bare hands, and there is no sign of the fighting slackening. The demonstrators are now acquiring weapons as Hungarian troops join the revolt.

Tonight Mr Ferenc Nagy, the new "Titoist" Prime Minister, undertook in a broadcast to begin negotiations for "the withdrawal of all Soviet troops stationed in Hungary at present". He said he would make the demand as soon as the armed revolt was suppressed.

He acknowledged that "some of the workers" had joined the rebels. "This was the result of the serious mistakes committed by the Hungarian government in the past," he said, and he promised that "democratisation will be carried out without delay".

He also made one promise which is certain to bring him into conflict with the Soviets. The political system, based on the predominance of the Communist party and the elimination of opposition parties, would, he said, be reformed to permit representation of "all democratic forces on the broadest basis".

Instructions were broadcast to Budapest citizens to "go home and stay there", and they were ordered to lock their houses, but travellers arriving at the Austrian border said that large areas of the Hungarian capital were in rebel hands. They spoke of men with oxy-acetylene torches destroying the most hated symbol of Soviet dominance in Hungary: the huge bronze statue of Stalin in Stalin Square.

One eyewitness spoke of a Russian tank opening fire on peaceful demonstrators, whose only weapons were Hungarian flags, but some told of seeing Hungarians riding on top of Russian tanks and armoured cars who said that the Russians told them that they had no intention of fighting the people and had orders to return to their bases.

The body of a dead Hungarian bears grim witness to Russia's invasion.

It seems that in many instances there has been genuine fraternisation between the Russian soldiers and the demonstrators, but the Russians have always obeyed orders to open fire.

In some parts of the capital the fighting has been so heavy that it resembles the grim days after the siege of the city in 1945 before it fell to the Red Army. In Madach Square, the Astoria Hotel has had all its windows broken, and holes made by tank-cannons gape in the walls of buildings.

The streets are littered with debris, with the cables of trams dangling down to the street. Many trams were dragged off their rails and used as barricades.

What makes this uprising even more significant is that it is not confined to the capital. Reports are coming in from all over Hungary of demonstrations which show that the whole nation is in revolt. In southern Hungary a revolutionary council has been formed in the province of Baranja, and radio reports speak of fighting against security police in this area.

Ominously, other reports speak of Soviet armoured forces on the march, with five divisions being brought up to the East German frontier (→ 31).

Poles demand Russian troop withdrawal

Oct 25. Thousands of young Poles demonstrated in the streets of Warsaw tonight in an outburst of feeling against Russian domination of their country and of support for the Hungarians who are trying to throw off the Russian yoke.

The Warsaw demonstrations are the culmination of days of unrest which saw Mr Khrushchev, the Russian leader, flying to the Polish capital at the head of a powerful delegation to tell the Poles that they have gone too far and too fast in their campaign for complete national independence and a separate Polish road to Socialism.

Mr Khrushchev also left Mr Gomulka, First Secretary of Poland's Communist Party, in no doubt of Russia's response if Poland persisted in her defiance of Moscow.

However, Mr Gomulka, recently rehabilitated after spending over three years in prison as a "Titoist", refused the Soviet demands to keep the Russian Marshal Rokossovski on the Polish Politburo, but the Marshal, born a Pole and now claiming Polish citizenship, remains Defence Minister.

Today demonstrators marched through central Warsaw shouting "Rokossovski to Moscow" and other anti-Soviet slogans. At times the demonstration threatened to get out of hand, and there were scuffles with Communist party workers armed with truncheons.

One of the fiercest clashes was outside the Hungarian Embassy, where the crowd shouted "We are with you, Hungarians". There were also rhythmic chants of "Katyn, Katyn, Katyn", recalling the massacre of 12,000 Polish officers in the Katyn forest during the war.

The Russians blame the Germans for this crime, but the Poles are sure that the Russians murdered their countrymen and will never forgive them.

Earlier, Mr Gomulka told a large crowd: "We have received from Mr Khrushchev assurances that the Soviet armies in Poland will return to their regular bases within two days." He ended by appealing: "Please leave the square in an orderly manner. Remember the women and children. Be disciplined. Prove what the proletariat of Warsaw are like. Enough of public meetings and demonstrating" (→28).

Gomulka – keeping Poland pure.

Hungarian rebels release jailed Cardinal

Oct 31. Cardinal Mindszenty, the Roman Catholic Primate of Hungary and leader of the opposition to Soviet domination, was brought back to Budapest today by rebel tank forces who stormed his prison last night and freed him after eight years of captivity.

The Cardinal, whose first act of freedom was to celebrate Mass, was obviously tired, but his large bright eyes had lost none of their intensity. A slight trembling of his hands was the only sign of the ordeals he has suffered and of the emotion he was trying to master.

He refused to make any political statement, emphasising that he must first bring himself up to date with developments before deciding on his next moves, but of the uprising itself he said: "I send my blessing to the Hungarian weapons that have won this glorious victory. God will bless these weapons which have brought us our freedom in the dire day of need."

Asked to comment on the claim made by Radio Budapest that he was "the only man who could save the country", the Cardinal merely said: "At last there is freedom of speech in Hungary and everyone can express his opinion" (→2/11).

Israel marches on Egypt

An Arab family stands silent as Israeli soldiers search their house.

Oct 29. Heavily-armoured Israeli forces today crossed the 120-mile border with Egypt, and swept into the Sinai Peninsula in a two-pronged drive. Tonight, they were reported to be within 20 miles of the Suez Canal. There are no reports of resistance by Egyptian forces. A communique issued in Cairo merely spoke of "activity by Israeli forces". Cairo international airport closed without explanation.

Some 30,000 men are believed to have spearheaded the attack. "Too big for a reprisal", said an Israeli official in Jerusalem, "and too small for a war." In fact, the Israelis are presenting the operation as a reprisal for Egyptian attacks on Israel's land and sea communications and for terrorist raids into Israel from bases in Sinai. The Israelis began mobilising in secret last week, but it was not until Sunday night, when they had some 400,000 reservists under arms, that the mobilisation was officially announced.

One question that remains unanswered at this stage is whether any of the Western powers had advance knowledge of Israeli intentions. In the 48 hours before the Israelis attacked, President Eisenhower sent two personal messages to David Ben-Gurion, the Israeli Prime Minister, appealing to him not to endanger peace. About the same time, the US State Department gave orders for the evacuation of American citizens from Israel and Egypt.

In London, Sir Anthony Eden called an urgent meeting of senior cabinet ministers in Downing Street. The Foreign Office said discussions were taking place with the US and France. Britain had followed the US in warning Israel not to start hostilities. The British view is that the three powers should "take action, both within and without the United Nations", to implement the 1950 joint declaration guaranteeing Arab-Israeli borders as they existed when the 1948 armistice ended fighting between Israel and the Arabs (→30).

Anglo-French forces bombard Suez

Young Arabs survey the ruins of Port Said, the Canal Zone town that bore the brunt of the Suez battles.

Oct 31. RAF Vickers Valiant and Canberra jet bombers took off from Cyprus this afternoon and, heading south, arrived over Egypt as dusk was closing in. Picking out targets marked by flares dropped by pathfinder aircraft, they began their bombing runs over military airfields near Cairo and in the Canal Zone. The Egyptians opened up with anti-aircraft guns but, according to the British pilots, the firing was wild and inaccurate. There was no opposition from fighters.

Despite the fact that there had been repeated warnings broadcast by the BBC Overseas Service to civilians to keep away from Egyptian airfields, the authorities seem to have been unprepared. "We could see the lights of Cairo clearly, and adjoining areas were also lit up," Flight Lieutenant John Slater, aged 34, captain of one of the Canberras, said. After his plane had passed, he said, the lights of Cairo and elsewhere went out suddenly.

The bombing followed the expiry of a 12-hour ultimatum delivered on Tuesday afternoon, when Britain and France called on Egypt and Israel to pull their forces back from the Canal. Israel agreed, but only on condition that Egypt also withdrew her forces. Colonel Nasser reacted angrily. He told the British ambassador, Sir Humphrey Trevelyan, that the Anglo-French demand was "an attack on the rights and dignity of Egypt". The Egyptian leader also called in the Soviet and American ambassadors and asked for the support of their governments.

The British and French have taken their stand on the vital necessity of keeping the Canal open to international traffic. The Israeli invasion on Monday, in the Anglo-French view, represents a threat to the Canal and must be dealt with, if necessary, by the use of force. Nasser's rejection of the ultimatum was obviously expected.

Well before the deadline expired a large British force, which had been assembling at Malta for the past month, left Valletta harbour with an escort of warships and sailed eastwards.

The isolation of the British and French on the world stage is emphasised by a resolution for the UN Security Council debate, introduced by the US. Without naming her two close allies, the US nevertheless "calls on all UN members to refrain from the use of force or threat of force and to refrain from giving aid to Israel" (→ 3/11).

Fury in US at British action over Suez

Oct 31. American officials have reacted to the Anglo-French action against Egypt with a degree of anger and bitterness without precedent in recent years. The Americans are convinced that, because Britain and France kept Washington in the dark, they must have been acting in colllusion with Israel.

Relations have been made worse by the Anglo-French veto of the US resolution, which the Soviet Union supported, in the Security Council. Washington has made it clear that if the British and French get into difficulties, they should not look to the US for help, but the respected Alsop brothers, in their syndicated column, blame Mr Dulles for procrastinating after Nasser seized the Canal. He believed "anything, including a major triumph for the violently anti-Western Nasser" was better than war.

1956

NOVEMBER

Su	Mo	Tu	We	Th	Fr	Sa
				1	2	3
4	5	6	7	8	9	10
11	12	13	14	15	16	17
18	19	20	21	22	23	24
25	26	27	28	29	30	

1. UK: The first Premium Bonds go on sale (→ 1/6/57).

2. Budapest: Nagy tells Soviet ambassador Yuri Andropov that Hungary will quit the Warsaw Pact and become neutral.→

3. Egypt: Israeli troops now control Gaza and Sinai (→ 10).

4. London: Hundreds of demonstrators demand Eden's resignation for his handling of the Suez crisis (→ 5).

5. New York: The UN votes to create a UN force for the Middle East (→ 7).

7. New York: The UN votes for Anglo-French and Israeli withdrawal from Egypt.→

7. London: Eden agrees to pull out of Suez if a UN force takes over.→

9. New York: The UN tells the USSR to withdraw from Hungary (→ 23).

10. Tel Aviv: Israel's foreign minister Golda Meir says the Gaza Strip is Israel's (→ 25).

13. Washington: The US Supreme Court declares invalid Alabama's law segregating blacks and whites on buses (→ 13/6/57).

18. Warsaw: Gomulka agrees to allow Soviet troops to remain in Poland (→ 20/1/57).

21. UK: Britain's first heavy water nuclear reactor opens at Harwell, Berkshire (→ 5/3/57).

22. Melbourne: The Duke of Edinburgh opens the 16th Olympic Games (→ 8/12).

23. Austria: Austrian troops clash with Soviet troops pursuing Hungarians trying to flee across the border.→

25. Egypt: The government begins expelling British, French and "Zionist" residents (→ 3/12).

30. Cuba: Insurgents under outlawed student leader Fidel Castro attack rural police stations (→ 2/12).

DEATHS

4. US musician Art Tatum (*13/10/10).

26. US musician Tommy Dorsey (*19/11/05).

Suez adventure is stranded in diplomatic desert

Egyptian life carries on undisturbed, as a British Marine looks on.

Allied forces seize control of Canal Zone

Nov 6. Royal Marine Commandos, brought ashore by naval helicopters, are this afternoon battling their way into the centre of Port Said in fierce house-to-house encounters with the Egyptian defenders. The French, watched by a large crowd of seemingly untroubled Egyptian civilians, landed at Port Fuad and are pressing south.

The Marine landings came after a successful paratroop assault on Gamel military airfield outside Port Said. There was some "tough fighting", according to General Sir Charles Keightley, Allied C-in-C, with the Egyptians deploying Russian tanks and 100mm self-propelled guns, but, according to the navigator of one of the transports, Egyptian soldiers began running away when the paratroops started to drop. The airfield control tower was in flames, having been hit by rocket- and cannon-firing RAF jet fighters. The Egyptians had placed barbed wire and oil drums across the runways.

With the airfield and the outskirts of Port Said under British control, the Egyptian Governor of the town said he wanted to surrender. Brigadier M.A.H. Butler, CO 16th Parachute Brigade, told the Egyptians to lay down their arms; all military operations by British and French forces were halted, but then the Governor received a phone call from Cairo and after a night of confusion called off the surrender.

Allied operations were resumed at dawn today. Warships lying offshore laid down a selective barrage before the Marine Commandos were put ashore. The docks were quickly taken over and the Egyptians retreated into the centre of the town, where they lodged their tanks in houses in an attempt to ambush the advancing Commandos. Another squadron of Egyptian tanks retreated to the golf course south of the town before giving battle. The Shell oil refinery is on fire.

Allied casualties have been light. Thirty men of the 16th Parachute Brigade were injured in the landings. An Army doctor, partly blinded in one eye by anti-aircraft fire, went on working at a casualty clearing station for four hours before being evacuated to Cyprus. The Egyptians lost 70 dead (→7).

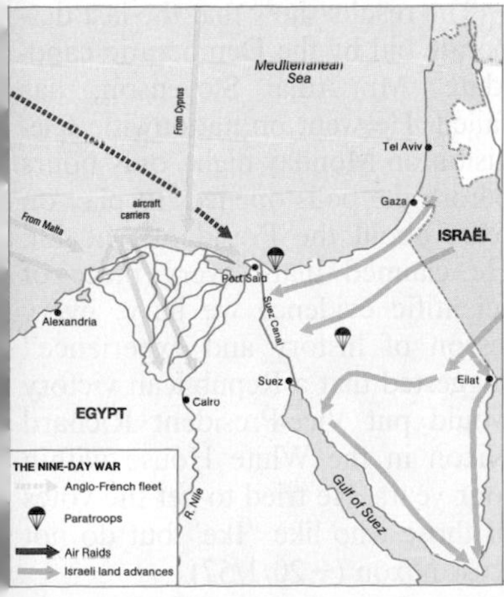

Port Said: a grief-stricken Arab woman runs to escape the Suez fighting.

UN imposes a cease-fire on the Allies

Nov 8. On the stroke of midnight all military operations by British and French forces in the Canal Zone came to a halt. Under the UN terms accepted by the allies, their troops will remain in place until an international force arrives to take over. In New York the UN Secretary-General, Dag Hammarskjoeld, began assembling 6,000 men from Sweden, Denmark, Norway, Canada, Colombia, Finland and India, ready to be dispatched as soon as the UN General Assembly has voted approval.

The Anglo-French forces claim to have occupied the greater part of the Canal. Supported by tanks, they pushed down to Ismailia before halting. The French claim that 95 per cent of the Egyptian air force has been destroyed. Egyptian land forces which tried to put up a resistance were brushed aside. Even so, the decision to call a halt before the complete occupation of the Canal represents a climbdown under UN and US pressure.

The sudden flurry of threats from the Soviet Union, including, in Marshal Bulganin's words, the use of "modern and terrible weapons", is not thought to have caused much concern in London and Paris, where there is an inclination to see the Soviet move as intended to deflect attention from events in Hungary.

Royal Navy frogmen have begun clearing blockships sunk by the Egyptians. There are at least 12 ships, including an Egyptian tank-landing craft at Ismailia. Whether the British will be allowed to continue operations after the UN force arrives is unclear (→25).

▷

US cash squeeze forced Suez pull-out

Nov 23. Under intense behind-the-scenes pressure from the US, the British government reluctantly agreed today to begin military withdrawal from Egypt.

Mr Selwyn Lloyd, the Foreign Secretary, told the United Nations General Assembly that troops will leave "as an act of faith" in UN intentions to ensure re-opening of the Suez Canal. To a hostile audience he repeated the claim that Britain has succeeded in "stopping a small war" in providing the right conditions for a UN force to go into the area and maintain peace.

In Parliament and Whitehall, turmoil continues. Tempers are high, nerves are frayed. Reports persist that the cabinet is split over how to minimise Britain's humiliation. Anglo-US relations are at an all-time low. In world money markets the run on the pound is alarming, and the US Treasury has bluntly told Mr Macmillan, the Chancellor of the Exchequer, that American financial help in preventing a total collapse of sterling depends on a British pull-out from Egypt. The Chancellor, formerly an advocate of the invasion, now rejects it.

That has been the decisive factor for the cabinet, but it is also now known that President Eisenhower and the Secretary of State, John Foster Dulles, have both shown great hostility to Sir Anthony Eden ever since he told them that, in the last resort, Britain and France would take military action.

Eden (r.), Dulles (l.) and France's Pineau start three-power talks on Suez.

Mr Selwyn Lloyd has again strongly denied accusations of Anglo-French collusion with Israel long before the fighting started. The United States believes that, after secret meetings in London and Paris between British and French leaders and military chiefs last month, there was a plan for Israel to attack Egypt, followed by Anglo-French intervention under the pretext of separating the combatants. In Parliament "Rab" Butler, now the acting Premier, rejected demands for an independent inquiry into the collusion charges.

MPs' emotions are running higher than at any time since World War Two. Commons sittings have been suspended several times in recent weeks on account of grave disorder. Some Tories agree with their opponents that the government's handling of the crisis has been a national disgrace (→3/12).

Britain hands over to United Nations in the Canal Zone

Nov 21. British troops were deployed to control the crowds and clear a way for the first of the United Nations forces, a company of Norwegians, who arrived in Port Said today to begin taking over the Canal from the Anglo-French force. A crowd of about 1,000 gathered at the railway station and surged forward, chanting "Nasser, Nasser", as the train pulled in. Egyptian police tried to control the crowd, but were nervous and uncertain. The British, on foot and in jeeps, moved ahead of the Norwegians, clearing a path, as young Egyptians shook their fists and shouted "British, go home, ours is victory".

The Norwegians, 20 officers and 175 other ranks, are due to be followed by troops from Denmark and other small countries to make up a 1,000-strong force, armed with rifles, pistols and machine-guns. It will be several weeks, though, before the UN force will be capable of taking over completely from the Allies (→3/12).

Eden, severely strained by Suez, flies to Jamaica for a rest

Nov 19. A midnight communique from 10 Downing Street said that Sir Anthony is suffering from "severe overstrain". Doctors have advised immediate rest. The Prime Minister will fly to Jamaica and stay there for three weeks. "Rab" Butler, the Leader of the House of Commons, takes temporary charge of the cabinet.

Sir Anthony's health has not been good for some years. It has cracked through overwork and the tensions of the Suez crisis. Colleagues have noted that he has been increasingly moody and short-tempered, and some have felt that vital decisions needed cooler judgment. In 1953 Sir Anthony had three major operations to remove a bile duct obstruction (→14/12).

10,000 people gathered in Trafalgar Square to demand "Law not war".

Americans still like "Ike" for President

Nov 6. President Eisenhower has won through to a second term with an even bigger majority than in 1952. He did better than expected in the urban north, even taking the Democratic stronghold of Chicago, and won some of the more marginal of the usually Democratic southern states.

The results show that the last desperate bid by the Democratic candidate, Mr Adlai Stevenson, has failed. He went on nationwide television on Monday night, only hours before the polls opened, to play on fears about the President's health. He claimed that "every piece of scientific evidence we have, every lesson of history and experience" suggested that a Republican victory would put Vice-President Richard Nixon in the White House within four years. He tried to get the votes of those who like "Ike" but do not trust Nixon (→20/1/57).

Soviet tanks crush Hungarian revolt

Nov 5. The Red Army has crushed the Hungarian Revolution. All the bright hopes of freedom from Soviet domination have died under the tracks of the heavy tanks which are flattening houses in search of single snipers. The Soviet assault has been irresistible. Tanks, aircraft, artillery and infantrymen have smashed the poorly-armed Hungarians.

An estimated 1,000 tanks attacked key points before dawn and, after heavy fighting with Hungarian army units dug in on the outskirts of the capital, the first Soviet forces entered Budapest soon after 6am.

Fighting in the city centred round the Defence Ministry and the Parliament Building, which fell before 9am. The fate of Mr Imre Nagy and his ministers, who were inside, is not yet known.

The last words heard from him were in a broadcast over Radio Budapest at 5.15am, when he told his people and the world of the Russian attack; by 8.10am Radio Budapest was silenced after broadcasting its last appeal: "Help Hungary ... Help ... Help ... Help ..."

It is known, however, that General Pal Maleter, commander of the Hungarian forces, was seized by the Russians while he was actually discussing the terms of the proposed withdrawal of Soviet troops from Hungary. It seems that these talks were merely a ruse covering the preparations for the assault.

News of the fighting came from a Hungarian reporter who tapped it out on a teleprinter in between firing at the Russians from the window of his office at the newspaper, Szabad Nep.

"The people have just turned over a tram to use as a barricade," he typed. "In the building young people are making Molotov cocktails and hand grenades to fight the tanks. We are quiet, not afraid. Send the news to the public of the world and say it should condemn the aggressors.

"The fighting is very close now and we haven't enough tommy guns. Heavy shells are exploding nearby. Above, jet planes are roaring but it doesn't matter.

"What is the United Nations doing? Give us a little encouragement. We will hold out to our last drop of blood ... The tanks are now firing towards the Danube. Our boys are on the barricades and calling for more arms and ammunition."

At 10.50am he reported that the heaviest fighting was going on at the Maria Theresa barracks. Five minutes later, the line was cut.

At lunchtime, Moscow Radio claimed that "the Hungarian counter-revolution has been crushed". It said that a "Revolutionary Workers and Peasants Government" had been formed under Mr Janos Kadar, a former "Titoist" who appears to have betrayed the Hungarians. The news of the ruthless crushing of the Hungarian uprising has dismayed the West.

President Eisenhower has sent a message to Marshal Bulganin, Russia's Prime Minister, expressing his shock, and the UN General Assembly has demanded the withdrawal of Russian troops and the entry of UN observers into Hungary.

It is not expected that these protests will have any effect. Faced with growing unrest in Eastern Europe, the Soviets have shown their iron fist (→9).

Rebel Hungarians brandish the national flag from atop a captured tank.

The revolt is over and a Russian officer bears down on this photographer.

Refugees from the uprising pour over Hungarian border

Nov 30. Refugees from the Hungarian uprising and the brutal Soviet repression following the crushing of the revolt are pouring across the Austrian border. The authorities in Vienna expect that the 100,000th refugee will actually cross the border tonight.

The flow continues almost unchecked, despite the increasing efforts by the Russian army to seal the border. Soviet troops are now manning the wooden watch-towers along the frontier which were abandoned when Hungary dismantled her western frontier barriers in the summer.

In Magyarovar, ten miles from the Austrian border, the Russians are warning the local people by loudspeaker of the danger from minefields. The increasing difficulty of getting across the border is reflected in the rising prices demanded by the professional guides who lead refugees to freedom.

The first of the refugees destined to settle in Britain are being flown here by planes which are carrying food and clothing out to the refugee camps in Austria. A spokesman for the British Council for Aid to Refugees says the first group will be mainly "professional people in small family groups" (→7/12).

Communists in the West quit the Party

Nov 13. The brutalities of the Russians in Hungary have thrown the British Communist Party into chaos. Ordinary members from all parts of the country are resigning in their hundreds in protest against the Russians' action. Leading figures, especially full-time trade union officials, are throwing away their membership cards.

Even the party-liners, who have obeyed the Kremlin line through all its twists and turns, cannot stomach the way in which Moscow crushed the uprising. Among the major defections are Mr J. Horner of the Fire Brigades Union and Alex Moffat of the National Union of Mineworkers.

1956  Melbourne

Chris Brasher wins gold

The Melbourne Olympic Games, the first to be held south of the Equator, were threatened before they started by heated political controversy – first in the wake of the British and French invasion of Suez, and later over the Soviet Union's part in crushing the Hungarian uprising.

Despite some withdrawals, the Games forgot the external pressures (except in a perhaps predictably ill-tempered water-polo semi-final between Hungary and the USSR) to display an unprecedented quality of sporting achievement.

It was a fine Games for the hosts. Australia dominated the swimming events, though the 17-year-old Judy Grinham, from Neasden, won the 100 metres backstroke to earn Britain her first swimming gold medal since 1924.

On the track, with many of the British high hopes reduced to a series of hard luck stories, the Australian women, led by Betty Cuthbert, were a spectacular success. With the powerful Hungarian track runners absent no one, not even Gordon Pirie at his most courageous, could match the resilience of Russia's Vladimir Kuts in the 5,000 or the 10,000 metres.

Then, in the 3,000 metres steeplechase final, Chris Brasher, the Cambridge graduate who came to Melbourne only as Britain's third string for the event, burst through a bunch of runners on the final lap to sprint away to victory.

Immediately there was controversy: Brasher was disqualified for interfering with another runner on the last lap. The appeal took three hours, but no athlete in the race was prepared to support the disqualification, and finally it was confirmed that Brasher would be presented with his gold medal the next morning: the first British track athlete to win an individual Olympic title since 1932.

Kuts comes home in the 10,000 m.

Two British champions – Judy Grinham (r.) and Margaret Edwards.

Men Athletics

100m
1. Robert Morrow USA 10.5
2. Thane Baker USA 10.5
3. Hector Hogan AUS 10.6

200m
1. Robert Morrow USA *20.6
2. Andrew Stanfield USA 20.7
3. Thane Baker USA 20.9

400m
1. Charles Jenkins USA 46.7
2. Karl-Friedrich Haas GER 46.8
3. Voitto Hellsten FIN 47.0
3. Ardalion Ignatyev URS 47.0

800m
1. Thomas Courtney USA *1:47.7
2. Derek Johnson GBR 1:47.8
3. Audun Boysen NOR 1:48.1

1500m
1. Ron Delany IRL *3:41.2
2. Klaus Richtzenhain GER 3:42.0
3. John Landy AUS 3:42.0

5000m
1. Vladimir Kuts URS *13:39.6
2. Gordon Pirie GBR 13:50.6
3. Derek Ibbotson GBR 13:54.4

10,000m
1. Vladimir Kuts URS *28:45.6
2. József Kovács HUN 28:52.4
3. Allan Lawrence AUS 28:53.6

Marathon
1. Alain Mimoun FRA 2:25:00.0
2. Franjo Mihalic YUG 2:26:32.0
3. Veikko Karvonen FIN 2:27:47.0

110m Hurdles
1. Lee Calhoun USA *13.5
2. Jack Davis USA 13.5
3. Joel Shankle USA 14.1

400m Hurdles
1. Glenn Davis USA =*50.1
2. Eddie Southern USA 50.8
3. Josh Culbreath USA 51.6

3000m Steeplechase
1. Christopher Brasher GBR *8:41.2
2. Sándor Rozsnyól HUN 8:43.6
3. Ernst Larsen NOR 8:44.0

4x100m Relay
1. USA **39.5 (Ira Murchison, Lemon King, Thane Baker, Robert Morrow)
2. URS 39.8 (Boris Tokaryev, Vladimir Sukharyev, Leonid Bartenyev, Yury Konovalov)
3. GER 40.3 (Lothar Knörzer, Leonhard Pohl, Heinz Fütterer, Manfred Germar)

4x400m Relay
1. USA 3:04.8 (Louis Jones, Jesse Mashburn, Charles Jenkins, Thomas Courtney)
2. AUS 3:06.2 (Leon Gregory, David Lean, Graham Gipson, Kevin Gosper)
3. GBR 3:07.2 (John Salisbury, Michael Wheeler, F. Peter Higgins, Derek Johnson)

20km Walk
1. Leonid Spirin URS 1:31:27.4
2. Atanas Mikenas URS 1:32:03.0
3. Bruno Junk URS 1:32:12.0

50km Walk
1. Norman Read NZL 4:30:42.8
2. Yevgeny Maskinskov URS 4:32:57.0
3. John Ljunggren SWE 4:35:02.0

High Jump
1. Charles Dumas USA *2.12
2. Charles Porter AUS 2.10
3. Igor Kashkarov URS 2.08

Pole Vault
1. Robert Richards USA *4.56
2. Robert Gutowski USA 4.53
3. Georgios Roubanis GRE 4.50

Long Jump
1. Gregory Bell USA 7.83
2. John Bennett USA 7.68
3. Jorma Valkama FIN 7.48

Triple Jump
1. Adhemar Ferreira Da Silva BRA *16.35
2. Vilhjálmur Einarsson ISL 16.26
3. Vitold Kreyer URS 16.02

Shotput
1. Parry O'Brien USA *18.57
2. William Nieder USA 18.18
3. Jiri Skobla TCH 17.65

Discus
1. Alfred Oerter USA *56.36
2. Fortune Gordien USA 54.81
3. Desmond Koch USA 54.40

Hammer
1. Harold Connolly USA *63.19
2. Mikhail Krivonosov URS 63.03
3. Anatoly Samotsvetov URS 62.56

Javelin
1. Egil Danielsen NOR **85.71
2. Janusz Sidlo POL 79.98
3. Viktor Tsibulenko URS 79.50

Decathlon
1. Milton Campbell USA *7937
2. Rafer Johnson USA 7587
3. Vassily Kuznyetsov URS 7465

Women Athletics

100m
1. Betty Cuthbert AUS 11.5
2. Christa Stubnick GER 11.7
3. Marlene Matthews AUS 11.7

200m
1. Betty Cuthbert AUS =*23.4
2. Christa Stubnick GER 23.7
3. Marlene Matthews AUS 23.8

80m Hurdles
1. Shirley de la Hunty AUS *10.7
2. Gisela Köhler GER 10.9
3. Norma Thrower AUS 11.0

4x100m Relay
1. AUS **44.5 (Shirley de la Hunty, Norma Croker, Fleur Mellor, Betty Cuthbert)
2. GBR 44.7 (Anne Pashley, Jean Scrivens, June Paul-Foulds, Heather Armitage)
3. USA 44.9 (Mae Faggs, Margaret Matthews, Wilma Rudolph, Isabelle Daniels)

High Jump
1. Mildred McDaniel USA *1.76
2. Maria Pissaryeva URS 1.67
2. Thelma Hopkins GBR 1.67

Long Jump
1. Elzbieta Krzesinska POL 6.35
2. Willye White USA 6.09
3. Nadezhda Dvalischvili URS 6.07

Shotput
1. Tamara Tyshkevich URS *16.59
2. Galina Zybina URS 16.53
3. Marianne Werner GER 15.61

Discus
1. Olga Fikotová TCH *53.69
2. Irina Beglyakova URS 52.54
3. Nina Ponomaryeva URS 52.02

Javelin
1. Inese Jaunzeme URS 53.86
2. Marlène Ahrens CHI 50.38
3. Nadezhda Konyayeva URS 50.28

Men Swimming

100m Freestyle
1. Jon Henricks AUS *55.4
2. John Devitt AUS 55.8
3. Gary Chapman AUS 56.7

400m Freestyle
1. Murray Rose AUS *4:27.3
2. Tsuyoshi Yamanaka JAP 4:30.4
3. George Breen USA 4:32.5

1500m Freestyle
1. Murray Rose AUS 17:58.9
2. Tsuyoshi Yamanaka JAP 18:00.3
3. George Breen USA 18:08.2

100m Backstroke
1. Davis Theile AUS *1:02.2
2. John Monckton AUS 1:03.2
3. Frank McKinney USA 1:04.5

200m Breaststroke
1. Masaru Furukawa JAP *2:34.7
2. Masahiro Yoshimura JAP 2:36.7
3. Charis Yunichev URS 2:36.8

200m Butterfly
1. William Yorzyk USA *2:19.3
2. Takashi Ishimoto JAP 2:23.8
3. György Tumpek HUN 2:23.9

4x200m Freestyle Relay
1. AUS **8:23.6 (Kevin O'Halloran, John Devitt, Murray Rose, Jon Henricks)
2. USA 8:31.5 (Richard Hanley, George Breen, William Woolsey, Ford Konno)
3. URS 8:34.7 (Vitaly Sorokin, Vladimir Strushanov, Gennady Nikolayev, Boris Nikitin)

Springboard Diving
1. Robert Clotworthy USA 159.56
2. Donald Harper USA 156.23
3. Joaquin Capilla Pérez MEX 150.69

Platform Diving
1. Joaquin Capilla Pérez MEX 152.44
2. Gary Tobian USA 152.41
3. Richard Connor USA 149.79

Water Polo

1. Hungary
2. Yugoslavia
3. Soviet Union

Women Swimming

100m Freestyle
1. Dawn Fraser AUS **1:02.0
2. Lorraine Crapp AUS 1:02.3
3. Faith Leech AUS 1:05.1

400m Freestyle
1. Lorraine Crapp AUS *4:54.6
2. Dawn Fraser AUS 5:02.5
3. Sylvia Ruuska USA 5:07.1

200m Breaststroke
1. Ursula Happe GER 2:53.1
2. Eva Székely HUN 2:54.8
3. Eva-Maria Ten Elsen GER 2:55.1

100m Backstroke
1. Judith Grinham GBR *1:12.9
2. Carin Cone USA 1:12.9
3. Margaret Edwards GBR 1:13.1

1956  Melbourne

100m Butterfly
1. Shelley Mann USA *1:11.0
2. Nancy Ramey USA 1:11.9
3. Mary Sears USA 1:14.4

4x100m Relay
1. AUS **4:17.1 (Dawn Fraser, Faith Leech, Sandra Morgan, Lorraine Crapp)
2. USA 4:19.2 (Sylvia Russka, Shelley Mann, Nancy Simons, Joan Rosazza)
3. SAF 4:25.7 (Jeanette Myburgh, Susan Roberts, Natalie Myburgh, Moira Abernathy)

Springboard Diving
1. Patricia McCormick USA 142.36
2. Jeanne Stunyo USA 125.89
3. Irene MacDonald CAN 121.40

Platform Diving
1. Patricia McCormick USA 84.85
2. Juno Irwin-Stover USA 81.64
3. Paula Jean Myers USA 81.58

Boxing

Flyweight
1. Terence Spinks GBR
2. Mircea Dobrescu ROM
3. John Caldwell IRL
3. René Libeer FRA

Bantamweight
1. Wolfgang Behrendt URS
2. Soon-Chun Song KOR
3. Frederick Gilroy IRL
3. Claudio Barrientos CHI

Featherweight
1. Vladimir Safronov URS
2. Thomas Nicholls GBR
3. Henryk Niedzwiedezki POL
3. Pentti Hämäläinen FIN

Lightweight
1. Richard McTaggart GBR
2. Harry Kurschat GER
3. Anthony Byrne IRL
3. Anatoly Lagetko URS

Light Welterweight
1. Vladimir Yengibaryan URS
2. Franco Nenci ITA
3. Henry Loubscher SAF
3. Constantin Dumitrescu ROM

Welterweight
1. Nicolae Linca ROM
2. Frederick Tiedt IRL
3. Kevin John Hogarth AUS
3. Nicholas Gargano GBR

Light Middleweight
1. László Papp HUN
2. José Torres USA
3. John McCormack GBR
3. Zbigniew Pietrzykowski POL

Middleweight
1. Gennady Schatkov URS
2. Rámon Tapia CHI
3. Gilbert Chapron FRA
3. Victor Zalazar ARG

Light Heavyweight
1. James Felton Boyd USA
2. Gheorghe Negrea ROM
3. Romualdas Murauskas URS
3. Carlos Lucas CHI

Heavyweight
1. T. Peter Rademacher USA
2. Lev Mukhin URS
3. Daniel Bekker SAF
3. Giacomo Bozzano ITA

Greco Roman Wrestling

Flyweight
1. Nikolai Solovyov URS
2. Ignazio Fabra ITA
3. Durum All Egribas TUR

Bantamweight
1. Konstantin Vyrupayev URS
2. Edvin Westerby SWE
3. Francise Horvath ROM

Featherweight
1. Rauno Mäkinen FIN
2. Imre Polyák HUN
3. Roman Dzneladze URS

Lightweight
1. Kyösti Lehtonen FIN
2. Riza Dogan TUR
3. Gyula Tóth HUN

Welterweight
1. Mithat Bayrak TUR
2. Vladimir Maneyev URS
3. Per Berlin SWE

Middleweight
1. Givy Kartoziya URS
2. Dimiter Dobrev BUL
3. Rune Jansson SWE

Light Heavyweight
1. Valentin Nikolayev URS
2. Petko Sirakov BUL
3. Karl-Erik Nilsson SWE

Heavyweight
1. Anatoly Parfenov URS
2. Wilfried Dietrich GER
3. Adelmo Bulgarelli ITA

Freestyle Wrestling

Bantamweight
1. Mustafa Dagistanli TUR
2. Mehdi Yaghoubi IRN
3. Mikhail Chakhov URS

Flyweight
1. Mirian Tsalkalamanidze URS
2. Mohamed-Ali Khojastépour IRN
3. Huseyin Akbas TUR

Featherweight
1. Shozo Sasahara JAP
2. Joseph Mewis BEL
3. Erkki Penttilá FIN

Lightweight
1. Emamali Habibi IRN
2. Shigeru Kasahara JAP
3. Alimbeg Bestayev URS

Welterweight
1. Mitsuo Ikeda JAP
2. Ibrahim Zengin TUR
3. Vakhtang Balavadze URS

Middleweight
1. Nikola Stanchev BUL
2. Daniel Hodge USA
3. Georgy Skhirtladze URS

Light Heavyweight
1. Gholam-Reza Takhti IRN
2. Boris Kulayev URS
3. Peter Blair USA

Heavyweight
1. Hamit Kaplan TUR
2. Yusein Mehmedov BUL
3. Taisto Kangasniemi FIN

Men Fencing

Foil Individual
1. Christian d'Oriola FRA 6
2. Giancarlo Bergamini ITA 5
3. Antonio Spallino ITA 5

Foil Team
1. Italy
2. France
3. Hungary

Epée Individual
1. Carlo Pavesi ITA 5/1/2
2. Guiseppe Delfino ITA 5/1/1
3. Eduardo Mangiarotti ITA 5/1/0

Epée Team
1. Italy
2. Hungary
3. France

Sabre Individual
1. Rudolph Kárpáti HUN 6
2. Jerzy Päwlowski POL 5
3. Lev Kuznyetsov URS 4

Sabre Team
1. Hungary
2. Poland
3. Soviet Union

Women Fencing

Foil Individual
1. Gillian Sheen GBR 6
2. Olga Orban ROM 6
3. Renée Garilhe FRA 5

Modern Pentathlon

Individual
1. Lars Hall SWE
2. Olavi Mannonen FIN
3. Väinö Korhonen FIN

Team
1. Soviet Union
2. USA
3. Finland

Men Canoeing

Kayak-1 1000m
1. Gert Fredriksson SWE 4:12.8
2. Igor Pissaryev URS 4:15.3
3. Lajos Kiss HUN 4:16.2

Kayak-2 1000m
1. Germany 3:49.6
2. Soviet Union 3:51.4
3. Austria 3:55.8

Kayak-1 10,000m
1. Gert Fredriksson SWE 47:43.4
2. Ferenc Hatlaczky HUN 47:53.3
3. Michael Scheuer GER 48:00.3

Kayak-2 10,000m
1. Hungary 43:37.0
2. Germany 43:40.6
3. Australia 43:43.2

Canadian-1 1000m
1. Léon Rotman ROM 5:05.3
2. István Hernek HUN 5:06.2
3. Gennady Bukharin URS 5:12.7

Canadian-2 1000m
1. Romania
2. Soviet Union
3. Hungary

Canadian-1 10,000m
1. Léon Rotman ROM 56:41.0
2. János Parti HUN 57:11.0
3. Gennady Bukharin URS 57:14.5

Canadian-2 10,000m
1. Soviet Union 54:02.4
2. France 54:48.3
3. Hungary 55:15.6

Women Canoeing

Kayak-1 500m
1. Yelisaveta Dementyeva URS 2:18.9
2. Therese Zenz GER 2:19.6
3. Tove Soby DEN 2:22.3

Rowing

Single Sculls
1. Vyacheslav Ivanov URS 8:02.5
2. Stuart Mackenzie AUS 8:07.7
3. John Kelly Jun. USA 8:11.8

Double Sculls
1. Soviet Union 7:24.0
2. USA 7:32.2
3. Australia 7:37.4

Coxless Pairs
1. USA 7:55.4
2. Soviet Union 8:03.9
3. Germany 8:11.8

Coxed Pairs
1. USA 8:26.1
2. Germany 8:29.2
3. Soviet Union 8:31.0

Coxless Fours
1. Canada 7:08.8
2. USA 7:18.4
3. France 7:20.9

Coxed Fours
1. Italy 7:19.4
2. Sweden 7:22.4
3. Finland 7:30.9

Eights
1. USA 6:35.2
2. Canada 6:37.1
3. Australia 6:39.2

Yachting

Finn
1. Paul Elvström DEN 7509
2. André Nelis BEL 6254
3. John Marvin USA 5953

Star
1. USA 5876
2. Italy 5649
3. Bahamas 5223

Dragon
1. Sweden 5723
2. Denmark 5723
3. Great Britain 4547

5.5m
1. Sweden 5527
2. Great Britain 4050
3. Australia 4022

Sharpie
1. New Zealand 6086
2. Australia 6086
3. Great Britain 4859

Cycling

Individual Road Race
1. Ercole Baldini ITA 5:21:17.0
2. Arnaud Geyre FRA 5:23:16.0
3. Alan Jackson GBR 5:23:16.0

Team Road Race
1. France 22
2. Great Britain 23
3. Germany (E + W Germany) 27

1000m Time Trial
1. Leandro Faggin ITA *1:09.8
2. Lasdilav Foucek TCH 1:11.4
3. Alfred Swift SAF 1:11.6

1000m Sprint
1. Michel Rousseau FRA 11.4
2. Guglielmo Presenti ITA
3. Richard Ploog AUS

2000m Tandem
1. Australia 10.8
2. Czechoslovakia
3. Italy

Team Pursuit 4000m
1. Italy 4:37.4
2. France 4:39.4
3. Great Britain 4:42.2

Equestrian Sports

Three-Day Event Individual
1. Petrus Kastenman SWE
2. August Lütke-Westhues GER
3. Frank Weldon GBR

Three-Day Event Team
1. Great Britain 355.48
2. Germany 475.91
3. Canada 572.72

Individual Dressage
1. Henri Saint-Cyr SWE 860.0
2. Lis Hartel DEN 850.0
3. Liselott Linsenhoff GER 832.0

Team Dressage
1. Great Britain 2475
2. Germany 2346
3. Switzerland 2346

Grand Prix Jumping Individual
1. Hans Günther Winkler GER -4
2. Raimondo D'Inzeo ITA -8
3. Piero D'Inzeo ITA -11

Grand Prix Jumping Team
1. Germany -40.00
2. Italy -66.00
3. Great Britain -69.00

Weightlifting

		2 Arm Press	2 Arm Snatch	2 Arm Clean and Jerk	Total
Bantamweight					
1. Charles Vinci	USA	=*105.0	=*105.0	132.5	**342.5
2. Vladimir Stogov	URS	=*105.0	=*105.0	127.5	337.5
3. Mahmoud Namjou	IRN	100.0	102.5	130.0	332.5
Featherweight					
1. Isaac Berger	USA	107.5	*107.5	*137.5	**352.5
2. Yevgeny Minayev	URS	**115.0	100.0	127.5	342.5
3. Marian Zielinski	POL	105.0	102.5	127.5	335.0
Lightweight					
1. Igor Rybak	URS	110.0	*120.0	*150.0	*380.0
2. Rafael Khabutdinov	URS	*125.0	110.0	137.5	372.5
3. Chang-Hee Kim	KOR	107.5	112.5	*150.0	370.0
Middleweight					
1. Fyodor Bogdanovsky	URS	*132.5	122.5	*165.0	**420.0
2. Peter George	USA	122.5	=*127.5	162.5	412.5
3. Ermanno Pignatti	ITA	117.5	117.5	147.5	382.5
Light Heavyweight					
1. Thomas Kono	USA	*140.0	*132.5	**175.0	**447.5
2. Vassily Stepanov	URS	135.0	130.0	162.5	427.5
3. James George	USA	120.0	130.0	167.5	417.5
Middle Heavyweight					
1. Arkady Vorobyov	URS	**147.5	137.5	=*177.5	**462.5
2. David Sheppard	USA	140.0	137.5	165.0	442.5
3. Jean Debuf	FRA	130.0	127.5	167.5	425.0
Heavyweight					
1. Paul Anderson	USA	167.5	=*145.0	*187.5	*500.0
2. Humberto Selvetti	ARG	*175.0	=*145.0	180.0	*500.0
3. Alberto Pigaiani	ITA	150.0	130.0	172.5	452.5

Men Shooting

Free Rifle, 3 positions
1. Vassily Borissov URS *1138
2. Allan Erdman URS 1137
3. Vilho Ylönen FIN 1128

Small Bore Rifle, 50m Prone
1. Gerald Ouellette CAN 600
2. Vassily Borissov URS 599
3. Gilmour Boa CAN 598

Small Bore Rifle, 3 positions
1. Anatoly Bogdanov URS *1172
2. Otakar Horinek TCH *1172
3. Nils Johan Sundberg SWE 1167

Rapid Fire Pistol, 50m
1. Stefan Petrescu ROM *587
2. Yevgeny Cherkassov URS 585
3. Gheorghe Lichiardopol ROM 581

Free Pistol, 50m
1. Pentti Linnosvuo FIN *556/26
2. Makhmud Umarov URS *556/24
3. Offutt Pinion USA 551

Mixed Shooting

Clay Pigeon
1. Galliano Rossini ITA *195
2. Adam Smelczynski POL 190
3. Alessandro Ciceri ITA 188/24

Running Deer Shooting, Single and Double Shot
1. Vitaly Romanenko URS *441
2. Per Olof Sköldberg SWE 432
3. Vladimir Sevryugin URS 429

Men Gymnastics

All-around Individual
1. Viktor Chukarin URS 114.25
2. Takashi Ono JAP 114.20
3. Yuri Titov URS 113.80

Combined Exercises Team
1. Soviet Union 568.25
2. Japan 566.40
3. Finland 555.95

Parallel Bars
1. Viktor Chukarin URS 19.20
2. Masami Kubota JAP 19.15
3. Takashi Ono JAP 19.10
3. Masao Takemoto JAP 19.10

Floor Exercises
1. Valentin Muratov URS 19.20
2. Nobuyuki Aihara JAP 19.10
2. William Thoresson SWE 19.10
3. Viktor Chukarin URS 19.10

Vault
1. Helmut Bantz GER 18.85
2. Valentin Muratov URS 18.85
3. Yuri Titov URS 18.75

Side Horse Vault
1. Boris Shakhlin URS 19.25
2. Takashi Ono JAP 19.20
3. Viktor Chukarin URS 19.10

Horizontal Bar
1. Takashi Ono JAP 19.60
2. Yuri Titov URS 19.40
2. Masao Takemoto JAP 19.30

Rings
1. Albert Azaryan URS 19.35
2. Valentin Muratov URS 19.15
3. Masao Takemoto JAP 19.10
3. Masami Kubota JAP 19.10

Women Gymnastics

All-Around Individual Competition
1. Larissa Latynina URS 74.933
2. Agnes Keleti HUN 74.633
3. Sofia Moratova URS 74.466

Combined Exercises Team
1. Soviet Union 444.80
2. Hungary 443.50
3. Romania 438.20

Asymmetrical Bars
1. Agnes Keleti HUN 18.966
2. Larissa Latynina URS 18.833
3. Sofia Muratova URS 18.800

Floor Exercise
1. Agnes Keleti HUN 18.733
2. Larissa Latynina URS 18.733
3. Elena Leustean ROM 18.700

Side Horse Vault
1. Larissa Latynina URS 18.833
2. Tamara Manina URS 18.800
3. Ann-Sofi Colling SWE 18.733
3. Olga Tass HUN 18.733

Beam
1. Agnes Keleti HUN 18.800
2. Tamara Manina URS 18.633
3. Eva Bosáková TCH 18.633

Team Exercise with Portable Apparatus
1. Hungary 75.20
2. Sweden 74.20
3. Poland 74.00

Basketball

1. USA
2. Soviet Union
3. Uruguay

Football

1. Soviet Union
2. Yugoslavia
3. Bulgaria

Hockey

1. India
2. Pakistan
3. Germany

(Key to symbols and abbreviations p. 1456)

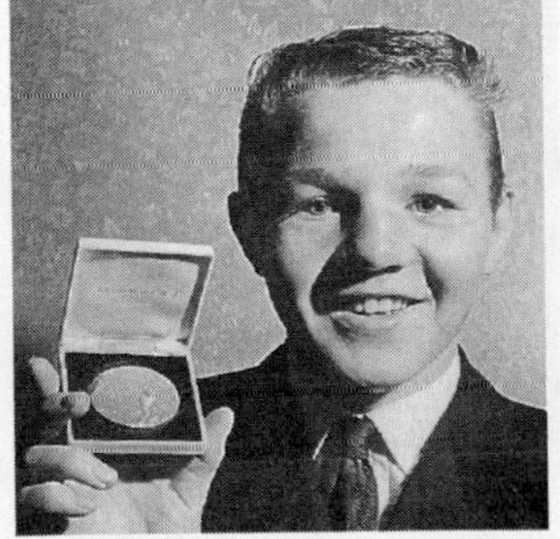

Terry Spinks is the first British boxer to win an Olympic gold medal in more than 20 years.

1956

DECEMBER

Su	Mo	Tu	We	Th	Fr	Sa
						1
2	3	4	5	6	7	8
9	10	11	12	13	14	15
16	17	18	19	20	21	22
23	24	25	26	27	28	29
30	31					

3. Washington: The US suspends its cultural exchange programme with the USSR.

3. Egypt: Britain and France announce their imminent withdrawal from Suez (→7).

4. London: The government says it has asked the US and Canada to waive interest due this month (→10).

5. S. Africa: 140 are arrested for alleged treason (→26/4/57).

7. Egypt: Anglo-French forces pull back from the front line (→20).

7. Budapest: Renewed strikes and fighting break out.→

10. Washington: The IMF authorises $1,300 million for Britain to bolster the economy (→7/2/57).

10. Stockholm: Nobel Prizes go to William Shockley, John Bardeen and Walter Brattain (US, Physics); Sir Cyril Hinshelwood (UK) and Nikolai Semenov (USSR, Chemistry); Andre Cournand (US), Werner Forsmann (W. Germany) and Dickinson Richards (US, Medicine); Juan Jimenez (Spain, Literature). No Peace Prize.

11. London: The government approves TV broadcasting between 6pm and 7pm.

14. London: Eden returns from his Jamaican rest cure (→9/1/57).

19. Cyprus: Proposals for a new constitution could lead to partition (→14/3/57).

20. Tel Aviv: Israel says it will not return Gaza to Egypt (→25/1/57).

28. Egypt: Divers start to remove a sunken ship blocking the Suez Canal (→4/1/57).

HITS OF 1956

Heartbreak Hotel.

Que sera sera.

I'll be home.

QUOTE OF THE YEAR

"We are not at war with Egypt, we are in an armed conflict."

Sir Anthony Eden, on the Suez Crisis, November 1956.

Castro is dead says the dictator Batista

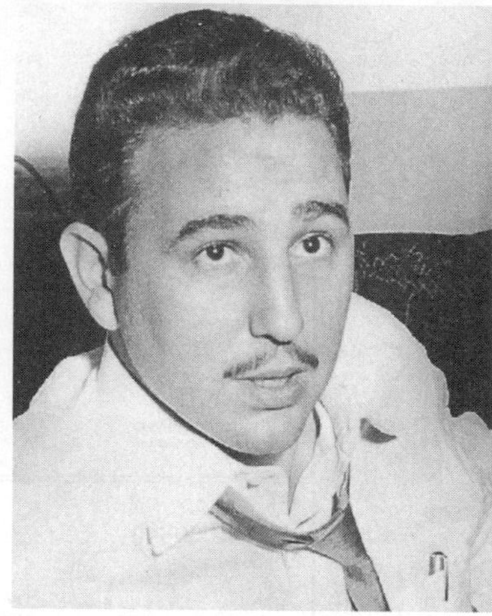

Fidel Castro, visiting New York.

Dec 2. Cuba's President Batista today claimed that his planes had killed the rebel leader, Fidel Castro, and his two brothers in a raid on Oriente province. Castro's rebellion began with an apparently suicidal frontal attack on the Moncada army post which killed 100 soldiers on July 26, 1953. He returned by yacht from Mexico last year with 80 followers. Wearing "26 de Julio" armbands, they have been fighting a guerrilla action since (→23/2/57).

Hungary put under Soviet martial law

Dec 10. Martial law has been clamped on Hungary and the Soviet army is threatening to turn its guns once again on the Hungarian people. These moves, in response to a call by the Budapest Workers' Council for a 48-hour general strike in protest against the actions of the Kadar regime, have stamped out the remnants of the freedom won by the Hungarians in their uprising against Soviet domination.

According to a decree signed by President Dobi last night, the Workers' Council has been dissolved, and summary courts are now to try people accused of inciting revolt, "jeopardising production", illegally possessing arms, murder and looting. These "extraordinary measures" had become necessary, said the decree, "owing to the continued activities of counter-revolutionary elements" (→18/2/57).

Arts: Dean brings delinquent to life

Only months after his death in his sports car, **James Dean** showed in his second film, "Rebel Without a Cause", what a loss he is to the Hollywood he despised. **Nicholas Ray's** picture, with its "chicken run" car race to the edge of a precipice, brings the affluent, alienated youth of California to vivid, delinquent life. Dean endows his portrayal of a "mixed-up kid" with awkward but touching vulnerability and loyalty to his friends.

A new and magnetic performer has appeared from France. In "Doctor at Sea" **Dirk Bogarde** surprises a girl whose face appears round a shower curtain, behind which she is clearly naked. **Brigitte Bardot** is the girl, or "sex-kitten". She attracted much attention when meeting the Queen at this year's Royal Command film.

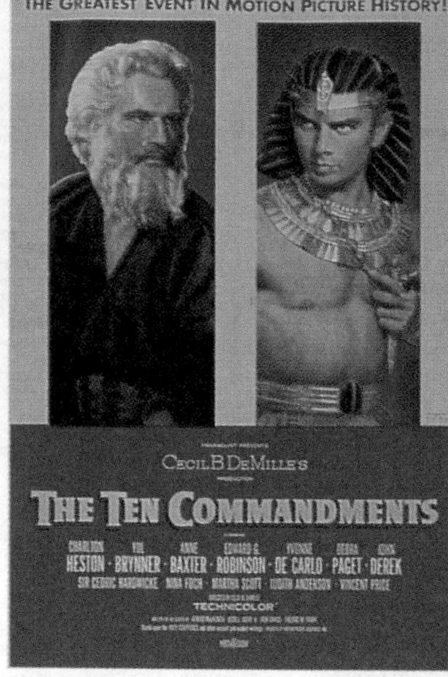

De Mille's "Ten Commandments".

A more substantial film of the year is "High Society", which combines the cool elegance of **Grace Kelly** with the eye-rolling charm of **Louis Armstrong** and features an amusing duet for **Bing Crosby** and **Frank Sinatra**, "Did You Evah?" Miss Kelly's chief competitor in the coolness stakes was **Deborah Kerr** as the English governess in "The King and I".

The London theatre has had a year of firsts: the first visit of the Bolshoi Ballet, headed by **Galina Ulanova**; of the Berliner Ensemble, headed by Brecht's widow, **Helene Weigel**; and of **Marilyn Monroe** on her honeymoon here with playwright **Arthur Miller**. They went to see his "A View from the Bridge".

At Stratford East, Theatre Workshop opened, directed by the charismatic **Joan Littlewood**. It presented a powerful play about Irish prison life by **Brendan Behan**, "The Quare Fellow". In Stratford-on-Avon the young director **Peter Hall** made his debut with "Love's Labours Lost", while in London he directed the French dancer-turned-actress **Leslie Caron** in **Colette's** "Gigi" – and then married her.

Two geniuses meet, as Salvador Dali paints Laurence Olivier costumed as "Richard III", the Shakespearean role he played in his latest film.

1957

JANUARY

Su	Mo	Tu	We	Th	Fr	Sa
		1	2	3	4	5
6	7	8	9	10	11	12
13	14	15	16	17	18	19
20	21	22	23	24	25	26
27	28	29	30	31		

1. West Germany: The Saarland returns to Germany under a 1956 agreement.

1. Cairo: Egypt abrogates the 1954 Anglo-Egyptian treaty, denying Britain use of the Suez Canal in war (→15).

4. London: A man upset by the shape of his nose is jailed for ten years for threatening a plastic surgeon with a gun.

7. Moscow: Chinese premier Chou En-lai arrives for talks.

9. London: Eden resigns as Prime Minister.→

9. UK: The Post Office introduces TV detector vans in a crackdown on licence-dodging.

11. London: Eden resigns from parliament (→7/4).

14. London: Macmillan's cabinet includes a new Ministry of Power; Peter Thorneycroft becomes Chancellor (→24/3).

15. Cairo: The government announces the nationalisation of all British and French banks.→

16. London: The Royal Ballet, created by charter from the Sadlers Wells Ballet, comes into being.

20. Washington: Eisenhower and Nixon are sworn in for a second term (→24/3).

20. Poland: National elections are held; Gomulka seems likely to win (→27/5).

23. Barbados: Pakistan's Hanif Mohammed scores 337 against West Indies in the longest-ever Test innings, 16 hours 10 minutes.

23. Monaco: Princess Grace has her first child, Caroline.

25. India: Kashmir joins India, defying a UN ruling.

25. New York: The UN demands Israeli withdrawal from Gaza and Aqaba (→1/2).

28. UK: Prince Charles has his first day at prep school.

DEATHS

14. US actor Humphrey Bogart (*25/12/1899).→

16. Italian conductor Arturo Toscanini (*25/3/1867).→

Macmillan becomes PM

Mr Macmillan is driven from Buckingham Palace as the new premier.

Jan 10. Harold Macmillan is Britain's new Prime Minister. His appointment at the age of 62 was announced this afternoon – nearly 20 hours after Sir Anthony Eden, three years younger, resigned from the post because his health was causing renewed anxiety.

The Queen consulted two Tory elders – Sir Winston Churchill and the Marquess of Salisbury – before sending for Mr Macmillan. Many politicians had expected "Rab" Butler, who has been Sir Anthony's deputy, to get the job.

There has been high drama and skulduggery overnight. Party whips finally reported that the party ranks would have split if Mr Butler won the power struggle. His lukewarm support for the Suez operations has told against him.

Deeply disappointed by this rejection, Mr Butler smiled enigmatically and said: "If my services are of value, they will be at Mr Macmillan's disposal." He is likely to become Home Secretary.

The immediate reaction from the Opposition to the new Premiership was a call from Mr Gaitskell for an immediate general election. This was brusquely rejected by Mr Macmillan. He sees post-Suez repairs to Anglo-US relations as his first job (→14).

Tough guy Bogart defeated by cancer

Jan 14. Humphrey Bogart, most people's favourite screen tough guy, died today at his home from throat cancer, aged 57. Despite his slight lisp, which he was told put him out of the running for stardom and was the result of a wound during Navy service, "Bogey" starred in over 50 films. He used the lisp, and his ability to pull back the lip in a snarl, to good effect.

His first gangster part was in "The Petrified Forest" in 1935. Having found the right combination of deadpan expression and monotone rasp, he went on using it for 20 years in such classics as "Casablanca", "The Big Sleep", which he made with Lauren Bacall whom he married, and "The African Queen", which won his Oscar.

Here's looking at you, Mr Bogart.

Britain drives the Yemenis from Aden

Jan 16. Invading Yemeni troops were sent fleeing from Aden today by a combined force of British soldiers and RAF planes firing rockets and cannons.

The soldiers, men of the Durham Light Infantry, used mortars to flush them out of houses they were occupying just inside the border with Aden, and then watched as the raiders were sent fleeing into scrubland over the border. Other Yemeni troops were removed from a nearby village which they had tried to invade (→8/3/58).

UN crews work to clear Suez Canal

Jan 4. Ships started to move through part of the Suez Canal again today, as UN-sponsored salvage crews cleared wreckage left by the recent conflict.

Two German tugs and their sister salvage vessels managed to move a 350-ton tower from the Firdan railway bridge to one side, and now six British ships and one French are working to clear 12 sunken ships blocking all but a slender channel to the sea at Port Said, so 13 ships, stranded further south, can get free (→10/2).

Toscanini, furious perfectionist, dies

Jan 16. Arturo Toscanini died today, three months short of his 90th birthday. As the most famous conductor of his time, he was also famous among players for his tantrums on the rostrum, his perfectionism, his shouts of "Vergogna!" (Shame!) when they failed to meet his exacting standard, but, as one of them put it, he made them play better than they knew they could.

In 1898, Toscanini took over La Scala, Milan. He had already given the first performances of "Pagliacci" and "La Boheme".

1957

FEBRUARY

Su	Mo	Tu	We	Th	Fr	Sa
					1	2
3	4	5	6	7	8	9
10	11	12	13	14	15	16
17	18	19	20	21	22	23
24	25	26	27	28		

1. Egypt: UN and Israeli troops clash in Sinai (→9).

4. Nicaragua: Acting President Luis Somoza is elected President.

5. Southampton: Fans greet Bill Haley as he arrives for a concert tour.→

7. London: The bank rate is cut to five per cent (→21/7).

9. Jerusalem: Thousands of Israelis protest at UN demands for a withdrawal of their troops from the Gaza Strip (→17).

10. Egypt: The Suez Canal is still reported to be impassable (→17).

13. London: Premiere of Sir William Walton's Cello Concerto.

13. London: Britain agrees to a six-month timetable for her withdrawal from Jordan (→14/4).

13. London: The government says it will boost Britain's output of nuclear weapons (→15/5).

15. Moscow: Andrei Gromyko succeeds Dmitri Shepilov as Foreign Minister.

17. Cairo: Nasser is reported to want to keep the Suez Canal closed to bring pressure on Israel to quit Gaza and Sinai.→

17. Portugal: The Queen and Prince Philip arrive on a state visit.

18. Budapest: The trial begins of people involved in the last year's uprising (→8/4).

18. London: BBC TV broadcasts the first of a new magazine series, "Tonight".

22. UK: The Vulcan bomber enters RAF service.

27. Washington: The US says Israel has agreed in principle to withdraw troops from Gaza and Aqaba (→1/3).

28. UK: Vauxhall launches its new Victor saloon which travels 40 miles per gallon.

DEATH

9. Hungarian commander and statesman Admiral Miklos Horthy von Nagybanya, Regent of Hungary 1920-44 (*18/6/1868).

Bill Haley and Comets set London rocking

Haley keeps rocking (second from right) as British fans join the frenzy.

Feb 7. Bill Haley and his Comets, who arrived at Southampton on the Queen Elizabeth to a heroes' welcome this week, last night gained another rapturous reception for their first London concert at the Dominion Theatre.

An audience of 3,000 hooted, sang, and clapped in time to the beat through "Rock Around the Clock", "Rip it Up", "Rockin' through the Rye", and the latest in his repertoire, "Don't Knock the Rock". As an added attraction, the saxophonist kneels on stage to play his instrument, while the bass player rides astride his bass.

Haley, whose record sales have reached 22 million, explains the wildfire success of rock and roll as follows: "Its appeal is its simplicity. Everyone wants to get into the act. With rock'n'roll they can join in." He believes its popularity has not yet reached its peak.

"I'm no ogre," he added. With his kiss-curl hanging limply over one eye, and plump looks, he does not seem one. He used to play for high school dances. He is 29, but makes up for it by exuberant energy on stage and his deafening beat.

One Haley song title has become a catch-phrase: "See you later, alligator", to which the reply is "In a while, crocodile". These greetings are said to be popular in Princess Margaret's set (→31/12).

Israel defies UN: holds on to Gaza

Feb 21. Despite a last-minute plea by President Eisenhower, Israel today rejected US and UN demands for an unconditional withdrawal of her troops from the Gaza strip and the Sharm el Sheikh area of the Gulf of Agaba. The 70-year-old white-haired Prime Minister, David Ben-Gurion, told the Israeli Knesset that they could not ignore the "grave and certain danger that Egypt would again interfere with Israel's freedom of navigation". He did hint, however, at further talks with the US, saying: "We hope the door is not finally closed" (→27).

Castro is waging war in Cuba jungle

Feb 23. The Cuban rebel leader, Fidel Castro, whom President Batista claimed to have had killed last December, is not only alive but directing his revolution from a secret jungle outpost. His guerrilla forces, which number only a few hundred, are effectively harrying Batista's army.

The main battle, however, is being fought in the cities; here young revolutionaries have been carrying out carefully planned acts of sabotage. Those caught have been savagely tortured by Batista's police.

1957

MARCH

Su	Mo	Tu	We	Th	Fr	Sa
					1	2
3	4	5	6	7	8	9
10	11	12	13	14	15	16
17	18	19	20	21	22	23
24	25	26	27	28	29	30
31						

1. Tel Aviv: Israel bows to UN and US pressure and agrees to pull out of Gaza and Aqaba (→11).

2. Gold Coast: The Duchess of Kent arrives for next week's independence ceremony.→

5. London: The government adopts a programme aimed at trebling nuclear energy production by 1965 (→29/5/58).

6. Ireland: De Valera, now aged 75, wins the general election.

8. Egypt: The Suez Canal reopens for smaller vessels (→15).

11. Cairo: Nasser claims Gaza and appoints a governor (→12).

12. Cairo: The US reminds Nasser that Gaza is now under UN control (→25).

14. Manchester: A BEA Vickers Viscount crashes, killing 22.→

14. Cyprus: EOKA offers a cease-fire.→

15. Cairo: Nasser decides to bar Israeli shipping from the Suez Canal (→25).

20. Bermuda: Eisenhower and Macmillan begin a four-day summit.→

22. San Francisco: The city is hit by the worst tremors since the great earthquake of 1906.

25. Rome: Six European nations create the Common Market and the European Atomic Pool, Euratom.→

25. Cairo: UN chief Dag Hammarskjold has talks with Nasser (→12/4).

28. Seychelles: Britain releases Archbishop Makarios, on condition he stays away from Cyprus (→4/4).

29. UK: Mrs G. Kohn's Sundew wins the Grand National.

30. Northern Ireland: Police uncover a plot to attack Royal Navy bases (→8/7).

DEATHS

11. US explorer Admiral Richard Byrd (*25/10/1888).

16. Rumanian sculptor Constantin Brancusi (*21/2/1876).→

Rome treaty creates Common Market

March 25. Six nations – France, West Germany, Italy, Belgium, Holland and Luxembourg – today signed the Treaty of Rome, setting up the European Common Market. This economic grouping of nations with a total population of 160 million will be developed in stages over 15 years. It aims at free movement of people, goods and money among the member states. Tariffs are abolished.

Millions of viewers watched the treaty-signing ceremony in a TV link-up and heard their leaders hailing a European renaissance.

In London, Mr Macmillan and his cabinet prepared for negotiations for establishing a wider continental trading structure which could embrace the Common Market, Britain and other countries.

They have already accepted that, without such new trading arrangements, the Market's development will be a threat to Britain, and could lead to new friction rather than greater European unity. So they are pushing for a European Free Trade Area, which would include the whole of Western Europe and would involve less surrender of sovereignty than joining the EEC.

The Prime Minister has said: "I do not conceal that there are great risks in this policy. Our industry will have to meet competition but there are also great prizes."

Caustic French diplomatic reaction is that Britain should have sought EEC membership in the first place. Privately, Mr Macmillan agrees.

Senior ministers of "The Six" meet to create a Common Market for Europe.

Ike and Mac make it up in Bermuda

March 24. Mr Macmillan and President Eisenhower claimed tonight to have re-established mutual confidence between their two governments. A communique on their four-day summit meeting in Bermuda showed that they have patched up Suez crisis quarrels and reached new agreements in several areas.

The meeting was the US leader's idea, and he talked cordially about "the long term bonds that bind together the British Empire and my country". In London the Foreign Office breathed more freely.

An "Ike-Mac" declaration condemned Soviet repression in Eastern Europe, applauded the project for a European Common Market, and referred to NATO as "the cornerstone of our policy in the West".

They also announced that the US will supply Britain with guided missiles, their warheads to be under American control (→21/7).

Ghana throws off "chains of imperialism"

March 6. The lowering of the Union Jack above the floodlit Parliament building in the capital, Accra, at midnight tonight signified the end of the British Gold Coast colony and the birth of the black state of Ghana. Dr Nkrumah, Prime Minister and self-styled liberator of his people, told a cheering crowd to rejoice at the casting-off of "the chains of imperialism".

The name Ghana is taken from an Islamic empire that existed in the Middle Ages in the Sudan, far distant from West Africa. Nkrumah wants to inspire people to emulate a past when Africans had wealth and power (→23/11/58).

Manchester crash grounds all Viscounts

March 17. British European Airways today grounded all its oldest Viscount turbo-prop airliners, following last week's crash at Manchester's Ringway airport in which 22 people were killed and houses demolished.

Experts now believe a failure in one of the wing flaps could have caused the crash – if a mechanical failure makes a flap extend on one side but not the other the aircraft would tilt over without warning. Five flights out of London airport were halted because of the instruction, and one Viscount on its way to Tel Aviv was stopped at Rome's Ciampino airport.

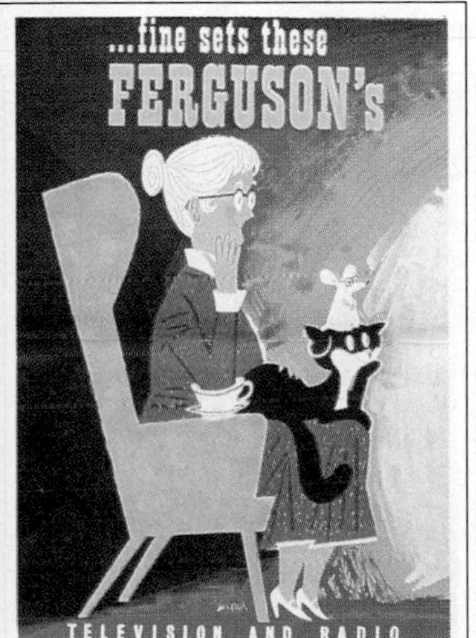
...fine sets these
FERGUSON's
TELEVISION AND RADIO

The television revolution gains momentum as everyone joins in.

Greece rejects new Cyprus peace plan

March 20. The Greek Government turned down an offer by NATO to mediate in the Cyprus dispute today. Within hours of the announcement of the offer, the Prime Minister, Mr Karamanlis, issued an uncompromising refusal even to sit down at the same conference table as the Turks.

In Cyprus, the Governor has rejected an EOKA offer of a ceasefire, because it was made in the hope that it might lead to the exiled Archbishop Makarios's return. He won't be allowed back until he renounces violence (→28).

Nurses and firemen search vainly for survivors after the Viscount crash.

1957

APRIL

Su	Mo	Tu	We	Th	Fr	Sa
	1	2	3	4	5	6
7	8	9	10	11	12	13
14	15	16	17	18	19	20
21	22	23	24	25	26	27
28	29	30				

1. Bonn: West German scientists refuse to work on nuclear weapons (→25).

2. S. Africa: Britain hands over the Simonstown naval base to South Africa.

3. UK: Tom Finney of Preston North End is voted Footballer of the Year.

4. Cyprus: The state of emergency is relaxed (→17).

4. London: The government says the last National Service call-up will be in 1960.

7. US: Eden enters a Boston clinic with liver disease (→3/6).

8. Budapest: Three leaders of the 1956 uprising are sentenced to death (→22).

8. Paris: The Queen arrives on a four-day state visit.

11. Singapore: The island is granted self-government from Britain (→23/8).

12. Riyadh: Saudi Arabia bars Israeli vessels from entering the Gulf of Aqaba (→12/4).

17. Athens: Greek premier Karamanlis welcomes Archbishop Makarios (→9/8).

22. Budapest: The government dissolves the Writers' Association as being partly behind last year's revolt (→5/7).

24. London: BBC TV broadcasts the first edition of an astronomy series "The Sky at Night" with Patrick Moore.

24. Jordan: Ibrahim Hashem forms a pro-Western government as unrest continues (→25).

25. Jordan: King Hussein proclaims martial law (→28).

25. Bonn: Adenauer rejects the idea of German neutrality (→7/5).

26. London: New council housing estates are reported to be unpopular among residents of the East End.

28. Jordan: King Hussein flies to Riyadh for talks with King Saud of Saudi Arabia (→16/6).

30. Beirut: The US Sixth Fleet arrives in response to current Middle East tension.

Hussein faces down Nasser-style coup

April 14. In an astonishing act of personal bravery, King Hussein of Jordan foiled a coup led by his army's Chief of Staff, General Abu Nuwar, aged 34. Although for long an intimate friend of the King's, Nuwar had been won over to the side of the former Prime Minister, Mr Nabulsi. Hussein dismissed Nabulsi five days ago, after he had declared his intention to set up a republic backed by Egypt and Syria.

Jordan still has no new government, and Nuwar planned to take advantage of the unrest and mount a Nasser-style coup. At noon yesterday the King learnt he had replaced the loyalist Armoured Regiment just north of Amman by the left-wing Fourth Infantry. During the night they cordoned off the capital.

On Sunday morning he called Nuwar to the Palace and drove with him to the scene of the rebellion. On the way he stopped an attempt on Nuwar's life by loyalist troops, and sent him back to the Palace under guard.

The King, at the wheel himself, then drove recklessly through heavy firing between loyalist and rebel troops to the Fourth Infantry headquarters. He walked in and told the rebel officers: "If I am a traitor, kill me." Instead they gave in; then the King drove back to the Palace where he dismissed and exiled Nuwar (→24).

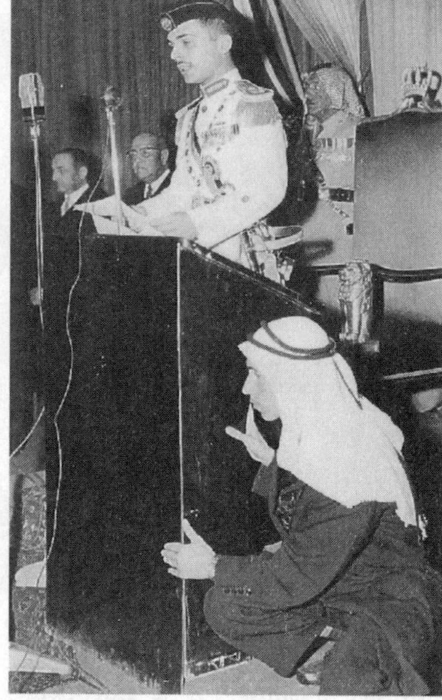

Hussein opens a new parliament.

Olivier displays finely-judged vulgarity

Laurence Olivier as Archie Rice.

April 11. John Osborne returned to the theatrical limelight last night with a new play that looks set to succeed on the scale of "Look Back in Anger". In "The Entertainer" he has created a third-rate music-hall comic called Archie Rice who struts the stage, cocky, hard-drinking, lecherous, and hollow inside.

This acting opportunity is seized upon by Laurence Olivier, making his first appearance in the Royal Court's seasons of "kitchen sink drama". He turns in a dazzling display of virtuosity.

Almost unrecognisable with his seedy bowler hat and gap-toothed smile, he sings, tap-dances and tells blue jokes to the "mike" with a finely-judged degree of vulgarity and tastelessness. "Thank God I'm normal," he sneers with whining innuendo, and bids farewell to the audience with a cynical: "Let me know where you're working tomorrow night and I'll come and see you" (→13/6).

Mao's 100 flowers continue blooming

April 24. The movement for greater freedom and internal reform in China, launched by Mao Tse-tung last year with the phrase "let 100 flowers bloom and 100 schools argue", is to continue. The Communist Party has now asked all critics of the government to come forward and explain their disenchantment.

Not wanting to follow the example set by de-Stalinisation in the USSR, the authorities appear to be seeking a political solution to the problems recognised by Mao in February. These include labour unrest, strikes, student demonstrations, peasant protests and the stoning of party officials. Government ministers who are not party members have complained that their role is merely symbolic.

Anglican church defies race laws

April 26. Widespread disobedience to the South African Government's race segregation laws is taking place, with the encouragement of such distinguished figures as the Anglican Bishop of Johannesburg, the Right Rev. Ambrose Reeve. He has told Africans to defy the new law that forbids a black man to attend a church in a white district without official permission. Cape Town University is continuing to accept black students in defiance of the Government's educational apartheid laws (→3/5).

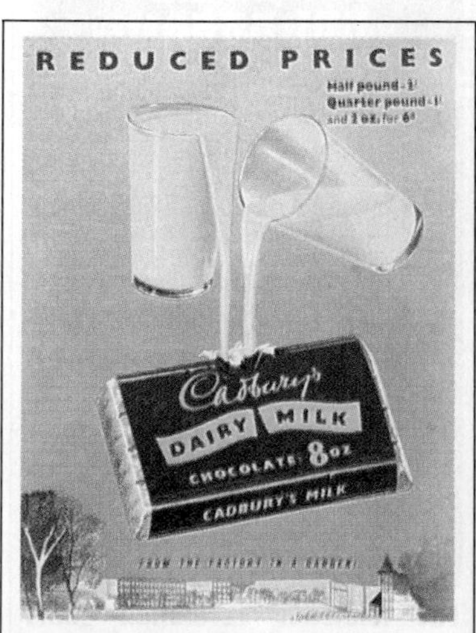

REDUCED PRICES
Cadbury's
DAIRY MILK
CHOCOLATE 8oz
CADBURY'S MILK

A cheaper glass-and-a-half.

1957

MAY

Su	Mo	Tu	We	Th	Fr	Sa
			1	2	3	4
5	6	7	8	9	10	11
12	13	14	15	16	17	18
19	20	21	22	23	24	25
26	27	28	29	30	31	

1. UK: 31 die when a troop plane crashes at Blackbush Airport in Hampshire.

3. Pretoria: South Africa drops "God Save the Queen" as its national anthem (→25/6).

6. New York: Eugene O'Neill wins a Pulitzer Prize for his play "Long Day's Journey into Night".

6. London: The Suez Canal Company resurrects the idea of a channel tunnel between Britain and France.

7. Bonn: Macmillan and Adenauer begin defence talks.

9. UK: Labour makes gains in local council elections.

12. Italy: 14 people are killed when the Marquis de Portago of Spain hits a crowd during the Mille Miglia motor race.

14. UK: Emergency petrol rationing ends.

15. Pacific: Britain's first hydrogen bomb is dropped on Christmas Island (→14/6).

16. London: The GPO announces plans for automatic trunk dialling by 1959.

19. Washington: The US puts off until 1958 its first artificial satellite launch, originally due in September (→6/12).

21. Paris: Premier Guy Mollet resigns after his government is defeated in the Assembly (→12/6).

23. London: The Church of England says that remarried divorcees can take the sacraments, if a bishop permits.

26. Paris: Algerian Muslim leader Ali Chekkal is assassinated at the French football cup final (→9/6).

27. Warsaw: Gomulka asks the USSR for economic aid (→6/10).

29. Madrid: Cupholders Real Madrid beat Italian side Fiorentina 2-0 in the second European Cup Final.

DEATHS

2. US politician Senator Joseph McCarthy (*14/11/08).

12. Austrian actor and film director Erich von Stroheim (*22/9/1885).

US writer refuses to fink on his friends

May 31. Arthur Miller, one of America's foremost playwrights, was convicted today of contempt of Congress for refusing to name names to the House of Representatives Un-American Activities Committee. He is liable to up to a year's imprisonment.

Called before the Committee last June, Miller answered every question about himself. He said his conscience did not permit him to name other allegedly Communist writers who had attended meetings with him and get them into trouble.

The Federal judge ruled that this was contempt, however laudable his motive may have been. Miller, on bail pending appeal, said: "I have no statement to make. Neither has my wife" (→7/8/58).

Injury foils Busby Babes' double bid

May 4. In a Cup Final made almost meaningless as a contest by one injury, Manchester United, already League champions, narrowly failed to become the first team this century to achieve a Cup-League double.

In the sixth minute of the game Peter McParland, the Aston Villa winger, charged United's goalkeeper Ray Wood. A clash of heads left Wood concussed and out of action, allowing Villa to score twice to win 2-1. The Football Association remains opposed to substitutes.

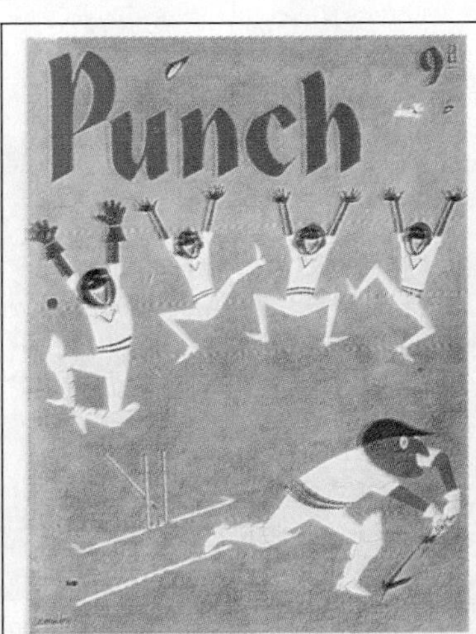

The cricket season starts again.

1957

JUNE

Su	Mo	Tu	We	Th	Fr	Sa
						1
2	3	4	5	6	7	8
9	10	11	12	13	14	15
16	17	18	19	20	21	22
23	24	25	26	27	28	29
30						

1. London: ERNIE picks the first premium bond prize winners.

3. Liverpool: Sir Anthony Eden says his active political life is over.

5. UK: Sir V. Sassoon's Crepello wins the Derby, ridden by Lester Piggott.

9. Algiers: Ten die when a bomb goes off in a casino (→1/7).

11. Canada: The Conservative Party under John Diefenbaker comes to power, ending 22 years of Liberal rule (→12/10).

12. Paris: Maurice Bourges-Manoury, a Radical, becomes premier.

13. New York: Premiere of the film "The Prince and the Showgirl" with Sir Laurence Olivier and Marilyn Monroe.

13. Washington: Vice-president Nixon and Dr Martin Luther King meet to discuss race issues (→3/9).

14. New York: The USSR says it wants a three-year ban on nuclear tests (→29/7).

16. Cairo: Jordan closes its embassy (→3/11).

19. London: ITV broadcasts the first in a new comedy series, "The Army Game" with Alfie Bass and Bill Fraser.

23. Cairo: Three Britons are jailed for spying (→30)

25. S. Africa: The African National Congress calls a one-day general strike (→23/1/58).

26. London: The Commonwealth summit ends.

27. UK: The Jodrell Bank radio telescope in Cheshire is reported near completion.

28. London: British Rail announces a loss of £16.5 million in 1956 (→3/10).

30. Cairo: Three Britons jailed for spying fly home after being released.

DEATHS

12. US band leader Jimmy Dorsey (*29/2/04).

28. German author Alfred Doblin (*10/8/1878).

Unspoilt Benidorm is new holiday spot

June 7. "The people are charming, not yet spoilt by easy money," wrote one travel writer today of a village called Benidorm on Spain's Costa del Sol. "The Germans are fond of it and they have built a magnificent hotel on the hill above it. It is a bed and breakfast place (only 110 pesetas a head)."

With limited foreign currency allowances at their disposal, more and more British holiday makers are being lured to Spanish resorts by the sun and low prices.

"New hotels are going up everywhere," the piece continues. "They are mostly cool, spick-and-span, well-fitted and flimsy with masses of private bathrooms, though in some places only salt water comes out of the taps."

Campaign to stop smoking launched

June 26. The special Medical Research Council report published tonight insists that the relationship between lung cancer and smoking is "one of direct cause and effect", and not just one of association as previously suggested. Earlier in the House of Commons John Vaughan Morgan, Parliamentary Secretary to the Ministry of Health, said that smokers must make up their own minds. He made it clear that there would be no attempt to ban smoking either by individuals or in public (→29/1/58).

Crabb's body found

June 26. The headless body of Royal Navy frogman Commander Lionel "Buster" Crabb has been found in the sea near Chichester Harbour, ending speculation that the former submariner was being held by the Soviet Navy. Crabb's underwater activities close to visiting Russian ships in Portsmouth Harbour caused a major diplomatic and political row just over a year ago.

In a statement, Crabb's mother insisted that her son had died "as he had lived, in the service of his own country and of no other".

1957

JULY

Su	Mo	Tu	We	Th	Fr	Sa
	1	2	3	4	5	6
7	8	9	10	11	12	13
14	15	16	17	18	19	20
21	22	23	24	25	26	27
28	29	30	31			

1. Washington: Senator John Kennedy calls on the US to aid Algerian independence (→21/11).

4. London: MPs vote themselves an increase in expenses of £750 a year.

5. Wimbledon: Lew Hoad beats Ashley Cooper to retain the Men's Singles title.→

5. London: The Commonwealth conference closes with a joint expression of concern over Hungary (→16/6/58).

9. Moscow: Ex-premier Malenkov is given the job of head of a hydro-electric power station in Kazakhstan (→31/8).

12. US: 20-year-old Harvard student Prince Karim is declared Aga Khan on the death of his grandfather.

15. London: A public inquiry opens into the redevelopment plans for the bombed area around St. Paul's Cathedral.

16. UK: Doctors express concern at the increased use of tranquillisers.

20. UK: Stirling Moss wins the British Grand Prix at Aintree, the first Briton to do so since 1923 (→8/9).

22. Israel: Shell and BP decide to quit Israel under pressure from Arab states (→29/10).

22. Oman: British troops move in to suppress an uprising against the sultan (→28).

23. UK: Picket line violence breaks out as a national bus strike takes effect (→15/8).

25. Tunisia: Premier Bourguiba ousts the Bey and becomes president (→21/11).

26. UK: Figures show that 1.5 million people are living alone, twice as many as in 1931.

28. Oman: The rebellion against the sultan is reported to be petering out (→11/8).

29. London: US Secretary of State Dulles arrives for talks on disarmament (→2/8).

DEATH

11. Ismaelite spiritual leader Aga Khan III (*2/11/1877).

Khrushchev foils coup

Khrushchev (l.), seen with Bulganin, during last year's visit to Britain.

July 3. Backed by the loyal Soviet military, Nikita Khrushchev has beaten off a challenge to his leadership and routed a so-called "anti-party group".

A stormy eight-day meeting of the policy-making Central Committee ended today with the removal from the ruling Politburo of Lazar Kaganovitch, Vyacheslav Molotov, and Georgi Malenkov, and the demotion of three other senior party officials. Essentially they were accused of attempting to halt the de-Stalinisation campaign launched last year.

The coup was engineered by Molotov, and Khrushchev was outvoted at a special Politburo meeting, but the Soviet Party leader quickly got in touch with Marshal Zhukov, who put the Army firmly on his side. Thus secured, Khrushchev next demanded a full session of the Central Committee and, having packed it with his supporters, ensured that the vote went unanimously in his favour (→9).

State of emergency declared in Ireland

July 8. The veteran Irish statesman Eamon de Valera, who formed his eighth administration in February, yesterday took the toughest decision of his political career, and issued a state of emergency proclamation which allows internment without trial in peacetime.

The security forces acted quickly. By last night 63 IRA men were behind bars at the Curragh military camp some 20 miles from Dublin. These are the men suspected of being responsible for the shootings and burnings that have happened over the last few months along the border with Northern Ireland. The Protestant Orangemen's marching season is about to start in the North, and the government felt it had to act quickly and without warning.

There are angry reactions on the Fianna Fail benches in the Dail over such drastic action, to which is added the belief that de Valera should be doing more about ending partition.

But the government was faced with the courts being unable to obtain convictions of known bombers and gunmen in the IRA's border campaign. The evidence has not been there, as witnesses are too frightened (→17/8).

Ibbotson recaptures mile record for Britain in 3m 57.2secs run

July 19. The mile world record has returned to Britain. In a superb race at White City, in London, in which the first four men all broke the magic four minutes, Derek Ibbotson of Huddersfield took on and beat the Olympic champion, Ron Delany of Ireland, and the new world 1,500 metres record holder, Stanislav Jungwirth of Czechoslovakia, in front of a television audience of some ten million.

Ibbotson broke the tape in three minutes 57.2 seconds, eight-tenths of a second faster than Australian John Landy's time three years ago when he became the second to break four minutes. Delany was nearly ten yards back, so exhausted that he had to be helped from the track; Jungwirth finished third and Ken Wood of Sheffield, also inside four minutes, fourth.

Derek Ibbotson cuts through the tape to notch up his world record mile.

First black wins a Wimbledon title

July 6. In a powerful display of controlled tennis throughout a fortnight in which she did not lose a single set, Althea Gibson of the United States became Wimbledon's first black champion as she beat Darlene Hard (with whom she later took the doubles title) 6-3, 6-2.

Neither played to their full potential in a scrappy final, but that should not detract from the achievement of the tall New Yorker who learned her tennis on the asphalt playgrounds of Harlem. She is promised a ticker-tape welcome on her return home.

Althea Gibson and Darlene Hard.

We've never had it so good, says 'Mac'

July 20. "Let us be frank about it. Most of our people have never had it so good." So Mr Macmillan told a cheering Conservative rally at Bradford today.

The Prime Minister is making a series of party speeches aimed at raising Tory morale which has been dented by recent poor by-election performances. The Treasury is also warning that there could be bad news for sterling soon.

Mr Macmillan asked his party faithful to rejoice over the difference in the standard of living compared with six years ago. Instead of austerity there is now, he said, an abundance of goods and freedom of choice: Tory policies work, he added (→ 19/9).

1957

AUGUST

Su	Mo	Tu	We	Th	Fr	Sa
				1	2	3
4	5	6	7	8	9	10
11	12	13	14	15	16	17
18	19	20	21	22	23	24
25	26	27	28	29	30	31

1. London: A £17 million expansion scheme for Heathrow Airport is unveiled.

2. London: The USSR gives a cool response to a US proposal for mutual inspections of military bases (→ 6/9).

3. Kuala Lumpur: Abdul Rahman is elected for a five-year term as first premier of independent Malaya.→

6. UK: 2,000 people a week are reported to be emigrating to the Commonwealth despite full employment at home.

8. UK: Myxomatosis is now reported to be rife in 11 counties.

9. Cyprus: The state of emergency is revoked (→ 28/10)

11. Oman: The rebel headquarters at Nizwa is taken by British troops (→ 16).

15. London: A dockers strike spreads; 12,000 are now out.

16. Oman: British troops leave as the anti-sultan rebellion has collapsed (→ 20).

17. Northern Ireland: 20 are arrested after a booby-trap bomb killed a policeman.

20. New York: The UN rejects an Arab motion condemning the British role in the Oman rebellion.

22. Edinburgh: A schoolboys' staging of "Hamlet" is coolly reviewed, but Derek Jacobi as Hamlet is "interesting".

23. Singapore: 23 alleged Communist plotters are arrested.

24. London: Chelsea FC cause a stir with their brilliant new star, 17-year-old Jimmy Greaves.

29. US: The "Drunkometer" is tested; it measures the amount of alcohol on the breath.

31. Moscow: Disgraced ex-foreign minister Molotov is appointed Soviet ambassador to Mongolia (→ 26/10).

DEATHS

7. US comedian Oliver Hardy (*18/1/1892).→

24. British violinist Albert Sammons (*23/2/1886).

Exasperated Olly, Stan's pal, is dead

Aug 7. Oliver Hardy, the corpulent, pompous and indignant half of the Laurel and Hardy partnership, died today, aged 65, following a stroke. Stan Laurel, his English-born partner, deeply affected, said: "He was like a brother to me."

Together they had made 200 pictures in the slapstick tradition in which they began 30 years ago. Hardy, always on the receiving end, weighed 20 stone. The contrast with Laurel's small figure and lugubrious personality made an immortal comedy partnership, which has lately found a new audience on television.

In 1947 they appeared at the London Palladium in the Royal Variety Show. Hardy had been married four times.

Laurel and Hardy - a fine mess.

Malaya independent as midnight chimes

Aug 30. Malaya, the last of Britain's major Asian colonies, is free. A bell tolled midnight over Kuala Lumpur as 170 years of British rule came to an end. As the union flag was lowered the new Chief Minister, Tengku Abdul Rahman, told a crowd of several thousand Malays, Chinese, Indians, Eurasians and Europeans that this was the greatest moment in the life of the Malayan people. He praised the troops who quelled the Communist rebellion, and called on the country to rid itself of terrorism so people could be free to move wherever they chose, unharassed, unafraid and undisturbed.

In a warm tribute to the British he said: "We were blessed with a good administration ... Let this legacy left by the British not suffer in efficiency or integrity in the years to come."

TV audiences soar as radio's slump

Aug 13. The BBC today announced a revamp of its radio programmes in a bid to stem the drift of its audience to television. Figures just released show that the evening audience for radio has declined by a million to 3.5 million in this year alone. Eight years ago the average nightly audience was eight million.

But television was then in its infancy, with transmissions only just beginning to spread beyond London. Now, as commercial television also begins to expand, six million people are estimated to watch BBC and ITV television programmes each evening. Radio planners hope that an earlier start to the Light Programme, plus hourly news summaries, will help them fight back.

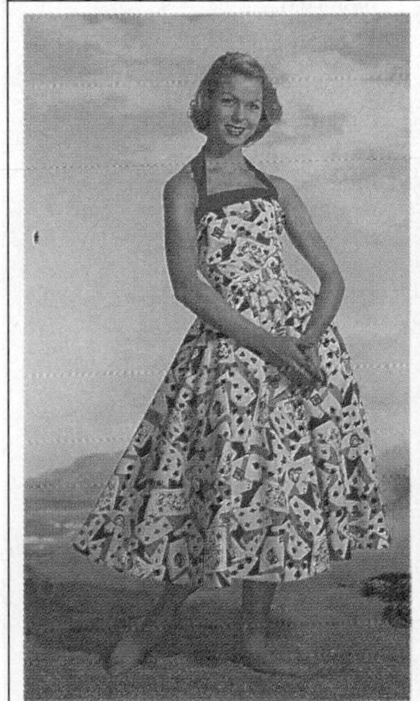

Diamonds are a girl's best friend, not to mention spades, hearts, clubs and the rest of the deck.

1957

SEPTEMBER

Su	Mo	Tu	We	Th	Fr	Sa
1	2	3	4	5	6	7
8	9	10	11	12	13	14
15	16	17	18	19	20	21
22	23	24	25	26	27	28
29	30					

1. Jamaica: 173 die in a rail crash.

3. US: The Federal District Court orders Little Rock, Arkansas, to end segregation in its schools immediately (→4).

4. US: Governor Faubus of Arkansas sends state troops to stop nine blacks going to a white school in Little Rock (→7).

6. London: The disarmament talks break up (→8/10).

7. US: The Federal court insists that desegregation in schools will not be postponed (→10).

8. Italy: Stirling Moss wins the Italian Grand Prix at Monza (→24/8/58).

10. Washington: The US government seeks an injunction to force Governor Faubus to end school segregation.→

12. Lebanon: Lebanese and Syrian troops clash on the border (→12/10).

13. London: Agatha Christie's "Mousetrap" becomes Britain's longest-running play as it has its 1,998th performance.

15. West Germany: Adenauer is re-elected by a large majority.

16. London: Paymaster General Reginald Maudling joins the cabinet in a government reshuffle.

19. London: New counter-inflation measures include a rise in the bank rate to seven per cent (→7/1/58).

21. Oslo: Prince Olav becomes King Olav V of Norway on the death of King Haakon VII.

23. Haiti: Dr Francois "Papa Doc" Duvalier wins the presidential election (→31/7/58).

26. New York: Hammarskjold is elected for another five-year term as UN Secretary-General.

DEATHS

20. Finnish composer Jean Sibelius, born Johann Julian Christian Sibelius (*8/12/1865).→

21. Norwegian King Haakon VII (*3/8/1872).

Troops end school ban

A white segregationist is led away by National Guardsmen in Arkansas.

Sept 25. Desegregation finally happened in Little Rock, Arkansas, today. Nine black children, three boys and six girls, hurried into the yellow brick Central High School, which was surrounded by over 1,000 US paratroopers, in full battle-dress with fixed bayonets and rifles at the ready. It was a quiet, orderly day in the school, but beyond the cordon about 1,500 whites demonstrated. At least seven were arrested and one man was knocked down as he tried to grab a soldier's rifle.

Most people still seemed stunned by President Eisenhower's decision yesterday to send in Federal troops and bring the state troops under Federal control. Earlier this month Governor Orval Faubus ordered the state militia to bar the entry of the black children to the school. He said he would never allow black children to enter a white school despite the order from the Federal District Court. He insisted that he was acting simply to preserve peace and to prevent bloodshed.

The troops kept the children away then while a crowd of over 400 white men and women jeered, booed, and shouted "Go home, niggers". The same strength of feeling still exists amongst whites in the South. This afternoon Governors of the southern states met at Sea Island, Georgia, and demanded withdrawal of the Federal troops "at the earliest possible moment", and an urgent meeting with the President. They see the move as a major threat to state rights, but the President is equally determined that the Federal laws shall be upheld even if the use of the armed forces is required (→20/8/58).

Liberalise homosexual laws, says report

Sept 4. Homosexual acts between consenting adult men in private should no longer be a criminal offence, says the long-awaited Wolfenden report, out today. It defines adult as over 21. The recommendation is bound to spark intense debate, and the Government is expected to wait several months to gauge public reaction before embarking on any legislative moves.

The report is the result of three years' work by the Commitee on Homosexual Offences and Prostitution, under the chairmanship of Sir John Wolfenden, vice-chancellor of Reading University.

It argues that the law ought to allow individual freedom of choice and action in matters of private morality, even if they are regarded as sinful or objectionable by some. Certain things are "not the law's business" (→14/11).

Jean Sibelius dies after a long silence

Sept 20. Jean Sibelius, national hero as well as chief composer in his native Finland, has died there at 91, after 30 years of silence. His Seventh Symphony, in one awe-inspiring movement, was written in 1924. He had promised an Eighth, which people assumed would be performed after his death. There was no Eighth Symphony.

He paid many visits to Britain which he said was the birthplace of his fame. Certainly English audiences showed a marked preference for his symphonies and tone poems over the music of Stravinsky or Schoenberg. His music was inspired by the forces of nature. "Others provide cocktails", he said, "I serve only plain water."

Jean Sibelius, Finland's composer.

Asian flu death toll continues to mount

Sept 23. A Ministry of Health spokesman stated today that the outbreak of Asian influenza remained essentially a mild one, although attacks have been complicated by pneumonia and bronchitis, resulting in additional deaths.

In 160 large towns of England and Wales, deaths from influenza rose from eight to 47 in the week ending September 14, while deaths due to pneumonia rose from 177 to 245, and those due to bronchitis from 128 to 158. Children are particularly affected and many are away from school (→1/10).

1957

OCTOBER

Su	Mo	Tu	We	Th	Fr	Sa
		1	2	3	4	5
6	7	8	9	10	11	12
13	14	15	16	17	18	19
20	21	22	23	24	25	26
27	28	29	30	31		

1. UK: An Asian flu vaccine is distributed (→4/11).

1. New York: The UN reports that half the world's population is underfed.

2. UK: Vauxhall introduces new Cresta and Velox models.

3. UK: 1,000 parish councillors ask the government to stop British Rail from closing branch lines.

6. Warsaw: Students riot against the government for the third day running.

8. Washington: Dulles says the US is willing to discuss the control of missiles with the USSR (→19/12).

12. Canada: The Queen arrives to open the Canadian parliament.→

12. Syria: Egyptian troops fly in, amid fears of an attack by Israel and Turkey (→1/2/58).

15. Moscow: Khrushchev writes to socialist parties in Europe urging action to end US and Turkish "aggression".

17. Moscow: The USSR says that its next artificial satellite will have an animal aboard (→3/11).

22. Saigon: Terrorist bombs injure 13 US servicemen and five civilians (→6/11).

23. Washington: Macmillan and Foreign Secretary Selwyn Lloyd have talks at the White House (→26/11).

25. UK: The first nuclear civil defence manual recommends wearing gloves and hats and using lots of soap and water.

26. Moscow: Marshal Georgi Zhukov is dismissed as minister of defence (→3/11).

28. Cyprus: Pro-EOKA street demonstrations are dispersed with tear gas (→28/1/58).

29. Tel Aviv: Premier Ben-Gurion and several ministers are hurt when a grenade is thrown into the Knesset.

DEATHS

24. French fashion designer Christian Dior (*21/1/05).→

26. Greek author Nikos Kazantzakis (*18/2/1885).

Russia is first in space

Oct 4. Russia today inaugurated the space age by launching a man-made satellite. The artificial moon, known as Sputnik-I, is now orbiting more than 500 miles above the earth, taking 95 minutes to complete each circuit at 18,000 miles an hour. The launch, the Russians claim, opens the way to interplanetary travel.

Two radio transmitters are operating on board. Their signals have already been picked up by the BBC, and by RCA in the United States. The transmissions are powerful enough to be detected by many amateur enthusiasts, too.

According to a Russian statement, the satellite is a sphere 22 inches in diameter, weighing 83.6 kilograms (185 pounds). This is six times heavier than the satellite the Americans plan to launch during the International Geophysical Year which runs to December 31 1958. The weight of the satellite points to a powerful launching rocket.

Dr Joseph Kaplan, chairman of the US National Committee for the IGY, hailed the Russian achievement as "fantastic". However, to be beaten into space by the Russians will be a severe blow to American pride. So far the Pentagon has not commented, saying it wanted to check details of the report. Besides scientific research, artificial satellites could have practical uses in such fields as weather forecasting and communications (→17).

Milk ban after severe fire at atom plant

Oct 17. A permanent shutdown of one of the piles at the Windscale atomic works in Cumberland has been ordered, following a serious fire in which substantial amounts of radioactivity escaped up the 500-foot chimney. Sales of milk, from a strip of land seven miles long and two wide, have been banned as it contains up to six times the permissible level of radioiodine.

The two Windscale piles are used to make plutonium for military purposes. They are fuelled with uranium rods in aluminium cans. The cans lie in channels in a stack of graphite blocks and are cooled by blowing air over them. The fire started when, for an unknown reason, some fuel rods overheated. Several cans burst, allowing radioactive material to escape. The fire was eventually extinguished by dousing the pile with water.

According to the Atomic Energy Authority, most of the radioactivity that escaped was carried out to sea by the wind, and there is no direct hazard to the public. Milk sales have been banned because of the possible danger to small children who drink large quantities.

Although nobody has been injured, and the Windscale plant is now back to normal operation, the fire is one of the most serious accidents yet in the short history of the atomic industry (→7/11).

Dumpa churna milka day? Thousands of gallons of contaminated milk from farms near Windscale are poured down the drains and out to the sea.

Queen pays visit to the White House

The Queen meets the President.

Oct 18. The visit of the Queen and Prince Philip to the United States has turned into a spectacular triumph all the way. In Washington, tens of thousands stood on footpaths till near midnight to see them return to the White House after entertaining President and Mrs Eisenhower to dinner.

Top Republicans pressurised the White House for invitations to the president's state banquet, and the lucky few were accommodated in every available space.

The visit marks the 350th anniversary of the first British settlers in Virginia. In a speech at Williamsburg, the colonial capital, she said: "There is a county in Virginia named after every English King and Queen from Elizabeth I to George III" (→23).

Labour keeps Bomb thanks to Bevan

Oct 3. The Labour Party conference voted overwhelmingly today against committing the next Labour government to renouncing the H-bomb. This happened after a sensational speech by Aneurin Bevan, the Shadow Foreign Secretary.

He was bitterly heckled by former comrades when he cried: "If you carry this (ban the bomb) resolution you'll send the British Foreign Secretary naked into the conference chamber." Nye is no longer the darling of the left (→6/3/58).

Dior, high priest of haute couture, dies

Oct 24. Christian Dior, the high priest of haute couture, died today in Italy. He was 52. The man who made fashion history with the New Look in his first collection originally began sketching dresses while stuck in bed, convalescing after a serious illness.

Backed by textile king Marcel Boussac, he opened his Paris house in 1947, and within eight years had a turnover of £5 million a year and a staff of 1,200 in subsidiaries in Britain, the US and South America. France awarded him the Legion of Honour for revitalising the fashion industry (→ 30/1/58).

Christian Dior and two creations.

Lords to take life and women peers

Oct 30. Government proposals for creating life peerages and admitting women to the House of Lords were announced today. The Earl of Home, leader of the Upper House, said the reforms are aimed at strengthening Parliament through practical improvement in their lordships' day-to-day working.

Some distinguished figures in many walks of life are known to be unwilling to accept a hereditary title. Legislation next year will allow such people to give a blood transfusion to an increasingly frail second chamber.

There is no sign yet of any inter-party agreement on more radical Lords' reform, affecting both composition and powers (→ 13/2/58).

1957

NOVEMBER

Su	Mo	Tu	We	Th	Fr	Sa
					1	2
3	4	5	6	7	8	9
10	11	12	13	14	15	16
17	18	19	20	21	22	23
24	25	26	27	28	29	30

3. Moscow: Marshal Zhukov loses his positions in the Party and his war record is dismissed as "self-aggrandisement" (→ 27/3/58).

3. Cairo: The government-controlled Egyptian radio calls for the assassination of King Hussein of Jordan (→ 26/12).

4. UK: The Asian flu epidemic is now abating.

6. Phnom Penh: Cambodia declares neutrality.

7. UK: At the Windscale inquiry, the UK Atomic Energy Authority is accused of misleading the public (→ 8).

8. UK: The Windscale inquiry blames the fire on bad judgement, wrong methods and faulty instruments (→ 19/12).

12. London: The GPO announces plans to introduce postcodes rather than addresses.

14. London: The Queen abolishes Court presentations of debutantes (→ 18/3/58).

14. London: The Church backs the recommendations of the Wolfenden Report on homosexuality (→ 4/12).

15. UK: 43 die when a plane crashes on the Isle of Wight.

19. London: The government proposes building a London to Dover motorway.

19. Prague: Antonin Novotny becomes Czech president following the death of Antonin Zapotocky on the 13th.

21. Morocco: King Mohammed and President Bourguiba of Tunisia plead for an end to the Algerian conflict (→ 12/2/58).

26. Washington: Eisenhower suffers a mild stroke (→ 1/3/58).

30. Jakarta: President Sukarno narrowly escapes an assassin's grenade (→ 1/12).

DEATHS

13. Czech statesman Antonin Zapotocky, President 1953-57 (*19/12/1884).

25. Mexican painter Diego Rivera (*19/12/1884).→

30. Italian tenor Beniamino Gigli (*20/3/1890).

Russian dog has her day in space

Little Laika, Russian dog in space.

Nov 3. A dog called Laika is now orbiting the earth in a Russian satellite. With a weight of 1,100 pounds the satellite is nearly six times as heavy as the original Russian satellite, Sputnik 1, launched last month and still in orbit.

Besides the equipment for supplying Laika with food, drink and air, and monitoring her condition, the new Sputnik contains apparatus for measuring cosmic rays and other conditions in space, 1,000 miles above the earth.

Laika's flight will provide information about how animals respond to prolonged weightlessness, so it could be a precursor to future manned spaceflights (→ 4/1/58).

Diego Rivera, left-wing Mexican painter of revolution Utopian Murals, has died in his native country at the age of 72.

1957

DECEMBER

Su	Mo	Tu	We	Th	Fr	Sa
1	2	3	4	5	6	7
8	9	10	11	12	13	14
15	16	17	18	19	20	21
22	23	24	25	26	27	28
29	30	31				

1. Jakarta: Sukarno calls a 24-hour boycott of Dutch business in protest at Dutch rule in West New Guinea (→ 2).

2. Amsterdam: Holland bars entry to Indonesians (→ 5).

4. London: The government rejects the recommendations of the Wolfenden Report.

5. Indonesia: All Dutch nationals are expelled.

6. US: The first US attempt to launch a satellite fails when the Vanguard Rocket explodes on take off (→ 20/2/58).

10. Stockholm: Nobel Prizes go to Chen Ning-yang and Tsung-dao Lee (US, Physics); Lord Alexander Todd (UK, Chemistry); Daniel Bovet (Italy, Medicine); Albert Camus (France, Literature); and in Oslo to Lester Pearson (Canada, Peace).

13. Iran: 2,000 are reported dead after an earthquake.

16. Paris: The first NATO heads of government meeting opens (→ 19).

19. UK: The Windscale inquiry concludes that the accident was caused by insufficient staffing.

19. Paris: The NATO conference ends with agreement to accept US nuclear missiles bases in Europe (→ 24/2/58).

20. US: Elvis Presley is called up to join the army (→ 24/3/58).

25. London: The Queen makes her first Christmas broadcast on television.

26. Cairo: Anti-Western demonstrations mark the opening of the Afro-Asian Solidarity Conference (→ 1/2/58).

DEATH

17. British author Dorothy Sayers (*13/6/1893).

HITS OF 1957

All shook up.

Love letters in the sand.

QUOTE OF THE YEAR

"Don't knock the rock."

Bill Haley, rock and roll star.

Fog causes rail tragedy

92 died and nearly 200 were injured in the Lewisham train disaster.

Dec 4. Ninety-two rail passengers are feared to have died and more than 100 seriously injured tonight when two trains crashed in thick fog in the evening rush hour at Lewisham in South London. It happened under a bridge which then collapsed on to the wrecked coaches. Ambulancemen, stationed only 200 yards away, were joined later by Royal Engineers in digging for survivors.

The collision had caused the tender and leading carriage of an express to Ramsgate to strike a bridge support, bringing down the 350-ton bridge. A third train was about to cross the bridge, but its driver had slowed down because of the fog and was just able to halt. All three trains had been packed.

Most of the injured were pinned down in the tangle of concrete and twisted metal. Then a fast steam train from Cannon Street to Ramsgate ran into the back of a ten-coach electric train going from Charing Cross to Hayes, Kent, standing at Lewisham station. British Rail said one of the drivers may have missed three warning lights in the gloom.

British rock and rollers fight US invasion

Tommy Steele: a British Elvis.

Dec 31. Rock and roll is no longer an entirely American phenomenon. A British version of it has emerged along with native singers such as Tommy Steele, a 20-year-old whose group has a hit record "Rock with the Cavemen".

He has been described by the journalist Colin MacInnes as "a gold-haired Robin Goodfellow in sky-blue jeans who jumps, skips, doubles up and wriggles as he sings. At a violent mop-shake of his head, the teenagers utter a collective shriek of ecstasy."

Other native discoveries are "skiffle king" Lonnie Donnegan and Marty Wilde. The prime showcases are the new teenage television audience shows, "Six-Five Special" (BBC) and "Oh Boy!" (ITV).

Arts: cats dig it all except the straights

Disengagement seems to be the motto of current writing on both sides of the Atlantic. America has produced a "Beat Generation", or "Beatniks", whose object is to drop out of the rat-race, and who scorn the materialistic way of life of the Eisenhower years.

Their inspiration is a book out this year, "On the Road" by **Jack Kerouac**, which describes an odyssey across America by rootless young hobos, hitch-hiking or driving borrowed or stolen cars, listening to modern jazz, or "bop", and uncritically accepting every kind of person or experience they meet on the way, however uncomfortable. "We dig it all," is Kerouac's philosophy, and he writes admiringly of "the mad ones, who are mad to live, mad to talk, mad to be saved, desirous of everything, the ones who never yawn but burn, burn, burn like fabulous yellow roman candles, exploding like spiders across the stars."

"Disengagement" was the title of a Beat Manifesto by **Kenneth Rexroth**, and Beat's best-known poem is "Howl!" by **Allen Ginsberg** – an incantation against materialism and the machine age. Another Beat, **William Burroughs**, wrote an account of his life called "Junkie". The Beats admire drugs and Zen philosophy equally.

They borrow the argot of modern jazz players, calling themselves "cats" who "dig" whatever is "hip" or "groovy". In an article on "hipsterism", **Norman Mailer** categorises the Beats as "white negroes". "If you don't dig, you lose your superiority over the square and so you are less likely to be cool."

In France, disengagement is cooler intellectually. Its leaders are men like this year's Nobel prizewinner, **Albert Camus**, who made his name with a novel called "The Outsider", whose hero calmly accepted "the benign indifference of the universe". From Paris this year comes "Endgame" by **Samuel Beckett**, a bleaker play than "Waiting for Godot", in which mankind is reduced to a tyrant and his slave. The old – his parents – spend the evening of their days in dustbins.

Laurence Olivier is the Prince, and Marilyn Monroe the showgirl.

Alec Guinness, in "The Bridge on the River Kwai", plays a prisoner of war living by iron discipline and the Geneva Convention.

1958

JANUARY

Su	Mo	Tu	We	Th	Fr	Sa
			1	2	3	4
5	6	7	8	9	10	11
12	13	14	15	16	17	18
19	20	21	22	23	24	25
26	27	28	29	30	31	

1. Albania: Albanian fighters shoot down a British freight plane that allegedly strayed into Albanian airspace.

3. Holland: The banks are nationalised.

3. West Indies: The British West Indies Federation is created (→22/4).

4. USSR: Sputnik I disintegrates as it enters the earth's atmosphere.

7. Washington: Texas Senator Lyndon Johnson calls for the US to overtake the USSR in space (→12).

8. US: The "Daily Worker", the last Communist newspaper in the US, closes down.

9. Moscow: Premier Bulganin calls for top-level East-West talks.

12. Washington: Eisenhower calls on the USSR to join in a ban on warfare in space (→31/5).

13. UK: Civil servant Irene Ferguson, now a man, gets the civil service's higher salary for men from today.

14. UK: Vickers signs a contract with BOAC to build a new airliner, the VC-10.

16. London: Studies show that the pre-war "suburban neurosis" is being diagnosed in the new housing estates.

20. London: The first radar speed checks are introduced.

23. Cape Town: The city's archbishop condemns "abhorrent apartheid legislation" (→17/4).

23. Mongolia: The USSR says a colossal earthquake here last month moved mountains and created new rivers and valleys.

24. Caracas: A civilian junta now rules Venezuela after the coup yesterday ousting dictator Marcos Perez Jimenez.

26. Israel: Moshe Dayan resigns as army chief of staff.

29. UK: A BMA report names cigarette smoking as the chief cause of lung cancer.

30. London: Ten die and 80 are injured in a rail crash at Dagenham.

Hillary beats Fuchs in new Polar trek

Sir Edmund Hillary (l.) and Dr Vivian Fuchs meet at the South Pole.

Jan 20. A British Polar expedition, led by Dr Vivian Fuchs, reached the South Pole by an overland route today – to be greeted by New Zealand rivals who had beaten them by 17 days. The Britons are attempting the first trans-Antarctic crossing, with the Pole their halfway mark.

Snow tractors, led by the Everest hero Sir Edmund Hillary, had roared into the American scientific base at the South Pole – after a "hell bent dash" from their final depot. Hillary's party were the first to reach the Pole overland since Captain Robert Falcon Scott 46 years ago. The New Zealand party had set out from Scott Base on McMurdo Sound. The British party travelled from Shackleton Base on the Vansee Sea.

Rivalry between the two expeditions was forgotten as Hillary drove out to meet the Britons, who are using "Weasel" tracked vehicles and snow-sleds for their 2,100-mile crossing. It has taken them eight weeks to reach the Pole – longer than estimated – because of soft snow, treacherous crevasses, bad weather and mechanical problems. Four of the nine vehicles in which they set out in November had to be abandoned (→2/3).

Ministers quit over money policy battle

Jan 7. "I thought," said Mr Macmillan loftily, "that the best thing to do was to settle up these little local difficulties and then turn to the wider vision of the Commonwealth."

Thus the Prime Minister today played down the sensational and simultaneous resignations of Peter Thorneycroft, the Chancellor of the Exchequer, and two other Treasury Ministers, Enoch Powell and Nigel Birch. He spoke at London Airport before leaving on a Commonwealth tour.

The Treasury trio quit in protest over the cabinet's refusal to peg next year's government spending at current levels (→20/3).

Yves St Laurent to wear Dior's mantle

Jan 30. A shy young ex-law student was today acclaimed the rightful heir to Dior. Rapturous scenes greeted the first Paris collection of 23-year-old Yves St Laurent. Crowds outside his salon became so dense that he had to make a "royal" appearance on the balcony.

The main feature of the collection, which St Laurent created at his mother's Algerian home, is the trapeze line.

100 Turks are hurt and 2 killed in anti-British riots in Cyprus

Jan 28. A British Army Land Rover drove at speed through a Turkish demonstration in Nicosia today – sparking off riots leaving seven dead and hundreds injured as the minority community erupted in fury. Despite a curfew thousands of Turks took to the streets, setting fire to garages and tobacco factories, overturning and burning police cars, and stoning security forces. The rioting ended only after an appeal by Rauf Denktash, a former solicitor-general and leader of the Turkish community.

Violence by the hitherto peaceful Turks marks a dangerous turn in the troubled island. The Governor, Sir Hugh Foot, is returning from a Baghdad Pact meeting in Ankara tonight (→8/6).

British soldiers are forced to use riot shields as Turkish Cypriots protest.

1958

FEBRUARY

Su	Mo	Tu	We	Th	Fr	Sa
						1
2	3	4	5	6	7	8
9	10	11	12	13	14	15
16	17	18	19	20	21	22
23	24	25	26	27	28	

1. Middle East: Egypt and Syria proclaim union as the United Arab Republic, or UAR, (→14).

5. London: Mayfair will be the first place in Britain to have parking meters when they are introduced (→26/3).

5. UK: Sir Adrian Boult and the BBC Symphony Orchestra perform the premiere of Michael Tippett's Second Symphony.

7. Munich: Matt Busby is reported to be fighting for his life in a Munich hospital (→21).

8. UK: David Lean's film "The Bridge on the River Kwai" wins three top British Film Academy awards (→27/3).

9. London: The Lord Chamberlain refuses a licence for Beckett's "Endgame" over an alleged blasphemy (→6/11).

12. Tunis: President Bourguiba demands the evacuation of all French troops (→13/5).

13. London: MPs give a second reading to the Life Peerages Bill (→23/7).

14. Amman: Jordan and Iraq sign an agreement for the union of the two kingdoms, backed by the US (→21).

20. US: An Atlas rocket explodes at Cape Canaveral, the fifth failed launch out of seven attempts (→9/3).

21. Munich: Manchester United and England star Duncan Edwards dies from his injuries (→3/5).

21. Cairo: Nasser becomes president of the UAR after a plebiscite (→8/3).

23. Havana: Cuban rebels seize Argentine racing champ Juan Fangio (→24).

24. London: The government says US missiles will be based in East Anglia, Yorkshire and Lincolnshire (→6/3).

24. Havana: Fangio is released after 28 hours in the hands of Cuban rebels (→12/3).

27. UK: 35 people are killed in a plane crash near Bolton.

28. US: 28 die when a school bus plunges off the road into a river in Tennessee.

Busby Babes killed in plane tragedy

The twisted wreckage on a Munich airport runway is a tragic memorial to Manchester United's footballers.

Feb 6. The whole city of Manchester is in mourning for the pride of English football, the Manchester United team, tragically destroyed today by a plane crash on a snow-covered Munich runway.

As the team began the last leg of their homeward trip from Belgrade, after qualifying for the European Cup semi-finals, their BEA Ambassador, after one abortive attempt, set off down the runway, tried to take off, hit a fence and an airport building, and broke in two.

Seven members of the superb squad, known as the "Busby Babes" after their manager Matt Busby, were killed, as well as eight journalists covering the match (including the former England goalkeeper Frank Swift), and three members of the club's staff.

Several other players and officials are very ill in a Munich hospital. They include the towering England left-half, Duncan Edwards; two other England internationals, Bill Foulkes and John Berry; and Matt Busby himself, who had done so much to weld this side into the most formidable in Europe.

Of the players who died, four were full internationals: the captain Roger Byrne (28), who had played left-back in every England match since his debut in 1954; Tommy Taylor (25), the centre-forward, with 18 England caps; the outside-left David Pegg (22), who won his first cap for England last May; and Bill Whelan (22), the inside-right, with four caps for the Irish Republic.

The others were the tiny (five feet seven inches) right-half Eddie Colman (21), the centre-half Mark Jones (24) and Geoff Bent (25).

Bulletins from the hospital have stressed concern over the condition of Matt Busby, as well as that of Edwards and Berry (→7).

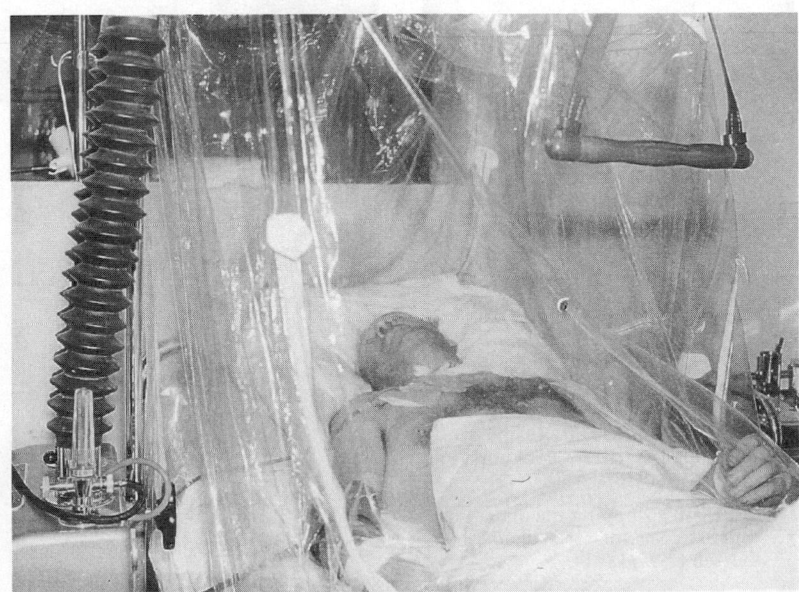

Matt Busby, Manchester United's manager, lies in an oxygen tent.

Duncan Edwards – dangerously ill.

▷

New group calls for Bomb to be banned

Feb 17. A new mass group calling for Britain to abandon nuclear weapons was formed at a meeting in Westminster's Central hall tonight.

The Campaign for Nuclear Disarmament was founded out of the old National Council for Abolition of Nuclear Weapon Tests, which started protest meetings attracting thousands last year calling for the Bomb to be banned.

Led by a committee including the Labour MP Michael Foot, the philosopher Bertrand Russell, the author J.B. Priestley and the journalist James Cameron, it has been given offices for free at 146 Fleet Street by the chairman of Horizon Holidays, Vladimir Raitz (→ 24).

US puts its first satellite into space

Feb 1. America finally followed Russia into space today, by putting a 30-pound satellite called Explorer into orbit. An earlier US attempt at launching a satellite failed last December, when the rocket blew up at launch.

The Jupiter C rocket used today is a modified military rocket, developed by a team which is led by Wernher von Braun, previously the chief scientist of Germany's wartime V-2 programme.

The grapefruit-sized Explorer, packed with miniaturised apparatus, is orbiting the earth at heights varying between 230 and 2,000 miles (→ 20).

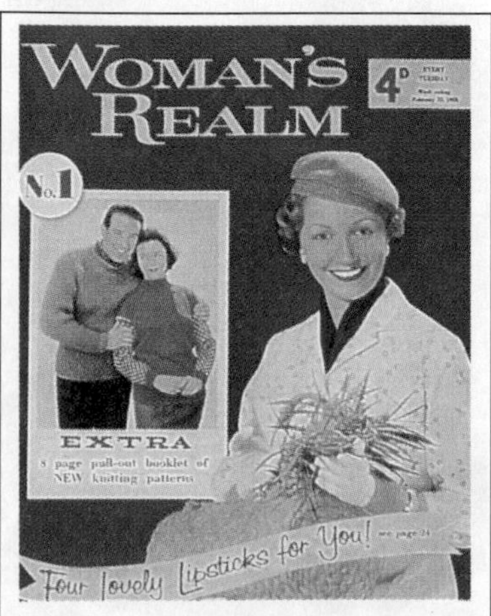

A new mass-market magazine.

1958

MARCH

Su	Mo	Tu	We	Th	Fr	Sa
						1
2	3	4	5	6	7	8
9	10	11	12	13	14	15
16	17	18	19	20	21	22
23	24	25	26	27	28	29
30	31					

1. Washington: Doctors report that Eisenhower is now fully recovered from his stroke.

1. Turkey: At least 220 people drown when a ferry sinks.

2. Athens: Constantine Karamanlis resigns as premier.

2. Antarctica: Dr Vivian Fuchs completes the first overland crossing of Antarctica.

6. UK: The TUC and Labour Party call for an end to H-bomb testing (→ 4/4).

8. Middle East: Yemen federates with the UAR (→ 2/5).

9. Washington: Secretary of State Dulles says the US is losing the space race (→ 2/4).

12. Havana: Batista suspends the constitution to fight Castro's rebels (→ 9/4).

14. Teheran: The Shah is to divorce Princess Soraya.

16. London: The Bishop of Woolwich says mothers who work full-time are the enemies of family life.

20. London: The bank rate is cut from seven to six per cent (→ 15/4).

25. Chicago: Sugar Ray Robinson becomes world middleweight champion for the fifth time.

26. London: Britain's first parking tickets are now being issued to motorists (→ 16/6).

27. US: "The Bridge on the River Kwai" wins three Oscars, with Alec Guinness named as best actor.

28. UK: Mark Bonham-Carter wins Torrington for the Liberals, their first by-election victory for 29 years.

29. UK: Mr D.J. Coughlan's Mr What wins the Grand National.

31. Birmingham: Work begins this week on a new £1.5 million shopping centre.

DEATHS

14. British suffragette Dame Christabel Harriette Pankhurst (*22/9/1880).

29. British shipping magnate and art collector Sir William Burrell (*9/7/1861).

Bulganin goes: Khrushchev supreme

March 27. With a simple administrative decision Nikita Khrushchev has toppled goateed Marshal Bulganin, his colleague and prime minister, and is now undisputed Soviet leader. By taking over Bulganin's job, the Soviet Communist Party secretary now occupies the two posts which Stalin held throughout World War Two.

Bulganin has been the straight man to the livelier and shrewder Khrushchev during the celebrated "B and K road shows" to several world capitals, including London. His name has been added to the black list of the "anti-party group" which tried to bring down Khrushchev last June. He was apparently kept on for reasons of decorum and expediency.

Khrushchev leaves the Lenin loco.

Debs come out at Palace for the last time

March 18. Debutantes who curtsied to the Queen and Prince Philip today made history. Presentation at Court for the daughters of the aristocracy and those prominent in the community is being discontinued.

It is felt at Buckingham Palace that this traditional practice is now archaic and not in keeping with the new Elizabethan age. Prince Philip is being credited with the change, but Buckingham Palace will not confirm or deny that his influence was decisive.

A girl needed a sponsor to be presented at the court; someone who also accompanied her on the day. They had to be women who had been presented themselves. Lately some of those ladies, now fallen on hard times, would seek out a rich and socially ambitous father and negotiate "a fee and expenses arrangement" to present his daughter.

Given such practices, and the drain the presentations make on the Queen's valuable time, it was inevitable that the party would soon be over.

A selection of the last debutantes to be presented at Buckingham Palace.

The King exchanges his guitar for a gun

March 24. Rock and roll's loss was the US Army's gain this morning, as Elvis Presley reported to a Memphis Draft Board for a two-year stint in the armed services.

The 23-year-old singer and actor, who has sold over 40 million records in the last two years, stands to see his existing $100,000 a month earnings drop to just $83.20 in the Army, but he remarked: "I think it will be a great experience for me."

As Presley joined up in Tennessee, accompanied by his parents and manager, Colonel Tom Parker, plus a sizeable press posse, many teenage fans were left distraught at the prospect of losing their idol until 1960.

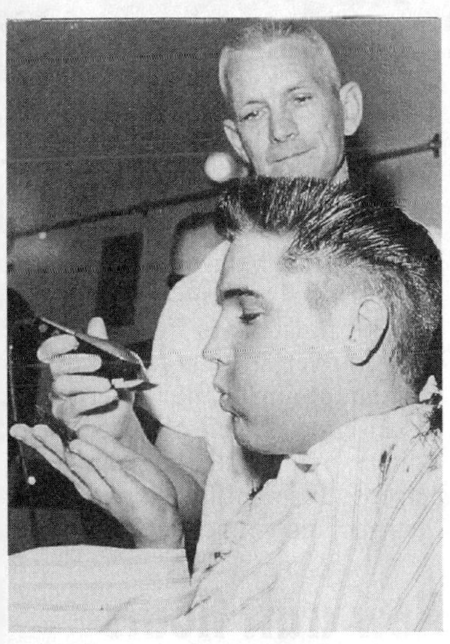

Short back and sides for the King.

Sobers' 365 not out is new Test record

March 2. The first visit to the West Indies by Pakistan's cricket team has produced record-breaking batting displays from both sides, and twice Len Hutton's Test match feats have been eclipsed.

First, in Barbados, Hanif Mohammad completed the longest innings in Test history, batting for 16 hours 13 minutes for his 337. Now, in Kingston, Jamaica, 21-year-old Garfield Sobers has broken Hutton's record Test score, hammering the Pakistan attack for a masterly 365 not out in little more than ten hours.

1958

APRIL

Su	Mo	Tu	We	Th	Fr	Sa
		1	2	3	4	5
6	7	8	9	10	11	12
13	14	15	16	17	18	19
20	21	22	23	24	25	26
27	28	29	30			

2. Washington: Eisenhower calls for a civilian-controlled US space agency (→29/7).

2. UK: Premiere of Vaughan Williams' Ninth Symphony.

4. London: 3,000 anti-nuclear protesters set out on a march to Aldermaston.→

6. US: Arnold Palmer wins the US Masters golf tournament.

7. UK: The Church of England gives its moral backing to family planning.

9. Havana: 40 are reported killed in street riots (→17/9).

10. UK: A Roman mosaic pavement has been unearthed at the site of a Roman villa in Sussex.

15. London: Chancellor Derick Heathcoat Amory's first budget cuts purchase tax, wine and cinema duties (→19/6).

17. S. Africa: The Nationalist Party wins its third successive general election (→2/9).

17. Brussels: King Baudouin opens the World's Fair.

18. Washington: Treason charges against poet Ezra Pound, who broadcast from Italy during the war, are dropped.

21. US: 49 die when two planes collide over Nevada.

21. Malta: Premier Dom Mintoff resigns in protest at Britain's aid limit to the island of £5 million (→24).

22. Trinidad: Princess Margaret opens the parliament of the new British West Indies Federation.

24. Malta: Britain's governor, Sir Robert Laycock, assumes full governmental power (→30).

27. UK: The Comet IV makes its maiden flight.

29. Cairo: Egypt agrees to pay £29 million compensation to the shareholders of the Suez Canal Company.

30. Malta: Laycock declares a state of emergency.

DEATH

18. French commander, General Maurice Gamelin (*20/9/1872).

CND marchers rally at nuclear weapons HQ

Journey's end for the anti-bomb marchers from London to Aldermaston.

April 7. To the sounds of a skiffle group playing "When the Saints Go Marching In", the 3,000 Easter anti-Hydrogen bomb marchers reached their goal today. The organisers say that 12,000 supporters of the new Campaign for Nuclear Disarmament attended the final rally at the gates of the Atomic Weapons Research Establishment at Aldermaston.

600-odd "hard core" marchers, who had walked the entire 50 miles from London, led the protesters along the last stretch past the barbed wire of the Aldermaston base. The crowd was for the most part young people, with students, bearded men and brightly-stockinged women prominent. But there were also earnest pram-pushing parents.

The meeting heard speeches from Stuart Morris of the Peace Pledge Union, Pastor Niemoeller from Germany, Mr Harold Steele and the US pacifist Beyard Rustin. A resolution was passed urging Britain, Russia and the United States to stop the manufacture testing and storage of nuclear weapons.

Some of the marchers set about a loudspeaker car which intercepted the procession to tell them they were "playing Khrushchev's game". But this was the only incident to mar a peaceful protest (→22/9).

Critics agree My Fair Lady is luverly

Julie Andrews and Rex Harrison backstage at "My Fair Lady".

April 30. "My Fair Lady", the musical by Alan J. Lerner based on "Pygmalion", Shaw's story of a cockney flower-seller turned into a lady by a professor of phonetics, reached Drury Lane last night after two years on Broadway. For once a show lived up to its advance publicity: the critics raved.

Frederick Loewe's score of hit numbers – "Wouldn't it be luverly?" and "I could have danced all night" – were despatched by Julie Andrews as a fiery but touching Eliza Doolittle. Rex Harrison, as the insufferably superior Higgins, offers a mixture of speech and song. Cecil Beaton's decor, especially the magnificent Ascot scene, is a triumph of Edwardiana.

1958

MAY

Su	Mo	Tu	We	Th	Fr	Sa
				1	2	3
4	5	6	7	8	9	10
11	12	13	14	15	16	17
18	19	20	21	22	23	24
25	26	27	28	29	30	31

2. Aden: Governor Sir William Luce declares a state of emergency.

3. London: Three months after Munich, Manchester United are in the FA Cup Final; they lose 2-0 to Bolton Wanderers.

4. Washington: Eisenhower rejects a Polish proposal for a nuclear-free zone in central Europe (→31).

7. London: The new high altar of St. Paul's is dedicated as the Empire War Memorial.

9. Pakistan: Premier Dr Khan Sahib is assassinated by a minor official.

12. UK: 160 square miles of Surrey countryside are to be established as an area of outstanding natural beauty.

14. Puerto Rico: Richard Nixon arrives, cutting short a South American tour because of his hostile reception.

19. UK: Premiere of the play "The Birthday Party" by Harold Pinter.

20. UK: BMC unveils its new sports car, the Austin Healey Sprite.

21. Paris: Premier Pierre Pflimlin sends General Henri Lorillot to negotiate with General Salan in Algiers.

27. UK: Jerry Lee Lewis cuts short his five-week tour after only two concerts; he leaves with his 13-year old wife.

28. Washington: The House of Representatives approves statehood for Alaska.

29. London: The CEGB says it has selected Dungeness in Kent as the site of its next nuclear power station (→29/9).

31. Moscow: The Kremlin agrees to early talks with the West aimed at ending nuclear test explosions (→23/7).

DEATHS

9. Pakistani statesman Khan Sahib, premier 1955-58 (*1882).

19. British actor Ronald Colman (*9/2/1891).

29. Spanish poet Juan Ramon Jimenez (*24/12/1881).

French Nationalists rebel in Algeria

May 13. While Pierre Pflimlin fought to get parliamentary approval of his Algerian policies in Paris yesterday, the French settlers in Algiers took matters into their own hands. Some 40,000 of them demonstrated against making any deal with the Algerian nationalists, seizing government buildings and setting up what they called a Committee of Public Safety.

This committee, half military, half civilian, has taken over the headquarters of the Ministry of Algeria which controls the administration of the country. Crowds of troops, police, firemen, students and settlers are surrounding the ministry, but there is complete disorder and nobody knows what is happening.

General Salan, C-in-C of the army in Algeria, declared in an emotional broadcast: "I have provisionally taken into my hands the destinies of French Algeria. I ask you to put your trust in the army and show your trust and determination."

In another broadcast from Algiers Radio, which is reported to have been taken over by paratroopers, a member of the Committee of Public Safety said: "We are waiting for news from Paris. We have reason to believe we have won the battle. Algeria will remain French forever. "Tonight, in yet another speech, the popular General Massu, commander of the Algiers military district, told the wildly cheering crowd of demonstrators "The Army is with you".

He read a telegram that he had sent to President Coty: "We await with vigilance the creation in Paris of a Government of Public Safety, alone capable of keeping Algeria as an integral part of Metropolitan France." Later General Massu declared: "We appeal to General de Gaulle to take the leadership of this Government of Public Safety."

Meanwhile, in Paris, the authorities were taking the strongest measures to prevent the Algerian turmoil spreading to France. Police arrested over 80 right-wing extremists, and tonight the government has in effect sealed off Algeria by banning all flights of "unofficial persons" between the territory and Metropolitan France (→21).

Hundreds of demonstrating "pieds-noirs" storm the Prefecture in Oran.

Algerian crisis prompts recall of de Gaulle

May 29. General de Gaulle has agreed to accept the post of Premier of France, but only on his own strict conditions, which will give him full powers for a "determined period" and a mandate to rewrite the Constitution.

There is little doubt that the National Assembly will grant him these powers for, with France on the verge of civil war over Algeria, the powerful figure of the wartime leader is generally considered the only man capable of stopping the country tearing herself apart.

Thousands of people swarmed in front of the National Assembly early this morning shouting "de Gaulle to power", while cars drove aimlessly round and round Paris sounding their horns in time with the shouting (→1/6).

De Gaulle: war hero and premier.

New craft floats on cushion of air

May 23. A new kind of vehicle which rides just above the ground on a cushion of air has been invented by Christopher Cockerell, a Suffolk boatbuilder. It has been named the Hovercraft.

The cushion of air is generated under the flat-bottomed vehicle with a fan of comparatively modest power. Inward-facing jets of air round the edge help to maintain the pressure of the cushion.

Besides being almost frictionless, air-cushion suspension would work just as well over water as over land, so Hovercraft would be amphibious. The government-backed National Research and Development Corporation is taking an interest in the invention (→16/4/59).

1958

JUNE

Su	Mo	Tu	We	Th	Fr	Sa
1	2	3	4	5	6	7
8	9	10	11	12	13	14
15	16	17	18	19	20	21
22	23	24	25	26	27	28
29	30					

1. Paris: De Gaulle takes over as premier.→

1. UK: "British Houdini" Alfred Hinds makes his third jailbreak, climbing a 20-foot wall in Chelmsford Prison.

4. UK: Sir V. Sassoon's Hard Ridden wins the Derby; it is jockey Charles Smirke's fourth Derby, equalling the record.

8. Cyprus: Four die and 70 are hurt in riots.→

9. UK: The Queen opens the new £7 million facilities at Gatwick Airport.

12. London: Britain says it will send paratroopers to Jordan to back up King Hussein's security forces (→20/7).

14. UK: Brilliant 17-year-old Christine Truman secures Britain the Wightman Tennis Cup for the first time in 28 years.

16. Belgium: Cheshire dentist Tony Brooks wins the European Grand Prix.

16. London: Yellow "No Waiting" lines come into force (→10/7).

17. Washington: The US slams the execution of Imre Nagy as a "shocking act of cruelty" (→23).

18. UK: Premiere of Britten's opera "Noye's Fludde".

19. London: The bank rate is cut from six to five per cent (→3/7).

23. Budapest: Yugoslavia and Poland protest at the execution of Imre Nagy.

23. India: Tamil leaders in Madras call on Nehru to lobby for better treatment of Ceylon's Tamil minority (→30).

25. Beirut: Lebanon asks the US to halt the flow of UAR arms to Lebanese rebels.

30. Ceylon: Tamils call for an independent state.

DEATHS

9. British actor Friedrich Robert Donat (18/3/05).

16. Hungarian statesman Imre Nagy (*7/6/1896).→

18. British cricketer Douglas Robert Jardine (*23/10/00).

De Gaulle's Algerian visit sows confusion

Prime Minister de Gaulle visits Algeria after the referendum is over.

June 4. General de Gaulle today addressed a vast, cheering crowd of the French settlers whose determination to keep Algeria French brought him to power three days ago, but his message gave them little comfort and when he finished speaking the cheers were muted.

Addressing the crowd from the balcony of Government House in Algiers, he said: "I have understood you. I know what has happened here. I see what you have wanted to do. I see that the road that you have opened in Algeria is that of renovation and of brotherhood."

The settlers, or "pieds-noirs", took heart from this, thinking that it implied his approval of their actions and a belief in "Algerie Francaise", but they grew restive when he told them with brutal frankness that the Algerian nationalists were courageous fighters, and that he accepted integration and equal rights for Europeans and Moslems, men and women, alike.

He insisted: "There are only Frenchmen, Frenchmen with full citizenship and the same obligations." And he held out the prospect of an amnesty for rebels: "To these men, I, de Gaulle, open the door of reconciliation" (→28/9).

Brilliant Brazil take home World Cup

June 29. At last the brilliance and skill of the Brazilian footballers has been matched by an equal discipline and determination, as they overwhelmed their Swedish hosts 5-2 to win the World Cup final in Stockholm today.

Despite all four home countries qualifying for the finals for the first time, it was France who produced the biggest surprise (by taking the third-place spot over Germany) and the top scorer (Just Fontaine, with 13 goals).

But Brazil were at their dazzling best, particularly their unstoppable winger, Garrincha, and the 17-year-old goal-scoring prodigy, Pele; even after going 1-0 down in the final they never looked anything but winners.

The Swedes fight off Brazil's Pele.

Curfew in Cyprus as peace plan rejected

June 20. In Athens, Archbishop Makarios, the exiled leader of the Greek-Cypriot community, tonight rejected a British peace plan, and once again Cyprus is under an island-wide curfew, as intercommunal warfare between the Greeks and Turks becomes a serious possibility.

The British plan called for a seven-year period for Cyprus under British rule, while a system of representative government was worked out by the two communities. Britain would retain responsibility for internal security.

The Greek community in Cyprus outnumbers the Turkish by four to one (→13/7).

A Turk is rescued by the British.

Hungary's former premier is hanged

June 16. Imre Nagy, the former Hungarian Prime Minister, has been executed, following a secret trial, nearly two years after the Hungarian uprising. Several other leaders of "free" Hungary have also been killed.

These executions are sure to arouse much anger in the Communist bloc as well as the West, for Mr Nagy had taken refuge in the Yugoslav Embassy in Budapest, and was handed over to the Kadar regime only after his safety had been guaranteed (→17).

1958

JULY

Su	Mo	Tu	We	Th	Fr	Sa
		1	2	3	4	5
6	7	8	9	10	11	12
13	14	15	16	17	18	19
20	21	22	23	24	25	26
27	28	29	30	31		

3. London: The Chancellor Mr Heathcoate Amory, announces a relaxation of the three-year-old credit squeeze (→ 20/11).

5. Wimbledon: Ashley Cooper beats Neal Fraser for the Men's Singles title; Althea Gibson beats Angela Mortimer in the Women's Singles final.

6. France: Mike Hawthorn wins the French Grand Prix.

8. London: The government says Britain is to buy a complete nuclear submarine propulsion plant from the US.

13. Cyprus: 31 have died in a week of violence (→ 31).

14. Baghdad: King Feisal, the Crown Prince and Iraq's prime minister are murdered in a Nasserite army coup (→ 19).

16. UK: Premiere of Peter Shaffer's play "Five-Finger Exercise".

18. UK: Prince Philip opens the Empire Games at Cardiff.

19. Cairo: Nasser signs a defence pact between the UAR and the new Iraqi regime (→ 20).

20. Jordan: King Hussein severs relations with the UAR.→

21. London: The government announces a big expansion in polio vaccination.

23. London: 14 women are on the list of Britain's first life peers (→ 21/10).

23. Moscow: Khrushchev accepts a US proposal for a summit at the UN.

26. London: Prince Charles is created Prince of Wales by the Queen.

29. Washington: The National Aeronautical and Space Administration, NASA, is created.

31. Cyprus: Eight die in a day of violence on the island (→ 4/8).

BIRTH

30. British athlete Daley Thompson.

DEATH

18. French aviator Henri Farman (*26/5/1874).

Superpowers jostle in Middle East

July 31. The Middle East flared into sudden and dangerous crisis this month in a chain of events which saw the monarchy in Iraq bloodily overthrown, British paratroops landing in Jordan, American Marines wading ashore at Beirut, and Russia impotently rattling her sabre in the United Nations.

The crisis started with a coup by a group of young Iraqi army officers, inspired by Colonel Nasser of Egypt, which destroyed the pro-Western regime of King Feisal of Iraq. The 23-year-old King was murdered, along with his powerful uncle, Crown Prince Abdulillah, and General Nuri el-Said, the Prime Minister, who was kicked to death by the Baghdad mob.

The coup immediately put pressure on Jordan, Iraq's partner in the Arab Union, and on Lebanon, where President Chamoun is fighting rebels funded and armed by Nasser. Frightened by the events in Iraq, President Chamoun demanded western aid "very quickly".

That aid did indeed come quickly for the next day, July 15, 1,700 Marines of the US Sixth Fleet waded ashore at Beirut, where they were greeted by bikini-clad Lebanese girls who handed out ice-creams to the Marines, sweating under the weight of their war kit. "It was", said one onlooker, "the most unopposed landing in the history of amphibious warfare."

Two days later RAF Beverly and Hastings transport aircraft landed some 2,000 British paratroopers at Amman airport in answer to a request for help from King Hussein.

At the same time Jordan complained to the UN that Syrian troops of the Nasser-led United Arab Republic had been massing to attack Jordan. The arrival of the British, said the Jordanian delegate, had "nipped this plot in the bud".

These swift moves by the United States and Britain have left Nasser and the Soviet Union fuming. Russia demanded that the UN must order the withdrawal of the British and American forces, but Mr Cabot Lodge, the American representative, argued that "if the United Nations cannot deal with indirect aggression, the United Nations will break up".

As locals stare, newly-landed American marines patrol a Beirut street.

King Feisal and Crown Prince Abdulillah of Iraq on a visit to London.

In the House of Commons "serious doubts" about the Government's action were expressed by Mr Gaitskell, and Mr Bevan said British policy should be conducted so as not to collide with Russia, but to a roar of Tory cheers Mr Macmillan won the vote by 314 to 251.

The latest shake of the Middle East kaleidoscope shows King Hussein breaking off diplomatic relations with the United Arab Republic because of President Nasser's support for the revolutionary regime in Iraq.

Troops are on the move all over the area. British reinforcements have been flown into Bahrein from Kenya to act as a fire brigade force in the event of trouble in the Persian Gulf. Other units have been sent to Malta and Cyprus.

The US has concentrated 44 warships off the Lebanese coast; and the Soviet Union has announced large-scale manoeuvres close to the Persian and Turkish borders.

Mr Khrushchev has also sent a message to Colonel Nasser, saying that Soviet "volunteers" are waiting to fly to his assistance. Nevertheless, the tension seems to be easing (→ 2/8).

Tibetans revolt against Chinese forces

July 31. The Tibetan revolt against the Chinese occupation forces has intensified recently. The death toll is now reckoned to top 300 a day, and it is estimated that 50,000 Chinese and 15,000 Tibetans have died since the latest outbreak of violence – the worst since the invasion in 1950 – began.

Over 150,000 guerrilla fighters are said to be fighting in the mountainous areas in East Tibet. They have blown up the bridges and roads leading into Tibet, and isolated all their troop garrisons so that they have to be supplied by airdrop. Chinese morale is said to be very low in the face of Tibetan success; they have already been defeated along the Lhasa-Chamdo highway.

The revolt is guided from India by a group of prominent Tibetan exiles, who have warned that the situation is moving rapidly beyond solution by peaceful means. India has consistently refused to recognise their struggle, because to do so would mean entering into open conflict with China.

Meanwhile officials of the Lhasa government in eastern Tibet, who supported the Dalai Lama two years ago, are now actively collaborating with the Chinese.

Peter Thomson wins Open in a play-off

July 5. Peter Thomson, the great Australian golfer, has won the Open Championship at Lytham St. Anne's, his fourth victory in five years.

This title proved the hardest of all, after David Thomas, the 23-year-old Sudbury professional, tied with Thomson on 278 at the end of the fourth round on Friday, to beat Eric Brown of Scotland and Christy O'Connor of Ireland by one stroke.

Only after a 36-hole stroke-play decider on Saturday, an exhausting climax to what is always a tense and draining week, did Thomson's experience and technique confirm his reputation as the best golfer in the world. He won the play-off by four clear strokes, ending the most thrilling championship for years.

Thomson round in a record 63.

Papa Doc crushes army rebellion

July 31. An attempted coup by the exiled Haitian leaders Louis Dejoie and Paul Magloire, executed by two army captains, has been crushed by President Francois Duvalier. The 100-strong rebel force had occupied army barracks in Port-au-Prince, across the street from the Presidential palace. Duvalier was supported by his palace guard and a core of loyal army officers.

Following the unrest, Haiti's Congress has granted Duvalier's request that he be allowed to rule by decree for six months, making him a virtual dictator.

Trial run of parking meters in Mayfair

July 10. London entered the pay-for-parking era yesterday, when a section of Mayfair opened its meters for business. Customers were wary and many spaces were vacant all day. Police claimed the traffic was smoother, but displaced parkers were to be found looking for kerb space in nearby unmetered streets.

Motorists complained about the lack of refunds for unused time. Commercial travellers said they had to pay over the odds, because they could not be sure how long their visits would last.

1958

AUGUST

Su	Mo	Tu	We	Th	Fr	Sa
					1	2
3	4	5	6	7	8	9
10	11	12	13	14	15	16
17	18	19	20	21	22	23
24	25	26	27	28	29	30
31						

1. London: Britain recognises the new regime in Iraq (→2).

2. Amman: King Hussein dissolves the Iraq-Jordan union of February (→4).

3. West Germany: British racing driver Peter Collins dies in the German Grand Prix.

4. Cyprus: EOKA chief Colonel Grivas orders a ceasefire (→12).

4. UAR: Syria seals its border with Jordan (→15/10).

7. US: Arthur Miller's conviction for contempt of Congress is overthrown.

12. London: Macmillan returns home after a peace mission to Greece, Turkey and Cyprus (→20).

14. Ireland: 99 people are feared dead when a Dutch airliner goes missing off the Irish coast.

20. US: Arkansas governor Faubus refuses to enforce the US Supreme Court's order to end schools segregation (→3/9).

20. Cyprus: Nearly 2,000 Greek Cypriots are held after a new British drive on EOKA (→7/9).

24. Portugal: Stirling Moss wins the Portuguese Grand Prix (→19/10).

25. London: The Midland Bank will be the first bank to offer personal loans from the beginning of next month.

30. Nottingham: 36 people are charged after police clashed with 500 Teddy Boys.

31. London: 13 arrests are made in the second night of fighting between white and black youths in Notting Hill (→9/9).

BIRTH

29. US pop star Michael Jackson.

DEATHS

24. South African leader Johannes Gerhardus Strijdom, Prime Minister 1954-58 (*14/7/1893).

26. British composer Ralph Vaughan Williams (*12/10/1872).→

Britain and Iceland set for fishing war

Aug 28. Britain and Iceland seem set for a fisheries war over the Reykjavik Government's unilateral declaration of a 12-mile fishing limit, to come into force next week. Talks between the two nations held during a NATO meeting in Paris broke down, and today efforts by the British ambassador to reach a solution met with failure.

British trawlers have just arrived off the present four-mile limit and begun fishing. Others are expected to arrive soon, supported by Royal Navy frigates. At home, Grimsby trawlermen are demanding sanctions against Iceland unless the dispute is resolved quickly, while the Icelandic Fisheries Minister said today his country would not sit at a conference table if his country was threatened (→2/9).

Thoroughly English Williams has died

The late Ralph Vaughan Williams.

Aug 26. No composer could be more thoroughly English than was Ralph Vaughan Williams, a country vicar's son who became a passionate collector of English folksong which inspired much of his music. He died yesterday aged 85.

His earliest works were songs like "Linden Lea" and the song-cycle "On Wenlock Edge". His Fantasias on Greensleeves and on a theme by Tallis were popular favourites. His Ninth Symphony was finished only this year. ▷

US hails sub that sailed under the Pole

Aug 27. New York gave a traditional ticker-tape welcome today to the crew of the nuclear submarine Nautilus after its epic first undersea voyage across the North Pole beneath the ice-cap.

The voyage took place last summer, but was only disclosed by the White House this month.

The submarine began its historic trip from Pearl Harbor on July 23 and cruised north through the Bering Strait. It dived under the Polar ice-cap off Alaska and continued under the North Pole, only raising its periscope once to check its bearings.

Its trip across the polar region took four days in all, with the North Pole reached at 11:45am on August 3. The submarine ended its voyage in Iceland on August 7. All the crew of the Nautilus have received citations and its skipper, Commander W.R. Anderson, was given the Legion of Merit medal.

Military experts believe that, far from just setting a new maritime record, the Nautilus' polar voyage has enormous strategic significance, as it could open the Arctic for the launching of guided missiles from submarines. Some believe it could have commercial implications and blaze a path for future cargo-carrying submarines.

Herb Elliott breaks two world records

Aug 28. Herb Elliott, the invincible Australian miler, has broken his second world record within a month. First, three weeks ago in Dublin, he took two-and-a-half seconds off the world mile record, leaving the field 15 yards behind.

Today at Gothenburg, Sweden, Elliott, who has never been beaten over a mile or its metric equivalent, took on the Czech world record holder Stanislav Jungwirth over 1,500 metres, beat him, too, by 15 yards, and lowered his record by an impressive two seconds to three minutes 36.00 seconds.

Stereo is the latest sound around town

Aug 27. A new phrase has gained currency among record buffs. "High Fidelity" does not refer to marriage vows, but to the latest advance in technique, stereophonic recording, now being made on disc as well as tape. Stereo or "hi-fi" equipment dominates this year's Radio Show. You require two loudspeakers, as well as other equipment, strategically placed about the room, taking up far more space than the old radiogram, but, just as LPs superseded the old 78s, it is said that stereo will mean the end of mono recording.

Replacing England's traditional chintzy, "lived-in" home interiors, modern designers advocate clean-cut, angular "contemporary" lines.

1958

SEPTEMBER

Su	Mo	Tu	We	Th	Fr	Sa
	1	2	3	4	5	6
7	8	9	10	11	12	13
14	15	16	17	18	19	20
21	22	23	24	25	26	27
28	29	30				

1. Iceland: British trawlers defy the Icelandic 12-mile limit which comes into force today.

1. S. Africa: Dr Hendrik Verwoerd is chosen to succeed Strijdom as premier.→

3. US: Martin Luther King is arrested for "loitering" in Alabama; he alleges police brutality (→4).

3. London: Macmillan says "utmost strictness" will be used to ensure impartiality in handling race clashes.→

5. US: Martin Luther King is fined $14 for refusing to obey a police officer (→20).

7. Cyprus: Grivas calls off last month's EOKA truce (→26).

7. Italy: Tony Brooks wins the Italian Grand Prix at Monza.

12. US: Arkansas Governor Faubus closes all four high schools in Little Rock.

15. UK: Nine youths are jailed for four years each for attacking blacks.

19. UK: The RAF takes delivery of its first US-built Thor missiles.

20. New York: A woman stabs Martin Luther King in Harlem.

22. UK: Anti-nuclear demonstrators led by Donald Soper stage a protest outside Aldermaston (→7/12).

24. Beirut: 30 die in street clashes (→25/10).

26. Cyprus: British army chief General Kendrew escapes an assassination attempt by EOKA terrorists (→29).

26. Rangoon: General Ne Win ousts premier U Nu in a coup.

28. Guinea: The French colony rejects the new constitution.→

29. London: The CEGB says its sixth nuclear power station will be built at Sizewell in Suffolk.

29. London: It is reported that the government is about to implement its plan for Cyprus (→2/10).

Hard-line Verwoerd takes over as PM

A new South African strongman.

Sept 2. A Dutch-born sociology professor with a reputation as a hard-line race segregationalist has become Prime Minister of South Africa, in succession to Johannes Strijdom, who died a week ago.

Dr Hendrik Verwoerd was brought to South Africa as a child. He studied at Stellenbosch University, later occupying the Chair of Sociology there. He founded the National Party newspaper, Die Transvaaler, in 1937, when he was 26. He has been Minister for Native Affairs for the past eight years. The National Party Parliamentary caucus chose him to take over from Strijdom at a two-hour meeting in Cape Town today.

Surrey are champs for seventh year

Sept 1. Once again Surrey have won cricket's county championship, their seventh successive title, marking the longest period of domination by a single county since the competition began in 1864.

Captained since 1956 by Peter May, Surrey's formidable bowling attack of Alec Bedser, Peter Loader, Jim Laker and Tony Lock is no less effective than it was in 1951-56, when Stuart Surridge was in command. Bedser was man of the match, taking four vital wickets from Sussex in ten balls.

Race riots flare in Notting Hill Gate

Sept 9. Race riots flared in Britain last night. Petrol bombs and thousands of milk bottles were thrown at police in West London, after white youths taunted black immigrants with racist slogans. Rioting continued through much of the night, and this morning the streets of Notting Hill Gate are strewn with broken glass and other debris.

Several people were badly hurt, and 59 people were being charged with carrying offensive weapons and other offences. The magistrate, E.R. Guest, said: "I feel that the peace should be kept in this neighbourhood which in my 13 years has never been so disgraceful."

The trouble started when a gang of white youths began demonstrating outside a house occupied by black people in Blenheim Crescent. They were met by a hail of milk bottles and a petrol bomb, which exploded on the pavement.

Within minutes, black men had began a counter-attack with iron bars. Although police broke this incident up and dispersed both mobs, sporadic fighting continued, with police advising black people to stay at home.

A black man and his girl friend were chased down Lancaster Road by a white mob shouting "Let's get the blacks", and in Bayswater black men were ambushed as they left a club in Ledbury Road. Three petrol bombs were thrown.

Special Branch officers were investigating the possibility of extreme right-wing inspiration behind the rioting.

Meanwhile, outside London, a television cameraman in Nottingham is being accused of starting a riot when a reconstruction got out of hand, and five men were imprisoned after disturbances in the St. Ann's Well Road area where white and black communities clashed.

As four policemen carried one screaming woman defendant from the court, the magistrate, Arthur Towney, said: "Lawlessness is not going to be tolerated in this city." The black population had nothing to do with the case, he added. The television cameraman had contributed to the rioting, it was said, by attempting to reconstruct a previous fight between two parties of youths. After he had lit a magnesium flare, "the mock fight, presumably staged for the benefit of the cameraman, developed into something more serious," said the prosecuting counsel.

Press and television reporters were told to consider carefully to what extent they had contributed to the riots (→15).

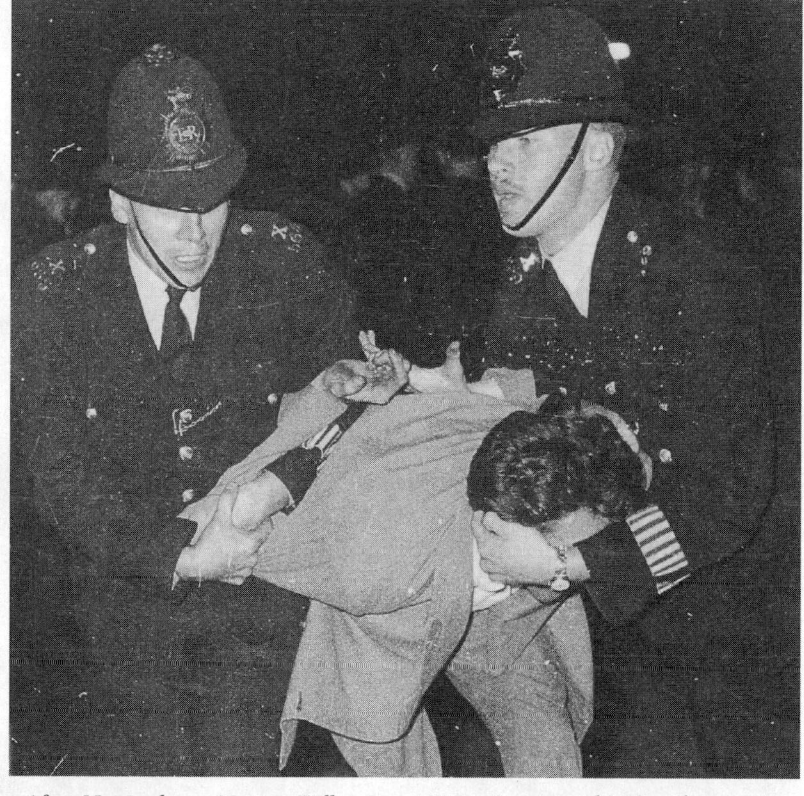

After Nottingham, Notting Hill – a race rioter is arrested in London.

Electors' vote gives extra powers to General de Gaulle

Sept 28. General de Gaulle today got a massive "oui" for his new constitution. A record number turned out for the referendum in France, Algeria and Francophone Africa, and initial returns show 80 per cent are in favour of the Fifth Republic. Even the most optimistic opinion polls had failed to predict that France and her Empire would give de Gaulle such a decisive vote of confidence. The Prime Minister now wields almost absolute powers.

The referendum was, in effect, three separate votes. Metropolitan France voted for presidential paternalism rather than parliamentary rule; Algeria wanted a negotiated settlement instead of all-out war; and France's black African territories – except Guinea – voted against complete independence, and for continued links with their colonial masters.

In Algeria, the rebel National Liberation Front failed to sabotage the ballot as it had threatened. Thanks to the army's vigilance, only a handful of Moslems were killed in sporadic incidents. The Vote Control Commission in Algiers reports that 83 per cent of those registered had voted, with 97 per cent in favour of the constitution. Some spectators have identified this as a demand for the full integration of Algeria into France, but de Gaulle stops short of this, saying only that Algerian Moslems who voted can now be considered Frenchmen with full rights (→2/10).

British trawlers defy Icelandic fishing ban

Sept 2. Two Icelandic gunboats seized a British trawler today, in the first battle of what appears to be a war over the cod within Iceland's newly-proclaimed 12-mile limit, but the gunboats had to abandon their prize, the Northern Foam, when a Royal Navy boarding party swung on board the trawler with grappling irons and reclaimed her – along with the Icelandic seamen trying to take her into port.

The Icelanders refused to accept their own men back, but their Foreign Minister, Mr Gudmundsson, still protested to the British Ambassador in Reykjavik over the Navy's action in "removing" his coastguard seamen from the Grimsby boat. That was followed by a demonstration by more than 1,000 people outside the British Embassy tonight.

The incident happened on the second day of the British challenge to the new fishing limit. A game of cat and mouse has developed, with gunboats trying to move in on any of the British trawlers that sail beyond Royal Navy protection.

Castro's promised offensive begins

Sept 17. Fidel Castro today launched his promised offensive against the Batista government. The rebels' radio station says that six columns have left Castro's mountain fort in Western Cuba.

Two of the columns were reported to be driving into Camaguey province in central Cuba. One of the groups was said to be led by Che Guevara, an Argentinian physician and chief aide to Castro; the other by Fidel's brother Raul (→9/11).

1958

OCTOBER

Su	Mo	Tu	We	Th	Fr	Sa
			1	2	3	4
5	6	7	8	9	10	11
12	13	14	15	16	17	18
19	20	21	22	23	24	25
26	27	28	29	30	31	

2. Guinea: Premier Sekou Toure declares an independent republic (→23/11).

4. Paris: The constitution of the Fifth Republic is officially declared (→28/11).

4. London: BOAC launches the first scheduled transatlantic jet service.→

6. Rome: Pope Pius XII suffers a stroke.→

10. Belgian Congo: Patrice Lumumba founds the Congolese National Movement (MNC).

10. Cyprus: 26 alleged EOKA terrorists are seized (→19/11).

14. London: Henry Cooper outpoints Zora Folley in a ten-round heavyweight bout.

15. Tunis: President Bourguiba breaks off relations with the UAR (→22/12).

16. Israel: Eight Israeli policemen are jailed for the slaughter of 48 Israeli Arabs.

20. Thailand: Military chief Sarit Thanarat seizes power in a bloodless coup.

21. London: The first women peers take their seats in the House of Lords.

22. London: Labour Minister Iain Macleod announces that compulsory arbitration in industrial disputes is to end.

23. Moscow: The USSR agrees to lend Nasser $100 million for the Aswan Dam project.

25. Beirut: The last US troops leave.

26. UK: The first paratroopers return from Jordan (→2/11).

29. Rome: Pope John XXIII makes a plea for world peace (→4/11).

31. Stockholm: Dr Ake Senning announces he has implanted the first internal heart pacemaker.

DEATHS

2. British birth control pioneer Marie Charlotte Carmichael Stopes (*15/10/1880).

9. Pope Pius XII, born Eugenio Pacelli (*2/3/1876).→

11. French painter Maurice de Vlaminck (*4/4/1876).

Progressive is Pope on twelfth ballot

Following his coronation as Pope John XXIII, the pontiff delivers the traditional blessing "Urbi et orbi".

Oct 28. After a major battle between progressive and conservative factions, Cardinal Angelo Giuseppe Roncalli, aged 76, was elected Pope on the twelfth ballot, and chose the title John XXIII. The news was heralded at 5.08 this evening, when the smoke from the Sistine Chapel chimney turned streaky yellow.

On Sunday night there had been a false alarm when, after the fourth ballot, the smoke looked snow-white under the glare of a dozen searchlights. News agencies flashed the news of a new Pope around the world. After Vatican officials had made contact with the traditionally sealed-off conclave by undisclosed means, a denial was put out on Italian radio.

Because of the sudden death of Cardinal Mooney of Detroit, an hour before the conclave, only 51 Cardinals voted. One of those, the exiled Archbishop of Peking, had to be carried in on a stretcher. For the first time in the history of the church, the Italians are outnumbered two to one in the conclave.

The new Pope owes his election to the support of the six French Cardinals. He was the first Papal Nuncio to visit liberated France, and stayed there until 1953. He was popular with the left for supporting worker-priests, banned by the Vatican, but he also became a firm friend of General de Gaulle.

For the past five years he has been Patriarch of Venice, where he continued to anger the ultra-conservative Papal Court. One group of leftish Christian Democrats, known to be his friends, had their newspaper banned by the Vatican earlier this year.

Cardinal Roncalli comes from a small village near Milan. His brothers still farm a small plot of land there, and he always joins them for his holidays (→29).

Some of Britain's Italian children kneel before a picture of Pius XII.

EOKA renews its violent campaign

Oct 2. EOKA terrorists stepped up their violent campaign in Cyprus today, two days after the Government said it was determined to implement its plan for the island, and killed a British civilian and wounded four policemen.

The civilian was shot in the back as he stood outside a chemists' shop in Larnaca. An immediate curfew was imposed.

Masked men shot dead a Greek Cypriot suspected of being an informer, leaving his body outside a cafe. Terrorists made four bombing attacks on army lorries wounding two soldiers.

When a bomb was lobbed at an army lorry near Famagusta, the sounding of the curfew siren was marked by hundreds of cars sounding the Enosis signal on their horns as security forces stood by with their latest weapons – tear gas and dye sprays.

Turkish youths rioted in Nicosia after reports of inter-village fighting in which six Turkish women and a Greek woman were injured.

The British plan allows for seven years of conciliation and political re-thinking by the two communities. Both Greeks and Turks have rejected the proposal, the Turks claiming it would create an "easy road to Enosis" – the union of Cyprus with Greece (→ 10).

Hawthorn first UK motor racing champ

Mike Hawthorn in the aftermath of his victory in the world championship.

Oct 19. Mike Hawthorn took second place to his fellow-countryman Stirling Moss in the Moroccan Grand Prix today, but became, by a single point, the first British motor-racing driver to hold the title of world champion.

Since the retirement of Juan Fangio earlier this year, it has been clear that a Briton was most likely to inherit his crown. Although the four Grand Prix victories by Moss, the 28-year-old from Tring, clearly suggest that he is the most accomplished driver, the championship's points system dictated that Hawthorn, the tall, blond extrovert from Farnham, Surrey, just a year older than Moss, needed only to finish better than fourth to become champion.

Moss, with the attack that has characterised his driving throughout the season, went flat out in his British-built Vanwall from the start, and led to the chequered flag. Hawthorn, presumably under orders from the Ferrari team, made no attempt to tangle with Moss, content to finish second in the knowledge that his one victory of the season, together with four other second places, were enough to give him the title.

Remarkably, the world's top five drivers are all Britons: Tony Brooks, Roy Salvadori and Peter Collins filled the next three places.

Pasternak may be exiled for Zhivago

Oct 31. "Dr Zhivago", the novel which has won the Nobel Prize for the Russian author, Boris Pasternak, has also brought him close to expulsion from his homeland. He has already been expelled as a "traitor" by the Soviet Writers' Union, which is petitioning that he be stripped of Soviet citizenship.

Pasternak, who declined the prize, has written an anguished letter to Mr Khrushchev pleading not to be sent abroad. In it he says: "I am tied to Russia by birth, by life and by work. Leaving my motherland would equal death for me."

"Dr Zhivago", basically a love story of the time of the Revolution, reflects its hero's disillusionment with what followed. After it was refused publication by the authorities, Pasternak sent the manuscript to Italy, where it came out in translation to world acclaim.

Boris Pasternak, banned laureate.

Bubble-cars add the sparkle to this year's British Motor Show

Oct 22. The vogue for unconventional runabouts continues at the latest Motor Show, with new models of bubble-car from Germany's Isetta and Messerschmitt. In Messerschmitt's TG500, now a fourwheeler, the driver sits alone in front, with one or two passengers behind. It does 52mpg, and is so stable it cannot be overturned (£654, including tax).

The familiar Isetta comes in several models, from a 300cc built in Brighton (£350) to a four-seat 600cc made in Germany (£676).

A Dutch debutante is the Daf, which offers gearing of near-continuous variability. By contrast the transatlantic look is long and low, spectacularly demonstrated by GM's Buick.

The Trojan three-wheeler estate van: under £300 and no purchase tax.

Jets begin regular Atlantic services

Oct 26. The Boeing 707 began flights across the Atlantic today, just 22 days after the British Comet jet began its transatlantic service for BOAC. The Pan American 707s are flying from New York to Paris, and will begin flights to Rome in two days' time. The British Overseas Airways Corporation jets fly from London to New York, but both airlines have gained from the easing of American noise rules.

1958

NOVEMBER

Su	Mo	Tu	We	Th	Fr	Sa
						1
2	3	4	5	6	7	8
9	10	11	12	13	14	15
16	17	18	19	20	21	22
23	24	25	26	27	28	29
30						

2. Jordan: The last British troops leave.

4. Rome: Pope John XXIII is crowned.

5. Washington: The Democrats win their biggest majorities in Congress since the 1930s.

6. London: The Lord Chamberlain ends the ban on plays about homosexuals.

6. Paris: De Gaulle invests Churchill with the Cross of Lorraine and the Order of Liberation.

9. Cuba: Castro frees 25 people held aboard a hijacked airliner (→30/12).

10. UK: Donald Campbell achieves a new water speed record of 248.62 mph.

13. London: George Brown loses his shadow cabinet seat.

19. Cyprus: British troops kill key EOKA figure Kyriakos Matsis.

20. London: The bank rate is cut from five to four per cent.

23. West Africa: Ghana and Guinea sign an agreement aimed at forming a Union of West African states (→28).

26. London: Vice-president Nixon attends the dedication of the American Memorial Chapel in St. Paul's Cathedral.

28. London: A government reshuffle gives junior posts to John Profumo, Julian Amery and Hugh Fraser.

28. Africa: Chad, Congo, Gabon, Mali, Mauritania and Senegal all became republics in the French Union this week (→31/12).

30. Paris: De Gaulle's Union for the New Republic (UNR) wins 198 out of 465 seats in the National Assembly (→21/12).

DEATHS

15. US actor Tyrone Power (*5/5/14).

24. British lawyer and statesman Edgar Algernon Robert Gascoyne-Cecil, Viscount Cecil of Chelwood, 1937 Nobel Peace Prize winner (*14/9/1864).

British housewives dangerously sedate

Nov 12. In his annual report on the state of the public health Sir John Charles, the chief medical officer of the Ministry of Health, warns against the increasing consumption of sedatives, stimulants and tranquillisers which, though of benefit in mental hospitals, could be harmful outside because of addictive qualities, as well as various side-effects. They may be used to avoid the anxieties of living, but "one test of a mature personality is the capacity to face reality and tackle difficult situations with courage and determination," said Sir John.

New forms of tranquilliser are being devised and he added: "The pity is that the energetic sales promotion devoted to the marketing of these agents is not always matched by adequate clinical trials".

Plan unveiled for cheap home loans

Nov 5. A £2,500 pre-1919 house for only £125 down, and up to 20 years to repay a six per cent mortgage: this is one example of how the Government's new homebuying plan announced today will work. Building societies will offer 95 per cent mortgages and local councils 100 per cent ones.

Legislation allowing the government to advance necessary funds to the societies will be introduced soon. This should help in making it easier for people to get mortgages on post-1919 property.

ALL-ROUND WARMTH
You'll bless the day Gas came to stay!

1958

DECEMBER

Su	Mo	Tu	We	Th	Fr	Sa
	1	2	3	4	5	6
7	8	9	10	11	12	13
14	15	16	17	18	19	20
21	22	23	24	25	26	27
28	29	30	31			

1. Chicago: 90 die in a school fire.

3. London: The government announces the closure of 36 pits and cuts in open-cast mining.

6. Japan: The world's largest oil tanker, capable of carrying 1,021,000 barrels, is launched at Kuri.

7. UK: RAF police and anti-nuclear protesters clash for the second day at the Thor rocket base at Swaffham (→21).

10. Stockholm: Nobel Prizes go to Pavel Cherenkov, Ilya Frank and Igor Tamm (USSR, Physics); Frederick Sanger (UK, Chemistry); George Beadle, Edward Tatum and Joshua Lederbreg (US, Medicine); Boris Pasternak (USSR, Literature); and in Oslo to Father Dominique Pire (Belgium, Peace).

13. New York: The UN rejects a motion calling for Algerian independence.

18. UK: John Betjeman wins the Duff Cooper Prize for his Collected Poems.→

21. UK: 21 anti-nuclear protesters are arrested at the Swaffham missile base.

22. Moscow: The USSR signs an agreement to give aid to the United Arab Republic.

23. Cairo: Nasser accuses Syrian Communists of opposing Arab nationalism.

30. New York: The sons of Cuban dictator Batista fly in amid reports his fall is near.

31. Africa: Ivory Coast, Niger, Central Africa, Upper Volta and Dahomey became French Union republics this month.

HITS OF 1958

Who's sorry now?

All I have to do is dream.

Magic Moments.

QUOTE OF THE YEAR

"How can you govern a country which produces 265 different kinds of cheese?"

General de Gaulle, appointed French premier 1958.

First motorway in Britain is opened

Dec 5. Britain's first stretch of motorway, the eight-mile Preston bypass in Lancashire, was opened today by the Prime Minister, Harold Macmillan. Afterwards he was driven four miles along it and declared it an historic occasion, "a token of what was to follow".

The road was a fine thing in itself, but it was also "the symbol of the opening of a new era of motor travel in the United Kingdom". The Government was determined to push ahead with an imaginative road programme, he said.

From now on, special traffic signs for use on motorways will be tested on the Preston bypass. They must be visible to high-speed drivers, and require letters as much as a foot high. The lettering will be white on a blue background.

Radiation belts circle the Earth

This year saw the first major scientific discovery of the space age, when American Explorer satellites revealed the presence of belts of radiation round the earth. Named after their discoverer, James Van Allen of the University of Iowa, the belts consist of charged particles from the sun, trapped in Earth's magnetic field.

An important new development in electronic miniaturisation was demonstrated this year: the integrated circuit, in which several components like transistors are built into a single tiny chip of silicon. In theory, there is no reason why thousands of components should not be combined in this way.

After an uncertain start, the Atoms for Peace conference held in Geneva achieved a major success with the superpowers agreeing to declassify much previously secret scientific information.

The year opened with the announcement of British experiments with a machine called Zeta which seemed to point the way towards harnessing the power of the H-bomb. The Americans are working on a similar project, but there is still a very long way to go before it becomes practicable.

De Gaulle is President

De Gaulle, the new president of France, greets M. Coty, his predecessor.

Dec 21. General Charles de Gaulle, France's Prime Minister, was today elected the first President of the Fifth Republic by an overwhelming majority of the electoral college. De Gaulle won 62,338 votes from the 80,508 "grand electors", easily defeating his Communist challenger M. Marrane's 10,354 votes. The Prime Minister will take over from President Coty on January 8.

Support for de Gaulle was especially strong in France's overseas possessions, where his Communist and Radical-Socialist opponents failed in many places to get a single vote. Among the elected local government representatives – the bulk of the electoral college – it is clear that Socialists, Radicals and Popular Republicans have all joined the Gaullist bandwagon.

The new President, who has been elected for seven years, is expected to name the Minister of Justice, Michel Debre, as his first Prime Minister. With ten days to go before the Common Market treaty comes into force, Debre is very keen that Britain should join the Market as a counter-balance to the growing power of West Germany.

General de Gaulle's Algerian policy is outlined in a letter published today. He warns against the use of "punitive or repressive measures", referring to allegations of torture made last year.

Arts: Davis may be hot but he blows cool

Jazz is evolving again in America. The summer jazz festival at Newport, Rhode Island, this year acclaimed the new sound made by **Miles Davis**, whose muted trumpet breathing melancholy messages in a pure, vibrato-less tone is the essence of "cool" modern style.

He and his quintet are the leading practitioners of the progressive jazz that grew out of "bop", as it was pioneered by the late **Charlie "Bird" Parker**, with whom Davis played when he was 18. Another small combo is the Modern Jazz Quartet (known as MJQ) led by the cerebral pianist **John Lewis**, whose inspiration is often Johann Sebastian Bach, and there is a new trio led by pianist **Oscar Peterson**.

John Coltrane, who plays tenor sax with Miles Davis and **Thelonius Monk**, saxophonist **Ornette Coleman**, drummer **Art Blakey** and his Jazz Messengers are all playing a new free-style jazz. The split between classicists like **Count Basie** and **Louis Armstrong** and the moderns looks permanent. The old master **Duke Ellington**, who made a triumphant UK tour this year, goes his own way. He has just recorded an ambitious new suite, "Black, Brown and Beige".

It is seldom that a poet catches on as fast as has **John Betjeman**, whose "Collected Poems" came out this year, won a literary prize and sold like a popular novel. His subjects are such things as old railways and churches, suburban gentility, and tough tennis-playing girls like Miss Joan Hunter Dunn of "A Subaltern's Love Song", but he manages to infuse his gentle mockery of a classridden England with a tragic consciousness of eternity.

Sweden has produced a film-maker of disquieting vision in **Ingmar Bergman**, whose "Wild Strawberries" and mediaeval-religious epic "The Seventh Seal" demonstrate his bleak but brilliant creation of images.

Jacques Tati is an artist-film-maker of a very different kind, from France. His character, M. Hulot, an eccentric observer of the follies of modern mechanical civilisation, has returned from his hilarious seaside holiday (1953) to the latest gadgetry of urban living in "Mon Oncle", which won a special prize at the Cannes Film Festival.

Betjeman, minstrel of Metroland.

Queen in Bristol talks to Edinburgh

Dec 5. The Queen made telecommunications history today, when she dialled the first trunk call on the new do-it-yourself system. The call was from Bristol to Edinburgh where the city's Lord Provost was waiting to speak to the Queen.

Accompanied by Prince Philip and the Postmaster-General, Mr Marples, the Queen then flipped the switch linking about 18,000 Bristol subscribers to the new service.

Eventually all parts of the country will be connected to the system, making it possible to call long distance without an operator.

Deadlock broken at nuclear test talks

Dec 8. After five weeks of deadlock the three-power talks in Geneva, aimed at creating a format under which nuclear tests can be banned, are finally making progress. Delegates from the US, the USSR and Great Britain have agreed on a draft test ban treaty, although experts admit there is still much work to be done.

The treaty sets up a control organisation which will administer the provisions of any future ban on nuclear weapons testing. Article 1 prohibits the tests; article 2 both establishes the control organisation and affirms that the three member nations will co-operate in ensuring that the provisions of the treaty are properly carried out.

According to Western observers, Russia, while agreeing with many US and UK views, also diverges from them in certain areas. A study of a list of detailed Russian demands shows, say these observers, that Russia does not really want a genuinely international control body. Instead, the Soviets are demanding a veto over any major decisions that such a body may reach.

Nevertheless, all the delegates are satisfied that after so lengthy a conference a real breakthrough has been achieved, and look forward to making the ban a reality.

Thalidomide drug causes birth defects

Dec 31. An epidemic of serious defects in newborn babies may have been caused by a drug called Thalidomide, widely prescribed for morning sickness in pregnancy. Most of the affected babies have one or more limbs seriously malformed or almost absent. About 7,000 babies have been born with the characteristic defects, the majority of them in Germany where the drug was developed. For some time doctors have been puzzled by the number of babies born with these malformations, which occur naturally very rarely.

1959

JANUARY

Su	Mo	Tu	We	Th	Fr	Sa
				1	2	3
4	5	6	7	8	9	10
11	12	13	14	15	16	17
18	19	20	21	22	23	24
25	26	27	28	29	30	31

1. UK: Alec Guinness is knighted in the New Year Honours.

7. London: Britain recognises Fidel Castro's regime (→10/2).

8. Paris: De Gaulle is inaugurated as first president of the Fifth Republic (→9/8).

8. Dublin: De Valera says he aims to quit as prime minister and run for president (→25/6).

9. London: Tube chiefs warn against staging strikes to protest at poor service, following sit-ins on the Northern Line (→21).

14. New Delhi: Nehru's daughter, Mrs Indira Gandhi, is standing for president of the Congress Party (→2/2).

16. London: Junior minister John Profumo joins the Foreign Office in a government reshuffle (→7/5).

16. Cairo: Britain unfreezes Egyptian assets in a finance agreement signed today with the United Arab Republic (→28/2).

20. UK: A doctor says obesity is now a bigger problem in Britain than malnutrition (→23).

21. Birmingham: 15,000 BMC workers are on strike (→29/4).

21. UK: The Preston bypass, Britain's first stretch of motorway, is closed due to frost damage (→29).

23. UK: A committee is to check possible links between leukaemia outbreaks and Windscale power station (→26).

26. London: The government announces a bill to improve care of the mentally ill (→5/3).

27. Moscow: Khrushchev claims the USSR has the lead in the space race, following the success of Lunik (→9/4).

29. UK: The worst winter fog since 1952 cripples transport throughout Britain (→3/2).

DEATHS

21. US film director Cecil Blount de Mille (*12/8/1881).→

22. British racing driver John Michael Hawthorn (*10/4/29).→

Castro's guerillas take power in Cuba

Jan 2. Rebel leader Fidel Castro today proclaimed a new government for Cuba with Santiago de Cuba, the town where he has his headquarters, as the provisional capital.

Dr Manuel Urrutia is to be President. He is due to fly in to Havana tomorrow, but it is already clear that all effective opposition has collapsed. The young leader, who was first ridiculed as a romantic young adventurer, has won his 25-month struggle against the dictator, General Fulgencio Batista.

Castro's army reached Camp Columbia, Batista's stronghold and army headquarters, this afternoon and met no opposition. Bands of his young followers, armed only with pistols, rifles and shotguns, have taken over all the main hotels in the last two days.

The beginning of the end came on New Year's Eve. While Havana was wining, dancing and gambling Batista called the leaders of the Senate and House to Camp Columbia. After toasting Cuba in champagne he told them he had decided to go. He blamed the rebels' guerrilla warfare and their "superior armament" for his defeat.

Cuba's new leader, revolutionary Fidel Castro, acknowledges the crowds.

News of his flight to the Dominican Republic spread slowly, and it was not confirmed on the radio until just before midday yesterday. People then poured out in their cars, sounding their hooters and brandishing the national flag in jubilation. Later in the day mobs sacked a Government newspaper office, set fire to a casino, looted stores and burned cars.

24.5m UK homes adjust their sets

Jan 22. Television's popularity in Britain continues to rise dramatically. In the last two years, according to a report issued today by the BBC, the number of people owning television sets has increased from 19 million to 24.5 million.

In effect, two-thirds of the adult British population of 37.8 million now own a TV, and they are also watching television for longer; around 12-and-a-half hours a week – an hour more than in 1957.

The report shows that people with a choice watch almost twice as many ITV programmes as they do BBC, even though there are still 7.5 million who can only receive the BBC.

The current viewing ratio is roughly 34 per cent for the BBC and 66 per cent for ITV, which is unchanged since last year. The report, was compiled from 300,000 interviews.

Movie mogul goes to meet his maker

Jan 21. Cecil B. de Mille, the man who made "colossal" the normal adjective to describe his pictures, has died at 77 in Hollywood, the hamlet which he discovered in 1913 when Sam Goldwyn sent him west to shoot "The Squaw Man", the first six-reel Western. He cabled back: "Want authority to rent barn in place called Hollywood for 75 dollars a month." He got it – but only for a month at a time.

De Mille won fame with his Biblical and Roman epics for Paramount. He proudly claimed that only one of his 70 films had been a box office failure. He used Barnum-style showmanship ("The Greatest Show on Earth") and relied on a formula of sensation, sex and religion. "The Ten Commandments" is still running. In the latest, "Samson and Delilah", Victor Mature pulls down the whole Paramount studio on top of him.

11 year-old Gail Bradley from Birmingham kept her hula-hoop spinning for a record 17 minutes at the Hammersmith Palais in London; not only that, but she turned round, knelt down, and tied up her shoelace while the hoop kept on going.

Racing driver Mike Hawthorn is dead

Mike Hawthorn, seen racing in 1952, who died in a crash this week.

Jan 22. Mike Hawthorn, the 29-year-old British racing driver, who had just retired after becoming world champion, has been killed, driving his own sports car, in a crash on the Guildford by-pass near his home in Surrey.

The ebullient, popular driver announced his arrival in 1952 by winning two races against some of the world's leading drivers at Goodwood. He was soon in the top class, and, driving for Jaguar, he won Le Mans in 1955, a year branded on the memory by the Mercedes crash that killed 85 spectators.

Most of his Grand Prix career he drove for Ferrari, for whom he clinched the world championship last October by a single point from his rival and compatriot Stirling Moss.

US and USSR race towards the moon

Jan 12. As a Soviet Lunik spacecraft flew past the moon into orbit round the sun today, the US Space Agency placed a contract for a capsule in which a man could orbit the earth. Although the Russians have made no comparable announcement, few space experts doubt that they, too, are planning to put a man into orbit.

In the meantime, the Russians continue to make the running in the superpower struggle for space supremacy. Their Lunik is the first spacecraft to escape from earth's gravity (→27).

Henry Cooper is new Empire champ

Jan 12. Despite the badly cut eye that has become almost a hallmark of Henry Cooper's boxing career, the 24-year-old from South London has won his first title. It comes after a frustrating year in which he lost three championship fights in a row. Tonight, after 15 punishing rounds at Earl's Court, he scored a well-deserved points victory over Blackpool's Brian London, to become British and Empire heavyweight champion.

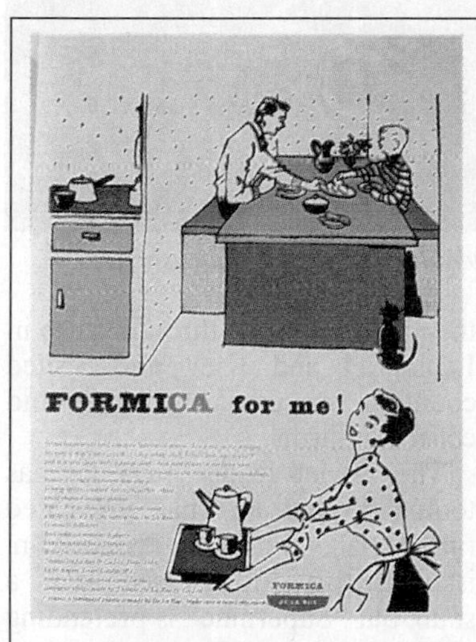

1959

FEBRUARY

Su	Mo	Tu	We	Th	Fr	Sa
1	2	3	4	5	6	7
8	9	10	11	12	13	14
15	16	17	18	19	20	21
22	23	24	25	26	27	28

2. Moscow: Khrushchev proposes a new East-West summit on Berlin (→9/4).

3. London: London Transport unveils details of a £50 million Victoria tube line from Victoria to Walthamstow (→17/3).

4. London: The Treasury drops all borrowing controls, ending the credit squeeze (→11).

4. UK: Tidworth garrison in Hampshire is raided by men who escape with a quantity of firearms (→31/3).

10. Havana: Castro, aged 30, becomes eligible for the Cuban presidency as the age qualification is cut to 30 (→16).

11. UK: Unemployment now stands at 620,728 (→1/4).

15. London: Archbishop Makarios arrives for talks on Cyprus with Macmillan (→17).

16. Havana: Castro takes the oath as Cuban premier (→22/3).

17. London: Twelve die when the plane bringing Turkish premier Mendares to the Cyprus talks crashes; Mendares survives.→

20. Nyasaland: British troops fly in as anti-British riots break out (→4/3).

21. Moscow: Macmillan arrives on official visit (→23).

23. Moscow: Macmillan and Khrushchev express willingness to expand Anglo-Soviet trade and cultural ties.→

26. Southern Rhodesia: A state of emergency is declared, dissolving African nationalist parties (→27).

28. Cairo: Britain and the United Arab Republic agree on the settlement of claims arising from the Suez crisis (→1/12).

BIRTH

16. US tennis player John Patrick McEnroe.

DEATHS

2. US singer Buddy Holly (*7/9/36).→

7. South African leader Dr Daniel Francois Malan, Prime Minister 1948-54 and institutor of apartheid (*22/5/1874).→

This was the day Buddy Holly died

Feb 3. Buddy Holly and two other rock singers died early today when a small plane carrying them crashed near Mason City, Iowa, in the United States. Holly, who was 22, toured Britain last year backed by the Crickets with whom he had recorded hits such as "That'll be the Day" and "Rave On".

At the time of his death he was performing solo, and was en route to a show tonight in North Dakota along with Richie Valens and J.P. "Big Bopper" Richardson. Both these singers had hits – Valens with "Donna" and the Big Bopper with "Chantilly Lace" – but it is Holly who will be most widely missed. He was the first pop star both to compose most of his own hits and to arrange them. His backing of guitars and drums – without brass – also pioneered a new sound.

Buddy Holly: a fall from grace.

Indira Gandhi new leader of Congress

Feb 2. Mrs Indira Gandhi, only daughter of Jawaharlal Nehru, India's Prime Minister, has been elected President of the ruling Congress Party. Her election comes as some surprise, for she is regarded as a shy person and will have to administer a party torn by internal quarrels. It is believed, however, that Mr Nehru, whose word is holy writ in the Congress Party, insisted on her appointment so that she could act as a peacemaker between the quarrelling factions (→25/8).

Rhodesia is under state of emergency

Feb 27. Claiming that Southern Rhodesia was faced with an imminent outbreak of violence instigated by African political agitators, Sir Edgar Whitehead, the colony's premier, today declared a state of emergency and ordered the detention of suspected trouble-makers. By tonight 435 people had been rounded-up – 88 per cent, according to police, of those whose names were on their lists.

But one of the key figures in the African nationalist movement, Joshua Nkomo, is out of the country, having left for Ghana to attend an All Africa Peoples Conference. It is thought unlikely that he will return (→21/7).

Dr Malan, architect of apartheid, dies

Feb 7. Dr Daniel Francois Malan, a lifelong campaigner for white supremacy in South Africa, and the Prime Minister who created a constitutional crisis by removing the mixed-race Coloured voters from the common electoral register, has died, aged 84.

He studied for the Dutch Reformed Church ministry and received his doctorate in Holland. He entered Parliament in 1919 as a National Party member but, dissatisfied with its lack of firmness on Afrikaaner principles, he founded a "purified" National Party to fight the 1943 election on a policy of pulling out of the war. He lost, but five years later his "white supremacy" message gave him victory (→18/6).

Australians win back the Ashes

Feb 5. Peter May's team, who began their Australian tour in such good form, have surrendered the Ashes which England have held for five years. Richie Benaud's leg-breaks, as well as his astute captaincy of an experienced team, assured Australia's victory in the fourth Test at Adelaide by ten wickets, and an unbeatable three-nil lead in the series.

Peace deal is hammered out for Cyprus

Feb 23. Full details of the agreement which ends the fighting in Cyprus, in which over 500 people have been kiled in the last four years, were published in a White Paper today. It was signed in Room 325 of the London Clinic where the Turkish Prime Minister, Mr Mendares, was taken after his Viscount aircraft crashed.

The agreement provides for a Republic to be established in Cyprus within a year. There will be a Greek-Cypriot President and a Turkish-Cypriot Vice-President. It ends 80 years of British rule – Cyprus became a British protectorate in 1878, and has been a Crown Colony since 1925.

Britain is to be allowed to retain her two military bases on the island, and will have substantial power to act if there is any threat to these bases, which are crucial to the defence of Britain's middle-eastern interests. Enosis, or union with Greece, which the EOKA resistance movement has been fighting for, is ruled out for ever. Young Cypriot supporters of EOKA protested at the terms when they got hold of the White Paper in Nicosia last night. They said Archbishop Makarios, still in London for the deal, would never agree to be President on such terms (→1/3).

Makarios stays at the Dorchester.

Supermac flies to Moscow for arms talks

Clad in suitably Soviet headgear, Mr Macmillan meets Mr Khrushchev.

Feb 28. Conspicuous in a tall white sheepskin hat, camera-conscious Mr Macmillan continued today on what he calls his "voyage of discovery" in the Soviet Union.

"Supermac" (as he is now nicknamed by the cartoonist Vicky) arrived in Russia nearly a week ago. He was Mr Khrushchev's guest at a dacha outside Moscow. Since then he has walked through slush in Leningrad and Kiev and visited countless museums, galleries and collective farms.

The Soviet leader says he has toothache and this has prevented further talks with the Prime Minister. British officials see it as a snub, but "Supermac" is pretending not to notice (→1/3).

1959

MARCH

Su	Mo	Tu	We	Th	Fr	Sa
1	2	3	4	5	6	7
8	9	10	11	12	13	14
15	16	17	18	19	20	21
22	23	24	25	26	27	28
29	30	31				

1. Moscow: Selwyn Lloyd and Andrei Gromyko have surprise talks (→3).

1. Cyprus: Makarios returns home to a rapturous welcome from Greek Cypriots (→9).

3. Washington: The Senate approves statehood for Hawaii.

3. Moscow: A communique at the end of Macmillan's visit says it allowed "a valuable exchange of views" (→21/4).

4. Nyasaland: Anti-British rioting continues as Hastings Banda and other nationalist leaders are arrested (→7/9).

5. UK: A BMA booklet on marriage is withdrawn because of a passage discussing whether chastity is outmoded (→27/5).

9. Cyprus: EOKA accepts the London agreement; Colonel Grivas retires (→17).

13. UK: A report on the Manchester United tragedy at Munich blames ice on the wings for the crash (→26/6).

17. Athens: Colonel Grivas is given a hero's welcome on his arrival from Cyprus (→14/12).

17. London: The government unveils plans for a road expansion scheme, estimated to cost £140 million annually (→3/4).

19. Washington: Macmillan arrives for talks on Berlin (→23).

21. UK: Mr J.E. Biggs's Oxo wins the Grand National.

22. Havana: Castro refuses to side with the US against the USSR (→15/4).

23. Washington: Macmillan's talks with Eisenhower end.

27. Madagascar: 3,300 are reported dead after the island was hit by a devastating hurricane (→26/6/60).

31. London: Burglars steal £10,000 from Sir Winston Churchill's home (→22/7).

DEATHS

3. US comedian Lou Costello (*6/3/1906).

26. US author Raymond Chandler (*23/7/1888).→

Dalai Lama flees from Chinese invaders

Disguised as a servant, the Dalai Lama makes a forced march to safety.

March 31. The Dalai Lama, spiritual leader of Tibet, has fled from Lhasa following China's brutal repression of the nationalists who are demanding independence from Chinese rule. Reports filtering out of Tibet say he has been smuggled out of the capital by Khamba warriors, and is making his way over the mountains by yak to sanctuary in India.

Chinese paratroops have been dropped south of the Brahmaputra river in an attempt to intercept him before he reaches the frontier. They have orders to capture him alive; in no circumstances must they kill him, for the Chinese know that if they harm him the whole of Tibet will rise against them.

Meanwhile the Panchen Lama, the second-ranking of Tibet's holy leaders, has gone over to the Chinese, and has sent the Peking government his congratulations on China's "tremendous" victory in suppressing the rebellion.

Fighting continues, however, at rebel forts covering the escape of the Dalai Lama (→19/4).

Chandler, bard of mean streets, dies

March 26. Unlikely as it sounds, Raymond Chandler, who has died aged 70, once contributed poems and essays to Bloomsbury magazines. Like P.G. Wodehouse, he was educated at Dulwich College.

He took up fiction in his mid-forties, and published his first Philip Marlowe story "The Big Sleep" in 1939. Nothing could have been further from the English country-house detective story. Chandler painted the mean streets, down which a man must go – nor was wise-cracking Marlowe any relation to Poirot or Wimsey, and there were only seven Marlowe novels.

Four years ago, after his wife died, Chandler attempted suicide. Ironically, the cartridges in his revolver were damp.

Dior's red cabbage dress comes garnished with toque and beads.

1959

APRIL

Su	Mo	Tu	We	Th	Fr	Sa
			1	2	3	4
5	6	7	8	9	10	11
12	13	14	15	16	17	18
19	20	21	22	23	24	25
26	27	28	29	30		

1. London: The Treasury says the British economy is stronger now than for many years (→7).

3. UK: Contractors bore test holes for a prospective Channel tunnel (→7/5).

5. Baghdad: The government moves towards nationalising foreign oil companies (→1/6).

7. London: The budget slashes income and purchase tax (→8).

7. US: David Niven and Wendy Hiller win Oscars.

8. London: Shadow Chancellor Harold Wilson leads the attack on the Budget (→14/5).

9. Bonn: Adenauer will not talk to East Germany (→11/5).

11. London: Bobby Charlton scores the only goal in England's 1-0 defeat of Scotland at Wembley.

14. UK: TV personality Robin Day is chosen as Liberal candidate for Hereford.

15. Washington: Secretary of State Dulles resigns through ill health (→27/5).

15. Washington: Castro arrives on an 11-day visit.→

17. Kuala Lumpur: Malaya signs a treaty of friendship with Indonesia (→2/8/60).

20. London: Sir Winston Churchill, 85, says he will stand again for parliament.

21. London: The government announces it is sending a trade mission to the USSR (→24/5).

22. Rome: Princess Margaret and the Queen Mother have an audience with Pope John (→7/8).

25. North America: Work on the St. Lawrence Seaway ends after five years (→26/6).

27. Peking: Veteran Communist Liu Shao-chi will succeed Mao as head of state; Mao stays head of the Party (→4/12).

30. London: The cabinet approves plans for British space research (→15/5).

DEATH

9. US architect Frank Lloyd Wright (*8/6/1869).→

Transport of the future will hover

Inventor Cockerell on the water.

April 16. The revolutionary new concept of a vehicle that will travel on a cushion of air – the Hovercraft – has moved from the drawing board into realistic development. Announced last year by its inventor a Suffolk boat-builder, Mr Christopher Cockerell, the concept has attracted interest from the government-backed National Research and Development Corporation. Now a two-ton hovercraft is under construction by Saunders Roe on the Isle of Wight. Trials are scheduled for June.

Future plans include a 100-ton hovercraft capable of carrying passengers and, after that, a 10,000-ton version which would be used for carrying freight (→26/8).

Me, a Communist? Never, says Castro

April 17. Fidel Castro, the new Premier of Cuba, is making a determined effort on his visit to Washington to quell American fears of a Communist threat. He assured Congressional leaders that he would uphold the mutual defence treaty. He promised that the US could keep its naval base at Guantanamo Bay.

He certainly impressed the American Society of Newspaper Editors. He won warm applause, particularly when he said "we are not Communists" (→18/5).

The genius Frank Lloyd Wright dies

April 9. Frank Lloyd Wright died today, just as his revolutionary spiral pudding-basin-shaped Guggenheim Museum on Fifth Avenue is ready to open. It is an astonishing work for a man of 89.

He was the best-known architect of his day and a non-conformist genius. Though trained by Louis Sullivan, "the father of the skyscraper", he made his name with long, single-storey "prairie houses" inspired by Japanese style. In Tokyo he built the Imperial Hotel, balancing each floor "like a teatray on a waiter's finger" to withstand earthquakes. In the 1923 'quake it was the only large building left standing.

NASA picks elite astronaut squad

April 9. The US National Aeronautics and Space Administration today announced the test pilots who have been chosen to participate in Project Mercury, NASA's manned space project. They are Scott Carpenter, Gordon Cooper, John Glenn, Virgil Grissom, Walter Schirra, Alan Shepard and Donald Slayton. All married and in their thirties, they will get no extra pay for hazardous duty (→30).

The swan who turned decoy duck

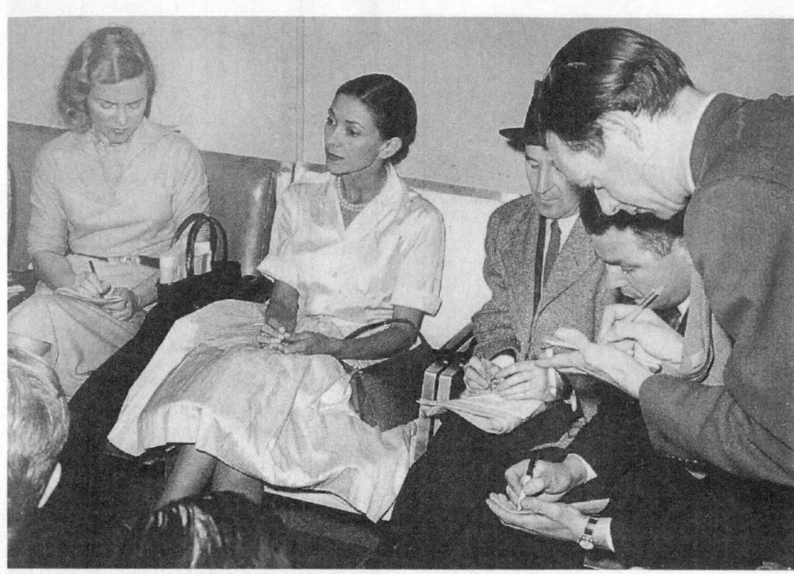

Prima ballerina Dame Margot Fonteyn tells the press about her arrest.

April 22. Dame Margot Fonteyn, aged 39, the Covent Garden ballet dancer, arrived in New York tonight looking none the worse for her day in a Panama City jail. Wearing a bright pink dress, she was gay and self-possessed as she parried questions from reporters about her real-life drama.

The Panamanian police are still hunting her husband, Dr Roberto Arias, a former Panamanian ambassador in London. He is suspected of planning a coup, with Cuban help, to overthrow the Government. It was timed to coincide with the one-day visit to Panama of Prince Philip in the royal yacht Britannia.

The police were tipped off that Dr Arias had refloated a launch loaded with rifles, machine guns, revolvers and grenades last week. His wife was supposed to have provided cover for his actions, but she managed to convince the police that she knew nothing.

The British shadow Foreign Secretary, Aneurin Bevan, had the last word. He told the Commons last night: "The British public did not appreciate, having seen her in the role of the swan, seeing her in the role of a decoy duck" (→28/6).

Happy team-mates carry captain Billy Wright shoulder-high after his hundredth match, against Scotland, results in a victory for England.

Workers walk out over chalk marks

April 29. One of Britain's biggest shipyards was at a virtual standstill today after an inter-union dispute over which workers draw a simple chalk mark. Nearly 2,000 men have been laid off at Cammell Laird in Birkenhead, after members of the Boilermakers' Society learned that a shipwright had been given the job of marking out where a steel plate should be cut, and walked out.

Previously its members had drawn the chalk marks on shore, but now plates are cut in the ship to save time. The company has refused to get directly involved in the dispute, but the strike by 1,800 men threatens to harm future orders at the yard (→1/7).

Dalai Lama finds sanctuary in India

April 19. The Dalai Lama has reached safety in India from his Chinese pursuers. He crossed the border into Assam yesterday, and today 7,000 Tibetans gave him a noble and moving welcome at the small West Bengal town of Siliguri.

His special train pulled into the station this morning to be greeted by Tibetan music weirdly amplified over the station loudspeakers. Then, after he had been tearfully greeted by his relatives, and received a long line of officials, he mounted a blue and white striped dais and the crowd began to throw katas – white silk scarves – into the air.

So many were being thrown up in this traditional Tibetan greeting that they formed a white mist over the heads of the people. The Dalai Lama, his boyish, bespectacled face reflecting his pleasure, stood smiling and waving while the shouts and chants grew louder.

The Dalai Lama speaks in India.

Then he rejoined the train to continue his journey to New Delhi where he will have talks with Mr Nehru. What must now be decided are the terms under which he will live in India. While welcoming him it is unlikely that the Indians will risk Chinese anger by allowing him to be politically active.

1959

MAY

Su	Mo	Tu	We	Th	Fr	Sa
					1	2
3	4	5	6	7	8	9
10	11	12	13	14	15	16
17	18	19	20	21	22	23
24	25	26	27	28	29	30
31						

1. Panama: Cuban troops who invaded earlier this week surrender.

2. London: Nottingham Forest beat Luton Town 2-1 in the FA Cup Final.

5. Washington: The World Bank warns that the "poverty gap" threatens the world more than the Cold War (→ 1/6).

6. London: A Picasso is sold for £55,000, a world record for a living artist.

7. UK: The Tories make gains in local elections (→ 20/6).

7. London: BR has plans to close down 230 stations (→ 8/7).

10. USSR: The first census in 20 years puts the Soviet population at 208,800,000 (→ 14/1/60).

11. Geneva: Foreign ministers of the Big Four meet to discuss German reunification (→ 1/7).

14. UK: Donald Campbell sets a water speed record of 260.35 mph.

14. UK: Mortgage rates drop to 5.5 per cent (→ 27/7).

15. UK: The Jodrell Bank radio telescope transmits radio messages to the US, via the moon (→ 28).

18. Havana: Cuba faces sweeping agrarian reforms (→ 30/6).

22. US: Alabama bans a children's book because it shows a black rabbit marrying a white one (→ 25).

24. London: Britain and the USSR sign a five year trade pact.

25. Washington: The US Supreme Court rules a Louisiana ban on mixed-raced boxing matches unconstitutional (→ 12/8).

27. London: A delegation of blacks urges the Home Office to defuse racial tension in Notting Hill (→ 28/2/60).

30. France: Work begins on a road tunnel beneath Mont Blanc (→ 9/8).

DEATH

24. US statesman John Foster Dulles (*25/2/1888).→

UK warns Iceland on Cod War tactics

An Icelandic navy boarding party approaches a British trawler in 1958.

May 6. Britain protested to the Icelandic Government today over the increasingly violent methods being used against her trawlers in the Cod War.

Iceland's gunboats have started firing live shells to drive off the British trawlers – last Thursday one missed the Hull fishing boat Arctic Viking by just three yards. Around 20 shots were fired, but the British vessel turned towards the gunboat and chased her.

The note, delivered to the Foreign Ministry in Reykjavik, also protests at the "dangerous manoeuvres" by the Icelandic coastguard ship, Maria Julia, which nearly collided with the British destroyer, Contest, during a recent incident.

The British protest went on to say that the Government took a "very serious view" of the shooting incident. It said the actions of the Icelandic ships were "dangerous and unseamanlike" and went beyond any measures necessary to identify the British vessels involved.

Meanwhile the Commons is putting pressure on the Government for firmer action against what one MP described as a "flagrant breach of diplomatic law" (→ 2/10/60).

The US statesman Foster Dulles is dead

Mr Dulles leaving hospital.

May 24. Today the maverick former US Secretary of State, John Foster Dulles, lost his two-year fight against cancer.

The architect of America's Cold War policy, Dulles took a hard line on Communism and threatened to use the nuclear bomb to meet Soviet aggression. Only in 1956 did he abandon his calls for the West to liberate eastern Europe, after the Allies had failed to aid Hungary during the uprising.

One obituary remarks that his attitude "may have denied the West advantageous moments for negotiation ... but without (his) crusading approach it is doubtful whether the peoples of the West could have maintained the will to go on fighting the Cold War" (→ 25/7).

Monkeys survive US space flight

May 28. Two monkeys have become the first animals to travel in space and return alive to earth. The Jupiter missile nose cone, in which they travelled 1,700 miles and reached a height of 360 miles, was picked up from the Atlantic by the US Navy today.

Able, a seven-pound rhesus monkey, and Baker, a one-pound squirrel monkey, were carefully monitored from the ground to see how they were affected by the stresses of spaceflight, particularly weightlessness and the violent accelerations of launch and re-entry into the atmosphere. Their performance at tasks in which they had been trained was followed, too. Such tests are essential preliminaries to the manned spaceflight for which the American space agency has already selected seven astronauts (→ 2/6).

New filters boost sales of cigarettes

May 27. Statements linking lung cancer and smoking have not affected sales, but may have influenced habits. This appears to be the lesson of figures released today by the Tobacco Manufacturers' standing committee. These show a marked trend towards smoking filter-tipped cigarettes, whose sales last year rose to £18.2 million from £10.1 million in 1957.

The value of all tobacco sales rose from £256 million to £260.8 million (→ 23/6).

1959

JUNE

Su	Mo	Tu	We	Th	Fr	Sa
	1	2	3	4	5	6
7	8	9	10	11	12	13
14	15	16	17	18	19	20
21	22	23	24	25	26	27
28	29	30				

1. Baghdad: Iraq renounces US military aid, saying it conflicts with its policy of neutrality (→25/6/61).

1. London: Macmillan launches World Refugee Year.

2. US: Able the rhesus monkey that orbited the earth, dies as an electrode is removed from its brain (→6/7).

3. West Germany: Real Madrid beat Stade de Reims 2-0 to win the European Cup at Stuttgart's Neckar Stadium.

3. UK: Sir H. de Trafford's Parthia wins the Derby.

5. London: The Queen opens a NATO conference (→28/12).

8. UK: Jockey Lester Piggott is suspended for rough riding.

9. US: The US Navy launches the nuclear sub George Washington, the first vessel equipped with Polaris missiles (→20/11).

13. US: Adlai Stevenson says he will not run for president in 1960 (→8/7).

17. London: Liberace wins £8,000 from the Daily Mirror after its "Cassandra" column implied he was homosexual.

18. Paris: Brigitte Bardot marries Jacques Charrier.

20. UK: Labour veteran Herbert Morrison announces he will retire after the next general election (→8/9).

22. London: Debenhams launch a £33.8 million takeover bid for Harrods (→7/7).

23. US: Louis Armstrong suffers a mild heart attack.

23. UK: Spy Klaus Fuchs is freed from jail; he will go to East Germany (→5/5/60).

26. Canada: The Queen and President Eisenhower inaugurate the St. Lawrence Seaway.

26. Italy: 68 die in the crash of a TWA airliner (→10/9/61).

28. Brazil: Margot Fonteyn is reunited with her husband Roberto Arias.

DEATH

23. French author Boris Vian (*10/3/20).

Sweden gets its first heavyweight champ

Patterson goes down for the seventh time as Johansson powers to victory.

June 26. In front of a disbelieving crowd at the Yankee Stadium in New York, the Swedish heavyweight Ingemar Johansson, who seven years ago was disqualified from an Olympic medal for "not fighting", battered the champion Floyd Patterson to the canvas seven times before the referee stopped the fight in the third round.

The Swede, who must defend the title against Patterson before he will even be paid for this one, becomes the first non-American world heavyweight champion since Italy's Primo Carnera 25 years ago.

Black women riot over slum clearances

June 18. Over 50,000 black South Africans, led by several thousand women protesting against a slum clearance scheme and a ban on home-brewed beer, burned houses, offices, beer halls and motor cars, and joined in running battles with police firing Sten guns. The slums at Cato Manor are to be demolished before plans are completed to move people to a new township, which means that they will be left temporarily homeless. The women forced the men to join the protest by dragging them from beer halls and beating them (→20/8).

Sticks and shoes litter the ground as baton-wielding police move in.

Ireland's grand old man goes upstairs

June 25. Behind the castellated walls of Dublin Castle today, Eamon de Valera took the oath as President of Ireland in a simple ceremony. Now 76, the most dominant figure in Irish politics this century steps up to the presidency – a strictly non-political job. It will be a big change from his 21 years as Prime Minister when he liked to make all the big decisions himself.

There was shock, and even tears, when "The Chief", as he was known to his Fianna Fail Party, announced his retirement earlier this year. He created the party himself in 1926 from a nucleus of those who had been jailed for their part in the civil war, then built it into Ireland's most consistently effective political machine (→6/10/61).

Land reform plans in Cuba worry US

June 30. Fidel Castro has brought in a new agrarian reform bill, which breaks up large landholdings and confiscates thousands of acres from Cuban and foreign property owners. Five cabinet ministers have resigned in protest, but Castro is unshaken, saying the policy is at the heart of the revolutionary spirit and that his regime is still solid.

The US government reacted with "serious concern" that proper compensation be paid to Americans, who owned many of Cuba's lucrative sugar plantations (→12/7).

Doctors to set up "spare parts" bank

June 23. A bank of spare parts from victims of road accidents and certain diseases, which will enable healthy kidneys or livers to be transplanted into patients, is planned at Hammersmith Hospital in London. It will involve a modification of the heart-lung machine, developed by David Melrose, to permit a kidney transplant next year. Transplant difficulties with bone, skin, and cornea are solved, but not those with a complete organ, except in twins (→21/10).

1959

JULY

Su	Mo	Tu	We	Th	Fr	Sa
			1	2	3	4
5	6	7	8	9	10	11
12	13	14	15	16	17	18
19	20	21	22	23	24	25
26	27	28	29	30	31	

1. UK: The TUC tells the "chalk mark" strikers to return to work (→ 1/9).

1. Bonn: Dr Heinrich Luebke is elected West Germany's second president (→ 17/11).

4. Wimbledon: Alex Olmedo of Peru beats Rod Laver for the Men's Singles title; Maria Bueno beats Darlene Hard in the Women's Single final.

6. USSR: A rabbit and two dogs are reported to have returned safely from space (→ 12/9).

7. London: House of Fraser launches a counter-bid for Harrods (→ 24/8).

8. Washington: Eisenhower says there is no reason why a Roman Catholic should not be elected president (→ 26/12).

8. London: BR are given the go ahead to raise rail fares by 50 per cent (→ 17/8).

12. Havana: Castro says the US is meddling in Cuban affairs by giving asylum to Cuba's ex-air force chief (→ 18).

17. Belgian Congo: The Congolese National Movement splits into two factions (→ 1/11).

18. Havana: Castro ousts President Urrutia and takes over the presidency (→ 26/11).

21. London: Macmillan is to set up a commission to review the Southern Rhodesian constitution (→ 14/10/60).

22. London: The crime rate in the city in 1958 rose by 21 per cent since 1957, according to new figures (→ 18/11).

27. UK: A study finds that the average male manual worker in Britain earns £13 2s 11d. a week (→ 1/8).

28. Norwich: Postmaster General Ernest Marples inaugurates the first post codes and post code sorting machine.

30. Laos: An anti-government Communist rebellion is reported to have broken out (→ 11/8).

DEATHS

6. German-born US artist George Grosz (*26/7/1893).

17. US singer Billie Holliday (*7/4/15).→

Nixon and Khrushchev debate in kitchen

Khrushchev tastes the fruits of capitalism – a glass of Pepsi-Cola.

July 25. The champions of American capitalism and Soviet communism slugged it out in an American kitchen in Moscow today. Richard Nixon, the American Vice-President, and Nikita Khrushchev, the Soviet First Secretary, argued about the virtues of the two systems, as well as foreign policy, for nearly an hour at an American exhibition, and agreed to differ on almost everything.

The impromptu summit got under way as Nixon tried to lure Khrushchev into a model American kitchen. Khrushchev said: "We've got all that in our kitchens. I've got everything in my home that you have there", but then his eye caught a glimpse of the array of electrical appliances, and he was lost. His legs steered him for a closer look and the "kitchen debate" got under way.

Subjects ranged from the merits of washing machines to nuclear weapons. Although both men spoke heatedly for the most part, they seemed to have still enjoyed the exchange (→ 2/8).

St. Laurent reveals the knees he hates

July 30. Yves St. Laurent today set aside his well-known dislike of knees, and raised hemlines in Paris. His new collection, aimed primarily at young women, with its puffed skirts and high, built-up hair styles, has been condemned as mere fancy-dress by some critics who claim that Dior's influence is waning.

Elsewhere in the fashion capital, skirts were much longer. Chanel showed new versions of her now-classic suits worn by models with the gamin look of top film star Audrey Hepburn (→ 21/9/61).

Commons uproar at Kenya camp deaths

July 28. "We will not abdicate," cried Alan Lennox-Boyd, the Colonial Secretary, during the fiercest parliamentary debating since the Suez crisis. It was about how Britain rules the shrinking Empire.

In the past 24 hours the Government has beaten off strong Opposition attacks on its response to serious unrest in Kenya and Nyasaland. These came after a judicial inquiry criticised security forces' action during Nyasaland riots, in which 51 Africans were killed, and also the circumstances in which 11 Mau Mau detainees died in Hola Camp in Kenya. The Labour MPs cried "Massacre", but Tories said "It was unavoidable" (→ 10/11).

Veteran radio man Greene heads BBC

July 7. Hugh Carleton Greene, a former journalist and the current head of news and curent affairs, is to be the next director-general of the BBC. He will succeed Sir Ian Jacob, whose seven-year tenure of the post expires this year. Greene, who will be paid an £8,000 salary, has yet to comment on his plans.

Greene, the brother of novelist Graham Greene, was the Daily Telegraph's chief correspondent in Germany up to 1939, when he was expelled. After a spell in the RAF he joined the BBC where he has stayed ever since (→ 17/9).

Billie Holliday has sung her last blues

July 17. Billie Holliday, one of the greatest ever singers of the blues, died today, aged only 44. With her personal emblem, the gardenia in her hair, and a voice that thrilled every devotee, Holliday delighted a world-wide audience with her interpretayions of a particularly American art form.

But singing as she did came from real experience, and Holliday's life, with its feckless lovers, its bouts of heroin addiction and its professional ups and downs, gave her, in the end, too much source material.

1959

AUGUST

Su	Mo	Tu	We	Th	Fr	Sa
						1
2	3	4	5	6	7	8
9	10	11	12	13	14	15
16	17	18	19	20	21	22
23	24	25	26	27	28	29
30	31					

1. UK: A report on teenage spending says that young working men have about £5 a week to spend (→28).

2. Warsaw: Vice-President Nixon arrives from Moscow (→15/9).

4. UK: Barclay's becomes the first British bank to order a computer for its branch accounts.

7. UK: Buckingham Palace announces that the Queen is expecting a third child early in the New Year (→8/2/60).

9. Paris: The 800-year-old central market of Les Halles is to be moved because it is costly and inefficient (→16/10).

10. UK: Violent storms lash the south of England (→21).

11. Washington: The US denies it has bases in Laos (→2/9).

13. Leicester: A fire at the Rolls-Royce factory causes £1 million of damage.

17. UK: Sodium road lighting is tested for the first time (→18).

18. UK: The proposed route of the M1 motorway is changed to save a forest (→6/11).

19. London: The Coal Board announces plans to close between 35 and 70 pits from 1960 and 1965 (→18/9).

20. S. Africa: White liberal MPs set up the anti-apartheid Progressive Party (→15/1/60).

21. London: Floods cause chaos in the city as three-quarters of an inch of rain falls in one hour.

25. New Delhi: Nehru warns China that India will defend Bhutan and Sikkim if they are attacked (→12/6/60).

26. Berlin: Eisenhower begins a European tour (→27).

27. London: Eisenhower arrives for talks with Macmillan.→

28. UK: Figures show that in 1957 the average household spent £1 8s 1d. a week on food (→20/10).

DEATH

19. British sculptor Sir Jacob Epstein (*10/11/1880).→

Here comes the Mini

Alec Issigonis, the inventor of the Mini, stands between his creations.

Aug 18. First pictures of British Motor Corporation's new mini-car reveal a compact four-seater. Its roominess is achieved by placing the four small wheels at the corners and mounting the engine sideways in front. There will be an Austin as well as a Morris version, differing only in front-end look. Both cars are capable of 70mph.

The pictures show an austere interior with pullstrings to open the two doors, and sliding fitment of the front door windows. Instruments are sparse. The bootlid is hinged at the bottom, forming a platform for a surprising amount of luggage.

The body design is essentially practical, with door hinges exposed, and styling minimal. But the car sits low on the road and gives a stable ride. It will cost around £500, with purchase tax (→1/9).

Transistors give radios a new look

Aug 26. The new models at the Earl's Court Radio Show, which opened today, are smaller and more economical than ever. Many manufacturers are using transistors in place of valves, allowing the size of sets to be reduced. The makers also claim that a transistor portable could run on the same batteries for a year, and that the new technology improves both tone and volume.

Prices start at £23 for a handbag-size model weighing just seven lbs, but the ultimate transistor is surely Roberts' £156 mink-covered portable, aimed perhaps at film stars, aristocrats, or arctic explorers.

Fraser takes over top people's store

Aug 24. Harrods of Knightsbridge, the department store which prides itself on supplying the needs of top people at home and abroad, conceded that House of Fraser now has enough shares to take them over. They had failed to do a deal with the neighbouring store, Debenham's, to block the bid from the Scottish accountant, Hugh Fraser, who will now take over the emporium – By Appointment.

Mob kept at bay as blacks go to school in Little Rock, USA

Aug 12. Just before two blacks, Jefferson Thomas and Elizabeth Eckford, were about to enter Central High School in Little Rock, Arkansas, this morning, 200 demonstrators marched on the building. They were were part of a 1,000-strong crowd which had gathered on the State Capitol at dawn to protest against desegregation. In defiance of the court order, Governor Orval Faubus told them: "I am with you all the way."

It was to this school that President Eisenhower sent the Federal troops in 1957. Today the local police stopped the march using truncheons and fire hoses, with enough water to soak the protesters but not sufficient to bowl them over. Over 20 people were arrested for violence or not obeying police orders (→9/2/60).

Johnny Gray, a black student, challenges white racists at Little Rock.

1959

SEPTEMBER

Su	Mo	Tu	We	Th	Fr	Sa
		1	2	3	4	5
6	7	8	9	10	11	12
13	14	15	16	17	18	19
20	21	22	23	24	25	26
27	28	29	30			

1. UK: Yorkshire wins the cricket county championship, ending Surrey's seven-year winning streak.

1. Birmingham: An unofficial strike at BMC halts production of the new Mini (→ 28/6/61).

2. Laos: The Communist rebel group Pathet Lao launches an offensive against the Laotian government (→ 9/8/60).

4. UK: The number of people going to university has doubled since 1939.

7. London: Lord Monckton will lead a study of the Nyasaland and Southern Rhodesian constitutions (→ 16/6/60).

8. Rome: Opera singer Maria Callas says she has split up with her husband, but denies a liaison with Aristotle Onassis.

12. USSR: The rocket Lunik II is launched at the moon.→

13. Italy: Stirling Moss wins the Italian Grand Prix.

15. Washington: Khrushchev arrives for a tour of the US.→

18. UK: 47 miners are trapped by a fire at Aughengeich Colliery near Glasgow.

20. UK: The last Spitfire to fly in the Battle of Britain remembrance display crashes.

22. New York: China may not join the UN (→ 23/9/60).

24. UK: Rolls-Royce launches its new £8,905 Phantom V.

25. US: Khrushchev and Eisenhower begin talks on Berlin (→ 25/12).

26. UK: Jockey Manny Mercer is killed in a parade before a race at Ascot.

27. Ceylon: Prime Minister Solomon Bandaranaike dies of wounds inflicted by a Buddhist monk two days ago (→ 21/7/60).

DEATHS

26. Sinhalese statesman Solomon West Ridgeway Dias Bandaranaike, Prime Minister of Ceylon 1956-59 (*8/1/1899).

28. German-born British humorist and musician Gerard Hoffnung (*22/3/1925).

Live from London, the "Ike and Mac" show

Mr Macmillan entertains President Eisenhower for television viewers.

Aug 31. The "Ike and Mac" show, the great Downing Street spectacular, hit Britain's TV screens tonight. Mr Macmillan and President Eisenhower were seen in apparently impromptu armchair conversation about matters great and small.

Their topics ranged from world peace to Britain's textile industry. The programme was the Prime Minister's idea. He steered it and took the time cues.

Mr Macmillan will probably call a general election soon, and the performance was seen as skilful electioneering. The US President, here on a five-day visit "to the land I love", drove with the Prime Minister through huge, cheering crowds most of the way from the airport to central London. Cynics noted that their zig-zag route took them through some marginal constituencies.

The President and Mrs Eisenhower go tomorrow to Balmoral to stay overnight with the Queen. On returning to London there will be a private "Ike-Mac" talk about arranging a four-power summit meeting with Mr Khrushchev and President de Gaulle (→ 4/4/61).

Epstein has power to shock to the end

Aug 19. Sir Jacob Epstein, Britain's best-known sculptor of the first half of the century, caused violent controversy with the massiveness and seeming crudity of his public statues, not to mention his emphasis on their sexual characteristics. It was a debate that lasted until his death today at 79. His sculpture of Christ, "Ecce Homo", has just been refused by Selby Abbey.

Born in New York of Russian stock, he took British nationality. Many of his works were defaced or tarred. His "Adam" (hugely endowed) and "Genesis" (enormously pregnant) were put on show at Blackpool. His "St. Michael and the Devil" is waiting to be unveiled at Coventry Cathedral.

Sir Jacob Epstein and his doves.

Algeria to decide her fate – de Gaulle

Sept 16. In a dramatic television address to the nation, President de Gaulle tonight offered the people of Algeria the right to choose their political future by referendum. Within four years of peace being restored, they could vote for the constitution of their choice. He defined peace as a time when less than 200 people a year died through terrorism.

He said that three alternatives faced Algeria. She might secede from France, choose to be integrated with it, or decide, as he recommended, upon independence in close association with France. This bold plan is bound to raise a storm of hostility among resentful French army officers, the settler population and their allies in France. Nor will it satisfy the rebels (→ 19/1/60).

Large screen takes beating from small

Sept 17. In the week the BBC announces the purchase of 20 American feature films to be shown on television, the Rank Organisation today disclosed a disastrous trend in cinema attendances. From 1950 to 1956, attendances dwindled from 1.396 million to 1.101 million, and this year's figures are already down on last year's by 14 per cent. Thus, as well as the 91 theatres shut down by Rank since 1956, and another 57 already ear-marked for the same fate, yet more cinema closures may soon have to come (→ 11/11).

Angry Khrushchev is denied Disneyland

Off duty in Hollywood, Mr Khrushchev meets the girls of "Can-Can".

Sept 20. Last night's Los Angeles banquet for the Soviet premier, Nikita Khrushchev, turned sour. He was angry even before the meal began because he was refused a visit to the Disneyland amusement park for security reasons. When Norris Poulson, the Los Angeles mayor, then made a hostile speech recalling Khrushchev's famous "We will bury you" remark, he exploded and threatened to take the next plane home.

The chill continued this morning when Mr Poulson did not turn up at the station to see the Soviet leader off. However, when the train drew into Santa Barbara there was an enthusiastic crowd of several hundred clapping and cheering and pushing forward to clasp his hand.

The ever-volatile Soviet leader responded promptly. He pushed through the guards to talk to the 350-strong press corps. He told them: "Well, I have seen some real Americans at last and it seems to me they are as good and kind as our Soviet people." The question now is: will his sunny mood last for the serious talks ahead with President Eisenhower about Berlin? (→25).

Mac sets date for a general election

Sept 8. There will be a general election on October 8. Mr Macmillan made the announcement today after a flying visit to the Queen at Balmoral. He said that he took the decision because the nation should have the chance to decide who will represent it at the approaching East-West summit conference.

The Tories will ask: "Do you want Supermac or Labour's less experienced Hugh Gaitskell?", and they reckon the answer will be an easy winner for them. Mr Gaitskell cut short a visit to Moscow and flew home tonight. He commented: "Labour victory is vital for the world" (→1/10).

Soviet rocket is first to hit moon

Sept 14. The Soviet Lunik II spacecraft crashed into the moon today, the first man-made object to reach our nearest neighbour in space.

During its 35-hour journey, Lunik II sent a stream of information back to earth about magnetic fields, radiation and the matter that even space contains. "We now know", commented a Soviet space expert, "that it is not a vacuum but contains gas, cosmic dust and some larger particles of matter."

This latest Soviet space spectacular seems to have been timed to coincide with a visit of Soviet premier Nikita Khrushchev to the US this week (→4/10).

1959

OCTOBER

Su	Mo	Tu	We	Th	Fr	Sa
				1	2	3
4	5	6	7	8	9	10
11	12	13	14	15	16	17
18	19	20	21	22	23	24
25	26	27	28	29	30	31

1. London: The Labour Party promises to abolish purchase tax if elected.→

2. UK: Jack Hawkins, Bryan Forbes, Richard Attenborough and others set up a new group, Allied Film Makers.

4. USSR: Lunik III is launched (→6).

6. USSR: Lunik III goes into orbit around the moon.→

7. London: Louis Leakey exhibits the skull of the earliest known precursor of man.

9. London: New women MPs include Tory Margaret Thatcher and Judith Hart for Labour (→14).

14. London: Macmillan's new ministers include Ernest Marples and Edward Heath (→16).

16. London: A Labour spokesman says nationalisation plans will win no votes (→28/11).

20. London: A Royal Mint report discusses decimalisation, and the possibility of introducing five and ten shilling coins (→19/11).

21. UK: A survey shows that a third of 15-year-old boys in Britain are regular smokers (→16/11).

23. London: A London School of Economics study recommends a new body for Greater London to replace the London County Council (→27).

23. India: Seventeen Indian soldiers are killed in a clash with the Chinese on the Kashmir border.

27. London: The Queen's Speech promises independence for Cyprus and Nigeria.

27. London: A housing official says slum clearance and rehousing causes misery for residents who are moved.

DEATHS

7. US singer Mario Lanza (*31/1/21).

14. British actor Errol Flynn (*20/6/09).→

16. US commander and statesman General George Catlett Marshall (*31/12/1880).

Errol Flynn buckles last swash at 50

Errol Flynn at the Savoy in 1954.

Oct 14. Errol Flynn, the hell-raising Hollywood swashbuckler who died today at only 50, was the son of a professor at London University and began acting at Northampton Rep. He went to Hollywood in 1935 and made a name as Captain Blood and Robin Hood. His reckless ways often landed him in court and in the newspapers, accused of seducing under-age girls. He also featured in many a night-club brawl. It was not his fault that Hollywood made him win the war in Burma practically single-handed. In private, when sober, Flynn could be charming, modest and witty. "The rest of my life will be devoted to women and litigation," he said recently.

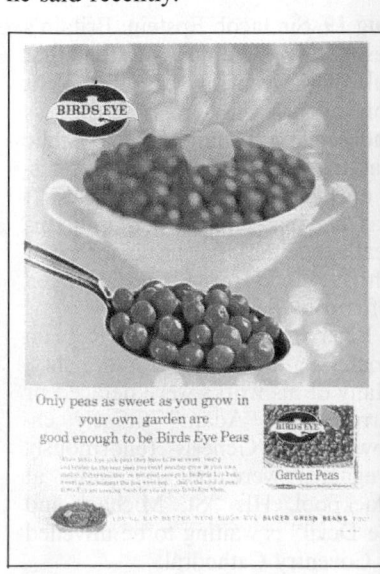

1959

NOVEMBER

Su	Mo	Tu	We	Th	Fr	Sa
1	2	3	4	5	6	7
8	9	10	11	12	13	14
15	16	17	18	19	20	21
22	23	24	25	26	27	28
29	30					

3. Israel: Ben-Gurion's Labour Party wins the general election (→14/3/60).

6. UK: Two lorry drivers die in the first fatal crash on the new M1 (→8).

8. Belgian Congo: Belgium flies in extra troops (→11/3/60).

8. UK: Sightseers flock to the M1 on the first Sunday since it opened, picnicking on the approach roads (→17).

10. Kenya: The state of emergency ends (→18/1/60).

11. London: The ITA rejects complaints that ITV shows too many advertisements (→26).

16. London: The Health Minister pledges £20 million for new hospitals (→20/1/60).

17. UK: Five police chiefs say the M1's design and operation is unsatisfactory (→19/9/60).

17. London: Macmillan begins talks with West Germany's Konrad Adenauer (→14/4/60).

18. London: The Home Secretary wants an enquiry into police relations with the government and public (→16/5/60).

19. London: The government says it will reintroduce £10 notes and put the Queen's head on notes for the first time (→17/3/60).

19. London: Archbishop of Canterbury Geoffrey Fisher says adultery ought to be a criminal offence (→24/2/60).

20. New York: The UN bans France's Saharan nuclear tests (→13/2/60).

26. London: The Lords oppose the introduction of commercial radio (→4/1/60).

26. Havana: Major Ernesto "Che" Guevara becomes head of the Cuban national bank (→10/2/60).

28. Blackpool: Gaitskell has a rough ride at the Labour Party Conference (→17/3/60).

DEATH

17. Brazilian composer Heitor Villa-Lobos (*5/3/1887).

Election victory is triumph for Supermac

Oct 9. The Government has been re-elected with a thumping majority in the general election. Trying to sound nonchalant, Mr Macmillan said today: "It has gone off rather well." The final seats tally will be Tories 365, Labour 258, Liberals 6, Others 1.

The Tories, who have now won three elections in a row and twice increased their overall majority, campaigned on "Supermac's" slogan: "You've never had it so good". Mr Gaitskell conceded Labour's defeat very early in the vote-counting, and put it down to his party's internal bickering. Privately he agreed with the Prime Minister, who remarked: "I think the class war is now obsolete."

The dejected Liberals only got six per cent of the vote. Two of their candidates were Oxford Union ex-presidents: Jeremy Thorpe was elected, and TV reporter Robin Day was defeated (→14).

Mr Macmillan's common touch.

Mitterrand's close brush with death

Oct 16. Senator Francois Mitterrand, a former French minister, narrowly escaped assassination tonight when right-wing hitmen chased his car through the streets of Paris. At the Luxembourg Gardens he jumped from his car and scrambled to safety over park railings. As he wormed down into a bed of geraniums, the raiders fired a burst into his new Citroen car (→3/12).

Dark side of moon filmed by Soviets

Oct 26. The first-ever pictures of the dark side of the moon, usually invisible from earth, have been sent back by the Soviet Lunik III spacecraft. It photographed more than 70 per cent of the far side in bright sunlight. One of the largest features has been named the Moscow Sea, but, according to Soviet scientists, the far side of the moon is "more monotonous" (→4/12).

Chairman Mao, with aide Liu Shao-tsi, arrives at Peking airport to bid farewell to his fellow Communist leader, Nikita Khrushchev.

Peace prize goes to a British Quaker

Noel-Baker, peace prize winner.

Nov 5. This year's Nobel Peace Prize has been awarded to Philip Noel-Baker, the Derby South MP. A Quaker, Noel-Baker helped draft the League of Nations covenant in 1919, and was a minister in the post-war Labour government. For over 40 years he has campaigned relentlessly to secure an international arms control treaty.

Ben Hur races onto the British screen

Nov 11. "Ben Hur", garlanded with more Oscars than any film has won before – 11, including two for its sound effects alone – has opened in Britain with suitable publicity. William Wyler's epic of ancient Rome ends with Charlton Heston's victory for the Christians in a spectacular chariot race.

Charlton Heston in "Ben Hur".

New trade pact tears Europe into two

Nov 20. Free Europe is now at sixes and sevens. In Stockholm today Britain, Austria, Denmark, Norway, Portugal, Sweden and Switzerland signed the European Free Trade Association (EFTA) agreement.

These "outer seven" nations plan trade co-operation and hope either to absorb or at least upstage the "inner six" Common Market countries. Negotiations are now expected between the rival trading blocs.

For Britain the attraction of EFTA is that its rules do not clash with existing Commonwealth tariff arrangements. The new organisation will work for wider and freer trade exchanges and the United States is reported to feel benevolent towards it.

Gunnar Lange, the Swedish Trade Minister, said that EFTA is not a closed club and that Russia and her satellites are eligible for membership. It is known, of course, that they will not apply.

Derick Heathcoat Amory, again Chancellor of the Exchequer in Mr Macillan's reshuffled cabinet, said Britain is "well pleased". In the coming negotiations with the Common Market, EFTA's first move will be to invite it to disband and join the seven.

This may well not happen, but holding the EFTA card strengthens Britain's hand in the diplomatic poker game (→28/4/61).

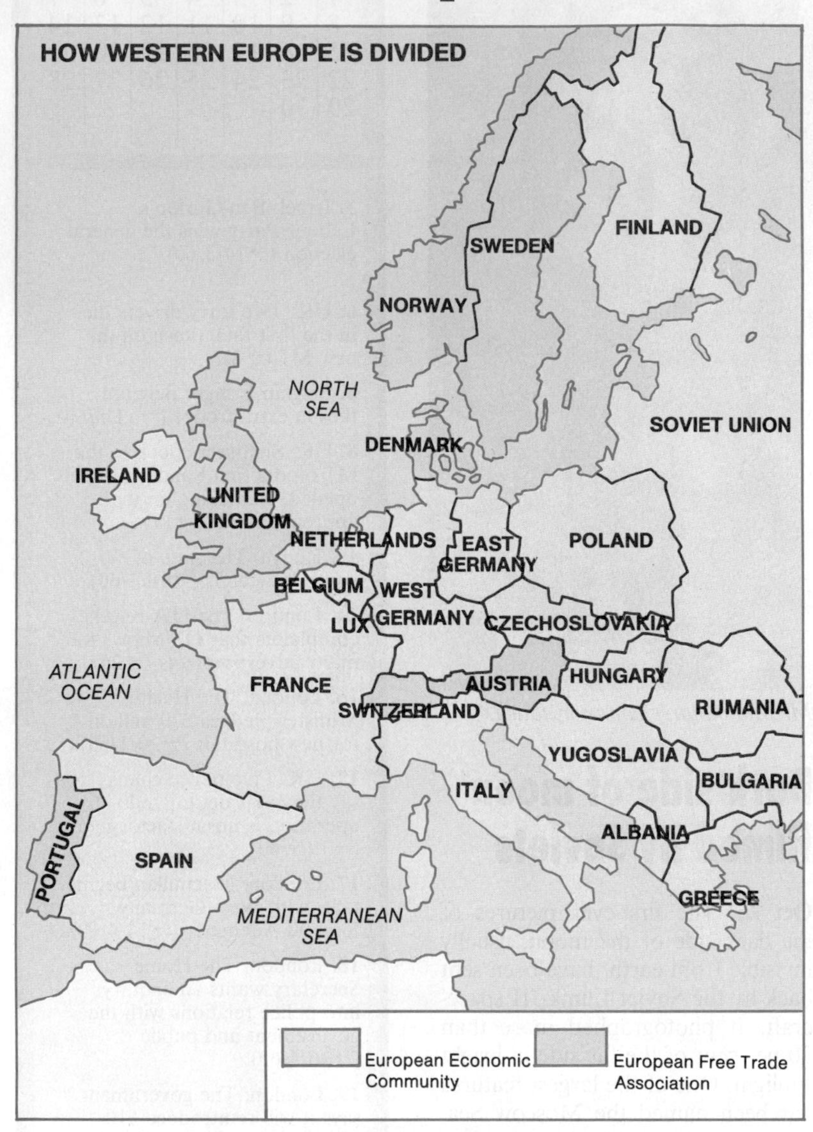

Nationalist leader arrested after anti-white Congo riots

Nov 1. Patrice Lumumba, the Congolese nationalist leader, is under arrest tonight following disturbances over the last two days. On Friday night thousands of Congolese, in full war paint, rampaged through Stanleyville chanting "Strangle the whites", after a meeting in a local cafe, called by 34-year-old Lumumba, broke up in disorder.

Charities to help Africans were special targets but finally black police, led by white officers, opened fire after a spear attack on a white lieutenant. Unofficial figures put the dead at 75. Disorders continued into Saturday, when police used grenades to drive back crowds advancing on the river port. Lumumba went into hiding, but was picked up after an intensive police hunt. Stanleyville radio said a man and a woman, not Belgians, who are believed to have influenced Lumumba, were also under arrest.

Lumumba, a former postal clerk who was gaoled for embezzlement, and who later became salesman for a brewery, helped to form the Mouvement National Congolais last year shortly before he attended the All-African Peoples Conference in Ghana in December. He returned to the Congo demanding immediate independence (→8).

Duty-free booze is perk for travellers

Nov 17. Passengers leaving Prestwick and Renfrew airports for overseas will now be able to buy duty-free wine and spirits. London airport is expected to be given the same facility soon. Customs and Excise has given its approval after rigorous security checks aiming at preventing an illicit home trade.

Travellers will be able to buy a bottle of whisky in the departure lounge. It will be marked "not for consumption on voyage" and handed to passengers as they board the aircraft. Such a service has been commonplace for years abroad, where it has proved a substantial foreign currency earner.

A workman cleaning up a stretch of Britain's first motorway, the M1, before it was opened this month.

1959

DECEMBER

Su	Mo	Tu	We	Th	Fr	Sa
		1	2	3	4	5
6	7	8	9	10	11	12
13	14	15	16	17	18	19
20	21	22	23	24	25	26
27	28	29	30	31		

1. London: Britain starts talks with Nasser (→ 10/1/60).

4. US: A monkey returns safely to earth from 55 miles out in space (→ 1/1/60).

9. UK: North Sea gales claim 27 lives as two ships sink.

10. Stockholm: Nobel Prizes go to Emilio Segre and Owen Chamberlain (US, Physics); Jaroslav Heyrovsky (Czechoslovakia, Chemistry); Severo Ochoa and Arthur Kornberg (Spain, Medicine); Salvatore Quasimodo (Italy, Literature); and in Oslo to Philip Noel-Baker (UK, Peace).

14. Cardiff: An archaeologist claims that Stonehenge is not of Druid origin.

18. Peking: Premier Chou En-lai proposes talks with Nehru on the Sino-Indian border row.

21. Teheran: The Shah is marries a former shepherdess Farah Dibah (→ 25/4/60).

21. UK: Oven-ready turkeys are popular this Christmas.

25. Moscow: Khrushchev calls for an East-West summit meeting next spring (→ 14/5/60).

26. New York: Governor Rockefeller will not run for president, Nixon is the Republican favourite (→ 31/1/60).

28. Paris: De Gaulle denies claims that France is intent on ruining the NATO pact.

DEATH

23. British Tory statesman Edward Wood, first Earl Halifax (*16/4/1881).

HITS OF 1959

Livin' Doll.

What do you want to make those eyes at me for?

QUOTE OF THE YEAR

" An article shall be deemed obscene if its effect...is, if taken as a whole, such as to tend to deprave and corrupt persons who are likely...to read, see or hear the matter contained or embodied in it."

Obscene Publications Act, Britain's first definition of obscenity since 1857.

Huge floods inundate the French Riviera

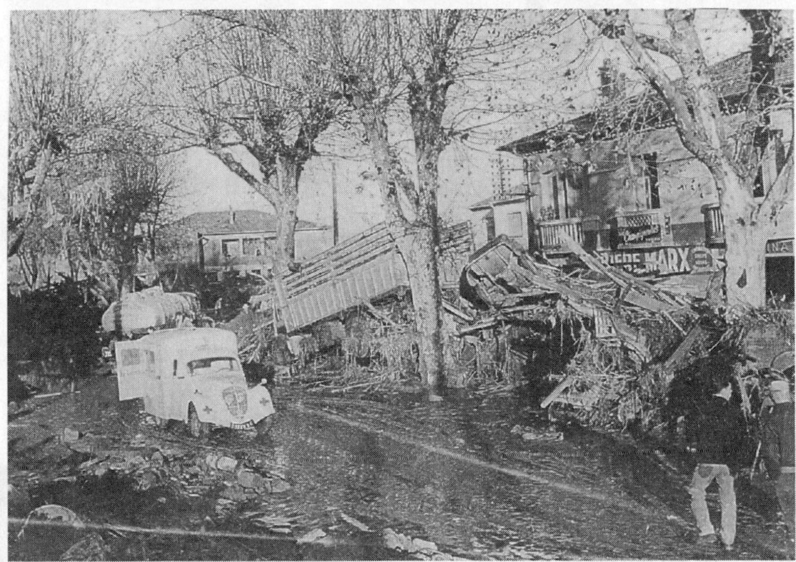

Houses lie shattered in Frejus, after it was hit by raging floodwaters.

Dec 3. Nearly 300 people are feared dead today after a dam collapsed and washed away part of a town on the French Riviera. A 15-foot high wall of water, mud and boulders swept down the valley into Frejus, where people warned two days ago that floodwater from recent storms had caused cracks in the bottom of the Malpasset dam.

The warnings went unheeded, and within minutes the town was devastated. Houses and a power station were washed aside by the raging torrent, a train was overturned, drowning dozens inside, and cars and lorries along a main coast road were submerged. Power and telephone lines were destroyed.

Rescue teams flown into the area by naval helicopters said that about ten square miles were underwater. One survivor said that water tore through the town for about an hour. "It hit like a hammer over a path of seven miles, tumbling houses and farms as if they were cards and tearing away the railway line as if it had been made of straw," he said. As troops dug out children's bodies from the mud, an official disaster inquiry began (→ 1/1/60).

Makarios is the new president of Cyprus

Dec 14. Thousands of people gathered in Metaxas Square, Nicosia, tonight to celebrate the victory of Archbishop Makarios in the election for the first President of the new Republic of Cyprus. They chanted his name, sounded motor horns and let off fireworks. Some staged a mock funeral for his Democratic Union opponent who won only 33 per cent of the vote.

In his speech the Archbishop first praised the "heroes and martyrs" of the liberation struggle, mentioning Colonel Grivas, the EOKA guerrilla leader. Then he insisted that fanaticism and antagonism must cease. Greeks and Turks must work together, he said, "in a spirit of great sincerity, with great respect for the natural rights of each other" (→ 16/8/60).

Archbishop Makarios in Athens.

Pu Yi is pardoned by the Communists

Dec 4. China's Supreme People's Court today pardoned 33 war criminals, including the former Emperor of China, Pu Yi, who reigned as a child from 1908 until 1912, when he abdicated. Peking radio said that, after ten years of reform through labour, the criminals "repented and acknowledged their crimes and showed that they are turning over a new leaf".

Pu Yi was resurrected from retirement in 1932, when Japan installed him as the puppet emperor of Manchuria. In 1945 he was seized by the Russians, and stood as a prosecution witness for them at the Tokyo war crimes trials in 1946.

Later he was turned over to the Chinese authorities, who kept him under house arrest in Fushun, near Mukden. There he was visited several times in recent years by foreign correspondents, who described him as an apathetic boiler-suited figure, eager to confess his past crimes against the people (→ 18).

Antarctic becomes a science reserve

Dec 1. In an unprecedented international agreement, a total of 12 countries have signed a treaty which says that no country shall claim any part of Antarctica as its own and establishes the continent as a preserve for scientific research.

The countries involved include Britain, the United States, the Soviet Union, and all other nations with claims on this last unexploited continent. The new treaty freezes all claims over sovereignty of sections of the continent, to stop it becoming the object of any territorial disputes. It also imposes a ban on all nuclear explosions, and prohibits the dumping of any nuclear waste there.

Each of the 12 nations has still to ratify the treaty before it becomes effective, but the document provides that it will then remain in force indefinitely and can only be changed by the unanimous agreement of all the signatories. It allows free access to all parts of Antarctica to scientists of all nations, but military bases are banned.

Demolition job is done on architects

Dec 18. Concern over Britain's architectural future was expressed today in the annual report of the Royal Fine Art Commission. Ugly new nuclear power stations in areas of natural beauty, the relentless spread of the suburbs into the country, and the "drabness", "mediocrity", if not "deplorably low standard", of much modern inner city architecture, were all targets for criticism from the Commission, whose members include John Betjeman and Henry Moore. And without a proper "master-plan" for all urban building, they pessimistically concluded, the outlook for big cities is "poor" (→2/6/60).

Merger plan by two UK airline giants

Dec 16. The Hawker Siddeley and de Havilland aircraft groups are merging to form the most powerful aircraft group in the country. The £220 million merger will be the biggest industrial link-up in Britain since the merger between Austin and Morris in 1952.

Hawker Siddeley, which makes everything from fighter planes to limousines, is offering £14 million for de Havilland, which makes the Blue Streak guided missile along with the Comet, Vampire, Sea Vixen jets and a significant loss last year.

Spencer, Cookham visionary, is dead

Dec 14. Sir Stanley Spencer, RA, died today, as he spent his life, in the village of Cookham on the Thames, where he set his visionary religious paintings. They included "Christ Preaching at Cookham Regatta" and "The Resurrection in Cookham Churchyard".

His ambulance service in Greece in the First War was recorded vividly in the Burghclere Chapel murals. In the Second War he recorded shipbuilding on the Clyde. He left the Academy when rejected in 1935 as too provocative, but rejoined. He was knighted earlier this year.

Arts: skylines fill with filing cabinets

One of the biggest changes the Fifties made was to the skylines of cities all over the West. The post-war "International Style" took off in 1951 with its most influential single building, the United Nations headquarters on the New York waterfront, a worldwide symbol of modernity. The up-ended glass-fronted box of the Secretariat was designed by a committee, but the credit for the concept is attributed to **Le Corbusier**.

In the Twenties he coined the slogan "the House – a Machine for Living In". Here was the Slab – a Filing Cabinet for Working In. Or that is what it inspired round the world as architects copied it, in steel frames hung with prefabricated glass and concrete sections. These are sprouting from capital city skylines like teeth, and are as indistinguishable from one another as tombstones.

Some architects have now refined the tower office block. Last year **Mies van der Rohe**, with his pupil **Philip Johnson**, produced New York's admired Seagram Building clad in bronze tinted glass. Another ex-Bauhaus teacher, **Marcel Breuer**, designed the long UNESCO building in Paris, now set off by a **Henry Moore** sculpture.

A new capital city on a virgin site is being completed in Brazil. The city of Brasilia is planned by **Lucio Costa** in sectors separated by parkland and joined by highways with no traffic inter-sections. The spectacular public buildings are by Brazilian **Oscar Niemeyer**.

Two very original films by French directors have created a new category – Nouvelle Vague or New Wave cinema. In "Hiroshima Mon Amour", **Alain Resnais** flashes forward and backward in time between a present-day and a past love affair and the nuclear devastation of the city. **Francois Truffaut**, formerly a film critic, has directed "Les Quatre Cents Coups" (slang for "Sowing Wild Oats"), in which an alienated boy of 12 lives on the streets and ends in a reformatory. We leave him on the run.

British films moved somewhat closer to reality (sex, cynicism and the ugliness of the industrial north) with "Room at the Top", made from **John Braine's** best-selling novel. **Laurence Harvey** plays Joe Lampton, who uses sex to get what he wants – "an Aston Martin, three-guinea shirts and a girl with a Riviera sun-tan" – along with a seat on the board.

Laurence Harvey uses Simone Signoret to find some "Room at the Top".

A slice of life in the raw was also served up at the Theatre Workshop in Stratford East by **Joan Littlewood** with "A Taste of Honey", by a young writer, **Shelagh Delaney**, which tells the story of a young Salford girl, pregnant by a black lover, and looked after by a homosexual, who is the most sympathetic character of her dingy world.

Starry acting at the other Stratford in the Memorial Theatre's last season under present management, **Paul Robeson** as Othello, **Charles Laughton** as King Lear, and **Laurence Olivier's** Coriolanus. Next year **Peter Hall** takes over.

The City of London opened its first new theatre for 300 years with the Mermaid – thanks to **Bernard Miles**, who made it a reality. At Covent Garden memorable nights: **Maria Callas** as Medea – "ranging the boards like a caged panther" and **Joan Sutherland** as Lucia di Lammermoor. **Margot Fonteyn** (now Dame) danced Ondine the sea spirit with the now "Royal Ballet".

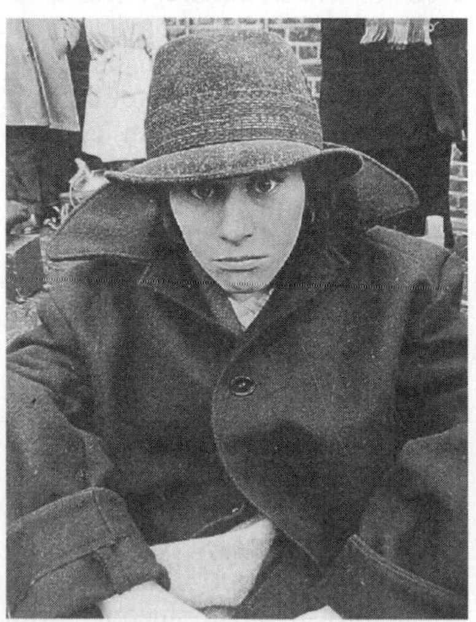

Rita Tushingham – fast becoming one of Britain's new film stars.

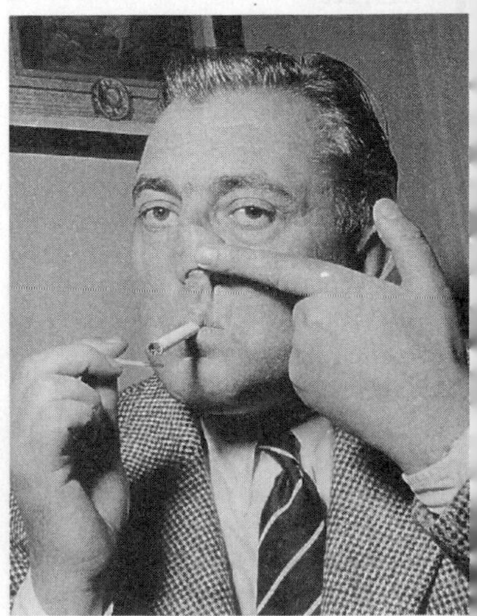

Jacques Tati as M. Hulot lights cigarettes in his very own way.

How five million teenagers took over the Fifties

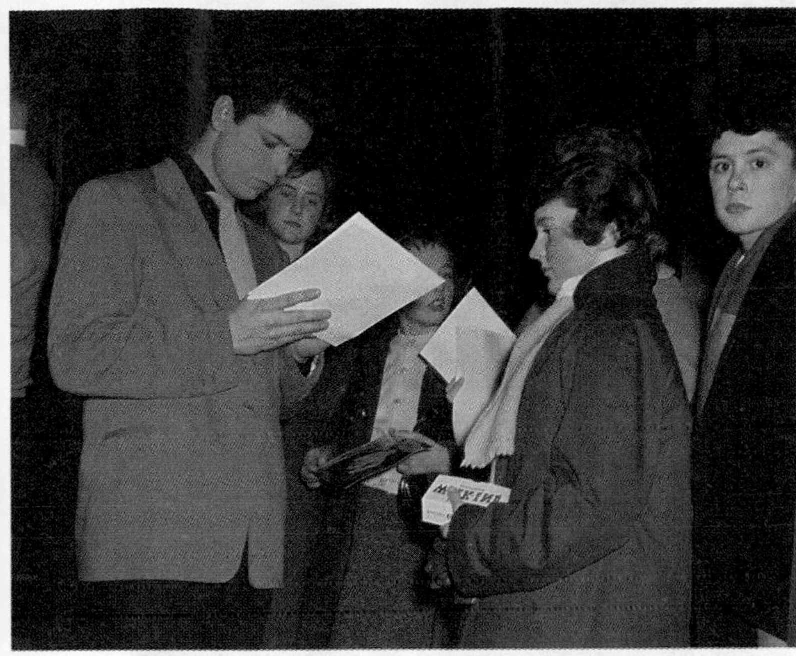

Cliff Richard, Britain's number one rock'n'roller, signing autographs.

Teddy boys hang around the jukebox at a south London coffee bar: frothy coffee and the latest hits proves a potent attraction.

When the Fifties began there were no "teenagers". As it draws to a close there are five million in Britain – and Britain knows it. They have not only got a name but found an identity and invented their own distinct teenage culture. They have, after all, £800 million a year to spend. Market research shows that they spend it on records, dressing up, cigarettes, cosmetics, bikes and going to the cinema.

In America they have their own cars or motor-bikes, and model themselves on **James Dean** or **Marlon Brando** – seen in "The Wild One" as an early Hell's Angel. Britain has its Teddy Boys, whose uniform of draped jackets with velvet collars, bootlace ties, drainpipe trousers and sideburns is the correct wear for gang skirmishes with flick-knives and bicycle chains. Some were prominent in provoking last year's Notting Hill riots.

Besides the adulation for **Bill Haley** and **Elvis Presley**, there is an alternative, home-grown music, spawned in the new coffee bars. Their essential attractions are a steaming Gaggia machine dispensing frothy coffee into glass cups, a jungle of cane furniture and rubber plants, and a juke-box. It was the coming of the seven-inch EP that made coffee bars work and nourished the sound of Skiffle.

Skiffle was an institution before rock'n'roll took hold. Three-chord guitar-players, making the rounds of the coffee bars, singing folk music, are supplemented by a bass made out of a tea-chest and broomhandle, and a wash-board to provide rhythm. They are likely to sing a **Lonnie Donegan** number, such as "Puttin' on the Style" or "Cumberland Gap". Donegan's hit, "Rock Island Line", climbed both British and American charts in competition with Elvis in 1956.

It was in a Soho basement coffee bar called "The Two I's" that Tommy Hicks was discovered playing skiffle by an agent, who marketed him as **Tommy Steele**. The agent, **John Kennedy**, and his partner, **Larry Parnes**, now have stables of hopeful singers with names like **Vince Eager**, **Billy Fury** and **Marty Wilde**. These were not their original names. There was a musical satire about the phenomenon, entitled "Espresso Bongo", in which the most successful of them all, **Cliff Richard**, whose real name was Harry Webb, played a talentless boy hopeful trying to get into the big time.

Colin MacInnes wrote a novel, "Absolute Beginners", in which London is seen through the eyes of a teenage narrator: "No one could sit on our faces no more because we'd loot to spend and our world was to be our world, the one we wanted." Rock'n'roll swept the under-18s off their feet (and there is even a rock'n'roll vicar who updates the hymn-tunes on television), but the over-18 student age-group is far more enthusiastic about traditional jazz. The "Trad" revival began at **Humphrey Lyttleton's** Club at 100 Oxford Street where "Humph", the ex-Guards Etonian, brings in the band with four thumps of his foot.

The early New Orleans purists have given way to less antiquarian bands led by players like **Ken Colyer** and **Chris Barber**, while some, like **Acker Bilk**, have taken the stand in bowler hats to show that it's British jazz they are playing. Trad rules the festivals. The Saints go marching in, nowadays, with the CND, on the road to or from Aldermaston.

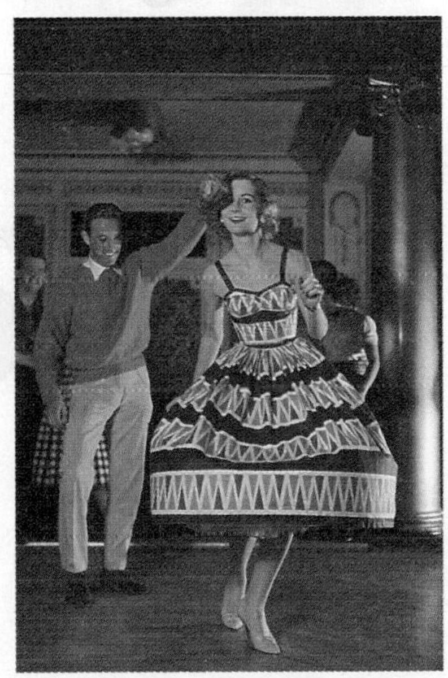

Dancing the night away at the Palais, in slacks and petticoats.

1960-1969

1960

JANUARY

Su	Mo	Tu	We	Th	Fr	Sa
					1	2
3	4	5	6	7	8	9
10	11	12	13	14	15	16
17	18	19	20	21	22	23
24	25	26	27	28	29	30
31						

1. US: The first meteorological satellite, Tiros I, is launched (→ 14/3).

1. France: The "New Franc" is introduced; it is worth 100 old francs (→ 11/5).

4. UK: A BBC survey finds that half the British population watch TV at peak times (→ 27).

10. Egypt: Nasser lays the foundation stone of the Aswan High Dam (→ 28/9/60).

14. Moscow: Khrushchev says the USSR will cut its armed forces by 1.2 million over the next two years (→ 1/2).

15. S. Africa: At the opening of parliament, uproar greets the new Progressive Party's call to end apartheid (→ 3/2).

17. Bonn: Adenauer, concerned at a new wave of anti-Semitism, says offenders should be thrashed (→ 23/5).

18. London: Africans boycott the Kenyan constitutional conference (→ 18/4/61).

19. Paris: De Gaulle recalls General Jacques Massu, a senior commander in Algeria, for criticising his policy there (→ 21).

20. London: The government announces curbs on the sale of "pep pills" (→ 7/6).

21. Paris: De Gaulle sacks Massu and bans him from returning to Algeria (→ 24).

24. Algiers: A state of siege is declared following an uprising by Europeans angry at the dismissal of Massu.→

26. Southern Rhodesia: Riots break out during a visit by Macmillan to the capital, Salisbury (→ 3/2).

27. London: The BBC says it wants a second TV channel (→ 1/6).

28. Rangoon: Burma signs a treaty with China (→ 3/11/61).

DEATHS

4. French author Albert Camus (*7/11/13).→

12. British author Nevil Shute, born Nevil Shute Norway (*17/1/1899).

24. Swiss pianist Edwin Fischer (*6/10/1886).

John Kennedy will run for President

Kennedy: a presidential hopeful.

Jan 31. Early this month, Senator John F. Kennedy of Massachusetts tossed his hat into the ring of presidential hopefuls. He now has campaign offices throughout the USA, headed by his brother Robert. His nearest rival, Minnesota's voluble Senator Hubert Humphrey, trails behind him in the opinion polls.

The bright young Senator resolved to run for President over five years ago, while he was hospitalised for a series of spinal operations. He first ran for the Democratic nomination in 1956, but was pipped as Adlai Stevenson's running mate by Estes Kefauver. Kennedy has two obstacles to overcome: his inexperience and his Catholicism, but his boyish, handsome smile might yet manage it (→ 6/3).

Civil war fear in Algeria

Jan 29. As France trembled on the edge of civil war, President de Gaulle appeared in General's uniform on television tonight to order his army to break the French settler insurrection in Algiers. He described it as "a foul blow against France". At this tense moment it is far from certain that army officers will order their troops into action against heavily armed part-time French militia, who for a week have occupied fortified positions in the public gardens by the university in central Algiers. Shortly before de Gaulle's dramatic intervention the Prime Minister, Michel Debre, flew to Algeria.

Already more than a score of Frenchmen have died in clashes between insurrectionists and Mobile Squads of the Gendarmerie. Paratroop and other line regiments recalled from their war against Algerian Moslem rebels now surround the barricades, but their commanders are reluctant to order them into action against compatriots. The fear is that either French will kill French, or the troops will not obey orders.

The crisis was caused by President de Gaulle's dismissal of General Jacques Massu as commander of the Central Algiers Region. The paratroop general, hero of French settlers and fighting soldiers, had criticised de Gaulle's offer of Algerian self-determination.

General Massu: paratroop leader.

Well-organised demonstrations brought more than 2,000 settler extremists to the barricades. Most were members of the militia, armed for self-protection against Algerian Moslems and led by a bearded student, Pierre Lagaillarde (→ 1/2).

Catholics forbidden to watch "unsafe" TV

Jan 24. Roman Catholics throughout the world are to be brought back to the straight and narrow path. The first synod ever held in Rome was opened by Pope John XXIII today. It is expected to make some new laws which, once approved by the Pope, are likely to be adopted in dioceses everywhere.

Catholics will be told not to watch films, television programmes or plays not considered "safe" by the Vatican. Women with bare arms or dressed in male clothing will not be allowed the sacrament. For priests, the new regime will be even tougher. They will not be allowed to smoke in public, and they will be forbidden to go to any cinemas or theatres (→ 7/2).

Camus, the existential outsider, is dead

Jan 4. French literature will be impoverished by the death, at only 46, of Albert Camus, who was killed when the car in which he was a passenger hit a tree. With Sartre he was a pillar of intellectual life in France, although they quarrelled when he renounced Communism.

Camus was born in Algeria, and brought up in a tenement where his mother was a charwoman. In 1942 he wrote "The Outsider" about a man who commits a murder as an "absurd" gesture of intellectual despair. Communism having failed him, Camus occupied the position of "outsider", and turned his existentialist confrontation with a meaningless universe into art.

He wrote "The Plague", "The Fall", and essays that compared man to Sisyphus and his stone.

1960

FEBRUARY

Su	Mo	Tu	We	Th	Fr	Sa
	1	2	3	4	5	6
7	8	9	10	11	12	13
14	15	16	17	18	19	20
21	22	23	24	25	26	27
28	29					

1. Algeria: The settlers' revolt ends after de Gaulle's appeal for loyalty (→ 2).

1. Moscow: Khrushchev opens a meeting of Communist leaders; the Chinese are absent (→ 12/4).

2. Paris: French MPs give de Gaulle emergency powers for one year (→ 10).

8. London: The Queen says that all her descendants not styled Royal Highness will be called Mountbatten-Windsor (→ 26).

9. US: A bomb goes off at the home of one of the first black pupils to attend Little Rock Central High School (→ 17).

10. Havana: 104 government opponents are jailed after the biggest mass trial since Castro came to power (→ 21).

10. Paris: De Gaulle announces plans to give Algerian Moslems a better deal (→ 9/12).

13. Africa: Despite UN and US opposition, France explodes an atomic bomb in the Sahara (→ 29/3).

15. London: The Kenyan conference accepts the constitutional plan of the Colonial Secretary' Iain Macleod.

17. US: Martin Luther King is arrested for perjury in connection with his state income taxes in 1956 (→ 1/3).

18. US: The Winter Olympics open at Squaw Valley, Idaho.

19. London: The Queen gives birth to a son (→ 26).

21. London: The Kenyan conference ends.

21. Havana: Castro nationalises private business (→ 7/8).

24. US: A survey finds that venereal diseases are increasing among teenagers (→ 27).

27. US: Connecticut bans "Playboy" magazine from newsstands (→ 17/8).

28. London: Mosleyites attack an anti-apartheid rally addressed by Hugh Gaitskell.

BIRTH

19. British Prince Andrew Albert Christian Edward.

Macmillan foresees wind of change

Feb 3. "The wind of change is blowing through this continent and, whether we like it or not, this growth of national consciousness is a political fact." They did not like it when Mr Macmillan used those words when addressing the South African Parliament in Capetown today.

The British Prime Minister, at the critical stage in his African tour, was accused by many white politicians of ignorant meddling.

He went on to warn his audience that the great issue in the rest of this century is whether the uncommitted peoples of Asia and Africa will swing to the Communist East or to the West. Pointedly he added: "We may sometimes be tempted to say to each other "Mind your own business". But in these days I would expand the old saying so that it runs 'Mind your own business but mind how it affects mine, too'."

Then Mr Macmillan urged South Africa's rulers to move towards policies of racial equality which Britain wants throughout the Commonwealth. Premier Verwoerd was loudly applauded when he retorted: "There has to be justice not only for the black man in Africa but also for the white man."

A new power-sharing constitution for Kenya, to give African nationalists experience prior to independence, will be announced by Britain within the next fortnight. The cabinet accepts that the pace of decolonisation is quickening, and that in another decade barely any of the empire will remain (→ 21/3).

Mr Macmillan greets Swazi warriors; later they gave him his own shield.

Princess Margaret to wed commoner

Princess Margaret and her fiance.

Feb 26. Princess Margaret, aged 29, is to marry Antony Armstrong-Jones, son of Ronald Armstrong-Jones, QC, and the Countess of Rosse. Mr Armstrong-Jones works as a photographer (→ 22/3).

Britain is to fund a supersonic aeroplane

Feb 22. The Government has agreed to fund a revolutionary supersonic airliner, capable of flying at 2,000mph. The new aircraft may well be built in collaboration with France or the United States, said the Aviation Minister, Duncan Sandys. The plane would fly between London and New York in little more than two hours.

The cost of developing the revolutionary new aircraft will be considerable. The estimate is that each will cost between £5 million and £6 million. All Britain's major aircraft groups have been given separate contracts to devise ways around particular problems. Hawker Siddeley-de Havilland and Vickers-Bristol-English Electric have been asked to study the airframe, while both Rolls-Royce and Bristol-Siddeley have been asked to develop engines (→ 21/10).

Biblical scrolls are found hidden in desert

Feb 7. Israeli archaeologists have made the most spectacular find of ancient biblical texts since the Dead Sea Scrolls were unearthed from Jordanian caves in 1947. The new discovery is of parchment scrolls, probably written about 1,700 years ago by Hebrew bands who had fled from the Roman occupation into hiding in the Judaean desert.

The scrolls, which contain at least 16 verses from Exodus, are a little frayed, but otherwise in excellent condition. They were covered by nearly a foot of dust, and have been preserved by the dry atmosphere. A coin found with them gives a clue to their age. It shows the head of the Roman Emperor Trajan, who died in AD 117. Scholars are comparing them with the Dead Sea Scrolls, which covered most of the Old Testament (→ 3/3).

1960

MARCH

Su	Mo	Tu	We	Th	Fr	Sa
		1	2	3	4	5
6	7	8	9	10	11	12
13	14	15	16	17	18	19
20	21	22	23	24	25	26
27	28	29	30	31		

1. US: One thousand black students stage a peaceful protest against segregation in Montgomery, Alabama (→9).

2. Kabul: Thousands of Afghans greet Khrushchev.

3. Rome: Pope John XXIII names the first black African, Japanese and Filipino cardinals (→2/12).

6. US: After the first primary, in New Hampshire, Kennedy and Nixon are favourites to be presidential candidates (→10/4).

6. Accra: Nkrumah announces that Ghana is to become a republic (→22/9/61).

9. US: Martin Luther King urges Eisenhower to intervene to defuse racial tension in Montgomery, Alabama (→16).

11. Belgian Congo: Riot police stand by as Patrice Lumumba is allowed to speak in public for the first time (→14).

14. Belgian Congo: Martial law is declared after unrest in which 14 people died (→17/5).

15. South Korea: Syngman Rhee is elected president for the fourth time (→19/4).

16. Washington: Eisenhower advises southern states to set up bi-racial talks to hear black grievances against segregation (→25/4).

17. UK: Labour loses the first two by-elections of the new parliament (→6/7).

17. UK: A new £1 note goes into circulation →13/8).

23. Paris: Khrushchev arrives on a visit and warns against the "rebirth of German militarism".

25. Johannesburg: All black political organisations are outlawed (→27).

26. UK: Miss W.H.S. Wallace's Merryman II wins the Grand National.

27. S. Africa: ANC leader Chief Luthuli launches a passbook-burning campaign by setting fire to his own pass (→30).

30. S. Africa: A state of emergency is declared as 30,000 blacks demand the release of their leaders (→1/4).

Police kill 56 at Sharpeville massacre

Dead bodies still lie as they fell at Sharpeville, after South African police opened fire and killed 56 blacks.

March 21. In one of the worst civilian massacres in South African history, 56 Africans died and 162 were injured when police opened fire today in the black township of Sharpeville in the Transvaal. In other disturbances, seven died and 209 were injured at the Langa township near Cape Town.

It happened on the first day of a campaign of civil disobedience against the pass laws, which require Africans always to carry identity cards. Instead of leaving their pass books at home and quietly surrendering to police, as directed by the Pan-African Congress, people gathered in crowds and went through townships kicking in doors and ordering those inside to join the demonstrations.

At Sharpeville, a crowd of 15,000 converged on the police station, to be met by a line of 75 armed police. When stones were thrown, and the crowd began to rush forward, the police opened fire. In a matter of minutes, the scene was like "a world war battlefield, with bodies sprawled all around," said one policeman. The African hospital at nearby Vereenigning was soon overflowing as ambulances, escorted by police motor cyclists, raced back and forth. Some injured were laid out on verandahs.

The police commander, Colonel D.H. Pienaar, said: "It started when hordes of natives surrounded the police station. If they do these things, they must learn their lesson the hard way" (→25).

Heads of Israel and West Germany talk

March 14. The first meeting between West German and Israeli leaders took place today in New York. David Ben-Gurion and Konrad Adenauer had friendly talks, but avoided the major issue of renewing diplomatic relations.

Adenauer said that Germany was pleased that its reparations were helping Israel. Said Ben-Gurion: "The Germany of today is not the Germany of yesterday. We remember the past not in order to brood upon it but in order that it shall never recur" (→31/1/61).

Jodrell Bank sets space-tracking record

March 14. The radio telescope at Jodrell Bank, Cheshire, has set a record in space-tracking, making contact with the American Pioneer 5 at a distance of 407,000 miles.

Jodrell was first in touch with the probe when it was 350,000 miles away yesterday. A spokesman said: "We sent a signal out at 2pm which switched on the transmitter in the satellite and tracked it for the next half hour. At 2.30 we sent a signal to turn the transmitter off." The previous record, about 290,000 miles, was achieved by Lunik III, which photographed the back of the moon last year (→2/4).

The Jodrell Bank radio telescope.

1960

APRIL

Su	Mo	Tu	We	Th	Fr	Sa
					1	2
3	4	5	6	7	8	9
10	11	12	13	14	15	16
17	18	19	20	21	22	23
24	25	26	27	28	29	30

1. S. Africa: The state of emergency is extended; Britain and France refuse to condemn South Africa at the UN (→ 7).

1. Southern Rhodesia: Nyasaland leader Dr Hastings Banda is released from jail.

4. London: The budget puts twopence on a packet of cigarettes.

5. US: "Ben Hur" wins a record ten Oscars.

5. London: A crowd of 100,000 cheer de Gaulle on the first day of his state visit to Britain.

6. London: Dr Richard Beeching is chosen to head a four-man team to study Britain's rail network.

7. UK: England cricketer, the Rev. David Sheppard, says he will not tour South Africa.

12. A UN report says that living standards in the Soviet bloc are rising (→ 4/5).

13. London: To uproar from MPs the government says it is to scrap Britain's £65 million Blue Streak missile project (→ 22/7).

13. UK: Stirling Moss loses his driving licence for a year for dangerous driving.

19. Seoul: Rhee declares martial law as police shoot dead 30 marchers protesting against "rigged" elections (→ 21).

21. Brazil: Brasilia is inaugurated as new capital of Brazil.

21. Seoul: Rhee's cabinet resigns after 115 protesters were reported killed by police.→

25. Iran: Up to 1,500 are feared dead when an earthquake hits the town of Lar.

25. US: Ten blacks are shot in the worst ever race riot in Mississippi after blacks gathered on a segregated beach (→ 28/5).

27. Africa: The French colony of Togoland becomes independent as Africa's smallest free nation.

30. Turkey: 3,000 have been arrested after three days of riots; a 24-hour curfew is imposed (→ 22/5).

Moroccan quake kills at least 1,000

Smashed shops and littered streets bear witness to the devastation.

March 1. First an earthquake, then a tidal wave, and finally widespread fire, today destroyed the Moroccan resort of Agadir and killed at least 1,000 people, including dozens of British tourists.

The 'quake was the worst in the country's history, and Crown Prince Moulay Hassan, who directed rescue work from amongst collapsed buildings, said he planned a new city built from the rubble: "the old one has ceased to exist."

Casualties are believed to run into thousands, and a shuttle of 50 ambulance planes began to fly them out of the stricken area. From the air, nothing higher than two-storey buildings could be seen standing.

A warning of the devastation came with a minor tremor late last night. Within 12 hours the main shock, recorded as far away as Moscow, levelled the sea-port.

Seconds later the tidal wave rolled a quarter of a mile into low-lying suburbs. As it receded a number of fires broke out in its wake. More than 40,000 people have been made homeless, and relief agencies have began an urgent evacuation of the ruins (→ 26/2/61).

Barrier will tame Thames floods

March 14. Within six years London could be protected from tidal flooding by a movable barrier across the River Thames. Engineers say it is feasible to build a swing bridge, or a lifting gate construction, to shut out freak surges of water from the North Sea which have in the past threatened to breach old defences. Seven years ago storms caused the water level to rise to within inches of causing widespread flooding.

A government study today says the barrier would currently cost about £17 million to build.

Macmillan signs a test treaty with US

March 29. Anglo-US agreement was reached today, in Camp David talks between President Eisenhower and Mr Macmillan, about new proposals to be put to Russia for a nuclear test ban treaty.

The next Western move will be to offer a short-term moratorium on small underground explosions in return for a formal treaty banning all other nuclear testing.

It is hoped to make progress with treaty negotiations before the East-West summit conference currently arranged for May (→ 13/4).

"Stop Kennedy" bid by Democrats

April 10. A coalition was formed today to "stop Kennedy", after his success in the Wisconsin primary last week. Led by Senator Robert Byrd, the group finds fault with Kennedy's youth and inexperience. Democrats are being urged to vote for Hubert Humphrey in next month's primary in West Virginia.

Kennedy's Catholicism is the unspoken issue. He was helped by Wisconsin's unique religious makeup: it is 32 per cent Catholic, compared with the average state's 23 per cent, but Kennedy plans to tackle the issue head on, declaring he believes church and state should be firmly separated (→ 17/5).

"Father" of Korean republic forced out

A student protester is arrested.

April 27. Syngman Rhee, the one-time strongman of South Korea, finally resigned today, following a week of rioting and bloodshed in the capital, Seoul. Students had taken to the streets to protest against irregularities in last month's elections which returned the 85-year-old president to office for the fourth time.

It is thought that 115 people were killed when the police, the most detested symbol of the Rhee regime, opened fire on the demonstrators. Rhee's position ultimately became untenable when his ally, the United States, criticised his "repressive measures" against demonstrations reflecting "popular dissatisfaction" (→ 19/5/61).

Flood of East Berliners flee to the West

Some of the refugees who are desperate to escape from East Berlin.

April 19. There has been a great influx of refugees, mainly small farmers, across the East German border into West Berlin during the Easter weekend. From Good Friday until noon today 5,056 people have applied to be recognised as refugees.

There has been nothing like this influx since the East Berlin rising in June 1953, and it stems from the completion of the Communist programme of forced collectivisation of small farms.

The resources of the West Berlin reception centre, which usually deals with about 300 people a day, have been severely strained. Two former camps have been reopened. Screening of the refugees for Communist "plants" has been temporarily abandoned, and the refugees are being flown to West Germany.

The sudden arrival of so many landless farmers will cause problems for West Germany. It will be difficult to assimilate them into the working population, and thousands of refugees are already waiting for land (→31/8).

General de Gaulle, President of France, inspects a guard of honour drawn from the Chelsea pensioners, veterans of Britain's forces.

Blacks riot in Durban

April 7. Undeterred by the emergency regulations and the nationwide round-up of their leaders, Africans today continued their mass protests against the country's apartheid laws. Army and commando units are standing by.

Outside Durban, police opened fire on a crowd of about 1,000, said to be attacking people who went to work in defiance of a Pan-Africanist Congress call for a general strike. One African was killed.

In another incident, a black crowd, armed with hatchets, iron bars and sticks, forced its way into the shopping centre of Durban. White women took refuge in shops and banks. Police opened fire when a section of the crowd headed for the central jail, where many African leaders have been detained. Three Africans were killed.

In the African township of Nyanga, near Cape Town, an African detective was hacked to death by a mob during a police round-up. The township was cordoned by troops. A soldier fired a single shot when a woman in a car sought permission to take her baby through the cordon to the hospital. The bullet struck the baby and killed it.

"My husband was driving," Mrs Eldina Manjati said. "With us in the car were Beatrice Manjati and her baby. We asked permission to leave the township to go to the Red Cross Hospital. This was refused. We asked permission to reverse, which was granted. As we did so the soldier fired" (→9).

A white officer attempts to calm down Africans during the Durban riots.

First weather lab is put into space

April 2. The first weather satellite has been launched by the United States. Called Tiros 1 it has already sent back pictures from a height of 450 miles showing the cloud cover over the north-eastern United States and part of Canada.

The 270-pound Tiros 1 is a prototype for weather satellites that will eventually give round-the-clock coverage of the entire globe. They are expected to lead to major improvements in weather forecasting by providing views of major weather systems from above. It is not practicable to obtain comprehensive information of this kind from the earth's surface (→22/8).

An attempt is made on life of Verwoerd

April 9. As Dr Hendrik Verwoerd, the South African Prime Minister, sat down after speaking at the Johannesburg Agricultural Show today, a white man in green sports jacket stepped forward. "Dr. Verwoerd," he said, and the Prime Minister turned, smiling. The man fired twice with a .22 pistol and Dr Verwoerd slumped forward onto a bank of microphones blood gushing from his mouth; doctors said he would make a good recovery. The gunman was David Pratt, a wealthy 52-year-old farmer, who this year was refused a visa to visit his second wife, who is living apart from him in Holland (→26/8).

1960

MAY

Su	Mo	Tu	We	Th	Fr	Sa
1	2	3	4	5	6	7
8	9	10	11	12	13	14
15	16	17	18	19	20	21
22	23	24	25	26	27	28
29	30	31				

3. London: The Commonwealth conference opens (→9).

4. Moscow: Leonid Brezhnev, aged 53, succeeds Marshal Voroshilov as head of state in a Kremlin reshuffle (→9/7/61).

6. Moscow: The Kremlin releases photographs of the US spy plane shot down earlier this week (→11).

6. London: Princess Margaret is married (→8/6/61).

7. London: Wolverhampton Wanderers beat Blackburn Rovers 3-0 in the FA Cup Final.

9. London: Commonwealth leaders have a "major showdown on apartheid" with South African representatives.

11. Washington: Eisenhower refuses to apologise for the U-2 episode, saying the US must guard against attacks (→8/7).

11. France: Mme de Gaulle launches the world's longest liner, the SS France (→4/6/61).

14. Paris: The Big Four summit opens.→

16. London: MPs give an unopposed second reading to a bill to curb Teddy Boys (→14/1/61).

17. Belgian Congo: Lumumba controls large areas of the colony as Belgian authority collapses (→17/6).

22. Ankara: The government closes all Turkish universities and colleges (→27).

24. Japan: At least 96 die in tidal waves triggered by earthquakes in Chile (→15/6).

26. China: A Chinese expedition says it has climbed Everest by the north face.

27. Ankara: Premier Adnam Mendares is ousted in a bloodless military coup (→17/9/61).

28. US: Martin Luther King is acquitted of perjury charges (→14/5/61).

29. Monaco: Stirling Moss wins the Monaco Grand Prix.

DEATH

30. Soviet author Boris Pasternak (*10/2/1890).→

Soviets claim US plane was spying

May 5. The Russians today admitted shooting down an American U-2 aircraft which, they claimed, had deliberately violated Soviet air space to wreck the forthcoming Summit talks.

The announcement by the Soviet leader, Mr Khrushchev, has prompted a sharp reaction in Washington where senators say the incident means a grim future for US-Soviet relations.

In Moscow the belief is that the plane was on a spying mission, but the Americans claim that the aircraft, piloted by Francis Gary Powers, a 30-year-old civilian, must have strayed off course, and was only carrying out weather research. Cameras on board were for taking pictures of clouds, according to the State Department in Washington (→6).

Debris from the alleged US spyplane, shot down over Russian territory.

Summit talks break up amid Soviet outrage at US spyplane

May 17. The great "summit that never was" finally fizzled out in Paris tonight after three days of bitter recrimination and diplomatic farce. The conference of the Big Four – Eisenhower, Khrushchev, Macmillan and de Gaulle – on which hopes were built for East-West rapprochement, had never really started.

There were only preliminary procedural meetings, and the Soviet leader adopted what his opposite numbers denounced as wrecking tactics. As Russia's price for allowing the conference to begin, he repeatedly and angrily demanded a public apology from President Eisenhower over the spyplane recently shot down over Russia. He also wanted a promise that there will never again be such an intrusion of Soviet air space. The US President rejected the demand, and expressed "complete disgust" at Mr Khrushchev's behaviour.

There have been some bizarre moments during efforts to rescue the conference. At one stage, the Soviet leader drove into the Paris suburbs and handed out ballpoint pens to startled children instead of turning up at the Elysee Palace where the others were waiting.

At another, in darkness, Mr Macmillan told staff "I'm off on a pub crawl" and clambered over the British Embassy garden wall on to the Elysee lawn on his way to see President de Gaulle (→4/6/61).

Khrushchev makes things clear.

Humphrey gives up

May 17. Hubert Humphrey gave up the fight for the Democratic nomination last week, after victories for John F. Kennedy in Nebraska and West Virginia. In today's Maryland primary, Kennedy swept up 70 per cent of the vote. Humphrey has promised his support for the Kennedy campaign. The fight against the Republicans, led by the Vice-President Richard Nixon, can now begin (→13/7).

Pasternak, Nobel Prize winner, is dead

May 31. Although Boris Pasternak, who died last night at his villa outside Moscow at Peredelkino, was chiefly known as the author of "Dr Zhivago", to his fellow-Russians he was primarily a lyric poet.

They have never had the chance to read his only novel, which won him the Nobel Prize that he declined under government pressure. It also brought him denunciation by the writers' union as a "traitor" who had sold his country for thirty pieces of silver. Pasternak said he would never touch the royalties from its publication abroad.

Although he refused to write to order, Stalin spared him the physical persecution that so many writers, especially Jewish ones, suffered. Under Stalin he published no more poetry except for his poetic translations of Shakespeare's plays. He was 70.

Israelis capture death camp organiser

May 23. Adolf Eichmann, the SS officer who master-minded the "Final Solution", Hitler's extermination of six million Jews, is in Israeli hands and will be put on trial for his life. Announcing this news to a startled Knesset today, Mr Ben-Gurion, the Prime Minister, described Eichmann as "one of the greatest of the Nazi war criminals".

Mr Ben-Gurion gave no details of how and where Eichmann had been caught, but reports in Israel speak of a daring operation carried out by the Israeli intelligence service, Mossad, to seize Eichmann from Argentina where he had been living under an assumed identity. The reports say he was flown to Israel on an official plane.

The Israelis have never ceased hunting for Eichmann who disappeared at the end of the war 15 years ago. They accuse him of being the "technician of death", the man who organised the transportation of the Jews from all over Europe to the gas chambers.

He fled, like so many other war criminals, along the SS escape route to the Argentine, where there were many Nazi sympathisers. His hunters have come close to him on a number of occasions, but each time he has been one jump ahead of them. Until now (→8/6).

Real Madrid's 5th European Cup win

May 18. In a great display of attacking football, Real Madrid beat Eintracht Frankfurt seven-three at Hampden Park, Glasgow, to win the European Cup for the fifth time in a row.

Before an enthralled crowd of 135,000, the brilliance of Real's midfield play gradually wore down Eintracht's non-stop attack, and the deadly finishing of the Argentinian Di Stefano (three goals) and the Hungarian Ferenc Puskas (four) emphatically drove home their superiority.

Kariba dam among wonders of world

May 17. The fabled Snake River God of the mighty Zambezi was tamed today when Queen Elizabeth the Queen Mother started the hydro-electric turbines of the Kariba dam. She said the "young and enterprising" Central African Federation of Rhodesia and Nyasaland had "created a marvel of modern engineering which in future may rank with the Seven Wonders of the Ancient World. I pray that Kariba may be the symbol of a new and wider understanding throughout the Federation."

Princess Margaret looks suitably radiant as she is driven by coach from Buckingham Palace to Westminster Abbey where she married Mr Anthony Armstrong-Jones, a fashionable commercial photographer.

1960

JUNE

Su	Mo	Tu	We	Th	Fr	Sa
			1	2	3	4
5	6	7	8	9	10	11
12	13	14	15	16	17	18
19	20	21	22	23	24	25
26	27	28	29	30		

1. London: Plans to introduce colour TV are "shelved indefinitely" (→22).

2. Washington: Eisenhower sends 120 USAF planes to south-east Asia (→26/10).

7. UK: The first NHS hearing aids are issued (→30/1/61).

8. Buenos Aires: The Argentine government demands the return of Adolf Eichmann from Israel (→20/12).

9. UK: One of Britain's oldest quality cars, the Armstrong Siddeley, is to go out of production, it is announced.

11. Rome: Ingrid Bergman's marriage to Roberto Rossellini is annulled.

12. New Delhi: 783 Sikhs are arrested while demonstrating for an independent Sikh state (→12/12/61).

15. Tokyo: One person killed in riots in protest at the new US-Japanese treaty (→12/10).

16. Nyasaland: The state of emergency is lifted (→4/8)

17. Belgian Congo: Joseph Kasavubu will be the colony's first president when it becomes independent this month (→21).

19. Belgium: Two British drivers, Bristow and Stacey, die in the Belgian Grand Prix; Stirling Moss is injured.

21. Zurich: West German Armin Hary runs the 100 metres in a record 10 seconds.

21. Belgian Congo: Lumumba is asked to be the first premier of independent Congo.→

22. London: The House of Lords urges the proposed "Press Council" to be "given some teeth" (→17/10).

22. Liverpool: Eleven die in a blaze in one of the city's biggest department stores.

24. Coventry: Epstein's last major work "St. Michael and the Devil" is unveiled at the Cathedral.

26. Africa: British Somaliland and French Madagascar become independent (→1/7).

28. UK: 28 miners die in a pit accident at the village of Six Bells, Monmouthshire.

Sino-Soviet split brought into open

June 22. The barely-concealed rift between the Soviet Union and China went public today, when Nikita Khrushchev launched a bitter attack on Mao Tse-tung and Chinese policies. Speaking at the Rumanian Party Congress in Bucharest, Khrushchev denounced the Chinese leader as another Stalin, and said the Chinese simply did not understand the meaning of modern war.

In turn, the Chinese speaker attacked Khrushchev as a "revisionist" who failed to grasp the true nature and real strength of imperialism. The two Communist giants have been sniping at each other for months in press articles, but this is the first time Khrushchev has told the Chinese just what he thought of them (→18/10).

Psycho opens to shower of applause

Tony Perkins as "Norman Bates".

June 30. Alfred Hitchcock, fastidious depicter of violence, has outdone himself in "Psycho". It leads up to a killing in a motel shower so suggestively that the horror can be left mainly to the audience's imagination.

The psychopath of the title is the motel owner, played by Anthony Perkins, who arouses our forebodings for the victim, Janet Leigh, from the moment she checks in.

Bitter birth for independent Congo

'ome of the 100,000 revellers who celebrated the Congo's independence.

Lumumba, the Congolese leader.

une 30. After 80 years of Belgian ule, the independence of the :ongo was proclaimed today in itterness and acrimony. Speaking t the ceremony in the Palais de la Jation, King Baudouin dwelt on ne benefits Belgium had bestowed n the Congo, a territory the size of ndia, but with a population of only 2 million. "For 80 years we sent ou the best of our sons," he said, s he presented the purple Order of eopold to the Congo's first Prime Ainister, the fiery 34-year-old atrice Lumumba, a former postal clerk. When Lumumba spoke, however, he launched into a furious denunciation of Belgian rule.

The assembled notables, perspiring in the sticky tropical heat and already bored with speeches, sat up as Lumumba cried: "We had to submit to ironies, insults and blows day and night because we were black. In towns there were magnificent houses for whites, while there were only broken-down hovels for blacks. A black man was not allowed into cinemas, restaurants and shops. The black man paraded on foot like a hen, while the whites travelled in luxury in motor cars." Throughout the King sat with hands clasped, gazing ahead.

Afterwards, a hasty meeting of Belgian ministers was held to consider whether the King should leave at once. He decided to carry on, but the official lunch was delayed. As a royal aide put it: "Who feels like food after having to stomach a speech like that?" The infant state has got off to an inauspicious start (→6/7).

Terrified spectators scramble vainly to escape as an aluminium tower crashes to the ground at the Indianapolis 500 race; two were killed.

Patterson first to regain a lost title

June 20. The world heavyweight title is back in the United States after just a year in European hands. Floyd Patterson delivered a merciless left hook to the head of Ingemar Johansson half-way through the fifth round of their return bout, to knock the champion out and administer the first defeat in the Swede's 23-fight career.

For Patterson the revenge was sweet, and made him the first heavyweight to regain a lost world title, a feat that has eluded such greats as James J. Corbett, Jim Jeffries, Jack Dempsey and Joe Louis.

Patterson's revenge on Johansson.

Jaguar buries its fangs in Daimler

June 19. Daimler, a household name since the firm was founded in 1896 to exploit the German Daimler patents, today changed hands. The firm has merged with the much-younger Jaguar whose chairman Sir William Lyons said: "Our urgent need for expansion will be met by this acquisition."

The price, undisclosed, is said to be near £3.5 million. The new factory acquired by Sir William is only a short drive away from his Coventry premises. Daimler cars will continue to be built, along with buses and armoured cars.

Plans to counter concern over high-rises

June 2. City planners in London today outlined eight rules by which they hope to control the spate of high-rise buildings which is transforming the capital's skyline. From the docklands in the East End to the South Bank in the heart of the city, blocks of flats and offices have been built on sites often left derelict by wartime bombing.

Now, planners from London County Council want new projects to meet various aesthetic standards, such as effects on existing buildings and open spaces. Although it is offices such as the new Shell building overlooking the Thames which prompted the rules, many ordinary Londoners are upset are being uprooted from close-knit communities to find themselves marooned in tower blocks in the sky.

1960

JULY

Su	Mo	Tu	We	Th	Fr	Sa
					1	2
3	4	5	6	7	8	9
10	11	12	13	14	15	16
17	18	19	20	21	22	23
24	25	26	27	28	29	30
31						

1. Africa: Newly independent Somaliland and the UN-run former Italian Somaliland unite as the republic of Somalia.

2. Wimbledon: Neale Fraser beats Rod Laver in the all-Australian men's singles final; Maria Bueno beats Sue Reynolds in the women's singles final.

3. France: Australia's Jack Brabham wins the French Grand Prix.

6. Congo: The Congolese Army mutinies against Lumumba's government and European settlers (→8).

8. Congo: The army mutiny ends as all white officers are dismissed; many whites flee the capital Leopoldville.→

8. Moscow: U-2 pilot Gary Powers is indicted as a spy (→19/8).

12. Moscow: Khrushchev vows to back Cuba in any effort to expel the US from its Guantanamo Bay naval base.

12. Africa: French Congo, Chad and the Central African Republic become independent from France.

13. Los Angeles: Kennedy wins the Democratic presidential nomination, beating Senator Lyndon Johnson (→15).

15. Congo: The first UN troops arrive (→28).

18. UK: Donald Campbell takes his new £1 million "Bluebird" car for its first test run.

22. Moscow: The Kremlin says that nuclear war is not inevitable (→21/10).

27. Chicago: Vice-President Nixon is the Republican presidential nominee (→26/9).

27. London: The Earl of Home becomes Foreign Secretary with Edward Heath as his deputy (→2/10).

28. Congo: UN chief Dag Hammarskjold arrives in Leopoldville (→3/8).

DEATH

6. British statesman Aneurin "Nye" Bevan (*15/11/1897).→

Kennedy launches idea of a New Frontier

John F. Kennedy (l.), with his younger brothers Robert (c.) and Edward.

July 15. Senator John F. Kennedy touched many chords of American history today when he said the nation must move to a "New Frontier". In his acceptance speech for the presidential nomination at the last session of the Los Angeles Democratic Convention he linked himself with the two great Democratic presidents of this century, Woodrow Wilson and Franklin Roosevelt.

He said: "Franklin Roosevelt's New Deal promised security and succour to those in need. But the New Frontier of which I speak is not a set of promises – it is a set of challenges." It was a direct appeal to the frontier spirit in which the early Americans settled the empty lands of the West. In an astute move to win votes in the South, Kennedy chose Texan Lyndon Johnson, as running mate (→27).

Chichester in record solo Atlantic trip

July 21. The solo Atlantic sailor Francis Chichester sailed into New York in Gypsy Moth II today, setting a new record of 40 days for the crossing from Plymouth.

The 58-year-old sailor, who has had lung cancer for two years, battled against hurricane-strength winds for part of the voyage. His clothes were tossed about so much in the 39-foot sloop's lockers that holes were worn in them; he had to abandon a plan to dine every evening in a dinner jacket because it became mouldy.

Gypsy Moth II nears New York.

Copper-rich Katanga splits from Congo and civil war begins

A white colonist, accused of possessing an illegal firearm, is arrested.

July 11. The 11-day-old Congo Republic is facing disintegration tonight after its richest province, copper-rich Katanga, declared its independence under Moise Tshombe, a three-times-bankrupt businessman.

Katanga, like the rest of the country, is in chaos, with Belgian paratroops, flown in three days ago, desperately seeking to halt an orgy of looting and killing. Ten Europeans have been killed by Congolese mobs in the provincial capital of Elisabethville in 24 hours.

When the Force Publique mutinied six days after independence, there was rioting, rape and looting. Belgians fled in their thousands over the River Congo to Brazzaville, bitterly accusing the Brussels government of betraying them, and the paras were sent in (→15).

Nye Bevan, orator and rebel, is dead

Nye Bevan: the people's friend.

July 6. Aneurin Bevan, the most controversial politician in the land, died of cancer today. He was 62. Parliament has lost its finest orator since Lloyd George and its most turbulent post-war figure.

Bevan could enthuse, beguile, seduce or enrage his audience with words. He was also a rasping demagogue who surprised himself with what he said.

Nye had a terrible urge to claw down his enemies. "Lower than vermin," he once screamed about the Tories. "A squalid nuisance," Winston Churchill called him.

His monument is the National Health Service. He was Minister of Health in the 1945 Labour Cabinet. Then he quarrelled with the party leadership and revelled in the role of chief rebel (→27).

First woman PM is elected in Ceylon

July 21. Mrs Sirimavo Bandaranaike, widow of the assassinated Prime Minister and leader of Ceylon's Sri Lanka Freedom Party, was sworn in today as the world's first woman Prime Minister. In the general election yesterday her party won 75 seats out of 150.

Mrs Bandaranaike, who entered politics only after the death of her husband last September, swore to carry on his "socialist programmes which reflect the national aspirations of the people".

1960

AUGUST

Su	Mo	Tu	We	Th	Fr	Sa
	1	2	3	4	5	6
7	8	9	10	11	12	13
14	15	16	17	18	19	20
21	22	23	24	25	26	27
28	29	30	31			

2. Malaya: The state of emergency is lifted.

3. Congo: Rebel Moise Tshombe mobilises Katangan troops against UN forces (→8).

4. London: Agreement is reached on a new constitution for Nyasaland (→15/1/61).

7. Havana: Castro nationalises all US-owned property in retaliation for "US economic aggression" (→3/1/61).

8. New York: UN chief Hammarskjold tells Belgium to pull out of the Congo (→14).

13. London: Beer goes up one penny a pint to 1/7d (→4/6/61).

14. Congo: Swedish troops replace Belgian forces (→16).

14. Portugal: Australian Jack Brabham wins the Portuguese Grand Prix to become Formula One world champion.

16. Congo: Lumumba declares martial law for six months (→5/9).

17. London: Penguin Books shelves plans to publish "Lady Chatterley's Lover", saying it expects legal action (→19).

19. USSR: A spaceship carrying two dogs is launched as a trial run for putting a man into space (→22).

19. London: Penguin Books is summonsed for planning to publish "Lady Chatterley's Lover" (→8/9).

22. USSR: Two dogs are safely retrieved when their spaceship returns to earth (→12/1/61).

22. Edinburgh: A satirical review called "Beyond the Fringe" opens at the Edinburgh Festival.

25. Rome: The Olympic Games open.

26. S. Africa: The state of emergency declared after the Sharpeville massacre is lifted (→5/10).

29. Amman: Jordanian premier Hazza Majali is assassinated with ten others by a time bomb (→2/5/61).

31. Berlin: The East Germans close the border with West Berlin.

Soviet court finds US pilot guilty of spying

Francis Gary Powers, shot down over Russia, stands trial for espionage.

Aug 19. A Soviet court today sentenced Francis Gary Powers, the American U-2 pilot, to ten years' detention for flying a spy mission over the Soviet Union. Powers, who was shot down near Sverdlovsk, the Soviet armaments centre in the Urals, will spend three years in prison and the rest in a labour camp. Powers, pleading guilty at the three-day trial, said he was sorry and had acted on orders from the Central Intelligence Agency.

His high-flying reconnaissance aircraft was shot down in May by a ground-to-air missile after flying over Soviet missile sites and arms factories from a US base in Pakistan. The flight led to the collapse of the summit in Paris, between President Eisenhower and Premier Khrushchev, and the cancellation of the president's planned visit to the Soviet Union (→8/1/61).

Ex-premier to head Laos again after coup

Aug 9. Prince Souvanna Phouma is to head a new government in Laos, following today's coup led by paratrooper Captain Kong Le. The Prince was briefly Prime Minister three years ago, when he formed a coalition with the pro-Communist Laos Patriotic Front. Since then Laos has been pro-Western, but it now seems that the government will be neutral. Captain Kong Le has pledged to "keep the nation, its religion, King and constitution in progress" (→29/12).

Three-way charter makes Cyprus free

Aug 16. Cyprus became a republic at midnight, with a 21-gun salute but little crowd enthusiasm. People stayed away in case there were riots. British rule now ends, and Archbishop Makarios becomes President, with the Turkish-Cypriot Dr Kutchuk as Vice-President. Sir Hugh Foot, the withdrawing British Governor, made an appeal for peace. "People who have been at the edge of hell do not want to go back," he said (→20/1/61).

1960 Rome

Sweltering Rome Olympics beamed to the world

The Rome Olympic Games, held at the height of a hot Mediterranean summer, against medical advice and to the detriment of many performances, was none the less a spectacular success; the first to get saturation TV coverage and to be watched world-wide.

Unfortunately, the correspondingly increased lure of Olympic glory became too powerful for some. A young Danish cyclist, Knut Jensen, collapsed, hit his head and died in the heat of the cycling road race; the post-mortem found that he had taken a stimulant drug before the race, which once again raised questions about the win-at-all-costs attitudes that have crept into the Olympic arena.

British performances were on the whole disappointing, partly because the team arrived too late to adjust properly to the heat. However, the 19-year-old Huddersfield clerk, Anita Lonsborough, won the 200 metres breaststroke with a superbly controlled swim, and another clerk, Don Thompson, the "Mighty Mouse" from Middlesex, prepared himself to perfection in a steam-filled bathroom at home to win the 50-kilometre walk.

The Tennessee beauty, Wilma Rudolph – a polio victim who could not walk properly until she was eight – won all three sprint golds for the USA, but her record-breaking 100 metres run of 11 seconds was disallowed because of a light following wind. American men, however, won no sprint events; Armin Hary of Germany won the 100 metres and, to fervent patriotic acclaim, Livio Berruti took Italy's only athletics gold medal in the 200 metres.

Athletes from the Antipodes dominated the middle distances. Young Peter Snell of New Zealand beat the world record holder to win the 800 metres; Herb Elliot of Australia took the 1,500 metres in a magnificent new world record; and Murray Halberg of New Zealand won the 5,000 metres.

Finally, along an Appian Way lit by flaming torches, an unknown Ethiopian, Abebe Bikila, barefoot and untroubled, led home the marathon runners to win the first track and field gold medal ever to go to Africa.

Wilma Rudolph (USA) shows off her golds for 100- and 200-metre sprints and 400-metre relay.

Barefooted Abebe Bikila of Ethiopia wins 26-mile marathon in a new record time. "I could have gone round again without any difficulty", he said.

Light-heavyweight Cassius Clay (USA) shows an unusual, fleet-footed style on his way to a boxing gold. Some say he may become World Champion.

Men Athletics

100m			
1. Armin Hary	GER	*10.2	
2. David Sime	USA	10.2	
3. Peter Radford	GBR	10.3	
200m			
1. Livio Berruti	ITA	=*20.5	
2. Lester Carney	USA	20.6	
3. Abdoulaye Seye	FRA	20.7	
400m			
1. Otis Davis	USA	**44.9	
2. Carl Kaufmann	GER	**44.9	
3. Malcolm Spence	SAF	45.5	
800m			
1. Peter Snell	NZL	*1:46.3	
2. Roger Moens	BEL	1:46.5	
3. George Kerr	JAM	1:47.1	
1500m			
1. Herb Elliot	AUS	*3:35.6	
2. Michel Jazy	FRA	3:38.4	
3. István Rózsavölgyi	HUN	3:39.2	
5000m			
1. Murray Halberg	NZL	13:43.4	
2. Hans Grodotzki	GER	13:44.6	
3. Kazimierz Zimny	POL	13:44.8	
10,000m			
1. Pyotr Bolotnikov	URS	*28:32.2	
2. Hans Grodotzki	GER	28:37.0	
3. David Power	AUS	28:38.2	
Marathon			
1. Abebe Bikila	ETH	2:15:16.2	
2. Rhadi Ben Abdesselem	MAR	2:15:41.6	
3. Barry Magee	NZL	2:17:18.2	
110m Hurdles			
1. Lee Calhoun	USA	13.8	
2. Willie May	USA	13.8	
3. Hayes Jones	USA	14.0	
400m Hurdles			
1. Glenn Davis	USA	*49.3	
2. Clifton Cushman	USA	49.6	
3. Richard Howard	USA	49.7	
3000m Steeplechase			
1. Zdzilaw Kryszkowiak	POL	*8:34.2	
2. Nikolai Sokolov	URS	8:36.4	
3. Semyon Rzhischin	URS	8:42.2	
4x100m Relay			
1. GER	**39.5		(Bernd Cullman, Armin Hary, Walter Mahlendorf, Martin Lauer)
2. URS	40.1		(Gusman Kosanov, Leonid Barteniev, Yuri Konovalov, Edvin Ozolin)
3. GBR	40.2		(Peter Radford, David Jones, David Segal, Neville Whitehead)
4x400m Relay			
1. USA	**3:02.2		(Jack Yerman, Earl Young, Glenn Davis, Otis Davis)
2. GER	3:02.7		(Hans-Joachim Reske, Manfred Kinder, Johannes Kaiser, Carl Kaufmann)
3. BWI	3:04.0		(Malcolm Spence, James Wedderburn, Keith Gardner, George Kerr)
20km Walk			
1. Vladimir Golubnichiy	URS	1:34:07.2	
2. Noel Freeman	AUS	1:34:16.4	
3. Stanley Vickers	GBR	1:34:56.4	
50km Walk			
1. Donald Thompson	GBR	*4:25:30.0	
2. John Ljunggren	SWE	4:25:47.0	
3. Abdon Pamich	ITA	4:27:55.4	
High Jump			
1. Robert Shavlakadze	URS	*2.16	
2. Valery Brumel	URS	2.16	
3. John Thomas	USA	2.14	
Pole Vault			
1. Donald Bragg	USA	*4.70	
2. Ronald Morris	USA	4.60	
3. Eeles Landström	FIN	4.55	
Long Jump			
1. Ralph Boston	USA	*8.12	
2. Irvin Roberson	USA	8.11	
3. Igor Ter-Ovanesyan	URS	8.04	
Triple Jump			
1. Józef Schmidt	POL	16.81	
2. Vladimir Goryayev	URS	16.63	
3. Vitold Keyer	URS	16.43	
Shotput			
1. William Nieder	USA	*19.68	
2. Parry O'Brien	USA	19.11	
3. Dallas Long	USA	19.01	
Discus			
1. Alfred Oerter	USA	*59.18	
2. Richard Babke	USA	58.02	
3. Richard Cochran	USA	57.16	
Hammer			
1. Vasily Rudenkov	URS	*67.10	
2. Gyula Zsivótzky	HUN	65.79	
3. Tadeusz Rut	POL	65.64	
Javelin			
1. Viktor Tsibulenko	URS	84.64	
2. Walter Krüger	GER	79.36	
3. Gergely Kulcsár	HUN	78.57	
Decathlon			
1. Rafer Johnson	USA	*8392	
2. Yang Chuan-Kwang	TAI	8334	
3. Vassily Kusnyetsov	URS	7809	

Women Athletics

100m			
1. Wilma Rudolph	USA	11.0	
2. Dorothy Hyman	GBR	11.3	
3. Giuseppina Leone	ITA	11.3	
200m			
1. Wilma Rudolph	USA	24.0	
2. Jutta Heine	GER	24.4	
3. Dorothy Hyman	GBR	24.7	
800m			
1. Lyudmila Shevtsova	URS	**2:04.3	
2. Brenda Jones	AUS	2:04.4	
3. Ursula Donath	GER	2:05.6	
80m Hurdles			
1. Irina Press	URS	10.8	
2. Carol Quinton	GBR	10.9	
3. Gisela Birkemeyer	GER	11.0	
4x100m Relay			
1. USA	44.5		(Martha Hudson, Lucinda Williams, Barbara Jones, Wilma Rudolph)
2. GER	44.8		(Martha Langbein, Annie Biechl, Brunhilde Hendrix, Jutta Heine)
3. POL	45.0		(Teresa Wieczorek, Barbara Janiszewska, Celina Jesionowska, Halina Richter)
High Jump			
1. Iolanda Balas	ROM	*1.85	
2. Jaroslawa Jozwiakowska	POL	1.71	
2. Dorothy Shirley	GBR	1.71	
Long Jump			
1. Vyera Krepkina	URS	*6.37	
2. Elzbieta Krzesinska	POL	6.27	
3. Hildrun Claus	GER	6.21	
Shotput			
1. Tamara Press	URS	17.32	
2. Johanna Lüttge	GER	16.61	
3. Earlene Brown	USA	16.42	
Discus			
1. Nina Ponomaryeva	URS	*55.10	
2. Tarama Press	URS	52.59	
3. Lia Manoliu	ROM	52.36	
Javelin			
1. Elvira Ozolina	URS	*55.98	
2. Dana Zátopková	TCH	53.78	
3. Birute Kalediene	URS	53.45	

Men Swimming

100m Freestyle			
1. John Devitt	AUS	*55.2	
2. Lance Larson	USA	*55.2	
3. Manuel Dos Santos	BRA	55.4	
400m Freestyle			
1. Murray Rose	AUS	*4:18.3	
2. Tsuyoshi Yamanaka	JAP	4:21.4	
3. John Konrads	AUS	4:21.8	
1500m Freestyle			
1. John Konrads	AUS	*17:19.6	
2. Murray Rose	AUS	17:21.7	
3. George Breen	USA	17:30.6	
100m Backstroke			
1. David Theile	AUS	*1:01.9	
2. Frank McKinney	USA	1:02.1	
3. Robert Bennett	USA	1:02.3	
200m Breaststroke			
1. William Mulliken	USA	2:37.4	
2. Yoshihiko Osaki	JAP	2:38.[illegible]	
3. Wieger Emile Mensonides	NETH	2:39.7	
200m Butterfly			
1. Michael Troy	USA	**2:12.[illegible]	
2. Neville Hayes	AUS	2:14.6	
3. J. David Gillanders	USA	2:15.3	
4x200m Freestyle Relay			
1. USA	**8:10.2		(George Harrison, Richard Blick, Michael Troy, F. Jeffrey Farrell)
2. JAP	8:13.2		(Makoto Fukui, Hiroshi Ishii, Tsuyoshi Yamanaka, Tatsuo Fujimoto)
3. AUS	8:13.8		(David Dickson, John Devitt, Murray Rose, John Konrads)
4x100m Medley Relay			
1. USA	**4:05.4		(Frank McKinney, Paul Hait, Lance Larrson, F. Jeffrey Farrell)
2. AUS	4:12.0		(David Theile, Terry Gathercole, Neville Hayes, Geoffrey Shipton)
3. JAP	4:12.2		(Kazuo Tomita, Koichi Hirakida, Yoshihiko Osaki, Keigo Shimizu)
Springboard Diving			
1. Gary Tobian	USA	170.00	
2. Samuel Hall	USA	167.08	
3. Juan Botella	MEX	162.30	
Platform Diving			
1. Robert Webster	USA	165.56	
2. Gary Tobian	USA	165.25	
3. Brian Phelps	GBR	157.13	

1960 Rome

Water Polo

1. Italy
2. Soviet Union
3. Hungary

Women Swimming

100m Freestyle
1. Dawn Fraser AUS *1:01.2
2. Susan Christine von Saltza USA 1:02.8
3. Natalie Steward GBR 1:03.1

400m Freestyle
1. Susan Christine von Saltza USA 4:50.6
2. Jane Cederqvist SWE 4:53.9
3. Catharina Lagerberg NETH 4:56.9

200m Breaststroke
1. Anita Lonsbrough GBR **2:49.5
2. Wiltrud Urselmann GER 2:50.0
3. Barbara Göbel GER 2:53.6

100m Backstroke
1. Lynn Burke USA *1:09.5
2. Natalie Steward GBR 1:10.8
3. Satoko Tanaka JAP 1:11.4

100m Butterfly
1. Carolyn Schuler USA *1:09.5
2. Marianne Heemskerk NETH 1:10.4
3. Janice Andrew AUS 1:12.2

4x100m Freestyle Relay
1. USA **4:08.9 (Joan Spillane, Shirley Stobs, Carolyn Wood, Susan Christine von Saltza)
2. AUS 4:11.3 (Dawn Fraser, Ilsa Konrads, Lorraine Crapp, Alva Colquhoun)
3. GER 4:19.7 (Christel Steffin, Heidi Pechstein, Gisela Weiss, Ursula Brunner)

4x100m Medley Relay
1. USA 4:41.1 (Lynn Burke, Patty Kempner, Carolyn Schuler, Susan Christine von Saltza)
2. AUS 4:45.9 (Marilyn Wilson, Rosemary Lassig, Janice Andrew, Dawn Fraser)
3. GER 4:47.6 (Ingrid Schmidt, Ursula Küper, Bärbel Fuhrmann, Ursel Brunner)

Springboard Diving
1. Ingrid Krämer GER 155.81
2. Paula Jean Pope USA 141.24
3. Elizabeth Ferris GBR 139.09

Platform Diving
1. Ingrid Krämer GER 91.28
2. Paula Jean Pope USA 88.94
3. Ninel Krutova URS 86.99

Boxing

Flyweight
1. Gyula Török HUN
2. Sergei Sivko URS
3. Kioshi Tanabe JAP
3. Abdelmoneim Elguindi EGY

Bantamweight
1. Oleg Grigoryev URS
2. Primo Zamparini ITA
3. Oliver Taylor AUS
3. Brunon Bendig POL

Featherweight
1. Francesco Musso ITA
2. Jerzy Adamski POL
3. Jorma Limmonen FIN
3. William Meyers SAF

Lightweight
1. Kazimierz Pazdzior POL
2. Sandro Lopopolo ITA
3. Richard McTaggart GBR
3. Abel Laudonio ARG

Light Welterweight
1. Bohumil Nemecek TCH
2. Clement Quartey GHA
3. Quincey Daniels USA
3. Marian Kasprzyk POL

Welterweight
1. Giovanni Benvenuti ITA
2. Yuri Radonyak URS
3. Leszek Drogosz POL
3. James Lloyd GBR

Light Middleweight
1. Wilbert McClure USA
2. Carmelo Bossi ITA
3. Boris Lagutin URS
3. William Fisher GBR

Middleweight
1. Edward Crook USA
2. Tadeusz Walesek POL
3. Ion Monea ROM
3. Evgeny Feofanov URS

Light Heavyweight
1. Cassius Clay USA
2. Zbigniew Pietrzykowski POL
3. Giulio Saraudi ITA
3. Anthony Madigan AUS

Heavyweight
1. Franco de Piccoli ITA
2. Daniel Bekker SAF
3. Günter Siegmund GER
3. Josef Nemec TCH

Greco Roman Wrestling

Flyweight
1. Dumitru Pirvulescu ROM
2. Osman Sayed EGY
3. Mohammad Paziraii IRN

Bantamweight
1. Oleg Karavayev URS
2. Ion Cernea ROM
3. Dinko Petrov BUL

Featherweight
1. Müzahir Sille TUR
2. Imre Polyák HUN
3. Konstantin Vyrupayev URS

Lightweight
1. Avtandil Koridze URS
2. Branislav Martinovic YUG
3. Gustav Freij SWE

Welterweight
1. Mithat Bayrak TUR
2. Günter Maritschnigg GER
3. René Schiermeyer FRA

Middleweight
1. Dimiter Dobrev BUL
2. Lothar Metz GER
3. Ion Taranu ROM

Light Heavyweight
1. Tevfik Kis TUR
2. Kralyu Bimbalov BUL
3. Givy Kartozlya URS

Heavyweight
1. Ivan Bogdan URS
2. Wilfried Dietrich GER
3. Bohumil Kubat TCH

Freestyle Wrestling

Bantamweight
1. Terrence McCann USA
2. Nezhdet Zalev BUL
3. Tadeusz Trojanowski POL

Flyweight
1. Ahmet Bilek TUR
2. Masayuki Matsubara JAP
3. Mohammad Seifpour IRN

Featherweight
1. Mustafa Dangistanli TUR
2. Stoncho Kolev BUL
3. Vladimir Rubashvili URS

Lightweight
1. Shelby Wilson USA
2. Vladimir Sinyavsky URS
3. Enyu Dimov BUL

Welterweight
1. Douglas Blubaugh USA
2. Ismail Ogan TUR
3. Muhammed Bashir PAK

Middleweight
1. Hasan Güngör TUR
2. Georgy Skhirtladze URS
3. Hans Yngve Antonsson SWE

Light Heavyweight
1. Ismet Atli TUR
2. Gholam Reza Takhti IRN
3. Anatoly Albul URS

Super Heavyweight
1. Wilfried Dietrich GER
2. Hamit Kaplan TUR
3. Savkus Dzarassov URS

Men Fencing

Foil Individual
1. Viktor Zhdanovich URS
2. Yuri Sissikin URS
3. Albert Axelrod USA

Foil Team
1. Soviet Union
2. Italy
3. Germany

Epée Individual
1. Giuseppe Delfino ITA
2. Allan Jay GBR
3. Bruno Khabarov URS

Epée Team
1. Italy
2. Great Britain
3. Soviet Union

Sabre Individual
1. Rudolf Kárpáti HUN
2. Zoltán Horváth HUN
3. Wladimiro Calarese ITA

Sabre Team
1. Hungary
2. Poland
3. Italy

Women Fencing

Foil Individual
1. Heidi Schmid GER
2. Valentina Rastvorova URS
3. Maria Vicol ROM

Foil Team
1. Soviet Union
2. Hungary
3. Italy

Modern Pentathlon

Individual
1. Férenc Németh HUN 5024
2. Imre Nagy HUN 4988
3. Robert L. Beck USA 4981

Team
1. Hungary (Férenc Németh, Imre Nagy, András Balczó)
2. Soviet Union (Igor Novikov, Nikolai Tatarinov, Hanno Selg)
3. USA (Robert L. Beck, Jack Daniels, George Lambert)

Men Canoeing

Kayak-1 1000m
1. Erik Hansen DEN 3:53.00
2. Imre Szöllösi HUN 3:54.02
3. Gert Fredriksson SWE 3:55.89

Kayak-2 1000m
1. Sweden 3:34.73
2. Hungary 3:34.91
3. Poland 3:37.34

Canadian-1 1000m
1. János Parti HUN 4:33.93
2. Aleksandr Silayev URS 4:34.41
3. Leon Rotman ROM 4:35.87

Canadian-2 1000m
1. Soviet Union 4:17.94
2. Italy 4:20.77
3. Hungary 4:20.89

4x500m Kayak-1 Relay
1. GER 7:39.43 (Paul Lange, Günter Perleberg, Friedhelm Wentzke, Dieter Krause)
2. HUN 7:44.02 (Imre Szöllösi, Imre Kemecsey, András Szente, György Mészáros)
3. DEN 7:46.09 (Helmuth Sörensen, Arne Höyer, Erling Jessen, Erik Hansen)

Women Canoeing

Kayak-1 500m
1. Antonina Seredina URS 2:08.08
2. Therese Zenz GER 2:08.22
3. Daniela Walkowiak POL 2:10.46

Kayak-2 500m
1. Soviet Union 1:54.70
2. Germany 1:56.66
3. Hungary 1:58.22

Rowing

Single Sculls
1. Vyacheslav Ivanov URS 7:13.86
2. Achim Hill GER 7:20.21
3. Teodor Kocerka POL 7:21.26

Double Sculls
1. Czechoslovakia 6:47.50
2. Soviet Union 6:50.49
3. Switzerland 6:50.59

Coxless Pairs
1. Soviet Union 7:02.01
2. Austria 7:03.69
3. Finland 7:03.80

Coxed Pairs
1. Germany 7:29.14
2. Soviet Union 7:30.17
3. USA 7:34.58

Coxless Fours
1. USA 6:26.26
2. Italy 6:28.78
3. Soviet Union 6:29.62

Coxed Fours
1. Germany 6:39.12
2. France 6:41.62
3. Italy 6:43.72

Eights
1. Germany 5:57.18
2. Canada 6:01.52
3. Czechoslovakia 6:04.84

Yachting

Finn
1. Paul Elvström DEN 8171
2. Aleksandr Chuchelov URS 6520
3. André Nelis BEL 5934

Star
1. Soviet Union 7619
2. Portugal 6665
3. USA 6269

Flying Dutchman
1. Norway 6774
2. Denmark 5991
3. Germany 5882

Dragon
1. Greece 6733
2. Argentina 5715
3. Italy 5704

5.5m
1. USA 6900
2. Denmark 5678
3. Soviet Union 5122

Cycling

Individual Road Race
1. Viktor Kapitonov URS 4:20:37.0
2. Livio Trapè ITA 4:20:37.0
3. Willy van der Berghen BEL 4:20:57.0

100km Team Time Trial
1. Italy 2:14:33.53
2. Germany 2:16:56.31
3. Soviet Union 2:18:41.67

1000m Time Trial
1. Sante Gaiardoni ITA 1:07.27
2. Dieter Gieseler BEL 1:08.75
3. Rostilav Vargashkin ITA 1:08.86

1000m Sprint
1. Sante Gaiardoni ITA 11.1
2. Leo Sterckx BEL
3. Valentino Gasparella ITA

2000m Tandem
1. Italy 10.7
2. Germany
3. Soviet Union

4000m Team Pursuit
1. Italy 4:30.90
2. Germany 4:35.78
3. Soviet Union 4:34.05

(In the race held to determine 3rd place, the Soviets were faster than the Germans).

Weightlifting

		2 Arm Press	2 Arm Snatch	2 Arm Clean an Jerk	Total
Bantamweight					
1. Charles Vinci	USA	=*105.0	=**107.5	132.5	=**345.0
2. Yoshinobu Miyake	JAP	97.5	105.0	=*135.0	337.5
3. Esmaiil Elmkhan	IRN	97.5	100.0	132.5	330.0
Featherweight					
1. Yevgeny Minayev	URS	=**120.0	=*110.0	=*142.5	=**372.5
2. Isaac Berger	USA	117.5	105.0	140.0	362.5
3. Sebastiano Manniironi	ITA	107.5	=*110.0	135.0	352.5
Lightweight					
1. Viktor Buschyev	URS	=*125.0	*122.5	150.0	**397.5
2. Howe-Liang Tan	SIN	115.0	110.0	*155.0	380.0
3. Abdul Wahid Aziz	IRK	117.5	115.0	147.5	380.0
Middleweight					
1. Aleksandr Kurynov	URS	135.0	*132.5	**170.0	**437.5
2. Thomas Kono	USA	*140.0	127.5	160.0	427.5
3. Gyözö Veres	HUN	130.0	120.0	155.0	405.0
Light Heavyweight					
1. Ireneusz Palinski	POL	130.0	=*132.5	*180.0	442.5
2. James George	USA	132.5	=*132.5	165.0	430.0
3. Jan Bochenek	POL	130.0	120.0	170.0	420.0
Middleweight					
1. Arkady Vorobyov	URS	152.5	*142.5	=*177.5	**472.5
2. Trofim Lomakin	URS	**157.5	130.0	170.0	457.5
3. Louis Martin	GBR	137.5	137.5	170.0	445.0
Heavyweight					
1. Yuri Vlassov	URS	*180.0	*155.0	**202.5	**537.5
2. James Bradford	USA	*180.0	150.0	182.5	512.5
3. Norbert Schemansky	USA	170.0	150.0	180.0	500.0

Equestrian Sports

Three-Day Event Individual
1. Lawrence Morgan AUS
2. Neale Lavis AUS
3. Anton Bühler SUI

Three-Day Event Team
1. Australia -128.18
2. Switzerland -386.02
3. France -515.71

Individual Dressage
1. Sergei Filatov URS 2144.0
2. Gustav Fischer SUI 2087.0
3. Josef Neckermann GER 2082.0

Grand Prix Jumping Individual
1. Raimondo D'Inzeo ITA -12
2. Piero D'Inzeo ITA -16
3. David Broome GBR -23

Grand Prix Jumping Team
1. Germany -46.50
2. USA -66.00
3. Italy -80.50

Men Shooting

Free Rifle, 3 positions
1. Hubert Hammerer AUT
2. Hans Spillman SUI
3. Vassily Borissov URS

Small Bore Rifle, 50m Prone
1. Peter Kohnke GER 590
2. James Hill USA 589
3. Enrico Forcella Pelliccioni VEN 587

Small Bore Rifle, 3 positions
1. Viktor Shamburkin URS =*1149
2. Marat Niyasov URS 1145
3. Klaus Zähringer GER 1139

Rapid Fire Pistol
1. William McMillan USA =*587/147
2. Pentti Linnosvuo FIN =*587/139
3. Aleksandr Zabelin URS =*587/135

Free Pistol, 50m
1. Alexei Gustchin URS *560
2. Makhmud Umarov URS 552/26
3. Yoshihisa Yoshikawa JAP 552/20

Mixed Shooting

Clay Pigeon
1. Ion Dumitrescu ROM 192
2. Galliano Rossini ITA 191
3. Sergei Kelinin URS 190

Men Gymnastics

All-around Individual
1. Boris Shakhlin URS 115.95
2. Takashi Ono JAP 115.90
3. Yuri Titov URS 115.60

Combined Exercises Team
1. Japan 575.20
2. Soviet Union 572.70
3. Italy 559.05

Parallel Bars
1. Boris Shakhlin URS 19.400
2. Giovanni Carminucci ITA 19.375
3. Takashi Ono JAP 19.350

Floor Exercises
1. Nobuyuki Aihara JAP 19.450
2. Yuri Titov URS 19.325
3. Franco Menichelli ITA 19.275

Long Horse Vault
1. Boris Shakhlin URS 19.350
1. Takashi Ono JAP 19.350
3. Vladimir Portnoi URS 19.225

Sidehorse
1. Boris Shakhlin URS 19.375
1. Eugen Ekman FIN 19.375
3. Shuji Tsurumi JAP 19.150

Horizontal Bar
1. Takashi Ono JAP 19.600
2. Masao Takemoto JAP 19.525
3. Boris Shakhlin URS 19.475

Rings
1. Albert Azaryan URS 19.725
2. Boris Shakhlin URS 19.500
3. Takashi Ono JAP 19.425
3. Velik Kaspazov BUL 19.425

Women Gymnastics

Combined Exercises Team
1. Soviet Union 382.320
2. Czechoslovakia 373.323
3. Romania 372.053

All-around Individual
1. Larissa Latynina URS 77.031
2. Sofia Muratova URS 76.696
3. Polina Astakhova URS 76.164

Asymmetric Bars
1. Polina Astakhova URS 19.616
2. Larissa Latynina URS 19.416
3. Tamara Lyukhina URS 19.399

Floor Exercises
1. Larissa Latynina URS 19.583
2. Polina Astakhova URS 19.532
3. Tamara Lyukhina URS 19.449

Side Horse Vault
1. Margarita Nikolayeva URS 19.316
2. Sofia Muratova URS 19.049
3. Larissa Latynina URS 19.016

Balance Beam
1. Eva Bosáková TCH 19.283
2. Larissa Latynina URS 19.233
3. Sofia Muratova URS 19.232

Basketball

1. USA
2. Soviet Union
3. Brazil

Football

1. Yugoslavia
2. Denmark
3. Hungary

Hockey

1. Pakistan
2. India
3. Spain

(Key to symbols and abbreviations p. 1456)

1960

SEPTEMBER

Su	Mo	Tu	We	Th	Fr	Sa
				1	2	3
4	5	6	7	8	9	10
11	12	13	14	15	16	17
18	19	20	21	22	23	24
25	26	27	28	29	30	

1. Tanganyika: Julius Nyerere is appointed the colony's first Prime Minister (→9/12).

5. Rome: US boxers, including Cassius Clay, win three gold medals at the Olympics.

5. Congo: President Kasavubu sacks Lumumba but he refuses to quit (→9).

6. UK: Ten skeletons are discovered in 3,800-year-old graves at Stonehenge.

8. London: Penguin faces trial for planning to publish "Lady Chatterley's Lover"; Penguin says the book is art (→20/10).

9. Congo: Lumumba's troops invade Katanga.→

12. Berlin: The post of East German president is abolished; premier Walter Ulbricht becomes head of state (→17/7/61).

16. US: Donald Campbell destroys "Bluebird" in a crash at 350 mph, but he is only slightly hurt.

19. London: 344 tickets are issued in central London on the first day of parking tickets and traffic wardens (→27).

20. UK: Lester Piggott wins his 1,000th race and 150th this season.

20. Congo: Mobutu appoints the Congo's third government since independence (→21/11).

23. New York: Khrushchev demands Hammarskjold's removal as UN chief and the UN's removal from the US (→29).

27. London: Europe's first moving pavement or "Travelator" opens at Bank tube station (→15/3/61).

28. New York: Macmillan meets Nasser at the UN (→20/6/61).

29. New York: Khrushchev heckles and thumps his desk during Macmillan's speech to the UN Assembly (→30).

30. New York: 15 new African nations are admitted to the UN (→12/10).

DEATH

27. British suffragette Estelle Sylvia Pankhurst (*1882).

Kennedy and Nixon draw in TV debate

Presidential hopefuls Kennedy and Nixon end their television debate.

Sept 26. Across the USA, millions tuned in tonight to see Richard Nixon and John Kennedy thrash out their differences in the first nationally televised debate between presidential candidates. The debaters clashed only mildly, and viewers questioned after the hour-long broadcast agreed that the competition ended in a draw. Most said they had not changed their minds, or that they were still undecided about whom to vote for on November 8.

If no real heat was generated, nor was the debate all sweetness and light. Vice-President Nixon accused his Democratic opponent of being a reckless spendthrift at the expense of the taxpayers, saying that his programme would cost many billions of dollars.

Senator Kennedy picked up the gauntlet and turned the spotlight on Nixon's allegedly uncaring policies. He said the Vice-President gave only "lip service" to an increase in the minimum wage to a dollar an hour, expanding school construction, and providing medical care for the aged.

The debate, held in a Chicago television studio, was carried by all major media outlets (→9/11).

Congo army takes over under Mobutu

Sept 14. The head of the Congolese army, Colonel Joseph-Desire Mobutu, marched into a downtown bar in Leopoldville this evening and said he had taken over, he had sacked the two Josephs – the Congolese President, Joseph Kasavubu, and the premier, Joseph Ileo – and was suspending parliament.

Mobutu, aged 31, acted after weeks of confusion, during which Kasavubu and Patrice Lumumba, the Congolese premier, tried various times to sack each other, then to arrest each other before Lumumba arrested the Public Prosecutor (→20).

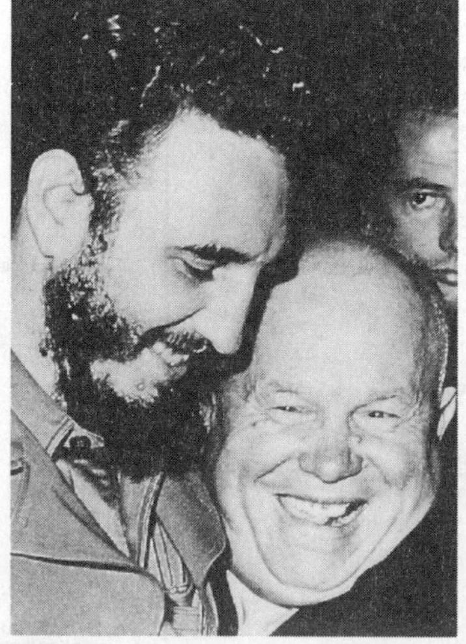

Cuba's Castro and Russia's Khrushchev embrace each other as comrades at the UN.

1960

OCTOBER

Su	Mo	Tu	We	Th	Fr	Sa
						1
2	3	4	5	6	7	8
9	10	11	12	13	14	15
16	17	18	19	20	21	22
23	24	25	26	27	28	29
30	31					

2. London: Anthony Wedgwood Benn resigns from Labour's National Executive Committee (→20).

2. Reykjavik: Iceland and Britain begin talks to settle their fishing dispute.

3. Nice: Brigitte Bardot leaves hospital after recovering from a suicide attempt.

5. S. Africa: The country's whites vote for a republic (→23/1/61).

9. UK: Southern England is hit by the worst flooding since 1953.

11. East Pakistan: Thousands die as the country is battered by a tidal wave and hurricane.

12. Tokyo: Protests follow yesterday's murder of Socialist leader Inejiro Asanuma by a right-wing student.→

14. Southern Rhodesia: 2,000 troops surround black townships (→17/2/61).

17. London: The News Chronicle is to close and merge with the Daily Mail (→25/1/61).

18. Moscow: Pravda prints its first attack on the Chinese Communists (→1/12).

19. London: A Royal Commission says the London County Council should be replaced by a Greater London Council.

20. London: Harold Wilson is to challenge Gaitskell for the Labour leadership (→3/11).

20. London: The Lady Chatterley trial opens at the Old Bailey; the judge tells the jury to read the book (→2/11).

21. UK: The Queen launches HMS Dreadnought, Britain's first nuclear submarine (→1/11).

21. UK: The Hawker P.1127 vertical take-off jet makes its first test flight.

22. US: Olympic boxing gold medallist Cassius Clay fights his first bout as a professional, in Louisville, Kentucky.

24. UK: Bertrand Russell resigns as leader of CND.

26. South Vietnam: The army clashes with Vietcong guerrillas (→10/4/61).

1960

Khrushchev in bid to bring UN to heel

Khrushchev's shoe takes a rest.

Oct 12. Two weeks ago, the United Nations General Assembly saw a furious Nikita Khrushchev heckle and thump his desk at Prime Minister Harold Macmillan. Today the Soviet leader cemented his reputation. When the Philippine delegate Lorenzo Sumulong accused the USSR of imperialism in Eastern Europe, Khrushchev waved his shoe in the air, slamming it down on the desk, calling his accuser "this jerk, this American stooge".

Later the US Assistant Secretary of State, Francis Wilcox, inspired another bout of brogue-brandishing, but the proceedings were finally adjourned in chaos after the Assembly's President, Mr Boland, smashed his gavel in rage at the insubordination of the Rumanian Foreign Minister (→27/10/61).

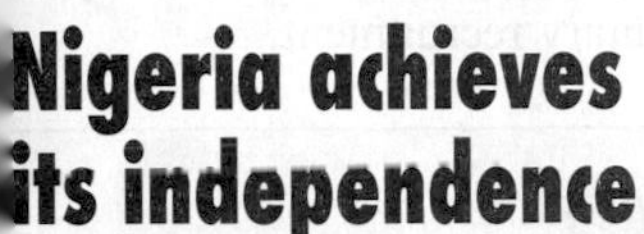

Nigeria achieves its independence

Oct 1. At the stroke of midnight last night, Britain's biggest colony became Africa's most populous independent state with 35 million people. It joins the Commonwealth under Prime Minister Sir Abubakar Tafawa Balewa, aged 48, a former schoolteacher, who spoke of the "affection and loyalty" Nigerians felt for Princess Alexandra, who is representing the Queen (→28/11).

Gaitskell will fight to save his Party

Oct 3. With sweat on his cheeks, and close to tears, Hugh Gaitskell told a largely hostile party conference today: "There are some of us who will fight and fight again to save the party we love."

The Labour leader's emotional speech failed to stop the conference from voting for unilateral nuclear disarmament, and the left-wing wants to get rid of him (→17).

Inejiro Asanuma, a Japanese MP, is assassinated at a political rally.

1960

NOVEMBER

Su	Mo	Tu	We	Th	Fr	Sa
		1	2	3	4	5
6	7	8	9	10	11	12
13	14	15	16	17	18	19
20	21	22	23	24	25	26
27	28	29	30			

1. London: Macmillan announces a bill to allow US nuclear submarines to use Holy Loch in Scotland (→7).

3. London: Gaitskell beats off Wilson's challenge to his leadership (→7).

4. UK: Severe flooding causes chaos in south-east England.

7. Moscow: Missiles appear for the first time at the annual parade in Red Square (→27/12).

9. UK: The world's first "hover-scooter" is demonstrated in Surrey.

10. UK: Penguin's first run of "Lady Chatterley's Lover", 200,000 copies, sells out on the first day of publication.

11. Saigon: Loyal troops crush a military coup attempt.

14. Central America: Nicaragua and Guatemala blame Cuba for recent unrest.

16. London: Broadcasting personality Gilbert Harding drops dead outside Broadcasting House.

17. UK: Viscount Stansgate dies; his son, MP Anthony Wedgwood Benn, succeeds to the title (→18).

18. UK: Michael Foot wins Nye Bevan's seat of Ebbw Vale in the by-election caused by his death (→23).

23. London: The new Viscount Stansgate returns his Letter Patent to the Queen in a bid to renounce his title (→16/3/61).

24. Congo: Lumumba escapes from the Congolese Army.

28. Lagos: Hundreds of students lobby Nigeria's parliament in protest at a planned defence pact with Britain.

DEATHS

5. US film pioneer and director Mack Sennett (*17/1/1880).

16. US actor Clark Gable (*1/2/01).→

16. British broadcaster Gilbert Charles Harding (*5/6/07).

17. British statesman William Wedgwood Benn, first Viscount Stansgate (*10/5/1877).

Wives or servants can read Lady C

Nov 2. Cheers and applause broke out in the Old Bailey courtroom today when a jury ruled that "Lady Chatterley's Lover", the novel banned for 30 years, is not obscene.

Penguin Books, who were prosecuted as a test case, have 200,000 copies ready to distribute at a price of 3s 6d. Sir Allen Lane, head of the firm, said it was now unlikely that there would be future prosecutions of any serious author.

During the six-day hearing Mr Mervyn Griffith-Jones, for the prosecution, said the book contained 13 "bouts" of sexual intercourse between Lady Chatterley and her husband's gamekeeper, Mellors, in many settings, "with the emphasis always on the pleasure, the satisfaction, the sensuality". One Anglo-Saxon word appeared 30 times, others 13 or 14. He asked the jury: "Is it a book you would wish your wife or your servant to read?"

Gable, the enduring heart-throb, dies

Clark Gable: "Frankly, my dear ..."

Nov 16. Clark Gable, the actor who once admitted "I can't emote worth a damn", despite playing the romantic hero of 90 films, has died, aged 59, following a heart attack while making his latest film "The Misfits". Gable, whose widow, and fifth wife, Kay Spreckels, is expecting a child in March, proved to be an unexpected and amazingly enduring heart-throb. ▷

Kennedy scrapes home

Still campaigning, John F. Kennedy addresses the crowds in New York.

Nov 9. After a night of uncertainty John Fitzgerald Kennedy emerged as the new President of the United States by a narrow margin. He obtained only 120,000 more in the popular vote than his Republican opponent, Vice-President Nixon.

Early returns favoured Kennedy, and shortly after midnight the several thousand Republicans waiting in the Los Angeles ballroom feared the worst. Standing next to his tearful wife, Pat, Nixon told them he thought he had lost. However, the pendulum then began to swing, and he did not formally concede until midday.

Kennedy walked into the Cape Cod Armoury at Hyannis, Massachusetts to accept. His pregnant wife, Jacqueline, was with him. He grinned and said: "So now my wife and I prepare for a new administration and a new baby."

At 43 Kennedy is the youngest man to win the Presidency. He is also the first Roman Catholic. His father is a self-made millionaire, who was wartime ambassador in London. Kennedy himself was brought up with Boston's elite, going to both Princeton and Harvard. He has many advisers from the East Coast universities and they are expecting government posts. It will be a big change from the businessmen who were favoured by President Eisenhower (→20/1/61).

Congolese army battles with UN troops

Nov 21. A battle between Congolese and UN troops took place tonight outside the house where the ambassador of Ghana, Nathaniel Welbeck, had barricaded himself in after refusing an order to leave the country.

The Congolese accused him of intriguing to bring back Patrice Lumumba, deposed as premier by Mobutu. UN troops from Tunisia and police from Ghana opened fire when the Congolese forces came near the house. A colonel and five other ranks were killed.

Firing continued into the early hours, with the Congolese using cannon and machine guns. Seven Tunisians are believed killed. The incident has soured already cool relations between Congo leaders and the UN force (→2/12).

1960

DECEMBER

Su	Mo	Tu	We	Th	Fr	Sa
				1	2	3
4	5	6	7	8	9	10
11	12	13	14	15	16	17
18	19	20	21	22	23	24
25	26	27	28	29	30	31

1. Moscow: The Soviet and Chinese Communist Parties admit serious differences.

2. Rome: The Pope has an historic meeting with the Archbishop of Canterbury, Dr Fisher.

2. UK: Vivien Leigh wins a divorce from Sir Laurence Olivier.

5. UK: Leyland Motors will take over Standard-Triumph International, it is announced.

9. Algiers: De Gaulle arrives on a visit.→

10. Stockholm: Nobel Prizes go to Donald Glaser (US, Physics); Willard Libby (US, Chemistry); Sir Burnet Macfarlane (Australia) and Peter Medawar (UK, Medicine); St. John Perse (France, Literature); and in Oslo to Albert Luthuli (South Africa, Peace).

15. Brussels: King Baudouin weds Dona Fabiola de Moran y Aragon of Spain (→23).

16. Addis Ababa: Haile Selassie returns as a coup staged two days ago collapses.

20. West Germany: Richard Baer, the last commandant of Auschwitz, is arrested.

23. Brussels: Fights break out in parliament amid nationwide strikes in protest at government austerity policies (→29).

27. Africa: France explodes a third atomic device in the Sahara (→1/2/61).

29. Belgium: King Baudouin cuts short his honeymoon to try to calm nationwide unrest (→6/1/61).

29. Vientiane: Laos appeals for UN aid against alleged North Vietnamese invaders.

HITS OF 1960

Cathy's Clown.

Please don't tease.

The girl of my best friend.

QUOTE OF THE YEAR

"[Politicians] are the same all over. They promise to build a bridge even when there is no river."

Nikita Khrushchev.

The last National Serviceman falls in

Dec 31. The last National Service men received their call-up cards today, bringing the total number of men enlisted under the scheme since it began in 1939 to 5,300,000. Of the 2,049 called-up today 1,99[illegible] will go into the army and 50 to the RAF; the intake of National Servicemen into the Royal Navy has always been small.

The last army intake are joining nine units in the Southern Command, based in Aldershot. They will remain there for a fortnight's basic training and then go on to other units to learn a trade. The air force recruits are all going through the RAF Reception Centre at Cardington, Bedfordshire. The ending of National Service means the forces will now have to rely entirely on voluntary recruitment.

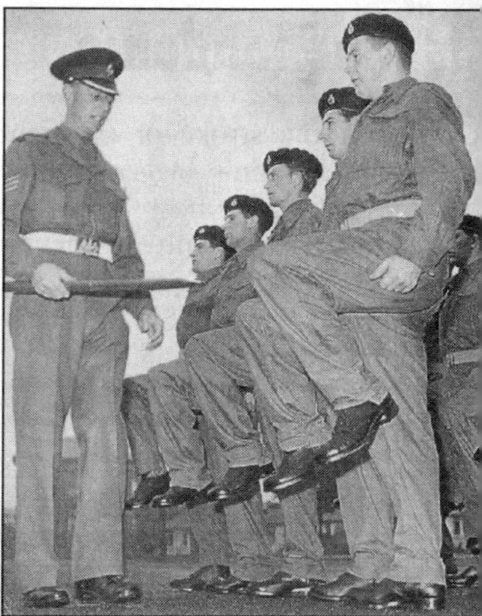

The last conscripts go on parade.

Test ends in a tie for the first time

Dec 14. With the scores level after five full days, Joe Solomon of the West Indies ran out Australia's Lindsay Kline off the seventh ball of Wes Hall's final over. For the first time in cricket history, a Test match had ended in a tie.

Australia had been close to victory, needing only six to win with three wickets left at the start of the last over. A catch at the wicket, a catch dropped, a run out, five scampered runs and finally Solomon's great throw completed the thrilling climax.

Lumumba is arrested

Former Congolese premier Lumumba and aides on their way to prison.

Dec 2. After a three-day manhunt Patrice Lumumba, the Congo's deposed premier, who escaped from house arrest in Leopoldville, was recaptured today 400 miles away at Port Francqui, on the road to his base at Stanleyville.

There troops loyal to Lumumba, expecting him to arrive at any moment, rounded up 1,000 European men, women and children and beat them up as a reprisal for Lumumba's house arrest. UN officials were present, but took no action to protect the Europeans. Lumumba was flown back to Leopoldville with his hands tied and driven to barracks in a lorry.

With his fiery rhetoric, Lumumba could count on support from young would-be revolutionaries, but his erratic behaviour as premier, at one moment mortgaging the Congo's vast mineral wealth to a shady American financier, the next calling on the Russians to come in, lost him the support of senior Congolese politicians. Now he faces trial for inciting the army to mutiny (→22/1/61).

Arts: Shakespeare becomes right royal

Theatrically speaking, this was a year of innovation. The Royal Shakespeare Company was inaugurated, directed by **Peter Hall** and led by **Peggy Ashcroft**. Two more innovations were three-year contracts for actors and the take-over of the Aldwych Theatre as the company's London home.

At Stratford, Ashcroft played Katharina in "The Taming of the Shrew" and opened the Aldwych season as "The Duchess of Malfi". **Peter O'Toole** played Petruchio and Shylock; in "Troilus and Cressida" the Trojan War was fought in a sand-pit. Stratford productions will transfer to London the following season.

The Old Vic, Shakespeare's traditional London home, struck back with a most original "Romeo and Juliet" directed by **Franco Zeffirelli**. The elaborate settings breathed Italy and the lovers were played as young as Shakespeare made them by newcomers **John Stride** and **Judi Dench**.

The first serious attempt at an English musical since Ivor Novello has bewitched the town. "Oliver!" is a jaunty version of "Oliver Twist" whose stars are the boy chorus of Fagin's pickpockets. **Lionel Bart's** numbers are infectiously hummable.

The theatre, post- "Look Back in Anger", has banished the West End stage voice. Regional and working-class accents are carefully nurtured. **Albert Finney**, from Salford, typifies the new breed of actor. He has scored a hit on stage as **Keith Waterhouse's** "Billy Liar", an undertaker's assistant with Walter Mitty dreams, and a huge success on screen as Arthur, the rebellious Nottingham factory worker of "Saturday Night and Sunday Morning", the film of the novel by **Alan Sillitoe**.

Three social misfits – a tramp and two strange brothers who give him temporary shelter – are the characters in "The Caretaker", by a new playwright, **Harold Pinter**. Pinter is clearly a disciple of **Samuel Beckett**. The laconic, hypnotic dialogue of his characters is causing as much heated debate as "Waiting for Godot" did five years ago.

The other high priest of the Theatre of the Absurd, **Eugene Ionesco**, provided **Laurence Olivier** with a surprise success in his play, "Rhinoceros". One by one, everyone turns into a rhinoceros, except his character, a little man who refuses to conform and is left searching the auditorium for a single human face.

D.H. Lawrence has been avenged for the neglect he suffered when alive. All 200,000 copies of "Lady Chatterley's Lover" sold out on the day they appeared. Audiences have also flocked to see **Ken Russell's** film of his better novel, "Sons and Lovers".

Riots follow warm Moslem welcome for de Gaulle in Algeria

Dec 13. Heavy-eyed but still sprightly after his perilous five-day campaigning journey through Algeria, President de Gaulle arrived back in Paris tonight. "There is only one policy for Algeria," he declared: self-determination and reconciliation.

His visit, planned to encourage acceptance of his referendum plan, had the extraordinary effect of pleasing the Arab population and provoking the anger of French settlers. While the Moslems massed to cry "Vive de Gaulle", French extremists rioted. The army, whose loyalty to the President is far from certain, was forced to intervene, and in clashes during the visit 123 people were killed.

Algerian gendarmes don riot gear as they clear the streets of protesters.

Science takes shine to laser's hot light

The laser, a light source of unprecedented intensity, made its debut this year. First demonstrated by **Theodore Maiman** of Hughes Aircraft in California, it is generating great interest among scientists, few of whom doubt that it will soon find many practical applications.

The Hawker P.1127, a British vertical-take-off aircraft, made its first flight this year. It uses an engine with swivelling nozzles to change from vertical to horizontal flight. And a new theory has proposed that particles like protons, hitherto considered to be fundamental, may be made of still more basic particles called quarks.

1961

JANUARY

Su	Mo	Tu	We	Th	Fr	Sa
1	2	3	4	5	6	7
8	9	10	11	12	13	14
15	16	17	18	19	20	21
22	23	24	25	26	27	28
29	30	31				

3. Washington: The US breaks off diplomatic relations with Cuba (→ 19/4).

3. UK: The millionth Morris Minor rolls off the production line.

6. Belgium: Sixty people are injured in Liege in violent protests against government austerity policies.

9. Moscow: Britain and the USSR sign a technology, culture and education agreement.

11. UK: British Rail orders an enquiry into why the Queen's train broke down, delaying her by nearly an hour.

12. Italy: The first Italian space rocket is launched (→ 31).

14. UK: Prison mutinies at Maidstone and Shrewsbury follow recent unrest at Wandsworth in London (→ 3/3).

18. Zanzibar: The pro-Western Afro-Shirazi Party win the elections by one vote; the opposition protests.

19. London: Dr Michael Ramsey becomes Archbishop of Canterbury on the retirement of Geoffrey Fisher (→ 20).

20. Cyprus: The Queen meets Archbishop Makarios (→ 16/2).

20. New Delhi: The Russian Orthodox Church is elected to the World Council of Churches (→ 2/4).

23. S. Africa: MPs give the first reading to a bill turning the country into a republic (→ 29/3).

24. Kenya: The lioness Elsa, heroine of Joy Adamson's book "Born Free", dies.

25. London: Thomson's buys the Daily Herald (→ 8/2).

31. US: A chimpanzee ascends 150 miles above the earth in an 18-minute flight to test the Mercury space capsule (→ 12/2).

31. Tel Aviv: Ben-Gurion resigns as Israeli Prime Minister.

DEATHS

10. US author Samuel Dashiell Hammett (*27/5/1894).→

17. Congolese statesman Patrice Lumumba (*2/7/25).

Kennedy sworn in as youngest President

Kennedy's inauguration: "Ask not what your country can do for you ..."

Jan 20. In a biting wind on a snow-covered Capitol Hill, power passed today from the oldest-ever US President to the youngest. John Fitzgerald Kennedy, aged 43, took the oath as 35th President on the family Douai Bible. General Eisenhower, aged 70, now a plain citizen, was the first to rise and shake his hand.

The ten-minute inaugural address set a high literary tone, which Americans are not used to in their Presidents. Kennedy said: "Now the trumpet summons us again ... against the common enemies of man: tyranny, poverty, disease and war itself." He appealed to the Soviets "that both sides begin anew the quest for peace". He proposed as a start genuine and polite negotiations on disarmament and nuclear inspection. "Civility isn't a sign of weakness," he said.

He also made it quite clear he was prepared to be tough with America's enemies. He warned them that those who tried to ride a tiger might finish up inside. He said: "Let the rest of the world know that this hemisphere intends to remain master in its own house."

He rose to a high pitch of eloquence which moved the Congress and the millions watching on television: "In your hands, my fellow citizens, more than mine, will rest the final success or failure of our course ... Ask not what your country can do for you – ask what you can do for your country." He showed a determination to bring in change, but with a respect for tradition. Though he said "the torch has been passed to a new generation of Americans", he added that that generation was "proud of our ancient heritage".

He also chose to return to formal dress for the ceremony, including the top hat. And in his opening words he used "my fellow citizens", the form used by the first President, George Washington. President Franklin Roosevelt preferred the cosier "my fellow Americans" and "my friends".

Contraceptive pill goes on sale in UK

Jan 30. After careful trials with combined female hormones, a progestogen-oestrogen mixture, Conovid, is now available for women as an oral contraceptive. One tablet is taken at night beginning on day five of the menstrual cycle and for the next 20 days.

Nausea, breast engorgement, premenstrual tension, headache and weight gain may occur in the first few months, but disappear later. When treatment is stopped the next cycle may be prolonged to 31 days, but soon becomes normal.

Experience with the equivalent of Conovid exceeds 7,000 cycles in over 1,000 women without a single pregnancy. The Ministry of Health may prescribe the drug through the National Health Service (→ 8/2).

Hammett, maestro of thrillers, is dead

Jan 10. Dashiell Hammett, who died today, started life as a detective with Pinkerton's agency, which equipped him to write the first authentic "private eye" stories. His characters, Sam Spade in "The Maltese Falcon" (1930) and Nick and Nora Charles, husband and wife team of "The Thin Man" (1934), were human and humorous. Both plots made fine movies.

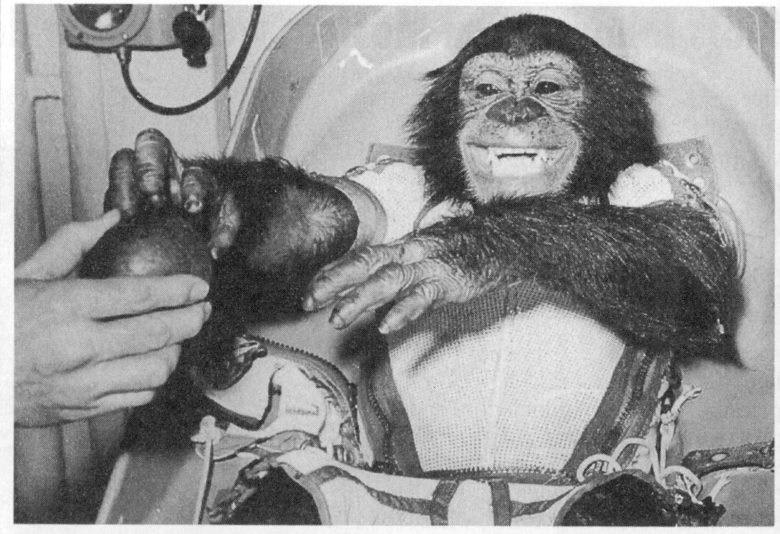

Ham, America's space chimp, back on board the recovery ship, gets an apple as his reward after a successful flight and splashdown, as experts prepare to "debrief" him when he arrives at Cape Canaveral.

1961

FEBRUARY

Su	Mo	Tu	We	Th	Fr	Sa
			1	2	3	4
5	6	7	8	9	10	11
12	13	14	15	16	17	18
19	20	21	22	23	24	25
26	27	28				

1. US: The first "Minuteman" intercontinental ballistic missile is fired (→3/4).

1. London: The Postmaster General announces plans to build a 507-ft GPO Tower in central London (→16/8).

3. Congo: Pro-Lumumba troops and UN forces engage in fierce fighting.→

5. Angola: Six die in a wave of nationalist unrest (→20/4).

6. London: Spurs captain Danny Blanchflower is the first person to refuse to appear on ITV's "This Is Your Life".

8. London: The Commons ends a debate on the NHS amid Labour fury at proposed increases in NHS charges (→4/12).

12. USSR: An "interplanetary space station" is launched, aimed at Venus (→9/3).

15. Belgium: A US skating team are among the 73 killed when a Sabena Boeing 707 crashes near Brussels.

16. Cyprus: The island applies to join the Commonwealth.

16. Oxford: Robert Graves is appointed Professor of Poetry.

17. London: Northern Rhodesian constitutional talks at Lancaster House reach deadlock.→

19. London: Police struggle with demonstrators marching on the Belgian embassy to protest at Lumumba's murder (→12/3).

24. UK: Jodrell Bank scientists say they sent telegraph signals to Australia by bouncing them off the moon.

25. Washington: Kennedy appoints academic Dr Henry Kissinger as a National Security Adviser.

26. Rabat: Hassan II succeeds as King of Morocco on the death of King Mohammed V.

28. Kenya: Tom Mboya wins the general election.

DEATHS

20. Australian composer Percy Grainger (*8/7/1882).

20. Moroccan King Mohammed V (*10/8/09).

Spy ring passed UK underwater secrets

Jan 8. Scotland Yard Special Branch officers today arrested five people, including a Canadian businessman, Gordon Lonsdale, on spying charges.

The charges relate to the passing on of secrets from the Navy's Underwater Warfare Establishment at Portland, Dorset. The group involves Peter and Helen Kroger, two Canadians living in Ruislip, along with two civil servants, Ethel Gee and Harry Houghton, thought to be connected with the base. Police arrested the group after watching Gee and Houghton pass a parcel to Lonsdale outside Waterloo Station. Police suspect that some of those charged may be Russians (→13/3).

Lonsdale: the accused spymaster.

French support de Gaulle's line on Algeria

Jan 8. Fifteen million French and Algerian voters answered "Yes" in today's referendum, and gave President de Gaulle a clear mandate to pursue his policy of home rule for Algeria. The resounding majority of over 75 per cent was expressing the hope that negotiations to end the long and increasingly unpopular Algerian war would begin very soon.

Good sense had prevailed, said the President, but the "no" votes came from five million people still determined to maintain that Algeria is French (→11/4).

Savage attacks on Europeans in Congo

Jan 22. Belgian paratroopers are flying to Stanleyville in the upper Congo today to rescue over 1,000 Europeans, victims of a reign of terror by supporters of the deposed premier, Patrice Lumumba.

Drunken troops are roaming the streets, beating up Belgian men and raping their wives. The local political boss, Antoine Gizenga, says the attacks are reprisals for the decision to hand Lumumba over to the pro-Western Katangan leader, Moise Tshombe (→3/2).

Eight Belgian soldiers kneel as their captors pose; later they were beaten.

Old bones tell tales of earliest humans

Feb 24. A new find of fossil bones in Tanganyika pushes the origins of human-like species back towards a million years ago. The bones, discovered by the British anthropologist Dr Louis Leakey in the Olduvai Gorge, have not been accurately dated yet, but according to Leakey they are much older than his previous find, the 600,000-year-old remains of "Nutcracker Man" with his powerful crushing molars.

The new find consists of a skull, a collarbone and parts of the hands and a foot of a child about 11 years old. The brain size is bigger and the teeth smaller than in Nutcracker man. A crack in the skull suggests that the child may have been murdered by a blow.

Leakey and an Olduvai skull.

Auntie says final "goodbye children"

Feb 8. "Children's Hour", a staple of BBC radio since 1922, is to be dropped in April. Various programmes for the young will replace it, including "Playtime", a daily broadcast on the Light Programme, and a Saturday morning feature, "Children's Favourites", also to be broadcast on the Light.

Competition from television has reduced audiences for "Children's Hour", which fell to 250,000 last year. New programmes are planned in an effort to gain young listeners, who will have nearly two hours of broadcasts every weekday (→11/6). ▷

Congo ex-premier dies while "escaping"

Feb 13. Patrice Lumumba, the Congo's controversial independence premier, has died in mysterious circumstances. Godefroid Munongo, Katanga's Minister of the Interior, called a Press conference in Elisabethville today to announce that Lumumba and two companions had been massacred by villagers after escaping from custody. He produced three death certificates, signed by a medical officer, which stated simply that the men had "died in the bush".

Mr Munongo said Lumumba and his companions were identified and then buried immediately on the spot. The villagers, who were not identified, were paid the £3,000 reward promised for the capture of the fugitives. He added: "I would be lying if I said the death of Mr Lumumba makes me sad. He was an ordinary criminal responsible for thousands of dead."

Mr Munongo's account is bound to be received with scepticism. Lumumba was transferred to Katanga because it was feared he would persuade his guards to let him escape. The European pilot who flew him there has said Lumumba was savagely beaten during the flight (→19).

President Tshombe of Katanga, speaking at the Elisabethville stadium.

Rhodesians refuse blacks greater say

Feb 21. Sir Roy Welensky, Prime Minister of the Central African Federation, tonight flatly rejected a British plan for increased African representation in the Northern Rhodesian Legislature. At the same time he ordered the call-up of 3,000 Territorial troops "to deal with any insurrection".

The British are determined to push ahead with reforms in the hope of persuading African leaders to accept the Federation, but Sir Roy claims the British are advancing the Africans too fast and are "debasing the franchise", bringing the risk of power slipping out of "responsible" hands (→26/6).

Two of the "stars" of Walt Disney's latest cartoon success – 101 Dalmatians, a story of canine misadventures, taken from author Dodie Smith's highly popular children's classic.

1961

MARCH

Su	Mo	Tu	We	Th	Fr	Sa
			1	2	3	4
5	6	7	8	9	10	11
12	13	14	15	16	17	18
19	20	21	22	23	24	25
26	27	28	29	30	31	

3. London: Edwin Bush is Britain's first suspected criminal to be identified by means of an "Identi-kit" picture (→24/8).

8. London: Colonial Secretary Iain Macleod says Malta is to be given self-government (→24/10).

9. USSR: A rocket containing a dog is successfully launched and lands safely (→12/4).

12. Congo: Congolese leaders agree to replace the existing republic with a federation of sovereign states (→26/4).

13. Kiev: 145 are reported killed when a dam bursts.

13. Nice: Picasso, aged 79, marries his 37-year-old model Jacqueline Roque.

13. London: Gordon Lonsdale and four others go on trial at the Old Bailey (→18/4).

15. London: Dr Richard Beeching is appointed to head British Railways (→8/5).

16. London: The Parliamentary Labour Party withdraws the whip from Michael Foot and four others (→17).

17. UK: Francis Pym wins a Cambridgeshire by-election for the Tories; (→21).

20. UK: The Shakespeare Memorial Theatre at Stratford-upon-Avon becomes the Royal Shakespeare Theatre.

21. London: The Commons Committee of Privileges disqualifies the new Viscount Stansgate from the Commons (→23).

23. Birmingham: Labour's Denis Howell wins the Small Heath by-election (→4/5).

25. UK: Mr C. Vaughan's Nicolaus Silver wins the Grand National.

29. S. Africa: The treason trial against 28 ANC leaders is dropped (→7/4).

DEATHS

6. British comedian George Formby, born George Hoy Booth (*26/5/04).

8. British conductor Sir Thomas Beecham (*29/4/1879).→

South Africa will quit Comonwealth

March 15. South Africa is leaving the Commonwealth when she becomes a republic on May 31. Dr Hendrick Verwoerd told his fellow prime ministers at their conference in London: "It is clear after the lead given by a group of Afro-Asian nations that we will be no longer welcome."

These nations had fiercely denounced his apartheid policies. The South African leader predicted that the Commonwealth will start to disintegrate if member countries meddle in each other's affairs.

Dr Verwoerd also said that South Africa's decision was taken partly to prevent embarrassment to Britain and the older members in their relations with the others.

In Cape Town there was gloomy white reaction, but the black leader, ex-chief Albert Luthuli, said: "I am overjoyed".

Beecham, musical grandee, is dead

The late Sir Thomas Beecham.

March 8. Sir Thomas Beecham, who died today aged 81, inherited a fortune from the family pill business and spent it on music. In his long life as a patron and conductor he founded four orchestras, including the Royal Philharmonic (1946), brought the Diaghilev Ballet to London, and above all conducted with a unique wit and brilliance.

US increases money and arms for Laos

President Kennedy gestures at a map of Indochina during the conference.

March 21. The United States is stepping up its military and financial aid to the government of Laos in its fight against the Pathet Lao Communist movement. Announcing that an additional 100 advisers are being sent to train the Laotian army, President John Kennedy told a press conference in Washington today that he would "back the Laotian government to the hilt".

American officials said that the increase in aid was designed specifically to counter the upsurge of rebel activity in the countryside where Pathet Lao guerrillas, supplied with Soviet arms, are attacking villages, killing officials and breaking down local administration. The US officials insist, however, that they are not engaged in an arms race with the Soviets.

Kennedy forms United States peace corps

March 1. President Kennedy today announced the formation of a Peace Corps of young men and women to work in the "great common cause of world developments". Unpaid volunteers will live with local people, speak their language, and help teach in their schools. "The life will not be easy but it will be rich and satisfying," said the President.

A pilot scheme led by his brother-in-law, Sargent Shriver, aims to have 500 to 1,000 volunteers placed by the end of the year, and if successful will be made permanent.

Britain's latest sports car: the Jaguar E-Type. It cruises at 100mph, can reach 150mph, and this solid-topped model will cost £2,196.

1961

APRIL

Su	Mo	Tu	We	Th	Fr	Sa
						1
2	3	4	5	6	7	8
9	10	11	12	13	14	15
16	17	18	19	20	21	22
23	24	25	26	27	28	29
30						

2. Israel: 40 Biblical scrolls are found in a cave in Judaea (→ 5/6).

3. London: 31 are arrested during an anti-nuclear protest outside the US Embassy (→ 3/9).

4. Washington: Macmillan arrives for talks with Kennedy.

7. New York: The UN votes 83-0 to censure South Africa for its racist policies (→ 24/5).

9. Persian Gulf: 150 people are feared dead after a fire sweeps through the British liner, Dara.

10. US: South African golfer Gary Player wins the US Masters by a single stroke.

11. France: De Gaulle says "Algerians are free to choose their own fate" (→ 22).

11. Jerusalem: The trial of Adolf Eichmann begins.→

17. London: Tottenham Hotspur win the League Championship (→ 8/5).

18. Kenya: Africans agree to join the Kenyan government in return for the release of Jomo Kenyatta (→ 14/7).

18. London: George Blake is charged under the Official Secrets Act; details of his alleged offences are withheld (→ 8/5).

20. New York: The UN tells Portugal to bring in reforms in Angola as a nationalist uprising nears its sixth week.→

22. Algiers: Rebel French army officers seize Algiers (→ 23).

23. Paris: De Gaulle assumes dictatorial powers, appealing for the nation's support against the Algerian rebellion.→

25. Paris: De Gaulle orders a blockade of Algeria (→ 26).

26. Algiers: The rebellion collapses; General Challe submits to Colonel Georges de Boissieu (→ 20/5).

28. Paris: It is revealed that Britain has applied to join the Common Market (→ 1/8).

DEATH

9. Albanian King Zog I, ruled 1928-39, 1944-46 (*8/10/1895).

Ex-Nazi Eichmann admits his role in the Final Solution

April 21. At the war crimes trial before a special Jerusalem court Adolf Eichmann, the former Nazi SS officer, reluctantly admitted today that he had played a part in "liquidating" German Jews. His qualified confession emerged during his interrogation by an Israeli police officer.

But the dull, birdlike, middle-aged accused man, on trial in a bullet-proof glass cage, also made excuses. He was "only a little sausage" in the wartime Nazi machine. "I was a transport officer and nothing more," he explained, and denied that he had been involved in killing Jews. That did not alter the fact that he organised transport to take them to places of extermination as part of Hitler's plan for the "Final Solution" to the Jewish problem.

"Not every person I evacuated was put to death," Eichmann told the court, "otherwise 2,400,000 Jewish survivors would not have been found after the war." He was reminded that those survivors owed their lives not to any kindness of his, but to the fact that Allied victory prevented further slaughter.

Eichmann is charged on 15 counts with conspiring to cause the death or persecution of millions of Jews. Twelve carry the death penalty (→ 20/6).

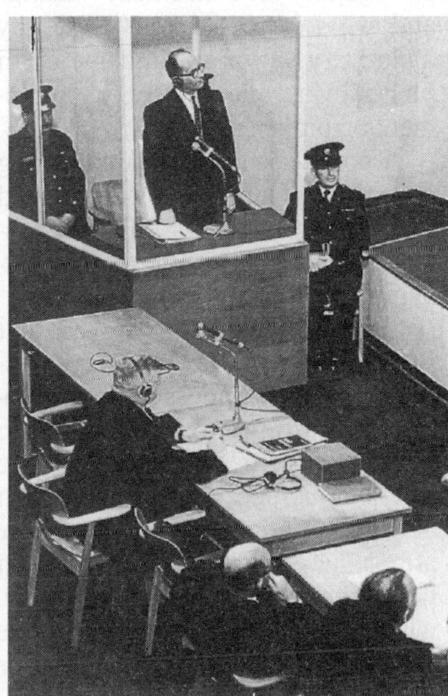

Eichmann has a bullet-proof trial.

▷

Soviet Union puts first man in space

April 12. The Soviet Union notched up another triumph today when 27-year-old Major Yuri Alexeyevitch Gagarin became the first man to fly in space. In a four-and-a-half-ton Vostok spaceship he orbited the earth and returned safely after a flight lasting 108 minutes.

Rumours that a spaceflight was imminent had been circulating in Moscow for some days, but the first definite news came at 10am, local time, when a radio announcer broke into a programme to say that Russia had put a man into space.

The Vostok spacecraft is believed to have been launched from the Tyuratam space centre in central Asia. Major Gagarin completed a single orbit of the earth, reaching a height of 190 miles, and then fired braking rockets. After orbiting, his spacecraft returned to earth by parachute.

Major Gagarin was born in March 1934 and brought up near Smolensk. He joined the Soviet Air Force school in Orenburg. Almost certainly he has experience as a test pilot. He met his wife, Valentina, while she was also at Orenburg as a medical student. They have two children, Yelena, aged 2, and Gala, who is only a few months old.

During the flight the "cosmonaut" was strapped to a couch and did little to fly his spacecraft. Instruments and television cameras monitored his responses to the stresses of his flight. He also reported regularly on instrument readings and what he could see. "The sky looks very very dark and the earth bluish" was one of his first comments from space.

"I could see seas, mountains, big cities, rivers and forests," he told the Soviet premier, Mr Khrushchev, who telephoned to congratulate him after his landing.

Gagarin's flight has proved that prolonged exposure to weightlessness, which is impossible to reproduce on earth, causes no immediate harm. Gagarin also survived the tremendous acceleration of launch and deceleration of re-entry to the atmosphere, rising to five to ten times the normal force of gravity, without damage. "I feel well. I have no injuries or bruises," he said after landing.

The Americans will not be ready to emulate the latest Soviet space feat until next year, though a brief sub-orbital flight into the fringes of space is planned for the near future. Like Gagarin, the American astronauts will do little to control their craft, which is far smaller than the Russian Vostok, another reflection of the superior rocket power developed by the Russians.

Russia has been celebrating after the flight with young people cheering and demonstrating in Moscow and other large towns. Radio Moscow and its Central Telegraph Office have been overwhelmed with messages of congratulations.

In the United States the reaction has been resigned and admiring. Gagarin's flight was "a fantastic, fabulous achievement" said the NASA chief, James Webb (→ 5/5).

Yuri Gagarin, Russia's pioneer cosmonaut, on board his spacecraft.

Cheering crowds march to welcome home their country's space hero.

Head of the rebel regime in Congo arrested by army

April 26. Troops loyal to the Cong central government today seize Moise Tshombe, the president c the breakaway province of Ka anga, after he walked out of a co ference to discuss the unity of th Congo state. Justin Bomboko, th Congolese Foreign Minister, sai Tshombe would be tried for hig treason; then a few hours late promised he would be freed an allowed to return to Elisabethville.

At the conference Tshombe ha attacked central government politi ians for giving in to UN demand that they be allowed to remov foreign advisers and officers fro Katanga. When his call to canc the agreement was ignored he lef and was arrested while boarding train (→ 22/6).

Nationalists kill whites in Angola

April 20. Several hundred white probably as many as 500, have bee hacked to death in a five-week-o uprising in Portugal's West Africa colony of Angola. "The atrociti are far more terrible than anythin that happened in the Belgia Congo," said an official, describin it as a full-scale revolutionary wa organised by experienced leader "This is a life or death struggle," h said. "Portugal cannot survive as nation without its African terr tories."

Diem is victorious in Vietnamese poll

April 10. President Ngo Di Diem, the strongly anti-Commu ist founder of the South Vietname Republic, won a crushing victory i today's election, which returne him to power for his second fiv year term as president.

The government machinery pr vented Communist attempts to e force a boycott of the electio reports say that about 85 per ce of the country's seven millic voters went to the polls (→ 14/11)

Invasion at Bay of Pigs

Fidel Castro, with Cuban leaders, prepares to resist the invasion.

April 19. Armed Cuban exiles, in a bid to overthrow the Marxist government of Fidel Castro, claimed to be within 70 miles of the capital, Havana, last night. The Cuban Revolutionary Council says its forces have set up an airstrip at the Bay of Pigs, but the Cuban authorities appear to be in control of the situation, using Russian-made tanks and MiG fighter planes. Havana Radio has announced 27 arrests and eight executions on conspiracy charges.

The invasion sparked off a wave of international tension as President Kennedy and the Soviet leader, Nikita Khrushchev, exchanged blunt personal messages. Khrushchev said that the organisers of the invasion were denying Cuba's right to self-determination, and appealed to the President to "put an end to the aggression against the Republic of Cuba". Russia, he promised, would give Castro "all necessary aid" to repel the invasion. In an oblique reference to Laos, he warned Kennedy that settlement could not be made in one area if trouble flared up in another.

The President told Khrushchev that he was "under a serious misapprehension with regard to events in Cuba" and warned that, although he has no plans to help the rebels, the USA would step in if Russia intervened. He has never made a secret of his admiration for the freedom fighters, and in the past has proposed helping them. US planes are reported to have been used in the Bay of Pigs landings.

Kennedy went on: "I have taken careful note of your statement that events in Cuba might affect peace in all parts of the world. I trust that this does not mean that the Soviet government ... is planning to inflame other areas of the world. I would like to think that your government has too great a sense of responsibility to embark on any enterprise so dangerous to general peace" (→ 1/5).

Vexed: Kennedy and Eisenhower.

Paris fears invasion by Algerian rebels

April 24. Paris is an armed camp tonight, standing by to repel airborne invasion by rebel French army units from Algeria. Sherman tanks surround the Presidential Elysee Palace. Freshly re-armed Gaullist and Socialist Resistance units guard strategic points.

This scratch army is reinforced by a 10,000-strong regiment of CRS riot police and Republican Guards, but these defences would be pitifully weak should crack paratroop regiments choose to risk civil war by trying to capture Paris.

Runways at Orly and Le Bourget airports remain blocked by trucks and buses, and the air force is under orders to shoot down any hostile French aircraft. A sea blockade of Algeria has been imposed and all commercial activity is frozen.

But there is every sign tonight that the two-day attempt by General Challe and three other officers, backed by paratroop regiments, to seize power in Algeria is crumbling. As President de Gaulle hit back at their plot, eight generals were arrested early this morning. All four senior rebel French commanders have been stripped of their rank. So, too, have the three activist colonels who carried out their orders.

A crucial factor in turning the tide against the rebellion may prove to be President de Gaulle's remarkable and moving broadcast to the nation tonight. Wearing his familiar army uniform, the old soldier who salvaged French honour in 1940 pulled out every emotional stop to save the Republic again. "Frenchmen and women, help me," he cried. "In the name of France I order the use of all means, I repeat all means, to bar the route to these men until they are defeated." He described Salan and his fellow rebels as a quartet of retired generals flouting the State, as "prejudiced, ambitious and fanatical".

The people of France have already displayed their loyalty in a nationwide symbolic strike. Popular feeling solidly opposes the army's attempt to impose its will on the nation. "We don't want Fascism here" is their slogan (→ 25).

De Gaulle salutes the dead.

Generals Jouhaud (l.), Salan (r.) and Challe: leaders of a coup in Algeria.

1961

MAY

Su	Mo	Tu	We	Th	Fr	Sa
	1	2	3	4	5	6
7	8	9	10	11	12	13
14	15	16	17	18	19	20
21	22	23	24	25	26	27
28	29	30	31			

1. Cuba: Castro proclaims Cuba a socialist nation and abolishes elections (→27/2).

2. Jordan: King Hussein announces he will wed Miss Gardiner, a telephonist from Stratford-upon-Avon.

4. Bristol: Viscount Stansgate (Anthony Wedgwood Benn) wins the by-election called by his elevation to the peerage.→

8. London: The Government announces plans to force pedestrians to cross the road at traffic lights (→14/6).

11. London: Macmillan says there will be an independent review of the security services after the Blake case (→13/6).

13. Washington: The US agrees to give more cash and military aid to South Vietnam.

14. US: A white mob attacks "freedom rider" integrationists at a bus station in Birmingham, Alabama.→

14. Monaco: Stirling Moss wins the Monaco Grand Prix.

18. London: The Government announces the creation of new universities at Canterbury, Colchester and Coventry.

19. Seoul: President Po Sun Yun resigns in the wake of a military coup two days ago.

20. France: A 30-day ceasefire is declared in Algeria as talks open with Algerian Moslem leaders at Evian-les-Bains (→5/7).

22. UK: The Post Office instals the first "pay-on-answer" phone boxes, with pips when coins are needed.

25. Washington: Kennedy says the US will aim to put the first man on the moon (→13/7).

28. London: The CEGB blames human error for a massive blackout of south-east England two weeks ago.

31. UK: Mrs A. Plesch's Psidium wins the Derby.

31. Pretoria: South Africa is declared a republic (→11/10).

DEATH

13. US actor Gary Cooper, born Frank James Cooper (*7/5/01).→

Blake receives record jail term for spying

May 8. George Blake, the former diplomat, received a record 42-year jail sentence at the Old Bailey today for spying. The 38-year-old self-confessed spy is said to have passed every document he could get hold of to the Russians over nine and a half years while working in Germany and the Lebanon.

Lord Chief Justice Parker said his treachery had "rendered much of this country's efforts completely useless."

Blake was captured by the Communists during the Korean War when he was British vice-consul in Seoul. He was held for three years and is thought to have been brainwashed (→11).

George Blake, jailed for 42 years.

The US puts a man (briefly) in space

May 5. Alan B. Shepard Jr, a commander in the US Navy, became the first American in space today with a 15-minute sub-orbital flight that took him 115 miles above the earth. He landed in the sea near the Bahamas, 360 miles from the Cape Canaveral launch site. He is said to be in "excellent" condition.

Shepard carried out some manoeuvres with his Mercury spacecraft, unlike Soviet cosmonaut Yuri Gagarin, who appears to have been only a passive observer during his orbital flight last month (→25).

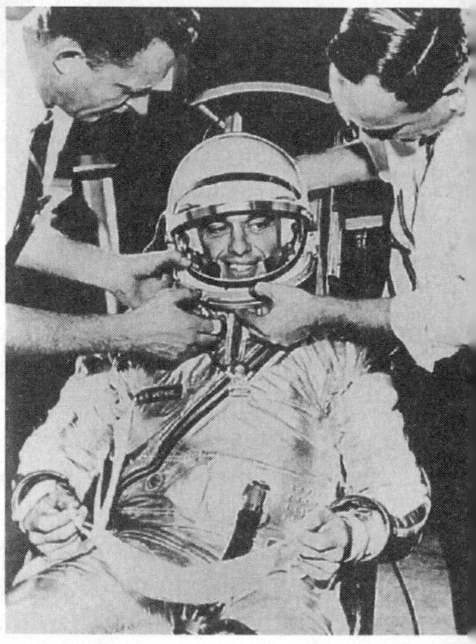

Alan Shepard: first for America, but still second to Yuri Gagarin.

Racists beat up liberal whites in US

May 25. Ugly racial violence continues today in Montgomery, Alabama, as black and white "freedom riders" systematically broke segregation laws on state and interstate buses. Mobs of angry whites, including members of the Ku Klux Klan, descended on the city to defend segregation. Governor John Patterson imposed martial law in an attempt to quell the rioting.

In the most violent outburst, over 1,000 whites attacked a bus full of freedom fighters with fists and clubs last week. At least 20 people were hurt. News reporters and cameramen were also attacked, their notes ripped up and equipment smashed. The riders were subsequently arrested for contempt of an injunction banning this form of protest.

Federal marshals were ordered into the city to protect a church meeting held by the integration leader, the Reverend Martin Luther King, as hundreds of whites gathered outside, shouting obscenities. Dr King said that blacks would "continue the struggle for freedom".

Tottenham win the double to become the team of the century

May 6. Tottenham Hotspur, with a two-nil Cup Final victory over Leicester City, have become the first team this century to achieve the FA Cup and League double.

Danny Blanchflower and his multi-talented side clinched the League title three weeks ago, but their Cup victory was hard work. Despite having their right-back Len Chalmers reduced to a hobble by a knee injury after 18 minutes, Leicester held firm, thanks in no small part to their young goalkeeper Gordon Banks, until three-quarters of the way through the game, when the England centre-forward, Bobby Smith, suddenly eluded his marker and shot Spurs into the lead. Nine minutes later the a double was in the bag with a headed goal by Terry Dyson.

Spurs captain Danny Blanchflower raises the Cup to celebrate the double.

Rebel peer is banned from the Commons

Wedgwood Benn, the reluctant peer, arrives at the House of Commons.

May 8. Anthony Wedgwood Benn, who doubled his majority in the Bristol South-East by-election caused by his succession to his father's peerage, was banned from the Commons today on arrival to claim his seat.

Labour's reluctant peer was told by the principal doorkeeper, a former regimental sergeant major, that force would be used if necessary to keep him out. This came after a vote in the House that Mr Benn, "otherwise Viscount Stansgate", should not be admitted to plead his case. So the position is upheld that, as a peer, Mr Benn cannot sit in the Commons, even though elected to it. He will now remain ineligible until there is a law enabling him to renounce his peerage.

Mr Benn was allowed to sit in the public gallery to hear MPs wrangling over his case. One of his supporters remarked: "King Charles I was at least given a hearing at his trial." However, everyone was most polite. "It was all so British," said a senior whip (→ 28/7).

Mandela eludes police round-ups

May 24. Seeking to head off a nationwide general strike called by black leaders, South African police are carrying out mass arrests of black activists. Today's drive brings the total detained to almost 10,000.

But the black nationalist leader Nelson Mandela, the key figure in organising the strike, was not at his home at Orlando, near Johannesburg, when police arrived. They were met by his wife, Winnie, who demanded to see their search warrant. They did not have one and had to return to police HQ for it.

Mrs Mandela said the police were polite when they rummaged through his drawers but found nothing. No whites have been arrested, but many Asians have (→ 31).

The eternal cowboy hero: Gary Cooper, who died this month at the age of 60, shows his meanest, Oscar-winning form in Fred Zinneman's "High Noon".

1961

JUNE

Su	Mo	Tu	We	Th	Fr	Sa
				1	2	3
4	5	6	7	8	9	10
11	12	13	14	15	16	17
18	19	20	21	22	23	24
25	26	27	28	29	30	

2. Albania: Eight Soviet submarines leave amid rumours of worsening Soviet-Albanian relations (→ 17/10).

4. France: The far right suffer setbacks in elections to the National Assembly (→ 30/8).

4. UK: Cigarettes go up a half-penny to around 1/9d. for ten (→ 25/7).

5. London: Dr Ramsey takes office as Archbishop of Canterbury.→

8. York: The Duke of Kent marries Katherine Worsley (→ 30).

13. London: A report blames lax security at the Admiralty for the Lonsdale spy ring.

14. London: The government announces the introduction of push-button controlled pedestrian crossings (→ 1/10).

15. Moscow: Khrushchev warns of "military conflict" if the West tries to reach Berlin against East Germany's will (→ 13/8).

19. Kuwait: Britain ends its protectorate of the oil-rich sheikdom, but will continue to lend military aid (→ 25).

20. Jerusalem: Eichmann gives evidence, but refuses to swear on the Bible (→ 14/8).

20. Cairo: Nasser approves a plan to move the ancient temple of Abu Simbel above the Aswan Dam's floodwaters (→ 28/9).

22. Congo: President Tshombe of Katanga is released (→ 13/9).

25. Baghdad: Iraq claims Kuwait (→ 1/17).

26. London: The government announces plans to give the vote to more, but not all, Northern Rhodesian Africans.

28. London: A judge declares a ballot by the Electrical Trades Union invalid as it was rigged by Communists (→ 4/9).

30. Glasgow: The Queen visits slums in the Gorbals (→ 3/10).

DEATH

6. Swiss psychoanalyst Carl Gustav Jung (*26/7/1875).→

Dr Ramsey created 100th Archbishop

Dr Ramsey – the 100th primate.

June 27. Dr Arthur Michael Ramsey, aged 56, was enthroned today as the 100th Archbishop of Canterbury. The 750-year-old marble throne of St. Augustine was moved to the altar steps so that the people in the nave, and those watching on television, could see the climax of the ceremony.

Dr Ramsey, previously Archbishop of York, said: "Today a man enters his task as the chief shepherd ... It is a task beyond all human strength, and many in the country are not so much hostile as indifferent and aloof." He hopes to win them back by giving more freedom in the words and form of church services.

Jung, the wise man archetype, is dead

June 6. Carl Gustav Jung, the Swiss psychoanalyst who broke with Freud to found his own school, has died aged 85. He classified men and women as either extroverts or introverts, and also rated them by four functions: sensation, feeling, thinking and intuition. Whereas Freud's symbolism was largely sexual, Jung found room for the magical and mystical, and believed in sub-personalities called archetypes. ▷

Stalemate in Vienna

Kennedy shakes hands with Khrushchev at a cordial meeting in Vienna.

June 4. An estimated 250,000 people cheered President and Mrs Kennedy along the route as they drove into town from London Airport today. They are staying overnight before returning to Washington after the Kennedy-Khrushchev summit meeting in Vienna.

The President, obviously nervous while in the Austrian capital, was relieved that his first venture in personal diplomacy is over without a dangerous explosion. He briefed Mr Macmillan on the outcome. Talks over two days between the US and Soviet leaders have changed almost nothing. They measured each other up, talked toughly, but made no serious new demands.

Test-ban talks are still deadlocked, but tension may have eased slightly over Berlin. The President said: "I made American policies crystal clear to remove the possibilities of war through miscalculation. That is something" (→15).

Towns emptying on this crowded isle

June 7. Britain's population has grown by nearly 2.5 million in the last ten years, according to the preliminary results of the 1961 census released today. The total figure is now 52,675,094, with the sharpest regional increases being recorded in the southern half of England. Overall there are fewer people living in towns and more in the suburbs or beyond, as people commute longer distances or retire to the country.

The higher population has been caused by nearly two million more births than deaths, and by a net gain of 353,000 through immigration. The result is a crowded island, with 790 people per square mile in England and Wales. This compares, for instance, with just 49 in the United States.

Pilate named on ancient tablet

June 19. The first archaeological evidence for the existence of Pontius Pilate has been discovered at Caesarea, ten miles south of Haifa. An Italian dig today found a stone slab, 30 by 24 inches, with two names on it. One is Pontius Pilate, the Roman Governor who ordered the crucifixion, and the other is the Emperor Tiberius.

Soviet ballet star in dramatic defection bid at Paris airport

June 16. The leading male dancer of the Kirov Ballet from Leningrad broke away from his company today at Le Bourget airport and ran to a group of French police, shouting "Protect me, protect me!".

The ballet company was about to fly from Paris to London to appear at Covent Garden, but Rudolf Nureyev, aged 23, was accosted in Customs by two burly Russians and told to return to Moscow immediately. Afterwards, under police protection, he was seen by Russian embassy officials who tried to change his mind about defecting.

They failed – he has been granted political asylum. Nureyev says he decided to stay of his own free will. In Russia he has been compared to Nijinsky.

Ballet star Rudolf Nureyev faces a new audience after his defection.

1961

JULY

Su	Mo	Tu	We	Th	Fr	Sa
						1
2	3	4	5	6	7	8
9	10	11	12	13	14	15
16	17	18	19	20	21	22
23	24	25	26	27	28	29
30	31					

1. Kuwait: British troops land in anticipation of an attack by Iraq (→5).

5. Algiers: 80 Arabs die when French troops open fire on Moslem demonstrators (→11).

5. Cairo: The United Arab Republic, backed by Moscow, calls for Britain to withdraw from Kuwait (→29/11).

8. Wimbledon: Rod Laver beats Charles McKinley in the men's singles final; Angela Mortimer beats Christine Truman.→

9. Moscow: Khrushchev says he has cancelled defence cuts and will increase military spending (→30/10).

11. France: Leaders of the failed Algerian coup, including General Salan, are sentenced to death in their absence (→11/8).

12. London: The government grants £1 million towards the establishment of a National Theatre.

13. London: Macmillan meets Yuri Gagarin and says he is "a delightful fellow".→

14. Kenya: Kenyatta is released (→21/8).

16. UK: Six people are killed and 116 hurt when a train full of holidaymakers crashes near Blackpool.

17. London: The government says a 43-letter phonetic alphabet will be taught to 1,000 children as an experiment.

21. US: Captain Virgil Grissom becomes the second US astronaut in a 16-minute flight 116 miles into space (→6/8).

25. London: A mini-budget puts fourpence on cigarettes and threepence on a gallon of petrol (→12/10).

25. Washington: Kennedy calls for increased defence spending.

28. London: The High Court quashes Viscount Stansgate's election victory and appoints his defeated opponent as MP (→9/10).

DEATH

2. US author Ernest Hemingway (*21/7/1899).→

Two Britons reach Wimbledon final

Mortimer – a winner for Britain.

July 8. For the first time since the long-skirted days of 1914, Britain provided both women finalists at Wimbledon, and was assured of the first British title-holder since Dorothy Round in 1937.

With Maria Bueno absent through illness, the 20-year-old Christine Truman, darling of Wimbledon since her Wightman Cup victory over the great Althea Gibson three years ago, was marginally favoured to beat Angela Mortimer, who had reached the final unseeded in 1958.

It was an awkward fall by Truman which decided the match. She lost the second set limping, rallied too late in the third, and saw the patient Mortimer take the title 4-6, 6-4, 7-5.

East Germans flood into West Berlin

July 17. Fears that the Communist regime in East Germany is about to cut the links between East and West Germany, and assume control of all access to West Berlin, follow the signing of a separate peace treaty with Russia, and have led to a massive flood of refugees leaving the East.

During the past 24 hours more than 1,800 have passed through the reception centres in West Berlin alone. Many of them are young families with their few belongings in net bags and suitcases (→ 8/8).

Britain bids to join the Common Market

July 31. Britain will now try to join the European Common Market. Mr Macmillan made the announcement in a tense House of Commons this afternoon. Cheers and angry cries on both sides immediately highlighted divisions within the parties on this momentous issue.

The Prime Minister said that the offer to negotiate for membership will depend on satisfactory arrangements to meet special needs, notably the interests of farmers, the Commonwealth, and Britain's fellow members of the European Free Trade Area (EFTA).

French reaction is already ominous. President de Gaulle is reported to be irked by Mr Macmillan's apparent insistence on special terms. Does he want the Common Market club rules radically changed? If so, Paris officials warned, negotiations may take a long time and France has a veto.

Mr Macmillan hopes for an early meeting with the French leader to clear the air, but first he plans a week's shooting holiday in Yorkshire. He has told Edward Heath, the deputy Foreign Secretary, to get ready to conduct the detailed negotiations. Also he has hinted to MPs that, if excluded, Britain may have to reduce her NATO defence spending. The other EFTA countries also announced today that they will make co-ordinated approaches to join the Market, which would create a single economic community of 300 million people. Some may join before Britain (→ 4).

Briton triumphant in middleweight bout

Paddington's Terry Downes, new middleweight champion of the world.

July 11. To the bewilderment of the crowd, and the astonished delight of his young cockney challenger, Paul Pender, the middleweight champion of the world, sat down in his corner at the end of the ninth round of his title defence at Wembley and declared that he had had enough. Terry Downes, of Paddington, was a world champion.

The ostensible reason for the 31-year-old Bostonian's retirement was a cut over the eye, though at the time his face looked less of a mess than that of Downes, who had absorbed the champion's persistent left jab for gruelling round after round.

But Downes had attacked hard with powerful hooks to the body, had slowed his opponent visibly, was marginally ahead on points, and looked better equipped to face the last six rounds. He is a worthy British successor to Randolph Turpin, who won the same world title in such spectacular fashion just ten years and one day ago.

Bell tolls for tough writer Hemingway

July 2. Ernest Hemingway was found shot through the head by his own 12-bore shot-gun early this morning. His fourth wife Mary, who was asleep upstairs at their home in Ketchum, Idaho, at the time, issued a statement saying that he was killed accidentally while cleaning the gun. He was in pyjamas and left no note.

Hemingway, stylistically the most influential and most imitated writer of his time, would have been 62 in three weeks. His father, a doctor with a love of hunting which he passed on to his son, shot himself when he was 57, and this incident was used in some of Hemingway's stories.

London goes wild over spaceman Yuri

July 14. Russia's first man in space, Major Yuri Gagarin, received an ecstatic welcome from British crowds today, while on a flying visit to the West. Following lunch with the Queen and Prince Philip at Buckingham Palace, and a tumultuous "press conference", attended by 1,000 inquisitive journalists, at Earl's Court, Major Gagarin is due to fly to Manchester to receive a gold medal from the Amalgamated Union of Foundry Workers.

Delighted by Gagarin's "film star" welcome, the British-Soviet Friendship Society considered the visit a landmark in East-West relations and told him he was "a missile surely guided at the hearts of the British people" (→ 21).

Gagarin – now London cheers too.

1961

AUGUST

Su	Mo	Tu	We	Th	Fr	Sa
		1	2	3	4	5
6	7	8	9	10	11	12
13	14	15	16	17	18	19
20	21	22	23	24	25	26
27	28	29	30	31		

1. Congo: Kasavubu appoints Cyrille Adoula premier.

4. London: MPs approve the government's proposal to join the Common Market (→ 10).

6. USSR: The USSR launches its second cosmonaut.→

8. Berlin: 1,741 East Germans have arrived in the last 24 hours (→ 13).

10. London: Britain formally applies for membership of the EEC.

11. Algeria: France ends the cease-fire originally imposed for 30 days in May during peace talks with Moslems rebels (→ 8/9).

13. Berlin: East Germany closes the Berlin border and blocks it with barbed wire (→ 16).

14. Jerusalem: Eichmann's trial ends (→ 15/12).

15. Nyasaland: Nationalist leader Dr Hastings Banda wins a general election.

16. Berlin: West Berlin mayor Willy Brandt appeals for calm, urging the US to take political action against the East (→ 17).

16. London: The GPO says its new tower will be 603 ft high, not 507 ft as originally planned.

17. Berlin: The three Western powers send notes to the USSR demanding an end to "illegal restrictions" in the city (→ 20).

20. Berlin: The East Germans erect a five foot concrete wall along the border to replace the barbed wire (→ 23).

21. Kenya: The last restrictions on Kenyatta's movements are lifted. →

23. Berlin: The Western powers place tanks and 1,000 troops along the wall.→

24. UK: A man is murdered and his girlfriend raped by a savage killer on the A6.

28. UK: The earliest extant Roman mosaics in Britain are discovered at Fishbourne.

30. France: 63 tourists are rescued from a stranded cable car after a jet sliced through its cable, killing six.

West is impotent as Berlin Wall rises

Aug 31. The wall which the Communists have built across Berlin, sealing off the Western sectors, is being made taller and stronger every day and, while the Western Powers are outraged by this swift and brutal action, it is becoming increasingly obvious that there is nothing they can do about it.

Mr Rusk, the US Secretary of State, has described the wall as "a flagrant violation of the right of free circulation throughout the city, in direct contravention of the Four-Power agreement reached in Paris on June 20, 1949". A British Foreign Office spokesman also insisted that the wall was contrary to the Four-Power status of Berlin.

None of these protests, however, seems likely to make a dent in the wall, which was put up to stop the swelling exodus of East Germans who were "voting with their feet" to seek a new life in the West.

The wall, made of pre-fabricated concrete blocks, went up with great rapidity. Early in the morning of the 13th, East German soldiers, armed with machine guns, sealed off the line dividing the sectors with rolls of barbed wire. Train services between the sectors were halted and the 50,000 East Germans who work in West Berlin were turned back.

Building materials stored in war-ruined buildings close to the line were brought forward, and work started immediately on the wall which now snakes across Berlin.

It was greeted with anger on both sides. East German police used hoses, truncheons and tear-gas on crowds milling around the closed crossing points. At the Brandenburg Gate 4,000 West Berliners jeered the East German troops, while at another point they trampled down the barbed wire, but fell back as the guards advanced with fixed bayonets.

The crowd shouted for the East Germans to "Hang old Goat-beard", their contemptuous name for Herr Walter Ulbricht, the East German Communist leader, and pleaded with the guards to "Put your guns away".

Herr Willy Brandt, the Mayor of West Berlin, is trying to calm the passions aroused by the division of the city. He has appealed to East Berliners not to revolt despite the provocation. In a broadcast to the East he promised them: "You cannot be held in slavery for ever."

But many East Germans are not waiting for future liberation. As the wall-builders strive to close off all loopholes, refugees are still finding secret ways through the war-ruins, gardens and backyards which run right up to the border. At least two families have swum across the city's canals to freedom.

Ominously, the border guards are now clearing strips of wooded country in the outskirts of the city in order to give themselves a clear field of fire at refugees trying to make their way through the trees.

Meanwhile, the harsh regulations, which have already caused so many people to flee, have been strengthened. A new order permits local authorities to assign anyone to work on the land, replacing those who have fled. Reports reaching the West suggest it is being used to impose forced labour on "undesirable political elements" (→25/10).

East German workers build the Berlin wall and split the city in two.

Still carrying his weapon, this East German soldier sprints to freedom.

1961

SEPTEMBER

Su	Mo	Tu	We	Th	Fr	Sa
					1	2
3	4	5	6	7	8	9
10	11	12	13	14	15	16
17	18	19	20	21	22	23
24	25	26	27	28	29	30

1. UK: Hampshire wins the County Cricket championship for the first time ever.

3. US: Britain and the US call for a ban on nuclear tests in the atmosphere (→ 7).

4. Portsmouth: The TUC expels the Electrical Trades Union for ballot-rigging (→ 29).

7. Portsmouth: The TUC votes against unilateral nuclear disarmament (→ 12).

10. Italy: 13 spectators at the Italian Grand Prix at Monza are killed when two cars collide and veer off the track.

10. Ireland: 86 die in a plane crash just after take off from Shannon Airport.

12. London: Nuclear protesters Bertrand Russell and Arnold Wesker are jailed.→

13. US: A Mercury capsule capable of carrying a man is put into a single orbit.

14. London: The first Mothercare shop opens, in Kingston.

17. Turkey: Ex-premier Adnam Menderes is hanged by Turkey's military rulers.

21. Paris: Dior heir Yves Saint Laurent says he will start his own fashion business.

22. Accra: Nkrumah sacks the British head of the Ghanaian army and takes over as Commander-in-Chief (→ 3/10).

28. Damascus: Syrian troops revolt against alleged Egyptian domination of the United Arab Republic or UAR (→ 30).

28. Stockholm: Up to 100,000 Swedes take to the streets to mourn Hammarskjold (→ 23/10).

29. London: The electricians' union is expelled from the National Executive Committee of the Labour Party.

30. Damascus: Syria declares independence from the UAR and orders the deportation of 27,000 Egyptians (→ 1/10).

DEATHS

17. Turkish statesman Adnam Menderes (*1899).

18. Swedish statesman Dag Hammarskjold, UN Secretary General 1953-61 (*29/7/05).→

Kenyatta released from British custody

Jomo Kenyatta, once the Mau Mau's figure-head, relaxes in his garden.

Aug 21. Jomo Kenyatta, Kenya's veteran nationalist leader, was today visited at his home outside Nairobi by a British District Commissioner and handed a gold signet ring and a black walking stick with a carved elephant's head handle.

These treasured possessions were returned to him to symbolise his return to freedom after nine years of detention and restriction. Kenyatta, now 71, was sentenced to hard labour in 1953 for running the secret terrorist organisation, the Mau Mau. African nationalists claimed that Kenyatta had been framed, and some Europeans remained sceptical about his guilt.

Though the British endeavoured to push ahead with political reform in the colony, influential African leaders refused to co-operate until Kenyatta was freed. Two years ago, the first cautious steps were taken to return him to public life. He was first released from prison, then moved to a new house built for him at Gatundu, 14 miles from Nairobi; but he was still under a detention order. Now that has been revoked.

He will meet African leaders tomorrow to discuss the forthcoming conference in London on the colony's future. The man whom a British governor called "a leader to darkness and death" seems to be coming out of the shadows.

Second Russian in orbit – 17 times

Aug 7. The Soviet Union's second cosmonaut, Major Gherman Titov, landed safely today some 500 miles south-east of Moscow, after orbiting the earth 17 times in just over 25 hours. Titov, aged 26, was said to be in excellent health. He flew in a five-ton Vostok spaceship, and was shown on Soviet television eating lunch and dinner, and sleeping for more than seven hours. Yuri Gagarin became the first Russian in space in April (→ 13/9).

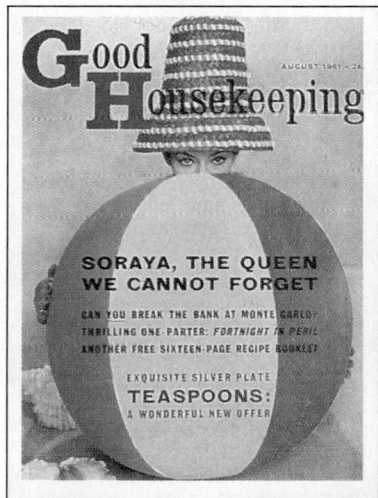

Good Housekeeping

SORAYA, THE QUEEN WE CANNOT FORGET

EXQUISITE SILVER PLATE TEASPOONS: A WONDERFUL NEW OFFER

Massive ban-the-bomb demo ends with arrest of 850

Sept 17. The biggest ban-the-bomb demonstration so far seen in London ended in violent clashes and the arrest of nearly 850 people today. Among them were Canon Collins, the chairman of the Campaign for Nuclear Disarmament, the playwright John Osborne, the jazz singer George Melly and the actress Vanessa Redgrave.

At one point more than 15,000 protesters jammed Trafalgar Square on a day that saw the Russians explode the 12th bomb in the present series. The clashes came as 3,000 police struggled to arrest demonstrators staging "sit down" protests.

Last week the philosopher Bertrand Russell was jailed for inciting a breach of the peace (→ 23/10).

Earl Russell sits down for peace.

UN crushes Congo Katangan rebels

Sept 13. The Katanga leader, Moise Tshombe, failed to keep a lunch date today with Dr Conor Cruise O'Brien, the UN representative in Elisabethville. Instead, he was in hiding from the Indian and Swedish UN troops which Dr O'Brien had ordered into action to suppress the Congo breakaway state. The death toll so far is 56, and Britain has queried the UN's authority for such action (→ 18).

UN chief Hammarskjold dies in air crash

Dag Hammarskjold and thirteen others died in this air crash in the jungle.

Sept 18. The DC-6 airliner carrying Dag Hammarskjold, the UN Secretary-General, was approaching Ndola airport in Northern Rhodesia early today when, without warning, it plunged to earth, tearing a wide swathe through the bush. Thirteen of the 14 passengers died, including Hammarskjold.

The UN Secretary-General had been flying to Ndola to meet Mr Tshombe, the Katanga leader, who fled to Northern Rhodesia when UN forces mounted their controversial action to end Katanga's secession. The Western powers have been highly critical of this operation, and Hammarskjold himself believed it should never have been launched. He had written to Tshombe agreeing to a meeting to work out a cease-fire.

But the sole survivor of the crash, an American security guard, said Hammarskjold had changed his mind about landing at Ndola, and had told the pilot to alter course. Soon afterwards there was an explosion and the plane went down.

In New Delhi, Mr Nehru, the Indian Prime Minister, suggested the crash might have been caused by sabotage. In New York, the Soviet delegate on the Security Council publicly dissociated his government from a joint communique praising Hammarskjold's leadership and diplomatic skill (→ 3/11).

Rebel general fails to kill de Gaulle

Sept 8. Raoul Salan, stripped of General's rank after organising the failed French rebellion in Algeria, was today named as the man responsible for an attempt on the life of President de Gaulle. A well-organised gang of the so-called Secret Army fired a plastic explosive charge, intended to blow up the President's car, near his country home at Colombey-les-Deux-Eglises.

"A joke in very bad taste," commented the President. Security men arrested one gang member, who named the others and said they were working for Salan (→ 20/10).

New York debut for newcomer Dylan

Sept 28. A surprising young talent with a frayed appearance and compelling stage presence is generating the kind of excitement in New York's Greenwich Village normally reserved for grizzled veterans of the folk music scene.

He is 20-year-old Bob Dylan, who is appearing this week at Gerde's Folk City. He sounds like a blend of the nasal drawl of Depression-era folk singers and the deep-throated growl of Southern blues. He sings his own vivid, haunting songs, and accompanies himself on guitar and harmonica.

1961

OCTOBER

Su	Mo	Tu	We	Th	Fr	Sa
1	2	3	4	5	6	7
8	9	10	11	12	13	14
15	16	17	18	19	20	21
22	23	24	25	26	27	28
29	30	31				

1. London: The last steam train runs on the London Underground.

3. Accra: Nkrumah announces the arrest of 50 opposition leaders, claiming they were plotting to kill him (→ 9/11).

3. London: The Queen creates Antony Armstrong-Jones Earl of Snowdon.

6. Dublin: Fianna Fail wins the Irish general election but loses its majority.

9. London: Youngest Tory woman MP Margaret Thatcher gets her first government job, as a parliamentary secretary.

11. New York: The UN Assembly censures S. Africa for the second time this year (→ 19).

12. UK: Smaller ten shilling notes come into circulation (→ 19/12).

12. Wellington: New Zealand MPs vote to abolish the death penalty.

17. Moscow: Khrushchev banishes pro-Chinese, Stalinist Albania from the Soviet Bloc (→ 10/12).

19. S. Africa: The Nationalists win the whites-only general election (→ 23).

23. USSR: A massive nuclear device, possibly as big as 30 megatons, is exploded.

23. Oslo: The late Dag Hammarskjold is to be awarded the 1961 Nobel Peace Prize posthumously.

24. Malta: The island gains independence from Britain.

25. Berlin: British and US tanks face Soviet tanks along the border in a row over Allied entry rights (→ 19/11).

27. New York: Mauritania and Mongolia join the UN.

30. Congo: The Congolese army begins an offensive to subdue the Katangan rebels (→ 14/11).

31. Algeria: 86 die in violent riots marking the seventh anniversary of the 1954 Moslem rebellion (→ 13/11).

DEATH

31. British painter Augustus John (*4/1/1878).→

Stalin moved from Red Square tomb

Oct 30. Russia's de-Stalinisation campaign came to a climax last night when the body of Joseph Stalin was secretly removed during the night from the great mausoleum in Red Square, where he had been laid to rest with great pomp beside Lenin in 1953, and dumped in a plot near the Kremlin wall. The decision to remove his corpse was taken at a Party congress after a woman delegate, imprisoned during pre-war purges, said she had "spoken" with Lenin in her heart; he had "said" it was unpleasant to lie near Stalin because of the harm he had done to the Party (→ 1/11).

Augustus John, fine portraitist, is dead

Oct 31. Augustus John looked like the flamboyant, operatic version of a painter, and lived up to it in his Bohemian ways. He died today at the age of 83. In early years he roamed England and Wales, where he was born, in a caravan, seeking the company of gipsies, whom he painted.

It was in portraits and portrait drawings that he showed his greatest mastery. His portraits of the cellist, Madame Suggia, of Shaw Thomas Hardy, T.E. Lawrence, W B. Yeats and Dylan Thomas fixed their images for posterity. He painted women and children sensitively but always maintained that his sister Gwen, who died in 1939, was the better painter.

Augustus John, sharp as ever.

Algerian troubles spread to French cities

Supporters of "Algerie Francaise" demonstrate in the streets of Paris.

Oct 20. A whiff of Algeria came to the streets of France today as thousands of slogan-shouting Moslem women staged passive demonstrations in Paris and Northern France. They were protesting against the curfew which has been imposed to cope with the growing dangers of terrorism in France.

Leaders of the National Liberation Front (FLN) had called them into the streets for a carefully planned public relations exercise, to show Parisians its disciplined control over the mass of the expatriate population. While the women marched, the men, many of whom work in France, went on strike.

Demonstrations began in outer Paris as hundreds of veiled Algerian women, many with babies in their arms, paraded through the North Paris suburbs, but late tonight more women in small groups surged from Metro stations into central Paris.

The women first appeared in force at Nanterre, a hotbed of FLN activity. They wanted to march on the local police headquarters, but reinforcements were rushed in. Shepherded by special squads armed with sub-machine guns, the women calmly allowed themselves to be ushered into waiting buses. More than 1,000 women and children are now being held for identity checks (→31).

Syrians rebel at union with Egypt

Oct 1. Syria, which recently merged with Egypt to form the United Arab Republic, is on the edge of civil war today. The First Army has revolted against the "tyranny and corruption" of Egyptian rule, and the soldiers have mutinied against their Egyptian officers, arresting Field Marshal Abdel Hakim Amer, Egypt's pro-consul in Syria.

The new army-installed government, headed by Dr Kuzbari, has seceded from the Union, supported by the civilians who resent nationalisation and the new restrictions on the economy. 5,000 Egyptian troops stationed in Syria are now marching on Damascus (→26/11).

Diem says Vietnam is engaged in war

Oct 16. With a renewed Viet Cong offensive expected during the dry season, due to begin within the next few weeks, South Vietnam's President Diam declared in Saigon today that the struggle against well-armed Communist insurgents was "no longer a guerrilla war, but a real war".

This war, Diem added, is being waged "by an enemy who attacks us with regular military units." The South Vietnamese leader told a group of his political supporters that the conflict has taken on a new dimension over the past 12 months, following the Communist failure at political subversion (→14/11).

1961

NOVEMBER

Su	Mo	Tu	We	Th	Fr	Sa
			1	2	3	4
5	6	7	8	9	10	11
12	13	14	15	16	17	18
19	20	21	22	23	24	25
26	27	28	29	30		

1. Moscow: Lenin's mausoleum re-opens after removal of Stalin's body.

2. London: Mosleyites attack MPs who oppose immigration controls (→23).

7. West Germany: Adenauer is elected for a fourth term as Chancellor.

9. Accra: The Queen arrives on a state visit to Ghana, which is going ahead despite a bombing wave in Accra.→

10. USSR: Stalingrad is renamed Volgograd (→11).

11. Moscow: Disgraced Stalinists Molotov, Malenkov and Kaganovich are expelled from the Communist Party (→12).

12. East Germany: All public memorials to Stalin are removed.

13. Algeria: Captured rebel leader Ben Bella, now on the 11th day of a hunger strike, is moved to a French hospital (→29/12).

14. New York: A UN report accuses Tshombe and Kasavubu of conspiring to murder Congo ex-premier Lumumba (→16).

16. Congo: The bodies of 13 Italian UN troops are sold in a market; U Thant orders punishment of those responsible (→1/12).

19. Berlin: The East Germans build tank traps along the Wall.

23. London: Gaitskell makes a fierce attack on Macmillan over the Immigration Bill.

24. London: De Gaulle arrives amid tight security for talks with Macmillan.

29. London: The Government issues a white paper outlining plans for the abolition of the London County Council.

29. New York: The USSR vetoes Kuwait's entry to the UN, pleasing the Iraqis, who claim Kuwait as part of Iraq.

DEATH

2. US author James Thurber (*8/12/1894).

Burmese diplomat to be new UN head

U Thant: the new man at the UN.

Nov 3. The United Nations general assembly and security council today unanimously chose experienced diplomat U Thant, 52, of Burma, to be the new Secretary-General. He will hold office until April 1963.

Meanwhile the crisis that led his predecessor, Dag Hammarskjold, to an untimely death, the Katangan secession in Congo, rumbles on and requires immediate attention.

Reports today indicated that President Moise Tshombe has violated the cease-fire by an air strike against Congolese government troops.

Tshombe, in turn, accused the United Nations of helping to transport Congolese troops to the Katanga border. U Thant will need all his diplomatic skill if he is to steer the United Nations away from military intervention and towards conciliation.

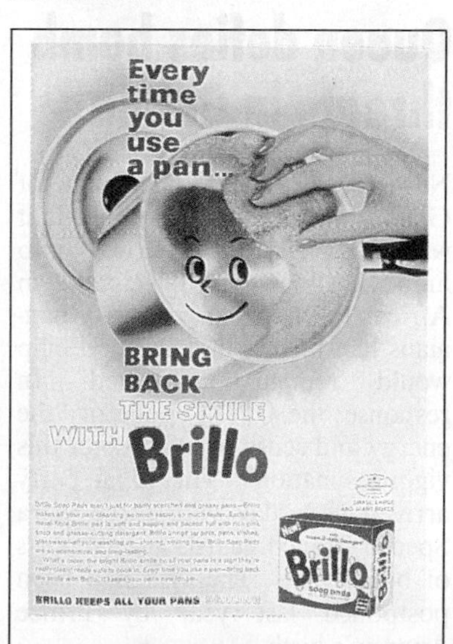

Britain tightens immigration curbs

Nov 1. The Government tonight announced new but flexible Commonwealth immigration controls. There is no stated annual quota. Entry will be curbed by a voucher system.

Immigrants will come to Britain as of right, provided they are self-supporting without a job, or have a voucher either showing they have a job to come to or guaranteeing they have skills which are needed.

It will be "first come, first served" in the voucher queue until the limit, possibly around 60,000, is reached. In 1959 Commonwealth immigrants totalled 21,000. This year the figure will be well over 100,000.

More US advisers for South Vietnam

Nov 14. The US announced today that it will increase the number of military advisers to South Vietnam to 16,000 over the next two years. The first phase will be implemented immediately, with the despatch of 200 Air Force instructors to join the 700 army training personnel already stationed there.

The military aid includes bombers, fighters, helicopters, radar, cars, trucks and generators. Medium-range bombers are due to arrive shortly, and a US ground crew has set up an airfield at Bienhoa, north-east of Saigon (→22/12).

Queen defies bomb threats in Ghana

Nov 10. President Nkrumah of Ghana told the Queen tonight that whatever might be blown into limbo by the wind of change in Africa, the personal regard Ghanaians had for her and Prince Philip would remain unaffected. In response, the Queen spoke of "the energy and sense of purpose of this vigorous nation". The royal party arrived yesterday with three extra Special Branch guards after reports of bomb plots. The visit had been postponed last year by Prince Andrew's birth.

1961

DECEMBER

Su	Mo	Tu	We	Th	Fr	Sa
					1	2
3	4	5	6	7	8	9
10	11	12	13	14	15	16
17	18	19	20	21	22	23
24	25	26	27	28	29	30
31						

3. UK: The south-east of England is plunged into darkness for two hours by an electrician's error.

4. London: The government says the birth control pill is now available on the NHS.

7. London: The LCC approves construction of 300-ft blocks of flats, Britain's highest, in Hammersmith.

9. Dar-es-Salaam: Tanganyika becomes independent.

10. Stockholm: Nobel Prizes go to Robert Hofstadter (US) and Rudolf Mossbauer (W. Germany, Physics); Melvin Calvin (US, Chemistry); Georg von Bekesy (US, Medicine); Ivo Andric (Yugoslavia, Literature); and in Oslo, posthumously to Dag Hammarskjold (Sweden, Peace).

10. Moscow: The USSR severs relations with Albania.

12. Goa: Portuguese civilians are evacuated amid fears of an Indian invasion (→17).

16. Venezuela: Kennedy begins a Latin American tour.

17. India: Indian troops invade the Portuguese enclaves of Goa, Daman and Diu.→

19. London: The government agrees to the principle of currency decimalisation.

22. South Vietnam: James Davis is the first US soldier killed by the Vietcong.

27. Havana: The first successfully hijacked airliner lands after being diverted by its Cuban hijacker.

29. Paris: De Gaulle says most French troops will leave Algeria in 1962.

HITS OF 1961

Wooden heart.

You don't know.

QUOTE OF THE YEAR

"I want to manage those four boys. It wouldn't take me more than two half-days a week."

Brian Epstein, record shop owner, later manager of a Liverpool pop group, "The Beatles".

UN fires Irish representative in the Congo

Conor Cruise O'Brien, during his time as UN representative in the Congo.

Dec 1. Dr Conor Cruise O'Brien, the Irish diplomat who provoked a storm of criticism last September when he ordered UN forces in Katanga to suppress the province's secession from the Congo, has been "released" from UN service. Dr O'Brien was in New York and about to return to Katanga, when he received the news. A UN spokesman said the Irish government had requested the move.

Dr O'Brien's dismissal had been expected several months ago, but then difficulties emerged. Though the Western Powers were highly critical of his actions in Katanga, Afro-Asian opinion was markedly in his favour. Soon after the military operation was launched, Dr O'Brien received a message of good wishes from President Nkrumah of Ghana. Dr O'Brien blames the British government for keeping up the pressure for his removal.

While in New York, Dr O'Brien was asked by a UN official who his female companion in Katanga was. "She is", said Dr O'Brien, "Maire MacEntee, and we are going to be married." Today Miss MacEntee, a member of the Irish delegation to the UN, resigned from the Irish foreign service (→21).

Congo rebel gives up plans for new state

Dec 21. After three months of clashes between UN forces and the Katangan gendarmes seeking to defend the province's secession from the Congo, Moise Tshombe has acknowledged defeat.

Today he gave a signed statement to Cyrille Adoula, the Congolese Prime Minister, recognising the authority of the central government and the constitutional validity of the Fundamental Law, which makes Katanga one of the Congo's six provinces. Tshombe also agreed to place his forces under the control of the Congolese President.

The agreement was reached after more than 18 hours of non-stop talks, during which orders were sent out for sandwiches, beer and whisky.

Tshombe at a police training camp.

Nazi Eichmann to hang

Eichmann: the Nazi is due to die.

Dec 15. Adolf Eichmann was sentenced today to be hanged for the murder of millions of Jews during the Nazi occupation of Europe. The sentence, in a Jerusalem court, came 19 months after his capture in Argentina by Israeli agents, who smuggled him out to face trial by the people he had tried to exterminate in the "Final Solution".

The former SS colonel, standing straight as a rod and immobile as a statue, looked into the judge's eyes and showed no emotion when Mr Justice Landau pronounced the words: "This court sentences the accused to death for crimes against the Jewish people, crimes against humanity and war crimes."

The sentence came as almost an anti-climax to the drama of the trial. There was no ceremony, no wearing of the black cap. The proceedings lasted only 15 minutes and the sentence was unanimous. As the court rose, Eichmann turned on his heel and left the dock.

Indians take back Goa after 400 years

Dec 19. Indian troops overran the Portuguese enclave of Goa today, forcing its Governor, General Silva, to surrender the territory which has been claimed by the Portuguese for the last 400 years.

The Portuguese stood no chance of resisting the Indian onslaught, in which air and sea power was used to support the invasion by heavily-armed Indian paratroopers. Yet in one episode of spectacular bravery, the Portuguese frigate Alfonso de Albuquerque went into battle against three Indian warships. Torn apart by shellfire, she was beached by her wounded captain; but bravery alone could not stop the formidable forces ordered to occupy Goa for India.

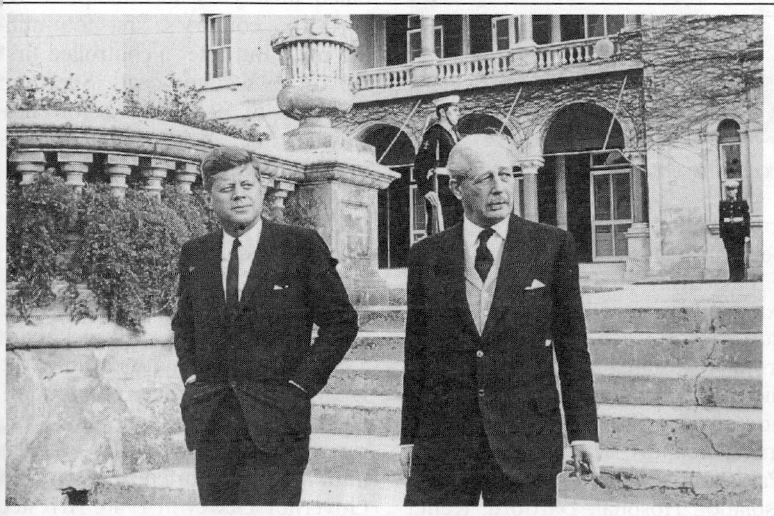

A very special relationship: President Kennedy consults with Prime Minister Macmillan, and professes great admiration for the older man.

Arts: faking madness as a sign of sanity

It has taken 16 years for a savage and brilliant satire on the Second World War to appear but here it is: "Catch 22" by **Joseph Heller** is the year's most talked-of book.

Heller served as a bombardier in the US Air Force, stationed on the island of Corsica. His hero, Captain Yossarian, based on the Italian island of "Pianosa", has decided he cannot face any more bombing missions. His determination to stay alive, by getting out of them, only proves to the authorities that he is sane enough to fly them. That is Catch 22.

This bitterly funny book does for the Second World War what Hasek did for the First in "The Good Soldier Schweik" (Schweik survived by pretending to be a simpleton). Heller exhibits the madness of his fellow officers in various forms – militarism, patriotism, discipplinarianism, ambition, greed for money, sex, or God.

Young men's debunking of a war they do not remember – and of much else in politics, religion, and the sacred cows of the British ruling classes – is a theme of "Beyond the Fringe", a new-style revue which unites the talents of four Oxbridge graduates, **Jonathan Miller, Alan Bennett, Peter Cook** and **Dudley Moore**. "They don't know the meaning of good taste," was one comment. True – that is why they are so exhilarating to the younger generation which is flocking to see them.

The stars of "Beyond the Fringe".

Also exhilarating is the film of the musical "West Side Story", which sets Romeo and Juliet-style star-crossed lovers among the gangs of New York; the dancing, directed by **Jerome Robbins** to the music of **Leonard Bernstein**, reaches new sizzling standards.

"Pop Art" is the label now being attached to the new movement arising which uses as subject matter the artefacts of urban life – advertisements, packaging, graffiti, motor car styling, movie posters.

A group of Pop artists emerged in this year's "Young Contemporaries" show: **David Hockney, Patrick Caulfield, Allen Jones, R.B. Kitaj** and **Peter Phillips. Peter Blake** and **Richard Hamilton** combined advertising images in collages back in 1956.

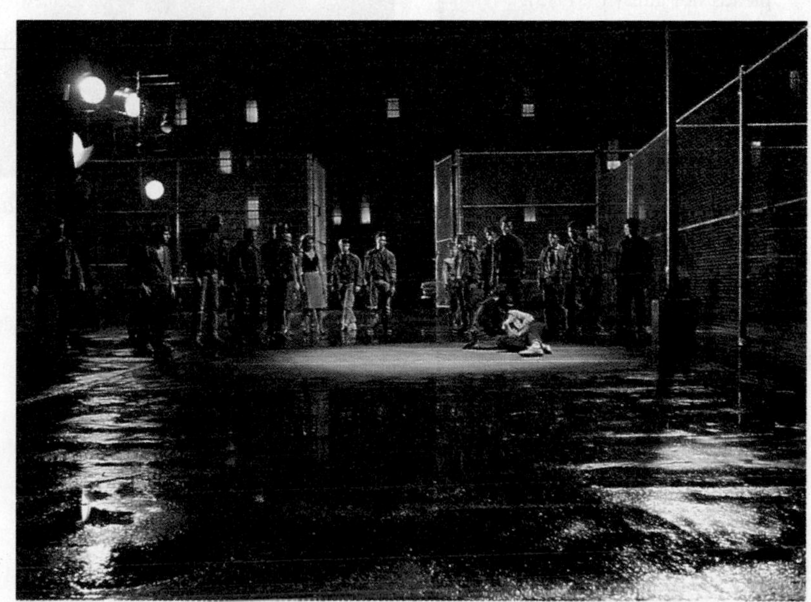

Sharks and Jets get ready for a rumble in Broadway's "West Side Story".

1962

JANUARY

Su	Mo	Tu	We	Th	Fr	Sa
	1	2	3	4	5	6
7	8	9	10	11	12	13
14	15	16	17	18	19	20
21	22	23	24	25	26	27
28	29	30	31			

1. Lebanon: The army arrests 400 for plotting to overthrow the government.

3. Rome: Fidel Castro is excommunicated by the Pope for his anti-clerical policies (→ 3/2).

8. Holland: 93 people are reported killed in a collision between two electric trams.

9. UK: The de Havilland Trident jet plane makes its maiden flight (→ 5/3).

11. Peru: Over 3,000 people are feared dead after a landslide (→ 7/2).

14. Brussels: The EEC nations reach agreement on a common agricultural policy (→ 15/2).

15. Madras: India beat England by 128 runs in the Fifth Test and win the series.

18. Paris: Valery Giscard d'Estaing is appointed Minister of Finance (→ 14/4).

18. Algeria: French troops kill 18 Moslem guerillas.→

21. London: Britain and Nigeria end their joint defence agreement (→ 1/10/63).

21. Tanganyika: President Julius Nyerere resigns because of opposition to his too "moderate" policies.

22. UK: The "A6 Murder" trial opens; James Hanratty pleads not guilty (→ 17/2).

24. Paris: World premiere of Francois Truffaut's latest film "Jules and Jim", starring Jeanne Moreau.

26. US: The rocket Ranger 3 strays off path; it will miss the moon by 20,000 miles (→ 20/2).

29. Algiers: 12 die when a bomb destroys the headquarters of a group opposed to the OAS (→ 5/2).

29. Geneva: Britain and America walk out of the nuclear test ban talks with the Soviet Union (→ 20/2).

DEATHS

16. British socialist historian Richard Henry Tawney (*30/11/1880).

24. French painter Andre Lhote (*7/7/85).

Algerian issue explodes on Paris streets

Jan 24. In response to a widespread daylight bombing campaign in France, President De Gaulle tonight ordered a security crackdown on OAS terrorists. To mark the anniversary of the settlers' revolt in Algiers, the OAS Secret Army, composed of right-wing fanatics and rebellious French soldiers, had exploded ten plastic devices in Paris, hitting political party offices and journalists' homes.

Fresh emergency measures to combat the OAS are to be applied immediately. All newspapers and radio are forbidden to publish terrorist communiques. Any editor breaking the ban is liable to be charged, and offending newspapers may be seized.

More than 50 OAS suspects are under arrest, but the organisation remains operational. Its aim is to terrorise the French people into rejecting the president's plan to restore peace in Algeria through a policy of self-determination. In Algeria it displayed its power today by forcing a general strike by the European population, while wreaths were placed to commemorate the uprising two years ago.

A plastic explosive bomb placed in a mail bag wrecked the Foreign Ministry office of George Gorse, the Secretary of State. It killed a driver and injured others. This outrage, which followed the kidnapping of Dr Mainguy, a Gaullist politician, has alarmed the government. The doctor was seized by three OAS men when he arrived at his suburban Paris surgery. Later he was freed by police (→ 29).

Smallpox outbreak claims British victims

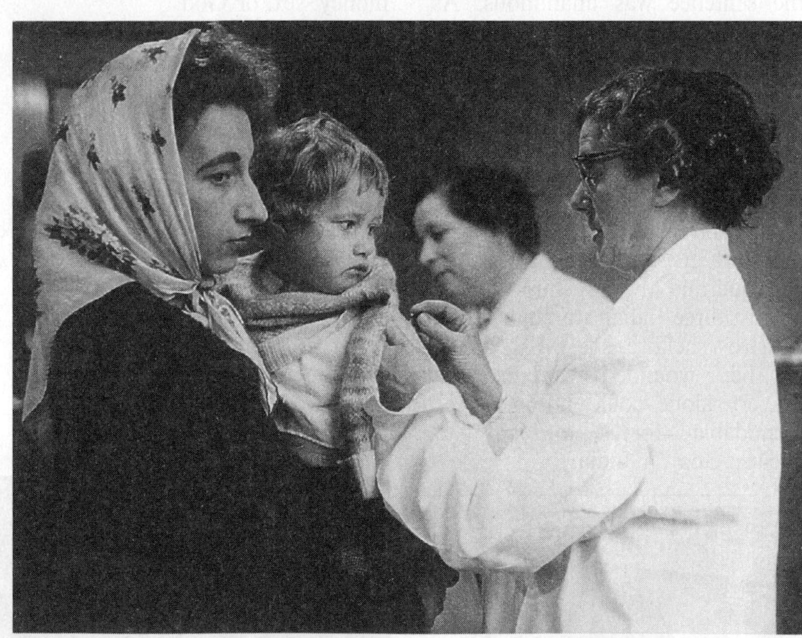

Thousands of children across Europe are receiving emergency vaccinations.

Jan 14. The death of a smallpox suspect in Otley, near Bradford, where four patients have already died, raises the number of deaths in the current outbreak to six.

Six possible victims in Oakwell Hospital, Birstall, near Leeds, are "quite ill". They include Dr J. Ainley, a pathologist, who conducted a post-mortem examination on a child who died of smallpox. Two more suspected cases have been reported and Dr J. Douglas, the Medical Officer of Health for Bradford, said that two children have been hospitalised.

Passengers on a BEA flight from Amsterdam were detained at London Airport when eight immigrants from Pakistan – where 13 have died from smallpox in the past 48 hours – felt ill, but they only had travel sickness. The condition of a Pakistani woman in Long Reach Isolation Hospital, Dartford, Kent, is unchanged. Dr Donald Johnson, MP for Carlisle, is demanding compulsory vaccination.

New Zealander sets world mile record

Peter Snell ends the fastest mile.

Jan 27. Peter Snell, New Zealand's Olympic 800 metres champion, who is trained by the outstanding Arthur Lydiard, broke the world mile record held by Herb Elliott, with a breathtaking final lap of 56.4 seconds on a grass track at Cook's Gardens, Wanganui.

There are no synthetic tracks in New Zealand and the race, in which Britain's Bruce Tulloh was favoured as a real challenge, was billed merely as an attempt to record the country's first four-minute mile. But after a controlled first lap of 60 seconds dead, Snell ran two each of 59 seconds before destroying the field, and Elliott's record in 3 minutes 54.4 seconds.

Luciano out of luck

Jan 26. Salvatore Luciano, better known as "Lucky", died in Italy of a heart attack today. As head of the US Mafia, he controlled prostitution, narcotics and gambling rings, and ran most of Al Capone's old rackets until he was deported by New York Governor Dewey in 1946. Arrested 25 times, he went to prison only twice. From his exile in Italy he ran a successful drugs ring (→ 27/9/63).

Yves St. Laurent sets up his own house

Jan 15. Yves St. Laurent, the Algerian-born wonder boy of fashion, has opened his own couture house in Paris. His successful first show there comes only two years after commentators were ready to write off his clothes as "fancy dress".

YSL, as he styles himself, was the protege of Christian Dior, taking over his salon at the age of 21, when its founder died in 1957. Apart from a brief flirtation with short skirts a couple of seasons ago, his main concern recently has been to make women look elegant and well-groomed. The shy, bespectacled couturier greatest success so far has been creating the "A" line in soft fabrics (→20/3).

St. Laurent with Zizi Jeanmaire.

More US aid and army units for Vietnam

Jan 4. President Kennedy today announced new measures to shore-up the government of South Vietnam which is increasingly under attack by communist guerrillas controlled by North Vietnam.

Already substantial military aid is in the pipeline to Saigon and two new regular US army divisions are to be formed in order, said the President, "to demonstrate in unmistakable terms our determination to resist Communist aggression". To complement this military aid, the US is also backing a "broad economic and social" programme to raise living standards in Vietnam whose infrastructure suffered badly during the Japanese occupation in the war and the subsequent revolt against the French.

The programme will cost appreciably more than last year's $136 million (→16/5).

MERSEYSIDE'S OWN ENTERTAINMENTS PAPER

MERSEY BEAT

NEMS
WHITECHAPEL AND GREAT CHARLOTTE STREET
THE FINEST RECORD SELECTIONS IN THE NORTH

Vol. 1 No. 13 JANUARY 4-18, 1962 Price THREEPENCE

Beatles Top Poll!

FULL RESULTS INSIDE

JOHN LENNON GEORGE HARRISON PAUL McARTNEY PETE BEST

Despite their success on Liverpool's music scene, the Beatles were rejected this month by the recording company, Decca, whose experts believe they will never make it to the music charts. Manager Brian Epstein and his proteges are considering producing their first album themselves.

1962

FEBRUARY

Su	Mo	Tu	We	Th	Fr	Sa
				1	2	3
4	5	6	7	8	9	10
11	12	13	14	15	16	17
18	19	20	21	22	23	24
25	26	27	28			

3. Washington: President Kennedy imposes an embargo on Cuban imports (→8/4).

4. Switzerland: Two climbers complete the first winter ascent of the Matterhorn's north face.

5. France: De Gaulle pledges in a TV broadcast that he will bring peace to Algeria (→8).

7. Karachi: England draw the Third Test and win the series against Pakistan (→16).

7. West Germany: 249 miners die and 146 are missing after a pit explosion in the Saar.

11. UK: An Essex schoolboy claims to have broken a world record by dancing The Twist non-stop for 33 hours.

13. Paris: A general strike is declared and 500,000 join the funeral march for eight people killed during rioting (→13).

14. Washington: Jackie Kennedy conducts a televised tour of the White House (→30/3).

15. West Germany: De Gaulle and Adenauer meet to discuss European unity (→17/4).

16. UK: At least 11 are feared dead after fierce gales (→21).

20. London: Six anti-nuclear protestors are jailed under the Official Secrets Act (→25).

21. Hamburg: 278 are feared dead after flooding (→3/9).

23. Paris: Delegates from 12 countries sign an accord to set up a European space research organisation (→16/3).

25. London: Bertrand Russell calls atomic tests "butchery" and attacks the conviction of anti-nuclear protestors (→14/3).

26. Northern Ireland: The IRA calls off its five-year campaign of violence (→20/4).

27. US: A government board of inquiry concludes that U-2 pilot Gary Powers did his best to follow orders (→6/9).

27. London: MPs pass a bill to restrict immigration from the Commonwealth (→1/7).

DEATH

17. German-born American conductor Bruno Walter (*15/9/1876).

Hanratty to hang for murder on A6

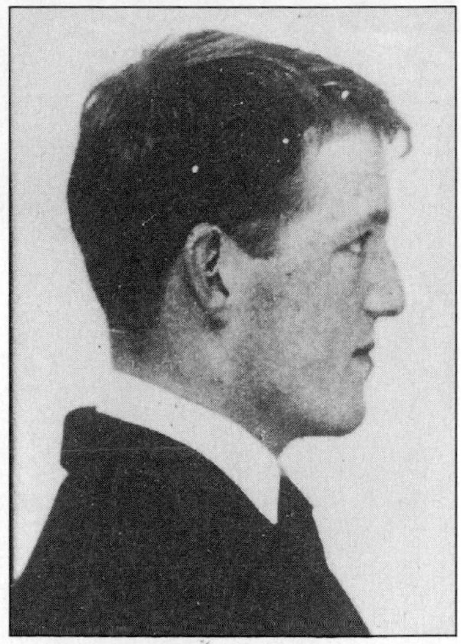

James Hanratty: guilty of murder.

Feb 17. James Hanratty was today sentenced to death for murdering Michael Gregsten, aged 36, in a lay-by at Deadman Hill near Bedford last year. His trial, lasting 21 days, was the longest murder case in British legal history and the jury retired for ten hours. But as Hanratty waited in the condemned cell he still claimed he was innocent and plans to appeal (→4/4).

Sunday Times gets colour supplement

Feb 4. A "colour supplement" was published today by the Sunday Times with features on Pop art and Mary Quant. Lord Thomson, the owner, believes it will be a winner. Most critics disagree.

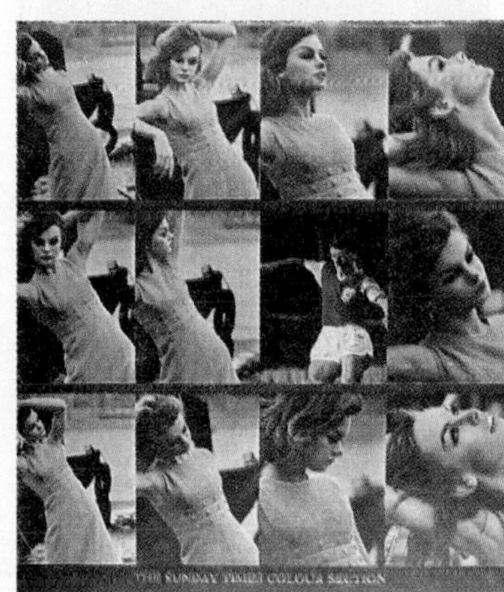

First colour supplement cover.

John Glenn orbits earth

American astronaut John Glenn back on earth after his space achievement.

Feb 20. Lieutenant-Colonel John H. Glenn today became the first American to orbit the earth. His Mercury capsule, called Friendship 7, lifted off from Cape Canaveral at 9.47am local time and then splashed down in the Atlantic off Puerto Rico five hours later, after circling the earth three times. "My condition is excellent," Glenn said as he went aboard the recovery ship, the USS Noa.

Glenn's flight was postponed ten times, first because of bad weather and difficult sea conditions in the recovery area, and then, at the last minute, for a power failure in a computer in Bermuda. But when the Atlas rocket bearing Friendship 7 finally lifted off the launch pad, thousands of people were on the nearby beaches to watch.

On his first orbit Glenn was able to see the lights of Perth in Australia, left on by the residents specially for him; by the end of it his spacecraft was surrounded by thousands of luminous particles.

A potentially serious problem arose just before re-entry, when instruments on the ground indicated that the heat shield had become loose. Without it the capsule would burn up on re-entry. As a precaution mission controllers decided not to jettison the retro-rocket package attached below the heat shield. In the event the heat shield remained in place and the capsule parachuted back safely (→23).

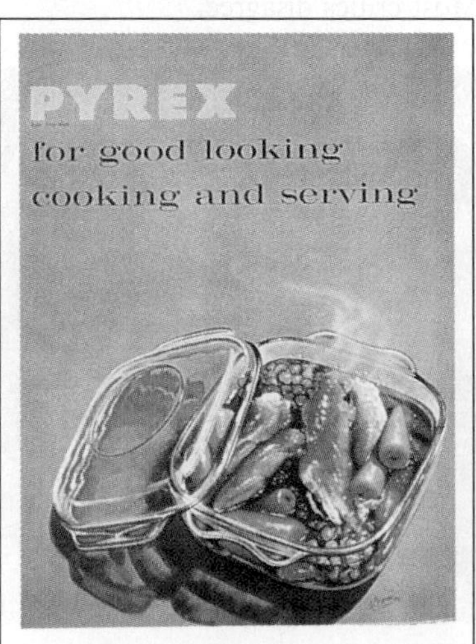

U-2 pilot Powers home in spy swap

Feb 10. U-2 Pilot, Francis Gary Powers, and Soviet KGB Colonel, Rudolph Abel, figured in a remarkable East-West spy swap on a Berlin bridge today, after months of secret negotiations. Powers flew over the Soviet Union on a spy mission in 1960, was shot down and received a ten-year sentence. Abel was the most important Soviet agent ever apprehended in the United States and was imprisoned for 30 years in 1957 (→27).

Eight die in protest over OAS bombings

Feb 8. France faced troubles tonight as eight people died after street fighting broke out in Paris at a banned mass demonstration of left-wingers led by French Communists.

The marchers assembled at the Bastille, chanting "OAS assassins" to protest at the Secret Army (OAS) bombing campaign that has been rocking the city. However, the government claims their real intention was to undermine President de Gaulle's authority. An official inquiry into the organisations which planned the march is under way.

Moderate demonstrators behaved peacefully. Some militant leftists, on the other hand, were out for trouble and attacked riot police with bottles, clubs and missiles. In police charges, 83 demonstrators were injured. The eight crushed to death, including women and a boy, were victims of panic when the mob was forced into the locked entrance of a Metro station.

Though police have broken an OAS cell in the capital, and despite the fact that 25,000 armed troops are on duty in Paris, the "plastiqueurs" or bombers, many of them renegade special forces' officers trained to fight Arab terrorism in Algeria, remain operational. They exploded ten charges today aimed at a number of targets, including Andre Malraux, the distinguished author who is now Minister of Culture (→13).

A victim of the Paris violence.

Killing spree follows Algeria peace talks

Feb 28. The OAS Secret Army of diehard French settlers and rebellious French officers, under ex-General Raoul Salan, today stepped up its desperate tactics to prevent Algerian independence and shot down a dozen Algerians in Algiers.

When progress in the peace talks between France and the provisional Algerian government was announced earlier in the month, the OAS began exploding scores of plastic bombs a day in the big cities. Their gunmen have murdered dozens of Moslem men and women. The aim of this wilful slaughter is to provoke a full-scale Arab uprising. Then the French army in North Africa would be forced into action to protect compatriot settlers.

The tactic is unlikely to succeed. So far the Arab population remains steady. French and Algerian negotiators have already agreed on terms, including a cease-fire, to end France's seven year war against Moslem nationalists. Today the Prime Minister, Michel Debre, sent 40,000 French troops into the city with orders to crush the terrorists. President de Gaulle is gambling all on the loyalty of the French army, albeit shaken by mutinies and revolts (→25/3).

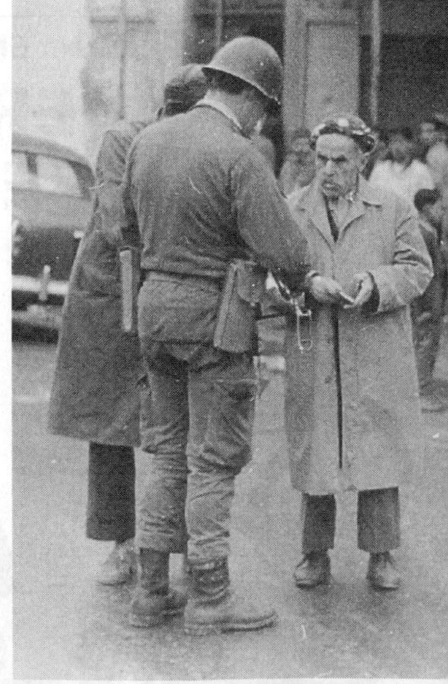
Algiers counts the bloody cost.

1962

MARCH

Su	Mo	Tu	We	Th	Fr	Sa
				1	2	3
4	5	6	7	8	9	10
11	12	13	14	15	16	17
18	19	20	21	22	23	24
25	26	27	28	29	30	31

1. New York: 93 die in a plane crash (→4).

2. India: President Nehru's Congress Party wins the general election with a big majority (→3/5).

2. Burma: The army seizes power in a coup.

3. South Atlantic: The British Antarctic Territory is created.

4. Cameroons: 110 are feared dead after the crash of a British DC-7 (→15).

4. Malta: The island becomes fully independent (→5/5/64).

5. Washington: The Supreme Court rules that airports must compensate nearby residents for disturbance (→20/7).

8. UK: Dick Taverne wins a by-election at Lincoln for the Labour Party (→15).

14. Geneva: East-West arms talks resume but are boycotted by the French (→24/4).

16. USSR: The first Cosmos satellite is launched (→26/4).

18. Israel: Fierce fighting on Syrian border (→16/6/63).

19. London: A 300-year-old skull is discovered beneath 10 Downing Street.

20. Paris: Yves St. Laurent wins a court case against the House of Dior fashion firm (→13/1/64)

25. Algeria: The OAS leader Edmond Jouhaud is arrested and flown to Paris (→26).

27. Syria: A military junta takes power after a coup by the army (→19/7).

28. Argentina: A military coup overthrows President Frondizi.

30. US: Edward Kennedy admits that he used a proxy to sit an exam at Harvard (→26/6).

31, UK: Mr N. Cohen's 12-year-old Kilmore wins the Grand National.

DEATHS

23. British politician Clement Davies (*19/2/1884).

25. Swiss scientist Auguste Piccard (*28/1/1884).

De Gaulle orders troops to crush the OAS

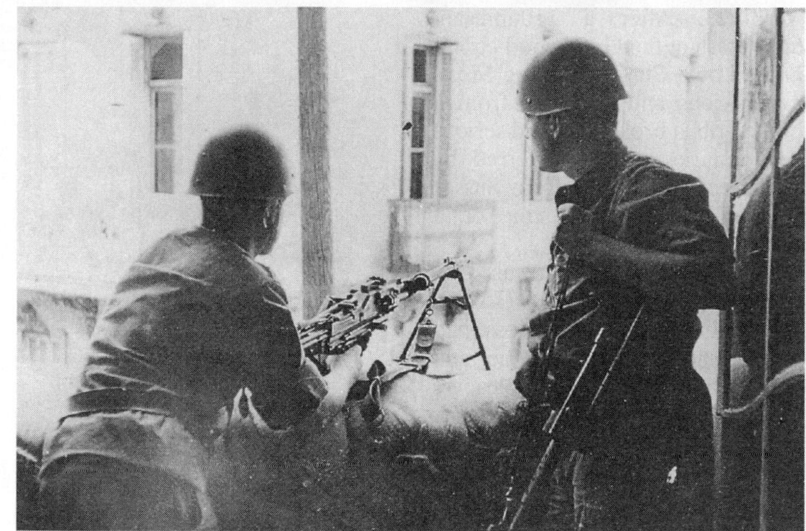

Soldiers keep guard as the Algerian fighting continues, despite a cease-fire.

March 26. The French army today launched a ruthless offensive, ordered by President de Gaulle, using every means to crush the armed insurrection in Algeria. The President yesterday told his cabinet that the most vital task facing France was to end what amounts to a civil war in Algeria.

The first success was the capture in Oran today of ex-General Edmond Jouhaud, one of the four OAS commanders, and 12 of his staff. It followed a seven-hour battle between infantry and tanks and a Secret Army gang which shot-up an army patrol. In the week since Louis Joxe for France, and Benyoussef Ben Kheddah, head of the provisional Algerian government, signed the Evian peace agreement, Algiers and Oran have turned into a battlefield.

Under the treaty a referendum will soon take place, allowing French and Algerians to decide whether the country shall be independent or keep its present status. But ex-General Salan has ordered his OAS extremists to make all-out war on Gaullist France and urged French troops to join him (→8/4).

Princess Grace may star in new movie

March 19. After a break of almost six years, actress Grace Kelly has announced her intention to resume her film career. The picture in question is "Marnie", a suspense thriller based on a novel by the British writer, Winston Graham, and directed by Alfred Hitchcock. It will be her first project since her marriage to Prince Rainier in 1956, when she became Princess Grace of Monaco. Since then, she has repeatedly denied any desire to return to films, which is why today's announcement came as a surprise. Some observers still suspect that the Princess will be persuaded to withdraw before shooting begins in July.

Goldwater darling of American right

March 7. Republican Senator Barry Goldwater was applauded by a massive conservative crowd at New York's Madison Square Gardens last night. The rally, organised by "Young Americans for Freedom", heard Goldwater attack President Kennedy and Communism. He declared: "Conservatism is young, virulent and alive: the wave of the future."

Liberals overturn huge Tory majority at Orpington by-election

March 15. The Liberals have triumphed in the most sensational by-election for a generation. They battered the Tories into humiliating defeat in suburban Orpington. A government majority of 14,760 in the 1959 general election was today turned into a Liberal one of 7,855.

Pundits are calling this massive voting swing the phenomenal climax in a recent run of Liberal polling successes. Some see the possibility now of a return to three-party politics in Britain after more than 30 years of a Tory-Labour duopoly of power.

It has still to be seen, however, whether the Liberals can repeat their feat in a nationwide contest. "It's a flash in the pan," growled Tory Party managers. "My God, it's incredible," said Liberal leader Jo Grimond (→5/4).

Eric Lubbock basks in public acclaim following his Orpington victory.

1962

APRIL

Su	Mo	Tu	We	Th	Fr	Sa
1	2	3	4	5	6	7
8	9	10	11	12	13	14
15	16	17	18	19	20	21
22	23	24	25	26	27	28
29	30					

1. Iraq: Hundreds are killed in fierce fighting between Kurdish rebels and the army (→24/5).

2. London: The first push-button controlled Panda crossings are introduced (→2/5).

4. UK: James Hanratty is hanged for the "A6 murder".

5. UK: William Rodgers wins a by-election at Stockton for the Labour Party (→10/5).

5. London: The Radcliffe report on security recommends banning Communists from the Civil Service (→31/7).

8. France: The Algerian peace accords receive a 90 per cent majority in a referendum.→

8. Cuba: 1,179 Bay of Pigs invaders are sentenced to 30 years in jail; Castro offers to ransom them for $62 million (→25/8).

9. Berlin: Two East Germans escape by driving a truck through the Berlin Wall (→5/5).

14. Paris: Premier Michel Debre resigns and is succeeded by Georges Pompidou (→20/6).

17. Paris: The French and Belgian governments call for Britain to be allowed to join the EEC (→11/9).

20. UK: The government says it will free jailed Irish terrorists following the IRA's peace offer.

24. Washington: Kennedy says atmospheric nuclear tests will be resumed (→9/7).

26. US: Ariel, Britain's first satellite, is successfully launched (→26).

26. US: The American rocket Ranger IV crashes onto the dark side of the moon (→24/5).

27. Washington: Macmillan arrives for discussions with President Kennedy.

30. Moscow: Pablo Picasso and President Nkrumah of Ghana are jointly awarded the Lenin Peace Prize.

30. London: The Metropolitan Police set up a frogman unit.

DEATH

5. British spy-chief Sir Percy Sillitoe (*22/5/1888).

Stirling Moss injured in 110mph crash

April 23. After a 110-mile-an-hour crash at the Goodwood circuit in his Lotus Climax, Stirling Moss, unconscious and suffering from a broken rib, a broken leg and serious head injuries, was transferred by high-speed ambulance from Sussex to the neuro-surgical unit of a London hospital.

Early in the 42-lap Formula One race, before a huge Bank Holiday crowd, the 32-year-old Moss had lost ground with gear trouble, and had set about pursuing the leaders with all the power he could coax from his car, equalling the track record as he passed all but the eventual winner, Graham Hill.

As he closed on Hill, Moss lost control as he approached a corner; the crash left the four-times world championship runner-up trapped for half-an-hour before he could be cut free.

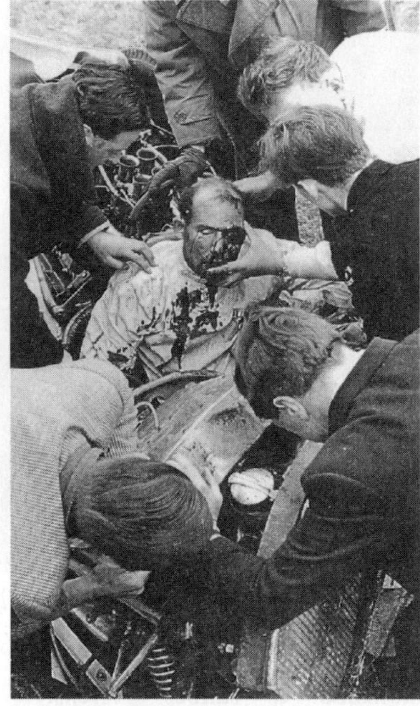

Rescuers rush to Moss's aid.

Budget benefits adults, but not the kids

April 9. Cuts in purchase tax on cars and domestic appliances announced this afternoon in the Budget seem certain to fuel the consumer boom. A ten per cent cut in the tax on cars brings a Mini down from £526 4s 9d to £495 19s 3d while prospective purchasers of a new Rolls-Royce will save £600.

Selwyn Lloyd, the Chancellor of the Exchequer, also revealed plans to reduce purchase tax on television sets, refrigerators and washing machines. Some observers voiced fears about a boom based on hire purchase credit and a growth of imports. Selwyn Lloyd says he is more worried about the reaction of his daughter to his new 15 per cent tax on ice cream and sweets (→29/5).

All the family can now enjoy an ever-widening choice of consumer goods.

French arrest head of OAS in Algiers

April 20. Raoul Salan, the former general who made war on France with his Secret Army, was today captured in Algiers. Promptly flown back to Paris, he is tonight in the Sante Prison. Outside, his supporters clashed with crowds of hostile demonstrators shouting "Death to the OAS".

Salan was arrested in the bathroom of a first-floor apartment in Central Algiers after being betrayed by one of his own men. With him were Madame Salan and her daughter, and his faithful ADC, ex-Captain Ferrandi.

Disguised with a Charlie Chaplin moustache and dyed hair, but still recognisable, he initially refused to admit who he was. He was then flown to a nearby air base (→2/5).

General Salan after his arrest.

Private Eye takes aim at public life

April 30. Peter Cook, one of the stars of the West End review "Beyond the Fringe", has come to the rescue of a new satirical magazine, "Private Eye". The magazine began publishing on a regular basis in February with a mixture of cartoons and articles lampooning people or institutions in the news. It has struck a chord with London's young intelligentsia, but financial difficulties soon arose. However Cook's support seems to assure the magazine of a future (→27/6).

1962

MAY

Su	Mo	Tu	We	Th	Fr	Sa
		1	2	3	4	5
6	7	8	9	10	11	12
13	14	15	16	17	18	19
20	21	22	23	24	25	26
27	28	29	30	31		

2. Algiers: 110 Moslems and Europeans are killed in an OAS terror campaign (→20)

2. London: The government warns it will fine pedestrians who don't use the new Panda crossings.

3. India: Hundreds of Moslems are killed in clashes with Hindus in West Bengal.

6. Laos: Communist guerrillas capture the government stronghold of Nam Tha.→

8. London: The last trolleybuses are taken out of service.

10. UK: The Conservative Party loses control of 30 councils (→15/6).

11. UK: Prince Charles begins his studies at Gordonstoun school in Scotland (→24/4/63).

13. Indonesia: President Sukarno escapes unhurt from assassination attempt (→15/8).

14. Yugoslavia: Vice-President Milovan Djilas is jailed for eight years for revealing details of talks with Stalin (→7/4/63).

16. South Vietnam: The government bans all unauthorized public gatherings.

17. Hong Kong: A barbed wire fence is erected to bar illegal Chinese immigrants.→

20. Algiers: An emergency airlift evacuates European settlers to France (→23).

24. Iraq: 200 die in fighting between rival Kurdish rebel groups (→8/2/63).

25. Stockholm: Two sisters, married to two brothers, give birth in the same hospital on the same day.

29. London: Share values fall by £1,000 million, the biggest slump since 1929 (→26/7).

30. Moscow: Khrushchev sees a Benny Goodman concert; says he is pleased but puzzled.

31. Chile: England lose 2-1 to Hungary in their first match in the World Cup soccer finals.

DEATHS

13. US painter Franz Kline (*23/5/10).

31. German Nazi Adolf Eichmann (*19/3/06).→

Eichmann hanged for his Nazi war crimes

May 31. Adolf Eichmann, "transport manager" of the Holocaust, in which six million Jews died, was executed just before midnight tonight. When told his appeal for clemency had been refused, he asked for a bottle of wine, wrote letters to his family and was visited by the Reverend William Hull, a nonconformist minister.

When he was taken to the scaffold, he refused the black hood, sent his greetings to Germany, Austria and Argentina "the countries I shall not forget", and told the official witnesses: "We shall meet again. I have believed in God. I obeyed the laws of war and was loyal to my flag" (→30/9/64).

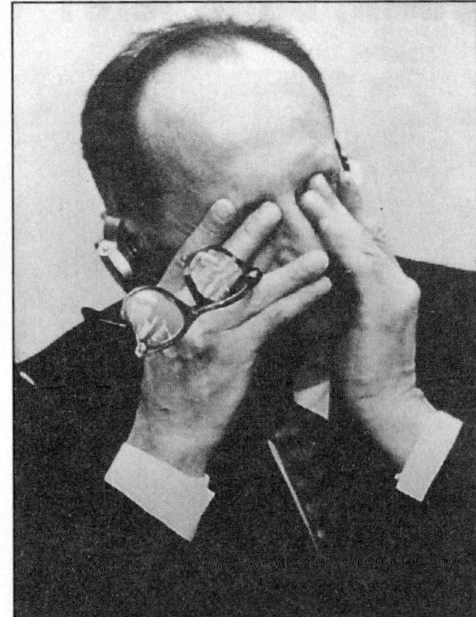

Adolf Eichmann at his trial.

Kennedy sends the US Marines into Laos

May 10. A United States force of 5,000 soldiers and marines from the Seventh Fleet is to be sent to Siam to counter the threat of the expanding military offensive in neighbouring Laos by the Communist Pathet Lao forces.

While America is acting independently in this action, it is expected that Washington will ask member states of the South-East Asian Treaty Organisation to send token forces to join the Americans.

The SEATO troops would be sent to Siam for political rather than military reasons. The Americans are confident their own men can deal with any incursion by the Pathet Lao, but they want to reassure the Siamese that they will be backed by the full weight of SEATO in any emergency. These moves reflect President Kennedy's new determination to exercise leadership where America's "vital interests" are involved, whether Allied governments are prepared to join him or not.

Preventing a Communist takeover in South East Asia is considered a "vital interest". The American government is determined to hold the line in Siam, South Vietnam and, if necessary, Cambodia (→23/7).

A young Chinese refugee, one of thousands, makes a vain attempt to escape from a lorry taking him back from Hong Kong to China.

Artistic triumph of Coventry Cathedral

May 25. The new Coventry Cathedral was consecrated today, 11 years after Sir Basil Spence won the competition to design it. It is a long, squat stone building joined by a pillared entrance porch to the old cathedral's blackened ruins, destroyed by German bombs in November, 1940.

The new building took six years and cost £1,350,000. It is dominated by a baptistery window set with richly stained glass designed by John Piper and by the giant tapestry by Graham Sutherland of Christ enthroned among the four Beasts of the Revelation. Both are over 70 feet high. Epstein's St. Michael commands the entrance, treading the Devil underfoot.

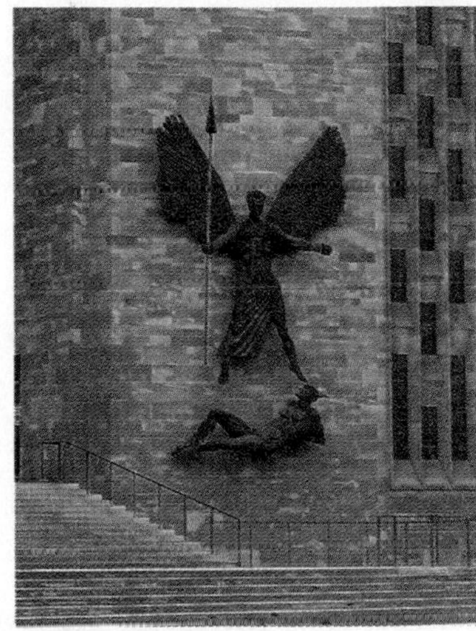

Epstein's St. Michael and Devil.

OAPs walk tall to freedom in West

May 5. A party of eleven elderly East Berliners held their heads high today when they stepped out from a tunnel dug under the Communist wall. They had been working on their underground passageway for more than two weeks and it was six feet high. As the escapers, including four women, came to the surface one yard beyond the barbed wire barrier at Frohnau in West Berlin, they were asked why the tunnel was so high. Their leader, a man of 81, said: "We did not want our wives to crawl, but to walk unbowed to freedom" (→13/8).

Tears as OAS chief given life sentence

May 23. To the amazement and indignation of France, Raoul Salan, the rebellious officer who brought France to the brink of civil war, today escaped death by firing squad. A Paris military tribunal found the self-confessed boss of the murderous OAS Secret Army guilty. But in view of unexplained "extenuating circumstances" it sentenced him only to life imprisonment.

The prosecution had demanded the death sentence and France expected no less. His fellow conspirator ex-General Jouhaud is already in the condemned cell.

Salan burst into tears as he heard the unexpected verdict. Then when full realisation of his escape from death and dishonour dawned upon him he broke into hysterical laughter.

The man who saved Salan is Maitre Tixier-Vignancour, an ultra-right barrister, who also defended Marshal Petain. He swayed the tribunal when he suggested that execution of the broken General would cause discord in France for a whole generation.

During the trial the Secret Army threatened to kill the judges if Salan were executed. Security forces have arrested a hit team sent from Algeria to kill President de Gaulle.

The court's decision is a setback for his policy of self-determination for Algeria by referendum. He remains determined to crush the OAS and punish the crimes of French insurgents there (→5/6).

Carpenter falls to earth, but where?

Astronaut M. Scott Carpenter.

May 24. America's second orbital spaceflight ended today with the capsule lost for nearly an hour after it had overshot the landing zone by 250 miles. However, Aurora 7 and its astronaut, Lieutenant Commander Malcolm Scott Carpenter, were eventually located and recovered safely, after Carpenter had spent three hours in an inflatable life raft.

Carpenter had not oriented the spacecraft correctly before firing the retro-rockets to slow it down for re-entry. He also fired the rockets a few seconds late. These were not the only problems during the flight. Carpenter's heavy use of the control jets to carry out manoeuvres used up more hydrogen peroxide fuel than expected, forcing a changeover from automatic to manual control (→26/8).

Prince Charles meets the headmaster on his first day at Gordonstoun.

1962

JUNE

Su	Mo	Tu	We	Th	Fr	Sa
					1	2
3	4	5	6	7	8	9
10	11	12	13	14	15	16
17	18	19	20	21	22	23
24	25	26	27	28	29	30

2. UK: The Metropole opens in Brighton, Britain's first legal casino.

3. Paris: 130 die in crash of an Air France Boeing 707 (→22).

5. Paris: General Edmond Jouhard appeals from jail for an end to the OAS terror campaign.→

6. UK: Larkspur wins The Derby; four jockeys are admitted to hospital after a seven-horse pile-up.

10. Chile: England lose the World Cup quarter final 3-1 to Brazil.→

11. US: Twentieth Century Fox scrap a new Marilyn Monroe film due to her repeated absences from the set.

12. San Francisco: Three prisoners dig their way out of Alcatraz using spoons.

14. France: Police arrest six OAS assassins sent to kill de Gaulle (→17).

15. UK: Tam Dalyell wins the West Lothian by-election for the Labour Party (→13/7).

17. Algiers: The OAS terror campaign ends after concessions by Moslem leaders (→3/7).

20. France: Breton farmers dump artichokes in the streets to protest at low prices (→9/8).

22. West Indies: 112 die when a French plane crashes (→27/11).

25. Washington: The Supreme Court outlaws "official prayers" in schools.

26. Wimbledon: The top seed Margaret Smith is beaten by 18-year-old Billie Jean Moffit.

27. London: A government committee suggests creating a new TV channel, BBC2 (→11/7).

27. Oxford: Charlie Chaplin receives an honorary Doctorate of letters from the university.

30. UK: First edition of "Police Five" on television.

DEATHS

2. British writer Victoria Sackville-West (*9/3/1892).→

13. British composer Eugene Goossens (*26/5/1893).

Sophia Loren is up on a bigamy charge

June 25. Film Star Sophia Loren and her producer husband, Carlo Ponti, are to face bigamy charges, a Rome magistrate announced today. The couple married by proxy in Mexico five years ago, after Ponti obtained a divorce there from his first wife. But Italian law, which does not recognise divorce, regards him as still being married.

The Oscar-winning actress has had to cancel plans to make a film in London later this year. But she has no intention of fleeing Italy. Currently on location in Leghorn, Miss Loren reacted by declaring: "I have never run away from anything."

Sophia Loren with Carlo Ponti.

The Gentlemen bow out to the Players

June 30. One of the last bastions of the amateur in British sport is set to crumble this year with the final match between the Gentlemen and the Players at Lord's. The cricket authorities have decided that next month's contest – the 137th in a sequence that began in 1806 – will be the last of its kind.

It was only in the last decade that a professional – Len Hutton – captained England and there are still formidable amateurs playing at the highest level, notably Ted Dexter. But the distinction is felt to be increasingly anachronistic. The Players lead by 68 victories to 41.

Brazil's football machine wins World Cup

The triumphant Brazilian team at the Chilean national stadium, Santiago.

June 17. Brazil's footballers, playing with all their natural verve and inventiveness, today conquered Czechoslovakia 3-1 in Santiago to retain the World Cup.

They did it, moreover, without their trump card Pele, who was reduced to a spectator after pulling a muscle in the group matches. His replacement, Amarildo, slotted perfectly into the machine, and scored twice in his first game.

England, the only one of the home countries to qualify for the finals, made heavy weather of their group matches. Nonetheless, with Bobby Charlton outstanding in the unfamiliar position of left-wing, they reached the quarter-finals. Then they met Brazil, for whom Garrincha was in masterly form, and lost 3-1.

The hosts, Chile, came through a vicious, ill-tempered group match against Italy, in which two Italians were sent off and at least one Chilean should have been, to become Brazil's 4-2 victims in the semi-final.

The Czechs disposed of the other surprise semi-finalists – Yugoslavia (for whom Jerkovic was the tournament's top scorer with five goals), but despite a heroic performance by their goalkeeper, Schroiff, in the final they fell to Brazil.

"Vita", the literary gardener, is dead

June 2. Victoria Sackville-West spent her childhood among the courtyards, galleries and secret passages of the great house of Knole at Sevenoaks. Her chief regret was that, as a woman, she could not inherit it. It inspired her friend Virginia Woolf to describe the house and its fictional owner in "Orlando", a sex-change fantasy.

"Vita", as she was known, died instead at Sissinghurst Castle nearby, whose ruins she and her husband, Sir Harold Nicolson made habitable and where she made a famous garden that will perhaps outlive her literary works.

OAS sets fire to Algerian oil fields

June 8. Desperate elements of the OAS today took the ultimate step in their scorched earth campaign by firing the oilfields. A plastic explosive charge set ablaze oil wells at Hassi Touareg, deep in the Sahara. This was the first sabotage attack on the oil resources which provide most of the country's wealth.

The OAS will stop at nothing in their attempts to cripple an independent Algeria. The campaign began with French terrorists burning Algiers University. Gunmen mowed down four Moslems in the streets (→14/6).

1962

JULY

Su	Mo	Tu	We	Th	Fr	Sa
1	2	3	4	5	6	7
8	9	10	11	12	13	14
15	16	17	18	19	20	21
22	23	24	25	26	27	28
29	30	31				

1. East Africa: The UN trusteeships of Rwanda and Burundi become independent.

2. Moscow: Khrushchev pledges that Russia will defend China from attack (→7/8).

5. Algeria: 50 die in fierce fighting between Moslems and Europeans in Oran (→25).

6. Algeria: Moroccan troops invade the border region of Tindouf.

7. Wimbledon: Karen Susman beats Vera Sukova and wins the Women's Singles.→

9. Pacific: US H-bomb test lights up the night sky from Hawaii to New Zealand (→12/11).

10. US: Martin Luther King is jailed for leading an illegal march in Georgia (→10/8).

11. UK: US frogman Fred Baldasare becomes the first person to swim the English Channel underwater.

15. France: Jacques Anquetil wins his third Tour de France.

17. US: An air force pilot sets a new record flying height of 59 miles in an X-15 plane.

18. Peru: The army seizes power and arrests President Prado (→6/1/63).

22. US: Valeri Brumel sets a new world high jump record of seven feet five inches.

23. Europe: 200 million viewers in 16 countries watch US TV programmes live by satellite for first time (→19/9).

23. Geneva: 14 nation conference agrees on a coalition government to rule Laos (→26).

25. Algeria: Civil war breaks out between Moslem factions (→3/8).

31. UK: Britain agrees to set up a Federation of Malaysia (→8/12).

DEATHS

4. British founder of the Glyndebourne Opera, John Christie (*14/12/1882).

6. US writer William Faulkner (*25/9/1897).

21. British historian George Trevelyan (*16/2/1876).

Mac carves up his cabinet colleagues

H. Macmillan – political axeman.

July 13. In an act of ferocious political butchery Mr Macmillan tonight sacked seven members of his cabinet. The dismissal of one-third of his most senior colleagues, including Selwyn Lloyd, the Chancellor of the Exchequer, came at short notice, just 24 hours after another huge Tory voting collapse in by-election polling.

The Prime Minister appears to have been panicked into action to save the government's skin at a time of increasing unpopularity over its pay restraint policies. His explanation is just that "now we need a broad reconstruction".

Liberal MP Jeremy Thorpe said of this Night of the Long Knives: "Greater love hath no man than this, that he lay down his friends for his life" (→26).

First hovercraft enters service

July 20. The world's first passenger hovercraft service opened today, across the estuary of the River Dee between Rhyl and Wallasey. Twenty-four passengers made the first trip, along with two mail-bags carrying 8,000 letters and cards from Rhyl organisations to their opposite numbers in Wallasey. The Queen and Prince Philip have been invited for a trip (→9/2/63). ▷

France proclaims independent Algeria

July 3. One hundred and thirty-two years of French rule in Algeria came to an end today with a brief declaration signed by Charles de Gaulle. He "solemnly recognised" the independence of the North African country that had been considered to be an integral part of France, so ending a conflict which recalled him from retirement to rule the Republic again.

The recognition followed Sunday's referendum when six million Algerians voted almost unanimously for independence in co-operation with France. Both Moslem and French citizens were enfranchised. The final vote in favour was 99 per cent. Jubilant Algerians cheered Benyoussef Ben Kheddah, their new Prime Minister, on his return to Algiers, but Ahmed Ben Bella, his quarrelsome deputy, refused to appear and flew off in a huff to Egypt to see his ally, President Nasser (→ 5).

The people rejoice as the Algerian flag flies free of France.

Act closes door to the Commonwealth

July 1. The Commonwealth Immigration Act became law on the stroke of midnight tonight. There were some remarkable scenes at Britain's airports as the new restrictions were enforced.

Seventy-four Jamaicans without entry certificate work permits were lucky. Their plane, delayed by bad weather, touched down at Belfast 56 minutes after the new rules applied. They were allowed to stay.

First refusals under the Act were three Pakistanis who were put aboard a return flight. Some Indians and Adenese were detained and await repatriation, and a young man went down on his knees and unsuccessfully begged a woman interpreter to be allowed to stay.

Many "beat the Act" immigrant flights have been arriving at Gatwick in the past few days. There were stringent medical checks, but very few exclusions.

Telstar brings Yves Montand live to US

July 11. Live trans-Atlantic television became a reality today, with the help of the Telstar communications satellite. A picture of the chairman of the American Telephone and Telegraph Co, which built Telstar, was relayed to the satellite from Andover in Maine. As Telstar came over the horizon, ground stations at Goonhilly, Cornwall, and in Brittany tried to pick up its signals. The French were successful first and obtained excellent pictures. Goonhilly only managed to lock on for the final minute. Later France sent live pictures of Yves Montand singing to the US. Britain sent a test card and an official greeting.

Telstar is the forerunner of satellites destined to make round-the-world television possible (→ 23).

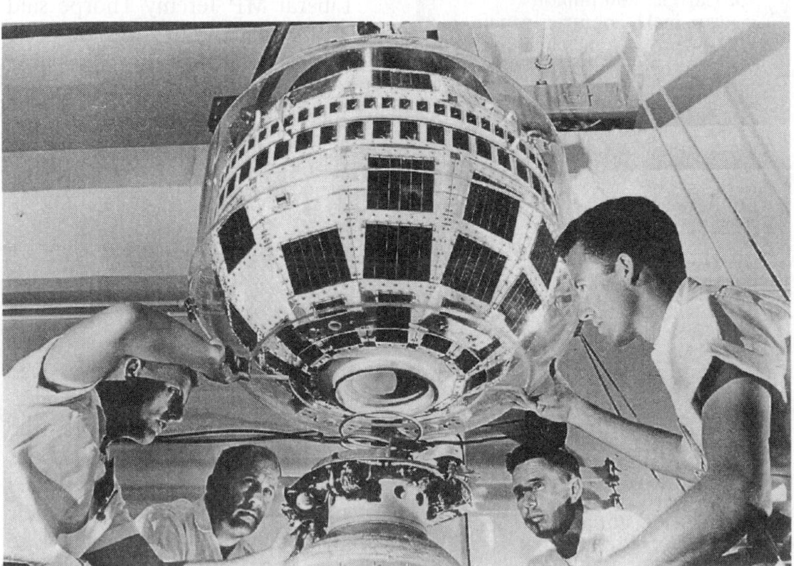

Technicians "mate" Telstar to the third stage of the Delta rocket.

Left and Right do power deal in Laos

July 26. The newly installed coalition government of Laos was reluctantly given the US seal of approval today when its leader, Prince Souvanna Phouma, flew to Washington to negotiate an aid package.

The new government, in which the middle-of-the-road Prince will try to hold together a cabinet composed of bitterly differing right-wing and Communist Pathet Lao ministers, was agreed in Geneva earlier this week.

The agreement was put together only after the neutralist and Pathet Lao factions told the International Control Commission that they were willing to enter into negotiations with the right-wing faction without conditions.

Previously they had demanded that the key posts of Defence and the Interior Ministry should go to the neutralists before they would begin the negotiations.

Prince Souvanna Phouma's welcome in Washington can only be described as cool. His left-inclined neutralism does not sit well with the Kennedy administration which distrusts him (→ 19/4/64).

Rod Laver retains his Wimbledon title

July 6. For the second year in succession Rod Laver, the red-headed Australian left-hander, proved himself incomparably the best player on the amateur circuit, taking the Wimbledon final in only 50 minutes with impressive ease from his fellow Australian Marty Mulligan 6-2, 6-2, 6-1.

Rod Laver: Wimbledon champion.

Mosleyites march through London again

July 31. More than 30 years after he first formed his own party, Sir Oswald Mosley, aged 62, again tried to address a meeting of the Union Movement in London's East End today.

It was, one could say, just like old times as Sir Oswald was knocked down and punched on the jaw, the target of a barrage of coins, oranges and other missiles. Police broke up the meeting only four minutes after it started, arresting 54 people on public order charges.

The incident follows a Mosleyite rally in Trafalgar Square last week which became violent after 15 minutes, as demonstrators stormed the plinth on which Mosley was due to speak. Speaking to the press afterwards, Mosley blamed the Government "for having lost control of the streets to Red anarchy".

Mosley's re-emergence is part of a return of right-wing extremism. A British Nazi party is preaching anti-Semitism, while the West Midlands town of Dudley today saw a gang of 400 whites march on the immigrant population. A police superintendent described them as "a pack of ravening wolves after their prey, shouting and brandishing weapons" (→ 2/9).

New pay judge Nicky finds few friends

July 26. The Government is to set up a National Incomes Commission, already nicknamed "Nicky", to judge wage claims in the light of the public interest. It will have no power to impose its views.

This latest move to encourage pay restraint was announced by Mr Macmillan today. It was denounced by the TUC as naive and dismissed by restless Government backbench MPs as a gimmick. Mr Macmillan said the "Nicky" idea is to encourage all-round self-discipline by giving the public the facts about pay deals. Mr Gaitskell called it an act of desperation.

As for Mr Macmillan's recent cabinet purge, the Labour leader said: "Not since Stalin liquidated the old Bolsheviks has there been such a successful process of elimination." The same restless Tories laughed (→ 5/11).

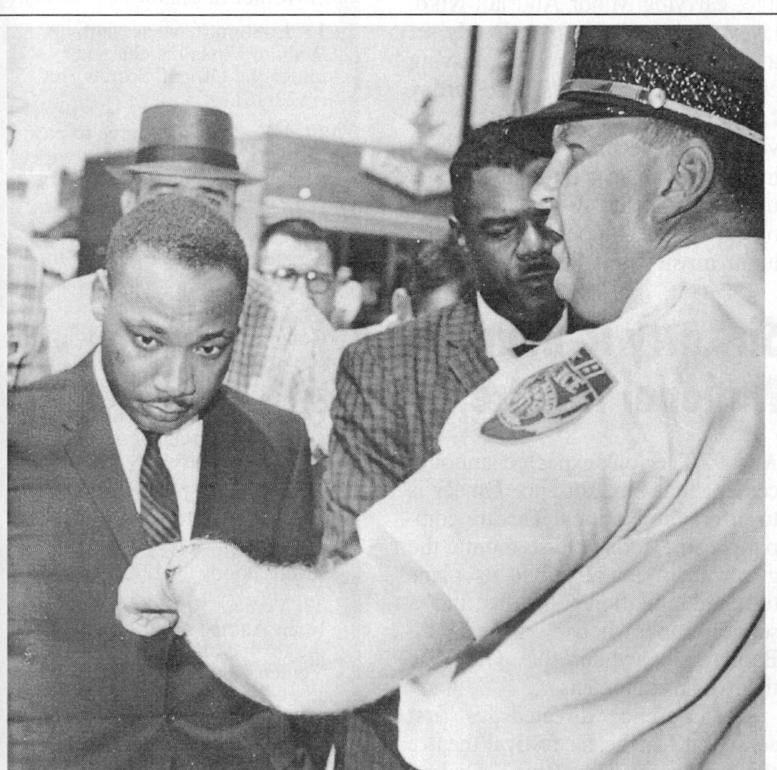

July 27. Dr Martin Luther King is arrested by Albany's police chief. His crime was to hold a prayer meeting on the steps of the city hall.

1962

AUGUST

Su	Mo	Tu	We	Th	Fr	Sa
			1	2	3	4
5	6	7	8	9	10	11
12	13	14	15	16	17	18
19	20	21	22	23	24	25
26	27	28	29	30	31	

1. Ghana: President Nkrumah escapes unhurt from an assassination attempt (→ 9/9).

3. Algeria: Rebel leader Ben Bella returns (→ 22).

6. Jamaica: The island gets its independence after 307 years of British rule.

7. USSR: The government announces plans to abolish single family houses in urban areas (→ 18/10).

8. London: US Nazi leader George Rockwell is arrested and ordered to leave Britain.

9. France: Arrest of politician Georges Bidault.

13. Berlin: East German guards fire tear gas to disperse protests by westerners at the Berlin Wall.→

14. Italy: The tunnel under Mont Blanc is completed.

15. Jakarta: The Dutch government agrees to cede western New Guinea to Indonesia (→ 1/10).

17. Los Angeles: Marilyn Monroe's death was probably a suicide, says the LA coroner.

19. Budapest: Party chief Janos Kadar purges 25 Stalinists.

20. New York: UN secretary-general U Thant presents a plan for independence for the Congo (→ 30/12).

25. Havana: Sea raid by US-based exiles opposed to Castro's government (→ 24/9).

26. US: The Mariner II space probe is launched towards Venus (→ 1/11).

29. Paris: De Gaulle says he plans to change the French constitution to permit direct presidential elections (→ 28/10).

31. Trinidad and Tobago: The islands become an independent nation within the British Commonwealth.

DEATHS

5. US actress Marilyn Monroe, born Norma Jean Baker (*1/6/26).→

9. German-born Swiss writer Hermann Hesse, 1946 Nobel Prize winner (*2/7/1877).

Wall guards watch as boy lies dying

Aug 20. Five thousand angry West Berliners protesting against the shooting of an 18-year-old East German boy trying to escape to the West, marched along streets near the Wall at midnight last night. Further protests are expected today, the first anniversary of the building of the "wall of shame".

The dead boy, Peter Fechter, was machine-gunned in the back as he tried to climb the wall and then bled to death while the East German guards looked on. There was nothing the West German police could do except throw him bandages as he cried out for help.

A wooden cross has been set up at the spot where he died. It is heaped with flowers and bears the words: "We accuse" (→ 18/9).

Police remove Fechter's body.

Bonington beats north face of Eiger

Aug 31. Chris Bonington, aged 27, and Ian Clough, aged 25, became the first Britons to conquer the north face of the Eiger today. Their two-day ascent was one of the fastest ever and just three hours later they were back in the safety of their hotel to declare: "It was a very enjoyable climb, with no difficulties." Yet tragedy was never far away on the fearsome 13,040-foot peak. While they neared the top, the north face claimed its 24th and 25th victims, one a Scot. ▷

Marilyn Monroe is found dead in her bed

Aug 5. Marilyn Monroe was found dead early today, lying naked in bed at her bungalow near Hollywood, clutching a telephone receiver. There was an empty bottle of Nembutal sleeping tablets on her bedside table.

Miss Monroe appears to have spent yesterday alone. At 5.15pm she telephoned her personal doctor, Ralph Greenson, about her sleeping problems. About 8pm she went to her bedroom saying "Goodnight, honey," to her housekeeper, Mrs Eunice Murray. At 3am, when she saw the bedroom light still on and could get no answer, Mrs Murray called Dr Greenson.

John Huston who directed her last film "The Misfits", written by Arthur Miller, her former husband, said: "Her great enemy was sleeplessness. Only God knows why she feared it so much."

In June she was fired from the filming of "Something's Got To Give". Twentieth Century Fox said that it had dropped its action against her for persistent absence.

After a troubled childhood spent with foster parents, Norma Jean Baker (her real name) married an aircraft worker at 16. She was divorced at 20 and became a photographer's model. Her talents as a comedienne soon got her bit parts in movies and her first featured role in "The Asphalt Jungle".

She went on to make 22 more films that earned her studio £70 million. Her second marriage to baseball star, Joe di Maggio, lasted nine months. She was married to Miller from 1956 to 1960.

In an article in this week's Life magazine, she talked of her troubles: "Everybody is always tugging at you. They would all like sort of a chunk of you" (→17).

Marilyn Monroe – the ultimate sex symbol in her youthful prime.

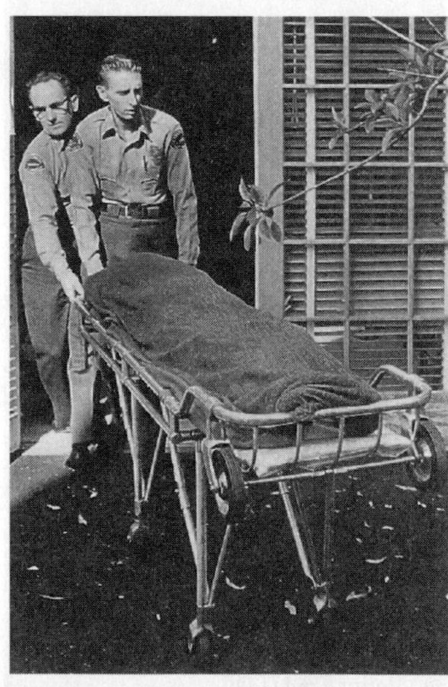

Marilyn's body is wheeled out on a stretcher from her LA home.

Martin Luther King is released from jail

Aug 10. City officials in Albany, Georgia, averted a march and widespread breaking of the segregation laws today by releasing Dr Martin Luther King and the Reverend Ralph Abernathy after two weeks in jail.

The two had been arrested after leading anti-segregationalists to Albany City Hall in a desperate attempt to secure meetings with officials which had been promised and postponed for eight months. When told that the Mayor was not in, Abernathy replied: "Then we'll just pray until they see fit to see us."

The police soon moved in and carried the group of 28 protestors off to jail for causing a disturbance. It was the third time since January that King and Abernathy have been arrested (→30/9).

De Gaulle escapes killer at crossroads

Aug 22. Secret Army hitmen almost succeeded today in what was their fourth attempt in 12 months to assassinate their arch-enemy President de Gaulle.

They ambushed his official Citroen DS at a crossroads near Versailles on the way to Villacoublay airport. From three points by the roadside they sprayed the car with bursts of sub-machine-gun fire, shattering the rear window and bursting two tyres.

The driver raced on for a mile and a half to a spot where the President, his wife and their son-in-law, Colonel de Boissieu, transferred to another car. General de Gaulle had just presided over a cabinet meeting to co-ordinate anti-terrorist measures.

Soviet space craft orbit side by side

Aug 12. Two Soviet cosmonauts are now orbiting the earth at the same time, in separate Vostok spacecraft. The first was launched two days ago, carrying Major Andrian Nikolayev on board. He has already set a space endurance record, having completed 31 orbits. Yesterday Lieutenant Colonel Pavel Popovitch, in a second Vostok, joined him in space. An attempt may be made to link the two spacecraft in orbit, a vital manoeuvre for future lunar missions (→26).

Sir Larry to head National Theatre

Aug 9. The long-expected announcement that Sir Laurence Olivier is to direct the National Theatre company came today. Last month the government made public its plans to build a national theatre and a separate opera house on the South Bank. Meanwhile the Old Vic theatre has been leased.

Sir Laurence directed his first season at Chichester festival theatre this summer. The Royal Shakespeare Company has withdrawn from plans to amalgamate with a national theatre.

1962

SEPTEMBER

Su	Mo	Tu	We	Th	Fr	Sa
						1
2	3	4	5	6	7	8
9	10	11	12	13	14	15
16	17	18	19	20	21	22
23	24	25	26	27	28	29
30						

1. Washington: A report suggests the world's population is now more than three billion.

2. London: Fierce street battle between fascists and East Enders (→6/10/63).

3. Iran: 20,000 feared dead in Iran's worst earthquake (→26).

4. Washington: Kennedy says he will take all steps necessary against Cuban aggression.→

4. Algiers: Cease-fire between rival Moslem groups (→17).

6. London: Soviet spy Dr Robert Soblen tries to commit suicide as he is being deported.

9. China: A U2 spy plane used by Taiwan is shot down (→26/10).

10. New York: Rod Laver wins the US tennis title and completes the Grand Slam.

11. London: Commonwealth premiers say they are against Britain joining the EEC (→16/12)

12. US: Richard Nixon launches his campaign to be Governor of California (→6/11).

13. London: Civil servant William Vassall is charged under the Official Secrets Act (→22/10).

14. UK: Distillers agree to pay £250,000 for research into damage done by thalidomide (→5/11).

18. East Berlin: 29 refugees escape by tunnelling under the wall (→8/9/64).

19. London: A Royal Commission recommends a Press Council (→24/11).

20. US: The Mississippi Governor defies a court order and refuses to allow a Negro to join the university.→

24. Aden: British troops fire tear gas at rioters (→10/12/63).

26. Barcelona: 323 die in severe floods (→22/2/63).

27. Yemen: Rebels assassinate Iman Ahmed after a week on the throne and establish a Free Yemen Republic (→7/10).

DEATH

3. US writer Edward Estlin Cummings (*14/10/1894).

Cuban crisis gives new powers to JFK

Sept 24. Congress today granted President Kennedy the power to call up 150,000 reservists if he considers it necessary. This means that he no longer has to go through the procedure of declaring a national emergency before summoning the reservists to the colours.

This move reflects the growing concern in Washington about the situation in Cuba and is a direct reply to Mr Khrushchev's threat that any American attack on Cuba would mean nuclear war. Meanwhile, the Secretary of State, Dean Rusk, has been giving Latin American governments details of Soviet missiles which the US says have been deployed in Cuba (→22/10).

Bomb blast rocks Nkrumah's party

Sept 9. As 2,000 guests danced at a party given by Ghana's President Kwame Nkrumah to celebrate his escape from last month's assassination attempt, an attack threatened his life once again. A girl was killed and several people were injured by a bomb outside the gates of his residence, Flagstaff House, in the capital Accra.

A new anti-Nkrumah organisation, the Kumasi Command, has been formed in Ashanti. The regime is under great pressure, and has been arresting left-wing militants throughout the country.

Riots as black goes to Deep South college

James Meredith leaves the registrar's office after his enrolment.

Sept 30. Angry whites stormed the University of Mississippi campus tonight protesting against the enrolment this morning of James Meredith, the first black student. The 750 Federal Marshals, headed by the deputy Attorney-General, were unable to prevent a riot and at least three people have been killed and over 50 injured.

Although the University Board of Trustees a week ago agreed to abide by the segregation law and admit Meredith, his admission was blocked by state troopers ordered in by Governor Ross Barnett. President John Kennedy promptly sent in the Federal Marshals to escort Meredith to school.

However, Barnett may not yet have given up. Last night he was urged to "rebel" by an all-white crowd at the Jackson football stadium. The "Ole Miss" college band was dressed in Civil War Confederate uniforms and the crowd all rose for the singing of "Dixie", the Southern battle song (→1/10).

Smith clamps down on black opponents

Sept 20. Southern Rhodesia headed for a showdown with the colony's black nationalist movement today, when the Prime Minister, Sir Edgar Whitehead, issued an order banning the Zimbabwe African People's Union as a terrorist organisation. Police began rounding up ZAPU leaders and steel-helmeted troops were deployed to guard airports, power stations and other vital installations.

Sir Edgar's action came after more than a year of violence and intimidation directed at blacks who, according to a government White Paper, show insufficient enthusiasm for ZAPU and its policies. African chiefs in rural areas have been prime targets. In the past nine months there have been over 30 petrol bomb attacks on Africans and their homes, and 18 African schools, as well as churches and welfare centres, have been burned.

The unrest has been taking place against a background of controversy over constitutional reform, with the white voters pressing for Britain to surrender its reserve powers to veto Southern Rhodesia legislation, in particular any that could affect the position of the African majority (→9/2/63).

Sonny Liston is new heavyweight champ with first round KO

Sept 25. Four clubbing punches within two minutes of the start of the fight in Comiskey Park, Chicago, saw Floyd Patterson stagger, drop against the ropes, and finally fall senseless to the canvas. The count reached ten before he could even move, and for the second time he had lost his world heavyweight title.

His conqueror this time was the huge, fearsome Sonny Liston, who many believed would never get the chance of a championship bout because of his dubious past record outside the ring.

But given the chance, there was never a moment when Liston looked like losing; in two minutes and six seconds Patterson was finished, and for the first time this century the challenger had beaten the world champion by a knockout in the first round.

Liston (r.) inflicts his first heavy blow of the fight on Patterson.

1962

OCTOBER

Su	Mo	Tu	We	Th	Fr	Sa
	1	2	3	4	5	6
7	8	9	10	11	12	13
14	15	16	17	18	19	20
21	22	23	24	25	26	27
28	29	30	31			

1. US: 200 are arrested during riots at Mississippi University as James Meredith attends his first classes (→25/2/63).

1. Indonesia: The UN takes control of west New Guinea from Holland (→18/5/64).

4. Italy: Huge crowds watch a Pope travel by train for the first time in 100 years.

5. UK: Ice cream makers Lyons Maid merge with two other firms to prepare for a "war of the cones" with Walls.

7. Yemen: First Egyptian troops arrive to support the government (→18/11).

8. London: Judge Elizabeth Lane becomes the first female judge to sit in the High Court.

9. Uganda: Independence is declared after 62 years of British rule.

10. US: The Mariner II space probe reveals the existence of solar winds.

11. India: 50 die as fighting breaks out along the border with China.→

14. Brussels: Riots as Flemish protesters call for proportional representation.

15. London: Amnesty International is created to investigate human rights abuses.

17. London: Hyde Park underpass opens creating huge traffic jams.

17. Saudi Arabia: King Saud names Prince Feisal as the new premier (→2/11/64).

18. Moscow: Nikolai Bukharin and Alexei Rykov, victims of Stalin's purges, are officially rehabilitated (→19/11).

22. South Africa: Nelson Mandela pleads not guilty to charges of treason, at the start of his trial (→7/11).

22. Washington: Kennedy says Russia has missile sites in Cuba and imposes an arms blockade.→

27. West Germany: Trial opens of three editors of "Der Spiegel" charged with treason.

28. France: De Gaulle's plans for direct presidential elections approved by referendum (→25/11).

World steps back from nuclear brink

Oct 28. The world took a step back from the brink of nuclear war today when Mr Khrushchev promised that the Russian missiles based in Cuba would be dismantled and shipped back to the Soviet Union. In return, President Kennedy promised that the United States would not invade Cuba and would lift the blockade imposed on Cuba by the US.

The two super-powers have been head-to-head for the past week in their game of nuclear poker while the rest of the world watched, fascinated, but hardly daring to breathe in case one of the players made a fatal mistake.

Now, it seems that Mr Kennedy has called Mr Khrushchev's bluff but is not pressing his advantage so that the Russian leader loses all credence in the Soviet Union.

In his message to President Kennedy, broadcast by Moscow Radio, Mr Khrushchev did not repeat his demand that missile bases in Turkey should be closed down as a condition of the Soviet withdrawal from Cuba. But he did accuse the US of sending a "spy-flight" over eastern Siberia yesterday.

In reply, Mr Kennedy apologised for the American flight over Siberia and greeted Mr Khrushchev's decision as "statesmanlike" and an "important contribution to peace". He said he would approach the UN Secretary General, U Thant, about "reciprocal measures" to assure peace in the Caribbean.

US officials, who said that American military action against Cuba was very close when the Russians backed down, insisted that Mr Kennedy had made no deal over either Turkey or Berlin in exchange for the withdrawal of the missiles.

It appears that the agreement was reached after several secret exchanges between Washington and Moscow in which the seriousness of the situation was acknowledged.

Military sources in Washington suggest that the US had two distinct advantages over the Soviets. The first was the ability to photograph the missile sites and so prove publicly they were not merely defensive and the second was their naval strength, which enabled the US to blockade Cuba without fear of Soviet intervention.

An aerial view of one of the Cuban medium-range missile bases.

A Soviet ship in the Caribbean showing missiles and their transporters.

World lets out a sigh of relief over Cuba

Oct 28. The world's reaction to the ending of the Cuban missile crisis today has been one huge sigh of relief, best summed up in the West by the British Foreign Secretary, the Earl of Home, who warmly welcomed Mr Khrushchev's decision to withdraw the Soviet missiles, but also hailed Mr Kennedy's diplomatic victory.

Perhaps the most disgruntled of the world's leaders was Dr Castro of Cuba, who was not consulted by the Russians about the withdrawal of the missiles. The Chinese are furious with Mr Khrushchev and have promised to "stand by Cuba through thick and thin".

There are some red faces among those leaders of the CND who fled from the demonstrations outside the American Embassy in London for a bolthole in western Ireland when war appeared imminent.

Earl Russell of CND argued that mankind owed a profound debt to the sanity of Mr Khrushchev. But others consider that it is Mr Kennedy who has won a contest in raw power politics (→2/11).

Heavy fighting on Indo-Chinese border

Oct 26. The simmering border dispute between China and India, high in the Himalayas, has flared into heavy fighting and today India has declared a state of emergency throughout the country which means that it is just one step removed from full war footing.

The announcement came after reports of fresh outbreaks of fighting with many casualties on the North East Frontier Agency border. Mr Nehru, India's Prime Minister, said tonight that the Chinese attack was not merely a border affair but was an "invasion of the whole of India even though war has not been declared".

Urging Indian students to join the National Cadet Corps, he said: "Let's show the world we are people of mettle. If China went unchecked it would lead to the imposition of the law of the jungle".

India is in need of money as well as men. Mr Desai, the Finance Minister, launched an appeal tonight for gold and silver ornaments to help raise foreign exchange for arms and equipment for the forces, which have been badly hit by an austerity programme (→ 16/11).

Vassall's "traitorous lust" leads to jail

Oct 22. A 38-year-old Admiralty clerk, William Vassall, was jailed for 18 years today for spying for the Soviet Union. The quietly-spoken vicar's son who passed secrets to the enemy for six years was described in court as a "traitorous tool of the Russians".

Vassall fell into their clutches during a posting to the British Embassy in Moscow. He was lured to a homosexual party, photographed in compromising situations and blackmailed. When he returned to London the Russians started paying him enough to double his £700 a year Civil Service salary.

Attorney General Sir John Hobson said: "He was entrapped by his lust and thereafter cash kept him crooked. He had neither the moral fibre nor the patriotism to alter his conduct." Some of the documents he photographed with a miniature camera and concealed in a secret compartment in his flat in Dolphin Square were said to be highly important (→ 2/11).

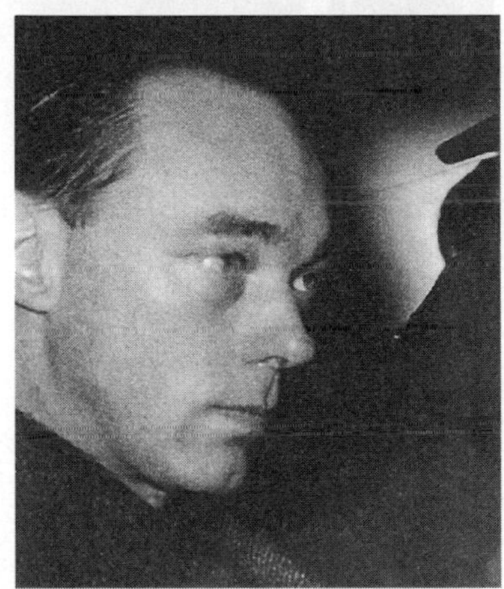

Vassall, former Admiralty clerk.

Paul Newman stars with Shirley Knight as the ill-starred young lovers in the film of Tennessee Williams' "Sweet Bird of Youth".

1962

NOVEMBER

Su	Mo	Tu	We	Th	Fr	Sa
				1	2	3
4	5	6	7	8	9	10
11	12	13	14	15	16	17
18	19	20	21	22	23	24
25	26	27	28	29	30	

1. USSR: Russia launches her first rocket towards Mars.

2. Washington: President Kennedy says all Soviet missile bases in Cuba have been destroyed (→ 20).

5. London: The government halves purchase tax on cars to boost the economy (→ 21/2/63).

6. US: Edward Kennedy is elected as a Senator for Massachusetts.

8. London: Thomas Galbraith resigns from the government after his letters to spy William Vassall are published (→ 11/12).

12. London: Macmillan is ready to sign a partial nuclear test ban treaty with the US and the Soviet Union (→ 7/12).

16. India: Chinese troops launch a major offensive in the frontier war.→

19. Moscow: Khrushchev says "we must learn from capitalist countries to imitate what...is good and profitable" (→ 5/3/63).

20. Washington: President Kennedy lifts the US blockade of Cuba (→ 26).

22. UK: Labour win the South Dorset by-election overturning a Tory majority of 8,000.

24. UK: First transmission of "That Was The Week That Was" by the BBC (→ 17/12).

25. France: De Gaulle's supporters win a majority in the National Assembly (→ 10/3/63).

26. Washington: The US agrees to remove its missile bases from Turkey.

28. Paris: The death sentence on ex-OAS leader, General Jouhaud, is commuted to life imprisonment (→ 15/2/63).

29. London: An agreement to build Concorde, a supersonic aircraft, is signed by France and Britain.

DEATHS

7. US ex-first lady and UN envoy Eleanor Roosevelt (*11/10/1884).

18. Danish nuclear physicist Niels Bohr (*7/10/1885).

28. Queen Wilhelmina of the Netherlands (*31/8/1880).

Briton arrested for spying in Budapest

Alleged spy Greville Wynne.

Nov 2. The Soviet KGB today seized a British businessman, Greville Wynne, in a Budapest park then flew him to Moscow to stand trial for espionage. Mr Wynne, aged 42, from Chelsea, had gone to Hungary to demonstrate a caravan trailer for exhibitions.

He was bundled into a car by KGB counter-intelligence agents after he had been throwing a party for Hungarian clients, and flown to the Soviet Union in a military aircraft for interrogation. He has visited Moscow on several occasions where he attended trade fairs and has many Soviet contacts (→ 8).

Acquittal in Belgian thalidomide trial

Nov 5. The trial in Belgium of a family and a doctor accused of the mercy-killing of Corinne van de Put, a thalidomide baby born without arms, has ended in the acquittal of all of the five defendants.

In the dock were the baby's mother, father, grandmother and aunt, together with Dr Jacques Casters. They did not deny poisoning the baby with barbiturates soon after her birth.

The prosecutor demanded that they be found guilty in the name of all parents who had accepted deformed children with love. But their acquittal has been welcomed both in Belgium and in a number of other countries.

Nelson Mandela is jailed for five years

Mandela, leading black activist.

Nov 7. In the Pretoria courthouse called the Old Synagogue, Nelson Mandela, the 44-year-old African nationalist leader known as the "Black Pimpernel" for his resourcefulness in evading arrest, was today jailed for five years.

He had been found guilty of incitement and leaving South Africa illegally. The court was told that Mandela had been the "mouthpiece and mastermind" behind a call for a national strike. When the strike failed, Mandela abandoned non-violent resistance and helped to found the Umkhonto we Sizwe (Spear of the Nation) movement.

He was smuggled out of South Africa to speak at an African freedom conference in Addis Ababa, just when Umkhonto began sabotage attacks (→ 12/7/63).

China wins border dispute with India

Nov 21. Chinese troops halted their advance into India today with the whole of the Assam Plains at their mercy, following their capture of Bomdila, a key defence and administrative position in the North-East Frontier Agency.

With victory secure, China has proposed a ceasefire and talks. An Indian Foreign Office spokesman said his country's attitude to these proposals was: "Let's wait and see". But India would seem to have little option; one division remains cut off and there is little to stop the Chinese debouching on to the rich, open plains.

1962

DECEMBER

Su	Mo	Tu	We	Th	Fr	Sa
						1
2	3	4	5	6	7	8
9	10	11	12	13	14	15
16	17	18	19	20	21	22
23	24	25	26	27	28	29
30	31					

4. US: Two British divers reach a world record depth of 1,000 feet underwater.

7. US: Britain's second underground nuclear test takes place in Nevada (→ 21).

8. Brunei: British troops clash with rebels opposing Malaysian Federation (→ 16/9/63).

10. Stockholm: Nobel Prizes go to Max Perutz and John Kendrew (UK, Chemistry); Francis Crick (UK), Maurice Wilkins (UK), James Watson (US, Medicine); Lev Landau (USSR, Physics); John Steinbeck (US, Literature); and in Oslo to Linus Pauling (US, Peace).→

12. Washington: President Kennedy says he favours an emergency phone link with the Kremlin (→ 20/6/63).

14. US: Mariner II sends back the first close-up pictures of the planet Venus (→ 7/5/63).

16. Paris: Talks between de Gaulle and Macmillan over Britain's entry into the EEC end in deadlock (→ 14/1/63).

17. London: A parliamentary committee recommends peers should be allowed to renounce their titles (→ 18/1/63).

24. Cuba: The government ransoms 1,113 exiles, captured in the Bay of Pigs invasion, for $53 million (→ 27/1/63).

25. Congo: Fighting breaks out between Katangese rebels and UN troops (→ 30).

30. Congo: President Tshombe flees into exile as UN troops advance into Katanga (1/1/63).

DEATH

15. British actor and film director Charles Laughton (*1/7/1899).→

HITS OF 1962

Stranger on the shore.

I remember you.

Rock a-hula baby.

QUOTE OF THE YEAR

"We're eyeball to eyeball and the other fellow just blinked."

Dean Rusk, US Secretary of State, on the Cuban crisis.

Satire angers ministers, but wins viewers

Stars of "That Was The Week That Was", topped by Millicent Martin.

Dec 17. The new Saturday night satire show, "That Was The Week That Was", which began three weeks ago, is getting into increasingly hot water for lampooning politicians, such as the Prime Minister, court officials like the Lord Chamberlain, and for portraying a group of cardinals at the Vatican Council singing "Arriverderci Roma".

The Postmaster-General has asked to see the script of the next programme and will take soundings from MPs – having not yet watched the show himself. One item which caused offence showed the Chancellor of the Exchequer, Mr Maudling, dismissing a delegation of the unemployed with the words: "Well, I can't spend all day talking to you – I've got work to do."

There were objections to a sketch in which a woman, played by the show's resident singer, Millicent Martin, loudly tells her man companion that his fly buttons are undone. Others object to the aggressive attitudes taken by the show's compere, David Frost, and its polemical journalist, Bernard Levin.

On Saturday the BBC received over 1,000 telephone calls six to four in favour. The BBC does not censor the programme (→ 15/1/63).

Deaths from smog reach 60 in London

Dec 6. A total of 60 deaths attributable to smog have occurred in London in the past three days. Of the 19 men and nine women aged between 37 and 86 who died yesterday, 20 collapsed indoors, six in the streets and two at work. Hundreds of out-patients could not be treated at hospitals in East London because ambulances, which usually transport them, could not be spared. The fog will last for at least another 24 hours and authorities have prepared for more victims.

KGB arrest contact of alleged UK spy

Dec 11. The Soviet KGB today arrested a colonel of Military Intelligence and accused him of passing secrets to Greville Wynne, the British businessman undergoing interrogation in Moscow. Oleg Penkovsky, aged 44, who also worked for a government scientific department, was said to have used "dead drops" to pass military, scientific and political secrets over a period of 16 months to Western agents in Moscow. A major spy trial is being prepared (→ 25/1/63).

Polaris for British subs

Dec 21. A multilateral NATO nuclear force is to be formed immediately. As part of it the US has offered to sell Polaris missiles to Britain and France for use in their submarines.

The deal was announced in a joint statement by President Kennedy and Mr Macmillan at the end of their conference in Nassau today. Britain's contribution to the force in subs and warheads will be over £350 million. The Anglo-US Skybolt rocket is abandoned.

The US President has sent a personal letter to President de Gaulle, who has not replied. France resents Anglo-US co-operation and the talk of their special relationship.

Mr Macmillan explained that except when "supreme national interests are at stake", the British units will be used for international defence of the Western alliance.

The political question now is just how independent is Britain's nuclear deterrent? The Nassau agreement is likely to become a major factor in negotiations about closer European integration (→16/1/63).

President Kennedy and Harold Macmillan clinch the Polaris deal.

Arts: Soviet critic wins official approval

Character actor Charles Laughton.

The surprise book of the year is a novel of the Soviet prison camps - "One Day in the Life of Ivan Denisovich". The biggest surprise is that it has been allowed to be published in the Soviet Union, unlike "Dr Zhivago" and countless other works. This occurred after Mr Khrushchev had read it and personally approved publication.

The author, **Alexander Solzhenitsyn**, was sent to the camps on almost the last day of the war for criticising Stalin in a letter sent to a friend from the army, in which he had been decorated for bravery. His book, a harrowing and detailed account of what political prisoners have to endure, is a best-seller in the West. Its publication is further sign of a "thaw" following the 20th Party Conference.

Astonishment reigned in New York galleries at exhibitions of paintings of Campbell's soup cans and of dollar bills, very realistically rendered by silk-screen process, and of large blow-ups of frames from comic strip cartoons of space warfare heroes, including their "thought balloons". The former are by **Andy Warhol**, a former commercial artist, the latter by **Roy Lichtenstein**. "Soft sculpture", gigantic enlargements of hamburgers, ice cream cones, washbasins and toilets made of stuffed vinyl in lurid colours, is being exhibited by **Claes Oldenburg**. All are manifestations of "Pop Art", American style, which is being featured in all the magazines.

The newly-completed Coventry Cathedral was the setting for the first performance of **Benjamin Britten's** "War Requiem" which movingly sets the bitter poems of **Wilfred Owen** in the context of the Requiem Mass.

Peter Brook's production of "King Lear" for the RSC is a breakthrough in style that makes Shakespeare's scenes between the King and his Fool (**Paul Scofield** and **Alec McCowen**) sound as bleakly contemporary as "Waiting for Godot".

Charles Laughton, who died at the age of 63, will be remembered for the way he used his personal grossness to theatrical effect as Henry VIII, Captain Bligh and the Hunchback of Notre Dame.

British scientists win Nobel Prizes

Four British scientists won Nobel Prizes this year for their structural studies of the molecules of life: **Max Perutz** and **John Kendrew** for work on proteins; **Francis Crick** and **Maurice Wilkins** (with **James Watson** of the US) for work on DNA.

Also of note this year was the discovery of quasars, super-bright objects whose energy source is unexplained. And on December 14 the American Mariner 2 spacecraft sent back, across 36 million miles of space, the first close-up pictures of Venus as it passed within 21,000 miles of the planet's surface.

Nyasaland is set to win independence

Dec 19. The nine-year-old Central African Federation is headed for disintegration after the announcement today by the British Government that Nyasaland is to be allowed to secede. The decision was branded as "treachery" by Sir Roy Welensky, the Federal Prime Minister. When the Federation was launched, Britain promised that secession by a member territory would not be permitted except by mutual agreement. But opposition to federation by Nyasaland's Dr Hastings Banda persuaded Britain to allow Nyasaland to go for independence on its own (→1/2/63).

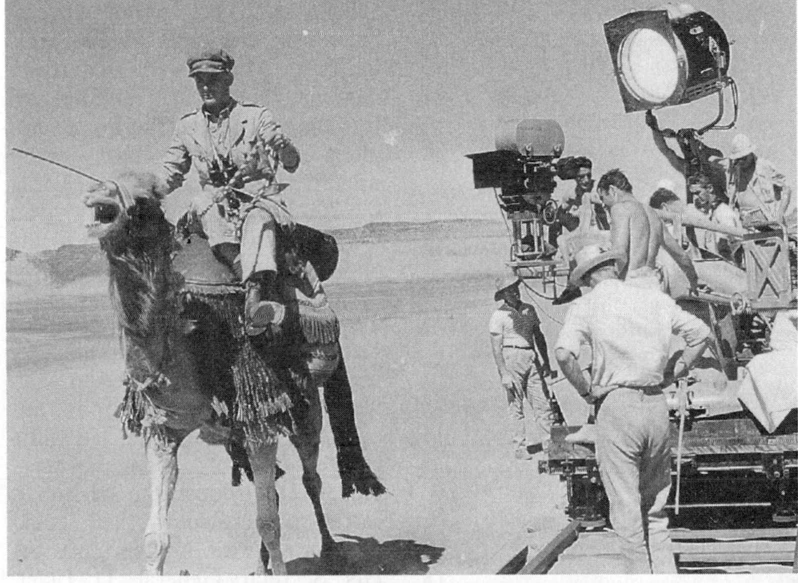

Peter O'Toole in the title role of the film "Lawrence of Arabia".

1963

JANUARY

Su	Mo	Tu	We	Th	Fr	Sa
		1	2	3	4	5
6	7	8	9	10	11	12
13	14	15	16	17	18	19
20	21	22	23	24	25	26
27	28	29	30	31		

1. Congo: President Tshombe appeals to the UN to declare a cease-fire (→ 9).

2. Vietnam: 50 die as Vietcong guerrillas shoot down five US helicopters in the Mekong delta.

6. Peru: 800 Communists are arrested by the military junta.

8. Washington: The "Mona Lisa" goes on show at the National Gallery.

9. Congo: President Tshombe is placed under house arrest by UN troops.→

13. Togo: The military seize power in a coup.

15. UK: The BBC ends its ban on mentioning politics, royalty, religion and sex in its comedy shows (→ 14/7).

16. Berlin: Khrushchev says a nuclear war would kill 800 million and warns that Russia has a 100 megaton bomb (→ 20).

16. Tunisia: 13 are sentenced to death for an assassination attempt against President Bourguiba.

17. London: Industrial action by electricity workers causes power blackouts.

17. Brussels: Students abduct the statue of "Mannikin Pis".

20. Moscow: Russia agrees to allow on-site inspection of nuclear tests (→ 20/2).

22. Paris: De Gaulle and Adenauer sign a political and military co-operation treaty.

25. London: A Daily Sketch journalist is jailed for refusing to reveal his sources to the Vassall tribunal (→ 4/2).

27. Cuba: The government claims to have broken up two US spy networks (→ 21/2).

30. London: Macmillan says de Gaulle is trying to dominate Europe (→ 11/2).

DEATHS

18. British Labour Party leader Hugh Gaitskell (*9/4/06).→

29. US poet Robert Frost (*26/3/1874).→

30. French composer Francis Poulenc (*7/1/1899).

De Gaulle dashes British EEC hopes

Jan 14. President de Gaulle got on his high horse and rebuffed both Britain and the United States today. He practically closed the door on Britain's Common Market entry and he rejected America's offer of Polaris missiles for France.

Speaking in a lofty tone, the French leader told a Paris news conference that Britain neither thinks nor acts like a Continental nation and is not yet qualified for full membership of the European Economic Community. Perhaps she could have some kind of junior associate status.

In Brussels, Edward Heath, Britain's chief Market negotiator, at once said that this is unacceptable, but negotiations must continue, even though de Gaulle indicated that the UK must sever her Commonwealth links as the price of EEC membership.

As expected in diplomatic circles, there is French resentment over the Anglo-US Polaris agreement. President de Gaulle said unequivocally: "We intend to have our own national defences." He added that an American-led Atlantic Community, which Washington seems to want, could very well try to swallow up the EEC.

In a final dig at Britain he said that "my friend Harold Macmillan" created the European Free Trade area only after trying to prevent the birth of the Common Market.

The Foreign Office maintains that President de Gaulle has bottled up feelings for a long time and may now feel better for having got them off his chest (→ 30).

De Gaulle stresses his opposition to Britain's entry of the EEC.

UN forces bring Katanga, the breakaway Congo state, to heel

Jan 15. After over two years, Moise Tshombe today bowed to UN pressures and announced the surrender of Katanga, the breakaway Congo state.

He said he was prepared to give allegiance to the central government, but he asked Cyrille Adoula, the Prime Minister, for an amnesty guaranteeing "security and liberty" for himself, members of his government and "all who have worked under their authority", including the 200 European mercenaries who have remained loyal to him to the end.

This is not the first time Tshombe has promised to end Katanga's secession. On previous occasions he has contrived to wriggle out of his promise; on this occasion, however, he has little choice. Most of Katanga is occupied by UN troops, with Tshombe's forces holding only the mining town of Kolwezi. In New York, the UN Secretary-General, U Thant, welcomed the news (→ 10/7/64).

A Belgian worker wounded when his car was shot at by United Nations troops as they advanced on the Katangan stronghold of Jadotville.

1963

FEBRUARY

Su	Mo	Tu	We	Th	Fr	Sa
					1	2
3	4	5	6	7	8	9
10	11	12	13	14	15	16
17	18	19	20	21	22	23
24	25	26	27	28		

1. Turkey: 67 die as a plane crashes into a market square (→ 12/9).

1. Nyasaland: Self-government begins with Hastings Banda as premier.

2. Finland: Penetti Nikula becomes the first pole vaulter to successfully jump five metres.

4. UK: Britain's worst learner driver, Margaret Hunter, is fined for driving on after her instructor jumped out shouting "this is suicide".

8. Baghdad: Army rebels seize power and execute premier Abdul Kassim (→ 18/11).

9. US: First test flight of the Boeing 727 (→ 14/10).

11. London: Macmillan says the cancellation of Princess Margaret's state visit to France is a snub for de Gaulle.

15. Paris: Police foil an assassination attempt against de Gaulle (→ 27).

17. West Berlin: Willy Brandt is overwhelmingly re-elected as mayor of the city (→ 23/4).

20. London: The government reveals plans to develop a new nuclear weapon to be launched from V-bombers (→ 7/4).

21. Washington: Kennedy warns Cuba after MiG fighters fire rockets towards a US boat (→ 27/4).

21. UK: New £5 notes are issued showing Britannia without her helmet (→ 26/3).

22. Libya: 300 die in an earthquake (→ 17/3).

25. Washington: The Supreme Court frees 187 Negroes jailed for protesting at segregation in South Carolina (→ 12/4).

27. Paris: OAS leader Antoine Argoud is found bundled-up and bruised in a van outside Notre Dame (→ 4/3).

DEATHS

7. Moroccan statesman Abdel Krim (*1884).

22. British businessman and founder of a retail chain, John Lewis (*22/9/1885).

Battling moderate, Gaitskell, is dead

Jan 18. Hugh Gaitskell, the Labour Party leader and apostle of new-style socialism, died in hospital tonight after a short illness, aged 56.

Doctors were puzzled when he failed to respond to treatment for a virus infection. His condition worsened unexpectedly and an artificial kidney was used in an attempt to save his life.

Gaitskell's strength was exhausted in the eight-year long ideological struggle for the soul of his party. Only lately did he achieve personal ascendancy. With his death Labour loses the electoral appeal of his integrity, personal charm and militantly moderate approach which middle-ground voters have liked (→ 14/2).

Labour leader Hugh Gaitskell.

Frost, poet of New England, is dead

Jan 29. Robert Frost, who was asked by President John Kennedy to read a poem at his inauguration, has died at 88. Called "the voice of New England", he settled there first as a cobbler and farmer.

The collection that made his name, "North of Boston", he was encouraged to publish by Rupert Brooke, whose clear imagery and straightforward emotion he shared. His work is permeated with the New Hampshire countryside and rural speech patterns.

Harold Wilson is elected as Labour leader

Feb 14. Harold Wilson was named tonight as Labour's new leader. In a ballot of the party's MPs he got 144 votes against 103 for George Brown, who was deputy leader under the late Hugh Gaitskell. James Callaghan came third in an earlier vote and was eliminated.

A bruising leadership battle has ended with inevitable calls for party unity. Wily and witty Mr Wilson, at 46 Labour's youngest leader, said: "My mandate is to lead to victory in the coming election and that is what I intend to do."

Mercurial Mr Brown said he looks forward to "frank talks" with Mr Wilson. He is still making up his mind whether to continue as No 2. He probably will. They will be uneasy partners prone to tiffs.

Mr Wilson promised to forget their differences. "They say I have a good memory. I intend to become famous for my short one," he quipped. MPs took bets about how long till the next row (→ 15/3).

Wilson takes up the challenge.

Newsmen go to jail for sheltering sources

Feb 4. Two journalists were jailed for contempt of court today. One of them, from the Daily Mail, got six months, the other, from the Daily Sketch, got three. Both had refused to disclose the sources of their information to the Government-appointed judicial tribunal investigating allegations of high-level incompetence in handling the case of John Vassall, the Admiralty spy.

Ten days ago another Daily Sketch journalist got a six-month sentence for a similar offence. In the High Court lawyers for the journalists argued that long-cherished freedom of the Press was involved and that the cases are constitutionally significant.

The judges ruled that discovery of the truth is an over-riding public policy and that the Press has no special privilege or immunity in withholding information required in the administration of justice. Relations between the Government and the Press are now extremely sour, each blaming the other (→ 3/3).

Doctor gives kidney from dead to living

Feb 14. Surgeons at Leeds General Infirmary have revealed that two months ago they successfully transplanted a kidney taken from a dead man, with the consent of relatives, into a living patient. In what is thought to be the first successful operation of this type, the kidney was cooled, special fluids circulated through it to preserve its function and then it was joined to the patient's blood vessels, by-passing his diseased kidneys (→ 29/4/64).

The Beatles record their first LP, "Please Please Me", as well as making their national TV debut on "Thank Your Lucky Stars".

Nkomo, Rhodesian rebel, is arrested

Nkomo, leader of banned ZAPU.

Feb 9. Six weeks after his release from detention under emergency regulations, Joshua Nkomo, Southern Rhodesia's black nationalist leader, was re-arrested today and charged under the Law and Order Maintenance Act. He will appear in court tomorrow, when the specific charges will be spelt out. Four other members of the Zimbabwe African People's Union were also arrested. The new Rhodesian Front government, which took over from Sir Edgar Whitehead's United Federal Party last month, has only one minister with experience of office. He is Ian Smith, once chief whip in the Federal Parliament. But the Front ministers have made it clear they are going to crack down hard on agitation by militant black nationalists (→ 1/4).

New racquet puts you on your metal

Feb 22. A tennis racquet made of steel, rather than the usual beech or ash, has been patented by one of the Four Musketeers of French tennis, Rene Lacoste, the former champion, who has also achieved fame marketing sports shirts.

A metal racquet produced in the 1930s failed to achieve popularity, but Lacoste's prototype, made in Britain, is expected to prove stronger and more durable than its wooden counterparts.

1963

MARCH

Su	Mo	Tu	We	Th	Fr	Sa
					1	2
3	4	5	6	7	8	9
10	11	12	13	14	15	16
17	18	19	20	21	22	23
24	25	26	27	28	29	30
31						

4. Paris: Six OAS members are sentenced to death for their assassination attempt on de Gaulle at Petit-Clamart (→ 16/9).

5. Moscow: The tenth anniversary of Stalin's death passes without any official recognition of it (→ 3/4/64).

7. London: Two journalists begin jail sentences for refusing to reveal their sources (→ 17/4).

8. Syria: Army seizes power in eighth coup since 1945 (→ 19/7).

10. Munich: Anti-Gaullist leader Georges Bidault applies for political asylum (→ 12).

12. France: Terrorists attack an express train (→ 27/1/64).

13. China: Mao invites Khrushchev to visit Peking (→ 9/5).

15. London: John Profumo has offered to resign from the government.→

17. Bali: 11,000 are killed by the eruption of the holy volcano on Mount Agung (→ 29/5).

18. New Zealand: England's cricket team win the Third Test to clinch the series.

21. London: The first automatically controlled tube trains are introduced.

23. US: Henry Carr runs 200 metres in a record 20.3 secs.

25. Los Angeles: Boxer Davey Moore dies after being severely injured in a fight with Sugar Ramos.

26. London: Mounted police disperse a demonstration by 4,000 jobless outside the Houses of Parliament (→ 21/1/64).

30. UK: Ayala wins the Grand National, four months after being bought by Mr P. Raymond for 40 guineas.

31. Guatemala: Coup overthrows President Miguel Fuentes.

DEATHS

4. US poet doctor William Carlos Williams (*17/9/1883).

16. British pioneer of the Welfare State Lord Beveridge (*5/3/1879).

"No impropriety", claims John Profumo

John Profumo, the Minister of War, with his wife, the actress Valerie Hobson.

March 22. In a personal statement John Profumo, Secretary of State for War, told MPs today that there was "no impropriety whatever" in his acquaintanceship with 21-year-old Christine Keeler, missing witness in a recent Old Bailey trial.

Grim-faced and pale, he added that he had last seen her in December, 1961, and that he will not hesitate to issue writs for libel and slander, if scandalous allegations are made or repeated outside the House of Commons about him having any connection with Miss Keeler's disappearance. Lobby correspondents were told that Mr Macmillan now regards the matter as closed.

Mr Profumo's statement came only hours after some Labour MPs spoke in the House about rumours connecting a government minister, whom they did not name, with Miss Keeler. They implied people in high places are concealing information.

Westminster is agog with rumours about Miss Keeler's meetings with Mr Profumo and about her knowing a Soviet diplomat. Mr and Mrs Profumo went to the races with the Queen Mother this afternoon (→ 24/4).

Missing: model Christine Keeler.

Suspected spy disappears from Beirut

March 3. "Kim" Philby, the former diplomat once accused of being the "Third Man" in the Burgess and MacLean spy scandal, made contact with his wife, Eleanor, by cable today, five weeks after disappearing from Beirut where he was working as a foreign correspondent.

Mrs Philby, who was waiting in vain for her husband at a diplomatic dinner party the night he vanished, remains mystified. The cable told her only that he is well and gave no indication of his whereabouts. It is now becoming increasingly certain that he has defected to the Soviet Union and was indeed the "Third Man" (→ 7).

Beeching's axe falls on BR branch lines

March 27. Savage cuts in Britain's rail network are proposed in the British Railways Board report published today. It will mean closing 2,128 stations, cutting the rail network by a quarter, scrapping 8,000 coaches and axing 67,700 jobs.

Passenger services north of Inverness will cease, and most of the branch lines in north and central Wales and in the West Country will be closed.

The report, "The Reshaping of British Railways", bears the personal stamp of the chairman, Dr Beeching, who was brought in from ICI by the Government to increase efficiency. Fierce opposition from the unions and from Conservative MPs representing the shires can be expected. But Dr Beeching is a determined man. He has even proposed closing Ballater, a station on the Balmoral line often used by the Royal Family (→3/3/64).

Beeching carrying his report.

Collapse of Central African Federation

March 29. Amid charges of betrayal from white politicial leaders, the British government finally abandoned its support for the ten-year-old Central African Federation. Mr Butler, Central African Affairs Minister, said today that Northern Rhodesia, like Nyasaland, will be allowed to secede. Southern Rhodesia, with a sizeable white community, is now expected to press for independence.

Hardest jail in US, Alcatraz, to close

March 21. The last 27 prisoners left Alcatraz Island, San Francisco, today. Opened as an army prison in 1909, and a federal jail for the most incorrigible convicts since 1934, the "Rock" has been worn away by the weather and the wind. The walls, which date back to the 18th century, have cracked and the concrete is decomposing. Future Al Capones will have to find alternative accommodation.

Alfred Hitchcock with two feathered extras from his film "The Birds".

1963

APRIL

Su	Mo	Tu	We	Th	Fr	Sa
	1	2	3	4	5	6
7	8	9	10	11	12	13
14	15	16	17	18	19	20
21	22	23	24	25	26	27
28	29	30				

1. N. Rhodesia: Joshua Nkomo is sentenced to six months hard labour (→20/12).

1. Australia: First issue of Oz, an underground "pyschedelic" magazine.

4. Hungary: 500 political prisoners are released.

7. Washington: Britain signs an agreement to buy 100 Polaris missiles from the US (→15).

7. Belgrade: A new constitution makes Tito president for life (→23/8).

9. US: Winston Churchill is awarded honorary American citizenship by Kennedy (→1/5).

9. Los Angeles: "Lawrence of Arabia" wins seven Oscars.

10. US: 129 are feared dead after the sinking of the US submarine Thresher in the Atlantic.

12. US: Martin Luther King is arrested for leading a civil rights march in Alabama (→25).

15. London: The Aldermaston marchers arrive for a protest by 70,000 against nuclear weapons (→17).

16. UK: Russian pianist Vladimir Ashkenazy is granted political asylum.

17. London: Special Branch arrest 20 CND activists in "Spies for Peace" for revealing classified military information (→25/7).

17. Moscow: British businessman Greville Wynne is charged with spying (→25).

21. Jordan: King Hussein dissolves the parliament after it passes a vote of no confidence in his government (→29).

24. London: Marriage of Princess Alexandra and Angus Ogilvy (→17/6).

24. London: Mandy Rice-Davies is arrested as she is about to leave the country (→5/6).

27. Moscow: Fidel Castro arrives to see Khrushchev (→29/6/64).

DEATH

23. Israeli president Itzhak Ben-Zvi (*6/12/1884).

Erhard to replace Adenauer in Bonn

Chancellor Ludwig Erhard.

April 23. Vice-Chancellor Ludwig Erhard, architect of West Germany's "economic miracle", is to succeed Konrad Adenauer as Chancellor when "der Alte" retires later this year. Herr Erhard is credited with providing the financial base on which Herr Adenauer has been able to restore Germany to the family of nations in his 14 years in office.

It is said of Herr Adenauer that he has taught Germans that it is possible to walk tall and straight even without wearing a uniform. However, his refusal to make any accommodation with the Soviet Union or even to acknowledge the existence of East Germany, which he described as the "so-called German Democratic Republic", left him increasingly isolated (→16/10).

Ministers cleared by Vassall tribunal

April 25. A judicial tribunal today cleared Lord Carrington, First Lord of the Admiralty, and his deputy, Tom Galbraith, of blame over the Vassall case.

Its report said that they were not remiss in failing to spot that William Vassall, the homosexual Admiralty clerk jailed for spying, was a security risk. Nor was there anything improper in the relationship between Mr Galbraith and Vassall who worked in the Minister's office and was befriended by him. Galbraith has resigned (→7/5). ▷

US governor will defy law on race issue

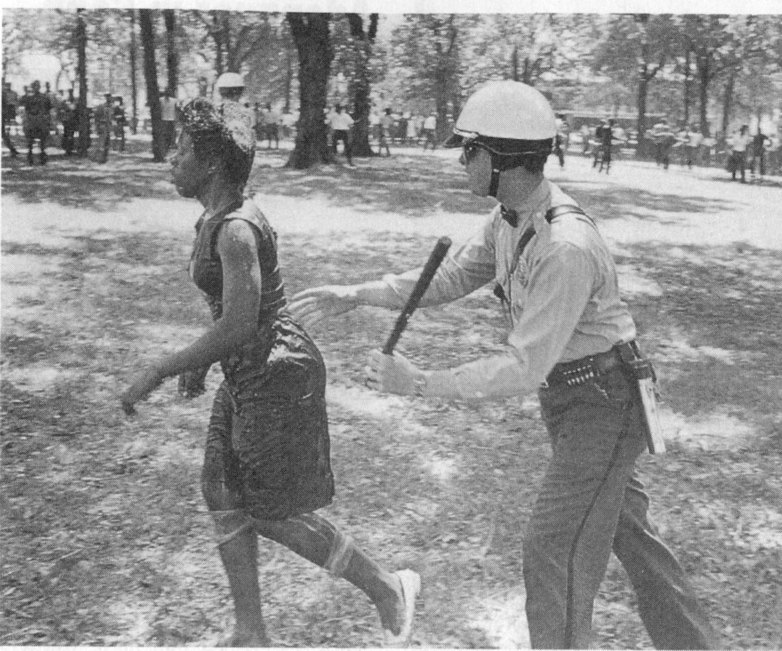

A policeman attempts to arrest a demonstrator in Birmingham, Alabama.

April 25. Another governor from the southern states is preparing to fight the federal government's attempts to enforce the desegregation laws. The US Attorney-General, Robert Kennedy, today met George Wallace, the Alabama governor, to try and persuade him to obey the law.

Wallace refused to withdraw his threat to defy federal authority. Kennedy said afterwards: "It's like a foreign country; there's no communication."

Tension between blacks and whites in the state is already high. Just two weeks ago the two Negro leaders, Dr Martin Luther King and Dr Ralph Abernathy led a march in Birmingham protesting against segregation. It was peaceful and disciplined, but the police arrested the two leaders and 58 others for parading without a permit.

The arrests angered the marchers and fighting then broke out between 2,000 blacks and the police. Many people were hurt, but through it all hundreds stood or sat singing, quietly but firmly, "We shall overcome"; this is now well established as the anthem of the civil rights movement (→5/5).

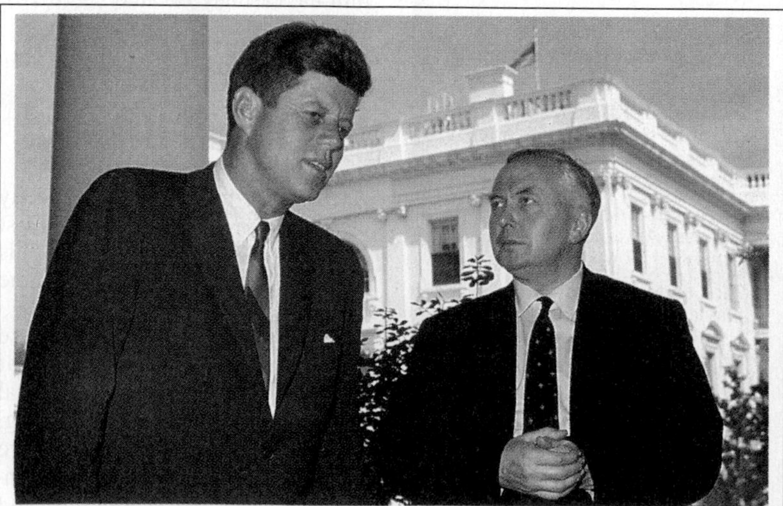

Harold Wilson outside the White House with President Kennedy during Wilson's first visit to the USA since he became leader of the Labour Party.

1963

MAY

Su	Mo	Tu	We	Th	Fr	Sa
			1	2	3	4
5	6	7	8	9	10	11
12	13	14	15	16	17	18
19	20	21	22	23	24	25
26	27	28	29	30	31	

3. Haiti: President Duvalier declares martial law after protests against his rule (→14/6/64).

5. US: 1,000 are arrested on a civil rights march in Alabama.

7. Moscow: Wynne's and Penkovsky's trial begins.→

7. US: Launch of the second Telstar satellite (→16).

9. Peking: China agrees to hold talks with Russia to try and resolve their differences (→5/7).

15. London: Chief Enharo is deported to Nigeria (→27).

15. Rotterdam: Tottenham beat Atletico Madrid 5-1 to become the first British team to win the European Cup Winners' Cup.

16. Pacific: US astronaut Major Gordon Cooper lands after 22 orbits of the earth in his Mercury capsule (→16/6).

18. US: Kennedy visits the South and praises civil rights demonstrators.→

22. London: Britain's first Communist peer, Lord Milford, sits in the House of Lords.

25. Addis Ababa: Leaders of 30 African nations found the Organisation of African Unity (→11/8).

25. London: Manchester United beat Leicester 3-1 to win the FA Cup.

26. Rome: Pope John XXIII suffers a relapse and is seriously ill (→19/6).

27. London: Home Secretary causes a major political storm by admitting he lied about the deportation of Chief Enharo.

27. Kenya: Jomo Kenyatta is elected premier in Kenya's first general election (→11/6).

29. UK: Mr M. Dupre's Relko wins the Derby.

29. East Pakistan: 10,000 die in a cyclone, and 500,000 are left homeless (→26/7).

DEATHS

8. British comedian Max Miller (*1895).

16. Soviet spy Oleg Penkovsky (*23/4/19).

Churchill will not seek re-election

May 1. Sir Winston Churchill will retire from the House of Commons at the next election. He is 88 and by October will have completed 60 years as an MP.

"My accident last year has decreased my mobility," he explained today. He broke his left thigh while on holiday in Monte Carlo last June. Sir Winston told his Woodford (Essex) constituency chairman: "I'm very sad."

Tonight he smiled and waved to a crowd awaiting his arrival at a Royal Academy banquet, resplendent in his Order of Merit sash. "I'll walk," he told his chauffeur and detective bodyguard. They said: "No, you won't." Reluctantly and smiling again, Sir Winston sat in his collapsible wheelchair.

Bond is a hit with his seductive stunts

Ursula Andress and Sean Connery in the first Bond film, "Dr No".

May 1. "From Russia With Love", a thriller about Ian Fleming's secret agent hero James Bond, is the biggest hit of the cinema so far this year. It stars Sean Connery as the suavely brutal Bond as 007 – "licensed to kill" – with a host of seductive girls and spectacular stunts.

Last year Bond made his screen debut in "Dr No", which took time to find an audience. But now there is a rush to exploit the 12 Bond adventures, and "Goldfinger" is being put into production.

Briton sentenced in Moscow spy trial

ʒreville Wynne takes the witness box during his trial in Moscow.

ɫay 11. A Moscow court today ıpplauded the death sentence pas-ꞏed on Colonel Oleg Penkovsky for ꞏupplying the West with up-to-late, high priority information on he innermost political and military ꞏecrets of the Soviet Union.

Greville Wynne, the British ɔusinessman who had acted as his 'go-between" with British and ⱯAmerican intelligence agents, eceived an eight-year sentence at he end of the four-day trial.

Penkovsky, who was a colonel in he GRU, the Soviet Military Intel-igence agency, spied for the West for 16 months, spanning a period of crisis between the regime of Nikita Khrushchev and the new administration of John Kennedy. He handed over more than 5,000 separate photographed items of secret military, political and economic intelligence.

Greville Wynne, who was Penkovsky's contact in Moscow, London and Paris, was given three years in prison and five in a labour camp. Eight British diplomats and five Americans were declared persona non grata in the USSR as a result of the case (→1/7).

Troops sent in to quell US race riots

May 18. President Kennedy today ent in Federal troops to try and quell the riots and violence in Alabama that have been going on poradically for two months. The most recent outbreak was provoked after 1,000 Negroes on a peace-ful protest march against segregat-on were arrested in Birmingham.

Behind the scenes, the US Attorney-General, Robert Ken-nedy, is working desperately to get a deal between white and black eaders. He asked the blacks to stop marching until a new city govern-ment takes over. But Dr Martin Luther King told him his plans vere "too little, too late" (→31).

Benn wins battle to renounce title

May 30. The Peerage Bill, allowing hereditary peers to renounce their titles for life and sit as MPs in the House of Commons, was published today, in time for reluctant peers like Anthony Wedgwood Benn to stand in the next general election.

Any MP succeeding to a peerage will have one month in which to disclaim it. Existing peers must decide within six months whether to become plain misters.

The new law is a personal triumph for Mr Wedgwood Benn who has been spearheading the campaign for reform. He is sure to be re-elected for his Bristol seat next time (→31/7).

1963

JUNE

Su	Mo	Tu	We	Th	Fr	Sa
						1
2	3	4	5	6	7	8
9	10	11	12	13	14	15
16	17	18	19	20	21	22
23	24	25	26	27	28	29
30						

1. US: Alabama Governor George Wallace vows to defy court order to open university to Negroes (→11).

4. US: Pan Am places an order to buy Concorde.

9. Belgium: Scottish farmer Jim Clark wins the Belgian Grand Prix in a Lotus Climax.

11. US: Kennedy orders National Guards to protect two Negroes enrolling at the University of Alabama (→15).

11. Nairobi: Kenya's National Assembly opens; Africa's first self-governing parliament (→12/12).

15. US: Shooting of civil rights leader Medgar Evans sparks rioting in the South (→18/8).

16. Jerusalem: David Ben-Gurion resigns as Israeli premier.

17. London: Macmillan faces fierce criticism during a debate on the Profumo affair.→

17. UK: Buckingham Palace admits that 14-year-old Prince Charles bought a cherry brandy in a hotel bar (→20/9).

19. Rome: 80 cardinals begin a conclave in The Vatican to choose a new Pope.→

19. UK: The first British-made oral contraceptive becomes available on prescription (→8/8).

20. Geneva: Russia and the US agree to establish a hot line phone link (→30/8).

20. UK: Merlyn Rees wins a by-election for Labour in South Leeds (→4/7).

21. Paris: France announces her withdrawal from the North Atlantic Fleet of NATO.

21. US: Athlete Bob Hayes sets a new world record by running 100 yards in 9.1 secs.

27. Ireland: Kennedy visits his ancestral home in Wexford County.

29. Rome: Coronation of Pope Paul VI (→5/1/64).→

DEATH

3. Pope John XXIII, born Angelo Giuseppe Roncalli (*25/11/1881).→

Russia puts first woman into space

June 16. The Soviet Union chalked up another first in outer space today when Lieutentant Valentina Tereshkova circled the earth in a Vostok spaceship. Miss Tereshkova, aged 26, and a former amateur parachute jumper, has spoken with Nikita Khrushchev, the Soviet leader, who expressed his "fatherly pride" in her success, called her "Valya" and promised she would receive a huge welcome on her return to earth.

Miss Tereshkova's space capsule is circling the earth near to another one, piloted by Colonel Bykovsky. This proximity suggests Soviet scientists were considering a rendezvous in space (→26/10).

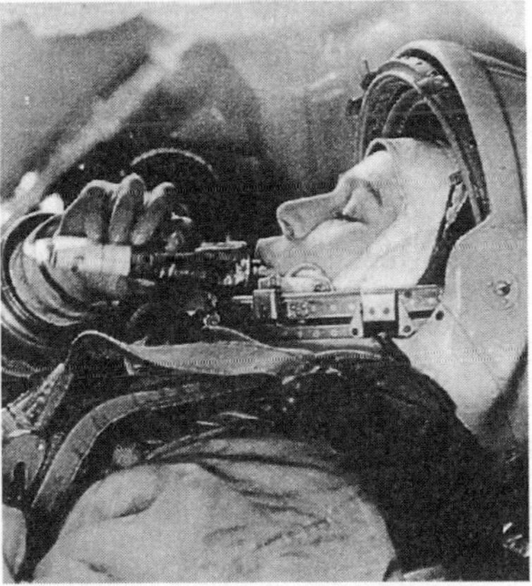

Valiant Valentina Tereshkova.

Tehran riots after Khomeini arrested

June 6. Martial law was declared in Tehran tonight after a day of rioting in which at least 20 people were killed. General Nassiri, the military governor, sent in tanks and troops with fixed bayonets to battle with mobs of religious rioters. Police were attacked and cars and buildings were set ablaze.

Disorders began after the arrest of Rouahallah Khomeini, a Moslem religious leader. He organised demonstrations against the Shah's land reform programme and votes for women, bitterly opposed by fanatical Mullahs. Reinforcements were called in to guard the Imperial Palace after an arrested holy man revealed that Khomeini's aim was to overthrow the monarchy.

Britain rocked by Profumo sex scandal revelations

Profumo quits after lying to the House

June 5. John Profumo, Secretary of State for War, resigned from the Government and from Parliament today. He admitted "with deep remorse" that ten weeks ago he had lied to the Commons in saying there had been no impropriety in his relationship with Christine Keeler. He reaffirmed, however, that it has involved no breach of security.

Mr Macmillan, on holiday in Scotland, wrote to him: "This is a great tragedy for you, your family and your friends."

The scandal, which is now rocking the Government and threatening the Prime Minister's position, finally broke when Mr Profumo decided it was time to confess to the Government chief whip. Earlier he had persisted in denying impropriety when his original statement to MPs was challenged by Dr Stephen Ward, the osteopath, at whose West End flat Mr Profumo met Miss Keeler. Denial became impossible when Dr Ward wrote privately to both the Prime Minister and Mr Wilson, the Opposition leader. Mr Macmillan's ministers accept tonight that the Government's image has been sadly tarnished. They are hoping that the Profumo confession and resignation will save it from more damage. The Opposition has other ideas (→10).

Profumo: the fallen minister.

Ward centre of sex and security circus

June 10. A key figure in the Profumo affair appeared in court today, accused of living off immoral earnings. Dr Stephen Ward, aged 50, was refused bail and told he would face further charges.

The osteopath and artist, whose subjects have included members of the Royal Family, is seen as the ringmaster of the sex and security circus, the link between high society and low life. It was at Ward's country cottage on Lord Astor's Cliveden estate that Profumo first saw Christine Keeler as she frolicked naked in the swimming pool.

It was Ward himself who tipped off MI5 when he became concerned by the fact that the former showgirl was also having a liaison with Soviet naval attache Eugene Ivanov. Miss Keeler, aged 21, is known to have had other exotic entanglements as well. It was an attempt by one ex-lover, John Edgecombe, to shoot her that first brought her and her life-style to public attention.

Another figure who may hold the key to many questions now being raised is blonde model Mandy Rice-Davies, aged 18, who wa[s] Ward's mistress and Christine Kee[l]ler's flatmate. In yet another twis[t] to the plot Miss Rice-Davies wa[s] previously the mistress of the notor[i]ious slum landlord Peter Rachma[n] whose name is now synonymou[s] with racketeering (→17).

Keeler: the naked temptress.

Supermac falls to earth with a bump

Ivanov: the Soviet connection.

June 30. Harold Macmillan is a broken man tonight. He was close to tears when nearly 30 Tory MPs refused to back the Government in defeating an opposition censure motion over security aspects of the Profumo Affair. Cabinet resignations have been narrowly averted. The Government staggers on but Supermac has suffered a severe dose of kryptonite. He told MPs: "I acted honourably." He had believed John Profumo's firm denial of impropriety with Christine Keeler.

The security services never told him of any security risk, he said. But many Tories agreed with Mr Wilson, the Opposition leader, who accused him of indolently gambling with national security for political reasons.

The role of Eugene Ivanov, the Soviet naval attache, is also worrying MPs. Six months ago Miss Keeler told the police that Dr Ward, osteopath friend of Profumo and Ivanov, asked her to find out when West Germany will get nuclear weapons. She ignored the request (→22/7).

Dr Stephen Ward returns to Brixton prison under police escort.

Buddhist protester goes up in flames

A fiery challenge: the self-immolation of Buddhist monk Quang Duc.

June 13. Buddhist protests in Vietnam reached a horrifying peak three days ago in Saigon, when a monk set fire to himself. His agonising ritual suicide was in protest at the unfair treatment which the Buddhists claim they suffer under the present government. A new, extreme wave of Buddhist rioting is now feared.

Broadly convinced of the rightness of the monk's case and that South Vietnam's mainly Buddhist population is being unfairly treated, the United States has warned President Diem that it will officially condemn his regime's behaviour unless he moves quickly to redress their grievances. Diem, a Catholic, heads a predominantly Catholic regime. His quarrel with the Buddhists got world-wide publicity last month, when Vietnamese soldiers fired on a Buddhist demonstration in Hue, killing nine.

According to Washington's experts, Saigon cannot beat the Viet Cong unless it first inspires confidence among its own people. That means getting the support of the Buddhist establishment. The current religious conflict is seen as a possibly irreparable blow to Diem's reputation, and is of deep concern to the US in its fight against the Viet Cong (→21/8).

The legacy of Pope John

June 21. In one of the shortest-ever conclaves, Cardinal Giovanni Battista Montini was elected Pope just before 11.30 this morning. It was only the third smoke signal from the iron stove pipe on the Sistine Chapel. The smoke was clearly white and priests in the Apostolic Palace threw open the windows of the papal apartments confirming that a Pope had been elected.

The shortness of the conclave reflects the desire for unity and continuity in papal policies. The Catholic world is still in a state of shock after the death of Pope John XXIII on June 3. In his tragically short reign of four years, he had become one of most loved Popes throughout the world.

In one of his boldest moves he had instituted an Ecumenical Council to consider the question of Christian unity. This had to be suspended in the last month of his life when he was fighting a painful struggle against cancer. His successor, who has chosen the name of Paul VI, is expected to restart it as soon as possible.

Pope John XXIII was both a theological liberal and an astute diplomat, able to carry more conservative figures along the path to reform. As the first papal legate to France after the war, he won the support of the left and progressives while forming a lasting personal friendship with General de Gaulle.

His Holiness Pope John XXIII.

The new Pope is also a liberal. He was born near Brescia and educated in his early years by the Jesuits. He was Pro-Secretary to Pope Pius and was later made Archbishop of Milan. Both these posts usually carry a cardinal's hat, but Montini did not get one because of his reputation as a liberal and innovator.

One of the first acts of Pope John after his election in 1958 was to make Montini a Cardinal. Now he is Pope he will have a chance to repay his mentor. His first important international act will be to receive President Kennedy on his trip to Rome, originally planned for yesterday, but postponed after the Pope's death (→29).

Cooper floors Clay, but cut eye beats him

First flooring for Cassius Clay – by British boxer Henry Cooper.

June 18. Henry Cooper, the British heavyweight champion, handed the cocksure Cassius Clay the biggest surprise of his professional life at Wembley, before bowing to the inevitable with a badly-cut eye.

The American, who predicted the fight would end in five rounds, and who had opened the cut over Cooper's eye early on, was cruising contemptuously to victory when, seconds before the end of round four, Cooper let go a desperate left hook and sent him sprawling on the seat of his pants.

The bell went at once, Clay recovered quickly, and in round five salved his embarrassment with a barrage that turned the trickle of blood into a flood.

After the conclave: the coronation of Pope Paul VI in St. Peter's, Rome.

"Ich bin ein Berliner" declares Kennedy

President Kennedy with Mayor Willy Brandt at the Brandenburg Gate.

June 26. The Kennedy eloquence was turned on full blast today to boost the morale of West Berliners. More than a million of them turned out to greet the US President and he did not disappoint them. "Ich bin ein Berliner" (I am a Berliner), he told them to roars of approval. "All free men, wherever they may live, are citizens of Berlin."

At Checkpoint Charlie, the crossing point to East Berlin, the Communists had hung signs condemning what they termed the fascist and militaristic revival in West Germany. Kennedy responded with a vigorous attack on Communism. He told them: "There are some who say in Europe and elsewhere, 'We can work with the Communists'. Let them come to Berlin. And there are even a few who say that it's true that Communism is an evil system, but it permits us to make economic progress. Let them come to Berlin."

Kennedy flew on to Dublin tonight, where huge crowds filled the airport and lined the streets to welcome him. He expressed pleasure in returning to his roots in a country whose sons and daughters had spread so far around the world, saying "this island still fulfils an historic assignment". He is expected to stay for three nights (→ 27).

Kennedy among a crowd of well-wishers during his visit to Cork, Ireland.

1963

JULY

Su	Mo	Tu	We	Th	Fr	Sa
	1	2	3	4	5	6
7	8	9	10	11	12	13
14	15	16	17	18	19	20
21	22	23	24	25	26	27
28	29	30	31			

3. London: The government announces the introduction of continental road signs (→ 26).

3. Nice: Court overturns Somerset Maugham's adoption of his secretary as his son.

4. UK: John Silkin wins the Deptford by-election for Labour.

5. Wimbledon: Charles "Chuck" McKinley beats Australian Fred Stolle to win the Mens' Singles title.→

5. Moscow: A delegation of Chinese party leaders arrive for discussions.→

9. London: 94 arrested in violent protests against the Greek King's visit (→ 14/11).

11. Ecuador: President Carlos Monray overthrown in a military coup.

12. South Africa: Security police arrest ex-ANC leader Walter Sisulu (→ 3/12).

14. UK: The BBC announces it is scrapping the TV panel show "What's My Line" (→ 13/11).

15. London: Nuclear physicist Giuseppe Martelli is acquitted of spying for Russia (→ 29).

16. London: The government proposes the creation of a Ministry of Defence.

19. Syria: 20 rebels are executed after government troops crush a coup attempt.

22. London: Trial of Stephen Ward begins.→

25. Moscow: A partial nuclear test ban treaty is agreed by Britain, the US and Russia (→ 8/8).

26. UK: 50mph speed limit is introduced, but ignored by most drivers.

29. Moscow: Philby is granted Soviet citizenship (→ 1/9).

31. London: Viscount Stansgate becomes the first peer to renounce his title; he is now Anthony Wedgwood Benn (→ 20/11).

DEATHS

22. British sculptor Frank Dobson (*18/11/1888).

23. Soviet painter Alexander Gerassimov (*12/8/1881).

Philby was "Third Man", MPs are told

July 1. The Government admitted today in a House of Commons statement that "Kim" Philby, the former Foreign Office colleague of the traitors Burgess and MacLean was, after all, the "Third Man". It was he who had tipped off MacLean, through Burgess, that the security service was on his trail. Both then fled to the Soviet Union.

Philby was named by Labour MP Marcus Lipton in 1955, but he was cleared by Harold Macmillan, then Foreign Secretary. Philby, however, had been forced to resign from the Foreign Office in 1951 and had gone to work in Beirut as a foreign correspondent. He vanished in January and is now assumed to be in Moscow (→ 15).

Australian woman wins at Wimbledon

July 8. Margaret Smith, the tall, powerful 20-year-old, who has brought all the power of the men's serve and volley technique to the women's game, overcame the pre-match nerves that cost her the last two Wimbledon championships to become the first Australian to win the women's title. Despite faltering in the second set, she rallied to beat the Californian teenager Billie Jean Moffitt 6-3, 6-4.

Australia's Margaret Smith.

Dr Ward takes overdose

July 31. Dr Stephen Ward was critically ill in hospital today after an apparent suicide bid at the end of his vice trial. He was found unconscious in a friend's flat in Chelsea two hours before the start of the trial's eighth and final day. The talented artist had swallowed an overdose of sleeping pills. Beside him were 12 letters and £150.

He was still in a coma when the jury returned a verdict of guilty on two charges of living on immoral earnings. His sentence has been postponed.

Throughout his trial Ward showed a steely resilience beneath the urbane charm, continually protesting his innocence. He claimed he was the victim of a campaign of villainy and that the authorities were determined to destroy him for his part in the Profumo Affair.

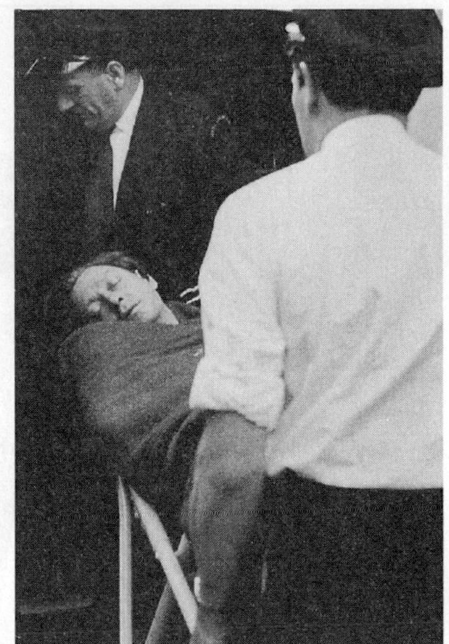

Ward is taken to hospital.

The court hearings lifted the lid on a twilight world where the famous and wealthy consorted with prostitutes, perverts and drug addicts. Members of the public queued for hours to hear details of orgies, two-way mirrors and black magic rituals.

They also heard how Ward arranged parties at his London flat and his Cliveden cottage, which brought together attractive young women of loose morals, like Christine Keeler and Mandy Rice-Davies, and important and influential men.

In his hour of need, however, he found himself virtually friendless. In his evidence Ward, a vicar's son and divorcee, admitted that he was a "connoisseur of love-making" and a "thoroughly immoral man". But he strenuously denied he had ever taken money from prostitution or for procuring girls. Testimony against him had been "a tissue of lies," he maintained (→ 3/8).

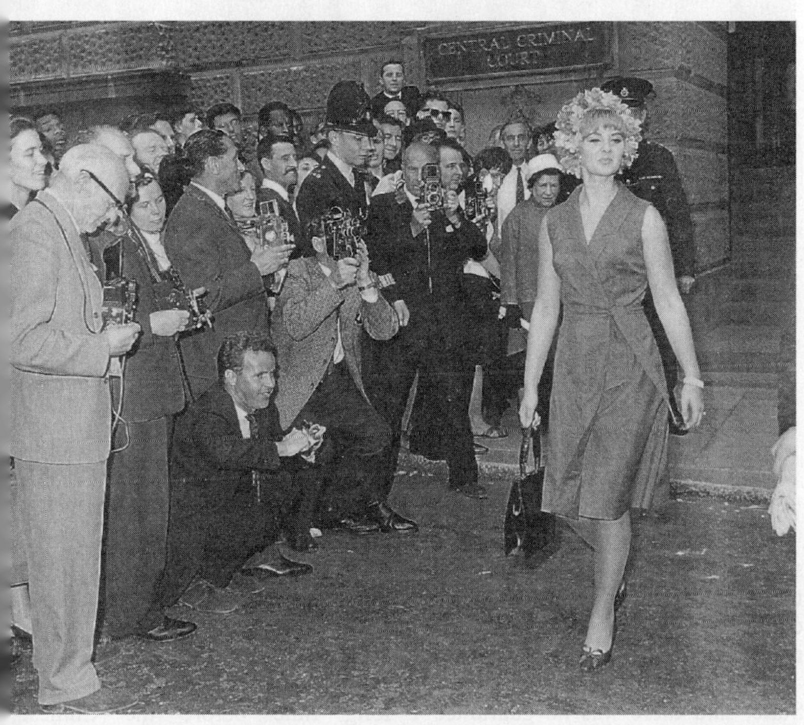

Mandy Rice-Davies leaves court after giving her evidence.

A quake makes half of Skopje homeless

July 26. Eighty shock waves from an earthquake today killed 1,000 people and destroyed the Yugoslav city of Skopje, which was virtually rebuilt following World War II.

Again hundreds of thousands are homeless. Once more the death toll is heavy and with more than 500 bodies believed to be buried in the ruins medical relief agencies warn of possible epidemics.

Sweden and the United States are flying in emergency supplies for the huge makeshift refugee camps out in the fields which are sheltering a vast exodus. A lucky few have found seats on rescue planes returning to Belgrade to pick up more equipment.

At 5.15am, the first shock struck the city, the provincial capital of Macedonia. Then for three hours the fearful tremors allowed nothing to stand still. A pilot due to fly out early today described how he woke to find his hotel swaying. "I watched the main railway station fall to bits. As I rushed outside buildings just collapsed everywhere. Screams were coming from under the ruins and the streets were filled with terror," he said.

Geologists say the epicentre was the middle of Skopje itself. The army social centre, the town hall, office blocks and hotels were flattened. At the city hospital, patients and staff jumped from upper floors as the building disintegrated.

Two German tourists are believed to be the only survivors out of 300 guests trapped inside an hotel as it toppled (→ 6/10).

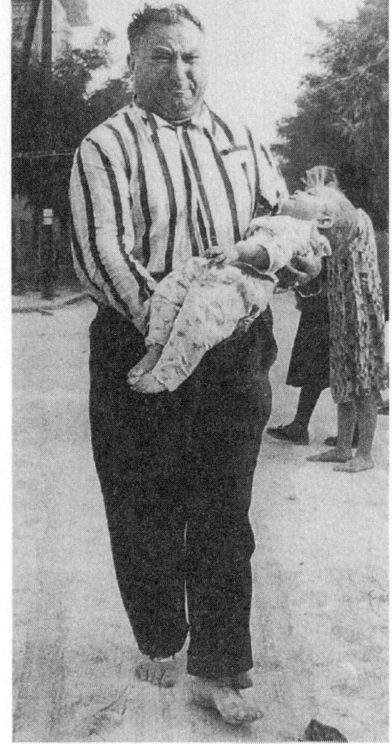

A tiny victim of the Skopje quake.

Rachman prompts slum housing probe

July 22. An independent inquiry is to be set up to investigate housing in London, particularly in the private rented sector. The announcement came today during a heated Commons debate, when Labour leader, Harold Wilson, denounced the rent-rackets run by "creatures of London's underworld growing fat by battening on human misery".

He attacked both the Government and the police, who had played "a curiously passive role in this shabby record of gangsterism".

The debate follows exposure of the practices of the late Peter Rachman, a slum landlord and associate of call-girl Christine Keeler, who made millions by buying cheap tenanted property and then using terror to force tenants from their homes.

Sino-Soviet split is now complete

July 21. The extent of the Sino-Soviet rift was again emphasised today when a strong delegation of Chinese party leaders packed their bags and went home after bitter and protracted "peace" talks in Moscow. The talks have followed months of intricate manoeuvring and savage press polemics with both sides claiming leadership of the Communist world.

Nikita Khrushchev, the Soviet leader, has shown what he thinks of the talks by ostentatiously absenting himself from Moscow and returning only to welcome Lord Hailsham and Averil Harriman, who arrived to negotiate a nuclear test ban treaty. Even if Khrushchev was now removed from office, the split between Moscow and Peking is likely to remain (→ 3/4/64).

1963

AUGUST

Su	Mo	Tu	We	Th	Fr	Sa
				1	2	3
4	5	6	7	8	9	10
11	12	13	14	15	16	17
18	19	20	21	22	23	24
25	26	27	28	29	30	31

3. London: Dr Stephen Ward dies after taking a drugs overdose.→

5. US: Craig Breedlove sets a new world land speed record of 407.45 mph.

8. UK: A government doctor says that sex change operations will never be possible (→23/6/64).

9. UK: The Post Office admits the Great Train Robbers stole £2.6 million (→13).

9. Washington: President Kennedy's second son dies 36 hours after his birth (→22/11).

11. Addis Ababa: The city is chosen as the headquarters of the Organisation of African Unity.

13. UK: Police find the Great Train Robbers hide-out, Leatherslade Farm (→22).

15. UK: Three Bristol footballers admit taking bribes to lose matches and are banned for life by the FA.

18. US: James Meredith, first Negro student at the University of Mississippi, receives his diploma (→28/8).

20. UK: The TV news in Wales is read by a female broadcaster for the first time.

21. Saigon: The army arrests 100 Buddhist monks (→25).

22. UK: Charlie Wilson is charged in connection with the Great Train Robberly (→4/9).

23. Yugoslavia: Khrushchev dances with Tito while on an official visit to Yugoslavia.

25. South Vietnam: 600 students are arrested for anti-government protests (→30).

26. London: West Indies win the Test series against England by three matches to one.

30. Rome: The Pope expresses his concern at events in Vietnam (→14/9).

DEATHS

22. British car tycoon Viscount Nuffield, born William Morris (*10/10/1877).→

31. French Cubist painter Georges Braque (*13/5/1882).

Great Train Robbery nets a million

Aug 8. In the most audacious crime in British history, a well-organised gang hijacked a train and escaped with mailbags worth well in excess of £1 million early today. At least 15 men, armed and wearing masks, carried out the ambush, but police immediately suspected the robbers had inside information.

They had faked a red track signal to stop the train at a secluded spot at Cheddington, Bucks., and the gang knew it was a special "travelling Post Office" laden with banknotes on their way to be destroyed. They also struck when normal high-security carriages had broken and had been taken out of service.

The robbery had been timed to the second. At 3.10am, with the train stopped, the engine and front two vans were uncoupled before being driven up the line. In the time it took the gang to smash their way in and overpower sorting staff, they had travelled 800 yards to where accomplices waited with a lorry. Twenty minutes later, 120 mailbags had been thrown to the road below and the gang had fled.

They left few clues in what has been dubbed "The Great Train Robbery". Police found one brown glove used to block out a green light and four large torch batteries which lit up the red stop signal.

The alarm was raised half-an-hour after their escape by train driver Jack Mills, and his fireman, David Whitby. Mills, aged 58, had been coshed repeatedly during the raid and Whitby was handcuffed after jumping down from the stationary train and finding telephone wires had been cut.

A full-scale inquiry into the security of Royal Mail trains has been ordered (→9).

Unloading mailbags from the remaining carriages of the robbed train.

Test ban treaty offers hope to children as yet unborn

Aug 8. Britons, Americans and Russians stood side by side in the Kremlin today to toast "peace and friendship among nations" as the Moscow Treaty banning nuclear weapon tests in the atmosphere, outer space and underwater was signed.

Lord Home, the British Foreign Secretary, described the event as a "great occasion for us all". Every family in the world could now hope to sleep free from the fear that the "health of their unborn children is in danger from man-made poisons in the air".

But it is also clear that the Test Ban treaty has not ended the Cold War overnight. President de Gaulle has made it clear that France will not agree to join the accord and the Soviet leader, Mr Khrushchev, warned that "a nuclear test ban does not mean disarmament and does not mean the end of the arms race". He told the Western powers today: "You do not like our social system and we don't like yours. No treaties can overcome the concrete contradictions between the two social systems."

Dean Rusk, the US Secretary of State, said there was no guarantee that the treaty would have any historical significance. The Soviet decision to sign the treaty is thought to be a reflection of their concern over Peking, although Mr Khrushchev believes it will be a long time before the Chinese develop nuclear weapons (→7/10).

The ceremony to mark the signing of the test ban treaty in Moscow.

"Hot line" opens to put Washington in touch with Moscow

Aug 30. A "hot line" between the Kremlin and the White House went into operation today, designed to reduce the risk of accidental war and reduce sudden East-West tensions. The opening of the direct communications link was announced in simultaneous statements by Washington and Moscow.

The Americans sent a standard test signal over the line and received one from the Soviet end. The link will be maintained round the clock, but will only be used only at times of emergency for diplomatic messages between the Soviet and American leaders. Each message will be encoded to prevent its interception along the 10,000-mile line.

A major reason for the link was the anxiety caused by delays in diplomatic communications during the 1962 crisis, when Nikita Khrushchev attempted to establish rocket bases in Cuba. Were direct communications available, such crises could be handled better.

Doubts surface over dead doctor's case

Aug 7. Scotland Yard are to investigate the evidence of prostitutes Vicky Barrett and Ronna Ricardo, key witnesses in the Stephen Ward vice trial. Barrett was today reported to have stated that she lied when she told the jury that she used the society osteopath's flat to have sex with men.

Ward, who was convicted of living off immoral earnings, took a fatal overdose after the judge's summing up. His funeral will be held tomorrow. Barrett is said to have broken down when she heard of his death and read a letter he had left pleading with her to tell the truth.

Her confession follows Ricardo's admission during the trial that she had given "completely untrue" evidence. Fresh inquiries into the case were disclosed after a report alleging perjury and conspiracy in the trial of Aloysius "Lucky" Gordon, Christine Keeler's boyfriend, was handed to the Director of Public Prosecutions (→ 5/9).

"I have a dream" says Luther King

Martin Luther King speaks of justice and equality: "a dream chiefly rooted in the American dream".

Aug 28. More than 200,000 people marched through Washington today in the biggest demonstration yet to press for civil rights. Negroes walked shoulder to shoulder with showbiz stars like Marlon Brando, Burt Lancaster, Judy Garland and Bob Dylan.

The peaceful tone was set by the Rev. Martin Luther King, who told the crowd by the reflecting pools of the Lincoln Memorial: "Let us not seek to satisfy our thirst for freedom by drinking from the cup of hatred and bitterness." The non-violent struggle would go on, he said, "until justice flows like water and righteousness like a stream".

President Kennedy told the civil rights leaders that they had advanced "the cause of 20 million Negroes". But the orator of the day was undoubtedly King, who told the huge crowd: "I still have a dream. It is a dream chiefly rooted in the American dream. I have a dream that one day this nation will rise up and live out the true meaning of its creed: 'We hold these truths to be self-evident, that all men are created equal'."

"I have a dream," he went on, "that the sons of former slaves and the sons of former slave owners would sit together at the table of brotherhood" in Georgia (→ 2/9).

Nuffield dies after making – and then giving away – millions

Aug 22. Britain's most successful car tycoon has died, aged 85. Lord Nuffield made a second career giving away the £27 million he had earned in the first.

Born William Morris, he started in business as an apprentice cycle mechanic. His greatest gift was to set up the Nuffield Foundation and endow it with £10 million of ordinary stock in his Morris Motors.

When car sales slumped after World War I, he achieved his most striking coup by cutting his prices by £100. He soon made a fortune with mid-price family cars. He became a baronet in 1929, and then a peer. He gave up his directorships ten years ago.

Lord Nuffield at the wheel of a 1911 Morris, one of his first cars.

1963

SEPTEMBER

Su	Mo	Tu	We	Th	Fr	Sa
1	2	3	4	5	6	7
8	9	10	11	12	13	14
15	16	17	18	19	20	21
22	23	24	25	26	27	28
29	30					

1. Moscow: British traitor Guy Burgess is reported to have died in obscurity several days earlier (→ 22/4/64).

2. US: Governor Wallace of Alabama orders state troopers to seal off Tuskegee High School to halt integration (→ 10).

5. UK: Christine Keeler is arrested and charged with perjury (→ 26).

7. UK: Sussex win the first one-day cricket final.

7. Venezuela: A grandmother gives birth to quins.

10. US: Kennedy takes control of Alabama's National Guard to implement the integration of its schools (→ 15).

12. France: 36 British tourists die in a plane crash in the Pyrenees (→ 29/11).

14. South Vietnam: The government begins arresting civilian leaders (→ 21).

16. Malaysia: The Federation of Malaysia is created; a mob of 10,000 burns down Britain's embassy in protest (→ 18).

16. Algiers: Ben Bella becomes the first President (→ 1/10).

17. UK: The early warning missile system at Flyingdales becomes operational.

18. Malaysia: Martial law is declared after widespread riots (→ 3/9/64).

20. UK: Princess Anne begins her classes at Benenden school (→ 29/2/64).

24. New Zealand: Doctors give the world's first successful blood transfusion to an unborn baby.

27. Washington: Joseph M. Valachi reveals the names of the key figures in organised crime to a Senate Committee.

30. US: 189 Negroes are arrested during a civil rights protest in Alabama (→ 8/3/64).

DEATHS

4. French statesman Robert Schuman (*29/6/1886).

19. New Zealand-born British cartoonist Sir David Low (*7/4/1891).

Negro girls killed by bomb in US church

Sept 15. Four Negro girls were killed and 23 people injured when a bomb exploded today during a church service in Birmingham, Alabama. The minister, J.H. Cross, was knocked out of the pulpit by the force of the explosion at the Sixteenth Street Baptist Church. It is a regular meeting place for Negro civil rights workers.

FBI agents have been sent from Washington to investigate the cause of the explosion. Birmingham has long been a focal point for clashes over de-segregation. George Wallace, the Alabama Governor, is a fierce opponent and has defied the law more than once. Last night riot squads were sent in to restore order after Negroes, shocked by the explosion, began throwing stones at the police. One Negro, aged 16, was shot dead by them and three others were wounded in the ensuing battle.

Dr Martin Luther King, the civil rights leader, is going to Birmingham to "plead with my people to remain non-violent in the face of this terrible provocation". He sent a telegram to Governor Wallace saying: "The blood of four little children and 13 others critically injured is on your hands. The irresponsible and misguided actions have created ... the atmosphere that induced continued violence and now murder" (→ 30).

Governor George Wallace.

Vietnam's hard-line worries US Congress

Sept 21. The US government has advised South Vietnam's President Ngo Dinh Diem to remove his brother Ngo Dinh Nhu from office. As police chief, Nhu is responsible for the recent crackdown on Buddhist leaders after religious demonstrations against the Diem regime.

Growing criticism from Congress of the repressive measures adopted by Diem could lead to a reduction in military and economic aid. Reflecting growing concern over developments in Saigon, President Kennedy sent out Defence Secretary Robert McNamara and General Maxwell Taylor to review the military effort (→ 2/11).

Ronald Biggs, suspected Great Train Robber, is arrested.

American Express launch card in UK

Sept 10. The banking giant, American Express, today launched its sterling credit card in Britain, five years after launching the original dollar equivalent in America.

The scheme allows selected "members" earning £2,000 or more a year to pay for goods and services on credit with a special card. It already has a rival in Britain – Diners' Club, which introduced the first-ever credit card to America in the early Fifties. The fee for joining American Express in Britain will be £3 12s 0d a year, and bills will be issued monthly.

Macmillan blamed by Profumo report

Sept 26. Harold Macmillan and his ministers failed in their handling of the Profumo Affair, the Denning report said today. Though security had not in fact been endangered, they had not dealt with the ex-War Minister's relationship with a call-girl even when it was affecting public confidence.

Hundreds of people scrabbled for the first copies of the report when it went on sale in London shortly after midnight. Lord Denning interviewed 160 people for his investigation, which completely clears some leading figures whose sexual proclivities had been the subject of gossip. One story centred on a man who served at dinner parties naked apart from a mask. Denning had interviewed him and he was not a minister (→ 1/10).

Clark is youngest world racing champ

Sept 9. Jim Clark, the modest young man from the Scottish Borders, has become the youngest driver to win the world championship. He won his first Grand Prix only last year, at the age of 26.

This season he has scored seven Grand Prix victories and astonished the Americans, who count the race as their personal preserve, by coming a close second in the gruelling Indianapolis 500.

Jim Clark and Colin Chapman, designer of the winning Lotus.

1963

OCTOBER

Su	Mo	Tu	We	Th	Fr	Sa
		1	2	3	4	5
6	7	8	9	10	11	12
13	14	15	16	17	18	19
20	21	22	23	24	25	26
27	28	29	30	31		

1. Nigeria: A republic is proclaimed with Dr Nnamdi Azikiwe as its first premier.

1. Algiers: President Ben Bella orders the nationalisation of all land owned by French settlers (→30/12).

3. Honduras: A military coup overthrows President Ramon Morales.

6. London: A crowd of 1,000 hurl eggs and apples at Nazi leader Colin Jordan after his wedding.

6. Haiti: 4,000 are feared dead after a hurricane strikes.

7. Washington: Kennedy signs the nuclear test ban treaty (→26/2).

10. UK: Macmillan announces he will resign as premier.→

10. Italy: 3,000 are feared drowned after a dam bursts in the Piave Valley (→10/11).

14. Washington: Pan Am and TWA place orders for 21 supersonic passenger planes.

16. West Germany: Dr Ludwig Erhard is elected Chancellor after the resignation of Konrad Adenauer.

17. Algeria: 10,000 Moroccan troops launch a fresh offensive against Algeria (→30).

20. London: The Earl of Home appoints his new cabinet; Enoch Powell and Iain Macleod refuse to serve in it (→23).

21. New York: The UN votes against admitting Communist China.

23. London: The Earl of Home renounces his six titles and becomes Sir Alec Douglas-Home (→8/11).

26. Moscow: Khrushchev says Russia won't race the US to put a man on the moon (→25/1/64).

30. Mali: Morocco and Algeria agree to a cease-fire (→20/2/64).

DEATHS

11. French artist Jean Cocteau (*5/7/1889).

11. French singer Edith Piaf, born Giovanna Gassion (*19/12/15).

Home is new Tory leader

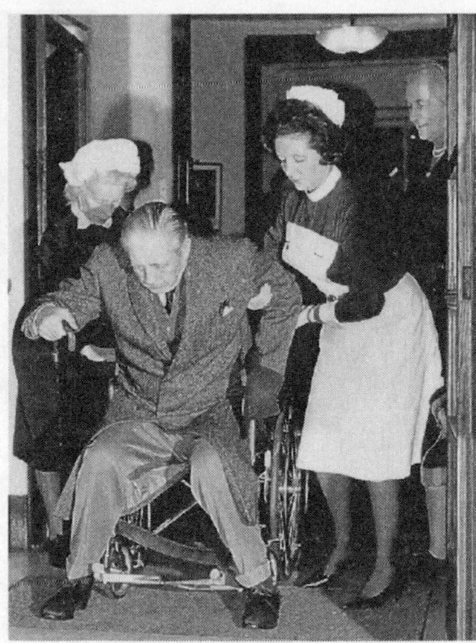

Harold Macmillan leaves hospital.

The Earl of Home, the new PM.

Oct 18. The Earl of Home is Britain's new Prime Minister. He will renounce his peerage. The Queen appointed him today on Mr Macmillan's advice and after consulting Sir Winston Churchill and other elder statesmen.

The Tory Party is still in a ferment which began with Mr Macmillan's resignation announcement from a hospital bed during last week's Tory Party conference at Blackpool. At once the town developed the frenzied atmosphere of an American convention. There has never been such a frenetic leadership struggle.

Lord Home emerged on top after a mysterious process of consultation. The deputy premier, Rab Butler, was widely expected to get the job. His backers are saying tonight that what they call a "magic circle" cooked up a plot to keep him out, supervised by Supermac.

Iain Macleod, leader of the Commons, and Enoch Powell, the Minister of Health, are among the government ministers refusing to serve under Lord Home. He is too lightweight, they say.

The process of consultation about leadership choice has been elaborate, but how much it counted for in the end only the magic circle knows (→20).

Report urges rapid growth in education

Oct 23. A massive expansion in British higher education is called for in the report published today by the committee headed by Lord Robbins, the economist. It proposes six brand-new universities and the immediate granting of university status to the ten Colleges of Advanced Technology. Existing universities will have to expand to at least three times their existing average size of 3,000 students.

All this can be achieved without a fall in standards, Robbins argues. He says that more than double the present number of 216,000 students in higher education are able enough to benefit from it.

Wilson's revolution will be white-hot

Oct 1. "We are redefining our socialism in terms of the scientific revolution," Party leader, Harold Wilson, assured Labour's conference in Scarborough today.

He continued: "The Britain that is going to be forged in the white heat of this scientific revolution will be no place for restrictive practices or outdated methods on either side of industry." It sounded exciting. Bemused delegates cheered. Details are awaited (→10).

Pop fans go wild as Beatlemania takes hold – yeah, yeah, yeah

Oct 31. They're calling it "Beatlemania" and there's no doubt that Britain is in love with the Beatles. This month screaming fans clogged the streets around the London Palladium when the Liverpool rock group starred in a TV show, caused traffic jams at airports (incidentally delaying the new Prime Minister) and bought enough copies of "She Loves You" to keep it at number one for four weeks.

Next month the "Fab Four", or "Mop Tops", as the press has dubbed its new heroes, reach their greatest pinnacle yet: they are due to top the bill at the Royal Variety Performance in London. Will the Royals also succumb to the charm of John, Paul, Ringo and George? Yeah, yeah, yeah (→4/11).

Sales of "She Loves You" pass a million: the Beatles win a gold record.

1963

NOVEMBER

Su	Mo	Tu	We	Th	Fr	Sa
					1	2
3	4	5	6	7	8	9
10	11	12	13	14	15	16
17	18	19	20	21	22	23
24	25	26	27	28	29	30

2. Canada: Archaeologists find Viking remains from 500 years before Columbus's arrival in America.

4. London: The Beatles star at the Royal Command Variety Performance (→ 30).

4. Germany: Russia blocks US troop convoy attempting to break through blockaded autobahn to West Berlin.

7. Washington: America recognises the new South Vietnamese government (→ 29/1/64).

8. UK: Sir Alec Douglas-Home is elected to the House of Commons in a by-election at Kinross (→ 6/12).

10. Japan: 616 die in two disasters; a pit explosion and a train crash (→ 19).

13. London: The BBC Board of Governors decides to take TW3 off the air (→ 28/12).

14. Greece: Hundreds of prisoners, jailed during the 1944-50 Communist revolt, are set free (→ 16/2/64).

18. Iraq: A military coup overthrows the Ba'athist government (→ 14/7/64).

19. Haiti: 500 are feared dead in floods and landslides (→ 10/2/64).

20. London: Viscount Hailsham renounces his peerage and becomes Quintin Hogg (→ 5/12).

20. Vienna: The detective who arrested Anne Frank during World War II is suspended from duty.

26. New York: Share values rise by $15 billion, Wall Street's biggest one-day rally.

29. Montreal: 118 die in a plane crash (→ 29/2/64).

31. Moscow: Soviet files on Lee Harvey Oswald are sent to the US to aid the investigation of Kennedy's assassination (→ 2/1/64).

DEATHS

22. US statesman John Fitzgerald Kennedy, President 1961-63 (*29/5/17).→

22. British novelist Aldous Huxley (*26/7/1894).→

John Kennedy is shot dead in Dallas

Nov 22. President Kennedy has been assassinated. He was shot in the head today as he drove through Dallas, Texas, in an open car on his way to a political festival. A number of shots were fired as crowds cheered him on a golden, sunny day. The 46-year-old President slumped in the car as his wife turned to help him. She cradled him in her arms, his blood staining her suit, as the car sped to nearby Parkland Hospital. Police motorcyclists, sirens blaring, cleared a path through the crowds

At the hospital he was given a blood transfusion as surgeons worked on his dreadful head wound. But it was to no avail. A Roman Catholic priest was called to administer the last rites and John Fitzgerald Kennedy, 35th President of the United States, died 25 minutes after being shot. Crowds waiting outside the hospital groaned as priests announced the President's death. Many collapsed in tears as they realised the full horror of what had happened in their city.

President and Mrs Kennedy drive through Dallas in the motorcade.

The Governor of Texas, John Connally, aged 46, was also wounded in the flurry of shots. Bullets struck him in the chest and head. Tonight his condition is described as "serious". The Vice-President, Lyndon Johnson, who was travelling in the car behind the President, escaped injury.

Eye-witnesses of the shooting reported seeing a rifle being withdrawn from a window in a building overlooking the President's route. Police later arrested Lee Harvey Oswald, chairman of a pro-Castro "Fair Play for Cuba" committee, who was seized in a cinema after a policeman had been killed nearby.

Oswald, a former US Marine, defected to the Soviet Union in 1959, but returned to America with his Russian wife last year. Police said he was the prime suspect in the assassination, but had denied the crime. He was later charged with the murder of a policeman.

The loss of the young and vibrant President will be keenly felt all over the world. Sir Winston Churchill said tonight: "This monstrous act has taken from us a great statesman and a valiant man."

Johnson is sworn in as the new President with Jackie beside him

Nov 22. Lyndon B. Johnson was sworn in as the 36th President of the United States this afternoon within hours of the assassination of President Kennedy. The new President will serve the remainder of Mr Kennedy's term of office until January 1965.

The oath of office was administered under the most dramatic circumstances in the presidential aircraft with Mrs Jacqueline Kennedy standing alongside the new President, her pink suit stained with her husband's blood.

The aircraft then took off for Washington bearing the murdered President's body and carrying his successor to assume the burden of office. When it arrived at Andrews Air Force Base, Mr Johnson, visibly shocked, said: "I will do my best, that is all I can do. I ask for your help, and God's" (→ 24).

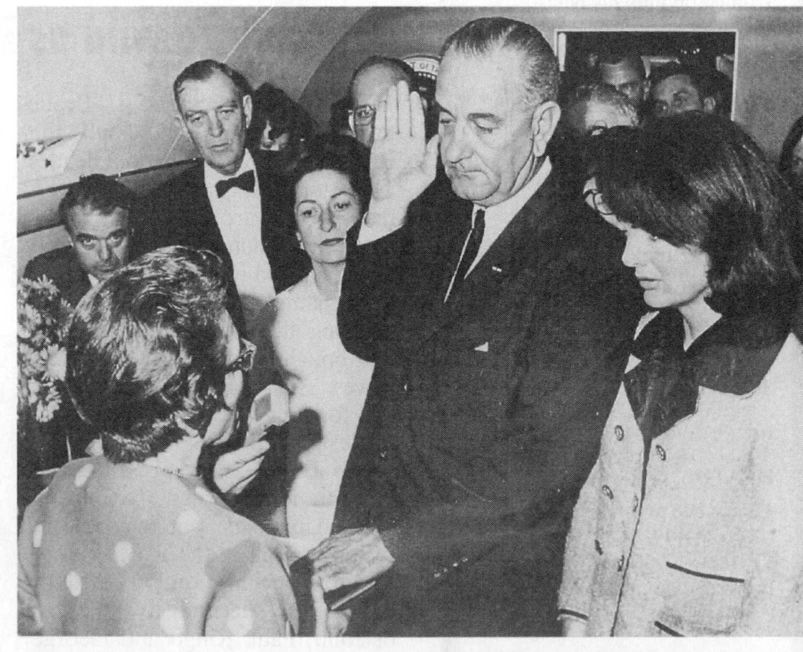
LBJ takes the oath aboard Air Force 1, with Jackie Kennedy at his side.

The moments of horror that killed a new Camelot

Shots ring out, and in the seconds that follow all is confusion in the presidential car, which keeps moving as the stricken Kennedy slumps.

Jackie Kennedy cradles her husband's head while John Connally, the Governor of Texas, looks on: he has been shot in the chest and head.

Then she reaches out to help a secret serviceman clamber into the car: he arrived too late to save the life of the fatally wounded President.

▷

Lee Harvey Oswald shot as millions watch on TV

Lee Harvey Oswald's captors appear paralysed by shock as Jack Ruby unloads his pistol into their prisoner at point-blank range.

Nov 24. Lee Harvey Oswald, the former Marine charged with the assassination of President Kennedy, was murdered today in the underground car park of Dallas police headquarters as he was being transferred to the County Gaol.

Millions of Americans, watching their television screens for their first glimpse of the man who shot their President, saw a burly man step from the crowd in the garage, stick a revolver into Oswald's ribs and pull the trigger.

The killer fired just one shot as the escorting police officers stood as if mesmerized. Oswald slumped forward with a rasping cry of agony and then he was dead. He died never having admitted that he was the killer of President Kennedy.

As Oswald was half-carried, half dragged through the swing doors into the police station, policemen jumped on his murderer who offered no resistance. He was later identified as Jack Rubinstein, the 52-year-old owner of a Dallas striptease club. Known as Jack Ruby, he was later charged with murdering Oswald. Police quoted him as saying: "I did it for Jackie Kennedy."

Ruby's relations with the Dallas police were such that during the past two days he has mingled freely with the reporters and cameramen allowed into Dallas City Hall while covering the story of the President's death. He even passed out invitation cards to his night-club to visiting journalists.

He was thus able to mingle, unchallenged, with the crowd watching Oswald being taken from the police headquarters. A police spokesman said: "We have no idea what Ruby's politics are. He was not connected with any group as far as we know."

Fantastic rumours are circulating in Dallas tonight about the reasons behind the assassination of the President and the murder of Oswald. One has it that Ruby wanted to silence Oswald because he was a co-conspirator. Another says that Oswald, thought to be a Marxist, is really a fanatical right-winger. In Wild West Dallas almost anything is believable (→ 14/3/64).

Kennedy buried as America mourns

Nov 25. In a mourning city, silent except for the tap of muffled drums and the tolling of a single bell, America's murdered President, John F. Kennedy, was buried today at Arlington National Cemetery where his widow lit an Eternal Flame alongside his grave.

President Kennedy's body was borne on a gun-carriage from the Capitol where he had lain in state, along streets lined with silent, weeping people. Mrs Kennedy, heavily veiled, walked behind her husband from the White House to St. Matthew's Roman Catholic Cathedral. With her walked the representatives of 93 nations, their presence demonstrating the respect in which America's slain young leader was held.

The Queen was represented by Prince Philip, sombre in admiral's uniform. Britain's Prime Minister Sir Alec Douglas-Home, Harold Wilson, the Leader of the Opposition, and Jo Grimond, the Liberal leader, mourned with statesmen from all over the world.

The Kennedy children, Caroline, who is six and John, who was three yesterday, were driven by car to the Cathedral. After the service John saluted as his father's coffin was carried back to the gun-carriage for the journey to the grave. Then he raised his hand again to wipe away a tear.

Six grey horses pulled the gun carriage. Behind them a soldier led a riderless horse with boots reversed in the stirrups, the traditional military symbol of a fallen warrior.

What remained at the end of this sad day was the memory of the quiet dignity of the ceremony and the sounds that accompanied it: the thud of the muffled drums, the plaintive melody of the pipes of the Black Watch, the solemn intonation of the funeral hymn "Dies Irae" and the solitary bugler sounding the "Last Post".

The funeral over, the new President invited a glittering array of Kings, Presidents and Prime Ministers to a reception tonight in the reception rooms of the State Department. He has let it be known that he wants to see as many as possible of the visiting leaders.

He conferred with President de Gaulle today and Sir Alec Douglas-Home will call on him tomorrow. Mr Johnson has already assured Mr Khrushchev that he will continue the late President's efforts to further world peace (→26).

John salutes his father's coffin, flanked by his mother and uncles.

Jack Ruby indicted for killing Oswald

Nov 26. Jack Rubinstein, known locally as Jack Ruby, was indicted by a grand jury in Dallas today for the murder of Lee Harvey Oswald, the man accused of assassinating President Kennedy. The strip-tease club owner was not in court to hear his lawyer say: "I think, as millions of other Americans think, that he should be given the Congressional Medal of Honour" (→29).

Commission to investigate assassination

Nov 29. A special commission is to be set up on President Johnson's orders to investigate all the circumstances surrounding the assassination of President Kennedy. The much respected Chief Justice, Earl Warren, has been appointed to head the commission.

A number of leading Senators and Congressmen will serve on the commission, along with Allen Dulles, former director of the CIA, and John McCloy, an aide to the murdered President. The official reason for the establishment of the commission is to prevent a number of investigations going over the same ground and to give the American people a single comprehensive report.

Another reason is to try to stem the flood of rumours about the killing. The Russians are being blamed, as are the Cubans, and the Mafia is said to have put out a "contract" on the President (→31).

Military coup ousts unpopular Diem in South Vietnam

Nov 2. Ngo Dinh Diem, the increasingly unpopular President of South Vietnam, was overthrown by a military coup last night. Both Diem and his influential brother, Ngo Dinh Nhu, are believed to have died when the army seized key points in Saigon. First reports from Saigon Radio say they committed suicide, but these reports are being greeted with some scepticism.

There has been a great deal of dissatisfaction with the way the brothers have been running South Vietnam and it is thought the United States will not be sorry at their removal – while regretting their deaths (→7).

Huxley, satirist and mystic, dies

Nov 22. Aldous Huxley, the satirist who turned mystic in Hollywood, has died there aged 69. He was a member of a family famous for its scientists and became a scientist-novelist with a coldly analytical approach to his characters. His frank amorality in such novels as "Antic Hay", shocked readers, as did "Brave New World" and its desolate picture of an antiseptic society. His essays culminated in "The Doors of Perception", which owed its mysticism to mescalin.

Iceland gets a brand new island

Nov 15. In a tumult of fire and smoke, this morning saw the birth of a new island - off the south coast of Iceland. Already 30 feet high, the land mass has appeared following a day of volcanic activity on the ocean floor. The island is still growing, spewing ash several thousand feet into the air with a 24,000-foot high column of smoke.

Scientists have warned of the danger to shipping and the local Vestmanna islanders should an explosion occur. But sightseers are queueing up in Reykjavik to fly over the site.

1963

DECEMBER

Su	Mo	Tu	We	Th	Fr	Sa
1	2	3	4	5	6	7
8	9	10	11	12	13	14
15	16	17	18	19	20	21
22	23	24	25	26	27	28
29	30	31				

3. S. Africa: Trial begins of Nelson Mandela, charged with treason (→20/4/64).

5. London: Quintin Hogg is elected to the Commons in a by-election (→9/4/64).

10. London: Roy James is arrested and charged in connection with the Great Train Robbery (→20/1/64).

10. Stockholm: Nobel Prizes go to Maria Goeppert-Mayer (US), Eugene Wigner (US), Johannes Jensen (Germany, Physics); Giulio Natta (Italy), Karl Ziegler (Germany, Chemistry); Alan Hodgkin (UK), Andrew Huxley (UK), John Eccles (Australia, Medicine); Giorgos Seferis (Greece, Literature); and in Oslo, to the International Committee of the Red Cross (Peace).

11. Los Angeles: Frank Sinatra Jr. is freed after his father pays a $240,000 ransom (→7/3/64).

20. Rhodesia: Joshua Nkomo is jailed for publishing a "subversive statement" (→13/4/64).

23. Atlantic: 919 are rescued from the blazing cruise liner Lakonia; 117 feared dead.

30. Paris: OAS leader Antoine Argoud is sentenced to life imprisonment (→13/3/64).

DEATHS

14. US blues singer Dinah Washington (*8/8/24).

28. German composer Paul Hindemith (*16/11/1895).

HITS OF 1963

She loves you

From me to you

In Dreams

QUOTE OF THE YEAR

"...called in MI5 because every time the chauffeur-driven Zis drew up at her front door, out of the back door into a chauffeur-driven Humber slipped..."

Robin Douglas-Home, in Queen magazine, the first press reference to the Profumo Affair.

How winds of change reshaped Africa

Dec 12. Kenya today became the 34th African territory to achieve independence, and its transition marks a significant turning-point for African nationalism.

Within the decade the once-dominant European rule has retreated into enclaves: in the north, Algeria, and at the other extreme, South Africa and Southern Rhodesia, all white settler territories. But so also was Kenya. The Duke of Edinburgh handed Kenya's instruments of independence to Jomo Kenyatta, who appealed to people of all races to join him in the Swahili rallying cry: "Harambee!" (Pull together). The omens are less favourable for the off-shore island of Zanzibar, which two days ago ceased to be a British protectorate. Now an Arab Sultan rules a largely African population.

When the then Prime Minister, Harold Macmillan, made his original "wind of change" speech in January 1960, that was the only country in black Africa to have gained independence. By the end of that year it had been joined by more than a dozen others. More followed in 1962 and Nyasaland and Northern Rhodesia are booked for next year. The transfer of power has been by no means easy or bloodless. Kenya was torn by a Mau Mau uprising in the 1950s which resulted in Jomo Kenyatta being jailed. The Belgian Congo was the scene of bitter internal fighting which even the intervention of United Nations' forces failed to quell earlier this decade.

Nor does it look like the violence is over. Black independence will be bitterly resisted by whites in southern Africa and elsewhere the blacks themselves are split (→10/11/64).

Keeler is jailed in tears

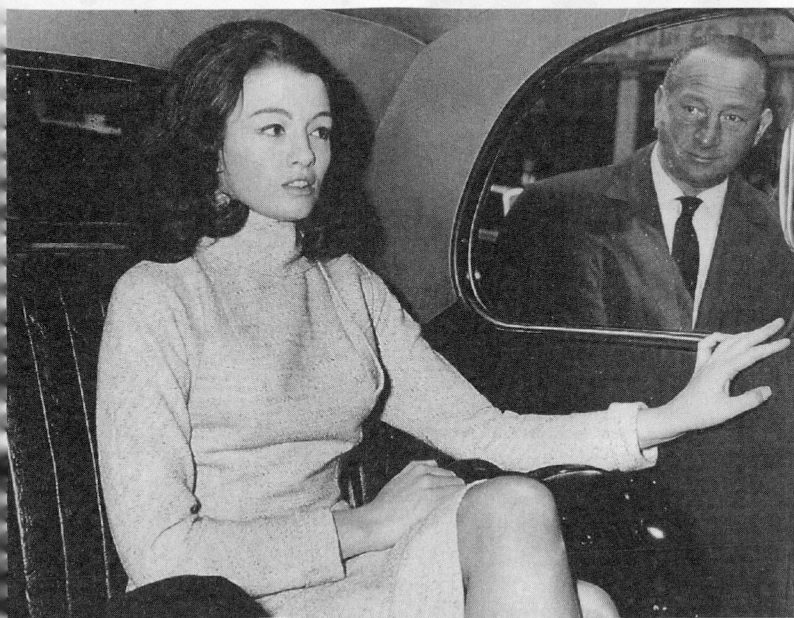
Christine Keeler arrives at the Old Bailey to hear her sentence.

Dec 6. Christine Keeler was jailed for nine months today after pleading guilty to perjury and conspiracy to pervert the course of justice. The 21-year-old brunette described by her counsel as "a central figure in a drama which has intrigued the world for the past 12 months", sobbed as she was led from the Old Bailey dock.

The charges arose out of the trial of her ex-boyfriend Aloysius "Lucky" Gordon, a West Indian jazz singer who was convicted of assaulting her. In court she had denied that two other men were present when the attack took place; in fact she was hiding them in a bedroom. She had not wanted to reveal her association with them.

In mitigation John Hutchinson said that the former nude showgirl had feared Gordon and had been dominated by Stephen Ward, who fashioned her in a perverted Prof. Higgins way. Keeler had bought herself a home and her parents a shop out of the £23,000 she got from a newspaper for her life story, the court was told.

Arts: 59-year wait for National Theatre

A National Theatre company at last became a reality on October 22 with its first performance: "Hamlet", uncut, directed by **Laurence Olivier**, with **Peter O'Toole** in the title role. It represented the first real advance in nearly 60 years of false starts since **William Archer** and **Harley Granville-Barker** produced detailed proposals in 1904.

In 1908 **Bernard Shaw** and other famous names supported plans for a "Shakespeare Memorial National Theatre". Over the next 40 years five sites were acquired and a bill, promising a million pounds for the building cost, was passed in 1949.

The foundation stone, laid by the then Princess Elizabeth in 1951, had to be moved to a new site on the South Bank as plans changed. Now an architect, **Denys Lasdun**, has been appointed. "Hamlet" has been joined by the transfer from Olivier's Chichester theatre of his magical production of "Uncle Vanya", with **Michael Redgrave**, and George Farquhar's Restoration comedy, "The Recruiting Officer", in which Olivier makes a telling appearance in a minor role.

France has lost its "little sparrow", the idolised singer **Edith Piaf**, who began her career at 15 singing in the streets and cafes. Her wild life, her multitude of lovers and her dependence on alcohol and morphine were summed up in her song "Je ne regrette rien". After hearing of her death, her friend and admirer **Jean Cocteau** had a heart attack and died.

Edith Piaf, who died this year.

Any and every art form stimulated Cocteau – novels ("Les Enfants Terribles"), plays ("The Eagle has two Heads"), films of fantasy ("Orphee", "La Belle et la Bete"), even opera and ballet, "Oedipus Rex" and "Parade"). For much of his life, he *was* the French avant-garde.

The French music world lost **Francis Poulenc**, its Stravinskyan parodist, and painting lost **Georges Braque**, co-originator with **Picasso** of Cubism and master of the art of still-life, which he refined all his life.

Grenade thrown at ministers in Aden

Dec 10. A state of emergency was declared throughout the South Arabian Federation tonight after a grenade was thrown into a group of local government ministers and British diplomats at Aden airport.

An Indian woman was killed and 39 injured, including the British High Commissioner, Sir Kennedy Trevaskis. The attack occurred as Sir Kennedy and the Aden ministers were preparing to fly to London for crucial talks on self-rule for the colony and the future of the base there. The frontier with the Yemen was closed and 100 Yemenis were rounded up and detained for deportation (→3/5/64).

TW3 becomes the TV show that was

Dec 28. The last "That Was The Week That Was", or "TW3", was transmitted last night. The BBC is taking it off the air 13 weeks earlier than planned, officially because 1964 will be election year. TW3's disrespect, already constantly under fire, would be too much for politicians to put up with.

The BBC governors were split over the decision. Some, like the Director-General, Hugh Carleton-Greene, supported the programme, others thought it an embarrassment. Its audience grew, to over 12 million. People paid it the rare compliment of coming home early from the pub to see it (→11/1/64).

Elizabeth Taylor in the title role of "Cleopatra", with Rex Harrison.

1964

JANUARY

Su	Mo	Tu	We	Th	Fr	Sa
			1	2	3	4
5	6	7	8	9	10	11
12	13	14	15	16	17	18
19	20	21	22	23	24	25
26	27	28	29	30	31	

1. Cyprus: Archbishop Makarios says he will abrogate treaties with Greece, Turkey and Britain (→28).

3. US: Barry Goldwater announces his candidacy for the US presidency (→14).

5. London: The first ticket collecting machine is installed on the Underground.

8. Washington: Johnson vows to wage "war against poverty".

12. Zanzibar: Nationalists overthrow the Sultan's regime and proclaim a people's republic (→22/4).

13. Calcutta: 200 die in Hindu-Moslem riots (→28/5).

14. US: Jacqueline Kennedy appears on TV to thank the nation for its sympathy (→15/7).

16. Cairo: 13 Arab states agree to try and stop Israel diverting the waters of the Negev (→24/3).

20. UK: The trial of the alleged Great Train Robbers begins (→27/3).

21. UK: Government figures show the average weekly wage is £16 14/11 (→21/2).

22. Northern Rhodesia: the nation's first premier, Kenneth Kaunda, is sworn in (→3/8).

23. London: Cecil King says he plans to relaunch The Daily Herald newspaper as The Sun (→28/3).

23. Uganda: British troops fly in to crush an army mutiny by soldiers angry at their low pay.

25. US: Launch of Echo C, the first joint US-Soviet space project (→29).

28. London: Turkish delegates walk out of Cyprus talks (→12/2).

29. South Vietnam: A military coup overthrows the junta of Major Van Minh (→13/2).

29. US: Launch of a Saturn rocket with a 10-ton payload, the heaviest ever (→3/2).

29. Austria: The ninth Winter Olympics open in Innsbruck.

DEATH

30. US actor Alan Ladd (*3/5/13).

Pope visits the cradle of Christianity

Pope Paul VI during his courageous visit to the Holy Land.

Jan 5. Exuberant Jerusalem crowds yesterday broke through the cordons of the Jordanian security forces and literally swept Pope Paul VI off his feet. Today, the second of his three-day "peace pilgrimage" to the Holy Land, the crowds were equally enthusiastic, but the extra police called in managed to maintain order for the most important event of the visit: the meeting with Patriarch Athenagoras, the head of the Eastern Orthodox Church, who flew in from Rhodes today.

The Orthodox Church broke away from Rome over 1,000 years ago and it is more than 500 years since the leaders of the two churches met.

Between them they represent 900 million Christians. "Is it not then a happy augury that today's meeting takes place in that land where Christ founded his church and shed His blood for her?" the Pope said.

His work for Christian unity done, the Pope went to Nazareth to celebrate mass at the Grotto of the Annunciation. He described it as "the school of the Gospel" where "everything speaks to us, everything has meaning" (→13/11).

Rag and bone men top the TV ratings

Jan 17. "Steptoe and Son", the comedy series about a family rag and bone business, has been declared Britain's most popular television show. Figures for the first episode of the latest series, compiled by the Television Audience Measurement organisation, claim that 26 million viewers in 9,653,000 homes tuned in. The shows are written by Ray Galton and Alan Simpson, creators also of "Hancock's Half Hour".

Wilfred Brambell as Albert Steptoe and Harry H. Corbett as Harold.

Mary Quant knocks the Paris fashion show as "out of date"

Jan 13. British designer Mary Quant today launched a stinging attack on Paris fashion which she described as "out of date". The ex-art student opened this country's first boutique, Bazaar, in Chelsea, with her public school husband Alexander Plunket-Greene, and has seized much of the fashion initiative from the couture houses.

Her bold designs and short skirts are aimed at young people whom she believes "are tired of wearing essentially the same as their mothers". She wants her designs to be fun and inexpensive.

At the beginning, what she calls her "absolutely 20th century" clothes were run up by a small team of machinists. Last year she went into mass production to meet the demand here and in the US. Other boutiques have sprung up in Chelsea, now all aimed at the young, particularly the Mods.

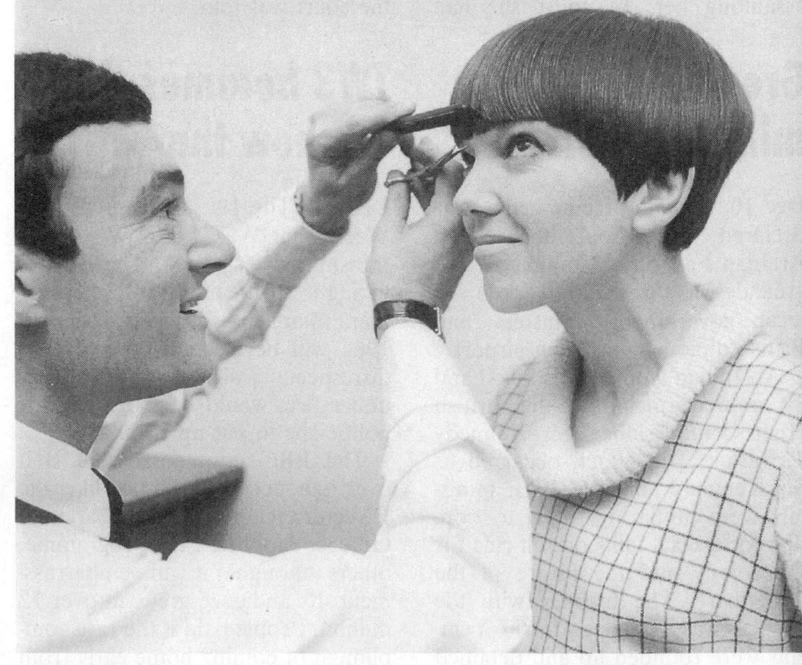

Sixties ikons: Mary Quant receives a haircut from Vidal Sassoon.

1964

FEBRUARY

Su	Mo	Tu	We	Th	Fr	Sa
						1
2	3	4	5	6	7	8
9	10	11	12	13	14	15
16	17	18	19	20	21	22
23	24	25	26	27	28	29

2. Austria: Nash and Dixon win the two-man bobsleigh at the Winter Olympics.

3. Moon: US spacecraft Ranger 6 crashes on the moon but fails to send back any pictures (→20/7).

5. Rwanda: Thousands of the Tutsi tribe are feared massacred by a rival tribe.

6. London: Britain and France agree to build a Channel Tunnel costing £160 million.

10. London: A magistrate declares "Fanny Hill" obscene and orders the confiscation of all copies of the book (→16/6).

10. Australia: 85 are missing feared dead after the sinking of the destroyer Voyager (→16/8).

13. North Vietnam: The government warns China will defend her against attack (→27/2).

16. Greece: George Papandreou wins the general election with a large majority (→6/3).

19. London: 1,500 British troops are flown out to Cyprus (→4/3).

19. UK: Actor Peter Sellers marries actress Britt Ekland.

20. Morocco: Algeria and Morocco reach agreement to end their border war.

21. UK: £10 banknotes are issued for the first time since World War II (→26/10).

23. London: The Beatles are mobbed by fans on their return to Britain (→21/5).

26. London: The Government announces plans for a fleet of five Polaris subs (→4/6).

29. UK: Princess Alexandra gives birth to a son (→10/3).

29. Italy: 84 die in the crash of a British holiday plane in the Alps (→11/5).

DEATHS

6. Philippine independence fighter Emilio Aguinaldo (*22/3/1869).

25. French aviation pioneer Maurice Farman (*21/3/1877).

Beatlemania grips US as Fab Four fly in

Beatle fans at San Francisco airport waiting to greet their idols.

Feb 8. The Beatles flew into Kennedy Airport in New York today and met their most ecstatic reception yet. Urged on by disc jockeys, who had been broadcasting constant updates on the progress of Pan Am flight 101, thousands of American teenagers packed the airport to scream their adulation. They broke through a police cordon, then formed a Beatles motorcade that followed their heroes all the way to the city's Plaza Hotel.

The Beatles, already superstars in Europe, are set to conquer America. Their song "I Want to Hold Your Hand" has gone to the top of the charts and tomorrow night's TV appearance on the Ed Sullivan Show, once the springboard for Elvis Presley, will put them into every American living-room (→23).

Greeks and Turks clash in Cyprus

Feb 12. Twenty Turks and one Greek Cypriot were killed in fighting in Cyprus today as the hostilities between the two communities worsened.

Late tonight Turkish Cypriots were reported to be mounting machine-guns on high buildings in Limassol to fire on the Greek quarter of the city. Throughout the day British troops were trying to arrange a cease-fire, but with only limited success. Greek Cypriot irregulars have occupied several streets, while many Turks have barricaded themselves into their homes. Other Turks have planted plastic booby-trap bombs on the roads and several British families are still thought to be trapped in parts of the city.

The Cyprus crisis has worsened in the past two weeks since the Turkish Prime Minister, Mr Inonu, walked out of the London conference on the troubled island requesting United Nations intervention to secure the rights of Turkish Cypriots.

The US Embassy was bombed and now more British troops have been flown in, to the protests of Mr Khrushchev, who has accused the West of attempting "occupation by NATO armed forces" (→19).

Clay confounds pundits to win when Liston throws in the towel

Feb 25. Dismissed as a no-hope braggart before the fight, which he began as the 7-1 underdog, Cassius Clay pulled off one of boxing's greatest surprises by beating the apparently invincible Sonny Liston to take the heavyweight championship of the world.

The weigh-in for the fight had degenerated into farce, with Clay whipping himself into a frenzy, screaming insults at the brooding, impassive champion, an exhibition which brought him a heavy fine – by which he seemed unimpressed.

Once the fight began, Clay's speed around the ring and his swift counter-punching clearly disconcerted Liston, but the Miami Beach audience were stunned into silence when the champion, complaining of a badly injured shoulder, refused to come out to fight the seventh round.

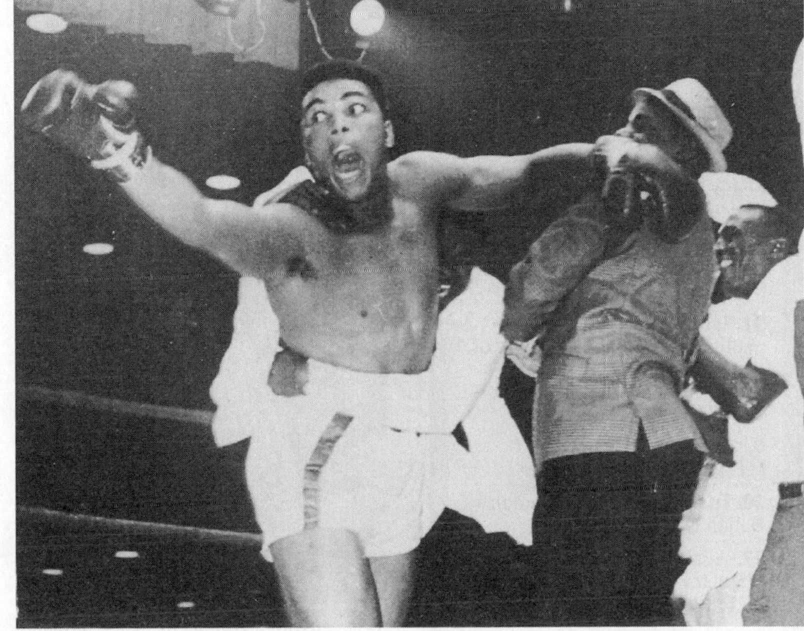

Cassius Clay – the new heavyweight boxing champion of the world.

1964

MARCH

Su	Mo	Tu	We	Th	Fr	Sa
1	2	3	4	5	6	7
8	9	10	11	12	13	14
15	16	17	18	19	20	21
22	23	24	25	26	27	28
29	30	31				

3. London: Mass closure of railway lines announced by the Government.

4. New York: UN Security Council decides to send a peace-keeping force to Cyprus (→9).

6. Greece: King Paul dies and is succeeded by Constantine XII (→18/9).

7. Los Angeles: Two men are jailed for life for kidnapping Frank Sinatra's son.

8. US: Malcolm X announces he is splitting from the Black Moslem movement to form his own group (→11/6).

9. Cyprus: British forces become involved in fighting between Greeks and Turks.→

10. London: Queen Elizabeth gives birth to her third son (→20/4).

11. Cambodia: The British embassy is wrecked in protests against Britain and US.

12. US: Union boss James Hoffa is sentenced to eight years in jail for jury-fixing.

13. Paris: De Gaulle meets Algerian President Ben Bella (→15/6).

19. Switzerland: Opening of the St. Bernard Tunnel through the Alps to Italy.

21. UK: Team Spirit wins the Grand National at the fifth attempt.

24. Egypt: Nasser orders the nationalisation of Shell and Anglo-Egyptian oil companies (→8/5).

28. UK: Radio Caroline begins transmissions from a ship in the North Sea (→21/4).

30. UK: Mods and Rockers fight each other on the beach at Clacton (→8/4).

31. UK: The Admiralty is abolished and becomes part of the Ministry of Defence.

DEATHS

6. Greek King, Paul I (*14/12/01).

20. Irish playwright Brendan Behan (*9/2/23).

23. Austro-Hungarian-born US actor Peter Lorre (*26/8/04).

United Nations troops fly into Cyprus

A woman grieves for her husband, killed in the fighting; her son offers comfort.

March 19. The newly-arrived United Nations force is expected to become fully operational in Cyprus this weekend, as it strives to keep the warring Greek and Turkish Cypriot communities apart.

Besides British and Canadian troops, soldiers from Finland, Sweden and Ireland have now arrived on the island. The final signal for the force to go into action will be given by the United Nations Secretary-General, U Thant. The force only has permission to stay for three months, but Whitehall is confident it will succeed.

One problem has been to get the two sides to agree to ceasefires and to stick by agreements. British troops themselves came under fire in the town of Ktima three days ago, after they arranged a ceasefire. The Greeks barred British reinforcements and refused to allow the evacuation of Turkish women and children (→10/5).

Ruby on death row for Oswald killing

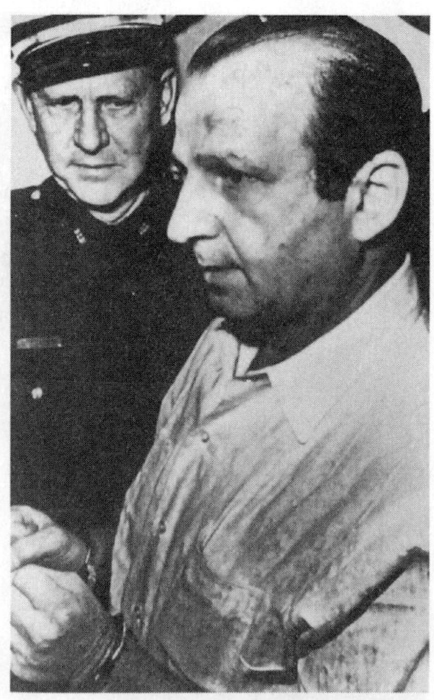

Jack Ruby, killer of Lee Harvey Oswald: destined for death row.

March 14. "We find the defendant guilty of murder with malice as charged in the indictment and assess his punishment as death," announced the jury in the trial of Jack Ruby, killer of Lee Harvey Oswald, the man accused of Kennedy's assassination. The prosecution thanked the jury for a fair verdict.

But Ruby's lawyers lambasted the jury before a television audience, calling the verdict a "violent miscarriage". His defence attorney, Melvin Belli, said he would appeal against the decision outside Dallas "where there is justice".

In the States, there has been a feeling that Dallas itself was on trial: would it be able to give Ruby justice? In England, there has been much interest in the sensational aspects of the trial and the unfamiliar legal system. Now the lengthy appeal process begins (→27/9).

Ten of the Great Train robbers guilty

March 27. Six months after Th Great Train Robbery and with 2 members of the notorious gang stil at large, a court today recorded th first convictions as a result of th hold-up.

Ten men were found guilty of th plot to steal mailbags worth mor than £2.6 million by ambushing travelling post office on the railwa line at Cheddington. The trial ha lasted 51 days and the 12-man jur at Buckinghamshire Assizes took record 66 hours to come to thei verdicts. Nine other defendants ar facing trial (→15/4).

White Paper plan to create new cities

March 19. A 20-year-plan to sto London "choking" was accepted i principle by the government today It will house, employ and transpor an extra 3.5 million people i South-east England, which alread contains 35 per cent of Britain' population. Three new cities ar planned near Bletchley, Newbur and Southampton. Six existin towns beyond the outskirts o London will be expanded.

March 15. Elizabeth Taylor and Richard Burton were married today in Montreal. Burton said he was "very, very happy"; Miss Taylor declined to comment.

1964

APRIL

Su	Mo	Tu	We	Th	Fr	Sa
			1	2	3	4
5	6	7	8	9	10	11
12	13	14	15	16	17	18
19	20	21	22	23	24	25
26	27	28	29	30		

3. Moscow: Former Foreign Minister Molotov is expelled from the Communist Party (→15/7).

5. Bhutan: Premier Jigme Dorji is assassinated.

8. London: 30 arrested after fights between Mods and Rockers in the capital (→18/5).

9. London: Labour wins the first elections to the Greater London Council (→7/5).

13. Los Angeles: Sidney Poitier becomes the first Negro to win an Oscar, for best actor in "Lilies of the Field".

14. London: The budget increases the price of a pint of beer to 2/1; cigarettes go up to 4/10 a packet.

15. UK: Ronald Biggs is found guilty of taking part in the Great Train Robbery (→16).

16. West Germany: Geraldine Mock completes the first solo round the world flight by a woman.

16. UK: 12 members of the Great Train Robbery gang are sentenced to a total of 307 years in jail (→13/7).

19. Laos: Right-wing army officers oust Prince Phouma's neutralist government from power.

20. London: The Queen's son is registered as Edward.

21. UK: BBC2 goes on the air; its first programme is "Play School" (→12/5).

22. Zanzibar: A surprise Act of Union between Tanganyka and Zanzibar is announced.

24. Yemen: Egyptian leader Colonel Nasser vows to expel the UK from all parts of the Arab world (→8/11).

29. UK: 136 cases of typhoid are reported in Aberdeen; the city's schools are closed.

DEATHS

5. US general Douglas MacArthur (*26/1/1880).

24. German biologist Gerhard Domagk, 1939 Nobel Prize winner (*30/10/1895).

Ian Smith is elected Rhodesia's PM

Ian Smith, Rhodesia's PM.

April 13. A butcher's son who flew (and crashed) Spitfires in the Western Desert and Italy in the Second World War today became Prime Minister of Southern Rhodesia. Ian Smith, aged 44, ousted Winston Field, who seemed to be dithering over independence. Field spoke of "serious disagreements" between himself and his party.

These disagreements were hinted at by Smith, who said he would seek to achieve a negotiated independence, but "we can visualise circumstances which might drive us to do something else".

More plainly, Smith is prepared to go for a unilateral declaration of independence if British governments continue to insist on the African majority being brought fully into the electoral process. Smith once said UDI would be only a "three-day wonder" (→4/6).

Spy swap brings Wynne back to UK

Wynne, back in Britain.

April 22. Greville Wynne, the British businessman jailed as a spy in Moscow, was freed today in a spy swap with the Russians. Mr Wynne was exchanged at a Berlin border checkpoint for Gordon Lonsdale, the KGB spymaster arrested in London in 1961 and sentenced to 25 years for his role in the Portland espionage ring.

Mr Wynne, who was sentenced to eight years, lost nearly three stones in weight during his 17 months in Russian prisons. He stood trial with Colonel Oleg Penkovsky, who was later shot for passing secrets to the West (→29/5).

Soviet leader slams former Chinese allies

April 3. Nikita Khrushchev today launched a vitriolic public attack on Russia's erstwhile brothers-in-arms, the Chinese Communists and their leader Mao Tse-tung. His speech in Budapest clearly signals a battle for the leadership of the Communist world. What began as an ideological dispute has become a tussle for allies amongst the emergent nations of Asia and Africa.

Mr Khrushchev accused China of trying to divide the working people of the world on the basis of colour and race. Such a view, he said, was "false and reactionary". Speaking of the dangers of a third world war, the Russian leader said the Chinese were "sowing the seeds of dangerous solutions when they claim that the atom bomb is no more than a paper tiger". Such attitudes, he said, benefited only the imperialists (→13/9).

Mandela admits to planning sabotage

April 20. Nelson Mandela, brought from jail to face trial with eight others accused of sabotage and conspiracy to overthrow the South African government by revolution, told a Pretoria court that his purpose was to rid the country of white domination. "I do not deny that I planned sabotage," he said. "We had either to accept inferiority or fight against it by violence."

While Mandela was serving a jail sentence for other offences, police raided the underground HQ of the African National Congress at Rivonia and found Mandela's diary of his African tour and notes on guerrilla warfare (→14/6).

The British pop group, the Rolling Stones, shocked the Montreux festival in Geneva by arriving in "dishevelled and bizarre" dress. But increasing numbers of fans like their raunchy style.

1964

MAY

Su	Mo	Tu	We	Th	Fr	Sa
					1	2
3	4	5	6	7	8	9
10	11	12	13	14	15	16
17	18	19	20	21	22	23
24	25	26	27	28	29	30
31						

2. London: West Ham beat Preston North End 3-2 to win the FA Cup Final.

3. Aden: Extra UK troops are flown in after reports of the decapitation of two British soldiers by Yemeni rebels.

4. New York: The Pulitzer committee decides there is no fiction, music or drama worthy of an award this year.

5. Malta: A referendum gives a narrow majority to a constitution for the island's independence (→21/9).

7. UK: Labour make big gains in the local elections (→15/9).

8. Egypt: Khrushchev arrives.→

10. Cyprus: British troops in the UN peace-keeping force are flown home (→9/8).

11. Philippines: 74 die in crash of US military plane (→23/11).

11. US: First flight of the 2,000mph B-70 bomber.

12. Taiwan: US reported to be training soldiers for possible use in Vietnam.

18. Indonesia: British tea and rubber estates are seized by the government.

21. UK: A BBC survey reveals the Beatles are Britain's most popular tourist attraction (→12/6).

22. British Guiana: State of emergency is declared as British troops fly out to restore order.

24. Peru: 135 die in a riot at a football match.

27. Vienna: Inter Milan win the European Cup, beating Real Madrid 3-1.

29. Moscow: Khrushchev admits Russia uses satellites for spying.

DEATHS

1. US band leader Spike Jones (*14/12/11).

2. US-born British politician Lady Nancy Astor, first woman MP (*19/5/1879).

11. Russian painter Michel Larionov (*3/6/1881).

27. Indian statesman Jawaharlal Nehru, Prime Minister 1947-62 (*14/11/1889).→

India's beloved leader, Nehru, dies

May 28. Jawaharlal Nehru, the Prime Minister of India since the country became independent in 1947, died at his home in New Delhi yesterday after a sudden heart attack. He was 74.

Mr Nehru was one of the architects of modern India and has guided the nation's fortunes with a gentle voice but a firm hand, and his loss will be felt keenly, not only in India but throughout the world.

Several members of the Indian parliament wept openly when the Steel Minister, Mr Subramaniam, rose to say: " I have grave news to announce to the House and the country. The Prime Minister is no more. The light is out".

As the news spread, thousands of people, wailing their grief, converged on the house where Mr Nehru lay in state in a room decorated with jasmine and green leaves. Two white lotuses, their stalks crossed, lay above his head.

Turbaned villagers, Buddhist monks in yellow robes and road-mender women in tattered skirts carrying naked babies, queued with officials, diplomats and princes in the unending procession passing Mr Nehru's body.

He will be cremated tomorrow evening on the banks of the Jumna River where statesmen from all over the world will mourn with the ordinary people. Sir Alec Douglas-Home flew to Delhi last night accompanied by Lord Mountbatten, the last Viceroy of India, representing the Queen, and George Brown, Labour's deputy leader. India's temporary Prime Minister is Gulzarilal Nanda (→9/6).

Women and children pay their last respects to India's first PM.

Mayhem at Margate as Mods and Rockers battle on beaches

May 18. In what is becoming something of a teenage ritual, gangs of Mods and Rockers clashed again this Whit weekend at a number of South Coast resorts. As reckless motorists accounted for 75 road deaths under the summer sun, youth gang-violence erupted in an orgy of hooliganism. In Brighton, where police dispersed 600 Mods, there were 76 arrests. In Margate two youths were stabbed and 51 arrested. Jailing four and imposing fines totalling £1900, the Margate magistrate dismissed the brawlers as "little sawdust Caesars". One paid his fine by cheque. Further clashes occurred at Southend, Bournemouth, Clacton (where there had also been disturbances at Easter) and even County Durham. Speaking for the Government, the Home Secretary, Henry Brooke, has promised firm action (→2/8).

Armed with sticks and bottles, hundreds of Mods race across Margate beach to do battle with Rockers.

Pharaohs tombs in danger from dam

May 14. President Nasser and the Soviet leader, Nikita Khrushchev, today joined hands to press a button that changed the course of the Nile. A huge sand barrage was blown up and the river diverted into a canal to allow the next stage of the Aswan High Dam to start.

The dam will increase Egypt's agricultural land by a third and double electric power output. But it will also raise the upstream level of the river 200 feet, inundating the ancient temples and tombs of the Pharaohs; a worldwide appeal is being made for funds to rescue the treasures.

Pop music all at sea with pirates

May 12. Pop fans who complain that they can't get enough of their favourite music can tune in to a new radio station as from today. Radio Atlanta, broadcasting on 200.6 metres, has started transmissions from "somewhere off the East Coast", joining Radio Caroline, Britain's first "pirate", which has been putting out its exclusively pop programmes since March.

Both stations operate legally from international waters. The GPO would still like to see them banned, but the Government prefers the blind eye (→ 2/7).

Over 100 die when soccer fans riot

May 24. An unpopular – not to mention unfortunate – decision by a referee at the Argentina v Peru match today sparked off a riot that left at least 135 people dead and over 500 injured when crowd panic led to a stampede. The trouble started when, with Argentina a goal ahead, Peru's equaliser was disallowed. Two fans descended to the pitch and assaulted the referee, who stopped play with two minutes to go. Furious Peru supporters broke up Lima stadium before going on an arson and looting spree. Police turned tear-gas and dogs onto the mob to restore order.

1964

JUNE

Su	Mo	Tu	We	Th	Fr	Sa
	1	2	3	4	5	6
7	8	9	10	11	12	13
14	15	16	17	18	19	20
21	22	23	24	25	26	27
28	29	30				

2. Jerusalem: Creation of the Palestine Liberation Organisation.

3. South Korea: Martial law is declared in Seoul after riots by 20,000.

3. UK: Jockey Scobie Breasley wins the Derby at the 13th attempt, on Santa Claus.

4. Australia: Britain's Blue Streak missile is launched from Woomera Range (→ 16/10).

4. Southern Rhodesia: Ian Smith warns that he will declare UDI if relations with Britain worsen (→ 26).

8. London: Christine Keeler is released from prison.

11. US: Martin Luther King is jailed for trying to force integration of a Florida restaurant.

12. Australia: A crowd of 300,000 greet the Beatles on their arrival in Adelaide (→ 6/7).

14. Haiti: Francois Duvalier is declared President for life.

15. Algeria: Withdrawal of all remaining French troops (→ 1/7).

16. New York: Nightclub comedian Lenny Bruce goes on trial for obscenity.

22. US: Francis Chichester sets a new record by crossing the Atlantic in under 30 days.

23. US: Three civil rights workers are reported missing after being arrested by the Mississippi police (→ 25).

23. Rome: The Pope attacks use of the contraceptive pill (→ 29/7).

25. US: Johnson orders 200 sailors to aid the search for the missing civil rights workers (→ 26).

26. Southern Rhodesia: A court lifts the restrictions on Joshua Nkomo (→ 6/9).

26. Washington: Civil rights leaders urge Johnson to take control over Mississippi (→ 2/7).

DEATHS

9. Canadian-born British newspaper tycoon Lord Beaverbrook (*25/5/1879).→

18. Italian painter Giorgio Morandi (*20/7/1890).

Mandela is sentenced to life for treason

June 14. Sentenced to life imprisonment for sabotage and plotting to overthrow the South African government, Nelson Mandela was today flown from Pretoria to Cape Town and taken out to Robben Island in Table Bay. Icy waters and swift-running currents make the island virtually escape-proof.

Mandela heard his sentence without visible emotion. As he left the dock he waved to his supporters in court. Police tried to smuggle him out of the building along with eight others sentenced at the same time, but were spotted by a waiting crowd of Africans, who ran along chanting "We have the strength", and making raised fist salutes.

Mandela was born in 1918 into the royal family of the Tembu tribe in the Transkei. He studied in Johannesburg, gained a law degree and opened the first African legal practice in the country. He took up the black nationalist cause in 1944.

In London the Labour frontbencher, Anthony Wedgwood Benn, joined a protest demonstration outside the South African embassy in Trafalgar Square (→ 18/8).

Lal Shastri sworn in as new Indian PM

In charge: Lal Bahadur Shastri.

June 9. The skilled veteran politician Lal Bahadur Shastri was sworn in as India's new Prime Minister in Delhi today, following the death of Jawaharlal Nehru.

Prime Minister Shastri, whose name means "learned in the scriptures", began his political life in Mahatma Gandhi's non-cooperation movement during the struggle against the British, and he has served several prison sentences for his political beliefs over the years. More recently, he has been India's Minister for Home Affairs and he has gained a reputation as a skilful mediator.

Nehru's daughter, 46-year-old Mrs Indira Gandhi, has been named as the new Minister of Information in Mr Shastri's cabinet.

Newspaper tycoon Beaverbrook dies

June 9. When Canadian-born Lord Beaverbrook died of cancer today, aged 85, it was no surprise. Recently this son of a New Brunswick Presbyterian minister remarked that he would soon become an apprentice again – whether in heaven or hell he did not know.

Born Max Aitken he was in turn, corner-cutting business tycoon, political king-maker, newspaper owner and war cabinet dynamo, and always a fanatical Empire zealot. He could be ruthless; he could be kind. Friends think he will be an impish master-craftsman in heaven.

Dressed for the occasion: two sisters display the latest fashion at the premiere of the film "London in the Raw".

1964

JULY

Su	Mo	Tu	We	Th	Fr	Sa
			1	2	3	4
5	6	7	8	9	10	11
12	13	14	15	16	17	18
19	20	21	22	23	24	25
26	27	28	29	30	31	

1. Algeria: An army leader in the Sahara rebels against Ben Bella's rule (→24).

2. UK: Radio Caroline and Radio Atlanta amalgamate to form the first national pirate radio station (→20/8).

3. Wimbledon: Roy Emerson beats Fred Stolle to win the Men's Singles; Maria Bueno beats Margaret Smith to win the Women's Singles.

8. Geneva: The International Commission of Jurists attacks Soviet repression of Jews.

10. Congo: Moise Tshombe is sworn in as premier (→21/8).

10. Liverpool: 300 injured as a crowd of 150,000 welcome the Beatles back to the city.

12. South Vietnam: Vietcong guerrillas inflict a major defeat on government forces in the Mekong Delta.

13. London: Appeal Court quashes 25 year jail sentences against two convicted Great Train robbers (→12/8).

14. Baghdad: The Iraqi government nationalises two British banks.

15. Moscow: Anastas Mikoyan succeeds Leonid Brezhnev as Soviet President (→15/10).

18. New York: Thousands riot in Harlem.→

20. US: NASA tests its first successful rocket engine (→31).

24. Algiers: 100 die in bomb blast on a ship in harbour.

27. Washington: Government announces plans to send 5,000 US advisers to Vietnam (→2/8).

28. US: Malcolm X founds Organisation for Afro-American Unity to seek independence for Negroes.

29. UK: The first Brook Advisory Clinic opens to give family planning advice to unmarried couples.

31. Moon: US satellite, Ranger 7, sends back first close-up pictures of the moon's surface (→30/11).

DEATH

11. French Communist Party leader Maurice Thorez (*28/4/1900).

LBJ signs sweeping Civil Rights Act

President Johnson shakes hands with King after signature of the bill.

July 2. President Lyndon Johnson showed his determination today to complete the work begun by President Kennedy, before his assassination, to end racial discrimination. He signed the Civil Rights Act of 1964, the most sweeping civil rights law in the history of the United States.

It prohibits racial discrimination in employment, places of public accommodation, publicly-owned facilities, union membership and federally-funded programmes. The president, himself a southerner, has worked hard to prevent the US Congress weakening the law.

On television tonight he called on all citizens to help "eliminate the last vestiges of injustice in America". He told them that the days of denying rights to negroes were over. "Let us close the springs of racial poison," he said (→18).

National Guard quell New York race riots

A confrontation in Harlem.

July 27. The third successive night of race riots in Rochester, New York State, has prompted Governor Nelson Rockefeller to send in National Guards equipped with rifles and armoured cars to quell the violence. Officials feared that the crash of a police helicopter on a building yesterday, killing two blacks, might be the catalyst for an escalation of the violence.

Law and order, in any serious meaning of the words, have broken down as looting mobs battle police with Molotov cocktails, stones and bricks; 500 arrests have been made and a curfew imposed.

Officials are at a loss to understand what caused the riots. Rochester has the lowest unemployment in the whole state, and the city fathers have been promoting racial harmony for years (→4/8).

Churchill leaves the House for last time

July 28. As a signal honour to Sir Winston Churchill, the House of Commons today passed a formal all-party motion recording the admiration and gratitude of Parliament for his heroic lifetime of service to the nation and the world.

Sir Winston, now 89 and frail, made his last appearance in the Commons yesterday. There was no demonstration. It was a sad occasion for everyone – not least for the old warrior himself, for it was his farewell to the place he loved and honoured. Afterwards party leaders went to his home and presented the motion inscribed on vellum. They stayed for a drink.

"Scottish Soldier" at Malawi's birth

July 6. A black-tarbushed band of the King's African Rifles played "A Scottish Soldier", as Nyasaland became the independent state of Malawi at midnight. The music was a reminder of Dr Banda's days as a student in Edinburgh, where he was an Elder of the Church of Scotland. Today, as Malawi's first Prime Minister, he said: "I want nothing but friendship between Britons and Malawians."

July 21. John White, Tottenham Hotspur's international inside-right, was killed by a flash of lightning when sheltering under a tree on an Enfield golf course.

Right-winger Goldwater to challenge LBJ

Barry Goldwater: "Extremism in the defence of liberty is no vice ..."

July 15. The Republican Party took a sharp right turn tonight. The national convention at the Cow Palace in San Francisco nominated Senator Barry Goldwater as its presidential candidate by a majority of 883 against 214 votes.

Goldwater's friends were busy tonight claiming that his extremist reputation was undeserved. The mood of the convention, however, was clear. An attempt by Governor Rockefeller to bring in a motion condemning the fanatical John Birch Society was shouted down by chants of "We want Barry" (→ 3/9).

Royalty joins fans at Beatles' first film

July 6. Ten thousand screaming teenagers thronged London's West End tonight as Princess Margaret arrived for the premiere of the Beatles' first film, "A Hard Day's Night", directed by Richard Lester. Revolving around a day in the group's life, the plot gives them a chance to display their acting skills, and show off comic talents (→ 10).

Police struggle with screaming Beatles fans outside the London Pavilion.

1964

AUGUST

Su	Mo	Tu	We	Th	Fr	Sa
						1
2	3	4	5	6	7	8
9	10	11	12	13	14	15
16	17	18	19	20	21	22
23	24	25	26	27	28	29
30	31					

2. North Vietnam: The US destroyer Maddox is fired upon in the Gulf of Tonkin.→

2. UK: Police are flown to Hastings to break up clashes between Mods and Rockers.

3. Northern Rhodesia: 150 are reported to have been massacred by Lumpa church sect members (→ 25).

4. US: The bodies of the three missing Mississippi civil rights workers are found (→ 2/10).

9. US: Johnson calls for Cyprus truce as Turkish planes renew attack.→

10. New York: Turkey and Greece accept a UN cease-fire in Cyprus (→ 18).

12. UK: Great Train Robber Charlie Wilson escapes from jail.

16. France: 13 children die when their coach crashes over a ravine in St. Bernard Pass (→ 29/9).

18. Switzerland: South Africa banned from the Olympics for apartheid policies (→ 17/11).

18. Cyprus: Greeks end their food blockade of the Turkish community (→ 11/10).

20. Washington: Johnson signs into law a $947.5 million anti-poverty bill.

21. Congo: Government forces drive rebels out of Bukavi and discover 300 bodies (→ 23).

21. London: Three women found guilty of indecency for wearing topless dresses.

23. Congo: 100 European mercenaries fly in to support government troops (→ 5/11).

25. N. Rhodesia: Kenneth Kaunda is elected President-designate of Zambia.→

30. UK: US reported to want the British island of Diego Garcia as a military base in the Indian Ocean.

DEATHS

3. US novelist Flannery O'Connor (*3/25/25).

12. British novelist Ian Fleming (*28/5/08).→

Fleming, man with golden pen, dies

Fleming, mastermind behind 007.

Aug 12. Ian Fleming, creator of James Bond, died of a heart attack today aged 56. He led a dilettante life at Eton, two European universities, as Reuters Moscow correspondent and as assistant to the head of Naval Intelligence.

In his first James Bond book, "Casino Royale" in 1953, he discovered the winning blend of sex, violence and gourmet-style living which he never varied – "snobbery with violence" it was once called.

Fleming married Lord Rothermere's former wife, Anne, after being cited in their divorce in 1952.

World population booming, says UN

Aug 30. The world's population is bulging by 63 million people a year – more than the populations of France and Czechoslovakia combined – according to the latest figures from the UN; and the rate of increase is accelerating.

The annual increase now averages 2.1 per cent. The rate ranges from 0.9 per cent in Europe and 1.6 per cent in North America to three or five per cent in some developing countries. Many experts fear the boom could jeopardise the battle against hunger and poverty in such nations. In mid-1962 the population was 3.1 billion. The most populated country is Communist China with 600 million.

US steps up action against Vietnam

Aug 7. With the smoke still rising from North Vietnamese installations bombed and rocketed by US carrier-borne planes, President Johnson has asked for and received approval from Congress to take "all necessary action" against the Communist regime in North Vietnam.

Both Houses voted almost unanimously to give the President the powers he wanted, but some members, while feeling duty-bound to approve the resolution, expressed fears that it would be used to commit US troops to an unwanted war.

The crisis arose from an attack by three North Vietnamese torpedo boats on the US destroyer Maddox in the Gulf of Tonkin last Sunday. The attack, with torpedoes and gunfire, did no damage and the torpedo-boats were driven off by the Maddox and rocket fire from carrier aircraft.

One of the Russian-built torpedo-boats was heavily damaged and lay dead in the water, while the other two, also damaged, limped to safety under cover of darkness.

President Johnson immediately ordered a retaliatory strike by carrier aircraft from the Ticonderoga and the Constellation. The Americans claim that 25 torpedo boats at four naval bases were destroyed or damaged and an oil installation was wrecked in raids along 100 miles of North Vietnamese coastline. Two US planes are missing.

Reporting his action next day, the President said: "To anyone who may be tempted to support or widen the present aggression, I say this: there is no threat to any peaceful power from the United States. But there can be no peace by aggression and no immunity from reply.

"The world must never forget that aggression unchallenged is aggression unleashed. We of the United States have not forgotten. That is why we have answered aggression with action."

A UN Security Council meeting, called after an American complaint of "deliberate attacks by the Hanoi regime on US vessels in international waters", heard the Russian delegate, Mr Platon Morozov, call on the US to halt her actions against North Vietnam or "bear the heavy responsibility for the consequences of such acts" (→ 14/9).

American-trained South Vietnamese combat troops prepare for action.

Turkish planes raid the north of Cyprus

Aug 9. The Turkish government tonight called off any further air strikes on Cyprus after a day of raids on Greek Cypriot positions in the north of the island by an estimated 64 jets.

The Turkish air force began attacking this morning, just two hours after Greek Cypriot forces resumed fighting around Kokkina, the last village still held by their Turkish enemies on the coast. A spokesman in Ankara said the situation of Turkish Cypriots in the area was "desperate" and that UN forces had left. "What alternatives does the Turkish government have except to attack?" he asked (→ 10).

Take-away TVs go on sale in the UK

Aug 20. A lighter, more transportable television set, with an 11-inch screen, and weighing only 16 lbs. was previewed today in London. Receiving both ITV and BBC on special 20-inch "rabbit's ear" aerials, it was hoped this new model would prove a useful second set for many families.

According to the suppliers, over half the 13 million British homes currently with television have up to four people living in them and some homes have even more. A second set, they suggested, might ease arguments over what to watch (→ 15/9)

Kaunda is the first Zambian President

Aug 25. In his teaching days Kenneth Kaunda often travelled by bicycle through the bush. Once finding his path blocked by a hungry-looking lion, he lifted the bike above his head, ready to throw. The lion stared at him and padded off. Since then, the 40-year-old African nationalist leader, son of a missionary and advocate of non-violence, has faced down many other lions, including the British one, and today, after an uncontested election, he became President of Zambia, his new name for Northern Rhodesia.

1964

SEPTEMBER

Su	Mo	Tu	We	Th	Fr	Sa
		1	2	3	4	5
6	7	8	9	10	11	12
13	14	15	16	17	18	19
20	21	22	23	24	25	26
27	28	29	30			

3. US: Robert Kennedy resigns as Attorney-General to run for the Senate (→ 3/11).

4. UK: Opening of the Forth Road Bridge, Europe's longest bridge.

4. Italy: Communist leader Togliatti's last testament calls for European Communists to be independent from Moscow.

6. London: Ian Smith arrives for talks on independence for Southern Rhodesia (→ 22/10).

8. Berlin: East Germans visit the West for the first time since the wall was built (→ 5/10).

9. Australia: US author William Willis completes his 200-day journey across the Pacific on a raft.

13. Peking: China is reported to be purging supporters of the Soviet Union (→ 6/11).

14. Saigon: Coup attempt by deposed General Lam Van Phat fails.

15. London: Sir Alec Douglas-Home announces a general election (→ 16/10).

15. UK: The Daily Herald newspaper ends publication and is replaced by The Sun (→ 28).

18. Athens: King Constantine marries Princess Anne-Marie of Denmark.

21. Malta: Becomes an independent member of the Commonwealth.

23. Paris: Unveiling of Marc Chagall's famous decorated ceiling at the Paris Opera.

27. UK: Maiden flight of the TSR-2, Britain's supersonic tactical strike plane.

28. UK: A survey reveals Radio Caroline has more listeners than BBC radio.

29. India: One thousand people are feared dead after a reservoir bursts (→ 24/12).

30. Munich: Himmler's aide Karl Wolff convicted of aiding the murder of 300,000 Jews.

DEATHS

18. Irish writer Sean O'Casey (*30/3/1880).

28. US comedian Harpo Marx, born Adolph (*23/11/1883).→

State of emergency declared in Malaysia

An Indonesian paratrooper shot dead by a security forces patrol.

Sept 3. A state of emergency was declared across Malaysia tonight and Prime Minister Tengku Abdul Rahman called for action by the United Nations after landings by Indonesian paratroops.

The airdrop is being seen as the most serious threat yet in the two years of conflict between the two countries. The Indonesian troops have landed at Labis, in Central Malaysia, one of the main trouble spots during the Communist insurrection, and with the current unrest and race riots in Singapore, they pose a real threat.

Earlier it was announced that Britain, Australia and New Zealand had agreed on the need for more defence and economic aid for Malaysia's armed forces. That announcement came after a two-hour cabinet meeting in Kuala Lumpur attended by Reginald Maudling, Britain's Chancellor of the Exchequer.

Some British defence officials are reported to be urging a full air and naval strike against Indonesian bases.

The Indonesians have always objected to the new state of Malaysia, especially to the inclusion of Borneo and the tiny sultanate of Brunei. They have protested at British "neo-colonialism" in the region and call Malaysia a "puppet" state.

Lyndon Baines Johnson, nominated as Democratic candidate for the presidency of the USA, sets off on the campaign trail. At the Democratic Convention in Atlantic City, he named Senator Hubert H. Humphrey from Minnesota as his choice for Vice-President.

Commission reports on killing of JFK

Sept 27. The Warren Commission's report on the assassination of President Kennedy, published today, blames the FBI, the Secret Service and the Dallas police force for serious failures in their duty to protect the President. But no substance has been found in the speculation that there was a conspiracy. The Commission said Lee Harvey Oswald, Kennedy's killer, and Oswald's murderer, Jack Ruby, both acted alone and on their own initiative.

The FBI had a dossier on Oswald, and knew that he had defected to Russia and worked in the book warehouse overlooking the President's route. But they never told the Secret Service, whose intelligence service was slammed for being inadequate and understaffed. The Commission made a series of recommendations to improve future security.

Harpo Marx, the silent one, is dead

Harpo, master of pantomime.

Sept 28. Harpo, the silent Marx brother, is dead after a heart operation at 70. As Adolph (his real name) he performed in the family vaudeville act with his brothers Julius (Groucho), Leonard (Chico) and Herbert (Zeppo) from 1918. Once they graduated to film, he never spoke another line but turned to mime and made his harp, on which he was a virtuoso player, his trademark.

1964

OCTOBER

Su	Mo	Tu	We	Th	Fr	Sa
				1	2	3
4	5	6	7	8	9	10
11	12	13	14	15	16	17
18	19	20	21	22	23	24
25	26	27	28	29	30	31

2. US: Two charged with murder of three Mississippi civil rights workers.

5. Berlin: 57 flee to the West using a tunnel under the Wall (→ 6).

6. East Germany: Amnesty for 10,000 political prisoners (→ 8).

7. Cairo: Congolese leader Tshombe held hostage by the Egyptians.

8. Bonn: West German government admits paying a ransom for release of East German prisoners.

10. Tokyo: Opening of the 18th Olympic Games (→ 14).

11. Cyprus: 15,000 demand the removal of British bases.

13. USSR: World's first three-man spacecraft returns to earth after a 24-hour space journey.

14. Tokyo: Mary Rand wins Britain's first gold medal of the Olympics, in the womens' long jump.→

15. US: Craig Breedlove sets world land speed record of 526.28 mph.

17. London: Wilson's cabinet includes Richard Crossman, James Callaghan, Denis Healey, Barbara Castle, and Roy Jenkins.

18. Moscow: New Soviet leaders call for a worldwide ban on nuclear tests.

22. Paris: Jean-Paul Sartre rejects a Nobel Prize saying it would reduce the impact of his writing.

22. Southern Rhodesia: Ian Smith sends an ultimatum on independence to Britain (→ 27).

26. London: Wilson warns of an economic crisis and imposes an import tax (→ 11/11).

29. Washington: The priceless Star of India is stolen.

DEATHS

10. US actor Eddy Cantor, born Edward Israel Iskowitz (*31/1/1892).

15. US composer Cole Porter (*9/6/1892).

20. US statesman Herbert Hoover, President 1929-33 (*10/8/1874).

Khrushchev deposed while on holiday

Oct 15. Nikita Khrushchev, the undisputed Soviet leader for more than six years, was ousted in a Kremlin coup today and packed off into retirement. Khrushchev, aged 70, who had been on holiday at his villa by the Black Sea, was brought down by his cronies in the ruling Politburo. He was succeeded as Communist party leader by Leonid Brezhnev, and as prime minister by Alexei Kosygin.

The announcement of the removal of Khrushchev came as a considerable shock to both the West and the Soviet people. But he was summoned to Moscow two days ago for a meeting of the Politburo and walked straight into a trap. The plotters secured the backing of the KGB and took precautions to ensure Khrushchev would be isolated.

The Politburo meeting turned out to be his trial. He was accused of growing wilfulness in his leadership by pushing through a whole series of hastily prepared schemes, disrupting industry, agriculture and the party organisation itself.

Khrushchev defended himself and demanded a meeting of the ostensibly policy-making Central Committee, as he had successfully done before in 1957. This time his opponents were more far-sighted and had already fixed the Central Committee: he lost the vote. A roly-poly, stout little man, fast on his feet, who began his working life as a pipe-fitter in a Donbass coal mine, Khrushchev has changed the Soviet Union irreversibly.

Nikita Khrushchev and Leonid Brezhnev outside Lenin's tomb.

Although he served Joseph Stalin faithfully for many years, he has broken up most of the labour camps for political prisoners and, to some extent, modified the power of the secret police.

His most famous feat of daring was his anti-Stalin speech in 1956, which led to turmoil in the Soviet Union and Eastern Europe as well as among the Communist parties of the world.

Khrushchev's vitality and drive were harnessed to selling a new Soviet image to the West of the necessity for a "peaceful co-existence" and co-operation. For all his faults the proper epitaph to Khrushchev's rule is that he probably left the Soviet Union a better place than he found it.

The Windmill's naked arms stop turning

Oct 31. The Windmill Theatre, a British institution as unchanging as saucy seaside postcards, has finally put up the shutters. All through the wartime air raids its proud boast was "We Never Closed". Now, permissiveness has left it behind.

The kind of titillation the Windmill girls provided was strictly limited by the law that permitted stage nudity only if it did not move. A Windmill girl known as Peaches was celebrated for having made an illegal dash from the stage on seeing a mouse when in mid-tableau.

The Windmill was known as a forcing house for new comedians. Peter Sellers and Tony Hancock first appeared between the nude acts and learned to hold an audience whose mind was elsewhere.

Revudeville bows out.

Martin Luther King to get Peace Prize

Oct 24. Dr Martin Luther King, the 35-year-old American black integration leader, was awarded the Nobel Peace Prize in Oslo today. The citation praises his leadership in the fight for civil rights and consistent adoption of the principle of non-violence. His books have won him recognition as the leading spokesman for black equal rights.

Dr King was in hospital for a check-up when he received the news. He said the award was "a tribute to the discipline, wise restraint and majestic courage of the millions of Negroes and white persons of good will ... seeking to establish a reign of justice and the rule of love" (→ 6/12).

China joins atomic club by exploding her first A-bomb

Oct 16. China became the fifth member of the nuclear club today when she exploded an atomic bomb at a test site in Sinkiang, a western province bordering the Soviet Union. China has not signed the 1963 partial test ban treaty. The other nuclear powers are the United States, Russia, Britain and France.

The Chinese test came as no surprise. Last month the US Secretary of State, Mr Dean Rusk, announced that one was imminent. But he said that it would be a long time before China had a stockpile of bombs and a delivery system.

The Russians helped the Chinese to build a reactor capable of producing the nuclear explosive plutonium, before the two countries fell out in 1959. The Chinese are also believed to have a gaseous diffusion plant for making the alternative nuclear explosive uranium 235. It is still not known which was used in the test, though analysis of the fallout will soon provide an answer.

The official announcement of the test from Peking said that it was "a major achievement of the Chinese people", carried out in the interests of national defence, and that China had been forced to develop nuclear weapons by the "ever increasing nuclear threat presented by the United States".

Labour wins power by a whisker

Oct 16. Labour is in power again tonight after 13 years of Tory rule. "Nice place we've got here," quipped Harold Wilson when he stepped inside 10 Downing Street as the new Prime Minister. Then he announced cabinet appointments at the start of a promised 100 days of dynamic action.

Labour's general election victory is by a whisker – Labour 317 seats, Tories 303, Liberals 9, the Speaker 1. So the overall majority is just four. There was nail-biting until almost the last results were declared this afternoon.

It has been a turning point election like those of 1906 and 1945. For the first time the main party leaders are men born in this century. Nearly half the electorate was too young to vote in 1945. There has been more sophisticated campaigning with greater use of broadcasting and other image-building techniques.

Above all there has been the striking contrast between the Tory and Labour leaders. Lord Home, derided by opponents as a remote 14th earl and leading a party battered by scandal, fared better than expected against thrusting, modern, grammar-school boy Wilson. Voters probably liked Lord Home's off-the-cuff remark: "Come to think of it, I suppose he's the 14th Mr Wilson."

Labour has been elected on a programme of "purposive planning". Its centrepiece will be a national economic plan, directed by a grandsounding First Secretary and Secretary of State for Economic Affairs, George Brown, who said triumphantly: "Brothers, we are on our way."

Steel, water and building land are scheduled for varying forms of public control. Labour is not committed to abandonment of Britain's nuclear deterrent, but the Anglo-Nassau agreement about Polaris submarines is to be "renegotiated". The left-wingers will be keener to do that than Mr Wilson is.

He says that he is "restless with remedies for the problems the Tories have criminally neglected". There are exciting political times ahead (→ 17).

Harold Wilson, Britain's first Labour Prime Minister since Attlee.

Female don wins Nobel chemistry prize

Oct 29. Professor Dorothy Crowfoot Hodgkin of Oxford has been awarded the 1964 Nobel Prize for Chemistry. Only two women have won the Prize before her: Marie Curie in 1911, and her daughter Irene Joliot-Curie in 1935.

Professor Hodgkin was awarded the Prize by the Royal Swedish Academy of Sciences for working out the structure of biologically important chemicals "by the difficult process of studying their behaviour while they were exposed to X-rays".

Among those chemicals whose structure she has determined in this way are penicillin, and vitamin B12, the antipernicious anaemia vitamin.

Professor Dorothy Hodgkin in her laboratory at Oxford University.

Wilson warns Smith that UDI is treason

Oct 27. White Southern Rhodesians were given a disagreeable shock today when Harold Wilson, Britain's newly-elected Labour Prime Minister, told them their government would be committing treason if it went ahead with its threat to go for a unilateral declaration of independence. Ian Smith, Rhodesian Prime Minister, said the warning amounted to "blackmail and intimidation". Previous Conservative governments have given Smith similar warnings, though in private. Today's public one was prompted by recent remarks made by Smith about gaining "independence by Christmas" (→ 6/11).

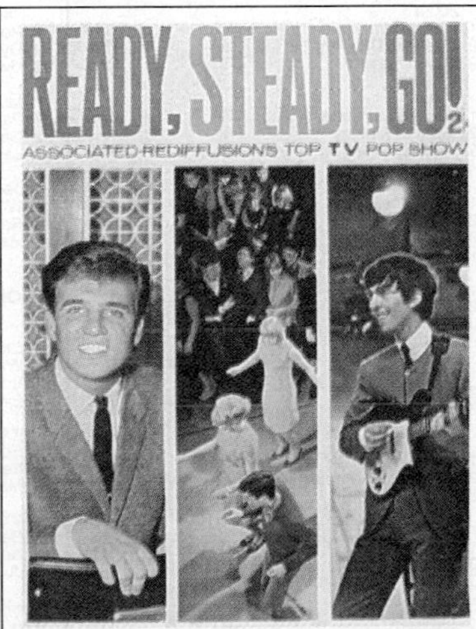

"Ready, Steady, Go!", ITV's first live pop programme, goes on the air. Fans dance in the studio while all the latest names in pop perform their hits.

1964 Tokyo

Oct 24. The Tokyo Olympic Games, the first to be held in Asia, were organised with great efficiency, marked by a general sense of goodwill, and distinguished by the best performance by a British athletics team since 1908.

It was a remarkable games for Olympic veterans. Abebe Bikila, Ethiopia's surprise victor at Rome four years earlier, retained his marathon title just five weeks after having his appendix removed; Peter Snell (New Zealand) retained his Rome 800 metres title, and added the 1,500 metres gold for good measure; Al Oerter (USA), discus champion in Melbourne and Rome, with damaged ribs strapped against the pain, took his third successive title; and so did Dawn Fraser, the Australian swimmer, an exceptional achievement for a 27-year-old in a sport where veteran status often begins at 20.

Only one of Britain's golden athletic achievements followed tradition: Ken Matthew's victory in the 20km walk was the latest in a string of British walking successes. The rest provided a series of trail-blazing firsts. Mary Rand, so disappointing as a teenage prodigy in Rome, took the first gold medal ever won by a British woman athlete with a world record in the long jump, and iced the cake with a silver in the pentathlon and a bronze as part of Britain's 4 x 100 metres relay team. Welshman Lynn Davies made it a long jump double to become the first British man to hold a field event title.

And as the climax to an extraordinary team performance, Ann Packer, disappointed with her own silver medal in the 400 metres, took on the 800 metres, very much her second event. She rounded the whole field on the final bend and broke the world record to take Britain's fourth gold medal.

Ken Matthews (UK) on his way to gold in 20,000 metres walk in a record time of 1hr 29min. 34sec.

Men Athletics

100m
1. Robert Hayes USA =*10.0
2. Enrique Figuerola CUB 10.2
3. Harry Jerome CAN 10.2

200m
1. Henry Carr USA *20.3
2. Otis Paul Drayton USA 20.5
3. Edwin Roberts TRI 20.6

400m
1. Michael Larrabee USA 45.1
2. Wendell Mottley TRI 45.2
3. Andrzej Badenski POL 45.6

800m
1. Peter Snell NZL *1:45.1
2. William Crothers CAN 1:45.6
3. Wilson Kiprugut KEN 1:45.9

1500m
1. Peter Snell NZL 3:38.1
2. Josef Odlozil TCH 3:39.6
3. John Davies NZL 3:39.6

5000m
1. Robert Schul USA 13:48.8
2. Harald Norpoth GER 13:49.6
3. William Dellinger USA 13:49.8

10,000m
1. William Mills USA 28:24.4
2. Mohamed Gammoudi TUN 28:24.8
3. Ronald Clarke AUS 28:25.8

Marathon
1. Abebe Bikila ETH **2:12:11.2
2. Basil Heatley GBR 2:16:19.2
3. Kokichi Tsuburaya JAP 2:16:22.8

110m Hurdles
1. Hayes Jones USA 13.6
2. Harold Blaine Lindgren USA 13.7
3. Anatoly Mikhailov URS 13.7

400m Hurdles
1. "Rex" Warren Cawley USA 49.6
2. John Cooper GBR 50.1
3. Salvatore Morale ITA 50.1

3000m Steeplechase
1. Gaston Roelants BEL *8:30.8
2. Maurice Herriott GBR 8:32.4
3. Yvan Belayev URS 8:33.8

4x100m Relay
1. USA **39.0 (Otis P. Drayton, Gerald Ashworth, Richard Stebbins, Robert Hayes)
2. POL 39.3 (Andrzej Zielinski, Wieslaw Maniak, Marian Foik, Marian Dudziak)
3. FRA 39.3 (Paul Genevay, Bernard Laide-, buer, Claude Piquemal, Jocelyn Delecour)

4x400m Relay
1. USA **3:00.7 (Ollan Cassell, Michael Larrabee, Ullis Williams, Henry Carr)
2. GBR 3:01.6 (Timothy Graham, Adrian Metcalfe, John Cooper, Robbie Brightwell)
3. TRI 3:01.7 (Edwin Skinner, Kent Bernard, Edwin Roberts, Wendell Mottley)

20km Walk
1. Kenneth Matthews GBR *1:29:34.0
2. Dieter Lindner GER 1:31:13.2
3. Vladimir Golubnichiy URS 1:31:59.4

50km Walk
1. Abdon Pamich ITA *4:11:12.4
2. Paul Nihill GBR 4:11:31.2
3. Ingvar Pettersson SWE 4:14:17.4

High Jump
1. Valery Brumel URS *2.18
2. John Thomas USA *2.18
3. John Rambo USA 2.16

Pole Vault
1. Fred Hansen USA *5.10
2. Wolfgang Reinhardt GER 5.05
3. Klaus Lehnertz GER 5.00

Long Jump
1. Lynn Davies GBR 8.07
2. Ralph Boston USA 8.03
3. Igor Ter-Ovanesyan URS 7.99

Triple Jump
1. Józef Schmidt POL *16.85
2. Oleg Fyedoseyev URS 16.58
3. Viktor Kravchenko URS 16.57

Shotput
1. Dallas Long USA *20.30
2. Randel "Randy" Matson USA 20.20
3. Vilmos Varju HUN 19.39

Discus
1. Alfred Oeter USA *61.00
2. Ludvik Danek TCH 60.52
3. David Weill USA 59.49

Hammer
1. Romuald Klim URS *69.74
2. Gyula Zsivotzky HUN 69.09
3. Uwe Beyer GER 68.09

Javelin
1. Pauli Nevala FIN 82.66
2. Gergely Kulcsár HUN 82.32
3. Janis Lusis URS 80.57

Decathlon
1. Willi Holdorf GER 7887
2. Rein Aun URS 7842
3. Hans-Joachim Walde GER 7809

Women Athletics

100m
1. Wyomia Tyus USA 11.4
2. Edith Mc Guire USA 11.6
3. Eva Klobukowska POL 11.6

200m
1. Edith Mc Guire USA *23.0
2. Irena Kirszenstein POL 23.1
3. Marilyn Black AUS 23.1

400m
1. Betty Cuthbert AUS *52.0
2. Ann Packer GBR 52.2
3. Judith Amoore AUS 53.4

800m
1. Ann Packer GBR *2:01.1
2. Maryvonne Dupureur FRA 2:01.9
3. Ann Chamberlain NZL 2:02.8

80m Hurdles
1. Karin Balzer GER 10.5
2. Tereza Ciepla POL 10.5
3. Pamela Kilborn AUS 10.5

4x100m Relay
1. POL 43.6 (Tereza Ciepla, Irena Kirszenstein, Halina Górecka, Eva Klobukovska)
2. USA 43.9 (Willye White, Wyomia Tyus, Marilyn White, Edith Mc Guire)
3. GBR 44.0 (Janet Simpson, Mary Rand, Daphne Arden, Dorothy Hyman)

High Jump
1. Iolanda Balas ROM *1.90
2. Michele Brown AUS 1.80
2. Taisiya Chenchik URS 1.78

Long Jump
1. Mary Rand GBR **6.76
2. Irena Kirszenstein POL 6.60
3. Tatiana Schelkanova URS 6.42

Shotput
1. Tamara Press URS *18.14
2. Renate Garisch GER 17.61
3. Galina Zybina URS 17.45

Discus
1. Tamara Press URS 57.27
2. Ingrid Lotz GER 57.21
3. Lia Manoliu ROM 56.97

Javelin
1. Mihaela Penes ROM 60.54
2. Márta Rudas HUN 58.27
3. Yelena Gorchakova URS 57.06

Pentathlon
1. Irina Press URS **5246
2. Mary Rand GBR 5035
3. Galina Bystrova URS 4956

Men Swimming

100m Freestyle
1. Donald Schollander USA *53.4
2. Robert McGregor GBR 53.5
3. Hans-Joachim Klein GER 54.0

400m Freestyle
1. Donald Schollander USA **4:12.2
2. Frank Wiegand GER 4:14.9
3. Allan Wood AUS 4:15.1

1500m Freestyle
1. Robert Windle AUS *17:01.7
2. John Nelson USA 17:03.0
3. Allan Wood AUS 17:07.7

200m Backstroke
1. Jed Graef USA **2:10.3
2. Gary Dilley USA 2:10.5
3. Robert Bennett USA 2:13.1

200m Breaststroke
1. Ian O'Brien AUS **2:27.8
2. Georgy Prokopenko URS 2:28.2
3. Chester Jastremski USA 2:29.6

200m Butterfly
1. Kevin Berry AUS **2:06.6
2. Carl Robie USA 2:07.5
3. Fred Schmidt USA 2:09.3

Ethiopian Abebe Bikila finishes the marathon 4 minutes ahead of the competition.

400m Individual Medley
1. Richard Roth USA **4:45.4
2. Roy Saari USA 4:47.1
3. Gerhard Hetz GER 4:51.0

4x100m Freestyle Relay
1. USA **3:32.2 (Stephen Clark, Michael Austin, Gary Ilman, Donald Schollander)
2. GER 3:37.2 (Horst Loffler, Frank Wiegand, Uwe Jacobsen, Hans-Joachim Klein)
3. AUS 3:39.1 (David Dickson, Peter Doak, John Ryan, Robert Windle)

4x200m Freestyle Relay
1. USA **7:52.1 (Stephen Clark, Roy Saari, Gary Ilman, Donald Schollander)
2. GER 7:59.3 (Horst-Günther Gregor, Gerhard Hetz, Frank Wiegand, Hans-Joachim Klein)
3. JAP 8:03.8 (Makoto Fukui, Kunihiro Iwasaki, Toshio Shoji, Yukiaki Okabe)

4x100m Medley Relay
1. USA **3:58.4 (H. Thompson Mann, William Craig, Fred Schmidt, Stephen Clark)
2. GER 4:01.6 (Ernst-Joachim Küppers, Egon Henniger, Horst-Günther Gregor, Hans-Joachim Klein)
3. AUS 4:02.3 (Peter Reynolds, Ian O'Brien, Kevin Berry, David Dickson)

Springboard Diving
1. Kenneth Sitzberger USA 159.90
2. Francis Gorman USA 157.63
3. Larry Andreasen USA 143.77

Platform Diving
1. Robert Webster USA 148.58
2. Klaus Dibiasi ITA 147.54
3. Thomas Gompf USA 146.57

Water Polo

1. Hungary
2. Yugoslavia
3. Soviet Union

Women Swimming

100m Freestyle
1. Dawn Fraser AUS *59.5
2. Sharon Stouder USA 59.9
3. Kathleen Ellis USA 1:00.8

400m Freestyle
1. Virginia Duenkel USA 4:43.3
2. Marilyn Ramenofsky USA 4:44.6
3. Terri Lee Stickles USA 4:47.2

200m Breaststroke
1. Galina Prozumenshikova URS *2:46.4
2. Claudia Kolb USA 2:47.6
3. Svetlana Babanina URS 2:48.6

100m Backstroke
1. Cathy Ferguson USA **1:07.7
2. Christine Caron FRA 1:07.9
3. Virginia Duenkel USA 1:08.0

100m Butterfly
1. Sharon Stouder USA **1:04.7
2. Ada Kok NETH 1:05.6
3. Kathleen Ellis USA 1:06.0

400m Individual Medley
1. Donna De Varona USA *5:18.7
2. Sharon Finneran USA 5:24.1
3. Martha Randall USA 5:24.2

4x100m Freestyle Relay
1. USA 4:03.8 (Sharon Stouder, Donna De Varona, Lillian "Pokey" Watson, Kathleen Ellis)
2. AUS 4:06.9 (Robyn Thorn, Janice Murphy, Lynette Bell, Dawn Fraser)
3. NETH 4:12.0 (Paulina van der Wildt, Catherina Beumer, Winnie Weerdenburg, Erica Terpstra)

4x100m Medley Relay
1. USA **4:33.9 (Cathy Ferguson, Cynthia Goyette, Sharon Stouder, Kathleen Ellis)
2. NETH 4:37.0 (Kornelia Winkel, Klena Bimolt, Ada Kok, Erica Terpstra)
3. URS 4:39.2 (Tatyana Savelyeva, Svetlana Babanina, Tatyana Devyatova, Natalya Ustinova)

Britain's Ann Packer is congratulated after her winning run in the 800m final.

Springboard Diving
1. Ingrid Engel-Krämer GER 145.0
2. Jeanne Collier USA 138.3
3. Mary Willard USA 138.1

Platform Diving
1. Lesley Bush USA 99.8
2. Ingrid Engel-Krämer GER 98.4
3. Galina Alekseyeva URS 97.6

Boxing

Flyweight
1. Fernando Atzori IT
2. Artur Olech PO
3. Stanislav Sorokin UR
3. Robert Carmody US

Bantamweight
1. Takao Sakurai JA
2. Shin-Cho Chung KO
3. Juan Fabila Mendoza ME
3. Washington Rodriguez UR

Featherweight
1. Stanislav Stepashkin UR
2. Anthony Villanueva PH
3. Heinz Schulz GE
3. Charles Brown US

Lightweight
1. Józef Grudzien PO
2. Velikton Barannikov UR
3. James Mc Court IR
3. Ronald Harris US

Light Welterweight
1. Jerzy Kulej PO
2. Yevgeny Frolov UR
3. Eddie Blay GH
3. Habib Galhia TU

Welterweight
1. Marian Kasprzyk PO
2. Richardas Tamulis UR
3. Pertti Purhonen F
3. Silvano Bertini IT

Light Middleweight
1. Boris Lagutin UR
2. Joseph Gonzales FR
3. Nojim Maiyegun NG
3. Józef Grzesiak PO

Middleweight
1. Valery Popenchenko UR
2. Emil Schulz GE
3. Franco Valle IT
3. Tandeusz Walasek PO

Light Heavyweight
1. Cosimo Pinto IT
2. Aleksei Kisselyov UR
3. Alexander Nikolov BU
3. Zbigniew Pietrzykowski PO

Super Heavyweight
1. Joseph Frazier US
2. Hans Huber GE
3. Giuseppe Ros IT
3. Vadim Yemelyanov UR

1964  Tokyo

Greco Roman Wrestling

Flyweight
1. Tsutomu Hanahara JAP
2. Angel Kerezov BUL
3. Dumitru Pirvulescu ROM

Bantamweight
1. Masamitsu Ichiguchi JAP
2. Vladien Trostyansky URS
3. Ion Cernea ROM

Featherweight
1. Imre Polyák HUN
2. Roman Rurua URS
3. Branislav Martinovic YUG

Lightweight
1. Kazim Ayvaz TUR
2. Valeriu Bularca ROM
3. Davis Gvantseladze URS

Welterweight
1. Anatoly Kolesov URS
2. Kiril Petkov BUL
3. Bertil Nyström SWE

Middleweight
1. Branislav Simic YUG
2. Jiri Kormanik TCH
3. Lothar Metz GER

Light Heavyweight
1. Boyan Radev BUL
2. Per Svensson SWE
3. Heinz Kiehl GER

Heavyweight
1. István Kozma HUN
2. Anatoly Roshin URS
3. Wilfried Dietrich GER

Freestyle Wrestling

Flyweight
1. Yoshikatsu Yoshida JAP
2. Chang Sun Chang KOR
3. Ali Akbar Heidari IRN

Bantamweight
1. Yojiro Uetake JAP
2. Hüseyin Akbas TUR
3. Aydyn Ibragimov URS

Featherweight
1. Osamu Watanabe JAP
2. Stancho Kolev BUL
3. Nodar Khokhashvili URS

Lightweight
1. Enyu Vulchev BUL
2. Klaus-Jürgen Rost GER
3. Iwao Horiuchi JAP

Welterweight
1. Ismail Ogan TUR
2. Guliko Sagaradze URS
3. Mohammad-Ali Sanatkaran IRN

Middleweight
1. Prodan Gardzhev BUL
2. Hasan Gungör TUR
3. Daniel Brand USA

Light Heavyweight
1. Aleksandr Medved URS
2. Ahmet Ayik TUR
3. Said Mustafov BUL

Heavyweight
1. Aleksandr Ivanitsky URS
2. Lyutvi Ahmedov BUL
3. Hamit Kaplan TUR

Judo

Lightweight
1. Takehide Nakatani JAP
2. Eric Hänni SUI
3. Oleg Stepanov URS
3. Aron Bogoyubov URS

Middleweight
1. Isao Okano JAP
2. Wolfgang Hofmann GER
3. James Bregman USA
3. Eui-Tae Kim KOR

Heavyweight
1. Isao Inokuma JAP
2. Alfred Douglas Rogers CAN
3. Anzor Kiknadze URS
3. Parnaoz Chikviladze URS

Open
1. Antonius Geesink NETH
2. Akio Kaminaga JAP
3. Klaus Glahn GER
3. Theodore Boronovskis AUS

Men Fencing

Foil Individual
1. Egon Franke POL
2. Jean-Claude Magnan FRA
3. Daniel Revenu FRA

Foil Team
1. Soviet Union
2. Poland
3. France

Epée Individual
1. Grigory Kriss URS 2 + 1
2. Henry Hoskyns GBR 2
3. Guram Kostava URS 1 + 1

Epée Team
1. Hungary
2. Italy
3. France

Sabre Individual
1. Tibor Pézsa HUN 2 + 1
2. Claude Arabo FRA 2
3. Umar Mavlikhanov URS 1 + 1

Sabre Team
1. Soviet Union
2. Italy
3. Poland

Women Fencing

Foil Individual
1. Ildikó Ujlaki-Retjő HUN 2 + 2
2. Helga Mees GER 2 + 1
3. Antonella Ragno ITA 2

Foil Team
1. Hungary
2. Soviet Union
3. Germany

Modern Pentathlon

Individual
1. Dr. Ference Török HUN
2. Igor Novikov URS
3. Albert Mokeyev URS

Team
1. Soviet Union
2. USA
3. Hungary

Men Canoeing

Kayak-1 1000m
1. Rolf Peterson SWE 3:57.13
2. Mihály Hesz HUN 3:57.28
3. Aurel Vernescu ROM 4:00.77

Kayak-2 1000m
1. Sweden 3:38.54
2. Netherlands 3:39.30
3. Germany 3:40.69

Kayak-4 1000m
1. Soviet Union 3:14.67
2. Germany 3:15.39
3. Romania 3:15.51

Canadian-1 1000m
1. Jürgen Eschert GER 4:35.14
2. Andrei Igorov ROM 4:37.89
3. Yevgeny Penyayev URS 4:38.31

Canadian-2 1000m
1. Soviet Union 4:04.64
2. France 4:06.52
3. Denmark 4:07.40

Women Canoeing

Kayak-1 500m
1. Lyudmila Khvedosyuk URS 2:12.87
2. Hilde Lauer ROM 2:15.35
3. Marcia Jones USA 2:15.68

Kayak-2 500m
1. Germany 1:56.95
2. USA 1:59.16
3. Romania 2:00.25

Rowing

Single Sculls
1. Vyacheslav Ivanov URS 8:22.51
2. Achim Hill GER 8:26.24
3. Gottfried Kottmann SUI 8:29.68

Double Sculls
1. Soviet Union 7:10.66
2. USA 7:13.16
3. Czechoslovakia 7:14.23

Coxless Pairs
1. Canada 7:32.94
2. Netherlands 7:33.40
3. Germany 7:38.63

Coxed Pairs
1. USA 8:21.23
2. France 8:23.15
3. Netherlands 8:23.42

Coxless Fours
1. Denmark 6:59.30
2. Great Britain 7:00.47
3. USA 7:01.37

Coxed Fours
1. Germany 7:00.44
2. Italy 7:02.84
3. Netherlands 7:06.46

Eights
1. USA 6:18.23
2. Germany 6:23.29
3. Czechoslovakia 6:25.11

Yachting

Finn
1. Wilhelm Kuhweide GER 7638
2. Peter Barrett USA 6373
3. Henning Wind DEN 6190

Star Class
1. Bahamas 5664
2. USA 5585
3. Sweden 5527

Flying Dutchman
1. New Zealand 6255
2. Great Britain 5556
3. USA 5158

Dragon Class
1. Denmark 5854
2. Germany 5826
3. USA 5523

5.5m Class
1. Australia 5981
2. Sweden 5284
3. USA 5106

Peter Snell (New Zealand) is the second man in Olympic history to win both 800m and 1500m.

Cycling

Individual Road Race
1. Mario Zanin ITA 4:39:51.63
2. Kjell Akerström Rodian DEN 4:39:51.65
3. Walter Godefroot BEL 4:39:51.74

100km Team Time Trial
1. Netherlands 2:26:31.19
2. Italy 2:26:55.39
3. Sweden 2:27:11.52

1000m Time Trial
1. Patrick Sercu BEL 1:09.59
2. Giovanni Pettenella ITA 1:10.09
3. Pierre Trentin FRA 1:10.42

1000m Sprint
1. Giovanni Pettenella ITA 13.69
2. Sergio Bianchetto ITA
3. Daniel Morelon FRA

2000m Tandem
1. Italy 10.75
2. Soviet Union
3. Germany

4000m Individual Pursuit
1. Jiri Daler TCH 5:04.75
2. Giorgio Ursi ITA 5:05.96
3. Preben Isaksson DEN 5:01.90

4000m Team Pursuit Race
1. Germany 4:35.67
2. Italy 4:35.74
3. Netherlands 4:38.99

Equestrian Sports

Three-Day Event Individual
1. Mauro Checcoli ITA
2. Carlos Moratorio ARG
3. Fritz Ligges GER

Three-Day Event Team
1. Italy +85.80
2. USA +65.86
3. Germany +56.73

Individual Dressage
1. Henri Chammartin SUI 1504
2. Harry Boldt GER 1503
3. Sergei Filatov URS 1486

Team Dressage
1. Germany 2558.0
2. Switzerland 2526.0
3. Soviet Union 2311.0

Grand Prix Jumping Individual
1. Pierre Jonquères d'Oriola FRA -9
2. Hermann Schridde GER -13.75
3. Peter Robeson GBR -16.0

Grand Prix Jumping Team
1. Germany -68.50
2. France -77.75
3. Italy -88.50

Men Shooting

Free Rifle, 300m. 3 positions
1. Gary Anderson URS **1153
2. Shota Kveliashvili URS 1144
3. Martin Gunnarsson USA 1136

Small Bore Rifle, 50m Prone
1. László Hammerl HUN **597
2. Lones Wigger USA **597
3. Tommy Pool USA 596

Small Bore Rifle, 3 positions
1. Lones Wigger URS **1164
2. Velichko Velichkov BUL 1152
3. László Hammerl HUN 1151

Rapid Fire Pistol, 25m
1. Pentti Linnosvuo FIN *592
2. Ion Tripsa ROM 591
3. Lubomir Nacovsky TCH 590

Free Pistol, 50m
1. Väinö Markkanen FIN =*560
2. Franklin Green USA 557
3. Yoshihisa Yoshikawa JAP 554/26

Weightlifting

		2 Arm Press	2 Arm Snatch	2 Arm Clean and Jerk	Total
Bantamweight					
1. Aleksei Vakhonin	URS	110.0	105.0	*142.5	**357.5
2. Imre Földi	HUN	*115.0	102.5	137.5	355.0
3. Shiro Ichinoseki	JAP	100.0	*110.0	137.5	347.5
Featherweight					
1. Yoshinobu Miyake	JAP	*122.5	*122.5	**152.5	**397.5
2. Isaac Berger	USA	*122.5	107.5	**152.5	382.5
3. Mieczyslaw Nowak	POL	112.5	115.0	150.0	377.5
Lightweight					
1. Waldemar Baszanowski	POL	132.5	*135.0	*165.0	**432.5
2. Vladimir Kaplunov	URS	=**140.0	127.5	165.0	**432.5
3. Marian Zielinski	POL	=**140.0	120.0	160.0	420.0
Middleweight					
1. Hans Zdrazila	TCH	130.0	*137.5	**177.5	=**445.0
2. Viktor Kurentsov	URS	135.0	130.0	175.0	440.0
3. Masashi Ouchi	JAP	140.0	135.0	162.5	437.5
Light Heavyweight					
1. Rudolf Plukfelder	URS	150.0	*142.5	182.5	*475.0
2. Géza Tóth	HUN	145.0	137.5	*185.0	467.5
3. Győző Veres	HUN	*155.0	135.0	177.5	467.5
Middle Heavyweight					
1. Vladimir Golovanov	URS	*165.0	=*142.5	180.0	*487.5
2. Louis Martin	GBR	155.0	140.0	180.0	475.0
3. Ireneusz Palinski	POL	150.0	135.0	*182.5	467.5
Heavyweight					
1. Leonid Zhabotinsky	URS	187.5	*167.5	**217.5	*572.5
2. Yuri Vlassov	URS	**197.5	162.5	210.0	570.0
3. Norbert Schemansky	USA	180.0	165.0	192.5	537.5

Mixed Shooting

Clay Pigeon
1. Ennio Mattarelli ITA *198
2. Pavel Senichev URS 194/25
3. William Morris USA 194/24

Men Gymnastics

All-around Individual
1. Yukio Endo JAP 115.95
2. Shuji Tsurumi JAP 115.40
3. Viktor Lisitsky URS 115.40
3. Boris Shakhlin URS 115.40

Combined Exercises Team
1. Japan 577.95
2. Soviet Union 575.45
3. Germany 565.10

Parallel Bars
1. Yukio Endo JAP 19.675
2. Shuji Tsurumi JAP 19.450
3. Franco Menichelli ITA 19.350

Floor Exercises
1. Franco Menichelli ITA 19.450
2. Viktor Lisitsky URS 19.350
2. Yukio Endo JAP 19.350

Long Horse Vault
1. Haruhiro Yamashita JAP 19.600
1. Viktor Lisitsky URS 19.325
3. Hannu Rantakari FIN 19.300

Side Horse
1. Miroslav Cerar YUG 19.525
2. Shuji Tsurumi JAP 19.325
3. Yuri Tsapenko URS 19.200

Horizontal Bar
1. Boris Shakhlin URS 19.625
2. Yuri Titov URS 19.550
3. Mirosalv Cerar YUG 19.500

Rings
1. Takuji Haytta JAP 19.475
2. Franco Menichelli ITA 19.425
3. Boris Shakhlin URS 19.400

Women Gymnastics

All-around Individual
1. Vera Cáslavská TCH 77.564
2. Larissa Latynina URS 76.998
3. Polina Astakhova URS 76.965

Combined Exercises Team
1. Soviet Union 380.890
2. Czechoslovakia 379.989
3. Japan 377.899

Asymmotric Bars
1. Polina Astakhova URS 19.332
2. Katalin Makray HUN 19.216
3. Larissa Latynina URS 19.199

Floor Exercises
1. Larissa Latynina URS 19.599
2. Polina Astakhova URS 19.500
3. Anikó Jánosi HUN 19.300

Side Horse Vault
1. Vera Cáslavská TCH 19.483
2. Larissa Latynina URS 19.283
2. Birgit Radochla GER 19.283

Beam
1. Vera Cáslavská TCH 19.449
2. Tamara Manina URS 19.399
3. Larissa Latynina URS 19.382

Basketball

1. USA
2. Soviet Union
3. Brazil

Football

1. Hungary
2. Czechoslovakia
3. Germany

Field Hockey

1. India
2. Pakistan
3. Australia

Men Volleyball

1. Soviet Union
2. Czechoslovakia
3. Japan

Women Volleyball

1. Japan
2. Soviet Union
3. Poland

(Key to symbols and abbreviations p. 1456)

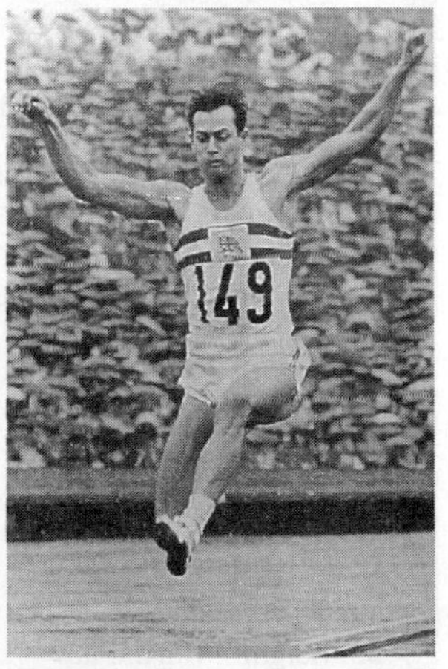

South Wales schoolteacher L. Davies jumps 26ft. 5.5in. to win a gold medal for Britain in the long jump event.

1964

NOVEMBER

Su	Mo	Tu	We	Th	Fr	Sa
1	2	3	4	5	6	7
8	9	10	11	12	13	14
15	16	17	18	19	20	21
22	23	24	25	26	27	28
29	30					

1. South Vietnam: The Vietcong launch major attack on the US base at Bien Hoa, destroying six planes.→

2. Saudi Arabia: King Saud deposed as ruler; replaced by his brother, Prince Feisal.

5. Congo: 2,000 government troops launch attack on rebels.→

6. Southern Rhodesia: White referendum overwhelmingly endorses Ian Smith's policy on independence (→16).

6. Moscow: Brezhnev meets Chinese leaders to try and heal the Sino-Soviet split.

8. Yemen: Cease-fire between Royalist and Republican forces.

9. London: Judy Garland gives a concert jointly with her daughter Liza Minnelli.

10. Kenya: One-party state declared.

11. London: Economy budget raises income tax by six per cent to pay for larger old age pensions (→25).

12. Prague: Antonin Novotny is re-elected President of Czechoslovakia.

13. Rome: Pope Paul VI gives his jewelled tiara to the world's poor (→2/12).

16. Southern Rhodesia: Joshua Nkomo and 16 of his followers are freed from jail.

17. London: The Government imposes an arms embargo on South Africa (→18/12).

18. Rome: Egyptian diplomats caught trying to smuggle a South Vietnamese attache out of the country in a crate (→19).

20. Rome: The Catholic Church agrees to exonerate Jews for their guilt in the crucifixion of Jesus.

23. Rome: 44 die in plane crash.

25. London: Eleven nations loan Britain £1,080 million to stem the slide in sterling's value.

25. Saigon: Martial law declared after student riots.

30. London: Sir Winston Churchill's 90th birthday.

LBJ sends Senator Goldwater packing

Nov 3. Lyndon B. Johnson swept back into the White House today with 60 per cent of the popular vote. His landslide win over his Republican opponent, Senator Barry Goldwater, shows that the US electorate prefers the man wooing the centre to the candidate of the far right.

The vice-presidential winner, Hubert Humphrey, called it "a mandate for unity, for a government that serves no special interest". It also reflects America's need for stability after the shock of the Kennedy assassination. Two of the late President's brothers won Senate seats – Robert, who as Attorney-General pushed hard for civil rights laws, in New York and Edward in Massachusetts.

Johnson, elected to his first term.

Paras in dramatic drop on Stanleyville

A helpful kick for a Congolese rebel.

Nov 26. Belgian paratroops swooped on Stanleyville, in the upper Congo, today after the Lumumbist rebel "President" Christophe Gbenye threatened that 1,500 white hostages would be "grilled alive".

Rebel troops, shouting "Piga! Piga!" (Swahili for kill) were shooting at the hostages when the paras raced into the centre of town: 30 hostages were killed, including two Belgian children, an American woman and two missionaries, an American and a Canadian.

The paras, in agreement with the Congo government, flew in from the Congo's Kamina military base. Moscow radio called the rescue "a criminal act" (→20/12).

Saigon begins new thrust on Vietcong

Nov 19. South Vietnamese forces today initiated the largest attack of the war, striking at a Communist stronghold in a forest 40 miles north-west of Saigon. Supported by 105 US army helicopters, 7,000 Vietnamese were airlifted to an area near Thudaumot. They met with no resistance, the guerrilla force having withdrawn from the area.

Vietnam's new premier, Tran Van Huong, has pledged "total war against the Communists"; it looks like it has just started (→25).

Lift off: the race is on for planet Mars

Nov 30. Two planetary probes, one American and one Russian, are heading to Mars. The Russian Zond 2 is already in trouble, with only half of its power source working. All is not well with the American Mariner 4, either. It has not locked on to Canopus, as intended, but on to a smaller nearby star. However, flight directors hope to be able to correct the error so that Mariner passes within 10,000 miles of Mars at the end of its seven and a half month voyage through space.

1964

DECEMBER

Su	Mo	Tu	We	Th	Fr	Sa
		1	2	3	4	5
6	7	8	9	10	11	12
13	14	15	16	17	18	19
20	21	22	23	24	25	26
27	28	29	30	31		

2. India: Two million greet the Pope's arrival in Bombay.

6. London: Martin Luther King preaches a sermon in St. Paul's Cathedral.

10. Stockholm: Nobel Prizes go to Nikolai Basov (USSR), Alexander Prokhorov (USSR), Charles Townes (US, Physics); Feodor Lynen (Germany), Konrad Bloch (US, Medicine); Jean-Paul Sartre (France, Literature); Dorothy Hodgkin (UK, Chemistry); and in Oslo to Martin Luther King (US, Peace).

15. Canada: Parliament adopts the Maple Leaf as the national flag.

18. S. Africa: British academic David Kitson is jailed for "revolutionary conspiracy".

20. Congo: Rebels massacre 15 British missionaries.

23. London: British Railways chief Lord Beeching is sacked by the Government.

24. Indian Ocean: A hurricane kills 7,000 in Ceylon and the Indian province of Madras.

29. London: An East End shooting incident is linked to the Kray brothers.

31. Australia: Donald Campbell sets world water speed record of 276.33mph.

DEATHS

1. British geneticist Professor John Haldane (*5/11/1892).

8. British businessman Lord Marks (*9/7/1888).→

9. British poet Dame Edith Sitwell (*7/9/1887).

HITS OF THE YEAR

I love you because

I won't forget you

It's over

QUOTE OF THE YEAR

"Join me and march along the road ... that leads to the Great Society, where no child will go unfed ... where every human being has dignity and every worker has a job."

Lyndon Johnson, campaigning for US President.

Kenya is now a republic

Kenya's President Jomo Kenyatta (r.) celebrates independence at last.

Dec 12. He was baptised Johnstone Kamau in August 1914; as a young man he was nicknamed "Piki-piki" after the sound of the motor cycle he rode round Nairobi; in England, he married an Englishwoman, wrote a book about the traditions of his tribe and called himself Jomo 'Burning Spear" Kenyatta. By the time the world at large heard of him he was cast as malevolent master of an anti-white terrorist society. But a year ago, when Kenya became independent, Jomo Kenyatta as Prime Minister asked Inspector Ian Henderson, the policeman who had arrested him years before, to stay on. Today, one year later, Kenya became a republic. At the ceremony in Nairobi, Malcolm MacDonald, British High Commissioner, described President Kenyatta as "the wisest old bird in the whole of Africa".

Diana Rigg and Patrick McNee are "The Avengers" on TV.

Death knell sounds for capital penalty

Dec 21. MPs voted tonight to abolish the death penalty for murder. Their vote – 355 to 170 – was so overwhelming that the House of Lords will not try to frustrate it.

The 1957 Homicide Act, which operates now, prescribes hanging for certain murders. Now, pending enactment of the new law, any murderers sentenced to death are likely to be reprieved by the Home Secretary.

Marks's spark gone

Dec 8. Lord Marks, who pioneered a revolution in British dress with the quality garments sold in Marks & Spencer, died today aged 76. He said his mission was "to glamorise the women and children at a price they can afford".

Arts: all the world's a stage for Britain

Shakespeare's quatercentenary year has established beyond dispute that in theatre England leads the world. The Royal Shakespeare Company's celebration of the 400th birthday took the form of "The Wars of the Roses", a serial constructed out of the history plays to make a bloody saga. Every effort is made to turn the playgoer's stomach. Queen Margaret of Anjou is capable of triumphantly smearing the blood of a dead child in its father's face. **Peter Hall's** direction and **Peggy Ashcroft's** Queen Margaret were the high watermark of the RSC seasons so far.

The National Theatre mounted a display of our greatest actor at the height of his powers – **Laurence Olivier**, playing Othello for the first time in his career. Olivier spent months lowering his voice by almost an octave, so that he can pad on stage "like a soft black leopard", gracefully barefooted, smelling a rose and rolling the whites of his eyes in a full-blooded negroid reading of the part.

For good measure the National put on a new hit play, "The Royal Hunt of the Sun" by **Peter Shaffer**, which presents Pizarro's conquest of the Incas of Peru in startling theatrical terms. And **Peter Brook** directed a section of the RSC in the "Marat-Sade" by **Peter Weiss**, which tells of the murder of Marat by Charlotte Corday as staged by the inmates of an asylum at Charenton, lead by the Marquis de Sade.

Peggy Ashcroft as Queen Margaret in the RSC's "Richard III".

In this extraordinary, grotesque play a new actress named **Glenda Jackson** achieved extreme intensity, as Corday. At the Royal Court, **Nicol Williamson** showed mesmeric powers of rhetorical soliloquy as a man on the brink of breakdown in "Inadmissible Evidence", **John Osborne's** strongest play since "Look Back in Anger".

In a rich theatrical year two Irish playwrights died: **Sean O'Casey**, the boy from the Dublin slums, and **Brendan Behan** who was only 41 when he died of drink. He had spent eight years in prison which provided him with the subject for "The Quare Fellow".

Laurence Olivier and Maggie Smith in the National's memorable "Othello".

1965

JANUARY

Su	Mo	Tu	We	Th	Fr	Sa
					1	2
3	4	5	6	7	8	9
10	11	12	13	14	15	16
17	18	19	20	21	22	23
24	25	26	27	28	29	30
31						

1. UK: Stanley Matthews is the first ever professional footballer to be knighted.

2. Djakarta: Sukarno announces that Indonesia will be the first country to quit the UN (→ 12).

7. UK: A two-week package holiday to the Costa del Sol can now cost from £66 16/-, to Greece from £93 17/-.

7. London: Ronnie and Reggie Kray are remanded in custody on a charge of demanding money with menaces (→ 9/3).

8. Johannesburg: Singer Adam Faith cancels concerts after being refused permission to play to multi-racial audiences.

12. Djakarta: Sukarno closes all UN offices in Indonesia (→ 8/8).

15. London: Sir Winston Churchill is gravely ill after a stroke (→ 25).

16. US: 30 people are killed when a US Air Force jet crashes into a house in Wichita, Kansas.

19. London: Wilson tells the French that Britain will continue with Concorde despite mounting costs (→ 18/11).

21. London: Patrick Gordon Walker, defeated in the general election, loses the Leyton by-election created for him (→ 22).

22. London: Gordon Walker resigns as Foreign Secretary and is replaced by Michael Stewart (→ 10/8/66).

25. London: MPs pay tribute to Churchill (→ 27).

27. London: Thousands queue all night to file past Churchill's bier as his lying-in-state begins in Westminster Hall.→

28. Holland: Protests greet Crown Princess Beatrix's announcement that she is to marry a German (→ 10/3/66).

DEATHS

4. US poet and dramatist Thomas Stearns Eliot (*26/9/1888).→

24. British statesman Sir Winston Leonard Spencer Churchill, PM 1940-45 and 1951-55 (*30/11/1874).→

World bids sad farewell to Churchill

Jan 30. Sir Winston Churchill was buried today in a village churchyard near his family's ancestral home at Blenheim Palace, Oxfordshire. This was how he wanted it. A simple graveside ceremony was the end to an extraordinary four days of homage on a grand scale which began when this man of many-sided genius died peacefully at the age of 90. The Queen led the nation in its mourning and spontaneous upsurge of affection and respect.

Representatives of 110 nations were at the state funeral service in St. Paul's Cathedral. They came eagerly to honour the giant of destiny whose inspired leadership was so much responsible for the survival of the free world.

For three days after his death Sir Winston lay in state in historic Westminter Hall in the heart of the Houses of Parliament. In hundreds of thousands the humble and the mighty filed past his coffin, by day and all through the night. At one stage the services' chiefs of staff in their own mark of respect took over the watch at the catafalque.

There was a solemn military procession to St. Paul's, where the throng of 3,000 mourners included the royal families of Europe and representatives of practically every country in the world. Old colleagues and opponents from war and peacetime were there in force to complete a scene of high dignity.

The coffin was then taken by launch from Tower Pier upriver to Waterloo Station on its way for burial. Everything was done with astonishing precision. Churchill would have approved. He took the precaution of making some of the arrangements himself some time ago. Live television coverage had the biggest audience ever recorded – 350 million in Europe alone.

Tributes to Sir Winston had come earlier from all quarters of the globe. "What he said and did will never die," said President Johnson. "In the war drama he was the greatest," said President de Gaulle. "The indefatigable champion of freedom," said the Pope.

It was in the House of Commons, where Churchill sat for more than 60 years, that the tributes were most moving. His old seat was left vacant as House veterans recalled his tempestuous career – the guns of Gallipoli and Flanders, the whine of air raid sirens, Dunkirk and the Normandy beaches.

"For now the noise of hooves thundering over the veldt, the clamour of hustings in a score of contests, the urgent warnings of the Nazi threat ... all are silent," said Harold Wilson. "There is a stillness and in that stillness, each has his memories." Tributes were similarly eloquent in the House of Lords where Lord Avon called for a national "Churchill Day". For Churchill, life was an endless adventure. Now there is a void in the nation.

The body of Sir Winston Churchill lies in state in Westminster Hall.

Guardsmen carry the coffin towards the steps of St. Paul's Cathedral.

Ireland's premiers meet for the first time

Terence O'Neill (c.) and Sean Lemass (r.) with Jack Lynch at Stormont.

Jan 15. In a move that surprised and stunned both Belfast and Dublin, the Prime Ministers of Northern Ireland and the Irish Republic met for the first time on Irish soil since their two parliaments were established in 1921.

Sean Lemass went to Belfast to lunch with Terence O'Neill at Stormont Castle. There was tension in the North prior to Lemass's arrival. His acceptance letter got delayed in the mail. It was addressed to Stormont Castle, Dublin. A postal worker crossed out Dublin and pencilled in: "Try Belfast".

The feeling in both capitals tonight is that, given 40 years of bitterness, the meeting showed great courage (→9/2).

Eliot, father of modernist poetry, dies

Jan 4. Thomas Stearns Eliot, whose poetry was once thought outrageous, died today loaded with honours, aged 76. He looked less like a poet than a banker (which he was).

His friend Ezra Pound called him "Possum" and he used the nickname for "Old Possum's Book of Practical Cats". He also mocked his dry, solemn persona in verse: "How pleasant to meet Mr Eliot – with his conversation so nicely restricted to What precisely and If and Perhaps and But."

Poems such as "The Waste Land" are thought to reflect his desperation at his marriage. His first wife, Vivienne, died in a mental home in 1947. Ten years later Eliot married his secretary.

LBJ is sworn in as new US President

Jan 20. Lyndon B. Johnson was sworn in today as 36th President of the US. He used his mother's bible held for him by his wife, dressed in a bright red coat and hat. He contrasted this occasion with the first time he took the oath, on an airliner in Dallas the day John F. Kennedy was killed. He promised a "Great Society" in which America held "no dominion over our fellow men, but man's dominion over tyranny and misery" (→5/3).

A girl's real gone on 'Crimplene'!

Uncrushably fashionable fabrics

1965

FEBRUARY

Su	Mo	Tu	We	Th	Fr	Sa
	1	2	3	4	5	6
7	8	9	10	11	12	13
14	15	16	17	18	19	20
21	22	23	24	25	26	27
28						

1. Addis Ababa: 200,000 Ethiopians greet the Queen at the start of her tour.

4. UK: Anthony Barber wins the Altrincham by-election for the Conservatives (→25).

6. South Vietnam: Seven US troops die in a Vietcong raid.→

9. Dublin: Captain O'Neill is the first Northern Irish premier to visit the city since 1921.

10. Moscow: War hero Marshal Zhukov is the first of Khrushchev's enemies to be rehabilitated.

11. UK: Ringo Starr marries Liverpool hairdresser Maureen Cox.→

16. London: British Rail publishes plans to slash the rail network by half, based on the Beeching report.

17. Gambia: The British colony becomes Africa's smallest independent state.

21. New York: Black Moslem leader Malcolm X is shot dead while beginning a speech to his followers (→5/3).

22. UK: The TSR-2 flies faster than the speed of sound for the first time.

22. India: Tension grows on the Sino-Indian border after reports of Chinese troop movements up to the frontier.

23. London: The government offers to help the UN set up a permanent peace-keeping force of up to six battalions.

23. UK: A whisky price war begins as Distillers sell scotch at 7/- a bottle (→26).

25. London: The Conservative Party decides that its future leaders will be elected by Tory MPs (→27/7).

26. UK: The whisky price war spreads to wine, now on sale for as little as 5/6d. a bottle (→6/4).

DEATHS

15. US singer Nat King Cole, born Nathaniel Adams Coles (*17/3/19).

23. British-born US comedian Stan Laurel, born Arthur Stanley Jefferson (*16/6/1890).→

Creeping blockade of Gibraltar begins

Feb 3. General Franco's "creeping blockade" of Gibraltar, designed to force Britain to give "the Rock" back to Spain, is beginning to take effect. Customs restrictions at the frontier have been intensified and action taken to prevent Spanish workers crossing the border.

Some Britons who work in Gibraltar have had their permits to live in Spain withdrawn, and tonight 450 of them are being housed in a transit camp.

The blockade is also badly delaying holiday traffic. Where 500 cars a day used to pass through the customs post of La Linea, only 14 are being allowed through, and tour operators are cancelling bookings to Gibraltar (→5/10/66).

Ron Clarke sets a record for 5,000m

Feb 1. For the second time in little more than a fortnight, the remarkable Australian running machine, Ron Clarke, has broken the 5,000 metres world record. In a runaway victory in Auckland in 13 minutes 33.6 seconds he trimmed more than a second off the time he set in Hobart last month. Clarke, who as a schoolboy lit the Olympic flame in the Melbourne stadium, also holds the world records at three miles, six miles and 10,000 metres.

Ringo Starr of the Beatles and wife Maureen at their wedding.

Cigarette ads to be banned from TV

Feb 8. Cigarette advertising is to be banned from television, it was announced in the Commons by the Minister of Health, Kenneth Robinson, today. Critics said discrimination between different media was illogical; television advertising would begin at night while cigarette advertising would continue to appear all day in newspapers. Manufacturers were also using coupons to distribute free cigarettes to young people. Mr Robinson said TV had been singled out because it was an effective form of advertising for adolescents and 20 per cent of those aged 11 to 15 watch television at 9pm.

Stan Laurel, the wistful one, is dead

Feb 23. Stan Laurel, the thin and wistful half of Laurel and Hardy, has gone at the age of 74 to join his old partner, who died in 1957. They spent 30 years together making 200 films. His real name was Jefferson. The son of an actor from Ulverston, Lancashire, he sailed on a cattle boat from Liverpool to America in 1910 where Charlie Chaplin persuaded him to try films in 1917. Later he was cast in a two-reeler with Oliver Hardy. The rest is slapstick history.

American planes pound North Vietnam

B-57 jet bombers have been enlisted to fly missions over North Vietnam.

Feb 11. American and South Vietnamese warplanes struck at North Vietnam today, blasting two barrack-areas believed to be used as transit depots for Viet Cong guerrillas who have been coming south to attack American installations.

The official explanation for the air-raids was that they were launched to counter "continued acts of aggression by Communist Viet Cong under the direction and with the support of Hanoi".

Altogether six targets were bombed and machine-gunned by 150 fighter-bombers, flying at little more than roof-top height. They left the barracks burning, and an American spokesman said the results were "quite successful". Three aircraft were lost. Two of them came down in the sea, and the third was wrecked when its landing gear collapsed coming in to Da Nang airfield, 80 miles south of the border. One of the pilots is missing.

Meanwhile, the Viet Cong have continued their attacks. About 100 of them tried to land from sampans on the beach at Qui Nonh, apparently to attack US troops engaged in rescue operations at a base blown up by guerrillas yesterday.

The Americans opened up with machine guns and artillery, but it wasn't until helicopter gunships raked the boats that they fled into the mangrove swamp (→ 30/3).

Alec Issigonis, inventor of the BMC "Mini", takes the wheel of the millionth vehicle to be produced; this one will go to Mr and Mrs Peter James, from Cheshire, who watched the ceremonial delivery of the car.

Luther King jailed after race protest

Feb 1. The civil rights leader Dr Martin Luther King and 300 supporters were arrested today in Selma, Alabama, for parading without a permit. They were protesting at the slow pace of electoral reforms intended to give them the vote. At the rally, King said: "If Negroes could vote, there would be no oppressive poverty ... our children would not be crippled by segregated schools and the whole community might live together in harmony."

The issue is crucial in Alabama, where blacks outnumber whites by six to four. At present only six per cent of eligible blacks are registered to vote (→ 5/3).

1965

MARCH

Su	Mo	Tu	We	Th	Fr	Sa
	1	2	3	4	5	6
7	8	9	10	11	12	13
14	15	16	17	18	19	20
21	22	23	24	25	26	27
28	29	30	31			

1. Cairo: The United Arab Republic signs a $100 million aid deal with East Germany.

2. UK: Roger Moore and Patrick McGoohan are Britain's top-earning actors, on £2,000 a week.

4. London: David Attenborough is appointed head of BBC2.

5. Washington: President Johnson has talks with Martin Luther King.

7. Bonn: Chancellor Erhard says West Germany will seek to establish diplomatic relations with Israel (→ 14).

9. London: The trial of the Kray twins begins (→ 6/4).

10. London: Zoo-keepers recapture Goldie the eagle (→ 15/12).

14. Aden: A British soldier dies in a grenade attack on a an army post (→ 25/9).

14. Tel Aviv: Jerusalem accepts West Germany's request to establish diplomatic relations (→ 13/5).

19. USSR: Leonov's spacecraft lands safely (→ 21).

21. US: Ranger 9, the last in the current series of US lunar explorations, is launched at Cape Kennedy (→ 23/4).

24. UK: David Steel, aged 26, wins Roxburgh, Selkirk and Peebles for the Liberals to become Britain's youngest MP.

25. Bonn: The Bundestag decides to extend the Statute of Limitations for War Crimes until January 1, 1970.

26. Congo: Moise Tshombe's party wins national elections (→ 25/11).

27. UK: Mrs M. Stephenson's Jay Trump wins the Grand National.

30. Saigon: At least six are feared dead after a bomb blast near the US embassy.→

DEATHS

6. British politician Herbert Stanley Morrison, Baron Morrison of Lambeth (*3/1/1888).

17. Egyptian King Farouk, ruled 1936-52 (*11/2/20).

LBJ sends the Marines into Vietnam

March 31. The conflict in Vietnam continues to escalate alarmingly. Following the bombing of targets in North Vietnam last month, in retaliation for Viet Cong raids on American bases, President Johnson has sent 3,500 US Marines into Da Nang to help protect the sprawling air base against guerrilla attack.

These two battalions of front-line troops are the first fighting soldiers America has committed to the war. All the others have been officially classed as "advisers" to the South Vietnamese forces.

The Viet Cong played their part in escalating the war yesterday by exploding a car bomb outside the US Embassy in Saigon, wrecking it, killing 21 people – including two Americans – and wounding 156. Mr Johnson is reported to have said at a private dinner in Washington: "I'm not going to tolerate this any longer" (→2/4).

This Vietnamese farmer allegedly failed to inform on Viet Cong guerrillas.

Japanese enter car races to kick off British sales drive

March 8. Japan is to compete in major British saloon car races this year. The move prepares the way for a major Japanese assault on the British domestic car market. Rising taxation and increasing competition in Japan is pushing the leading car companies to develop new overseas markets.

Two 1.5 litre saloons are already on their way to Britain from Isuzu, one of the oldest and largest Japanese car companies. The 1,600cc GT is claimed to have a top speed of over 100mph and will be a competitor for the British Ford Cortinas which have dominated this class in recent years. British drivers are likely to be invited to race the cars here and on the continent. They will race under the banner of Nippon Racing.

25,000 in Alabama civil rights march

March 28. A month of civil rights protests in Alabama came to a climax today, when Dr Martin Luther King led 25,000 marchers to the steps of the state Capitol in Montgomery to present a petition of black grievances to Governor Wallace. As the marchers gathered in Selma, 50 miles away, last week, large bombs were discovered at a black church, a funeral parlour and a leading black lawyer's home. To prevent further attacks, President Johnson gave the marchers the protection of nearly 3,000 troops, plus FBI and local police assistance.

On March 10, in Selma, a demonstration led by six nuns in defiance of a police ban – imposed after a white gang injured three liberal clergymen – was halted after less than a hundred yards. A week later, 3,000 protesters marched peacefully on Selma's courthouse, but a later demonstration in Montgomery by college students was broken up by club-swinging, mounted state troopers (→30/5).

Dr Martin Luther King and his wife set out on the civil rights march.

Russian cosmonaut somersaults in space

March 18. A Russian cosmonaut left his spaceship today to float in space 300 miles above the earth, attached to his craft only by a thin cord. The spacewalker, Colonel Alexei Leonev, remained outside the Voshkod 2 spacecraft for about ten minutes, during which time he travelled some 3,000 miles. The other crew member, Colonel Pavel Belyaev, remained inside while Leonev took pictures with a cine camera and tried out various tools.

Viewers in the USSR and in Europe watched the spacewalk on television, seeing Leonev emerge in an orange spacesuit and turn a somersault. The timing of the Soviet space feat was probably influenced by a flight of the American Gemini spacecraft planned for next week (→19).

Crowds cheer Goldie's bid for freedom

March 7. Thousands thronged Regent's Park today to see Goldie, London Zoo's Golden Eagle, on his tenth day of liberty. The scenes resembled a Bank Holiday rather than a wintry Sunday, with traffic jams in the area from midday to dusk.

Goldie is enjoying his freedom, regaining strength in the wings he has not used properly for five years. He hopped from tree to tree, occasionally descending to eat a titbit offered by his visitors.

Aged seven, Goldie is young – the average lifespan of an eagle is 43. A spokesman for the Zoo said he could survive indefinitely by eating one of the park's ducks when hungry (→10).

Still uncaptured in Regent's Park.

1965

APRIL

Su	Mo	Tu	We	Th	Fr	Sa
				1	2	3
4	5	6	7	8	9	10
11	12	13	14	15	16	17
18	19	20	21	22	23	24
25	26	27	28	29	30	

2. Paris: Wilson and de Gaulle meet for talks on Vietnam.→

2. Washington: The US decides to increase its military and financial aid to South Vietnam.→

6. London: The budget puts 4/- on a bottle of whisky and 1d. on a pint of beer.

6. London: The Kray twins are cleared at the Old Bailey of running a protection racket (→19).

7. London: The Home Secretary announces that incitement to racial hatred is to be outlawed (→8/11).

9. London: Liberal MP Eric Lubbock returns to the boxing ring after 13 years and is knocked out in two minutes.

10. Moscow: Richard Nixon arrives on a visit to the USSR.

11. Teheran: A machine-gun attempt on the Shah's life fails, but three others are killed (→26/10/67).

14. Jersey: 26 people die in a Dakota Airways plane crash.

18. UK: Police are on the alert as Mods and Rockers converge on seaside resorts; 56 are arrested in Brighton.

19. London: Reggie Kray marries at a celebrity wedding; Judy Garland and Barbara Windsor send messages (→4/8/66).

23. USSR: The first Soviet communications satellite, Molnya-1, is launched.

25. Dominican Republic: The army ousts President Donald Reid Cabral and pleads for US aid against Communist rebels.→

26. Rhodesia: The government says it will deport 500,000 African citizens if Britain imposes a trade embargo (→7/5).

28. Rome: Wilson is the first Labour prime minister to meet the Pope.

DEATHS

21. British physicist Edward Appleton, 1947 Nobel Prize winner (*6/9/1892).

27. US broadcaster Edward R. Murrow (*25/4/08).

US Marines go to aid of Dominican coup

US Marines in Dominica question a civilian passing their checkpoint.

April 30. A new military junta seized power in the Dominican Republic today, and immediately called for more American troops to help them fight off the leftish guerrilla forces. Yesterday a force of 550 Marines landed to protect US citizens and property; they fought a minor battle with snipers who were attacking the American Embassy in Santo Domingo, the capital of the Caribbean island.

Today an additional 1,000 Marines began moving in, together with 2,500 men of the 82nd Airborne Division. Their arrival was denounced by Cuba's premier, Fidel Castro.

Hundreds of people have been killed in the civil war which has been raging sporadically on the island since 1963. In that year President Juan Bosch was deposed because Communists infiltrated his government. His successor, Donald Reid Cabral, has now been overthrown.

In the past week of intense fighting at least 400 people have been killed and over 1,200 injured. The trouble is believed to have started when groups of armed civilians tried to take power and set up a Castro-style regime. At the same time some army units were seeking to restore Juan Bosch to power. The first task of the new junta will be to restore order (→5/5).

Chaired from the field by Russia's Yashin and Hungary's Puskas, Sir Stanley Matthews finally says farewell to football at the age of fifty.

Julie Andrews wins Oscar in film debut

April 6. At a Hollywood Academy Awards ceremony tonight, dominated by British success, Julie Andrews won an Oscar for the best actress of the year for her lead role in "Mary Poppins". In all, the film won five Oscars, and "My Fair Lady", starring the veteran British actor, Rex Harrison, won eight, including best film of the year. The triumphs prompted MC Bob Hope to remark: "Welcome to Santa Monica on the Thames."

Julie Andrews, Oscar winner.

European protest at Vietnam grows

April 27. There is growing protest in Europe, both in the streets and the legislatures, about the escalating American involvement in the Vietnam war. There have been a number of violent demonstrations in Paris, with police fighting running battles with demonstrators marching on the US Embassy shouting "US assassins" and "Peace in Vietnam".

President de Gaulle has condemned foreign intervention in the war and the Prime Minister, Mr Wilson, infuriated the Americans last month when he made no mention in the Commons of the blowing up of the US Embassy in Saigon.

The Pope has also expressed his unease at the growth of the war, saying: "Once again humanity must tremble for the fate of peace. The hour is grave" (→16/6).

1965

MAY

Su	Mo	Tu	We	Th	Fr	Sa
						1
2	3	4	5	6	7	8
9	10	11	12	13	14	15
16	17	18	19	20	21	22
23	24	25	26	27	28	29
30	31					

2. London: Scotland Yard appeals for world help in catching the three train robbers still at large (→ 20/6/66).

4. France: Common Market finance ministers endorse Britain's application to the IMF for a £500 million loan (→ 13/11/67).

5. Dominican Republic: Both sides sign a truce in the civil war (→ 3/6).

6. London: Labour gains a four-vote majority after the debate on steel nationalisation (→ 9/11).

9. USSR: The space station Lunar V is launched (→ 12).

12. USSR: The space station Lunar V fails to land on the moon (→ 3/6).

12. East Pakistan: Over 10,000 are reported dead after a violent cyclone.

13. Bonn: West Germany and Israel establish relations; nine Arab states break diplomatic ties with West Germany (→ 19/8).

16. China: The second Chinese nuclear bomb is detonated in Sinkiang province (→ 23/6).

18. West Germany: The Queen begins a state visit (→ 27).

19. London: West Ham win the European Cupwinners' Cup, beating TSV Munich 2-0.

24. London: The Government announces that Britain is to switch to the metric system (→ 1/3/66).

27. West Berlin: The Queen visits the Berlin Wall.

28. Rhodesia: A state of emergency is declared in several areas (→ 29/10).

30. US: Vivian Malone is the first black to graduate from Alabama University (→ 13/8).

31. US: Britain's Jim Clark is the first non-American to win the Indianapolis 500 (→ 27/6).

DEATH

21. British aircraft pioneer Geoffrey de Havilland (*27/7/1882).

Queen dedicates Runnymede field to JFK

Jackie Kennedy brings her children, Caroline and John, to Runnymede.

May 14. No greater tribute could be paid by Britain to the late John Kennedy, America's 35th president, assassinated in 1963. Under sullen skies, close to the spot on which the Magna Carta was signed, the Queen dedicated an acre of wood and grassland "in perpetuity to the American people ... in memory of a man whom in death my people still mourn and whom in life they loved and admired". Among the trees, a simple memorial of Portland stone carries the late President's famous declaration in his inauguration speech: "We shall pay any price, bear any burden, support any friend or oppose any foe in order to assure the survival and success of liberty."

The Prime Minister, Harold Wilson, said that President Kennedy should be forever identified with "this historic meadow".

Liverpool win FA Cup for first time

May 1. After a tense, fluctuating final at Wembley, that threatened for more than an hour and a half to end in total stalemate, Liverpool and Leeds United conjured up three goals in extra time and, to the delighted chants of their loyal, irreverent but thoroughly good-natured fans, Bill Shankly's Liverpool won the FA Cup for the first time in the club's history.

For all Liverpool's undoubted promise, they had started the game as marginal outsiders to Don Revie's highly talented Leeds side, but a goal by Roger Hunt broke the tension three minutes into extra time, and though Leeds's Billy Bremner, equalised, his fellow Scot, Ian St. John, sealed Liverpool's triumph nine minutes from time.

Rhodesian electors vote for "cowboys"

May 7. In a stunning political somersault, Rhodesia's white electors have abandoned their traditional loyalties and thrown their support behind the "cowboy" Rhodesian Front party, launched only three years ago. In today's general election, the Front made a clean sweep of all the 50 European seats, with an average swing in its favour of over 30 per cent.

The result sets Rhodesia on course for confrontation with Britain. The Front's commitment to keeping political power in white hands, in order, as it says, to maintain "civilised standards", is seen in London as, at best, out of tune with the times, and, at worst, positively dangerous.

The Front was born of disillusionment with the old establishment politicians, who are now accused of letting down white Rhodesians by being too compliant when Britain dismantled the Central African Federation. Though Front politicians have little experience of government, they have the backing of a small but powerful group of "cowboys" – wealthy tobacco farmers and cattlemen, who sustain the Front with their money and their notions of white supremacy (→ 28).

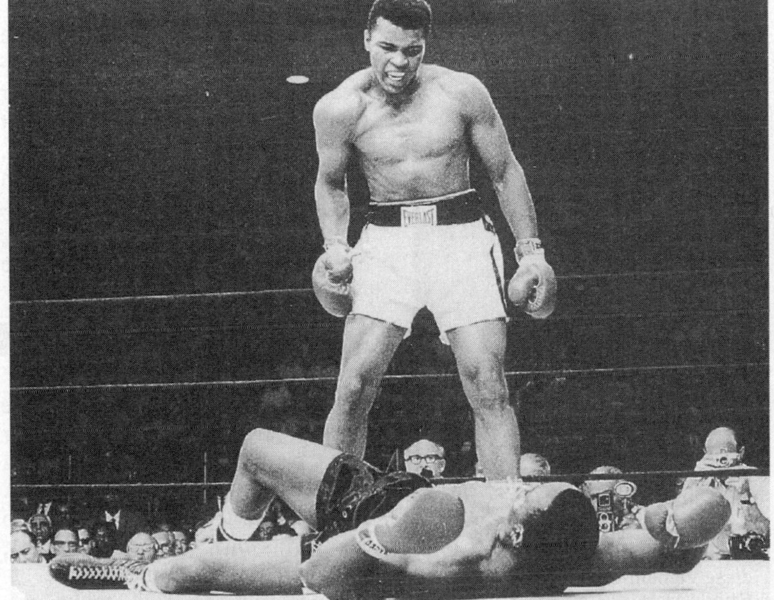

The count reached 22 after Cassius Clay refused to retreat to a neutral corner, and there may be an official inquiry, but challenger Sonny Liston was obliterated in the first round of this championship fight.

1965

JUNE

Su	Mo	Tu	We	Th	Fr	Sa
		1	2	3	4	5
6	7	8	9	10	11	12
13	14	15	16	17	18	19
20	21	22	23	24	25	26
27	28	29	30			

1. New York: Governor Nelson Rockefeller abolishes the death sentence in the state.

1. Japan: Around 250 miners are feared dead in a pit explosion.

2. London: With the Speaker's casting vote, MPs approve a bill to impose a Corporation Tax on company profits.

3. Washington: Johnson withdraws all US Marines from the Dominican Republic.

7. Moscow: Major Squires, a British officer who disappeared in Berlin in 1947, is discovered to be working for the USSR.

10. London: A ceremony at St. Paul's Cathedral marks the 750th anniversary of Magna Carta.

11. London: The Queen's Birthday Honours includes an OBE for "Dixon of Dock Green" star Jack Warner.→

14. UK: Two OBEs return their honours to Buckingham Palace in protest at the award of MBEs to The Beatles.

16. Paris: De Gaulle condemns US intervention in south-east Asia and Latin America (→19).

18. London: The Government announces it will introduce a legal blood alcohol limit for drivers (→21/12).

19. Saigon: General Nguyen Van Thieu becomes head of state and Air Marshal Nguyen Cao Ky, aged 34, premier.

20. Peking: China denounces Wilson's peace mission to Vietnam.→

21. Algiers: Riot police disperse supporters of jailed ex-President Ben Bella.

22. Tokyo: Japan and South Korea establish diplomatic relations.

23. Washington: Robert Kennedy proposes a nuclear arms limitation treaty (→29/10).

25. London: The Commonwealth Conference ends with disagreement on Vietnam and Rhodesia.→

27. France: Jim Clark wins the French Grand Prix (→1/8).

US troops are sent into battle in Vietnam

June 29. American troops have gone onto the offensive for the first time in Vietnam. In a joint operation with South Vietnamese forces they overran a network of trenches and tunnels in a Viet Cong stronghold 30 miles east of Saigon.

Most of the 173rd Airborne Brigade were flown into the area yesterday by 130 helicopters, but only light contact was made as the guerrillas melted into jungle and deep swamp infested with leeches.

Despite its lack of results the operation was important because it marks the the beginning of the regular commitment of American troops in an offensive role.

It follows the announcement three weeks ago that US forces had been authorised to give "combat support" to Vietnamese troops. While this is qualified, in that the Vietnamese must request assistance and the Americans must operate alongside South Vietnamese troops, it is felt in Saigon that the Americans will soon become the major partners (→4/7).

Two more victims of the war.

Wilson's Vietnam peace hopes dashed

June 23. Russia has now joined China and North Vietnam in rejecting the Commonwealth peace mission proposed by Harold Wilson. So this eye-catching diplomatic initiative is now aborted.

The British Prime Minister won the agreement of his Commonwealth counterparts at their London conference last week that he should lead a team to Hanoi, Peking, Moscow and Washington in search of settlement of the Vietnam war. The premiers of Ghana, Nigeria, Trinidad and Ceylon were named as his companions. However, Mr Kosygin today told a group of Commonwealth ambassadors that Russia has no authority to conduct peace talks.

It is clear that the Kremlin is refusing co-operation because it fears a Chinese accusation that it is betraying a revolutionary struggle. Mr Wilson's support for American policy in Vietnam would also make him an unwelcome visitor to Moscow. Labour left-wingers talked of "a Wilson stunt come unstuck" (→25).

Austere colonel ousts flamboyant Bella

June 20. President Ben Bella, the ill-fated Algerian leader jailed for years by the French, is tonight a prisoner again in a Sahara outpost. He was seized in a lightning coup led by his own Defence Minister, Colonel Houari Boumedienne.

A column of T-34 tanks surrounded the Villa Joly, his official residence, before dawn, and soldiers burst into the president's bedroom. Colonel Boumedienne had persuaded Ben Bella that the troops and armour had entered the capital to take part in a film about Algeria's war of independence.

The austere Boumedienne disapproved of the President's flamboyant style and frequently quarrelled with him. His popular coup was timed to coincide with the arrival of Third World leaders for the jamboree planned to glorify Ben Bella's foreign policy (→21).

Old guard protest at MBEs for Beatles

June 15. Somehow the words, John Lennon, MBE, have an unexpected ring to them. And while the MBEs for all four Beatles in the Birthday honours list has delighted pop fans, it has outraged others. Some members of the Order of the British Empire are returning the insignia of the order as a protest against the awards to the Beatles. They feel that these honours, presumably suggested by the Prime Minister, Harold Wilson, diminish the value of their own award.

Although every holder remains a member of the order, no matter what they choose to do with the actual insignia, at least nine people have chosen to protest against what one of them calls the "cheapening" of their honour by sending it back to the Palace. The first to return his OBE was Mr Hector Dupuis, a Canadian MP, who said the awards placed him on the same level as "vulgar nincompoops" (→29/7).

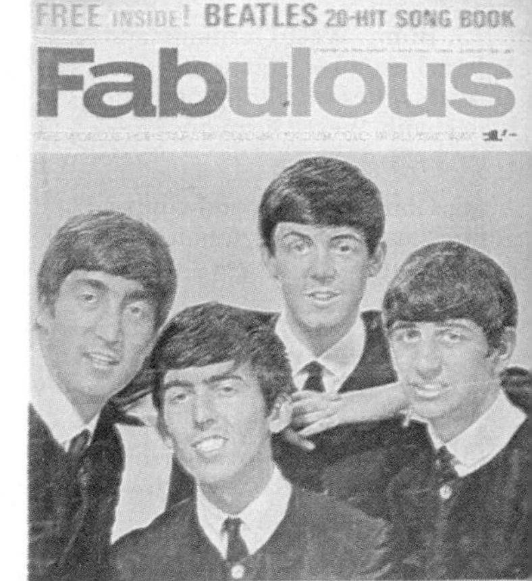

The controversial Beatles, MBE.

Churchmen protest over Sunday ferry

June 6. A demonstration by 50 island crofters failed to stop the first Sunday ferry crossing from the mainland to the Isle of Skye yesterday. The islanders viewed the crossing as a "desecration of the biblical Sabbath", and sat in the road leading from the harbour trying to block cars. Seven constables removed one 20-stone crofter.

First US astronaut takes a walk in space

High above a blue-tinged Earth, Major Ed White walks through space.

June 3. Major Edward White today became the first American to walk in space. He spent 14 minutes outside the Gemini 4 spacecraft, four minutes longer than the first spacewalker of all, Colonel Alexei Leonev of the Soviet Union, in March.

However, another part of Gemini 4's mission was cancelled – an attempt at a space rendezvous with the final stage of the spacecraft's Titan 2 launcher. Rendezvous in orbit is a key manoeuvre in American moon-landing plans.

White climbed out of the spacecraft while it was over the United States. "He looked great," commented his partner, Major James McDivett. White took photographs and manoeuvred on his tether, using a compressed oxygen gun to propel himself. He was so excited by his spacewalk that he had to be persuaded back into Gemini by McDivett.

The flight is scheduled to last four days, during which Gemini 4 will orbit the Earth 62 times. "The Soviet people sincerely congratulate the two cosmonauts and the American scientists," said a spokesman on Moscow TV (→15/7).

M.J. Ternywck, a happy owner, leads in his horse Sea Bird II, ridden by T.P. Glennon, after it won the 1965 Derby at Epsom. Meadow Court, ridden by Lester Piggott, was second and I Say took third place.

1965

JULY

Su	Mo	Tu	We	Th	Fr	Sa
				1	2	3
4	5	6	7	8	9	10
11	12	13	14	15	16	17
18	19	20	21	22	23	24
25	26	27	28	29	30	31

3. Wimbledon: Roy Emerson beats Fred Stolle in the Men's Singles final; Margaret Smith beats Maria Bueno for the Women's Singles title.

4. Washington: Martin Luther King calls for an end to the Vietnam War (→9).

9. Washington: Johnson predicts that the situation in Vietnam will get worse (→13).

13. Washington: Johnson orders more troops to Vietnam.→

14. London: US statesman and ambassador to the UN Adlai Stevenson collapses and dies in the street from a heart attack.

15. US: The probe Mariner IV, launched last November, sends back pictures of Mars (→29).

16. France: De Gaulle and Italy's President Saragat officially open the Mont Blanc tunnel.

20. London: The Lords unexpectedly approves a bill to abolish hanging by a majority of 100 (→8/11).

22. London: Figures show that 1964 was the worst year this century for crime in the capital.

22. London: Sir Alec Douglas-Home resigns as Tory leader.→

26. London: The GPO says it is switching to numbers-only telephones in anticipation of international direct dialling.

29. London: Premiere of the Beatles' film, "Help" (→15/8).

29. US: Mariner IV's final photos of Mars show the planet's moon-like surface (→29/8).

30. UK: Figures show that ITV's "Coronation Street" is the most popular weekly TV programme (→16/9).

31. Bhutan: King Jigme Wangchuk escapes an assassination attempt.

DEATHS

14. US statesman and diplomat Adlai Stevenson (*5/2/00).

19. Korean statesman Syngman Rhee, first President of South Korea 1948-60 (*26/4/1875).

One-time boxing champ is shot dead

Freddie Mills – tragic victim.

July 24. Freddie Mills, the former light-heavyweight champion of the world, has been found shot dead in a car in London's Soho, aged 43.

As a professional fighter for 14 years Mills was rarely considered to rank in the highest class, and it was only a powerful pair of shoulders, and a lasting belief that he could beat anybody, that took him to the very top and, in a bruising fight with Gus Lesnevich, to the world title.

His subsequent ventures – a night club, a Chinese restaurant, regular TV appearances – brought some financial trouble, but confirmed his popularity.

London lecturer is jailed for spying

July 23. Gerald Brooke, a university lecturer who smuggled pamphlets into the Soviet Union while on a tourist visit, was sentenced to five years' imprisonment by a Moscow court today.

Brooke, aged 28, who pleaded guilty to anti-Russian activities, had been held by the KGB security police for more than three months. The pamphlets were produced by a Russian emigre organisation which had apparently been infiltrated by the KGB.

Edward Heath is elected as Tory leader

Fellow Conservatives gather to applaud their new leader, Edward Heath.

July 27. Edward Heath became the Conservative Party leader today. It was a double-first occasion. He is the first one elected by his fellow MPs and the first grammar schoolboy in the job. Mr Heath got 150 votes against 133 for Reginald Maudling and 15 for Enoch Powell. It was a surprise result. About 25 Tories either made a late switch or never intended to honour pledges of support given to Mr Maudling.

At 49 Mr Heath is his party's youngest leader since the middle of last century. He sees his first task as restoring party morale, which has been sagging ever since a young Liberal, David Steel, captured a Scottish Borders constituency from the Tories in a by-election in March. Sir Alec Douglas-Home decided then that it was time for him to resign as leader and make way for more vigorous management.

He personally constructed leadership election rules, which have now been used, instead of the mysterious "magic circle" process from which Tory leaders always emerged in the past.

Sir Alec's departure was sudden. He told his MPs: "I would never allow disunity over myself", and out he went. Now begins a less relaxed era in politics. Leadership by the aristocracy is out. The grammar schoolboys' takeover is complete. There will be nasty fights in the playground now (→ 6/10).

Another 50,000 US troops to Vietnam

July 28. President Johnson today announced that he was going to send another 50,000 troops to Viet nam "almost immediately". Speaking at a nationally televised news conference, he said the United States was involved in Vietnam because "we have learned at a terrible and brutal cost that retreat does not bring safety and weakness does not bring peace".

US troop strength in Vietnam will therefore be raised to 125,000 men, with 35,000 recruits being called up each month (→ 30/10).

Margot Bryant (l.) and Violet Carson chat about life on ITV's serial "Coronation Street".

1965

AUGUST

Su	Mo	Tu	We	Th	Fr	Sa
1	2	3	4	5	6	7
8	9	10	11	12	13	14
15	16	17	18	19	20	21
22	23	24	25	26	27	28
29	30	31				

1. West Germany: Jim Clark wins the world motor racing championship (→ 2/10/66).

2. France: Forest fires sweep the Riviera.

8. Indonesia: The first Indonesian rocket is launched (→ 1/10).

9. France: Francois Mitterrand says he will run for president (→ 4/11).

9. Athens: 10,000 anti-monarchist demonstrators chant slogans against King Constantine II (→ 21/4/67).

10. Blackpool: South African Karen Muir, 12, swims 110 yards backstroke in a world record 68.7 seconds.

10. London: The Queen cancels Kim Philby's OBE.

13. Los Angeles: Troops move into the city on the third day of rioting by blacks.→

15. New York: 55,000 attend the Beatles' concert at the Shea Stadium (→ 26/10).

19. West Germany: Auschwitz victims protest at light terms for 16 ex-warders found guilty of murder; only six get life.

19. Jerusalem: Protests greet the arrival of West Germany's first ambassador to Israel.

19. London: The Home Secretary orders an enquiry into the case of Timothy John Evans, hanged in 1950 (→ 22/11).

20. West Germany: Willy Brandt's Socialists make gains as Chancellor Erhard's Christian Democrats are re-elected.

21. UK: Charlton Athletic's Keith Peacock becomes the first substitute to appear in the Football League.

25. India: Indian troops cross the Kashmir cease-fire line after Pakistani "infiltrators".→

29. US: The space capsule Gemini V splashes down after eight days in space (→ 15/12).

DEATH

27. Swiss-born French architect Charles Edouard Jeanneret, alias Le Corbusier (*6/10/1887).→

Singapore to cut link with Malaysia

Aug 9. Britain recognised Singapore tonight after the island's surprise secession from Malaysia. Talks between the two prime ministers, Tengku Abdul Rahman of Malaysia and Lee Kuan Yew of Singapore, failed to avert the break which is the result of antagonism between Malay and Chinese races.

Singapore's 1,700,000 Chinese claim Malays were given preferential treatment by Malaysia's federal government. However, Lee Kuan Yew said continued economic co-operation was essential, otherwise Singapore would have to "seek a living by trading with the devil".

The 214-square mile island state is the principal British base in south-east Asia, and its continued use by 50,000 servicemen seems assured. The Chinese population greeted the news by bursting fire-crackers in the streets.

Wedding bells for media star Bailey

Aug 18. With Mick Jagger as best man, no wedding is exactly normal, but today's register office marriage of the photographer David Bailey and the beautiful French actress Catherine Deneuve summed up for many people the magic that has made London the capital of contemporary style. Bailey, the son of an East Ham tailor, is one of the "new aristocrats", a success built not on birth, but on pure talent.

Bailey and bride – beautiful people.

Race riots flare in Watts

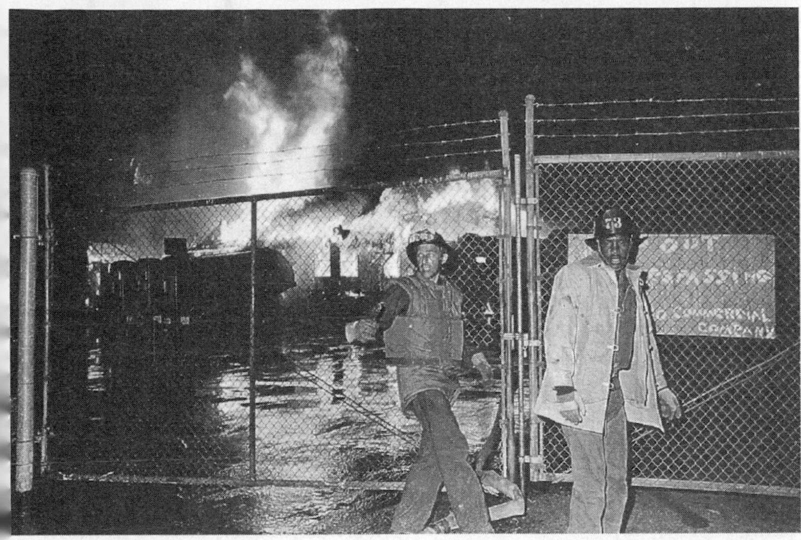

Black and white firemen unite to fight the flames in the Watts ghetto.

Aug 15. In Los Angeles a police patrol arrested a black man for drunken driving. Within hours, Watts, an area of the city which is mainly inhabited by blacks, was in flames, with roof-top snipers ignoring a curfew and shooting at police. Fire and ambulance men were enlisted to contain the worst outbreak of racial rioting in the United States since the War.

As 20,000 steel-helmeted national guardsmen patrolled a "relatively calm" Watts yesterday, the cost of the rioting became clear. Twenty-eight people, some of them children, have died, and 676 people have been wounded, including 70 police, 26 firemen and four national guardsmen.

Watts was named as a "disaster area" last night by President Lyndon Johnson, who said that the rioting "strikes from the hand of the Negro the very weapons with which he is achieving his own emancipation". Some black spokesmen in Watts claimed that excessive police brutality had sparked off the rioting. Others blamed the disturbances on soaring temperatures during an unusually hot Californian summer.

Cornell Henderson, a black worker for the Congress of Racial Equality, admitted that "young hoodlums and agitators" were involved, but added: "There were a lot of others who were just discontented and took advantage of the situation for emotional release." Governor Edmund Brown flew back from a Greek holiday last night, but his plans to tour the district were cut short by the danger from snipers.

Terrified residents blamed the police for failing to call the national guard in sooner, particularly to support firemen who wore flak-jackets as they tried to fight over 1,000 fires, 300 of them described as "major". Police have arrested 2,157 looters – few liquor shops in the area have been left undisturbed – and damage is estimated at more than $175 million.

As tension continues, despite a lull in rioting, authorities are hoping that a break in the heatwave – with even a chance of rain – is at hand. Dr Martin Luther King, the black civil rights leader, plans to visit Watts soon (→ 7/6/66).

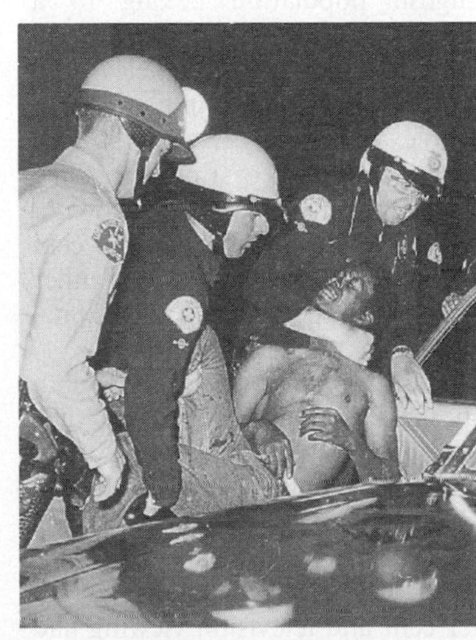

Los Angeles police arrest a rioter.

Radical architect, Le Corbusier, has died

Aug 27. The high priest of the Modern Movement in architecture, Le Corbusier, is dead, his name both revered and reviled. His book "Towards a New Architecture" published in 1923 created the elitist, purely functional theory of architecture, which eliminated ornament and, some would say, human values altogether.

The monument to his theories is the Unite d'Habitation outside Marseilles, completed in 1952 and little loved by those who have been rehoused there. It is a mammoth-sized human beehive raised on stilts to accommodate a self-sufficient community with its own shops and schools, with swimming pools and sports grounds on the roof.

One Corbusier-designed city was built – the new capital of the Punjab, Chandigarh, a geometrical plan of blocks, with cool vaulted space beneath them, but his most admired building is a chapel at Ronchamps, France. Le Corbusier (real name Charles Edouard Jeanneret) was Swiss and aged 77. His imitators around the world gave pre-fabricated tower-block building a bad name.

Revered and reviled: Le Corbusier seen here in his Paris studio.

Kashmir clashes fan fears of border war

Aug 31. Pakistan tonight claimed that more than 200 Indian troops have been killed in fighting in Kashmir, where Pakistan has a long-standing claim to part of the mountain territory. The Pakistanis say Kashmiris loyal to President Ayub Khan are involved in the fighting, after India sent troops to disputed outposts earlier this month. Pakistan says India's action is pushing the two countries nearer to war, and the UN Secretary-General, U Thant, says the United Nations may need to step in to stop the conflict escalating.

The dispute began in 1949 when Kashmir was divided between the two countries, with India receiving the wealthier portion (→ 1/9).

First woman High Court judge appointed

Aug 12. Judge Elizabeth Lane, aged 60, today became the country's first woman High Court judge. She will sit in the Probate, Admiralty and Divorce Division and be addressed as Your Lordship in court. The appointment is her fourth legal first: she was the first woman county court judge, the first woman divorce commissioner and the first woman to preside over one of the Courts of the Inner London Sessions.

Judge Lane became a barrister in 1940, and made legal history six years later when she argued a murder appeal in the Lords. Her new job means a salary increase of £2,700 up to £8,000 (→ 30/9/65).

Judge Elizabeth Lane in her robes.

1965

SEPTEMBER

Su	Mo	Tu	We	Th	Fr	Sa
			1	2	3	4
5	6	7	8	9	10	11
12	13	14	15	16	17	18
19	20	21	22	23	24	25
26	27	28	29	30		

1. New York: UN Secretary-General U Thant appeals to India and Pakistan to end their clashes in Kashmir (→ 8).

2. London: The death of the Speaker of the Commons cuts Wilson's majority to two (→ 28).

2. Israel: David Ben-Gurion is expelled from the Mapai party.

6. India: Indian troops launch a full-scale invasion of Pakistan as the Pakistanis mount air-raids on New Delhi (→ 20).

10. Moscow: Brezhnev calls for an end to the Indo-Pakistani conflict (→ 13).

10. US: Yale University says a map dating from 1440 appears to prove that the Vikings discovered North America.

11. Paris: De Gaulle announces that France will leave NATO in 1969 (→ 12/4/66).

13. India: The Pakistanis bomb Bombay (→ 20).

16. London: Wilson marks the tenth anniversary of ITV, saying he enjoys "Coronation Street".

20. New York: The UN Security Council orders India and Pakistan to stop fighting.→

24. Mauritius: The island becomes independent within the Commonwealth (→ 7/11).

27. New York: The Argentine foreign minister restates to the UN his country's claim to the Falkland Islands.

28. Blackpool: Wilson tells the Labour Party he would rather fight another election than do a deal with the Liberals.

29. UK: Aston Martin presents the DB6, its first four-seater.

30. UK: EMI begins selling LP records through 3,000 grocers for 12/6d. each.

30. London: Judge Elizabeth Lane is sworn in as Britain's first High Court judge.

DEATH

4. German-born French doctor, musician, theologian and missionary Dr Albert Schweitzer, 1952 Nobel Prize winner (*14/1/1875).→

India and Pakistan at war over Kashmir

Sept 22. Pakistani war planes today raided the Sikh holy city of Amritsar,.as the war between India and Pakistan took a turn for the worse just hours before UN observers are due to start monitoring a cease-fire in the border conflict. The war, which began at the beginning of the month over rival claims on Kashmir, is the biggest threat to world peace since the 1939-45 conflict, according to Britain's Prime Minister, Harold Wilson.

The United Nations Secretary-General, U Thant, appealed for a halt to the fighting as soon as Pakistani troops crossed the 1949 cease-fire line into Jammu three weeks ago, but the battle has since moved from the mountains to the cities, with India invading Pakistan and striking at Lahore 15 miles across the border, followed by a Pakistani air raid on Bombay.

Mr Bhutto, Pakistan's Foreign Minister, has said his country is ready to fight "for a thousand years", while India claims to have destroyed about half Pakistan's total of 400 tanks in the fighting around Lahore.

Pakistan has offered to withdraw its troops from Kashmir if a plebiscite is held, an act which India claims is merely designed to wreck the UN peace moves. At the same time China and Russia are sabre-rattling, with Moscow condemning "incendiary statements" from Peking (→ 19/1/66).

The Indian army prepare their guns for an assault on Pakistani troops.

Nasser protests at curfew in Aden

Sept 25. President Nasser of Egypt today cancelled a meeting with a British Foreign Minister, George Thomson, in protest at Britain's suspension of the constitution in Aden. Egypt believes the timing of the suspension, while Mr Thomson was in Cairo, was designed as personal snub to President Nasser, who is on the record as supporting anti-British activities in Aden.

The constitution was suspended, and the British High Commissioner took over personal rule, after Aden ministers refused to condemn the guerrilla National Liberation Front for its assassination of the Speaker of the Aden parliament. The situation could not continue where ministers "gave moral support to the other side," he said (→ 7/10).

English believe in God, but prefer TV

Sept 19. Ninety-four per cent of the English population belong to a church, according to a Gallup poll commissioned by ABC Television. It is based on a sample of 2,211 people of whom two-thirds said they are Church of England. Only two per cent said they did not believe in God. Another 14 per cent were undecided, and the rest either believed in a personal God or a vital spirit.

A fifth claimed to go to church on most Sundays, but when they were asked about last Sunday only ten per cent had been to church, while 79 per cent had watched television. Compared with a 1957 survey, church-going had fallen by 14 per cent and television viewing had risen by 49 per cent.

Saint of Lambarene buried by his lepers

Albert Schweitzer, always working.

Sept 4. In a grave dug by lepers on the fringes of the primaeval forest, Dr Albert Schweitzer, The Saint of Lambarene, as he was called, was laid to rest today, aged 90. Hospital workers and lepers wept and prayed as African girls piled tropical flowers on the coffin. A choir sang "Ach bleib mit Deiner Gnade" (Rest with Your Grace).

When he was 3l, Schweitzer, a doctor of philosophy, theology and music, gave up everything to study medicine and then establish a hospital in Equatorial Africa. The 1952 award of the Nobel Peace Prize brought him worldwide acclaim. More recently critics claimed his hospital facilities were primitive and his attitude towards Africans dismissive.

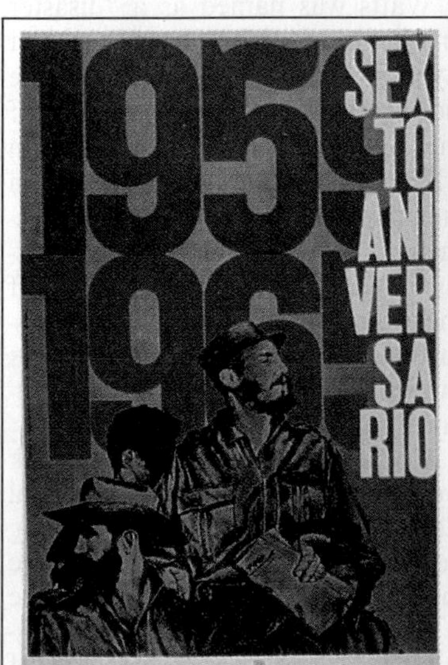

Six years of Cuban revolution.

Ready, Steady, Go: pop cults start here

Cathy McGowan, uncrowned queen of television's rock and roll ravers.

Sept 15. What makes a hit television show? What sends a pop song to the top of the charts? Whatever it is, the two magic ingredients come together on ITV's "Ready Steady Go", which has just begun its third but possibly last series as Britain's most popular and influential live music show.

RSG, as devotees call it, arrived on screen in August 1963, just as Beatlemania took hold of Britain. Rock groups played live in front of an audience which, dressed in whatever was the latest trend, gave the programme a uniquely fashionable and unpredictable feel. One of the hosts, Cathy McGowan, soon became known as "Queen of the Mods", and for millions of teenagers the show's boast ("the weekend starts here") became true.

The list of bands which have gained their big break on the Friday evening show include the Rolling Stones, the Kinks, the Animals, Manfred Mann and the Who. As well as these top British artists, RSG has featured major American acts like Ike and Tina Turner, Stevie Wonder and James Brown.

According to producer Vicki Wickham, the secret of RSG's success is that they book only acts that they like; where they are on the charts doesn't matter, though a spot on the show is often a pointer to success.

Julie Christie, already well-known for her role in "Billy Liar", stars in "Darling", the story of an amoral, narcissistic London model girl.

1965

OCTOBER

Su	Mo	Tu	We	Th	Fr	Sa
					1	2
3	4	5	6	7	8	9
10	11	12	13	14	15	16
17	18	19	20	21	22	23
24	25	26	27	28	29	30
31						

3. Washington: Johnson says all refugees from Castro's Cuba are welcome to come to the US (→ 4).

4. Havana: Castro reveals that Che Guevara has left Cuba "to fight imperialism abroad" (→ 10/10/67).

4. New York: Pope Paul VI becomes the first Pope to visit the western hemisphere as he arrives to address the UN (→ 15).

6. London: Heath says he will take Britain into the EEC if he is elected (→ 30/11/66).

7. Aden: Police use tear gas to disperse demonstrating students (→ 1/3/67).

8. Madrid: The International Olympic Committee says East and West Germany will compete separately in 1968.

12. Moscow: Eight Soviet soccer stars are banned from playing for life for being "incorrigible drunks".

14. London: Bertrand Russell tears up his Labour Party card in protest at British support for the US in Vietnam.

15. Rome: The Vatican Council says that all Jews cannot be blamed for the death of Christ (→ 8/12).

17. UK: A body found in a shallow grave in the Pennines is identified as missing schoolgirl Lesley Ann Downey (→ 21).

21. UK: Police discover a boy's body in the Pennines.→

26. London: The Queen writes to Ian Smith saying she hopes a negotiated solution is possible to the Rhodesian crisis.→

27. London: 36 die when an airliner crashes on landing at Heathrow Airport.

28. London: The Murder (Abolition of the Death Penalty) Bill passes its final stages (→ 8/11).

29. US: The US explodes an 80 kiloton H-bomb over the Aleutian Islands (→ 17/1/66).

30. Vietnam: US planes bomb a friendly village by mistake, killing 48 and injuring 55 (→ 24/12).

Two charged with "Moors murders"

Ian Brady, an alleged killer.

Oct 28. Police used decoy cars to foil demonstrators outside a Cheshire courthouse today as Ian Brady, aged 27, and Myra Hindley, aged 23, were charged with the murder of a ten-year-old girl. The body of Lesley Ann Downey was found after a police search on Saddleworth Moor 13 days ago, and an intensive search continues for further bodies. RAF photo-reconnaissance bombers have been called in to assist.

Among the crowd of 200 outside the court at Hyde were Lesley Ann's father and uncle, who tried to wrench open the door of the decoy car as it drove past. Others in the crowd shouted insults at the vehicle. Neither Brady, a stock-clerk, nor Hindley, a typist, spoke during the hearing (→ 19/4/66).

Wilson fails to stop Smith's UDI gamble

Oct 29. Harold Wilson's dramatic flight to Rhodesia, in an attempt to head off Ian Smith's gamble on a "unilateral declaration of independence", has failed. After a midnight confrontation between the two prime ministers, a British spokesman said "The door can still be considered ajar". In fact, Mr Smith did not budge an inch from his demand that the colony be granted independence, with the white voters keeping political power. The British say the black majority must have a voice (→ 5/11). ▷

John, Paul, George and Ringo get gongs

The Beatles, MBE, line up after seeing the Queen at Buckingham Palace.

Oct 26. The Beatles duly received their MBEs today, but the scenes outside Buckingham Palace were hardly as decorous as such occasions usually merit. Driven in a Rolls-Royce, the four Beatles swept through the gates, accompanied only by their manager Brian Epstein.

As they made their way to the Royal Investiture, crowds of teenage girls struggled with hundreds of police, specially brought in to control the excitement. As bemused tourists stared, the youngsters screamed, shouted, waved banners, and generally proved that nowhere is immune to Beatlemania.

Inside the Palace, far from the frenzy, the Beatles, like everyone else attending the Investiture, enjoyed the pomp and circumstance of this great occasion. As the Lord Chamberlain called their names, they stepped forward to meet Her Majesty and receive their honours.

The Queen was reported to have asked them: "How long have you been together now?" Quipped Ringo: "Forty years" (→ 1/6/67).

Map shows Vikings discovered America

Oct 11. Published today is a map of a large island west of Greenland, inscribed "Vinland – a new land discovered by Bjarni and Leif Eriksson, extremely fertile, even having vines". Bjarni and Leif were Vikings, who sailed the "Western Ocean" in the 11th Century.

The map shows Vinland to have a sea passage to an inland bay like Hudson's Bay and a deep estuary to the south like the St.Lawrence. It was drawn on parchment which has been dated to 1440, some 50 years before Columbus landed.

It was found in 1957 in a vellum volume about a mediaeval expedition to China, and given to modern Vinland's Yale University.

Sukarno survives a coup in Indonesia

Oct 1. President Ahmed Sukarno of Indonesia today survived an attempted coup believed to have been started by Communists. Details are still not clear, but it appears that loyal army units headed by the Defence Minister, General Nasution, put down a rebellion which was started by a lieutenant-colonel in the Palace Guard.

First reports say six senior military officers were kidnapped by the plotters and forced to make radio announcements that Sukarno had been toppled. Sukarno proclaimed Indonesia's independence in 1945, but today his formula for retaining power by striking a balance between the army and the Communists looks shaky (→ 12/3/66).

Tallest building in Britain is opened

Oct 7. The slim 620-foot Post Office Tower, the tallest building in Britain, was opened today by the Prime Minister. It has Europe's fastest lifts to the public viewing gallery and a revolving circular restaurant. Anthony Wedgwood Benn, who is the Postmaster-General, called it the Big Ben of the 20th Century (→ 22/8/66).

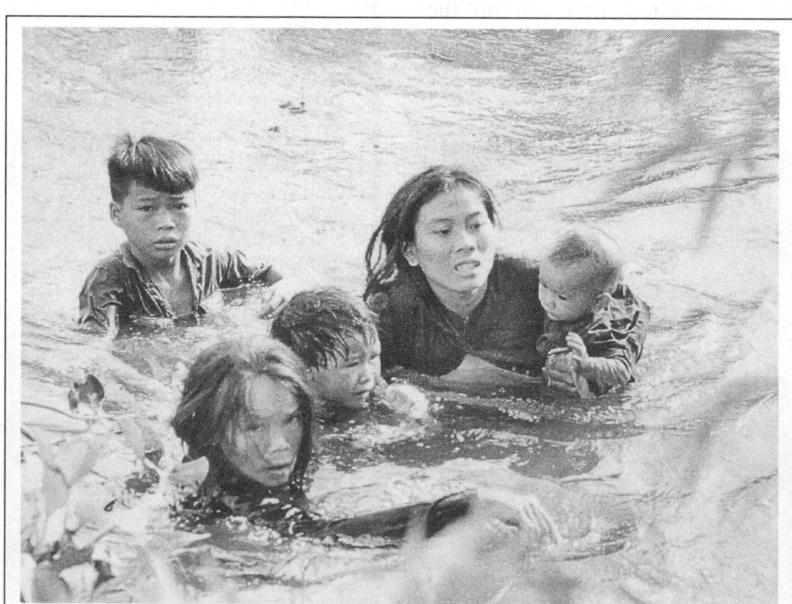

A Vietnamese mother wades across a river with her four children, as they all seek to escape the bombs raining down from American aircraft.

1965

NOVEMBER

Su	Mo	Tu	We	Th	Fr	Sa
	1	2	3	4	5	6
7	8	9	10	11	12	13
14	15	16	17	18	19	20
21	22	23	24	25	26	27
28	29	30				

1. UK: Seven die as hurricane-force winds batter Britain.

4. Paris: De Gaulle will stand for re-election as President (→ 19/12).

5. Rhodesia: Ian Smith declares a state of emergency, insisting it is not a prelude to declaration of independence.→

8. London: The Murder (Abolition of the Death Penalty) Bill and Race Relations Bill become law (→ 27/4/67).

9. US: The biggest power cut in American history blacks out New York City and parts of nine states.

9. London: Wilson drops plans for steel nationalisation (→ 28/7/67).

12. Rhodesia: Britain's governor, Sir Humphrey Gibbs, defies Smith's order to resign (→ 12).

12. New York: The UN condemns Rhodesian UDI (→ 16).

16. London: The Southern Rhodesia Bill, authorising sanctions against Ian Smith's regime, gets Royal Assent.→

18. London: Provisional timetables for Concorde flights are issued: London to New York in three hours, Tokyo in 13.

22. US: Cassius Clay beats Floyd Patterson in Las Vegas to keep his world heavyweight boxing title (→ 21/5/66).

22. London: The inquiry into Timothy John Evans' conviction begins (→ 18/10/66).

24. London: The government introduce an experimental 70mph speed limit on motorways (→ 17/5/66).

26. Africa: France launches its first satellite, A1 "Asterix".

DEATHS

6. French-born US composer Edgar Varese (*22/12/1883).

16. Irish statesman William Thomas Cosgrave, first President of the Executive Council of the Irish Free State (*6/6/1880).→

White Rhodesia breaks with Britain

Ian Smith, the premier of Rhodesia, at a press conference at the Commonwealth Relations Office last month.

Nov 11. Rhodesia, Britain's last colony in Africa, is on a war footing tonight after Ian Smith, the Prime Minister, issued the long-expected Unilateral Declaration of Independence. He chose 11am on Remembrance Day, the anniversary of the 1918 armistice, for his radio broadcast.

He read a proclamation that echoed the 18th-century American Declaration of Independence: "Whereas in the course of human affairs history has shown that it may become necessary for a people ... to assume amongst other nations the separate and equal status to which they are entitled ..." In this context, the "people" are not the four million Africans in the colony, but the 220,000 whites.

Mr Smith's government has assumed wide powers to impose rationing, control currency transfers abroad, and impose censorship of press, radio and television. The Governor, Sir Humphrey Gibbs, sacked by Mr Smith, has responded by sacking Mr Smith. In London, Mr Wilson announced that all ties with the rebel regime have been broken, that economic sanctions will be imposed, but that armed force will not be used.

The white Rhodesians' UDI has been widely denounced as a foolhardy adventure; for Mr Wilson in 10 Downing Street it poses a particularly painful dilemma. Commonwealth leaders in black Africa are already calling on Britain to take immediate and decisive action to crush the rebellion, but many people in Britain have close relatives in Rhodesia; would they support tough measures – by a Labour government, too – against their kith and kin? (→ 12)

Wilson draws up economic sanctions to bring Rhodesia to heel

Nov 16. Parliament sat until nearly 2am today in a rush to pass emergency legislation imposing sanctions against Ian Smith's illegal breakaway regime in Rhodesia. Lord Gardiner, the Lord Chancellor, described Mr Smith's action as 'one of the most irresponsible acts in the history of the Commonwealth". MPs talked of treason.

Government ministers told MPs and peers that the unilateral declaration of independence must be countered swiftly and effectively by action to restore constitutional rule, but they have decided against the use of British military force and will rely instead on moral and economic pressure. The cabinet has accepted expert Whitehall advice that sanctions can work without imposing great suffering on Rhodesians remaining loyal to the Crown. The broad plan is to starve Rhodesia of overseas credits, and there will also be no customers for her tobacco crop. In Salisbury the Smith regime appealed to the Rhodesian armed forces and civil service for their loyalty.

The rebel leader said: "My government is the only one in a position to maintain law and order." He claimed that before Mr Wilson visited Salisbury on the eve of the UDI declaration the Queen told him "Don't sell the white man down the river". In Downing Street this was denounced as a lie.

As the Queen's representative Sir Humphrey Gibbs, the Governor of Rhodesia, said again that he will not yield to Smith regime pressure on him to resign. He has reported to Whitehall that he is now isolated in Government House, but is not under house arrest. Mr Smith said: "We have no governor and British ministers are unscrupulously trying to manipulate the Queen. She is our Queen. We are loyal to the Queen of Rhodesia" (→ 1/12).

Sir Humphrey Gibbs, the Queen's beleaguered man in Rhodesia, has been awarded the KCVO.

Housewife to probe TV sex and violence

Nov 29. New demands for BBC-TV's cleansing were made today by the housewife and "Clean Up TV" campaigner Mrs Mary Whitehouse, when she announced the setting-up of the National Viewers' and Listeners' Association. Formed to tackle "BBC bad taste and irresponsibility", the NVLA claims to have nearly 500,000 supporters. Mrs Whitehouse called for the BBC to be made more accountable both financially and in the way it monitors the morality of its output. She cited a recent play showing a crucifix being used as a pipe rack as an example of "bad taste".

Whitehouse: self-appointed censor.

Mobutu in replay of Congo army coup

Nov 25. General Joseph-Desire Mobutu, the Congolese army commander, who briefly took power in the 1960 post-independence chaos, staged a replay in Leopoldville today. After weeks of squabbling between would-be prime ministers, Mobutu stepped in and announced the sacking of President Joseph Kasavubu and the imposition of army rule for five years. He then went along to the National Assembly and told the bemused deputies that the army would nonetheless "remain out of politics". Though various regional rebellions by left and right wing regimes appear to have been quashed, the underlying tensions remain (→ 31/5/66).

Customs act as minis rise out of tax reach

Nov 5. Customs men have clamped down on rising skirts. Mini-skirts made famous by models like Jean "The Shrimp" Shrimpton have forced them to change their regulations. Until now length determined whether a dress was a woman's, and liable to ten per cent purchase tax, or a child's and so tax-free.

But they've become so short that officials are worried traders will pass one off as the other. From January 1, a dress will be taxed on bust size, too, it was announced today. Anything over 32 inches will be classed as a woman's dress.

The appeal of the mini, launched by the French designer Courreges and popularised by British talents like Mary Quant, has not only shocked the tax man. Moral watchdogs have condemned it as a reflection of declining standards and the rise of the permissive society.

Yet despite the raised eyebrows the hemline shows no signs of falling. Young women, and some older ones, see it as the fashion epitome of their new freedoms, particularly, since the advent of the Pill, sexual ones.

Jean Shrimpton's hemline shocked racegoers in Melbourne this month.

Cosgrave, first President of Ireland, dies

Nov 16. W.T. Cosgrave, the first President of the Irish Free State and always affectionately known as "WT", died today, aged 85.

He ruled the Free State for ten years from 1922, after the two men preferred before him – Arthur Griffith and Michael Collins – both died. He held the fledgling state together through the civil war and dealt fearlessly with the gunmen. He was as good a judge of horses as of men, always an asset in Ireland, and regularly spent Saturdays riding to hounds or at top race meetings.

Haltered together by strips of cloth, a chain of Viet Cong prisoners is led by US Marines, who captured the guerrillas close to Da Nang.

1965

DECEMBER

Su	Mo	Tu	We	Th	Fr	Sa
			1	2	3	4
5	6	7	8	9	10	11
12	13	14	15	16	17	18
19	20	21	22	23	24	25
26	27	28	29	30	31	

1. London: Wilson says Britain has offered Zambia military aid and proposes tougher Rhodesian sanctions.→

3. US: A white jury convicts three Ku Klux Klansmen of murdering Viola Liuzzo.

8. Rome: The Vatican Council ends after three years.

9. Moscow: Nikolai Podgorny succeeds Anastas Mikoyan as Soviet head of state (→ 8/4/66).

10. Stockholm: Nobel Prizes go to Sin-Itiro Tomonaga (Japan), Julian Schwinger (US) and Richard Feynman (US), all Physics; Robert Woodward (US, Chemistry); Francois Jacob, Andre Lwoff and Jacques Monod (France, Medicine); Mikhail Sholokhov (USSR, Literature); and in Oslo to UNICEF (Peace).→

15. London: Goldie the eagle escapes from London Zoo for the second time this year.

21. London: Plans for a Road Safety Bill include legal alcohol limits and random breath-tests (→ 29/1/66).

22. London: Roy Jenkins becomes Home Secretary and Barbara Castle Minister of Transport in a reshuffle.

24. Vietnam: Both sides agree to a Christmas truce (→ 8/1/66).

27. Rhodesia: Petrol rationing is introduced (→ 12/1/66).

30. Manila: Ferdinand Marcos is sworn in as the sixth President of the Philippines.

DEATHS

16. British author William Somerset Maugham (*25/1/1874).→

22. British journalist and broadcaster Richard Frederick Dimbleby (*25/5/13).→

HITS OF 1965

Tears.

A walk in the black forest.

QUOTE OF THE YEAR

"Political power grows out of the barrel of a gun."

Mao Tse-tung, from "Quotations from Chairman Mao Tse-tung", 1965.

Richard Dimbleby dies of cancer

The master of ceremonies is dead.

Dec 22. He was known jokingly as "gold microphone-in-waiting" and relished the title. Richard Dimbleby, Britain's outstanding broadcaster, died today of cancer at the age of 52. Dimbleby was a unique commentator, covering every major Royal occasion – the Coronation and the weddings of Princess Margaret and Princess Alexandra among them – during 27 years with the BBC.

As a war correspondent, Richard Dimbleby broadcast from a Lancaster bomber during a 1,000-bomber raid over Germany, and covered the fall of Berlin, using a smuggled transmitter. He also took part in the first transatlantic satellite transmission (→ 4/1/66).

De Gaulle wins but by lowest margin

Dec 19. Although he was elected for seven more years, Charles de Gaulle suffered a setback today in the second round of the presidential election. His majority was the lowest since he founded the Fifth Republic.

In the first round there was no clear majority, a sign of waning popularity. More than half the voters backed de Gaulle today, but a surprisingly large number in southern and central France favoured his Socialist rival, Francois Mitterrand (→ 15/2/66).

Oil rig collapses: 13 die

Dec 27. An oil rig with 32 men on board collapsed and sank today as 20-foot waves smashed into the North Sea structure. Two of the rig's ten legs buckled in the rough seas, and 13 members of the crew drowned when they were thrown into the icy water. Snow storms later hampered attempts by RAF divers to locate anyone still trapped inside the giant Sea Gem rig, the pride of British Petroleum's fleet.

Survivors said there had been no warning that the £2.5 million oil platform, 40 miles east of Grimsby, was in danger of capsizing. Many had been in their bunks at the end of the night shift when the deck suddenly tilted into the sea. For a moment its fall was arrested and some crewmen jumped clear, but others were still fighting for a way out as the rig completely inverted.

There had been no time for an SOS alert, but a passing British steamer saw the legs buckle and men waving a white sheet. Coastguards were called out and they launched a major rescue operation involving lifeboats and helicopters.

One rig crewman, Larry Burton, aged 23, said: "I was thrown out of bed and then made a dash for the top of the platform. It went down like hell." BP said an inquiry would establish the cause.

US astronauts meet in space rendezvous

Dec 15. Two American Gemini spacecraft achieved the first rendezvous in space today. They then flew side-by-side, only six to ten feet apart, for two orbits.

Gemini 7, crewed by Frank Bormann and James A. Lovell Jr, had been in orbit for 11 days when Gemini 6, with Walter P. Schirra Jr and Thomas P. Stafford blasted off from Cape Kennedy at 8.37am. During the next few hours Schirra fired the rocket motors several times to edge into the higher orbit of the other craft.

The meeting finally came over the Pacific, during Gemini 6's fourth orbit. After four hours side-by-side, Gemini 6 manoeuvred back to a lower orbit and will return to earth tomorrow. Gemini 7 will remain aloft for three more days (→17/3/66).

The Gemini 6 rocket is launched.

UNICEF is awarded Nobel Peace Prize

Dec 10. To honour its achievements for the world's children, UNICEF – the United Nations Children's Fund – was awarded the Nobel Peace Prize in Oslo tonight.

The fund, founded 19 years ago, is dedicated to providing care for deprived infants. Other Nobel awards included the literature prize to Russian writer Mikhail Sholokhov for "And Quiet Flows the Don", a war novel.

Wilson staunches flow of Smith's oil

Dec 17. Five weeks after the illegal declaration of independence by Rhodesia, the British government today tightened the screws on the rebel colony by imposing oil sanctions and asking other countries to join in. Edward Heath, leader of the Conservative opposition in the House of Commons, called it a "grave development" and said it could cause "individual hardship" to Rhodesians (→27).

Arts: Maugham slides off razor's edge

On his 90th birthday **William Somerset Maugham** declared: "There are moments when I have such an eagerness for death that I could fly to it as to the arms of a lover. It seems to offer the final absolute freedom." On his 91st birthday last January he said "Oh hell, another birthday". He will not have to face any more. He died on December 16, after being taken ill at the Villa Mauresque, his luxurious home at Cap Ferrat.

Maugham was one of the richest authors alive, having sold more than 80 million copies of his works. "The Razor's Edge" alone sold 2.5 million, but the only novel of his that he would admit to being any good was the semi-autobiographical "Of Human Bondage".

In 1959 he sailed on a sentimental journey to the East – Bangkok, Malaya, Japan – where so many of his short stories, such as "Rain", are set. Many judges rate them above his novels. In them his storytelling gifts in plain, swift prose were unsurpassed.

An agnostic, a pessimist and a sardonic observer of human frailty, Maugham's philosophy was a bleak and lonely stoicism. His family relationships were never happy. His own parents died in his infancy. He divorced Syrie, daughter of Dr Barnardo, who, he said, "terrorised" him. A few years ago he adopted Alan Searle, his secretary and companion of 30 years, as his "son". The courts annulled the adoption and legitimised the claim of his daughter, Lady John Hope.

Somerset Maugham has died at 91.

When he was 77, Maugham appeared on television to read his stories. He would have been ideal for BBC 2, the second BBC network, which opened this year promising alternative intelligent programmes, especially in the arts, with the "Late Night Line-Up" discussion programme often focusing on new works.

The Royal Opera House this year witnessed the delayed first performance of **Schoenberg's** epic Biblical opera "Moses und Aron" (written in 1932); the partnership of **Fonteyn** and **Nureyev** in "Romeo and Juliet" by **Prokofiev** now choreographed by **Kenneth Macmillan**; and what proved to be the last performance by **Maria Callas** on any stage – in "Tosca", last year's sensation.

Dusty Springfield, voted top female singer, at the Royal Variety Show.

Steve McQueen starred this year as "The Cincinnati Kid" and is now one of Hollywood's top stars.

1966

JANUARY

Su	Mo	Tu	We	Th	Fr	Sa
						1
2	3	4	5	6	7	8
9	10	11	12	13	14	15
16	17	18	19	20	21	22
23	24	25	26	27	28	29
30	31					

1. Central African Republic: Colonel Jean Bokassa takes office following a coup earlier this week.

4. London: 4,000 attend a memorial service in Westminster Abbey for Richard Dimbleby.

7. London: Britain, Canada and Australia are to mount drought relief operations in central Africa and Rhodesia.

11. Nigeria: Commonwealth leaders begin a conference on Rhodesia in Lagos.→

12. Rhodesia: Three visiting Labour MPs are jostled and jeered at by a white crowd in the capital, Salisbury (→13).

13. Rhodesia: The regime expels the three visiting Labour MPs (→20).

17. UK: Leading bakers put one penny on the price of a standard loaf, which now costs around 1/3d halfpenny.

19. Canberra: Menzies resigns as Prime Minister of Australia after a record 16 years in office (→21/6).

20. London: The Queen commutes the death sentence on a black prisoner in Rhodesia (→31).

24. France: 117 die when an Air India airliner crashes into Mont Blanc (→4/2).

28. Los Angeles: Film actress Hedy Lamarr is arrested for shoplifting.

31. Vietnam: US planes resume bombing raids after a 37-day pause (→7/2).

31. London: The Board of Trade bans nearly all trade between Britain and Rhodesia (→15/3).

DEATHS

1. French statesman Vincent Auriol, President 1947-53 (*27/8/1884).

11. Indian statesman Lal Bahadur Shastri, PM 1964-66 (*2/10/04).→

11. Swiss sculptor Alberto Giacometti (*10/10/01).

16. Nigerian statesman Alhaji Sir Abubakar Tafawa Balewa, PM 1960-66 (*10/12/12).→

Indian Prime Minister, Lal Shastri, dies

Jan 11. Mr Lal Bahadur Shastri, India's Prime Minister, died of a heart attack at Tashkent in the early hours of this morning, shortly after signing a new agreement for peace with Pakistan. He was struck down soon after returning to his quarters from a farewell banquet given by Mr Kosygin, the Russian Prime Minister, who had acted as mediator between Mr Shastri and the Pakistan President, General Ayub Khan. His body will be flown to New Delhi to be burnt on the banks of the Jumna where Nehru and Gandhi were cremated.→

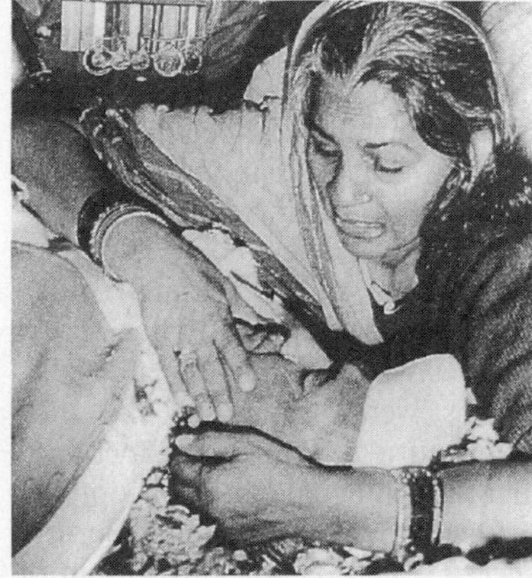

Mrs Shastri mourns her husband.

Nehru's daughter Indira is new Indian PM

Jan 19. Mrs Indira Gandhi, daughter of Mr Nehru and newly-elected Prime Minister of India, pledged tonight that she would "strive to create what my father used to call a climate of peace". She added that she would honour the peace agreement with Pakistan signed in Tashkent by her predecessor, Mr Shastri, only hours before he died.

Mrs Gandhi, aged 48, beat Morarji Desai, 69, the former Finance Minister, by 355 votes to 199, to be elected premier. Crowds gathered outside Parliament House cheered her wildly when the result became known (→27/3).

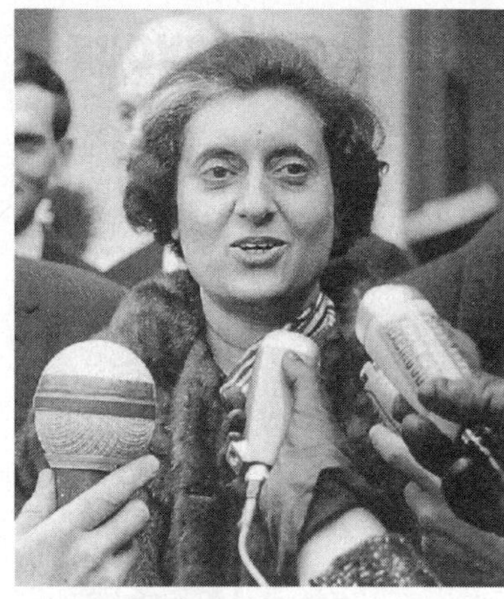

India gains a new Gandhi.

UDI will be over in "weeks not months"

Jan 12. A fierce verbal duel between Mr Wilson and Sir Albert Margai, the British and Sierra Leone prime ministers, occupied all the afternoon at the Commonwealth conference in Lagos today.

When Sir Albert called for immediate British military action against rebel Rhodesia, Mr Wilson jumped up and put a series of questions: "How many divisions did Sir Albert think would be needed? How would the troops be conveyed to landlocked Rhodesia? Would the they be ferried across the Zambezi under fire?" Mr Wilson said any expedition against Rhodesia would cost the lives of many thousands of Africans as well as Europeans.

After suggesting that those who advocated military action should examine the facts, Mr Wilson went on to argue that economic sanctions were already beginning to bite. Indeed, they "might well bring the rebellion to an end within a matter of weeks rather than months".

Though Britain has officially cut all ties with the rebel colony, that has not put an end to visits. Three Labour MPs have turned up in Salisbury on a "fact-finding mission". After a talk with Mr Smith, the Prime Minister, they announced they would hold a meeting in a hotel. About 400 whites crowded into the banqueting hall and shouted insults: "Communists", "Stupid nits", "Liars" and "You're yellow". The crowd surged forward, chanting South African rugby war cries; the MPs were grabbed, and beer and itching powder was poured on them. Plain-clothes policemen moved in (→13).

H-bomb is missing after mid-air crash

Jan 17. The nightmare of a nuclear accident became a reality today when an American B-52 bomber, carrying nuclear weapons, collided with a K-C 135 fuel tanker aircraft in mid-air over Spain.

Eight of the 14 crew on board the huge aircraft were killed, and an H-bomb, with an explosive capacity of more than a million tons of TNT, has fallen into the Atlantic Ocean off southern Spain.

Emergency measures were immediately implemented by the Pentagon in Washington. The American Strategic Air Command has despatched a squad of aircraft and 1,000 soldiers to look for the missing bomb, but so far without success (→14/2).

New "breath test" for drunken drivers

Jan 29. A bill permitting random roadside breathalyser tests was published yesterday. It sets a limit of 80 milligrammes of alcohol in 100cc of blood. It becomes an offence to drive or try to drive with higher levels. A driver behind the wheel of a stationary car will be exempt, but he may have to prove he intended to wait until fit to proceed.

The motoring organisations object to the proposals as infringements of liberty. The Pedestrians' Association welcomes them.

George Harrison with his new wife, Patti Boyd; they met on set of "A Hard Day's Night".

US troops launch biggest offensive of war

US physician Thomas Cole, his own head severely wounded, works on.

Jan 8. The "Iron Triangle", a Viet Cong jungle stronghold 20 miles north-west of Saigon, was attacked today by 8,000 US troops in the biggest American offensive of the Vietnam war. The area, riddled with tunnels, was pounded by B-52 heavy bombers and artillery before the troops went in. Observers say it was one of the heaviest barrages yet laid down in this war and it was an entirely American affair.

The old guidelines of US troops not being allowed to conduct offensives except at the request of the South Vietnamese have been swept away. Indeed, officials said the operation was kept secret from the Vietnamese for fear of betrayal by Viet Cong agents in the army (→31).

Politicians killed in Nigerian army coup

Jan 16. Just ten days after the Commonwealth conference on rebel Rhodesia was held in Lagos, Nigeria, the Nigerian government has been overthrown in a military coup. At least 50 politicians and army officers have been killed. "We wanted to get rid of rotten and corrupt ministers and political parties," said Major Chukwuma Nzugwa, who led the coup. He is an Ibo from Eastern Nigeria; many of those killed, including the Prime Minister, Sir Abubakar Tafawa Balewa, are Hausa Moslems from the North. A backlash seems inevitable (→24/2).

Former chief Tafawa Balewa.

1966

FEBRUARY

Su	Mo	Tu	We	Th	Fr	Sa
		1	2	3	4	5
6	7	8	9	10	11	12
13	14	15	16	17	18	19
20	21	22	23	24	25	26
27	28					

1. London: The Government increases its squeeze on bank lending.

3. London: The Companies Bill, under which firms would have to reveal donations to political parties, is published.

4. Japan: 133 are killed when an airliner crashes in Tokyo Bay (→5/3).

7. US: Johnson and South Vietnamese premier Nguyen Cao Ky open talks in Honolulu (→15).

9. London: The Government announces plans for a prototype fast-breeder reactor at Dounreay, in Scotland.

10. UK: Actor Jack Hawkins leaves hospital 17 days after an operation for throat cancer.

10. UK: Watneys puts a penny on a pint of bitter, which now costs 1/8d.

14. Spain: It is reported that an H-bomb lost when a US bomber crashed last month has been found (→7/4).

15. Paris: De Gaulle offers Ho Chi Minh French aid in finding a settlement of the Vietnam war (→8/4).

19. London: Christopher Mayhew resigns as Navy Minister over "dangerously mistaken" defence policies.

22. Kampala: Prime Minister Milton Obote jails five ministers, seizing "all powers of the government of Uganda" (→10/3).

23. Rome: Premier Aldo Moro forms a new cabinet.

24. US: Governor George Wallace's wife, Lurleen, enters the race to succeed him as Alabama governor (→3/5).

27. UK: Shell Oil reports it has struck oil in the Trucial State of Muscat and Oman.

28. London: Wilson calls an election for March 31 (→1/4).

DEATHS

1. US actor and director Buster Keaton, born Joseph Francis Keaton (*4/10/1895).→

20. US commander Admiral Chester William Nimitz (*24/2/1885).

Nkrumah is toppled during peace trip

Feb 24. Ghana's President, Kwame Nkrumah, was welcomed in Peking today by a 2l-gun salute, and then told by Chinese Communist leaders that back home people were dancing in the streets after the army had seized power and overthrown his regime. Grim-faced, he said he would continue with his peace mission to Vietnam.

Nkrumah, the self-styled Osagyefo or Redeemer, won independence for Ghana in 1957, but his dictatorial rule alienated the people. The only resistance to the army's coup came from the 200-strong Russian-trained bodyguard at Flagstaff House, the presidential palace in Accra. Over 1,000 political prisoners have been freed (→3/6).

Melancholy comic, Buster Keaton, dies

Buster Keaton, filming in 1921.

Feb 1. It will always be debated whether Chaplin or stone-faced Buster Keaton, who died today aged 70, is the greater silent film comedian. Keaton began as part of his parents' slapstick act and was nicknamed "Buster" by Houdini.

In Hollywood he made only ten feature films, from 1920-29, in which he piles disaster upon disaster, on steamboats, railway trains, liners or waterfalls. To each he reacts with ever more acrobatic but deadpan frenzy. Words are superfluous to his style, which finished with the coming of sound. ▷

Laker forms airline for cut-price tours

Feb 8. Freddie Laker, the man who turned British United Airways into Britain's largest independent carrier, is setting up an all-jet airline catering for the booming package holiday trade.

Mr Laker, aged 43, has bought three BAC One-Eleven 75-seater airliners at cost of £4 million. He started in the airline business with his £40 RAF pay-off in 1946, and is now reported to have amassed a personal fortune of more than £1 million. "I will make possible cheaper and longer holidays by efficiency and speedier travel," he said.

Demo at banned War Game showing

Feb 8. Supporters of the Campaign for Nuclear Disarmament picketed a showing of "The War Game", the controversial film about an H-bomb attack on Britain made by Peter Watkins for the BBC but banned from television transmission by the Corporation.

Before the showing at the National Film Theatre, Kenneth Adam, the BBC's director of television, said that the BBC had taken its decision "carefully, reluctantly, I hope responsibly, I know independently". Opponents of the BBC's ban blame government influence for the decision.

Soviet writers are jailed for slander

Feb 14. Two Russian writers, Andrey Sinyavsky and Yuri Daniel, were sent to a labour camp for seven and five years today for "slandering the Soviet state". Their offence was to have smuggled their novels, which were suppressed, to the West to be published.

Both of them made history by refusing to plead guilty. "We had no wish to damage our country," said Daniel in court. John Gollan, secretary of the British Communist Party, said the trial had done a greater disservice than anything the two might have written.

1966

MARCH

Su	Mo	Tu	We	Th	Fr	Sa
		1	2	3	4	5
6	7	8	9	10	11	12
13	14	15	16	17	18	19
20	21	22	23	24	25	26
27	28	29	30	31		

1. London: Chancellor of Exchequer James Callaghan says Britain will switch to decimal currency in 1971 (→ 1/3/67).

3. London: The BBC announces plans to broadcast in colour next year (→ 1/7/67).

3. Guinea: President Sekou Toure steps down; Nkrumah becomes "President of Ghana and Guinea" (→ 4).

4. Accra: Britain and the US recognise the new Ghanaian regime, which severs ties with Guinea.

5. Japan: 130 die when a British Boeing 707 crashes into Mount Fuji (→ 31/8).

7. London: The Government says it will abolish National Assistance and create a new Ministry of Social Security.

8. Dublin: An IRA bomb destroys the Nelson Column.

10. Amsterdam: Anti-German protests mar the wedding of Princess Beatrix to former diplomat Claus von Amsberg.

10. Kampala: Obote abolishes the post of President.

12. Djakarta: Sukarno hands over power to the army under General Suharto after a bloodless coup (→ 11/8).

15. Madagascar: The RAF is granted a base from which to patrol the African coast for Rhodesian sanctions-busters (→ 4/4).

20. London: The World Cup goes missing from Westminster Central Hall (→ 27).

25. Switzerland: Four Germans and a Scot reach the top of the Eiger by the north face "direct route" for the first time.

26. UK: Mr S. Levy's Anglo wins the Grand National.

27. Washington: Mrs Gandhi arrives for talks with Johnson (→ 12/3/67).

29. Moscow: Brezhnev opens the 23rd Party Congress with a call for the US to end its involvement in Vietnam (→ 8/4).

31. S. Africa: Verwoerd's National Party retains power after the whites-only general election.

Pope and Archbishop end 400-year rift

The Pope and the Archbishop, after worshipping together at St. Peter's.

March 23. The first official meeting for 400 years between the heads of the Roman Catholic and Anglican churches took place in Rome today. The Pope and the Archbishop of Canterbury embraced and exchanged a "kiss of peace" in the Sistine Chapel. Both men made speeches in Latin and English. Pope Paul said: "You rebuild a bridge, which for centuries has lain fallen between the Church of Rome and the Church of Canterbury; a bridge of respect, of esteem and of charity."

There was an unofficial meeting in 1960 when Archbishop Fisher met the previous Pope. Today's meeting is part of a three-day visit to Rome by Dr Ramsey which represents a much more serious attempt at Christian unity. In private the two men have been dealing with such difficult issues as the Vatican line on mixed marriages.

Fierce opposition still exists. This morning three British ministers interrupted Dr Ramsey while he was celebrating Communion. They took off their coats showing display aprons with the words "Archbishop Ramsey is a traitor to Protestant Britain".

Arkle wins third Cheltenham Gold Cup

March 17. Arkle, the great Irish steeplechaser, today celebrated St. Patrick's Day in truly masterful style at Cheltenham, winning the Gold Cup, National Hunt racing's greatest prize, for the third year in succession, and putting in yet another convincing bid for consideration as the greatest jumper of all time.

This victory was no hard-fought battle, as had been his great tussles with Mill House in the last two Gold Cups. This time, despite a blunder at the 11th fence, which perturbed neither Pat Taaffe, his jockey, nor the champion himself, Arkle strolled home 30 lengths in front of a despairing field to record his 25th victory for his owner, Anne, Duchess of Westminster.

Arkle – the punters' number one.

First space docking by US astronauts

March 17. Astronauts Neil Armstrong and David Scott on board the US Gemini 8 spacecraft docked with the final stage of their Agena launcher today, the first time this crucial space manoeuvre has been successfully completed. Rendezvous and docking in orbit round the moon are vital for the success of the American moon landing planned for before 1970.

However, half an hour after the docking one of Gemini's small thruster rockets started firing in error, making the spacecraft spin and roll uncontrollably. Armstrong had to undock prematurely and land in the Pacific, two days earlier than scheduled (→4/4).

A man and his dog find lost World Cup

March 27. The World Cup, stolen a week ago from a stamp exhibition in Westminster Hall and subsequently the subject of a ransom demand to the Football Association, has been found in a South London garden by a mongrel called Pickles.

David Corbett, a Thames lighterman, saw his dog tearing at an object wrapped in newspaper. The bundle contained the solid gold Jules Rimet trophy, for which 16 nations will be battling in England in July, and whose loss caused great embarrassment in the football hierarchy (→30/7).

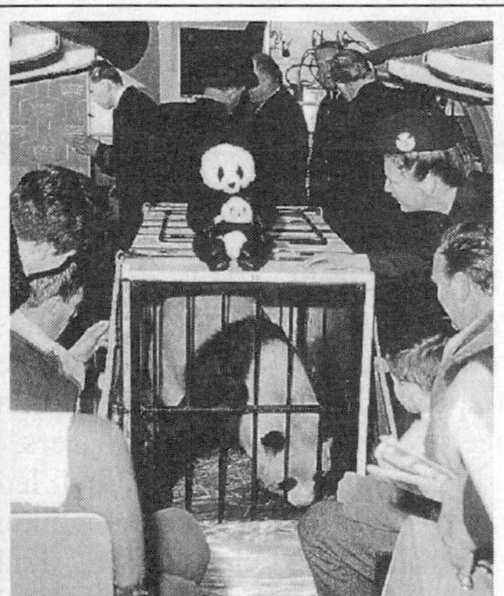

Chi-Chi, a giant panda, set off to meet a possible mate, An-An, but love failed to bloom, despite much human encouragement.

1966

APRIL

Su	Mo	Tu	We	Th	Fr	Sa
					1	2
3	4	5	6	7	8	9
10	11	12	13	14	15	16
17	18	19	20	21	22	23
24	25	26	27	28	29	30

1. UK: The British Airports Authority is formed.

4. USSR: The Soviet craft Luna X goes into orbit round the moon (→6/6).

4. Mozambique: A Greek tanker, laden with oil believed bound for Rhodesia, is intercepted by the Royal Navy (→22/7).

5. UK: Shell says a recent oil find off Great Yarmouth is of "considerable importance" (→1/6).

8. Vietnam: The US begins to evacuate Americans from Da Nang.

8. UK: Figures show that the number of illegitimate births in England and Wales has nearly doubled in the last ten years.

9. France: Sophia Loren marries Italian producer Carlo Ponti, despite the fact he is still married in Italy.

12. Paris: US Secretary of State Dean Rusk says France is not vital to NATO (→30/6).

14. UK: The Sussex Downs are designated an Area of Outstanding Natural Beauty.

18. US: "The Sound of Music" wins the Oscar for Best Film.

19. London: Selwyn Lloyd and Ernest Marples are out as Heath reshuffles the shadow cabinet.

19. London: Myra Hindley and Ian Brady go on trial at the Old Bailey for the "Moors Murders" (→6/5).

21. London: The State Opening of Parliament is televised for the first time.

25. London: Leslie O'Brien succeeds Lord Cromer as Governor of the Bank of England.

30. UK: Hoverlloyd begins the first regular cross-Channel hovercraft service, between Ramsgate and Calais.

DEATHS

2. British author Cecil Scott Forester, born Cecil Smith (*27/8/1899).

10. British author Evelyn Arthur St. John Waugh (*28/10/03).→

Storm clouds loom for triumphant Labour

Mr Wilson plays a little football with some young constituents in Huyton.

April 1. Labour now has a secure grip on power, with an overall majority of 96 after the general election. Harold Wilson said today, on his return to 10 Downing Street, "Now we have a clear mandate". In the new House of Commons there are 363 Labour, 253 Tory, 12 Liberals and two others.

This means that parliament can now settle down, instead of living in the shadow of an impending election as it has done during the near-stalemate situation of the last 18 months.

Mr Wilson hinted at once at unpopular measures which may be needed for Britain's economic health. However, the Rhodesia crisis was at the top of the Number 10 agenda tonight. Mr Wilson reckons that the illegal Smith regime may be readier for a settlement now it has had to abandon hopes of dealing with a Tory government.

The election has left Labour apparently in total command of British politics, with Mr Wilson having captured much of the middle ground, but economic problems persist, and a clash is obviously looming between government and unions over incomes restraint.

So, despite the new parliamentary arithmetic, Labour may be heading into stormy weather at a time when a Tory recovery could begin under Mr Heath (→23/5).

Julie Christie and Omar Sharif star in David Lean's "Dr Zhivago".

Brezhnev becomes top Soviet leader

April 8. Leonid Brezhnev, the Soviet Communist Party leader, emerged today clearly on top in the Kremlin after a reshuffle and a change of labels. Brezhnev, who had formed a collective leadership when Nikita Khrushchev was ousted in 1964, has taken the new title of general secretary. The new Soviet pecking order indicates that following him in order of importance, are Alexei Kosygin, the Prime Minister, Nikolai Podgorny, the President, and Mikhail Suslov, the party's leading ideologist.

Brezhnev is a long-time party machine man who, although owing his career to Khrushchev, was the leading organiser of the coup against him. There are already indications that many of the Khrushchev reforms will be slowed and even reversed (→ 12/6).

Australian troops fly into Vietnam

April 19. The advance party of the 4,500-man Australian task force being sent to fight alongside the Americans in Vietnam left Sydney last night. Among them were the first National Servicemen to leave Australia since World War II. An Army spokesman said: "This is a highly professional and specialised group so the proportion of National Servicemen is extremely low." Qantas has cancelled 16 flights to London, switching its Boeings to ferry the troops to Vietnam (→ 15/5).

Three modern girls modelling hair by Mary Quant and, of course, mini-skirts all round.

His novels will be a Waugh memorial

Waugh: the novelist as aristocrat.

April 10. Evelyn Waugh, the purest stylist among English novelists of his time, has died aged 62 at Combe Florey, Somerset, where he lived the life of a diehard Catholic squire. He repelled the 20th Century, refusing to have radio or television. He even affected an ear trumpet.

Youthful gaiety in the face of preposterous behaviour was the kernel of his early fiction, culminating in "A Handful of Dust" and "Scoop". His later novels, from "Brideshead Revisited" onwards, are marred for many by excessive Catholic nostalgia. Once he allowed his mask to slip, in "The Ordeal of Gilbert Pinfold", who heard voices vilifying him. It was a self-portrait.

The lost H-bomb is found in one piece

April 7. The missing American H-bomb was discovered on the Atlantic sea-bed today, to the great relief of the State Department. The weapon, which fell off a B-52 bomber two months ago, was discovered by a midget submarine. It is said to be intact. The US and Spain have been concerned that it might leak radiation, but American officials recently plunged into the Atlantic surf to "prove" that the water was safe.

1966

MAY

Su	Mo	Tu	We	Th	Fr	Sa
1	2	3	4	5	6	7
8	9	10	11	12	13	14
15	16	17	18	19	20	21
22	23	24	25	26	27	28
29	30	31				

1. Italy: Britain's John Surtees wins the Syracuse Grand Prix in Sicily (→ 22).

3. US: Governor Wallace's wife wins the Democratic nomination for Governor of Alabama (→ 16/1/67).

4. London: Doctors and dentists are to get pay rises of ten to 35 per cent; the average GP now earns £4,000 a year.

6. Peking: Mao is reported to be recovering from a heart ailment (→ 13/8).

11. Barcelona: Police beat up 100 priests protesting at police brutality.

13. Johannesburg: 3,000 students demonstrate against the banning of student leader Ian Robertson.

14. London: Everton beat Sheffield Wednesday 3-2 in the FA Cup Final.

15. Washington: 8,000 Vietnam protesters encircle the White House for two hours (→ 14/6).

17. London: Transport Minister Barbara Castle says the 70 mph speed limit will continue until 1967 (→ 12/7/67).

17. UK: Ex-world middleweight champion Randy Turpin is found shot dead in his Leamington Spa flat.

18. London: Home Secretary Jenkins says that the number of police forces in England and Wales will be cut by 68.

21. London: Cassius Clay beats Henry Cooper in the sixth round to retain the world heavyweight championship (→ 30/4/67).

22. Monaco: Jackie Stewart wins the Monaco Grand Prix.→

25. UK: Lady Zia Wernher's Charlottetown wins the Derby.

26. London: The Government announces an enquiry into the shipping dispute (→ 28/6).

31. Congo: Four former ministers are sentenced to death for treason and murder (→ 30/6).

DEATH

17. British boxer Randolph Turpin (*7/6/28).

State of emergency for seamen's strike

May 23. The Government declared a state of emergency today to ensure maintenance of essential supplies and services during the seamen's strike, which is causing mounting congestion at the ports. There is deadlock in negotiations between employers and seamen's leaders over the length of the working week without overtime payment. It is 56 hours at present, and the unions are demanding a reduction to 40.

Mr Wilson said that the Government will set up an independent inquiry regardless of the outcome of the dispute. He considers that port strike committees are under communist influence – what he calls "a tightly-knit group of politically-motivated men" (→ 26).

Hill in 144mph win of Indianapolis 500

Graham Hill beats the Americans.

May 30. Graham Hill, the former world champion racing driver, has won the great American showcase of speed, the Indianapolis 500, in a race dominated by British drivers.

Jackie Stewart of Scotland led with only eight laps remaining when his Lola failed, leaving Hill and Jim Clark to battle out the final miles before Hill, at an average speed of 144mph in his Lotus-Ford, forged ahead to become the first man to win the race first time.

Moors murderers are sentenced to life

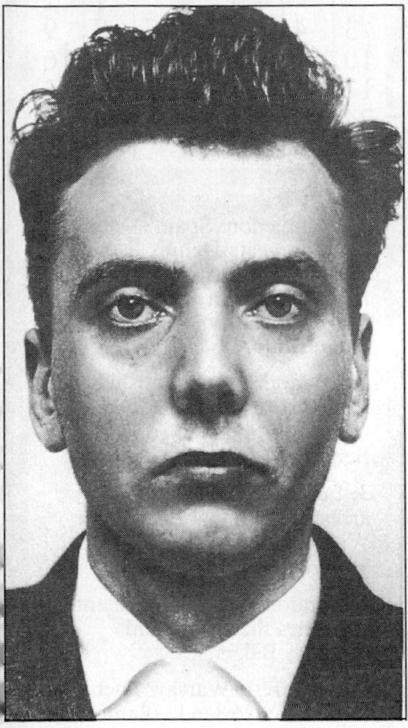
Ian Brady: mastermind of murder.

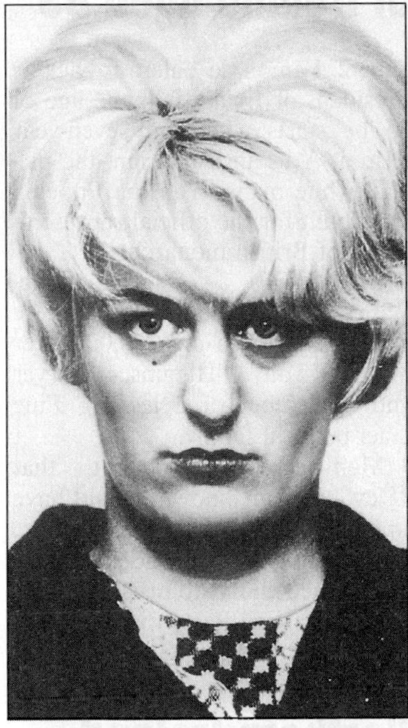
Myra Hindley: a willing helper.

May 6. It was a late-night telephone call to the police by a terrified witness that led to the convictions of the Moors murderers, Ian Brady and Myra Hindley, tonight.

Brady, aged 28, was sentenced to three concurrent terms of life imprisonment for the murders of Edward Evans, aged 17, and two children, Lesley Ann Downey, aged ten, and John Kilbride, aged 12. Hindley received two concurrent life sentences for the murders of Evans and Lesley Ann.

Police are continuing to search for the bodies of at least two other missing children on the Pennine moors. During the trial, the all-male jury heard harrowing tape recordings of Lesley Ann's ordeal and viewed nude pictures taken of the child by the couple before her murder. These had been found in suitcases traced through a left luggage ticket found in Myra Hindley's Communion prayerbook.

Police were alerted by a call from Hindley's brother-in-law, David Smith, who had witnessed the killing of Evans with an axe. Police searched Brady's house and found Evans's body in a blanket.

Holding a white flag, this monk walks between troops firing tear gas at Buddhist demonstrators against the government of Marshal Ky.

1966

JUNE

Su	Mo	Tu	We	Th	Fr	Sa
			1	2	3	4
5	6	7	8	9	10	11
12	13	14	15	16	17	18
19	20	21	22	23	24	25
26	27	28	29	30		

1. UK: Philips Petroleum is reported to have made the richest North Sea gas strike yet.→

1. UK: The AA announces its first subscription increase since it was formed in 1905, from two to three guineas annually.

6. UK: The BBC broadcasts the first episode of a comedy series called "Till Death Us Do Part" (→ 8).

7. US: Ex-actor Ronald Reagan wins the Republican nomination for Governor of California (→ 8/11).

8. London: Tories ask for the script of "Till Death Us Do Part", which called Heath a "grammar school twit" (→ 25/11).

11. UK: Mary Quant and Peter Sellers get OBEs.

12. USSR: Khrushchev makes his first public appearance in a year to vote.

14. Washington: A US pilot and drug addict admits downing two South Vietnamese planes while high on drugs.→

14. UK: Scotland's Walter McGowan beats Italian Salvatore Burruni to become world flyweight boxing champion.

20. London: James White gets 18 years for his part in the Great Train Robbery.

21. Australia: Opposition leader Arthur Calwell is wounded in an assassination attempt.

25. US: James Meredith rejoins civil rights marchers near Jackson, Mississippi (→ 31/7).

28. London: Wilson names Communists who, he claims, are using the seamen's strike to gain power in the NUS (→ 29).

29. UK: Seamen decide to end their strike on July 1.

29. UK: Barclay's Bank introduces Barclaycard, the first British credit card (→ 27/6/67).

30. Congo: The capital Leopoldville is renamed Kinshasa (→ 13/3/67).

30. Paris: France formally leaves NATO (→ 26/10).

Unmanned space ship lands on moon

June 6. Gemini 9 splashed down safely today after failing to dock with an independently-launched satellite. However, the disappointment was offset by the triumphant success of the unmanned Surveyor space-craft, which had soft-landed on the moon three days before.

Surveyor, and its Soviet predecessor of four months ago, have removed one of the great uncertainties about the moon: the nature of its surface. Some astronomers had suggested that it is covered with deep, fine dust in which anything attempting to land would be swallowed up.

"The area where Surveyor landed," said one of the project scientists, "would support the weight of a walking man. The dust, if any, is either not extremely soft, or not very deep" (→ 14/8).

Folk's a'changing: Dylan goes electric

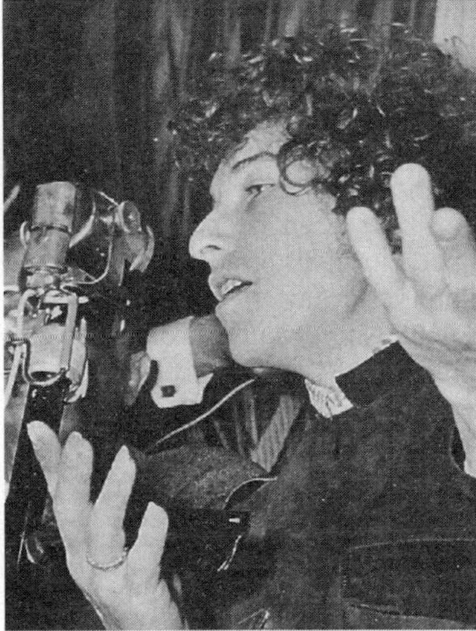
Bob Dylan at the Olympia, Paris.

June 1. Folk singer Bob Dylan shocked his audience tonight when he came up with something no protest lyric could ever rival: an electric back-up band. Appearing at the Royal Albert Hall, he delighted the crowd with a selection of their favourite songs, accompanied on an electric guitar, but when he introduced the group, the Band, for the second half, the folk fans booed and jeered. Less purist listeners were more rapturous. ▷

Race barrier busting black is shot in back

James Meredith lies wounded on a Mississippi road after the shooting.

June 7. James Meredith, the first Negro to brave the colour bar at the University of Mississippi in 1962, was shot in the back and legs yesterday just after he entered Mississippi on a civil rights march. He was carrying only a bible. "There are a million Negroes in Mississippi. I think they'll take care of me," he said just before the shooting.

Meredith was under constant Federal guard while he was at the university. Two people were shot in the riots of his early days there. He had only been back to Mississippi once since his graduation in 1963 until yesterday.

The shots came from a wood shortly after a car carrying whites waving the Confederate flag had passed the marchers. The police have arrested a man found near the scene with a shotgun. Meredith was taken to hospital in Memphis, Tennessee. His condition is satisfactory.

Today Dr Martin Luther King, the civil rights leader, led the march starting from the point on US Highway 51 where Meredith was gunned down. From his hospital bed Meredith said he planned to rejoin the 225-mile march as soon as the doctors let him out. He said: "The day for the Negro man being a coward is over" (→25).

Biggest North Sea gas find to date

June 2. Philips Petroleum disclosed today that its test well in Block 48/30, 80 miles off the mouth of the Humber, indicates a gas flow of "up to 17 million cubic feet a day". That is equal to 3.5 per cent of daily British gas consumption. Shell-Esso, which does not publish flow figures until exhaustive tests are done, announced a significant find in the adjoining block last month. Trade sources believe their find is even bigger. It now seems certain that this area is at least as gas rich as the BP field further north, and that soon all British gas will be natural (→23/11).

Ronald Reagan, the former film star, wins the Republican nomination to be Governor of California as wife Nancy looks on.

De Valera President of Ireland aged 83

June 2. Eamon de Valera is back as President of Ireland. At the age of 83 he starts a second seven-year term at Arus an Uactarian, the palatial white mansion in the Phoenix Park built for the official representatives of British monarchs.

But it was a close-run thing. With over one million votes cast, he had a majority of only 10,000 over his rival Tom O'Higgins, a lawyer and a member of a leading Fine Gael political family.

Many people thought that "Dev", as he is known, would have stepped down before the election. His meeting with President Kennedy seemed climax to his career, but the Fianna Fail Party that he created wished him to restand (→9/11).

Northern Ireland PM bans the UVF

June 6. After a Catholic youth was shot dead in Belfast at the weekend, the Northern Ireland Prime Minister, Terence O'Neill, cut short his visit to Paris to return home. He surprised Stormont by announcing a ban on the Ulster Volunteer Force. The UVF was formed by Lord Carson, KC, to confront the British Army should Whitehall try to impose an all-Ireland parliament on the North. The Force is revered by hardline Protestants.

US bombs hit Hanoi for the first time

June 30. US bombers have raided Hanoi and its port of Haiphong for the first time. Previously American policy has been to stay clear of the North Vietnamese capital while hammering military targets in the country. The bombers hit five large fuel storage areas and are estimated to have wiped out half of North Vietnam's vital oil storage capacity.

Although these were military targets, the raids prompted strong protests in Britain where left-wing Labour MPs have been demanding that Mr Wilson's government dissociate itself from US policy in Vietnam (→3/7).

1966

JULY

Su	Mo	Tu	We	Th	Fr	Sa
					1	2
3	4	5	6	7	8	9
10	11	12	13	14	15	16
17	18	19	20	21	22	23
24	25	26	27	28	29	30
31						

2. Wimbledon: Spain's Manuel Santana beats Dennis Ralston of the US in the Men's Singles final; Billie-Jean King beats Maria Bueno for the Women's Singles title.

3. London: Frank Cousins resigns as Minister of Technology; Anthony Wedgwood Benn succeeds him.

3. London: 31 people are arrested during anti-Vietnam War protests in Grosvenor Square (→7).

4. London: The Government publishes the Prices and Incomes Bill.→

7. Bucharest: Warsaw Pact states offer to send volunteers to North Vietnam if Hanoi wants them (→30).

9. UK: American Jack Nicklaus wins the British Open Championship.

11. UK: BMC and Jaguar announce they are to merge as British Motor Holdings (→27/9).

14. London: The bank rate is raised one per cent to seven per cent (→26/1/67).

14. US: Brigitte Bardot marries Guenther Sachs.

17. Moscow: Kosygin accompanies Harold Wilson on a tour of an industrial fair.

19. US: Frank Sinatra marries Mia Farrow in Las Vegas.

22. UK: 11 die when a pleasure boat crashes on the River Mawddach, Merionethshire (→1/8).

22. Lusaka: The Zambian government is to resume sending copper through Rhodesia.

27. UK: The TUC general council votes to back Wilson's wage freeze (→4/10).

28. UK: Florence Nagle, 70, wins a 20-year fight to be the first woman in Britain granted a licence to train racehorses.

30. Vietnam: US planes bomb the demilitarised zone between North and South Vietnam (→26/8).

DEATH

23. US actor Montgomery Clift (*17/10/20).

Welsh Nationalist MP takes seat in House for first time

July 21. Gwynfor Evans, the Welsh Nationalist victor in the Carmarthen by-election, was today sworn-in as an MP – in English. He had been expected to refuse to take the oath of allegiance except in Welsh; but, having signed on, he then asked if he could do it again in his native tongue. No, said Mr Speaker. Why not, asked Mr Evans? Because other folk would not know what he was saying, said Mr Speaker. That was that. Mr Evans is the first nationalist MP from Wales. The first Scottish Nationalist won a by-election in 1945, but was defeated later that year.

Record set for the mile in California

July 17. Jim Ryun, the spindly 19-year-old student from Wichita, Kansas, has broken the world mile record in Berkeley, California, slicing a remarkable 2.3 seconds off Michael Jazy's year-old record.

In a race hastily arranged after political wrangles over Vietnam had led to the cancellation of a US-Poland match Ryun, who runs over 100 miles each week, spurted on the last lap to a new record of 3 minutes 51.3 seconds.

Race riots flare up in US

Members of the National Guard on the march through a riot-torn city.

July 31. America is scarred with racial unrest. The streets of Chicago, New York and Cleveland have seen deaths and injuries as black gangs and police have clashed.

Over 4,000 National Guardsmen were called into Chicago to stop a persistent sniper campaign against the police. Two blacks were killed, and six policemen injured, in the final shootout. Today, 54 people were hurt when angry whites hurled bricks at civil rights protesters marching through an all-white neighbourhood.

The situation in Brooklyn, New York City, has become so ugly that 1,000 more policemen have been sent in to keep the peace. Black, white and Puerto Rican gangs have been fighting in the streets for a week, resulting in at least two deaths. Mayor John Lindsay has pleaded with leaders of the gangs to try to talk out their differences. "It won't do any good to demonstrate violently in the streets," he said.

In Cleveland, the death of a young black mother by police gunfire sparked off more rioting. Two have died and 30 been injured in the fighting so far.

Richard Burton and his wife Elizabeth Taylor star in the film of Edward Albee's "Who's afraid of Virginia Woolf?" set on an American campus.

Man charged with murder of 8 nurses

July 19. Corazon Amurso, the sole survivor of the mass slaying of eight student nurses in Chicago last week, today identified 24-year-old Richard Speck as the murderer.

The nurses all shared a dormitory at the South Chicago Community Hospital. Miss Amurso escaped death by rolling under a bed and groping to a window ledge where she screamed: "They are all dead! My friends are all dead! My God, I'm the only one alive!"

Speck was arrested at a Chicago hotel, bleeding profusely from self-inflicted cuts on his wrist. He has been charged with murder, but may be too weak to stand trial.

Wilson imposes pay and wages freeze to beat the crisis

July 20. A six-month standstill on wages and dividends, followed by another six months of severe restraint, was announced by the Prime Minister today. Other crisis moves are prices frozen for 12 months, increases in purchase tax, cuts in holiday currency allowances, and more hire purchase curbs. Faced with runaway inflation, Mr Wilson said grimly: "The time has come to call a halt."

The cabinet has been in turmoil over incomes policy ever since Frank Cousins, former Transport Workers' Union leader, angrily resigned as Minister of Technology nearly three weeks ago. He accused Mr Wilson of double-talk, and he refused to stomach pay restraint legislation now being rushed into law and providing sanctions against unions defying the rules.

Mr Wilson prepares to broadcast.

The battle lines are now drawn for a trial of strength between the unions and the cabinet, which is split. Tonight its number two man, the volatile George Brown, who is economic supremo, offered his resignation for at least the fifth time in the past 48 hours.

Under the strain of events he has been tired and emotional. He has been having stormy conversations with cabinet colleagues, and friends fear his truculence is getting out of hand. However, at midnight he appeared at the door of Number 10 with a piece of paper in his hand and read out: "We have decided it is my duty to stay" (→27).

England beat Germany to win the World Cup 4-2

July 30. England, the fathers of football and early missionaries of the game, have played host to the world of football and celebrated the occasion by winning the World Cup for the first time.

In a fluctuating final at Wembley Stadium the red-shirted England team, managed with laconic intensity by Alf Ramsey and captained by West Ham's Bobby Moore, beat a superbly organised West German team 4-2 in extra time.

Of the 16 nations that reached the final stages, two of the best equipped teams, Brazil and Hungary, were drawn in the same group – and it was the holders, Brazil, who failed, losing both Pele (after crippling tackles from Bulgarian defenders in their opening game) and two matches – to Hungary and the delightful Portuguese.

In the north-east of England the USSR romped through, but the cautious Italians suffered the biggest upset, losing 1-0 to the unknown North Koreans.

Argentina and West Germany qualified in the Midlands, and Uruguay, who had drawn 0-0 with England in the showpiece opening match, came through to the quarter-finals with the hosts, who had found better form in beating Mexico and France.

England reached the semi-finals with a 1-0 victory over Argentina, who had their captain Rattin sent off for continuous dissent, to meet Portugal, who had the shock of their lives in going 3-0 down to the astonishing North Koreans before Eusebio (who was to end the tournament as top scorer with eight goals) brought them to their senses and a 5-3 victory.

Exultant Bobby Moore, England's captain, brandishes the World Cup as the team carry him from the field.

Russia and West Germany contested a bruising semi-final, which the Germans won 2-1, and with it the right to meet England who, growing in confidence match by match, beat Portugal by the same score with Bobby Charlton outstanding.

The Germans took an early lead in the final, but Geoff Hurst equalised and then his West Ham colleague Martin Peters put England ahead, only to see Germany snatch a scrambled goal on the stroke of full time. Extra time was frenetic, until Hurst slammed a shot against the underside of the crossbar; the ball bounced down over the goal line (or, as all Germany believes, on to it) and the goal was awarded.

In the dying seconds Hurst completed his hat-trick to put the issue beyond doubt and to set the celebrations in train (→ 1/1/67).

HOW THE TEAMS LINED UP
ENGLAND
Banks
Cohen
Wilson
Stiles
Charlton (J)
Moore
Ball
Charlton (R)
Peters
Hurst
Hunt
Emmerich
Held
Seeler
Overath
Beckenbauer
Halle
Schnellinger
Schulz
Weber
Hottges
Tilkowski
WEST GERMANY

Hurst scores his third, and England's fourth goal, to seal the victory.

1966

AUGUST

Su	Mo	Tu	We	Th	Fr	Sa
	1	2	3	4	5	6
7	8	9	10	11	12	13
14	15	16	17	18	19	20
21	22	23	24	25	26	27
28	29	30	31			

1. UK: 31 people are lost off the Cornish coast in the pleasure boat Darlwyne.

1. US: Charles Whitman, 25, shoots dead 12 at Texas University in Austin, before being killed by a policeman (→2).

1. Nigeria: Lieutenant-Colonel Yakubu Gowon seizes power in a coup (→3/10).

2. Washington: Johnson urges firearms curbs to prevent further tragedies like the Austin massacre.

3. US: Comedian Lenny Bruce dies of a drugs overdose.

4. London: The Kray twins are taken in for questioning by police conducting a murder investigation (→8/5/68).

7. West Germany: Jack Brabham wins the German Grand Prix (→4/9).

10. London: George Brown succeeds Michael Stewart as Foreign Secretary.

14. US: A spacecraft Orbiter 1 is reported to be in orbit around the moon (→15/11).

15. London: John Whitney is charged with the murder of three policemen (→17).

17. Glasgow: John Duddy is arrested in connection with the London police murders (→12/8).

22. London: Plans are announced for a 385-foot, 34-floor skyscraper in the West End called Centre Point.

23. UK: The Cotswolds are designated an Area of Outstanding Natural Beauty.

26. Vietnam: 20 US soldiers die when US planes napalm Americans by mistake (→30).

27. Plymouth: Francis Chichester sets off on a lone round-the-world voyage (→27/1/67).

30. Peking: China pledges more aid to Ho Chi Minh's government (→5/9).

31. Yugoslavia: 92 die when a British airliner crashes.

DEATH

3. US comedian Lenny Bruce (*13/10/26).

Mao proclaims a Cultural Revolution

Aug 13. China is being turned upside down by a "great proletarian cultural revolution" designed to bring the country closer to Mao Tse-tung's concept of the ideal Communist state.

The new campaign is taking many forms, but is being spearheaded by hundreds of thousands of students organised into bands of Red Guards.

Since the cultural revolution was launched at a mass rally in Peking, Red Guards have been moving across the country, parading with portraits of Mao and carrying little red books of quotations from his works. Their aim is to arouse townspeople and villagers to recapture the victorious 1949 revolutionary zeal, and ferret out those who have departed from Mao's ideals.

The chief targets of the campaign are Communist Party officials, and workers in artistic and educational institutions guilty of "revisionist" attitudes and "bourgeois reactionary thinking". Schools are being shut and hundreds of teachers and other intellectuals are being paraded by Red Guards through the streets wearing dunces' caps.

Everywhere are the words of Mao, written in 1927: "A revolution is not a dinner party, or writing an essay, or painting a picture, or doing embroidery ... a revolution is an insurrection, an act of violence by which one class overthrows another" (→9/1/67).

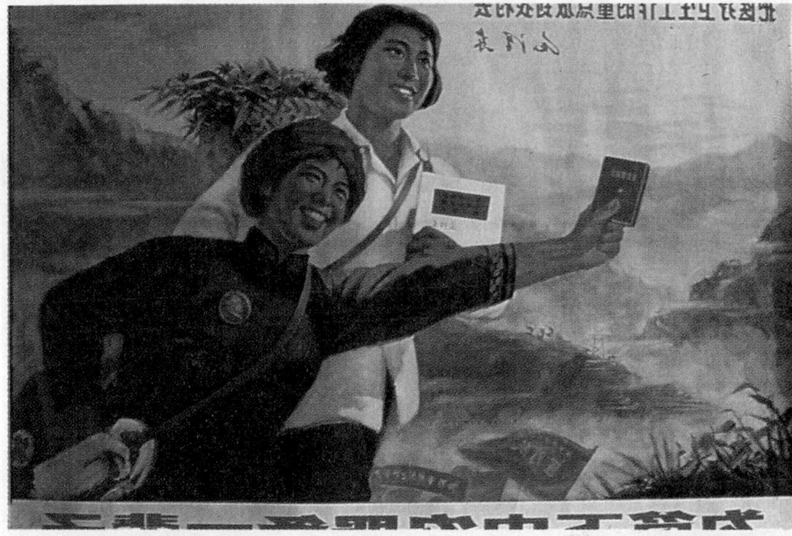

Idealised Red Guards wave Chairman Mao Tse-tung's Little Red Book ...

... and nature imitates art as flesh-and-blood activists clutch their texts.

Peace deal ends Malaysian bush warfare

Aug 11. Three years of bush warfare between Indonesia and Malaysia came to an end today, with the increasingly powerless President Sukarno apparently the only person unhappy about the outcome.

The Indonesian President hardly spoke in Djakarta today as the two countries agreed to "normalise relations". He failed to see his Malaysian guest, the vice-premier Tun Abdul Razak, to the doors of his palace, and had no gift to present to him after accepting a silver tea-set.

Sukarno has lost a lot of prestige in this war, which was fought sporadically in jungle battles. He is also in a weak position following the attempted coup put down by the army last October. Army leaders had been carrying out secret talks with Kuala Lumpur for some time, and operations against Malaysia were abandoned several months ago. The army can no longer be bothered with Sukarno's anti-imperialist rhetoric, and senior officers seem more concerned with building up their own power base.

The war was largely an attempt by Sukarno to get British forces out of the region, but it also raised the issue of whether or not its former Borneo colonies, now known as Sabah and Sarawak, should be included in Malaysia (→22/2/67).

German crisis over Starfighter crashes

Aug 26. The West German air force has been thrown into a tailspin by the horrific number of US-built Starfighter jets which have crashed. Sixty of the jets have been destroyed so far on training missions and several senior officers in the Federal Ministry of Defence have been forced to resign.

Word of the trouble with the aircraft bought from America leaked out when the Inspector-General of the Air Force, Werner Panitzki, criticised the Defence Minister in a newspaper interview. Panitzki was immediately suspended.

▷

Policemen shot dead on London street

Grim-faced fellow police officers look down on the shrouded corpses.

Aug 12. One of Britain's biggest manhunts was underway today for gunmen who shot three policemen dead within sight of a London jail. Every available officer was called in to help track down the killers, who jumped from a car while being followed by the detectives.

Christopher Head, aged 30, and David Wombwell, aged 25, were each killed by a single shot as they approached the suspects. The driver, Geoffrey Fox, aged 41, was killed as he sat at the steering wheel. He had no time to radio to base, but before he died he had managed to scribble the registration number of the gang's car in his notebook. Last night the murder squad was said to be closing in on the killers.

They are believed to have links with the criminal underworld, and senior Scotland Yard detectives suspect the dead officers had come across a planned breakout from Wormwood Scrubs prison.

Children who were playing in quiet Braybrook Street, Shepherd's Bush, as the gunmen opened fire, are under armed guard (→ 15).

The Hawker Siddeley Harrier, the world's first vertical take-off and landing aircraft, was revealed at this month's Farnborough Air Show.

1966

SEPTEMBER

Su	Mo	Tu	We	Th	Fr	Sa
				1	2	3
4	5	6	7	8	9	10
11	12	13	14	15	16	17
18	19	20	21	22	23	24
25	26	27	28	29	30	

2. UK: Yorkshire become County Cricket Champions (→ 18/9/67).

5. Washington: Johnson offers to set a date for US withdrawal from Vietnam when North Vietnam leaves (→ 18).

10. London: The West End's longest-running musical "Oliver!" ends its run of six years, three months.

13. S. Africa: Balthazar Johannes Vorster is sworn in as Prime Minister (→ 19).

15. UK: The Queen Mother launches Britain's nuclear submarine, HMS Resolution, at Barrow (→ 29/3/67).

18. New York: UN Secretary-General U Thant says a UN force cannot end the Vietnam conflict (→ 28).

19. US: Singer Joan Baez leads black children to an all-white school in Mississippi (→ 16/10/67).

19. S. Africa: A bill is introduced that would abolish all inter-racial political parties.

25. Japan: 174 are reported dead after a typhoon.

27. UK: BMC lays off 7,000 workers, and plans over 11,000 redundancies on November 11 (→ 3/10).

28. South Vietnam: The US accidentally bombs a friendly village, killing 28 (→ 26/10).

30. Bechuanaland: The colony gains independence as Botswana (→ 3/10).

30. Falklands: The Argentinian "invaders" surrender to a Catholic priest.

DEATHS

6. Dutch-born South African leader Dr Hendrik Frensch Verwoerd, Prime Minister 1958-66 (*8/9/01).→

6. US birth control pioneer Margaret Sanger, born Margaret Higgins (*14/9/1883).

25. British circus owner William George "Billy" Smart (*23/4/1893).

28. French poet and author Andre Breton (*18/2/1896).→

Brabham is racing champ in own car

Jack Brabham takes the applause.

Sept 4. Jack Brabham of Australia has become the first man to win the world drivers' championship in a car he built himself. At the Italian Grand Prix at Monza, Brabham watched from the pits as John Surtees, who needed victory to challenge his lead, retired after 32 laps with engine trouble.

Lord Thomson to buy up the Times

Sept 30. Lord Thomson of Fleet, the Canadian press and television magnate, has bought The Times, subject to Monopolies Commission consent. It will be linked with the Sunday Times which he already owns. Thomson made his money through Scottish Television, which he called a "licence to print money", and thinks he can make The Times profitable again (→ 21/12).

A Canadian to run The Times?

1966

OCTOBER

Su	Mo	Tu	We	Th	Fr	Sa
						1
2	3	4	5	6	7	8
9	10	11	12	13	14	15
16	17	18	19	20	21	22
23	24	25	26	27	28	29
30	31					

2. New York: Jim Clark wins the US Grand Prix (→ 23).

3. Basutoland: The colony becomes independent as the Kingdom of Lesotho.

4. London: The Government invokes a price and wage freeze under the new Prices and Incomes Act.

5. Spain: Franco bans all traffic to and from Gibraltar (→ 10/9/67).

11. UK: Jensen presents its latest models, the FF and Interceptor.

11. London: The GPO says all British homes and businesses will have postcodes, starting in Croydon on November 5.

17. Rhodesia: Ex-premier Garfield Todd is released from the restriction order imposed by the Smith regime (→ 13/11).

20. UK: Figures show unemployment stands at 437,229, up 100,000 on last month (→ 24/11).

21. UK: Over 130 people, mainly children, are buried by a coal slag heap at Aberfan, near Merthyr Tydfil.→

23. Mexico: John Surtees wins the Mexican Grand Prix (→ 4/6/67).

24. New Delhi: Mrs Gandhi, Nasser and Tito head a conference of "non-aligned" nations.

26. Paris: NATO decides to transfer its headquarters from Paris to Brussels.

27. London: Wilson says he will make no more recommendations for honours for political services.

29. UK: The British Army drops its colour bar.

31. UK: Strikes in protest at planned redundancies close all BMC factories in England and Wales.→

DEATHS

18. French cosmetics expert Elizabeth Arden (*31/12/1884).

22. British churchman Dr Hewlett Johnson, the "Red Dean" of Canterbury (*25/1/1874).

Verwoerd, father of apartheid, is knifed

Sept 6. Seven minutes after taking his seat in the House of Assembly today the South African Prime Minister, Dr Hendrik Verwoerd, was assassinated by a Bible-quoting parliamentary messenger.

Demetrio Tsafendas, of Greek and Portuguese parents, pulled a long stiletto from his belt and stabbed Verwoerd four times in the chest. He had started work as a messenger about a month ago. Colleagues said they often heard him talking about guns and repeating passages from the Bible. He speaks six languages, including English, German and Afrikaans.

Verwoerd, aged 64, became Prime Minister in 1958 and survived a previous attempt on his life in 1960, when a demented white farmer, whose wife had left him, fired at point-blank range, wounding Verwoerd in the mouth.

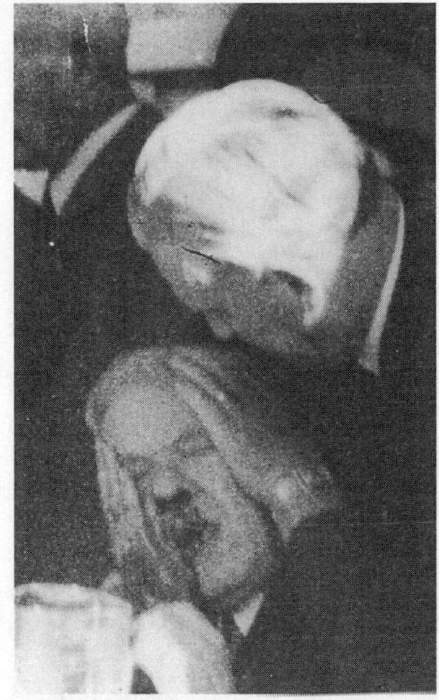

The 1960 attack Verwoerd survived.

As Minister for Native Affairs for eight years from 1950, Verwoerd had a key role in constructing the network of laws and regulations designed to keep whites, blacks and mixed-race coloureds entirely segregated – at home, at work, and in personal relations. Ironically, his assassin was critical of the government because, he said, it was "doing too much for the coloureds and nothing for the poor whites" (→ 13).

Founder of Surrealism, Andre Breton, dies

Sept 28. It was a poet, Andre Breton, who wrote the Surrealist Manifesto in 1924, calling for self-expression "free of all control exercised by reason, aesthetics or morals". He died today having seen the Surrealism he pioneered become more a visual than a literary movement, through the paintings of Magritte and Dali and the films of Bunuel and Cocteau.

As a medical student in the First World War, Breton was struck by the poetic quality of the ravings of shellshocked patients. He studied Freud, tried automatic writing, edited a Surrealist journal and, in 1930, turned Communist.

Argentinians raid Falkland Islands

Sept 29. Gunmen attacked the British Ambassador's residence in Buenos Aires where Prince Philip is staying tonight after a day in which 20 Argentinian nationalists "invaded" the Falkland Islands in a hijacked airliner. The invaders were still surrounded on the airfield at Port Stanley, the islands' capital, tonight. In Buenos Aires, the embassy raiders opened up fire from two darkened cars. Argentina claims sovereignty over the islands in the South Atlantic which it calls the Malvinas (→ 30).

King Rameses must be moved as the Aswan Dam takes shape.

Spy George Blake breaks out of jail

Blake when he returned from Korea.

Oct 22. Russia was suspected of masterminding the dramatic escape today of the double agent George Blake, who scaled the outer wall of Wormwood Scrubs jail in London by using a homemade rope ladder, strengthened by ten pairs of size 13 knitting needles.

A pink chrysanthemum left outside was the only other clue to who had helped his bid for freedom, which is a significant propaganda coup for the Soviets. Blake, serving 42 years for spying, may be aboard a Communist ship (→ 20/11).

Belated pardon for the hanged Evans

Oct 18. The Queen has granted a free pardon to Timothy John Evans, the 25-year-old lorry driver, who was hanged in 1950 for murdering his wife and daughter in the house occupied by the mass murderer, John Reginald Christie.

The Queen acted on the advice of the Home Secretary after a High Court judge found that Evans was "probably innocent" of the offence. Evans's pardon, unprecedented in the history of British justice, follows a massive campaign by opponents of capital punishment. ▷

Coal tip buries generation of children

Oct 27. A teddy bear was thrown into a mass grave today and a police sergeant burst into tears. Aberfan had begun the grim business of burying its children. On a hillside, in the very shadow of the slag heap that had moved, burying the local school and killing 116 children and 28 adults, ashen-faced parents wept as 82 victims were interred.

As a huge workforce continues to clear thousands of tons of the slurry and slag that engulfed the school and part of the village, the Government has promised a "high level" inquiry.

George Thomas, the Minister of State for Wales, said: "A generation of children has been wiped out in the village. South Wales has an abundance of tips of this character and it is essential that we should know the cause of the disaster and whether it could be repeated."

It was mid-morning when the giant tip began its deadly slide towards the village. An avalanche of black slag demolished the school in a matter of seconds. A ten-year-old girl survivor described the scene thus: "We heard a noise and we saw all the stuff flying about. The desks were falling about and the children were shouting and screaming. We couldn't see anything but then the dust began to go away."

An army of rescuers – many of them parents – toiled throughout the day and night to reach the victims. The headmistress was brought out alive. The deputy headmaster was found dead with the bodies of five children in his arms.

The Prime Minister, Harold Wilson, who had walked through the slurry to the school, said: "I don't think any of us can find words to describe this tragedy."

Debris from the local colliery was being tipped on to the slag heap when the disaster happened, and the National Coal Board is facing accusations that it had been warned that the village was in danger. Merthyr Tydfil's Borough Council had previously rejected a request for an examination of the tip's condition.

Lord Robens, the Coal Board chairman, said that a natural spring, previously unknown, was a possible cause. Water pouring into the tip had created what he called "a water bomb" (→3/8/67).

Anguished parents watch as a policeman carries out one young survivor.

A row of miniature coffins bears grim witness to the horror of Aberfan.

LBJ pays surprise visit to Vietnam

Oct 26. President Johnson swept in and out of the massive US base at Cam Ranh Bay today in a surprise trip from Manila. Speed, secrecy and stratagems were used to protect him from Viet Cong attack.

For over two hours, in boiling heat, he mixed with the sweaty, grubby soldiers of an army too preoccupied with war for spit and polish. They treated their Commander-in-Chief with easy informality.

This made the visit less a publicity stunt than an emotional experience for Mr Johnson, who genuinely agonises over the soldiers. His voice broke during a speech and he was deeply affected as, subdued and soaked in sweat, he returned to his jet for the flight back to Bangkok to continue his 17-day tour of the South Pacific (→1/11).

Troops rampage in Nigerian tribal riots

Oct 3. The long-standing hostility between Nigeria's Moslem Hausas in the North and the Christian Ibos from the East erupted in wholesale killings over the week-end. Mutinous troops roamed the ancient city of Kano, hunting Ibos and shooting on sight. Upwards of 1,000 people are believed to have died. Relations between the two communities worsened after the military coup last July, when an Ibo army commander took power. The Hausas struck back and installed a Northerner as leader (→30/5/67).

Car strike closes all BMC factories

Oct 31. Production of Austin and Morris cars was brought to a standstill today as strike action against the management's redundancy plans intensified. Last month British Motor Corporation announced the dismissal of 12,000 of its 109,000 workers, in the hope of restoring profitability. Most of the redundancies, due to take effect next week, are in the Austin and Morris car sections, whose 24,000 workers were idle today (→11/11).

1966

NOVEMBER

Su	Mo	Tu	We	Th	Fr	Sa
		1	2	3	4	5
6	7	8	9	10	11	12
13	14	15	16	17	18	19
20	21	22	23	24	25	26
27	28	29	30			

1. Seoul: A huge crowd greets Johnson on the last stop of his Far Eastern tour (→16).

4. Italy: At least 21 deaths are reported in floods; Florence is cut off.→

8. US: Republican candidate Ronald Reagan is elected Governor of California (→2/1/67).

8. US: Edward Brooke is the first black senator elected since direct senatorial elections were introduced in 1911 (→13/6/67).

9. UK: Rootes introduces the Hillman Hunter (→17/1/67).

11. UK: The unofficial stoppage at BMC over redundancies ends.

13. London: Supporters of Ian Smith stage a Remembrance Sunday demonstration outside 10 Downing Street (→2/12).

15. US: James Lovell and Edwin "Buzz" Aldrin splashdown after five days orbiting in Gemini 12, the last Gemini mission.

16. US: Johnson has surgery to remove a throat polyp and to repair a small hernia.

20. Berlin: Escaped British spy George Blake is reported to have turned up in East Berlin.

23. UK: BP says it has struck the best gas-producing areas yet in the North Sea, 40 miles east of the Humber (→12/12).

24. UK: Figures show that unemployment has risen from 437,229 to 531,585 in the last month.

25. Washington: FBI chief J. Edgar Hoover says all evidence suggests that Oswald acted alone in killing Kennedy (→3/1/67).

25. UK: Warren Mitchell, star of "Till Death Us Do Part", is named best TV actor of 1966.

27. Moscow: The Soviet Communist Party denounces the Chinese leadership.

30. US: NASA releases close-up photos of the moon taken by Orbiter 2 (→27/1/67).

30. London: Wilson urges building up the European economy to avoid US economic domination (→2/5/67).

Masterpieces destroyed in Florence flood

A statue of the Virgin gazes mutely as clean-up crews work in Florence.

Nov 9. Art treasures damaged in the worst storms in northern Italy for nearly 1,000 years today became the focus of rescue work by teams of restoration specialists, who have recovered priceless books, paintings and sculptures from galleries awash with rivers of mud and silt. Rain has fallen for 40 hours non-stop.

As the human toll from the disaster rose to an unofficial 180, the Mayor of Florence tearfully spoke of an "incalculable" loss to the nation's arts heritage. Other experts value it at £58 million.

Two thirds of the city is under six feet of water after the River Arno burst its banks, and the bronze Door of Paradise was swept away from the cathedral.

Thousands of books at the National Library are soaked in green slime, and the Uffizi Gallery fears 130,000 photographic negatives of masterpiece paintings are lost.

There is hope many treasures can be saved by salvage work now being hurriedly, although not always conventionally, carried out. Companies are drying sodden documents on equipment designed to dry tobacco leaves.

Astronaut Buzz Aldrin takes a walk in space during the flight of the Gemini 12 spacecraft.

Saigon is shelled by the Viet Cong

Nov 1. The Viet Cong bombarded Saigon today, using Russian-made Katyusha rockets that wailed in over the suburbs to strike haphazardly into the heart of the city. These rockets are fired from simple bamboo stands erected at the edge of the jungle, and the Viet Cong are always far away by the time the defending forces track down their firing positions. Katyushas used like this are not a serious military weapon, but they effectively spread terror among civilians. They carry a heavy warhead, and have inflicted a number of casualties in Saigon's teeming streets (→19/1/67).

UK scientists going down brain drain

Nov 7. The number of British scientists and engineers emigrating to the United States has increased sharply in recent years. According to a survey by the US National Science Foundation, the outflow rose by 22 per cent between 1962 and 1964. The proportion of scientists to engineers leaving is roughly one to two. The figures do not include doctors, who are also believed to be leaving for the United States in large numbers.

According to Gregory Henderson of the United Nations Institute for Training and Research, Britain is the nation most seriously affected by the brain drain. The number of scientists and engineers emigrating to the United States from other Western European nations is falling.

Jack Lynch is new Eire Prime Minister

Jack Lynch, Ireland's new leader.

Nov 9. Jack Lynch, aged 49 and a lawyer, but better known as an All-Ireland footballer and hurley player, is the new Irish Prime Minister. This morning the Fianna Fail Party gave him 52 votes, as against 19 cast for the Industry and Commerce Minister George Colley.

A quietly-spoken, shrewd politician from the city of Cork, he is expected to advance further the thaw in North-South relations begun by his predecessor Sean Lemass, who is retiring as premier.

1966

DECEMBER

Su	Mo	Tu	We	Th	Fr	Sa
				1	2	3
4	5	6	7	8	9	10
11	12	13	14	15	16	17
18	19	20	21	22	23	24
25	26	27	28	29	30	31

1. Bonn: Christian Democrat Kurt Kiesinger is sworn in as Chancellor in the first coalition with the Social Democrats.

2. Mediterranean: Harold Wilson and Ian Smith open talks on Rhodesia aboard the cruiser, HMS Tiger.→

5. London: Transport union chief and ex-Minister of Technology Frank Cousins resigns as Labour MP for Nuneaton.

8. Greece: 280 are feared lost when a ferry sinks in a storm.

10. Stockholm: Nobel Prizes go to Alfred Kastler (France, Physics); Robert Mulliken (US, Chemistry); Peyton Rous and Charles Huggins (US, Medicine); Shmuel Agnon (Israel) and Nelly Sachs (Sweden, Literature); no Peace Prize.

12. UK: The Gas Council-Amoco group has made a further successful North Sea gas strike, it is reported.

16. New York: The UN tells all members to put an oil embargo on Rhodesia (→20).

20. London: Wilson says majority rule is first condition for a Rhodesian settlement, hopes for which are now slim (→22).

21. London: The Monopolies Commission approves Thomson's takeover of The Times (→12/1/67).

22. Salisbury: Rhodesia leaves the Commonwealth (→9/2/67).

28. Australia: The Davis Cup stays in Australia for the third year running as India loses in the final.

DEATH

15. US animator and showman Walt Disney (*5/12/01).→

HITS OF 1966

Distant drums.

Strangers in the night.

Spanish Flea.

QUOTE OF THE YEAR

"In a decade dominated by youth, London has burst into bloom. It swings; it is the scene."

Time magazine "London: The Swinging City", April 15, 1966.

Terms to end UDI declared "repugnant"

Ian Smith makes it clear that he will not accede to England's demands.

Dec 6. After a ten-hour cabinet meeting in Salisbury, Ian Smith, leader of the rebel Rhodesian regime, announced the rejection of British proposals for ending the 13-month-old dispute. "The fight goes on," he said.

Mr Wilson put the terms to Mr Smith during a series of meetings held aboard the cruiser Tiger, sailing off Gibraltar. These called for Mr Smith to repudiate UDI, surrender control of the armed forces and bring at least two Africans into the cabinet. Mr Smith castigated the terms as "repugnant".

Britain will now ask the UN Security Council to impose mandatory sanctions on Rhodesian exports. These are certain to be agreed, but will have limited effect, since Rhodesia has found obliging foreign partners to handle its exports (→16).

King of cartoons, Walt Disney, dies

Dec 16. You may not immediately recognise the names of Michele Topolino, Miguel Ratonicito and Miki Kuchi as anyone you know. They are. They are what people in Italy, Spain and Japan call Mickey Mouse, demonstrating the universal appeal of Walt Disney, who died yesterday, aged 65. Disney supplied the idea and the voice, his partner Ubbe Iwerks the drawing.

Mickey was followed by the orchestrated mayhem of Donald Duck, Goofy and Pluto in the Silly Symphonies, which went into colour with the "Three Little Pigs" in 1933. "Snow White" and her seven dwarfs were the first full-length feature in 1937 (still the best for many). After that the studio became an industry.

After Cinderella, Alice, Peter Pan and Mary Poppins, it seemed that no well-loved children's classic was safe from the somewhat sickly charms of Disneyfication in Disneyland (opened in 1955). Handing "The Jungle Book" to a writer, he said: "The first thing I want you to do is not to read it."

Arts: something strange is happening, but is it really art?

A "Happening", the sort of event by which the Sixties may be remembered, took place over "Nine Evenings" at the New York City Armory in October, staged by **Robert Rauschenberg**, who is famed for adding radio sets, billboards and junk to his paintings.

One Happening was set on an indoor tennis court lit by 48 lamps. Each time a tennis player hit the ball his racket gave out an amplified "Boinggg" and turned out one of the lamps. When they were all extinguished, 700 people filed on to the court, made visible by infra-red TV cameras, talking quietly among themselves. When they left, an "artist" crossed the court carrying a canvas bag, in which a woman sang softly. End of Happening.

Rauschenberg and the composer **John Cage**, whose piece 4'33" (four minutes, 33 seconds) consists of a player sitting at a closed piano for that length of time while the audience provides the sounds, have joined with some engineers to set up EAT – Experiments in Art and Technology, using video tape, lasers and computer programmes.

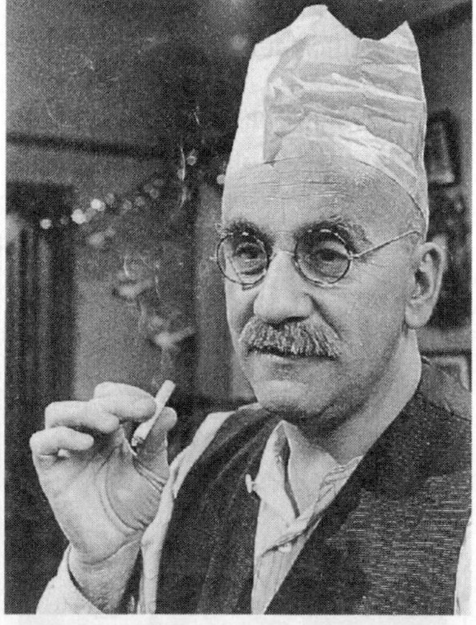

Warren Mitchell is "Alf Garnett", named best TV actor of the year.

Strange evenings in the theatre: **Peter Brook** staged his anti-Vietnam war show "US" with the RSC in London – not so much a play as a collection of theatrical shock tactics. At one stage actors representing the maimed war victims, with paper bags over their heads, descend into the audience moaning pitifully. A searchlight is turned on the patrons to see who will assist them to find the exits.

The Royal Court has been prosecuted for presenting a play banned by the Lord Chamberlain. It is "Saved", by **Edward Bond**, in which a gang of aimless louts stone a baby's pram, killing the baby. In "Loot", a farce by a new author, **Joe Orton**, the hero uses his mother's coffin to hide stolen banknotes. Her sheeted body is on stage to be used as a comic property. Orton's bad taste is accompanied by dialogue of surprising delicacy.

Death is the theme of **Truman Capote's** gruesome and chilling non-fiction novel, or "faction", "In Cold Blood". He spent some months with the two young killers of a Kansas family while they awaited execution.

The year that London became the swinging capital

Fashion: Carnaby Street adds style

London has become the fashion capital of the world as far as young people are concerned. At its centre lie three streets – The King's Road in Chelsea, put on the map by Mary Quant; Kensington Church Street, where designer Barbara Hulanicki runs a "total look" boutique called Biba; and Carnaby Street, not so long ago, a run-down back alley behind Regent Street.

Today Carnaby Street has become a mecca for clothes fanatics of both sexes. It owes its success to John Stephen, a Glaswegian who decided that men's clothes should be as much fun as women's.

His first boutique selling pink hipsters paved the way for dozens more, making the street a major draw both for British youth and overseas tourists who come to stare at the parade of long-haired young men – many in the latest Eastern-style kaftans and beads – and their mini-skirted girlfriends. The girls either wear their hair similarly long – and always straight – or cropped into the angular cut made popular by hair stylist Vidal Sassoon.

The rising star of the scene is a 17-year-old model Twiggy, a six and a half stone Cockney with huge eyes and waif-like looks, who can now earn ten guineas an hour as a model.

Twiggy: less is presumably more.

A hippie girl, and a junior version, enjoy the sunshine in Hyde Park.

Lifestyles: the pill, pot and freedom

This, if we are to believe Time Magazine, has been the year of "Swinging London". The cover story of its April 15 issue told an international audience: "In this century, every decade has its city... and for the Sixties that city is London".

Maybe we shouldn't believe everything we read in the papers, but there's no doubt that London is doing its best to live up to its billing. The keywords are "uninhibited", "now" and, above all, "young". Certainly there can never have been a better place to be in your teens and twenties.

Traditionalists may bridle at such descriptions as "the new aristocracy", and the media, which has climbed merrily onto Time's bandwagon, prefer "the meritocracy". Yet ever since the Beatles made it clear that youth culture was here to stay, and the Labour government opted to promote the mood, the capital has been taken over by successful young people. Artists, models, photographers, rock stars, fashion designers, all dedicated to serving, and dictating the hip young style.

Social revolution with its mini-skirt and contraceptive pill isn't for everyone. What America calls the "baby boom" generation has come out to play, but its mystified elders are clinging desperately to fast eroding traditions. For the young those "standards" are merely "uncool"; morality, totem of the old, is the dirty word now.

Music: British rock rules the pop world

For rock fans 1966 has provided a mix that, more than ever, shows the ever-widening gap between traditional mass-appeal and the trendier young. And while such "family favourites" as Ken Dodd and the Bachelors continue to fill the charts, it is among the shelves of LPs that youthful interest can often be found. None more so than "Aftermath", from the Rolling Stones – an album that epitomises this year of "Swinging London".

Not that the rockers don't hit the charts as well. The year started with Beatles "Day Tripper" at number one and "Paperback Writer" and "Eleanor Rigby" both went to the top. Other youth culture successes included hits for the Who, the Kinks, and the Small Faces.

Ironically, it was America which provided the highlight of the year with the tour of Bob Dylan. His introduction of an electric backing group appalled the traditionalists of the folk scene, but the less purist loved it.

Dylan's hardcore fans come from what is known as the "underground", and it is here that a number of new bands are emerging, although they may never reach the charts. Those in the know tip the weirdly named Pink Floyd and the Soft Machine.

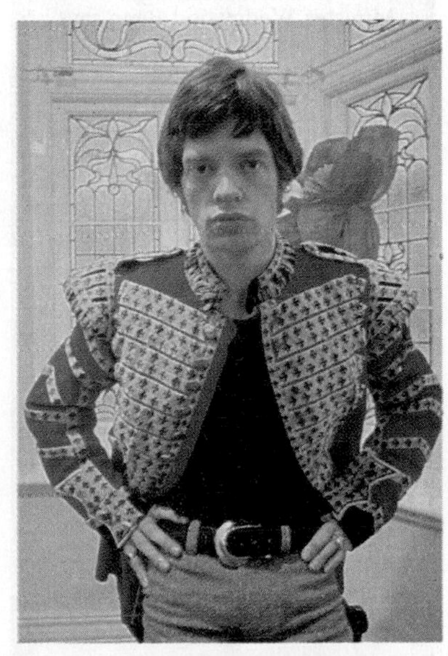

Jagger: you're under my thumb.

1967

JANUARY

Su	Mo	Tu	We	Th	Fr	Sa
1	2	3	4	5	6	7
8	9	10	11	12	13	14
15	16	17	18	19	20	21
22	23	24	25	26	27	28
29	30	31				

1. UK: Alf Ramsey is knighted and Bobby Moore gets an OBE in the New Year Honours.

2. US: Ronald Reagan is sworn in as Governor of California (→ 12/9).

3. US: Jack Ruby, killer of Lee Harvey Oswald, dies of a blood clot in the lung.

4. UK: The BBC's "Ken Dodd Show" topped the list of the most popular Christmas TV programmes.

7. UK: BBC TV begins on BBC1 its acclaimed adaptation of John Galsworthy's epic, "The Forsyte Saga".

9. Shanghai: An open rebellion against Mao is reported to have broken out (→ 17/4).

11. UK: The Society for the Protection of Unborn Children is formed.

12. UK: Britain's largest new town will occupy 22,000 acres of rural Buckinghamshire and be called Milton Keynes.

12. London: William Rees-Mogg becomes editor of The Times, Harold Evans editor of The Sunday Times.

16. US: George Wallace's wife is sworn in as Governor of Alabama.

17. London: Jo Grimond resigns as leader of the Liberal Party.→

17. London: Technology Minister Wedgwood Benn says the US car firm Chrysler will be allowed to take over Rootes.

20. Monaco: A Mini Cooper wins the Monte Carlo Rally.

26. London: The bank rate is cut from seven per cent to 6.5 per cent, ending a sterling crisis (→ 16/3).

27. Malta: Premier Borg Olivier tells Britain to "get out" (→ 20/3).

27. UK: Lone yachtsman Francis Chichester is awarded a knighthood.

31. London: A porter dies as students break into a meeting calling for Rhodesian Walter Adams to resign as head of the London School of Economics (→ 13/3).

Flash fire kills astronauts on launch pad

"Gus" Grissom (l.), Ed White (c.) and Roger Chaffee died in the capsule.

Jan 27. Three American astronauts died today in a fire which swept through their spacecraft during a launch pad rehearsal. "Gus" Grissom, Ed White and Roger Chaffee were in their Apollo spacecraft going through a simulation of the launch which was to have put them into earth orbit next month.

The fire, probably started by a spark from faulty electrical equipment, was boosted by the pure oxygen atmosphere in the capsule and engulfed its interior within minutes. The ground crew were unable to open the hatch, which could not be freed from inside, in time for the astronauts to escape.

The disaster is a serious setback to the Apollo programme, with its goal of landing men on the moon before 1970 (→ 9/4).

US Vietnam deaths reach a new high

Jan 19. More American soldiers died in Vietnam last week than in any other week of the war. The casualty list reveals that 144 men were killed, 1,044 were wounded and six are listed as missing in action. This increase reflects not only the deepening American involvement in the war, but also the vicious nature of the guerrilla war being fought in the jungle and the paddy fields. Most of the American casualties are being caused by mines and booby traps rather than open warfare.

Cathy Come Home sparks housing row

Jan 11. The controversial TV play, "Cathy Come Home" was repeated tonight despite complaints from local authority officials that it was "full of blunders". The play's harrowing portrayal of a young homeless couple shocked Britons when it was first shown and led to the establishment of a new charity, Shelter, to help the homeless. Author Jeremy Sandford says "Cathy" was based on a real girl.

Donald Campbell dies when Bluebird somersaults at 300mph

Jan 4. Frogmen halted their search for the body of Donald Campbell tonight after his jet-powered Bluebird leapt into the air, somersaulted and plunged into Coniston Water during an attempt to break the world water-speed record. Campbell was within a fraction of a second of beating his own record of 276.33mph when the disaster occurred. The boat reared into the air as over the radio Campbell said: "She's going – she's going. I'm almost on my back." His helmet, shoes, oxygen mask and teddy bear mascot were found at the spot where the boat plunged – but no sign of Campbell.

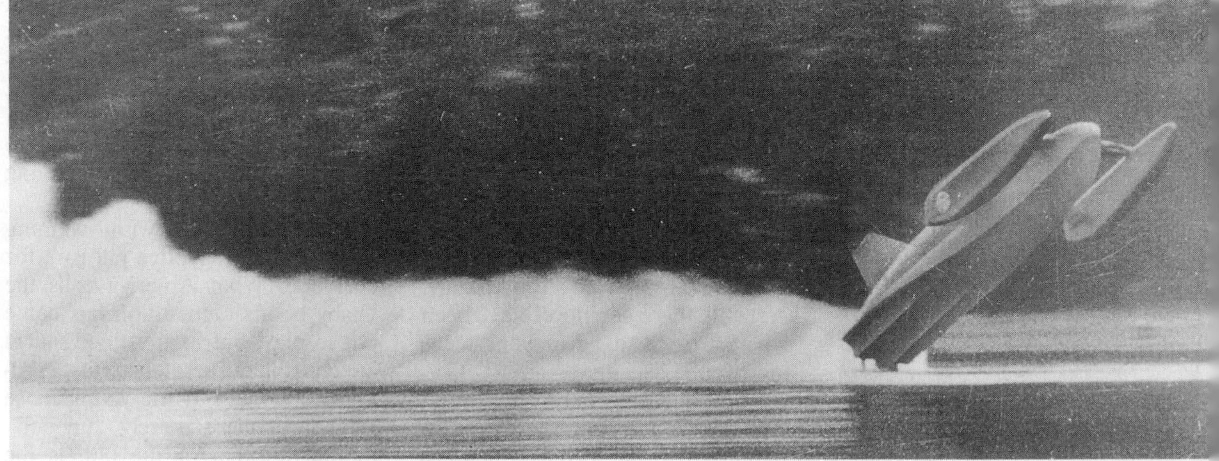

Bluebird makes her fatal somersault and record-breaker Donald Campbell loses his life on Coniston Water.

Jeremy Thorpe is new Liberal leader

The Liberals' new young leader.

Jan 18. Jeremy Thorpe, an extrovert 34-year-old Old Etonian and television personality, is the new leader of the Liberal Party. He got the job today after a hurried ballot of the 12 Liberal MPs to choose a successor to Jo Grimond, another Old Etonian who says he is now too deaf to lead.

It was only yesterday that Mr Grimond quit, and there were protests from constituency Liberals of being "undemocratically" bounced by two taxi-loads of MPs into having their new leader. An earlier Mr Thorpe, MP, was beheaded in the 14th century.

"Boys' Own" folds in a unisex world

Jan 16. The Boys' Own Paper, home of the rattling good yarn for generations, is closing down on its 88th anniversary because "market changes" have made it uneconomic. In its heyday, the 1890s, it had a circulation of 190,000 a week. Now it is only 24,000. Its best-known serial featured the detective Sexton Blake. On the BOP contributors' list were R.M. Ballantyne, G.A. Henty, Algernon Blackwood and Arthur Conan Doyle.

1967

FEBRUARY

Su	Mo	Tu	We	Th	Fr	Sa
			1	2	3	4
5	6	7	8	9	10	11
12	13	14	15	16	17	18
19	20	21	22	23	24	25
26	27	28				

1. UK: Students protest against a Government decision to increase fees for overseas students (→ 23).

5. UK: The Musicians' Union bans the Rolling Stones' "Let's spend the night together" from Eamonn Andrews' TV show.

5. Nicaragua: Anastasio Somoza is elected President.

6. London: Soviet premier Alexei Kosygin arrives on an official visit.

9. Salisbury: Rhodesia ends Commonwealth tariff preferences (→ 4/3/68).

12. Switzerland: Dougal Haston and Mike Burke are first Britons to climb the Matterhorn's north face in winter.

13. London: Teenagers run wild at Heathrow as they try to get a glimpse of The Monkees pop group.

14. London: 100 Labour MPs stage a revolt, voting to condemn the renewed bombing of North Vietnam.→

16. US: British films "Georgy Girl", "A Man for all Seasons" and "Alfie" win top honours at the Golden Globe awards.

20. UK: Viyella International announces the closure of two Lancashire cotton mills.

22. Djakarta: President Sukarno hands over power to Suharto, but retains his title.

23. London: Over 30 Labour MPs abstain in a vote of censure of government increases in overseas student fees.

25. US: Police recapture "Boston Strangler" Albert DeSalvo, who escaped from a prison mental ward yesterday.

26. UK: 30 people are held in police drug raids in the West Country.

28. London: 62 Labour MPs revolt on the Defence White Paper, cutting Wilson's majority to 39 (→ 18/7).

DEATHS

8. British publisher Sir Victor Gollancz (*9/4/1893).

18. US nuclear scientist Dr. J. Robert Oppenheimer (*22/4/1904).

US launches major attack on Viet Cong HQ

Feb 26. American troops today launched Operation Junction City, their biggest assault of the war, when more than 25,000 men attacked the Viet Cong stronghold known as War Zone C, which runs right up to the Cambodian border.

It is here that Nguyen Huu Tho, chairman of the political wing of the Viet Cong, has his HQ. It is also the terminal of the Ho Chi Minh supply trail from the north.

Paratroopers were used for the first time in Vietnam, jumping less than five miles from the Cambodian border. From the air, the whole area was a fantastic scene of criss-crossing aircraft, billowing smoke, parachutes dotting the jungle and soldiers hacking their way through the undergrowth (→ 10/3).

US troops land near Kontum.

Fraud charges after insurance collapse

Savundra: no truck with peasants.

Feb 10. Five days after an extraordinary television interview with David Frost, Dr Emil Savundra was arrested tonight and charged with fraud. Savundra is the former chairman of the Fire, Auto and Marine Insurance company which collapsed last year with losses estimated at £1.4 million.

During the interview, Savundra met some of his victims. "I do not want to cross swords with the peasants," he told Frost.

Bill to put birth control on the rates

Feb 17. A bill for birth control on the rates was given an unopposed second reading in the House of Commons today. It will empower local authorities directly or through voluntary bodies to give "medical examinations and advice on contraception and supply pills and appliances to men and women". Each authority will decide on charges and whether to treat the unmarried.

During the debate Labour MP Leo Abse called for a monopolies inquiry into contraceptives since some which sold for 1s 3d cost only 3d to make (→ 4/4).

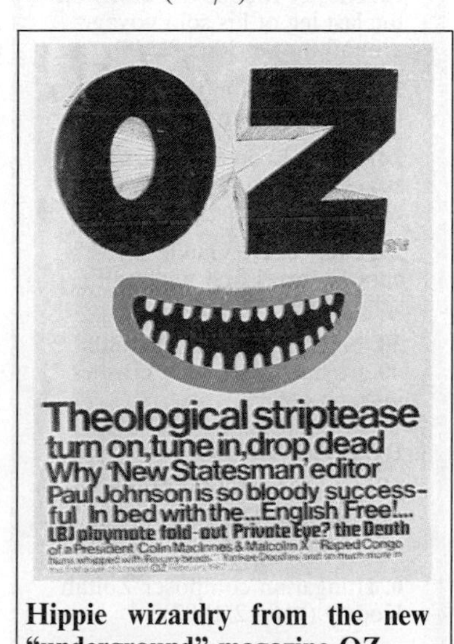

Hippie wizardry from the new "underground" magazine OZ.

1967

MARCH

Su	Mo	Tu	We	Th	Fr	Sa
			1	2	3	4
5	6	7	8	9	10	11
12	13	14	15	16	17	18
19	20	21	22	23	24	25
26	27	28	29	30	31	

1. London: The Decimal Currency Bill is published (→ 23/4/68).

1. London: The Queen opens the Queen Elizabeth Hall and the Purcell Room.

4. London: QPR are the first Third Division club to win a Wembley final, beating West Brom 3-2 for the League Cup.

6. UK: The police begin the trial use of helicopters.

10. Vietnam: The US bombs a major industrial installation for the first time (→ 1/4).

12. India: Mrs Gandhi is re-elected Prime Minister.

13. Congo: Moise Tshombe is sentenced to death in absentia (→ 1/7/67).

13. London: LSE students stage an all-night sit-in to protest at the suspension of two students.→

15. London: Emanuel Shinwell resigns as chairman of the Parliamentary Labour Party.

16. London: The bank rate is cut to six per cent (→ 12/4).

17. UK: A star-grading system for petrol is introduced this month.

19. UK: An oil tanker, the Torrey Canyon, runs aground off Land's End and begins spilling its oil cargo (→ 24).

20. Atlantic: Sir Francis Chichester rounds the Horn on the last leg of his solo voyage around the world (→ 28/5).

24. UK: Oil from the Torrey Canyon begins to wash ashore.→

24. Sierra Leone: The army seizes power in a bloodless coup.

29. France: De Gaulle launches France's first nuclear submarine.

30. New Orleans: 18 die and 40 are hurt when a jet crashes into a motel.

DEATHS

5. Iranian statesman Dr Mohammed Mossadegh, premier 1951-53 (*1880).

6. Hungarian composer Zoltan Kodaly (*16/12/1882).

Stricken oil tanker bombed by RAF

March 30. Fighter aircraft blasted the wreck of the oil tanker Torrey Canyon again today, in a final attempt to destroy the oil which has fouled Cornish beaches in what has been described as the "greatest peacetime threat to Britain". Sea Vixens, Buccaneers and Hunters dropped 48 incendiary bombs and 1,200 gallons of napalm on what remains of the 61,263-ton tanker, which ran aground on the Seven Stones Reef between Land's End and the Scilly Isles.

After he returned from watching the bombing, Air Vice-Marshal John Lapsley said today: "We are satisfied beyond reasonable doubt that the source of the oil on the ship is now destroyed." Divers will check the wreck over tomorrow to make sure no more oil is trapped in its tanks.

More than 100 miles of coastline have been polluted by some of the 100,000 tons of oil the vessel carried, which spilled out as she split her back. The Prime Minister, Harold Wilson, even held a crisis mini-cabinet meeting of ministers at RAF Culdrose in Cornwall, as it rapidly became clear bombing and setting fire to the oil was the only way to halt its spread and save what is left of the West Country's tourist prospects this summer.

The wrecked tanker, pounded by the force of the Atlantic waves.

Hunger strikers at LSE call off their fast but sit-in goes on

March 19. Thirteen hunger strikers, who have refused food for five days in protest against the suspension of two student leaders at the London School of Economics, have abandoned their fast. However, although the suspensions have been lifted, the battle for student rights at the college is far from over.

The two leaders, David Adelstein and Marshall Bloom, were suspended for three months this week, following their holding of a banned meeting on January 31, protesting against the appointment of Walter Adams, former head of University College Rhodesia, as the LSE's new director.

Since the suspension the LSE has been in turmoil, with more than 1,000 students occupying the school. They are leaving now, but will be back if necessary.

Protesting students mass in an LSE lecture theatre to attack the appointment of Walter Adams, the former principal of a college in Rhodesia.

British troops open fire on Aden rioters

British soldiers take on an Arab demonstrator in the Crater district.

March 1. British troops opened fire on rioters in Aden tonight as a bomb, believed to have been planted by an Arab servant, killed a British woman at a government official's dinner party.

Earlier a crowd of 15,000 attending the funeral of an assassinated local government minister killed by two Arabs who opened fire on the procession. They were thrown from the roof of a mosque. Aden was paralysed for much of the day by strikes in protest at the assassination, as rival groups blamed each other for his death (→ 30/4).

Thalidomide firm is charged in Germany

March 14. Nine executives of Chemie Gruementhal, the German company that launched the drug known in Britain as thalidomide, were charged in Aachen today with a series of offences. They include causing bodily harm, causing death by negligence, and contravening drug laws. The trial could last a year.

Stalin's daughter, Svetlana, has defected

March 9. In a remarkable ideological about-turn, Svetlana Alliluyeva, the daughter of the late Soviet dictator Joseph Stalin, has defected to the West. Svetlana, aged 41, walked into the American embassy in Delhi and applied for asylum. Stunned officials quickly granted it and she is almost certain to live in the United States.

Svetlana had been let out of the Soviet Union in great secrecy to take the ashes of her Indian husband to India. Although Stalin has been disgraced since his death in 1953, his daughter's defection will be a blow to the Kremlin and will be used as a propaganda coup by the West (→ 21/4).

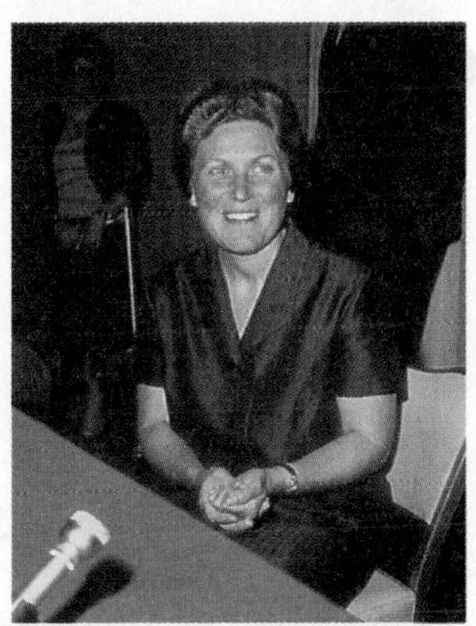

Svetlana, happy away from home.

1967

APRIL

Su	Mo	Tu	We	Th	Fr	Sa
						1
2	3	4	5	6	7	8
9	10	11	12	13	14	15
16	17	18	19	20	21	22
23	24	25	26	27	28	29
30						

1. New York: UN Secretary-General U Thant renews his call for an end to the war in Vietnam (→ 7).

3. Aden: Three Arabs die as British troops clash with 1,200 demonstrators; 11 soldiers are hurt (→ 30).

3. London: Calder and Boyars is sent for trial for publishing the allegedly obscene "Last Exit to Brooklyn" (→ 23/11).

4. London: The Government says it will not ban the contraceptive pill, which may cause thrombosis, as the risk is "very slight" (→ 29/7/68).

7. France: 129 people are arrested during anti-Vietnam protests against US Vice-President Hubert Humphrey (→ 15).

9. Washington: An inquiry into the Apollo 1 disaster in January says it was probably caused by faulty wiring (→).

10. US: Elizabeth Taylor wins an Oscar for "Who's Afraid of Virginia Woolf"; "A Man for All Seasons" wins six Oscars.

12. UK: The pound reaches parity with the dollar for the first time in a decade (→ 4/5).

14. UK: Tories win nine counties and a 14-seat majority on the GLC, controlling London for the first time since 1934.

15. US: More than 200,000 protest in New York and San Francisco against the Vietnam War (→ 6/5).

17. Peking: President Liu Shao-chi is accused of leading a coup attempt against Mao in February (→ 15/5).

21. US: Svetlana Alliluyeva Stalin arrives "to seek self-expression".

26. London: A Picasso is sold for $532,000, a record for a living artist.

30. Aden: Nine Arab schoolchildren die and 14 are hurt when their bus runs over a landmine (→ 20/6).

DEATH

19. German statesman Konrad Adenauer, first Chancellor of the German Federal Republic 1949-63 (*5/1/1876).→

Germany's old fox, Adenauer, is dead

Germany's post-war inspiration.

April 19. Konrad Adenauer, who led Germany to respectability and economic prosperity out of the moral and physical ruination of the war, died at his home at Rhondorf near Bonn today. He was 91.

Flags were lowered to half-mast and church bells tolled in mourning for Germany's first post-war Chancellor and elder statesman. Known affectionately by some as Der Alte, "the old man", others thought of him as "the old fox".

Constantly under attack by the Soviet Union as a "revanchist", he refused to bow to the Kremlin's pressure and continued to work for the reunification of Germany.

He will be given a state funeral in Cologne Cathedral and will be buried in the family grave in Rhondorf churchyard.

Ombudsman clocks on with a warning

April 1. Sir Edmund Compton prepared to start work today as Britain's first Ombudsman, and said that he expects to deal with up to 7,000 complaints a year. These will be referred to him by MPs on behalf of people claiming to have had a raw deal from government departments. "I shall investigate ministries from the minister downwards," warned Sir Edmund, whose past work as auditor-general has often uncovered Civil Service shortcomings. ▷

Army colonels take power in Greece

April 21. Athens is under curfew and martial law tonight, after a junta of right-wing army officers seized power from the democratic government. Troops commanded by Colonel Georges Papadopoulos occupied government buildings in the capital. They appointed a civilian ex-minister to head a cabinet of officers. "We shall suppress any resistance", he stated.

The military claim to be acting in the name of King Constantine, who tonight swore in the new government. Greeks suspect that the Queen Mother encouraged the coup. Junta leaders declared that they struck to save Greece "from internal enemies". Georges Papandreou, a former Prime Minister, is under arrest, and so is his son Andreas, who was himself suspected of plotting a left-wing coup to stop the next general election (→13/12).

Soviet cosmonaut plunges to his death

At the funeral Valentina Komarova kneels to kiss her husband's picture.

April 24. Vladimir Komarov, aged 40, the Soviet cosmonaut, was killed today when his Soyuz spacecraft crashed to earth after coming out of orbit. A Kremlin commission will investigate the tragedy, the world's first space-flight disaster.

According to American sources, the spin of the capsule, after it had re-entered the earth's atmosphere, may have caused the parachute to snarl up. Why Komarov did not use the automatic ejector, with which all Soviet spacecraft are fitted, is unexplained.

Komarov was the first cosmonaut to fly in the big new Russian Soyuz spacecraft. During his 24 hours in orbit there were a number of indications that all was not well. A brief announcement at the beginning of the flight was followed by 13 hours of silence.

According to American observers, Komarov made an unsuccessful attempt to bring his craft down during its 16th orbit. During the 18th he succeeded and re-entered the atmosphere normally, but disaster struck in the last few miles of his descent.

All 47 American astronauts have signed a telegram of sympathy to Russia's cosmonauts.

Ali stripped of title for refusing draft

April 30. Muhammad Ali, previously Cassius Clay and unquestionably the best heavyweight boxer in the world, has been stripped of his world title by all the American boxing associations for formally refusing to be inducted into military service.

Ali, who is 25, and who has rejected the name Clay since joining the Black Moslem sect, faces a minimum jail sentence of five years if he is found guilty of draft evasion, but the champion, who has defended his title successfully nine times since dramatically taking the crown from Sonny Liston in February 1964, says that as a minister in the Black Moslem faith, he "cannot be true to my belief in my religion" by accepting the country's call to arms.

"I ain't got no quarrel with them Viet Congs," he protested (→8/5).

Two dead lords are a hit for Stoppard

April 12. The National Theatre put its faith in a first play by a new playwright last night, and it came up trumps. Tom Stoppard's "Rosencrantz and Guildenstern are Dead" explores what these two characters do between their appearances in "Hamlet". They debate the mystifying goings-on at Elsinore and their own shadowy existence. The play is funny and philosophical, and got a rapturous reception.

Stoppard: philosophical wit.

Winner of Grand National at 100-1

April 8. A pile-up of riderless, fallen and baulked horses at the 23rd fence turned the Grand National into near farce today, and allowed Foinavon, a rank outsider ridden by John Buckingham, to thread his way through and romp home to win the world's most famous steeplechase at the staggering price of 100-1.

Race relations laws may be strengthened

April 27. Roy Jenkins, the Home Secretary, is considering whether the race relations laws can be strengthened; so he told MPs today after publication of the first annual report of the Race Relations Board.

The Board called for more legislation to cover jobs, financial facilities, housing and behaviour in public places. It said that the coloured population – now estimated at one million – may rise to three million by the year 2000, and it warned that inertia and inaction now could create huge social problems for the future. Mark Bonham-Carter, the chairman of the Race Relations Board, argues for effective legal sanctions to back educational and conciliation work.

He says: "No country has a better chance than Britain of handling the influx of aliens in a civilised and constructive fashion."

However, MPs complained that both employers and the TUC are "alarmingly complacent". Mr Jenkins said that police forces at least are not, and are striving for closer co-operation with immigrant communities. He is studying US race relations (→4/2/68).

Barefooted Sandie Shaw wins the Eurovision Song Contest.

1967

MAY

Su	Mo	Tu	We	Th	Fr	Sa
	1	2	3	4	5	6
7	8	9	10	11	12	13
14	15	16	17	18	19	20
21	22	23	24	25	26	27
28	29	30	31			

1. London: Ten men make off with £700,000 in gold bars from a security van in Britain's biggest-ever bullion raid.

2. London: Wilson says Britain will apply for membership of the EEC.→

4. UK: The bank rate is cut to 5.5 per cent (→19/10).

5. US: Ariel 3, the first all-British satellite, is launched.

6. Hanoi: Three captured US pilots are displayed at the International Press Club (→12/8).

8. US: Muhammad Ali is indicted for refusing the draft.

10. London: The Road Safety Bill, introducing compulsory breath tests, becomes law (→12/7).

14. Liverpool: The Roman Catholic Cathedral of Christ the King is opened.

15. Peking: A mob ransacks a British diplomat's home as anti-British demonstrators march through the city.→

18. UAR: The UN agrees to withdraw its 3,400-man peace-keeping force from the Israeli border (→22).

20. London: Tottenham Hotspur beat Chelsea 2-1 in the FA Cup Final.

22. Brussels: 322 people die when a fire sweeps through "L'Innovation" department store.

22. Cairo: Nasser says he will close the Tiran Strait on the Gulf of Aqaba to Israeli shipping (→30).

25. London: Enoch Powell calls Britain "the sick man of Europe" (→21/4/68).

28. UK: 520,000 people have signed a petition against the Medical Termination of Pregnancy Bill (→14/7).

30. Cairo: The UAR and Jordan sign a military alliance (→1/6).

DEATHS

12. British poet John Masefield, Poet Laureate 1930-67 (*1/6/1878).

30. British actor Claude Rains (*10/11/1889).

De Gaulle rebuffs Wilson

President de Gaulle doesn't need to whisper about his views on England.

May 16. President de Gaulle today repeated his "Non" in characteristically roundabout way. Just two days after Britain has applied again for Common Market membership, the French leader said that there will be boundless joy in France when Britain joins, but it cannot be yet, can it? At a rare news conference, the French President spoke of "formidable obstacles" to the application. It is another velvet veto.

Despite this, Mr Wilson told MPs the application will be pursued with all vigour and determination. The Government won a Commons majority of 488 votes to 62 for this move. It is the biggest vote in the parliamentary records for the past 100 years. However, 62 anti-Marketeers – half of them Labour, half Tory – smiled contentedly on hearing about de Gaulle's new brush-off. The President called for an end to the Anglo-US special relationship, dismantling of the sterling area and proof that the British have begun to think like good Europeans. Then it will be "Oui" (→27/11).

Rolling Stones in court on drugs charges

Jagger and Richard leave court.

May 10. In two separate incidents three members of the Rolling Stones rock group are currently facing trials for drug use. After a raid on February 12 on guitarist Keith Richard's home in Sussex, Richard, the lead singer Mick Jagger and an art gallery owner, Robert Fraser, all appeared today before Chichester magistrates charged with drug offences. After pleading not guilty, they await a jury trial.

Another member of the band, the guitarist Brian Jones, was arrested today in London after police raided his Kensington apartment; with another man he, too, faces drugs charges (→27/6).

Biafra is to break away from Nigeria

May 30. After the massacres of recent months, the Ibo people no longer believed their lives and property were safe in Nigeria, the Ibo leader, Colonel Odumegwu Ojukwu, said today when he announced the secession of the Eastern Region and proclaimed its independence as the Republic of Biafra. Of a total Nigerian population of about 50 million, some 12 million live in the Eastern Region, though many of those are not Ibos.

Lieutenant-Colonel Yakubu Gowon, the Federal leader in Lagos, described the secession as a "bloody disaster". He had tried hard to persuade Colonel Ojukwu to remain in Nigeria, and as a final desperate measure had divided the four-region federation into 12 states to accommodate the country's major tribal groups, but for Ojukwu and his Ibos it was too late (→7/7).

Peking orders UK diplomat to leave

May 22. The diplomatic squabble between Britain and China continued today when Peking expelled a British diplomat and shut down the Shanghai consulate. The move is part of the war of nerves which China is waging over its claims of sovereignty to Hong Kong, where it has organised anti-British demonstrations (→30/8).

Elvis Presley marries his long-time sweetheart Priscilla Beaulieu; the cake had six tiers.

Great welcome for solo OAP yachtsman

Francis Chichester greets the crowds as he ends his world voyage.

May 28. Amid tumultuous cheers Francis Chichester, the lone yachtsman, ended his epic 28,500-mile voyage round the world in Plymouth tonight. At 8.56pm his yacht, Gipsy Moth IV, crossed the finishing line, to a victory salute from hundreds of welcoming craft, after 119 days at sea, sailing non-stop from Sydney.

The slight and bespectacled Chichester, who had previously sailed the Atlantic three years ago in Gipsy Moth III, was initially greeted on board by his family – his wife and their son, Giles – before coming ashore at the Royal Western Yacht Club.

Walking very deliberately, after so long at sea, he then greeted the Lord Mayor of Plymouth at a special reception. There was a "welcome home" message, too, from the Queen and Prince Philip, and a telegram of congratulations from the Prime Minister, Harold Wilson.

Later, "looking as if he had just been away for the weekend", as one reporter remarked, the 65-year-old yachtsman was taken to the local Guildhall in an open Rolls-Royce, and cheered by thousands on his way. Chichester's arrival had come ten hours later than expected, but now, he declared, the first thing he wanted was "the best dinner from one of the best chefs, in the best company I can have" (→4/7/68).

Three hippie poster artists with a selection of their products.

Celtic score a first for British soccer

May 25. Glasgow Celtic have triumphed where the great English teams of the 1950s and early 1960s all failed: they have won the European Champions' Cup.

In the heat of Lisbon, Jock Stein's team conceded an early penalty to Internazionale of Milan, and fought the toughest defence in Europe for nearly an hour before Tommy Gemmell equalised. Eight minutes from the end, Celtic's non-stop attack found a hole in Inter's defence, Steve Chalmers stuck out a boot, and it was left to the captain Billy McNeill to raise the huge trophy in victory.

1967

JUNE

Su	Mo	Tu	We	Th	Fr	Sa
				1	2	3
4	5	6	7	8	9	10
11	12	13	14	15	16	17
18	19	20	21	22	23	24
25	26	27	28	29	30	

1. Tel Aviv: Moshe Dayan is appointed Israeli defence minister (→2).

1. UK: The Beatles' LP "Sergeant Pepper's Lonely Hearts Club Band" is released (→27/8).

2. Tel Aviv: Israel agrees to sign an Anglo-US declaration asserting the right of free passage in the Gulf of Aqaba.→

3. France: 88 die when a British airliner crashes in the Pyrenees.→

4. Holland: Jim Clark wins the Dutch Grand Prix in a new Lotus-Ford (→1/10).

9. Cairo: The Egyptian assembly refuses to accept Nasser's resignation (→10).

13. Washington: Thurgood Marshall is appointed the first black member of the US Supreme Court.

17. China: The first Chinese H-bomb is detonated.

20. Aden: Eighteen Britons are shot dead in a police mutiny (→30/11).

26. Rome: The Pope names 27 new cardinals, including the Archbishop of Krakow, Karol Wojtyla.

27. UK: Mick Jagger and Keith Richard are found guilty of drug offences (→29).

27. UK: Barclays Bank introduces Britain's first cash-dispensing machine.

29. UK: Keith Richard gets one year, Mick Jagger three months for drug offences (→31/7).

DEATHS

3. British author Arthur Mitchell Ransome (*18/1/1884).

3. British commander Marshal of the Royal Air Force Arthur William Tedder, Lord Tedder (*11/7/1890).

7. US author and critic Dorothy Parker (*22/8/1893).

10. US actor Spencer Tracy (*5/4/1900).→

29. US actress Jayne Mansfield (*19/4/1932).

Old time movie star Spencer Tracy dies

Tracy: grand old man of film.

June 10. When Katharine Hepburn stepped into his kitchen to say good morning to Spencer Tracy today, she found him sitting at the table, head bowed. Her dearest friend was dead, at the age of 67.

They met in 1942, and made nine films together, reflecting their own relationship of teasing and embattled affection. Tracy separated from, but did not divorce, his wife, with whom he founded a deaf school.

Tracy's weatherbeaten looks and gritty integrity won him two Oscars, as the fisherman of "Captains Courageous" and, in 1938, as the padre who created "Boys' Town" for delinquents such as poker-playing Mickey Rooney.

Holiday plane crash death total hits 160

June 4. Two plane loads of holidaymakers have died within 12 hours of each other, with the loss of 160 lives in all. The first tragedy occurred yesterday when a DC-4 plane owned by Air Ferry Ltd, carrying 83 holidaymakers to the Costa Brava, crashed into the Pyrenees just 40 miles from Perpignan in southern France.

Then, today, a British Midland Airways Argonaut hit the ground four miles from Manchester as it attempted to land after the pilot reported "trouble with the rpm's". A total of 78 people returning from Majorca were killed.

Israel is triumphant in six-day war against Arabs

Day 1: the attack

June 5. The growing tension between Israeli and the Arab states erupted into all-out war today, as Israeli planes launched pre-emptive strikes against the Arab air forces, destroying 374 planes and gaining supremacy in the skies. On the ground, Israel captured the Sinai capital of El Arish, fought fierce tank battles with Egypt along a 200 mile desert front, and clashed with the Jordanian Army in Jerusalem.

Day 2: the advance

June 6. Israel was heading for total victory today as her troops swept across the Sinai peninsula towards the Suez Canal, took the Gaza Strip from Egypt and the biblical towns of Bethlehem and Hebron from Jordan. Colonel Nasser accused the US and Britain of aiding Israel and three Arab states immediately cut of oil supplies in retaliation while the UN Security Council called for an immediate cease-fire.

Day 3: Jerusalem

June 7. Israeli paratroopers prayed at the Wailing Wall in Jerusalem today after capturing it from the Jordanians in fierce house to house fighting, while thousands of Jews caused a near-riot as they rushed to visit the holy site which politicians vow will remain Israel's for ever. Jordan accepted the UN cease-fire, having also lost Jericho and most of the West Bank, and Israeli troops advanced across the Sinai to the Suez Canal and took the Egyptian fortress of Sharm el Sheikh.

Advancing Israeli troops pass trucks full of Arab prisoners as their vehicles penetrate the Mitla Pass.

Day 4: the victory

June 8. Egypt admitted defeat and accepted the UN cease-fire today. The counter-offensive launched by President Nasser's troops had failed, leaving the remnants of her army in the Sinai trapped behind enemy lines. Earlier, Israel killed ten US sailors in a torpedo attack on the communications ship Liberty, after mistakenly identifying it as an Egyptian ship.

Day 5: Nasser out

June 9. Colonel Nasser announced his resignation as Egypt's President in a TV broadcast today only to have it rejected by the National Assembly after mass rallies in Cairo and Beirut urging him to stay on. On the northern front, Israel began an all-out offensive only hours after Syria accepted the UN cease-fire, bombing Damascus and advancing into the Golan Heights.

Day 6: cease-fire

June 10. Fighting in the Middle-East ended today as Israel finally observed the UN cease-fire and halted her 12-mile advance into Syria at Keneitra. Within the space of just six days she has taken Arab territory many times larger than Israel, and will now face the dilemma of how she can control their hostile populations. Western nations are also pondering the implications of Arab states using oil as a political weapon. Many families have more immediate concerns, though: total war casualties are estimated as at least 100,000.

Dayan: Israel's military planner.

Jews celebrate their return to the liberated Wailing Wall in Jerusalem.

Duchess of Windsor meets Queen in public

History is made as the Queen Mother greets the once-estranged Duke.

June 7. A simple slate plaque was unveiled by the Queen today in memory of her grandmother Queen Mary (1867-1953). It is set in the wall of Marlborough House, Queen Mary's home for much of her life.

But what fascinated onlookers was the presence of the Duchess of Windsor, who, for the first time, was attending an official ceremony involving other members of the Royal Family.

For 30 years relations between the Duke and Duchess and members of the Royal Family have been distinctly cool. Queen Mary felt that the Duke's duty was to remain as monarch. Queen Elizabeth the Queen Mother blamed the early death of her husband, King George VI, on the abdication. He became monarch at the shortest of short notice and toiled diligently in a job for which he had not been trained until his death in 1952.

But today both the Duke and Duchess were warmly greeted by the Queen and the Queen Mother.

The Beatles hold the sleeve of their latest album ("Sergeant Pepper's Lonely Hearts Club Band") their new-style "concept" album which is widely tipped by critics and fans alike to prove their greatest success ever, with its blend of singalong, musical virtuosity and psychedelia.

1967

JULY

Su	Mo	Tu	We	Th	Fr	Sa
						1
2	3	4	5	6	7	8
9	10	11	12	13	14	15
16	17	18	19	20	21	22
23	24	25	26	27	28	29
30	31					

1. UK: BBC 2 begins regular colour broadcasting; the first seven hours is mostly coverage of Wimbledon.

1. Algeria: Moise Tshombe's plane is hijacked to Algiers on a flight from Ibiza to Majorca (→21).

3. UK: ITV launches a new regular daily half-hour news programme, "News at Ten".

5. Tel Aviv: Dayan announces the annexation of Gaza.

7. Nigeria: Government troops invade the oil-rich breakaway region of Biafra.→

8. Wimbledon: Australian John Newcombe beats Wilhelm Bungert for the Men's Singles title; Billie Jean King beats Ann Jones in the Ladies' Singles final.

9. Hong Kong: Four die in clashes between police and Communist rioters.

12. London: Transport Minister Barbara Castle says the 70 mph speed limit is to stay.

15. Canada: De Gaulle arrives in Quebec.→

16. London: 5,000 attend a "Legalise Pot 1967" rally in Hyde Park.

17. UK: The "Keep Britain Tidy" group launches Britain's first Anti-Litter Week.

21. Algiers: Tshombe is ordered to be extradited to the Congo, where he is under a death sentence for treason.

25. London: Judith Hart replaces Margaret Herbison as Minister of Social Security.

27. London: The Sexual Offences Bill becomes law.

28. London: The British Steel Corporation is formed.

DEATHS

8. British actress Vivien Leigh (*5/11/1913).→

17. US saxophonist John Coltrane (*23/9/1926).

21. British actor Basil Rathbone (*13/6/1892).

21. South African black leader Albert John Luthuli, 1960 Nobel Peace Prize winner (*1898).

British cyclist dies on Tour de France

Simpson: strain proved too much.

July 23. Tommy Simpson, the most successful road-race cyclist Britain has produced, died on the notorious Mont Ventoux on the 13th stage of the Tour de France.

The 29-year-old from Durham, world road-race champion in 1965 and the first Englishman ever to wear the coveted yellow jersey in the Tour de France, was lying in overall seventh place at the start of the Marseilles-Avignon stage.

The heat on the mountain stage was intense and, three miles from the towering summit of the Ventoux, Simpson fell, remounted, then collapsed unconscious by the roadside. He was flown to Avignon by helicopter, but died in hospital on arrival.

Rolling Stones to stay out of prison

July 31. Rolling Stones Mick Jagger and Keith Richard walked free today, after appeal court judges quashed the prison sentences that followed their recent trial on drugs charges. After leaving the court, Mr Jagger gave a press conference before being helicoptered to an undisclosed destination in Essex, where he was filmed for television in conversation with a number of "Establishment" figures.

Europeans flee Biafra

July 16. Some 2,000 Britons and 800 Americans are fleeing from Biafra in cars and canoes as Nigerian federal troops step up their two-pronged drive into the breakaway eastern region, but it's not an easy journey. Fred McKinnon, a British oil-drilling executive, said his group encountered 31 road blocks before they reached Onitsha to cross the Niger by canoe.

The Nigerian forces, pushing into rebel territory from the north, have captured the university town of Nsukka, and in the south they have taken Ogoja.

The Federal leader, Yakubu Gowon, now promoted to General, says the military successes are largely due to skilful use of artillery, backed up by determined infantry action. But the Biafrans have been more successful than the Federal government cares to admit. The rebels initially knocked the Federal forces off balance with a powerful thrust on the central front. That has now been held, but the Federals have still to make an in-depth penetration into Biafra.

Most of Nigeria's oil is produced in the area now held by the Biafran forces under Colonel Ojukwu, and he is insisting that British oil companies operating the concessions must now pay him the royalties. When Shell-BP was reported to be ready to pay up, the Federal authorities retaliated by blockading all oil exports. Before the war, Britain took about ten per cent of her oil from Nigeria.

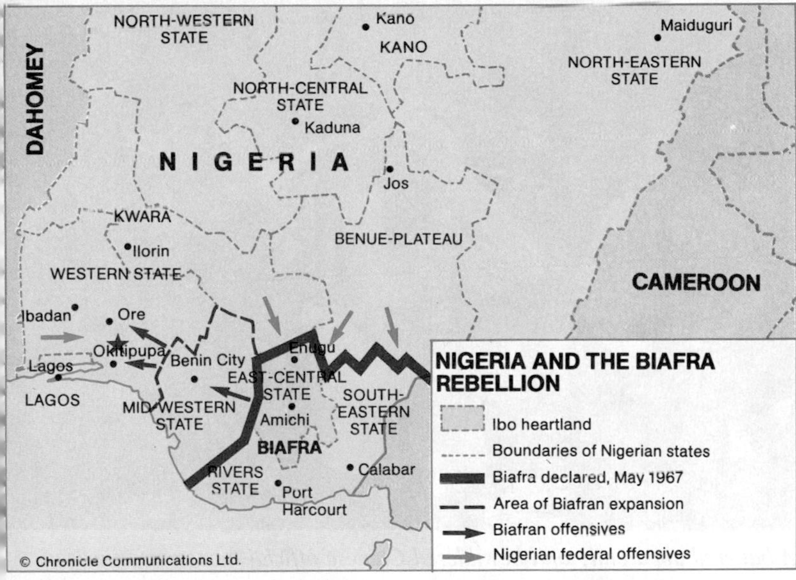

Race riots sweep through American cities

A city block stands gutted after a night of racial turmoil in Detroit.

July 27. As paratroops from the 101st and 84th Airborne divisions restored order in the riot-torn streets of Detroit, President Lyndon Johnson today announced the appointment of a high-level commission to look into the causes of the recent urban rioting in American cities.

The Detroit riot began on July 24th when police were called to a noisy party at a "blind pig", or illegal drinking shop, to welcome a black soldier home from Vietnam.

Relations between blacks and the police in Detroit have been poor since the race riot of 1943, and have deteriorated recently after two incidents in which black women were shot by policemen. Before the rioting was brought under control, at least 38 people had been shot, most of them black rioters and looters shot by police and the National Guard.

While this is the most serious riot in recent years, rioting has broken out in dozens of US cities since 1964. Just this week, two were killed and many injured when thousands of Puerto Ricans looted shops in New York. The presidential commission will be led by Otto Kerner, the Governor of Illinois, with Mayor Lindsay of New York as Vice-Chairman.

Abortions are to be legal in Britain

July 14. The controversial bill to legalise abortion cleared its third reading in the Commons today after 64 hours of debate, the longest continuous sitting for 16 years. It is expected to become law later this year.

The bill is the second this month to have aroused passionate feelings. The bill to legalise homosexual acts between adult men went through ten days ago. Supporters see it as a liberalising and humane measure, opponents as a decline into degeneracy.

Britain withdraws from East of Suez

July 18. Britain is to withdraw her forces from East of Suez by the mid-1970s. The forces will be cut by 20 per cent, and all soldiers, sailors and airmen will be pulled out of Singapore and Malaysia in a few years time, according to the new defence estimates. Despite these cuts, Britain will still be spending over £2 billion a year on defence by the mid-seventies, but Conservative MPs called the move a "recipe for disaster", and warned that it presented an open invitation for China to take over the Far East.

The Queen dubs Francis Chichester, the lone yachtsman, a knight.

De Gaulle boosts Free Quebec hopes

July 31. President de Gaulle today added fuel to the flames of controversy which have been raging since his recent visit to Canada. He said he had observed in his visit to French-speaking Quebec "their will to control their own destiny, if possible, in all respects". He said Canada owed her origin to France, and referred to "a century of oppression which followed the British conquest".

The French President was invited by the Quebec premier, Mr Daniel Johnson. While there he raised the hopes of the separatists who want complete independence. He told them France would help their fight for freedom. He cut short his visit without going on to Ottawa to see the Federal premier, Mr Lester Pearson. Today he said it was Mr Pearson's fault for saying that a totally free Quebec was unacceptable.

Vivien Leigh, cat-like beauty, dies

Vivien Leigh, the saddest star.

July 8. Vivien Leigh, whose delicate cat-like beauty won her the role of Scarlett O'Hara over all the sirens of Hollywood, died today of tuberculosis at the early age of 53. In 1940 she and Laurence Olivier were married and became the royal couple of the stage, but her depressive mental illness was intensified by playing Blanche in "A Streetcar Named Desire", her best performance. She divorced Olivier in 1960.

1967

AUGUST

Su	Mo	Tu	We	Th	Fr	Sa
		1	2	3	4	5
6	7	8	9	10	11	12
13	14	15	16	17	18	19
20	21	22	23	24	25	26
27	28	29	30	31		

1. Ottawa: Canadian Prime Minister Lester Pearson dismisses de Gaulle's challenge on Quebec.

2. London: The £8 million Dartford Tunnel under the Thames opens.

3. UK: The Aberfan Disaster inquiry blames the Coal Board.

6. Tel Aviv: Israel and Jordan agree a scheme for the repatriation of 175,000 Arab refugees to occupied land.

9. Nigeria: Biafran troops cross the River Niger and invade the Mid-Western Region of Nigeria.

12. Washington: Johnson authorises a new list of bombing targets in North Vietnam.

14. UK: Most pirate radio stations close in advance of the Marine Broadcasting Act.

15. UK: The Marine Broadcasting Act comes into force, banning pirate radio stations.

17. UK: Coventry FC manager Jimmy Hill announces he is quitting to pursue a career in television.

17. US: Muhammad Ali marries an orthodox Moslem and reaffirms his commitment to Islam.

20. London: Three gunmen attack the US Embassy with automatic rifles.

23. Belgium: Eddy Merckx becomes world cycling champion.

25. US: George Rockwell, founder of the US Nazi Party, is shot dead by a sniper.

28. London: Herbert Bowden is appointed chairman of the Independent Television Authority.

29. US: Ex-child star Shirley Temple Black announces she is standing for Congress.

DEATHS

1. British poet Siegfried Lorraine Sassoon (*8/9/1886).

9. British playwright John Kingsley "Joe" Orton (*1/1/1933).

15. Belgian artist Rene Magritte (*21/11/1898).→

Anglo-Chinese battles of the embassies

Aug 30. In the latest round of the Anglo-Chinese war of the missions, China early today barred all members of the British Mission in Peking from leaving the country without official permission. The Chinese action follows the extraordinary pitched battle yesterday in the Marylebone mews where the Chinese Mission office is located.

Tension erupted into violence after an argument about a police car parked near the Mission garage in the mews off Portland Place. A chanting group of about 30 Chinese diplomats wielding baseball bats, iron bars and axes rushed out and hurled themselves at the police and press photographers. The police, using dustbin lids as shields, counter-attacked with truncheons; one person was hurt on each side.

The trouble began in Peking when Red Guards set fire to the British Mission, looted the home of Mr Hopson, the Charge d'Affaires, and beat up several members of the Mission. The British Government responded by putting restrictions on movements of the Chinese diplomats in London. The police car that sparked yesterday's most undiplomatic fracas was checking those movements.

Last night the Foreign Office said that the day's "deplorable incidents" were a deliberate attempt by the Chinese to provoke violence by the British police and so justify their own actions.

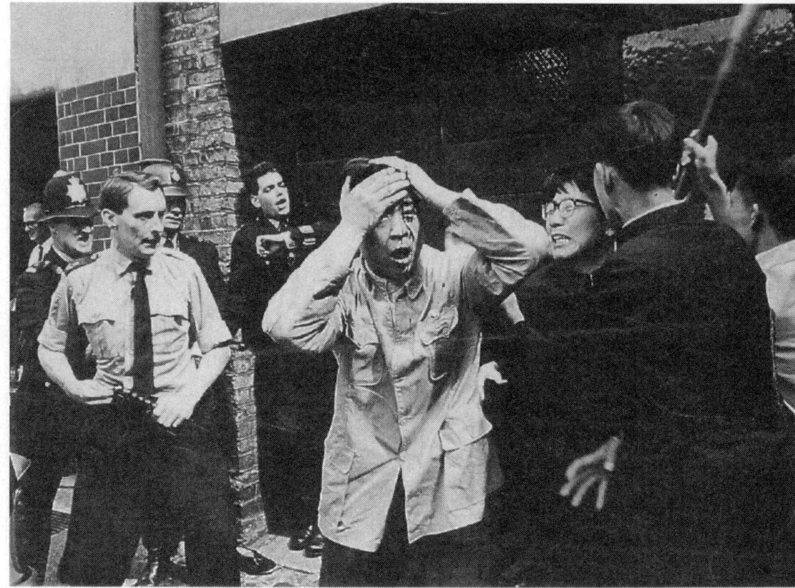

A battered apparently and bewildered Chinese official nurses his injuries.

This isn't about the death of Magritte

Aug 15. Rene Magritte, the Belgian Surrealist, painted an extremely solid-looking pipe and underneath it the message "This is not a pipe". He was pointing out the difference between images and reality. His art explores the gap between the two, often wittily, as when you realise that the view out of the window is partly a painting on an easel placed in front of the window; but what is behind the canvas? The same view – or something else? Magritte left us with no answers to his enigmas when he died today aged 69.

Majority verdicts to be allowed in court

Aug 21. Criminal courts in future will be able to convict a defendant even though some jurors believe he is innocent. Majority verdicts will be accepted from next month where jurors have tried and failed to reach unanimous decisions, Home Office ministers announced today. Other changes being introduced under the Criminal Justice Bill include a ban on ex-prisoners serving on criminal juries, provision for sentences to be suspended, corporal punishment in jail to be ended, and higher fines for many offences.

Flower power blooms at Woburn Festival

The hippies were out in force at Woburn's Festival of the Flower Children.

Aug 31. As the hippies wander home happily from Woburn Abbey, where for the past three days the Duke of Bedford has been hosting the "Festival of the Flower Children", there's no doubt that this really has been the Summer of Love. The hippie headquarters may be in San Francisco, but LSD guru Timothy Leary's gospel of "Turn on, tune in and drop out" has certainly spread across the Atlantic.

Garlanded in flowers, beads, bells, a kaleidoscope of multi-coloured clothing, entertained by their own music, dancing at their own clubs, living in a world where they make the rules, for the young, being a hippie is truly "where it's at".

Whether flowers, psychedelic drugs and "love" offer any real answers to the problems of the modern world remains debatable. What is certain is that, for large numbers of the young, they're a better solution than most.

Beatles' manager, Epstein, is found dead

Aug 27. Brian Epstein, the former Liverpool record store owner who discovered and then managed the Beatles, is dead. He was found this afternoon when his butler broke into the locked bedroom of his house in London's Belgravia. Mr Epstein appeared to have taken an overdose of sleeping pills. Police said foul play was not suspected.

As crowds of pop fans filled the street outside, and many of Epstein's friends and associates arrived to speak to the police, the Beatles, who have been involved in five days of meditation with the Maharishi Mahesh Yogi in Wales, broke off their retreat to return immediately to London. John Lennon, visibly shocked, said: "I do not known where we would have been without Brian."

Epstein: from the murky Cavern to the glitter of the West End.

1967

SEPTEMBER

Su	Mo	Tu	We	Th	Fr	Sa
					1	2
3	4	5	6	7	8	9
10	11	12	13	14	15	16
17	18	19	20	21	22	23
24	25	26	27	28	29	30

1. Khartoum: An Arab summit lifts the oil embargo on western states imposed during the Six-Day War.

3. Sweden: Traffic switches to driving on the right.

3. South Vietnam: General Nguyen Van Thieu is elected President, with Nguyen Cao Ky as Vice-President.

4. London: The jury at the Joe Orton inquest is told that Orton was hammered to death by Kenneth Halliwell.

4. London: 17 ex-pirate DJs are to join the BBC; Tony Blackburn and John Peel will work on Radio 1 (→30).

6. Warsaw: De Gaulle arrives on a visit, the first to Poland by a French president.

8. UK: The families of the Aberfan tragedy victims are to get £5,000 each, it is announced.

11. London: The Tories announce that Anthony Barber will succeed Edward du Cann as Party Chairman.

12. US: Governor Reagan of California urges escalation of the Vietnam War to bring it to a swift end.

18. UK: Yorkshire Cricket Club turns down an offer to tour Rhodesia.

21. UK: The Conservatives capture Walthamstow and Cambridge from Labour in by-elections.

23. Moscow: The USSR signs an aid pact with North Vietnam.

25. Paris: Britain, France and West Germany sign an agreement to co-operate on an "Airbus" airliner.

27. UK: The Queen Mary arrives at the end of her last cruise.

30. UK: BBC Radios 1,2,3 and 4 begin broadcasting in place of the Light and Third Programmes and the Home Service.

DEATH

18. British nuclear physicist Sir John Douglas Cockcroft (*27/5/1897).

Gibraltar votes to keep ties with UK

Sept 10. In a referendum today the people of Gibraltar voted overwhelmingly to stay British and reject General Franco's sovereignty claims. There were flag-waving scenes of enthusiasm when the result was announced – 12,138 for staying with Britain and 44 for joining Spain.

Ninety-five per cent of those eligible to vote did so, and there were queues outside the four polling stations two hours before they opened. Spain is now expected to sever remaining links with Gibraltar. Five thousand dockyard workers will be forbidden to cross from Spain, and the Algeciras ferry will be out of action. Air travel will be more difficult, but the Union Jack will fly high.

Queen launches the QE2 at Clydebank

Sept 20. Bellowing sirens mixed with the cheers of 100,000 people today as the Queen named the new £29 million Cunard liner, Queen Elizabeth II, at Clydebank. She pressed a button to release a bottle of champagne as the 58,000-ton liner moved down the slipway. She said the liner, which 2,000 workmen will transform into a floating town over the next 14 months, represented the best standards of British engineering, management and workmanship.

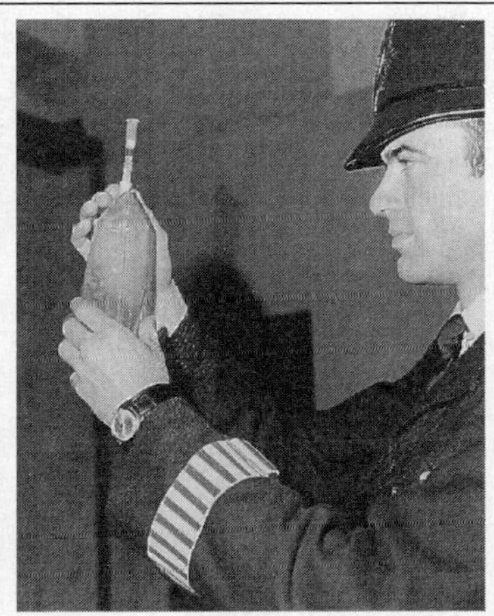

A policeman looks carefully at a new hazard for road-users – the bag of breathalyser crystals.

1967

OCTOBER

Su	Mo	Tu	We	Th	Fr	Sa
1	2	3	4	5	6	7
8	9	10	11	12	13	14
15	16	17	18	19	20	21
22	23	24	25	26	27	28
29	30	31				

1. US: Jim Clark wins the US Grand Prix.

3. Hanoi: North Vietnam rejects a US offer of peace talks.

4. Nigeria: Federal troops take Enugu, the capital of Biafra.

5. London: The British Lawn Tennis Association proposes to abolish the distinction between amateurs and professionals.

8. Cambridge: Prince Charles begins his course at Trinity College this week.

9. UK: Rootes announces its new Sunbeam Rapier.

10. Oxford: Six undergraduates are suspended for taking drugs.

12. Mediterranean: 66 die when a BEA Comet crashes 170 miles west of Cyprus.

16. US: Singer Joan Baez is arrested at an anti-Vietnam War protest in California (→ 20).

19. London: The bank rate rises from 5.5 to 6 per cent.

25. London: The Medical Termination of Pregnancy Bill, renamed the Abortion Bill, is passed by Parliament.

26. Tehran: Coronation of the Shah.

27. London: The Abortion Bill becomes law.

30. London: Rolling Stone Brian Jones is jailed for nine months on a drugs charge.

31. Southampton: The Queen Mary leaves for the last time, bound for Long Beach, California.

31. London: Brian Jones is released on bail pending an appeal.

DEATHS

8. British statesman Clement Richard Attlee, first Earl Attlee, PM 1945-51 (*3/1/1883).→

9. Argentine-born Cuban revolutionary Ernesto "Che" Guevara (*14/6/28).→

9. French author Andre Maurois (*26/7/1885).

17. Chinese ruler Pu Yi, last Emperor of China (*1906).

Anti-war demo at Pentagon turns violent

Anti-Vietnam demonstrators taunt the ranks of US military police.

Oct 21. A peaceful rally against the Vietnam war turned violent today as demonstrators, after meeting at the Lincoln Memorial, crossed the Potomac and surrounded the Pentagon. Although Viet Cong flags flew in the crowd, the gathering at the Memorial had been peaceful, but at the Pentagon the crowd tried to rush lines of armed soldiers and US federal marshals. No shots were fired, but many demonstrators were hit over the head with truncheons and rifle butts.

The demonstrators – some stoned on drugs, many in fancy dress, and including young women with bare breasts – taunted the soldiers, who in some cases beat them severely. The novelist Norman Mailer was among more than 250 people arrested during the demonstration.

Attlee, unassuming reformer, is dead

Oct 8. The most unassuming Prime Minister in British history died today, aged 84. Clement Richard (later Earl) Attlee, led Labour's first majority governments from 1945 to 1951, presiding over a social revolution and giving India independence. As Churchill's deputy in the wartime coalition, he did much to keep the wheels of government turning – an achievement better appreciated now than then.

Years later he said: "It was a state of life to which I never expected to be called." His route to socialism was through good works in London's East End.

Naked Ape is most sexy primate alive

Oct 12. Dr Desmond Morris, once curator of mammals at the London Zoo, has written a study of man as if he were reporting on the orang-utan. He calls it "The Naked Ape", since man is the only species of ape without a hairy coat, but he is, says Morris, "the sexiest primate alive". He illuminates man's behaviour by comparison with other animals.

Revolutionary hero, Che Guevara, is shot in Bolivian jungle

Oct 10. The body of Ernesto "Che" Guevara, the Argentine-born hero of Latin American revolutionaries, is on public display today at Villa Grande in Bolivia. Formal identification confirmed claims by Bolivian troops that he was finally shot dead yesterday. Six other guerrillas, including five Cubans, were killed in the same action, when the army cornered his band.

Since he disappeared on clandestine operations two years ago there have been many false reports of his capture or death. Regis Debray, the French writer on trial for aiding underground groups, admitted seeing Guevara this year in Bolivia.

"Che" Guevara, the 39-year-old firebrand, was formerly the confidant of Fidel Castro. In 1965 he left to establish guerrilla groups in Latin America. His death will be a blow to the morale of guerrilla groups across the continent.

Gloating Bolivian officers poke and prod at the dead guerrilla's body.

1967

NOVEMBER

Su	Mo	Tu	We	Th	Fr	Sa
			1	2	3	4
5	6	7	8	9	10	11
12	13	14	15	16	17	18
19	20	21	22	23	24	25
26	27	28	29	30		

1. Washington: Johnson says Vietnam war protests do not aid peace (→ 14).

2. UK: Winifred Ewing wins the Hamilton by-election to become the first Scottish Nationalist MP since 1945.

4. UK: 37 die when a Spanish airliner crashes near London.

5. London: 53 are feared dead and 90 hurt in a train crash at Hither Green, south-east London.

7. UK: Hugh Scanlon is elected head of the engineering union, the AEU.

8. Leicester: Radio Leicester, the BBC's first local station, opens.

9. London: Bernard Haitink gives his first concert as principal conductor of the London Philharmonic.

10. London: MPs approve the Countryside Bill, which allows local authorities to set up Country Parks.

13. London: Britain is reported to have received $250 million in international credits to bolster the pound.→

14. Washington: Secretary of State Rusk says an escalation of the Vietnam war cannot be avoided.→

14. Moscow: Kim Philby gives his first interview to Western journalists.

18. Detroit: Michigan Governor George Romney says he will run for President.

23. London: The book "Last Exit to Brooklyn" is found to be obscene.

27. Paris: De Gaulle vetoes British entry into the Common Market.

28. UK: All horse-racing is suspended owing to the foot-and-mouth epidemic.

29. London: Roy Jenkins becomes Chancellor in succession to James Callaghan, who becomes Home Secretary.

DEATH

20. Polish-born US biochemist Casimir Funk, inventor of the term "vitamin" (*23/2/1884).

The pound is devalued

Nov 19. The worst financial crisis for nearly 20 years has ended with another devaluation of sterling. The exchange rate for the pound was today brought down from two dollars 80 cents to two dollars 40 cents – a fall of 14.3 per cent. At the same time the credit squeeze is to be tightened, with the Bank Rate hoisted to eight per cent and taxes increased by £200 million. Arrangements have been made for big new foreign loans and credits.

These emergency moves have come after several days of rumour, confusion and wild speculation in world money markets. They involve a complete reversal of government policy during the last three years. James Callaghan, the Chancellor of the Exchequer, who recently called devaluation "a flight into escapism", is expected to resign soon.

Mr Wilson, in a television broadcast tonight, presented the measures as the key to economic expansion and boom times by 1969. He also struck a patriotic note. "We're on our own now. It means Britain first," he said. Explaining devaluation, the Prime Minister said: "It does not mean, of course, that the pound here in Britain in your pocket or purse or in your bank has been devalued."

Wilson with Chancellor Callaghan.

Year	US dollars
1900	4.87
1920	3.66
1925	4.82
1931	3.69
1934	5.04
1940	4.03
1950	2.80
1967	2.40

The fall, rise and fall of the pound in US dollars during the 20th Century.

After 128 years UK troops leave Aden

Nov 30. Arabs surged into the port city of Aden today to celebrate the end of 128 years of colonial rule and the formation of the new People's Republic of South Yemen. Britain has been struggling against rebellion in the colony for four years and talks with the National Liberation Front, which is expected to form the first government, were only concluded in Geneva two days ago. The East India Tea Company seized control of Aden in 1839, to stop pirate attacks on ships sailing for India.

Outbreak of foot-and-mouth hits UK

Nov 21. Efforts to check the spread of foot-and-mouth disease have led to the slaughter of 134,000 animals in Britain, the highest number since the outbreak in 1923. The figure was announced by the Government today amid farming fears that the disease is showing no sign of being stamped out. Experts confirmed 71 new farms had been hit, taking the total to 746 in a month. Cheshire, Shropshire and Northamptonshire are the latest counties to be badly affected.

US air force steps up bombing raids against North Vietnam

Nov 21. Despite the growing protests in the United States against the war in Vietnam, American warplanes have returned to the attack on North Vietnam with increased ferocity. B-52 heavy bombers based in Thailand have bombed a large military supply depot three miles from the centre of Hanoi, and carrier-based aircraft have struck at a shipyard at Haiphong. It has been admitted that these raids have caused civilian casualties.

Other aircraft operating from bases in South Vietnam are supporting US troops engaged in fierce fighting in the Central Highlands near the Cambodian border. Using napalm, bombs and machine-gun fire, they are clearing the ground for the advancing troops and protecting them with close-range bombing when they are attacked.

Citizens of Hanoi take shelter as the American bombs continue to fall.

1967

DECEMBER

Su	Mo	Tu	We	Th	Fr	Sa
					1	2
3	4	5	6	7	8	9
10	11	12	13	14	15	16
17	18	19	20	21	22	23
24	25	26	27	28	29	30
31						

1. UK: Tony O'Connor becomes Britain's first black headmaster, at Warley School in Worcestershire.

4. London: Britain announces a ban on meat from countries with foot-and-mouth disease.

9. Bucharest: Nicolae Ceausescu becomes Rumanian premier.

10. Stockholm: Nobel Prizes go to Hans Bethe (US, Physics); Manfred Eigen (West Germany), Ronald Norrish (UK) and Sir George Porter (UK), all for chemistry; Ragnar Granit (Sweden), Haldan Hartline (US) and George Wald (US, Medicine); Miguel Asturias (Guatemala, Literature). No Peace Prize.

12. London: Brian Jones will not go to jail for his drugs offence, but he is put on probation and fined £1,000.

14. Athens: King Constantine flees to Rome.

17. Australia: Greengrocer Alec Rose ends a 14,500-mile lone voyage from Britain.

18. Moscow: British traitor Kim Philby is hailed as a hero of the USSR.

19. Australia: John McEwen is sworn in as acting Prime Minister (→9/1/68).

21. London: Premiere of "Half a Sixpence", with Tommy Steele.

26. Indochina: The North Vietnamese attack Laos.

30. Hanoi: Ho Chi Minh sends a New Year greeting to US anti-war protesters.

DEATH

29. US jazz musician Paul Whiteman (*28/3/1890).

HITS OF 1967

Release Me.

All you need is love.

The Last Waltz.

QUOTE OF THE YEAR

"No Viet Cong ever called me nigger."

Muhammad Ali, refusing to fight in Vietnam.

Man is given new heart

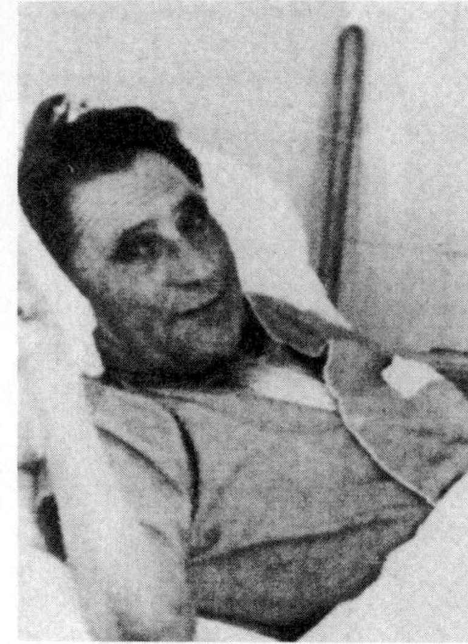

Recipient Washkansky...

and miracle-worker Barnard.

Dec 21. Louis Washkansky, the world's first heart transplant patient, died today in Cape Town, South Africa, after leaving for 18 days with the heart of a 25-year-old woman who was killed in an auto accident. Doctors at Groote Schuur Hospital said the 53-year-old grocer died after a steady deterioration that began when he developped lung complications several days ago. The transplanted heart continued to beat until the end.

The transplant was performed on Dec 3 by a team headed by Dr. Christiaan N. Barnard, who trained in the USA and continued animal experiments on heart transplants in South Africa. The operation was performed when Washkansky, who had suffered a series of heart attacks, was so weakened that he would have lived only a few days.

Fast food at home: 1st microwave oven

Dec. Cooks are now wondering how popping frozen food in an oven and seeing it sizzle in an instant could possibly be appealing.

New microwave oven.

Counter-coup by Greek King flops

Dec 13. King Constantine of Greece fled to Rome late tonight after the failure of his ill-organised attempt to topple the military junta. Mistakenly convinced that the Third Army Corps was loyal to him, the King flew to its Northern HQ, but there was no popular response to his broadcast appeal to all democrats for help in dismissing the military government which seized power eight months ago.

The Air Force failed to rally, and senior Royalist army officers were promptly arrested. Recrimination has followed the King and Queen to their exile home in Italy. The left accused the King of cowardice; junta supporters said he had fallen into "great error". All were agreed that his flight marks the end of the monarchy in Greece.

Tennis finally goes open at Wimbledon

Dec 14. Despite threats of suspension from the international game, the Lawn Tennis Association has voted to end the distinction between amateurs and professionals in lawn tennis. From the start of the Bournemouth hard court championships on April 22 next year all competitors, including those at Wimbledon, will be known simply as "players". It means champion Rod Laver will be back at Wimbledon for the first time in six years. Only five people voted against the proposal.

Supersonic Concorde is triumph of Anglo-French co-operation

Dec 11. The world's first supersonic airliner, the Anglo-French Concorde, was rolled out of its hangar in Toulouse today as both countries celebrated a triumph in international co-operation. Now the final squabble over whether or not the aircraft's name should end in an "e" has been resolved, there seems little to stop the new aircraft. It has been ordered by 16 airlines, although whether or not they will all take up their options to buy remains to be seen. Much will depend on its final cost.

The band plays on as Concorde 001, the first prototype, is rolled out.

Rock: pop music gets into sex and drugs

Posters, a Mini Moke, hippies – I mean, that's a real heavy scene, man.

Ballad singers **Engelbert Humperdinck** and **Tom Jones** may have sold records by the million this year, but in terms of rock and roll, they are strictly for the "straights" and the old: 1967 has been the year of Flower Power, and the music that appealed most to the young has made that clear.

Hippie or not, it's been impossible to avoid the world of love and peace or its centre in California. **Scott McKenzie** hymned the psychedelic glories of "San Francisco", backed up by the **Flowerpot Men** who urged the world "Let's Go To San Francisco".

Love and peace remained synonymous with drugs and, for all their denials, the **Beatles'** astonishing LP, "Sergeant Pepper's Lonely Hearts Club Band", seemed riddled with LSD references. The **Rolling Stones** temporarily abandoned their tried and tested Rhythm and Blues background for their own essay in psychedelia, "Their Satanic Majesties Request", as well as their love and peace singles "We Love You" and "Dandelion".

The hippie single has to be **Procul Harum's** "Whiter Shade of Pale", which spent five weeks at number one, but the most important debut of the year has been the **Jimi Hendrix Experience**, two British sidesmen led by a hugely talented American guitarist.

Arts: New Anthems are concrete example

One of the leading composers of electronic music (or Musique Concrete), **Karlheinz Stockhausen**, has produced a composition which lasts all evening. "Anthems", for electronic and concrete sounds, is divided into four parts, each featuring the national anthem of a different country, accompanied by sounds ranging from the recorded cries of jungle animals to the heavy breathing of the orchestral players themselves. "Music is a state of being," Stockhausen declares. "It is a means to a new awareness."

A new awareness of the quiet horror of life seems to be inherent in **Francis Bacon's** new paintings on exhibition. His portraits of popes, seemingly imprisoned in transparent cubes, have been succeeded by portraits of himself or of his companion **George Dyer**. The figures are placed on stools in the middle of ambiguous, menacing rooms, their faces distorted as if by wearing a stocking mask or blurred by revolving at high-speed. Whatever the cause, the effect conveyed is close to agony.

Francis Bacon's "Pope No 2".

British films and players have had a good year, with "A Man for all Seasons" sweeping the board of American film awards, including six Oscars. **Paul Scofield** was voted best actor for his cool but moving portrayal of Sir Thomas More.

The enigmatic "Blow Up", although directed by the Italian **Michelangelo Antonioni**, is as English as the Swinging London which it presents, complete with stripping games and marijuana parties. Its hero (**David Hemmings**) is, of course, a fashion photographer. The team which made the heartless and trendy "Darling" – director **John Schlesinger**, writer **Frederick Raphael** and actress **Julie Christie** – have turned to Thomas Hardy for their next subject. "Far From the Madding Crowd", his novel of what was then considered Swinging Wessex, earned a U-certificate.

Richard Burton and **Elizabeth Taylor** seem natural casting as a feuding, but mutually attracted couple. They rise to it in **Franco Zeffirelli's** "Taming of the Shrew", just as they did in the gameplaying of **Edward Albee's** "Who's Afraid of Virginia Woolf?", which won Miss Taylor her second Oscar.

President Johnson visits Vietnam's Cam Ranh Bay to see the troops he calls "my boys", who are fighting America's war in Vietnam.

Australia's Prime Minister drowns in surf

Dec 17. Harold Holt, Australia's Prime Minister, apparently drowned today while swimming in the sea near his holiday home at Portsea, Victoria, just 30 miles from Melbourne.

Holt was known as a strong swimmer and skindiver, but a spokesman revealed that the Prime Minister nearly drowned in a similar incident just a few weeks ago.

Hundreds of divers, including teams from the civilian rescue services and navy frogmen, joined the hunt for Mr Holt.

Holiday-makers watched and waited while soldiers checked the beaches along a 30-mile front while out at sea surface craft helped the divers in their efforts. Every available helicopter was mustered to the search, including a number of those ready to go to help Australian forces in Vietnam.

America's President Johnson has requested immediate notification of any news. The Queen has also expressed her deep concern.

If Mr Holt is not found alive, Lord Casey, Australia's Governor-General, will appoint an interim Prime Minister. The most likely choice will be the current vice-premier, John McEwen. Mr McEwen is a member of the minority Country Party, which shared in a coalition government with Mr Holt's Liberal Party.

1968

JANUARY

Su	Mo	Tu	We	Th	Fr	Sa
	1	2	3	4	5	6
7	8	9	10	11	12	13
14	15	16	17	18	19	20
21	22	23	24	25	26	27
28	29	30	31			

1. London: Cecil Day Lewis becomes Poet Laureate, a post vacant since the death last year of John Masefield.

2. Cape Town: Dr Christiaan Barnard performs the world's second heart transplant (→2/5).

2. US: Actress Sharon Tate marries Roman Polanski.

5. Washington: Dr Benjamin Spock is indicted for his anti-draft activities (→14/6).

9. Canberra: John Gorton becomes Prime Minister on his election as leader of the Liberal Party.

12. Moscow: Writers Alexander Ginsburg and Yuri Galenkov are jailed for "slandering the state".

14. Edinburgh: Malcolm Muggeridge resigns as rector of the university over plans to offer the Pill free to students.

15. London: A bill is published making "irretrievable breakdown of marriage" sole ground for divorce.

15. UK: 20 die as hurricane-force winds lash Scotland.

17. London: Michael Foot leads 41 Labour MPs in a revolt against spending cuts of £712 million (→31).

17. UK: British Motor Corporation and Leyland say they will merge as British Leyland Motor Corporation.

23. North Korea: The Pueblo, a US intelligence ship, is seized and its crew held as spies.→

23. London: The Port of London says it will close London Docks and sell St. Katherine Docks to the GLC.

25. Canada: Escaped Great Train Robber Charles Wilson is arrested.

26. UK: The National Provincial Bank and the Westminster Bank announce a merger as Britain's biggest bank (→9/7).

31. London: Wilson stays away from a meeting of Labour MPs that decides to suspend 24 rebels (→20/2).

31. Mauritius: The island becomes independent of Britain after days of race riots.

Tet offensive hits at heart of Saigon

Jan 31. Taking advantage of the traditional truce during the Tet (New Year) celebrations, the Viet Cong today launched a coordinated series of heavy attacks against most of the major cities in South Vietnam. Saigon itself became a battlefield, with Viet Cong suicide teams shooting it out in the streets with American troops and South Vietnamese armed police.

One of the first targets was the US Embassy where Viet Cong, dressed in South Vietnamese uniforms, blew a hole in the wall, shot the guards and occupied the building. A swarm of helicopters landed American troops on the roof, and they fought their way room by room through the Embassy, finally clearing it after six hours against fanatical opponents.

President Thieu's Palace was also attacked, and a determined attempt was made to seize the radio station, which went off the air early today. Cholon, the Chinese suburb of Saigon, is believed to have fallen to the Viet Cong, who have many sympathisers in its mean streets.

Reports are coming in of similar attacks all over the country. Thirty aircraft have been destroyed at Da Nang, America's biggest airbase, and Bien Hoa, the headquarters 20 miles outside Saigon, has been cut off from the capital. Casualties have been heavy on both sides.

This assault has taken the Americans and the South Vietnamese completely by surprise. It seems that the Viet Cong, who have shown signs of defeat recently, have gathered all their forces for a last desperate attack designed to undermine the government and rally the people to their cause (→24/2).

A Viet Cong guerrilla is taken prisoner by US military police in Saigon.

US spy ship seized by North Koreans

Jan 24. North Korean patrol boats last night attacked, boarded and captured the Pueblo, an American "spy ship", killing and wounding a number of her crew. The North Koreans accused the Pueblo, officially described as an "intelligence auxiliary ship", of "provocative acts" within their 12-mile limit, and of opening fire on the four patrol boats which surrounded her.

A converted freighter, packed with electronic listening devices but with few guns, the Pueblo is commanded by Lieutenant-Commander Lloyd Butcher. America's first diplomatic efforts to secure the release of the Pueblo and her crew have failed. Russia has refused to intervene, and the North Koreans say they intend to keep them.

There can be no doubt about the gravity of the situation. Mr Dean Rusk, the US Secretary of State, said last night that it could be interpreted as an act of war (→2/2).

Trevor Nunn takes over as head of RSC

Jan 31. Peter Hall is handing over direction of the Royal Shakespeare Company later this year to Trevor Nunn, it is announced today. Hall's first actions when appointed eight years ago were to rename the company, give it a London home at the Aldwych Theatre, and campaign for an Arts Council grant, which it got in 1963. He was 29. Nunn is 28 and also comes from Suffolk and Cambridge University (→23/2).

Trevor Nunn (r.) jokes with his predecessor, theatre director Peter Hall.

New liberal leader heads Czechoslovakia

Jan 5. After a bitter behind-the-scenes struggle, the Czechoslovak Communist Party has produced a new leader with a reputation as a reformer and – in East European terms – a liberal.

Alexander Dubcek, aged 46, a Communist official since the war-time years underground, ousted the pro-Moscow stalwart, Antonin Novotny, to become the first Slovak to lead the party. The power shift will open the way for long-delayed economic reforms.

Dubcek is also expected to ease the heavy-handed party controls on the press and encourage more candour in political discussions. Novotny briefly talked of holding on by using the army (→13/3).

A victory smile for Dubcek.

"I'm backing Britain" campaign takes off

All together in the national debt.

Jan 1. Government statements on the economy may be gloomy, against a background of continuing inflation, but today saw the launch of a new movement that defies worry and aims to replace fears by optimism and positive action. Five typists, all employed at Colt Heating and Ventilation Ltd., of Surbiton in Surrey, declared "I'm Backing Britain" and promised to work an extra half hour every day, free of charge, as their way of improving the situation.

The new movement has met an enthusiastic welcome. Politicians and the press have joined in praising the women, and suggested that, if everyone adopted this selfless attitude, Britain may yet become great once more. Edmund Dell, a junior minister for economic affairs, intends to visit Surbiton on a "fact-finding mission", and the Labour Party plans a poster featuring the slogan. Also quick to cash in is TV's Bruce Forsyth, who promises a record, titled, unsurprisingly, "I'm Backing Britain".

Beatles set up shop in Apple boutique

Jan 31. One month from its launch, the public is still flocking into the Beatles' Apple boutique, their £100,000 psychedelic shop in London's West End. Not many of the beautiful clothes, made from exotic fabrics by the fashionable Dutch hippie designers Simon and Marijke, who call themselves "The Fool", actually get bought – they're too expensive for those outside Swinging London's elite – but if nothing else, Apple makes a great tourist attraction.

US nuclear bomber in Greenland crash

Jan 28. A US B-52 bomber carrying four nuclear bombs crashed into the ice off Greenland today while trying to make an emergency landing. The US Defence Department said the bombs were not armed, so there was no chance of a nuclear explosion at the crash site near the US airbase at Thule. However, it is not immediately clear what has happened to the bombs – whether they are scattered across the surface of the ice or have plunged into the 800-feet deep water below.

1968

FEBRUARY

Su	Mo	Tu	We	Th	Fr	Sa
				1	2	3
4	5	6	7	8	9	10
11	12	13	14	15	16	17
18	19	20	21	22	23	24
25	26	27	28	29		

1. US: Former Vice-President Richard Nixon says he will run for president (→8).

2. Pyongyang: The North Koreans refuse to release the US ship Pueblo (→24/12).

4. UK: 96 Kenyan Asian refugees fly in (→13).

5. Atlantic: 19 Hull trawlermen die when their boat sinks off Iceland; 60 have now died in three tragedies in a month.

6. France: The Winter Olympics open in Grenoble.

8. US: Democrat George Wallace says he will seek the presidency (→14/3).

11. Paraguay: President Stroessner is re-elected.

13. UK: Kenyan Asians are now flying in at the rate of 1,000 to 1,500 a week (→19).

15. Atlantic: The Royal Navy's first Polaris missile is tested successfully.

19. UK: The Home Office launches an anti-theft drive based on the slogan "Watch Out! There's a thief about"

19. London: The Government says 61,377 Commonwealth immigrants arrived in 1967, 11,000 more than in 1966 (→22).

20. London: MPs pass a bill to raise National Insurance rates and end free secondary school milk; Tories and 46 Labour MPs abstain (→15/3).

20. Barbados: England bowler Fred Titmus loses four toes in a boating accident.

22. London: Callaghan announces legislation to restrict entry of Commonwealth citizens with British passports.→

23. London: MPs approve the Theatres Bill, abolishing the censorship powers of the Lord Chamberlain (→27/9).

26. Shrewsbury: 22 people die in a fire at a mental hospital.

DEATHS

17. British actor-manager Sir Donald Wolfit (*20/4/1902).

20. British film director Anthony Asquith (*9/11/1902).

Work vouchers plan in emergency bill to stem Asian tide

Feb 22. New legislation is to be rushed through parliament to stem the tide of Asian immigrants from East Africa. At least 2,500 holding British passports have arrived in Britain in the last three weeks, and tens of thousands more want to leave Kenya. In future they will be subject to a quota of 1,500 work vouchers a year. They will be allowed to bring wives and families.

James Callaghan, the Home Secretary, said today: "We have a responsibility to our own people at home as well as to a million holders of British passports abroad." In Kenya there is now a great stampede to get out ahead of the new restrictions (→1/3).

Safe passage for another refugee.

Three golds go to Jean-Claude Killy

Feb 17. Jean-Claude Killy, the pin-up boy of French sport and alpine skier supreme, today completed his clean sweep of medals in the Winter Olympic Games at Grenoble.

After victories in the downhill and the giant slalom, he seemed to have lost the special slalom, in atrocious, foggy conditions, to a superb final run by Karl Schranz, but Schranz was disqualified for missing two gates and, despite frantic Austrian appeals, Killy won his third gold to emulate the feat of the great Toni Sailer in 1956. ▷

Americans hit back after Tet disaster

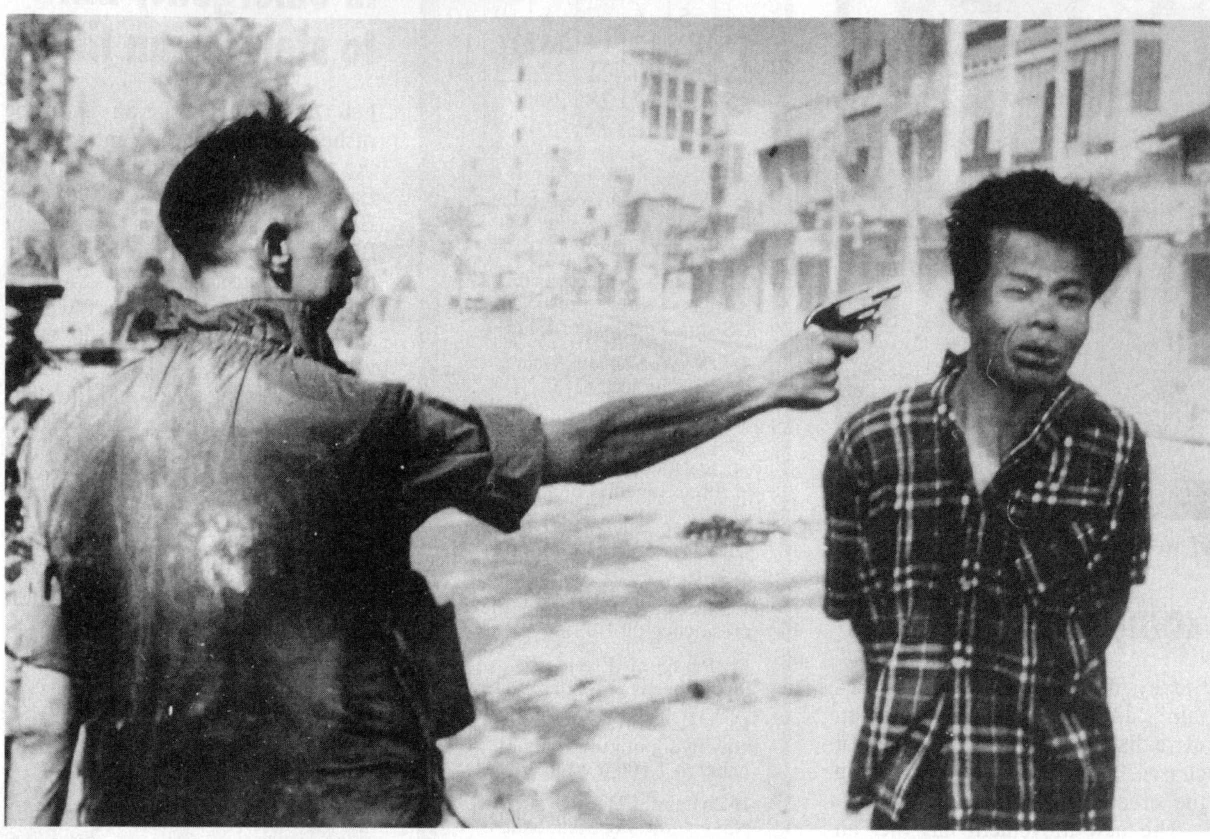

South Vietnamese army General Loan kills a suspect in public: "Buddha will understand," he said.

Feb 24. At 2.30 this afternoon, in drizzling rain, a four-wheeled "mule" mounted with a recoilless rifle drove casually alongside the inner wall of the citadel of the old Imperial City of Hue. It marked its target with a burst of tracer and then blew down the three gates leading to the Imperial Palace.

A South Vietnamese platoon advanced in open order, while a heavy machine-gun barked out covering fire. They went to ground in a ditch, drew breath and then, as the machine-gun tore chunks out of the palace walls, they went up and over the top, across the moat and, cheering wildly, tore through the breached gates.

That was how the Americans and the South Vietnamese finally recaptured Hue, the Communists' greatest prize of the Tet offensive. Seized by Viet Cong guerrillas and North Vietnamese regulars, this northern city became the symbol of Communist success.

They slaughtered all opposition, murdering local officials and replacing them with their own "cadres", and declared Hue, always restive under Saigon's rule, to be "liberated". Its recapture demonstrates the way in which the US and South Vietnamese forces have fought back after the disaster of the Tet offensive, defeating the Viet Cong in the field. It is not in the field, however, where the offensive has done its greatest damage. It is on television in American homes.

No matter how often General Westmoreland claims to be winning, pictures relayed from Saigon such as that of an army chief executing a prisoner in cold blood have seriously affected the American will to continue (→16/3).

American troops shelter behind a tank in the savage fighting for Hue.

1968

MARCH

Su	Mo	Tu	We	Th	Fr	Sa
					1	2
3	4	5	6	7	8	9
10	11	12	13	14	15	16
17	18	19	20	21	22	23
24	25	26	27	28	29	30
31						

1. London: The Commonwealth Immigrants Bill gets Royal Assent (→9/4).

2. US: Lockheed presents the world's largest aircraft, the Galaxy.

4. Salisbury: The Rhodesian appeal court overturns the Queen's reprieve of three blacks sentenced to death (→6).

8. Poland: Police clash with students demonstrating for greater freedom (→12).

10. New Zealand: 200 are feared dead when a car ferry capsizes in Wellington harbour in a severe storm.

12. Warsaw: 300 are arrested during further riots.

13. Prague: Dubcek relaxes press censorship and arrests the former head of the Czech secret police (→22).

14. Washington: Robert Kennedy says he will not back Johnson for re-election.→

16. Washington: Johnson decides to send between 35,000 and 50,000 more troops to Vietnam.→

19. London: The budget raises purchase tax and the duty on petrol, cigarettes, spirits and gambling (→3/4).

21. UK: Figures show that road deaths fell by 23 per cent in the three months after the introduction of breath tests.

22. Prague: Antonin Novotny resigns as President (→9/5).

27. London: Michael Stewart says Britain will not transfer sovereignty of the Falklands without the islanders' consent.

28. UK: The Tories win four by-elections, taking three seats from Labour; Kenneth Baker is new Tory MP for Acton.

29. UK: Rolls-Royce wins a £150 million order for RB2-11 engines from Lockheed, Britain's biggest aviation contract.

30. UK: Mr J. Manners' Red Alligator wins the Grand National.

DEATH

27. Soviet cosmonaut Yuri Gagarin (*9/3/1934).→

LBJ will not run again

"I will not stand, even if asked."

March 31. President Lyndon Johnson tonight stunned America by going on television and announcing that he will not be a candidate for re-election in 1968.

As the incumbent president, and as an exceptionally determined politician, it was universally assumed that he would run for four more years in the White House, and generally accepted that he would probably succeed. So it came as a complete shock tonight when, at the end of a TV speech about the Vietnam war, the President added some words that were not in the text handed out to reporters.

He added, in words that are certain to become historic: "I shall not seek and I will not accept the nomination of my party as President." He suggested that there was "a division in the house", and said that he was withdrawing in the name of national unity. Political setbacks may also have influenced the president's decision.

Two weeks ago, while he beat Eugene McCarthy in New Hampshire, McCarthy received 40 per cent of the vote. That same day Senator Robert Kennedy joined the race for the Democratic nomination (→27/4).

Robert Kennedy to run for White House

March 16. Senator Robert Kennedy, brother of the assassinated John Kennedy, announced today that he is a candidate for the presidency. Although Senator Kennedy has been considering running for months, his decision comes as a surprise. Senator Kennedy was placed in an acute dilemma when Senator Eugene McCarthy won 40 per cent of the votes in the New Hampshire primary on Tuesday. Kennedy is also opposed to the war, but thought President Johnson was invincible. McCarthy has proved how many Democrats oppose the war, and Kennedy decided to act.→

George Brown quits as Foreign Secretary

Brown: a rather chastened figure.

March 15. After twenty-four hours of threats, sulks and high farce, George Brown tonight resigned as Foreign Secretary. He accused Mr Wilson of running the cabinet in a dictatorial fashion.

So ends the ministerial career of Britain's most wayward politician. His erratic behaviour has sorely tried the patience of even his closest friends. He was at home asleep instead of being at an important cabinet meeting today. This was after quarrelling with colleagues and generally making a fool of himself during an all-night sitting at the Commons. The new Foreign Secretary is the cabinet's most staid member, Michael Stewart (→27).

Violent anti-Vietnam war demo in London

Police charge protesters on the day Vietnam came to Grosvenor Square.

March 17. Police foiled attempts by angry demonstrators to storm the American Embassy in London at the end of a rally protesting at United States military involvement in the Vietnam war. In Grosvenor Square the scene was a battlefield as police and protesters traded punches in the worst scenes of violence in the capital for years.

Three hundred arrests were made and 90 policemen were hurt, many seriously, in the trouble. For one and a half hours they held a cordon in front of the embassy, despite repeated charges by youths using banners as battering rams. Skirmishes broke out across the square's gardens and lawns, with officers bringing down the fleeing protesters with rugby-tackles amid the daffodils and shrubs.

Tonight's rally began in Trafalgar Square, where an 80,000 strong crowd was addressed by the actress and peace campaigner Vanessa Redgrave. The protesters then marched to Grosvenor Square, where they hurled paint and stones at the embassy before turning their attention to the bland facade of the nearby Europa Hotel (→13/5).

First man in space dies in air crash

March 27. Colonel Yuri Gagarin, the world's first spaceman, was killed today when an obsolete MiG-15 jet trainer he was flying lost height and crashed into the ground 40 miles north of Moscow. He was 34. Another member of Russia's space team died with him.

Gagarin became a national hero after his pioneer orbital flight in a Vostok capsule on April 12, 1961, which lasted 108 minutes and beat America into space. Medals were heaped upon him and he was given a triumphal ceremony in Red Square where thousands lined the streets to cheer him. He was followed into space by a series of Soviet and American launches. He will be buried in the Kremlin Wall.

In Jacksonville this month, Tony Jacklin became the first English golfer to win a major US tournament for more than 20 years.

1968

APRIL

Su	Mo	Tu	We	Th	Fr	Sa
	1	2	3	4	5	6
7	8	9	10	11	12	13
14	15	16	17	18	19	20
21	22	23	24	25	26	27
28	29	30				

3. London: A white paper proposes a 3.5 per cent ceiling on pay rises (→30/9).

4. US: Dr Martin Luther King is shot dead in Memphis (→5).

5. US: Dr Ralph Abernathy takes over as leader of King's Southern Christian Leadership Conference.→

5. London: Barbara Castle heads the new Department of Employment and Productivity, absorbing the Labour Ministry.

6. Canada: Pierre Trudeau becomes Liberal premier in succession to Lester Pearson, who has retired (→25/6).

9. London: Publication of the Race Relations Bill, which aims to protect non-whites.→

11. Washington: Johnson signs the Civil Rights Bill, making it illegal to refuse housing on the grounds of race.→

12. West Germany: Thousands of students riot following the attempted killing of student leader Rudi Dutschke.→

16. London: Britain withdraws from the European Launcher Development Organisation, a major space project.

18. London: It is announced that US oil tycoon Robert McCullough has bought London Bridge for £1 million.

19. Washington: The FBI says it is seeking James Earl Ray, alias Eric Galt, for the murder of Martin Luther King (→8/6).

20. S. Africa: 122 die when a London-bound Boeing 707 crashes.

23. UK: The first decimal coins come into circulation, for five New Pence (1/-) and ten New Pence (2/-) (→10/5).

26. London: Police seize LSD worth £1.5 million in Britain's biggest drug haul (→26/8).

27. US: Hubert Humphrey says he will run for President (→7/5).

DEATHS

4. US civil rights leader Dr Martin Luther King (*15/1/1929).→

7. British racing driver Jim Clark (*4/3/1936).→

Martin Luther King is gunned down

King's aides point in the direction of the shots, but the killer is long gone.

Coretta King weeps at the funeral.

April 9. More than 150,000 people followed the body of Dr Martin Luther King to burial in Atlanta today. The coffin was drawn by two mules on a plain wooden farm cart. Among the mourners were Mrs Jacqueline Kennedy and the Vice-President, Hubert Humphrey.

Dr King pronounced his own eulogy. Mrs King asked for a tape of his last sermon to be played. Anticipating his own death, Dr King asked that he be remembered because he "gave his life for love".

Dr King was shot dead last Thursday in Memphis, where he had gone to lead a dustmen's strike. The son of a prominent Negro preacher in Atlanta, he was educated at Morehouse College there, and in Boston, where he studied theology and became a disciple of Gandhi. He first came to prominence when he led a bus boycott in Montgomery, Alabama, in 1956. In 1963 he became nationally known by leading mass protests in Birmingham, and through his "I have a dream" speech to the march on Washington. Since then Dr King and his Southern Christian Leadership Conference had begun to concentrate on poverty, both white and black, North and South.

Dr King was shot dead by an unknown white assassin, who escaped in a white Mustang car. He leaned over the motel balcony to speak to his friend, the Reverend Jesse Jackson; his last words were "Be sure to sing "Precious Lord" tonight, and sing it well." (→19)

Luther King's death triggers black riots in major US cities

April 11. President Johnson today postponed a planned trip to Hawaii, and promised to appear before Congress on Monday to announce legislation to ease racial tension, which has boiled over since the murder of Dr Martin Luther King. Within hours of his death, there were riots in dozens of towns and cities last night, from California to Kalamazoo. As soon as blacks heard the news on transistor radios, they began to riot.

In New York, Mayor Lindsay was stoned by a black crowd in Harlem. In Detroit two policemen were shot, and a white youth was burned to death in Tallahassee, Florida. Some of the worst rioting was in Washington, where mobs burned and looted within 300 yards of the White House (→12/8).

An apprehensive National Guardsman is silhouetted against burning ruins.

Enoch Powell foresees a "river of blood"

April 21. "As I look ahead I am filled with foreboding. Like the Roman, I see the River Tiber foaming with much blood." With this classical quotation Enoch Powell, the Tory Shadow Minister of Defence, today triggered fierce controversy over race relations.

In a Birmingham speech which has immediately isolated him from his party leadership, he said that Britain must be "mad, literally mad as a nation" to allow 50,000 dependants of immigrants into the country each year. The present situation, he argued, is like a nation "busily engaged in heaping up its own funeral pyre".

Mr Powell's speech took other senior Tories by surprise. The Opposition leader, Edward Heath, considers that it is racialist and inflammatory. He will sack Mr Powell from the shadow cabinet. However, politicians in all parties are uneasily aware that the speech probably expresses the fears of very many people. Mr Powell says he chose his words carefully, and he denies that he is either being irresponsible or seeking to incite racial prejudice (→6/5).

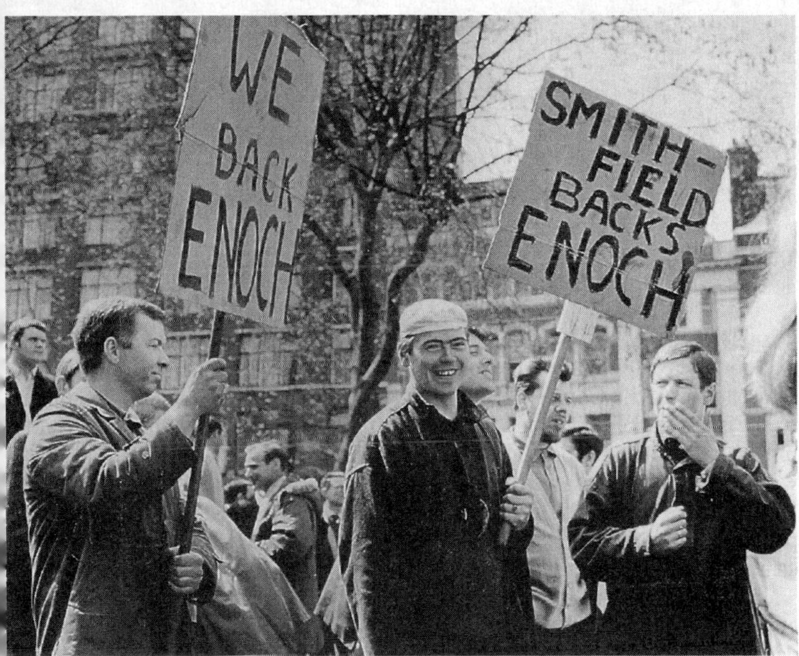

English racism takes to the streets as the bummarees march for Powell.

Motor racing champ is killed in smash

April 7. Jim Clark, twice world champion Formula One Driver and already leader in this year's championship, was killed instantly in a minor Formula Two Race at the Hockenheim circuit in West Germany today, when his Lotus-Cosworth went out of control on a straight and skidded into trees at 125mph.

Clark, a farmer's son from the Scottish Borders, was considered by his fellow-drivers to be the best of his generation; he drove his whole Grand Prix career for Lotus, winning a remarkable 25 races in only seven seasons (→26/5).

Student riots after Dutschke shooting

April 15. The attack on left-wing student leader Rudi Dutschke, who has been shot and wounded in the head and body, has triggered off a wave of student riots across Europe. The gunman has claimed that he was hoping to emulate the recent assassination of Dr King.

West German demonstrators targeted the Axel Springer newspaper group, accusing the right-wing press of creating an intolerant climate which made the shooting inevitable. Similar protests have arisen in Italy, Holland and Britain, where Springer offices were attacked.

1968

MAY

Su	Mo	Tu	We	Th	Fr	Sa
			1	2	3	4
5	6	7	8	9	10	11
12	13	14	15	16	17	18
19	20	21	22	23	24	25
26	27	28	29	30	31	

2. US: 1,000 set out on a Poor People's March from Memphis to Washington.

2. Cambridge: Britain's first liver transplant is made (→16).

5. Paris: 500 are arrested and the Sorbonne is closed as French students riot.→

6. UK: A Gallup Poll suggests 74 per cent of Britons support Enoch Powell on immigration (→10/10).

7. US: Robert Kennedy wins his first primary in Indiana (→14).

8. London: Charlie, Reggie and Ronnie Kray and 18 others are arrested (→9).

9. London: 21 people, including the Krays, are charged with offences including conspiracy to murder and fraud.

10. London: A seven-sided 50 New Pence coin is to replace the ten shilling note.

14. US: Robert Kennedy wins his second successive primary in Nebraska (→28).

16. UK: Alex Smith, aged 15, becomes Britain's first lung transplant patient (→28).

17. Prague: Soviet premier Kosygin arrives for talks to heal the rift between Dubcek and the Kremlin (→15/7).

18. London: West Bromwich Albion beat Everton 1-0 in the FA Cup Final.

22. UK: Bobby Charlton scores a record 45th goal for England in his 85th cap.→

22. Paris: Premier Georges Pompidou survives a vote of censure by 11 votes (→24).

24. Lyons: The student unrest claims its first victim when a policeman is killed by a lorry.→

26. Monaco: Briton Graham Hill wins the Monaco Grand Prix (→6/10).

28. US: Eugene McCarthy causes an upset when he beats Robert Kennedy in the Oregon primary (→5/6).

28. UK: Lung transplantee Alex Smith dies (→17/6).

29. UK: Mr R.R. Guest's Sir Ivor wins the Derby.

22-storey block of flats just unzips

Ronan Point after it collapsed.

May 16. Three people were killed today when all the corner flats in a 22-storey tower block collapsed. A full-scale inquiry was ordered by the Home Secretary, Mr Callaghan.

Rescuers in Newham, east London, said floors crumbled like a house of cards. The block, called Ronan Point, is made out of prefabricated slabs, and the Greater London Council has said it might ban system-built designs in future if the construction is found at fault. A gas explosion on the 18th floor is blamed for starting the collapse.

Manchester United win European Cup

May 29. The European Cup has come to Britain for the second year in succession. Manchester United, the team rebuilt by Matt Busby from the ruins of the Munich air crash of 1958, beat Benfica of Portugal in a thrilling final at Wembley today.

With the score 1-1 at full time, United attacked from the start of extra time and, within ten minutes, after goals by Bobby Charlton, George Best and the young Brian Kidd on his 19th birthday, they had sealed the match, and the coveted cup, with a 4-1 victory (→7/6). ▷

How the "month of the barricades" shook France

Torn-up cobblestones and wrecked cars litter this Paris street, the aftermath of a night of bitter fighting between demonstrators and the police.

Rioting students battle against police

May 7. In the last two days, Paris has seen the worst street-fighting since the Liberation in 1944. Up to 30,000 students, locked out of their own campus yesterday by the Sorbonne rector, Jean Roche, have fought the tear gas of the riot police with barricades, bricks, paving stones and Molotov cocktails.

The trouble has been fermenting for some time. On March 20, six students were arrested after an anti-American demonstration; the next day, a mass sit-in at the Nanterre campus began. Last Friday, the police (whose alleged brutality is said to have sparked off the violence) forcibly evicted the students, who were led by Daniel Cohn-Bendit.

All day yesterday, the Latin Quarter was the arena for running street fights centred on the Boulevard St. Germain. Nearly 1,000 people were injured, including 345 policemen harassed by student "commando squads". Today, a huge crowd sang the Communist anthem, the Internationale, at the Arc de Triomphe. Later the barricades, and the violence, reappeared (→ 24).

Workers back students with snap strikes

May 21. France is at a virtual standstill today. No sector of the economy (not even the Cannes Film Festival) is unscathed, with up to ten million workers – about half the workforce – taking action. The French have a host of grievances: poor state salaries, censorship, discrimination and centralisation.

The workers first joined the students a week ago today, when a one-day general strike was called to support student demands for an amnesty. Snap strikes grew in the following days, with rail and air travel heavily disrupted and managers held hostage in their own factories.

Two days ago, with two million on strike, President de Gaulle returned from a state visit to Rumania and told an emergency cabinet meeting: "Yes to reform, No to fouling the bed". Yesterday, the growing strike action caused the franc to plummet, and a rush on gold. The Communist Party has pledged to "eliminate the Government", but de Gaulle is taking steps to regain power and plans a referendum next month.→

Student protesters brandish revolutionary slogans and the red flag.

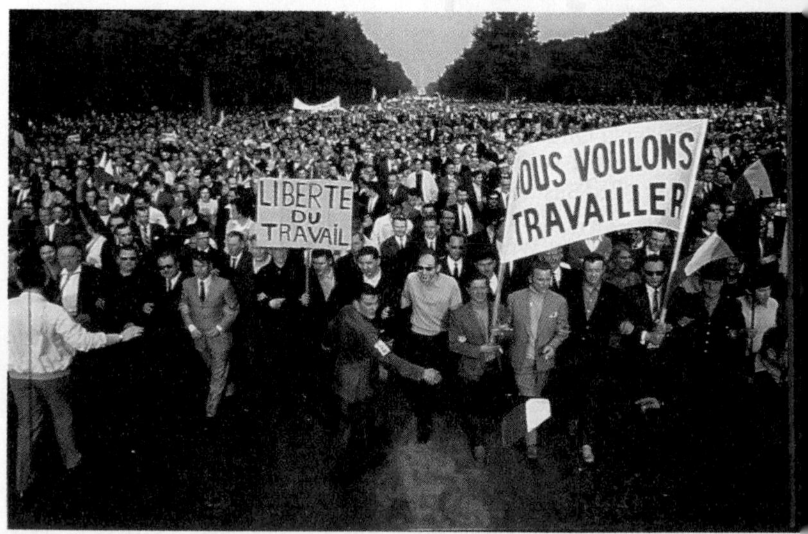

French trade unionists on parade; their banner says "We want to work".

De Gaulle strikes back

May 30. President de Gaulle, who has come under the most intense pressure to resign in the face of a sustained strike and strong political opposition, today told France that he would not quit. In a vigorous six- minute radio broadcast he defended his position, warning that he intended neither to give up his legitimate presidential powers nor to drop his Prime Minister, Georges Pompidou.

France, he said, was threatened by an illegal Communist dictatorship. Prefects throughout the country would be given full powers as "Commissioners of the Republic" to suppress any subversion. Strict exchange controls, imposed by the Ministry of Finance, apply from midnight tonight, to halt the flow of capital from France. If necessary, stronger measures would be taken, warned the President.

De Gaulle then dissolved the National Assembly and called a general election. He remains the "sole custodian" of the State, but the chaos on the streets has weakened his power. The referendum planned for June 16 has been postponed, a concession unthinkable in the heyday of Gaullism. The vote – for or against a programme of universal but undefined reforms – has long been regarded as pointless by all but the hard-core Gaullists. In any case, the general strike has made it impossible to print or distribute the ballot papers.

It is thought that de Gaulle's strong stand has been made possible by the full backing of the military. Unconfirmed reports say that the president spent much of yesterday extracting pledges of support from the army, and that motorised units and paratroops are already in position at possible trouble-spots to nip any moves towards impending civil war in the bud.

France's left-wing and union movement have denounced the President's speech. Francois Mitterrand, the leader of the Federation of the Left, accused him of provoking civil war: "The voice we have just heard is that of dictatorship; the French people will silence that voice" (→ 12/6).

The CRS attack the barricades.

Supporters of President de Gaulle show their own flag – the Tricolour.

Students "sit in" at Hornsey college

May 30. A "state of anarchy" has been declared at Hornsey College of Art, where today the students, following in the footsteps of their fellows at the London School of Economics and other British universities, have taken over the college building.

They are complaining against what they see as short-comings in the college's academic set-up, and the way in which student affairs are administered. The students have evicted the college principal, Harold Shelton, and intend to "sit in" until their demands for major changes are met.

The first heart is transplanted in UK

May 3. A crowd cheered and clapped outside the National Heart Hospital, Marylebone, when a team of 18 doctors and nurses led by Donald Ross, the senior surgeon, stood on the steps and announced Britain's first successful heart transplant operation on a man of 45. The donor was Patrick Ryan, a 26-year-old labourer, who had suffered a bad fall. Transferred from King's College Hospital to the Heart Hospital the transplant was performed immediately after his death. The patient's reaction to the implant over the next ten to fourteen days is critical.

Talks begin about Vietnam peace deal

May 13. American and North Vietnamese diplomats met in Paris today to discuss the setting-up of talks to end the war. The first day of these "talks about talks" was devoted, as expected, to mutual recrimination, with Xuan Thuy, the Communist delegate, accusing America of "monstrous crimes", and Averell Harriman, for the US, alleging "aggression".

The talks, in which South Vietnam is not taking part, were made possible by President Johnson's promise to stop the bombing of North Vietnam above the 20th Parallel, but what emerged in the acrimonious exchanges today was that the North Vietnamese would discuss nothing of substance until the US makes a total and unconditional end to the bombing of North Vietnam (→ 2/6).

Troops fighting in Saigon.

Soviet troops move up to Czech border

May 9. Alarmed by the liberalising tide released by the new Czechoslovak Communist leadership, the Russians have begun moving troops and tanks through Poland and East Germany up to the Czech frontier.

Fears of an invasion have been heightened by reports of a hastily called meeting in Moscow during the weekend, which included all the Soviet East European satellite countries except Rumania and Czechoslovakia.

When Alexander Dubcek took over as Czech Communist leader at the beginning of the year, the whole country, but especially Prague, was launched into an exhilarating springtime of freedom: real news in the papers and on TV and radio; exposures of corruption in high places; criticism of housing conditions, low wages, bureaucratic oppression. Although Dubcek is insisting that Czechoslovakia will remain a loyal ally of the Soviet Union, Moscow is far from being reassured (→ 17).

1968

JUNE

Su	Mo	Tu	We	Th	Fr	Sa
						1
2	3	4	5	6	7	8
9	10	11	12	13	14	15
16	17	18	19	20	21	22
23	24	25	26	27	28	29
30						

2. Saigon: A bomb wounds the Mayor of Saigon and seven South Vietnamese officials (→27/10).

3. New York: Artist Andy Warhol is shot and seriously hurt by Valeria Solanis, an actress in one of his films.

5. Los Angeles: Robert Kennedy is shot in the head at a rally.→

7. UK: Matt Busby gets a knighthood.

8. US: Robert Kennedy is buried in Arlington Cemetery (→2/8).

11. London: French student leader Danny Cohn-Bendit arrives on a short visit.

12. Paris: De Gaulle bans open-air demonstrations.→

13. London: A royal commission recommends setting up a permanent Industrial Relations Commission.

14. US: Dr Spock and three others are found guilty of encouraging draft evasion.

17. UK: Frederick West, Britain's first heart transplant patient, dies.

20. US: Jim Hines sets a new record for the 100 metres of 9.8 seconds.

20. London: Wilson announces plans to reform the composition and structure of the House of Lords.

24. UK: 1,000 trains are cancelled as the National Union of Railwaymen begins a work-to-rule.

25. Canada: Pierre Trudeau's Liberal Party celebrates its biggest general election victory in ten years.

30. London: Women machinists at Ford's Dagenham plant call off a strike for equal pay, but say the dispute goes on.

DEATHS

6. US politician Robert Francis Kennedy (*20/11/1925).→

14. Italian poet Salvatore Quasimodo, 1959 Nobel Prize winner (*20/8/1901).

24. British comedian Anthony John Hancock (*12/5/1924).→

Bobby Kennedy is shot

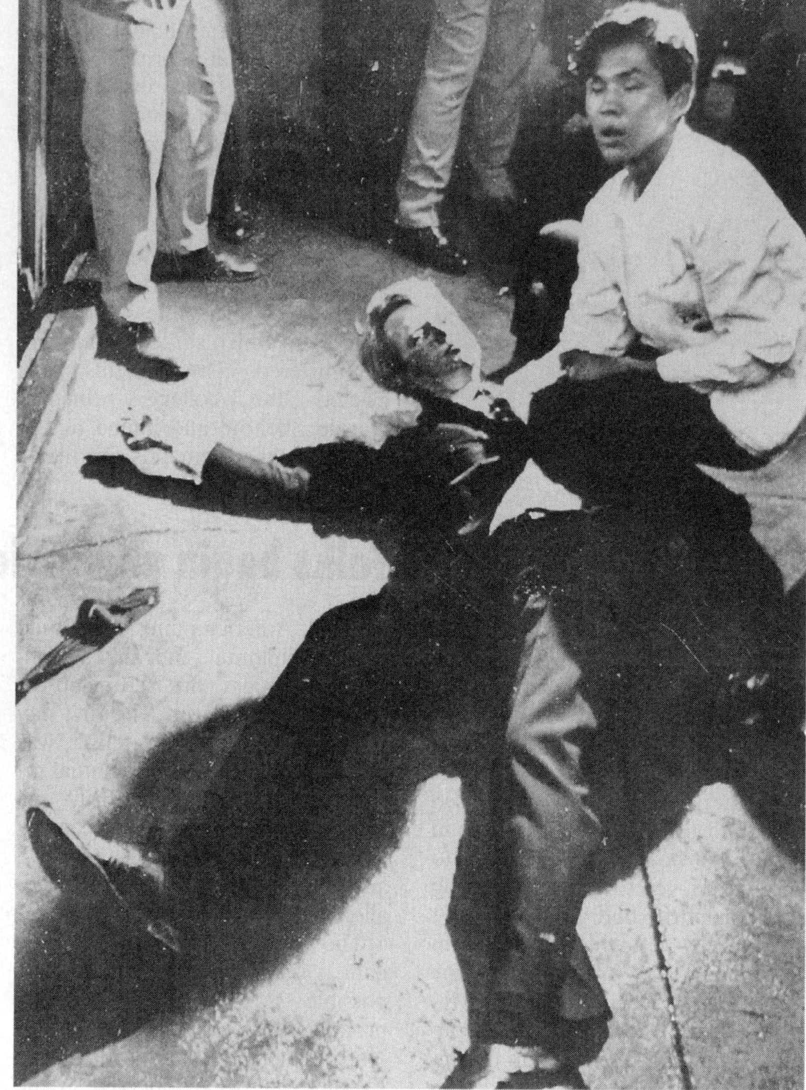

Bobby Kennedy lies prostrate as a kitchen porter kneels in vain at his side.

June 6. Senator Robert Kennedy was shot and fatally wounded early yesterday in the Ambassador Hotel in Los Angeles, hours after winning the California Democratic primary election. Surgeons at the Good Samaritan Hospital fought for Kennedy's life for 20 hours. One surgeon, Dr Henry Cuneo, said that because he was shot with a small-calibre .22 gun he might have survived if the bullet had hit a centimetre away from where it did.

It was just before midnight when Senator Kennedy arrived at the hotel to make a brief, light-hearted speech, thanking his campaign volunteers for their part in his victory in the California primary, where he won 50 per cent of the vote, easily defeating his chief rival, Senator Eugene McCarthy. He left the ballroom accompanied by bodyguards, including the professional football player, Roosevelt Grier, and the Olympic decathlon champion, Rafer Johnson, as well as by political aides and a television reporter who wanted to interview him. Then, as he was taken through a kitchen passage, a small man, later identified as Sirhan Sirhan, a 24-year-old Palestinian immigrant, fired five shots before he was seized.

Senator Kennedy, a former US attorney-general, was a late entrant to the Democratic primary campaign and infuriated supporters of Senator Eugene McCarthy, who saw him as cashing-in on the anti-war movement. The California primary has therefore been bitter, ending in an angry television debate hours before Kennedy's death.

A young Arab male is held for killing of Bobby Kennedy

June 7. A Palestinian Arab immigrant, Sirhan Sirhan, has been charged in Los Angeles with murdering Senator Robert Kennedy and assaulting five other people. Sirhan, who suffered a broken finger and a sprained ankle during arrest, shouted out immediately after shooting Kennedy "I did it for my country!"

This week is the anniversary of the Six Days' War between Israel and the Arab countries. In his election campaign Kennedy had expressed support for Israel in general, and for maintaining arms supplies to Israel (→8).

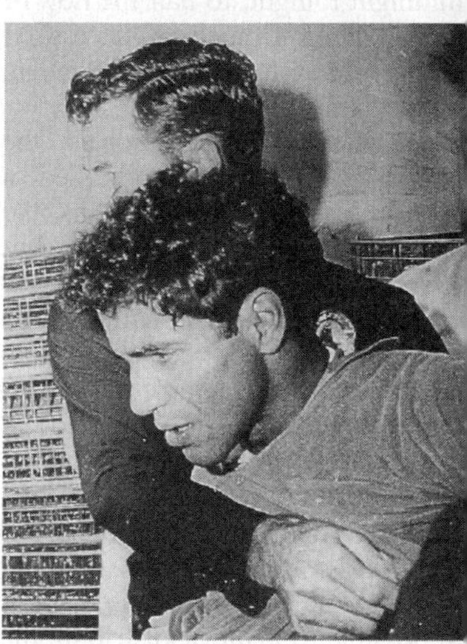

Sirhan Sirhan, Kennedy's killer.

King fugitive is arrested in London

June 8. James Earl Ray, who is wanted by the FBI for the murder of Dr Martin Luther King, was arrested in London yesterday. Ray, who is 40, was en route for Brussels after telephoning a newspaper about enlisting as a mercenary.

He arrived in Toronto on April 8, four days after Dr King was murdered. He then obtained a Canadian passport in the name of Ramon George Sneyd and flew to London. The ease with which he obtained money to buy a Mustang car and to travel to five countries in the past year has raised suspicions that Ray was a hired gunman.

Voters give a big majority to de Gaulle

Riot police chase protestors as the electors back their President again.

June 30. France's general election has resulted in a landslide victory for President Charles de Gaulle. Early returns indicate that the Gaullist UD-V party has achieved a clear majority over all the other parties put together. The Communists and the Federation of the Left, who had called for de Gaulle's resignation during the Paris riots in May, saw their share of seats in the National Assembly slashed by more than half.

Thus the President, whose regime was all but dead a month ago, now has a solid vote of confidence and more parliamentary style than any government since the war. Le Monde, the French newspaper, summed up de Gaulle's electoral triumph by commenting that "the Communists are being blamed for barricades they did not build, and for strike pickets they did not command".

The poll was preceded by clashes between pro- and anti-de Gaulle militants. In the worst incident, an 18-year-old Communist was shot dead at point-blank range by men alleged to be Gaullists. Demonstrations also took place in the Latin Quarter of Paris as the polls opened today. Students built barricades and set fire to them, shouting, "elections are treason" (→ 10/7).

Tony Hancock, comedy maestro, is dead

June 24. Tony Hancock was probably the most popular comedian in the country during the run of his radio show "Hancock's Half Hour", which transferred to television in 1956. His character, intolerant, indignant and with pretensions to a culture he did not understand, was part of himself. "You take your own weaknesses and exploit them," he once explained. Unfortunately, he believed he could dispense with anyone else's contribution, including his scriptwriters'. He committed professional suicide long before his actual suicide today in a Sydney hotel room.

Tony Hancock: tears of a clown.

1968

JULY

Su	Mo	Tu	We	Th	Fr	Sa
	1	2	3	4	5	6
7	8	9	10	11	12	13
14	15	16	17	18	19	20
21	22	23	24	25	26	27
28	29	30	31			

1. Europe: Common Market countries remove their last customs barriers.

1. London: 36 nations sign a Nuclear Non-Proliferation Treaty in London, Moscow and Washington.

2. London: Dr David Owen, aged 30, becomes the government's youngest member as Under-Secretary for the Navy.

3. Washington: General Westmoreland is sworn in as US Army chief of staff.

5. UK: Lone yachtsman Alec Rose is knighted.

8. London: Britain is promised $2,000 million credit by 12 countries to bolster the pound.

9. London: The Queen opens the Hayward Gallery on the South Bank.

9. London: The Monopolies Commission vetoes a planned merger of Lloyd's, Barclay's and Martin's Banks (→ 25).

10. US: Dr Spock and three others are sentenced to two years in jail for encouraging draft-dodging.

10. Paris: Maurice Couve de Murville becomes premier in succession to Pompidou.

13. UK: Gary Player wins the British Open golf title.

15. Warsaw: Leaders of five Warsaw Pact states meet to discuss Czechoslovakia (→ 18).

18. Prague: Dubcek says there will be "no retreat" from the new "democratic process" (→ 22).

22. Moscow: Soviet leaders invite Dubcek to "friendly bilateral talks" at Cierna in eastern Czechoslovakia.→

25. UK: Barclay's Bank merges with Martin's Bank (→ 13/9).

30. Czechoslovakia: Talks between Dubcek, Brezhnev and other East Bloc leaders end with little agreement (→ 9/8).

DEATHS

21. US dancer Ruth St. Denis (*20/1/1878).

28. German nuclear physicist Otto Hahn (*8/3/1879).

Russian tanks put heat on the Czechs

July 29. With over 1,000 Russian tanks and 75,000 troops waiting just across the border, Soviet and Czech leaders met today in the small frontier village of Cierna to try to resolve their differences over the "Prague Spring".

While Alexander Dubcek, the Czech leader, talks of remaining a loyal Soviet ally while giving socialism a human face, Leonid Brezhnev, the Soviet leader, claims American spies are in Czechoslovakia to prepare for a West German invasion. So Brezhnev is demanding that large Soviet forces should be allowed into Czechoslovakia to protect it against a Western threat (→ 30).

Round-the-world sailor comes home

Alec Rose comes home in triumph.

July 4. Yachtsman Alec Rose, aged 59, returned home to his home town of Portsmouth and a massive celebration today after sailing around the world in his tiny ketch Lively Lady. His 28,500-mile adventure had taken him 354 days. After being cheered by 250,000 on the quayside, Mr Rose, a greengrocer, said he had come close to death between New Zealand and Cape Horn (→ 5).

Papal encyclical says No to birth control

July 29. Pope Paul today dashed the hopes of many of the world's 530 million Catholics by refusing to make any concessions to liberal opinion on birth control. In an encylical entitled Humanae Vitae (Of Human Life), he declared that any form of artificial birth control was against the Divine Will.

While the announcment is not necessarily "infallible" it has the weight of the Pope's authority, which means that any Catholics disobeying it open themselves to the possibility of excommunication.

Usually papal decisions are accepted without public quibbling by the Church leadership. Today many Catholic leaders around the world were saying they were disappointed by the decision. Some were openly critical.

Typical of them was Archbishop Roberts, the Jesuit, who said the Pope had gone against most of his own experts, adding: "Protestants have been discussing this for 50 years and are almost unanimous in saying contraception is not forbidden by Divine Law."

Hopes have been raised in recent years because of the growing number of Catholic bishops in Third World countries which have population problems. Many expected the Pope to bow to their problems if only for the sake of keeping them solidly Roman Catholic (→22/8).

Rod Laver wins the first open Wimbledon

Rod Laver on the Centre Court.

July 6. The first Open Wimbledon proved a resounding success – both in terms of the public response, and for the two triumphant singles champions.

Rod Laver carried on as he left off as an amateur six years ago, powering his way to the final without ever looking in serious trouble, and winning it, as he had done in both 1961 and 1962, in straight sets, 6-3, 6-4, 6-2 over his fellow-Australian Tony Roche.

In the women's competition, Billie Jean King re-emphasised her mastery of grass-court play, beating the tall, jovial Australian Judy Tegart 9-7, 7-5 to become the first woman since Maureen Connolly to win three titles in a row.

"Last Exit" is not obscene says court

July 31. "Last Exit to Brooklyn", the book that followed "Lady Chatterley's Lover" into the dock at the Old Bailey, and which was found guilty of obscenity by an all-male jury last year, has now had the conviction quashed on appeal because of flaws in the summing-up. The jury had not been given proper guidance on the defence of publication "for the public good".

This novel by Hubert Selby Jr is set in a world of prostitutes, pimps and homosexuals living brief, violent lives in New York.

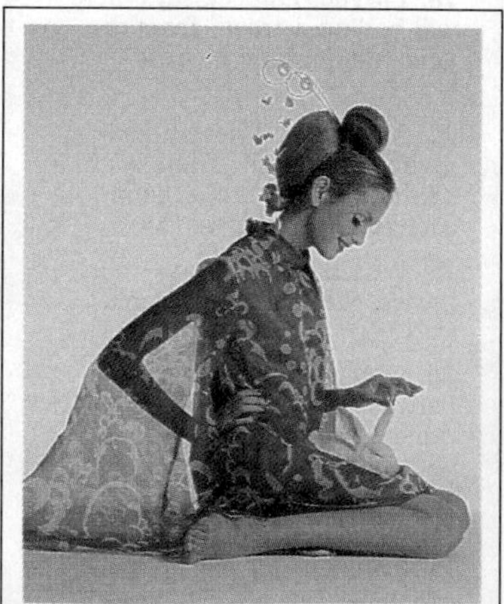

Flowers in her hair, a rabbit on her lap, model Twiggy gives her version of "love and peace".

1968

AUGUST

Su	Mo	Tu	We	Th	Fr	Sa
				1	2	3
4	5	6	7	8	9	10
11	12	13	14	15	16	17
18	19	20	21	22	23	24
25	26	27	28	29	30	31

1. US: Nixon calls for the US role in Vietnam to be scaled down (→8).

2. Los Angeles: Sirhan Sirhan pleads not guilty to the murder of Robert Kennedy.

3. UK: The Countryside Act, allowing local authorities to designate country parks, comes into force.

5. US: Governor Reagan of California says he will run for President (→8).

8. Miami: Nixon wins the Republican nomination for President; Spiro Agnew will be his running-mate (→10).

9. West Germany: 48 die when a British Eagle Airways Viscount hits the Munich to Nuremberg autobahn.

9. Prague: Marshal Tito arrives on a visit (→16).

10. Washington: Senator George McGovern says he will run for the Democratic presidential nomination (→6/11).

12. Los Angeles: Rioting breaks out in the Watts district.

16. Prague: Dubcek signs a 20-year pact with Rumania (→21).

18. UK: South African Test cricketer Colin Bland is refused entry because he has a Rhodesian passport.

21. Czechoslovakia: Tanks from the USSR and four other Eastern Bloc states cross the Czech border.→

22. Bogota: Pope Paul VI arrives in Colombia on the first visit by a Pope to Latin America.

23. Czechoslovakia: Czechs stage a one-hour general strike to protest at the Soviet invasion (→24).

24. Moscow: Dubcek and Czech premier Cernik hold extended talks with Soviet leaders (→12/9).

26. Oxford: The Professor of Pharmacology says heroin addiction is now "a major - emergency" (→18/10).

30. Washington: Johnson warns the USSR against intervention in Rumania.

Nigerians mount an assault on Biafrans

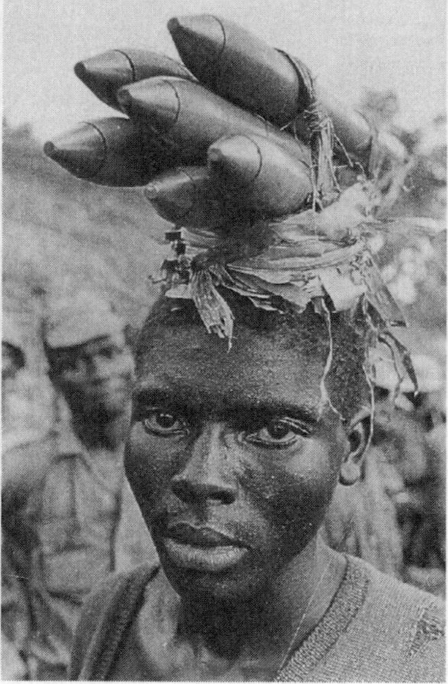

More shells for the war in Biafra.

Aug 19. One of Nigeria's most dashing commanders, Col. Benjamin Adekunle, known as "The Scorpion", is directing what is expected to be the final assault on Biafra. Federal troops were reported tonight to be within 15 miles of the rebel stronghold of Aba and the main road to the north, which is used as an airstrip and is the only supply link with the outside world. Radio Biafra says "major offensives" have been launched on all sectors. It claimed that over 2,000 men, women and children had been massacred, but General Gowon, the Federal leader, says "my boys" are behaving correctly (→3/9).

D'Oliveira dropped from cricket tour

Aug 28. The MCC selectors have stirred up a serious controversy by omitting Basil d'Oliveira, Worcestershire's South African-born Cape Coloured all-rounder, from the South African winter tour.

D'Oliveira appeared a certainty for the tour after his innings of 158 against Australia last week. The MCC argues that the team was picked on merit, but faces fierce accusations that his omission constitutes appeasement to the apartheid policies which drove him to England in 1960 (→17/9).

Russian tanks roll in to crush the Prague spring

Aug 22. Several hundred thousand Soviet troops, accompanied by token units of other Warsaw Pact countries, are today fighting to turn the Prague Spring of freedom into a Moscow winter of oppression. Fires are raging in the Czech capital as scattered bands of young Czechs fight the Soviet armour with guns, sticks and sometimes bare hands.

People can be seen climbing on Soviet tanks and arguing with the men inside. Emil Zatopek, the Olympic gold medallist, appeared in his Colonel's uniform and told a crowd of several hundreds the Russians had to go home. When Russians arrived to take over Prague radio, crowds blocked their way. An ammunition lorry exploded, setting fire to buildings and Russian tanks. Several hundred people were injured and scores are believed to have died.

Russian officers entered the HQ of the Czechoslovak Communist Party, brought out Alexander Dubcek and other liberal Communist leaders, and took them away in an armoured troop carrier. The National Assembly has been occupied, and the Czech news agency, which gave the world the first news of the invasion, has been shut.

To the last, Dubcek and the reformers clung to the belief that the Russians would not invade. Details of a meeting of the party's 20-member Presidium have been given by the clandestine radios that have started up. At the meeting on Tuesday night, three hard-liners called for the abandonment of the reform programme. The others heatedly rejected the proposal. Then someone answered a telephone call and said "The Russians have begun to invade".

Dubcek was stunned. "How could they do this to me?" he cried. "My entire life has been devoted to cooperation with the Soviet Union. This is my own profound personal tragedy." Only the three hard-liners showed no surprise at the news. Some party members quite evidently were warned. Hours before the invasion began, the party newspaper "Rude Pravo" dropped its liberal role of recent weeks and attacked the Dubcek reforms. The Russians now say the invasion was necessary to prevent Dubcek restoring capitalism in the country. Something like a "Brezhnev Doctrine" is being invoked to give Moscow the right to use force to stop any East European country slipping away.

Tass, the official Soviet news agency, says the Czechs are showing gratitude for the timely arrival of Soviet troops (→ 23).

Czech Davids taunt the Russian Goliath as tanks move into Prague, pitting their armour against bare hands.

People of Prague attempt to convince the Russian invaders of their cause.

A desperate Czech bares his chest in an attempt to halt the invasion.

▷

"Gestapo" jibe as police run wild at Chicago convention

Aug 29. The Democrats nominated Vice-President Hubert Humphrey as their presidential candidate here today, but the nomination, ending the bitterest primary campaign in recent years, took second place to the violence of Mayor Richard Daley's Chicago police.

Officers used truncheons, mace and tear-gas on demonstrators marching from Grant Park to oppose the Vietnam war. Later they dragged at least two delegates from the convention floor, and national television recorded them brutally beating demonstrators and others outside the Hilton Hotel.

On the floor Senator Ribicoff complained to Mayor Daley's face about "gestapo tactics on the streets of Chicago". According to lip-readers, the mayor's response was unprintable.

Vice-President Humphrey was nominated easily over his rivals Senator Eugene McCarthy and Senator McGovern, who was supported by many of those delegates who had supported Senator Robert Kennedy, murdered in Los Angeles in June after winning the California primary. The divisions within the peace wing of the Democratic party guaranteed its defeat. A minority plank, calling for peace in Vietnam, was defeated by 1,567 to 1,041.

Happier times: Hubert Humphrey, the Democrat's man for the White House, on a visit to London.

1968

SEPTEMBER

Su	Mo	Tu	We	Th	Fr	Sa
1	2	3	4	5	6	7
8	9	10	11	12	13	14
15	16	17	18	19	20	21
22	23	24	25	26	27	28
29	30					

1. London: The first part of the £80 million Victoria Line is opened between Walthamstow and Highbury.

2. Iran: At least 11,000 people are reported to have been killed in earthquakes in the past two days.

3. Lagos: General Gowon agrees to let the Red Cross fly relief supplies into Biafra for ten days from September 5 (→29).

6. UK: GEC announces its £892 million merger with English Electric.

8. US: Virginia Wade beats Billie Jean King to become the first women's Open champion of the US.

13. Prague: Press censorship is reimposed (→19).

13. UK: The big banks announce they will close on Saturdays from July 1969; shops and the police protest.

15. UK: Hundreds of homes are evacuated as south-east England is hit by the worst floods since 1953.

16. UK: Two-tier post comes into force: a first-class letter costs 5d., second-class 4d.

19. Prague: Foreign Minister Jiri Halek resigns in protest at Soviet demands (→4/10).

19. London: The Government announces that the Foreign Office and the Commonwealth Office will merge next month (→6/10).

24. London: The England cricket tour of South Africa is officially cancelled.

26. UK: Jaguar unveils its new XJ-6 luxury saloon.

26. Lisbon: Marcello Caetano takes over as premier from Antonio Salazar, who has been in a coma for ten days.

27. London: 13 members of the cast of "Hair" face the audience naked the day after play censorship is abolished.

29. Nigeria: 55 Nigerian troops die when a Red Cross DC-4 crashes.

30. UK: The Labour Party Conference votes to urge the repeal of the Government's wage restraints.

Vorster bans MCC tour of South Africa

Sept 17. The day after Basil d'Oliveira, England's Cape Coloured all-rounder, was picked for this winter's MCC tour as a replacement for the injured Tom Cartwright, South Africa reacted by cancelling the four-month tour.

In a statement read out to a Nationalist Party meeting in Bloemfontein, Mr Vorster, the Prime Minister, claimed the touring party was "no longer a cricket team, but a team of troublemakers for South Africa's separate development policies". D'Oliveira's original omission from the team last month was greeted by protests from anti-apartheid groups, and when Cartwright was declared unfit he was the logical replacement (→24).

D'Oliveira: belated selection.

Prague is gripped by a Moscow winter

Sept 12. As the last Soviet tanks disappeared from the streets of Prague today, the Czechs were beginning to count the cost of the return to "socialist solidarity" with Moscow. Strict censorship of press, radio and television has been imposed. All meetings and processions that "endanger socialism" are banned. Vasiliy Kuznetov, of the Soviet Politburo, is in Prague as Moscow's viceroy, giving orders to Czech party leaders (→19).

Epidural promises painless childbirth

Sept 11. A new method of relieving pain in childbirth, called the epidural technique, has been reported today. It involves the injection of anaesthetic into the space outside the membrane surrounding the spinal cord through a small tube inserted into the mother's lower back. Most of the over 500 mothers who have had it so far have asked for it again. A woman can read a paper while having a baby, with a mirror to watch the birth.

The mini has reached such heights that cleaners charge by the inch.

1968

OCTOBER

Su	Mo	Tu	We	Th	Fr	Sa
		1	2	3	4	5
6	7	8	9	10	11	12
13	14	15	16	17	18	19
20	21	22	23	24	25	26
27	28	29	30	31		

3. UK: Booker McConnell and the Publishers' Association announce a £5,000 prize for 1968's best British novel.

4. Prague: More press curbs are imposed as it is revealed that Warsaw Pact troops will stay in the country (→28).

6. US: Jackie Stewart, Graham Hill and John Surtees come 1st, 2nd and 3rd in the US Grand Prix (→3/11).

9. Gibraltar: Wilson and Ian Smith meet for talks aboard HMS Fearless.→

10. UK: Enoch Powell warns that immigrants may "change the character of England" (→25).

12. Mexico City: The Olympic Games open (→27).

16. London: The Foreign and Commonwealth Offices merge.

16. UK: Labour MP Robert Maxwell launches a £26 million bid for the News of the World organisation (→23).

17. London: Judith Hart joins the Government as Paymaster-General.

18. UK: John Lennon and his girlfriend Yoko Ono are arrested on drugs charges (→28/11).

18. UK: John Lennon appears in his first solo film role in "How I Won The War".

23. UK: News Ltd., owned by Australian Rupert Murdoch, enters the battle to buy the News of the World.

25. London: The Race Relations Bill gets Royal Assent (→26/11).

28. Prague: Tens of thousands of Czechs take to the streets to protest against the Soviet occupation (→7/11).

31. Washington: Johnson says he has ordered a halt to US bombing of North Vietnam (→1/11).

DEATHS

13. British publisher Sir Stanley Unwin (*19/12/1884).

20. British comedian Bud Flanagan, born Chaim Reeven Weintrop (*14/10/1896).

Peaceful demo dispels revolution fears

Most people opted for a peaceful march, but there was still some violence.

Oct 27. An estimated 250,000 people marched on the US Embassy in Grosvenor Square today, in the year's second demonstration against the war in Vietnam, but the day on which revolution was scheduled – or feared – to arrive on the streets of London turned out something of a damp squib. Despite forebodings in the press, everything has passed off almost amicably. Perhaps not all the marchers chose to link arms with the police in a chorus of "Auld Lang Syne" but, other than a few arrests, the march encountered few problems (→31).

Wilson reveals the deal Smith rejected

Oct 15. Harold Wilson reported to Parliament today on his abortive talks with Rhodesia's rebel leader, Ian Smith, aboard HMS Fearless at Gibraltar.

It appears that the Prime Minister went further than before to open the door for the Salisbury regime's return to legality and the dropping of sanctions, but it was not far enough to satisfy Mr Smith's hard-line colleagues.

The British offer is now for Mr Smith to form a broad-based government, including Africans, which will be accepted as legitimate "while unimpeded progress is made towards majority rule".

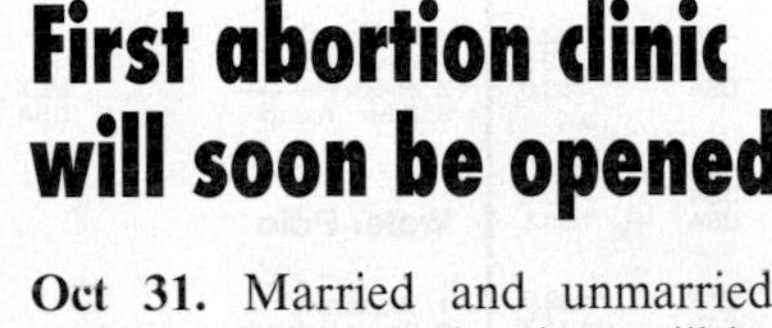

First abortion clinic will soon be opened

Oct 31. Married and unmarried women who want abortions will be able to get help at a "sympathetic" new clinic opening in London next week. Launching the Pregnancy Advisory Service today, chairman Alan Golding said that where there were legal grounds for abortion the clinic would supplement the efforts of a woman's GP.

Although the Abortion Act had changed the law, it had not changed the attitudes of certain doctors or increased NHS facilities.

100 Catholics hurt in Londonderry riot

Oct 6. Riot police broke up a demonstration by 800 Roman Catholics and sympathisers last night, after two days of bloody street battles in Londonderry. Armoured cars, high-pressure water hoses and repeated baton charges finally restored order. Some 100 demonstrators and several police constables were taken to hospital.

The march, which took place in defiance of a ban imposed by the Home Affairs Minister, William Craig, deteriorated swiftly into violence as the police tried to halt it.

The Catholics, their student supporters and trade unionists were protesting against sectarian discrimination in housing and employment (→30/11).

The first sextuplets are born in Britain

Oct 2. Of Britain's first sextuplets, born at the Birmingham Maternity Hospital to Sheila Ann Thorns, two boys and three girls are still alive; one girl died soon after birth. They were 2 months premature, weighed between 2 pounds and 2 pounds and ten ounces, and were delivered by a caesarean. Mrs Thorns had been given fertility drugs and her specialist said that we "shall be guarding against any similar occurence in the future". The couple had kept the pregnancy secret and it was "a great shock" to Mr Thorns' mother.

Jackie K becomes "Jackie O" on "the happiest day of my life".

▷

1968 Mexico

Beamon leaps into Olympic history

Oct 27. Controversy dogged the Mexico City Olympic Games from first to last. Even before the opening ceremony, a student riot in the city was brutally put down by the authorities; and the berets, black gloves and clenched-fist salutes of the American "Black Power" athletes severely embarrassed the US Olympic Association and led to some athletes being summarily expelled from the Games.

Mexico City's altitude (about 7,000 feet) created a parallel controversy: would the thin air be dangerous for competitors in endurance sports? And would it distort performances in the explosive events?

The results gave the answers. Every running event under 800 metres (with the exception of David Hemery's incomparable world record victory for Britain in the 400 metres hurdles) was won by a black American sprinter in, or near, a world record time.

Three more Americans made history. Bob Beamon's long jump, advancing the world record by almost two feet, is predicted by experts to outlast the century; A. Oerter achieved the impossible in the discus with his fourth gold medal in four consecutive Games; and Dick Fosbury justified his new, and seemingly dangerous, head-first-on-the-back-of-the-neck style of high jumping with a gold medal.

However, his coach has issued a warning: "Kids imitate champions but if they imitate Fosbury he will wipe out an entire generation of high jumpers because they will all have broken necks."

Tommie Smith and John Carlos give the victory to Black Power.

Men Athletics

100m
1. Jim Hines USA **9.9
2. Lennox Miller JAM 10.0
3. Charlie Green USA 10.0

200m
1. Tommie Smith USA **19.8
2. Peter Norman AUS 20.8
3. John Carlos USA 20.0

400m
1. Lee Evans USA **43.8
2. Larry James USA 43.9
3. Ronald Freeman USA 44.4

800m
1. Ralph Doubell AUS =**1:44.3
2. Wilson Kiprugut KEN 1:44.5
3. Thomas Farrell USA 1:45.4

1500m
1. Kipchoge Keino KEN *3:34.9
2. Jim Ryun USA 3:37.8
3. Bodo Tümmler FRG 3:39.0

5000m
1. Mohamed Gammoudi TUN 14:05.0
2. Kipchoge Keino KEN 14:05.2
3. Naftali Temu KEN 14:06.4

10,000m
1. Naftali Temu KEN 29:27.4
2. Mamo Wolde ETH 29:28.0
3. Mohamed Gammoudi TUN 29:34.2

Marathon
1. Mamo Wolde ETH 2:20:26.4
2. Kenji Kimihara JAP 2:23:31.0
3. Michael Ryan NZL 2:23:45.0

110m Hurdles
1. Willie Davenport USA *13.3
2. Ervin Hall USA 13.4
3. Eddy Ottoz ITA 13.4

400m Hurdles
1. David Hemery GBR **48.1
2. Gerhard Hennige FRG 49.0
3. John Sherwood GBR 49.0

3000m Steeplechase
1. Amos Biwott KEN 8:51.0
2. Benjamin Kogo KEN 8:51.6
3. George Young USA 8:51.8

4x100m Relay
1. USA **38.2 (Charles Greene, Melvin Pender, Ronnie Ray Smith, Jim Hines)
2. CUB 38.3 (Hermes Ramirez, Juan Morales, Pablo Montes, Enrique Figuerola)
3. FRA 38.4 (Gérard Fénouil, Jocelyn Delecour, Claude Piquemal, Roger Bambuck)

4x400m Relay
1. USA **2:56.1 (Vincent Matthews, Ronald Freeman, Larry James, Lee Evans)
2. KEN 2:59.6 (Daniel Rudisha, Munyoro Nyamau, Naftali Bon, Charles Asati)
3. FRG 3:00.5 (Helmar Müller, Manfred Kinder, Gerhard Hennige, Martin Jellinghaus)

20km Walk
1. Vladimir Golubnichiy URS 1:33:58.4
2. José Pedraza MEX 1:34:00.0
3. Nicolai Smaga URS 1:34:03.4

50km Walk
1. Christoph Höhne GDR 4:20:13.6
2. Antal Kiss HUN 4:30:17.0
3. Larry Young USA 4:31:55.4

High Jump
1. Dick Fosbury USA *2.24
2. Ed Caruthers USA 2.22
3. Valentin Gavrilov URS 2.20

Pole Vault
1. Bob Seagren USA *5.40
2. Claus Schiprowski FRG *5.40
3. Wolfgang Nordwig GDR *5.40

Long Jump
1. Bob Beamon USA **8.90
2. Klaus Beer GDR 8.19
3. Ralph Boston USA 8.16

Triple Jump
1. Viktor Saneyev URS **17.39
2. Nelson Prudencio BRA 17.27
3. Giuseppe Gentile ITA 17.22

Discus
1. Alfred Oerter USA 64.78
2. Lother Milde GDR 63.08
3. Ludvik Danek TCH 62.92

Shotput
1. Randy Matson USA 20.54
2. George Woods USA 20.12
3. Eduard Gushchin URS 20.09

Hammer
1. Gyula Zsivotzky HUN *73.36
2. Romuald Klim URS 73.28
3. Lázár Lovász HUN 69.78

Javelin
1. Janis Lusis URS *90.10
2. Jorma Kinnunen FIN 88.58
3. Gergely Kulcsar HUN 87.06

Decathlon
1. Bill Toomey USA 8193
2. Hans-Joachim Walde FRG 8111
3. Kurt Bendin FRG 8064

American Bob Beamon soars to victory in the long jump with a span of 8.90 metres.

Women Athletics

100m
1. Wyomia Tyus USA **11.0
2. Barbara Ferrell USA 11.1
3. Irena Szewinska POL 11.1

200m
1. Irena Szewinska POL **22.5
2. Raelene Boyle AUS 22.7
3. Jennifer Lamy AUS 22.8

400m
1. Colette Besson FRA =*52.0
2. Lillian Board GBR 52.1
3. Natalya Pechenkina URS 52.2

800m
1. Madeleine Manning USA *2:00.9
2. Ilenea Silai ROM 2:02.5
3. Maria Gommers NETH 2:02.6

80m Hurdles
1. Maureen Caird AUS *10.3
2. Pam Kilborn AUS 10.4
3. Chi Cheng TAI 10.4

4x100m Relay
1. USA **42.8 (Barbara Ferrell, Margaret Bailes, Mildrette Netter, Wyomia Tyus)
2. CUB 43.3 (Marlene Elejade, Fulgencia Romay, Violetta Quesada, Miguelina Cobián)
3. URS 43.4 (Lyudmila Zharkova, Galina Burkharina, Vyera Popkova, Lyudmila Samotysova)

High Jump
1. Miloslava Rezkova TCH 1.82
2. Antonina Okorokova URS 1.80
3. Valentina Kozyr URS 1.80

Long Jump
1. Viorica Viscopoleanu ROM **6.82
2. Shelia Sherwood GBR 6.68
3. Tatyana Talisheva URS 6.66

Shotput
1. Margitta Gummel GBR **19.61
2. Marita Lange GBR 18.78
3. Nadezhda Chizhova URS 18.19

Discus
1. Lia Manoliu ROM *58.28
2. Liesel Westermann FRG 57.76
3. Jolán Kleiber HUN 54.90

Javelin
1. Angéla Németh HUN 60.36
2. Mihaela Penes ROM 59.92
3. Eva Janko AUT 58.04

Pentathlon
1. Ingrid Becker FRG 5098
2. Liese Prokop AUT 4966
3. Annamária Toth HUN 4959

Men Swimming

100m Freestyle
1. Michael Wenden AUS **52.2
2. Ken Walsh USA 52.8
3. Mark Spitz USA 53.0

200m Freestyle
1. Michael Wenden AUS *1:55.2
2. Donald Schollander USA 1:55.8
3. John Nelson USA 1:58.1

400m Freestyle
1. Michael Burton USA *4:09.0
2. Ralph Hutton CAN 4:11.7
3. Alain Mosconi FRA 4:13.3

1500m Freestyle
1. Michael Burton USA *16:38.9
2. John Kinsella USA 16:57.3
3. Gregory Brough AUS 17:04.7

100m Backstroke
1. Roland Matthes GDR *58.7
2. Charles Hickcox USA 1:00.2
3. Ron Mills USA 1:00.5

200m Backstroke
1. Roland Matthes GDR *2:09.6
2. Mitchell Ivety USA 2:10.6
3. Jack Horsley USA 2:10.9

100m Breaststroke
1. Donald McKenzie USA 1:07.7
2. Vladimir Kosinsky URS 1:08.0
3. Nicolai Pankin URS 1:08.0

200m Breaststroke
1. Felipe Munoz MEX 2:28.7
2. Vladimir Kosinsky URS 2:29.2
3. Brian Job USA 2:29.9

100m Butterfly
1. Douglas Russell USA *55.9
2. Mark Spitz USA 56.4
3. Ross Wales USA 57.2

200m Butterfly
1. Carl Robie USA 2:08.7
2. Martin Woodroffe GBR 2:09.0
3. John Ferris USA 2:09.3

200m Individual Medley
1. Charles Hickcox USA *2:12.0
2. Gregory Buckingham USA 2:13.0
3. John Ferris USA 2:13.3

400m Individual Medley
1. Charles Hickcox USA 4:48.4
2. Gary Hall USA 4:48.7
3. Michael Holthaus FRG 4:51.4

4x100m Freestyle Relay
1. USA **3:31.7 (Zachary Zorn, Stephen Rerych, Mark Spitz, Kenneth Walsh)
2. URS 3:34.2 (Semyon Belits-Geiman, Viktor Mazanov, Georgy Kulikov, Leonid Illyichev)
3. AUS 3:34.7 (Gregory Rogers, Robert Windle, Robert Cusack, Michael Wenden)

4x200m Freestyle Relay
1. USA 7:52.3 (John Nelson, Stephen Rerych, Mark Spitz, Don Schollander)
2. AUS 7:53.7 (Gregory Rogers, Graham White, Robert Windle, Michael Wenden)
3. URS 8:01.6 (Vladimir Bure, Semyon Belits-Geiman, Georgy Kulikov, Leonid Illyichev)

4x100m Medley Relay
1. USA **3:54.9 (Charles Hickcox, Donald McKenzie, Douglas Russell, Kenneth Walsh)
2. GDR 3:57.5 (Roland Matthes, Egon Henninger, Horst-Günther Gregor, Frank Wiegand)
3. URS 4:00.7 (Yuri Gromak, Vladimir Kossinsky, Vladimir Nemshilov, Leonid Illyichev)

Springboard Diving
1. Bernie Wrightson USA 170.15
2. Klaus Dibiasi ITA 159.74
3. James Henry USA 158.09

Platform Diving
1. Klaus Dibiasi ITA 164.18
2. Alvaro Gaxiola MEX 154.49
3. Edwin Young USA 153.93

Water Polo

1. Yugoslavia
2. Soviet Union
3. Hungary

Women Swimming

100m Freestyle
1. Jan Henne USA 1:00.3
2. Susan Pedersen USA 1:00.3
3. Linda Gustavson USA 1:00.3

200m Freestyle
1. Debbie Meyer USA *2:10.5
2. Jan Henne USA 2:11.0
3. Jane Barkman USA 2:11.2

400m Freestyle
1. Debbie Meyer USA *4:31.8
2. Linda Gustavson USA 4:35.5
3. Karen Moras AUS 4:37.0

800m Freestyle
1. Debbie Meyer USA *9:24.0
2. Pamela Kruse USA 9:35.7
3. Maria Teresa Ramirez MEX 9:38.5

100m Breaststroke
1. Djurdjica Bjedov YUG *1:15.8
2. Galina Prozumenshikova URS 1:15.9
3. Sharon Wichman USA 1:16.1

200m Breaststroke
1. Sharon Wichman USA *2:44.4
2. Djurdjica Bjedov YUG 2:46.4
3. Galina Prozumenshikova URS 2:47.0

100m Backstroke
1. Kaye Hall USA **1:06.2
2. Elaine Tanner CAN 1:06.7
3. Jane Swagerty USA 1:08.1

200m Backstroke
1. Pokey Watson USA *2:24.8
2. Elaine Tanner CAN 2:27.4
3. Kaye Hall USA 2:28.9

100m Butterfly
1. Lynette McClements AUS 1:05.5
2. Ellie Daniel USA 1:05.8
3. Susan Shields USA 1:06.2

200m Butterfly
1. Ada Kok NETH *2:24.7
2. Helga Lindner GDR 2:24.8
3. Ellie Daniel USA 2:25.9

200m Individual Medley
1. Claudia Kolb USA *2:24.7
2. Susan Pedersen USA 2:28.8
3. Jan Henne USA 2:31.4

400m Individual Medley
1. Claudia Kolb USA *5:08.5
2. Lynn Vidali USA 5:22.2
3. Sabine Steinbach GDR 5:25.3

4x100m Freestyle Relay
1. USA *4:02.5 (Jane Barkman, Linda Gustavson, Susan Pedersen, Jan Henne)
2. GDR 4:05.7 (Gabriele Wetzko, Roswitha Krause, Uta Schmuck, Martina Grunert)
3. CAN 4:07.2 (Angela Coughlaw, Marilyn Corson, Elaine Tanner, Marion Lay)

4x100m Medley Relay
1. USA *4:28.3 (Kaye Hall, Catie Ball, Ellie Daniel, Susan Pedersen)
2. AUS 4:30.0 (Lynette Watson, Lynette McClements, Judy Playfair, Janet Steinbeck)
3. FRG 4:36.4 (Angelika Kraus, Ute Frommater, Heike Hustede, Heidi Reineck)

Springboard Diving
1. Sue Gossick USA 150.77
2. Tamara Pogoscheva URS 145.30
3. Keala O'Sullivan USA 145.23

Platform Diving
1. Milena Duchková TCH 109.59
2. Natalya Lobanova URS 105.14
3. Ann Peterson USA 101.11

Boxing

Light Flyweight
1. Francisco Rodriguez VEN
2. Yong-ju Jee KOR
3. Harlan Marbley USA
3. Hubert Skrypczak POL

Flyweight
1. Ricardo Delgado MEX
2. Artur Olech POL
3. Servilio Oliveira BRA
3. Lee Rwabwago UGA

Bantamweight
1. Valery Sokolov URS
2. Eridari Mukwanga UGA
3. Eiji Morioka JAP
3. Kyou-Chull Chang KOR

1968 Mexico

Featherweight
1. Antonio Roldan MEX
2. Albert Robinson USA
3. Philipp Waruinge KEN
3. Ivan Mihailov BUL

Lightweight
1. Ronald Harris USA
2. Józef Grudzien POL
3. Calistrat Cutov ROM
3. Zvonimir Vujin YUG

Light Welterweight
1. Jerzy Kulej POL
2. Enrique Requeiferos CUB
3. Arto Nilsson FIN
3. James Wallington USA

Welterweight
1. Manfred Wolke GDR
2. Joseph Bessala CAM
3. Vladimir Mussalimov URS
3. Mario Guilloti ARG

Light Middleweight
1. Boris Lagutin URS
2. Rolando Garbey CUB
3. John Baldwin USA
3. Günther Meier FRG

Middleweight
1. Christopher Finnegan GBR
2. Aleksei Kisselyov URS
3. Agustin Zaragoza MEX
3. Alfred Jones USA

Light Heavyweight
1. Dan Poznyak URS
2. Ion Monea ROM
3. Georgi Stankov BUL
3. Stanislaw Dragan POL

Heavyweight
1. George Foreman USA
2. Ionas Chepulis URS
3. Giorgio Bambini ITA
3. Joaquin Rocha MEX

Greco Roman Wrestling

Flyweight
1. Peter Kirov BUL
2. Vladimir Bakulin URS
3. Miroslav Zeman TCH

Bantamweight
1. János Varga HUN
2. Ion Baciu ROM
3. Ivan Kochergin URS

Featherweight
1. Roman Rurua URS
2. Hideo Fujimoto JAP
3. Simeon Popescu ROM

Lightweight
1. Munji Mumemura JAP
2. Stevan Horvat YUG
3. Petros Galaktopoulos GRE

Welterweight
1. Rudolf Vesper GDR
2. Daniel Robin FRA
3. Károly Bajkó HUN

Middleweight
1. Lothar Metz GDR
2. Valentin Olenik URS
3. Branislav Simic YUG

Light Heavyweight
1. Boyan Radev BUL
2. Nicolai Yakovenko URS
3. Nicolae Martinescu ROM

Heavyweight
1. István Kozma HUN
2. Anatoly Roshin URS
3. Petr Kment TCH

Freestyle Wrestling

Flyweight
1. Shigeo Nakata JAP
2. Richard Sanders USA
3. Surenjav Sukhbaatar MON

Bantamweight
1. Yojiro Uetake JAP
2. Donald Behm USA
3. Abutaleb Talebi IRN

Featherweight
1. Masaaki Kaneko JAP
2. Enyu Vulchev BUL
3. Shamseddin Seyed-Abassy IRN

Lightweight
1. Abdollah Movahed IRN
2. Enyu Todorov BUL
3. Sereeter Danzandarjaa MON

Welterweight
1. Mahmut Atalay TUR
2. Daniel Robin FRA
3. Dagvasuren Purev MON

Middleweight
1. Boris Gurevitch URS
2. Munkbat Jigjid MON
3. Prodan Gardzhev BUL

Light Heavyweight
1. Ahmet Ayik TUR
2. Schota Lomidze URS
3. Jószef Csatári HUN

Heavyweight
1. Aleksandr Medved URS
2. Osman Duraliev BUL
3. Wilfried Dietrich FRG

Men Fencing

Foil Individual
1. Ionel Drimba ROM 4
2. Jenö Kamuti HUN 3
3. Daniel Revenu FRA 3

Foil Team
1. France
2. Soviet Union
3. Poland

Epée Individual
1. Gyözö Kulcsár HUN 6
2. Grigory Kriss URS 4
3. Gianluigi Saccaro ITA 4

Epée Team
1. Hungary
2. Soviet Union
3. Poland

Sabre Individual
1. Jerzy Pawlowski POL 5
2. Mark Rakita URS 4
3. Tibor Pézsa HUN 3

Sabre Team
1. Soviet Union
2. Italy
3. Hungary

Women Fencing

Foil Individual
1. Yelena Novikova URS 4
2. Maria Del Pilar Roldan MEX 3
3. Ildikó Ujlaki-Retjö HUN 3

Foil Team
1. Soviet Union
2. Hungary
3. Romania

Modern Pentathlon

Individual
1. Björn Ferm SWE 4964
2. András Balczó HUN 4953
3. Pavel Lednev URS 4795

Team
1. Hungary 14325
2. Soviet Union 14248
3. France 14188

Men Canoeing

Kayak-1 1000m
1. Mihály Hesz HUN 4:02.63
2. Aleksandr Shaparenko URS 4:03.58
3. Erik Hansen DEN 4:04.39

Kayak-2 1000m
1. Soviet Union 3:37.54
2. Hungary 3:38.44
3. Austria 3:40.71

Kayak-4 1000m
1. Norway 3:14.38
2. Romania 3:14.81
3. Hungary 3:15.10

Canadian-1 1000m
1. Tibor Tatai HUN 4:36.14
2. Detlef Lewe FRG 4:38.31
3. Vitaly Galkov URS 4:40.42

Canadian-2 2000m
1. Romania 4:07.18
2. Hungary 4:08.77
3. Soviet Union 4:11.30

Women Canoeing

Kayak-1 500m
1. Lyudmila Pinayeva URS 2:11.09
2. Renate Breuer FRG 2:12.71
3. Victoria Dumitru ROM 2:13.22

Kayak-2 500m
1. West Germany 1:56.44
2. Hungary 1:58.60
3. Soviet Union 1:58.61

Rowing

Single Sculls
1. Henri Jan Wienese NETH 7:47.80
2. Jochen Meissner FRG 7:52.00
3. Alberto Demiddi ARG 7:57.19

Double Sculls
1. Soviet Union 6:51.82
2. Netherlands 6:52.80
3. USA 6:54.21

Coxless Pairs
1. GDR 7:26.56
2. USA 7:26.71
3. Denmark 7:31.84

Coxed Pairs
1. Italy 8:04.81
2. Netherlands 8:06.80
3. Denmark 8:08.07

Coxless Fours
1. GDR 6:39.18
2. Hungary 6:41.64
3. Italy 6:44.01

Coxed Fours
1. New Zealand 6:45.62
2. GDR 6:48.20
3. Switzerland 6:49.04

Eights
1. FRG 6:07.00
2. Australia 6:07.98
3. Soviet Union 6:09.11

Yachting

Finn
1. Valentin Mankin URS 11.7
2. Hubert Raudaschl AUT 53.4
3. Fabio Albarelli ITA 55.1

Star
1. USA 14.4
2. Norway 43.7
3. Italy 44.7

Flying Dutchman
1. Great Britain 3.0
2. FRG 43.7
3. Brazil 48.4

Dragon
1. USA 6.0
2. Denmark 26.4
3. GDR 32.7

5.50m
1. Sweden 8.0
2. Switzerland 32.0
3. Great Britain 39.8

Cycling

Individual Road Race
1. Pierfranco Vianelli ITA 4:41:25.24
2. Leif Mortensen DEN 4:42:49.71
3. Gösta Pettersson SWE 4:43:15.24

100km Team Time Trial
1. Netherlands 2:07:49.06
2. Sweden 2:09:26.60
3. Italy 2:10:18.74

1000m Time Trial
1. Pierre Trentin FRA **1:03.91
2. Niels-Christian Fredborg DEN 1:04.61
3. Janusz Kierzkowski POL 1:04.63

1000m Sprint
1. Daniel Morelon FRA 10.68
2. Giordano Turini ITA
3. Pierre Trentin FRA

2000m Tandem
1. France 9.83
2. Netherlands
3. Belgium

4000m Individual Pursuit
1. Daniel Rebillard FRA 4:41.71
2. Mogens Frey Jensen DEN 4:42.43
3. Xaver Kurmann SUI 4:39.42

The time of the race held to determine 3rd place were better than those of the final.

4000m Team Pursuit
1. Denmark 4:22.44
2. FRG 4:18.94
3. Italy 4:18.35

The West German team was the winner, but was first disqualified for having been pushed at the start, and then placed second.

The times of the race held to determine third place were better than those of the initial race.

Equestrian Sports

Three-day Event Individual
1. Jean-Jacques Guyon FRA
2. Derek Allhusen GBR
3. Michael Page USA

Three-day Event Team
1. Great Britain -175.93
2. USA -245.87
3. Australia -331.26

Individual Dressage
1. Ivan Kizimov URS 1572
2. Josef Neckermann FRG 1546
3. Reiner Klimke FRG 1537

Team Dressage
1. FRG 2699
2. Soviet Union 2657
3. Switzerland 2547

Grand Prix Jumping Individual
1. William Steinkraus USA -4
2. Marion Coakes GBR -8
3. David Broome GBR -12/0/35.3

Grand Prix Jumping Team
1. Canada -102.75
2. France -110.50
3. FRG -117.25

Shooting

Free Rifle, 300m, 3 positions
1. Gary Anderson USA **1157
2. Vladimir Kornev URS 1151
3. Kurt Müller SUI 1148

Small-Bore Rifle, 50m prone
1. Jan Kurka TCH **598
2. László Hammerl HUN **598
3. Ian Ballinger NZL 597

Small-Bore Rifle Combined, 3 positions
1. Bernd Klingner FRG 1157
2. John Writer USA 1156
3. Victor Parkhimovich URS 1154

Rapid-Fire Pistol
1. Józef Zapedzki POL *593
2. Marcel Rosca ROM 591/147
3. Renart Suleimanov URS 591/146/148

Free Pistol, 50m
1. Grigory Kossykh URS *560/30
2. Heinz Mertel FRG *526/26
3. Harald Vollmar GDR 560

Clay Pigeon
1. John Braithwaite GBR *198
2. Thomas Garrigus USA 196/25/25
3. Kurt Czekalla GDR 196/25/23

Skeet
1. Yevgeny Petrov URS =**198/25
2. Romano Garagnani ITA =**198/24/25
3. Konrad Wirnhier FRG =**198/24/23

Weightlifting

		2 Arm Press	2 Arm Snatch	2 Arm Clean and Jerk	Total
Bantamweight					
1. Mohammad Nassiri	IRN	112.5	105.0	**150.0	=**367.5
2. Imre Földi	HUN	*122.5	105.0	140.0	=**367.5
3. Henryk Trebicki	POL	115.0	107.5	135.0	357.5
Featherweight					
1. Yoshinobu Miyake	JAP	=*122.5	117.5	=**152.5	392.5
2. Dito Shanidze	URS	120.0	117.5	150.0	387.5
3. Yoshiyuki Miyake	JAP	=*122.5	115.0	147.5	385.0
Lightweight					
1. Waldemar Baszanowski	POL	135.0	=*135.0	*167.5	*437.5
2. Parviz Jalayer	IRN	125.0	132.5	165.0	422.5
3. Marian Zielinski	POL	135.0	125.0	160.0	420.0
Middleweight					
1. Viktor Kurentsov	URS	*152.5	135.0	**187.5	*475.0
2. Masashi Ouchi	JAP	140.0	*140.0	175.0	455.0
3. Károly Bakos	HUN	137.5	132.5	170.0	440.0
Light Heavyweight					
1. Boris Selitsky	URS	150.0	*147.5	*187.5	=**485.0
2. Vladimir Belyayev	URS	152.5	*147.5	185.0	=**485.0
3. Norbert Ozimek	POL	150.0	140.0	182.5	472.5
Middle Heavyweight					
1. Kaarlo Kangasniemi	FIN	*172.5	**157.5	187.5	*517.5
2. Jaan Talts	URS	160.0	150.0	**197.5	507.5
3. Marek Golab	POL	165.0	145.0	185.0	495.0
Heavyweight					
1. Leonid Zhabotinsky	URS	*200.0	*170.0	202.5	=*572.5
2. Serge Reding	BEL	195.0	147.5	212.5	555.0
3. Joe Dube	USA	*200.0	145.0	210.0	555.0

Men Gymnastics

All-around Individual
1. Sawao Kato JAP 115.90
2. Mikhail Voronin URS 115.85
3. Akinori Nakayama JAP 115.65

Combined Exercises Team
1. Japan 575.90
2. Soviet Union 571.10
3. GDR 557.15

Parallel Bars
1. Akinori Nakayama JAP 19.475
2. Mikhail Voronin URS 19.425
3. Vladimir Klimenko URS 19.225

Floor Exercises
1. Sawao Kato JAP 19.475
2. Akinori Nakayama JAP 19.400
3. Takeshi Kato JAP 19.275

Long Horse Vault
1. Mikhail Voronin URS 19.000
2. Yukio Endo JAP 18.950
3. Sergei Diomidov URS 18.925

Side Horse
1. Miroslav Cerar YUG 19.325
2. Olli Eino Laiho FIN 19.225
3. Mikhail Voronin URS 19.200

Horizontal Bar
1. Mikhail Voronin URS 19.550
1. Akinori Nakayama JAP 19.550
3. Eizo Kenmotsu JAP 19.375

Rings
1. Akinori Nakayama JAP 19.450
2. Mikhail Voronin URS 19.325
3. Sawao Kato JAP 19.225

Women Gymnastics

All-around Individual
1. Vera Cáslavská TCH 78.25
2. Zinaida Voronina URS 76.85
3. Natalia Kuchinskaia URS 76.75

Combined Exercises Team
1. Soviet Union 382.85
2. Czechoslovakia 382.20
3. GDR 379.10

Asymmetric Bars
1. Vera Cáslavská TCH 19.650
2. Karin Janz GDR 19.500
3. Zinaida Voronina URS 19.425

Floor Exercises
1. Larissa Petrik URS 19.675
1. Vera Cáslavská TCH 19.675
3. Natalia Kuchinskaia URS 19.650

Side Horse Vault
1. Vera Cáslavská TCH 19.775
2. Erika Zuchold GDR 19.625
3. Zinaida Voronina URS 19.500

Balance Beam
1. Natalia Kuchinskaia URS 19.650
2. Vera Cáslavská TCH 19.575
3. Larissa Petrik URS 19.250

Basketball

1. USA
2. Yugoslavia
3. Soviet Union

Hockey

1. Pakistan
2. Australia
3. India

Men Volleyball

1. Soviet Union
2. Japan
3. Czechoslovakia

Women Volleyball

1. Soviet Union
2. Japan
3. Poland

Soccer

1. Hungary
2. Bulgaria
3. Japan

(Key to symbols and abbreviations p. 1456)

Dick Fosbury won the high jump gold, clearing 2.24 metres with his trademark backwards flop.

1968

NOVEMBER

Su	Mo	Tu	We	Th	Fr	Sa
					1	2
3	4	5	6	7	8	9
10	11	12	13	14	15	16
17	18	19	20	21	22	23
24	25	26	27	28	29	30

1. London: The Family Law Reform Bill is published; it aims to lower the age of adulthood from 21 to 18.

3. Mexico: Graham Hill wins the Mexico Grand Prix to become world motor racing champion.

4. Italy: Over 100 people are now known to have died in flooding in the north of the country.

5. US: Shirley Chisholm becomes the first black woman to be elected to the House of Representatives.

6. UK: 2,300 lose their jobs when the British Eagle airline stops flying.

7. Prague: Crowds burn Soviet flags and battle with police (→17).

8. London: Bruce Reynolds, the last unapprehended Great Train Robbery suspect, is arrested.

14. London: Heath appoints Margaret Thatcher as Shadow Transport Minister.

17. Prague: Students occupy the city's university in protest at government repression.

18. Glasgow: At least 20 people die in a warehouse fire.

24. Falklands: Lord Chalfont becomes the first member of a British government to visit the islands.

26. UK: The Race Relations Act comes into force (→25/12).

28. UK: John Lennon is fined £150 for possession of cannabis.

30. Northern Ireland: Loyalist extremists take over the centre of Armagh.

30. UK: The Trades Descriptions Act comes into force.

DEATHS

6. French conductor Charles Munch (*26/9/1891).

17. British author and artist Mervyn Laurence Peake (*9/7/1911).

25. US author Upton Sinclair (*20/9/1878).

28. British author Enid Mary Blyton (*11/8/1897).

Nixon is US President

Vice-President Agnew and President Nixon acknowledge the applause.

Nov 6. Richard Nixon was elected President of the United States yesterday, eight years after he just failed to beat John F. Kennedy in 1960. Mr Nixon, a Californian who has moved to New York, and his vice-presidential running-mate, Spiro T. Agnew, the Governor of Maryland, together beat the incumbent Vice-President, Hubert Humphrey of Minnesota, whose vice-presidential partner was Senator Edmund Muskie of Maine.

Mr Nixon won 301 votes in the electoral college, as compared to 191 for the Vice-President and 46 for former Alabama Governor George Wallace, running as an American Independent.

The margin in the popular vote was much closer: only a little more than half a million votes, with 31.785 million for Nixon, 31.274 million for Humphrey and nearly ten million votes going to George Wallace.

In the last days before the election, it appears from the polls that Hubert Humphrey was rapidly overhauling Nixon (→2/12).

A view from the batsman's end of England and Yorkshire's fast bowler "Fiery" Fred Truman, who announced his retirement from the game this month.

LBJ orders bombing to stop in Vietnam

Nov 1. President Johnson today ordered a total and unconditional end to the bombing of North Vietnam, in an attempt to breathe life into the stalled peace talks in Paris. In a televised speech the President said: "What we now expect – what we have a right to expect – are prompt, productive, serious and decisive negotiations in an atmosphere conducive to peace".

In return, the North Vietnamese have agreed to allow the South Vietnamese to take part in the Paris talks. This move has been generally welcomed in America, although some cynics claim it is a ploy to improve Vice-President Humphrey's chances in this month's Presidential election (→18/12).

1968

DECEMBER

Su	Mo	Tu	We	Th	Fr	Sa
1	2	3	4	5	6	7
8	9	10	11	12	13	14
15	16	17	18	19	20	21
22	23	24	25	26	27	28
29	30	31				

1. Israel: Jordanian bridges are blown up by Israeli raiders.

2. Washington: Nixon names Henry Kissinger as National Security Adviser.

6. London: Tory chiefs ban Enoch Powell from making a planned speech on Rhodesia.

10. Stockholm: Nobel Prizes go to Luis Alvarez (US, Physics); Lars Onslager (US, Chemistry); Robert Holley, Har Khorana and Marshall Nirenberg (US, Medicine); Yasunari Kawabata (Japan, Literature); and in Oslo to Rene Cassin (France, Peace).

16. Bristol: An 11-day sit-in at Bristol University ends.

18. Phnom Penh: The Cambodians say they will release 11 US prisoners.

19. London: Colin Davis is chosen to succeed Georg Solti as director of the Royal Opera House.

20. Madrid: Franco banishes Prince Carlos, the pretender to the Spanish throne.

21. US: Apollo 8 is launched from Cape Kennedy.→

25. London: The Queen calls for racial tolerance in her Christmas message.

29. UK: Cunard postpones the first voyage of the QE2 because she is still unfit for sailing.

DEATH

20. US author John Steinbeck (*27/2/1902).

HITS OF 1968

I pretend.

Wonderful world.

Those were the days.

QUOTE OF THE YEAR

"Longevity has its place. But I'm not concerned about that right now. I want to do God's will and he's allowed me to go up to the mountain, and I've looked over and I've seen the Promised Land."

Martin Luther King, speaking on April 3, 1968, the night before his assassination.

Astronauts orbit Moon

The Moon, as seen by the astronauts as Apollo 8 rounds it.

Dec 27. After a six-day flight that included ten orbits of the moon, the American Apollo 8 spacecraft splashed down in the Pacific today, only 5,000 yards from the recovery ship. The crew – Frank Bormann, James A. Lovell and William Anders – "look great and are very happy" according to the Apollo flight surgeon Dr Charles Berry.

The flight went according to plan. The launch of the giant Saturn V rocket was on time, putting Apollo into earth orbit. There the final stage of the launcher was re-ignited to put the spacecraft on course for the moon. After a journey of a quarter of a million miles Apollo's own engines were fired to slow it down, allowing it to enter the moon's gravity.

In a moment of high tension, communications were lost as Apollo disappeared behind the moon. Later, after the astronauts had read from the bible on Christmas Eve, Apollo's engines were fired again to put it on an earth trajectory, heading for the 35-mile wide window for re-entry. The flight was a "giant step," said the Apollo programme director, General Sam Phillips.

Arts: the audience not let down by Hair

The long-desired abolition of stage censorship by the Lord Chamberlain was followed on the very next night by the premiere of "Hair", the "Tribal-Love-Rock" musical from America in which the cast, having divested themselves of their clothes under blankets, stand up and face the audience naked just before the lights go down.

The lights did not have far to go it was dim enough already, but the first-night audience went wild with enthusiasm at this new "breakthrough" in Sixties permissiveness. Stage nudity is now with us, along with "Hair's" deafening beat, psychedelic light effects, showers of confetti, and barrages of "the" four-letter word in chorus. The show is a celebration of the hippie values – sexual free-for-all, hashish and hatred (of authority and of the Vietnam war). There is a song extolling long hair.

Oddly enough television, or at least its most popular serial, is firmly anchored in 1906, not 1960. "The Forsyte Saga", **John Galsworthy's** detailed documentary indictment of Edwardian affluence, possessiveness and obsession with ownership, even of people, is the most ambitious serial TV has yet mounted, and commands huge audiences for the Nation's newest channel, BBC2. **Eric Porter** as Soames Forsyte holds the nation in thrall.

Books from America include "The Armies of the Night" by **Norman Mailer**, an account of the peace march on the Pentagon last October by pacifists, hippies, anarchists, academics, the poet **Robert Lowell** and, most important, himself. "Myra Breckinridge" by **Gore Vidal** is a notorious "pornographic" exposure of sex in Hollywood, whose heroine changes sex. "Couples" by **John Updike** is also about the American obsession with sex; it is set in an affluent Connecticut village where commuters play marital musical chairs.

Mia Farrow in "Rosemary's Baby" one of this year's successful films.

How trivial this would seem to **Alexander Solzhenitsyn**, whose banned novels circulate secretly in home-typed copies in Russia. We can now read smuggled texts of "Cancer Ward", whose dying inmates epitomise Soviet society, and "The First Circle", set in a prison for dissident scientists. It includes a blistering portrait of Stalin, walled-up in the Kremlin fearing anyone he has left alive.

Captured spy ship crew comes home

Dec 24. The crew of the spy ship Pueblo was released today after eleven months captivity in North Korea. The Pueblo was boarded and captured by the North Koreans, who claimed the Pueblo was operating in their territorial waters. The North Koreans made great propaganda play with "confessions" of spying by the crew, but far more damaging was their capture of coding and surveillance equipment which the captain did not have time to destroy.

An 11-year-old girl gets a life sentence

Dec 17. A senior judge highlighted the lack of specialised medical care for prisoners with mental disorders today, when he sentenced a girl of eleven to be detained for life for the manslaughter of two tiny boys. Mary Flora Bell strangled them with a friend, but was found not guilty on a murder charge after doctors said she suffered from a psychopathic illness. Mr Justice Cusack said: "It is a most unhappy thing there is no hospital suitable for this girl."

"Hair" makes its "statement of youth" to the flocking coach parties.

1969

JANUARY

Su	Mo	Tu	We	Th	Fr	Sa
			1	2	3	4
5	6	7	8	9	10	11
12	13	14	15	16	17	18
19	20	21	22	23	24	25
26	27	28	29	30	31	

1. UK: Sir Learie Constantine becomes Britain's first black life peer.

4. UK: Up to 50 die when an airliner crashes into houses near Gatwick (→3/7/70).

6. Belfast: The Northern Ireland government uses "B Specials" to aid the Royal Ulster Constabulary (→27).

9. Washington: NASA picks Neil Armstrong and Edwin "Buzz" Aldrin for the first moon landing (→24/2).

12. London: Police battle with 4,000 demonstrators trying to take over Rhodesia House and South Africa House (→5/11).

14. UK: Sir Matt Busby announces his retirement as Manchester United manager.

15. UK: QE2 sailings are cancelled because of more trouble with her turbines.

17. London: Barbara Castle publishes her White Paper on industrial relations, "In Place of Strife" (→11/2).

19. Prague: Angry crowds gather after hearing of Jan Palach's immolation.

20. Washington: Nixon is sworn in as President.

23. London: Home Secretary James Callaghan says the existing penalties for cannabis will stay (→27).

24. UK: Ford unveils a new sports saloon, the Capri.

27. London: MPs condemn the Wootton proposals to alter cannabis laws (→27/4/70).

27. Northern Ireland: Protestant leader Ian Paisley is jailed for three months for unlawful assembly (→3/2).

30. London: Callaghan bans the immigration of fiances of Commonwealth citizens (→9/4).

30. London: "The Dales", the BBC's longest-running radio show, will end on April 25 (→23/2).

DEATH

11. British author Richmal Crompton Lamburn, known as Richmal Crompton (*15/11/1890).

Ulster police clash with civil rights march

No surrender: police lines halt civil rights marchers in Londonderry.

Jan 3. Violence flared in Londonderry last night at the end of a 73-mile civil rights march from Belfast. Police used armoured water cannons to disperse several hundred Catholics who had trapped their arch-opponent, the Rev Ian Paisley and his supporters, in the city's Guildhall.

Mr Paisley's car was overturned and set on fire as the crowd, shouting "We want Paisley," attacked the Guildhall with stones and other missiles. Despite appeals for calm by civil rights leaders, dozens of windows were shattered and an angry mob tried to break through the wrought-iron gates. The foyer of a nearby hotel was turned into a casualty station early this morning with over 20 injured people – several of them young girls – being treated for minor injuries.

In Claudy, nine miles away, the riot squad was called to a pitched battle in the town centre between loyalist extremists and militant supporters of the march. A civil rights leader said: "It has been a very nasty and disappointing affair. Everyone is very upset."

Ulster's Roman Catholic community is demanding "one man, one vote" in the province, claiming discrimination in local government laws under which only householders are allowed to vote. They also claim unfairness by Protestant-controlled councils in the allocation of council houses (→6).

Exodus of Kenyan Asians to hit UK

Jan 1. Thousands of Asians will be on their way to Britain from Kenya in the next few months because the Kenya government is taking away their trading licences in order to encourage African businessmen. All the Asians carry British passports, but they are entitled to enter Britain only if they are unemployed or have been ordered to leave Kenya. The loss of a trading licence effectively makes them unemployed. With wives and children, they number over 15,000. A year ago, about 10,000 came from Kenya. In the next few years about 35,000 are expected (→30).

Cut pot penalties says drug report

Jan 10. In their report published today, the Home Office Advisory Committee on Drug Dependence, headed by Lady Wootton of Abinger, recommends that the penalties for smoking cannabis should be substantially reduced. The Committee firmly rejects any suggestions that cannabis should be legalised or its use encouraged, but they believe new legislation is required to separate the control of the "soft" drug cannabis from the "hard" drugs such as heroin which lead to addiction (→23).

Flames from Jan Palach's sacrifice burn in the heart of Czechs

Jan 26. The student Jan Palach is dead, but his spirit burns in the hearts of Czechs throughout the country. Tonight, several thousand young people crowded into central Prague to obliterate newly-painted signs reading "Red Army Square" and replace them with "Jan Palach Square". Hour after hour they chanted: "Russians Go Home."

Jan Palach, aged 21, died in hospital two days after he set fire to himself in Wenceslas Square in protest against the Russian invasion. A woman announcer who gave out the news in a TV bulletin was in tears. Before he died, he said: "My act has fulfilled its purpose, but let nobody else do it." He was buried yesterday (→25/2).

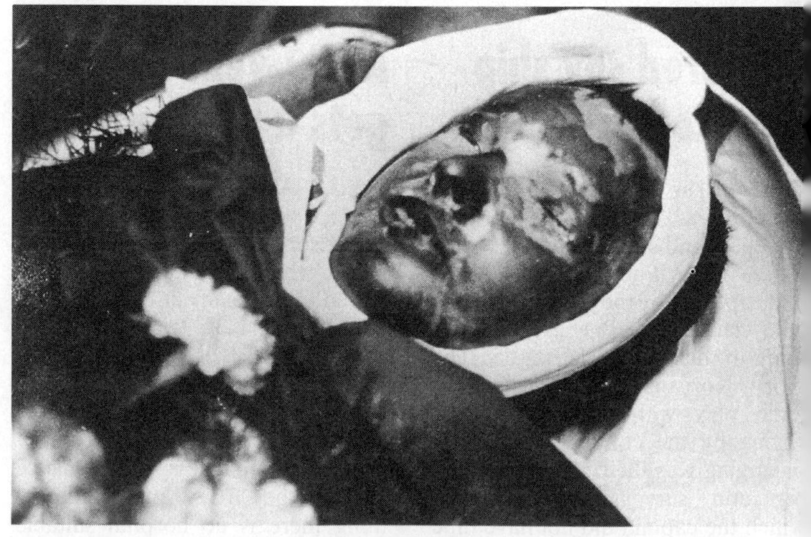

The body of Jan Palach after his self-immolation in Wenceslas Square.

1969

FEBRUARY

Su	Mo	Tu	We	Th	Fr	Sa
						1
2	3	4	5	6	7	8
9	10	11	12	13	14	15
16	17	18	19	20	21	22
23	24	25	26	27	28	

3. Belfast: Prime Minister O'Neill calls an election for February 24.→ 0

3. London: The director of the LSE keeps it closed for "the immediate future" (→ 19/4).

7. Nigeria: Up to 300 die when a bomb rips through a market in Biafra (→ 12).

8. US: Boeing's 747 airliner, the largest commercial aircraft in the world, makes its maiden flight (→ 2/3).

11. UK: 1,600 women workers at Ford win equal pay with their men colleagues (→ 20).

14. UK: Marty Feldman is named TV personality of 1968.

15. Vietnam: The US calls a truce for Tet, the lunar new year.

18. UK: Pop stars Lulu and Maurice Gibb get married.

20. London: Lloyd's of London will admit women from January 1970 (→ 27).

21. Vietnam: A week-long truce ends (→ 24/4).

23. UK: Ex-Test cricketer, the Rev. David Sheppard, is appointed Bishop of Woolwich.

23. UK: BBC2 begins a new series called "Civilisation", presented by Sir Kenneth Clark (→ 25/4).

24. US: The unmanned Mariner 6 is launched on a voyage to Mars (→ 13/3).

25. Prague: Jan Zajic becomes the latest Czech protester to burn himself to death (→ 28/3).

27. UK: Vic Feather becomes acting general secretary of the TUC (→ 5/11).

28. Los Angeles: Sirhan Sirhan, on trial for Bobby Kennedy's murder, is refused a request to be executed (→ 6/3).

DEATHS

2. British-born US actor, Boris Karloff, born William Pratt (*23/11/1887).

23. Saudi Arabian King Abd el-Aziz Ibn Saud, ruled 1953-64 (*15/1/02).

26. Israeli statesman Levi Eshkol, premier 1963-69 (*25/10/1895).

Murdoch wins News of the World battle

Jan 1. Hambros Bank claimed victory tonight for the News of the World directors in the battle to fight off the takeover bid from Robert Maxwell's Pergamon Press. This will give effective control to Rupert Murdoch's News Ltd of Australia.

The struggle began in October when Maxwell made a £26 million bid with the support of Professor Derek Jackson's family who own 25.5 per cent of the shares. The deal was fiercely opposed by the Carr family, who owned around 30 per cent of the shares and who run the company.

Stafford Summerfield, the editor, wrote an editorial saying the News of the World was "as British as roast beef" which was seen as a deliberate slight on Mr Maxwell's Czech origins. The Carrs set up a deal with Murdoch and beat Maxwell in a share-buying spree (→ 30).

Rupert Murdoch, the victor.

Court ban on LSE student ringleaders

Jan 30. Thirteen students, the alleged ringleaders of this week's clashes at the London School of Economics (LSE) and the University of London Union (ULU), were banned today in the High Court from entering the LSE without official permission for one week. They include David Adelstein and Martin Tomkinson, both of whom took part in disturbances at the college two years ago. The current problems began on January 24 when students destroyed a number of internal iron gates, designed to prevent sit-ins at the LSE's Houghton Street building.

At the demonstration which followed, the police made 25 arrests. On January 27, 1,000 LSE students occupied the ULU buildings, intending to establish an "LSE in exile" before being expelled by the college rugby team. It is hoped that the High Court decision will calm the situation (→ 3/2).

Showdown: police ring the LSE and begin to arrest protesting students.

Yassir Arafat is the new leader of PLO

Feb 3. The Palestine National Congress, meeting in Cairo today, appointed Yassir Arafat to be the new head of the Palestine Liberation Organisation. A short, bald and dynamic man, founder in 1963 of the military resistance movement Fatah, he escaped capture by the Israelis two years ago while organising cells in Jerusalem.

Fatah will now dominate the PLO. Arafat, as the new head of the 11-man committee responsible for organising all operations against Israel, can concentrate on making guerrilla warfare. Only the PFLP, the Popular Front for the Liberation of Palestine, a group led by the Marxist, George Habash, is going its own way (→ 9/2/70).

Arafat wants a Palestinian state.

Wilson faces Biafra protest in Germany

Feb 12. African students performed a war-dance in the snow-covered streets of Bonn and chanted "Wilson, murderer", as the British Prime Minister arrived for two days of talks with the West German Chancellor, Dr Kiesinger. The students were protesting against British support for the Nigerian government in the war with breakaway Biafra. "I respect their strength of feeling, even though I know rather more of the facts of this question," said Mr Wilson (→ 6/4).

Human egg is made fertile in test-tube

Feb 13. For the first time human eggs taken from women volunteers have been fertilised in test-tubes outside the body. The breakthrough is revealed in a report by R.G. Edwards and B.D. Bavister of the Physiological laboratory at Cambridge University, who collaborated with Patrick Steptoe, a specialist in obstetrics and gynaecology at Oldham General Hospital.

The eggs from the patients, together with human sperm, were washed in a nutrient fluid and brought together at body temperature. Out of a total of 56 eggs 18 were fertilised. The method was first tried out with rabbits' eggs.

The researchers prefaced their remarkable achievement with a warning that "problems of embryonic development are likely", meaning that there was a possibility that deformed foetuses might be produced.

Although the technique could be employed to treat certain types of infertility in older women "a higher incidence of mongols and abortions would thus be expected in these patients", they warned. It is clear that additional research needs to be done before these results can be applied (→17/8).

Goon Show fan Prince Charles takes time off from his academic studies at Cambridge and assumes a somewhat unprincely role in a university revue.

Ulster PM's future hangs in the balance

On the stump: the Rev. Ian Paisley begins his campaign at Bannside.

Feb 24. Ulster's Prime Minister, Terence O'Neill, has won the election and Stormont's composition is much as before, but his political future hangs in the balance.

All his old enemies within the Unionist Party are back, including Brian Faulkner, his former deputy, who resigned his office before the election. Even his own Bannside constituency delivered a shock, giving 38 per cent of the vote to his arch enemy – the Rev. Ian Paisley, hardest of hardliners. For 23 years it has returned O'Neill unopposed.

His problem now is to convince both the Roman Catholics that he is serious about reform and his own grassroots that he will safeguard the Union (→18/4).

Nixon comes to London to see Wilson

Feb 24. President Nixon and Mr Wilson met for the first time today when the US leader made a brief visit to London. They exchanged promises of straight dealing and they were reported to have got on very well together. A Wilson aide was asked the question which once plagued Nixon in America: "Would you buy a used car from this man ?" He replied: "I believe I would."

President Nixon meets British PM Harold Wilson at Downing Street.

1969

MARCH

Su	Mo	Tu	We	Th	Fr	Sa
						1
2	3	4	5	6	7	8
9	10	11	12	13	14	15
16	17	18	19	20	21	22
23	24	25	26	27	28	29
30	31					

2. France: The Anglo-French Concorde makes its maiden flight (→9/4).

2. USSR: Soviet and Chinese troops clash on the border.→

4. London: The longest-ever Old Bailey trial ends with Kray twins and four others found guilty of murder (→5).

6. Los Angeles: Sirhan Sirhan claims he does not remember killing Kennedy (→23/4).

7. London: The Queen opens the new Victoria Line from Victoria to Walthamstow.

10. Memphis: James Earl Ray pleads guilty to the murder of Martin Luther King and is jailed for 99 years (→3/3/70).

12. UK: Paul McCartney marries Linda Eastman (→12).

12. UK: George Harrison is arrested for illegal possession of cannabis (→9/4/70).

13. US: Apollo 9 splashes down safely after the first test of the lunar module (→16/5).

17. Tel Aviv: Golda Meir becomes Israeli premier (→10/7).

18. Budapest: Eastern Bloc leaders hold their first meeting since the Soviet invasion of Czechoslovakia.

22. London: Soccer hooligans run riot on the Tube, causing thousands of pounds worth of damage.

25. Karachi: President Ayub Khan resigns as the army, under General Yahya Khan, takes control (→8/12/70).

29. UK: Mr T. McKoy's Highland Wedding wins the Grand National.

31. UK: All BOAC flights are grounded as pilots strike over pay and productivity.

31. Anguilla: Britain signs a truce with rebel leaders.

DEATHS

11. British author John Wyndham, born John Wyndham Parkes Lucas Beynon Harris (*10/7/1903).

28. US commander and statesman, General Dwight David Eisenhower, President 1953-61 (*14/10/1890).

Gangland bosses, Kray twins, are jailed

The twins, Ronald (l.) and Reginald, their mother and grandfather.

March 5. Gangland twins Ronald and Reginald Kray, who were said to have terrorised the East End of London, were given life sentences today after being found guilty of murder. The judge, Mr Justice Melford Stevenson, said they should not be released for 30 years. Four members of their underworld "firm" were also convicted.

The 35-year-old brothers gained a reputation for violence while also commanding a cult following. They were arrested after George Cornell, aged 38, was shot in the head at the Blind Beggar pub and Jack "The Hat" McVitie, also 38, was lured to a flat and then stabbed in the face, chest and throat. The jury took nearly seven hours to find Ronald guilty of both killings and convict his twin of the knife attack.

The 39-day trial was the longest murder hearing at the Old Bailey. Ronald, his face more plump and wearing glasses, and his brother sat impassively in the dock. Charles Kray, their elder brother, and other gang members were convicted of being accessories. One of them turned to the public gallery as he was led away and called out menacingly: " I will see you later" (→7/4).

Israel elects Golda Meir

March 7. Golda Meir, the Grand Old Woman of Israeli politics, will succeed her old poltical friend, Levi Eshkol, as Prime Minister of Israel. Today her candidature was officially accepted by the Labour Party. In the central committee 287 voted for her and 47 abstained. On Sunday President Shazar will begin consultations with other parties to prepare the way for her formal appointment.

Within the Labour Party, the opposition to Mrs Meir centred round supporters of General Moshe Dayan, the Defence Minister. They believe that he would be a more suitable head of the government in troubled times, even though he did not put himself forward as a candidate.

An ultra-religious group, whose adherents advise Jewish men not to look upon "strange women", also declared themselves to be against the choice. Mrs Meir, a widowed 70-year-old grandmother who was once a schoolteacher in America, served as Foreign Minister for ten years before resigning because of ill health (→17).

Israel's first woman premier.

UK invades the tiny island of Anguilla

March 19. British paratroopers and Royal Marines invaded the tiny Caribbean island of Anguilla today and won the moment they stepped ashore. There was no resistance at all from the the rebel "Republican Defence Force" set up by self-styled President Ronald Webster.

The British troops will soon be replaced by 40 police constables flown out from London. Many of the 6,000 population were on the streets to welcome the troops ashore – their impending arrival had been broadcast by the BBC.

The invaders handed out leaflets saying an "orderly administration" would be set up, and hinting that the government no longer wanted to link the island with the hated neighbouring St. Kitts-Nevis federation (→31).

Sino-Soviet clash on a frozen river

March 29. Soviet and Chinese troops have fired on each other in another clash over a disputed island in the middle of the Ussuri river, which forms the border between the two.

Since 31 Russian soldiers and an unknown number of Chinese were killed in the fighting earlier this month, there have been several further clashes. However, the Soviets are currently in control of the island which Moscow calls Damansky. The Chinese say it is used as a staging-post for shelling targets in Manchuria. The fighting has strained relations between the two countries (→11/9).

Czechs joyful after defeating Russians

March 28. Jubilant Czechs have taken to the streets to celebrate the defeat of Russia – at ice hockey. Today's 4-3 Czech victory over the USSR in the world ice hockey championships in Stockholm follows a 2-0 win last week, and has sparked an eruption of nationalism that goes far beyond sport. In Prague and other cities, where Soviet tanks brought a rapid winter to last year's liberal Spring, Czechs have flaunted their joy under the very noses of the occupying army. And when the medals ceremony was shown on television tonight sound and vision went dead – as the Soviet flag was raised (→17/4).

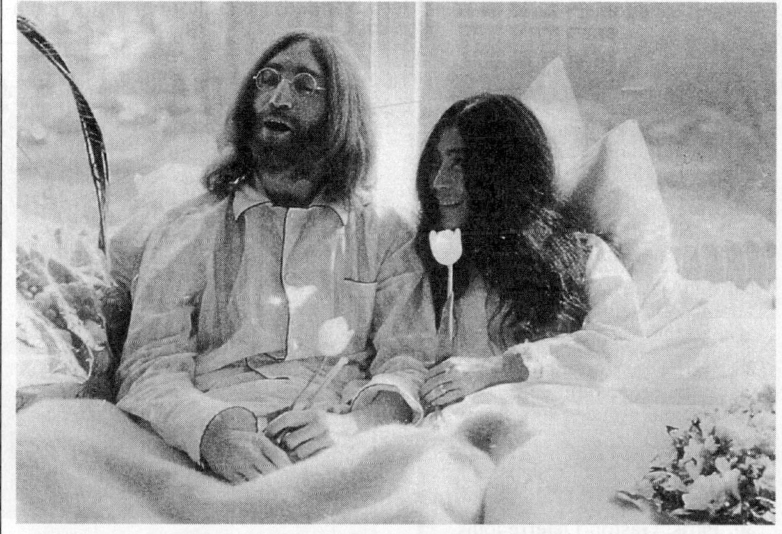

"Make love not war": Beatle John Lennon and artist Yoko Ono, his wife of one week, in the presidential suite of the Hilton Hotel, Amsterdam, where their honeymoon has become a "bed-in" for peace.

1969

APRIL

Su	Mo	Tu	We	Th	Fr	Sa
		1	2	3	4	5
6	7	8	9	10	11	12
13	14	15	16	17	18	19
20	21	22	23	24	25	26
27	28	29	30			

1. Washington: Many foreign leaders attend Eisenhower's funeral.

1. Paris: France formally withdraws from NATO's command structure.

2. Accra: Lt.-Gen. Joseph Amkrah, head of the military junta, resigns following a corruption enquiry.

7. UK: 25 paintings worth £300,000 are stolen from the home of Tate Gallery trustee Sir Roland Penrose (→ 2/7).

9. Wolverhampton: Sikh busmen win a two-year battle to be allowed to wear their turbans at work (→ 9/6).

14. US: Katharine Hepburn gets a record third Oscar for Best Actress, winning jointly with Barbra Streisand.

19. France: Student leader Daniel "The Red" Cohn-Bendit is deported to West Germany.

22. Southampton: The QE2 leaves on her first commercial voyage four months late, owing to technical problems.

22. UK: A single-handed round-the-world yacht race is won by Robin Knox-Johnston.

23. Nigeria: Federal troops capture Umuahia (→ 30/6).

24. UK: British Leyland announces its new 1500 Austin saloon, called the "Maxi".

25. UK: 500 more troops are to be sent to Northern Ireland in the next few days (→ 28).

25. UK: The BBC ends its 21-year old daily serial "The Dales" (→ 18/5).

26. London: Manchester City beat Leicester City 1-0 to win the FA Cup Final.

28. Belfast: Prime Minister Terence O'Neill quits as leader of the Unionist Party (→ 29).

28. UK: The Monopolies Commission recommends allowing any retailer to sell alcohol.

29. Belfast: O'Neill resigns as Prime Minister (→ 1/5).

30. Paris: Gaston Deferre joins Georges Pompidou as a presidential candidate (→ 15/6).

Biafrans begin to evacuate their last town

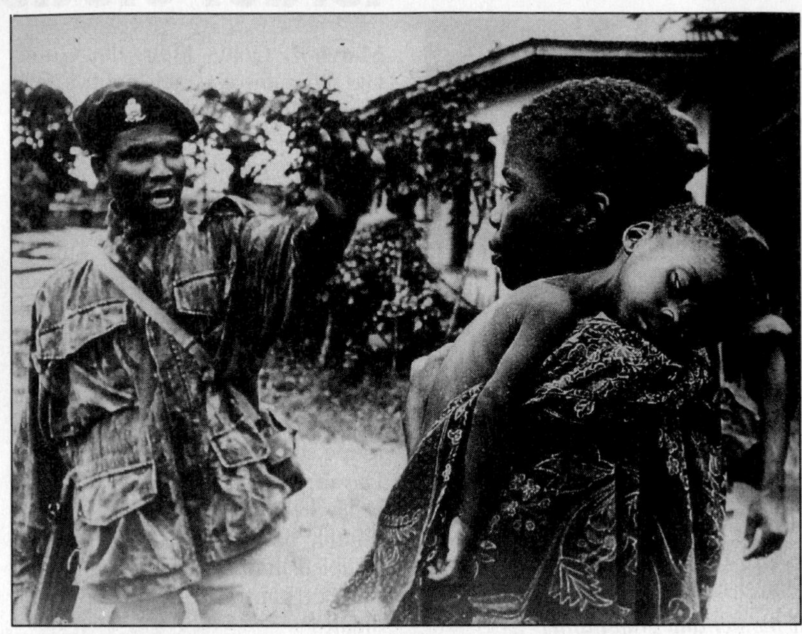

A federal soldier confronts an Ibo refugee carrying her dead child.

April 6. Just when the Biafran rebels had lost hope and were beginning to evacuate their last town, the French airlift of arms resumed. Last night, at the Uli airstrip – a stretch of motorway that lights up only when a plane is heard overhead – over 40 four-engined cargo planes came in to land. Some had Red Cross markings, but many had not,and according to a French "specialist" who has operated in the Congo, the three-week hold-up of arms supplies has definitely ended.

Despite their new lease of life, the Biafran authorities are continuing the evacuation of children and wounded from Umuahia to neighbouring Dahomey and Gabon. All available lorries and cars have been seized to make the journey without lights through the rain-soaked forest to the airstrip. Old British-made lorries used by traders and still carrying such slogans as "Love thy neighbour" have been pressed into service, along with trucks from mission stations.

Umuahia, a key road and rail communications centre, has served as the administrative capital of Col Ojukwu's Biafran regime since the fall of Port Harcourt a year ago. Three days ago, Federal forces came within seven miles of the town before they were stopped (→ 23).

Black students evacuate a building at Cornell University, USA, after a 36-hour occupation; the activists accuse the university of racism and are demanding the establishment of a separate black college.

Ulster civil rights worker elected MP

April 18. Northern Ireland yesterday elected Bernadette Devlin, 22 next week, as the Westminster MP for the Mid-Ulster constituency. The result is a triumph for the province's civil rights movement.

Miss Devlin, a civil rights worker and psychology student at Queen's University in Belfast, scored a 4,211 majority over her Unionist opponent, Anne Forrest, widow of the former incumbent. Unionist support rallied from all over the province in a vain attempt to beat the determined Miss Devlin, who is a fiery orator. "It proves that clinical efficiency never beats honest-to-God enthusiasm for a good cause," said Miss Devlin (→ 20).

Devlin – an Irish firebrand.

The Kremlin's man in power in Prague

April 17. The "normalisation" campaign picked up momentum in Czechoslovakia today with the rounding-up of thousands of "anti-social elements" and the sacking of Alexander Dubcek from the Communist Party leadership. In his place the Russians have installed a dependable apparatchik, Gustav Husak, who, like Janos Kadar in Hungary, was out of favour and in prison during the later Stalin years. Husak said on TV that everything that stands between Czechoslovakia and the Soviet Union must be cleared away (→ 2/5).

Britain's Concorde roars into the air

Concorde 002, the British-built prototype of the Anglo-French supersonic airliner, noses its way into flight.

April 9. Concorde 002 pointed her long nose into the air and took off on her maiden flight today with the dreams of two nations and a £360 million investment behind her. The supersonic plane landed just 21 minutes later with a slight bounce and pilot Brian Trubshaw declared it a "wizard flight". The British Concorde's first flight, from Filton, Bristol, comes just over a month after the French aircraft 001 took off.

Some say the four Rolls-Royce Olympus engines, which barely got out of first gear today reaching only 202 mph, are quieter than those on a VC-10, but noise levels twice those permitted in the US were recorded. The supersonic aircraft should be in service by 1974 and Britain and France hope to sell over 400, making some £4,000 million by the 1980s (→ 1/10).

Referendum says No to de Gaulle and so he resigns

April 28. Charles de Gaulle, the great soldier-statesman who twice in a lifetime saved his country from disaster, was today rejected by the voters of France. At the age of 78 he had staked his political career on winning a constitutional referendum.

However, as soon as the final figures showed that only 47 per cent of the 29 million voters had supported him, he issued a statement from his home at Colombey-les-deux-Eglises: "I am ceasing the exercise of my functions as President of the Republic. The decision takes effect at noon."

Twice during the campaign President de Gaulle had made it clear that if his proposals to abolish the senate and reorganise regional administration were rejected he would step down. The Prime Minister, Maurice Couve de Murville, warned the nation in a TV broadcast that it must now take the consequences of the decisive "non". He said: "A new page will be turned in the history of France" (→ 30).

RFK's killer is sent to the gas chamber

April 23. Sirhan Bishara Sirhan, who shot Senator Robert F. Kennedy last June, was sentenced to death in the gas chamber by a Los Angeles jury today. Sirhan killed Kennedy in a crowded Los Angeles hotel as he was celebrating his victory in the presidential primary. Sirhan, aged 25, a Palestinian Arab, hated Bob Kennedy because of his threat to send jet bombers to help Israel (→ 20/7).

Successor to Mao elected by Chinese

April 1. The Chinese Communist Party Congress today chose Lin Piao, the present Defence Minister, to be the successor to Chairman Mao Tse-tung when he eventually retires. The 1,500 delegates are assembled in Peking in the cause of "youth, unity and victory". Meanwhile, Red Guards are celebrating what they call the victorious conclusion of the cultural revolution (→ 16/11/71).

Rioting firebombers set Belfast ablaze

April 20. British troops have been called in to guard key installations in Northern Ireland, the Ulster cabinet announced tonight, as firebombers struck at nine Belfast post offices and attacked the city's main bus station. Explosions also damaged Belfast's main reservoir – causing a serious water shortage at a time when the fire brigade was fighting "too many fires to keep track of" (→ 25).

Trouble spreads to Derry: police join battle with stone-throwing youths.

Vietnam's US death toll now tops Korea

April 24. The toll of American dead in the Vietnam war has now risen to 33,641 and so exceeds the number of those killed in Korea. This sad record has brought a new outburst against the war. Thousands marched up Sixth Avenue in the first protest against the four-month-old Nixon administration. The President himself has signalled his determination to "bring the boys home" by announcing cuts in heavy bomber operations and in ammunition supplies for "budgetary reasons". He has set himself a strict timetable to reach agreement at the Paris peace talks. But meanwhile the killing goes on (→ 4/9).

1969

MAY

Su	Mo	Tu	We	Th	Fr	Sa
				1	2	3
4	5	6	7	8	9	10
11	12	13	14	15	16	17
18	19	20	21	22	23	24
25	26	27	28	29	30	31

2. New York: Two university campuses are closed because of student rioting (→21/9).

2. Czechoslovakia: Over 1,000 Czechs have been detained in two days of arrests (→21/8).

3. Toronto: Jimi Hendrix is arrested for possession of heroin (→2/7).

5. London: NHS charges for spectacles and dental treatment are to rise (→11/2/70).

6. Belfast: Ian Paisley is freed under a wide-ranging amnesty announced today (→3/8).

8. UK: The Tories make sweeping gains in borough elections (→13).

9. Rome: The Vatican says St. Christopher and 30 other "saints" are being dropped from the liturgical calendar (→17/3/70).

13. Malaysia: A state of emergency is declared in Selangor state after racial clashes (→30/8/70).

16. USSR: The spacecraft Venera 5 sends back data about Venus before crashing on the planet (→18).

18. US: Apollo 10 is launched at the moon with three astronauts aboard in a rehearsal for a moon landing in July (→21).

18. Monaco: Graham Hill wins the Monaco Grand Prix for a record fifth time.

21. US: Apollo 10 orbits the moon (→22).

22. UK: Christopher Chataway wins at Chichester for the Tories (→26/6).

22. US: Apollo 10 dips to within 9.4 miles of the moon's surface (→24).

24. US: Apollo 10 begins its return to earth (→26).

25. Khartoum: The government is overthrown in an army coup (→1/4/70).

26. Pacific: Apollo 10 splashes down safely (→13/7).

DEATH

2. German statesman Franz von Papen, Chancellor 1932 (*29/10/1879).

New premier is elected in Ulster

May 1. By a single vote Major James Chichester-Clark yesterday became the new leader of the Ulster Unionists and succeeds his rival, Captain Terence O'Neill, as Prime Minister of Northern Ireland.

He got 17 votes as against 16 for Brian Faulkner, a former deputy prime minister. Ironically O'Neill's was the crucial vote: "I supported the man who opposed me for six months rather than the one who opposed me for six years."

O'Neill, scion of what Burke's Peerage calls "the oldest traceable family left in Europe", was proud that his last speech as Prime Minister was to commend one-man, one-vote in local elections. But it was the speech many of his party did not want to hear (→6).

At the helm: Chichester-Clark.

Union curbs split the Labour cabinet

May 13. Mr Wilson ostentatiously dropped James Callaghan, the Home Secretary, from his inner cabinet today. The Prime Minister would like to throw him out of his team altogether, but does not dare. Mr Callaghan is siding with the TUC in opposing strike-curbing plans announced in a controversial White Paper, "In Place of Strife".

The Labour Party is now in turmoil over the plans proposed by the Employment Secretary, Barbara Castle. At least 100 of its MPs are rebelling. It is now known that a fortnight ago there was an attempted coup by Labour left-wingers to topple Mr Wilson (→22).

Sir Kenneth Clark is Lord of Civilisation

May 18. "Civilisation", a 13-part BBC TV series charting the artistic and aesthetic progress of Western man from the Middle Ages, ended its run tonight. Presented by Sir Kenneth Clark, whose knowledge and personal philosophies, whether discussing Mediaeval paintings or a Victorian suspension bridge, delightfully illuminated a potentially overpowering subject, the series has been judged one of the best things ever made for television. It is now hoped that Clark, who maintains "human sympathy is worth more than ideology" and that "order is better than chaos" will make a sequel (→25/8).

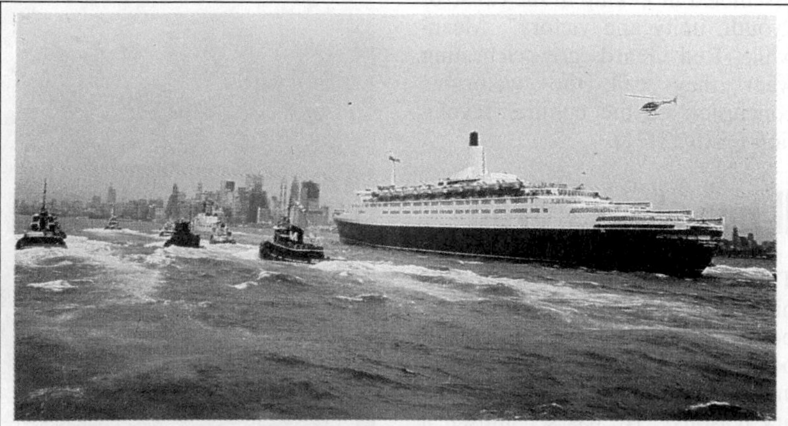

The QE2 arrives in New York at the end of her maiden crossing of the Atlantic; technical problems delayed the voyage by four months.

1969

JUNE

Su	Mo	Tu	We	Th	Fr	Sa
1	2	3	4	5	6	7
8	9	10	11	12	13	14
15	16	17	18	19	20	21
22	23	24	25	26	27	28
29	30					

2. South China Sea: 56 US sailors are missing after an Australian aircraft-carrier cuts a US destroyer in two.

4. Mr A. Budgett's Blakeney wins the Derby.

7. UK: The Maltings concert hall at Snape in Suffolk is destroyed by fire.

9. London: Enoch Powell proposes the repatriation of immigrants from Britain (→30/12).

13. UK: John Betjeman is knighted, Daphne du Maurier and Anna Neagle get DBEs and Basil D'Oliveira an OBE.

15. France: Georges Pompidou is elected President (→20).

18. London: Wilson drops penal clauses from the Industrial Relations Bill, and postpones the bill until next session.

20. Paris: Pompidou takes office and appoints Jacques Chaban-Delmas premier (→28/2/70).

24. Rhodesia: Sir Humphrey Gibbs resigns as Governor (→2/3/70).

25. Wimbledon: Pancho Gonzales beats Charlie Pasarell in the longest-ever singles match: 22-24, 1-6, 16-14, 6-3, 11-9.

26. Birmingham: Wallace Lawler wins the Ladywood by-election becoming the city's first Liberal MP for 83 years (→9/10).

29. Algeria: Moise Tshombe, former Congo premier and Katangan president, dies in jail (→27/10/71).

DEATHS

16. British commander Field Marshal Earl Harold Rupert Leofric George Alexander, first Earl Alexander of Tunis (*10/12/1891).

21. US tennis player Maureen "Little Mo" Connolly (*17/9/34).

22. US actress Judy Garland, born Frances Ethel Gumm (*10/6/22).→

29. Congolese statesman Moise Tshombe (*10/11/19).

Nigeria bans Red Cross relief flights

June 30. The four million people remaining in beleaguered Biafra are facing starvation in the wake of the Nigerian government's ban on night flights by the Red Cross. The British government has expressed "deep concern" to the Nigerians at the stopping of food and medicines two weeks ago.

The Nigerians say the Biafran rebels have been using night flights by the Red Cross as a cover for the delivery of arms. In Lagos today the relief agencies were told by a Nigerian official that relief flights would be allowed into Biafra each day between 8am and 5pm, after cargoes had been checked at Nigerian airfields by international teams. The Biafrans refuse to allow daylight flights to their airstrip at Uli. A few planes operated by Joint Church Aid are still flying in by night with medical supplies from Sao Tome.

Three Privy Councillors have appealed to the British government to step-up relief supplies and join other countries in an embargo on arms to both sides. In his reply to them – Jeremy Thorpe, the Liberal leader, Hugh Fraser, a former Conservative minister, and James Griffiths,former deputy leader of the Labour Party – the Foreign Secretary, Michael Stewart, said if Britain stopped arms for the Nigerian government it would be interpreted as support for the Biafran rebels (→13/7).

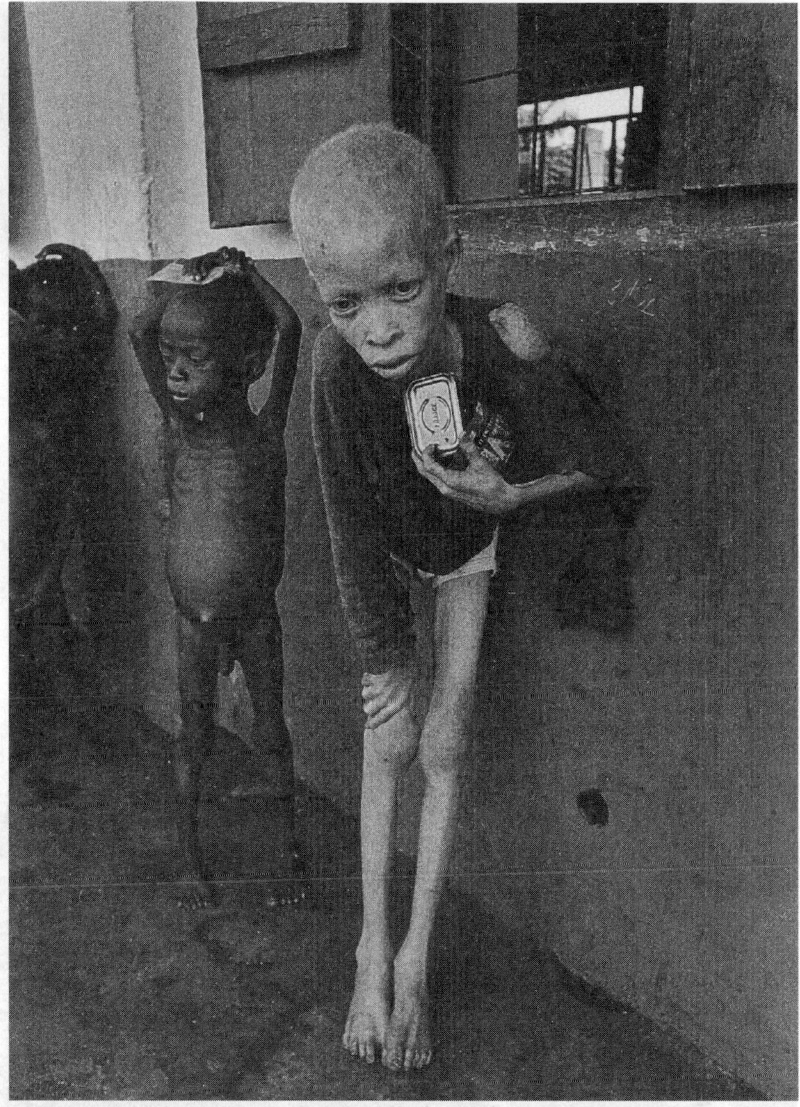

Biafra's children are caught in the crossfire of political wrangling over aid.

High-grade oil has been discovered in the North Sea

June 20. High-grade crude oil has been discovered on the borders of the British and Norwegian sectors of the northern North Sea, according to a company involved in exploratory drilling. Whether these finds in such deep and difficult waters are commercially viable is not yet clear.

For the moment, the main oil companies involved – Shell-Esso, Total and BP on the British side and Phillips on the Norwegian – are saying nothing. It is now ten years since Shell-Esso first discovered a massive natural gas field off the Dutch coast (→19/10/70).

Spanish lay siege to Rock of Gibraltar

June 8. Spain began a siege of Gibraltar tonight as General Franco ordered the land frontier closed in a move aimed at crippling the Rock's economy and forcing its people to their knees. The Algeciras ferry remains the only link with Spain and that may close soon. But as the last Spanish workmen packed up their tools, said goodbye to their friends and crossed the border, spirits in the colony remained high. "What sort of people do they think we are?" asked Chief Minister, Sir Joshua Hassan (→4/7).

Judy Garland goes over that rainbow

June 22. Judy Garland said she had found peace in London, when she got married for the fifth time last March. But today she was found dead at her flat. She was 47 and her career was a ruin, haunted by the ghost of a heart-stopping voice.

Her last cabaret season here was, like her emotions, unpredictable. Sometimes she showed up late, sometimes unsteady on her feet and uncertain of her lyrics.

Her real name was Frances Gumm and she went on stage aged two. She had many other successes besides Dorothy in "The Wizard of Oz", but "Over the Rainbow" was her signature tune. She never found the bluebirds.

Judy Garland: a star is dead.

Casanova fears fail to stop divorce law

June 13. An easier end to unhappy marriages came a step nearer today when the Divorce Reform Bill was given its third reading in the Commons by a two to one majority. It will mean that a divorce can be obtained after two years separation, if both husband and wife consent, or after five years apart without consent. Opposition to the Bill has centred on fears for the financial position of women – Lady Summerskill has called it a "Casanova's Charter" – and it will not be implemented before further legislation is passed giving women a bigger stake in matrimonial assets (→17/10).

Brazilian soccer star, Pele, who has just scored his 1,000th goal.

1969

JULY

Su	Mo	Tu	We	Th	Fr	Sa
		1	2	3	4	5
6	7	8	9	10	11	12
13	14	15	16	17	18	19
20	21	22	23	24	25	26
27	28	29	30	31		

2. UK: Rolling Stone Brian Jones drowns in his swimming-pool at Hartfield, East Sussex.

2. London: Demolition workers find £300,000 worth of paintings stolen from Sir Roland Penrose (→ 18/12).

4. Madrid: Franco offers Gibraltarians Spanish nationality.

5. Wimbledon: Rod Laver beats John Newcombe in the all-Australian Men's Singles final.

7. UK: A coroner says Brian Jones died "of alcohol and drugs" (→ 16/8).

10. Paris: Pompidou will maintain France's embargo on jets to Israel (→ 7/10/71).

13. USSR: An unmanned spacecraft is launched towards the moon (→ 16).

16. US: Apollo 11 is launched at Cape Kennedy (→ 21).

20. Cairo: The UAR claims to have shot down 19 Israeli planes in clashes along the Suez Canal and in Sinai (→ 3/8).

24. Pacific: Apollo 11 splashes down safely (→ 26).

24. Moscow: Jailed Briton Gerald Brooke is exchanged for two Soviet spies (→ 24/10).

25. US: Senator Kennedy pleads guilty to leaving the scene of an accident (→ 30).

30. London: Two thalidomide boys win a total of £33,600 damages in the High Court (→ 23/3/70).

30. US: Senator Kennedy announces he is dropping plans to run for president in 1972 (→ 29/4/70).

31. US: Mariner 6 sends back close-up pictures of Mars (→ 14/11).

DEATHS

2. British rock musician Brian Jones (*28/2/1944).

5. German architect Walter Gropius (*18/5/1883).

25. German artist Otto Dix (*2/12/1891).

28. US composer Frank Loesser (*29/6/1910).

The first man sets foot on the moon

Neil Armstrong, the first man on the moon, is reflected in the visor of his companion, Edwin "Buzz" Aldrin.

July 21. Today man set foot on the moon for the first time. At 3.56am British Summer Time, the American astronaut Neil Armstrong, commander of Apollo 11, watched by hundred of millions of television viewers round the world, stepped off the ladder of the lunar module, Eagle, onto the moon. "That's one small step for a man, one giant leap for mankind," he said.

"The surface is like a fine powder," he reported. "It has a soft beauty all its own, like some desert of the United States." Soon Armstrong was joined by fellow astronaut Edwin "Buzz" Aldrin and the two experimented with moving in the moon's low gravity, collected samples of dust and rock, took pictures, and planted the Stars and Stripes before returning to the lunar module.

The climax of the Apollo 11 mission came four days after blast-off from Cape Kennedy. After an uneventful flight, Apollo went into orbit round the moon. Armstrong and Aldrin transferred to the lunar module and fired their engine to start their descent. A tense final few minutes, when they had to avoid a boulder-filled crater with fuel running low, and they were down. "Houston. Tranquility Base. The Eagle has landed," said Armstrong.

The two astronauts are scheduled to remain on the moon's surface for a bit less than a day. Tomorrow they will lift off, rendezvous with Apollo 11, which has remained in orbit round the moon with Michael Collins on board, transfer to the main spacecraft taking their moon samples with them, jettison the lunar module, and fire their engine to put them on course back to earth (→ 24).

Armstrong takes one small step for a man

Astronauts Armstrong, Collins and Aldrin with their rocket to the moon.

The lunar module floats above the moon, with the earth rising behind.

Edwin Aldrin sets up one of NASA's experiments close to the lunar module.

A disputed soccer match ends in war

July 14. El Salvador's troops invaded Honduras last night and its planes bombed military targets at the international airport and cities south and west of Tegucigalpa. Honduras ordered an immediate counter-attack and its planes took off from the military airport to do battle.

The two countries broke off diplomatic relations two weeks ago after violent clashes at a soccer match between their national teams. The violence reflects long-standing hostility. Honduras resents the influx of Salvadorans across the border into their sparsely populated farmland while El Salvador claims Honduras has persecuted these settlers.

Nigeria allows in the relief flights

July 13. General Gowon, the Nigerian leader, today agreed to ease the air blockade of rebel Biafra to permit a Red Cross airlift of desperately needed medical supplies. The General was warned by Red Cross officials that the undernourished Biafrans have become highly vulnerable to infection, and epidemics could run out of control unless relief was provided at once.

But the Nigerians are still refusing to allow food supplies to be flown into Biafra, except on their terms. They say relief planes must leave from Nigerian airfields after inspection by neutral teams. The Biafrans refuse to agree "to any plans which subject relief to Nigerian whims" (→2/11).

Tony Jacklin is the British Open champion

July 12. Tony Jacklin today became the first Briton to win the British Open since Max Faulkner in 1951. He needed a par (or better) at the last hole. After a perfect tee-shot down the narrow 18th fairway at Lytham St. Anne's, 25-year-old Jacklin pitched on to the green with a seven-iron, putted to within a few inches of the hole – and took his par to give him 72 for the final round and the Championship.

Despite relentless pressure from a distinguished chasing bunch, which included three former Open champions, Jacklin's nerve never faltered, and a huge gallery on the final day roared him down the final fairways to the title.

Tony Jacklin clutches his trophy.

Scientists have first look at moon rock

July 26. Like the astronauts themselves, the rocks collected on the moon during the Apollo 11 mission have been put in quarantine. For the time being, frustrated geologists eager to get their hands on the moon samples can only look at them through a window. The rocks are covered with a blackish dust, so will yield little information of value until they have been scrubbed clean.

Fears that organisms from the moon could infect animals and plants on earth lie behind the quarantine measures. Remote though the possiblity of life on the moon is, if it does exist it could run riot in the more favourable conditions on earth. Terrestrial animals and plants will be exposed to the 15 pounds of moon rocks for 50 to 90 days before samples are released.

Geologists hope that the moon rocks will help to solve some of the outstanding mysteries about the moon: are the craters volcanic or the result of meteorite impacts? How like the earth is the moon geologically?

Young girl drowns when Senator Edward Kennedy crashes car on Chappaquiddick

A frogman searches Edward Kennedy's car hours after the accident.

July 20. Senator Edward Kennedy is expected to appear in court today for failing to report an accident in which a woman passenger in his car, Mary Jo Kopechne, drowned.

Miss Kopechne, aged 27, was found in the back seat of the Senator's car which lay submerged in water alongside a bridge on Chappaquiddick island in New England. She and another young woman on Kennedy's staff had been at a party at Kennedy's cousin, Joseph Gargan's house on the island which adjoins Martha's Vineyard.

Mystery surrounds the eight hours between the time of the accident and Senator Kennedy's appearance at Martha's Vineyard police station to report it. Dominic Arena, the police chief, said he was told of the accident by two boys. He put on swimming trunks and dived into about eight feet of water and found Miss Kopechne's body.

"I phoned my office," said Mr Arena, "and told them to get hold of Ted Kennedy at once". He added that the Senator was "extremely distressed" but said he wanted to co-operate. Miss Kopechne was once the secretary to the Senator's brother, Robert, assassinated last year (→25).

Ann Jones is Wimbledon ladies' champion

Ann Jones defeats Billie Jean.

July 4. For only the second time since the Second World War, Britain has a Wimbledon singles champion. To crown a superbly fought tournament in which she overcame determined challenges from Nancy Richey and Margaret Court on the way to the final, Ann Jones beat the redoubtable Billie Jean King, of the United States, 3-6, 6-3, 6-2 to earn a rapturous Centre Court reception.

For the 30-year-old Mrs Jones, it was the climax to a distinguished career. Formerly Ann Haydon, a talented international table-tennis player, she triumphed at her 14th Wimbledon, having previously lost in the 1967 final – to Mrs King.

Rolling Stones play for free in Hyde Park

July 5. In the largest of this summer's series of free pop concerts in Hyde Park, the Rolling Stones played today to an estimated 250,000 people. As television crews recorded the event, and London's Hell's Angels ran security, Mick Jagger, decked out in a white, frilly dress and a brass-studded leather collar, delivered a eulogy to Brian Jones, the Stones' former guitarist, who died three days ago.

As Jagger intoned lines from Shelley's "Adonais", and clouds of white butterflies spread out from the stage, the crowd fell silent. Then, the obsequies over, the Rolling Stones turned back, as triumphantly as ever, to playing rock 'n roll (→7).

Mick Jagger – magnetic performer.

General Franco names his heir apparent

July 22. "Before God and history", General Franco today named Prince Juan Carlos his heir as head of state and future King of Spain. The General, now 77, showed signs of emotion and shed a few unexpected tears as he presented the 31-year-old Prince to the Cortes in Madrid.

He said the Prince, whom he had chosen over the head of his father, the legitimate pretender to the throne, Don Juan of Bourbon, would "succeed me" with the title of King. This would be done at a moment of Franco's own choosing. Not unexpectedly, the Cortes approved Franco's proposals. The open vote was 491 in favour and 19 against with nine abstentions.

The new law of succession provides a new and original title for Juan Carlos. He will become Prince of Spain. In the past the heir to the throne was known as Prince of the Asturias, the equivalent to Britain's Prince of Wales. The new heir is an officer in the Spanish army.

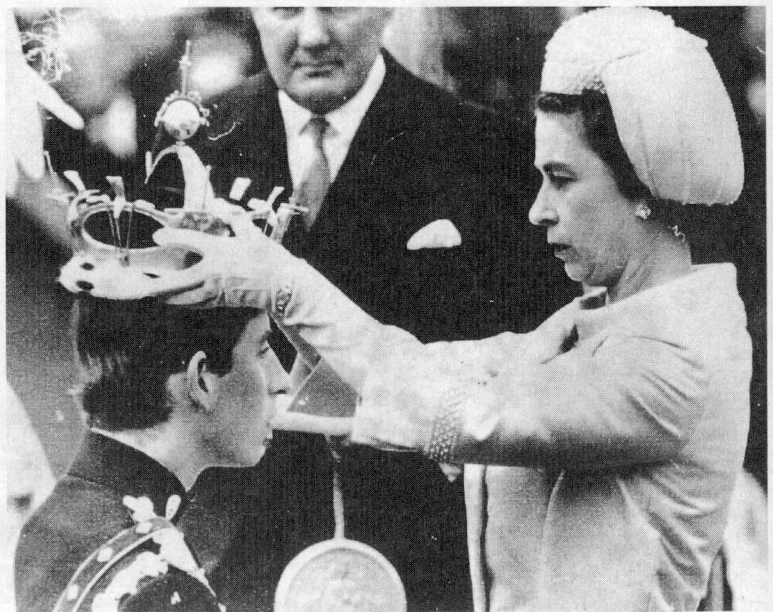

July 1. The Queen places the gold coronet on her 20-year-old son's head during his investiture as Prince of Wales at Caernarvon Castle.

1969

AUGUST

Su	Mo	Tu	We	Th	Fr	Sa
					1	2
3	4	5	6	7	8	9
10	11	12	13	14	15	16
17	18	19	20	21	22	23
24	25	26	27	28	29	30
31						

2. Bucharest: Nixon arrives on the first visit by a US President to a Communist country in nearly 25 years (→4/1/71).

3. Belfast: Armoured cars crush barricades as new sectarian violence flares.

3. Tel Aviv: Israel will keep territories captured in 1967 (→10/2/71).

8. UK: Handley Page, oldest aircraft manufacturer in Britain, calls in the receiver.

10. Los Angeles: two more murders take place near the home of Sharon Tate (→24/12).

12. Londonderry: 112 are treated in hospital in the city's worst night of rioting since the current troubles began.→

14. UK: 16 die when a bus crashes on a hill near Stanhope, County Durham.

16. UK: Troops begin to patrol streets of Belfast in Falls Road and Ardoyne areas (→19).

17. Cape Town: Dr Philip Blaiberg dies a record 19 months 15 days after receiving a heart transplant (→13/11).

17. US: The Woodstock festival ends; around 400,000 attended (→13).

19. Northern Ireland: Lt.-Gen. Sir Ian Freeland, Ulster army chief, takes over control of the "B Specials" (→22).

21. Prague: Tanks enter the city after protests mark the anniversary of the Soviet invasion (→28/9).

22. Northern Ireland: The "B Specials" are ordered to hand in their arms (→10/9).

25. London: Rupert Murdoch has made a bid to take over The Sun newspaper (→5/9).

31. US: Rocky Marciano, the only world heavyweight champ who never lost a professional fight, dies in a plane crash.

DEATHS

17. German-born US architect Ludwig Mies van der Rohe (*27/3/1886).

31. US boxer Rocky Marciano, born Rocco Francis Marchegiano (*1/9/1923).

Ulster Catholics cheer British troops

Troops are expected to restore order as violent confrontations, such as this in Londonderry, intensify.

Aug 15. British troops were cheered as they ringed the predominantly Catholic Bogside district of Londonderry with barbed wire tonight. The soldiers were deployed after a week of furious sectarian fighting in Northern Ireland, in which five people have been killed and hundreds injured.

It seems inevitable that British soldiers will also be sent into the streets of Belfast where sten-guns and rifles were used in gun battles which raged in the Falls Road and Shankhill Road.

The decision to use British troops was greeted with widespread relief in Ulster, although the Irish government tonight repeated its view that their involvement was not acceptable. The Ulster cabinet had asked for them "to prevent a breakdown of law and order".

British ministers hope that the intervention is a "limited operation" with the soldiers being withdrawn as soon as law and order is restored. The Government has insisted that the troops remain under the control of the Army chief in Northern Ireland who has been instructed "to take all necessary steps, acting impartially between citizen and citizen". One factor in the renewed troubles has been what is widely seen as the partisan attitude of the Protestant "B Specials" police reservists.

Rioting flared in Londonderry towards the end of the annual Orangemen's "Apprentice Boys" parade, which many Catholics regard as provocation. As police used tear-gas to clear hundreds of rioters, petrol bombs were hurled and hidden snipers opened fire.

More petrol bombs were used in Belfast, where police fought to separate Protestant and Catholic mobs. A loyalist commando squad made frequent sorties into Catholic "territory". A boy of nine was among the victims, shot through his kitchen window (→16).

A petrol bomb ignites a police vehicle in a Londonderry street.

▷

Sharon Tate killed in Hollywood massacre

Aug 9. Sharon Tate, the actress wife of film director Roman Polanski, has been brutally murdered, along with four others, at the couple's mansion in exclusive Beverly Hills. As well as Miss Tate, who was eight months pregnant, the victims included fashionable hair stylist Jay Sebring, coffee heiress Abigail Folger and writer Voytec Frykowski. A fifth victim, an unnamed young man, was found at the seat of Sebring's car.

Several of the bodies had been viciously mutilated and the word "Pig" has been smeared in blood across the front door. Telephone wires to the house were cut. Other than Miss Tate, the victims seem to have been attempting to escape from their attacker when they were shot down.

Police have arrested William Garretson, aged 19 and the mansion's caretaker, for the killings, but he has denied any guilt and experts privately accept that the murders, which have terrified fashionable Hollywood, were certainly the responsibility of a gang. One senior police official said: "You just have to take a look at the murder scene to know that one man alone couldn't do this" (→10).

Sharon Tate with Roman Polanski.

Rock fans flock to festival in Isle of Wight

Aug 31. In his first concert after the three years of semi-retirement that followed his near-fatal motorcycle crash, Bob Dylan tonight played for 150,000 ecstatic fans at the second Isle of Wight Festival of Music. Backed by The Band, Dylan sang such favourites as "Tambourine Man" and "Subterranean Homesick Blues" in a two-hour set. Celebrities like Jane Fonda, Roger Vadim and assorted rock stars joined the long-haired crowd who had paid £2 10s hoping to enjoy three days of sex, dope and rock and roll. Some obviously did. Naked, painted bodies abounded, the scent of cannabis wafted above makeshift tents and the joint never stopped rocking (→26/10).

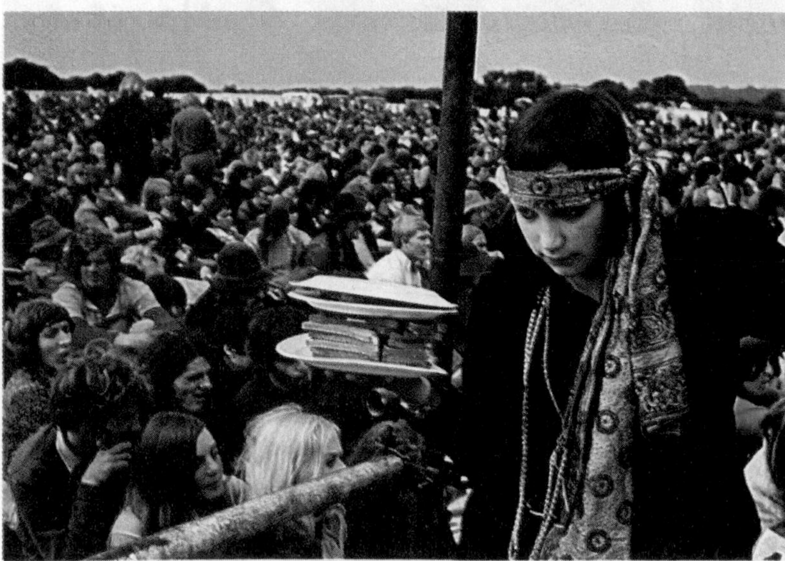

On the menu at the Isle of Wight Festival: drugs, rock ... and sandwiches.

1969

SEPTEMBER

Su	Mo	Tu	We	Th	Fr	Sa
	1	2	3	4	5	6
7	8	9	10	11	12	13
14	15	16	17	18	19	20
21	22	23	24	25	26	27
28	29	30				

2. London: The London Contemporary Dance Company begins its first season.

3. UK: The TUC votes for the repeal of the 1966 Prices and Incomes Act.

4. Vietnam: The Viet Cong call a three-day truce in memory of Ho Chi Minh.→

5. UK: ITV makes its first colour transmissions (→26).

6. Washington: The US recognises Gaddafi's regime (→14/11).

7. Italy: Jackie Stewart wins the Italian Grand Prix to secure the world Formula One championship.

8. New York: Rod Laver wins the US Open to achieve his second tennis Grand Slam.

10. Northern Ireland: There are now 7,000 troops in the province (→12).

11. Peking: Soviet premier Kosygin has surprise talks with China's leader, Chou en-lai.

12. UK: The Cameron Report, set up in March, blames Ulster extremists for the current disturbances (→28).

12. Washington: Richard Nixon orders B-52 bombing raids of North Vietnam to continue (→24).

13. Tirana: Albania announces its intention to leave the Warsaw Pact.

18. Greece: Briton Lillian Board wins the 800m gold at the European Games in a record 2 minutes 1.4 seconds.

24. Hanoi: Ton Duc Thang is elected to succeed Ho Chi Minh as President (→15/10).

26. London: Murdoch says he will pay £250,000 for the Sun if a deal with the unions can be made within a fortnight (→5/10).

28. Prague: The Communist Party expels Dubcek from its presidium (→9/10).

DEATHS

3. North Vietnamese statesman Ho Chi Minh (*19/5/1890).→

Uncle Ho, revered, and ruthless, dies

Ho Chi Minh, a ruthless fighter.

Sept 3. President Ho Chi Minh of North Vietnam has died after what Radio Hanoi described as "a grave and very sudden heart attack" following weeks of illness. He was 79.

"Uncle" Ho with his goatee beard and gentle smile was a revered figure in Asia, but behind the smile there was a man of complete ruthlessness who was prepared to sustain a war first against the French colonial power and then against the might of the US to unite Vietnam under Communist rule.

Diplomats in Paris did not expect his death to have any immediate effect on the deadlocked talks. They thought Hanoi's envoys would continue with the same intransigent arguments they have used for months (→12).

Stewart is world motor racing champ

Sept 7. After one of the closest Grands Prix in history, with five cars crossing the line within a second-and-a-half of each other, Jackie Stewart today opened up an unassailable 36-point lead in the drivers' table to clinch his first world championship.

After 68 laps of the super-fast Monza track, the 30-year-old Scot – always distinguishable by the Stewart tartan band round his crash helmet – pipped Austria's Jochen Rindt by a fifth of a second to win the Italian Grand Prix and to clinch the vital points.

Gaddafi throws out king and takes power

Muammar Gaddafi, leader of the Libyan revolution and the new republic.

Sept 1. A group of revolutionary army officers seized power in Tripoli today while King Idris of Libya, the 70-year-old monarch, was abroad in Turkey. A Royal spokesman said the coup was "of no importance", but Crown Prince Hassan Rida, in a broadcast from Libya, renounced his title and supported the new regime. The plotters, led by a subaltern named Muammar Gaddafi, have proclaimed a republic in the name of "freedom, socialism and unity", dedicated to the struggle against colonialism. They have warned opponents that they would be court-martialled and shot (→ 6).

Little Biba grows into a department store

Sept 16. Dolly birds got their very own department store today with the opening of Biba in Kensington High Street. The store marks a new high in the fortunes of designer Barbara Hulanicki, who began selling her clothes, just five years ago.

Mail-order success was rapidly followed by the opening of a boutique almost in the shadow of the latest venture. The opulent store not only features the ultra-modern clothes that made her a cult, but also a wide range of household goods including satin sheets at £17 a set (→ 10/1/71).

Biba's queen Barbara Hulanicki, designer doyenne of the "dolly girls".

Troops erect peace wall

Sept 28. Warring factions in Belfast woke to find themselves separated by a six-feet-high barbed wire "peace wall" today. Royal Engineers, supported in places by the Royal Ulster Constabulary, are building the huge barricade between the Protestant stronghold near the Shankhill Road and the predominantly Catholic area of the Falls Road.

At the same time, a traffic curfew was imposed on the riot area, allowing only essential vehicles – ambulances, fire-engines and clergymen's cars – through heavily guarded checkpoints. As the "peace wall" grows, other troops have begun to remove illegal barricades throughout the city.

Lt.-Gen. Sir Ian Freeland, GOC Northern Ireland and Director of Operations, dismissed suggestions that his troops were creating a "Berlin Wall" situation. He stressed that it was a "very temporary" operation, although many Ulster politicians are convinced that troops will be patrolling the barrier for years to come.

Major James Chichester-Clark, the Northern Ireland Prime Minister, has appealed for the voluntary removal of illegal barricades, but only two out of several hundred have been taken down (→ 10/10).

Police storm peaceful squat in Piccadilly

Police storm the ramparts of "Hippie Hall" under a torrent of plastic balls.

Sept 21. A task-force of 200 police stormed 144 Piccadilly today, evicting 250 hippie squatters and ending the week-long occupation of the century-old, 100-room mansion in London's West End.

They tricked "Dr John Moffatt", leader of the squatters, into allowing them into the building, ostensibly to check on the squatters' health. Once inside a senior officer blew his whistle and the police squad rushed in. Truncheons were drawn, and the defenders threw slates and water-filled balloons, but after four minutes the 'battle' was over. 150 squatters were taken to West End Central police station where 30 were later charged.

The hippies based their claim to the building on centuries-old squatter's rights, but failed to occupy the building long enough to gain legal possession. The bailiffs had a repossession order, but the police, acting under the drug laws, moved first. Squatters who act legally, however, will not face police raids so this may be seen by radicals as a solution to the housing problem (→ 29/4/70).

1969

OCTOBER

Su	Mo	Tu	We	Th	Fr	Sa
			1	2	3	4
5	6	7	8	9	10	11
12	13	14	15	16	17	18
19	20	21	22	23	24	25
26	27	28	29	30	31	

1. Sweden: Olof Palme is elected leader of the Social Democratic Party and Swedish Prime Minister.

1. France: Concorde 001 breaks the sound barrier for the first time (→23/1/70).

5. UK: The BBC transmits the first in a new "nutty, zany and oddball" series called "Monty Python's Flying Circus" (→15).

9. London: Reg Prentice resigns as Technology Minister three days after his appointment (→17).

9. Prague: The Czech government bans individuals from travelling to the West (→15/12).

10. Belfast: The Ulster government says the "B Specials" are to be disbanded (→12).

14. UK: The seven-sided 50 New Pence coin comes into circulation (→17/12).

15. London: The print unions allow Murdoch's purchase of The Sun (→25/11).

17. London: The Divorce Reform Bill is passed, making total breakdown of marriage sole grounds for divorce.

17. London: James Callaghan, the Home Secretary, returns to the "inner cabinet" (→21).

21. London: Heath appoints Margaret Thatcher as shadow education spokesman (→30).

24. UK: 47 are hurt when prisoners at Parkhurst riot in protest at the early release of the Soviet spy Peter Kroger (→15/1/70).

27. UK: All wildlife in a 3,000-acre area around Camberley, Surrey, is to be destroyed after a rabid dog bit two people.

27. UK: P&O says it will cease passenger services to India from February 1970, after 130 years.

30. Nairobi: Kenyatta bans the Kenya People's Union, following the arrest of its leader, Oginga Odinga.

DEATH

21. US author Jack Kerouac (*12/3/1922).

Willy Brandt elected German Chancellor

Social Democrat Willy Brandt, the new Chancellor of West Germany.

Oct 21. Herr Willy Brandt today became the first German Social Democrat Chancellor for 39 years. The Christian Democrats have held power in West Germany since the war. Today they mustered 235 votes against the 251 votes from Brandt's coalition of Social and Free Democrats.

Brandt won by a margin of only two votes above the minimum. On hearing the news he smiled and said it was "better than only one". That was a reference to the size of the victory in 1949 by Dr Adenauer, the first post-war chancellor. Brandt, who has been a popular Mayor of Berlin and who has many friends in the British Labour Party, will have enough margin to govern.

On most issues the 50 Free Democrats are likely to vote with him. Nor does he have anything to fear from by-elections because in Germany MPs who die are replaced by party colleagues. Nevertheless, the Christian Democrats are likely to try to split the coalition on the spread of nuclear weapons, which Brandt opposes (→19/3/70).

Army fires tear-gas at Ulster Protestants

An RUC member fires tear-gas.

Oct 12. British troops used tear-gas on a stone-throwing mob of 500 Protestants in the Shankhill Road district of Belfast today and seized arms, ammunition and a "pirate" radio station in a two-hour swoop. Sixty-nine people were arrested. For the first time since the beginning of the latest outbreak of Ulster violence, troops have been ordered to shoot back at snipers and bombers.

The 1st Parachute Regiment flew into Northern Ireland yesterday to reinforce the existing hard-pressed garrison on a weekend when three people – including a policeman – have been killed and 66 injured.

The British and Ulster governments confirmed today that a new reserve force will replace the controversial "B" Special police force which has frequently been accused of bias in the Protestants' favour and of brutality (→22/12).

Millions protest in US at Vietnam war

Oct 15. Millions of Americans across the country demonstrated today against their country's involvement in the Vietnam war.

They marched, held rallies and read aloud the roll of the 40,000 American dead. In the main their protests were non-violent. But in Washington police fought about 100 black students who tried to get into the White House.

This "Vietnam Moratorium" was the biggest anti-war demonstration ever organised in America. Those who took part included the old and the young, blacks and whites, rich and poor, though some supporters of the war drove with their headlights on to express their support for the President (→19/11).

Knees disappear beneath the maxi

The other extreme to the mini.

Oct 13. Just when it seemed skirts could get no shorter, coats have plunged to the ankles. The "maxi" look is proving a success with women of all ages who see it as a romantic – and warm – alternative to the mini. There is also the "midi" where the hemline hovers half-way between knee and ankle. Clearly, any length now goes.

1969

NOVEMBER

Su	Mo	Tu	We	Th	Fr	Sa
						1
2	3	4	5	6	7	8
9	10	11	12	13	14	15
16	17	18	19	20	21	22
23	24	25	26	27	28	29
30						

1. Lebanon: The Lebanese government and the PLO agree a cease-fire following recent clashes.

3. London: Work begins on the National Theatre after over a century of arguments and delays.

5. UK: Farmworkers minimum wages will go up 15/- to £13 3/- (→9/2/70).

7. S. Africa: 64 die in a mine explosion (→15).

10. London: Sir David Rose, Governor-General of Guyana since 1966, is killed by falling scaffolding.

11. UK: Barracuda Tankers, owners of the Torrey Canyon, pay Britain and France £3 million compensation.

14. US: Apollo 12 is launched at Cape Kennedy (→24).

14. Libya: Gaddafi nationalises all foreign banks (→16/1/70).

15. Swansea: Anti-apartheid protesters battle with police at a Springbok match (→19/5/70).

19. Washington: A sergeant claims US soldiers massacred women and children in a South Vietnamese village (→23).

19. London: MPs approve a Bill to set up a new "Ulster Defence Regiment" to replace the "B Specials".

20. Nigeria: 87 die when a Nigeria Airways VC-10 crashes in the jungle.

23. Saigon: Officials report that the US is escalating bombing raids on neighbouring Laos (→24).

25. London: The Government authorises 12 new local radio stations (→26/2/70).

27. New York: The Rolling Stones play at Madison Square Gardens.

30. Vienna: Austria and Italy formally end their dispute over the German-speaking South Tyrol region of North Italy.

DEATH

18. US diplomat Joseph P. Kennedy, father of John, Robert and Edward (*6/9/1888).

300,000 Nigerians face famine due to row

Nov 2. More than 300,000 people in refugee camps near the Nigerian war zone are facing starvation because of a quarrel between the Nigerian government and the International Red Cross. When the Red Cross stopped its work last month it was spending £250,000 a month importing food to feed refugees. Since then no food whatever has been brought in, and lack of funds means the stocks remaining cannot be transported to the camps.

Because the Red Cross was flying relief missions to refugees in rebel Biafra, it was ordered out of Nigeria by the Federal government. A Nigerian rehabilitation commission was supposed to take over the relief programme, but so far it has not even met to draw up plans. Dr John Berall, an American doctor who is adviser to the Nigerian Red Cross, says: "We have to face it that many people are going to die" (→11/1/70).

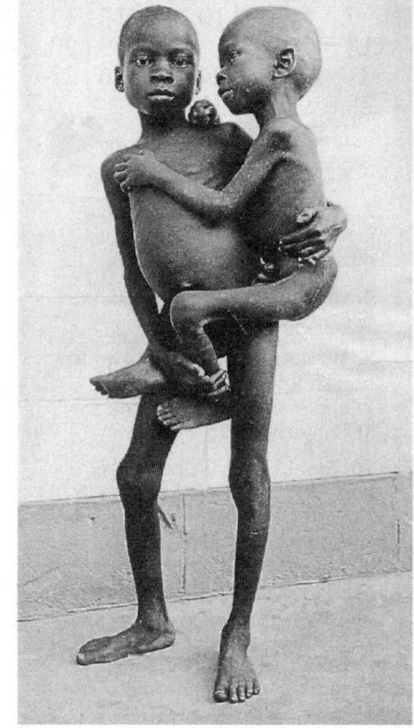

The Biafra tragedy continues.

Royals may go into the red, says Philip

Nov 9. Prince Philip said that the Royal Family may have to leave Buckingham Palace next year – "if we go into the red". Speaking on an American TV programme, he said that the problem is that the Queen's allowance of £475,000 a year is "based on costs of 18 years ago". He maintained there was no question of "bad housekeeping".

The practice is to fix the monarch's allowance at the beginning of a reign. But as the Queen's reign looks like being a long one, Parliament may have to review the allowance at intervals. "We sold off a small yacht and I may have to give up polo," he said (→11/2/70).

Woman has quins after fertility drug

Nov 13. John Hanson was on a routine visit to his wife at Queen Charlotte's Maternity Hospital, London, when he was told that she had given birth to quin girls of whom the heaviest was three pounds and seven ounces. They had been delivered by an emergency Caesarean operation. Mrs Irene Mary Hanson, 33 this week, thought she would never have a baby, but became pregnant after taking gonadotrophin, a fertility drug, in March (→19/12).

Americans make a second moon landing

Nov 24. America's second manned mission to the moon ended triumphantly today when Apollo 12 splashed down in the Pacific within sight of the recovery ship.

On board were astronauts Charles Conrad and Alan Bean, who spent 32 hours on the moon's surface, and Richard Gordon who orbited the moon in the parent spacecraft. During their stay on the surface Conrad and Bean made two moon walks totalling eight hours and taking them more than 1,000 feet from the lunar module.

They collected 50 pounds of samples, set out scientific instruments, and inspected an unmanned Surveyor spacecraft that landed three years before (→17/4/70).

Anti-apartheid demo greets the Springboks at Twickenham

Nov 5. An anti-apartheid protest today disrupted the rugby tour by the South African Springbok team at Twickenham. Police had been expecting trouble and a contingent of 400 officers protected the ground against a mass invasion by the 300 demonstators who had infiltrated the terraces.

But at half-time one protester tried to climb a goalpost while an accomplice, in shorts with the letters AA for anti-apartheid, sprinted towards the visitors before he was tackled by policemen. Before the kick-off demonstrators shouted "Seig Heil" to the tourists. John Taylor, a Wales and British Lions player, has refused to play against the tourists (→7).

Police remove an anti-apartheid protester from the Twickenham ground.

US officer charged with the massacre of 109 Vietnamese

Nov 24. Lieutenant William Calley will be tried by a court martial on murder charges arising from his part in the massacre at Mylai in 1968, the US Army announced today. Lt. Calley is charged with killing at least 109 "Oriental human beings", one of them approximately two years old. If convicted he faces either the death penalty or life imprisonment.

Last night on nationwide television Paul Meadlo, a member of Lt. Calley's platoon, said he had fired about 70 rounds into a group of 45 Vietnamese men, women and children. He thought he had been ordered to guard the villagers. But when Calley came to inspect them later, he allegedly said: "How come they ain't dead?"

The first report of the massacre came from a soldier, Ronald Ridenhour, aged 23, who wrote letters to President Nixon and members of Congress. More recently, an army photographer, Ron Haeberle, wrote an article in a Cleveland paper with photographs of the bodies.

When GIs fired at the women, he wrote: "The bones were flying in the air chip by chip" (→8/12).

Danish sex fair is seminal happening

Nov 1. Thousands of visitors streamed into Copenhagen today with just one thing on their mind – sex. They were coming for the opening of a six-day long "Sex Fair", which promised free love, live sex shows and hours of pornographic movies.

It was made possible by the fact that this year Denmark abolished all censorship of film and TV – they freed books in 1967. Consequently, the rest of the world has come to regard the Danes as international advocates of pornography. They, however, don't see themselves like that. On the contrary, they suggest that the more you prohibit pornography, the more titillating you make it. Hence the Sex Fair which they say will be joyful rather than prurient.

1969

DECEMBER

Su	Mo	Tu	We	Th	Fr	Sa
	1	2	3	4	5	6
7	8	9	10	11	12	13
14	15	16	17	18	19	20
21	22	23	24	25	26	27
28	29	30	31			

2. Aberdeen: 98 people are arrested after pitch invasions during a Springbok match.

4. Chicago: Police shoot dead two Black Panthers.

8. Washington: Nixon vows to punish anyone guilty of killing Vietnamese civilians at Songmy (→25/1/70).

10. Stockholm: Nobel Prizes go to Murray Gell-Mann (US, Physics); Sir Derek Barton (UK) and Odd Hassell (Norway), both Chemistry; Max Delbruck, Alfred Hershey and Salvador Luria (US, Medicine); Samuel Beckett (Ireland, Literature); and in Oslo to the International Labour Organisation (Peace).

13. Washington: The Supreme Court orders four southern states to end segregation completely by February 1970.

15. Prague: Dubcek is made ambassador to Turkey (→21/3/70).

17. London: The Superannuation and Social Insurance Bill is published; it aims to create earnings-based pensions (→14/4/70).

19. Uganda: Obote is shot in the head (→2/1/70).

23. UK: 294 people died from flu last week (→8/1/70).

26. London: A BBC "World at One" poll names Harold Wilson "Man of the Decade", followed by Enoch Powell.

30. UK: The Race Relations Board finds Wolverhampton Council guilty of racial discrimination (→9/8/70).

DEATH

3. Soviet statesman and commander Marshal Kliment Voroshilov (*4/2/1881).

HITS OF 1969

My way.

Gentle on my mind.

QUOTE OF THE YEAR

"This is the greatest week in the history of the world since the Creation."

Richard Nixon, greeting the returned moon astronauts.

Bernadette Devlin sentenced to prison

Devlin smashes rocks in Bogside.

Dec 22. An Ulster magistrate found Bernadette Devlin MP guilty of incitement to riot in Bogside yesterday and sentenced her to six months imprisonment. Miss Devlin, who is now 22, became the youngest member of parliament this year when she was elected as independent member for mid-Ulster. She is now free on bail pending an appeal.

The mini-skirted MP was cheered by supporters as she left the court to the sound of "We shall Overcome" and other protest songs. Earlier, her defence counsel, Dingle Foot QC, had told the court that Miss Devlin's actions during the Bogside riot could be compared with "the roles of Joan of Arc and Florence Nightingale". She had played a responsible role, he claimed, and had been concerned with the safety of women and children (→29/3/70).

Terrorist bombings in Milan and Rome

Dec 12. Thirteen people were killed and at least 100 injured today when a bomb devastated a bank in Milan. At almost the same time three bombs exploded in Rome, injuring at least 14 people. Another bomb was found later in Milan near the city's La Scala opera house.

The explosion at Milan's National Agricultural Bank occurred in a third-floor waiting room, occupied at the time by around 100 people. "In the smoke I saw a body flying from the public section above the counter and falling one yard away from me," said Michele Carlotto, a 27-year-old clerk.

Four men have been detained by police in Rome. No organisation has claimed responsibility, but the marxist "Red Brigade" is inevitably suspected.

Vasectomy will be a snip in Birmingham

Dec 19. A sterilisation clinic for men will open in Birmingham early next year and enable a simple vasectomy operation to be performed under local anaesthesia for around £16.

There is already a six-month waiting-list, but no decision on a location or opening date. Plans for another West Midlands clinic are also being discussed. Together with the clinic in Cardiff, the new one in Birmingham will be the second run by the Family Planning Association. Its spokesman said: "Sterilisation is a much less serious operation for a man and men are beginning to realise this" (→2/2/70).

Edward Heath, leader of the Opposition, enjoys a favourite pastime aboard his new fibreglass sloop, Morning Cloud.

"Family" arrested for movie star slayings

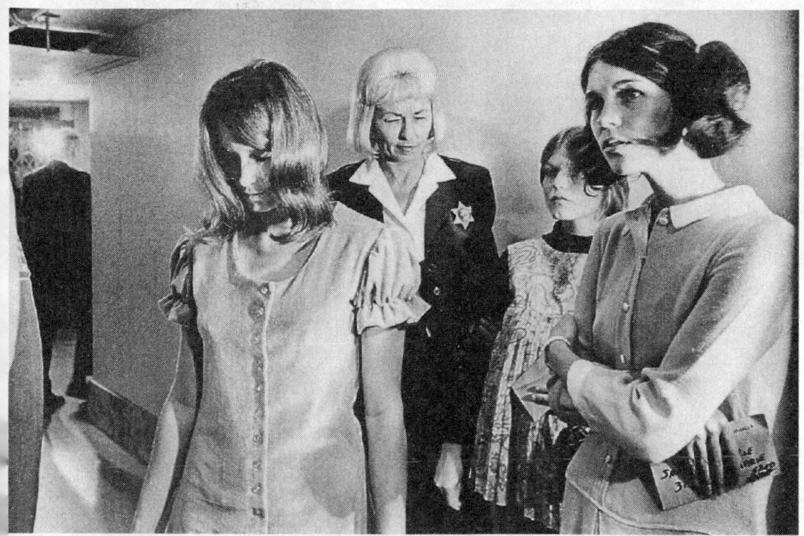
Three members of the Manson commune arrive at court to hear charges.

Dec 24. Today, more than four months after seven brutal slayings at a house in Los Angeles shocked America, four members of a so-called hippie commune have been arrested and charged with the first degree murder of actress Sharon Tate, supermarket tycoon Leno LaBianca and five others.

The commune, which calls itself "The Family", is led by Charles Manson, aged 35, a veteran convict who preyed on the young drifters of Los Angeles, wooing them from the streets and taking them to a hideout in the desert, 20 miles from the city.

The commune members are mainly teenage girls, all absolutely devoted to Manson, and three of them – Patricia Krenwinkel, Susan Atkins and Leslie van Houten – are to be tried alongside him. One male member, Charles "Tex" Watson is also charged.

Little is known as yet about "The Family", but investigators have already uncovered tales of bizarre and perverted goings-on. Manson, who calls himself "Jesus Christ", apparently used his own charisma, mixed with liberal doses of LSD and other drugs, to orchestrate an orgiastic lifestyle notorious in hippie circles for mingling satanism with other fantasies (→4/8/70).

Manson – eyes of a crazed killer?

Peers consign death penalty to history

Dec 18. Nobody will ever again go to the gallows in Britain for murder. That is the meaning of a decision in the House of Lords tonight. After heated debate the peers accepted that the law passed in 1965 to abolish the death penalty – technically for an experimental period – should now continue indefinitely. The House of Commons took the same view two days ago.

Dr Michael Ramsey, the Archbishop of Canterbury, said:"Abolition of capital punishment once and for all will help create a more civilised society. It will rebound to the advantage and honour of the nation." As usual for discussion of this subject, there was no party pressure on MPs and peers as to their vote. However, opinion polls continue to register strong support for the death penalty, so the debate continues (→12/9/71).

Arts: Easy riding, rebellious drop-outs fill the screen and win awards for Britain

It was a year for off-beat, drop-out films of which British directors proved themselves masters. "Midnight Cowboy", a tale of two ill-assorted hustlers, inspired **John Schlesinger** to direct a brilliant evocation of living off your wits in or near the New York gutter, with fine performances from **Jon Voight** and **Dustin Hoffman** (following up his impressive debut in "The Graduate" last year) as a sickly, undersized street boy of rat like cunning.

"Easy Rider", the odyssey of a pair of hippies by motor bike from Los Angeles to New Orleans, was almost a companion piece, featuring **Peter Fonda**, son of **Henry**, and introducing **Jack Nicholson**.

Lindsay Anderson won the major prize at Cannes – a rare event for Britain – with his showily directed "If", set at an English public school where discontent turns into armed rebellion. **Karel Reisz** directed "Isadora", a portrait of **Isadora Duncan** in blowsy, sad middle age, for which **Vanessa Redgrave** won the best actress award at Cannes. The brittle Edinburgh schoolmistress, whom Miss Redgrave created on stage, was played in the film of "The Prime of Miss Jean Brodie" by **Maggie Smith** in an Oscar-winning performance.

Both actresses appear among the star-laden cast assembled by actor **Richard Attenborough** for his debut as director of "Oh What a Lovely War!", the musical lampoon of the First World War which was one of **Joan Littlewood's** finest stage productions.

Dustin Hoffman and Jon Voight hustling in "Midnight Cowboy".

Another new director to note is **Ken Russell**, who turned from a notable career making films for television to the cinema for D.H. Lawrence's "Women in Love". It was made memorable by **Glenda Jackson's** powerful Gudrun and the nude wrestling scene between the two men friends.

The Nobel Prize for Literature went this year to **Samuel Beckett**, the Irish poet and playwright who composes. A new award for fiction, the Booker Prize, worth £6,000, was won by **P.H. Newby**, controller of BBC's Radio Three.

Dennis Hopper and Peter Fonda take to the road in: "Easy Rider".

1970-1979

1970

JANUARY

Su	Mo	Tu	We	Th	Fr	Sa
				1	2	3
4	5	6	7	8	9	10
11	12	13	14	15	16	17
18	19	20	21	22	23	24
25	26	27	28	29	30	31

1. UK: The age of majority is reduced from 21 to 18 (→13/3).

1. London: The minimum fare on the Underground is to rise by 50 per cent to one shilling at the end of 1970.

2. UK: England cancels the first part of its planned East African tour because of Ugandan government "pressures".

2. UK: The FA suspends Manchester United star George Best for a month for disreputable behaviour.

7. UK: The England tour of East Africa collapses as Kenya cancels the matches due to be played there (→1/5/70).

8. UK: 4,000 are now known to have died of Asian flu in the week ending January 2.→

11. Nigeria: The last Biafran airstrip is reported out of action as federal troops launch a final assault on Biafran rebels (→12).

12. Nigeria: Biafra capitulates (→13).

13. London: The Government announces an extra £5 million to aid Biafran refugees.

15. London: Labour MP Will Owen is charged under the Official Secrets Act with passing secrets (→24/9/71).

16. Libya: Gaddafi becomes premier (→7/12/71).

18. London: Karl Marx's grave in Highgate is daubed with swastikas and damaged in a bid to blow it up.

19. India: The country's first nuclear power station opens (→2/9).

23. Ivory Coast: The Biafran leader Ojukwu is granted political asylum.

26. UK: Mick Jagger is fined £200 for possession of cannabis; Marianne Faithfull is found not guilty (→7/6).

27. Warsaw: Three British diplomats are expelled (→18/11).

DEATH

29. British historian Sir Basil Henry Liddell Hart (*31/10/1895).

Biafran revolt is crushed

General Ojukwu announces Biafra's surrender to the federal government.

Jan 21. Furious controversy over conditions in the former territory of Biafra has erupted in the seven days since the rebels surrendered to the Nigerian federal government. Western journalists who were allowed to visit the territory have reported widespread starvation, looting and rape. The Spanish Princess Cecile de Bourbon-Parma, who fled from Biafra shortly before the surrender, says: "There was massacre all the way as the federal troops advanced. The people were separated into three groups, men, women and children. The men were all killed." The women were allegedly raped, and often killed, while the fate of the children is unknown.

Lord Hunt, Britain's special envoy, who visited the territory, said on his return to London that the reports were "exaggerated and irresponsible". It was true that some soldiers had misbehaved, but it was not general. Relief supplies were getting through and thousands of displaced people were returning home looking "in no way undernourished" (→23).

Hong Kong flu kills 2,850 in one week

Jan 16. Influenza due to the Hong Kong A2 virus killed 2,850 people in Britain in the week ending January 9, the highest weekly figure since 1933. In the week ending December 26 there were 1,421 deaths with 731 on Christmas and Boxing Day and 2,400 in the next week.

Despite this overall increase in the total number of deaths, a more detailed look at the figures suggests that the epidemic has passed its peak in the south, where the number of deaths has fallen substantially, although more deaths have been reported in north-west England.

Anti-war protesters in Whitehall clash

Jan 25. A torchlit peace procession to Whitehall became violent tonight when 2,000 marchers were turned away from Downing Street, where they wanted to deliver a petition condemning a visit to America by the Prime Minister because of US involvement in the Vietnam war. Senior police officers were knocked to the ground as placards were used for bonfires in nearby Parliament Square. March organisers said they were angry at the Washington trip by Harold Wilson (→8/2).

First Jumbo lands at Heathrow to launch new era in jet travel

Jan 23. A giant jet airliner, known as a "Jumbo", landed at Heathrow airport today. Owned by Pan Am, it weighs 350 tons and carries 362 passengers – twice as many as a Boeing 707. The airport's facilities could scarcely cope and a lot of luggage went astray in the crush.

Lost luggage was not the only problem. The plane arrived three hours late because an engine had to be changed before it could take off from New York, and then the plane's onward flight to Frankfurt had to be cancelled because of bad weather.

There are fears that schedules at the airport may be seriously disrupted by the turbulence caused by the giant jet (→12/9).

The first wide-bodied Boeing 747 "Jumbo Jet" lands at Heathrow.

1970

FEBRUARY

Su	Mo	Tu	We	Th	Fr	Sa
1	2	3	4	5	6	7
8	9	10	11	12	13	14
15	16	17	18	19	20	21
22	23	24	25	26	27	28

2. Munich: The first nerve transplant is performed (→15/7).

3. London: Police seize Andy Warhol's film "Flesh" from the Open Space theatre.

8. Saigon: A bomb wrecks the National Press Centre (→26).

9. Moscow: PLO leader Yassir Arafat arrives for talks.

10. Munich: One person dies and 11 are hurt in an Arab attack on a London-bound Israeli El Al airliner (→1/3).

11. London: The Government announces plans to decentralise the NHS under 90 new health authorities.

11. London: Prince Charles takes his seat in the Lords (→19).

16. New York: Joe Frazier knocks out Jimmy Ellis to become world heavyweight boxing champion.

17. West Germany: "Anastasia" loses her 50-year fight to prove she is the daughter of Czar Nicholas II.

19. London: Buckingham Palace says that Prince Charles will join the Navy (→23/6).

23. UK: Rolls-Royce asks the Government for £50 million to develop the R.B. 211-50 Airbus jet engine.

26. South Vietnam: Five US Marines are arrested for killing 11 women and children (→1/3).

26. London: Rupert Murdoch sacks Stafford Somerfield as editor of the News of the World (→13/8).

28. Chicago: Pompidou gets a hostile reception from a crowd of 10,000 demonstrators (→2/3).

DEATHS

2. British philosopher Bertrand Arthur William Russell, third Earl Russell (*18/5/1872).→

11. British cartoonist Henry Mayo Bateman (*15/2/1887).

15. British commander Air Chief Marshal Hugh Caswall Tremenheere Dowding, first Baron Dowding (*24/4/1882).

25. US artist Mark Rothko (*25/9/1903).

Russell, passionate thinker, dies at 97

Bertrand Russell, a serious thinker.

Feb 2. "Three passions have governed my life: the longing for love, the search for knowledge and unbearable pity for the sufferings of mankind." Bertrand Russell prefaced his autobiography with these words two years ago. His long, passionate life ended today at 97.

Those who knew Russell as the ardent disarmer, president of CND and then of the Committee of 100, who went to prison at 88 for his beliefs, knew only a third of him. His search for knowledge resulted in his reducing the principles of mathematics to logic and ended with his magnificent "History of Western Philosophy" in 1946.

His third passion, for love, took him through four marriages and many more love affairs.

Bill aims to give women equal pay

Feb 9. A bill giving women equal pay with men by 1976 passed its second reading unopposed in the Commons today. And Employment Secretary Barbara Castle warned bosses that women would still expect to keep their special privileges in such matters as pregnancy.

She believed the bill would lead to a better use of labour and greater efficiency. However, one backbencher said that he feared many women would lose their jobs if employers had to pay them the higher rate (→26/11).

1970

MARCH

Su	Mo	Tu	We	Th	Fr	Sa
1	2	3	4	5	6	7
8	9	10	11	12	13	14
15	16	17	18	19	20	21
22	23	24	25	26	27	28
29	30	31				

1. UAR: 32 Egyptians die in Israeli air raids (→2/4).

2. Rhodesia: The rebel colony becomes a republic (→9).

2. New York: Nixon meets Pompidou and apologises for anti-French protests (→12/11).

3. US: Police break up white mobs attacking buses carrying black children (→12/5).

5. Washington: The Nuclear Non-Proliferation Treaty goes into effect (→24/8).

8. Oxford: Premiere of Samuel Beckett's play "Breath", lasting only a minute.

9. Washington: The US will close its consulate in Rhodesia (→16/4).

9. US: Troops disperse "assaults" on two forts near Seattle by American Indians.

12. UK: The quarantine period for cats and dogs is extended to a year as an anti-rabies move.

13. UK: Tom King trebles the Tory majority in the first by-election in which 18-year-olds can vote (→18/5).

17. UK: The Sunday Telegraph's editor is summonsed under the Official Secrets Act.

19. East Germany: Willy Brandt and Willi Stoph hold the first meeting between East and West German leaders (→21/5).

21. Prague: Dubcek is suspended from the Communist Party (→6/5).

22. Phnom Penh: Cambodia appeals to Britain and the USSR to stop the invasion of its territory (→30).

23. UK: 18 thalidomide children are awarded damages totalling £369,709 (→30/7).

24. UK: Henry Cooper beats Jack Bodell to regain the British heavyweight boxing title.

29. Londonderry: Troops seal off the Catholic Bogside area after clashes with stone-throwing rioters (→10/4).

30. Phnom Penh: Premier Lon Nol asks for US arms after Viet Cong incursions (→30/4).

US planes bomb the Ho Chi Minh trail

March 1. President Nixon has authorised General Abrams to intensify the pounding of the Ho Chi Minh trail in eastern Laos by B-52 heavy bombers. More than 200 sorties a day are being launched in order to cut the supplies streaming down the trail to the North Vietnamese forces in Laos.

These forces have mounted a major assault on the land-locked kingdom and have overrun the Plain of Jars. The fall of Laos would jeopardise the security of the American forces in Vietnam and also threaten Thailand. The big question is whether American airpower alone can prevent the Communists taking control of Laos (→18).

New Bible sells one million in a day

March 17. There was such demand for the New English Bible, which went on sale yesterday, that the publishers, the Oxford and Cambridge University Presses, had exhausted their entire output of a million copies by the end of it. It is being reprinted at the rate of 20,000 copies a week. The edition with the Apocrypha, costing 35 shillings, is in the most demand (→22/6). ▷

Army coup ousts Cambodian leader

March 18. Cambodia's neutralist head of state, Prince Sihanouk, was ousted today by right-wing leaders, impatient at his failure to remove the threat posed by 50,000 North Vietnamese and Viet Cong troops active within Cambodia's borders.

The Prince learned of the coup from Mr Kosygin, the Russian Prime Minister, while in Moscow to ask the Soviets to put pressure on Hanoi to pull out its troops.

The coup came after a week of skirmishing between the right and left factions in the Cambodian government and followed the sacking of the North Vietnamese and Viet Cong missions by a mob of frenzied youths (→22).

Damages award to thalidomide victims

March 23. Eighteen children born with defects caused by their mothers taking the drug thalidomide during pregnancy were awarded damages of almost £370,000 in the High Court today. The figure includes damages to their parents for shock and loss of earnings. The judgement was against Distillers (Biochemicals) which sold the drug under licence from Germany. The amount which individual children will receive depends on the severity of their disability. The five worst cases, born with "flipper" arms, will get £28,800 (net) each (→30/7).

Makarios survives assassination bid

March 8. The Greek Cypriot leader, Archbishop Makarios, escaped unhurt today as terrorists raked his helicopter with machine-gun fire as he left the presidential palace.

They were lying in wait on the roof of a school near the palace and the archbishop's pilot received three bullet wounds in his stomach yet still managed to land the helicopter. Police arrested three men linked to the outlawed National Front which wants Enosis – union with Greece.

1970

APRIL

Su	Mo	Tu	We	Th	Fr	Sa
			1	2	3	4
5	6	7	8	9	10	11
12	13	14	15	16	17	18
19	20	21	22	23	24	25
26	27	28	29	30		

1. Sudan: Hadi al Mahdi, leader of an abortive coup last week, is killed trying to flee to Ethiopia (→22/7/71).

2. Israel: Israeli and Syrian troops fight their biggest battle since the six-day war (→8).

4. UK: Mr A. Chambers' Gay Trip wins the Grand National.

5. Guatemala City: West Germany's kidnapped ambassador is found murdered near the city (→10/5).

7. US: John Wayne wins an Oscar for Best Actor in the film "True Grit".

8. UAR: At least 30 children die when Israeli bombers attack the Delta village of Bahr al Bakar (→13/5).

10. Athens: Premier Papadopoulos releases 350 prisoners as part of "liberalisation measures" (→28/8/70).

11. London: Chelsea and Leeds United draw 2-2 in the FA Cup Final.

14. London: The budget raises tax allowances, exempting two million people from income tax (→16/7).

16. Northern Ireland: The Rev. Ian Paisley wins the Bannside by-election (→26/6).

16. Salisbury: Clifford Dupont is sworn in as the first President of the Republic of Rhodesia (→24/11/71).

18. UK: British Leyland announces that the Morris Minor, Britain's longest-running car, will cease production by 1971.

21. UK: Bernice Rubens wins the Booker Prize for her novel "The Elected Member".

27. UK: US actor Tony Curtis is fined £50 for possession of cannabis.

29. US: Seven people are shot in student rioting at Ohio State University (→28/5).

29. US: The judge at the Chappaquiddick inquest says he doubts the truth of Senator Kennedy's testimony.

29. London: Chelsea beat Leeds 2-1 to win the replayed FA Cup Final.

Nixon sends US troops into Cambodia

Cambodian soldiers keep low as they meet heavy Communist resistance.

April 30. President Nixon tonight sent US combat troops to attack communist bases in Cambodia. This announcement, which is certain to arouse bitter controversy, was made in a surprise television address to the nation

Aware of the political trouble in store, Mr Nixon argued that: "This is not an invasion of Cambodia. The areas in which these attacks will be launched are completely occupied by North Vietnamese forces.

"Tonight," he went on, "American and South Vietnamese units will attack the headquarters for the entire Communist military operation in South Vietnam. This key control centre has been occupied by the North Vietnamese and Viet Cong for years in blatant violation of Cambodia's neutrality."

He said that members of his own Republican Party had warned him that his action would lose "all chance of winning the November election". Others said that the move against the enemy sanctuaries would make him a one-term president. "No one," he insisted, "is more aware than I am of the political consequences."

But he went on: "I would rather be a one-term president than a two-term president at the cost of seeing America become a second-rate power and accept the first defeat in its history" (→4/5).

Beatles go to court to divorce each other

April 9. An era is over. The Beatles, erstwhile "Fab Four", one-time psychedelic pioneers and most recently squabbling businessmen, have finally dissolved the partnership that for many young people was the most influential phenomenon of the past decade.

Today Paul McCartney issued a writ in the High Court calling for the dissolution of "the business carried on ... as the Beatles and Co." and effectively ended a creative alliance that might justifiably be said to have changed the world.

The real reasons for the split are debatable, but the foursome, notably songwriting partners Lennon and McCartney, have not been happy for some time (→31/12).

Paul forsook the Beatles in favour of his family and his farm.

1970

MAY

Su	Mo	Tu	We	Th	Fr	Sa
					1	2
3	4	5	6	7	8	9
10	11	12	13	14	15	16
17	18	19	20	21	22	23
24	25	26	27	28	29	30
31						

1. Kampala: Obote announces nationalisation of all major industries (→25/1/71).

5. Washington: Nixon promises to remove all US troops from Cambodia in three to seven weeks (→15/8).

6. Prague: Czechoslovakia signs a 20-year treaty of friendship with the USSR (→26/6).

10. London: A bomb is found on an airliner at Heathrow after blasts at three European airports (→6/9).

12. US: Six blacks die in racial violence in Georgia (→2/8).

13. Lebanon: Israeli troops withdraw after a 32-hour raid in which 30 Arabs died (→29/5).

15. Washington: Ann Hays and Elizabeth Hoisington become the first women generals in the US Army.

15. Holland: The International Olympics Committee bars South Africa from the 1972 Olympics.

16. France: Robert Altman's film, M*A*S*H, wins first prize at the Cannes Film Festival.

18. London: Wilson calls a general election for June 18 (→18/6).

19. London: The MCC says the South Africa tour of England will go ahead (→22).

21. West Germany: Leftists and neo-Nazis clash as Brandt meets East German leader Stoph for the second time.→

22. Salisbury: Ian Smith begins informal talks with South African premier John Vorster.

26. Bogota: England footballer Bobby Moore is held for stealing a gold bracelet.→

27. Ceylon: Mrs Bandaranaike is re-elected Prime Minister.

28. Paris: Maoist students riot in the Latin Quarter.

29. Tel Aviv: The Israeli Army claims it has killed 11 guerrillas from Jordan (→4/8).

31. UK: The great racehorse Arkle dies.

Happy landing for crippled spacecraft

April 17. The cliff-hanging flight round the moon of Apollo 13 ended happily today when the capsule splashed down in the Pacific with its crew – James Lovell, John Swigert and Fred Haise – safe and well. For 90 hours Apollo 13 had travelled through space crippled by an explosion in the service module – which contains the main engine and consumables like oxygen – with vital supplies running low and the crew's lives hanging by a thread. The planned moon landing was abandoned, but Apollo, unable to turn back, had to continue round the moon. The astronauts had to take refuge in the cramped lunar module, which was unaffected by the explosion, for most of the flight. They returned to the main spacecraft only for the final re-entry into the earth's atmosphere (→19/6).

Troops in Ulster to kill petrol bombers

April 10. The British Army announced the adoption of a new "get tough" policy in Northern Ireland today with a warning by a commander that "anyone throwing a petrol bomb after a warning was liable to be shot dead in the street". As 500 more soldiers flew in to reinforce the 6,000 troops already in Ulster, the GOC, General Sir Ian Freeland, said that there were "sinister people" behind the youths and teenagers who had caused the latest outbreaks of violence (→16).

George C. Scott is "Patton".

US anti-war protesters shot at Kent State

A student screams in horror as she realises her colleague has been killed.

May 4. Four students, two of them girls, were shot dead by National Guard soldiers at Kent State University in Ohio today. The Guard shot into a crowd of anti-war demonstrators injuring 11 of them, on the third day of violent rioting at a hitherto non-political university.

Two black students were also shot dead at Jackson State University in Mississippi.

President Nixon called on all American Universities, students, teachers and administrators alike, to stand firmly for the right of peaceful dissent. He deplored the deaths of the students, he said, but commented that "when dissent turns to violence it invites tragedy". National Guard called to the university to break up an unruly demonstration used bayonets and teargas the night before last. Then, last night, they fired into the unarmed crowd.

The President's decision to send troops into Cambodia, which sparked off the current round of student demonstrations, now looks like leading to a constitutional crisis. Senator George McGovern, a Democrat on the foreign relations committee, has moved a resolution to cut off money for the war appropriations. But even senators and congressmen not as committed against the war as McGovern are troubled by the President's bypassing of congress in his widening of the war (→5).

Ex-Irish ministers up on gun charges

May 28. The mystery £30,000 arms find at Dublin airport acquired a political dimension today when two cabinet ministers, dismissed by Prime Minister Jack Lynch, appeared in a Dublin court. They were later released on bail. Charles Haughey and Neil Blaney are former finance and agriculture ministers. Both were named in Irish security reports of arms smuggling to Ulster. Both denied any involvement (→2/7).

Government to bail out Rolls-Royce

May 19. The Government is lending £20 million to Rolls-Royce to help it out of its financial problems arising from the huge cost of developing new aero-engines. The Government has already put up £47 million for the R.B. 211 which has been ordered for the Lockheed TriStar and the BAC One-Eleven. The Industrial Reorganisation Corporation will have a representative on the board who will be monitoring the loan.

England soccer captain accused of theft

May 28. Bobby Moore, captain of the England football team, today rejoined the World Cup squad in Mexico after he was held for two days in Colombia accused of theft. The owner of a jewellery shop in a Bogota hotel had said the player stole a gold bracelet. Moore, aged 29, said after his release: "I am very happy to be a free man once again and pleased the accusations have been shown to be unfounded."

He was freed provisionally as police want to make further enquiries. He must report regularly to Colombian officials in Mexico and has agreed to attend their embassy in London in 30 days to hear the result of the case. But the judge who released him said: "I hope everything goes well for you and that you score many goals." Moore has only six days before he leads his team out in Mexico for their first match (→14/6).

Bobby Moore: future uncertain.

Massacre journalist receives press prize

May 4. Seymour Hersh, the American reporter who first told the world about the Mylai Massacre, has won a Pulitzer Prize for international reporting. Mylai is a South Vietnamese hamlet where, in 1968, US troops butchered more than 350 men, women and children while allegedly looking for Viet Cong. A court martial has begun (→14/12).

Inter-German talks end in stalemate

May 21. Hopes for closer ties raised by March's historic first meeting of Willy Brandt and the East German premier Willy Stoph were dampened last night when their second summit in Kassel ended. Herr Stoph insists that Bonn fully recognise East Germany, but the West Germans, who aim for eventual reunification, refuse to concede.

Rocket attack on Israeli school bus

May 22. In a terrorist attack, described by Golda Meir, the Israeli Prime Minister, as "premeditated murder" eight Jewish children were killed today. Four adults also died when a school bus, driving along a lonely road near the Lebanese frontier, came under rocket fire.

This is the 140th terrorist raid in the border area this year. Responsibility was claimed by the Popular Front for the Liberation of Palestine General Command, a group led by former Syrian army officer, Ahmed Jibril. It alleged that "Zionist experts" were on the bus (→29).

South African tour cancelled by MCC

May 22. South Africa's cricketers will not tour England this summer. Though the Cricket Council had reaffirmed a determination for it to proceed, it came under strong pressure from the Home Secretary, James Callaghan, to cancel the tour, due to begin next week.

Today Lord's accepted that it had "no alternative" but to withdraw the invitation to the South African team. The announcement signals a triumph for Peter Hain and his anti-apartheid "Stop the '70 Tour" campaign, which had threatened disruptions should the tour go ahead (→22/2/71).

1970

JUNE

Su	Mo	Tu	We	Th	Fr	Sa
	1	2	3	4	5	6
7	8	9	10	11	12	13
14	15	16	17	18	19	20
21	22	23	24	25	26	27
28	29	30				

2. UK: Emanuel Shinwell becomes a life peer at 85.→

4. UK: Charles Engelhard's Nijinsky, ridden by Lester Piggott, wins the Derby.

4. Tonga: The islands become independent of Britain.

7. New York: The Who perform their rock opera "Tommy" at the Metropolitan Opera House (→21/8).

8. Buenos Aires: President Ongania is overthrown in an army coup (→23/3/71).

14. Mexico: West Germany beat England 3-2, knocking them out of the World Cup.

17. UK: Rover announces its new four-wheel-drive "Range Rover".

18. UK: George Brown loses his Belper seat to Tory Geoffrey Stewart-Smith (→19).

19. USSR: Soyuz 9 cosmonauts land safely after a record 17 days in space (→6/11).

21. London: Sir Alec Douglas-Home becomes Foreign Secretary, Reginald Maudling Home Secretary and Iain Macleod is Chancellor (→8/7).

23. Cambridge: Prince Charles is awarded a 2:2 in history (→27/5/71).

24. Dallas: A memorial to John F. Kennedy is unveiled close to the place of his assassination.

26. Prague: Dubcek is expelled from the Communist Party.

29. UK: Caroline Thorpe, wife of the Liberal leader, dies in a car crash.

30. Luxembourg: Britain, Ireland, Denmark and Norway open talks on their entry into the Common Market (→30/3/71).

DEATHS

7. British author Edward Morgan Forster (*1/1/1879).→

11. Russian statesman Alexander Kerensky, Soviet leader March-October 1917 (*4/5/1881).

21. Indonesian statesman Ahmed Sukarno, President 1945-67 (*6/6/1901).

E.M. Forster makes his final connection

The Empire's novelist, E.M. Forster.

June 8. Apart from some short stories, E.M. Forster, who died yesterday aged 91, had published no fiction since "A Passage to India" in 1924 – and even that book was largely written, like his other four novels, by 1910. No one has explained the long silence that followed but, despite his small output and the lapse of over 40 years, he was acknowledged to be among the two or three major novelists of his time.

"Only connect" he inscribed on the title page of "Howard's End". Above all he valued personal relations: "If I had to choose between betraying my country or my friend, I hope I should have the guts to betray my country."

June 24. John Lill, from Leyton in Essex, has won joint first prize in the International Tchaikovsky Competition in Moscow.

Surprise election victory for Heath

New Prime Minister Edward Heath arrives at Number 10, promising "strong and honest government".

June 19. The Tories are back in power tonight with Edward Heath installed as Prime Minister. The general election result was totally unexpected. Nearly all opinion pollsters had signalled an easy Labour victory. There is egg on their faces now.

On the doorstep of 10 Downing Street Mr Heath promised "strong and honest government". Half-a-mile away at Labour headquarters a painful inquest began. Has Harold Wilson lost office through complacency? Party strengths in the new House of Commons are: Tories 330, Labour 287, Liberals 6 and Others 7.

In a presidential-style campaign Mr Wilson cast himself as a calm, Baldwinesque figure – the man in charge who has brought Britain through many setbacks into the economic sunshine. Big pay rises won by many people in the past six months led to improved opinion poll ratings for Labour and the party relied too much on them.

Mr Heath attacked Labour as men of straw trampled over by greedy, strike-prone unions responsible for rising prices. Industrial strife has proved a more potent electoral factor than Labour's portrayal of the Tories as "Yesterday's Men" (→21).

Methodist Church to allow women to become ministers

June 22. Women will soon be able to become full ministers of the Methodist Church, it was announced today. The decision is to be ratified at the Methodist Conference which opens in Manchester on Friday. They are to have equal pay and their status will be equal to men in every respect.

It is hoped the move will help to inject new life into the Methodist movement. Church membership has fallen by 11.2 per cent to 651,139 over the last ten years. The number of ministers has fallen from 3,448 to 3,149. The one bright spot is collections, which have risen by more than 50 per cent (→23/11).

Laurence Olivier is awarded a peerage

June 15. In today's Birthday Honours List, Sir Laurence Olivier is given a life peerage "for services to the theatre". It is the first time an actor has been ennobled, making it a comparable honour to the first theatrical knighthood conferred on Henry Irving in 1895. He is currently appearing as Shylock.

Ulster MP loses her appeal and is jailed

June 26. Violence flared in Ulster today after police "ambushed" Bernadette Devlin MP and took her to prison where she is starting a six-month sentence for incitement to riot. The 23-year-old independent member for Mid-Ulster was arrested at a road block on her way to a meeting. She had intended to give herself up "by appointment" later, supporters claimed.

The police action incensed a crowd of over 1,000 who were waiting in the Bogside to hear the MP's speech. Troops were stoned and petrol bombs hurled before troops used CS gas to disperse the mob. Twenty soldiers were injured.

Earlier, Miss Devlin was refused leave to appeal to the Lords. She will remain an MP (→3/7).

Tony Jacklin is first Briton to win the US Open for 50 years

June 21. Four immaculate rounds of golf, in conditions which destroyed the concentration of the world's best, has brought Tony Jacklin the US Open Championship – a full 50 years after Ted Ray last brought it back to Britain.

Jacklin joins only two other golfers who have held the British and US Opens within the same 12 months – the great Bobby Jones and Ben Hogan – and the £12,500 he has won in Minneapolis this week is only a fraction of the fortune that awaits as he and his agent exploit his titles to the full.

Those spectators who braved the intense heat were united in praise of Jacklin's coolness: the only golfer in the tournament to finish all four rounds under par, he beat the runner-up Dave Hill (USA), by a margin of seven strokes.

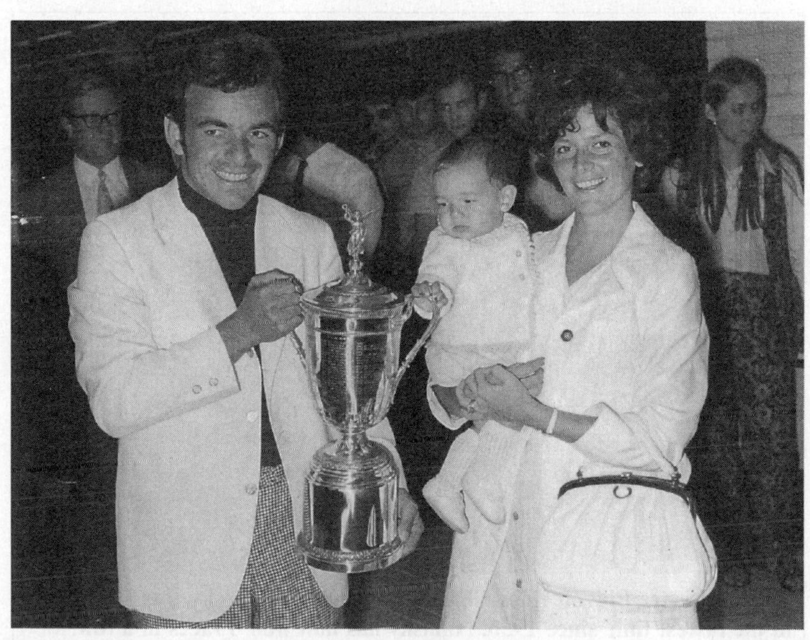

Tony Jacklin holds the US Open trophy – with a little help.

European effort plays supporting role to Latin inspiration as Brazil win World Cup

June 21. Four minutes of characteristic genius in Mexico City's Aztec Stadium proved beyond all doubt that Brazil are the best football team in the world.

These four minutes – studded by goals from Gerson and Jairzinho – saw them progress from a slightly shaky 1-1 to an imperious 3-1 lead halfway through the second half. They relegated Italy to also-rans, provided the platform for their captain, Carlos Alberto, to gild the lily with his first goal of the tournament, and gave Brazil a 4-1 victory and the Jules Rimet Cup for the third time. This means that they keep that particular gold ornament for ever.

It was a thoroughly deserved victory, rarely in doubt after Pele had almost scored with a piece of inspired opportunism from the centre circle in the first moments of their first match. After their narrow victory in a splendidly contested group match with the cup holders, England, comfortable victories against Peru and Uruguay took them to the final.

The other finalists had been less predictable. In the heat of Leon, England apparently had their quarter-final against West Germany sewn up at 2-0 when they made two unsettling substitutions, allowed the Germans to equalise and went out in extra time to a goal from the irrepressible Gerd Mueller (eventually the tournament's top scorer with 10 goals).

Bobby Moore: sick as a parrot.

The Germans themselves succumbed 4-3 to Italy in the semi-final (a thriller with five goals coming in extra time and with the injured Franz Beckenbauer playing the last period with his arm in a sling), but in the event all the European effort had been spent for the privilege of becoming sacrificial victims to the incomparable Brazilians (→ 20/8).

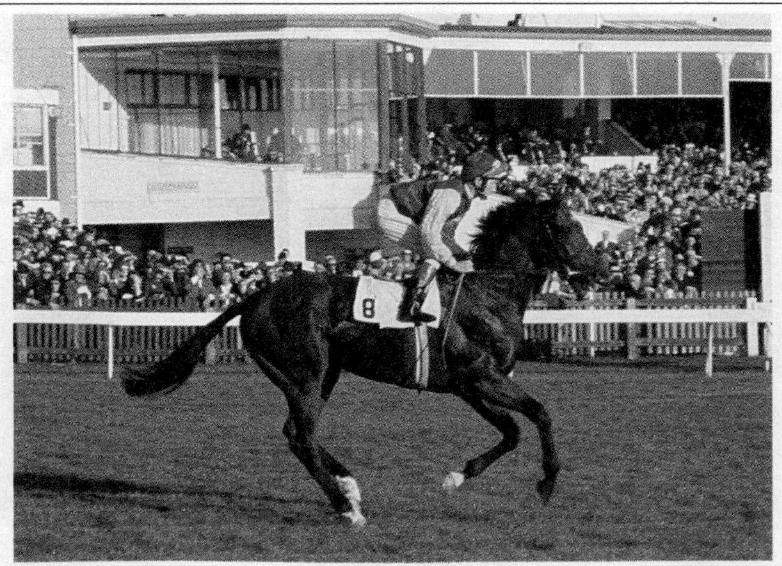

June 4. Lester Piggott rides Charles Engelhard's Nijinsky to a Derby win in the fastest time since 1936. Nijinsky has now won 8 races in a row.

1970

JULY

Su	Mo	Tu	We	Th	Fr	Sa
			1	2	3	4
5	6	7	8	9	10	11
12	13	14	15	16	17	18
19	20	21	22	23	24	25
26	27	28	29	30	31	

2. Dublin: Ex-minister Neil Blaney is cleared of gun running charges (→ 23/10).

3. Spain: A British Comet airliner carrying 112 holiday-makers and crew crashes, killing all on board (→ 9/8).

4. Wimbledon: Margaret Court beats Billie Jean King 14-12, 11-9 in the longest Women's Singles final; John Newcombe beats Ken Rosewall in the all-Australian Men's Singles final.

8. London: Roy Jenkins becomes deputy leader of the Labour Party (→ 20).

10. France: David Broome becomes the first Briton to win the world showjumping championship.

12. UK: Jack Nicklaus wins the British Open Golf Championship.

13. Northern Ireland: Orange Day parades pass off peacefully after the UK's biggest ever security operation (→ 2/8).

16. London: Heath declares a state of emergency as dockers stage their first national strike since 1926 (→ 29).

21. UAR: The Aswan Dam is completed (→ 28/9).

25. Muscat: Sultan Said bin Taimur of Oman is overthrown by his son.

29. UK: The dockers vote to accept an increased pay offer and return to work next month (→ 15/2/71).

30. UK: 28 thalidomide children are awarded damages totalling £485,000 (→ 18/12).

DEATHS

8. British publisher Sir Allen Lane, born Allen Lane Williams (*21/9/02).→

8. British artist Dame Laura Knight, born Laura Johnson (*4/8/1877).

20. British politician Iain Norman Macleod (*11/11/13).→

27. Portuguese leader Antonio de Oliveira Salazar, dictator 1933-69 (*28/4/1889).→

29. British conductor Sir John (Giovanni Battista) Barbirolli (*2/12/1899).

Troops on standby as dockers strike

July 16. Troops are being put on standby today in case they have to keep British ports open following the start of a national docks strike. They could be sent in under the state of emergency declared by the Government in an attempt to break the deadlocked pay dispute.

A full independent inquiry has also been ordered into the wages of seamen, who yesterday voted to continue their fight for a basic weekly wage of £20. The unions and employers are preparing for a stoppage lasting six weeks at least.

British industry now fears overseas trade will be badly hit, although food manufacturers warned against panic buying (→ 29).

Portuguese dictator, Salazar, is dead

Salazar, ruler of Portugal.

July 27. Antonio d'Oliviera Salazar who became dictator of Portugal because, it was said, he was good at bookkeeping, has died at the age of 81. He was appointed Finance Minister after an army coup in 1926, but resigned because the generals would not accept his proposals for restoring the country's finances after a century of deficits. He was brought back two years later on his own terms, and in his first year produced a budget surplus. He became Prime Minister and remained in office until a stroke forced him to resign two years ago. A farmer's son and a lifelong bachelor, he adopted two girls (→ 3/6/71).

Troops battle with IRA snipers in Belfast

As the marching season arrives in Belfast, British troops try to keep order.

July 3. A fierce gun battle between 1,500 British troops and IRA snipers continued in Belfast today after a night of violence in which three civilians – one of them a sniper – were killed and 10 soldiers wounded. Meanwhile, bombs have been exploding throughout the city.

Over 50 streets were placed under curfew with a low-circling army helicopter warning people that they would be arrested if they stayed on the streets. Women and children were evacuated from the area as troops searched buildings.

The latest trouble began after a police raid had uncovered a cache of arms including 15 pistols, a rifle, sub-machine gun and ammunition. A crowd gathered near the house in the Falls Road area and refused to disperse. Troops used CS gas, fired by a makeshift "catapult", after they were attacked by groups of youths brandishing iron bars.

A newspaper office was badly damaged by a bomb thrown from a passing car and other bombs were thrown at a Catholic Church and petrol station (→13).

Penguin's boss, Sir Allen Lane, is dead

July 7. The man who made the paperback revolution, Sir Allen Lane, died today having made the name Penguin, which he chose for his imprint, a household word.

Lane, who was 67, did not invent the paperback book, but he made it widely acceptable, indeed the most popular form of serious reading matter. In 1935 he could persuade only one London store to display the first titles. By afternoon they were sold out – to the staff.

It was the design plus the excellence of the titles reprinted that made Penguins such a success. There are now over 100 paperback imprints, but Penguin is still the common name for the type.

Sir Allen Lane picks up a Penguin.

New sex revue Oh! Calcutta! a bit limp

The Tynans arrive for the premiere.

July 18. The uninhibited sex revue, "Oh! Calcutta!", devised by Kenneth Tynan, opened last night at the Round House, a converted engine shed near Euston, without raising the promised head of steam. A fashionable, exotically-clad audience greeted sketches about knickers, lesbians and orgies with polite laughter. Two dances were performed totally naked by a man and a woman. "It is a mistake to promise more than you can perform," was one critic's comment, "in sex and even more in comedy."

Heart now pumps to a nuclear beat

July 15. The heart-beat of a 56-year-old woman is now normal after a pacemaker, driven by a nuclear battery designed by atomic scientists at Harwell, was placed under the skin above her right breast in an hour-and-a-half-long operation at the National Heart Hospital, London. If her heart rate is too slow it will raise it to 70 beats per minute but it will cease to act when the rate is normal. It is designed to last 10 years.

The power source is plutonium in a capsule sealed in a steel cylinder. Dr M.J. Poole, a Harwell physicist, said there is no radioactivity when a two-ton weight or intense heat is applied to the capsule, so there is no risk if a patient is burned or cremated (→25/7/71).

Iain Macleod's death comes as shock to Heath Government

July 20. Iain Macleod, the Chancellor of the Exchequer, had a heart attack and died suddenly tonight at his official residence in Downing Street. He was 56. This is a crushing blow to Mr Heath's government, formed only a month ago. Mr Macleod was its main ideas man, its finest fighting orator and one of its shrewdest tacticians. He was the champion of the Tory left.

Since a wartime injury Mr Macleod suffered spinal trouble and arthritis and he had learned to live with constant discomfort. His untimely death will force the Prime Minister into a major cabinet reshuffle before his team has had time to settle down. It is thought that Anthony Barber, who ran the Tory election campaign as party chairman, will be the new Chancellor (→6/8).

The late Iain Mcleod (2nd from r.) was Edward Heath's first Chancellor.

1970

AUGUST

Su	Mo	Tu	We	Th	Fr	Sa
						1
2	3	4	5	6	7	8
9	10	11	12	13	14	15
16	17	18	19	20	21	22
23	24	25	26	27	28	29
30	31					

2. US: Mississippi has its first inter-racial wedding.

2. Belfast: The army uses rubber bullets for the first time (→ 12).

4. Tel Aviv: Israel refuses to withdraw to its pre-1967 borders (→ 4/1/71).

6. UK: George Brown gets a peerage in Wilson's Dissolution Honours (→ 15/10).

7. Moscow: The USSR signs a non-aggression treaty with West Germany.

9. Peru: 99 die in a plane crash (→ 30/7/71).

9. London: Police and blacks clash in Notting Hill (→ 14).

12. London: Dame Sybil Thorndyke opens the Young Vic theatre.

12. Londonderry: Troops fire CS gas and rubber bullets at stone-throwing rioters in the Bogside.→

13. UK: The magazines "Harper's Bazaar" and "Queen" merge (→ 19).

14. UK: The Community Relations Commission accuses Britain's beat policemen of being racially prejudiced (→ 15/2/71).

15. South Vietnam: A US Marine is jailed for five years for murdering 15 Vietnamese (→ 28/9).

19. UK: "Coronation Street" is 1,000 episodes old tonight (→ 16/9).

24. UK: Part of Windscale nuclear power station is sealed off because of a radioactive leak (→ 12/2/71).

26. UK: The second Isle of Wight Pop Festival begins (→ 18/9).

27. UK: Wages rose on average by 9.9 per cent in the first seven months of this year.

30. Amman: The Jordanian Army launches an attack on guerrillas in the capital (→ 14/9).

30. Kuala Lumpur: Tengku Abdul Rahman, Malayan premier since 1957, announces his retirement (→ 22/9).

Nixon blunders into Manson trial gaffe

Aug 4. Charles Manson, on trial for the brutal mass murder in Los Angeles last August of actress Sharon Tate and four others, today gleefully showed jurors a newspaper bearing the headline "Nixon declares Manson guilty". The judge confiscated the paper and warned the jury not to be swayed by it.

The President had said at a press conference that Manson was "guilty directly or indirectly of eight murders without reason". Mr Nixon immediately tried to clarify his gaffe, in the end retracting it altogether (→ 25/1/71).

England's captain not guilty of theft

Aug 20. Three judges in Colombia today cleared the England soccer captain Bobby Moore on charges of stealing an emerald bracelet from a hotel shop in the capital Bogota. In London, the player held a party to celebrate. He had been waiting for three months to hear whether they would reject the claim which led to him being held for two days as his team mates trained in Mexico for the World Cup.

New Ulster Party to speed reform

Aug 21. Within months of the formation of the non-sectarian Alliance Party, Ulster is to have another opposition party as the government staggers from crisis to crisis. The Social and Democratic Labour Party, aimed at speeding vital reforms, is to be led by Gerry Fitt, an MP at both Westminster and Stormont (→ 21/10).

The Range Rover has four-wheel drive and a V8 engine for £2,000.

1970

SEPTEMBER

Su	Mo	Tu	We	Th	Fr	Sa
		1	2	3	4	5
6	7	8	9	10	11	12
13	14	15	16	17	18	19
20	21	22	23	24	25	26
27	28	29	30			

1. Jordan: King Hussein escapes an assassination attempt (→ 14).

2. New Delhi: Parliament abolishes the privileges of 279 maharajahs (→ 3/11/71).

4. Chile: Socialist leader Salvador Allende Gossens is elected President (→ 22/10).

5. Italy: Austrian racing driver Jochen Rindt dies in a crash in a qualifying race before the Italian Grand Prix (→ 4/10).

6. Europe: Four airliners bound for New York are hijacked; one is blown up (→ 9).

9. Jordan: A BOAC VC-10 is forced to land after being hijacked.→

10. UK: An organisation is formed to provide shelter for homeless and alcoholics, called the Cyrenians.

12. London: Complaints about noise greet Concorde's first landing at Heathrow.

14. Jordan: Palestinian guerrillas are reported to have taken control of Irbid, the second largest Jordanian city.

16. UK: George Gale is appointed editor of "The Spectator" in succession to Nigel Lawson (→ 18/2/71).

18. London: Rock star Jimi Hendrix dies of a drugs overdose (→ 4/10).

22. Kuala Lumpur: Abdul Razak succeeds Abdul Rahman as premier.

28. US: Students at Kent State University in Ohio burn their draft cards in memory of the students killed in May (→ 12/11).

28. Cairo: Nasser dies of a heart attack (→ 1/10).

DEATHS

18. US musician Jimi Hendrix (*27/11/42).

25. German author Erich Maria Remarque (*22/6/1898).

28. Egyptian statesman Colonel Gamal Abdel Nasser, (*15/1/1889).

28. US author John Dos Passos (*14/1/1896).

Court clinches only second Grand Slam

Triumphant: Margaret Court.

Sept 13. Australia's Margaret Court today became only the second woman in tennis history to complete the testing Grand Slam of the four major tennis championships when she won the United States Open tennis title at Forest Hills, New York. Her three-set victory over the American Rosie Casals means she has emulated the feat of the great Maureen Connolly in 1953.

The 27-year-old from New South Wales is now indisputably number one in the world, having already won the Australian Open, the French Open and Wimbledon.

Sept 4. Natalia Makarova, star of the visiting Kirov Ballet, has defected. Her friends say the reason is not politics, but love.

Hijacked jets blown up in the desert

The Arab terrorists blow up the three jets in Jordan. They released many passengers, but 40 are still hostage.

Sept 12. Urgent efforts are being made to secure the release of 56 hostages, including eight Britons, after their Palestinian captors blew up three hijacked airliners in the baking heat of Dawson's Field in the Jordanian desert today.

Nine explosions shattered the British, Swiss and American aircraft as they sat in the so-called "Liberation Airport", in reality a disused RAF wartime airstrip. Tonight smoke still curls up into the velvet sky from the skeletons of the three planes. Only the tails remain to distinguish them.

Their fiery end came as the climax to a story which started with the mass hijacking of three aircraft six days ago. The hijackers seized a TWA Boeing 707, a Pan Am Boeing Jumbo and a Swissair DC-8 over North Europe. They flew the Jumbo to Cairo, apparently because they feared it could not land in the desert and blew it up after releasing the passengers and crew.

Another attempted hijack on the same day failed when the crew of an El Al Boeing 707 overpowered two would-be hijackers, killing one. The El Al pilot landed his plane at Heathrow to seek help for a wounded steward and, after some argument, handed over the captured hijacker, Leila Khaled, to the British police. She is being held at a London police station. Her arrest prompted the hijack of a BOAC VC-10 and it was that aircraft which exploded with the Swiss and American planes at Dawson's Field today.

The armed men who met the hijackers at Dawson's Field released 255 passengers before destroying the planes, but are holding the remaining 56 at a secret location.

Believed to belong to the Popular Front for the Liberation of Palestine, they are demanding the release of Leila Khaled in exchange for their British hostages (→ 30).

Britain exchanges terrorist for hostages

Sept 30. All the hostages taken in the mass hijack by Palestinian terrorists have now been released and, in accordance with the deal worked out with The Popular Front for the Liberation of Palestine, Leila Khaled, captured in her attempt to seize an El Al plane over the Thames Estuary, was taken from Ealing police station tonight and put on an RAF Comet to be flown to Beirut.

The Comet landed at Munich and Zurich to pick up three terrorists held by the Germans and three by the Swiss whose release was also demanded in exchange for the freeing of the hostages.

While the safe return of the hostages is welcomed, there is much unease about the capitulation of the Western governments to the terrorists' demands.

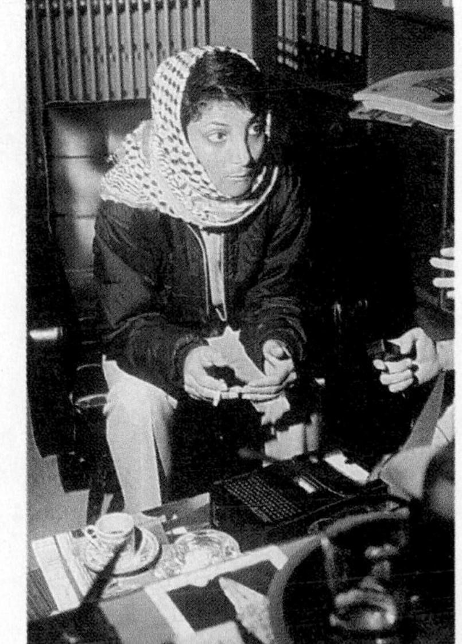

Leila Khaled: held in Britain.

Palestinians face a Black September as Jordan evicts PLO

Sept 27. An armed truce in the war waged by the army against Palestinian guerrillas in Jordan was arranged today at President Nasser's Cairo conference.

Symbolically both King Hussein and Yassir Arafat, the PLO leader, wore gun belts as they signed. The King made concessions, but the losers are the Palestinian guerrillas, evicted from their strongholds. For them it is "Black September".

The conflict, which began ten days ago, was provoked by the aggressive behaviour of the PLO, based in the Kingdom. They had seized control of northern Jordan and dominated the approaches to Amman, the capital. Furthermore, the recent mass hijackings of Western airliners ended in three of the planes being blown up at Dawson's Field in Jordan while Syria manoeuvered a brigade of tanks up to the border in support.

Fearful that the war was going to spread, King Hussein appealed to the US who put their forces on alert while he declared a military government. Field Marshal Habis al-Majali was appointed Commander-in-Chief with orders to clear out the Palestinians, which he did in just 10 days (→ 10/1/71).

PM's wife publishes slim poetic volume

Sept 21. A slim volume of "Selected Poems" by Mary Wilson, price 12 shillings, caused a stir when it went on sale in Oxford Street today. Long queues of purchasers waited to have their copies signed by the author. Her husband, puffing a pipe, kept in the background.

Mrs Wilson said the excitement of seeing her work in print was tremendous but did not compare with the excitement of being at Number Ten. She admitted she had not written any poetry lately, but hoped to now that they had moved out.

She said her love poems were written "a very long time ago – let's leave it at that". And so was the one about "crowded rooms thick with whisky fumes".

1970

OCTOBER

Su	Mo	Tu	We	Th	Fr	Sa
				1	2	3
4	5	6	7	8	9	10
11	12	13	14	15	16	17
18	19	20	21	22	23	24
25	26	27	28	29	30	31

1. Cairo: 46 die as thousands of mourners mob Nasser's funeral cortege.→

4. Austria: Jochen Rindt, who died last month, becomes world motor racing champion posthumously.

4. Los Angeles: Rock singer Janis Joplin is found dead of a drugs overdose (→12/5/71).

5. Montreal: French Canadian separatists kidnap British diplomat James Cross (→10).

9. Phnom Penh: Cambodia is declared a republic.

10. Fiji: The islands become independent of Britain.

10. Montreal: Two men kidnap the Quebec Labour and Immigration Minister, Pierre Laporte.→

15. London: Heath creates two ministries, the Departments of Trade and Industry and of the Environment (→22).

15. Melbourne: 33 die when the West Gate Bridge, Australia's biggest, collapses.

16. Cairo: Sadat becomes UAR President (→15/1/71).

18. Canada: The body of kidnapped minister Pierre Laporte is found (→2/12).

21. Northern Ireland: Bernadette Devlin is released from jail (→9/2/71).

21. Philippines: Nearly 800 people are believed to have died in a typhoon (→20/11).

22. London: Kenneth Baker wins the St. Marylebone by-election for the Tories (→19/11).

22. Chile: A state of emergency follows a bid to murder the army chief (→13/11).

25. UK: Racing driver Jack Brabham announces his retirement.

31. Belfast: Troops come under machine-gun fire in the second consecutive night of Belfast rioting.

DEATHS

4. US singer Janis Joplin (*19/1/1943).

10. French statesman Edouard Daladier (*18/6/1884).

Nasser's successor is the moderate Sadat

Oct 5. Anwar Sadat, oldest and closest colleague of the late Gamal Abdel Nasser was today nominated to succeed him as President of Egypt by the central committee of the Arab Socialist Union. Next week parliament will probably approve their choice and later in the month a plebiscite will be held.

Nasser, the hero of both Arab nationalism and Third World statesmen and the most powerful figure in the Middle East, died a week ago after a heart attack, some say of a broken heart. He was deeply depressed by disunity in the Arab world after presiding over the conference attempting to reconcile Jordan and the Palestinian guerrillas. Millions of weeping Egyptians attended his funeral.

Since then Anwar Sadat has been acting President. Aged 51, and considered to be a moderate, he is experienced in government, though not nearly so flamboyant as his old friend. He helped Nasser to plot the 1952 coup which threw out King Farouk.

The new President is expected to take a more moderate line in regional politics (→16).

The Cairo crowds bid farewell to their leader Gamal Abdel Nasser.

Soviet writer in row over a Nobel Prize

Author Alexander Solzhenitsyn.

Oct 9. A first-class literary row is brewing in Russia because of the Nobel Prize award to Alexander Solzhenitsyn, the banned author of "Cancer Ward" and "The First Circle".

He says he will travel to Stockholm to receive it if he is allowed to. But the Writers' Union, which expelled him last year, is expected to put pressure on him to refuse it, as it did with Boris Pasternak.

Last year Solzhenitsyn wrote an open letter to the Union protesting strongly at the state censorship of Soviet literature. He is staying at the dacha of the cellist, Mstislav Rostropovich (→17/12).

Irish politician not guilty in gun trial

Oct 23. Amid cheers and jubilation the Irish High Court today acquitted Charles Haughey, the former Finance Minister, and four others of importing arms illegally. The main defence was that the guns were part of an officially authorised intelligence operation for the Irish Army. Another former minister, Neil Blaney, was acquitted of the same charge in July.

The Prime Minister, Jack Lynch, said from New York that he did what he believed to be his duty in dismissing Haughey from his cabinet. The reputation of his government appears to have suffered some damage from the affair.

790 couples from Korea and all parts of the world, members of the controversial Unification Church, were married by their leader Sun Myung Moon in a mass ceremony at the Changchung gym in Seoul.

Trudeau gets tough with Quebec rebels

Oct 16. Pierre Trudeau, the Canadian Prime Minister, has acted decisively to deal with the steadily worsening Quebec separatist problem. In the early hours of this morning he declared a state of "insurrection" in the province and invoked war emergency powers. He outlawed the Quebec Liberation Front (FLQ) which has kidnapped Pierre Laporte, the Quebec Minister of Labour and James Cross, a British diplomat.

At dawn 1,500 parachute troops moved in to take over strategic points in the Montreal area. Police arrested 250 FLQ supporters, including Robert Lemieux, who had been negotiating for the release of the hostages (→18).

Kidnapped minister Pierre Laporte.

Major oil field is found in North Sea

Oct 19. British Petroleum tonight announced the first major find of oil in the British sector of the North Sea. The test well, 110 miles east of Aberdeen, in 350 feet of water produced oil at the rate of 4,700 barrels a day. Drilling has only recently started off Scotland, which the oilmen always thought was the most promising area. So the hope will be that BP has found a field as big as Norway's Ekofisk, discovered in June and now thought capable of supplying 10 per cent of Britain's needs (→3/2/71).

1970

NOVEMBER

Su	Mo	Tu	We	Th	Fr	Sa
1	2	3	4	5	6	7
8	9	10	11	12	13	14
15	16	17	18	19	20	21
22	23	24	25	26	27	28
29	30					

1. France: 146 die in a fire at a dance hall at Saint-Laurent-du-Pont, near Grenoble.

3. Chile: Allende is sworn in as President; he promises "socialism within liberty".

6. US: NASA puts a satellite into orbit which it claims can detect missile launchings anywhere in the world (→31/1/71).

10. London: Henry Cooper knocks out Jose Manuel Ibar to regain the European heavyweight championship.

12. US: The court martial begins of Lt. William Calley, accused of leading the Mylai massacre in 1968 (→7/12).

13. Paris: The Place de l'Etoile is renamed Place Charles de Gaulle (→26/7/71).

13. Damascus: The President and premier are arrested as Defence Minister General Hafez al-Assad seizes power (→12/8/71).

18. Warsaw: Poland signs a treaty of reconciliation with West Germany (→20).

19. London: Tory candidate Cecil Parkinson wins Iain Macleod's seat of Enfield West in a by-election (→16/2/71).

20. London: Britain formally recognises the Oder-Neisse Line as Poland's western frontier (→16/12).

20. London: Missiles are thrown at the stage during the Miss World contest (→7/2/71).

23. Rome: Pope Paul VI bars cardinals over 80 from voting in papal elections (→27).

25. Tokyo: Yukio Mishima calls for a return to militarism before committing hara-kiri in the Defence Ministry.

27. Manila: A knife-wielding man is seized as he tries to attack Pope Paul.

DEATHS

9. French statesman and commander General Charles de Gaulle, head of government 1944-46, President 1958-69 (*22/11/1890).

25. Japanese author Yukio Mishima (*14/1/1925).

Typhoon kills 150,000

The survivors fish out victims' bodies from a flooded field.

Nov 20. It is now feared that more that 150,000 people died in the typhoon and tidal wave which last week brought death and disaster to East Pakistan. Only now, as the waters recede, is it possible to see fully the devastating effect the storm has had.

The tidal wave, as high as a two-storey building, has changed the map of the delta, sweeping away islands and making others uninhabitable. Whole communities have been destroyed and all their people and livestock killed.

One week ago, Ali Husain, a 25-year-old soldier, had 90 people in his family all living in a compound in the village of Medua. Today only 20 are alive. "We were all sleeping when it hit at midnight," he said. "I caught hold of a palm tree and hung on until the waters went down around dawn." A massive international aid effort is now getting under way.

British and American planes flew into Dacca today carrying vehicles, helicopters, food and medical supplies. The Royal Navy is also on its way; the assault ship Intrepid and the repair ship Triumph are sailing for Dacca to set up a supply and communications centre to co-ordinate the flow of aid.

It may yet be some time before help can reach the outlying districts, however. Roads have been washed away and the current is still too swift in some of the channels for relief boats to get through.

The greatest fear now is that with thousands of bodies still unburied and rotting in the blazing sun, disease will sweep through the starving survivors.

Gay Lib holds first public demo in UK

Nov 27. The Gay Liberation Front, formed recently to combat prejudice and discrimination against homosexuals, held its first demonstration in London today. It wants gay men and women to be able to express their feelings openly and without shame.

One man said: "We don't want to be a freak show, we just want to be the same as anybody else." The Front has 250 members so far, including heterosexuals. In America it is already a powerful lobby.

Strikes at highest level since 1926

Nov 26. The first year of Mr Heath's government has been marked by more working days lost by strikes than at any time since 1926, the year of the General Strike.

Figures published today show that 8.8 million days have already been lost this year, with the engineering industry worst hit, mainly by many small stoppages. But there have also been major disputes involving dockers, national newspapers and local authorities (→3/12).

France mourns de Gaulle

De Gaulle's coffin, draped in the Tricolour, arrives at Colombey.

Nov 12. Charles de Gaulle, who so often in life managed to get his own way, exerted his influence from the grave today. He had left explicit instructions that his funeral was to be a simple ceremony at his home village of Colombey-les-Deux-Eglises, unattended by any members of the present government.

He had, however, invited "the men and women of France and of elsewhere ... to do my memory the honour of accompanying my body to the grave". They came in their tens of thousands and pressed against the barriers in the narrow streets.

Just before 3pm the plain, light-oak coffin, draped with the Tricolour flag, left for the church on a French Army reconnaissance vehicle. The bells of Colombey rang out along with the bells of churches all over France. In the church there were only his widow and immediate family and a few friends from the Free French army and de Gaulle's post-war government.

The ceremony was, according to a French radio commentator, "grandiose in its rustic simplicity". His grave is a plain white marble slab, the twin to that of his retarded daughter, Anne, beside whom he had asked to be buried.

In contrast, over 6,000 people crowded into Notre Dame in Paris for the pomp and ceremony of a full Requiem Mass. It was like a roll-call of the leaders of the world, past and present. They included President Pompidou, President Nixon, Soviet President Podgorny, Britain's Prince Charles, Edward Heath, Harold Macmillan and Lord Avon, Mrs Gandhi, Queen Juliana, the Shah of Iran and the Emperor of Ethiopia.

In the evening hundreds of thousands braved the cold, the wind and the pouring rain to march up the Champs Elysees to the Arc de Triomphe in silent respect. Only twice in the past have such crowds been seen: in May 1958, when they gathered to cheer de Gaulle's election as President, and in August 1944, when they turned out for the liberation of Paris by de Gaulle and the Free French forces (→13).

The architect of modern France.

1970

DECEMBER

Su	Mo	Tu	We	Th	Fr	Sa
		1	2	3	4	5
6	7	8	9	10	11	12
13	14	15	16	17	18	19
20	21	22	23	24	25	26
27	28	29	30	31		

2. London: MPs reject a move to keep British Summer Time in winter.

3. London: Publication of the Industrial Relations Bill.

10. Stockholm: Nobel Prizes go to Hannes Alfven (Sweden) and Louis Neel (France), both Physics; Luis Leloir (Argentina, Chemistry); Sir Bernard Katz (UK), Ulf von Euler (Sweden) and Julius Axelrod (US), all for Medicine); Alexander Solzhenitsyn (USSR, Literature); Paul Samuelson (US, Economics) and in Oslo to Norman Borlaug (US, Peace).

13. Laos: A US bomber carrying top secret equipment is reported to have been shot down (→13/2/71).

16. Poland: Six people have been killed in two days of rioting at the port of Gdansk.

17. Moscow: Pravda slams Solzhenitsyn as "alien and hostile" to the Soviet people.

18. West Germany: Thalidomide victims are awarded over £11 million compensation.

23. Warsaw: Gierek pledges to freeze food prices for two years and aid poorer families (→7/2/71).

28. Canada: The alleged killers of Quebec Labour Minister, Pierre Laporte, are arrested.

31. UK: Paul McCartney files a suit against Lennon, Starr and Harrison to dissolve "The Beatles and Co."

DEATH

14. British commander Field Marshal William Joseph Slim, first Viscount Slim (*6/8/1891).

HITS OF 1970

Yellow river.

The wonder of You.

In the summertime.

QUOTE OF THE YEAR

"We are all the President's men."

Dr Henry Kissinger, justifying the US invasion of Cambodia.

Abducted consul freed in Quebec

James Cross is greeted by his family.

Dec 3. James Cross, who was kidnapped by the Quebec Liberation Front (FLQ) nearly two months ago, was released today. Pierre Trudeau, the Canadian Prime Minister, who had spoken to him on the telephone, said he was in good health, adding: "The nightmare is over."

Cross was kidnapped at the same time as Pierre Laporte, the Quebec Minister of Labour, whose body was found in a car boot a few days later. Today, Cross was released into the custody of a Cuban diplomat. His three kidnappers are being flown to Havana and he will be freed when they arrive (→28).

We followed orders say massacre GIs

Dec 14. Soldiers who appeared as defence witnesses in the trial of Lieutenant William Calley testified today that they believed that their commanding officer, Captain Ernest Medina, had given them orders to kill every living human being in the hamlet of Mylai, where 567 men, women and children were massacred by US troops in 1968.

Lt. Calley is pleading not guilty to charges that he was responsible for the massacre, the details of which remained an Army secret until the Pulitzer Prize-winning journalist Seymour Hersh revealed them in the New York Times in November 1969. Calley, too, says he was only following orders.

Poland rocked by riots

Dec 20. After a week of anti-government riots over food price rises, with militiamen opening fire on workers, the Polish Communist Party leader, Wladyslaw Gomulka, has resigned. His successor is Edward Gierek, aged 57, a former miner with a reputation as a good administrator.

The rioting, which began in the Baltic port of Gdansk with a dockers' demonstration against rises in the price of meat and other items, rapidly got out of control. Crowds set fire to the local Communist Party HQ and other public buildings. Dozens of shops were looted. As the rioting spread to other Baltic towns, the militia were called out and ordered to open fire. A Swedish journalist who was in the area, which has now been sealed off to foreigners, says he was told that at least 300 people, including women and children, died in the Gdansk clashes.

Gomulka's departure comes 14 years after anti-government riots in Poznan forced his predecessor, Edward Ochab, to quit and brought him to power with a reputation as a reformer (→23).

British Olympic athlete dies of cancer

Dec 26. The outstanding British runner, Lillian Board, has died in a Bavarian clinic after a long fight against cancer at the tragically early age of 22. The courage with which she tackled her illness moved her admirers as much as her running had excited them.

Her defeat by inches in the Olympic 400 metres final in Mexico City served only to spark a new determination in her. In 1969, in the European Championships in Athens, she switched to the 800 metres, won a superbly controlled final, and followed it triumphantly by anchoring Britain's relay team and inching past her Olympic conqueror Colette Besson in the final straight for her second gold.

Lillian Board in her prime.

Arts: Monty Python off to a flying start

What begins as a minority taste often becomes a cult and so has "Monty Python's Flying Circus", which slipped into a late-night religious slot on BBC2 last year. Now on BBC1 it is television's nearest equivalent to radio's Goon Show.

Its humour, recognisably British, is of the obsessively straight-faced kind. **John Cleese**, a Guards officer type with a ramrod bearing and rigid upper lip, maintains decorum in the face of absurdity, as when demonstrating "silly walks" devised by a government department. Pythonesque humour scorns common sense as when a pet-dealer tries to sell a dead parrot.

An anti-war novel in the guise of science fiction comes from **Kurt Vonnegut** who, like his hero, experienced the destruction of Dresden by obliteration bombing and firestorm in February 1945, as a prisoner of war in an underground coldstore. When he emerged, the city and 135,000 civilians were gone. "Slaughterhouse Five" treats this event with the laconic, deadpan detachment which is his trade-mark.

C.P. Snow began his sequence of novels, "Strangers and Brothers", in 1940. The eleventh volume, "Last Things" has brought its hero, Lewis Eliot, and his career to a conclusion. It is a saga about power and the way it is exercised in "the corridors of power" (Snow's term). He is best at describing the machinations of Cambridge dons ("The Masters") and the consciences of scientists working on atomic weapons ("The New Men").

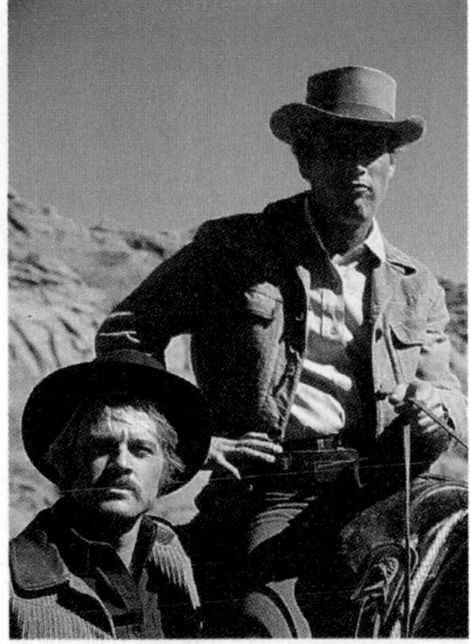
Newman and Redford as "Butch Cassidy and the Sundance Kid".

Sir Frederick Ashton, Britain's best-known choreographer, retired from directing the Royal Ballet after seven years. His best-known ballets for the company include "Ondine", "La Fille Mal Gardee", "Marguerite and Armand", which began the **Fonteyn-Nureyev** partnership, and "The Dream" which launched that of **Antoinette Sibley** and **Anthony Dowell**. **Kenneth Macmillan** succeeds him.

Germaine Greer, an Australian, challenged the masculine world with an erudite and witty analysis of the way it stereotypes women's roles – "The Female Eunuch".

Strikes fail to stop bill to curb unions

Dec 15. MPs voted tonight to set up an Industrial Relations Court with power to fine unions for ignoring new procedures for settling disputes without strikes. The legislation was approved against a background of widespread labour unrest, including disruption of electricity supplies.

The Government's plans have similar strike-curbing elements to the action which the Labour government abandoned last year. The Prime Minister, Edward Heath, says the country is sick of wildcat disputes. Mr Wilson agrees, but dislikes the remedy (→20/1/71).

Elections threaten to divide Pakistan

Dec 8. In a surprising landslide victory. Mr Zulfikar Ali Bhutto, the former Foreign Minister, has emerged from Pakistan's first free elections as the undisputed leader of West Pakistan while the Bengali nationalist, Shaikh Mujibur Rahman, has scored an equally complete victory in East Pakistan.

These two regional leaders take opposite views on all major issues in Pakistan so the election will divide the country into two entities, as far apart politically as they are geographically. With no hope of compromise, Pakistan faces a period of crisis (→26/3/71).

Sir Frederick Ashton, who has retired, with Dame Margot Fonteyn.

1971

JANUARY

Su	Mo	Tu	We	Th	Fr	Sa
					1	2
3	4	5	6	7	8	9
10	11	12	13	14	15	16
17	18	19	20	21	22	23
24	25	26	27	28	29	30
31						

1. UK: The new divorce law comes into force, making "irretrievable breakdown of marriage" sole grounds (→11).

2. Tel Aviv: Israeli scholars say they have found the skeleton of a man who died by crucifixion.

4. Cairo: Sadat admits that six Soviet soldiers died in an Israeli raid on an Egyptian missile site (→1/2).

4. Washington: Nixon warns Soviet submarines to keep away from Cuba.

7. Moscow: A Soviet official rules that long hair is legal in the USSR.

10. Jordan: The Jordanian Army deports 384 Palestinian guerrillas (→14/7).

11. UK: The first divorce is granted under the Divorce Act.

15. UAR: Sadat and Soviet President Podgorny open the Aswan High Dam (→18/4).

18. US: George McGovern pledges to withdraw all US troops from Vietnam if elected President in 1972 (→13/2).

22. Singapore: The Commonwealth Conference ends with disagreement over UK arms sales to South Africa.

27. London: The Angry Brigade claims responsibility for a string of bomb attacks in a letter to The Times (→28/4).

28. Kampala: Idi Amin bans all political activity but releases 55 political prisoners (→5/2).

29. Mozambique: Hundreds are feared dead after a cyclone.

31. US: NASA launches the Apollo 14 moonshot, modified to prevent the problems that aborted Apollo 13 (→5/2).

DEATHS

5. US heavyweight boxer Sonny Liston (*8/5/32).

10. French fashion designer Gabrielle "Coco" Chanel (*19/8/1883).→

Angry Brigade bomb minister's house

Jan 14. An anonymous letter, sent to Fleet Street newspapers by an extremist group calling themselves The Angry Brigade, claims responsibility for the bombing of the home of Robert Carr, the Secretary of State for Employment. Mr Carr, his wife and younger daughter, escaped unharmed when two time-bombs exploded shortly after 10pm two days ago outside his Hertfordshire home. They shattered windows, blew out the front door and damaged the minister's official Daimler.

The Angry Brigade have previously claimed responsibility for machine-gunning the Spanish Embassy in London, and for planting bombs near a BBC van during the Miss World contest and at the Department of Employment offices in Westminster (→27).

Robert Carr's wrecked kitchen.

Manson convicted of Tate murders

Jan 25. "You won't outlive this, old man," was murderer Charles Manson's response to the judge when a Los Angeles jury found him and three co-defendants guilty of the murders of the pregnant actress, Sharon Tate, and four others at her Beverly Hills home in August 1969.

At the end of a trial lasting 121 days, Manson, the drug-crazed king of a California hippie commune, was also found guilty of masterminding the murder of a Los Angeles couple, the LaBiancas. In the latter case, he strolled on the beach munching peanuts as his "family" carried out his instructions. The trial was marked by Manson's wild rantings about race war. The prosecution are now pressing for the death penalty (→29/3).

British envoy is kidnapped in Uruguay

Jan 8. The British Ambassador to Uruguay was kidnapped by urban guerrillas of the left-wing Tupamaros movement today as he was being driven from his home to the Embassy.

The gun-toting terrorists used five cars to force 53-year-old Mr Jackson's Daimler limousine off the road and then drove him away to their hideout, having dragged the chauffeur out of the car and beaten him unconscious. They also staged a diversionary incident on the other side of the capital, Montevideo, to distract the attention of the police.

It is the first time a British diplomat has been kidnapped in Latin America and fears for his safety are compounded by the fact that he suffers from a heart ailment. Tonight about 12,000 troops and police began a search. A Brazilian diplomat and an American agricultural expert have been held hostage for several months (→9/9).

Coup puts Idi Amin in power in Uganda

Jan 25. President Milton Obote of Uganda, who has been attending the Commonwealth conference in Singapore, has been overthrown by his army commander, General Idi Amin, who accused Obote of corruption, tribalism and economic policies to benefit the rich and hurt the poor. Amin, a 45-year-old former army boxing champion, promised free elections, an early return to civilian rule and the release of all political prisoners held on "false or unspecified charges" (→28).

Ousted: Uganda's Milton Obote.

Coco Chanel, fashion revolutionary, dies

Style leader for half a century.

Jan 10. The legendary designer, Gabrielle "Coco" Chanel, died today in her suite at the Paris Ritz. She was 87. In the 1920s, Chanel almost single-handedly revolutionised the way women looked, freeing them from corsets and putting them into simple, yet elegant styles: little chemises, softly tailored suits.

She launched bobbed hair, suntans and costume jewellery. Her No.5 perfume, named after her lucky number, became a world best-seller. After a comeback in the 1950s, Chanel suits became synonymous with French chic. Beautiful and ruthless, Chanel had many admirers among the rich, but she never married.

Sixty-six die as football barriers collapse

The buckled rails at Ibrox Park ...

... led to this scene of icy carnage.

Jan 2. Two hundred football fans were crushed as crowd barriers at the Ibrox Park stadium in Glasgow collapsed today. By the time rescuers had forced a path through the mangle of twisted metal poles on the terracing to reach the heap of bodies, they found 66 people were dead.

Seconds before the disaster, the home fans had been elated when their team, Glasgow Rangers, equalised against their fierce local rivals, Glasgow Celtic. As those at the back surged forward – some pushing themselves onto heads in front – barriers gave way and a mass of fans swept to the foot of the terraces. An inquiry into ground safety is expected.

Postmen go on strike for the first time

Jan 20. Motor bikes, vans, taxis and even pigeons were zooming around the country today delivering urgent letters and parcels. Virtually all of the 230,000 postal workers had laid down their bags at midnight. But the Conservative government, determined to be tough, had waived the ban on private services, leaving the field open for any fast-moving entrepreneur. Even the police helped by sending summonses by police car. The postmen want a 19.5 per cent pay rise, but the Post Office says this would mean an unacceptable 9d. letter rate (→ 1/3).

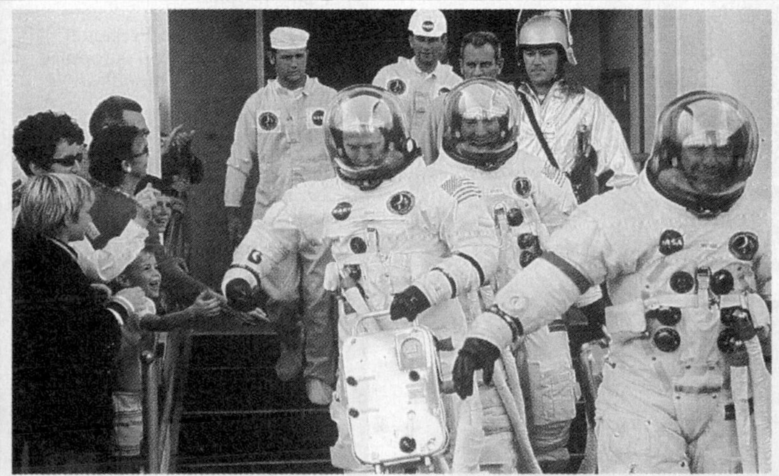
Jan 31. Apollo 14 astronauts Roosa, Mitchell and Shepard make their way to the launch-pad for another NASA mission to the moon.

1971

FEBRUARY

Su	Mo	Tu	We	Th	Fr	Sa
	1	2	3	4	5	6
7	8	9	10	11	12	13
14	15	16	17	18	19	20
21	22	23	24	25	26	27
28						

1. Lebanon: Israeli troops cross the border to attack "terrorist bases" (→ 6/3).

3. Teheran: 11 OPEC states threaten to increase oil prices without prior consultation with buyer countries.

4. UK: Rolls-Royce declares itself bankrupt.→

5. US: Apollo 14 lands safely on the moon; two astronauts walk on its surface (→ 30/5).

5. London: Britain recognises Idi Amin's government in Uganda (→ 20).

7. Switzerland: A referendum gives women the vote in national elections (→ 28).

7. Warsaw: Gomulka is suspended from the Communist Party Central Committee as part of a major purge.

11. Moscow: Britain is among 40 nations which sign a treaty banning nuclear weapons from the seabed.

13. US: Vice-President Agnew hits three spectators with his first two shots at Bob Hope's Desert Classic golf match.

15. London: Enoch Powell predicts an "explosion" unless there is a massive repatriation scheme for immigrants (→ 24).

16. London: Peter Walker outlines plans for sweeping reorganisation of local government (→ 13/5).

18. London: Rupert Murdoch takes control of London Weekend Television (→ 8/3).

20. Entebbe: Amin declares himself President, promotes himself to general and ends the state of emergency.→

22. Cape Town: South African MPs cheer when they learn Britain will sell seven helicopters to South Africa (→ 3/3).

24. London: The Immigration Bill, published today, will end the right of Commonwealth workers to settle in Britain.

26. Belfast: Two policemen die in hospital after being shot on patrol (→ 11/3).

28. Liechtenstein: The tiny state's male electorate refuse to give the vote to women.→

British currency is getting a new point

Feb 15. After centuries of dealing in the illogical – yet lovable – pounds, shillings and pence, Britons found themselves battling with decimal currency today. Despite a claim by Lord Fiske, chairman of the Decimal Currency Board, that "all was going well", many found difficulty in understanding the new system.

So it is goodbye to symbols such as 1/- (meaning one old shilling or five new pence) and "p" replaces "d" for pence. Many mourned the end of the half-crown coin (now 12.5 pence). Many more found it hard to adjust to the concept of a ten pence coin which equalled a florin (two shillings) and most worried that shops would use the change to mark up prices (→ 19/4).

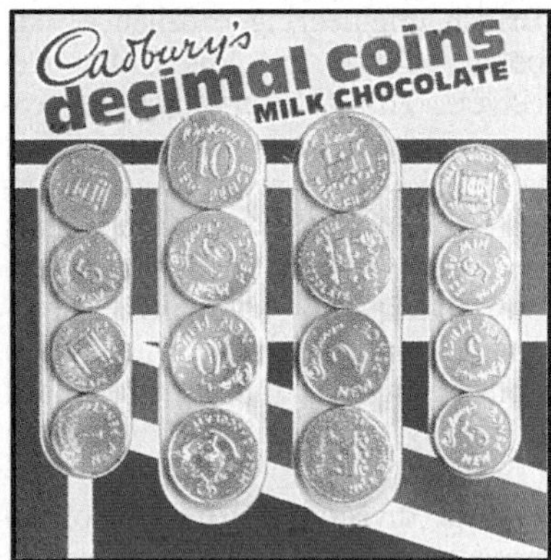

Everything is going decimal.

Attack on Laos by South Vietnamese

Feb 13. South Vietnamese troops swept into Laos today in a determined effort to disrupt the Communist supply routes along the Ho Chi Minh trail. American warplanes, and guns fired from bases in Vietnam, gave support to the advance, but US ground troops and advisers were under orders not to cross the border.

Initial reports say the 12,000-man force was encountering little resistance and was finding many caches of arms. Among the booty are four tanks, 45 lorries and 290 assorted weapons. Unconfirmed reports say the troops have reached Tchepone, an important Communist headquarters (→ 29/3).

Rolls-Royce is bankrupt

British prestige and pride take a bashing with the collapse of Rolls-Royce.

Feb 4. Rolls-Royce, the symbol of British engineering excellence, has collapsed into the hands of a Receiver. The Conservative government, which came to power last year pledged to return state industry to private ownership, has decided in the national interest to buy back the company's aero-engine and aero-space activities and to put them into a nationalised company to be called Rolls-Royce (1971) Ltd. The Rolls-Royce luxury car division will be sold off to private enterprise. The company has been brought down by a disastrous contract to design and manufacture the RB.211 jet engine for the new Lockheed Tristar.

Rolls-Royce was so keen to get the order that it allowed Lockheed to drive an impossibly hard bargain on price and penalty clauses. The project has also been beset with technical problems, involving the use of carbon fibre.

The Government has been aware since last November that Rolls had problems, but their extent only became clear last week.

First British soldier is killed in Ulster

Feb 9. A British soldier was shot dead during rioting in Ulster tonight, the first to be killed since British troops moved into the province in August, 1969. He was killed during an attack by gelignite bombs and machine-gun fire as his unit moved into the Ardoyne district of the city. Two civilians and five other soldiers were wounded.

An army spokesman said that one of the civilians died after troops of the First Parachute Regiment had opened fire on petrol bombers who had set fire to an armoured personnel carrier. Eight soldiers inside escaped unhurt.

Sporadic bombings and attacks on troops and police continued throughout Northern Ireland tonight with innocent bystanders – including two girls and a youth – being injured by machine-gun fire as they made their way home through the Belfast rush-hour traffic.

A sinister new development in the conflict was revealed tonight as police investigated what appears to be a second Ulster sectarian killing, in which the body of a young Protestant, shot in the head, was dumped near Aldergrove Airport last night. Scotland Yard detectives are assisting the local police forces with their inquiries (→26).

Idi Amin of Uganda promotes himself to general and president

Feb 20. Just one month after he seized power, Uganda's dictator, Major-General Idi Amin, today promoted himself to the rank of full general and appointed himself President. A 13-point declaration by leaders of the armed forces endorsed Amin's policies and agreed that he needed to remain in power for five years before elections could be held "in a mood of tranquillity and mutual respect".

The state of emergency imposed by the former President, Dr Milton Obote, has been lifted, but meetings and other political activities are banned and offenders will be "dealt with severely". Amin has ordered the return of the body of King Freddie, the Kabaka of Buganda, who died in exile in London. He will be given a state funeral.

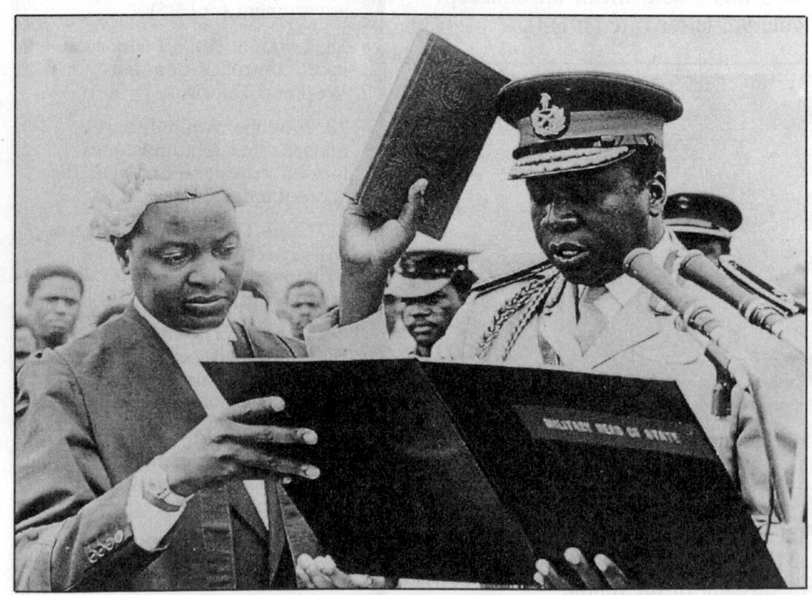

Major-General Idi Amin takes the oath of office in Kampala.

1971

MARCH

Su	Mo	Tu	We	Th	Fr	Sa
	1	2	3	4	5	6
7	8	9	10	11	12	13
14	15	16	17	18	19	20
21	22	23	24	25	26	27
28	29	30	31			

1. UK: 1.5 million workers stage a one-day strike to protest at the Industrial Relations Bill (→8).

4. Canada: Prime Minister Trudeau secretly marries 22-year-old Margaret Sinclair.

6. Cairo: Sadat says he will not extend the cease-fire with Israel which ends today.

8. London: Associated Newspapers announce the closure of the Daily Sketch after 62 years of publication (→9).

8. UK: The postal strike ends when workers vote 14-1 to return to work (→18).

9. London: London Weekend appoints a new chief executive after the IBA tells Murdoch he cannot run LWT and a national paper (→29).

11. Belfast: Following the murder of a milkman in front of his children two days ago, three troops are shot dead (→20).

12. Ankara: The army forces premier Suleyman Demirel to resign.

16. London: Henry Cooper retires after losing his British, European and Commonwealth titles to Joe Bugner.

18. UK: 1.5 million workers stage a second one-day strike in protest at the Industrial Relations Bill (→10/6).

20. Belfast: Ulster Prime minister James Chichester Clark resigns.→

23. Buenos Aires: President Roberto Levingston is toppled by the army in a bloodless coup.

24. London: Lord Olivier takes his seat in the Lords.

29. US: The jury in the trial of Charles Manson votes to send Manson and three women accomplices to the gas chamber.→

29. London: The Government plans Britain's first 60 commercial radio stations (→1/5).

DEATHS

8. US actor and comedian Harold Lloyd (*20/4/1893).

16. US Republican politician Thomas Dewey (*24/3/1902).

Split in Pakistan sparks civil war

March 26. Civil war erupted in East Pakistan today following the broadcast by Sheikh Mujibur Rahman declaring the independent state of Bangladesh. The Sheikh, who won overwhelming support for his nationalist policies in the elections held three months ago, claimed that West Pakistan troops and "the entire police force" had been surrounded in six cities.

Initial reports say that Dacca, capital of the eastern wing, has become a battlefield with tanks and guns in action. The fighting is said to have broken out when West Pakistan troops attempted to disarm men of the East Pakistan Rifles at their barracks in Dacca (→ 5/4).

Rebel Sheikh Mujibur Rahman.

Manson family is sentenced to death

March 29. Murderer Charles Manson and three of his "family" were sentenced to death today in a Los Angeles courtroom for the first degree murders of Sharon Tate, her three guests, a passer-by and Leon and Rosemary LaBianca, in August 1969. Manson, Leslie van Houten, Susan Atkins and Patricia Krenwinkel theoretically face the gas chamber.

In fact, since the death penalty is not currently in use in California, all four will be starting indeterminate sentences on death row.

Calley is guilty of the massacre at Mylai

Lt. William Calley (c.), found guilty of murdering 20 Vietnamese at Mylai.

March 29. Lieutenant William Calley was today found guilty at a court martial of murdering Vietnamese civilians at Mylai in 1968. Calley was found guilty of murder on three charges by a jury of six officers at Fort Benning, Georgia. They rejected his defence that he had been obeying orders.

The jury reduced the number of those Calley was found to have killed in the first two charges. In the fourth the charge was reduced to assault with intent to kill. The jury, which deliberated for 13 days, must now decide Calley's sentence, which can only be either death or life imprisonment.

Three of Calley's senior officers remain to be tried, but two of his juniors have been acquitted and charges have been dropped against 19 others.

Calley said yesterday: "I will be extremely proud if Mylai shows the world what war is" (→ 1/4).

Senate blasted by Laos protest bomb

March 1. Washington was shocked today by the first serious act of sabotage against a federal building for many years. A bomb exploded in the Senate wing of the Capitol half an hour after a telephoned warning, blasting doors off their hinges, shattering windows and cracking walls and floors throughout the building. The person who gave the warning said the device had been planted in protest at current US actions in support of the South Vietnamese invasion of Laos.

Three weeks ago, South Vietnam launched a major operation to try and cut the North Vietnamese supply line, known as the Ho Chi Minh trail. The US is backing the push into Laotian territory with air and artillery cover, but South Vietnamese losses are heavy.

March 6. In London, 4,000 women joined Britain's biggest women's lib march from Hyde Park to No.10 Downing St.

Faulkner becomes new PM of Ulster

March 23. Brian Faulkner, who has worked for over a decade to become Prime Minister of Northern Ireland, finally made it today. After his victory he was buoyant and assured, in striking contrast to the clouds of gloom and doom that now hang over Ulster politics.

James Chichester-Clark, his predecessor, resigned, having been clearly out-manoeuvred on security matters by the British, especially Defence Secretary Lord Carrington. In Parliament he failed utterly to justify his policies in the face of onslaughts by the Rev. Ian Paisley. As a cabinet minister Faulkner has won widespread praise for his competence (→ 11/3).

Winnie Mandela is jailed for a year

March 3. Winnie Mandela, 36, wife of Nelson Mandela, leader of the banned African National Congress, was today sent to jail for a year by a court in Johannesburg. She was found guilty of receiving visitors at her home. A government banning order forbids her to see anyone at her home except a doctor and her two children. Mrs Mandela lodged an appeal and was freed on bail. Her husband is serving a life sentence on Robben Island in Table Bay, Cape Town, for conspiracy to overthrow the South African government by force (→ 22/4).

VAT nudges Britain towards the EEC

March 30. Two years from now purchase tax will be abolished and replaced by value added tax, it was announced today in the first Tory budget since 1964. The switch to VAT will bring Britain into line with the Common Market and is seen in Whitehall as another sign of the Government's eagerness to join the EEC. As for the rest of the budget, it is a tax-cutting bonanza. "Cautious reflation," argued the Chancellor, Anthony Barber. "A nudge in the right direction," said the TUC (→ 10/5).

1971

APRIL

Su	Mo	Tu	We	Th	Fr	Sa
				1	2	3
4	5	6	7	8	9	10
11	12	13	14	15	16	17
18	19	20	21	22	23	24
25	26	27	28	29	30	

1. Washington: Nixon orders the release of Lt. Calley while his conviction for the Mylai Massacre is reviewed (→7).

3. UK: The Grand National is won by Mr F. Pontin's Specify.

5. East Pakistan: Thousands are reported dead in continuing violence; foreigners are being airlifted out.→

7. Washington: Nixon vows to end US involvement in Vietnam and says 100,000 troops will leave by December (→2/5).

11. Londonderry: 10 British soldiers are hurt in riots.→

14. Washington: Nixon eases the trade boycott of China to allow exports of non-military goods (→26).

15. London: The City gives the go-ahead for the building of the £17 million Barbican Arts Centre (→26).

18. Cairo: The UAR, Libya and Syria form a Federation of Arab Republics (→2/9).

19. UK: Figures show unemployment at 814,819, the highest since May 1940 (→14/6).

20. US: The IRA claims it caused the explosion which sank a Royal Navy launch in Baltimore harbour (→26/5).

22. Pretoria: Vorster says South Africa will allow mixed-race sport at international level (→27).

23. USSR: Three cosmonauts are put into orbit in Soyuz 10.

26. Washington: A presidential commission recommends the US seek Chinese entry to the UN in the near future.

28. London: The Times receives a letter bomb from the Angry Brigade.

28. London: The Government says it will study ways to redevelop London's declining docklands.

DEATHS

6. Russian composer Igor Fedorovich Stravinsky (*17/6/1882).→

21. Haitian dictator Dr Francois "Papa Doc" Duvalier (*14/4/1907).→

Pakistan wreaks its vengeance

April 17. The Pakistan army is exacting a bloody revenge on the rebels who last month declared East Pakistan to be the independent state of Bangladesh. The battered and demoralised forces of the "Liberation Army" abandoned their provisional capital of Chaudanga without a fight yesterday and thousands of refugees, fearing for their lives, streamed out of the town towards the Indian border.

There is good reason for their fear. The Pakistan troops are not bothering to distinguish between civilians and fighters; in Dacca alone, some 7,000 people died in two days and nights of indiscriminate shelling.

The attack was aimed at the university and the populous Old City where Sheikh Mujibur Rahman, the separatists' leader, has his strongest following and the industrial outskirts of the city. At the university the burning bodies of students were still lying on their beds. Their dormitories had been hit by tank fire in a surprise attack.

Resistance to the army has been negligible. The green, red and yellow flag of Bangladesh has been torn down from government buildings and replaced by the national flag of Pakistan. Army lorries and armoured cars patrol streets deserted except for the dogs feeding off the sprawled bodies of people caught in the crossfire.

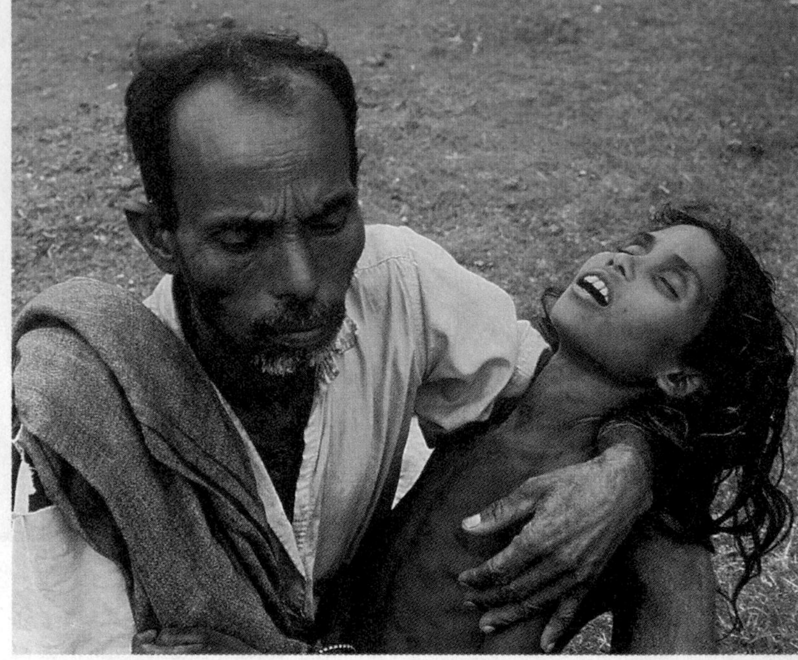

Wholesale slaughter greets the attempted birth of a nation, Bangladesh.

All this is in sad contrast to the high spirits with which the Bangladesh rebels celebrated their independence. Today there is deep bewilderment and bitterness about the indifference, as the Bengalis see it, of the rest of the world to their plight.

Muhammed Eunus Ali, a member of the provincial assembly, asked foreign correspondents: "Why do you do nothing to help us? The outside world says this is an internal affair. How can you say this when thousands of people are being killed? This is not an internal affair. This is a pogrom."

The army has won a war, but destroyed a country. And the story is not over yet (→5/5).

Stravinsky, musical revolutionary, dies

April 6. Igor Stravinsky, the Russian who revolutionised the sound of 20th Century music, died in New York today aged 88. After a Russian Orthodox funeral his body will be flown to Venice for interment on the island of San Michele.

Stravinsky wrote more great ballet scores than anyone since Tchaikovsky, whom he met. He studied under Rimsky-Korsakov but his first ballet, "The Firebird", transformed 19th Century orchestration. It was to write it that he left Russia for Paris at Diaghilev's invitation in 1910. His next scores, for "Petrushka" and "The Rite of Spring", began "modern" music with their hard-edged clarity and rhythm. In 1962 Stravinsky revisited Russia at the age of 80 and was received with honour.

Stravinsky conducting in London.

Provisionals break from Official IRA

April 10. The increasing split within the Irish Republican movement was evident today with two separate marches organised in Belfast to commemorate the Easter Rising of 1916 in Dublin. First on the scene were around 7,000 people organised by the new "provisional" wing of the IRA; then, an hour later, came around 3,500 in the traditional or "official" parade to Milltown Cemetery.

Leaders of the two groups had met earlier today to try and avert open clashes on the streets. The provisional wing of the IRA is believed to be responsible for the more militant campaign of violence now being waged against British forces in Northern Ireland (→20).

1971

MAY

Su	Mo	Tu	We	Th	Fr	Sa
						1
2	3	4	5	6	7	8
9	10	11	12	13	14	15
16	17	18	19	20	21	22
23	24	25	26	27	28	29
30	31					

1. UK: The Daily Mail appears for the last time as a broadsheet newspaper (→11).

2. Washington: Police expel 30,000 anti-war protesters from the banks of the River Potomac (→30/6).

3. East Berlin: Erich Honecker becomes general secretary of the Communist Party in succession to Walter Ulbricht.

5. New Delhi: India appeals for urgent aid for 1.8 million Bangladeshi refugees.→

10. London: 100 Labour MPs defy party policy and sign a declaration supporting British entry into the EEC (→21).

11. UK: The Daily Sketch, Britain's oldest tabloid paper, closes down (→19/6).

12. France: Mick Jagger marries Bianca Perez Morena de Macias in St. Tropez (→1/8).

13. UK: Labour makes big gains in local elections, and takes over the GLC (→15/6).

18. London: The Government announces plans to charge between 10-20 new pence for entry to museums and art galleries.

21. Athens: Chelsea wins the European Cup Winners' Cup, beating Real Madrid 2-1.

21. Paris: Heath and Pompidou end talks, saying the road is clear for British entry to the Common Market (→24/6).

23. Monaco: Jackie Stewart wins the Monaco Grand Prix.

26. Belfast: A soldier is killed and several hurt by a bomb (→8/7).

27. UK: British golfers win the Walker Cup for the first time since 1938.

27. UK: Richard Crossman blasts the Queen's request for a Civil List rise as "truly regal cheek" (→20/8).

28. Cairo: Sadat signs a 15-year friendship treaty with the USSR (→2/9).

30. US: Mariner 9 is launched towards Mars (→7/6).

DEATH

19. US poet Ogden Nash (*19/8/1902).

Baby Doc follows in footsteps of Papa

"Baby Doc" addresses Haiti.

April 22. Francois Duvalier, 61, President of Haiti, died last night and was immediately succeeded by his son, Jean-Claude, a 19-year-old law student.

Elected by the popular vote in 1957 and known fondly as "Papa Doc", the elder Duvalier soon became a ruthless dictator with a private army, the Tontons Macoutes. In 1964 he declared himself President for life. It remains to be seen whether Jean-Claude, called "Baby Doc", will relax at all his father's reign of terror.

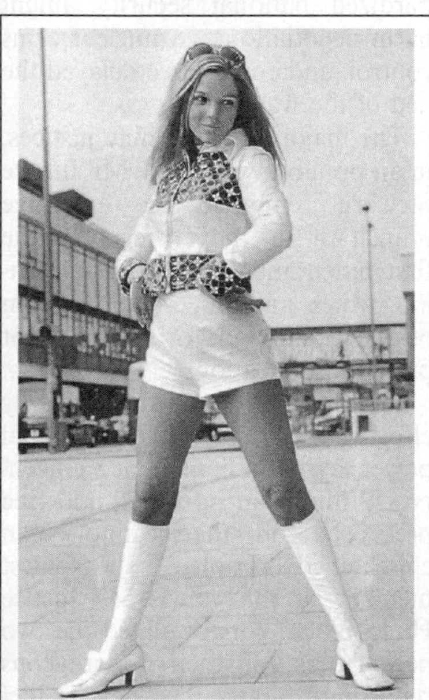

Ladies in hot pants, we are told, will only be allowed to enter the Royal Enclosure at Ascot if the "general effect" is satisfactory.

Sadat foils a coup and purges opponents

May 16. Egyptians poured into the streets of Cairo today to celebrate President Anwar Sadat's broadcast announcement that he had defeated an attempt to overthrow him. Thousands of people demanded the death penalty for those "heads of sedition and conspiracy" plotting a coup. Sadat is moving quickly to consolidate his hold on the country.

The rebels, led by Vice-President Ali Sabry, opposed his plan for a political solution to the conflict with Israel. Among the purged cabinet members and senior officials are Sharawy Gomaa, the Interior Minister, and General Mohammad Fawiz, War Minister. The heads of both of the Egyptian intelligence services have also been swiftly replaced (→28).

Anwar Sadat, on the warpath.

Millions flee from East Pakistan war

May 14. Nearly two million refugees from the fighting in East Pakistan have fled across the border into India where the overworked medical service is struggling to cope with them. The great fear is that the monsoon rains will bring an outbreak of cholera.

"They don't even have straw huts for shelter," said a doctor at one camp, "and it is doubtful whether we could control a cholera epidemic under these conditions. They will die like flies." Food is desperately short, with people waiting hours for a meagre rice ration. A few lucky children get half a cup of milk (→4/6).

Arsenal win FA Cup and League double

May 8. A dramatic 20-yard goal by Charlie George nine minutes from the end of extra time today gave Arsenal the FA Cup. It is only the second League and Cup double this century, emulating Tottenham Hotspurs' feat of 1961.

It was a scrambled 1-0 victory over Tottenham last week that gave Arsenal the League title by a single point over Leeds United. In the tense Cup Final against Liverpool at Wembley, they came close to defeat, going 1-0 down in the first period of extra time. But a scrappy goal touched in by Eddie Kelly, and George's decisive strike clinched the Double.

Controversially sold to an American consortium, London Bridge was transported brick by brick and reassembled at Lake Havasu, Arizona.

1971

JUNE

Su	Mo	Tu	We	Th	Fr	Sa
		1	2	3	4	5
6	7	8	9	10	11	12
13	14	15	16	17	18	19
20	21	22	23	24	25	26
27	28	29	30			

1. UK: It is reported that more people than ever before are refusing to fill in their census returns.

3. Lisbon: A terrorist bomb goes off as NATO foreign ministers begin talks.

4. India: The cholera epidemic in West Bengal is reported to be out of control (→6).

6. India: Mrs Gandhi seals the border with Bangladesh to keep out the refugees (→2/8).

7. USSR: Soyuz 11 docks with the Salyut space station (→30).

8. UK: British Rail approves plans to develop a high-speed "Advanced Passenger Train".

10. UK: Joe Gormley defeats Mick McGahey to become president of the National Union of Mineworkers (→4/8).

11. UK: Terence Rattigan gets a knighthood in the Birthday Honours.

15. UK: Local authorities protest at Education Secretary Mrs Thatcher's plans to end free school milk (→17/11).

17. Malta: Dom Mintoff's Socialists win the general election (→30).

19. UK: Figures show that "Opportunity Knocks" is Britain's most popular TV show, watched by 6.6 million (→9/11).

20. London: Britain grants asylum to space expert Anatol Fedoseyev, one of the most important defectors since 1945.

23. London: The Government says it will extend British motorways by 1,000 miles by the 1980s.

28. Washington: The Supreme Court clears Muhammad Ali of draft-dodging.

30. Malta: Dom Mintoff scraps the 10-year defence treaty with Britain (→20/7).

DEATHS

4. Hungarian philosopher, critic and politician Gyorgy Lukacs (*13/4/1885).

16. British broadcasting pioneer John Charles Walsham Reith, first Baron Reith (*20/7/1889).

EEC agrees terms for UK

June 24. "The back of the negotiations is broken. We have a very satisfactory deal," Geoffrey Rippon, the cabinet's EEC negotiator, told MPs this afternoon. Pro-Marketeers cheered, anti-Marketeers groaned. And everybody knew there will be much more haggling yet.

After a year's tough bargaining Mr Rippon said that there is now agreement on arrangements for British participation with a place equal to that of France, Germany and Italy. He claimed that plans for a transitional period will fully safeguard the interests of not only British farmers and fishermen but also New Zealand's dairy industry.

As for Britain's annual subscription, MPs were told that it will be around £100 millions in 1973 and rising to £200 in 1977. "It is fair and right that we should pay our proper part," said Mr Rippon, in replying to complaints that these sums are higher than expected.

Since President de Gaulle's death France has raised fewer obstacles to Britain joining the EEC, but there is still uneasiness in French government circles. "Things will never be quite the same again," one official said tonight in commenting on the agreement with Britain. The length and complexity of the negotiations has induced boredom in all the capitals. "Can't things be more simply explained?" one MP asked Mr Rippon unavailingly (→4/11).

Cosmonauts found dead in spaceship

June 30. Three Russian cosmonauts were found dead in their spacecraft after an apparently normal flight and landing, Tass announced today. The three – Victor Passayev, Vladislav Volkov and Georgi Dubrovolsky – went into space on June 6 and had established a space endurance record. During their flight they linked their Soyuz spacecraft to an orbiting Salyut laboratory, returning to Soyuz shortly before an apparently normal descent. But all were dead when the recovery team reached them (→2/7).

"Lame duck" policy dooms shipbuilders

June 14. The Government is forcing Upper Clyde Shipbuilders into liquidation, John Davies, the Trade and Industry Secretary, announced in Parliament today. The decision was attacked by Anthony Wedgwood Benn, who as Labour's Technology Minister put £20 million of public funds into the ailing Scottish company. Mr Davies is following his policy of not investing in "lame ducks" – an expression borrowed from Mr Wedgwood Benn who used it three years ago about industry rescues (→19/7).

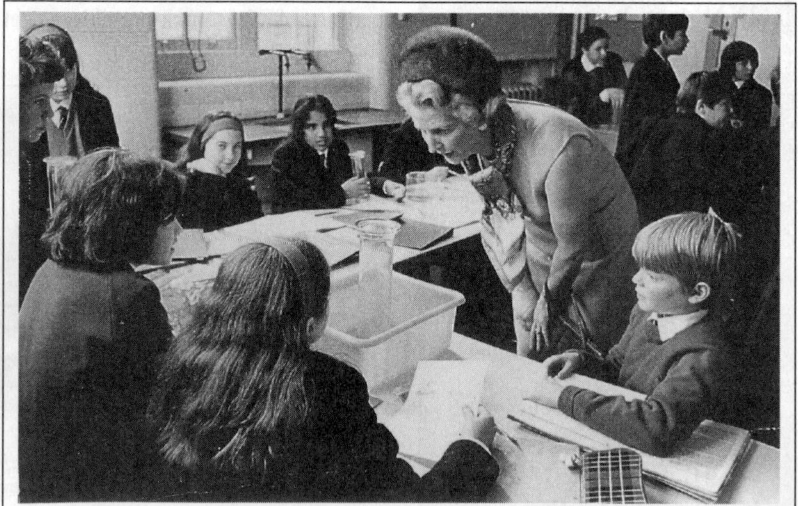

Education Secretary Mrs Margaret Thatcher, who has refused to allow local councils to continue to supply free school milk on the rates.

US press right to print secret papers say Supreme Court

A pleased Pentagon researcher.

June 30. The Supreme Court of the United States decided today that the New York Times and Washington Post are at liberty to publish the secret "Pentagon Papers" on the Vietnam war.

Both newspapers published long extracts from a secret government study of the origins of the war and continuing policy. The Justice Department prosecuted them, on the grounds that publication had jeopardized national security, might harm negotiations on nuclear arms control, and could have delayed the end of the war.

The majority of the nine justices, in an opinion written by Mr Justice Stewart, reminded the executive branch of the government of the first amendment to the Constitution, which guarantees the freedom of the press and forbids restraint prior to publication.

Mr Stewart argued that the only effective restraint on presidential power lay in an enlightened citizenry. "Without an informed and free press," he said "there cannot be an enlightened people." The oldest member of the court, Mr Justice Hugo Black, congratulated the two newspapers for their "courageous reporting". But the new Chief Justice, Warren Burger, was in the dissenting minority. Mr Arthur O. Sulzberger, owner of the New York Times, hailed the judgement as a "landmark" (→15/9).

1971

JULY

Su	Mo	Tu	We	Th	Fr	Sa
				1	2	3
4	5	6	7	8	9	10
11	12	13	14	15	16	17
18	19	20	21	22	23	24
25	26	27	28	29	30	31

1. Portsmouth: Three men are trapped when the submarine HMS Artemis sinks in the harbour.→

2. Moscow: Ten of thousands pay their respects to the dead Soyuz 11 cosmonauts (→26).

2. Portsmouth: Three sailors are rescued from the Artemis.

3. Wimbledon: John Newcombe beats Stan Smith in the Men's Singles final.

6. London: The Government announces that crash helmets are to become compulsory for motorcyclists.

8. Londonderry: A 19-year-old youth is killed in the worst rioting in two years (→12).

10. UK: Lee Trevino wins the British Open Golf Championship.

10. Morocco: King Hassan crushes a coup attempt.

12. Belfast: Seven explosions rock the city centre (→11/8).

14. Jordan: The Jordanian Army launches an all-out attack on Palestinian guerrillas in the country (→15/12).

19. London: A mini-budget slashes purchase tax and abolishes all hire-purchase controls (→1/9).

20. Malta: Anglo-Maltese defence talks collapse after Mintoff demands £20 million annual rent for British bases (→13/8).

22. Khartoum: General Gaafar al-Numeiry is restored to power in a counter-coup four days after being overthrown.

26. US: Apollo 15 is launched carrying three astronauts and a moon-vehicle (→31).

26. France: Riot police on the Riviera order hundreds of topless women to put their bikini tops back on (→16/10).

29. Yugoslavia: Tito is re-elected for another five-year term (→28/10).

30. Japan: 162 die in the worst recorded plane crash (→2/10).

DEATH

6. US singer and trumpeter Louis Armstrong (*4/7/1900).

Astronauts go for drive on the moon

James Irwin checks the Lunar Roving Vehicle or "moon buggy", with Mount Hadley in the background.

July 31. Two astronauts went for a drive on the moon today, picking their way between boulders and craters and covering several miles in their moon "rover", with its communications aerial like an insideout parasol. On board were David Scott and James Irwin, two of the crew of Apollo 15. The third member, Alfred Worden, remains in orbit above. Apollo 15's lunar module Falcon touched down in the Sea of Rains yesterday.

Scott and Irwin left it this morning, becoming the seventh and eighth men to walk on the moon, but the first to drive there. Although their vehicle's front wheel steering did not work, they were able to manoeuvre with the rear wheels. During their drive they turned on TV cameras which gave high quality colour pictures back on earth, showing the astronauts collecting samples on the rim of Elbow Crater. Further trips in the moon rover are scheduled (→7/8).

First heart and lung transplant is made

July 25. A report from South Africa claims that a combined heart and lung transplant has been performed by Christian Barnard, the surgeon who carried out the first human heart transplant in December, 1967.

But Donald Ross, a surgeon at the National Heart Hospital, London, said he knew of no medical development that could justify resumption of transplants. The combined transplant is important, he said "But at the moment we can't even transplant the lungs alone with a reasonable chance of success. With both together the chance is even less. However, I shall be very pleased to be proved wrong."

Graceful Goolagong surprises Wimbledon

July 2. Australia once again took the women's singles title at Wimbledon, though not in the way the experts had expected. The reigning champion, Margaret Court, sailed through to the final as number one seed, only to be stopped in her tracks by a 19-year-old part-aboriginal girl, Evonne Goolagong.

Despite arriving with the French clay-court title under her belt, Miss Goolagong was hardly fancied to match the power of the Courts and the Kings who have reigned at Wimbledon in recent years. Yet, with a graceful ease that enchanted the crowd and the television audience, she beat Billie Jean King in the semi-final and Margaret Court in the final, both in straight sets.

The unflappable Miss Goolagong.

1971

AUGUST

Su	Mo	Tu	We	Th	Fr	Sa
1	2	3	4	5	6	7
8	9	10	11	12	13	14
15	16	17	18	19	20	21
22	23	24	25	26	27	28
29	30	31				

2. Pakistan: The Pakistani army kills 95 Indian soldiers in a border clash.

4. London: MPs approve the Industrial Relations Bill.

5. US: George Wallace says he will run for President in 1972.

6. UK: Chay Blyth returns from the first solo voyage round-the-world in a westerly direction.

7. Pacific: Apollo 15 splashes down safely (→13/11).

9. New Delhi: India and the USSR sign a 20-year defence pact.

11. Plymouth: Edward Heath leads Britain to victory in the Admiral's Cup.→

12. Damascus: Syria breaks off relations with Jordan.

13. Malta: NATO pulls its Mediterranean headquarters out of the island.

15. UK: Harvey Smith wins the British Showjumping Derby but is disqualified for making a two-finger gesture (→17).

15. Bahrain: The emirate becomes independent and signs a friendship treaty with Britain.

17. UK: Harvey Smith's disqualification is overturned.

18. Northern Ireland: Troops shoot dead a deaf mute who ignored an order to stop (→22).

20. UK: Prince Charles gets his wings at RAF Cranwell (→5/11).

22. Bolivia: Right-wing rebels seize power in an army coup.

22. Belfast: An IRA bomb destroys the gates of Crumlin Road prison in protest at alleged brutality (→2/9).

24. London: Crowds invade the pitch as India beat England for their first ever victory in Britain.

28. Greece: 25 die and 1150 are rescued when fire breaks out aboard the Greek liner Haleanna.

DEATH

14. German car manufacturer Georg von Opel (*18/5/1912).

Riots flare in Ulster after internment

Aug 11. Three hundred suspected IRA supporters have been arrested in dawn raids this week in Ulster, as a massive crackdown on terrorists and extremists began. The IRA responded savagely and violently – killing 12 and injuring a large number within a few hours.

The 300 face internment without trial under new emergency powers. Many are being held in a Royal Naval ship in Londonderry, others in local prisons as squads of detectives begin interrogations.

In a further attempt to defuse the situation, the Government has banned all processions – except Remembrance Day Parades – in the province, including the provocative "Apprentice Boys" demonstration in Londonderry.

Ulster's Prime Minister, Brian Faulkner, described the organisations concerned as "those who have murdered in cold blood, created situations which have led to death or injury to people quite uninvolved in disorder, maimed numerous people including young children and put at risk their jobs and the whole future of entire communities."

The internment policy has received a cool reception from the Irish government whose Prime Minister, Jack Lynch, described the move as "a deplorable evidence of the political poverty of Ulster's policies". In London, the shadow Home Secretary, James Callaghan, called for a "Council of All-Ireland" as Ulster faced its worst crisis since 1921. Among today's casualties were a priest, shot while giving the last rites to a dying man, a 15-year-old boy shot by soldiers as he threw a petrol bomb and a soldier shot by a sniper and shot again as he lay on the ground (→12).

The British Army searches suspected terrorists for arms.

IRA threaten to start bombing mainland

Aug 16. As an army chief claimed yesterday that the hard core of IRA gunmen in Ulster had been "virtually defeated", police and Special Branch men stepped up surveillance at British ports for known terrorists. Intelligence sources believe that frustrated IRA "provisionals" are planning a bombing campaign on the British mainland and extra security has been ordered at all military establishments.

In Belfast, Joe Cahill, the city's IRA chief, gave a surprise press conference to refute the army's claim. Only 30 IRA men had been interned, he said – "no more than a pin-prick" (→18).

At the press conference: provisional IRA leader Paddy Cahill (in cloth cap).

Gunmen burn down 7,000 Ulster homes

Aug 12. In four days of violence in Belfast 5,000 Catholics and 2,000 Protestants have had their homes burnt to the ground. In new terror tactics gunmen shot their way into homes, sprinkled the furniture with petrol and set it alight. Some owners were forced into the streets with only the clothes they wore and a loaf of bread and a bottle of milk.

The homeless are being cared for at 18 halls and schools in the city. Many have walked out into the countryside in search of a bed, while others have taken trains to the South where they are being accommodated in camps.

After a cabinet meeting in Dublin, the Irish premier, Jack Lynch, called for the abolition of the Ulster government. Some form of power-sharing between Protestants and Catholics was the only hope for the future, he said (→16).

Best sent off as soccer referees get tough

Aug 18. George Best, Manchester United's wayward genius, has become one of the first victims of the "Referees' revolution" – sent off for persistently arguing with the referee at Stamford Bridge during United's 3-2 defeat of Chelsea.

Best's dismissal gives a clear indication that the FA's determination to bring players' conduct on English grounds into line with that expected on the continent has been put firmly in the hands of League referees. The indulgence so often shown in this country to tactical fouls – the so-called "professional fouls" – deliberate handling of the ball, and abuse of officials will now be replaced with unprecedented severity.

George Best leaves the pitch.

Rock stars raise cash for Bangladesh

Aug 1. Led by the former Beatle, George Harrison, some of rock music's finest artists played and sang for charity tonight at two sold-out shows at Madison Square Garden, New York. More than 40,000 fans attended the two performances, and Harrison hopes to send around $250,000 to help refugees from Bangladesh. Performers included sitar master Ravi Shankar, Eric Clapton and Ringo Starr.

Heath leads Britain to Admiral's Cup win

Aug 11. Edward Heath, skipper of the sloop Morning Cloud, led Britain to team victory in the Admiral's Cup, as all three British yachts completed the 605-mile Fastnet Race – the gruelling climax to the Cup's all-round test of ocean racing – comfortably ahead of their nearest challengers. The Prime Minister, who had elected to race despite the Irish crisis, was at the helm of Morning Cloud as she sailed into Plymouth, the last of the victorious team to finish after losing part of her spinnaker gear off the Scillies.

At the tiller, the Prime Minister sails through the crisis in Ireland.

1971

SEPTEMBER

Su	Mo	Tu	We	Th	Fr	Sa
			1	2	3	4
5	6	7	8	9	10	11
12	13	14	15	16	17	18
19	20	21	22	23	24	25
26	27	28	29	30		

1. UK: 1d. and 3d. coins cease to be legal tender (→23/11).

1. UK: Caledonian-British United Airways changes its name to British Caledonian Airways.

2. Cairo: The UAR reverts to the name Egypt as it joins a Federation of Arab Republics with Syria and Libya.

2. Belfast: 39 are hurt in six bomb blasts; the headquarters of the Unionist Party is wrecked (→3).

3. Belfast: An IRA sniper's bullet kills an 18-month-old girl.→

6. London: The AA says it now costs from £8 to £9 a week to run a family car.

8. Washington: The Kennedy arts centre opens with the premiere of Bernstein's Mass for the late President.

9. New York: Inmates at Attica jail revolt and hold 32 guards hostage.→

12. London: Thieves tunnel into a branch of Lloyd's Bank and steal £500,000.

13. UK: Ten die and 60 are hurt in the worst ever series of motorway accidents.

14. Leningrad: Duke Ellington gets an enthusiastic welcome for his first concert in the USSR.

15. Saigon: 15 die in a bomb blast in a nightclub (→22).

16. Tokyo: Three die as police clash with demonstrators trying to stop the building of Tokyo's second airport.

22. US: Captain Ernest Medina is cleared of all charges connected with the Mylai Massacre (→3/10).

29. London: Chelsea beat Jeunesse Hautcharage 13-0 in the European Cup Winners Cup second round, a European record of 21-0 on aggregate.

30. Belfast: The Official IRA condemns a pub bombing by the Provisionals in which two people were killed (→7/10).

DEATH

11. Soviet statesman Nikita Khrushchev (*17/4/1894).→

Britain expels 90 Russians for spying

Sept 24. Ninety Russian diplomats and officials were expelled from Britain today for spying, following revelations made by a senior KGB defector. The move, which was initiated by the Foreign Secretary, Sir Alec Douglas-Home, is bound to worsen already tense Anglo-Soviet relations. But the British government claims it cannot tolerate the current "hive of Russian intelligence activity" in London.

As a result of the expulsions, the Soviet government is likely to eject British diplomats from Moscow. A visit by Sir Alec to Moscow next year is also in jeopardy (→8/10).

A one-way trip for Russian officials.

Embattled cardinal ends embassy exile

Sept 28. The Roman Catholic Primate of Hungary, Cardinal Jozsef Mindszenty, now aged 79, ended his self-imposed exile today and flew to Rome. The Cardinal was sentenced to life imprisonment by the Communist regime in 1949 on charges of high treason. He was freed during the 1956 rising and after that failed took refuge in the US embassy in Budapest.

He refused to leave there until the charges against him were withdrawn. They have still not been, but the Pope pleaded with him to come to Rome before he died (→18/10). ▷

42 die as prisoners revolt in US prison

Sept 30. A prison riot in New York state which left 32 inmates and ten warders dead is to be investigated by an independent inquiry team, it was announced today. They will study the causes of the revolt which began three weeks ago at the Attica State Correction Facility and lasted for four days. More than 1,000 prisoners took guards hostage, smashed windows and set fire to the building before troops stormed in.

Members of the inquiry team have been chosen for their expertise in the law and penal matters. One member is a former convict who was once sentenced for forgery and drugs offences.

Nikita Khrushchev dies in obscurity

Sept 11. Nikita Khrushchev, the Soviet leader who was ousted seven years ago, died in obscurity in Moscow today, aged 77. He ruled Russia from 1956 to 1964 and was responsible for a dramatic reappraisal of Stalin's image. But his other reforms have been largely curtailed or reversed. He will not be given a state funeral nor be buried at the Kremlin Wall.

British ambassador freed by guerrillas

British Ambassador Geoffrey Jackson is welcomed after his safe release.

Sept 9. Geoffrey Jackson, the 56-year-old British Ambassador to Uruguay, who has been held captive for eight months by the left-wing Tupamaros guerrillas, was released tonight. He was let out of a car on a street corner in the Montevideo suburb of Nuevo Paris.

Father Jose Maria told how he heard a knock on his church door at 8pm and found Mr Jackson standing there, blindfolded, clean-shaven and dressed in a light-weight suit. "He looked very well," he said. Mr Jackson took Communion and offered thanks in the Church of St. Francis of Assisi, while waiting for British officials to collect him. He was then taken to the British hospital.

Earlier this week there was a mass breakout from prison of Tupamaros guerrillas and in Montevideo today it was being said that this might have been "arranged" as part of a deal to secure the ambassador's release. Uruguayan officials, unsurprisingly, deny this.

Premiers meet as Ulster's troubles claim their 100th victim

Sept 7. The death of the 100th victim of the troubles in Ulster yesterday gave a special urgency to today's talks at Chequers between the Prime Minister, Edward Heath, and his Irish opposite number, Jack Lynch.

She was Annette McGavigan, aged 14, who was shot dead in the streets of Londonderry by a bullet from a high velocity rifle when she was caught in the crossfire between the Army and IRA rooftop snipers. As the shooting started, Annette had told a friend that she was going out in the street to find a rubber bullet to add to her collection of riot souvenirs.

William Craig, a right-wing Unionist leader, told a rally in Larne yesterday that there was a desperate need for a new force of 20,000 men to defend Ulster (→ 30).

Peter Gallagher buries his baby daughter Angela, murdered in the troubles.

1971

OCTOBER

Su	Mo	Tu	We	Th	Fr	Sa
					1	2
3	4	5	6	7	8	9
10	11	12	13	14	15	16
17	18	19	20	21	22	23
24	25	26	27	28	29	30
31						

2. Belgium: A British airliner crashes, killing all 63 passengers and crew.

3. UK: Jackie Stewart retains the world motor racing championship.

3. South Vietnam: Nguyen Van Thieu wins another four-year term as President (→ 12/11).

4. Brighton: The Labour Party Conference votes 5-1 against British entry to the EEC on the terms agreed by Heath.→

7. Tel Aviv: Israel bars entry to 21 black Jewish-Americans.

7. Northern Ireland: Another 1,500 troops are sent to the province (→ 23).

8. Peking: Emperor Haile Selassie of Ethiopia has a meeting with Mao.

8. Moscow: The USSR expels five Britons and bars entry to 13 more in response to Britain's expulsion of Russians.

10. US: The US wins the Davis Cup tennis trophy.

16. New York: The French secret service is implicated during investigations into a drug-trafficking scandal.

18. Ottawa: Soviet premier Kosygin is attacked by a man crying "Long Live Hungary!" (→ 23)

23. Northern Ireland: Five people, including two sisters, are shot dead by British soldiers (→ 31).

23. Rome: Exiled Hungarian primate Cardinal Mindszenty leaves to live in Vienna.

26. Argentina: Bobby Fischer beats Tigran Petrosian for a chance to play world chess champion Boris Spassky.

27. Kinshasa: Congo changes its name to Zaire.

28. Washington: Nixon meets Marshal Tito.

30. UK: An opinion poll indicates that most Britons oppose Britain's entry into the Common Market.

31. Singapore: 17 Royal Navy warships leave as Britain's naval Far East Command comes to an end.

US defeated in UN: China in, Formosa out

Oct 25. In a snap vote in the United Nations late tonight the United States policy on the two Chinas was overwhelmingly defeated. The US was hoping that the UN would allow the nationalist regime in Formosa, which the US has consistently supported, to keep its seat, while at the same time admitting Communist China, with whom it is seeking to make peace.

Albania forced a decision on a joint motion expelling Formosa, which the US failed to avoid being put to the vote. When the result of 76 votes against 35 was declared the Tanzanian delegate led a victory dance in front of the Assembly. George Bush, the US delegate, called it "a moment of infamy".

Britain voted against the US. Their delegate, Sir Colin Crowe, said: "It represents a return to reality. It was the right result." In Formosa, President Chiang Kai-shek renewed his vow to overthrow China's Communist regime and said the UN had "bowed to the forces of evil". The Peking government is expected to take its seat next month. President Nixon is due to visit China next year (→15/11).

London crowds greet Hirohito in silence

Prince Philip accompanies Emperor Hirohito to London Zoo.

Oct 9. Emperor Hirohito arrived in Britain on a state visit today to be greeted by large, but curiously silent, crowds as he drove to Buckingham Palace. The Queen told the Emperor: "We cannot pretend that the past did not exist. We cannot pretend that relations between our two peoples have always been peaceful and friendly."

Former prisoners-of-war of the Japanese have called for a boycott of Japanese goods in protest at the Emperor's visit.

Commons votes for UK to join the EEC

Oct 28. By a 356-244 vote MPs tonight approved the cabinet's decision in principle to join the Common Market. Most Tories were for joining, most Labour against. But 69 Labour pro-Marketeers supported Mr Heath's government while 39 Tories voted against (→30).

Post Office Tower is blasted by a bomb

Oct 31. Fears of a new terrorist campaign in the capital have been sparked by a bomb which ripped through the Post Office Tower in central London at 4.30 this morning. The blast tore through an observation platform just under the revolving restaurant, showering debris onto the streets below.

1971

NOVEMBER

Su	Mo	Tu	We	Th	Fr	Sa
	1	2	3	4	5	6
7	8	9	10	11	12	13
14	15	16	17	18	19	20
21	22	23	24	25	26	27
28	29	30				

1. India: Over 5,000 are reported killed and a million homes destroyed when a cyclone hits the state of Orissa.

1. Belfast: Two policemen are shot dead (→7).

3. Washington: Mrs Gandhi arrives for talks with US leaders (→21).

7. Northern Ireland: The IRA shoots dead two off-duty soldiers in County Armagh (→10).

9. London: The BBC is inundated with complaints after a boy uses a four-letter word on "Woman's Hour".

10. Belfast: Two local women are tarred and feathered for dating British soldiers (→12).

12. Washington: Nixon says 45,000 more US troops will be withdrawn from Vietnam by next February (→26/12).

12. Northern Ireland: The Government announces that the Ulster police are to be armed with automatic weapons.→

13. US: NASA says Mariner 9 has gone into orbit around Mars.

15. New York: Delegates from China take their seats at the UN for the first time (→21/12).

16. Peking: Reports emerge that Mao's heir Lin Piao died in a plane crash fleeing to the USSR on September 13.

17. London: Roy Jenkins beats Michael Foot to remain as Labour deputy leader after defying Labour's EEC policy.

18. London: The Queen meets John Profumo for the first time since 1963, at the opening of a residential home (→2/12).

21. India: 90 Indian troops die in border clashes with the Pakistanis.→

23. London: Anthony Barber says £160 million of public money is to go towards cutting unemployment.

28. Rome: 100,000 demonstrators take part in an anti-Fascist march.

29. UK: Seven die in the worst-ever multiple crash on the M1.

Princess Anne wins Sportswoman title

Royalty's sporting superstar.

Nov 5. Princess Anne has been named Sportswoman of the Year by the British Sportswriters Association. The Princess, now aged 21, has emerged as one of Britain's most accomplished all-round riders, and proved her skill in September by winning the European Three-Day Event championship on her horse, Doublet, at Burghley.

She comfortably headed the poll ahead of the world showjumping champion, Ann Moore, and tennis player, Virginia Wade (→18).

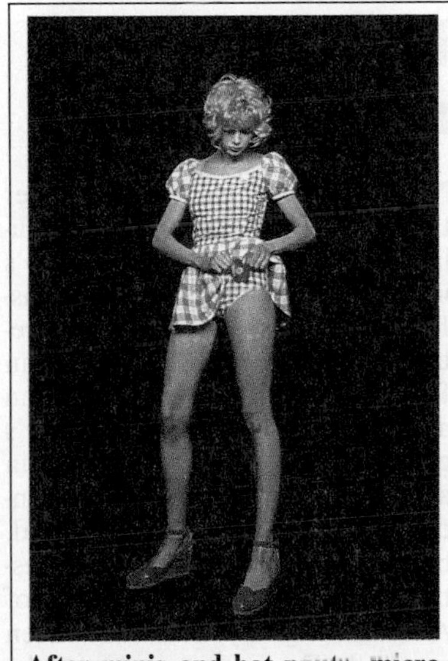

After minis and hot pants, micro skirts are the logical next step.

India and Pakistan clash over border

Nov 23. The continuing clashes along the border between India and East Pakistan are threatening to erupt into full-scale war. Pakistan said tonight: "We have been attacked by India. We are fighting back. We do not know whether a state of war exists."

A Pakistan military spokesman said Indian guns were pounding the airport at Jessore, nearly 30 miles inside East Pakistan, in the second day of heavy fighting. In New Delhi, the Indian government met in emergency session after the shooting down of three Pakistani Sabres over Indian territory (→ 3/12).

Report says Ulster suspects ill-treated

Nov 16. A Government committee has admitted "ill-treatment" but refuted "physical brutality" by security forces to detainees in Ulster. In a report published today, the committee headed by Sir Edmund Compton, Northern Ireland's ombudsman, found that some prisoners were forced during interrogation to stand for hours at a time, others kept in black hoods, subjected to continuous noise and deprived of sleep for long periods. The committee investigated charges by 40 detainees, but only one man gave evidence (→ 20).

Deal to end British rift with Rhodesia

Nov 24. Six years and 13 days after the Rhodesian government unilaterally proclaimed the colony's independence, Sir Alec Douglas-Home, the British Foreign Secretary, and Ian Smith, Rhodesian Prime Minister, today signed an agreement to restore the territory's constitutional links with Britain and pave the way for legal independence. Details were not revealed, but opposition Labour critics question whether the crucial question of African majority rule has been resolved. The settlement has to be approved by "the Rhodesian people as a whole".

1971

DECEMBER

Su	Mo	Tu	We	Th	Fr	Sa
			1	2	3	4
5	6	7	8	9	10	11
12	13	14	15	16	17	18
19	20	21	22	23	24	25
26	27	28	29	30	31	

1. London: MPs approve the Rhodesian settlement.

3. Karachi: Pakistan launches a full-scale war against India; Mrs Ghandi declares a state of emergency (→ 6).

6. New Delhi: India recognises Bangladesh; Pakistan breaks off diplomatic relations with India (→ 9).

9. Dacca: 300 children die when Indian planes bomb an orphanage (→ 14).

10. Stockholm: Nobel Prizes go to Denis Gabor (UK, Physics); Gerhard Herzberg (Canada, Chemistry); Earl Sutherland (US, Medicine); Pablo Neruda (Chile, Literature); Simon Kuznets (US, Economics); and in Oslo to Willy Brandt (W. Germany, Peace).

12. Northern Ireland: Stormont Senator Jack Bernhill is shot dead by the IRA.

14. Dacca: The official government of East Pakistan resigns as Indian troops close in on the city.→

15. London: The Jordanian ambassador escapes a machine-gun attack on his car by Black September guerrillas.

20. Karachi: Zulfikar Ali Bhutto succeeds President Yahya Khan, who resigned yesterday.

25. Seoul: A hotel fire kills 156 people.

26. Vietnam: The US resumes air raids on North Vietnam.

31. Iraq: The government expels thousands of Iranians.

DEATH

18. US golfer Bobby Jones (*17/3/1902).

HITS OF 1971

Chirpy, chirpy, cheep, cheep.

My sweet Lord.

Maggie May.

QUOTE OF THE YEAR

"The most potent weapon in the hands of the aggressor is the mind of the oppressed."

Steve Biko, South African black leader, in a speech.

Kurt Waldheim chosen as new UN chief

Austria's Kurt Waldheim.

Dec 21. A little-known Austrian career diplomat was today appointed UN Secretary-General. After three secret ballots in the Security Council, Dr Kurt Waldheim received 11 votes, with the US, the Soviet Union and France supporting him and Britain abstaining.

Dr Waldheim, aged 53, joined the Austrian Foreign Ministry in the autumn of 1945. His UN career began in 1955 when he was sent to New York to negotiate Austria's entry to the world organisation; in 1964 he became Austrian ambassador to the UN. In Vienna, the officially released biographical notes made no mention of Dr Waldheim's career before he joined the Foreign Ministry in the autumn of 1945.

Queen very amused by large pay rise

Dec 2. The Queen's allowance is to be doubled from £475,000 to £980,000. The rise comes after a study by an all-party Commons select committee. Most of it will go on the wages and salaries of her 375 full-time and 100 part-time staff. The Queen is said to be pleased and a little surprised by the size of the increase.

BP's holdings in Libya nationalised

Dec 7. Libya nationalised the £80 million British Petroleum assets in the country and withdrew all her deposits from British banks tonight. The country's new strong man, Colonel Gaddafi, aged 29, said the move was because Britain had failed to prevent the Persian occupation of three Persian Gulf islands earlier this week.

Christmas bombing campaign hits Ulster

Dec 20. It looks like a bleak holiday for Northern Ireland as the IRA steps up its bombing campaign of major centres like Belfast and Londonderry, now thronged with Christmas shoppers. The whole country has been especially outraged by the bombing of a Belfast public house which killed 15 people and injured another 13.

The British Army has hotly denied allegations by a Republican MP that British intelligence agents were responsible for the outrage, which reduced McGurk's Bar to a heap of rubble. The charge was made by Paddy Kennedy – an opposition MP abstaining from parliamentary duties.

Others have blamed a militant loyalist group for the explosion which killed ten men, three women, a girl and a boy of 13 (→ 12/12).

Yuletide terror, from the IRA.

India defeats Pakistan

Dacca race-track is the scene of public torture, then execution by bayonet.

Dec 17. The two-week war between India and Pakistan ended today in defeat for Pakistan when President Khan swallowed his pride and accepted Mrs Gandhi's cease-fire ultimatum. Pakistan was stunned by his capitulation. Only last night he was insisting that the war would go on until victory had been won despite the loss of East Pakistan.

The President's position must now be in jeopardy as public reaction against the military regime begins to mount. Not only has the regime lost East Pakistan, it has lost the war to the hated Indians.

In the Eastern wing Pakistan's commander, General "Tiger" Niazi, stripped off his badge of rank and surrendered his revolver to the Indian GOC, Lieutenant-General Aurora. In New Delhi it was said that the surrender documents were "in the highest terms of gallantry and chivalry".

General Aurora allowed the vanquished Pakistani troops to keep their arms to avoid being butchered by the bitterly resentful population. Revenge-seeking bands of guerrillas continued to roam the streets yesterday, despite the Indian commander's call for a bloodless transfer of power.

Machine-guns rattled in the heart of Dacca throughout the night and the cheers of the crowds celebrating the birth of Bangladesh turned to screams as fighting broke out between the victorious Mukti Fouj guerrillas and the "razakars" who collaborated with Pakistan.

One razakar, his gun blazing, leaped to his death from the roof of a building as the mob closed on him. Others were hunted down in the streets and slaughtered. Three were killed at the gates of the British High Commission.

India's total casualties in the war were given as 10,633, including 2,307 dead. Pakistani casualties are not yet known but they are believed to be much heavier.

Arts: Man with golden obbligato is dead

The death of **Louis Armstrong** on July 6 ended the first great era of jazz. "Satchmo" was 71 and had been blowing his horn since he was 13, when he learned to play cornet in a home for waifs and strays in New Orleans. Serving his apprenticeship at street funeral parades, he was taken up by **"King" Oliver** and went with his band to Chicago.

It was Louis's brilliant improvisation and personality playing that turned jazz into a soloist's art. From playing with bands – his Hot Five and Hot Seven – he turned to playing in front of them. "They played the tune, he sang the words, then blasted the roof off with his golden obbligato," wrote **Philip Larkin**. "He spoke to the heart of Greenlander and Japanese alike. He had world stature."

He was also described as "the voice of his people, speaking on a horn". The birth of Bop and modern jazz passed him by – he was not an originator. Instead, he made his recording of "Hello Dolly!" the Number One hit of 1964. He was proud of that.

Pop Art, the phenomenon of the Sixties, reached period status this year when the big retrospective of **Andy Warhol** reached the Tate Gallery. Warhol has long left off painting dollar bills, Campbell's soup cans, Brillo boxes, and multiple images of **Jackie Kennedy** or **Marilyn Monroe**. He left the donkey work to his "factory", with its motley crew of weird, drug-taking hangers-on, one of whom, **Valerie Solanas**, shot and nearly killed him in 1968. Warhol became primarily a film-maker – "Chelsea Girls" and "Flesh" were shown privately in London last year. But most of all, he has become a full-time celebrity.

Violence is this year's flavour of the cinema. "The French Connection" took the car chase to the ultimate conclusion and "A Clockwork Orange" was a **Stanley Kubrick** fantasy, owing little to **Anthony Burgess's** novel. **Visconti** was faithful to **Thomas Mann** in his "Death in Venice", although it made Von Aschenbach a composer, not a writer, and drenched the lingering visual images in Mahler.

Peter Brook once more set the theatre by the ears with his circus-ring production of "A Midsummer Night's Dream", which reached London after its triumphs in Stratford and the US. Brook's Puck, in yellow pantaloons, juggles with the love-juice swinging from a trapeze.

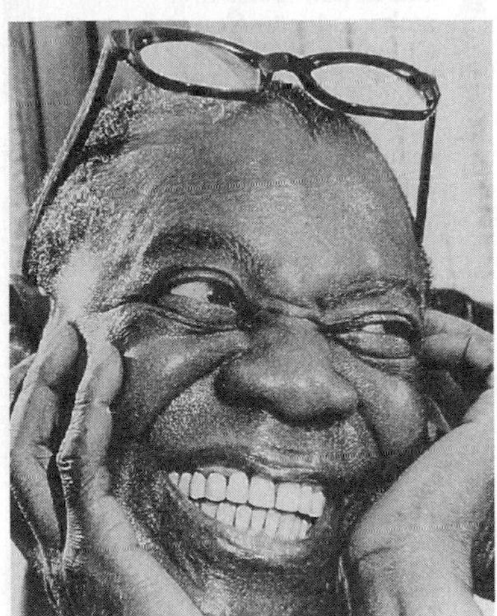

The brilliant smile of a brilliant trumpet-player, Louis Armstrong.

Major airlines threaten to boycott Seoul

Dec 28. All foreign airlines flying into Seoul have joined in a threat to ban tourist flights to the South Korean capital after a Christmas Day fire in a tourist hotel killed 156 and injured 70 others.

Thirty-eight of the victims died jumping from the upper floors of the 22-storey Taeyunyak Hotel, which, like many of the tourist hotels in central Seoul, is not fitted with an outside fire escape and possesses only a minimum of fire-fighting equipment. The fire is believed to have begun when a gas cylinder blew up in a coffee shop on the second floor, which meant that guests on upper storeys had almost no chance of fleeing the flames and heavy smoke as it spread rapidly up the two-year-old building.

The world's major airlines have threatened to halt all flights to Seoul unless the government makes sure that the city's hotels are adequately equipped to avoid a repetition of the tragedy. Meanwhile, the South Korean police say they will issue warrants against the hotel's owner, general manager and coffee shop manager, accusing them of severe negligence.

1972

JANUARY

Su	Mo	Tu	We	Th	Fr	Sa
						1
2	3	4	5	6	7	8
9	10	11	12	13	14	15
16	17	18	19	20	21	22
23	24	25	26	27	28	29
30	31					

3. Belfast: IRA bomb in a department store injures 55 women and children (→27).

5. Washington: Nixon signs a bill granting $5.5 billion to begin space shuttle research (→2/3).

9. Washington: Richard Nixon announces he will stand for re-election as President (→16/5).

9. Hong Kong: Fire destroys the liner Queen Elizabeth, the former symbol of Britain's maritime glory.

9. UK: Miners' strike begins; government urges shops to ration coal supplies (→9/12).

13. London: Britain cuts diplomatic ties with Taiwan and appoints her first ambassador to Communist China (→21/2).

13. UK: Naval officer David Bingham jailed for 21 years for selling secrets to Russia (→29/9).

14. Denmark: King Frederik IX dies and is succeeded by Princess Margrethe.

17. Israel: 350 Soviet Jews arrive.

18. Brussels: Negotiations over British entry into the EEC are completed.→

20. UK: Unemployment rises above a million (→21/3).

24. Moscow: The Soviet Union recognises Bangladesh as a separate nation.

25. London: World's first kidney and pancreatic tissue transplant (→25/1/74).

27. Northern Ireland: Gun battle between IRA and British troops along the Irish border (→30).

30. Pakistan: Government quits the Commonwealth in protest at British plans to recognise Bangladesh.

30. Bolivia: Klaus Barbie, the Gestapo's "Butcher of Lyons", arrives from Peru (→10/3).

DEATHS

1. French actor and singer Maurice Chevalier (*12/9/1888).

14. King Frederik IX of Denmark (*11/3/1899).

Paratroopers fire on Derry marchers

Jan 30. An end to the conflict in Ulster seemed further away than ever today after a civil rights march turned into a riot and British paratroopers opened fire in Londonderry's Bogside, killing 13 men and youths and wounding a further 17.

Opposition MPs described the killings as a "Bloody Sunday" and "mass murder by the British Army", but Major-General Robert Ford, the Army chief, said: "There is absolutely no doubt that the Parachute Battalion opened up only after they were fired on."

The shooting began after a crowd, which tried to storm a street barrier, was dispersed with rubber bullets and purple dye, sprayed from a water cannon. A reporter at the scene said that more than 100 youths hurled sticks, stones and iron bars at the soldiers.

He described a running battle which went on "for more than ten frightening minutes". He said: "I was one of more than 1,000 people lying flat on their faces as the shooting continued".

Many witnesses claimed that the first shots were fired by a loyalist sniper as the MP, Bernadette Devlin, was being introduced. Major-General Ford agreed that the dead "might not have all been killed by our troops". The IRA declared that their immediate policy was "to kill as many British soldiers as possible" (→2/2).

Two of the thirteen victims of "Bloody Sunday" lie on a Bogside street.

Ian Smith arrests former Rhodesian PM

Jan 18. Policemen drove up to the Shabani farm of Garfield Todd, the former Rhodesian Prime Minister, this evening, and told him that he and his daughter Judith were under arrest. The Todds were told the authorities believed they were a threat to public order.

The arrests follow violent demonstrations by Africans against an agreement between Sir Alec Douglas-Home, Britain's Foreign Secretary, and the Rhodesian leader, Ian Smith, for granting legal independence to Rhodesia. Mr Todd, aged 63, and Judith, aged 28, have been campaigning against the agreement (→22/8).

Tugs pour water onto the burning Queen Elizabeth as she stands in Hong Kong harbour; arson is suspected as the cause of the fire on board the former pride of the Cunard fleet, now a floating university.

Sheikh Mujibur to head Bangladesh

The Sheikh talks to journalists.

Jan 12. Sheikh Mujibur Rahman, released from nine months of imprisonment only two days ago, was sworn in today as Prime Minister of the new state of Bangladesh. Given a triumphant homecoming from West Pakistan, he will lead a parliamentary democracy based on British lines (→4/2).

And then there were 10: Britain joins EEC

Jan 22. The Six became Ten today with the signing of the Treaty of Brussels which will bring Britain, Ireland, Denmark and Norway into the European Community as from January 1 next year. The new community will have a population bigger than the United States, a gross national product of nearly £400 billion a year, and 41 per cent of world trade.

The signing did not pass without incident. As the Prime Minister, Edward Heath, went into the Egmont Palace, a plastic bag full of black printer's ink was thrown over him by demonstrators who objected to the Covent Garden redevelopment plans. This was nothing at all to do with the Common Market, but there was also a group of anti-Market demonstrators whose Union Jack was torn in a scuffle with the Belgian police.

The signing is a personal triumph for Edward Heath, who has been active throughout Britain's ten-year struggle for membership. He first had to carry his own party and country, and then to get special terms for Commonwealth butter, meat and sugar (→17/2).

Mr Heath is splattered with ink.

After years of supplication, Britain finally joins the Common Market.

Divorces soar after reform of the law

Jan 19. Petitions for divorce in Britain rocketed from 72,000 to over 100,000 last year, Sir George Baker, President of the Family Division, said today. The rise follows the new 1971 Divorce Reform Act, which allows divorce after set separation periods: two years if both partners consent and five if one doesn't.

Coup turns Ghana into dictatorship

Jan 13. A 40-year-old colonel, trained at the Mons Officer Cadet School in Aldershot, today seized power in Ghana, deposing the Prime Minister, Dr Kofi Busia, who is in London for medical treatment. Colonel Ignatius Acheampong, accusing Dr Busia of arbitrary rule, said he was forming a National Redemption Council.

1972

FEBRUARY

Su	Mo	Tu	We	Th	Fr	Sa
		1	2	3	4	5
6	7	8	9	10	11	12
13	14	15	16	17	18	19
20	21	22	23	24	25	26
27	28	29				

2. Tokyo: Winter Olympics begin.

4. London: Britain recognises Bangladesh as an independent nation (→19/3).

6. Northern Ireland: Civil rights march takes place in Newry (→21).

9. London: State of emergency declared by the Government.→

11. US: Life magazine claims Clifford Irving's autobiography of Howard Hughes is a fake (→13/3).

13. North Vietnam: Intensive bombing campaign by US Air Force (→24).

15. London: 12 nations sign an international convention to stop dumping at sea (→1/4/73).

17. London: Commons pass bill to bring Britain into the EEC (→23/4).

18. US: Californian Supreme Court rules that death penalty is unconstitutional (→8/3).

18. UK: Wilberforce court of inquiry recommends £6 per week pay increase for miners (→25).

21. Peking: Nixon arrives in China.→

21. London: Official inquiry begins into the "Bloody Sunday" killings (→22).

22. Qatar: Crown Prince seizes power in a bloodless coup.

23. Aden: Arab terrorists hijack Lufthansa jumbo flying to New Delhi (→25).

24. Paris: North Vietnamese walk out of Paris peace talks in protest at US bombing campaign (→30/3).

25. UK: Miners vote 27-1 in favour of pay settlement (→2/3).

25. Aden: Hijacked hostages released after West German government pays a $3 million ransom (→9/5).

28. Paris: Demonstrators fight with riot police (→27/6).

DEATHS

5. US poet and critic Marianne Moore (*15/11/1887).

15. US writer Edgar Snow (*19/7/1905).

Britain gropes in the dark as miners' strike start to bite

Feb 16. Total electricity blackouts lasting nine hours were imposed today over virtually the whole country as the crisis over the miners' pay dispute deepens. Since last week industry has officially been working a three-day week, with householders asked to heat only one room.

Power stations are almost all working below capacity, with 12 shut down completely to save fuel. The position has been made graver by the decision, announced today by Ray Buckton of the train drivers' union, that his members will not move oil trains past miners' pickets.

All now hinges on the report of Lord Wilberforce's three-man court of enquiry. It has completed its investigations of the miners' pay claim in less than 48 hours, and will report to the Government by the end of the week (→18).

Newly born, power strike or not.

British Embassy in Dublin is destroyed

Feb 2. A day of anti-British demonstrations in Dublin ended tonight with the burning down of the British Embassy. Firemen were only allowed to tackle the blaze when the roof collapsed.

The demonstration was called as a protest against Sunday's killings of 13 Londonderry Catholics by British Paras (→6).

Treaty crowns Nixon's trip to China

President and Mrs Nixon, obviously enjoying themselves, during their walk along the top of the Great Wall.

Feb 22. President Nixon today urged China to join the United States in a "long march together" on different roads to world peace. The President spoke as a guest of the Chinese Prime Minister, Chou En-lai, at a banquet in the Great Hall of the People in Peking. Earlier he was welcomed by Chou En-lai at the airport, and by Chairman Mao Tse-tung at his house in Peking's Forbidden City.

The speed with which Mr Nixon and his national security adviser, Dr Henry Kissinger, were received by Chairman Mao augurs well for the outcome of the "serious and frank" talks they have begun with Chou En-lai. The biggest single obstacle to the improvement in relations, which it is clear that both sides want, is the status of Taiwan, where the US recognises the Nationalist regime. China insists that diplomatic relations cannot be re-established until the Taiwan problem is solved.

IRA bomb Para headquarters at Aldershot: seven are killed

Feb 22. Six civilians and a priest were killed in an IRA bomb attack on the 16th Parachute Brigade at Aldershot at lunchtime today. The IRA claimed responsibility for the blast, which they said was in revenge for the death of 13 civilians in last month's "Bloody Sunday" battle. No warning was given before the 50-pound bomb, planted in a stolen car, went off.

Five of the dead were women domestic workers preparing food in the kitchens. The others were a gardener, and Catholic padre, Captain Gerry Weston, awarded the MBE for brave service in Ulster. The Army is now tightening security in all its premises, signalling the end of "open barracks" like Aldershot (→ 1/3).

Paratroopers check through the debris of their bomb-devastated barracks.

1972

MARCH

Su	Mo	Tu	We	Th	Fr	Sa
			1	2	3	4
5	6	7	8	9	10	11
12	13	14	15	16	17	18
19	20	21	22	23	24	25
26	27	28	29	30	31	

2. UK: Power cuts end after 20 days of blackouts due to the miners' strike.

3. Jamaica: Michael Manley's Labour Party wins the general election.

7. UK: Soldier tells inquiry into "Bloody Sunday" deaths that he "shot to kill" (→ 21).

8. US: A bomb explodes aboard TWA jet after a phone call demanding $2 million (→ 5/5).

10. Vienna: Jury frees Walter Dejaco, the designer of Auschwitz's gas chambers (→ 7/1/73).

14. Nicaragua: Millionaire recluse Howard Hughes meets President Somoza (→ 16/6).

15. India: Mrs Gandhi's supporters win big majority in state elections (→ 3/7).

19. Bangladesh: Treaty of friendship signed with India (→ 7/3/73).

21. Paris: Yves St. Laurent launches his autumn collection, stressing "Le Look Anglais".

21. London: Income and purchase taxes are reduced in the Budget; a Rolls-Royce is now £340 cheaper (→ 23/6).

22. Washington: Senate passes the Equal Rights Amendment (→ 1/2/73).

26. London: Britain signs seven-year pact with Malta to retain her military bases there.

27. El Salvador: 100 feared dead in failed revolt against the government.

28. Belfast: 100,000 Protestants protest against direct rule (→ 3/4).

29. UK: Transport Workers' Union fined for breaking the new Industrial Relations Act (→ 9/4).

29. Berlin: West Berliners to enter the East for the first time in 20 years (→ 3/6).

30. Vietnam: North launches heaviest attack against South for four years (→ 2/4).

30. Turkey: Terrorists kill three British hostages as police storm their hide-out.

Heath imposes direct rule for Ulster

March 25. By Easter the Stormont Parliament of Northern Ireland will be taken over by the British government and the province will be administered from Whitehall. The intention of Edward Heath, the Prime Minister, is that direct rule will last for at least a year, and the hope is that within that period it will be possible to get both sides working together.

The Prime Minister in a TV broadcast last night said that he saw the new arrangements as giving "a fresh start" to the people of Northern Ireland. His voice was very emotional as he spoke directly to the Irish: "Now is your chance. A chance for fairness, a chance for prosperity, a chance for peace: a chance at last to bring the bombings and killings to an end."

The new Secretary of State, William Whitelaw, will be for all practical purposes the British Consul in Ulster.

Dublin has signalled its approval by restoring diplomatic relations, severed in January. Opposition leaders Harold Wilson and Jeremy Thorpe have promised their support in getting the legislation through. But the Unionists, led by Brian Faulkner, the Prime Minister of Northern Ireland, have angrily condemned the move as a concession to IRA violence. Their Westminster colleagues will oppose the bill.

Loyalist Ulstermen demonstrate against the winding up of Stormont rule.

Shoppers maimed in Belfast bomb blast

March 21. A hoax call in Belfast deliberately steered shoppers and other pedestrians towards a massive explosion today. Six people died and 146 were injured as they observed instructions by security forces to avoid a bomb in a major shopping street. Two off-duty policemen – one of them a Catholic – were shepherding the shoppers to what they thought was "safety" when they and four civilians were blown to pieces.

One witness said: "To see the people crying and to see their wounds was terrible" (→25).

This lucky girl survived the blast, but six other victims were less fortunate.

PM vows to aid boy held in Turkish jail

March 2. The Prime Minister, Edward Heath, vowed tonight to do everything possible to help Timothy Davey, the 14-year-old London boy who has been sentenced to six years in a Turkish jail for conspiring to sell cannabis. Heath said the Turkish government had been "made aware of the deep feelings in this country" over the matter, in view of the boy's age, and he hoped they would show mercy (→11/4).

Army interrogation techniques banned

March 1. The Parker Committee on interrogation procedures in Northern Ireland, set up last November, has now submitted its report. Suspected terrorists, it is alleged, have been hooded and subjected to sleeplessness and constant noise by the security authorities. The recommendation that "intensive" questioning techniques in Ulster should cease is now being considered by the Government (→7).

US launches space probe to Jupiter

March 2. The American Pioneer 10 Spacecraft, launched today, is heading for the most distant goal in space research yet – Jupiter. If all goes well Pioneer will pass within 100,000 miles of the giant planet in December next year, making close-up observations and photographing two-thirds of its surface over a period of four days.

One of the mysteries on which it may throw light is the nature of the Red Spot, a conspicuous feature of the planet. After passing Jupiter, Pioneer will eventually become the first spacecraft to leave the solar system. It has four nuclear generators to power it on its epic journey (→20/4).

Autobiography of Hughes is a hoax

March 13. One of the hoaxes of the century was exposed today when author Clifford Irving admitted to a New York court that he fabricated the "autobiography" of the millionaire recluse Howard Hughes.

Irving was paid $750,000 by McGraw Hill, the publishers, for what he claimed were transcripts of 100 secret interviews with Hughes, some in his own writing. Time Magazine bought the serial rights.

Then the telephone rang. It was Howard Hughes, to say that he did not know Irving from Adam. Irving had gambled on his belief that Hughes, not seen in public for years, would not have the capacity to denounce him (→14).

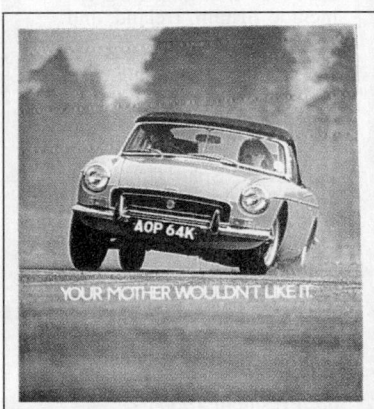

YOUR MOTHER WOULDN'T LIKE IT.

The romance of the sports car is given a fresh meaning by MG.

1972

APRIL

Su	Mo	Tu	We	Th	Fr	Sa
						1
2	3	4	5	6	7	8
9	10	11	12	13	14	15
16	17	18	19	20	21	22
23	24	25	26	27	28	29
30						

2. South Vietnam: Communist forces capture half of Quangtri province (→ 14).

3. Belfast: Catholic women demonstrate in support of the IRA (→ 13).

4. Moscow: Russia refuses a visa for a Swedish official to present Nobel Prize to Solzhenitsyn.

4. London: Police seize arms in raids on 40 East End homes in big operation against organised crime (→ 1/2/74).

6. Cairo: Egypt cuts ties with Jordan in protest at her efforts to build links with Israel (→ 21/6).

9. UK: Merseyside dockers vote to defy court ban on their industrial action (→ 21/7).

10. Argentina: Assassination of General Juan Sanchez and abduction of a Fiat director (→ 17/11).

11. Sweden: Paul McCartney is fined for importing cannabis (→ 19/5/74).

13. Northern Ireland: 23 explosions in the worst day of violence since imposition of direct rule (→ 19).

15. North Vietnam: US launches massive bombing raids on Haiphong (→ 25).

19. UK: "Bloody Sunday" inquiry says troops were provoked, but some fired recklessly (→ 21/5).

20. Moon: Apollo 16 lands (→ 27).

23. France: Referendum approves enlarging EEC to include Britain, Ireland, and Denmark (→ 11/5).

25. Washington: White House says US will resume Vietnam peace talks if North halts her attacks (→ 1/5).

27. Pacific: Splashdown of Apollo 16 (→ 11/7).

DEATHS

9. US Secretary of State and Supreme Court judge James Byrne (*2/5/1879).

27. Ghanaian statesman Kwame Nkrumah, PM 1957-60, President 1960-67 (*21/9/1909).

Nixon steps up bombing of North Vietnam

Citizens of Hanoi inspect the aftermath of another American bomb raid.

April 14. American bombers, including B-52 Strato-Fortresses, pounded Hanoi, the North Vietnamese capital, and its port, Haiphong, today. The targets for the radar-directed planes were fuel dumps and warehouses in Hanoi and port installations in Haiphong, where Russian ships are unloading weapons for the Communist forces in their drive south. This is the first time the US has raided this area since March 1968, and stems from the invasion of the south by North Vietnamese troops. President Nixon signalled the raids last week when he described the invasion as a "naked attack" and sent 20 more B-52s to bolster his 700-plane strike force (→ 15).

Oxford ivory towers to get female touch

April 27. Five of Oxford University's 24 all-male colleges plan to admit women for the first time, it was revealed today. The experiment, to run for an initial five years from October 1974, will involve Brasenose, Jesus, Wadham, Hertford and St. Catherine's – some of the oldest all-male colleges in the University. In all they will allot up to 100 places for women in two years' time.

Trains are at a premium as some railwaymen work to rule, so one commuter made sure that, dignified or not, he would get a seat.

Jenkins quits over referendum plan

April 11. Roy Jenkins resigned as Labour's deputy leader tonight. This was in protest against the decision by Harold Wilson's shadow cabinet to support a call by Tory antiMarket rebels for a referendum on whether Britain should join the Common Market.

Other prominent Labour pro-Marketeers joined him in quitting the Opposition's front-bench team. They included Harold Lever, David Owen and George Thomson. All of them accused their party leader, who had previously criticised the referendum idea, of inconsistency and opportunist vacillation (→ 5/11).

Roy Jenkins, after his resignation.

Couple are first to row across Pacific

April 22. John Fairfax and his girlfriend, Sylvia Cook, landed safe and well on Hayman Island off Australia's Queensland coast tonight, having rowed across the Pacific. They were last seen off the Solomon Islands nearly eight weeks ago, and were feared lost in one of the two cyclones that have swept through the area since.

Their epic voyage has taken them 361 days, starting at San Francisco. Fairfax rowed the Atlantic alone in 1969. Cook is a former London secretary from Ewell, Surrey.

1972

MAY

Su	Mo	Tu	We	Th	Fr	Sa
	1	2	3	4	5	6
7	8	9	10	11	12	13
14	15	16	17	18	19	20
21	22	23	24	25	26	27
28	29	30	31			

1. US: New York Times awarded Pulitzer Prize for publishing Pentagon Papers (→ 3).

3. Vietnam: 150,000 evacuate Hue as Communist forces draw near (→ 10).

3. Burundi: Hundreds killed in tribal uprising (→ 22/6).

5. Italy: 115 die as Alitalia DC-8 crashes (→ 18/6).

6. London: Leeds beat Arsenal 1-0 in the FA Cup final.

9. Jerusalem: Israeli troops storm hijacked jet and free 92 passengers held hostage by Black September guerrillas.

10. Vietnam: US bombs Hanoi and other northern towns; martial law declared in the south (→ 11/8).

11. Argentina: 63 British sailors feared dead in sinking of UK ship.

11. Ireland: Referendum approves entry into EEC (→ 25/9).

13. Japan: 118 die in department store fire.

16. Washington: George Schultz appointed as US Secretary for the Treasury.

18. Paris: Duke of Windsor meets the Queen despite being seriously ill.→

22. Moscow: Nixon arrives in the Soviet Union.→

26. Rotterdam: Amsterdam's Ajax beat Inter Milan 2-0 to win the European Cup.

26. UK: Travel firm Thomas Cook is denationalised.

30. Dublin: Official IRA declare cease-fire, but Provisional IRA say they will continue fighting until British withdraw (→ 12/6).

DEATHS

2. US FBI chief John Edgar Hoover (*1/1/1895).→

22. British poet laureate and novelist Cecil Day Lewis (*27/4/1904).

22. British actress Dame Margaret Rutherford (*11/5/1892).

28. British ex-King Edward VIII, the Duke of Windsor (*23/6/1894).

Gunman fires shots at Governor Wallace

May 16. George Wallace, the segregationist Governor of Alabama, was tonight critically ill in a suburban Washington hospital after an assassination attempt.

A white gunman fired five shots at Governor Wallace as he campaigned in the Maryland Democratic primary election for President. A bullet lodged near Wallace's spine, others in the abdomen and leg. Three other people were hit.

An eyewitness said the gunman kept shouting "Hey, George!" Then he "stuck his gun in his stomach and fired". The Justice Department said last night that Arthur Bremer, aged 21, had been arrested for the shooting (→ 11/7).

George Wallace on the hustings.

Bomb disposal men parachute onto QE2

May 18. Bomb disposal experts parachuted onto the QE2 in mid-Atlantic tonight, after a warning that six bombs were on board. A caller told Cunard's New York office that his accomplices on board, a terminal cancer patient and an ex-convict with a death wish, would detonate the bombs unless a $350,000 ransom was paid.

Cunard, with a 65,000-ton luxury liner and the lives of 1,438 passengers and 950 crew at risk, say they will pay up, but are taking no risks. The unruffled passengers carried on playing bridge after watching the spectacular descent.

Terrorists massacre 25 at Tel Aviv airport

Chaotic aftermath of a massacre.

May 30. Three Japanese killers launched a kamikaze terror raid on passengers at Lod International Airport, Tel Aviv, late last night. Twenty-five people were killed, including a dozen Christian pilgrims to the Holy Land from Puerto Rico.

The hit team arrived on an Air France flight, and passed controls into the baggage hall where they calmly took assault rifles and grenades from their bags and opened fire into the screaming crowds.

Two of them were shot and the third arrested. They are from the Japanese Red Army, trained in Lebanon by Wadi Hadad's Popular Front for the Liberation of Palestine (PFLP). It was their first joint operation (→ 2/6).

FBI director dies after 50-year reign

May 2. John Edgar Hoover, the founder, and for almost 50 years director, of the Federal Bureau of Investigation (FBI), died today in Washington, aged 77.

Hoover first came to public attention as the leader of the "G-men" against the gangs of the 1930s. He greatly developed the use of technical methods of detection, including fingerprints, files and a modern forensic laboratory. After the war, the FBI transferred its attention from Nazi to Soviet spies.

In the 1960s he feuded with both Robert Kennedy and Martin Luther King, but his power was so great that eight presidents retained his services (→ 29/6).

Rangers win the European trophy

May 24. Twenty thousand Glaswegians sang, roared and virtually colonised Barcelona as Glasgow Rangers achieved their first major European honour, the Cup Winners' Cup.

The local police were almost as baffled as Moscow Dynamo as Rangers took an irretrievable 3-0 lead and, at every goal, were enveloped by hordes of delighted fans racing on to the pitch. Dynamo scored twice but failed to deny the the Scots their triumph.

Borne by eight airmen, the Duke of Windsor's coffin comes home.

Nixon and Brezhnev sign Moscow pact

One-time cold warrior Richard Nixon beams as he greets Mr Brezhnev.

May 29. President Nixon and Mr Leonid Brezhnev, the Soviet Communist Party Leader, today acknowledged their major differences, but agreed to do their utmost to avoid military confrontations. At the end of a week-long summit in Moscow the two men signed a document on the basic principles of relations aimed at reducing the danger of a nuclear war.

The talks emphasised the differences between Moscow and Washington on several major international issues, especially the Vietnam war, but there was some agreement on the idea of "reciprocal reductions" in the strength of the NATO and Warsaw Pact forces in Central Europe.

Mr Nixon, who was making the first visit to Moscow by an American President, said in a television address to the Soviet people, for whom he had "great respect", that if the arms race went unchecked there would be no winners, only losers (→ 7/7).

Rival vigilantes battle it out in Belfast

May 21. The crack of gunfire echoed through Belfast's streets today as snipers from both communities fought a running battle. Eight people – one a girl of 13 – were killed as Catholic gunmen from the Ballymurphy Estate exchanged a withering hail of shots with armed Protestants in the adjoning Springmartin Estate.

Three hundred British paratroopers have moved into the district in an attempt to drive a wedge between the two hostile communities. Armoured cars crossed the firing line, and troops took up positions facing both ways, but to little effect.

With the onset of darkness, the battle increased in intensity. Street lights were turned out and families huddled in darkened houses. In the streets, bands of vigilantes hijacked vehicles and set fire to double-decker buses, pushing them into the roads as barricades.

The violence follows the Protestant bombing of a Ballymurphy bar in which a total of 71 people were injured (→ 30).

Masked vigilantes search a youth.

1972

JUNE

Su	Mo	Tu	We	Th	Fr	Sa
				1	2	3
4	5	6	7	8	9	10
11	12	13	14	15	16	17
18	19	20	21	22	23	24
25	26	27	28	29	30	

1. Baghdad: Iraq nationalises London-based Iraq Petroleum Company (→ 1/6/73).

2. Frankfurt: Arrest of the terrorist Andreas Baader.→

3. Berlin: UK, US, USSR and France sign first major accord on the city's status (→ 3/9).

4. US: Black militant Angela Davis acquitted on charges of kidnapping, conspiracy and murder (→ 23/11).

7. UK: Lester Piggott rides Mr J. Galbreath's horse Roberto to victory in the Derby.

8. Rhodesia: 422 miners feared dead after a pit explosion.

11. Tripoli: Colonel Gaddafi says Libya is giving aid to the IRA (→ 2/8).

12. Belfast: Three civilians killed in gun battle between IRA, Army and Protestants (→ 22).

13. Mediterranean: Israeli and Egyptian warplanes clash for the first time in 22 months.

16. London: Court of Appeal quashes fine on Transport Workers' Union and blocks arrest of three dockers for contempt of court.

16. New York: Clifford Irving jailed for 30 months for writing fake Howard Hughes biography.

17. Tokyo: Resignation of Eisaku Sato, Japanese head of state since 1964 (→ 13/3/73).

18. US: Jack Nicklaus wins the US Open, his 13th major golfing victory.

22. Burundi: Thousands of Hutu tribesmen feared killed in reprisal for failed uprising.

27. Northern Ireland: Official IRA begin cease-fire (→ 30).

27. France: Socialist leader Francois Mitterrand forms pact with Communist Party (→ 5/7).

29. Washington: Supreme Court rules death penalty is unconstitutional (→ 15/7/73).

30. Belfast: Protestant groups begin erecting barricades in the city (→ 10/7).

DEATH

8. US blues singer Jimmy Rushing (*26/8/1902).

Duke of Windsor is buried in England

The Duchess in mourning.

June 5. The Duke of Windsor, who as Edward VIII gave up the throne for "the woman I love", was laid to rest today in English soil at Frogmore, near the garden where he played as a boy.

The two-day lying-in-state at St. George's Chapel in Windsor was the only popular spectacle marking the occasion. Thousands gazed silently at the coffin of English oak with its single sheaf of white lilies from the Duchess. The 75-year-old widow sat with the Queen and Prince Philip for the funeral service, screened off from the remainder of the congregation.

Last night the Duchess, slim, frail and alone, left Heathrow, not even pausing at the top of the steps for a last look at the land her husband had given up for her (→ 28/8).

Pound will float on the money markets

June 23. Anthony Barber, the Chancellor of the Exchequer, shocked world financial markets today at 7.55am with a decision to float the pound. The Government is believed to have spent £1,000 million in an effort to stop the slide in the pound caused by speculators selling in the wake of Britain's inflation and industrial unrest (→ 26/9).

Burglars caught in Watergate offices

June 17. Five men were arrested at gunpoint in the Democratic National Committee's offices in the Watergate complex in Washington early this morning. Police said they were attempting to "bug" the opposition party's headquarters with sophisticated electronic surveillance equipment including miniature microphones.

One of the men, James McCord, is the "security co-ordinator" of the Republican committee to re-elect President Nixon. He is a former CIA employee. Two of the others arrested are believed to have had contacts with the CIA and with anti-Castro groups in Florida.

Already it seems that the break-in may become an election issue. Senator Hubert Humphrey, a Democratic candidate, says President Nixon owes the country "an explanation and an apology".

The chairman of the Democratic National Committee, Lawrence O'Brien, said: "This raises the ugliest questions about the integrity of political processes" (→ 1/7).

118 die in worst-ever crash at Heathrow

A solitary Policeman keeps watch over the wreckage of the Trident.

June 18. The worst disaster in British aviation history happened at 5.15pm today. All 118 people aboard a BEA Trident died when the airliner crashed in a field near Staines, minutes after taking off from Heathrow on a flight to Brussels. The plane was full after a scramble for seats caused by tomorrow's threatened pilots' strike.

Eye-witnesses say they heard an enormous thud as the tail broke off and the plane then simply dropped out of the sky, engines spluttering. People who ran to the scene were shocked by the utter silence, no cries for help coming from the wreckage. Only two people were dragged out alive and both died within hours. A Catholic priest administered the last rites to about 60 of the victims (→ 14/8).

These children were playing in their village when American planes dropped napalm, supposedly on the Viet Cong; screaming in pain, one girl with her clothes burnt off her back, they run from their burning homes.

Top "Red Army" terrorist captured

June 16. Ulrike Meinhof, the last leading member of the terrorist "Red Army Faction" still free, was today caught by West German police in Hanover. Andreas Baader, Holger Meins and Carl Raspe were apprehended 15 days ago after a gun battle with police in Frankfurt. The arrests were the result of the biggest German manhunt since 1945.

In the last few weeks, the Baader-Meinhof gang's bombing campaign has caused the deaths of four people, serious injuries to another 36, and a great deal of damage to property (→ 17/7).

Provos and British agree to cease-fire

June 22. The Government has responded favourably to a cease-fire offer by the Provisional IRA, William Whitelaw, the Northern Ireland Secretary, announced tonight. In a statement, the IRA said said it would suspend operations next Monday – "provided that a public reciprocal response is forthcoming from the armed forces of the British Crown".

Mr Whitelaw said the British Army would "reciprocate" in unspecified ways. The IRA leadership is hoping for "meaningful talks between the major parties in the conflict" (→ 27).

Top Syrians taken in Israeli reprisal

June 21. An Israeli patrol making a reprisal raid into Lebanon today was amazed to capture a Syrian general and four colonels from the intelligence service. They were the most senior Syrians to be taken since the Six-Day War in l967.

Israelis seized them when they stormed into the small village of Ramiyeh, a mile and a half from the frontier. Syria said the officers were on an exchange visit to the Lebanese army. Israel struck by land and air at PLO bases in revenge for the terror attack on Lod airport last month (→ 15/10).

1972

JULY

Su	Mo	Tu	We	Th	Fr	Sa
						1
2	3	4	5	6	7	8
9	10	11	12	13	14	15
16	17	18	19	20	21	22
23	24	25	26	27	28	29
30	31					

1. Washington: John Mitchell resigns as Nixon's campaign manager (→ 15/9).

3. Iceland: Bobby Fischer arrives for chess match after British banker adds $125,000 to prize money.→

3. New Delhi: India agrees to withdraw her troops occupying 5,000 square miles of Pakistan (→ 8/4/73).

5. Paris: Gaullist premier Jacques Chaban-Delmas resigns (→ 22/2/73).

6. London: Government sets up inquiry into allegations of corruption by architect John Poulson.→

7. Moscow: US signs science and technology cooperation pact with the Soviet Union (→ 3/10).

8. Wimbledon: Stan Smith beats Ilie Nastase to win the Men's Singles; Billie Jean King beats Evonne Goolagong to win the Women's Singles.

10. London: Home Secretary William Whitelaw admits he secretly met IRA leaders (→ 14).

11. Washington: Apollo 15 astronauts reprimanded for smuggling philatelic souvenirs to the moon and back (→ 11/12).

13. US: George McGovern wins Democratic nomination for President (→ 4/8).

14. Belfast: Four die in fierce fighting after IRA abandon two-week-long cease-fire (→ 18).

15. UK: Lee Trevino wins the British Open golf title.

17. Israel: Japanese terrorist Kozo Okamato jailed for life for airport massacre (→ 4/8).

18. Cairo: Sadat orders the USSR to withdraw her advisers from Egypt (→ 2/2/74).

18. Northern Ireland: A sniper kills the 100th British soldier to die in the province (→ 21).

21. London: Four dockers jailed for contempt of court (→ 28).

21. Belfast: 11 die and 130 are injured in IRA bomb attacks.→

28. UK: Nationwide dock strike begins, despite release of jailed dockers (→ 3/8).

British troops smash Ulster's no-go areas

July 31. In a dawn action named "Operation Motorman", 12,000 troops, supported by tanks and bulldozers, smashed Ulster's "no-go" areas yesterday, ending months of anarchy by extremists from both sides. Late last night police were patrolling districts of Belfast, Londonderry and other main towns which Republican leaders had termed "free Ulster". With guns trained to the rear, tanks moved up as troops began dismantling barricades. In Belfast they were helped by some Catholics and by members of the Ulster Defence Association.

The Army had allowed for as many as 40 civilian casualties in the operation, but their worst fears proved unfounded. Two youths were shot dead and two others injured in a series of short gun battles in Londonderry, but no servicemen were injured. However, the Army had hoped to snare some IRA terrorists when they raided selected addresses but, although 24 people were arrested for having weapons and explosives, they believe the leaders escaped into the Irish Republic.

A British soldier patrols in Ulster.

The worst violence occurred in Claudy, a village nine miles from Londonderry, where six people died when three terrorist car bombs exploded (→ 9/8).

Shock therapy row forces Eagleton to quit

A beleaguered George McGovern.

July 31. Senator Thomas Eagleton of Missouri, chosen only 18 days ago by Senator George McGovern, the Democratic presidential candidate, as his vice-presidential running-mate, has now withdrawn.

Just under a week ago Senator Eagleton admitted he had undergone electric shock therapy twice for depression. At first there were press rumours of a drinking problem. Then McGovern's staff discovered Eagleton had been been in hospital three times for nervous exhaustion.

The resignation is embarrassing for McGovern because he has repeatedly said that he is "1000 per cent" for Eagleton (→ 13).

Home Secretary quits in building scandal

July 18. Reginald Maudling, the Home Secretary, resigned today because of his involvment with John Poulson, the Yorkshire architect. Two weeks ago the Liberal Party raised the issue of the "allegations of financial corruption in public life" in the Poulson bankruptcy hearings. There is now to be a police inquiry and, since the Home Secretary is responsible for the police, Mr Maudling felt he had to resign.

He was chairman of a Poulson company and, although he received no payment, his children and his wife's East Grinstead theatre charity did benefit (→ 22/6/73).

Fischer scores first win in chess battle

July 17. Bobby Fischer, the temperamental contender for the world chess championship in Reykjavik, arrived 15 minutes late for his adjourned match against Russia's Boris Spassky to find an emptying hall and his adversary gone.

Spassky had resigned after opening Fischer's sealed 41st move, Bishop to Queen six, and gone back to his hotel without waiting to shake hands. It is his first defeat at the hands of the 29-year-old American, making the score 2-1 to Spassky. The fourth game in the series starts tomorrow; Fischer needs another 11 and a half games to win the title (→ 1/9).

Fischer arrives for the match.

Top minister died in crash says Mao

July 27. China's Chairman Mao Tse-tung has revealed that his chosen successor, Marshal Lin Piao, died in an air crash last year after fleeing the country in the wake of an abortive coup. Mao said that Lin died when a Chinese Trident airliner crashed in Mongolia in September as he was trying to escape to the Soviet Union. There has since been an official silence about the fate of the marshal. Mao gave no other details of the alleged plot, but reports say Lin was betrayed by his own daughter.

1972

AUGUST

Su	Mo	Tu	We	Th	Fr	Sa
		1	2	3	4	5
6	7	8	9	10	11	12
13	14	15	16	17	18	19
20	21	22	23	24	25	26
27	28	29	30	31		

1. Manila: 356 feared dead in severe flooding.

2. Libya: Sadat and Gaddafi announce plans for federation of Egypt and Libya (→23/7/73).

4. Italy: Black September attack transalpine oil pipeline causing $35 million of damage (→5/9).

4. US: Arthur Bremer jailed for 63 years for shooting George Wallace (→5).

5. Washington: John Kennedy's brother-in-law, Sargent Shriver, chosen as Democrats' vice-presidential candidate. (→2)

9. Belfast: British troops clash with the Protestant Ulster Defence Association for the first time (→19/11).

14. East Berlin: 156 die in plane crash (→24/9).

16. UK: Transport Workers' Union calls off national dock strike (→9/10).

16. Morocco: Failed coup attempt against King Hassan by air force officers (→13/1/73).

17. Holland: World Court rules Iceland should not extend her exclusive fishing zone to 50 miles (→12/9).

20. Vietnam: Southern troops abandon the provincial capital of Queson (→22/9).

22. US: Nixon renominated for President by Republicans (→11/11).

22. Munich: International Olympics Committee expels Rhodesia (→9/1/73).

26. Munich: Opening of the 20th Olympic Games (→31).

28. UK: Prince William of Gloucester killed in an air race (→17/10).

31. Munich: Swimmer Mark Spitz wins five gold medals (→3/9).

DEATHS

26. British yachtsman Sir Francis Chichester (*17/9/1901).

29. German singer and originator of "Lili Marlene" Lale Andersen (*23/3/1905).

US combat troops withdraw from Vietnam

Jeremiah Purdie, a wounded US soldier, is led from a Vietnam battlefield.

Aug 11. The last American ground combat unit in South Vietnam, the 3rd Battalion of the 21st Infantry, packed up its weapons today and left the huge base at Da Nang where the US Marines landed in March 1965 in a "purely defensive role". Within days that role had been changed and the Marines went on the offensive in a war which has cost the United States over 45,000 dead and more than $100 billion.

America's role in the ground war is now at an end. President Nixon, faced with growing domestic unrest, is determined that the war should be "Vietnamised"and all the American troops brought home.

However, this does not end America's involvement in the air war. In the past 24 hours B-52 Stratofortress bombers have carried out the heaviest raids of the war against supply routes feeding the Communists' invasion of the South (→20).

Clydebank shipyard deal faces the axe

Aug 3. Wayne Harbin, the Texan president of Marathon Manufacturing, last night threatened to pull out of the bid for the bankrupt Clydebank shipyard if the unions did not sign the deal by Monday. Harbin flew in early today expecting to complete the deal, which will provide 2,000 jobs for making oil-rigs and platforms.

Last night the boilermakers' union had still not agreed to an arbitration clause. It was their president, Danny McGarvey, who suggested the deal after Upper Clyde Shipbuilders collapsed with debts of £17 million (→16).

Solzhenitsyn urges human rights fight

Aug 24. "One word of truth shall outweigh the whole world" declares Alexander Solzhenitsyn in the Nobel lecture he has not been able to deliver, published today.

He appeals to writers and artists to expose the suppression of human rights and literature throughout the world. He does not name the Soviet Union (→10/12/74).

Amin to expel 50,000 Asians to Britain within three months

Aug 6. Uganda's military dictator, General Idi Amin, caused consternation in London today when he declared that 50,000 Asians with British passports are to be expelled to Britain within three months. Speaking in Kampala, General Amin said the Asians were "sabotaging the economy". A British Home Office official, expressing surprise at Amin's move, said: "We always thought that Amin was a decent chap. After all, he served in the British Army for more than 15 years."

The Asians, who have been settled in East Africa for over a century, form the most prosperous community in Uganda. Last night some were expressing pleasure at their imminent expulsion, since they would be able to enter Britain without delay, instead of having to wait to be included in the 3,500 annual quota (→14/9).

General Idi Amin: British officials thought he was "a decent chap".

1972

SEPTEMBER

Su	Mo	Tu	We	Th	Fr	Sa
					1	2
3	4	5	6	7	8	9
10	11	12	13	14	15	16
17	18	19	20	21	22	23
24	25	26	27	28	29	30

2. Montreal: 22 killed in nightclub bomb attack.

3. West Germany: First air link to East Germany begins (→8/11).

8. Lebanon: Israeli planes bomb ten guerrilla bases in revenge for Munich massacre (→19).

8. Phnom Penh: Rioters attack food markets looking for rice (→17/3/73).

12. North Sea: Icelandic gunboat sinks two British trawlers in first hostilities of the Cod War (→25/10).

14. Washington: US halts $3 million loan to Uganda after Idi Amin praises Hitler (→18).

14. Rome: Pope Paul VI abolishes the tonsure, the circular shaving of the head for monks.

18. Uganda: Invasion by exiles from Tanzania repelled (→21).

19. London: Israeli diplomat killed by letter bomb from Black September; four more are intercepted by police (→29/10).

19. London: Heavy penalties for pornographers proposed by the Longford Committee (→21/6/73).

22. South Vietnam: No US military deaths reported this week for the first time since March 1965 (→11/10).

23. Manila: Martial law declared after attack on minister (→17/5/73).

24. US: 22 die in crash of a private plane into an ice cream parlour in California.

25. Norway: Government resigns after referendum votes against joining the EEC.

29. London: Abolition of Section Two of the Official Secrets Act recommended by the Franks Committee.

DEATH

14. Geoffrey Francis Fisher, Lord Fisher of Lambeth, Archbishop of Canterbury 1945-61 (*5/5/1887).

Israeli Olympic compound is stormed

Sept 5. At dawn today a band of "Black September" Arab guerrillas broke into the Israeli building in the Olympic village near Munich where 10,000 athletes are staying. Over 250 plain clothes police had been brought into the village, following a tip-off of trouble ahead, but none of them saw the Arabs scale the fence.

They burst into the Israeli building with sub-machine guns blazing at 5.10am. Moshe Weinberg, aged 33, a wrestling coach, was killed instantly. Yosef Romano, a weightlifter, was mortally wounded as he held a door shut while two of his teammates escaped through the window. Another 15 also escaped through the windows and side doors. Ten were taken hostage, but one of them, Gad Tsabari, suddenly made a dash for freedom. He wove in and out, dodging bullets. An onlooker said: "He went so fast he would have beaten Borzov, the Russian gold medallist."

The guerrillas demanded the release of 200 Palestinians held in Israeli jails and a safe passage out of Germany. Within hours the Olympic Village was surrounded by 12,000 police. The Olympic Games were suspended and the remaining Israeli team members said they would leave Munich because security measures were inadequate.

The West German Chancellor, Willy Brandt, flew in to take personal charge of negotiations with the terrorists. They were told they would be flown with their hostages to an Arab country. They were taken by helicopter to the Furstenfeld military airport 25 miles from Munich.

Just before midnight the guerrillas and their hostages began to walk across the tarmac to a waiting Boeing 727 aircraft. Suddenly all the airport lights were turned out and German police sharpshooters opened fire.

The rescue attempt failed tragically. In the gun battle all nine hostages were killed, as well as four Arabs and one policeman. Three Arabs were captured and one escaped into the nearby woods.

The guerrillas' name recalls September 1970 when Palestinian organisations were expelled from Jordan by King Hussein. They were responsible for the assassination of Jordan's premier, Wasfi Tell, in Cairo last November, and for the hijack of a Belgian jet last spring (→8).

A masked commando surveys the scene from outside the Israeli building.

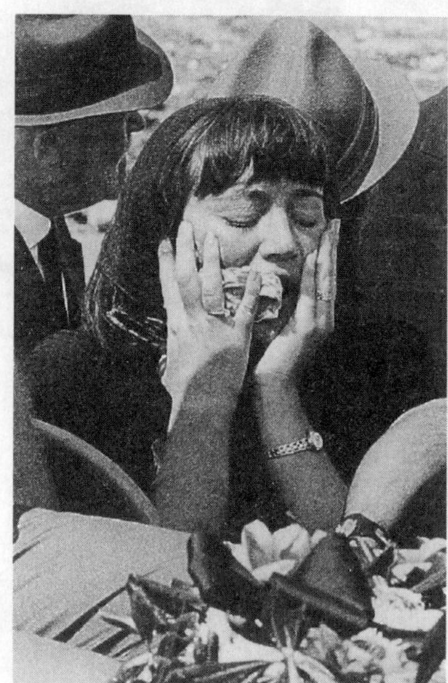

A weeping mourner at Tel Aviv.

German officials acquiesce as a guerrilla dictates his group's demands.

Ugandan Asians flee gauntlet of terror

Sept 21. Asians expelled from Uganda are arriving penniless at Heathrow Airport after being robbed by General Amin's soldiers and officials. Narshi Vadher, a microbiologist, said every shilling was taken from his family as they boarded the plane. Premilla Ladve, an 18-year-old secretary, said £35 was taken from the six in her family. Mr Praful Patel, a member of the British Resettlement Board, said: "I am getting reports all the time of assaults, plundering, threats and bullying."

Tonight, the airlift to London came to a virtual halt after a day of chaos and panic caused by Amin's troops running riot. Asians queuing for passports outside the British High Commission in Kampala fled at the sight of troops coming down the street in lorries. Many Asian families with passports and exit visas are afraid to run the gauntlet of army roadblocks on the 20-mile drive from Kampala to the airport.

The soldiers were set loose after Uganda's Chief Justice gave a judgment which angered Amin. Soldiers seized the judge at gunpoint and took him away yesterday. He has not been seen since. All Kampala's judges have stopped work and some are in hiding (→5/10).

Some of the Asian refugees.

Fischer is first US world chess champ

Sept 1. Bobby Fischer became the world chess champion today by beating the Russian master Boris Spassky, and lived up to his unpunctual reputation by turning up an hour late for the award ceremony.

The decisive 21st game was replayed after Spassky said he had sealed a wrong move, moving his Queen instead of his King. Fischer replied that Spassky was doomed either way, and pulled out a pocket chess set to prove it. Fischer's inventive style has breathed new life into the game, but the Reykjavik crowd still prefers Spassky.

Watergate charges against Nixon aides

Sept 15. Two former White House aides, Howard Hunt and Gordon Liddy, were among seven men indicted in Washington today on charges of conspiring to break into Democratic headquarters in the Watergate building on June 17.

Liddy was a presidential assistant before he went to work for President Nixon's re-election. Hunt is a former CIA officer who writes espionage thrillers. The other five men were caught in the Watergate. A spokesman said there was "absolutely no evidence" that others were involved (→30/1/73).

Keep down pay rises, Heath urges Britain

Sept 26. The Prime Minister, Edward Heath, put forward radical proposals for a voluntary prices and incomes policy in his talks today with the TUC leader, Vic Feather, and the CBI president, Michael Clapham. Meanwhile he called for a £2 limit on pay rises and a five per cent peg on prices.

In a hard-hitting speech to the Press Club tonight Mr Heath said: "We are not prepared to allow inflation to take control of events, with all that would mean for people's lives and for our future." Big pay demands are already in the pipeline. The power workers are asking for an extra £5.50, the dustmen for £4, and the miners for between £4.50 and £7 (→23/10).

Swimmers and gymnasts star at Munich

Sept 11. The shadow of the terrorist gunmen that lay over the last days of the Munich Games took much of the gilt from a superbly staged festival, but it did not prevent a host of new heroes emerging from the least likely quarters.

Never before had the swimmers been much more than a curtain-raiser, yet in Munich the 22-year-old Californian Mark Spitz won seven gold medals – the greatest haul by any athlete in any games.

Never before had the gymnasts evoked more than wonder at their almost unattainable fitness, yet here a cheeky, waif-like bundle of energy, Olga Korbut of the USSR, captivated the crowd with her vulnerable brilliance and proved herself a world-class entertainer.

Never before, until finals night, had the Olympic boxing competition been a focus for world attention, yet at Munich the handsome Cuban giant Teofilo Stevenson was daily attracting professional offers (all brusquely rejected) as he cruised to his gold medal.

In the athletics arena, too, the order was changing. The Africans consolidated the advance they had shown in Mexico City, with the great Kipchoge Keino dabbling in new territory – the steeplechase – and winning it, and John Akii-Bua of Uganda taking the 400m hurdles in a world record.

In the sprints the United States was eclipsed with two double gold medal performances, by the Russian Valery Borzov and the powerful East German Renate Stecher; and in the longer track events the Finns, after 20 years in decline, threw up a surprise winner of the 1500m in Pekka Vasala, and a true world-beater in Lasse Viren, who won both the 10,000m and 5,000m, the former despite falling to the track in the early stages of the final.

For Britain, yachting and eventing gold medals did not entirely make up for failures on the track, though there were few spectators, even among the Germans cheering their own favourite Heide Rosendahl, who were not delighted by the pentathlon victory – in her third Games – by the ever-smiling Mary Peters, who hails from Northern Ireland.

Olga Korbut, gymnast supreme.

America's Mark Spitz, winner of a record seven gold medals in the pool.

1972  Munich

Men Athletics

100m
1. Valery Borzov URS 10.14
2. Robert Taylor USA 10.24
3. Lennox Miller JAM 10.33

200m
1. Valery Borzov URS 20.00
2. Larry Black USA 20.19
3. Pietro Mennea ITA 20.30

400m
1. Vincent Matthews USA 44.66
2. Wayne Collett USA 44.80
3. Julius Sang KEN 44.92

800m
1. David Wottle USA 1:45.9
2. Yevgeni Arzhanov URS 1:45.9
3. Mike Boit KEN 1:46.0

1500m
1. Pekkha Vasala FIN 3:36.3
2. Kipchoge Keino KEN 3:36.8
3. Rod Dixon NZL 3:37.5

5000m
1. Lasse Viren FIN *13:26.4
2. Mohammed Gammoudi TUN 13:27.4
3. Ian Stewart GBR 13:27.6

10,000m
1. Lasse Viren FIN **27:38.4
2. Emiel Puttemans BEL 27:39.6
3. Miruts Yifter ETH 27:41.0

Marathon
1. Frank Shorter USA 2:12:19.8
2. Karel Lismont BEL 2:14:31.8
3. Mamo Wolde ETH 2:15:08.4

110m Hurdles
1. Rodney Milburn USA =**13.24
2. Guy Drut FRA 13.34
3. Thomas Hill USA 13.48

400m Hurdles
1. John Akii-Bua UGA **47.82
2. Ralph Mann USA 48.51
3. David Hemery GBR 48.52

3000m Steeplechase
1. Kipchoge Keino KEN *8:23.6
2. Benjamin Jipcho KEN 8:24.6
3. Tapio Kantanen FIN 8:24.8

4x100m Relay
1. USA **38.19 (Larry Black, Robert Taylor, Gerald Tinker, Eddie Hart)
2. URS 38.50 (Alexandr Kornciuk, Vladimir Lovetski, Yuri Silov, Valeri Borzov)
3. FRG 38.79 (Jobst Kirscht, Karlheinz Klotz, Gerhard Wucherer, Klaus Ehl)

4x400m Relay
1. KEN 2:59.8 (Charles Asati, Hezakiah Nyamau, Robert Ouko, Julius Sang)
2. GBR 3:00.5 (Martin Reynolds, Alan Pascoe, David Hemery, David Jenkins)
3. FRA 3:00.7 (Gilles Bertould, Daniel Valasques, Francis Kerbiriou, Jacques Carette)

20km Walk
1. Peter Frenkel GDR *1:26:42.4
2. Vladimir Golubnichiy URS 1:26:55.2
3. Hans Reimann GDR 1:27:16.6

50km Walk
1. Bernd Kannenberg FRG *3:56:11.6
2. Veniaman Soldatenko URS 3:58:24.0
3. Larry Young USA 4:00:46.0

High Jump
1. Yuri Tarmak URS 2.23
2. Stefan Junge GDR 2.21
3. Dwight Stones USA 2.21

Pole Vault
1. Wolfgang Nordwig GDR *5.50
2. Robert Seagren USA 5.40
3. Jan Johnson USA 5.35

Long Jump
1. Randy Williams USA 8.24
2. Hans Baumgartner FRG 8.18
3. Arnie Robinson USA 8.03

Triple Jump
1. Viktor Saneyev URS 17.35
2. Jörg Drehmel GDR 17.31
3. Nelson Prudencio BRA 17.05

Shotput
1. Wladyslaw Komar POL *21.18
2. George Woods USA 21.17
3. Hartmut Briesenick GDR 21.14

Discus
1. Ludvik Danek TCH 64.40
2. Jay Silvester USA 63.50
3. Rickard Bruch SWE 63.40

Hammer
1. Anatoly Bondarchuk URS 75.50
2. Jochen Sachse GDR 74.96
3. Vasily Khmelevski URS 74.04

Javelin
1. Klaus Wolfermann FRG *90.48
2. Ianis Lusis URS 90.46
3. William Schmidt USA 84.42

Decathlon
1. Nikolai Avilov URS 8454
2. Leonid Litvinenko URS 8035
3. Ryszard Katus POL 7984

Women Athletics

100m
1. Renate Stecher GDR 11.07
2. Raelene Boyle AUS 11.23
3. Silvia Chibas CUB 11.24

200m
1. Renate Stecher GDR =**22.40
2. Raelene Boyle AUS 22.45
3. Irena Szewinska POL 22.74

400m
1. Monika Zehrt GDR *51.08
2. Rita Wilden FRG 51.21
3. Kathy Hammond USA 51.64

800m
1. Hildegard Falck FRG *1:58.55
2. Niole Sabaite URS 1:58.65
3. Gunhild Hoffmeister GDR 1:59.19

1500m
1. Lyudmila Bragina URS **4:01.4
2. Gunhild Hoffmeister GDR 4:02.8
3. Paola Cacchi ITA 4:02.9

100m Hurdles
1. Annelie Ehrhardt GDR **12.59
2. Valeria Bufanu ROM 12.84
3. Karin Balzer GDR 12.90

4x100m Relay
1. FRG =**42.81 (Christiane Krause, Ingrid Mickler, Annegret Richter, Heide Rosendahl)
2. GDR 42.95 (Evelyn Kaufer, Christina Heinich, Bärbel Struppert, Renate Stecher)
3. CUB 43.36 (Marlene Elejarde, Carmen Valdes, Fulgencia Romay, Silvia Chibas)

4x400m Relay
1. GDR **3:23.0 (Dagmar Käsling, Rita Kühne, Helga Seidler, Monika Zehrt)
2. USA 3:25.2 (Mable Fergeson, Madeline Manning, Cheryl Toussaint, Kathy Hammond)
3. FRG 3:26.5 (Anette Rückes, Inge Bödding, Hildegard Falck, Rita Wilden)

High Jump
1. Ulrike Meyfarth FRG =**1.92
2. Yordanka Blagoeva BUL 1.88
3. Ilona Gusenbauer AUT 1.88

Long Jump
1. Heide Rosendhal FRG 6.78
2. Diana Yorgova BUL 6.77
3. Eva Suranova TCH 6.67

Shotput
1. Nadezhda Chizhova URS **21.03
2. Margitta Gummel GDR 20.22
3. Ivenka Hristova BUL 19.35

Discus Throw
1. Faina Melnik URS *66.62
2. Argentina Menis ROM 65.06
3. Vassilika Stoeva BUL 64.34

Javelin
1. Ruth Fuchs GDR *63.88
2. Jacqueline Todten GDR 62.54
3. Kathy Smith USA 59.94

Pentathlon
1. Mary Peters GBR **4801
2. Heide Rosendahl FRG 4791
3. Burglinde Pollak GDR 4768

Men Swimming

100m Freestyle
1. Mark Spitz USA **51.22
2. Jerry Heidenreich USA 51.65
3. Vladimir Bure URS 51.77

200m Freestyle
1. Mark Spitz USA **1:52.78
2. Steven Genter USA 1:53.73
3. Werner Lampe FRG 1:53.99

400m Freestyle
1. Bradford Cooper AUS *4:00.27
2. Steven Genter USA 4:01.94
3. Tom McBreen USA 4:02.64

1500m Freestyle
1. Michael Burton USA **15:52.58
2. Graham Windeatt AUS 15:58.48
3. Douglas Northway USA 16:09.25

100m Backstroke
1. Roland Matthes GDR *56.58
2. Mike Stamm USA 57.70
3. John Murphy USA 58.35

200m Backstroke
1. Roland Matthes GDR =**2:02.82
2. Mike Stamm USA 2:04.09
3. Mitchell Ivey USA 2:04.33

100m Breaststroke
1. Nobutaka Taguchi JAP **1:04.94
2. Tom Bruce USA 1:05.43
3. John Hencken USA 1:05.61

200m Breaststroke
1. John Hencken USA **2:21.55
2. David Wilkie GBR 2:23.67
3. Nobutaka Taguchi JAP 2:23.88

100m Butterfly
1. Mark Spitz USA **54.27
2. Bruce Robertson CAN 55.56
3. Jerry Heidenreich USA 55.74

200m Butterfly
1. Mark Spitz USA **2:00.70
2. Gary Hall USA 2:02.86
3. Robin Backhaus USA 2:03.23

200m Individual Medley
1. Gunnar Larson SWE **2:07.17
2. Tim McKee USA 2:08.37
3. Steven Furniss USA 2:08.45

400m Individual Medley
1. Gunnar Larson SWE *4:31.98
2. Tim McKee USA *4:31.98
3. András Hargitay HUN 4:32.70

4x100m Freestyle Relay
1. USA **3:26.42 (Dave Edgar, John Murphy, Jerry Heidenreich, Mark Spitz)
2. URS 3:29.72 (Vladimir Bure, Viktor Mazanov, Viktor Aboimov, Igor Grivennikov)
3. GDR 3:32.42 (Roland Matthes, Wilfried Hartung, Peter Bruch, Lutz Unger)

4x200m Freestyle Relay
1. USA **7:35.78 (John Kinsella, Frederick Tyler, Steven Genter, Mark Spitz)
2. FRG 7:41.69 (Klaus Steinbach, Werner Lampe, Hans-Gunter Vosseler, Hans Fassnacht)
3. URS 7:45.76 (Igor Grivennikov, Viktor Mazanov, Georgy Kulikov, Vladimir Bure)

4x100m Medley Relay
1. USA **3:48.16 (Mike Stamm, Tom Bruce, Mark Spitz, Jerry Heidenreich)
2. GDR 3:52.12 (Roland Matthes, Klaus Katzur, Hartmut Flöckner, Lutz Unger)
3. CAN 3:52.26 (Eric Fish, William Mahony, Bruce Robertson, Bob Kasting)

Springboard Diving
1. Vladimir Vasin URS 594.09
2. Franco Cagnotto ITA 591.63
3. Craig Lincoln USA 577.29

Platform Diving
1. Klaus Dibiasi ITA 504.12
2. Richard Rydze USA 480.75
3. Franco Cagnotto ITA 475.83

Water Polo

1. Soviet Union
2. Hungary
3. USA

Women Swimming

100m Freestyle
1. Sandra Neilson USA *58.59
2. Shirley Babashoff USA 59.02
3. Shane Gould AUS 59.06

200m Freestyle
1. Shane Gould AUS **2:03.56
2. Shirley Babashoff USA 2:04.33
3. Keena Rothhammer USA 2:04.92

400m Freestyle
1. Shane Gould AUS **4:19.44
2. Novella Calligaris ITA 4:22.44
3. Gudrun Wagner GDR 4:23.11

800m Freestyle
1. Keena Rothhammer USA **8:53.68
2. Shane Gould AUS 8:56.39
3. Novella Calligaris ITA 8:57.46

100m Breaststroke
1. Catherine Carr USA **1:13.58
2. Galina Stepanova URS 1:14.99
3. Beverley Whitfield AUS 1:15.73

200m Breaststroke
1. Beverley Whitfield AUS *2:41.71
2. Dana Schoenfield USA 2:42.05
3. Galina Stepanova URS 2:42.36

100m Backstroke
1. Melissa Belote USA *1:05.78
2. Andrea Gyarmati HUN 1:06.26
3. Susie Atwood USA 1:06.34

200m Backstroke
1. Melissa Belote USA **2:19.19
2. Susie Atwood USA 2:20.38
3. Donna Gurr CAN 2:23.22

100m Butterfly
1. Mayumi Aoki JAP **1:03.34
2. Roswitha Beier GDR 1:03.61
3. Andrea Gyarmati HUN 1:03.73

200m Butterfly
1. Karen Moe USA **2:15.57
2. Lynn Colella USA 2:16.34
3. Ellie Daniel USA 2:16.74

200m Individual Medley
1. Shane Gould AUS **2:23.07
2. Kornelia Ender GDR 2:23.59
3. Lynn Vidali USA 2:24.06

400m Individual Medley
1. Gail Neall AUS **5:02.97
2. Leslie Cliff CAN 5:03.57
3. Novella Calligaris ITA 5:03.99

4x100m Freestyle Relay
1. USA **3:55.19 (Sandra Neilson, Jennifer Kemp, Jane Barkman, Shirley Babashoff)
2. GDR 3:55.55 (Gabriele Wetzko, Andrea Eife, Elke Sehmisch, Kornelia Ender)
3. FRG 3:57.93 (Jutta Weber, Heidemarie Reineck, Gudrun Beckmann, Angela Steinbach)

4x100m Medley Relay
1. USA **4:20.75 (Melissa Belote, Catherine Carr, Deena Deardurff, Sandra Neilson)
2. GDR 4:24.91 (Christine Herbst, Renate Vogel, Roswitha Beier, Kornelia Ender)
3. FRG 4:26.46 (Silke Pielen, Verena Eberle, Gudrun Beckmann, Heidi Reineck)

Springboard Diving
1. Micki King USA 450.03
2. Ulrika Knape SWE 434.19
3. Marina Janicke GDR 430.92

Platform Diving
1. Ulrika Knape SWE 390.00
2. Milena Duchková TCH 370.92
3. Marina Janicke GDR 360.54

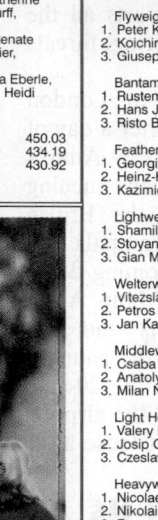

Mary Peters, from Northern Ireland, won the women's pentathlon gold for Great Britain.

Boxing

Light Flyweight
1. György Gedó HUN
2. U Gil Kim PRK
3. Ralph Evans GBR
3. Enrique Rodriguez ESP

Flyweight
1. Georgi Kostadinov BUL
2. Leo Rwabwogo UGA
3. Leszek Blazynski POL
3. Douglas Rodriguez CUB

Bantamweight
1. Orlando Martinez CUB
2. Alfonso Zamora MEX
3. George Turpin GBR
3. Ricardo Carreras USA

Featherweight
1. Boris Kousnetsov URS
2. Philip Waruinge KEN
3. András Botos HUN
3. Clemente Rojas COL

Lightweight
1. Jan Szczepanski POL
2. László Orbán HUN
3. Samuel Mbugua KEN
3. Alfonso Pérez COL

Light Welterweight
1. Ray Seales USA
2. Angel Angelov BUL
3. Zvonimir Vujin YUG
3. Isaaka Daborg NIG

Welterweight
1. Emilio Correa CUB
2. János Kadji HUN
3. Jesse Valdez USA
3. Dick Tiger Murunga KEN

Light Middleweight
1. Dieter Kottysch FRG
2. Wieslaw Rudkowski POL
3. Alan Minter GBR
3. Peter Tiepold GDR

Middleweight
1. Uyacheslav Lemechev URS
2. Reime Vitanen FIN
3. Marvin Johnson USA
3. Prince Amartey GHA

Light Heavyweight
1. Mate Parlov YUG
2. Gilberto Carillo CUB
3. Janusz Gortat POL
3. Isaac Ikhouria NGA

Heavyweight
1. Teófilo Stevenson CUB
2. Ion Alexe ROM
3. Peter Hussing FRG
3. Hasse Thomsen SWE

Greco Roman Wrestling

Light Flyweight
1. Gheorge Berceanu ROM
2. Rahim Aliabadi IRN
3. Stefan Angelov BUL

Flyweight
1. Peter Kirov BUL
2. Koichiro Hirayama JAP
3. Giuseppe Bognanni ITA

Bantamweight
1. Rustem Kazakov URS
2. Hans Jurgen Veil FRG
3. Risto Björlin FIN

Featherweight
1. Georgi Markov BUL
2. Heinz-Helmut Wehling GDR
3. Kazimierz Lipien POL

Lightweight
1. Shamil Khisamutdinov URS
2. Stoyan Apostolov BUL
3. Gian Matteo Ranzi ITA

Welterweight
1. Vitezslav Mácha TCH
2. Petros Galaktopoulos GRE
3. Jan Karlsson SWE

Middleweight
1. Csaba Hegedus HUN
2. Anatoly Nazarenko URS
3. Milan Nenadic YUG

Light Heavyweight
1. Valery Rezantsev URS
2. Josip Corak YUG
3. Czeslaw Kwiencinski POL

Heavyweight
1. Nicolae Martinescu ROM
2. Nikolai Iakovenko URS
3. Ferenc Kiss HUN

Super Heavyweight
1. Anatoly Roshin URS
2. Alexander Tomov BUL
3. Victor Dolipschi ROM

Freestyle Wrestling

Light Flyweight
1. Roman Dimitriev URS
2. Ognyan Nikolov BUL
3. Ebrahim Javadi IRN

Flyweight
1. Kiyomi Kato JAP
2. Arsen Alakhverdiev URS
3. Hyong Kim Gwong PRK

Bantamweight
1. Hideaki Yanagida JAP
2. Richard Sanders USA
3. László Klinga HUN

Featherweight
1. Zagalav Abdulbekov URS
2. Vehbi Akdag TUR
3. Ivan Krustev BUL

Lightweight
1. Dan Gable USA
2. Kikuo Wada JAP
3. Ruslan Ashuraliev URS

Welterweight
1. Wayne Wells USA
2. Jan Karlsson SWE
3. Adolf Seger FRG

Middleweight
1. Levan Tediashvili URS
2. John Peterson USA
3. Vassile Iorga ROM

Light Heavyweight
1. Ben Peterson USA
2. Gennady Strakhov URS
3. Károly Bajkó HUN

Heavyweight
1. Ivan Yarigin URS
2. Khorloo Baianmunkh MON
3. József Csatári HUN

Super Heavyweight
1. Aleksandr Medved URS
2. Osman Duraliev BUL
3. Chris Taylor USA

Judo

Lightweight
1. Takao Kawaguchi JAP
2. Yong-Ik Kim PRK
3. Jean-Jacques Mounier FRA

1972 Munich

Welterweight
1. Toyakazu Normura JAP
2. Anton Zajkowski POL
3. Dietmar Hötger GDR
3. Anatoli Novikov URS

Middleweight
1. Shinobou Sekine JAP
2. Seung-Lip Oh PRK
3. Jean-Paul Coché FRA
3. Brian Jacks GBR

Light Heavyweight
1. Shota Chochoshvili URS
2. David Starbrook GBR
3. Chiaki Ishii BRA
3. Paul Barth FRG

Heavyweight
1. Willem Ruska NETH
2. Klaus Glahn FRG
3. Motoki Nishimura JAP
3. Givi Onashvili URS

Open Category
1. Willem Ruska NETH
2. Vitali Kusnezov URS
3. Jean-Claude Brondani FRA
3. Angelo Parisi GBR

Men Fencing

Foil Individual
1. Witold Woyda POL
2. Jenő Kamuti HUN
3. Christian Noël FRA

Foil Team
1. Poland
2. Soviet Union
3. France

Epée Individual
1. Csaba Fenyvesi HUN
2. Jacques la Degaillerie FRA
3. Győző Kulcsár HUN

Epée Team
1. Hungary
2. Switzerland
3. Soviet Union

Sabre Individual
1. Viktor Sidiak URS
2. Péter Maróth HUN
3. Vladimir Nazlymov URS

Sabre Team
1. Italy
2. Soviet Union
3. Hungary

Women Fencing

Foil Individual
1. Antonella Ragno-Lonzi ITA
2. Ildikó Bóbis HUN
3. Galina Gorokhova URS

Foil Team
1. Soviet Union
2. Hungary
3. Romania

Modern Pentathlon

Individual
1. András Balczó HUN 5412
2. Boris Onischenki URS 5335
3. Pavel Lednev URS 5328

Team
1. Soviet Union 15968
2. Hungary 15348
3. Finland 14812

Men Canoeing

Kayak-1 1000m
1. Aleksandr Shaparenko HUN 3:48.06
2. Rolf Peterson SWE 3:48.38
3. Géza Csapó HUN 3:49.38

Kayak-2 1000m
1. Soviet Union 3:31.23
2. Hungary 3:32.00
3. Poland 3:33.83

Kayak-4 1000m
1. Soviet Union 3:14.02
2. Hungary 3:15.07
3. Norway 3:15.27

Canadian-1 1000m
1. Ivan Patzaichin ROM 4:08.94
2. Tamás Wichmann HUN 4:12.42
3. Detlef Lewe FRG 4:13.63

Canadian-2 1000m
1. Soviet Union 3:52.60
2. Romania 3:52.63
3. Bulgaria 3:58.10

Kayak Slalom
1. Siegbert Horn GDR 268.56
2. Norbert Stattler AUT 270.76
3. Harald Gimpel GDR 277.95

Canadian Slalom
1. Reinhard Eiben GDR 315.84
2. Reinhold Kauder FRG 327.89
3. Jamie McEwan USA 335.95

Canadian Two-Man Slalom
1. German Democratic Republic 310.68
2. German Federal Republic 311.90
3. France 315.10

Women Canoeing

Kayak-1 500m
1. Yulia Ryabchinskaya URS 2:03.17
2. Mieke Jaapies NETH 2:04.03
3. Anna Pfeffer HUN 2:05.50

Kayak-2 500m
1. Soviet Union
2. German Democratic Republic
3. Romania

Kayak Slalom
1. Angelika Bahamnn GDR 364.50
2. Gisela Grothaus FRG 398.15
3. Magdalena Wunderlich FRG 400.50

Rowing

Single Sculls
1. Yuri Malishev URS 7:10.12
2. Alberto Demiddi ARG 7:11.53
3. Wolfgang Güldenpfennig GDR 7:14.45

Double Sculls
1. Soviet Union 7:01.77
2. Norway 7:02.58
3. German Democratic Republic 7:05.55

Coxless Pairs
1. German Democratic Republic 6:53.16
2. Switzerland 6:57.06
3. Netherlands 6:58.70

Coxed Pairs
1. German Democratic Republic 7:17.25
2. Czechoslovakia 7:19.57
3. Romania 7:21.36

Coxless Fours
1. German Democratic Republic 6:24.27
2. New Zealand 6:25.64
3. German Federal Republic 6:28.41

Coxed Fours
1. German Federal Republic 6:31.85
2. GRD 6:33.30
3. Czechoslovakia 6:35.64

Eights
1. New Zealand 6:08.94
2. USA 6:11.61
3. GDR 6:11.67

Sprint
1. Daniel Morelon FRA 11.69/11.25
2. John Nicholson AUS
3. Omari Phakadze URS

2000m Tandem
1. Soviet Union -/10.52/10.60
2. GDR
3. Poland

4000m Individual Pursuit
1. Knut Knudsen NOR 4:45.74
2. Xaver Kurmann SUI 4:51.96
3. Hans Lutz FRG 4:50.80

4000m Team Pursuit
1. German Federal Republic 4:22.14
2. GDR 4:25.25
3. Great Britain 4:23.78

Equestrian Sports

Three Day Event Individual
1. Richard Meade GBR 57.73
2. Alessandro Argenton ITA 43.33
3. Jan Jönsson SWE 39.67

Three Day Event Team
1. Great Britain 95.53
2. USA 10.81
3. German Federal Republic -18.00

Individual Dressage
1. Liselott Linsenhoff FRG 1229.00
2. Elena Petushkova URS 1185.00
3. Josef Neckermann FRG 1177.00

Team Dressage
1. Soviet Union 5095.0
2. German Federal Republic 5083.0
3. Sweden 4849.0

Grand Prix Jumping Individual
1. Graziano Mancinelli ITA
2. Ann Moore GBR
3. Neal Shapiro USA

The USA basketball team mistakenly celebrate a win over the USSR; the game is not over.

Yachting

Finn
1. Serge Maury FRA 58.0
2. Ilias Hatzipavlis GRE 71.0
3. Victor Potapov URS 74.7

Star
1. Australia 28.1
2. Sweden 44.0
3. German Federal Republic 44.4

Flying Dutchman
1. Great Britain 22.7
2. France 40.7
3. German Federal Republic 51.1

Soling
1. USA 8.7
2. Sweden 31.7
3. Canada 47.1

Dragon
1. Australia 13.7
2. GDR 41.7
3. USA 47.7

Cycling

Individual Road Race
1. Hennie Kuiper NETH 4:14.37
2. Kevin Clyde Sefton AUS 4:15:04
3. Bruce Biddle NZL 4:15:04

100km Team Time Trial
1. Soviet Union 2:11:17.8
2. Poland 2:11:47.5
3. Belgium 2:12:36.7

1000m Time Trial
1. Niels Fredborg DEN 1:06.44
2. Daniel Clark AUS 1:06.87
3. Jürgen Schütze GDR 1:07.02

Grand Prix Jumping Team
1. German Federal Republic -32.00
2. USA -32.25
3. Italy -48.00

Shooting

Free Rifle, 300m, 3 Positions
1. Lones Wigger USA 1155
2. Boris Melnik URS 1155
3. Lajos Papp HUN 1149

Small-Bore Rifle, 50m, Prone
1. Ho Jun Li PRK **599
2. Victor Auer USA 598
3. Nicolas Rotaru ROM 598

Small-Bore Rifle, 3 positions
1. John Writer USA **1166
2. Lanny Bassham USA 1157
3. Werner Lippoldt GDR 1153

Moving Target
1. Lakov Zhelezniak URS **569
2. Helmut Bellingrodt COL 565
3. John Kynoch GBR 562

Clay Pigeon (Trench)
1. Angelo Scalzone ITA **199
2. Michel Carrega FRA 198
3. Silvano Bassigni ITA 195

Skeet
1. Konrad Wirnhier FRG 195
2. Yevgeny Petrov URS 195
3. Michael Buchheim GDR 195

Rapid Fire Pistol, 25m
1. Józef Zapedzki POL *595
2. Ladislav Falte TCH 594
3. Victor Torshin URS 593

Free Pistol, 50m
1. Ragnar Skanaker SWE *567
2. Dan Iuga ROM 562
3. Rudolf Dollinger AUT 560

Men Archery

1. John Williams USA **2528
2. Gunnar Jarvil SWE 2481
3. Kyösti Laasonen FIN 2467

Women Archery

1. Doreen Wilber USA **2424
2. Irena Szydlowska POL 2407
3. Imma Gaptchenko URS 2403

Men Gymnastics

All-around Individual
1. Sawao Kato JAP 114.650
2. Eizo Kenmotsu JAP 114.575
3. Akinori Nakayama JAP 114.325

Combined Exercises Team
1. Japan 571.25
2. Soviet Union 564.05
3. GDR 559.70

Parallel Bars
1. Sawao Kato JAP 19.475
2. Shigeru Kasamatsu JAP 19.375
3. Eizo Kenmotsu JAP 19.250

Floor Exercises
1. Nikolai Andrianov URS 19.175
2. Akinori Nakayama JAP 19.125
3. Shigeru Kasamatsu JAP 19.025

Long Horse Vault
1. Klaus Köste GDR 18.850
2. Viktor Klimenko URS 18.825
3. Nikolai Andrianov URS 18.800

Side Horse
1. Viktor Klimenko URS 19.125
2. Sawao Kato JAP 19.000
3. Eizo Kenmotsu JAP 18.950

Horizontal Bar
1. Mitsuo Tsukahara JAP 19.725
2. Sawao Kato JAP 19.525
3. Shogoru Kasamatsu JAP 19.450

Rings
1. Akinori Nakayama JAP 19.350
2. Mikhail Voronin URS 19.275
3. Mitsuo Tsukahara JAP 19.225

Women Gymnastics

All-around Individual
1. Lyudmila Tourischeva URS 77.025
2. Karin Janz GDR 76.875
3. Tamara Lazakovitch URS 76.850

Combined Exercises Team
1. Soviet Union 380.50
2. GDR 376.55
3. Hungary 368.25

Asymmetric Bars
1. Karin Janz GDR 19.675
2. Olga Korbut URS 19.450
3. Erika Zuchold GDR 19.450

Floor Exercises
1. Olga Korbut URS 19.575
1. Lyudmila Tourischeva URS 19.550
3. Tamara Lazakovitch URS 19.450

Side Horse Vault
1. Karin Janz GDR 19.525
2. Erika Zuchold GDR 19.275
2. Lyudmila Tourischeva URS 19.250

Balance Beam
1. Olga Korbut URS 19.400
2. Tamara Lazakovitch URS 19.375
3. Karin Janz GDR 18.975

Handball

1. Yugoslavia
2. Czechoslovakia
3. Romania

Soccer

1. Poland
2. Hungary
3. GDR

Hockey

1. Germany
2. Pakistan
3. India

Basketball

1. Soviet Union
2. USA
3. Cuba

Men Volleyball

1. Japan
2. GDR
3. Soviet Union

Women Volleyball

1. Soviet Union
2. Japan
3. North Korea

(Key to symbols and abbreviations p. 1456)

Weightlifting

		Press	Snatch	Clean and Jerk	Total
Flyweight					
1. Zygmunt Smalcerz	POL	*112.5	100.0	125.0	337.5
2. Lajos Szücs	HUN	107.5	95.0	127.5	330.0
3. Sándor Holczreiter	HUN	112.5	92.5	112.5	327.5
Bantamweight					
1. Imre Földi	HUN	*127.5	107.5	142.5	**377.5
2. Mohammed Nassiri	IRN	*127.5	100.0	142.5	370.0
3. Gennady Chetin	URS	120.0	107.5	140.0	367.5
Featherweight					
1. Norair Nurikian	BUL	*127.5	117.5	**157.5	=**402.5
2. Dito Shanidze	URS	**127.5	120.0	152.5	400.0
3. János Benedek	HUN	125.0	120.0	145.0	390.0
Lightweight					
1. Mukharbi Kirzhinov	URS	147.5	=*135.0	**177.5	**460.0
2. Mladen Kuchev	BUL	**157.5	125.0	167.5	450.0
3. Zbigniew Kaczmarek	POL	145.0	125.0	167.5	437.5
Middleweight					
1. Yordan Bikov	BUL	160.0	140.0	185.0	**485.0
2. Mohamed Trabulsi	LIB	160.0	140.0	172.5	472.5
3. Anselmo Silvino	ITA	155.0	140.0	175.0	470.0
Light Heavyweight					
1. Leif Jenssen	NOR	*172.5	*150.0	185.0	*507.5
2. Norbert Ozimek	POL	165.0	145.0	187.5	497.5
3. György Horváth	HUN	160.0	142.5	*192.5	495.0
Middle Heavyweight					
1. Andon Nikolov	BUL	180.0	155.0	190.0	*525.0
2. Atanas Chopov	BUL	180.0	145.0	192.5	517.5
3. Hans Bettembourg	SWE	182.5	145.0	185.0	512.5
Heavyweight					
1. Jaan Talts	URS	*210.0	165.0	205.0	*580.0
2. Alexander Kraichev	BUL	197.5	162.5	202.5	562.5
3. Stefan Grutzner	GDR	185.0	162.5	207.5	555.0
Super Heavyweight					
1. Vassily Alexeyev	URS	*235.0	*175.0	*230.0	*640.0
2. Rudolf Mang	FRG	225.0	170.0	215.0	610.0
3. Gerd Bonk	GDR	200.0	155.0	217.5	572.5

1972

OCTOBER

Su	Mo	Tu	We	Th	Fr	Sa
1	2	3	4	5	6	7
8	9	10	11	12	13	14
15	16	17	18	19	20	21
22	23	24	25	26	27	28
29	30	31				

2. Denmark: Referendum votes 2-1 in favour of joining the EEC (→21).

5. Somalia: Tanzania and Uganda sign peace pact to end their border war (→9/7/73).

6. Mexico: 147 die and 700 are injured in a train crash.

10. London: John Betjeman is appointed poet laureate.

11. North Vietnam: US bombing raid destroys French embassy in Hanoi (→19).

12. UK: Students shout insults at the Queen during her visit to Stirling University (→23/1/74).

13. Chile: Plane crash strands survivors in the Andes without food supplies (→14).

14. Moscow: 170 die in the Soviet Union's worst civil air disaster (→3/12).

15. Lebanon: Israeli air attacks on guerrilla bases (→30).

17. Yugoslavia: Queen arrives on state visit, the first to a Communist state by a British monarch (→2/3/73).

17. South Korea: Martial law declared in Seoul (→5/8/74).

19. Paris: Kissinger holds peace talks with envoy from North Vietnam.→

22. UK: England's goalkeeper Gordon Banks damages his eyesight in a car crash.

23. UK: Access credit cards introduced (→25).

25. Iceland: Boycott of British goods announced as part of the Cod War (→19/1/73).

25. London: The pound sinks to record low of $2.36 (→6/11).

27. UK: First episode of the TV series, "Colditz".

30. Syria: 50 feared dead after Israeli bombing raid (→22/2/73).

DEATHS

1. British anthropologist Dr Louis Leakey (*7/8/1903).

26. Russian-born US aviation pioneer Igor Sikorsky (*25/5/1889).

Nixon and Gromyko to curb nuclear race

Oct 3. In the White House today Richard Nixon put his signature to two agreements with the Soviet Union which he described as the "first step" towards ensuring a generation of peace. Andrei Gromyko, the Soviet Foreign Minister, spoke of the new accords as "a significant achievement in restraining the arms race".

The first agreement, known as SALT (Strategic Arms Limitation Treaty), limits the US and the Soviet Union to 200 defensive anti-ballistic missiles to be installed at two sites. The other agreement is an interim one on limiting each side's offensive missiles.

Moscow will continue to have a three-to-two superiority in the number of missiles, but the US will have more missiles with multiple warheads. The SALT negotiations were concluded during President Nixon's summit meeting with the Soviet leader Leonid Brezhnev in Moscow last May. Mr Nixon looks forward to an era of detente, underpinned by a web of agreements on trade, cultural and scientific links as well as arms control. After today's signing, Mr Nixon and Mr Gromyko announced they had agreed to open a new round of arms limitation talks in Geneva.

Three days ago, Mr Nixon set up a special ceremony to put his signature to a Congressional resolution endorsing the accords with Moscow. In the midst of all the high-level diplomacy for disarmament and detente, the President has not forgotten he is up for re-election next month (→16/6/73).

Shipworkers win jobs as "work-in" ends

Oct 9. Clydeside workers were planning a victory celebration tonight after they had agreed to end their 15-month "work-in". It began following the collapse of Upper Clyde Shipbuilders. Men declared redundant still reported for work and were paid by a fighting fund raised by the workers, which still has £60,000 in it.

Today Marathon, the Texas company which is taking over the Clydebank yard for building oil-rigs, agreed to take on 1,000 men due to be laid off next month. Wayne Harbin, the Marathon president, has threatened to pull out several times, but today concessions on both sides produced agreement. The unions now expect the entire Clydebank workforce to be taken on by Marathon (→13/2/73).

Leader Jeremy Thorpe with the new MP for Rochdale, Cyril Smith – every inch a Liberal.

Europe's big three look towards union

Oct 21. Weary but pleased after 13 hours of continuous negotiation, the leaders of Europe's three largest nations have proclaimed that European Union will be here by 1980. President Pompidou of France said: "We have the will to make our countries move towards a broader and deeper union."

Edward Heath, the British Prime Minister, said: "We have shown this is a Europe for the people." And Chancellor Willy Brandt underlined West Germany's support for political union.

First moves are likely to be in forging a common foreign policy, with regular meetings of foreign ministers, and in moving towards economic and monetary union and a common currency (→1/1/73).

Vietnam peace is close – Kissinger

Kissinger – on the verge of peace.

Oct 26. Henry Kissinger today declared that "peace is at hand" in Vietnam, and said that a cease-fire could be arranged in just one more session of the Paris peace talks.

This statement by President Nixon's adviser on national security has been welcomed in the United States as a sign that the talks are making progress, but it was also greeted more cynically by some who point out that Mr Nixon is waging an election campaign in which Vietnam is a major issue.

Mr Nixon has promised he will achieve "peace with honor and not peace with surrender", but his Democratic opponent, George McGovern, argues that anti-war activists, not Nixon, will be credited with ending the war (→7/11).

Germans give in to Arab terrorists

Oct 29. The "Black September" guerrilla group, which massacred 11 Israeli athletes at the Olympic Games last month, struck again today. Two Arabs armed with pistols and hand grenades hijacked a Lufthansa Boeing 727 as it flew over Turkey at 6am. They demanded the release of their three colleagues still held for the Olympic massacre. The West German government, unwilling to risk a repetition of last month's bloody battle, gave in (→10/11).

1972

NOVEMBER

Su	Mo	Tu	We	Th	Fr	Sa
			1	2	3	4
5	6	7	8	9	10	11
12	13	14	15	16	17	18
19	20	21	22	23	24	25
26	27	28	29	30		

1. East Germany: 171 political prisoners released.

2. Washington: American Indians seize federal office in protest at government neglect of them.

3. Chile: Allende forms new People's Front government to end wave of strikes (→ 20/3/73).

8. Bonn: West and East Germany agree treaty to normalise relations (→ 19).

10. London: 12 letter bombs sent to Jews by Arab terrorists (→ 6/12).

13. London: 57 nations sign pact to control dumping at sea.

15. London: Kidney donor card scheme announced by the Government (→ 1/4/74).

17. Argentina: Juan Peron returns after 17 years in exile (→ 6/6/73).

17. London: High Court bans Sunday Times from printing articles on thalidomide (→ 29).

19. West Germany: Willy Brandt's SPD government re-elected to power with increased majority (→ 7/6/73).

19. Ireland: Provisional IRA leader Sean MacStiofain arrested by Special Branch (→ 26).

22. Vietnam: First US B-52 shot down (→ 18/12).

23. UK: John Berger wins Booker Prize; says he will share it with the Black Panther Movement (→ 15/10/74).

26. UK: Race Relations Act comes into force; employers can no longer discriminate on grounds of colour.

26. Dublin: Hospital shoot-out as police stop IRA from freeing their captured leader (→ 1/12).

DEATHS

1. US poet Ezra Pound (*30/10/1885).

30. British author Sir Compton Mackenzie (*17/1/1883).

It's Nixon by a landslide

Four more years – the Republican winners, and their wives, enjoy success.

Nov 7. President Richard Nixon obliterated the challenge from the Democratic candidate, Senator George McGovern, today when he won re-election by a huge majority. He lost only Massachusetts and the District of Columbia. In the popular vote, Nixon won 47 million votes, against 29 million for the Democratic candidate, while in the electoral college McGovern won only 17 votes, against 520 for Nixon. In a televised address tonight Mr Nixon called on Americans to "get on with the great tasks that lie before us", and pledged himself to work for "peace with honor in Vietnam". Spiro Agnew is again to be Nixon's Vice-President.

Only 55.7 per cent of eligible voters used their votes, the lowest percentage since President Truman was elected in 1948 (→ 26/12).

Heath puts 90-day freeze on wages, prices and rents

Nov 6. The Government today announced an immediate compulsory prices and wages freeze. This follows the failure of the CBI and TUC to agree on a voluntary deal to curb inflation.

The Prime Minister, Edward Heath, told MPs that the standstill, initially for 90 days but with a possible 60-day extension, will also cover dividends and rents. Emergency legislation will be rushed through Parliament. The Prime Minister confessed disappointment at having to go back on a promise not to repeat the last Labour government's statutory wage control. Leading a few Tory rebels, Enoch Powell asked him: "Have you taken leave of your senses?". Vic Feather, the TUC General-Secretary, said: "It would have been wiser to continue discussions".

Mr Heath acted after a total of 64 hours of negotiations with leaders of both sides of industry failed to produce a pay restraint deal. Many "beat the freeze" wage settlements were hurriedly cobbled together immediately before the Prime Minister's announcement. These included 16 per cent for Fleet Street printers (→ 17/1/73).

US tries to bomb North Vietnam back to the conference table

Nov 7. American hopes of peace in Vietnam are rising, in the belief that the intensified US bombing campaign has done so much damage to the North Vietnamese economy that Hanoi will soon be forced to agree to a cease-fire.

It is suggested that the damage is so great that President Nixon will be able to win better terms from the Communists than was thought possible before the offensive started. "Even if the bombs don't coerce the enemy into successful peace talks," said one officer, "they're destroying his will to fight."

Others dispute this assessment, doubting that the bombing will drive Hanoi to weakness at the conference table and suggesting that its political repercussions in America will weaken the United States' position at the table (→ 22).

Massive craters link piles of rubble amidst the ruins of bombed Hanoi.

Cash for victims of thalidomide drug

Nov 29. Three million pounds of public money is to be made available for the benefit of congenitally disabled children, including the victims of the drug thalidomide.

Announcing the move the Minister of Health, Sir Keith Joseph, said it was not intended as compensation but as a supplement to services already being provided. Various legal cases involving Distillers (Biochemicals), who marketed the drug in Britain, are still sub judice. As soon as they are resolved the Government will consider donating a sum similar to the £3 million in trust (→13/12).

Oldest human skull is found in Kenya

Nov 9. A skull 2.6 million years old with human characteristics found in Kenya may be the earliest "missing link" in human ancestry yet discovered. The skull, found in fragments near Lake Rudolf, was shown in London today by Richard Leakey, director of the National Museum of Kenya.

The brain capacity of the skull is 800cc, much higher than that of other early hominids, though it is well below the 1450cc of modern man. It could be a link between the ape-like australopithecines and the more recent homo erectus, an undoubted human ancestor.

Top Soviet scientist joins protest group

Nov 20. One of Russia's greatest nuclear physicists, the Academician Andrei Sakharov, has joined 50 other Soviet civil rights campaigners and liberal intellectuals in urging the Kremlin to abolish the death penalty and free all political prisoners. Sakharov, who has been in the forefront of the human rights movement in the Soviet Union, has formed a committee for the campaign. Another member is Mstislav Rostropovich, the cellist; but despite their efforts, the KGB is continuing its current crackdown on dissidents (→26/3/73).

1972

DECEMBER

Su	Mo	Tu	We	Th	Fr	Sa
					1	2
3	4	5	6	7	8	9
10	11	12	13	14	15	16
17	18	19	20	21	22	23
24	25	26	27	28	29	30
31						

1. Dublin: Two die in bomb blasts; Dail votes through tough anti-terrorist law (→4/1/73).

2. Australia: Labour Party wins general election (→24/11).

3. Canary Islands: 155 die in the worst crash in Spanish aviation history (→24).

4. Honduras: Army topples President Ramon Cruz.

7. UK: Liberals overturn big Tory majority to win Sutton and Cheam by-election (→18/1/73).

10. Stockholm: Nobel Prizes go to John Schrieffer, John Barden, Leon Cooper (US, Physics); Christian Anfinsen, Stanford Moore, William Stein (US, Chemistry); Rodney Porter (UK), Gerald Edelman (US), both Medicine; Heinrich Boell (Germany, Literature); Kenneth Arrow (US), Sir John Hicks (UK, Economics). No Peace Prize.

11. Moon: Two Apollo 17 astronauts land (→14/5/73).

13. UK: Distillers offers £11.25 million compensation to the thalidomide victims (→5/1/73).

18. North Vietnam: Massive bombing of Hanoi by B-52s (→30).

22. UK: Manchester United appoint Tommy Docherty as their new manager.

29. US: Life Magazine is published for the last time.

DEATHS

23. Soviet aviation pioneer Andrei Tupolev (*10/11/1888).

26. US statesman Harry S. Truman, President 1945-53 (*8/5/1884).→

HITS OF 1972

Amazing grace

Mouldy old dough

Puppy love

QUOTE OF THE YEAR

"Today I am one trillionth part of history."

Arthur Bremer, on his attempt to assassinate George Wallace.

Day of mourning as Harry S. Truman dies

Dec 26. Harry S. Truman, the 33rd President of the United States, died today in a hospital in Kansas City. He was 88. Truman was catapulted into the presidency as a virtual unknown when Franklin D. Roosevelt died in 1945. Truman, the Vice-President, said he felt as if the moon and the stars had fallen on him. As a senator he was attacked for his links with the Democratic political machine. Yet this former haberdasher from Missouri proved a courageous president. He stood up to Stalin, built up US military power and US alliances, and defied the pollsters to be re-elected in his own right in 1948 to lead America in the Korean War (→20/1/73).

Truman plays for Lauren Bacall.

Nixon orders halt to Hanoi bombing

Dec 30. President Nixon today ordered the suspension of the American air offensive against Hanoi, capital of North Vietnam, after 12 days of the heaviest raids of the whole war by B-52 Stratofortress bombers. This blitz was mounted in order to bomb the North Vietnamese negotiators back to the table at the Paris peace talks.

In spite of considerable losses of American aircraft, this tactic seems to have worked. There is a hint of progress in the air which is expected to become more tangible when Henry Kissinger, now Secretary of State, meets Le Duc Tho, Hanoi's representative, in Paris next week (→15/1/73).

Angry Brigade are jailed for ten years

Dec 6. Four members of the Angry Brigade, the revolutionary group, who were involved in a series of bombings between 1968-71, were each jailed for ten years at the Old Bailey today. Sentencing John Barker, James Greenfield, Anna Mendelson and Hilary Creek, all in their early twenties, Mr Justice James said: "I am sorry to see such intelligent and educated people in your situation. Undoubtedly a warped understanding of sociology has brought you to the state in which you are."

Four others were acquitted after the 111-day trial in which the jury took 52 hours to reach the majority verdicts (→20/2/73).

One of the new "Granada" cars which are to be built in a number of Ford factories throughout Europe; this one comes from Spain.

Earthquake kills 10,000

What remains of Managua, after the earthquake hit Nicaragua's capital.

Dec 25. Up to 10,000 people are feared dead after the Nicaraguan capital of Managua was shattered by earthquake tremors lasting two hours today. The quake sparked off huge fires. Survivors who joined a massive exodus from the rubble described their ordeal as like "the end of the world". Buzzards are circling overhead as relief workers burn bodies with petrol and dig rough graves. In the stifling, dusty air the stench of decomposing corpses has become unbearable.

Despite the extent of the chaos in the city, where two-thirds of all buildings were destroyed, scores of families refuse to join the refugees, but the government is planning to force them to leave their homes by cutting off food supplies. Troops are prepared to clear the ruins at gunpoint if necessary, as looting is spreading amid the rubble.

Westerners caught up in the quake included the industrialist and reclusive millionaire Howard Hughes, one of 3,000 Americans. He is reported to be safe, and 100 Britons also escaped injury during Managua's third big earthquake in 76 years.

Arts: Betjeman is dumbfounded Laureate

The appointment of a new Poet Laureate to succeed the late **C. Day Lewis** came as a surprise – not least to the Laureate himself. **Sir John Betjeman** said he was "dumbfounded". "When I was asked if I would accept, I thought there were better poets than me and they might be annoyed," he explained.

But there is no more popular choice than Betjeman, whose work sells better than any living poet has since Tennyson. His evocations of the Middlesex suburbs, gymkhana girls, seaside golf, church mice and "How to Get On in Society" may be written to entertain, but there is a sombre and melancholy strain in much of his work. His verse autobiography, "Summoned by Bells" (1960), was far from the blithe personality he shows on television.

"Poetry should be life-enhancing. It should also be turned on the enemies of the public, such as developers and people who think only in terms of money," he declared.

Sir Compton Mackenzie, who died at the age of 89 with about 100 books to his name, came from a family of actors – the Comptons – and no one knew better than he how to play the part of a man of letters, with his pointed beard, constant pipe and elegant drawl.

"Sinister Street", a novel of his schooldays and young manhood, made his name in 1913 because its outspokenness upset the libraries. His memory had perfect recall from the age of two. His autobiography ran to an unwieldy ten volumes.

King Tut: exhibition of the year.

The talents of **Andrew Lloyd-Webber** and **Tim Rice**, first noticed in a musical, "Joseph and his Technicolour Dreamcoat", have moved from the Old to the New Testament in "Jesus Christ Superstar" – a hit whose title caused religious picketing on the first night. Hero of the show: Judas Iscariot. Like the devil he has the best tunes.

Film of the year: **Francis Ford Coppola's** "The Godfather", in which **Marlon Brando** plays the murderous Mafia chief as a good Italian family man.

Andes plane crash survivors ate the dead

Dec 29. Sixteen survivors of a Uruguayan plane, which crashed in the Andes on October 13, only stayed alive by eating the bodies of passengers who died. Speaking at a press conference in Montevideo today, Sr Alfredo Delegado told reporters: "If Jesus, in the Last Supper, offered his body and blood to all the apostles, he was giving us to understand that we must do the same."

Of the 45 people on board, 29 died in the crash. The remainder, mainly members of a rugby team, the Old Christians, were trapped for ten weeks on a remote Andean mountain. Finally, two of them made a ten-day forced march down the mountain to find help. When rescuers arrived at the crash site, they found six butchered corpses. The 16 men had eaten all their food within 48 hours of the crash and their leader, a medical student, Roberto Canessa, convinced them they could live only by taking in protein. Such protein is found in human bodies, and they kept alive by eating one every five days. Before starting their grim task, the men marked out a gigantic cross in the snow, to justify themselves before God. Theologians agree that cannibalism was justifiable in these circumstances and the Archbishop of Montevideo attended the press conference. Nonetheless, opinions in Uruguay remain sharply divided (→22/1/73).

Woody Allen in "Everything you always wanted to know about sex ..."

1973

JANUARY

Su	Mo	Tu	We	Th	Fr	Sa
	1	2	3	4	5	6
7	8	9	10	11	12	13
14	15	16	17	18	19	20
21	22	23	24	25	26	27
28	29	30	31			

1. Europe: Britain, Ireland, and Denmark become members of the EEC (→ 8/6).

4. Londonderry: 400 children attack British troops (→ 28).

7. US: Hitler's car is sold for $153,000 at an Arizona auction (→ 4/4).

9. Rhodesia: Government closes Zambian border to try to halt guerrilla attacks (→ 6/7).

11. UK: The Open University awards its first degrees to 867 students.

12. Cairo: Yassir Arafat re-elected PLO leader (→ 2/5).

13. Morocco: 13 air force officers executed for assassination attempt on King Hassan.

15. US: Nixon orders a halt to the bombing of Vietnam.→

17. London: "Phase II" of the Government's pay and prices freeze announced (→ 22).

17. Manila: President Marcos extends his term of office indefinitely.

18. UK: Eleven Clay Cross councillors are surcharged for refusing to increase council house rents (→ 12/4).

19. UK: A British super tug is sent to protect fishing boats from Icelandic gunboats (→ 18/3).

20. Washington: President Nixon sworn in for a second term in office (→ 22).

22. Nigeria: 180 die in crash of pilgrimage plane (→ 5/3).

22. London: Share values fall £4,000 million in a day (→ 22/3).

23. Iceland: 7,000 evacuated as volcano erupts.

28. Londonderry: Troops use plastic bullets to break up riots marking anniversary of "Bloody Sunday" (→ 4/2).

30. US: Pan Am and TWA scrap plans to buy 13 Concordes.

DEATHS

22. US statesman Lyndon Baines Johnson, President 1963-69 (*27/8/1908).→

26. US actor Edward G. Robinson (*12/12/1893).

Peace treaty brings Vietnam war to end

Negotiators attend the Multinational Conference on Vietnam in Paris.

Jan 23. A cease-fire is to be declared in Vietnam. An agreement to stop the shooting has at last been hammered out at the Paris peace talks. Announcing this in a television broadcast to the American people, President Nixon said tonight it was an agreement to end the war and bring peace with honour to Vietnam and south-east Asia. The treaty stipulates that:

1. Fighting will stop at midnight British time on Saturday.

2. A force of 1,160 officers and men from Canada, Poland, Hungary and Indonesia will supervise the truce.

3. An international conference is to be held within 30 days of the cease-fire to guarantee the peace.

4. Within 60 days, all American troops and military advisers will be withdrawn and all military prisoners on either side will be freed.

Mr Nixon said the people of South Vietnam will be guaranteed the ability to settle their own political future. He insisted that the objectives for which America had fought during the war had been attained.

It is clear, however, that the North Vietnamese do not see the agreement in the same way as Mr Nixon. Le Duc Tho, Hanoi's chief negotiator, said in Paris that he regarded it as a victory: "Right has triumphed over wrong" (→ 4/2).

White House aides guilty of conspiracy

Jan 30. Gordon Liddy and James McCord Jr, both former aides to the committee to re-elect President Nixon, were today convicted of conspiring to spy on the Democratic party headquarters in the Watergate building during the election campaign.

McCord, a former CIA officer and a security consultant to the Republican national committee, was one of five men arrested inside the Democrats' offices. Liddy, a lawyer, was counsel to the committee and head of its financial subcommittee.

Judge Sirica has set March 23 as the day for sentencing (→ 8/2).

LBJ dies, a political victim of Vietnam

Jan 22. Former President Lyndon Johnson died of a heart attack today in Texas. He was 64. Johnson became president when John Kennedy was assassinated in 1963. He immediately put his legendary energy and political skill to work to pass an ambitious package of social legislation which he called the "Great Society". He became more and more deeply involved in Vietnam, and in March 1968 announced his withdrawal from the election campaign (→ 8/8).

Supermarkets back thalidomide victims and boycott Distillers

Jan 5. A leading supermarket chain has banned goods produced by Distillers from its stores because of delays in providing compensation for thalidomide children. A Distillers subsidiary marketed the drug in Britain.

Distillers have been under great pressure to provide realistic compensation for the thalidomide victims. The damages awarded by the courts do not begin to cover the costs of caring for them, particularly allowing for inflation.

The new boycott move, by the Wrenson group, which controls David Greig and Redmans supermarkets, will affect many leading brands of whisky, gin, vodka and brandy (→ 30/7).

Eddie Freeman, a victim of thalidomide, playing chess with his father.

1973

FEBRUARY

Su	Mo	Tu	We	Th	Fr	Sa
				1	2	3
4	5	6	7	8	9	10
11	12	13	14	15	16	17
18	19	20	21	22	23	24
25	26	27	28			

1. London: Women allowed on the Stock Exchange floor for the first time (→ 17/9).

4. Belfast: Nine die in disturbances.→

4. Vietnam: Inspection teams to monitor the truce (→ 14).

5. S Africa: 20,000 black workers go on strike (→ 11/6).

8. Washington: Federal prosecutor orders fresh inquiry into Watergate burglary (→ 26).

8. Cyprus: Makarios re-elected for a third term as President (→ 15/7/74).

12. US: Dollar devalued by ten per cent to stem its fall in value; foreign exchange markets closed around the world.

13. UK: Gas workers begin nationwide strike over pay (→ 27).

16. Washington: US Army court upholds death sentence on Lieutenant Calley for Mylai massacre (→ 27/3).

20. London: Two Pakistanis, holding dummy pistols, are shot dead by police (→ 2/3).

21. Laos: Two sides sign pact aiming to end the war (→ 16/4).

22. France: Coffin of wartime leader Marshal Petain recovered two days after its theft (→ 5/4).

25. Israel: Government agrees to pay compensation for shooting down the Libyan passenger plane (→ 10/4).

26. Washington: Publisher and eleven reporters from three newspapers subpoenaed to testify on Watergate (→ 3/4).

27. UK: Rail workers' and civil servants' strikes begin (→ 1/5).

27. US: American Indians seize ten hostages at Wounded Knee in protest at government neglect of Indians (→ 8/5).

DEATHS

11. German physicist Hans Jensen, 1963 Nobel Prize winner (*25/6/1907).

22. British born Irish writer Elizabeth Bowen (*7/6/1899).

74 die as Israel shoots down Libyan plane

An Israeli soldier patrols through the wreckage of Libya's Boeing 727.

Feb 22. Israeli jets yesterday shot down a Libyan Boeing 727 airliner. Seventy-four passengers and crew perished as the doomed plane crashed into the Sinai desert. Amid worldwide expressions of horror at the attack, Israel's Defence Minister, General Moshe Dayan, today defended the action of his fighter pilots. "There is no reason to feel guilty," he said. Israel claims that the airliner was instructed to land as it flew over a military airfield, but Cairo ground control, in radio contact with the plane, denied that the French captain had been warned. His voice on tape said: "We are shot by a fighter" (→ 25).

American and Vietnam exchange POWs

Feb 14. The exchange of prisoners of war taken on the battlefields of Vietnam started today when a US plane carrying 20 former POWs touched down at Travis Air Force Base in California. The first man down the gangway was Captain Jeremiah Denton, a naval airman. There were emotional scenes as families ran to kiss and hug fathers and husbands whom they feared were lost forever. However, despite the joy, there is still much confusion about how many US prisoners are held in the "Hanoi Hilton" and other camps (→ 16).

Viet Cong prisoners, all seriously wounded, prepare to return to the North.

Ulster paralysed by a general strike

Feb 7. Unionist supporters demonstrated their full strength in Northern Ireland today, crippling the province with a general strike which hit power supplies, industry, commerce and transport. Shipyards were silent, with masked men threatening violence to any one who dared cross picket lines. No buses or trains ran anywhere in Ulster. Electricity supplies were limited to "essential purposes".

Shops which ignored the call to close were petrol-bombed, while the deserted city-centre was the scene of looting and arson. Four men died in shooting incidents.

The British government was powerless to prevent the day of action, despite appeals by the Northern Ireland Office for a return to work. A state of emergency has been declared (→ 3/3).

Brave Bugner falls to Ali in Las Vegas

Feb 14. Joe Bugner, the tall, blond British holder of the European heavyweight championship, fought the fight of his life in Las Vegas today before losing a 12-round contest on points to Muhammad Ali – no longer world champion since his long ban and his subsequent defeat by Joe Frazier, but still a formidable fighter, determined to challenge again for the world title.

The Hungarian-born Bugner was cut above the eye early in the fight, and again near the end, but he never flinched from the attack, and received a warm ovation from the British fans.

Jeans are the signs of the times.

1973

MARCH

Su	Mo	Tu	We	Th	Fr	Sa
				1	2	3
4	5	6	7	8	9	10
11	12	13	14	15	16	17
18	19	20	21	22	23	24
25	26	27	28	29	30	31

1. Ireland: Fianna Fail loses election to Fine Gael-Labour coalition after 16 years in office (→26/4).

2. Sudan: Three diplomats shot dead by Black September terrorists (→5/8).

2. UK: Princess Anne says there is no romance between her and Captain Mark Phillips (→16).

5. France: 68 die in collision of two Spanish planes (→10/4).

7. Bangladesh: Government of Sheikh Mujibur wins first general election (→29/1/74).

9. Northern Ireland: 90-1 majority in favour of staying in UK, in referendum boycotted by most Catholics (→20).

10. Bermuda: Assassination of Governor Richard Sharples; state of emergency declared.

13. Japan: 10,000 commuters go on the rampage in protest at railway strike.

14. London: Marriage of Liberal leader Jeremy Thorpe to the Countess of Harewood.

16. London: Queen opens the new London Bridge (→29/5).

17. Cambodia: 20 die in failed assassination attempt against President Lon Nol (→31/5).

18. North Sea: Icelandic gunboat fires live ammunition at British tug (→24/4).

22. UK: Counter-Inflation bill becomes law (→1/4).

26. Dissident Andrei Sakharov interviewed by the KGB (→14/4/74).

27. North Vietnam: Release of last US prisoners of war (→29).

28. Los Angeles: Marlon Brando rejects his Oscar in protest at Hollywood's degradation of American Indians.

29. South Vietnam: Departure of the last US troops (→17/7).

31. UK: Red Rum wins the Grand National in record time of nine minutes 1.9 seconds.

DEATHS

6. US writer Pearl S. Buck (*26/6/1892).

26. British playwright Sir Noel Coward (*16/12/1899).→

Fresh IRA bombing campaign hits London

March 3. One person was killed, and about 250 injured, today when two bombs exploded in central London. Terrorists of the Irish Republican Army are suspected of planting the explosives in cars outside the Old Bailey and at the Agriculture Ministry in Whitehall.

The blasts coincide with Ulster's referendum on the future of British rule in the province, and police fear they signal the start of a bombing campaign on the mainland. The toll would have been far worse if Scotland Yard had not acted on a tip-off and defused two other car bombs, also placed in the West End. Last night, as part of an intensive police operation, ten people were arrested at Heathrow (→9).

An injured lawyer is guided away.

CIA "conspired to stop Allende" in Chile

March 20. Further dramatic evidence emerged today of the plot by the Central Intelligence Agency to prevent the election of a Marxist government in Chile. William Merriam, a vice-president of International Telephone and Telegraph, revealed that the plot was hatched at a secret meeting between the director of the CIA, William Broe, and the president of ITT, Harold Geneen, in 1970. Merriam was giving evidence to the Senate panel headed by the Democrat Frank Church which is investigating the activities of multinational corporations. He told them that the plan involved providing anti-Marxist propaganda and inciting violence to provoke an anti-Marxist coup. The plan was designed to prevent the election of Salvador Allende as president. It failed because of the widespread support Allende had amongst the intelligentsia of Chile. Nevertheless, the CIA continued to work towards destabilising the government (→29/6).

Captain Robert L. Atrim, one of the first POWs to return from North Vietnam, is greeted by members of his unrestrainedly joyful family.

Coward, theatre's blithe spirit, dies

March 26. It has been the custom recently to call Noel Coward, who died today at his home in Jamaica aged 73, "The Master". Ironically, he had joined the Establishment.

"Private Lives" was revived after many years, and was a revelation to those who had dismissed it without having seen it; it was now a classic. In 1964 the National Theatre asked him to direct "Hay Fever".

In 1966 he returned to the West End stage in "A Song at Twilight" as an ageing writer whose homosexual past is threatened with exposure. It all proved he had in him more than "a talent to amuse".

Coward – the blithest of spirits.

Trials without jury proposed for Ulster

March 20. Trials without juries and a parliament elected by proportional representation are among the plans for Northern Ireland proposed by the British government. Although ministers have been reluctant to abandon the principle of trial by jury, they have accepted it as inevitable given the danger of intimidation of witnesses.

Politicians in Westminster broadly welcomed the proposals for Ulster which were outlined in a white paper published yesterday by William Whitelaw, the Northern Ireland Secretary of State. These include a new Ulster Assembly with 80 members (→16/4).

1973

APRIL

Su	Mo	Tu	We	Th	Fr	Sa
1	2	3	4	5	6	7
8	9	10	11	12	13	14
15	16	17	18	19	20	21
22	23	24	25	26	27	28
29	30					

1. UK: VAT introduced (→8/10).

1. India: Government campaign to save the tiger from extinction.

3. Washington: Gordon Liddy sentenced to 18 months in jail for not answering jury's questions (→19).

5. Paris: Pierre Mauroy forms his second government (→13/3/74).

8. India: Troops annex the independent Himalayan kingdom of Sikkim (→9/4/74).

10. Lebanon: 40 die in Israeli raid in revenge for terrorist attacks in Cyprus.

11. Bonn: West Germany closes file on Nazi war criminal Martin Bormann after his death is confirmed (→29/10).

12. UK: Labour makes big gains in local elections (→10/5).

16. Dublin: IRA chief Sean MacStiofain freed from jail (→22).

16. Laos: US resumes bombing campaign.

17. Afghanistan: Republic proclaimed after army-backed coup ousts the government.

19. Washington: John Dean says he will not be made a scapegoat for Watergate.→

22. Belfast: Provisional IRA chief David O'Connell appears at an Easter rally, but police are unable to catch him (→19/5).

24. North Sea: Icelandic gunboat opens fire on two British trawlers (→21/5).

27. Moscow: Andrei Gromyko and Yuri Andropov promoted to Politburo.

26. Ireland: Government sells surplus butter to the poor for 8p a pound (→24/6).

27. Washington: Judge reveals White House aides tried to get psychiatric records on leaker of Pentagon Papers.→

DEATH

8. Spanish painter Pablo Picasso (*25/10/1881).→

Top Nixon aides quit over Watergate

April 30. The White House today announced the resignation of four of President Nixon's top aides in the spreading Watergate scandal. The four aides who have resigned are "H.R. Bob" Haldeman, President Nixon's chief of staff; John Ehrlichman, Haldeman's closest ally and Nixon's chief domestic affairs adviser; Richard Kleindienst, the Attorney-General of the United States since last year; and John Dean, legal counsel to the President.

On April 17, Kleindienst disqualified himself from dealing with matters relating to the Watergate break-in because of his "close personal and professional relationship" with some of those who were being mentioned in connection with the scandal. Elliott Richardson, the Secretary of Defence, is to be the new Attorney-General.

In a televised address to the nation yesterday President Nixon accepted responsibility for the Watergate incident, but denied any personal involvement in either the break-in or the cover-up. He did, however, concede that there had been "an effort to conceal the facts", and announced that the Attorney-General, Mr Richardson, would have the power to appoint a special prosecutor to look into the whole affair. After the speech, the President told reporters to "give me hell every time you think I'm wrong".

"H.R. Bob" Haldeman.

John D. Ehrlichman.

The resignations came after six weeks of dramatic revelations in Washington, beginning on March 17, the day James McCord, one of the convicted conspirators in the original break-in, wrote to Judge Sirica charging that senior White House officials had been involved in covering up the true scope of the scandal. Five days later Patrick Gray, acting director of the FBI, said that Dean had "probably lied" to FBI investigators (→7/5).

Picasso, the giant of modern art, is dead

Pablo Picasso: productive recluse.

April 8. Pablo Picasso died today at his chateau at Mougins where he lived reclusively with his second wife, Jacqueline. He was 91 years old and had a heart attack.

He was not only the most influential painter of the century, but the most prolific. His output is estimated at 140,000 paintings and drawings, 100,000 engravings and 300 sculptures. No-one knows how many of his works he retained in his private collection or what will happen to it now.

Picasso never ceased his restless experiments, which produced the Blue and Rose paintings of circus performers, Cubism and collages, neoclassical and Surrealist works, the immense "Guernica" and the savage distortions of the war years. Then came comparative serenity when he settled on the Riviera and took up ceramics at Vallauris.

He was still working. He had promised 100 of his latest works for exhibition at the Avignon Festival. His creative energy was without equal among painters.

Looking at some children's paintings he once said: "When I was their age I could draw like Raphael. It has taken me a lifetime to learn how to draw like them."

Vatican knew of Nazi death camps

April 4. Documents released by the Vatican today show how much the Church knew about the holocaust. One report by Archbishop Roncalli, later Pope John XXIII, to Monsignor Montini, now Pope Paul VI, revealed a meeting with a Hitler envoy which referred to Polish death camps. Montini was then secretary to Pope Pius XII (→11).

105 shoppers die in day trip crash

April 10. A day-shopping trip to Switzerland for a West Country women's club (mainly from four Somerset villages) ended in tragedy today, when their plane overshot the runway at Basle in driving snow, and crashed into a mountain, killing 105 out of the 144 passengers and crew. At least 50 of the dead were mothers (→4/6).

1973

MAY

Su	Mo	Tu	We	Th	Fr	Sa
		1	2	3	4	5
6	7	8	9	10	11	12
13	14	15	16	17	18	19
20	21	22	23	24	25	26
27	28	29	30	31		

1. UK: 1.6 million join TUC one-day strike in protest at the Government's pay restraint policy (→3/9).

2. Lebanon: 29 die as civil war between army and Palestinian guerrillas begins (→19/9).

7. Washington: Carl Bernstein and Bob Woodward win the Pulitzer Prize for their investigation of Watergate (→10).

8. US: Rebel Indians end their occupation of Wounded Knee.

10. Washington: Nixon aides John Mitchell and Maurice Stans indicted for perjury.→

14. US: Skylab launched into orbit (→25).

16. Greece: AC Milan beat Leeds United 1-0 to win the European Cup-Winners' Cup.

18. London: Inquiry into Lonhro's affairs announced by the Government.

19. Northern Ireland: Nine die in violent clashes (→12/6).

21. North Sea: British gunboat chases Icelandic frigate in first Royal Navy action of the Cod War (→24).

22. Washington: Nixon admits White House cover-up of Watergate (→25/6).

22. London: John Conteh beats Chris Finnegan to become British light heavyweight champion.

24. Iceland: British embassy stormed by rioters protesting at Royal Navy's action (→29/8).

25. US: Skylab's first crew is launched into space to join the space station (→7/6).

30. Yugoslavia: Ajax Amsterdam beat Juventus 1-0 to win the European Cup for the third year running.

31. Washington: Senate votes to cut off funds for the bombing of Cambodia (→30/6).

DEATHS

18. US politician Jeannette Rankin, first woman in Congress (*11/6/1880).

26. French painter and sculptor Jacques Lipchitz (*22/8/1891).

Ministers resign in British sex scandal

Lord Lambton – acknowledges the affair, but rejects any security risk.

May 24. Two government ministers have resigned after admitting that they associated with prostitutes. They are Earl Jellicoe, the Lord Privy Seal and Tory leader in the House of Lords, and Lord Lambton, a Defence Under-Secretary. Their extra-mural activities were spotted by the secret service.

The Prime Minister, highly embarrassed by another Tory sex scandal, told MPs today that the Security Commission has been asked to verify that there have been no security breaches or blackmail attempts. He is confident that there have been none.

The scandal broke when photographs of Mr Lambton taken by a call-girl's husband were sold to newspapers. By then he was already under surveillance (→12/7).

Princess Anne to wed Mark Phillips

May 29. Princess Anne, only daughter of the Queen, is to marry Lieutenant Mark Phillips, aged 24, of the Dragoon Guards, it was revealed today when they officially announced their engagement at the Badminton horse trials (→28/8).

Princess Anne and fiance Phillips.

Lonrho's capitalism rebuked by Heath

May 15. "It is an unpleasant and unacceptable face of capitalism." With those carefully-chosen words Mr Heath today condemned Lonrho, the international mining and trading company, for some of its business practices. He spoke in the Commons as the Government faced questions from MPs about references during a High Court case to a £350,000 company-owned house and payments into a Cayman Islands tax haven.

The Prime Minister added that the Lonrho affair is not typical of British industry, but he considers that it must weaken the Government's counter-inflation efforts. It was disclosed in court that Duncan Sandys, a former Tory cabinet minister, repaid £44,000 to Lonrho on finding that a contract offered to him had been arranged without approval of the company's board of directors (→18).

No charges against Pentagon leaker

May 11. A Federal judge dismissed all charges against Dr Daniel Ellsberg in the Pentagon Papers case today on the grounds of "improper government conduct". Ellsberg had been prosecuted for espionage, theft, and conspiracy, along with Anthony Russo, for copying the secret official history of the Vietnam war, and giving it to the New York Times.

Judge William Matthew Byrne said that government misconduct had made a fair trial impossible. Howard Hunt and Gordon Liddy, two of the former White House aides convicted in the Watergate affair, had broken into Ellsberg's psychiatrist's office (→17).

Liberals win control of Liverpool council

May 10. The Liberals will control Liverpool when the new metropolitan district councils come into operation next year. This was the most eye-catching result in today's elections. The Liberal leader, Jeremy Thorpe, crowed "We are the champions." It was the party's first advance in local government in living memory (→1/10).

America's Skylab space station orbiting high above the Earth. US astronauts Kerwin, Conrad and Weitz are due to rendezvous with the station, taking with them replacement solar panels.

1973

JUNE

Su	Mo	Tu	We	Th	Fr	Sa
					1	2
3	4	5	6	7	8	9
10	11	12	13	14	15	16
17	18	19	20	21	22	23
24	25	26	27	28	29	30

1. Athens: Greek government abolishes the monarchy and proclaims a republic (→19/8).

1. Geneva: OPEC agrees a 6.1 per cent oil price increase with the oil companies (→9/8).

3. Jerusalem: Israel frees 56 Arab prisoners in exchange for three captured pilots (→13/9).

6. UK: The 25-1 outsider Morston wins the Derby.

6. Argentina: Kidnapping of British businessman Charles Lockwood (→23/9).

7. Space: Skylab astronauts fix broken solar panels (→24/9).

8. UK: Enoch Powell hints public should oppose EEC entry by voting Labour.

8. Madrid: General Franco appoints Admiral Luis Blanco as President after ruling Spain alone for 34 years (→21/12).

11. S. Africa: 1,500 students expelled from university after demanding appointment of a Coloured rector (→15/10).

12. Northern Ireland: Car bomb attack kills six in the Protestant town of Coleraine.→

16. US: Brezhnev arrives for a nine-day visit.→

21. Washington: Supreme Court gives US states the power to censor obscene material.

22. Wimbledon: Tennis stars announce boycott of the tournament over suspension of Yugoslav player (→7/7).

22. New York: UN Security Council approves admission of East and West Germany.

24. Ireland: President Eamon de Valera resigns, aged 90, the world's oldest head of state (→13/3/74).

29. Chile: Revolt against President Allende crushed with support of the military (→12/9).

30. Cambodia: Communist guerrillas launch major attack towards Phnom Penh (→25/7).

DEATHS

10. US poet William Inge (*3/5/1913).

26. British dancer John Cranko (*15/8/1927).

Senate begins hearings on Watergate

Sam Ervin and his fellow investigators look into the Watergate Affair.

May 17. The Senate select committee's hearings into the Watergate affair began today in the ornate Senate caucus room. The hearings are televised and the chairman, Senator Sam Ervin of North Carolina, is on his way to be a star.

Judge Ervin, as he is called after a state judicial appointment, is a homespun man with a strong southern accent, and he imposed his personality from the first speech.

If the allegations about the Watergate burglars were true, Senator Ervin said, what they were trying to steal was "not the jewels, money or other property of American citizens, but something much more valuable – their most precious heritage, the right to vote in a free election". Senator Howard Baker of Tennessee, the senior Republican on the committee, said it was for the people to decide what Watergate meant.

The first witness, Robert Odle, testified that the head of the Richard Nixon re-election plan, Jeb Stuart Magruder, had concealed a file within hours of the Watergate break-in. Tomorrow the committee will hear a crucial witness, James McCord, one of the Watergate burglars (→22).

Second division Sunderland win FA Cup

May 5. A well-worked first-half goal, 90 minutes of non-stop harassing, tackling, running and spoiling, and one goalkeeping save that had to be seen a dozen times on the TV replays to be believed – these were the ingredients of one of the biggest Cup Final upsets of the century.

Sunderland of the Second Division, managed by the engaging Bob Stokoe, held on against relentless pressure for the best part of an hour to their one-goal lead against Don Revie's formidable Leeds United. Only after Jim Montgomery's double reflex save from Cherry and Lorimer, when it seemed certain that Leeds would equalise, did the fairy-tale outcome seem possible – the first FA Cup win by a Second Division club for 42 years.

Skipper Bobby Kerr lifts the Cup after Sunderland's shock victory.

Architect quizzed in corruption case

June 22. John Poulson, a leading architect engaged in building contracts in the public sector, was tonight being questioned about allegations of conspiracy. Police called at his Pontefract home just days before he was due to face bankruptcy proceedings which have already linked him with many well-known names. Poulson, aged 63, sought contracts with councils, health authorities and nationalised industries (→5/10).

John Poulson outside Leeds court.

Spate of tit-for-tat murders in Ulster

June 26. A loyalist vigilante group, styling themselves "The Ulster Freedom Fighters", have claimed responsibility for a series of sectarian murders in Northern Ireland.

After two men – one a 17-year-old youth called Daniel Ruse – were shot dead in Belfast, a caller to a newspaper described one of the killings thus: "We gave him two in the back and one in the head. There will be more."

The IRA retaliated by killing a Pakistani civilian – who supplied troops with tea and sandwiches – and a Unionist candidate in the coming Ulster Assembly election, who was shot in his Belfast sitting room (→22/7).

Nixon knew about Watergate cover-up

Dean: Nixon ignored his warnings of a "cancer" in the White House.

June 25. In long-awaited testimony to the Senate Watergate committee, President Nixon's counsel, John Dean, said that Nixon had taken part in the cover-up of illegality for eight months.

He said he had warned the President that the effort to cover up the White House's involvement in the break-in at the Democratic party headquarters and other illegal acts was "a cancer growing on his presidency". Dean said, though, that the President did not "realize or appreciate at any time the implications of his involvement".

Dean's testimony was explosive. He accused the President of actively taking part in the cover-up of the burglary; of saying it would be possible to find $1 million in hush money; and of trying to find others, including a former Attorney-General, to take the rap.

Dean also said that the organisers of the cover-up were two top Nixon aides, "Bob" Haldeman and John Ehrlichman.

Brezhnev leaves US with good feelings

June 24. Mr Leonid Brezhnev, the Soviet leader, concluded a week-long trip to the United States today which both he and President Nixon hailed as a "further milestone" toward an improvement in their relations. Mr Brezhnev, who had met Hollywood stars at a pool party in California, and held long conversations with Mr Nixon, said he was leaving the United States with a "good feeling". Mr Nixon said that improved US-Soviet relations could build an era of peace for all the peoples of the world. It was agreed to hold another summit sometime next year (→27/6/74).

"Concordski" crash at Paris air show

June 4. Tragedy struck at the Paris International Air Show today when the main attraction, a Russian Tupelov-144 supersonic airliner, exploded in mid-air, killing its six crew immediately. Nine more people were killed and 28 injured when fragments of the wrecked craft landed on the nearby town of Goussainville. Experts say that pilot error was almost certainly to blame for the disaster.

Brandt makes the first visit by a West German leader to Israel

June 7. Herr Willy Brandt today paid tribute to the six million Jews who died in the Nazi concentration camps, as he began the first visit ever made by a West German Chancellor to Israel. He was visibly moved at the Yad Vashem memorial and laid a wreath on the vault containing ashes taken from the gas chambers.

Mrs Golda Meir, the Israeli Prime Minister, who greeted him at Lod airport, said: "Mr Chancellor, you are being welcomed in Israel with the esteem due to one who, in the darkest period for the human race and especially for the Jewish people, joined forces with those who fought the Nazis."

Other Israelis were not so welcoming. About 200 hundred young protesters shouted "German murderer" at him in Jerusalem.

Germany's Brandt (l.) talks with Moshe Dayan, Israeli's Defence Minister.

1973

JULY

Su	Mo	Tu	We	Th	Fr	Sa
1	2	3	4	5	6	7
8	9	10	11	12	13	14
15	16	17	18	19	20	21
22	23	24	25	26	27	28
29	30	31				

3. New York: Elizabeth Taylor says she has separated from Richard Burton.

6. Rhodesia: Guerrillas kidnap 270 children and staff from a Catholic mission school (→11/12/74).

7. Wimbledon: Jan Kodes beats Alex Metreveli to win the Men's Singles; Billie Jean King beats Chris Evert to win the Women's Singles.

9. Uganda: Idi Amin orders arrest and expulsion of 112 Peace Corps workers (→25/3/74).

11. Paris: 121 die in crash of Brazilian plane (→31/1/74).

15. US: Kidnap of Paul Getty III, Paul Getty's grandson (→14/12).

17. London: Britain recognises the Hanoi government (→23/10).

19. US: Nixon says he won't hand over White House tapes to Senate investigators (→29/8).

21. South Pacific: French test H-bomb near the Mururoa Atoll (→18/5/74).

22. Ireland: Mass arrests by troops and police on both sides of the border (→29).

23. Libya: Colonel Gaddafi withdraws his resignation as Libya's leader (→12/1/74).

25. US: New York court rules US must halt illegal bombing of Cambodia (→3/9).

29. Belfast: Police fire plastic bullets in clashes with rioters (→31).

30. UK: Eleven-year battle over thalidomide compensation ends with £20 million court settlement (→25/10/74).

31. Belfast: First meeting of the Ulster Assembly (6/8).

DEATHS

1. British novelist Nancy Mitford (*28/11/1904).

2. US film actress and pin-up girl Betty Grable (*18/12/1916).

8. English cricketer Wilfred Rhodes (*29/10/1877).

19. US Kung Fu film star Bruce Lee (*27/11/1940).

Senate hears Nixon has bugged himself

July 17. A middle-level White House aide revealed today that President Nixon installed listening devices in the Oval office.

The revelation makes it certain that a titanic legal battle will be joined over whether or not the Senate investigating committee can have access to the tapes. Since the committee's hearings are being televised, if the committee can get the tapes, the whole nation will have conclusive evidence whether or not the President is telling the truth when he says he was not involved in ordering or covering up illegal activities.

Alexander Butterfield, who was in charge of routine administration in the White House, testified that listening devices were installed in the president's Oval office and in other offices and on the telephones used by the President in the summer of 1970; that the devices were still in place; and that tapes recorded by them were kept by the White House.

Members of the Watergate Committee confer over the new revelations.

Wimbledon boycott by the star players

July 7. A row between the International Lawn Tennis Federation and the Association of Tennis Professionals, over players' contracts, exploded into the unthinkable: a ban by the ATP on its members playing at Wimbledon.

A total of 79 players, including 13 of the 16 men's seeds, withdrew just before the start of the fortnight. Consequently the singles draw, led by the rebels Ilie Nastase and Yorkshire's Roger Taylor, had a distinctly threadbare look.

The main beneficiary was the new second seed, Jan Kodes of Czechoslovakia, who beat Taylor in the semi-final, and became one of the most unlikely champions by beating Russia's first Wimbledon finalist, Alex Metreveli 6-1, 9-8, 6-3.

Free Bahamas bank on off-shore riches

July 10. After more than 300 years of British rule, the 700 islands of the Bahamas, off the east coast of Florida, last night became independent. The Prince of Wales handed the documents of sovereignty to Lynden Oscar Pindling, the islands' first black Prime Minister, elected in 1967.

The great majority of the 185,000 population are black. Many of the white minority, fearing political and economic instability, have emigrated after selling their property at give-away prices, but Mr Pindling says: "Despite the inevitable ups and downs, we know we are going to make it." He says he plans to develop the islands as a major international investment and banking centre for "off-shore" funds.

1973

AUGUST

Su	Mo	Tu	We	Th	Fr	Sa
			1	2	3	4
5	6	7	8	9	10	11
12	13	14	15	16	17	18
19	20	21	22	23	24	25
26	27	28	29	30	31	

3. UK: Summerland disaster death toll rises to 50.

5. Athens: Arab terrorists open fire at airport, killing three and injuring 55 (→5/9).

6. UK: Kenneth Littlejohn claims he was an MI6 spy inside the IRA.→

9. UK: Petrol rationing coupons stockpiled amid fears of an oil crisis (→27).

14. Washington: US bombing of Cambodia officially ends.

16. Moscow: Soviets denounce children's TV show Sesame Street as "imperialistic".

19. Athens: President Papadopoulos ends martial law.

19. Mozambique: Portuguese army admits to the massacre of civilians (→11/9/74).

20. London: Fire bombs go off in two West End stores.→

21. Londonderry: Inquest returns open verdict on 13 victims of Bloody Sunday.

25. UK: 180 arrested in soccer violence on the first day of the new football season.

25. London: Doctors report using the first "CAT scan" (→11/10/79).

27. Saudi Arabia: Government announces cut in oil supplies to US to try to force change of attitude on Israel (→12/10).

28. Mexico: At least 500 feared dead in an earthquake.

28. USSR: Princess Anne visits Russia, the first member of the Royal Family to do so (→14/11).

29. Washington: Nixon refuses court order to hand over the tapes of White House conversations (→19/11).

29. North Sea: Icelandic gunboat engineer dies in collision with Royal Navy vessel (→7/9).

DEATHS

1. East German head of state Walter Ulbricht (*30/6/1893).

6. Cuban dictator and exile Fulgencio Batista (*16/1/1901).

31. US film director John Ford (*2/1/1895).

US Vice-President in bribery probe

Agnew: another troubled official.

Aug 8. Vice-President Spiro Agnew today revealed that he is under investigation on charges of bribery by government contractors in his home state of Maryland.

The Vice-President is being investigated by a federal grand jury in Baltimore on charges of bribery, extortion, and tax fraud.

Mr Agnew went on television and denounced the charges as "damned lies". He said he had "nothing to hide", and that he did not expect to be indicted as a result of the investigation.

Before running for Vice-President in 1968, Mr Agnew was Governor of Maryland and before that he was the county executive in Baltimore.

Gordon Banks, goalkeeper for Stoke City and England; now he may quit top-class soccer after a car-crash has damaged his sight.

▷

Thirty die as flames engulf holiday centre

Shocked holiday-makers can only watch as the fire engulfs Summerland.

Aug 2. An entertainment complex packed with hundreds of holiday-makers was tonight destroyed in an inferno which killed 30 people at Douglas, in the Isle of Man. Eighty people were hurt, many with serious burns.

Summerland, built at a cost of £2 million and said to be the largest "funland" in the world, was destroyed within minutes. As the flames raced through its upper floors there was little time for people to escape, and some people were trampled in the crush.

How the blaze started is not known – and why it spread so quickly will be a key question for the inevitable inquiry. Certainly flames soon engulfed the theatre, funfair, solarium, discotheque and restaurant, all crowded during the height of the summer season. Every fire engine on the island was called to the blaze. Hours later a huge pall of smoke hung over the centre.

One woman said: "I was knocked down in the stampede. I was flat on my stomach and there was a kiddie underneath me." Another said: "People had to kick their way through windows" (→ 3).

Carl Bernstein (l.) and Bob Woodward, the two Washington Post reporters whose dedication uncovered the complexities of Watergate.

MI6 linked to bomb attacks in Dublin

Aug 13. The Defence Minister, Lord Carrington, refused to comment today on a claim by a convicted bank robber – Kenneth Littlejohn – that he had been employed by MI6. Littlejohn made the allegation at his Dublin trial at which he was sentenced to 20 years.

Some Ulster MPs said last night that the Littlejohn affair might help to explain the planting of bombs in Dublin – leading to anti-IRA laws – and called for an inquiry into intelligence activities in the Irish Republic (→ 20).

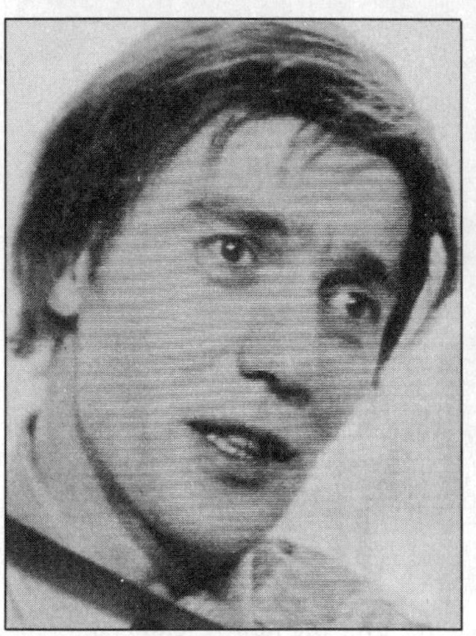

Littlejohn – wearing a wig for TV.

Irish troubles hit mainland shoppers

Aug 29. The Irish troubles spread to the West Midlands tonight when two carrier-bag bombs exploded simultaneously in the main shopping street of Poplar Road, Solihull. Police say it was extraordinary that no one was injured by the blasts, which could be heard two miles away.

The bombs, relatively small at about ten pounds but capable of killing a man, were planted in the doorways of a bank and a building society. They were fitted with timers set to detonate at pub closing-time.

In London, an incendiary device was found hidden inside a carpet at top people's store, Harrods. IRA spokesmen have denied responsibility for the bombing campaign.

1973

SEPTEMBER

Su	Mo	Tu	We	Th	Fr	Sa
						1
2	3	4	5	6	7	8
9	10	11	12	13	14	15
16	17	18	19	20	21	22
23	24	25	26	27	28	29
30						

1. Atlantic: World's deepest undersea rescue frees two Britons trapped inside mini-sub Pisces III.

3. UK: 20 trade unions expelled from the TUC for obeying the new Industrial Relations Act (→ 26/10).

3. Cambodia: Convoy reaches the besieged capital of Phnom Penh (→ 26/12).

5. Paris: Black September terrorists seize the Saudi Arabian embassy (→ 28).

7. North Sea: Royal Navy frigate accused of throwing carrots at an Icelandic gunboat.

10. London: Bomb explosions at two main-line train stations. (→ 23).

12. London: Government gives go-ahead for a Channel Tunnel.

15. Sweden: Crown Prince Carl Gustav becomes King on the death of his father, Gustav VI Adolf.

19. Jordan: King Hussein declares a general amnesty and releases Palestinian prisoners (→ 27/11).

23. UK: Bomb disposal expert killed by an IRA bomb in Birmingham (→ 31/10).

23. Argentina: Juan Peron re-elected President 18 years after he was ousted from power by a military coup (→ 6/11).

24. Pacific: Second Skylab crew returns to earth after their 59 day mission (→ 16/11).

26. London: England beats Austria 7-0 in soccer international.

28. Vienna: Palestinian terrorists attack train and seize hostages (→ 18/12).

DEATHS

2. British author John Ronald Reuel Tolkien (*3/1/1892).→

11. Chilean statesman Salvador Allende, President 1970-73 (*26/7/1908).→

15. Swedish King Gustav VI Adolf (*11/11/1882).

28. British poet Wystan Hugh Auden (*21/2/1907).→

Jackie quits Grand Prix while on top

Sept 7. With his third world championship assured, and on the eve of his 100th Grand Prix race, Jackie Stewart, the most successful driver in Formula One history, has pulled out of the United States Grand Prix and announced his retirement.

His decision came immediately after his Tyrrell-Ford team-mate, Francois Cevert, was killed during practice at Watkins Glen. Despite Stewart's constant campaigning for the highest safety standards, he always made it clear that racing is not the be-all and end-all of his life. And with 27 victories in 99 Grand Prix starts since 1965, he has nothing left to prove (→ 14).

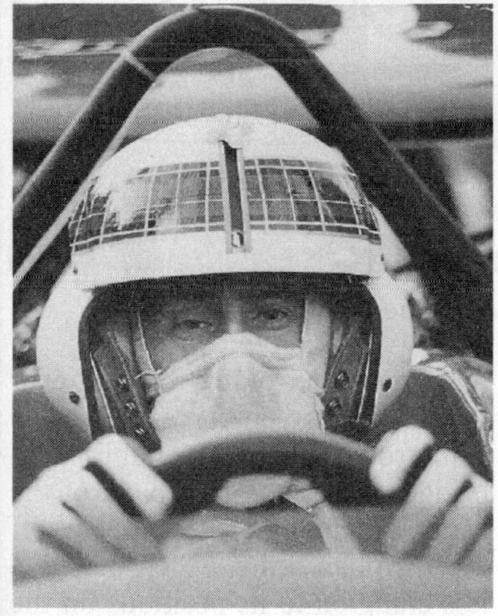

Jackie Stewart quits at the front.

Equality promised to women workers

Sept 17. Measures to tackle discrimination against women – at work and in general – were unveiled by the Government today in a report called "Equal Opportunities for Men and Women" which is expected to pave the way for a change in the law. It proposes the setting up of a new body, the Equal Opportunities Commission, which will investigate particular cases and initiate complaints. In employment, training and education, the report called for a legally-backed right for women to be treated on equal terms with men. Robert Carr, the Home Secretary, sees it as an "historic occasion" in the annals of women's rights.

Chile's Marxist leader is killed in coup

Chile's President Allende, flanked by his bodyguards, at the palace.

Sept 11. President Allende of Chile, the world's first democratically-elected Marxist head of state, died today during a military coup which overthrew his government. The revolt, led by commanders of the armed forces and the paramilitary police, marked the climax of three years of opposition from the political right and centre to the Allende government. A communique issued by the coup leaders tonight says they acted "to free the country from the Marxist yoke".

Air Force planes attacked the presidential palace with rockets and bombs, and it was assaulted by tanks after the President rejected a demand that he should resign. Some reports say he committed suicide when he saw defeat was inevitable. Others say he was shot down, sub-machine gun in hand, defending the palace. President Allende, supported by members of the Presidential Guard and civilian police, held out for more than two hours while the palace, set on fire by bombs, blazed around him. In mounting this coup the armed forces shattered a long tradition of non-intervention in the nation's political affairs. It is being suggested by Mr Allende's friends that the coup was instigated by American big business and the CIA (→ 11/10).

W.H. Auden, voice of the Thirties, is dead

Sept 28. The poet W.H. Auden came back from long years in America last year to live at his old Oxford college, Christ Church. He was not home for long. He died in Vienna today, aged 66.

Auden, Spender and Isherwood were the voice of English poetry in the Thirties, combining everyday language with leftish, near-Communist views and concern in the Spanish Civil War. In 1939 he and Isherwood went to the US.

Better than anyone he caught the anxiety of the Thirties – "The shallow hopes of that low, dishonest decade", as he memorably put it. His great facility led him to write too much. His admirers agree that early Auden is the best.

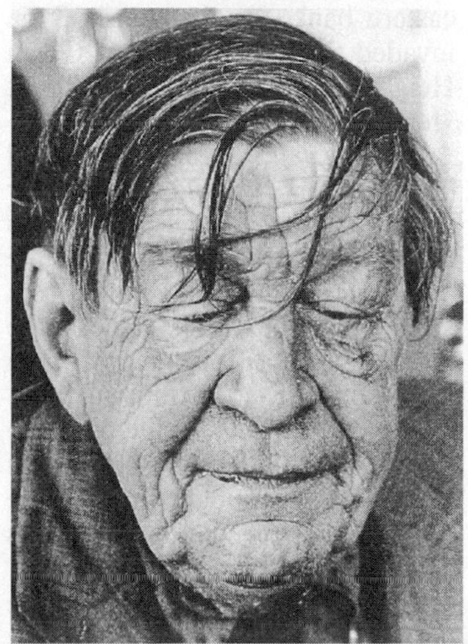

W.H. Auden, a thirties icon.

Israel and Syria fight air battle

Sept 13. In the greatest air battle since the Six-Day War, Israel claimed to have shot down 13 Syrian planes today for the loss of one fighter. Syrian MiG 21s scrambled as Israeli squadrons of Mirages and Skyhawks winged in over the Syrian border. Mass dogfights developed high over the Mediterranean and sonic booms could be heard in Beirut. General Nejamin Peled, the Israeli commander, claimed that the Syrians fired as his planes flew over the sea. The battle is seen as a warning to President Hafez Assad as he returned from talks in Egypt with President Sadat (→ 6/10).

J.R.R. Tolkien, Lord of the Rings, dies

Sept 3. J.R.R. Tolkien, a quiet scholar of Anglo-Saxon, suddenly became a best-seller in his seventies. When he died yesterday aged 81 he was rich. Not that he cared.

After writing a story about a Hobbit for his children, he began to construct an imaginary world called Middle Earth. After 12 years it had grown to 500,000 words. Published as "The Lord of the Rings", it caused a great stir when the US paperback appeared in the Sixties and sold a million copies a year.

Japanese car sales go into overdrive

Sept 15. For the first time, foreign cars are outselling the British Leyland range. Figures released today show that they took a record 32 per cent of the British market this August. The Japanese Datsun company made nearly 1 in 20 of all cars sold, topping runners-up Renault, Fiat and Volkswagen by a good margin. Japanese cars, rare ten years ago, now have an enviable reputation.

Lord Stokes, British Leyland's chairman, has urged the government to take action to stem the tide of imports. Peter Walker, the Secretary for Trade and Industry, says he is willing to discuss car export restrictions with the Japanese.

1973

OCTOBER

Su	Mo	Tu	We	Th	Fr	Sa
	1	2	3	4	5	6
7	8	9	10	11	12	13
14	15	16	17	18	19	20
21	22	23	24	25	26	27
28	29	30	31			

1. UK: Denis Healey vows Labour will tax rich until "the pips squeak" (→9/11).

5. UK: Dan Smith arrested and charged with corruption over the Poulson affair (→11/2/74).

6. Israel: Egypt and Syria launch an attack on two fronts.→

8. London: Heath announces Phase III of his pay policy, including a seven per cent limit on pay increases (→6/12).

11. Chile: At least 2,000 now feared dead following the military coup.

12. Vienna: OPEC begins oil price negotiations with the oil companies.→

14. Thailand: Government resigns after shooting of 400 students by troops.

15. S. Africa: Government extends racial segregation to all private gatherings.

17. London: England draw 1-1 with Poland and fail to qualify for World Cup soccer finals.

19. Spain: 500 feared dead after severe floods.

19. Washington: Nixon refuses to surrender Watergate tapes, despite Appeal Court order to do so (→23).

23. Paris: Vietnamese envoy Le Duc Tho refuses Nobel Peace Prize, saying there is still no peace in his country (→20/1/74).

23. UK: Derby County football team demonstrate in support of their sacked manager, Brian Clough.

26. UK: Troops provide emergency 999 service in Glasgow as firemen go on strike (→13/11).

29. Bolivia: Nazi fugitive Klaus Barbie is released after eight months' detention.

DEATHS

2. Finnish long-distance runner Paavo Nurmi (*13/6/1897).

22. Spanish cellist Pablo Casals (*29/12/1876).

26. British MI5 chief Sir Roger Henry Hollis (*2/12/1905).

Israel counters Yom Kippur offensive

An Israeli soldier gazes down on his wounded friend, their tank in the background, as the war rages on.

Oct 17. Egyptian troops were today fighting Israeli troops in the Sinai desert in one of the fiercest battles since the Second World War, 11 days after they launched a shock attack across the Suez Canal on the holiest day in the Jewish calendar. As Israeli soldiers prayed in their bunkers to celebrate Yom Kippur, the Egyptians built pontoon bridges to cross the canal and stormed the supposedly impregnable "Bar-Lev line", gaining control of most of the eastern bank. Simultaneously Syria invaded the Israeli-occupied Golan Heights, rapidly capturing Mount Hermon and advancing 15 miles.

Although Egypt and Syria had been building up their forces for several days in advance, Israel was taken completely by surprise by the attack. Troops were mobilised from synagogues and Israel Radio broke its traditional silence during Yom Kippur to broadcast instructions. Forces were rushed to the northern front, where the Arab advance was threatening the kibbutzim, and the air force launched bombing raids against Damascus.

Israeli troops retook all of the Golan Heights during the first six days of the war and began their advance into Syria proper. In Sinai, Egyptian troops consolidated their positions on the east bank as President Sadat called the crossing of the Suez Canal "a miracle at any military level". On October 14, the 100,000-strong Egyptian forces launched a massive offensive eastwards, which rapidly became a tank battle of unparalleled violence and ferocity – one of the biggest ever fought. As Israeli forces began to gain ground, they also established a bridgehead on the west bank of the canal which threatened to cut off the Egyptian army, which nonetheless clung on to its positions on the east bank, the first-ever military gain won from Israel during any war with the Arabs (→26).

Blindfolded Egyptians are led off to a prison on the banks of the Canal.

US forces are put on world-wide alert

Oct 26. President Nixon announced today that he had placed US forces throughout the world on military alert after he "received information that the Soviet Union was planning to send a very substantial force" to the Middle East to relieve the beleaguered Egyptian Third Army, trapped in the Sinai desert. Nixon said the alert was intended to show this would not be tolerated.

The alert started yesterday, but the President said the crisis was "defused" within a few hours by a message from Mr Brezhnev, and both superpowers then supported a UN Security Council motion which finally ended the Yom Kippur war. The new cease-fire is being policed by UN peacekeeping troops, unlike the previous one which, although agreed to by the Egyptians and the Israelis on October 22, failed to end the fighting.

Mr Nixon, watched by his wife Pat, talks to a group of Italian visitors.

Fears of a Soviet effort to aid the Third Army, which is still holding 450 square miles of territory on the east bank of the Suez Canal, arose after the failure of its offensive aimed at breaking out of the Israeli encirclement of their positions. The Israeli troops, who now have a 500-square mile bridgehead on the west bank of the Canal, had refused to allow through emergency medical supplies for the trapped Egyptians in a bid to force their surrender. On the northern front, the Israeli troops advanced to within 20 miles of the Syrian capital of Damascus and retook Mount Hermon before the cease-fire (→31).

Sheikhs massively increase price of oil

Oct 17. The oil states sent shivers through the Western world today as they increased oil prices by 70 per cent and cut back production in protest at US support for Israel in the Yom Kippur war. The decision is a warning to the other Western nations to choose between their oil supplies and support for Israel, as well as an attempt to pressurise the US to change its policy. It also marks an end to the negotiation of price increases, with the Arab oil states indicating that from now on they will decide them unilaterally.

The oil companies had offered to raise prices by 15 per cent, but the ten oil producers rejected this and announced a 70 per cent rise with a five per cent per month cut in production. As news came through later in the day of Nixon's request for $2,200 million in emergency aid for Israel, three states – Abu Dhabi, Libya and Qatar – rushed to impose a complete oil embargo on the US. They were then quickly followed by the other oil producers.

The decision caused panic in Western Europe, which depends on the Arab producers for 80 per cent of its oil, and must now prepare for petrol rationing. In Britain, the effects of the petrol price rises will cause severe problems for the Government's anti-inflation policy and the £409 million rise in the bill for oil imports will worsen the balance of payments deficit (→4/11).

Sheikh Yamani: man of power.

US and Europe split over policy on Israel

Oct 31. The war in the Middle East has led to a crisis within NATO as its European members, under the pressure of an oil embargo, split from the US in their policy towards the Arab-Israeli conflict. When the Americans organised a huge airlift of arms for Israel, four European members of NATO refused to let the US use bases on their territory or fly through their airspace; West Germany publicly rebuked the US for doing so; and Britain privately warned she would not co-operate.

All were anxious to avoid the oil embargo against the US widening to cover them, as it did Holland, when the Dutch government came out in support of Israel. US officials attacked the Europeans for their attitude. "There wasn't one country in Europe which wouldn't have let Israel go under," said a Pentagon official, while a spokesman for the US Secretary of State, Dr Henry Kissinger, warned US bases might be pulled out of Europe (→11/11).

Helicopter plucks IRA men from jail

Oct 31. IRA terrorists hi-jacked a helicopter and forced the pilot to land in a prison exercise yard today. Three Provisional IRA leaders were snatched to freedom in a split-second operation.

The helicopter had been chartered by a "Mr Leonard" and flown to a remote field, allegedly to pick up a film crew. Instead, the pilot found himself flying at gunpoint to Mountjoy Prison, Dublin.

The three men were waiting. Among them is Seamus Twomey, regarded as the most dangerous IRA man ever to operate in Ulster, who was serving a three-year sentence for his IRA membership and receiving stolen money (→14/11).

BBC radio gets a rival after 50 years

Oct 8. The London Broadcasting Company – the first-ever legal competition for BBC Radio – went on the air today. The new commercial station, which breaks the BBC's 50-year radio monopoly, will broadcast to the London area 24 hours a day. Its diet of news and current affairs will be complemented tomorrow by a second London station, Capital Radio's music and entertainment.

LBC, which celebrated its inauguration with the release of 1,000 carrier-pigeons, hopes to gross at least £1 million a year.

Casals, best cellist in the world, dies

Oct 22. Pablo Casals, the world's greatest cellist for some 70 years, died today in Puerto Rico, aged 96. A Catalan, he was an ardent Republican and after the Spanish Civil War said he would never set foot in Spain until democracy was restored. He settled in Prades, a village in the Pyrenees on the French side of the border, where his music festivals and playing attracted audiences from around the world. At the age of 80 he married a pupil in her twenties, Marta Montanez. He played to Queen Victoria in 1899. ▷

Nixon sacks the Watergate prosecutor

Oct 23. President Nixon today consented to turn over tapes demanded as evidence by Judge Sirica, who was asked to order the president to do so by the special Watergate prosecutor, Archibald Cox. The tapes are believed to contain records of conversations in which the President is alleged to have discussed the cover-up of illegal actions with his staff.

The way the President has handled the matter of the tapes, however, has been disastrous and for the first time there is now a widespread belief in Washington that he faces possible impeachment.

On Saturday night he ordered the Attorney-General, Elliot Richardson, to dismiss Cox. Richardson refused, and resigned. The President then ordered his deputy, William Ruckelshaus, to fire Cox, and he, too, refused. Finally the Solicitor-General, Robert Bork, agreed to do so.

The request for the tapes was made both by the special prosecutor and by the US Court of Appeal. The refusal to comply with their requests, and what is being called the "Saturday night massacre", have reinforced allegations of a cover-up and could be grounds for impeachment, say some members of Congress (→1/11).

Agnew out in tax deal, Ford takes over

Oct 12. Vice-President Spiro T. Agnew today resigned after agreeing not to contest a federal charge of tax evasion. Gerald Ford, the Republican leader in the House of Representatives, was appointed in his place.

The appointment will be popular. Mr Agnew has been investigated by a federal grand jury in Maryland on charges that, while governor of the state and chief executive of the county which includes the city of Baltimore, he both accepted and extorted bribes and evaded taxes.

Under the terms of an agreement to spare him imprisonment, Mr Agnew, who denounced the charges as "damned lies" when they were made, agreed to plead no contest to a charge of failing to report $29,500 of income while Governor of the state of Maryland. The Justice Department requested leniency, and the judge fined Agnew only $10,000 and sentenced him to three years' probation.

Under the new 25th Amendment, Mr Ford's appointment must be ratified by both houses of Congress. As a moderate minority leader, he is not expected to have any difficulty (→6/12).

North Vietnam's Le Duc Tho (l.) with America's Dr Henry Kissinger: the two men are to share this year's Nobel Peace Prize for their efforts in leading their respective countries towards a cease-fire in Vietnam.

1973

NOVEMBER

Su	Mo	Tu	We	Th	Fr	Sa
				1	2	3
4	5	6	7	8	9	10
11	12	13	14	15	16	17
18	19	20	21	22	23	24
25	26	27	28	29	30	

1. Washington: Nixon names Leon Jaworski as Watergate special prosecutor (→9).

1. UK: Last issue of the underground magazine, Oz.

3. Ethiopia: 100,000 feared dead as the result of a famine (→26/2/74).

4. Kuwait: Arab oil producers tighten embargo with further 25 per cent cut in supplies (→29).

6. Buenos Aires: Peronistas launch campaign to regain the Falklands from Britain (→29/6/74).

9. Washington: Six Watergate burglars convicted and sentenced (→26).

9. UK: Liberals and Scottish Nationalists each win a seat in parliamentary by-elections (→1/3/74).

11. Egypt: Israel and Egypt sign cease-fire agreement, the first-ever pact between the two nations (→30).

13. UK: State of emergency declared as power workers and miners begin industrial action.→

14. UK: Eight IRA terrorists found guilty of London car bombings (→22).

16. Space: Skylab's third crew dock with the space station (→8/2/74).

18. Athens: Martial law imposed after nine die in riots.→

24. Australia: Aborigines granted the vote.

25. Northern Ireland: 200th British soldier killed in the province (→9/12).

27. Algiers: PLO recognised as the sole legal representative of the Palestinian people

29. London: Saudi oil minister Sheikh Yamani says Britains's oil supplies are safe (→23/12).

30. Egypt: Fierce fighting with Israel along the Suez Canal cease-fire line (→2/12).

DEATHS

13. German-Italian conductor and composer Bruno Maderna (*21/4/1920).

13. French fashion expert Elsa Schiaparelli (*10/9/1896).

Power-sharing deal agreed in Ulster

Whitelaw: power-broker.

Nov 22. William Whitelaw, the Northern Ireland Secretary, yesterday persuaded Protestant and Roman Catholic politicians in Belfast to agree to take part in a power-sharing executive. It is a real breakthrough after decades of deep divisions which have kept the two communities totally separate. Only a few days ago there was no more than a vague hope that both sides would agree to serve together.

Precise details are being worked out, but the new executive will take overall control of domestic administration in the six counties. For the time being the British government will be in charge of policing, internment of terrorists and the courts.

The success is a triumph for William Whitelaw, who was given a warm welcome in the Commons this afternoon. Labour MPs seemed as genuinely pleased as Conservatives (→25).

Nixon's secretary wipes tape in error

Nov 26. President Nixon's secretary, Rose Mary Woods, gave evidence today in a federal court that through some "terrible mistake" she caused an 18-minute gap in one of the Watergate tape recordings. She told the court she pressed the wrong button. Mr Nixon said it did not matter (→4/1/74).

Princess Anne marries

The bride and groom, flanked by young royals, appear on the balcony.

Nov 14. A smiling Princess Anne on the arm of her father, Prince Philip, walked to the high altar of Westminster Abbey today where she married Captain Mark Phillips.

Just as for other young princesses before her, it was an occasion of pride and pageantry, both for the two families and for Londoners. Many had slept overnight in The Mall, thawing their frost-cold bodies in the morning with bacon and sausages cooked on picnic stoves.

It was a full military ceremony. Captain Phillips awaited the bride in a splendid and ornate uniform of scarlet and blue, designed for The 1st Queen's Dragoon Guards.

As the bride and groom are world-class riders – she a European gold medallist and he an Olympic one – there were a great many of their sporting friends in the Abbey among the 1,500 guests.

The atmosphere beforchand was one of excitement and whispered gossip. Then it changed abruptly to hushed silence as the notes of the organ announced the arrival of the bride.

She wore a Tudor-style wedding dress, with high collar, slim waist and mediaeval sleeves. The all-over embroidery of silver and pearls on the full skirt sparkled in the TV lights.

She had only two attendants, her youngest brother, Prince Edward, and her cousin Lady Sarah Armstrong-Jones. The bride and the groom smiled at one another repeatedly. No one could recall seeing the Princess smile so often and so warmly.

After the wedding lunch, the Princess and her husband left Buckingham Palace for the first night of their honeymoon at White House Lodge in Richmond Park. Tomorrow they fly to Barbados where they will join the royal yacht for 18 days of sailing in the Atlantic and the Pacific (→20/3/74).

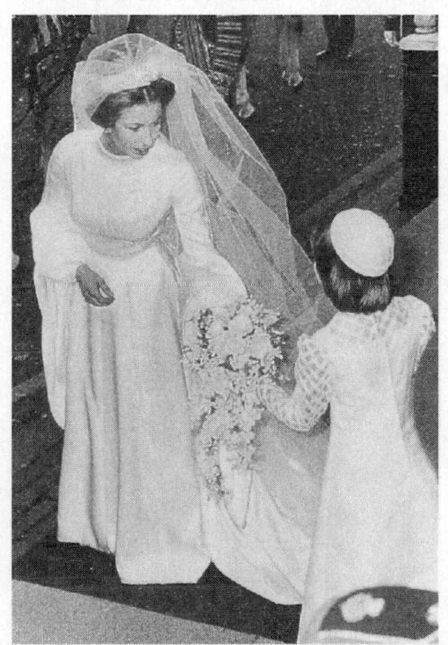
Anne's bouquet goes to bridesmaid, Lady Sarah Armstrong-Jones.

Army coup ousts Greek President

Nov 25. The Greek armed forces seized power in Athens today, overthrowing the government of President George Papadopoulos which they accused of "weakness" and dragging the country towards an "electoral adventure".

A broadcast proclamation said the Greek people should rest assured that the armed forces would tackle the job properly and take over the country until the situation had been "cleansed".

This language smacks of the original "Colonels' Coup" of 1967, and indeed, radio broadcasts tonight are saying the army takeover is "a continuation of the revolution of April 21, 1967". The coup follows weeks of unrest during which at least ten people have died and tanks were used to smash down the iron gates of the Athens Polytechnic to evict 5,000 students protesting about the lack of academic freedom.

Mr Papadopoulos declared martial law and dozens of people were arrested. Today's coup, however, seems to have been carried out without bloodshed.

Tanks rolled into central Athens before dawn and troops with fixed bayonets took up positions round government buildings. It was efficiently done. Tonight, Athens is under curfew (→24/7/74).

Tanks mass in the streets of Athens as the Colonels take control.

Petrol rationing is on the cards in Britain

Nov 26. Peter Walker, the Secretary for Trade and Industry, told the House of Commons today that the Government is printing sixteen million petrol ration books. Drivers will have to collect them from post offices, starting next Thursday.

Mr Walker stressed that the Government had not yet decided rationing was necessary, but they had to act now to get the books out before the Christmas postal rush begins. So far there has been no fall in crude oil supplies to Britain, but there is a worldwide shortage of refined petroleum products.

Companies all around the world have been hoarding petrol in case the Middle Eastern crisis gets worse. Already 200 petrol stations in England have had to close down through shortage of petrol.

How much the petrol ration would be has not been revealed, but the last time petrol was rationed – during the Suez crisis of 1956 – motorists were allowed 200 miles of motoring per month.

Special arrangements are planned for essential business use and for other priority users. These include doctors, vets, nurses and midwives, priests, undertakers, probation officers and the disabled. If rationing is introduced, anyone who can make out a good case will be able to apply for a supplementary allowance (→5/12).

1973

DECEMBER

Su	Mo	Tu	We	Th	Fr	Sa
						1
2	3	4	5	6	7	8
9	10	11	12	13	14	15
16	17	18	19	20	21	22
23	24	25	26	27	28	29
30	31					

2. Israel: Clashes with Syria on the Golan Heights for the first time since the cease-fire (→ 18/1/74).

5. UK: Government imposes compulsory 50mph speed limit to save fuel (→ 14).

6. London: Share values fall £2,000 milion as Arab funds are withdrawn from banks (→ 26/3/72).

6. Washington: Gerald Ford sworn in as Vice-President (→ 11/6/74).

10. Stockholm: Nobel Prizes go to Leo Esaki (Japan), Ivar Giaever (US), Brian Josephson (UK), all Physics; Ernst Fischer (West Germany), Sir Geoffrey Wilkinson (UK), both Chemistry; Konrad Lorenz (Austria), Karl von Frisch (West Germany), Nikolaas Tinbergen (UK), all Medicine; Wassily Leontief (US, Economic Science); Patrick White (Australia, Literature); and in Oslo to Henry Kissinger (US, Peace), awarded jointly to Le Duc Tho (Vietnam) who declined.

14. Uganda: Idi Amin starts "Save Britain" fund to help Britain out of economic crisis.→

18. Kuwait: Arab terrorists end hijack after killing 31 (→ 30).

23. Iran: Arab oil producers double oil prices (→ 25/1/74).

28. Paris: Solzhenitsyn's "The Gulag Archipelago" is published.

DEATHS

1. Israeli statesman David Ben-Gurion, premier 1948-63 (*16/10/1886).

20. Spanish statesman Luis Carrero Blanco, premier 1973 (*4/3/1903).→

HITS OF 1973

Eye level

Tie a yellow ribbon

Blockbuster.

QUOTE OF THE YEAR

"There will be no whitewash at the White House."

Richard Nixon, in TV speech on Watergate, April 30.

Britain goes onto a three-day week

Dec 17. Anthony Barber, the Chancellor of the Exchequer, this afternoon unveiled his pre-Christmas crisis budget, designed to cope with what he described as "the gravest situation by far since the end of the war". It cut a massive £1,200 million from public spending, including axing one in five of the schools and colleges due to be built in 1974-5.

There is growing speculation at Westminster that, unless the disputes now paralysing industry, involving the coal mines, railways and power stations, are settled soon after Christmas, Mr Heath will be forced to call a general election. He needs both a strong new mandate for his policies and an answer to the question "who rules the country – an elected government or the unions?"

The immediate crisis has been caused by the decision by miners' leaders to continue an overtime ban, without balloting their members. Coal supplies to power stations are already down by 40 per cent.

Industry and commerce is to be limited to five days' electricity consumption in the fortnight to December 30 and three days a week in the New Year. Except over Christmas and the New Year, all television services will close down at 10.30pm.

The mini-budget, however, was more immediately concerned with the effects of OPEC's massive oil price increases, shown in November's £270 million trade gap. As Mr Heath said in his broadcast last week: "If we have to have oil and pay more for it, the country will have less to spend on other things from abroad".

Edward Heath: under pressure.

Len Murray: voice of the TUC.

The Chancellor's priority has been to cut the nation's demand for non-oil imports in order to cope with the higher OPEC prices. His measures today, therefore, included tighter hire purchase and credit controls and a ten per cent surcharge on surtax. He has also responded to criticism of the speculative property boom by raising the tax on development gains from 30 to 50 per cent. This is expected to bring in about £80 million a year, but is a less severe measure than many had expected.

Mr Barber's measures did not include any of the expected increases in VAT or duties on drink, cigarettes and petrol. He is clearly anxious not to push the cost of living index above the "threshold" point where it would trigger automatic pay increases all round under Phase III of the Government's current prices and incomes policy.

The Shadow Chancellor, Denis Healey, told Mr Barber he should tax the rich and the profits of private business rather than slash public services (→ 10/1/74).

Gunman shoots Marks and Spencer boss

Dec 30. Joseph Sieff, head of the Marks and Spencer chain and a top Jewish figure in Britain, was shot and badly wounded by a terrorist gunman tonight. Police say fanatics from an Arab group, such as Black September, probably wanted to end his support for the Zionist cause.

The gunman forced his way into Mr Sieff's home in St. John's Wood, London, and fired at him from close range. As police launched a nationwide hunt, Mr Sieff, aged 68, was undergoing emergency surgery to remove a bullet from his jaw. Two years ago he received death threats over his fund-raising trips to Israel (→ 11/4/74).

Mr Joseph Sieff – still in hospital.

Kidnapped oil heir Getty III is set free

Dec 14. John Paul Getty III, the teenage grandson of the American oil tycoon, has finally been freed by Italian kidnappers who held him in captivity for six months. At one point they cut off his right ear and sent it through the mail to further their demand for a ransom of about $750,000.

Meanwhile, the oil giant Exxon has announced that it will pay a ten-million-dollar ransom to Argentinian kidnappers for the release of the American executive Victor S. Samuelson, seized almost a week ago at a Buenos Aires refinery (→ 5/2/74).

Council of Ireland to link North and South

Dec 9. There was a dramatic moment in the history of Ireland yesterday when political leaders from London, Dublin and Belfast agreed to the setting up of a Council of Ireland.

It is to be a two-tier, seven-a-side Ministerial Council and a 30-a-side Consultative Assembly. The Council, which will deal with problems common to all of Ireland, will be drawn in equal numbers from the Irish parliament and the new Northern Ireland Assembly.

A very similar type of Council of Ireland was provided for in the treaty which set up the two parliaments in Ireland in the 1920s, but it was never established because of the objections of Ulster Unionists.

The announcement came after four days and nights of talking at a meeting called by Edward Heath, the Prime Minister, at the Civil Service College at Sunningdale. Mr Heath said: "I believe our agreement will mean a better future not only for Northern Ireland but for Southern Ireland as well."

The way is now open for the British government to give full powers to the Northern Ireland Executive from January 1, but major difficulties still lie ahead. Precisely how policing and law enforcement in Northern Ireland should be carried out has yet to be agreed, and many Northern Catholics and Protestants are unhappy about the agreement which is to be lodged with the United Nations.

Faulkner, (l.) and Liam Cosgrave.

The signatories of the agreement, in addition to Edward Heath, were Liam Cosgrave, the Irish premier; Brian Faulkner, chief executive-designate of Northern Ireland; Gerry Fitt, leader of the Social Democratic and Labour Party; and Olivier Napier, leader of the Alliance Party.

A major point in it is that if a future majority of the people of Ulster wish to become part of the united Ireland the British will support them. Equally the status of the North will not be changed unless the people there agree (→8/1/74).

Two Rhodesian policemen patrol for rebels: terrorists in the eyes of the police, freedom fighters as the blacks see themselves.

Spanish premier is killed by a bomb

Dec 20. Spain's Prime Minister, Admiral Luis Carrero Blanco, was assassinated today when a huge bomb hurled his car over the 65-foot tall church where he had just attended Mass. The bomb had been planted in a tunnel dug under the road from the cellar of a building on the route he regularly took to church. The car landed on a second-floor balcony.

Admiral Carrero, a close friend as well as political right-hand man of General Franco, was alive when he was taken from the wreckage, but died shortly after reaching hospital. ETA, the Basque underground separatist movement, claimed all responsibility (→22/1/74).

Arts: Nancy Mitford becomes simply non

Nancy Mitford was the eldest of the six Mitford sisters, and her death at 68 removes the most high-spirited writer on the English upper classes bar **P.G. Wodehouse**. The eccentric upbringing of the Mitford menage was the background to her novels "The Pursuit of Love" and "Love in a Cold Climate".

Their father, Lord Redesdale, appeared as a ferocious Philistine who believed "abroad is bloody and foreigners are fiends". **Lord Berners**, the eccentric composer who painted his doves and had a piano keyboard in his Rolls, was thinly disguised as "Lord Merlin".

In later years she lived at Versailles and wrote a biography of Louis XIV. She remained a presence in English life through her book "Noblesse Oblige", a guide to "U and Non-U" (upper-class and not) use of language. She revealed to her fascinated readers that to use words like "mirror", "serviette" and "sweet" (for "looking glass", "napkin" and "pudding") betrayed your lowly social origin.

The year saw a curious mixture of best-sellers. **Frederick Forsyth**, a former BBC reporter, whose "The Day of the Jackal" – a "faction" about the attempted assassination of President de Gaulle – was a sell-out in paperback, followed it with another best-seller, "The Odessa File", about the SS men's escape organisation. **Grahame Greene** introduced the Latin-American concept of "machismo" in his story of "The Honorary Consul" who was taken hostage by mistake.

Peter Hall: appointed to be next director of the National Theatre.

An unexpected best-seller was entitled "Small is Beautiful – a Study of Economics as if People Mattered". In it the economist **E.F. Schumacher** put forward an alternative technology to save the planet from human greed.

"The Sting" brought **Paul Newman** and **Robert Redford** together again, but its real star was the long-dead **Scott Joplin** whose relaxed piano rags on the soundtrack revived the taste for Ragtime.

Robert Redford (r.) and Paul Newman – best buddies in "The Sting".

1974

JANUARY

Su	Mo	Tu	We	Th	Fr	Sa
		1	2	3	4	5
6	7	8	9	10	11	12
13	14	15	16	17	18	19
20	21	22	23	24	25	26
27	28	29	30	31		

1. Israel: Golda Meir's Labour government re-elected to office (→ 10/4).

2. UK: 18 national museums and galleries begin charging for admission.

4. US: Nixon rejects court subpoenas of 500 tapes and papers (→ 15).

6. UK: First-ever professional football matches played on a Sunday, due to the power shortage.

9. Cambodia: Government troops launch offensive against Khmer Rouge (→ 11/2).

10. UK: Train drivers' strike cripples rail services (→ 4/2).

12. Tunisia: Unification treaty signed with Colonel Gaddafi of Libya (→ 14/8).

15. Washington: Court told there are five gaps on the Watergate tapes (→ 14/2).

18. Israel: Military separation agreement signed with Egypt (→ 23).

22. Spain: Peseta allowed to float on foreign exchanges (→ 19/7).

23. Egypt: Israel begins troop withdrawals from west bank of Suez Canal (→ 18/2).

25. S. Africa: Dr. Christiaan Barnard performs first heart transplant without removal of existing organ (→ 15/5).

25. North Sea: Major oil find disclosed by British Petroleum (→ 18/3).

29. Bangladesh: Report reveals seven babies are born a minute, 10,000 a day (→ 22/2).

31. Belfast: Two Catholic workers killed for refusing to kneel before hooded gunmen (→ 4/2).

DEATHS

6. Mexican painter David Siqueiros (*29/12/1896).

25. British author James Pope-Hennessy (*20/11/1916).

31. US film producer Samuel Goldwyn (*27/8/1882).

Protestants split on power-sharing deal

Ian Paisley: for God and Ulster.

Jan 22. The Northern Ireland Assembly was reduced to an unworkable shambles today as hard-liners protested vigorously at Protestants sharing power with Catholics in the new Executive Council. Unionists spat at Unionists, the mace was seized and passed from hand to hand, and police forcibly removed the Reverend Ian Paisley.

The crisis follows Brian Faulkner's resignation as leader of the Unionist Party, although he remains as chief executive of the disrupted "cabinet" (→ 31).

Dr Spock is blamed for revolting youth

Jan 23. Dr Benjamin Spock, whose best-selling guide to child-rearing, "The Common Sense Book of Baby and Child Care", has long been the paediatric "bible" for millions of British and American families, was blamed today for much of the contemporary youth rebellion.

Spock's book has sold more than 25 million copies since it appeared in 1946. Faithful readers followed his advice: to relax traditional controls and let children have their own way.

Now critics are united in laying all the ills of the so-called "permissive society" at Spock's door, but the doctor stresses that any problems stem from people misinterpreting his original theory (→ 15/6).

1974

FEBRUARY

Su	Mo	Tu	We	Th	Fr	Sa
					1	2
3	4	5	6	7	8	9
10	11	12	13	14	15	16
17	18	19	20	21	22	23
24	25	26	27	28		

1. Brazil: Great Train robber Ronald Biggs arrested (→ 4).

2. Cairo: Sadat sacks powerful editor Mohammed Heikal.

4. UK: 81 per cent of miners vote for a national strike (→ 24).

4. Brazil: Government refuses to extradite Ronnie Biggs to UK because he has a Brazilian child.

5. US: Patty Hearst kidnapped in California.→

5. UK: Police, in raids, seize arms caches belonging to Protestant extremists (→ 12).

8. US: Astronauts return from Skylab after 84 days in orbit: man's longest-ever space flight (→ 29/3).

10. Iran: 70 die in border clash with Iraqi troops.

11. UK: John Poulson and William Pottinger jailed for five years on seven corruption charges (→ 15/3).

11. UK: Four-star petrol rises to 50p a gallon, the fourth rise in a year.

12. UK: 10 injured by IRA bomb in Buckinghamshire (→ 11/3).

14. Washington: Special prosecutor Leon Jaworski says Nixon won't surrender key Watergate tapes (→ 19).

15. China: Foreigners banned from travelling within the country.

18. Washington: Four Arab nations propose plan for truce in the Golan Heights (→ 17/3).

19. Washington: Two of Nixon's ex-cabinet ministers go on trial for perjury before a grand jury (→ 2/3).

22. Dacca: Bangladesh is recognised by its former ruler, Pakistan (→ 11/8).

24. London: £1 million Vermeer painting stolen from Kenwood House gallery (→ 6/5).

28. Egypt: Diplomatic ties with the US restored after a seven-year break.

Election called as miners snub Heath

Feb 7. Who runs Britain – the Government or the miners? That is the issue on which the Tories are asking the nation to vote on February 28. In announcing tonight the date of the general election, Mr Heath said that some miners' leaders "want to change our whole democratic way of life".

The Prime Minister unsuccessfully appealed to the miners to call off their all-out strike for the duration of the campaign. Labour's Harold Wilson accused Mr Heath of "making a run for it" in the hope that the strike will divert voters from the Government's economic failures.

This election campaign will be the shortest for 40 years. The 10.30pm curfew on television programmes recently imposed on account of the electricity shortage will be lifted (→ 6/3).

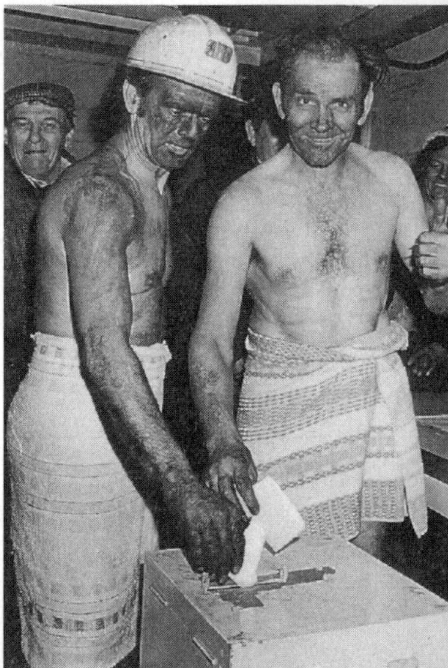

Kent miners ballotting for a strike.

Bomb rips troop bus apart on M62

Feb 4. Eleven people are feared dead after an explosion early today blew apart a coach carrying servicemen and their families on the M62 near Bradford. Bodies were thrown 250 yards; at least one of the dead was a child. Ten ambulances were needed to take the survivors to hospital. Police believe the blast was caused by a bomb.

Author Solzhenitsyn is sent into exile

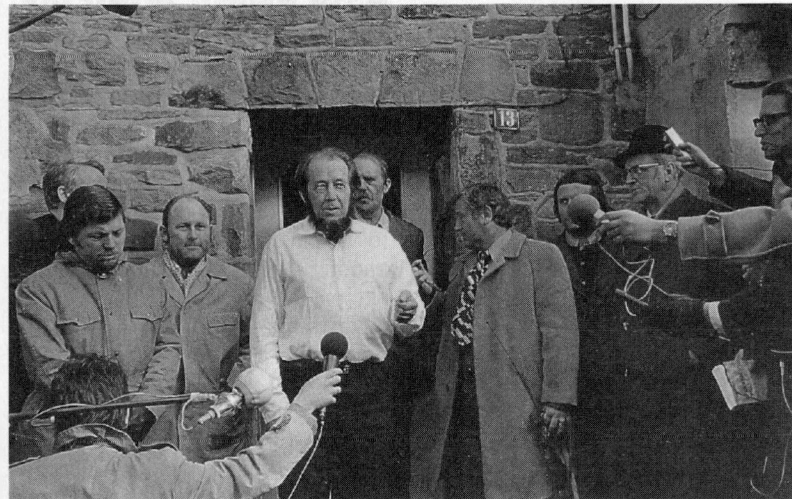

Solzhenitsyn at the home of his friend, the German author Heinrich Boell (r.).

Feb 14. Alexander Solzhenitsyn was expelled from his homeland and deprived of his Soviet citizenship today. It was the Kremlin's response to the publication abroad of his exposure of conditions in Soviet labour camps under Lenin and Stalin.

"The Gulag Archipelago" came out in Paris six weeks ago after the KGB had obtained a copy of the manuscript by brutal interrogation of a woman friend of the author. She subsequently committed suicide. Solzhenitsyn had held up publication for five years to protect victims whose names appear in it. Last evening KGB men forced their way into the Solzhenitsyns' flat in Gorky Street in Moscow, and dragged him away after a struggle in which his wife, Natasha, and her mother tried to protect him. He was taken to Lefortovo prison and today put on a plane to Frankfurt.

From Frankfurt he was driven to the country cottage of the German author, Heinrich Boell. Tonight Moscow announced that his family could join him. Mrs Solzhenitsyn said she and her three sons would follow him into exile.

Patty Hearst seized by revolutionaries

Feb 22. Patty Hearst, the 19-year-old heiress who was abducted from her San Francisco apartment on February 4, is in the hands of an extremist left-wing group, the self-styled Symbionese Liberation Army. Hearst attends the University of California's Berkeley campus. Her father, the millionaire publisher Randolph Hearst, has revealed that, in a series of ransom notes, the group have demanded that foodstuffs be distributed to the poor of San Francisco. On an accompanying tape Hearst calls herself "a prisoner of war", and it is feared by FBI analysts that she may have been brainwashed.

The SLA are hard-line revolutionaries, linked with the killing last year of a school superintendent in Oakland (→ 10/3).

Communists shell Cambodian capital

Feb 11. Communist-led rebels showered artillery fire into a densely-populated area of Phnom Penh today, killing 159 and wounding 46. The vicious shelling of the Cambodian capital ended an eight-day ceasefire in the civil war, and was the heaviest attack in almost two years.

Officials estimate that 73 bombs were launched in the midday barrage, which lasted for half an hour. Fast winds swept flames started by the explosions towards the dry, wooden buildings of the city's poor district. A section of the neighbourhood nearly a quarter of a mile long was destroyed.

President Nixon has promised Premier Lon Nol and his troops the maximum possible aid in the fight against the rebels.

1974

MARCH

Su	Mo	Tu	We	Th	Fr	Sa
					1	2
3	4	5	6	7	8	9
10	11	12	13	14	15	16
17	18	19	20	21	22	23
24	25	26	27	28	29	30
31						

2. Washington: Grand Jury says Nixon was involved in Watergate cover-up (→ 15).

6. UK: Miners' strike ends with 35 per cent pay increase (→ 8).

7. Ethiopia: First-ever general strike begins against Haile Selassie's rule (→ 12/9).

8. UK: Return to five-day working week (→ 26/6).

10. San Francisco: Hearst family receives tape from abducted Patty urging them to do more to free her (→ 15/4).

11. Dublin: Kenneth and Keith Littlejohn, allegedly MI6 spies inside the IRA, escape from prison (→ 20).

11. UK: Dr Ramsey says he will retire as Archbishop of Canterbury (14/5).

13. Dublin: Premier Cosgrave becomes first Irish leader to concede Northern Ireland is a province under UK control.

13. Paris: Inauguration of Charles de Gaulle airport (→ 3/4).

17. Israel: Sixth day of border clashes with Syria in the Golan Heights (→ 19/4).

18. Austria: Arab oil states lift oil embargo on US (→ 2/4).

20. Northern Ireland: Police shoot dead two British soldiers (→ 20/4).

21. London: Ian Ball charged for murder attempt on Princess Anne; says he did it to show lack of mental care facilities (→ 13/6).

22. Vietnam: Communists call for new truce and fresh general elections (→ 15/9).

25. Uganda: 50 army officers killed after failed coup attempt against Amin (→ 4/6).

29. UK: 50mph motorway speed limit restored.

29. US: Space probe Mariner 10 takes first close-up pictures of the planet Mercury (→ 3/7).

30. UK: Mr N. le Mare's horse, Red Rum, wins the Grand National for the second time.

Heath seeks to do deal with Liberals to hang on to power

March 1. The political crisis is acute today as the Prime Minister tries to avoid the Tory government's resignation. Labour has won 301 seats in the general election and the Tories 297: neither party can command an overall majority.

Within his constitutional rights, Mr Heath told the Queen tonight that he will negotiate with Liberal leader Jeremy Thorpe over the weekend for Liberal support. If he fails, Mr Heath will resign and Labour will be back in office.

Britain's political fate is thus now in the hands of 14 Liberal and nine Scottish and Welsh Nationalist MPs holding the balance of power in the new parliament. Mr Heath is ready to offer Scottish and Welsh parliaments to the Nationalists, if he can first secure Liberal backing with a promise of an electoral reform inquiry (→ 6).

Liberal leader Jeremy Thorpe.

Corrupt architect jailed for 7 years

March 15. The architect John Poulson was today jailed for seven years at the end of a trial in Leeds which took the lid off corruption in public life. The jail term is to run concurrently with the five year sentence he was given last month. Mr Poulson, who is 63, gave away more than £500,000 in suits, holidays and flowers to win contracts.

Report says Nixon knew of Watergate

March 15. A federal grand jury has concluded that President Nixon was involved in a conspiracy to cover up White House involvement in the burglary at the Democratic Party headquarters in June 1972.

The grand jury found that the President was an "unindicted co-conspirator" in the cover-up of illegalities. Seven former White House and election campaign officials were named in a sealed report to a federal judge; this will also be shown to the House of Representatives judiciary committee, which is considering impeachment proceedings against the President.

Britain fails to star in Michelin Guide

March 22. No restaurant in Britain or Ireland is worth a detour, let alone a special visit, according to the first "Michelin Guide" to British hotels and restaurants published today. A Chinese restaurant is among 25 awarded one star ("good in their class") compared to 549 in France, where there are also 17 three-star ("worth a journey") and 58 two-star restaurants (→22/4).

DC-10 crashes outside Paris, killing 344

French rescue services carry away the bodies after 344 died in the crash.

March 3. All 344 passengers on board a Turkish Airlines flight from Paris to London have perished in the world's worst air disaster. At least 200 of the dead were British.

Eye-witnesses report that the wide-bodied DC-10 airliner came down very fast and very low before bursting into a massive fireball. The plane was totally destroyed after it ploughed into the thick Forest of Ermonville, cutting a swathe nearly a mile long, before exploding.

Several bodies, and part of the fuselage, fell seven miles away from the main wreckage, indicating that the trouble started with structural failure at an altitude of over 10,000 feet. Experts say the likely cause was an explosion, possibly an engine disintegrating. The "black box" or flight recorder has been recovered, but is badly damaged.

The passengers' corpses are mutilated beyond recognition. The forest, a favourite picnic spot for Parisians, is strewn with human limbs, articles of clothing, charred wallets and passports. Ambulance men are still collecting fragments of bodies in plastic bags.

Harold Wilson is new Prime Minister

March 6. Labour is back in government – but without real power. Mr Wilson now begins his third and most difficult term as Prime Minister with his party outnumbered in the House of Commons. He will try to survive without a pact, but another general election seems likely later this year.

He said: "All I can say is my prayers." This was after Mr Heath had bowed to the inevitable and resigned when the Liberals rejected his offer of coalition with a cabinet post for their leader, Jeremy Thorpe. The new government's

Mr Wilson returns to number 10.

first act has been to end the miners' four-week-old strike by conceding practically all their pay demands. They will get rises ranging from £6 to £15 a week. These represent nearly twice the increases allowable under the Tory government's pay code.

Mr Wilson has made James Callaghan Foreign Secretary in the new government and Denis Healey Chancellor of the Exchequer. Two key posts go to left-wingers – Michael Foot at Employment and Anthony Wedgwood Benn at Industry.

More than six million people voted Liberal in this latest election. The party secured 23.6 per cent of all votes cast. This is its best performance since 1935 and gives them great leverage in the weeks to come. Looking around the Commons tonight, Mr Thorpe said: "We are all minorities now" (→8/4).

Princess Anne shot at, but unhurt in kidnap attempt in the Mall

March 20. Princess Anne escaped a kidnap attempt by a gunman who tonight ambushed her car and then fired six shots at the vehicle. One bullet passed between her and her husband, Captain Mark Phillips, but both were unhurt.

A police bodyguard, the chauffeur, a policeman patrolling the Mall and a passing taxi passenger who tried to tackle him were seriously wounded. The attacker slewed his car across the path of the Princess's limousine and planned to demand a £1 million ransom, but he was foiled as he tried to drag her from the car when the bodyguard drew a pistol. After the gunman fired he fled into St. James's Park before being arrested by police reinforcements.

Safely back at Buckingham Palace, the Princess was "thankful to be in one piece" (→21).

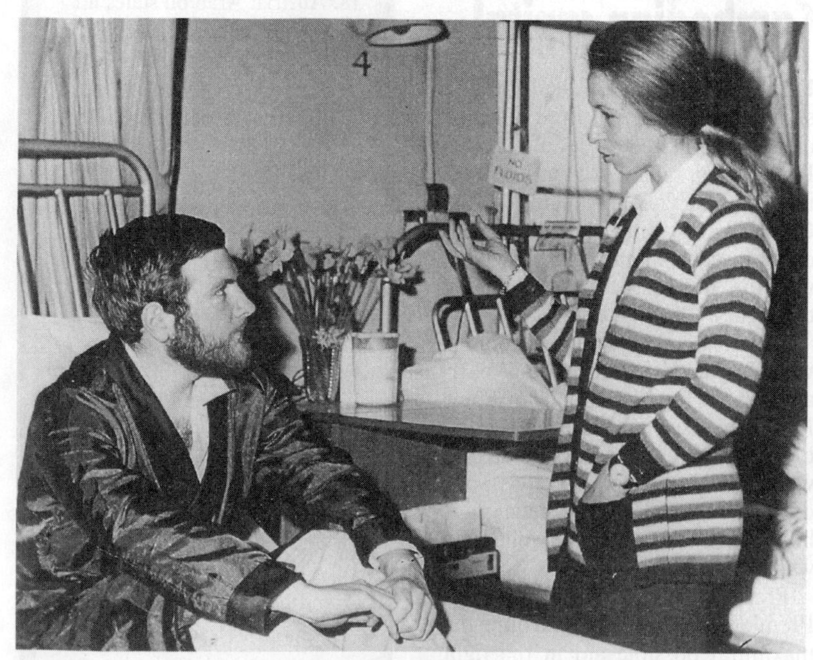
Princess Anne talks to one of the men who saved her from a kidnapper.

1974

APRIL

Su	Mo	Tu	We	Th	Fr	Sa
	1	2	3	4	5	6
7	8	9	10	11	12	13
14	15	16	17	18	19	20
21	22	23	24	25	26	27
28	29	30				

1. UK: Free family planning for all becomes available on the National Health Service.

2. North Sea: Burmah Oil announce discovery of huge Ninian oil field (→10/7).

3. Los Angeles: Seven Oscars for "The Sting" and an Oscar for Glenda Jackson as best actress in "A Touch of Class".

8. London: Political storm over alleged dealings in the property market by some Wilson aides (→3/9).

9. New Delhi: Pact signed to repatriate 195 Pakistani prisoners of war (→5/6).

10. Jerusalem: Golda Meir resigns as premier because of divisions within the Labour Party (→22).

11. Israel: 18 die in Arab guerrilla raid on village of Qiryat Shemona (→16/5).

14. Moscow: Andrei Sakharov calls on Soviet leadership to renounce Marxism.

19. Syria: First air battle with Israel since the Yom Kippur war (→31/5).

20. Belfast: Catholic man shot dead: 1,000th victim of unrest in Northern Ireland (→26).

22. Indonesia: Pan-Am plane crashes in Bali with 107 on board; most are feared dead (→27).

22. Jerusalem: Yitzhak Rabin chosen as new leader of the Labour Party (→3/6).

26. Ireland: Armed gang steal paintings worth £8 million from country house (→3/5).

27. Leningrad: 100 die in Soviet airliner crash (→20/11).

28. Washington: First post-war trial of cabinet ministers ends in acquittal of Maurice Stans and John Mitchell (→30/5).

28. Portugal: Socialist leader Mario Soares returns after four years in exile (→10/8).

DEATHS

2. French statesman Georges Pompidou, President 1969-74 (*5/7/1911).→

5. British politician Richard Crossman (*15/12/1907).

Heiress Patty Hearst turns bank robber

The rich girl turns revolutionary.

April 15. In a dramatic turnaround today, Patty Hearst, the heiress victim of a kidnap by the revolutionary Symbionese Liberation Army, appears to have joined her captors and raided a bank.

A hidden camera in the San Francisco bank shows Hearst, complete with carbine, along with the rest of the heavily-armed gang. Only the sight of another woman apparently training her gun on Hearst might imply that the heiress was taking part under duress.

The FBI has issued a warrant for the arrest of all the gang, including Hearst, who earlier this month issued a seemingly voluntary pro-SLA statement, in which she revealed her new "revolutionary" name: "Tania".

Winds of change blow through the shires

April 1. Towns with charters going back to the Middle Ages and counties chronicled in the Domesday Book disappear today in the greatest reorganisation of local government in England and Wales since 1888. Only ten of the 45 English counties and just one of the 13 Welsh counties survive unchanged, although even that, Montgomery, is renamed Gwent.

Four English counties go altogether: Cumberland, Rutland, Huntingdonshire and Westmorland. Yorkshire retains three counties, but they are no longer called "Ridings". Much of the former East Riding awakens today as part of "Humberside", for instance.

This is one of four new counties in England and six in Wales. With new "metropolitan counties" and district councils, too, the changes are intended to make local government more efficient – once the dust settles.

A streaker at Twickenham inspires a novel use for a police helmet.

Pompidou dies of mysterious illness

The late Georges Pompidou.

April 2. Georges Pompidou, President of France, died tonight at his home in Paris after a long illness. The actual cause of death was not given, though for some months there had been speculation about his illness, which gave him a pale and bloated face.

Pompidou tried to make light of it. He told Henry Kissinger, the US Secretary of State: "Every time someone shakes my hand I feel they are trying to take my pulse." Pompidou was de Gaulle's successor. Whoever follows him will continue the move away from Gaullism Pompidou began (→19/5).

Coup in Portugal promises freedom

April 25. General Antonio Spinola, the sacked hero of Portugal's African wars, took control of the country today after a dawn military coup had toppled Dr Caetano's right-wing regime. The coup, mounted by young officers weary of the 13-year-old colonial wars, was relatively bloodless. Three people were reported dead and 39 wounded.

It was only when the action was over that the rebels asked General Spinola to join them, and his position did not become clear until he had broadcast as head of the "Junta of Salvation". He promised the restoration of full civic liberties to the Portuguese people and an early opportunity for them to elect a new president (→28).

1974

MAY

Su	Mo	Tu	We	Th	Fr	Sa
			1	2	3	4
5	6	7	8	9	10	11
12	13	14	15	16	17	18
19	20	21	22	23	24	25
26	27	28	29	30	31	

1. UK: Sir Alf Ramsey sacked as England's soccer manager.

3. Ireland: Gang threatens to destroy £8 million of stolen paintings unless the Price sisters are released from jail (→ 17).

4. London: Liverpool beat Newcastle United 3-0 to win the FA Cup final.

6. Brazil: Ronald Biggs freed from jail (→ 21/7).

11. China: 20,000 feared dead in an earthquake in Sichuan and Yunnan provinces.

13. Italy: Retention of divorce laws approved in referendum.

14. UK: Dr Donald Coggan named as the new Archbishop of Canterbury.

15. US: Dalkon Shield intra-uterine contraceptive device taken off the market amid fears of health hazards.

16. West Germany: Helmut Schmidt becomes the new Chancellor.

19. Turkey: Release of London schoolboy, Timothy Davey, 17, jailed for drugs offences.

20. UK: 500th episode of the BBC-TV series, "Z Cars".

23. Israel: Capture of six Arab terrorists preparing to kidnap Jewish women and children (→ 4/8).

26. London: Mass hysteria grips audience at concert by David Cassidy.

27. Paris: Jacques Chirac appointed premier.

29. Holland: Feyenoord beat Tottenham Hotspur 4-2 on aggregate to win the UEFA Cup.

30. Washington: Congressional Committee warns Nixon he may be impeached for refusing to surrender Watergate tapes (→ 24/7).

31. Israel: Truce signed with Syria in the Golan Heights after Kissinger's mediation.

DEATH

24. US jazz musician Duke Ellington, born Edward Kennedy Ellington (*29/4/1899).

16 children die in Arab-Israeli cross-fire

Burial for the latest victims in the Middle East's bitter war of attrition.

May 16. Sixteen children were killed today in a fierce battle between Israeli troops and Palestinian terrorists holding 90 people hostage in a school at Maalot. Seventy other people were wounded.

Negotiations for the release of the hostages, conducted by the French and Rumanian ambassadors, hinged on the broadcast of a code word, but the raiders became suspicious and opened fire on the children. Just then an Israeli rescue force led by General Moshe Dayan went in.

An angry crowd gathered at the schoolhouse only six miles from the Lebanese border and called for revenge. There were also indignant shouts of "Where was our security?" A child who escaped said that teachers had told them to jump through a window when firing began (→ 23).

Strikers topple power-sharing executive

May 28. Jubilant Protestants danced in Belfast streets tonight as the chief executive, Brian Faulkner, resigned with fellow-members of his power-sharing executive. Ulster now faces direct rule from Westminster.

A general strike, sponsored by militant Unionists, had paralysed the province, bringing Ulster to the brink of complete collapse. Despite this, Harold Wilson's government declined to use British troops to break the strike. The executive had only come into existence at the beginning of this year. Within weeks, its position was undermined by the success of its opponents in the February general election.

During the seven-day strike Ulster faced severe power cuts, food shortages, street barricades, limited petrol supplies, intimidation of workers and isolated shooting at security forces. A "back-to-work" march, sponsored by official trade unions, was a flop with only 250 people turning up to be pelted with eggs, tomatoes and assorted missiles. The unions claimed that workers had been threatened by men in paramilitary uniforms (→ 7/6).

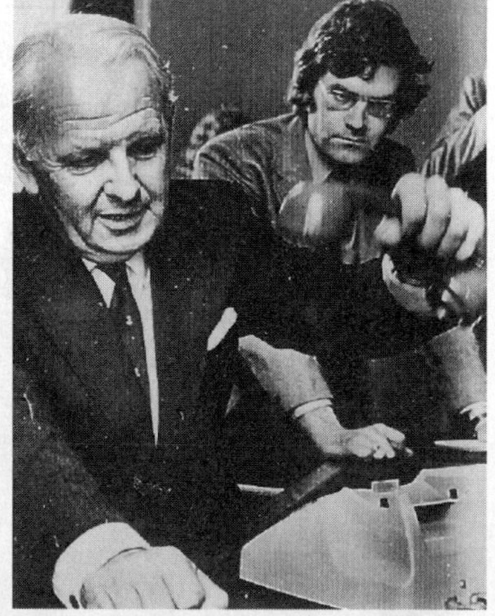

Brian Faulkner makes a final call.

Brandt resigns in German spy row

May 6. Willy Brandt, the West German Chancellor and architect of Ostpolitik – detente with the Communist bloc – resigned tonight after an East German spy was discovered working in his office. The spy, Gunter Guillaume, had been a close aide to the Chancellor since 1970, despite warnings that he was under suspicion as a security risk.

Brandt was the first Social Democrat Chancellor in West Germany's 25-year post-war history. He is said to have been depressed in recent months. His successor is likely to be the former Defence Minister, Helmut Schmidt (→ 16).

Chancellor Brandt under attack.

Dublin car bombs kill 23 in rush hour

May 17. The full savagery of the Northern Ireland conflict came to Dublin today when three car bombs went off during the rush hour, killing 23 people and seriously injuring more than 100. An hour later, another car vanished in a huge explosion which killed a further five and injured 20 in the border town of Monaghan.

All four cars had Ulster registrations; two of them had been hijacked from Protestant areas in Belfast.

In Dublin a police witness said: "Blood was flowing down the pavement. I never believed such horror could exist." Dublin has been declared a disaster area (→ 28).

1974

JUNE

Su	Mo	Tu	We	Th	Fr	Sa
						1
2	3	4	5	6	7	8
9	10	11	12	13	14	15
16	17	18	19	20	21	22
23	24	25	26	27	28	29
30						

3. Jerusalem: Yitzhak Rabin becomes new Israeli PM.

4. Africa: 250,000 killed in Uganda since Idi Amin took power, says International Committee of Jurists.

5. UK: Mrs N. Phillips' horse Snow Knight, 50-1 outsider, wins the Derby (→ 13/10).

5. India: 10,000 at risk from smallpox outbreak.

7. UK: The Price sisters end their six-month hunger strike in jail (→ 17).

11. Austria: Kissinger says he will resign unless cleared of wiretapping allegations (→ 12/12).

13. London: Prince Charles makes maiden speech in House of Lords, the first such Royal speech in 90 years.

15. London: Student dies in fighting between left and right wingers in Red Lion Square (→ 29/8).

16. Damascus: Nixon and Assad announce resumption of diplomatic ties.

18. Luxembourg: Gaston Thorn appointed PM.

20. Lebanon: 16 die in Israeli air attacks on Palestinian refugee camps (→ 29/10).

21. UK: Inflation soars to post-war record of 16 per cent.

25. Ireland: Dr. Bridget Rose Dugdale jailed for nine years for art theft (→ 14/7).

26. UK: Labour government and TUC finalise the "Social Contract" to restrain pay increases (→ 31/7).

27. Moscow: Nixon arrives for meeting with Brezhnev (→ 24/11).

29. Argentina: Isabel Peron takes effective control of the government after her husband becomes ill (→ 1/7).

DEATHS

10. British Prince Henry William Frederick Albert, Duke of Gloucester (*31/3/1900).

18. Soviet World War II commander Marshal Georgi Zhukov (*1/12/1896).

Giscard d'Estaing is French President

France's new conservative leader.

May 19. By a narrow margin Valery Giscard d'Estaing was today elected President of France in the second round of the elections. As an Independent Republican candidate, he scored nearly 51 per cent of the votes. His Socialist rival, Francois Mitterrand, with Communist support, got 49 per cent.

President Giscard campaigned on a reformist programme and promised a rise in basic wages. Union leaders threatened labour troubles (→ 27).

India joins nuclear club with Bomb test

May 18. The Rajasthan Desert gained a new hill and a 26-acre crater today as India detonated her first nuclear device in an underground test. India is the sixth nation to have the atom bomb.

Indira Gandhi, the Prime Minister, said that the purpose of the blast was peaceful, with potential use in mining or bringing water to the desert, but experts say India could be only two years away from military nuclear capability. She already has the Russian SAM delivery system and MiG-23 fighter planes. The expensive nuclear programme has gone ahead even though over 200 million Indians live below the poverty line.

Huge chemical explosion at Flixborough

A charred metal skeleton is all that remains after the massive blast.

June 10. Twenty-eight people were killed today in a massive explosion at a chemical plant on Humberside. Flixborough, a community of 200 that had overcome fears of danger because of the employment at the factory, within seconds was turned into a ghost village of devastation.

About 100 stone-built houses were wrecked. An acrid cloud later hung over the lush countryside and silent streets evacuated by families who pledged never to return. The factory was left a grotesque ruin of blackened steel frames.

The shattering violence had hit at 4.53pm without warning. Two brothers buried in the rubble of their home remember watching television and then recovering in hospital. Four miles away in Scunthorpe people were hurled to the ground.

A high-level inquiry is expected now, to seek ways of siting potentially dangerous industrial processes further away from homes. A build-up of vapour at the nylon factory is being blamed by experts.

Those who died were working near the plant's central control room. A red emergency light and a factory hooter had signalled trouble, but before workers had time to react two blasts ripped the factory apart and it roared into flames.

President Nixon, his mind on more pressing matters, shakes hands with a few of the crowd who have turned out during his trip to Belgium.

▷

Soviet ballet star defects in Toronto

June 30. Another leading dancer from the Soviet Union, Mikhail Baryshnikov, defected from the Bolshoi company on tour in Toronto last night. He broke away from his party and ran towards a waiting car, chased by presumed KGB men. Canadian police helped him into the vehicle.

Baryshnikov, a Latvian-born star aged 26, wants to stay in the West to continue dancing. Three weeks ago two former stars of the Kirov Ballet, Valery Panov and his wife, were allowed to leave after two years' harassment because they had applied to emigrate to Israel. In London a committee for their release had threatened to disrupt the Bolshoi performances.

IRA bomb damages Westminster Hall

Firemen tackle the Commons fire.

June 17. Nowhere is safe now. IRA terrorists have breached the high security arrangements at the Palace of Westminster to plant a 20-pound bomb in the 877-year-old Westminster Hall, scene of the lying-in-state of British sovereigns.

Eleven people were injured and the Hall was badly damaged by the blast and subsequent fires. Police suspect the bomber could have sneaked in with labourers employed on building the Commons' new underground car park (→25).

1974

JULY

Su	Mo	Tu	We	Th	Fr	Sa
	1	2	3	4	5	6
7	8	9	10	11	12	13
14	15	16	17	18	19	20
21	22	23	24	25	26	27
28	29	30	31			

1. San Francisco: First shop opened in the US by fashion designer Laura Ashley.

3. USSR: Two-man spacecraft launched into orbit (→26/8).

5. UK: Don Revie becomes England's new soccer manager.

8. Canada: Trudeau's Liberal Party overwhelmingly returned to power in general election.

10. Holland: Arabs end oil boycott against the Dutch.

11. London: First big property deal by Arabs in Central London.

13. UK: Gary Player wins the British Open Golf championship.

14. UK: Terrorist bombs explode in Birmingham and Manchester (→17).

15. Cyprus: Greek officers in the National Guard stage dawn coup.→

17. London: Bomb explosion at the Tower of London kills one and injures 41 (→16/9).

19. Spain: Franco hands over power to Prince Juan Carlos as his health deteriorates (→2/9).

21. UK: Police national computer starts operating.

22. Belfast: Harland and Wolff shipyard taken over by the government.

24. Washington: Supreme Court forces Nixon to hand over Watergate tapes (→27).

27. Washington: House Judiciary Committee votes first article of impeachment against Nixon.→

31. London: Trade Union and Industrial Relations Bill comes into force, repealing the Tories' Industrial Relations Act (→17/9).

DEATHS

1. Argentinian statesman Juan Domingo Peron, President 1943-55, 1973-4 (*10/8/1895).→

5. British novelist Georgette Heyer (*16/8/1902).

9. US politician and judge Earl Warren, Chief Justice of the Supreme Court (*19/3/1891).

Peace deal signed to end Cyprus conflict

July 30. In Geneva, it was all smiles today as the British Foreign Secretary, James Callaghan, clinched an agreement to bring peace and a new constitution to Cyprus. The deal, signed by both Greek and Turkish foreign ministers, calls for an immediate ceasefire and the establishment of a security zone between Turkish and Greek troops.

On the island, however, the fighting goes on. Turkey has established a beachhead around Kyrenia, on the north coast, through which it is pouring armour, troops and heavy artillery. President Glafcos Clerides said this week that he would have no hesitation in asking Greek Cypriots to fight "to the last drop of Greek blood" against any build-up of the Turkish presence.

Greek irregular troops are defending the zone occupied by the Turkish invaders, who staged a big eastward push yesterday to enlarge their territory in advance of today's ceasefire. The Turks are accused of looting and intimidation in the occupied zone. Today the Turkish command stopped UN relief convoys from entering to bring food to the besieged inhabitants (→15/8).

Trapped foreign nationals run to the helicopter that will evacuate them.

Civilians oust the colonels in Greece

July 24. Seven years of military rule by the Colonels ended in Greece today with the announcement that the ex-premier, Constantine Karamanlis, was returning from exile in France to form a new government.

The President, General Phaeton Gizikis, said: "In view of the exceptional circumstances with which our motherland is faced, the armed forces have decided to entrust the government of the country to a civilian government."

The news was greeted with jubilation. Around 100,000 people, shouting "Democracy!", flocked to Athens' Constitution Square. There is even speculation that ex-King Constantine may be recalled to the throne (→16/8).

Nixon must deliver tapes, says Court

July 30. The Supreme Court of the United States, by eight votes to one, ruled that in the case of US versus Nixon the president must hand over the additional tape recordings which have been demanded by the special prosecutor who wants them as evidence in the trial of six former Nixon aides.

The President tried to withhold them on grounds of "executive privilege", an extension of the tradition that the president's staff cannot be made to testify to Congress.

Chief Justice Warren Burger, a Nixon appointee, found the privilege was not absolute. The decision opens the way for impeachment, for which the House judiciary has voted 27-11 (→8/8).

Efficient West Germany win World Cup

July 7. Despite conceding a penalty to the rampaging Dutch in the first minute of the final, the efficient West Germans, playing on home soil and captained by the masterly Franz Beckenbauer, recovered to lead 2-1 by half-time and hang on to win their second World Cup.

England were eliminated in the qualifying rounds by Poland, who beat Brazil for third place and provided the final's top scorers in Lato (seven goals) and Szarmach (five). Scotland went out in the group matches, despite not losing a game, and it was left to Holland, with Johan Cruyff and Johan Neeskens to the fore, to provide the strongest challenge to the hosts.

Cruyff shows the Dutch sorrow.

Peron is dead: long live his wife Isabel

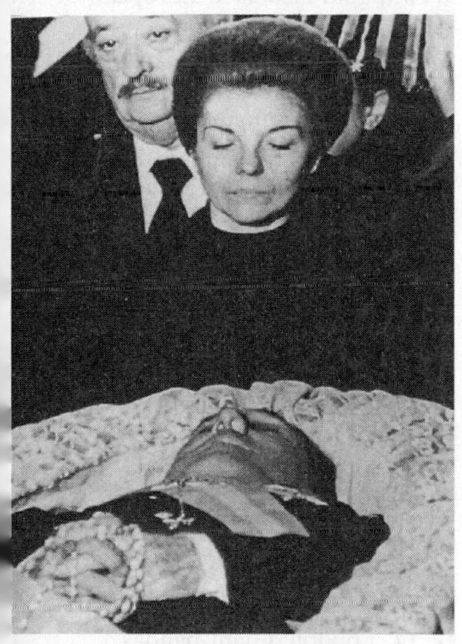

Isabel Peron watches at the coffin.

July 1. President Juan Domingo Peron, aged 78, died today after a 16-day illness. He handed over power on Saturday to his wife, who is now the first woman President of Argentina, or of any Latin-American country. Senora Isabel Peron was in tears when she told of Peron's death on television, saying he "gave his life for national and continental unity" and calling on God to "show me the road ahead".

She will need all the help she can get if she is to survive. She does not have the popular support enjoyed by Peron's first wife, the legendary Evita, who forged the alliance with the unions which enabled Peron to take dictatorial powers. An army coup is feared now.

Evert and Connors' Wimbledon love match

July 6. Youth ushered in a new era at Wimbledon with two exciting young talents – as closely involved with each other off-court as they are dedicated on it – taking the singles for the first time.

The 19-year-old Chrissie Evert, from Florida, beat the surprise Russian finalist Olga Morozova (who defeated Billie Jean King to get there) 6-0, 6-4. Meanwhile her brash fiance, the 21-year-old fireball from the Mid-West, Jimmy Connors, outgunned and outran the sentimental favourite, Ken Rosewall, now 39 and close to retirement, 6-1, 6-1, 6-4.

Loving victors Connors and Evert.

1974

AUGUST

Su	Mo	Tu	We	Th	Fr	Sa
				1	2	3
4	5	6	7	8	9	10
11	12	13	14	15	16	17
18	19	20	21	22	23	24
25	26	27	28	29	30	31

4. Italy: 12 die in neo-Fascist attack on express train (→8/9).

8. London: Government says capital transfer and wealth taxes will be introduced (→19).

10. Portugal: Two-year plan to give independence to Angola announced (→26).

11. Bangladesh: 2,500 feared dead and ten million homeless after monsoon floods half the country.

14. West Germany: First flight of UK-German-Italian multi-role combat aircraft.

14. Libya: Gaddafi arrests 500 Egyptian troops after Cairo refuses to return 40 planes.

15. South Korea: President Park Chung-hee's wife shot by an assassin.

16. Athens: Leftist leader Andreas Papandreou returns after seven years in exile (→18/11).

19. London: FT share index slumps below 200 points for the first time in 16 years (→5/9).

23. US: US Marshals attack spectators at trial of Indians for Wounded Knee occupation.

23. UK: Colonel David Stirling launches ultra-right anti-strike militia.

26. USSR: Soyuz 15 launched into orbit to dock with space station.

26. Algiers: Portugal signs pact to give independence to her two West African colonies (→30/9).

28. UK: Liberal leader Jeremy Thorpe begins election campaign by hovercraft (→30).

29. UK: Eight-hour battle between hippies and police at illegal Windsor pop festival.

30. UK: Thorpe's hovercraft is wrecked on a Devon beach.

DEATHS

13. Irish playwright and novelist Kate O'Brien (*3/12/1897).

22. Polish-born British biologist Dr. Jacob Bronowski (*18/1/1908).

Greek Cypriots flee from Turkish tanks

Turkish cypriot Rauf Denktash.

Aug 15. Turkish tanks rumbled into the Greek Cypriot port of Famagusta today to link up with Turkish Cypriot fighters. The Turkish airforce supported the invasion with napalm and high explosive bombing attacks.

The 12,000 Greek-Cypriot inhabitants have streamed out of Famagusta, as it was strafed and bombed, in a seven-mile long convoy, leaving it wide open to the advancing Turks who are now poised for a final assault tomorrow morning.

The town's population had just a handful of national guardsmen to defend them. Most have now taken refuge at the nearby British base of Dhekelia (→2/9).

40,000 stranded as holiday giant fails

Aug 16. Around 40,000 British holidaymakers are stranded today after the giant leisure group, Court Line, owner of Clarksons and Horizon Holidays, collapsed last night. At least 100,000 more people have holidays booked with one of the tour operators; they are unlikely to get their money back.

Yesterday 5,000 people flew out only hours before the group ceased operations at 7pm. Trade Secretary Peter Shore promised that all those stranded abroad will get home, but he can do nothing for those who lose booked holidays. ▷

Nixon is first US President to resign

Aug 8. President Richard Nixon, facing impeachment by Congress for "high crimes and misdemeanours" in the Watergate scandal, today announced his resignation.

He will be succeeded by his newly appointed Vice-President, Gerald Ford. Ford was until recently the Republican minority leader in the House of Representatives. He was appointed Vice-President after the previous incumbent, Spiro Agnew, resigned after pleading guilty to tax evasion charges.

Mr Nixon was re-elected by an overwhelming majority in November 1972 after his brilliant opening of relations with China. On June 17 1972, however, five burglars were caught putting listening devices on telephones in the Democratic party headquarters.

Gradually, a whole series of illegal or unethical acts on the part of the Nixon White House and the Republican campaign were revealed. Mr Nixon stubbornly refused to admit wrong-doing, but the Senate investigating committee and special prosecutors uncovered convincing evidence of Mr Nixon's involvement in covering up wrong-doing.

After the Supreme Court found against him and held that he must hand over tapes of his private conversations with aides to the courts, impeachment proceedings were only a matter of time, and Mr Nixon, defiant to the last, chose to resign rather than wait for Congress to impeach him (→ 9).

Richard Nixon, with wife Pat and daughter Tricia, resigns the presidency.

Gerald Ford is sworn in as new President

Aug 9. President Gerald Ford was today sworn in as President of the United States in place of Richard Nixon, who resigned on August 8 after he no longer had enough votes to avoid impeachment for his part in the Watergate cover-up.

Mr Ford, who is 60, has been the Republican congressman for the Grand Rapids district of Michigan for many years and has been more recently the Republican minority leader in the House, where he has the reputation of being a conservative, but easy-going politician. He became Vice-President after Spiro Agnew resigned, pleading guilty to tax evasion (→ 20).

Gerald Ford, from Vice-President to the leader of the Western world.

Rockefeller chosen as Vice-President

Aug 20. President Gerald Ford today chose the Governor of New York, Nelson Rockefeller, as his Vice-President. He said he thought Rockefeller would be "a good partner for me and for the country". Governor Rockefeller, whose family controls vast wealth as a result of his grandfather's control of Standard Oil, ran for president in 1964 and 1968 as a moderate Republican (→ 16/9).

Jail terms for Dean and J. Ehrlichman

Aug 2. Two of President Nixon's aides, John Dean and John Ehrlichman, have been sentenced to jail terms for their roles in the Watergate affair. Ehrlichman was sentenced to a maximum of five years and Dean received a maximum of four years. They had made futile respective appeals of innocence and for compassion (→ 8).

1974

SEPTEMBER

Su	Mo	Tu	We	Th	Fr	Sa
1	2	3	4	5	6	7
8	9	10	11	12	13	14
15	16	17	18	19	20	21
22	23	24	25	26	27	28
29	30					

1. Yugoslavia: 150 die in train crash.

1. Nicaragua: General Somoza appointed President.

2. Cyprus: Mass grave of 60 bodies of Turks uncovered (→ 7/12).

2. Madrid: Franco resumes controlling Spain after recovering from his illness.

3. Northern Ireland: Enoch Powell adopted as Official Unionist candidate for South Down (→ 11/10).

4. Italy: Britons Alan Pascoe, David Jenkins, and Steve Ovett win gold medals in European championships (→ 8).

6. London: Government White Paper outlines plans to outlaw sexual discrimination.

8. Greece: 88 die in crash of US Boeing 707; Palestinian guerrillas claim responsibility.

8. Italy: Britons Ian Thompson and Brendan Foster win gold medals on last day of championships.

10. China: Chou En-lai resigns as PM (→ 31/10).

11. Mozambique: 100 feared dead in two days of violence (→ 20).

12. UK: Inflation pushes the cost of a Mini up to £1,000 a car.

14. London: Giant pandas Chia-Chia and Ching-Ching arrive in the zoo.

15. Vietnam: 71 die when hijacker blows up plane.

16. Belfast: IRA shoot dead a judge and a magistrate (→ 5/10).

17. UK: Nurses receive pay rises of up to 58 per cent.

20. Honduras: Cyclone Fifi kills 10,000.

20. Mozambique: Transitional government led by Frelimo liberation movement takes office (→ 21/10).

23. UK: First transmissions of Ceefax Teletext information service on BBC-TV.

29. Moscow: 10,000 visit officially sanctioned modern art show.

Selassie, Lion of Judah, has lost his pride

Sept 12. A shabby second-hand Volkswagen pulled up outside the royal palace in Addis Ababa today and an old man in a dark suit was bundled into the back seat. He was the Emperor of Ethiopia, His Imperial Majesty Haile Selassie, King of Kings, Lion of Judah, now overthrown in a coup by middle-ranking army officers, who are so unsure of themselves that for the time being they are unnamed.

They accuse Selassie of corruption and of allowing the people to live in poverty, and they promise to hold free elections in the near future. The deposed Emperor began his reign almost 60 years ago with a programme of modernisation, but was exiled after the war with Italy in the 1930s.

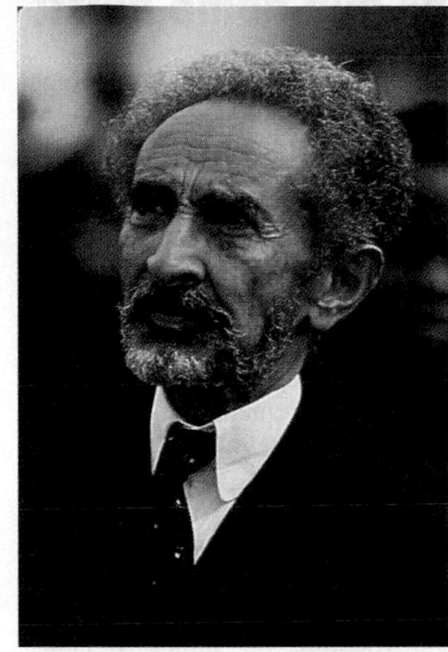

Selassie: no longer King of Kings.

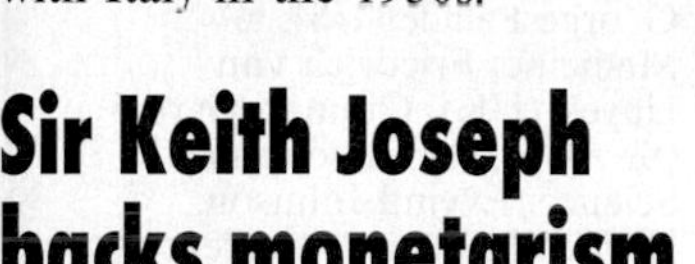

Sir Keith Joseph backs monetarism

Sept 5. Sir Keith Joseph, the shadow Home Secretary, today urged control of the money supply to check galloping inflation. An influential right-wing Tory figure, he rejected the full employment policies of post-war governments. Edward Heath retorted that mass unemployment is a greater social evil than inflation. Will he sack Sir Keith? "That would be preposterous," he said (→ 19/10).

Ford gives pardon to disgraced Nixon

Sept 16. President Ford has pardoned his predecessor, Richard Nixon, who resigned the presidency last month, though special prosecutors and a grand committee of the House of Representatives all suspect him of criminal acts.

Opinion remains sharply divided, with some feeling former President Nixon has suffered enough, others that Ford has weakened his authority by the pardon (→ 12/10).

Young rebels force out Portuguese leader

Spinola: ousted by radicals.

Sept 30. General Spinola, who has ruled Portugal for the past five months, resigned as president today with his power eroded by the increasingly radical young leaders of the Armed Force Movement.

In an emotional resignation speech to the Council of State, General Spinola declared: "I find myself incapable of faithfully executing the programme of the Movement. My sense of loyalty prevents me from betraying my people, for whom new forms of slavery are being prepared under the flag of a false freedom."

General Spinola has been succeeded as president by his deputy, General Francisco da Costa Gomez, but he is looked on as a stopgap.

1974

OCTOBER

Su	Mo	Tu	We	Th	Fr	Sa
		1	2	3	4	5
6	7	8	9	10	11	12
13	14	15	16	17	18	19
20	21	22	23	24	25	26
27	28	29	30	31		

1. London: Britain's first McDonald's hamburger restaurant opens in south London.

5. UK: Five die and 65 injured by IRA bombs in two Guildford pubs (→ 8).

8. Stockholm: former Eire foreign minister Sean MacBride wins Nobel Peace Prize (→ 10/12).

11. London: IRA bombs go off in Pall Mall and Marble Arch (→ 16).

12. Washington: Resignation of Watergate special prosecutor Leon Jaworski.

13. India: Worst famine in 20 years feared.

15. US: Students injured in racial fighting after court order for integration of Boston's schools.

19. UK: Sir Keith Joseph makes controversial speech calling for better birth control amongst the poor (→ 21).

21. Mozambique: 48 killed in racial violence.

21. UK: Wages have risen by a record 20.7 per cent in the last 12 months.

22. London: Bomb explodes close to Edward Heath in Central London (→ 28).

23. Russia: Moscow is chosen as site for the 1980 Olympics.

25. UK: Government awards £5 million to thalidomide children to offset taxation of their trust fund.

28. London: Bomb explodes under car of Sports Minister Denis Howell (→ 4/11).

29. Zaire: Muhummad Ali regains world heavyweight championship, knocking out George Foreman.

29. Morocco: Arab leaders pledge billions of dollars in aid to frontline states for war against Israel.

31. Hong Kong: Communist newspaper confirms death of China's former head of state Liu Shao-chi.

DEATH

24. Soviet violinist David Oistrakh (*30/9/1908).

Labour win power with tiny majority

Oct 11. Labour has won by the narrowest of overall majorities – just three seats. "This is viable and my government can endure," said Harold Wilson after Britain's second general election this year. For survival he is relying on clever parliamentary footwork.

The final seats tally tonight is Labour 319, Tories 276, Liberals 13, Nationalists 14 and Others 13. The Prime Minister called for national unity to tackle the gravest economic crisis since the last war. Unlike the defeated Mr Heath, who offered co-operation with other parties if he won, Mr Wilson is not asking anyone outside Labour's ranks to share in government.

The defiant Mr Heath, in trouble with his own side now, says he will stay on (→ 25).

Political leaders enter the House.

Maze prison is set on fire by rioters

Oct 16. Republican prisoners set fire to their Maze Prison tonight and turned on their guards in protest against new restrictions which had been imposed on visitors. As troops were flown in to the prison grounds by helicopter, news of the disturbances brought sympathisers on to the streets in Republican Belfast where bonfires were lit and buses stoned (→ 22). ▷

Conteh wins light-heavyweight title

Conteh wins world boxing crown.

Oct 1. After 15 punishing rounds at Wembley against one of the hardest punchers around, John Conteh of Liverpool won on points to take the world light-heavyweight title, the first British holder since Freddie Mills nearly 25 years ago.

The 23-year-old Conteh, with only 26 professional fights behind him, needed all the strength and concentration he could muster to grind down his experienced Argentinian opponent, Jorge Ahumada, and succeed to Greg Foster's vacant title.

Documents stolen from Wilson's home

Oct 25. Some of the Prime Minister's personal papers, including tax documents, are missing from his home in fashionable Lord North Street, Westminster. No state papers are involved. Scotland Yard said: "We are treating the loss as theft."

Curiously, there is no evidence that the house was broken into. Mr Wilson suspects that ultra-right MI5 men in a plot to discredit him may have been the burglars. Friends think he is allowing his imagination to run away with him.

On returning to the premiership last March, Mr Wilson decided not to live in Downing Street. "I don't want to live above the shop any more," he explained (→ 6/11).

1974

NOVEMBER

Su	Mo	Tu	We	Th	Fr	Sa
					1	2
3	4	5	6	7	8	9
10	11	12	13	14	15	16
17	18	19	20	21	22	23
24	25	26	27	28	29	30

3. South Korea: 88 die in hotel fire.

4. UK: Judith Ward jailed for 30 years for the M62 bombing (→ 7).

6. London: Government lifts disqualification and surcharge of rebel Clay Cross councillors (→ 24/12).

7. London: IRA Woolwich pub bomb kills one and injures 28 (→ 15).

8. UK: Ronald Milhench jailed for forgery, attempted fraud, and firearms offences.

10. West Germany: Top West Berlin judge murdered in revenge for death of Baader-Meinhof terrorist (→ 29).

13. New York: Yassir Arafat addresses the UN and says: "Do not let the olive branch fall from my hands".

14. UK: Police search Sussex coves for the missing Lord Lucan.

15. Coventry: IRA terrorist James McDade killed by his own bomb.→

18. Athens: Premier Karamanlis wins first free elections in a decade (→ 8/12).

22. UK: Arrest of five Irishmen who left Birmingham after the pub bombings (→ 29).

24. USSR: Ford and Brezhnev reach broad agreement on limiting strategic nuclear weapons.

26. UK: Miss World, Helen Morgan, resigns, fearing she will be named in divorce case.

29. West Germany: Terrorist leader Ulrike Meinhof jailed for eight years.

29. London: Prevention of Terrorism Act becomes law (→ 17/12).

DEATHS

7. British novelist Eric Linklater (*8/3/1899).

13. Italian film director Vittorio de Sica (*7/7/1902).

24. Irish-born US writer Cornelius Ryan (*5/6/1920).

25. Burmese UN Secretary-General U Thant (*22/1/1909).

Seventeen killed by pub bomb blasts

Nov 21. IRA terrorists tonight killed 17 people by blowing up two Birmingham pubs packed with young drinkers. Devices exploded simultaneously at the Mulberry Bush and the Tavern in the Town, bringing tons of rubble down on to the bars. Up to 120 injured customers were taken to hospital, many by taxis helping ambulancemen, and firemen dug with their bare hands to rescue victims pinned beneath masonry.

The twin outrage, the worst yet by the IRA on the British mainland, appears to be in revenge for a ban on a hero's funeral being staged in the Midlands for James McDade, who was killed last week by his own bomb in Coventry (→ 22).

Police want Lucan for nanny's murder

The Lucans, but where is he now?

Nov 7. In London's gaming society he was known as "Lucky", but luck seems to be running out for Richard John Bingham, the seventh Earl of Lucan, who is being sought by police in Britain and Europe for the alleged murder of his child's nanny, Sandra Rivett and an attack on his estranged wife.

The nanny's battered body was discovered after Lady Lucan, suffering from head wounds, staggered into a Belgravia public house near their home screaming: "He's murdered my nanny! My children, my children!" (→ 14)

1974

DECEMBER

Su	Mo	Tu	We	Th	Fr	Sa
1	2	3	4	5	6	7
8	9	10	11	12	13	14
15	16	17	18	19	20	21
22	23	24	25	26	27	28
29	30	31				

3. UK: Government says it will cut defence spending by £4,700 million over ten years, and reduce forces east of Suez.

7. Cyprus: President Makarios returns to the island.

8. Athens: Greece votes to become a republic and abolish the monarchy.

10. Stockholm: Nobel Prizes go to Sir Martin Ryle, Antony Hewish (UK, Physics); Paul Flory (US, Chemistry); Albert Claude (Belgium), Christian-Rene de Duve (Belgium), George Palade (US), all Medicine; Friedrich von Hayek (UK), Gunnar Myrdal (Sweden), both Economic Science; Eyvind Johnson, Harry Martinson (Sweden, Literature); and in Oslo to Eisaku Sato (Japan) and Sean MacBride (Ireland), both Peace.

11. Rhodesia: Premier Ian Smith agrees immediate cease-fire with black nationalists.

12. US: Georgia Governor James Carter announces his candidature for president (→ 19).

17. London: IRA bombs kill one, injure five (→ 18).

18. Northern Ireland: Government agrees to pay £42,000 compensation to victims of Bloody Sunday (→ 22).

19. US: Nelson Rockefeller sworn in as Vice-President.

22. London: IRA bombers attack Edward Heath's house.

26. Australia: Cyclone shatters the city of Darwin.

29. Pakistan: 4,700 killed by an earthquake.

DEATH

14. US journalist Walter Lippman (*23/9/1899).

HITS OF 1974

She

Seasons in the sun

Tiger feet

QUOTE OF THE YEAR

"Who loves ya, baby?"

Telly Savalas, in the TV series "Kojak".

Vanishing MP turns up Down Under

John Stonehouse enters the court.

Dec 24. A Labour MP and former minister, whose clothes were found on a Miami beach, is in custody in Australia tonight as police examine what appears to be a false passport.

John Stonehouse, a former Postmaster-General, is claiming the right to stay in Australia – "to establish a new life". British police are investigating the affairs of a Bangladesh bank of which Stonehouse was chairman.

Solzhenitsyn collects Prize four years late

Dec 10. The exiled Russian author, Alexander Solzhenitsyn, collected the Nobel Prize he was awarded four years ago at a Stockholm ceremony today – and then left his medal behind on his seat. He thanked the Swedish Academy for having honoured his empty chair when he was being harassed in the Soviet Union. The Communist bloc countries boycotted the ceremony.

Since the prize was announced, Solzhenitsyn's fame has become world-wide through the publication this year of translations of "The Gulag Archipelago", his two-volume exposure of the Soviet labour camps from 1918-1956, in which he spent eight years himself.

The "Gulag" – an acronym for the camp administration – has been officially unknown in the USSR. He speaks for all the victims of the Communist regime, under Lenin as well as Stalin, who have been enslaved in some part of its chain of camps, many of them never to emerge again.

Better late than never – Solzhenitsyn receives his Nobel Prize at last.

Soaraway inflation has Britain reeling

Dec 31. As the year ends, galloping inflation has Britain in its grip. A vicious circle of price rises and wage increases has pushed up the cost of living by 20 per cent this year, and industry is stunned by crippling wage demands and rises in the costs of raw materials. The price of steel, for example, has gone up by 45 per cent this year.

Figures issued in September showed that wages had gone up by 20 per cent in the previous year; December's figures give a record annual rise of 26 per cent. The government has been unable to keep its own wage bill under control, with local government workers awarded a 13.5 per cent increase, senior civil servants 28 per cent and teachers 32 per cent. Bakers went on strike for a 66 per cent wage claim.

The Chancellor Denis Healey's November budget boosted the rate of inflation, by dropping price control for nationalised industries and applying a prohibitive VAT rate at the petrol pump, adding to the rise in oil prices which has fuelled the worldwide inflationary spiral. A gallon of four-star petrol cost 42p in January; now, motorists are paying 72p, and grimly expecting the 80p gallon in the New Year.

Arts: Great composer Duke Ellington is buried under honours

Duke Ellington's death in May (he was 75 and had lung cancer) brought home to many that he was America's greatest composer, with some 3,000 works to his credit. He held the presidential Medal of Freedom, the highest civilian award in the US, and honorary degrees from 15 universities. Two African republics issued stamps in his honour. The musical world, from **Leonard Bernstein** to **Miles Davis**, paid its tributes to him.

The albums featuring his orchestra stretched jazz far beyond the limits of the small improvising group without losing its character, although his scores became as complex as classical ones. His instrument was not really the piano but the orchestra.

He kept his very expensive payroll of virtuoso musicians together by writing popular hits like "Sophisticated Lady" and "Satin Doll" and playing in night clubs, but in recent years he regarded his "Sacred Concerts", played in cathedrals from San Francisco to Coventry, or his "New Orleans Suite" (1970 record of the year), as his important works. In 1970 he toured Europe, the USSR and Latin America.

David Hockney was honoured by an exhibition at the Paris Musee des Arts Decoratifs, and designed Glyndebourne's production of "The Rake's Progress".

"The Ascent of Man", a book based on the popular-science television series, was a best-seller in its field. Its author and presenter, **Dr Jacob Bronowski**, died in August. Television's most esteemed comedy duo, **Morecambe and Wise**, invited as their guest **Glenda Jackson**, who has won her second Oscar for "A Touch of Class".

Morecambe and Wise, Britain's top comedy duo, with their Christmas guest, Glenda Jackson as Cleopatra.

Genetic engineering soon to be a reality

This was the year it became clear that practical genetic engineering will soon be a reality. Biologists in the United States have shown it is possible to chop up the genetic material DNA, to stick fragments from different sources together, introduce these artificial genes into simple organisms like bacteria, and make them multiply. The long-term possibilities are endless: new drugs, improved plant and animal breeding, treatment for hereditary diseases among them.

However, also this year, a new environmental alarm was sounded. The ozone layer, high in the atmosphere, which protects us against harmful ultra-violet radiation from the sun, may be threatened by chlorofluoro-carbons, chemicals used as propellants in aerosols.

1975

JANUARY

Su	Mo	Tu	We	Th	Fr	Sa
			1	2	3	4
5	6	7	8	9	10	11
12	13	14	15	16	17	18
19	20	21	22	23	24	25
26	27	28	29	30	31	

1. Washington: Nixon aides Mitchell, Haldeman and Ehrlichman are convicted of trying to cover up Watergate.

2. UK: Charlie Chaplin and P.G. Wodehouse are knighted in the New Year Honours (→4/3).

5. Australia: 17 people die when a ship rams the Tasman Bridge in Hobart, Tasmania.

6. Washington: The Pentagon is reported to want a squadron of the new AWAC early-warning planes.

7. UK: OPEC are reported to have agreed to a ten per cent rise in the price of crude oil.

9. London: The Government announces pay rises of up to 74 per cent for 14,000 hospital workers (→20).

10. Portugal: The Government agrees to give Angola its independence.→

10. UK: Two workers at Windscale have died this week, apparently of leukaemia (→5/2).

14. UK: 17-year-old Lesley Whittle, left £82,000 by her father, is kidnapped from her home in Shropshire (→7/3).

17. UK: Britain's last major typewriter maker, Imperial Typewriters, says it will close (→31/7).

20. UK: Wage inflation reaches 28.5 per cent, a quarter of pay rises are breaking the Social Contract (→13/2).

20. London: The Government abandons the Channel Tunnel.

23. London: Wilson says there will be a referendum on EEC membership soon (→18/12).

25. London: The Tory leadership battle begins between Heath and ex-Education Secretary Mrs Thatcher (→4/2).

27. UK: Five IRA bombs go off in London; 19 are hurt in a blast in Manchester (→16/2).

29. UK: A colour TV licence goes up £6 to £18, black and white £1 to £7 (→30/7/77).

31. London: Publication of the Industry Bill to create a National Enterprise Board.

New heavy attack on Cambodian capital

The suffering continues: blood and fire add to Phnom Penh's agony.

Jan 4. The Communist Khmer Rouge forces have begun a siege of the Cambodian capital, Phnom Penh with a heavy rocket and artillery attack and the guerrillas are already nibbling at the city's outer defences. Rebel pressure is building up to the north and west as the North Vietnamese army sweeps on through Laos, South Vietnam and Cambodia.

The first objective of the besiegers will be Neak Luong, the important ferry town on the Mekong river. Once they have that the capital will be cut off from supplies and its fall will be inevitable.

Arrangements are already being made to evacuate non-essential members of the 200 strong American embassy and the many employees of American companies supporting the Cambodian war effort.

No one really knows what to expect if the city does fall to the Khmer Rouge. Its leader, Pol Pot, is a man of mystery who has fought in the jungle for five years without making any clear statement of his political intentions.

The new Archbishop of Canterbury, Dr. Donald Coggan, aged 65, dressed in full regalia, with the cathedral in the background.

Burmah Oil crash greases share slide

Jan 2. More than £1,000 million was wiped off share values today as the City reacted gloomily to the collapse of Burmah Oil, Britain's second largest oil company.

The Financial Times ordinary share index dropped to a 20-year low of 149.7, gold plummetted $11.50 to $174.50 an ounce and sterling dropped on all foreign exchanges.

A surprise loss made last year on tanker operations has meant that Burmah cannot service huge debts incurred to finance an ambitious acquisitions programme. The Bank of England and the Government have bailed it out. But City analysts say there could be more "lame ducks" this year.

Freedom for Angola after 13 year fight

Jan 16. Just 400 years after they founded the city of Luanda as the capital of Angola, the Portuguese today agreed to give the colony its independence. A bitter liberation war has been going on for 13 years, but not until the military coup in Lisbon last April did the prospect of independence appear on the horizon. The soldiers have promised to hand over power to the Angolans in November. There are, however, three rival liberation movements, who have been inclined to fight each other rather than the Portuguese. Lisbon is sending an soldier to Luanda to try to persuade the three to join a coalition government.

The future of independent Angola?

IRA truce called off after only 25 days

Jan 16. After 25-day lull in its campaign of bombing and murder, the IRA said it would call off the ceasefire at midnight. Observers are convinced that "hawks" in the Provisional terrorist movement have overcome "doves" who were looking for a political solution.

Ulster Secretary Merlyn Rees denounced the move. "I will not be influenced by any views which are backed by the bomb and the bullet," he said. Police are stepping up security against renewed IRA activity in Britain.

1975

FEBRUARY

Su	Mo	Tu	We	Th	Fr	Sa
						1
2	3	4	5	6	7	8
9	10	11	12	13	14	15
16	17	18	19	20	21	22
23	24	25	26	27	28	

2. Ethiopia: Government planes attack rebel positions outside Asmara, the Eritrean capital (→ 21/3).

4. London: Heath resigns as Tory leader after Thatcher's shock 130-119 victory in the first ballot of Tory MPs.→

5. London: The Government approves two new nuclear power stations at Sizewell, in Suffolk, and Torness Point, in Lothian (→ 10/6).

13. UK: Miners accept pay rises of up to 35 per cent.

13. Cyprus: Turkish Cypriot leader Rauf Denktash declares Turkish Cyprus independent.

16. Ireland: IRA prisoners at Portlaoise jail call off a hunger strike (→ 5/4).

17. London: The Coal Board says coal prices will go up by 30 per cent next month (→ 25/3).

18. London: Maudling is recalled as shadow Foreign Secretary in Thatcher's new shadow cabinet (→ 25).

24. Kathmandu: 29-year-old King Birendra is crowned as the world's only Hindu monarch.

25. London: Lord Thorneycroft becomes chairman of the Conservative Party.

26. London: MPs approve a £420,000 rise in the Civil List by a majority of 337 (→ 1/7).

26. London: Off-duty policeman Stephen Tibble is shot dead chasing a suspected burglar.→

27. West Berlin: Peter Lorenz, leader of the city's Christian Democratic Party, is kidnapped at gunpoint (→ 2/3).

DEATHS

14. British scientist and philosopher Sir Julian Sorell Huxley (*22/6/1887).→

14. British-born US author Sir Pelham Grenville Wodehouse (*15/10/1881).

24. Soviet statesman Nikolai Bulganin (*11/6/1895).

28. British music and cricket writer Sir John Frederick Neville Cardus (*2/4/1889).

Underground crash at Moorgate kills 35

Firemen try to reach a survivor in the wreckage of the underground train.

Feb 28. A tube train today rammed into the end of a dead-end tunnel, killing the driver and 34 passengers. As rescue workers prepared for a long fight to bring all the injured out of the mangle of compressed carriages, a full-scale investigation was set up into the Moorgate tube disaster, the worst-ever on the London Underground.

The key question is why the driver, Leslie Newson, aged 56, accelerated into the blind tunnel when his 8.37am commuter train from Drayton Park should have been braking. It sped past platform nine at twice the usual speed of 15mph and then ran out of track.

The first three of the six coaches telescoped at the end of the 80-yard tunnel after crashing through sand piles and over the buffers. Many of the dead have been found beneath the first carriage; the first 15 feet has compacted down to two feet and is embedded in the end wall.

All day teams of doctors, firemen and nurses wrestled with the wreckage, in dust and withering heat, attempting to reach those still alive. A teenage policewoman was carried out after 12 hours. One of her feet had been pinned down by the tangle of metal and had to be amputated at the scene.

One young doctor who spent hours in the tunnel said: "If there's a hell, I've seen it."

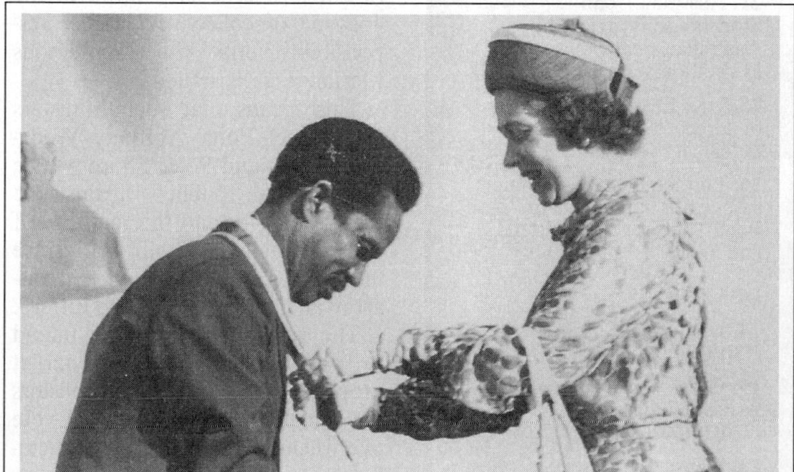

Feb 19. More than 10,000 Barbadians cheer as the Queen knights their cricketing hero, Gary Sobers, in a ceremony at Bridgetown racecourse. Sir Garfield said afterwards that he would remain "one of the lads".

Margaret Thatcher is new Tory leader

Feb 11. Margaret Thatcher, wife of a wealthy businessman and mother of twins, today became the first woman leader of a British political party at the age of 49. Her victory over four male rivals in the fight to succeed Edward Heath in the Tory leadership was overwhelming.

She won the votes of 146 MPs against 79 for William Whitelaw and fewer than 20 apiece for Sir Geoffrey Howe, James Prior and John Peyton.

Women of all parties were exultant. Mr Heath sulked. Mrs Thatcher tried to conceal her ectasy. "I beat four chaps. Now let's get down to work", she said. Mr Whitelaw, close to tears, promised: "We unite behind her".

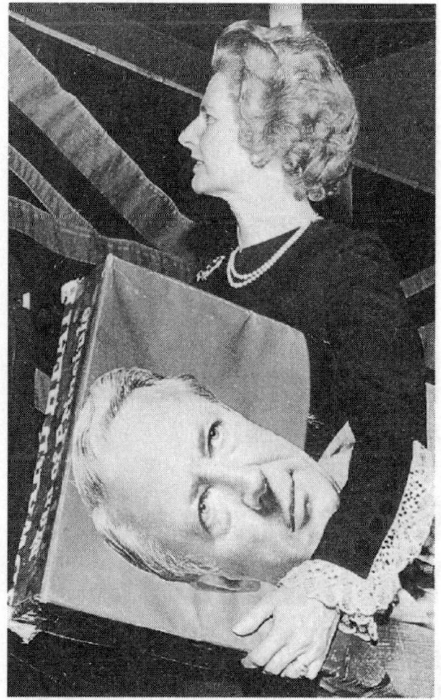

Mr H is carried off by Mrs T.

Nixon aides jailed for Watergate role

Feb 21. Four of President Nixon's senior aides were sentenced to jail today for conspiracy to obstruct justice in the Watergate affair.

Former Attorney-General John Mitchell, chief of staff H.R. Haldeman, and domestic adviser John Ehrlichman, were sentenced to terms of up to eight years. Robert Mardian, formerly an assistant Attorney-General, received a shorter sentence. ▷

Shot policeman was killed by IRA man

Feb 27. A nationwide hunt is under way for an IRA gunman who shot a 21-year-old policeman in a London street. Motorcycle officer PC Stephen Tibble, had joined detectives chasing a suspect. He was shot twice at point-blank range.

During a round-up of known sympathisers, police have uncovered an IRA bomb "factory" in a Hammersmith basement – an indication that the IRA is preparing a new series of bombing outrages in London and the provinces.

A Scotland Yard commissioner said the find was "the breakthrough we have waited for".

PC Stephen Tibble: killed off-duty.

Boffin of the Brains Trust, Huxley, dies

Feb 15. Sir Julian Huxley, one of the country's best known scientists, died today at his home in London, aged 87. He was a member of a distinguished family. Darwin's famous advocate Thomas Huxley was his grandfather, the novelist Aldous Huxley was his brother.

Julian Huxley made important contributions to biology, particularly evolution and genetics, but it was as a teacher, writer and populariser that he became known to a wide public. He collaborated with H.G. Wells on a highly successful book called "The Science of Life", was a popular contributor to the Brains Trust radio panel during the Second World War and became the first director-general of UNESCO after it.

1975

MARCH

Su	Mo	Tu	We	Th	Fr	Sa
						1
2	3	4	5	6	7	8
9	10	11	12	13	14	15
16	17	18	19	20	21	22
23	24	25	26	27	28	29
30	31					

1. Nairobi: 27 Kenyans die when a bomb rips through a bus station.

2. West Germany: Four Baader-Meinhof prisoners are flown to Frankfurt as part of a deal to free Peter Lorenz (→24/4).

4. Rhodesia: Zimbabwe African National Union leader Ndabaningi Sithole is arrested (→1/6).

6. UK: The General Medical Council says overseas doctors who join the NHS will have to sit English tests after May.

9. Washington: Two aides of the late Robert Kennedy claim he said the CIA had a contract with the Mafia to kill Castro (→19/5).

11. London: The Government says direct-grant grammar schools will be phased out by the end of 1976.

15. Glasgow: Troops move in to clear 70,000 tons of refuse that have piled up during a nine-week dustmen's strike.

19. South Vietnam: Thousands of refugees are fleeing from the northern provinces as North Vietnamese troops advance.→

20. London: A warrant is issued for the arrest of John Stonehouse on charges of theft, forgery and deception (→21).

21. Addis Ababa: The monarchy is abolished.

21. Australia: John Stonehouse is arrested by Australian police on an extradition warrant (→20/10).

25. UK: Electricity prices rise by a record 33 per cent (→13/5).

26. London: The Government says it will nationalise the Belfast shipyard of Harland and Wolff.

DEATHS

14. US actress Susan Hayward (*30/6/1918).

15. Greek shipping magnate Aristotle Onassis (*20/1/1906).

28. British composer Sir Arthur Edward Drummond Bliss, Master of the Queen's Musick 1953-75 (*2/8/1891).

Key Vietnam cities fall

March 29. Da Nang, South Vietnam's second largest city, fell to the North Vietnamese army today. It is a prize of major military importance. With its sprawling complex of land, sea and air bases stuffed full of American-supplied equipment, its loss is a terrible blow to the South Vietnamese efforts to halt the onrushing Communist forces.

This represents an advance of 50 miles in the three days since the ancient imperial capital of Hue fell to an attack by Communist tanks and infantry. The survivors of the rearguard were evacuated by boat to Da Nang but now that fortress has also fallen and the North Vietnamese are pushing on inexorably towards Saigon.

Reports from Da Nang suggest that there was no real defence of the city with civil and military officials abandoning their posts as anarchy broke out among hungry, looting, demoralised troops and terror-stricken refugees.

One lone telex operator stuck to his post. One of his last messages was: "There is pandemonium everywhere". Almost the entire 1st and 2nd Divisions were said to be out of control, rampaging through the city. Some people clung to the undercarriages of planes in their efforts to escape and fell to their deaths in the sea.

A family flees from the Communists.

Cabinet is split on Common Market

March 18. By 16 votes to seven the Cabinet today decided to advise the nation to vote in the coming referendum to keep Britain in the Common Market. To prevent a fatal Government split, Mr Wilson was forced to accept suspension of the doctrine of collective Cabinet responsibility until the momentous Market issue is settled.

This means that such ministers as Michael Foot, Anthony Wedgwood Benn and Peter Shore will be free to argue publicly against the Prime Minister and the majority of their colleagues. It is 40 years since there was comparable Cabinet disarray and an "agreement to differ".

The rebel ministers now intend to wage a vigorous anti-Market propaganda war. Opinion pollsters are signalling that Britain will vote overwhelmingly for Market membership.

Mr Wilson said that he is not over-enthusiastic about the Cabinet's majority view and he will not resign if the vote is "No".

Arise, Sir Charlie: Chaplin is knighted

March 4. The Queen today conferred a knighthood on one of the best-known expatriate Englishmen, Charles Chaplin, now aged 85 and living in Switzerland after finding fame and fortune in the United States.

The Tramp becomes a Knight.

King Faisal killed by crazed nephew

March 25. A mentally deranged Arab prince today assassinated his uncle, King Faisal of Saudi Arabia, during a ceremony in his palace at Riyadh. The murder of the most powerful and moderate of Islamic leaders threw the Arab world into chaos.

It has also alarmed the US who fear it may upset the balance of power in the region, especially coming soon after the breakdown of Henry Kissinger's Middle East peace mission. A younger brother, Crown Prince Khalid, succeeds to the Throne. The King was shot as he received his subjects on the Prophet's birthday. His killer, Prince Museid, aged 31, studied in the US in the 1960's (→18/6).

King Faisal in his prime.

Black Panther kills kidnapped heiress

March 7. The body of a young heiress, kidnapped from her Shropshire home 52 days ago by a man known as the Black Panther, was found in a 60-foot drain shaft today. She appears to have been strangled.

Lesley Whittle was discovered dead only a few feet away from a spot where the killer had arranged to meet her brother, Ronald. Under police guidance Mr Whittle took a £50,000 ransom to a country park in Staffordshire, but the kidnapper failed to show (→15/12).

Right wing Lisbon coup foiled by army

March 12. Jubilant left-wing officers today swiftly asserted their power in Portugal after the bungled coup attempt by the former President, General Antonio de Spinola, who has now fled to Spain. The soldiers have set up a Supreme Revolutionary Council with sweeping powers for transforming the economic and political life of the country. A spokesman said centre and left "fringe groups" that did not accept the armed forces programme would be banned (→26/4).

Iraq launches new assault on the Kurds

March 31. The Iraqi army has launched a general assault on mountain positions in northern Iraq held by Kurdish rebels. Six divisions, with artillery and armoured support, have been unleashed against forces led by Mustafa al-Barzani, the separatist leader.

For 20 years the Kurds have been engaged in sporadic guerrila warfare. This time, according to statements in Baghdad, the Iraqi leadership intends to destroy the guerrillas for ever.

The way for a new offensive was paved by last month's agreement with the Shah of Iran, who also has trouble with the Kurds. It is part of a new attempt to end Iran-Iraq border disputes.

Kurdish leader Mustafa al-Barzani.

1975

APRIL

Su	Mo	Tu	We	Th	Fr	Sa
		1	2	3	4	5
6	7	8	9	10	11	12
13	14	15	16	17	18	19
20	21	22	23	24	25	26
27	28	29	30			

1. South Vietnam: The towns of Qui Nhon and Nha Trang fall to the Communists (→3).

3. Washington: Ford says US losses in South Vietnam do not mean the US will not honour its commitments elsewhere.

3. Phnom Penh: The US begins the evacuation of its embassy staff.→

5. UK: Mr R. Guest's L'Escargot wins the Grand National.

5. Belfast: Nine die and 79 are hurt in a series of bomb attacks (→28).

9. London: Wilson sacks Industry Minister Eric Heffer for opposing British EEC membership (→26).

11. UK: International Semi-Conductor of the US buys the car firm of Aston-Martin Lagonda for £1.05 million.

13. Cambridge: The "hooded rapist" claims his sixth victim (→6/5).

16. Moscow: Ex-KGB chief Alexander Shelepin is expelled from the Politburo.

21. Saigon: President Thieu resigns with a blistering attack on the US (→23).

23. London: Foreign Secretary orders the closure of the British embassy in Saigon and the evacuation of staff.→

24. Stockholm: Three people die as Baader-Meinhof terrorists seize the West German embassy and blow it up (→21/5).

26. UK: Labour votes two to one to leave the EEC (→6/6).

28. Belfast: Billy McMillan, the Official IRA's commander in the city, is shot dead (→2/5).

DEATHS

5. Chinese statesman Chiang Kai-shek, president of Nationalist China at various times 1926-49, of Taiwan 1950-75 (*31/10/1887).→

12. US-born French entertainer Josephine Baker (*3/6/1906).→

15. British actor, comedian and writer Michael Henry Flanders (*1/3/1922).

Chiang, Nationalist Chinese head, dies

April 5. Gen. Chiang Kai Shek, President of Nationalist China and the last of the great wartime leaders, died tonight in Taipeh, capital of his island redoubt of Formosa, where he held out following his defeat by the Communists in 1949. He was 87 years old.

Despite losing diplomatic recognition by most countries as Red China became accepted, he always considered himself the legitimate President of that vast country and its millions of people.

His death opens the way for the United States, his ally, to end its "two Chinas" policy by recognising Peking as the only legitimate government of China.

The irony of the situation is that Nationalist Formosa has become rich while the Communist mainland remains desperately poor.

Karpov is champ as Fischer stays away

Anatoly Karpov: the new champion.

April 3. Anatoly Karpov, aged 23, today became the youngest world chess champion by default when the current holder, American Bobby Fischer, failed to meet the entry deadline for a match in Manila. Behind the no-show lay Karpov's rejection of Fischer's condition that, in the event of an evenly-played game, the Russian must win by two clear points overall (→19/10/78).

Cambodia falls to Communist forces

As Phnom Penh falls, the bombs fill the air with thick smoke: the people have learned to live with war.

April 17. Cambodia fell under the control of the Communist Khmer Rouge forces today when the capital, Phnom Penh, surrendered after a siege lasting three and a half months. The guns fell silent when the defending forces were ordered to cease fire. Within an hour, the black uniformed insurgents were taking control of a city festooned with thousands of white flags.

Smiling soldiers from the opposing armies embraced each other, according to reports sent out before communications were cut, and initially there was no indication of the feared bloodbath of revenge.

However, the Khmer Rouge later made their position plain when a broadcast, monitored in Bangkok, announced: "We enter as conquerors and are not here to talk about peace with the traitors of the Phnom Penh clique." Another broadcast said the leaders of the defeated forces were fit "only for hanging".

The puzzle for Western diplomats now is to discover who will be running the country. Prince Norodom Sihanouk, who was ousted as premier five years ago, is titular head of the Cambodian government in exile in Peking. But he is reported to have said that Khieu Samphan, his deputy premier and commander of the "Armed Force of National Unity in Cambodia" would exercise direct power with other Khmer Rouge leaders.

Prince Sihanouk said he would continue to represent Cambodia abroad and would guarantee "Cambodian policies of non-alignment". But in Cambodia power grows out of the barrels of the Khmer Rouge guns, and the enigmatic Pol Pot controls those guns.

It is his victory, and after a war which has devastated the country, killing a quarter of a million people in the past five years, he will not easily hand over the reins of power to a government in exile (→15/6).

NHS is putting the squeeze on pay beds

April 3. A senior National Health Service official admitted today that nearly half the 5,000 pay beds in NHS hospitals have been permanently closed. This is despite undertakings given by Barbara Castle, Social Services Secretary, that they would be phased out gradually.

The Labour government has been under pressure from health service unions to get rid of the beds, which are provided for private patients. They believe that the pay beds drain away resources from the public sector, lengthening waiting-lists.

Many pay beds have been closed temporarily because of a shortage of nurses. But health service unions have reached agreement with many hospitals that such beds should remain permanently closed.

Buzz from bleepers

April 8. Radio-operated bleepers to tell people on the move that they are wanted are to be made generally available in London. Doctors, salesmen and service engineers are expected to be major users. The bleep is activated by a call to a special number. A radio signal then triggers the device, which is about the size of a cigarette packet, alerting the user to call his office.

Christian Lebanese Phalangists battle with Palestinians

April 15. Private armies of warlike irregulars manned road blocks throughout Beirut today after three days of fighting. Ninety people have been killed in sectarian clashes between right-wing Christian Phalangists and Palestinians, which began when Phalangists massacred 27 Palestinians by shooting at a crowded bus.

Households are running short of food and business is at a standstill; the country is on the edge of civil war. President Suleiman Franjieh is hesitant to call in the Lebanese mixed army of Christians and Moslems for fear that, in a country deeply divided on religious lines, the army would side with the Christians against Palestinians, who are now established in Beirut (→29/6).

Baker, the darling of the Folies, dies

April 11. Josephine Baker, from St. Louis, was the darling of the Folies Bergeres in the Twenties, celebrated for the gyrations of her exciting legs, and her songs – not to mention her G-string adorned with bananas and the leopard which she walked in the Champs Elysees. She became a French citizen, a member of the Resistance, and foster mother to a "rainbow family" of many children. When she died yesterday at 68 there were 12 of them.

Enchanting to the very end.

Panic at US Embassy as Saigon falls

April 31. The war in Vietnam is over. Saigon surrendered almost without a struggle today as North Vietnamese tanks rolled into the city and knocked down the gates of the presidential palace.

Convoys of lorries carrying thousands of jubilant Communist troops drove through the city. The guerrillas, some of them teenage girls, exchanged waves and banter with the Saigon population. However, fear of the Communists and their regime remains paramount. One police colonel marched up to the war memorial, saluted, then shot himself.

Thousands have been trying to escape by boat, but have been turned back by North Vietnamese tanks firing warning shots across their bows. Some air force pilots have loaded their planes with relatives and flown them to Thailand.

All the Americans have gone in a mass evacuation which ended in heart-rending scenes at the US embassy, long the symbol of American power in Vietnam, as masses of people swarmed round it, desperate to get a place on the shuttle service of helicopters lifting people from the roof to safety on board warships in the South China Sea.

The last 11 Marines of the unit which had been guarding the embassy were plucked from the roof after an angry mob opened fire and trapped them inside. They were the last of the Americans, foreigners and well-connected Vietnamese to be lifted to safety.

When it became apparent there would be no more helicopters, the mob sacked the embassy. Thus ended America's 15-year involvement in Vietnam (→4/5).

Panic and fighting surrounds the last refugee plane to leave Nha Trang.

Armed to the teeth, Communist forces enter central Saigon at noon.

Socialists sweep to power in elections held in Portugal

April 26. The Socialists emerged as the biggest party after Portugal's first free elections for 50 years. The elections, for a Constituent Assembly, recorded a 91 per cent turnout, and the Socialists received over 2,000,000 votes. The left-of-centre Popular Democrats came second with 1,490,000 votes, and the Communists are in third place with 709,000.

Alvaro Cunhal, the Communist leader, played down his party's poor showing by saying: "In a revolutionary process the vote is not the only or even the most significant expression of the strength and influence of a party." Mario Soares, the Socialist leader, expressed regret that the Communists in practice held more power than the voting showed, because they had established themselves in local government immediately after the 1974 military coup (→24/6).

Unemployment hits the million mark

April 24. The number of jobless in Britain has passed the million mark with the biggest monthly increase since the Second World War, according to figures released today. The total out of work has shot up by nearly 124,000 on the March figure to reach 1,012,949 – four per cent of the working population.

Unemployment normally falls at this time of year, but this April has seen the seasonally adjusted total soar by 38,000, representing an alarming increase in "hard-core" unemployment.

Chancellor Denis Healey's warning that higher wage claims would mean higher unemployment is proving to be true. Rail workers are pressing for 30 per cent more and doctors have just been awarded 38 per cent, with pay rises in the last year averaging 32 per cent. But the unions are reluctant to shoulder the blame. Hugh Scanlon, of the Engineers, said the figures were "disappointing, alarming and an absolute tragedy". He called for a reversal of the last budget (→24/7).

Operation Baby Lift flies Vietnam orphans to UK for adoption

April 6. One hundred and five orphans from South Vietnam arrived in Britain tonight on board a chartered airliner. The children were met by a fleet of ambulances and, warmly wrapped in winter clothes, were then taken by volunteers to a special reception centre.

Immigration procedures were carried out on board the aircraft to cause as little delay as possible to the children, many of them very young babies. Some would-be parents, who had waited for hours for the plane to arrive, were disappointed as the children were whisked to the Ockendon Venture homes.

There was, however, a feeling of great relief that the children had arrived safely, following the disaster in Saigon two days ago when 140 orphans on their way to a new life in America were killed when a Galaxy, the world's largest aircraft, crashed soon after taking off from Saigon.

Not everybody has welcomed the children's arrival. Tom Litterick, Labour MP for Selly Oak, said that many of them are not orphans and "child-stealing" is not too strong a phrase to describe what is happening. "Many have parents who have left them temporarily at orphanages because they cannot afford to feed them," he said.

1975

MAY

Su	Mo	Tu	We	Th	Fr	Sa
				1	2	3
4	5	6	7	8	9	10
11	12	13	14	15	16	17
18	19	20	21	22	23	24
25	26	27	28	29	30	31

1. London: The Government introduces a bill to nationalise the shipbuilding and aircraft industries.

2. London: Nine IRA members are jailed for ten to 15 years for running a year-long Birmingham bomb campaign (→11/7).

3. London: West Ham beat Fulham 2-0 in the FA Cup Final.

4. Northern Ireland: Ulster Unionists win a resounding victory in elections to the Ulster Convention (→8).

4. Hong Kong: 4,000 South Vietnamese refugees arrive after being rescued from a sinking ship.

6. Cambridge: A seventh woman falls victim to the "hooded rapist" (→8/6).

8. Belfast: The Northern Ireland Convention meets for the first time.

13. UK: Inflation reaches 21 per cent.→

14. London: Frank Sinatra wins substantial damages from the BBC over a programme linking him to the Mafia.

19. Washington: A probe into CIA activities learns there is documentary proof of a plot to kill Castro.

21. Stuttgart: The trial of the Baader-Meinhof terrorist gang opens.

23. UK: ITV programmes are blacked-out by a technicians strike.

24. USSR: Two cosmonauts are launched towards the Salyut 4 space station (→19/7).

26. UK: Evel Knievel suffers spinal injuries when his car fails in an attempt to jump 13 buses.

28. UK: Prince Charles is installed as Great Master of the Order of the Garter.

DEATHS

6. Hungarian prelate Cardinal Jozsef Mindszenty (*29/3/1892).→

20. British sculptor Dame Jocelyn Barbara Hepworth (*10/1/1903).→

Day trip ends in worst road crash

May 27. A tourist coach plunged off a moorland road into a ravine on the Yorkshire Dales today killing 32 elderly passengers. It was the worst-ever road disaster in Britain.

The driver also sustained fatal injuries, but before he died he described how first the gears and then the brakes had failed. Firemen fought for several hours to cut casualties free.

His wife was among the party of 45 women from Thornaby, Teesside on a sightseeing tour which had been arranged between neighbours and friends. She survived.

Only two passengers escaped being trapped in the wreckage of the upturned coach after it had crashed through a three-foot stone wall and landed 16 feet below on its roof. The accident happened at the foot of a notorious mile-long, one-in-six gradient hill in Wharfedale known as Devil's Bridge.

The pound sinks while prices soar

May 16. Rampant inflation has led to a widespread belief that the Government has lost control of the economy. The pound sank like a stone this week on the foreign exchanges to lose 25.2 per cent of its 1971 value, as investors fled from sterling. The Bank of England sat firmly on the sidelines, making no moves to buy sterling and stop the downward slide.

Figures released today show the annual rate of inflation is approaching a record 22 per cent, and poised to leap even higher next month, as the effects of the March budget begin to filter through (→13/6).

Barbara Hepworth is killed in a fire

Barbara and her 1957 "Requiem".

May 21. Britain's leading woman sculptor, Dame Barbara Hepworth, died in a fire at her studio at St. Ives late last night. Police were beaten back by the flames when they tried to reach her. Firemen later found her body in the bedroom attached to the studio where she lived alone. She was 72 years old.

Barbara Hepworth studied with Henry Moore, both being from Yorkshire, and married the sculptor John Skeaping and then the painter Ben Nicholson. She made abstract sculpture of beautiful texture, some for open-air sites in Cornwall. Her "Single Form" outside the UN building is a memorial to her friend Dag Hammarskjold.

Embassy Cardinal has died in exile

May 6. Cardinal Jozsef Mindszenty, former Archbishop and Primate of Hungary, died today in exile in Vienna, aged 83. He was a fierce opponent of Communism and in 1948 was arrested for high treason. He was tortured for 29 days by the Communist secret police, being made to stand naked in a cold damp cell, beaten with a rubber hose and forced to watch obscene orgies. He was released in the 1956 revolution and, when that was crushed, lived in the US embassy in Budapest for 15 years.

He refused to go along with the Vatican's conciliatory stance towards Communist regimes and so was finally dismissed as Primate by Pope Paul in 1974.

1975

JUNE

Su	Mo	Tu	We	Th	Fr	Sa
1	2	3	4	5	6	7
8	9	10	11	12	13	14
15	16	17	18	19	20	21
22	23	24	25	26	27	28
29	30					

1. Salisbury: Rhodesian police shoot dead 11 blacks during riots (→25/8).

3. New York: Pele signs a $7 million three-year contract with the New York Cosmos.→

4. UK: Dr C. Vitadini's Grundy wins the Derby.

8. UK: Van driver Peter Cook is arrested in connection with seven rapes in Cambridge.

9. London: The Commons is broadcast live by radio for the first time.

10. London: Industry Minister Wedgwood Benn is switched to Energy in a direct swap with Eric Varley (→18).

11. Uganda: A tribunal finds British author and lecturer Denis Hills guilty of "treason" for criticising Idi Amin (→20).

12. Athens: Greece officially applies for membership of the Common Market.→

13. UK: Inflation reaches 25 per cent (→11/7).

13. UK: Ex-minister John Profumo is made a CBE in the Queen's birthday honours.

15. Cambodia: Thousands are reported to have died under the Khmer Rouge (→19/7).

16. S. Africa: Britain and South Africa terminate the 1955 Simonstown naval agreement (→18/6/76).

18. Riyadh: The mentally ill prince who assassinated King Faisal is publicly beheaded.

19. UK: Over 100 striking stable-boys march around Ascot racecourse on Gold Cup Day (→15/7).

20. Uganda: Amin rejects an appeal for the release of Denis Hills (→11/7).

24. New York: A Boeing 727 crashes at the edge of Kennedy Airport, killing 109.

24. Mozambique: The colony becomes independent of Portugal (→3/3/76).

26. London: Peter Bottomley wins Woolwich West for the Tories in the first by-election of the present parliament.

29. Beirut: 40 die as new street battles erupt (→16/9).

Gandhi is guilty in election fraud case

Found guilty: Indira Gandhi.

June 12. Mrs Indira Gandhi, the Indian Prime Minister, was today found guilty in the Allahabad High Court of electoral corruption. Her election to the Lok Sabha, the Indian House of Commons, was declared null and void by Justice Jag Mohan Lal Sinha, who barred her from public office for six years.

The case arose out of accusations that Mrs Gandhi had illegally obtained the help of government officials to construct rostrums and supply power for loudspeakers in her election campaign. Mrs Gandhi, the world's most powerful woman politician, is to appeal to the Supreme Court (→ 19/4/76).

June 3. Pele, the king of soccer, signs a 3-year contract with the New York Cosmos for $7 million.

Britons say "Yes" to joining the Market

June 6. The British people have voted overwhelmingly for continued membership of the European Common Market. Referendum results completed tonight show 67.2 per cent in favour and 32.8 per cent against.

Nearly 26 million votes were cast and a majority said "No" in only two of the 68 counties – Shetland Islands and Western Isles.

The referendum campaign was fought by rival umbrella groups covering all the main parties. However, the strongest anti-EEC force was a left-wing Labour "No to Europe" group. The Tories worked for a "Yes" vote.

After initial fears of apathy the voting turn-out was nearly up to general election standards. Other fears of problems over vote-counting on a county basis proved equally groundless. "More than in a general election, the referendum is open to mischief," said Sir Philip Allen, the chief electoral officer.

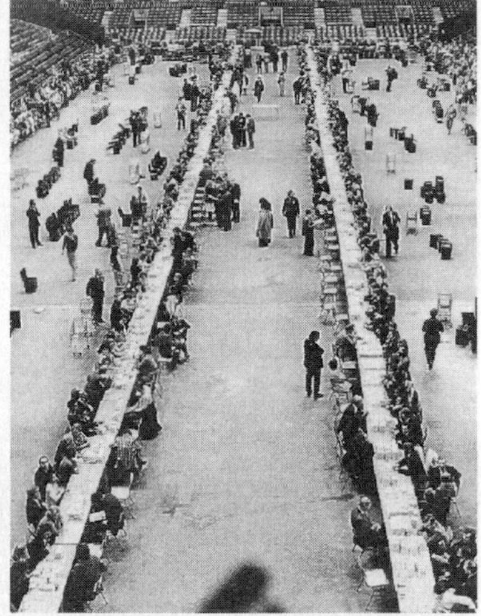

Counting the referendum votes.

Maximum security was in force to safeguard ballot boxes against any hi-jacking attempts.

The referendum went smoothly, but most politicians think it is un-British and it will be a long time before there is another (→ 12).

Oil begins to flow from the North Sea

June 18. Britain's first North Sea oil flowed ashore today from a Liberian tanker to BP's Isle of Grain refinery. The oil came from the Argyll field in the North Sea, 200 miles east of Edinburgh. Tony Benn, the Energy Secretary, who went to the ceremony in a Russian-built hydrofoil, triumphantly held up a bottle of crude oil in the air and said: "I hold the future of Britain in my hand" (→ 27/6/77).

Inquest finds Lucan is guilty of murder

June 19. A London jury named Lord Lucan as the killer of his child's nanny today, and the missing earl faces a murder trial at the Old Bailey if he returns to Britain. "Lucky" Lucan disappeared in November after the battered body of Sandra Rivett was found at his home. The Countess of Lucan told the jury that her husband had tried to strangle her. Lucan's friends are convinced that he has committed suicide.

Suez Canal reopens after eight years

June 5. Eight years to the day after Egypt's crushing defeat by Israel, the Suez Canal reopened today for international maritime traffic. Ships' sirens sounded and thousands of Egyptians cheered at the ceremony in Port Said. Anwar Sadat, who succeeded Gamal Abdul Nasser as Egyptian President in 1970, said the opening of the canal was a gesture of peace; he also pledged to "liberate" the Sinai Peninsula, which Israeli forces conquered in 1967.

Unofficially, however, Sadat is said to have told the US President, Gerald Ford, that he is willing to negotiate with Israel on the future of Sinai and to discuss a peace treaty between the two countries, even though all Arab states have in the past refused to acknowledge Israel's right to exist. Sadat has dropped his plan for a full-scale peace conference.

West Indians win cricket's first World Cup

June 21. An invaluable innings of 102 by their captain, Clive Lloyd, and some spectacular outfielding by the whole team, saw the West Indies beat Australia by 17 runs at Lord's today and take cricket's first World Cup.

The tournament, based on a series of 60-over, one-day matches, proved a remarkable success with seven national teams and a representative East Africa side. These were whittled down to semi-finals in which West Indies easily pegged back New Zealand, and Australia utterly outplayed England, with left-arm seamer Gary Gilmour taking six for 14 in his 12 overs.

In the final, Australia made a fine attempt to match the West Indies' 291, but five brilliant run-outs – three by the young prodigy Vivian Richards – assured the West Indies of an historic victory.

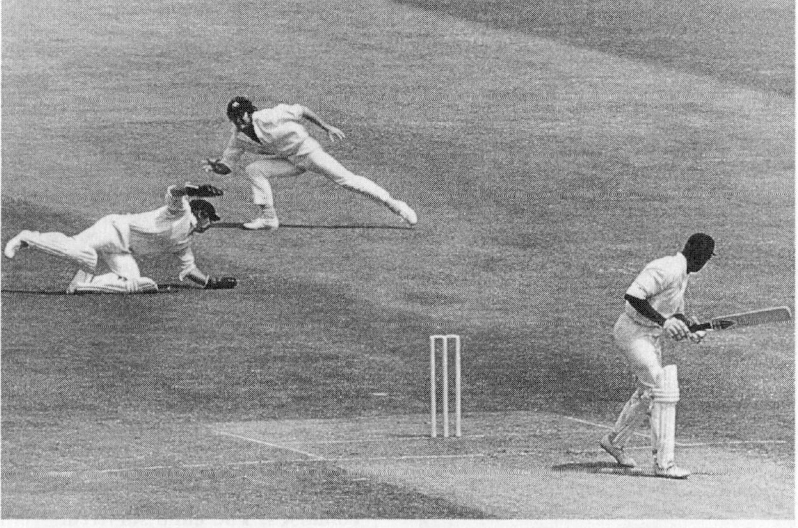

Australian keeper Rodney Marsh dives for a missed catch off Clive Lloyd.

1975

JULY

Su	Mo	Tu	We	Th	Fr	Sa
		1	2	3	4	5
6	7	8	9	10	11	12
13	14	15	16	17	18	19
20	21	22	23	24	25	26
27	28	29	30	31		

1. London: Denis Healey gives employers and unions a week's ultimatum to accept a ten per cent voluntary pay rise limit.→

4. Jerusalem: A bomb goes off in a busy square at the height of the pre-Sabbath rush, killing 13 and injuring 72.

5. Wimbledon: Billie Jean King beats Evonne Cawley for her sixth Women's Singles title; Arthur Ashe beats Jimmy Connors to become the first black Men's Singles champion.

8. Washington: Ford says he will run for President in 1976 (→20/11).

8. Bonn: Itzhak Rabin arrives on the first visit to Germany by an Israeli premier.

11. London: The prosecution in the Birmingham bomb trial concedes the six accused were seriously assaulted in custody (→31).

13. UK: Tom Watson of the US wins the British Open Golf championship.

15. UK: Stable-boys end an 11-week strike, accepting a 19 per cent pay rise to £37 a week.

18. UK: Graham Hill announces his retirement from motor racing (→29/11).

23. London: Newham North East Labour Party rejects minister Reg Prentice as candidate in the next election.

24. Pacific: The Apollo astronauts splash down safely.

24. UK: Unemployment now stands at 1,147,633, the highest since March 1940 (→21/8).

29. Lagos: General Gowon is deposed in a bloodless coup while he is at an African summit in Uganda.

31. Northern Ireland: Three of the Dublin group, Miami Showband, die in an ambush near Newry, County Down (→10/8).

31. Helsinki: 33 nations are present at the opening of the largest summit conference in European history (→1/8).

DEATH

2. British actor James Robertson Justice (*15/6/1905).

Handshakes in space as US meets USSR

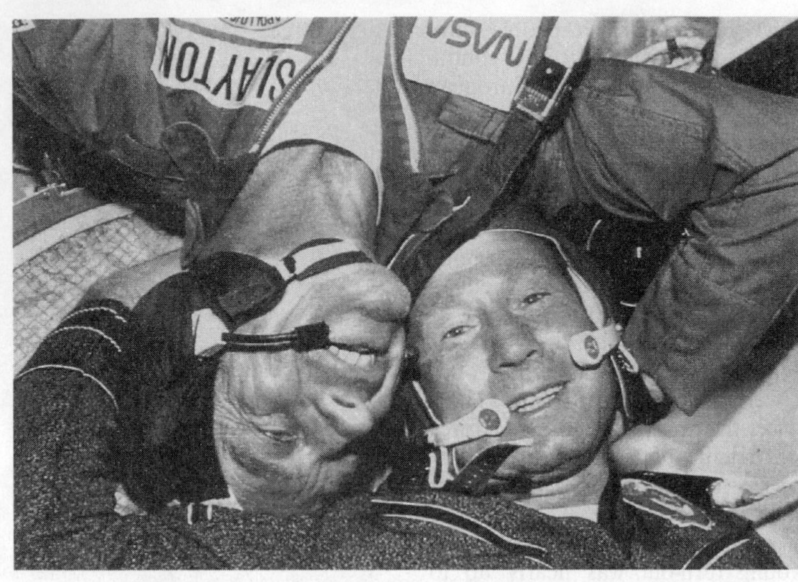

Apollo astronaut Deke Slayton (l.) greets Soyuz cosmonaut Alexei Leonov.

July 19. The symbolic Russian-American joint spaceflight ended today when the American Apollo and the Russian Soyuz undocked and went into separate orbits. The Russians will land tomorrow, the Americans remaining in space for five more days.

The flight, agreed in 1972 as part of a detente package and in preparation ever since, started four days ago with the launch of the two craft. The Russians showed their launch live on TV for the first time.

The day before yesterday, Apollo and Soyuz docked 140 miles above the Atlantic. The commanders, Tom Stafford and Alexei Leonov, shook hands through the hatches of their spacecraft and exchanged greetings in each other's languages. During the ensuing two days the crews, each consisting of three men, moved from one spacecraft to the other, appeared on television together, carried out joint experiments, and shared meals. Later they flew in formation close together while making observations of the sun and the earth (→24).

July 23. Diana Bryant plunges to her death as a Boston fire escape collapses. The child survived.

Pay rises in UK to be limited by law

July 11. Desperate measures were taken by the Government today to save the nation from economic catastrophe. In the struggle against inflation, now running at 26 per cent, Mr Wilson said there can only be "rough justice".

Wage increases will be limited to £6 per week with a total freeze on incomes above £8,500 per year. Price controls will be extended and cash limits applied to Government spending programmes.

An emergency law, bitterly resented by the trade unions, will be made to reinforce voluntary pay curbs. Denis Healey, Chancellor of the Exchequer, said: "Something had to be done to bring this madman's merry-go-round of inflation to a stop" (→24).

Ancient clay army is dug up in China

July 11. Chinese archaeologists have uncovered a "terra-cotta army" of 6,000 life-sized and life-like warriors, with their chariots, spears and horses drawn up in battle formation, near the ancient Chinese capital of Xian. The figures guard the tomb of the first Ch'in emperor, who died in 206 BC.

Ch'in Shih-huang-ti unified the country and gave it its Western name, China. He expended the lives of hundreds of thousands of labourers in building the Great Wall and imposed a draconian system of law. The artisans who knew the secrets of his tomb were walled up inside it. It was discovered by peasants digging for water.

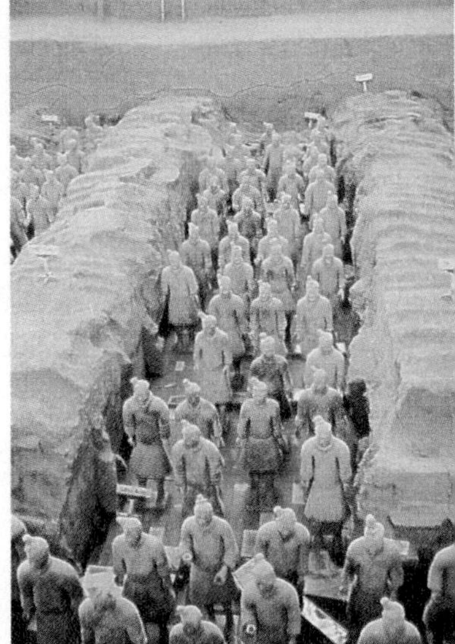

Still parading after 2,000 years.

Cambodians tell of "human buffalos"

July 19. Appalling stories of atrocities in Cambodia, ruled by the Pol Pot regime, are emerging from refugees who slip across the border into Thailand. They tell of townspeople being driven into the countryside and shackled to ploughs instead of water buffalo. They till the land with their bare hands and work from dawn to dusk with only a cup of rice to eat. Many people die in the fields and thousands, maybe hundreds of thousands, are being summarily executed by Pol Pot's followers (→9/9).

Lord Sainsbury is on terrorist hit list

Wanted: the terrorist "Carlos".

July 1. Scotland Yard and French police are tonight hunting Carlos, an international killer working for Palestinian terrorists. They began liaising after the discovery of his "safe-house" in London. Small-arms and grenades had been hidden there together with a hit list naming prominent people in Britain. On the list were Yehudi Menuhin, Bernard Delfont and Lord Sainsbury.

Hills' head is off the chopping block

July 1. Uganda's military dictator, Idi Amin, today gave way to international pressure and granted Denis Hills, the 61-year-old British author and lecturer, an unconditional reprieve from the firing squad. Hills had enraged Amin by describing him as a "village tyrant" in a manuscript discovered by Ugandan police in Hills' home (→ 1/7/76).

No more money for British bike firm

July 31. The Labour government refused today to give more money to the Norton Villiers Triumph motor cycle firm. This reverses the policies of Tony Benn, former Industry Secretary. He gave £24 million to NVT and £5 million to the Meriden workers' co-operative to save the Triumph (→ 11/8).

1975

AUGUST

Su	Mo	Tu	We	Th	Fr	Sa
					1	2
3	4	5	6	7	8	9
10	11	12	13	14	15	16
17	18	19	20	21	22	23
24	25	26	27	28	29	30
31						

3. Morocco: 188 die when a Boeing 707 crashes.

4. Tokyo: Seven Red Army members are freed when terrorists vow to blow up the US embassy in Malaysia (→ 7).

5. UK: Foresters say Dutch elm disease, which affects over three million trees in the south and Midlands, is spreading (→ 30/10).

7. London: The capital has its hottest day for 35 years with temperatures of 32 degrees C.

7. Malaysia: Ten Japanese terrorists who took over the US embassy leave for Libya.

10. Belfast: Four-year-old Siobhan McCabe becomes the 1,271st person to die in six years of violence (→ 13).

13. Belfast: Four die and 23 are hurt in a raid on a bar in the Shankill Road used by the Ulster Volunteer Force (→ 3/10).

15. UK: Middlesex spin bowler Edmonds takes five Australian wickets for 17 in his test debut at Headingley (→ 19).

19. UK: Test Match is abandoned after a group seeking the release of jailed cabbie George Davis dig up the pitch (→ 23/9/77).

21. UK: 1.25 million are jobless (→ 3/9).

24. Athens: Death sentences on ex-premier Papadopoulos and two other 1967 coup leaders are commuted to life.

25. Rhodesia: Talks between the government and black leaders open in railway carriages near the Victoria Falls (→ 26).

26. Rhodesia: The black/white talks collapse (→ 28/9).

29. Madrid: Two alleged Basque terrorists are sentenced to death by garrotting (→ 27/9).

DEATHS

9. Soviet composer Dmitri Shostakovich (*25/9/1906).

27. Ethiopian Emperor Haile Selassie, reigned 1916-74 (*23/7/1892).

29. Irish statesman Eamon de Valera, premier 1932-48, 1951-54, 1957-59; President 1959-73 (*14/10/1882).→

Human rights pact signed in Helsinki

Aug 1. Two years of dogged negotiations between the Western powers and the Soviet bloc reached a climax in Helsinki today, with champagne glasses raised and leaders of 35 European countries, plus the US and Canada signing the final pact on security and co-operation.

The 30,000-word pact recognises Europe's post-war boundaries and, by implication, Moscow's hegemony in Eastern Europe. In return, the West has secured from the Soviet leader, Leonid Brezhnev, a pledge to uphold human rights and the free movement of people and ideas across frontiers. President Gerald Ford said he hoped that this time "we mean what we say". People were tired, he said, of having "hopes raised and then shattered by empty words and unfulfilled pledges".

Brezhnev, evidently a sick man and slurring his words as he read from a prepared text, said: "No one should try to dictate to other peoples the manner in which they ought to conduct their internal affairs."

Delegates of the 35 countries will meet in Belgrade in two years' time to debate whether the promises have been kept.

De Valera, supreme nationalist, dies

De Valera: rebel and statesman.

Aug 29. Eamon de Valera, who dominated Irish politics for 60 years, has died. He was 92. Known as "Dev" to friend and foe alike he was born in the US, the son of a Spanish father and an Irish mother.

A quiet man who seldom took a drink, he was in striking contrast to the usual gregarious Irish politician. His bearing was that of an aloof Spanish grandee with a passion for advanced mathematics.

His exploits in "The Troubles" included a dramatic escape from Lincoln jail, making him a hero with the IRA, an organisation he was later, as premier, to outlaw.

At 76, and nearly blind, he was elected President of Ireland – and again at 83. "Dev" was a nationalist first, last, always.

British Leyland to be state-controlled

Aug 11. British Leyland, the only major British-owned motor company, passed into Government ownership today. The company, which produces Austin, Morris, Rover and Jaguar cars and Leyland commercial vehicles, was the subject of a devastating Government inquiry headed by Lord Ryder earlier this year.

Ryder was highly critical of the present management, but he produced a plan, backed by the then Industry Secretary, Tony Benn, to pump £1,400 million of Government money into the company. Management control will be exercised through Lord Ryder's National Enterprise Board (→ 11/9).

Bangladesh leader is killed in coup

Aug 15. Sheikh Mujibur Rahman, the "Father of Bangladesh" was shot dead by army officers in a dawn coup in Dacca today. The Bengali soldiers, brutalised by the nine-month guerrilla struggle for freedom from Pakistan, and by the near-anarchy reigning in Bangladesh today, butchered the Sheikh, his wife, his two elder sons and two other members of his family.

The new President is a civilian, Khandakar Mostaque Ahmed. He was Commerce Minister in Sheikh Mujibur's government. He is regarded as an army stooge.

Whites flee Angola as civil war looms

Aug 12. With independence for Portugal's West African colony of Angola still three months away, a mass flight of panic-stricken whites is under way, while thousands of black refugees are streaming into Luanda and other towns, telling of murder, rape and looting by rival armies of "freedom fighters". Most of Angola's half-million whites are expected to have left by November. No transition government exists and Portugal's High Commissioner, General Ferreira do Macedo, has spoken of total social and economic collapse (→ 10/11).

Walker runs mile in under 3min 50

Aug 12. John Walker, the 23-year-old New Zealander who came so close to spoiling Filbert Bayi's runaway victory in the Commonwealth Games 1,500 metres last year, has added another record to the list of his country's athletic achievements.

At Gothenburg in Sweden tonight, he beat a world-class mile field to break Bayi's world record and become the first man to run a mile in under 3min 50sec. Barely 21 years ago people were wondering whether the four-minute mile would ever be run. Now, having led from start to finish, Walker has set a new target: 3min 49.4sec.

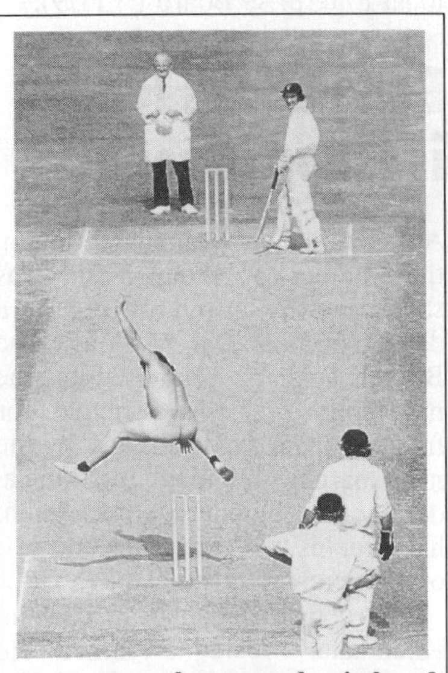

Not even the sacred pitch of Lord's is streak-proof, it seems.

1975

SEPTEMBER

Su	Mo	Tu	We	Th	Fr	Sa
	1	2	3	4	5	6
7	8	9	10	11	12	13
14	15	16	17	18	19	20
21	22	23	24	25	26	27
28	29	30				

1. Egypt: Israel and Egypt reach an interim accord, orchestrated by Kissinger, on Israeli withdrawal from Sinai.

3. UK: The TUC votes two to one to accept a voluntary pay rise limit of £6 a week (→ 7/11).

5. London: Two die and 63 are hurt when a bomb explodes at the Hilton Hotel.

8. UK: Scottish captain Billy Bremner is banned from playing soccer for Scotland after an alleged brawl in Copenhagen.

9. Cambodia: Prince Sihanouk returns from exile.

11. UK: The last Wolseley car rolls off the production line.

14. Amsterdam: Rembrandt's "The Night Watch" is slashed a dozen times.

15. Port Moresby: Papua New Guinea becomes independent of Australia.

17. West Indies: Hurricane Eloise causes widespread devastation.

23. San Francisco: Patty Hearst signs an affidavit saying she was coerced into committing robbery (→ 20/3/76).

24. Nepal: Britons Dougal Haston and Doug Scott are the first to climb Everest by the south-west face (→ 29).

27. Madrid: Five convicted Basque terrorists are shot despite protests from the rest of Europe.→

28. UK: Ten Territorial Army soldiers drown in an accident during an exercise on the River Trent.

28. Rhodesia: Joshua Nkomo is elected President of the United African National Council (→ 19/3/76).

29. Nepal: Mike Burke, one of the British team which climbed Everest last week, dies while attempting a second climb.

30. UK: Denis Healey is ousted from the Labour Party National Executive Committee and replaced by Eric Heffer.

30. Manila: Muhammad Ali beats Joe Frazier to retain his world heavyweight title (→ 30/4/76).

Beirut torn by civil war

The gunfighters move into the shells of Beirut's once smart apartments.

Sept 16. The fragile fabric of life in Beirut, the elegant Lebanese capital, was finally ripped apart today as Christians and Moslems in this sectarian country viciously fought it out on the streets.

A great pall of black smoke hangs over the stricken city. Day and night the warring groups blast at each other; the chatter of automatic weapons mingling with the crump of mortar bombs and scream of rockets and artillery shells.

Lebanon's 25,000-strong army is the only force which can end the fighting. But a government, sharply divided on sectarian lines, has not dared to order it into action. Rashid Karami, the Prime Minister, fears that this Christian-dominated force might turn on the Moslems and their Palestinian allies. Late tonight he had a narrow escape when a rocket almost destroyed his car as he visited the Arab suburb of Chiah, scene of some of the heaviest fighting.

The war began as a result of the activities of heavily-armed Palestinian groups who were driven from Jordan five years ago. Three times this year there have been outbreaks of fighting, ending in fragile ceasefire arrangements (→ 22/1/76).

Ford escapes two assassination bids

Sept 22. President Ford escaped assassination for the second time in 17 days today when a woman fired a gun at him as he left a hotel in San Francisco. His assailant was Sara Jane Moore.

Earlier in the month, on September 5, a dishevelled girl called Lynette "Squeaky" Fromme, pointed a pistol at Ford in Sacramento. She was a member of the "Family", a cult led by Charles Manson, the leader of the group convicted of murdering actress, Sharon Tate, wife of the director Roman Polanski, and six other people in Hollywood in 1969.

Czech tennis star defects to the West

Sept 9. The young Czechoslovakian tennis champion Martina Navratilova has requested political asylum in the United States. The 18-year-old left-hander, who last week reached the semi-finals of the US Open at Forest Hills, has been granted a temporary stay in America while her case is examined.

Navratilova said she was seeking asylum because of the interference in her career by the Czech sports authorities, but the opportunity to keep her high tennis earnings, rather than pay it all into a state fund as at present, must also have been a factor.

Kidnapped Hearst on robbery charge

Sept 18. Patty Hearst, the newspaper tycoon's daughter who turned from kidnap hostage to "urban guerrilla" after being snatched by the Symbionese Liberation Army 19 months ago, was refused bail today by a San Francisco court, following bank robbery charges. Miss Hearst, who apparently came to embrace the SLA's ideals and clenched-fist salutes, was arrested with other SLA members after an intensive FBI hunt (→ 23).

Troubled heiress Patty Hearst.

Executions in Spain spark wide protests

Sept 28. There were demonstrations in Europe today protesting at the execution of five Basque "urban guerrillas" by Spain. In Holland the Spanish embassy was set on fire; a bomb exploded outside the embassy in Turkey; and Sweden's premier, Olof Palme, described the Franco government as "bloody murderers" (→ 21/10).

Hostages are held in Spaghetti House

Sept 28. Armed raiders were today holding seven Italians hostage in the basement of a restaurant after they bungled a robbery. They burst into the Spaghetti House at 2am but the gang panicked when a worker kicked the takings under a counter. Armed police who have laid siege to the area are refusing demands to let them go free (→ 3/10).

1975

OCTOBER

Su	Mo	Tu	We	Th	Fr	Sa
			1	2	3	4
5	6	7	8	9	10	11
12	13	14	15	16	17	18
19	20	21	22	23	24	25
26	27	28	29	30	31	

1. London: Attorney-General Sam Silkin fails in his bid to halt publication of the Crossman Diaries.

3. Belfast: Ulster Secretary, Merlyn Rees, bans the Ulster Volunteer Force (→ 3).

3. Dublin: The Irish government refuses to free three IRA prisoners for Dutch businessman Tiede Herrema, kidnapped today (→ 21).

3. London: Spaghetti House siege ends with hostages freed unharmed.

5. Austria: Niki Lauda becomes world motor racing champion (→ 1/8/76).

9. London: One person dies and 20 are hurt when a bomb goes off outside Green Park tube station in Piccadilly.

10. Botswana: Richard Burton and Elizabeth Taylor remarry in a remote village.

14. London: Peers approve a state-sponsored maternity pay fund as part of the Employment Protection Bill.

16. Morocco: King Hassan says he will lead an army of 350,000 unarmed Moroccans to claim the Spanish Sahara (→ 14/11).

20. London: John Stonehouse addresses the Commons for the first time since his disappearance (→ 7/4/76).

21. Madrid: Franco has a heart attack (→ 30).

21. Ireland: Police begin a vigil at the house in County Kildare where Herrema is being held captive (→ 7/11).

26. London: Young Liberal leader Peter Hain is charged with stealing £490 from a bank in Putney (→ 9/4).

30. Madrid: Prince Juan Carlos takes over as provisional head of state during Franco's illness (→ 20/11).

31. Belfast: Provisional Sinn Fein leader Seamus McCusker is shot dead, apparently by the Official IRA (→ 4/11).

DEATH

22. British historian Arnold Joseph Toynbee (*14/4/1889).

Soviet dissident wins Nobel Peace Prize

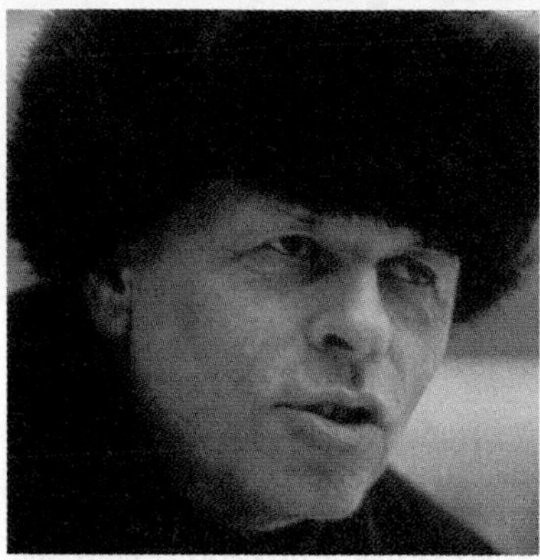

Soviet scientist Andrei Sakharov.

Oct 9. Dr Andrei Sakharov, the Soviet Union's foremost dissident and human rights campaigner, was today awarded the Nobel Peace Prize. He said he was "shocked, stunned, happy, surprised and delighted". Dr Sakharov, aged 54, said he would use the prize money for the benefit of political prisoners in the Soviet Union, and indicated he would be prepared to travel to Oslo to collect the award. But the Soviet authorities ruled out giving him a visa to leave the country, despite having signed the Helsinki declaration which promised freer East-West contacts.

Dr Sakharov has been described as the "father of the Soviet H-bomb". He fell out of favour when he protested against the Soviet testing of nuclear weapons in 1958, and has since been working at a scientific institute.

As a founding member of the Soviet Human Rights Committee and the author of countless civil rights appeals, he has frequently been the object of harassment by the KGB (→ 12/11).

Protestant revenge killings hit Ulster

Oct 2. Protestant fury erupted in Ulster today with a wave of revenge killings for IRA atrocities. Eleven people died, six of them Catholics, including two sisters in a bottling factory. And a car bomb exploded prematurely killing four militant Unionists sitting inside the car.

A Republican spokesman accused the Ulster Volunteer Force of trying to provoke further IRA violence. "There are people on both sides who have a vested interest in this fighting," he said (→ 3).

Elm disease kills 6.5 million trees

Oct 30. The face of rural England is being transformed by Dutch elm disease. According to a report published today by the Forestry Commission, 6.5 million elms have been destroyed. The disease, which is spread by a fungus, was first detected in France in 1918. It was noticed again in England in the late 1960s. Since then, originally isolated outbreaks have coalesced and the disease, so far confined to southern England, appears to be advancing northwards.

Oct 23. Firemen tackle the smouldering remains of a car bomb which exploded outside the London home of Hugh Fraser, a Tory MP. It killed a passer-by, Professor Gordon Fairley, a renowned cancer specialist.

1975

NOVEMBER

Su	Mo	Tu	We	Th	Fr	Sa
						1
2	3	4	5	6	7	8
9	10	11	12	13	14	15
16	17	18	19	20	21	22
23	24	25	26	27	28	29
30						

1. North Sea: Three die and six are hurt in a fire aboard the Ekofisk A oil-rig.→

3. Washington: Vice-President Nelson Rockefeller says he will not be Ford's running-mate in the 1976 election (→20).

4. London: Merlyn Rees says people convicted of terrorist crimes after next February will no longer have special status (→18).

7. London: Britain asks the IMF for £1,000 million (→2/1/76).

9. Morocco: King Hassan calls off the 350,000-strong march into the Spanish Sahara which began three days ago.→

10. Lisbon: Portugal announces it is quitting Angola after five centuries (→14).

12. Moscow: Andrei Sakharov is denied a visa to go to Oslo for his Nobel Peace Prize (→14/4/76).

14. Angola: Soviet advisers are reported to have arrived in the country.→

18. London: Two die and 23 are hurt in the second IRA restaurant bomb blast in the capital this month (→27).

19. London: Ruth Prawer Jhabvala wins the Booker Prize for "Heat and Dust".

20. Miami: Ex-Governor of California Ronald Reagan says he will run for president (→20/1/76).

20. Madrid: General Franco dies.→

25. Madrid: King Juan Carlos declares a general amnesty to mark his accession.

27. London: Campaigner Ross McWhirter is shot dead by Irish gunmen at his home (→6/12).

DEATHS

7. British prelate Cardinal John Carmel Heenan, eighth Archbishop of Westminster 1963-75 (*26/1/1905).

20. Spanish leader General Francisco Franco, head of state 1936-75 (*4/12/1892).→

29. British racing driver Norman Graham Hill (*15/2/1929).→

Angola is torn apart by a civil war

Nov 24. Two weeks after Angola gained its independence from Portugal an estimated 40,000 people are reckoned to be dead and over a million are homeless. Rival gangs of "liberation" fighters are roaming the bush, raiding farms and villages, in a bitterly contested three-sided civil war.

In and around Luanda, the capital, the Marxist MPLA (People's Movement for the Liberation of Angola) has a precarious hold and is under threat from Holden Roberto's FNLA (National Angolan Liberation Front), which has its base in neighbouring Zaire, while to the south, Jonas Savimbi's UNITA (National Union for the Total Independence of Angola) holds sway.

The power struggles could well be resolved in favour of the Marxist MPLA if the reports of Russian intervention are confirmed. Moscow was the first to recognise the MPLA regime and now Western intelligence sources are saying that 400 Soviet military "advisers", including fighter pilots and tank commanders, have arrived in Luanda.

Other reports speak of Russians arriving in Brazzaville, across the Congo River, and assembling weapons before shipping them to the MPLA forces. It is also believed that Castro is flying in Cuban troops to stiffen the MPLA forces. The MPLA, for its part, claims that Savimbi's UNITA in the south is being backed by South African forces and white mercenaries. In Washington, William Colby, director of the CIA, has told a Senate committee that the US is supplying the two anti-Marxist movements, FNLA and UNITA, with rifles, machine-guns, ammunition and lorries in order to keep a balance of power (→10/1/76).

Soldiers of the Soviet-backed MPLA, on their way to clash with the FNLA.

IRA hostage freed unhurt after 36 days

Nov 7. An IRA kidnap victim walked to freedom today after a 36-day ordeal. His IRA captors surrendered to police who had besieged a house in County Kildare for the past 19 days.

Industrialist Tiede Herrema was unharmed, although, during the siege, he had pleaded "with a gun at my head" to police not to storm the house.

Police have charged Marian Coyle and Eddie Gallagher with abduction.

Dr Herrema holds up a bullet, given to him by his abductor Eddie Gallagher.

CIA plotted deaths of foreign leaders

Nov 20. The Senate select commitee on intelligence, chaired by Senator Frank Church, Democrat of Idaho, today published its long-awaited report on the CIA and assassination attempts abroad.

The committee ignored last-minute appeals from CIA director, William Colby, and a personal letter from President Ford. It found that the CIA had indeed directly plotted the death of two foreign leaders, President Fidel Castro of Cuba and Patrice Lumumba in the Congo.

In two other cases, those of General Rafael Trujillo in the Dominican Republic, and Ngo Dinh Diem in South Vietnam, the CIA was involved in plotting and the men were murdered, but no direct link could be made with the CIA. The committee could find no proof that the CIA was involved in the murder of General Schneider in Chile in 1970.

Queen opens North Sea pipeline and the oil flows ashore

Nov 3. Queen Elizabeth II today opened the first underwater pipeline to bring North Sea oil ashore. The pipeline runs 110 miles on the seabed from BP's Forties Field and 127 miles underground to the Grangemouth refinery on the Firth of Forth. When full production is reached, the pipeline will supply 400,000 barrels a day, about one quarter of Britain's oil needs.

This is only the first of major North Sea oil fields to come on stream. Proved oil reserves are now valued at £200,000 million and the Prime Minister, Harold Wilson, who was at today's ceremony, said: "We expect to be self-sufficient in oil by 1980."

Ex-racing champ dies in air crash

Nov 29. Graham Hill, twice world motor racing champion and one of Britain's most urbane, durable and popular sportsmen, was killed along with five members of the Lotus grand prix team when the light aircraft he was piloting crashed in freezing fog near Elstree Airport tonight.

Hill, who was 46, won the championship with BRM in 1962 and with Lotus in 1968. He was returning from testing a car in the south of France for an end-of-season dinner-dance.

Spain agrees to get out of the Sahara

Nov 14. An army of 350,000 chanting Moroccans, armed only with copies of the Koran, poured across the border into Spanish Sahara last week in response to King Hassan's call for them to "liberate" the territory. When they came up against Spanish machine-guns and tanks, they stopped and prayed. Today the King called them home, saying the affair will be settled by diplomacy. Spain, apparently, has now agreed to relinquish its desert colony.

Monarchy returns to Spain following death of General Franco

Exit General Franco ...

... Enter the protege groomed to rule, Spain's new King Juan Carlos.

Nov 22. Don Juan Carlos Borbon y Borbon was sworn in before the Cortes, the Spanish Parliament, today as the first occupant of the Spanish throne since his grandfather Alfonso XIII went into exile in 1931. Don Juan was groomed for the throne by General Franco, strongman of Spain from the Civil War until his death two days ago.

Now Franco's carefully laid plans for his succession come into effect. But his tutelage of the new King extends even beyond death. He left a message which was read on television by the Prime Minister, Senor Arias, calling on the people to offer his successor the same affection and loyalty he had enjoyed.

Yet in language unchanged over the decades, the "Caudillo" warned Juan Carlos and his people to be constantly vigilant against the ever alert "enemies of Spain and Christian civilisation".

One of the first duties of the King and his young wife, Queen Sophia, will be to preside over the burial of Franco in the "Valley of the Fallen". There, under the huge cathedral hewn out of the mountainside, Franco will join the men who died under his command during the Civil War.

With Franco gone, Spain faces a period of uncertainty in a fast-changing world. It will be King Juan Carlos's task to reconcile needed change with Spain's innate conservatism. He acknowledged the pressure for reform in his speech to the Cortes today. Without committing himself to change, he said he would encourage "far-reaching improvements" (→25).

Constitutional crisis in Australia as Prime Minister is sacked

Nov 11. Australia's controversial left-wing Labour Prime Minister, Gough Whitlam, was dismissed from office today in an unprecedented intervention by Sir John Kerr, the Governor-General.

After a month of parliamentary turmoil, set off by the opposition Liberal and Country parties, which combined to block Labour's budget in the Senate, Sir John told Mr Whitlam that any Prime Minister who could not get the money for carrying on the government had either to resign or call an election.

Ironically, Sir John was appointed to the traditionally ceremonial role of the Queen's representative on Whitlam's recommendation. A Liberal caretaker government has been formed. Elections will be held next month (→13/12).

Gough Whitlam addresses reporters in Canberra after his sacking.

1975

DECEMBER

Su	Mo	Tu	We	Th	Fr	Sa
	1	2	3	4	5	6
7	8	9	10	11	12	13
14	15	16	17	18	19	20
21	22	23	24	25	26	27
28	29	30	31			

3. US: Scientists claim uterine cancer is linked to oestrogen, taken for period pains.

4. Amsterdam: Moluccans seize Indonesia's consulate.→

6. London: IRA gunmen take a married couple hostage.→

7. East Indies: Indonesian troops seize Dili, capital of Portuguese Timor.

10. Stockholm: Nobel Prizes go to Niels Bohr (Denmark), Ben Mottelson (Denmark) and James Rainwater (US), all Physics; Sir John Cornforth (UK) and Vladimir Prelog (Switzerland), both Chemistry; David Baltimore, Renàto Dulbecco and Howard Temin (US, Medicine); Eugenio Montale (Italy, Literature); Leonid Kantorovich (USSR) and Tjalling Koopmans (US), both Economics; and in Oslo to Yelena Bonner for Andrei Sakharov (USSR, Peace).

13. Australia: The Liberals, under Malcolm Fraser, win the general election.

15. West Germany: Gunther Guillaume, an ex-aide to Willy Brandt, gets 13 years for spying for East Germany.

15. UK: Bradford joiner Donald Nielson, 39, is charged with killing Lesley Whittle (→21/7/76).

21. Vienna: Six gunmen take 60 hostage at OPEC talks.→

27. India: 372 miners die in a huge blast in Bihar state.

DEATH

7. US author Thornton Wilder (*17/4/1897).

HITS OF 1975

Bye bye baby.

Sailing.

Bohemian Rhapsody

QUOTE OF THE YEAR

"Television brought the brutality of war into the comfort of the living room. Vietnam was lost in the living rooms of America, not on the battlefields of Vietnam."

Marshall McLuhan, media guru.

Women's Year ends with equality laws

Dec 31. International Women's Year ends today with two major breakthroughs in Britain. The Sex Discrimination Act and the Equal Pay Act, which came into force two days ago, have been hailed as the biggest step forward for women since they won the vote.

It will now be against the law to discriminate against them in employment, training, education, trade union activities and in the supply of goods, facilities and services to the public. One of the most controversial aspects is the ban on discriminatory adverts: bosses, for instance, will no longer be able to request "pretty" secretaries.

The Act, however, does not give women equality in pensions, taxes or social security benefits. Private clubs are also exempt, as are certain types of job: in mining, prisons, religious organisations and midwifery. Though aimed primarily at liberating women, the law also applies to sex discrimination against men. The Equal Opportunities Commission has been set up to monitor the situation and take offenders to court.

Row at missionary position on fibre

British bowels came under close scrutiny this year thanks to the proselytising work of two missionaries, who pushed such humble foods as potatoes and cabbage into the limelight with a book entitled, "Refined Carbohydrate Foods and Diseases: some implications of dietary fibre".

Authors **Denis Burkitt** and **Hubert Trowell** noticed when they were in Uganda that certain diseases such as constipation, appendicitis, and bowel cancer, common in Western countries, are far less frequent in Africa because of a diet containing little refined foods such as white flour and sugar.

Unsurprisingly the flour advisory bureau, for one, was not impressed: "unjustified and inaccurate criticisms of suggestions of harmfulness without valid evidence." The BMJ said the evidence was "circumstantial".

Arts: Humanity is left a message short

P.G. Wodehouse died within six weeks of receiving his belated knighthood, so his many admirers never had to get used to calling him Pelham, always shortened to "Plum". He will remain "P.G." in literary history, a stylist venerated by such peers as **Evelyn Waugh** and **Hilaire Belloc**. His writing, which he referred to as "my stuff" and which he re-wrote and polished time and again, had, he admitted, no message for humanity. "Unless I discover one soon," he wrote late in life, "humanity is likely to remain a message short."

Wodehouse lived at Remsenburg on Long Island with his wife Ethel and a family of stray cats and dogs. He became an American citizen in 1955 and had not set foot in England since before the Second World War, when he was living at Le Touquet and was interned by the Germans in Upper Silesia.

On his release from the camp at 60, he agreed to broadcast five talks to neutral America in 1941 – lighthearted descriptions of prison life. With a touch of hysteria the British authorities represented him as a man who had gone over to the enemy. On the direct orders of the Minister of Information Duff Cooper, the protesting BBC broadcast a Post-Script by "Cassandra" of the Daily Mirror (**William Connor**) accusing Wodehouse.

At this point, almost no one had heard or read the broadcasts. **George Orwell** and **Evelyn Waugh** both wrote in his defence but for years the vague possibility of prosecution kept him out of England. The Blandings Castle saga, like the Jeeves-Wooster saga, inhabits an immortal fantasy world where wars have no place.

One novel sequence in which war does intrude has just been concluded by **Anthony Powell**. "A Dance to the Music of Time", 12 novels which are really one, follows its characters through the years from 1914 to the Seventies. Among the 300 characters are some very recognisable people such as **Field Marshal Montgomery**.

A saga about the English in India, "The Raj Quartet" by **Paul Scott**, has ended with the violence of Partition. Englishwomen's reactions to India, then and now, are the subject of "Heat and Dust" for which **Ruth Prawer Jhabvala** won the Booker Prize.

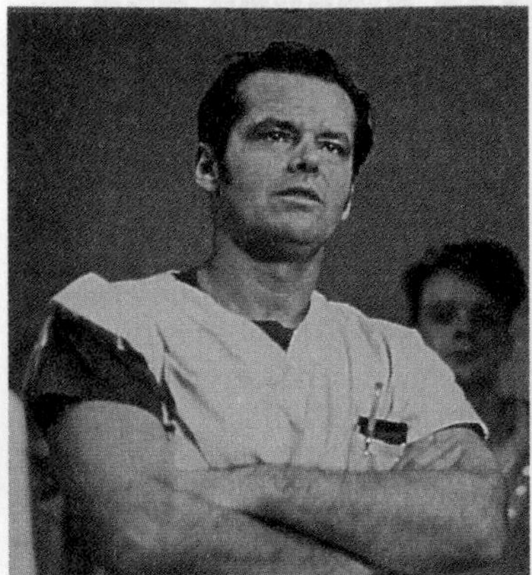

"One Flew Over The Cuckoo's Nest" is a hit for Jack Nicholson.

Two satirical novels were set on university campuses by authors who are themselves academics: "Changing Places" by **David Lodge** and "The History Man", by **Malcolm Bradbury**.

"Upstairs Downstairs", the epic television serial about the households on either side of the green baize door in Eaton Place, reached its end in 1930, with Hudson, the butler, played by **Gordon Jackson**, remaining loyal to the class system to the end. "Ramsay MacDonald is a disgrace to Scotland," he said.

Viewers were offered something completely different when **John Cleese** of Monty Python fame appeared as Basil, the manic and incompetent hotel manager of "Fawlty Towers".

Blue-collar rock hits America and Bruce Springsteen is its "Boss".

International terrorists hold Europe to ransom

Armed police cover detectives running into the flats at Balcombe Street.

Carlos walks free from Algiers airport after the Austrians let him go.

Vienna: Palestinians raid OPEC summit

Dec 22. The Austrian government capitulated early today to the gang of pro-Palestinian terrorists led by the infamous Venezuelan killer, Carlos, who yesterday seized 70 hostages, including 11 oil ministers at the Vienna headquarters of the Organisation of Petroleum Exporting Countries.

Dr Kreisky, the Austrian Chancellor announced that the terrorists would be flown to an undisclosed destination, taking with them the oil ministers, among them the powerful Sheikh Yamani of Saudi Arabia. One member of the gang, a German, who was seriously wounded in the attack will also go.

An Austrian police inspector and a Libyan security guard were killed in cold blood by the heavily-armed terrorists and a police spokesman in Vienna said the feeling was that with two dead already, a capitulation was the only reasonable move open to the authorities.

London: IRA gunmen seize hostages

Dec 12. The Balcombe Street siege ended peacefully today – six days after four IRA gunmen took a husband and wife hostage in their Marylebone flat. TV viewers saw police, wearing bullet-proofed flak jackets and training pistols on every move, bring Mr John Matthews, aged 54 and his 53-year-old wife, Sheila, to safety and take the hooded gunmen into custody.

Later, the IRA men were said to be undergoing "intensive questioning" about the murders of television personality, Ross McWhirter, and a London policeman in February.

The siege began when gunmen burst into the Matthews' council flat after a car chase and a running gun battle through the West End. The men declared they were IRA in a 999 call to Scotland Yard; a major alert was called and adjoining homes were evacuated for police marksmen. The four men barricaded themselves and their hostages in one room in the flat. A telephone link was established between police and the IRA men and a long series of negotiations began with the gunmen demanding an aircraft to fly them and their hostages to Ireland.

Police negotiator, Detective Superintendent Peter Imbert, made it clear to the men that there would be no deals. Scotland Yard's policy was to wear the men down. They refused demands for food; and only a limited amount of drinking water was lowered to the sitting room from a flat above.

The siege ended suddenly – two and a half hours after the men asked to talk. Later, the Matthews were safe in hospital – "tired but unharmed and drinking gallons of tea" (→4/1/76).

Amsterdam: Moluccans storm consulate

A blindfolded hostage.

Dec 19. The armed South Moluccan gang, which stormed the Indonesian Consulate in Amsterdam, were talked-out peacefully today after a 15-day siege. One of their 25 hostages jumped to his death from a window.

The affair ended in bizarre fashion with the seven-man gang laying down their firearms and walking out, having been persuaded by a psychiatrist to give in. Police surrounding the building were surprised to hear hostages and captors singing in English, "Happy birthday".

Another Moluccan gang last week hijacked a train, killing two before they gave in. The terrorists, from a former Dutch colony, want independence from their new master, Indonesia (→29/5/77).

1976

JANUARY

Su	Mo	Tu	We	Th	Fr	Sa
				1	2	3
4	5	6	7	8	9	10
11	12	13	14	15	16	17
18	19	20	21	22	23	24
25	26	27	28	29	30	31

1. Saudi Arabia: 82 die when a Lebanese airliner crashes (→ 10/9).

2. UK: Hurricane-force winds up to 105 mph cause widespread havoc, leaving 22 dead.

4. Northern Ireland: Five SDLP men are murdered in two shootings in Armagh (→ 5).

5. Northern Ireland: Ten Protestant workmen are shot dead in a bus ambush.→

7. Atlantic: The frigate HMS Andromeda is rammed by an Icelandic gunboat (→ 19).

10. Addis Ababa: African states meet to discuss the war in Angola (→ 26).

14. London: Malaysian premier Abdul Razak dies while visiting the capital.

15. Switzerland: John Curry wins the men's European figure skating championship (→ 11/2).

19. London: Britain agrees to withdraw her naval protection ships from Icelandic waters pending talks (→ 19/2).

20. US: Ex-Governor of Georgia, Jimmy Carter, takes the lead in the race for Democratic presidential candidate (→ 19/8).

24. Moscow: The USSR attacks the "Iron Lady", Margaret Thatcher (→ 25/2).

26. Angola: Soviet-built MiG fighters join the conflict (→ 28).

28. UK: Two abortion charities get permission to provide abortion to out-patients.

28. UK: 128 British mercenaries fly out to Angola (→ 14/2).

DEATHS

5. Irish statesman John Aloysius Costello, premier 1948-51, 1954-57 (*20/6/1891).

8. Chinese statesman Chou En-lai, premier 1949-76 (*1898).→

12. British author Dame Agatha Christie (*15/9/1890).→

23. US singer, actor and black activist Paul Robeson (*9/4/1898).

Beirut factions reach a peace agreement

Palestinian refugees mourn the victims of a Phalangist massacre.

Jan 22. Hopes of a temporary end to the civil war in Lebanon were strengthened today when rival factions signed a Syrian-sponsored accord. President Assad strengthened his position by backing an all-out assault by left-wing Arab militias on the Christians in the east. He allowed the Palestine Liberation Army to march in from Syria to support it.

A Syrian peace delegation of ministers and generals is conferring with Lebanese leaders, trying to achieve a stand-off of rival forces through deals to give Moslems a greater say in Lebanese government. Despite that, the country is in chaos and fighting continues almost everywhere.

Moslem soldiers in the Lebanese army are deserting while thousands of Christians, after the massacre at Damour, south of Beirut, are fleeing to safety in the east. Meanwhile Moslems claim to have cut supply lines to Christians besieged in the Holiday Inn (→ 16/5).

Chou En-lai, Mao's quieter deputy, dies

Chinese charmer, Chou En-lai.

Jan 8. Chou En-lai, Premier of the People's Republic of China since the Communist victory in 1949 and the right-hand man of Chairman Mao for half a century, died today in Peking, aged 77.

Premier Chou had enormous personal charm and captivated all the men and women he met, but despite his sophistication and deep understanding of Western ways he made no secret of being a dedicated and, when necessary, a ruthless revolutionary.

He was, however, an outstanding negotiator and was prepared to mask his true feelings and even suffer fools gladly in the pragmatic interests of Red China. It was his eyes that gave him away. While the rest of his face smiled warmly, his eyes remained cold (→ 7/2).

First SAS units go to Northern Ireland

Jan 7. Troops from the elite Special Air Service were today ordered into the "bandit country" of South Armagh where 15 Protestants and Catholics have died in sectarian revenge attacks this week.

They will follow troops of the 600-strong "spearhead battalion", which is also being sent to the area, bringing the total Ulster garrison to about 15,200. The SAS will be used mainly for surveillance duties. Gerry Fitt, the SDLP MP, has said their presence "will not be helpful".

Meanwhile, in Belfast, loyalist paramilitary and political leaders are planning revenge for the killings of 10 Protestant workers gunned down in South Armagh by the IRA as they were returning from work in a mini-bus (→ 5/3).

Christie, Queen of crime fiction, dies

Mysterious Mrs Christie.

Jan 13. The Queen of the detective story, Dame Agatha Christie, died yesterday at 85, just after publishing Poirot's last case, "Curtain", in which the Belgian's "little grey cells" are laid to rest. The lights were dimmed outside the St. Martin's theatre where "The Mousetrap" is in its 25th year.

Dame Agatha was Britain's richest author with worldwide sales of her 80 books topping 300 million. She divorced her first husband, Colonel Christie and married the archaeologist, Sir Max Mallowan.

1976

FEBRUARY

Su	Mo	Tu	We	Th	Fr	Sa
1	2	3	4	5	6	7
8	9	10	11	12	13	14
15	16	17	18	19	20	21
22	23	24	25	26	27	28
29						

2. Birmingham: The Queen opens the £45 million National Exhibition Centre.

3. London: Labour's George Thomas is chosen to succeed Selwyn Lloyd as Speaker of the House of Commons.

4. South Atlantic: An Argentine destroyer fires shots across the bows of the Shackleton, a British research ship.

6. Washington: Lockheed says it paid $1.1 million to Dutch Prince Bernhard and $3 million to Japanese officials (→8).

7. Peking: Hua Kuo-feng becomes acting premier (→15/6).

8. Guatemala: 12,000 are now thought to have died in a massive earthquake last week (→6/5).

8. Holland: The government launches an enquiry into Lockheed's claim that it bribed Prince Bernhard (→26/8).

12. London: Britain's only major women's hospital staffed by women, the Elizabeth Garrett Anderson, is to close.

17. London: Sir Hugh Casson is elected 17th President of the Royal Academy.

17. London: Basil Hume is chosen to succeed the late Cardinal Heenan as Archbishop of Westminster.

18. London: The Race Relations Bill is published; it would make it an offence to incite racial hatred (→9/6).

19. Reykjavik: Iceland breaks off relations with Britain over the fishing dispute (→24).

24. UK: The Royal Navy sends a fourth gunboat to Iceland (→1/6).

25. Moscow: Party officials prepare to issue thousands of posters of Thatcher as the "Wicked Cold War Witch".

27. London: The Post Office announces the end of Sunday collections and Saturday afternoon post office opening.

DEATH

23. British artist Laurence Stephen Lowry (*1/11/1887).→

Brace of Concordes carry passengers

Concorde gets a final check-up.

Jan 21. The age of supersonic air travel began today as two Concordes took off simultaneously from London and Paris on their first commercial flights. The British Airways Concorde touched down in Bahrain after three hours 38 minutes, while the Air France flight to Rio de Janeiro was late because the President of Senegal arrived late when it refuelled. Hopes of flying into the US slumped when a lawyer, hired to win landing rights, admitted "Concorde is noisy as hell" (→24/5).

Bankruptcies hit a record level in UK

Jan 2. More people went broke last year than ever before, making 1975 the worst year for financial failures in British history. The High Court made 1,875 winding-up orders, an increase of 110 per cent on 1973's total of 883 orders.

Millionaires whose jet-set lives have crumbled include company director Robert Woods, who lost £3 million in four months, and property dealer David Hart who accumulated £1 million in debts. Farmer Christopher Reeves blamed his wife for spending his £1.8 million inheritance, but the Inland Revenue and the VAT man are the usual culprits (→5/3).

Cuban-backed forces winning in Angola

UNITA armed forces chief Samuel Chiwale smiles in spite of MPLA gains.

Feb 14. Soviet T-54 tanks, driven by Cuban troops and backed by MiG fighter planes, are sweeping all before them as they drive into southern Angola, stronghold of the anti-Marxist and Western-backed UNITA nationalist movement.

The UNITA leader, Jonas Savimbi, has fled into the bush with his last remaining forces. The Marxist MPLA regime in Luanda has now gained control of all key points in the vast country, thanks to massive help from Russia and her Cuban ally. It is estimated that some 15,000 Cuban troops are in action.

Refugees, many of them sick and wounded, are pouring into South West Africa. One column of them, 43 miles long and estimated to number 100,000, has been observed moving south, with Cuban forces rapidly closing in behind them. Among the refugees are about 10,000 Portuguese women.

The swift turn of events makes it virtually certain that the white mercenaries, most of them British, will be engulfed. Some who returned to London three days ago have told how 14 of their comrades were shot by their Greek-Cypriot commander because they wanted to come home, saying the war was lost (→11/6).

Holland will probe Lockheed bribery

Feb 8. Holland was shocked tonight at the news that there is to be an official inquiry into allegations that Prince Bernhard, the husband of Queen Juliana, accepted a bribe of £550,000 to clinch the sale of Starfighter jets to Holland. Dutch people find it incredible that their royal family, one of the richest monarchies in the world, could accept a cash bribe.

Significantly, although Prince Bernhard has denied the charge, the government has not issued a denial. The allegation surfaced last week in the Senate investigation in Washington into the Lockheed aircraft firm (→26/8).

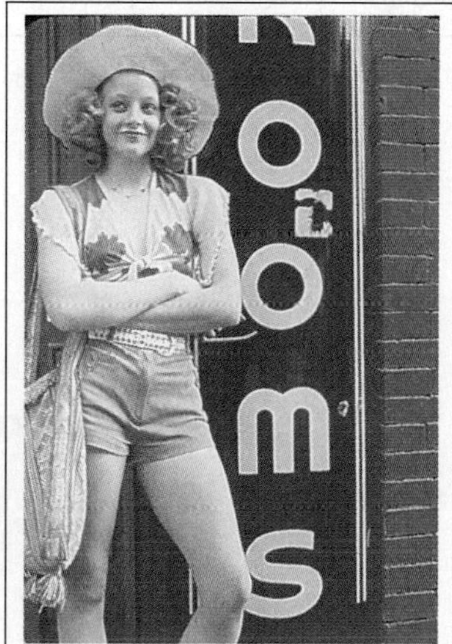

Jodie Foster plays a child prostitute in Martin Scorsese's chilling success, "Taxi Driver".

John Curry glides to Winter Olympic gold

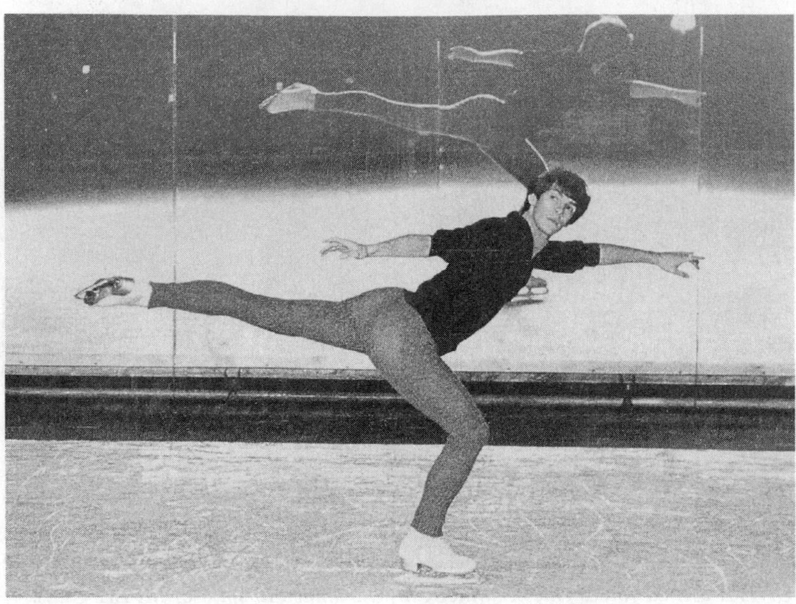
Grace under pressure: John Curry combines art with athleticism.

Feb 11. With a display of free skating that combined balletic grace with athletic agility, John Curry of Birmingham decisively won the men's figure skating gold medal at the Innsbruck Winter Olympic Games today. It was a performance which owed as much to artistic integrity as to Curry's competitive drive.

He is the first Briton to win a medal of any sort in the men's skating events, and his victory may well prove a watershed in competitive figure skating in Europe. This has become increasingly dominated by the technical expertise, allied to physical strength and spectacular jumping ability, perfected by the Eastern bloc countries.

Curry's skating contrasts dramatically with this view. His figures are of a high standard, but his boyhood ambitions to be a ballet dancer (quashed at an early age by his father) are apparent in all his free programmes. Though in his formative years as a competitor he tended to be marked down by hide-bound judges for his low-key choice of music and this balletic style, he has outclassed all his contemporaries, in the eyes of all but the most determinedly antagonistic judges, in the depth and brilliance of his presentation (→4/3).

Feb 18. Two art students contemplate the Tate Gallery's newest exhibit. The gallery refuses to reveal the price of Carl Andre's pile of bricks, but many members of the public have offered their own valuations.

Queen awards OBE to stricken cellist

Feb 25. Cellist Jacqueline du Pre went to Buckingham Palace yesterday to receive her OBE from the Queen, in a wheelchair pushed by her husband, the pianist and conductor, Daniel Barenboim.

Miss du Pre was stricken with multiple sclerosis two years ago and had to give up her concert career at its zenith. She now gives private classes.

She made her public debut at 16 and studied with Paul Tortelier in Paris and Mstislav Rostropovich in Moscow. She was closely associated with the Elgar cello concerto, which she played at her first Festival Hall concert in 1962. She and Barenboim were married five years ago.

L.S. Lowry, northern fantasy artist, dies

Lowry: the man and his art.

Feb 24. L.S. Lowry, who died yesterday, painted a vision of the northern industrial townscape which most people accepted as real. But it was a poetic vision painted by artificial light between 10pm and 2am with no shadows, which he thought spoilt its clarity. His spindly-legged crowds inhabit clean white streets and he rearranged the mills and viaducts from imagination. He learned to paint at evening classes and all his life worked for a Manchester property company as a rent collector and later chief cashier. He kept this secret for fear of being thought an amateur painter.

1976

MARCH

Su	Mo	Tu	We	Th	Fr	Sa
	1	2	3	4	5	6
7	8	9	10	11	12	13
14	15	16	17	18	19	20
21	22	23	24	25	26	27
28	29	30	31			

1. London: MPs approve the Road Traffic Bill, which aims to make the wearing of seat belts compulsory.

2. London: Lord George-Brown resigns from the Labour Party in protest at closed shop legislation (→2/4).

3. Mozambique: President Machel puts the country on a war footing and seizes Rhodesian assets (→19).

4. Stockholm: John Curry wins the men's figure skating world championship.

5. UK: The pound falls below $2 for the first time, closing at $1.9820 (→28).

5. Belfast: Rees dissolves the Ulster Convention (→17/5).

9. Italy: 42 skiers die when a cable car plunges to the ground in the Dolomites.

11. Washington: Nixon says he ordered the CIA to prevent the election of Allende.

15. London: A tube driver is shot dead chasing a gunman moments after a bomb goes off in a train near West Ham.

16. UK: Norman Scott tells a court of when he first "went to live with Jeremy Thorpe" (→10/5).

19. Rhodesia: Constitutional talks collapse (→20/4).

20. London: Oxford win the Boat Race in a record 16 minutes 58 seconds.

25. London: Michael Foot beats Jim Callaghan by six votes in the first ballot for the Labour leadership (→5/4).

26. Cairo: Sadat bans Soviet warships from Egyptian ports (→19/1/77).

28. Cambridge: A group of economists predict economic recession up to 1980 and beyond (→14/5).

DEATHS

14. US choreographer Busby Berkeley (*29/11/1895).

24. British commander Field Marshal Bernard Law Montgomery, first Viscount Montgomery of Alamein (*17/11/1887).

Wilson springs a surprise and quits No.10

In a room at the Ministry of Defence, Harold Wilson meets the press.

March 16. Harold Wilson is resigning from the premiership. The announcement came without warning this morning. He drove to Buckingham Palace, told the Queen and then instructed his press secretary: "Tell the lobby correspondents you've got a little story that might interest them."

The news has stunned and baffled the political world. Speculation about what lies behind it has raged throughout the day. Mr Wilson says that he decided a long time ago to retire about now. He has led the Labour Party for 13 years and has lost some of his old india-rubber resilience. He is both physically and mentally exhausted. It could be as simple as that.

But in the parliamentary lobbies both friends and foes indulged in colourful theories about him "getting out before some balloon he knows about bursts". But what? Mr Wilson just smiled (→25).

Isabel Peron thrown out in bloodless coup

March 24. President Isabel Peron, aged 45, was deposed in the small hours this morning in a bloodless coup by Argentine's military leaders. Isabel, who has held office since the death of her husband in 1974, was flying in a helicopter from Government House to her home in a Buenos Aires suburb. The crew flew instead to the metropolitan airport, where she was arrested by a general. She drew her revolver, but was quickly disarmed.

The coup, which had been forecast for days by Buenos Aires newspapers, met no opposition. The junta's first task is to revive the tottering economy and control inflation which topped 475 per cent in the last year.

Princess Margaret and Snowdon split

March 19. Princess Margaret, the Queen's only sister, and her husband, the Earl of Snowdon, are to separate after fifteen years of marriage. The official announcement came from the Princess's home, Kensington Palace.

Separations such as the Princess and her husband have decided on are unusual in royal circles. But it allows for such decisions as access to their two children to be decided behind closed doors (→25/2/78).

Patty Hearst guilty of armed robbery

March 20. American newspaper heiress, Patricia Hearst, was found guilty today of assisting her kidnappers, the Symbionese Liberation Army, in an armed bank robbery. The San Francisco jury were unconvinced by her defence that she was brainwashed by her captors, who locked her in a cupboard for weeks and bombarded her with propaganda. Miss Hearst has taken the Fifth Amendment, refusing to testify against herself (→24/9).

1976

APRIL

Su	Mo	Tu	We	Th	Fr	Sa
				1	2	3
4	5	6	7	8	9	10
11	12	13	14	15	16	17
18	19	20	21	22	23	24
25	26	27	28	29	30	

1. UK: The Coal Board gets the go-ahead to build the world's largest pit near Selby in Yorkshire.

2. UK: British Rail sacks 27 employees for failing to comply with its closed shop policy.

3. UK: Mr P. Raymond's Rag Trade wins the Grand National.

7. London: John Stonehouse resigns from Labour Party, putting the Government in a minority of one (→14).

8. London: Anthony Crosland becomes Foreign Secretary in a cabinet reshuffle (→6/5).

9. London: Young Liberal leader Peter Hain is acquitted of stealing £490 from a Putney bank.

14. London: Stonehouse joins the English National Party (→6/8).

14. Moscow: Andrei Sakharov and his wife Yelena Bonner are arrested on a charge of hitting a policeman (→27/7).

17. Athens: Prime Minister Karamanlis proposes a non-aggression pact with Turkey.

19. New Delhi: Mrs Gandhi proposes a resumption of ties with Pakistan (→1/9).

25. Bradford: 26 people are arrested after clashes break out at a National Front march.

26. UK: Actor Sid James collapses on stage in Sunderland and dies later in hospital.

30. US: Muhammad Ali beats Jimmy Young to keep his heavyweight title after a 15th round decision (→24/5)

30. Uganda: Ex-RAF pilot Bob Astles is under arrest for "spreading false rumours" (→29/6).

DEATHS

1. German-born French artist Max Ernst (*2/4/1891).

5. US tycoon Howard Hughes (*24/12/1905).→

25. British film director Sir Carol Reed (*30/12/1906).

26. South African-born British actor and comedian Sidney James (*6/5/1913).

Rhodesia calls up its white reservists

April 20. Ian Smith's illegal UDI regime in Rhodesia today called up several thousand white reservists after black guerrillas blew up the key rail link to South Africa.

The railway was repaired within 24 hours, but the main road to the South African frontier at Beit Bridge remains closed after three Easter holiday-makers were gunned down.

Security has deteriorated rapidly since neighbouring Mozambique became an independent Marxist state and began giving refuge to the guerrillas, who are believed to have penetrated 100 miles or more into Rhodesia to strike at road and rail links (→6/6).

Portugal elects new Socialist premier

Mario Soares and floral tributes.

April 25. Two years after the military coup engineered by middle-ranking left-wing officers, Portugal today got a democratically elected Prime Minister. He is Dr Mario Soares, a lawyer who spent six years in exile during the Salazar dictatorship. His Socialists won 38 per cent of the popular vote in the first free elections in 50 years, but he has had to accept support from the Communists, who gained 12 per cent, in order to put together a parliamentary majority and form a government. ▷

James Callaghan is new Prime Minister

April 5. James Callaghan became Prime Minister tonight. The Queen appointed him two hours after the ruling Labour Party made him its leader. He defeated Michael Foot, the left-wingers' champion, by 176 to 137 in the final vote for the job. Earlier, Denis Healey, the Chancellor of the Exchequer, was eliminated from the contest.

Mr Callaghan, who is 64, called for Labour unity and said that the Government will serve out its full term. Defeated left-wingers defiantly rejected the appeal to close ranks. They met immediately to plan new attacks on the Government's economic policy. Denis Healey, still Chancellor, vowed "even more vigorous" action to halt inflation (→8).

Mr Callaghan takes over at No. 10.

Reclusive tycoon, Howard Hughes, dies

April 5. Howard Hughes, the world's most notorious recluse, died today of a stroke as his private jet flew him from Mexico to Texas. Hughes, aged 70, was preparing to see specialists about an undisclosed ailment. His fortune is estimated at $1.5 billion.

Hughes, the source of many bizarre rumours, went underground in the early Sixties, living out a hideaway life around the world in a series of hotels, many of which he bought in his endless efforts to obtain perfect privacy.

His real life often outdid those rumours. Inheritor at 18 of the Hughes Tool Co, makers of a patented oil well drill, he turned his father's millions into many more, expanding his interests into Hollywood, breaking world aviation records, running commercial airlines, designing military aircraft, and buying lucrative Las Vegas real estate.

Howard Hughes stands in the cockpit of the all-wooden "Spruce Goose".

1976

MAY

Su	Mo	Tu	We	Th	Fr	Sa
						1
2	3	4	5	6	7	8
9	10	11	12	13	14	15
16	17	18	19	20	21	22
23	24	25	26	27	28	29
30	31					

1. London: Second division Southampton beat Manchester United 1-0 in the FA Cup Final (→4).

4. UK: Liverpool are League champions for a record ninth time.

6. UK: Tories make sweeping gains in local elections (→26).

6. Italy: 2,000 are feared dead and 80,000 homeless after a series of earthquakes in northern Italy (→29/7).

9. Stuttgart: Terrorist leader Ulrike Meinhof is found dead in her cell after apparently committing suicide (→28/4/77).

11. UK: London cab driver George Davis is released from jail after serving one year of a 17-year sentence.

12. London: Jo Grimond takes over as interim Liberal leader (→18).

14. UK: Inflation has dropped to 18.9 per cent (→21).

17. Northern Ireland: Ten people are dead and 56 hurt after one of the province's most violent weekends (→21/7).

18. London: Liberal MP David Steel receives alleged proof of a South African smear campaign against the Liberals (→7/7).

21. UK: Sterling has lost 12.5 per cent of its value on foreign currency markets in the past three months (→3/6).

24. US: Two Concordes land at the end of the first commercial transatlantic supersonic flights.

24. Munich: Muhammad Ali knocks out Richard Dunn to retain his heavyweight boxing title (→28/9).

27. London: The Commons is suspended in disorder after the Government wins a crucial division by one vote (→10/11).

31. Lebanon: Over 2,000 Syrian troops cross the border (→9/6).

DEATH

26. British soprano Dame Maggie Teyte, born Margaret Tate (*17/4/1888).

Row over Wilson's odd Honours list

May 26. "Disgusting". This was an infuriated Labour reaction today to Sir Harold Wilson's resignation Honours list which was mysteriously leaked in advance.

On his advice, the Queen has given a knighthood to James Goldsmith, the financier said to be a Tory supporter, and a life peerage to Sir Joseph Kagan, maker of Gannex raincoats favoured by the former premier.

The original list, revised by Sir Harold, is thought to have been even more controversial; it was drawn up by Lady Falkender (Mrs Marcia Williams), his political secretary, and others (→13/2/77).

Former political secretary Marci[a] Williams is now Lady Falkender.

Homosexual claims force Thorpe to quit

May 10. Jeremy Thorpe resigne[d] from the Liberal Party leadershi[p] today. He could no longer stan[d] what he called "a sustained pres[s] witchhunt and campaign of deni[-] gration". Mr Thorpe, who is 47 said: "No man can effectively lea[d] a party if the greater part of his tim[e] has to be devoted to answering alle[-] gations and countering plots and in[t]rigues." He repeated earlier ca[t]egorical denials of claims by a[n] unemployed male model that the[y] once had a homosexual relationshi[p] (→12).

Renewed fighting breaks out in Lebanon

A woman questions a masked gunman as an Arab family flees the carnage.

May 16. Yet another truce in the 13-month-long Lebanese civil war collapsed today as a barrage of shells crashed into the centre of shattered Beirut. Some of them cut into a crowd waiting by a cinema at a "Green Line" crossing point, killing 15 people and injuring a further 35.

This cease-fire, the 30th of its kind to be negotiated during the thirteen-month long civil war in Lebanon, lasted a scant 48 hours.

In what has been the worst night of violence during this bloody, attritional conflict, Christians and Moslems exchanged artillery and rocket fire from their respective strongholds in the suburbs. At one stage, the Phalangist radio reported a shell was falling every three minutes.

In the last two months President Assad has sent more than 40,000 troops to Lebanon in attempts to bring peace. Included in this force are 15,000 Syrian regulars, backed up by a number of PLO fighters who are stiffening the Moslem militias.

Assad is again hoping to negotiate a cease-fire, but experts believe that nothing permanent can be achieved until the PLO agree (→ 31).

This parched, cracked surface is usually the Pitsford Reservoir in Northampton, another victim of this summer's all-consuming drought.

1976

JUNE

Su	Mo	Tu	We	Th	Fr	Sa
		1	2	3	4	5
6	7	8	9	10	11	12
13	14	15	16	17	18	19
20	21	22	23	24	25	26
27	28	29	30			

1. Oslo: Britain and Iceland sign an agreement to end the third Cod War.

3. UK: Sterling falls to a new low of $1.71 (→ 7).

6. Rhodesia: Former Prime Minister Sir Garfield Todd has his first day of unrestricted freedom in four years (→ 24/9).

7. London: The Government is to receive loans from 10 nations of £3,000 million to support sterling (→ 24/8).

9. London: Police chief Robert Mark points to the police's poor relations with black youths (→ 31/8).

11. Angola: 13 mercenaries go on trial for murder, looting and other crimes.→

15. Peking: The government says Mao will no longer meet foreign leaders (→ 9/9).

16. Beirut: US ambassador Francis Meloy and an aide are kidnapped and killed (→ 20).

20. Beirut: 263 Britons and Americans are evacuated (→ 26/8).

21. London: Two Arabs buy the Dorchester Hotel for £9 million (→ 4/11/77).

26. London: The city has a record temperature of 95 degrees F (35°C) (→ 14/7).

27. Greece: Six Palestinians hijack an Air France Airbus with over 250 passengers on board (→ 29).

28. Seychelles: The islands become independent after 162 years of British rule (→ 5/6/77).

29. Uganda: The Airbus hijackers, now at Entebbe airport, demand the release of 53 Palestinians (→ 4/7).

30. London: Spaghetti House siege leader, Franklin Davies, gets 21 years; two accomplices also get long jail terms.

DEATHS

6. US oil tycoon Jean Paul Getty (*15/12/1892).

9. British actress Dame Agnes Sybil Thorndike (*24/10/1882).

25. US singer and songwriter Johnny Mercer (*18/11/1909).

Syria turns on its Palestinian allies

June 9. Fresh and bloody battles developed in Lebanon today as a column of Syrian troops 5,000-strong launched a full-scale attack down the Damascus highway.

Spearheaded by tanks and jets, the Syrians began the assault on Palestinian guerrilla strongholds in the mountains. Simultaneously their Moslem allies began hammering Palestinian units in Beirut with their Russian-made missiles. Among the targets were Palestinian camps at Sabra and Chatilla.

Having originally intervened against the Christians, President Assad has now decided to turn on the Palestinians. The US Navy has evacuated 263 Americans from Beirut (→ 16).

Palestinian children join the fight.

Record Derby win for Lester Piggott

June 2. Lester Piggott proved himself today to be the all-time master of the greatest (and the most taxing) of the racing classics, winning the Derby at Epsom for a record seventh time on the French-trained Empery. This beats the six winners of Jim Robinson back in the 1830s and Steve Donoghue, whose six Derby triumphs included two wartime victories at Newmarket. ▷

Blacks revolt in Soweto

June 18. Three days and nights of rioting, burning and looting in South Africa's black townships have left 100 dead and over 1,000 injured. After John Vorster, the Prime Minister, announced that the security forces had been told to restore order "at all costs", police have been opening fire on crowds without warning. "My patience is at an end," said Brigadier J.F. Visser, Police Commissioner for the Witwatersrand, Johannesburg.

The riots were set off by a directive from the Transvaal Education Authority that Afrikaans and English must be used equally for instruction in black secondary schools. Afrikaans, the language of the Dutch-descended section of the white community, is seen by blacks as the language of oppression. "It is the language of pass laws, permits and police," a black social worker said.

In some of the demonstrations, children wearing school uniforms have been led through the townships by their parents, stoning, looting and burning. The front page of a Johannesburg newspaper carries a picture of a girl of about 12 lying dead in the street. Two white men have been killed; they were dragged from their cars and beaten and stoned (→13/8).

This child was shot by the police.

Mercenaries to be executed in Angola

June 28. Three British ex-paratroopers and an American were sentenced to death by firing squad at the close of the trial of 13 white mercenaries in Luanda today. The nine others were given jail sentences of between 16 and 30 years. They came to Angola to join the fight against the Marxist MPLA regime, but were rounded up by the victorious Cuban forces. Passing sentence, the judge, Comrade Ernesto da Silva, condemned the mercenaries, telling them that they had spread "fear, shame and outrage" wherever they went (→10/7).

European mercenaries facing their accusers: four are to be executed.

1976

JULY

Su	Mo	Tu	We	Th	Fr	Sa
				1	2	3
4	5	6	7	8	9	10
11	12	13	14	15	16	17
18	19	20	21	22	23	24
25	26	27	28	29	30	31

1. London: "Black Panther" Donald Nielson is found guilty of murdering heiress Lesley Whittle (→21).

3. Wimbledon: Chris Evert beats Evonne Cawley in the Women's Singles final.→

7. Washington: The Queen arrives on a bicentenary tour of the US (→17).

7. Uganda: 75-year-old Briton Dora Bloch, one of the hijack passengers, has not been seen since the Entebbe raid (→28).

10. Italy: A safety valve bursts at a chemical factory at Seveso, near Milan, releasing a cloud of poison gas.→

10. Angola: Four mercenaries, three British and one American, are shot by firing squad (→18/3/77).

13. Brussels: Roy Jenkins is appointed president of the European Commission (→3/1/77).

14. London: Publication of the Drought Bill to tackle Britain's worst drought in 250 years (→6/8).

17. Montreal: The Queen opens the Olympic Games.→

21. Ireland: British ambassador Christopher Ewart-Biggs is killed when his car is wrecked by a landmine (→9/8).

21. London: Donald Nielson gets five life sentences for murder.

27. Tokyo: Ex-Prime Minister Kakuei Tanaka is arrested for his involvement in the Lockheed bribery scandal (→16/8).

27. Amsterdam: Soviet chess star Victor Korchnoi asks for political asylum (→21/12).

28. London: Britain breaks off diplomatic relations with Uganda (→4/8).

29. UK: Southend Pier, the world's longest, is severely damaged by fire.

30. London: "Private Eye" editor Richard Ingrams sent for trial on criminal libel charges brought by Goldsmith.

DEATH

22. British archaeologist Sir Robert Eric Mortimer Wheeler (*10/9/1890).

Borg becomes idol of Wimbledon fans

July 3. To the delight of the teenage girls who have mobbed his every move since he made his first impact on Wimbledon, the 20-year-old Bjorn Borg, his long blond hair held in place by a headband, today beat Ilie Nastase of Rumania 6-4, 6-2, 9-7 to become the youngest champion for 45 years.

Borg, the first Swede to win the singles title, has been a member of his country's Davis Cup team since he was 15. Last year he won the French title, and this week his superb technique has been equal to anything his more experienced opponents could produce.

Nastase (l.) and new champ Borg.

Chinese city hit by a huge earthquake

July 29. The world's most violen[t] earthquake for 12 years devastate[d] a Chinese city today. Tangshan wa[s] hit by tremors which registered 8.[2] on the Richter scale and in Peking 100 miles away, shock waves rattled buildings. Hundreds of peopl[e] are feared dead in the ruined city[.] Any homes still standing wer[e] brought down by a second powerfu[l] tremor. One woman said her hote[l] split in two only seconds after sh[e] escaped and joined the city's on[e] million population heading for shelter at makeshift camps (→24/11).

Israelis free hostages in Entebbe raid

July 4. In a brilliant feat of arms, Israeli commandos flew 2,500 miles to Uganda on Saturday night and rescued over 100 hostages held by pro-Palestinian hijackers at Entebbe airport. Most of the hostages were Israeli citizens or Jews.

Ugandan soldiers and the hijackers guarding the hostages in a terminal building were taken completely by surprise as three giant Hercules transport planes came in to land and Israeli commandos stormed out. In a 35-minute battle, 20 Ugandan soldiers and all seven hijackers – five Palestinians and two German terrorists – died; three hostages and one Israeli commando were killed.

The Israeli raid came only hours before a deadline set by the hijackers for killing the hostages if demands for the release of 53 pro-Palestinian terrorists held in jails in Israel and four other countries were not met. During the fighting, the Israeli destroyed 11 Russian-built MiG fighters – a quarter of Uganda's air force. Civil aircraft and the hijacked Air France Airbus were shot up. The Israelis put the released hostages aboard the Hercules transports and returned to Israel, stopping at Nairobi to refuel.

The Ugandan dictator, Idi Amin, who had been giving help to the hijackers, is reported to have been in a state of shock after the raid. Later, having recovered, he congratulated his troops for "repulsing the invaders" (→ 7).

Exhausted, but very relieved, some of the hostages talk to the press.

Evacuation ordered as chemical release sparks cancer scare

July 29. Large-scale evacuations have been ordered by the police in the neighbourhood of Seveso near Milan, following an accident at a chemical plant. The accident released a small quantity of a weed-killer called TCDD. However, the danger comes from an impurity called dioxin sometimes produced during the manufacture of TCDD.

Dioxin produces a blistering skin rash even in minute doses, and is suspected of causing cancer and other conditions, too. It is also extremely persistent; dioxin contamination may take years to disappear.

Since the accident occurred over two weeks ago the contaminated area has been steadily increasing in size. Some 250 people, out of 1,500 tested, have shown signs of being affected by dioxin (→ 17/8).

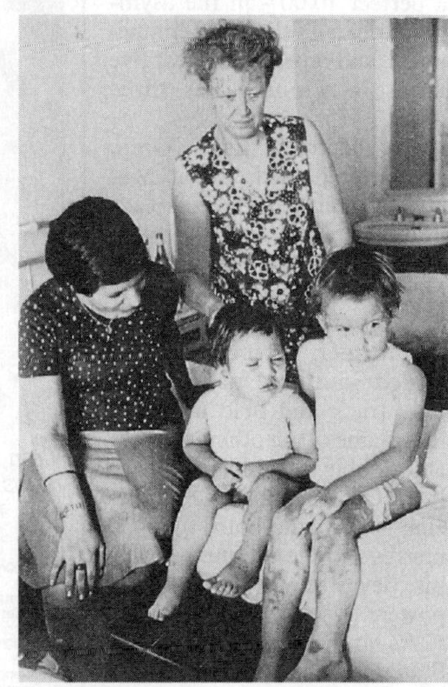

Two sisters display skin rashes.

Carter wins the Democratic nomination

July 15. The Democratic convention in New York today chose former Governor Jimmy Carter of Georgia as their presidential candidate and approved Carter's choice of Walter "Fritz" Mondale, a liberal from Minnesota, as his vice-presidential running-mate. In a harmonious convention, Carter scored easily over Governor "Jerry" Brown of California and Rep "Mo" Udall of Arizona.

"Born-again" presidential campaigner Jimmy Carter glad-hands the fans.

US in the grip of bicentennial fever

July 4. America celebrated its 200th birthday today in a mood of festive introspection. A million people in Washington cheered as lasers wrote in the sky: "1776-1976: Happy Birthday, USA". 10,000 people became US citizens in mass ceremonies, and 15 tall ships sailed into New York harbour. Vice-President Rockefeller sounded a gloomy note and warned that the country's problems might be "insurmountable".

Earthmen get first close look at Mars

July 20. America's Viking spacecraft landed on Mars today and sent back to Earth the first close-up pictures of the planet's surface.

The craft landed on the Chryse Plain after an 11-month journey. It will be analysing soil and searching for living organisms.

David Steel to lead the Liberal Party

July 7. David Steel, son of a Presbyterian minister, was today elected Liberal Party leader. He got 12,541 votes against 7,032 cast for John Pardoe in a ballot of party members. It is the first time that any political leader has been chosen in this grassroots way (→ 24/3/77).

1976  Montreal

Nadia steals glory as Games survive the African boycott

July 31. As the Queen and Prince Philip arrived to open the Montreal Olympic Games, a political crisis was resulting in a boycott by almost all the African athletes. They were withdrawn by their governments because of the International Olympic Committee's refusal to discipline New Zealand over its continued links with South Africa on the rugby field.

Their absence cost the Games dear in the athletics arena - particularly in the long-distance events - and in the boxing ring. But, as always at such a wide-ranging festival, absentees were forgotten as records began to tumble.

As at Munich, the gymnastics provided the early headlines as the mantle of Olga Korbut was assumed by an even younger genius - 14-year-old Nadia Comaneci of Rumania. She was awarded the first maximum score in Olympic history - a perfect 10.00 - in the asymmetric bars in the team competition, and repeated the feat five times in winning her three golds.

On the track, Lasse Viren, double gold medallist at Munich, established a special place in the history books by repeating the 10,000 metres and 5,000 metres double in two masterly displays of distance running (in the former, Brendan Foster trailed in third for Britain's only track and field medal of the Games). Another remarkable double was achieved by the huge Cuban, Alberto Juantorena, who won both the 400 metres and the 800 metres with his devastating, long-striding power.

As at Munich, the United States lost the sprint titles - to Hasely Crawford, a Trinidadian, and Don Quarrie, of Jamaica - but responded with impressive victories in the decathlon, with the photogenic Bruce Jenner, and the 400 metres hurdles, with a world record from the exciting young Edwin Moses.

In the swimming pool the American men, even without Mark Spitz, carried all before them. Only in the 200 metres breaststroke did they falter as David Wilkie's world record gave Britain her first men's swimming gold medal for 68 years.

Men Athletics

100m		
1. Hasely Crawford	TRI	10.06
2. Donald Quarrie	JAM	10.08
3. Valéry Borzov	URS	10.14
200m		
1. Donald Quarrie	JAM	20.23
2. Millard Hampton	USA	23.29
3. Dwayne Evans	USA	20.43
400m		
1. Albert Juantorena	CUB	44.26
2. Fred Newhouse	USA	44.40
3. Herman Frazier	USA	44.95
800m		
1. Alberto Juantorena	CUB	**1:43.50
2. Ivo van Damme	BEL	1:43.86
3. Richard Wohlhuter	USA	1:44.12
1500m		
1. John Walker	NZL	3:39.17
2. Ivo van Damme	BEL	3:39.27
3. Paul-Heinz Wellmann	FRG	3:39.33
5000m		
1. Lasse Viren	FIN	13:24.76
2. Dick Quax	NZL	13:25.16
3. Klaus-Peter Hildenbrand	FRG	13:25.38
10,000m		
1. Lasse Viren	FIN	27:40.38
2. Carlos Lopes	POR	27:45.17
3. Brendan Foster	GBR	27:54.92
Marathon		
1. Valdemar Cierpinski	GDR	*2:09:55.0
2. Frank Shorter	USA	2:10:45.8
3. Karel Lismont	BEL	2:11:12.6
110m Hurdles		
1. Guy Drut	FRA	13.30
2. Alejandro Casanas	CUB	13.33
3. Willie Davenport	USA	13.38
400m Hurdles		
1. Edwin Moses	USA	**47.64
2. Michael Shine	USA	48.69
3. Yevgeny Gavrilenko	URS	49.45
3000m Steeplechase		
1. Anders Gärderud	SWE	**8:08.02
2. Bronislaw Malinowski	POL	8:09.11
3. Frank Baumgartl	GDR	8:10.36
4x100m Relay		
1. USA		38.33
2. German Democratic Republic		38.66
3. Soviet Union		38.78
4x400m Relay		
1. USA		2:58.65
2. Poland		3:01.43
3. German Federal Republic		3:01.98
20km Walk		
1. Daniel Bautista Rocha	MEX	*1:24:40.6
2. Hans Reimann	GDR	1:25:13.8
3. Peter Frenkel	GDR	1:25:29.4
High Jump		
1. Jacek Wszola	POL	*2.25
2. Greg Joy	CAN	2.23
3. Dwight Stones	USA	2.21
Pole Vault		
1. Tadeusz Slusarski	POL	=*5.50
2. Antti Kalliomacki	FIN	=*5.50
3. David Roberts	USA	=*5.50
Long Jump		
1. Arnie Robinson	USA	8.35
2. Randy Williams	USA	8.11
3. Frank Wartenberg	GDR	8.02
Triple Jump		
1. Viktor Saneyev	URS	17.29
2. James Butts	USA	17.18
3. Joao de Oliveira	BRA	16.90
Shotput		
1. Udo Beyer	GDR	21.05
2. Yevgeny Mironov	URS	21.03
3. Aleksandr Baryshnikov	URS	21.00
Discus		
1. Mac Wilkins	USA	67.50
2. Wolfgang Schmidt	GDR	66.22
3. John Powell	USA	65.70
Hammer		
1. Yuri Sedykh	URS	77.52
2. Aleksei Spiridonov	URS	76.08
3. Anatoli Bondarchuk	URS	75.48
Javelin		
1. Miklos Németh	HUN	**94.58
2. Hanun Siitonen	FIN	87.92
3. Gheorghe Megelea	ROM	87.16
Decathlon		
1. Bruce Jenner	USA	**8617
2. Guido Kratschmer	FRG	8411
3. Nikolai Avilov	URS	8369

Viren Lasse, the "Flying Finn", races to the gold in the 5,000 and 10,000 metre events; he runs 13:24.8 and 27:40.4.

Modern Pentathlon

Individual		
1. Janusz Pyciak-Peciak	POL	5520
2. Pavel Lednev	URS	5485
3. Jan Bártu	TCH	5466
Team		
1. Great Britain		15.559
2. Czechoslovakia		15.451
3. Hungary		15.395

Women Athletics

100m		
1. Annegret Richter	FRG	11.08
2. Renate Stecher	GDR	11.13
3. Inge Helten	FRG	11.17
200m		
1. Bärbel Eckert	GDR	*22.37
2. Annegret Richter	FRG	22.39
3. Renate Stecher	GDR	22.47
400m		
1. Irena Szewinska	POL	**49.29
2. Christina Brehmer	GDR	50.51
3. Ellen Streidt	GDR	50.55
800m		
1. Tatyana Kazankina	URS	**1:54.94
2. Nikolina Shtereva	BUL	1:55.42
3. Elfi Zinn	GDR	1:55.60
1500m		
1. Tatyana Kazankina	URS	4:05.48
2. Gunhild Hoffmeister	GDR	4:06.02
3. Ulrike Klapezynski	GDR	4:06.09
100m Hurdles		
1. Johanna Schaller	GDR	12.77
2. Tatiana Anisimova	URS	12.78
3. Natalya Lebedeva	URS	12.80
4x100m Relay		
1. German Democratic Republic		*42.55
2. German Federal Republic		42.59
3. Soviet Union		43.09
4x400m Relay		
1. German Democratic Republic		**3:19.23
2. USA		3:22.81
3. Soviet Union		3:24.24
High Jump		
1. Rosemarie Ackermann	GDR	*1.93
2. Sara Simeoni	ITA	1.91
3. Yordanka Blagoeva	BUL	1.91
Long Jump		
1. Angela Voigt	GDR	6.72
2. Kathy McMillan	USA	6.66
3. Lidia Alfeyeva	URS	6.60
Shotput		
1. Ivanka Hristova	BUL	21.16
2. Nadezhda Chizhova	URS	20.96
3. Helena Fibingerová	TCH	20.67
Discus		
1. Evelyn Schlaak	GDR	*69.00
2. Maria Vergova	BUL	67.30
3. Gabriele Hinzmann	GDR	66.84
Javelin		
1. Ruth Fuchs	GDR	*65.94
2. Marion Becker	FRG	64.70
3. Kathy Schmidt	USA	63.96
Pentathlon		
1. Siegrun Siegl	GDR	4745
2. Christine Laser	GDR	4745
3. Burglinde Pollak	GDR	4740

Men Swimming

100m Freestyle		
1. Jim Montgomery	USA	**49.99
2. Jim Babashoff	USA	50.81
3. Peter Nocke	FRG	51.31
200m Freestyle		
1. Bruce Furniss	USA	**1:50.29
2. John Naber	USA	1:50.50
3. Jim Montgomery	USA	1:50.58
400m Freestyle		
1. Brian Goodell	USA	**3:51.93
2. Tim Shaw	USA	3:52.54
3. Vladimir Raskatov	URS	3:55.76
1500m Freestyle		
1. Brian Goodell	USA	**15:02.40
2. Bobby Hackett	USA	15:03.91
3. Stephen Holland	AUS	15:04.66
100m Backstroke		
1. John Naber	USA	**55.49
2. Peter Rocca	USA	56.34
3. Roland Matthes	GDR	57.22
200m Backstroke		
1. John Naber	USA	**1:59.15
2. Peter Rocca	USA	2:00.55
3. Dan Harrigan	USA	2:01.35

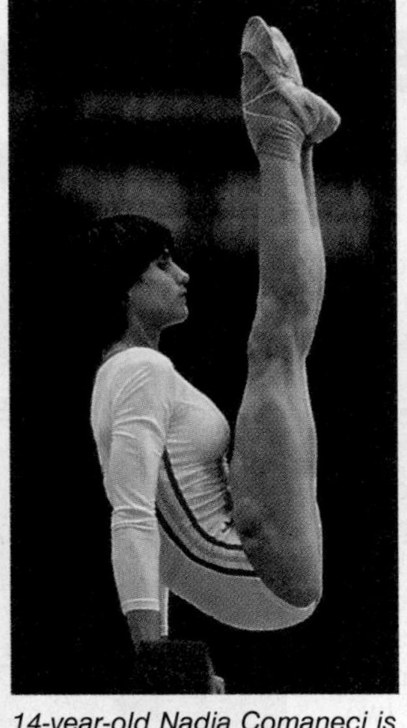
14-year-old Nadia Comaneci is the latest gymnastic star.

100m Breaststroke		
1. John Hencken	USA	**1:03.11
2. David Wilkie	GBR	1:03.43
3. Arvidas Ivozaytis	URS	1:04.23
200m Breaststroke		
1. David Wilkie	GBR	**2:15.11
2. John Hencken	USA	2:17.26
3. Rick Colella	USA	2:19.20
100m Butterfly		
1. Matt Vogel	USA	54.35
2. Joe Bottom	USA	54.50
3. Gary Hall	USA	54.65
200m Butterfly		
1. Mike Bruner	USA	**1:59.23
2. Steve Gregg	USA	1:59.54
3. Bill Forrester	USA	1:59.96
400m Individual Medley Relay		
1. Rod Strachan	USA	**4:23.68
2. Tim McKee	USA	4:24.62
3. Andrei Smirnov	URS	4:26.90
4x200m Freestyle Relay		
1. USA		**7:32.22
2. Soviet Union		7:27.97
3. Great Britain		7:32.11
4x100m Medley Relay		
1. USA		**3:42.22
2. Canada		3:45.94
3. German Federal Republic		3:47.29
Springboard Diving		
1. Phil Boggs	USA	619.05
2. Giorgio Cagnotto	ITA	570.48
3. Aleksandr Kosenkov	URS	567.24
Platform Diving		
1. Klaus Dibiasi	ITA	600.51
2. Gregory Louganis	USA	576.99
3. Vladimir Aleynik	URS	548.61

Water Polo

1. Hungary
2. Italy
3. Netherlands

Women Swimming

100m Freestyle		
1. Kornelia Ender	GDR	**55.65
2. Petra Priemer	GDR	56.49
3. Enith Brigitha	NETH	56.65
200m Freestyle		
1. Kornelia Ender	GDR	**1:59.26
2. Shirley Babashoff	USA	2:01.22
3. Enith Brigitha	NETH	2:01.40
400m Freestyle		
1. Petra Thümer	GDR	**4:09.89
2. Shirley Babashoff	USA	4:10.46
3. Shannon Smith	CAN	4:14.60
800m Freestyle		
1. Petra Thümer	GDR	**8:37.14
2. Shirley Babashoff	USA	8:37.59
3. Wendy Weinberg	USA	8:42.60
100m Breaststroke		
1. Hannelore Anke	GDR	1:11.16
2. Lyubov Rusanova	URS	1:13.04
3. Marina Koshevaia	URS	1:13.30
200m Breaststroke		
1. Marina Koshevaia	URS	**2:33.35
2. Marina Iurchenia	URS	2:36.08
3. Lyubov Rusanova	URS	2:36.22
100m Backstroke		
1. Ulrike Richter	GDR	*1:01.83
2. Birgit Treiber	GDR	1:03.41
3. Nancy Garapick	CAN	1:03.71
200m Backstroke		
1. Ulrike Richter	GDR	*2:13.43
2. Birgit Treiber	GDR	2:14.97
3. Nancy Garapick	CAN	2:15.60
100m Butterfly		
1. Kornelia Ender	GDR	=**1:00.13
2. Andrea Pollack	GDR	1:00.98
3. Wendy Boglioli	USA	1:01.17
200m Butterfly		
1. Andrea Pollack	GDR	*2:11.41
2. Ulrike Tauber	GDR	2:12.50
3. Rosemarie Gabriel	GDR	2:12.86
400m Individual Medley Relay		
1. Ulrike Tauber	GDR	**4:42.77
2. Cheryl Gibson	CAN	4:48.10
3. Becky Smith	CAN	4:50.48
4x100m Medley Relay		
1. GDR		**4:07.95
2. USA		4:14.55
3. Canada		4:15.22
4x100m Freestyle Relay		
1. USA		**3:44.82
2. GDR		3:45.50
3. Canada		3:48.81
Springboard Diving		
1. Jennifer Chandler	USA	506.19
2. Christa Köhler	GDR	469.4
3. Cynthia Potter	USA	466.83
Platform Diving		
1. Elena Vaytsekhovskaya	URS	406.5
2. Ulrike Knape	SWE	402.6
3. Deborah Wilson	USA	401.0

Boxing

Light Flyweight (48kg)	
1. Jorge Hernandez	CU
2. Byong-Uk Li	PR
3. Orlando Maldonado	PU
3. Payao Pooltarat	TH
Flyweight (51kg)	
1. Leo Randolph	US
2. Ramon Duvalon	CU
3. David Torosyan	UR
3. Leszek Blazynski	PO
Bantamweight (54kg)	
1. Yong-Jo Gu	PR
2. Charles Money	US
3. Patrick Cowdell	GB
3. Victor Rybakov	UR
Featherweight (57kg)	
1. Angel Herrera	CU
2. Richard Nowakowski	GD
3. Leszek Kosedowski	PO
3. Juan Paredes	ME
Lightweight (60kg)	
1. Howard Davis	US
2. Simion Cutov	RO
3. Vasily Solomin	UR
3. Ace Rusevski	YU
Light Welterweight (63.5kg)	
1. Ray Leonard	US
2. Andrés Aldama	CU
3. Vladimir Kolev	BU
3. Kazimierz Szczerba	PO
Welterweight (67kg)	
1. Jochen Bachfeld	GD
2. Pedro Gamarro	VE
3. Reinhard Skricek	FR
3. Victor Zilbermann	RO
Light Middleweight (71kg)	
1. Jerzy Ribicki	PO
2. Tadija Kacar	YU
3. Victor Savchenko	UR
3. Rolando Garbey	CU
Middleweight (75kg)	
1. Michael Spinks	US
2. Rufat Riskiev	UR
3. Alec Nastac	RO
3. Luis Martinez	CU

Alberto Juantorena of Cuba se a new world record of 1:43.5 in the 800 metres.

1976 Montreal

Light Heavyweight (81kg)
1. Leon Spinks USA
2. Sixto Soria CUB
3. Costica Dafinoui ROM
3. Janusz Gortat POL

Heavyweight (more than 81kg)
1. Téofilo Stevenson CUB
2. Mircea Simon ROM
3. Johnny Tate USA
3. Clarence Hill BER

Weightlifting

Flyweight (52kg)
1. Aleksandr Voronin URS =**242.5
2. György Köszegi HUN 237.5
3. Mohammad Nassiri IRN 235.0

Bantamweight (56kg)
1. Norair Nurikian BUL **262.5
2. Grzegorz Cziura POL 252.5
3. Kenkichi Ando JAP 250.0

Featherweight (60kg)
1. Nikolai Kolesnikov URS =**285.0
2. Georgi Todorov BUL 280.0
3. Kazumasu Hirai JAP 275.0

Lightweight (67.5kg)
1. Piotr Korol URS *305.0
2. Daniel Senet FRA 300.0
3. Kazimierz Czarnecki POL 295.0

Middleweight (75kg)
1. Yordan Mitkov BUL *335.0
2. Vartan Militosyan URS 330.0
3. Peter Wenzel GDR 327.5

Light Heavyweight (less than 82.5kg)
1. Valeri Shary URS *365.0
2. Trendafil Stoichev BUL 360.0
3. Péter Baczako HUN 345.0

Middle Heavyweight (less than 90kg)
1. David Rigert URS *382.5
2. Lee James USA 362.5
3. Alanas Shopov BUL 360.0

Heavyweight (110kg)
1. Yuri Zaitsev URS 385.0
2. Krustiu Semerdzhiev BUL 385.0
3. Tadeusz Rutkowski POL 377.5

Super Heavyweight (more than 110kg)
1. Vassily Alexeyev URS 440.0
2. Gerd Bonk GDR 405.0
3. Helmut Losch GDR 387.5

Greco Roman Wrestling

Light Flyweight (48kg)
1. Alexei Shumakov URS
2. Gheorghe Berceanu ROM
3. Stefan Angelov BUL

Flyweight (53kg)
1. Vitaly Konstantinov URS
2. Nicu Ginga ROM
3. Koichiro Hirayama JAP

Bantamweight (57kg)
1. Pertti Ukkola FIN
2. Ivan Frgic YUG
3. Farhat Mustafin URS

Featherweight (62kg)
1. Kazimierz Lipien POL
2. Nelson Davidian URS
3. László Réczi HUN

Lightweight (68kg)
1. Suren Nalbandyan URS
2. Stefan Rusu ROM
3. Heinz Helmut Wehling GDR

Welterweight (74kg)
1. Anatoly Bykov URS
2. Vitezslav Mácha TCH
3. Karl-Heinz Helbing FRG

Middleweight (82kg)
1. Momir Petkovic YUG
2. Vladimir Cheboksarov URS
3. Ivan Kolev BUL

Light Heavyweight (90kg)
1. Valeri Rezantsev URS
2. Stoyan Ivanov BUL
3. Czeslaw Kwiecinski POL

Heavyweight (100kg)
1. Nikolai Balboshin URS
2. Kamen Goranov BUL
3. Andrzej Skrzydlewski POL

Super Heavyweight (more than 100kg)
1. Aleksandr Kolchinsky URS
2. Alexander Tomov BUL
3. Roman Codreanu ROM

Freestyle Wrestling

Light Flyweight (48kg)
1. Hasan Isaev BUL
2. Roman Dmitriev URS
3. Akira Kudo JAP

Flyweight (less than 52kg)
1. Yuji Takada JAP
2. Aleksandr Ivanov SOV
3. Hae-Sup Jeon KOR

Bantamweight (less than 57kg)
1. Vladimir Umin URS
2. Hans-Dieter Brüchert GDR
3. Masao Arai JAP

Featherweight (less than 62kg)
1. Jum-mo Yang KOR
2. Zeveg Oidov MON
3. Gene Davis USA

Lightweight (less than 68kg)
1. Pavel Pinigin URS
2. Lloyd Keaser USA
3. Yasaburo Sugawara JAP

Welterweight (less than 74kg)
1. Juchiro Date JAP
2. Mansour Barzegar IRN
3. Stanley Dziedzic USA

Middleweight (less than 87kg)
1. John Peterson USA
2. Viktor Novoyilov URS
3. Adolf Seger FRG

Light Heavyweight (less than 90kg)
1. Levan Tediashvili URS
2. Benjamin Peterson USA
3. Stelica Morcov ROM

Heavyweight (less than 100kg)
1. Ivan Yarygin URS
2. Russell Hellickson USA
3. Dimo Kostov BUL

Super Heavyweight (more than 100kg)
1. Soslan Andiev URS
2. Jozsef Balla HUN
3. Ladislau Simon ROM

Judo

Lightweight (less than 63kg)
1. Hector Rodriguez CUB
2. Eun-Kyung Chang KOR
3. József Tuncsik HUN
3. Felice Mariani ITA

Welterweight (less than 70kg)
1. Vladimir Nevzorov URS
2. Koji Kuramoto JAP
3. Patrick Vial FRA
3. Marian Talaj POL

Middleweight (less than 80kg)
1. Isamu Sonoda JAP
2. Valery Dvoinikov URS
3. Slavko Obadov YUG
3. Young-Chul Park KOR

Light Heavyweight (less than 90kg)
1. Kazuhiro Ninomiya JAP
2. Ramaz Harshiladze URS
3. David Starbrook GBR
3. Jürg Röthlisberger SUI

Heavyweight (less than 95kg)
1. Sergei Novikov URS
2. Günther Neureuther FRG
3. Allen Coage USA
3. Sumio Endo JAP

Open
1. Haruki Uemura JAP
2. Keith Remfry GBR
3. Shota Chochoshvilli URS
3. Jeaki Cho KOR

Men Fencing

Foil Individual
1. Fabio Dal Zotto ITA
2. Aleksandr Romankov URS
3. Bernard Talvard FRA

Foil Team
1. German Federal Republic
2. Italy
3. France

Epée Individual
1. Alexander Pusch FRG
2. Jürgen Hehn FRG
3. Győzö Kulcsar HUN

Epée Team
1. Sweden
2. German Federal Republic
3. Switzerland

Sabre Individual
1. Viktor Krovopuskov URS
2. Vladimir Nazlymov URS
3. Viktor Sidiak URS

Sabre Team
1. Soviet Union
2. Italy
3. Romania

Women Fencing

Foil Individual
1. Ildikó Schwarczenberger HUN
2. Consolata M. Collino ITA
3. Yelana Belova URS

Foil Team
1. Soviet Union
2. France
3. Hungary

Men Canoeing

Kayak-1 500m
1. Vasile Diba ROM 1:46.41
2. Zoltán Sztanity HUN 1:46.95
3. Rüdiger Helm GDR 1:48.30

Kayak-2 500m
1. German Democratic Republic 1:35.87
2. Soviet Union 1:36.81
3. Romania 1:37.43

Kayak-1 1000m
1. Rüdiger Helm GDR 3:48.20
2. Géza Csapó HUN 3:48.84
3. Vasile Diba ROM 3:49.65

Kayak-4 1000m
1. Soviet Union 3:08.69
2. Spain 3:08.95
3. German Democratic Republic 3:10.76

Canadian-1 500m
1. Aleksandr Rogov URS 1:59.23
2. John Wood CAN 1:59.58
3. Matija Ljubek YUG 1:59.60

Canadian-2 500m
1. Soviet Union 1:45.81
2. Poland 1:47.77
3. Hungary 1:48.35

Canadian-1 1000m
1. Martija Ljubek YUG 4:09.51
2. Vassily Urchenko URS 4:12.57
3. Tamás Wichmann HUN 4:14.11

Canadian-2 1000m
1. Soviet Union 3:52.76
2. Romania 3:54.28
3. Hungary 3:55.66

Women Canoeing

Kayak-1 500m
1. Carola Zirzow GDR 2:01.05
2. Tatiana Korshunova URS 2:03.07
3. Klára Rajnai HUN 2:05.01

Kayak-2 500m
1. Soviet Union 1:51.15
2. Hungary 1:51.69
3. German Democratic Republic 1:51.81

Men Rowing

Single Sculls
1. Pertti Karppinen FIN 7:29.03
2. Peter-Michael Kolbe FRG 7:31.67
3. Joachim Dreifke GDR 7:38.03

Double Sculls
1. Norway 7:13.20
2. Great Britain 7:15.26
3. German Democratic Republic 7:17.45

Quadruple Sculls
1. German Democratic Republic 6:18.65
2. Soviet Union 6:19.89
3. Czechoslovakia 6:21.77

Coxless Pairs
1. German Democratic Republic 7:23.31
2. USA 7:26.73
3. German Federal Republic 7:30.03

Coxed Pairs
1. German Democratic Republic 7:58.99
2. Soviet Union 8:01.82
3. Czechoslovakia 8:03.82

Coxless Fours
1. German Democratic Republic 6:37.42
2. Norway 6:41.22
3. Soviet Union 6:42.52

Coxed Fours
1. Soviet Union 6:40.22
2. German Democratic Republic 6:42.70
3. German Federal Republic 6:46.96

Eights
1. German Democratic Republic 5:58.29
2. Great Britain 6:00.82
3. New Zealand 6:03.51

Britain's David Wilkie – first at 200m breaststroke, and second at 100m breaststoke.

Women Rowing

Single Sculls
1. Christine Scheiblich GDR 4:05.56
2. Joan Lind USA 4:06.21
3. Elena Antonova URS 4:10.24

Double Sculls
1. Bulgaria 3:44.36
2. German Democratic Republic 3:47.86
3. Soviet Union 3:49.93

Coxed Fours
1. German Democratic Republic 3:29.99
2. Bulgaria 3:32.49
3. Soviet Union 3:32.76

Quadruple Sculls
1. German Democratic Republic 3:29.99
2. Soviet Union 3:32.49
3. Romania 3:32.76

Coxless Pairs
1. Bulgaria 4:01.22
2. German Democratic Republic 4:01.64
3. FRG 4:02.35

Coxed Fours
1. German Democratic Republic 3:45.08
2. Bulgaria 3:48.24
3. Soviet Union 3:49.38

Eights
1. German Democratic Republic 3:33.32
2. Soviet Union 3:36.17
3. USA 3:36.68

Yachting

Finn Monotype
1. Jochen Schümann GDR 35.4
2. Andrei Balashov URS 39.7
3. John Bertrand AUS 46.4

Flying Dutchman
1. German Federal Republic 34.7
2. Great Britain 51.7
3. Brazil 52.1

Soling
1. Denmark 46.7
2. USA 47.4
3. German Democratic Republic 47.4

Tempest
1. Sweden 14.0
2. Soviet Union 30.4
3. USA 32.7

470 (men only)
1. German Federal Republic 42.4
2. Spain 49.7
3. Australia 57.0

Tornado
1. Great Britain 18.0
2. USA 36.0
3. German Federal Republic 37.7

Cycling

Individual Road Race
1. Bernt Johansson SWE 4:40.52
2. Giuseppe Martinelli ITA 4:47.23
3. Mieczyslaw Nowicki POL 4:47.23

100km Team Time Trial
1. Soviet Union 2:08.53
2. Poland 2:09.13
3. Denmark 2:12.20

1000m Time Trial
1. Klaus-Jürgen Grünke GDR 1:05.92
2. Michel Vaarten BEL 1:07.51
3. Niels Fredborg DEN 1:07.61

1000m Sprint
1. Anton Tkác TCH
2. Daniel Morelon FRA
3. Hans-Jürgen Geschke GDR

4000m Individual Pursuit
1. Gregor Braun FRG 4:47.61
2. Herman Ponsteen NETH 4:49.72
3. Thomas Huschke GDR 4:52.71

4000m Team Pursuit
1. German Federal Republic 4:21.06
2. Soviet Union 4:27.15
3. Great Britain 4.22.41

Equestrian Sports

Three-Day Event Individual
1. Edmund Coffin USA 114.99
2. John Plumb USA -125.85
3. Karl Schultz FRG -129.45

Three-Day Event Team
1. USA -441.00
2. German Federal Republic -584.60
3. Australia -599.54

Individual Dressage
1. Christine Strückelberger SWE 1486
2. Harry Boldt FRG 1435
3. Reiner Klimke FRG 1395

Team Dressage
1. German Federal Republic 5155
2. Switzerland 4684
3. USA 4647

Grand Prix Jumping Individual
1. Alwin Schockemöhle FRG 0
2. Michel Vaillancourt CAN -12
3. François Mathy BEL -12

Grand Prix Jumping Team
1. France
2. German Federal Republic
3. Belgium

Shooting

Small-Bore Rifle, 50m, Prone
1. Karlheinz Smieszek FRG =**599
2. Ulrich Lind FRG 597
3. Gennadi Luschikov URS 595

Small-Bore, Combined, 3 Positions
1. Lanny Bassham USA 1162
2. Margaret Murdock USA 1162
3. Werner Seibold FRG 1160

Rapid-Fire Pistol, 25m
1. Norbert Klaar GDR *507
2. Jürgen Wiefel GDR 596
3. Roberto Ferraris ITA 595

Skeet
1. Josef Panacek TCH =*198
2. Eric Swinkels NETH =*198
3. Wieslaw Gawlikowski POL 196

Free Pistol 50m
1. Uwe Potteck GDR **573
2. Harald Vollmar GDR 567
3. Rudolf Dollinger AUT 562

Clay Pigeon Individual
1. Donald Haldeman USA 190
2. Armando Silva Marques POR 189
3. Ubaldesco Baldi ITA 189

Moving Target
1. Aleksandr Gazov URS **579
2. Aleksandr Kedyarov URS 576
3. Jerzy Greszkiweicz POL 571

Men Archery

1. Darrell Pace USA **2571
2. Hiroshi Michinaga JAP 2502
3. Giancarlo Carlo Ferrari ITA 2495

Women Archery

1. Luann Ryon USA **2499
2. Valentina Kovpan URS 2460
3. Zebiniso Rustamova URS 2407

Men Gymnastics

All-around Individual
1. Nikolai Andrianov URS 116.650
2. Sawao Kato JAP 115.650
3. Mitsuo Tsukahara JAP 115.575

Combined Exercises Team
1. Japan 576.8
2. Soviet Union 567.4
3. German Democratic Republic 564.6

Parallel Bars
1. Sawao Kato JAP 19.675
2. Nikolai Andrianov URS 19.500
3. Mitsuo Tsukahara JAP 19.475

Floor Exercises
1. Nikolai Andrianov URS 19.450
2. Vladimir Marchenko URS 19.425
3. Peter Kormann USA 19.300

Long Horse Vault
1. Nikolai Andrianov URS 19.450
1. Mitsuo Tsukahara JAP 19.375
3. Hiroshi Kajiyama JAP 19.275

Side Horse
1. Zoltan Magyar HUN 19.700
2. Eizo Kenmotsu JAP 19.575
3. Nikolai Andrianov URS 19.525

Horizontal Bar
1. Mitsuo Tsukahara JAP 19.675
1. Eizo Kenmotsu JAP 19.500
3. Eberhard Gienger FRG 19.475
3. Henry Boërio FRA 19.475

Rings
1. Nikolai Andrianov URS 19.650
2. Aleksandr Dityatin URS 19.550
3. Dan Grecu ROM 19.500

Women Gymnastics

All-around Individual
1. Nadia Comaneci ROM 79.275
2. Nelli Kim URS 78.675
3. Lyudmila Tourischeva URS 78.625

Combined Exercises Team
1. Soviet Union 466.00
2. Romania 462.35
3. German Democratic Republic 450.00

Asymetric Bars
1. Nadia Comaneci ROM 20.000
2. Teodora Ungureanu ROM 19.800
3. Márta Egervári HUN 19.775

Floor Exercises
1. Nelli Kim URS 19.850
2. Lyudmila Tourischeva URS 19.825
3. Nadia Comaneci ROM 19.750

Side Horse Vault
1. Nelli Kim URS 19.800
2. Lyudmila Tourischeva URS 19.650
3. Carola Dombeck GDR 19.650

Balance Beam
1. Nadia Comaneci ROM 19.950
2. Olga Korbut URS 19.725
3. Teodora Ungureanu ROM 19.700

Men Basketball

1. USA
2. Yugoslavia
3. Soviet Union

Women Basketball

1. Soviet Union
2. USA
3. Bulgaria

Football

1. German Democratic Republic
2. Poland
3. Soviet Union

Men Hand-Ball

1. Soviet Union
2. Romania
3. Poland

Women Hand-Ball

1. Soviet Union
2. GDR
3. Hungary

Field Hockey

1. New Zealand
2. Australia
3. Pakistan

Men Volleyball

1. Poland
2. Soviet Union
3. Cuba

Women Volleyball

1. Japan
2. Soviet Union
3. Korea

(Key to symbols and abbreviations p. 1456)

1976

AUGUST

Su	Mo	Tu	We	Th	Fr	Sa
1	2	3	4	5	6	7
8	9	10	11	12	13	14
15	16	17	18	19	20	21
22	23	24	25	26	27	28
29	30	31				

1. West Germany: World champion Niki Lauda is seriously burned in an accident in the German Grand Prix.→

4. Madrid: King Juan Carlos pardons about 90 per cent of Spanish political prisoners.

4. Uganda: Five students die during an anti-Amin protest at Makerere (→7/2/77).

6. London: The Drought Bill receives Royal Assent (→24).

9. Belfast: SDLP leader Gerry Fitt drives a Republican mob from his house at gunpoint (→11).

11. Belfast: A third child dies after being hit by a car hijacked by the IRA yesterday (→2/9).

16. Tokyo: Ex-Prime Minister Tanaka is indicted on charges of accepting bribes from Lockheed (→26).

17. Italy: A growing number of women in the Seveso area are seeking abortions to avoid having deformed children.

19. US: Gerald Ford wins the Republican presidential nomination (→23/9).

23. Cairo: Arab terrorists hijack a plane, but release the 100 passengers on board.

24. UK: 1.5 million are reported to be jobless (→28/9).

24. London: Callaghan puts Dennis Howell in charge of co-ordinating Government drought measures.→

26. Holland: Prince Bernhard resigns from most of his positions following a report on the Lockheed affair.

26. Lebanon: Over 40,000 have died so far in the civil war (→19/10).

27. London: Stonehouse resigns as an MP.

DEATHS

2. German film director Fritz Lang (*5/12/1890).

4. Canadian-born British newspaper owner Roy Herbert Thomson, first Baron Thomson of Fleet (*5/6/1894).

19. British actor and director Alastair George Bell Sim (*9/10/1900).

Women's peace movement starts in Ulster

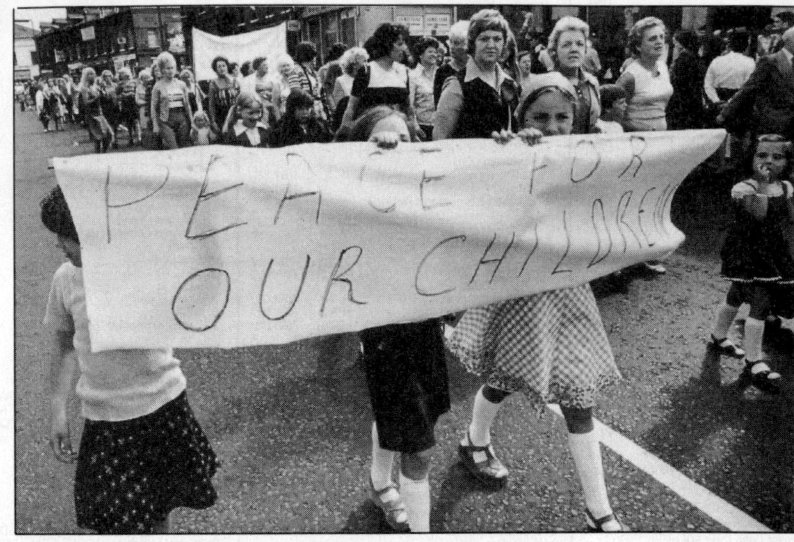

The women and children of Belfast march for the greatest goal of all.

Aug 8. A women's peace movement was launched in Northern Ireland yesterday at a rally of 20,000 Protestants and Roman Catholics. "Everybody has failed so far to get the two sides together and to bring us peace," said Mairead Corrigan, one of the organisers. "I believe it is time for the women to have a go, and see what the women of both sides, working together, can do."

Miss Corrigan is the aunt of the three Maguire children killed in a recent outbreak of violence. They were hit by a car careering out of control, after the terrorist driver had been shot and killed by the Army.

The children were crushed to death when the vehicle mounted the pavement, pushing them against a fence. The youngest of the three was a boy of six months in his pram. What began as a spontaneous protest against these deaths is becoming something like a movement with plans to build community halls where Roman Catholics and Protestants can meet and play together (→9).

Stonehouse guilty of fraud and theft

Aug 6. John Stonehouse – a man once tipped as a future leader of the Labour Party – was in a police cell tonight, branded as a forger, thief and liar. The former minister is beginning a seven-year sentence for fraud. Stonehouse, who organised an elaborate "disappearance", leaving his clothes on a Miami beach before turning up in Australia under an assumed name and carrying a false passport, had been found guilty on 19 counts.

His mistress, Sheila Buckley, who had helped him, was freed with a two-year suspended sentence. The judge told Stonehouse: "You falsely accused other people of cant, hypocrisy and humbug, when you must have known all the time your defence was the embodiment of all those things" (→27).

Riot mars Notting Hill carnival

Aug 31. Fierce race riots broke out in London's Notting Hill tonight at the end of the traditional three-day Caribbean carnival.

By the end the happy festival had given way to a toll of 68 arrests, 36 buildings looted or wrecked and 35 police cars damaged. Up to 350 officers were injured, several with stab wounds, and 150 people were hurt among the crowd.

Fighting first erupted as police tried to arrest a suspected pickpocket among a large gathering of black youths. One young officer was hit with a brick and when colleagues went to help, a scuffle developed into skirmishes up and down the Portobello Road. When a mob marched on the Notting Hill police station officers came out armed with dustbin lids.

Winnie Mandela is held as riots spread

Aug 13. Winnie Mandela, wife of the jailed black nationalist leader, Nelson Mandela, was among the 20 black South Africans picked up by police in raids in Soweto, Port Elizabeth and Grahamstown. The police raids came as rioting in the black townships, which began last June, reached new peaks of violence and spread from Johannesburg to Cape Town.

In townships outside Capetown thousands of blacks, many of them children, raided liquor stores and plunged into a drunken orgy of violence and fire-raising. Police fired into the crowds and 29 people are reported dead (→15/9).

England hammered by Viv Richards

Aug 13. In a savage display of aggressive batting in the fifth Test at the Oval, Vivian Richards, the West Indies batting sensation from Antigua, brought his own score to 291, the highest innings in an England-West Indies Test match in this country. It gave him an aggregate for the series of 829 runs, a total bettered only three times before. And to complete the record-breaking, the West Indies total of 687 for eight was also their highest-ever total against England.

The end of a great innings.

Phew, what a scorcher!

Aug 31. A few drops of rain made headline news today. At Lord's, the crowd cheered when rain stopped play – if only for 15 minutes – and in Somerset, a vicar asked his congregation to give thanks to the Almighty for a downpour.

The rain was the first hint of the end of a heatwave which delighted Britons, worried the Government, threatened industry and left millions in the West of England and Wales without tap-water for much of the day.

There had not been a summer like it this century; temperatures soared and all parts of the UK basked in record hours of sunshine. Suddenly it was a time of barbecues, bikinis in Hyde Park, endless queues for ice creams and cold drinks ... and drought.

Industry suffered water rationing, and several companies in the Midlands were forced to curtail their working week. Forest fires raged in the south – and firemen watched impotently as hundreds of acres of the New Forest and other woodland were destroyed.

With no sign of a break in the weather, the Government was becoming increasingly worried by a potentially disastrous national water shortage. Reservoirs were drying up and their clay bottoms were cracking in the heat.

Householders were advised to use their bath water to water their gardens, to avoid overflushing their lavatories and to place bricks in their cisterns. Dirty cars were patriotic and draconian penalties were introduced for the use of garden hoses.

The avuncular Sports Minister, Denis Howell, was created "Minister for Drought" and warned that unless consumption was cut by a half all over Britain, the country would almost certainly face water rationing until Christmas. Then, today, the rains came and Britons could complain, once more, about their awful climate (→1/9).

Making the most of the sun.

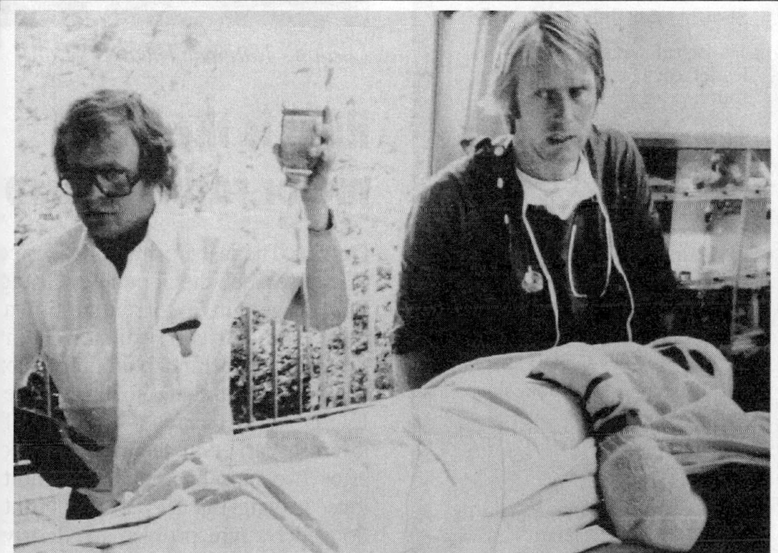

Aug 1. Seriously injured and badly burnt, Austrian racing driver Niki Lauda is rushed to hospital after crashing in the German Grand Prix.

1976

SEPTEMBER

Su	Mo	Tu	We	Th	Fr	Sa
			1	2	3	4
5	6	7	8	9	10	11
12	13	14	15	16	17	18
19	20	21	22	23	24	25
26	27	28	29	30		

1. New Delhi: Mrs Gandhi asks for sweeping new powers (→22/3/77).

1. UK: 750,000 homes in Yorkshire are to have their water mains supply replaced with communal standpipes.

3. UK: After 65 hours of rioting protests at Hull jail end; damage is put at £1 million.

6. Paris: Vietnam tells the US that six of the 12 pilots it claims are still missing were killed in action (→12/11).

10. London: Roy Mason replaces Merlyn Rees as Ulster Secretary; Rees becomes Home Secretary (→10/10).

10. Yugoslavia: 176 die in the world's worst mid-air disaster when two planes collide (→13/10).

11. Belgrade: Tito is reported to be seriously ill.

14. London: Slater Walker Securities announces a loss of £42 million last year; its shares slide from 16p to 8p.

15. Cape Town: 250,000 non-whites stage a strike (→25/10).

17. UK: The first women cadets are admitted to Dartmouth Naval College.

20. Sweden: A coalition defeats Olof Palme's Socialists, who leave office for the first time in 30 years.

23. US: Ford and Carter have their first televised debate (→14/11).

24. US: Patty Hearst is jailed for seven years for armed robbery (→9/5/77).

28. UK: The pound falls to $1.64.→

28. New York: Muhammad Ali beats Ken Norton to retain his world heavyweight boxing title (→29/9/77).

DEATHS

9. Chinese statesman Mao Tse-tung, chairman of the Communist Party, 1949-76 (*26/12/1893).→

21. British publisher Sir William Alexander Roy Collins (*23/5/1900).

Britain goes cap-in-hand to the IMF

Sept 29. Britain has applied to borrow $3.9 billion (£2.3 billion), its maximum entitlement, from the International Monetary Fund to prop up the pound. Sterling collapsed on Tuesday, falling four cents to $1.63, and causing the Chancellor of the Exchequer, Denis Healey, to turn back from Heathrow minutes before he was due to take off for a Commonwealth financial conference in Hong Kong.

Markets have taken fright at left-wing demands at Labour's party conference in Blackpool, despite the fact that the Prime Minister, James Callaghan, made an uncompromising speech on Tuesday in which he declared that the option of cutting taxes and boosting Government spending "no longer exists" (→7/10).

South Africa eases sports segregation

Sept 23. In what opponents of apartheid see as a major breakthrough, and upholders of white supremacy have categorised as the "thin end of the wedge", South Africa has decided to permit multi-racial teams to represent the country in international sport. But the strict segregation of sporting clubs, the basis of any national sides, is to remain indefinitely.

Rhodesia will be a multi-racial state

Sept 24. In a 20-minute radio and TV broadcast tonight, Ian Smith stunned his white Rhodesian supporters by announcing a two-year plan for transition to black majority rule. It was, in effect, the end of 11 years of illegal independence.

Mr Smith's government is to be replaced at once by a Council of State, with half white and half black members and a white chairman. Mr Smith, who often said black rule would never come in his lifetime, has been under heavy pressure from the US Secretary of State, Dr Henry Kissinger, and the South Africans (→3/10). ▷

Chairman Mao has died

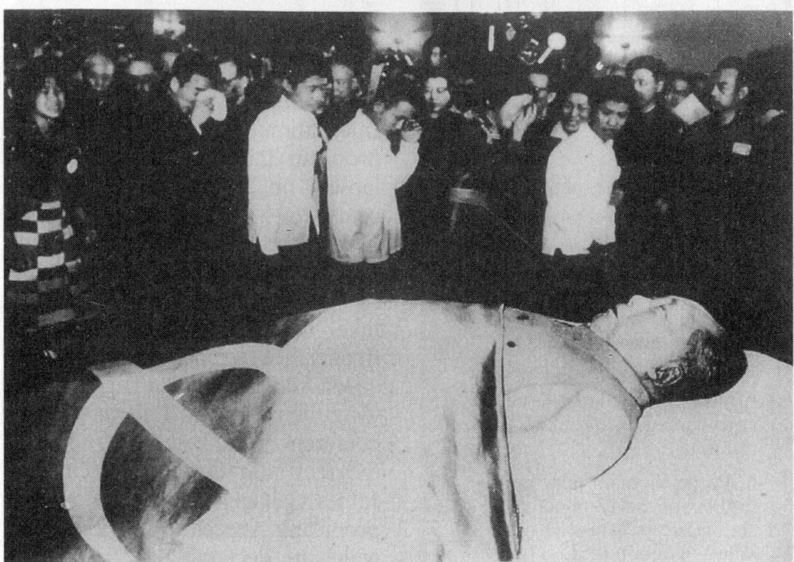

Weeping Chinese citizens pay tribute to their great leader.

Sept 9. Chairman Mao Tse-tung, the God-like leader of Communist China and its 800 million people, or a quarter of the world's population, died today at the age of 82.

It was Mao, who, facing defeat by the Nationalist forces of General Chiang Kai-shek, led his followers on the "Long March" to safety in the mountains of Yenan, from where they emerged to defeat the Nationalists and, in 1949, to turn China Communist.

The announcement of his death, accompanied by mournful martial music, said Mao had "struggled with his illness" and "fought to the last breath". It is believed he died after a series of strokes.

Within minutes several hundred mourners, some sobbing openly, gathered in the Square of Heavenly Peace. Wreaths were placed on the Revolutionary Martyrs Monument and several mourners prostrated themselves before it.

But there was little of the hysteria that might have been expected at the passing of such a giant. Orders were given long ago that when his time came life was to continue normally under the legacy of Mao's thoughts as embodied in his "Little Red Book".

The indications are, however, that already a power struggle has broken out among Mao's would-be successors, the "radical Maoists" led by his widow, Chiang Ching, and the "moderate Communists". The radicals, who preach the gospel of continuing class struggle, accuse the moderates of being "capitalist roaders" and "bourgeois reactionaries". The moderates argue that economic progress should not be blocked by over-zealous insistence on proletarian purity (→ 11/10).

Man who invented cat's eyes is dead

Sept 2. Percy Shaw had a bright idea one night on his way home from the pub. He died today, aged 86, but his brain-wave lives on: the reflector studs set in the middle of the road known as "cat's eyes". The idea was beautifully simple, transforming road safety at night, yet using no fuel and never requiring cleaning. It made a fortune for Mr Shaw, a labourer's son.

Britain is guilty of torture in Ulster

Sept 2. The Irish Republic has angered Britain by its determination to press for allegations of torture in Northern Ireland to be heard by the European Court of Human Rights.

A European Commission found today that "deep interrogation" techniques employed in Ulster constitute inhuman treatment and torture (→ 10).

1976

OCTOBER

Su	Mo	Tu	We	Th	Fr	Sa
					1	2
3	4	5	6	7	8	9
10	11	12	13	14	15	16
17	18	19	20	21	22	23
24	25	26	27	28	29	30
31						

3. Rhodesia: Black leader Bishop Abel Muzorewa returns to a tumultuous welcome after 15 months in exile (→ 31).

4. UK: The world's fastest diesel rail services begin as BR introduces its HS-125 train, capable of 125 mph.

6. Bangkok: The army seizes power after violent clashes between police and students.

7. UK: The Bank of England raises its minimum lending rate from 13 to 15 per cent (→ 8).

7. Washington: The US and Panama agree to renegotiate the 1903 Panama Canal Treaty (→ 6/9/77).

8. UK: Building societies put up mortgage interest rates to 12.25 per cent (→ 3/1/77).

10. Belfast: The women's peace movement founders are attacked by a mob (→ 28).

11. Peking: Mao's widow Chiang Ching and three others are arrested and charged with plotting a coup (→ 14).

13. Bolivia: 102 die when a Boeing 707 crashes onto a main street in Santa Cruz (→ 27/3/77).

14. Peking: Hua Kuo-feng is confirmed as Mao's successor.→

15. London: Two men are jailed for life for murdering three members of the Miami Showband in July 1975 (→ 28).

19. Beirut: "Black September" leader Ali Hassan Salameh is found dead (→ 16/3/77).

25. S. Africa: Transkei becomes the first black "homeland" or "Bantustan" to be given "independence" (→ 28/12).

28. Belfast: Provisional Sinn Fein vice-president Maire Drumm is shot dead (→ 27/11).

28. Geneva: A conference on Rhodesia opens (→ 31).

31. Mozambique: Rhodesian commandos launch a fierce raid across the border (→ 14/12).

DEATHS

14. British actress Dame Edith Evans (*8/2/1888).

22. British artist Edward John Burra (*29/3/1905).

Three years late, Britain has got its National Theatre

Oct 26. The National Theatre on the South Bank was officially opened by the Queen last night after years of delay. The huge concrete complex has been under construction since 1969 to the design of Denys Lasdun. It was expected to open in 1973 and is still unfinished. Its final cost is £16 million.

Lord Olivier made his only appearance in the building to welcome the Queen from the stage of the amphitheatre named after him. The Olivier Auditorium opened three weeks ago with Marlowe's "Tamburlaine the Great" and the conventional proscenium theatre, the Lyttleton, last March with "Hamlet". Albert Finney played the lead in both plays, directed by Peter Hall, the NT's director.

The Queen watched Goldoni's "Il Campiello" – badly received by the critics – and her theatre-loving sister, Princess Margaret, saw Tom Stoppard's "Jumpers". Later they visited the unfinished Cottesloe studio theatre.

Lasdun's National Theatre.

Hunt is the world motor racing champ

Oct 24. The last Formula One race of the season, the Japanese Grand Prix, began in a torrential downpour with Britain's James Hunt three points behind Niki Lauda of Austria in the championship table. Lauda, badly scarred after a horrific crash earlier in the year, retired after two laps in appalling conditions, leaving the 29-year-old Hunt dogged by tyre problems but driving furiously through the spray, to take third place for McLaren and the world championship by a single point (→ 2/10/77).

Mao's widow condemned as "dog dung"

Effigies of the Gang of Four are paraded on the streets of Peking.

Oct 23. Chairman Mao Tse-tung's widow, the former actress, Chiang Ching, and her three fellow radicals in the Chinese politburo have been jailed for plotting to take over the government. A report from the official news agency in Peking said the members of the "Gang of Four" were "filthy and contemptible like dog's dung". Orchestrated processions all over China today celebrated their downfall.

The way now seems open for Hua Kuo-feng to assume power as chairman of the party. Little is known about this functionary who became premier on Chou En-lai's death (→22/7/77).

Ford gets in a tangle over Eastern Europe

Oct 7. President Gerald Ford perpetrated a spectacular gaffe and endangered his election prospects by seeming to deny Soviet domination over Eastern Europe.

Last night, in a TV debate with his Democratic opponent, Jimmy Carter, the President said: "There is no Soviet domination of Eastern Europe and there never will be under a Ford administration."

Jimmy Carter retorted he would like to see Ford convince Polish-Americans and Czech-Americans that their countries do not live under Soviet domination (→2/11).

Gerald Ford asserts that the Soviet Union does not dominate Eastern Europe.

1976

NOVEMBER

Su	Mo	Tu	We	Th	Fr	Sa
	1	2	3	4	5	6
7	8	9	10	11	12	13
14	15	16	17	18	19	20
21	22	23	24	25	26	27
28	29	30				

2. Paris: A bomb goes off at the home of National Front leader Jean-Marie Le Pen.

4. UK: The Tories win Workington and Walsall North from Labour in by-elections (→31/3/77).

6. London: An exiled Soviet scientist claims hundreds died in an atomic waste explosion in the USSR in 1958 (→17).

10. London: The Government is defeated on the Dock Work Regulation Bill (→22).

12. Paris: Vietnam and the US begin their first formal talks since the Vietnam War (→15).

14. US: Jimmy Carter's home church in Plains, Georgia, ends its colour bar.

15. New York: The US vetoes Vietnam's application to join the UN.

17. China: The Chinese detonate their most powerful nuclear device to date (→26/11).

17. UK: 40,000 strike in protest at public sector cuts.

20. US: Dr Kissinger meets President-elect Carter for a foreign policy briefing (→20/1/77).

22. London: Peers reject the aircraft and shipbuilding nationalisation bill; Callaghan vows to reintroduce it (→6/12).

24. Turkey: 6,000 are reported dead after an earthquake near the Soviet border (→4/3/77).

26. Bucharest: The Warsaw Pact invites the West to join in an agreement barring first use of nuclear weapons (→7/4/78).

27. UK: The four millionth Mini rolls off the assembly line this week.

30. London: The Government publishes a bill to create separate assemblies in Scotland and Wales (→16/12).

DEATHS

18. US artist and photographer Man Ray (*27/8/1890).

19. British architect Sir Basil Urwin Spence (*13/8/1907).

23. French author and politician Andre Malraux (*3/11/1901).→

Malraux, literary man of action, dies

Andre Malraux: action man.

Nov 23. The death of Andre Malraux deprives France of a man of letters who was also a man of action. As an archaeologist working in Indochina, Malraux witnessed Chiang Kai-shek's revolution and the purge of Chinese Communists which followed. This was the inspiration for his novel "La Condition Humaine". The coming of the Nazis to power inspired "Days of Contempt" while taking part in the Spanish Civil War led to "Days of Hope", later a film. He spent the war in the Resistance.

After the war he became de Gaulle's Minister of Culture and ordered the cleaning of the public buildings of Paris.

Eight jailed for record bank raid

Nov 16. An eight-man gang was jailed today for robbing £8 million from deposit boxes at the Bank of America in London's Mayfair. It was the world's biggest bank haul, but an Old Bailey judge said he was determined they should not benefit from their record-breaking crime.

Lennie Minchington, known by the underworld as "King of the Keys" because of his safe-breaking, was given a 25-year sentence.

Judge King-Hamilton said that it would be a "sad day if robberies of this magnitude were the norm. If the money has been salted away, it can stay salted."

Jimmy Carter is elected US President

Nov 2. Jimmy Carter of Plains, Georgia, was today elected President of the United States. His Vice-President will be Walter Mondale.

Carter beat the incumbent Republican President, Gerald Ford, by 297 electoral college votes to 240. In the popular vote, Carter won by the narrow margin of 40.8 million votes to 39.1 million.

Carter's victory demonstrated the shrewdness of picking a southerner. The South and border States gave him more than half his electoral college votes.

President Ford was damaged in his re-election effort by his decision to pardon his predecessor, President Nixon, and also by his gaffe in denying, in one of the TV debates, Soviet domination of Eastern Europe.

Carter, for his part, was given a searching examination by the media, who found him a strange candidate, and seized on such "issues" as a candid interview in "Playboy" magazine. But Carter's election owed more to economic difficulties and to the harm done to the Republicans by Watergate and the Nixon pardon.

Rosalyn Carter: tears and pride.

Ulster's peace women lead London march

Mrs Williams (l.) and Miss Corrigan (r.) are joined by Joan Baez and others.

Nov 27. Mrs Jane Ewart-Biggs, widow of the British Ambassador who was murdered by the IRA in Dublin, was one of the leaders of a 30,000-strong peace march which wound through London today. With her, at the head of the column, were Betty Williams and Mairead Corrigan, the co-founders of the three-month-old Ulster Peace Movement.

It was one of the movement's most striking demonstrations so far, with an impressive range of supporters. The Archbishop of Canterbury and Cardinal Hume were among the speakers at a Trafalgar Square rally which was attended by contingents from Europe and America. Folksinger Joan Baez linked arms with fellow demonstrators as they marched from Hyde Park. As counter-demonstrators shouted "Troops Out", Miss Corrigan told the rally: "The world is here today. This is one of the most important rallies we have had" (→10/12).

1976

DECEMBER

Su	Mo	Tu	We	Th	Fr	Sa
			1	2	3	4
5	6	7	8	9	10	11
12	13	14	15	16	17	18
19	20	21	22	23	24	25
26	27	28	29	30	31	

1. London: The Criminal Law Bill is published; it aims to end jury trials for minor crimes such as petty theft.

3. Dublin: Dr Patrick Hillery is installed as President.

7. London: MPs approve the bill to nationalise the aircraft and shipbuilding industries.

7. New York: The UN Security Council approves a second term for UN chief Waldheim.

10. Stockholm: Nobel Prizes go to Burton Richter and Samuel Ting (US, Physics); William Lipscomb (US, Chemistry); Baruch Blumberg and Carleton Gajdusek (US, Medicine); Saul Bellow (US, Literature); Milton Friedman (US, Economics); and, announced later in Oslo, to Mairead Corrigan and Betty Williams (UK, Peace) (→10/10/77).

14. Geneva: The Rhodesian conference is adjourned.→

17. Qatar: OPEC states agree to a 15 per cent rise in oil prices, 10 per cent higher than the Saudis and Emirates want.

17. London: Ian Trethowan is appointed Director-General of the BBC.

21. Moscow: 45 Jews are arrested as "ringleaders" of a planned symposium on Jewish culture.

24. Tokyo: Takeo Fukuda is elected Prime Minister.

28. S. Africa: Winnie Mandela is released as the deaths from Christmas rioting rise to 26.

DEATH

4. British composer Edward Benjamin Britten, Baron Britten (*22/11/1913).→

HITS OF 1976

Save your kisses for me.

Don't go breaking my heart.

Dancing Queen.

QUOTE OF THE YEAR

"A lie can be half-way around the world before the truth has got its boots on."

James Callaghan, attacking the media, November 1, 1976.

Devolution plan for Scotland and Wales

Dec 16. The Government's controversial legislation to set up mini-parliaments for Scotland and Wales was approved in principle by MPs tonight, but this is no guarantee that the constitutional changes will ever be enacted. A long parliamentary fight over the devolution proposals is already scheduled.

There are divisions within parties and feelings are running high. Opponents of reform say that disintegration of the United Kingdom looms. Supporters say that backing for Scottish and Welsh nationalists demanding full independence will grow unless limited home rule is conceded.

With its Commons majority now wafer-thin, the Government fears that its survival depends on satisfying the devolutionists. The Queen is mildly alarmed (→3/2/77).

Britten, the first musical peer, dies

Britten takes the sun at Aldeburgh.

Dec 5. Benjamin Britten, who died at Aldeburgh, Suffolk, yesterday aged 65, last June become the first musician to be made a life peer. His large output included several important pieces written for children. "The Young Person's Guide to the Orchestra", "Let's Make an Opera" and the opera "Noye's Fludde" His vocal works were mostly composed for his life-long companion Peter Pears.

Rhodesian terror gang kill 27 Africans

Wives and families stare horrified at the carnage after the massacre.

Dec 20. A guerrilla gang, crossing into Rhodesia from Mozambique, moved in on a British-owned tea estate and lined up the African workers and their families. The men were taken into the bush and gunned down with Russian AK automatic rifles: 27 died and two escaped by throwing themselves into a river in pitch darkness. The women and children were later taken to a guerrilla camp in Mozambique. The guerrillas, who have been seeking to drive the white farmers from the Eastern Highlands, had earlier told the Africans to stop working, but they had refused. In the past four years 716 civilians have been killed by guerrillas, 61 of them white (→2/1/77).

Chat show host out in Sex Pistols TV row

Dec 3. Thames TV presenter Bill Grundy was suspended tonight after rock music's notorious Sex Pistols ran riot on ITV's "Today" show.

The band, who have won a reputation for physical and verbal excess, were scheduled to talk about punk rock, of which they are the leading exponents. When one of the band's members used an obscenity, Grundy foolishly told him to repeat it. Then the interview turned into a tirade by what Grundy termed "a foul-mouthed set of yobs". Pistols manager Malcolm McLaren agreed that the band were yobs "and proud of it" (→6/1/77).

The Sex Pistols: the group adults love to hate enjoy a quiet can of lager.

Arts: fine art taken in by fraud squad

"We consider them a work of art," said the Tate Gallery director, **Sir Norman Reid**, of the 120 fire bricks laid in an oblong and entitled "Low Sculpture", by an American "artist" from whom the gallery purchased them. A few days later a disgruntled visitor poured blue dye over the bricks and they were withdrawn from view.

It has been a bad year for the credibility of the fine arts. A sudden glut of landscapes, apparently by **Samuel Palmer**, the 19th century water-colourist, have been selling in the sale-rooms for as much as £15,000 apiece. Then a picture restorer, **Tom Keating**, wrote to "The Times" to claim that he had been faking Samuel Palmers for 25 years. He said he was surprised that his "crude daubs" had been accepted as authentic. He later claimed that dealers paid him "pitifully small" fees for pictures in the styles of many famous artists and sold them for high prices after signatures had been added.

BBC2 began a serial epic based on **Robert Graves's** "I, Claudius" and "Claudius the God", an imaginative account of the early Roman empire narrated by the emperor, played with nervous, shambling charisma by **Derek Jacobi**. "The Naked Civil Servant", a Thames TV play by **Philip Mackie** adapted from the autobiography of **Quentin Crisp**, won the Prix Italia. It was directed by **Jack Gold** with **John Hurt** as the embattled homosexual.

Sylvester Stallone wrote, and stars in, boxing box-office hit "Rocky".

Viewers also saw the last of "Dixon of Dock Green", in which **Jack Warner**, now 80, has been playing PC (later Sgt) Dixon, created by **Ted** (later **Lord) Willis**, for 21 years. They are now clamouring for more of a very different character, Basil Fawlty, created last year by **John Cleese**, as the manic manager of a small hotel, "Fawlty Towers".

Miss Marple also made her exit as a crime-solver in **Agatha Christie's** posthumous "Sleeping Murder". And **Jeffrey Archer**, an MP who resigned because of bankruptcy, made his debut as an author with "Not a Penny More, Not a Penny Less", about a swindle.

Sergeant Dixon (played by Jack Warner) has said his last "Goodnight all" after 21 years under the blue lamp, fighting the villains of Dock Green.

1977

JANUARY

Su	Mo	Tu	We	Th	Fr	Sa
						1
2	3	4	5	6	7	8
9	10	11	12	13	14	15
16	17	18	19	20	21	22
23	24	25	26	27	28	29
30	31					

2. Salisbury: Ian Smith rejects the peace proposals of British envoy Ivor Richard (→ 31).

3. Washington: The IMF approves a £2,300 million loan to Britain to halt the fall in the value of sterling (→ 14/3).

5. London: Roy Jenkins resigns as an MP.

6. London: EMI sacks the Sex Pistols for their outrageous behaviour.

8. Moscow: Several people are killed when a bomb explodes on the Moscow underground.

9. Paris: Abu Daoud, said to be behind the 1972 Munich Olympics massacre, is arrested.→

10. UK: Clive Sinclair introduces his £175 two-inch screen TV.

14. UK: Police in Macclesfield shoot dead an escaped prisoner after he kills four people in Chesterfield.

17. Sydney: 80 die in a train crash.

19. Cairo: Sadat imposes a curfew after two days of rioting at food price rises that have left 44 dead (→ 12/3).

20. Washington: Carter is inaugurated as President (→ 24/2).

23. UK: Anti-hunting saboteurs dig up the grave of legendary Lake District huntsman John Peel.

26. London: A report on industrial democracy proposes worker-directors on all company boards.

29. London: Seven IRA bombs go off in the capital's West End (→ 4/2).

31. Rhodesia: It is revealed that 400 mission children have been kidnapped for guerrilla training by nationalists (→ 7/2).

DEATHS

14. British statesman Robert Anthony Eden, first Earl of Avon, Prime Minister 1955-57 (*12/6/1897).→

14. British actor Peter Finch (*28/9/1916).

14. US author Anais Nin (*21/2/1907).

Roy Jenkins to take over as head of EEC

Jan 3. Roy Jenkins, Home Secretary and former Labour deputy leader, has resigned from the cabinet and from parliament to become the first British president of the EEC Commission in Brussels.

Mr Jenkins, a passionate European, is disillusioned over the present state of domestic politics and uneasy about his own party's reservations over Common Market membership.

His friends say that he hopes to return to Westminster after a few years to spearhead efforts to form a "third force" alliance of politicians occupying the middle ground (→ 5).

Jenkins: new EEC president.

Eden, dogged by Suez debacle, is dead

Lord Avon and his dog Nipper.

Jan 14. The Earl of Avon (formerly Sir Anthony Eden) whose premiership ended in physical collapse and the catastrophic Suez miscalculation, died today aged 79. The one-time debonair and heroic worker for world peace had spent the last 20 years in seclusion, suffering from recurring illnesses.

Tonight the Queen called him "a man of courage and integrity". It is known that he had prepared a defence of his handling of the Suez affair for publication after his death. It has been his personal tragedy that the brave and successful chapters of his earlier career as Churchill's Foreign Secretary were largely forgotten.

Let's do it says Gary Gilmore and it's done

Jan 17. Murderer Gary Gilmore today became the first convict to be executed in the United States for ten years. "Let's do it," were his final words before walking out in front of a firing squad at the Utah State Prison warehouse, so ending a lengthy campaign across America against return of the death penalty.

Gilmore, found guilty of murdering two students at the Brigham Young University last year, had wanted to be executed. But as he waited for the sentence to be carried out his case became a focus of protest. An earlier stay of execution was lifted by the US Court of Appeals and 18 minutes after an icy sunrise, four shots were fired into a target pinned over his heart.

Gilmore at the courthouse.

Czech liberals draw up rights charter

Jan 9. In a striking demonstration of opposition to the Communist regime imposed by the Russians after the 1968 Prague Spring, 240 Czech scholars, writers and former politicians yesterday signed a document calling for civil rights for the people. The document, known as Charter 77, says that though the Czechoslovak government signed the Helsinki accords guaranteeing democratic freedoms, these are still denied to the people. Today, several of the most prominent dissidents were arrested (→ 13/3).

French set free a PLO terrorist leader

Jan 12. Israel today asked the European Community to denounce France for releasing an arrested Palestinian leader. Abu Daoud, a founder of Black September, is accused of organising the Munich Olympics terror attack in which 11 Israelis were killed. He was arrested three days ago in Paris.

A hastily convened court found no grounds for holding him, pending West German extradition proceedings. He was expelled to Algiers. Israel withdrew its ambassador; Yigal Allon, the Foreign Minister, described the release as "a shameful capitulation".

Acropolis attacked by aerial pollution

Jan 10. The Acropolis, home of the crowning glories of the Greek capital, Athens, and a place of pilgrimage both for tourists and scholars from all over the world, is facing a serious threat to its fabric from pollution. A rescue fund, sponsored by UNESCO, has been launched.

The Acropolis is 2,400 years old, the site of the Parthenon and a number of other temples to the goddess Athene. In this time it has survived all the elements and several invasions. But 20th century pollution, notably from the exhausts of the city's cars, may succeed where wind, weather and barbarian have failed.

1977

FEBRUARY

Su	Mo	Tu	We	Th	Fr	Sa
		1	2	3	4	5
6	7	8	9	10	11	12
13	14	15	16	17	18	19
20	21	22	23	24	25	26
27	28					

3. London: The Government says it will hold referenda in Scotland and Wales on devolution (→4/5).

4. Liverpool: Police discover an IRA bomb factory (→8).

6. UK: Today is the Silver Jubilee of the Queen's accession (→7/6).

7. London: Amnesty International says that Idi Amin has executed thousands since he came to power.→

8. Strasbourg: Britain defends itself against claims it tortured IRA suspects in Ulster (→10).

10. London: The IRA terrorists involved in the Balcombe Street siege are jailed for life for six murders (→11/3).

13. London: Lady Falkender admits she put forward names for Wilson's resignation Honours List.

13. UK: Foreign Secretary Tony Crosland suffers a massive stroke.→

17. London: The Government announces it is to spend £6 million on the development of solar power.

21. London: 38-year-old Dr David Owen becomes the youngest Foreign Secretary since Anthony Eden (→14/4).

24. Washington: Carter cuts aid to Argentina, Uruguay and Ethiopia because of their poor human rights records (→6/3).

24. London: The Tories win the Westminster by-election (→24/3).

25. Kampala: Amin orders all US citizens in the country to meet him and forbids them to leave the country (→1/3).

26. UK: British Leyland chiefs say they will shut down plants to put an end to strikes (→1/3).

27. Paris: Rebel Catholics occupy a church in protest at the Vatican's ban on the Latin Mass.

DEATH

19. British author and politician Charles Anthony Raven Crosland (*29/8/1918).→

Ugandan Archbishop dies in terror wave

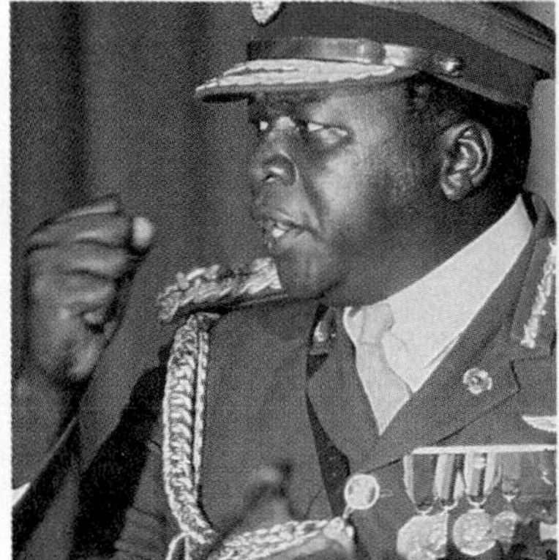

Idi Amin: the joke's long over.

Feb 18. Uganda's six-year reign of terror under Idi Amin entered a new dimension of horror this week with the killing of the Archbishop of Uganda, the Most Reverend Janani Luwum, who was last seen two days ago being dragged away from a rally in Kampala, along with two former cabinet ministers, by troops chanting "Kill them! Kill them!". Amin today issued a statement saying the three men died in a Land Rover crash outside the capital. Nobody believes him.

In London, the Archbishop of Canterbury, Dr Donald Coggan, said Archbishop Luwum was a man of great courage and gentleness. He had criticised the "summary killing of great numbers of civilians" in Uganda, but "such criticism was always peaceable and open".

The latest round of killings by Amin appears to have been set off by protests from a group of non-commissioned army officers, who objected to all positions of power being held by men from Amin's Kakwa tribe. Within days, bullet-riddled bodies were seen floating down the Malaba River on the Uganda-Kenya border. Reports reaching Nairobi say about 130 people have died (→25).

Black guerrillas kill white missionaries

Feb 7. In what Church leaders described as the "most insane and brutal" atrocities of Rhodesia's four-year war, an African guerrilla gang has massacred seven white missionaries (three Jesuits and four Dominican nuns) at St. Paul's Roman Catholic Mission, near Mrewa, 37 miles east of Salisbury. The attack took place yesterday evening, some hours after the Sunday services had finished (→14/4).

Hi-tech arts centre hits classical Paris

Feb 2. Traditional Paris architecture is nowhere more elegant than in the 18th century Quartier du Marais, where the new Pompidou Centre for the arts has arrived like a bombshell – a glass-walled laboratory, covered in brightly coloured tubing with exterior escalators climbing up one side of it. Joint architects of this "high tech" design are Englishman Richard Rogers and Italian Renzo Piano.

Labour intellectual Tony Crosland dies

Crosland: unfulfilled possibilities.

Feb 19. Tony Crosland, the Foreign Secretary, died today. He was 58 and had been in a coma since suffering a massive stroke a week ago.

The Labour Party is thus robbed of one of its most powerful intellects and attractive apostles of moderation. He published a seminal book, "The Future of Socialism", which tried to redefine Socialist beliefs in modern terms. To party traditionalists he seemed a dangerous revisionist while the left saw him as a rightist.

Crosland had hoped to swop jobs with Denis Healey, the Chancellor of the Exchequer, before long. Now Mr Callaghan faces an emergency cabinet reshuffle (→21).

The Space Shuttle, destined to be America's spacecraft of the 1980s, makes its maiden flight on top of a Boeing 747. Soon the shuttle will begin gliding tests and in 1979 will begin a series of orbital flights.

1977

MARCH

Su	Mo	Tu	We	Th	Fr	Sa
		1	2	3	4	5
6	7	8	9	10	11	12
13	14	15	16	17	18	19
20	21	22	23	24	25	26
27	28	29	30	31		

1. London: Callaghan warns British Leyland to stop its strikes or it will get no more Government money.

1. Kampala: Amin tells Americans they are free to leave the country (→15/5).

4. Rumania: Hundreds are feared dead in a massive earthquake (→25/4).

6. Washington: Israeli premier Yitzhak Rabin arrives for Middle East peace talks with Carter (→25/4).

7. Pakistan: Bhutto wins parliamentary elections (→23).

11. Belfast: 26 members of the outlawed Ulster Volunteer Force are jailed (→2/4).

12. Cairo: Sadat says he will not allow a single inch of Arab land to remain under Israeli occupation (→24/7).

13. Prague: "Charter 77" leader Jan Potocka dies after police interrogation.

14. London: The Government says prices in Britain have risen 69.5 per cent since 1974 (→29).

16. Beirut: Kamal Jumblatt, leader of the Druze Moslems in the civil war, is assassinated (→6/11/77).

18. Zaire: Troops are flown to Shaba province in a bid to halt the advance of forces invading from Angola (→4/4).

23. Pakistan: Riots erupt in Lahore amid accusations that Bhutto rigged the general election result (→21/4).

25. Paris: Gaullist leader Jacques Chirac is elected Mayor of Paris.

28. US: "Rocky" wins an Oscar as best film; the late Peter Finch is best actor, Faye Dunaway best actress.

29. London: The budget cuts income tax from 35p to 33p in the pound, dependent on union pay claim restraint (→4/4).

29. Tenerife: A Dutch official admits the KLM 747 had not been cleared for take-off.

31. UK: The Tories win the by-election for Roy Jenkins' old seat of Stechford with a 17.4 per cent swing (→5/5).

574 die in Jumbo crash

The two Jumbos burn on the runway, as dazed survivors rest yards away.

March 27. Two Jumbo jets collided on the ground in the Canary Islands tonight, killing 574, in the worst tragedy in aviation history. The aircraft, belonging to KLM and Pan Am, had both been diverted to Tenerife from Las Palmas because of a bomb explosion there, when the American jet turned onto the runway just as the other aircraft was taking off.

Tonight more than 70 survivors, many with horrific burns, were being treated in hospital. All 248 passengers on the KLM jet died, while survivors on the Pan Am jumbo described how passengers on the upper deck fell on top of them in flames. Jim Naik, from California, said: "I heard an explosion. Then the ceiling caved in. A piece of the ceiling fell on my wife, and as I was trying to unfasten her seat belt there was another explosion.

"People just started raining down from the lounge above on top of me. It was just like a movie. It was the flames that did it."

Eye-witnesses described the scenes as "horrifying" as the two entangled jets burst apart in flames. Radio and television stations on the island broadcast urgent appeals for all doctors and medical personnel to rush to hospitals because of an "utmost emergency". It is not clear yet who was responsible for the accident (→29).

Mrs Gandhi routed in Indian elections

March 22. The Indian general election is turning into a disaster for the Prime Minister, Mrs Indira Gandhi, who has crashed to defeat in her own constituency of Rae Bareli while her son, Sanjay, has been heavily beaten in the neighbouring seat of Amethi. The latest returns indicate that Mrs Gandhi's Congress party is going to be ousted from office by Morarji Desai's Janata party. The defeat of Mrs Gandhi and her unpopular son is looked upon as a vote against the much-hated state of emergency 21 months ago (→3/1/78).

BL gives ultimatum to striking workers

March 15. British Leyland today told their 3,000 striking toolmakers that if they did not return to work on Monday they would be sacked. Some 40,000 BL workers have been laid off by the dispute. Today's ultimatum from the state car company has the full backing of the Labour government. The Prime Minister, James Callaghan, warned the workers that there would be no more state money unless industrial discipline was restored. He told them that foreign firms were "simply waiting to pour cars into this country" (→15/4).

Liberals prop up Labour government

March 24. The tiny Liberal Party tonight saved the tottering Labour government's skin by helping to vote down a Tory "no confidence" motion which seemed likely to force an immediate general election.

To keep office Mr Callaghan has been forced into a Lib-Lab pact which now gives the Liberals a say in Government policy.

Her hopes for an election foiled, Mrs Thatcher denounced the Prime Minister and Mr Steel, the Liberal leader, as "timid men fearful of the fate they know awaits them". David Penhaligon, Cornish Liberal MP, put it differently. "Turkeys don't volunteer for Christmas", he said (→28/9).

Why is Ayckbourn a National farce?

Ayckbourn – the National farceur.

March 17. One of the plays commissioned for the opening of the National Theatre, "Bedroom Farce" by Alan Ayckbourn, opened last night with great success. Set in three bedrooms side-by-side, on the night of a disastrous party, it exploits the gaucheness, embarrassments and sexual hang-ups of three middle-class couples. It is the first Ayckbourn play to be performed at the National, after a series of hits in the West End.

1977

APRIL

Su	Mo	Tu	We	Th	Fr	Sa
					1	2
3	4	5	6	7	8	9
10	11	12	13	14	15	16
17	18	19	20	21	22	23
24	25	26	27	28	29	30

2. London: Tory Ulster spokesman Airey Neave says Provisional Sinn Fein should be banned (→1/5).

3. Washington: Sadat arrives for talks with Carter on peace in the Middle East (→25).

4. London: The Government introduces a bill giving the Prices Commission power to freeze prices (→15).

4. Kinshasa: Zaire breaks off relations with Cuba, accusing Castro of involvement in the Angolan invasion of Shaba.

8. Tel Aviv: Premier Rabin says he will not stand for re-election, following revelations of illegal US deposits (→22).

10. London: Yemeni officials are shot dead by an Arab gunman (→4/1/78).

14. Cape Town: Foreign Secretary David Owen has talks with Ian Smith during a tour of southern Africa (→18).

15. UK: Miners demand an end to the Social Contract as industrial unrest grows in many sectors (→2/7).

15. Brazil: A row breaks out after Great Train robber Ronald Biggs attends a drinks party on a Royal Navy ship.

18. London: Dr Owen returns from his African trip; he is cautious about the prospects for a Rhodesian settlement.

22. Tel Aviv: Rabin resigns after his wife is fined for her illegal US bank accounts; Shimon Peres takes over. (→18/5).

23. London: National Front marchers clash with anti-Nazis (→13/8).

25. Washington: King Hussein arrives for talks on a Middle East peace settlement (→26/7).

28. Stuttgart: Terrorists Andreas Baader, Gudrun Ensslin and Jan-Carl Raspe are jailed for life plus 15 years (→12/11).

29. UK: British Aerospace is formed to run Britain's nationalised aviation industry.

DEATH

11. French poet Jacques Prevert (*4/2/1900).

Vast oil slick from North Sea blowout

Rescue equipment and fire-fighting tugs attempt to quell the Ekofisk fire.

April 30. An oil slick of more than 1,000 square miles is threatening the Scottish east coast after a North Sea drilling platform blew out of control. Eight days after disaster struck the Bravo rig in Norway's Ekofisk Field, experts were able to place a seal in position, but by then seven million gallons of crude oil had spewed on to the waves. Four earlier attempts, using hydraulically-operated rams failed as insufficient pressure was applied.

Paul "Red" Adair, renowned in America for high-risk fire-fighting operations, was then called in and today he declared the vast flow of crude oil had been tamed. However, fish stocks are still bound to be badly damaged by the slick, which the Norwegian government regards as the worst pollution catastrophe since oil prospecting began in the North Sea.

Although ecologists are preparing for the Scottish coastline to be badly hit, officials say they expect most marine life to be saved by a change in wind direction. Before the oil reaches the coast it is likely to be broken up by the waves.

More than 100 platform workers were rescued after taking to their lifeboats when oil gushed 150 feet into the air as a drilling valve was being changed.

Pakistan put under state of martial law

April 21. Martial law was imposed tonight on the chief Pakistani cities of Karachi, Hyderabad and Lahore. It appears that Mr Bhutto, the beleaguered Prime Minister, feared a total breakdown in law and order. There are indications that the army might extend its control to the rest of the country.

The announcement came on the eve of a general strike called by the opposition Pakistan National Alliance, which has been campaigning for the resignation of Mr Bhutto and for a fresh general election under the supervision of the army and the judiciary (→5/7).

Mr Bhutto – under the gun.

Red Rum is first horse to pull off the Grand National hat trick

April 2. With the confident jumping and the untroubled stamina that has made him a favourite of racegoers, Red Rum galloped away to his third Grand National victory today, the first horse to win this most challenging of steeplechases more than twice.

For five consecutive years the 12-year-old bay gelding, trained by Ginger McCain on Southport sands, has sailed over the fearsome Aintree fences; he won in 1973 and 1974, came second in 1975 and 1976, and this year (in a National that had already made history by allowing the first woman jockey to take her place at the start) he carried Tommy Stack home 25 lengths clear of the field (→31/3/78).

Grand National star Red Rum returns to the Aintree winner's enclosure.

1977

MAY

Su	Mo	Tu	We	Th	Fr	Sa
1	2	3	4	5	6	7
8	9	10	11	12	13	14
15	16	17	18	19	20	21
22	23	24	25	26	27	28
29	30	31				

1. Northern Ireland: Army reinforcements arrive in anticipation of a loyalist general strike from tomorrow (→3).

3. Northern Ireland: Paisleyite thugs are said to be intimidating non-strikers after a weak response to the strike call (→16).

4. London: The Queen's Jubilee Speech indirectly criticises Scottish and Welsh nationalism (→7/6).

5. UK: The Tories make gains in local elections, winning control of the Greater London Council (→8/7).

7. London: A seven-nation economic summit opens.→

8. Amsterdam: The trial begins of art dealer Peter Menten, accused of murdering Polish Jews in 1941 (→14/12).

9. US: Patty Hearst is freed on five years probation (→2/11).

11. London: Ex-police pornography squad chief Wallace Virgo is found guilty of taking bribes from Soho vice kings.

15. UK: Liverpool win the League Championship for a tenth time (→21).

16. Northern Ireland: The IRA says it has kidnapped, interrogated and killed an officer it claims was in the SAS.

19. Nairobi: Kenyatta bans big game hunting in an effort to conserve wildlife (→22/8/78).

21. Wembley: Manchester United beat Liverpool 2-1 in the FA Cup Final.→

23. Holland: South Moluccan terrorists take over a primary school and hijack a train with 161 passengers (→29).

24. Moscow: President Podgorny is dropped from the Politburo (→16/6).

27. Ottawa: Pierre and Margaret Trudeau announce their formal separation.

29. Holland: Moluccan terrorists have freed many train hostages, but still hold 56 (→11/6).

DEATH

10. US actress Joan Crawford, born Lucille le Sueur (*23/3/1908).

Packer's piracy splits the world of cricket

May 13. A revolutionary deal worked out in secret during the winter, has seen an Australian TV boss and publisher, Kerry Packer, sign up 35 of the world's best cricketers to play in a series of internationals in Australia this autumn.

The proposals have shaken the administration of the game at Lord's as well as in Australia, New Zealand, Pakistan and the West Indies. They are seen as a direct threat to official Test cricket and the first-class game.

Eighteen players from Australia and 17 from other countries have signed, with Ian Chappell and Tony Greig contracted to lead the teams (→26/7).

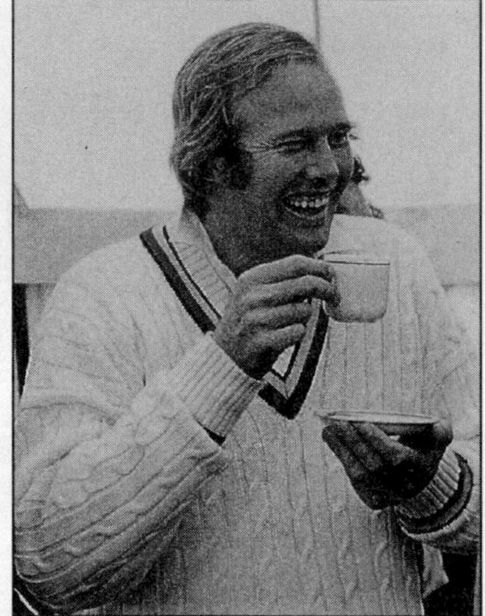

England's rebel leader Tony Greig.

La Passionara comes home to Spain

Ibarruri: Spain's exiled icon.

May 13. Dolores Ibarruri, the fervent Communist who became renowned as "La Passionara" during the Spanish Civil War, has been allowed to return to her homeland after 38 years in exile, most of them spent in Moscow. It was her fiery oratory that inspired the Republicans to fight on against Franco's conquering army. "It is better to die on your feet," she shouted, "than live on your knees." She must, however, carry a measure of responsibility for the anarchy and violence which led to the civil war. At 81, she is returning to politics.

Nigel Short qualifies for chess final at 11

May 29 Nigel Short, England's chess prodigy, set a new record for his sport today when at just eleven years old he qualified as the youngest ever competitor in a national chess championship.

Short, from Atherton, near Manchester, learned to play at the age of six and since then has made a meteoric rise through the chess world, beating many senior players. His greatest triumph to date was defeating Viktor Korchnoi, one of the world's top players, during a simultaneous exhibition by the Russian grandmaster.

Prior to today, the youngest national qualifier was the 12-year-old Cuban Capablanca, later a major chess star. Now Nigel Short seems set to follow suit.

Nigel Short: pre-teen prodigy.

Ex-terrorist Begin takes over in Israel

May 18. Menachem Begin, the right-wing former leader of the Jewish terror group, Irgun Zvai Leumi, which fought against the British, today became Prime Minister of Israel. His Likud Party in opposition for 29 years finally succeeded in defeating the ruling Labour Party. Its beaten leader, Shimon Peres, declared: "It is a tough blow."

Likud won more seats in the election than any other party. It adopted a hawkish policy towards the Arabs and Palestinians which won votes from the new majority of immigrants from North Africa and the Middle East (→26/7).

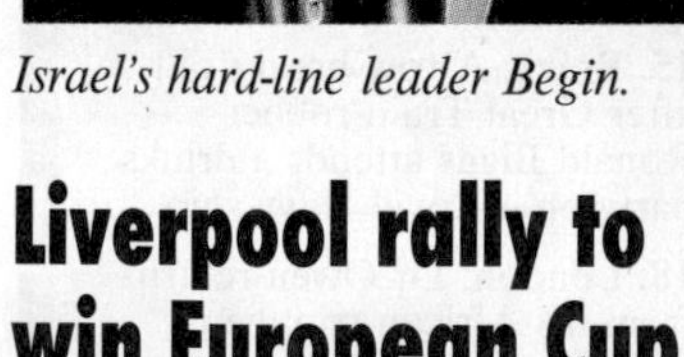

Israel's hard-line leader Begin.

Liverpool rally to win European Cup

May 25. Liverpool have crowned 13 consecutive seasons of European competition by joining Manchester United on the roll of European champions. At the Olympic Stadium in Rome, in a performance which fully lived up to the tournament's reputation, they beat the German champions, Borussia Moenchengladbach 3-1.

After controlling the game from mid-field throughout the first half, they went ahead through Terry McDermott, but lost the initiative soon after half-time, when Simonsen equalised for Borussia.

Then a fine headed goal by Tommy Smith, playing his last game for the club, and a penalty by Phil Neal after Kevin Keegan had been fouled, sealed the game for Bob Paisley's team.

Pledges on economy at London summit

President Carter waves as his host Jim Callaghan beams for the camera.

May 8. The free world's major industrial nations tonight pledged joint action to prevent global economic breakdown and chaos. After a twoday meeting at 10 Downing Street, the leaders of Britain, the United States, France, West Germany, Italy, Japan and Canada declared: "Our most urgent task is to create more jobs while continuing to reduce inflation." They accepted stated economic growth targets and agreed to take corrective measures if necessary to achieve them.

As the conference host and chairman, Mr Callaghan, said: "It is intolerable that there should be 15 million unemployed in our seven countries." For the US, President Carter warned his opposite numbers: "Now we must act as well as talk."

Critics claim whiff of nepotism at No. 10

May 13. Peter Jay, the journalist son-in-law of the Prime Minister, was today named as Britain's next ambassador to Washington. Charges of nepotism were immediately hurled at Mr Callaghan and indignantly rejected by his aides. Mr Jay, aged 40, worked as a civil servant in the Treasury before joining "The Times" and then ITV's "Weekend World". Now he has Britain's top diplomatic job.

All the best of Saturday morning movies comes back in "Star Wars".

1977

JUNE

Su	Mo	Tu	We	Th	Fr	Sa
			1	2	3	4
5	6	7	8	9	10	11
12	13	14	15	16	17	18
19	20	21	22	23	24	25
26	27	28	29	30		

1. UK: Lester Piggott has his eighth Derby win, on The Minstrel.

4. UK: Artist Francis Bacon turns down the award of a Companionship of Honour.

4. London: Damage estimated at £15,000 is caused when fans dig up the Wembley pitch after Scotland beat England 2-1.

5. Seychelles: President James Mancham is deposed in a coup while he is in London for the Commonwealth Conference.→

6. UK: Beacons are lit across the nation to begin the Queen's Silver Jubilee festivities.→

8. London: Commonwealth leaders issue a warning to southern African whites to change or face more bloodshed (→15).

10. US: Martin Luther King's killer James Earl Ray breaks out of jail in Tennessee (→13).

13. Washington: Carter gives the go-ahead to Laker's proposed "Skytrain" (→26/9).

13. US: James Earl Ray is recaptured.

15. London: Commonwealth leaders issue a communique attacking Idi Amin's human rights violations.

16. Moscow: Brezhnev takes over as President following the sacking of Podgorny.

17. Ireland: Jack Lynch's Fianna Fail sweeps to victory in the general election (→23).

20. London: Home Secretary Merlyn Rees pleads to the unions for calm as picket line violence grows at Grunwick.→

23. Dublin: Cosgrave resigns as premier.

26. East Africa: Djibouti, France's last African colony, becomes independent.

30. London: Trafalgar House takes over Beaverbrook Newspapers.

DEATHS

3. Italian film director Roberto Rossellini (*8/5/1906).

16. German-born US scientist Wernher von Braun (*23/3/1912).→

Spain's first polling day for 41 years

June 15. Spain went to the polls today in the country's first democratic election for 41 years. With 70 per cent of the votes counted, the Prime Minister, Adolfo Suarez, would now appear to have won a working majority with his Democratic Centre coalition sure of 170 seats in the 350 seat lower house.

The poll was orderly and good humoured, far removed from the anarchy and bloodshed which marked the elections leading up to the civil war. Elections were banned by General Franco but restored by King Juan Carlos, and tonight his faith in the democratic process seems to be justified (→28/7).

Suarez: victor for democracy.

Seychelles leader is ousted by left wing

June 6. James Mancham, 37-year-old President of the Indian Ocean Seychelles Islands, who is in London for the Commonwealth Conference, learned today he had been overthrown. The islands became independent only a year ago, when Mr Mancham promised to make his 60,000 people prosperous by creating a playground for the world's tourists. The coup leader who has replaced him, Marxist Albert Rene, aged 41, says he will free the islanders of "capitalists and foreign countries". Five British policemen on secondment there are being deported. ▷

Britons celebrate the Queen's Jubilee

Her Majesty prays at St. Paul's.

The Queen and the Lord Mayor of London take a Jubilee "walkabout".

June 7. A week of festivities was sparked off by the Queen last night when she lit a giant bonfire in Windsor Great Park. It marked the start of celebrations to mark her 25 years on the throne. As the flames brightened the darkness in the park, over 100 other bonfires were lit by Lords Lieutenant, Mayors and Bishops from Land's End to Saxavord in the Shetlands. Many were on the same sites as those used in 1588, when Queen Elizabeth I ordered the lighting of bonfires to warn of the Spanish Armada.

The climax of the Silver Jubilee celebrations came today when the Queen and Prince Philip rode in a carriage procession to St. Paul's Cathedral for a service of Thanksgiving. This was followed by a banquet at the Guildhall with the sun shining through the stained glass windows on to gold plate.

Afterwards the Queen and Prince Philip went on a City walkabout. A small boy who approached the Queen with an autograph book was deterred by an equerry who told him: "The Queen only signs Acts of Parliament." He settled for a conversation with Prince Philip instead.

Picket violence at the Grunwick strike

June 20. Seventeen people were arrested today in the worst clashes between pickets and police at the Grunwick film-processing laboratories. The unions, supported by hundreds of students, have been demonstrating daily against the firm's refusal to have trade unions. Milk bottles were thrown today at the bus taking the workers in.

Von Braun, rocket pioneer, is dead

June 16. Wernher von Braun, the German-born leader of the team that built the American Saturn 5 moon rocket, died today in Virginia. He was 65. During the Second World War he led the group that developed the V-2 rocket used to bombard London; he went to work in the US after the war.

Dutch Marines storm besieged train

June 11. Dutch Marines today stormed the train at Assen in which South Moluccan terrorists have been holding 55 hostages for a record 20 days. Six of the terrorists were killed and two of the hostages lost their lives in the hail of bullets which riddled the train in the dawn attack. In the school siege at Bovensmilde 15 miles away, four terrorists surrendered and their four hostages were freed (→13/3/78).

A South Moluccan terrorist waves his national flag alongside the train.

1977

JULY

Su	Mo	Tu	We	Th	Fr	Sa
					1	2
3	4	5	6	7	8	9
10	11	12	13	14	15	16
17	18	19	20	21	22	23
24	25	26	27	28	29	30
31						

2. UK: The miners demand £135 for a four-day week, despite appeals from Joe Gormley for pay restraint.→

6. Washington: Carter calls on Arab nations to establish links with Israel.

8. UK: The Tories win Saffron Walden in a by-election.

10. France: 31 die in torrential rain in the south-west.

11. Washington: Carter gives Martin Luther King's widow a Medal of Freedom awarded to him posthumously.

11. London: The newspaper "Gay News" is found guilty of blasphemy and fined £1,000.

12. UK: The average house price in London and the south-east is £16,731.

13. New York: Looting and vandalism is rife as the city is blacked out by a massive power failure.

16. Mogadishu: The Somali government expels all Soviet advisers (→23/11).

18. Salisbury: Smith calls a general election (→6/8).

19. UK: The TUC refuses to set any levels for wage claims.

20. London: A report recommends splitting the Post Office into separate postal and telecommunications companies.

21. Sri Lanka: Mrs Bandaranaike loses a general election to Julius Jayawardene.

22. Peking: The "Gang of Four" is expelled from the Communist Party and Teng Hsiao-ping is rehabilitated (→29/10/78).

24. Cairo: Sadat orders Egyptian troops to observe an immediate cease-fire in border clashes with Libya (→26/12).

28. Madrid: The Spanish government requests to join the EEC.

30. UK: Colour TV licences are to go up to £21, black and white to £9.

DEATH

2. Russian-born US writer Vladimir Nabokov (*23/4/1899).

Begin snubs US and gives go ahead to West Bank settlers

July 26. Israeli-American relations were plunged into crisis today when Menachem Begin snubbed President Carter. The new right-wing Prime Minister gave his official blessing to the creation of three Israeli settlements on the occupied West Bank of the Jordan, despite a plea from the President not to do so. They are all to be set up on land conquered from the Kingdom of Jordan in the Six-Day War of 1967.

Britain and the US insist that the territory should be returned to Jordan and that the status of the West Bank eventually be decided at a Middle East peace conference.

Menachem Begin and his Likud Party, however, claim that Israel did not occupy the West Bank but "liberated" it. He makes a point of referring to the area in Biblical terms as Judaea and Samaria which he claims are part of an ancient Jewish homeland.

The installation of Jewish settlements on Arab land is bound to increase the hatred of Israel simmering among the Arab population. There have been frequent anti-Israeli demonstrations, especially in the towns of Nablus and Ramallah (→ 17/8).

Pakistan premier ousted

July 5. Zulfikar Ali Bhutto, the Prime Minister of Pakistan, was overthrown and arrested today by General Zia ul-Huq the man Mr Bhutto had appointed Chief of Staff of the Army. The coup is the result of four months of unrest, in which hundreds have died and Mr Bhutto was forced to declare martial law in major cities.

The trouble stemmed from the overwhelming victory which his People's Party won in March. The elections, it was said, had been rigged. Mr Bhutto admitted some irregularities but it is doubtful if they would have affected the result. Now the army has stepped in. General Zia will probably head the new government (→ 18/3/78).

Zia: Pakistan's army strongman.

Social contract dead as wage claims soar

July 13. The Government tonight abandoned the so-called social contract with the trade unions on which the Prime Minister once said its survival depended.

Feeling disillusioned and let down, Mr Callaghan said he could only now appeal for union common sense in keeping wage increases as near to ten per cent as possible if they will not operate their "solemn and binding" voluntary pledge about a stated percentage. This signalled that formal pay control is finally buried.

Denis Healey, the Chancellor, is now preparing another mini-budget with tax cut incentives to unions to moderate claims as part of the fight against inflation. Left-wing unions are unmoved. Railwaymen have put in a 63 per cent claim and similar ones are on the way. A wages avalanche looms (→ 19).

Virginia Wade wins Wimbledon to give Britain a Jubilee victory

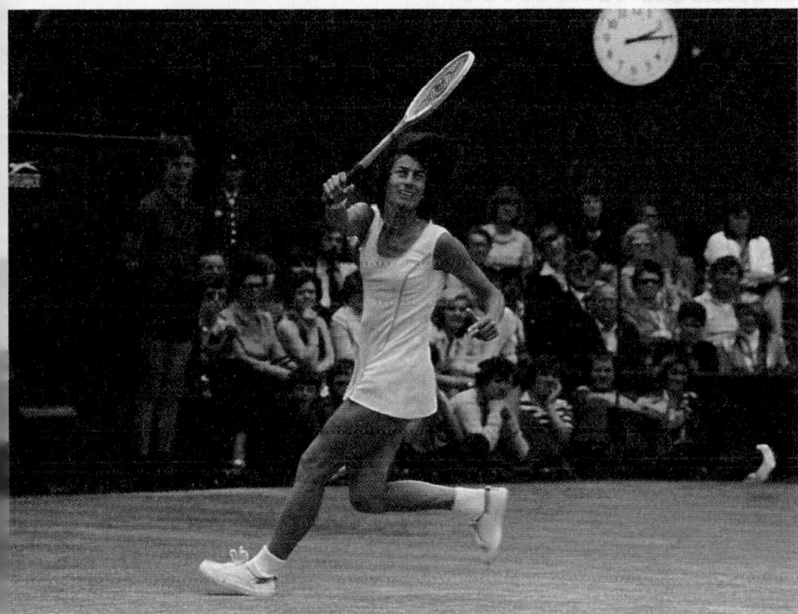

Virginia Wade on her way to becoming Wimbledon's ladies' champion.

July 1. Wimbledon's centenary year began with a breathtaking parade of past champions, headed by Kitty Godfree (winner in 1924) and Jean Borotra (1926), and climaxed as all Britain hoped it would with Virginia Wade, at last delivering what she had promised for so long.

A splendid semi-final victory by the 31-year-old Wade over the reigning champion, Chris Evert, set up the possibility of an all-British final, but Sue Barker could not match the solid force of the Dutch champion Betty Stove.

The final was a nervous, tense affair, full of errors forced by the grandeur of an occasion marked by the presence of the Queen in her Jubilee year, and only after losing the first set did Wade ride to victory on the cheers of an ecstatic Centre Court crowd.

Test stars face ban as cricket declares war against Packer

July 26. A deep split between the world's leading cricketers and the game's administrators now seems inevitable, with the International Cricket Conference's ultimatum to all those who have signed for Kerry Packer's pirate circus.

Following the initial moves – such as the sacking of Tony Greig from England's captaincy – the ICC has now threatened to ban from Test cricket, and by implication from the whole first-class game, all players who do not revoke their Packer contracts. The players have indicated that they will fight this ban in court (→ 3/8).

Mocking butterfly expert has died

July 2. Vladimir Nabokov was the most cosmopolitan of novelists, born in St. Petersburg, studying at Cambridge, living as an emigre in Berlin and Paris and writing in Russian, French and English. He settled in Boston as a research fellow at Harvard in entomology – he was a butterfly expert – and died today an American citizen.

There was nothing American about his style, full of cool mockery, parody and ingenuity. "Lolita" made his name but "Pale Fire" and "Ada" enjoyed greater critical esteem.

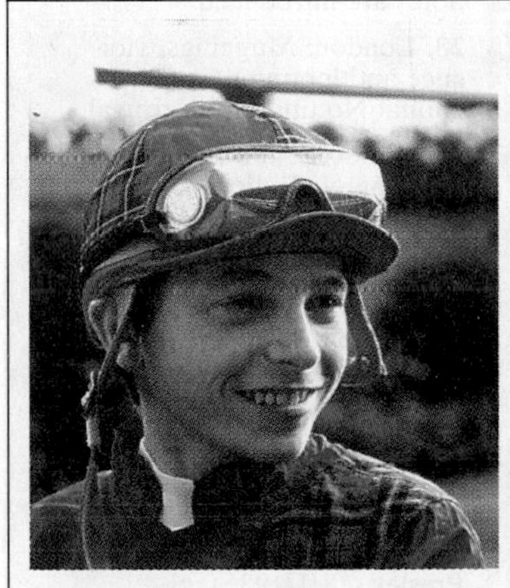

Jockey Steve Cauthen, aged 17, has broken records for victories in America; now he is planning to start riding in Britain.

1977

AUGUST

Su	Mo	Tu	We	Th	Fr	Sa
	1	2	3	4	5	6
7	8	9	10	11	12	13
14	15	16	17	18	19	20
21	22	23	24	25	26	27
28	29	30	31			

3. London: Kerry Packer takes the English cricket authorities to court (→ 25/11).

3. Cyprus: Archbishop Makarios dies of a heart attack.

5. Northern Ireland: Firebombs cause damage estimated at £1 million (→ 10).

6. Salisbury: 12 Rhodesians die when a bomb rips through a crowded Woolworth's store (→ 21).

10. Northern Ireland: The Queen arrives on her first official visit for 11 years.

12. US: The space shuttle makes its first test flight, gliding from the back of a NASA jet to land safely (→ 20).

13. Helsinki: Steve Ovett wins the 1,500 metres at the European championships.

15. Birmingham: An anti-National Front march turns into a riot as police clash with demonstrators (→ 22/7/78).

17. Israel: The Israelis set up three new settlements on the occupied West Bank (→ 13/11).

18. US: Hubert Humphrey is reported to be suffering from terminal cancer (→ 13/1/78).

20. US: The Voyager 2 probe is launched towards Jupiter, Saturn and possibly Uranus.

21. Rhodesia: 16 people are massacred by guerrillas at Umtali (→ 31).

23. UK: New smaller pound notes are introduced.

28. London: Muggings, violence and looting mar the annual Notting Hill Carnival.

31. Rhodesia: Ian Smith wins the general election with 80 per cent of the overwhelmingly white electorate's vote (→ 24/11).

DEATHS

3. Cypriot leader Archbishop Makarios, born Michael Mouskos, President of Cyprus 1959-74, (Greek Cyprus only) 1974-77 (*13/8/1913).

16. US singer Elvis Aaron Presley (*8/1/1935).→

19. US actor and comedian Julius "Groucho" Marx (*2/10/1890).→

Elvis, the king of rock and roll, is dead

Elvis: the King is dead, and while rock lives on, there are no pretenders.

Aug 16. Elvis Presley, for more than twenty years the undisputed "King" of rock and roll, has died at the age of 42. He was found dead today at Graceland, the Memphis, Tennessee mansion where he lived, surrounded by an entourage of family and friends.

The initial cause of death appears to be a drug overdose, and rumours are already suggesting that the entertainer was fatally addicted to tranquillisers and barbiturates.

Presley took the world by storm in 1956 when a hip-shaking stage act earned him the name "Elvis the Pelvis" and records like "Heartbreak Hotel" and "Hound Dog" revolutionised the pop charts.

Tutored by his manager, "Colonel" Tom Parker, a one-time carnival huckster, Presley grossed lifetime earnings of up to $1,000 million, from records, films, and allied merchandising. Early fans saw his style soften after he served in the US Army in 1958, but the hits never stopped and he kept performing, usually in Las Vegas hotels, until his death.

Geoff Boycott scores a hundred centuries

Aug 11. In only the second match since his return to Test cricket after a self-imposed exile of 30 matches, Geoffrey Boycott scored the 100th century of his career in the most august of circumstances – in a Test against Australia in front of his own Yorkshire crowd at Headingley, Leeds.

The third Yorkshireman to achieve the century of centuries (after Herbert Sutcliffe and Len Hutton) and the first man to complete it during a Test match, Boycott has become a controversial figure through his self-absorbed application to compiling runs. But in the stern arena of an Ashes series there is no harder fighter, and the achievement was inevitable once he had survived the early onslaught of Australia's pace attack (→ 15/1/78).

Boycott: a cricketing centenarian.

Ulster riot shields are used in London

Aug 13. Fifty-six police were hurt today as rioting raged in Lewisham, South London. The local station was besieged by protesters angry that National Front supporters had marched in the area. Smoke bombs, stones and ammonia were thrown at officers and when the driver of a police van was injured the crowd rounded on it chanting "Kill, Kill".

They were driven back by officers, who for the first time hid behind riot shields normally seen on the streets of Northern Ireland. David McNee, the Metropolitan Police Commissioner, said the violence was planned by extremists hoping to halt the march (→ 15).

Police march off an anti-Fascist.

Marx is in a place that accepts him

Aug 20. You would not suppose that the perfect way to set off a repertoire of outrageous insult would be a frock coat, a crouching walk, waggling eyebrows, leering eyeballs and a cigar. Yet that is the combination which made Groucho Marx, who died yesterday aged 86, an American institution, enjoyed around the world for his rasping voice, terrible puns and total amorality.

Alone of the Marx Brothers, he went on after their last film, "Love Happy" in 1949, to a radio and TV career as a quiz-show host.

1977

SEPTEMBER

Su	Mo	Tu	We	Th	Fr	Sa
				1	2	3
4	5	6	7	8	9	10
11	12	13	14	15	16	17
18	19	20	21	22	23	24
25	26	27	28	29	30	

2. UK: Inflation has dropped to 11 per cent (→ 17/2/78).

5. West Germany: Terrorists kidnap Hans Martin Schleyer, the head of the Association of German Employers (→ 19/10).

6. Panama: Carter and President Torrijos sign a treaty transferring the Panama Canal to Panama in 1999.

6. UK: Figures show that for the first time Britons are buying more imported cars than British ones.

9. US: A study shows that murder is the leading cause of death for young black Americans.

12. S. Africa: Black rights leader Steve Biko dies in detention (→ 15).

15. S. Africa: 1,200 students are arrested when they gather to mourn Steve Biko (→ 25).

19. US: Film director Roman Polanski is jailed for three months for having sex with a 13-year-old girl.

23. London: George Davis, subject of a campaign in 1975 to free him from jail, is arrested during a bank raid (→ 24/7/78).

25. S. Africa: 15,000 attend Steve Biko's funeral (→ 20/10).

28. London: David Steel gets backing for the Lib-Lab pact from Liberal MPs, except Cyril Smith (→ 25/4/78).

29. New York: Muhammad Ali retains his world heavyweight title after 15 rounds against Ernie Shavers (→ 15/2/78).

DEATHS

4. German-born British economist Ernst Friedrich Schumacher (*16/8/1911).→

12. South African black leader Steve Biko (*18/12/1946).

13. British-born US conductor Leopold Stokowski (*18/4/1882).

16. Greek soprano Maria Callas, born Maria Kalogeropoulos (*2/12/1923).→

16. British rock musician Marc Bolan (*30/9/1947).

Skytrain promises cheap flights for all

Cheap flight entrepreneur Freddie Laker waves off the first Skytrain.

Sept 26. Freddie Laker personally thanked his passengers for "helping to prove me right" today as his first cut-price Skytrain service to New York took off from Gatwick. Most passengers had queued for more than 24 hours to pay £59 for the first walk-on, no-frills flight. The normal single fare to New York is £186.

For an extra £1.75 passengers were offered a meal of pate, beef in red wine, apple pie, cheese and biscuits and a small bottle of wine. Later Mr Laker walked down the cabin of the DC-10 aircraft, decked out inside with Union Jacks, and thanked all 272 passengers for having faith in his ability to provide a service which promises cheap flights for all. Then he got down to planning his next service – a cut-price flight to Australia.

He accused the six major airlines which fly the Transatlantic route of trying to make Skytrain fail, claiming they "dared to go for me with a knife and tried to slit my throat". Mr Laker added: "All they have managed to do is to improve our licence and open the floodgates for lower-price air travel all over the world."

He then announced that he had made £2,176 clear profit from the first flight (→ 3/6/78).

Mysterious Pol Pot makes trip to China

Sept 28. Pol Pot, the enigmatic leader of the Khmer Rouge in Cambodia, arrived in Peking today for talks with Hua Kuo-feng, who is both Prime Minister of China and Chairman of the Communist Party.

Pol Pot's visit is the first he has made outside Cambodia since the end of the war in Indochina. His rule in Cambodia is absolute and is enforced ruthlessly. Refugees fleeing across the border tell horrific stories of the annihilation of the country's middle class.

The reason for his visit is to discuss aid from China and it underscores the increasing co-operation between the two countries. Doubtlessly their strained relations with Vietnam will be discussed.

Small but beautiful economist is dead

Sept 4. E.F. "Fritz" Schumacher, economic guru and author of the best-selling book "Small Is Beautiful", died today on his way to a conference in Switzerland. He was 66. His influential collection of essays rejected traditional ways of aiding the Third World, by imposing capitalism, proposing instead systems of "intermediate" or "appropriate" technology whereby impoverished communities could help themselves.

Maria Callas, the Prima Donna supreme, dies at fifty-three

Sept 17. Maria Callas, the opera singer with a fan following to rival any pop star's, ended her life a tragic and solitary figure. When she died yesterday in her Paris flat of a heart attack at 53, she had been abandoned by her lover, Aristotle Onassis, and by her voice.

Tosca was her last stage role in 1965. At Covent Garden people queued for 48 hours to see it. It was her last performance anywhere. Her unique voice was often imperfect, but her intense dramatic impact as Norma, Madame Butterfly, Violetta or Gilda showed that opera demands more than flawless notes – something that her records can only hint at.

Maria Callas accepts the applause at the Royal Festival Hall.

1977

OCTOBER

Su	Mo	Tu	We	Th	Fr	Sa
						1
2	3	4	5	6	7	8
9	10	11	12	13	14	15
16	17	18	19	20	21	22
23	24	25	26	27	28	29
30	31					

2. Austria: Niki Lauda wins the world motor racing championship.

3. New Delhi: Mrs Gandhi is arrested on two charges of corruption (→3/1/78).

5. Dublin: Former head of the IRA Seamus Costelloe is murdered.

8. London: Reg Prentice applies to join the Tories, saying there are too many Marxists in the Labour Party.

8. London: 800 corpses remain unburied as undertakers go on strike (→3/11).

10. Italy: 16 deaths are reported after three days of violent storms.

12. Luxembourg: England beat Luxembourg 2-0, but it is unlikely they will qualify for the World Cup (→25/6/78).

14. London: 14 injured in a pub bomb explosion.

19. France: The body of kidnapped German industrialist Hans Martin Schleyer is found in a car boot in Alsace (→12/11).

21. UK: BL chief Sir Richard Dobson resigns after a speech in which he referred to "bribing wogs" is published (→25).

23. Pretoria: Vorster says there will be no moves towards black majority rule, regardless of international pressure (→3/11).

25. UK: Michael Edwardes is appointed British Leyland chief in succession to Richard Dobson (→1/2/78).

27. London: Jeremy Thorpe denies ever having had a homosexual relationship with Norman Scott (→3/6/78).

28. UK: Police in Yorkshire appeal for help in finding a vicious murderer of women known as the "Yorkshire Ripper" (→16/9/78).

29. Warsaw: Polish leader Edward Gierek and primate Cardinal Wyszinski meet for the first time in 20 years.

DEATH

14. US actor Harry "Bing" Crosby (*2/5/1904).→

Commandos storm hijacked jet in Somalia

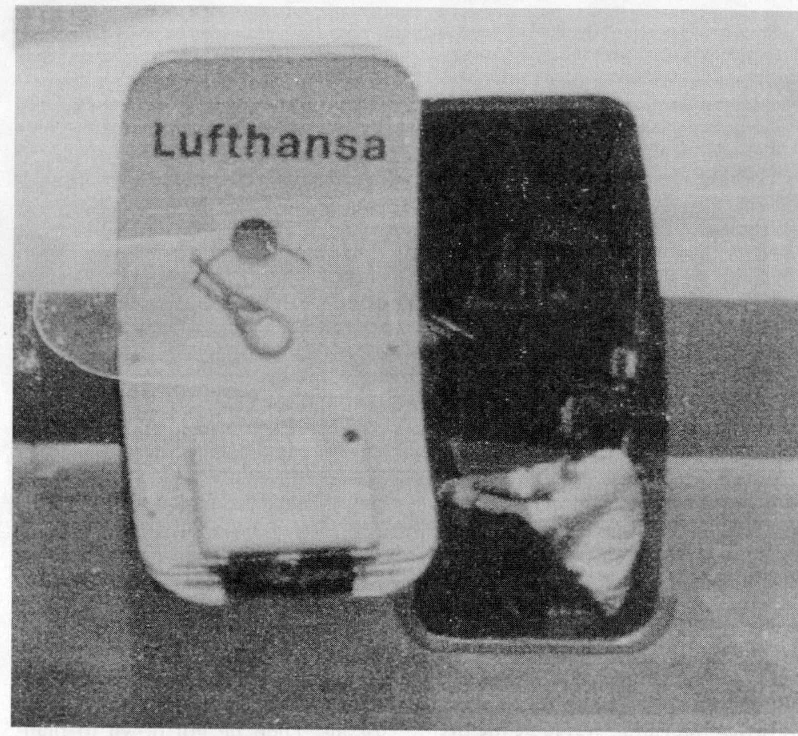

In the doorway of the hijacked jet a gunman threatens the German pilot.

Oct 18. Troops of a crack German anti-terrorist unit stormed the hijacked Lufthansa airliner at Mogadishu airport today, killing three of the four Palestinian terrorists and freeing all the hostages unharmed, just an hour before the terrorists' deadline for blowing up the plane and its 86 passengers.

Two British SAS men led the assault, throwing "flash-bang" grenades into the aircraft to stun the terrorists, before the Germans burst through the plane doors and "took out" the hijackers in a classic anti-terrorist exercise.

It ended the sweltering, terrifying, five-day ordeal of the passengers, but came too late to save the pilot, Jurgen Schumann, who was shot and dumped out of the plane.

The Palestinians hijacked the plane to reinforce the demands of their Baader-Meinhof allies who have kidnapped the industrialist Hans Martin Schleyer and are demanding the release of jailed Baader-Meinhof leaders (→19).

Bing dies playing in his green heaven

Oct 14. Bing Crosby collapsed and died of a heart attack on a golf course near Madrid today aged 75, after winning a match by one hole. His wife Kathryn said at the news: "I can't think of any better way for a golfer who sings for a living to finish the round."

Radio made Crosby the most popular "crooner" in America by 1934. During the war his film career blossomed, making the "Road" films with Bob Hope and Dorothy Lamour. More than 20 of his records sold a million with "White Christmas" selling 30 million.

South Africa clamps down on the press

Oct 20. Faced with continued unrest in the townships and a growing boycott of state schools by black children and teachers, the South African authorities today arrested at least 60 people and banned two black newspapers and 18 black organisations. In another move against the press, Donald Woods, the editor of the "East London Daily Despatch" and a long-time critic of apartheid, was served with an order banning him from taking part in politics, being quoted or published, or meeting more than one person at a time (→23).

Nobel for Peace Women of Ulster

Oct 10. The two women who founded the Northern Ireland Peace Movement, Betty Williams, aged 34, and Mairead Corrigan, aged 24, have won the Nobel Peace Prize. The announcement came today as Mrs Williams was attending the Women of the Year lunch at the Savoy Hotel in London.

Excited as a schoolgirl and with tears of joy streaming down her face, she rushed off to telephone Miss Corrigan. "We're absolutely shattered, it was beyond our wildest dreams," said Mrs Williams. The award is actually that for 1976 for which they were nominated by West German parliamentarians. The nomination papers arrived after the closing date, so today's belated announcement came as a complete surprise. The prize is worth £80,000, but it has not been decided how the money will be spent.

Nureyev stars in Russell's Valentino

Oct 4. Rudolf Nureyev turns film star, in the surprising role of another Rudolph, in "Valentino", premiered last night. Valentino started life as a dancer and was celebrated for his tango. Ken Russell's biographical fantasy shows Nureyev tangoing with Nijinsky, his great ballet predecessor.

Nureyev portraying his namesake.

1977

NOVEMBER

Su	Mo	Tu	We	Th	Fr	Sa
		1	2	3	4	5
6	7	8	9	10	11	12
13	14	15	16	17	18	19
20	21	22	23	24	25	26
27	28	29	30			

1. USSR: The supersonic airliner TU-144 makes its first scheduled flight.

2. San Francisco: Three judges uphold Patty Hearst's conviction for bank robbery (→29/4/78).

3. London: Industrial action blacks out the state opening of Parliament; Callaghan warns of trouble this winter (→29).

4. New York: The UN puts a mandatory and permanent ban on arms sales to South Africa (→14).

9. Lebanon: 68 are reported dead after an Israeli air raid (→13/6/78).

12. Munich: Ingrid Schubert, a founder of the Baader-Meinhof gang, kills herself (→15/9/78).

13. Tel Aviv: Begin invites Sadat to come to Israel and address the Knesset, the Israeli parliament (→18).

14. UK: Firemen strike for 30 per cent wage increase (→16/1/78).

14. Pretoria: Police officers swear they did not assault Steve Biko, but admit leaving him naked and shackled (→2/12).

15. London: Princess Anne has a seven pound, nine ounce baby (→8/12).

18. Jerusalem: Sadat becomes the first Arab leader to visit Israel.→

25. Manila: Jailed Marcos opponent Benigno Aquino is sentenced to death for subversion and murder.

26. Cairo: Sadat calls for Middle East peace talks involving the US and USSR (→5/12).

29. UK: Swan Hunter shipyard loses a £52 million order because fitters cannot agree on overtime; 700 jobs go (→21/12).

DEATHS

18. Austrian statesman Kurt von Schuschnigg, Chancellor 1934-38 (*14/12/1897).

30. British playwright Sir Terence Mervyn Rattigan (*10/6/1911).→

Sadat talks to Knesset

Egypt's President Anwar Sadat addresses members of Israel's parliament.

Nov 21. "No more war; no more bloodshed" was the slogan agreed today by President Sadat and Menachem Begin at the end of a momentous visit to Israel by the Egyptian statesman.

But as Anwar Sadat, the "hero of peace", returned to a tumultuous welcome in Cairo, it became clear that wide differences persist despite the wave of mutual goodwill. The miracle is that it took place at all and that the two sides agreed to continue talking. Addressing the Knesset, President Sadat declared that he wanted a permanent peace arrangement for the Middle East. "I have not come here for a separate agreement between Egypt and Israel," he said, arguing that such a deal would not bring durable and just peace.

The Israelis rejoiced at the prospect of peace, but were less happy at the idea of withdrawing from Arab territory conquered in the 1967 war, or granting a homeland for Palestinians (→26).

Packer wins his cricket circus court case

Nov 25. Kerry Packer and his contracted players have won their High Court action against the cricket authorities seeking to ban them from first-class cricket because of their involvement in the cricket circus in Australia.

In the High Court Mr Justice Slade ruled that a proposed ban on players who took part in the Australia v Overseas X1 series was illegal, as it represented an unreasonable restraint of trade and an inducement for players to break their contracts with Packer.

The verdict represents a clear victory for Mr Packer and for the three players, all currently playing in Australia, who sued the authorities jointly: Tony Greig, John Snow and Mike Procter.

Kerry Packer at the Dorchester.

One-man one-vote principle accepted by Rhodesian PM

Nov 24. Almost 90 years of white rule in Rhodesia was approaching its end today after Ian Smith announced plans for a constitutional conference to prepare for black majority rule based on universal adult suffrage.

He spoke after secret meetings with tribal chiefs and two black leaders, Bishop Abel Muzorewa and the Rev. Ndabaningi Sithole. "We want to bring to an end the madness which exists today, where Rhodesians are killing Rhodesians," said Mr Smith. But his talks have not included Joshua Nkomo and Robert Mugabe, the leaders of the black nationalist movements whose guerrilla armies have been doing the killing (→15/2/78).

The playwright for Aunt Edna has died

Nov 30. Sir Terence Rattigan, who died today at his home in Bermuda, began his career with a golden touch. His first West End play, "French Without Tears" in 1936, ran for over 1,000 performances.

He fell out of favour with the critics in the Fifties for purveying drawing room comedy. He said he wrote for "Aunt Edna" who came to town to be entertained, not lectured. But his best plays, "The Browning Version" and "The Deep Blue Sea" probe human pain.

Arab oil money is buying up London

Nov 4. London councillors have set up a working party to examine ways of curbing the number of houses being bought by foreigners, mostly Arabs. Since the oil price boom, many Arabs have bought property in London – from flats to the Dorchester Hotel. What is worrying local councils is that houses are often bought as a tax dodge and are left empty for months on end at a time when there is an acute shortage of homes for people to live in the capital.

1977

DECEMBER

Su	Mo	Tu	We	Th	Fr	Sa
				1	2	3
4	5	6	7	8	9	10
11	12	13	14	15	16	17
18	19	20	21	22	23	24
25	26	27	28	29	30	31

2. London: Menachem Begin arrives on a visit to Britain (→16).

4. Malaysia: A hijacked Malaysian airliner crashes near Singapore, killing 100.

5. Cairo: Sadat severs ties with Syria, Libya, Algeria and South Yemen, opponents of his peace moves (→16).

8. London: Princess Anne names her son Peter Mark Andrew.

10. Stockholm: Nobel Prizes go to Philip Anderson (US), Sir Nevill Mott (UK) and John van Vleck (US), all Physics; Ilya Prigogine (Belgium, Chemistry); Roger Guilleman, Andrew Schally and Rosalyn Yalow (US, all Medicine); Vicente Aleixandre (Spain, Literature); Bertil Ohlin (Sweden) and James Meade (UK, Economics); and in Oslo to Amnesty International (based in UK, Peace).→

16. Washington: Begin tells Carter Israel is ready to return the Sinai to Egypt (→26).

21. UK: The TUC narrowly votes to support the Government's wages policy (→2/2/78).

26. Egypt: Sadat and Begin end two days of talks in Ismailia, vowing to continue peace talks despite discord on key issues.

31. Phnom Penh: Cambodia breaks off relations with Vietnam (→7/1/78).

DEATHS

12. British politician Clementine Ogilvy Spencer Churchill, first Baroness Churchill of Chartwell (*1/4/1885).

25. British actor and director Sir Charles Spencer Chaplin (*16/4/1889).→

HITS OF 1977

Don't give up on us.

Don't cry for me, Argentina.

Mull of Kintyre.

QUOTE OF THE YEAR

"You can't reheat a souffle."

Paul McCartney, denying talk of The Beatles' re-formation.

South African police cleared of Biko death

Brandishing Biko's picture, a protester demonstrates outside the inquest.

Dec 2. Twelve weeks after Steve Biko, the South African black consciousness leader, was found foaming at the mouth and dying in a police cell at Port Elizabeth, a magistrate today ruled that police could not be held responsible for his death.

Biko, aged 30, was arrested on August 18 and kept naked in leg irons and handcuffs before his interrogation which lasted five days. According to police evidence, the irons and handcuffs were removed "to make him feel at ease".

Biko, it is claimed, became violent and threw a chair at police. During a struggle, the prisoner "collided with walls and tables" and he began to speak incoherently with a lisp. After being found injured in his cell, Biko was driven, naked and manacled, 750 miles to Pretoria, where he died of brain injuries in a prison hospital.

Stanley Kentridge, the lawyer who represented the Biko family at the three-week inquest, had argued that one or more of the eight police who interrogated Biko should be charged with at least culpable homicide. He said two white doctors had joined a conspiracy of silence with police (→1/1/78).

French foot bill for Bokassa's coronation

Bokassa – self-styled Napoleon.

Dec 4. The more he thought about it, the more Jean-Bedel Bokassa, President of the impoverished Central African Republic, and former sergeant in France's colonial army, liked the idea. If Napoleon could do it, why not Bokassa?

He ordered an embroidered coronation uniform, imported white horses to pull his coach, spent $2 million on a crown, and today, to the accompaniment of tribal drums and Mozart's music, he was crowned Emperor of the Central African Empire (pop. two million; per capita annual income $250).

All told, he spent about $30 million and French President Giscard d'Estaing footed the bill. "We ask the French for money, get it and waste it," he said.

Amnesty win the Nobel Peace Prize

Dec 10. Amnesty International, the London-based organisation which campaigns for prisoners and human rights in general across the world, has been awarded this year's Nobel Peace Prize. The citation refers to the group's efforts in "securing the ground for freedom".

Amnesty, founded in 1961 by lawyer Peter Benson, developed from a newspaper article on "The Forgotten Prisoners", calling for action to free men and women imprisoned for their political or religious beliefs. Since then it has brought together people from all countries and every walk of life to campaign together for the maintenance of human rights.

US offers help with Arab-Israel pact

Dec 30. President Jimmy Carter, on a six-nation visit, today offered to help negotiate an Arab-Israeli pact. Speaking in Warsaw, he said that he favoured an arrangement for a Palestinian homeland on the West Bank and involving Jordan. He is considering a meeting in Egypt with Anwar Sadat, whose Middle East peace initiative is flagging. Next week he visits Saudi Arabia and could go via Cairo (→4/1/78).

Like any other fond grandmother the Queen offers her hand to her first grandchild, Peter Phillips, resting after his christening.

Vietnam exodus begins

Some of the so-called "boat people" who risk every danger to escape.

Dec 3. Refugees are fleeing from the Communist regime of what was South Vietnam in ever-increasing numbers. Something like 1,500 a month are slipping away from isolated beaches in craft completely unsuitable for the open sea. But so desperate are these "boat people" to escape that they are prepared to risk certain hardship and possible death.

They risk not only storm and shipwreck, but also pirates who board them at sea, raping and killing and stripping the survivors of all their meagre possessions. Many of them have no chance of reaching friendly land, but hope that passing ships will pick them up before they sink.

This can prove embarrassing to ships' captains unable to find a country willing to take them, and some skippers are ignoring the plight of the boat people.

Many countries are responding, however, to this world problem. America, Australia, Canada, Germany, France and Britain have all accepted Vietnamese, who are proving to be admirable, hard-working citizens (→31).

Chaplin, cinema's greatest clown, is dead

Chaplin's wife, Oona, at the grave with some members of her family.

Dec 25. Sir Charles Chaplin, or "Charlie" as the world knew him, died on Christmas morning at his home in Switzerland, aged 88. As the "Little Fellow" or "The Tramp", he was loved by people of all nations, a sign of comic genius.

Chaplin's Dickensian childhood in the streets and institutions of South London was left behind when he went to America with Fred Karno in 1910 and was spotted by Mack Sennett. A six-minute short, "Kid Auto Races in Venice", became part of cinema history because in it he invented the tramp costume to liven it up. The tramp last appeared in "Limelight". In 1972 Chaplin returned from exile to receive a special Academy Award in Hollywood (→2/3/78).

Arts: outer space is big at the box office

It was a year glutted with space sensationalism in the cinema. The Force was with "Star Wars" which took an all-conquering $185 million at the box office for director **George Lucas**, even outdoing **Steven Spielberg's** "Jaws". But Spielberg had the lucrative "Close Encounters of the Third Kind", which cost $20 million in special UFO effects. **John Williams** wrote the music for both movies.

Closer encounters with real life were provided by **Woody Allen** in "Annie Hall". He played, of all things, a Jewish comedian horrified by life's embarrassing and tricky moments in a screen love affair with **Diane Keaton**. In real life they had separated before the film appeared.

Richard Burton gave his best performance for years in "Equus" by **Peter Shaffer** as the psychiatrist trying to understand the mind of a boy who blinds horses. **Fellini's** "Casanova" gave **Donald Sutherland** the task of seducing a nun, a circus giantess and a mechanical doll – an unappetising assignment.

"Saturday Night Fever" enthused a young following with its energetic disco dancing among the lads of Brooklyn epitomised by **John Travolta**. The Best Picture award for 1976 releases went for the first time to a sporting film, "Rocky", though not to **Sylvester Stallone**, who wrote and starred in it. Best actor was judged to be **Peter Finch**, who died in January, as the rebel news commentator in "Network".

The most impressive book published was a translation from the Colombian author **Gabriel Garcia Marquez**, who now lives in Spain and is celebrated for "A Hundred Years of Solitude". His new novel is "The Autumn of the Patriarch". The Patriarch is the dictator of an anonymous Latin-American country, who lies dead in his palace but returns to life. The novel pours out like angry music in sentences that roll on for pages of vivid images of cruelty, evil and corruption.

Christopher Isherwood, so autobiographical in his novels, finally came straight out with his homosexuality in "Christopher and his Kind", as **Tennessee Williams** did in his "Memoirs" two years ago. An autobiography of a different kind came from **J.B. Priestley**. "Instead of the Trees" shows what a fine essayist he still is.

John Travolta starred in the disco film "Saturday Night Fever".

Steven Spielberg's fantasy "Close Encounters of the Third Kind."

1978

JANUARY

Su	Mo	Tu	We	Th	Fr	Sa
1	2	3	4	5	6	7
8	9	10	11	12	13	14
15	16	17	18	19	20	21
22	23	24	25	26	27	28
29	30	31				

1. Bombay: An Air India Boeing 747 explodes in mid-air, killing 213.

3. New Delhi: Mrs Gandhi is expelled from the Congress Party (→ 19/12).

4. Cairo: Sadat and Carter call for a Palestinian role in the Middle East peace process (→ 18).

7. Phnom Penh: Cambodia admits over 3,000 of its troops have died in border clashes with Vietnam.

9. Iran: 60 die in anti-Shah riots in the Moslem holy city of Qom (→ 11/5).

12. UK: 17 seamen are feared dead in severe gales.

15. Karachi: Geoff Boycott becomes England captain for the first time, taking over from the injured Mike Brearley.

16. UK: Firemen's strike, which saw troops deployed in Glasgow, ends with 10 per cent pay award and reduced working hours.

18. Cairo: Sadat recalls his peace delegation from Cairo, demanding a shift in Begin's position on the Palestinians (→ 3/2).

23. Paris: Gunmen kidnap Baron Edouard Empain, a leading European industrialist (→ 27).

23. Ethiopia: Fighting resumes between the Ethiopians and Somalis in the Ogaden Desert (→ 9/2).

29. Stockholm: Sweden becomes the first country to pass a law against aerosol sprays which affect the ozone layer.

30. UK: Mrs Thatcher says many Britons fear being "swamped by people with a different culture" (→ 13/2).

31. London: Foreign Secretary Dr Owen apologises to the Saudis for British criticism of the execution of a Saudi princess.

DEATHS

13. US politician Hubert Humphrey (*27/5/1911).

22. English cricketer Herbert William Sutcliffe (*24/11/1894).

South African editor swims to freedom

Editor Donald Woods and his family arrive to seek asylum in Britain.

Jan 1. Donald Woods, the South African newspaper editor who was banned from continuing his work after he attacked the government over the death of Steve Biko, the black-consciousness leader, has escaped to Lesotho, hitch-hiking 300 miles and then swimming a flooded river.

Police had told him not to leave his home in East London, where he had edited the "Daily Despatch", but he decided to risk getting caught. "I stuck on a stage moustache and dyed my grey hair black and then climbed over the back fence," he said.

He hitched rides from white drivers, posing in turn as an Afrikaner with no English, then as an Australian and finally as a German tourist. He swam the 75-yard-wide Tele River into the independent kingdom of Lesotho.

Friends of Donald Woods in East London said he finally decided to escape when he began to fear for the safety of his family. Recently, a T-shirt bearing a portrait of Steve Biko was posted to his home, and when his five-year-old daughter, Mary, put it on she burned her eyes, face and arms. The shirt had been impregnated with acid. His wife and five children are joining Woods in Lesotho and will fly with him to London. He is planning to write a book on Biko.

PLO delegate shot on a London street

Jan 4. An Arab gunman today murdered the PLO's London representative, Said Hammami. He fired three automatic pistol shots into Hammami's head as he sat alone in his West End basement office. The assassin escaped in the shopping crowds after being chased by Arab students from nearby offices.

Hammami, aged 35, was known as a moderate within the PLO. The Scotland Yard anti-terrorist chief, Commander James Nevill, believes that the murderer was acting for Palestinian extremists, possibly the group led by Abu Nidal.

Churchill's portrait destroyed by widow

Jan 12. Lady Churchill's executors revealed last night that she gave orders for the portrait of her husband by Graham Sutherland to be burned about 18 months after it was painted. She was distressed to see how much the portrait, which they both disliked, preyed on his mind.

It was presented to him by the members of both Houses of Parliament in 1954. In his speech he called it "a remarkable example of modern art" but privately commented, "It makes me look half-witted, which I ain't."

1978

FEBRUARY

Su	Mo	Tu	We	Th	Fr	Sa
			1	2	3	4
5	6	7	8	9	10	11
12	13	14	15	16	17	18
19	20	21	22	23	24	25
26	27	28				

1. UK: The unions agree to the British Leyland "survival plan" put forward by BL chairman Michael Edwardes.

2. London: It emerges that the Government is blacklisting companies which breach pay guidelines (→ 17).

3. Washington: Sadat arrives for talks with Carter (→ 8/8).

8. Northern Ireland: A car booby trap kills a UDR man and his daughter (→ 17).

9. Somalia: A state of emergency is declared in preparation for war with Ethiopia.→

13. London: Anna Ford starts work as ITN's first woman newscaster.

13. London: Edward Heath slams Thatcher's remarks on immigration for causing an "unnecessary national row".

15. US: Leon Spinks becomes the first boxer to beat Muhammad Ali for the world heavyweight boxing title (→ 17/9).

17. UK: Inflation falls to 9.9 per cent, the first time in nearly five years it has been in single figures (→ 2/10).

18. Belfast: 20 IRA suspects are arrested for the Le Mons restaurant bombing.

19. Cyprus: 15 Egyptian commandos die in a raid to free 30 hostages held on a plane at Larnaca Airport.

20. UK: South-west England suffers its worst blizzards for many years.

24. Washington: Archaeologist Mary Leakey announces the discovery of four million-year-old human-like footprints.

25. London: Princess Margaret and her friend Roddy Llewellyn leave for a holiday on the island of Mustique (→ 10/5).

25. Belfast: Leading Republican Gerry Adams is charged with membership of the IRA (→ 6/9).

27. Managua: Ten die in clashes between troops and anti-government rebels (→ 28/9).

Plan for blacks to win power in Rhodesia

Feb 15. The Rhodesian white leader, Ian Smith, and three black leaders, including Bishop Abel Muzorewa, today produced their plan for moving the country over to black majority rule.

All citizens over 18 years will be allowed to vote in elections for a 100-member Assembly, but 28 of the seats will be reserved for whites for ten years. Mr Smith, looking more relaxed than he has for weeks, said an interim government could be formed in the next few days.

The settlement was immediately criticised by the US State Department and by Andrew Young, US ambassador to the United Nations. Mr Young said he believed it to be unworkable and likely to lead to a bloodbath, because Joshua Nkomo and Robert Mugabe, the two black nationalists whose supporters are fighting the guerrilla war, have not been brought into the deal.

In London, the Foreign Office was less sceptical than the Americans and referred to statements by Dr David Owen, the Foreign Secretary, which left open the possibility of Britain accepting an "internal" Rhodesian settlement (→3/3).

Under the hot sun, a Rhodesian soldier interrogates some captured rebels.

Somalia mobilises against Ethiopians

Feb 11. Somalia is reported to be preparing to send regular forces into the Ogaden, a Somali-speaking province of Ethiopia, after peasant guerrillas have begun inflicting defeats on Ethiopian units. Behind this move lies a surprising big-power switch in the Horn of Africa. The Russians, who have been backing Somalia with arms and military advisers, have now begun to leave the country in large numbers, having transferred their support to the new regime in Ethiopia. Somalia, meanwhile, has been making secret approaches to Washington, which has promised to supply "defensive" weapons. Until the coup in 1974 put a left-wing regime in power, Ethiopia was receiving arms from the Americans (→9/3).

Bomb in a Belfast restaurant kills 14

Feb 17. At least 14 people died tonight when a bomb exploded at the Le Mons restaurant and hotel near Belfast tonight. Four hundred people were in the building at the time, 50 of them children attending the annual prize-giving of a junior motor cycle club.

The hotel was at its busiest when an anonymous telephone call warned of a bomb. Staff had just begun to clear the hotel when a bomb exploded on a window-sill outside the dining room. Immediately, flames swept through the building, killing people trapped in the wreckage. Many guests leapt from windows, their clothes on fire.

Eight people are still missing, so the death toll could rise. Many of the victims are children (→18).

1978

MARCH

Su	Mo	Tu	We	Th	Fr	Sa
			1	2	3	4
5	6	7	8	9	10	11
12	13	14	15	16	17	18
19	20	21	22	23	24	25
26	27	28	29	30	31	

2. USSR: Czech Vladimir Remek becomes the first man in space from neither the USSR nor the US.

3. Salisbury: Ian Smith and three black leaders sign an agreement to end white rule by the end of the year (→7).

7. Zambia: 38 die in a cross-border raid by Rhodesian troops (→21).

9. Mogadishu: Somalia accepts defeat in the Ogaden War and withdraws from Ethiopian territory.

11. Israel: Arab terrorists murder at least 37 Israelis in a machine-gun attack on a bus.→

13. Holland: Moluccan gunmen take 72 people hostage in a government building in Assen.→

17. Damascus: Syria says it is ready to intervene to support Palestinians fighting Israelis in south Lebanon (→21).

21. Lebanon: The Israelis call a cease-fire (→28).

21. Salisbury: Absolute white rule ends as Rhodesia's first three black government ministers are sworn in.→

25. London: Oxford wins the Boat Race after the Cambridge boat sinks a mile from the finish.

25. Pakistan: Bhutto appeals against his death sentence.

26. Paris: Belgian industrialist Baron Empain is released by his kidnappers.

28. Lebanon: UN troops take up positions along the Litani River (→3/4).

29. English Channel: French naval helicopters fail in a bid to sink the Amoco Cadiz with depth charges.

30. UK: The Tories reveal that they have hired their first advertising agency since the 1950s, Saatchi and Saatchi (→6/4).

30. Rome: Aldo Moro's Christian Democratic Party rejects any deal with the former premier's abductors.

31. UK: It is announced that three-times Grand National winner Red Rum is to retire.

Red Brigade kidnap Italian ex-premier

March 18. Red Brigade terrorists today released a picture of Aldo Moro, the former Italian Prime Minister kidnapped two days ago, threatening to put him on trial before an underground "people's court". In violent language they denounced Moro's Christian Democrat Party as "the central power of imperialistic government".

Six gunmen, dressed in airline uniform, ambushed Moro's car in central Rome. They machine-gunned escorting police cars, killing five guards (→30).

Bhutto is sentenced to die for murder

March 18. Mr Bhutto, the deposed Prime Minister of Pakistan, was today sentenced to death by hanging after being found guilty in the High Court at Lahore of ordering the political assassination of one of his opponents in 1974.

His lawyers have seven days in which to appeal against the sentence. If the appeal fails, the right of clemency rests with President Choudry, acting on the advice of General Zia ul-Huq, the country's military ruler. But as it was Zia who deposed Bhutto and ordered his arrest, little mercy is expected from that quarter (→25).

Androgyne chameleon David Bowie, a mysterious star of films and rock and roll.

Stricken tanker spews oil on beaches

March 24. The super-tanker, Amoco Cadiz, finally split in two off the coast of Brittany today, spilling the last 50,000 tons of her 220,000 tons of crude oil into the Channel. Marine pollution experts believe the spill is the worst in history and with 70 miles of Brittany coastline already affected. oil from the stricken ship has now started to move towards the Channel Islands.

It is currently about 25 miles from Jersey but if the wind changes there will be little to stop it affecting the holiday island's beaches. A fleet of 19 British vessels is spraying dispersant chemicals on the slick while on the Brittany coast the foul black slime covers beaches, harbours and boats.

French officials are investigating claims that the disaster was caused by an argument about financial terms between the tanker's captain and the master of a West German tug called to the rescue after the ship's steering broke in heavy seas. During the argument the towline broke and the ship drifted onto rocks. The captains of the tanker and the tug have been taken into custody by French police.

While French riot police fired smoke bombs at a crowd of 2,000 students demonstrating against the pollution of the sea in Brest, a British Minister, Stanley Clinton Davies, flew over the slick for talks with his French counterpart. He said: "I am absolutely appalled, particularly by the sight of those lovely beaches" (→29).

The Amoco Cadiz splits in half, battered ceaselessly by Atlantic waves.

The oil slick has fouled beaches the length of the Brittany coast.

Guerrillas reject Ian Smith's peace deal

March 28. In an attempt to wreck the internal political settlement between Ian Smith and moderate black leaders, a powerful force of guerrillas loyal to Robert Mugabe has crossed into Rhodesia from Mozambique. For the past week, black and white troops of the Rhodesian army have been fighting running battles with the guerrillas. Reports from border areas say the main guerrilla units include five high-ranking field commanders. Leaflets printed in Shona and Ndbele, the main vernacular languages, have been found, calling on Rhodesian blacks to reject the settlement with Smith (→24/6).

Dutch Marines foil hostage shootings

March 14. Dutch Marines stormed a government building at Assen today and rescued 71 hostages, just before two of them were to be killed by their South Moluccan captors. The terrorists, who want their island home in Indonesia returned to them, had selected two local officials for death.

They had already killed one official when they took over the building 27 hours before. They shot him and threw his body out of the window. The authorities are hoping this will be the last of the Moluccans' forlorn campaign. They are killing and dying for nothing.

Chaplin's coffin is stolen from grave

March 2. Grave-robbers today stole the body of Charlie Chaplin from the Swiss cemetery where he was buried three months ago. The police are baffled; a ransom is thought to be the likely motive, but the thieves left behind no demands.

Marks on the ground at the graveyard in Cosier-sur-Vevey showed the heavy casket had been dragged several feet before being heaved on to a truck. At least four men must have carried out the operation. Chaplin died aged 88 on Christmas Day last year (→17/5).

Israel launches raid in Lebanon as reprisal for bus attack

March 14. More than 7,000 Israeli assault troops, backed by armour and artillery, stormed into southern Lebanon today to strike at Palestinian camps and bases in the biggest-ever cross-border operation.

A spokesman said the attack was more than just a retaliation raid and that the Israelis would stay there "for quite a while".

Action was promised after seaborne Palestinians raided the coast road south of Haifa, hijacking three buses. They killed 30 civilians and 80 were wounded. Menachem Begin vowed to cut off the evil arm of terrorism (→17).

One of three burnt-out buses, all hijacked by Palestinian terrorists.

1978

APRIL

Su	Mo	Tu	We	Th	Fr	Sa
						1
2	3	4	5	6	7	8
9	10	11	12	13	14	15
16	17	18	19	20	21	22
23	24	25	26	27	28	29
30						

1. UK: Mrs D. Whitaker's Lucius wins the Grand National.

3. London: The BBC begins permanent radio broadcasting from the House of Commons (→ 6).

3. Lebanon: The Israelis announce they are beginning to withdraw their troops (→ 9/6).

6. Paris: Premier Raymond Barre forms a new cabinet.

7. Washington: Carter decides to postpone production of the neutron bomb (→ 25).

10. Washington: Arkady Shevchenko, the highest-ranking Soviet official at the UN, defects (→ 18/5).

13. Glasgow: Donald Dewar retains Cowcaddens for Labour in a by-election (→ 4/5).

15. Italy: Dozens die and 100 are injured when two trains collide between Bologna and Florence.

15. UK: Joyce McKinney, accused of kidnapping and sexually abusing a Mormon missionary, disappears (→ 20/6).

16. Rome: The Italian government appeals for Aldo Moro's abductors to spare his life (→ 20).

18. Washington: The Senate approves the Carter-Torrijos treaty, giving Panama control of the Canal in 1999.

20. Rome: Aldo Moro's captors issue a photograph of him to prove he is still alive.→

24. Washington: The Supreme Court turns down Patty Hearst's appeal for a review of her sentence (→ 4/10).

24. US: ITV's "Upstairs, Downstairs" is the first foreign programme to win the top US TV award, the Peabody.

25. London: David Steel says the Lib-Lab pact will end with the current parliamentary session.

25. Moscow: Brezhnev says the USSR will join the US in deferring production of neutron weapons (→ 26/5).

30. Washington: Menachem Begin arrives for talks with Carter.

Italy's agony over doing hostage deal

Moro: photographed in captivity.

April 20. An anguished debate continued in the Italian cabinet today about how to respond to demands from the Red Brigade kidnappers of Aldo Moro who have threatened to murder the senior Christian Democrat statesman unless imprisoned members of their group are released. The ugly choice now facing the government is whether to negotiate or take the blame for Moro's eventual murder. Despite massive police efforts, his whereabouts remain a mystery, five weeks after his capture (→ 7/5).

Afghan President is killed in a coup

April 30. The full horror of the bloodbath in which the army took over Afghanistan three days ago was revealed last night when the country's new Soviet-backed rulers announced that almost the whole of the leadership of the ousted moderate regime had been wiped out, as well as the president, Mohammed Daoud. The fighting left the centre of Kabul littered with bodies. The KGB is alleged to have been heavily involved.

Birching outlawed

April 25. Britain faces a constitutional poser tonight after the European Court ruled that birching is degrading. Corporal punishment has been abolished, but birching is still used in the Isle of Man and the Channel Islands.

1978

MAY

Su	Mo	Tu	We	Th	Fr	Sa
	1	2	3	4	5	6
7	8	9	10	11	12	13
14	15	16	17	18	19	20
21	22	23	24	25	26	27
28	29	30	31			

3. Jamaica: Police fire over spectators who invade the pitch during a Test match between the West Indies and Australia.

4. UK: Labour holds its ground in local elections, but the Tories make gains in London (→ 31).

6. London: Arsenal beat Manchester United 3-2 in the FA Final Cup.

7. Rome: 26 are arrested in the hunt for Aldo Moro after the Red Brigade threatened to carry out a "death sentence".→

8. New York: David Berkowitz is charged with six "Son of Sam" murders (→ 12/6).

10. Italy: Aldo Moro is buried in a funeral from which all public leaders are barred (→ 13).

13. Rome: Pope Paul attends a requiem for Aldo Moro (→ 23/6).

14. Morocco: Roddy Llewellyn says he will never marry Princess Margaret.→

16. Peking: King Juan Carlos of Spain arrives on the first visit to China by a European monarch.

16. London: The Government abandons plans for compulsory metrication.

17. Switzerland: Charlie Chaplin's coffin is found buried ten miles from its original grave.

18. Moscow: Human rights activist Yuri Orlov is jailed for seven years (→ 14/7).

20. Paris: Three terrorists are shot dead as they try to shoot their way onto an El Al airliner at Orly airport.

26. New York: Pierre Trudeau tells the UN Canada will end its nuclear weapons capability.

31. UK: Labour beats the Scottish Nationalists to win a by-election at Hamilton.

DEATHS

9. Italian statesman Aldo Moro (*23/9/1916).→

15. Australian statesman Sir Robert Gordon Menzies, Prime Minister 1939-41, 1949-66 (*20/12/1894).

Paratroopers try to rescue Europeans stranded in Zaire

May 21. French and Belgian paras who flew to the rescue of 3,000 whites trapped in the Zaire copper town of Kolwezi today, found more than 150 bodies lying in the blood-stained streets. A girl of about 16 was still clutching her handbag. She had been beheaded. A woman, with an expression of terror, had her fingers in her ears.

The horror began last week when former Katangese gendarmes, who had been living in neighbouring Angola, invaded southern Zaire, as they have done on previous occasions, and occupied Kolwezi and the airport. Many of the Zairean troops sent to dislodge the gendarmes, instead joined them, getting high on drugs and going on the rampage. Zaire's President Mobutu then called on France and Belgium to help.

Some of the 150 corpses in Zaire.

Europeans to play in the Ryder Cup

May 30. After more than 50 years as a match (all too often one-sided) between the USA and Great Britain and Ireland, the Ryder Cup has been opened to European golfers, allowing such players as Severiano Ballesteros to represent Europe in the biennial series. ▷

Body of kidnapped Italian minister found

Photographers gather for pictures of the assassinated ex-premier.

May 9. The body of Aldo Moro, a senior Italian statesman, who five times served as Prime Minister, was found today wrapped in blankets and stuffed into a small Renault car in central Rome.

His Red Brigade captors, who shot him dead with a burst from a machine-pistol, made a final grim political joke. They left the car halfway between the headquarters of his Christian Democrat Party and those of the Italian Communist Party. On the day he was kidnapped the two parties were to become allies in government. Among the first of the politicians, to pay their respects, was Francisco Cossiga, the Interior Minister.

With tears in his eyes he raised a corner of the coat covering the body of his old party colleague and friend. His had been the painful task of refusing to negotiate for Moro's life.

The terrorists forced Moro to write pathetic letters begging political friends to negotiate. His family bitterly accused them of abandoning him (→ 10).

A protester against Japan's new Tokyo International airport is engulfed in flames as the Molotov cocktail he is about to throw explodes.

Opposition to Shah is growing in Iran

May 11. Thousands of demonstrators, whipped up by religious leaders, marched through Tehran today shouting "Down with the Shah" as the ferment, which has brought rioting to other parts of Iran, erupted in the capital.

The rioting has forced the Shah to cancel the visit to Hungary and Bulgaria which he and the Empress Farah were to have begun today. He claims to "have a cold", but it is transparently clear that the situation has become so serious it demands his presence in Tehran.

It seems that he is preparing to crackdown on the rioters. The government says the unrest, caused by a "few thousand" opponents, will no longer be tolerated (→ 8/9).

Princess Margaret seeking a divorce

May 10. Princess Margaret is seeking a divorce from the Earl of Snowdon. Two years ago the couple decided to separate. The two children of the marriage are with their mother. It is understood that under a financial settlement Lord Snowdon gets a central London house. Since the separation he has been expanding his photographic and artistic work.

Divorce will not affect the Princess's official position and she will continue her public engagements (→ 14).

European Cup is kept by Liverpool

May 30. Liverpool have joined the distinguished ranks of Real Madrid, Benfica, Inter Milan, Ajax Amsterdam and Bayern Munich by winning the European Champions' Cup for the second year running.

In the final at Wembley Stadium, with a performance rather less assured than last year's victory in Rome, a goal by Kenny Dalglish, their most expensive player who was signed last year as a replacement for Kevin Keegan, earned Bob Paisley's team a 1-0 victory over FC Bruges of Belgium.

1978

JUNE

Su	Mo	Tu	We	Th	Fr	Sa
				1	2	3
4	5	6	7	8	9	10
11	12	13	14	15	16	17
18	19	20	21	22	23	24
25	26	27	28	29	30	

1. Moscow: US officials say they have found electronic bugging devices in the US embassy.

3. UK: Jeremy Thorpe is interviewed by detectives investigating a plot to kill male model Norman Scott (→ 4/8).

3. UK: Freddie Laker is knighted (→ 27/7).

7. UK: The Earl of Halifax's Shirley Heights wins the Derby.

8. UK: Naomi James arrives home after a round-the-world trip, shaving two days off Sir Francis Chichester's time.

9. Lebanon: Israeli commandoes raid an alleged PLO naval base (→ 13).

12. New York: Berkowitz gets 25 years to life for each of six "Son of Sam" murders.

13. Lebanon: The Israelis withdraw the last of their troops in the south (→ 1/7/78).

15. Rome: President Giovanni Leone resigns after press allegations of corruption and tax evasion (→ 8/7).

15. S. Africa: The government disbands its information department amid accusations of misuse of public funds (→ 28/9).

16. Rome: The Pope bans Prince Michael of Kent from marrying his Catholic fiancee in a Catholic church (→ 30).

20. London: Joyce McKinney, the runaway kidnapper of a Mormon missionary, is jailed for one year in her absence.

23. Rome: 29 are jailed and 16 freed at the end of a trial of Red Brigade terrorists (→ 8/7).

24. US: Astronomers announce the discovery of a black hole in the constellation Scorpio.

24. North Yemen: A parcel bomb kills President Ahmed al-Ghashmi.

26. Paris: Three groups claim responsibility for a bomb that caused serious damage to part of the Palace of Versailles.

30. Vienna: Prince Michael of Kent marries Austrian Baroness Marie von Reibnitz.

Missionaries massacred

June 24. In the worst massacre of Rhodesia's six-year bush war, 12 Britons, including wives and children, one a three-week-old baby, were bayonetted and bludgeoned to death last night at a lonely mission station near Vumba, in the Eastern Highlands. The bodies were found today scattered across a cricket pitch.

The gang arrived about 8pm and rounded up the missionaries and their families. One middle-aged woman, her hair in pink curlers, was raped before having an axe buried in her skull. A man had his face hacked open. The children had been kicked and bayonetted. One white man, warned by his black servant, barricaded himself in his bedroom and survived.

After the massacre the 20-strong gang, armed with Soviet AK-47 rifles and calling themselves soldiers of Robert Mugabe's Zimbabwe African National Liberation Army, rounded up the mission's 250 black children and denounced the peace settlement reached by Ian Smith and moderate black leaders.

The victims were from the Elim Pentecostal Mission Church, which has its headquarters in Cheltenham, Glos. The missionaries, who did not wish to be identified with Rhodesia's white regime, had refused to accept protection from the security forces (→2/9).

Abusive MPs upset listeners to radio

June 6. Parliament is in danger of becoming a monumental laughing-stock because it sounds like a zoo. After the first three days of live radio broadcasting of MPs at work, William Price, the Government minister in charge of the project, said this afternoon that the great majority of listeners "are appalled by the bellowing, abuse, baying, hee-hawing and the rest". He warned: "We have a public relations disaster on our hands. We really must behave. The nation cannot stand this shock."

North Sea offers UK oil self-sufficiency

June 27. Britain is now the 16th biggest oil-producing nation. Figures released today show that output last month topped the one-million-barrels-a-day mark for the first time. Current output is equal to 56 million tons a year and represents 60 per cent of the country's current demand for oil.

New discoveries of oil in the North Sea are still being made. It is now clear that not only will Britain be self-sufficient in oil in two years time, but that it will soon become a significant oil exporter.

New boy Botham is the best all-rounder

Ian Botham: on his way to the top.

June 19. In the finest all-round performance ever recorded by an England Test player, Ian Botham beat Pakistan virtually single-handedly at Lord's and established himself, at the age of 22, as an exciting force in international cricket for years to come.

Botham's powerfully-struck century in England's innings was capped by bowling figures of eight for 34 when Pakistan followed on – the best analysis for an England bowler since Jim Laker in 1956.

In his seven Test matches to date, the young Somerset all-rounder has scored three centuries and captured five wickets in an innings five times (→28/7).

Argentina wins the World Cup at home

Kempes scores to give Argentina a 3-1 World Cup victory over Holland.

June 25. A long, but ultimately triumphant World Cup tournament saw the host nation lifting the trophy in a stadium packed with delirious fans. Argentina played some inspired football and consigned Holland, who fought well in the absence of Johan Cruyff, to the disappointment of runners-up position for the second World Cup in succession.

The final was splendidly contested, with Argentina emphasising their superiority only in extra-time, as Mario Kempes (the tournament's top scorer with six goals) fashioned two clinching goals for a 3-1 victory.

Brazil, the only team to complete the tournament undefeated, beat Italy (who had themselves beaten Argentina in a group match) 2-0 for third place, and it was left to some of the minor nations to reflect on success or embarrassment in the early rounds.

The Scots, who travelled in high hopes under the management of Ally MacLeod, had a nightmare week as the group matches began. They missed a penalty and conceded three goals to lose to the unfancied Peruvians; they had their winger, Willie Johnstone, sent home after admitting taking "pep pills"; and they could only draw 1-1 with the unknowns of Iran. Ally's Army drifted despondently home – as did Mexico, humbled 3-1 by Tunisia.

The giants of Europe and South America are still dominating the tournaments; but the fast-growing world of football is still capable of putting out its tongue at the traditional masters.

Is it a man? A bird? No, it's a stylish re-creation of "Superman", with Christopher Reeve (and special effects) fighting evil in Metropolis.

1978

JULY

Su	Mo	Tu	We	Th	Fr	Sa
						1
2	3	4	5	6	7	8
9	10	11	12	13	14	15
16	17	18	19	20	21	22
23	24	25	26	27	28	29
30	31					

1. Beirut: 22 die in heavy fighting between Syrian peacekeeping troops and Christian militiamen.

3. Peking: China cancels all aid to Vietnam and recalls its advisers (→ 11).

4. Wimbledon: Ilie Nastase is knocked out of the Men's Singles and banned for three months for bad behaviour.→

6. UK: 11 die in a fire on the Penzance to London sleeper.

7. Wimbledon: Martina Navratilova beats Chris Evert for the Women's Singles title.→

7. Solomon Islands: The colony becomes independent of Britain.

8. Italy: Sandro Pertini is elected Italy's first Socialist President by an overwhelming majority.

10. Moscow: The trials open of leading dissidents Anatoly Shcharansky and Alexander Ginsburg.→

11. Peking: China cuts off all economic and technical aid to Albania.

15. UK: Jack Nicklaus wins his third British Open gold championship.

18. S. Africa: The authorities refuse to give Nelson Mandela the thousands of 60th birthday cards he has received (→ 20/9).

21. London: The Government announces a new pay increase guideline of five per cent; the unions reject it as unrealistic (→ 2/10).

24. London: George Davis, released from jail after a campaign protesting his innocence, gets 15 years for robbery.

27. London: The popularity of Laker's Skytrain causes chaotic scenes at Gatwick Airport.

28. London: David Gower scores his first Test century on the first day of the second Test against New Zealand (→ 29/9).

31. Paris: Two French security men die in a shoot out with guards at the Iraqi embassy.

BIRTH

26. Louise Brown, the world's first "test-tube" baby.→

First baby is born from a test-tube

July 26. Around midnight it was announced that the world's first test-tube baby, weighing five pounds twelve ounces, had been delivered by a Caesarean operation at Oldham District General Hospital, Greater Manchester.

Patrick Steptoe, a pioneer of test-tube baby research, who is in charge of the mother, said: "All examinations showed that the baby is quite normal. The mother's condition after delivery was also excellent." Mrs Lesley Brown, the mother, was said to be "enjoying a well-earned sleep".

The embryo was implanted in her womb last November, after one of her eggs was fertilised in a test-tube by her husband's sperm. She was sterile because blocked Fallopian tubes prevented any eggs from her ovaries reaching her uterus.

Mr Steptoe had spent more than 12 years perfecting the technique in his laboratory, where he works with Dr Robert Edwards, a Cambridge physiologist.

The child's financial future should be comfortable as the newspaper rights have been sold for £300,000.

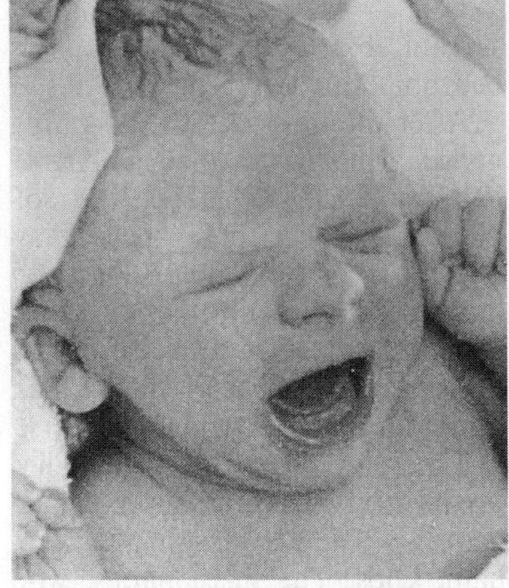

Louise Brown: life in a test-tube.

Explosion in Spanish campsite kills 200

July 11. Nearly 200 holidaymakers were killed today when a liquid gas tanker exploded in the middle of a crowded camp-site on the Spanish coast. Among 200 injured are many who are so badly burned they are not expected to survive. Most had been lazing in their swimwear in the afternoon sun.

Some victims, who include British tourists, were hurled 100 yards into the sea by the force of the blast. It tore through the camping site leaving a deep crater 60 feet long. The disaster struck at San Carlos de la Rapita when the tanker lorry lost control on the main coast road and careered into the tents and caravans parked in rows.

One survivor described the scene of devastation that was left behind as a "holocaust of flame". As the lorry's load erupted, it set off a chain of explosions throughout the site as bottled gas used by campers ignited.

An exploding tanker killed 188 tourists at this Spanish campsite.

Hat-trick for Bjorn Borg at Wimbledon

July 8. With a straight-sets victory over Jimmy Connors, Bjorn Borg became the first player in the modern era to record a hat-trick of men's singles titles at Wimbledon. It was a far more decisive victory for 22-year-old Borg than last year's five-set struggle.

The last man to perform the feat, Fred Perry in 1934-5-6, said that the treble required a combination of form, fitness, luck, belief, ability – and a bit more luck. The Swede had all this, plus an ice-cool temperament in moments of crisis.

Bjorn Borg wins his third title.

Russian dissidents get hard labour

July 14. The Soviet government's crackdown on human rights campaigners intensified today when heavy sentences were passed on three dissidents for "treason and anti-Soviet agitation".

The best known was Anatoli Shcharansky, a founder member of the Helsinki Group set up to monitor Soviet observance of human rights agreements. He was sent to prison and labour camp for 13 years. Shcharansky, who had been trying for years to emigrate to Israel, told the court: "As the Jews say 'next year in Jerusalem'."

In a separate trial Alexander Ginsberg, a fund-raiser for families of political prisoners, received an eight-year sentence.

1978

AUGUST

Su	Mo	Tu	We	Th	Fr	Sa
		1	2	3	4	5
6	7	8	9	10	11	12
13	14	15	16	17	18	19
20	21	22	23	24	25	26
27	28	29	30	31		

3. Canada: The Queen opens the Commonwealth Games at Edmonton.

6. Rome: Pope Paul VI dies of a heart attack (→12).

8. Europe: The continent is lashed by gales and torrential rain.

8. Washington: The White House says Carter will meet Begin and Sadat in the US next month (→18/9).

10. France: Peugeot-Citroen announces it is buying Chrysler's European operation.

12. Rome: 200,000 people attend Pope Paul's funeral.→

14. Bucharest: Hua Kuo-feng arrives in Rumania on the first trip to Europe by a Chinese Communist Party chief.

19. Iran: 377 are killed when a fire begun by Shi'ite extremists engulfs a cinema in Abadan (→8/9).

20. London: An Arab terrorist and an air hostess die in a machine-gun and grenade attack on an El Al aircrew.→

24. West Germany: A 100-pound bomb is found at a British Army barracks.

28. London: Disturbances and bottle-throwing mar the end of the Notting Hill Carnival.

31. London: The Bingham Inquiry concludes that Shell and BP broke the oil sanctions on Rhodesia.

31. Kenya: Prince Charles refuses to talk to Idi Amin at Kenyatta's funeral (→30/10).

31. Manchester: Express Newspapers announce plans for a new national daily, possibly called "Daily Star".

DEATHS

6. Pope Paul VI, born Giovanni Battista Montini, reigned 1963-78 (*26/9/1897).

14. British cartoonist Nicolas Clerihew Bentley (*14/6/1907).

22. Kenyan statesman Jomo Kenyatta, born Kamau wa Ngengi and baptised Johnstone Kamau (*1891).→

26. French actor Charles Boyer (*28/8/1897).

Cardinals elect a Pope who was a peasant

Aug 26. Albino Cardinal Luciani was elected Pope this morning on the fourth ballot, after one of the quickest papal elections in recent history. He has chosen the name of John Paul I, in homage to his two immediate predecessors. He is a strong supporter of the drive towards ecumenicism begun by Pope John XXIII and continued by Pope Paul VI who died on August 6.

Cardinal Luciani, currently Patriarch of Venice, is an Italian of peasant origins. He is believed to be a moderate, capable of securing the support of both liberal and conservative wings of the Roman Catholic church (→3/9).

Pope Paul VI lies in state.

Israeli reprisal after Heathrow shootings

Aug 21. Israeli jets struck back in anger today with raids on Palestinian guerrilla bases in Lebanon in revenge for Sunday's terrorist attack on an El Al airline bus in London. Palestinian gunmen from the Popular Front for the Liberation of Palestine opened fire on the airline crew bus in front of the Europa Hotel. They also threw grenades, killing an air hostess and wounding others.

General Mordechai Hod, president of El Al, attacked the British for refusing to allow his security men to carry firearms.

Jomo Kenyatta, Kenya's "Old One", dies

Aug 22. Long queues gathered outside State House, Nairobi, today to file past the body of Jomo Kenyatta, Mzee (the Old One), as Kenya's President was known. He is dressed in his pin-striped blue suit, with his ceremonial silver fly whisk resting in his hand. Many in the crowd wept and women fainted. Kenyatta, who was about 80, led Kenya to independence in 1963. Once condemned as a terrorist, he gave his country political stability and prosperity (→31).

Daley Thompson in Canada won the decathlon gold medal at the Commonwealth games in Edmonton: his first title, but unlikely to be the last.

Ex-Liberal leader "plotted murder"

Aug 4. A magistrate's court today heard Jeremy Thorpe, the former Liberal leader, deny that he had a homosexual affair with a man he had allegedly plotted to have killed. Thorpe and three other men are accused of conspiring to kill Norman Scott, a former male model.

Thorpe has denied making a payment of £5,000 to a former airline pilot, Andrew Newton, who claims that he was hired to kill Scott. He admitted befriending Scott, but says his compassion and kindness was repaid with "malevolence and resentment" (→20/11).

Balloon sets record in Atlantic crossing

Aug 19. Three exhausted Americans stepped onto French soil tonight after completing the first balloon crossing of the Atlantic in a six-day, 3,200-mile voyage, at the mercy of icy winds and freezing rain.

The helium-filled balloon, Double Eagle II, carrying Ben Abruzzo, Maxie Anderson and Larry Newman, landed in a field 55 miles west of Paris. There have been 17 previous attempts.

The trio, who flew from Maine and lived off hot dogs and tins of sardines, will have an audience with President Carter next week.

"Christ imprinted" shroud displayed

Aug 25. The ancient linen cloth, revered by many Catholics as Christ's shroud, went on public display today for the first time in 45 years. More than two million people are expected to flock to see it on the high altar of St. John's Cathedral in Turin.

The shroud clearly shows the imprint of a long-haired, bearded man with blotches which could be bloodstains on the right wrist. It is protected by a bullet-proof screen, which also keeps out ultra-violet rays to prevent deterioration during the 43-day exhibition. Usually it is locked in a silver casket.

1978

SEPTEMBER

Su	Mo	Tu	We	Th	Fr	Sa
					1	2
3	4	5	6	7	8	9
10	11	12	13	14	15	16
17	18	19	20	21	22	23
24	25	26	27	28	29	30

1. Tel Aviv: Begin says he will press for a mutual defence treaty between Israel and the US.→

2. Salisbury: Ian Smith reveals he held secret talks with nationalist leader Joshua Nkomo last month.→

3. Rome: Pope John Paul I is crowned.→

6. Belfast: Gerry Adams is freed after a judge rules there is not enough evidence that he is a member of the IRA.

10. Salisbury: Ian Smith imposes a form of martial law in parts of Rhodesia (→30).

12. Paris: Monique Pelletier is appointed France's first minister for women.

15. London: German Baader-Meinhof terrorist Astrid Proll is arrested (→24).

16. Iran: 20,000 are feared dead after a minute-long earthquake.

16. UK: Police attribute two more murders to the "Yorkshire Ripper", bringing the number of victims to ten.

17. New Orleans: Muhammad Ali beats Leon Spinks to win the world heavyweight championship a record third time.

20. S. Africa: Prime Minister Vorster announces his resignation "for health reasons".→

20. UK: Police launch a massive manhunt after newspaper boy Carl Bridgewater is murdered.

24. Dortmund: A West German policeman dies in a shoot-out with Baader-Meinhof terrorists.

29. UK: Geoff Boycott is sacked as captain of Yorkshire Cricket Club.

30. Rhodesia: 300 have died in the bloodiest month so far in the guerrilla war (→22/10).

DEATHS

15. German aircraft engineer Willy Messerschmitt (*26/6/1898).

30. Pope John Paul, born Albino Luciani, reigned 1978 (*17/10/1912).→

Carter hosts Israeli-Egyptian summit

Sept 18. The "Spirit of Camp David" triumphed today when President Anwar Sadat of Egypt and Menachem Begin, the Prime Minister of Israel, announced that they had reached agreement on the signing of a peace treaty.

The agreement is a triumph, not only for the leaders of the two warring nations, but also for President Jimmy Carter of the United States, who brought them together and kept the talks going when it seemed certain they would fail.

Mr Begin praised Mr Carter for achieving "a great victory" and pointedly said he had "worked harder than our forefathers did in Egypt building the pyramids".

The agreement, which came unexpectedly and only after hours of persuasion by Mr Carter shuttling between Sadat in Dogwood Lodge and Begin in Birch Lodge, brings hope that the two major combatants in the Middle East will now be able to settle their differences round the conference table rather than on the battlefield.

The terms of the agreement are embodied in two separate documents which the two leaders are to sign in an official ceremony with Mr Carter. However, much work remains to be done. The Israelis still refuse to withdraw from all occupied Arab land. What they have done is to promise to give up the Sinai, which they have held since the Six-Day War in 1967, and, according to one source, to "recognize the legitimate rights of the Palestinians". More talks will have to be held to discuss the future of the occupied territories of the West Bank and the Gaza Strip.

In return, the Egyptians have agreed to move towards opening normal diplomatic relations with Israel, a move which will horrify those in the Arab world who are dedicated to its destruction.

There are grave dangers in this agreement for both Begin and Sadat. The withdrawal from the Sinai, which many Israelis regard as a vital buffer against invasion from Egypt, will rouse fierce criticism from those who fear the Egyptians are still committed to destroying them. Their hardline Prime Minister's exchange of strategic territory for promises will be looked upon with horror.

The danger for Sadat is even greater. Already regarded as a traitor by militant Arabs for his dramatic flight to Jerusalem last year, this agreement will intensify hostility towards him (→27/10).

The peace treaty signed, Sadat and Begin embrace as Carter grins.

Mid-air collision between airliner and small plane kills 150

Sept 25. At least 150 people have died in one of America's worst air disasters when a light aircraft collided with an airliner over San Diego and both crashed onto houses.

All 135 passengers on the Pacific Southwest Airlines 727, and the student pilot of the light aircraft, died immediately; others were killed on the ground as burning wreckage crashed onto homes, which are still being checked for bodies.

The collision occurred after both pilots were warned that other aircraft were dangerously close. Investigators believe the pilot of the light aircraft may not have seen the jet because he could have been wearing a hood to simulate foul weather conditions while he practised instrument landings.

Blazing and out of control, the airliner plunges towards the ground.

Rhodesian rebels shoot air crash victims

Sept 4. An Air Rhodesia Viscount airliner with 56 people on board crashed in remote bush country near Lake Kariba this evening, after being hit by a Russian SAM-7 heatseeking missile. Both starboard engines were blown off by what a passenger described as a "thunderous explosion".

Some time after the 18 survivors had staggered from the wreckage and begun looking to their injuries, a guerrilla gang appeared and said they would get them water and help. Then they opened fire with their AK-7 assault rifles. One woman was gunned down as she was tearing strips from her dress to bandage people.

There were eight survivors of the massacre. Five, including a girl of four, had left the scene of the crash to seek help from local villagers. Three others were hiding in the bush and looked on helplessly as, first, the people were killed and, then, the plane was looted. The area around Kariba has been infiltrated by Joshua Nkomo's guerrillas, Cuban-trained and Russian-armed. A guerrilla source said the attack on the airliner had been a "military operation" because the airliner ferried troops (→ 10).

New Pope dies after only 33 days in office

Sept 30. Pope John Paul was found dead at 5.30am today by his private secretary. He is thought to have died of a heart attack after only 33 days in office. The news shocked Catholics because, at 65, he was young for a pope and his breezy style gave no clue to his underlying poor health. It was the shortest papal reign since Stephen II died two days after his election in 752.

The second election will put a severe strain on the Vatican. Apart from the difficulty of finding a candidate to keep liberals and conservatives happy, there is strong pressure from the Third World to appoint a non-Italian Pope. The 26 Italian Cardinals will fiercely resist this trend, but today they only have a quarter of the votes (→ 16/10).

The cortege of Pope John Paul I.

Iran under martial law

Rioters carry off a wounded man after the demonstrations in Tehran.

Sept 8. The Shah imposed martial law on Tehran and 11 other cities today after mass demonstrations against his rule. The announcement led immediately to bloody clashes on the streets. Fanatical Shias burned down two cinemas and destroyed scores of vehicles. It is thought that 58 people died in fighting between the mob and the Defence Forces, and a further 208 were injured.

The demonstrations which led to martial law being imposed, were organised by fundamental religious leaders who are opoposed to the Shah's programme of modernisation, but they were supported by leftists who proclaimed themselves "Islamic Socialists" and "Islamic Republicans".

Criticisms of the Shah centre on his attempts to turn Iran into a "Western" country, concentrating his efforts on arms spending and modernising the cities. In the meantime, he has neglected Iran's predominantly peasant population.

The Shah's future now seems to depend on the loyalty of the army, and while its conscript troops show no signs of rebellion, it is certain that since many of them are in close contact with their families, some of the anti-Establishment emotions are bound to rub off (→ 31/10).

Deadly brolly kills Bulgarian defector

Sept 29. In one of the most bizarre murders ever, a Bulgarian defector has been killed by being stabbed with a poisoned umbrella point. Mr Georgi Markov died on September 15, four days after the tip was jabbed into his thigh as he waited at a bus stop on Waterloo Bridge in central London. Before he fell into a coma, Mr Markov, an author and BBC broadcaster, told friends he had been jabbed from behind.

Today police said the umbrella tip contained an alloy ball no bigger than a pin head and filled with an unknown chemical (→ 2/10).

US urges Nicaraguan President to resign

Sept 28. President Anastasio Somoza of Nicaragua has agreed to step down at last, according to top political sources in Managua. He had five hours of talks today with US President Carter's roving envoy, William Jorden. The US thinks that his position has become insupportable and he must resign soon if a takeover by the Marxist Sandinista National Front is to be averted.

Somoza has had to make many concessions to the Sandinista guerrillas, who last month seized control of the National Palace. The economic condition of the country is deteriorating rapidly and Somoza has lost the support of conservative businessmen.

Today, in Cuba, Senor Tomas Borges, one of the Sandinista founders, said they would fight on until the Somoza dynasty, which has ruled for 41 years, was ousted. So far more than 1,500 have died in the fighting between the guerrillas and Somoza's National Guard.

Borges was in Cuba to see President Fidel Castro, but he said afterwards that there was no hope of getting Cuban armed support. He said the Sandinistas wanted a government of national unity and would be prepared to have conservatives in it.

South Africa elects a hawk as premier

Sept 28. South Africa's new Prime Minister is Pieter Willem Botha, the 62-year-old Defence Minister with a reputation as a hawk on such issues as South West Africa or Namibia. "We shall go forward in faith and humble obedience to God," he said after his election. "We will not bend on our knees before Marxism or revolution." He promised to apply a "positive policy" towards improving the relations between South Africa's different racial groups "taking into account the inalienable right of self-determination of all peoples".

1978

OCTOBER

Su	Mo	Tu	We	Th	Fr	Sa
1	2	3	4	5	6	7
8	9	10	11	12	13	14
15	16	17	18	19	20	21
22	23	24	25	26	27	28
29	30	31				

1. Washington: Soviet Foreign Minister Gromyko has a meeting with Carter to discuss strategic arms limitations (→29).

2. London: Bulgarian defector Vladimir Simeonov dies in mysterious circumstances less than a month after Georgi Markov.

4. US: Emily and William Harris are jailed for ten years for kidnapping Patty Hearst.

8. US: American Mario Andretti becomes world Formula One motor racing champion.

9. London: "Miss World" founder Eric Morley resigns from Mecca with a £200,000 "golden handshake".

12. New York: Ex-Sex Pistols guitarist Sid Vicious is arrested and charged with murdering his girlfriend Nancy Spungen.

17. UK: The environmentalist group Greenpeace prevents a cull of grey seals with its boat, Rainbow Warrior.

23. London: The Government publishes plans to replace GCE "O" Levels and CSEs with a single exam.

27. Oslo: The Nobel Prize committee announces that Begin and Sadat will share this year's Nobel Peace Prize (→29).

27. UK: A gunman runs amok in the West Midlands, killing four and wounding two before being captured by police.

29. Paris: Gromyko says to award the Nobel Peace Prize to Begin and Sadat is "something of a joke" (→10/12).

30. Uganda: Fighting is reported in the west of the country, apparently between Ugandan and Tanzanian troops (→1/11).

31. Iran: Oil production is virtually at a standstill due to a wave of anti-Shah strikes (→5/11).

31. Madrid: The Cortes, Spain's parliament, approves a new constitution guaranteeing full democratic rights (→18/11).

DEATHS

9. Belgian singer Jacques Brel (*8/4/1929).

21. Soviet politician Anastas Mikoyan (*25/11/1895).

Polish Cardinal is now Pope John Paul II

The Catholic Church's first non-Italian Pope for 400 years greets the crowds.

Oct 16. Cardinal Karol Wojtyla of Poland tonight became the first non-Italian Pope since Adrian VI of Holland in 1542. The Italian crowd of 200,000 in St. Peter's Square was momentarily stunned by the news. However, when the new Pope broke with tradition and addressed them in Italian instead of Latin they gave him a standing ovation.

The result came on the eighth ballot after two days of the conclave and represents a victory for the Third World cardinals who wanted a non-Italian Pope. The new Pope has chosen the name of John Paul II in honour of his short-lived predecessor who died after only 33 days in office.

He is a fierce anti-Communist and his election will be seen as a challenge to Poland's Communist government. He is Archbishop of Cracow and second in Poland's Catholic hierarchy to Cardinal Wyszynski, who stood with him on the balcony tonight.

The new Pope is 58, the youngest pontiff this century. He has a round, open face, short silver hair and a broad smile which delighted the crowd tonight. He is the son of an army NCO and speaks English, French and German as well as Italian.

France is new home for exiled Khomeini

Oct 6. The Ayatollah Khomeini, the Iranian religious leader who has sworn to bring down the Shah, has been granted asylum in France, after being expelled from Iraq.

The Ayatollah was first deported from the holy city of Qom in 1963 because of his revolutionary preaching. He found refuge in Iraq in the city of Najaf, which is equally holy to his Shia followers and, protected by the Iraqi government which had its own quarrel with the Shah, he carried on his revolutionary work.

However, the Iraqis, anxious to mend their fences with the Shah, ordered him out and he had nowhere to go until President Giscard d'Estaing offered him asylum. It is a move which could prove embarrassing to France.

Rhodesian forces kill 1,200 in 4 days

Oct 22. Rhodesian security forces striking deep inside Mozambique, have killed more than 1,200 men in two separate attacks on guerrilla camps. The Rhodesians claim to have destroyed the guerrillas' chances of mounting a rainy season offensive. It is also hoped that these heavy raids will reinforce the internal political settlement between Ian Smith and moderate black leaders and weaken the opposition by exiled militant leaders (→24/11).

Mao's Little Red Book is no longer Chinese Communists' bible

Oct 29. The late Chairman Mao Tse-tung's "Little Red Book", once the bible of Chinese Communism, was denounced in the "People's Daily" today. The official party paper, which used to lavish fulsome praise on Chairman Mao, said the effect of the book was to give him a "God-like" status.

The book, which incorporated Mao's thoughts on many subjects, had been translated into 80 languages and at one time rivalled the Bible as the world's best-seller. In China, it became obligatory for everyone to carry a copy and his words were invested with a spurious infallibility.

Mao, surrounded by Red Book-wielding acolytes, in his infallible days.

1978

NOVEMBER

Su	Mo	Tu	We	Th	Fr	Sa
			1	2	3	4
5	6	7	8	9	10	11
12	13	14	15	16	17	18
19	20	21	22	23	24	25
26	27	28	29	30		

1. London: Callaghan says this winter is "make or break time" for the Government (→14/12).

1. Kampala: Amin announces he is annexing 710 square miles of Tanzania.

4. UK: Many bakers impose bread rationing as a bakers' strike leads to panic buying (→10).

6. Tehran: The Shah appoints as Prime Minister his chief of staff, General Azhari (→28).

7. Pretoria: Information Minister Connie Mulder resigns as the "Muldergate" scandal grows.

10. UK: Panic bread buying stops as most bakers go back to work.

15. London: Thatcher brings Norman St. John Stevas and John Biffen into the shadow cabinet.

16. Sri Lanka: 202 die in the crash of an Icelandic Airways DC-8.

18. Washington: Congressman Leo Ryan is reported to have been killed on a visit to the Jonestown sect in Guyana.→

18. Madrid: 12 right-wing army officers are arrested for planning a coup (→6/12).

20. UK: Committal proceedings begin against Jeremy Thorpe for allegedly plotting to murder Norman Scott (→13/12).

20. London: Buckingham Palace announces that Prince Andrew is to join the Navy.

24. Salisbury: Martial law is extended to three-quarters of Rhodesia.

26. Belfast: The deputy governor of the Maze Prison is shot dead by terrorists (→20/12).

28. Tehran: The government bans religious marches (→10/12).

30. London: Publication of "The Times" and "Sunday Times" is suspended because of an industrial dispute.

DEATH

15. US anthropologist Margaret Mead (*16/12/1901).

Soviet chess champ beats the defector

Karpov – the new chess king.

Oct 19. Anatoly Karpov of the Soviet Union retained the world chess championship title today by defeating the Russian defector Viktor Korchnoi.

His victory came in the 22nd game of a three-month series, when Korchnoi lost after 21 draws. Korchnoi claimed his chances of victory had been thwarted by "hostile" Soviet thought-waves and favouritism. Karpov himself was asleep when his rival conceded.

Now 27, the champion secured the title by default three years ago, when American Bobby Fischer, failed to meet the entry deadline for a match. After this victory he left without comment.

TUC votes against the incomes policy

Oct 2. The trade unions spearheaded a massive vote of condemnation of the Government's incomes policy at the Labour Party conference today. But Mr Callaghan, who has been threatening to resign, will stagger on with his latest five per cent pay limit.

Without much hope, he is appealing to the TUC for talks on alternatives for checking inflation. The conference contemptuously ignored cabinet warnings that the pay policy vote could settle the result of the next general election (→1/11).

Mass suicide in Guyana

Some of the 913 members of the People's Temple, victims of cyanide.

Nov 29. In what may be the modern world's largest instance of mass suicide, some 913 members of an American religious cult, the People's Temple, have been found dead, deep in the jungles of Guyana. The gruesome discovery follows that of the bodies of US Congressman Leo Ryan and five others near the campsite.

The cultists, all of whom lived in an agricultural commune known as Jonestown, appear to have been poisoned, and survivors, who have been hiding in the jungle, claim that the cult's leader, the Rev. Jim Jones, forced them all to drink a mixture of soft drink Kool-Aid, laced with cyanide. A note, signed by Jones, explains the deaths as "an act of revolutionary suicide".

Quite how Jones induced his followers to kill themselves remains a mystery. But rumours coming from the commune told how the former Methodist preacher, who founded the Temple in 1957 and moved 1,000 of its members to Guyana in 1976, had turned from a philanthropist into a dictator, often rehearsing the cultists in such acts of self-destruction.

When Ryan and his party came to investigate, say survivors, Jones first killed them, and then ordered the suicide. His own body, with a bullet in its head, was among the corpses.

Iranian PM resigns after heavy rioting

Nov 5. The Iranian Prime Minister, Jaffer Sharif-Emami, resigned tonight after two days of mob rule in Tehran, with crowds rampaging through the capital, setting fire to scores of buildings, including the British Embassy.

Clouds of black smoke spiralled over the city and fires blazed as darkness fell. There were shots in the university area and also in the bazaar, the heart of the disturbances. Tanks are on the streets amid reports of Soviet troop movements on the border (→6).

Muldergate scandal rocks South Africa

Nov 3. The resignation of South Africa's Information and Interior Minister, Connie Mulder, has become inevitable in the wake of revelations that he set up a secret £37 million fund "to outsmart and neutralise" the country's enemies. Much of the money, according to a judge's report, was used for unsuccessful business ventures, films that lost money, and to buy a block of flats in Cape Town. The "Citizen" newspaper was launched to counter the influence of the liberal "Rand Daily Mail" (→7).

1978

DECEMBER

Su	Mo	Tu	We	Th	Fr	Sa
					1	2
3	4	5	6	7	8	9
10	11	12	13	14	15	16
17	18	19	20	21	22	23
24	25	26	27	28	29	30
31						

1. El Salvador: Guerrillas kidnap two British bankers.

5. London: Britain announces it will not join the EEC's new European Monetary System.

5. Moscow: The USSR signs a 20-year treaty of friendship with Afghanistan.

6. Spain: A referendum endorses the new democratic constitution.

10. Stockholm: Nobel Prizes go to Peter Kapitsa (USSR), Arno Penzias (US) and Robert Wilson (US), all Physics; Peter Mitchell (UK, Chemistry); Werner Arber (Switzerland), Daniel Nathans (US) and Hamilton Smith (US), Medicine; Isaac Bashevis Singer (US, Literature); Herbert Simon (US, Economics); and in Oslo to Menachem Begin (Israel) and Anwar Sadat (Egypt), both Peace.→

14. London: The Government ends its blacklist of firms breaching its pay guidelines.

19. New Delhi: Indian MPs vote to jail Mrs Gandhi for contempt of the chamber.

21. Northern Ireland: Three soldiers are shot dead.

24. Peking: Two victims of Mao's purges are honoured.

29. Teheran: Opposition leader Shahpur Bakhtiar becomes premier.

DEATHS

8. Israeli stateswoman Golda Meir, born Golda Mabovich, Prime Minister 1969-74 (*3/5/1898).→

27. Algerian statesman Houari Boumedienne, President 1965-78 (*16/8/32).→

HITS OF 1978

Rivers of Babylon.

You're the one that I want.

Summer nights.

QUOTE OF THE YEAR

"No satisfying solution to the Iranian political problem is possible without the disappearance of the Pahlevi dynasty."

Ayatollah Ruhollah Khomeini.

Millions march in Iran against Shah

Dec 10. Millions of Iranians poured onto the streets in cities across the country today to reinforce the ever-growing clamour for the abdication of the Shah and an end to the month-old military government.

In Tehran it was estimated that a quarter of the city's population of 4,500,000 joined in a huge demonstration which must have dismayed the beleaguered Shah. There is no doubt that he knew what was going on, for his officers kept watch on the march from their helicopters.

Thirty or more abreast, the marchers formed a procession over five miles long on the tree-lined avenue which runs through the city centre. There was no violence. The crowds of men, women and children were kept in order by marshals.

Troops in tanks and armoured cars patrolled near the route but they kept a discreet distance from the demonstrators, and on this occasion they were not needed.

Dr Karim Sanjhabi, leader of the National Front opposition party, who was released from prison only a few days ago, took part in the march. He said later that: "This great human scene ignored the massacres we have seen in recent times and threats of all kinds to show the justice of their cause."

Many of the demonstrators carried pictures of the exiled Ayatollah Khomeini and as they marched they chanted "Khomeini great, Shah bad" (→29).

Arms clapping, voices shouting slogans – Iran protests against the Shah.

Golda Meir, Jewish lioness, has died

Dec 8. Golda Meir, the first woman Prime Minister of Israel, died this afternoon at the age of 80. She had suffered from leukaemia for more than 12 years. She was described as a "stalwart lioness, one of the great women of the Jewish world" by Shimon Peres.

Golda Meir, Israeli leader.

Operation Santa to save Xmas shoppers

Dec 20. To foil the IRA threat to continue their Christmas bombing campaign in British cities, more than 2,000 uniformed police – many of them armed – have been drafted into London's West End. All police leave in the Metropolis has been cancelled and troops with automatic rifles are patrolling Heathrow Airport.

The move – called "Operation Santa" – follows explosions and attempted bombings in Southampton, Bristol, Liverpool, Manchester and Coventry. In London, one bomb went off late at night outside the Oasis swimming baths in Holborn, followed by two more in Bedford Street and a car bomb outside the YMCA, but no one was hurt.

As Christmas shoppers pour into city centres, all department store employees have been warned to remain especially vigilant and shoppers can expect to be searched on entry (→21).

Sadat and Begin share Nobel Peace Prize

Dec 10. The Nobel Peace Prize, jointly awarded this year to President Sadat of Egypt and Prime Minister Begin of Israel for their efforts to bring peace to the Middle East, was presented in Oslo today in a strangely muted ceremony.

Only Mr Begin was there, for Mr Sadat had other business in Cairo with US Secretary of State Cyrus Vance and the ceremony was held for security reasons in the fortress-like Akershus Castle. There was good cause for the precautions for demonstrators were on the streets, criticising the awards and demanding a Palestinian homeland.

The low-key ceremony reflected the way in which the "Spirit of Camp David" has turned sour since the two award-winners agreed to make peace three months ago.

Profound differences still exist between Israel and Egypt, and it will take more than an award in the name of a dynamite manufacturer to ease the still-explosive situation in the Middle East.

Thorpe to face Old Bailey murder trial

Jeremy Thorpe walks with his wife Marion during the hearing in Devon.

Dec 13. Despite a vigorous denial from the dock, magistrates at Minehead in Devon, found today that there was a prima facie case against Jeremy Thorpe, the former leader of the Liberal Party, and committed him for trial at the Old Bailey.

Thorpe is accused with three other men of conspiracy and incitement to murder Norman Scott, a former male model. Bail was allowed, but Thorpe had to remain in custody until his friend, Lord Avebury had signed a surety for £5,000 in London. After the charges were read out to him, Thorpe told the court: "I plead not guilty and will vigorously defend this matter."

Algeria's President Boumedienne dies

Dec 27. Houari Boumedienne, President of Algeria, died today after a long illness, aged 56. A hero of the independence war against France, he overthrew his friend Ben Bella in the 1965 coup and was subsequently elected head of state.

The late Houari Boumedienne.

Man is not guilty of raping his own wife

Dec 27. An American man has been cleared of raping his wife in what was seen as an important test case in establishing women's sexual rights. It is believed to be the first time a wife has charged a husband with rape while still living under the same roof.

The couple in the case were Greta and John Rideout, from Oregon in the north-west of the United States. Greta Rideout charged her husband with beating her and forcing her to have sex. John Rideout admitted beating her, but said the sex was voluntary.

After a three-hour deliberation, a jury found him not guilty. Unsure whom to believe, they considered the case not proven. "I don't think justice was done," said Greta afterwards. Feminists argue that marriage does not give a man the right to force his wife to have sex, if she does not wish to do so.

Arts: De Chirico, Surrealism's herald, dies

Giorgio de Chirico was a paradoxical figure in 20th century art. He was the forerunner of Surrealism, but did not like the artists who followed in his footsteps. He created some of the most evocative dream landscapes ever painted but denied they came from dreams.

He made everyday objects unfamiliar by combining them oddly and releasing their "metaphysical" nature which he called "the daemon in everything". Oddest of all, long before he died this year, aged 89, he gave up painting his dreamscapes in favour of a naturalistic (and quite boring) style.

He was a master of the intriguing title. "A Song of Love", for instance, shows an antique sculptured head alongside a large red rubber glove pinned to the wall in a setting of empty arches and a steam engine glimpsed behind a wall. The steam engine and factory chimney belching smoke were favourite symbols of his "metaphysical alphabet", like the phallic cannon and cannonballs. All were combined in empty townscapes where sinister shadows appear from around corners lit by an eerie, brilliant moonlight. It is a nightmare country that he depicts, heavy with anxiety. And all this dates from the years 1910-1917, long before anyone else had set foot in such territory.

The Nobel Prize for Literature went to **Isaac Bashevis Singer**. The Polish writer who lives in New York, writes in Yiddish and then translates his stories of the lost way of life of European Jews under pressure of persecution. "Enemies, A Love Story" is typical of his novels and his short stories are superb.

"Evita": D. Essex and E. Page.

"Evita" gave the **Rice-Lloyd Webber** partnership another hit opera-musical. Eva Peron's life has drama enough to sustain it, but her greed and hypocrisy were not allowed to spoil the sentiment of "Don't Cry for Me, Argentina".

"A Little Night Music", with **Stephen Sondheim's** most popular score, has been filmed with **Elizabeth Taylor** as the immoral actress, after its success on Broadway and in London. "Julia" is **Lillian Hellman's** story of a childhood friend who was killed by the Nazis in the Thirties, played by **Vanessa Redgrave**. Television took the Thirties and turned its major crisis into a soap opera for superior persons in "Edward and Mrs Simpson".

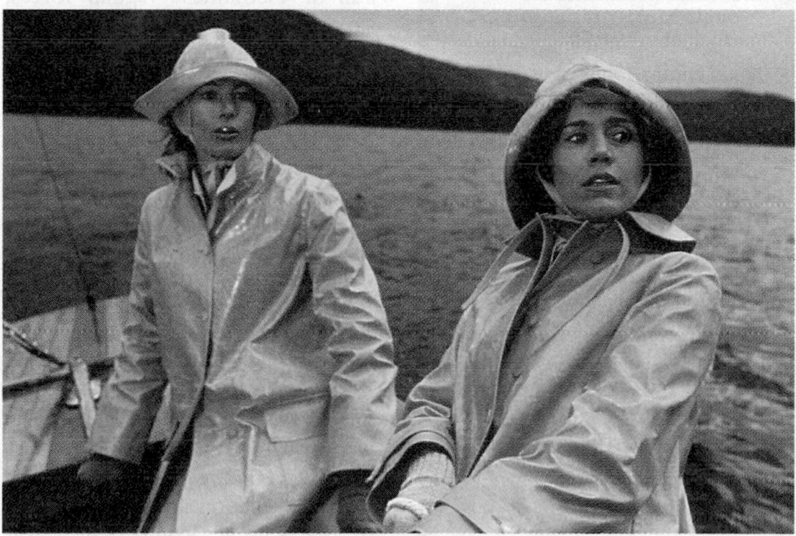

Vanessa Redgrave and Jane Fonda (r.) film Lillian Hellman's story "Julia".

1979

JANUARY

Su	Mo	Tu	We	Th	Fr	Sa
	1	2	3	4	5	6
7	8	9	10	11	12	13
14	15	16	17	18	19	20
21	22	23	24	25	26	27
28	29	30	31			

2. Cambodia: The Vietnamese attack along a 200-mile front.→

2. London: An inquest decides that Georgi Markov died from a poison metal pellet twice as deadly as cobra venom (→21/8).

5. UK: A lorry drivers' strike causes heating oil and fresh food shortages (→10).

10. London: Callaghan returns from a four-nation summit on Guadeloupe and denies Britain is facing chaos (→15).

12. Tehran: Bakhtiar says the Shah will leave Iran within a week (→16).

14. Washington: Carter asks Congress to make Martin Luther King's birthday a national holiday (→9/8).

15. UK: One-day rail strikes begin (→18).

16. Tehran: The Shah leaves Iran.→

18. London: The Government announces a voluntary picketing code to avoid declaring a state of emergency (→22).

19. Washington: Ex-Attorney General John Mitchell, the last Watergate conspirator still in jail, is released on parole.

22. UK: A 24-hour public employees' strike hits hospitals and schools.→

22. Beirut: A car bomb kills Abu Hassan, allegedly behind the 1972 Olympics massacre.

24. Cape Town: Former information minister Dr Connie Mulder resigns from parliament (→4/6).

26. Tehran: Troops kill 35 in the worst outbreak of violence since the Shah left Iran (→1/2).

29. Washington: Carter commutes Patty Hearst's jail sentence (→1/2).

30. Rhodesia: The country's whites approve the new black-dominated constitution in a referendum.→

31. Algeria: Colonel Benjedid Chadli is elected President (→4/7).

DEATH

26. US Republican politician Nelson Rockefeller (*8/7/1908).

Shah is driven into exile

Iranian troops, with pictures of Ayatollah Khomeini, join the revolt.

Jan 16. The Shah of Iran fled from his capital today, driven into exile by supporters of Ayatollah Khomeini, who has masterminded the downfall of the "Peacock Throne" from his own exile in Paris.

When the news was broadcast that the Shah had flown to Egypt, jubilant Iranians danced in the streets and on the rooftops. Soldiers, waving flowers instead of guns, joined in the celebrations while men and women clambered over tanks which a few days ago were trying to crush their demonstrations.

Tehran became a vast traffic jam of hooting cars plastered with photographs of the Ayatollah. Among the first targets for the celebrating mob were the statues of the Shah and his father, the former Cossack sergeant who seized the throne in 1925. They were toppled from their plinths and smashed.

As the Shah left he was asked how long he would be away. He replied "I don't know"; but his people knew (→26).

Oil tanker explodes in Ireland: 49 die

Jan 8. An oil tanker, unloading its 120,000 ton cargo at Bantry Bay in Ireland, was ripped apart by a series of explosions today, killing 49 people. The blasts rocked the town; seven of the victims were local shore workers.

Officials from the ship's owners, Total, said they had no clues as to what caused the disaster. Witnesses said the tanker had discharged half its load when it became a massive fireball at 1am. A police officer said: "The whole ground shook and it was like hell itself." Tugs fought the blaze, but were pushed back as burning oil spread.

Rhodesian whites vote for black rule

Jan 30. White Rhodesians today turned their backs on their 13-year long struggle to hold on to power and voted overwhelmingly to approve a new constitution that will lead to an African-dominated government. Of the 94,000 registered voters, almost 90 per cent cast a vote, 80 per cent of them in favour. They loyally followed Ian Smith, even though he was asking them to vote for the eventuality he had firmly resisted in 1965 when he had declared UDI for Rhodesia (→12/2).

Cambodia falls to Vietnamese as tanks roll into Phnom Penh

Jan 8. Vietnamese regular forces, supported by tanks and fighter planes, have crushed the lightly-armed troops of the Khmer Rouge regime in Cambodia and have occupied the capital, Phnom Penh. It seems clear that this is no punitive expedition designed to stop the murderous excesses of the Khmer Rouge leader, Pol Pot, but a full-scale occupation of Cambodia.

Hanoi Radio has announced the formation of a government by a group calling itself the Cambodian National United Front for National Salvation, under Heng Samrin who is known to be a protege of Hanoi.

Observers are now waiting for China's reaction to the overthrow of the Khmer Rouge which was aided by Peking (→2/4).

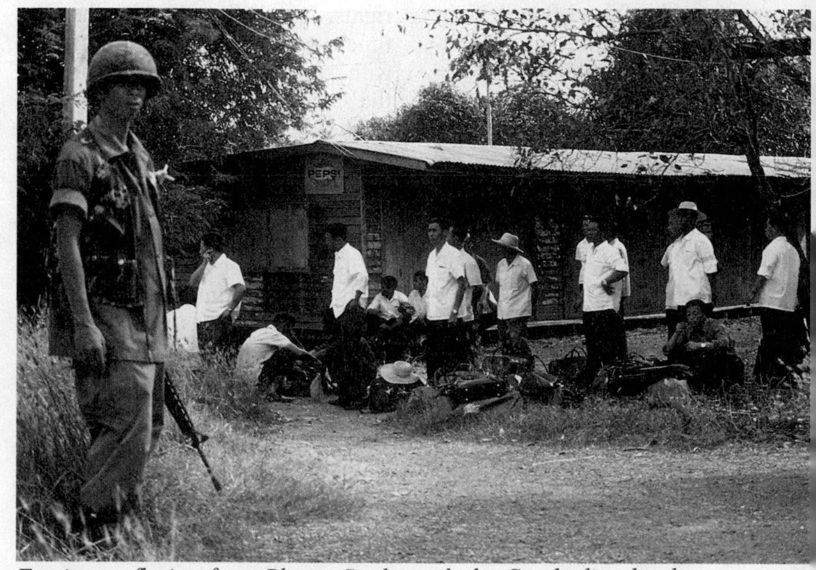

Foreigners fleeing from Phnom Penh reach the Cambodian border.

Rubbish piles up in winter of discontent

Clapham Common in London: now being used as an emergency dump.

Jan 31. Dustbins overflowing. Streets piled with rubbish. Hospitals turning away patients, including cancer sufferers. Disruption of food and petrol supplies. Hundreds of thousands of workers laid off.

That is the state of much of Britain today as industrial chaos continues. There have even been isolated cases of cemetery workers refusing to dig graves. Cabinet ministers are beginning to count the economic and, for Labour, the likely electoral cost of Britain's winter of discontent.

Union leaders have told James Callaghan, the Prime Minister, that they cannot curb many of the widespread unofficial, but sometimes paralysing, strikes which have erupted in the past two months. These have been in protest against the five per cent limit on pay rises demanded by the Government. Many settlements have been reached at three or four times that level, and the pay restraint policy is in tatters.

The cabinet, which backed away from declaring a state of emergency because it feared union backlash, appealed again tonight to "dirty job" public service workers to desist from more strikes.

Opposition politicians continued to attack Mr Callaghan for having said he saw no chaos. That was on landing at London Airport from a four-power summit conference in Guadeloupe. "He was puffing and posturing in the sunny Caribbean while Britain shuddered to a freezing, strike-bound halt," said the Tory MP Norman Tebbit (→1/2).

James Callaghan dressed for a sunshine summit with (l. to r.) Helmut Schmidt, Jimmy Carter and Giscard d'Estaing, in tropical Guadeloupe.

1979

FEBRUARY

Su	Mo	Tu	We	Th	Fr	Sa
				1	2	3
4	5	6	7	8	9	10
11	12	13	14	15	16	17
18	19	20	21	22	23	24
25	26	27	28			

1. Liverpool: Grave-diggers call off a strike which has prevented the burial of many bodies (→12).

1. US: Patty Hearst is released from prison.

2. New York: Ex-Sex Pistol Sid Vicious dies of a heroin overdose.

6. Pakistan: The Supreme Court upholds the death sentence passed on ex-Prime Minister Bhutto (→9).

8. Washington: The US breaks off relations with Nicaragua (→6/6).

9. Pakistan: Brezhnev and the Pope send appeals for the life of Bhutto (→10).

9. UK: A fallopian tube is transplanted successfully for the first time (→11/10).

10. Karachi: General Zia ul-Haq announces the introduction of Islamic laws (→14).

12. UK: Over 1,000 schools close owing to a heating oil shortage caused by the lorry drivers' strike (→14).

12. Rhodesia: Nationalist guerrillas use missiles to bring down an Air Rhodesia airliner, killing 59 (→13/4).

14. Pakistan: The Supreme Court grants Bhutto a stay of execution (→4/4).

14. Kabul: US ambassador Adolph Dubs is kidnapped and shot dead (→27/12).

16. Tehran: Four of the Shah's generals are executed (→22).

17. China: Troops invade Vietnam "to teach her a lesson".→

22. Iran: Over 100 die when Kurdish tribesmen clash with Khomeini followers (→26).

23. West Indies: St. Lucia becomes independent of Britain (→27/10).

26. London: The Old Bailey trial of Tom Keating, accused of forging old masters, ends due to his poor health.

DEATH

12. French film director Jean Renoir (*15/9/1894).

Ayatollah Khomeini comes back to Iran

The Ayatollah greets the faithful.

Feb 1. The Ayatollah Khomeini made a victorious return to Iran today after 14 years in exile, and immediately sent his multitude of supporters into a frenzy of excitement by denouncing the Shah's left-over government as illegal.

He threatened to arrest its members if they continued in office and to bring them before special courts. In words that left little room for conciliation he said: "I will strike with my fists at the mouths of this government. From now on it is I who will name the government."

Although the Ayatollah appeared physically frail and aged, there was no doubting the power of his words. The crowd rose to him and chanted themselves hoarse with cries of "God is Great" (→22).

Francis becomes a million-pound man

Feb 9. Trevor Francis, the 24-year-old Birmingham City forward, today became Britain's first million-pound footballer. In the biggest deal ever negotiated between two Football League clubs, he has signed with Brian Clough's Nottingham Forest for £1 million.

Despite Forest's current success as League champions, their gates remain disappointingly low, and the capture of such a talented player is expected to boost the current average of 30,000. ▷

Troops clash on Vietnam-Chinese border

Chinese troops move into North Vietnam as they launch their invasion.

Feb 17. Chinese and Vietnamese forces are fighting each other in a vicious border war today after China launched a punitive expedition in which, according to Hanoi, they poured across the border and overran nearly all Vietnam's border posts.

China made it plain yesterday that her aims were limited. An official statement said that her forces would withdraw "after counter-attacking the Vietnamese aggressors as they deserve".

In the past six months, say the Chinese, Vietnam had made more than 700 armed provocations against China. "We do not want a single inch of Vietnamese territory, but neither will we tolerate wanton incursions into Chinese territory. All we want is a peaceful and stable border."

The background to the quarrel is complex, involving Chinese opposition to the Vietnamese invasion of Cambodia, and Vietnam's new treaty of cooperation with Russia. The Kremlin has already warned China to withdraw.

Unions and Labour do sweetheart deal

Feb 14. An uneasy peace pact between government and unions was more or less sealed today. It was dubbed the St. Valentine's Day Agreement, and is aimed at repairing the huge electoral damage suffered by Labour in the recent "winter of discontent". Whether it is the product of true love is doubtful.

The pact, announced by James Callaghan in Parliament, sets out long-term plans for reducing inflation without insisting on any "norm" for pay rises this year. This was branded by the Tories as a climbdown. "Nothing but a boneless wonder," said Mrs Thatcher.

The Tories are now 20 per cent ahead in the opinion polls. Having decided against an election last year, Mr Callaghan is boxed in. He prays for union restraint at least until the nation votes later this year. Even the more militant union leaders are now expected to avoid more industrial disruption over the next few months while Labour struggles to recover.

Health workers on the march.

1979

MARCH

Su	Mo	Tu	We	Th	Fr	Sa
				1	2	3
4	5	6	7	8	9	10
11	12	13	14	15	16	17
18	19	20	21	22	23	24
25	26	27	28	29	30	31

1. Iran: Ayatollah Khomeini says there is no place for democracy in Iran (→8).

4. Uganda: Tanzanian forces advance on the Ugandan capital Kampala (→11).

5. Peking: The Chinese have begun to withdraw from Vietnam.

7. UK: Industrial action by a million local government workers ends as Professor Clegg is appointed to study their pay.

11. Uganda: Libyan troops arrive to aid Amin (→25).

13. Cairo: Carter wins the Egyptian government's approval of all key points in the Middle East peace treaty.

16. Northern Ireland: The Bennett Committee reports that prisoners have been injured in police custody (→17/4).

17. London: Nottingham Forest beat Southampton 3-2 to retain the League Cup.

19. Iran: A cease-fire is declared after further clashes between Kurdish rebels and Iranian troops (→1/4).

22. The Hague: Sir Richard Sykes, British ambassador to Holland, is shot dead.

22. Tel Aviv: The Knesset approves the peace treaty with Egypt by 95 votes to 18 (→26).

23. London: Financier Jim Slater is found guilty of 15 offences involving deals worth over £4 million.

24. Pakistan: The Supreme Court rejects an appeal to lift the death sentence on Bhutto.

25. Uganda: A curfew is imposed in Entebbe as rebel troops arrive on the outskirts of the city.→

29. London: Callaghan calls a general election for May 3 (→4/5).

29. Liverpool: Liberal David Alton wins the Edge Hill by-election with a 32 per cent swing from Labour.

DEATH

30. British politican Airey Middleton Sheffield Neave (*23/1/1916).→

Commons car bomb kills Thatcher aide

March 30. A terrorist bomb today killed Airey Neave, a Tory MP who was a senior aide to Mrs Thatcher, as he drove out of an underground car park at the House of Commons. As Tory spokesman on Ulster, he advocated a tough line on security to combat the IRA and had known he was a possible target. Police fear his assassination may be the start of a terror campaign in the run-up to the general election.

Party officials are to introduce new security measures to guard all top politicians. The bomber planted a sophisticated device which went off as the car moved. Mr Neave was freed from the wreckage, but died minutes later (→17/4).

Wreckage of Airey Neave's car.

Amin flees Uganda as regime crumbles

March 29. Idi Amin's regime of buffoonery and murder in Uganda collapsed today when he took to his heels with the remnants of his troops, leaving the capital, Kampala, besieged by forces of the Tanzanian-backed Uganda Liberation Front. Libyan troops flown in by Colonel Gaddafi delayed the issue for only a few days. Amin is believed to be making for his Kakwa tribal stronghold in northern Uganda; latterly his soldiers were fighting among themselves instead of facing the invaders (→4/4).

Atomic leak crisis in US

March 31. A potentially explosive bubble of hydrogen gas inside a crippled reactor at the Three Mile Island nuclear power station in Pensylvania is posing a new threat of nuclear disaster. If it explodes the reactor's containment could be breached, releasing large amounts of radioactivity. The state governor, Richard Thornburgh, has recommended the evacuation of children and pregnant women living within five miles of the plant.

Some melting of the core has probably occurred already. Experts have not ruled out the possibility of a complete meltdown, but they claim that the accident is being brought under control. A general evacuation is not thought to be necessary. The cause of the accident two days ago has still not been definitely established, but a combination of defective equipment and operator error was probably responsible.

Apparently valves controlling the flow of cooling water failed to function correctly, and plant operators compounded the fault by taking the wrong corrective action. The result was that part of the core was left without cooling water and the exposed fuel melted. More water is now being introduced to cool the overheated core.

Very little radioactivity has escaped into the general environment, but the reactor building is badly contaminated. President Carter is to visit the scene of the accident tomorrow (→6/4).

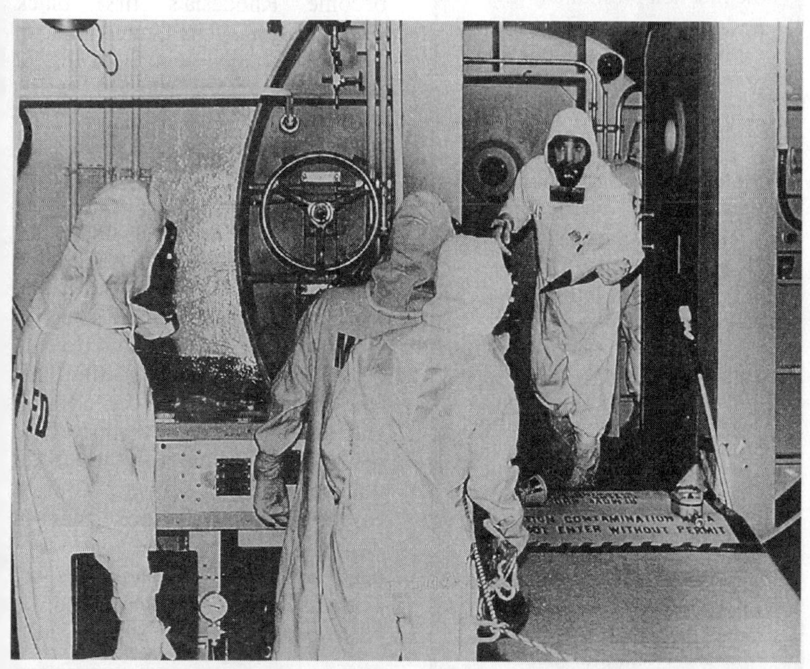

Technicians check the damage at the Three Mile Island atomic plant.

Egypt and Israel sign peace treaty in US

Menachem Begin, Jimmy Carter and Anwar Sadat at the White House.

March 26. After 30 years of hostility and four major wars, Israel and Egypt today signed a peace treaty. The ceremony took place on the lawn of the White House in Washington with President Carter, the benevolent sponsor of the deal, smiling amiably and joining hands with Anwar Sadat, President of Egypt, and Menachem Begin, the Prime Minister of Israel. "Peace has come," said President Carter. "We have won, at last, the first step of peace, a first step on a long and difficult road."

Just how difficult became clear as Mr Begin insisted in emotional language that all Jerusalem must remain an indivisible part of Israel. Anwar Sadat remained equally firm in his references to the next stage of the accord, which involves the vexed question of Palestinian autonomy. However, a great storm is clearly brewing in the Arab world against what is seen as a betrayal. Even on the White House lawn, Arab demonstrators in a nearby park could be heard shouting "Sadat is a traitor".

The hardline presidents of Syria and Iraq, backed by Jordan's more moderate King Hussein, are to summon a Middle East summit conference to oppose the settlement. They believe the accord represents a sell-out on the Palestine issue and are threatening to sever all diplomatic links with Egypt.

Saudi Arabia is likely to endorse measures by the radical states against Egypt and to consider halting its financial aid on which Sadat depends.

The first symbolic act is likely to be the expulsion of Egypt from the Arab League. Yassir Arafat, the PLO leader, has threatened to "eliminate" the Egyptian President (→2/4).

Women in Iran fear future under Islam

March 8. Iranian women, regarded as the freest in the Middle East, chose today, International Women's Day, to brave the snow and the Ayatollah Khomeini's wrath to show their fear of their future under the new strict Islamic laws. They marched to the Palace of Justice in Tehran demanding the right to dress as they please – "freedom not the chador" (→19).

Scots say Aye, Welsh Nay, to home rule

March 2. Wales has voted massively against having its own mini-parliament. Scotland has voted unenthusiastically for having one, but by well below the prescribed 40 per cent acceptability test.

Referendum results announced tonight mean that devolution is dead. The Government, with its fragile grip on power, may soon be, too. Its life depends on not alienating eleven Scottish Nationalist MPs who demand home rule and will not now get it. In Scotland there was a 33 per cent vote for an Assembly in Edinburgh and 31 per cent against. In Wales 12 per cent said "Yes" to a Cardiff Assembly and 47 per cent said "No". The rest of the voters stayed silent.

Overall this amounts to a massive thumbs-down to changing the United Kingdom constitution. It is also a snub to James Callaghan's government whose days are numbered.

Lee Marvin's lover seeks "palimony"

March 10. The film star Lee Marvin may pay a high price for parting from his girlfriend Michelle Triola Marvin, who assumed the actor's name. The former singer is suing Marvin for "palimony" of up to half of the £3.6 million he made while they were living together from 1964-70. She claims to have abandoned her career to be his loyal companion (→18/4).

Government falls over home rule vote

March 28. The Labour Government fell at 10.19pm tonight – the first one forced out of office by a parliamentary vote for half a century. There will be a general election on May 3.

The Tories carried a "no confidence" vote by a majority of one. With dignified defiance, but knowing in his heart that his premiership is nearly over, Mr Callaghan said: "Now that the House of Commons has declared itself we shall take our case to the country."

Mrs Thatcher, pale and trembling with excitement, demanded Parliament's quick dissolution. The election announcement will come tomorrow. As the fateful Commons sitting ended a group of Labour MPs led by Neil Kinnock, a Welsh left-winger, sang The Red Flag. The death blow for Labour came when Liberals, Scottish Nationalists and most Ulster Unionists joined in a strange alliance. This grew out of the Nationalists' determination to kill the Government for its refusal to go ahead with home rule for Scotland legislation.

With its weak Commons voting strength, it is remarkable that Mr Callaghan's government has lasted so long. He kept it going through wheeling and dealing with minor parties and by means of the Lib-Lab pact which lasted 18 months up to last autumn. Now Labour moves into an election to face the nation's verdict on the so-called winter of discontent. The political weather looks good for the Tories (→29).

Rings round Jupiter as well as Uranus

March 7. The planet Jupiter has rings – like its neighbour Saturn. The US spacecraft, Voyager 1, has sent back a picture showing a faint ring, estimated to be 5,000 miles wide and 18 miles thick. It is presumably composed of rocky debris like the rings of Saturn, say scientists at the Jet Propulsion Laboratory in Pasadena, California.

The picture, the first big surprise of the Jupiter fly-past, was taken with an 11-minute exposure 16 hours before the spacecraft's closest approach to the planet. Uranus, too, has rings, though like those of Saturn these were discovered by earthbound astronomers with telescopes (→19/8).

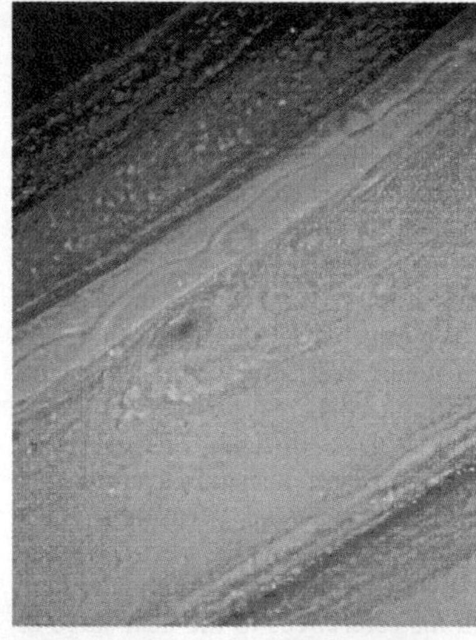

Jupiter's rings, from Voyager 1.

Grenada coup ousts absentee premier

March 13. Sir Eric Gairy, the Prime Minister of Grenada, was toppled in a coup yesterday. The moderate-left New Jewel Movement, led by Maurice Bishop, aged 33, armed with shotguns, pistols and rifles took over the radio station, while Sir Eric was away in New York at the UN. One policeman was killed in the coup. They set up a headquarters for the People's Revolutionary Army and appealed for the island's 110,000 inhabitants to keep calm.

Welsh win crowns victorious decade

March 17. With a crushing second-half performance, Wales defeated England 27-3 at Cardiff today to clinch the Triple Crown for the fourth successive year, and the championship for the second year running. The victory capped a superb decade for Wales – from the core of the great Lions' Squad in 1971 under John Dawes, through the ascendancy of Gareth Edwards and Phil Bennett, to their current run under the greatest full-back in the world, J.P.R. Williams.

1979

APRIL

Su	Mo	Tu	We	Th	Fr	Sa
1	2	3	4	5	6	7
8	9	10	11	12	13	14
15	16	17	18	19	20	21
22	23	24	25	26	27	28
29	30					

1. Iran: Khomeini declares an Islamic republic before the results of a referendum on the subject are fully known (→7).

1. Malta: The last Royal Navy warship leaves, ending British military ties with the island.

2. Cairo: Begin becomes the first Israeli Prime Minister to visit Egypt (→4/6/81).

4. Kampala: Clashes occur in the suburbs as anti-government forces surround the city.→

4. Halifax: The "Yorkshire Ripper" claims his 11th victim, the first non-prostitute (→2/9).

6. Washington: The US says eight reactors by Babcock and Wilcox, builders of Three Mile Island, may keep operating (→9).

6. S. Africa: Dr Connie Mulder is expelled from the ruling National Party.

7. Tehran: Ex-premier Amir Hoveida is executed (→7/5).

9. US: Officials say the Three Mile Island crisis is over (→18/5).

13. Zambia: Rhodesian troops destroy the home of nationalist leader Joshua Nkomo in a cross-border raid.→

17. Northern Ireland: Four policemen are killed by a 1,000-pound bomb, the IRA's most powerful yet (→12/7).

18. US: A judge orders Lee Marvin to pay $104,000 "palimony" to his former lover Michelle Triola Marvin.

23. London: 300 are arrested in clashes at a National Front rally in Southall; teacher Blair Peach is seriously hurt (→24).

24. London: Blair Peach dies; Scotland Yard will look into claims he was killed by the Special Patrol Group (→30/10).

26. Strasbourg: The Human Rights Court says a ban on a "Sunday Times" piece on thalidomide breached the right of free expression.

DEATH

4. Pakistani statesman Zulfikar Ali Bhutto, Prime Minister 1971-77 (*5/1/1928).→

First black PM is elected in Rhodesia

Muzorewa on the campaign trail.

April 24. A 54-year-old Methodist bishop educated in the United States, Abel Muzorewa, is set to become Rhodesia's first black Prime Minister. His United African National Council won 51 of the 72 black seats in the 100-seat parliament in which 28 seats are reserved for whites.

The Bishop said that, as the country now had a people's government, British sanctions should be lifted and the guerrilla war called off. "We expect all countries in the world to recognise us," he said.

But Robert Mugabe and Joshua Nkomo, exiled leaders of the bush war, have denounced the election and are pledged to overthrow the new regime. Britain and the US do not recognise it either. Tonight Bishop Muzorewa's spokesman in Zambia, Robert Hove, was shot dead outside his home in Lusaka. The assassins are believed to be Nkomo supporters (→29/5).

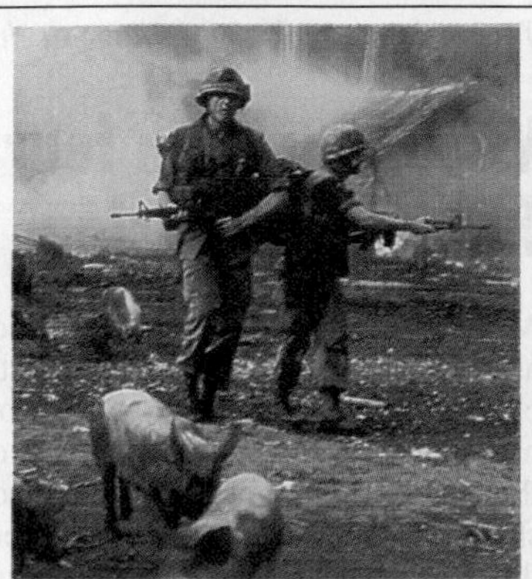

Robert de Niro goes to war – in Michael Cimino's Vietnam movie "The Deer Hunter".

Vietnamese reveal Pol Pot's mass graves

April 2. Gruesome evidence of the mass murders carried out by the Khmer Rouge regime of Pol Pot in Cambodia has been discovered near the town of Stung Treng in the north-east of this once beautiful, but now fearful country.

The new Phnom Penh administration, put into power by the invading Vietnamese, has announced that 2,000 skeletons, tied together with ropes and weighted with stones, have been found in a lake south of the town.

More bones and piles of skulls have been found in shallow ditches dug in a nearby forest. Awful as these discoveries are, they are believed to represent only a small fraction of the hundreds of thousands of people who were murdered or worked to death on starvation rations by Pol Pot's commissars.

One of the problems for the new administration is that they have no records of those who were forced out of the towns to die in the jungle. Whole families, tribes and villages were wiped out, and refugees who survived are too frightened to return to their homes. There is no doubt, however, that a frightful calamity has befallen the people of Cambodia (→30/7).

This pile of bones represents only a fraction of Khmer Rouge's victims.

New Uganda leader backs rule of law

April 13. Thousands of whooping and stamping Ugandans lined the 20-mile route from Entebbe airport to the capital Kampala as Yusuf Lule returned from exile to become president after the Tanzanian-backed overthrow of Idi Amin.

Arriving in the war-torn capital, where shops and offices had been looted, Mr Lule, aged 57 and a former vice-chancellor of Kampala's Makerere University, went directly to the parliament building to take the oath of office beneath the Ugandan flag. He said: "We must not indulge in the evil acts of the regime we have removed. Respect for life and individual rights must be paramount. The rule of law must be established" (→27/5/80).

Ex-premier Bhutto hanged in Pakistan

April 4. Zulfikar Ali Bhutto, the deposed Premier of Pakistan, was hanged in the early hours of today and buried before news of his death reached his followers. Convicted of the murder of a political opponent, Mr Bhutto is widely viewed as the victim of a judicial murder set up by the military ruler, General Zia.

The news of his death brought thousands of demonstrators onto the streets screaming for revenge against Zia. Mourners attending a prayer meeting were whipped into a frenzy of sorrow and anger when they were told that, as he stood on the scaffold with the hangman's noose around his neck, his last words were "O Lord, help me, for I am innocent".

1979

MAY

Su	Mo	Tu	We	Th	Fr	Sa
		1	2	3	4	5
6	7	8	9	10	11	12
13	14	15	16	17	18	19
20	21	22	23	24	25	26
27	28	29	30	31		

1. Washington: Republican George Bush says he will run for President in 1980 (→4/3/80).

3. UK: Jeremy Thorpe loses his seat in the election.→

4. UK: Labour makes widespread gains in local elections, and wins control of the GLC (→5).

5. London: Lord Carrington is Foreign Secretary, Sir Geoffrey Howe becomes Chancellor and William Whitelaw Home Secretary (→10).

7. Tehran: Khomeini lowers the age of marriage for girls to 13, for boys to 15 (→8/6).

8. Manchester: Ten die and 47 are hurt when fire breaks out in a branch of Woolworth's.

10. London: Tony Benn says he will not stand for the shadow cabinet to allow him greater freedom of expression (→15).

12. Wembley: Ipswich Town beat Arsenal 1-0 in the FA Cup Final.

15. London: Thatcher outlines her government's plans: lower taxes and public spending and curbs on union power (→17).

18. US: The estate of nuclear worker Karen Silkwood wins $10.5 million for atomic contamination she suffered in 1974.

21. London: Thatcher wins her first division as MPs approve proposals to sell off parts of nationalised industries (→25).

23. Ottawa: Trudeau concedes victory to Progressive Conservative leader Joe Clark in the Canadian general election (→4/6).

25. UK: Milk goes up to 15p a pint (→27).

27. UK: The situation in Iran provokes panic buying of petrol, with prices hitting £1.22 a gallon (→12/6).

29. Salisbury: Muzorewa is sworn in as Rhodesia's first black premier (→1/6).

DEATH

29. Canadian-born US actress Mary Pickford, born Gladys Smith (*9/4/1893).

Ex-Liberal leader on murder charge

Norman Scott at the Old Bailey.

May 18. A one-time male model told an Old Bailey jury today of an alleged homosexual relationship with Jeremy Thorpe, the former Liberal leader. Norman Scott, aged 39, said that Thorpe had twice seduced him at the MP's mother's home in Surrey.

Thorpe, aged 50, is accused with three other men of conspiring to murder Scott. The prosecution is alleging that Thorpe saw disclosure of the relationship as a threat to his political ambitions.

Scott claimed that Thorpe had hugged him and called him "poor bunny" before getting into bed with him (→22/6).

Nottingham Forest win European Cup

May 30. Just three months after joining the club as Britain's first million-pound footballer, Trevor Francis marked his first appearance in the European Cup by heading home a superbly worked goal seconds before half-time.

Against the unfancied but resilient Swedish champions Malmo, Nottingham Forest held on to their lead to bring the Cup to England for the third successive year. ▷

Thatcher wins election

Margaret Thatcher rejoices as Tory government returns to Britain.

May 4. The Tories rule Britain again and the nation has its first woman Prime Minister. On the threshold of 10 Downing Street, a triumphant 53-year-old Margaret Thatcher said this afternoon: "Where there is discord may we bring harmony ... where there is despair may we bring hope."

Having quoted from St. Francis of Assisi she went inside to embark on what she promised will be complete transformation of the British economic and industrial climate.

It has been a watershed general election, with a difference of two million votes between the major parties. The final seats tally is Tories 339, Labour 269, Liberals 11, Ulster parties 12 and Nationalists four. This gives the new Government an overall majority of 43. "I feel an aura of calm," the new Prime Minister said as she began to pick her team.

There will be no place in it for ex-premier Edward Heath whom she ousted from the Tory leadership. He is refusing her offer to make him ambassador in Washington. The TUC will be another problem for her. Tonight it showed its teeth and growled "keep your hands off the unions". With early union-curbing laws likely, it warned that "persecution begets resistance".

DC-10s grounded in wake of air crash

May 29. All DC-10 airliners in both Britain and the United States were grounded today following the disaster in Chicago four days ago when an engine ripped off the wing of an aircraft on take-off.

A total of 273 people died in the worst crash in American history and since then inspections have found weaknesses in many DC-10 engine mounts. Two Laker Airways DC-10s flying to the United States turned back to Gatwick as soon as the order was made.

The US Federal Aviation Administration said the flaws found were both "grave and potentially dangerous".

Cathedral massacre shocks El Salvador

May 10. Some 20,000 mourners walked through the streets of San Salvador today, in a funeral procession for 17 of the 24 people killed by police and soldiers two days ago when they opened fire on a crowd of 300 demonstrating peacefully outside the Metropolitan Cathedral. The group had been showing its support for the members of the anti-government Popular Revolutionary Bloc, who occupied the cathedral and also the Costa Rican and French embassies, where they held six hostages. Mentioning previous massacres, a woman said: "This is the first time they've fired on a cathedral" (→3/7).

1979

JUNE

Su	Mo	Tu	We	Th	Fr	Sa
					1	2
3	4	5	6	7	8	9
10	11	12	13	14	15	16
17	18	19	20	21	22	23
24	25	26	27	28	29	30

1. Salisbury: Rhodesia is renamed Zimbabwe-Rhodesia (→4/7).

2. Warsaw: Pope John Paul II is welcomed in his native land on the first visit by a Pope to a Communist country.→

4. Ottawa: Joe Clark is sworn in as Prime Minister (→18/2/80).

5. London: The Archbishop of Canterbury, Dr Coggan, says he will retire to give way for a younger man (→25/3/80).

6. UK: The 200th Derby is won by Sir Michael Sobell's Troy with the biggest winning margin in 54 years.

6. Managua: President Somoza declares a state of siege (→21).

10. UK: The Tories win 60 and Labour 17 of Britain's 81 Euro-seats, but Socialists are the largest European group (→25/9).

12. London: Howe's first budget cuts the standard tax rate by 3p and lowers the top rate from 83 to 60 per cent (→23/7).

15. Vienna: Carter and Brezhnev meet for the first time.→

18. London: Neil Kinnock, with no previous government experience, becomes shadow education spokesman (→2/10).

20. US: Opposition to Somoza grows after the screening of an ABC reporter being murdered by Nicaraguan troops (→20/7).

21. Malaysia: The government begins turning back Vietnamese refugees into international waters.

25. Belgium: General Haig, chief of Allied Forces in Europe, narrowly escapes assassination by a car bomb (→12/12).

26. US: Muhammad Ali is to retire (→31/12).

28. Geneva: OPEC agrees to a 15 per cent oil price rise, which would put up to 13p a gallon on petrol in Britain.

DEATH

11. US actor John Wayne, born Marion Morrison (*26/5/1907).→

The Duke rides the range in the sky

June 11. John Wayne lost his fight against cancer today and America is mourning a symbol of manhood. Wayne, who was 72, began his career under his real name, Marion Morrison, nicknamed "Duke", as a student on vacation. He met and worked for the director John Ford, who became his father figure.

It was Ford's first big Western, "Stagecoach", that made Wayne's newly-adopted name. By 1950, after a series of war movies, he was the top box-office actor in America and also the highest-paid. He won his Oscar in "True Grit" as a one-eyed US marshal running to fat. He was married three times and had seven children.

Wayne – never a shot in anger.

Slush fund scandal forces Vorster out

June 4. The so-called Muldergate scandal, named after Dr Connie Mulder, the former Information Minister, today forced the resignation of South Africa's President John Vorster. The report of a judicial commission says Mr Vorster had "full knowledge of all the irregularities" in the Information Department, which set up a secret fund to promote South Africa's interests abroad. Millions of pounds went missing and Dr Eschel Rhoodie, a Department head, has disappeared after accusations of mishandling funds (→3/10).

Brezhnev and Carter sign SALT treaty

June 18. In the baroque splendour of Vienna's Hofburg Palace, the leaders of the two superpowers, Jimmy Carter and Leonid Brezhnev, today signed the SALT-2 arms limitation treaty. "A victory in the battle for peace," President Carter said. "We are helping to defend the most sacred right of every man, the right to live," said Mr Brezhnev.

The treaty restricts each side to a ceiling of 2,250 strategic nuclear missiles by 1981, requiring Moscow to dismantle about 270 launchers and allowing Washington to bring 190 more into service, but no limitation has been placed on the number of warheads.

The treaty faces fierce opposition in the US Senate, where a two-thirds majority is required for ratification. Senator Henry Jackson has described the agreement as "a new Munich", because he believes it does not actually restrain the Russian arms build-up.

Though official NATO reaction in Brussels was favourable, European members of the alliance are anxious over the implications for their security. Though SALT-2 restricts the intercontinental missiles, it will leave Western Europe exposed to the threat posed by Russia's massive build-up of SS-20 medium range mobile missiles.

Brezhnev and Carter shake hands after signing the arms treaty in Vienna.

After the signing, Mr Carter flew to Washington to address Congress.

Mr Brezhnev, a sick man, seemed on the point of collapse as he tottered along the carpeted runway to his plane. Waving slowly and mechanically, he was assisted up the plane steps (→ 17/6/81).

Jury finds Thorpe innocent of murder plot after 52 hours

June 22. Jeremy Thorpe's ordeal ended today as a jury – after three days of deliberation – found the former Liberal leader not guilty of plotting a murder. Thorpe, who had spent two nights in Brixton Prison waiting to hear the verdict, was also cleared of a charge of inciting others to kill Norman Scott. Three other men, George Deakin, David Holmes – a former deputy treasurer of the Liberal Party – and John le Mesurier, were also found not guilty.

During the 31 days of the trial, the prosecution had claimed that the disclosure of an alleged homosexual relationship between Thorpe and Scott would have imperilled Thorpe's political future.

Outside the court, an ebullient Thorpe faced a mass of press and television reporters and described the verdict as "fair, just and a complete vindication" (→ 10/10).

Millions waving Catholic icons greet Pope in Communist Poland

June 2. More than two million Poles lined the streets from the airport to Warsaw today to welcome Pope John Paul II in the first visit of a Pope to a Communist country since the end of World War II.

In place of the usual red flags and pictures of Communist leaders were pictures of Christ, the Virgin Mary and Vatican flags. People threw roses, carnations and irises into his path and cheered and shouted, "Long live the Pope".

Earlier, the Pope had walked slowly down the steps of the Boeing jet and immediately knelt down. "I have kissed the ground of Poland on which I grew up, and the land from which, through the inscrutable design of Providence, God called me to the chair of Peter in Rome, the land to which I am coming today as a pilgrim," he said.

He was welcomed by Cardinal Wyszynski, Primate of Poland, and President Jablonski. When asked about the political significance of the visit he told journalists: "Communism and capitalism are realities, but underneath stand the people. This is a human reality."

Poland may be Communist, but the crowds still gather for John Paul II.

More than a quarter of a million people crowded into Victory Square in the middle of Warsaw for an open air mass. Many wept openly as the Pope blessed them from a raised dais in front of a 30 ft cross draped in red stoles.

Although Poland is officially atheist, millions still follow the traditional Catholic faith. The government has bowed to the inevitable in meeting the Pope and in today's brilliant sunshine all was peace and harmony.

Euro elections are a bore, say Britons

June 8. The British people have regarded the first direct elections for the European Parliament as a great bore. Fewer than one in three registered voters (32 per cent) bothered to go to the polls. Voting turn-out was also low in other Common Market countries in the greatest multi-national transaction in democracy that the world has known.

Sixty Tories, 17 Labour and one Scottish Nationalist have been elected for the 78 Euro constituencies in mainland Britain. This landslide victory for the Tories was on the cards after their return to power at Westminster last month.

The turn-out would probably have been higher if the elections had been held before Britain's own general election and thus treated as a rehearsal. In the event, Labour hardly bothered to campaign. For ardent Europeans it is galling that the level of interest is comparable to that shown in filling a council seat in a local government district election (→ 10).

1979

JULY

Su	Mo	Tu	We	Th	Fr	Sa
1	2	3	4	5	6	7
8	9	10	11	12	13	14
15	16	17	18	19	20	21
22	23	24	25	26	27	28
29	30	31				

2. Wimbledon: 16-year-old Tracy Austin knocks Billie Jean King out of the Ladies' Singles in straight sets (→7).

3. El Salvador: Two British bankers are released by guerrillas seven months after the payment of a ransom (→15/11).

4. London: Thatcher moves to normalise relations with Zimbabwe-Rhodesia (→1/8).

5. Tehran: The government announces the nationalisation of most of the remaining big industry in private hands (→9).

7. Wimbledon: Martina Navratilova beats Chris Evert in the Ladies' Singles final; Bjorn Borg beats Roscoe Tanner in the Men's Singles final.

9. Tehran: Khomeini announces an amnesty for all jailed under the Shah except murderers and torturers (→23).

12. London: Thatcher attacks the BBC for an interview on "Tonight" with an INLA terrorist (→2/8).

13. US: The Federal Aviation Authority lifts its grounding of DC-10s.

17. Oslo: Sebastian Coe runs a mile in a record 3 minutes 48.95 seconds (→15/8).

19. Lisbon: Maria Pintassilgo becomes Portugal's first woman Prime Minister.

22. Indonesia: 750 are feared dead after a tidal wave hits the island of Lomblen.

23. London: The cabinet agrees to public spending cuts of £4,000 million (→22/10).

23. Iran: Khomeini bans broadcast music, saying it corrupts youth (→23/8).

27. Lusaka: The Queen arrives on a state visit to Zambia (→1/8).

30. Phnom Penh: The new regime accuses Pol Pot's government of murdering three million Cambodians (→19/8).

DEATH

29. German-born US philosopher Herbert Marcuse (*19/7/1898).→

Sandinistas are victorious in Nicaragua

Some of the Sandinista rebels who have overthrown Nicaragua's rulers.

July 20. General Anastasio Somoza Debayle, whose family have ruled Nicaragua since 1933, finally gave in today to the Sandinista rebels. He resigned and flew into exile. He left a country devastated by civil war with fighting still going on in parts of the country. Thousands of people have been killed over the last two months and half a million, one-fifth of the country's population, have been displaced from their homes.

Somoza claimed he had been ousted by a Communist conspiracy. In fact, he had lost the support of conservatives and the business community and of the country's most powerful ally, the United States. It was US officials who worked out the plan to replace Somoza by a five-man junta including businessmen as well as the Sandinistas.

Francisco Uryco Malianos, the President of the Chamber of Deputies, is to be the transitional President. There was a last-minute hitch when he at first declined to surrender power to the junta.

There is widespread relief that the authoritarian regime of Somoza is at an end, but many difficulties lie ahead. How long the Marxist Sandinistas will be able to work harmoniously with a business group, which is dedicated to fostering private enterprise, is an open question.

July 5. The Isle of Man celebrated the 1,000th anniversary of its Parliament or "Tynwald" with a ceremony attended by the Queen. Meanwhile the beaches saw a recreation of the first Viking landings on the island.

Seve Ballesteros wins British Open

July 20. Fully 72 years after Arnaud Massy of France beat the giants of the day at Hoylake, Spanish golfer Severiano Ballesteros today become only the second golfer from the continent of Europe to capture the British Open Championship.

In a final round of aggression, luck and cool opportunism, marked by a succession of huge wayward drives and almost unbelievable recoveries, the 22-year-old from Pedrena, in Northern Spain, mastered a cruel, blustery wind at Lytham St. Anne's to record a 70 – the best of the day among the leading contenders – and beat the holder, Jack Nicklaus, by three clear strokes.

Spain's golfing hero, Ballesteros.

Marcuse, father of New Left, is dead

July 29. Herbert Marcuse, the guru of the student revolutionary movements of the Sixties, has died aged 81. He denounced the "repressive monolith" of Western capitalist society and proposed in its place an intoxicating mixture of permissive sex and radical politics. His books "One Dimensional Man" and "Eros and Civilisation", inspired the New Left, but the revolutionary coalition of urban blacks, students and white intellectuals he hoped for has yet to come about.

Algerian hero freed after 14 years' jail

Ben Bella, freed after 14 years.

July 4. Ahmed Ben Bella, confined under guard for 14 years after being overthrown as President of Algeria, was released today. Now 62, he was once the hero of Algerian independence, even though he was captured by the French when they forced down his aircraft. He spent most of the war in French detention before returning in triumph.

A former French army sergeant, he became a flamboyant statesman amongst Third World politicians and guerrilla leaders. It was a style which did not suit his old comrade Houari Boumedienne, who deposed him in 1963. The newly-elected President, Chadli Benjedid, sees Ben Bella as yesterday's man, too old to be a threat.

Nigeria seizes BP in sanctions row

July 31. Britain reacted with shock and anger today at the sudden seizure of British Petroleum's Nigerian assets by the country's military regime. "I can think of nothing more counter-productive and less likely to succeed than an attempt of this kind to move government policy on South Africa," said Lord Carrington, the Foreign Secretary. BP officials said the company, which has lost nine per cent of its oil supplies, was being used as a "political football".

1979

AUGUST

Su	Mo	Tu	We	Th	Fr	Sa
			1	2	3	4
5	6	7	8	9	10	11
12	13	14	15	16	17	18
19	20	21	22	23	24	25
26	27	28	29	30	31	

1. Lusaka: Commonwealth leaders begin talks amid deep divisions on Zimbabwe-Rhodesia.→

2. Northern Ireland: An IRA landmine kills two soldiers, bringing to 301 the number of Army deaths since 1969 (→27).

3. Equatorial Guinea: One of the world's most brutal dictators, Francisco Nguema, is overthrown in a coup.

6. Mauritania: The government concedes defeat in the former Spanish Sahara to the Polisario guerrilla movement.

9. US: Ku Klux Klansmen begin a 50-mile "white rights" march from Selma to Montgomery, Alabama (→18/5/80).

14. Norwich: John Stonehouse is released from prison.

15. USSR: 150 die in a collision between two Aeroflot airliners over the Ukraine (→28/11).

17. UK: The Fastnet death toll reaches 18.

19. USSR: Two cosmonauts return to earth after a record 175 days in space (→11/10/80).

21. UK: Essex become County Cricket Champions for the first time.

23. Iran: Fighting resumes between Iranian troops and Kurdish rebels, after 18 Kurds were executed on August 21 (→23/10).

26. Salisbury: Muzorewa announces that the country is to be renamed Zimbabwe (→7/9).

28. Ireland: Dowager Lady Brabourne dies of injuries from the bomb that killed Mountbatten (→30).

30. Dublin: Two are charged with the murder of Lord Mountbatten (→5/9).

DEATHS

16. Canadian statesman John George Diefenbaker, Prime Minister 1957-63 (*18/9/1895).

27. British commander and statesman Admiral of the Fleet Louis Francis Albert Victor Nicholas Mountbatten, first Earl Mountbatten of Burma (*25/6/1900).→

Thatcher does U-turn on Rhodesian deal

The Queen and Mrs Thatcher at the Lusaka Commonwealth Conference.

Aug 5. A new initiative by Mrs Thatcher, the British Prime Minister, aimed at resolving the Rhodesia-Zimbabwe issue, was unanimously endorsed by the Commonwealth Conference in Lusaka, Zambia, today.

When she arrived last week, Mrs Thatcher was still inclined to accept the so-called internal settlement which has put Bishop Muzorewa in power in Salisbury, but in talks with five key Commonwealth states, Australia, Jamaica, Nigeria, Tanzania and Zambia, she agreed that the exiled leaders of the independence struggle must be part of any settlement.

Britain will now produce a constitution providing for "genuine" black majority rule, and prepare a plan for supervising elections in Rhodesia-Zimbabwe attended by Commonwealth observers (→26).

Seb Coe completes hat-trick of records

Aug 15. Sebastian Coe lit up the night sky of Zurich tonight with the greatest in a series of performances that in the space of six weeks have established the slender 22-year-old Briton as the world's greatest talent in middle-distance running – with only the possible exception of his compatriot, Steve Ovett, the European 1,500 metres champion.

Last month in Oslo, Coe cut a full second off Alberto Juantorena's time to set a world 800 metres record of 1 minute 42.33 seconds. A fortnight later, back in Oslo for the Golden Mile, he captured John Walker's world record in 3 minutes 48.95 seconds. A week ago he won the Europa Cup 800 metres in Turin and today, at the Weltklasse Games in Zurich, he ran a blistering last lap on his own to trim Filbert Bayi's 1,500 metres world record to 3 minutes 32.1 seconds – the first man simultaneously to hold the three records.

Coe sets record number three.

▷

Lord Mountbatten killed by IRA bomb

Aug 27. For more than 30 years, Earl Mountbatten of Burma had spent every August in the quiet fishing village of Mullaghmore, County Sligo. He and his family were familiar faces and well-liked by villagers with whom they mixed freely. He never felt the need of a bodyguard.

It was the middle of the morning when Earl Mountbatten and members of his family drove from their Irish home, Classiebawn Castle, down to the harbour and set out for a day's fishing in their 30-foot boat, Shadow V.

The boat had hardly left the harbour mouth when it was ripped apart by an IRA bomb. Earl Mountbatten, aged 79, statesman and warrior, was killed instantly. His grandson, Nicholas, aged 14, and a 15-year-old boatman, Paul Maxwell, also died in the blast.

Lord Mountbatten's daughter, Lady Brabourne, her son Timothy and her mother-in-law, the Dowager Lady Brabourne, were all said to be "critical" in an intensive-care ward.

Eyewitnesses described a "roaring" explosion which blew the boat high in the air, smashing it into tiny pieces of wood. The party's fishing lines, anoraks and plimsolls floated on the water as the bodies were recovered.

In a statement tonight, the IRA claimed responsibility for "the execution of Lord Louis Mountbatten" and said that the boat had been blown up by remote control. The bomb contained 50 pounds of explosives.

As news of the murders was broken to the Queen, who was said to be "deeply shocked" by the death of her cousin, the outrage was condemned throughout the world. In Mullaghmore, one fisherman said: "He was our friend, not an enemy. Everyone here liked him and will mourn him greatly."

President Carter said he was "profoundly shocked and saddened" by the murders. Senator Edward Kennedy said that "no cause is served by those committing these senseless acts of violence that have plagued Ireland".

"This is mass murder and nothing can justify it," declared Cardinal Tomas O'Fiaich, the Roman Catholic Primate of Ireland. The Irish Deputy Prime Minister, George Colley, said: "I know all Irish people will join me in condemning this cowardly and heartless outrage" (→28).

Earl Mountbatten's corpse is carried ashore from his boat at Mullaghmore.

Army's worst day at hands of IRA

Aug 27. At Warrenpoint, Co Down, an IRA bomb, containing more than half a ton of explosives hidden in a haycart, exploded as an Army convoy drove past today. Fifteen soldiers were killed and eight more "very seriously" injured, said an Army spokesman.

A helicopter was damaged in a further explosion, but managed to fly the wounded to hospital. A gun battle ensued between troops and IRA men across a nearby loch. The death toll was the worse suffered by the army in any single incident and brings the total of soldiers killed in the province since 1969 to 316.

Lord Mountbatten: a much-loved hero

Mountbatten visiting Canada.

Aug 27. The Royal Family was said to be "deeply shocked" by the murder of Earl Mountbatten. The former Viceroy of India was a cousin of the Queen, Prince Philip's uncle, and served as mentor to the Prince of Wales in his later years.

"Dickie" Mountbatten held a unique position in the British establishment. He entered the Royal Navy in 1913, and in World War II became supreme Allied commander in South-east Asia, retaking Burma. Appointed Viceroy by the Attlee government, he presided over the transfer of power to India and Pakistan. The Indian Government has announced a week of mourning for Lord Mountbatten.

Khmer Rouge chief Pol Pot condemned to die for genocide

Aug 19. Pol Pot, the leader of the Khmer Rouge regime overthrown by the invading Vietnamese seven months ago, has today been sentenced to death for the genocide of the Cambodian people during his four years in power.

Millions of skulls in mounds dotting the Cambodian countryside testify to the ferocity of Pol Pot's campaign to wipe out Cambodia's middle class and intellectuals, and there is no doubt that the new Vietnamese-supported government will kill him if they can catch him.

But with his henchman, Leng Sari, who has also been condemned to death, the mass-murderer has vanished into the jungle (→26/9).

14 die as storm hits Fastnet yacht race

Aug 14. Fourteen yachtsmen died as savage Atlantic storms brought havoc to the Fastnet international sailing race today. At least 25 of the 330 yachts between the southern Irish coast and Cornwall were sunk or disabled. Lifeboats, trawlers and tugs joined with helicopters in a huge rescue in force 11 hurricane winds, saving 125 yachtsmen.

Yet some crews, from 18 nations, in the larger craft, were continuing the race. Bottles of champagne for toasting the winners of the Admiral's Cup were instead handed out among relatives to ease their grief (→17).

Granny wins nude sunbathing battle

Aug 9. Following a campaign by a nude bathing fan and grandmother, Mrs Eileen Jakes, Brighton today became the first British seaside resort to open a special area for naturist swimmers near the town centre. Mrs Jakes, aged 47, said she was "overwhelmed" by the new nudist beach, but opposing local councillors still fear the 200-metre stretch of shingle might attract "undesirables" to the resort.

1979

SEPTEMBER

Su	Mo	Tu	We	Th	Fr	Sa
						1
2	3	4	5	6	7	8
9	10	11	12	13	14	15
16	17	18	19	20	21	22
23	24	25	26	27	28	29
30						

2. UK: The "Yorkshire Ripper" murders his 12th victim; police warn "no woman is safe now" (→2/10).

5. UK: Nationwide mourning marks the state funeral of Lord Mountbatten (→16/10).

6. Poland: A dissident group called KOR calls for the right of workers to go on strike (→14/8/80).

7. Mozambique: Over 300 are reported killed in raids by Zimbabwe-Rhodesian troops (→10).

10. UK: BL announces it is to end production of all MG models.

10. London: Nkomo, Mugabe, Muzorewa and Smith attend a conference on the future of Zimbabwe-Rhodesia (→27).

12. London: The Government announces that the postal service is to be split from the telephone network (→14/7/80).

14. London: Plans are announced for the revitalisation of London's docklands (→17/9/81).

16. East Germany: Two families cross to the West in a hot-air balloon made from curtains and sheets.

20. Central African Empire: Bokassa is overthrown by ex-President David Dacko, who abolishes the Empire (→10/10).

25. Strasbourg: The European Court rules that France is acting illegally in restricting imports of British lamb (→30/11).

27. Mozambique: Zimbabwe-Rhodesian troops launch a cross-border raid, despite the London talks (→18/10).

29. Ireland: Pope John Paul II arrives on the first papal visit to Ireland.→

29. Equatorial Guinea: Dictator Nguema is sentenced to death for genocide.

DEATHS

8. US actress Jean Seberg (*13/11/1938).→

27. British actress and entertainer Dame Gracie Fields, born Grace Stansfield (*9/1/1898).

Pope makes peace appeal on Irish visit

Pope John Paul II waves from the "Popemobile" as he tours Ireland.

Sept 30. It was an occasion touched with magic when Pope John Paul flew to Ireland today to visit a people who have clung to the Roman Catholic faith through centuries of tribulations.

His Jumbo jet, St. Patrick, flew to the Tuskar Rock lighthouse, off the south-east coast, to rendezvous with two Irish Air Force jets which escorted it low over an excited countryside; men doffed their hats, women waved, and some dropped to their knees.

In Phoenix Park one and a quarter million people with upturned faces watched the plane descend to Dublin Airport. Two hours later His Holiness arrived in the park himself to celebrate Mass with 40 cardinals and bishops.

Then he led a huge service outside Drogheda where the congregation included 250,000 people from Northern Ireland, among them Gerry Fitt MP, leader of the Social Democratic and Labour Party.

The Pope told the largely young audience: "On my knees I beg you to turn away from violence. Further violence will only drag down to ruin the land you claim to love and the values you claim to cherish" (→1/10).

President Carter entered this six-mile race in Maryland, but the pace proved too hot, and Carter had to leave the race.

Fred and David hit US and Puerto Rico

Sept 12. The second hurricane in a week scythed across the southern American state of Florida today. As it crashed ashore from the Gulf of Mexico it sent 500,000 people fleeing inland and caused damage estimated at £45 million.

In Mobile, Alabama, hundreds of homes were flattened by 130mph winds. Power to dozens of communities was cut and many roads were blocked. Despite the chaos a large death toll was averted by a huge evacuation of the coastline as Hurricane Frederick closed in.

A similar operation last week saved lives when Hurricane David hit. It had led to 1,000 deaths in Puerto Rico, the Dominican Republic and Haiti.

Yorkshire Ripper claims 12th victim

Sept 2. A killer known as the "Yorkshire Ripper" today claimed his 12th victim with the murder of a girl student. He has succeeded in evading capture during a four-year reign of terror, and detectives at the centre of one of Britain's biggest manhunts issued a warning that no woman was safe to be out on the streets at night on her own.

By attacking Barbara Leach, aged 20, a student from Bradford University, the murderer had proved he was now picking off his victims at random, police said. Her mutilated body was found on the fringes of the city's red light district, but unlike 8 of the Ripper's other victims she had no links with vice. He struck as she walked by.

FBI smeared name of dead actress

Sept 8. Jean Seberg, the small-town girl from Iowa whom Otto Preminger chose to play St. Joan out of 80,000 applicants, was found dead in the back of a parked car in Paris yesterday. She disappeared ten days ago with a blanket and a tube of pills. She was almost 41 years old.

Her ex-husband, the author Romain Gary, claimed that she had been made suicidal by the FBI after she took up the cause of the Black Panthers. They spread rumours that she was pregnant by a Panther. Her still-born baby was white.

Jean Seberg: harassed by the FBI.

Big aid effort for Cambodia launched

Cambodian refugees huddle together in a camp across the Thai border.

Sept 26. The Red Cross and the United Nations Children's Fund (UNICEF) today launched a massive food and medical aid operation in Cambodia in order to save an estimated two million lives.

They are reported to have received promises of cooperation from both the official Cambodian regime, installed after a Vietnamese invasion toppled Pol Pot's Khmer Rouge, and the Khmer Rouge itself, which still holds power in large parts of the country.

The initiative comes as Vietnam is reported to have launched its second major offensive of the year in Cambodia, adding to the already desperate burden of the Cambodian people. Vietnam intends to wipe out the 30,000-odd men still loyal to the Khmer Rouge, whose main bastions are close to the Thai border.

There is a steady stream of refugees flowing across the border into Thailand, which is expected to swell rapidly. Disease and famine are taking their toll, but Vietnam says reports of food shortages are exaggerated, and has ridiculed Western plans to send aid to areas controlled by the Khmer Rouge. It denies the existence of such areas, more for propaganda purposes than anything else.

Aid officials, however, say they have got approval from both Hanoi and Phnom Penh for relief flights to land in Phnom Penh.

Surrounded by the sailors to whom he owed a lifelong allegiance, Earl Mountbatten's coffin, draped with a flag, moves through the streets. Thousands of mourners lined the streets of London to pay a last tribute.

1979

OCTOBER

Su	Mo	Tu	We	Th	Fr	Sa
	1	2	3	4	5	6
7	8	9	10	11	12	13
14	15	16	17	18	19	20
21	22	23	24	25	26	27
28	29	30	31			

1. Boston: Pope John Paul arrives on a US tour (→ 6).

2. Brighton: The Labour Party Conference votes for mandatory re-selection of Labour MPs (→ 21/3/80).

2. UK: Yorkshire Police launch a £1 million publicity campaign to try to find the "Yorkshire Ripper" (→ 19/11).

3. UK: South Africa's Barbarians rugby team begin a British tour amid widespread protests (→ 26/5/80).

6. Washington: Carter welcomes the Pope; they issue a joint appeal for peace (→ 2/5/80).

10. UK: Jeremy Thorpe says he will not stand for Parliament again.

10. France: The satirical paper "Le Canard Enchaine" claims ex-Emperor Bokassa gave Giscard diamonds (→ 24/12/80).

14. Bonn: 100,000 demonstrators march against nuclear power stations.

15. El Salvador: A military coup topples President Carlos Romero (→ 7/3/80).

16. Ireland: Desmond O'Hare, one of the most wanted men in Ulster, is arrested (→ 23/11).

18. London: Guerrilla leaders accept Britain's Rhodesian charter (→ 7/11).

21. London: Unions and management at "The Times" and "The Sunday Times" reach agreement on a settlement (→ 12/11).

22. London: The Government says it will outlaw "insider trading" (→ 1/11).

26. Seoul: President Park Chung Hee is "accidentally" shot dead by his intelligence chief (→ 27/5/80).

27. West Indies: St.Vincent and Grenada become independent of Britain (→ 27/3/81).

30. London: Martin Webster of the National Front is found guilty of inciting racial hatred (→ 27/5/80).

DEATH

30. British air engineer Sir Barnes Neville Wallis (*26/9/1887).

Nobel Prize for the CAT scan inventor

Nobel scientist Hounsfield.

Oct 11. Godfrey Hounsfield, a 60-year-old British scientist who never went to university, was today named as joint winner of the Nobel Prize for Medicine for his invention of the EMI body scanner. He got the idea for the scanner while walking. "I always get quite a lot of ideas rambling," he said.

His invention is also known as a CAT scanner – standing for computerised axial tomography. This enables pictures of the body to be produced electronically, without the invasive techniques of X-rays. The scanner allows bleeding, clots, abscesses and growths to be diagnosed more easily, and has proved particularly valuable in assessing brain problems.

A body scanner currently costs £341,000, and sales have already boosted British exports by over £200 million. Godfrey Hounsfield, head of the EMI research laboratories in Hayes, Middlesex, shares the Nobel Prize with Allan Cormack, an American (→ 14/1/80).

Women's marathon time-barrier bust

Oct 21. Grete Waitz, the trailblazing long-distance runner from Norway, has broken one of the most formidable barriers in women's athletics, beating two-and-a-half hours for the 26 miles 385 yards of the New York Marathon. Despite 74-degree heat, and in only her second attempt at the distance, the 26-year-old won in two hours 27 minutes 32.6 seconds

1979

NOVEMBER

Su	Mo	Tu	We	Th	Fr	Sa
				1	2	3
4	5	6	7	8	9	10
11	12	13	14	15	16	17
18	19	20	21	22	23	24
25	26	27	28	29	30	

1. London: The Government announces £3,500 million spending cuts and an increase in prescription charges (→13).

2. Ireland: Security forces seize £500,000 worth of weapons for the IRA from US sympathisers.

4. New York: Iranian students protest against the ex-Shah's presence in the US.→

5. Dublin: The trial begins of two men accused of murdering Lord Mountbatten (→23).

7. Stockholm: The King says his successor will be his eldest child, whether male or female.

9. UK: Four men are found guilty of murdering newspaper boy Carl Bridgewater.

9. London: Newscaster Reginald Bosanquet resigns from ITN.

12. UK: "The Times" appears for the first time in almost a year.

13. UK: The miners reject a 20 per cent pay increase and warn they will take action to secure their 65 per cent claim (→22).

17. Tehran: Khomeini orders the release of all women and black US hostages (→21).

20. Saudi Arabia: Gunmen seize the Grand Mosque in Mecca, Islam's holiest shrine.→

21. Tehran: The Iranians warn that if the US attacks Iran all the embassy hostages will die "on the spot" (→23).

22. UK: Building societies put the mortgage rate up 3.5 per cent to a record 15 per cent (→20/12).

23. Tehran: Economics and Foreign Minister Abol Hassan Bani-Sadr declares void all Iranian foreign debts (→4/2).

23. Dublin: Thomas McMahon is jailed for life for killing Lord Mountbatten (→16/12).

26. Saudi Arabia: 160 die when an airliner carrying Mecca pilgrims explodes (→9/1/80).

28. Antarctica: 257 are feared dead when a DC-10 crashes into a mountain (→25/4/80).

Sick Shah flies to US for treatment

Oct 23. The exiled Shah of Iran is recovering in a New York hospital from an operation to remove his gall bladder. It has also been admitted that he has cancer of the lymph glands. During the operation surgeons took tissue samples to determine the rate at which the cancer is spreading through his body.

While the operation was being performed, a group of demonstrators gathered in response to the urging of Iran's "hanging judge", Ayatollah Khalkhali, for Moslems to drag him out of his hospital bed and dismember him (→4/11).

Chairman Hua wins Thatcher's praise

Chairman Hua under royal guard.

Oct 28. Chairman Hua Kuo-feng, the first leader of Communist China to visit Britain, was welcomed by Mrs Thatcher on his arrival in London today.

The Prime Minister pulled out all the stops. She said: "The great and historic nation of China has a crucial role to play in world affairs." The aim of British diplomacy is to get China divorced irrevocably from Russia.

Mrs Thatcher is ready to offer Chairman Hua favourable trade terms. In Moscow, Pravda criticised him for visiting the West; Russia fears that Britain and France will sell arms to China (→29/2/80).

Iran takes US hostages

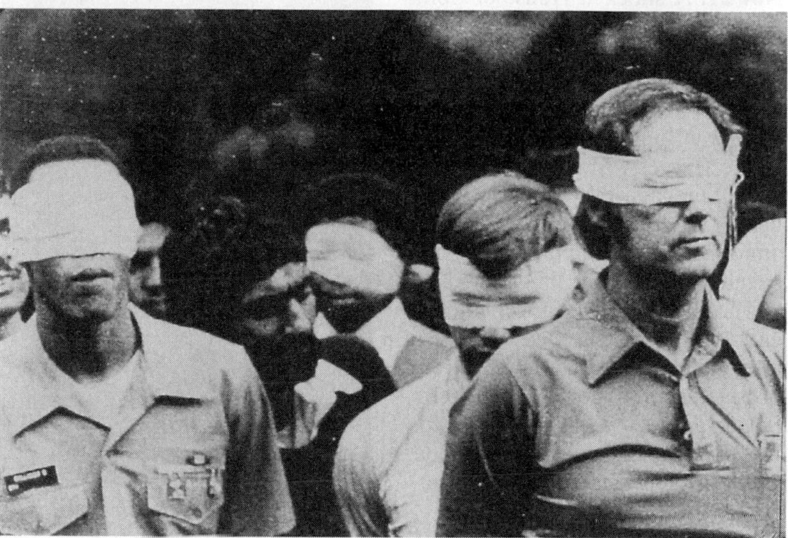

Blindfolded members of the US embassy are escorted by Iranian radicals.

Nov 4. Fanatical followers of the Ayatollah Khomeini stormed the United States Embassy in Tehran today, brushed aside the Marine guards, occupied the building, and took nearly 100 embassy staff and Marines hostage.

Tonight the hostages, women among them, are being held under close guard behind the locked gates of the sprawling embassy, once the seat of American power in the Middle East.

Some of the hostages were blindfolded and handcuffed before being led to a basement room, according to a Revolutionary Guard, one of those supposed to be protecting the Americans when the "students" swarmed over the embassy's walls.

Outside, thousands of demonstrators chanted anti-American slogans and gave some indication of what might happen to the Shah if President Carter gave in to their demands to send him back. An improvised gallows was hoisted above the crowd to thunderous applause. From it dangled a notice saying "For the Shah".

The cheers turned to shouts of hate as two American flags were burned. A placard said "USA, we want the Shah soon". Another boasted "When Khomeini fights, Carter trembles".

The attitude of the Ayatollah is crucial to the development of what threatens to be a dangerous situation. When Revolutionary Guards occupied the embassy earlier this year, he ordered them out, but he has made no move to intervene in today's events, and some of the occupiers claim they are acting on his authority (→17).

American Embassy stormed in Pakistan

Nov 21. Islamic anti-American fervour spread to Pakistan today when a huge mob stormed the US embassy in Islamabad. The attackers swarmed all over the building as the 110 Americans trapped inside barricaded themselves in a third-floor vault.

Using rifles snatched from Pakistani police guards, some of the mob opened fire down the air shafts on the roof. One of their bullets killed a 20-year-old Marine guard.

President Zia ordered troops into the grounds and they fought their way through the shrieking crowds to rescue the Americans. The Pakistani ruler later telephoned President Carter and expressed his deep regret at the incident.

It was, however, more than an isolated incident; other US buildings across the country were raided and the British Council library in Rawalpindi was badly damaged. The ostensible reason for the attacks was a rumour that American agents were behind last Tuesday's seizure of the Grand Mosque in Mecca (→24).

Queen's art adviser was a Russian spy

Blunt – Russia's "Fourth Man".

Nov 21. A shocked House of Commons heard today that the Queen's distinguished art adviser was a spy for the Russians. In a written answer, Mrs Thatcher named Sir Anthony Blunt as the "fourth man" in the Burgess, MacLean and Philby affair. As the disclosure was being made, Buckingham Palace announced that Blunt, aged 72, had been stripped of his knighthood.

The PM said that, under interrogation, Blunt admitted in 1964, after being granted immunity from prosecution, to being a long-term Soviet agent – a talent-spotter for Russian Intelligence in pre-War Cambridge. Blunt is abroad, apparently "tipped off" (→ 26/3/81).

Saudi troops recapture mosque in Mecca

Nov 24. In a violent and dramatic assault Saudi Arabian troops today stormed renegade Shi'ite fanatics embattled in the Great Mosque at Mecca, the holiest place in Islam. Moslems fought Moslems in a bloody battle within sight of the Kabaa, a holy building swathed in black cloth which contains the stone given to the Prophet Ismael by the Angel Gabriel.

Before launching the attack King Khaled had sought the approval of religious leaders. A week ago strong Royal forces equipped with armoured personnel carriers surrounded the mosque in which 500 heavily armed Shi'ites were holding hostage thousands of pilgrims.

They had orders not to take prisoners, but it is reported that a 27-year-old theology student leader, convinced that he is the messianic Mahdi, was arrested and is under interrogation. His Shi'ite followers are members of the same sect of Islam as the Ayatollah Khomeini and the Iranian revolutionaries who overthrew the Shah. Saudi Arabia fears that the attack in Mecca may be the beginning of an attempt to overthrow its own monarchy which follows the orthodox Sunni sect of Islam (→ 26).

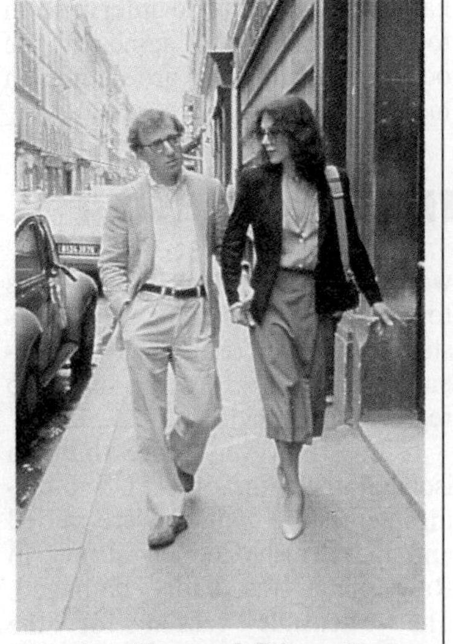
Woody Allen and Diane Keaton stroll down a SoHo street, setting for his film "Manhattan".

Thatcher demands large EEC rebate

Nov 30. "I was not prepared", said Mrs Thatcher in Dublin tonight, "to settle for a third of a loaf." She had asked for the whole loaf – a £1,000 million rebate on what she argued is Britain's unfairly high subscription for Common Market membership.

At an EEC summit meeting, other government leaders offered £350 million. She indignantly rejected this and said that they had to come up with a better proposal within three months. This was the Prime Minister's first encounter with her European opposite numbers. She was rebuffed, but will continue to ask for more (→ 18/3/80).

1979

DECEMBER

Su	Mo	Tu	We	Th	Fr	Sa
						1
2	3	4	5	6	7	8
9	10	11	12	13	14	15
16	17	18	19	20	21	22
23	24	25	26	27	28	29
30	31					

2. Tripoli: The US embassy is attacked and set on fire by 2,000 demonstrators.

4. Iran: A referendum confirms Khomeini as absolute ruler (→ 15).

7. Dublin: Charles Haughey is elected to succeed Jack Lynch as Prime Minister (→ 30/6/81).

7. London: Lord Soames is appointed transitional British Governor of Rhodesia.→

10. Stockholm: Nobel Prizes go to Sheldon Glashow (US), Steven Weinberg (US) and Abdus Salam (Pakistan), all Physics; Herbert Brown (US) and George Wittig (West Germany), both Chemistry; Allan Cormack (US) and Godfrey Hounsfield (UK), both Medicine; Odysseus Elytis (Greece, Literature); Theodore Schultz (US) and Sir Arthur Lewis (UK), both Economics; and in Oslo to Mother Teresa (India, Peace).

15. US: The ex-Shah leaves for exile in Panama after being refused entry to Mexico (→ 22).

16. Northern Ireland: Two remote-control bombs kill five troops (→ 10/2/80).

20. London: The Housing Bill, obliging councils to sell their houses to tenants who want to buy them, is published (→ 2/1/80).

22. Iran: A state of emergency is declared in Baluchistan as fighting with rebels continues (→ 31).

26. Salisbury: Patriotic Front guerrillas return from exile to a rapturous welcome (→ 13/1/80).

HITS OF 1979

Bright eyes.

I don't like Mondays.

We don't talk anymore.

QUOTE OF THE YEAR

"The intensity of a conviction that a hypothesis is true has no bearing over whether it is true or not."

Sir Peter Medawar, scientist, in his book "Advice to a Young Scientist", 1979.

Mother Teresa gets Nobel Peace Prize

Mother Teresa, friend to the poor.

Dec 10. Mother Teresa, the frail and ceaseless campaigner for the world's poor, was awarded the Nobel Peace Prize tonight. The charitable movement which she founded in India now comprises 700 shelters and clinics.

She began her work with the poor of India in 1946, after leaving the relative comfort of a Calcutta convent which she had joined at 18. Born in Albania in 1910, Mother Teresa's enthusiasm for her mission seems never to have waned with advancing years.

Dubbed a "living saint", her achievement has brought world leaders to her door for advice.

Fears of inflation as oil prices double

Dec 31. Oil prices have doubled this year. In December 1978 the average price for crude oil was roughly $12 a barrel; today the average is about $26. The high cost is bound to increase inflation in the short term and depress industrial output in oil-importing countries like Britain.

This month the ministers of the Organisation of Petroleum Exporting Countries (OPEC), meeting in Venezuela, failed to agree on a single price, meaning that importers will pay as much as $40 a barrel for Iranian crude. OPEC is set to reduce output in 1980, which will mean still higher prices (→ 27/3).

Invasion of Afghanistan

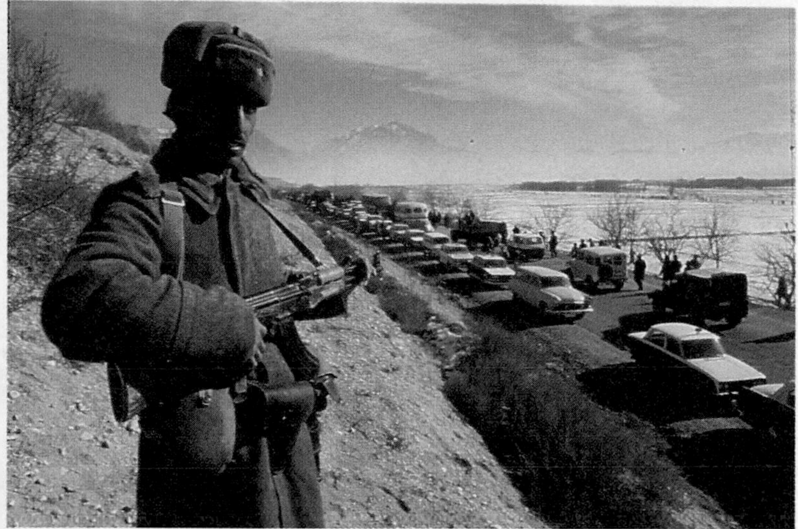

A Soviet soldier looks on as cars move down a road in Afghanistan.

Dec 27. The Soviet move into Afghanistan has become an invasion, with a rapid build-up today of Red Army divisions and the fall of the government in Kabul. The new Afghan leader was named as Babrak Karmal, who has been in exile in Eastern Europe.

The invasion began on Christmas Eve when a crack Soviet unit seized Kabul airport. This opened up the way for a massive airlift of Soviet troops and equipment. At the same time at least four motorised rifle divisions rolled across Afghanistan's northern border, and sped south, covered by several squadrons of Soviet fighters. In Kabul, a special KGB hit squad assaulted the city's Darulaman Place, gunning down the Communist leader Hafizullah Amin and his immediate family.

The Kremlin is claiming that its forces were "requested to render urgent political, moral, military and economic assistance" to Afghanistan.

But Afghans have traditionally vigorously resisted foreign pressure and interference. The Soviet Union may therefore find it difficult to subdue them and install a new government (→2/1/80).

Zimbabwe peace deal signed in London

Dec 21. After 14 years and one month of illegal independence, Rhodesia (or Zimbabwe as it will be known) today became a British colony again and looked forward to an end to the guerrilla war. At Lancaster House in London, Robert Mugabe and Joshua Nkomo, exiled leaders of the war, joined Bishop Muzorewa, the caretaker premier, in signing an accord for a cease-fire and new elections.

Lord Soames, the new (and last) British Governor, has arrived in Salisbury with British troops. Today he declared an amnesty for the black guerrillas and for the white rebels who declared UDI. In New York the UN Security Council lifted sanctions imposed on Rhodesia 13 years ago (→26).

Guerrilla fighters on their way to the British cease-fire headquarters.

Arts: mole-hunting makes compulsive TV

"Tinker Tailor Soldier Spy" has shown that there is no more compulsive medium for the spy story, than television. The BBC lavished every attention on **John Le Carre's** 1974 novel: the casting – notably **Alec Guinness**, teasingly inscrutable as molehunter George Smiley in his bowler hat – adaptation by **Arthur Hopcraft**, direction by **John Irvin**, even the theme music, were striking.

It was a vintage year for TV entertainment, with the revival of "Fawlty Towers", with **John Cleese** rising to new heights of paranoia, and **John Mortimer's** study of a cantankerous barrister, "Rumpole of the Bailey", played with crusty gravitas by **Leo McKern**.

The most original comedy programme since Monty Python also made its bow – "Not the Nine O'Clock News", featuring the new faces of **Rowan Atkinson, Mel Smith, Griff Rhys-Jones** and **Pamela Stephenson**, with a savage line in subversive humour.

Hollywood has produced its delayed shock reactions to the Vietnam war in three disquieting pictures. Its effect on three small-town youths from Pennsylvania is the subject of "The Deer Hunter", with **Robert De Niro** as the survivor who has to come to terms with it as a veteran. "Coming Home" shows the war's legacy to a paraplegic played by **Jon Voight**. "Apocalypse Now" is the attempt by **Francis** Ford Coppola of "Godfather" fame to compare Vietnam with Conrad's story "Heart of Darkness". Brilliant and disturbing photography of violence, helicopters going into the attack to the strains of Wagner, suggests that to some its horrors are attractive.

Coppola's "Apocalypse Now".

The theatrical talking-point of the year was **Peter Shaffer's** "Amadeus", which explored the death of Mozart through the eyes of his mediocre rival and putative murderer Salieri. **Paul Scofield** returned to the National Theatre as Salieri, with **Simon Callow** as the giggling, dirty-minded Mozart, under **Peter Hall's** direction.

Dustin Hoffman in "Kramer vs Kramer": turning divorce into drama.

1980 – 1989

1980

JANUARY

Su	Mo	Tu	We	Th	Fr	Sa
		1	2	3	4	5
6	7	8	9	10	11	12
13	14	15	16	17	18	19
20	21	22	23	24	25	26
27	28	29	30	31		

2. Washington: Carter asks the Senate to delay the nuclear arms treaty because of the invasion of Afghanistan (→29).

2. UK: The first national steel strike since 1926 begins (→17).

3. Kenya: Naturalist Joy Adamson, author of "Born Free", is killed, apparently by a lion.

4. Tehran: UN Secretary-General Kurt Waldheim cuts short a mission to Iran when Khomeini refuses his request to see US hostages (→25).

7. India: Mrs Gandhi wins the general election (→23/6).

9. Saudi Arabia: 63 of the terrorists who seized the Grand Mosque are executed (→28/3).

13. Salisbury: Joshua Nkomo returns to Zimbabwe-Rhodesia for the first time in three years (→27).

14. Washington: The US Surgeon General warns that lung cancer is now the leading killer cancer among women (→16).

17. UK: British Steel will axe 11,287 jobs in Wales by the end of March (→14/2).

20. Belgrade: Tito's left leg is amputated to avoid the spread of gangrene (→16/2).

24. Stockholm: Robin Cousins wins the European Figure Skating Championship.

25. Tehran: Bani Sadr is appointed premier (→29).

25. Tokyo: Paul McCartney is deported after spending nine days in jail suspected of importing marijuana (→6/6).

27. Salisbury: ZANU leader Robert Mugabe returns after five years in exile (→9/2).

31. Amsterdam: Queen Juliana says she will abdicate in favour of her daughter Beatrix (→30/4).

DEATHS

3. Austrian-born naturalist Joy Adamson (*20/1/1920).

18. British photographer and designer Sir Cecil Walter Hardy Beaton (*14/1/1904).→

29. US comedian Jimmy Durante (*10/2/1893).

Moslems protest against Afghan invasion

A Moslem fighter from the Afghan mujahideen, waiting for the Soviets.

Jan 29. As the number of Soviet troops in Afghanistan following last month's invasion climbed to over 80,000, the Moslem world today sharply rebuked the Kremlin and called for a Soviet withdrawal.

The Islamic conference, meeting in Islamabad, represents 36 countries, some of whom traditionally have good relations with Moscow. But it condemned Russia's intervention as a flagrant violation of international law and demanded the immediate and unconditional withdrawal of the Soviet troops.

Meanwhile there are increasing reports of fierce fighting between Soviet and Afghan army units on the one hand and Afghan rebel forces, known as the mujahideen, on the other. Much of this fighting is well away from Soviet bases. Moscow's "limited contingent", however, is being obliged to take on a progressively greater burden for the overall military effort than it originally planned.

The mujahideen can be expected to step up their opposition and the Russians may discover that the reliability and effectiveness of the Afghan armed forces has been over-estimated.

The invasion will provide the Red Army with an invaluable testing ground for new weapons and tactics, but it has already affected Soviet relations with the United States, and the cause of detente (→22/2).

Local people came down to the sea to look at the Greek cargo ship "Athina B", which ran aground near Brighton after a Channel storm.

Dissident Sakharov faces internal exile

Jan 22. Dr Andrei Sakharov, the Soviet Union's most prominent dissident, was arrested today, stripped of all state honours and exiled to Gorky, a Volga city 250 miles east of Moscow closed to foreigners. Dr Sakharov and his wife were seized by the KGB security police in a Moscow street and given two hours to pack before being flown to Gorky. Earlier this month he spoke out against the Soviet invasion of Afghanistan. His arrest has caused a storm of protest in the West (→22/11/81).

Beaton, exquisite style arbiter, dies

My fair gentleman: Cecil Beaton.

Jan 18. Sir Cecil Beaton, the arbiter of style for his generation, died today at his exquisite 17th-century home at Broadchalke, Wiltshire, aged 76. He made his name in the Twenties by his elegantly exhibitionist photographs of the Sitwells. He was chief illustrator of Vogue and his royal portraits were as romanticised as Winterhalter's.

His stage and film designs for "Gigi" and "My Fair Lady" had dazzling opulence and won him Oscars, while his Diaries charted his (platonic) love for Garbo.

Eagle swapped for maple to aid Iran flight

Even the children of Iran are recruited to make anti-US propaganda.

Jan 29. Six American diplomats, who had been in hiding in the Canadian embassy in Tehran ever since their own embassy was occupied nearly three months ago, arrived in America last night after making a daring escape from Iran.

Their getaway was largely engineered by the CIA, which made the crucial forgeries of Iranian visa stamps which were then put into Canadian passports to enable the Americans to leave the country.

The Iranians are furious with the Canadians and Mr Ghotbzadeh, the Foreign Minister, threatened tonight that the Canadians would be made to pay "sooner or later, somewhere in the world", for smuggling the Americans out of Tehran.

His threat was shrugged aside by the Canadians (→4/2).

Secrets of the natural virus killer cracked

Jan 16. Scientists working at Boston's Harvard University today announced that they have successfully synthesised interferon, a natural virus-fighting agent, by genetic engineering.

The substance was first discovered by British scientists in 1957, working at the National Institute for Medical Research at Mill Hill. The researchers, Drs Isaacs and Lindemann, noted interferon's ability to restrict the growth of common cold and other viruses. The race to isolate it started then.

Recent tests in Sweden suggest that interferon could be valuable in treating cancer; it has arrested the growth of certain tumours. But it is too early to assume that the effect observed in the laboratory will work in the human body.

Britain tops league for women at work

Jan 3. Half of Britain's married women now go out to work – the highest proportion of any Common Market country. The dramatic increase from one in five in 1951 is revealed in a survey by Durham University Business School. At the end of 1978, 9.1 million women had jobs, mainly part-time in the service sector.

A Belfast tragedy, but with a legacy

Jan 21. Anne Maguire, the death of whose three children in 1976 sparked off Northern Ireland's Peace People movement, was found dead with her throat and wrists cut in her Belfast home today. Foul play is not suspected.

Mrs Maguire's sister, Mairead Corrigan, co-founded the movement with Betty Williams.

1980

FEBRUARY

Su	Mo	Tu	We	Th	Fr	Sa
					1	2
3	4	5	6	7	8	9
10	11	12	13	14	15	16
17	18	19	20	21	22	23
24	25	26	27	28	29	

3. US: At least 14 prisoners are murdered by rioting convicts at the New Mexico state penitentiary (→4).

4. Tehran: Bani Sadr becomes Iran's first President (→7).

4. US: The death toll in the New Mexico prison riot approaches 50 as the National Guard restores order.

7. Tehran: Bani Sadr gets increased powers from Khomeini to deal with the US hostage captors (→17).

10. Belfast: Nobel Prize winner Betty Williams, co-founder of the Peace People, resigns "for family reasons".

12. US: The Winter Olympics open at Lake Placid, New York State.

13. UK: Sixpence pieces will cease to be legal tender after June 30.

14. London: Thatcher says state benefit to strikers is to be halved.→

16. Belgrade: Tito is in hospital with weakened kidneys (→8/5).

17. New York: UN Secretary-General Waldheim completes the formation of a commission to look into the ex-Shah's activities (→8/3).

17. UK: The Greek cargo ship Athina B is refloated a month after being stranded on a Brighton beach in a storm.

18. Canada: Trudeau is returned to power in a general election (→20/5).

22. Tel Aviv: The government says it will replace the Israeli pound with a new unit, the shekel (→30/6).

27. Zimbabwe-Rhodesia: The general election begins (→4/3).

29. Peking: Liu Shao-chi, Mao's ex-heir who was sacked in 1964 and died trying to flee China, is rehabilitated.

DEATHS

17. British artist Graham Vivian Sutherland (*24/8/1903).→

22. Austrian artist Oskar Kokoschka (*1/3/1886).

Former Rhodesian premier arrested

Feb 9. Garfield Todd, Prime Minister of Rhodesia from 1953 to 1958 and a long-time supporter of black majority rule, was arrested today when he went to his local police station at Shabani to intercede for a black schoolmaster accused of assisting terrorists. A policeman told Mr Todd: "Let's get down to the nitty-gritty. You are being arrested on the same charges."

After being held for more than four hours he was remanded "out of custody", it is believed after pressure from the Governor, Lord Soames. Mr Todd blamed his arrest on "the Rhodesian white establishment" (→27).

Joshua Nkomo and Garfield Todd.

Martial law after Afghanistan riots

Feb 22. Mounting opposition to the Soviet military presence in Afghanistan led today to anti-Soviet riots in the capital, Kabul, and the imposition of martial law. Three Moslem demonstrators were shot dead in the worst riots since last December's invasion of the country.

There are also reports of increased rebel attacks on Soviet convoys taking supplies and ammunition to towns under government control. President Leonid Brezhnev today called for an end to outside interference in Afghanistan (→21/6).

Striking steel managers blast their bosses

Hundreds of striking pickets outside Hadfield's steel works in Sheffield.

Feb 15. Hopes for an early end to the seven-week-old national steel strike received a setback today when a major rift appeared on the management side. Leaders of the 11,500 middle managers of the British Steel Corporation passed an unprecedented vote of no confidence in the top management, calling it "incompetent".

The attack came at a special conference in Leamington Spa which was attended by top managers up to the level of Bob Scholey, chief executive and deputy chairman. They are seeking an urgent meeting with Sir Keith Joseph, the Industry Secretary, to tell him that the present Board is incapable of restoring the corporation, now losing over £2 million a day, to profitability. Earlier this week, the British Steel chairman, Sir Charles Villiers, was pelted with rotten eggs, fish and fruit by strikers in Middlesbrough.

The strike began in the nationalised steel sector where the workers are fighting the management plans to close down plants. These include the Llanwern and Port Talbot steelworks in South Wales, whose closure is scheduled for March 31 with the loss of 11,287 jobs.

The strike now involves the private steel firms as well. Lord Denning declared this was illegal in the Court of Appeal, but his decision was overturned by the Law Lords early this month (→ 15/2).

Britain's top artist, Sutherland, dies

Feb 17. Graham Sutherland, who died today aged 76, was regarded by such critics as Kenneth Clark as Britain's leading painter. Ironically he is now best known for a picture that no longer exists – his portrait of Churchill which was destroyed by Lady Churchill because it made them both unhappy. He described this as "an act of unparallelled vandalism".

Sutherland's other portraits – of Somerset Maugham, Helena Rubinstein and Lord Beaverbrook – were not "happy" pictures either, but severe and penetrating. His landscapes were also discomfiting.

Last time it was Curry, now skater Cousins can look forward to fame and fortune after scoring a victory in the Olympics.

1980

MARCH

Su	Mo	Tu	We	Th	Fr	Sa
						1
2	3	4	5	6	7	8
9	10	11	12	13	14	15
16	17	18	19	20	21	22
23	24	25	26	27	28	29
30	31					

4. US: Edward Kennedy defeats Carter in the Massachusetts primary (→ 17/7).

7. El Salvador: A state of siege is declared (→ 30).

8. Washington: Carter refuses to apologise for past US actions in Iran in return for the release of the hostages.→

11. Salisbury: Nkomo is home affairs minister in Mugabe's first cabinet, which includes two whites (→ 11/4).

13. West Germany: Robin Cousins wins a silver medal in the World Figure Skating Championships.

16. US: Britain's Alan Minter outpoints Vito Antuofermo of the US for the world middleweight boxing championship.

18. London: Thatcher says she will withhold VAT payments to the EEC if it does not cut Britain's budget contribution (→ 28/4).

20. UK: German industrialist Thomas Niedermeyer, kidnapped in Belfast in 1973, is buried two weeks after his body was found.

21. UK: The Underhill Report reveals a plan to control the Labour Party by Trotskyites called "Militant Tendency" (→ 9/6).

23. Panama: The ex-Shah leaves for Cairo just 24 hours before Iran was due to serve a request for his extradition (→ 17/4).

25. Canterbury: Robert Runcie is enthroned as Archbishop of Canterbury (→ 12/11).

26. London: The budget raises tax allowances and duties on petrol, drink and tobacco (→ 1/4).

29. UK: Mr R. Stuart's Ben Nevis wins the Grand National.

31. UK: BL agrees to sell its MG works at Abingdon to a consortium headed by Aston Martin-Lagonda.

DEATHS

26. French philosopher Roland Barthes (*12/11/1915).

31. US athlete Jesse Owens (*12/9/1913).

Mugabe is elected Zimbabwe premier

March 4. Robert Gabriel Mugabe, aged 52, the Roman Catholic mission boy who became a schoolteacher and a Marxist revolutionary, is Prime Minister of the new state of Zimbabwe. His Zimbabwe African National Union won 57 of the 80 black seats in the 100-member Assembly. The 20 white seats have been won by Ian Smith's Rhodesian Front. Mugabe's rival, Joshua Nkomo, won 20 seats, all in his Matabeleland tribal base.

Mugabe spent 11 years in detention for his commitment to armed resistance to white rule. Since his election victory he has played down Marxism, emphasised moderate socialism and said private business can continue (→ 11).

Mugabe's supporters at a rally.

Britain rejects plea for Olympic boycott

March 25. In spite of pressure from the Government, the British Olympic Association has voted by a large majority not to boycott the Olympic Games in Moscow this summer. The American Association, under pressure from President Carter, has agreed not to send a team to Moscow in response to the Soviet invasion of Afghanistan. Despite pleas from Mrs Thatcher, the BOA has left the decision to the individual sporting bodies. Most are committed to competing (→ 7/4).

Twenty killed during Salvador funeral

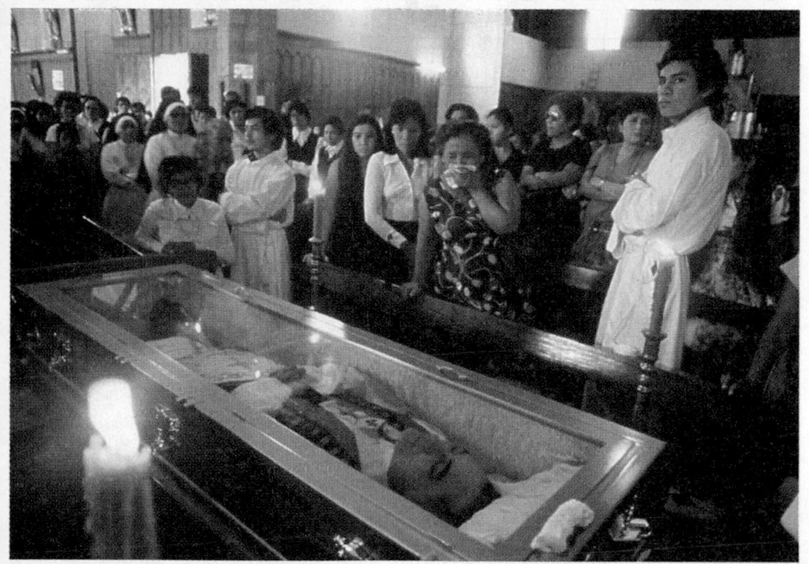

Salvadorean mourners gather round the corpse of Archbishop Romero.

March 30. Over 20 people were killed and more than 200 were wounded during a service in the Cathedral of San Salvador today when four bombs exploded and snipers with automatic rifles fired into the crowd of 50,000 in the plaza outside the cathedral.

The crowd had gathered for the funeral Mass for Archbishop Oscar Arnulfo Romero who was shot by four gunmen last week while he was saying Mass for his dead mother at the high altar.

Romero was a champion of economic and social reforms, but he had been a vocal critic of both left-wing and right-wing extremists in El Salvador. A right-wing paramilitary group has been blamed for his assassination. Today, a government spokesman, Jose Napoleon Duarte, blamed leftist guerrillas for the bombing and the shooting in the square.

Today's violence erupted just as the highly emotional Mass, conducted by a special delagate of the Pope, Cardinal Ahumada of Mexico, was ending. Observers said that left-wing marchers pulled out submachine guns and fired on the snipers.

Many of the dead were trampled to death in the wild stampede which began when the shooting started. One witness said: "They didn't know which way to run. They were just running into each other." The service was suspended and the Archbishop was hastily buried in the crypt (→29/11).

100 die in rig tragedy

March 27. An oil platform used as a floating hotel for North Sea rig workers capsized today, with half the 200 men aboard feared dead. Most were trapped inside as one of five supporting legs buckled and the Alexander Kielland collapsed into the sea. About 50 men were in the cinema when the platform began to topple. Rescue teams say they hope some will still be alive in air pockets, and diving bells are being sent to the disaster scene.

It took just 15 minutes for the huge platform to overturn in stormy seas 240 miles off the coast. Helicopters, planes and at least 13 ships have gone to the rescue.

A spokesman for Phillips Petroleum, the owners, said: "Men just tumbled into the cold water. It was getting dark. We fear a great disaster." Seven people are known to be dead, but dozens of bodies were seen several hundred yards away.

Some survivors were flown ashore, and others were taken to another production platform for emergency medical treatment.

The Alexander Kielland "hotel" is a semi-submersible platform with five air-filled steel legs. Each is six yards wide, but Phillips say one of them broke, probably after being hit by a strong wave.

The disaster came at 6.30pm. One survivor, Mr Tom Greenwood, said: "Metal screeched as it began to keel over. Suddenly men were cut and bleeding" (→23/6).

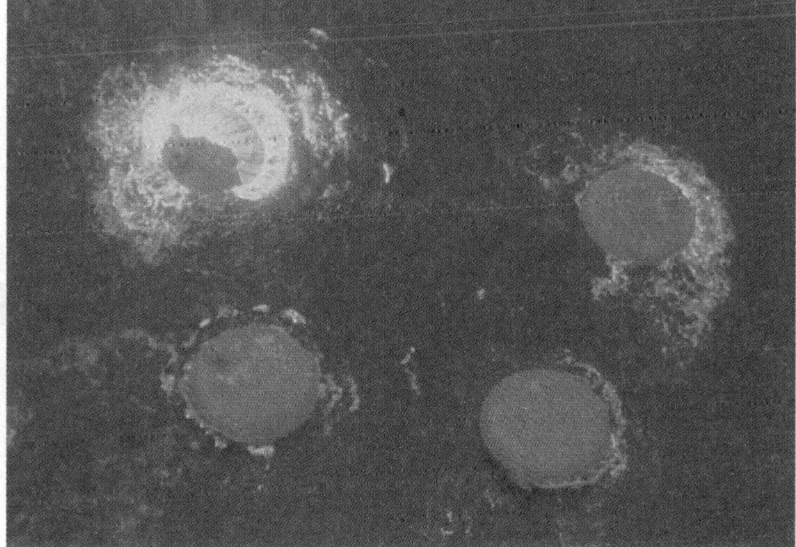

Four upturned feet mark the submerged oil rig Alexander Kielland.

Best-selling doctor is found shot dead

March 11. Scandal hit Westchester County, a wealthy suburb of New York, tonight after Dr Herman Tarnower, aged 69, the author of the best-selling "Complete Scarsdale Medical Diet" was found shot dead in his home. Shortly afterwards Mrs Jean Harris was apprehended leaving Tarnower's estate. Mrs Harris, a 59-year-old girls' school headmistress, had known Tarnower for 14 years, and was credited in his book. She is being held by police in connection with the doctor's murder (→20/3/81).

Khomeini supports US hostage takers

March 10. Dr Waldheim, the UN Secretary-General, today ordered the UN Commission trying to resolve the problem of the American diplomatic hostages held in Tehran to leave Iran. This follows the Ayatollah Khomeini's refusal to allow the Commission to see the hostages unless its members first "expressed a view" about the "crimes" of the Shah and America, the "Great Satan".

The Ayatollah's stand injects a new and serious element into the fate of the hostages for, until now, he has always insisted that they were being held by the "students" who occupy the embassy and not by the Iranian government.

Jody Powell, press secretary to President Carter, reflected the growing mood of disillusion with Khomeini tonight when he said: "The Iranian government's ability to function as a government and fulfil the commitments it has made is now seriously in doubt."

In Tehran, a "student" spokesman insisted that when the Commission revealed the results of its work and "it is in favour of Iran and they prove that they are truthful, then they can come back to Iran and meet all the hostages" (→23).

Release of Britons kidnapped in Italy

March 22. The teenage kidnap victim Annabel Schild was reunited with her mother today just a week after the Pope made a passionate appeal for her release. The 15-year-old daughter of the London electronics engineer Rolf Schild had been held for seven months by Sardinian bandits.

Her mother, Mrs Daphne Schild, was freed in January earlier this year, after Mr Schild's negotiators handed over 500 million lire (about £262,000). Eight men are now in prison.

1980

APRIL

Su	Mo	Tu	We	Th	Fr	Sa
		1	2	3	4	5
6	7	8	9	10	11	12
13	14	15	16	17	18	19
20	21	22	23	24	25	26
27	28	29	30			

1. UK: The steel strike is called off (→22).

4. Buenos Aires: Argentina is reported to be increasing links with the Falkland Islands (→20/3/81).

5. London: Oxford wins the Boat Race in a finish equalling the closest ever, except for the dead heat in 1877 (→4/4/81).

7. UK: 400 march to protest at the decision to site Cruise missiles in East Anglia (→19/9).

7. UK: The British Equestrian Federation decides not to send a team to Moscow (→19/7).

10. Madrid: Spain agrees to re-open the Gibraltar border.

11. Salisbury: Dr Canaan Banana is chosen to be the first President of Zimbabwe.→

13. US: Spaniard Severiano Ballesteros becomes the youngest golfer to win the Masters.

14. US: "Kramer vs. Kramer" wins an Oscar for best film; Alec Guinness wins one for "lifetime achievement".

17. Washington: Carter says military action will be his only choice if Iran fails to free the US hostages.→

22. UK: Unemployment tops 1.5 million for the first time since 1978 (→1/5).

22. Liberia: 13 leading ministers of the previous government are publicly executed by firing squad.

25. Tenerife: 146 die when a Boeing 727 crashes (→19/8).

28. Luxembourg: The EEC is in disarray after failing to solve the problems of Britain's budget contributions (→30/5).

30. London: Three gunmen seize 20 hostages at the Iranian embassy and demand freedom for 91 Arabs in Iran (→5/5).

30. Amsterdam: Rioters clash with police during the coronation of Queen Beatrix.

DEATHS

15. French philosopher and writer Jean-Paul Sartre (*21/6/1905).→

29. British film director Sir Alfred Joseph Hitchcock (*13/8/1899).→

Desert fiasco ends hostage rescue bid

April 25. An attempt by America's crack Delta Force to rescue the 53 diplomatic hostages being held by the Iranians in the US embassy in Tehran ended in fiery disaster in the early hours of this morning when a helicopter of the assault force collided with a tanker aircraft on the ground in the Iranian desert.

The rescue attempt, codenamed "Operation Eagle Claw" and led by Colonel "Charging" Charlie Beckwith, had already been aborted because mechanical failures meant that Delta did not have enough helicopters to carry out the mission. The machines were refuelling to go home when the accident occurred.

Eight Americans died and their bodies were left in the flaming wreckage 200 miles south-east of the Iranian capital where the militants holding the hostages tonight threatened to kill them if there was another rescue attempt.

Appearing on breakfast-time television, President Carter told a shocked nation: "It was my decision to attempt the rescue operation, it was my decision to cancel it when a problem developed in the placement of our rescue team. The reponsibility is purely my own."

Iranian troops and Revolutionary Guards gather around the wreckage.

The fiasco in the desert will be a bitter personal and political blow for the President. After months of criticism for vacillating in the hostage crisis, Mr Carter is now facing even greater scorn for not being able to mount the daring rescue mission successfully.

The Ayatollah Khomeini added to his misery tonight calling the mission "an act of stupidity" which would have sent the hostages "to hell" (→30).

Union Jack lowered for last time in Africa

April 18. At midnight last night Britain's last African colony, the embattled land of Rhodesia, saw the Union Jack lowered and the red-starred flag of Zimbabwe raised as a bugler sounded the Last Post. Prince Charles, representing the Queen, presented the instruments of sovereignty to the President, the Rev Canaan Banana.

Robert Mugabe, the Prime Minister, spoke of black and white reconciliation. "If yesterday you hated me, today you cannot avoid the love that binds you to me and me to you," he said (→6/8).

Ian Smith, former Prime Minister, listens as Rhodesia becomes Zimbabwe.

Sartre's being is now nothingness

April 15. France is mourning her post-war intellectual guru, Jean-Paul Sartre, dead at the age of 74, whose funeral filled Paris's streets. While working in the Resistance, Sartre wrote his most influential work "Being and Nothingness" and also his plays "Huis Clos" and "Crime Passionnel" (about a Communist dilemma – should you kill for the Party against your own judgment?).

After the war, Sartre became the outstanding voice on the left-wing and the Left Bank, whose disciples communed in the Cafe de Flore. With his lifelong companion, Simone de Beauvoir, he edited the monthly "Les Temps Modernes" and published his doctrine of Existentialism – that man, in a godless universe, gives meaning to his existence only by his own acts of moral choice and commitment.Though he broke with Communism, Sartre joined the demonstrations of 1968. He refused the Nobel Prize in 1964.

Hitchcock, master of suspense, dies

April 29. Alfred Hitchcock (Sir Alfred for a brief four months until his death today, aged 80) was the only film director who was instantly recognisable to the public. His portly figure was unmistakable in brief appearances in his films.

He was the son of a Leytonstone greengrocer who directed the first British "talkie", "Blackmail", in 1929. After such successes as "The Thirty-Nine Steps" and "The Lady Vanishes", he went to Hollywood and won an Academy Award with his first picture there, Daphne du Maurier's "Rebecca", in 1940. "Rear Window" and "Psycho" were among many later successes which demonstrated his mastery of suspense.

Hitch: East End to West Coast.

Diplomatic row at princess' TV death

April 23. An outraged Saudi Arabia came close to breaking off diplomatic relations with Great Britain today following the showing of an ITV film, "Death of a Princess", which alleged a free-wheeling lifestyle existed in their strict Islamic society.

A formal apology by Britain has failed to cool the Saudis' fury, and the Council of Ministers in Jeddah has asked for the withdrawal of the British Ambassador and a review of future economic relations (→22/5).

1980

MAY

Su	Mo	Tu	We	Th	Fr	Sa
				1	2	3
4	5	6	7	8	9	10
11	12	13	14	15	16	17
18	19	20	21	22	23	24
25	26	27	28	29	30	31

1. UK: Ian MacGregor is named as chairman of the British Steel Corporation (→12).

2. Kinshasa: Pope John Paul arrives in Zaire on the first leg of an African tour (→4).

4. Kinshasa: Nine worshippers are trampled to death trying to see the Pope (→17/10).

8. Belgrade: Tito is buried.→

10. London: Second division West Ham beat Arsenal 1-0 in the FA Cup Final.

11. Tehran: Protesters use a sledgehammer to smash the tomb of Reza Shah Pahlavi, the ex-Shah's father (→30/6).

12. London: An industrial tribunal rejects the claim by BL shop steward "Red Robbo" Robinson of unfair dismissal (→14).

14. UK: Today is a "Day of Action" called by the TUC (→16).

16. UK: Inflation rises to 21.8 per cent (→30).

18. Miami: The National Guard is called in after five people are killed in race riots.

20. Canada: Quebec votes against a move to take the French-speaking province out of the federation.

22. London: Lord Carrington publicly apologises to Saudi Arabia for the programme "Death of a Princess" (→8/8).

26. S. Africa: Police arrest 52 demonstrating churchmen (→16/6).

27. UK: An inquest jury finds that Blair Peach died through "misadventure", implying the police used reasonable force.

27. Uganda: Ex-President Milton Obote returns.

28. Spain: Nottingham Forest beat Hamburger SV 1-0 to retain the European Cup.

30. London: The Government says it will ban "insider dealing" from next month (→12/6).

DEATH

4. Yugoslav commander and statesman Marshal Tito, born Josip Broz, President of Yugoslavia 1946-80 (*25/5/1892).→

Volcano erupts in US killing eight people

Mount St. Helens: seconds later, half the mountain seemed to explode.

May 19. At least eight people lost their lives today in an eruption of Mount St. Helens, a long-dormant volcano in the north-western United States. The explosion, at 8.39am local time, blew the top off the 9,677-foot peak. The 60,000-foot column of ash from the eruption darkened the skies in Walla Walla 160 miles away.

Mount St. Helens had been emitting smoke and ash for several weeks before it erupted and geologists had been monitoring it carefully. Most local residents had been evacuated, but the eruption caused floods and mudslides in the valley of the Toutle River, which was not thought to be in danger and where most of the deaths occurred. Many fires were also ignited in surrounding forests. Two earthquakes that occurred shortly before the eruption may have set it off.

One of the volcano's eight victims.

Communists unite in tribute to Tito

May 8. Leaders from more than 100 countries, including the Soviet Union and China, paid their respects today to Yugoslavia's President Tito who has died just three days short of his 88th birthday. Once leader of the partisans in the Second World War, he broke with Stalin in 1948. Today old rifts were forgotten, though, and Tito was praised for uniting the country's diverse elements.

Modern medicine wipes out smallpox

May 8. For centuries smallpox has been feared as a deadly and untreatable infection in every country, but today the World Health Organisation claims that it has been eliminated as a human disease as a result of international preventive health measures. However, even when strictly controlled, the smallpox virus can still be dangerous, as was shown by a laboratory accident in Birmingham in 1978 (→14/10).

SAS storm embassy to free hostages

Who dares wins: black track-suited members of the SAS toss stun grenades as they enter the embassy.

May 5. The Special Air Service made a spectacular assault on the terrorist-occupied Iranian embassy in Knightsbridge tonight, killing four of the five gunmen who took over the building six days ago and rescuing the surviving 19 hostages. The once-elegant building, set on fire by the explosive charge used to blow in the armoured first-floor window, is now a gutted ruin.

The assault became inevitable when the gunmen, demanding the release of political prisoners in Iran, started to shoot the hostages. They killed Abbas Lavasani, the Iranian Press Attache, dumped his body on the steps, and threatened to murder a hostage every thirty minutes.

It was now that the Counter-Revolutionary Warfare team of the SAS came "to the aid of the civil power". Anyone watching the snooker championships, or a John Wayne film, on television suddenly found themselves switched to a real-life drama.

Black-uniformed figures wearing balaclavas and carrying submachine guns appeared on the balcony of the embassy; others, caught by a camera smuggled round the back of the building by ITN, abseiled from the roof to break in through the rear windows.

The men in the front fitted a frame of explosives to the window and blew it in. The curtains caught fire and almost immediately the flames which were to gut the building licked into Prince's Gate. Simeon Harris, a BBC sound recordist taken hostage when applying for a visa, scrambled to safety through the flames as a second explosion rocked the building and a flurry of gunshots echoed through fashionable Knightsbridge.

PC Lock: survivor of terror.

Inside the building the terrorists opened fire on their hostages, killing one Iranian diplomat and severely wounding another. A third was saved when a bullet struck a coin in his pocket.

The terrorist leader, known as "Own", would certainly have killed the first SAS man into the building if he had not been tackled by PC Trevor Lock who had been on duty at the embassy when the gunmen took over. PC Lock had kept his revolver concealed throughout the siege. As he grappled with "Own" the SAS man ordered him away, then shot "Own" dead.

The SAS men worked their way through the building, picking off the terrorists with short bursts of machine-gun fire and bundling the hostages none too gently to safety. The only terrorist to survive was protected by women hostages who pleaded for his life. It was all over in 11 minutes (→ 11).

Korean students crushed by army

May 27. The Korean army, in a skilful display of force and tactics, crushed a student revolt in Kwangju at dawn today. An entire division and two special regiments were used to surround the rebels and round up the ringleaders. Compared to recent bloody battles, where special forces used bayonets and knives to quell resistance, today's manoeuvres went off peacefully.

Eye-witnesses say that at least 10 students were killed and many soldiers wounded in the action, which ends a ten-day protest against martial law and the arrest of the opposition leader Kim Dae Jung (→ 17/9).

Guerrillas killed in Angola border clash

May 23. In one of the fiercest clashes of the bush war on the South-West Africa/Namibia border with Angola, five white South African soldiers and 81 black nationalist guerrillas have been killed. The South African Defence Force HQ in Pretoria said their men died when they walked into an ambush.

"A hectic firefight started and the security forces went over to the offensive immediately," the statement said. "The terrorists were driven back and fled. The security forces followed them and in the ensuing contact 81 terrorists were shot dead."

Britain wins big cut in payments to EEC

May 30. Britain's annual payment into the Common Market kitty will be drastically reduced. It is now running at £1,100 million and will be down to around £250 million by 1981. This was agreed by EEC foreign ministers after lengthy haggling in Brussels today. A delighted British spokesman said: "It would be crazy not to accept this." French and West German contributions will be increased to compensate. A French newspaper said: "Waterloo is not so far from Brussels." Yet Mrs Thatcher will still ask for more (→ 19/8).

1980

JUNE

Su	Mo	Tu	We	Th	Fr	Sa
1	2	3	4	5	6	7
8	9	10	11	12	13	14
15	16	17	18	19	20	21
22	23	24	25	26	27	28
29	30					

2. Jordan: Three bombs on the occupied West Bank maim two Arab mayors.

4. London: BBC musicians strike in protest at the corporation's plans to axe five orchestras.

4. UK: Mrs A. Plesch's Henbit wins the Derby.

6. London: Two Malaysians who headed a multi-million pound drug smuggling ring are jailed for 14 years.

9. London: Roy Jenkins hints at plans for a new radical centre-left party.

11. London: The Government plans to send 200 Marines to aid diplomatic moves to end a revolt in the New Hebrides.

12. UK: Over 650 pounds of cannabis are discovered in a crate bound for the Moroccan embassy in London.

12. UK: British Steel announces the closure of its Consett works on September 30 with the loss of 3,700 jobs.

13. Italy: UEFA fines the FA £8,000 for the Turin riots.

16. S. Africa: Police and blacks clash in Soweto on the anniversary of the 1976 revolt.

19. Baghdad: Iraqi police kill three terrorists in the British embassy compound.

21. Moscow: The Soviet news agency Tass reports that troops are being withdrawn from Afghanistan.

24. UK: Unemployment now stands at 1.6 million, the highest since the war.

29. Iceland: Vigdis Finnbogadottir becomes the country's first woman President.

30. Tel Aviv: Begin suffers a mild heart attack in the Knesset and is rushed to hospital.

30. Cairo: The ex-Shah has an operation to drain fluid from his lungs.

DEATHS

7. US writer Henry Miller (*20/1/1891).→

7. US artist Philip Guston (*27/6/1913).

Ten million face famine in East Africa

June 12. Over ten million people in East Africa are threatened by what Britain's Disasters Emergency Committee describes as the "world's worst famine". The committee is trying to raise £5 million to provide immediate relief. In Brussels, Common Market officials have decided to send food and drugs worth £300,000 to Uganda.

Two years of drought, combined with at least half a dozen local wars, have led to widespread crop failures and a massive refugee problem. The famine area extends from northern Kenya, through Uganda, to Somalia, Ethiopia, Sudan and Djibouti. Some two million people are reckoned to be refugees.

In Somalia, said to have "the biggest refugee problem in the world today", an estimated 500 people are dying each day in refugee camps. In the Karamoja area of northern Uganda, between 400 and 500 people, mostly children, are dying each day. A million refugees have struggled to Sudan from Ethiopia, Zaire, Chad and Uganda. Drought is also returning to the Sahel states of Mauritania, Senegal, Gambia, Upper Volta, Mali, Niger and Chad, where famine killed at least 250,000 in 1973.

Young victims are still starving.

Cape Town looting spree leaves 42 dead

June 18. Residents in the Coloured – or mixed race – townships outside Cape Town took the law into their own hands today, and started shooting at gangs of thugs known as "skollies" who were roaming the streets looting and fire-raising. At least 42 people have been killed and 200 injured. During last night the Cape Flats area was reported to be in a state of siege, with rioters burning cars and shops and throwing up barricades.

The Police Commissioner, Gen. Mike Geldenhuys, sent two plane-loads of riot police from Pretoria to Cape Town and told them to shoot to kill. Police insist the troublemakers are "hooligans, not school or bus boycotters".

Korean students are herded together by the police after protesting against the death sentence passed on opposition leader Kim Dae Jung.

Cruise missiles are to be based in UK

June 17. American-owned Cruise missiles are to be based at a US Air Force airfield at Greenham Common, near Newbury in Berkshire and later at a disused military base at Molesworth, Cambridgeshire. This follows NATO's decision to counter Soviet SS-20 rockets now being moved into Eastern Europe.

A total of 160 of the mobile missiles will be based here as a result of the NATO decision. Britain is the first NATO country to say that it will take the missiles and the Government's announcement seems bound to cause protest action by anti-nuclear groups.

Sir Billy, king of the redcoats, dies

June 12. It was a dull, rain-soaked holiday in Skegness in 1932 that prompted Billy Butlin to open what he called a "holiday camp" two years later – offering outdoor and indoor entertainment to the masses. For £3 a head, he provided a chalet, four meals a day, and free entertainment, with red-coated staff acting as cheerleaders, guides and baby-sitters.

The idea caught on. Butlin Holidays attracted millions and Sir Billy, who died today aged 80, became the head of a £55 million empire. In 1964 he was knighted for services to charity.

Miller's lustful tale comes to its end

June 7. Henry Miller proved that if you outlive your detractors, you will end up respected. The author of the "obscene" and explicit (for their day) "Tropic of Cancer" and "Tropic of Capricorn", smuggled out of France under plain cover in the Thirties, was 89 when he died today. He was an honoured guest at literary congresses, at which he beat other authors at ping-pong.

Miller was from Brooklyn. He gave up his job at Western Union to go to Paris and be a writer in 1924. He went on to Greece and wrote "The Colossus of Maroussi". ▷

Gandhi's son and heir dies in plane crash

Indira Gandhi mourns her son Sanjay, who died when his aircraft crashed.

June 23. Sanjay Gandhi, the 33-year-old younger son of Mrs Indira Gandhi, died today when the light aircraft he was piloting crashed on the outskirts of New Delhi. People who saw the crash say the Pitts aerobatic biplane he was flying looped the loop several times before its fatal dive. Captain Subash Saxena, a flying instructor, also died in the crash.

Gandhi's death brought to an end a meteoric five-year career in politics, in which he had become the man thought most likely to succeed his mother as Prime Minister of India, and so perpetuate the political dynasty founded by his grandfather, Pandit Nehru, India's first prime minister.

His closeness to his mother and her devotion to him were legendary, and when she declared the much-hated state of emergency in 1975 he wielded extraordinary power. He sponsored an economic and social development programme which bordered on ruthlessness.

His family-planning drive, in particular, aroused bitter controversy and was largely responsible for his mother's humiliating defeat in the 1977 election, but he helped her regain power and last week was made general secretary of the Congress Party, a stepping-stone to the Premiership.

Mrs Gandhi has one other son, Rajiv, an Indian Airlines pilot, who has never shown any interest in politics. His mother may now require him to do so.

West's leaders plan oil consumption cut

June 23. The seven major industrial nations of the free world today agreed to cut their oil consumption substantially by 1990 in order to be less dependent on Arab whims.

A communique issued by the government leaders of Britain, the United States, France, West Germany, Italy, Japan and Canada after a summit meeting in Venice stated that they will try to halve present consumption by doubling coal output and making more use of nuclear energy. The Big Seven also pledged the highest priority for public health and safety in using nuclear power.

English soccer fans riot in Turin streets

June 12. Turin police fired tear gas to break up rioting British soccer supporters during England's opening match today in the European championship. Play was halted for five minutes to allow footballers to recover from the effects of the gas. About 100 youths charged across terraces to fight with Belgian fans whose team had just equalised.

England's manager, Ron Greenwood, broadcast an appeal for calm and his team spoke of their shame at the fans' behaviour. Riot police moved in with baton charges and scores of Britons were thrown out of the ground (→ 13).

1980

JULY

Su	Mo	Tu	We	Th	Fr	Sa
		1	2	3	4	5
6	7	8	9	10	11	12
13	14	15	16	17	18	19
20	21	22	23	24	25	26
27	28	29	30	31		

1. UK: Hopes fade for BL's MG offshoot as Aston Martin fails to raise money to buy it.

4. Wimbledon: Evonne Cawley, nee Goolagong, beats Chris Lloyd for her second Women's Singles title.→

5. Tehran: Iranian women protest to the President about the imposition of the Islamic rules for female dress (→ 11).

10. London: A fire causes huge damage to Alexandra Palace in North London.

11. Tehran: Richard Queen, a US hostage, is released on medical grounds (→ 18).

14. London: Transport secretary Norman Fowler unveils plans to sell off Sealink and British Rail hotels (→ 4/2/81).

18. Paris: Shahpur Bakhtiar, the Shah's last Prime Minister, escapes an assassination bid (→ 27).

19. Moscow: Brezhnev opens the 22nd Olympic Games.→

22. UK: Unemployment stands at 1,896,634, the highest since 1936 (→ 29).

23. London: The BBC reaches agreement with musicians to end their strike, which has lasted almost two months.

24. New Hebrides: 200 Anglo-French marines land on the rebel island of Espiritu Santo and end its revolt peacefully.

29. London: Thatcher announces the creation of seven "Enterprise Zones" in areas of high unemployment (→ 27/8).

31. UK: Shirley Williams, Bill Rodgers and Dr David Owen urge Labour members to join them against the far left (→ 1/10).

DEATHS

13. Botswanan statesman Sir Seretse Khama, first President of Botswana 1966-80 (*1/7/1921).

24. British actor and comedian Richard Henry "Peter" Sellers (*8/9/1925).→

27. Iranian monarch Shah Mohammed Reza Pahlavi, ruled 1941-79 (*26/10/1919).→

For fifth time Borg wins at Wimbledon

July 5. Bjorn Borg, the Swedish tennis ace known for his ice-cool temperament, today wept after he won his fifth successive men's title at the Wimbledon championships.

As he sank to his knees the tears streamed down his face. By beating the American John McEnroe in a four-hour five-set duel, Borg wins a place in sporting history.

He said afterwards: "My ambition is to be remembered as the greatest player of all time. I guess you could say I have come close."

McEnroe said: "I wish Borg would let someone else have a go at the title for a change."

Sweden's invincible Bjorn Borg.

World leaders shun funeral of the Shah

July 27. The deposed Shah of Iran died of cancer today in Cairo after living the last 18 months of his life in troubled exile. He is to be buried in a Cairo mausoleum after a state funeral which President Sadat said would show "all honours and due respect", but without any of the world's leaders being present.

President Sadat's decision not to invite heads of state offered a diplomatic let-out for countries unwilling to risk antagonising the revolutionary regime in Iran where Tehran Radio declared "the bloodsucker of the century" had died (→ 4/8).

Ex-actor Reagan to run

Republican conventioneers boost their candidate's presidential chances.

July 17. Ronald W. Reagan was chosen by the Republican Party in Detroit yesterday as its presidential candidate, and immediately called on Americans "not simply to trust me, but to trust your values – our values" in order to face what he called "this unprecedented calamity" of the American hostages in Tehran.

Reagan ignored calls to choose former President Ford as his vice-presidential running-mate, and opted for George Bush, the former head of the CIA.

Mr Reagan, who served two terms as Governor of California, started his career as a radio announcer before going to Hollywood where he became a film star of the second magnitude and the host of a 1950s TV show.

Reagan is a strong conservative who came to national political prominence with a speech made for Senator Goldwater in 1964 (→ 14/8).

Peter Sellers, man of many voices, dies

July 24. By sad coincidence Peter Sellers died today, a fortnight after his latest film, "Being There", was hailed as one of his finest comedy performances. In it he plays a character who is a complete blank, on whom others project their wishes. Sellers, who hid behind his brilliant gift for mimicry, was said to be rather like this in private life. His extravagance and four marriages seemed to bring no contentment.

He got his first radio part by ringing a producer and convincing him that he was Kenneth Horne. He enjoyed "The Goon Show", in which he invented so many voices, more than anything. Later came his shop steward, Indian doctor, and incompetent Inspector Clouseau.

Jobless rising as UK slides into recession

July 1. Redundancies in Britain are reaching 40,000 a month as industry prepares to weather what could be the worst depression since the war. Economists feel it is inevitable that unemployment will reach two million by next summer.

Manufacturing industry reports a falling-off in orders this year of between 10 and 40 per cent, and is cutting back on production and stocks to preserve cash. In the badly-hit car industry, Lucas Industries is axing 3,000 jobs in Birmingham, and 900 are at risk at MG Cars, where a rescue consortium failed today in a bid to buy the company from British Leyland.

The Government's monetary and anti-inflation policy is blamed by the unions for weakening Britain's industrial base.

Ovett and Coe lead Britain's gold rush as Moscow Olympics eclipse the boycott

July 19-Aug 3. Many of the performances at Moscow's Olympic Games were clearly distorted by the absence of Americans, West Germans and Kenyans; but the Games went ahead, the organisation both inside and outside the stadiums was far better than athletes and visitors had feared, and the Games, as always, provided feats of brilliance for all competing nations to savour.

Allan Wells: fastest at 100 metres.

The high-profile gymnastic events saw the now mature Nadia Comaneci all but eclipsed by an even tinier, more elf-like dynamo from Russia, Yelena Davydova. Teofile Stevenson of Cuba won his third consecutive heavyweight boxing gold medal, while in swimming – apart from a breaststroke gold medal for the engaging baldheaded Briton, Duncan Goodhew – the Soviets and East Germans let few medals pass them by.

In the athletics stadium, there was enough drama to erase talk of boycotts. The Soviet Union's own Viktor Saneyev, with three Olympic triplejump titles to his name, failed by a whisker to add a fourth, and two Poles – Malinowski in the steeplechase and Kozakiewicz in the pole vault – delighted their supporters by beating the Russians in the Soviet capital.

Britain's athletes celebrated in style. The 28-year-old Scot Allan Wells became the first Briton since Harold Abrahams in 1924 to win the 100 metres, and he very nearly held off the fast-finishing challenge of Italy's Pietro Mennea to clinch an historic sprint double. Daley Thompson, the brash young son of a Nigerian father and a Scottish mother, waltzed away with the decathlon, the first Briton ever to win the title.

For many the highlight of the Games were the first clashes in two years between the world's two greatest middle-distance runners, Britain's Steve Ovett and Sebastian Coe. Each won gold, although not in the event most would have predicted. In the 800 metres, the world-record-holder Coe lost concentration early in the second lap and could not earn himself more than a silver medal behind Ovett's gold.

Inconsolable for a day, Coe then responded with a perfectly judged 1,500 metres in which Ovett had been unbeaten for over three years, striking on the final bend to take his gold, leaving Ovett with a bronze.

Sebastian Coe, his mouth gaping with effort, wins the 1,500 metres final.

▷

1980 Moscow

Men Athletics

100m
1. Allan Wells GBR 10.25
2. Silvio Leonard CUB 10.25
3. Peter Petrov BUL 10.39

200m
1. Pietro Mennea ITA 20.19
2. Allan Wells GBR 20.21
3. Donald Quarrie JAM 20.29

400m
1. Viktor Markin URS 44.60
2. Rick Mitchell AUS 44.84
3. Frank Schaffer GDR 44.87

800m
1. Steve Ovett GBR 1:45.4
2. Sebastian Coe GBR 1:45.9
3. Nikolai Kirov URS 1:46.0

1500m
1. Sebastian Coe GBR 3:38.4
2. Jürgen Straub GDR 3:38.8
3. Steve Ovett GBR 3:39.0

5000m
1. Miruts Yifter ETH 13:21.0
2. Suleiman Nyambui TAN 13:21.6
3. Kaarlo Maaninka FIN 13:22.0

10,000m
1. Miruts Yifter ETH 27:42.7
2. Kaarlo Maaninka FIN 27:44.3
3. Mohammed Kedir ETH 27:44.7

Marathon
1. Waldemar Cierpinski GDR 2:11.03
2. Gerald Nijboer NETH 2:11.20
3. Satymkul Dzhumanazarov URS 2:11.35

110m Hurdles
1. Thomas Munkelt GDR 13.39
2. Alejandro Casanas CUB 13.40
3. Aleksandr Puchkov URS 13.44

400m Hurdles
1. Volker Beck GDR 48.70
2. Vassily Arkhipenko URS 48.86
3. Gary Oakes GBR 49.11

3000m Steeplechase
1. Bronislaw Malinowski POL 8:09.7
2. Filbert Bayi TAN 8:12.5
3. Eshetu Tura ETH 8:13.6

4x100m Relay
1. URS 38.26 (Vladimir Muravyov, Nikolai Sidorov, Aleksandr Aksinin, Andrei Prokofiev)
2. POL 38.33 (Krzystof Zwolinski, Zenon Licznerski, Leszek Dunecki, Marian Woronin)
3. FRA 38.53 (Antoine Richard, Pascal Barré, Patrick Barré, Hermann Panzo)

4x400m Relay
1. URS 3:01.1 (Remigius Valiulis, Mikhail Linge, Nikolai Chernetsky, Viktor Markin)
2. GDR 3:01.3 (Klaus Thiele, Andreas Knebel, Frank Schaffer, Volker Beck)
3. ITA 3:04.3 (Stefano Malinverni, Mauro Zuliani, Roberto Tozzi, Pietro Mennea)

20km Walk
1. Maurizio Damilano ITA *1:23.35
2. Pyotr Pochinchuk URS 1:24.45
3. Roland Wieser GDR 1:25.58

50km Walk
1. Hartwig Gauder GDR *3:49.24
2. Jorge Llopart ESP 3:51.25
3. Yevgeni Ivchenko URS 3:56.32

High Jump
1. Gerd Wessig GDR **2.36
2. Jacek Wszola POL 2.31
3. Jörg Freimuth GDR 2.31

Pole Vault
1. Wladyslaw Kozakiewicz POL **5.78
2. Konstantin Volkov URS 5.65
2. Tadeusz Slusarski POL 5.65

Long Jump
1. Lutz Dombrowski GDR 8.54
2. Frank Paschek GDR 8.21
3. Valeri Podluzhniy URS 8.18

Triple Jump
1. Jaak Uudmae URS 17.35
2. Vikter Saneyev URS 17.24
3. Joao Carlos de Oliveira BRA 17.22

Shotput
1. Vladimir Kiselyov URS *21.35
2. Aleksandr Barishnikov URS 21.08
3. Udo Beyer GDR 21.06

Discus
1. Viktor Rashchupkin URS 66.64
2. Imrich Bugár TCH 66.38
3. Luis Delis CUB 66.32

Hammer
1. Yuri Sedykh URS **81.80
2. Sergei Litvinov URS 80.64
3. Yuri Tamm URS 78.96

Javelin
1. Dainis Kula URS 91.20
2. Aleksandr Makarov URS 89.64
3. Wolfgang Hanisch GDR 86.72

Decathlon
a1. Daley Thompson GBR 8495
2. Yuri Kautsenko URS 8331
3. Sergei Zhelanov URS 8315

Women Athletics

100m
1. Lyudmila Kondratyeva URS 11.06
2. Marlies Göhr GDR 11.07
3. Ingrid Auerswald GDR 11.14

200m
1. Bärbel Wöckel GDR *22.03
2. Natalya Bochina URS 22.19
3. Merlene Ottey JAM 22.20

400m
1. Marita Koch GDR *48.88
2. Jarmila Kratochvilová TCH 49.46
3. Christina Lathan GDR 49.66

800m
1. Nadezhda Olizarenko URS ***1:53.4
2. Olga Mineyeva URS 1:54.9
3. Tatyana Providokhina URS 1:55.5

1500m
1. Tatyana Kazankina URS *3:56.6
2. Christiane Wartenberg GDR 3:57.8
3. Nadezhda Olizarenko URS 3:59.6

100m Hurdles
1. Vera Komisova URS *12.56
2. Johanna Klier GDR 12.63
3. Lucyna Langer POL 12.65

4x100m Relay
1. GDR ** 41.60 (Ingrid Auerswald, Marlies Göhr, Romy Müller, Bärbel Wöckel)
2. URS 42.10 (Vera Komisova, Vera Anisimova, Lyudmila Maslakova, Natalya Bochina)
3. GBR 42.43 (Heather Hunte, Kathryn Smallwood, Beverley Goddard, Sonia Lannaman)

4x400m Relay
1. URS 3:20.2 (Tatyana Prorochenko, Tatyana Goistchik, Nina Zyuskova, Irina Nazarova)
2. GDR 3:20.4 (Gabriele Löwe, Barbara Krug, Christina Lathan, Marita Koch)
3. GBR 3:27.5 (Linsey MacDonald, Michelle Probert, Joslyn Hoyte-Smith, Janine MacGregor)

High Jump
1. Sara Simeoni ITA *1.97
2. Urszula Kielan POL 1.94
3. Jutta Kirst GDR 1.94

Long Jump
1. Tatiana Kolpakova URS *7.06
2. Brigitte Wujak GDR 7.04
3. Tatiana Skachko URS 7.01

Shotput
1. Ilona Slupianek GDR 22.41
2. Svetlana Krachevskaya URS 21.42
3. Margitta Pufe GDR 21.20

Discus Throw
1. Evelin Jahl GDR *69.96
2. Maria Petkova BUL 67.90
3. Tatyana Lesovaya URS 67.40

Javelin
1. Maria Colon Ruenes CUB 68.40
2. Saida Gunba URS 67.76
3. Ute Hommola GDR 66.56

Pentathlon
1. Nadezhda Tkachenko URS **5083
2. Olga Rukavishnikova URS 4937
3. Olga Kuragina URS 4875

Men Swimming

100m Freestyle
1. Jörg Woithe GDR 50.40
2. Per-Alvar Homertz SWE 50.91
3. Per Johansson SWE 51.29

200m Freestyle
1. Sergei Kopliakov URS *1:49.81
2. Andrei Krylov URS 1:50.76
3. Grame Brewer AUS 1:51.60

400m Freestyle
1. Vladimir Salkinov URS *3:51.31
2. Andrei Krylov URS 3:53.24
3. Ivar Stukolkin URS 3:53.95

1500m Freestyle
1. Vladimir Salkinov URS **14:58.27
2. Aleksandr Chaev URS 15:14.30
3. Max Metzker AUS 15:14.49

100m Backstroke
1. Bengt Baron SWE 56.63
2. Viktor Kuznetsov URS 56.99
3. Vladimir Dolgov URS 57.63

200m Backstroke
1. Sándor Wladár HUN 2:01.93
2. Zoltán Verrasztó HUN 2:02.40
3. Mark Kerry AUS 2:03.14

100m Breaststroke
1. Duncan Goodhew GBR 1:03.34
2. Arsen Miskarov URS 1:03.82
3. Peter Evans AUS 1:03.96

200m Breaststroke
1. Robertas Julpa URS 2:15.85
2. Albán Vermes HUN 2:16.93
3. Arsen Miskarov URS 2:17.28

100m Butterfly
1. Pär Arvidsson SWE 54.92
2. Roger Pyttel GDR 54.94
3. David Lopez ESP 55.13

200m Butterfly
1. Sergei Fesenko URS 1:59.76
2. Philip Hubble GBR 2:01.20
3. Roger Pyttel GDR 2:01.39

400m Individual Medley
1. Aleksandr Sidorenko URS *4:22.89
2. Sergei Fesenko URS 4:23.43
3. Zoltán Verrasztó HUN 4:24.24

4x200m Freestyle Relay
1. URS 7:23.50 (Sergei Kopliakov, Vladimir Salnikov, Ivar Stukolkin, Andrei Krylov)
2. GDR 7:28.60 (Frank Pfütze, Jörg Woithe, Detlev Grabs, Rainer Strohbach)
3. BRA 7:29.30 (Jorge Lutz Fernandes, Marcus Mattioli, Cyro Marques, Djan Garrido Madruga)

4x100m Medley Relay
1. AUS 3:45.70 (Mark Kerry, Peter Evans, Mark Tonelli, Neil Brooks)
2. URS 3:45.92 (Victor Kuznetsov, Arsen Miskarov, Yevgeny Seredin, Sergei Kopliakov)
3. GBR 3:47.71 (Gary Abraham, Duncan Goodhew, David Lowe, Martin Smith)

The controversy over the Soviet Union's invasion of Afghanistan was forgotten when the Russians put on their opening pageant.

Springboard Diving
1. Aleksandr Portnov URS 905.025
2. Carlos Giron MEX 892.140
3. Giorgio Cagnotto ITA 871.500

Platform Diving
1. Falk Hoffmann GDR 835.650
2. Vladimir Aleynik URS 819.705
3. David Ambartsumyam URS 817.440

Water Polo

1. Soviet Union
2. Yugoslavia
3. Hungary

Women Swimming

100m Freestyle
1. Barbara Krause GDR **54.79
2. Caren Metschuk GDR 55.16
3. Ines Diers GDR 55.65

200m Freestyle
1. Barbara Krause GDR *1:58.33
2. Ines Diers GDR 1:59.64
3. Carmela Schmidt GDR 2:01.44

400m Freestyle
1. Ines Diers GDR *4:08.76
2. Petra Schneider GDR 4:09.16
3. Carmela Schmidt GDR 4:10.86

800m Freestyle
1. Michelle Ford AUS *8:28.90
2. Ines Diers GDR 8:32.55
3. Heike Dähne GDR 8:33.48

100m Breaststroke
1. Ute Geweniger GDR 1:10.22
2. Elvira Vasilkova URS 1:10.41
3. Susanne Nielsson DEN 1:11.16

200m Breaststroke
1. Lina Kaciusyte URS *2:29.54
2. Svetlana Varganova URS 2:29.61
3. Yulia Bogdanova URS 2:32.39

100m Backstroke
1. Rica Reinisch GDR **1:00.86
2. Ina Kleber GDR 1:02.07
3. Petra Riedel GDR 1:02.64

200m Backstroke
1. Rica Reinisch GDR **2:11.77
2. Cornelia Polit GDR 2:13.75
3. Birgit Treiber GDR 2:14.14

100m Butterfly
1. Caren Metschuck GDR 1:00.42
2. Andrea Pollack GDR 1:00.90
3. Christiane Knacke GDR 1:01.44

200m Butterfly
1. Ines Geissler GDR *2:10.44
2. Sybille Schönrock GDR 2:10.45
3. Michelle Ford AUS 2:11.66

400m Individual Medley
1. Petra Schneider GDR **4:36.29
2. Sharron Davies GBR 4:46.83
3. Agnieszka Czopek POL 4:48.17

4x100m Freestyle Relay
1. GDR 3:42.71 (Barbara Krause, Caren Metschuck, Ines Diers, Sarina Hülsenbeck)
2. SWE 3:48.93 (Carina Jungdahl, Tina Gustafsson, Angeta Martens-son, Agneta Eriksson)
3. NETH 3:49.51 (Cornelia van Bentum, Wilma van Velsen, Reggie de Jong, Annelies Maas)

4x100m Medley
1. GDR **4:06.67 (Rica Reinisch, Ute Geweniger, Andrea Pollack, Caren Metschuck)
2. GBR 4:12.24 (Helen Jameson, Margaret Kelly, Ann Osgerby, June Croft)
3. URS 4:13.61 (Yelena Kruglova, Elvira Vasilkova, Alla Grishchenkova, Natalya Strunnikova)

Springboard Diving
1. Irina Kalinina URS 725.910
2. Martina Proeber GDR 698.895
3. Karin Guthke GDR 684.245

Platform Diving
1. Martina Jäschke GDR 596.250
2. Servard Emirzyan URS 576.465
3. Liana Tsotadze URS 575.925

Boxing

Light Flyweight
1. Shamil Sabyrov URS
2. Hipolito Ramos CUB
3. Ismail Hjuseinov BUL
3. Byong Uk Li PRK

Flyweight
1. Peter Lessov BUL
2. Victor Miroshnichenko URS
3. János Váradi HUN
3. Hugh Russell IRL

Bantamweight
1. Juan Hernandez CUB
2. Bernardo José Pinango VEN
3. Michael Anthony GUY
3. Dumitru Cipere ROM

Featherweight
1. Rudi Fink GDR
2. Adolfo Horta CUB
3. Krzysztof Kosedowski POL
3. Viktor Rybakov URS

Lightweight
1. Angel Herrera CUB
2. Viktor Demianenko URS
3. Richard Nowakowski GDR
3. Kazimierz Adach POL

Light Welterweight
1. Patrizio Oliva ITA
2. Serik Konakbaev URS
3. Anthony Willis GBR
3. José Aguilar CUB

Welterweight
1. Andrés Adalma CUB
2. John Mugabi UGA
3. Karl Heinz Krüger GDR
3. Kazimierz Szczerda POL

Light Middleweight
1. Armando Martinez CUB
2. Aleksandr Koshkin URS
3. Detlef Kästner GDR
3. Ján Franek TCH

Middleweight
1. José Gomez CUB
2. Victor Savchenko URS
3. Valentin Silaghi ROM
3. Jerzy Rybicki POL

Light Heavyweight
1. Slobodan Kacar YUG
2. Pawel Skrzeck POL
3. Herbert Bauch GDR
3. Ricardo Rojas CUB

Heavyweight
1. Teófilo Stevenson CUB
2. Pyotr Zaev URS
3. István Levai HUN
3. Jürgen Fanghänel GDR

Weightlifting

Flyweight
1. Kanybek Osmanoliev URS *245.00
2. Bong-Choi Ho PRK 245.00
3. Gyong Si Han PRK 245.00

Bantamweight
1. Daniel Nunez CUB 275.00
2. Yurik Sarkisian URS 270.00
3. Tadeusz Dembonczyk POL 265.00

Featherweight
1. Viktor Mazin URS *290.00
2. Stefan Dimitrov BUL 287.50
3. Marek Seweryn POL 282.50

Lightweight
1. Yanko Roussev BUL **342.50
2. Joachim Kunz GDR 335.00
3. Mincho Pachov BUL 325.00

Middleweight
1. Assen Zlatev BUL **360.00
2. Aleksandr Pervy URS 375.50
3. Nedelcho Kolev BUL 345.00

Light Heavyweight
1. Yurik Vardanyan URS **400.00
2. Blagoi Blagoev BUL 372.50
3. Dusan Poliacik TCH 367.50

Middle Heavyweight
1. Peter Baczako HUN 377.50
2. Roumen Aleksandrov BUL 375.00
3. Frank Mantek GDR 370.00

100kg
1. Ota Zaremba TCH *395.00
2. Igor Nikitin URS 392.50
3. Alberto Blanco CUB 385.00

Heavyweight
1. Leonid Taranenko URS *422.50
2. Valentin Hristov BUL 405.00
3. György Szalai HUN 390.00

Super Heavyweight
1. Sultan Rakhmanov URS =*440.00
2. Jürgen Heuser GDR 410.00
3. Tadeusz Rutkowski POL 407.50

Greco Roman Wrestling

Light Flyweight
1. Zaksylik Ushkempirov URS
2. Constantin Alexandru ROM
3. Ferenc Seres HUN

Flyweight
1. Vakhtang Blagidze URS
2. Lajos Rácz HUN
3. Mladen Mladenov BUL

Bantamweight
1. Shamil Serikov URS
2. Józef Lipień POL
3. Benni Ljungbeck SWE

Featherweight
1. Stylianos Mygiakis GRE
2. István Tóth HUN
3. Boris Kramorenko URS

Lightweight
1. Stefan Rusu ROM
2. Andrzej Supron POL
3. Lars-Erik Skiöld SWE

Welterweight
1. Ferenc Kocsis HUN
2. Anatoly Bykov URS
3. Mikko Huhtala FIN

Middleweight
1. Gennady Korban URS
2. Jan Dolgowicz POL
3. Pavel Pavlov BUL

Light Heavyweight
1. Norbet Növényi HUN
2. Igor Kanygin URS
3. Petre Dicu ROM

Heavyweight
1. Georgi Raikov BUL
2. Roman Bierla POL
3. Vasile Andrei ROM

Super Heavyweight
1. Aleksandr Kolchinsky URS
2. Aleksandr Tomov BUL
3. Hassan Bchara LIB

1980  Moscow

Freestyle Wrestling

Light Flyweight
1. Claudio Pollio ITA
2. Se Hong Jang PRK
3. Sergei Kornilaev URS

Flyweight
1. Anatoly Beloglazov URS
2. Wladyslaw Stecyk POL
3. Nermedin Selimov BUL

Bantamweight
1. Sergei Beloglazov URS
2. Ho Pyong Li PRK
3. Dugasuren Ouinbold MON

Featherweight
1. Magomedgasan Abushev URS
2. Miho Doukov BUL
3. Georges Hadjiioannidis GRE

Lightweight
1. Saipulla Absaidov URS
2. Ivan Yankov BUL
3. Saban Sejdi YUG

Welterweight
1. Valentin Angelov BUL
2. Jamtsying Davaajav MON
3. Dan Karabin TCH

Middleweight
1. Ismail Abilov BUL
2. Magomedhan Aratsilov URS
3. István Kovács HUN

Light Heavyweight
1. Sanasar Oganesyan URS
2. Uwe Neupert GDR
3. Aleksander Cichon POL

Heavyweight
1. Ilja Mate URS
2. Slavcho Chervenkov BUL
3. Julius Strnisko TCH

Super Heavyweight
1. Soslan Andiev URS
2. József Balla HUN
3. Adam Sandurski POL

Judo

Extra Lightweight
1. Thierry Rey FRA
2. Carbenell Rodriguez CUB
3. Tibor Kincses HUN
3. Aramby Emizh URS

Half Lightweight
1. Nikolai Solodukhin URS
2. Tsendying Damdin MON
3. Iliyan Nedkov BUL
3. Janusz Pawlowski POL

Lightweight
1. Ezio Gamba ITA
2. Neil Adams GBR
3. Karl-Heinz Lechmann GDR
3. Ravdan Davaadalai MON

Half Middleweight
1. Shota Khabareli URS
2. Juan Ferrer CUB
3. Bernard Tchoullouyan FRA
3. Harald Heinke GDR

Middleweight
1. Jürg Röthlisberger SUI
2. Isaac Azcuy CUB
3. Detleef Ultsch GDR
3. Aleksandr Iatskevich URS

Half Heavyweight
1. Robert van de Walle BEL
2. Tengiz Khubuluri URS
3. Dietmar Lorenz GDR
3. Henk Numan NETH

Heavyweight
1. Angelo Parisi FRA
2. Dimitur Zapryanov BUL
3. Vladimir Kocman TCH
3. Radomir Kovacevic YUG

Open Category
1. Dietmar Lorenz GDR
2. Angelo Parisi FRA
3. András Ozsvár HUN
3. Arthur Mapp GBR

Men Fencing

Foil Individual
1. Vladimir Smirnov URS 4
2. Pascal Jolyot FRA 4
3. Aleksandr Romankov URS 3

Foil Team
1. France
2. Soviet Union
3. Poland

Epée Individual
1. Johan Harmenberg SWE 4
2. Erno Kolczonay HUN 3
3. Philippe Riboud FRA 3

Epée Team
1. France
2. Poland
3. Soviet Union

Sabre Individual
1. Viktor Krovopuskov URS 4
2. Mikhail Burtsev URS 4
3. Imre Gedovari HUN 3

Sabre Team
1. Soviet Union
2. Italy
3. Hungary

Women Fencing

Foil Individual
1. Pascale Trinquet FRA 4
2. Magda Maros HUN 3
3. Barbara Wysoczanska POL 3

Foil Team
1. France
2. Soviet Union
3. Hungary

Modern Pentathlon

Individual
1. Anatoly Starostin URS 5568
2. Tamás Szombathelyi HUN 5502
3. Pavel Lednev URS 5382

Team
1. Soviet Union
2. Hungary
3. Sweden

Men Canoeing

Kayak-1 500m
1. Vladimir Parfenovich URS 1:43.43
2. John Sumegi AUS 1:44.12
3. Vasile Diba ROM 1:44.90

Kayak-1 1000m
1. Rüdiger Helm GDR 3:48.77
2. Alain Lebas FRA 3:50.20
3. Ion Birladeanu ROM 3:50.49

Kayak-2 500m
1. Soviet Union 1:32.38
2. Spain 1:33.65
3. German Democratic Republic 1:34.00

Kayak-2 1000m
1. Soviet Union 3:26.72
2. Hungary 3:28.49
3. Spain 3:28.66

Kayak-4 1000m
1. German Democratic Republic 3:13.76
2. Romania 3:15.35
3. Bulgaria 3:15.46

Canadian-1 500m
1. Sergei Postrekhin URS 1:53.37
2. Lyubomir Lyubenov BUL 1:53.49
3. Olaf Heukrodt GDR 1:54.38

Canadian-1 1000m
1. Lyubomir Lyubenov BUL 4:12.38
2. Sergei Postrekhin URS 4:13.53
3. Eckhard Leue GDR 4:15.02

Canadian-2 500m
1. Hungary 1:43.39
2. Romania 1:44.12
3. Bulgaria 1:44.83

Canadian-2 1000m
1. Romania 3:47.65
2. German Democratic Republic 3:49.93
3. Soviet Union 3:51.28

Women Canoeing

Kayak-1 500m
1. Birgit Fischer GDR 1:57.96
2. Vania Gesheva BUL 1:59.48
3. Antonina Melnikova URS 1:59.66

Kayak-2 500m
1. German Democratic Republic 1:43.88
2. Soviet Union 1:46.91
3. Hungary 1:47.95

Men Rowing

Single Sculls
1. Pertti Karppinen FIN 7:09.61
2. Vassily Yakusha URS 7:11.66
3. Peter Kersten GDR 7:14.00

Double Sculls
1. German Democratic Republic 6:24.33
2. Yugoslavia 6:26.34
3. Czechoslovakia 6:29.07

Coxless Pairs
1. German Democratic Republic 6:48.01
2. Soviet Union 6:50.50
3. Great Britain 6:51.47

Coxed Pairs
1. German Democratic Republic 7:02.54
2. Soviet Union 7:03.35
3. Yugoslavia 7:04.92

Quadruple Sculls
1. German Democratic Republic 5:49.81
2. Soviet Union 5:51.47
3. Bulgaria 5:52.38

Coxless Fours
1. German Democratic Republic 6:08.17
2. Soviet Union 6:11.81
3. Great Britain 6:16.58

Coxed Fours
1. German Democratic Republic 6:14.51
2. Soviet Union 6:19.05
3. Poland 6:22.52

Eights
1. German Democratic Republic 5:49.05
2. Great Britain 5:51.92
3. Soviet Union 5:52.66

Women Rowing

Single Sculls
1. Sanda Toma ROM 3:40.69
2. Antonina Makhina URS 3:41.65
3. Martina Schröter GDR 3:43.54

Double Sculls
1. Soviet Union 3:16.27
2. German Democratic Republic 3:17.63
3. Romania 3:18.91

Coxless Pairs
1. German Democratic Republic 3:30.49
2. Poland 3:30.95
3. Bulgaria 3:32.39

Coxed Fours
1. German Democratic Republic 3:19.27
2. Bulgaria 3:20.75
3. Soviet Union 3:20.92

Quadruple Sculls
1. German Democratic Republic 3:15.32
2. Soviet Union 3:15.73
3. Bulgaria 3:16.10

Eights
1. German Democratic Republic 3:03.32
2. Soviet Union 3:04.29
3. Romania 3:05.63

Yachting

Monotype Finn
1. Esko Rechardt FIN 36.7
2. Wolfgang Mayrhofer AUT 46.7
3. Andrei Balashov URS 47.4

Flying Dutchman
1. Spain 19.0
2. Ireland 30.0
3. Hungary 45.7

Soling
1. Denmark 23.0
2. Soviet Union 30.4
3. Greece 31.1

Star
1. Soviet Union 24.7
2. Austria 31.7
3. Italy 36.1

470
1. Brazil 36.4
2. German Democratic Republic 38.7
3. Finland 39.7

Tornado
1. Brazil 21.4
2. Denmark 30.4
3. Sweden 33.7

Cycling

Individual Road Race
1. Sergei Sukhoruchenkov URS 4:48.28
2. Czeslaw Lang POL 4:51.26
3. Yuri Barinov URS 4:51.29

100km Team Time Trial
1. Soviet Union 2:01.22
2. German Democratic Republic 2:02.53
3. Czechoslovakia 2:02.54

1000m Sprint
1. Lutz Hesslich GDR
2. Yave Cahard FRA
3. Sergei Kopylov URS

Steve Ovett (center) celebrates victory in the 800-metre finals; Sebastian Coe (left) later beat Ovett in the 1,500-metre race.

1000m Time Trial
1. Lothar Thoms GDR **1:02.955
2. Aleksandr Panfilov URS 1:04.845
3. David Weller JAM 1:05.241

4000m Individual Pursuit
1. Robert Dill-Bundi SUI 4:35.66
2. Alain Bondue FRA 4:42.96
3. Hans-Erik Orsted DEN 4:36.54

4000m Team Pursuit
1. Soviet Union 4:15.70
2. German Democratic Republic 4:19.68
3. Czechoslovakia

Equestrian Sports

Three-Day Event Individual
1. Federico Roman ITA -108.60
2. Aleksandr Blinov URS -120.80
3. Yuri Salnikov URS -151.60

Three-Day Event Team
1. Soviet Union -457.00
2. Italy -656.20
3. Mexico -1172.85

Individual Dressage
1. Elisabeth Theurer AUT 1370
2. Yuri Kovshov URS 1300
3. Viktor Ugryumov URS 1234

Team Dressage
1. Soviet Union 4383.0
2. Bulgaria 3580.0
3. Romania 3346.0

Individual Grand Prix Jumping
1. Jan Kowalczyk POL -8
2. Nikolai Korolkov URS -9.50
3. Joaquin Perez de las Heras MEX -12

Team Grand Prix Jumping
1. Soviet Union -20.25
2. Poland -56.00
3. Mexico -59.75

Shooting

Small-Bore Rifle, 50m, Prone
1. Károly Verga HUN =**599
2. Hellfried Heilfort GDR =**599
3. Petur Zapianov BUL 598

Small-Bore Rifle, Combined, 3 Positions
1. Viktor Vlasov URS **1173
2. Bernd Hartstein GDR 1166
3. Sven Johansson SWE 1165

Rapid-Fire Pistol, 25m
1. Corneliu Ion ROM 596/443
2. Jürgen Wiefel GDR 596/442
3. Gerhard Petritsch AUT 596/146

Free Pistol
1. Aleksandr Melentov URS **581
2. Harald Vollmar GDR 568
3. Ljubcho Diakov BUL 565

Clay Pigeon
1. Luciano Giovannetti ITA 198
2. Rustam Yambulatov URS 196
3. Jörg Damme GDR 196

Skeet
1. Hans-Kjeld Rasmussen DEN 196
2. Lars-Göran Carlsson SWE 196
3. Roberto Castrillo CUB 196

Moving Target
1. Igor Sokolov URS 589
2. Thomas Pfeffer GDR 589
3. Aleksandr Gazov URS 587

Archery

Men Archery
1. Tomi Poikolainen FIN 2455
2. Boris Isachenko URS 2452
3. Giancarlo Ferrari ITA 2449

Women Archery
1. Keto Losaberidze URS 2491
2. Natalya Butuzova URS 2477
3. Paivi Marilouto FIN 2449

Men Gymnastics

All-around Individual
1. Aleksandr Dityatin URS 118.650
2. Nikolai Andrianov URS 118.225
3. Stoyan Deltchev BUL 118.000

Combined Exercises Team
1. Soviet Union 598.60
2. German Democratic Republic 581.15
3. Hungary 575.00

Parallel Bars
1. Aleksandr Tkatchyov URS 19.775
2. Aleksandr Dityatin URS 19.750
3. Roland Brückner GDR 19.650

Floor Exercises
1. Roland Brückner GDR 19.750
2. Nikolai Andrianov URS 19.725
3. Aleksandr Dityatin URS 19.700

Long Horse Vault
1. Nikolai Andrianov URS 19.825
2. Aleksandr Dityatin URS 19.800
3. Roland Brückner GDR 19.775

Horse
1. Zoltán Magyar HUN 19.925
2. Aleksandr Dityatin URS 19.800
3. Michael Nikolay GDR 19.775

Horizontal Bar
1. Stoyan Deltchev BUL 19.825
2. Aleksandr Dityatin URS 19.750
3. Nikolai Andrianov URS 19.675

Flying Rings
1. Aleksandr Dityatin URS 19.875
2. Aleksandr Tkatchyov URS 19.725
3. Jiri Tabak TCH 19.600

Women Gymnastics

All-around Individual
1. Yelena Davydova URS 79.150
2. Nadia Comaneci ROM 79.075
3. Maxi Gnauck GDR 79.075

Combined Exercises Team
1. Soviet Union 394.90
2. Romania 393.50
3. German Democratic Republic 392.55

Asymmetric Bars
1. Maxi Gnauck GDR 19.875
2. Emilia Eberle ROM 19.850
3. Maria Filatova URS 19.775
3. Steffi Kräker GDR 19.775
3. Melita Rühn ROM 19.775

Floor Exercises
1. Nadia Comaneci ROM 19.875
1. Nelli Kim URS 19.875
3. Natalya Shaposhnikova URS 19.825
3. Maxi Gnauck GDR 19.825

Side Horse Vault
1. Natalya Shaposhnikova URS 19.725
2. Steffi Kräker GDR 19.675
3. Melita Rühn ROM 19.650

Balance Beam
1. Nadia Comaneci ROM 19.800
2. Yelena Davydova URS 19.750
3. Natalya Shaposhnikova URS 19.725

Men Basketball

1. Yugoslavia
2. Italy
3. Soviet Union

Women Basketball

1. Soviet Union
2. Bulgaria
3. Yugoslavia

Football

1. Czechoslovakia
2. German Democratic Republic
3. Soviet Union

Men Handball

1. German Democratic Republic
2. Soviet Union
3. Romania

Women Handball

1. Soviet Union
2. Yugoslavia
3. German Democratic Republic

Men Hockey

1. India
2. Spain
3. Soviet Union

Women Hockey

1. Zimbabwe
2. Czechoslovakia
3. Soviet Union

Men Volleyball

1. Soviet Union
2. Bulgaria
3. Romania

Women Volleyball

1. Soviet Union
2. German Democratic Republic
3. Bulgaria

(Key to symbols and abbreviations p. 1456)

1980

AUGUST

Su	Mo	Tu	We	Th	Fr	Sa
					1	2
3	4	5	6	7	8	9
10	11	12	13	14	15	16
17	18	19	20	21	22	23
24	25	26	27	28	29	30
31						

1. London: Attorney-General Sir Michael Havers announces the introduction of tighter rules for jury vetting.

1. Ireland: 17 die and 51 are seriously hurt when the Dublin to Cork express jumps the rails at 70 mph.

4. London: 56 Iranians are arrested during a protest outside the US embassy in Grosvenor Square (→ 9/9).

6. Salisbury: Cabinet minister Edgar Tekere is charged with the murder of a white farmer.

8. Saudi Arabia: Surgeon Richard Arnott and his wife Penelope are freed and allowed to return to Britain (→28).

12. Mexico: A giant panda gives birth to the first cub born naturally in captivity.

14. Poland: Workers at the Lenin shipyard in Gdansk strike in support of a dismissed colleague (→17).

15. Atlantic: The wreck of the Titanic is reported to have been located 12,000 feet beneath the surface of the sea.

16. London: 37 die when fire breaks out in two nightclubs.

17. Gdansk: Striking shipyard workers issue a 16-point manifesto of their demands (→23).

19. Saudi Arabia: 301 die when a Lockheed Tristar lands in flames at Riyadh Airport (→1/12/81).

22. Jerusalem: Archaeologists say they have found the palace of either King David or King Solomon.

23. Warsaw: The Polish government agrees to negotiate directly with striking Gdansk shipworkers (→24).

24. Warsaw: Premier Edward Babiuch is replaced by Jozef Pinkowski in a government shake-up.→

27. East Germany: Steve Ovett sets a new 1500 metres world record of three minutes 31.4 seconds.

28. London: The Foreign Office denies a cover-up in the case of Helen Smith, who died at a party in Saudi Arabia in 1979 (→9/6/81).

Polish strikers triumph

Members of Solidarity, Poland's independent trade union, demonstrate.

Aug 30. After two months of strikes and demonstrations, Polish workers have wrested far-reaching concessions from their Communist rulers. An agreement signed today by Lech Walesa, the strike leader in the Lenin shipyards at Gdansk, and Mieczyslaw Jagielski, the deputy Prime Minister, provides for independent trade unions, the right to strike, an easing of censorship and the release of political prisoners.

"We are now co-masters of this land," Walesa said at a shipyard meeting to call off the strikes. Jagielski said there were no victors and no vanquished, but there is no hiding the fact that the Party leadership has experienced defeat of a kind that has almost certainly never happened before in the Soviet bloc.

Whether the Polish authorities will be allowed to keep their promises must be open to question in the light of today's denunciation of the Polish strikers in "Pravda", the Soviet Party newspaper, which accuses them of having links with "reactionary Polish emigrants and subversive centres abroad".

UK unemployment tops two million

Aug 27. Unemployment in Britain has topped two million for the first time since 1935 according to figures published today. The total was up by 105,000 on July and officials fear that the total may soon reach 2.5 million. Mrs Thatcher, the Prime Minister, blamed the rise on wage inflation. "We have paid ourselves 22 per cent more for producing four per cent less," she said. The monetarist policy was "absolutely right" and, she added, the Government would not be panicked into introducing emergency measures.

French fishermen block Channel ports

Aug 18. French fishermen have blocked Channel ports in a protest over subsidies, trapping 1,500 British tourists. Two British ferries are on either side of the blockade of fishing vessels in Cherbourg after one broke through the blockade to the strains of "Land of Hope and Glory" from its loudspeakers.

The ferry captains' plans to crash through again last night were scotched by an order from their company, Townsend Thoresen, that to do so would mean "a serious risk of loss of life".

Carter beats off the Kennedy challenge

Aug 14. President Carter was duly endorsed as the Democratic Party's candidate, but not until Senator Edward Kennedy, in a speech widely regarded as the best of his career, had called for unity – and at the same time bitterly divided the party into Kennedy and Carter fans.

The speech has not only made the President, in the eyes of Kennedy supporters at least, seem pale by comparison, it has also drawn attention to the differences between the President's conservative economic programme and Kennedy's more radical proposals. Carter asked for Kennedy's help, saying "I can win much better with him", but again chose Walter Mondale as his running-mate.

Bomb blast kills 84 at Bologna station

Aug 2. Eighty-four people were killed and hundreds injured by a bomb blast in the crowded railway station at Bologna in northern Italy today. It was Europe's most lethal and devastating terrorist outrage. A suitcase packed with at least 90 pounds of high explosive had been left in a waiting room. When it exploded it left a crater five feet deep.

"It was a monstrous act," said a security man. A right-wing group, the Armed Revolutionary Nuclei, claimed responsibility for the explosion. It came after an Italian court sent eight neo-Fascists for trial, accused of causing a train explosion at Bologna six years ago which killed 12. Communists control the city administration, making it a target for Fascist attacks.

The wreckage of Bologna station.

1980

SEPTEMBER

Su	Mo	Tu	We	Th	Fr	Sa
	1	2	3	4	5	6
7	8	9	10	11	12	13
14	15	16	17	18	19	20
21	22	23	24	25	26	27
28	29	30				

1. Gdansk: Striking Lenin shipyard workers return to work (→5).

3. Peking: Chairman Hua resigns the premiership.

5. Switzerland: The world's longest road tunnel, the 10-mile Goschenen-Airolo tunnel, opens.

5. Warsaw: Stanislaw Kania replaces Edward Gierek as Polish Communist Party leader.→

9. Tehran: The British embassy is closed.→

11. Chile: A referendum finds 69.14 per cent of voters in favour of an eight-year extension of Pinochet's term.

16. Moscow: The USSR demands the return of a Soviet soldier who has sought asylum in the US embassy in Kabul.

17. Seoul: Opposition leader Kim Dae Jung is sentenced to death by a military tribunal (→23/1/81).

19. US: One person dies in a fuel explosion in an underground nuclear missile silo at Damascus, Arkansas (→26/10).

20. Tehran: The Iranian government has begun to call up army reservists (→21).

21. Baghdad: Iraq says it has shot down an Iranian Phantom F-4 fighter and sunk eight warships.→

22. UK: A tiger at John Aspinall's private zoo is shot dead after killing the second keeper in a month.

25. Baghdad: Iraq claims it has captured the Iranian city of Khorramshahr and cut a rail link (→16/11).

26. Munich: At least eight are killed and 60 hurt when a bomb goes off at the annual beer festival (→3/10).

27. UK: Alan Minter loses his world middleweight title to Marvin Hagler of the US in the third round.

29. London: Jeremy Isaacs is chosen to head the new fourth television channel.

30. Israel: The shekel replaces the pound as Israel's unit of currency (→18/12).

Iraq attacks the Iranian oil installations

An Iraqi soldier watches as distant Abadan goes up in smoke and flames.

Sept 24. The simmering border war between Iraq and Iran flared into full-scale hostilities today, with Iraqi troops and tanks crashing across the border in a dawn thrust to encircle Abadan. Tonight the oil refinery at Abadan, the world's largest, is blazing, its tanks ruptured by Iraqi artillery and bombs.

The Iraqi attack, after months of border trouble, which culminated last week with the revocation by Iran of the 1975 border treaty, was obviously carefully prepared and is on a large scale.

As well as Abadan and its port of Khorramshahr, the Iraqi army, well-equipped with Russian weapons, has struck at a number of places further north where it claims to have advanced up to ten miles into Iranian territory.

The fighting immediately raised fears that oil supplies to the rest of the world from both Iran and Iraq will be threatened. However, oil stocks are so high in the West that there is no immediate prospect of shortages, but a lengthy stoppage of supplies could provide a lever to force up prices.

The rest of the world is viewing the fighting with concern, but both Russia and the United States last night made it clear that they intend to remain strictly neutral (→25).

Army coup in Turkey "to save democracy"

Turkey's new boss, General Evren.

Sept 14. General Kenan Evren, chief of the Turkish general staff, today announced that he intended to become President – a clear indication that the army means to hold on to the power it seized in a coup three days ago.

General Evren told strikers to go back to work or risk going to prison. All offices and government departments are instructed to start business as usual tomorrow. His National Security Council has arrested some MPs, including the head of an extreme right-wing party. When Evren and six other officers seized power they wanted to save democracy in a faction-ridden nation.

Deported Iranians carried on to plane

Sept 9. Two Iranian students were deported from Britain today after taking part in a violent demonstration outside the American embassy in London last month. Both of them were unwilling to climb the aircraft's steps and had to be half-carried up them. As they were pushed aboard the plane they shouted anti-American slogans.

At the same time the British embassy in Tehran has been closed. Douglas Hurd, a Foreign Office minister, said the risks of the four remaining diplomats being taken hostage were too great (→21/1/81).

Close of play for commentator Arlott

Sept 2. With the last session of the Centenary Test match at Lord's came the end of a momentous era in English cricket. John Arlott, whose Hampshire burr has become synonymous with the radio broadcasting of the game since he first described a match on the air 35 years ago, concluded his last stint of characteristic live commentary. He left the commentary box to applause from the entire crowd, led from the field by the Australian captain Greg Chappell.

Prince Charles's latest girlfriend, Diana Spencer, posed somewhat unwisely with some of the nursery children in her care.

Creation of "Solidarity" union in Poland

Sept 22. Polish workers, who last month won the right to organise free trade unions, today launched their central organisation and called it Solidarity, with Lech Walesa, the Gdansk shipyard worker, as its leader.

The strikes that won substantial concessions from the Polish government have also brought about the downfall of Edward Gierek, the party leader for ten years. He is said to be suffering "serious disturbances of the heart". His successor, named after a hastily-called meeting of the party's central committee, is Stanislaw Kania, aged 53, the party official responsible for overseeing the security forces.

He says the strikes were not against socialism, but against the mistakes of the party.

Solidarity leader Lech Walesa.

Ex-dictator of Nicaragua is assassinated

Sept 17. Anastasio Somoza Debayle, the deposed dictator of Nicaragua, was assassinated today in a fashionable street in Asuncion, the capital of Paraguay. His Mercedes-Benz was ambushed by a small group with a bazooka and automatic weapons. Somoza, aged 54, and his chauffeur and bodyguard died instantly.

Somoza, who has been drinking heavily during his 13-month exile, was on his way to his daily jog at the time of the attack. Several men have been arrested by Asuncion police who say they are connected with the Sandinistas. In Nicaragua there was dancing and cheering in the streets when the news came through. The ruling junta expressed "joy at the death of an evil man", but said the Sandinistas had "nothing to do directly" with the killing.

The Somoza family had ruled Nicaragua for 44 years until the former President was ousted by a combination of the Sandinistas, local businessmen and US government influence. He has been under trial in absentia for some months in Nicaragua for alleged atrocities.

Loyal supporters carry the coffin of Nicaragua's former leader Somoza.

1980

OCTOBER

Su	Mo	Tu	We	Th	Fr	Sa
			1	2	3	4
5	6	7	8	9	10	11
12	13	14	15	16	17	18
19	20	21	22	23	24	25
26	27	28	29	30	31	

1. UK: The Labour Party votes to extend the franchise for leadership elections beyond the parliamentary party.→

1. London: It is announced that the "London Evening News" will close at the end of the month (→22).

3. UK: The Housing Act comes into force, allowing council tenants to buy their homes (→10).

3. Paris: Four die when a bomb goes off at a synagogue.

8. UK: British Leyland launches the Mini Metro.

10. UK: Thatcher tells the Conservative Party conference she is "not for turning" on her economic policies (→24/11).

11. USSR: A team of cosmonauts return to earth after a record 185 days in space aboard Salyut 6 (→8/11).

14. Pyongyang: North Korea's Communist Party appoints Kim Jong Il as heir to his father, President Kim Il Sung.

17. US: Mount St. Helens in Washington state erupts for the third time in 24 hours.

17. Rome: The Queen meets the Pope on the first state visit to the Vatican by a British monarch (→15/11).

21. UK: William Golding wins the Booker Prize for "Rites of Passage".

22. London: Lord Thomson says "The Times" and "Sunday Times" will close next March unless sold (→27/1/81).

23. Spain: 48 children and three adults die in an explosion at a Basque primary school (→15/3/81).

23. Moscow: Kosygin resigns after 16 years as premier.

26. London: 60,000 protesters take part in Britain's biggest anti-nuclear demonstration for nearly 20 years (→24/10/81).

28. London: The DPP decides not to prosecute the National Theatre over the play "The Romans in Britain".

31. Jamaica: Edward Seaga's Labour Party beats Michael Manley's People's National Party in a general election.

Callaghan resigns as Labour leader

Oct 15. James Callaghan today announced his resignation as Labour Party leader. A bitter battle for the succession between the party's left and right wings has begun. The ex-premier, who is 68, said that he wants to hand over to someone bringing "fresh vigour and a fresh eye to our problems".

In truth, his patience is exhausted. He is wounded and tired by the recrimination and splenetic feuding which have engulfed Labour and the unions in the past few years and which made the party's defeat in last year's election inevitable. The leadership fight is likely to be between Denis Healey, backed by the right, and Michael Foot, champion of the left.

Second Nobel puts Briton top of elite

Frederick Sanger in Cambridge.

Oct 14. The British biochemist Dr Frederick Sanger has won a second Nobel Prize. Only two others have been so honoured: the legendary Marie Curie, and the American physicist Professor John Bardeen. Dr Sanger, who works for the Medical Research Council in Cambridge, received his first prize for unravelling the structure of insulin, the first protein to be analysed in full. His new prize – to be presented in December – is for similar work on the hereditary material DNA. He will share the prize with two Americans.

Algerian earthquake kills at least 20,000

Corpses and shattered homes bear mute witness to the Algerian disaster.

Oct 11. Two big earthquakes today destroyed most of the Algerian city of El Asnam. Two towns were also badly hit and government officials say up to 20,000 people may have died.

Two housing complexes, the main hospital, a large department store and the central mosque collapsed. The tremors were so strong that scientists in Sweden said seismological instruments broke.

It was believed to be 7.3 on the Richter scale, the most violent ever in that part of Algeria. As the second, weaker quake hit, huge fissures appeared in the roads.

It is the second time the city has been devastated by an earthquake; in 1954, 1,600 were killed and the city's market was rebuilt with foundations designed to withstand such tremors. Now it is again in ruins. As a weeping television announcer told his countrymen of the catastrophe, rescue helicopters flew into the stricken area with relief food supplies.

Reagan-Carter TV debate is a draw

Oct 28. Both Republicans and Democrats claimed victory after President Jimmy Carter and his Republican challenger, Ronald Reagan, met in their third TV debate in Cleveland last night.

The two candidates kept the tone civil as they debated for 90 minutes, standing less than ten feet from one another, in front of a TV audience of 80 million.

It is not thought the debate will have convinced many voters. The President kept Mr Reagan on the defensive much of the time, and called his plan for tax cuts "ridiculous", but Mr Reagan scored when he dismissed as scaremongering Carter's warnings that he would cut free medical care for the old. "There you go again, Jimmy," he said (→4/11).

Polish church plans to back Solidarity

Oct 19. The Roman Catholic hierarchy, which was praised recently by Poland's Communist rulers for "patriotic prudence and concern for the nation's welfare", today openly threw its support behind the newly launched Solidarity trade-union organisation. Though the authorities solemnly promised to allow free trade unions to operate, they have still not given official recognition to the six-million-strong Solidarity.

The Polish Primate, Cardinal Stefan Wyszynski, told union leaders who visited him in his private chapel: "I am with you. You will survive and hold out." From the outset the Polish clergy and Pope John Paul (the former Cardinal Karol Wojtyla) have supported the Solidarity movement (→7/11).

1980

NOVEMBER

Su	Mo	Tu	We	Th	Fr	Sa
						1
2	3	4	5	6	7	8
9	10	11	12	13	14	15
16	17	18	19	20	21	22
23	24	25	26	27	28	29
30						

2. Tehran: Iran's parliament approves four conditions laid down by Khomeini for the release of the US hostages.

5. Washington: The Republicans control the Senate for the first time in 26 years (→20/1/81).

7. Warsaw: Kania accuses Solidarity of abusing the right to strike (→11/2).

8. US: NASA reports that the Voyager 1 space probe has discovered a 15th moon around Saturn (→14/4/81).

12. London: The Queen opens the General Synod, praising the Church of England's new Alternative Service Book.

13. London: Denis Healey is Labour deputy leader (→3/12).

15. Cologne: Pope John Paul arrives on a visit to West Germany (→13/5/81).

16. Iran: 500 Iranians are reported to have died in an Iraqi attack on the town of Susangerd.

19. UK: Student Jacqueline Hill is confirmed as the 13th victim of the "Yorkshire Ripper" (→25).

23. Italy: A severe earthquake devastates a wide area in the south of the country (→25).

24. London: Howe announces a cut in the minimum lending rate from 16 to 14 per cent (→16/1/81).

25. Italy: 3,000 are now believed to have died in the earthquake (→4/1/81).

25. UK: A team of detectives is sent to Yorkshire to assist the county's police in the search for the "Ripper".

29. El Salvador: 20 die in violence following the murder of prominent leftists (→27/12).

DEATHS

7. US actor Steve McQueen (*24/3/1930).→

9. Irish journalist and humorist Patrick Gordon Campbell, third Baron Glenavy (*6/6/1913).

22. US actress Mae West (*17/8/1892).

Screen tough guy McQueen is dead

McQueen – Hollywood speedster.

Nov 7. Steve McQueen, the screen's tough guy par excellence, stayed tough to the end. Fighting "inoperable" cancer, he got married for the third time, to a model of 25, and went to Mexico for treatment. He died of a heart attack following an operation. McQueen's obsession with racing bikes and cars stood him in good stead in such films as "Bullitt" and "The Great Escape".

Dallas turns Britain into soap addicts

Nov 19. "Who shot JR?" The topic has been discussed by newspapers and even replayed on the TV news, such is Britain's addiction to the US TV series "Dallas". The suspense ended tonight. The soap opera's baddie was shot by Kristen.

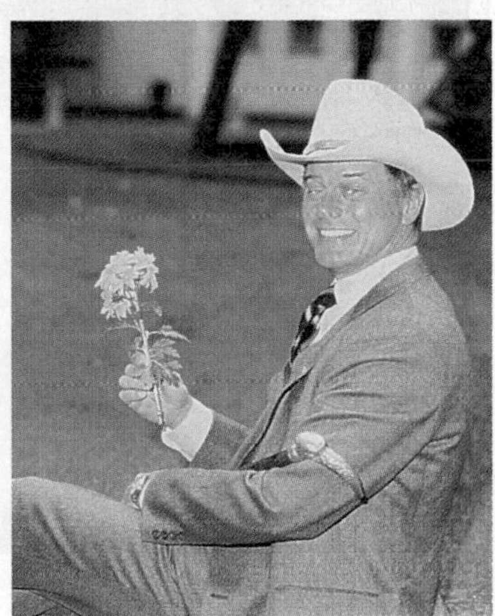

"J.R." – the man you love to hate. ▷

Reagan defeats Carter

Nov 4. Governor Ronald Reagan, the Republican candidate, and his vice-presidential running mate, George Bush, trounced President Carter and Walter Mondale in the presidential election today.

President Carter could only carry six States out of the 50. He was the first elected sitting President to be defeated since Hoover in 1932. Reagan won 43.9 million votes, Carter only 35.4 million.

Carter's popularity suffered from the energy crisis and petrol queues, but it was his failure to free the US hostages in Tehran which sealed his electoral fate.

Ronald Reagan.

Michael Foot is the new Labour leader

Nov 10. Michael Foot became Labour's leader tonight – and the party kept its fingers crossed. The 67-year-old veteran left-winger's victory over Denis Healey, a former Chancellor of the Exchequer, in the contest to succeed James Callaghan was unexpected. It was by 139 votes to 129 in a ballot of Labour MPs.

In the parliamentary lobbies there is speculation that Mr Foot's appointment may hasten the defection of some moderates who talk about leaving to form a new centre party. The Tories are pleased about Labour's choice. They regard Mr Foot as "easy meat".

British boxer dies after a title fight

Nov 4. Johnny Owen, the shy young Welsh bantamweight, has died in Los Angeles after being knocked out by the Mexican Lupe Pintor during their contest for the world crown. He had been in a coma ever since the fight some six weeks ago.

The thin, almost weedy, 24-year-old from Tredegar hardly looked like a world-class fighter, but he commanded enormous affection throughout Wales. He survived into the 12th round against the champion before falling to an overwhelming rain of punches. He never regained consciousness.

Saturn's rings, seen from Voyager 1: pictures show they form a complex of concentric circles, deep-space rings within rings.

1980

DECEMBER

Su	Mo	Tu	We	Th	Fr	Sa
	1	2	3	4	5	6
7	8	9	10	11	12	13
14	15	16	17	18	19	20
21	22	23	24	25	26	27
28	29	30	31			

3. London: Thatcher axes 192 "quangos", bringing to 400 the number she has wound up (→ 5/1/81).

8. Salisbury: Cabinet minister Edgar Tekere is cleared of murdering a white farmer (→ 15/2/81).

10. Stockholm: Nobel Prizes go to James Cronin and Val Fitch (US, Physics); Paul Berg (US), Walter Gilbert (US) and Frederick Sanger (UK), all Chemistry; Baruj Benacerraf (US), Jean Dausset (France) and George Snell (US), all Medicine; Czeslaw Milos (US, Literature); Lawrence Klein (US, Economics); and in Oslo to Adolfo Perez Esquivel (Argentina, Peace).

14. Liverpool and New York: Thousands of fans hold a 10-minute vigil for John Lennon (→ 6/1/81).

16. London: IRA bomber Gerard Tuite and two others escape from Brixton Prison.

24. Bangui: Bokassa is sentenced to death in absentia.

28. London: Southern TV and Westward TV lose their IBA franchises; TV-AM wins the breakfast TV franchise.

DEATHS

3. British politician Sir Oswald Mosley (*16/11/1896).→

8. British musician John Winston Lennon (*9/10/1940).→

18. British playwright Ben Travers (*12/11/1886).→

18. Soviet statesman Alexei Kosygin, premier 1964-80 (*20/2/1904).

24. German commander Grand Admiral Karl Doenitz, briefly Fuehrer, 1945 (*16/9/1891).

HITS OF 1980

Don't stand so close to me.

Woman in love.

Crying.

QUOTE OF THE YEAR

"The lady's not for turning."

Margaret Thatcher, at the Conservative Party conference, October 10, 1980.

American nuns are killed in Salvador

Dec 27. Mystery still surrounds the killing of three American nuns and a lay missionary in El Salvador earlier this month. Yesterday more violence erupted when 1,000 leftist guerrillas opened fire on government forces. Since October 1979 over 9,000 people, mostly civilians, have been killed in the fighting.

American aid was suspended after the death of the nuns which forced a government crisis. The exiled President, Jose Napoleon Duarte, has returned to lead a new four-man junta which is trying to stop the fighting (→ 11/1/81).

Mosley, a star who lost his way, dies

Mosley, the home-grown Fuehrer.

Dec 3. Sir Oswald Mosley, friend of Hitler and Mussolini and loathed for trying to bring Fascism to Britain, died today, aged 84.

He was born into high society – rich, handsome and physically brave. He became a Socialist. He took office in a Labour government and was tipped as a future premier. Then, in the 1930s, he formed the British Union of Fascists whose quasi-military Blackshirts marched with thuggery in London's Jewish districts and elsewhere.

Mosley was interned during the war against the dictators whose example he wanted the British people to follow.

John Lennon shot dead

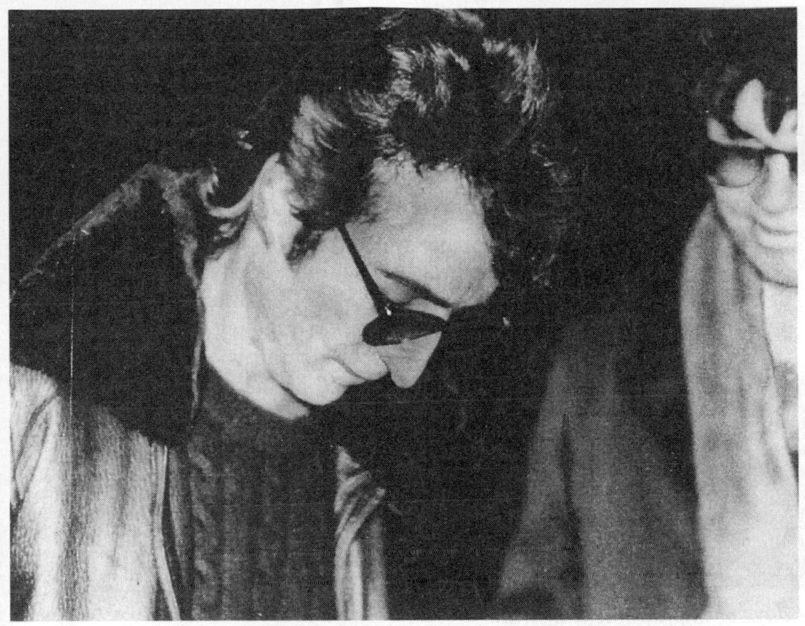

John Lennon signs an autograph for Mark Chapman – his murderer.

Dec 8. John Lennon, who as one of the Beatles helped shape the music and the philosophies of a generation, was shot dead late tonight outside the Dakota building, his home in New York.

Lennon, aged 40, had driven back from a recording session and was walking with his wife Yoko Ono into the building when he was approached by Mark David Chapman, aged 25. Chapman, to whom Lennon had given his autograph earlier in the day, shot the musician five times at point-blank range, using a .38 revolver purchased at a gunshop in Honolulu.

Lennon was rushed to Roosevelt Hospital for surgery, but failed to recover. After the shooting Chapman seemed pleased, and read "Catcher in the Rye" while waiting to be arrested. He is being held under high security in the Tombs Prison tonight. Police say that after flying from Hawaii he stalked Lennon for three days before carrying out the shooting.

West warns Soviets stay out of Poland

Dec 11. NATO leaders last night issued a warning to the Soviet Union that intervention in Poland's internal affairs would destroy detente between East and West. The warning came after a meeting between Soviet and Warsaw Pact officials in Moscow over the labour crisis stemming from Poland's approval for independent unions. Solidarity leader Lech Walesa condemned "irresponsible strikes".

There are fears of an invasion following a concentration of Soviet troops on the Polish border. NATO warned that if the Soviets intervene it would react "in the manner that the gravity of this development would require" (→9/2/81).

IRA hunger strikers begin to eat again

Dec 12. The campaign for political status in Ulster jails is ending. Seven hunger strikers, including one who is close to death, today asked for food. Mrs Thatcher, the Prime Minister, was attending a staff Christmas party at Downing Street when she heard the news.

It is hard to say exactly why the campaign is ending, as both sides are giving totally contradictory reasons. The most likely one is that Charles Haughey, the Irish Prime Minister, was able to convince the leaders that the families of the prisoners wanted it to end.

Recently the European Commission on Human Rights rejected the case for political status.

Arts: Regency-style log wins the Booker

Literature has dominated the year in the arts, both in itself and as the material for stage and screen. The Booker Prize was won by **William Golding** for "Rites of Passage", a vivid reconstruction of a voyage to Australia in a man o' war of Nelson's times. It takes the form of a log of the voyage kept in the language of Regency England.

A strong contender for the prize was "Earthly Powers", also a tour de force by another master of language, **Anthony Burgess**. An aged homosexual writer narrates his life story in a series of scenes that mix fictitious and real events and people. James Joyce's Paris, Mussolini's Italy, Nazi Germany, Papal Rome, Hollywood and a sinister love-cult in California which commits mass suicide are among the set-pieces.

Graham Greene produced a curiosity, "Dr Fischer of Geneva", whose greedy party guests are induced to play Russian Roulette with his crackers, one of which is a bomb. His more admired novel, "The Human Factor", about treachery and conscience in an unappealing British Secret Service, was made into a film by **Otto Preminger** with a script by **Tom Stoppard**. So was **Gunter Grass's** masterpiece, "The Tin Drum", which views the rise of the Nazis through the clear eyes of a boy who refuses to grow up.

Ben Travers, a farceur supreme, who died on December 18.

There were contrary opinions about how far such novels could be translated to the screen, but none about "Nicholas Nickleby" which the Royal Shakespeare Company staged with verve. The eight-hour adaptation by **David Edgar** was acclaimed as an artistic triumph and a box-office sell-out.

"The Romans in Britain", by **Howard Brenton**, outraged the National Theatre's backers, the GLC, which half-threatened to withdraw its grant. When the Director of Public Prosecutions declined to take it to court for obscenity (a scene of the simulated homosexual rape of a Briton by a Roman soldier), **Mrs Mary Whitehouse** said she would.

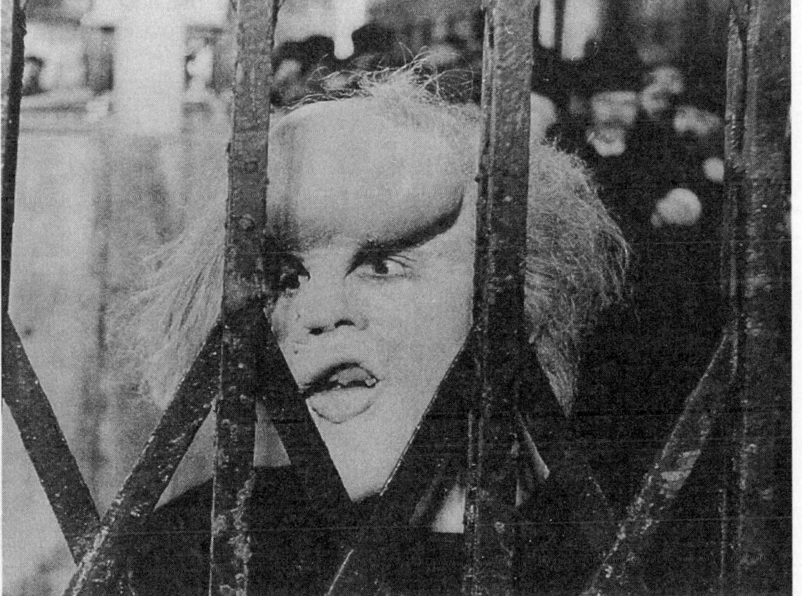

John Hurt, transformed by skilful makeup into "The Elephant Man".

1981

JANUARY

Su	Mo	Tu	We	Th	Fr	Sa
				1	2	3
4	5	6	7	8	9	10
11	12	13	14	15	16	17
18	19	20	21	22	23	24
25	26	27	28	29	30	31

1. Brussels: Greece joins the EEC (→13/8).

2. UK: The Queen is upset at the press invasion of Sandringham, sparked by rumours of Prince Charles' engagement (→24/2).

3. London: Anti-vivisection protesters attack the homes of Oxford and Cambridge scientists.

4. UK: Yorkshire police hold a suspect for the "Ripper" murders; they are "totally delighted".→

5. London: Thatcher sacks Norman St. John Stevas as Leader of the Commons; Francis Pym takes over (→25).

6. New York: Mark Chapman pleads insanity to the charge of murdering Lennon (→22/6).

11. El Salvador: The junta declares martial law (→30/4).

14. London: Publication of the Nationality Bill, which would replace the current citizenship with three new categories.

16. UK: Inflation is down to 15.1 per cent (→26).

18. London: Ten die and over 30 are injured when a fire bomb is thrown into a West Indian party in Deptford (→25).

20. Washington: Reagan is inaugurated as 40th President (→26/2).

23. Seoul: The death sentence on opposition leader Kim Dae Jung is commuted to life imprisonment.

25. London: Another person dies from injuries received during the Deptford fire (→2/3).

26. London: Industry Secretary Keith Joseph announces an extra £990 million state aid for British Leyland (→10/2).

26. London: Nine Labour MPs declare their support for the SDP "Gang of Four" (→27).

27. London: Bill Rodgers resigns from the shadow cabinet (→4/2).

DEATHS

6. British author Archibald Joseph Cronin (*19/7/1896).

23. US composer Samuel Barber (*9/3/1910).

Iran releases hostages

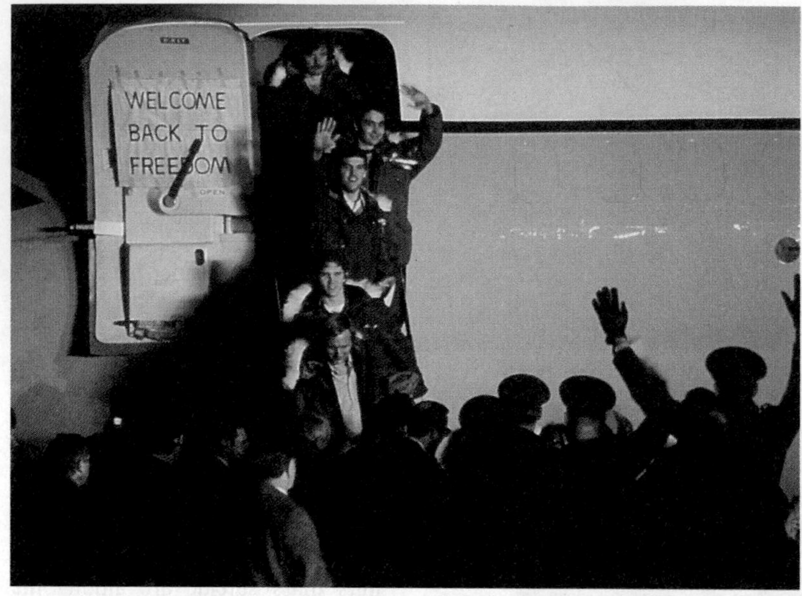

American embassy staff return from 444 days of imprisonment in Iran.

Jan 21. After 444 days of captivity the US hostages taken by Iranian "students" who stormed the US embassy in Tehran have been released and in the early hours of this morning, exhausted but smiling, they stepped to freedom in Algiers.

First off the Algerian aircraft which had flown them from Tehran was Bruce Laingen, the charge d'affaires and the senior diplomat to be held captive, flanked by the two women hostages, Kathryn Koob and Elizabeth Ann Swift. The two women wore yellow ribbons, the American symbol of coming home, in their hair.

One by one the hostages shook hands as an improvised reception line formed. There were kisses, hugs, laughter. All 52 seemed well. Last to disembark were the Marines who had guarded the embassy.

All across the United States the news was greeted with the pealing of bells and the sounding of sirens. In New York, where a huge sign had recorded their days of captivity, a new sign now reads "Free at last, thank God, free at last". And it added: "Never again".

However, the Ayatollah Khomeini humiliated President Carter to the very end by delaying the hostages' departure from Tehran Airport until the President's term of office ended with the inauguration of President Reagan (→4/2).

The new President and Mrs Reagan wave to crowds after the inauguration.

Charges brought in Ripper murder case

Jan 5. A long-distance lorry-driver was today charged with murder by police investigating the Yorkshire Ripper killings. Peter Sutcliffe, aged 35, made a five-minute appearance at Dewsbury court accused of murdering Jacqueline Hill, a Leeds student whose body was found in the city two months ago.

Sutcliffe, thick-set, with curly black straggling hair and a short beard, stood in the dock with head bowed as the charge was read out. More than 100 reporters filled the oak courtroom, while outside a crowd of 1,000 jeered and shouted "Hang him". He was remanded in custody for a week. Meanwhile workmates said he was "highly thought of by everyone" (→29/4).

Sutcliffe on his wedding day.

Ex-Ulster MP shot by Loyalist gunmen

Jan 16. Three men smashed their way into a remote farmhouse in Ulster today and fired seven shots into Mrs Bernadette McAliskey – the former Westminster MP Bernadette Devlin. Mrs McAliskey, who was dressing two of her three children at the time, was "critically ill" in a Belfast hospital tonight. Her husband, Michael, also shot, was said to be "stable".

Friends said that Mrs McAliskey had feared an attack because of her championing of the cause of IRA prisoners in the H-block of the Maze Prison (→1/3).

Gang of Four break with Labour Party

The founder members of the breakaway Council for Social Democracy.

Jan 25. The prototype of a new radical party out to change the face of British politics was launched tonight by four former cabinet ministers. Roy Jenkins, Shirley Williams, David Owen and William Rodgers will now be thrown out of the Labour Party for forming a Council for Social Democracy. From Dr Owen's London dockland home they issued what they are calling the Limehouse Declaration. In this, the breakaway Gang of Four condemned Labour for drifting towards extremism and called for a classless crusade for social justice. A new party will be formed this summer (→26).

Murdoch is allowed to buy "The Times"

Jan 27. Rupert Murdoch's "conditional" agreement to buy "The Times" and "Sunday Times" from the Canadian-based Thomson Organisation, announced on January 22, is to go ahead without the investigation normally required by the Monopolies Commission. John Biffen, the Trade Secretary, told the House of Commons today that the delay involved in such an enquiry would risk the permanent closure of "The Times" (→12/2).

Smokers poison air

Jan 16. A research study into lung cancer has found that the death rate was twice as high in the women married to men who smoked 20 or more cigarettes a day than in those married to non-smokers, even if they do not smoke themselves. According to the Takeshi Hirayama National Cancer Research Institute in Tokyo, the effect of such passive or involuntary smoking is a third to a half that of direct smoking.

Mao's widow guilty of cultural crimes

The mightily fallen Mrs Mao.

Jan 25. Chiang Ching, the 67-year-old widow of Mao Tse-tung, was dragged shouting from a courtroom in Peking today after being given a suspended death sentence for committing "counter-revolutionary" crimes during the Cultural Revolution (→28/2).

1981

FEBRUARY

Su	Mo	Tu	We	Th	Fr	Sa
1	2	3	4	5	6	7
8	9	10	11	12	13	14
15	16	17	18	19	20	21
22	23	24	25	26	27	28

3. Norway: Gro Harlem Brundtland becomes the country's first woman Prime Minister.

4. London: The Gang of Four publishes a list of 100 sympathisers among MPs (→9).

4. London: A verdict of justifiable homicide is returned on the terrorists who died in the Iranian embassy siege (→10/6).

8. Athens: 24 die in a stampede at a football match.

9. London: Shirley Williams resigns from Labour's national executive committee (→26/3).

10. London: The Coal Board announces plans to close 50 pits employing 30,000 miners (→17).

12. London: Rupert Murdoch reaches agreement with the unions on his takeover of "The Times" and "Sunday Times" (→18).

12. Athens: Ex-King Constantine returns for the first time in 14 years for the funeral of his mother, Queen Frederika (→18/10).

15. Zimbabwe: Over 300 people have died in a week in clashes between ZANLA and ZIPRA guerrillas.→

17. UK: South Wales miners begin an unofficial strike.→

18. London: Harold Evans is appointed editor of "The Times", while Frank Giles takes over as editor of the "Sunday Times".

24. Spain: Tejero abandons his coup attempt; rebel General Milano del Bosch and 19 other officers are arrested (→27).

26. Washington: Thatcher meets President Reagan for the first time (→6/3).

27. Madrid: Thousands take part in a march condemning the coup and supporting Spanish democracy.

28. Peking: China announces new austerity measures which include some encouragement of private business.

DEATH

9. US rock singer Bill Haley (*6/7/1925).

Charles and Di are to marry in July

Feb 24. After an announcement yesterday that the Prince of Wales, aged 32, is to marry beautiful Lady Diana Spencer, aged 19, events took a new and informal turn.

The Prince invited the press to chat to him and Diana in the Palace sitting room where he proposed, prior to her recent visit to Australia – "I wanted to give her a chance to think about it and if it was all going to be too awful."

Diana's father, Earl Spencer, said: "Prince Charles telephoned and asked: 'Can I marry your daughter?' Very surprisingly she has said yes" (→5/5).

Charles and Di – the official shot.

The St. Valentine's Day disco tragedy

Feb 14. Forty-nine people, most of them teenagers, died tonight when fire gutted a Dublin disco during a St. Valentine's Day dance. A further 130 victims were badly injured. The Irish state radio played solemn music as the full scale of the tragedy left a country in mourning.

Flames spread so fast through the Stardust Club that there was little chance to escape. Those who managed to battle their way out of the dance floor found iron bars and shutters across windows, while the main exits were blocked by people forcing their way in to try to find loved ones. ▷

Mugabe uses force against former ally

Feb 15. Ten months after white Rhodesia became independent Zimbabwe with a black government, Robert Mugabe, the Prime Minister, is using white-led air and ground forces to crush a rebellion by guerrilla supporters of Joshua Nkomo, his former ally in the liberation struggle.

At least 300 people are reported dead and, with the mortuary in Bulawayo overflowing, bodies are being stored in refrigerated coaches in a siding at the railway station.

The regular forces were sent in after fighting broke out between Mugabe and Nkomo supporters at camps in Nkomo's Matabeland tribal base. Rival guerrilla units were recently integrated in preparation for induction into the regular army, but Nkomo's men say members of Mugabe's Shona tribe are getting favoured treatment in independent Zimbabwe.

Thatcher steps up privatisation drive

Feb 4. The Government announced today that it will sell half of the shares in British Aerospace, the civil and military aircraft business nationalised in 1977. This is part of Mrs Thatcher's drive to "privatise" nationalised industries, and will raise £150 million of which the Treasury will keep £50 million with the company receiving the rest.

City experts expect far more applications from small investors than can be satisfied. Employees of the company will get priority and preferential terms if they apply.

The British Aerospace offer for sale is just a modest instalment of what Mrs Thatcher and her policy planners are scheduling for the next few years if the Tories win a second term. Future transfers envisaged to the private sector include British Gas, British Electricity, British Telecommunications and the Trustee Savings Bank. In the meantime the Government is promising to expose state-owned organisations to greater competition. "You're seeing a quiet revolution," said a Thatcher aide.

Guardia Civil takes Spanish MPs hostage

Lt-Col. Antonio Tejero brandishes his pistol on the tribunal of the Cortes.

Feb 23. King Juan Carlos, dressed in military uniform, told the Spanish people in a television broadcast early today that he had ordered the armed forces to "take all necessary measures" to put down an attempted coup by a right-wing group of the paramilitary Guardia Civil.

The guards, led by the moustachioed Lieutenant-Colonel Tejero de Molina, burst into the Cortes, the Spanish parliament, this afternoon and, firing sub-machine guns into the ceiling, took the cabinet and some 350 MPs hostage.

The first result of the King's tough four-minute speech was that the Francoist General, Jaime Milans del Bosch, who appeared to be behind the attempted coup, ordered his troops back to their barracks from the positions they had taken up in Valencia.

The general had earlier declared a state of emergency in eastern Spain in which he said his regulations would remain in force until other instructions came from the king, or, he added significantly, "from some other superior authority". The King's broadcast seems to have ended his ambitions.

Thatcher's U-turn over miners' strike

Feb 18. In the first major U-turn by Mrs Thatcher's Conservative government, more state money was promised for the coal mines today. Pressure has been building up for a national miners' strike since the Coal Board released a plan to close 50 pits and lose 30,000 jobs a week ago. Already 26,000 men in the more militant areas of South Wales have come out on strike.

The Government is anxious to avoid the kind of head-on clash with miners that brought down the government of Edward Heath. They may have succeeded. Today Joe Gormley, the miners' president, said a strike was no longer necessary. Other NUM leaders are waiting for details (→23/4).

Torvill and Dean win first Euro title

Feb 6. With a free dance performance of originality and almost revolutionary dramatic expression, the young Nottingham pairing of Jayne Torvill, aged 23, and Christopher Dean, aged 22, today won back for Britain the European ice dancing title. This has been in Soviet hands – latterly those of the former world champions Moiseeva and Minenkov – for 12 years.

Moderate general takes over as Poland's new Prime Minister

Feb 9. The continuing strikes and demonstrations, which have dragged Poland to the brink of economic collapse, tonight brought down the Prime Minister of only five months. At a turbulent meeting of the Communist Party's ruling Central Committee, Pinkowski was sacked and replaced by the Defence Minister, General Jaruzelski.

Though the general received his training in the Soviet Union, he is seen as a moderate in the context of Soviet bloc politics. Even so, the appointment reflects the party leadership's concern at the continuing unrest, and is an acknowledgement of the critical role the armed forces will play in the event of a showdown with the Solidarity movement.

General Jaruzelski, flanked by fellow members of the Warsaw Pact.

1981

MARCH

Su	Mo	Tu	We	Th	Fr	Sa
1	2	3	4	5	6	7
8	9	10	11	12	13	14
15	16	17	18	19	20	21
22	23	24	25	26	27	28
29	30	31				

1. Northern Ireland: IRA prisoner Bobby Sands begins a hunger strike.→

2. London: 17 police are hurt and 23 people arrested during a protest at police handling of the Deptford fire (→3/4).

6. Washington: Reagan announces plans to cut 37,000 federal jobs (→13).

9. London: John Lambe, the "M5 Rapist" who admitted 16 attacks, receives 12 life sentences.

11. London: Britain agrees to grant independence to Belize by the end of the year.

13. Washington: Reagan assigns $1.5 million to aid the inquiry into 21 murdered or missing Atlanta children (→30).

13. London: Tom O'Carroll, head of the Paedophile Information Exchange, gets two years for corrupting public morals (→18).

15. Damascus: 101 Pakistan Airways hostages are freed after 13 days, on the release of 54 opponents of General Zia.

18. London: Sir Peter Hayman is named in the Commons as the diplomat mentioned in the Old Bailey paedophile trial.

20. Buenos Aires; Isabel Peron is jailed for eight years for corruption.

20. New York: Jean Harris gets 15 years for killing Scarsdale Diet doctor Herman Tarnower.

26. London: The Gang of Four formally launch the Social Democratic Party (→7/5).

29. London: Dick Beardsley of the US wins the first London Marathon; Joyce Smith wins the women's trophy.

DEATHS

9. British intelligence chief Sir Maurice Oldfield (*16/11/1915).

23. British motor sportsman Mike Hailwood (*4/4/1940).→

23. British commander Field Marshal Sir Claude John Eyre Auchinleck (*21/6/1884).

30. US publisher De Witt Wallace, founder of Reader's Digest (*12/11/1889).

Reagan wounded in assassination bid

March 30. President Reagan was shot in the chest by a 25-year-old disc jockey today as he left a Washington hotel where he had been speaking to a trade union audience.

The 70-year-old President was hit three inches from his heart by a bullet which lodged in his left lung. It was successfully removed at George Washington hospital, and Mr Reagan is said to be in a stable condition with an "excellent" chance of recovery.

Three other men were wounded: Jim Brady, the President's press secretary; a Secret Service agent; and a Washington policeman.

All four were shot by John Hinckley III, the son of a Denver oil executive. He is a former Yale student who dropped out and had been working as a disc jockey.

Most of the President's top White House staff hurried the few blocks to the hospital. Mrs Nancy Reagan, wearing a cherry-red coat, was driven to the hospital and ran indoors. When she was taken in to see her husband, he quoted a quip from a 1930s film: "Honey, I forgot to duck". As he was being given an anaesthetic before the operation, Mr Reagan said to the surgeons: "I hope you guys are Republicans."

In the near-panic which seized the Government after the news of the assassination attempt, the Secretary of State, Alexander Haig, made what may prove to be a damaging mistake. He told a press conference that, after the President and the Vice-President, Mr Bush, he, as Secretary of State, was in control.

Unfortunately, under the US constitution, the Speaker of the House of Representatives, currently "Tip" O'Neill, comes next in the order of succession. Mr Haig's agitated appearance on television did nothing to reassure viewers.

The President was leaving the hotel and walking to his limousine, waving to a crowd of onlookers, when Hinckley fired six shots from 10 feet away. He was pinned against a wall as Secret Servicemen threw the President bodily into a car, which raced to the hospital. He fired a .22 revolver: a .45, one doctor said, "would have blown him away". Congress closed for the day, as did Wall Street (→27/4).

The President waves as he leaves the hotel, then (middle photo) looks up in surprise before (lower photo) his aides push him to his car and safety.

Armed Secret Service agents stand guard as police tend the wounded while in the background the assailant is surrounded by other security officers. ▷

IRA hunger striker stands for parliament

March 15. Events in troubled Northern Ireland took an ominous turn today as a 27-year-old convicted terrorist – on hunger strike with three others in the Maze Prison – was put up as a Republican candidate in a by-election.

Bobby Sands, serving a 14-year sentence for a firearms offence, has been fasting for two weeks. The protest stems from a demand by IRA prisoners for "prisoner of war" status involving segregation from loyalist supporters in the Maze. The strike is believed to have been carefully timed to coincide with the traditional commemoration of the 1916 Dublin Easter rising.

Sands, said to be the "commander" of the IRA prisoners, played a major role in last December's hunger-strike when he acted as negotiator. That strike ended after 55 days. He has spent much of the past eight years in prison for terrorist offences. After his release from a five year sentence, he was arrested after a bombing attack and received 14 years (→ 11/4).

Bike king Hailwood dies in a car crash

March 23. Mike Hailwood, the finest exponent of motor-cycle racing that Britain has ever produced, died today in a motor accident two miles from his home in Warwickshire. His nine-year-old daughter was also killed when his car collided with a lorry.

Hailwood, who was only 40, had become synonymous with motorcycling success worldwide, winning nine world championships as well as 14 Tourist Trophy titles on the notorious Isle of Man circuit.

In 1968 "Mike the Bike" retired at the top to drive Formula One racing cars. A TT comeback at the age of 37 brought one last victory before he retired for good.

Motorbike champ Mike Hailwood.

Was ex-MI5 chief really a Soviet spy?

March 26. The British establishment was shaken today by a report alleging that the former head of MI5 was in fact a "mole" for the KGB. Sir Roger Hollis – who headed the security service from 1956 until 1965 – was named as the likely suspect.

In a forthcoming book "Their Trade is Treachery", the writer Chapman Pincher claims that MI5 men had agitated for an inquiry after concern about the scale of Soviet penetration into the organisation.

Lord Trend, formerly the Cabinet Secretary Sir Burke Trend, who conducted the inquiry, questioned Sir Roger and said that he was the most likely suspect. Sir Roger died in 1973.

Solidarity calls for a national strike

March 27. Millions of Polish workers defied their Communist masters today and staged a four-hour general strike that paralysed industry from the Baltic shipyards to the Silesian coalfield. The strike was called by the independent trade union, Solidarity, in protest at police treatment of union activists.

It was also a calculated demonstration of strength directed at hardliners in the Communist leadership, who are resisting the concessions made to Solidarity last year. "We cannot back down until the hardliners make their exit," Lech Walesa, the Solidarity leader, told a Warsaw rally. The party hardliners are said to be demanding martial law (→ 7/4).

1981

APRIL

Su	Mo	Tu	We	Th	Fr	Sa
			1	2	3	4
5	6	7	8	9	10	11
12	13	14	15	16	17	18
19	20	21	22	23	24	25
26	27	28	29	30		

1. US: Robert De Niro wins an Oscar for "Raging Bull" and Sissy Spacek one for "Coal Miner's Daughter".

3. London: At least 80 people, including 40 police, are injured when 300 skinheads and 400 Asians clash in Southall (→ 4).

3. UK: The report on the Alexander Kielland disaster sharply criticises the design of the North Sea hotel platform.

7. Moscow: The USSR calls off Warsaw Pact exercises to ease tension in Poland (→ 7/6).

13. London: Thatcher condemns the Brixton riots as "utterly wrong...unjustified... criminal".

13. London: As new violence erupts in Brixton, Whitelaw announces an inquiry headed by Lord Scarman (→ 13/5).

14. US: The space shuttle Columbia lands after its three-day maiden flight (→ 19/6).

19. Belfast: The first shipment of De Lorean DMC12 sports cars leaves for New York (→ 6/10).

20. Belfast: Clashes worsen as Bobby Sands passes the 51st day of his hunger strike (→ 5/5).

23. UK: Unemployment has reached 2.5 million (→ 30/5).

26. France: Giscard is ahead of Socialist leader Mitterrand after the first ballot of the presidential election (→ 10/5).

27. US: A Maryland judge rules that ex-Vice-President Agnew took bribes, and orders their repayment (→ 28/8).

27. UK: James Goldsmith's news magazine, "Now!", closes after less than two years of publication.

30. Washington: The House of Representatives says aid to El Salvador will be cut if indiscriminate killings do not stop (→ 9/5).

DEATHS

8. US commander General Omar Nelson Bradley (*12/2/1893).

12. US boxer Joe Louis Barrow (*13/5/1914).

Jockey beats cancer and wins National

Bob Champion and victor Aldaniti.

April 4. With half the packed Aintree stand cheering, and the other half fighting back tears of emotion, Aldaniti led the Grand National from start to finish today to complete a stirring tale of courage by both the horse and his 32-year-old jockey Bob Champion.

For Aldaniti, years of tendon trouble and a broken hock bone were forgotten as he led the field home. For Champion, the triumph was even more dramatic: in 1979 he was given eight months to live when cancer was diagnosed, and his fight back to health caught the imagination of the racing world.

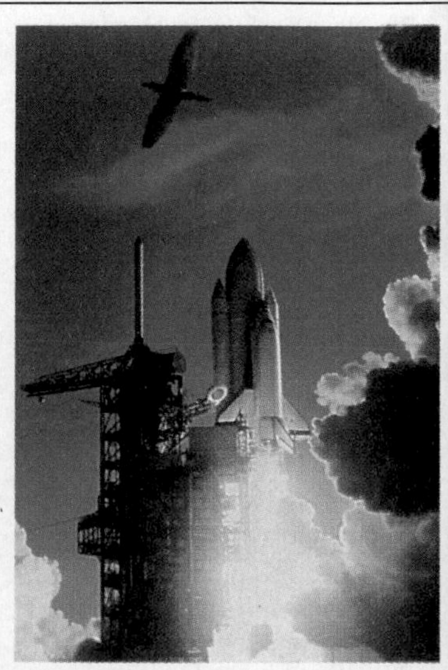

The space shuttle Columbia, the world's first reusable spacecraft, takes off on its first flight.

Brixton is ablaze as black youths riot

April 4. Hundreds of youths, both black and white, turned the south London streets of Brixton into a battleground tonight as they fought skirmishes with the police and indulged in an orgy of looting, vandalism and arson.

After a second night of violence in this major centre of London's black population, 213 people have been arrested and 201 police have been injured. Members of the fire and ambulance services, as well as press and TV journalists, have also been attacked.

Both sides are offering predictably polarised explanations. The Metropolitan Police Commissioner, Sir David McNee, claims that police community relations are as good as can be expected, and that the riots have been promoted by outside agitators. He denied suggestions of police harassment of black youths, but stressed that the level of crime in Brixton demands "a strong police presence".

Black leaders reject his analysis, and claim that the riots were the inevitable result of years of heavy-handed policing. Young blacks feel themselves the victims of continual pressure from what they see as a racist police force.

The violence came as the direct result of "Operation Swamp 81", a high-intensity crackdown on street crime which flooded the area with police and compounded an already tense situation. When one youth was arrested in Wiltshire Road and a crowd attempted to free him, the confrontation escalated and the riots began (→ 13/4).

A police van burns, overturned by rioters on Brixton's "front line".

Angry police surround a black youth whom they suspect of looting.

IRA hunger striker wins a by-election

April 11. Hunger-striker Bobby Sands – close to death after 42 days of fasting in the Maze prison – won the Fermanagh and South Tyrone by-election today, giving the IRA a major propaganda boost. The convicted terrorist is reported to have lost two stones in weight and is unable to take water.

With 30,492 votes, Sands had a majority of 1,446 over his Unionist opponent, although 3,280 spoiled papers suggest that many Catholics feared intimidation when they went to the polls.

The militant Republican movement is likely to exploit Sands' victory to the full, demanding the release of a democratically-elected MP (→ 20).

Oxford win with first woman cox

April 4. The first woman cox in the history of the Boat Race, Susan Brown, steered her crew to victory today. The 22-year-old biochemist's Oxford team led from the start, and were eight lengths in front at the finishing point in Mortlake where Susan helped carry the boat ashore.

Miss Brown, a student from Honiton in Devon, has trained six hours a day for the past six months on the water and in the gym. She said: "Now I will have to get back to work."

Sue Brown – after Oxford's win.

Sutcliffe confesses to the Ripper killings

April 29. Peter Sutcliffe admitted today that he was the Yorkshire Ripper who attacked and killed 13 women during a four-year reign of terror. He denied murdering them, but admitted to manslaughter on the grounds of diminished responsibility.

But the judge, Mr Justice Boreham, said he was uneasy about the pleas and ruled a jury should decide the defendant's state of mind. The 34-year-old lorry driver from Bradford had also admitted murder attempts on seven other women. Sutcliffe arrived at the Old Bailey in an armoured prison van escorted by police cars. He stared straight ahead as 20 charges were read out.

On a desk in front of him lay an array of hammers, screw-drivers, pieces of rope, and knives, which police say were the tools of his vicious trade. Behind him sat two of his victims who survived to give evidence against him.

Sutcliffe's wife, Sonia, aged 30, sat three feet away from him and turned pale as he confessed to carrying out the killings (→ 22/5).

Davis is the World Snooker Champion

April 20. Steve Davis, the ginger-headed snooker player from South London, has reached the pinnacle of the game at the age of 23, beating Doug Mountjoy 18-12 at Sheffield to win the world championship. Managed with flair and foresight by Barry Hearn at Romford, Davis has crowned a momentous season, in which he won the English professional title and three other classic tournaments, by capturing the biggest prize of all.

1981

MAY

Su	Mo	Tu	We	Th	Fr	Sa
					1	2
3	4	5	6	7	8	9
10	11	12	13	14	15	16
17	18	19	20	21	22	23
24	25	26	27	28	29	30
31						

1. US: Tennis star Billie Jean King admits having a lesbian affair with the woman who is suing her for support.

5. Belfast: Bobby Sands dies (→12).

5. London: A parcel bomb is found addressed to Prince Charles (→11/6).

7. UK: Labour makes gains in local elections, winning control of the GLC (→8).

8. London: Ken Livingstone is elected leader of the GLC (→16/6).

9. London: Manchester City and Tottenham Hotspur draw 1-1 in the 100th FA Cup Final (→14).

9. El Salvador: Six soldiers arrested for the murders of five US nuns and a missionary.

12. Belfast: Francis Hughes is the second IRA hunger striker to die.→

13. London: An inquest jury returns an open verdict on the deaths of 13 people killed in the Deptford fire (→20/6).

14. London: Spurs beat Manchester City 3-2 in the FA Cup Final replay.

18. Italy: Italians vote 2:1 to liberalise abortion laws (→26).

19. Northern Ireland: A bomb kills five soldiers (→21).

21. Belfast: Patrick O'Hara is the fourth IRA hunger striker to die, after Ray McCreesh's death yesterday (→22).

22. Northern Ireland: Two die after being hit by plastic bullets (→10/6).

22. London: Peter Sutcliffe is jailed for life after an Old Bailey jury finds he is a murderer, not mentally ill.

26. Rome: The government resigns following revelations of links between ministers and the illegal masonic lodge P-2.

30. London: The People's March for Jobs arrives from Liverpool, but is forbidden to march down Whitehall (→25/6).

DEATH

28. Polish primate Cardinal Stefan Wyszynski (*3/8/1901).

Pope is shot as he blesses the crowds

May 13. Pope John Paul II was shot by a Turkish gunman today, but after a five-hour operation surgeons said they hoped he would make a full recovery. The Pope was driving in his white, open-top jeep-style vehicle through a crowd of 20,000 in St. Peter's Square. It was his weekly audience in which he blesses the crowds. He was hit by four bullets, two of which lodged in the lower intestine. Two women standing near him were also hit, and one was seriously injured.

The gunman, who used a Browning 9mm pistol, was seized by police as the Pope's jeep drove off at high speed. One witness said: "It was awful. There was blood on the Pope's cassock." Another said the gunman might have been drugged: "He had a crazy stare." The police had to surround the assassin, Mehmet Ali Agca, aged 23, to stop him being lynched by the outraged crowd.

Agca, of Armenian extraction, escaped from a Turkish jail where he was being held for the murder of a Turkish newspaper editor. Italian police found a letter in his Rome boarding house, saying he planned to kill the Pope "to demonstrate to the world the imperialistic crimes of the Soviet Union and the United States". Apparently he was protesting against Soviet action in Afghanistan and US involvement in El Salvador. Turkish authorities say they had warned Interpol about Agca. He arrived in Rome three days ago with false papers claiming he was a student at the International University in Perugia. He was staying near the Vatican.

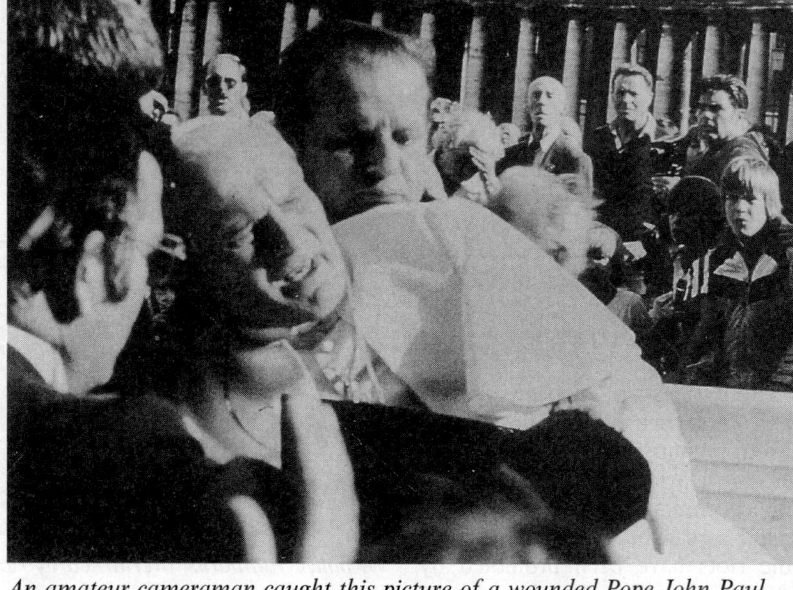

An amateur cameraman caught this picture of a wounded Pope John Paul.

Marley, apostle of reggae music, dies

May 11. Bob Marley, the dreadlocked Rastafarian who, with his group The Wailers, took reggae from the slums of Jamaica to the stages of the world, died today in Miami of cancer at the age of 36. Always politically engaged, Marley capitalised on his fame to pursue his commitment to black rights around the world.

Bangladesh leader killed in army coup

May 30. President Ziaur Rahman of Bangladesh was assassinated before dawn this morning in the government guest house at Chittagong in what would appear to be an attempted coup mounted by Major General Manzur Ahmed, commander of the Chittagong garrison. General Arshad, Chief of Staff, has called upon Ahmed to surrender.

Mitterrand becomes President of France

May 10. Young Paris went wild tonight after the news that Francois Mitterrand had succeeded in his third attempt to be President. There was dancing in the Place de la Bastille, red flags were hung from the balconies and lines of cars blared their horns to celebrate the end of 23 years of right-wing governments in France. The crowds chanted "Mitterrand – President. Giscard – unemployed."

Mitterrand, widely regarded as the founder of the modern French Socialist Party, won a decisive victory with over 52 per cent of the vote. As soon as he takes office he is expected to call new elections for the National Assembly, which now has a right-wing majority.

Mitterrand promises to be radical at home and conservative in foreign affairs. He has promised nationalisation of banks and insurance companies, wealth taxes, higher wages and an end to unemployment. He is a firm supporter of NATO and attacked the former President, Giscard d'Estaing, for being too soft on the Soviet Union. The open question is whether he will be forced to bring the Communists into his government.

Giscard hands over to Mitterrand.

1981

JUNE

Su	Mo	Tu	We	Th	Fr	Sa
	1	2	3	4	5	6
7	8	9	10	11	12	13
14	15	16	17	18	19	20
21	22	23	24	25	26	27
28	29	30				

3. UK: The Aga Khan's Shergar wins the Derby by 10 lengths, the greatest margin this century.

3. Rome: Pope John Paul II leaves hospital (→22/7).

4. Egypt: Sadat and Begin meet in Sinai.

7. Warsaw: Polish Communist Party leaders call a meeting for crisis talks (→15/7).

7. Iraq: The Israelis bomb a nuclear plant near Baghdad.→

9. London: King Khaled of Saudi Arabia arrives on a state visit.

10. Tehran: Khomeini sacks President Bani Sadr as head of Iran's armed forces (→20).

11. London: The Queen opens the Nat West Tower, Europe's tallest building.

17. Washington: Relations with Moscow are strained as Reagan agrees to sell arms to China.

19. French Guiana: Two satellites are launched aboard a European rocket (→12/11).

20. London: 500 youths riot in Peckham (→5/7).

20. Tehran: Impeachment proceedings begin against Bani Sadr (→28).

21. France: The Socialists win control of the National Assembly in a general election (→18/9).

21. London: One dies and 16 are hurt in a fire at Goodge Street tube station.

22. New York: Mark Chapman pleads guilty to the murder of John Lennon (→24/8).

25. London: Defence Secretary John Nott announces defence cuts, including the closure of Chatham dockyard (→2/7).

28. Tehran: 72 politicians and officials are killed by a bomb at the HQ of the Islamic Republican Party (→30/8).

29. Beijing: Chairman Hua Guofeng (Hua Kuo-feng) is replaced by Hu Yaobang as party chairman.

29. London: "Tiny" Rowland is given the go-ahead to buy "The Observer".

Belfast riots follow hunger striker's death

As vehicles burn, a masked rioter stands defiant in a Belfast street.

May 12. The eight days of rioting that followed the death of the hunger-striker Bobby Sands reached a crescendo today when the Government announced the death of a second prisoner. Francis Hughes, once described as "Ulster's most wanted man" died after a 59-day fast in the Maze Prison.

News of Hughes's death was spread through the Republican areas of Belfast by banging dustbin lids and whistle-blowing, sparking the stoning of police and troops. A soldier was set on fire by a petrol bomb. An IRA gunman was shot dead. Rioting continued in Londonderry, and in Dublin police baton-charged a mob of 2,000 attempting to storm the British Embassy.

Two other prisoners have been refusing food in the Maze for 53 days. A third man took the place of Sands last Saturday, and a further IRA man is likely to begin a hunger-strike, replacing Hughes.

In London, Mrs Thatcher restated her determination not to grant political status to prisoners who are demanding special conditions as "prisoners of war", but in Dublin the Prime Minister, Mr Haughey, claimed the recent events confirmed that Northern Ireland was "no longer a viable political entity".

Hughes, a terrorist since the age of 16, is believed to have carried out over 30 killings (→19)

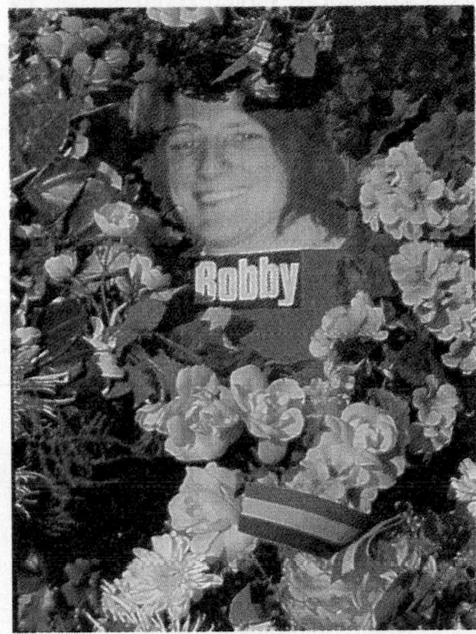

Sands – a propagandist suicide.

Liverpool win their third European Cup

May 27. Liverpool are back at the top of the European tree. In a tense, fluctuating match at the Parc des Princes in Paris, they took the lead with a goal by Alan Kennedy just nine minutes from the end of the game to beat Real Madrid 1-0 and lift the trophy for the third time in five years. It was a triumphant night for the Merseyside fans who had travelled in their thousands, many without a ticket, for a chance of seeing the match, though they did not all escape trouble; twice the Paris riot police made baton charges at fans who had been hurling missiles at them outside the stadium.

Israelis claim they can build A-bomb

June 24. In the wake of Israel's attack on Iraq's nuclear reactor in Baghdad, General Moshe Dayan has claimed that Israel has the capacity to make nuclear bombs. The former Defence Minister said that if the Arabs produced nuclear weapons, so must Israel. "We should not be the first ones, but we shouldn't be too late," he said.

The Israelis may have such weapons already, though the subject is publicly taboo. Certainly they have the scientific know-how. Their attack on the Iraqi reactor was the world's first air-strike against a nuclear plant. It destroyed the reactor, which was nearing completion but had not been stocked with nuclear fuel (→17/7).

Liberals and SDP form an alliance

June 16. Firm moves were made by Liberal and Social Democrat leaders today to form an alliance to fight the next general election as a single organisation. They agreed on pact rules for submission to party conferences in the autumn. David Steel, the Liberal leader, and the SDP's president, Shirley Williams, then knelt together on a Westminster lawn, not in prayer but to pose for photographs.

They chirped lovingly about breaking the two-party system and forming a coalition government in the next parliament. They will also co-operate in by-elections (→16/7).

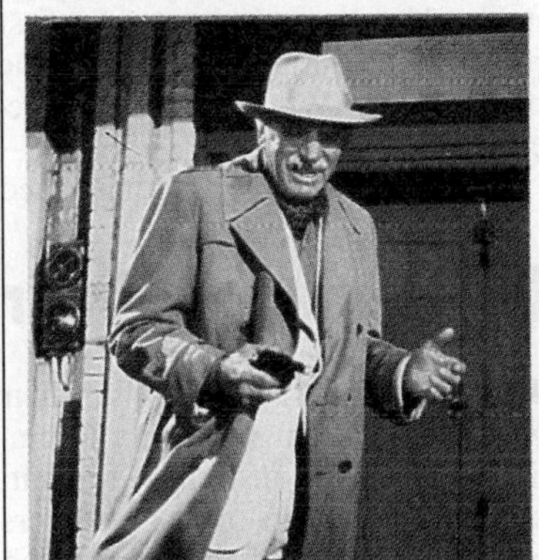

Gun-toting Burt Lancaster, one of Hollywood's elder statesmen, in the film "Atlantic City".

▷

Blank shots fired at Queen in the Mall

Police run forward as they hear six blank shots fired at the Queen.

June 30. For one fleeting moment the Queen's face shook with shock after a youth had fired six blank shots at her as she rode down the Mall for the Trooping of the Colour today. She lent forward to reassure her black mare, Burmese, by patting her on the neck. Then, calm and unruffled, she rode on towards the parade ground.

In the afternoon, Marcus Sargeant, an unemployed youth from Folkestone, appeared in court and was charged under the Treason Act 1842 of wilfully discharging a gun with intent of harming Her Majesty. Under the Act, he could be sentenced for anything from six months to six years.

Before the ceremony, police examined invitations of those with stands-tickets and even turned out handbags for a close look, but the people concerned were VIPs – the gunman was among the crowds on the Mall (→ 29/7).

Fitzgerald becomes Irish Prime Minister

June 30. Dr Garret Fitzgerald, a 55-year-old academic, is the new Irish Prime Minister, heading a coalition of his own Fine Gael party and Labour.

In a speech to the Dail today he made Northern Ireland his first priority: "Nothing else can come before that. We will seek to re-establish links."

He comes from a distinguished political dynasty. Desmond Fitzgerald, his father, was Foreign Minister in the first Free State government of W.T. Cosgrave.

Two women have been notably influential in his career. One was his mother, a Northern Presbyterian, the other his wife Joan, whose keen political insight brings a grass-roots touch to a sometimes rarefied academic approach (→ 6/11).

IRA men shoot their way out of prison

June 10. Eight IRA men shot their way out of the high-security Crumlin Road Prison in Belfast tonight, after holding ten prison officers hostage. They used three smuggled handguns and injured two prison officers in an exchange of fire as they dashed from the main gate. Two of the escapees were wearing prison officers' uniforms, taken from their hostages.

The men were due to hear verdicts tomorrow in what has become known as the M60 machine-gun case, in which an American-made M60 was supposedly used in the murders of an SAS man and a policeman (→ 8/7).

1981

JULY

Su	Mo	Tu	We	Th	Fr	Sa
			1	2	3	4
5	6	7	8	9	10	11
12	13	14	15	16	17	18
19	20	21	22	23	24	25
26	27	28	29	30	31	

2. London: The Government announces cuts in university grants, threatening 12,000 places next year (→ 23/9).

3. Wimbledon: Chris Lloyd beats Hana Mandlikova in the Women's Singles final.→

5. Liverpool: Rioting erupts in the Toxteth area (→ 10).

7. Washington: Judge Sandra O'Connor becomes the first woman appointed to the US Supreme Court.

7. UK: Ian Botham quits as England cricket captain in anticipation of being sacked.→

8. Belfast: Joseph McDonnell is the fifth IRA hunger striker to die (→ 13).

10. UK: Riots break out in London, Birmingham, Reading, Wolverhampton, Preston, Hull and Ellesmere Port.→

13. Belfast: IRA hunger striker Martin Hurson dies (→ 18).

15. London: Violence flares again in Brixton following a series of police raids (→ 20).

15. Warsaw: Ex-premier Edward Gierek is expelled from the Polish Communist Party (→ 7/8).

16. UK: Labour holds on to Warrington in a by-election, but Roy Jenkins of the SDP slashes its majority (→ 8/9).

18. Dublin: 120 people are hurt during demonstrations in support of the IRA.→

20. Liverpool: Michael Heseltine begins a fact-finding tour of Merseyside to examine the city's problems (→ 5/8).

22. Rome: Mehmet Ali Agca is jailed for life for trying to kill the Pope (→ 15/9).

24. Lebanon: The Israelis and the PLO call a cease-fire (→ 14/12).

29. Tehran: Disgraced president Bani Sadr leaves to seek refuge in France.

30. Gambia: President Sir Dawda Jarawa, in London for the Royal Wedding, is deposed in a coup (→ 6/8).

31. Panama: President Omar Torrijos dies in a plane crash.

Borg's winning run ended by McEnroe

July 4. Bjorn Borg's record-breaking run at Wimbledon is over. After a string of 41 victories stretching back to 1976, Borg finally fell today to the man he beat in last year's final, John McEnroe.

The tension was every bit as nerve-racking this year, with the initiative changing hands throughout the three hours and 22 minutes of the match. Eventually, the 22-year-old McEnroe gained the upper hand to win 4-6, 7-6, 7-6, 6-4, though the American could lose almost a third of his £27,000 winnings in fines awarded for his behaviour on court.

John McEnroe abuses his racket.

Israeli planes bomb heart of Beirut

July 17. Israeli jets today launched a ferocious air onslaught on Lebanon as a reprisal against Palestinian guerrillas. They struck at the centre of Beirut where panic broke out after a half-hour raid.

Whole apartment blocks collapsed and it looked as though the Lebanese capital had been struck by an earthquake. More than 150 people, mostly civilians, perished, and hundreds were wounded.

President Reagan deplored the attacks. Washington decided to hold up delivery of four new F-16 fighter-bombers to Israel. "If that is the price, we have no regrets," said Yitzhak Shamir, Israel's Foreign Minister (→ 24).

World's eyes watch Royal Wedding

July 29. Today, 700 million TV viewers worldwide watched the Prince of Wales marry Lady Diana Spencer, the kindergarten helper, at St. Paul's Cathedral.

Public admiration for the Prince and for his courage in speaking out on environmental matters, and affection for his beautiful and shy bride, made it a particularly happy and warm event.

Their love, which had blossomed from their first meeting in a ploughed field where the Prince, a friend of the bride's eldest sister, had gone on a shoot, culminated in today's rich pageantry. It was, said Dr Robert Runcie, the Archbishop of Canterbury, "the stuff of which fairy tales are made".

The first view of the bride as she left Clarence House, home of the Queen Mother, was of a serene young girl in a wedding dress which was a billowing affair of ivory silk with puffed sleeves. She waved a hand occasionally as the horse-drawn carriage trotted down the Mall, but most of the waving to the excited crowds was done by her proud father, Earl Spencer, a former equerry to the Queen.

In keeping with tradition, the bride was one minute late at St. Paul's, arriving at 11.01. Walking up the crimson carpeted steps, she passed huge banks of purple and pink flowers, the Spencer family tiara sparkling beneath the batteries of TV lights. Prince Charles, in naval uniform, stopped joking with his brothers, Prince Andrew and Prince Edward, and took his place beside her at the high altar. Prince Philip smiled, the Queen looked blissfully happy. The couple made their vows in clear, soft voices, with slight slips by both, to the amusement of the congregation.

Afterwards they rode to Buckingham Palace in a horse-drawn carriage, past cheering crowds, for the wedding breakfast. Then they appeared on the Palace balcony where they kissed to a roar of approval from the crowd.

As they drove off on their honeymoon, a cluster of blue balloons and a sign which read "Just Married" bobbed up and down on the back of the 70-year-old landau drawn by a pair of Windsor Greys – the work of his brothers (→14/9).

Britain's favourite balcony scene: a kiss for the Prince and Princess.

The ceremony is over and the happy couple proceed down the aisle.

Red Cross bid to end Ulster hunger strikes is a failure

July 19. Hopes of a settlement of the bitter hunger-strike crisis in Northern Ireland faded today when fasting prisoners rejected attempts by a Swiss Red Cross team to mediate with the British government. In fact, both sides proved intransigent, as the Northern Ireland Office has also refused to negotiate on the issue. Two more prisoners, Kieran Docherty and Kevin Lynch, are close to death.

The death of another hunger-striker, Joseph McDonnell, ten days ago has brought Anglo-Irish relations to a low ebb, with the Republic's Prime Minister threatening to delay the dialogue between the two countries (→2/8).

Botham inspires England to victory

July 21. In one of the most remarkable reversals in Test history, England recovered from the near-certainty of an innings defeat (and odds against victory of 500 to one) to turn the tables on Australia.

Ian Botham, in his first Test after relinquishing the captaincy to Mike Brearley, blasted an unforgettable 149 not out as England's last three second innings wickets amassed 221. Australia, chasing only 130 to win, collapsed against the speed of Bob Willis, whose eight for 43 saw England home by just 18 runs.

Economic woes dog the Ottawa summit

July 21. Inflation and high unemployment were again bracketed today as the twin curses of the industrialised free world, but in highlighting them at their Ottawa summit meeting, the leaders of Britain, the United States, France, West Germany, Italy, Japan and Canada confessed that there is no early relief in sight. Nor did they agree on any new action. Mrs Thatcher took comfort in claiming that Britain's monetary policies are now being copied.

Riots hit British cities

Police crouch as Toxteth's rioters attack them with a barrage of missiles.

July 13. In scenes reminiscent of America's "long hot summers" of ghetto rioting in the late Sixties, Britain's towns and cities this week have suffered the worst outbreaks of civil unrest this century.

On July 10, in what has been called "Britain's night of anarchy", youths rampaged through the high streets and side roads of such disparate areas as Liverpool, north, south and west London, Wolverhampton, Birmingham, Reading, Luton, Chester, Hull and Preston.

This weekend's riots are seen as the latest episode in a chain of such incidents, which can be traced back to disturbances in the St. Paul's area of Bristol in 1980 and, more immediately, to April's events in Brixton. This time the violence left London for the provinces, starting with the ghetto area of Toxteth in Liverpool, where on July 5 the police were forced to withdraw when they admitted that the mob had gone "out of control".

This weekend's incidents, while equally disturbing, have simply continued the process, and are judged to have as many "copy-cat" elements as they have of genuine spontaneity. Some self-confessed rioters have admitted that they have no greater motivation than enjoying the excitement.

The authorities, represented by the Government and the police, and the communities involved, notably local black leaders, have reacted differently to the riots. While the former concentrate on the effects of the violence – looting, arson, damage to property, injuries to the police – the latter draw attention to what they see as its causes, notably unemployment, poor housing, racism and police harassment.

The most vociferous response is coming from right-wing Tory backbenchers who blame all the riots, by no means accurately, on the black community. Although police and other eye-witnesses have spoken of the large-scale involvement of white youths, these MPs are demanding immediate curbs on immigration, which the Home Secretary, William Whitelaw, has hitherto left relatively untouched (→ 15).

Police use riot gear to face youths.

1981

AUGUST

Su	Mo	Tu	We	Th	Fr	Sa
						1
2	3	4	5	6	7	8
9	10	11	12	13	14	15
16	17	18	19	20	21	22
23	24	25	26	27	28	29
30	31					

2. Belfast: Kieran Docherty is the eighth IRA hunger striker to die, following the death of Kevin Lynch yesterday (→ 8).

5. Liverpool: Heseltine announces a package of measures to help depressed areas of Merseyside (→ 15/9).

6. Gambia: The coup bid against President Jarawa ends when British SAS men free 25 hostages still held by rebels.

7. Poland: A million Solidarity members go on strike in protest at the Polish food and economic crises (→ 3/9).

8. Belfast: Thomas McElwee is the ninth IRA hunger striker to die (→ 20).

11. Europe: Thousands are stranded in airports as the US air-traffic controllers dispute causes huge delays to flights.

13. North Sea: 13 die when a helicopter ferrying gas rig workers crashes.

13. Strasbourg: The human rights court says British Rail was wrong to sack three men who would not join a union.

17. UK: England go 3-1 up in the test series against Australia, retaining the Ashes.

19. Switzerland: Sebastian Coe runs the mile in 3 minutes 48.53 seconds, breaking the world record by 0.3 seconds.→

20. Belfast: Michael Devine is the tenth IRA hunger striker to die (→ 21).

21. Northern Ireland: Owen Carron, Bobby Sands's agent, wins the Fermanagh and South Tyrone by-election (→ 3/10).

24. New York: Chapman is jailed for life for killing John Lennon.

27. London: Moira Stuart is appointed the BBC's first black woman newsreader.

28. Kenya: Paul Nakwale Ekai is found guilty of murdering "Born Free" author Joy Adamson in January 1980.

DEATHS

14. Austrian conductor Karl Bohm (*28/8/1894).

19. British singer and actress Jessie Matthews (*11/3/1907).→

World records fall to Coe and Ovett

Aug 28. An astonishing ten days of middle-distance running has ended with Sebastian Coe recapturing the world mile record from his compatriot Steve Ovett by over a second in an electrifying run in Brussels.

A little over a week ago Coe set the ball rolling in Zurich, to clip Ovett's year-old record by 0.3 seconds to 3 minutes 48.53 seconds. Within a week Ovett had got the record back, trimming a further 0.13 seconds off the time in Koblenz. Now, two days later, the record is Coe's again. A crowd of 40,000 at the Heysel Stadium cheered every step of his final 600 metres, and he crossed the line, his style still smooth and easy, to post a new time of 3 minutes 47.53 seconds.

Matthews, singer and diarist, is dead

Matthews: I'm worried about Jim.

Aug 21. Jessie Matthews, who began her career dancing to a barrel organ, became a musical comedy star second only to Gracie Fields between the wars.

She was one of C.B. Cochran's Young Ladies, and partnered Sonnie Hale in "Wake Up and Dream" by Cole Porter. Their hit song was "Let's Do It". Hale was married to Evelyn Laye, who cited Jessie Matthews in her divorce.

She made a come-back as the eponymous heroine of the radio series Mrs Dale's Diary from 1963-69. She died yesterday, aged 74.

Not guilty plea to Reagan killing bid

Hinckley is driven to his trial.

Aug 28. John Hinckley today pleaded not guilty to charges of attempting to kill President Reagan and two other men outside a Washington hotel last March. A federal grand jury indicted him four days ago.

Judge Barrington Parker signed an order declaring Hinckley mentally competent to participate in the proceedings. The order states that the defendant understands the charges against him and is capable of assisting his lawyer in preparing his defence.

Two top Iranians die in bomb blast

Aug 30. The President and Prime Minister of Iran were assassinated today by a bomb which exploded during a meeting at the house of Dr Mohammed Javad Bahomar, the Prime Minister. Both he and Mohammed Ali Rejai were killed outright.

Three others also died and Iran has gone into official mourning. Cinemas and other places of entertainment have been closed while preparations are being made for a massive funeral procession.

The Ayatollah Khomeini is in no doubt about the source of the bomb. He told a weeping crowd that the blame lay with exiled Iranian leaders who "head terrorists, who direct these people and force them to carry out sabotage".

The Ayatollah thundered: "There is no place in this nation for deviants from Islam."

1981

SEPTEMBER

Su	Mo	Tu	We	Th	Fr	Sa
		1	2	3	4	5
6	7	8	9	10	11	12
13	14	15	16	17	18	19
20	21	22	23	24	25	26
27	28	29	30			

1. UK: Garages begin selling petrol by the litre.

3. Moscow: The USSR says military manoeuvres near the Polish border are "normal" (→6).

6. Gdansk: Solidarity holds its first national congress (→15).

8. London: 16 Islington Labour councillors join the SDP, after the defection of Labour MP Michael O'Halloran (→14).

9. UK: Geoff Boycott is suspended for the rest of the cricket season for remarks he made on television.

10. Spain: Picasso's "Guernica" returns after spending 40 years on show in New York.

14. London: Thatcher sacks three "Wets", sends Jim Prior to Ulster and appoints Cecil Parkinson as Tory chairman.

14. London: 17-year-old, Marcus Sarjeant is jailed for five years for firing blanks at the Queen.

15. Rome: The Pope says trade unions are "indispensable in the struggle for social justice".→

15. Liverpool: Heseltine approves a £10 million scheme to redevelop the city's derelict South Dock (→25/11).

18. Paris: Mitterrand abolishes the guillotine.

18. UK: Steel tells delegates at the Liberal conference to "go back to your constituencies and prepare for government."

20. Tehran: The government reports that it has executed 149 "leftist militants" (→29).

23. London: The stock market suffers the second worst fall in its history (→12/10).

26. Warsaw: Poland refuses visas to US trade union leaders invited for a visit (→18/10).

29. Iran: Four of Iran's military chiefs are killed in a plane crash (→4/10).

DEATH

1. German architect Albert Speer (*19/3/1905).

Moscow slams "anti-Soviet" Solidarity

Sept 18. Leaders of Poland's Communist Party today revealed details of a grim warning, received from Moscow a week ago, that the time had come to bring the Solidarity free trade union movement to heel. It was given maximum publicity in the Polish press and on radio and television. The warning, by the Soviet Politburo, complained bitterly about a wave of "anti-Sovietism and anti-Communism".

What seemed to have angered the Kremlin particularly is the resolution passed by a Solidarity meeting calling for free trade unions to be allowed in all Soviet-bloc countries. "This so-called message to the working people of Eastern Europe, adopted at Gdansk, has become an outrageous provocation," Moscow said, and compared the anti-Soviet hostility in Poland to "the hysteria of some of the imperialist states".

In a passage that comes close to delivering an ultimatum to the Polish comrades, the message from the Soviet Politburo goes on: "We expect the Polish Communist Party leadership and the Polish government immediately to take determined radical steps to cut short the malicious anti-Soviet propaganda and actions hostile to the Soviet Union."

Healey pips Benn for Labour deputy

Sept 27. Denis Healey kept his job as Labour deputy leader by a whisker tonight. He beat off the challenge of the party's left-wing darling, Tony Benn, by a majority of less than one per cent. Mr Benn whooped: "Now I'm on the incoming tide." Mr Healey said: "No, you're not. The majority voted for sanity." The struggle for the soul of the party continues.

Christy Brown, who wrote by toes, dies

Sept 7. The amazing life of Christy Brown, the crippled Irish novelist who could only type with the toes of one foot, ended yesterday in a choking fit. He was 48 years old.

Cerebral palsy from birth caused him to be treated as a vegetable until he seized a chalk with his foot and began to draw. In 1970 he brought out his best-selling autobiography "Down All Our Days".

London docks die but rebirth is planned

Sept 17. London's Royal Docks were axed today in a move which means the end of London as a major world port. The number of dockers is now down to 6,000 compared with 30,000 in 1956. The latest move releases 900 acres of land in Newham and all the talk now is of redevelopment. Earlier this week Michael Heseltine, the Environment Secretary, announced a £10 million project to redevelop Liverpool's derelict South Docks. Even more ambitious plans are in the pipeline for the London docklands.

France's high-speed TGV train makes the journey from Paris to Lyons in just two hours 40 minutes, cutting the old journey time by half.

1981

OCTOBER

Su	Mo	Tu	We	Th	Fr	Sa
				1	2	3
4	5	6	7	8	9	10
11	12	13	14	15	16	17
18	19	20	21	22	23	24
25	26	27	28	29	30	31

1. Beirut: A bomb goes off at a PLO office, killing 50.

3. Belfast: The hunger strike formally ends after seven months and ten deaths (→17).

6. Belfast: John DeLorean begins a libel action after the Government denies it is investigating his car firm.

7. Cairo: Hosni Mubarak becomes acting President (→9).

8. USSR: A British salvage crew arrives in Murmansk with gold bars from HMS Edinburgh, sunk in 1943.

9. Egypt: Menachem Begin arrives for Sadat's funeral on the 12th (→10/11).

12. UK: British Leyland announces the closure of three plants with the loss of 2,850 jobs (→15).

12. UK: A report says that one in eight children now lives in a single-parent family.

15. UK: Norman Tebbit tells Tories: "My father did not riot. He got on his bike and looked for work."

17. London: Royal Marines chief Lt.General Sir Steuart Pringle is injured when a bomb goes off under his car (→26).

18. Greece: The Pasok Socialist Party of Andreas Papandreou sweeps to power in a general election.

18. Warsaw: Jaruzelski succeeds Kania as party leader (→4/11).

22. London: Liberal Bill Pitt captures Croydon North-West from the Tories in the Alliance's first by-election win (→26/11).

26. London: An army explosives expert dies when the bomb he was trying to defuse in Oxford Street goes off (→13/11).

30. London: Mark Lyons, head of the euthanasia group, EXIT, is jailed for two and a half years for abetting suicide.

DEATH

6. Egyptian statesman Mohamed Anwar el-Sadat, President 1970-81, (*25/12/1918).→

Sadat is assassinated

One of the gunmen who used automatic weapons to assassinate Sadat.

Oct 6. A state of emergency was declared in Cairo tonight after an Egyptian lieutenant assassinated Anwar Sadat. Wearing black ceremonial uniform at a military parade the Egyptian President was shot down by bursts of automatic fire.

Four uniformed men jumped from an armoured vehicle, hurling grenades and firing bursts at the President. He rose to his feet as the shooting began and, hit by five bullets, collapsed in a pool of blood. At the time of the attack all eyes were turned to the sky as air force jets roared past at the end of an anniversary march-past. The armoured vehicle slowed down and then swung out of the parade line towards the saluting base where President Sadat had been sitting.

In the ensuing gun battle, presidential guards killed one assassin. The rest, including the officer, were arrested. The conspirators killed five people on the saluting base and a number of others, including foreign envoys attending the parade, were wounded.

Hosni Mubarak, the Egyptian Vice-President and chosen successor of Sadat, moved swiftly tonight to take firm control. Troops and riot police were out in force in the capital, though there are no signs of any attempted coup. The Vice-President promptly declared that Egypt would stand by her treaties, including the one with Israel which outraged much of the Arab world.

A Libyan-backed group in Tripoli has claimed responsibility for the murder, but it seems more likely that the assassins belonged to an extremist Islamic group, such as the Moslem Brotherhood.

Four American presidents pay tribute to the dead Egyptian leader: Gerald Ford, Richard Nixon and Jimmy Carter flank President Ronald Reagan.

Soviet submarine is stranded in Sweden

Oct 30. Sweden today stepped up its guard on the Soviet submarine stranded on rocks near its sensitive Karlskrona naval base. Stockholm believes Soviet warships waiting outside Swedish waters may try to snatch the obsolete Whisky Class submarine which ran aground while on an intelligence-gathering mission.

Swedish negotiators have already boarded the submarine to try to convince her commander, Captain Piotr Juzcin, to leave for interrogation, but each time a political commissar on the damaged vessel is the man issuing the orders.

Europe-wide demos say "No" to nukes

Oct 24. Britain today witnessed what is believed to be the biggest anti-nuclear demonstration in 20 years as more than 150,000 people marched to Hyde Park to protest at the siting of Cruise missiles here.

Similar demonstrations are planned in other European cities today as part of a burgeoning campaign by nuclear disarmers. In London the column of marchers was so long that many only arrived in Hyde Park long after the speeches by the Labour leader, Michael Foot, and CND secretary, Bruce Kent, were over (→30/11).

BT says stop it will stop telegrams stop

Oct 19. British Telecom announced today that it will scrap the telegram. By next autumn BT intend to have replaced the time-honoured system for sending news of triumphs and disasters with the "tele-message". This will arrive by first post the next day, but the original message won't be accepted over a Post Office counter; instead, it must come from a telephone or Telex. It will cost less than a telegram (£3 plus VAT for up to 50 words) and will involve the loss of around 1,400 jobs, but BT claims that last year the 2.89 million telegrams cost them £50 million.

1981

NOVEMBER

Su	Mo	Tu	We	Th	Fr	Sa
1	2	3	4	5	6	7
8	9	10	11	12	13	14
15	16	17	18	19	20	21
22	23	24	25	26	27	28
29	30					

1. UK: British Leyland's 58,000 workers begin a strike over pay (→ 8/12).

4. Warsaw: Jaruzelski proposes a "National Alliance Council" of the government, the Church and Solidarity (→ 15/12).

5. Sweden: The Soviet submarine is released by the Swedish authorities.

6. London: Thatcher and Irish premier Garret Fitzgerald agree to increase the links between Britain and Ireland.

12. US: The space shuttle Columbia is launched, becoming the first spacecraft to be used more than once (→ 14).

13. London: A bomb explodes at the home of Attorney-General Sir Michael Havers while he is away (→ 14).

14. US: The space shuttle lands after curtailing its mission owing to a fuel cell failure.

18. London: England beat Hungary 1-0 at Wembley to qualify for the World Cup finals in 1982.

20. Italy: Anatoly Karpov wins the world chess championship.

21. Cairo: The alleged assassins of Sadat go on trial.

22. USSR: Andrei Sakharov and Yelena Bonner begin a hunger strike at their home in Gorky (→ 14/12).

24. North Sea: Two oil-rigs break from their moorings and drift in hurricane-force winds.

26. UK: Shirley Williams wins the Crosby by-election for the SDP, overturning a 19,272 Conservative majority.

30. Geneva: NATO and Warsaw Pact countries begin talks on limiting medium-range nuclear missiles.

DEATHS

10. French film director Abel Gance (*25/10/1889).

16. US actor William Holden (*17/4/1918).

29. US actress Natalie Wood (*20/7/1938).

Belfast Unionist MP is murdered by IRA

Nov 14. Politicians in Northern Ireland believe that the IRA is determined to provoke full-scale sectarian strife in the province after the cold-blooded killing today of a Unionist MP.

Three gunmen, posing as workmen in white overalls, shot down Robert Bradford, the Official Unionist MP for Belfast South and a Methodist minister, at his home. A social worker was also killed.

A joint statement by police and the army said that the intention of the IRA and other terrorist organisations was to create strife in the community. "Today's murders should be seen in that light," it added. Gerry Fitt, the SDLP MP, said the IRA was seeking a full-scale civil war.

Bradford, a victim of the gunmen.

BL and Honda plan saloon car link up

Nov 12. British Leyland today announced a new deal with the Japanese car and motor cycle giant, Honda. They are planning the joint development of a middle-range executive car for the 1990s, at present code-named "Project XX". The new car will slot in between the group's Triumph and Jaguar car ranges.

The big saving will be in the mass production of matching components in both countries. There will be one basic design but the external appearance of the cars will be different, suiting customer demand in Japan and Britain. The British car will be made at either Longbridge or Cowley.

Mubarak assumes the mantle of Sadat

Mubarak, a new leader for Egypt.

Nov 10. The Vice-President, Hosni Mubarak was tonight chosen to be Egypt's next President in a ballot of the country's parliament. The vote at the People's Assembly was unanimous, although there were some abstentions, indicating muted opposition in the country. Mubarak is a former commander in the Air Force and a fighter pilot.

His election is a sign that Anwar Sadat's foreign policy will be continued, with a stricter regime at home, but Israel may well find her negotiations with Egypt becoming tougher. Mustafa Khalil, a former Prime Minister, is expected to be Mubarak's Vice-President.

Unholy row looms over women priests

Nov 12. The Church of England's General Synod today voted overwhelmingly to admit women to Holy Orders as deacons. The decision will take about two years to implement. As deacons, women will be able to style themselves Reverend and conduct baptisms, funerals and weddings; they will not be able to administer Holy Communion. The move, backed by the Archbishop of Canterbury, Dr Runcie, is seen as a major step towards admitting women to the priesthood and is bound to fan the flames of controversy.

Race and police led to riots, says study

Nov 25. "Racial disadvantage" and a wholesale breakdown of trust in the authorities lay at the heart of last April's Brixton riots, according to Lord Scarman's report "The Brixton Disorders", published today. He called for urgent action.

Citing "a disease threatening our society", Lord Scarman said that both police and community leaders were responsible for the riots. Black youths were harassed, and the riots were their response, but the police, despite black allegations, were not all racists.

A prototype De Lorean car, sporting its distinctive gull wings, is wheeled out on display in 1981; now its maker is under investigation.

1981

DECEMBER

Su	Mo	Tu	We	Th	Fr	Sa
		1	2	3	4	5
6	7	8	9	10	11	12
13	14	15	16	17	18	19
20	21	22	23	24	25	26
27	28	29	30	31		

1. France: 178 die when a Yugoslav DC-9 crashes.

2. UK: A TV licence goes up £12 to £46 for colour, £3 to £15 for black and white.

8. UK: Arthur Scargill is elected president of the National Union of Mineworkers.

9. London: Heseltine announces £95 million aid for the inner cities.

10. Stockholm: Nobel Prizes go to Nicolaas Bloembergen (US), Arthur Schawlow (US) and Kai Siegbahn (Sweden), all Physics; Kenichi Fukui (Japan) and Roald Hoffmann (US), both Chemistry; David Hubel, Torsten Wiesel and Roger Sperry (US, all Medicine); Elias Canetti (UK, Literature); James Tobin (US, Economics); and in Oslo to the UN High Commission for Refugees (Geneva, Peace).

13. London: Two Iranians die when a bomb they are carrying explodes near Marble Arch.

14. USSR: The Sakharovs end their hunger strike when their daughter-in-law is given a visa to join her husband in the US.

17. Poland: Seven are reported killed when troops open fire on demonstrating workers (→ 20).

20. Washington: Poland's ambassador to the US is granted political asylum (→ 28).

28. Poland: 900 miners at Piast in Silesia end a two-week underground strike.

DEATH

27. US pianist Hoagy Carmichael (*22/11/1899).

HITS OF 1981

Stand and deliver.

Under pressure.

Imagine.

QUOTE OF THE YEAR

"If we resign today we will bury our hopes for freedom for many years to come. Several thousand people cannot overcome ten million."

Solidarity, a message to Polish workers, December 1981.

Poles face martial law

Dec 15. At least 14,000 trade union activists have been arrested since General Jaruzelski clamped martial law on Poland in the early hours of Sunday. Strikes are reported to be continuing, and troops with armour have moved into key factories to break up sit-ins and to make arrests.

It is officially admitted that seven people have been killed resisting martial law in the Silesian coalfields. About 300 strikers and police have been injured in clashes at the Gdansk shipyards, the power base of the Solidarity leader, Lech Walesa, now under arrest.

Jaruzelski moved swiftly late on Saturday, cutting links with the West and deploying troops and armour to set up road blocks and occupy strategic installations, before he appeared on radio and TV the next day to announce the formation of a Military Council of National Salvation. He claimed that strikes, protest demonstrations and crime had brought the country "to the border of mental endurance ... the verge of an abyss". He promised that martial law would not mean a return "to the false methods and practices" of the past.

In an apparent gesture to public opinion, the authorities announced that Edward Gierek, the party boss sacked last year, is among a number of leading Communists arrested for "abusing their posts for personal profit". In a sermon in the Jesuit Church in Warsaw, Cardinal Josef Glemp criticised martial law, but appealed to Poles not to start fighting each other (→ 17).

Soldiers in the Warsaw traffic enforce the new regime of martial law.

"Froth Blowers" thwarted in Seychelles

Dec 2. The 44 burly tourists who left the plane at Pointe Larue airport in the Seychelles identified themselves as members of the "Froth Blowers" looking forward to a golfing and drinking holiday. They might have got away with it, too, if one of the "golf" bags had not opened – to expose a gun.

Police identified the leading "Froth Blower" as Colonel "Mad Mike" Hoare, notorious as a Congo mercenary in the 1960s. This time the aim was to overthrow the left-wing regime of Albert Rene, who came to power in a coup in 1977, but with their cover blown the "Froth Blowers" set about escaping. They shot up the airport and, boarding an Air India jetliner, ordered the pilot to fly to South Africa.

The South African authorities released all but five of the hijackers. The five, including Hoare, were charged with kidnapping, a lesser crime than hijacking, which carries a mandatory sentence. Appearing in court in Pretoria in beach shirts, they smiled and waved at the public. After a brief hearing they were released on bail and told not to talk to the media.

Alert is sounded as illness erodes immune defences

Dec 31. Alarming reports from Los Angeles, San Francisco and New York suggest that a new type of lung infection and skin cancer may be common in homosexuals. It appears to destroy the body's immune system, so that after a period of weight loss the victim succumbs to infections.

Although doctors have identified what appears to be a new disease, they have yet to devise a cure. Nor does this as yet unnamed disease appear to be confined to homosexuals. Of 152 similar cases reported this year, one involved an intravenous drug user, suggesting that sharing needles could spread the disease.

Boycott sets record for Test Match runs

Dec 23. As Geoffrey Boycott took his score to 86 not out against India at Delhi today, he became the most prolific run-scoring batsman in Test history, passing the record of 8,032 held by the great West Indies all-rounder Gary Sobers. Boycott is not the fastest of batsmen (his runs took him nearly 452 hours), but the fact that he had bowed out of Test cricket for three years in the 1970s can only hint at the totals he might have accumulated in an unbroken career.

Boycott hails another 50 runs.

Rawlings is back in second Ghana coup

Ghana's leader Jerry Rawlings.

Dec 31. The African state of Ghana seems split today as rival factions battle for power. The first sign of trouble came when Jerry Rawlings turned up at an all-ranks dance at Burma Camp outside Accra. He had held power briefly in 1979 and there has been speculation that he was about to strike again.

President Hilla Limann seemed unconcerned. He, too, was at Burma Camp, dancing the night away. Then, at 11am the next day, Rawlings was on the radio announcing his takeover and attacking the Limann government as "a pack of criminals". Unofficial reports say 70 soldiers have died in clashes with Limann loyalists.

16 perish in Cornish lifeboat tragedy

Dec 20. The eight-strong crew of the Cornish Penlee lifeboat today drowned as they battled in vain to save eight people from a wrecked coaster in hurricane-lashed seas.

The lifeboat had managed to save four passengers from the 1,400-ton Union Star, only for them to die as they were dashed on rocks. A search by Royal Navy helicopters and fishing ships found no sign of any survivors.

At the tiny harbour of Mousehole, the dead lifeboatmen's neighbours and friends stood ready to replace them. It is thought the lifeboat was holed during a collision with the ship in 60-foot waves.

Golan Heights are Israel's, says Begin

Dec 14. Israel is planning to annex the Syrian mountain territory of the Golan Heights which it captured during counter-attacks in the Yom Kippur War. Menachem Begin, the Prime Minister, claims that this is now part of Israel. However, the United States reacted sharply to the proposed move. Larry Speakes, the White House spokesman said: "We have made known to the Israeli government our deep concern over any effort to change the status of the Golan Heights unilaterally."

Arts: aristocrats triumph on the screen

There has been no more sumptuous television serial than Granada's "Brideshead Revisited", which fascinated many this autumn. Based by **John Mortimer** on **Evelyn Waugh's** 1945 novel, it was shot with great devotion to detail at Castle Howard, Yorkshire, in Oxford and in Venice.

As the 11 hour-long episodes unwound, some found it a cloying and snobbish account of heavy drinking in an effete, if noble, family. It was notable for two cameos, by **Laurence Olivier** as the dying Lord Marchmain and by **John Gielgud** as the acidly restrained father of the narrator, played by **Jeremy Irons**.

Another theatrical knight effortlessly hypnotised viewers – **Alec Guinness**, who returned to the name part in "Smiley's People", even less scrutable than before. He also collected a personal Oscar for lifetime achievement in the cinema, just as Olivier did last year.

It was a good year for British films, led by "Chariots of Fire" whose heroes were the forgotten runners, **Harold Abrahams** and **Eric Liddell**, victors at the 1924 Olympics despite the snubs of the Olympic committee. "The French Lieutenant's Woman" was adapted by **Harold Pinter** from **John Fowles** novel of Victorian passion and shame. **Meryl Streep** as the lady's companion who is seduced and **Jeremy Irons** as her lover (and victim?) were more at home in 1867 than in the present day, when, as actors in the film, they were shown having a love affair. While Fowles' tale was set and shot on the sombre undercliff at Lyme Regis, in Hardy's "Tess", directed by **Roman Polanski** with **Nastassia Kinski** in the title role, the all-important Wessex landscape was in fact Brittany.

Meryl Streep who starred as "The French Lieutenant's Woman".

The most celebrated theatrical shows have shunned the human face. "Cats", a ballet-musical by **Andrew Lloyd-Webber** set to **T.S. Eliot's** Old Possum poems as lyrics, relies on feline make-up, sinuous dancing, and wailing and jumpy music. At the National, **Peter Hall's** production of the Oresteia of Aeschylus is played entirely in large and somewhat disconcerting Greek masks.

Britain's challenger in the new generation of fast express trains – the Advanced Passenger Train – showing its special tilting mechanism which enables it to travel at high speed without new track being put down.

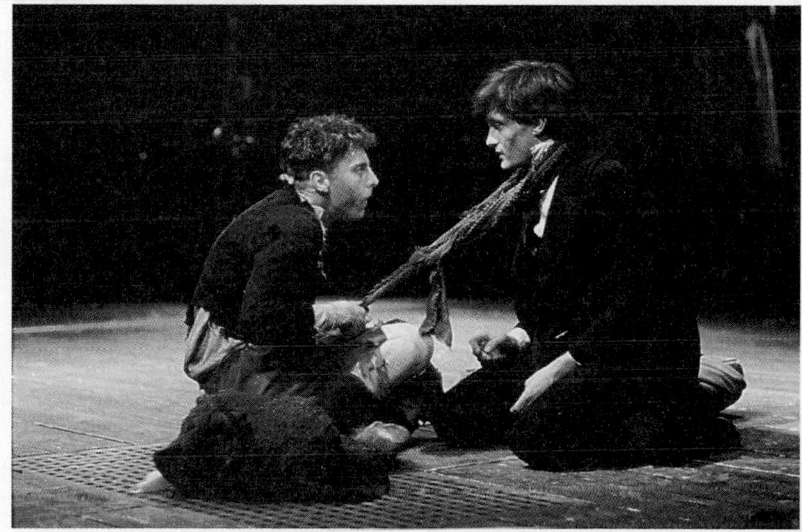
Roger Rees (r.) is Nicholas in the RSC's production of "Nicholas Nickleby".

1982

JANUARY

Su	Mo	Tu	We	Th	Fr	Sa
					1	2
3	4	5	6	7	8	9
10	11	12	13	14	15	16
17	18	19	20	21	22	23
24	25	26	27	28	29	30
31						

1. UK: Three ITV stations, Central, TV South and TV South West, go on the air for the first time (→ 4/3).

5. UK: The families of the victims of the Penlee lifeboat disaster are to share the £2 million proceeds of the appeal.

7. Washington: Reagan says registration of young men for possible military draft will continue (→ 1/2).

11. Albania: Premier Mehmet Shehu is reported to have died in a dinner-table shoot-out involving Enver Hoxha.

11. London: Hailsham rebukes a judge who said a rape victim was guilty of "contributory negligence" for hitch-hiking.

12. Africa: Mark Thatcher goes missing in the Sahara on the Paris-Dakar rally (→ 14).

14. Washington: The death toll from the Air Florida crash now stands at 78.

14. Africa: Mark Thatcher is rescued after being spotted by a search plane.

18. S. Africa: Colonel "Mad Mike" Hoare and 44 others are charged with hijacking a plane after the Seychelles coup bid (→ 27/7).

21. UK: Miners vote against strike action and in favour of the Coal Board's offer of a 9.3 per cent pay increase (→ 2/11).

21. London: Nicholas Fairbairn, Solicitor-General for Scotland, resigns.

26. Washington: Secretary of State Alexander Haig has eight hours of talks with Soviet Foreign Minister Gromyko (→ 15/6).

27. Dublin: The Fine Gael-Labour coalition collapses over stiff rises in duty on beer, petrol and cigarettes (→ 20/2).

28. Padua: Troops storm a flat to free US Brigadier-General James Dozier, 42 days after he was abducted.

30. Bristol: Serious disturbances break out in the St. Paul's district.

31. Tel Aviv: Israel agrees to accept a UN peacekeeping force in Sinai with troops from four European nations (→ 21/4).

Unemployment tops the three million mark

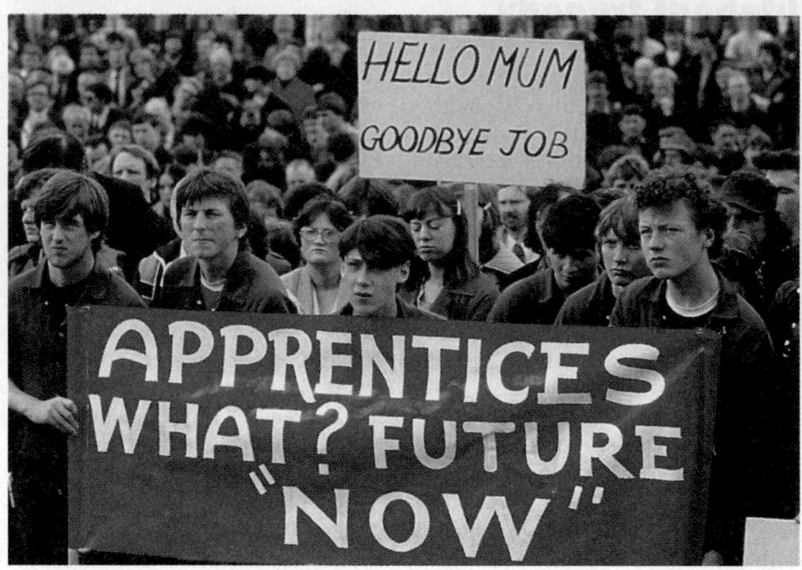

Young people, badly hit by growing unemployment, march for jobs.

Jan 26. Unemployment in Britain is now above three million for the first time since the 1930s. Mrs Thatcher faced strong criticism of her government's economic policies in the House of Commons this afternoon, when the figures were announced by Norman Tebbit, the Employment Minister.

The total was up 130,000 on December, the highest monthly rise since the present set of records began in 1948. The so-called "wet" wing of the Tory party – notably Sir Ian Gilmour and Norman St. John Stevas, both dismissed by Mrs Thatcher from her cabinet, and the former premier, Edward Heath – is saying that the figures must be reduced substantially if the Government is to have any hope of re-election. The Confederation of British Industry also joined calls for action by the Chancellor, Sir Geoffrey Howe, in his March budget to increase public sector investment to make more jobs.

Mr Tebbit blamed the sharp rise on the recent severe weather. The Prime Minister, her voice husky with a cold, drew attention to some positive signs, like increased job vacancies and a much higher level of productivity (→ 4/2).

Plane crashes in sight of the White House

The frozen river gives up its dead.

Jan 13. About 78 people died today when a passenger jet crashed on take-off from Washington's National Airport, slicing into cars and a truck before it plunged over a bridge into the frozen Potomac River. The twin-engined Air Florida jet took off after the airport re-opened as a snowstorm eased a little. Officials said six people died on the bridge and 18 survivors were treated in hospital.

Joseph Stiley, a surviving passenger, said the plane began to stall as soon as it lifted off the runway. Several survivors were plucked from the river by helicopter as rescue vehicles were forced to drive along pavements outside the White House to avoid huge traffic jams caused by the disaster.

Spain calls off its siege of Gibraltar

Jan 8. Spain has agreed to lift its 12-year siege of Gibraltar in return for talks on the colony's future. The deal, announced today after a meeting in London between the Spanish premier, Calvo Sotelo, and Mrs Thatcher, means that Spain will no longer demand the return of "the Rock" on the understanding that Britain lift its unstated but very real opposition to Spain's NATO and EEC membership.

The deal ending the annoying, if not crippling, siege will not be greeted with any enthusiasm by Spain's nationalists, who want Gibraltar back, or by those Gibraltarians who fear moves towards integration with Spain.

Price rises spark Polish food riots

Jan 31. Polish housewives shopping for basic foods today found that prices had doubled, trebled and in some instances increased fivefold. The new prices set off riots in the Baltic shipyards at Gdansk and over 200 people were arrested in battles with police. The city was sealed off, an 8pm to 5am curfew imposed, private cars banned and all public entertainment and sports suspended (→ 9/2).

Jan 4. Erika Roe displays her enthusiasm for rugby at the England v Australia match.

1982

FEBRUARY

Su	Mo	Tu	We	Th	Fr	Sa
	1	2	3	4	5	6
7	8	9	10	11	12	13
14	15	16	17	18	19	20
21	22	23	24	25	26	27
28						

1. Washington: Reagan says the US will send emergency assistance to the El Salvador government (→10).

4. London: Tebbit appoints industry adviser David Young to be head of the Manpower Services Commission.

5. London: Laker Airways collapses, leaving 6,000 passengers stranded.→

9. Madrid: The EEC and US tell Moscow that East-West talks in Spain will end until martial law in Poland is lifted (→17).

10. El Salvador: The army surrenders six soldiers to a civilian court to face charges of murdering three US nuns (→25/3).

12. London: Murdoch transfers control of The Times and Sunday Times to his company News International (→12/3).

14. France: The Socialist government begins nationalisation of banks and other major industries.

14. UK: The Animal Liberation Front raids laboratories and releases beagles used for experiments (→30/11).

17. Poland: The government launches a new crackdown, arresting 3,500 for violating martial law (→1/3).

22. UK: The firm Mercury receives a licence to operate telephones in competition with British Telecom.

23. Uganda: 69 are reported killed in a failed coup.

24. Denmark: Greenland votes to withdraw from the EEC.

25. Strasbourg: The European Court outlaws corporal punishment for children whose parents disapprove.

27. London: The D'Oyly Carte Opera Company gives its last Gilbert and Sullivan performance, at the Adelphi.

28. Johannesburg: Geoff Boycott and 11 others arrive, despite a ban on playing cricket in South Africa (→19/3).

DEATH

17. US jazz pianist Thelonius Monk (*10/10/17).

Laker's cut-price airline does a nose-dive

Feb 7. Offers of help are pouring in to rescue Laker Airways which collapsed three days ago, but there are fears that Sir Freddie's dream of a major airline for cut-price travel may have crashed for ever.

A merchant bank, which has suggested it can raise £25 million to rescue the airline, and a ten-year-old boy with 16p are among those who have tried to help. An anonymous businessman, who claimed Sir Freddie has done more for enterprise in Britain than anyone in the past 25 years, offered £1 million. Even Prince Michael of Kent sent a telegram offering his backing, but there are doubts that the support will help.

The £230 million crash is expected to be followed by increased fares from Laker's larger rivals, who always resented the airline's policy of trying to undercut them. Factors blamed for the collapse include the recession, high interest rates on the cash Sir Freddie had to borrow to run his fleet of DC-10s and the rise in the value of the dollar against sterling.

The crash came when the banks decided they could no longer support the company. They thought it would be better if it failed now rather than risk even more costly trouble at the height of the summer. Sir Freddie was said to be "in a state of misery" as he stalked around Gatwick Airport watching passengers being turned away (→27/5/83).

Luxury car firm is in a financial pile-up

De Lorean's sports cars line up for a cash injection that never came.

Feb 19. John De Lorean's dream of producing luxury sports cars in Belfast was finally shattered today when his company was put into receivership. James Prior, the Ulster Secretary, made it clear that there would be no more state cash for the ailing firm. The minimum loss of taxpayers' money is £17.8 million, the size of the original investment in 1978.

The low-slung, aero-dynamic styled, fibre-glass sports car was aimed at the US luxury market. De Lorean hoped to sell 20,000 of them at $25,000 each. Today the receivers said that 8,500 would have been a more realistic target. The project was a curious alliance between the flamboyant former boss of General Motors and the Labour government, hoping to boost jobs in Northern Ireland. Mr Prior said there had been "very considerable management and marketing mistakes" in the running of the company.

At a press conference in New York, Mr De Lorean came under heavy fire. Asked "Are you a con man? Is your conscience clear?" he replied: "My conscience is very, very clear." He admitted, however, that the company needed a further £16 million to £27 million to survive (→19/10).

Irish election won by Charles Haughey

Feb 20. The Irish Republic will have another hung parliament when the Dail meets next month. But despite the inconclusive results of this week's general election it is Charles Haughey who will be the new premier.

He will succeed Dr Garret Fitzgerald, whose coalition government was brought down last month by an independent MP voting against the budget. It will be Haughey's second term of office. In 1979 he took over the premiership mid-term when Jack Lynch resigned. He faces the prospect of difficult economic circumstances without an overall parliamentary majority (→9/3).

Zimbabwe premier ousts his partner

Feb 17. The 22-month-old coalition government of Africa's newest independent state, Zimbabwe, was brought to an abrupt end tonight, when Robert Mugabe, the Prime Minister, dismissed the veteran nationalist, Joshua Nkomo, and two other ministers from his cabinet. The dismissals follow the discovery of large caches of arms on farms owned by Nkomo.

Mugabe has accused Nkomo of plotting a coup against his government. Business firms owned by Nkomo have been seized as "unlawful organisations". Nkomo said tonight that the coup allegations were "an excuse to get rid of me and smear my reputation" (→18/4).

Bingo war boosts sales of tabloids

Feb 1. Sales of tabloid newspapers rose by 540,000 to 13 million in the second half of last year, thanks to bingo. However, almost all of the increase was in sales of the "Sun", now 4.1 million. Industry experts say that the newspapers have spent £16 million on the bingo war, whereas the rise in sales will bring in only an extra £6 million. Moreover, the circulation tends to fall again as soon as the bingo promotion stops.

1982

MARCH

Su	Mo	Tu	We	Th	Fr	Sa
	1	2	3	4	5	6
7	8	9	10	11	12	13
14	15	16	17	18	19	20
21	22	23	24	25	26	27
28	29	30	31			

1. Moscow: Jaruzelski arrives for talks about the situation in Poland (→28/4).

4. London: The Government gives the go-ahead to satellite television (→2/11).

4. Ireland: IRA bomb suspect Gerard Tuite, who escaped from Brixton Prison, is arrested (→13/5).

6. Cairo: Five men are sentenced to death for the murder of Sadat (→15/4).

9. Dublin: Haughey is sworn in as Prime Minister (→4/11).

15. London: Director Michael Bogdanov goes on trial for his "indecent" production of "The Romans in Britain" (→18).

18. London: The "Romans in Britain" trial is stopped by the Attorney-General "in the public interest".

19. South Georgia: An Argentine scrap-metal dealer lands and plants an Argentinian flag.→

20. S. Africa: Dr Andries Treurnicht launches the ultraright-wing Conservative Party (→10/8).

22. US: The space shuttle Columbia is launched on its third mission (→16/11).

24. Bangladesh: General Ershad seizes power in a coup.

25. Glasgow: Roy Jenkins wins the Hillhead by-election for the SDP (→3/6).

26. Cambridge: The first test-tube twins are born.

28. Iran: The Iranians gain ground in the heaviest fighting of the Gulf War (→24/5).

29. US: Jane Fonda accepts the Oscar for best actor for her ill father, Henry; "Chariots of Fire" is best film.→

DEATHS

8. British statesman Richard Austin "Rab" Butler, Baron Butler of Saffron Walden (*9/12/1902).

29. German composer Carl Orff (*10/7/1895).

All civil rights suspended in Nicaragua

March 25. Nicaragua has declared a state of emergency for a month, which gives the Sandinista government sweeping powers to arrest suspects and censor the press. They fear a US-inspired attack to coincide with the elections in neighbouring El Salvador. They say anti-Sandinista exiles in Honduras and Miami are being prepared.

The Defence Minister, Commander Humberto Ortega, announced a civil defence scheme to "defend the towns brick-by-brick and house-by-house". The government is planning to build air-raid shelters in case of "a foreign attack".

The new American ambassador in Managua, Anthony Quaiton, has denied that the US is planning any such attack (→14/4/83).

Sandinistas show their strength.

Rebel cricketers banned for three years

March 19. The Test and County Cricket Board has cracked down hard on the 15 English players currently engaged on the "rebel" tour of South Africa as an "Invitation XI".

All 15, most of whom played Test cricket for England, have been banned from international cricket for three years as a gesture, in the words of the TCCB statement, "to protect our legitimate and important objectives towards achieving multi-racial cricket". It is hoped that the Board's action will now save the Indian and Pakistani tours of England scheduled to take place this summer.

The players include former Test stars, Geoff Boycott and Derek Underwood, but the current England regulars, Graham Gooch and John Emburey, are the ones likely to suffer the greatest loss (→9/7).

March 29. "Gimme!" says David Puttnam as Loretta Young hands him the Oscar for his production "Chariots of Fire", voted best film.

Scrap dealers stir row in Falklands

March 31. The British nuclear submarine Spartan is heading for the Falkland Islands in the South Atlantic as tension mounts over the illegal landing of Argentinian scrap-metal merchants on the neighbouring South Georgia where they have hoisted the Argentine flag.

Publicly, the Foreign Office is playing down the situation, but there is an unmistakable whiff of crisis in Whitehall tonight. It is feared that the Argentinians are using the "scrap merchants" to bolster their claim to the British islands. Argentine warships are in the vicinity while Britain has only the ice-patrol vessel, HMS Endurance, in the area (→2/4).

The Barbican arts centre is opened

The Barbican Centre: flats and arts.

March 4. The Barbican Centre, the long-awaited arts complex financed by the City of London, was opened by the Queen last night after an 11-year building period during which the cost has escalated from an estimated £19 million in 1971 to an actual £153 million.

The centre houses the London Symphony Orchestra's concert hall, the Royal Shakespeare Company's new theatre, a library and art gallery. Its main drawback is the difficulty of finding your way to it through the Barbican walkways.

1982

APRIL

Su	Mo	Tu	We	Th	Fr	Sa
				1	2	3
4	5	6	7	8	9	10
11	12	13	14	15	16	17
18	19	20	21	22	23	24
25	26	27	28	29	30	

2. London: Britain breaks off diplomatic relations with Argentina.→

3. UK: Mr F. Gilman's Grittar wins the Grand National.

4. Falklands: The Argentinians say they have overrun the last British military unit on the islands (→4).

4. South Atlantic: Argentine troops take South Georgia.→

7. Washington: Secretary of State Haig says he will mediate in the Falklands crisis (→7).

7. London: Thatcher announces the imposition of a 200-mile "exclusion zone" around the Falklands (→8).

8. London: Haig holds talks with Thatcher (→10).

10. Brussels: The EEC approves a ban on Argentinian imports in support of Britain (→12).

12. Falklands: The British 200-mile war zone comes into force; Argentinian forces evacuate the area (→19).

14. Rome: 63 people go on trial for the kidnap and murder of ex-premier Aldo Moro.

15. Cairo: The five found guilty of killing Sadat are executed.

17. Ottawa: The Queen signs an act transferring sovereignty of the 1867 Canadian constitution from Britain to Canada.

18. Zimbabwe: The capital Salisbury is renamed Harare (→19/2/83).

19. London: The Government rejects Haig's plan for an end to the Falklands crisis (→24).

21. Tel Aviv: The Israeli cabinet votes to withdraw from Sinai on Sunday.→

24. South Atlantic: The first Briton to die in the campaign is killed in the crash of a Sea King helicopter.→

28. Warsaw: Martial law is relaxed, the curfew is lifted and one third of political prisoners released (→4/5).

29. Buenos Aires: The Galtieri junta rejects the Haig peace plan.→

Argentinians invade Falkland Islands

April 2. Argentina today invaded and captured the Falkland Islands, overwhelming the single company of Royal Marines guarding the islands' capital, Port Stanley. An emergency session of parliament has been called for today, the first Saturday sitting since the Suez crisis, and Mrs Thatcher will make a statement detailing Britain's response to the invasion.

The Defence Secretary, John Nott, told a press conference today that Britain was already assembling a task force of up to 40 warships and 1,000 commandos, but said the fleet was not yet under orders to sail. Among the warships are the aircraft carriers, Invincible and Hermes.

It would, however, take such a force at least two weeks to get to the Falklands, 8,000 miles away, while the Argentinians, only 400 miles from their bases, would have ample time to build up strong defences.

First reports suggest that they have already put a formidable force ashore, led by elite troops of the "Buzo Tactico", who forced the Royal Marines to surrender after a spirited defence of Government House, in which three Argentinians were shot. The Marines suffered no casualties, but were ordered to surrender by Governor Rex Hunt. The news that the "Malvinas", as Argentina calls the islands, had been occupied was greeted with tremendous enthusiasm in Buenos Aires. In Whitehall, the feeling is one of shock and outrage (→4).

Outnumbered Royal Marines are forced to surrender by the Argentinians.

UN backs Britain's Falklands protest

April 3. A move to brand Britain as the villain of the Falklands conflict failed in the United Nations Security Council tonight when its members demanded a cessation of hostilities and an immediate withdrawal of the Argentinian invasion force to be followed by negotiations.

Panama, which had urged the Council to name Britain as the aggressor, cast the only vote against the British resolution. It was passed by 10 votes to one. Significantly, Russia and China, who could have vetoed the resolution, abstained, as did Spain and Poland.

Britain had carried out its most intensive lobbying operation for many years and until the last minute there was uncertainty about the intentions of a number of delegates.

In the end, however, the explanation by Argentina's Foreign Minister, Nicanor Costa Mendez, that his country had merely "recovered" its own territory, thus ending "one of the last vestiges of imperialism", was not accepted by the Security Council (→4).

Argentina celebrates taking the Malvinas

April 3. Cheering crowds gathered outside the Casa Rosada presidential palace in Buenos Aires today to celebrate the recapture of the islands that the Argentinians call "Las Malvinas". General Galtieri, the leader of the ruling junta, said the military leaders had "only interpreted the sentiment of the Argentine people". And for once, there was no dissent: men and women wept tears of joy as internal divisions, for a while at least, were forgotten. In a broadcast to his people, General Galtieri promised no disruption to the lives of the islanders and said he wanted good relations with Britain (→4).

Buenos Aires: General Leopoldo Galtieri acknowledges the crowd's applause. ▷

Task force sets sail for South Atlantic

Aboard the task force's flagship HMS Hermes, the huge hangar is crammed with Harrier jets and helicopters.

April 5. The Royal Navy Task Force set sail for the Falklands today amid a fervour of patriotic flag-waving and military music. The decks of the two carriers, HMS Hermes and HMS Invincible, were lined by sailors and crammed with Harrier jump-jets as they left Portsmouth. It was a display which Mrs Thatcher wanted the world, and more particularly, the Argentinians to see. Its message: Britain meant business.

Other ships are leaving Plymouth to link up with yet more naval forces from Gibraltar. It is Britain's greatest display of naval strength since Suez, and it is far from complete yet. Already it includes frigates, destroyers, troop carriers, landing ships and supply vessels. On board are Royal Marines, Paratroopers and men from the Special Forces. Invisible, but already despatched, are submarines. It has all been assembled in days, with seamen and dock workers toiling round the clock.

It was proposed last Wednesday by Admiral Sir Henry Leach, the First Sea Lord, and endorsed by the cabinet on April 2. Some ministers voiced worries about the 8,000-mile line of communication between Britain and the South Atlantic. Some recalled Suez and feared the political dangers of summoning the forces home short of victory.

Mrs Thatcher felt she had no choice but to respond to Argentina's military aggression and backed the Royal Navy's proposal.

Will he come back alive?

Whether it will frighten the Argentinians into a diplomatic settlement or lead to military conflict, nobody knows. Captain Jeremy Black, of HMS Invincible, said: "Nobody wants to get involved in military action, but we are training to do so if the nation requires it."

Feelings among the men were stirred by newspaper pictures of the Royal Marines who, after their valiant defence of Port Stanley, were forced to lie on the ground by their Argentinian captors. From the Harrier pilots to the junior ratings there was a determination to "bloody the nose" of the Argentinians, if necessary.

Ironically, some of the workers who prepared the fleet had received redundancy notices during the week as part of the Government's defence cuts. The two carriers had also faced limited futures: HMS Hermes, the flagship, was destined to be scrapped in the mid-1980s while HMS Invincible has been sold to Australia. All that was forgotten today, as the ships eased out of Portsmouth Harbour. "Come back safely," said one banner. It spoke for all the families (→7).

Thatcher rocked by Falklands invasion as ministers resign

April 5. Lord Carrington resigned as Foreign Secretary today. In a bombshell statement he said: "I accept responsibility for a very great national humiliation." That was how he described Argentina's invasion of the Falklands.

Mrs Thatcher, shaken by the invasion and the surrender of the island's governor, said that she accepted Lord Carrington's decision "with a heavy heart". She rejected an offer to quit by John Nott, the Defence Secretary, but accepted the resignations of two other Foreign Office Ministers, Humphrey Atkins and Richard Luce.

As a British task force sailed off towards the Falklands, Lord Carrington said that the Argentine occupation is an affront to Britain. Although he rejected much criticism about having misread the situation, he now accepted that Argentina took its decision to invade a week ago. Because his efforts for a diplomatic solution of the crisis had failed, he had to go "as a matter of honour".

In a cabinet reshuffle, Francis Pym, the Leader of the Commons, becomes the new Foreign Secretary. Rejecting calls for her own resignation, the Prime Minister tried tonight to steady Tory morale. On restoring British sovereignty over the Falklands she quoted Queen Victoria: "Failure? The possibility does not exist".

Lord Carrington: a political victim of "a great national humiliation".

Rejoice! Marines take South Georgia

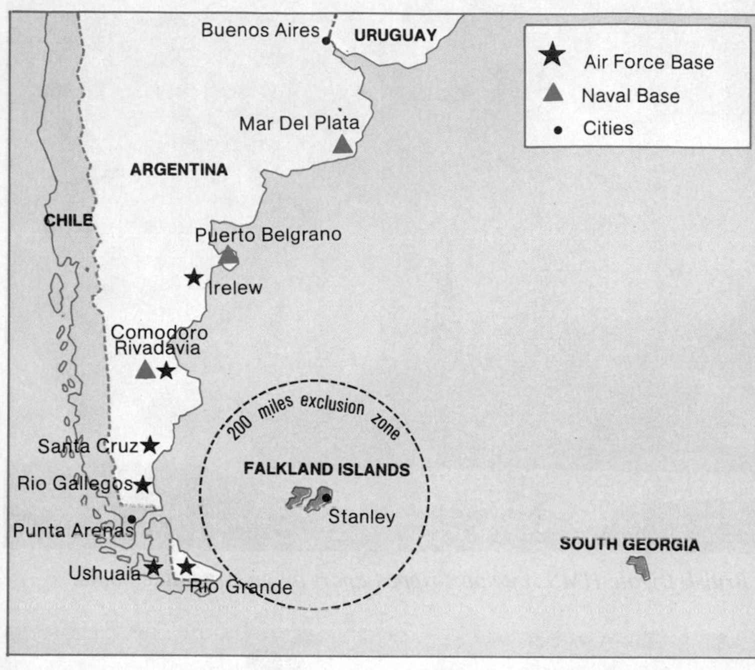

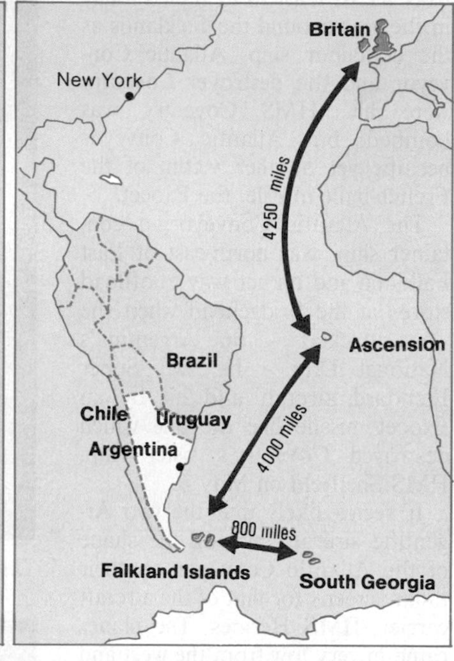

April 25. Royal Marine commandos have recaptured South Georgia, the island in the South Atlantic invaded by Argentina three weeks ago. Announcing the news tonight, the Defence Secretary, John Nott, said there was only limited resistance and no British casualties.

Standing beside him outside No. 10 Downing Street, the Prime Minister said: "Let us congratulate our armed forces and the Marines. Rejoice, rejoice."

Earlier she had told the Queen of the "wonderful news" of the victory. The repossession of the Antarctic island came after members of the elite Special Boat Squadron landed there last week to spot places for an attack. They worked their way across the frozen mountain range on one side of South Georgia until they found the Argentinians.

As the main force was preparing to go ashore, two Royal Navy helicopters attacked the Argentine submarine, Santa Fe, near the main old whaling base of Grytviken, inflicting severe damage with rockets and putting it out of action while it tried to run for shelter.

The action is not being seen in London as heralding the end of negotiations with Buenos Aires. South Georgia has a symbolic rather than a political or military significance. After marking time near Ascension Island, the main Task Force is now heading south towards the Falklands where a maritime exclusion zone has been declared by Britain. It seems certain that the British presence, until now, has been through submarines, although the Ministry of Defence will not confirm this (→ 29).

Israel defies Jewish zealots to return the Sinai to Egypt

April 25. The last Israeli army units withdrew from Sinai today and rolled back across the frontier. The Egyptian flag flies once again over the desert peninsula occupied by Israelis since its conquest in 1967. The handover was arranged under the terms of the Camp David agreement to end the state of war between Egypt and Israel.

Ironically, the final stages of the withdrawal were complicated, not by the Egyptians, but by a score of diehard Jewish zealots at Yamit, a border settlement. These fanatical followers of the extremist Rabbi Meir Kahane barricaded themselves in an underground bunker and threatened to commit mass suicide. The rabbi was allowed through a cordon of troops and persuaded his supporters not to kill themselves.

By then, however, they had been reinforced by thousands of sympathisers from the surrounding district. In the end, army units wielding pick-handles moved in to clear out the settlers and shepherd them back into Israel.

The desert town has now been evacuated and its buildings razed by bulldozers to prevent settlers from drifting back. This will also ensure that the place cannot be used as a guerrilla base (→ 29/6).

Israeli forces, covered in foam, prepare to eject suicidal Jewish extremists from Yamit in Sinai.

US backs Britain over Falklands as diplomatic moves fail

lexander Haig (c.) joins Mrs Thatcher and Foreign Secretary Francis Pym.

April 30. President Reagan today pledged American support for Britain, "our closest ally", in the Falklands crisis. Branding the Argentinians as "aggressors", he ordered economic sanctions against them and offered to supply Britain with war material.

America's abandonment of its neutral role resulted from Argentina's "failure to accept a compromise", said Alexander Haig, the US Secretary of State. Although he stressed there would be no direct US involvement should fighting start, the propaganda effect will be invaluable to Britain, while the economic sanctions will sap Argentina's ability to wage war (→ 1/5).

1982

MAY

Su	Mo	Tu	We	Th	Fr	Sa
						1
2	3	4	5	6	7	8
9	10	11	12	13	14	15
16	17	18	19	20	21	22
23	24	25	26	27	28	29
30	31					

1. Falklands: The RAF bombs the airport at Stanley (→3).

2. South Atlantic: The Argentine cruiser General Belgrano is sunk; hundreds are feared dead.→

4. Falklands: HMS Sheffield is sunk by an Exocet; 21 die (→7).

4. Poland: Restrictions are reimposed after widespread pro-Solidarity demonstrations beginning on May Day (→21/7).

7. London: Britain warns that all Argentine forces more than 12 miles off Argentina will be liable to attack (→12).

12. Portugal: A man tries to attack the Pope at the Shrine of Fatima.→

12. UK: The requisitioned liner QE2 leaves for the Falklands with 5 Infantry Brigade (→17).

13. Brussels: The EEC calls for a ban on the use of rubber bullets by British troops in Northern Ireland (→20/7).

17. Brussels: The EEC renews sanctions against Argentina for a week; Italy and Ireland lift them altogether (→21).

18. US: Unification Church founder Sun Myung Moon is found guilty of income tax fraud.

21. Falklands: British troops establish a beachhead in San Carlos Bay; HMS Ardent sunk.→

23. Falklands: HMS Antelope sunk and seven Argentine aircraft shot down in battles at San Carlos.→

24. Brussels: Eight EEC nations vote to continue the trade boycott of Argentina.→

28. London: Spurs beat QPR 1-0 in the FA Cup Final replay.

28. Spain: Diego Maradona of Boca Juniors and Argentinos Juniors is bought by Barcelona for a record £5 million (→1/7/84).

30. Madrid: Spain joins NATO (→28/10).

DEATH

29. Austrian actress Romy Schneider (*23/9/1938).

Exocets change shape of war at sea

May 25. At least 24 men died today in the seas around the Falklands as the container ship, Atlantic Conveyor and the destroyer Coventry were hit. HMS Coventry was bombed, but Atlantic Conveyor became yet another victim of the French-built missile, the Exocet.

The Atlantic Conveyor, a container ship, was north-east of East Falkland and on her way to offload stores at the bridgehead when she was attacked – on Argentina's National Day – by two Super Etendard aircraft and hit by an Exocet missile like the one which destroyed Coventry's sister ship, HMS Sheffield on May 4.

It seems likely that the two Argentine aircraft mistook the shape of the Atlantic Conveyor on their radar screens for that of the aircraft carrier, HMS Hermes. The planes came in very low from the west and were only detected at the last minute by electronic equipment, but not by radar. The container ship's cargo had originally included Harrier jump-jets and Chinook helicopters. If these had been lost, the Argentinians could have dealt Britain a crippling blow.

Exocet attacks began with the loss of the Sheffield, again with the enemy aircraft flying too low to be registered on radar and firing from a range of about 20 miles while still effectively unhittable. The Sheffield was the first major British warship to be lost for 37 years and news of the attack stunned politicians and public alike. The Falklands crisis had become a shooting war and one moreover posing new technological challenges.

For Admiral Sandy Woodward, the Task Force commander, the potency of the Exocet attacks make it far more difficult to protect the fleet. The Sheffield was on what was called "picket duty" around the two aircraft carriers, Hermes and Invincible. The Exocets have ushered in a new era in maritime warfare, to which nobody yet has the answer.

Some Conservative MPs were so alarmed by the threat that they called for revenge attacks against Argentinian bases on the mainland. Government sources are reluctant to countenance this degree of escalation. It would almost certainly lose Britain the support it enjoys at the UN for the right of "self-defence" against the original Argentinian aggression.

The British position has already been brought into question by the attack on Argentina's only cruiser, General Belgrano, on the night of May 2. The warship was sunk by the submarine Conqueror outside an exclusion zone set up by Britain.

Some 362 men are feared dead after the Belgrano was sunk in what the Buenos Aires government called "a treacherous act of armed aggression". Despite its position outside the exclusion zone, Mrs Thatcher insists that it had represented "a very obvious threat to British forces".

The British frigate HMS Antelope: ripped apart by an Argentine bomb.

The Argentinian cruiser, General Belgrano: doomed by British torpedoes.

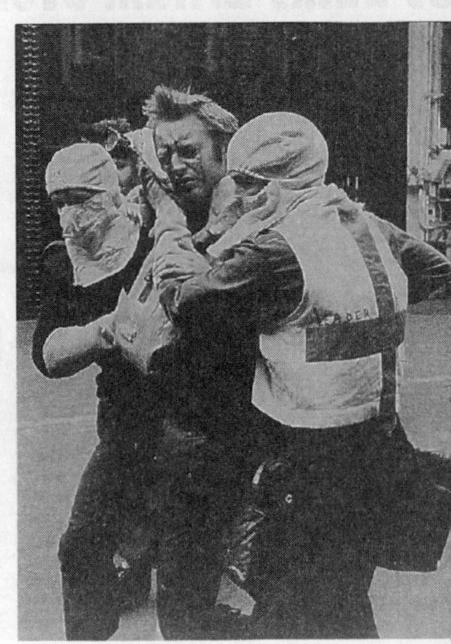

One of HMS Sheffield's survivors.

Troops land in Falklands

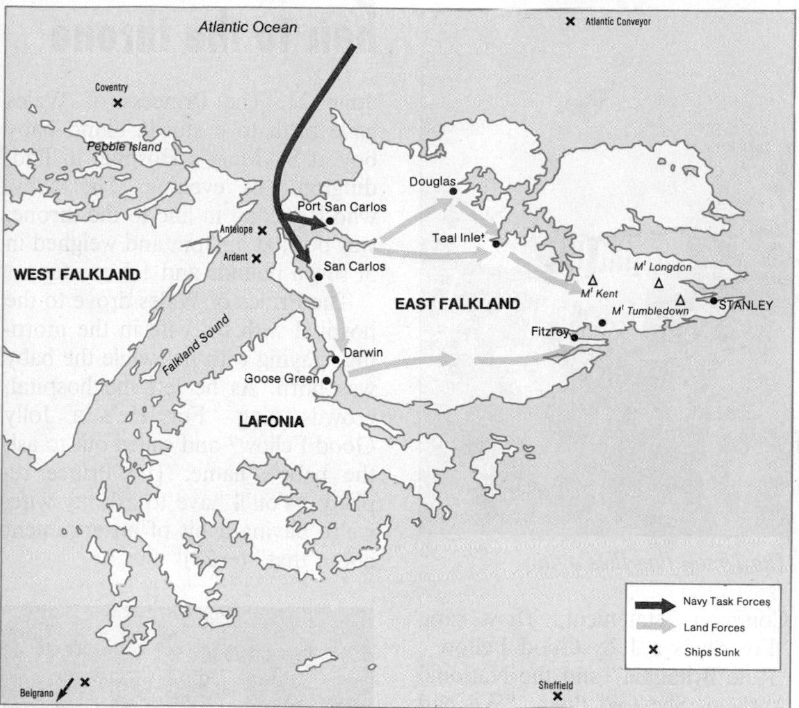

May 29. British troops today claimed victory in the first land battle of the Falklands War, just over one week after Marines and paratroopers stormed ashore at San Carlos. Seventeen paratroopers died in the attack on Goose Green, including their commanding officer, but the victory will come as a welcome respite after sustained Argentinian air attacks.

Two Royal Navy ships, Ardent and Antelope, were sunk by low-flying aircraft in what the soldiers are calling "bomb alley". British sources claim that as many as 23 Argentinian planes have been shot down, but the beach-head has been established. So far, there has been no counter-attack by Argentinian land forces, and the troop ships, including the requisitioned liner Canberra, have been able to discharge the British forces.

The landing on the Falklands was crucial to the success of the British military campaign. Until May 21, when the first forces went ashore at the sheltered inlet of San Carlos Water, there had been only raids by the Special Forces and air strikes against Argentinian airfields. The landing, approved by the war cabinet on May 19, had to be undertaken without superiority either in the air or, in terms of numbers, on the ground. Yet to delay would risk falling foul of the worsening South Atlantic winter.

The men went ashore from the landing-craft, darting through the heather in case of snipers on the land and digging in. Argentinian jets were screaming through the ships assembled in the bay, but there were few attacks on the forces on land and, although slow, the build-up of supplies was completed. Now the forces are fanning out towards Stanley.

The soldiers are making a two-pronged assault on the Falklands capital, trekking – or "yomping" as the Marines call it – across rugged terrain. So far, only the paras have encountered resistance. At Darwin and Goose Green they were outnumbered by three to one in what Field Marshal Sir Edwin Bramall, Chief of the General Staff, has called "an epic battle".

Lieutenant-Colonel Herbert 'H' Jones of 2 Para died leading a charge on a sub-machine-gun post which was holding up their advance. Twelve bloody hours later his 450 men had triumphed, leaving the Argentinians with 250 dead and 1,200 taken prisoner. Islanders released from the recreation hall at Goose Green, where they had been held for 30 days, threw their arms around the British troops and offered them cups of tea (→1/6).

Pope in first visit to Britain for 450 years

May 29. In dazzling sunshine today Pope John Paul II reached the climax of his historic visit to Britain as he stepped into the nave of Canterbury Cathedral. His is the first visit of a Pope to Britain since 1531. For the first time since Britain broke away from the Catholic Church at the time of Henry VIII, a Pope and an Archbishop of Canterbury prayed together at Canterbury.

So great was the emotion that the congregation clapped loudly as the Pope entered to a fanfare of trumpets. Prince Charles was there to represent the Head of the Church of England, but the Prime Minister was kept away because of the Falklands crisis.

The two church leaders prayed together at the tomb of St. Thomas a Becket, who was brutally murdered there by the King's men in 1170 for standing up for the rights of the church. They lit candles for two modern martyrs, a priest who gave his life to save a condemned man at Auschwitz, and a Ugandan Archbishop killed by Idi Amin. Later they announced a commission to study reunification of the two churches (→2/6).

The Pope and the Archbishop.

Sophia Loren is put in jail for tax evasion

May 19. A prison cell awaited film actress Sophia Loren today, as she flew back to her native Italy to begin a month-long sentence for tax evasion. The crime, which the 47-year-old actress attributed to "a little error" by her accountant, dates back to around 1970, and undeclared earnings of £2,500.

Originally a Rome court awarded Loren a four-month suspended jail sentence, but this was later changed to a month in prison plus a very large fine. When starting her sentence, at a women's prison 30 miles north of Naples, the actress claimed that a month behind bars was ultimately preferable to a lifetime in exile from her homeland and family (→5/6).

Loren: less to smile about in jail.

Iran is recapturing ground lost to Iraq

May 24. Triumphant Iranian communiques today claimed their greatest victory in the war with Iraq. According to Tehran Radio, revolutionary forces have entered the city of Khorramshahr, an important oil port. If this is confirmed, it will mean that Ayatollah Khomeini's men have succeeded in winning back almost all territory captured by Iraq in the early stages of the war.

News of the Iraqi defeat spread alarm down the Gulf. Saudi Arabia and the small oil states fear the spread of Shi'ite revolution to their patriarchal cities and therefore back Iraq (→15/9).

1982

JUNE

Su	Mo	Tu	We	Th	Fr	Sa
		1	2	3	4	5
6	7	8	9	10	11	12
13	14	15	16	17	18	19
20	21	22	23	24	25	26
27	28	29	30			

1. Falklands: 5 Infantry Brigade land at San Carlos (→ 8).

2. Cardiff: The Pope ends his tour of Britain (→ 23/6/83).

3. London: Bruce Douglas Mann, ex-Labour SDP MP, loses Mitcham to the Tories in a by-election (→ 2/7).

3. London: Israeli ambassador Shlomo Argov is shot and seriously wounded (→ 4).

4. Lebanon: Israeli jets bomb guerrilla targets in retalitioan for London attack on envoy (→ 6).

5. Italy: Sophia Loren is released from prison.

6. Lebanon: Israel launches major invasion by land, sea and air.→

8. London: Reagan becomes the first US President to address a joint session of Parliament.→

8. Falklands: Sir Galahad and Sir Tristram are hit by Argentine air attacks at Fitzroy near Bluff Cove (→ 11).

9. UK: The 20p coin goes into circulation (→ 22/4/83).

11. Falklands: The Ministry of Defence says 42 British troops died at Fitzroy (→ 14).

19. London: Italian banker Roberto Calvi is found hanged from Blackfriars Bridge (→ 23/7).

20. Brussels: The EEC lifts its trade boycott of Argentina (→ 5/7).

21. US: John Hinckley is found not guilty of trying to kill Reagan, on mental grounds (→ 9/8).

25. Washington: Haig quits as Secretary of State; George Shultz takes over.

28. London: Charles and Diana's son is named William Arthur Philip Louis (→ 16/9/80).

DEATHS

10. German film director Rainer Werner Fassbinder (*31/5/46).

13. Saudi Arabian King Khaled, ruled 1975-82 (*1913).→

Argentinians surrender

June 14. British forces are now in command of the Falkland Islands and the Argentinian invaders are flying the white flag over Port Stanley. A jubilant Mrs Thatcher told the cheering House of Commons late tonight that the victory had been won by an operation which was "boldly planned, bravely executed and brilliantly accomplished".

The end to the fighting came when British troops broke the last ring of defences round Port Stanley at Tumbledown Mountain, Wireless Ridge and Mount Longdon. After hard fighting against well dug-in defenders, the British soldiers saw large numbers of the enemy streaming back to Stanley, and soon white flags began to blossom like flowers.

Contact was made between a Spanish-speaking British officer and Major-General Menendez, the Argentine commander. A cease-fire was agreed and the hopelessness of his position was explained to General Menendez.

Shortly afterwards the British Land Forces' commander, Major-General Jeremy Moore, was able to signal London: "The Falkland Islands are once more under the government desired by their inhabitants. God Save the Queen."

Mrs Thatcher was greeted by cheering crowds at the entrance to Downing Street after making her Commons statement. They sang "For She's a Jolly Good Fellow", "Rule Britannia" and the National Anthem. She told them: "We had to do what we had to do. Great Britain is great again."

There is a price to be paid for greatness, however, and last night the Ministry of Defence released the names of the 56 servicemen killed or missing after the devastating Argentine air attacks on the landing ships Sir Galahad and Sir Tristram at Fitzroy last Tuesday. The known death toll for the campaign as a whole is 255 Britons and 652 Argentinians.

The Union flag flies again.

Princess Diana has given birth to an heir to the throne

June 21. The Princess of Wales gave birth to a sturdy blond baby boy at St. Mary's Hospital in Paddington this evening. The baby, who is second in line to the throne, was born at 9:03pm and weighed in at seven pounds and 1.5 ounces.

The Prince of Wales drove to the hospital with his wife in the morning, staying with her while the baby was born. As he left the hospital, crowds sang "For He's a Jolly Good Fellow" and called out to ask the baby's name. The Prince replied: "You'll have to ask my wife, we're having a bit of an argument about that" (→ 28).

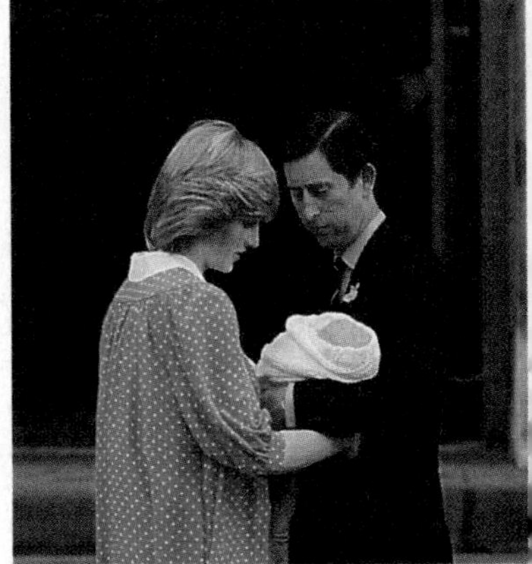

Prince Charles gingerly hands his first-born son to Princess Diana.

Galtieri ousted after Falklands defeat

June 17. General Galtieri has paid the price for his army's defeat in the Falklands. He was ousted from his position as President of Argentina after 12 out of 14 senior generals voted at a meeting in Buenos Aires to use only diplomacy and not force to "regain the Malvinas".

Galtieri's disgrace is complete. The handsome cavalryman, who was hailed as his country's hero only two months ago, has also been stripped of his post as commander-in-chief of the army.

General Alfredo Saint Jean, the hard-line Minister of the Interior of the military junta, has been made interim President, but the post will probably go to a civilian, possibly the Foreign Minister, Nicanor Costa Mendez (→ 20).

Argentine captives are searched.

Saudi monarch dies, the reluctant king

June 13. King Khaled, the reluctant monarch of Saudi Arabia, died today in Taif aged 69. He ascended the throne in 1974 after the assassination of his half-brother, King Faisal, by a crazy nephew. In accordance with Arab tradition the King was buried in an unmarked grave after evening prayer.

Khaled ibn Abdul Aziz was a quiet and authoritative ruler active in international affairs, especially in his attempts to control world oil prices. He had been ill for some time and underwent open-heart surgery in America. The new King will be his brother Prince Fahd who has been the power behind the throne for some time.

Israel invades Lebanon

An armed Israeli soldier chases away protesting Lebanese in Sidon.

June 29. With Israeli troops at the gates of Beirut Menachem Begin, the Prime Minister, today offered to allow encircled Palestinian guerrillas to leave the city with their weapons. This is a dramatic shift in the declared aim of the invasion to destroy the PLO's leadership and its armed forces. Only two days ago Israel was demanding that all 15 terrorist organisations must hand over their weapons to the Lebanese army.

The invasion began early in June. One day after the Israeli ambassador in London had been shot by Palestinian gunmen, Israel's jets bombed guerrilla targets in reprisal raids. Then, on June 6, a force of 20,000 men crossed the border and drove northwards into Lebanon. Two days later advance units were in sight of Beirut. Fierce fighting developed at Tyre and Sidon and in Damur. Other columns cut the Damascus-Beirut highway, clashing with the Syrian army deployed there in strength.

In air battles the Israelis claim to have shot down 61 MiGs while Syria says that it knocked down 19 Israeli warplanes. What is certain is that Israel is isolated diplomatically. Faced with threats of Soviet intervention to aid Syria, plus American disapproval, Prime Minister Begin has been forced to modify his demands (→27/7).

June 8. President Reagan, used to galloping through the Hollywood studios as a cowboy, takes things rather more gently in Windsor Home Park as he takes a dawn canter alongside his hostess, the Queen.

1982

JULY

Su	Mo	Tu	We	Th	Fr	Sa
				1	2	3
4	5	6	7	8	9	10
11	12	13	14	15	16	17
18	19	20	21	22	23	24
25	26	27	28	29	30	31

2. London: Roy Jenkins is elected leader of the SDP.

4. Wimbledon: Martina Navratilova beats Chris Lloyd in the Women's Singles final; Jimmy Connors beats John McEnroe in the Men's Singles final.

5. London: Lord Franks is appointed to chair the government's inquiry into the events leading to the Falklands War (→11).

5. Madrid: England draw 0-0 with Spain and are knocked out of the World Cup.→

7. Oslo: David Moorcroft of Coventry sets a new world record of 13 minutes 00.41 seconds for the 5,000 metres (→8/9).

9. London: Botham scores 208, his highest Test score, against India (→30/12).

11. Southampton: The Prince of Wales welcomes the liner Canberra back from the Falklands (→12).

12. London: Britain declares an end to hostilities in the South Atlantic and says it will repatriate Argentine prisoners (→22).

15. Hereford: Geoffrey Prime is charged under the Official Secrets Act with passing government secrets (→11/11).

19. London: The Queen's bodyguard, Michael Trestrail, resigns after admitting a homosexual affair.

21. Warsaw: The government releases 1,227 people in detention (→13/8).

22. Falklands: Britain lifts the 200-mile exclusion zone (→26).

23. London: An inquest jury returns a verdict of suicide on Italian banker Roberto Calvi (→27/6/83).

26. London: At the Falklands remembrance service, Archbishop Runcie says "War has always been detestable" (→26/8).

27. S. Africa: Col "Mad Mike" Hoare and 40 others are jailed for hijacking a plane after the Seychelles coup bid.

31. France: 46 children die in a coach collision near Dijon.

Intruder gets into Queen's bedroom

July 7. The Queen woke with a start early this morning to find a dishevelled man sitting on her bed in the royal suite in Buckingham Palace, drinking from a bottle of wine that he'd taken from her cellar and wanting a chat. The Queen obliged, hoping to disarm her unwanted guest, but it was not until Michael Fagan, aged 30, asked for a cigarette that she was able to summon help.

Fagan was remanded in custody, charged with theft of the wine while trespassing. The incident has highlighted lax security at the Palace. Recently, a party of German tourists climbed a barbed-wire fence and camped out in the Queen's gardens.

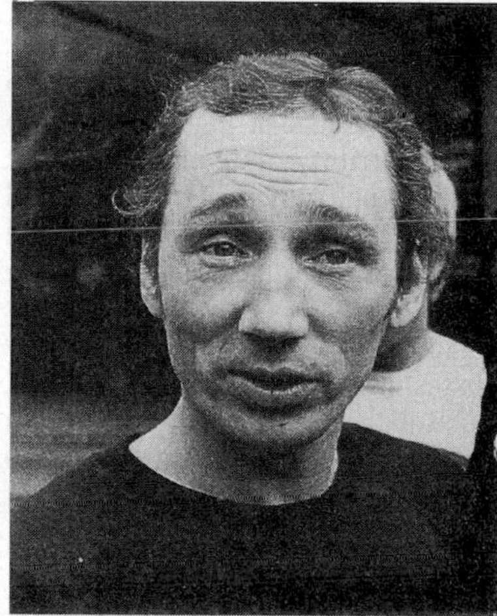
Fagan, guilty of lese-majeste.

Tom Watson holds UK and US Opens

July 19. Tom Watson of the United States has achieved another of his golfing ambitions, becoming only the fifth man to win both the US and British Opens in the same year.

On the notorious undulations of Royal Troon he captured the Open Championship by a single stroke from Peter Oosterhuis and Nick Price to equal his feat last month at Pebble Beach. He now joins four other Americans who have achieved the rare double – Bobby Jones (twice), Gene Sarazen, Ben Hogan and Lee Trevino. Watson has now won four British Opens, all of them on Scottish courses (→11/4/83). ▷

Israeli boats and planes blast Beirut

July 27. Israel kept up its pressure on Beirut today when its aircraft blasted Palestinian positions in the shattered city. Gunboats cruising off the once fashionable Corniche coast joined tanks and guns in the hills ringing the Lebanese capital in the bombardment.

It is estimated that 120 people were killed, making it one of the bloodiest days since Israel began the siege of Beirut six weeks ago. It is not known if the Israelis are still using the American-made cluster bombs they dropped at the start of the invasion. In the city ordinary bombs kill just as well.

Iran launch first offensive into Iraq

July 14. An Iranian army group today launched a night attack into Iraqi territory and claimed to be within nine miles of the great oil port of Basra. Both sides reported that hard fighting was still going on. Baghdad army headquarters claimed to have inflicted heavy losses in counter-attacks. In Iran, Ayatollah Khomeini broadcast an appeal calling on the Iraqi people to rise and overthrow President Saddam Hussein.

IRA bombs explode in the Royal Parks

The sad aftermath of the IRA's car bomb attack in Hyde Park.

July 20. Horror has come to London on a sunny summer's day. As a detachment of the Blues and Royals trotted along South Carriage Road in Hyde Park today, on their way to the colourful guard-changing at Horseguards' Parade, a car-bomb exploded a few yards away. Two guardsmen were killed and 17 spectators injured. Seven army horses were either killed by the blast or had to be destroyed.

A Knightsbridge hairdresser described the scene: "I ran across and it was just a carnage of horses, a pile of men and horses with blood spurting from their wounds."

Two hours later, as the band of the Royal Green Jackets were playing a selection from "Oliver", another bomb exploded under the bandstand in Regent's Park, killing six soldiers and injuring a further 24. One bandsman was hurled nearly 50 yards, his dismembered body impaled on the park railings. Thirteen Green Jackets were critically ill in hospital tonight.

For many animal lovers, numbed by the scale and callousness of this latest attack, the focus of attention tonight is a horse called Sefton - recovering after an eight-hour operation to remove shrapnel. The IRA has admitted responsibility for the killings (→21/10).

Italy wins World Cup with a 3-1 victory over West Germany

July 11. Three goals in the second half of an ill-tempered final in Madrid today clinched Italy's third World Cup victory, but their first since 1938. Paolo Rossie, the tournament's top scorer with six goals, opened the scoring for Italy but they had missed a penalty before finally cruising to a 3-1 victory over West Germany.

The Germans had qualified for the final by means of a negative draw with a disappointed, but far from disgraced England team, and then a thriller with France which was settled by the World Cup's first penalty shootout. France had earlier ended a brave campaign by Northern Ireland. Italy had beaten the favourites Brazil before beating Poland in the semi-final with two goals from Rossi.

Top of the world: Italy hold the World Cup after beating West Germany.

1982

AUGUST

Su	Mo	Tu	We	Th	Fr	Sa
1	2	3	4	5	6	7
8	9	10	11	12	13	14
15	16	17	18	19	20	21
22	23	24	25	26	27	28
29	30	31				

1. London: The Government creates Britoil to take over from the British National Oil Company (→19/11).

1. Nairobi: President Arap Moi announces the crushing of an attempted coup by junior air force officers.

4. Beirut: 250 are reported killed as the Israelis send armoured forces into the west of the city (→12).

9. Washington: Hinckley is sentenced to be detained indefinitely for shooting Reagan.

9. Paris: Six die when unidentified gunmen hurl a grenade into a Jewish restaurant.

10. Namibia: 216 South African and SWAPO guerrillas are reported killed in clashes on the Angolan border (→9/12).

12. Beirut: Israeli jets carry out an 11-hour air raid on West Beirut (→21).

12. Brussels: The EEC protests at Reagan's ban on companies working on the Siberian oil pipeline to Western Europe (→1/9).

16. Leeds: An inquest opens into the death of British nurse Helen Smith in Saudi Arabia in 1979 (→9/12).

21. Beirut: The PLO begins to evacuate the city (→23).

23. Beirut: Christian militia leader Bashir Gemayel is elected President of Lebanon.→

26. Poland: Cardinal Glemp calls for the release of Lech Walesa (→6/9).

26. Buenos Aires: The government lifts the ban on political parties (→11/10).

29. UK: American Ashby Harper, 65, becomes the oldest person to swim the English Channel.

DEATHS

12. US actor Henry Fonda (*16/5/1905).→

21. Swazi King Sobhuza II, ruled Swaziland 1899-1982 (*22/7/1899).

29. Swedish actress Ingrid Bergman (*29/8/1915).→

Israelis drive the PLO out of Beirut

Beirut: a city shattered by war.

PLO fighters lining up to leave Beirut, driven out by the victorious Israelis.

Aug 31. Yassir Arafat, leader of the Palestine Liberation Organisation, left Beirut yesterday amid scenes of chaos, abandoning his power base in the shattered Lebanese capital after 12 years. He said: "I am leaving this city, but my heart is here. I am leaving to continue the struggle, so that we can win the war."

His departure was the culmination of the evacuation of the PLO from Beirut, following their defeat by the Israelis. Seven thousand of them have now left, chanting and firing their guns in the air, as if victorious rather than beaten. They are being dispersed to Syria, Jordan, Sudan, North and South Yemen, Algeria, Iraq and Tunisia, where Arafat will set up his new headquarters. Despite his brave words he will find it difficult to carry on the struggle from there, for with the loss of his base in Lebanon there is no border across which his guerrillas can strike.

He left by ferry for Athens for talks with Prime Minister Papandreou. But before he sailed away he issued a long farewell message to the Lebanese people, thanking them for the sacrifices they had made in the cause of the Palestinian revolution.

"No matter how much I try," he said, "I am still unable to express my gratitude and feelings and admiration towards you and towards this country which has embraced our people with love and affection."

Many Lebanese, looking at the destruction inflicted on their once-beautiful country because of the presence of the Palestinians, take a different view (→10/9).

Tear gas and water cannons break up Polish demonstrations

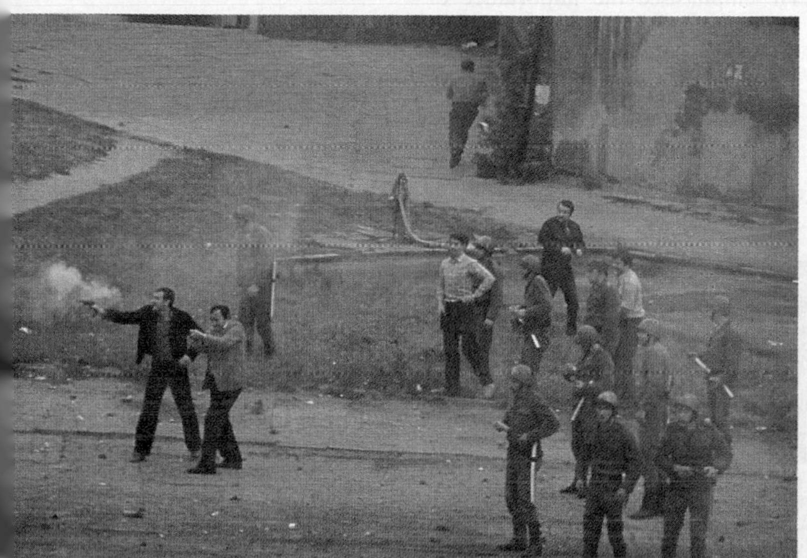
Soldiers and plain-clothes police fire on a Solidarity demonstration.

Aug 13. Poland began its ninth month under martial law today with clashes between police and demonstrators in Warsaw and other cities. The biggest battles took place in Gdansk, stronghold of the Solidarity trade union organisation. Some 10,000 workers marched through the city chanting Solidarity songs, after laying flowers at the foot of three big crosses marking the spot where workers were shot dead during protest marches in 1970. When the crowd made for the Communist Party HQ, which rioting strikers set alight in 1970, police turned on water cannons and fired tear-gas grenades. Solidarity leaders, in hiding, have called for more demonstrations against martial law (→26).

Doctors can still use controversial drug

Aug 8. In a letter to doctors today the Committee on Safety of Medicines said that they could continue to treat patients with the controversial anti-rheumatic drug Opren and that pharmacists will still hold stocks, even though the manufacturers, Dista Products, are prohibited from promoting or supplying it.

In the letter, Professor Abraham Goldberg, the chairman of the committee, went on merely to advise doctors not to treat new patients with Opren and not "to represcribe the drug without good reason."

Most of the deaths, it was claimed, had been in elderly women who had developed jaundice soon after starting on Opren.

Two stars, Fonda and Bergman, die

Aug 30. Ingrid Bergman died last night of cancer on her 67th birthday in her Chelsea flat overlooking the Thames. Her third husband, Lars Schmidt, was with her. Her romance with Roberto Rossellini, by whom she had a child in 1948, scandalised her American fans and the US Senate called her "a powerful force for evil". She won two Academy Awards.

Her death comes only two weeks after that of Henry Fonda, who was 77. He won his first Oscar this year for "On Golden Pond" in which he appeared with his daughter Jane. They had been estranged during her stand against the Vietnam war.

Double Oscar winner Bergman.

1982

SEPTEMBER

Su	Mo	Tu	We	Th	Fr	Sa
			1	2	3	4
5	6	7	8	9	10	11
12	13	14	15	16	17	18
19	20	21	22	23	24	25
26	27	28	29	30		

1. Washington: The US says it will ease sanctions against countries helping to build the Siberian oil pipeline.

6. Berne: Gunmen seize the Polish embassy, demanding an end to martial law (→9).

8. Athens: Daley Thompson wins the decathlon in the European Games (→14/8/83).

9. Berne: Police free the Polish embassy hostages (→8/10).

10. Morocco: Arab leaders say all Middle East states have a right to security – the first implicit recognition of Israel (→14).

13. Australia: Lindy and Michael Chamberlain, who claim a dingo killed their baby, go on trial for murder (→29/10).

14. Beirut: President-elect Gemayel is killed by a bomb.→

15. Tehran: Ex-Foreign Minister Sadegh Ghotbzadegh is found guilty of plotting to overthrow the government (→1/10).

17. Bonn: The coalition of Social Democrats and liberal Free Democrats collapses after governing for 13 years (→1/10).

19. Sweden: Olof Palme's Social Democrats return to power in a general election.

22. Peking: Thatcher arrives on a visit (→25).

23. Oxford: Nigel Lawson says: "No industry should stay in state ownership unless there is an overwhelming case."

25. Peking: Thatcher begins talks on Hong Kong (→1/8/84).

30. London: Lord Denning delivers his last judgement as Master of the Rolls.

DEATHS

1. Polish statesman Wladyslaw Gomulka, premier 1956-70 (*6/2/1905).

5. British airman Group Captain Sir Douglas Robert Steuart Bader (*21/2/1910).

14. US-born actress and Princess of Monaco Grace Patricia Grimaldi, nee Kelly (*11/12/1929).→

Beirut is plunged into a blood bath

Civilians massacred in refugee camps

Sept 18. Lebanese Christian militia yesterday began a bloody massacre in the Palestinian refugee camps of Sabra and Chatila in West Beirut. Hundreds have been killed in the slaughter which was carried out in revenge for the assassination four days ago of Bashir Gemayel, the President-elect of Lebanon.

Men, women and children were ruthlessly shot down and their bodies lie in hideous piles in the mean streets of the camps. Whole families were dragged out of their houses and butchered by Gemayel's vengeful followers. The Israeli army is being blamed for allowing the killers to go about their dreadful work. The first reaction of the Israelis is to deny involvement; they say they allowed the right-wing Phalangists into the camp to search for Palestinian guerrillas.

In Jerusalem embarrassed Israeli officials said: "As soon as we knew of the massacre we took all possible measures to prevent its continuation." But the sight of the innocent dead sprawled in the squalid camp will not sit easy on Israeli consciences. Only three days ago, Yassir Arafat had an audience with the Pope, who spoke of "the suffering of the Palestinian people".→

Some victims of the massacre.

Sects back Gemayel as new president

Sept 23. Amin Gemayel was sworn in as Lebanon's President today after being elected in a rare display of Moslem and Christian harmony. Mr Gemayel, aged 40, succeeds his younger brother, Bashir, who was assassinated before he could take up the post.

The new president promised to stop the vicious circle of violence in his country. It will be a difficult promise to keep. The swearing-in ceremony had to be conducted in the military academy because the bullet-ridden parliamentary building is unsafe, and as he spoke an arms dump blew up.→

Bashir Gemayel, sectarian victim.

Marines to act as Beirut peace-keepers

Sept 28. President Reagan announced last night that US Marines are to resume their peace-keeping role in Beirut, which was interrupted by the Israeli invasion of Lebanon a month ago. Their mission will last, he said, until the Lebanese government is in full control and "able to preserve order". He said on TV that he believed all Israeli and Syrian forces would be withdrawn "rapidly" with the US, French and Italian peace-keeping contingents overseeing the peace until the Lebanese "tell us we can go home". He emphasised the importance of maintaining a military presence in the area (→25/10).

French soldiers disembark for their peace-keeping mission in Lebanon.

Big demo in Israel over the massacres

Sept 25. Israel's biggest-ever political rally protested today about the massacre of Palestinian refugees in the Sabra-Chatila camps and called for Begin's government to resign. Some 300,000 people cheered Opposition leader, Shimon Peres, when he said that Israel would not stay silent about the massacre. "You have been silent, Mr Begin," said Mr Peres. "You wanted us to be silent as well. You tried to say that the height of patriotism is a conspiracy of silence".→

1982

OCTOBER

Su	Mo	Tu	We	Th	Fr	Sa
					1	2
3	4	5	6	7	8	9
10	11	12	13	14	15	16
17	18	19	20	21	22	23
24	25	26	27	28	29	30
31						

1. Iraq: The Iranians launch an offensive against Iraq as the Gulf War enters its third year (→ 2).

2. Tehran: 60 die in a bomb blast in the city (→ 7/2/83).

2. UK: The Inland Telegram service ends.

3. Spain: Three colonels are arrested for trying to stage a coup.→

6. London: Sid Weighell resigns as general secretary of the NUR in a row over his alleged misuse of the rail union's vote.

8. Brighton: Thatcher tells the Conservative conference: "The National Health Service is safe with us."

9. Rome: A two-year-old boy dies in a machine-gun attack on a synagogue.

11. London: The full Falklands honours list is published; over 800 people are to receive awards (→ 4/11).

12. Mustique: Prince Andrew cuts short a holiday with actress Koo Stark owing to excessive media attention.

13. US: Two gold medals taken from Jim Thorpe for being paid for a baseball game are restored posthumously.

19. Los Angeles: John De Lorean is arrested and charged with possession of cocaine (→ 19).

19. Belfast: The Government announces the closure of the De Lorean car plant with the loss of 1,500 jobs (→ 8/11).

21. Northern Ireland: Sinn Fein's Martin McGuinness and Gerry Adams are elected in the first Ulster Assembly poll (→ 11/11).

25. Jerusalem: Defence Minister Ariel Sharon says he only learnt of the Beirut massacres 24 hours after they happened (→ 1/12).

29. Melbourne: Lindy Chamberlain is jailed for life for murdering her daughter, at the end of the "Dingo Baby" trial.

DEATH

4. Canadian pianist Glenn Gould (*25/9/1932).

Princess Grace is killed in car crash

A tragic end to a fairytale life.

Sept 15. Princess Grace of Monaco died last night of head injuries received when her car plunged 120 feet off a mountain road due, it is believed, to brake failure. Neither she nor her daughter, Princess Stephanie, beside her was wearing a seat belt.

After appearing in three Hitchcock films, Grace Kelly, of a rich Philadelphia family, wed Prince Rainier III of Monaco in 1956 and gave up her screen career. Her last film was "High Society". She was 52 years old (→ 18).

Age cannot wither them ... 20 years on, the Stones and Mick Jagger are still Rolling.

Socialists win landslide victory in Spain

Gonzalez, the triumphant victor.

Oct 28. The Socialist Party has won a landslide victory in the Spanish general election, sweeping to power Felipe Gonzalez who, at the age of 40, will become Europe's youngest Prime Minister.

Not all the results are in, but the returns show that the Socialists will have at least 200 seats in the 350-seat Congress of Deputies. The centre parties have completely collapsed, while the right-wing Alianza Popular has won 100 seats, 10 times as many as it held in the previous parliament.

Amid emotional celebrations by those who saw the election as the final victory of the Civil War, 45 years ago, Senor Gonzalez described it as a triumph "for democracy and the Spanish people".

Heave ho and up Mary Rose rises

Oct 11. It was the year 1545 and the French fleet was heading across the channel. As the Mary Rose, Henry VIII's flagship, sailed out to do battle, she suddenly capsized and sank, taking most of her crew to the bottom.

For 400 years, the wreck of the Mary Rose lay under the Solent mud – until today when, with infinite slowness, the remains of her hull were raised to the surface in an operation which has taken 22 years since divers first confirmed her presence.

Since then, scores of Tudor artifacts and weapons have been raised from the sea bed. Now her remains will be preserved in a museum in Portsmouth.

New conservative Chancellor in Bonn

Oct 1. The West German parliament today threw out Chancellor Schmidt and elected Helmut Kohl, the leader of the Christian Democrats in his place. In a bitter speech Herr Schmidt questioned the rules which gave them the right to remove him without an election.

Schmidt's Social Democrats ruled with the help of a minority party, the Free Democrats, who switched sides when Schmidt refused to cut spending on the social services. Today's move brings the right-wing Christian Democrats back to power for the first time for sixteen years. Herr Kohl, aged 52, said his first priority would be to tackle economic problems and reduce unemployment (→ 6/3/83).

Polish parliament outlaws Solidarity

Oct 8. Riot police appeared on the streets of Warsaw tonight as Poland's Communist-controlled parliament was voting to ban the two-year-old Solidarity free trade union organisation. Of the 460 deputies, ten voted against and nine abstained.

The government promised to set up a new trade union body that would be independent of the government, though not of the party. In Warsaw, a statement was issued on behalf of the now underground Solidarity branch. It said the ban would be defied, but it also called on workers not to be led into mass protests at the present time. "We cannot allow the enemy to impose on us the time and forms of the fighting," it said.

In London, the Foreign Office said the Solidarity ban was "a further obstacle to the restoration of normal relations" between the two countries (→ 10/11).

1982

NOVEMBER

Su	Mo	Tu	We	Th	Fr	Sa
	1	2	3	4	5	6
7	8	9	10	11	12	13
14	15	16	17	18	19	20
21	22	23	24	25	26	27
28	29	30				

2. UK: The miners reject a call for industrial action by 6:4 in a national ballot (→ 28/2).

2. UK: Channel Four goes on the air (→ 2/12).

4. New York: The UN passes a resolution calling for negotiation on the sovereignty of the Falklands (→ 8/1/83).

4. Dublin: Haughey's government collapses after losing a vote of confidence in the Dail.

7. UK: Police find a pair of trousers stolen from Sir Geoffrey Howe while he was asleep on a train.

8. Los Angeles: John De Lorean pleads not guilty to charges of drug dealing (→ 18/7).

10. Poland: A general strike called by Solidarity meets with a poor response.→

11. Belfast: The SDLP and Sinn Fein boycott the opening of the Northern Ireland Assembly (→ 16).

16. US: The space shuttle returns to earth after its fifth mission, the first on which it launched a satellite (→ 24/6/83).

16. Northern Ireland: Two policemen, a hardline Loyalist and a Catholic shopkeeper are shot dead in a day of violence.

19. London: Only 30 per cent of shares are sold in the Britoil privatisation.

22. UK: The pound slides to $1.581 after the Government says it will not intervene to support it (→ 25/1/83).

25. Rome: A Bulgarian airline official is arrested on suspicion of complicity in the plot to kill the Pope last year.

30. London: A letter bomb addressed to Thatcher from the Animal Welfare Militia explodes in Downing Street.

DEATHS

5. French film director and actor Jacques Tati, born Jacques Tatischeff (*9/10/1908).

10. Soviet statesman Leonid Brezhnev, leader 1964-82 (*19/12/1906).→

16. British comedian Arthur Bowden Askey (*6/6/1900).

Leonid Brezhnev is dead

Grief shows on the faces of senior party members as they shoulder his coffin.

Nov 10. President Leonid Brezhnev, Soviet leader for the past 18 years, died today and will be succeeded by Yuri Andropov, until recently the long-serving head of the KGB.

Brezhnev died of a heart attack, aged 75, and will be given a state funeral in Red Square which will be attended by statesmen and political leaders from more than 70 countries. The Kremlin obituary hailed him as a "true continuer of Lenin's great cause and an ardent champion of peace and Communism" whose name will live forever.

Brezhnev toppled Khrushchev in a clinical coup in October 1964 and quickly became "first among equals". He was only the fourth leader of the Soviet Communist party since the 1917 Revolution, and the most predictable and conservative, opting for continuity rather than reform.

He failed to solve the country's deepening agricultural and economic problems, but brought the Soviet Union to full superpower status and strategic parity with the United States.

Andropov, aged 61, was for 15 years chief of the KGB, in charge of foreign espionage operations and internal security. He has long experience of Communist Party management, international relations and during his reign at the KGB became adept at crushing dissent (→ 28/9/83).

Lust proves to be downfall of a spy

Nov 11. In the words of the Lord Chief Justice, Geoffrey Prime, aged 44, was a "ruthless and rationally motivated spy". But it was his lust for young girls and a tip-off from his wife that finally exposed Prime, who was jailed for 35 years at the Old Bailey today

Prime, a former linguist at the Government's top secret communications centre, had been positively vetted four times before he was arrested on a sexual assault charge. He confessed his spying activities to his wife, Rhona, who found a miniature camera and high-powered radio transmitter hidden in their home. Mrs Prime "agonised for two weeks" before telling the police.

Soviet and Afghan troops die in tunnel

Nov 9. Several hundred Soviet and Afghan troops have been burnt alive or suffocated in a fire inside the Salang Pass tunnel, which links Afghanistan by road with the Soviet Union.

The fire began after two vehicles collided in the mile-and-a-half-long tunnel. Soviet troops mistook the incident for a rebel attack and closed the tunnel trapping traffic inside.

Lech Walesa surprised at being set free

Free again to speak his mind.

Nov 12. From his place of detention in a state-owned hunting lodge in Eastern Poland, Lech Walesa, the Solidarity leader, wrote to General Jaruzelski. The time had come, he said, to "reach some kind of understanding". Today, four days later, Walesa is a free man after almost a year in detention. He says he wrote the letter because he wanted to persuade Solidarity leaders outside not to risk losing influence with the people by seeking to stage demonstrations that would no longer win mass support. He says he gave no promises to the authorities and is surprised by his release (→ 10/3/83).

In "Sophie's Choice", Meryl Streep plays a US immigrant tortured by the memory of her life and actions under Nazi rule.

1982

DECEMBER

Su	Mo	Tu	We	Th	Fr	Sa
			1	2	3	4
5	6	7	8	9	10	11
12	13	14	15	16	17	18
19	20	21	22	23	24	25
26	27	28	29	30	31	

1. Beirut: Druze leader Walid Jumblatt escapes a bomb blast near his car that kills four.→

5. London: The GLC invites Danny Morrison and Gerry Adams of Sinn Fein on a visit to London (→8).

8. London: The Government bans Morrison and Adams from travelling to Britain (→9/8/83).

9. Lesotho: 41 die in a raid by South African troops against alleged guerrilla bases (→20/5/83).

9. Leeds: The Helen Smith inquest returns an open verdict on the nurse's death in 1979.

10. Stockholm: Nobel Prizes go to Kenneth Wilson (US, Physics); Aaron Klug (UK, Chemistry); Sune Bergstrom (Sweden), Bengt Samuelson (Sweden) and John Vane (UK), all Medicine; Gabriel Marquez (Colombia, Literature); George Stigler (US, Economics); and in Oslo to Alva Myrdal (Sweden) and Alfonso Robles (Mexico, Peace).

15. Gibraltar: The border with Spain is re-opened after 13 years.

19. UK: Townsend Thoresen's European Gateway car ferry collides with another ship near Harwich, killing five.

30. Melbourne: England beat Australia by three runs in the fourth Test, one of the smallest margins in an Ashes match (→7/1/83).

DEATH

20. Russian-born US pianist Artur Rubinstein (*28/1/1887).→

HITS OF 1982

Come on Eileen.

Fame.

Eye of the tiger.

QUOTE OF THE YEAR

"Christ might be described as an under-privileged, colonial, working-class victim of political and religious persecution."

HRH Prince Philip, in "A Question of Balance".

Greenham women head anti-Cruise drive

Another non-violent protester is pulled away from the base, resisting passively.

Dec 12. More than 20,000 women clasped hands to encircle the air-base at Greenham Common today in protest at the planned siting of 96 US Cruise missiles there next year.

The "embrace of the base" was organised by the Peace Camp women who have been staging a round-the-clock vigil at the Berkshire camp since September. The council has twice tried to evict them and several have been jailed.

Because the action was aimed at showing the strength of anti-nuclear feeling among the women of Britain, men, including CND leader Bruce Kent, were asked to keep a low profile. The women, many of them with children, sang anti-war songs and lit candles as the circle was completed to a great shout of "Freedom".

Some tied toys and baby-clothes to the wire, others pinned up photographs of war victims and peace poems. Huge cobwebs of cotton were woven into the fence representing the campaign's symbol of a tiny missile trapped in a web.

Police expect more direct action today when the women plan to blockade the base completely and confront American servicemen as they arrive for work (→1/4/83).

GLC put in jeopardy by Sinn Fein visit

Dec 13. The future of the Greater London Council, the largest local authority in the world, is under threat today. This follows a row last week when two leaders of Sinn Fein, the political wing of the IRA, invited to London by the GLC, were banned by the Government from entering the country under the Prevention of Terrorism Act.

Ministers were angered by the refusal of Ken Livingstone, the Labour leader of the GLC, to withdraw the invitation after the Ballykelly pub bombing, in which 11 died. It is the latest in a series of decisions known to have angered Mrs Thatcher, prompting Government plans to abolish the GLC.

British troops set off for the Lebanon

Dec 12. Britain is to send an armoured reconnaissance unit of 80 men to serve with the multilateral force of the United States, France and Italy aiming to keep the warring factions of Beirut apart. The United Kingdom was asked to contribute to the force two months ago, but has only just agreed to do so. This follows a visit by the Lebanese Foreign Minister, Elie Salem, to London.

Extra-Terrestrial is set to invade Britain

Spielberg (r.) and his creation.

Dec 9. "ET" stands for Extra Terrestrial and for thousands of Britain's children, there will be an extra treat this Christmas: an encounter with Steven Spielberg's latest film success, "ET".

Spielberg, who has already carved himself a name among the Hollywood greats, recycling the ever-popular worlds of heroic adventure and space fantasy with "Raiders of the Lost Ark" and "Close Encounters of the Third Kind", now crosses science fiction with fairy-tales in this story of an alien space creature, accidentally abandoned on earth, and the children who befriend him.

Already a smash hit in the US, this charming, evocative film is set to succeed here too.

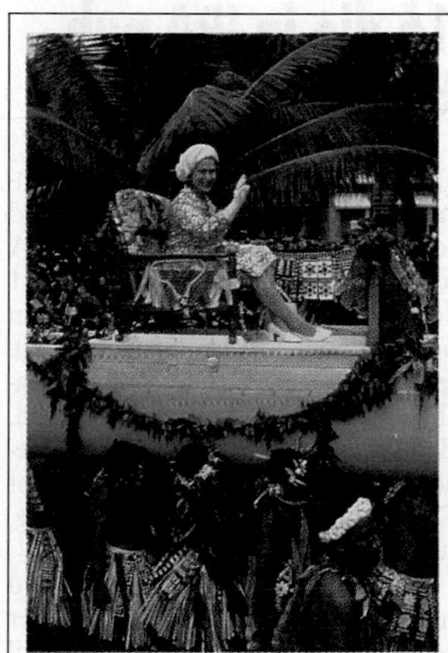

The Queen starts her visit to Tuvalu in the Pacific by being lifted ashore by grass-skirted locals. It's all in a day's work.

Man has artificial heart

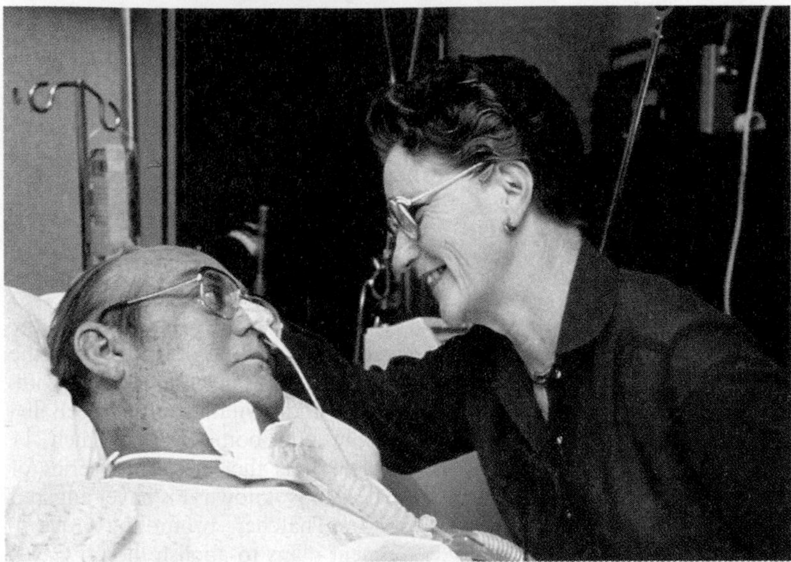

Barney Clark recovers from the surgery that gave him a mechanical heart.

Dec 22. Barney Clark, a 61-year-old American dentist, stood unaided today, 19 days after two chambers of his failing heart had been replaced by a mechanised aluminium and polyurethane pump.

Two days after the operation, performed by William DeVries in Salt Lake City, Utah, he had a second one to repair his lungs, damaged when air was pumped in during the first. He also had seizures from changes in his fluid and salt levels and was given chicken soup and carrots by a tube. A week ago part of his new heart had to be replaced because a valve had broken due to metal fatigue.

Dr DeVries is the only American surgeon allowed to perform human operations with artificial hearts. It was agreed before the operation that Mr Clark could end his own life if conditions became unbearable.

His new heart is now linked by six-foot hoses to an air compressor and mobile power supply giving him a "life tethered to a grocery cart" (→24/3/83).

16 die in IRA pub bombing in Ulster

Dec 6. After years of condemnation, Irish leaders found it hard to find words for the latest IRA atrocity in which 16 people – 11 soldiers and four young women among them – were killed in a village pub's disco. The Roman Catholic Primate, Cardinal O'Fiaich, denounced the bombing as "gruesome slaughter" and the Bishop of Derry described it as a "shocking, horrible, blasphemous thing".

Fury at the attack was reflected in Parliament, where Mrs Thatcher said that it was "the product of evil and depraved minds" and denounced a proposed visit to Britain by leaders of Sinn Fein, the IRA's political wing, at the invitation of the Greater London Council (→8).

**** and **** row at Channel 4

Dec 2. William Whitelaw, the Home Secretary, tonight voiced his concern about the "bad language, political bias and many other undesirable qualities" which he says people have found on the new Channel Four programmes.

Almost from the day it went on the air last month, Britain's fourth TV channel has been dogged by controversy. Established to cater for minorities, some critics felt that programmes were nonetheless too concerned with groups such as homosexuals and feminists. Low viewing figures a are problem for the channel's beleaguered boss, Jeremy Isaacs, but against that there has been praise for arts and current affairs shows (→17/1/83).

Arts: homosexual rape case called off

The private prosecution for obscenity brought against the director of the National Theatre production of "The Romans in Britain" two years ago ended in some confusion at the Old Bailey with both sides claiming victory. The charge against **Michael Bogdanov** of procuring an obscene act in a scene involving the homosexual assault by a Roman on a Celtic Briton was brought by **Mrs Mary Whitehouse** under the Sexual Offences Act. It was stopped on the direction of the Attorney-General.

The inimitable film director and innovator of genius, **Jacques Tati**, has died, leaving only five full-length films, but in them a whole personal and distinctive world which transcends national frontiers, especially prized in Britain.

Tati's eccentric, silent Monsieur Hulot, of the short raincoat, hat, pipe and angular walk, creates chaos in any mechanical environment, thereby standing for unamenable human awkwardness at war with the conformity of the 20th century. He dispenses with dialogue in favour of noise and dispenses almost entirely with actors in favour of real people whom he found on the streets where he was shooting – such as the inhabitants of the seaside town of St. Marc-sur-Mer, in Brittany, where M Hulot enjoyed his famous holiday.

A brilliant mime, as he showed in his sporting sketches of boxers, tennis players, riders and their horses, Tati planned every frame of his pictures in advance. To have created the funniest firework display, traffic pile-up, and house-full of frustrating gadgets is quite a legacy. Tati as Hulot lives as a successor to Chaplin's or Keaton's screen characters: he has the gift of making everyone else look absurd.

Artur Rubinstein brandishes a cast of those famous hands, now stilled.

The death of **Artur Rubinstein** aged 95, removed not only the greatest romantic pianist since **Paderewski**, but also one of the world's most unabashed bon viveurs. As a Pole he was naturally admired for his Chopin interpretations which seemed to get more refined with the years.

A scene from "The Romans in Britain", which brought director Michael Bogdanov to the Old Bailey when Mrs Mary Whitehouse took offence.

A silicon-hungry world gets chips with everything

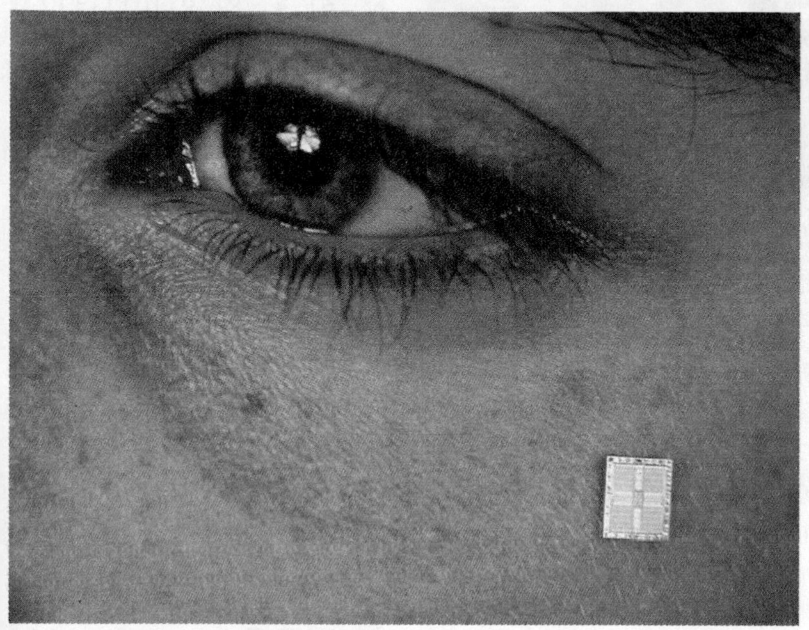

64 kilobytes of computer memory sits like a beauty spot on a girl's cheek.

In the home: new toys and new tools

A major step in the revolution in our daily lives was taken ten years ago when the first true pocket calculator, called the Sinclair Executive, appeared. In the ensuing decade the micro-chip at the heart of the calculator became increasingly indispensable. We were soon having chips with everything.

It's happened fast. The once exotic calculator soon became cheap and commonplace, and Clive Sinclair's £100 ZX home computer was the novelty. Now home computers are increasingly common.

The chip itself is a minute piece of silicon into which transistors, resistors and other electronic components are built by a process a bit like stencilling. Every year the number of components per chip has increased. The single-chip computer is already a reality.

Besides the innovation of calculators and computers a whole new world of electronic games opened up. The first were simple tennis-style games, knocking a blip back and forwards, but the latest ones – fast-moving action games in colour – demonstrate the increasing power of the chip.

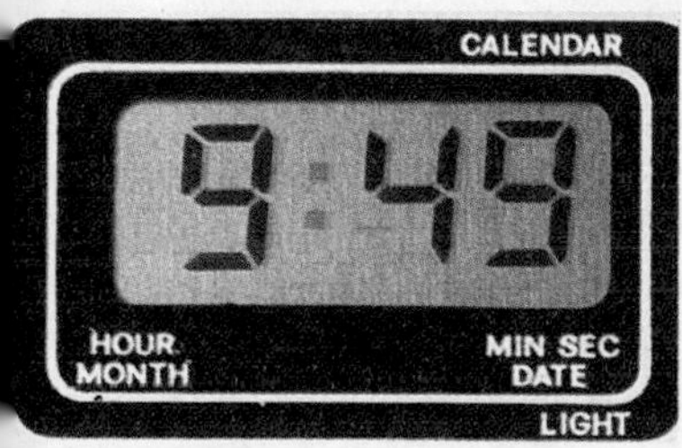

The liquid crystal display is now commonly found on wristwatches.

Chips have not only become more powerful, they have got cheaper too. Designing a chip and getting it into production is expensive, but beyond this stage chips can be turned out in vast numbers at very low cost. The Sinclair Executive cost £70, while today £7 buys a far more powerful machine.

As well as giving us new toys and tools, the chip has transformed everyday objects based on earlier technologies, like the watch and hi-fi. Few watches are driven by clockwork now and where people on the move once listened to tinny transistor radios they can now carry a high quality personal stereo. The video recorder, once very bulky and the preserve of TV studios, now transforms TV viewing in millions of homes.

In the future the biggest changes are likely to come in the information field with link-ups between phones, TV and computers – all plugged into banks, shops, libraries and all dependent on the chip.

In the workplace: the microprocessor is improving itself

Hair-thin glass fibres are beginning to replace conventional cables in the world's telephone networks. Carrying signals coded as pulses of light, a single fibre can carry thousands of simultaneous telephone conversations or dozens of television channels.

On car production-lines robots assemble, weld and paint tirelessly and precisely, displacing for better or worse, production-line workers. Human operators have supervisory roles only.

In offices secretaries with word-processors can redraft documents painlessly, correcting mistakes and moving blocks of text with no need to retype everything. When finished, the documents can be laid-out with a sophistication quite impossible with a typewriter.

Silvery discs like gramophone records, etched with tiny pits by laser beams, can store information so densely that one can hold the equivalent of the Encyclopaedia Britannica several times over.

These are a few of the new developments in the work-place and what they all have in common is that they are based on the silicon chip which, especially in the form of a micro-processor or computer on a single chip, is now found in most industries.

Complicated electronic controls used to be tailor-made for a particular job and so were very expensive. But the micro-processors have changed all that. They are general purpose devices which can be made very cheaply in huge numbers and then programmed to do different jobs.

In fact, the day is fast approaching when most complex control tasks in industry, from guiding coal cutting machines in mines and steel-making at the heavy end, down to the production of new micro-processors themselves at the light end, will be controlled by micro-processors.

Not only are computers controlling industrial processes, they

Fibre optics: better than wires.

are also playing an even greater part in design, too. A draughtsman working at a screen may now have computing power on tap in quantities that would have been unbelievable a decade ago.

He can carry out many humdrum tasks semi-automatically. He can modify a drawing painlessly, rotate it to see it from a different angle, zoom in on part of it to add detail. And he can have a huge library of basic and specialised engineering information ready to be called directly to his screen. One of the fields where computer-aided design is particularly advanced is micro-electronics. Computers are helping to design new and better computers.

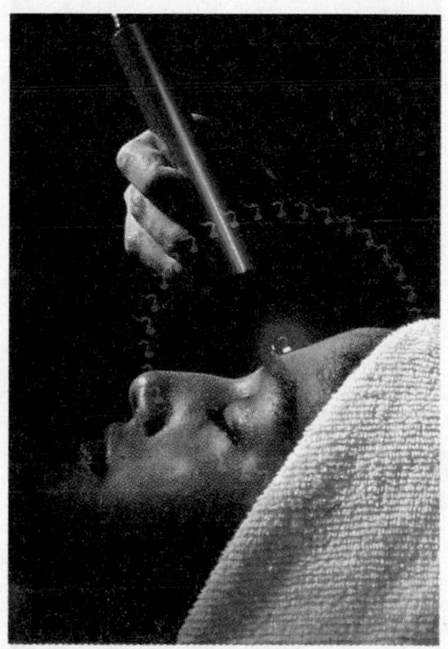

Lasers enter the operating theatre.

1983

JANUARY

Su	Mo	Tu	We	Th	Fr	Sa
						1
2	3	4	5	6	7	8
9	10	11	12	13	14	15
16	17	18	19	20	21	22
23	24	25	26	27	28	29
30	31					

1. London: Britain bans Danish trawlers from fishing in British waters (→ 6).

5. Blackpool: A policeman and two policewomen die trying to save a man who jumped into the sea after his dog.

6. London: Michael Heseltine is appointed Defence Secretary in succession to Sir John Nott.

6. UK: Danish trawler captain Kent Kirk is arrested for illegally entering British waters.

7. Melbourne: Australia win the Test series against England 2-1, regaining the Ashes (→ 3/10).

8. Falklands: Thatcher arrives on a four-day visit.→

10. New Caledonia: Two policemen die in clashes with Melanesians seeking independence for the French colony.

14. London: Police open fire on Stephen Waldorf, believing him to be escaped prisoner David Martin (→ 17).

17. London: Whitelaw says of the Stephen Waldorf shooting: "Nothing like this must ever happen again." (→ 28)

17. UK: Early morning TV begins with the BBC's "Breakfast Time" (→ 1/2).

19. Bolivia: Klaus Barbie, the notorious wartime SS chief of Lyons, is arrested (→ 6/2).

19. London: Two policemen are charged with shooting Waldorf and freed on bail (→ 28).

20. UK: The Serpell Report on British Rail recommends drastic cuts in the network.

25. UK: The pound slides to a record low of $1.517 (→ 3/2).

28. London: Escaped prisoner David Martin is re-arrested (→ 19/10).

31. UK: From today it is compulsory to wear a seat belt in the front seat of a car.

DEATHS

11. Soviet statesman Nikolai Podgorny (*18/2/1903).

24. US film director George Cukor (*7/7/1899).

Nigeria throws out one million workers

A Nigerian soldier encourages immigrants to leave for their homelands.

Jan 30. More than a million Ghanaian migrant workers are on the move tonight, pouring over the border out of Nigeria in lorries, buses and taxis, some even walking. Others are thronging the Lagos airport. Another 100,000 or more are encamped at the docks, awaiting boats; their luggage, including transistors and video recorders, piled beside them.

Two weeks ago, the Nigerian government announced that all unskilled foreign workers must be out of the country by the end of the month "or take the consequences". The government has been under pressure to help unemployed Nigerians crowded in the slums of Lagos. Ghanaians are often ready to work for less money than Nigerians; they have also been accused of turning to crime. Skilled workers, whose hasty exit would upset Nigeria's shaky economy, have been given a month to leave.

As well as the Ghanaians, there are about 700,000 other West Africans who were drawn to Nigeria by the oil boom. Now they are fleeing from a country hit by the collapse in oil prices to homelands whose economic problems are even worse than Nigeria's, and often compounded by drought and political instability.

Whitewash charge on Falklands report

Jan 18. Mrs Thatcher and her cabinet are not to blame for Argentina's invasion of the Falklands last year. Triumphantly the Prime Minister today reported to Parliament this verdict of Lord Franks and five other privy councillors after a six-month inquiry.

"Whitewash," yelled Labour MPs. A pro-Tory factor for the next election campaign is now established. The report stated that the Government could neither have foreseen nor prevented the invasion. It also said that successive British governments gave the impression of being no longer interested in defending the Falklands (→ 12/4).

Bjorn Borg retires at the age of 26

Jan 22. At the age of 26, at the very height of what has become an astonishingly lucrative career, Bjorn Borg has retired from tennis.

With five Wimbledon titles to his name, as well as five French Opens, he became the most difficult player in the world to beat. Of the major championships he contested, only the US Open eluded him, with four finals, two against Connors and two against McEnroe, going against him.

A request to reduce his tournament-playing commitments was refused by the tennis authorities, so he has decided to give up the professional game altogether and retire to the south of France.

1983

FEBRUARY

Su	Mo	Tu	We	Th	Fr	Sa
		1	2	3	4	5
6	7	8	9	10	11	12
13	14	15	16	17	18	19
20	21	22	23	24	25	26
27	28					

1. UK: ITV's breakfast television service TV-am begins broadcasting (→ 18/3).

1. London: The Thames Flood Barrier is raised for the first time in a flood alert.

3. UK: Unemployment stands at a record 3,224,715 (→ 15/3).

6. France: Barbie, expelled by Bolivia yesterday, is imprisoned in Lyons and charged with crimes against humanity (→ 16/8).

9. Ireland: 1981 Derby winner Shergar is kidnapped; a £2 million ransom is demanded.

10. UK: The remains of 17 people are found at a house in north London.→

13. Turin: 64 die in a theatre fire.

15. Beirut: The Lebanese army takes control of East Beirut from the Christian militia (→ 19/4).

15. UK: The BL Metro is now Britain's best-selling car.

16. Australia: 68 die in the country's worst bush fires; arson is suspected.

16. London: Habitat buys Heal's for £5 million.

19. Harare: Nkomo is held by police eight hours before he is due to board a plane to Czechoslovakia (→ 13/3).

20. India: Over 600 Moslem refugees in Assam are massacred in the worst sectarian violence since partition (→ 6/10).

22. UK: Britain's first national water strike ends.

24. London: Labour's Peter Tatchell loses the Bermondsey by-election to Liberal Simon Hughes.

26. UK: Pat Jennings becomes the first player in England to appear in over 1,000 first-class football matches.

28. UK: Yorkshire and South Wales miners are called out on strike in protest at planned pit closures (→ 3/3).

DEATH

25. US playwright Tennessee Williams, born Thomas Lanier Williams (*26/3/1911).

1983

MARCH

Su	Mo	Tu	We	Th	Fr	Sa
		1	2	3	4	5
6	7	8	9	10	11	12
13	14	15	16	17	18	19
20	21	22	23	24	25	26
27	28	29	30	31		

1. US: The Queen and Prince Philip meet Reagan on his ranch.

3. UK: The NUM executive calls a national strike ballot, against the wishes of Arthur Scargill (→ 28).

5. Australia: Bob Hawke's Labour Party returns to power in a general election.

5. London: Three Arabs are sentenced to 35 years in jail for the attempted murder of the Israeli ambassador last year.

6. West Germany: Chancellor Kohl retains power in an election which gives the Greens their first seats.

10. Gdansk: Shipyard workers demand the restoration of Solidarity (→ 22/4).

11. Moscow: The funeral takes place of ex-spy Donald MacLean, believed to have died three days ago (→ 26).

14. London: The 13 members of OPEC all agree to cut oil prices for the first time in the organisation's 23-year history.

15. London: The Budget raises tax allowances and cuts taxes by £2,000 million.

17. London: The second letter bomb sent to 10 Downing Street in three days is defused.

18. London: Peter Jay resigns as chairman of TV-am (→ 19/4).

22. Jerusalem: Belfast-born Opposition MP Chaim Herzog is elected President of Israel (→ 28/8).

24. US: Artificial heart recipient Barney Clark dies, after the failure of all his vital organs except his heart.

26. London: Anthony Blunt dies of a heart attack.

28. London: Labour MPs protest at British Steel chief Ian MacGregor's appointment as head of the Coal Board (→ 1/9).

DEATHS

3. Hungarian-born author Arthur Koestler (*5/9/1905).→

8. British composer Sir William Turner Walton (*29/3/1902).→

15. British author Dame Rebecca West (*21/12/1892).

Sharon should quit over camp killings

Feb 8. The Israeli war hero "Arik" Sharon should resign or be sacked from his post as Defence Minister, according to the findings of the government inquiry into the Beirut massacre of Palestinian refugees.

The report said that Mr Sharon bore "personal responsibility" for the decision to allow Israel's allies of the Lebanese Christian Phalangist militia into the refugee camps last September.

It also blamed the Prime Minister, Menachem Begin, who shared "a certain degree of responsibility". But it made no recommendations against him (→ 15).

Civil servant may have murdered 16

Feb 11. Dennis Andrew Nilsen, a civil servant, was today accused of murder, following the discovery of dismembered human remains in a sewer pipe in London.

Two heads, a hand and other pieces of flesh were recovered from under the garden of a Hornsey bedsitter. Remains of up to 14 other bodies are expected to be discovered at a house in Willesden Green.

Police think the killings took place over a five-year period and probably all involved the deaths of young men with no fixed addresses who would not have been reported as missing (→ 24/10).

Iranian forces cross the border into Iraq

Iran bombards the Iraqi front line with artillery as its troops press forward.

Feb 7. Six Iranian divisions are today battling forward across the frontier in a mass attack on Iraqi fortifications. As many as 200,000 men, most of them ill-trained but fanatical Revolutionary Guards, are slogging forward through sand and winter desert mud. The offensive developed on a 40-kilometre front near Ammara, south-east of Baghdad, where the Iranians claim to have broken through. Iraq is fighting back with helicopter-borne reserves and air attacks (→ 4/5).

The symphony Mozart composed at nine

Feb 5. An unknown Mozart symphony has been found amongst old papers in Odense, Denmark. It is a symphony written when Mozart was nine years old.

The 42-page manuscript is divided into three movements, an allegro, an andantino and a rondo. The work is in A minor. Professor Jens Larsen, a Mozart specialist at Copenhagen University, said today: "It is not what one would call a major work, but it is a charming chamber symphony written with the boyish hand of a great composer."

William Walton, UK composer, is dead

Sir William, a popular composer.

March 8. Sir William Walton died today at his villa on Ischia, where he had lived with his Argentinian wife Susana since 1958. His deft and witty "Facade" music (1923), written originally to accompany Edith Sitwell's poems, remained his most popular success.

"Belshazzar's Feast", an oratorio for massive forces, followed in 1931 and in 1935 his first Symphony, whose "modern" dissonances and cross-rhythms pleased audiences. His opera "Troilus and Cressida" was not a success, but his scores for Olivier's "Henry V" and its sequels were serious film music.

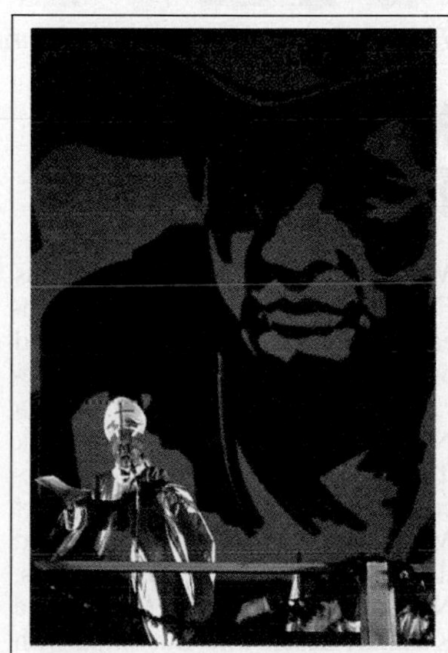

March 4. The Pope, visiting Nicaragua, assails the Sandinistas and the "People's Church". There is only one church, he says.

Reagan urges "Star Wars" for defences

March 23. President Reagan today proposed a revolutionary defence system dubbed "Star Wars" to build a futuristic missile shield across America to protect it from Soviet attack. The move comes only days after he dubbed the Soviet Union the "Evil Empire" saying peace could only come through strength.

White House officials said the new scheme, which will require years of research, might include laser beams, microwave devices and particle beams directed from satellites or the earth.

In a television address from the White House, the President spoke of "a vision of the future which offers hope" that the US could stop relying on the policy of massive retaliation to counter the threat of a Soviet nuclear attack. He said the system would render nuclear weapons "impotent and obsolete". But he warned that the technological breakthroughs "may not be accomplished before the end of this century".

A senior administration official claimed that President Reagan's proposal represented no threat to the Soviets and did not violate the Anti-Ballistic Missile Treaty signed more than a decade ago because it did not ban research and development. The Russians are unlikely to agree (→ 28/9).

The Queen amuses the President during this month's visit to the USA.

Nkomo on the run from Mugabe raids

March 13. Zimbabwe's notorious Fifth Brigade security force, trained by the North Koreans, swooped on the Bulawayo home of the veteran African nationalist, Joshua Nkomo, and proceeded to ransack it, killing the chauffeur in the process. A spokesman for Robert Mugabe, the Prime Minister, said they were looking for bandits. Nkomo, aged 66, fled across the Kalahari desert into Botswana with his family. Today he flew into London, a bitter and disappointed man after almost 40 years devoted to the liberation of his people. He said Mugabe wanted to kill him.

Koestler exercises his right to suicide

March 4. Arthur Koestler and his wife Cynthia were found dead side-by-side in their armchairs at home in Kensington yesterday. They had committed suicide. Koestler, who was 77, was suffering from leukaemia and advanced Parkinson's Disease. He was a vice-president of the Voluntary Euthanasia Society.

Koestler's masterpiece of Communist exposure, "Darkness at Noon", caused a sensation in 1941 when the Stalinist terror was not widely known. A Hungarian-born cosmopolitan, he made himself a major literary and intellectual figure in his adopted country.

1983

APRIL

Su	Mo	Tu	We	Th	Fr	Sa
					1	2
3	4	5	6	7	8	9
10	11	12	13	14	15	16
17	18	19	20	21	22	23
24	25	26	27	28	29	30

1. London: The Government expels three Russians named as KGB agents by a Soviet defector (→ 5).

4. London: Gunmen get away with £7 million from a Security Express van, the biggest cash haul in British history.

9. UK: Mr B.R.H. Burrough's Corbiere wins the Grand National, trained by Jenny Pitman, the first woman to train a National winner.

11. US: Richard Attenborough's "Gandhi" wins eight Oscars, the most ever by a British film.→

11. US: Seve Ballesteros becomes US Masters golf champion (→ 22/7).

12. Buenos Aires: The government of President Reynaldo Bignone orders the arrest of ex-President Galtieri (→ 6/7).

14. Washington: Reagan denies that sending covert aid to Nicaraguan rebels is illegal (→ 27/4).

17. London: Britain's Michael Gratton wins the men's London Marathon; Grete Waitz of Norway is first woman home.

19. London: Anna Ford and Angela Rippon are sacked from TV-am (→ 8/12).

22. Gdansk: Lech Walesa returns to work at the Lenin shipyard (→ 1/5).

22. UK: The £1 coin comes into circulation (→ 1/2/84).

24. Tel Aviv: The Israelis say they are preparing to withdraw from some parts of Lebanon (→ 26/6).

24. Vienna: Bruno Kreisky, Europe's longest-serving head of government, resigns after losing his majority.

26. Stockholm: The government warns the USSR it will sink any submarine that enters Swedish waters illegally.

27. Washington: Reagan appeals to Congress to support increased aid to the El Salvadorean government (→ 4/5).

DEATH

4. US actress Gloria Swanson (*27/3/1899).

Car bomb destroys US Beirut embassy

April 19. Cranes and bulldozers were brought in today by rescue workers searching frantically for survivors still unaccounted for among the ruins of the US Embassy in Beirut. In a suicide attack yesterday a terrorist drove up to the building in a truck loaded with 300 pounds of explosive. He perished in the explosion, along with at least 40 others, including eight Americans.

Several groups claimed that they had carried out the bombing. The most likely one is Islamic Jihad, a pro-Iranian network of fanatical Shi'ites. Suicide bombing is a deadly technique adopted by Lebanese Moslems who believe that a martyr's death is a passport to paradise (→ 24).

Experts go to war over Hitler diaries

Stern reveals those diaries.

April 25. Are they, could they be, the most remarkable historical find of the century? Or have the "Sunday Times" and a leading historian been hoaxed by a clever forger?

Extracts from 60 volumes of diaries, allegedly written by Adolf Hitler, are being published in the German magazine "Stern" today. Lord Dacre, formerly Professor Hugh Trevor-Roper, is convinced they are authentic. Other experts are more sceptical. Times Newspapers will not confirm paying £1 million for them (→ 6/5).

Fourteen miles of protest at Greenham

CND supporters hold hands for peace between Burghfield and Greenham.

April 1. Today, thousands of CND supporters poured into Berkshire's "nuclear valley" to form a 14-mile human chain linking Greenham, Aldermaston and Burghfield. They included actress Julie Christie and the veteran peace campaigner, 92-year-old Lord Brockway.

The day was peaceful apart from a few attempts to scale the wire and rush the gates. But both the 1,000 Thames Valley police and the Ministry of Defence wanted no arrests and no one was charged.

The Defence Secretary, Michael Heseltine, said the protesters were travelling a "naive and reckless road". A mass "die-in" is planned in Glasgow tomorrow to symbolise the cost of nuclear war (→3/6).

Mario Soares win turns Portugal socialist

April 25. The Socialist Party will be the biggest single political group in the new Portuguese parliament as a result of today's election. Although the party, led by Mario Soares, failed to win an overall majority, it will dominate the new assembly.

Soares, who lived in exile in France during the old dictatorial regime, will become prime minister in a coalition government of Socialists and Social Democrats. The heaviest losers were Catholic Democrats, who ruled the country for three years in turbulent alliance with the Social Democrats. The election was the tenth since the 1978 revolution.

Oscars for "Gandhi": Sir Richard Attenborough and Ben Kingsley.

1983

MAY

Su	Mo	Tu	We	Th	Fr	Sa
1	2	3	4	5	6	7
8	9	10	11	12	13	14
15	16	17	18	19	20	21
22	23	24	25	26	27	28
29	30	31				

1. Poland: May Day demonstrators in 20 cities call for the restoration of Solidarity (→23/6).

2. UK: Steve Davis regains the world professional snooker championship from Cliff Thorburn.

6. Bonn: After examination by experts, the "Hitler Diaries" are declared a fake (→14).

8. UK: London tube driver Christopher Hughes wins the BBC's Mastermind quiz.

9. London: Thatcher calls an election for June 9 (→11).

11. London: Unilateral nuclear disarmament and EEC withdrawal feature in Labour's new manifesto, adopted today (→18).

14. West Germany: Konrad Kujau, alleged author of the "Hitler Diaries", surrenders to the police (→27).

16. London: the first wheel clamps are introduced, in the boroughs of Kensington and Chelsea and Westminster.

18. London: The Tory manifesto is published; it includes plans to abolish the GLC and six metropolitan counties (→25).

21. London: Manchester United and Brighton draw 2-2 after extra time in the FA Cup Final (→26).

25. Egypt: 500 die when a Nile steamer sinks in crocodile-infested waters.

25. Cardiff: Callaghan sparks a fierce row when he attacks Labour's plans to abandon Polaris missiles (→9/6).

26. London: Manchester United beat Brighton 4-0 in the FA Cup Final replay.

27. West Germany: Gerd Heidemann, the reporter who "discovered" the "Hitler Diaries", is arrested.

29. London: A Rembrandt worth £1 million is stolen from Dulwich Gallery.

DEATHS

21. British historian Lord Kenneth Clark (*13/7/1903).→

31. US boxer Jack Dempsey (*24/6/1895).

Reagan sides with Contra "terrorists"

May 4. For the first time today President Reagan backed the aims of the Contra rebels, who are fighting to overthrow the Marxist Sandinista government of Nicaragua. Previously the US government has maintained that their covert aid for the Contras was to help halt the flow of weapons.

Reagan said the Sandinistas had betrayed their revolutionary principles. Theirs was "government out of the barrel of a gun", he said. He questioned their right to retain power and said he would be happy for US support for the Contras to be open, not secret (→28/7).

"Civilisation" Clark has died at eighty

May 21. Kenneth Clark will be best remembered as the cultural mandarin of television who presented the series "Civilisation". But his long career in art began as director of the National Gallery at the age of 31.

He championed Henry Moore and Graham Sutherland in their early days. Later he was first chairman of the Independent Television Authority and was hissed in the Athenaeum for his pains. A wealthy connoisseur, he died at his home, Saltwood Castle. He was made a life peer in 1969.

Iran expels Soviet diplomats as spies

May 4. Iran today expelled 18 Russian diplomats and banned the country's Tudeh Communist party. These moves follow the televising of confessions to spying for Russia by leading members of the Tudeh.

At first sight this would seem to reflect the antagonism of Iran's fundamentalist Islamic government to atheistic Communism. But it owes more to pragmatic politics than to religion, for a defector from the Soviet embassy in Tehran is known to have revealed how the KGB has been using the 2,000 strong Tudeh party to infiltrate the government of the Ayatollah Khomeini. The purge followed (→25/7). ▷

Car bomb rocks South African air force HQ

Bloodshed in apartheid's heartland: a victim of the car bomb in Pretoria.

May 20. A blue Alfa-Romeo parked outside the multi-storey HQ of the South African Air Force in Pretoria exploded at about 4.30 this afternoon, at the height of the evening rush-hour. Employees, both black and white, were thronging the pavement as they came out of the building. At least 16 people were killed and 190 injured. It was the worst single terrorist attack yet in South Africa and Louis le Grange, the Minister for Law and Order, blamed it on the exiled black nationalists in the African National Congress (→29/6).

No-frills flights cut fares to New York

May 27. Passengers can fly from Gatwick to New York from today for less than the cost of a first-class return from London to Edinburgh. At £99 the cut-price fare from the US airline People Express is £76 cheaper than a stand-by ticket from British Airways. Experts say that People Express has cut its own profit margins so tightly that its 747s will have to be two-thirds full just to break even. But the airline says the market for no-frills flights (meals cost extra) has been untapped since the collapse of Sir Freddie Laker's Skytrain (→22/6/84).

May 14. Mount Etna's lava flow is diverted by a huge explosive charge to make an artificial avalanche. The aim is to send it into a channel that has been dug by bulldozers, thus saving the towns of Nicolosi and Belpasso.

1983

JUNE

Su	Mo	Tu	We	Th	Fr	Sa
			1	2	3	4
5	6	7	8	9	10	11
12	13	14	15	16	17	18
19	20	21	22	23	24	25
26	27	28	29	30		

1. UK: Lester Piggott wins his record ninth Derby on Mr G. Wragg's Teenoso.

1. UK: The first prosecution of a "video nasty" is made under the Obscene Publications Act (→3/2/84).

3. UK: 752 have been arrested in four days of protests outside Upper Heyford US Air Force base (→22/10).

4. USSR: Over 100 die when a passenger ship rams a rail bridge over the Volga.

6. Washington: Bernadette Devlin McAliskey is refused a visa by the State Department.

10. London: Computer tycoon Clive Sinclair is knighted.

11. London: Howe becomes Foreign Secretary and Lawson Chancellor; Pym is sacked and Whitelaw made a peer (→12).

12. London: Foot resigns as Labour leader; Neil Kinnock is favourite to succeed him (→13).

13. London: Roy Jenkins resigns as SDP leader, recommending Dr Owen as his successor (→16).

14. Chile: Thousands of people take part in nationwide protests against the rule of General Pinochet.

15. London: Tory backbencher Bernard Weatherill is chosen to succeed George Thomas as Speaker of the Commons.

16. London: Thatcher scraps her "Think Tank", the Central Policy Review Staff (→14/9).

19. Warsaw: The government warns the Church to keep out of politics.→

20. Wimbledon: John McEnroe argues with the umpire on the first day of the championships.

25. Washington: George Shultz reaffirms US support for President Marcos of the Philippines (→21/8).

27. London: A second inquest into the death of Italian banker Roberto Calvi returns an open verdict.

29. S. Africa: The government extends the banning of Winnie Mandela (→3/11).

NASA's Sally rides into space history

Challenger's latest space rider.

June 24. America's first woman in space returned safely to earth today as the Challenger space shuttle touched down at Edwards Air Force Base in California. Sally Ride, a 32-year-old physicist, was one of five crew members aboard the shuttle for the almost flawless six-day flight.

Challenger's return was witnessed by 250,000 spectators, many wearing T-shirts that read, "Ride, Sally, Ride". During the mission Sally gave a preview of the days when satellites will be returned to earth for servicing by placing one in orbit and then retrieving it.

Arafat blasts Assad as he leaves Syria

June 26. The Palestine Liberation Organisation was in deep trouble today after the expulsion from Damascus of its leader, Yassir Arafat. Split into rival warring factions by its defeat in Beirut at the hands of Israel, the PLO is facing the worst crisis in its 18-year existence.

Arafat openly accused the Syrians of lying about their alliance with what he calls mutinous Palestinian elements led by Sa'id Mousa. Attacks on his men by rebel Palestinian groups could not have been mounted, said Arafat, without the help of President Assad.

Thatcher triumphs again

June 10. The Tories are back in power tonight with their widely-predicted landslide general election victory. It has been a personal triumph for Mrs Thatcher, whose personality dominated the campaign.

She is the first Prime Minister for more than 30 years to gain re-election after a full term in office. The final election score is: Tories 397 seats, Labour 209, Liberal-Social Democratic Alliance 23, Others 21.

The overall Tory majority of 144 is the biggest since Labour's victory in 1945. Outside London, Labour is now almost wiped out as an electoral force in the south. The Alliance is runner-up in two-thirds of Tory-won constituencies. But even with 25 per cent of all votes cast the Liberals and Social Democrats have failed to make a breakthrough in terms of seats.

Mrs Thatcher said: "It is wonderful," while Labour's leader, Michael Foot, called the result a national disaster. For the Alliance, David Steel said: "We demand an inquiry into the unfair voting system." Mr Foot and Roy Jenkins, who led the Alliance with the grand title of prime minister-designate, intend to resign from their posts in the next few days (→11).

Maggie celebrates a landslide.

Liberal Pope backs Polish freedoms

June 23. For his last appointment at the end of an eight-day visit to his native land, Pope John Paul II flew in a white helicopter to the Polish skiing resort of Zakopane in the Tatra mountains. There he walked with Lech Walesa, leader of Solidarity, the outlawed free trade union movement. The meeting lasted 40 minutes. Two days ago the Pope told a congregation of almost two million at Katowice, Poland's industrial heartland, that people had a right to join free trade unions. "This right is not given to us by the State," he said. "It is a right given by the Creator." Tonight the Pope is back in Rome (→21/7).

Not Poles apart: the Pope embraces Solidarity's Lech Walesa, and his ideals.

1983

JULY

Su	Mo	Tu	We	Th	Fr	Sa
					1	2
3	4	5	6	7	8	9
10	11	12	13	14	15	16
17	18	19	20	21	22	23
24	25	26	27	28	29	30
31						

3. Wimbledon: John McEnroe beats Chris Lewis for the Men's Singles title; Martina Navratilova beats Andrea Jaeger in the Women's Singles final.

6. London: The Government announces a rise in defence spending, including £624 million for the Falklands (→7).

7. London: The new Chancellor, Nigel Lawson, announces public spending cuts of £500 million.

11. Ecuador: 119 die when an airliner flies into a mountain.

11. London: The satirical magazine "Private Eye" pays Sir James Goldsmith £85,000 libel damages and costs.

13. UK: Neil Kinnock escapes unhurt when his car overturns on the M4 near Newbury (→2/10).

13. London: After a long debate, MPs vote 361-245 against the restoration of the death penalty.

16. UK: 20 die in Britain's worst helicopter crash, off the Scilly Isles.

19. UK: Fossil remains of a previously unknown species of carnivorous dinosaur are found in a Surrey clay pit.

21. UK: Sir Harold Wilson, Jo Grimond and Gerry Fitt are among 17 new life peerages announced today.

22. Washington: Robert MacFarlane replaces Philip Habib as Reagan's roving envoy in the Middle East.

25. Sri Lanka: Over 100 are reported killed in racial violence between Sinhalese and Tamils.→

27. Lisbon: Seven die when Armenian terrorists storm the Turkish ambassador's residence.

28. Washington: The House of Representatives votes to end covert aid to Nicaraguan rebels by September 30 (→8/9).

DEATHS

29. British actor James David Graham Niven (*1/3/1910).→

29. Spanish film director Luis Bunuel (*22/2/1900).

100 killed in race riots in Sri Lanka

July 27. Racial violence has led to the death of at least 100 people in Sri Lanka in the past few days, with Tamil-owned shops being set on fire and their owners beaten to death by mobs of Sinhalese youths rampaging through the streets seeking revenge for the murder of 13 government troops.

The soldiers were killed outside Jaffna in the Tamil-dominated north by "Tamil Tigers" who are demanding their own state of "Eelam" in this beautiful but troubled island. More than 20,000 fearful refugees from the violence are now crammed into makeshift relief centres around the capital.

High Court says yes to teenage lovers

July 26. Anti-pill campaigner, Victoria Gillick, wept today after a High Court judge refused to rule that it was illegal for a doctor to supply contraceptive pills to girls under 16 without their parents' consent. Mother-of-ten Mrs Gillick said; "I no longer have the rights I thought I had to protect my own children."

The judge said his decision would be "deeply disturbing" to many, but he believed doctors took such measures only in "exceptional circumstances".

July 17. Tom Watson, on his way to winning his fifth British Open.

Niven, the perfect gentleman, is dead

July 30. David Niven died yesterday of a muscular wasting disease at his home in Switzerland aged 73. He had lost the use of his left hand but was debonair to the end.

At 19, Niven was commissioned from Sandhurst, but left the army to go to Hollywood, as an extra: "Anglo-Saxon type 2008". His career later blossomed as an ever-relaxed, well-mannered Englishman, notably as Phileas Fogg in the star-studded "Around the World in 80 Days" and as the disgraced ex-major in "Separate Tables". His autobiography "The Moon's a Balloon" was a best-seller.

David Niven: debonair to the end.

Iraq swelters awaiting Iran's offensive

Iran's popular art reflects her bloodlust and political obsessions.

July 25. The Iraqis are waiting under the burning summer sun along the Iranian border for the much-publicised offensive, promised by the Ayatollah Khomeini. Their tanks and artillery are ready, the ammunition dumps are full, the troops are dug into the ruins of the towns along the border as they look east, waiting for the Iranian guns to open the campaign.

The Iraqis are seasoned soldiers after three years of bloody war and they know how to conduct themselves under fire. But they know that when the Iranians attack it will not be according to the manual of war, for the Iranians come on, oblivious to their losses, seeking martyrdom in the cause of Iran, the Ayatollah and Allah. The Iraqis speak with wonder of the young boys and old men who march through minefields, opening the way for the regular soldiers to attack the Iraqi positions.

The first skirmish of the campaign was fought two days ago, when a sudden Iranian onslaught drove the Iraqis out of Haj Omran in Kurdistan. But it is down in the south, among the heat and the flies and the bloated bodies on the banks of the Euphrates, between the battered oil towns of Iraqi Basra and Iranian Abadan, that this murderous war will flame into action. The Ayatollah intends to break the Iraqi army and humiliate President Saddam Hussein (→24/5/84).

KGB "tried to kill" Pope, claims Agca

July 9. Mehmet Ali Agca, the Turkish terrorist who is serving a life sentence for the attempted assassination of Pope John Paul II in May 1981, claimed today that the KGB and agents of the Bulgarian secret service were behind the plot in which he badly wounded the Pope.

In a prison interview with an Italian news agency he said that Sergei Ivanov Antonov, the Bulgarian airline official who is already under arrest for complicity in the shooting, was his accomplice. He was not explicit about the role played by the KGB and the Soviet news agency, Tass, disdainfully calls his claims "threadbare" (→27/12).

Compulsory ballots in new strike law

July 12. Trade unions will be compelled by law to hold secret ballots of members before calling strikes. They will also be obliged to conduct elections for their top union jobs.

Early government legislation was promised today to implement these changes, which were foreshadowed in the Tory manifesto. Norman Tebbit, the Employment Secretary, told MPs: "This will give the community more protection against irresponsible industrial action."

He said that he aimed also at getting more democracy within the unions and he promised that more reforms are on the way (→3/9).

Martial law lifted by Polish leaders

July 21. In a move intended to demonstrate to the West that Poland is returning to normal, Gen Jaruzelski today lifted martial law, 19 months after imposing it during a December weekend in order to crackdown on Solidarity, the free trade union movement. But many of the martial law regulations have been incorporated in the civilian legal code, so life will not be much easier for Poles. Jaruzelski, however, says his gesture is "proof of the goodwill of the authorities". He also had a warning: "Any attempts at anti-socialist activities will be muzzled no less decisively than before" (→7/9).

1983

AUGUST

Su	Mo	Tu	We	Th	Fr	Sa
	1	2	3	4	5	6
7	8	9	10	11	12	13
14	15	16	17	18	19	20
21	22	23	24	25	26	27
28	29	30	31			

4. Rome: Bettino Craxi is sworn in as Italy's first Socialist Prime Minister.

6. Washington: The US says it is sending two AWACS and F-15 planes to aid Chad against the Libyans.→

9. Belfast: Rioting follows the fatal shooting of an unarmed youth; an army officer is charged with murder (→14).

9. Chad: The first French paratroopers arrive.

10. Helsinki: The first athletics world championships begins.→

12. Santiago: The Chilean government says 17 people have been killed in anti-Pinochet rioting.

12. Buenos Aires: The government releases British assets frozen during the Falklands War (→10/12).

14. France: The police seize a large consignment of arms bound for the IRA.

16. Washington: The US admits Klaus Barbie was protected by the US Army after the war.

20. Washington: The US lifts its ban on the sale of parts for the Siberian pipeline to the USSR.

20. UK: Radio Caroline returns to the air three years after its previous ship sank in the North Sea.

21. Ireland: 13 die when two trains collide.

22. Manila: Marcos accuses his enemies of trying to spread panic throughout the Philippines (→27).

27. Manila: Crowds of mourners mob the hearse carrying the coffin of murdered opposition leader Benigno Aquino (→31).

28. Tel Aviv: Begin announces his resignation as Prime Minister (→1/9).

28. Beirut: US troops return fire for the first time when they come under attack in fighting near Beirut airport.→

31. Manila: Cory Aquino addresses a crowd of three million Filipinos at her husband's funeral (→29/9).

Britain's Thompson is triple champion

Aug 14. A healthy absence of political wrangling, superb organisation and an expert Helsinki crowd has made the first World Athletics championships a great success.

In a week of outstanding performances, the most prominent were the American Carl Lewis, (golds in the 100m, long jump and 4 x 100m relay) and two women double champions, Mary Decker of the USA (1,500m and 3,000m) and the Czech Jarmila Kratochvilova (400m and 800m).

For Britain Steve Cram emerged triumphantly from the shadow of Coe and Ovett to win the 1,500m title, and Daley Thompson added the world title to his Olympic and Commonwealth titles.

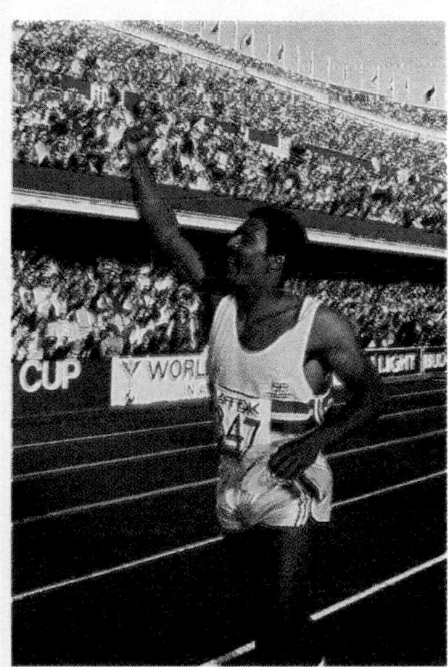

Daley Thompson gets his gold.

Opposition leader gunned down in Manila

Security men lift Aquino's body into a van; his assassin lies to the left.

Aug 21. Benigno Aquino, the only opposition leader who is a serious rival to President Marcos of the Philippines, was gunned down as he stepped from a jet at Manila airport today. Aquino, once jailed by Marcos, was returning from a three-year self-exile in the US to fight the election. He had been warned he might be arrested.

As soon as the aircraft taxied to a halt, two guards arrested him. As they hustled him towards a van there was a fusillade of shots. Government sources said he was shot in the head by a lone assassin, dressed as a maintenance worker, who was immediately shot by guards. Aquino always wore a bullet-proof vest, but as he told reporters on the plane: "If they hit me in the head, I'm a goner" (→22).

Tanker blaze threatens massive pollution

Aug 6. The Castillo de Belver, a Spanish supertanker fully laden with 200,000 tons of crude oil, has caught fire and split in two off the Cape coast of South Africa. A huge oil slick, 20 miles long and three miles wide, now threatens the whole area. Two men are still missing from the blazing wreck after helicopters hovered just ten feet above the burning deck to rescue the crew of 36. South Africa is taking emergency clean-up measures.

The Castillo de Belver pollutes air and sea off the South African coast.

France sends men and arms to Chad

Aug 7. With invading Libyan forces occupying a third of the poverty-stricken Sahara republic of Chad, France today acted to help her former colony, sending paratroops, helicopters and anti-aircraft weapons to reinforce the 500 "military instructors" already there.

Chad's see-saw civil war, with Goukouni Oueddei and Hissen Habre taking turns to overthrow each other, took a sinister turn when Libya's Gaddafi sent in his so-called Islamic Legion and annexed a broad strip of northern Chad. The US has promised Habre, currently the President, £16 million in military aid, half of it to be spent on sending 2,000 Zairean troops to Chad (→9).

Chad fights back against Libya.

Western forces are attacked in Beirut

Aug 31. Two American Marines and three French soldiers have been killed in the factional fighting of the past two days, as the peace-keeping forces become increasingly sucked into the Beirut maelstrom.

The American embassy buildings on the seafront are under sustained attack from Shia and Druze militiamen and the Marine guards are replying with small arms fire. A British patrol has also come under fire for the first time, but sustained no casualties (→12/10).

"Supergrass" turns tables on IRA men

Aug 5. Evidence by a "supergrass" led to sentences totalling more than 4,000 years on 22 members of an IRA cell today. The cell's leader, Kevin Mulgrew, aged 27, was sentenced to 963 years for conspiracy to murder, attempted murder and other crimes – all in addition to the life sentence which he is already serving.

The key witness, Christopher Black, is a self-confessed bully, perjurer, failed assassin and robber, the court was told (→9).

1983

SEPTEMBER

Su	Mo	Tu	We	Th	Fr	Sa
				1	2	3
4	5	6	7	8	9	10
11	12	13	14	15	16	17
18	19	20	21	22	23	24
25	26	27	28	29	30	

1. UK: Ian MacGregor takes over as chairman of the National Coal Board (→ 12/3/84).

1. Tel Aviv: Yitzhak Shamir is chosen to succeed Begin as leader of the Likud Party and Prime Minister (→ 10/10).

3. Washington: The US Census Bureau says the world's population stands at 4,721,887,000.

7. Blackpool: Scargill attacks Solidarity as "an anti-Socialist organ who desire the overthrow of a Socialist state" (→ 5/10).

8. Nicaragua: Rebel aircraft attack the capital Managua, bombing the airport and residential areas (→ 7/1/84).

9. Buenos Aires: President Bignone pardons former President Isabel Peron.

11. UK: The SDP conference votes against a merger with the Liberals for at least five years.

14. London: John Selwyn Gummer is chosen to succeed Cecil Parkinson as chairman of the Conservative Party (→ 5/10).

16. Washington: The CIA denies that the South Korean airliner was spying.

24. Italy: Executives of the company responsible for the 1976 Seveso disaster are jailed for up to five years.

25. Northern Ireland: 134 IRA prisoners break out of the Maze Prison.

28. Moscow: Andropov rejects Reagan's proposal to limit medium-range nuclear missiles in Europe (→ 24/11).

29. Manila: Marcos shuts down a newspaper for hinting that army officers were involved in the murder of Aquino (→ 30).

30. Manila: The chief justice of the Philippines resigns from the panel investigating the Aquino murder (→ 14/10).

DEATH

10. South African leader Balthazar Johannes Vorster, Prime Minister 1966-78, President 1978-79 (*13/12/1915).

Soviets shoot down Korean airliner

Sept 6. The Soviet Union admitted tonight that military chiefs ordered a fighter pilot to "stop the flight" of Korean Airlines' Boeing 747 flight 007. The Kremlin hopes the statement will ease the tension with the West following the missile attack on the aircraft as it flew over Sakhalin Island off Siberia, with the loss of 269 lives last week.

The Soviet Union claims the aircraft was on a spy flight over sensitive military installations on the island, but had so far come up with a variety of excuses for blasting it out of the sky. Today's statement said: "The Soviet government expresses regret over the death of innocent people and shares the sorrow of their bereaved relatives and friends." However, it still criticised the US government, saying "the entire responsibility for this tragedy rests wholly and fully" with America's leaders.

It was almost a week after the plane disappeared from radar screens on a flight from New York to Seoul before the Soviets gave an explanation. First reports suggested it had been forced to land by Soviet jet fighters.

The Soviet statement insisted that the jet was flying without navigation lights, in the depths of night with bad visibility, and was not answering signals. But today the US played a tape at the UN of what the fighter pilot said: "I am closing in on the target ... I am in lock-in. I have executed the launch. The target is destroyed" (→ 16).

Soviet spokesman Nikolai Ogarkov gives the Soviet analysis of events at a rare press conference by Russian military officers held in Moscow.

Oblivious to political wrangling, Koreans mourn lost relatives and friends.

NHS is forced to privatise services

Sept 8. From today the NHS will have to allow private contractors to tender for cleaning, catering and laundering services to see if they can do it more cheaply. Norman Fowler, the Social Services Secretary, has said that he believes that this will save between £90 and £180 million a year.

Mr Ron Keating, assistant general secretary of the National Union of Public Employees, called the instruction "a sword of Damocles hanging over 250,000 support jobs in the NHS".

Australia wins Cup – after 132 years

Sept 26. After 132 years and 24 vain challenges the America's Cup has finally left the United States. Throughout Australia, and among the vociferous contingent of Australian supporters in Newport, Rhode Island, the celebrations began as Alan Bond's Australia II, captained by John Bertrand, came from 3-1 down to defeat the American defender Liberty, skippered by Dennis Conner, in today's final race in the series of seven.

The Americans, who have held the trophy in New York Yacht Club since 1851, have vowed to seek revenge.

The Australians edge ahead to win the America's Cup from the US.

1983

OCTOBER

Su	Mo	Tu	We	Th	Fr	Sa
						1
2	3	4	5	6	7	8
9	10	11	12	13	14	15
16	17	18	19	20	21	22
23	24	25	26	27	28	29
30	31					

3. UK: Geoff Boycott is sacked by Yorkshire Cricket Club (→ 21/1/84).

5. London: Cecil Parkinson admits having had a relationship with his secretary, Sara Keays.→

6. New Delhi: Gandhi sacks the state government of Punjab as religious and political violence continue (→ 21/5/84).

7. London: Thatcher says the GLC and metropolitan counties will be abolished in 1986.

9. Rangoon: South Korean foreign minister Lee Bum Suk and three other ministers are killed in a bomb blast.

10. Tel Aviv: The Knesset confirms Yitzhak Shamir's appointment as Prime Minister (→ 24/11).

11. Blackpool: Home Secretary Leon Brittan says child or police murderers face a minimum 20 years in jail.

12. Washington: Reagan approves a bill to keep the US Marines in Beirut for another 18 months.→

14. Manila: Marcos announces a new inquiry into the death of Benigno Aquino (→ 27/11).

16. London: Norman Tebbit succeeds Parkinson as Trade and Industry Secretary (→ 31/11).

19. Washington: The Senate approves a bill to make Martin Luther King's birthday a national holiday (→ 2/11).

19. London: The two detectives who shot Stephen Waldorf are cleared of attempted murder (→ 17/3/84).

20. Grenada: The armed forces seize power following the murder of Prime Minister Maurice Bishop.→

24. London: At Dennis Nilsen's trial it is revealed he has confessed to 15 or 16 murders.

28. New York: The US vetoes a UN resolution deploring the invasion of Grenada (→ 6/11).

DEATH

10. British actor Sir Ralph David Richardson (*19/12/1902).→

Kamikaze raids kill 299

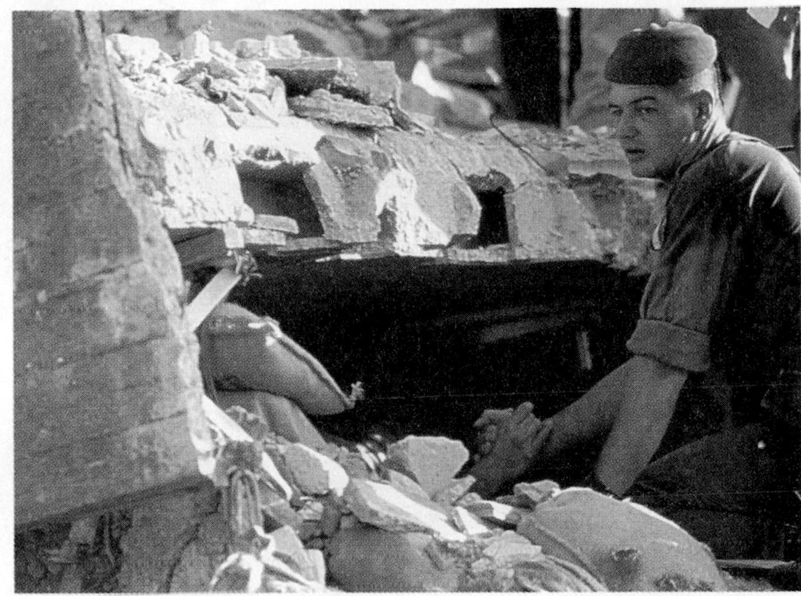

A French soldier gives comfort to a colleague trapped in the rubble.

Oct 23. In two co-ordinated suicide missions in Beirut today, fanatical Shia terrorists drove trucks filled with explosives into the headquarters of the French and American peace-keeping forces and killed themselves along with 241 Marines and 58 French paratroopers.

The first attack came soon after dawn, when a red truck was seen gathering speed in the parking area of the airport and heading for the fence, beyond which lay the four storey building housing the Marines' headquarters.

It crashed through two barricades, drove round a third and crashed into the lobby of the building and blew up. The building was full of sleeping men and one Marine survivor said: "There was carnage like I have not seen since Vietnam."

Three minutes later, the second "kamikaze" bomb destroyed the residential block used by the French a few miles to the north. This eight-storey building folded like a pack of cards, trapping sleeping soldiers between the concrete floors. Tonight the rescue work continues with bulldozers and bare hands as soldiers search desperately for comrades who might still be alive in the rubble (→ 4/11).

Minister Parkinson quits and admits to Sara's love child

Oct 14. Cecil Parkinson has resigned from the cabinet in disgrace. His fight to stay as Trade and Industry Secretary was over when his jilted mistress, Sara Keays, who is expecting his child in January, made a statement to "The Times" to "put the record straight".

A week ago Mr Parkinson said that he had withdrawn an offer to marry Miss Keays, his former secretary, and that he and his wife had decided to stay together. Miss Keays disputed his version of events. Mrs Thatcher originally saw no reason for her colleague to resign. Many grassroots Tories, some ministers and Church leaders did. He just had to go (→ 16).

Neil Kinnock is new leader for Labour

Oct 2. Neil Kinnock, a fiery 41-year-old left-winger, was today picked as Labour's new leader by an overwhelming majority of the party's electoral college votes. Roy Hattersley, a right-winger, will be his deputy on what they are calling "our dream ticket".

Earlier, Mr Kinnock slipped on Brighton beach and got his trousers wet. "Bet it wouldn't happen to Maggie," he quipped (→ 15/1/84).

Anti-nuclear demonstrators march in several European capitals

Oct 22. A huge CND demonstration halted central London today in protest at the plan to base US Cruise missiles in Britain. It was the biggest anti-nuclear rally in two decades, with crowds estimated at between 250,000 and 400,000.

Marchers, lead by CND's Bruce Kent and Joan Ruddock, packed Hyde Park to hear Labour's new leader, Neil Kinnock, tell them: "This is the movement for life." His wife and two children were there.

Similar scenes were repeated across Europe. A million West Germans staged the largest demonstration of post-war years, and in Paris 10,000 people formed a "human chain" (→ 3/12).

Dummy missiles form part of the West German anti-nuclear protest.

US Marines go ashore in Grenada

Oct 27. Resistance to the US invasion of Grenada collapsed last night as more American troops, including 800 Marines, moved in to boost the attacking force. But the political storm shows no sign of abating. Even President Reagan's most stalwart ally, Mrs Thatcher, is angry about the invasion of what was a British colony.

The Prime Minister telephoned President Reagan in the early hours to try and get him to call it off, asking him to consider the Soviet propaganda value of the US intervening in another country's affairs. The UN Security Council voted to approve a resolution "deeply deploring" the invasion as "a flagrant violation of international law."

US troops hold Cuban and Grenadan prisoners at the airfield.

The US action came after the island's Prime Minister, Maurice Bishop, had been placed under house arrest by the military commander, General Hudson Austin. This move was backed by deputy prime minister, Bernard Coard, but thought by the US to have been inspired by the presence of many Cuban troops on the island. A group of friends freed Bishop, but when they marched to a military base to demand the freedom of other colleagues they were arrested again. Bishop is now missing, feared dead.

President Reagan has given several reasons for attacking, from the construction of a new airport which could be used for military jets, to the protection of Americans living in Grenada, including 1,000 attending a medical school in St. Georges, the island capital. Another motive was to send a message to other small Latin American countries that the US will not tolerate Marxism in its backyard.

The Marines have been deployed against an estimated 600 Cubans. There have been air strikes, but no word yet on casualties. Details are sparse because the press has been barred from covering the early days of the invasion (→28).

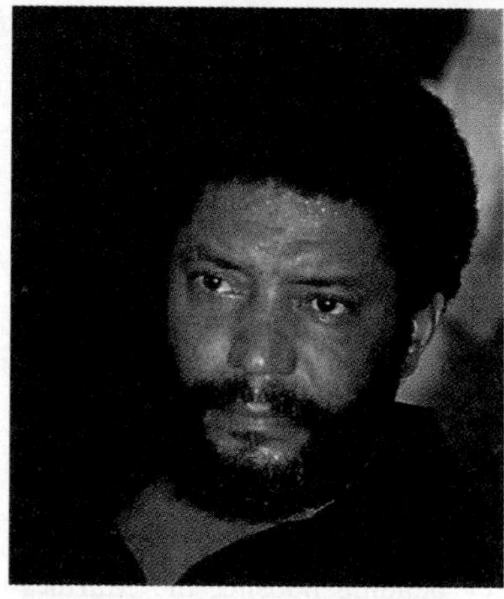

Maurice Bishop: the missing PM.

Peace Prize award for Solidarity chief

Oct 5. It was two in the morning. Lech Walesa, the Polish Solidarity leader, was awakened by the phone ringing. "Lech!" the caller, an old friend, cried, "You've won the Nobel Prize." "Yeah," Lech growled and went back to sleep. But the phone was ringing again a few minutes later. And for the rest of the night it never stopped. In Oslo, the Nobel Committee said Walesa had made "a massive personal effort" in trying to get workers the right to a free trade union. A Polish official spokesman attacked the Nobel Committee as "politically motivated". Walesa said he would give the £100,000 prize to a Catholic agricultural fund (→31/12).

Ralph Richardson, acting knight, dies

Oct 10. Sir Ralph Richardson was loved not only as an actor of uncanny powers but as a great English eccentric. Until just before his death today at 80 he was riding his powerful motor-bike round Regent's Park, where he lived, with his parrot on his shoulder. Its wings were clipped and he wanted it to enjoy the sensation of flying, he explained. Sir Ralph's greatest role was his Falstaff in 1945, which he refused to repeat. He never liked his own work or his face – "I've seen better-looking hot cross buns," he said.

Biking it to the pearly gates.

Thousands die as earthquake tremors ravage Turkish villages

465 died in one village, including all five of this woman's children.

Oct 30. Rescuers toiled in heavy rain and bitter cold today to try to reach a remote area of east Turkey where an earthquake is feared to have killed 2,000 people.

The epicentre of the tremors was at Pasinler and hundreds of simple, low houses collapsed. In the nearby Hasankale village 200 out of 300 houses were in ruins, many with families trapped inside. Ten hours later more than 500 bodies were recovered. But the earthquake was the same force as one seven years ago in the area, when almost 4,000 died.

One survivor said: "A strong humming came from the earth and our houses were like cradles swinging from side to side. There was no escape" (→6/11).

1983

NOVEMBER

Su	Mo	Tu	We	Th	Fr	Sa
		1	2	3	4	5
6	7	8	9	10	11	12
13	14	15	16	17	18	19
20	21	22	23	24	25	26
27	28	29	30			

1. London: New Treasury Minister John Moore says "no state monopoly is sacrosanct" (→28).

2. Washington: Reagan signs the bill to make Martin Luther King's birthday a national holiday.

3. S. Africa: A referendum of whites comes out in favour of power-sharing with coloureds and Indians but not blacks (→20/2/84).

4. Lebanon: 39 Israeli troops die when an Arab suicide bomber drives a lorry full of explosives into their camp (→21/12).

6. Turkey: Turgut Ozal wins the general election aimed at returning the country to civilian rule.

9. Amsterdam: Brewing magnate Alfred Heineken is kidnapped (→30).

12. Belfast: Gerry Adams is elected leader of Sinn Fein (→20).

15. Cyprus: Turkish Cypriot leader Rauf Denktash declares an independent Turkish Republic of Cyprus.

16. Luxembourg: English fans riot after England beat Luxembourg 4-0, but fail to qualify for European finals.

18. London: A report commissioned by the Metropolitan Police says some officers are "racists and bullies".

20. Northern Ireland: Gunmen burst into a Protestant chapel and open fire, killing three and wounding seven.→

24. Moscow: Andropov says the USSR will increase the submarine missiles aimed at the US because of Cruise (→13/2/84).

27. Manila: Thousands of anti-Marcos protestors take to the streets on the birthday of the late Benigno Aquino (→21/8/84).

28. London: The Government says it will end the opticians' monopoly on the sale of glasses.

30. Holland: Police free kidnapped brewer Alfred Heineken in a raid.

Arafat trapped as PLO factions wrangle

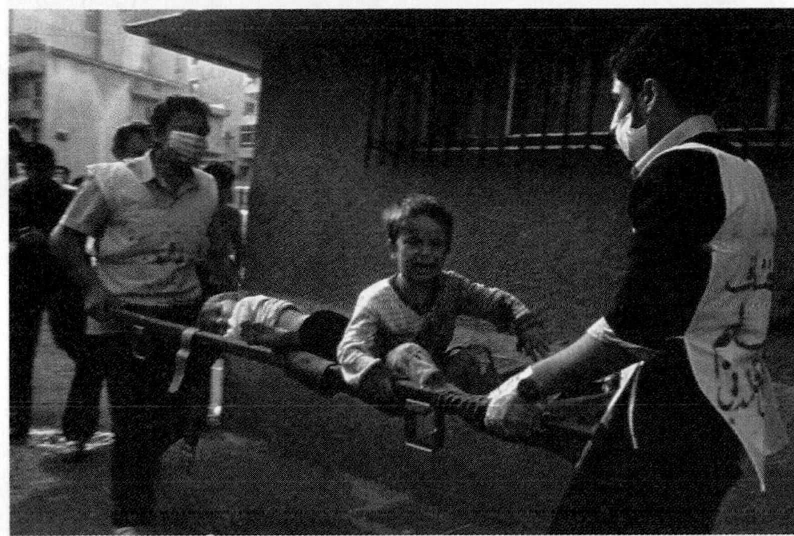

Once again, the innocent suffer as a result of internecine warfare.

Nov 24. Today Israel freed 4,800 Palestinian prisoners in exchange for just six Israeli soldiers held in Tripoli in the Lebanon. Among the Palestinians were over a hundred serving long sentences for terrorism, including Teresa Halasan, serving life for hijacking a Sabena airliner and a couple who have killed dozens of Israelis in bombings.

Mr Moshe Arens, Israeli Defence Minister admitted: "We paid a heavy price but there was no other way to free our prisoners from the hell of Tripoli."

About a thousand of the Palestinians flew to Algiers and it is believed that PLO leader, Yassir Arafat, will try to get them back to the Lebanon, where he is under great pressure from Syria, as soon as possible.

UK honour for India's "Angel of Mercy"

Nov 24. Mother Teresa of Calcutta, who has devoted her life to caring for the poverty-stricken children and orphans of India, was today presented with the insignia of the Order of Merit by the Queen.

At the ceremony, in the grounds of the Presidential Palace in New Delhi, Mother Teresa said: "This is not for me. This honour is for the poor." The shining medal with its blue and maroon ribbon formed a stark contrast to Mother Teresa's humble nun's habit. After the ceremony, she returned to a children's home to continue her work.

The richest woman in the world pays tribute to one of the poorest.

Greenham protest as Cruise arrives

Nov 15. Three hundred demonstrators – mostly women – were arrested as they blocked the entrance to the House of Commons tonight. They had planned to "invade" parliament in protest against the arrival of the first American Tomahawk missiles at Greenham Common airbase in Berkshire.

Earlier Michael Heseltine, the Defence Secretary, was sprayed with red paint and shouted down by students at Manchester. In the past 48 hours, 141 women peace campaigners have been arrested at Greenham. The Government says a joint Anglo-US decision is needed before missiles are fired.

Millions grabbed in airport bullion haul

Nov 26. A highly-organised gang today carried out Britain's biggest robbery when they stole gold bars worth £25 million from Heathrow Airport. It took an hour to load the three-ton haul into a lorry.

But police say the raid was so well-planned that the six-man gang may have immediately melted the gold down and smuggled it out of the country.

It was taken from the Brinks-Mat security warehouse, where the gang broke through a formidable array of alarms and then held up the six guards inside.

Unionists abandon Ulster's Assembly

Nov 22. The Official Unionist Party, furious over the killing of three elders at a church mission hall in South Armagh on Sunday, is to pull out of the Northern Ireland Assembly.

Party leaders failed to get their demands met at a meeting with the Ulster Secretary, Jim Prior, yesterday. They demanded the detention of Gerry Adams, the West Belfast MP who said last week that the "armed struggle must go on". They also wanted "saturation coverage" by the security forces for communities in the border area (→4/12).

Windscale cancer cases to be investigated

Nov 2. The Government today ordered an inquiry into claims that a high incidence of cancer is to be found around the UK nuclear power station at Windscale. The claims were made in a programme by Yorkshire TV which reported that the incidence of leukaemia among children in the three villages close to the plant were five to ten times the national average. The programme claimed that in the past 20 years a quarter of a ton of plutonium had been discharged into the sea from the plant, enough to give 250 million people a lethal dose if dispersed through the atmosphere.

The inquiry follows a report earlier in the year by the National Radiological Protection Board, the official watchdog, which suggested that the health hazards of the fire at Windscale 25 years ago had been played down. At the time it was said there was no danger, now it is estimated that the fall-out from the fire could have caused 260 thyroid cancers, 13 of them fatal.

The inquiry, which is to be headed by Sir Douglas Black, was welcomed by British Nuclear Fuels: "We have nothing to hide."

Body of ex-premier found in Grenada

Caribbean troops escort ex-Deputy Prime Minister Bernard Coard to jail.

Nov 6. About 100 bodies, including that of the former Prime Minister Maurice Bishop, have been discovered by US troops on the island of Grenada. The US believe that Bishop was killed two weeks ago, but could only find his body now all resistance has been crushed. Sixteen US soldiers were also killed in the fighting and 630 Cubans taken prisoner. As many as 47 mental patients are feared to have died when a US air attack hit a hospital.

It is now known that the island's British Governor, Sir Paul Scoon, had appealed to the Organisation of East Caribbean States urging intervention.

Six at a time for a mum in a billion

Nov 18. A 31-year-old Liverpool woman today gave birth to sextuplets. The babies, all girls, weighed in at around two pounds each. They are in intensive care at a maternity hospital in the city, but doctors are said to be happy with their health. Their mother, Mrs Janet Walton, is said to be satisfactory. She had been having fertility drug treatment and now becomes a mum-in-a-billion.

The babies were born eight weeks early and delivered within five minutes of each other by Caesarean section. Doctors had delayed their arrival as long as possible.

1983

DECEMBER

Su	Mo	Tu	We	Th	Fr	Sa
				1	2	3
4	5	6	7	8	9	10
11	12	13	14	15	16	17
18	19	20	21	22	23	24
25	26	27	28	29	30	31

3. UK: Women peace campaigners break into the Greenham Common base (→ 4/3/84).

4. Northern Ireland: Two IRA gunmen are shot dead in an SAS ambush without raising their weapons (→ 28/1/84).

6. London: Swede Lars Ljunberg has Britain's first heart and lung transplant.

7. Madrid: 93 die when two airliners collide on the runway.

8. London: Peers vote to allow the Lords to be televised for an experimental period.

10. Stockholm: Nobel Prizes go to Subhrahmanyan Chandrasekhar (US) and William Fowler (UK, Physics); Henry Taube (US, Chemistry); Barbara McLintock (US, Medicine); William Golding (UK, Literature); Gerard Debreu (US, Economics): and in Oslo to Danuta Walesa for Lech Walesa (Poland, Peace).

12. Kuwait: Seven die when a car bomb explodes outside the US embassy.

17. Madrid: 83 die in a fire at a disco.

18. US: Ex-President Ford makes his acting debut in the soap opera "Dynasty".

21. Beirut: 15 French troops die when a bomb-laden lorry is driven into their post (→ 18/1/84).

31. Brussels: The EEC lifts the sanctions imposed on the USSR after martial law was declared in Poland (→ 4/5/84).

DEATH

25. Spanish artist Joan Miro (*20/4/1893).

HITS OF 1983

Karma Chameleon.

Uptown girl.

Every breath you take.

QUOTE OF THE YEAR

"I am extraordinarily patient, provided I get my own way in the end."

Margaret Thatcher.

Arafat leads PLO out of Lebanon

Dec 20. For the second time in 16 months Yassir Arafat has been forced to evacuate his Palestine Liberation Forces from Lebanon. In August last year he led his men from Beirut. Today, hemmed in by the Syrian army and rebel Palestinian guerrillas, Arafat and 4,000 PLO loyalists left Tripoli, their last Lebanese stronghold.

After a bloody three-week war of the camps, which cost 700 lives, the United Nations Security Council arranged the evacuation. With guns blazing away into the empty sky, Arafat and his followers headed for Tunisia. "This is part of the long march to Jerusalem, capital of Palestine," said Arafat.

Arafat holds court at Tripoli port.

The Pope forgives his jailed attacker

Dec 27. Mehmet Ali Agca, the Turkish "Grey Wolf", fell on his knees in his prison cell before the Pope today and kissed the hand of the man he had tried to assassinate. During their emotion-filled meeting he begged forgiveness for his crime; the Pope, who was making a Christmas visit to Rome's Rebibbia prison, willingly granted it. When he emerged from the cell, the visibly moved pontiff said: "I spoke with a brother of ours in whom I have total trust. What we told each other is a secret between us." He left a small religious gift for his would-be killer (→ 9/6/84).

Alfonsin ends military rule in Argentina

Raul Alfonsin, Argentina's first civilian President for eight years.

Dec 10. The restoration of democracy in Argentina was greeted with great joy today when Senor Raul Alfonsin was inaugurated as the first civilian President for eight years. A moderate man, it is hoped that he will be able to wipe out the excesses of the military junta.

He told the people: "These are difficult times. But we do not have a single doubt. We will move forward." He lost no time in announcing that the former military rulers will be brought to justice for spreading "terror, pain and death throughout Argentine society". Mrs Thatcher took the opportunity to send a conciliatory goodwill message to the new President and, in what will be seen as a major shift in British policy, she opened the door to diplomatic and trade negotiations, frozen since the Falklands war 18 months ago.

The message, relayed through the Swiss embassy in Buenos Aires, said: "We can all take pleasure in the restoration of democracy to Argentina, believing that it will bring freedom and justice to all your people. Today brings new hope to your country."

Dec 17. Smoke billows from the famous terracotta building and debris litters the street after an IRA bomb exploded outside Harrods.

Arts: Channel Four harvests top awards

Channel Four, now on the air for just over a year, was given the brief to "innovate". So far it has brought in a promising harvest. The King Lear that **Laurence Olivier** promised to do on the stage was finally unveiled on Channel Four in a production by Granada. Not surprisingly it won an international Emmy award as Best Drama.

"Film on Four" is one of the fields of innovation and "The Ploughman's Lunch" with a screenplay by novelist **Ian McEwan** directed by **Richard Eyre** was another award winner. The Channel succeeded in bringing the RSC's teeming "Nicholas Nickleby" to the small screen (an international Emmy) and the animated cartoon film of **Raymond Briggs's** "The Snowman" collected more awards.

A troupe of iconoclastic "alternative comedians" calling themselves "The Comic Strip" were given a budget and came back with the notorious "Five Go Mad in Dorset", which reduced **Enid Blyton's** Famous Five to absurdity. We shall probably hear more of **Rik Mayall, Adrian Edmondson, Dawn French, Jennifer Saunders, Nigel Planer** and **Peter Richardson**.

Another Famous Five came to grief with the opening of TV-am, soon after the BBC began "Breakfast Time". Its expensively engaged presenters, **David Frost, Angela Rippon, Anna Ford, Robert Kee** and **Michael Parkinson** failed to attract sufficiently high audiences and most soon departed.

Actor Kenneth Branagh, who was superb in "Another Country".

For the first time for many years the Nobel Prize went to an English author, **William Golding**, while in the Academy Awards "Gandhi" swept the board collecting an unprecedented eight Oscars for Britain. **Sir Richard Attenborough** who directed and **Ben Kingsley** as Gandhi got two of them.

The compact disc has made its appearance, promising clearer and truer sound – at a price – and claiming to supersede other forms of recording. Each 4.75-inch disc has a playing time of just over an hour. It offers the advantages of no background noise, full frequency range and no wearing out or scratching. But players are expensive.

Glowing pink and strange, like something escaped from a giant's toybox or surgical store, is another of the creations of Christo, the "Wrapper".

1984

JANUARY

Su	Mo	Tu	We	Th	Fr	Sa
1	2	3	4	5	6	7
8	9	10	11	12	13	14
15	16	17	18	19	20	21
22	23	24	25	26	27	28
29	30	31				

1. Brunei: The sultanate becomes fully independent of Britain.

3. Damascus: A US airman shot down over Lebanon is freed following an appeal from the Rev. Jesse Jackson (→ 14).

6. UK: The anti-smoking group ASH says over a million people have given up smoking in the last two years.

7. Central America: Costa Rica, El Salvador, Honduras and Guatemala draft a plan for peace in the region (→ 10/4).

9. London: Sarah Tisdall, a 23-year-old Foreign Office clerk, is charged under the Official Secrets Act (→ 23/3).

10. Washington: Chinese premier Zhao Zhiyang has talks with Reagan (→ 29).

10. Karachi: Opposition leader Benazir Bhutto, daughter of the late premier, is freed from house arrest.

13. UK: At least six people die in hurricane-force winds (→ 24).

14. Damascus: President Assad says Syrian troops will not leave Lebanon while US and other troops remain (→ 18).

15. UK: Tony Benn is chosen as Labour candidate in the Chesterfield by-election (→ 1/3).

18. Beirut: Gunmen murder Malcolm Kerr, the head of the American University (→ 6/2).

21. UK: Yorkshire Cricket Club reverses its decision to sack Geoff Boycott (→ 31/5).

24. UK: 17 die after abandoning the stricken freighter Radiant Med in a gale off Guernsey.

26. Belfast: The governor of the Maze Prison resigns following criticism in a report on last year's IRA breakout (→ 14/3).

28. London: Leading Soviet writer Oleg Bitov is granted asylum in Britain.

29. Washington: Reagan says he will seek re-election.

DEATH

20. US actor and athlete Johnny Weissmuller (*2/6/1904).

New Nigerian leader after bloodless coup

Jan 1. Once again the generals have emerged from their barracks to overturn a civilian government and promise to rid Nigeria of corruption and rescue the country's floundering economy. General Mohammed Buhari, aged 41, named head of the new military regime, announced that President Shehu Shagari and other politicians and officials had been arrested and would face charges of corruption.

Shagari, a former schoolteacher, was first elected President in 1979 when free elections were held after 13 years of military rule. He had recently been re-elected, but stories of ministers allegedly holding upwards of £7 billion in foreign bank accounts have caused widespread discontent (→ 4/3).

New leader Mohammed Buhari.

Death toll hits 75 in Tunisian food riots

Jan 6. Habib Bourguiba, hero of Tunisia's independence struggle, and the country's President for the past 27 years, last week allowed his Prime Minister to increase the price of bread by 125 per cent, from eight to 18 cents a loaf, in an effort to narrow a yawning budget deficit. Then he left for his country home outside Tunis.

Today the death toll after a week of rioting reached 75, a dusk-to-dawn curfew has been imposed, schools have been closed and public transport halted. The Government has blamed drought and two years of recession for its economic problems. The Tunisian ambassador to France claims the riots have little to do with food prices, but were instigated by Moslem fundamentalists who oppose Bourguiba's moderate pro-Western policies and support for negotiations with Israel.

This is Boy George, Britain's latest pop idol. He wears pretty frocks and heavy make-up, yet he remains totally masculine. Especially when he opens his mouth to sing – really rather well.

Acid rain threat to UK countryside

Jan 2. Acid rain is seriously contaminating Britain's lakes and rivers, according to an environmental report published today. Scotland and the Lake District are identified as the areas most at risk, with fish stocks declining and woodland habitats also losing some of their bird, plant and animal life.

Although today's report comes from a private pressure group, its message will be reinforced next week with the publication of an official study into what it says is a growing problem. Acid rain is caused by sulphur dioxide and nitrous oxide from smoke, dissolving in water droplets. These fall as rain contaminated by sulphuric and nitric acid. It is a problem now afflicting much of Europe.

1984

FEBRUARY

Su	Mo	Tu	We	Th	Fr	Sa
			1	2	3	4
5	6	7	8	9	10	11
12	13	14	15	16	17	18
19	20	21	22	23	24	25
26	27	28	29			

1. London: The halfpenny coin is to be phased out by the end of 1984.

1. London: Tebbit announces that Nissan will build a pilot plant in Britain before making a long-term commitment (→ 28/3).

5. Birmingham: Kidnapped Indian diplomat Ravindra Mhatre is found shot dead near his home.

6. Beirut: President Gemayel orders a 24-hour shoot-on-sight curfew as open civil war erupts in the city (→ 7).

7. Washington: Reagan orders the withdrawal of the US peacekeeping force.→

9. Beirut: 400 Britons are among over 500 civilians evacuated from the city (→ 17).

10. London: After many years of refusing a peerage, Harold Macmillan accepts a hereditary earldom on his 90th birthday (→ 13/11).

15. UK: Comedian Tommy Cooper dies after collapsing on stage.

17. Beirut: Lebanese opposition leaders reject a reconciliation plan put forward by President Gemayel (→ 23).

20. Maputo: The Mozambique government agrees a formal peace pact with South Africa outlawing cross-border raids (→ 16/3).

21. London: Thatcher says most workers at GCHQ have accepted the offer of £1,000 to give up their union rights (→ 6/8).

23. Beirut: Rebel Lebanese Army soldiers appear in West Beirut under Shi-ite and Druze leaders (→ 26).

26. Beirut: The last US Marines leave (→ 29).

29. New York: The USSR vetoes a French proposal to send a UN force into Beirut (→ 12/3).

DEATH

9. Soviet statesman Yuri Andropov, leader 1982-84 (*15/6/1914).→

Peace keepers quit war-torn Lebanon

Feb 8. British troops of the international peace-keeping force in Lebanon were flown out by helicopters today to a Royal Navy ship. American and Italian contingents of the four-nation force – the fourth are the French – are also abandoning Beirut to the local militias.

Sir Geoffrey Howe, the British Foreign Secretary, said the withdrawal had been ordered because they could no longer fulfil their peace-keeping role in such dangerous conditions. For the time being the 115-strong British unit will stay aboard HMS Reliant, off the Lebanese coast. British civilians have been urged to leave (→9).

Francome makes it a thousand wins

Feb 29. On the modest back of a hitherto unremarkable horse called Observe, John Francome rode into history to join the great Stan Mellor in the most distinguished club – so far with only two members – in National Hunt racing: the jockeys who have ridden 1,000 winners in hurdles and steeplechases. His milestone was reached at Worcester in the 4,576th race of a career that began 14 years ago – with a winner, of course.

Feb 7. The first untethered space walk took place today from the US space shuttle Challenger. The era of human satellites is here.

Andropov dead: Chernenko is new leader

The Soviet Union buries its ruler of only 15 months, in Red Square.

Feb 13. The Soviet Union again has a new leader. Konstantin Chernenko was named Soviet Communist Party chief today within hours of the burial on Red Square of Yuri Andropov, who had ruled Russia for only 15 months.

Andropov died after a long struggle with kidney disease. He last appeared publicly in mid-August and has had the shortest Kremlin tenure in history. His main achievement has been to bring fresh blood into Soviet leadership circles, creating a team of younger top officials on which the party could build for the rest of the century. Nevertheless, Chernenko at 72 is the oldest man ever to take over as Soviet leader and his appointment is a victory for Russia's old-guard bureaucracy.

Chernenko, a stocky white-haired Siberian, was a close associate of former Soviet leader Leonid Brezhnev, and is known to suffer from emphysema. It would appear that the Soviet Communist Party has chosen to risk another succession crisis in the next year or two rather than pass power now to a younger man who could begin getting to grips with Soviet economic problems. One man widely tipped to take over when Chernenko goes is the "youthful" 52-year-old Mikhail Gorbachev (→11/4).

New leader Konstantin Chernenko.

Canadian Prime Minister Trudeau quits

Feb 29. Pierre Trudeau, the Prime Minister of Canada and the dominant Liberal Party leader for 15 years, resigned today. He said that now was "the appropriate time for someone else to assume this challenge". He succeeded Lester Pearson in 1968 and has been in power ever since, with the exception of a brief period of Conservative government in 1979. He pursued an independent foreign policy and led Canada to recognise Communist China in 1970.

His informal style and flamboyant wife often got him into trouble with friends and enemies alike (→4/9).

Valentine's victory for British ice pair

Feb 14. To the pulsating rhythms of Ravel's "Bolero", Jayne Torvill and Christopher Dean today skated off with the Olympic gold for ice dancing. The audience rose to their feet at the Olympic rink in Sarajevo, the flowers came raining on to the ice, and the judges – all nine of them awarded Jayne Torvill and Christopher Dean maximum points for artistic impression.

It was an overwhelming St. Valentine's Day victory for the young Nottingham pair, in an event which had been dominated by Soviet skaters throughout its short existence as an Olympic sport. They now have only their world championship to defend before starting a lucrative professional career.

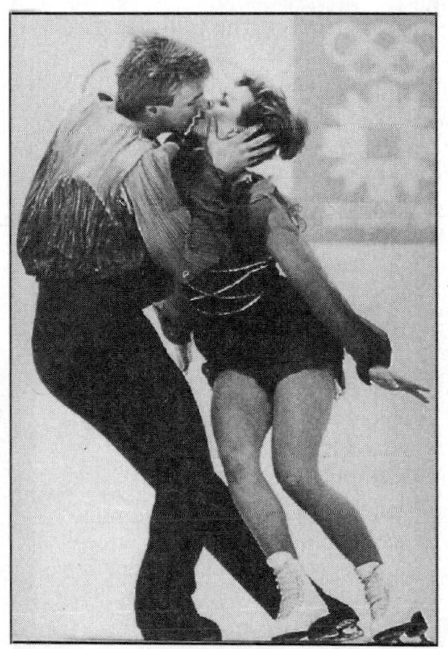

A sizzling, erotic performance.

"Video nasty" man is sent to jail

Feb 3. David Hamilton-Grant, the distributor of the "video nasty" "Nightmares in a Damaged Brain", was jailed today for 18 months after being found guilty of possessing copies of an obscene video cassette for gain. The US video features a variety of sexual perversions, climaxing in murder. Video tapes for watching on TV at home have become increasingly popular, but some MPs have expressed concern about pornography as well as the violence of the "nasties".

1984

MARCH

Su	Mo	Tu	We	Th	Fr	Sa
				1	2	3
4	5	6	7	8	9	10
11	12	13	14	15	16	17
18	19	20	21	22	23	24
25	26	27	28	29	30	31

1. UK: Tony Benn is returned to Parliament in the Chesterfield by-election.

4. Nigeria: As many as 1,000 are feared dead after a week of religious rioting in the northern city of Yola (→ 10/7).

7. London: Stephen Waldorf, shot in error in 1982, gets £120,000 compensation from the Metropolitan Police.

12. Geneva: President Gemayel opens a conference for peace and reconciliation in the Lebanon (→ 5/7).

12. UK: A nationwide miners' strike begins.→

13. London: The Budget raises tax thresholds.

14. Northern Ireland: Sinn Fein leader Gerry Adams is shot and seriously wounded by Loyalist gunmen (→ 17).

16. S. Africa: The government signs a peace accord with Mozambique (→ 2/6).

17. Ireland: INLA leader Dominic McGlinchey is arrested after a shoot-out and extradited to Ulster (→ 12/8).

18. London: Oxford wins the Boat Race in a record 16 minutes 45 seconds.

20. Brussels: An EEC summit collapses because of disagreement over Britain's budget payments.

21. UK: Brenda Dean becomes the first woman to head a major union when she is elected leader of SOGAT '82.

27. UK: Peter Sutcliffe is transferred from Parkhurst to Broadmoor.

28. Athens: British diplomat Kenneth Whitty is shot dead.

28. UK: Nissan chooses Washington New Town, near Sunderland, as the site for its pilot car plant.

31. UK: Mr R. Shaw's Hello Dandy wins the Grand National.

DEATHS

1. US actor Jackie Coogan (*26/10/1914).

5. Italian singer Tito Gobbi (*24/10/1915).

Violence flares as pit strike splits miners

March 15. Only 21 of Britain's 174 mines are working normally tonight. Strikes against the Coal Board's 5.2 per cent pay offer and its programme of pit closures began in Yorkshire and Scotland and have now been made official. The Coal Board chairman, Ian MacGregor, has warned that a prolonged stoppage could accelerate pit closures.

The pits in Nottinghamshire, which is the country's second largest coalfield, have become the focus of attention. It is here that resistance to going on strike without a national ballot seems greatest and many miners are continuing to work. Aware that this could undermine the impact of the strike, large numbers of militant strikers are travelling to Nottinghamshire in order to picket the working pits.

This has already led to violence and clashes with not only the police but new laws against secondary picketing. One Yorkshire "flying picket" died today outside Ollerton Colliery. It seems death was caused by a chest injury and not a blow from a brick or truncheon, but his death has intensified the bitterness of the dispute. Yorkshire miners continue to defy a High Court injunction, granted under the 1980 Employment Act, confining them to pits in their own area. More than 3,000 police officers are available to help the Nottinghamshire police ensure that miners who wished to work could do so (→ 5/4).

Gary Hart scores in Democratic primaries

Could Hart be the next President?

March 27. Senator Gary Hart took another step closer to winning the Democratic presidential nomination with a strong victory in the Connecticut primary today.

Fifty-three per cent of the delegates, including the majority of the key trade union and Jewish votes, voted for Hart compared with 29 per cent for his nearest rival, Walter Mondale. Hart now has all six New England states, and is girding his loins for the crucial New York State primary.

Hart says a key factor in his success is his call for an immediate US military withdrawal from central America. Senator Mondale has not backed this policy (→ 12/7).

March 17. The Cambridge boat-race crew head for the bank, after their cox steered them into a moored barge, damaging the boat just slightly.

Civil servant jailed for whistle-blowing

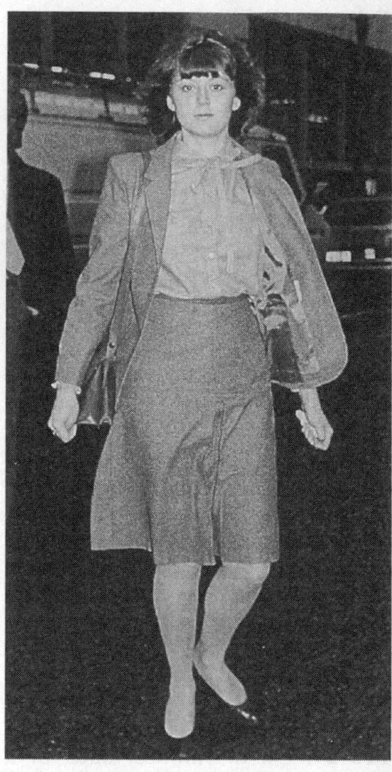

Sarah Tisdall goes to court.

March 23. A 23-year-old Foreign Office clerk, who passed a secret document to "The Guardian", was jailed for six months at the Old Bailey today. Sarah Tisdall, who had worked in Sir Geoffrey Howe's private office, admitted copying a document which revealed details about the arrival of Cruise missiles.

"The Guardian's" editor, Peter Preston – criticised for not destroying the evidence – described the sentence as "savage".

Scientists warn of greenhouse effect

March 5. Concern is growing that carbon dioxide, produced by burning fossil fuels, will affect the climate. Carbon dioxide acts like the glass of a greenhouse, trapping the sun's heat, and the amount in the atmosphere is growing. The latest pointer to its effects comes from scientists at the University of East Anglia who have found that 1981 and last year were among the warmest on record. A warmer climate could damage agriculture and cause flooding by melting the polar ice caps.

1984

APRIL

Su	Mo	Tu	We	Th	Fr	Sa
1	2	3	4	5	6	7
8	9	10	11	12	13	14
15	16	17	18	19	20	21
22	23	24	25	26	27	28
29	30					

1. London: The Metropolitan Police say some officers will be allowed to carry automatic weapons.

1. Los Angeles: Singer Marvin Gaye is shot dead during an argument with his father.

4. UK: Bailiffs backed by 300 police clear the main women's peace camp at Greenham Common (→ 12/9).

5. UK: Nottinghamshire miners reject an NUM executive recommendation not to cross picket lines (→ 9).

9. UK: 100 are arrested at Nottinghamshire and Derbyshire pits in some of the worst violence of the strike (→ 12).

10. Washington: The Senate votes against the mining of Nicaraguan ports (→ 10/5).

11. Moscow: Chernenko is elected Soviet President by the Supreme Soviet.

12. UK: Scargill vetoes a proposal for a national ballot of miners on whether to continue their strike (→ 23/5).

13. UK: Seven servicemen serving in Cyprus are charged under the Official Secrets Act.

16. London: MI5 traitor Michael Bettaney is jailed for 23 years.

17. London: WPC Yvonne Fletcher is shot dead during an anti-Gaddafi protest outside the Libyan People's Bureau.→

23. Africa: Famine relief agencies are reported to be striving to provide aid to 150 million in 24 countries.

26. Beijing: Reagan arrives on a six-day visit.

27. UK: 30 Libyan diplomats leave Britain (→ 9/6).

DEATHS

1. US singer Marvin Gaye (*2/4/1939).

5. British commander Marshal of the RAF Sir Arthur Travers "Bomber" Harris (*13/4/1892).

17. US commander General Mark Clark (*1/5/1896).

26. US bandleader William "Count" Basie (*21/8/1904).→

UK expels Libyans after embassy killing

Police cover the embassy, but the killers of Yvonne Fletcher get away.

April 22. Despite police fury and public anger at the shooting of a young policewoman outside the Libyan embassy, in St. James' Square, London, the Libyan diplomats and others under siege in the embassy are to be allowed to leave the country. The Government has given students and professional diplomats, holed up in the "People's Bureau", seven days to quit.

Policewoman Yvonne Fletcher was shot when police were accompanying a demonstration outside the embassy. Although her body was removed soon afterwards, her hat remains on the pavement in the square, a sad reminder to millions of television viewers who have followed the progress of the siege.

In protest against the embassy being used for "terrorist activities", Britain has broken off diplomatic relations with Colonel Gaddafi's Libya. As the Libyans prepare to leave – taking vital evidence away in diplomatic bags – their opposite numbers in Tripoli have been warned to "consider their safety". The Home Secretary, Leon Brittan, has admitted that the Government has no means of establishing the identity of Yvonne Fletcher's murderer (→ 27).

Jack Nicholson and Shirley Maclaine, Oscar winners.

South African Zola will run for Britain

April 6. Zola Budd, the 17-year-old South African distance runner who beat Mary Decker's 5,000 metres world record in January, is to receive a British passport, and will thus be eligible to run for Great Britain in the Los Angeles Olympic Games this summer.

The campaign to establish British citizenship for Budd, and so beat the world ban on South African athletes, was launched by the "Daily Mail" and expedited with unprecedented speed – 13 days from application to approval. This may provoke controversy amongst Third World countries (→ 8/8).

US jazz bandleader Count Basie dies

April 26. "Count" Basie (real name William) was one of the most economical pianists in jazz history. He learned his playing from Fats Waller, who got him his first job as an accompanist. He formed his own band in the Swing era and its distinctive sound was its jumping beat (Basie's "One O'Clock Jump" was their signature tune), its horn power and Basie's laconic piano.

His second band, formed in 1951, was even more famous on films, television and touring Europe. Basie was asked to play for the inauguration of President Kennedy. Last year jazz celebrities paid him tribute. Today he died of cancer, aged 79.

Brilliant Basie in the 1950s.

Virus that causes AIDS is discovered

April 23. The discovery of the AIDS virus was announced in Washington today by Margaret Heckler, the US Health and Human Services Secretary. She hoped that a blood test would be available in six months and a vaccine ready for testing in two years.

American and French scientists have been searching separately for the virus. In the US, Robert Gallo, National Cancer Institute, claimed it was of a type named HTLV-III whilst the Pasteur Institute in Paris went for one called LAV. Recent work shows that both these viruses are the same (→ 18/11).

1984

MAY

Su	Mo	Tu	We	Th	Fr	Sa
		1	2	3	4	5
6	7	8	9	10	11	12
13	14	15	16	17	18	19
20	21	22	23	24	25	26
27	28	29	30	31		

2. UK: TUC general secretary Len Murray announces that he will retire this autumn (→4/9).

4. Warsaw: Jaruzelski signs a 15-year economic pact with the USSR (→21/7).

6. Paris: The French government ends no-passport trips by Britons after 30 years.

8. London: The Thames Barrier is officially opened.

13. Angola: Sixteen Britons are freed by rebels after 11 weeks.

18. Moscow: Yelena Bonner tells the US embassy her husband Andrei Sakharov is on hunger strike (→6/8).

19. London: Everton beat Watford 2-0 in the FA Cup Final.

23. UK: The first talks between Scargill and NCB chairman MacGregor break down after an hour.→

23. UK: Nine die in an explosion at Abbeystead pumping station in Lancashire.

24. El Salvador: Five former soldiers are found guilty of murdering three US nuns and a missionary in 1980.

24. Managua: The first elections since 1979 will be in 12 weeks (→1/9).

30. UK: Scargill is arrested and charged with obstruction at Orgreave Colliery (→7/6).

30. Italy: Liverpool draw 1-1 with A.S. Roma, then beat them 4-2 on penalties to win the European Cup.

31. UK: Viv Richards scores 189 not out for the West Indies against England, the highest-ever one-day innings.

DEATHS

4. British actress Diana Dors, born Diana Fluck (*23/10/1931).

8. US publisher Lila Bel Wallace (*25/12/1889).

19. British poet Sir John Betjeman, Poet Laureate 1972-84 (*6/4/1906).→

28. British comedian Eric Morecambe, born Eric Bartholomew (*14/5/1926).→

Riot police battle miners at Orgreave

At Orgreave coking plant, police give chase to local miners and supporters from across the nation.

May 29. Forty-one policemen and 28 picketing miners were injured today in South Yorkshire, outside the Orgreave coking plant. The pitched battles are by far the most violent incidents to date in the 12-week-long coal strike. For the first time police wore full riot gear. Order was only restored after several charges by mounted police across a barley field.

Police blamed the violence on the presence of Arthur Scargill, the NUM president, who has been at Orgreave for the past two days. The pickets, though, again failed to prevent convoys of lorries taking coke to British Steel's Scunthorpe works. The miners are increasingly bitter that steel workers are crossing their picket lines to work normally. Mr Scargill said afterwards that South Yorkshire was like a "police state which you might expect to see in Chile, but not here".

Today's display of determination by the miners comes on the eve of resumed talks between the union and the Coal Board. Ian MacGregor, its chairman, will not initially take part in them, as animosity between him and Mr Scargill is partly blamed for the collapse of talks a week ago. Mr Scargill then described him as "a butcher sent to destroy the industry".

The Coal Board, however, is still insisting that discussion will have to be about cutting output by four million tonnes a year and the closure of up to 20 "uneconomic" pits with 20,000 job losses by natural wastage within 12 months. Mr Scargill's position remains that he will only discuss the future of the industry on the basis of no further pit closures and no job losses. His position is weakened by the continued working of many Nottinghamshire miners and the summer slump in demand for coal (→30).

Soviets to boycott Los Angeles Olympics

May 8. Just 12 weeks before the opening ceremony of the Los Angeles Olympic Games, the Soviet Union – in a move that has been half-expected for four years, yet which will still come as a bitter disappointment – has announced that it will not be sending a team to the Games.

Ostensibly the Russians have pulled out because of concern about the lack of security for their athletes and officials, but most will see the Soviet decision as a direct tit-for-tat retaliation for the US-led boycott of the Moscow Games four years ago.

Sadly for Los Angeles, the absentees are unlikely to be confined to the Soviet Union; it is generally expected that all the Eastern European nations, and some Third World countries, will come under pressure to follow suit (→28/7).

World Court rules against US action

May 10. The International Court of Justice in The Hague today ruled that the US should cease immediately any supportive military action against the Sandinista government of Nicaragua. The mining of the ports was particularly condemned. The United States has already said it will not recognise the court judgment (→24/5).

Betjeman, Britain's best loved poet, dies

May 19. Sir John Betjeman died at his Cornish home today aged 78, long after being incapacitated by a stroke. He is mourned not only as Britain's most popular poet but as the nation's television "Teddy-Bear", who used his following to defend the kind of England that he loved against the developers, speculative builders and vandals.

He fought for the appreciation of old churches, railway stations like Liverpool Street, the remaining landscape of Middlesex, Bucks and his beloved Cornwall, everything threatened by what he memorably called "ghastly good taste" and modernists who believed that "decoration is unnecessary and collects dust". He lived to see the Victorian architecture which he championed appreciated once more (→20/9).

Betjeman, in the Cornwall he loved.

Iranian regime is censured by Arabs

May 24. Iranian warplanes today attacked an oil tanker off the Saudi Arabian coast. This was Tehran's first response to this week's action by the Arab League, condemning Iran for aggression against Iraq in the Gulf War. A majority of League members warned Iran to stop attacks in international waterways. The statement was a triumph for King Hussein of Jordan, a loyal ally of Iraq. Syria and Libya did their best to stifle criticism of Iran.

Rival sects clash in fresh Bombay riots

May 21. India's never-ending problem of religious strife has flared again with five days of bloody rioting between Hindus and Moslems in and around Bombay. Over a hundred people have died so far in the riots, which seem to have their origin in the bitter rivalry between two of the district's senior politicians, one Hindu, the other Moslem. Mrs Gandhi, touring the area, pointed out that "it is the poor who always suffer" and appealed for peace and religious tolerance (→2/6).

Eric Morecambe dies as final curtain falls

May 29. A heart attack ended the career of 58-year-old comedian Eric Morecambe last night at the end of a charity show he gave at his friend Stan Stennett's Tewkesbury theatre. After six curtain calls, Morecambe collapsed in the wings. He died in hospital without regaining consciousness.

The partnership of Morecambe (real name Bartholomew) and Ernie Wise began in 1941. Their television partnership reached its peak in the Seventies with audiences of 20 million. Such diverse individuals as Sir Alec Guinness and Sir Harold Wilson were happy to be made fools of by them.

One of Britain's funniest men.

1984

JUNE

Su	Mo	Tu	We	Th	Fr	Sa
					1	2
3	4	5	6	7	8	9
10	11	12	13	14	15	16
17	18	19	20	21	22	23
24	25	26	27	28	29	30

2. India: The Indian army launches an offensive against Sikhs seeking regional autonomy for the Punjab.→

2. London: President Botha arrives amid protests on the first visit by a South African leader for 23 years (→4/5).

3. Bermuda: Nineteen people are missing after the British barque Marques sinks off the island in the Tall Ships race.

6. UK: Mr L. Miglietti's Secreto wins the Derby.

7. London: 120 are arrested when fighting breaks out outside Parliament during a mass lobby by striking miners (→15).

9. Italy: A judge says Mehmet Ali Agca was hired by the Bulgarians to kill the Pope in a plot to undermine Solidarity.

12. UK: A civil servant and mother wins the right to do her Home Office job on a part-time basis.

14. UK: Michael Hancock wins Portsmouth South from the Tories in a surprise victory for the Alliance.

15. UK: A miner picketing a Yorkshire power station is killed by a lorry (→1/8).

20. London: Education Secretary Keith Joseph approves a new GCSE exam to replace 'O' Levels and CSEs.

21. UK: Solicitors are to be allowed to advertise their services and charges from the beginning of October.

22. UK: The first Virgin Atlantic flight to New York, costing £99 single, leaves Gatwick.

26. Havana: Castro frees 22 jailed Americans after talks with the Rev Jesse Jackson.

28. UK: The magazine "Titbits" closes after 104 years.

DEATHS

11. Italian statesman Enrico Berlinguer (*25/5/1922).→

22. US film director Joseph Losey (*14/1/1909).

30. US author and playwright Lillian Hellman (*20/6/1907).

Thatcher fights to quell terror gangs

June 9. Leaders of the seven major industrial nations – Britain, the United States, France, West Germany, Italy, Japan and Canada – tonight endorsed plans for closer international co-operation against state-sponsored terrorism.

They acted on the initiative of Mrs Thatcher. She called for "relentless action" in the wake of the Libyan embassy siege in London which followed the killing of a policewoman. There will now be a crackdown on terrorists masquerading as diplomats.

The seven-nation statement stopped short of endorsing military action against states such as Libya. There is also scepticism about economic sanctions.

Leukaemia threat near atom plant

June 3. The level of childhood leukaemia is ten times the national average around the Sellafield nuclear reprocessing plant in West Cumbria, according to a government report chaired by Sir Douglas Black and published today. In nearby Bootle and Haverthwaite the level is five times the average. No definite link has been found, but the food and milk consumed by the victims may be checked (→23/7).

June 6. The leaders of France and Germany show their countries' friendship on the 40th anniversary of the D-Day landings.

▷

Missiles explode as Soviet base burns

June 22. A massive explosion, which some Western intelligence agencies thought was a nuclear blast, has destroyed a Soviet naval arsenal in Northern Russia.

The explosion at the Soviet Northern Fleet's depot at Severomorsk, near Murmansk, destroyed a third of the fleet's stockpile of surface-to-air missiles and killed an unknown number of Russians. The explosion was detected by American spy satellites.

A United States official said the blast was only the latest and the worst of a series of similar mishaps at Soviet military installations over the last six months.

New UK law means quicker divorces

June 14. A new divorce law, enabling couples to end a marriage after one year instead of three as at present, completed its final stages in the Commons today. The Matrimonial and Family Proceedings Bill will make courts consider the financial support of children the first priority, rather than the open-ended maintenance of the spouse.

It also provides for a "clean break" where both partners are self-sufficient. Opponents have argued it will lead to divorces where couples might have been reconciled if given more time.

Berlinguer, Italian statesman, is dead

June 11. Enrico Berlinguer, one of the greatest post-war leaders of Communism in Europe, died today of a cerebral haemorrhage, aged 62. He joined the Italian Communist Party just before the Second World War and by 1972, when he became general secretary, it was the largest in Western Europe.

As a leader of the European Communist movement, he fought to reduce the Soviet grip on the party and he worked with the late Aldo Moro to forge an alliance with the Christian Democrats in what he called an "historic compromise".

Indian troops storm Sikh Golden Temple

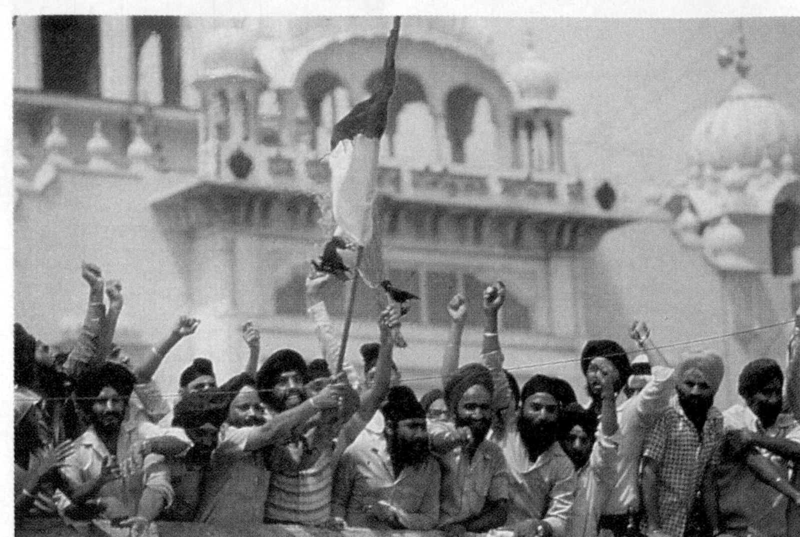

Militant Sikhs demonstrate for their own state of Khalistan.

June 6. Indian troops today stormed the Golden Temple in Amritsar, the holiest of Sikh shrines, after a four-day siege of the temple complex, which had been taken over by heavily-armed Sikh militants led by Sant Jarnail Singh Bhindranwale, the high-priest of Sikh extremists.

The Indian authorities had hoped to carry out "Operation Blue Star" with few casualties, but such was the ferocity of the Sikh resistance that 90 soldiers and 712 extremists died in the battle. Among the dead were Bhindranwale and his military leaders, two former major generals, Narinder Singh Bhuller and Shahbeg Singh.

The Sikhs, a warrior sect, were well-prepared. They fought from strong fortifications and a maze of tunnels and manholes. The strength of their resistance emphasised both their fanatical zeal and the failure of the intelligence services properly to assess their strength.

Finally tanks and commandos had to be sent in. They were ordered not to harm the golden-domed Harmandir Sahib, but the other holy sanctuary of Akal Takht, where Bhindranwale held out to the last, was heavily damaged.

Mrs Gandhi was forced to take action to stop the murderous activities of the extremists, who are demanding their own state of Khalistan, but the assault on the temple will enrage all Sikhs. There are already reports of mutinies among Sikh troops (→ 31/10).

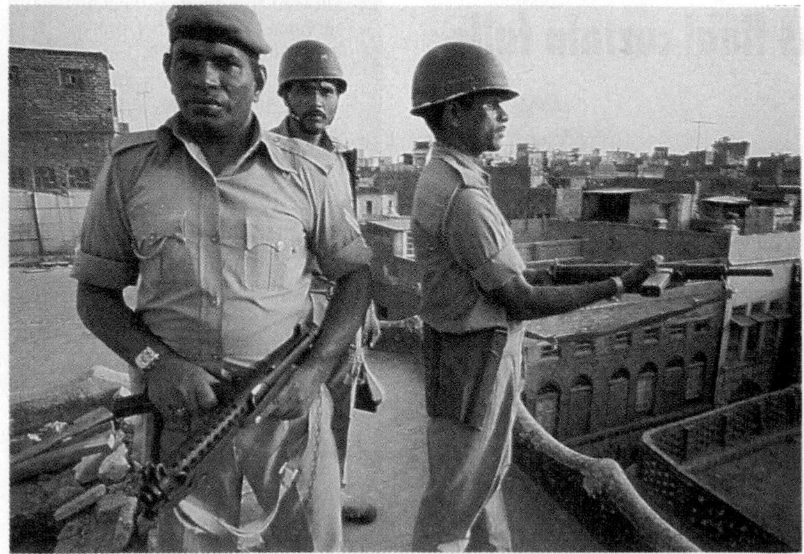

Indian troops stand guard after storming the Golden Temple enclosure.

1984

JULY

Su	Mo	Tu	We	Th	Fr	Sa
1	2	3	4	5	6	7
8	9	10	11	12	13	14
15	16	17	18	19	20	21
22	23	24	25	26	27	28
29	30	31				

1. Argentina: Soccer star Diego Maradona is to join Naples for around £1 million.

4. UK: The Government announces the abolition of dog licences.

5. Beirut: the Lebanese army tears down the Green Line, the five miles of barricades that divides the city (→ 20/9).

5. Moscow: Vyacheslav Molotov is reinstated as a member of the Communist Party.

6. UK: Dr David Jenkins of Leeds University is consecrated as Bishop of Durham (→ 22/9).

8. Wimbledon: John McEnroe beats Jimmy Connors to win the men's singles final.→

12. London: Robert Maxwell buys the Mirror newspaper group for £113.4 million.

17. Paris: Laurent Fabius succeeds Pierre Mauroy as Prime Minister.

18. UK: The Government says Sealink is to be bought by the Bermuda-based group, Sea Containers.

18. Westminster: A report by the Commons public accounts committee slams the misuse of public funds by the De Lorean car company in Ulster (→ 16/8).

21. Warsaw: Poland's parliament approves an amnesty for 652 political prisoners to mark 40 years of Communism (→ 19/10).

22. UK: Seve Ballesteros wins his second British Open Golf Championship.

23. UK: A Government inquiry says radiation from Sellafield is not the cause of cancer in local children.

28. Los Angeles: The 23rd Olympic Games open (→ 8/8).

30. UK: 11-day-old Holly Roffey becomes the world's youngest heart transplant patient (→ 17/8).

30. UK: At least 13 die when a crowded Edinburgh-Glasgow commuter train crashes near Falkirk.

DEATH

27. British actor James Mason (*15/5/1909).→

York Minster set ablaze

The night sky lights up as 700 years of history go up in smoke.

July 9. A bolt of lightning, but of natural and not heavenly origins, was blamed for the fire which devastated the 700-year-old York Minster today.

As experts assessed the damage at more than £1 million, the Archbishop of York dismissed as "ridiculous" assertions that linked the disaster to last week's consecration of the controversial Rt Rev. David Jenkins as the Bishop of Durham, seen by church stalwarts as dangerously liberal. Rather, added Dr Runcie, the Archbishop of Canterbury, it was "a miracle" that the fire had destroyed only the south transept, and that the world-famous Rose Window had survived.

Although the building was fully protected against lightning, and had a number of fire detectors, the sheer speed of the spread of the flames defeated the fire services. The highly inflammable lead roof and dry old timbers helped intensify the blaze.

Most of the cathedral's treasures were saved from the fire by relays of clergy who risked the flames and showers of molten lead to salvage priceless artefacts. Only when the beams supporting the roof started to collapse were they forced to give up.

Like most church buildings, the Minster is properly insured and its policy will "more than cover the cost of repairs". But the Government has promised additional money and a fund for public donations has been set up. Repairs will take at least two years.

Democrats pick woman to back Mondale

July 12. The Democratic presidential candidate, Walter Mondale today chose as his vice-presidential running mate a New York Congresswoman, Geraldine Ferraro. She is the first woman ever chosen to run for Vice-President by either major party.

Mr Mondale's choice was seen as at once politically astute and a sign of the desperation with which he seeks to avoid annihilation by President Reagan, who stands many points ahead in the polls.

"She's a woman, she's ethnic, she's a Catholic," said one of Mondale's advisers, explaining the calculation that had led to her choice. Mrs Ferraro worked as a teacher before studying law and becoming an assistant prosecutor in Queens, a substantially Italian part of New York City. She is married to a real estate developer and is 48.

In 1968 and 1972 women played an important part in the insurgencies that almost overthrew the Democratic Party's traditional leadership. Democrats are therefore concerned not to alienate women voters.

That is specially important this year, since one of the few signs of weakness in President Reagan's political armour is the "gender gap" – according to some polls, the Republicans will get 10 per cent fewer women's votes than Democrats. So such experienced politicians as Speaker "Tip" O'Neill and Governor Mario Cuomo of New York support the choice (→6/11).

Mondale and Ferraro join forces on the Democratic platform.

Jogging champ dies while on the run

July 21. James F. Fixx, the man who turned America on to jogging has died while running. He collapsed and died of a heart attack while jogging in Vermont. He was 52. His best-selling book, "The Complete Guide to Running", combined medical information about exercise with practical advice on everything from choosing shoes to avoiding dogs. Fixx took up running because of his family's history of heart disease. Jogging disciples believe he prolonged his life.

Nigerian minister found in diplomatic bag

July 10. A major diplomatic row with Nigeria erupted today when Scotland Yard charged four men with drugging and kidnapping Umaru Dikko, a former Nigerian transport minister. The four, a Nigerian diplomat and three Israelis, are alleged to have seized Dikko when he left his home in West London and bundled him into a van after a violent struggle.

Four hours later, customs officers at Stansted airport became suspicious when they were asked to pass two crates as diplomatic luggage. The Foreign Office was contacted and armed police of Scotland Yard's anti-terrorist unit ringed the airport. The crates were opened in the presence of a diplomat from the Nigerian High Commission. A heavily drugged Dikko was found in one of them.

Dikko, deposed in the military coup six months ago, fled to Britain and asked for political asylum. In Lagos, the military regime put him on a wanted list after accusing him of being one of the "economic saboteurs" in the civilian government which had brought Nigeria to the brink of bankruptcy.

Navratilova wins a fifth Wimbledon

July 7. In the centenary year of the women's championship at Wimbledon, the number one seed and odds-on favourite, Martina Navratilova, overcame the Centre Court heat and the challenge of her closest and most persistent rival, Chris Evert Lloyd, to win her fifth singles title – and her third in succession – 7-6, 6-2.

Since the war, only Billie Jean King has won as many titles as the 27-year-old Czech-born Navratilova, now an American citizen. ▷

McDonald's killer massacres 20 people

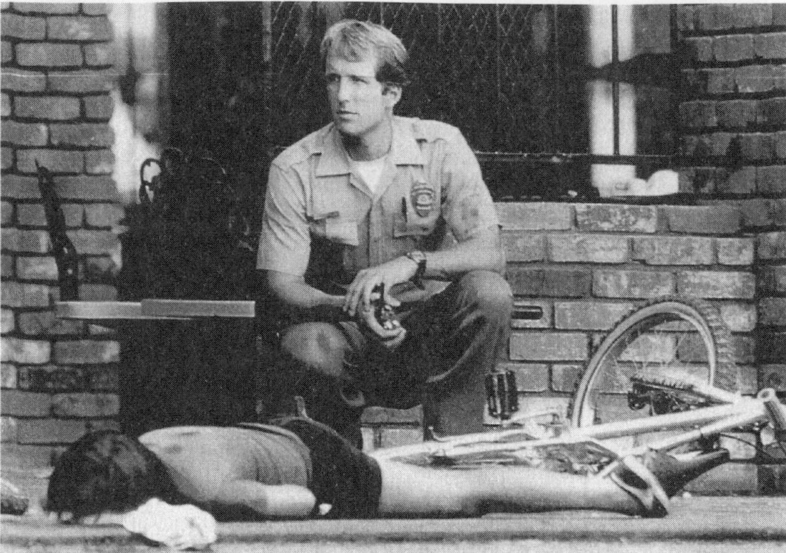

A San Diego policeman squats over the body of one of the gunman's victims.

July 18. A gunman slaughtered 20 people and wounded 16 others at a McDonald's hamburger restaurant in California today. Before being shot dead himself by police marksmen he explained his motive for the killings. "I don't like Mondays," he said.

He was later identified as Oliver Huberty, aged 41, married with two children and a grudge against the San Ysidro community after he was dismissed from his job as a security guard. Armed with three guns, he strode into the restaurant at 4pm and began firing at anybody who fell into his sights. Even when children ran across his path he kept pulling the triggers of a shotgun, pistol and a semi-automatic rifle. Sixteen of his victims lay inside and four were on the pavement.

By the time he was felled by a police gunman he had achieved a grisly place in the record books; it was the largest death toll by a single gunman in a single day in America.

Until today Huberty was an unknown, having moved with his family into the town just north of the Mexican border town less than a year ago. Police described it as the most "sickening and most horrendous massacre".

James Mason, British leading man, dies

July 27. James Mason was, until his middle years, one of the most underestimated British actors. He made his mark during the war as the villain of costume melodramas like "The Man in Grey" and "The Wicked Lady", but he showed his quality as an IRA gunman on the run in "Odd Man Out". He became a top draw in English films.

Hollywood was slow to appreciate Mason's capacity for silky-voiced menace which so appealed to women. He found his forte as "Rommel – Desert Fox" (and in many more German roles). He was further tested as Shakespeare's Brutus, Nabokov's Humbert Humbert and in Chekhov's "The Seagull". He died at Lausanne at the age of 75.

Smoothly menacing James Mason.

1984

AUGUST

Su	Mo	Tu	We	Th	Fr	Sa
			1	2	3	4
5	6	7	8	9	10	11
12	13	14	15	16	17	18
19	20	21	22	23	24	25
26	27	28	29	30	31	

1. UK: Legal moves to seize the assets of the South Wales miners begin as they fail to meet a deadline for a fine (→ 9/9).

1. Hong Kong: Sir Geoffrey Howe announces a framework of the deal for the handover of Hong Kong to China in 1997 (→ 26/9).

2. Strasbourg: The European Human Rights Court condemns phone-tapping authorised by the Home Secretary.

6. London: The Appeal Court overturns a High Court ruling that the GCHQ union ban was illegal.

6. USSR: Sakharov has ended the hunger strike aimed at getting his wife medical treatment abroad (→ 23).

8. UK: British Rail's Advanced Passenger Train makes its first journey since it was withdrawn owing to technical faults in 1981.

12. Belfast: One person dies when police try to seize Martin Galvin of the US pro-IRA group Noraid at a meeting (→ 29/9).

16. Los Angeles: John De Lorean is acquitted of plotting to distribute cocaine worth £18 million.

17. UK: Month-old heart transplant patient Holly Roffey dies.

19. UK: 13 die when a Vickers Varsity plane crashes at Uttoxeter on its way to an air show.

23. USSR: Yelena Bonner is reported to have joined her husband Sakharov in internal exile for slandering the USSR.

27. Washington: Reagan says the first ordinary US citizen to go into space on the shuttle will be a schoolteacher (→ 5/9).

31. Kabul: 28 die in a bomb attack at the airport.

DEATHS

5. British actor Richard Burton (*10/11/1925).→

14. British author and playwright J.B. (John Boynton) Priestley (*13/9/1894).→

25. US author Truman Capote (*30/9/1924).

Ponting is charged after Belgrano leak

Aug 18. A senior civil servant at the Ministry of Defence, Clive Ponting, was charged tonight with an offence under the Official Secrets Act. The charge is understood to be connected to information sent to Labour MP, Tam Dalyell, about the sinking of the Argentinian cruiser, General Belgrano, in 1982.

Mr Ponting, aged 38, is an assistant secretary at the Ministry of Defence and heads a defence secretariat which advises the Government on naval policy. Mr Dalyell has been campaigning on the case of the Belgrano, arguing that ministers misled MPs about its sinking during the Falklands War.

British novelist J.B. Priestley is dead

J.B. Priestley relaxes at home.

Aug 15. All the preparations had been made for J.B. Priestley's 90th birthday celebrations, when he died just too soon for them at his home near Stratford-upon-Avon yesterday. Highly gifted as an all-rounder of letters, essayist, novelist, playwright and social historian, Priestley's Yorkshire common sense and common touch shows through all his work. "English Journey" articulated what his countrymen were thinking in the depressed Thirties, and his radio "Post-Scripts" expressed their feelings in 1940. His favourite subject was "the English". No one knew them better.

Filipinos march against dictator Marcos

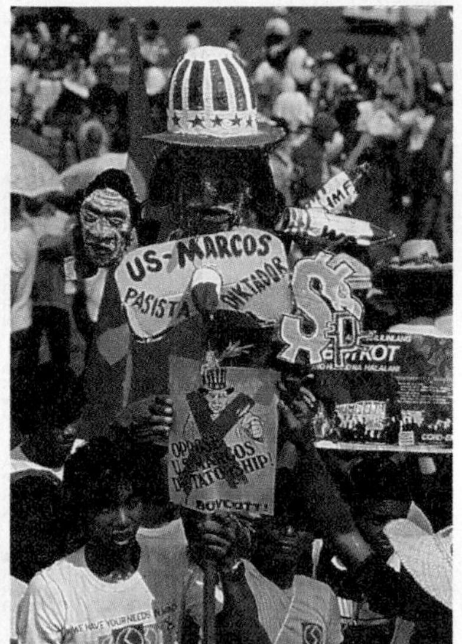

The US and Marcos, both to blame.

Aug 21. Over 900,000 Filipinos took to the streets of Manila today to protest against the government of President Marcos, and to mark the death of the opposition leader who was gunned down just one year ago. His widow, Corazon Aquino, made a passionate speech to the main rally in Rizal Park, calling for Marcos' resignation and denouncing his economic policies and record on human rights.

Some 2,000 troops were present but the demonstration was entirely non-violent. There was a fierce anti-American tone. The posters proclaimed "Down with the US-Marcos Dictatorship" and anyone who spoke in English was booed until they changed to the native tongue, Tagalog (→24/10).

Britain is hit by the BMX bike cult

Aug 14. BMX mania has hit Britain, ten years after the craze began in the US. BMX ("bicycle motocross") machines now make up a third of total cycle sales, and are worth about £100 million. Besides the brightly-coloured, chunky-tyred bikes themselves (costing between £100 and £300 and selling to five to 16-year-olds), there is a BMX culture, with "gangs", events and accessories.

Nuclear scare when French ship sinks

Aug 28. Fears were growing of nuclear pollution in the North Sea tonight as a ship carrying 450 tons of uranium collided with a ferry and capsized off Belgium. The owners of the cargo ship, the Mont Louis, have now admitted she was carrying radioactive material. The environmental group Greenpeace said: "The accident in the North Sea proves that it is not safe to transport nuclear materials by sea."

Richard Burton, actor and jet-setter, dies

Richard Burton and daughter Kate.

Aug 5. Richard Burton, who died of a stroke in Geneva today, was 58, but looked much older. "He loved women, he loved booze and he loved fame," said a friend. Burton's beginnings with the Old Vic company were brilliant, but remained unfulfilled. His childhood poverty as youngest of 13 children in a Welsh pit village tempted him to the lure of riches in indifferent Hollywood films, in which his magnificent voice was wasted.

His five marriages included two to Elizabeth Taylor, on whom he lavished jewels like an Indian prince. They got together in "Cleopatra" (1963) the most expensive flop ever made, but later turned in searing performances together in "Who's Afraid of Virginia Woolf?"

Lewis tops the bill in Olympics spectacular

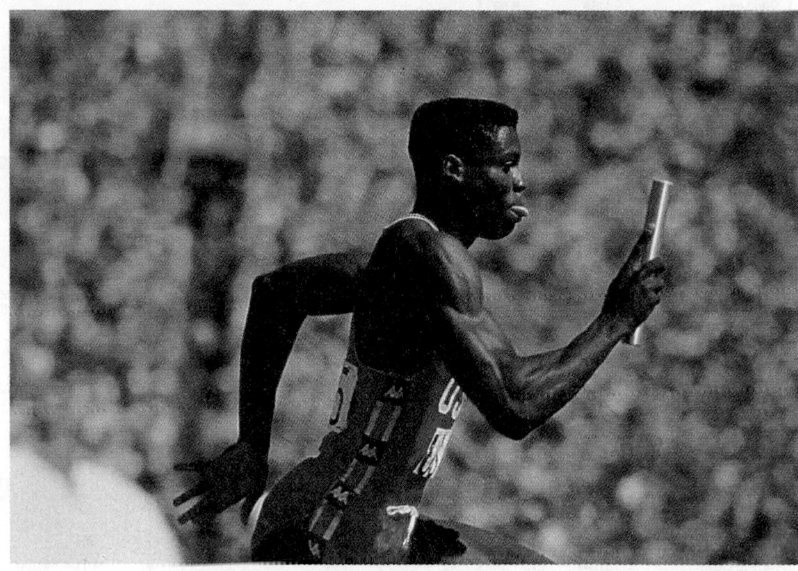
Carl Lewis, on his way to a sprint relay world record and a gold medal.

Aug 8. The Los Angeles Olympics will be remembered for its spectacle, its string of American victories in the absence of almost the entire Eastern bloc (only the Rumanians broke ranks to participate), and two dramatic controversies close to the end.

For the first time an Olympic track medallist (the Finn, Martti Vainio, who came in second in the 10,000 metres) was disqualified after a positive drugs test; and the US 3,000 metres favourite, Mary Decker, tripped over the heels of South African-born British runner, Zola Budd, and left the track in a welter of tears and recrimination.

Americans won medals in sports where they had rarely prospered in the past – notably gymnastics and cycling – but their authentic hero, Carl Lewis, delivered the goods as expected, emulating Jesse Owen's feat of 1936 by winning gold in both sprints, the long jump and, in a world record, the sprint relay.

Britain hailed her first gold medallist in a throwing event, Tessa Sanderson in the javelin, but reserved the biggest accolade for two great comebacks. Daley Thompson retained his decathlon title with his usual panache; and Sebastian Coe, after two years of illness and injury, repeated his Moscow medals – the 800 metres silver behind the Brazilian, Joaquim Cruz, and the 1,500 metres gold ahead of Steve Cram.

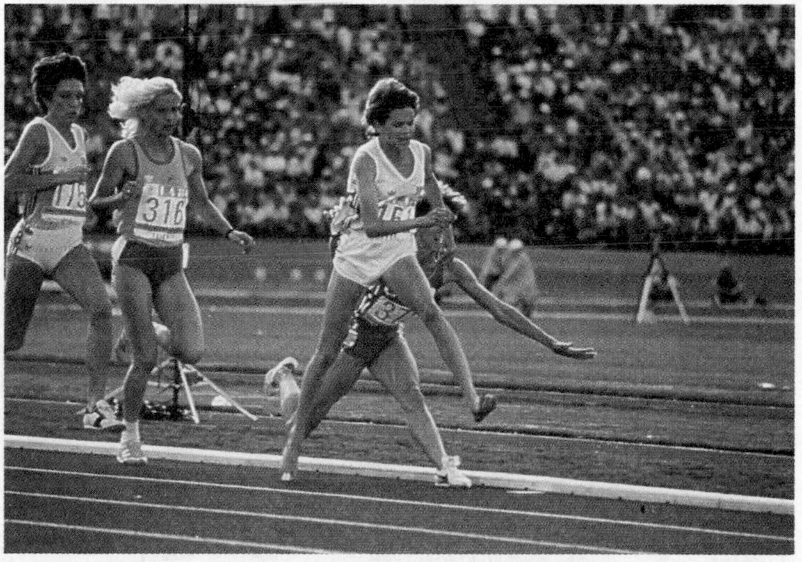

Mary Decker trips over Zola Budd's heel in the 3,000 metres final.

1984 Los Angeles

Men Athletics

100m
World Record: 9.93
Olympic Record: 9.95
1. Carl Lewis USA 9.99
2. Sam Graddy USA 10.19
3. Ben Johnson CAN 10.22

200m
World Record: 19.72
Olympic Record: 19.83
1. Carl Lewis USA *19.80
2. Kirk Baptiste USA 19.96
3. Thomas Jefferson USA 20.26

400m
World Record: 43.86
Olympic Record: 43.86
1. Alonzo Babers USA 44.27
2. Gabriel Tiacoh CIV 44.54
3. Antonio McKay USA 44.71

800m
World Record: 1:41.73
Olympic Record: 1:43.50
1. Joaquim Cruz BRA *1:43.00
2. Sebastian Coe GBR 1:43.64
3. Earl Jones USA 1:43.83

1500m
World Record: 3:30.77
Olympic Record: 3:34.91
1. Sebastian Coe GBR *3:32.53
2. Steve Cram GBR 3:33.40
3. José Abascal ESP 3:34.30

5000m
World Record: 13:00.41
Olympic Record: 13:20.34
1. Said Aouita MAR *13:05.09
2. Markus Ryffel SUI 13:07.54
3. Antonio Leitao POR 13:09.20

10,000m
World Record: 22.04
Olympic Record: 27:38.34
1. Alberto Cova ITA 27:47.54
2. Michael McLeod GBR 28:06.22
3. Mike Musyoki KEN 28:06.46

Marathon
1. Carlos Lopes POR 2:09.21
2. John Treacy IRL 2:09.56
3. Charles Spedding GBR 2:09.58

110m Hurdles
World Record: 12.93
Olympic Record: 13.24
1. Roger Kingdom USA *13.20
2. Gregory Foster USA 13.23
3. Arto Bryggare FIN 13.40

400m Hurdles
1. Edwin Moses USA 47.75
2. Danny Harris USA 48.13
3. Harald Schmid FRG 48.19

3000m Steeplechase
World Record: 8:05.4
Olympic Record: 8:08.02
1. Julius Korir KEN 8:11.80
2. Joseph Mahmoud FRA 8:13.31
3. Brian Diemer USA 8:14.06

4 x 100m Relay
1. USA 37.83** (Sam Graddy, Ron Brown, Calvin Smith, Carl Lewis)
2. JAM 38.62 (Albert Lawrence, Gregory Meghoo, Donald Quarrie, Ray Stewart)
3. CAN 38.70 (Ben Johnson, Tony Sharpe, Desai Williams, Sterling Hinds)

4 x 400m Relay
Worl Record: 2:56.16
Olympic Record: 2:56.16
1. USA 2:57.91 (Sunder Nix, Ray Armstead, Alonzo Babers, Antonio McKay)
2. GBR 2:59.13 (Kriss Akabusi, Gary Cook, Todd Bennett, Philip Brown)
3. NGR 2:59.32 (Sunday Uti, Moses Ugbusien, Rotimi Peters, Inocent Egbunike)

20km Walk
1. Ernesto Canto MEX *1:23.13
2. Raúl González MEX 1:23.20
3. Maurizio Damilano ITA 1:23.26

50km Walk
1. Raúl González MEX *3:47.26
2. Bo Gustafsson SWE 3:53.19
3. Alessandro Bellucci ITA 3:53.45

High Jump
World Record: 2.39
Olympic Record: 2.36
1. Dietmar Mögenburg FRG 2.35
2. Patrik Sjöberg SWE 2.33
3. Zhu Jianhua CHN 2.31

Pole Vault
World Record: 5.90
Olympic Record: 5.78
1. Pierre Quinon FRA 5.75
2. Mike Tully USA 5.65
3. Earl Bell USA 5.60

Long Jump
1. Carl Lewis USA 8.54
2. Gary Honey AUS 8.24
3. Giovanni Evangelisti ITA 8.24

Triple Jump
World Record: 17.89
Olympic Record: 17.39
1. Al Joyner USA 17.26
2. Mike Conley USA 17.18
3. Keith Connor GBR 16.87

Shotput
World Record: 22.22
Olympic Record: 21.35
1. Alessandro Andrei ITA 21.26
2. Michael Carter USA 21.09
3. Dave Laut USA 20.97

Discus
World Record: 71.86
Olympic Record: 68.28
1. Rolf Danneberg FRG 66.60
2. Mac Wilkins USA 66.30
3. John Powell USA 65.46

Hammer
World Record: 86.34
Olympic Record: 81.80
1. Juha Tiainen FIN 78.08
2. Karl-Hans Riehm FRG 77.98
3. Klaus Ploghaus FRG 76.68

Javelin
World Record: 104.80
Olympic Record: 94.58
1. Arto Härkönen FIN 86.76
2. David Ottley GBR 85.74
3. Kenth Eldebrink SWE 83.72

Decathlon
World Record: 8798
Olympic Record: 8618
1. Daley Thompson GBR =*8798
2. Jürgen Hingsen FRG 8673
3. Siegfried Wentz FRG 8412

Women Athletics

100m
World Record: 10.79
Olympic Record: 11.01
1. Evelyn Ashford USA *10.97
2. Alice Brown USA 11.13
3. Merlene Ottey-Page JAM 11.16

200m
World Record: 21.71
Olympic Record: 22.03
1. Valerie Brisco-Hooks USA *21.81
2. Florence Griffith USA 22.04
3. Merlene Ottey-Page JAM 22.09

400m
World Record: 47.99
Olympic Record: 48.88
1. Valerie Brisco-Hooks USA *48.83
2. Chandra Cheeseborough USA 49.05
3. Kathryn Cook GBR 49.42

800m
World Record: 1:53.28
Olympic Record: 1:53.43
1. Doina Melinte ROM 1:57.60
2. Kim Gallagher USA 1:58.63
3. Fiat Lovin ROM 1:58.83

1500m
World Record: 3:52.47
Olympic Record: 3:56.56
1. Gabriella Dorio ITA 4:03.25
2. Doino Melinte ROM 4:03.76
3. Maricica Puica ROM 4:04.15

3000m
World Record: 8:26.78
Olympic Record: 8:43.32
1. Maricica Puica ROM *8:35.96
2. Wendy Sly GBR 8:39.47
3. Lynn Williams CAN 8:42.14

100m Hurdles
World Record: 12.36
Olympic Record: 12.56
1. Benita Fitzgerald-Brown USA 12.84
2. Shirley Strong GBR 12.88
3. Kim Turner USA 13.06
3. Michèle Chardonnet FRA 13.06

400m Hurdles
World Record: 53.58
Olympic Record: 55.17
1. Nawal el Moutawakel MAR *54.61
2. Judi Brown USA 55.20
3. Cristina Cojocaru ROM 55.41

4 x 100m Relay
World Record: 41.53
Olympic Record: 41.60
1. USA 41.65 (Alice Brown, Jeanette Bolden, Chandra Cheeseborough, Evelyn Ashford)
2. CAN 42.77 (Angela Bailey, Marita Payne, Angella Taylor, France Gareau)
3. GBR 43.11 (Simone Jacobs, Kathryn Cook, Beverley Callender, Heather Oakes)

4 x 400m Relay
World Record: 3:15.92
Olympic Record: 3:19.23
1. USA *3:18.29 (Lillie Leatherwood, Sherri Howard, Valerie Brisco-Hooks, Chandra Cheeseborough)
2. CAN 3:21.21 (Charmaine Crooks, Jillian Richardson, Molly Killing-beck, Marita Payne)
3. FRG 3:22.98 (Heike Schulte-Mattler, Ute Thimm, Heide Gaugel, Gaby Bussmann)

High Jump
World Record: 2.07
Olympic Record: 1.97
1. Ulrike Meyfarth FRG *2.02
2. Sara Simeoni ITA 2.00
3. Joni Huntley USA 1.97

Long Jump
World Record: 7.43
Olympic Record: 7.06
1. Anisoara Stanciu ROM 6.96
2. Valeria Ionescu ROM 6.81
3. Susan Hearnshaw GBR 6.80

Shotput
World Record: 22.53
Olympic Record: 22.41
1. Claudia Losch FRG 20.48
2. Mihaela Loghin ROM 20.47
3. Gael Martin AUS 19.19

Discus
World Record: 73.26
Olympic Record: 69.26
1. Ria Stalman NETH 65.36
2. Leslie Deniz USA 64.86
3. Florenta Craciunescu ROM 63.64

Javelin
World Record: 74.73
Olympic Record: 68.40
1. Tessa Sanderson GBR *69.56
2. Tiina Lillak FIN 69.00
3. Fatima Whitbread GBR 67.14

Heptathlon
1. Glynis Nunn AUS *6390
2. Jackie Joyner USA 6385
3. Sabine Everts FRG 6363

Marathon
1. Joan Benoit USA 2:24.52
2. Grete Waitz NOR 2:26.18
3. Rosa Mota POR 2:26.57

Men Swimming

100m Freestyle
World Record: 49.36
Olympic Record: 49.99
1. Ambrose Gaines USA *49.80
2. Mark Stockwell AUS 50.24
3. Per Johansson SWE 50.31

200m Freestyle
World Record: 1:47.55
Olympic Record: 1:48.03
1. Michael Gross FRG **1:47.44
2. Michael Heath USA 1:49.10
3. Thomas Fahrner FRG 1:49.69

400m Freestyle
World Record: 3:48.32
Olympic Record: 3:51.31
1. George DiCarlo USA *3:51.23
2. John Mykkanen USA 3:51.49
3. Justin Lemberg AUS 3:51.79

1500m Freestyle
World Record: 14:54.76
Olympic Record: 14:58.27
1. Michael O'Brien USA 15:05.20
2. George DiCarlo USA 15:10.59
3. Stefan Pfeiffer FRG 15:21.11

100m Backstroke
World Record: 55:19
Olympic Record: 55:49
1. Richard Carey USA 55:79
2. David Wilson USA 56:35
3. Mike West CAN 56:49

200m Backstroke
World Record: 1:58.86
Olympic Record: 1:58.99
1. Richard Carey USA 2:00.23
2. Frederic Delcourt FRA 2:01.75
3. Cameron Henning CAN 2:02.37

100m Breaststroke
World Record: 1:02.13
Olympic Record: 1:02.16
1. Steve Lindquist USA **1:01.65
2. Victor Davis CAN 1:01.99
3. Peter Evans AUS 1:02.97

200m Breaststroke
World Record: 2:14.58
Olympic Record: 2:15.11
1. Victor Davis CAN **2:13.34
2. Glenn Beringen AUS 2:15.79
3. Etienne Dagon SUI 2:17.41

100m Butterfly
World Record: 53.38
Olympic Record: 53.78
1. Michael Gross FRG **53.08
2. Pablo Morales USA 53.23
3. Glenn Buchanan AUS 53.85

200m Butterfly
World Record: 1:57.05
Olympic Record: 1:58.72
1. John Sieben AUS **1:57.04
2. Michael Gross FRG 1:57.40
3. Rafael Vidal Castro VEN 1:57.51

200m Individual Medley
World Record: 2:02.45
Olympic Record: 2:08.60
1. Alex Baumann CAN **2:01.42
2. Pablo Morales USA 2:03.05
3. Neil Cochran GBR 2:04.38

400m Individual Medley
World Record: 4:17.53
Olympic Record: 4:22.89
1. Alex Baumann CAN **4:17.41
2. Ricardo Prado BRA 4:18.45
3. Robert Woodhouse AUS 4:20.50

4 x 100m Medley Relay
World Record: 3:40.42
Olympic Record: 3:42.22
1. USA 3:39.30** (Richard Carey, Steve Lundquist, Pablo Morales, Ambrose Gaines)
2. CAN 3:43.23 (Mike West, Victor Davis, Tom Ponting, Sandy Goss)
3. AUS 3:43.25 (Mark Kerry, Peter Evans, Glenn Buchanan, Mark Stockwell)

4 x 100m Freestyle Relay
World Record: 3:19.26
Olympic Record: 3:19.94
1. USA 3:19.03** (Christopher Cavanaugh, Michael Heath, Matthew Biondi, Ambrose Gaines)
2. AUS 3:19.68 (Gregory Fasala, Neil Brooks, Michael Delany, Mark Stockwell)
3. SWE 3:22.69 (Thomas Leidstrom, Bengt Baron, Mikael Om, Per Johansson)

4 x 200m Freestyle Relay
World Record: 7:20.40
Olympic Record: 7:18.87
1. USA 7:15.69** (Michael Heath, David Larson, Jeffery Float, Bruce Lawrence Hayes)
2. FRG 7:15.73 (Thomas Fahrner, Dirk Korthals, Alexander Schowtka, Michael Gross)
3. GBR 7:24.78 (Neil Cochran, Paul Easter, Paul Howe, Andrew Astbury)

Springboard Diving
1. Gregory Louganis USA 754.41
2. Tan Liangde CHN 662.31
3. Ronald Merriott USA 661.32

Platform Diving
1. Gregory Louganis USA 710.91
2. Bruce Kimball USA 643.50
3. Li Kongzheng CHN 638.28

Water Polo

1. Yugoslavia
2. USA
3. German Federal Republic

Women Swimming

100m Freestyle
World Record: 54.79
Olympic Record:
1. Carrie Steinseifer USA 55.92
1. Nancy Hogshead USA 55.92
3. Annemarie Verstappen NETH 56.08

200m Freestyle
World Record: 1:57.75
Olympic Record: 1:58.33
1. Mary Wayte USA 1:59.23
2. Cynthia Woodhead USA 1:59.50
3. Annemarie Verstappen NETH 1:59.69

400m Freestyle
World Record: 4:06.28
Olympic Record: 4:08.76
1. Tiffany Cohen USA *4:07.10
2. Sarah Hardcastle GBR 4:10.27
3. June Croft GBR 4:11.49

800m Freestyle
World Record: 8:24.62
Olympic Record: 8:28.90
1. Tiffany Cohen USA *8:24.95
2. Michele Richardson USA 8:30.73
3. Sarah Hardcastle GBR 8:32.60

100m Backstroke
World Record: 1:00.86
Olympic Record: 1:00.86
1. Theresa Andrews USA 1:02.55
2. Betsy Mitchell USA 1:02.63
3. Jolanda De Rover NETH 1:02.91

200m Backstroke
World Record: 2:09.91
Olympic Record: 2:11.77
1. Jolanda De Rover NETH 2:12.38
2. Amy White USA 2:13.04
3. Aneta Patrascoiu ROM 2:13.29

100m Breaststroke
World Record: 1:08.51
Olympic Record: 1:10.11
1. Petra Van Staveren NETH *1:09.88
2. Anne Ottenbrite CAN 1:10.69
3. Catherine Poirot FRA 1:10.70

200m Breaststroke
World Record: 2:28.36
Olympic Record: 2:29.54
1. Anne Ottenbrite CAN 2:30.38
2. Susan Rapp USA 2:31.15
3. Ingrid Lempereur BEL 2:31.40

100m Butterfly
World Record: 57.93
Olympic Record: 59.05
1. Mary T. Meagher USA 59.26
2. Jenna Johnson USA 1:00.19
3. Karin Seick FRG 1:01.36

200m Butterfly
World Record: 2:05.96
Olympic Record: 2:10.44
1. Mary T. Meagher USA *2:06.90
2. Karen Phillips AUS 2:10.56
3. Ina Beyermann FRG 2:11.91

200m Individual Medley
World Record: 2:11.73
Olympic Record: 2:14.47
1. Tracy Caulkins USA *2:12.64
2. Nancy Hogshead USA 2:15.17
3. Michele Pearson AUS 2:15.92

400m Individual Medley
World Record: 4:36.10
Olympic Record: 4:36.29
1. Tracy Caulkins USA 4:39.24
2. Suzanne Landsells AUS 4:48.30
3. Petra Zindler FRG 4:48.57

4 x 100m Medley Relay
World Record: 4:05.79
Olympic Record: 4:06.67
1. USA 4:08.34 (Theresa Andrews, Tracy Caulkins, Mary T. Meagher, Nancy Hogshead)
2. FRG 4:11.97 (Svenja Schlicht, Ute Hasse, Ina Beyemann, Karin Seick)
3. CAN 4:12.98 (Reeman Abdo, Anne Ottenbrite, Michelle Mac-Pherson, Pamela Rai)

4 x 100m Freestyle Relay
World Record: 3:42.71
Olympic Record: 3:42.71
1. USA 3:43.43 (Jenna Johnson, Carrie Steinseifer, Dara Torres, Nancy Hogshead)
2. NETH 3:44.40 (Annemarie Verstappen, Elles Voskes, Desi Reijers, Conny Van Bentum)
3. FRG 3:45.56 (Iris Zscherpe, Susanne Schuster, Christiane Pielke, Karin Seick)

Springboard Diving
1. Sylvie Bernier CAN 530.70
2. Kelly McCormick USA 527.46
3. Christina Seufert USA 517.62

Platform Diving
1. Zhou Jihong CHN 435.51
2. Michele Mitchell USA 431.19
3. Wendy Wyland USA 422.07

Synchronised Swimming Individual
1. Tracie Ruiz USA 198.467
2. Carolyn Waldo CAN 195.300
3. Miwako Motoyoshi JAP 187.050

Synchronised Swimming Duet
1. Candy Costie, Tracie Ruiz USA 195.584
2. Sharon Hambrook, Kelly Kryczka CAN 194.234
3. Saeko Simura, Miwako Motoyoshi JAP 187.992

Boxing

Light Flyweight
1. Paul Gonzales USA
2. Salvatore Todisco ITA
3. Keith Mwila ZAM
3. Marcelino Jose Bolivar VEN

Flyweight
1. Steven McCrory USA
2. Redzep Redzepovski YUG
3. Eyup Can TUR
3. Ibrahim Bilali KEN

Bantamweight
1. Maurizio Stecca ITA
2. Hector Lopez MEX
3. Dale Walters CAN
3. Pedro Nolasco DOM

Featherweight
1. Meldrick Taylor USA
2. Peter Konyegwachie NGR
3. Targut Aykac TUR
3. Omar Catari Peraza VEN

Lightweight
1. Pernell Whitaker USA
2. Luis Ortiz PUR
3. Martin Ndongo Ebanga CMR
3. Chil-Sung Chun KOR

Light Welterweight
1. Jerry Page USA
2. Dhawee Umponmaha THA
3. Mircea Fulger ROM
3. Mirko Puzovic YUG

Welterweight
1. Mark Breland USA
2. Young-Su An THA
3. Joni Nyman ROM
3. Luciano Bruno YUG

Light Middleweight
1. Frank Tate USA
2. Shawn O'Sullivan CAN
3. Manfred Zielonka FRG
3. Christophe Tiozzo FRA

Middleweight
1. Joon-Sop Shin KOR
2. Virgil Hill USA
3. Mohamed Zaoui ALG
3. Aristides Gonzalez PUR

Light Heavyweight
1. Anton Josipovic YUG
2. Kevin Barry NZL
3. Mustapha Moussa ALG
3. Evander Holyfield USA

Heavyweight
1. Henry Tillman USA
2. Willie DeWit CAN
3. Angelo Musone ITA
3. Arnold Vanderlijde NETH

Super-Heavyweight
1. Tyrell Biggs USA
2. Francesco Damiani ITA
3. Robert Wells GBR
3. Salihu Azis YUG

Weightlifting

Flyweight (less than 52kg)
1. Zeng Guoqiang CHN 235.0
2. Zhou Peishun CHN 235.0
3. Kazushito Manabe JPN 232.5

Bantamweight (less than 56kg)
1. Wu Shude CHN 267.5
2. Lai Runming CHN 265.0
3. Masahiro Kotaka JPN 252.5

Featherweight (less than 60kg)
1. Chen Wieqiang CHN 282.5
2. Gelu Radu ROM 280.0
3. Wen-Yee Tsai TPE 272.5

Lightweight (less than 67.5kg)
1. Yao Jingyuan CHN 320.0
2. Andrei Socaci ROM 312.5
3. Jouni Gronman FIN 312.5

Middleweight (less than 75kg)
1. Karl-Heinz Radschinsky FRG 340.0
2. Jacques Demers CAN 335.0
3. Dragomir Cioroslan ROM 332.5

Light Heavyweight (less than 82.5kg)
1. Petre Becheru ROM 355.5
2. Robert Kabbas AUS 342.5
3. Ryoji Isaoko JPN 340.0

Middle Heavyweight (less than 90kg)
1. Nicu Vlad ROM *392.5
2. Dumitru Petre ROM 360.0
3. David Mercer GBR 352.5

Heavyweight (100kg)
1. Rolf Milser FRG 385.0
2. Vasile Gropa ROM 382.5
3. Pekka Niemi FIN 367.5

Heavyweight (less than 110kg)
1. Norberto Oberburger ITA 390.0
2. Stefan Tasnadi ROM 380.0
3. Guy Carlton USA 377.5

Super-Heavyweight (more than 110kg)
1. Dinko Lukin AUS 412.5
2. Mario Martinez USA 410.0
3. Manfred Nerlinger FRG 397.5

1984  Los Angeles

Judo

Extra Lightweight
1. Shinji Hosokawa JPN
2. Jae-Yup Kim KOR
3. Edward Liddie USA
3. Neil Eckersley GBR

Half Lightweight (less than 65kg)
1. Yoshiyuki Matsuoka JPN
2. Jung-Oh Hwang KOR
3. Josef Reiter AUT
3. Marc Alexandre FRA

Lightweight (less than 71kg)
1. Byeong-Keun Ahn KOR
2. Ezio Gamba ITA
3. Luis Onmura BRA
3. Kerrith Brown GBR

Half Middleweight (less than 78kg)
1. Frank Wieneke FRG
2. Neil Adams GBR
3. Michel Nowak FRA
3. Mircea Fratica ROM

Middleweight (less than 86kg)
1. Peter Seisenbacher AUT
2. Robert Berland USA
3. Seiki Nose JPN
3. Walter Carmona BRA

Half Heavyweight (less than 95kg)
1. Hyoung-Zoo Ha KOR
2. Douglas Vieira BRA
3. Bjarni Fridriksson ISL
3. Günter Neureuther FRG

Heavyweight (more than 95kg)
1. Hitoshi Saito JPN
2. Angelo Parisi FRA
3. Yong-Chul Cho KOR
3. Mark Berger CAN

Open Category
1. Yasuhiro Yamashita JPN
2. Mohamed Rashwan EGY
3. Mihai Cioc ROM
3. Arthur Schnabel FRG

Men Fencing

Foil Individual
1. Mauro Numa ITA
2. Matthias Behr FRG
3. Stefano Cerioni ITA

Foil Team
1. Italy
2. German Federal Republic
3. France

Epée Individual
1. Philippe Boisse FRA
2. Björne Väggö SWE
3. Philippe Riboud FRA

Epée Team
1. German Federal Republic
2. France
3. Italy

Sabre Individual
1. Jean-Francois Lamour FRA
2. Marco Marin ITA
3. Peter Westbrook USA

Sabre Team
1. Italy
2. France
3. Romania

Women Fencing

Foil Individual
1. Luan Jujie CHN
2. Cornelia Hanisch FRG
3. Dorina Vaccaroni ITA

Foil Team
1. German Federal Republic
2. Romania
3. France

Modern Pentathlon

Individual
1. Daniele Masala ITA 5469
2. Svante Rasmuson SWE 5456
3. Carlo Massullo ITA 5406

Team
1. Italy 16060
2. USA 15568
3. France 15565

Greco-Roman Wrestling

Light Flyweight
1. Vincenzo Maenza ITA
2. Markus Scherer FRG
3. Ikuzo Saito JPN

Flyweight
1. Atsuji Miyahara JPN
2. Daniel Aceves MEX
3. Dae-Du Bang PRK

Bantamweight
1. Pasquale Passarelli FRG
2. Masaki Eto JPN
3. Haralambos Holidis GRE

Featherweight
1. Weon-Kee Kim PRK
2. Kent-Olle Johansson SWE
3. Hugo Dietsche SUI

Lightweight
1. Vlado Lisjak YUG
2. Tapio Sipila FIN
3. James Martinez USA

Welterweight
1. Jouko Salomäki FIN
2. Roger Tallroth SWE
3. Stefan Rusu ROM

Middleweight
1. Ion Draica ROM
2. Dimitrios Thanopoulos GRE
3. Soren Claesson SWE

Light Heavyweight
1. Steven Fraser USA
2. Ilie Matei ROM
3. Frank Andersson SWE

Heavyweight
1. Vasile Andrei ROM
2. Greg Gibson USA
3. Jozef Tertelje YUG

Super Heavyweight
1. Jeffrey Blatnick USA
2. Refik Memisevic YUG
3. Victor Dolipschi ROM

Freestyle Wrestling

Light Flyweight
1. Robert Weaver USA
2. Takashi Irie JPN
3. Gab-Do Son PRK

Flyweight
1. Saban Trstena YUG
2. Jong-Kyu Kim PRK
3. Yuji Takada JPN

Bantamweight
1. Hideaki Tomiyama JPN
2. Barry Davis USA
3. Eui-Kon Kim PRK

Featherweight
1. Randy Lewis USA
2. Kosei Akaishi JPN
3. Jung-Keun Lee PRK

Lightweight
1. In-Tak You PRK
2. Andrew Rein USA
3. Jukka Rauhala FIN

Welterweight
1. David Schultz USA
2. Martin Knosp FRG
3. Saban Sejdi YUG

Middleweight
1. Mark Schultz USA
2. Hideyuki Nagashima JPN
3. Chris Rinke CAN

Light Heavyweight
1. Lou Banach USA
2. Joseph Atiyeh SYR
3. Vasile Puscasu ROM

Super Heavyweight
1. Bruce Baumgartner USA
2. Bob Molle
3. Ayhan Taskin TUR

Men Canoeing

Kayak-1 500m
1. Ian Ferguson NZL 1:47.84
2. Lars-Erik Moberg SWE 1:48.18
3. Bernard Bregeon FRA 1:48.41

Kayak-1 1000m
1. Alan Thompson NZL 3:45.73
2. Milan Janic YUG 3:46.88
3. Greg Barton USA 3:47.38

Kayak-2 500m
1. Ian Ferguson, Paul MacDonald NZL 1:34.21
2. Per-Inge Bengtsson, Lars-Erik Moberg SWE 1:35.26
3. Hugh Fisher, Alwyn Morris CAN 1:35.41

Kayak-2 1000m
1. Hugh Fisher, Alwyn Morris CAN 3:24.22
2. Bernard Bregeon, Patrick Lefoulon FRA 3:25.97
3. Bary Kelly, Grant Kenny AUS 3:26.80

Kayak-4 1000m 1. NZE – 2. SWE – 3. FRA

Canadian-1 500m
1. Larry Cain CAN 1:57.01
2. Henning Jakobsen DEN 1:58.45
3. Costica Olaru ROM 1:59.86

Canadian-1 1000m
1. Ulrich Eike FRG 4:06.32
2. Larry Cain CAN 4:08.67
3. Henning Jakobsen DEN 4:09.51

Canadian-2 500m
1. Matija Ljubek, Mirko Nisovic YUG 1:43.67
2. Ivan Potzaichin, Toma Simionov ROM 1:45.68
3. Enrique Miguez, Narcisco Suarez ESP 1:47.71

Canadian-2 1000m
1. Ivan Potzaichin, Toma Simionov ROM 3:40.60
2. Matija Ljubek, Mirko Nisovic YUG 3:41.56
3. Didier Hoyer, Eric Renaud FRA 3:48.01

Women Canoeing

Kayak-1 500m
1. Agneta Andersson SWE 1:58.72
2. Barbara Schüttpelz FRG 1:59.93
3. Annemiek Derckx NETH 2:00.11

Kayak-2 500m
1. Agneta Andersson, Anna Olsson SWE 1:45.25
2. Alexandra Barre, Sue Holloway CAN 1:47.13
3. Josefa Idem, Barbara Schüttpelz FRG 1:47.32

Kayak-4 500m
1. ROM 1:38.34 (Agafia Constantin, Nastasia Ionescu, Tecla Marinescu, Maria Stefan)
2. SWE 1:38.87 (Agneta Andersson, Anna Olsson, Eva Karlsson, Susanne Wiberg)
3. CAN 1:39.40 (Alexandra Barre, Lucie Guay, Sue Holloway, Barbara Olmsted)

Men Rowing

Single Sculls
1. Pertti Karppinen FIN 7:00.24
2. Peter-Michael Kolbe FRG 7:02.19
3. Robert Mills CAN 7:10.38

Double Sculls
1. USA 6:36.87
2. Belgium 6:38.19
3. Yugoslavia 6:39.59

Coxless Pairs
1. Romania 6:45.39
2. Spain 6:48.47
3. Norway 7:12.81

Coxed Pairs
1. Italy 7:05.99
2. Romania 7:11.21
3. USA 7:12.81

Quadruple Sculls
1. German Federal Republic 5:57.55
2. Australia 5:57.98
3. Canada 5:59.07

Coxless Fours
1. New Zealand 6:03.48
2. USA 6:06.10
3. Denmark 6:07.72

Coxed Fours
1. Great Britain 6:18.64
2. USA 6:20.28
3. New Zealand 6:23.68

Eights
1. Canada 5:41.32
2. USA 5:41.74
3. Australia 5:43.40

Women Rowing

Single Sculls
1. Valeria Racila ROM 3:40.68
2. Charlotte Geer USA 3:43.89
3. Ann Haesebrouck BEL 3:45.72

Double Sculls
1. Romania 3:26.75
2. Netherlands 3:29.13
3. Canada 3:29.82

Coxless Pairs
1. Romania 3:32.60
2. Canada 3:36.06
3. German Federal Republic 3:40.50

Coxed Quadruple Sculls
1. Romania 3:14.11
2. USA 3:15.57
3. Denmark 3:16.02

Coxed Fours
1. Romania 3:19.30
2. Canada 3:21.55
3. Australia 3:23.29

Eights
1. USA 2:59.80
2. Romania 3:00.87
3. Netherlands 3:02.92

Yachting

Windglider
1. Stephan van den Berg NETH 27.7
2. Randall Scott Steele USA 46.0
3. Bruce Kendall NZE 46.4

Finn
1. Russell Coutts NZL 34.70
2. John Bertrand AUS 37.00
3. Terry Neilson CAN 37.70

Flying Dutchman
1. USA 19.70
2. Canada 22.70
3. Great Britain 48.70

Soling
1. USA 33.70
2. Brazil 43.40
3. Canada 49.70

Star
1. USA 29.70
2. German Federal Republic 41.40
3. Italy 43.50

470
1. Spain 33.70
2. USA 43.00
3. France 49.40

Tornado
1. New Zealand 14.70
2. USA 37.00
3. Australia 50.40

Men Cycling

Individual Road Race
1. Alexi Grewal USA 4:59.57
2. Steve Bauer CAN 4:59.57
3. Dag Otto Lauritzen NOR 5:00.18

100km Team Time Trial
1. Italy 1:58.28
2. Switzerland 2:02.38
3. USA 2:02.46

1000m Time Trial
1. Fredy Schmidtke FRG 1:06.10
2. Curtis Harnett CAN 1:06.44
3. Fabrice Colas FRA 1:06.65

1000m Sprint
1. Mark Gorski USA
2. Nelson Vails USA
3. Tsutomu Sakamoto JPN

4000m Individual Pursuit
1. Steve Hegg USA 4:39.35
2. Rolf Gölz FRG 4:43.82
3. Leonard Harvey Nitz USA 4:44.03

4000m Team Pursuit
1. Australia 4:25.99
2. USA 4:29.85
3. FRG 4:25.60

Points Race
1. Roger Ilegems BEL
2. Uwe Messerschmidt FRG
3. José Manuel Youshimatz MEX

Women Cycling

Road Race
1. Connie Carpentier USA 2:11:14
2. Rebecca Twigg USA 2:11:14
3. Sandra Schumacher FRG 2:11:14

Equestrian Sports

Three-day event Individual
1. Mark Todd, Charisma NZL
2. Karen Stives, Ben Arthur USA
3. Virginia Holgate, Priceless GBR

Three-day Event Team
1. USA
2. Great Britain
3. FRG

Individual Dressage
1. Reiner Klimke, Ahlerich FRG
2. Anne Grethe Jensen, Marzog DEN
3. Otto Hofer, Limandus SUI

Team Dressage
1. FRG
2. Switzerland
3. Sweden

Grand Prix Jumping Individual
1. Joe Fargis, Touch of Class USA
2. Conrad Homfeld, Abdullah USA
3. Heidi Robbiana, Jessica V SUI

Grand Prix Jumping Team
1. USA
2. Great Britain
3. FRG

Mary Lou Retton won the gold for all-around gymnastic ability.

Men Shooting

Small-Bore Rifle, 50m, Prone
1. Edward Etzel USA =*599
2. Michel Bury FRA 596
3. Michael Sullivan GBR 596

Small-Bore Rifle, Combined, 3 Positions
1. Malcolm Cooper GBR =*1173
2. Daniel Nipkow SUI 1163
3. Alister Allan GBR 1162

Rapid-Fire Pistol
1. Takeo Kamachi JPN 595
2. Corneliu Ion ROM 593
3. Rauno Bies FIN 591

Free Pistol
1. Xu Haifeng CHN 566
2. Ragnar Skanaker SWE 565
3. Wang Yifu CHN 564

Trap Shooting
1. Luciano Giovannetti ITA 192
2. Francisco Boza PER 192
3. Daniel Carlisle USA 192

Skeet
1. Matthew Dryke USA =*198
2. Ole Riber Rasmussen DEN 196/25
3. Luca Rossi Scribani ITA 196/23

Moving Target
1. Li Yuwei CHN 587
2. Helmut Bellingrodt COL 584
3. Huang Shiping CHN 581

Women Shooting

Sport Pistol
1. Linda Thom CAN 585/198
2. Ruby Fox USA 585/197
3. Patricia Dench AUS 583/196

Small-bore Rifle, Three Positions
1. Wu Xiaoxuan CHN 581
2. Ulrike Holmer FRG 578
3. Wanda Jewell USA 578

Air Rifle
1. Pat Spurgin USA 393
2. Edith Gufler ITA 391
3. Wu Xiaoxuan CHN 389

Men Archery

1. Darrell Pace USA *2616
2. Richard McKinney USA 2564
3. Hiroshi Yamamoto JPN 2563

Women Archery

1. Hyang-Soon Seo KOR *2568
2. Li Lingjuan CHN 2559
3. Jin-Ho Kim KOR 2555

Men Gymnastics

All-around Individual Competition
1. Koji Gushiken JPN 118.700
2. Peter Vidmar USA 118.675
3. Li Ning CHN 118.575

Combined Exercises Team
1. USA 591.40
2. People's Republic of China 590.80
3. Japan 586.70

Floor Exercises
1. Li Ning CHN 19.925
2. Lou Yun CHN 19.775
3. Koji Sotomura JPN 19.700
3. Philippe Vatmone FRA 19.700

Parallel Bars
1. Bart Conner USA 19.950
2. Nobuyuki Kajitani JPN 19.925
3. Mitchell Gaylord USA 19.850

Side Horse Vault
1. Li Ning CHN 19.950
1. Peter Vidmar USA 19.950
3. Timothy Daggott USA 19.825

Long Horse Vault
1. Lou Yun CHN 19.950
2. Mitchell Gaylord USA 19.825
2. Koji Gushiken JPN 19.825
2. Li Ning CHN 19.825
2. Shinji Morisue JPN 19.825

Horizontal Bar
1. Shinji Morisue JPN 20.000
2. Tong Fei CHN 19.975
3. Koji Gushiken JPN 19.950

Rings
1. Koji Gushiken JPN 19.850
1. Li Ning CHN 19.850
3. Mitchell Gaylord USA 19.825

Women Gymnastics

Combined Exercises Team
1. Romania 392.02
2. USA 391.20
3. People's Republic of China 388.60

All-around Individual Competition
1. Mary Lou Retton USA 79.175
2. Ecaterina Szabó ROM 79.125
3. Simona Pauca ROM 78.675

Asymmetric Bars
1. Ma Yanhong CHN 19.950
1. Julianne McNamara USA 19.950
3. Mary Lou Retton USA 19.800

Floor Exercises
1. Ecaterina Szabo ROM 19.975
2. Julianne McNamara USA 19.950
3. Mary Lou Retton USA 19.775

Side Horse Vault
1. Ecaterina Szabó ROM 19.875
2. Mary Lou Retton USA 19.850
3. Lavinia Agache ROM 19.750

Beam
1. Simona Pauca ROM 19.800
1. Ecaterina Szabó ROM 19.800
3. Kathy Johnson USA 19.650

Rhythmic Competition
1. Lori Fung CAN 57.950
2. Doina Staiculescu ROM 57.900
3. Regina Weber FRG 57.700

Men Basketball

1. USA – 2. SPA – 3. YUG

Women Basketball

1. USA – 2. KOR – 3. CHN

Soccer

1. FRA – 2. BRA – 3. YUG

Men Handball

1. YUG – 2. FRG – 3. ROM

Women Handball

1. YUG – 2. KOR – 3. CHN

Men Hockey

1. PAK – 2. FRG – 3. GBR

Women Hockey

1. NETH – 2. FRG – 3. USA

Men Volleyball

1. USA – 2. BRA – 3. ITA

Women Volleyball

1. CHN – 2. USA – 3. JPN

(Key to symbols and abbreviations p. 1456)

1984

SEPTEMBER

Su	Mo	Tu	We	Th	Fr	Sa
						1
2	3	4	5	6	7	8
9	10	11	12	13	14	15
16	17	18	19	20	21	22
23	24	25	26	27	28	29
30						

1. Tripoli: Gaddafi says he has sent arms to Nicaragua to help the Sandinistas fight the US (→5/11).

3. Philippines: Up to 1,000 are feared dead in a typhoon.

4. UK: Norman Willis is elected to succeed Len Murray as TUC general secretary.

4. Canada: Progressive Conservative leader Brian Mulroney defeats Prime Minister John Turner in a general election.

5. US: The new space shuttle Discovery returns from its six-day maiden flight.

7. UK: 22 people have died from salmonella-type poisoning at a hospital in Wakefield in the last ten days.

9. Edinburgh: NCB chairman Ian MacGregor arrives for talks with Scargill with a carrier bag over his head (→21).

10. London: Douglas Hurd becomes Ulster Secretary; new peer Lord Young becomes minister without portfolio.

12. London: The High Court grants an eviction order against the Greenham Common peace camp.

16. London: Princess Diana goes home 22 hours after having her second son, Henry Charles Albert David.

18. Moscow: Ex-defector Oleg Bitov claims at a press conference he was kidnapped by British agents.

21. UK: Maltby Colliery near Rotherham is the scene of some of the worst violence in the miners strike so far (→28).

22. UK: The new Bishop of Durham calls Coal Board chief Ian MacGregor an "imported, elderly American" (→27).

27. London: Dr Runcie confirms he has written to Ian MacGregor regretting the Bishop of Durham's remarks (→1/10).

28. London: The High Court rules the pit strike unlawful (→10/10).

29. Ireland: A massive IRA arms haul is seized aboard an Irish trawler off the south-west coast (→12/10).

China and UK agree Hong Kong deal

Sept 26. Sovereignty over Hong Kong will revert to China in 1997, but the colony will keep its free enterprise system for at least 50 years after that. These were key elements of an agreement initialled in Peking today about the future of the territory when the British lease runs out.

It marked the end of two years of hard negotiation and it was hailed in Whitehall as a triumph. The stipulation about Hong Kong keeping its capitalist life-style is seen in Western circles as acceptance by China's Communist leaders that they need to keep strong financial and commercial contacts with Britain and the free world's other trading nations.

In Peking diplomats insisted that capitalist and socialist systems can work within one country and that the deal can be copied in ultimate reunification of Taiwan with China.

Sir Geoffrey Howe, the Foreign Secretary, assured MPs: "The colony's future is assured." About 20,000 Hong Kong Chinese have a right to settle in Britain, but the Foreign Office played down the prospect of mass exodus to this country. Its emphasis tonight was on making the agreement work – however surprising the nature of it (→19/12).

Prince Charles wins "carbuncle" battle

Sept 20. The National Gallery extension designed for Trafalgar Square, which Prince Charles likened to "a monstrous carbuncle on the face of a much-loved friend", was rejected today by the Environment Secretary. Mr Jenkins said its proposed 100-foot tower would be an "unwelcome intrusion".

Prince Charles made his feelings known in a speech to architects earlier this year. He called the winning design "a vast municipal fire station" asking: "Why has everything got to be vertical, straight, unbending and functional?"

US embassy hit again by Beirut bombers

Lebanese troops survey the destruction caused by one kamikaze Moslem.

Sept 20. Forty people were killed when an Islamic suicide bomber blasted himself and his explosive-packed car in an attack on the US embassy in East Beirut today. Both the American ambassador and his visiting British colleague, David Meirs, were wounded in the attack. This was the third attack on American property in Beirut. All were carried out by Islamic Jihad, a network of Shi'ite fanatics. The driver of the car-bomb zig-zagged at speed through the dragons' teeth roadblocks. Rifle fire from militia guards failed to stop him.

Peres to be Israel's new prime minister

Sept 14. The Knesset, Israel's parliament, today approved an unusual scheme for power-sharing in the cause of national unity. Shimon Peres of the Labour Party has been sworn in as prime minister, but halfway through the regular 50-month term of office he will hand over to Yitzhak Shamir, the leader of the right-wing Likud Party.

Until then, Shamir will serve as deputy to Peres and as foreign minister. The arrangement is intended to solve the political impasse in which neither party can deal with national problems.

The Prince and Princess of Wales show off their second son, Prince Henry, known to all as Harry.

Mob hacks Sharpeville mayor to death

Sept 4. South Africa's new constitution, which came into effect yesterday, and gives limited political power to Asians and coloureds of mixed race, but has nothing for blacks, was marked by violent rioting in five black townships outside Johannesburg. Overnight, the death toll rose to 29. In Sharpeville, the deputy mayor, Sam Dlamini, was hacked to death by a mob of youths, doused in petrol and burned. Some observers say the riots are a protest against rent increases and poor educational facilities. Others claim that most of the rioting and looting was the work of drunken youths (→16/10).

1984

OCTOBER

Su	Mo	Tu	We	Th	Fr	Sa
	1	2	3	4	5	6
7	8	9	10	11	12	13
14	15	16	17	18	19	20
21	22	23	24	25	26	27
28	29	30	31			

1. UK: The Bishop of Durham launches an attack on Thatcher's social policies.

1. London: Johnson Matthey Bankers, which has £150 million loan losses, is bought by the Bank of England.

5. UK: Police and customs men seize £7.2 million worth of drugs in Europe's biggest ever haul of cannabis.

9. Jordan: Mubarak becomes the first Egyptian leader to visit an Arab state since the peace treaty with Israel.

10. London: The High Court fines the NUM £200,000 and Arthur Scargill £1,000 for contempt of court (→16).

14. Brighton: The Grand Hotel death toll rises to four.

15. UK: The pound closes at $1.2060.

16. UK: The pit deputies union NACODS votes to go on strike (→24).

16. Oslo: The Nobel Peace Prize is awarded to Bishop Desmond Tutu (→10/12).

18. UK: Veteran Labour peer Manny Shinwell celebrates his 100th birthday.

19. Poland: Pro-Solidarity priest Jerzy Popieluszko is kidnapped (→27).

21. Portugal: Niki Lauda becomes world motor racing champion for the third time.

23. Manila: A civilian panel studying the Aquino murder rejects the army's claim that the killer acted alone.→

24. UK: NACODS calls off its threatened strike (→6/11).

25. Brussels: The EC grants £1.8 million famine aid to Ethiopia (→1/11).

27. Warsaw: The interior minister says one of his agents has confessed to killing Father Popieluszko.→

DEATHS

21. French film director Francois Truffaut (*6/2/1932).→

31. Indian stateswoman Indira Gandhi, born Nehru, Prime Minister 1966-77, 1980-84 (*19/11/1917).→

IRA bomb blasts Tory conference HQ

Oct 12. An IRA bomb intended to assassinate most of the British cabinet devastated the Grand Hotel, Brighton, at 2.54am today. Most top Tories were staying in the hotel during the Tory Party conference. The Prime Minister narrowly escaped death in the blast, which killed at least three people.

Those who died included one MP, Sir Anthony Berry, and the wife of the government chief whip, John Wakeham. More than 30 people were pulled – badly injured – from the rubble. Among them were Norman Tebbit, the Trade and Industry Secretary, his wife and Mr Wakeham.

Mrs Thatcher had a lucky escape. A bathroom which she had been in two minutes earlier was wrecked. The bedrooms of other government ministers were showered with masonry as a 20-pound bomb exploded and sliced four floors out of the centre of the building.

It was the most devastating terrorist attack ever perpetrated against British politicians. Hours later the IRA gloated: "Today we were unlucky, but remember we have only to be lucky once."

The hotel and a neighbouring one were evacuated within minutes of the blast. Police escorted Mrs Thatcher and her husband out of the town. More bombs were feared. Dazed cabinet members wandered about the Brighton front in their pyjamas as firefighters, hampered by darkness, searched the charred hotel for bodies. Mrs Thatcher said: "Life must go on" (→14).

A hole gashes the Grand Hotel's facade where the blast destroyed four floors.

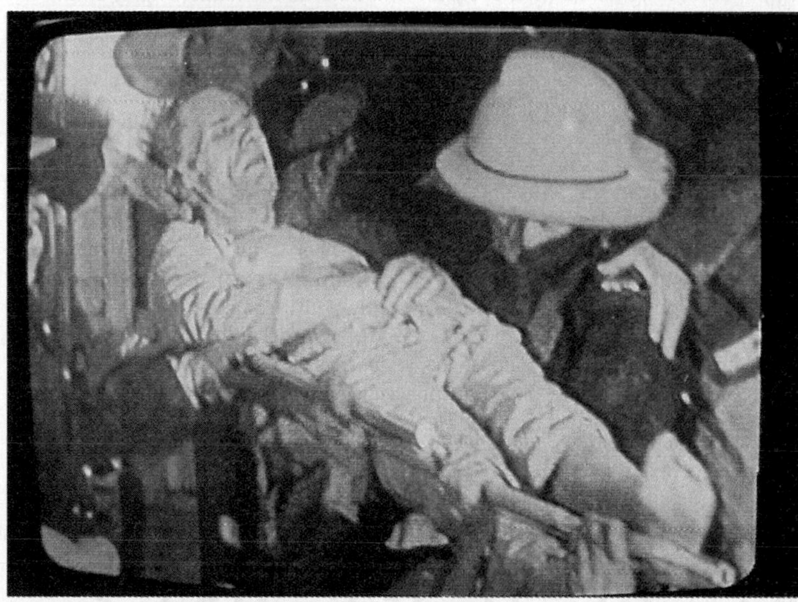

As seen on TV, Industry Minister Norman Tebbit is freed by firemen.

China sets off down the capitalist road

Oct 28. China set off down the capitalist road today after 35 years of Communism, during which former capitalists were executed, imprisoned and "re-educated". Now, with its economy and industry in a woeful state of inefficiency, the Communist Party Central Committee is looking to free enterprise to solve the economic problems which beset China's vast population.

The reforms announced by the Central Committee include plans to allow a million state-owned enterprises greater independence, to encourage competition and to allow the pricing of many products to be determined by the market forces of supply and demand – a process which is an anathema to Communist doctrine.

The Committee also promised to increase foreign trade and to give industrial plant managers more autonomy from the dead hand of state bureaucracy. One of the forces behind the reforms is the dramatic success of an incentive programme for China's millions of small farmers.

French film-maker Truffaut has died

Oct 21. The most charismatic French film director, Francois Truffaut, who founded the "New Wave" and is best known for "Jules et Jim", died of cancer today aged 52. His own troubled and rebellious youth inspired his series of films about his fictional self, Antoine Doinel. The first of them, "Les Quatre Cents Coups", won him a director's prize at Cannes festival, which he had pilloried when he was a film critic. ▷

Mrs Gandhi shot dead

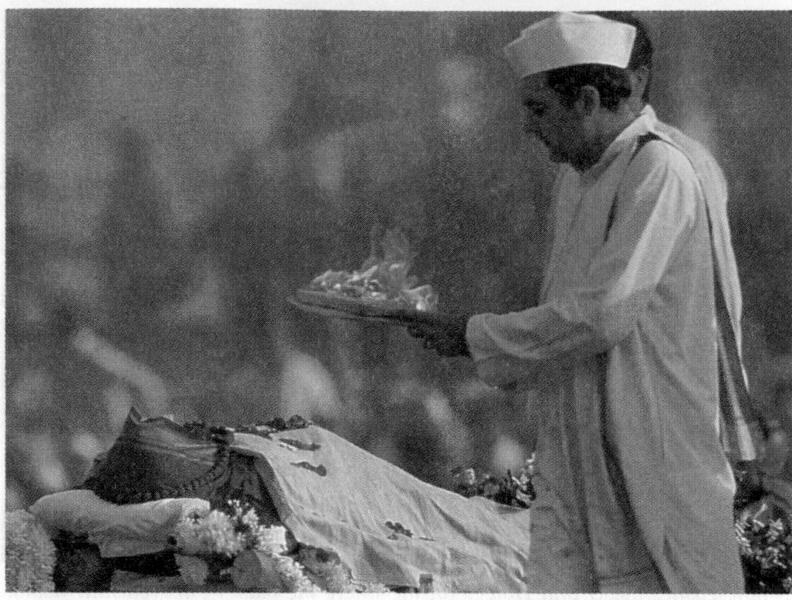

Rajiv Gandhi lights his mother's pyre and inherits the leadership of India.

Oct 31. Mrs Indira Gandhi, Prime Minister of India, was assassinated today, shot down by her Sikh bodyguards as she walked in the garden of her New Delhi home. There is no doubt that her murder was an act of revenge for "Operation Blue Star", the storming of the Sikhs' holiest shrine at Amritsar last June.

Sikhs, even those opposed to the extremists who had occupied the Golden Temple, regarded Mrs Gandhi's action as a desecration and she had been warned about the dangers of keeping her Sikh bodyguards. But she was sure of their loyalty, and now she has paid the price. One of her assassins was killed and the other wounded. The 66-year-old Prime Minister, who had a stormy political career, was shot ten times as she walked to a meeting with Peter Ustinov, who is making a TV documentary about her.

Mrs Gandhi's son, Rajiv, aged 40, was sworn in as her successor within hours of her death. As midnight approached he broadcast an appeal for calm as violence flared across the nation.

Prophetically, the night before her death, Mrs Gandhi told a political rally: "I don't mind if my life goes in the service of the nation. If I die today, every drop of my blood will invigorate the nation" (→1/11).

Baboon's heart for 15-day-old Baby Fae

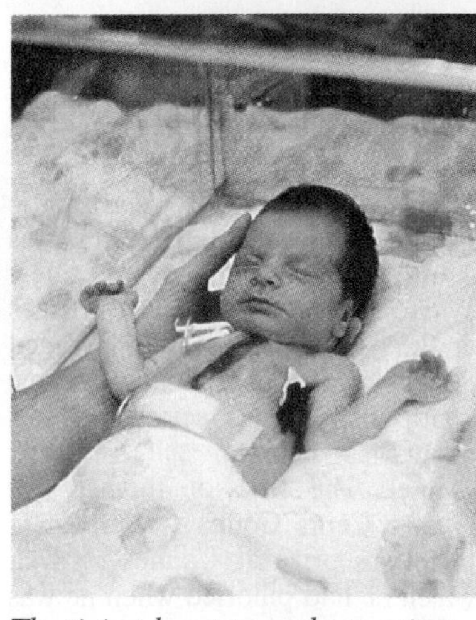

The tiniest heart transplant patient.

Oct 26. A 15-day-old baby, identified as "Baby Fae", now has a baboon's heart, which was transplanted to replace a defective heart in a five-hour operation by Leonard L. Bailey at Loma Linda University Medical Center in California. It is the first time a baboon's heart has been used in this way and at present the infant is in a critical state.

Although Dr Bailey has been criticised, he defends this operation as very useful. A hospital spokesman said Baby Fae's immature immune system was less likely to cause rejection and that "she will live a long life with this heart" (→13/11).

Solidarity priest "beaten to death"

Oct 30. The body of Father Jerzy Popieluszko, the 37-year-old Warsaw priest and friend of the Solidarity free trade union movement who was kidnapped 11 days ago by three policemen, was found tonight in a reservoir in central Poland. He appeared to have been bound and beaten to death.

In recent weeks Father Popieluszko had become the best-loved priest in Poland. Wearing jeans and a white polo shirt, he would talk with workers; then in church, in his robes, he would hold masses for Solidarity, attended by 10,000 people spilling out of the church into the park. "If we lack freedom, it is because we submit to falsehood," he said. "It's because we don't expose it every day" (→3/11).

Padre of Gdansk shipyard.

Military link found to Aquino shooting

Oct 24. The assassination a year ago of Benigno Aquino, the Philippine opposition leader, was most likely the work of the armed forces, concluded the five-member investigating panel today. They rejected the government story that he was killed by a lone gunman hired by Communists. The head of the panel blamed an air force general; the others thought the chief of the government's armed forces was implicated.

1984

NOVEMBER

Su	Mo	Tu	We	Th	Fr	Sa
				1	2	3
4	5	6	7	8	9	10
11	12	13	14	15	16	17
18	19	20	21	22	23	24
25	26	27	28	29	30	

1. New Delhi: Rajiv Gandhi is sworn in as Prime Minister by President Zail Singh amid anti-Sikh riots (→3).

3. India: Mrs Gandhi is cremated as violence continues.→

3. Warsaw: 200,000 attend the funeral of Father Popieluszko (→27/12).

5. UK: 800 miners return to work.→

5. Nicaragua: Daniel Ortega is elected President.

6. London: The Government admits the log of HMS Conqueror, the submarine which sank the Belgrano, is missing.

11. Washington: Reagan formally accepts the privately-funded Vietnam Memorial for the US nation.

12. London: Lawson announces that no more English one-pound notes will be issued after the end of this year.

13. London: Harold Macmillan, first Earl of Stockton, makes his maiden speech in the Lords.

13. US: Baboon heart transplant patient "Baby Fae" is beginning to suffer heart and kidney failure (→15).

15. US: "Baby Fae" dies.

19. UK: 2,282 miners return to work, bringing the number of working miners to around 62,000 (→20).

20. UK: The North Wales branch of the NUM decides to end its strike (→30).

20. UK: The flotation of 51 per cent of the shares of British Telecom is launched (→28).

23. Korea: Three North Korean troops die in a clash with UN troops at the demilitarised zone.

23. London: Hundreds of people flee from smoke-filled tunnels when fire breaks out at Oxford Circus tube station.

28. UK: The British Telecom share offer closes (→18/12).

30. UK: Two miners are charged with murdering cab driver David Wilkie, killed by a concrete block dropped on his car (→14/12).

Aid to Ethiopia thwarted

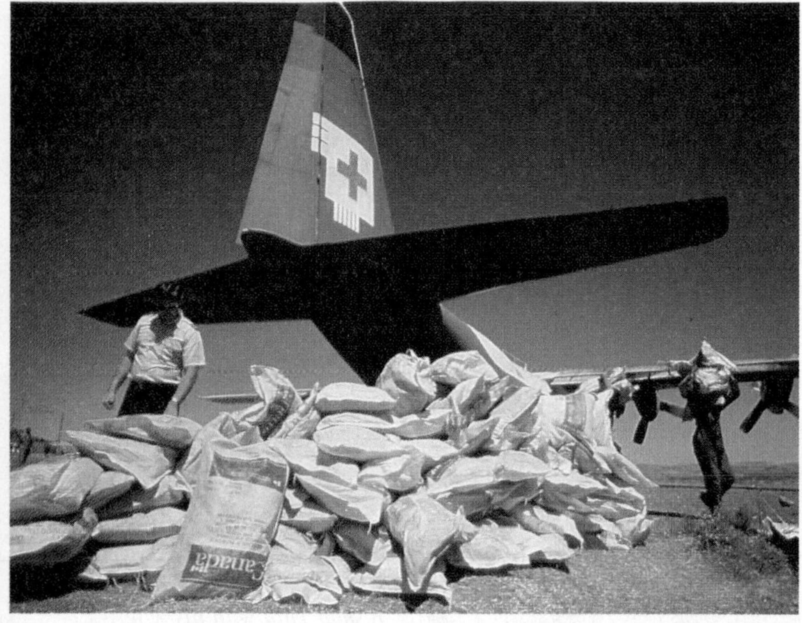

The Red Cross ferries food aid from Canada with all possible speed.

Nov 1. Attempts by Britain and other Western countries to airlift desperately needed food and medical supplies to Ethiopia are being frustrated by bureaucracy and mistrust in the country's capital, Addis Ababa.

As RAF transport aircraft stand-by to airlift wheat to the stricken country – in which at least 900,000 people are almost certainly doomed and the lives of six million others threatened – arguments continue about the choice of airports.

The Ethiopian government is urging the RAF to fly directly to the small runway at Assab or to the former French colony of Djibouti. British logistics experts have asked to fly to the airport at Addis Ababa, from where supplies can be flown to the famine areas or transported by lorry.

So far, only one British relief plane – chartered by a newspaper – has touched down with 20 tons of supplies. The horrific scale of the famine was revealed in a moving BBC television report by Michael Buerk. The sight of emaciated children clinging to parents close to death has brought an "unbelievable" response from the British public (→ 14/12).

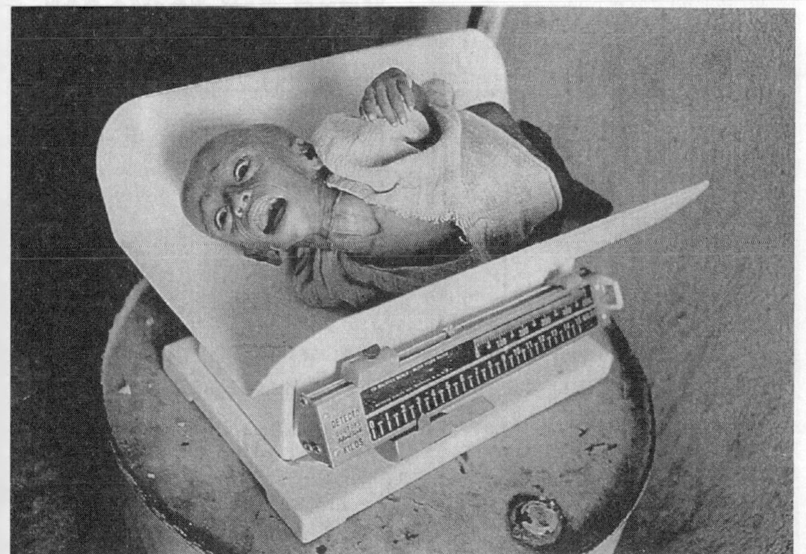

Aid may be too late for this two-year-old, weighing in at only 6.5 pounds.

Courts rule to sequestrate NUM assets

Nov 6. A Dublin High Court judge today froze £2.7 million of the funds of the National Union of Mineworkers. The order covered £8.7 million, but by the time the judge was reached on Sunday night £6 million had been transferred.

The court orders follow last month's High Court decision that the strike, now in its 35th week, was illegal. The NUM was fined £200,000 and its president, Arthur Scargill, £1,000. The judge gave the union 14 days to pay and threatened to seize their assets if they failed to pay in time.

The NUM contests the High Court decision. It maintains that the strike is fully in accordance with Rule 41. Although the miners' strike has not been universally popular in the trade union movement, there is considerable sympathy for the miners over the latest moves, which involve the courts determining how union rules shall be applied.

The Labour Party leader, Neil Kinnock, has called on the miners to respect the rule of law. "The only way to get power to change laws and right injustice for the people is to win elections to that power," he said. Today he declined to attend any rallies supporting the miners. Meanwhile, the Coal Board is claiming a "surge" back to work, with 55 of the 174 pits now working (→ 19).

Four policemen are alleged to have attacked this picket at Maltby.

India torn by riots as Rajiv takes power

Nov 4. Bloody riots swept across India today as Hindus took their revenge on Sikhs for the murder of Mrs Gandhi, who was herself killed in revenge for ordering the attack on the Sikhs' holiest shrine, the Golden Temple of Amritsar.

The riots took their customary form with innocents slaughtered in the most horrific fashions in the teeming city slums. Reports tell of whole families being butchered or burnt alive in their houses. Others, fleeing, have been hunted down and torn to pieces by mobs.

At least 1,000 people have died in the four days since Mrs Gandhi was murdered. Her son, Rajiv, the former airline pilot who succeeded her, has ordered the army into the cities to quell the violence.

Cynics say the bloodletting was inevitable and the people had to work off their anger. But the Sikhs are warriors and there is no doubt they will retaliate (→ 29/12).

Stalin's daughter goes home to Russia

Nov 2. Joseph Stalin's daughter, Svetlana Alliluyeva, has returned to the Soviet Union after 17 years in the West where she has been insisting she enjoyed a "perfectly free life." Miss Alliluyeva slipped out of Britain with her daughter Olga, aged 13, who had been going to a school in Essex.

She defected to the West in 1967 while taking her late husband's ashes to be buried in an Indian village. Her defection was seen as a considerable propaganda blow to the Soviet Union, and the Kremlin may now be in a position to recoup. While in the West she married, and subsequently divorced, an American businessman, and wrote two books about her experiences which were widely sold. She and her daughter had lost their Soviet citizenship which might now be restored.

Reagan romps to victory

Nov 6. President Reagan today won a stunning victory in the US presidential election. He beat his Democratic opponent, Walter Mondale, in all but one of the 50 states. Mr Reagan and Mr Bush won more than 59 per cent of the vote.

The President led in every major block of voters except blacks, Jews and trade unionists. The choice of Geraldine Ferraro, a Roman Catholic woman, made no difference to Mondale's fortune; Mr Reagan led among both women and Catholics.

Mrs Ferraro's impact on the result was hampered by the disclosure of her and her husband's financial problems. But it is doubtful whether any recent event could have altered the result.

With the improvement in the economy, President Reagan's popularity was enough to preserve Republican control of the Senate, but the Democrats still control the House of Representatives.

As Mr Reagan arrived to celebrate his victory in Los Angeles, supporters shouted his campaign slogan: "Four more years!" Mr Reagan said: "I think that's been arranged."

AIDS deaths after blood transfusions

Nov 18. Two people in Britain are now known to have died from AIDS after blood transfusions. In one case Terence McStay, a 33-year-old laboratory worker, received plasma from the US, which may have contained the AIDS virus, when he was treated for haemophilia at a hospital in Newcastle-upon-Tyne.

Blood donors will now be vetted more carefully and high-risk groups, like homosexuals and hard-drug addicts, rejected. Officials say imported blood should no longer be necessary in 12 months time. Meanwhile, methods of testing blood for AIDs are being investigated.

Gas inferno kills hundreds in Mexico

Nov 19. At least 260 people were killed and 500 others seriously hurt in Mexico City when a gas plant exploded today. Many of the dead were pulled from the rubble of a crowded supermarket.

Flames rose 300 feet above the processing plant and wooden shacks in nearby slum communities ignited. A thick black cloud hung over the Ecatepec industrial suburb several hours later. Television and radio stations put out appeals for blood, clothing and food.

Police said a series of explosions began when a lorry carrying cooking gas cylinders caught fire at the propane plant.

Frozen in death: this is one of two sailors found in the Arctic this year, perfectly preserved yet believed by Owen Beattie, professor of anthropology from the University of Alberta, to have been dead for 136 years.

1984

DECEMBER

Su	Mo	Tu	We	Th	Fr	Sa
						1
2	3	4	5	6	7	8
9	10	11	12	13	14	15
16	17	18	19	20	21	22
23	24	25	26	27	28	29
30	31					

3. London: Two Brinks-Mat robbers are jailed for 25 years each.

6. London: Roger de Grey is elected 21st President of the Royal Academy in succession to Sir Hugh Casson.

7. Sri Lanka: Over 100 people, mainly Tamils, are reported to have died earlier this week after a landmine ambush.

10. Stockholm: Nobel Prizes go to Carlo Rubbia (Italy) and Simon van der Meer (Holland), both Physics; Bruce Merrifield (US, Chemistry); Niels Jerne (Denmark), Georg Kohler (West Germany) and Cesar Milstein (UK), all Medicine; Jaroslav Seifert (Czechoslovakia, Literature); Sir Richard Stone (UK, Economics); and in Oslo to Bishop Desmond Tutu (South Africa, Peace).→

14. UK: Arthur Scargill is fined £250 with £750 costs for obstruction.

18. London: The Government announces the privatisation of the Trustee Savings Bank.

19. UK: Ted Hughes is appointed John Betjeman's successor as Poet Laureate.→

19. Beijing: Britain and China sign the treaty returning Hong Kong to China in 1997.

22. Malta: Dom Mintoff resigns as Prime Minister.

27. Poland: Four police officers go on trial for the murder of Father Popieluszko.

29. India: Rajiv Gandhi wins the general election by a landslide.

DEATH

28. US film director Sam Peckinpah (*21/2/1925).

HITS OF 1984

Do they know it's Christmas?

I just called to say I love you.

Two Tribes.

QUOTE OF THE YEAR

"You ain't seen nothing yet."

President Reagan, re-elected November 1984.

Bishop Tutu given Nobel Peace Prize

Bishop Tutu with his wife.

Dec 10. The Nobel Peace Prize ceremony was held up for 20 minutes in Oslo today after police received a bomb threat. When the all clear was given, Desmond Tutu, the Anglican Bishop of Johannesburg, received the prize for his non-violent struggle against apartheid.

"I have just got to believe God is around," he said. "If He is not, we in South Africa have had it." Later, he told a story going the rounds back home. When President P.W. Botha was told that Bishop Tutu had committed suicide, he answered: "Oh, I didn't know he'd been arrested."

Band Aid rocks for hungry Ethiopians

Dec 14. In an unprecedented example of co-operation, Britain's top rock stars have come together to help the starving refugees of Ethiopia, suffering both from famine and a bitter civil war.

Calling themselves Band Aid, the rock stars, who have all been enlisted by Boomtown Rats singer, Bob Geldof, have produced a single: "Do They Know It's Christmas?" which has already topped the charts.

Only Mrs Thatcher, who has refused to drop a possible VAT bill of £500,000, has proved immune to their charitable appeal.

Fatal gas leak at Bhopal

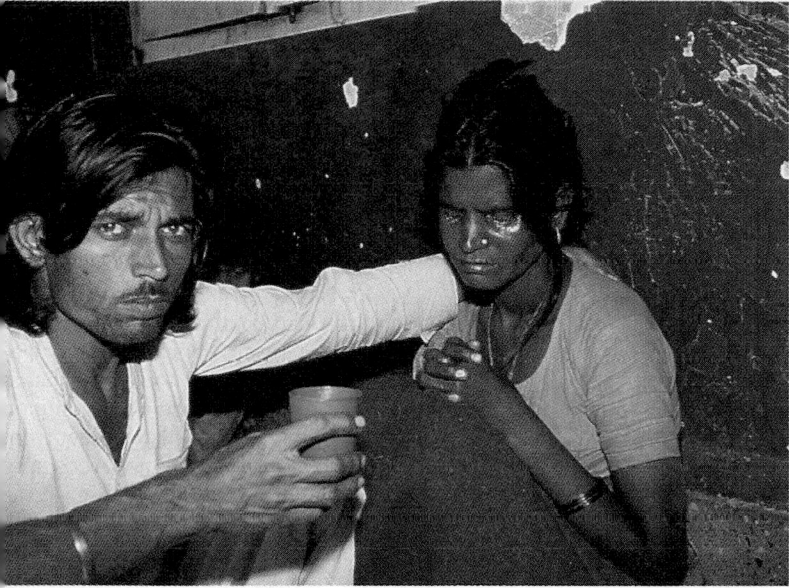

A survivor of the Bhopal disaster waits to find out if she can still see.

Dec 10. A leak from a chemical factory's storage tank has killed at least 2,000 people in the central Indian city of Bhopal. The foul-smelling methyl isocyanate gas which it released has affected a further 200,000; many have been blinded, many more are suffering from liver and kidney failure. Doctors believe that most will face long-term health effects.

The government has called for volunteers to fly to Bhopal to help the army and militia in the grim task of clearing bodies and dead animals from the streets. Ever since the disaster, the skies over Bhopal have glowed red from hundreds of funeral pyres.

As the Indian government declared Bhopal a disaster area, anger is mounting at the American Union Carbide company which runs the plant. A newspaper reported that at least four similar, but smaller, leaks had occurred at the Bhopal plant, which produces pesticides for Third World countries.

The company has pledged itself to treat compensation claims as it would do if the accident had happened in America.

Dec 16. At Chequers, Mikhail Gorbachev and his wife Raisa listen carefully to Mrs Thatcher. Mr Gorbachev is in England as the head of a 30-strong Soviet delegation on an eight-day fact-finding tour.

Arts: Poet Laureate is the violent type

The new Poet Laureate is **Ted Hughes**, bard of the savagery of nature rather than of its beauty – of hawks diving to the kill, thrushes stabbing worms, tomcats biting heads off chickens, pikes devouring each other, and of men dying in battle.

His first volume of verse, "The Hawk in the Rain" was an instant success in 1957. His poetry celebrates power and violence. "What excites my imagination is the war between vitality and death," he explains. It will be interesting to see what he makes of the task of getting excited by state occasions.

Hughes is a carpenter's son from the Bronte country. He was married to **Sylvia Plath**, the poet who committed suicide in 1963.

Theatrical excitement at Stratford – the RSC has discovered a new Richard III in **Anthony Sher**, who does not pale in comparison with memories of **Laurence Olivier**. He plays the king on arm-crutches, calling up Shakespeare's image of a "bottled spider", free of its bottle and scuttling around the stage.

The National Theatre's reply is the charismatic **Ian McKellen** as Coriolanus and a revival of their hit production of **Frank Loesser's** classic musical "Guys and Dolls".

With the arrival of 1984, **George Orwell's** prophetic novel was filmed for the second time, with **Richard Burton** as the inquisitor. **Albert Finney** dominated the screen in two bravura parts: the alcoholic hero of alcoholic author **Malcolm Lowry's** "Under the Volcano"; and in "The Dresser" as a touring actor-manager of the old school just managing to give his last performance of King Lear. The original play was by **Ronald Harwood**, himself once dresser to **Sir Donald Wolfit**.

Elfin eccentric Michael Jackson helps the forces of law and order.

Television honours went to "The Jewel in the Crown", the lavish Granada series adapted from **Paul Scott's** "Raj Quartet" – another triumph for **Peggy Ashcroft** and for newcomer **Tim Pigott-Smith.**

The Rock phenomenon **Michael Jackson** this year brought out "Thriller", which broke all records for records, with sales topping 37 million. Jackson is aged 26.

Tom Hulce plays the composer Mozart in Milos Forman's film of Peter Shaffer's play "Amadeus". No prizes for guessing who wrote the score.

1985

JANUARY

Su	Mo	Tu	We	Th	Fr	Sa
		1	2	3	4	5
6	7	8	9	10	11	12
13	14	15	16	17	18	19
20	21	22	23	24	25	26
27	28	29	30	31		

2. Washington: The US officially withdraws from UNESCO (→ 5/12).

4. UK: P&O sells its Channel car ferry fleet to European Ferries (Townsend Thoresen).

7. UK: Nine striking miners are jailed for arson (→ 25/2).

8. Washington: Reagan names Donald Regan as White House Chief of Staff.

10. London: Eight die when a gas explosion wrecks a block of flats in Putney, south London, early this morning.

14. UK: Emergency government action to halt the slide in the pound fails; it closes at a new low of $1.1105 (→ 18).

15. Brazil: Tancredo de Almeida Neves is elected Brazil's first civilian President in 21 years (→ 21/4).

16. London: The Dorchester Hotel is bought by the Sultan of Brunei.

18. London: The Financial Times-Stock Exchange share index breaks through 1,000 points for the first time (→ 11/2).

23. Manila: Army Chief of Staff General Fabian Ver is among 26 charged with murdering Benigno Aquino (→ 1/2).

24. New York: A jury clears "Time" magazine of libelling former Israeli Defence Minister Ariel Sharon (→ 8/3).

26. Venezuela: Pope John Paul II begins a 12-day visit to South America (→ 27/5).

29. Oxford: University dons refuse to grant Mrs Thatcher an honorary degree (→ 18/7/87).

31. Finland: Finnish divers hoist a strayed Soviet missile from Lake Inari (→ 5/2).

DEATHS

16. German-born British philanthropist and musician Sir Robert Mayer (*5/6/1879).

26. British journalist and author Mark James Walter Cameron (*17/6/1911).

26. British diplomat and broadcaster William David Ormsby Gore, 5th Baron Harlech (*20/5/1918).

Court order is lifted on surrogate baby

Jan 12. One-week-old Baby Cotton, the child at the centre of the surrogate birth row, was flown to America today with the couple who want to be her parents. The move came after a High Court judge ruled they were the best people to look after her.

The couple, professionals in their thirties, paid £14,000 to an agency, and Mrs Kim Cotton, a 28-year-old mother of two, was artificially inseminated with the man's sperm. The case highlighted public concern over such deals, and Barnet Council in North London issued a place of safety order when the baby was born eight days ago. Six months ago the Warnock committee recommended the banning of commercial surrogacy (→ 31/3/87).

The surrogate mother Kim Cotton.

Israel halts airlift of Ethiopian Jews

Jan 3. Thousands of Falashas, black Jews of a tribe which for centuries lived in Ethiopia, have been flown in secret to Israel. Most of the 25,000, reputed to be descendants of the lost tribe of Dan, were rescued from a country now threatened by famine. News of the covert rescue was disclosed today as the Jewish Agency announced that the airlift had been halted.

As a result of leaks in the US, Israel was forced to admit that a covert operation had been going on for years. Rescue planes flew from Sudan which does not recognise Israel. There was indignation in the Arab world when the fact of Sudanese co-operation emerged.

Sinclair takes himself for a ride on his C5

Sir Clive Sinclair riding in his C5.

Jan 10. The electronics genius Sir Clive Sinclair unveiled his answer to Britain's traffic problems today – a low-slung, lightweight, single-seat, 31-inch high, battery and pedal-powered tricycle called the C5. It has a range of 20 miles before recharging and will cost £399. Sir Clive predicted that by the end of the century "the petrol engine will be seen as a thing of the past".

Motoring correspondents were notably less enthusiastic, however. One described it as a "fun-machine that can hardly be regarded as serious, everyday, all-weather transport" (→ 29/3).

Major rail disaster kills 390 in Africa

Jan 13. In the third worst rail disaster ever, and the worst in Africa, 390 people were killed and 370 injured as an Ethiopian train bound for Addis Ababa fell into a ravine.

The engineer, who has been arrested, apparently failed to slow down as the train rounded a curve on a bridge 35 feet up. The rear car derailed first, crashing through a guard rail and pulling the rest of the train with it. The damage to the track has severed a vital link between Addis Ababa and the port of Djibouti.

Gun charge only for subway vigilante

Jan 25. Bernhard Goetz, who has admitted shooting four black youths on the New York subway, is to face illegal weapon charges only, a grand jury decided today. The prosecution intends to press on for attempted murder charges.

Goetz claims he acted in self-defence after being threatened by the youths. Goetz is a hero for many New Yorkers sick of being intimidated by muggers; his action echoed movies such as "Death Wish". Others regard him as a dangerous criminal whose action shows his racial prejudice (→ 17/6/87).

The arctic weather puts the beach at Nice under a blanket of snow.

1985

FEBRUARY

Su	Mo	Tu	We	Th	Fr	Sa
					1	2
3	4	5	6	7	8	9
10	11	12	13	14	15	16
17	18	19	20	21	22	23
24	25	26	27	28		

1. Paris: 13 nations and the World Bank set up a fund for Africa (→ 7/7).

1. Manila: The alleged murderers of Aquino go on trial (→ 11/11).

5. UK: 200 protesters are evicted from outside a Cruise missile base at Molesworth in Cambridgeshire (→ 1/3).

7. Poland: Four police officers are jailed for the murder of Father Popielusko (→ 1/5).

10. UK: Nine die in a multiple crash on the M6.

11. UK: The pound falls below $1.10.→

11. West Germany: 17 RAF bandsmen are among 19 killed when their bus collides with a petrol tanker near Munich.

12. London: The leader of an Israeli gang which bungled the kidnapping of Nigerian Umari Dikko is jailed for 14 years.

14. London: Clive Ponting is told that despite his acquittal he can never work for the MoD again (→ 16).

14. London: Doctors must not give contraceptive advice to girls under 16 (→ 20).

16. London: Ponting resigns from the MoD (→ 24/10).

19. Spain: 150 die when an Iberia Airlines Boeing 727 crashes near Bilbao.

19. Dublin: The Dail passes an emergency bill to allow the seizure of up to £5 million of IRA assets (→ 20).

20. Washington: Thatcher tells Congress she supports "Star Wars" and appeals for Americans to end aid to the IRA (→ 28).

20. Dublin: The Dail passes a bill to legalise shop sales of contraceptives (→ 17/10).

25. UK: 3,807 miners go back to work; only 51 per cent are still on strike (→ 3/3).

26. London: Michael Fairley, the hooded rapist known as the Fox, is given six life sentences.

28. Northern Ireland: Nine RUC men are killed in an IRA mortar attack on a police station in Newry (→ 7/3).

South African police clash with squatters

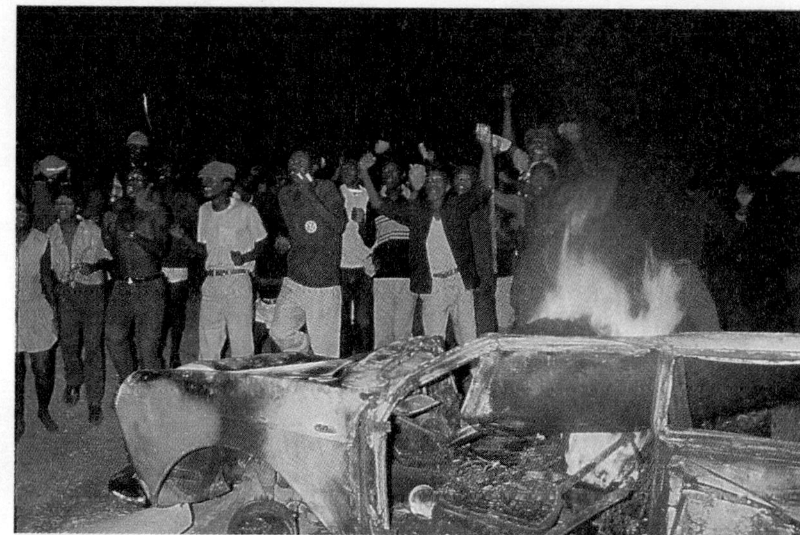

A burning car lights up the faces of South African squatters at barricades.

Feb 18. At least eight people have been killed and several hundred hurt in clashes between police and black squatters in the windswept Cape Flats district north of Cape Town. The authorities are trying to move some 100,000 squatters to the Kayelitsha new township further from the city.

The squatters, many of whom come from the distant Transkei and Ciskei tribal homelands, refuse to budge. Attempts to move them have led to demonstrations, with squatters setting up barricades and burning car tyres. Police retaliate with rubber bullets and tear gas. Rival gangs of skollies (hoodlums), known as Witdoeke (vigilantes) and Comrades, take advantage of the disorder to fight running battles among the shanties, shooting, burning and looting. Social workers claim police are encouraging the vigilantes in order force the squatters to move (→ 21/3).

Pound falls to its lowest value ever

Feb 22. The one-dollar pound came closer today, as sterling fell in London to a record low of $1.0765. Last month's emergency rise of four and a half points in base interest rates to 14 per cent has not yet stopped the slide, which has devalued the pound by 27 per cent in the last year.

Gibraltar siege is ended by Spanish

Feb 4. A Spanish police officer unlocked a pair of green iron gates at the border between Spain and Gibraltar tonight, and so ended the 16-year siege imposed on "the Rock" by General Franco in a vain effort to force Britain and the unwilling population of Gibraltar to transfer sovereignty to Spain.

Tempers flare as chess match is called off

Feb 15. The hard-fought world chess championship ended in chaos in Moscow tonight with the champion and his challenger glowering at each other with undisguised fury. The International Chess Federation abandoned the five-month series on the grounds that it "had exhausted the physical, if not the psychological resources, not only of the participants but of all those connected with the match". The champion, Anatoly Karpov, angrily denied reports that he was close to a breakdown while the challenger, Gary Kasparov, claimed that he was being deprived of victory.

Observers believe that the Soviet Chess Federation may have influenced the decision. Karpov is a favourite of the chess establishment.

Terry Waite frees Britons from Libya

Feb 5. Terry Waite, the special representative of the Archbishop of Canterbury, has won the freedom of four Britons held hostage by the Libyan government for nearly nine months. The Libyan Foreign Minister today assured Mr Waite, a gentle giant of a man, that the four men will be released tomorrow at a ceremony to mark the opening of the General People's Congress which will be addressed by Mr Waite.

At her home in Suffolk tonight, Mrs Carol Russell, wife of one of the men, said: "Thank God for the Church and Terry Waite. They showed they cared – unlike the Foreign Office."

Jury rejects judge and clears Ponting

Feb 11. Clive Ponting, the senior civil servant accused of breaking the Official Secrets Act by giving information about the Falklands War to an MP, was acquitted today at the Old Bailey. He had argued that he acted out of "his duty to the interests of the state". The judge had said that a civil servant owed his duty to the Government. The jury rejected this view, to the surprise of the Government which now faces a parliamentary row (→ 14).

Clive Ponting freed in secrets case.

1985

MARCH

Su	Mo	Tu	We	Th	Fr	Sa
					1	2
3	4	5	6	7	8	9
10	11	12	13	14	15	16
17	18	19	20	21	22	23
24	25	26	27	28	29	30
31						

1. Washington: The Pentagon accepts the theory that nuclear war would lead to years of "nuclear winter" (→ 7/4).

7. London: Two IRA men are jailed for 35 years for planning the month-long IRA bombing campaign in London in 1981 (→ 24/6).

8. Beirut: A massive car bomb kills 62 people (→ 10).

10. Moscow: Chernenko dies.→

10. Lebanon: 12 Israeli soldiers die when a terrorist drives a lorry full of explosives into a troop column (→ 17/4).

11. London: The Government announces a rise in prescription charges of 40p to £2.

11. London: The Egyptian Al-Fayed brothers win control of House of Fraser, owners of Harrods (→ 9/4/87).

13. Moscow: Chernenko is buried in Red Square (→ 2/7).

17. Washington: Reagan agrees to a joint US-Canadian study of acid rain.

21. S. Africa: Riot police shoot dead 17 blacks at Langa township on the 25th anniversary of Sharpeville (→ 15/4).

23. UK: Three-year-old Ben Hardwick, Britain's youngest liver transplant patient, dies.

26. US: Milos Forman's film "Amadeus" wins eight Oscars; actor Ben Kingsley wins one for "Gandhi".

28. London: The bill to scrap the GLC and Metropolitan counties passes its final Commons stages (→ 16/7).

29. UK: Production of the Sinclair C5 electric tricycle is suspended (→ 14/10).

30. UK: The Duchess of Westminster's Last Suspect wins the Grand National.

DEATHS

10. Soviet statesman Konstantin Chernenko, leader 1984-85 (*24/9/1911).

21. British actor Sir Michael Scudamore Redgrave (*20/3/1908).

28. Russian-born French painter Marc Chagall (*7/7/1887).

Mikhail Gorbachev is new Soviet leader

Mikhail Gorbachev, the new leader of the Soviet Union with his wife, Raisa.

March 11. Mikhail Gorbachev attained supreme power in the Soviet Union today, becoming head of the Communist Party on the death of Konstantin Chernenko. Gorbachev, at 54, is the youngest member of the ruling Politburo and is seen as a potential reformer. In his first official pronouncement he praised detente with the West and called for a reduction in arms stockpiles.

Gorbachev was named as party general secretary four hours after the announcement of the death of Chernenko, who was 73 years old and had been leader for only 13 months. He had been regarded as the heir apparent for some time, and is being seen as an unusually welleducated and open-minded Kremlin leader with an interest in moderation and reform.

Gorbachev is young enough to lead the Soviet Union into the 21st century, and provide continuity badly needed after the deaths of three leaders – Brezhnev, Andropov, and now Chernenko – since 1982. He began working life driving a harvester in his native North Caucasus, but by 1955 had graduated in law from Moscow University. He became a Communist party organiser and rose swiftly (→ 13).

AIDS screening for UK blood donors

March 15. Britain's two million blood donors are to be tested for the AIDS virus under a new scheme announced yesterday. In future, no blood donation will be used unless it has been screened, which should end public fears of catching the killer virus from transfusions. The tests, which have only now become available, cost only around £2 a head to carry out, which health authorities will be expected to meet from existing resources as the Government is not putting up extra cash, says Health Minister Kenneth Clarke. A total of 132 people in Britain had AIDS at the end of 1984, compared to four reported cases in 1981 (→ 11/4).

Iran and Iraq both claim to have won

March 18. Iraq and Iran are both claiming victory in the biggest battles yet fought in the Gulf war. The fighting erupted six days ago with a carefully planned Iranian offensive north of Basra. The Iranians say they have broken the Iraqi lines, and the Iraqis admit that at one stage Revolutionary Guards threatened the road to Baghdad, but now, they claim, the "invaders have been annihilated" (→ 19/2/86).

Shouts of "scab" greet miners' union vote to end national strike

March 3. There were scenes of fury and anguish outside the headquarters of the Trades Union Congress as the National Union of Mineworkers decided to call off the year-long national strike. Shouts of "scum, scabs, traitors" greeted the delegates, who voted 98 to 91 to return to work on Tuesday. They agreed to go back without an amnesty for those miners dismissed during the dispute.

In effect the strike was broken before today's meeting. There has been a steady trickle of miners back to work over the last few months. The Prime Minister, Mrs Thatcher, claims "a famous victory", but the NUM President, Arthur Scargill, was last night denying it was a defeat for him (→ 26/5).

A Kent miner returns to work under the watchful eye of the police.

1985

APRIL

Su	Mo	Tu	We	Th	Fr	Sa
	1	2	3	4	5	6
7	8	9	10	11	12	13
14	15	16	17	18	19	20
21	22	23	24	25	26	27
28	29	30				

1. London: The Government plans to ban alcohol from "problem" football grounds in England and Wales (→ 11/5).

7. China: The Chinese are bemused by the pop duo Wham!, who arrive to give two concerts.

7. Moscow: Gorbachev announces a 10-month freeze in deployment of medium-range missiles aimed at Europe (→ 19/11).

11. UK: An 18-month-old boy becomes the first British baby to die of AIDS (→ 25/7).

14. Tirana: Ramiz Alia is chosen to succeed Hoxha as Albanian leader.

15. S. Africa: The government says it will end the ban on mixed marriages (→ 15/6).

21. London: Britain's Steve Jones wins the men's London Marathon; Ingrid Kristiansen wins the women's race.

21. Brazil: President-elect Neves dies on the eve of his inauguration as Brazil's first civilian President since 1964.

22. UK: Nissan negotiates a single-union deal with the engineering union AUEW at its new Washington plant.

24. Washington: The House of Representatives rejects Reagan's request for aid to the Contra rebels in Nicaragua (→ 30).

27. London: The only short story Lord Byron is known to have written is discovered by his publishers, John Murray.

28. UK: Denis Taylor wins the Embassy world snooker championship.

29. London: The Government announces a computerised screening programme in a bid to cut cervical cancer deaths.

30. Washington: Reagan tells Congress he plans a total trade embargo on the Sandinista regime in Nicaragua (→ 27/6/86).

DEATH

11. Albanian leader Enver Hoxha, head of state 1944-85 (*16/10/1908).

Lebanese cabinet falls after Beirut battle

A fighter in West Beirut remains defiant in the midst of devastation.

April 17. Lebanon plunged into a new crisis today when the Prime Minister Rashid Karami, a Sunni Moslem, resigned following the victory of the Shia Moslems, led by the Justice Minister Nabih Berri, in a bloody battle for control of west Beirut.

The battle, which lasted for more than 15 hours and left at least 20 dead and 150 wounded, toppled the Sunnis from their traditional position as leaders of the Moslem community and demonstrated that the Shias, once the underdogs in Lebanon, have become a force to be reckoned with. Karami's government of National Unity, formed a year ago, never really exercised control over the country, but it was a forum in which the leaders of rival factions could meet to discuss their differences. Now even that fragile arrangement has disappeared.

Mr Karami has agreed to stay on as head of a caretaker team at the request of the Christian President, Amin Gemayel, but political sources say it is now up to Syria, the power broker in the Lebanon, to intervene to bring some sort of order to the chaos in Beirut (→ 22/5).

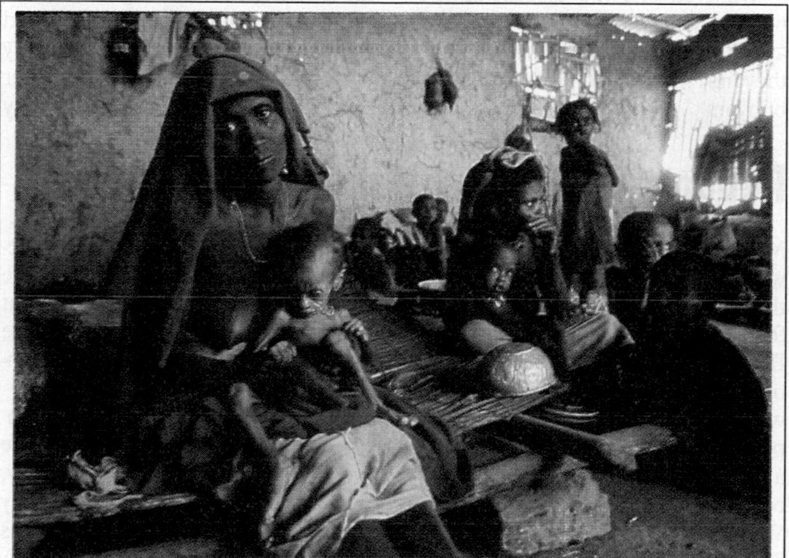

A starving Ethiopian mother waits listlessly in a makeshift refugee camp for some food so that she can feed herself and her poorly nourished child.

Murdoch becomes a Hollywood mogul

April 8. Rupert Murdoch, whose multi-national media empire spans Britain, America and Australia, has now added to newspapers and television a Hollywood studio, the one prize that has hitherto eluded him.

Today's purchase of 50 per cent of the loss-making Twentieth Century-Fox Film Corporation cost Murdoch £209 million, but it marks another stage in the growth of Mr Murdoch's global empire with interests in newspapers, magazines and television. Next comes satellite broadcasting in which owning rights to films could be crucial (→ 23/9).

Black Britons move into a few top jobs

April 30. The recent appointment of Britain's first black council leader, Bernie Grant, and first black bishop, Wilfred Wood, gives some hope to those who fear that racial origin impedes professional progress in this country.

Guyana-born Mr Grant, aged 41, who took up office at the Labour-controlled London Borough of Haringey ten days ago, originally came to England in 1963 as a mining student. The Venerable Wilfred Wood, aged 49, Archdeacon of Southwark since 1982, was born in Barbados and moved to London in 1962, where he was ordained priest in St. Paul's Cathedral. He will be consecrated Bishop of Croydon. Though there have been black Anglican bishops before, they have all served overseas.

Coke: variations on the Real Thing

April 23. Coke is it. Or is it? America's cool customers are to be offered a new formula for their favourite soft drink which will hit local stores next month. "New Coke" will look the same, but will it taste the same? If it is new, can it still be The Real Thing? Many, including jubilant rivals Pepsi, are convinced New Coke will fall flat, despite all the advertising hype.

1985

MAY

Su	Mo	Tu	We	Th	Fr	Sa
			1	2	3	4
5	6	7	8	9	10	11
12	13	14	15	16	17	18
19	20	21	22	23	24	25
26	27	28	29	30	31	

1. Gdansk: 10,000 Solidarity supporters clash with police during a May Day march (→31/5/86).

2. UK: The Liberal-SDP Alliance makes big gains in local council elections.

8. Strasbourg: Reagan speaks to the European Parliament on the 40th anniversary of the end of the War in Europe.

10. India: 59 die and 150 are hurt in attacks by Sikh extremists (→23/6).

11. Birmingham: A man is killed during violent clashes at a Birmingham City-Leeds United football match.→

13. Philadelphia: 11 die and 200 are made homeless in a fire started when police bomb a house occupied by gunmen.

16. London: Home Secretary Brittan announces new police and court powers to combat picket line and mob violence.

16. UK: Two South Wales miners are jailed for life for the murder of taxi driver David Wilkie (→3/10).

17. Japan: 62 miners die in a firedamp explosion at Yubari in northern Japan.

18. London: Manchester United beat Everton 1-0 to win the FA Cup Final.

22. Lebanon: A car bomb kills over 50 people in Christian East Beirut.→

26. Spain: At least 34 die when two oil tankers explode at the port of San Roque.

27. Rome: Eight men accused of trying to kill the Pope go on trial (→18/6).

28. Strasbourg: The European Human Rights Court finds Britain guilty of sex discrimination in its immigration policy (→2/7).

30. Brussels: British soccer teams are banned from Belgium after the Heysel tragedy, in which 38 died (→31).

31. London: The FA bans English clubs from playing in Europe next season (→2/6).

31. Bangladesh: The death toll from the cyclone is now put at 10,000.

Soccer fans die in Bradford inferno

The crowd is transfixed in horror as a stand at the Bradford football ground turns into a blazing inferno.

May 11. Fire swept through the packed main stand of Bradford City football ground today, killing over 40 soccer fans. Many deaths are thought to have been caused by crushing and trampling as spectators rushed for safety. More than 150 people were taken to hospital with burns, cuts and bruises.

What caused the disastrous fire nobody yet knows, but it spread at appalling speed half-way through the first half. The crowd was in buoyant mood for the match against Lincoln City as the home team was celebrating promotion to the Second Division. Then flames started to appear and billowed quickly through the wooden stand, driven by strong winds.

"In a matter of seconds, flames appeared, and seconds after that the whole of the roof at the back of the stand was well alight and the stand was engulfed in flames," said Police Superintendent Barry Osborne. A Bradford supporter said: "The smoke was absolutely choking, you couldn't breathe."

The heat was so intense that hair and clothes caught fire. Blazing rafters from the roof crashed down on the fans as they ran onto the pitch to escape the flames. Many of those killed were elderly or very young spectators trampled by more able-bodied fans.

Fans later expressed concern that the exit gates and turnstiles at the back of the stand were padlocked. The gates were smashed down, but the delay claimed many lives.

Reagan's cemetery visits anger US Jews

May 5. President Reagan made what he called "a painful walk into the past" today, when he visited the former Nazi concentration camp at Belsen and then went on to the Bitburg war cemetery, where he laid a wreath. It was the second visit that provoked controversy, in Germany and at home, because the cemetery contains the graves of 49 SS men. When Mr Reagan arrived at the US base near Bitburg he was met by protesting Jews.

He acknowledged that with his visit to the cemetery he had risked re-opening old wounds. "This I regret very much," he said, "because this should be a time of healing. But from the terrors of the past we have built 40 years of peace and reconciliation."

At Belsen, where 50,000 prisoners died, Mr Reagan, with his wife Nancy beside him, said: "Today, we have been grimly reminded why the commandant of this camp was named "The Beast of Belsen". Above all we are struck by the monstrous incomprehensible horror of it all."

Legionnaire's lung infection kills 31

May 10. Over 30 people have died in Staffordshire as a result of Legionnaire's disease, a lung infection which was named after an outbreak at a 1976 American Legion convention. Now the victims are out-patients attending the Stafford District General Hospital and the cause appears to be germs spread from the hospital's cooling towers. In the last month 132 people have been admitted for treatment, of whom 31 have died.

Beirut camps undergo fresh assaults

May 25. Hundreds of men, women and children have died in a ferocious assault upon the Palestinian strongholds in Beirut by Syrian-backed Shi'ite militiamen. The battle for control of the Chatila and Sabra camps began when Amal, the Shi'ite private army, swarmed in to disarm Palestinian fighters. The camps, which were the scene of a massacre inflicted by Christian Lebanese militia during the Israeli invasion three years ago, are located in south Beirut.

Today bearded Amal irregulars, equipped with AK-47 assault rifles, fought it out in the back streets of the shanty towns, overwhelming the PLO defenders, desperate to protect their families, while Red Cross ambulances were refused entry. Even by Lebanese standards the battles are exceptionally vicious and bloody.

Nabih Berri, commander of the Amal forces, blames Yassir Arafat for attempting to re-build the power-base in Beirut he lost last year by pumping in money and key men. Simultaneously, however, he is now moving towards peace negotiations with Israel, a process bitterly opposed by Syria and PLO defectors of the National Liberation Front.

To counteract these schemes the Syrian President, Hafez el Assad, organised an all-out attack on the camps. Using his Amal allies in the assault he hopes to break Palestinian power there once and for all and to establish Syrian rule. The Shi'ite offensive is the most cynical of Syria's actions in Lebanon (→ 7/6).

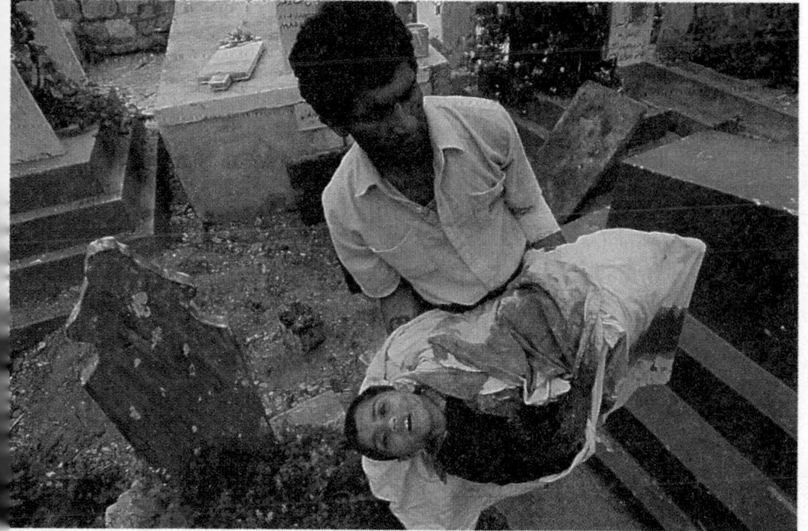

A man cradles the body of a young PLO fighter killed in the camp massacre.

Soccer rampage kills 41

Spectators are crushed as Liverpool fans riot at Heysel Stadium, Brussels.

May 29. British football hooliganism reached a hideous climax in a Belgian stadium tonight, when Liverpool fans went on a rampage which left 41 Italian and Belgian supporters dead and at least 350 injured. Disaster came when a wall and safety fence collapsed as British fans charged towards supporters of the Juventus team after a running battle in the stands at the Heysel Stadium in Brussels, scene of the European Cup Final.

Many victims were trampled to death; many more were crushed by the weight of their fellow supporters. Even as police and ambulance men struggled to revive victims the fighting continued, with flagpoles and metal bars used as weapons; bottles, cans and pieces of concrete were hurled through the air.

As a priest gave the last rites in a car park carpeted with bodies, riot-police on horse-back rode to the ground to separate the fighting fans.

For many Europeans, shocked over the years by mounting violence by flag-waving British hooligans, Britain's reputation has reached its nadir. Many politicians believe that the Heysel disaster will see British football teams banned from the continent.

In London, the Prime Minister, Margaret Thatcher, said that those responsible had brought "shame and dishonour" to the community and football (→ 30).

BBC's king of the castaways is dead

May 30. The ever-courteous host of 1,790 castaways on the radio programme "Desert Island Discs", Roy Plomley, died suddenly yesterday. Listeners learned with surprise that he was aged 71. He and his programme, which he devised, had been a regular fixture since 1941. No other BBC programme has run as long with the same presenter.

The simple formula, of asking a guest to choose eight records, one book, and one luxury, appealed to all. Princess Margaret and Mrs Thatcher had both been castaways.

Tidal wave and cyclone batter Bangladesh

May 28. Thousands of bodies are floating in the Bay of Bengal following the cyclone and tidal wave which battered the coast of Bangladesh three days ago. It is still difficult to estimate the full extent of the disaster because so much of the low-lying land is under water, and some of the coastal islands have been swept away, along with the inhabitants and their livestock.

So far 3,000 bodies have been recovered, and unofficial estimates say that as many as 40,000 people have died. At least 12,000 people are missing from the seven islands hit by the full force of the 45-foot tidal wave which came raging in from the sea, destroying everything in its path.

President Ershad, who has cancelled a visit to China, described the disaster as the "worst tragedy in Bangladesh's history". He has put the armed forces on war footing to mount the rescue operation. Helicopters are dropping food and drinking water to survivors, and naval ships are battling through heavy seas to reach cut-off islands.

One report said survivors on bamboo rafts and floating rooftops were being stalked by sharks and crocodiles (→ 31).

Bruce Springsteen, "the Boss" of rock and roll, touring Europe.

1985

JUNE

Su	Mo	Tu	We	Th	Fr	Sa
						1
2	3	4	5	6	7	8
9	10	11	12	13	14	15
16	17	18	19	20	21	22
23	24	25	26	27	28	29
30						

1. UK: Police arrest 300 members of a "Peace Convoy" heading for Stonehenge for midsummer.

2. Switzerland: UEFA bans English clubs from playing in Europe "indefinitely" (→16/1/86).

5. UK: Lord Howard de Walden's Slip Anchor wins the Derby.

6. Brazil: A skeleton, allegedly that of the notorious Auschwitz doctor Josef Mengele, is exhumed.→

7. Lebanon: Israeli-backed militiamen seize 21 Finnish troops of the UN peacekeeping force (→14).

8. UK: Barry McGuigan beats Panamanian Eusebio Pedroza to win the WBA featherweight boxing championship.

9. Sri Lanka: Over 100 Tamils are reported to have been killed in the past week by security forces (→3/5/86).

11. Israel: 21 die, most of them children, when their bus is hit by a train between Tel Aviv and Haifa.

14. Beirut: Gunmen hijack a TWA airliner after taking off from Athens and demand the release of over 700 prisoners in Israel (→19).

15. S. Africa: The country's first mixed marriage is celebrated (→21/7).

18. Rome: Mehmet Ali Agca denies making a deal to implicate the USSR in the plot to kill the Pope (→8/8).

19. Beirut: A car bomb explodes in the city centre, killing 52.→

24. UK: Keith Castle, Britain's longest surviving heart transplant patient, dies six years after receiving his heart (→17/12/86).

29. London: Patrick Magee is charged with the murder of the people who died in the Brighton bomb last October (→30/7).

DEATH

2. British statesman George Alfred Brown, Baron George-Brown of Jevington (*2/9/1914).

Terrorists stage new wave of attacks

Shi'ite hijackers meet the press outside the plane they held for 16 days.

Beirut: TWA hostages freed after 16 days

June 30. The 16-day ordeal of the 39 Americans held hostage by Shia terrorists who hijacked a TWA airliner to Beirut ended today with roses and carnations being given to the hostages by their captors as they were freed. The tired, relieved Americans were driven in a Red Cross convoy to Damascus before flying to a US base in West Germany for an emotional reunion with their families.

The details of the arrangements for their release remain unclear, but while both the United States and Israel insist that they have done no deal with the terrorists, Israel will tomorrow release the 700 Lebanese Shias whose freedom was demanded by the hijackers.

President Reagan left no doubt about his attitude towards the terrorists, who brutally murdered a young US sailor during the hijacking. Waiting until after the hostages had been freed, he said: "We will not rest until justice has been done. Terrorists be on notice. We will fight back against you in Lebanon and elsewhere" (→17/8).

Venice: EEC plans war on terrorists

June 28. Mrs Thatcher, in her sternest mood, today led the heads of the ten Common Market governments into war against terrorism.

At the start of the EEC meeting in Milan she told them that much more impetus should be put behind agreements providing for the boycotting of airports that fail to meet security standards, and that people convicted of terrorist crimes should be barred from EEC nations. The ease with which the terrorists boarded the TWA airliner at Athens was clearly in her mind.

London: IRA plan seaside bombings

June 24. An IRA campaign to bring terror to Britain's holiday resorts this summer has been foiled. Anti-terrorist Branch detectives are questioning 12 people, following a raid on a Glasgow tenement in which they found a list of places where bombs with long-delay timing devices were to be planted to explode at the height of the holiday season. One bomb on the list, at the Rubens Hotel near Buckingham Palace, has been found (→29).

Irish Sea: mystery bomb kills 325 as Air India jumbo crashes

June 23. A terrorist bomb is believed to have caused the destruction of an Air India Boeing 747 flying from Canada which plunged into the sea about 120 miles off Ireland at 8.15 this morning. All 325 people on board are feared dead.

Disaster came so suddenly that the pilot had no time to send out a Mayday signal. The jumbo simply disappeared off the radar. By nightfall 130 bodies had been recovered from the wreckage-littered sea which one searcher described as "a floating graveyard".

It is suspected that Sikh extremists are responsible, and the disaster is being linked to an explosion among baggage from Canada at Japan's Narita airport (→10/7).

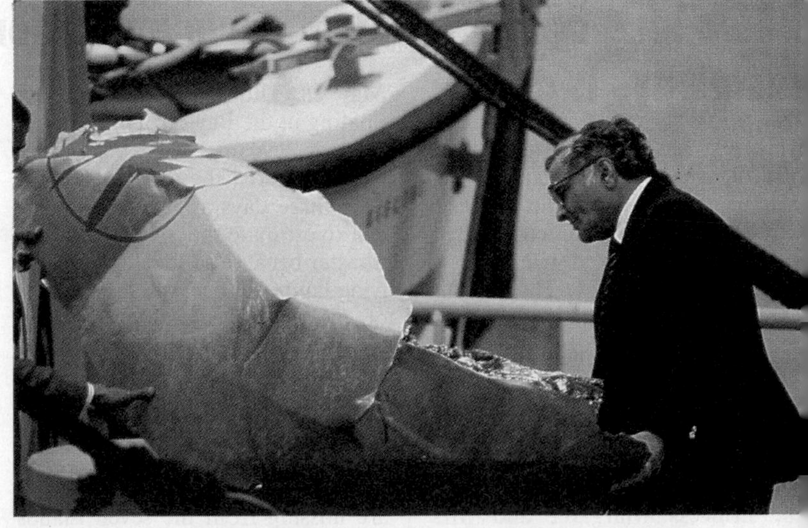

A section of the wreckage of the Air India plane that exploded in mid-air.

"Angel of Death's" corpse is identified

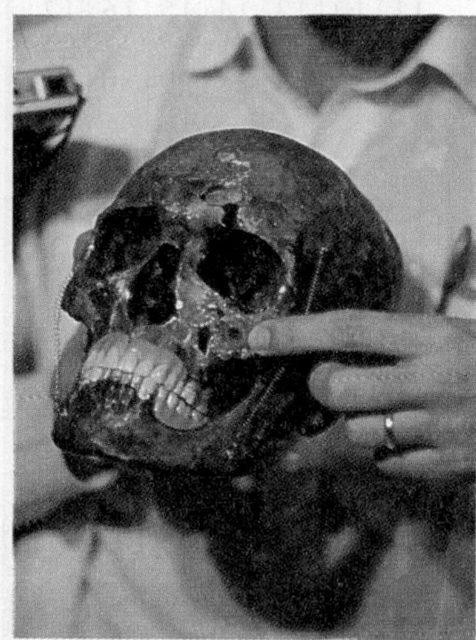

The exhumed skull of Mengele.

June 21. The 40-year hunt for Josef Mengele, the Auschwitz "Angel of Death", believed to have been responsible for 400,000 deaths by torture in Nazi concentration camps, came to an end today when investigators from the US, West Germany and Brazil said they were 99 per cent certain they had identified his body. Three weeks ago, Brazilian police opened a grave outside Sao Paulo, smashed open a coffin and removed bones and shreds of clothing. He apparently died in a swimming accident six years ago when he was 67. Police said an Austrian couple had admitted sheltering Mengele (→ 8/7).

A jubilant Barry McGuigan just after he has beaten Panamanian Eusebio Pedroza for the WBA world featherweight boxing title.

1985

JULY

Su	Mo	Tu	We	Th	Fr	Sa
	1	2	3	4	5	6
7	8	9	10	11	12	13
14	15	16	17	18	19	20
21	22	23	24	25	26	27
28	29	30	31			

2. Moscow: Eduard Shevardnadze becomes Foreign Minister in place of Gromyko, who becomes Soviet president (→ 2/3/86).

2. London: The Church of England General Synod approves the ordination of women deacons (→ 10).

5. UK: Liberal Richard Livesey captures Brecon and Radnor from the Tories (→ 18/4).

6. Wimbledon: Martina Navratilova beats Chris Lloyd in the Women's Singles final.→

8. West Germany: The originators of the "Hitler Diaries" are jailed for forgery.

10. Ireland: Searchers recover the voice recorder from the Air India jet which crashed into the sea last month (→ 20/8).

10. Nairobi: 10,000 women meet for an international conference on progress in women's rights (→ 14/4/86).

16. London: The Local Government Bill, abolishing the GLC and other metropolitan counties, becomes law (→ 31/3/86).

17. UK: The Live Aid appeal reaches £50 million (→ 8/12).

19. Austria: Large quantities of Austrian wine are revealed to contain a toxic substance similar to anti-freeze.

23. S. Africa: Police say 441 have been detained under emergency laws (→ 1/8).

23. New Zealand: A French man and woman are indicted in connection with the Rainbow Warrior sinking (→ 26/8).

25. Paris: US actor Rock Hudson goes into hospital to be treated for AIDS (→ 13/9).

27. Kampala: President Milton Obote is overthrown in a bloodless coup (→ 17/1/86).

30. London: The BBC drops a documentary in its series "Real Lives" containing an interview with Sinn Fein's Martin McGuinness (→ 7/9).

Live Aid rocks the world for the hungry

A gigantic Bowie looms over the thousands packing Wembley for Live Aid.

July 13. Bob Geldof, the man who last Christmas brought together Britain's rock superstars to help Ethiopia's hungry, has done it again, on an international scale. Following the Band Aid single, which raised tens of thousands of pounds, two monster concerts – one in Wembley Stadium, the other in JFK Stadium in Philadelphia – have raised a staggering £40 million, all to help Africa's famine-stricken poor.

More than 1.5 billion people in 160 countries watched the concerts on TV, as rock's elite, such as Dire Straits, David Bowie, Mick Jagger and Queen, turned out for free to play and urge the audience to give generously. Only the USSR resisted transmitting the "global jukebox".

Now Geldof, who watched the Wembley show with the Prince and Princess of Wales, taking time out to appear on TV, calling on our generosity in impassioned, if uninhibited, language, has been put forward for the Nobel Peace Prize. MPs in Sweden and Britain have proposed the singer as a tribute to his "unique effort to save suffering Africans" (→ 17).

Greenpeace ship in mystery blast

July 10. Rainbow Warrior, the international protest ship belonging to the environmental action group Greenpeace, was badly damaged by two explosions in Auckland Harbour today.

Two blasts, 60 seconds apart, tore the ship's hull apart below the waterline. Nine people on board, including one Briton, escaped, but a Portuguese photographer, Fernando Pereira, was killed.

Police in New Zealand have not yet ascertained the cause of the explosions, but suspect sabotage was the cause. The Rainbow Warrior was to have led a flotilla of seven peace vessels into the French nuclear test site at Muroroa Atoll in the Pacific for a Bastille Day protest action.

Reagan talks tough on terrorist states

July 8. President Reagan today branded five nations – Iran, Libya, North Korea, Cuba and Nicaragua – as members of a "confederation of terrorist states" that was carrying out "outright acts of war" against the United States.

Speaking to the American Bar Association, the President said: "The American people are not ... going to tolerate these attacks from outlaw states run by the strangest collection of misfits, looney tunes and squalid criminals since the advent of the Third Reich."

The President failed to mention Syria's leading role in international terrorism, as a gesture of thanks to its President Hafez el Assad for helping in the release of 39 hostages in Beirut this week.

Botha takes steps to "protect blacks"

Several laughing South African police detain a suspected black activist.

July 21. Claiming that "law-abiding black people" were the victims of "thuggery and violence", South Africa's President P.W. Botha last night announced that a state of emergency was being imposed on 30 magisterial districts, where more than a year of unrest has left at least 500 dead. Police swooped on black townships, set up road-blocks, and detained at least 113 people identified as black activists and white community leaders involved in the township unrest. The South African Council of Churches condemned the move as "a desperate act" aimed at stemming "the tide of liberation" (→23).

Unseeded Becker wins Wimbledon at 17

July 7. With a triumphant roar of "Ja" that reverberated round the Centre Court, the 17-year-old West German Boris Becker today celebrated his defeat of Kevin Curren, 6-3, 6-7, 7-6, 6-4, to become the youngest Wimbledon men's champion in history. Becker, who left the tournament last year in a wheelchair after badly injuring himself during a third round match, powered through the draw with an acrobatic serve-and-volley game to become the first German, and the first unseeded player, to win the title.

Boris Becker, playing dirty, stretches for a backhand against Kevin Curren.

Cram and Lyle give British sport a lift

July 27. In a triumphant week for British sport, a runner stole the headlines from a golfer as Steve Cram won the Dream Mile in Oslo with all the assurance he displayed at the world championships two years ago. He took more than a second off Sebastian Coe's world record, reducing the mark to a formidable 3 minutes 46.32 seconds.

Earlier, the glory had all been Sandy Lyle's, as the 27-year-old Scot became the first British Open champion since Tony Jacklin 16 years ago. At Royal St. George's, Sandwich, Lyle clinched the title by a single stroke from the American Payne Stewart, with all the favourites well down the field.

Oxford degree for 13-year-old genius

July 4. The young maths genius, Ruth Lawrence, won a first-class degree at Oxford today at the age of 13. She completed the course in only two years, and her marks were the highest of all the students. Her performance was described by her tutors as "staggering".

The child prodigy from Huddersfield in Yorkshire said: "I don't think I'm a genius. It came out of a lot of hard work." She cannot collect her certificate for another year until she has completed the residential qualification; she plans to stay on in Oxford for at least a further three years to undertake research.

Tourists die after Italian dam bursts

July 19. Over 260 people are feared dead after floods from a burst dam engulfed a village in the Italian Dolomites. Fifty-five million gallons of water escaped from the dam, sweeping through the Fiemme valley and devastating the hamlet of Stava at lunchtime today. At least 200 people, including entire families, are still missing as rescue workers and distraught relatives continue to dig for survivors; 66 bodies have been recovered from the river of grey mud.

1985

AUGUST

Su	Mo	Tu	We	Th	Fr	Sa
				1	2	3
4	5	6	7	8	9	10
11	12	13	14	15	16	17
18	19	20	21	22	23	24
25	26	27	28	29	30	31

1. Washington: The House of Representatives votes to impose sanctions on South Africa (→10).

2. US: 133 die when an airliner crashes at Fort Worth airport.→

4. Hungary: Steve Cram sets a world record for the 2,000 metres of four minutes 51.39 seconds.→

4. Ireland: Thousands are flocking to Ballinspittle after reports that a statue of the Virgin Mary moves.

8. Rome: Pope John Paul II leaves on a seven-nation African tour (→3/2/86).

10. S. Africa: Leading anti-apartheid campaigner, the Rev. Allan Boesak, is arrested as 40 die in riots.→

11. UK: 100 yachts are forced to retire from the Fastnet race owing to fierce gales.

15. Atlantic: The Virgin Atlantic Challenger sinks two hours short of a record Atlantic crossing (→29/6/86).

16. S. Africa: Bishop Tutu says the chances of peaceful change in South Africa are "virtually nil" (→23).

17. Beirut: A car bomb kills 50 and injures 120 (→1/10).

20. UK: Amstrad launches its PCW 8256 word processor (→7/4/86).

20. India: Sikh leader Harchand Singh Longowal is murdered (→22/1/86).

23. S. Africa: Six blacks are killed in clashes with security forces; 500 children are detained for boycotting school.

23. Bonn: It is revealed that the ex-head of West German counter-intelligence was an East German spy.

24. Birmingham: Five-year-old John Shorthouse is shot dead by police during a raid (→4/7/86).

26. Paris: A report clears the French government and secret service of involvement in the Rainbow Warrior sinking (→22/9).

28. UK: The 55th victim of the Manchester air disaster dies in hospital.

Three air crashes in a month kill 711

Aug 22. A horrific fire on a holiday flight from Manchester today brought the grisly total of dead in air crashes this month to 711, and made 1985 the worst year yet for air fatalities. The British Airtours Boeing 737 burst into flames when its pilot aborted a take-off at the last minute, apparently after an engine exploded. About 80 people slid down chutes to safety, while 54 were unable to escape the smoke and flames which turned the rear of the plane into an inferno.

In the second tragedy a Japanese Boeing 747, tightly-packed with 517 passengers and crew, crashed and burst into flames on a remote wooded mountainside near Tokyo. The crash, thought to be caused by a faulty rear door, is the worst in history involving a single aircraft. The aircraft had only been in the air for 30 minutes when air traffic controllers received an emergency message that the plane was losing altitude.

In the third disaster a Delta Airlines jet crashed on landing at Dallas-Fort Worth airport during a thunderstorm, killing 140 of the 161 people on board (→28).

Firemen on the wreckage of British Airtours Boeing 737 in which 54 died.

Journalists make news by striking

Aug 7. Radio and television journalists went on strike today in protest against the banning of "Real Lives", a programme about Republican and Protestant extremists in Northern Ireland, by the BBC after Government pressure. The BBC's World Service was off the air for the first time ever (→9/10).

Zola Budd speeds to a world record

Aug 26. In an invitation race staged at Crystal Palace, without any prior publicity that might have attracted anti-apartheid demonstrations, the South African-born Zola Budd today broke Ingrid Kristiansen's 5,000 metres world record by more than ten seconds to set a new mark of 14 minutes 48.07 seconds.

Botha moves to crush hopes of reform

Aug 15. South Africa's President P.W. Botha tonight disappointed his friends overseas with a refusal to consider immediate and major reforms in the country's apartheid system. In a speech that had been preceded by hints that sweeping changes would be announced, Mr Botha told a meeting of his National Party in Durban he would press ahead with his reform programme, but there would be no "unparalleled scurry". He would not give in to "hostile pressure and agitation from abroad", which only encouraged militants (→16).

1985

SEPTEMBER

Su	Mo	Tu	We	Th	Fr	Sa
1	2	3	4	5	6	7
8	9	10	11	12	13	14
15	16	17	18	19	20	21
22	23	24	25	26	27	28
29	30					

2. London: Hurd goes to the Home Office, Brittan to the DTI, Tom King to Ulster and Lord Young to Employment (→3).

3. London: Jeffrey Archer becomes deputy chairman of the Tory Party under chairman Norman Tebbit (→18).

6. S. Africa: Botha closes half the "Coloured" schools in the Western Cape, where 30 have died in a week of clashes (→11).

9. London: Liverpool and Lambeth Labour councillors are told to pay £250,000 surcharges for not setting a rate (→5/3/86).

11. Portugal: 150 die in a head-on train collision.

11. S. Africa: The government says it will restore citizenship to 15 million blacks living in "homelands" (→16/10).

13. Switzerland: The World Health Organisation says AIDS has reached epidemic proportions (→26).

18. UK: Opinion polls put the Alliance in the lead by 9.5 per cent over Labour, with the Tories third (→23/9/86).

19. Mexico City: Thousands are feared dead in the most devastating earthquake this century.→

20. Detroit: John De Lorean is indicted on a charge of defrauding investors (→17/12/86).

23. US: Rupert Murdoch buys the rest of Twentieth Century-Fox (→29/12).

26. London: The Government says it has allotted £1 million to be spent on countering the spread of AIDS (→21/11).

27. UK: A High Speed Train travels from Newcastle to London in a record two hours 19 and a half minutes.

28. London: Youths go on the rampage in Brixton after a black woman, Cherry Groce, is shot during a police raid (→29).

29. London: Rioting erupts in Brixton for a second day; 209 have now been arrested (→1/10).

DEATH

17. British fashion designer Laura Ashley (*7/9/1925).→

Ryder Cup comes to Europe at long last

Victorious Tony Jacklin with cup.

Sept 15. A booming drive, a dead safe second shot and a perfect, curling putt on the 18th hole at The Belfry today gave Sam Torrance of Scotland victory over Andy North, and clinched the vital point which ensured that Europe's golfers would recapture the Ryder Cup from the United States – the first time it had been wrested from their grasp for 28 years.

The eventual margin of victory by the European team – consisting of seven Britons, four Spaniards and a German – was a decisive 16.5 to 11.5, a triumph of tactics and leadership for the Europeans' non-playing captain, Tony Jacklin.

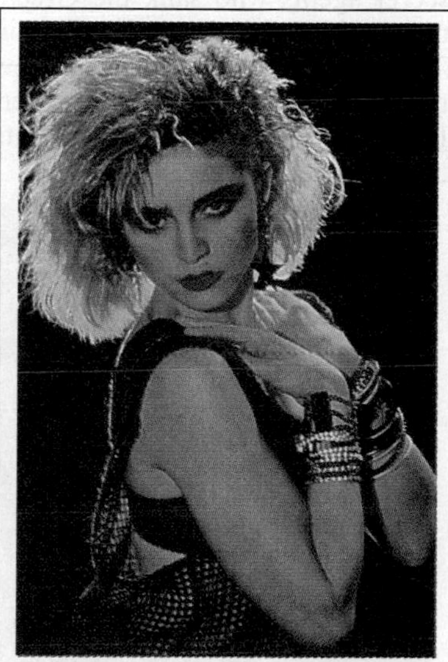

The incredible Madonna in black string vest and bra feeling like a happy virgin with her big hit.

Babies plucked alive from Mexico quake

Buildings in Mexico City hurled onto the street like toys by an earthquake.

Sept 22. With the death toll from last Thursday's earthquake reaching 2,000, and the baseball stadium turned into a giant morgue, news of a miracle heartened Mexico City's rescue workers today.

Fifty-eight new-born babies have been rescued from the city's largest maternity ward, which was flattened by the quake. A Red Cross worker told of how a muffled baby's cry started a desperate excavation which revealed a cavity in the rubble. There, rescuers found the quake's youngest survivors covered in grime and dirt. Many of them only knew peace for an hour or two. Meanwhile, the horror continues. Mexicans are filing through the mortuaries, searching the mangled corpses for missing relatives and friends.

Minister quits in Rainbow Warrior affair

Sept 22. The French government admitted tonight that it was French secret agents who sank the Greenpeace ship, Rainbow Warrior, in Auckland Harbour, killing a crew member. The Prime Minister, Laurent Fabius, said that the agents were acting "under orders". Greenpeace has frequently tried to foil French nuclear tests in the Pacific.

The affair has led to the resignation of the French Defence Minister and demands for the sacking of the head of the secret service (→3/11).

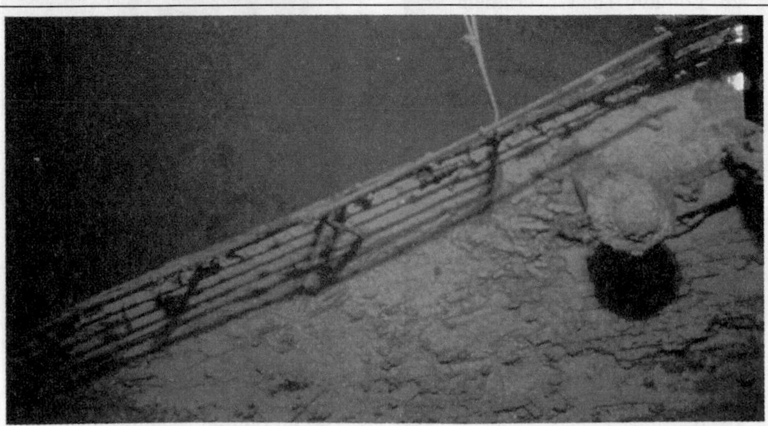

A part of the ghostly deck of the great doomed liner, the Titanic, finally located and photographed this summer 12,000 feet down in the Atlantic.

USSR and UK in tit-for-tat spy swaps

Sept 18. Britain today called a ceasefire in the Anglo-Soviet battle of tit-for-tat expulsions of diplomats and journalists triggered off by the defection of a KGB spy master. The extraordinary diplomatic row has ended with the score even at 31 expulsions each.

It began with the defection of Oleg Gordievski, who headed the KGB at the Soviet Embassy in London, but had also been working for British intelligence for several years. He named 25 Soviet spies operating in London, who were promptly expelled by the Foreign Office. In retaliation Moscow ordered out 25 Britons. Then Britain reacted by expelling more Russians.

Laura Ashley falls to an early death

Sept 17. The fashion empress Laura Ashley, whose romantic styles dressed a generation, has died after a fall at her home. She was 60. The Welsh-born mother-of-four began by designing tea-towels on her kitchen table; by the time she died she was deputy chairman of a multi-million pound international business employing 4,000 people.

The appeal of her flowery clothes lay in their affordability as well as their timelessness. Coupling her flair with her husband's business drive, they branched out into furnishings and wallpapers to give even city homes a country air.

Only one in three still smokes in UK

Sept 17. Barely one person in three of the adult British population now smokes, according to a Government survey published today. Smoking amongst men has shown the biggest drop – down from 52 per cent in 1972 to 36 per cent today. Women smokers have fallen from 41 to 32 per cent over the same period. Those who do still smoke are also smoking fewer cigarettes: 115 a week for men, for instance, as against 129 in 1972.

1985

OCTOBER

Su	Mo	Tu	We	Th	Fr	Sa
		1	2	3	4	5
6	7	8	9	10	11	12
13	14	15	16	17	18	19
20	21	22	23	24	25	26
27	28	29	30	31		

1. UK: Riots break out in Toxteth and Peckham.→

1. Tunisia: At least 50 have died in an Israeli air raid on PLO offices near Tunis (→7).

3. London: Sir Robert Haslam is appointed to succeed Ian MacGregor as NCB chairman next year (→19).

7. Mediterranean: Arab gunmen hijack an Italian cruise liner, the Achille Lauro.→

9. London: Self-confessed terrorist Dominic McGlinchey wins an appeal against his conviction for murder (→15/11).

14. UK: Sir Clive Sinclair's crisis-ridden company TPD, makers of the C5 electric tricycle, calls in a receiver (→7/4/86).

17. London: The Law Lords reject a ban on giving the pill to under-16s, won after a campaign by Mrs Victoria Gillick.

19. UK: Nottinghamshire and South Derbyshire miners vote to set up a Union of Democratic Mineworkers (→31).

21. UK: 13 die in Britain's worst motorway accident when a coach bursts into flames in an M6 pile-up.

24. London: Three of the seven servicemen accused of passing on secrets in Cyprus are acquitted (→25).

25. London: Two more are acquitted in the Cyprus secrets trial (→28).

28. London: An Old Bailey jury clears the last two Cyprus secrets trial defendants (→2/2/87).

31. London: Life sentences on two miners jailed for murdering a cab driver are changed to eight years for manslaughter (→12/11/87).

DEATHS

2. US actor Rock Hudson, born Roy Scherer (*17/11/25).→

10. US actor and director Orson Welles (*6/5/15).→

10. US actor Yul Brynner, born Taijde Khan (*11/7/20).

Policeman hacked to death in London riot

The Metropolitan Police tactical firearms squad deployed for the first time.

Oct 7. Mob fury came to North London tonight as several hundred black youths rioted after the death of a black woman during a police search of her flat. PC Keith Blakelock, aged 40, was hacked to death; he is understood to have been a former community policeman.

Another constable was shot in the stomach with a revolver, and three more policemen, together with three members of a television news team, were hit by shotgun blasts and concrete blocks thrown from upper storeys. Although police reinforcements, including marksmen, have been rushed to the area from all parts of London, the battle of Broadwater Farm, a prize-winning housing development, looked set to continue after several charges by police using batons and shields were repulsed by petrol bombs and stones and burning cars.

The ferocity of tonight's rioting, in which over 200 policemen are known to have been injured, will strengthen demands for the use of plastic bullets in similar circumstances (→15/1/87).

Oct 2. Rock Hudson died, aged 59, after a year-long battle against AIDS. A romantic leading man in films such as "Pillow Talk", his illness – and revelations about his homosexuality – shocked millions of fans.

Thatcher boycotts apartheid sanctions

Oct 21. "Tiny", said Mrs Thatcher, well-satisfied and holding up a finger and thumb a centimetre apart to show television cameras. She was describing how much difference there will be in future in Commonwealth sanctions against South Africa. A Commonwealth Prime Ministers' conference in Nassau ended today with Britain's leader hardly budging in her resistance to demands by the other countries for full-scale economic sanctions.

This contrasts with growing pressure for reform from South Africa's own business leaders. A delegation this month met exiled leaders of the African National Congress in Zambia and came home persuaded that business could live with a black government (→2/11).

Hijacker freed by Italy

Oct 17. The freeing by Italy of Mohammed Abbas, the man who masterminded the capture by Palestinian pirates of the cruise ship Achille Lauro, has outraged President Reagan, and today it provoked the fall of Bettino Craxi's government in Italy. Expressing indignation at the release of the man who planned the operation, James Baker, the US Treasury Secretary, said: "The Administration would love to get its hands on Mr Abbas. He's a known terrorist."

The saga began ten days ago when PLO terrorists seized the 25,000-ton liner heading from Alexandria to Port Said and demanded the release of 50 Arab prisoners held in Israeli jails, threatening otherwise to blow up the ship and its 454 passengers. Then they murdered an elderly and crippled New York Jew named Leon Klinghoffer for arguing.

This single act horrified American opinion, and Special Forces were deployed in the eastern Mediterranean, ready to storm the ship, if necessary; but after complicated negotiations, involving Arafat's PLO and the Egyptian government, the pirate captain, "Commandant Omar", surrendered on condition that he and his men were flown to Tunis. However, American jet fighters then intercepted their Egyptian airliner and forced it to land in Sicily where US forces, flown into the NATO installation with orders to seize the terrorists, clashed with Italian Carabinieri, who were asserting their right to arrest the hijackers on Italian territory. The Italians prevailed, and later allowed Mohammed Abbas to slip away to Yugoslavia (→24/11).

Hijack leader Mohammed Abbas.

Citizen Welles, film-making genius, dies

Oct 10. Orson Welles was the one undoubted directorial genius that Hollywood has known, other than Chaplin. Unfortunately he insisted on behaving like one, alienating studio heads, and never received the financial backing he needed. At his death at the age of 70 yesterday he left eight or nine brilliant, but flawed films. People always hoped for another masterpiece like his first, "Citizen Kane" – but that was a lot to ask.

Welles's Shakespearean trilogy came nearest – especially his Falstaff in "Chimes at Midnight". His performances in other people's pictures were often unforgettable – Harry Lime in "The Third Man", Cardinal Wolsey in "A Man for All Seasons" and the General in "Catch 22". He was a child prodigy. By the age of ten he had read all Shakespeare. By 16 he was on the stage. The second of three wives was Rita Hayworth with whom he made "The Lady from Shanghai".

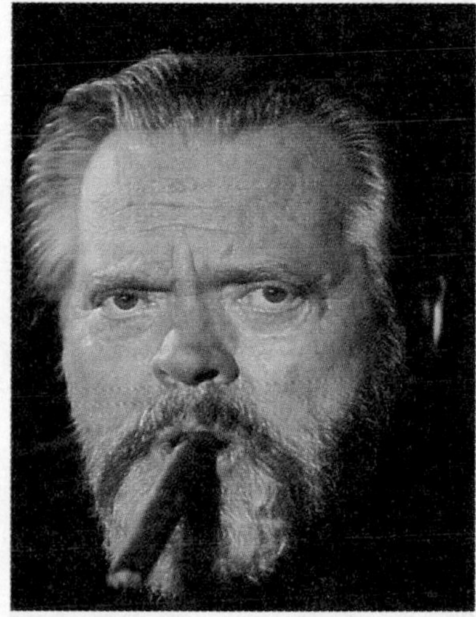

Orson Welles with the inevitable cigar clamped between his teeth.

1985

NOVEMBER

Su	Mo	Tu	We	Th	Fr	Sa
					1	2
3	4	5	6	7	8	9
10	11	12	13	14	15	16
17	18	19	20	21	22	23
24	25	26	27	28	29	30

1. UK: The new technique of "genetic fingerprinting" has been used for the first time to prove paternity.

2. S. Africa: The government put severe restrictions on press reporting (→21).

3. New Zealand: Two French agents plead guilty to sinking the Greenpeace ship, Rainbow Warrior (→21).

7. Colombia: Over 50 die when police and troops storm the palace of justice in Bogota to end a 27-hour siege by gunmen.

11. Philippines: Marcos calls a presidential election for early next year in a bid to calm growing unrest (→2/12).

15. London: Treasury Minister Ian Gow resigns in protest at the Anglo-Irish agreement.→

18. London: An Anglo-French summit ends with agreement to build a fixed link between Britain and France (→20/1/86).

19. Geneva: Reagan and Gorbachev open talks.→

21. S. Africa: 13 blacks are killed in clashes with the police at Mamelodi township (→25/12).

21. New Zealand: The two French agents who sank the Rainbow Warrior are jailed for ten years.

24. Malta: 59 die when Egyptian commandos storm an Egyptian airliner kidnapped by Palestinian gunmen (→13/12).

25. London: Habitat and British Home Stores announce they are to merge in a deal worth £1.5 billion.

27. Moscow: Gorbachev calls his meeting with Reagan "a positive start" (→1/1/86).

27. London: MPs approve the Anglo-Irish accord; Ulster Unionists begin to resign in protest (→11/12).

29. UK: Cricketer Ian Botham completes a charity walk from John O'Groats to Land's End for leukaemia research (→29/5/86).

DEATH

17. Cambodian leader Lon Nol (*13/11/1913).

Summit stirs optimism

Reagan and Gorbachev delighted to find they understand each other better.

Nov 21. In their Geneva meetings, which ended today, President Reagan and Mr Gorbachev spent six hours together with only interpreters present. The private sessions were the longest in 14 US-Soviet summits going back 30 years. The two leaders agreed to work for a 50 per cent cut in their strategic nuclear arsenals, and to explore the possibility of an agreement on medium-range missiles.

They agreed on the importance of resolving "humanitarian cases in the spirit of co-operation" – a reference to emigration permits for Soviet Jews. They also agreed to implement measures to avoid incidents like the 1983 Soviet shooting down of a South Korean airliner. After the meeting, Mr Reagan flew home to address Congress on what he called "our fireside summit".

He said the two powers had made a fresh start. "I cannot claim we had a meeting of minds on such fundamentals as ideology or national purpose, but we understand each other better," he said.

Before leaving for Moscow, Mr Gorbachev held an unprecedented 95-minute press conference. "The world has become a safer place," he said. He was "very optimistic" about the future (→27).

Nov 9. Outsider Gary Kasparov waits to play against Anatoly Karpov whom he beat to become the youngest world chess champion ever at 22.

Two villages buried in Colombian mud

Nov 13. A long-dormant volcano erupted in Colombia tonight, spewing rocks, water, mud and ash over four sleeping towns. Up to 20,000 people are feared to have died in the destruction.

The Nevado del Ruiz volcano, 80 miles west of Bogota, has been quiet since 1845. Tonight it came back to life with a vengeance. Nearby towns have been covered with a layer of ash and rock 28 inches thick, and a 70-square-mile area has been declared a disaster zone. The town of Armero, with a population of 50,000, has all but disappeared under a torrent of hot mud. Ash and smoke are being carried some 300 miles.

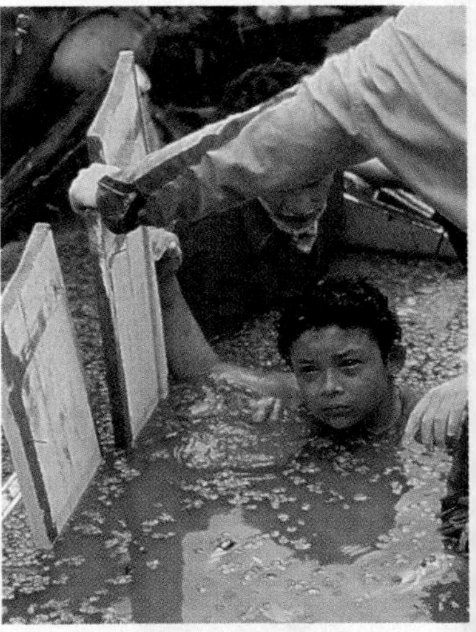

Just mud where once was a home.

Anglo-Irish deal signed on Ulster

Nov 15. Margaret Thatcher and Dr Garret FitzGerald, the Irish Prime Minister, signed an agreement in Belfast today which could prove momentous in the history of Ireland. The Anglo-Irish Agreement gives the Republic a consultative role in the running of Northern Ireland for the first time.

An inter-governmental conference of ministers and civil servants, with its own secretariat in Belfast, will meet regularly to discuss political, legal and security matters. Mrs Thatcher said the agreement recognises the interests of the two Ulster communities (→15).

1985

DECEMBER

Su	Mo	Tu	We	Th	Fr	Sa
1	2	3	4	5	6	7
8	9	10	11	12	13	14
15	16	17	18	19	20	21
22	23	24	25	26	27	28
29	30	31				

2. Manila: Cory Aquino says she will run for President (→ 7/1/86).

8. Sudan: Princess Anne appeals for immediate famine aid to the Sudan after a week-long visit (→ 25/5/86).

9. Buenos Aires: Ex-President Videla is jailed for life for human rights violations.

10. Stockholm: Nobel Prizes go to Klaus von Klitzing (West Germany, Physics); Aaron Hauptmann and Jerome Karle (US, Chemistry); Joseph Goldstein and Michael Brown (US, Medicine); Claude Simon (France, Literature); Franco Modigliani (US, Economics), and in Oslo to International Physicians for the Prevention of Nuclear War (US and USSR, Peace).

11. Belfast: 38 police are injured in clashes with Loyalists during the first Anglo-Irish conference (→ 16/1/87).

13. Cyprus: Briton Ian Davison, who joined the PLO, gets life for killing three Israelis.

19. Washington: Edward Kennedy says he will not run for President in 1988 (→ 16/3/87).

23. S. Africa: Six whites die in a bomb blast at a shopping centre near Durban (→ 2/1/86).

29. London: Rupert Murdoch orders his new Wapping plant to be prepared for operations (→ 16/2/86).

DEATHS

2. British poet Philip Arthur Larkin (*9/8/1922).

7. British poet and author Robert Ranke Graves (*24/7/1895).

HITS OF 1985

The power of love.

I know him so well.

Dancing in the street.

QUOTE OF THE YEAR

"I am not prepared to lead white South Africans ... on a road to abdication and suicide."

President P.W. Botha.

Two airports hit by terrorist attackers

Dec 30. Arab terrorists today staged simultaneous assaults with grenades and automatic weapons on Israeli airline check-in desks at Rome and Vienna airports. Twelve people among the holiday travellers were killed and over a hundred were wounded. Security guards returned fire, and in the ensuing gun battles four raiders were shot dead. One who admitted working for Abu Nidal, the renegade Palestinian faction leader. Although they claimed that the attacks were in revenge for Israel's recent air attack on PLO headquarters in Tunis, the PLO denied involvement (→ 15/4/86).

UK gives up as UNESCO member

Dec 5. Britain today pulled out of UNESCO, the scientific and cultural arm of the United Nations which it helped to found 40 years ago. Timothy Raison, the Overseas Development Minister, told the House of Commons that the £6.4 million saved would be spent on Third World Aid projects which were "thoroughly worth doing", unlike much of UNESCO's work.

The Government, like the US which left UNESCO a year ago, claims an anti-Western bias and financial extravagance by its boss, Mr M'Bow. Labour Party leaders disagree.

Compact discs start to gain popularity

Dec 31. Compact discs have finally started to catch on in a big way, two years since their launch in 1983. Then the public largely ignored the silver discs, smaller than an LP, but offering music of infinitely higher quality.

You could grind them underfoot, smear them with honey, and still they would play. That's what the makers said, but it's taken a while, and an influx of cheaper CD players, to interest music fans. At the moment, though, it is the older, wealthier punters who are doing the buying.

Arts: Paris bridge in under-cover job

Parisians woke one September morning this year to find that the Pont Neuf had been shrouded in 40,000 square yards of canvas by **Christo**, the Bulgarian artist who regards packaging as an artistic activity. Starting with a humble magazine and a bicycle, he progressed to wrapping public buildings, a stretch of coastline, even an island.

The death of **Marc Chagall** at 97 removes the last great figure of the Ecole de Paris and one of its most lyrical. He was born Moyshe Shagal in Vitebsk and first went to Paris in 1910. After the Russian revolution he served briefly as "arts commissar" of his birthplace, but returned to Paris in 1923. His work never lost its Russian and peasant-poet's eye-view. Lovers fly through the air in ecstasies, and humans and animals mix on terms of equality.

English poetry suffered a double blow with the deaths of **Robert Graves** and **Philip Larkin**. Graves had lived on Majorca, the seigneur of the village of Deya, since 1929, when he published his autobiography "Goodbye to All That". There he wrote his historical novels about the Emperor Claudius and other figures like Milton's wife. He said he could not write poetry unless he was in love – he had a tempestuous affair with the American poet, Laura Riding, for years. Some of the best modern love poetry is his. He was aged 90.

Philip Larkin, a shy, reclusive poet, spent the major part of his working life as librarian of Hull University. He published only four slimmish volumes, but won high esteem with "The Whitsun Weddings" and his last collection, "High Windows". He could also be wryly funny, as in the verse beginning: "Sexual intercourse began in 1963 – which was rather late for me."

The theatre lost one of its subtlest actors, **Sir Michael Redgrave**, known for the sensitivity and intelligence of his Hamlet and other Shakespearean roles, his definitive Uncle Vanya, and fine film parts, including the schoolmaster in "The Browning Version".

The year's stage hits have been "Les Miserables", a musical version of Hugo's novel, and "Pravda", a sour satire on the tabloid press, with **Anthony Hopkins** as an odious press tycoon.

Robert Graves, author of some of the best love poetry, at home in Deya.

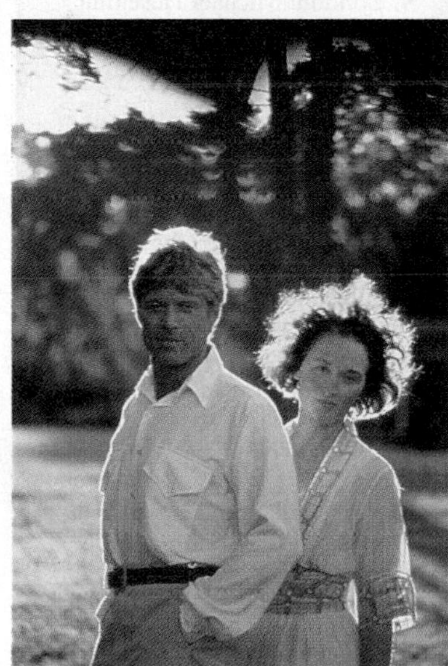

Robert Redford and Meryl Streep in Kenya making "Out of Africa".

The lyrical painter Marc Chagall who died this year, aged 97.

1986

JANUARY

Su	Mo	Tu	We	Th	Fr	Sa
			1	2	3	4
5	6	7	8	9	10	11
12	13	14	15	16	17	18
19	20	21	22	23	24	25
26	27	28	29	30	31	

1. Moscow/Washington: Gorbachev and Reagan extend New Year's greetings to each other's nations (→15).

2. London: England's cricket tour of Bangladesh is cancelled at the last minute in a row over ties with South Africa.→

6. US: The launch of the space shuttle Columbia is delayed owing to a faulty valve.→

8. London: Permanently-armed police begin patrolling Heathrow Airport.

9. London: Michael Heseltine resigns from the cabinet over the row within the Government over Westland Helicopters.→

13. Aden: Fierce fighting is reported following an attempted coup.→

15. Moscow: Gorbachev proposes a 15-year timetable to eliminate all nuclear arms by the end of the century (→13/4).

16. UK: A report into football violence by Mr Justice Popplewell says "we can never suppress soccer thugs completely" (→8/8).

16. Amsterdam: Escaped IRA prisoners Brendan McFarlane and Gerard Kelly are arrested by Dutch police (→24).

17. Uganda: Heavy fighting is reported between government forces and troops of the National Resistance Army (NRA) (→25).

20. US: The Martin Luther King national holiday is observed for the first time.

22. New Delhi: Three Sikhs are sentenced to death for murdering Mrs Gandhi (→10/8).

24. Northern Ireland: Unionists are re-elected in 14 of 15 seats contested as a referendum on the Anglo-Irish deal (→22/3).

25. Uganda: Yoweri Museveni, backed by the NRA, ousts the government of President Tito Okello.

28. London: The Government issues a green paper on plans to replace the rates with a "community charge" (→17/11/87).

Space shuttle explodes on take-off

The Challenger's seven astronauts.

Just 72 seconds after lift-off, at 2,000mph, Challenger's fuel tank exploded.

Jan 28. The American space shuttle Challenger exploded seconds after lift-off today, killing its crew of seven. Among them was Christa McAuliffe, a schoolteacher selected as the first to fly in the "citizen in space" programme. Her husband and children, along with the families of other astronauts, witnessed the disaster.

Challenger was 72 seconds into its flight, travelling at nearly 2,000 mph at a height of ten miles, when it was suddenly enveloped in a red, orange and white fireball as thousands of tons of liquid hydrogen and oxygen fuel exploded. Photographs taken by chase planes reveal that there was a prelude: a small tongue of flame appeared on one of the external booster rockets soon after lift-off and was quickly followed by another. Then a halo of flame grew round the base of the booster just before the explosion. However, the crew reported nothing abnormal. The flight had been postponed five times, three of them because of bad weather. The temperature the night before launch fell to eight degrees Fahrenheit below freezing and the vehicle was covered with icicles which had to be chipped off by hand. Whether the highly unusual conditions had anything to do with the disaster is unknown.

The tragedy has dealt a devastating blow to the shuttle programme, already in difficulties because of cost overruns. These are the first American fatalities in space, though three astronauts died in a launch-pad fire in 1967 (→2/2).

Britain and France give Chunnel go-ahead

Jan 20. There really is going to be a Channel Tunnel at last. Mrs Thatcher and President Mitterrand confirmed the project at a ceremony in Lille today. Work will begin next year on a rail-only link between Britain and France, with the first trains due to run in 1993. An additional road tunnel is planned for the year 2000.

An Anglo-French construction and operating company will be financed initially by banks in many countries. The tunnel will cost nearly £5 billion, and will be 31 miles long.

There will be four trains an hour in each direction, with through services from London to Brussels and Paris. Fares – at present prices – will be £50 per car. Ferry operators are threatening a price war, and rural communities in Kent plan to fight the proposals (→12/2).

Coup in Lesotho is pro-South African

Jan 20. South African forces three weeks ago imposed a virtual blockade on landlocked Lesotho, after claiming black nationalist terrorists were finding refuge there. Today the people of Lesotho awoke to find that General Justin Lekhanya, aged 47, had seized power and formed a government. Within hours the blockade was lifted (→18/2).

1986

FEBRUARY

Su	Mo	Tu	We	Th	Fr	Sa
						1
2	3	4	5	6	7	8
9	10	11	12	13	14	15
16	17	18	19	20	21	22
23	24	25	26	27	28	

2. US: NASA says the space shuttle's solid fuel booster rockets had no sensors to warn of trouble (→9/3).

2. Over 34 deaths are reported as blizzards and freezing weather sweeps much of Western Europe.

3. Calcutta: Pope John Paul II meets Mother Teresa (→29/3).

5. London: The Government publishes a white paper advocating the privatisation of the water industry.

6. London: The Government drops plans to sell Austin-Rover to Ford due to post-Westland backbench pressure.

7. Philippines: Widespread intimidation and violence mars the presidential election, leaving over 30 dead (→9).

7. Australia: "Dingo Baby" Lindy Chamberlain is freed from jail after new evidence undermines her conviction.

9. Manila: Vote-counters walk out in protest at Marcos' falsification of the election results (→15).

12. Canterbury: Thatcher and Mitterrand sign a treaty to build a Channel Tunnel.

15. Manila: The opposition walks out of the Philippine parliament when Marcos says he has won the election (→22).

16. Lisbon: Dr Mario Soares succeeds General Eanes as Portugal's first civilian President in 60 years.

22. Manila: Defence Minister Juan Ponce Enrile and chief of staff Fidel Ramos resign and urge Marcos to quit.→

23. New Zealand: Two Maori activists throw eggs at the Queen during a visit to Auckland.

26. Manila: President Aquino names her cabinet as Marcos arrives in Hawaii (→6/7).

28. US: Car worker John Demjanjuk is extradited to Israel to stand trial for alleged war crimes (→16/2/87).

DEATH

28. Swedish statesman Olof Palme (*30/1/1927).→

Leon Brittan resigns over Westland leak

Jan 24. The Westland Affair – the most sordid and public cabinet row for years – reached a climax this afternoon with the resignation of a second senior member of Mrs Thatcher's team. Leon Brittan surrendered to fierce pressure from influential Tory MPs and resigned as Trade and Industry Secretary.

This followed his admission that he had authorised the leaking of a government law officer's letter criticising Michael Heseltine's actions while Defence Secretary. Ten days ago Mr Heseltine created turmoil by resigning "on a point of honour". He marched out sensationally in the middle of a cabinet meeting when Mrs Thatcher insisted that his public statements must be vetted by her officials.

Mr Heseltine just after resigning.

The bitter squabble over the future of the Westland helicopter company centred on Mr Heseltine's campaign on behalf of a European consortium wanting to underpin it. Mr Brittan favoured greater American participation. Bernard Ingham, the Prime Minister's controversial press secretary, knew about the leak. Mrs Thatcher said that she did not. Her style of government is now the issue, and her critics are on the warpath (→6/2).

Britannia evacuates refugees from Aden

Beached foreigners, fleeing the civil war in Aden, wait to be rescued by boat.

Jan 23. The royal yacht, Britannia, steamed into the Arabian Sea port of Djibouti today with 440 passengers who never thought they would flee to safety in such style. In six days of rescue off the beach of strife-torn Aden, Britannia has carried up to 1,082 Britons, Bangladeshis, East Germans, Japanese and others to safety. Britannia was on her way to Australia when she was diverted. In a further twist, the evacuees were told to assemble in the Russian Embassy near the beach before they were taken offshore to safety.

"This operation has done an awful lot of good for Britain's reputation," said her master, Rear Admiral John Garnier.

Swedish PM is shot dead in the street

Swedish premier, Olof Palme.

Feb 28. Olof Palme, the Prime Minister of Sweden, was assassinated in Stockholm tonight as he walked home from a visit to a cinema. His wife was wounded in the attack by a lone gunman, whose age is estimated at around 35.

It was just before midnight when the gunman struck. Mr Palme, aged 59, was hit in the chest and then the attacker fired another shot into his wife's back. The gunman ran off before any attempts could be made to capture him. The couple were rushed to hospital, but Mr Palme died despite extensive efforts to save him. No organisation has yet claimed responsibility (→12/3).

Pickets clash with police at Wapping

Feb 16. Police wearing riot gear clashed with 5,000 pickets outside Rupert Murdoch's printing plant in Wapping last night, as the protesters sought to stop the distribution of the "News of the World" and "Sunday Times".

Several policemen and pickets were hurt in what was the worst violence since Mr Murdoch switched production of his newspapers to the Wapping plant without union agreement over manning levels. Over 2,000 print workers are on strike, but the papers are still being produced. ▷

Aquino forces Marcos to flee Manila

Ferdinand and Imelda's farewell.

Corazon Aquino being sworn in as the new President of the Philippines.

Feb 25. Ferdinand Marcos, President of the Philippines for 20 years, was finally toppled from power today by Mrs Corazon Aquino, widow of the opposition leader assassinated by Marcos troops in 1983. Installed as the new president in a Manila country club, she said that the "long agony was over". Later on television she said: "A new life starts for our country - a life filled with hope, and I believe, a life that will be blessed with peace and progress."

At midday Marcos went ahead with a ceremony to install him as President for another six years, but it was boycotted by his own Prime Minister and the television broadcast was blacked out. Nine hours later Aquino supporters stormed his Malacanang Palace, and Marcos and his family fled to the roof. They were snatched to safety by four American helicopters, who dived in out of the darkness, searchlights blazing. Marcos, a sick man, was lifted off on a stretcher and taken to the US Navy hospital in Guam for a check-up.

The beginning of the end for Marcos came when he declared he had won the February 7 election. World opinion was outraged because the polls had been rigged so blatantly by his supporters. However, the United States, which backed his long rule, did not finally withdraw their support from him until last Saturday.

On that day the Defence Minister, Juan Ponce Enrile, and the army chief of staff, General Fidel Ramos, revolted against Marcos and took over the military camp which houses the Defence Ministry. It was clear then that Marcos was finished (→26).

Gorbachev attacks wasted Brezhnev years at Congress

Feb 2. Mikhail Gorbachev, the new Soviet leader, today ushered in an era of change in Soviet life. In a major speech to the 27th Communist Party congress he mounted a large-scale assault on the country's bureaucracy and blamed his predecessors, and particularly the former President Leonid Brezhnev, for "years of stagnation".

Gorbachev, aged 55, was addressing his first party congress since taking power last March, and said it marked an "abrupt turning point". In his frank review of the state of the nation he said major problems had been ignored, and a major overhaul of the country's hide-bound centralised economic system was essential.

Gorbachev attacked "armchair managers, hack workers, idlers and grabbers", and said there were party officials who had lost touch with life. Officials should be held accountable for their actions and the people should be given more information by which to judge them.

Gorbachev has used his first year in office to replace hundreds of party and government officials whom he maintains have grown old and corrupt under Brezhnev's patronage (→23/12).

Iran captures key town to win major victory in the Gulf War

Iranian soldiers killed in the battle for the vital port of Faw in Iraq.

Feb 19. In an eleven-day offensive Iranian forces, spearheaded by Revolutionary Guards, have captured the Iraqi oil port of Faw. Today they took Western correspondents there to prove the point, just as the Iraqi airforce counter-attacked heavily. Iran now controls both banks at the mouth of the Shatt al Arab, which connects Basra, the great Iraqi port, to the Gulf.

In this significant victory Iranian commanders claim to have destroyed 570 tanks and captured 140. It began when an Iranian column feinted towards Khorramshahr to the north and drew off Iraqi reserves before launching the main attack. Iraq is accused of using mustard gas in a desperate attempt to hold off the attackers (→2/7).

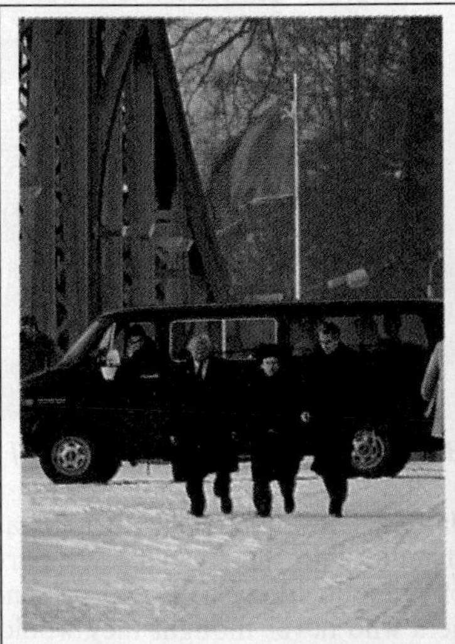

Feb 11. Anatoly Shcharansky, the Soviet human rights activist, freed after eight years in jail, is escorted to the West across the Glienicke Bridge in Berlin.

1986

MARCH

Su	Mo	Tu	We	Th	Fr	Sa
						1
2	3	4	5	6	7	8
9	10	11	12	13	14	15
16	17	18	19	20	21	22
23	24	25	26	27	28	29
30	31					

2. Canberra: The Queen signs the Australia Bill, formally severing the nation's last constitutional ties with Britain.

5. London: The High Court rules to disqualify and fine 81 Liverpool and Lambeth councillors for failing to set a rate (→ 8/5).

9. US: US Navy divers find the crew compartment of the space shuttle (→ 26).

12. Spain: In a triumph for Prime Minister Gonzalez, a referendum backs continued membership of NATO.

12. Sweden: Acting premier Ingvar Carlson is elected to succeed Olof Palme as Prime Minister.

16. France: Jean-Marie Le Pen's National Front makes large gains in the general election.→

19. London: Buckingham Palace announces the engagement of Prince Andrew and Sarah Ferguson.

24. UK: Over eight are killed as hurricane-force winds sweep across Britain (→ 16/10/87).

26. Moscow: The USSR names seven asteroids after the crew members of the space shuttle Columbia (→ 9/4).

29. Rome: Three Bulgarians and three Turks are cleared through lack of evidence of plotting to kill the Pope.

29. London: The world's first test-tube quins are born.

31. Mexico: 166 are feared dead when a Boeing 727 crashes in mountains.

31. London: A woman dies in a fire which damages the south wing of Hampton Court Palace, designed by Wren.

DEATHS

14. British author and broadcaster Sir Huw Pyrs Wheldon (*7/5/1916).

17. British soldier Lieutenant-General Sir John Bagot Glubb, known as Glubb Pasha, commander of the Arab Legion 1939-56 (*16/4/1897).

30. US actor James Cagney (*17/7/1899).→

Riots as Baby Doc is thrown out of Haiti

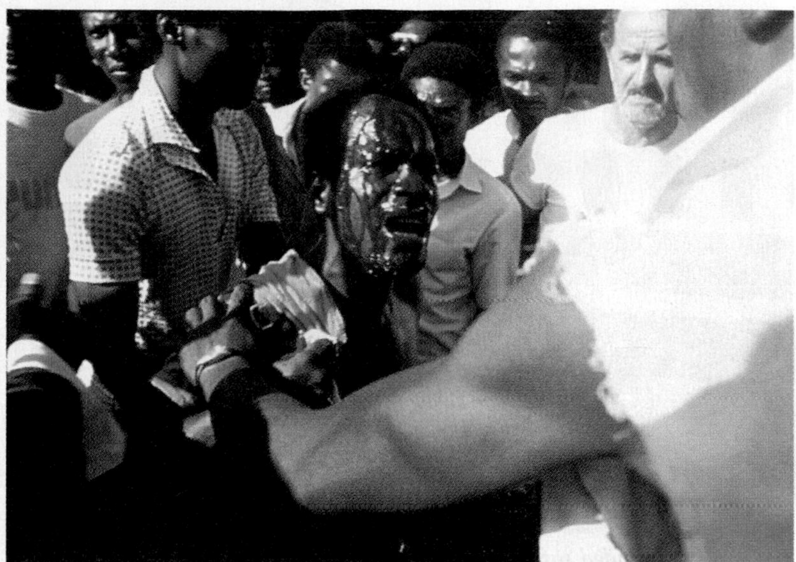

Haitians take revenge on the Tontons Macoutes after "Baby Doc" flees.

Feb 7. Thousands of jubilant Haitians swarmed on to the streets of Port-au-Prince this morning after hearing on the 7am radio news that their President had fled during the night. Jean-Claude Duvalier, the 34-year-old self-styled President-for-life, known as "Baby Doc", was an even more hated figure than his father, "Papa Doc".

Between them they ruled Haiti for 28 years, using the ruthless Tontons Macoutes secret police to murder their opponents. Last night the jubilation turned to violence. Tontons Macoutes were lynched, shops looted, and "Papa Doc's" coffin was dragged through the streets. "Baby Doc" has fled to France, taking with him an estimated £100 million (→ 29/11/87).

Jean-Claude Duvalier late of Haiti.

South Africa bars TV men from riots

Feb 18. Four days of fighting between black youths and police and security forces in the Alexandra township outside Johannesburg have left 19 dead, according to official figures, but blacks living in the township say the true figures are 80 dead and 300 injured. Police say there have been 130 separate violent incidents since last Saturday. Alexandra, which is flanked by an industrial zone and a white suburb, has been cordoned by security forces with reporters and TV men being kept out (→ 2/4).

Mafia gangsters go on trial in Sicily

Feb 10. The biggest ever Mafia trial began in Palermo today amid the sort of security normally reserved for military manoeuvres. Armoured cars and steel-helmeted security guards were on hand to prevent any bid to free the 474 alleged gangsters from the £18 million fortress-like court building. The trial was made possible when Tommaso Buscetta broke the Mafia code of silence to spill the beans on his ex-colleagues, who face hundreds of charges of murder, extortion, drug-running and prostitution (→ 16/12/87).

Extradition farce running in Dublin

March 24. Evelyn Glenholmes, aged 27 and top of Scotland Yard's most wanted list, walked free from a Dublin court for the second time yesterday, to the fury of both the British and Irish governments. Yet again the warrants for her extradition were found to be faulty. The Irish Justice Minister, Alan Dukes, blamed the British Attorney-General, Sir Michael Havers, for the blunder which has made both governments so angry.

Miss Glenholmes is wanted for questioning about the bombing of the Grand Hotel in Brighton in 1984, when Mrs Thatcher and members of her cabinet came close to being killed (→ 23/6).

Tough guy Cagney can't beat final rap

Cagney, who ended up a nice guy.

March 30. It was a compliment to James Cagney, who died today at his farm, aged 86, that generations of young males imitated his sneer, the menacing tapping of his fist with his other palm and his drawl through clenched teeth – "Jest don't make me mad, see?" He was the most attractive of bad guys in the gangster movies of the Thirties.

In "The Public Enemy" he added to his legend of meanness by picking up a half-grapefruit from the table and squashing it into the face of a female companion. In later pictures he joined the good guys. ▷

Curious cohabiting in Elysee Palace

March 20. France today moved into a new political era and they already have a word for it – "cohabitation". For the first time this century there is a right-wing Prime Minister and a Socialist President. Jacques Chirac, the Neo-Gaullist leader, became Prime Minister today as a result of the right's victory in Sunday's elections.

President Mitterrand will have to rule with him, although Chirac is determined to roll back the Socialist programme, particularly on nationalisation of key firms. The tension is heightened by the fact that Chirac intends to run against Mitterrand in the presidential election of 1988.

End of the road for largest local council

March 31. The Greater London Council – the largest local government unit in the world – was abolished tonight. The metropolitan county council areas of Greater Manchester, Merseyside, Tyne and Wear, South Yorkshire, West Yorkshire and West Midlands also died. The Government said that the abolished authorities – especially the Labour-controlled GLC – were unnecessary and wasteful. Their powers now pass to the smaller districts or borough councils.

Prince Andrew and Sarah Ferguson kiss for the photographers on their engagement.

1986

APRIL

Su	Mo	Tu	We	Th	Fr	Sa
		1	2	3	4	5
6	7	8	9	10	11	12
13	14	15	16	17	18	19
20	21	22	23	24	25	26
27	28	29	30			

2. S. Africa: Bishop Tutu calls for international sanctions against South Africa.

4. London: Rupert Murdoch offers his Gray's Inn Road plant to the print unions if they end the Wapping dispute.

5. UK: Mr P. Luff's West Tip wins the Grand National.

7. London: Sir Clive Sinclair sells his computer business to Amstrad boss Alan Sugar.

9. US: Federal safety inspectors say the crew cabin of the space shuttle remained intact until it struck the water.

10. Pakistan: Benazir Bhutto returns, demanding an end to martial law and free elections.

14. London: Rebel Tories force the Government to drop plans for Sunday trading.

17. Lebanon: Three British hostages are murdered in retaliation for Britain's role in the US attack on Libya.

18. UK: Brewing giant Guinness wins a takeover battle for the Distillers group.

20. Moscow: Pianist Vladimir Horowitz returns to Russia for the first time in 61 years.

22. London: Flooding damages treasures in the Victoria and Albert Museum.

22. UK: King Juan Carlos arrives on the first visit to Britain by a Spanish monarch for 81 years.

24. London: The Government drops plans to sell the Land Rover group to a US buyer.

29. UK: The Duchess of Windsor is buried at Windsor.

DEATHS

14. French author Simone de Beauvoir (*9/1/1908).→

15. French author and playwright Jean Genet (*19/12/1910).

23. English cricketer Jim Laker (*9/2/1922).

23. US film director Otto Preminger (*5/12/1906).

24. US-born British Duchess Wallis Warfield Simpson, Duchess of Windsor (*19/6/1896).→

Bomb explodes while plane is in the air

The plane still landed safely after a bomb blew this hole in the fuselage.

April 2. A bomb exploded in mid-air on board a TWA Boeing 727 and sucked four people to their deaths while on a flight from Rome to Athens today. A shepherd reported seeing bodies tumbling from the sky and Greek police later found three bodies and an aircraft seat near the town of Argos. A fourth body was recovered from the sea. The victims were a man, a grandmother and her daughter and child. Nine others were injured.

There was speculation that the explosion was the first act of retaliation by Libyan-backed terrorists following last week's United States naval action against Libyan boats and aircraft in the Gulf of Sirte.

A Greek government spokesman said: "the blast was caused by a bomb placed in a piece of luggage aboard the plane." The blast tore a hole nine feet by three feet in the fuselage and the plane was saved from destruction only because it had descended to 11,000 feet on its landing run to Athens (→5).

GI discotheque is bombed in Berlin

April 5. A bomb exploded in La Belle discotheque, packed with American soldiers, in West Berlin in the early hours of this morning. Two people, a black American soldier and a Turkish woman, are known to have died and scores more were injured. Rescue teams are still searching for more casualties in the rubble.

A disc jockey said: "There was an unbelievably loud bang, then I found myself in the cellar as the floor had collapsed. It was a horrible picture. There were limbs scattered around the rubble. It was bad, really bad".

The 7,000 US servicemen stationed in West Berlin have been on high security alert following last month's clash between American and Libyan forces in the Gulf of Sirte (→15).

Boyfriend of duped bomb girl arrested

April 18. Anti-terrorist detectives tonight arrested Nezar Hindawi, the Jordanian wanted by Scotland Yard in connection with the attempt to plant a bomb on an El Al jumbo jet at Heathrow. The search for Hindawi began when his pregnant lover, Ann Marie Murphy, was stopped as she was about to board the plane for Tel Aviv.

A ten-pound bomb was found in the false bottom of her holdall. It had been timed to explode when the aircraft with its 360 passengers was airborne, possibly over London. Detectives soon realised that she was an innocent dupe who would have died in the blast.

Hindawi was arrested after being recognised when he checked into a hotel in West Kensington. The owner, who knows Hindawi, telephoned the police.

US launches air strike against Libya

April 15. United States aircraft, some of them F-111s flying from bases in Britain, attacked targets in Libya early this morning. Correspondents in Tripoli reported that the southern part of the city was enveloped in smoke, and that the attack appeared to have been aimed at targets in the harbour.

Mr Reagan's spokesman, Larry Speakes, said: "US forces have executed a series of carefully-planned air strikes against terrorist targets in Libya." He justified the bombing by accusing Libya of direct responsibility for acts of terrorism aimed at Americans, especially the bombing of La Belle discotheque in West Berlin 10 days ago.

"In the light of this reprehensible act of violence," said Mr Speakes, "and clear evidence that Libya is planning future attacks, the US has chosen to exercise its rights of self-defence ... Every effort was made to avoid civilian casualties."

The attacks began after a huge increase in coded radio traffic between US ships and planes off the Libyan coast had been noticed. The attacking forces seem to have been both carrier-based aircraft, operating in the Mediterranean, and the British-based bombers, which would have refuelled in mid-air.

The use of these aircraft from British bases will raise questions about how much control Britain has over them. It is unlikely that they would have been used without the British government's permission. Mrs Thatcher is certain to face fierce criticism (→17).

A baby is carried out of the ruins in Tripoli after the US air strike.

Guinness heiress unharmed after a week-long kidnap

April 16. After a six-hour siege of a house in a fashionable Dublin road, police today freed the kidnap victim Mrs Jennifer Guinness, aged 48, after six days of captivity. The wife of a merchant banker and an international yachtswoman, she saw her husband pistol-whipped before she was bundled into a car by three masked men. They demanded a £2,000,000 ransom.

Three men, two of them wanted for questioning about the murder of a policeman in Yorkshire two years ago, were in custody tonight. Police are satisfied that the IRA was not involved. Mrs Guinness dissuaded the kidnappers from taking her daughter Gillian too.

During her captivity, Mrs Guinness told reporters, she had concealed a tyre lever under her pillow. "I was determined to come out of this mentally and physically intact. If they were going to shoot me, I was going to be shot intact."

Duchess dies and will have royal farewell

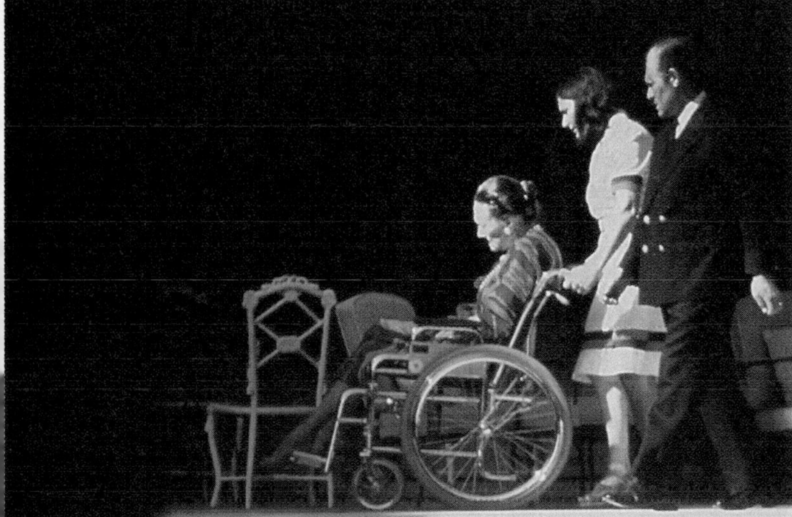

The last ever photo of the Duchess of Windsor, taken in her large garden.

April 24. The Duchess of Windsor, for whom King Edward VIII gave up his throne in 1936, died today in Paris. She was 89. The Duchess had been ill for some years, crippled with arthritis and partly paralysed.

She died at the fine mansion near the Bois de Boulogne which was rented to the Duke by the City of Paris in 1953 for a peppercorn rent of about £25 a year.

The funeral service at St. George's Chapel in Windsor on Tuesday will be attended by the Queen and other members of the royal family. The Duchess will then be laid to rest at Frogmore beside her husband (→29).

Mayor Eastwood to clean up Carmel

April 8. The Hollywood actor Clint Eastwood, aged 55, won a landslide victory today as the new Mayor of the Californian resort of Carmel. Long known as a hard-liner, Eastwood vowed to "build bridges" between the two warring factions of merchants and residents in Carmel (population 4,700) where he has lived for 14 years. As mayor he will be paid $200 a month, but he will also continue to make films.

Stalin's daughter is back in America

April 15. Svetlana Alliluyeva, the daughter of Joseph Stalin, is on the move again and heading back to the United States. Svetlana originally defected to the West in 1967 with her daughter. They returned to Moscow in 1984. Olga says she is delighted to be back in the West and does not regret her "Russian experience".

De Beauvoir, early feminist, is dead

Simone de Beauvoir.

April 14. Simone de Beauvoir, who inspired the women's movement with "The Second Sex" in 1949, has died in Paris, aged 78. At the Sorbonne she came second to Jean-Paul Sartre in philosophy. She said of him: "It was the first time I had felt intellectually inferior to anyone" (→26/2/87).

Soviet reactor is on fire

Technicians fly over the stricken reactor measuring radioactive emissions.

April 30. A Russian nuclear reactor is ablaze after what could turn out to be the world's worst civil nuclear disaster. The Soviet Union admitted this today – four days after the accident occurred – as high radiation levels were detected in Scandinavia.

According to the brief Russian statement, the Number 4 reactor at Chernobyl power station in the Ukraine is affected. The other three reactors in the plant have been shut down. Two people have been killed and nearby places evacuated, the statement on Soviet television said.

Pictures taken by American satellites indicate that the top of the reactor was blown off in an explosion. The graphite moderator of the reactor is on fire and the Russians have asked for help in fighting it from Sweden and West Germany, but offers of assistance, including one from the International Atomic Energy Agency, of which Russia is a member, have been refused.

How much radioactivity has escaped is unknown, but if the core is exposed, as the pictures suggest, it will be substantial. Russian reactors do not have containment buildings, normal in the West, to prevent the release of radioactivity after an accident. Local reports say 15,000 people have been moved from Pripyat, but life in Kiev, 60 miles from Chernobyl, seems normal. There is no immediate danger to Western Europe, though in the long term radiation from fallout could cause cancers (→ 14/5).

Lorries arrive to start cleaning up.

1986

MAY

Su	Mo	Tu	We	Th	Fr	Sa
				1	2	3
4	5	6	7	8	9	10
11	12	13	14	15	16	17
18	19	20	21	22	23	24
25	26	27	28	29	30	31

1. Johannesburg: 1.5 million black workers go on strike (→ 19).

4. Austria: Ex-UN Secretary-General Kurt Waldheim tops the first ballot of the presidential election (→ 8/6).

5. Sheffield: 150-1 outsider Joe Johnson becomes Embassy World Snooker Champion.

8. UK: Labour makes large gains in local elections (→ 12/6).

10. London: Britain expels three Syrian diplomats after Syria refuses to let them be quizzed on the El Al bomb (→ 11).

10. London: Liverpool beat Everton 3-1 in the FA Cup Final.

11. Damascus: Three British diplomats are expelled in a tit-for-tat move (→ 6/9).

14. Europe: A sharp drop in the number of US tourists coming to Europe this year is reported.

17. Seoul: Students confront police during anti-government demonstrations (→ 7/2/87).

19. S. Africa: South African forces carry out raids on Zambia, Zimbabwe and Botswana.→

21. London: Kenneth Baker succeeds Sir Keith Joseph as Education Secretary.

25. Worldwide: 30 million join in Bob Geldof's latest idea, a "Race Against Time" to raise money for Sportaid.

25. S. Africa: 30,000 blacks are forcibly expelled from their homes at Crossroads squatter camp near Cape Town (→ 12/6).

29. UK: Cricketer Ian Botham is banned from first class cricket for two months for admitting smoking cannabis (→ 7/7).

31. Warsaw: Zbigniew Bujak, the fugitive underground leader of Solidarity, is arrested (→ 11/9).

DEATH

9. Nepalese climber Tensing Norgay, alias Sherpa Tensing, (*1914).

Sri Lanka rocked by separatist violence

May 3. Twenty people died and 24, including five Britons, were injured when a bomb ripped an airliner in half at Colombo airport early today. The device was apparently timed to explode shortly after the TriStar would have taken off for the Maldives, but an unforeseen 15-minute delay prevented further carnage. Sri Lankan officials blame Tamil separatists for planting the bomb, the latest in a series of outrages that have marked the Tamils' three-year campaign for a separate state. Today's slaughter is believed to have been timed to sabotage current mediation efforts by the Indian government.

Tokyo summit calls for war on terror

May 5. Government leaders of the seven leading industrial nations meeting in Tokyo today issued a new declaration of war on international terrorism. They singled out Libya for its role in fomenting such violence, and also agreed to ostracise, and ban arms sales to, all nations supporting terrorism. As if to reinforce their message, a salvo of locally-made Japanese terrorist rockets was fired at the state guest house where the leaders are staying. They missed.

Prince Charles and Diana greet the torch bearer at the start of The Race Against Time, raising money for Africa.

Fear of melt-down at Chernobyl reactor

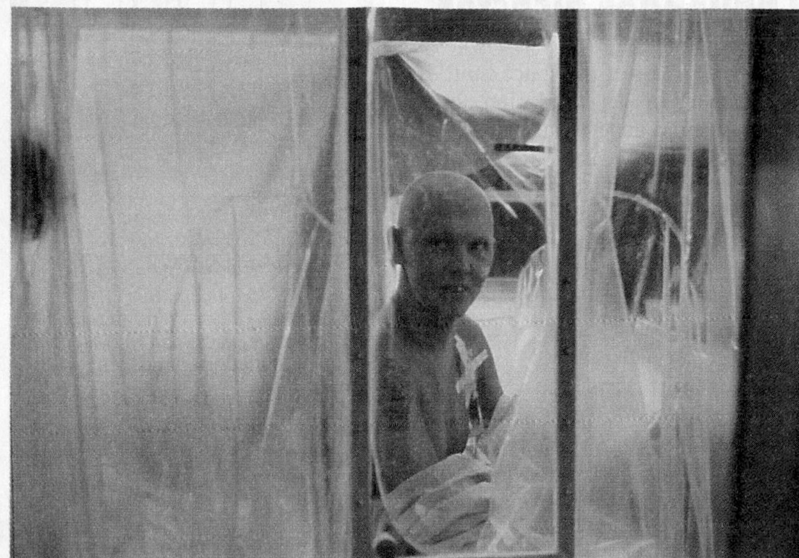

A victim of the reactor fire being cared for by a US doctor, Robert Gale.

May 14. The extent of the threat posed by the nuclear reactor at Chernobyl in the Soviet Union, seriously damaged in an explosion last month, is still uncertain. According to a German expert, Dr Thomas Roser, the molten white hot core may be melting its way through the concrete floor of the reactor, on its way to contaminating the Dnieper river. However, the Soviet academician Yevgeny Velikhov says the reactor is no longer a hazard, though he admitted that the danger of a meltdown had existed earlier. Work is under way to encase the reactor in concrete. Pictures of the empty town of Chernobyl, shown on Soviet television last night, suggest that the authorities regard the situation as under control (→20/6).

White extremists break up Botha meeting

May 22. Right-wing white extremists, wearing swastika-style armbands and brown uniforms, broke into a public hall in Pietersburg, Transvaal, tonight, and stopped a meeting that was to have been addressed by Pik Botha, the South African Foreign Minister. Twelve people were injured when police threw tear gas into the hall and caused panic. Supporters of the governing National Party accused local police of encouraging the white extremists (→25).

The extreme right-wing leader, Terre Blanche, surrounded by supporters.

1986

JUNE

Su	Mo	Tu	We	Th	Fr	Sa
1	2	3	4	5	6	7
8	9	10	11	12	13	14
15	16	17	18	19	20	21
22	23	24	25	26	27	28
29	30					

3. Sri Lanka: Tamil separatists claim responsibility for three bombs which killed 50 people (→17/2/87).

4. UK: The Aga Khan's Shahrastri wins the Derby.

8. Peru: President Garcia Perez escapes an assassination attempt.

12. UK: Austin-Rover is renamed the Rover Group.

12. UK: Ex-deputy leader of Liverpool council Derek Hatton is expelled from the Labour Party (→12/3/87).

13. Johannesburg: Bishop Tutu meets Botha for the first time in six years to protest against the state of emergency (→16).

16. S. Africa: Millions of blacks stay away from work on the tenth anniversary of the Soweto uprising (→9/7).

17. Madrid: Three die in a bomb attack by the Basque separatist group ETA (→19/6/87).

20. UK: The slaughter and movement of lambs in parts of Cumbria is temporarily banned because of Chernobyl fall-out (→21/8).

23. UK: 13 die in a crash on the M4 near Maidenhead.

23. London: Patrick Magee gets eight life sentences for the Brighton and other bombings (→24).

24. Belfast: Police carry Ian Paisley kicking and screaming out of the Ulster Assembly after it is dissolved (→12/7).

27. The Hague: The World Court says Reagan broke international law by aiding Nicaraguan Contra rebels (→7/12).

29. UK: Richard Branson crosses the Atlantic in record time in the Virgin Atlantic Challenger II.

DEATHS

3. British actress Dame Anna Neagle, born Florence Marjorie Robertson (*20/10/1904).

13. US clarinettist Benny Goodman (*30/5/1909).

14. Argentine author Jorge Luis Borges (*24/8/1899).

Waldheim elected Austrian President

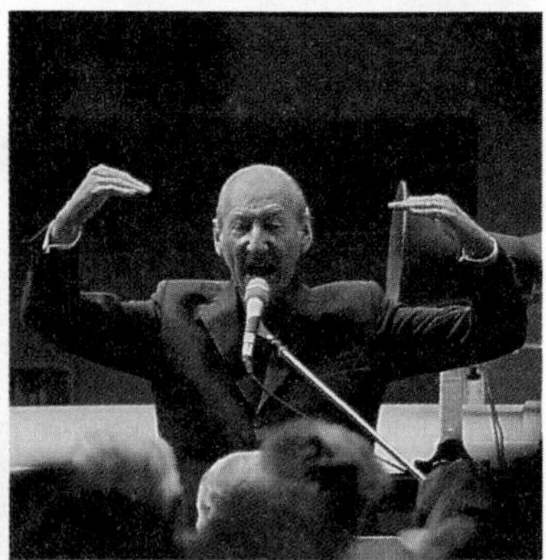

New President Kurt Waldheim.

June 8. Dr Kurt Waldheim, shrugging off accusations that he had been involved in Nazi wartime atrocities in the Balkans, was elected President of Austria today with a decisive victory over his Socialist Party rival, Kurt Steyrer.

Dr Waldheim said his task was to heal the wounds that had been opened in Austrian society. He predicted that the furore over his wartime activities would soon die down because there was nothing incriminating in his past.

The Conservatives, who supported Dr Waldheim, were jubilant. Dr Michael Graft described the result as "a landslide" and said the issue of Dr Waldheim's past played only a minor role. It is not, however, likely to go away and could prove embarrassing (→25/6/87).

Irish voters say No to new divorce laws

June 27. The Irish people have rejected a constitutional change which would allow divorce in the Republic. The proposal of Dr Garret FitzGerald's government was rejected in a referendum by 935,842 votes to 538,729.

Dr FitzGerald hoped that, by allowing divorce, the Republic would be more acceptable to northern Protestants. Ministers felt that the change, if it had come about, would have lessened bitterness and tensions between the north and the south of Ireland.

Dr FitzGerald said: "I accept the decision of the people, but I regret it" (→20/1/87).

South Africa declares state of emergency

Rioters gathered in a shanty town are armed with sticks and long knives.

June 12. In a nationwide sweep by South African security forces at dawn today, hundreds of black activists, trade unionists and church workers were rounded up in an attempt to prevent widespread unrest on the tenth anniversary of the black uprising on June 16 in Soweto township. Several hours after the arrests, President P.W. Botha disclosed that an indefinite nationwide state of emergency had been declared to curb mounting violence by "revolutionaries supported by the African National Congress".

A limited emergency was declared a year ago, and Mr Botha was preparing to lift it by putting through parliament security laws that would give the police much the same wide powers of arrest and detention as they have under a state of emergency, but Coloured (mixed race) and Asian MPs in the recently-created three-chamber parliament blocked the move.

The new emergency was declared just as the Commonwealth Eminent Persons' Group, reporting on their visit to South Africa, predicted a "bloodbath" if political reform was delayed (→13).

Faulty ring caused Challenger disaster

June 9. The loss of the space shuttle Challenger in an explosion last January could have been prevented, according to the 256-page report on the disaster by the presidential commission of inquiry published today. A faulty seal on one of the solid-fuelled booster rockets, which allowed hot gases to escape, was the probable cause of the explosion.

The report says the National Aeronautics and Space Administration had enough warnings of the hazard last year to require a change in the seal design. The manufacturers of the booster were also at fault, adds the report.

Stalker taken off Ulster investigation

June 30. John Stalker, the deputy chief constable of Manchester, was today suspended from duty, pending investigation of his alleged association with "known criminals". Mr Stalker, aged 47, has been on leave since the end of May when he was taken off a two-year inquiry into allegations of a "shoot to kill" policy by the Royal Ulster Constabulary (→22/8).

"Hand of God" helps Argentina to victory in the World Cup

June 29. The second World Cup to be staged in Mexico will always be remembered for the influence of the Argentinian captain Diego Maradona. It was his blatant fisted goal that helped beat England in the quarter-final ("The hand of God", he later called it), his two goals that beat Belgium in the semi-final, and West Germany's preoccupation with keeping him quiet that allowed Argentina to find gaps in the German defence in the ill-tempered final which proved decisive in the 3-2 victory.

Both Scotland and Northern Ireland departed early, though England survived a shaky start to mount a worthwhile challenge – with Gary Lineker emerging as the tournament's top scorer with six goals – before their fateful encounter with Maradona.

Diego Maradona, Argentina's soccer hero, gets his hands on the World Cup.

1986

JULY

Su	Mo	Tu	We	Th	Fr	Sa
		1	2	3	4	5
6	7	8	9	10	11	12
13	14	15	16	17	18	19
20	21	22	23	24	25	26
27	28	29	30	31		

2. Gulf War: The Iranians capture the border town of Mehran (→18/1/87).

4. UK: A policeman is acquitted of the manslaughter of five-year-old John Shorthouse, killed in a raid.

6. Wimbledon: Martina Navratilova beats Hana Mandlikova for the Women's Singles title; Boris Becker beats Ivan Lendl in the Men's Singles final (→22).

6. Manila: A pro-Marcos coup attempt fails (→23/11).

7. Kuala Lumpur: A Briton and an Australian are the first foreigners to be hanged under Malaysia's stiff anti-drug law (→29).

9. London: Thatcher restates her opposition to sanctions against South Africa, saying they hurt blacks most (→13).

12. Northern Ireland: 100 are injured in Orange Day clashes between Protestants and Catholics (→7/8).

13. UK: Native South Africans Zola Budd and Annette Cowley are banned from the Commonwealth Games (→1/8).

17. Washington: The Senate ratifies an Anglo-US extradition treaty.

20. UK: Greg Norman wins the British Open Golf Championship.

21. UK: A report says 20 per cent of children are now born outside marriage.

22. Prague: Martina Navratilova plays tennis in Czechoslovakia for the first time since her defection in 1975.

27. Paris: Greg Lemond becomes the first American to win the Tour de France.

29. London: Pop singer Boy George is convicted of possessing heroin (→11/11/87).

30. US: Divers report that a split seam, not a hole, caused the Titanic to sink.→

30. London: Estate agent Suzy Lamplugh is reported missing.

DEATH

26. US politician and diplomat Averell Harriman (*15/11/1891).

1986

AUGUST

Su	Mo	Tu	We	Th	Fr	Sa
					1	2
3	4	5	6	7	8	9
10	11	12	13	14	15	16
17	18	19	20	21	22	23
24	25	26	27	28	29	30
31						

100-year-old lady celebrates her facelift

July 4. The Statue of Liberty celebrated her 100th birthday today by re-opening her newly-refurbished doors to visitors. America's great symbol of hope is now restored to full health. The first visitor on Independence Day was, perhaps appropriately, an English tourist.

America certainly gave her a splendid party. This morning President Reagan surveyed 20 US warships and 21 from other nations in New York harbour, while a newly-scrubbed Miss Liberty looked on. He took lunch with the French President, Francois Mitterrand, whose country delivered the statue as a gift 100 years ago. Jet fighters from France performed an aerobatic tribute, and tonight she glowed in a brilliant firework display.

Statue of Liberty's birthday bash.

Publication of spy's revelations banned

July 11. Newspapers were today banned from publishing information received from Peter Wright, a former senior MI5 officer. A High Court judge said that Britain's security services must be seen to be leak-proof.

He granted injunctions sought by the Government which is bringing a court case against Mr Wright in Australia where he has lived for ten years. It wants to stop publication of his memoirs. Mr Wright says they contain nothing new (→28/11).

Rivets blamed for sinking of Titanic

July 30. Divers who have found the wreck of the Titanic on the Atlantic sea-bed have challenged what was long held to be the cause of the liner's sinking in 1912. Dr Robert Ballard, leader of the investigating team, said today that the Titanic was not sunk by an enormous gash in the hull torn by an iceberg. It was more likely, he added, that the hull of the supposedly unsinkable liner simply buckled on impact, with the rivets popping "quietly but lethally" out of place.

July 23. Showered with confetti and surrounded by pageantry, Prince Andrew and Sarah Ferguson, the Duke and Duchess of York, ride in the Honeymoon Carriage, after being married in Westminster Abbey.

1. Washington: A Senate group votes for strict sanctions against South Africa (→4).

4. London: A Commonwealth summit ends with Thatcher agreeing only to voluntary sanctions on South Africa (→18).

7. Ireland: Democratic Unionist deputy leader Peter Robinson is arrested at a Loyalist protest in the republic (→13).

8. English Channel: Manchester United and West Ham "fans" fight a pitched battle aboard a cross-Channel ferry (→20/1/87).

10. El Salvador: Scores are feared dead when an earthquake topples buildings in the capital, San Salvador.

10. India: The general who ordered the storming of the Sikh Golden Temple in 1984 is shot dead in Poona (→30/11).

13. Dublin: IRA suspect Gerard O'Reilly is freed due to an error in an extradition warrant (→16/1/87).

18. S. Africa: According to the government, 8,501 have been detained under the state of emergency regulations.→

21. Moscow: The report into the Chernobyl disaster blames the plant's technicians for ignoring safety rules.

22. US: Nuclear processing firm Kerr-McGee agrees to pay $1.3 million to the estate of Karen Silkwood.

22. Manchester: Stalker is reinstated as deputy chief constable after a probe clears him of associating with criminals (→19/12).

27. Washington: A report says the US accidentally dropped a 42,000-ton hydrogen bomb on New Mexico in 1957 (→12/3/87).

31. Los Angeles: 67 are killed when two planes collide in mid air.

DEATH

31. British sculptor Henry Moore (*30/7/1898).→

Police shoot eight as fresh rioting erupts in Soweto

Aug 27. At least 12 people are dead and 70 are injured, including five policemen, after a night of rioting in the black township of Soweto, outside Johannesburg. The trouble started when police used tear gas to halt a crowd of 500 or more marching on the offices of Soweto council to protest against evictions in the wake of an 11-week rent boycott, but police claim black youths set up barricades to prevent evictions, and then turned on the homes of black councillors, setting fire to them and hacking one councillor to death. Black militants say councillors are traitors (→7/9).

Lake of death kills 1,500 in Cameroons

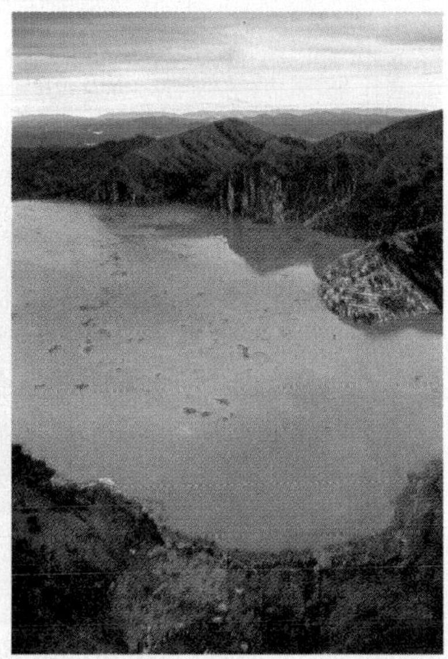

The highly poisonous Lake Nios.

Aug 26. Fifteen hundred people died today in the Cameroons when a deadly mixture of carbon dioxide and hydrogen gas escaped from a volcanic lake near the town of Wum. The odourless gas poured out of a fissure near Lake Nios, some 200 miles north of the capital Yaounde, and filled Nios village, killing people as they slept. Only two of the 700 inhabitants survived; other lakeside villages were similarly devastated. Teams of French and Israeli rescuers are flying in to help.

▷

Moore, grand old man of sculpture, dies

Aug 31. More than any other artist, Henry Moore, who died today, put Britain on the map of 20th century art. He was to sculpture what Picasso was to painting: he reinvented it. Countries around the world honoured him with exhibitions and commissions.

In earlier years he was often ridiculed for piercing holes through the middle of his figures, which enhanced their three-dimensional effect. In his Reclining Figures he was influenced by the carvings of early cultures other than Greek, which he pointed out was only a small fragment of man's sculpture.

A miner's son from Castleford, Yorkshire, he said he enjoyed the "hard navvying" of working with stone. He had a cottage-workshop near the Carrara quarries as well as his home at Much Hadham, Herts. His drawings are highly prized.

Moore: sculptor as navvyman.

Riots flare as Bhutto's daughter is jailed

Rioting supporters of Miss Benazir Bhutto hurl stones at government forces.

Aug 14. Riots erupted in cities across Pakistan today as supporters of Miss Benazir Bhutto demonstrated against the government of President Zia on the country's Independence Day. Three people were shot dead and Miss Bhutto, daughter of the hanged former premier, Zulfikar Ali Bhutto, was arrested.

Miss Bhutto led a procession of more than 8,000 people from her home in Karachi, but police stopped the marchers after they had gone only a few hundred yards and dispersed them with baton charges and tear gas. Miss Bhutto was arrested later, after addressing a rally of supporters at which she called for the resignation of President Zia's regime. She will be held in jail for 30 days under the public order law.

The three people who died were in a crowd of 2,000 which marched on a police station in Lahore. They were protesting about the banning of a major series of rallies planned by Miss Bhutto's Pakistan People's Party, working with other opposition parties in the Movement for Restoration of Democracy to get rid of President Zia.

1986

SEPTEMBER

Su	Mo	Tu	We	Th	Fr	Sa
	1	2	3	4	5	6
7	8	9	10	11	12	13
14	15	16	17	18	19	20
21	22	23	24	25	26	27
28	29	30				

2. USSR: 400 are feared dead when a Soviet liner sinks in the Black Sea.

2. Harare: Leaders of the "Non-aligned" nations begin talks.

5. Karachi: Over 17 die when Pakistani commandos storm a hijacked US airliner; 300 passengers and crew escape.

6. Istanbul: Arab gunmen open fire on worshippers in a synagogue, killing 21 (→7/10).

7. Cape Town: Tutu is enthroned as Archbishop of Cape Town, the first black head of southern African Anglicans.→

10. London: Mrs Edwina Currie becomes a health minister in a reshuffle of junior ministerial positions (→23).

11. Warsaw: The Polish government announces the release of 225 political prisoners.

12. Washington: The House of Representatives votes to impose economic sanctions on South Africa (→25).

16. S. Africa: 177 black miners die in a fire at the Kinross gold mine.

21. UK: Prince Charles admits on TV that he talks to his plants.

23. Eastbourne: The Liberal Assembly votes against the leadership to scrap Britain's nuclear deterrent (→22/12).

23. UK: Edwina Currie says people in the north have generally poorer health because of ignorance.

24. UK: Four million people have applied for shares in the Trustee Savings Bank in Britain's most popular flotation ever (→14/11).

25. S. Africa: The government tightens press restrictions (→29).

28. US: Londoner Lloyd Honeyghan beats Don Curry to become world welterweight boxing champion (→28/10/87).

29. Washington: The House of Representatives overrides Reagan's veto of sanctions against South Africa (→2/10).

Nissan opens a car factory in the UK

Sept 8. Nissan, the Japanese car manufacturer, today opened a new plant near Sunderland, and said it would be increasing its British output to 100,000 cars a year. Several areas of Britain had sought to woo the Japanese, despite worries about the effect on the British motor industry.

Mrs Thatcher, who opened the plant, welcomed Nissan's commitment to Britain. and the 2,000 jobs it provides. Her government will provide £100 million in regional aid towards Nissan's expenditure of £380 million.

Zimbabwe's aid cut for rudeness to US

Sept 2. It was a moment of triumph for Robert Gabriel Mugabe, Zimbabwe's Prime Minister, as he welcomed Rajiv Gandhi of India, Fidel Castro of Cuba, Daniel Ortega of Nicaragua and some 50 other stars of the non-aligned movement. The bad news was that the US had just stopped all $20 million of aid after a Mugabe minister delivered a furious tirade against the US at a meeting attended by former President Jimmy Carter, who walked out. The US accused Mr Mugabe's government of lacking "diplomatic civility".

Kim Basinger and Mickey Rourke take time off from their constant coupling in the box-office smash "9 ½ Weeks".

Arab bomb blitz shakes Parisian shoppers

Chaos and carnage on the Paris streets after an Arab bomb attack.

Sept 17. A bomb hurled from a speeding BMW car into a Paris department store today killed four and wounded 44, including many children. "This is a bloody massacre," said a fireman as panic broke out in the busy Left Bank street. It was the fifth bomb in a week long Arab terrorist onslaught which has shaken Parisians.

Last week Jacques Chirac, the Prime Minister, announced tough new measures against terrorism. Visas are now required for all non-EEC visitors, and armed soldiers patrol the Paris streets.

US deny deal on newsman freed in USSR

Sept 29. A month-long US-Soviet confrontation ended today when the Soviet Union released Nicholas Daniloff, an American journalist accused of spying. Daniloff flew from Moscow with his wife, insisting the case had been fabricated by the KGB to secure the release of a Russian United Nations employee, Gennadi Zakharov, arrested for spying. Although the Reagan administration insisted no deal had been done to swap Zakharov for Daniloff, the US has agreed not to press charges against the Russian and allow him to return home. A group of Soviet dissidents is also to be freed, under the deal.

Geoffrey Boycott is fired by Yorkshire

Sept 23. After a career of 24 years as Yorkshire's – and for much of that time England's – most successful opening batsman since the war, Geoffrey Boycott has been sacked by his county.

In recent years the relationship between Yorkshire and their dedicated run-machine, who is the most prolific scorer in test history, has become increasingly stormy. Although he topped the county's batting averages last season, at the age of 45, the committee voted overwhelmingly today for a clean break with their former captain.

Sept 7. Desmond Tutu enthroned as Archbishop of Cape Town.

1986

OCTOBER

Su	Mo	Tu	We	Th	Fr	Sa
			1	2	3	4
5	6	7	8	9	10	11
12	13	14	15	16	17	18
19	20	21	22	23	24	25
26	27	28	29	30	31	

2. Washington: The Senate overrides Reagan's veto on sanctions against South Africa.→

2. India: Gandhi escapes an assassination attempt.

4. Nicaragua: US Air Force pilot Eugene Hasenfus is captured after his cargo plane is shot down.

6. Moscow: Kasparov beats Karpov to retain the world chess championship.

7. Tunisia: Arafat says the PLO will move headquarters from Tunis to Yemen (→15).

9. London: An angry crowd surrounds Notting Hill police station after a black man dies in police custody.

11. Tanzania: Mother Teresa escapes unhurt from a plane crash which kills six.

12. Beijing: The Queen arrives on the first visit to China by a British monarch.

15. Jerusalem: A soldier is killed and 70 hurt in a grenade attack at the Wailing Wall (→24).

17. Switzerland: Birmingham gets only eight votes as Barcelona is chosen to host the 1992 Olympic Games.

20. Tel Aviv: Shimon Peres hands over the premiership to his coalition partner Yitzhak Shamir (→20).

20. London: Israeli nuclear technician Mordechai Vanunu is reported to have been kidnapped (→9/11).

22. UK: Kingsley Amis wins the Booker Prize for his novel "The Old Devils" (→12/1986).

24. London: Syrian Nezar Hindawi is jailed for 45 years for plotting to blow up an El Al airliner (→24).

24. London: Britain breaks off relations with Syria after the Hindawi verdict (→2/11).

28. UK: Jeremy Bamber is jailed for life for killing five of his family in the hope of inheriting a fortune.

DEATH

16. Belgian violinist Arthur Grumiaux (*21/3/1921).

American firms pull out of South Africa

Oct 22. General Motors today became the fourth big US business to abandon operations in South Africa. The others are Honeywell, IBM and Warners. General Motors said they have been losing money in their South African plant, but their decision has clearly been influenced by this month's overwhelming vote for sanctions by the Senate, despite President Reagan's appeal for delay. The US will now ban imports of South African iron, steel, coal, uranium, textiles and farm produce; new loans and investments are also banned (→24/11).

Top oil minister is fired by Saudi king

Oct 28. Sheik Yamani, Saudi Arabia's oil minister for 24 years, was given his marching orders today by King Fahd. Ahmed Zaki Yamani was effectively at the helm of the Organisation of Petroleum Exporting Countries, which the Saudis were instrumental in founding in 1960. Although he engineered the 1973 oil embargo that led to a tenfold rise in oil prices, he was seen as a moderate in OPEC. Recently he is reported to have sold Saudi oil at less than OPEC rates, which may have prompted his dismissal.

Big Bang splutters into a damp squib

Oct 27. The London Stock Exchange's "Big Bang" got off to a shaky start today when its new computerised dealing system failed for an hour at 8.30am, unable to cope with the huge rush of enquiries. Frustrated dealers went back on to the Stock Exchange floor to do business in the traditional way.

Big Bang applies not merely to the introduction of computers but also the scrapping of many controls which previously applied. It allows foreign companies into the Exchange, and ends the system of fixed commission rates on deals. The big institutions have already halved their payments to brokers (→3/12). ▷

Star Wars spike summit

Reagan and Gorbachev sit with the shadow of Star Wars between them.

Oct 13. A non-existent US weapon, the "Strategic Defence Initiative", has scuppered the superpowers' arms control talks at Reykjavik in Iceland, which ended today without any agreement.

President Reagan and Mr Gorbachev, meeting in an isolated villa, had started off by agreeing to remove intermediate nuclear forces from Europe and cut them by 80 per cent in Soviet Asia, to halve strategic weapons, and to work towards a new test ban treaty.

Gorbachev then made the whole deal conditional on Reagan keeping SDI, the outer-space defence shield better known as "Star Wars", in the laboratory. Reagan said he had promised never to trade away SDI.

His counter-proposal, that both sides eliminate all ballistic missiles by 1996, and then rely on Star Wars technology, fell at the same hurdle: Gorbachev's insistence that the US drop SDI, and Reagan's refusal.

There was a definite frost in the air as the leaders went their separate and gloomy ways; but before the stalemate, good progress had been made on how to count weapons, and the President invited the Soviet leader to Washington for further talks.

Archer quits, but denies sex charges

Oct 26. Jeffrey Archer resigned as deputy chairman of the Tory Party today on account of newspaper allegations that he had tried to pay a prostitute to go abroad to avoid a scandal.

The best-selling novelist and former MP stated that he felt obliged to resign "for lack of judgement and that alone". He strongly denied that he had ever met the prostitute, and said that he had foolishly fallen into a reprehensible trap to get him to offer her money.

Mr Archer said that Mrs Thatcher had been "extremely gracious and kind" when he told her about the incident. MPs regard it as bizarre (→ 24/7/87).

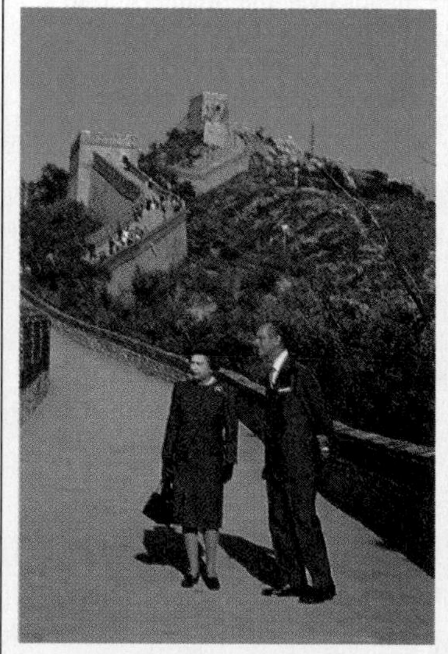

Oct 14. The Queen and the Duke of Edinburgh sight-seeing on the Great Wall; she is the first British monarch to visit China.

1986

NOVEMBER

Su	Mo	Tu	We	Th	Fr	Sa
						1
2	3	4	5	6	7	8
9	10	11	12	13	14	15
16	17	18	19	20	21	22
23	24	25	26	27	28	29
30						

2. Beirut: US hostage David Jacobsen is freed after 18 months following the intervention of Terry Waite.→

3. Mozambique: Joaquim Chissano is chosen to succeed President Machel, killed in a plane crash in South Africa.

4. Washington: The Democrats win control of the Senate.

6. London: Lawson announces a £4.6 billion rise in public spending.

9. Tel Aviv: The Israelis admit they hold Mordechai Vanunu, the nuclear technician believed kidnapped in Britain.

12. Berne: The Swiss agree to pay compensation for damage caused by the Rhine chemical spillage.

14. London: The Government rushes through tougher rules against insider dealing on the Stock Exchange (→ 17).

17. Paris: Renault chief executive Georges Besse is shot dead by unidentified gunmen.

17. London: Share prices tumble after New York financier Ivan Boesky confesses to insider dealing (→ 1/12).

20. UK: Police search Saddleworth Moor for two missing children, feared killed, after Myra Hindley broke her silence (→ 1/7/87).

23. Manila: Aquino sacks Defence Minister Juan Ponce Enrile for plotting the return of Marcos (→ 29/1/87).

24. London: Barclays Bank announces it is "disinvesting" from South Africa, where it is the biggest bank (→ 30/12).

27. London: A secret report reveals that George V's doctor hastened the sick king's death with cocaine and morphine.

30. India: 24 die when Sikh extremists slaughter passengers on a bus in the Punjab.

DEATHS

8. Soviet statesman Vyacheslav Molotov (*9/3/1890).

29. British-born US actor Cary Grant, born Alexander Archibald Leach (*18/1/1904).→

Grant, nonchalant matinee idol, dies

Nov 29. A matinee idol is known by the quality of his leading ladies and Cary Grant had the best – beginning with Mae West who invited him to "come up and see me sometime" in "She Done Him Wrong". She done him nothing but good. He starred with every female star of note. The chemistry worked especially well with Katharine Hepburn, Ingrid Bergman, Grace Kelly and Sophia Loren. He married for the fifth time at the age of 77.

Cary Grant's real name was Archibald Leach. Behind his poised nonchalance lay a troubled youth in Bristol. He died today, aged 82.

Cary Grant: a man for all ladies.

Cabinet secretary apologises to court

Nov 28. Sir Robert Armstrong, Britain's Cabinet Secretary, apologised to an Australian court today for unintentionally giving misleading evidence. He said he had been "economical with the truth".

Sir Robert is the Government's chief witness in an action to try to suppress publication of the memoirs of Peter Wright, the former MI5 officer. He explained that there had been some misunderstanding. In a dramatic courtroom clash Mr Wright's lawyer demanded of him "Can any of your evidence be trusted?" The case goes badly for Her Majesty's Government (→ 12/7/87).

Washington hit by Irangate row

Nov 30. The "Irangate" saga erupted into a new crisis for the Reagan administration today with the resignation of Admiral John Poindexter as the President's National Security Adviser and the dismissal of Lieutenant-Colonel Oliver North, a member of the National Security Council staff. "Ollie" North, a much-decorated Marine officer, known to White House cynics as the President's "Swashbuckler in Chief", was linked to the transfer of some $30 million profit from the Iran weapons sales to Contra rebels fighting the left-wing Sandinista government in Nicaragua.

The affair began early this month after Terry Waite, the special representative of the Archbishop of Canterbury, secured the release of Mr David Jacobsen, an American hostage held for 18 months in Beirut by Shia supporters of Iran.

America insisted that no deal had been done with the Iranians to secure Mr Jacobsen's release, but a Beirut magazine then revealed that Oliver North had set up an arms-for-hostages deal with the Iranians, incidentally using Mr Waite as an innocent pawn in the deal. Mr Reagan was forced to admit that he had been involved in secret diplomacy with Iran for 18 months to try to free American hostages, and that he had authorised the transfer of "small amounts" of arms to Tehran. Now it has emerged that Oliver North not only made a profit on the deal but passed it on to the Contras when Congress cut off official US funds for the rebels.

Seeking to contain the damage, a grim-faced Mr Reagan today announced a review of the National Security Council. Still insisting his overtures to Iran had not been a mistake, he said: "I was not fully informed of one of the activities undertaken in connection with this initiative" (→27/1/87).

Anglican envoy, Terry Waite, smiles delightedly as freed hostages embrace.

Tyson is youngest heavyweight champ

Nov 22. With a speed not seen in the heavyweight ring since the early days of Muhammad Ali, and with an awesome punch that will have all his potential challengers thinking twice, Mike Tyson has reached the top of the most lucrative tree in sport at the age of only 20 – younger than any of his predecessors. In less than two rounds of controlled aggression in Las Vegas today he tore the WBC world heavyweight title from the champion, Trevor Berbick (→1/8/87).

The new world heavyweight champion triumphantly displays his trophies.

Chemical spill may strip Rhine of life

Nov 10. In one of the worst ecological disasters in recent years, the River Rhine, once a mythical symbol of purity, has been massively polluted after firemen, fighting a blaze at the Sandox chemicals plant at Basle in Switzerland, washed some thirty tons of highly toxic liquid pesticides into the river.

The full scale of the disaster was only appreciated when fishermen began hauling hundreds of thousands of dead fish from the river, all victims of the floating chemicals. Some of these chemicals are being gradually diluted, but quantities of non-soluble mercury are moving almost as a solid body.

The Swiss government has promised to pay substantial compensation to all those whose livelihoods suffer, but Germany's powerful ecology lobby is demanding that tough new anti-pollution legislation be passed (→12).

Safe sex is way to beat AIDS says big new ad campaign

Nov 21. The Government today launched the biggest-ever health campaign in Britain, in a bid to combat the growing menace of AIDS. So far there have been 548 cases in Britain and 278 deaths – and the numbers are doubling every ten months.

An estimated 30,000 are infected with the virus, with a third expected to develop the disease. Acquired Immune Deficiency Syndrome attacks the body's defence system and there is no cure. The main victims so far have been male homosexuals and drug users, but there are fears that the disease could spread to the general population through sexual contact.

The £20 million campaign has the slogan "AIDS – Don't Die of Ignorance". Leaflets to 23 million households will hammer home the messages: stick to one partner or use condoms and, for drug users, never share needles (→7/1/87).

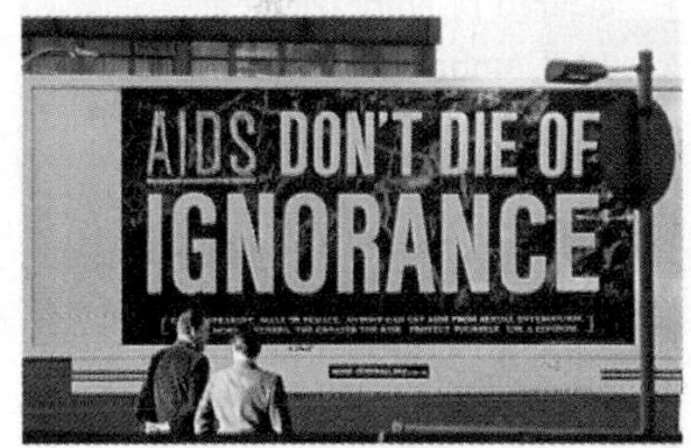

A very expensive word to the wise.

45 die as oil-rig helicopter crashes

Nov 6. Forty-five people are feared dead after a helicopter crashed into the North Sea two miles off the Shetland Islands in the worst civilian helicopter crash in history.

The Chinook, which was carrying Shell oil workers back from the Brent oil field to Sumburgh airport, disintegrated on impact. In spite of an immediate air-sea rescue operation, only two of the 47 passengers and crew survived. The rescued men owe their lives to a coastguard helicopter passing the scene at the time, which was able to pull them out only seconds after they entered the water.

1986

DECEMBER

Su	Mo	Tu	We	Th	Fr	Sa
	1	2	3	4	5	6
7	8	9	10	11	12	13
14	15	16	17	18	19	20
21	22	23	24	25	26	27
28	29	30	31			

3. UK: Four million apply for British Gas shares (→30/1/87).

7. Washington: Reagan authorises the use of US helicopters to ferry Honduran troops into battle against Nicaragua (→20/2/87).

9. UK: The NSPCC says cases of child sexual abuse have doubled in the last year (→29/6/87).

10. Stockholm: Nobel Prizes go to Ernst Ruska (West Germany), G. Binnig (West Germany) and H. Rohrer (Switzerland), all Physics; Dudley Hershbach (US), Yuan Tseh-Lee (US) and John Polanyi (Canada), all Chemistry; S. Cohen (US) and R. Levi-Montalcini (Italy), both Medicine; Wole Soyinka (Nigeria, Literature); J. Buchanan (US, Economics); and in Oslo to Elie Wiesel (US, Peace).→

17. Detroit: John De Lorean is cleared of embezzlement.

17. Cambridge: Davina Thompson becomes the world's first triple heart, lungs and liver transplant patient.

19. Manchester: John Stalker resigns from the police.

22. UK: Truro's Liberal MP David Penhaligon is killed when a van hits his car (→26/2/87).

30. South Africa: Oil giant Esso says it is disinvesting (→12/4/87).

DEATH

29. British statesman Maurice Harold Macmillan, first Earl of Stockton, Prime Minister 1957-63 (*10/2/1894).→

HITS OF 1986

Don't leave me this way.

Every loser wins.

I want to make up with you.

QUOTE OF THE YEAR

"Ideology is the curse of public affairs because it converts politics into a branch of theology and sacrifices human beings on the altar of dogma."

Arthur Schlesinger, US historian, 1986.

Macmillan bows out from earthly stage

Dec 29. "Supermac" died tonight at the age of 92. Harold Macmillan, first Earl of Stockton, was one of the political giants of the century – philosopher, wit, showman and master of manoeuvre – all rolled into one.

Macmillan was Prime Minister from 1957 to 1963, a period epitomised in his famous slogan "You've never had it so good". Following his "wind of change" speech he presided over the rapid liquidation of the old British Empire.

He was born rich and married a duke's daughter, but for much of his life was a rebel against his party establishment. In later life he became a national father-figure. It was a role he played superbly from his stage in the Lords (→5/1/87).

Harold Macmillan posing at home.

Chinese students lead democracy demos

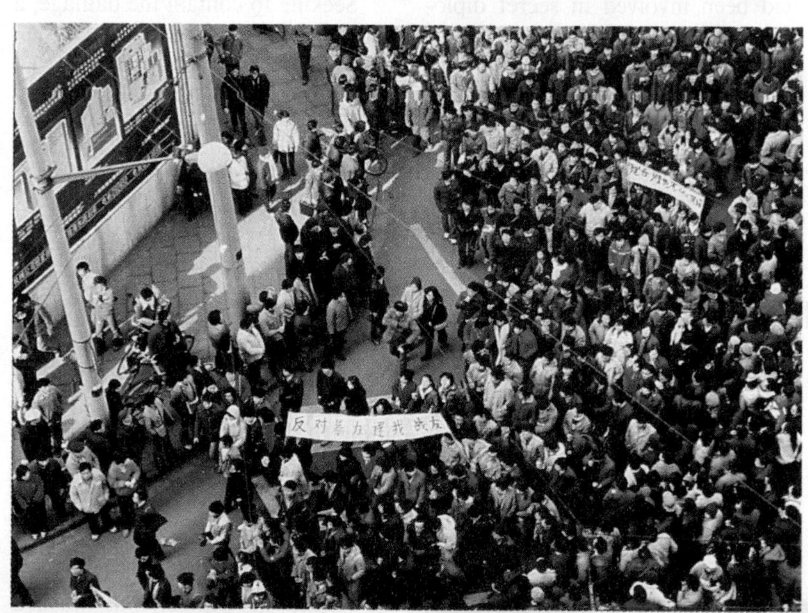

Chinese students gather in Shanghai to demonstrate for more democracy.

Dec 21. Chinese students are holding huge demonstrations in several cities demanding democratic reforms, including freedom of the press. In the latest demonstration more than 50,000 students gathered today in Shanghai's People's Square, carrying posters reading "Give us democracy" and "Long Live Freedom".

The wave of protests began two weeks ago in the central Chinese city of Hefei, and now appears to be out of the control of the authorities. The demonstrations in Shanghai were triggered off by the beating of a student at a pop concert and a tough warning by the city's mayor that action would be taken against young people taking their grievances to the streets.

China is now experiencing the most dramatic student unrest since the ill-fated "Democracy Wall" movement of 1979.

Some observers believe it is being orchestrated by supporters of the Chinese leader Deng Xiao-ping. He is believed to be planning reforms involving the separation of the powers of party and government (→1/1/87).

City probe not good for Guinness shares

Dec 1. The shares of Guinness, the beer and spirits group, plunged by over £300 million today after a Department of Trade inquiry was announced "to examine circumstances suggesting misconduct". Guinness is by far the most important company to be probed in this way. The inquiry relates to the bitterly fought takeover bid for Distillers, and arises from evidence given during the investigation in New York of the US share dealer Ivan Boesky (→9/1/86).

Halley's Comet tops the scientific year

February this year saw Halley's Comet come the closest to the sun on its latest 75-yearly visit. It was barely visible to the naked eye, but for space researchers the visit was a triumph. Observations from spacecraft, notably the European Giotto which sent back close-up pictures, provided much new information.

The year of 1986 will also be remembered as the year of the discovery of high temperature superconductors. These are materials that lose all resistance to an electric current at very low temperatures. Their practical usefulness is limited by the expense of refrigeration, but with the new materials this cost will be much lower.

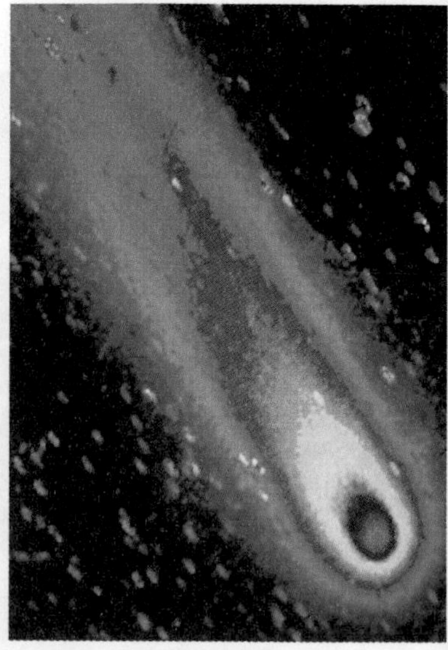

Halley's Comet captured close up.

Soviets free Sakharov

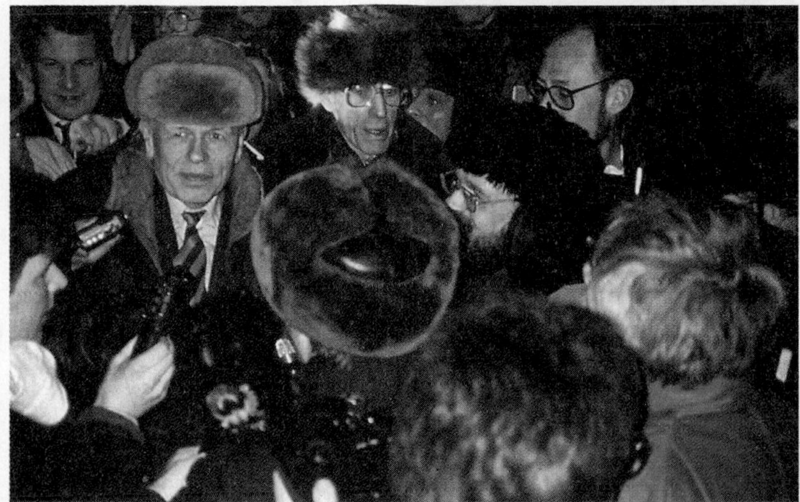

Sakharov is mobbed at Moscow station as he arrives home from exile.

Dec 23. The Soviet authorities have released Dr Andrei Sakharov, the spiritual father of the Soviet dissident movement, from internal exile in Gorky. He had been sent there without trial in January 1980, but today he and his wife returned to Moscow by train. He had been telephoned by Mikhail Gorbachev and told that they were no longer banished. Dr Sakharov said he had raised the question of human rights in Russia with the Soviet leader urging him to free all other dissidents from prison and labour camps (→29/1/87).

Super-light plane circles globe non-stop

Dec 12. The experimental aircraft Voyager landed safely today after flying round the world on one tank of fuel – in nine days, three minutes and 44 seconds. The strange-looking aircraft, with engines front and rear, set records for the endurance of its two-person crew and for distance flown without refuelling. The pilot, Richard Rutan, hopes the flight will lead to more fuel-efficient flying, and described the feat as "the last major event of atmospheric flight". His co-pilot Jeana Yeager said on her return to earth "I never really felt frightened", but she was nursing some bruises received while aloft.

The curious-looking Voyager on its record-breaking, round-the-world flight.

Arts: first literature Nobel goes to Africa

For the first time in its 85-year history, the Nobel Prize for Literature has been awarded to an African writer, the Nigerian **Wole Soyinka**. The Swedish Academy has been criticised for awarding the prize only to white Western authors. Soyinka said: "Finally African literature has been recognised."

Best known in Britain for his plays, such as "The Road" and "The Trials of Brother Jero", Soyinka was educated at Leeds University and was play-reader for the Royal Court Theatre, which presented his work. He also adapted Euripides for the National.

At the height of the Biafran war, Soyinka attempted to act as intermediary and was arrested as a "Biafran spy". He spent two years in jail confined alone to a small cell. The result was his bitter book of prison writings, "The Man Died".

The Booker Prize was won by **Kingsley Amis**, once mistakenly dubbed one of the "angry young men" and now, on the strength of his latest novel, "The Old Devils", an angry old man of letters (he is 64). It expresses ire at ageing, while his last book, "Stanley and the Women", was a hymn to misogyny.

Christopher Isherwood, who has died in California aged 81, went to America with **W.H. Auden** in 1939. Neither was quite forgiven for not coming back. Isherwood became a screenwriter for MGM in Hollywood, and an American citizen. His early, much-praised autobiography, "Lions and Shadows", was completed by "Christopher and his Kind", which frankly acknowledged his homosexuality.

Kingsley Amis wins the Booker Prize having been short-listed twice before.

The Oxford English Dictionary, whose first section, A – ANT, was published in 1884, is complete. The last volume of the Supplement, making 16 volumes defining half a million English words, came out in May. The original editor, **Sir James Murray**, hoped to finish it in his lifetime, but died while still on the letter T. The present editor, **Dr Robert Burchfield**, is now retiring. The next edition will be on computer. Meanwhile, there is no need for dictionaries of slang or of swear-words – they are all in the OED, which costs, complete, £1,095.

Bob Hoskins with stars on his eyes is the decent driver in "Mona Lisa".

1987

JANUARY

Su	Mo	Tu	We	Th	Fr	Sa
				1	2	3
4	5	6	7	8	9	10
11	12	13	14	15	16	17
18	19	20	21	22	23	24
25	26	27	28	29	30	31

1. Beijing: Thousands of students march on Tienanmen Square in the biggest demonstration since 1976.→

2. London: Douglas Hurd orders a report into New Year's Eve violence in which over 50 police were hurt.

5. UK: Lord Stockton is buried in the village of Horsted Keynes.

7. UK: The Army urges 600 troops to take AIDS tests after a tour of Kenya (→4/2).

9. London: Ernest Saunders resigns as Guinness chief executive over the DTI probe into the Distillers' takeover.→

12. London: Richard Eyre is named to succeed Sir Peter Hall as director of the National Theatre.

12. UK: Prince Edward resigns from the Royal Marines.→

15. London: A policeman is cleared of criminal charges in shooting Cherry Grose, sparking a riot in Brixton (→19/3).

16. Ireland: Ulster MP Peter Robinson is fined £15,000 for leading Loyalists on an "invasion" of an Irish village (→24/3).

18. Gulf War: The Iranians claim their troops have reached Basra in Iraq (→18/5).

20. Dublin: Dr FitzGerald's coalition collapses (→18/2).

20. UK: Police in eight counties arrest 26 alleged football hooligans after a mass operation.

25. Puerto Rico: 96 die when a hotel collapses.

25. West Germany: Kohl wins a general election with a greatly reduced majority.

27. Washington: Reagan says he "regrets" the secret arms deal with Iran (→10/2).

29. London: BBC Director-General Alasdair Milne resigns "for personal reasons" (→26/2).

30. London: South African envoy Dennis Worrall quits to stand against the government in the whites-only election.

30. UK: The flotation of British Airways begins (→2/3).

Archbishop's envoy kidnapped in Beirut

Terry Waite in happier days negotiating for the release of other hostages.

Jan 21. Fears are beginning to be expressed about the safety of Terry Waite, the special representative of the Archbishop of Canterbury, who is in Beirut negotiating for the release of foreign hostages held by supporters of the Hezbollah "Party of God", the militant followers of the Ayatollah Khomeini.

The tall, bearded Mr Waite left his seafront hotel in Moslem West Beirut yesterday evening, and dismissed his armed Druze guards. They were reluctant to allow him to go without protection, but he insisted he was safe and was being taken to see the hostages.

The Druze, waiting for him to reappear, say that his mission will take some time, but it is obvious that they are growing anxious about him. Walid Jumblatt, the Druze leader, has been contacting Shia commanders asking for news.

Some observers believe his disappearance from public view could mean that he is making progress in his efforts to secure the freedom of the hostages. Others, however, believe his absence bears a more sinister interpretation.

They point out that, while Mr Waite is known to be a scrupulous negotiator, he has been tainted in Middle Eastern minds by his involvement in the Irangate affair. Even though he was an innocent dupe of Colonel North, he has the CIA label attached to him, and they fear that he is now a hostage (→2/2).

Noddy can't play with golly any more

Jan 2. Ideological purity has reached the superficially cosy world of the nursery – actually a reactionary hotbed of ageism, sexism and racism, say some critics, and none more so than Enid Blyton's Noddy books, admit her publishers, Macdonald's, today.

In an attempt to excise any taint of racism at least, all new editions of Noddy will be shorn of the traditional black golliwogs, who will be replaced by neutral gnomes.

Traditionalists are appalled, and claim that such "sanitisation" will destroy many classics.

Chinese Communist Party has new boss

Jan 16. Six weeks of huge student demonstrations demanding more democracy in China led today to the resignation of Hu Yao-bang, the colourful and outspoken Communist party leader. He was replaced by Zhao Ziyang, the Chinese Prime Minister.

Hu had come under increasing pressure for failing to halt the demonstrations. He was replaced for making "mistakes on major political principles". The move is seen as a victory for the conservatives, who had denounced the students for being sympathetic to "bourgeois liberalism". China's paramount leader remains Deng Xioa-ping (→2/11).

Guinness brews up a head of scandal

Jan 21. The City was shocked today when Gerald Ronson, the popular head of the Heron International group, paid back the £5.8 million his group received for "support" during the Guinness bid for Distillers. The scandal surrounding the share dealings, now the subject of a Department of Trade inquiry, has already led to the sacking of Ernest Saunders, the Guinness chairman, and Roger Seelig, a top man at the merchant bankers Morgan Grenfell. City men fear others may be involved, too (→7/5).

Forty years after Dior's New Look revolutionised fashion, a massive "homage" in Paris shows the latest creations and the best of the old.

1987

FEBRUARY

Su	Mo	Tu	We	Th	Fr	Sa
1	2	3	4	5	6	7
8	9	10	11	12	13	14
15	16	17	18	19	20	21
22	23	24	25	26	27	28

2. Beirut: Terry Waite is reported to be held "under arrest".→

4. US: Flamboyant pianist Liberace dies, officially of a brain tumour, unofficially of AIDS.

4. Australia: Dennis Conner of the US wins back America's Cup from the Australians.

5. London: SOGAT calls off its picket of Murdoch's Wapping plant (→30/6).

7. Seoul: 35,000 police charge students protesting peacefully against a student's death in police custody (→20/6).

10. Moscow: Gorbachev pardons 140 dissidents (→20).

10. Washington: Ex-security adviser Robert McFarlane, implicated in the Irangate scandal, attempts suicide.→

11. London: An Old Bailey jury clears Cynthia Payne of running a brothel in the "sex on the stairs" case.

12. UK: Health Minister Edwina Currie says "good Christians won't get AIDS" (→4/5).

17. London: Tamils seeking asylum strip to their underwear in protest against plans to return them to Sri Lanka (→21/4).

20. USSR: Jewish dissident Joseph Begun is freed (→12/11).

20. Washington: A Senate committee votes to halt US aid to Nicaraguan Contra rebels.

24. UK: Six alleged Nazi war criminals are living in Britain, according to leading Nazi hunters (→11/5).

25. UK: Sir Yehudi Menuhin, now a naturalised Briton, is appointed to the Order of Merit.

26. London: The SDP's Rosie Barnes wins Greenwich in a by-election (→13/3).

26. London: Michael Checkland is appointed Alasdair Milne's successor as Director-General of the BBC.

DEATH

22. US artist Andy Warhol (*6/8/1928).→

Aquino suppresses pro-Marcos uprising

After the failed counter-coup, a body becomes part of the debris.

Jan 29. Corazon Aquino, the President of the Philippines, put down another rebellion against her government today. Her troops fired tear gas into one of the main radio and television stations in Manila which had been occupied by a heavily armed rebel group for two days. A few minutes later they all surrendered.

Although they had held the station, they had been prevented from broadcasting by loyal officials who had cut off the electricity. The takeover was part of a series of carefully orchestrated attacks on key military bases and broadcasting stations. Rebels assaulted the Villamor air force base near Manila airport in the south of the city. They were routed in ten minutes of heavy fighting in which two rebels were killed and 50 captured.

General Fidel V. Ramos said today that government troops are now in control of all the target areas. Most of the rebels were supporters of the former President, Ferdinand Marcos. Others were sympathetic because they feel Aquino is being too soft on the Communists (→29/8).

Gorbachev calls for greater democracy

Jan 29. Mikhail Gorbachev, the Soviet leader, today called for greater democracy in the Soviet Communist Party which, he said, had to bear heavy responsibility for the economic and social stagnation of the last 20 years.

Gorbachev told a plenary meeting of the party's policy-making central committee that there had to be greater "control from below" and voters should have a choice of candidates in elections for local soviets, or councils.

Gorbachev's reforms are based on perestroika, or reconstruction, and glasnost, or openness. However, his radical plans to unravel the fabric of the Soviet government can be expected to arouse opposition from party stalwarts (→10/2).

Jan 12. Prince Edward, seen here in the dress uniform of the Royal Marines, caused an upset today when he resigned his commission.

Irangate inquiry criticises Reagan

Feb 26. The Tower Commission investigating US arms sales to Iran reported today that, although President Reagan did not deliberately mislead the American people, he seemed to be unaware of important aspects of the operation.

"The President made mistakes," said the Commission's chief, ex-senator John Tower. "He should have followed up more and monitored this operation more closely." Reagan refused to comment on the report, promising to make a statement when he had digested its full contents.

The report goes on to criticise the White House chief of staff, Donald Regan, for general "chaos", and Lieutenant-Colonel Oliver North for concealing information about the plan he had hatched (→17/7).

Warhol exceeds 15-minute fame limit

Andy Warhol, who never explained.

Feb 23. Andy Warhol died during an operation last night, although many of his fans refuse to believe it; will he re-appear at his funeral? It would be an Andy thing to do. His famous prediction that in the future "everyone will be famous for 15 minutes" was greatly exceeded in his case. His "factory" turned out Pop Art, films and tape-recordings without end. Sphinx-like, he never explained the Warhol myth. Smart. ▷

Beirut gunmen attack UN relief lorries

One of the relief lorries unloading supplies for a shattered Palestinian camp.

Feb 13. Shi'ite Moslem militia today attacked two UN relief agency lorries attempting to take food to starving inhabitants of a besieged Palestinian stronghold in Beirut.

As the convoy approached the Bourj al Barajneh camp, the Amal militia shot out the tyres of the leading vehicles. A relief worker was killed and another injured. Vital supplies of flour and milk powder for the 30,000 trapped inside lay scattered in the road.

Conditions inside the camp are appalling. It has been under siege for three months by Shi'ite guerrillas, determined to break the power of Arafat's PLO in Beirut. Pauline Cutting, a British surgeon working in the hospital there, said that people inside were so desperately hungry that they were eating stray dogs, cats and even rats. A 12-year-old boy who managed to escape said: "There is even a shortage of animals now."

Miss Cutting reported by radio that seven people were killed and many more wounded when Amal put down artillery fire on the camp yesterday. She and the other foreign medical people had decided to stay on, despite Medical Aid's evacuation plans. "We have decided to remain with the Palestinians, to live or die with them" (→8/4).

Haughey to become Irish premier again

Feb 18. With the votes still being counted in the Irish general election the Prime Minister, Dr Garret Fitzgerald, conceded defeat tonight. When the Dail meets in three weeks time, Charles Haughey will become Prime Minister for the third time; but he will be relying on the support of up to three Independents to stay in office. Dr Fitzgerald said tonight that he would give the new government every support in furthering the work of the Anglo-Irish agreement on Northern Ireland. The first priority for Mr Haughey will be to revive the economy: one-third of all tax revenue is now used simply to service the national debt (→10/3).

Church of England votes for women

Feb 26. The Church of England's General Synod today gave the go-ahead for the ordination of women priests by voting overwhelmingly for legislation suggested by the House of Bishops. The move brings the possibility of a major schism a step closer.

Die-hard opponents like the Bishop of London, Dr Graham Leonard, are now talking of joining the Roman Catholic or Orthodox Churches. A leading layman and government minister, John Selwyn Gummer, has vowed to leave if the plan goes ahead, but the Archbishop of Canterbury said that no legislation could be enacted before 1991, and appealed for unity.

Raid on BBC sparks "police state" charge

Feb 2. MPs clashed in the Commons today after members of the Special Branch raided the BBC offices in Glasgow and removed two vanloads of material allegedly gathered while making the controversial programme about the secret Zircon spy satellite project, for the series on Britain's "Secret Society", which has recently been banned indefinitely.

Ignoring Government claims that the police acted independently, Opposition MPs branded the raid as the action of "a second-rate police state infused by illiberalism and incompetence" and a major threat to democracy.

Officials are still desperate to discover the highly-placed source who supposedly leaked top-secret information on Zircon to the investigative journalist and programme-maker Duncan Campbell.

Meanwhile, the Government is reportedly considering legal action against the "New Statesman" magazine, which published extracts from Mr Campbell's banned script last week (→19/9).

Jerusalem trial begins of alleged guard at Nazi death camp

Feb 16. "I am not a human monster," said John Demjanjuk, a 66-year-old Ukrainian retired car worker from Cleveland, Ohio, when he appeared in a Jerusalem court today charged with war crimes. He is accused of being an attendant at the Nazi death camp at Treblinka. If found guilty he could be hanged. He denies that he was the man known to camp inmates as "Ivan the Terrible" and claims that it is a case of mistaken identity.

This is the second war crimes trial in Israel in 25 years. Demjanjuk, who was extradited from the US, faced angry relatives of the Treblinka victims. One man shouted: "He strangled my entire family with his bare hands" (→24).

John Demjanjuk, charged with war crimes, puts a brave face on it in court.

Broom cupboard is worth small fortune

Feb 13. A snip at £36,500, say the estate agents. The property, no more than a converted broom cupboard 5 feet 6 inches wide by 11 feet long, is up for sale and the normally-sized Grace Newbold of Milton Keynes is bidding hard.

What makes the self-contained dwelling so attractive is not the Laura Ashley wallpaper, nor the single radiator, nor even the shower, wash-basin and lavatory contained in a minuscule cupboard. It is opposite Harrods, and that's good enough for Miss Newbold, it seems. The agents are recommending it to people who "like eating out". It has no cooker.

1987

MARCH

Su	Mo	Tu	We	Th	Fr	Sa
1	2	3	4	5	6	7
8	9	10	11	12	13	14
15	16	17	18	19	20	21
22	23	24	25	26	27	28
29	30	31				

2. London: Japan is given three weeks to open its money markets to British firms or risk expulsion from the City (→6).

3. UK: NHS prescription charges rise 20p to £2.40.

6. UK: The pound is at its highest for four years at $1.5870 (→1/4).

9. London: Thatcher announces urgent safety measures for ferries and a fund for survivors and victims' families.

10. Dublin: Haughey takes over as Taioseach (Prime Minister) for the third time.

12. London: The Government gives the go-ahead to the Sizewell B nuclear processing plant in Suffolk (→29).

13. UK: Liberal Matthew Taylor wins Truro in the by-election caused by the death of David Penhaligon (→6/8).

15. Budapest: 1,500 people take part in a march to call for liberal reforms.

16. Boston: Massachusetts Governor Michael Dukakis enters the 1988 presidential race.

19. London: Winston Silcott, a ring-leader of the Tottenham riot, is jailed for life for murdering PC Blakelock.

24. West Germany: The IRA says it planted the bomb at Britain's Rheindalhen base injuring 31 yesterday (→25/4).

26. Brussels: The EEC agrees to sell surplus butter to the USSR for 6p a pound.

27. Washington: Labour leader Neil Kinnock meets Reagan for what are reported to be frosty talks (→12/6).

31. London: Thatcher says her talks with Gorbachev pave the way for the removal of Cruise from Europe by 1988 (→4/4).

31. US: A judge denies rights of parenthood to a woman who agreed to act as a surrogate mother.

DEATH

3. US actor and comedian Danny Kaye, born David Daniel Kaminski (*18/1/1913).→

Car ferry capsizes: 200 feared dead

March 6. Two hundred cross-channel passengers were feared dead tonight after a car ferry capsized in the bitterly cold waters off Zeebrugge. The Herald of Free Enterprise, belonging to Townsend Thoresen, rolled over and sank a mile outside the Belgian port. First indications are that the bow doors were open enabling water to pour into the car deck.

The 7,951-ton roll-on-roll-off ferry had just left the port around 7.00pm bound for Dover when she sank, leaving one third of the hull still above water. The disaster happened so swiftly there wasn't time to send an SOS, but Dutch and Belgian ships and helicopters were soon on the scene picking up survivors.

Divers immediately went into the submerged section of the hull to try to free trapped passengers. They witnessed scenes of appalling tragedy. One Dutch diver said he saw up to 20 dead bodies huddled together. A Belgian naval officer, Jacques Thas, said: "Dead bodies are on the bridge, on the side of the ship and in cabins." The divers had to climb down through the side of the ship while passengers, many with tales of selfless heroism to relate, struggled to climb out through broken windows.

For them it was a race against time before they succumbed to exposure. Passengers described constant screams as the ship went over, with people grabbing fixed furniture to avoid slipping into the water, then watching others slowly lose their grip and perish.

Alan Hawkes, a lorry driver from Peterlee, County Durham, said: "We could see members of the crew badly injured. Then suddenly the portholes were broken and lights shone through. They lowered a rope for the children but we couldn't tie the children up. Then they sent down a bag and we were able to get the children into it and see them lifted to safety" (→9).

The stricken ferry being held in place while rescuers search for victims.

Mrs Thatcher gets warm welcome going walkabout in Moscow

March 29. Mrs Thatcher was mobbed by welcoming crowds when she went walkabout in Moscow today. Although everything was stage-managed, ordinary Russians seemed genuinely pleased to see her.

There were cries of "Thank you for coming", much hand-shaking and some cheek-kissing. In a supermarket she bought a loaf and a tin of pilchards for no apparent reason.

During a four-day visit she is having disarmament talks with Mr Gorbachev. She rebuked a BBC reporter for asking if her trip has anything to do with electioneering. She snapped at him: "Enlarge your view" (→31).

Mrs Thatcher waves to the Moscow crowds who are obviously fascinated.

The gentle jester, Danny Kaye, dies

Danny Kaye in "The Court Jester".

March 3. Daniel Kaminski, son of a Ukrainian tailor, shortened his name to Danny Kaye when he went on stage and stopped the show with 54 Russian names in a song gabbled at breakneck speed. In 1948, he wowed them at the London Palladium. His first film "Up in Arms" started a Kaye cult.

He will always be associated with James Thurber's Walter Mitty, whose secret life he enacted so exhilaratingly. From 1950 he worked tirelessly as roving ambassador for UNICEF, performing for needy children without the help of language. He died today, aged 74.

Councillors to pay for not setting rate

March 12. Forty-seven Labour councillors who failed to set a legal rate for Liverpool in 1985 were disqualified from office for five years today when the Law Lords dismissed their appeal against penalties imposed by the District Auditor.

They could also face bankruptcy, as they must pay both their surcharge and the costs of the extended litigation. The Liberal Alliance will take over the running of Liverpool's council.

But Derek Hatton, the Militant ex-deputy leader of the council, said defiantly that Labour would be back at the next local elections, and that the Labour movement would meet the penalties imposed on him and his colleagues (→27).

1987

APRIL

Su	Mo	Tu	We	Th	Fr	Sa
			1	2	3	4
5	6	7	8	9	10	11
12	13	14	15	16	17	18
19	20	21	22	23	24	25
26	27	28	29	30		

1. London: MPs vote against the restoration of hanging by 342-230.

1. UK: Keith Best, Tory MP for Ynys Mon (Anglesey), admits he made multiple applications for British Telecom shares (→18/5).

5. UK: It is revealed that two of the Queen Mother's cousins have been in a mental home since 1941.

6. UK: Mr J. Joel's Maori Venture wins the Grand National.

7. Belgium: The Herald of Free Enterprise is refloated; divers retrieve 50 more bodies (→15).

9. London: The Government orders an inquiry into the Al-Fayed brothers £650 million purchase of Harrods.

12. S. Africa: Tutu says he will breach emergency laws by praying for the release of detainees (→6/5).

15. Canterbury: A memorial service is held for victims of the Zeebrugge tragedy (→27).

16. London: Right-wing Tory MP Harvey Proctor is charged with gross indecency (→20/5).

21. Colombo: Tamil separatists are believed to be behind a bomb attack which leaves over 100 dead.→

22. London: Jim Callaghan is appointed to the Order of the Garter (→30/7).

23. London: Thatcher confirms that ex-MI5 chief Sir Maurice Oldfield was a practising homosexual.

25. Northern Ireland: Senior Ulster judge Sir Maurice Gibson and his wife are killed by a remote control bomb (→8/5).

27. UK: The Zeebrugge inquiry hears on its first day that Townsend Thoresen gave "inherently dangerous orders" (→8/10).

29. Tel Aviv: Moslem demands for an "Islamic Palestine" are growing in Israel.

30. London: The Law Lords approve the sterilisation of a 17-year-old mentally subnormal girl.

Argentinian President ends army revolt

April 19. President Alfonsin of Argentina tonight personally ended the three-day revolt of some of his most senior army officers. He flew in a helicopter to the Campo de Mayo military base, 20 miles from Buenos Aires, where the rebels were in control. The men, their faces covered with camouflage paint, were armed with rifles, pistols and grenades, but instead of using them they responded to his brave personal appeal.

Alfonsin flew back to the capital and told a wildly cheering crowd of 400,000 in the Plaza de Mayo that the crisis was over. "The house is in order. There is no blood in Argentina," he told them. He said the rebels would be detained and brought to justice.

The rebel leader, Colonel Aldo Rico, is a Falklands war veteran who, like many in the army, wants to stop the human rights trials of officers alleged to have committed crimes under the former military regime. It is thought that Alfonsin is ready to make some concessions to their feelings. Tonight there were unconfirmed reports that the army chief of staff, General Hector Rios Erenu, whom the rebels disliked, had resigned.

Alfonsin during the army revolt.

EastEnders "puts nation in moral peril"

April 5. The "Clean Up TV" campaigner, Mrs Mary Whitehouse, today launched a furious attack on the BBC's immensely popular soap series, "EastEnders", claiming its bad language and general portrayal of low moral values to be a "peril" to viewers and their children.

She cited a recent episode where two homosexuals embraced as "the height of irresponsibility", and told a National Viewers' and Listeners' Association annual convention that the BBC's managing director, Mr Bill Cotton, was living in "cloud cuckoo land" if he thought the series could be justified, especially as it went out at a time "when young children will be watching". Some episodes "could have torn viewers' sensitivities to shreds". The BBC did not comment.

"Dirty" Den and Angie entertaining some of the regulars in the "Queen Vic".

1987

MAY

Su	Mo	Tu	We	Th	Fr	Sa
					1	2
3	4	5	6	7	8	9
10	11	12	13	14	15	16
17	18	19	20	21	22	23
24	25	26	27	28	29	30
31						

1. UK: The Government's search for a nuclear waste dumping site switches to the sea bed (→ 7/7).

4. UK: A new Government-backed anti-AIDS campaign is launched (→ 10/8).

7. London: Ex-Guinness chief Saunders is remanded on bail on a charge of attempting to pervert the course of justice (→ 26).

8. Northern Ireland: Eight IRA men die when an attempt to attack an RUC post in Loughgall is foiled (→ 8/11).

9. Poland: 183 die when a Polish airliner crashes on a flight from Warsaw to New York.

11. London: Thatcher calls an election for June 11 (→ 12/6).

11. Lyons: The trial of Klaus Barbie opens (→ 3/7).

16. London: A Tottenham Hotspur own goal gives Coventry City a 3-2 victory in the FA Cup Final.

17. Fiji: Governor-General Ratu Sir Penaia Ganilau refuses to recognise Rabuka's takeover (→ 24).

18. London: Tory MP Keith Best is arrested and charged with deception over his application for Telecom shares (→ 1/7).

20. London: Harvey Proctor admits taking part in sex sessions with teenage male prostitutes.

22. London: One of Mozart's notebooks fetches £2.3 million at Sotheby's.

24. Fiji: Ganilau is now reported to be in charge of the provisional government (→ 30/9).

26. London: Ernest Saunders quits as a director of Guinness (→ 17/7).

29. Tehran: A British diplomat is beaten up in response to the arrest of an Iranian envoy for shoplifting in Manchester (→ 10/6).

DEATH

14. US actress Rita Hayworth, born Margarita Carmen Cansino (*17/10/1918).

Gorbachev makes new offer on arms cuts

Mikhail Gorbachev on a visit earlier in the month to Czechoslovakia.

April 14. The Soviet leader, Mikhail Gorbachev, today laid down another challenge to President Reagan by offering to remove all the Soviet Union's short-range missiles from Eastern Europe as part of a major agreement on medium-range missiles. The offer could pave the way for an early accord on arms cuts between the Soviet Union and the United States.

So far the White House has only said that the Soviet proposals were "interesting", but it seems likely they will throw the Americans off-balance as they go further than President Reagan has been prepared to contemplate (→ 1/5).

Syrian troops end siege of refugee camp

April 8. Syrian troops have finally broken through a Shi'ite Amal militia siege of the Chatila Palestinian camp in Southern Beirut. A cease-fire has been arranged, and food distributed to the 3,000 inhabitants, many of whom are ill and starving. In February the Syrians put an end to fighting between rival Moslem forces in West Beirut, and it is hoped that by acting as a buffer in Chatila between the groups they will bring an end to the bitter "war of the camps," which has claimed 800 dead and 3,000 wounded since it erupted last November (→ 1/6).

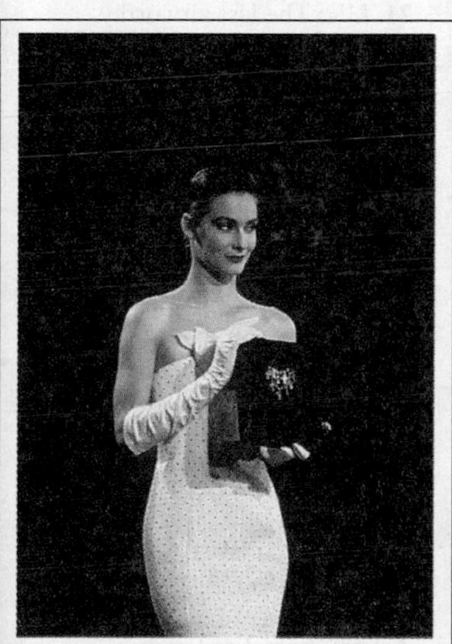

April 3. Duchess of Windsor's jewels are sold for £31,380,197.

Rebel Tamil bases hit after bus bomb

April 22. Sri Lankan war-planes today launched strikes on outposts of the Tamil separatists, following the bomb which claimed 105 lives in a Colombo bus station this week. The government said the attacks would continue until the rebels stopped killing innocent civilians and agreed to peace talks.

The Tamils have been seeking autonomy for their northern part of the island since the 1950s, but only turned to violence recently, after having protested against years of discrimination by the Sinhalese majority (→ 14/8).

Donna involved in affairs of the Hart

May 8. The presidential hopes of the former Senator, Gary Hart, ended today, after one of the shortest campaigns in history. He announced he was withdrawing from the campaign, in which he was the Democratic front-runner, after newspaper exposure of his relationship with Donna Rice, a 29-year-old model.

The Miami Herald reported that Hart, who is married, saw Miss Rice on a yacht called "Monkey Business", and spent the night with her in Washington. Hart said that the press should ignore candidates' private lives.

Ms Donna Rice hard at work.

Fiji coup aims to cut Indian power

May 14. Fiji's Governor-General, Ratu Sir Penaia Ganilau, declared a state of emergency in the former British colony today, after troops led by 38-year-old Lieutenant-Colonel Sitiveni Rabuka entered parliament and arrested the Prime Minister, Timoci Bavadra, and 27 members of the Indian-dominated government.

Rabuka explained that the coup is intended to eliminate the danger of racial clashes between native Fijians and the Indian community. The populations are about equal, but Fijians resent Indian political dominance (→ 17). ▷

Iraqi Exocet blasts US frigate in the Gulf

May 18. The American frigate Stark, patrolling the Gulf north of Bahrain, was today hit by two Exocet missiles fired by Iraqi Mirage jets. The surprise attack by aircraft not considered hostile killed 28 sailors and crippled the ship.

President Reagan at once launched a vigorous protest and demanded an immediate explanation from Baghdad. Apparently the aircraft had wrongly identified the frigate as Iranian; but questions were immediately asked about the warship's state of radar watch readiness in dangerous waters.

The only warning came too late, from a visual sighting by a sailor. Two missiles were fired from a distance of 12 miles, which led naval experts to conclude that two aircraft were involved. Only one

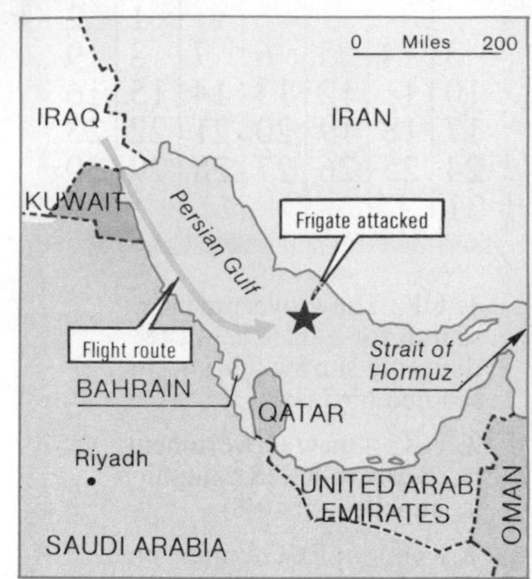

Exocet exploded. The other warhead remained embedded in the superstructure as the Stark, abandoned by her crew of 200, was towed to Bahrain. Tonight she was reported still on fire (→3/7).

West German lands next to the Kremlin

May 28. A 19-year-old West German flew through the Soviet Union's air defences today and landed his light aircraft on Red Square. Mathias Rust flew the four-seater Cessna single-handed from Helsinki to Moscow, before swooping over the Kremlin, the Lenin Mausoleum and St. Basil's Cathedral and putting the aircraft down on the upward slope near the Kremlin Wall. Rust got out of the cockpit and signed autographs for an amused and amazed crowd of Russians who had been strolling in Red Square. Rust had only 24 hours flying time to his credit and his flight through heavily-defended Soviet air space has embarrassed the military (→4/9).

Militant whites oust South African liberals

May 6. South Africa's ruling National Party (NP) today began its 40th year in power with another easy election win, gaining 123 of the 166 seats in the House of Assembly – but not without a disagreeable shock from the hard-line no-concessions-to-blacks Conservative Party (CP). This won 22 seats and displaced the liberal Progressive Federal Party as the official Opposition in the Assembly.

The CP, formed five years ago by rebels who consider the NP has gone soft on apartheid, was fighting its first general election. Its success amounts to a rebuff from white voters for President Botha's cautious attempts at reform.

The elections were marked by a massive million-strong strike of blacks in protest at being excluded from the electoral process. At the predominantly white, but liberal, Witswatersrand University, Johannesburg, students invited Winnie Mandela, wife of the jailed black nationalist leader, Nelson Mandela, to come and speak to them. Police moved in to stop the speech, using whips and firing tear gas, and arresting 120 students (→26/7).

South Korean protesters, wearing shirts and headbands and carrying light staves, pit themselves against the steel and plastic of the riot police.

Rust, after landing in Red Square.

Official "vandals" smash phone boxes

May 2. As British Telecom push forward with their modernisation plans, conservationists are complaining bitterly about what they call the company's "official vandalism" – the wholesale destruction of hundreds of traditional red telephone kiosks.

In an attempt to beat new conservation laws, scheduled for 1988, BT has been ripping out many of the kiosks, classic English landmarks since the 1930s, and replacing them with plastic booths.

1987

JUNE

Su	Mo	Tu	We	Th	Fr	Sa
	1	2	3	4	5	6
7	8	9	10	11	12	13
14	15	16	17	18	19	20
21	22	23	24	25	26	27
28	29	30				

1. Beirut: Prime Minister Rashid Karami is assassinated by a bomb in the helicopter in which he is travelling (→22/7).

3. UK: Mr. L. Freidman's Reference Point wins the Derby.

8. Venice: World leaders gather for the first day of an economic summit (→10).

10. Venice: The economic summit ends with leaders backing growth.

10. London: Britain expels two Iranian envoys after the mistreatment of British envoy Edward Chaplin (→17).

12. Northern Ireland: Enoch Powell loses his seat.→

12. UK: Princess Anne is given the revived title "Princess Royal" for the monarch's eldest daughter.

17. New York: Subway vigilante Goetz is cleared of attempted murder but convicted of owning an illegal gun.

17. London: Four more Iranian envoys are expelled (→23/9).

18. UK: Unemployment has fallen below three million.

19. Barcelona: 15 die in a car bomb explosion caused by the Basque separatist group ETA.

20. Seoul: Anti-government street protests continue (→18/12).

21. UK: The last airworthy Bristol Blenheim bomber crashes onto a golf course.

25. Rome: The Pope welcomes Austrian President Waldheim.

26. London: Denis Healey announces his retirement from Labour's front bench (→28/9).

30. Brussels: Thatcher comes under attack from EEC leaders when she refuses to increase Britain's EEC payments.

30. London: Rupert Murdoch buys the "Today" newspaper from the Lonrho group.

DEATHS

3. Spanish guitarist Andres Segovia (*21/2/1893).

22. US dancer and actor Fred Astaire, born Frederick Austerlitz (*10/5/1899).→

1987

JULY

Su	Mo	Tu	We	Th	Fr	Sa
			1	2	3	4
5	6	7	8	9	10	11
12	13	14	15	16	17	18
19	20	21	22	23	24	25
26	27	28	29	30	31	

1. London: Geoffrey Collier, a director of merchant bank Morgan Grenfell, is fined £25,000 for insider dealing (→25/8).

1. UK: Police find the body of one of the missing victims of Moors murderers, Hindley and Brady (→4/8).

2. Italy: Pornography star Ilona Staller is elected to the Italian parliament.

5. Wimbledon: Martina Navratilova beats Steffi Graf for a record sixth Women's Singles title in a row; Pat Cash beats Ivan Lendl in the Men's Singles final.

7. West Germany: 30 people die when a tanker lorry crashes into a restaurant in a small town and bursts into flames.

7. USSR: Six former technicians at the Chernobyl plant go on trial for causing last year's accident.

12. UK: Nigel Mansell wins the British Grand Prix.

12. London: Contempt proceedings begin against the "Sunday Times" for printing "Spycatcher" extracts (→23/9).

13. Cleveland: Six children put in care in the child abuse affair are returned to their parents (→11/8).

16. London: British Airways announces that it is buying British Caledonian for £237 million (→6/8).

17. London: Ernest Saunders is ordered to repay £5 million to Guinness (→13/10).

18. Oxford: The university refuses Mrs Thatcher an honorary degree for the second time.

22. London: A Palestinian cartoonist who lampooned Arafat is shot and gravely wounded in Chelsea (→12/12).

24. London: Jeffrey Archer wins a libel action against the "Daily Star" over his pay-off to prostitute Monica Coghlan.

30. UK: Jim Callaghan and Roy Jenkins receive life peerages; ex-Liberal MP Clement Freud is knighted.

Mrs Thatcher is elected for a third term

June 12. The Tories have swept back to power in another historic general election victory. Tonight Mrs Thatcher is the first Prime Minister for over a century to face the prospect of a third consecutive full term of office backed by a massive parliamentary majority.

The final election scorecard reads Tories 375 seats, Labour 229, Alliance 22, Others 24. The Tories feel serene. Opposition parties are shattered.

Neil Kinnock said that Labour must embark on a fundamental reappraisal. The party has failed to break out of its inner-city, Scottish and Welsh strongholds. The Alliance began to crack up almost before all the results were declared, with the Social Democrats' leader David Owen accusing David Steel, the Liberal leader, of trying to "bounce" the SDP into a merger.

Mrs Thatcher smiled and called her hat-trick "a fantastic triumph". She talked about winning a fourth term in 1992. Her position in the political history books is already secure with three (→26).

Fred Astaire, king of the hoofers, dies

June 22. "Can't act. Can't sing. Slightly bald. Can dance a little." So ran the verdict on the first screen test of Fred Astaire (born Austerlitz), and it showed sublime ignorance of the reputation he already had as a stage dancer with his sister Adele, in New York and London. Adele had just married into the English peerage, and he needed a partner; in 1933 he found her in Ginger Rogers.

For two decades he personified blithe perfection of dress, of rhythm and of style. He admitted afterwards that he disliked wearing top hat, white tie and tails. He retired several times, only to re-emerge partnering Judy Garland or reunited with Rogers.

Racehorses were his life in retirement, and in 1980 he was married again, to Robyn Smith, a leading jockey. He died today, aged 88.

Fred Astaire and Ginger Rogers.

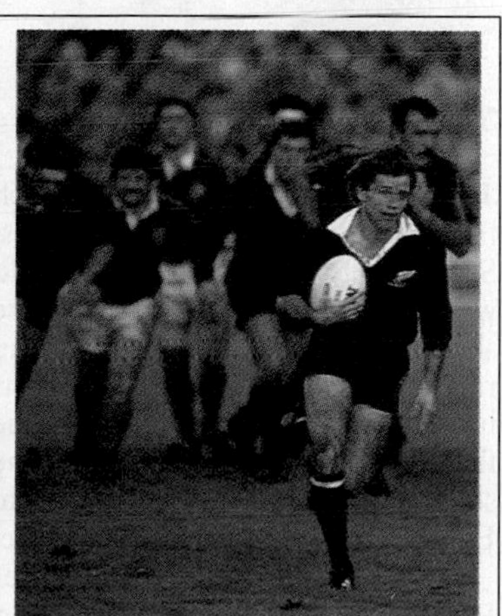

June 20. The All Blacks power to a win over the French in rugby's first World Cup final.

Doctor in child sex abuse case accused

June 29. Dr Marietta Higgs, the paediatrician at the centre of the Cleveland child sex abuse storm, was today accused by the Labour MP Stuart Bell of conspiring with a social worker to keep police away from her cases.

Some 202 children in Mr Bell's constituency have been taken into care this year, following examinations by Dr Higgs and a colleague. Parents of 17 of them are now seeking their return through the courts as concern grows over methods used for diagnosis (→13/7).

Ollie North wraps himself in the flag at Irangate hearing

Ollie North: new patriotic hero.

July 17. President Reagan's National Security Adviser, Rear Admiral John Poindexter, today told Congress he authorised the diversion of money from arms sales to Iran to the Contra rebels in Nicaragua. "The buck stops with me," he said. Earlier Lieutenant-Colonel Oliver North, Poindexter's assistant, had said he assumed, but did not know, that the President knew of the diversion.

Colonel North's patriotic defence of his actions has made him a hero for many. Telegrams poured in supporting him, and "God bless Ollie North" T-shirts were on sale. Fawn Hall, North's beautiful secretary, called him "every secretary's dream of a boss", and said "sometimes you just have to go above the written law" (→18/11).

Two Britons win both Golf Opens

July 28. British golf stands higher in the world than it has done for three-quarters of a century. Today 23-year-old Laura Davies became the first Briton to win the US Women's Open, just a week after Nick Faldo, at 29, achieved his own life's ambition at Muirfield by winning the Open Championship by a single stroke.

▷

Barbie gets life for his inhuman crimes

July 3. Applause and cheering broke out in court as the former SS officer Klaus Barbie, the "Butcher of Lyons" was found guilty today on all charges for his part in wartime atrocities. The court in Lyons sentenced him to life imprisonment for deporting 844 members of the Resistance and Jews during the Nazi occupation. At least 373 of them were murdered in the gas ovens of Nazi concentration camps.

The 73-year-old, once a swaggering bully in this city, listened to the verdict in silence with hands in pockets in the bullet-proof dock. His lawyer had threatened to name Resistance traitors, but did not do so, during the 37-day trial (→17/8).

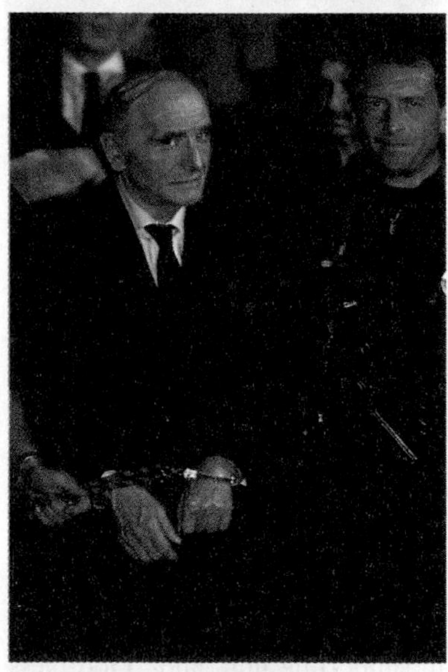

Handcuffed Klaus Barbie on trial.

Over 700 die from heatwave in Greece

July 26. The Greek government announced a state of emergency today, as the death toll from a national heatwave rose to over 700. Hospitals and military clinics were struggling to handle an influx of casualties as temperatures continued to soar.

Over a million visitors from Britain come to Greece each year, but so far the only British death reported has been Mrs Catherine Boyle, aged 46, of Oxfordshire. She was taken to hospital suffering from dehydration and died yesterday.

Rioting Iranian zealots killed in Mecca

Iranian pilgrims, bearing pictures of the Ayatollah, marching in Mecca.

July 30. Unprecedented rioting erupted in Mecca today when Iranian zealots disrupted the Hajj, the annual Moslem pilgrimage to the Holy City of Islam. Scores of Iranians died when Saudi police opened fire on the rioters. Other pilgrims and a number of Saudis died when the Iranians attacked them with knives and bricks.

There is no doubt that the Iranians went to Mecca under orders to cause trouble because Saudi Arabia supports Iraq in the Gulf War, and because the Ayatollah Khomeini regards the Saudi royal family as heretics.

Today's clash exploded after the Iranian "hajjis" gathered for a political demonstration, forbidden under Saudi law. When the Saudi police stopped their march, the Iranians started a running battle in which they set fire to police cars before the police opened fire on them.

Tehran radio accused the Saudi police of provoking the riot by beating pilgrims during a demonstration by more than 155,000 Iranians, some of whom set fire to effigies of President Reagan. It said the pilgrims chanted slogans denouncing the United States, the Soviet Union and Israel.

When the news of the deaths of the Iranians broke, demonstrators in Tehran took to the streets and vented their anger on the Saudi embassy.

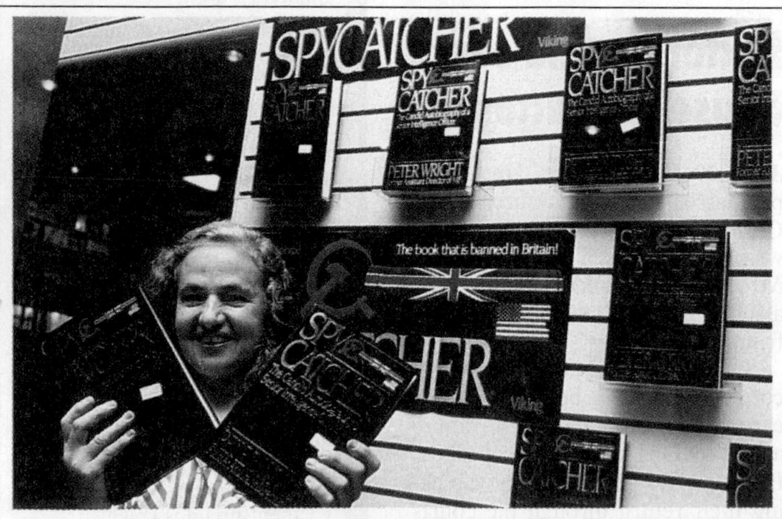

In Britain "Spycatcher" is banned, but anyone can buy it in America.

Thatcher says no to Royal Navy in Gulf

July 31. Mrs Thatcher has dealt a snub to her closest ally, President Reagan, by turning down a request to send minesweepers to the Gulf to clear the way for American warships and tankers.

Britain is against the whole White House plan to reflag Kuwaiti tankers as American ships and then escort them to the head of the Gulf, fearing it may only provoke the Iranians. The Government would much rather see them cool down and accept a cease-fire.

Britain is also worried about how long it would take the ships to get there, and the problem of protecting them. The reflagged tanker Bridgeton has already hit an Iranian mine (→29/9).

Irish cyclist wins the Tour de France

Stephen Roche on a victory lap.

July 26. Almost lost in the bunch that swept up the Champs Elysees, Stephen Roche, the 27-year-old who has raced for so long in the shadow of Ireland's great road racer Sean Kelly, threw up his arms in joy today. He had become the first Irish cyclist, and only the second from outside continental Europe, to win the Tour de France.

Roche overtook the race leader Pedro Delgado of Spain in yesterday's time trial to lead by just 40 seconds – a tiny margin, but one which Delgado could not dent on the final run into Paris.

1987

AUGUST

Su	Mo	Tu	We	Th	Fr	Sa
						1
2	3	4	5	6	7	8
9	10	11	12	13	14	15
16	17	18	19	20	21	22
23	24	25	26	27	28	29
30	31					

1. US: Mike Tyson beats Tony Tucker to become undisputed world heavyweight boxing champion.

4. UK: Moors murderer Ian Brady claims he committed five more killings.

6. UK: The SDP votes to merge with the Liberals; Dr Owen resigns as leader (→27).

6. London: The Department of Trade and Industry refers the British Airways takeover of British Caledonian to the Monopolies Commission.

10. UK: One person a day is now reported to be dying of AIDS (→2/9).

10. Sweden: Life Guards Captain Simon Hayward is jailed for five years for drugs smuggling.

11. UK: The Cleveland child abuse inquiry opens.

14. Sri Lanka: A soldier in a guard of honour attacks Indian Prime Minister Gandhi with his rifle butt.

15. UK: The world-famous Amadeus Quartet announces it will break up, following the death of viola player Peter Schidlof.

17. West Berlin: Rudolf Hess is found dead in Spandau after apparently killing himself with electrical flex.

21. London: The Government says it may tighten firearms laws as the 16th victim of the Hungerford massacre dies (→22/9).

25. New York: The Dow Jones share index reaches a record 2,722 points (→30/9).

27. London: Scottish MP Robert Maclennan emerges as the new leader of the SDP (→30).

30. Portsmouth: Dr Owen forms a breakaway SDP.

DEATHS

17. German Nazi Rudolf Hess, Hitler's deputy 1933-41 (*26/4/1894).

28. US film director John Huston (*5/8/1906).→

29. US actor Lee Marvin (*19/2/1924).

Gunman on rampage

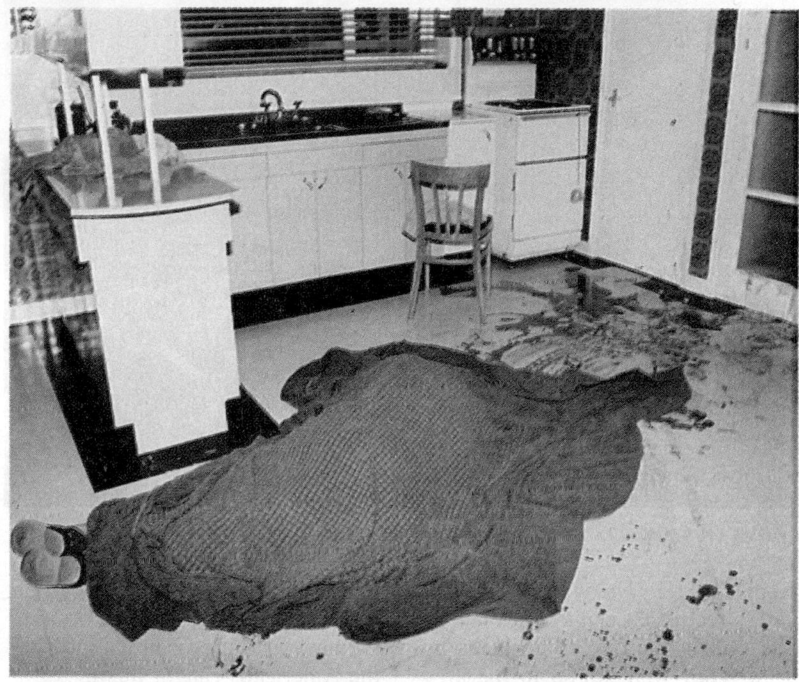

Jack Gibbs lies in his kitchen, where neighbour Michael Ryan shot him.

Aug 20. A silence hangs over the pretty town of Hungerford after yesterday's nightmare of slaughter that left 14 dead and 15 wounded. It was at lunchtime that pensioner Myra Rose, walking in Savernake Forest, met two toddlers who told her calmly: "A man in black has shot our Mummy." Susan Godfrey was Michael Ryan's first victim. Ryan, aged 27, then returned to his home in nearby Hungerford where he first shot his mother and then set fire to the house. A neighbour, Jack Gibbs, was next to die and the carnage had begun ...

Eventually Ryan, holed up in the local school, turned his gun upon himself. Ryan had a licence for several pistols and rifles. Why he should turn them on neighbours and strangers is a mystery which Hungerford, stunned with grief, understands least of all.

Aug 30. Canada's Ben Johnson (in red) powers his way past American Carl Lewis in Rome to set a world 100 metres record of 9.83 seconds.

New peace plan for Central America

Aug 8. The presidents of Costa Rica, El Salvador, Guatemala, Honduras and Nicaragua today signed an agreement in Guatemala City. The accord is based on proposals put forward earlier this year by Oscar Arias Sanchez, the President of Costa Rica.

Each government is to declare an amnesty, restore the freedom of the press and of political association, hold internationally-observed elections, arrange a ceasefire with guerrilla groups, and prohibit rebels from using bases in one country to attack another. The accord sets a deadline of November 7 for a ceasefire and for implementing these reforms (→10/12).

Huston, a grizzled eminence, is dead

The great director John Huston.

Aug 28. No one, except Orson Welles, made a more impressive debut as a film director than John Huston, who died today aged 81. He kicked off with "The Maltese Falcon", then "The Treasure of the Sierra Madre" in which he cast his father, Walter (both won Oscars). Then came "The African Queen".

Behind his grizzled eminence lay his early life as a screenwriter, gambler, boxer and hell-raiser, with five failed marriages. He sought consolation in hunting with the Galway Blazers, of which he was joint Master.

1987

SEPTEMBER

Su	Mo	Tu	We	Th	Fr	Sa
		1	2	3	4	5
6	7	8	9	10	11	12
13	14	15	16	17	18	19
20	21	22	23	24	25	26
27	28	29	30			

2. London: The Government launches a new, more explicit campaign warning of AIDS.

4. Moscow: Mathias Rust gets four years in a labour camp for violating Soviet airspace.

5. UK: Eight die in an M6 pile-up near Manchester.

7. UK: Ford announces it has bought the luxury sports car company Aston Martin.

9. Bonn: Erich Honecker arrives on his first visit to the Federal Republic.

11. London: The Government announces plans to abolish the Inner London Education Authority.

13. UK: The Jockey Club approves Sunday racing.

19. UK: A search begins for a possible Soviet mole at GCHQ following a series of leaks (→ 10/11).

22. London: The Government bans automatic weapons of the type used by Hungerford killer Michael Ryan.

23. Sydney: Britain loses an appeal against a court decision to allow the publication of "Spycatcher" in Australia (→ 24).

24. London: Thatcher says she will take the "Spycatcher" case to the Australian High Court.

25. UK: The biggest Iron Age burial site in Britain has been discovered in Yorkshire.

28. Brighton: The Labour Party conference backs a call by Kinnock for a rethink of key Labour policies (→ 9/10).

30. Fiji: Colonel Rabuka agrees to talks with Ganilau, Bavadra and Kamisese Mara before declaring a republic (→ 1/10).

30. London: Former MP Keith Best is jailed for four months for share-cheating (→ 5/10).

DEATH

16. British politician Arthur Christopher John Soames, Baron Soames of Fletching, last Governor of Rhodesia 1979-80 (*12/10/20).

US sweeps up Iranian mines in the Gulf

Mines on board the Iranian ship, Iran Ajr, boarded by the US Navy.

Sept 29. US Navy minesweepers today recovered eight mines laid in the Gulf's main shipping lanes by Iran. They were found in the area where an Iranian mine-laying ship, the Iran Ajr, was intercepted by an American helicopter patrol on Monday. Ten primed mines were found on board the ship by US commandos, but many more are thought to have been laid before the Americans caught them.

The Gulf is described as "extremely tense" today, and Iran has stepped up its patrolling of the Straits of Hormuz (→ 18/10).

House prices widen North-South divide

Sept 24. Soaring house prices are widening the gulf between North and South in Britain, according to a regional survey published today. This shows that the typical semi-detached house in London has gone up by 26.8 per cent over the last year – or by £53 a day.

Anyone moving from the North or the Midlands to work in London will now need a pay rise of at least 25 per cent simply in order to maintain living standards. The average house price in the capital now costs five and a half times annual salary, compared to two and a half in the West Midlands and two and a third in the North.

Europe keeps Ryder Cup playing in US

Sept 27. After a day of almost unbearable tension at Muirfield Village in Ohio, with the gap between the two teams closing inexorably hole by hole, the Irishman Eamonn Darcy today sank a fiendish downhill put to beat Ben Crenshaw and retain the Ryder Cup for Europe.

A big European lead, built with confident golf in the four-balls and foursomes, was whittled away by the Americans in the singles on the final afternoon, but the Europeans held on staunchly in the crucial matches to win 15-13 – the first defeat at home for America since the series began in 1927.

Pledges made to save ozone layer

Sept 16. More than 70 nations have agreed on measures to reduce the threat to the earth's ozone layer. This layer, high in the atmosphere, screens out harmful ultra-violet radiation from the sun. Evidence is growing that it is affected by long-lived chemicals called chlorofluorocarbons, used as propellants for aerosols, and in refrigerators and air conditioners.

Under the new agreement, drawn up at a conference in Montreal, use of chlorofluorocarbons will be frozen at existing levels right away and reduced by half by 1999.

Daley defeated, but Fatima hits gold

Sept 6. British hopes of a gold haul at the World Athletics Championships in Rome faded away during a week of superb performances, headed by the world record 9.83 seconds by which Ben Johnson of Canada beat Carl Lewis in the 100 metres.

Two of Britain's defending champions, Daley Thompson in the decathlon and Steve Cram in the 1,500 metres, were pushed back to ninth and eighth place respectively. The gloom was relieved only on the final day by Fatima Whitbread. Her throw of 76.64 metres took the javelin gold medal.

"Crocodile Dundee", a big box office romantic comedy, stars Paul Hogan.

Storm of the century lashes England

Oct 16. Yesterday evening, a viewer called the BBC and asked the weatherman if there was going to be a hurricane. He laughed off the suggestion. Within hours, south-east England was being battered by winds gusting up to 110mph causing greater havoc than any other storm this century. Northern France was also lashed by the hurricane-force winds.

In England the storm has killed at least 17 people and left a £300 million trail of destruction from Cornwall to East Anglia. Hotels and houses collapsed. Railway lines and roads are blocked by thousands of fallen trees, with no services running south of Rugby or Peterborough. A 6,000-ton ship was washed on to the beach in Sussex; and most of south-east England was without electricity for at least some time. Many areas are likely to be without power for several days to come.

In London, the fire brigade dealt with a record 6,000 emergency calls in 24 hours. Kew Gardens lost a third of its trees. Sevenoaks in Kent lost six of the oaks which gave it its name; and casualty wards in every London hospital were filled with casualties from flying slates and other debris.

The Meteorological Office is under fire from both the public and politicians for its failure to predict the hurricane. A computer misreading is being blamed for the poor forecast. "We could have got it better," a Meteorological Office spokesman said (→18).

The morning after: the havoc wrought in the London suburb of Orpington

Kew Gardens lost a third of its trees, some of which are irreplaceable.

US hits Iranian oil platforms in the Gulf

Oct 18. The US fleet in Gulf waters has struck back hard in retaliation for Iranian attacks on shipping. Four American destroyers blasted two Iranian offshore platforms with a thousand shells. Both are in international waters and were used as bases for Iranian gunboats marauding against Gulf tankers.

A 20-minute warning was given so that the crew could evacuate. A few hours later Special Forces landed on a third sea platform, five miles away, and destroyed radar and communications equipment. The naval raids, which left the platforms ablaze and badly damaged, followed last week's Iranian attack with a Chinese-built shore-to-ship Silkworm missile on the Sea Island City, a Kuwaiti tanker flying the American flag.

President Reagan described the 90-minute bombardment as a "prudent yet restrained response" to offensive Iranian operations. The British government was told about it in advance. Caspar Weinberger, the US Defence Secretary, warned Tehran that, if the attacks did not stop, even stronger measures might be ordered.

Prosecutions may follow ferry sinking

Oct 8. The Transport Secretary, Paul Channon, tonight warned that nobody was immune from possible public prosecution, after the inquest into the Herald of Free Enterprise disaster returned unlawful killing verdicts on the 187 victims.

The Director of Public Prosecutions will now decide whether or not charges should be made, following an official inquiry, which accused the ferry company of "sloppiness from top to bottom", and demands for directors to be charged (→31/12). ▷

1987

OCTOBER

Su	Mo	Tu	We	Th	Fr	Sa
				1	2	3
4	5	6	7	8	9	10
11	12	13	14	15	16	17
18	19	20	21	22	23	24
25	26	27	28	29	30	31

1. Los Angeles: The city is rocked by an earthquake that leaves six dead and 100 hurt.

1. Fiji: Rabuka declares himself head of state.→

3. UK: SAS troops storm Peterhead jail in Scotland to free a prison officer held hostage by inmates (→4).

4. UK: Prisoners at Perth begin a protest against prison conditions, seizing a warder.

5. London: A court quashes share cheat Tory MP Keith Best's four-month jail term.

9. Blackpool: Thatcher tells the Tory Conference she wants at least seven more years (→2/11).

9. Tibet: The death toll from a month of anti-Chinese riots now stands at six.

11. UK: A huge sonar exploration of Loch Ness has failed to find the Monster.

13. London: Heron boss Gerald Ronson is charged with the theft of £6 million from Guinness (→15).

14. Bristol: Four people are shot dead by a man upset that his girlfriend has left him.

15. London: Morgan Grenfell director Roger Seelig is arrested for stealing £2.95 million from Guinness.

18. UK: 250,000 homes in southern England still have no electricity after the storm (→19).

19. UK: Four die when a train falls off a bridge swept away by a swollen river in Wales.

22. London: Share prices plummet again after a day of optimism (→26).

26. London: City institutions plead with the Government to halt the BP flotation as share prices continue to plunge (→30).

28. London: Lloyd Honeyghan loses his world welterweight boxing crown.

30. London: A 23-year-old trainee accountant on £6,400 a year owes £1 million from stock market deals.

DEATH

19. British cellist Jacqueline du Pre (*26/1/45).

Bottom falls out of the Stock Market

A distraught dealer discovers that he is unable to get out of his position.

Oct 19. Fifty billion pounds, or ten per cent, was wiped off the value of publicly-quoted companies in London today by a tidal wave of selling that began when dealers reached their desks at 7am and never stopped. It has been the worst day for shares this century. The previous sharpest one-day fall was on March 1, 1974, after Labour's indecisive election victory, when shares fell 7.1 per cent.

The crash followed Wall Street's panic performance last Friday and heavy selling today in Tokyo. No market escaped the shockwaves. The Hong Kong market is to close all week, while Wall Street today had its worst day ever, with the Dow Jones industrial average falling 508 points to 1,739, wiping 22.5 per cent off share values, almost double the drop on the worst day of the Great Crash in October 1929. John Phelan, chairman of the New York Stock Exchange, said: "This is the nearest thing to a financial meltdown I've ever come across."

It is the end of the bull market of the last five years, which has seen a three and a half fold rise in average share prices. The collapse is blamed by analysts variously on the US budget and trade deficits, rising interest rates, and computer-controlled "programme trading" (→22).

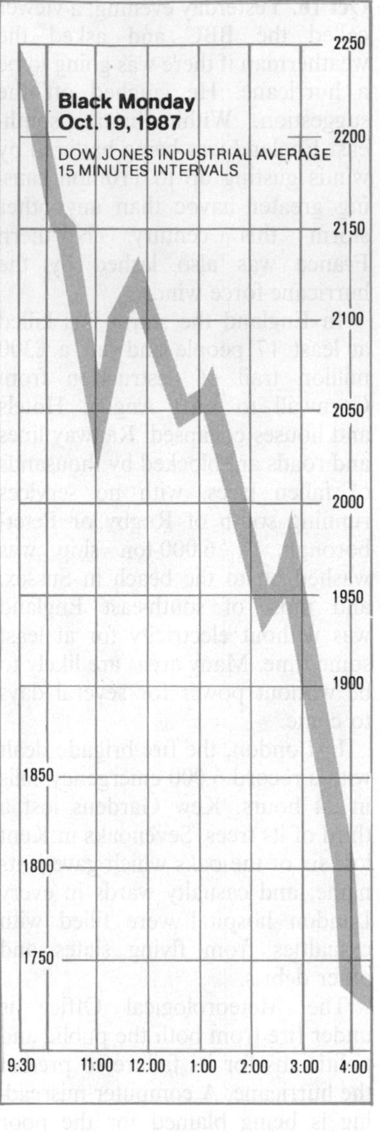

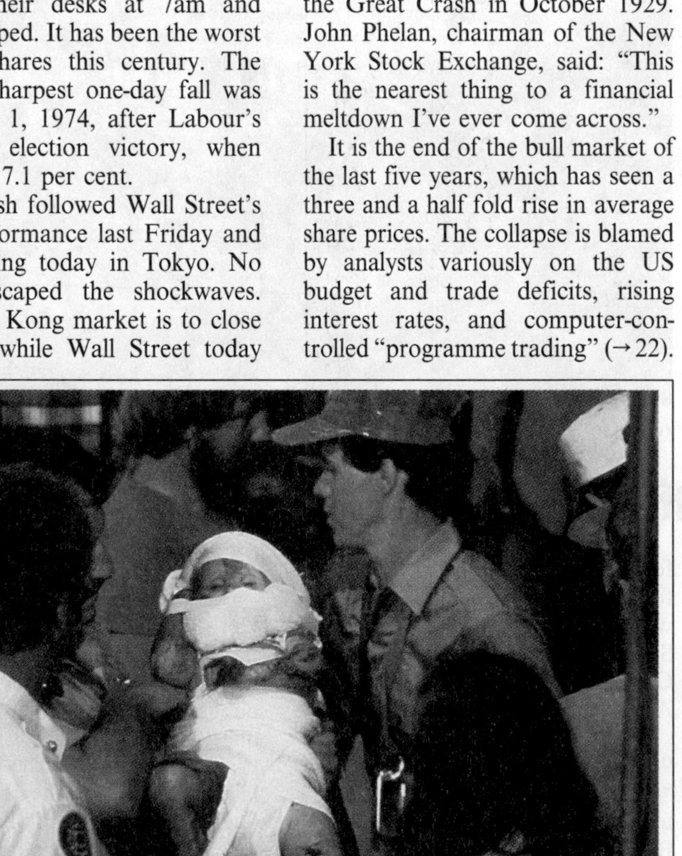
Oct 16. Eighteen-month-old Jessica McClure, who was stuck in an abandoned well shaft for over 57 hours, is brought out exhausted and dirty but alive. Inhabitants of her home town kept a round-the-clock vigil.

Lester Piggott falls at the tax hurdle

Oct 23. Lester Piggott, the most spectacularly successful British jockey of all time, appears to have met one rival he just cannot beat: the tax inspectors of the Inland Revenue. Today at Ipswich Crown Court Piggott was jailed for three years after admitting tax evasion totalling £3.1 million.

Piggott, who will be 52 next month, was estimated to have acquired a personal fortune worth £20 million during a career which brought him over 5,000 winners, including a record nine Derby victories. He retired in 1985 and turned to training.

Indian paratroops fight pitched battle with rebels

Oct 12. House-to-house battles raged through the Tamil stronghold of Jaffna, in Sri Lanka, as 6,000 Indian soldiers fought Tamil separatist guerrillas.

Paratroopers, tanks and helicopter gunships are all being used in the offensive, which is intended to purge the city of the extremist Liberation Tigers of Tamil Eelam organisation.

The Indian army is in Sri Lanka to enforce a ceasefire between the rebels and government forces. The Tigers, however, have sworn to fight to the last man.

Fiji chooses to quit the Commonwealth

Oct 15. Fiji, a Pacific island linked to Britain since 1874, left the Commonwealth today when the Queen accepted the resignation of the Governor-General, Ratu Sir Penaia Ganilau, and acknowledged, albeit reluctantly, Lieutenant-Colonel Sitiveni Rabuka's declaration of a republic.

Although the Queen personally broadcast a warning to the Fijians last month that such a declaration would be treasonable, the revolution, following the coup in May, has apparently taken root; so when Sir Penaia resigned voluntarily, to ease the crisis, she had to accept it.

Fiji's new leader Colonel Rabuka.

1987

NOVEMBER

Su	Mo	Tu	We	Th	Fr	Sa
1	2	3	4	5	6	7
8	9	10	11	12	13	14
15	16	17	18	19	20	21
22	23	24	25	26	27	28
29	30					

2. Beijing: Deng Xiaoping, 83, retires as Party General-Secretary, but his influence is expected to continue.

2. London: Peter Brooke is appointed to succeed Norman Tebbit as Chairman of the Conservative Party.

4. UK: Peter de Savary buys Land's End for £6.7 million.

7. Tunis: Colleagues of the frail and senile President Habib Bourguiba, 84, remove him from office after 31 years.

9. UK: Free dental check-ups are to be scrapped under new Government proposals (→24).

10. London: The government says it is looking at ways of reforming the Official Secrets Act.

11. New York: Van Gogh's "Irises" sells for a record $53.9 million (→12/1987).

11. Southampton: Customs men make Europe's biggest ever haul of cocaine, with a street value of £51 million.

12. UK: Arthur Scargill says he will seek re-election as NUM president to get a new mandate from the miners.

17. London: The Government says the community charge or "poll tax" will be introduced on April 1, 1990.

17. London: Michael Grade is named as successor to Jeremy Isaacs as head of Channel Four.

23. Ireland: 40 are held after police raids for IRA arms north and south of the border.

24. London: The Government announces that free eye tests are to be abolished.

25. Zimbabwe: 16 missionaries are massacred by guerrillas near Bulawayo.

27. Mauritius: 160 passengers die when an airliner crashes into the Indian Ocean.

29. Haiti: The presidential election is cancelled by the provisional government.

DEATH

5. Irish broadcaster and author Eamonn Andrews (*19/12/22).

Ulster bomb blast on Remembrance Day

Dazed and terrified, the surviving marchers hurry from the explosion.

Nov 8. As marchers assembled for the annual Remembrance Day parade in the town of Enniskillen, County Fermanagh, an IRA bomb exploded in a disused school, killing 11 people, including three married couples. Sixty-three people were injured, some critically. The IRA has admitted responsibility and apologised, blaming the British Army for triggering the bomb with a high-frequency scanning device.

The Northern Ireland Secretary, Tom King, dismissed the IRA statement. "There is not a shred of truth in it and I think people will recognise it for the contemptible document it is," he said.

The carnage at Enniskillen followed the pattern of so many atrocities in Northern Ireland, with shocked relatives combing through the debris for relatives and operating theatres working to capacity throughout the district.

Gordon Wilson, aged 60, lost his daughter Marie, a nurse, in the explosion, and was buried with her in the wreckage. Father and daughter comforted each other, holding hands. "When I asked her for the fifth time if she was all right, she said "I love you Daddy"," he said. "Then I knew there was something wrong." Marie died on a life-support machine five hours later.

And yet Gordon Wilson forgave his daughter's killers. "I shall pray for those people tonight and every night," he said.

A few days later, mourners gather at the War Memorial to bury the dead.

Party boss, critical of Gorbachev, fired

Nov 12. Moscow's Communist party boss, Boris Yeltsin, has been sacked after criticising Mikhail Gorbachev, the Soviet leader, for tolerating the slow pace of his reforms. Yeltsin, a candidate member of the ruling Politburo, has been given a minor ministerial post. He is a protege of Gorbachev and an outspoken supporter of the policies of perestroika (reconstruction) and glasnost (openness).

The dismissal stems from a bitter confrontation at a party meeting when Yeltsin strongly attacked Yegor Ligachev, the number two man in the Kremlin and leading ideologist, for opposing the Gorbachev reforms.

NHS row over hole-in-the-heart baby

Nov 25. The hole-in-the heart baby David Barber was stable today after his long-awaited operation at Birmingham Children's Hospital. Five previous operations had to be cancelled due to a lack of intensive-care nurses. His mother failed in her bid to get a High Court order compelling the hospital to operate, but the plight of seven-week-old David has highlighted what Opposition politicians are calling a crisis in the National Health Service. Mrs Thatcher says more money is being spent than ever (→5/12).

Australia win World Cup for first time

Nov 8. England's innings failed to find the necessary impetus in the World Cup final today in Calcutta, and fell just seven runs short of the required 254, to give Australia the trophy for the first time. Australian opener David Boon was man of the match with his innings of 75.

The tournament, co-hosted by India and Pakistan, lost much of its local appeal at the semi-final stage, when Australia surprisingly outmanoeuvred Pakistan in Lahore, and England, with a century by Graham Gooch, beat India in Bombay (→9/12).

Thirty die as Tube fire hits King's Cross

King's Cross Underground's incinerated booking hall after the flash fire.

Nov 19. Firemen, forensic scientists and doctors are still trying to assess the damage, identify the charred corpses and discover the cause of last night's inferno at King's Cross Underground station in which 30 people died.

The fire started on a wooden escalator and flashed, with searing heat and thick smoke, through the ticket hall. The escalators carried passengers to the heart of the blaze, and death.

One survivor described how trains disembarked passengers onto smoke-filled platforms: "A thing, I suppose a person, came stumbling down the stairs, his hair was all burnt off, his head was smoking and his skin blistering. He held his hands in front of him and there was smoke coming off them."

Surgeons at University College Hospital said the injuries included some of the worst flash burns they had ever seen. "I think the fact that we have only seven patients is a reflection of the severity of the accident. So few survived to reach hospital," said a doctor.

London Regional Transport (LRT) is strongly denying that its recently-privatised cleaning methods are inadequate, allowing inflammable fluff, which became soaked in machine oil, to accumulate under the escalator. Staff cuts and inadequate training have also been blamed. It emerged today that no sprinkler system was in operation at King's Cross and that LRT ignored recommendations made in 1984 to install one. Paul Channon, the Transport Secretary, has announced a public inquiry into the disaster.

Irangate report blames President

Nov 18. The Congressional report on the Iran-Contra affair, America's worst political scandal since Watergate, lays the ultimate responsibility for the widespread government corruption and deceit on President Reagan. The report does not claim that the president knew that the profits of arms sales to Iran were donated to the Nicaraguan Contras, but makes it clear that if he did not know, then he certainly should have.

"Yuppies" put cash before compassion

Nov 12. Compassion is out, conspicuous consumption in, and the Puritan work ethic back at the helm as far as Britain's under-25s are concerned, according to a new survey published today by the advertising agency McCann Erichson.

Money, above all, is what the "Yuppies" – Young, Upwardly-Mobile Persons – want, to the dismay of critics who condemn those they call "Thatcher's Children" for selfishness.

1987

DECEMBER

Su	Mo	Tu	We	Th	Fr	Sa
		1	2	3	4	5
6	7	8	9	10	11	12
13	14	15	16	17	18	19
20	21	22	23	24	25	26
27	28	29	30	31		

3. UK: The Church of England directory, Crockford's, criticises Dr Runcie (→8).

5. Birmingham: Hole-in-the-heart baby David Barber dies 11 days after his operation.

8. Oxford: Dr Gareth Bennett, who killed himself yesterday, is revealed as the author of the Crockford's attack on Runcie.

9. Lahore: Play is halted between England and Pakistan after Mike Gatting rows with umpire Shakoor Rana.→

10. Stockholm: Nobel Prizes go to Alex Muller and Georg Bednorz (Switzerland, Physics); Jean-Marie Lehn (France), Charles Pedersen (US) and Don Cram (US), all Chemistry; Susumu Tonegawa (Japan, Medicine); Joseph Brodsky (US, Literature); Robert Solow (US, Economics) and in Oslo to Oscar Arias Sanchez (Costa Rica, Peace).

16. Palermo: 338 are convicted in the biggest ever Mafia trial.

19. Israel: 18 have died in new Arab unrest (→25).

20. Philippines: 1,500 die when a ferry sinks.

25. Israel: The Israelis launch a crackdown on Arab rioters.

31. UK: Zeebrugge heroes are on the Honours List.

31. Worldwide: 1987 is shortened by one second to allow for an adjustment of the Gregorian calendar.

DEATH

10. Russian-born US violinist Jascha Heifetz (*2/2/1901).

HITS OF 1987

Never gonna give you up.

Nothing's gonna stop us now.

China in your hand.

QUOTE OF THE YEAR

"How do we prevent the use of nuclear weapons? By threatening to use nuclear weapons. And we can't get rid of nuclear weapons, because of nuclear weapons."

Martin Amis, "Einstein's Monsters", 1987.

Uprising looms on Israel's West Bank

Dec 12. As Christmas and its associated goodwill approaches in the Holy Land, it becomes increasingly apparent that the level of Arab hostility on the Israeli-occupied West Bank is reaching unprecedented heights.

Palestinians living in the occupied territories have never accepted Israeli rule since it was established after the Six-Day War in 1967, but their resentment has escalated substantially since the invasion of Lebanon in 1982.

Neither Israel's right-wing government nor the PLO seems willing to give ground, and many observers are convinced that the new protests are leading inexorably to a full-scale civil uprising (→19).

Cricket row turns to diplomatic incident

Dec 12. It was definitely not cricket: the England captain Mike Gatting and the Pakistani umpire Shakoor Rana locked in public confrontation in a test match. Both parties accused the other of abusive language and the crisis escalated. With play stopped in the test and the tour in jeopardy, it threatened to cause a diplomatic rift. English officials today ordered Gatting to apologise, leaving his team complaining of "betrayal" (→9/6/88).

After the success of "Terminator", Arnold Schwarzenegger hunts an alien in "Predator".

Missile treaty is signed

Reagan's damp farewell to Gorbachev after signing the historic arms deal.

Dec 8. President Reagan and the Soviet leader, Mr Gorbachev, made history today as they signed the first-ever treaty to cut the size of their nuclear arsenals. The accord, signed at the Washington summit, provides for the dismantling of all Soviet and American medium- and shorter-range missiles.

The Soviet leader seemed exceptionally eager to go on and conclude a more far-reaching reduction in superpower arsenals. Even before the two men put their names to the treaty, they began talks in the Oval Office about a possible future deal, reducing long-range missile stocks by half. But the new treaty still needs to be ratified by the US Senate, where some hawkish senators are threatening to cause problems.

Once approved the treaty will require the dismantling, within three years, of all 1,752 Soviet and 859 American missiles with ranges of 300 to 3,400 miles.

Observers were struck by the friendly banter between the two men, considering the frostiness of the Iceland summit last year. President Reagan repeated his Russian saying: "Doverai no proverai" – "Trust but verify". "You repeat that at every meeting," joked Mr Gorbachev.

Koreans riot over "corrupt" election

Dec 18. Roh Tae Woo has been declared the winner of the first presidential election to be held in South Korea for 16 years, but his victory has been greeted with rioting by angry students who claim the election was corrupt.

Both the President's opponents, Kim Yung Sam and Kim Dae Jung, who split the opposition vote, say the election was fraudulent, with Kim Yung Sam calling the vote "a coup d'etat in the name of election". Roh Tae Woo is trying to calm the dissenters, saying that his policies will "reflect the wishes" of the many who opposed him.

Kasparov is chess champ by a whisker

Dec 19. The charismatic Gary Kasparov, aged 24, retained his title as world chess champion in Seville tonight with a powerful series of attacks on his arch-rival Anatoly Karpov's queen. After three hours of play Kasparov had tied up his opponent's pieces, leaving him no choice but to resign.

The series was tied at 12 games all, but Kasparov, the challenger, wins the title under international rules. The victory is not likely to be popular in the Kremlin. Kasparov, doubly alien to the authorities as an Armenian Jew, has frequently criticised the rules as unfair.

Arts: flower prices go through the roof

The value put on paintings at auction soared out of the realms of the believable this year. Prices have been accelerating sensationally as the Eighties wear on. In 1976 the record price for a British painting at auction was £340,000, for **Turner's** Bridgewater Sea Piece. By 1980 his panorama of Venice by night called "Juliet and her Nurse" reached a record £2.6 million. In 1984 his unfinished seascape of Folkestone owned by the late **Kenneth (Lord) Clark** made £7.3 million. A year later this record passed to **Mantegna** – £8.1 million for his "Adoration of the Magi".

But the climb of the Impressionists and Post-Impressionists has left the old masters behind. It began with **Manet**, whose study of roadmenders at work in a Paris street, the Rue Mosnier, fetched £7.7 million, while **Degas'** yawning laundrywomen at their ironing made nearly £7.5 million. Then **Van Gogh's** painting of the old-fashioned wooden bridge at Trinquetaille jumped the record up to £12.6 million, just as a start.

Next Christie's sold the "Sunflowers", which used to hang in **Gauguin's** bedroom at his home in Arles, for £24,750,000, trebling Mantegna's record at a stroke. The buyer turned out to be a Japanese insurance firm, Yasuda Fire and Marine; but the new record only stood for eight months before Van Gogh's "Irises" was knocked down by Sotheby's in New York for an astonishing £30 million. Van Gogh didn't see a franc for either of

Anthony Hopkins and Judi Dench in the National's "Cleopatra".

them. Auction fever seems to have been general.

Mozart's manuscript book containing symphonies number 22 to 30 in his hand went for £2.5 million, eclipsing all manuscript records except one – the richly-illuminated **Henry the Lion** Gospel which fetched £8 million in 1983.

Nor has there been a jewellery sale to rival that of the **Duchess of Windsor's** collection in Geneva, which was forecast to raise £5 million for the Pasteur Institute of Medical Research. The total for the two-day sale was £31 million in wild bidding which reflected the associations more than the style of the items he gave her. Her engagement ring, inscribed "We are Ours now", made over a million pounds. **Elizabeth Taylor** and **Joan Collins** were among the buyers.

Van Gogh's "Sunflowers" being knocked down for £24 million at Christie's.

1988

JANUARY

Su	Mo	Tu	We	Th	Fr	Sa
					1	2
3	4	5	6	7	8	9
10	11	12	13	14	15	16
17	18	19	20	21	22	23
24	25	26	27	28	29	30
31						

1. London: Cabinet papers out today show Macmillan's government suppressed the 1957 Windscale fire report.

5. UK: A report published today shows that wealth is growing much faster in the south than in the north.

8. Nigeria: Mrs Thatcher ends her African tour amid protests at Kano in the Moslem north.

10. London: Viscount Whitelaw resigns as Leader of the House of Lords.

13. New York: Doctors reveal that one in every 61 babies born last month in New York City had AIDS.

15. Jerusalem: Israeli soldiers battle with Palestinians outside Islam's Noble Sanctuary in the heart of the city.→

17. Nicaragua: President Ortega offers a cease-fire to US-backed Contra rebels, hoping to stop American aid.

19. UK: Christopher Nolan, who has no speech or muscular coordination, wins the Whitbread Book of the Year Prize for his autobiography, "Under the Eye of the Clock".

22. London: Liberal MP David Alton's Bill to reduce the time limit on abortions wins a majority of 45 on its second reading (→6/5).

24. UK: Arthur Scargill is narrowly re-elected as President of the National Union of Mineworkers.

25. London: Mrs Thatcher announces a radical review of the National Health Service (→3/2).

28. London: An appeal by six Irishmen convicted of the Birmingham pub bombing in 1975 is rejected at the Old Bailey.

DEATHS

7. British actor Trevor Wallace Howard (*29/9/1916).

15. Irish statesman and co-founder of Amnesty International Sean McBride (*26/1/1904).

28. East German nuclear spy Dr Emil Julius Klaus Fuchs (*29/12/1911).

Israel takes tough line in Gaza uprising

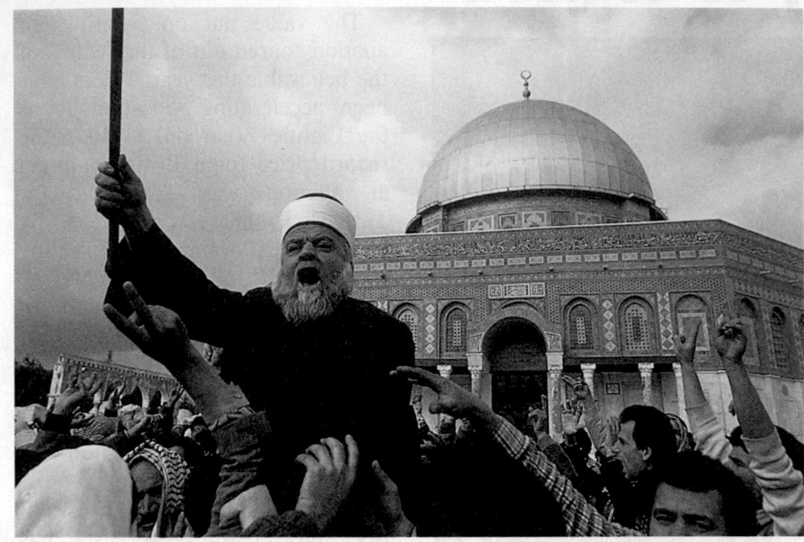

An Imam leads Palestinian demonstrations at the Dome of the Rock.

Jan 20. Defiant Palestinians call it the intifada or uprising, Israeli politicians and soldiers like to dismiss it as a minor local difficulty. Whatever the description, the demonstrations by West Bank and Gaza Arabs against the occupying authorities are proving to be Israel's severest test since the Six-Day War of 1967.

As the world's media transmit grim scenes of conflict, with stone-throwing men, women and children pitting themselves against Israeli rifles, clubs and rubber bullets, the situation has been intensified by a full-scale commercial strike. With most shops shut, essential food is in short supply. Speaking yesterday to angry Palestinians at the Jelazoun refugee camp in Gaza, the Israeli Defense Minister, Yitzhak Rabin, emphasised that there would be no softening of the government's position. If demonstrations continued, they would be met with "might, power and beatings."

Forbidding foreign charities to send in food to the beleaguered Palestinians, he said: "If they want to strike and not supply food they should not cry afterwards that there's a food shortage. There is no food shortage, there is an attempt by use of threats to prevent the population from getting food" (→1/2).

Manchester nurses strike for more pay

Jan 7. More than 50 nurses at the North Manchester General Hospital went on a strike today over proposed cuts in their payments for "unsocial hours". The nurses, all members of the National Union of Public Employees, are unimpressed by a scheme to offer higher pay to nurses with specialist skills.

Although the Royal College of Nursing maintains its opposition to strikes, the Manchester action heightens the controversy currently surrounding the Governement's policy on the National Health Service. Much of this focuses on the plight of very ill children unable to have surgery because of a shortage of qualified nurses (→25/1).

David Steel to quit as Liberal leader

Jan 23. David Steel will not stand for the leadership of a merged Liberal and Social Democratic Party. "I have been a leader for 12 years and I have no wish to go on any longer," he said today. The Liberal leader was speaking as his own and SDP officials prepared membership ballots on whether the two former Alliance parties should merge.

Mergers still seem likely, despite opposition from the former SDP leader Dr David Owen. Mr Steel's own position was weakened by proposals prepared jointly with the current SDP leader, Robert Maclennan. These included putting VAT on food and were withdrawn after protests by Liberal MPs.

1988

FEBRUARY

Su	Mo	Tu	We	Th	Fr	Sa
	1	2	3	4	5	6
7	8	9	10	11	12	13
14	15	16	17	18	19	20
21	22	23	24	25	26	27
28	29					

1. Israel: Jewish settlers on the West Bank kill two Palestinians (→26).

3. London: Hundreds of nurses march on Parliament in support of pay claims and more money for the NHS (→21/4).

5. Russia: Mr Gorbachev rehabilitates 21 "un-persons" executed and erased from history by Stalin.

7. Brazil: At least 127 are feared killed by floods and mud-slides in the Rio de Janeiro area.

9. London: MPs vote for experimental televising of the House of Commons.

10. Bangladesh: Eighty people are reported killed and 1,000 injured during violence caused by the local elections.

15. Canada: Pirmin Zurbriggen of Switzerland wins the Olympic men's downhill ski championship.→

17. US: Vice-President George Bush wins the New Hampshire Republican primary, followed by Senator Robert Dole (→11/3).

18. Russia: Mr Gorbachev sacks Boris Yeltsin following his complaints last year about the slow pace of reform.

21. US: Jimmy Swaggart, America's leading television evangelist, confesses that he consorted with a prostitute.

26. Israel: Palestinians refuse to meet US Secretary of State George Shultz as he begins a Middle East peace mission (→16/4).

28. USSR: Armenians call for Nagorny Karabakh in Moslem Azerbaijan to become part of Soviet Armenia (→2/3).

29. S. Africa: Archbishop Tutu arrested for defying law banning demonstrations outside parliament (→15/3).

DEATHS

14. American composer Fritz Loewe (*10/6/1901).

15. American physicist and Nobel Prize winner Richard Phillips Feynman (*11/5/1918).

1988

Waldheim rides out storm over Nazi past

Feb 11. Kurt Waldheim, the former UN Secretary-General, today made it clear he is determined to ride out the storm over his Second World War record and continue as President of Austria. Waldheim, a German army intelligence officer in the Balkans, has been accused of complicity in the deaths of thousands of Jews, Yugoslavs and Italians. A panel of historians, set up by the Austrian government, refused to condemn him outright, but said Waldheim "let slip parts of the past into oblivion, and if that was not possible, made them appear harmless". However, polls show that 70 per cent of Austrians think he should not resign (→ 15/3).

Waldheim: riding the storm.

Genuine stars shine in artificial snow

Feb 29. After all the worries about artificial snow and far-flung locations, the Winter Olympics ended today in Calgary with a spectacular display of ice-skating before 70,000 enthusiastic Canadians.

The XVth Winter Olympiad had been a huge popular success and thrown up genuine stars in the Finnish ski-jumper Matti Nykanean, East Germany's vivacious free skater Katarina Witt, and Switzerland's downhill ski champion Pirmin Zurbriggen. Russia topped the medal table, but it was a Briton who finished last who won the hearts – ski-jumper Eddie "the Eagle" Edwards from Cheltenham.

Ferry strike throws UK ports into chaos

Feb 4. Britain's ferry ports are in chaos today as seamen continued their strike, despite calls by their union leader for a return to work. With only French or Belgian-owned Channel ferries operating, over 1,500 lorries are choking the roads to Dover. The dispute began after 162 seamen were sacked by the Isle of Man Steam Packet Company. Members of the National Union of Seamen, fearing redundancies by other companies, stopped work. Sealink and P&0, claiming they were not party to the dispute, won injunctions against the union and the union's funds could be seized (→ 15/3).

Feb 5. Red-nosed London bobbies put charity before dignity by wearing the symbol of Comic Relief, a campaign to combat famine in Africa.

1988

MARCH

Su	Mo	Tu	We	Th	Fr	Sa
		1	2	3	4	5
6	7	8	9	10	11	12
13	14	15	16	17	18	19
20	21	22	23	24	25	26
27	28	29	30	31		

1. UK: British Aerospace makes a surprise bid for the state-owned Rover car firm.

3. Geneva: Afghanistan and Pakistan agree a nine-month timetable for Soviet withdrawal from Afghanistan (→ 7/4).

4. Beirut: Two Oxfam officials are seized by an unnamed Palestinian group (→ 8).

8. Beirut: Oxfam officials, Peter Coleridge and Omar Treboulsi, released unharmed.

10. Tibet: The Chinese army moves into the capital, Lhasa, after nationalist violence breaks out over the weekend.

11. US: George Bush leads the Republican presidential candidate race after 17 states held their primary elections today (→ 27).

15. S. Africa: President Botha rules that the Sharpeville Six, who took part in the killing of a black councillor, must die.

15. UK: P&O European Ferries announce that 2,300 striking Dover seamen are to be sacked (→ 9/5).

17. UK: Ford abandons its plans for a new electronics plant in Dundee, depriving the area of 1,000 new jobs (→ 31).

19. Cardiff: France win a share in the Five Nations' rugby championship by beating Wales.

20. Iran: 54 men die in an Iraqi attack on an Iranian oil terminal at Kharg island (→ 1/4).

23. USSR: Troops move into Soviet Armenia and arrest nationalist activists (→ 21/5).

25. London: British and Irish ministers announce plans for closer co-operation in fight against terrorism (→ 30/9).

27. US: Jesse Jackson wins 55 per cent of the votes in the Michigan Democratic caucus (→ 19/4).

29. UK: Plans for Britain's biggest skyscraper, in London's docklands, are unveiled.

31. UK: Last-ditch efforts by TUC leader, Norman Willis, to save the proposed new Ford plant in Dundee fail.

Russia sends army into Azerbaijan

March 2. Russian troops have moved into the industrial city of Sumgait in Soviet Azerbaijan, and a curfew has been ordered, after what official sources describe as "hooligans" launched a series of race riots. A number of people have been hurt. This outburst is the latest example of the problems that have developed in the USSR's southern provinces where rival Christian and Moslem groups are engaged in intense ethnic rivalry.

Nationalist campaigners in Christian Armenia are demanding the return of Nagorny Karabakh, a largely Christian enclave within Moslem Azerbaijan. The events in Sumgait are the Azerbaijani response to what they see as an unacceptable grab for their land (→ 23).

Royal ski party in avalanche tragedy

Prince Charles in Switzerland.

March 10. The Prince of Wales narrowly escaped death this afternoon near Klosters in Switzerland. An avalanche swept one member of the royal ski party to his death and seriously injured another as what the Prince described as "a whirling maelstrom" caught them as they skied off-piste. The dead man is Major Hugh Lindsay, aged 34, a former equerry to the Queen. The injured woman is Mrs Palmer-Tomkinson, wife of one of the Prince's oldest friends (→ 27/6).

SAS shootings spark bloody reprisals

IRA trio gunned down in Gibraltar

March 7. Three members of an IRA "active service unit" were gunned down by British soldiers wearing civilian clothes in a Gibraltar street yesterday. The shootings – at point-blank range in broad daylight – are believed to have been carried out by members of the SAS after security forces had feared the IRA members were planning to set off a car bomb.

Gibraltar police and Ministry of Defence spokesmen in London initially had indicated that a planted bomb had been found, but this was today denied by the Foreign Secretary, Sir Geoffrey Howe. He said the soldiers opened fire because they concluded from the IRA trio's movements "that their own lives and the lives of others were under threat". The dead three were identified as Sean Savage, Mairead Farrell and Daniel McCann; the IRA has confirmed that they were on "active service".

MPs generally welcomed the action to prevent a bomb outrage, but some eye-witnesses disputed official claims that the soldiers had given warning before firing. The three dead were unarmed, although a search for explosives has now spread to Spain (→ 16).

Moments before death: Corporal Wood draws his gun, but to no avail.

Crazed mob lynches two British corporals

March 19. In full view of television cameras, two British soldiers blundered at high speed into an IRA funeral cortege in West Belfast today – to meet their deaths after several horrifying minutes at the hands of a lynch mob.

No explanation was given by the Army as to why the two men were driving through a staunchly Republican area of the city at the very time when burials of people killed in the shootings at Milltown cemetery earlier this week were taking place. Corporal Derek Wood, aged 24, and Corporal Robert Howes, aged 23, were caught up in the melee and unable to escape. Both were members of the Signals Regiment, although they were in plain clothes at the time of the attack.

The windows of their Volkswagen car were smashed and, although the soldiers drew their guns, they were bludgeoned before being driven off in a car. They were apparently taken to some waste ground where, despite spirited resistance observed by a hovering, but helpless Army helicopter, the soldiers were stripped and then shot.

Father Alec Reid, a local priest, administered last rites to the men, kneeling over the soldiers' battered bodies on the ground. "Our parish is seen as dripping in the blood of murders," he said, reflecting the public revulsion over the public and barbaric nature of the killings.

The Army rejected the IRA's claims that the corporals were "SAS soldiers on a dirty-tricks operation", and said Corporal Howes had only arrived in Northern Ireland last week. Tonight, the policy of "no policing" at funerals is under urgent review (→ 25).

Loyalist assassin fires on IRA mourners

March 16. A Loyalist gunman opened fire indiscriminately and hurled grenades into a crowd of mourners at an IRA funeral in Belfast today, killing three people and injuring 50. The shooting occurred when the bodies of the three IRA members killed by the SAS in Gibraltar ten days ago were being lowered into their graves at Milltown cemetery. Panic ensued as shots exploded, with mourners diving for cover behind gravestones. The gunman fled across fields before being overtaken and beaten up before police intervened. Loyalist organisations denied involvement, but the unprecedented attack on a funeral has undoubtedly raised tension (→ 19).

The gunman at Milltown cemetery.

1988

APRIL

Su	Mo	Tu	We	Th	Fr	Sa
					1	2
3	4	5	6	7	8	9
10	11	12	13	14	15	16
17	18	19	20	21	22	23
24	25	26	27	28	29	30

1. Iraq: Iran claims Iraq dropped mustard gas on Kurdish villages in north-west Iraq.

3. India: Rajiv Gandhi seals the border between the Punjab and Pakistan.

5. London: The Home Office says the British passport will be phased out to be replaced by a European one.

7. Geneva: Mr Gorbachev says he will sign the Geneva peace accord enabling Soviet troops to leave Afghanistan (→ 16/5).

9. Aintree: Rhyme 'n' Reason, trained by David Elsworth and ridden by Brendan Powell, wins the Grand National.

12. China: The National People's Congress votes to allow capitalist-style private enterprise.

16. Tunisia: Abu Jihad, military commander of the PLO, is murdered; Israeli gunmen are suspected.

18. Israel: John Demjanjuk is convicted in Jerusalem of being Ivan Grozny, a notorious SS guard at Treblinka.

20. Algiers: Hostages from the Kuwaiti Airlines Jumbo are released; the captors go free.

21. UK: Nurses are offered pay rises averaging 15 per cent, with more for specialist skills.

23. Beirut: A vegetable truck packed with explosives kills 54 in Tripoli marketplace.

25. France: Francois Mitterrand leads Jacques Chirac in the first round of the presidential elections (→ 10/5).

29. Poland: Thousands of steel workers strike after huge price increases (→ 5/5).

DEATHS

14. British politician/author John Stonehouse (*28/7/1925).

15. British actor and comedian Kenneth Williams (*22/2/1926).

23. British churchman Lord Ramsey, former Archbishop of Canterbury (*14/11/1904).

28. British politician/pacifist Fenner Brockway (*1/11/1888).

Dukakis set to win Democratic race

April 19. Governor Michael Dukakis of Massachusetts was tonight heading for victory in the New York primary election and a commanding lead in the Democratic race for the presidential nomination. He fought off a spirited challenge from the Reverend Jesse Jackson whose victory in the Michigan Democratic caucuses last month stunned party managers.

Dukakis cannot match Jackson's oratorical skills, or his passion, but he has outlasted the many other Democratic hopefuls who started the race. His Republican rival next November seems certain to be Vice-President George Bush, who has overcome early setbacks to beat Senator Robert Dole and the TV evangelist Pat Robertson (→ 21/7).

Hijacked plane now set down in Cyprus

April 9. The Kuwaiti airliner hijacked four days ago at Mashad in Iran was allowed to land at Cyprus's Larnaca airport tonight after authorities at Beirut airport had refused to let it touch down there.

The hijackers, who are demanding the release of 17 men jailed in Kuwait, hold some 50 crew and passengers, including members of Kuwait's royal family (→ 20).

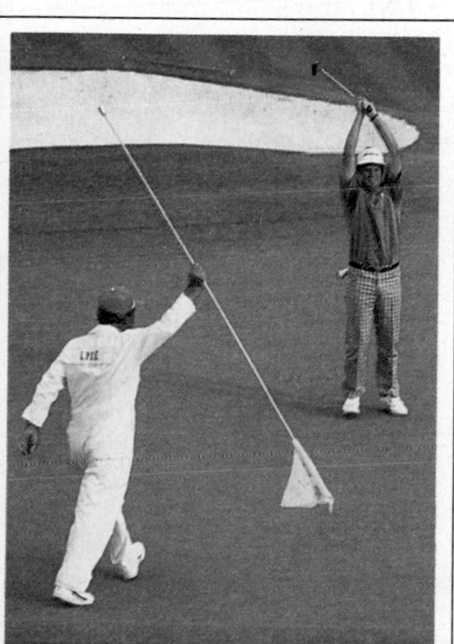

April 10. Sandy Lyle celebrates victory in the US Masters championship to become the first Briton to win the coveted golf title.

1988

MAY

Su	Mo	Tu	We	Th	Fr	Sa
1	2	3	4	5	6	7
8	9	10	11	12	13	14
15	16	17	18	19	20	21
22	23	24	25	26	27	28
29	30	31				

2. Holland: A police hunt begins in northern Europe after the IRA kill three British servicemen.

3. Lebanon: Israeli troops occupy four villages just short of Syrian army positions (→ 9).

5. Poland: Riot police smash shipyard and steelwork strikes.

6. London: David Alton's controversial bill to reduce the legal limit for abortions is talked out of Parliament.

6. UK: Graeme Hick scores 405 not out for Worcestershire, the highest cricket innings in England this century.

9. Dover: Lorry drivers block berths of P&O striking ships, claiming that French drivers have been given preference.

9. Beirut: The Syrian army threatens to intervene to stop fighting between Amal and Hezbollah militia.

10. UK: Athlete Zola Budd flies home to South Africa, exhausted by rows over her eligibility for England.

14. Iran: Iraq attacks Iran's Larak oil terminal (→ 25).

16. Kabul: The Communist President, Mr Najibullah, thanks Soviet troops preparing to leave Afghanistan.

18. India: Sikh militants give up their siege of the Golden Temple at Amritsar after 10 days.

21. USSR: Communist Party bosses in Armenia and Azerbaijan are sacked after unrest in Soviet Transcaucasia (→ 25/6).

25. Iran: Iraq takes Basra from Iran, a defeat which marks a reversal of fortunes in the Gulf War (→ 3/7).

26. Liverpool: The Tate Gallery opens a new wing at Liverpool's refurbished former Albert Dock.

31. UK: The BBC's controversial Falklands film, "Tumbledown", is broadcast despite Ministry of Defence concern.

DEATH

11. British spy H.A.R. "Kim" Philby (*1/1/1912).

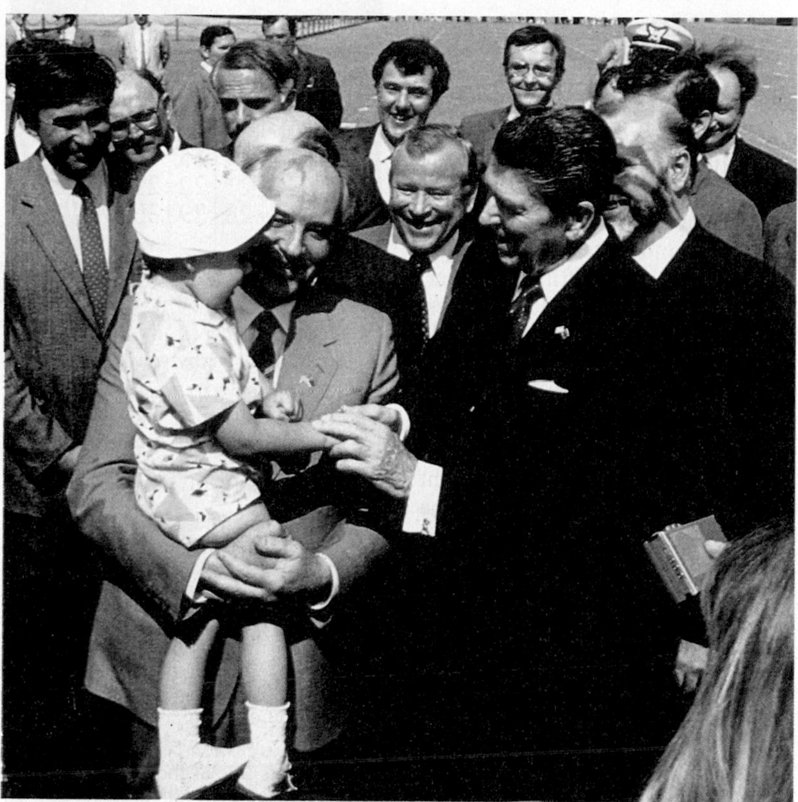

Gorbachev and Reagan find common political ground in Red Square.

Reagan woos minds of the "evil empire"

May 31. On his first visit to the capital of what he once called "an evil empire", President Reagan has praised President Gorbachev for his *glasnost* and *perestroika* reforms, but irritated the Soviet leader by calling for more progress in human rights. Nevertheless, the formalities of signing the Intermediate Nuclear Forces Treaty have been completed and there was talk of a possible agreement on strategic arms.

Mr Reagan made his foray into human rights when, flanked by a huge bust of Lenin, he addressed 1,000 students at Moscow University. Despite his strictures, he told students that they were living in one of the most hopeful times in their country's history.

Today, in an unprecedented news conference for the foreign press, Mr Gorbachev ticked off the President for his "propaganda gambits", but he, too, was capable of generosity; his four meetings with Mr Reagan, he acknowledged, "have made huge breaches in the walls of the Cold War fortress".

Longer time should please gentlemen

May 20. Nearly 75 years after the demands of the First World War's munitions factories put paid to Britain's traditional day-long drinking hours, a new law will soon see the end of the country's limited opening time. A new Licensing Act received its royal assent today, and as from summer, Britain's 65,000 pubs will be able to stay open from 11am to 11pm on weekdays, although hours will still be restricted on Sundays.

Nancy's astrologer dictates to Reagan

May 3. A film star in the White House is one thing, a star-gazer quite another. But according to the tell-tale memoirs of the former Chief of Staff, Donald Regan, President Reagan used his wife Nancy's astrologer for advice on "virtually every major move and decision". Such moves apparently included the timing of last year's summit meeting with Mikhail Gorbachev and a wide range of decisions vital to national interest. ▷

Mitterrand returns as French President

May 10. Francois Mitterrand was re-elected President of France today, taking 54 per cent of the popular vote and defeating his right-wing opponent, the Prime Minister, Jacques Chirac. The Socialist President, first elected in 1981, set aside party politics to declare: "Our first duty is to national solidarity and national cohesion." M. Chirac took defeat with dignity, but Jean-Marie Le Pen, leader of the extreme right National Front, condemned "the stupidest right in the world" for Mitterrand's success. Le Pen won 14 per cent of the vote in the first round of the contest.

Francois Mitterrand (r.) with his likely new premier, Michel Rocard.

Celtic's late winner clinches the double

May 14. Britain's domestic football seasons reached their traditional climax today with the two Cup Finals, but the two teams of the season experienced contrasting fortunes. In Scotland, Celtic duly completed a Cup and League double by beating Dundee United 2-1 at Hampden Park, thanks to Frank McAvennie who scored the winner one minute from time. There was no such reprieve for Liverpool at Wembley, where their dream of the double became a nightmare as their expensive stars tumbled to a drab 1-0 defeat against humble Wimbledon.

1988

JUNE

Su	Mo	Tu	We	Th	Fr	Sa
			1	2	3	4
5	6	7	8	9	10	11
12	13	14	15	16	17	18
19	20	21	22	23	24	25
26	27	28	29	30		

1. Epsom: Ray Cochrane rides Kahysi, owned by the Aga Khan, to a Derby win.

1. Australia: The British government fails to stop the publication of "Spycatcher", by the ex-MI5 agent, Peter Wright (→13/10).

2. UK: Chancellor of the Exchequer Nigel Lawson increases interest rates from 7.5 to 8 per cent (→25/8).

3. Moscow: Andrei Sakharov, Russia's famous dissident, calls for human rights at an officially-sanctioned press conference (→26/10).

4. France: Steffi Graf wins the women's title at the French Open, beating Natalia Zvereva (→2/7).

9. UK: Mike Gatting is sacked as England cricket captain for "irresponsible" off-field behaviour during a Test match.

9. Seoul: Students demanding union with North Korea battle with police (→15/8).

11. London: 80,000 celebrate Nelson Mandela's 70th birthday at Wembley Stadium.

12. Stuttgart: Ireland beat England 1-0 in the opening match of the European Nations' Championships (→25).

15. Peter Clowes, accused of diverting funds from Barlow Clowes International, is arrested.

16. UK: Plans for the ordination of women in 1993 are published (→5/7).

18. Turkey: The Prime Minister, Turgut Ozal, survives an assassination attempt.

23. UK: Thatcher rules out Britain joining a proposed European central bank (→6/7).

25. USSR: Armenians in Nagorny Karabakh vote to end their five-week-old strike (→22/9).

27. Switzerland: A magistrate blames the royal party for the avalanche that killed Major Hugh Lindsay last March.

DEATH

8. British writer/broadcaster Russell Harty (*5/9/1934).

Dusk-to-dawn curfew imposed in Burma

Demonstrators stage another protest against General Ne Win's regime.

June 21. The Burmese government tonight imposed a dusk-to-dawn curfew on the capital, Rangoon, after student protesters burnt down a police station, set fire to policemen's homes and wrecked cinemas. Five policemen were killed and 26 injured. One demonstrator was also killed in what is described as the worst violence in the past quarter century.

The students are demonstrating against Burma's increasing economic problems, which have caused food shortages in some areas of the country. Their anger is particularly directed against the 26-year-long rule of General Ne Win, whose Socialist government is accused of corruption and incompetence. Government defences have been substantially undermined by the clandestine circulation of letters written to Ne Win by his former deputy, Brigadier Aung Gyi, who apparently leaked the correspondence himself. In his letters, Aung Gyi demanded that the general should act against food shortages, government corruption and human rights violations. Aung Gyi himself is now believed to be in prison.

Today's measures, which are scheduled to last for the next two months, have also closed the universities and forbidden students from the provinces to enter Rangoon. Experts doubt if they will have any real effect on the troubles (→4/8).

Dutch footballers win Europe's crown

June 25. Dutch skill finally landed a national football title today when, after nine years of being runners-up, the Netherlands beat the Soviet Union 2-0 in Munich to win the European Nations' championship. The flamboyant Ruud Gullit and Marco van Basten gave the Dutch a deserved victory in a tournament which, for England, was a disaster on and off the pitch. Its team lost all three matches, while the fans battled with police in German cities. English gloom was in contrast to Irish joy: the Republic's team not only beat England, but almost qualified for the semi-finals.

June 8. Broadcaster Russell Harty died today after a long struggle against hepatitis in a Leeds hospital. He was 53.

1988

JULY

Su	Mo	Tu	We	Th	Fr	Sa
					1	2
3	4	5	6	7	8	9
10	11	12	13	14	15	16
17	18	19	20	21	22	23
24	25	26	27	28	29	30
31						

2. Wimbledon: Steffi Graf wins the Women's Singles final, beating Martina Navratilova 5-7, 6-2, 6-1 (→ 10/9).

4. Wimbledon: Stefan Edberg beats Boris Becker, 4-6, 7-6, 6-4, 6-2 in the Men's final delayed by rain.

5. UK: The Church of England Synod votes to go ahead with plans for ordination of women (→ 1/8).

6. Strasbourg: Jacques Delors, President of the EC, says European economic unity is on the way (→ 21/9).

11. Greece: Nine people die and 78 are injured when terrorists open fire on a Greek ferry, the City of Poros.

12. UK: The Texan oilman, Red Adair, boards the burning Piper Alpha oil-rig.

14. UK: The Tories just keep Kensington in the first by-election since Mrs Thatcher won her third term.

18. Zimbabwe: President Mugabe apologises to Neil Kinnock for his detention by soldiers on arrival in the country.

18. UK: Spanish golfer Seve Ballesteros wins his third British Open championship.

21. Atlanta: Dukakis accepts presidential candidacy at the Democratic convention (→ 19/8).

22. Iraq: As the UN plans peace for the Gulf, Iraq launches a new attack (→ 8/8).

24. Paris: Spanish cyclist Pedro Delgado wins the Tour de France.

28. UK: Paddy Ashdown, an ex-Royal Marine commando, is elected leader of the Social and Liberal Democrats.

29. UK: The Education Reform Bill receives royal assent (→ 2/11).

31. Nigeria: The cargo ship Karin B sails for Italy, loaded with toxic waste (→ 30/8).

DEATH

20. British cartoonist and journalist Charles Mark Edward Boxer (*19/5/1931).

Over 150 feared dead in oil-rig fire

July 6. More than 150 workers are feared to have been killed tonight in a massive explosion on Occidental Petroleum's Piper Alpha oil-rig, situated in the North Sea some 120 miles off Wick. Only 70 of the rig's 227 workers are thought to have survived the blast, described by one as "like an atomic bomb going off" and which brought the sea to near boiling-point. NATO warships have joined the rescue operation.

Survivors told of a whistle of escaping gas, then "a big bang" which shook the whole rig. It wiped out the control room, seriously hampering escape operations. Ten minutes later came the second explosion, when flames more than 500 feet high engulfed the platform, reducing it to a couple of molten stumps of metal and two twisted derricks.

Some men leapt 200 feet into a sea covered in blazing oil, where high-speed rescue dinghies dodged the flames as best they could. Some, who had never learnt to swim, drowned as helpless rescuers looked on. Others were too shocked to move. "Some of the boys just gave up the ghost," says a rigger, James MacDonald, who realised "either I stay here and get roasted alive or I get out". He chose to jump into the scalding sea. The rig passed a regulation safety check just eight days ago (→ 12).

Fires still rage on Piper Alpha, preventing efforts to board the platform.

US warship shoots down Iranian airliner

July 3. The US guided-missile cruiser Vincennes today shot down an Iran Air Airbus on a regular flight over the Gulf. All 286 people on board were killed. The Vincennes at first claimed that it had shot down an attacking F-14 Tomcat fighter, following earlier skirmishes with the Iranian navy. But it soon emerged that the ship's captain, Will Rogers, had made a terrible mistake.

There is now serious concern in Washington that sophisticated weapons systems could not tell the difference between the Tomcat and an aircraft almost three times as large. Amid outrage in Tehran, the Prime Minister, Mr Mousavi, said that the United States will "not be exempt from the consequences" (→ 22).

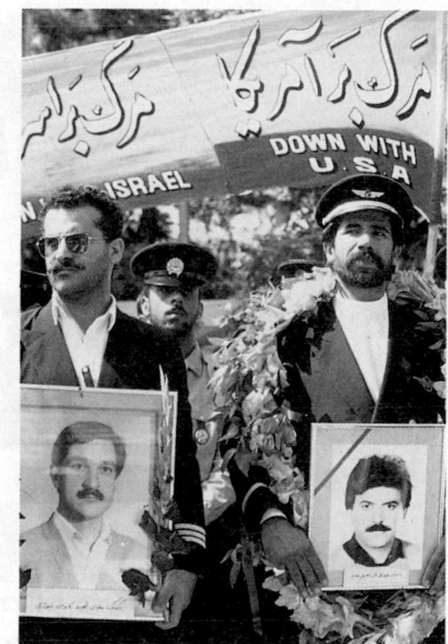

Anger and sorrow in Tehran.

Thousands turn out for Jacko's UK tour

July 16. The American rock star Michael Jackson played to a full house of dedicated fans at Wembley Stadium tonight at the start of his British tour. Despite all the hype and some hostile press coverage, "Wacko Jacko" proved himself to be a supreme entertainer.

Jackson first hit the headlines as the 11-year-old singer in his family group, the Jackson Five. Now, 18 years on, he is rumoured to be worth 600 times his weight (8.5 stone) in gold. For one hour on stage Jackson earns £700,000, but the 75,000 fans watching him dance his way through hits like "Billie Jean" and "Thriller" seemed to think this a fair price.

1988

AUGUST

Su	Mo	Tu	We	Th	Fr	Sa
	1	2	3	4	5	6
7	8	9	10	11	12	13
14	15	16	17	18	19	20
21	22	23	24	25	26	27
28	29	30	31			

1. London: Anglican bishops vote for ordination of women at the Lambeth Conference (→24/9).

2. China: Floods kill at least 250 people in the east (→4/11).

4. Rangoon: Anti-government demonstrators defy martial law to protest (→12).

11. Sudan: 13 hours of rain lead to flooding which leaves 1.5 million homeless.

12. Rangoon: President Sein Lwin resigns after five days of rioting (→8/9).

12. S. Africa: Nelson Mandela is taken from prison to hospital with tuberculosis.

15. Seoul: Riot police stop students from marching to meet North Korean colleagues on the eve of the Olympics (→3/11).

17. Pakistan: The military ruler President Zia ul-Haq is killed when his plane explodes in mid-air (→30/11).

20. UK: Six British soldiers die when a land-mine explodes under their bus in Northern Ireland.

21. India: An earthquake measuring 6.7 on the Richter scale kills 500 on the border with Nepal.

25. UK: The Government's announcement of a £2.2 million trade deficit leads to an increase in interest rates (→18/11).

28. West Germany: 33 die when Italian air force jets collide at an air show.→

30. UK: Virginia Bottomley, junior Environment Minister, bans the toxic waste-laden Karin B from landing.

31. Poland: Lech Walesa calls for miners, shipyard and transport workers to end their strikes (→11/11).

DEATHS

14. Italian racing car magnate Enzo Ferrari (*18/2/1898).

17. Pakistani President Zia ul-Haq (*12/8/1924).

19. British ballet choreographer Sir Frederick Ashton (*17/9/1904).

Cease-fires herald the end of two wars

Aug 8. Cease-fires were announced today which herald the end of two prolonged world conflicts. In New York, the UN Secretary-General announced that Iran and Iraq have agreed a truce after eight years of bloody clashes in the Gulf War. Almost simultaneously, an end to an even longer war – 20 years of bush warfare over the future of Angola and Namibia – was signalled by statements released after months of negotiations between Angola, Cuba and South Africa. The Gulf War truce is due to come into effect on August 20, but a timetable for the withdrawal of the 50,000 Cuban troops backing Angola's Marxist government has still to be worked out (→22/12).

Unknown senator chosen by Bush

Aug 19. George Bush said he has chosen "an inspiring young leader" as his vice-presidential running mate, but so far his choice of Senator Dan Quayle has generated controversy and astonishment rather than the excitement sought by the Bush campaign team.

The 41-year-old senator from Indiana is little known outside his state, and was a rank outsider amongst the vice-presidential candidates. Besides his inexperience, Senator Quayle is accused of having used family influence to avoid service in Vietnam (→13/10).

Seal virus spreads to British waters

Aug 10. The disease that has killed thousands of seals along the northwest coast of continental Europe has now reached British seas. Sick seal pups are being rescued from around the Wash, where there is the biggest concentration of common seals.

Marine biologists from North Sea countries are now meeting in London to discuss the epidemic. Most experts see pollution as only a minor contributory factor. Luckily the 90,000 grey seals in British waters appear to be less susceptible to the disease.

Aug 28. An Italian air force jet crashes after a mid-air collision at a display at Ramstein, West Germany, killing 33 and injuring hundreds.

1988

SEPTEMBER

Su	Mo	Tu	We	Th	Fr	Sa
				1	2	3
4	5	6	7	8	9	10
11	12	13	14	15	16	17
18	19	20	21	22	23	24
25	26	27	28	29	30	

2. Chile: Isabel Allende, daughter of the former President, flies home after the ban on political exiles returning is lifted (→6/10).

7. UK: The postal strife escalates, with only Belfast sorting office now working normally.

8. Rangoon: Diplomats are evacuated as rioters sack government buildings (→19).

9. New Delhi: Half the English cricket team will be denied visas because of links with South Africa.

13. London: The Cuban ambassador and one of his envoys are expelled following a shooting incident in Bayswater.

14. Lesotho: The Pope's visit is marred by guerrillas hijacking a bus carrying 70 Roman Catholics.

15. Yugoslavia: Serbians demonstrate against Albanian persecution of Serbs in the province of Kosovo (→4/10).

16. UK: Worcestershire win England's County Cricket championship.

19. Rangoon: The army, which took power yesterday, shoots 100 demonstrators.

21. Bruges: Thatcher attacks a centralised European government as a "nightmare".

22. USSR: Moscow sends in tanks again to quell unrest in the Armenian capital, Yerevan.

24. Seoul: Ben Johnson breaks his own world record, winning the Olympic 100 metres final in 9.79 seconds.→

29. US: The space shuttle Discovery goes into orbit, putting the US back into the space race.

30. USSR: Mr Gorbachev retires President Andrei Gromyko, Russia's former Foreign Minister (→1/10).

30. Gibraltar: An inquest jury decides that the IRA gang shot dead last March were lawfully killed by SAS soldiers.

DEATH

12. British illustrator Roger Hargreaves, creator of the "Mister Men" (*7/6/1918).

Millions homeless in Bangladesh floods

Sept 4. Bangladesh, a nation seemingly dogged by natural disasters, has suffered a new one. Massive floods have overwhelmed two-thirds of the country, leaving more than 20 million people homeless. At least 300 people have died.

A quarter of this year's crops have been washed away and roads and dykes have been breached. Hard-pressed relief services, still struggling to cope with the aftermath of last month's monsoon which killed at least 700 people, are further hampered by the floods; the international airport cannot be used and the railways, supposedly built three feet above any possible high-water mark, are totally submerged.

As relief agencies attempt to tackle this new disaster, the main priority is to establish where help is needed most and to deliver it as efficiently as possible. The Information Minister, Mahabur Rahmanthe, is appealing for helicopters to provide emergency aid. "We are hoping for an inspired response," he said. "No other country in the region has suffered so much damage from natural calamity".

The streets of Dacca, the capital city, are obliterated by flood waters.

Steffi Graf wins the "Grand Slam"

Sept 10. Steffi Graf today became only the fifth person to win the "Grand Slam" of the four top tennis tournaments in the same calendar year by beating Gabriela Sabatini 6-3, 3-6, 6-1 to clinch the US Open. Miss Graf, who is still only 19, only twice lost a set in the four top championships (→ 30).

US Anglicans elect first woman bishop

Sept 24. The Rev. Barbara Harris was tonight chosen to be the first woman bishop in America. She said she hoped to use "her peculiar gifts as a black woman and a woman priest". The election will certainly cause trouble in the Church of England which is deeply divided on the question of women priests.

"Gilbert" wreaks havoc in West Indies

Sept 16. Hurricane Gilbert, the worst storm the Western world has seen this century, has tonight hit the coast of Mexico for the second time. Hundreds of thousands of people have been made homeless, and damage costs are estimated at several billion dollars since the storm became a hurricane on September 10. Gilbert had swept through Dominica, Haiti, Venezuela and Jamaica before hitting Mexico for the first time on Wednesday at a terrifying 175 miles per hour. The storm is only now beginning to weaken.

Drugs tarnish Olympics

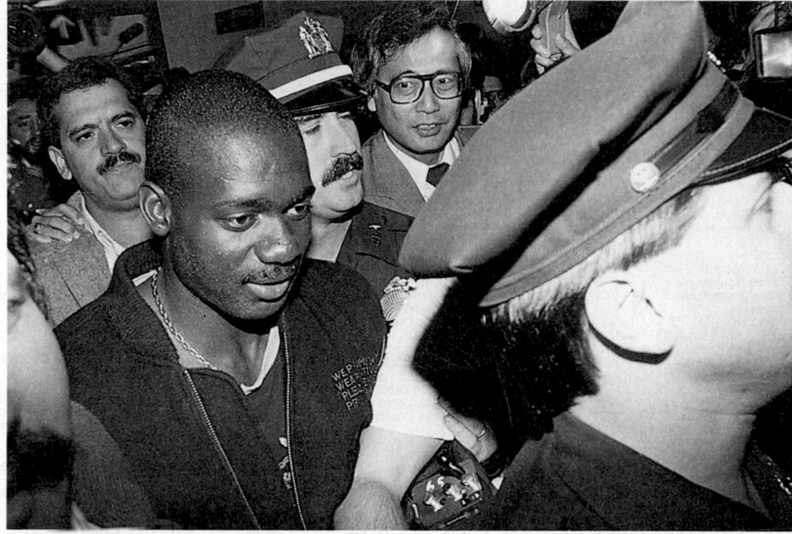

Gold turned to ashes: Ben Johnson passes through New York airport.

Sept 30. Ben Johnson, acclaimed as a hero when he set a world record winning the Olympic 100 metres final last Saturday, is now the villain of world sport. The fastest man on earth has been stripped of his gold medal after being found guilty of using drugs. Johnson has flown home to Canada in disgrace, but the scandal of drug-taking has not ended with his departure.

Nine athletes have been disqualified from the Olympics in Seoul, South Korea, after failing drug tests. Among them is Britain's Kerrith Brown, who today lost his judo bronze medal. And the shadow of drugs fell over even the innocent. Florence Griffith-Joyner, the American sprinter who won both the 100 and 200 metres, was greeted with rumours about drugs which were rebutted by tests.

If "Flo-Jo" was the brightest of the new stars, Seoul also saw the eclipse of many older stars. Edwin Moses failed to win the 400 metres hurdles, while fourth was the best that Britain's Daley Thompson and Steve Cram could manage. Carl Lewis added the long jump to the 100 metres which he won through Johnson's disqualification (Linford Christie similarly moved up to a silver), but he was second in the 200 metres and watched in dismay as the US relay team was disqualified.

In global terms the stars were the distance runners of Africa and the swimmers of East Germany, although the USSR easily topped the medals table. For Britain, there was gold for swimmer Adrian Moorhouse, but no golds in the athletics stadium. It was less publicised sports, such as rifle-shooting, rowing, yachting and hockey, which provided the British heroes.

Probably the most predictable gold medallist was Steffi Graf, fresh from completing her Grand Slam of major tournaments, as tennis returned to the Olympics for the first time since 1924. One of the bravest winners was Greg Louganis of the United States, who became the first person to retain an Olympic spring-board diving title. Louganis hit a board on his descent into the water. The injury required stitches, but Louganis came back to win the gold.

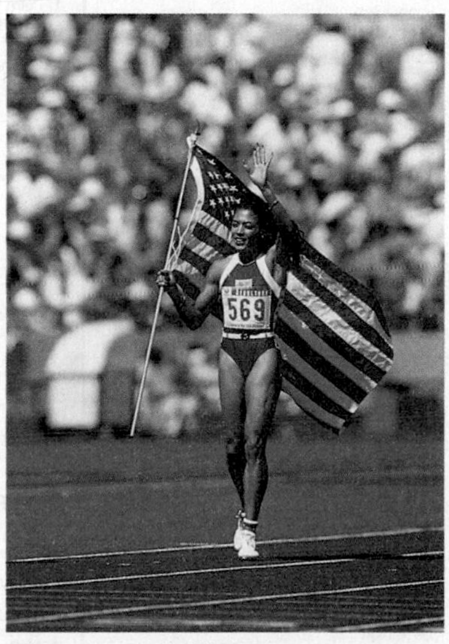

Florence Griffith-Joyner: black, beautiful and a triple champion.

1988 Seoul

Men Athletics

100m
1. Carl Lewis USA 9.92
2. Linford Christie GBR 9.97
3. Calvin Smith USA 9.99

200m
1. Joe DeLoach USA 19.75
2. Carl Lewis USA 19.79
3. Robson Da Silva BRA 20.04

400m
1. Steven Lewis USA 43.87
2. Butch Reynolds USA 43.93
3. Danny Everett USA 44.09

800m
1. Paul Ereng KEN 1:43.45
2. Joaquim Cruz BRA 1:43.90
3. Said Aouita MOR 1:44.06

1.500m
1. Peter Rono KEN 3:35.96
2. Peter Elliott GBR 3:36.15
3. Jens-Peter Herold GDR 3:36.21

5.000m
1. John Ngugi KEN 13:11.70
2. Dieter Baumann FRG 13:15.52
3. Hans Joerg Kunze GDR 13:15.73

10.000m
1. M. Brahim Boutaieb MOR 27:21.46
2. Salvatore Antibo ITA 27:23.55
3. Kipkemboi Kimeli KEN 27:25.16

3.000m Steeplechase
1. Julius Kariuki KEN 8:05.51
2. Peter Koech KEN 8:06.79
3. Mark Rowland GBR 8:07.96

110m Hurdles
1. Roger Kingdom USA 12.99
2. Colin Jackson GBR 13.28
3. Tony Campbell USA 13.38

400m Hurdles
1. Andre Phillips USA 47.19
2. El Hadj Dia Ba SEN 47.23
3. Edwin Moses USA 47.56

High Jump
1. Guennadi Adveienko URS 2.38m
2. Hollis Conway USA 2.36m
3. Rudolf Povarnitsine URS 2.36m
Patrick Sjoeberg SWE 2.36m

Britain wins hockey gold.

Long Jump
1. Carl Lewis USA 8.72m
2. Mike Powell USA 8.49m
3. Larry Myricks USA 8.27m

Pole Vault
1. Serguei Bubka URS 5.90m
2. Rodion Gataulline URS 5.85m
3. Grigori Yevgorov URS 5.80m

Triple Jump
1. Christo Markov BUL 17.61m
2. Igor Lapchine URS 17.52m
3. Alexandre Kovalenko URS 17.42m

Shotput
1. Ulf Timmermann GDR 22.47m
2. Randy Barnes USA 22.39m
3. Werner Gunthoer SUI 21.99m

Discus
1. Jurgen Schult GDR 68.82m
2. Romas Ubartas URS 67.48m
3. Rolf Danneberg FRG 67.38m

Hammer
1. Serguei Litvinov URS 84.80m
2. Youri Sedykh URS 83.76m
3. Youri Tamn URS 81.16m

Javelin
1. Tapio Korjus FIN 84.28m
2. Jan Zelezny TCH 84.12m
3. Seppo Raty FIN 83.26m

Marathon
1. Gelindo Bordin ITA 2 h 10:32
2. Douglas Wakihuru KEN 2 h 10:47
3. Ahmed Salah DJI 2 h 10:59

Decathlon
1. Christian Schenk GDR 8 488 pts
2. Torsten Voss GDR 8 399 pts
3. Dave Steen CAN 8 328 pts

4 x 100m Relay
1. URS 38.19 (Bryzguin, Krylov, Mouraziev, Savin)
2. GBR 38.28 (Bunney, Regis, McFarlane, Christie)
3. FRA 38.40 (Marie-Rose, Sangouma, Quenerve, Moniniere)

4 x 400m Relay
1. USA 2:58.16 (Everett, S. Lewis, Robinzine, Reynolds)
2. JAM 3:00.30 (Davis, Morris, Graham, Cameron)
3. FRG 3:00.56 (Dobeleit, Itt, Vaihinger, Luebke)

20km Walk
1. Jozef Pribilinec TCH 1 h 19:57
2. Ronald Weigel GDR 1 h 20:00
3. Maurizio Damilano ITA 1 h 20:14

50km Walk
1. Vlasheslav Ivanenko URS 3 h 38:29
2. Ronald Weigel GDR 3 h 38:56
3. Hartwig Gauder GDR 3 h 39:45

Women Athletics

100m
1. Florence Griffith-Joyner USA 10.54
2. Evelyne Ashford USA 10.83
3. Heike Drechsler GDR 10.85

200m
1. Florence Griffith-Joyner USA 21.34 (world rec.; prev. rec. 21.71 by Koch and by Drechsler)
2. Grace Jackson JAM 21.72
3. Heike Drechsler GDR 21.95

400m
1. Olga Brysguina URS 48.65
2. Petra Mueller GDR 49.45
3. Olga Nazarova URS 49.90

800m
1. Sigrun Wodars GDR 1:56.10
2. Christine Wachtel GDR 1:56.64
3. Kim Gallagher USA 1:56.91

1.500m
1. Paula Ivan ROM 3:53.96
2. Lailoute Baikauskaite URS 4:00.20
3. Tatiana Samoilenko URS 4:00.24

3.000m
1. Tatiana Samoilenko URS 8:26.53
2. Paula Ivan ROM 8:27.15
3. Yvonne Murray GBR 8:29.02

10.000m
1. Olga Bondarenko URS 31:05.21
2. Elizabeth McColgan GBR 31:08.34
3. Helena Joupieva URS 31:19.82

100m Hurdles
1. Jordanka Donkova BUL 12.38
2. Gloria Siebert GDR 12.61
3. Claudia Zaskiewicz FRG 12.75

400m Hurdles
1. Debbie Flintoff-King AUS 53.17
2. Tatiana Ledovskaia URS 53.18
3. Helen Fiedler GDR 53.84

High Jump
1. Louise Ritter USA 2.03m
2. Stefka Kostadinova BUL 2.01m
3. Tamara Bykova URS 1.99m

Long Jump
1. Jackie Joyner-Kersee USA 7.40m
2. Heike Drechsler GDR 7.22m
3. Galina Tchistyakova URS 7.11m

Shotput
1. Natalia Lissovskaia USA 7.40m
2. Kathrin Neimke GDR 21.07m
3. Meisu-li CHN 21.06m

Discus
1. Martina Hellman GDR 72.30m
2. Diana Gansky GDR 71.88m
3. Tzvetanka Hristova BUL 69.74m

Javelin
1. Petra Felke GDR 74.68m
2. Fatima Whitbread GBR 70.32m
3. Beate Koch GDR 67.30m

4 x 100m Relay
1. USA 41.98 (Brown, Echols, Griffith-Joyner, Ashford)
2. GDR 42.09 (Moller, Behrendt, Lange, Gohr)
3. URS 42.75 (Kondratieva, Maltschugina, Jirova, Pomochtchnikova)

4 x 400m Relay
1. URS 3:15.18 World rec.; prev. rec. 3:15.92 (Ledovskaia, Nazarov, Piniguina, Bryzguina)
2. USA 3:15.51 (Howard, Dixon, Brisco, Griffith-Joyner)
3. GDR 3:18.29 (Neubauer, Emmelmann, Busch, Muller)

Heptathlon
1. Jackie Joyner-Kersee USA 7 291 pts (World rec.; own prev. rec. 7 215 pts)
2. Sabine John GDR 6 897 pts
3. Anke Behmer GDR 6 858 pts

Marathon
1. Rosa Mota POR 2 h 25:40
2. Lisa Martin NZL 2 h 25:53
3. Kathrin Doerre GDR 2 h 26:21

Men Rowing

Sculls
1. Thomas Lange GDR 6:49.86
2. Peter-Michael Kolbe FRG 6:54.77
3. Eric Verdonck NZL 6:58.66

Coxed Pairs
1. G. Abbagnale, C. Abbagnale ITA 6:49.86
2. M. Streit, D. Kirch GDR 7:00.63
3. S. Redgrave, A. Holme GBR 7:01.95

Double Sculls
1. R. Florijn, N. Rienks HOL 6:21.13
2. B. Schwerzmann, U. Bodenmann GDR 6:22.59
3. A. Martchenko, V. Iakoucha URS 6:22.87

Coxless Pairs
1. A. Holmes, S. Redgrave GBR 6:36.94
2. D. Neagu, D. Dobre ROM 6:38.06
3. B. Presern, S. Mujkic YUG 6:41.01

Coxless Fours
1. GDR 6:10.74
2. ROM 6:13.58
3. NZL 6:15.78

Quadruple Sculls (Coxed)
1. ITA 5:53.37
2. NOR 5:55.08
3. GDR 5:56.13

Quadruple Sculls (Coxless)
1. GDR 6:03.11
2. USA 6:05.53
3. FRG 6:06.22

Eights
1. GDR 5:46.05
2. URS 5:48.01
3. USA 5:48.26

Women Rowing

Sculls
1. Jutta Behrendt GDR 7:47.19
2. Anne Marden USA 7:50.28
3. Magdalena Gueorguieva BUL 7:53.65

Coxless Pairs
1. O. Homeghi, R. Arba ROM 7:28.13
2. L. Berberova, R. Stoyanova BUL 7:31.95
3. L. Hannen, N. Payne NZL 7:35.68

Double Sculls
1. M. Schroeter, B. Peter GDR 7:00.48
2. V. Coeanu, E. Lipa ROM 7:04.36
3. S. Madina, V. Ninova BUL 7:06.03

Coxed Fours
1. GDR 6:56.00
2. CHN 6:58.78
3. ROM 7:01.13

Quadruple Sculls (Coxless)
1. GDR 6:21.06
2. URS 6:23.47
3. ROM 6:23.81

Eights
1. GDR 6:15.17
2. ROM 6:17.44
3. CHN 6:21.83

Basketball

Men
1. Soviet Union – 2. Yugoslavia – 3. United States

Women
1. United States – 2. Yugoslavia – 3. Soviet Union

Boxing

48kg
1. Ivailo Hristov BUL
2. Michael Carbajal USA
3. Robert Isaszegi HON
Leopoldo Serantes PHI

51kg
1. Kwang-Sun Kim KOR
2. Andreas Tews GDR
3. Timofei Skriabin URS
Mario Gonzalez MEX

54kg
1. Kennedy McKinney USA
2. Alexandar Hristov BUL
3. Phajol Moolsan THA
Jorge Julio Rocha COL

57kg
1. Giovanni Parisi ITA
2. Daniel Dumitrescu ROM
3. Abdelhack Achik MOR
Lee Jae-hyuk KOR

60kg
1. Andreas Zuelow GDR
2. George Cramne SWE
3. Nerguy Enkhbat MGL
Romallis Ellis USA

63.5kg
1. Viatcheslav Janovski URS
2. Graham Cheney AUS
3. Lars Myrberg SWE
Reiner Gies FRG

67kg
1. Robert Wangila KEN
2. Laurent Boudouani FRA
3. Jan Dydak POL
Kenneth Gould USA

71kg
1. Park Si-Hun KOR
2. Roy Jones USA
3. Raymond Downey CAN
Richard Woodhall GBR

75kg
1. Henry Maske GDR
2. Egerton Marcus CAN
3. Chris Sande KEN
Hussain Shad Syed PAK

81kg
1. Andrew Maynard USA
2. Nourmagomed Chanavazov URS
3. Henryk Petrich POL
Damir Skaro YUG

91kg
1. Ray Mercer USA
2. Baik Hyun-Man KOR
3. Arnold Vanderlijde HOL
Andrzej Golota POL

More than 95kg
1. Lennox Lewis CAN
2. Riddick Bowe USA
3. Janusz Zarenkiewicz POL
Alexandre Mirochnitchenko URS

Men Canoeing

Canadian-1 (500m)
1. Olaf Heukrodt GDR 1:56.42
2. Mikhail Slivinskii URS 1:57.26
3. Martin Marinov BUL 1:57.27

Canadian-2 (500m)
1. V. Reineski, N. Jouravski URS 1:41.77
2. M. Dopierala, M. Lbik POL 1:43.61
3. P. Renaud, J. Bettin FRA 1:43.81

Canadian-1 (1.000m)
1. Ivan Klementiev URS 4:12.78
2. Joerg Schmidt GDR 4:15.83
3. Nikolai Boohlov BUL 4:18.94

Canadian-2 (1.000m)
1. V. Reineski, N. Jouravski URS 3:48.36
2. O. Heukrodt, I. Spelly GDR 3:51.44
3. M. Dopierala, M. Lbik POL 3:54.33

Kayak-1 (500m)
1. Zsolt Gyulay HUN 1:44.82
2. Andreas Staehle GDR 1:46.38
3. Paul McDonald NZL 1:46.46

Kayak-2 (500m)
1. I. Ferguson, P. McDonald NZL 1:33.98
2. I. Nagaev, V. Denissov URS 1:34.15
3. A. Abraham, F. Csipes HUN 1:34.32

Kayak-1 (1.000m)
1. Greg Barton USA 3:55.27
2. Grant Davies AUS 3:55.28
3. André Wohllebe GDR 3:55.55

Kayak-2 (1.000m)
1. G. Barton, N. Bellingham USA 3:32.42
2. I. Ferguson, P. McDonald NZL 3:32.71
3. P. Foster, K. Graham AUS 3:33.76

Kayak-4 (1.000)
1. HUN 3:00.20
2. URS 3:01.40
3. GDR 3:02.37

Women Canoeing

Kayak-1 (500m)
1. Vania Guecheva BUL 1:55.19
2. Birgit Schmidt GDR 1:55.31
3. Izabella Dylewskia POL 1:57.38

Kayak-2 (500m)
1. B. Schmidt, A. Nothnagel GDR 1:43.46
2. V. Guecheva, D. Paliiska BUL 1:44.06
3. A. Derckx, A. Cox HOL 1:46.00

Kayak-4 (500m)
1. GDR 1:40.78
2. HUN 1:41.88
3. BUL 1:42.63

Men Cycling

100km Team Time Trial
1. GDR 1 h 57:47
2. POL 1 h 57:54
3. SWE 1 h 59:47

Team Pursuit
1. URS 4:13.31
2. GDR 4:14.09
3. AUS 4:16.02

Sprint
1. Lutz Hesslich GDR
2. Nikolai Kovch URS
3. Gary Neiwand AUS

1.000m
1. Alexandre Kiritchenko GDR 1:04.499
2. Martin Vinnicombe AUS 1:04.784
3. Robert Lechner FRG 1:05.114

Individual Pursuit
1. Giantauras Umaras URS
2. Dean Woods AUS
3. Bernd Dittert GDR

30km Points Race
1. Dean Frost DEN
2. Leo Peelen HOL
3. Marat Ganeev URS

Individual Road Race
1. Olaf Ludwig GDR 4 h 32:22
2. Bernd Groene FRG
3. Christian Henn FRG

Women Cycling

Sprint
1. Erika Salumiae URS
2. Christa Rothenburger-Luding GDR
3. Connie Paraskevin-Young USA

Individual Road Race
1. Monique Knol HOL 2 h 52:
2. Jutta Niehaus FRG
3. Laina Zilporitie URS

Equestrian Sports

Grand Prix Jumping Individual
1. Pierre Durand/"Jappeloup" FRA 1.25 pts
2. Greg Best/"Gem Twist" USA 4 pts
3. Karsten Huck/"Neponuk" FRG 4 pts

Grand Prix Jumping Team
1. FRG 17.25 pts (Beerbaum, Brinkmann, Hafemeister, Sloothaak)
2. USA 20.50 pts (Best, Jacquin, Kursinski, Fargis)
3. FRA 27.50 pts (Bourdy, Cottier, Robert, Durand)

Individual Dressage
1. Nicole Uphoff/"Rembrandt" FRG 1.521 pts
2. Margitt Otto-Crépin/"Corlandus" FRA 1.462 pts
3. Christine Stueckelberger/"Gauguin de Lulle" SUI

Team Dressage
1. FRG 4.302 pts (Klimke, Linsenhoff, Theodorescu, Uphoff)
2. SUI 4.164 pts (Hofer, Stueckelberger Ramseier, Schatzmann)
3. CAN 3.969 pts (Ishoy, Pracht, Smith, Nicoll)

Three-day event (Individual)
1. Mark Todd/"Charisma" NZL 42.60 pts
2. Ian Stark/"Sir Watte" GBR 52.80 pts
3. Virginia Leng/"Master Craftsman" GBR 62.00 pts

Three-day event (Team)
1. FRG 225.95 pts (Erhorn, Baumann, Kaspareit, Ehrenbrink)
2. GBR 256.80 pts (Philips, Straker, Leng, Stark)
3. NZL 271.20 pts (Todd, Knighton, Bennie, Pottinger)

Men Fencing

Foil Individual
1. Stefano Cerioni ITA
2. Udo Wagner GDR
3. Alexandre Romankov URS

Sabre Individual
1. Jean-François Lamour FRA
2. Janusz Olech POL
3. Giovanni Scalzo ITA

Epée Individual
1. Arnd Schmitt FRG
2. Philippe Riboud FRA
3. Andrei Chouvalov URS

Foil Team
1. URS (Romankov, Mamedov, Aptsiaouri, Ibraguimov, Koretskil)
2. FRG (Gey, Weidner, Behr, Schreck, Endres)
3. HUN (Ersek, Szekeres, Szelei, Gatai, Bua)

Sabre Team
1. HUN (Nebald, Szabo, Consgradi, Bujdoso, Gedeovari)
2. URS (Mindirgassov, Bourtsev, Pogossov, Alchan Koriakine)
3. ITA (Cavaliere, Scalzo, Marin, Dallabarba, Meglio)

Epée Team
1. FRA (Lenglet, Strecki, Riboud, Henry, Delpha)
2. FRG (Borrmann, Fischer, Gerull, Pusch, Schmitt)
3. URS (Chouvalov, Tichko, Kolobkov, Reznitchenko, Tikhomirov)

Women Fencing

Foil Individual
1. Anja Fichtel FRG
2. Sabine Bau FRG
3. Zita Funkenhauser FRG

Foil Team
1. FRG (Fichtel, Funkenhauser, Bau, Weber, Klug)
2. ITA (Vaccaroni, Zalaffi, Traversa, Gandolfi, Bortolozzi)
3. HUN (Janosi, Stefanek, Szocs, Kovacs, Tuschak)

Soccer

1. Soviet Union – 2. Brazil – 3. FRG

Men Gymnastics

All-round Individual Competition
1. Vladimir Artemov URS 119.125 pts
2. Valeri Lioukine URS 119.025 pts
3. Dimitri Bilozertchev URS 118.975 pts

All-round Team Competition
1. URS 593.35 pts
2. GDR 588.45 pts
3. JPN 585.60 pts

Horizontal Bar
1. Valeri Lioukine URS 19.900 pts
Vladimir Artemov URS 19.900 pts
3. Holger Behrendt GDR 19.800 pts
Marius Gherman ROM 19.800 pts

Horse
1. Dimitri Bilozertchev URS 19.950 pts
Zsolt Borkai BUL 19.950 pts
Lubomir Gueraskov URS 19.950 pts

Rings
1. Dimitri Bilozertchev URS 19.925 pts
Holger Behrendt BUL 19.925 pts
3. Sven Tippelt GDR 19.875 pts

Vault
1. Lou Yun CHN 19.875 pts
2. Sylvio Kroll GDR 19.862 pts
3. Park Jong-Hoon KOR 19.775 pts

Parallel Bars
1. Vladimir Artemov URS 19.925 pts
2. Valeri Lioukine URS 19.900 pts
3. Sven Tippelt GDR 19.750 pts

Floor Exercise
1. Sergei Kharkov URS 19.925 pts
2. Vladimir Artemov URS 19.900 pts
3. Lou Yun CHN 19.850 pts
Yukio Iketani JPN 19.850 pts

Women Gymnastics

All-round Individual Competition
1. Elena Chouchounova URS 79.662 pts
2. Daniela Silivas ROM 79.637 pts
3. Svetlana Boguinskaia URS 79.400 pts

All-round Team Competition
1. URS 395.475 pts
2. ROM 394.125 pts
3. GDR 390.875 pts

Vault
1. Elena Boguinskaia URS 19.905 pts
2. Gabriela Potorac ROM 19.830 pts
3. Daniela Silivas ROM 19.818 pts

Floor Exercise
1. Daniela Silivas ROM 19.937 pts
2. Svetlana Boguinskaia URS 19.887 pts
3. Diana Doudeva BUL 19.850 pts

1988  Seoul

Beam
1. Daniela Silivas ROM 19.924 pts
2. Elena Chouchounova URS 19.875 pts
3. Phoele Mills USA 19.837 pts
Gabriela Potorac ROM 19.837 pts

Asymetric Bars
1. Daniela Silivas ROM 20.000 pts
2. Dagmar Kersten FRG 19.987
3. Elena Chouchounova URS 19.962 pts

Apparatus
1. Lobatch URS 60.000 pts
2. Dounavska BUL 59.950 pts
3. Timoshenko URS 59.875 pts

Rhythmic Competition
1. Lobatch URS 60.000 pts
2. Dounavska BUL 59.950 pts
3. Timoshenko URS 59.875 pts

Weightlifting

52kg
1. Sevdalin Marinov BUL 270.0kg
2. Chun Byung-Kwan KOR 260.0kg
3. He Zhuoqiang CHN 257.5kg

56kg
1. Oksen Mirzoian URS 292.5kg
2. He Yingiang CHN 287.5kg
3. Liu Shoubin CHN 267.5kg

60kg
1. Naim Suleymanoglou TUR 342.5kg
2. Stefan Topourov BUL 312.5kg
3. Ye Huanming CHN 287.5kg

67.5kg
1. Joachim Kunz GDR 340.0kg
2. Israel Militosian URS 337.5kg
3. Li Jinhe CHN 325.0kg

75kg
1. Borislav Guidikov BUL 375.0kg
2. Ingo Steinhoefel GDR 360.0kg
3. Alexander Varbanov BUL 357.5kg

82.5kg
1. Israil Arsamakov URS 377.5kg
2. Istvan Messzi HUN 370.0kg
3. Lee Hyung-Kun KOR 367.5kg

90kg
1. Anatoli Khrapatyi URS 412.5kg
2. Nail Moukhamediarov URS 400.0kg
3. Slawomir Zawada POL 400.0kg

100kg
1. Pavel Kouznetsov URS 425.0kg
2. Nicu Vlad ROM 402.5kg
3. Peter Immesberger FRG 395.0kg

110kg
1. Youri Zakharevitch URS 455.0kg
2. Jozsef Jacso HUN 427.5kg
3. Ronny Weller GDR 425.0kg

More than 110 kg
1. Alexandre Kourlovitch URS 462.5kg
2. Manfred Nerlinger FRG 430.0kg
3. Martin Zawieja FRG 415.0kg

Handball

Men
1. Soviet Union – 2. South Korea – 3. Yugoslavia

Women
1. South Korea – 2. Norway – 3. Soviet Union

Hockey

Men
1. Great Britain – 2. FRG – 3. Netherlands

Women
1. Australia – 2. South Korea – 3. Netherlands

Judo

60kg
1. Kim Jae-Yup KOR
2. Kevin Asano USA
3. Shinji Hosokawa JPN
Amiran Totikachvili URS

65kg
1. Lee Kyung-Keum KOR
2. Janusz Pawlowski POL
3. Bruno Carabetta FRA
Yosuke Yamamoto JPN

71kg
1. Marc Alexandre FRA
2. Sven Loll GDR
3. Gueorgui Tenadze URS
Michael Swain USA

78kg
1. Waldemar Legien POL
2. Frank Wieneke FRG
3. Torsten Brechot GDR
Bachir Varaev URS

86kg
1. Peter Seisenbacher AUT
2. Vladimir Chestakov URS
3. Akinobu Osako JPN
Ben Spijkers HOL

95kg
. Aurelio Miguel BRA
2. Marc Meiling FRG
3. Robert Van de Walle BEL
Dennis Steward GBR

More than 95kg
. Hitoshi Saito JPN
. Henry Stoehr GDR
. Cho Yong-Chul KOR
Grigori Veritchev URS

Greco-Roman Wrestling

48kg
. Vincenzo Maenza ITA
. Andrzej Glab POL
. Bratan Tzenov BUL

52kg
. Jon Ronningen NOR
2. Atsuji Miyahara JPN
3. Lee Jae-sute KOR

57kg
1. Andras Sike HUN
2. Stoyan Balov BUL
3. Charalambos Holidis GRE

62kg
1. Kamandar Madjidov URS
2. Jivko Vanguelov BUL
3. An Dae-hyun KOR

68kg
1. Levon Djoufalakian URS
2. Kim Sung-moon KOR
3. Tapio Sipilae FIN

74kg
1. Kim Young-nam KOR
2. Daoulet Tourlykhanov URS
3. Jozef Tracz POL

82kg
1. Mikhail Mamiachvili URS
2. Tibor Komaromi HUN
3. Kim Sang-kyu KOR

90kg
1. Atanas Komchev BUL
2. Harri Kosteka FIN
3. Vladimir Popov URS

100kg
1. Andrezj Wronski POL
2. Gerhard Himmel FRG
3. Dennis Koslowski USA

130kg
1. Alexandre Kareline URS
2. Ranguel Guerovski BUL
3. Tomas Johansson SWE

All-In Wrestling

48kg
1. Takashi Kobayashi JPN
2. Ivan Tzonov BUL
3. Serguei Karamchatzov URS

52kg
1. Mitsuru Sato JPN
2. Saban Trstena YUG
3. Vladimir Togouzov URS

57kg
1. Sergei Beloglazov URS
2. Mohammadian IRN
3. Noh Kyung sun KOR

62kg
1. John Smith USA
2. Stephan Sarkissian URS
3. Simeon Chterev BUL

68kg
1. Arsen Fadzaev URS
2. Park Jang-soon KOR
3. Nate Carr USA

74kg
1. Kenneth Monday USA
2. Adlan Varaev URS
3. Rakhmad Sofiadi BUL

82kg
1. Han Myung-woo KOR
2. Nemci Gencalp TUR
3. Joseph Lohyna TCH

90kg
1. Makharbek Khardartsev URS
2. Akira Ota JPN
3. Kim Tae-woo KOR

100kg
1. Vasile Puscasu ROM
2. Leri Khabelov URS
3. Bill Scherr USA

130kg
1. David Gobedjichvili URS
2. Bruce Baumgartner USA
3. Andreas Schroeder GDR

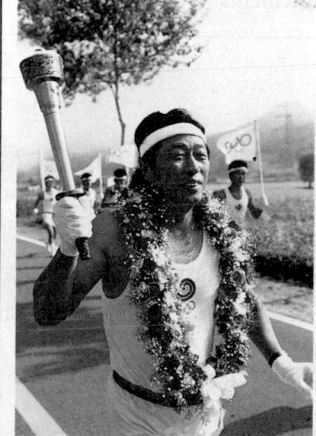

Olympic flame.

Men Swimming

50m – Freestyle
1. Matt Biondi USA 22.14
(world rec.; prev. rec. 22.23 by Jager)
2. Tom Jager USA 22.33
3. Guennadi Prigoda URS 22.71

100m – Freestyle
1. Matt Biondi USA 48.63
2. Christopher Jacobs USA 49.08
3. Stephan Caron FRA 49.62

200m – Freestyle
1. Duncan Armstrong AUS 1:47.25
(world rec.; prev. rec. 1:47.44 by Gross)
2. Anders Holmertz SWE 1:47.89
3. Matt Biondi USA 1:47.99

400m – Freestyle
1. Uwe Dassler GDR 3:46.95
(world rec.; prev. rec. 3:47.38 by Wojdat)
2. Duncan Armstrong AUS 3:47.15
3. Artur Wojdat POL 3:47.34

1 500m – Freestyle
1. Vladimir Salnikov URS 15:00.40
2. Stephan Pfeiller GDR 15:02.69
3. Uwe Dassler GDR 15:06.15

100m – Backstroke
1. Daichi Suzuki JPN 55.05
2. David Berkoff USA 55.18
3. Igor Polianski URS 55.20

200m – Backstroke
1. Igor Polianski URS 1:59.37
2. Frank Baltrusch GDR 1:59.60
3. Paul Kingsman NZL 2:00.48

100m – Butterfly
1. Anthony Nesty SUR 53.00
2. Matt Biondi USA 53.01
3. Andy Jameson GBR 53.30

200m – Butterfly
1. Michael Gross FRG 1:56.94
2. Benny Nielsen DEN 1:58.24
3. Anthony Mosse NZL 1:58.28

100m – Breaststroke
1. Adrian Moorhouse GBR 1:02.04
2. Karoly Guttler HUN 1:02.05
3. Dmitri Volkov URS 1:02.20

200m – Breaststroke
1. Josef Szabo HUN 2:13.52
2. Nick Gillingham GBR 2:14.12
3. Sergio Lopez ESP 2:15.21

200m – Individual Medley
1. Tamas Darnyi HUN 2:00.17
(world rec.; own prev. rec. 2:00.56)
2. Patrick Kuehl GDR 2:01.61
3. Vadim Tarotchouk URS 2:02.40

400m Individual Medley
1. Tamas Darnyi HUN 4:14.75
(world rec.; own prev. rec. 4:15.42)
2. David Wharton USA 4:17.36
3. Stefano Battistelli ITA 4:18.01

4 x 100m Medley Relay
1. USA 3:16.53
2. URS 3:18.33
3. GDR 3:19.82

4 x 200m Medley Relay
1. USA 7:12.51
2. GDR 7:13.68
3. FRG 7:14.35

4 x 100m Freestyle Medley
1. USA 3:36.93
2. CAN 3:39.28
3. URS 3:39.96

Water-Polo

1. Yugoslavia – 2. United States – 3. Soviet Union

Women Swimming

50m – Freestyle
1. Kristin Otto GDR 25.49
2. Yang Wenyi CHN 25.64
3. Katrin Meissner GDR 25.71
Jill Sterkel USA 25.71

100m – Freestyle
1. Kristin Otto GDR 54.93
2. Zhuang Yong CHN 55.47
3. Catherine Plewinski FRA 55.49
(France rec.; own prev. rec. 55.53)

200m – Freestyle
1. Heike Friedrich GDR 1:57.65
2. Sylvia Poll CRC 1:58.67
3. Manuela Stellmach GDR 1:59.01

400m – Freestyle
1. Janet Evans USA 4:03.85
2. Heike Friedrich GDR 4:05.94
3. Anke Moehring GDR 4:06.62

800m – Freestyle
1. Janet Evans USA 8:20.20
2. Astrid Strauss GDR 8:22.09
3. Julie MacDonald AUS 8:22.93

100m – Backstroke
1. Kristin Otto GDR 1:00.89
2. Krisztina Egerszegi HUN 1:01.56
3. Cornelia Sirch GDR 1:01.57

200m – Backstroke
1. Krisztina Egerszegi HUN 2:09.29
2. Kathrin Zimmermann GDR 2:10.61
3. Cornelia Sirch GDR 2:11.45

100m – Butterfly
1. Kristina Otto GDR 59.00
2. Birte Weigang GDR 59.34
3. Qiuan Hong CHN 59.45

200m – Butterfly
1. Katleen Nord GDR 2:09.29
2. Birte Weigang GDR 2:09.91
3. Mary T. Meagher USA 2:10.80

100m – Breaststroke
1. Tania Dangalakova BUL 1:07.95
2. Antoaneta Frankeva BUL 1:08.74
3. Silke Hoerner GDR 1:08.83

200m – Breaststroke
1. Silke Hoerner GDR 2:26.71
2. Huang Xiaomin CHN 2:27.46
3. Antoaneta Frankeva BUL 2:28.34

200m – Individual Medley
1. Daniela Hunger GDR 2:12.59
2. Helena Dendeberova URS 2:13.31
3. Noemi Lung ROM 2:14.85

400m – Individual Medley
1. Janet Evans USA 4:37.76
2. Noemi Lung ROM 4:39.40
3. Daniela Hunger GDR 4:39.76

4 x 100m Medley Relay
1. GDR 3:40.53
2. HOL 3:43.39
3. USA 3:44.25

4 x 100m Individual Medley
1. GDR 4:03.73
2. USA 4:07.90
3. CAN 4:10.49

Daley Thompson.

Synchronized Swimming Individual
1. Carolyn Waldo CAN 200.150 pts
2. Tracie Conforto Ruiz USA 197.633 pts
3. Mikako Kotani JPN 191.159 pts

Synchronized Swimming Duet
1. Canada 197.717 pts
2. United States 197.284 pts
3. Japan 190.159 pts

Men Diving

Springboard Diving
1. Greg Louganis USA 730.80 pts
2. Tan Liangde CHN 704.88 pts
3. Li De Liang CHI 665.28 pts

High Diving
1. Greg Louganis USA 638.61 pts
2. Xiong Ni CHN 637.47 pts
3. Jesus Mena MEX 594.39 pts

Women Diving

Springboard Diving
1. Galo Min CHN 580.23 pts
2. Li Qing CHN 534.33 pts
3. Kelly McCormick USA 533.19 pts

High Diving
1. Xu Yannei CHN 445.20 pts
2. Michele Mitchell USA 436.95 pts
3. Wendy Williams USA 400.44 pts

Modern Penthatlon

Individual
1. Janos Martinek HUN 5 404 pts
2. Carlo Massullo ITA 5 379 pts
3. Vakhtang Iagorachvili URS 5 367 pts

Team
1. Hungary 15 886 pts
2. Italy 15 571 pts
3. Great Britain 12 276 pts

Tennis

Men's Singles
1. Miloslav Mecir TCH
2. Tim Mayotte USA
3. Stefan Edberg SWE
Brad Gilbert USA

Men's Doubles
1. Ken Flach, Robert Seguso USA
2. Emilio Sanchez, Sergio Casal ESP
3. Stefan Edberg, Anders Jarryd SWE
Miloslav Mecir, Milan Srejber TCH

Women's Singles
1. Steffi Graf FRG
2. Gabriela Sabatini ARG
3. Manuela Maleeva BUL
Zina Garrison USA

Women's Doubles
1. Pam Shriver, Zina Garrison USA
2. Jana Novotna, Helena Sukova TCH
3. Steffi Graf, Claudia Kohde Kilsch FRG
Elizabeth Smylie, Wendy Turnbull USA

Table Tennis

Men's Singles
1. Yoo Nam-Kyu KOR
2. Kim Ki-Taik KOR
3. Erik Lindh SWE

Men's Doubles
1. Chen Long Can, Wei Quingguang CHN
2. Ilija Lupulescu, Zoran Primorac YUG
3. Ahn Jae Hyung, Yoo Nam Kyu KOR

Women's Singles
1. Chen Jing CHN
2. Li Huifen CHN
3. Jiao Zhimin CHN

Women's Doubles
1. Hyun Jung Hwa, Yang Young-ja KOR
2. Chen Jing, Jiao Zhimin CHN
3. Jazna Fazlic, Gordana Perkucin YUG

Men Shooting

Free Pistol
1. Sorin Babii ROU 660 pts
2. Ragnar Skanaker SWE 657 pts
3. Igor Bassinski URS 657 pts

Rapid-Fire Pistol
1. Afanasi Kouzmine URS 698 pts
(world rec.)
2. Ralf Schumann GDR 696 pts
3. Zoltan Kovacs HUN 693 pts

Airgun
1. Taniou Kiriakov BUL 687.9 pts
2. Erich Buljung USA 687.9 pts
3. Xu Maifeng CHN 684.5 pts

Small-Bore Rifle, Prone
1. Miroslav Varga TCH 703.9 pts
2. Cha Young-Chul KOR 703.8 pts
3. Attila Zahonyi HUN 701.9 pts

Airgun, 10m
1. Goran Maksimovic YUG 695.6 pts
2. Nicolas Berthelot FRA 694.2 pts
3. Johann Riederer FRG 694 pts

Small-Bore Rifle, 3 positions
1. Malcolm Cooper GBR 1279.3 pts
2. Alister Allan GBR 1275.6 pts
3. Kirill Ivanov URS 1275 pts

Moving Target
1. Tor Heiestad NOR 689 pts
2. Huang Shiping CHN 688 pts
3. Guennadi Avramenko URS 686 pts

Trap Shooting
1. Dimitri Monakov URS 222 pts
2. Miroslav Bednarik TCH 222 pts
3. Frans Peeters BEL 219 pts

Skeet
1. Axel Wegner GDR 222 pts
2. Alfonso De Izuarrizaga CHI 221 pts
3. Jorge Guardiola ESP 220 pts

Women Shooting

Airgun, 10m
1. Jasna Sekaric YUG 489.5 pts
2. Nino Saloukvadze URS 487.9 pts
3. Marina Dobrancheva URS 485.2 pts

Sport Pistol
1. Nino Saloukvadze URS 690 pts
2. Tomoko Hasegawa JPN 686 pts
3. Jasna Sexaric YUG 686 pts

Small-Bore Rifle, 3 positions
1. Silvia Sperber FRG 685.6 pts
2. Vessela Letcheva BUL 683.2 pts
3. Valentina Tcherkassova URS 681.4 pts

Airgun
1. Irina Chilova URS 498.5 pts
2. Silvia Sperber FRG 497.5 pts
3. Anna Maloukhina URS 495.5 pts

Archery

Men individual
1. Jay Barrs USA 338 pts
2. Park Sung-Soo KOR 336 pts
3. Vladimir Echeev URS 335 pts

Men team
1. South Korea 986 pts
2. United States 972 pts
3. Great Britain 968 pts

Women individual
1. Kim Soo-Nyung KOR 344 pts
2. Wang Hee-Kyung KOR 332 pts
3. Yun Young-Sook KOR 327 pts

Women team
1. South Korea 982 pts
2. Indonesia 952 pts
3. United States 952 pts

Men Yachting

Finn Class
1. Jose Luis Doreste ESP 36.1 pts
2. Peter Holmberg VI 40.4 pts
3. John Cutler NZL 45 pts

470 Class
1. Thierry Peponnet-Luc Pillot FRA 34.7 pts
2. Tynou et Thomas Tyniste URS 46 pts
3. John Shadden-Charlie McKee USA 49 pts

Flying Dutchman Class
1. DEN 31.4 pts
2. NOR 37.4 pts
3. CAN 48.4 pts

Soling Class
1. GDR 11.7 pts
2. USA 11.4 pts
3. DEN 52.7 pts

Tornado Class
1. FRA – 2. NZL – 3. BRA

Windsurfing
1. Bruce Kendall NZL 35.4 pts
2. Jan D. Boersma ANE 42.7 pts
3. Michael Gebhardt USA 48 pts

Star Class
1. GBR – 2. USA – 3. BRA

Women Yachting

470 Class
1. USA – 2. SWE – 3. URS

(Key to symbols and abbreviations p. 1456)

1988

OCTOBER

Su	Mo	Tu	We	Th	Fr	Sa
						1
2	3	4	5	6	7	8
9	10	11	12	13	14	15
16	17	18	19	20	21	22
23	24	25	26	27	28	29
30	31					

1. USSR: Mikhail Gorbachev is appointed President.

2. Pakistan: 300 die in ethnic clashes in Karachi and Islamabad.

4. Belgrade: Workers besiege parliament demanding the government's resignation (→ 19/11).

6. Blackpool: Labour's annual conference reaffirms commitment to unilateral nuclear disarmament in defiance of Kinnock.

6. Chile: The military dictator, General Pinochet, is defeated in the election and his cabinet resigns.

9. Riga: Latvians vote to form a Popular Front aimed at loosening ties with Moscow.

12. Algiers: A referendum will be held on the President's proposed political reforms.

13. US: Michael Dukakis fails to close the gap on opponent George Bush in the second and final TV debate (→ 8/11).

14. Stockholm: Naguib Mahfouz of Egypt becomes the first Arabic novelist to win the Nobel Prize for Literature.

16. St. Andrew's: Ireland, seeded eight out of 16 nations, wins golf's Dunhill Cup.

20. UK: The Government announces plans to end a suspect's right to remain silent.

21. Greece: The cruise ship Jupiter sinks outside Piraeus harbour: 14 are missing.

24. UK: The cabinet agrees to a shake-up of the legal profession, reducing barristers' monopoly on court work.

28. Prague: Riot police with tear gas meet freedom demonstrators in Wenceslas Square (→ 13/11).

31. UK: Kinnock calls Mrs Thatcher a cheat, following her decision to freeze child benefit for the second year.

DEATHS

2. British inventor of the Mini motor car, Sir Alexander Arnold Constantine Issigonis (*18/11/1906).

9. British footballer Jackie Milburn (*1924).

Russian dissidents may be freed at last

Oct 26. Mikhail Gorbachev has promised to free all those regarded by the West as political prisoners by the end of the year. The news came from the West German Chancellor, Helmut Kohl, who has just ended four days of talks in Moscow with the Soviet leader. Mr Kohl said the talks had achieved results "beyond my expectations" and certainly Mr Gorbachev's apparent move is a remarkable gesture for a regime which until recently denied that any political prisoners existed.

Gorbachev's move would appear to be the logical extension of his increasingly friendly relations with Andrei Sakharov, the world's best-known dissident. Gorbachev freed the nuclear scientist from his internal exile in 1987 and held a public meeting with him last January. Sakharov has responded by praising Gorbachev as "an outstanding statesman" and presenting him with a list of some 200 political prisoners still languishing in prison camps and psychiatric hospitals.

While few doubt that Gorbachev's promise will hold good, and that some "politicals" will indeed be released, the major question is how many. Despite Sakharov's list, the Soviet spokesman Gennady Gerasimov claims that there are only "a dozen or two" still in prison.

What will certainly force the issue is Mr Gorbachev's desire to stage a human rights conference in Moscow in 1991. To get Western support for that plan he will need to demonstrate that, in Russia, human rights begin at home.

Turin Shroud is a "mediaeval fake"

Fake – but still a mystery.

Oct 13. The Turin Shroud, revered for centuries as one of Roman Catholicism's most sacred relics, has been declared a fake. Carbon-dating tests conducted at Oxford University and elsewhere have proved that the linen of the Shroud, once believed to have wrapped the newly-crucified Christ, actually dates from between 1260 and 1390.

The Church accepts the technical evidence, but even the scientists cannot explain how this blood-stained piece of mediaeval cloth is imprinted with the image of a crucified man. Relics were often faked, but this process was surely beyond even the cleverest forger.

Lords vote against "Spycatcher" ban

Peter Wright: best-selling spy.

Oct 13. The long battle to ban the publication of "Spycatcher", the memoirs of the former MI5 man Peter Wright, is over. The British government today lost the final round of its legal warfare when, in a unanimous decision, the House of Lords rejected the Government's effort to bar any mention of the book in Britain's media. Last year's injunctions against three newspapers are lifted. The Lords stressed, however, that this decision came only because the book was already so widely available. They denied that its evidence of MI5's law-breaking justified publication.

Charles slams new buildings in London

Oct 28. Prince Charles today renewed his attack on architects for inflicting "terrible damage" on our cities. In a BBC "Omnibus" TV film, which he both wrote and narrated, the Prince compared the British Library to "an academy for secret police" and the National Theatre to "a nuclear power station", and lamented the "jostling scrum of skyscrapers round St. Paul's". Architects are shocked, but much of the public appears pleased by his statements (→ 2/11).

Two wales stranded in Alaskan ice fight for air through two holes kept open by Eskimoes as rescuers race to carve a channel to the open sea.

1988

NOVEMBER

Su	Mo	Tu	We	Th	Fr	Sa
		1	2	3	4	5
6	7	8	9	10	11	12
13	14	15	16	17	18	19
20	21	22	23	24	25	26
27	28	29	30			

2. London: Architects hit back at Prince Charles, blaming planners and politicians for disastrous buildings.

3. Seoul: 24,000 police protect ex-President Chun Doo Hwan from a student lynch mob.

4. China: Warning is given that 20 million peasants are at risk following droughts and floods.

4. Maldives: Indian troops thwart an attempted coup by 400 Tamil mercenaries in Male.

7. UK: Three new TV channels, plus a shake-up for the BBC and ITV, are announced.

8. China: Nearly 1,000 people are feared dead after an earthquake near the Burmese border.

9. US: The Air Force makes public its Lockheed F-117A "Stealth" fighter plane which radar cannot detect.

10. Glasgow: Scottish Nationalists win the Govan constituency from Labour in a by-election shock.

11. West Germany: The President of the Bundestag, Phillip Jenninger, resigns after his pro-Nazi speech yesterday.

15. UK: The Education Secretary, Kenneth Baker, says that national testing will place greater emphasis on grammar.

18. S. Africa: Four well-known anti-apartheid campaigners are found guilty of treason.

24. London: Police clash with students demonstrating against Government plans to bring in student loans.

29. Belgium: The Government rejects Britain's plea to extradite Patrick Ryan, a former priest accused of IRA terrorist offences (→ 13/12).

30. New York: The PLO leader, Yasir Arafat, is refused a US entry visa to address the UN (→ 14/12).

DEATH

19. Greek ship owner Christina Onassis (*11/12/1950).

George Bush is elected US President

Nov 8. Vice-President George Bush won the American presidential election comfortably today. The Republican candidate carried 40 states against only ten for his Democratic opponent, Governor Michael Dukakis of Massachusetts. The President-elect and his controversial running mate, Senator Dan Quayle, received 54 per cent of the popular vote.

The Dukakis campaign, which had held an 18-point lead in August, rallied in the final fortnight, but it was too little, too late. Americans appear to have believed the promise made by Bush not to raise taxes more than the claim by Dukakis and his running mate, Senator Lloyd Bentsen, that the US economy was in trouble.

Hail to the new chief: George Bush celebrates his victory over Dukakis.

First reactions in Washington are that the Bush administration will not be very different from the Reagan administration. After running a surprisingly abrasive campaign, the new President can expect a difficult relationship with Congress where the Democrats have strengthened their control.

Even his fellow Republican, Senator Robert Dole, whom Bush beat in rough primary campaigns, is unlikely to offer any favours.

Mr Bush has already appointed his campaign manager and close friend, Jim Baker, the former Treasury Secretary, as his Secretary of State. Mr Bush hopes for an early summit with Russia's Mikhail Gorbachev, but he is wary of allowing the Soviet President an easy opportunity for a propaganda coup. At home, his priority will be to persuade the financial markets that he can reduce the US trade deficit without breaking his campaign promise not to raise taxes.

Thatcher speaks out for Polish freedom

Nov 11. Margaret Thatcher visited Poland's Gdansk shipyard today, and in one of those paradoxes of ideology the Prime Minister, who is often reviled by British trades unionists, was cheered to the echo by their Polish cousins and praised by the Solidarity leader, Lech Walesa, as she congratulated them on their struggle for freedom. In talks with the Polish leader General Wojciech Jaruzelski, she called on him to establish "a real dialogue with all sections of society including Solidarity". The General promised "a new phase of democratic, humanistic socialism". Afterwards, Mrs Thatcher visited the grave of Father Jerzy Popieluszko, killed by the secret police in 1984.

West meets East: Margaret Thatcher and Solidarity leader, Lech Walesa.

Bhutto wins seat in Pakistan assembly

Nov 30. Benazir Bhutto, whose Pakistan People's Party won the country's first democratic election in 11 years two weeks ago, took her seat as Prime Minister in Pakistan's National Assembly today. Her triumph is the culmination of a nine-year battle to topple General Zia ul-Haq who died in a mid-air explosion earlier this year, and who had her late father, Zulfikar Ali Bhutto, executed in 1979.

Miss Bhutto will have little enough time for rejoicing. Her country remains divided, and her chief rival, the Zia appointee, Naraz Sharif, refuses even to attend the Assembly, preferring to operate from his power base in the Punjab. The army, who backed General Zia, must be placated at once.

Politics apart, the new Prime Minister faces urgent problems. The economy is badly depressed, and there is widespread corruption and poverty and a desperate need for land reform (→ 31/12).

Ethnic unrest rocks Communist world

Estonia: Moscow reforms spurned

Nov 16. The Baltic state of Estonia, which has been ruled by the Soviet Union since World War II, joined the growing movement towards national self-determination within the USSR today.

In an unprecedented act of defiance its Assembly, meeting in the capital Tallinn, voted to reject the Soviet premier's plans to reform the constitution, demanding instead a unique Estonian constitution under which the Assembly can choose to reject or accept Moscow's legislation.

The Assembly has resisted demanding absolute independence, but does insist upon the "sovereignty of Estonia", with all human rights guaranteed, private property allowed and all lands and natural resources turned over to Estonian control. This runs directly in the face of the Gorbachev plan, which leaves all regional economic planning in Moscow's hands.

Estonia's Communist Party has backed the nationalist surge, but its leader Vaino Valjas is keen to enlist the support of the country's 1.5 million Russians – 40 per cent of the population. "The future," he says, "is in the hands of us all."

Striking Yugoslav car workers besiege Belgrade's parliament building.

Serbia: a million rally for independence

Nov 19. In their latest protest against attacks on the Serbian community by ethnic Albanians in the Yugoslav province of Kosovo, one million Serbs demonstrated in the Yugoslav capital, Belgrade, today.

Slobodan Milosevic, the charismatic leader of Serbia's Communist Party, denounced "secret meetings, agreements made in restaurants and a lot of dirty slyness" which he said were standing in the way of solving the Kosovo crisis. Milosevic, whom critics see as using the crisis to advance his own ambitions, has been spearheading Serbian demands for justice ever since demonstrations began in July. Kosovo, ruled for two centuries by a Serbian king, is seen as the home of Serbian culture.

The protesters are also complaining about problems in the Yugoslav economy. With annual inflation at 200 per cent, the Serbs have been the first to organise strikes and rallies, rejecting a wage freeze and demanding reforms (→ 30/12).

Dubcek speaks out against 1968 invasion

Nov 13. Alexander Dubcek, once the architect of Czechoslovakia's shortlived experiment in freedom – the "Prague Spring" of 1968 – attacked the Soviet Union's repression of his reforms today, although he did not say a critical word.

Receiving an honorary degree from Bologna University, Mr Dubcek distributed to the press the full text of his speech. In it, he savaged the stifling of his efforts and the 20 years of "economic stagnation, sterility and incalculable moral loss" that followed.

But no such sentiments were offered from the podium. Instead, Dubcek offered a carefully uncontroversial address, ensuring that nothing would anger the Party diehards taking notes in Prague.

Dubcek: a prophet before his time.

Georgia: freedom campaign grows

Nov 23. Georgia, in the Soviet Union's Transcaucasian south, is the latest Soviet republic to join the drive for greater national freedom and an end to control from Moscow. Like Estonia and Lithuania, Georgia has rejected Mr Gorbachev's plans for a reformed constitution and called on the Soviet leader to "take account of the demands of the Georgian community".

Two-thirds of Georgia's 5.3 million people are ethnic Georgians, who cherish a reputation for asserting their own independence in the face of foreigner invaders. Only Stalin, a native son, managed to crush their aspirations, absorbing them into the USSR in 1921.

Likud party wins Israel's election

Nov 2. Prime Minister Yitzhak Shamir's right-wing Likud party, has won Israel's first general election by the smallest possible margin. Likud gained one more seat in the Israeli parliament, the Knesset, than Shimon Peres' Labour Party. With so tiny a majority, Mr Shamir will be forced to look for allies among the Knesset's minority parties, notably a number of ultra-religious groups which increased their seats in the Knesset from 13 to 18. It is expected that they will try to impose strict religious sanctions on the normally secular state in return for their support. Meanwhile, the PLO has called the results "a fatal blow for peace".

Inflation fuelled by mortgage rate rise

Nov 18. The pace of inflation is quickening, according to official statistics released tonight. It was running at 6.4 per cent in the year to October – the highest rate since 1985. Higher mortgage payments are largely responsible. These have risen as the Government has increased interest rates from eight to 12 per cent during the course of the year in an attempt to control inflation. Imports have also soared to record levels, but Nigel Lawson, the Chancellor of the Exchequer, believes higher interest rates will soon curb consumer demand.

HOW INFLATION HAS RISEN

Monthly rise in retail price index over previous year

6,4% 6,2 6,0 5,8 5,6 5,4 5,2 5,0 4,8 4,6 4,4 4,2 4,0 3,8 3,6 3,4 3,2

M J J A S O N D J F M A M J J A S O

1987 1988

1988

DECEMBER

Su	Mo	Tu	We	Th	Fr	Sa
				1	2	3
4	5	6	7	8	9	10
11	12	13	14	15	16	17
18	19	20	21	22	23	24
25	26	27	28	29	30	31

2. Bangladesh: A cyclone has killed over 1,200.

3. UK: Junior Health Minister Edwina Currie says most of UK egg production is infected with salmonella (→ 16).

6. UK: 2,400 jobs are lost with the Government closure of the last remaining ship-building yard on Wearside.

10. Stockholm: Nobel Prizes are awarded to Sir James Black (UK), Gertrude Elion and George Hitchings (both US) for Medicine; Naguib Mahfouz (Egypt), Literature; Maurice Allais (France), Economics; Leon Lederman, Melvyn Schwartz and Jack Steinberger (all US), Physics; Robert Huber, Hartmut Michel and Johann Deisenhofer (all West Germany), Chemistry; and in Oslo the Peace Prize to the UN peace-keeping force.

20. Sri Lanka: Prime Minister Ranasinghe Premadasa has won yesterday's violent presidential election.

22. New York: South Africa, Cuba and Angola sign treaties for the phased withdrawal of Cuban troops from Angola.

26. UK: Three North Sea oilfields are shut down when a storage vessel breaks free in gale-force winds.

30. UK: Scottish detectives fly to Germany as the hunt begins for the bombers responsible for the Lockerbie air disaster.

30. Yugoslavia: The Government resigns after a year of economic crisis and ethnic unrest in Serbia.

DEATH

6. American singer Roy Orbison (*23/4/1936).

HITS OF 1988

The Only Way Is Up

I Should Be So Lucky

Mistletoe And Win

QUOTE OF THE YEAR

"There is no such thing as collective guilt."

Kurt Waldheim, President of Austria on his wartime past.

Gorbachev slashes Red Army troops

Dec 7. Mikhail Gorbachev today unwrapped his Christmas present for the world – unilateral troop cuts of 500,000 men, or ten per cent of Soviet military strength, within the next two years. The troop cuts were the centrepiece of a dramatic speech by President Gorbachev to the United Nations in which he called for "a new world order" in international relations.

It was the first speech by a Russian leader to the UN General Assembly since Khrushchev's shoe-banging appearance in 1960. Today Mikhail Gorbachev used words alone to surprise his audience which applauded enthusiastically. Not only is the scale of troop cuts unprecedented, but never before has a Soviet leader embraced so warmly the prospect of international cooperation.

Gorbachev in New York: he offers troop cuts and "a new world order".

President Reagan, who met his Soviet counterpart for lunch after the UN speech, said he "heartily approved" of the speech. European leaders generally responded positively to Mr Gorbachev's vision of a continent that one day may not be divided into two military blocs.

NATO's chiefs were more wary, pointing out that Warsaw Pact forces would still retain numerical supremacy despite the cuts. Nor is military unease confined to the West. Marshal Sergei Akhromeyev, the chief of the Soviet general staff, has retired, ostensibly for health reasons, but more likely because of his opposition to Mr Gorbachev's cuts in the armed forces. Six tank divisions, with 5,000 tanks based in East Germany, Hungary and Czechoslovakia, will be disbanded, with a further 5,000 tanks taken out of service in the western Soviet Union. Eight hundred combat aircraft and 8,500 artillery systems will also go. In all, one quarter of Soviet tanks and artillery in Europe will be scrapped.

Assault and landing forces will also be reduced, including specialist units for crossing rivers. This heralds a potentially seismic shift in Soviet strategy which until now has been based on offensive capabilities which NATO was formed to counter.

Although troop cuts were the most dramatic element in the Soviet President's speech, it was also a tour de force as a review of global problems. He talked about a UN peace-keeping force in Afghanistan, unveiled proposals for tackling Third World debts, and called for diplomatic initiatives to combat environmental damage.

Armenian earthquake wipes cities off "the face of the earth"

Dec 10. Over 100,000 people are feared to have died in Armenia after the worst earthquake the region has ever seen hit last Wednesday. The quake, which happened near the Turkish border in northern Armenia, measured 6.9 on the Richter scale; anything over six is considered serious.

The town of Spitak, which had a population of 50,000, has been utterly destroyed. In Leninakan, a city of 300,000, 80 per cent of the apartment blocks collapsed, burying their occupants alive.

President Gorbachev cut short his American trip to visit the area. In Leninakan, he said: "Now the important thing is to save everyone who can be saved".

Armenian women grieve over their families and friends lost in Leninakan.

▷

Britain is shocked by two disasters in nine days

Rescue workers battle to free people from the horror of enmeshed trains.

A huge crater and charred houses are what's left of one Lockerbie street.

Faulty signals blamed in train tragedy

Dec 12. Thirty-six people are feared to have died today when a packed commuter train piled into the back of another just outside Clapham Junction, the world's busiest railway junction, in south-west London. Seconds later, an empty train ploughed into the wreckage, and only quick thinking by its guard prevented a fourth train from joining the pile-up.

It was Britain's worst railway disaster for more than 20 years, with over 100 people injured in addition to those who died. Tonight signal failure appears to be the most likely cause of the tragedy, with British Rail admitting: "The fail-safe mechanism did not work."

The accident occurred at 8.13 this morning when the 6.30 train from Bournemouth crashed into the rear of the 7.18 from Basingstoke to Waterloo. The Bournemouth train sheared into the air and onto its side in a cloud of flying glass and metal, only to crash into an empty train travelling south on the adjoining track. It was the guard of this train who ran back to stop a fourth train, packed with passengers, from joining the wreckage. Survivors spoke later of the devastating moment of impact. "The roof split open and the bogeys came up through the floor. Everything went dark and furniture and debris flew around," said Mike Clarke, who was in the buffet car of the Bournemouth train.

Rescue workers were hampered by the location of the crash in a deep cutting. As the tangled trains were prised apart, doctors crawled towards trapped people to give life-saving transfusions and pain-killing drugs. More than 1,000 people were on the trains and over-crowding, as well as signal failure, will be examined at an inquiry.

Red for danger: the worst crashes

MAY 1915: 227 people killed in a collision between a troop train and a passenger train near Gretna Green in the Scottish Borders.
OCTOBER 1952: 112 people killed and 340 injured at Harrow and Wealdstone station when a Perth to Euston express ran into another train, with a Euston to Manchester express hitting the wreckage.
DECEMBER 1957: 92 people killed and 173 injured when two trains collided in thick fog under a bridge which then collapsed at Lewisham.
NOVEMBER 1967: 49 people killed and 78 injured when a Hastings to Charing Cross train was derailed at Hither Green, south London.

American jet crashes on Scottish town

Dec 22. A Pan American jumbo jet crashed onto the town of Lockerbie in the Scottish Borders last night, killing all 259 passengers on board and at least 11 people on the ground to make it Britain's worst air disaster. As accident investigators began examining the wreckage, it emerged today that US embassies had received a warning that a Pan Am flight would be a terrorist target for a bomb.

The plane, flying from Heathrow to New York, broke up in mid-air so suddenly that the crew was unable to send any message and so dramatically that wreckage was scattered over large areas of Lockerbie and the surrounding countryside. Bodies were strewn around the town and fields, often mutilated beyond recognition. Twisted fragments of metal litter streets and gardens. On a hillside three miles away lies the nose of the aircraft, largely intact, while in the town a wing has gouged a deep crater, totally destroying half a dozen houses in Sherwood Crescent.

Flight 103 had originated in Frankfurt and then, after a stop at London's Heathrow Airport, took off 25 minutes late at 6.25pm for New York. The plane – the 15th Boeing 747 to be built and now 19 years old – was at its cruising height of 31,000 feet and crossing the Scottish border towards the North Atlantic when, at 7.19pm, it disappeared from radar screens. There were high winds, but no other aircraft was in the area at the time.

Minutes later what eye-witnesses described as a "fireball" fell from the sky over Lockerbie. "The whole sky lit up and it was virtually raining fire," said Mike Carnahan. As the Fire Brigade battled to control dozens of fires, RAF helicopters flew medical teams to Lockerbie, a market town with a population of 2,500. Today, they have been joined by soldiers and policemen who are combing the area not only for bodies but also for clues to the cause of the disaster. If it does turn out to be a bomb, the crash will focus renewed attention on airport security.

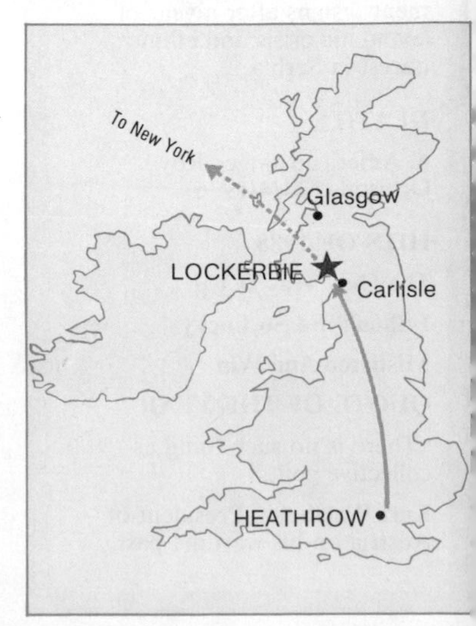

US to open historic dialogue with Arafat

Arafat: fighter turned diplomat

Dec 14. After years of refusing to deal with the Palestine Liberation Organisation, the United States said today it was ready to open "substantive dialogue" with them. This follows an announcement by PLO chairman that effectively removed all the US objections by renouncing "totally and absolutely .. all forms of terrorism, including individual, group and state terrorism". He also accepted UN resolutions 242 and 338, recognising Israel's right to exist within secure borders. George Shultz, the US Secretary of State, welcomed the statement as a major step towards direct talks between Israel and the Palestinians. Israel is appalled and said the US should not be fooled by "cheap words".

Edwina resigns after storm in egg cup

Dec 16. Edwina Currie, the junior Health Minister, has been forced to resign in the wake of angry protests from farmers over her claim that most British eggs are infected with salmonella. Sales of eggs have slumped and the taxpayers may end up paying over £10 million in compensation to egg-producers.

Currie's career has been marked by statements calculated to offend. In her opinion, northeners die of "ignorance and crisps", cervical cancer is the result of "being far too sexually active" and "good Christian people ... will not catch AIDS". However, health experts agree that Britain is facing its worst ever outbreak of salmonella.

Edwina: "I have no regrets".

Irish refuse to extradite Ryan

Dec 13. Ireland today refused to extradite Patrick Ryan, the former priest accused of terrorist offences, on the grounds that he would not receive a fair trial in Britain. Mrs Thatcher said this decision was a "great insult" to the British people, but the Labour leader, Neil Kinnock, blamed the Prime Minister for her vitriolic attacks on Ireland and on Belgium, which had also refused to extradite Mr Ryan to Britain. However, he may still face trial in the Irish Republic.

Bhutto and Gandhi seal nuclear treaty

Dec 31. Today India and Pakistan signed their first agreement for 16 years. After an historic meeting in Islamabad, the two prime ministers, Rajiv Gandhi and Benazir Bhutto, signed a pact in which both sides pledge not to attack each other's nuclear establishments.

The agreement, which is Miss Bhutto's first diplomatic move since her election last month, is more important to the Pakistanis who are thought to be near to possessing a nuclear bomb.

Arts: Salome unveils in year of Tempest

Artistic inflation: a Picasso sells for a world record sum of £20.9 million.

The most discussed opera of the year was Covent Garden's production of "Salome", in which **Sir Peter Hall** directed his then wife, **Maria Ewing**. Physically as well as vocally striking, she removed all seven veils and bared herself to the audience as well as to Herod.

Hall, meanwhile, was also directing "The Tempest", whose near-naked Caliban, streaked with dirt, was judged suitable for inspection by the Queen on her 25th anniversary visit to the newly-renamed Royal National Theatre. This was only one of four productions of "The Tempest" in a boom year for Shakespeare. The National and RSC had the hot competition of **Kenneth Branagh's** Renaissance Company's sell-out tour, **Jonathan Miller's** Old Vic company and **Derek Jacobi's** "Richard II". By the end of the year, **Sir Peter Hall** was directing **Vanessa Redgrave** in the first production of his new non-subsidised West End company.

David Hockney's owlish high profile ensured big attendances for his retrospective at the Tate Gallery. Is he rivalling his idol Picasso in versatility? asked the critics. Not yet anyway in price; a Tokyo department store paid £20.9 million at Christie's for "Acrobat and Young Harlequin". Even the amateur works of **Sir Noel Coward** fetched £780,000.

To judge from media coverage, you might conclude that **Joan Collins** was the most significant new novelist of the year, although **Melvyn Bragg** did not lack column inches for his biography of **Richard Burton**. Australian **Peter Carc** won the Booker Prize for his novel "Oscar and Lucinda", while scientist **Dr Stephen Hawking** was the year's least likely best-seller with "A Brief History of Time".

Bernardo Bertolucci's film "The Last Emperor" netted nine Oscars, the most by any single film since "West Side Story", but tops at British box offices was a modern morality tale, "Fatal Attraction". **John Cleese** scored a transatlantic hit with "A Fish Called Wanda", while repeats of "Fawlty Towers" still made TV's top ten. Top of the TV pops, though, was "Neighbours", a twice-daily soap opera whose success with the Poms baffled even its Aussie makers.

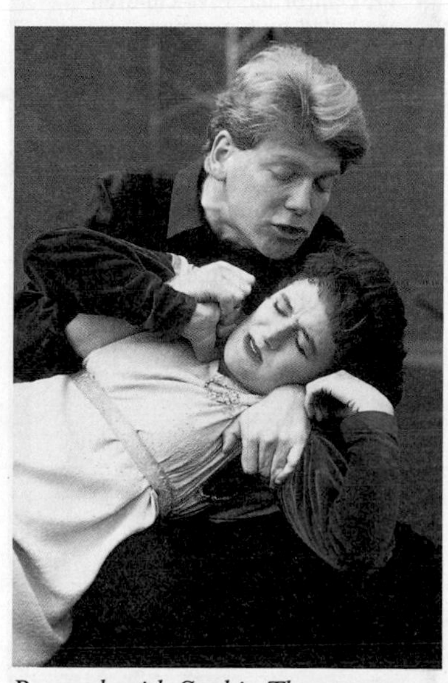
Branagh with Sophie Thompson.

1989

JANUARY

Su	Mo	Tu	We	Th	Fr	Sa
1	2	3	4	5	6	7
8	9	10	11	12	13	14
15	16	17	18	19	20	21
22	23	24	25	26	27	28
29	30	31				

2. Sri Lanka: Ranasinghe Premadasa is sworn in as president (→16/2).

4. UK: The BMA backs a campaign to cut the working week of junior doctors by 14 hours.

5. US: Serious conspiracy charges are dropped against Oliver North, the former White House aide (→4/5).

6. India: Two Sikhs are hanged for the murder of Indira Gandhi.

8. Paris: At 14-nation talks, the USSR says that it will destroy its chemical weapons.

8. UK: At least 40 people die when a British Midlands jet crashes on a motorway (→11).

10. USSR: Mikhail Gorbachev warns the Communist Party that it has no God-given right to rule (→28/3).

11. Hungary: A law is enacted allowing the formation of political parties (→15/3).

14. Belgium: Paul Vanden Boeynants, a former prime minister, is kidnapped (→14/2).

14. Tunis: William Waldegrave is the first British minister to meet Yassir Arafat, the PLO leader (→23/3).

15. USSR: Moscow imposes direct rule on Nagorny Karabakh, the Armenian enclave in Azerbaijan.

17. California: Five children are killed by a gunman.

22. Poland: Solidarity agrees to government terms to end an eight-year ban on the union (→17/4).

28. London: Violence erupts at an anti-Rushdie demonstration in Hyde Park (→15/2).

30. Lebanon: Amal and Hizbollah, the rival Shia groups, sign a pact ending their year-long feud.

DEATHS

7. Japanese Emperor Hirohito (*29/4/1901).→

23. Spanish artist Salvador Dali (*11/5/1904).→

27. British aviation pioneer Thomas Sopwith (*17/1/1888).

Japan mourns Hirohito

Jan 7. The Imperial Son of Heaven, Michinomiya Hirohito, Emperor of Japan for 62 turbulent years, died today at the age of 82. His son, Crown Prince Akihito, automatically succeeds to the Chrysanthemum Throne, although he will not be crowned for at least two years. Hirohito saw Japan evolve from a fiercely militaristic state, defeated in World War II, into one of the world's most powerful economies. In 1945 he admitted to his shattered people that he was not a god incarnate. Some countries wanted him tried for war crimes, but General MacArthur, the US supreme commander, chose to rule Japan through its emperor (→24/2).

Hirohito, ruler of Japan for 62 years.

Over 1,000 die in Soviet earthquake

Jan 23. At least two villages were buried by landslides and over 1,000 people killed when an earthquake measuring 5.5 on the Richter scale struck the Soviet Central Asian republic of Tajikistan at dawn today. The death toll from the shock, which comes only six weeks after the Armenian quake disaster, is expected to rise much higher.

Vast areas of agricultural land have been covered by mud and thousands of cattle destroyed. This will hit hard in a republic which is already one of the poorest in the Soviet Union, and where two-thirds of the population of five million live on the land.

Bradford Moslems burn Salman Rushdie's "Satanic Verses"

Jan 14. "The Satanic Verses", a novel by Salman Rushdie, was publicly burnt at a Moslem demonstration in Bradford today. There is growing unrest among Moslems in the city, who plan a march on W.H. Smith's bookshop, which has now withdrawn the book from display.

Banned as blasphemous in India, Pakistan and Saudi Arabia, the novel came out in Britain last year and has been on the bestseller lists for three months. Its title refers to verses cut from the Koran by the Prophet Mohammed because he believed they were inspired by Satan. Rushdie says "The Satanic Verses" concerns the struggle between secular and religious views of life (→28).

Rushdie's "blasphemous" book is set ablaze outside Bradford City Hall.

Bush signals a more compassionate era as Reagan bows out

President Bush shares a joke with his former boss at the inauguration.

Jan 20. George Herbert Walker Bush today placed his hand on the same Bible as that used for George Washington's swearing-in 200 years ago and became the 41st President of the United States. He thanked his predecessor for "the wonderful things you have done for America". Ronald Reagan, the old master of the one-liner, said simply: "Carry on." But in his inauguration speech, Bush said "a new breeze is blowing" and implied that his administration would be more compassionate than its predecessor. "We are not the sum of our possessions," he said (→26/2).

Pilot shut down "wrong engine" in crash

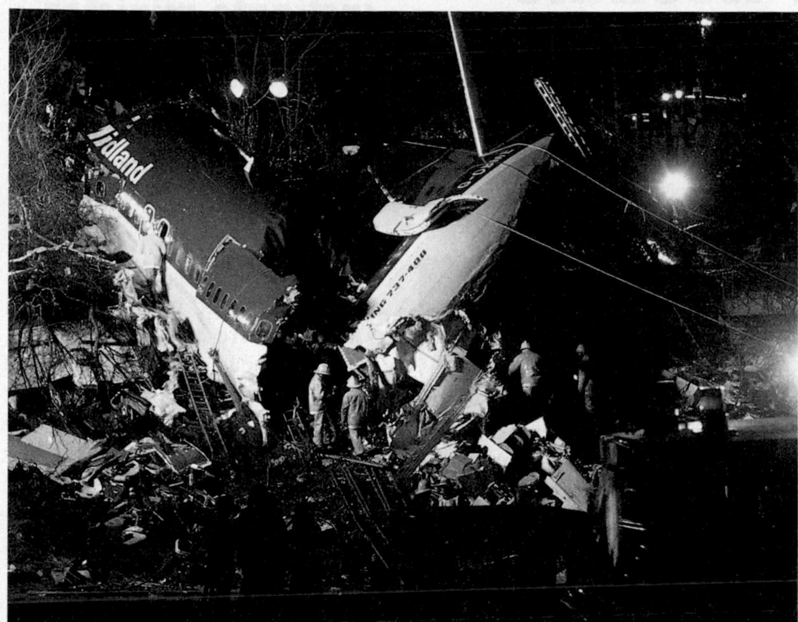

Rescuers fought through the night to free survivors trapped in the wreckage.

Jan 11. Preliminary evidence from the inquiry into the crash three days ago of a British Midland Boeing 737 suggests that the pilot shut down the wrong engine after reporting a fire 15 minutes after leaving Heathrow for Belfast. Forty-four of the 117 passengers and eight crew were killed when the plane ploughed into an embankment on the M1 motorway near Kegworth, less than half a mile from East Midlands airport where the pilot, Captain Kevin Hunt, was attempting to make an emergency landing. It was Britain's second major air disaster in under a month. The jet – delivered to the airline just 12 weeks ago – broke in two, littering the motorway with debris. Accident investigators, already busy with the bombing of Pan Am Flight 103, which crashed onto Lockerbie three weeks ago, have found no evidence of a fire or mechanical trouble in the starboard (right) engine which Captain Hunt had shut down after reporting a fire.

However, there was evidence of a fire in the other engine, MPs were told today by Paul Channon, the Transport Secretary. Captain Hunt is in hospital recovering from a broken back. It now seems likely that Boeing will be ordered by US aviation authorities to carry out systems checks on all 1,755 Boeing 737s it has delivered to airlines.

US jets shoot down two Libyan MiGs

Jan 5. US Navy jets shot down two Libyan MiG-23 fighters yesterday about 70 miles off the Libyan coast. The Pentagon said that they fired in self-defence, but the Libyan leader, Colonel Muammar Gaddafi, called it "premeditated aggression". He threatened revenge for what he called "US terrorism" and demanded an emergency meeting of the UN Security Council. A US military spokesman said that two F-14 Tomcats fired air-to-air missiles after the Libyan fighters approached in a hostile manner.

Police take control of Wandsworth jail

Jan 30. More than 200 police officers were drafted into Wandsworth Prison in south London today when warders walked out after refusing to work new shift patterns. They patrolled the jail under the direction of 36 senior prison staff and had to deal with several disturbances, including two small fires and an assault on an assistant governor. Members of the Prison Officers' Association in the jail claimed that the Home Office had imposed new working practices while negotiations were still in progress.

1989

FEBRUARY

Su	Mo	Tu	We	Th	Fr	Sa
			1	2	3	4
5	6	7	8	9	10	11
12	13	14	15	16	17	18
19	20	21	22	23	24	25
26	27	28				

1. London: The Guardian Angels, a group of New York subway vigilantes, arrive to set up a London branch.

3. S. Africa: F.W. de Klerk succeeds P.W. Botha as the National Party leader (→ 14/8).

3. Paraguay: A coup ousts the dictator, Alfredo Stroessner.

8. Azores: A Boeing 707 crashes, killing 144 people.

9. UK: Neil Kinnock confirms Labour plans to drop unilateral nuclear disarmament.

10. Jamaica: Michael Manley, the former premier, wins a landslide victory in elections.

12. Belfast: Pat Finucane, a leading solicitor who specialised in IRA cases, is shot dead.

14. Belgium: Paul Vanden Boeynants, the ex-premier, is freed for a £1 million ransom.

16. Sri Lanka: The ruling United National Party wins elections after a campaign that cost at least 700 lives.

17. London: Eight top V&A scholars are made redundant.

20. UK: IRA bombs destroy a Shropshire barracks (→ 20/3).

21. S. Africa: Two of Winnie Mandela's former bodyguards are charged with murder.

22. Iran: Envoys are withdrawn by Britain and the EC in the Rushdie affair (→ 16/3).

24. Japan: Prince Philip represents Britain at the funeral of Hirohito.

24. Pacific: A Boeing 747 cargo door blows off at 22,000 feet, sucking 16 to their deaths.

26. London: More than 15,000 people protest at plans to build a high-speed rail link to the Channel Tunnel (→ 8/3).

28. Yugoslavia: Troops are moved into the ethnic hotspot of Kosovo (→ 24/3).

DEATHS

2. British wartime spymaster Sir William Stephenson, known as "Intrepid" (*11/1/1896).

17. French couturier Guy Laroche (*1921).

27. Austrian polymath Konrad Lorenz (*7/11/1903).

Satellite TV on the air, but no dishes

Feb 5. Rupert Murdoch's £25 million Sky TV satellite network was launched today, doubling the number of channels available in Britain. Celebrations were muted, however, by the near-impossibility of obtaining the necessary dish aerials. It is estimated that only 50,000 people are able to receive the new broadcasts of movies, sport, news and general entertainment.

Murdoch dismissed claims that more channels will undermine quality and blamed class snobbery for opposition to his plans. He said: "In America there are 30 channels, amazing documentaries, excellent serials. When I arrive here all I find late at night is snooker."

However, Bryan Gould, Labour's trade spokesman, is calling for the Monopolies Commission to investigate Rupert Murdoch's media empire.

First woman bishop consecrated in US

The new bishop makes history.

Feb 11. The first woman bishop in Anglican history was consecrated today. The ceremony, which risks heightening the schism in the church over the role of women, was performed at the Boston Episcopal church in the United States. Traditionalists who objected to the Right Reverend Barbara Harris's consecration were booed by an 8,000-strong congregation, but the controversy is not over. ▷

Khomeini orders death of Rushdie

Feb 15. In an unprecedented move, Ayatollah Khomeini, the leader of Iran, has ordered the execution of Salman Rushdie, the British author accused of blaspheming Islam. In an edict broadcast yesterday on Tehran radio, the ayatollah said: "I inform the proud Moslem people of the world that the author of 'The Satanic Verses' book, which is against Islam, the Prophet and the Koran, and all those involved in its publication who were aware of its content, are sentenced to death."

"The Satanic Verses", which was published in Britain last September, has already been publicly burnt by angry Moslems. At least five people died in Pakistan at the weekend during a rally against the book. Rushdie, who lives in London, said that the strong reaction to the novel was based on a misunderstanding: "It is not true that this book is a blasphemy against Islam. I doubt very much that Khomeini or anyone else in Iran has read it."

In support of Khomeini's edict, thousands of Iranians marched on the British embassy in Tehran today, chanting "Death to England" and "Death to America". The demonstration was part of a day of mourning in Iran to protest against "The Satanic Verses". Senior political figures endorsed the call for the author's execution, and the Revolutionary Guard said that it was ready to carry out the order. In another development, the head of a wealthy Islamic charity organisation offered a $1 million reward to any non-Iranian who would "punish this mercenary of colonialism for his shameful act".

Meanwhile, Rushdie has cancelled a three-week tour of the US to promote his book and gone into hiding under police guard. Experts on Islam and terrorism have warned that he may need protection for the rest of his life. Security has also been stepped up at the London offices of his publishers, Viking Penguin, who have issued a statement regretting the distress caused to Moslems by the novel but confirmed that they plan to go ahead with a paperback edition (→22).

Angry Iranians show their determination to win retribution from the West.

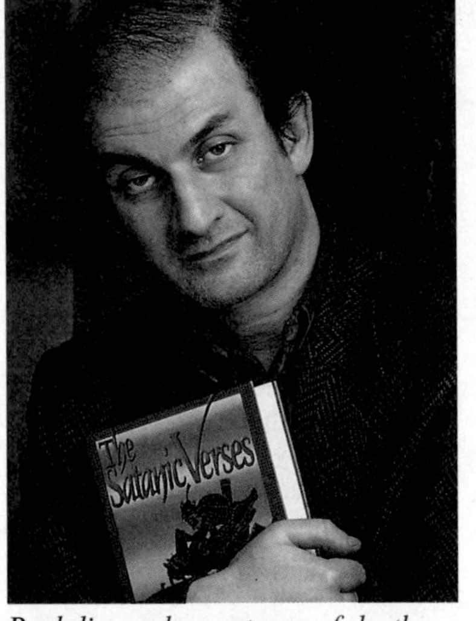

Rushdie: under sentence of death.

Lockerbie families castigate minister

Feb 23. Relatives of the victims of the Lockerbie air disaster have demanded the resignation of Paul Channon, the British Transport Secretary. This follows a statement by the US Federal Aviation Authority that it issued only 16 warnings about terrorism last year, whereas Mr Channon had implied that such warnings were so numerous that Heathrow had not been alerted about the specific threat to Pan Am flights from Frankfurt. A week ago police confirmed that a bomb hidden in a radio-cassette player caused last December's disaster, when a Jumbo jet crashed on Lockerbie, killing 270 people. It is believed that the bomb was loaded onto a Boeing 727 at Frankfurt in West Germany, which connected with the 747 flight from London to New York (→16/3).

Tyson halts Bruno

Feb 25. A brave challenge by the British boxer Frank Bruno for the world heavyweight title ended in the fifth round in Las Vegas today. The referee stopped the fight after Mike Tyson, the defending champion, had battered Bruno with a series of uppercuts to the chin. Bruno caught the mighty Tyson with one good blow and battled gamely, but otherwise was on the receiving end of the punishment.

Row over dissident faces Bush in China

Feb 26. George Bush's first visit to China as US President has been upset by a row over an astrophysicist. Fang Lizhi, a leading advocate of free speech and democratic reform, was stopped by police on his way to a party given by the Americans for their Chinese hosts and told that he was not on the guest list – a claim later denied by the Americans. Zhao Ziyang, the Communist Party General-Secretary, tonight slated dissidents who back "the multi-party, parliamentary politics of Western countries" and threaten Chinese reform by playing into the hands of hardline conservatives.

Last Soviet troops leave Afghan soil after ten-year occupation

Massed Soviet tanks prepare to begin their final withdrawal from Kabul.

Feb 15. The Soviet occupation of Afghanistan drew to a close today when General Boris Gromov, the Soviet commander, became the last soldier to leave Afghan soil. It is almost a fortnight since the final big Soviet army convoy began its homeward journey, leaving only a handful of personnel to wind up an unhappy ten years. Over a million have died, while six million more – nearly half the 1979 population – have fled to refugee camps in Pakistan and Iran. The Soviets suffered 46,000 casualties, including 16,000 killed, in a war that proved expensive, unpopular at home and damaging to Moscow's international relations (→8/3).

1989

MARCH

Su	Mo	Tu	We	Th	Fr	Sa
			1	2	3	4
5	6	7	8	9	10	11
12	13	14	15	16	17	18
19	20	21	22	23	24	25
26	27	28	29	30	31	

2. Brussels: The European Community agrees to ban the use of ozone-destroying chlorofluorocarbons by 1999.

2. Venezuela: Troop reinforcements arrive in Caracas, where 200 people have died in riots.

2. Lebanon: Four Palestinians are killed in an ambush in Israel's border security zone.

4. UK: Five people die in a rail crash at Purley, Surrey.

6. UK: Two people are killed in a rail crash at Glasgow.

8. Afghanistan: Mujahedin guerrillas attack Jalalabad (→21/6).

9. US: The Senate rejects the nomination of Senator John Tower as Defence Secretary.

11. Lebanon: The Christian General Michel Aoun vows to drive the Syrians out of Lebanon (→2/4).

15. Budapest: A rally calls for democracy and a withdrawal of Soviet troops (→2/5).

16. US: Pan Am says it was alerted about the type of bomb which resulted in the Lockerbie disaster (→10/5/90).

16. Riyadh: The Islamic Conference Organisation fails to back Iran on Rushdie.

18. Paris: France win the Five Nations' rugby championship.

20. El Salvador: Alfredo Cristiani's right-wing Arena Party wins elections (→16/11).

20. Northern Ireland: The IRA kills two top Royal Ulster Constabulary officers.

23. Tunis: The PLO holds its first formal talks with the new US administration.

24. Yugoslavia: Much of Kosovo's autonomy is forcibly surrendered to Serbia (→22/1/90).

31. UK: Family doctors campaign against government NHS reforms (→15/10).

31. US: Joseph Hazelwood, the captain of the Exxon Valdez, is fired after failing an alcohol test.

DEATH

14. Former Empress Zita of Austria (*9/5/1892).

Captain held as oil spill ravages Alaska

Salvage vessels with the damaged Exxon Valdez after she was refloated.

March 25. The captain and two crew members of an oil tanker have been subpoenaed by the US Coast Guard in Alaska following the worst oil spillage in US history. High winds are hindering efforts to mop up oil gushing from the tanker, and state officials are considering declaring a state of emergency.

The 987-foot supertanker Exxon Valdez ran aground on a reef yesterday, shortly after leaving the port of Valdez, the terminus of the Alaskan oil pipeline; eleven million gallons of crude oil poured out into Prince William Sound, an area rich in marine wildlife and economically crucial to local fishing communities. According to an estimate by Alaska state authorities, the slick covers 50 square miles and is continuing to spread. Officials are not yet able to identify the cause of the accident.

However, Joseph Hazelwood, the captain of the ship, and two other crew members have been ordered to be available to face federal investigations into the disaster. Exxon Shipping, the owners of the Exxon Valdez, confirmed that the captain had been in his cabin, one deck below the bridge, at the time of the accident.

Exxon says that all possible resources are being used to clean up the huge spillage and promises to take financial responsibility. But the company has come under fire from state sources and environmental groups for its allegedly slow response to the disaster (→31).

Soviet party bosses humiliated in polls

Yeltsin basks in a stunning victory.

March 28. Communist hardliners have been roundly humiliated in the first Soviet poll to put a toe into the water of real democracy. In elections to the Congress of People's Deputies, hundreds of Brezhnevite local Communist leaders were rejected in favour of reformers. A quarter of seats were allotted by the Communist Party, but elsewhere alternatives to the party's candidates were allowed for the first time in Soviet history. The biggest upsets occurred in Leningrad and the Ukraine. The leading reformer Boris Yeltsin – who believes that Mikhail Gorbachev is moving too slowly – won his seat with 90 per cent of the vote (→25/4).

BR reveals Channel Tunnel link route

March 8. British Rail said today that the rail link between the Channel Tunnel and King's Cross and Waterloo will traverse Peckham in south London. Despite plans to put much of the route in tunnels, and proposals to compensate householders living along the route, widespread hostility is expected – adding to opposition from Kent residents who fear that the link will blight their county. BR also faces problems over who will pay for the £1.7 billion project, whose costs have risen £500 million before work has even begun. The Channel Tunnel Bill bans the use of public money (→31/10).

Bloody riots mark Tibet anniversary

March 10. Despite a news blackout and the "evacuation" of tourists, reports reaching the West from the Tibetan capital, Lhasa, tell of at least 16 dead and thousands arrested in demonstrations to mark the 30th anniversary of the first anti-Chinese uprising. The last tourists to leave the capital talked of people being "dragged from their homes" by police and soldiers. Unrest began when Buddhist monks staged a protest against Chinese rule, which sparked riots and looting. China has ruled Tibet since 1950.

March 16. Gold Cup for a grey: Desert Orchid ridden by Simon Sherwood wins at Cheltenham.

1989

APRIL

Su	Mo	Tu	We	Th	Fr	Sa
						1
2	3	4	5	6	7	8
9	10	11	12	13	14	15
16	17	18	19	20	21	22
23	24	25	26	27	28	29
30						

2. Beirut: Christian areas suffer one of their worst attacks for 14 years (→16/8).

5. Vietnam: A withdrawal of all Vietnamese troops from Cambodia is declared (→26/9).

6. UK: The dock labour scheme is to end (→11/7).

6. Namibia: The UN proposes a truce to end fighting which imperils independence (→12/9).

7. Norwegian Sea: A Soviet submarine catches fire and sinks, with the loss of 42 lives.

8. UK: Little Polveir wins the Grand National.

9. USSR: Police clash with demonstrators in Georgia calling for independence from Moscow (→29/8).

13. West Bank: Israelis are accused of a massacre in the village of Nahhalin (→7/5).

18. Brussels: Britain is formally declared in breach of laws on drinking water.

18. UK: Hillsborough claims its 95th victim, 14-year-old Lee Nichol (→4/8).

20. Atlantic: A gun turret blows up on the US battleship Iowa, killing 47 sailors.

21. Paris: Three Ulster Loyalists are held for trying to trade British defence secrets for South African arms (→5/5).

25. USSR: Gorbachev purges the top ranks of the Communist Party; Andrei Gromyko is among the 110 ousted (→25/5).

28. Bangladesh: Up to 1,000 people are killed in a tornado.

27. UK: The jockey Peter Scudamore achieves a record 200 victories in a season.

29. Brussels: Fourteen Liverpool football fans receive jail terms for their part in the 1985 Heysel stadium disaster.

DEATHS

12. US boxer Sugar Ray Robinson (*1922).

15. Chinese liberal reformer Hu Yaobang (*1915).→

19. British novelist Daphne du Maurier (*13/5/1907).

26. US comedienne Lucille Ball (*6/8/1911).

Hillsborough disaster claims 94 lives

April 15. A police officer ordered a gate to be opened at a football stadium today to allow in a tightly-packed crowd of fans to watch an FA Cup semi-final. The result was the worst-ever disaster in Britain's sporting history.

Ninety-four people perished and 170 were injured when Liverpool supporters rushed on to the already crowded centre section of the west stand at Hillsborough in Sheffield, during a match between Liverpool and Nottingham Forest. Victims were crushed in the entrance tunnel, on the steps up to the terraces and against the perimeter fence.

In horrific, chaotic scenes, dead and badly-injured supporters – most of them from Liverpool – were passed over the fence onto the pitch. Others scrambled to safety on the balcony above. Within minutes the match was abandoned, and the pitch became like a battlefield, with police, ambulancemen and fans working frantically to revive the dying and cope with countless broken arms and legs.

Nottingham fans at the far end of the stadium initially jeered, unaware of the scale of the disaster and convinced that Liverpool fans were rampaging. With police struggling to keep order, the Liverpool manager, Kenny Dalglish, made an appeal over the stadium's public address system: "I think everyone knows there have been a few problems. Please try to be calm. We are doing our best for you."

As ambulances appeared on the pitch and fans ripped advertising hoardings from their mountings for use as makeshift stretchers, the crowd hushed and watched as the frantic efforts continued. A doctor appealed for a defibrillator – a resuscitation device – to be told that none was available. An oxygen bottle was found to be empty.

One man was seen to be given mouth-to-mouth resuscitation as ambulance workers pumped his heart. The crowd applauded when he appeared to come to life, only to be stilled again when his head sagged finally.

As the pitch was slowly cleared of the dead and injured, survivors talked of the horror of the crush. Wayne Adams, aged 17, was five rows from the front on the terrace.

Helpless supporters trapped at the perimeter fence as the tragedy unfolds.

"It was mainly youngsters standing in front of me," he said. "I realised it was serious when I saw one of the lasses standing near me just turn blue in the face. She went down. She was dead. That was it."

Peter Wells, one of 30 St John Ambulance volunteers at the scene of the disaster, told of helping a young girl in her twenties: "I was trying to hold her mouth through the wire mesh to keep her breathing going, but there was nothing we could do. She died."

Liverpool is in deep mourning tonight. Many of the dead are teenagers. The youngest is a boy of ten (→18).

April 23. An estimated two million mourners have filed into the Anfield ground during the past week, transforming the Liverpool stadium into a shrine.

Queen accepts invitation to Soviet Union

April 7. During a lunch at Windsor Castle today, the Queen accepted an invitation from Mikhail Gorbachev, the Soviet leader, to visit Moscow. No date was fixed and it could be two years away. She will be the first British monarch to go to Russia since the 1917 Communist revolution and the murder of her family's cousins, the Romanovs.

Mrs Thatcher said towards the end of the three-day visit to Britain by Mr Gorbachev that a turning-point had been reached in Anglo-Soviet relations. She told him: "You have provided us with an occasion we shall never forget and it is the start of something big."

The timing of the Queen's visit will depend on the progress of Gorbachev's policies of perestroika and glasnost. Mrs Thatcher is still counselling caution. Her press secretary annoyed the Queen's advisers at Buckingham Palace last year when he hinted that the Prime Minister might veto the trip which was then being tentatively mooted in Moscow. However, it was said in Downing Street tonight that the royal visit now has her full blessing. Mr Gorbachev has also invited Mrs Thatcher to Moscow again.

An historic handshake at Windsor.

Poland lifts eight-year ban on Solidarity

April 17. Hundreds of supporters of Solidarity cheered and gave "V" for victory signs today when an eight-year ban on the Polish trade union was lifted by a Warsaw court. Solidarity now has around six weeks to prepare for Poland's first experiment with democracy for 60 years. Under a deal hammered out after several weeks of round-table talks with the Communist government, Solidarity will be allowed to contest one third of seats in elections to a lower house and all seats in a new senate. There will also be elections to a new senate and presidency. Lech Walesa, Solidarity's leader, said: "I am happy we have now returned to the road of democracy and freedom" (→ 5/6).

Britain's Nick Faldo secures the US Masters golf championship.

Pet rottweilers kill an 11-year-old girl

April 14. An 11-year-old Scottish girl was savaged to death today by two rottweiler dogs. Kelly Lynch was walking the dogs, owned by the father of her school friend Lorraine Simpson, on the Dunoon seashore of the Firth of Clyde when they launched their unprovoked attack. A woman tried to pull the dogs off the young girl, but she too was mauled. Lorraine called her father, but before he could reach the spot Kelly was dead. The tragedy has fuelled fears in Britain about the recent huge growth in ownership of potentially dangerous dogs such as rottweilers and pit bull terriers.

1989

MAY

Su	Mo	Tu	We	Th	Fr	Sa
	1	2	3	4	5	6
7	8	9	10	11	12	13
14	15	16	17	18	19	20
21	22	23	24	25	26	27
28	29	30	31			

1. Europe: Battles between police and anti-government demonstrators mar May Day in Prague, Berlin and Istanbul.

2. Hungary: Troops begin to destroy the border fence with Austria (→ 16/6).

2. Netherlands: The Christian Democrat-led coalition falls.

3. UK: A three-day rooftop protest by prisoners at Risley remand centre ends.

4. US: Oliver North is found guilty of three minor charges in the Iran-Contra affair (→ 5/7).

5. UK: Three South African diplomats are ousted for trying to acquire missile secrets.

8. Hungary: The veteran leader Janos Kadar is removed from all powerful posts (→ 16/6).

12. UK: BBC unions launch a campaign of strikes in support of a 16 per cent pay claim.

13. Beirut: Jackie Mann, a 74-year-old Briton, is abducted.

15. Argentina: The Peronist candidate Carlos Menem wins the presidential election (→ 30).

17. Prague: The dissident playwright Vaclav Havel is freed after four months in jail for inciting unrest (→ 24/11).

19. UK: Inflation rises to eight per cent (→ 6/10).

20. China: Martial law is declared in Beijing (→ 9/6).

21. USSR: Eleven Britons are expelled in a growing spy row.

25. USSR: Mikhail Gorbachev is elected President (→ 29/8).

26. England: Arsenal win the football league championship by beating Liverpool in the final minute of the season.

27. UK: Lord Mackay, the Lord Chancellor, is suspended from the Free Presbyterian Church of Scotland.

30. Bonn: A bold US arms control initiative is saluted at Nato's 40th-birthday summit.

30. Argentina: More than 1,000 are arrested in food riots.

31. US: Jim Wright resigns as Speaker of the House of Representatives after charges of financial corruption.

Thatcher celebrates ten years in power

May 5. Mrs Thatcher yesterday quietly celebrated ten years as Prime Minister. But while the political pundits were busy assessing her first decade in Downing Street, voters in the Vale of Glamorgan gave the biggest swing to Labour in a by-election – 12.5 per cent – since 1935, turning a Tory majority of 6,251 into a Labour one of 6,028. Ministers dismissed the defeat as "mid-term blues" as newspapers pondered whether the Thatcher years have nearly run their course. Writers of all political hues agreed that she has been a strong leader who has radically changed the nation. But there the consensus ends (→ 19/6).

The PM and her first grandchild.

Liverpool snatch FA Cup in extra time

May 20. Liverpool, who considered quitting the competition after the Hillsborough tragedy, today paid a fitting tribute to the fans who died by winning the FA Cup, beating Merseyside rivals Everton 3-2. There was drama to the end as Everton snatched a last-minute equaliser to force the game into extra time. The Liverpool substitute Ian Rush then scored his second goal of the match for the trophy.

Celtic won the Scottish FA Cup final, beating Glasgow Rangers 1-0; Joe Miller scored (→ 26).

Democracy marchers upstage Gorbachev

One man speaks for the massed ranks of protesters in Tiananmen Square.

May 16. In the austere vastness of Beijing's Great Hall of the People, Mikhail Gorbachev today shook hands with the Chinese leader, Deng Xiaoping – ending 30 years of estrangement between the two mighty Communist nations. It was an historic moment – but totally overshadowed by the extraordinary events taking place a few hundred yards away, with up to half a million students and pro-democracy supporters from every walk of life occupying Tiananmen Square.

The incredible has happened in a country where discipline and respect for authority are paramount. Throughout the day processions flowed into the square, the marchers carrying banners in support of the students. Many of their slogans openly defied the country's leaders. Beijing's democracy rallies have so far been peaceful. Police have stood back, many of them clearly sympathetic to the crowds. Events could take an ominous turn, however, if any of the 3,000 hunger-striking students should die; 12 lives are said to be in danger.

The Chinese leadership appears impotent – and embarrassed in the presence of the Soviet leader – in the face of such protest. Zhao Ziyang, the head of the Communist Party, has promised to "enhance democracy, oppose corruption and expand openness" (→ 20).

Actors campaign to save Rose Theatre

May 15. Cheers filled the Commons today as the Environment Secretary, Nicholas Ridley, announced a one-month "breathing space" in the building works due to bury the site of the historic Rose Theatre in Southwark, south London. This follows an all-night vigil and dawn protest by actors and archaeologists led by two theatrical dames, Peggy Ashcroft and Judi Dench; forming a human wall to stop the developer's lorries entering the site, they sang "We Shall Overcome". The Rose, where Shakespeare performed, is the only Elizabethan theatre ever uncovered (→ 12/10).

Libel record broken

May 24. The wife of the mass sex-killer Peter Sutcliffe was awarded £600,000 damages today against the satirical magazine Private Eye. This is £100,000 more than the record British libel sum awarded to the novelist Jeffrey Archer and 100 times greater than any single sum received by any of the families of the victims of Sutcliffe, the "Yorkshire Ripper". The magazine had claimed that Sonia Sutcliffe sold the story of her life for £250,000. "If this is justice," said Eye editor Ian Hislop, "I'm a banana." He plans to appeal (→ 19/10).

Anti-Noriega candidates bludgeoned in Panama poll violence

May 10. Demonstrators in Panama City protesting against ballot-rigging in last Sunday's presidential election got a brutal beating today from paramilitary forces in the pay of General Manuel Noriega, the Panamanian dictator. Guillermo Endara, the opposition candidate for President, was hit with iron bars and taken to hospital drenched with blood; Guillermo Ford was among Vice-Presidential candidates who were also attacked.

"Pineapple Face" Noriega claims victory in the poll, which he rigged so blatantly that not even government television stations are reporting the results. These events will not be lost on the US, which wants the thuggish general to face drug-trafficking charges (→ 1/9).

Guillermo Ford, an opposition Vice-Presidential candidate, is attacked and beaten by a pro-government supporter while on a tour of Panama City.

1989

JUNE

Su	Mo	Tu	We	Th	Fr	Sa
				1	2	3
4	5	6	7	8	9	10
11	12	13	14	15	16	17
18	19	20	21	22	23	24
25	26	27	28	29	30	

1. UK: University lecturers accept a six per cent pay offer, ending a five-month dispute.

4. USSR: Up to 800 people are feared dead when a gas blast causes the USSR's worst rail disaster 750 miles from Moscow.

7. UK: Nashwan, ridden by Willie Carson, wins the Derby.

9. Hong Kong: Shares crash in response to the massacre of students in China.

12. USSR: At least 100 people are reported to have died in ethnic violence in the Central Asian republic of Uzbekistan.

12. Bulgaria: In one of Europe's largest population shifts for 50 years, thousands of persecuted ethnic Turks are leaving the country (→ 18/11).

16. Hungary: Five executed leaders of Hungary's uprising in 1956, including Imre Nagy, are reburied (→ 31/8).

16. Ireland: Fianna Fail loses seats in a general election (→ 29).

19. Poland: Solidarity wins 99 seats in the new 100-seat senate (→ 19/7).

19. Greece: Andreas Papandreou offers to resign as premier after an election defeat for his Pasok Party (→ 28/9).

21. Afghanistan: The siege of Jalalabad ends after 15 weeks.

25. China: Zhao Ziyang and other leading reformers are stripped of their posts.

25. UK: The government turns down pleas to provide a haven in Britain after 1997 for 3.25 million Hong Kong citizens (→ 22/12).

27. UK: Australia win the Second Test at Lord's to take a 2-0 lead in the series (→ 1/8).

28. UK: A second national one-day rail strike coincides with a virtual shutdown of the London tube (→ 12/7).

29. Ireland: Charles Haughey resigns as premier (→ 12/7).

DEATHS

4. Iranian leader Ruhollah Khomeini (*1902).→

27. British philosopher A.J. Ayer (*29/10/1910).

Crackdown follows Chinese massacre

One man who stopped the tanks: his name is unknown, but his act of defiance wins admiration around the world.

June 9. In a horrific show of force, China's leaders have vented their fury and frustration on student dissidents and their pro-democracy supporters. Several hundred people are thought to have been killed and thousands wounded when the People's Liberation Army moved on Beijing's Tiananmen Square, firing indiscriminately.

When, late on Saturday night, the army turned on its own people, it was with a cold brutality that spilt Chinese blood on the Avenue of Eternal Peace after the advancing troops met a hail of stones and petrol bombs. Twenty-six people died in the first encounter, but the real savagery was yet to come.

As the first armoured vehicles smashed their way through a ring of burning buses into Tiananmen Square itself, the student occupiers began to fight. By now, Beijing was in a state of siege, with fires burning across the city. Screams of agony rang out as scores of injured were carried to hospitals, many overflowing with dead and dying. It was after one in the morning when the troops lined up for their final assault on the square. They marched towards the students, shooting at will, climbing over bodies and still shooting. Then came the tanks. A merciless crackdown is now under way throughout China as hundreds of "counter-revolutionaries" are rounded up and dragged, cowed and bruised, to be tried in people's courts. Some students are accused of the murder of soldiers who mowed down their comrades on that night of terror.

Unseen during the days of protest, the prime minister, Li Peng, and the aged leader Deng Xiaoping – whom many believed dead – have emerged to praise the troops who put down the demonstrations in Beijing and elsewhere (→25).

Monetary union comes closer in Madrid

June 27. Mrs Thatcher reaffirmed today that Britain wants closer economic and monetary union in Europe. She also signalled greater willingness to join the European Monetary System – but did not say when.

At a summit meeting in Madrid, European Community leaders accepted that the British premier is willing to compromise. Any deal would include a fixed exchange rate regime built around the German mark, but it would not include plans for a common currency.

In moving towards conciliation with Britain's partners and abandoning the idea of a floating pound, Mrs Thatcher seems to have yielded to pressure from within her government, especially at the Treasury and the Foreign Office (→20/11).

Bonn hails "Gorby"

June 13. President Gorbachev – voted the most popular politician among West Germans – has joined Chancellor Kohl in signing a Bonn declaration putting Soviet-German relations on a new plane. Greeted by crowds chanting "Gor-by, Gor-by", the Soviet leader offered peace and reconciliation in Europe in return for the economic help his reforms so urgently need.

Labour and Greens share the glory in European elections

June 19. Labour and the Greens have received a great boost in elections to the European Parliament. In its first national poll win since 1974, the Labour Party took 45 of Britain's 78 European seats, against 32 for the Conservatives; the remaining seat went to the Scottish Nationalists. But perhaps the most remarkable showing was made by the Green Party, which won 2.3 million votes – 15 per cent of the total – mainly at the expense of the former Alliance parties, although Britain's voting system denies the Greens seats at Strasbourg.

The Tories have paid dearly for appearing divided about the future of Europe and running a lacklustre and negative campaign – one slogan suggested that Britons would not stand "a diet of Brussels". The Labour leader, Neil Kinnock, declared the result "a rehearsal for things to come". Left-wing parties will have a working majority in the new European Parliament if they can woo the Green group, now doubled in strength, which could hold the balance. The final seats tally is: Socialists 181, European People's Party 123, Liberals 44, Communists and allies 41, Greens 39, Democrats 34, European Right 22, Democratic Alliance 19 and Independents 15 (→5/7).

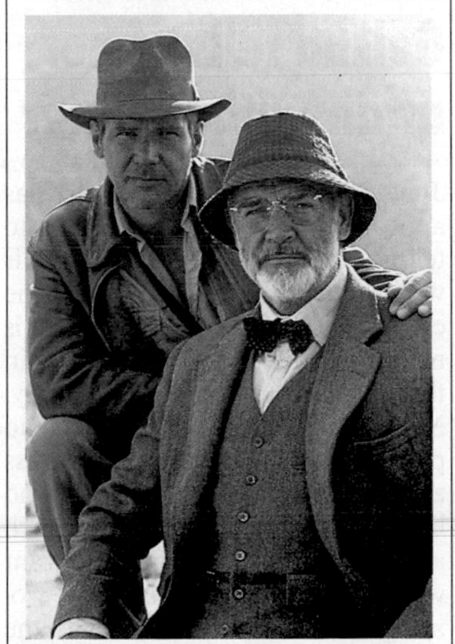

Indiana meets 007: Harrison Ford is joined by Sean Connery in the new Indiana Jones film.

Khomeini's funeral is marked by hysteria

June 6. Iran today bade farewell to Ayatollah Ruhollah Khomeini in much the same way as it greeted him ten years ago, when he returned from exile to lead the country's Islamic revolution: with unfettered mass hysteria. He died two days ago at the age of 86.

His body was to have been paraded for 15 miles through Tehran to a burial site south of the capital for "martyrs of the revolution". Iran's clerical leaders scrapped this plan as it became clear that around two million mourners, weeping and beating themselves in grief, had filled the streets soon after dawn.

Instead, the body was flown to the cemetery by helicopter, where, after a perilous landing, it was beset by mourners. In the ensuing melee the ayatollah's bier was jostled so much that his body was half exposed, as people tore at his shroud. Guards eventually got the dead man back into the helicopter and the funeral was postponed until late afternoon. This time the body was in a metal coffin, and the graveside had been cleared of all except Revolutionary Guards and officials.

Iran's President, Ali Khamenei, was appointed the country's new spiritual leader yesterday, while Ali Akbar Hashemi Rafsanjani, the Speaker of the Iranian parliament, is tipped to succeed Khamenei as President later this year (→29/7).

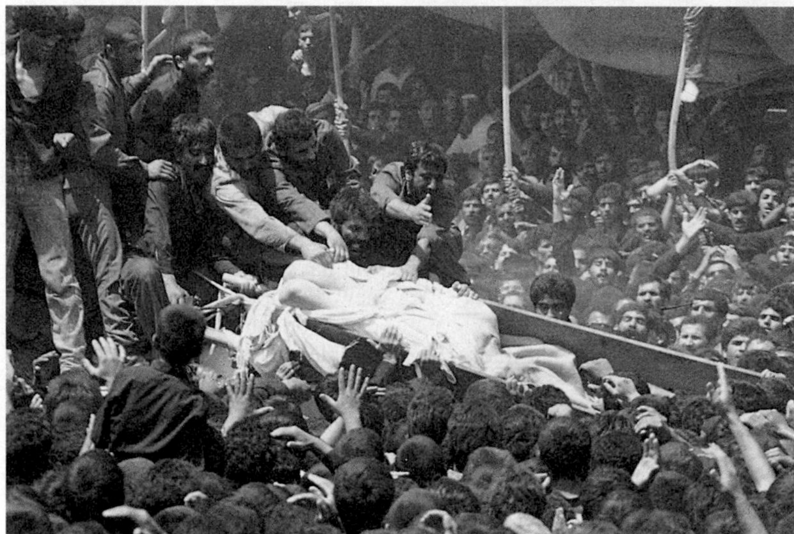

The ayatollah's body is half exposed as frantic mourners tear at his shroud.

Geisha tells of her affair with premier

June 25. A former geisha girl has appeared on television in Japan to tell astounded viewers of her affair with Sosuke Uno, who became the country's new premier earlier this month. Apologising for the pain that would be caused to his family, Mitsuko Nakanishi said that Uno paid her £15,000 to be his mistress and described him as a man who liked to humiliate underlings, such as the manageress of a restaurant whom he addressed as "old woman". Miss Nakanishi broke the geisha code of silence with her revelations, but maintained that "he is a public figure and people have a right to know" (→24/7).

Solidarity triumphs over Communists

June 5. In the first free election in Eastern Europe for 40 years, Polish voters have delivered a spectacular snub to the Communist government of General Wojciech Jaruzelski. Solidarity, the free trade union and democratic movement, captured one-third of seats – all it was allowed to contest – in yesterday's elections to the lower house of Poland's parliament. The government has called on Solidarity to join a coalition, but in a fortnight it will be contesting every seat in elections to a new senate. It could then be Lech Walesa, Solidarity's leader, who calls the shots, not General Jaruzelski (→19).

1989

JULY

Su	Mo	Tu	We	Th	Fr	Sa
						1
2	3	4	5	6	7	8
9	10	11	12	13	14	15
16	17	18	19	20	21	22
23	24	25	26	27	28	29
30	31					

2. Hanover: An IRA bomb kills a British soldier (→7/9).

4. Belgium: A Soviet MiG-23 fighter plane crashes after flying pilotless from Poland.

5. US: Oliver North is given a suspended jail term and fined.

8. UK: The House of Lords passes a bill privatising the water industry in England and Wales (→9/12).

9. Wimbledon: Steffi Graf wins the ladies' tennis final, beating Martina Navratilova 6-2, 6-7, 6-1. Boris Becker wins the men's title, beating Stefan Edberg 6-0, 7-6, 6-4.

11. UK: Dockers begin a strike in protest at the dock labour scheme abolition (→1/8).

12. UK: Rail workers stage a fourth one-day strike.

19. Poland: Jaruzelski is elected to the new post of executive President (→24/8).

20. US: A United Airlines DC-10 crash in Iowa kills 107.

21. UK: The comedian Ken Dodd is acquitted of defrauding the Inland Revenue.

24. Japan: Sosuke Uno resigns as premier after the defeat of his ruling Liberal Democratic Party in elections (→10/8).

27. Sweden: Christer Pettersson, an alcoholic and a drug addict, is jailed for the 1986 murder of the then premier, Olof Palme (→12/10).

27. UK: Rail workers accept a pay offer and call off their campaign of one-day strikes.

29. Iran: Hashemi Rafsanjani wins the presidential election.

31. Lebanon: Arab terrorists claim to have killed a US hostage in retaliation for Israel's kidnapping of pro-Iranian Sheikh Obeid (→3/8).

DEATHS

2. Soviet statesman Andrei Gromyko (*18/7/1909).

6. Hungarian leader Janos Kadar (*26/6/1912).

11. British actor Lord Olivier (*22/5/1907).→

16. Austrian conductor Herbert von Karajan (*20/11/1918).

Olivier makes exit from life's stage

Early days, with Vivien Leigh.

July 11. Lord Olivier, the grand old man of the stage, died in his sleep today surrounded by his family. He was 82. This evening, London theatres dimmed their lights for him; at the National, of which he was the first director, audiences stood in silent tribute. Judged the greatest actor of his time, Laurence Olivier triumphed in Shakespeare and was one of the last actor-managers, working at the St. James's Theatre with his second wife, Vivien Leigh. He founded and led the National Theatre company (1963-73) and was the first actor to be made a peer. His 60 films included "Henry V", and "The Entertainer" with his third wife, Joan Plowright.

Hottest summer in Britain since 1976

July 22. Weather experts forecast no respite from the intense heat that has all but dried up water supplies to 500,000 people in south-east London and Kent. Already 100,000 people in the area have been without water for a week, and residents are being told to boil drinking water because of fears of disease. Six million people around the country are watching their garden plants die as hose-pipe bans continue. Temperatures today hit the record-breaking levels of 1976, with 93F (34C) recorded at Heathrow. Mediterranean resorts are having a mild summer compared with Britain.

Late deal keeps Haughey in power

July 12. An eleventh-hour pact with the small right-of-centre Progressive Democrat (PD) party has allowed Charles Haughey to remain Ireland's Prime Minister. The deal ends the political crisis caused by last month's election, in which Haughey's ruling Fianna Fail party fell short of an absolute majority in the Dail, the Irish parliament. Des O'Malley, the PD leader, held out for cabinet posts as a condition for sharing power and, just an hour before the Dail was due to vote on Haughey's re-election, the veteran premier gave way. Of the six PD MPs, two – including O'Malley – are in the new cabinet.

Haughey celebrates his re-election as premier after a power-sharing deal.

Row blows up over cabinet reshuffle

July 25. Margaret Thatcher is tonight embroiled in an unseemly row following a cabinet reshuffle which has wounded and angered senior colleagues. It began yesterday when Sir Geoffrey Howe was replaced as Foreign Secretary by John Major, the Chief Secretary to the Treasury. She offered Howe the job of Home Secretary; he turned it down in favour of becoming leader of the Commons, insisting that he should also be made Deputy Prime Minister. Douglas Hurd, the Home Secretary, is cross that his job was offered to someone else, and now the ministers are squabbling over country houses (→ 26/10).

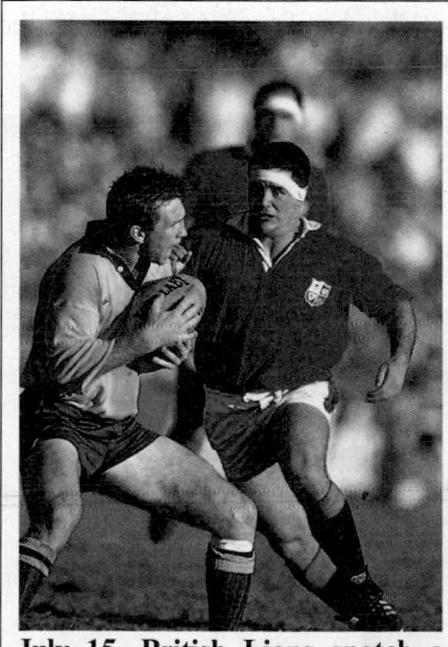

July 15. British Lions snatch a 2-1 rugby series win in Australia.

Botha is a suprise visitor for Mandela

July 8. The South African President, P.W. Botha, had a meeting three days ago with Nelson Mandela, the jailed African National Congress (ANC) leader, it was announced today. Leaders of the main opposition groups were surprised at the news of what is officially described as a "courtesy visit". Liberals hope that the meeting will be a prelude to Mandela's release and the eventual recognition of the ANC. Radical black politicians, however, suspect that it is some kind of a set-up. The far-right Conservative Party said that the government is planning a "sell-out" to black extremists (→ 14/8).

France indulges in revolutionary fever

July 14. Celebrations to mark the bicentenary of the French Revolution reached a festive climax in Paris tonight when an especially grand version of the traditional Bastille Day parade was followed by a lavish pageant, watched on television by hundreds of millions worldwide. The pageant embraced "national" displays from around the globe. Britain upset the festivities somewhat last week when Margaret Thatcher denied that the Revolution had inspired human rights: "Good heavens no. We had the Magna Carta in 1215."

1989

AUGUST

Su	Mo	Tu	We	Th	Fr	Sa
		1	2	3	4	5
6	7	8	9	10	11	12
13	14	15	16	17	18	19
20	21	22	23	24	25	26
27	28	29	30	31		

1. UK: The three-week-old dock strike is called off.

3. Lebanon: Terrorists lift their threat to kill a hostage, Joseph Cicippio (→ 30/4/90).

4. UK: An interim report on the Hillsborough disaster lays the blame on police action.

6. UK: British male athletes win the European Cup.

8. New Zealand: Geoffrey Palmer succeeds David Lange as Prime Minister.

9. Belfast: Seamus Duffy, aged 15, dies from a plastic-bullet wound during riots.

10. Japan: Toshiki Kaifu is sworn in as the country's premier (→ 19/2/90).

10. UK: British ports ban the import of highly toxic PCBs.

14. S. Africa: P.W. Botha resigns as President (→ 7/9).

14. Birmingham: The West Midlands serious crimes squad is disbanded after allegations of police corruption.

16. Beirut: A cease-fire begins between the Lebanese army and the Syrians with their Moslem militia allies (→ 22/9).

19. UK: A massive Shell oil leak in the Mersey threatens thousands of migrating birds.

23. USSR: A 180-mile chain in the Baltic states marks the 50th anniversary of the Soviet-Nazi pact (→ 24/2/90).

30. Northern Ireland: Loyalist groups claim to have received leaks on IRA suspects from security forces (→ 8/10).

31. Hungary: The exodus of 20,000 East Germans to the West is approved (→ 11/9).

31. UK: Worcestershire win the County Cricket title.

31. UK: Princess Anne and Mark Phillips are to separate.

DEATHS

21. Kenyan conservationist George Adamson (*1906).

23. British psychiatrist R.D. Laing (*7/10/1927).

24. Polish-born artist Feliks Topolski (*1907).

29. British naturalist Sir Peter Scott (*14/9/1909).

Scientists amazed by space pictures of Neptune's moon

Aug 25. Seasoned space scientists gasped in amazement today at the latest pictures – of Neptune's moon Triton – beamed to earth by the spacecraft Voyager 2. Triton has hitherto been thought remarkable for two reasons: it has an atmosphere, and it orbits Neptune in a different direction from the planet's other seven moons, six of them discovered by Voyager which sent back brilliantly clear pictures of Triton's surface. This is covered by pink glaciers, probably of methane, with white ice at the equator. Voyager 2 has taken 12 years to reach Neptune – arriving 1.4 seconds behind schedule – and has revealed that the planet has great storms, 400mph jet streams and five rings rather than three.

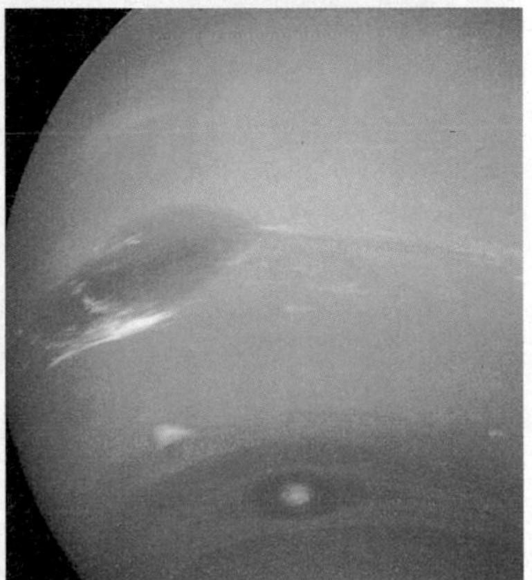

Voyager 2's view of Neptune itself.

Rebels plan cricket tour of South Africa

Aug 1. Sixteen English cricketers, headed by the former Test captain Mike Gatting, walked into a storm today by announcing that they will tour South Africa this winter. The news coincided with England's comprehensive defeat in the fourth Test at Old Trafford; Australia cruised to a 3-0 lead, regaining the Ashes. Under the terms of an international cricketing agreement of last January, the tourists will all face a five-year ban from international cricket. Two – Neil Foster and John Emburey – were on duty yesterday (→ 30/1/90).

Poland elects first non-Communist PM

Aug 24. Poland today became the first country in the Soviet bloc to elect a non-Communist Prime Minister. The parliament voted decisively for Tadeusz Mazowiecki – a Catholic editor and an adviser to Lech Walesa, the Solidarity leader – who was interned for a year by the Communist authorities under martial law. After the vote the Prime Minister sat with his head bowed as he received a standing ovation. Lech Walesa said from his home in Gdansk: "Hopes are turning in the direction of a man who has devoted all his life to the struggle for Poland" (→12/9).

Nationalist unrest troubles Gorbachev

Aug 29. The Soviet President, Mikhail Gorbachev, is facing a major nationalist challenge around the rim of the Soviet Union. In the Baltic republics of Lithuania, Latvia and Estonia there has been a surge of public support for outright independence, and in other regions ethnic tensions are mounting. Georgians and Abkhazians, Azerbaijanis and Armenians are at each others' throats in the south; there are strikes in Moldavia over local culture and riots in the Central Asian republic of Uzbekistan which have left at least 100 dead and thousands homeless (→13/12).

Sixty feared dead after party boat sinks

A diver comes up from inspecting the Marchioness after she was raised.

Aug 20. A night of joy ended in catastrophe this morning when, just before two o'clock, the Thames pleasure boat Marchioness was hit from behind by the 1,880-ton dredger Bowbelle. Around 150 people were enjoying a 26th-birthday party on the Marchioness when the collision occurred near Blackfriars Bridge in the heart of the capital. One moment they were dancing or admiring the view; the next they were plunged into fast-moving tidal water or entombed in the vessel as she keeled over, sinking within seconds.

Seventy-six people are known to have survived, and so far 26 bodies have been recovered. The final death toll, however, could be as high as 60. "It was like a tank running over a Mini," said a director of Tidal Cruises, the owners of the Marchioness. One of the survivors, Eric Wilson, a waiter, described what happened: "There was a massive jolt. The boat swivelled to the left and tipped sharply on its side. People were screaming and shouting: "Jump into the water!" I jumped. I saw the ship that hit us sailing away, a great dark hulk, something out of a horror movie."

The party was to celebrate the birthday of Antonio de Vasconcellos, an extrovert figure with fashionable friends in photography, modelling and the City.

1989

SEPTEMBER

Su	Mo	Tu	We	Th	Fr	Sa
					1	2
3	4	5	6	7	8	9
10	11	12	13	14	15	16
17	18	19	20	21	22	23
24	25	26	27	28	29	30

1. US: Bush cuts relations with Panama after Francisco Rodriguez, a Noriega puppet, is made President (→5/10).

4. East Germany: Police break up a demonstration by people seeking free emigration to the West.

4. UK: Hundreds of children are sent home from school owing to a lack of teachers.

7. West Germany: Heidi Hazell, a British soldier's wife, is shot dead in Dortmund in an IRA "mistake".→

10. Hong Kong: Cholera causes 4,400 Vietnamese boat people to be moved from Tai Ah Chau Island (→13/12).

10. Danube: Up to 162 people drown in a collision between a pleasure cruiser and a tug.

12. Poland: The first cabinet for 40 years not dominated by Communists is elected.

12. Namibia: Anton Lubowski, a senior white official of Swapo, is killed.

13. S. Africa: Cape Town sees the biggest anti-apartheid march for 30 years (→15/10).

13. UK: 19,000 ambulance staff ban overtime in a pay dispute (→23/10).

17. UK: A new newspaper, the "Sunday Correspondent," makes its debut.

20. Scotland: 300,000 people in Strathclyde have defaulted on the poll tax (→9/2/90).

22. Lebanon: The Christian leader General Michel Aoun abandons his "war of liberation" against Syria.

27. UK: David Owen admits that his party, the Social Democrats, is no longer a national force (→3/6/90).

28. Greece: Andreas Papandreou, the former premier, is committed for trial on charges relating to bank fraud.

DEATHS

4. Belgian novelist Georges Simenon (*13/2/1903).

22. US songwriter Irving Berlin (*11/5/1888).

28. Former Philippines leader Ferdinand Marcos (*11/9/1917).

Deal bomb kills ten Marine bandsmen

Sept 22. Early morning practice at the Royal Marines' School of Music was almost over. It was 8.26am. "I heard music playing and then it went bang and there was glass everywhere," said one witness after an IRA bomb ripped through the barracks in Deal, Kent, killing ten bandsmen and injuring 22. As marines clawed through the rubble to reach trapped survivors, recriminations began over poor security at the school – provided by a private firm, it has been called "pathetic".

Tom King, the Defence Secretary, has promised a full review of the security arrangements and assured the "godfathers of Northern Ireland" that the fight against terrorism would go on (→26/10).

Runcie under fire over visit to pope

Sept 30. Pope John Paul II and Dr Robert Runcie, the Archbishop of Canterbury, attended vespers together today at Rome's church of San Gregorio. But Runcie's historic visit is running into problems. His offer to recognise the "universal primacy" of the pope has angered many Protestants. He insists that he means "spiritual", not political, primacy, but this does not satisfy those for whom Rome is a spiritual enemy. At home Dr Runcie is at the centre of a political row over an attack he made on Britain's "Pharisees", who disparage the poor, the unsuccessful and the unemployed.

Dr Runcie and Pope John Paul II.

American coast hit by Hurricane Hugo

Sept 21. The weather satellites saw it first: a swirling mass of disturbed air and sea in the Atlantic, moving ominously at a steady 25mph, gaining strength and threatening the Caribbean. The weathermen dubbed it Hugo and issued urgent warnings of the most dangerous hurricane for a decade.

In Puerto Rico and the Virgin Islands, 25 were killed, hundreds injured and 100,000 made homeless within hours. Some 12,000 people lost their homes on Montserrat. Last night, Hugo hit the American mainland, lashing the coasts of South Carolina and Georgia. But with shops boarded up, schools closed and 100,000 people evacuated, the nation was prepared.

Bush gives billions to anti-drugs war

Sept 5. In his first TV address to the nation, President Bush announced a plan worth $7.86 billion to halve drug use in the US by the year 2000. "Drugs are sapping our strength as a nation," he said. "Our most serious problem today is cocaine and, in particular, crack." States will impose harsher penalties for drug use. The US will give £200 million in aid to drug-exporting countries such as Colombia, Bolivia and Peru. Money will also be spent on more prisons and more police to control the $110 billion drug trade.

Sept 24. Europe, led by Tony Jacklin (above), draw with the US to retain golf's Ryder Cup.

Hungary opens refugee floodgates

Sept 11. The Hungarians today opened their border with Austria, enabling an estimated 60,000 East Germans – ostensibly "holidaying" in Budapest – to reach West Germany. The action follows a previous decision to relax border controls and allow a batch of 20,000 East Germans through.

After weeks of talks with Bonn and East Berlin, Hungary made the move unilaterally, at a time of high tension in East German domestic politics. Last week police in Leipzig broke up demonstrations demanding economic and political reforms, including the right of free passage to the West.

East Germans in Hungary greeted the news with cheers and clapping, followed by feverish packing. But the East German news media have accused West Germany of conducting a provocative campaign to lure the fugitives to the West, and smeared Budapest with the taint of Judas for accepting "pieces of silver" from Bonn in return for allowing them to leave (→1/10).

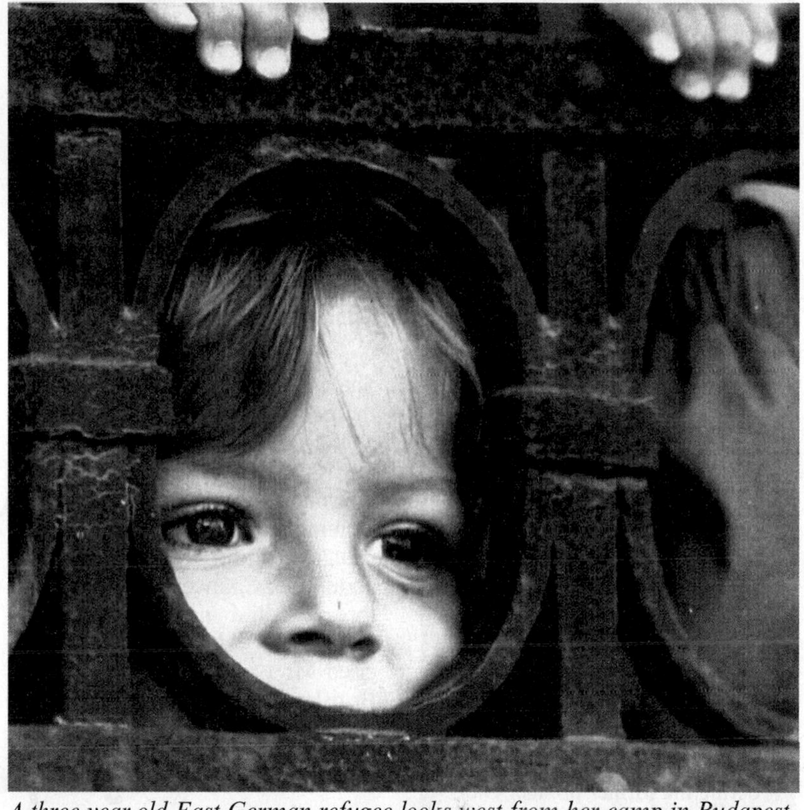

A three-year-old East German refugee looks west from her camp in Budapest.

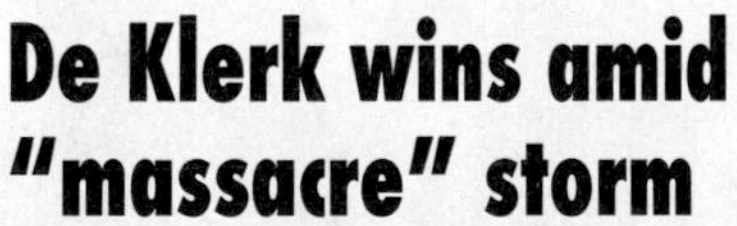

De Klerk wins amid "massacre" storm

Sept 7. South Africa's ruling National Party today marked its 11th consecutive election victory, amid allegations that police last night killed 23 people in areas near Cape Town. Anti-apartheid leaders said that the "massacre" followed protests by black and "coloured" (mixed-race) youths against the exclusion of most South Africans from the whites-only poll. Police – who have used clubs, water cannon and whips against demonstrators during several weeks of organised protest in the run-up to the election – deny the charges. On election day an estimated three million black workers staged strikes in the country's major cities.

F.W. de Klerk, who in February replaced P.W. Botha as the National Party leader, won 93 of the 166 seats in parliament. He thus still has a comfortable majority, despite losing 13 seats to the anti-apartheid Democratic Party (33 seats) and 17 to the pro-apartheid Conservative Party (39 seats) (→13).

Vietnamese leave Cambodia to its fate

Sept 26. The last Vietnamese troops in Cambodia headed home today, ending Hanoi's 11-year occupation of the country.

It was in 1978 that Vietnam drove out the Khmer Rouge regime of Pol Pot and installed a government which the West, despite its revulsion at Pol Pot's mass murders, has never recognised. Hanoi wants its withdrawal to lead to internationally supervised talks between the government and its opponents, including the ex-ruler Prince Sihanouk and the Khmer Rouge. The alternative – a civil war which could return Pol Pot to power – terrifies Cambodians.

The Vietnamese say farewell to Cambodia after over a decade of occupation.

1989

OCTOBER

Su	Mo	Tu	We	Th	Fr	Sa
1	2	3	4	5	6	7
8	9	10	11	12	13	14
15	16	17	18	19	20	21
22	23	24	25	26	27	28
29	30	31				

1. West Germany: About 7,000 East Germans arrive on special trains from various East European countries.→

5. Panama: An attempt to oust Noriega fails (→21/12).

6. UK: Interest rates go up to 15 per cent (→26/1/90).

7. Hungary: The Communist leaders vote to become Social Democrats.→

8. Belfast: Twenty-eight UDR members are held in an inquiry into leaks about Republican suspects.

11. Poland: England draw 0-0 with Poland to reach the 1990 World Cup football finals.

12. London: The remains of Shakespeare's Globe theatre are found on Bankside.

12. Sweden: The conviction of Christer Pettersson for murdering the former premier Olof Palme is overturned on appeal.

14. New York: Wall Street shares suffer their second biggest fall on record.

15. S. Africa: Eight jailed nationalists, including Walter Sisulu, are freed (→8/1/90).

15. UK: The Government says that it will impose new contracts on GPs (→7/6/90).

17. Lausanne: A 103-nation conference votes for a global ban on trading in ivory.

19. UK: The £600,000 damages award to Sonia Sutcliffe against "Private Eye" is overturned on appeal.

23. Kuala Lumpur: Thatcher is alone among Commonwealth leaders in opposing sanctions against South Africa.

26. West Germany: The IRA kills an RAF corporal and his young child (→16/5/90).

30. Spain: The Socialists, led by Felipe Gonzalez, secure their third election victory.

31. UK: British Rail puts off plans for a new rail link to the Channel Tunnel (→1/12/90).

DEATHS

6. US film actress Bette Davis (*5/4/1908).

20. British actor Sir Anthony Quayle (*7/9/1913).

Lawson resigns in day of high drama

Principal players: (l. to r.) Nigel Lawson, the ex-Chancellor; Alan Walters, the Prime Minister's guru; John Major, Foreign Secretary, now Chancellor.

Oct 26. Nigel Lawson, the Chancellor of the Exchequer, resigned tonight. The British government is plunged into its greatest agony and turmoil of the Thatcher years.

A day of high drama began with a bitter breakfast-time row between the Prime Minister and Mr Lawson. He said that his position was untenable. It had been undermined by constant public sniping from Mrs Thatcher's personal economic adviser, Professor Sir Alan Walters. She must promise to sack him by the end of the year or Mr Lawson would quit now. The Prime Minister asked him to reconsider. In the afternoon she answered teasing Commons questions about Sir Alan's position. She said nothing about the Chancellor's resignation threat – and nothing about disowning Sir Alan for having criticised Mr Lawson's backing for full British membership of the European Monetary System. Lawson was livid. He stormed into 10 Downing Street, his resignation letter in his hand, as soon as Mrs Thatcher returned from the House.

The letter said: "Successful conduct of economic policy is possible only if there is full agreement between the Prime Minister and the Chancellor of the Exchequer." Tonight Mrs Thatcher named John Major, her recently-appointed Foreign Secretary, to succeed Mr Lawson, and moved Douglas Hurd from the Home Office to the Foreign Office. Tories asked if the Government was falling apart, and the odds shortened against Mrs Thatcher facing a challenge for the leadership this winter (→23/11).

State of emergency declared as quake shatters San Francisco

A house lists like a sinking ship and ruins smoulder in San Francisco.

Oct 19. The quake that San Francisco's seismologists and seers have been predicting with irrepressible regularity finally erupted today, killing an estimated 273 people and doing $1 billion-worth of damage. It was 5.04pm local time when the earthquake, measuring 6.9 on the Richter scale, struck. Homes and offices were wrecked, fires broke out and vital services were cut off. Most of the deaths came when a half-mile part of the double-decker Interstate 880 highway collapsed, crushing vehicles on the lower deck. The last major earthquake here was in 1906, when 2,000 people died in a tremor measuring 8.3 on the scale. Experts warn that another "Big One" is yet to come.

British woman's death in Kenya was the result of "foul play"

Oct 27. An inquest into the death of Julie Ward, the British woman whose charred remains were found last year in a Kenyan game park, has concluded that the 28-year-old was the victim of "foul play". She was not, as the Kenyan police maintained, killed by wild animals. "Those sharp cuts described by the pathologist were man-made," said the chief magistrate, dismissing the theory that Miss Ward abandoned the Suzuki vehicle in which she was travelling alone in the Masai Mara park, lit a fire and was knocked into it during a struggle with an animal.

Suspicious actions by park wardens and police failure to investigate evidence were highlighted at the inquest. To get to where she was found, Miss Ward would have had to walk six miles through rocky bush, crossing a road. The ashes of the fire containing her remains bore traces of a petrol-like substance. There was no blood at the scene.

John Ward, Julie's father, who has spent many thousands of pounds pursuing the case, said he had got the verdict required.

East German crisis forces out Honecker

On their way to a new life: East German refugees set out for the West.

Oct 18. Erich Honecker, the leader of East Germany for 18 years, was ousted today by his own Communist Party, which is confronting its greatest crisis since it took power 40 years ago. He is succeeded by Egon Krenz, aged 52, who also has a reputation as a hardliner.

Honecker has paid the price for repudiating reforms in the face of a mounting tide of protest and a continuing haemorrhage of East Germans to the West. President Gorbachev, on a visit to East Berlin ten days ago for East Germany's 40th anniversary, advised him to heed the "impulses" of the times.

For East Germany those "impulses" began in May, when Hungary took down part of the "Iron Curtain" along the Austrian border. During the summer thousands of East Germans headed for Hungary in the hope of crossing the frontier into Austria and then to West Germany. The flow became a flood last month when Budapest officially sanctioned their departure.

Hundreds more East Germans have been cramming into the West German embassy in Prague, and the exodus – 100,000 may have left already – has triggered huge demonstrations in East Germany itself, with protesters calling for freedom of travel and political reforms. Krenz – the man sent to congratulate China's leaders for how they handled the pro-democracy movement – has a hard task (→4/11).

Oct 5. The Nobel Peace Prize is awarded to the Dalai Lama, the exiled spiritual leader of Tibet.

Police take over in ambulance dispute

Oct 23. Seven million Londoners are facing life without a regular ambulance service. From today, their emergency calls are being answered by the police, who lack both skill and equipment, backed up by Red Cross and St. John Ambulance teams. Ambulance crews began a work-to-rule at 7am in support of their current pay claim. Management promptly stopped their pay and declared the crews "off-duty", but ambulance staff say that they will answer emergencies whether they are paid are not. Both sides are calling for talks, before the dispute leads to loss of life (→8/11).

Hungarians declare birth of new republic

Oct 23. Over 60,000 people gathered outside the Budapest parliament building today to hear the acting President, Matyas Szuros, proclaim the birth of a new Hungarian republic. On the 33rd anniversary of the 1956 Hungarian uprising against Soviet rule, the country has finally turned its back on Marx and Lenin.

Thousands rally outside parliament.

In the last few weeks, Hungarian politicians have approved a series of radical changes to the constitution. The ruling Communist Party changed its name to the Socialist Party and promised free elections – the first since 1947 – for next year; MPs introduced the secret ballot; Soviet-style trappings of the Communist state, such as workers' militias, are to be dissolved. Now both Parliament and President are to be elected by the people. Previously-banned opposition groups, such as the New Democrats and the Democratic Forum, have hardened into political parties and assembling candidates. But, for the moment, veteran leaders such as Miklos Nemeth, Rezso Nyers and Imre Poszgay are carrying the torch of reform (→23/1/90).

Guildford Four are freed after 14 years

Gerard Conlon responds to an ecstatic crowd just minutes after his release.

Oct 20. The appeal court took half an hour yesterday to overturn the convictions of four alleged terrorists found guilty of pub bombings in 1975. The convictions of the Guildford Four had been based on police lies and fabricated confessions. Gerard Conlon, aged 35, Carole Richardson, aged 32, and Patrick Armstrong, aged 39, were freed at once, after serving 14 years for a crime that they did not commit. Paul Hill, aged 35, was released today. A judicial inquiry has been ordered into the case. Allegations that senior detectives had tampered with, and even concocted, confessions came to light in May, during inquiries by the Avon and Somerset police. The court's decision also has implications for members of the Maguire family, relations of Conlon convicted after he apparently named them as bomb-makers.

1989

NOVEMBER

Su	Mo	Tu	We	Th	Fr	Sa
			1	2	3	4
5	6	7	8	9	10	11
12	13	14	15	16	17	18
19	20	21	22	23	24	25
26	27	28	29	30		

1. Pakistan: Benazir Bhutto, the premier, narrowly survives a no-confidence vote.

3. UK: Peter Brooke, the Northern Ireland Secretary, hints at talks with Sinn Fein.

4. East Germany: Spreading dissent across the country culminates in a million-strong protest in East Berlin (→7).

6. New York: David Dinkins is elected as the city's first black mayor.

7. East Germany: The entire cabinet resigns (→8).

8. East Germany: A new politburo is appointed; Hans Modrow, a liberal reformer, becomes Prime Minister.→

12. Berlin: Over a million East Berliners visit the West after more crossing points are opened in the Wall (→22/12).

17. Prague: Police beat up and detain hundreds at the biggest protest rally for 20 years.→

18. Paris: European Community heads agree urgent aid packages for Eastern Europe.

20. Brussels: The European Commission modifies plans for a Social Charter for workers' rights (→9/12).

21. UK: Proceedings in the House of Commons are televised for the first time.

21. UK: Ambulance crews start a ban on all but accidents and emergencies (→13/1/90).

25. Hong Kong: Deportation threats spark riots among Vietnamese boat people (→13/12).

25. Lebanon: Elias Hrawi is sworn in as President.

27. Czechoslovakia: A strike turns into an anti-Communist celebration (→7/12).

30. West Germany: A terrorist bomb kills Alfred Herrhausen, the head of Deutsche Bank.

DEATHS

5. Russian-born pianist Vladimir Horowitz (*1/10/1904).

12. Spanish republican heroine Dolores Ibarruri, known as "La Pasionaria" (*1896).

22. Lebanese President Rene Moawad (*1925).→

Troops man ambulances as dispute grows

An Army ambulance crew delivers an elderly patient to a London hospital.

Nov 8. Army and RAF ambulances are out on the streets of London tonight in the latest twist to the ambulance workers' dispute. The decision to send in troops follows yesterday's suspension of London's 2,500 crew members, who are working to rule in a national campaign for better pay and conditions. Kenneth Clarke, the Health Secretary, said yesterday that he had reluctantly called in the military because ambulance crews could not guarantee emergency cover. But the ambulance men's negotiator Roger Poole insisted that his members, who remain at their posts despite the suspensions, will "maintain accident and emergency cover if they are allowed to do so" (→21).

"Sir Nobody" runs for Tory leadership

Nov 23. Mrs Thatcher is to face her first challenge to the Tory Party leadership since she ousted Edward Heath 14 years ago. The contest will be forced by Sir Anthony Meyer, a backbencher of liberal views. He says he is ready to withdraw in favour of a better-qualified candidate, but so far appears undeterred by either the derision of the tabloid press ("Sir Nobody") or pleas for party loyalty. Only Tory MPs can vote for the leader. While no one doubts that Mrs Thatcher will win, the number of votes against, and abstentions, will reflect her hold on the party (→5/12).

Sir Anthony and his wife, Barbadee.

Plans for nuclear power sale ditched

Nov 9. The British nuclear power industry was dealt a major blow today by a Government statement that nuclear power stations will not now be sold off to private investors along with the rest of the electricity industry. Plans for the development of pressurised water reactors have also been shelved, following predictions that nuclear power will cost at least three times as much as fossil-fuel electricity. The announcement marks a U-turn in Government policy and is widely seen as an attempt to save the electricity privatisation programme from collapse.

Gandhi faces big loss in Indian poll

Nov 27. The supremacy of the dynasty which has ruled India for most of its 42 years of independence is under threat tonight as Rajiv Gandhi, the Prime Minister, faces defeat in the general election which ended last Sunday. Gandhi's Congress Party is likely to win about 200 of the 545 seats in the Lok Sabha, India's lower house, compared with the 415 seats it won five years ago. This will leave Congress 70 seats short of an absolute majority. A minority government could be formed by an opposition coalition led by Janata Dal, which held power from 1977 to 1980 (→2/12).

Irish and Scots reach World Cup finals

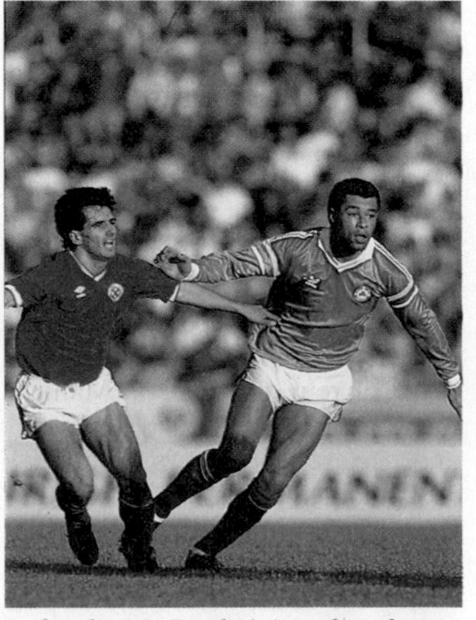

Ireland's McGrath (r.) in fine form.

Nov 15. Sales of the stuff which is good for you soared in Dublin last night, and drams aplenty flowed in Edinburgh. The reason? Ireland and Scotland have won their way to the World Cup finals to be held in Italy next year. Ireland, who have been trying to qualify for 55 years, beat Malta 2-0 in Valletta last night, with John Aldridge scoring both goals. Meanwhile at Hampden Park the Scots, needing only one point to qualify, battled it out with Norway. Scotland led 1-0 from half-time with a goal by Ally McCoist. But a powerful 40-yard equaliser from Norway's Johnsen had the 60,000 crowd praying for the final whistle.

The Berlin Wall becomes a gateway to the West

Excited crowds of Germans from both East and West celebrate the symbolic destruction of the world's most notorious monument to repression.

Nov 10. The 28-mile-long scar cutting across central Berlin – the ugliest symbol of a divided world – has no meaning any more. Few thought to see it happen in their lifetimes, but last night, at the stroke of midnight, thousands lining both sides of the Berlin Wall gave a great roar and began to pour through checkpoints and to climb up and over it. They danced and trumpeted on the top. They hacked at the loathed monument to repression, loosening chunks of masonry. "I'm no longer in prison!" one young man shouted. They crowded onto the West Berlin streets, spraying champagne and sounding car horns until long past dawn.

It all began quietly. With mass protests and the flight of refugees continuing unabated – and Egon Krenz, the new East German leader, intent on showing sincerity about reform – Gunter Schabowski, the East Berlin party boss, yesterday held a press conference. He declared that, starting from midnight, East Germans would be free to leave the country, without special permission, at any point along the border, including the crossing-points through the Wall in Berlin. The news travelled quickly through both parts of the divided city; at Checkpoint Charlie in West Berlin a crowd formed early, taunting East German border guards with cries of "Open the gate!". When midnight struck, the first East Berliners came through.

Today East German bulldozers moved in to open new crossing-points for the hundreds of thousands of East Berliners who have swarmed to the West for their first taste of freedom for 28 years.

The Berlin Wall rose in August 1961 after East Germany sealed off the border between East and West Berlin to stem a growing tide of refugees. In the six weeks before a six-foot-high concrete barrier topped with barbed wire was erected in the Potsdamer Platz, over 45,000 had crossed into West Berlin – adding to the more than two and a half million who had fled since 1949. At least 75 people have since met often violent deaths while trying to escape over the Wall.

This morning, standing at the spot where, in 1963, President John F. Kennedy declared: "*Ich bin ein Berliner*", the Mayor of West Berlin, Walter Momper, said: "The Germans are the happiest people in the world today" (→12).

Hopes and fears rise from broken Wall

Many world leaders expressed delight at the opening of the Wall. Some, such as George Bush, were "elated". In London, Margaret Thatcher heralded the news as "a great day for freedom", and Francois Mitterrand talked of "these happy events". The West German Chancellor, Helmut Kohl, was clearly concerned that his country would be swamped by newcomers: "Our interest must be that the East Germans stay at home." The USSR praised the move as "symbolic" but warned the Bonn government against changing its borders. The threat to the existing balance of the European Community was in many minds – as was the spectre of a reunified Germany.

Prague in ecstasy as leadership quits

Nov 24. Czechs and Slovaks – massed in their tens of thousands to salute the return to Prague of Alexander Dubcek – erupted in joy tonight at the news that Milos Jakes, the Communist Party boss, and the entire ruling Politburo had quit. Crowds streamed through the city chanting "Dubcek! Dubcek!" and the name of the playwright Vaclav Havel, the leading opposition figure in Czechoslovakia.

The announcement of the resignations followed a special meeting of the Communist Party central committee. Jakes, a hardliner, is replaced by Karol Urbanek, the party leader of the Czech republic, who has no link with the 1968 Soviet-led invasion of the country.

Even before the changes became known, it was clear that support for the government had collapsed. The marches that began just a week ago have mushroomed into a huge popular movement affecting many cities, although centred on the capital. The crowds thronging Wenceslas Square have grown daily, as determination mounted to oust the repressive Communist leadership. Addressing a crowd of 200,000 tonight, Dubcek – who has emerged from 20 years' obscurity, which began after the crushing of his 1968 "Prague Spring" – declared: "We have been too long in darkness. Once already we have been in the light, and we want it again" (→27).

Joy sweeps Prague's Wenceslas Square as the news of the resignations breaks.

Alexander Dubcek and Vaclav Havel join to toast "a free Czechoslovakia!".

Nov 22. Lebanese women express their grief at the assassination of Rene Moawad, President for under three weeks. Moawad and 23 others were killed by a massive bomb hidden in a shop window. His death is seen as one of the worst disasters in Lebanon's recent bloody history (→25).

Death toll mounts in El Salvador war

Nov 16. Over 650 people have died in six days of fighting between left-wing rebels and government troops, in the worst outbreak of violence since El Salvador's civil war began ten years ago.

The suddenness and intensity of the guerrilla attacks have shocked the government, which is using helicopter gunships against the rebels. Many civilians have died in the crossfire, and brutal death squads are active. Early this morning a right-wing death squad entered a university in the capital, San Salvador, and murdered six Jesuit priests together with their cook and her 15-year-old daughter.

Bulgaria sees vast democracy march

Nov 18. In the largest political demonstration seen in Bulgaria since the war, 100,000 people rallied today in the heart of the capital, Sofia. Not satisfied by the reforms introduced since the ousting of Todor Zhivkov, their leader for 35 years, they were demanding free elections, a new constitution and the sacking of the remaining hardliners in the Politburo. Zhivkov, aged 78 – the longest-serving Communist boss in Eastern Europe – was replaced a week ago by the foreign minister, Petar Mladenov. With his departure the Iron Curtain opened a little wider (→16/12).

Olympic gymnast flees from Rumania

Nov 29. The top Rumanian gymnast Nadia Comaneci, who won the hearts of millions in 1976, somersaulting from one gold medal to the next at the Montreal Olympics, crossed the border into Hungary last night and asked for political asylum. She is now reported to be heading for Austria. By the time she retired in 1984, Comaneci had won 21 gold medals. Her defection is an embarrassment to Rumania's hardline President, Nicolae Ceausescu, who received her personally after her successes (→31/12).

Peer awarded £1.5 million in libel case

Nov 30. A £1.5 million libel award – almost three times the previous record – was today made to Lord Aldington, a 75-year-old former deputy chairman of the Tory Party.

The defendants, Nigel Watts and Count Nikolai Tolstoy, had circulated a pamphlet to MPs, peers and Lord Aldington's neighbours describing him as a man with "the blood of 70,000 men, women and children on his hands" for ordering the repatriation of Yugoslavs and Cossacks after the war, knowing that it would result in their deaths.

Both defendants, who plan to appeal, face financial ruin as a result of the award.

1989

DECEMBER

Su	Mo	Tu	We	Th	Fr	Sa
					1	2
3	4	5	6	7	8	9
10	11	12	13	14	15	16
17	18	19	20	21	22	23
24	25	26	27	28	29	30
31						

2. India: V.P. Singh of Janata Dal becomes Prime Minister.

5. UK: Thatcher beats Meyer in the Tory leadership poll; 60 Tory MPs did not vote for her.

6. East Germany: Egon Krenz is ousted as head of state.→

7. Philippines: Rebel troops end a bid to topple Aquino.

7. Montreal: Fourteen women students are massacred.

7. Czechoslovakia: Marian Calfa replaces Ladislas Adamec as premier (→10).

9. UK: The sale of shares in the water industry is 5.7 times over-subscribed.

10. Stockholm: Nobel Prizes are presented to Norman Ramsay (US), Hans Dehmelt (US) and Wolfgang Paul (West Germany), all Physics; Sidney Altman and Thomas Cech (US, Chemistry); Michael Bishop and Harold Varmus (US, Medicine); Camilo Jose Cela (Spain, Literature); Trygve Haavelmo (Norway, Economics); and in Oslo to the Dalai Lama (Peace).

10. Czechoslovakia: Gustav Husak resigns as President after swearing in a majority non-Communist government.→

14. Chile: Patricio Aylwin is elected President.

24. Panama: Manuel Noriega takes refuge in the papal nunciature (→4/1/90).

28. Australia: The country's first fatal earthquake kills 11.

DEATHS

14. Soviet physicist Andrei Sakharov (*21/5/1921).→

22. Irish writer Samuel Beckett (*13/4/1906).→

25. Rumanian leader Nicolae Ceausescu (*26/1/1918).→

HITS OF 1989

Ride on Time.

Swing the Mood.

Too Many Broken Hearts.

QUOTE OF THE YEAR

"We have become a grandmother."

Margaret Thatcher.

Superpowers declare end of Cold War

Dec 3. At the end of their shipboard summit off Malta – transformed into near-farce by tempestuous weather – Mikhail Gorbachev and George Bush hailed the start of a new era in superpower relations. They envisaged wide new arms cuts and a chance for Moscow to play a full role in the world economy. According to the Soviet spokesman, Gennady Gerasimov, the Cold War ended at 12.45pm today (11.45am British time). Later, Bush gave the thumbs-up sign to a reporter who asked if he agreed.

After a stormy but amicable summit, Bush and Gorbachev speak to the press.

The US and Soviet leaders detailed plans to sign two arms control pacts in June next year. One would halve strategic nuclear weapons; the other would reduce conventional forces in Europe. There is also hope for agreement on chemical weapon destruction. They remained split on naval forces and the Soviet supply of arms to Nicaragua. Bush pledged to end curbs on US-Soviet trade once the USSR opened its borders. He also proposed observer status for Moscow in the General Agreement on Tariffs and Trade (Gatt), the body that regulates international trade. Although Eastern European issues pervaded the talks, the leaders strove to avoid public comment that could be interpreted as outside interference. On his way to Malta, Gorbachev had the first ever meeting between a Soviet Communist leader and a pope (→3/6/90).

Vietnamese boat people are sent home

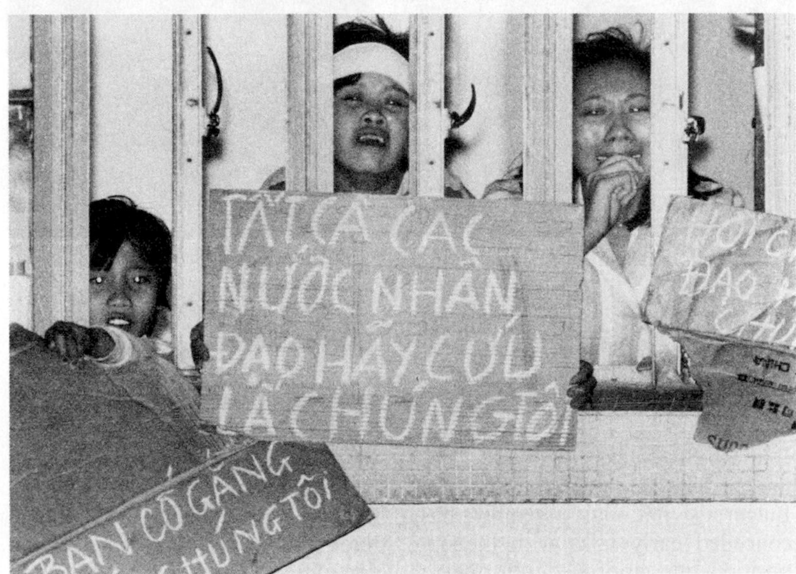

Tears of misery and fear from Vietnamese boat people about to be deported.

Dec 13. At dawn yesterday a Cathay Pacific jet carrying 51 Vietnamese boat people landed at Hanoi airport. The 25 adults and 26 children on board were the first to be returned from the British colony of Hong Kong under a mandatory repatriation scheme for Vietnamese not considered to be real refugees.

The Hong Kong government insisted that no force was used, but the clandestine, early-morning deportation by 150 police in full riot gear has sparked opposition fury in Britain and an international outcry. Although the operation has now been temporarily suspended, Hong Kong said it planned eventually to send home 44,000 Vietnamese. Today 6,000 boat people in camps in Hong Kong held peaceful protests against the repatriation.

Tory MPs split over Hong Kong policy

Dec 22. Government proposals to admit up to 225,000 Hong Kong citizens to Britain were today attacked by Norman Tebbit, a former Tory minister, who believes that as many as 50 Tory MPs will vote against the "vast wave of immigrants". This could scupper the government's majority, as Labour also opposes the plan, which embraces only professional and business figures. Douglas Hurd, the Foreign Secretary, says the move is to "anchor" key people in Hong Kong until 1997, when China takes control of the colony (→4/4/90).

Flu forces red alert

Dec 11. So many have fallen victim to Britain's worst flu epidemic for 14 years that 20 health authorities have declared "red alerts", cancelling all routine hospital admissions. The number of medical staff ill with the virus has added to pressure on beds. The estimate of those infected is up 24 per cent on last week, but vaccine is so scarce that only the sick and elderly are getting it. ▷

Death throes of Communist rule rock Eastern bloc

Ceausescu executed by a firing squad

Dec 31. Church bells in Rumania are tonight ringing out an old year unimaginable two weeks ago. Out went the dictator Nicolae Ceausescu and his wife Elena: executed on Christmas Day by firing squad after being found guilty by an army tribunal of "crimes against the people", including genocide leading to an alleged 60,000 deaths. Out went the hated Securitate secret police: defeated by the Rumanian army – whose support for protesters was crucial – after a week of bloody street-fighting. Out went the Communist Party: abolished yesterday as the ruling National Salvation Front planned free elections.

Civil war erupted in Rumania ten days ago, ending Ceausescu's 24 years of tyrannical rule and causing the President and his wife to flee their burning palace in Bucharest by helicopter – only to be swiftly recaptured. What had begun on 16 December as a small protest in Timisoara had toppled the most dictatorial regime in Eastern Europe. The final death toll is not known, but a grave containing 4,630 bodies has been found in Timisoara and, apart from the fighting in Bucharest, there has been bloodshed in other cities (→ 1/1/90).

Securitate forces still loyal to Ceausescu fire on army tanks in Bucharest.

The dictator executed: as shown on television screens around the world.

Wall breached at Brandenburg Gate

Dec 22. To the cheers of tens of thousands on each side, the leaders of East and West Germany opened the Berlin Wall at the Brandenburg Gate today. Helmut Kohl walked through a gap made during the night, to become the first West German Chancellor to set foot in East Berlin. He was greeted by the East German Prime Minister, Hans Modrow, and the two walked side by side through the central arch of the 200-year-old monument. Built in celebration of Prussian power, the Brandenburg Gate, topped by a bronze statue of horses pulling a chariot, symbolised German unity until Hitler's defeat in World War II. It subsequently became the most potent reminder of the Cold War division of Europe.

"The burning stench of war must never again be smelt here," said Mr Modrow, who went on to hail the downfall of Nicolae Ceausescu in Rumania. Mr Kohl avoided any provocative reference to the possible reunification of Germany. Three days earlier Modrow and Kohl agreed in Dresden to cooperate to save East Germany's shaky economy and establish a "community of treaties" between the two German states (→ 9/3/90).

Playwright Havel is to be Czech leader

Dec 29. The playwright Vaclav Havel – a leading figure in his country's recent transformation – took office today as Czechoslovakia's new President. "I shall not fail your trust," he told crowds in Prague, "and I shall lead this country to free elections." The installation of the first non-Communist head of state for over 40 years represents the greatest triumph of Czechoslovakia's democratic revolution. It follows the election yesterday of Alexander Dubcek, the architect of the 1968 Prague Spring, as chairman of the federal assembly, which remains Communist-dominated (→ 5/7/90).

Sofia signals end of Communist power

Dec 16. Six weeks after the fall of the hardline leader Todor Zhivkov, Bulgaria's national assembly has conceded early talks with the opposition and approved reforms to abolish the political monopoly of the Communist Party in the new year. It has also agreed to liberalise laws on public gatherings, amend the penal code and grant an amnesty. Today's moves bring the country into line with other reforming states in Eastern Europe. They come in the wake of mounting popular demonstrations for change, which culminated yesterday in a siege of the parliament building in Sofia by 50,000 marchers (→ 1/2/90).

Gorbachev makes shock offer to quit

Dec 13. Mikhail Gorbachev threatened to resign during a fierce row at last weekend's plenary meeting of the Communist Party's central committee, it was claimed in Moscow today. Regional party chiefs led an attack on the Soviet leader, according to an article in today's Moscow News. They fear that the pace of reform is too fast, and some accuse him of selling out to the West. Ironically, this week Gorbachev also faces demands from progressives for an end to one-party rule. So far he has fended off both attacks, but regional unrest and economic woes still threaten his grip on power (→ 22/1/90).

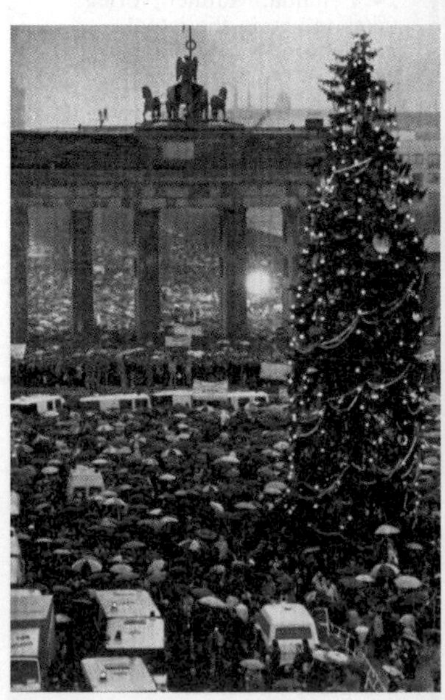
In time for Christmas: Berlin's Brandenburg Gate is thrown open.

US troops oust Noriega

America's quarry: Manuel Noriega.

Dec 21. American troops have invaded Panama, ousted the dictator Manuel Noriega and installed a new government headed by Guillermo Endara. Panama City is a battleground, with the Americans claiming almost total control. Some 200 civilians, 19 Americans and 59 Panamanian soldiers are believed to have died in the fighting. Yesterday President Bush said that a series of attacks by Noriega's paramilitary "dignity battalions", culminating in the murder of an American soldier, triggered his decision to order the invasion. "General Noriega's reckless threats and attacks ... created an imminent danger to Americans in Panama," he said. So far, he has been supported by Congress and US public opinion.

The US Army swept through the streets of Panama City today, mopping up pockets of resistance and continuing the search for Noriega. President Bush wants him to stand trial in the US on drug-trafficking charges and has offered a $1 million (£660,000) reward for information leading to his capture.

The failure to net Noriega is proving embarrassing. It is thought that he is still in Panama City, possibly in the Cuban or Nicaraguan embassy. If he is not found soon, the US faces the prospect of a prolonged urban guerrilla war. With up to 12 US citizens believed held hostage, the struggle is far from over (→24).

Thatcher makes lone stand at Strasbourg

Dec 9. Margaret Thatcher brushed aside the claim that Britain was isolated at the European Community summit in Strasbourg today as "absolute nonsense". The charge came after EC leaders voted by 11-1, with Britain against, to hold talks next year about changes to the Treaty of Rome for economic and monetary union. By the same margin, they approved the Community Social Charter guaranteeing basic workers' rights. Mrs Thatcher insisted that Britain would play a full role in the Community despite differences on a number of issues.

Agreement was reached, however, on a formula for West German reunification, which accepted the right of the German people to "regain unity through free self-determination". It was also agreed to set up a Bank of Europe to help Eastern Europe (→20/6/90).

Sakharov, symbol of the Soviet soul, dies

Dec 14. Andrei Sakharov, the 68-year-old Soviet nuclear physicist and radical, died tonight at his home in Moscow. When his wife, Yelena Bonner, went to wake him from a nap at 10.30pm she found him dead on the floor of his study after a heart attack.

Since 1975, when he won the Nobel Peace Prize, Sakharov's name has been associated around the world with the struggle for human rights. A top nuclear physicist, who was campaigning for a ban on nuclear testing as early as 1955, he was reduced as a dissident to a lowly academic job. In 1980 he was sent into internal exile in Gorky, where he lived until he was recalled to Moscow by Mikhail Gorbachev in 1986.

He was a firm believer in the multi-party system and was elected in 1989 to the Congress of the People's Deputies, emerging as the unofficial opposition spokesman.

Arts: some great names pass into legend

Emma Thompson and Kenneth Branagh in a new film version of "Henry V".

The performing arts lost some of their "greats" in 1989. Apart from **Lord Olivier** and **Anthony Quayle**, a King Lear of actor-managers, death claimed the entertainers **Tommy Trinder**, **Harry Worth**, **Harry Corbett** and, in the US, **Lucille Ball**, the first international star produced by TV. The year ended with the death of the Nobel prize-winning Irish writer **Samuel Beckett** – one of the greatest dramatist this century. The chief stage money-spinners were musicals: "Aspects of Love" and "Miss Saigon". There were some notable performances: **Ian McKellen's** evil Iago, **John Wood's** ravaged Prospero and Solness, **Judi Dench's** volatile Madame Ranevskaya, and even **Dustin Hoffman's** offbeat, if lightweight, Shylock.

Deaths also dominated music: **von Karajan**, succeeded at the Berlin Philharmonic by **Claudio Abbado**, the pianists **John Ogdon** and **Vladimir Horowitz** and the composer **Lennox Berkeley**. Ageing rockers such as **The Who** went on tour, but **Kylie Minogue** and **Jason Donovan** ruled the charts. Opera relied on special effects: **Michael Tippett's** near-rock opera "New Year" used saxophones, electric guitars and a spaceship. "Carmen" filled Earl's Court with a Spanish fiesta and **Maria Ewing**. **Luciano Pavarotti** filled the London Arena.

Literature lost the veterans **Georges Simenon** and **Daphne du Maurier**, and the gifted novelist and travel writer **Bruce Chatwin** at the age of 48. **Kazuo Ishiguro** won the Booker Prize for "The Remains of the Day".

Art saw the death of **Salvador Dali**, while London hosted four **Andy Warhol** retrospectives.

In a year of hyped films, topped by "Batman", the ubiquitous **Kenneth Branagh** bore comparison with Olivier as a Shakespeare film-maker with his "Henry V". "Rain-man", starring **Dustin Hoffman** and **Tom Cruise**, won four Oscars. The screen goddess **Bette Davis** died. **Peter Brook** filmed the Hindu epic "The Mahabharata" for cinema and television, but a bigger TV audience followed **Michael Palin** "Around the World in 80 Days" and later bought the book.

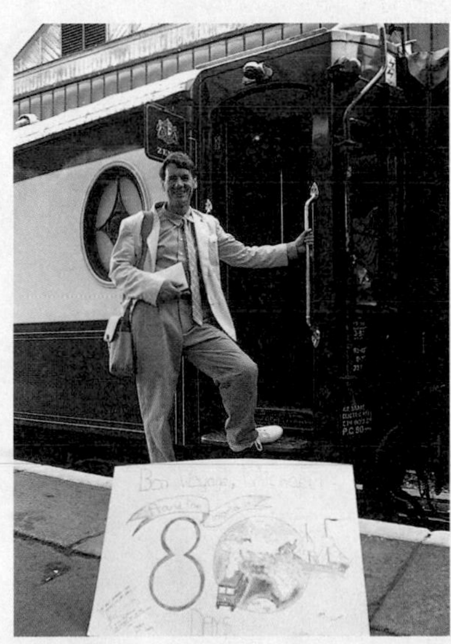

Michael Palin boards the train for his epic and hugely popular voyage.

1990 – 1999

1990

JANUARY

Su	Mo	Tu	We	Th	Fr	Sa
	1	2	3	4	5	6
7	8	9	10	11	12	13
14	15	16	17	18	19	20
21	22	23	24	25	26	27
28	29	30	31			

1. Rumania: The secret police are abolished (→28).

3. UK: Norman Fowler, the Employment Secretary, resigns from the Cabinet.

4. Miami: Manuel Noriega is charged with drug trafficking.

6. Iraq: The army displays new missiles with a 400-mile range (→2/4).

7. USSR: Soviet troops intervene in clashes between Georgians and Ossetians (→13).

8. S. Africa: Winnie Mandela says that the jailed ANC leader, Nelson Mandela, will be released soon (→2/2).

9. UK: The Government gives £2.2 million for research into bovine spongiform encephalopathy (BSE), known as "mad cow disease".

11. UK: By the end 1989, 1,612 people had died of AIDS (→8/3).

13. London: 50,000 rally to back ambulance workers (→30).

13. USSR: Over 25 people are killed in riots in Baku, the capital of Azerbaijan.→

15. East Berlin: A mob sacks the secret police headquarters.

19. Washington: Mayor Marion Barry is arrested on charges of using "crack" cocaine.

21. Kashmir: Thirty die as police fire on crowds calling for independence from India.

22. Yugoslavia: The Communists vote to abandon the one-party system (→23/12).

23. Hungary: The Red Army leaves Hungary after 45 years of occupation (→9/4).

26. UK: Britain's trade deficit for 1989 was a record £20.31 billion (→14/2).

25. UK: Gale-force winds kill 46 people and injure many more.

30. UK: Thousands strike for 15 minutes in support of the ambulance workers (→23/2).

DEATHS

21. American actress Barbara Stanwyck (*1907).

25. American actress Ava Gardner (*24/12/1922).

Gorbachev confronts growing unrest

Jan 22. President Mikhail Gorbachev set about re-establishing firm rule in Azerbaijan today as the republic buried its dead after a bloody takeover by the Soviet army. An estimated one million mourners attended the funerals of some 60 people who were killed when tanks smashed their way into the republic's capital, Baku, four days ago.

The army was ordered into the republic in an attempt to end the murderous undeclared war between the Azerbaijanis and the Armenians, and to put down a separatist insurrection by Azerbaijani nationalists. The tensions that had been building in Soviet Transcaucasia for months erupted at a nationalist rally. In the ensuing pogroms in Baku, Armenian homes were set on fire and looted, and scores of Armenians were killed or injured. In the disputed Azerbaijani region of Nagorny Karabakh, where Armenians are in the majority, roads were blocked and trains halted. Gorbachev also faces mounting unrest in the Baltic republic of Lithuania, where nationalists are agitating for outright independence. In a recent visit to Vilnius, the Lithuanian capital, the Soviet President warned that a break with Moscow could lead to tragedy, adding that his personal fate depended on the success of his reform policies in the republics (→7/2).

The Soviet leader explains his position to people on the streets of Vilnius.

Rebel cricketers face riots in South Africa

Protesters at a Cape Town rally.

Jan 30. More than 100 people were reported injured today after 24 hours of rioting had greeted 16 English cricketers in Bloemfontein. Violent protests have followed the cricketers, led by the former England captain Mike Gatting, ever since they arrived in Johannesburg 11 days ago in defiance of a ban on tours to segregated South Africa.

Matches have been played before all-white audiences while police fired tear-gas and rubber bullets to quell crowds. The rioting in Bloemfontein is said to have been South Africa's worst for four years. Mike Gatting has said he backs peaceful protests, but his attempts to keep sport and politics apart now seem doomed as well as naive.

Drug scandal hits Welsh weightlifters

Jan 31. Two Welsh weightlifters left Auckland in disgrace today after using performance-boosting drugs at the Commonwealth Games. Ricky Chaplin and Gareth Hives were stripped of their medals and banned for life after tests had detected the drugs.

The individual star of the games was Hayley Lewis, a 15-year-old Australian who won five gold medals for swimming – the best ever achieved by a woman in the history of the games. Australia headed the medals table, with England second. Linford Christie ran his fastest-ever 100 metres, and Peter Elliott won the 1,500 metres.

Rumanian opposition parties jostle to succeed Ceausescu

Jan 28. Just over a month after Rumania's hated dictator Nicolae Ceausescu and his wife Elena were executed by firing squad, the country is still in turmoil as opposition parties take their political arguments onto the streets of Bucharest. Today a 40,000-strong mob trying to force its way into parliament clashed with police and troops, while others laid siege to the offices of the ruling National Salvation Front (NSF) in Victory Square. The party bussed in thousands of supporters, armed with sticks and chains, to defend its headquarters.

Opposition parties complain that although the interim President and NSF leader Ion Iliescu has promised democracy, he is denying them the chance to stand on equal terms with the ruling party in the free elections planned for May. They accuse the NSF of attempting to use old Stalinist methods to establish a one-party state, similar to Ceausescu's old regime (→2/2).

1990

FEBRUARY

Su	Mo	Tu	We	Th	Fr	Sa
				1	2	3
4	5	6	7	8	9	10
11	12	13	14	15	16	17
18	19	20	21	22	23	24
25	26	27	28			

1. Bulgaria: A coalition government takes over from Communist rule (→3/4).

2. Rumania: Four leaders of the Ceausescu regime are jailed for suppressing last December's revolt (→6/5).

4. Egypt: Gunmen attack a tour bus, killing 15 Israelis.

4. New Zealand: Richard Hadlee becomes the first cricketer to take 400 Test wickets.

7. Moscow: The Soviet Communist Party votes to abandon one-party rule (→25).

8. UK: The House of Lords votes to allow experiments to continue on human embryos.

9. UK: Labour backs an income-related property tax to replace the poll tax (→16).

13. Tokyo: James "Buster" Douglas knocks out Mike Tyson to become the world heavyweight boxing champion.

14. UK: Mortgage rates rise to 15.4 per cent (→12/4).

15. Madrid: Argentina and Britain establish full diplomatic relations, severed in 1982 during the Falklands War.

16. UK: A poll shows that 73 per cent of voters are against the poll tax (→28).

19. Japan: The Liberal Democrats, led by Toshiki Kaifu, win the general election.

20. UK: Environmentalists attack the Government for proposing to spend £12.4 billion on new roads.

24. USSR: The first multi-party elections since 1917 are held, for the new Lithuanian parliament (→3/3).

26. Merseyside: Ambulance crews begin an all-out strike.

28. UK: Eighteen Oxfordshire Tory councillors resign over Government rules that forced their poll tax up from £253 to £412 (→2/3).

DEATHS

8. US rock singer Del Shannon (*30/12/1939).

14. British photographer Norman Parkinson (*21/04/1913).

South Africa enters new era of hope

Ban lifted on anti-apartheid parties

Feb 2. F.W. de Klerk, South Africa's President, today lifted the 30-year-old ban on the African National Congress (ANC) and the South African Communist Party. He also ended restrictions on over 30 other anti-apartheid organisations, opening a new era of hope for South Africa. Mr de Klerk also promised to release political prisoners, of whom the most famous is Nelson Mandela, the leader of the ANC, from jail as soon as possible. He announced the lifting of press restrictions and the suspension of the death penalty. The ANC said that it was only the start of a long road towards ending apartheid and minority white rule in this majority black country (→11).

Mandela, a free man, and his wife Winnie salute supporters outside the prison.

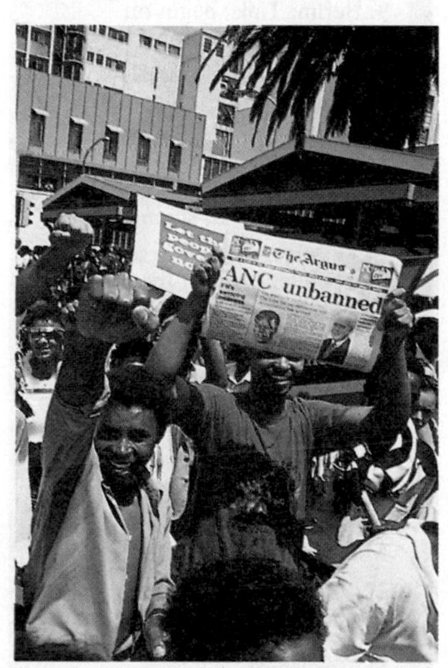

Jubilant black South Africans.

Nelson Mandela is freed after 27 years

Feb 11. Free at last, Nelson Mandela walked out of Victor Verster prison, near Cape Town, this afternoon. Two thousand people – the most that the authorities would allow – erupted with joy as the white-haired, grey-suited figure emerged. In his first statement for a quarter of a century, he said: "I greet you in the name of peace, democracy and freedom for all."

He thanked all who had campaigned for his release and praised President F.W. de Klerk as a man of integrity, but he endorsed the African National Congress's recent calls for armed resistance if necessary. Later, he addressed a 50,000-strong rally in Cape Town at greater length. But what he said seemed less important than the mere fact that he was there.

It is almost 26 years since the black nationalist leader was sentenced to life imprisonment for sabotage and plotting to overthrow the South African government. Successive Pretoria rulers are said to have offered to release him if he softened his demands and renounced the use of violence to achieve political change, he never recanted. In prison, he became a symbol of the black struggle. Freed, he now has the chance to be an active part of it again (→4/5).

Tory MP suspended

Feb 19. An all-party committee today found John Browne, the Tory MP for Winchester, guilty of failing to disclose his outside business interests. By keeping quiet about his dealings with Lebanese businessmen, a Saudi bank and a satellite television company, he was in breach of House of Commons rules, and he now faces possible deselection for his constituency. Mr Browne denied any dishonesty.

Long-running ambulance dispute ends

Feb 23. Britain's ambulance union leaders today agreed a formula with management to end their bitter six-month dispute, during which police and troops manned emergency services. The deal was described by Roger Poole, the chief union negotiator, as giving "staggering" pay rises. It will now be put to a ballot of ambulance workers. Some crews are furious that one of their key demands – for a long-term pay mechanism – has not been met in the settlement. Workers on Merseyside have voted for an indefinite strike from Monday. Both sides are claiming victory in the negotiations, however. The Government says that the two-year package will put just 13 per cent on the pay bill, while according to the unions the basic pay of qualified ambulance staff will be 17.6 per cent higher at the end of the deal (→26).

Soviet rally demands democratic reforms

A protester tears up a poster of Lenin, the architect of the Soviet Union.

Feb 25. Hundreds of thousands of Soviet citizens took to the streets of Moscow and several other major cities today demanding more political and economic reforms. The demonstrations came just two and a half weeks after an historic vote by the central committee of the Soviet Communist Party to abandon the Communists' guaranteed monopoly on power. There were unprecedented security precautions, but all the rallies passed off peacefully.

The 200,000-strong march in Moscow was thought to be the biggest such non-official event since the Bolshevik revolution. Demonstrations were also held in cities in the Ukraine and Byelorussia, where Communist Party conservatives face defeat in forthcoming elections, and in Georgia (→ 15/3).

Nicaragua votes to oust the Sandinistas

Feb 26. President Daniel Ortega of Nicaragua today conceded victory to Violeta Chamorro in a stunning outcome to the country's first truly free elections since his Sandinista movement took power in 1979. Ortega said that the Sandinistas would "respect and heed" the unexpected vote in the poll, which was set up as part of a peace plan for Central America. With close to 80 per cent of the votes counted, the Sandinistas remain the largest single party in the country, with 40 per cent support. However, 55 per cent of voters backed Senora Chamorro's National Opposition Union (UNO), an alliance of anti-Sandinista parties ranging from far left to far right.

"Stay childless," nuclear workers told

Feb 21. Men working at Britain's nuclear plants may be advised by doctors not to have children. New evidence has indicated a firm link between male workers' exposure to radiation at the Sellafield plant in Cumbria and the incidence of leukaemia in their children.

Dr Roger Berry, the health and safety director at British Nuclear Fuels (BNF), which runs Sellafield, was asked at a press conference what advice he would give to a male employee worried about this risk. "Workers who want individual counselling can get it," he said, but added ominously: "If they are so worried, the advice could be: don't have children."

A spokesman for the environmental pressure group Greenpeace led wide condemnation of the remarks, saying: "It is outrageous that Dr Berry can even consider advising parents not to have children. It is not for the workers to change their ways but for BNF to stop its dangerous practices."

1990

MARCH

Su	Mo	Tu	We	Th	Fr	Sa
				1	2	3
4	5	6	7	8	9	10
11	12	13	14	15	16	17
18	19	20	21	22	23	24
25	26	27	28	29	30	31

2. Glasgow: The Queen inaugurates the city's year as "cultural capital of Europe".

2. London: The Tory-controlled Wandsworth council sets the country's lowest poll tax, £148 per head (→ 8).

3. Lithuania: The Baltic state's first free elections are won by a pro-independence party (→ 11).

5. UK: Arthur Scargill is accused of using NUM funds to pay personal debts (→ 20/7).

8. London: Police clash with rioters in Hackney during one of many nationwide protests as local councils set their poll taxes.→

8. UK: It is revealed that more than 3,000 Britons have fully-developed AIDS (→ 11/4).

9. Berlin: Talks begin on German reunification (→ 24/4).

9. UK: Customs officials seize 116lbs of heroin – the biggest-ever haul in Britain.

10. Iraq: Farzad Bazoft, an Iranian-born British journalist, is found guilty of spying.→

11. Vilnius: Lithuania seeks independence from the Soviet Union.→

15. Moscow: Mikhail Gorbachev is elected executive President of the USSR (→ 1/5).

17. UK: Scotland beat England 13-7 at Murrayfield to take rugby's "grand slam".

20. UK: The Chancellor, John Major, delivers his first budget.

22. UK: In a by-election, Labour wins the normally safe Tory constituency of Mid-Staffordshire.

23. UK: The Duchess of York gives birth to a daughter, Eugenie Victoria.

28. Heathrow: Customs men intercept a cargo of electrical detonators for nuclear weapons bound for Iraq.

31. UK: Oxford win the 136th Boat Race by two lengths.

DEATHS

12. British cookery writer Jane Grigson (*13/03/1928).

21. British scientist, author and collector Lord (Victor) Rothschild (*31/10/1910).

Soviet troops seize Lithuanian rebels

Lithuania claims its independence.

March 31. Three weeks after the tiny Baltic republic of Lithuania unilaterally declared its independence from Moscow, the Soviet army has intervened by rounding up deserters and seizing control of the Communist Party headquarters in the capital, Vilnius. Soviet paratroopers have arrested some 20 young Lithuanians who had left their army units and taken refuge in a psychiatric hospital. Vitautas Landsbergis, Lithuania's President, condemned the raid as a gross violation of sovereignty and accused the West of "collusion" in a fresh betrayal of Lithuania – annexed by Stalin in 1940 – by not putting pressure on President Gorbachev to leave the republic in peace (→ 17/4).

New York disco fire kills eighty-seven

March 25. A fierce fire in a New York discotheque has claimed the lives of 87 people. There was only one survivor – the disc jockey, who escaped with severe burns. The Happy Land disco in the Bronx was officially closed three months ago, but an eviction order was never enforced and, like some 700 other nightclubs in New York, it continued to open illegally. Police suspect arson and have arrested a man who started a fight in the club shortly before the fire broke out.

Poll tax riot in London

March 31. On the eve of the introduction of the community charge or poll tax – the government's replacement for the rates – in England and Wales, a huge march and rally in central London today turned into a full-scale riot, with hundreds of arrests and widespread violence. It is the climax to a month of protests as councils set poll taxes.

The trouble, at the end of a peaceful demonstration, started when mounted police baton-charged the 300,000-strong crowd in an attempt to clear Trafalgar Square. Tempers rose on both sides. Small groups of extremist agitators and hooligans set buildings and cars on fire and looted shops all the way to Oxford Circus. The rioting petered out at about midnight. But if the experience in Scotland, where the poll tax began a year ago, is repeated, resistance will continue in the form of refusing to pay (→ 11/5).

The poll tax rally erupts in chaos.

Iraqis hang British journalist for spying

March 15. Farzad Bazoft, an Iranian-born journalist working for the Observer newspaper in Iraq, was hanged today in Baghdad. Bazoft, aged 31, was sentenced to death five days ago by a military court which had found him guilty of espionage.

Iraq's President Saddam Hussein rejected a personal appeal from Margaret Thatcher to spare the reporter's life. Bazoft was arrested when he visited an Iraqi military base to check reports of an explosion in which 700 people were said to have died. After seven weeks in captivity, he "confessed" on videotape to spying. Daphne Parish, a 52-year-old British nurse who drove him to the site, was sentenced to 15 years' imprisonment (→ 16/7).

March 27. Daniel Day Lewis wins the Oscar for Best Actor for his role in "My Left Foot".

West Indies lose long unbeaten run

March 1. It has taken 16 years and 29 matches to do it, but England has finally beaten the West Indies in a test match in the Caribbean. The England team, led by Graham Gooch, romped to a nine-wicket victory to take a 1-0 lead in the five test series. The win has made heroes of relative youngsters such as the bowlers Angus Fraser and Devon Malcolm; old stalwarts of the 1980s, like Ian Botham and David Gower, were not in the team. Viv Richards, the West Indian captain, will be determined to wreak revenge following his team's shock defeat by a team labelled as "nohopers" when they left England.

1990

APRIL

Su	Mo	Tu	We	Th	Fr	Sa
1	2	3	4	5	6	7
8	9	10	11	12	13	14
15	16	17	18	19	20	21
22	23	24	25	26	27	28
29	30					

2. Baghdad: President Saddam Hussein says that if Israel attacks Iraq he will retaliate with chemical weapons.→

3. Bulgaria: Petar Mladenov is elected President of a new, non-Socialist republic (→ 22/11).

4. UK: The Hong Kong Nationality Bill is introduced, proposing to allow 50,000 Hong Kong people to obtain UK passports.

7. Sweden: More than 150 people are killed when the ferry Scandinavian Star catches fire en route from Norway to Denmark.

7. UK: Mr Frisk wins the Grand National in record time.

11. UK: Figures show that AIDS cases from heterosexual intercourse have doubled in the last year (→ 27/7).

12. UK: Inflation rises to 8.1 per cent (→ 15/6).

13. UK: The makers of the alleged supergun, Sheffield Forgemasters, say that 44 tubes are already in Iraq (→ 20)..

17. USSR: Moscow imposes an economic blockade on Lithuania (→ 4/5).

18. Beirut: Eleven children die in an attack on a school bus.

20. Greece: Greek customs authorities arrest Paul Ashwell, a lorry driver taking tubing bound for Iraq (→ 9/7).

21. UK: Baroness Susan de Stempel is jailed for theft and defrauding her aged aunt.

24. Bonn: West and East German leaders agree on 1 July for economic union (29).

25. Manchester: The last rebel prisoners are evacuated from Strangeways Prison.

25. Westminster: MPs vote to reduce the upper time limit for abortions from 28 weeks to 24.

29. USSR: Mikhail Gorbachev rules out Soviet support for a unified Germany in NATO (→ 1/7).

DEATHS

2. British sports commentator Peter Jones (*7/2/1930).

15. Swedish-born actress Greta Garbo (*18/09/1905).

Communists lose in Hungarian election

April 9. Decades of Communist rule ended in Hungary today when, in the final round of free elections, the people voted in favour of the traditionalist Hungarian Democratic Forum. A majority for the Forum – together with its allies, the Christian Democratic People's Party – is assured in a new parliament. Its president, Joszef Antall, is expected to become the country's next prime minister. Antall said that one of his main priorities would be to take the country into Europe while maintaining many of its ties with the Soviet Union.

US hostage release raises Beirut hopes

Robert Polhill: a free man.

April 30. The release of a second American hostage in ten days has raised hopes that all Westerners held by Lebanese militiamen might soon be freed. Last week Robert Polhill was set free from his Beirut cell. Today Frank Reed, the US college administrator held hostage by the Iranian-backed Islamic Jihad organisation since September 1986, was released.

President Bush has thanked Syria for facilitating Reed's release and Iran for bringing its influence to bear. But the Iranians may be looking for a more solid reward, such as the freeing of Iranian assets frozen by the US since the occupation of the American embassy in Tehran in 1979 (→ 30/8). ▷

Deaths feared in Strangeways Prison riot

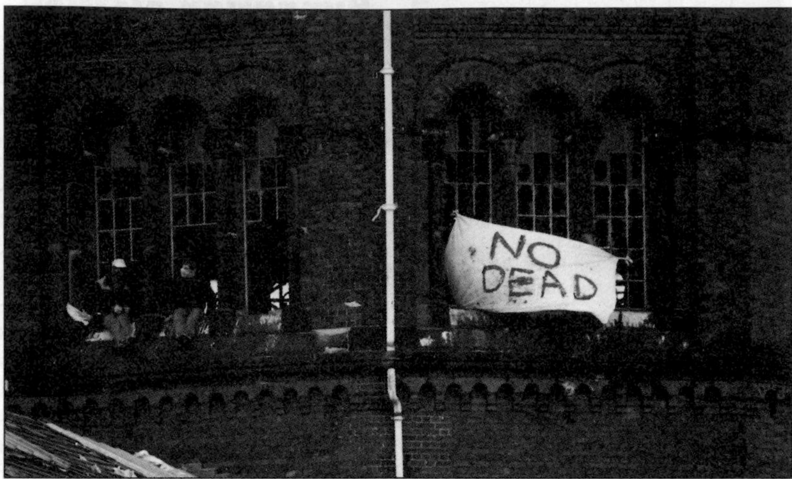

Rebel inmates now in control contradict claims of any deaths in the riot.

April 1. A riot in Manchester's Strangeways Prison erupted today during Sunday morning prayers in the chapel. The prisoners quickly overpowered the guards and took their keys, opening cells throughout the prison and releasing around 1,000 men. Seven hundred are still on the loose within Strangeways.

Prison staff, overwhelmed by the speed of the riot, are urging police to storm the building, but David Waddington, the Home Secretary, prefers a low-key approach. Fires have already gutted the chapel and gymnasium, while prisoners are busy hurling slates from the roof onto the police below.

Those evacuated have alleged that so-called "rule 43" prisoners – sex offenders normally segregated in "E" wing for their own protection – have been severely beaten by rioters, and unconfirmed rumours say some men have died.

The riot is mainly a protest against the appalling conditions which keep prisoners – even those on remand – locked up three to a cell for 23 hours a day. As one roof-top rioter shouted: "We are having no more" (→25).

Faldo and Hendry win sports awards

April 30. It has been a mixed, if dramatic, month for Britain's top sportsmen. Heading the individual honours was Nick Faldo, who became only the second golfer to win the US Masters tournament in successive years. Championships were also won by Stephen Hendry, at 21 the youngest-ever world snooker champion, and Nigel Benn, the new world middleweight boxing titleholder.

England's cricketers returned from the West Indies without a trophy, however. They finally lost the test series 2-1 after rain had denied them a good chance of victory in Trinidad. Top team honours within Britain have gone to Wigan (rugby league) and Liverpool and Glasgow Rangers (football). Nottingham Forest retained the Littlewood's Cup.

Iraqi "supergun" is seized in Britain

April 11. Customs officers in Britain today seized what are said to be parts of a massive cannon bound for Iraq's growing war machine. Eight sections of barrel labelled "petroleum piping" were stopped at Teesport. Experts believe that the components are part of a "supergun" which could launch rockets into space or fire a three-foot-wide nuclear shell for hundreds of miles. Sheffield Forgemasters, the manufacturers, maintain that they are oil pipes and point out that the government passed them for export.

Two weeks ago, a joint Anglo-US operation caught an Iraqi trying to smuggle 40 "krytons" – tiny capacitors needed to detonate nuclear weapons – to Baghdad. The capacitors, which had been ordered from a Californian company, were being delivered via London (→13).

1990

MAY

Su	Mo	Tu	We	Th	Fr	Sa
		1	2	3	4	5
6	7	8	9	10	11	12
13	14	15	16	17	18	19
20	21	22	23	24	25	26
27	28	29	30	31		

1. UK: A four-year-old girl receives over 200 stitches after being savaged by two pet dogs.

2. UK: English football fans planning to attend the World Cup are warned to behave or face a two-year ban on any match abroad.

4. Riga: The Baltic state of Latvia votes for independence from Moscow (→29/6).

6. USSR: Moldavia opens its border with Rumania for the first time in 50 years (→14/6).

6. S. Africa: P.W. Botha resigns from the National Party over government talks with the ANC (→2/11).

8. UK: Billy Cartman is the sixth Briton to die building the Channel Tunnel.

10. UK: The ministry of agriculture says that a cat put down five weeks ago was suffering from BSE or "mad cow disease".→

10. UK: Pan Am pays £10 million in compensation to the families living in Lockerbie.

12. Glasgow: Aberdeen beat Celtic on penalties to win the Scottish Cup Final.

12. Colombia: Three separate terrorist car bombings kill 39 people in Bogota and Cali.

16. London: A booby-trapped minibus explodes, killing an army sergeant (→28).

17. London: Manchester United beat Crystal Palace 1-0 in the FA Cup Final replay.

21. Rumania: Ion Iliescu's National Salvation Front wins in free elections.

21. Israel: A man posing as a soldier shoots dead seven Palestinian workers.

23. UK: The government announces a £1.8bn current account deficit for April.

30. France: British beef and live cattle imports are banned.→

DEATHS

8. Irish churchman Cardinal Tomas O Fiaich (*2/11/1923).

16. US entertainer Sammy Davis Jr (*08/12/1925).→

22. British comedian Max Wall (*1908).

Tories suffer local election battering

May 11. The government has announced a near-record increase in inflation. Prices last month were 9.4 per cent above what they were in the same month a year ago, the highest level since May 1982. Analysts expect that inflation will soon exceed the 10.1 per cent figure inherited by Mrs Thatcher when she came to power in 1979, declaring the conquest of inflation to be the main plank of her economic policy.

Two months of protests over the poll tax, or community charge, took their toll of the Conservative Party last week, as their candidates took a battering in local elections in England and Wales. Labour gained 304 net seats, with an average swing of 11 per cent – more than enough to put Neil Kinnock into Downing Street.

Two Tory victories in boroughs which set low levels of poll tax – Westminster and Wandsworth – led Mrs Thatcher to claim that "the message about the community charge is beginning to work". But the combination of bad economic news and a drubbing at the polls have prompted some Tories to wonder whether the Iron Lady is suffering from metal fatigue (→14/8).

May 16. Sammy Davis Jr, the entertainer and member of Hollywood's "rat pack" of the 1950s, dies of throat cancer.

Red Square crowd jeers Gorbachev

Mikhail Gorbachev (r.) and Prime Minister Nikolai Ryzhkov quit the scene.

May 1. One of the most solemn occasions in the Soviet calendar, the May Day celebrations in Red Square, ended in humiliation today for President Gorbachev. Members of the pro-democracy Moscow Voters' Association led a number of other opposition groups in jeering and whistling at the party leaders standing on the balcony of the Lenin mausoleum. A furious and embarrassed Mr Gorbachev led his colleagues in a rapid retreat to the Kremlin.

The protesters did not pull their punches. Banners referred to "70 years of dirt on the Soviet people" and demanded "Gorbachev, hands off Soviet power". This slogan no doubt alludes to the election of Gorbachev as executive President of the Soviet Union on March 15 – in a secret ballot with himself as the sole candidate.

The hecklers at today's rally, who included Baltic and Russian nationalists and fledgling opposition parties, were taking advantage of the increased tolerance of political dissent. According to radical politicians, they also represent the discontent of millions of ordinary citizens with the painful process of economic reform (→30/5).

Meeting brings new hope to South Africa

May 4. The historic talks between Nelson Mandela, the leader of the African National Congress (ANC), and South Africa's President F.W. de Klerk ended today with a message of hope. The Cape Town meeting was the first time that government and ANC leaders had ever sat round the same table. Afterwards, the two men said that they had agreed on a number of initiatives to create a peaceful climate for negotiations on South Africa's future.

It is just over three months since the 30-year ban on the ANC was lifted, and – nine days later – Mandela was freed from prison. In the wake of these events, five leading ANC figures returned to South Africa on April 27 after 30 years' exile. Mandela called the talks with the government "the realisation of a dream" (→6).

A light moment before talks begin.

Australians killed by IRA "mistake"

May 28. Two Australians were machine-gunned down in the main square of Roermond (in Holland, near the German border) last night. IRA gunmen evidently believed that Stephen Melrose and Nick Spanos, both aged 24, were British servicemen. In fact, they were both London-based lawyers, visiting Holland as tourists. As they left their UK-registered car to take photographs, another car pulled up and two men opened fire. They were killed in front of the two women whom they were with. The IRA today issued a statement apologising for its "mistake" (→13/7).

Yelstin elected as Russian President

May 30. Boris Yeltsin, the leading Soviet radical, has been elected President of the republic of Russia. The poll confirms him as the major rival of his former ally, President Gorbachev, who sacked Yeltsin from the post of chief of Moscow's Communist Party in 1987. Yeltsin got his own back today, defeating a candidate favoured by Gorbachev. Yeltsin can now negotiate with Gorbachev from a position of great strength. The Russian republic is enormous, and with its industrial and mineral resources and population of 280 million, it wields great influence in Soviet politics (→1/6).

Minister puts beefburgers to family test

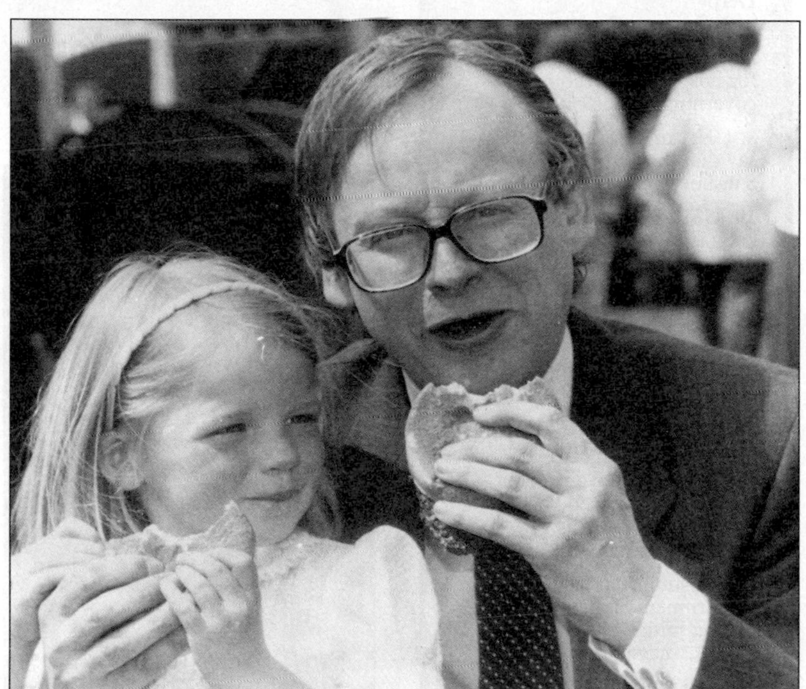
Cordelia and John Gummer have no worries as they eat their beefburgers.

May 19. In an attempt to calm public fears that bovine spongiform encephalopathy (BSE) – also known as "mad cow disease" – can be passed on to humans Britain's Agriculture Minister, John Gummer, munched his way through a £1.60 beefburger for the benefit of newspaper and television cameras. And to make an even better "photo opportunity", he then roped in his four-year-old daughter Cordelia to eat another burger in public. "Delicious" was the Gummer family's verdict. It is not certain, however, that the minister's critics will be silenced by this public show of gastronomic confidence. Several town councils have withdrawn beef products from school meals, but the government has rejected proposals to ban the use of certain offals in pet food.

Some domestic pets have already been infected with BSE, a brain disease which has spread rapidly through Britain's cattle herds. Beef sales have plummeted as some vets warned that humans could catch it. The Government denies any risk.

1990

JUNE

Su	Mo	Tu	We	Th	Fr	Sa
					1	2
3	4	5	6	7	8	9
10	11	12	13	14	15	16
17	18	19	20	21	22	23
24	25	26	27	28	29	30

1. Lichfield: An IRA attack leaves one army recruit dead and two others wounded (→26).

3. France: Eleven British tourists die in a coach crash.

3. USSR: At least 40 people die in ethnic clashes between Uzbeks and Kirghiz.

3. Washington: Presidents Bush and Gorbachev agree on new arms cuts (→19/11).

4. Beijing: Violence marks the first anniversary of the Tiananmen Square massacre.

6. Epsom: Quest for Fame, ridden by Pat Eddery, wins the Derby.

7. UK: The British Medical Association opposes proposals for hospitals to become self-governing bodies (→1/8).

8. UK: Animal rights activists say that they attacked a Salisbury vet with a car bomb.

10. UK: A 13-month-old baby is injured when a car bomb planted in an animal psychologist's car explodes.

14. Bucharest: The government busses in club-wielding miners to quell opposition on the streets.

15. UK: The inflation rate reaches 9.7 per cent (→14/9).

20. UK: The Government unveils its proposed "hard Ecu", a step towards a single European currency.→

22. Westminster: The Government launches a £15 million initiative to stop homelessness.

26. London: An IRA bomb damages the Carlton Club, a haunt of Tory MPs (→20/7).

27. Brussels: The European Commission orders British Aerospace to pay back to the Government some £33 million in illegal "sweeteners".

29. USSR: Lithuania suspends its declaration of independence for 100 days.

DEATHS

2. British actor Sir Reginald Carey "Rex" Harrison (*05/03/1909).→

29. US writer Irving Wallace (*19/03/1916).

Earthquake devastates northern Iran

June 22. A devastating earthquake has brought death and destruction to more than 100 square miles of north-west Iran. Upwards of 40,000 people are feared dead, and some 100,000 have been injured. The provinces of Zanjan and Gilan near the Soviet border were the centre of the tremors, which measured 7.7 on the Richter scale. But shocks were felt as far away as Azerbaijan, where some buildings were destroyed. Although Iran's foreign policy has been resolutely anti-Western, President Ali Akbar Rafsanjani said that his country would welcome help "from whatever source". He then declared three days of national mourning. The EC has responded with a $1 million package of instant aid.

A mother mourns her children after the earthquake in which over 40,000 died.

SDP remnant stops working as a party

Dr David Owen breaks the bad news.

June 3. The Social Democratic Party is no more, announced its leader, Dr David Owen, today. With just 6,200 members, it has become too small to function effectively, he explained. The SDP was launched in 1981 with a promise to "break the mould" of British politics. In 1988, when the party voted to merge with the Liberals to become the Liberal Democrats, Owen and his supporters stood aloof. They have since been sidelined by both the merged party and the revitalised Labour Party.

Euro-currency plan infuriates Thatcher

June 26. Mrs Thatcher was isolated at the European summit, which ended today in Dublin, over her opposition to greater economic and monetary unity within the community. In particular, she totally opposed the plans proposed by Jacques Delors, the President of the European Commission, for a single currency and central bank.

The Delors plan attacked national sovereignty and failed to recognise the differences between the economies of the members of the community, she argued. The only way forward, she said, was the British proposal for the "hard Ecu" – a pan-European currency designed to coexist with national currencies. This view was rejected by Chancellor Kohl of West Germany and President Mitterrand of France. The proposed moves towards economic and political union were, said Mr Kohl, "the next step in the direction of a United States of Europe". A weary Mitterrand added somewhat tetchily that they could always rely on the British Prime Minister to ensure that "the debates are long and that the decisions taken are always retaken" (→5/10).

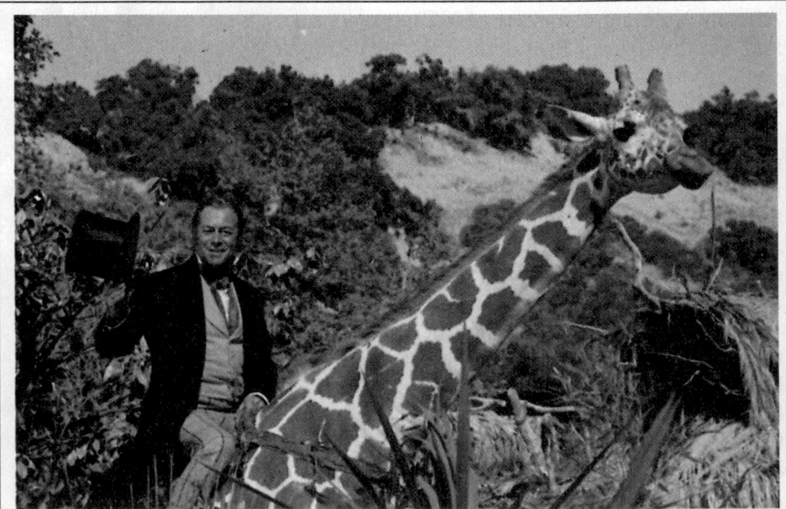

June 2. Rex Harrison, one of Britain's greatest film actors, dies. Here he is seen in one of his best-loved roles, as the remarkable Dr Doolittle.

1990

JULY

Su	Mo	Tu	We	Th	Fr	Sa
1	2	3	4	5	6	7
8	9	10	11	12	13	14
15	16	17	18	19	20	21
22	23	24	25	26	27	28
29	30	31				

1. Germany: The Deutschmark becomes the official currency of both East and West Germany (→23/8).

3. Liberia: President Samuel Doe offers to resign as rebels overrun the country (→5/8).

5. Albania: Serbs and Albanians clash violently.

5. Czechoslovakia: Vaclav Havel is re-elected for a two-year term as President.

7. Italy: England lose 2-1 to Italy, taking fourth place in the World Cup.→

8. Wimbledon: Stefan Edberg beats Boris Becker to win the men's title and Martina Navratilova wins a record ninth ladies' singles title by beating Zina Garrison.

9. Lebanon: Eleven people are killed in an Israeli air raid.

9. Baghdad: President Saddam Hussein denies that Iraq has a nuclear capability (→24).

10. UK: A British Airways pilot is sucked halfway out of his cockpit after his windscreen blows out.

11. UK: The case of the Maguire family, convicted of running an IRA bomb factory in 1976, is referred to the Court of Appeal (→26/6/1991).

15. Pakistan: More than 38 people are killed by a bomb blast at Hyderabad.

16. Baghdad: Daphne Parish, the British nurse sentenced to 15 years' jail for spying, is released.

20. UK: The NUM sues Arthur Scargill for £1.4 million in allegedly missing funds.

20. UK: An IRA bomb explodes at the London Stock Exchange.→

24. Iraq: Saddam Hussein sends 30,000 troops to the Iraqi-Kuwait border (→2/8).

27. Geneva: Reports show that AIDS is now the main cause of death for women aged between 20 and 40 (→15/10).

DEATH

14. British film actress Margaret Lockwood (*15/09/1916).

Foul play mars Germany's World Cup win

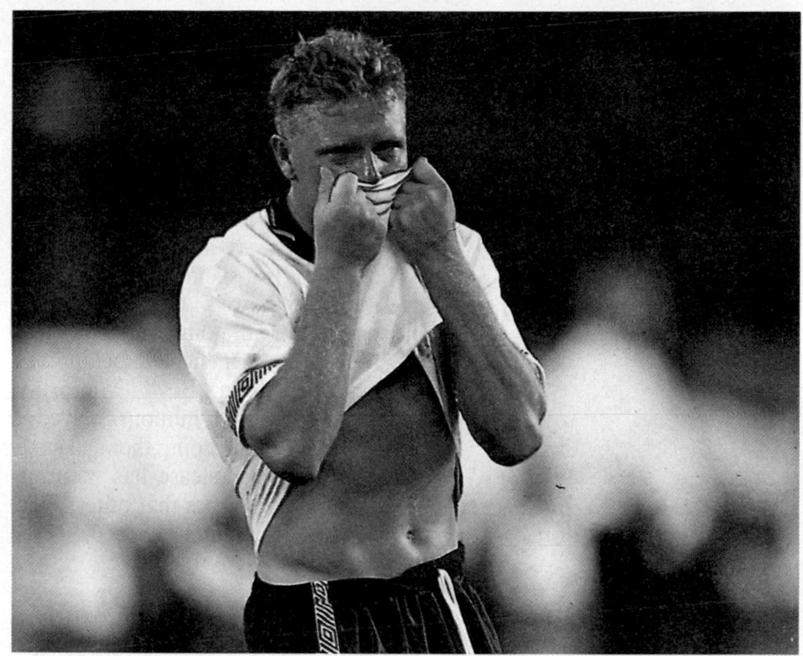

The agony and the despair: tears from Gascoigne as England's hopes end.

July 8. West Germany tonight won football's World Cup, but few outside Germany will recall the victory over Argentina with much pleasure. A penalty decided a final in Rome littered with fouls; two Argentinians were sent off.

Both semi-finals were also decided by penalty shoot-outs, after the games had ended in draws. In the first, the host nation Italy lost to Argentina, and in the second, it was England's turn to suffer the agony of defeat after drawing 1-1 with West Germany. England's performance in the tournament was their best for 24 years. After a lacklustre start the English players grew in confidence, with Paul Gascoigne and David Platt emerging as new stars. At the end Gascoigne (or "Gazza" as he became known) was in tears. The Republic of Ireland also exceeded expectations, reaching the quarter-finals for the first time before losing 1-0 to Italy. No joy for Scotland, though; they went out in round one.

Yeltsin resigns as Gorbachev is cheered

July 13. Boris Yeltsin, the President of the powerful Russian republic, shocked delegates gathered in the Kremlin for the 28th congress of the Communist Party when he announced his resignation from the party yesterday. He blamed the slow pace of reform for his decision. It was a bad moment for President Gorbachev, already under fire from conservatives accusing him of "losing" Eastern Europe. Gorbachev has done well to force through vital reforms in the face of outspoken criticism from both reformers and the old guard of hardline Communists. The congress rewarded his promise that "no one will be permitted to wreck perestroika" with a standing ovation after his closing speech this afternoon (→24/9).

Yeltsin walks away from the party.

Minister quits after "Hitler" outburst

July 14. Nicholas Ridley, the Secretary for Trade and Industry, resigned today over remarks he made in this week's "Spectator" magazine. Mr Ridley described proposals for monetary union in Europe as "a German racket to take over the whole of Europe". As for handing over sovereignty to the European Commission in Brussels, Ridley said that "you might just as well give it to Adolf Hitler". It became obvious that a man with such views could not negotiate Britain's trading links with Europe. His resignation has forced the fifth cabinet reshuffle in a year.

Teenagers accused of drug smuggling

July 19. Two teenage English girls were arrested at Bangkok airport last night as they tried to board a flight to Amsterdam. Patricia Cahill, aged 17, and Karyn Smith, aged 19, have been charged with attempting to smuggle £4 million worth of heroin out of Thailand. If they are found guilty, they could face sentences of life imprisonment.

The two girls were carrying 44 pounds of the drug hidden in shampoo bottles and coffee and tea containers. The girls' parents are astonished. They had been under the impression that their daughters were in Scotland (→20/12).

IRA car bomb kills outspoken Tory MP

July 30. Ian Gow, the Conservative MP for Eastbourne, was murdered today by an IRA car bomb at his home in the Sussex village of Hankham. He had driven just a few feet when a four-pound bomb, planted under the front seat of his vehicle, exploded. He died before he could be taken to hospital. A former Northern Ireland minister, Gow knew that he was a target for the terrorists. He will be greatly missed by his fellow MPs, among them the Prime Minister, Margaret Thatcher, to whom he was once a parliamentary secretary (→19/9).

1990

AUGUST

Su	Mo	Tu	We	Th	Fr	Sa
			1	2	3	4
5	6	7	8	9	10	11
12	13	14	15	16	17	18
19	20	21	22	23	24	25
26	27	28	29	30	31	

1. UK: Hospital waiting lists are, at 881,000, the highest for six years.

3. UK: A record heatwave brings temperatures of up to 37.1C (98.8F).

4. Saudi Arabia: Saudi forces go onto full alert as Iraqi troops breach the neutral zone at the Kuwaiti border (→8).

5. Liberia: US Marines rescue US citizens from the civil war (→9/9).

8. US: President Bush warns Iraq not to cross the border into Saudi Arabia (→10).

11. Sri Lanka: Tamil rebels massacre 144 Moslems in the continuing ethnic violence.

12. Pakistan: Benazir Bhutto is offered an amnesty from corruption charges if she withdraws from politics.

12. Kuwait: Iraqi troops shoot dead Douglas Croskery, a British businessman trying to escape into Saudi Arabia (→17).

14. Bridport: Seven-year-old Gemma Lawrence, who was snatched from her parents' holiday caravan, is found safe and well.

14. UK: Figures show that one Briton in five is evading paying the poll tax.

15. S. Africa: At least 150 people are killed in township battles between Zulu and Xhosa tribesmen (→9/9).

20. Kuwait: Iraqi soldiers take 82 Britons hostage (→22).

22. Amman: Overwhelmed by refugees, Jordan closes its border with Iraq (→23).

23. East Germany: MPs choose October 3 as the date for reunification (→12/9).

27. Baghdad: Saddam Hussein says that all Western women and children held hostage are free to leave (→2/9).

30. UK: Petrol prices go up to 225.9p a gallon (→17/10).

DEATHS

9. British footballer and manager Joe Mercer (*09/08/1914).

18. US singer Pearl Bailey (*29/03/1918).

Freed Irish hostage tells of Beirut "hell"

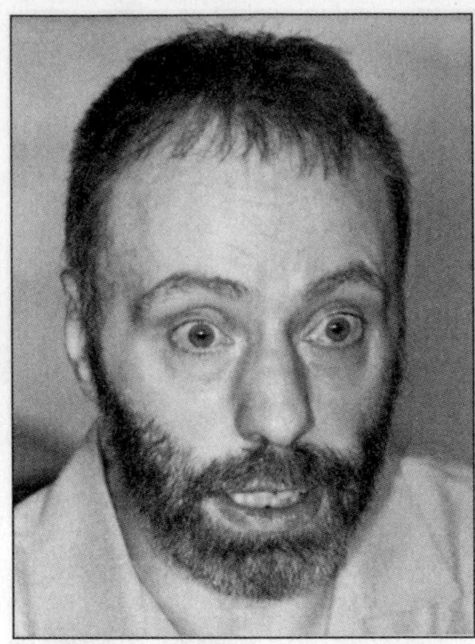

Brian Keenan after his release.

Aug 30. Brian Keenan, the Irish hostage freed a week ago, today spoke of his 1,597 days of captivity in Beirut – and confirmed that at least one British hostage, John McCarthy, is alive. Keenan faced the press in Dublin to give a moving description of his ordeal.

"Hostage is a crucifying aloneness ... it is a silent, screaming slide into the bowels of ultimate despair," he said, going on to pay tribute to the men he left behind, especially "John Boy" McCarthy, whose sense of humour played a major part in keeping them all sane. Mr Keenan's release has naturally given rise to hopes that other Western hostages might be freed.

Britain's schools "sell children short"

Aug 20. A leading British academic today called for a royal commission to investigate what he claims is a crisis in the country's education system. Sir Claus Moser, Vice-President of the British Association for the Advancement of Science, said in a speech to the association's annual conference that Britain was selling its schoolchildren short.

Sir Claus, who is also the warden of Wadham College, Oxford, said that in Britain today "hundreds of thousands of children have educational experiences not worthy of a civilised nation". He singled out what he said were ten years of government cuts in education spending for particular attack. These had compounded the problems of a demoralised and underskilled teaching profession, so that only one child in three stays on at school or college after the minimum leaving age of 16. Even fewer choose to undertake any form of higher education, said Sir Claus.

The speech seems certain to increase the attention being given to education by all the political parties in the run-up to the next general election.

Benazir Bhutto sacked as Pakistan's PM

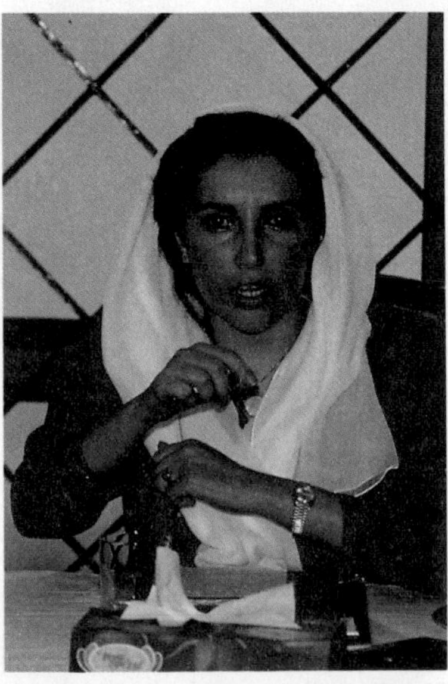

No longer in charge: Miss Bhutto.

Aug 8. Benazir Bhutto was sacked as Prime Minister of Pakistan today, and her government dissolved, after a rule of just 20 months. She described the action, taken by President Gulam Ishaq Khan, as a "constitutional coup d'etat", but the president accused the government of "wilfully undermining the workings of the constitution" and "scandalous horse-trading for personal interest". Tonight Miss Bhutto's home is surrounded by soldiers in scenes reminiscent of the arrest of her father, Zulfikar Ali Bhutto, on the orders of President Zia. Her father was executed, she was arrested, and Zia was later killed in a bomb attack on his plane. Today's events show that democracy is still fragile (→12).

Guinness case ends with guilty verdicts

Former chairman Ernest Saunders.

Aug 28. Three of the four businessmen at the centre of a massive fraud were sentenced today after a jury found them guilty of theft, false accounting and supporting the price of shares during Guinness's takeover of Distillers four years ago.

Ernest Saunders, the former chairman of Guinness, was jailed for five years for what Mr Justice Henry called "dishonesty on a massive scale". Gerald Ronson, the garage and property tycoon, was fined £5 million and jailed for a year, while the stockbroker Tony Parnes received 18 months' imprisonment. The fourth defendant, Sir Jack Lyons, was too ill to be sentenced today (→25/9).

Ninety years young: the Queen Mother receives flowers from children outside Clarence House as Britain celebrated her 90th birthday on 4 August.

West prepares for battle as Iraq conquers Kuwait

Tanks roll over Kuwait's puny defences

Aug 2. Iraq's massive army has invaded its oil-rich neighbour, Kuwait. Tanks and aircraft massed near the border simply rolled over meagre Kuwaiti defences, and although some resistance is still reported in the capital, Kuwait City, it seems certain to be crushed soon. Government buildings and telecommunications centres have already been captured, and the Dasman Palace, home to the Kuwaiti royal family, is said to be "crawling with Iraqi tanks". The emir, Sheikh Jaber al-Sabah, has fled to the safety of Saudi Arabia. The invasion of Kuwait, a country less than one-twentieth the size of Iraq and with one-ninth of its population, has been prompted by what Saddam Hussein, Iraq's President, sees as Kuwait's theft of £2.4 billion worth of oil from a disputed field.

Saddam also accuses Kuwait of deliberately exceeding Opec quotas in order to lower the price of oil, thus damaging Iraq's economy. World leaders have rushed to condemn the invasion, but it is unlikely that words will deter Saddam (→4).

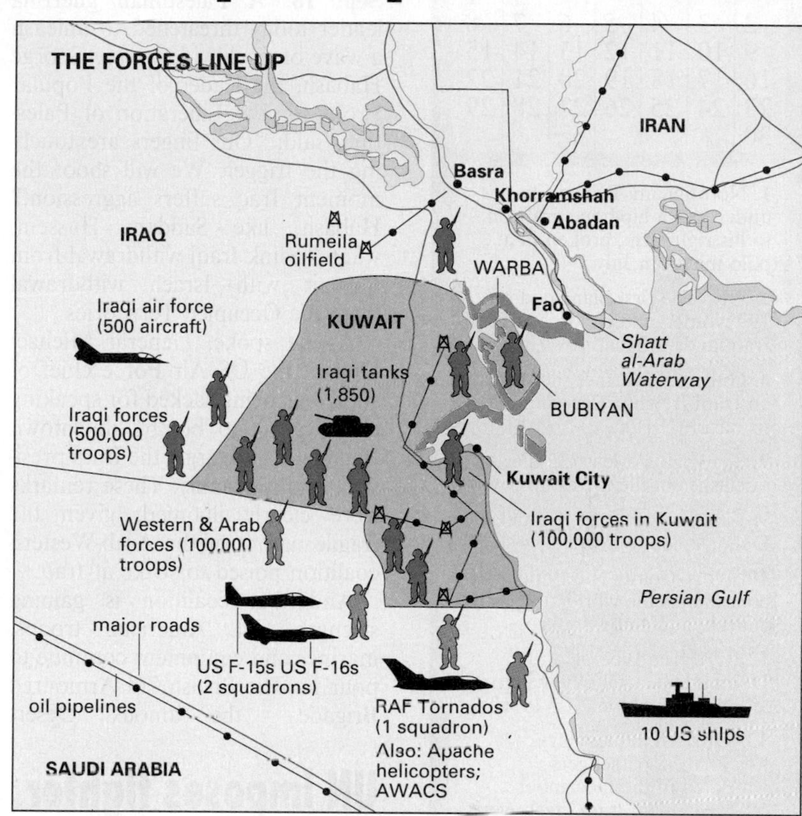

Saddam annexes Kuwait into Iraq

The Iraqi President and henchmen.

Aug 10. As members of the Arab League met in Cairo today to demand Iraq's withdrawal from Kuwait, Saddam Hussein called on all Gulf Arabs to rise up to topple their wealthy leaders and free Mecca from "the spears of the Americans and the Zionists".

Just two days ago the Iraqi President defied the UN to announce that Kuwait was now part of Iraq in an "eternal merger". Foreign embassies in Kuwait have been given two weeks to move to Baghdad, and, in an alarming new development, the Iraqis have transported hundreds of Britons and Americans from Kuwait to Baghdad. Saddam says that their lives will be in danger if the West takes any military action against him (→12).

Iraq drops claim on Iran to free troops

Aug 17. President Bush was today reported to have asked King Hussein of Jordan to show himself out of the building after "very frank, open and candid" discussions at the President's holiday home in Maine. The King, caught between economic dependence on the West and a population that mostly supports Saddam Hussein – who is posing as the saviour of the Palestinians – has been striving to secure peace in the area. But US troops and armaments continue to pour into the region to defend Saudi Arabia.

Saddam, meanwhile, yesterday surprised observers by ending ten years of conflict with Iran, buying peace with his arch-enemy in order to concentrate Iraq's forces against the international army now being mustered in Saudi Arabia following the invasion of Kuwait.

Iraq and Iran reached a truce in 1988, after eight years of war which claimed a million lives. Today Saddam Hussein offered a formal peace treaty which concedes all Iran's key demands. It was hailed by Ali Akbar Velayati, the foreign minister in Tehran, as the "biggest victory" in his country's history.

Iraq's territorial claims along the border and the Shatt al-Arab waterway – which ostensibly prompted its 1980 invasion of Iran – will be abandoned, freeing 300,000 men to be redeployed along its southern borders (→20).

Iraq's TV hostage parade causes outrage

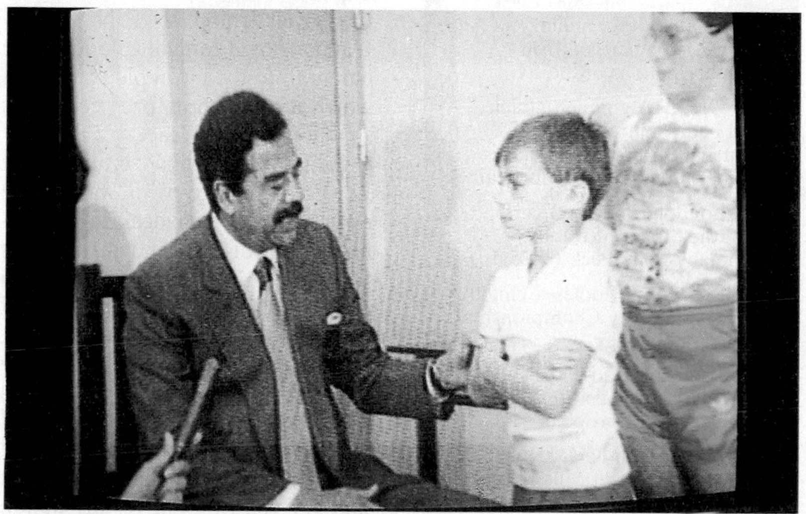
Six-year-old Stuart Lockwood edges away from his captor Saddam Hussein.

Aug 23. Saddam Hussein appeared on the world's television screens today in an attempt to allay fears about the treatment of Western hostages. Dressed in a casual suit, the Iraqi President was seen telling 15 British hostages that they were "heroes of the peace" whose presence in Iraq would help avert a war.

The idea was to prove that the hostages – or "guests", as Saddam prefers to call them – were relaxed and content with their lot, but they looked ill at ease – none more so than six-year-old Stuart Lockwood, who tried to squirm away as Saddam tried to ruffle the boy's hair. Concern for their safety continues to grow. Hundreds of Britons and Americans have been brought from Kuwait to be detained in Baghdad (→27).

1990

SEPTEMBER

Su	Mo	Tu	We	Th	Fr	Sa
						1
2	3	4	5	6	7	8
9	10	11	12	13	14	15
16	17	18	19	20	21	22
23	24	25	26	27	28	29
30						

1. Nottingham: Prince Charles undergoes a hip-bone graft on to his right arm, broken in a polo match in July.

2. UK: The first planeload of 199 women and children from Iraq lands at Heathrow (→ 4).

4. Gulf: US Marines intercept an Iraqi freighter carrying tea to Basra (→ 15).

9. S. Africa: At least 35 die in clashes in the townships.

9. Liberia: President Samuel Doe is killed by rebels.

10. Ivory Coast: The Pope consecrates the world's biggest church, at Yamoussoukro.

12. UK: The Liberal Democrats unveil a new logo, a "bird of freedom" (→ 19/10).

13. UK: An inquest jury says that 35 passengers who died in the December 1988 Clapham train crash were unlawfully killed.

15. Kuwait: Thousands flee to Saudi Arabia when Iraq opens the border for a day (→ 17).

17. Europe: Iraqi military attaches are expelled from member nations of the EC.→

19. UK: IRA gunmen attack and badly injure Air Chief Marshal Sir Peter Terry, a former Governor of Gibraltar.

20. London: Police officers raid the offices of trading company Polly Peck (→ 25/10).

20. Brighton: Middlesex clinch cricket's County Championship by beating Sussex.

21. Baghdad: Iraq expels 40 diplomats in retaliation for expulsions in Europe (→ 25).

25. London: Sir Jack Lyons is fined £4 million for his role in the Guinness fraud.

27. UK: Britain and Iran agree to resume relations.

30. Moscow: The USSR re-opens diplomatic relations with Israel, broken in 1967.

DEATHS

6. English cricketer Sir Leonard Hutton (*23/06/1916).→

7. British historian Alan John Percival Taylor (*25/03/1906).

Fears grow of Arab terrorist wave as Gulf tension heightens

Sept 18. A Palestinian guerrilla leader today threatened to unleash a wave of worldwide terror. George Habash, the leader of the Popular Front for the Liberation of Palestine, said: "Our fingers are touching the trigger. We will shoot the moment Iraq suffers aggression." Habash, like Saddam Hussein, wants to link Iraqi withdrawal from Kuwait with Israeli withdrawal from the Occupied Territories.

As he spoke, General Michael Dugan, the US Air Force chief of staff, was being sacked for speaking about plans to bomb "downtown Baghdad" and target the Iraqi president and his family. These remarks were clearly ill-timed, given the fragile nature of the Arab-Western coalition poised to strike at Iraq.

And that coalition is gaining strength fast. American troops, marines and equipment continue to pour in. The British 7th Armoured Brigade – the famous "Desert Rats" – is soon to leave for the Gulf. France has replied to the Iraqi looting of its embassy in Kuwait by sending an extra 4,000 men to Saudi Arabia. The Allied effort has been boosted by George Bush and Mikhail Gorbachev's united opposition to Iraq's occupation to Kuwait and its seizure of Western hostages (→ 21).

US troops on patrol take a welcome break in the heat of the day.

UN imposes tighter sanctions on Iraq

Sept 25. With the full backing of the Soviet Union, the UN Security Council voted tonight to add an air embargo to the naval blockade with which it plans to enforce economic sanctions against Iraq.

Eduard Shevardnadze, the Soviet Foreign Minister, who was in the chair, was unequivocal in his denunciation of Iraq and his support for military action, if necessary, to end the crisis. He said that the Iraqi invasion of Kuwait was an "affront to mankind" and warned that the UN had the power to suppress acts of aggression by force "if the illegal occupation continues". He added that Moscow was willing to make a military contribution to any action under the UN umbrella.

Javier Perez de Cuellar, the UN Secretary-General, still hopes for a peaceful settlement, but the Security Council – meeting at foreign-minister level for only the third time in its 45-year history – voted by 14-1 to warn Iraq of "potentially severe consequences" if it did not withdraw from Kuwait. Despite this clear UN verdict Saddam Hussein, however, shows no sign of compliance (→ 23/10).

Germany gets back its full sovereignty

Sept 12. The Second World War was finally laid to rest in Moscow today when the four Allied powers – France, Britain, the US and the USSR – signed the treaty which handed back full sovereignty to East and West Germany, which will soon be united. More than 45 years of division, occupation and the dangers of the Cold War were wiped away with a few strokes of the pen. A date for German reunification was agreed three weeks ago when the East German parliament voted in favour of October 3. Spokesmen from East and West greeted the decision with joyous relief, for it has taken months of fierce argument to settle on a timetable (→ 3/10).

Anglo-French "lamb war" is stepped up

Sept 7. A French lorry driver was savagely assaulted this morning in Kent in an incident linked by police with recent attacks by French farmers on lorry drivers carrying British meat and livestock. The French driver was dragged from his cab and beaten by three men armed with wooden staves. Feelings in France are increasingly hostile to the current scale of British lamb imports. A week ago 100 farmers tried to stop a consignment of lamb leaving Calais, while a lorry-load of British lambs was seized in southern France. Yesterday 400 more British lambs were seized and burnt.

Sept 6. Sir Leonard Hutton, the record-breaking cricketer who led England to victory in the 1950s, dies at the age of 74.

1990

OCTOBER

Su	Mo	Tu	We	Th	Fr	Sa
	1	2	3	4	5	6
7	8	9	10	11	12	13
14	15	16	17	18	19	20
21	22	23	24	25	26	27
28	29	30	31			

2. UK: Police seize two suspected IRA "hit-men" at Stonehenge.

6. Philippines: Government troops crush an attempted coup after only 48 hours.

11. UK: The former British Prime Minister Edward Heath announces that he will go to Iraq to plead for the release of British hostages (→21).

12. UK: Inflation reaches 10.9 per cent (→13/12).

13. US: The UN condemns Israel for the killings on Temple Mount.

15. UK: Latest figures show that the rate of increase of heterosexual AIDS cases is higher than that among homosexuals or intravenous drug users (→11/12).

17. UK: Petrol prices fall by 9.6 pence per gallon.

19. UK: The Liberal Democrats win the previously safe Tory seat of Eastbourne.

21. Baghdad: Edward Heath meets Saddam Hussein to negotiate the release of British hostages.→

21. Japan: Ayrton Senna of Brazil wins the world Formula One motor racing championship.

23. US: President Bush says that there is no room for a negotiated peace in the Gulf.

24. Northern Ireland: The IRA attacks two border posts, forcing drivers to carry bombs in their cars, then blowing them up by remote control.

24. UK: Under intense pressure, the Government announces an extra £1 a week in child benefit.

25. UK: Polly Peck, the £2 billion multinational trading group, goes into receivership with debts of £1.3 billion.

28. USSR: Troops intervene in Moldavia to keep Gaugaz Turks and Moldavians apart.

DEATHS

4. British actress Jill Bennett (*24/12/1931).

14. US composer and conductor Leonard (Louis) Bernstein (*25/08/1918).→

Gorbachev acquires tough new powers

Sept 24. The Soviet parliament has voted overwhelmingly to give President Mikhail Gorbachev sweeping new powers. The parliamentary decree will allow Mr Gorbachev to direct the reform of the Soviet economy more closely and introduce measures to speed up the process of decentralisation.

Time, however, may not be on the president's side. Another winter of food shortages and industrial unrest is looming, while the "fast track" plan to create a free market system within 500 days is being slowed down. The government is now asking President Gorbachev to produce a compromise plan for a more gradual transformation to be presented by the middle of next month (→17/11).

Gorbachev: reform champion.

Inflation hits peak

Sept 14. Inflation in Britain has reached 10.6 per cent, according to figures released today. This is higher than the rate which Mrs Thatcher inherited when she came to power in 1979 and stands as an acute embarrassment to a government which has always dedicated itself to combating inflation as economic enemy number one. The rise was greater than had been expected – and only a third of last month's increase can be blamed on higher petrol prices caused by the Gulf crisis (→12/10).

German dream of unity becomes reality

East and West Germany, divided for 45 years, are reunited at last.

Oct 3. Germany is one nation again. Its rebirth was ushered in at midnight with a triumphant peal from the Freedom Bell at Schoneberg city hall. A roar went up from the thousands of cheering, weeping people, who hugged each other with joy and waved a forest of black, red and gold flags. Forty-five years after the end of the Second World War, Germany was free and united in liberty.

As fireworks exploded, it was hard to believe that it was only 11 months since the hated Wall dividing East and West began to disintegrate and the Soviet Union loosened its iron grip. The future may hold many difficulties, but tonight there is only joy (→2/12).

Sterling joins other European currencies

Oct 5. The Government has surprised the City – and its political opponents – by announcing that it will apply for membership of Europe's exchange rate mechanism (ERM). This will link sterling to other European currencies, despite the Prime Minister's known hostility to greater economic and monetary union. The move was coupled with a one per cent cut in interest rates. The decisions will certainly be welcomed at next week's Tory Party conference (→28).

Fighting evil in the sewers: Sky TV has made stars of Michelangelo, Donatello, Leonardo and Raphael – the Teenage Mutant Hero Turtles.

Palestinians die in Jerusalem rioting

Oct 8. Israeli police have shot dead 21 Palestinians during riots around the Western Wall and the al Aqsa mosque in Jerusalem. The police opened fire with tear-gas, rubber bullets and live rounds after the Arabs threw stones at Jews praying at the Western Wall. Israel has said the police were provoked, but Palestinians say it was "a massacre." There has been international condemnation of Israel's actions, and much discussion of their potential effect on the Gulf crisis. Some of the Arab members of the coalition ranged against Iraq could be swayed by an appeal for solidarity against Israeli aggression (→ 13).

Israeli soldiers stand guard over Palestinians after the riot on Temple Mount.

Heath returns from Iraq with hostages

Going home: rescued Britons drink a toast to their rescuer, Edward Heath.

Oct 23. Edward Heath, the former British Prime Minister, took off from Baghdad tonight with 33 Britons and two pet dogs whose release he won from Saddam Hussein in 48 hours of talks. The Iraqi President has also promised to free about 30 more Britons.

Mr Heath's rescue mission, seen by some as an attempt to embarrass Mrs Thatcher, was widely criticised because of its potential propaganda value to Saddam. What is more, he has failed to reach his target, which was to bring home 200 hostages. The mostly sick and elderly hostages freed today, however, are just relieved to be going home and have nothing but praise for Mr Heath. Elder statesmen of other countries are now thought to be planning similar missions (→ 18/11).

Thatcher is isolated on European policy

Oct 28. European leaders surprised and annoyed Margaret Thatcher at the Rome summit today by moving with unexpected speed to set deadlines for the next stages of economic and monetary union. The British Prime Minister was isolated in her opposition and outspoken in her defiance. "Cloud cuckoo land," she said dismissively, vowing to veto moves towards a single European currency in order to retain the pound.

Mrs Thatcher said that the British parliament would never agree to abolish the pound and accused the European leaders of ducking short-term problems such as farm subsidies by taking refuge in "grandiose" words about long-term schemes. Her European counterparts took little notice, however, and set January 1994 as the deadline for a European central bank, with a single currency likely by the end of the century. Mrs Thatcher's tough talking and rigid policies will alarm the City – and some of her cabinet colleagues (→ 1/11).

Irish premier sacks his deputy in order to save his government

Oct 31. Charles Haughey, the Irish Taoiseach or Prime Minister, today jettisoned his deputy in order to save his government. He sacked Brian Lenihan one hour before facing a vote of no confidence, forced by opposition parties after revelations that Lenihan had made calls to the Irish President in 1982 to try to delay a general election. The Progressive Democrats, the junior party in Ireland's coalition government, threatened to withdraw their support if Lenihan stayed in the cabinet. Today Haughey reluctantly acquiesced, firing his closest ally and winning the crucial vote by a majority of three (→ 9/11).

1990

NOVEMBER

Su	Mo	Tu	We	Th	Fr	Sa
				1	2	3
4	5	6	7	8	9	10
11	12	13	14	15	16	17
18	19	20	21	22	23	24
25	26	27	28	29	30	

1. Westminster: Sir Geoffrey Howe, the Deputy Prime Minister, resigns.→

2. S. Africa: The Government says that all political prisoners are to be freed (→ 1/2).

7. India: V.P. Singh, the Prime Minister, resigns after losing a vote of confidence.

12. Kuwait: Kuwaiti citizens are given two weeks to take up Iraqi identity cards.

14. France: The Government announces an extra £450 million for education after 200,000 students take to the streets.

17. Moscow: President Gorbachev wins increased powers after Soviet MPs force an emergency debate (→ 20/12).

17. UK: Newspaper polls show that the Tories would win more votes if led by Michael Heseltine (→ 22).

18. Baghdad: Saddam Hussein says he will release Western hostages in a trickle (→ 22).

19. Paris: NATO and Warsaw Pact countries agree to slash their conventional weapons armouries (→ 1/8/91).

22. Bulgaria: At least 20,000 protesters call for the government's resignation (→ 29).

22. Saudi Arabia: President Bush spends Thanksgiving Day with US troops in the desert.→

22. UK: Another 15,000 British troops are sent to the Gulf.→

22. UK: John Major and Douglas Hurd announce their candidacies for the Tory leadership. →

28. UK: Britain re-opens diplomatic links with Syria.

29. Bulgaria: Andrei Lukanov resigns as Prime Minister.

29. Bonn: Germany begins airlifting food supplies to the USSR as several cities suffer severe shortages (→ 1/12).

DEATHS

4. US actress Mary Martin (*01/12/1913).

14. British writer and broadcaster Malcolm Muggeridge (*24/03/1903).

Conservatives join forces to oust Mrs Thatcher

Howe speech opens door for challenge

Nov 13. Sir Geoffrey Howe, who resigned from the Government two weeks ago because he could no longer agree with policy on Europe, today delivered a resignation speech of astonishing vehemence. The man who had served the Prime Minister faithfully for eleven years accused her of having a "nightmare vision" of a Europe "teeming with ill-intentioned people scheming to extinguish democracy". Mrs Thatcher's implacable opposition to European economic union undermined all her colleagues' attempts at negotiation, he said: "It's rather like sending your opening batsmen to the crease to find ... that their bats have been broken before the game by the team captain" (→ 14).

Time to go? Mrs Thatcher checks her watch as Tory MPs vote for a leader.

Heseltine bids to topple wounded leader

Nov 14. Confirming rumours that have been rife for weeks, Michael Heseltine today announced his candidacy for the leadership of the Conservative Party - and fired the first shots by demanding an urgent review of the poll tax.

"I am now persuaded that I would have a better prospect than Mrs Thatcher of leading the Conservatives to a fourth electoral victory and preventing the ultimate calamity of a Labour government," he explained. Mr Heseltine resigned as defence secretary in 1986 after losing a row with the Prime Minister over the future of the Westland helicopter company, in which he backed a European rescue plan. Now it is once again Europe which has raised his hackles (→ 17).

The challenger: Michael Heseltine.

Thatcher opts to make it a dignified exit

Nov 22. Two days ago she failed, by four votes, to win outright the first ballot of the Tory leadership contest. Today, aware that her supporters were drifting away to the Heseltine camp, Mrs Thatcher decided to quit rather than see her record-breaking premiership end in an undignified defeat.

At a tearful meeting this morning, the Prime Minister announced her decision to her cabinet colleagues. "It's a funny old world," she told them. Then she went to Buckingham Palace to inform the Queen, as the nation came to terms with her defeat at the hands of her own party. This afternoon, in an extraordinary end to her career, Mrs Thatcher was on brilliant form as she fought off a censure debate in the Commons. "I'm enjoying this," she crowed as she parried Labour's attacks with wit and charm. Many Tory backbenchers were then left wondering whether they had not made a mistake in ousting her (→ 27).

Major triumphs in three-way battle to become Prime Minister

Nov 27. John Major has won the battle to become Britain's new Prime Minister. His opponents, Douglas Hurd and Michael Heseltine, withdrew after he won 185 votes from Tory MPs, compared with Hurd's 56 and Heseltine's 131.

Aged 47, he is Britain's youngest Prime Minister this century. He has been in the cabinet for only three years and Chancellor of the Exchequer for just 13 months. The son of a music-hall entertainer, he left school at 16 with ambitions to be a professional cricketer, but then politics attracted him. As Mrs Thatcher's preferred candidate, Mr Major is already fighting off accusations that she will remain as a "back-seat driver". His first task, though, is to unite the party (→ 28).

A beaming John Major becomes Britain's youngest Prime Minister at 47.

Tears mark end of the Thatcher years

Nov 28. A purple-clad Margaret Thatcher today left 10 Downing Street for the last time as Prime Minister. Fighting back tears, she said that it was time for a new chapter to open.

The chapter that has just closed, on the other hand - entitled "Thatcherism" - has been a long and eventful one. Since coming to power in 1979 Mrs Thatcher has attacked, and in many cases destroyed, Britain's sacred cows. The power of the trade unions was crushed, and free enterprise became the new god. The market ruled. Many people got rich. Others did less well as the welfare state was changed (→ 28/6/91).

▷

Bush offers talks as UN sets a deadline

Getting ready for war in the desert: a British soldier hurls a grenade.

Nov 30. President Bush today sought to open high-level talks with Iraq. The surprise move comes in the wake of yesterday's crucial UN resolution, which gives Saddam Hussein until January 15 to pull his troops out of Kuwait. If he does not, the US-led alliance ranged against him is authorised to use force to liberate Kuwait. Today's invitation to talks is a U-turn by Mr Bush, who has so far refused to countenance any contact with Iraq until it leaves Kuwait. Even as he issued it, however, he made it clear that neither the Iraqi withdrawal nor the freeing of all the hostages held by Iraq were negotiable. Saddam might well ask what is the point of the meeting (→ 10/12).

Ireland opts for untraditional president

Nov 9. Mary Robinson was tonight confirmed as the first woman President of the Republic of Ireland. The 46-year-old liberal lawyer will occupy a post traditionally filled by elderly conservative men. Standing as an independent, she beat her nearest rival, Fianna Fail's Brian Lenihan, by 86,566 votes, days after he was sacked as deputy premier. Robinson has spent the years since 1985, when she resigned from the Labour Party, campaigning for civil and women's rights. She says that she will use the office of President – which brings few powers but vast prestige – to speak up for the disadvantaged in society.

The new President, Mary Robinson.

Emperor Akihito is enthroned in Japan

Nov 12. Festivities have begun in Tokyo for the first coronation of an emperor for 60 years. Akihito, aged 56, was today seated on the "August Heavenly Throne" left empty since the death in January 1989 of his father, Hirohito. Over the next four days, 2,500 guests will be treated to seven court banquets. In ten days' time comes the next – and secret – part of the ceremony. This is the *daijosai*, when Akihito ascends to the heavenly realm and becomes a living god.

1990

DECEMBER

Su	Mo	Tu	We	Th	Fr	Sa
						1
2	3	4	5	6	7	8
9	10	11	12	13	14	15
16	17	18	19	20	21	22
23	24	25	26	27	28	29
30	31					

1. Leningrad: Food rationing is introduced (→ 14).

2. Germany: In the first elections of the reunited country, Helmut Kohl is elected Chancellor.

9. Poland: Lech Walesa wins a landslide victory in the presidential elections.

10. Stockholm: Nobel Prizes go to Jerome Friedman (US), Henry Kendall (US) and Richard Taylor (Canada), Physics; Elias James Corey (US), Chemistry; Joseph Murray and Donnall Thomas (US), Medicine; Octavio Paz (Mexico), Literature; Harry Markowitz, William Sharpe and Merton Miller (US), Economics. Mikhail Gorbachev (USSR) is to collect the Peace Prize next year.

11. UK: The Government makes £42 million compensation available to the 1,200 haemophiliacs infected with the AIDS virus by blood transfusions (→ 2/5/91).

14. Italy: The EC agrees to send food aid to the USSR.

14. Baghdad: Saddam Hussein refuses to meet US officials before January 12 (→ 3/1/91).

20. Thailand: Karyn Smith, aged 19, is sentenced to 25 years for trafficking in heroin.

22. Saudi Arabia: The Prince of Wales visits British troops.

23. Yugoslavia: Slovenia votes for independence (→ 9/3/91).

27. USSR: Gennady Yanayev is elected Vice-President.

DEATHS

2. US composer Aaron Copland (*14/11/1900).

10. US industrialist Armand Hammer (*21/05/1898).

18. French cellist Paul Tortelier (*21/03/1914).

HITS OF 1990

Nothing Compares 2 U.

Sacrifice.

QUOTE OF THE YEAR

"It's a funny old world."

Margaret Thatcher, November 22.

Gorbachev shocked as top ally quits

Dec 20. Eduard Shevardnadze, the USSR's highly-respected Foreign Minister, has stunned politicians at home and abroad by announcing his resignation. "Dictatorship is coming," he warned, speaking to a suitably amazed Soviet parliament. He went on to say that he could not reconcile himself "to what is happening in our country and the trials awaiting our people".

Although Mr Shevardnadze claimed "no one knows ... what kind of dictator will come", the finger clearly points to the Soviet president, Mikhail Gorbachev. Until today one of Gorbachev's closest allies, Shevardnadze has joined the growing chorus of dissent against him as his reforms take effect (→ 27).

Shevardnadze: old ally who quit.

Retailers feel chill

Dec 13. Proof of the recession in Britain can be seen in any high street, where sales have begun during what is normally the peak Christmas period. Consumer confidence is low because unemployment is rising (figures out today showed the biggest monthly jump since 1981, to a total of 1,762,000) and interest rates stay high. Manufacturing output has also fallen for six successive months, but ministers are resisting calls for further cuts in interest rates because of sterling's weakness within the European exchange rate mechanism.

Channel tunnellers meet

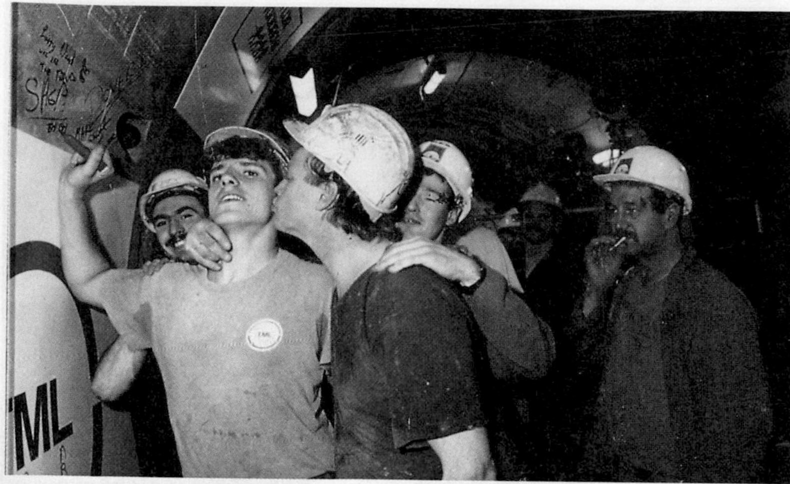

French and English tunnellers celebrate as they join up under the Channel.

Dec 1. There were celebrations deep under the English Channel at 11.15 this morning as the last inch (or centimetre) of chalk separating England from France was bored through by two tunnel workers, Philippe Cozette and Graham Fagg. The occasion was marked, perhaps ominously, by champagne on the French side and mineral water on the English side. Today's breakthrough was in the service tunnel; the train tunnels should be joined up by autumn 1991. But the project still has problems ahead. British Rail has been denied permission to build a high-speed rail link from the tunnel to central London.

Iraq starts to free foreign hostages

Dec 10. Iraq has started to free all 3,400 foreign hostages held since the invasion of Kuwait – fulfilling one of the central demands of the UN Security Council. President Saddam Hussein may have concluded that his "human shield" plan was unlikely to deter attack, and that the chances of peace on his own terms would be greater if he made concessions before opening a dialogue with the US.

Britons held at strategic installations during the crisis started to arrive home today with new stories of Iraq's determination to wipe out Kuwait. Almost everything useful in the country – food, industrial machinery, cameras and even paving stones – has been loaded onto trucks bound for Iraq. The hostages describe how they lived at gunpoint in ramshackle accommodation at munitions dumps, steelworks, power stations and even inside a dam. They survived on cucumbers, rice and tomatoes, and entertained themselves by playing card games and telling stories (→ 14).

Trade war fears as economic talks fail

Dec 7. Four years of negotiations designed to lower trade barriers and thereby boost the world economy are in jeopardy tonight after the final round of talks broke down in Brussels. A potential trade war was averted only by setting a new deadline, but there is no sign of a solution to the deadlock on farm subsidies, regarded by US negotiators as the nub of the problem.

Over 100 nations have been involved in the talks, held under the auspices of the General Agreement on Tariffs and Trade (Gatt), but most were left on the sidelines this week at the final discussions. The United States and the European Community both blame each other for the impasse. The European leaders' offer to cut subsidies by 30 per cent – which prompted noisy protests from farmers – was rejected by the US as being too little. With negotiations now in disarray, the danger is that protective tariffs and regional trade blocs will start to grow again and intensify the downward spiral of recession.

Arts: theatres close, but the past enthrals

If you want to get noticed in the literary field nowadays, write a biography, not a novel. The novelist **Peter Ackroyd** made the jump on a Victorian scale with his 1,000-page biography of Charles Dickens, which read like a novel in places and included imaginary dialogues with its subject. A far thinner volume provided fascinating detection on "The Invisible Woman" in Dickens's life, Ellen Ternan. Its author, **Claire Tomalin**, unlike Ackroyd, did not believe that their friendship was a chaste one.

Other literary biographies of note included portraits of an uncuddlesome A.A. Milne by **Ann Thwaite**, the wayward Jean Rhys by **Carole Angier** and the Raj novelist Paul Scott by **Hilary Spurling**. The year that saw the demise of the novelists **Lawrence Durrell, Patrick White, Alberto Moravia, Rosamund Lehmann** and **Roald Dahl**, as well as the historian **A.J.P. Taylor** and the essayist **Malcolm Muggeridge**, provided biographers with abundant new prey.

Financial crisis closed the Royal Shakespeare Company's London home at the Barbican for the winter with a deficit of £4 million, while the Royal Opera House, £3 million in the red, cancelled new productions. The West End theatre struggled with a crop of musicals that did not break even or were costly flops. **Arthur Miller**, now 75, was the most successful playwright, with five of his plays produced.

The operatic highlight of the year was neither **Sir Michael Tippett's** latest, "New Year", nor farewell galas for **Dame Joan Sutherland** at Sydney and Covent Garden, but the World Cup concert, in the open air in Rome, of "The Three Tenors" – **Domingo, Carreras** and **Pavarotti** – outsinging each other to a world-wide television audience. There can be no-one left, however tone-deaf, who does not recognise Puccini's "Nessun Dorma".

Cannes awarded its Palme D'Or to **David Lynch's** surreal film, "Wild at Heart", despite the very strong competition of **Martin Scorsese's** "GoodFellas". The biggest money-spinner was the romantic hit "Ghost", but European cinema provided the year's most memorable films – "Cyrano de Bergerac", embodied by **Gerard Depardieu**, and "Cinema Paradiso" from Italy's **Giuseppe Tornatore**.

Patrick Swayze and Demi Moore throw a pot in the hit film "Ghost".

Three tenors and a conductor: Domingo, Carreras, Mehta and Pavarotti.

1991

JANUARY

Su	Mo	Tu	We	Th	Fr	Sa
		1	2	3	4	5
6	7	8	9	10	11	12
13	14	15	16	17	18	19
20	21	22	23	24	25	26
27	28	29	30	31		

1. UK: Norman Lamont, the Chancellor of the Exchequer, warns that war in the Gulf could mean tax increases (→ 30).

2. UK: Fewer drivers than last year were found positive in Christmas holiday alcohol tests.

3. London: Eight Iraqi diplomats are expelled after a "We'll hit British targets" threat by Baghdad (→ 9).

5. British Isles: Thirteen people die as 100-mph winds bring havoc and power cuts.

6. London: The Prime Minister, John Major, says that the poll tax will not be abolished (→ 1/3).

9. Baghdad: Foreign diplomats shred documents and pull out as war looms (→ 10).

10. Geneva: Last-ditch talks to prevent war between James Baker, the US Secretary of State, and the Iraqi Foreign Minister, Tariq Aziz, fail (→ 16).

13. Lithuania: Soviet troops open fire on unarmed civilians in the capital, Vilnius, killing at least 13 people.→

14. Tunis: Abu Iyad (Salah Khalaf), the deputy leader of the Palestine Liberation Organisation, is assassinated.

15. UK: Ten thousand NHS hospital beds are prepared for up to 7,000 casualties of the Gulf War.

16. Gulf: Operation "Desert Storm" to liberate Kuwait begins with US air raids at midnight GMT.→

18. Israel: Iraqi Scud missiles hit Tel Aviv and Haifa.→

20. Moscow: A crowd of 100,000 demonstrates outside the Kremlin over violence in Lithuania, expressing support for Boris Yeltsin (→ 19/2).

30. UK: With the cost of the war already at £1.25 billion, British ministers appeal to their allies for financial help.

31. Saudi Arabia: Allied forces recapture the border town of Khafji from Iraqi troops.→

DEATH

13. British yachtsman Sir Alec Rose (*13/7/1908).

"Desert Storm" launches Gulf War

The Allies show their air superiority as anti-aircraft fire lights up the Baghdad sky during the second night of bombing.

Jan 17. Baghdad is shuddering under the impact of heavy bombs and missiles, with thick palls of smoke drifting across the city as waves of Allied planes pound Saddam Hussein's capital. The January 15 deadline for Iraq to leave Kuwait has passed, and the war that everyone tried to avoid has begun.

Operation "Desert Storm" was launched last night when an F-117 Stealth fighter evaded Iraqi radar and destroyed Saddam's telecommunications centre with a 2,000-lb "smart" bomb. Then map-reading Tomahawk cruise missiles flew as if on rails along Baghdad streets to hit Saddam's palace.

Specially-equipped aircraft confused radar defences while missiles locked onto anti-aircraft rocket batteries; then Allied aircraft hammered 300 high-value targets. Over 1,300 sorties have now been flown.

UN Secretary General Javier Perez de Cuellar, France and King Hussein of Jordan all offered compromise deals; all foundered on Saddam's intransigence. "We are preparing for the crushing of evil heads," declared Latif Jassim, his Information Minister. "If Mr Bush makes the mistake of attacking us he will repent it for ever."

It may be the Iraqis who are repenting. They face an Allied force of 700,000 with contingents from 30 countries; 420,000 come from the US, 25,000 from Britain. In the air the Allies have massive superiority, with 2,200 combat aircraft and 530 attack helicopters (→ 18).

RAF changes tactics in high-tech war

Jan 24. The RAF tactic of bombing Iraqi airfields from a height of 33 yards, regarded by the Americans as suicidal, is to be abandoned after the loss of five Tornadoes.

The pilots, admired for their courage, fly through a wall of flak from anti-aircraft guns to drop JP 233 "dispenser" bombs which scatter mines with delayed-action fuses on the runways. "Going up in front of you is just a mass of fire," said one pilot. "If it doesn't hit you, you can breathe again."

Now, like the Americans, they will use laser-guided bombs from high altitude. The RAF insists that the new tactic is because all the airfields have been damaged (→ 9/2).

Captured Tornado pilot John Peters.

Oil disaster feared as Gulf slick grows

Jan 30. Iran called today for a joint international effort to clean up the vast amounts of oil currently spilling into the Gulf, most of it deliberately released by Iraq. The oil has been pouring into the sea from a Kuwaiti pumping station and five Iraqi tankers for over a week now in an apparent attempt by President Saddam Hussein to prevent an Allied amphibious landing. As a huge slick – at least ten miles long and two wide – heads south, it spells disaster for the region's rich coastal and marine wildlife. The US calls Iraq's action "environmental terrorism" (→ 22/2).

Iraq fires Scuds against Israel and Saudi Arabia in bid to widen the Gulf conflict

Jan 31. President Bush is coming under intense pressure from Israel to allow it to attack Iraq in retaliation for the 26 Scud missiles that have so far fallen on Israeli cities. The prospect of such action fills Western leaders with dread.

If Saddam Hussein can provoke Israel into attacking him he will have succeeded in linking his invasion of Kuwait with the Palestinian problem, making it difficult for the Arab members of the US-led coalition to continue fighting.

The attacks on Israel began on day two of the war when eight Scud missiles landed in Tel Aviv and Haifa. Unfounded fears that the missiles might carry gas or chemical warheads caused people to wait in gas masks for an hour after the explosions. The missiles have also been used regularly to attack the Saudi Arabian capital, Riyadh. So far the actual physical damage inflicted by the ageing yet still deadly Russian-built Scuds has been slight. This is mainly because the US Patriot anti-missile missile, or "Scudbuster", has proved effective, lighting up the night sky over Tel Aviv and Riyadh with spectacular explosions.

President Bush has promised the "darndest search-and-destroy operation that has ever been undertaken" to wipe out Scud launchers, but – as the Israelis wryly observe – so far it has been "less than complete". Israel's Defence Minister, Moshe Arens, has said that Israel knows where the surviving launchers are and has plans to destroy them. The deputy Foreign Minister, Benjamin Netanyahu, warned: "We will act when our considerations deem appropriate and in the manner we deem fit" (→15/2).

Damage by Scud attacks on Tel Aviv, made to provoke Israel to retaliate.

Civilians killed as Soviets move in Baltics

Jan 15. Soviet troops stormed a police academy in the Latvian capital of Riga at dawn today as the crackdown on the Baltic states spread from Lithuania, where at least 13 people died in violence at the weekend. Latvians followed the example of Lithuanians by barricading key buildings against further attack. Tension is rising, too, in Estonia, where Boris Yeltsin, the leader of the Russian republic, met leaders of the three Baltic states to give support for their sovereignty. Moscow's attempts to bring the Baltic states to heel as a warning to other restive republics has been widely criticised within the Soviet Union and by Western leaders.

Lithuania remains the prime battleground. Those civilians who died in the capital, Vilnius, were killed when Soviet troops opened fire on crowds trying to prevent the takeover of the radio and television centre last weekend (→20).

1991

FEBRUARY

Su	Mo	Tu	We	Th	Fr	Sa
					1	2
3	4	5	6	7	8	9
10	11	12	13	14	15	16
17	18	19	20	21	22	23
24	25	26	27	28		

1. S. Africa: Cries of "traitor" greet President F.W. de Klerk's announcement that the last apartheid laws are to be abolished (→15/4).

5. Johannesburg: Winnie Mandela goes on trial for her part in allegedly kidnapping four youths (→14/5).

9. Gulf: Allied bombers have flown more than 44,000 sorties in the Gulf War (→13).

9. World: Fear of terrorist bombs is hitting air travel.

12. London: Fine powdery snow is blamed for the failure of British Rail's new trains.

15. London: Opinion polls show John Major to be most popular premier for years.

15. Gulf: TV companies are accused of being "used" by Iraqi propagandists.

15. Gulf: A peace offer by Saddam Hussein is dismissed as "cruel hoax" by Bush (→22).

16. London: Seven thousand gay rights protesters march to a rally in Hyde Park; it is the largest such protest in Britain since 1988.

18. London: One man is killed and 43 people are injured in an IRA bombing at Victoria Station.

19. Moscow: The Russian leader Boris Yeltsin accuses Mikhail Gorbachev of "bringing the Soviet Union to dictatorship" (→30/4).

22. Gulf: President Bush tells Saddam Hussein to "withdraw from Kuwait or face full-scale land attack tomorrow" (→24).

22. Gulf: Iraqi forces begin setting Kuwaiti oilfields on fire, raising fears for the environment (→6/3).

24. Gulf: Allied tanks begin to race north with the aim of encircling the Iraqi army.→

25. UK: Government law officers say that they can no longer support the convictions of the "Birmingham Six" for murder as satisfactory (→14/3).

DEATH

21. British dancer Dame Margot Fonteyn (*18/5/1919).→

IRA blasts mortars at Downing Street

Feb 7. The cabinet had a lucky escape today when the IRA fired a mortar into the garden of 10 Downing Street, shattering windows in the room just 13 yards away where John Major and ministers were meeting. Two other bombs overshot, landing harmlessly. The mortars were launched from a home-made device in a van whose driver had parked in Whitehall seconds earlier before escaping on a motor cycle. After the blast Mr Major remarked: "I think we had better start again somewhere else" (→18).

Hundreds killed in a Baghdad bunker

Feb 13. The US handed Saddam Hussein a propaganda gift in the early hours today when Stealth bombers killed up to 400 civilians, mainly women, children and old men, sheltering inside what was thought to be a command bunker in Baghdad. In the devastatingly accurate attack one bomb blew a hole in the roof and another went through the hole, exploding inside. Foreign reporters were woken and taken to the grisly scene by officials; pictures of the tragedy, shown worldwide, have deeply embarrassed the US (→15).

Feb 21. Dame Margot Fonteyn, top British ballerina, dies aged 71 in Panama. At the age of 50 she could dance like a teenager. She is seen here in "Swan Lake".

100-hour land war crushes the forces of Saddam

Artillery and tanks signal night attack

Feb 24. Allied tanks crashed across the Saudi border in the early hours of this morning behind a devastating artillery barrage. After a month of intensive air attacks – over 97,000 sorties have been flown – the land war to drive Saddam Hussein out of Kuwait has begun.

First reports tell of a stunning victory, with Britain's 1st Armoured Division and the US 7th Corps advancing for eight hours without serious opposition. Overhead, swarms of Allied aircraft queue up to demolish bunkers and dug-in tanks; on the ground special forces teams guide the advancing colums and mark targets for the warplanes.

The two senior commanders make an odd couple. The burly American Norman Schwarzkopf seems like a "dirty boots" soldier but has an incisive military mind, while the smaller Sir Peter de la Billiere looks like an academic but is the most decorated serving British soldier (→25).

Republican Guard units are crushed

Feb 26. Two of Saddam Hussein's elite Republican Guards divisions have been surrounded in southern Iraq. Some Iraqi tanks managed to slip away, but the trap has now been sprung.

"This is it," said an American official, "we have them checkmated. If they go back to Basra, the airforce will kill them. If they try for the other side of the Tigris, the bridges are down. If they flee north to Baghdad they will run into the US Army, and if they move south they run into coalition forces."

The Republican Guard, better equipped, trained and paid than the rest of the Iraqi forces, and most feared by the Allies, have taken a terrible hammering for the past month from unceasing raids by ancient B-52 bombers each of which carries up to 108 500-pound bombs and can "sanitise" an area of over 2,000 square yards (→27).

Hundreds of Iraqi prisoners in Saudi Arabia await transfer to PoW camps.

Fleeing Iraqi convoys stand silent after the Allied attack on the road to Basra.

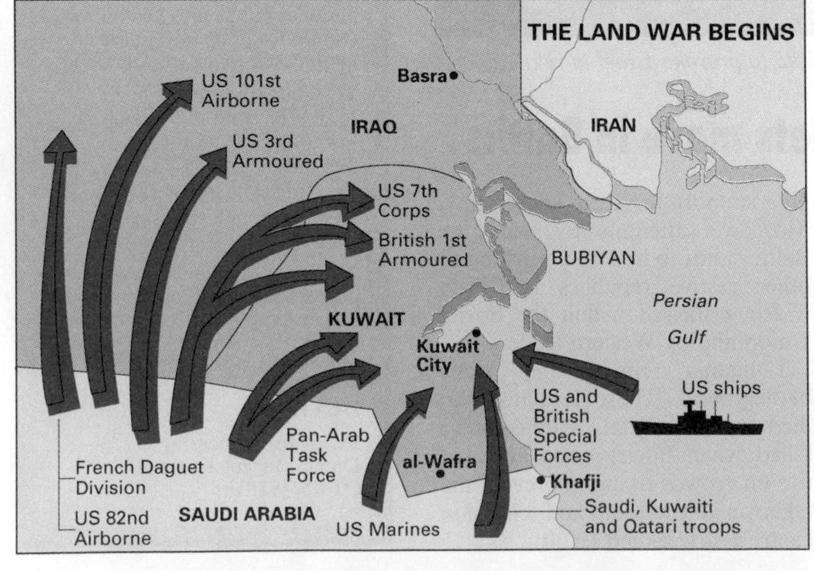

Weary Iraqi troops flee from Kuwait

Feb 25. The Iraqi army is fleeing from Kuwait. Baghdad Radio has announced that it is leaving in accordance with the Soviet cease-fire plan – one already rejected by the Allies. They leave behind scenes of physical and human devastation.

More than 150 of Kuwait's oil wells have been set on fire, and clouds of black smoke blanket the desert, turning day into night. It is an act of wanton destruction with no military value, although the environmental impact is incalculable.

Humans have fared little better, according to an Amnesty International report which drew a "horrifying picture of widespread arrests, torture, summary executions, and mass, extrajudicial killing."

The withdrawal came as the British 1st Armoured Division and the US 7th Corps moved to encircle the Republican Guard to the west. So far more than 270 Iraqi tanks have been destroyed and more than 25,000 troops captured (→26).

Bush orders Allied troops to cease fire

Feb 27. The Gulf War is over. At 9pm in Washington President Bush went on nationwide television to declare: "Kuwait is liberated. Iraq's army is defeated. I am pleased to announce that at midnight tonight, exactly 100 hours since ground operations commenced and six weeks since the start of Operation Desert Storm, all United States and coalition forces will suspend offensive combat operations."

It is not a complete victory. Saddam still rules in Baghdad and retains some military capability, but President Bush could not ignore the growing disquiet at the slaughter of Iraqi soldiers in "turkey shoots". And if they were not dying, the weary Iraqi forces were surrendering by the thousands to the Allies, whose technological superiority was becoming almost embarrassing. With Kuwait free, Mr Bush called it a day (→28).

1991

MARCH

Su	Mo	Tu	We	Th	Fr	Sa
					1	2
3	4	5	6	7	8	9
10	11	12	13	14	15	16
17	18	19	20	21	22	23
24	25	26	27	28	29	30
31						

1. UK: Anne-Marie Dawe, aged 22, becomes the RAF's first female navigator.

3. USSR: Latvians and Estonians vote for independence (→ 20/8).

4. Kuwait: The Crown Prince kisses the ground on his return to freed Kuwait (→ 16/3).

6. Canterbury: Dr George Carey is formally elected as the new archbishop.

6. Paris: Five Irishmen are jailed for a plot to smuggle Libyan arms to the IRA (→ 9/6).

6. Cambridge: Scientists say that Kuwait's burning oil wells could affect human health.

7. King's Lynn: The biggest hoard of gold and silver found in Britain this century is declared crown property.

7. Gulf: Saddam Hussein releases nine British and 26 other prisoners of war (→ 3/8).

9. Belgrade: Riot police fire on anti-Communist protesters in the worst violence in Yugoslavia since 1945 (→ 7/5).

10. Rome: The Rome football club, Lazio, offers £6 million for Paul Gascoigne.

15. UK: Unemployment tops two million (→ 16/8).

20. New York: Property tycoon Donald Trump announces a $10 million settlement with his ex-wife.

22. Ethiopia: Millions of people are threatened by starvation and civil war (→ 30/5).

23. Southport: John Major outlines plans for a charter protecting citizens against corporate abuse (→ 22/7).

28. UK: Scientists predict that "mad cow" disease may persist to the end of the decade.

31. UK: New NHS legislation, including hospital "trusts", comes into effect (→ 16/10).

DEATH

24. Sir John Kerr, former Australian Governor-General (*24/9/1914).

27. Ralph Bates, British actor (*12/2/1940).

Kuwait celebrates its liberation from Iraq

An overjoyed Kuwaiti celebrates his country's freedom from Iraqi occupation.

Feb 28. After six months and 25 days of brutal occupation by Iraqi forces, Kuwait is tonight wild with celebrations of its liberation by the Allies. In the capital, Kuwait City, the jubilation is taking place in a town without power and shrouded in the smoke of burning oil wells – just two legacies of Saddam's rule.

As Allied armoured columns rolled into the city, they were greeted by huge cheering crowds. Young men fired rifles into the air, and the Kuwaiti flag, banned under Iraqi rule, flew everywhere as locals set about destroying all traces of the occupier. Huge gaudy portraits of Saddam were shredded with bullets and Iraqi banknotes burnt. But the joy is mixed with violent anger. Everyone has a tale of torture or murder, and Iraqi troops, when they had orders to withdraw, embarked on an orgy of murder, kidnapping, looting and destruction. Many hostages may have died on the road to Basra, where Allied planes slaughtered Iraqi columns retreating with their plunder.

Kuwait's Sheikh Jaber al-Sabah, in exile in Saudi Arabia, has declared three months of martial law and put the Crown Prince in charge of restoring order. He has the tough job of reining-in former resistance fighters now dealing out summary justice to suspected collaborators, especially Palestinians (→ 4/3).

"Friendly fire" killed most Allied troops

Feb 28. Out of the 16 British troops who died in the Gulf, nine were killed by the Americans. They died when two A-10 tankbusting aircraft mistook British Warrior armoured vehicles carrying men of the Royal Fusiliers and the Queen's Own Highlanders for retreating Iraqis. Their relatives are demanding an enquiry.

The Americans also suffered from "friendly fire", which claimed 35 of their 148 deaths. Officials blame these errors on the featureless terrain, the need to fight in rain and darkness, and the long range of the weapons. The body count for the rest of the coalition was 28. By contrast the number of Iraqi deaths is estimated at 50,000, with 100,000 wounded (→ 7/5).

A British footsoldier in action.

"Birmingham Six" are freed by court

March 14. Six Irishmen jailed in 1975 for the murder of 21 people in a bomb outrage were set free today. The "Birmingham Six" had served 16 years for their alleged part in the IRA Birmingham pub bombings of 1974 – the worst mass murder in recent British history. The court of appeal has now upheld the men's claim that officers of the West Midlands police invented or distorted evidence against them. Today's events raise serious doubts about bias in British courts: this is the third acknowledged miscarriage of justice involving Irish people in the past 18 months (→ 26/6).

Unionists agree to Ulster peace talks

March 25. Leaders of Unionists in Northern Ireland today said that they would join talks about the future of the province with not only the nationalists but also the British and Irish governments. It will be the first time that hard-line Unionists had talked with Irish ministers. The agreement is a triumph for the patient diplomacy of Peter Brooke, the Northern Ireland Secretary, but he is the first to warn that many hurdles remain on the road to any agreement (→ 22/5).

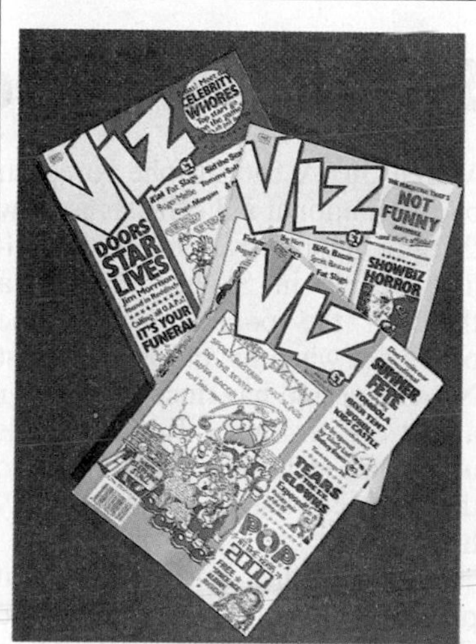

March 5. "Viz", an anarchic and raunchy comic, is a bestseller. Its sales of 1.13m copies per issue are now among the highest for any magazine in Britain.

Chaos grows in aftermath of war

West plays it tough on diplomatic deal

March 16. At their summit meeting in Bermuda today John Major, the British Prime Minister, and President Bush discussed a very tough cease-fire resolution being prepared for the UN Security Council which will leave strict economic sanctions in place, enabling the Allies to keep pressure on President Saddam Hussein without renewing military action.

The summit was preceded by intense diplomatic activity. Mr Major went to secure Soviet support – stopping off in the Gulf to thank British troops – while Mr Bush visited France, and the eight Arab members of the coalition forming a Gulf peace-keeping force. The pressure for a tough line seems to have come from John Major.

He wants penalties imposed on Iraq's oil revenues to pay for Saddam's Kuwaiti adventure, the destruction of Iraq's chemical weapons, the release of Kuwaiti hostages and Iraq's assurance that it will recognise Kuwait's sovereignty for ever. At a joint press conference Mr Bush said he did not "rule in or out" further military action but added that it was difficult to foresee normal relations with Iraq while Saddam was in power.→

Kurdish families abandon their homes, fearing attacks by Saddam's soldiers.

Internal revolts grow in war-torn Iraq

March 23. Kurdish families are fleeing from their homes to the "safety" of the mountains along the Turkish and Iranian borders, with little to protect them from the bitter cold as the fighting grows between Saddam's soldiers and the Kurdish peshmerga guerrillas.

Earlier this month Shia rebels, who owe allegiance to Iran's ayatollahs rather than to Saddam, raised the flag of revolt across southern Iraq. In four major cities Ba'ath Party officals were lynched; disillusioned troops turned their guns on government offices and defaced portraits of Saddam.

The expected US aid never came, and the Republican Guard, despite the hammering it had taken in the war, crushed the uprising, leaving its forces free to move north against the rebellious Kurds.

Now led by Saddam's hated cousin, Ali Hassabn al-Majid, they have taken 5,000 women and children hostage and are using napalm and helicopter gunships to terrorise the peshmerga who are threatening Iraqi oilfields (→ 1/4).

Poll tax is ditched as Tories lose seat at key by-election

March 21. The British government laid the hated poll tax to rest today when the Environment Secretary, Michael Heseltine, unveiled a new property tax to replace it.

Once heralded as the flagship of Margaret Thatcher's third term of office, the poll tax had shrunk to an electoral albatross, sparking riots around the country and dragging the party to a poor second in the traditionally safe Tory seat of Ribble Valley in the by-election earlier this month.

Details of the new tax are still being worked out, but it will seek to reflect both the number of adults in each household and the property's value – houses will be allocated to one of seven bands. Several Tory MPs have expressed fears that the new tax will create millions of new losers, thereby offsetting any electoral gains from people hit hardest by the old poll tax.

This was why Norman Lamont, the Chancellor of the Exchequer, sprang a surprise in his budget speech this week by raising VAT in order to reduce poll tax bills by an average of £140 a head this year. This £4.25 billion interim relief while the new tax is worked out has caused chaos for local councils, who must now recall poll tax bills already sent to householders.

Seven million feared to be at risk as new famine hits Africa

March 30. A catastrophe foreseen by international aid officials is now threatening the lives of seven million people in Sudan – about a third of the population. Famine broke out when the crops failed last November and has since raged over a vast area from the Red Sea Hills in the east to Darfur, 1,000 miles to the west. No one knows how many have died.

Western relief workers dole out porridge to refugees in the squalid shanties outside the capital, Khartoum, but such efforts are too little, too late. Huge amounts of grain are required, yet foreign aid was refused up until last month by the military junta, which suspected the West's motives for offering it.

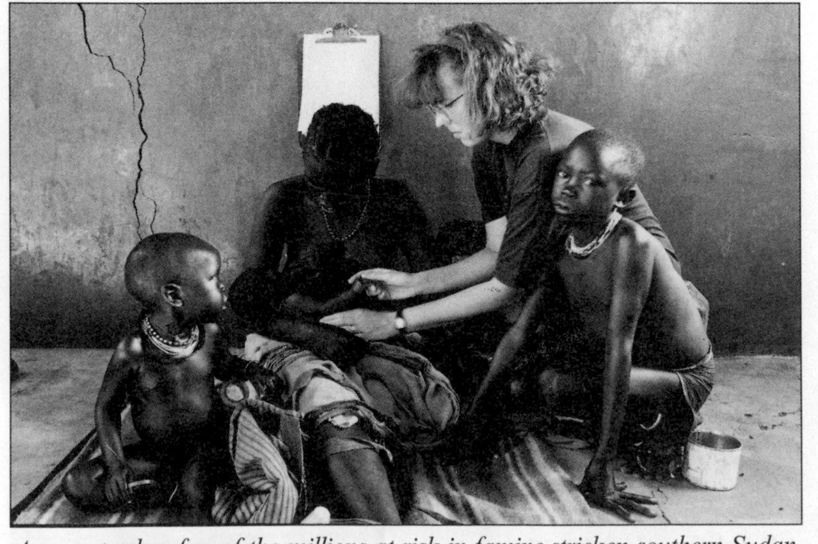

A nurse tends a few of the millions at risk in famine-stricken southern Sudan.

England complete the "grand slam"

March 16. England's rugby union team today ended 11 barren years by winning the Five Nations' championship at Twickenham. England end the season undefeated, although France made them work hard for the "grand slam". A magnificent try by Saint-Andre had given France a first-half lead, but England fought back with a try by Underwood and five successful kicks by Hodgkinson. With two minutes to go, a run by Mesnel and a conversion by Camberabero closed the gap to just 21 points to 19. A relieved yet exultant England hung on until the final whistle and victory (→ 5/10).

1991

APRIL

Su	Mo	Tu	We	Th	Fr	Sa
	1	2	3	4	5	6
7	8	9	10	11	12	13
14	15	16	17	18	19	20
21	22	23	24	25	26	27
28	29	30				

1. Ankara: The Turkish government seeks UN help as its troops turn away thousands of refugees from Iraq (→ 8).

2. Florida: A 30-year-old woman complains to police that she was sexually assaulted on the Kennedy estate (→ 9/5).

2. Tehran: Roger Cooper, a British businessman, is released after five years in prison.

4. Kirkwall: Nine children taken into council care through fears of sexual abuse are returned to their families.

6. Liverpool: Seagram wins the Grand National.

8. Luxembourg: John Major outlines his plan for a "safe haven" for Kurds in Iraq.→

8. Jerusalem: The Israeli government agrees in principle to attend a Middle East peace conference (→ 13/9).

8. UK: Plans are announced to form a new "super league" for English football.

9. Tblisi: Georgia, Stalin's province, votes for independence from the Soviet Union.

11. UK: London Zoo may close for lack of subsidy.

14. Augusta: The Welshman Ian Woosnam wins the US Masters golf championship.

15. Strasbourg: European Community foreign ministers agree to end sanctions against South Africa (→ 10/7).

19. Winchester: The first man to be convicted in England for raping his wife while they were still living together is sent to jail.

21. Iraq: Saddam Hussein defies the Allies and moves his police into Kurdish areas (→ 15/7).

23. Monte Carlo: Former tennis champion Bjorn Borg of Sweden is easily beaten in his first comeback match.

30. Bangladesh: A cyclone causes severe flooding (→ 3/5).

DEATHS

3. British novelist Graham Greene (*2/10/1904).→

16. British film director Sir David Lean (*25/3/1908).

Kurds flee from Saddam

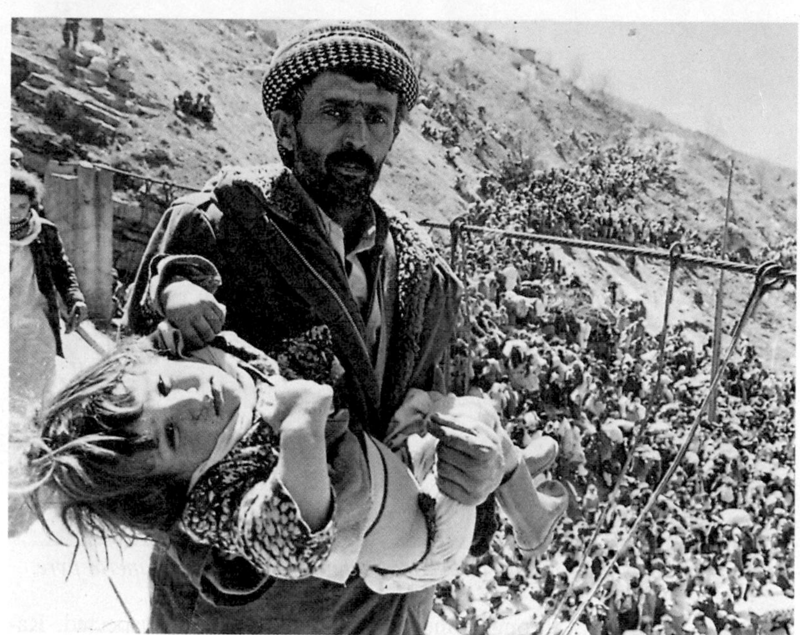

Kurdish refugees await their turn as a father carries his child over the Tigris.

April 19. Several thousand British, American and French troops will move into northern Iraq within 24 hours to prepare camps for the 500,000 Kurdish refugees who have fled the vicious fighting between Saddam's forces and the peshmerga and are living in appalling conditions on the Turkish border.

The move follows an international outcry over the refusal by the British and American governments to help the refugees, whose plight has been making heart-breaking nightly TV news stories, on the grounds that they had no powers to intervene in Iraq's internal affairs.

Margaret Thatcher was among those calling for action: "It should not be beyond the wit of man to get planes there with tents, food and warm blankets. It's not a question of legal niceties." Ten days ago John Major put forward a plan for establishing a safe haven for the refugees inside Iraq which won support from the European Community and the United Nations.

The US then agreed to renewed military action if Iraq attempted to prevent relief agencies from aiding the Kurds by banning all Iraqi military activity in northern Iraq. A spokesman said that the Americans had drawn a "line in the sky" along the 36th parallel: Iraqi aircraft entering the 90-mile-deep zone will be shot down.

As the relief work gets under way A-10 ground attack aircraft circle overhead, and US tanks are only five miles away (→ 21).

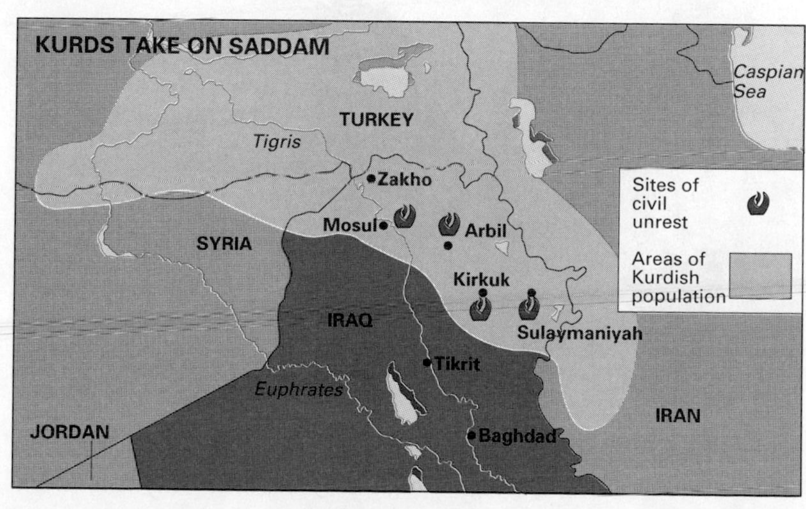

Graham Greene is dead at age of 86

April 3. Graham Greene, Britain's leading novelist for over 30 years, died today at Vevey in Switzerland aged 86. He began his writing career as a journalist on "The Times", and his nose for issues and eye for colour were put to marvellous use in his novels. Many had foreign settings, such as "The Power and the Glory", "Our Man in Havana", "The Quiet American", "The Comedians", "The Honorary Consul" and "Travels With My Aunt".

Greene called himself a Catholic agnostic, and works such as "Monsignor Quixote" explore the theme of the doubting outsider. Several books were turned into screenplays, such as "Brighton Rock" and "The Third Man". He was, controversially, among the best modern writers not to win the Nobel Prize.

Graham Greene: leading novelist.

Soviet leaders fix timetable for polls

April 30. President Mikhail Gorbachev and his chief rival, Boris Yeltsin, have agreed on a timetable for the forthcoming elections for the Soviet presidency – the first direct and free ones ever held for this post. Unlike Gorbachev, whose popularity shrinks as the food queues lengthen, Yeltsin's chances look good: he is already well set to be voted President of the Russian republic in June elections (→ 13/6).

1991

MAY

Su	Mo	Tu	We	Th	Fr	Sa
			1	2	3	4
5	6	7	8	9	10	11
12	13	14	15	16	17	18
19	20	21	22	23	24	25
26	27	28	29	30	31	

1. Beijing: The labour leader Han Dongfang is freed after 22 months in prison without trial (→ 5/9).

2. Geneva: The World Health Organisation says 40 million people will have the HIV virus by the year 2000.

3. London: The Islamic community rejects Salman Rushdie's return to Islam.

4. US: President Bush suffers a mild heart attack after jogging.

6. S. Africa: More than 60 people die in black township street battles.

7. Belgrade: Serbia calls up its army reservists (→ 29/6).

7. US: The US Air Force blames a British air controller for the deaths of nine British troops in the Gulf War.

9. US: William Kennedy Smith, a nephew of Senator Edward Kennedy, is charged with rape (→ 11/12).

15. Rotterdam: Manchester United win the European Cup-Winners' Cup by beating Barcelona 2-1.

16. Paris: Edith Cresson, aged 57, is appointed France's first woman Prime Minister.

18. UK: Tottenham beat Nottingham Forest 2-1 to win the FA Cup, while Motherwell beat Dundee United 4-3 in the Scottish Cup Final.

21. UK: American pit bull terriers face an import ban after the latest savage attack on a child (→ 10/6).

22. Belfast: The Northern Ireland Secretary, Peter Brooke, reports "excellent progress" in attempts to arrange all-party talks (→ 18/6).

23. UK: After urging national pay restraint, the Bank of England Governor, Robin Leigh-Pemberton, is awarded a 17 per cent pay rise.

30. Addis Ababa: A new government is formed by the rebel Ethiopian People's Revolutionary Front.

31. Northern Ireland: Three soldiers die when a lorry carrying a 2,000-pound bomb explodes at an army base.

Rajiv Gandhi is killed

A mourner holds up a picture of his assassinated leader at the funeral pyre.

May 24. Thousands thronged the flower-strewn streets of New Delhi today for the funeral of Rajiv Gandhi, assassinated three days ago by a suicide bomber at a Congress Party election rally near Madras in the southern state of Tamil Nadu. The former Prime Minister's body, covered by an Indian flag, was borne on a gun carriage to the cremation ground and laid on a sandalwood pyre which his son Rahul, in accordance with Hindu tradition, lit with a flaming torch. Seven years ago Rajiv did the same at the funeral of his mother, murdered by Sikh extremists; the identity of Rajiv's killers is unknown, but Tamil guerrillas are suspected. Rajiv's grief-stricken widow, Sonia, and daughter, Priyanka, placed sandalwood sticks around the body as thousands of mourners looked on. They included the Prince of Wales, Douglas Hurd, the Foreign Secretary, the Labour leader Neil Kinnock and US Vice-President Dan Quayle.

To many it seemed that the political dynasty which, with short intervals, has led India since independence was passing at last. Rahul is 20 and Priyanka 19, too young to lead this turbulent nation. The Italian-born Sonia has resisted pressure to assume her husband's mantle.

Winnie Mandela is sentenced to prison

May 14. Winnie Mandela, the wife of the deputy ANC leader Nelson Mandela, was stunned today when a judge sentenced her to six years in prison for complicity in the kidnapping and beating of four black youths, one of whom was later found dead. She has been released on bail pending her appeal.

Mrs Mandela denied knowing anything of the kidnappings and beatings, which were carried out by her thuggish bodyguards, euphemistically called Mandela United Football Club. The brutality of the "club", coupled with her own increasingly dictatorial manner in recent years, have alienated many of her former supporters.

Briton ends orbit

May 26. Britain's first astronaut, 27-year-old Helen Sharman, returned to earth today in Soviet Central Asia after a flight of over three million miles. The food scientist at a Mars chocolate factory beat 13,000 rivals to endure a 17-month training programme and win her place on the Soyuz TM-12 spacecraft. She was launched on May 18 to rendezvous with a Soviet orbital station. Today she said: "I could easily have spent another two weeks up in space. I was having a wonderful time."

Bangladesh floods increase the strain on relief agencies

A fisherman and his family trudge through heavy mud after the cyclone horror.

May 3. Chittagong's beaches are strewn with swollen and decomposing corpses, and each day brings more: victims of the 145-mph cyclone that struck Bangladesh three days ago, leaving at least 125,000 dead and ten million homeless.

The West has promised £12 million, compared with the £32 million needed, but relief agencies are stretched to the limit and reports are coming in of "donor fatigue". The year has seen a succession of disasters such as the Georgian earthquake – 100 dead and 100,000 homeless – and Saddam Hussein's persecution of Shi'ites and Kurds in Iraq – one and a half million more refugees – while in Africa 29 million people are facing famine.

1991

JUNE

Su	Mo	Tu	We	Th	Fr	Sa
						1
2	3	4	5	6	7	8
9	10	11	12	13	14	15
16	17	18	19	20	21	22
23	24	25	26	27	28	29
30						

3. Co. Tyrone: Three suspected IRA terrorists are shot dead in an SAS ambush.

3. London: Prince William has an operation on his skull after being hit by a golf club.

4. Albania: A general strike brings down the hardline Communist government after 22 days (→ 8/8).

4. UK: The British Army will lose a quarter of its manpower in new Government cuts.

5. Epsom: Generous wins the Ever Ready Derby.

5. Stockholm: The Nobel prize-winner, Mikhail Gorbachev, pleads with the West not to set conditions for helping the USSR.

9. Tripoli: In an attempt to improve relations with Britain, Libya breaks all links with the IRA.

10. UK: The House of Commons approves the bill to curb fighting dogs (→ 12/8).

10. Leeds: England win a Test match at home against the West Indies for the first time for 22 years (→ 13/8).

12. London: Five homosexual couples are "married" in Trafalgar Square in a Gay Rights demonstration.

15. Philippines: Half a million people are evacuated as Mount Pinatubo threatens to erupt.

21. Durham: Millions of TV viewers watch in horror as a planning officer is shot dead on camera.

26. London: The Court of Appeal overturns the conviction of the Maguires, now serving their 16th year on IRA charges.

28. Westminster: Margaret Thatcher says she will retire as an MP at the next general election (→ 17/10).

30. Luxembourg: European leaders leave decisions on political and monetary union to the next summit (→ 11/12).

DEATHS

14. British actress Dame Peggy Ashcroft (*22/12/1907).→

14. British actor Lord (Bernard) Miles (*27/9/1907).

Violence as civil war looms in Yugoslavia

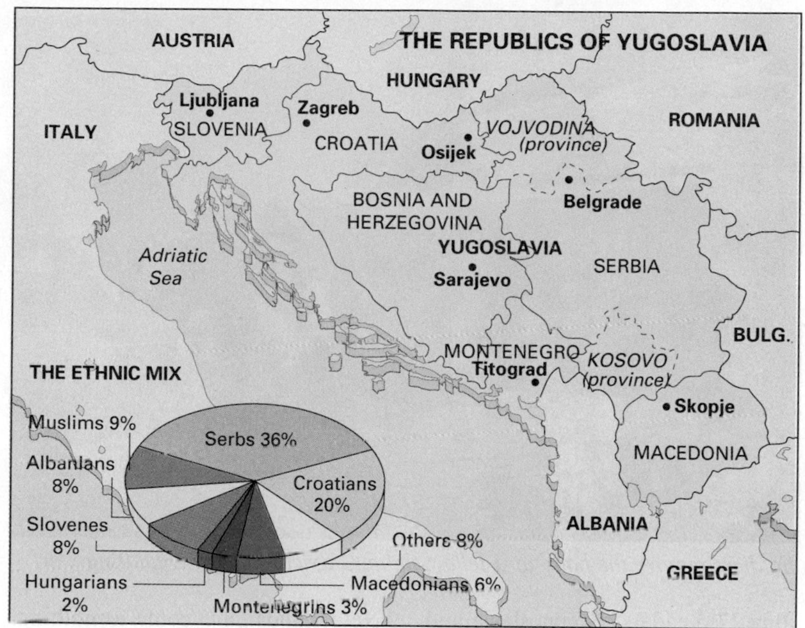

June 29. The phoney war in Yugoslavia is over as the Serbian-dominated federal army tries to suppress independence bids in Slovenia and Croatia. Jets screech over the Slovenian capital, Ljubljana, and tanks roam the streets. Thirty people have been killed in the last two days, and the main radio transmitter has been destroyed. The Slovenians in turn have downed two federal helicopters. In Croatia there is more fighting; airports and borders are closed, and tourists have been warned to stay away.

The fighting in Slovenia is taking place despite an announcement by the defence ministry in Belgrade that the army was halting offensive action after securing most of the border points.

Slovenia and Croatia have both declared independence. They have democratically-elected presidents and a much higher standard of living than the other four republics. Serbia, which traditionally is the toughest and most powerful republic by virtue of its control of the army, is determined to prevent the break-up of the country. A European Community delegation to Belgrade has threatened to halt aid if the fighting does not stop (→ 2/7).

Boris Yeltsin is elected Russian President

Yeltsin: won 60 per cent of the votes.

June 13. In the first free elections of Russia's 1,000-year history Boris Yeltsin has been voted to be the first President of the largest Soviet republic. He won about 60 per cent of the votes in a poll which saw official Communist candidates severely defeated. Yeltsin, aged 60, has promised a democratic multi-party system and faster moves towards a free market economy. Two of his supporters won elections to be mayors of Moscow and Leningrad, where a majority also voted to change the city's name back to that of the Czarist capital, St. Petersburg. Yeltsin's triumph, and Russia's power, will make clashes likely with Mikhail Gorbachev, the Soviet President (→ 4/7).

Parties to meet for first time for years

June 18. For the first time for 15 years political parties in Northern Ireland met for formal discussions today about the future of the province. It was the first stage of a three-stage process devised by Peter Brooke, the Northern Ireland Secretary; talks with the Irish and British governments are scheduled to follow today's opening sessions in Belfast, although the road to the negotiating table has already been bedevilled by arguments about the role of Dublin and the identity of an independent chairman. That the Ulster politicians are talking at all is a tribute to Mr Brooke's patience and to their own desire to avoid being blamed for the collapse of this political initiative (→ 4/7).

Naked Wren guilty

June 13. A Wren was found sitting naked on the bunk of another officer aboard a warship serving in the Gulf, a court martial was told today. HMS Brilliant was the first Royal Navy ship to carry female personnel at sea, and Sub-Lt. Jacqueline Ramsay was one of four officers chosen for this controversial break with tradition. Sub-Lt. Ramsay, who is 25, and Lt. Mark Davies, aged 29, denied having intercourse but were fined £750 each and severely reprimanded.

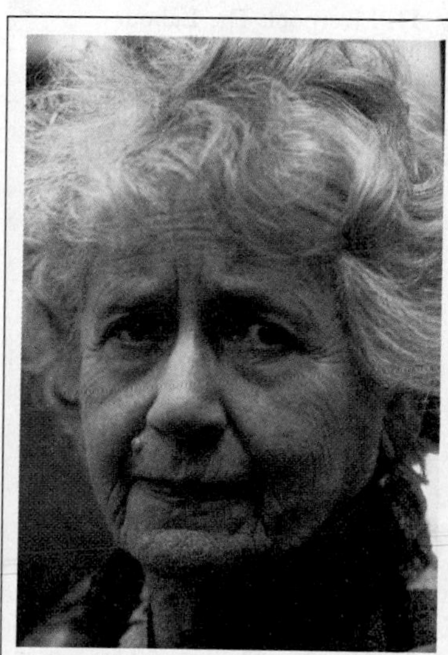
June 14. Dame Peggy Ashcroft, a star actress for 50 years, died today aged 83. One of her last films was "A Passage to India".

1991

JULY

Su	Mo	Tu	We	Th	Fr	Sa
	1	2	3	4	5	6
7	8	9	10	11	12	13
14	15	16	17	18	19	20
21	22	23	24	25	26	27
28	29	30	31			

2. Yugoslavia: The Serbian-led army rejects Slovenia's peace offer.→

3. London: Buckingham Palace dismisses talk of the Queen's wealth of £6.6 million as "exaggerated".

4. Moscow: The former Soviet Foreign Minister Eduard Shevardnadze announces plans for a new democratic movement (→17).

4. Belfast: Loyalist paramilitaries call off the cease-fire after the peace talks collapse (→17/8).

5. UK: The Labour leader, Neil Kinnock, plans a purge of Militants after defeating a left-wing candidate in the Walton by-election.

5. UK: The Bank of England orders the closure of the Bank of Commerce and Credit International (BCCI).→

7. Wimbledon: Michael Stich wins the Men's Singles to complete a German double after Steffi Graf had won the Womern's Singles title.

9. UK: Local councils are said to have invested around £30 million in BCCI.→

10. Leeds: Yorkshire cricket club breaks with tradition to allow outsiders to play for the county.

11. Liverpool: The Labour MP Terry Fields is jailed for failing to pay his poll tax.

14. UK: Nigel Mansell wins the British Grand Prix for his 17th Grand Prix victory, more than any other Englishman.

15. Iraq: Allied forces depart as the UN's "safe havens" end.

19. Cape Town: A minister admits that police have funded the conservative Zulu Inkatha tribal party.

22. UK: John Major launches a "citizen's charter" to improve public services.

25. Milwaukee: Police claim that Jeffrey Dahmer, aged 31, cut up 18 victims and ate parts of their bodies.

31. UK: The Sheikh of Abu Dhabi deposits £50 million in a London bank to help British depositors in BCCI.

European leaders seek Yugoslav peace

Soldiers remove the body of a fellow fighter, a victim of the escalating war.

July 27. Leaders of Yugoslavia and four of its neighbours are meeting in Dubrovnik in an attempt to halt Yugoslavia's apparently inexorable slide into a civil war between Serbs and Croats. Clashes last week between the army and the Croatian National Guard left at least 50 dead.

Despite the spectre of the murderous civil war between these two communities in the 1940s hanging over the proceedings, few of those involved – from Italy, Austria, Hungary and Czechoslovakia – have much confidence in their peace-making abilities. Previous attempts by the foreign ministers of Portugal, Luxembourg and The Netherlands have come to nothing. The Serbian President, Slobodan Milosevic, who is supported by the federal army, has called on all Serbs to be "ready for war" to protect the 600,000 Serbian minority living in the Croatian republic. On the Croatian side, their Information Minister, Hrvoje Hitrec, has predicted a war that would make the recent violence in Slovenia look like a "Disneyland".

The latest fuel to the flames is a report of a huge shipment of tanks, boats, guns and helicopters from Lebanon arriving at the Adriatic port of Bar, which should be a boost to the relatively poorly armed Croatian forces (→6/8).

West offers Soviet Union limited help

July 17. Mikhail Gorbachev made history again today when he became the first Soviet leader to attend a G7 economic summit. Tangible aid to the floundering Soviet economy was, however, limited. A six-point package of assistance held the promise of integrating the Soviet Union more closely into the world economy but gave little of the immediate financial aid Mr Gorbachev had hoped for. The G7 countries had been divided as what their response should be – wait and see because the reforms so far are not radical enough, or allow international bodies like the IMF to become involved (→19/8).

South Africa rejoins international sport

July 10. After 21 years as the pariah of international sport for its now vanishing apartheid policy, South Africa will once more be able to play world-class cricket and take part in the Olympic Games. Colin Cowdrey, who was at the crease at the finish of the last England-South Africa Test, announced the end of the boycott by the International Cricket Council at Lords. The Olympic boycott had been dropped in Lausanne earlier in the week.

The move was welcomed by the South African swimming coach Sam Ramsamy who spent 18 years in exile in Britain and led the boycott campaign.

Bank's doors close

July 20. Embarrassment over the Bank of Commerce and Credit International (BCCI) intensified today with the revelation that the Arab terrorist leader Abu Nidal had used it in London.

The bank was closed by the Bank of England earlier this month following evidence of fraud, a move which was criticised for being far too late; the auditors, Price Waterhouse, had warned of fraud in one of BCCI's subsidiaries four years ago, and last year BCCI was found guilty in Florida of laundering $32 million of drug money (→31).

July 30. Soaked by the torrential rain, the Princess of Wales was among celebrities at Pavarotti's free 30th anniversary celebration concert in Hyde Park. A crowd of around 150,000 listened in the downpour.

1991

AUGUST

Su	Mo	Tu	We	Th	Fr	Sa
				1	2	3
4	5	6	7	8	9	10
11	12	13	14	15	16	17
18	19	20	21	22	23	24
25	26	27	28	29	30	31

3. UK: British pilots tell of torture by their Iraqi captors.

5. Middlesborough: A two-year-old girl is savaged by a rottweiler (→ 12).

6. Yugoslavia: The leaders of Serbia and Croatia agree an unconditional cease-fire (→ 26).

7. Ontario: Indigenous Canadians are to be given the right to govern themselves.

8. Italy: Thousands of Albanian refugees swarm ashore at Bari to seek asylum.

12. UK: From today, fighting dogs must be muzzled and cannot be bred or sold.

13. Edinburgh: As a protest over proposals for the design of the National Museum of Scotland, the Prince of Wales resigns as its patron.

13. London: England win the final Test against the West Indies to square the series.

16. London: The Bank of England backs Government claims that the worst of the recession is over (→ 13/9).

17. Northern Ireland: Sectarian violence has claimed seven lives in seven days (→ 15/11).

20. Estonia: Parliament of the republic votes for independence from the USSR (→ 27).

24. USSR: Ukraine leads the other republics in a move to secede from the Union.→

26. USSR: Thousands gather in Red Square to mourn three victims of the coup (→ 29).

26. USSR: Nikolai Kruchina, involved in the coup, commits suicide.→

27. Brussels: The European Community recognises the independence of Baltic states.

28. Newry: Two Catholics sought by the IRA seek sanctuary in the cathedral.

29. USSR: The Soviet parliament suspends all Communist activities.→

29. London: Princess Diana attends the funeral of friend who died of AIDS.

29. Cardiff: Riots break out on the Ely estate between police and local people (→ 3/9).

President Gorbachev toppled by coup

Yeltsin defies the Soviet hardliners

Aug 19. Hardline Communists have today toppled President Gorbachev. After a sudden and dramatic dawn coup they are now locked in a trial of strength with Boris Yeltsin, the Soviet leader's long-time political partner who became his greatest rival. Yeltsin has now rallied to support Gorbachev, calling on the people to resist the coup.

But the plotters have moved to enforce their authority by putting tanks on the streets of Moscow and banning demonstrations under a state of emergency. Leaders of the coup [*see below*] said that they had taken power because Mr Gorbachev, who had been in office for six and a half years, was "unwell". In fact, he is under house arrest in the Crimea where he was on holiday.

Mr Yeltsin, the President of the Russian republic, made public his defiance by climbing on top of a tank near the Russian parliament to denounce a "cynical attempt at a right-wing coup". Calling for the reinstatement of Gorbachev he urged soldiers to mutiny and workers to strike. Thousands of people surged onto the streets to support the man who has proclaimed himself the champion of democracy within the Soviet Union. But will his voice be heard? The coup leaders are trying to regain control of the press, radio and TV (→ 21).

A defiant Yeltsin waves to his supporters, calling on them to resist the coup.

The Communists who turned against Gorbachev and his reforms

Leaders of the coup: Boris Pugo, Gennady Yanayev and Oleg Baklanov.

Aug 19. Members of the self-styled "committee for the state of emergency" met secretly on Sunday to plan the coup and overthrow the man who had appointed them – Mikhail Gorbachev. Their frontman and nominally the new head of the USSR is Gennady Yanayev, Gorbachev's Vice-President and a party official. Other leading members of the "gang of eight" include the KGB chief Vladimir Kryuchkov, Prime Minister Valentin Pavlov, Defence Minister Dmitri Yazov, Interior Minister Boris Pugo and a senior party official, Oleg Baklanov (→ 21). ▷

Communist rule ends as Russian coup collapses

Three die as tanks roll through streets

Aug 21. Mikhail Gorbachev is on his way back to Moscow tonight after the coup mounted against him disintegrated in the face of popular resistance led by Boris Yeltsin. Thousands in Moscow, Leningrad and other cities answered Yeltsin's call to raise barricades against tanks and troops. Three died early today when tanks moved on the White House, the Russian parliament building, from where Yeltsin was orchestrating the defiance.

But the assault was half-hearted, with many army and KGB officers openly sympathetic to Yeltsin. The collapse of the coup was signalled this afternoon when the defence ministry ordered all troops to withdraw from Moscow. The jubilant crowds raised "V for Victory" signs and chanted Yeltsin's name. Inside the White House the Russian President said the plotters would be brought to trial and claimed personal command of Soviet armed forces within Russia (→ 23).

Gorbachev caught in a power struggle

Aug 23. Boris Yeltsin has moved quickly to consolidate his authority within an apparently crumbling Soviet Union. He humbled Mikhail Gorbachev in the Russian parliament by forcing the reinstated Soviet President to read out a list of alleged coup supporters – a who's who of the Soviet establishment including many supposed Gorbachev allies. Yeltsin then suspended the Russian Communist Party.

Gorbachev has found himself on the defensive since he returned to Moscow after 60 hours of house arrest. His power base has been the Soviet Communist Party, but its role in the coup has unleashed a torrent of public criticism. The party's central committee building in Moscow has been closed and sealed off. Senior figures are resigning, if not arrested and facing trial, leaving Gorbachev with a battle to retain his authority (→ 26).

A Soviet army officer shows the white flag of surrender during the violence.

Yeltsin (r) forces Gorbachev to read out names of coup backers in parliament.

More republics join a rush for freedom

Aug 31. The Soviet Union appears to be disintegrating in the wake of the abortive coup. Seven Soviet republics have opted for independence since the coup collapsed, joining the three Baltic states in their determination to run their affairs without domination from Moscow.

Boris Yeltsin's Russia is by far the largest of those wishing to break away, with a population of 145 million people. But Ukraine, too, has mighty economic potential and would become the fifth largest nation in Europe. Western leaders are watching events closely, not least because of doubts over who now controls nuclear weapons.

Mikhail Gorbachev is struggling to retain a role for a central government, but his position has been undermined by the discrediting of his former allies in the Soviet government and the Communist Party, which was suspended two days ago by the Soviet parliament (→ 5/9).

Coup leaders face trials for treason

Aug 31. Fourteen leading Soviet Communists are now behind bars in Moscow awaiting trial for their role in the failed coup against President Gorbachev. They have all been charged with treason, which carries a sentence of ten years in prison or the death penalty.

All seven surviving members of the committee which headed the coup are among those arrested – the eighth, the former Interior Minister Boris Pugo, committed suicide. The others arrested come from the top ranks of the army, the KGB and the Communist Party. One arrest that dealt a particularly heavy blow to Gorbachev was that of his longtime friend Anatoli Lukyanov, a former speaker of the Soviet parliament. Many others have been fired, including a former chief of the armed forces, a former foreign minister and the heads of the Tass news agency and the state television service.

Israel holds key to new hostage deal

John McCarthy flies to hero's welcome

Aug 17. As the euphoria surrounding the release of the longest-held British captive in Lebanon, the journalist John McCarthy, begins to subside, Israel is emerging as a key to future hostage releases. The hostage-takers insist that progress depends on Israel freeing Arab prisoners, including the prominent Shi'ite cleric, Sheikh Obeid.

A fit and smiling McCarthy flew home on August 8 to a tremendous welcome after being held by the group Islamic Jihad for five years and three months. He said that other hostages, including the Briton Terry Waite, were in good shape, and later handed a letter to the UN Secretary-General, Javier Perez de Cuellar, empowering him, without being precise, to act for Islamic Jihad. Hopes that the hostage episode was ending grew when a long-term American prisoner, Edward Tracy, was freed this week, as was a French aid worker held for three days. With ten Western hostages left, eyes are looking to the Israelis for a gesture. But they refuse to free a single Arab until they know the fates of seven of their servicemen held by Hizbollah (→25/9).

Happy to be back: John McCarthy throws up his hands to greet his friends.

Fighting intensifies as Yugoslavia slips closer to civil war

Aug 26. Cluster bombs were met with petrol-soaked blankets as Yugoslavia slid further into civil war today. The federal army, together with Serbian guerrillas, launched a fierce assault on the key city of Vukovar in eastern Croatia. Cluster bombs killed dozens of the 50,000 inhabitants of the city, whose population is roughly divided between Serbs and Croats.

The defenders are less well armed but undaunted. Lacking anti-tank weaponry, the Croatians are being advised on how to tackle tanks. Lights and periscopes should be shot out, declare newspaper features, portholes stuffed with petrol-soaked blankets and set alight, and bundles of hand-grenades should be rolled under the tank's belly while Molotov cocktails are tossed at the engine.

Air force jets bombed Vinkovci, 20 miles away, while the Serbs near Split, on the Adriatic, have called up men under 60. Three weeks ago Yugoslavia's eight state presidents declared an "unconditional and absolute cease-fire", but so many details were left unclear that it has not held. Meanwhile the Soviet Union has warned Europe against armed intervention (→20/9).

Moscow treaty will cut nuclear arsenal

Aug 1. Nine years of talks were successfully concluded yesterday when Presidents Bush and Gorbachev signed START, the Strategic Arms Reduction Treaty, at the Kremlin. The treaty, which will cut the superpowers' nuclear arsenals by up to a third, was signed with pens made from scrapped missiles.

The occasion was very amicable but also serious, as Mr Gorbachev stressed. The Soviet leader called the treaty "a moral achievement" which replaced "militarised thinking" with "normal human thinking". Mr Bush agreed and gave the impression that as far as he was concerned the danger of a nuclear war between the West and the USSR was over.

Powell's long leap takes the world record

Mike Powell leaps 8.95 metres to gold and into the record books.

Aug 30. The longest-surviving world record in athletics was broken today when Mike Powell of the United States leapt 8.95 metres to erase the mark set by Bob Beamon at the Mexico Olympics of 1968. Carl Lewis, unbeaten in major championships at the long jump for a decade, also beat the old record, but his 8.91 metres was wind-assisted. Some consolation for Lewis will be his victory (and world record) in the 100 metres at the world championships in Tokyo. He won in 9.86 seconds, with six of the finalists clocking less than ten seconds in the greatest sprint race of all time.

Scotland's Liz McColgan was the sole British gold medallist, winning the 10,000 metres today by more than 20 seconds.

Aug 17. Arnold Schwarzenegger as fans saw him in a midnight preview: the first British screening of "Terminator 2: Judgment Day" in London's West End.

1991

SEPTEMBER

Su	Mo	Tu	We	Th	Fr	Sa
1	2	3	4	5	6	7
8	9	10	11	12	13	14
15	16	17	18	19	20	21
22	23	24	25	26	27	28
29	30					

3. UK: Police Federation leaders call for the return of the Riot Act after late-night fighting breaks out in Cardiff, Birmingham and Oxford.→

5. Moscow: The Congress of People's Deputies votes to wind up the USSR in favour of a looser federation of sovereign states (→ 2/12).

5. Beijing: John Major criticises the Chinese government's record on political prisoners.

9. UK: The Keith Prowse ticket agency collapses with losses of £9 million.

13. UK: Figures today show that the annual rate of inflation has dropped to 4.7 per cent (→ 19/12).

13. US: President Bush angers Israel by refusing a $10bn loan guarantee for housing in the Occupied Territories (→ 31/10).

16. UK: The all-male Magic Circle lifts its ban on women.

17. UK: The case of Judith Ward, convicted for a 1974 IRA coach bombing in which 11 people died, is sent to the Court of Appeal (→ 11/5/92).

20. The Hague: European Community ministers defer a decision on sending a peace-keeping force to Yugoslavia.→

21. London: The boxer Michael Watson faces brain surgery after collapsing in the ring after a world-title fight last night against Chris Eubank.

25. Wiltshire: Jackie Mann, aged 77, returns to Britain after two and a half years as a hostage in Beirut (→ 18/11).

29. Baghdad: UN inspectors investigating Iraq's nuclear programme are allowed to leave after being besieged in a car park for a week.

30. Dublin: An inquiry begins into various business scandals which allegedly have links with the Irish government (→ 18/10).

30. UK: John Major lets it be known that there will be no general election this year.

DEATH

28. US jazz musician Miles Davis (*25/5/1926).→

Archbishop blames deprivation for riots

Police hope for a new Riot Act to prevent scenes like this in Tyne and Wear.

Sept 20. Church and State were on a collision course today after the Archbishop of Canterbury blamed social deprivation for a wave of inner city riots this month. This view contrasts strongly with that of government ministers who argue that criminal behaviour – not unemployment or poverty – is to blame for riots in four British cities.

Cardiff was the first troublespot, when a dispute between two shopkeepers escalated into fighting between 300 people and 200 police in riot gear. Late-night fighting then broke out in Birmingham and Oxford, where the focus was a police crack-down on "hotting" – racing stolen cars. But the worst of the riots occurred on Tyneside, where for three nights hundreds of youths set buildings ablaze, looted shops, set up barricades and taunted the police to catch them in stolen vehicles. With the Police Federation calling for a return of the Riot Act to give police stronger powers, the Government says that the Church should be giving young people a moral lead, not excusing them.

Trumpeter Miles Davis plays his last solo

"Cool" jazz: the late Miles Davis.

Sept 28. The death today of Miles Davis, aged 65, robbed jazz of both its foremost living exponent and the inventor of a new trumpet sound – languid, haunting, melancholy. He played without looking at the audience (often turning his back on it) and left the stage without waiting for applause.

Many placed him above both Louis Armstrong and Dizzy Gillespie, who with Charlie Parker was his original inspiration. He studied music at the Juilliard School in New York but left – because it was "too white" – to play bebop in the clubs of 52nd Street. He developed what became known as "cool" jazz, a subtle and sophisticated style, exemplified in albums like "Kind of Blue" and "Milestones".

Yugoslav violence thwarts peace bid

Sept 29. An attack on a Red Cross convoy rescuing mental patients is the latest violation of Yugoslavia's nominal cease-fire. The Red Cross has suspended operations. The cease-fire has supposedly been in operation since September 7 when a peace conference, to try to settle the bitter dispute between Serbia and Croatia, opened in The Hague.

So far the militarily superior Serbian forces have occupied nearly a third of Croatia in a bid to crush the republic's drive for independence, but Serbia's success has alarmed its neighbours and provoked an international backlash. The European Community has shied at sending in a peace-keeping force but wants greater protection for the 80 EC monitors in the country (→ 12/10).

A Croatian policeman under attack.

Ryder Cup lost by final missed putt

Sept 29. The Ryder Cup reached a gripping climax today as Bernhard Langer of Germany attempted to sink a five-foot putt to beat his American opponent, Hale Irwin. He had fought back from two holes down with four to go on this testing new course on Kiawah Island, but he missed by an inch, and the Americans recaptured a trophy they had lost to Europe in 1985.

1991

OCTOBER

Su	Mo	Tu	We	Th	Fr	Sa
		1	2	3	4	5
6	7	8	9	10	11	12
13	14	15	16	17	18	19
20	21	22	23	24	25	26
27	28	29	30	31		

1. Haiti: A military coup forces Jean-Bertrand Aristide, the President, to flee.

3. UK: Sir Allan Green, the Director of Public Prosecutions, resigns after an incident in a red-light district of London.

3. Stockholm: Nadine Gordimer, the South African novelist, wins the Nobel Prize for Literature (→ 10/12).

5. Twickenham: The rugby World Cup begins (→ 2/11).

6. US: Elizabeth Taylor marries for the eighth time.

7. US: Judge Clarence Thomas, a nominee for the Supreme Court, is accused of sexual harassment (→ 15).

9. UK: The Government chooses a route to Stratford for the high-speed rail link to the Channel Tunnel.

12. Dubrovnik: The mediaeval "pearl of the Adriatic" comes under fire by federal troops.→

15. US: The Senate elects Judge Thomas to the Supreme Court by 52 votes to 48 after televised hearings into charges of sexual harassment.

16. Texas: A 35-year-old man kills 22 people in a restaurant.

16. UK: A further 99 hospitals and health units are to become self-governing trusts.

17. UK: Margaret Thatcher's memoirs are bought for £2.5 million.

18. Brussels: Britain is angered by a European Commission demand that it halts seven building projects on environmental grounds.

20. US: David Duke, a former Ku Klux Klan leader, qualifies for the second round as a Republican candidate for the governorship of Louisiana.

22. London: The Nigerian author Ben Okri wins the Booker Prize for his novel "The Famished Road".

29. Hong Kong: Britain agrees to return over 60,000 "boat people" to Vietnam (→ 8/11).

31. UK: The Queen's speech opening a new session of Parliament signals more money for public services.

Dubrovnik under siege

A concentrated Serbian attack on Dubrovnik threatens "a unique heritage".

Oct 26. Dubrovnik, "the pearl of the Adriatic", is coming under concentrated attack from the Yugoslav army. The historic mediaeval heart of the city, once Yugoslavia's most famous tourist attraction, is being shelled by troops of the Serb-dominated federal army. The city is now besieged, with a naval blockade stopping supplies to the 50,000 Croatian inhabitants who are already without electricity or water.

The federal army had said that it intended to spare the city – designated a "world heritage site" by Unesco – from all-out assault by trying to starve out the lightly-armed Croatian forces. But the collapse of moves to establish a ceasefire between the Croats and Serbs brought a change of tactics.

World attention has focussed on the threat to Dubrovnik's unique heritage of Venetian architecture and baroque churches. However, aid organisations are more concerned about the plight of the civilian victims of the civil war. Other towns along the Adriatic coast are also being pounded from land and sea, while in the north the Croatian border town of Vukovar seems close to collapse after months of resistance to the Serbs (→ 15/11).

Adams is record-breaking number one

Oct 27. The Canadian singer Bryan Adams was toppled from the top of the pops today after a record-breaking run of 16 weeks at number one. His recording of "(Everything I do) I do it for you" comfortably beat the previous record, which goes back to the pre-rock era of 1955 when Slim Whitman spent 11 weeks at number one with "Rosemarie". Nobody else ever got into double figures, although Paul McCartney was one of four singers or groups with nine weeks at the top. Quite why Adams has had such a hit nobody seems to know. His previous seven singles failed to reach the top 40. And even though this one is sung in Kevin Costner's "Robin Hood" film, it is heard only over the closing titles.

Bryan Adams, surprise chart topper.

Haughey survives vote of confidence

Oct 18. Charles Haughey, the Irish Prime Minister, today confirmed his legendary reputation as the great survivor of Dublin politics. Bruised by financial scandals in the state sector, battered in the opinion polls and subjected to direct attack by his party's deputies, it seemed that Haughey's third term as taoiseach was in jeopardy. But a last-minute deal between his Fianna Fail party and the Progressive Democrats, its coalition partners, enabled Haughey to survive today's vote of no confidence in the Dail (parliament). However, his position remains less secure than at any time since he returned to office as Prime Minister in 1987.

Haughey: criticism from all sides.

Burmese prisoner wins Nobel Prize

Oct 14. The Nobel Peace Prize was awarded today to Aung San Suu Kyi, a frail 46-year-old woman who has been kept under house arrest for the past 15 months in Burma. Her detention was ordered by the Burmese military leaders who refuse to recognise the electoral victory won by her National League for Democracy in May 1990. In its award, the Nobel committee says she is providing "one of the most extraordinary examples of civil courage in recent years". The Burmese leaders are unmoved: the detention continues (→ 2/11).

Madrid hosts historic Middle East summit

Oct 31. Months of diplomacy and superpower cooperation came to fruition today when Arabs and Israelis sat down together in Madrid to begin a conference designed to bring peace to the Middle East. James Baker, the US Secretary of State, has spent months cajoling and twisting arms to bring all parties to the negotiating table. Today he succeeded, with Presidents Bush and Gorbachev acting as conference co-chairmen.

The US President opened the first session with an appeal for Arabs and Israelis to forgive and forget, but his words were soon lost in a flurry of bitter invective. The quarrel rested on what was always going to be the main stumbling block: what the Arabs see as the Occupied Territories. Israeli Prime Minister Yitzhak Shamir insisted: "The issue is not territory, but our existence." The Syrian Foreign Minister, Farouk al-Sharaa, replied by saying the Israelis must return "every inch of Arab land occupied by force".

The lands in question are the Golan Heights, the West Bank and Gaza Strip, a 440-square mile "security zone" in South Lebanon, and Jerusalem. The Palestinians, who are not formally represented in Madrid, are particularly critical of the Israeli policy of allowing settlers to make homes in these disputed territories.

Israel's Shamir: bitter invective.

Thatcher says sorry to axed ITV boss

Oct 17. Margaret Thatcher has apologised to one of the victims of a shake-up in Britain's commercial television system caused by changes which her government introduced. Four ITV companies are to lose their licences from 1993, including Thames, the largest supplier of weekday programmes to the ITV network. Some companies found themselves to be winners despite being outbid, while others lost even though they made higher bids than their rivals. One of the latter losers was the breakfast station TV-am, whose chief, Bruce Gyngell, today revealed Mrs Thatcher's handwritten note saying that she was "mystified and heartbroken".

Reporter sacked in "Mirror" spy storm

Oct 28. Nicholas Davies, the journalist accused last week of being an Israeli spy and an arms dealer, was sacked today as foreign editor of the "Daily Mirror" because he had damaged the "reputation and integrity" of the newspaper by lying about a meeting with an arms dealer in Ohio. But the "Mirror" still denies that Davies and its proprietor, Robert Maxwell, have close links with the Israeli secret service, Mossad, as alleged by the American writer Seymour Hersh in his book "The Samson Option". After questions were asked in the Commons, Mr Hersh arrived in Britain to promote his book and to receive a libel writ from Maxwell (→5/11).

1991

NOVEMBER

Su	Mo	Tu	We	Th	Fr	Sa
					1	2
3	4	5	6	7	8	9
10	11	12	13	14	15	16
17	18	19	20	21	22	23
24	25	26	27	28	29	30

2. Burma: The Nobel prize-winner Aung San Suu Kyi is said to be critically ill on hunger strike (→10/12).

4. UK: British Rail blames leaves on lines for delays.

8. UK: The former Tory minister Nicholas Ridley says people should vote for anti-European candidates, regardless of party (→23).

8. Hong Kong: Vietnamese "boat people" struggle against police forcing their return.

8. US: America is shocked by the news that the basketball star Earvin "Magic" Johnson has AIDS (→24).

12. Tenerife: Experts are reported to be uncertain about the cause of Robert Maxwell's death (→7/12).

13. Warsaw: England draw with Poland to qualify for the European Football Finals.

14. UK: Two Libyans are named as suspects for the 1988 explosion which blew up a Pan Am jet over Lockerbie.

15. Yugoslavia: The 13th cease-fire in recent months is proclaimed (→23).

15. New York: Shares on Wall Street experience their biggest fall for two years.

15. St. Albans: Two IRA bombers blow themselves up near an Army band concert.

18. Damascus: Terry Waite and Tom Sutherland are released.→

23. UK: Margaret Thatcher attacks her successor's government as "arrogant and wrong" in refusing to have a referendum on a single European currency (→11/12).

24. London: Ian Richter returns home after more than five years in an Iraqi jail.

25. UK: Winston Silcott, serving life for a policeman's murder in the 1985 Broadwater Farm riots in Tottenham, is cleared by the Appeal Court; two other men are expected to be cleared.

DEATH

24. British rock star Freddie Mercury (*5/9/1946).→

Wallabies celebrate World Cup victory

Nov 2. The Australians are the new world champions of rugby union. They beat England today in a final at Twickenham that was a splendid showcase for the game. A month of matches in England, Scotland, Wales, Ireland and France had brought two hard-fought semi-finals between old rivals. The Wallabies won the battle of the southern hemisphere by knocking out the defending world champions, New Zealand. England meanwhile beat Scotland at Murrayfield 9-6.

England, who had been criticised for relying too much on forward power, played a more open game today, but it is the Australian team which has proved itself the supreme masters of open rugby in this tournament. Deservedly, they won 12-6, although England made them fight all the way.

Queen star Freddie succumbs to AIDS

Nov 24. Freddie Mercury, the lead singer of the rock group Queen, died today of AIDS. He was 45 and had been one of the most flamboyant stars of the pop world, a master showman with a powerful voice who headed one of the most successful bands of the last 20 years. In 1975, Queen's "Bohemian Rhapsody" introduced the first video to promote a pop single. Mercury, a bisexual, won praise for admitting he had AIDS.

Singing for Live Aid at Wembley.

Publisher Robert Maxwell drowns at sea

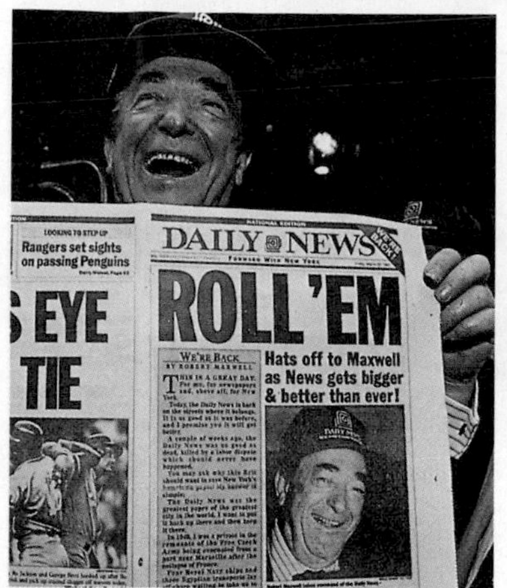

Maxwell holds up the first copy of the "News" under his ownership.

Nov 5. Robert Maxwell, the British publishing tycoon who disappeared from his yacht off the Canary Islands in the early hours of this morning, has been found dead. His naked body was picked up by a helicopter and taken to the island of Gran Canaria where it was identified by his wife, Elisabeth, and one of his sons, Philip. He was 68.

The Spanish authorities have begun an enquiry on board his yacht, the "Lady Ghislaine", to determine whether he died accidentally or killed himself, overcome by the financial problems of his empire or the accusations of links with the Israeli secret service. A Czech refugee in the Second World War, he was briefly a Labour MP and built up a global publishing empire, bouncing back from criticism in the 1970s to own publishing companies and leading newspapers such as the British "Daily Mirror" and New York's "Daily News". But his companies in Britain and the United States are saddled with huge debts to increasingly anxious banks. Shares in his British companies have been suspended (→ 12).

Terry Waite is released

A cheery wave of freedom from Terry Waite as he arrives at RAF Lyneham.

Nov 19. Terry Waite came home today after spending nearly five years as a hostage chained to a wall in Beirut. He was released yesterday along with the Scottish-born American, Tom Sutherland. Mr Waite, the last remaining British hostage in Lebanon, was welcomed at a rainy RAF Lyneham in Wiltshire by the Archbishop of Canterbury and his predecessor, Lord Runcie, whose envoy he had been.

Minutes after walking down the steps of the plane Terry Waite delivered a forceful, emotional account of his imprisonment and the Christian faith which had sustained him, interspersed with jokes about lacking shoes big enough for him. He had seen no one and spoken to no one except his guards for four years. Then one day he was given a postcard sent by an unknown well-wisher. It showed a stained-glass window depicting John Bunyan in Bedford jail. "I thought, my word Bunyan, you're a lucky fellow. You've got a window out of which you can look, see the sky and here I am in a dark room. You've got pen and ink, you can write, but here am I, I've got nothing and you've got your own clothes and a table and chair" (→ 4/12).

Biblical names top those of the royals

Nov 24. The Bible outscored the British royal family when it came to influencing children's names in the 1980s, according to a survey of 180,000 children published today.

James was the top boy's name, with Matthew in second place. Joshua, Joseph and Luke all rose in popularity while royal names languished – William was 21st, Harry 58th and Charles 62nd. Among the girls the biblical influence was less marked, with Sarah, Laura and Emma the top names. However Rebecca, Hannah and Rachel still outscored Elizabeth, Anne, Margaret and Diana, none of which made the top ten. Nor did that chosen by the Princess Royal for her daughter – Zara.

Croatian city falls to Serbian-led army after three month siege

Nov 23. After a three-month siege by the Serbian-led Yugoslav federal army, the Croatian city of Vukovar has surrendered. The battle for the border town, which had a population of 50,000, has been the most ferocious so far in Yugoslavia's civil war. As many as 5,000 people, most of them civilians, are feared to have been killed by the federal army's intense air and artillery bombardments. This continued unabated while world opinion focused on the threat to the port of Dubrovnik. Its 15th-century fortress, for long a major tourist attraction as "the pearl of the Adriatic", has come under heavy fire. Peace moves there have brought an uneasy lull while the army switches to Osijek (→ 17/12).

Smoke and flames rise from the ancient city of Dubrovnik after heavy attack.

More troops sent to embattled Belfast

Nov 15. More troops and police were sent to patrol dangerous areas in and around Belfast today after two nights of tit-for-tat killings by Republican and Loyalist gunmen left seven people dead. In the past five weeks, some 20 people have died, including two soldiers killed by an IRA bomb attack on Musgrave Park military hospital. The reinforcements include 1,400 members of the Ulster Defence Regiment and 300 regular soldiers. The killings have stirred demands for the reintroduction of internment without trial, but the government is cautious, knowing that it would be resisted by Nationalists north and south of the border (→ 21/12).

1991

DECEMBER

Su	Mo	Tu	We	Th	Fr	Sa
1	2	3	4	5	6	7
8	9	10	11	12	13	14
15	16	17	18	19	20	21
22	23	24	25	26	27	28
29	30	31				

1. UK: Shops across England and Wales open and defy the Sunday trading laws.

2. Ukraine: Voters in the former Soviet republic vote for independence (→20).

4. US: Pan Am stops flying when a financial rescue plan fails to save the airline.

10. Stockholm: Nobel Prizes are awarded to Pierre-Gilles de Gennes (France, Physics); Richard Ernst (Switzerland, Chemistry); Erwin Neher and Bert Sakman (Germany, Medicine); Nadine Gordimer (South Africa, Literature); Ronald Coase (Britain, Economics); and in Oslo to the sons of Aung San Suu Kyi (Burma, Peace).

15. Red Sea: Over 400 people die when an Egyptian ferry sinks.

17. Blackpool: Fire destroys the famous Fun House.

17. Netherlands: EC foreign ministers bow to German pressure to recognize the independence of Croatia and Slovenia next year.

20. New York: Governor Mario Cuomo says he will not run for the US presidency.

20. Australia: Bob Hawke is ousted as premier by Paul Keating.

21. Belfast: Four people die in sectarian violence.

25. UK: The Queen, in her Christmas broadcast, hints that she will not abdicate.

27. Sweden: All 129 people on board survive when their SAS DC-9 crashes after take-off.

DEATHS

8. Cricket commentator John Arlott (*25/02/1914).

14. Judith Hart, Labour politician (*18/9/1924).

HITS OF 1991

(Everything I do) I do it for you.

I'm too sexy.

QUOTE OF THE YEAR

"The great, the jewel and the mother of battles has begun."

Saddam Hussein.

Gorbachev goes, Soviet Union ends

A last call to President Bush.

Army nuclear specialists show Yeltsin (centre) the "Nuclear Button" controls.

Dec 25. Mikhail Gorbachev resigned today. He was the first and, it turned out, the last Soviet executive President, and he bowed out amid warnings about the future of the country which he had led for almost seven years. The death knell for the Soviet Union sounded on December 8 when Russia, Byelorussia and the Ukraine announced their vision of a Commonwealth of Independent States. Then, on December 21, the leaders of eight other republics backed the commonwealth. Only Georgia and the three Baltic states remain outside.

Events in what for 70 years was the centre of the Communist empire have moved this month with bewildering speed. Boris Yeltsin, the President of Russia, forced the pace, seeking US recognition and signing decrees taking over the Soviet Foreign Ministry and the Kremlin itself. Yet there has been none of the euphoria which greeted the collapse of the hard-line Communist coup last August.

Whoever runs the republics, they face daunting economic problems which James Baker, the US Secretary of State, has warned could cause a "social explosion". The West is also concerned about other forms of potential explosion: the 27,000 nuclear weapons now lacking any clear central control. So far leaders of the republics have failed to agree on defence policy, although Yeltsin initially has inherited control of the Soviet nuclear armoury. He has sought to reassure the West that he would use his new power responsibly, but there are also fears within the commonwealth that Russia is too powerful. Ukraine, the second largest state, has clashed with Russia over control of the Black Sea fleet, and several former republics have protested over the effects of Yeltsin's plans to end price controls.

In his ten-minute resignation speech on television Mikhail Gorbachev said he had no regrets about the democratic movement which he had launched in 1985, but added: "The old system fell apart before the new one began to work." He said he supported the independence of the republics but opposed "dismembering this country and disuniting the state" as entailed by the new commonwealth. As he spoke, the red flag was lowered for the last time over the Kremlin (→30/1/92).

Kennedy nephew acquitted in rape trial

Dec 11. William Kennedy Smith, a nephew of Senator Edward Kennedy, was today found not guilty of raping a 30-year-old woman at his family's Florida estate last March. The trial had been televised live and, besides lurid tales of late-night drinking and casual sex, had sharpened public debate about "date rape" and the difficulty of proving sexual assault. The defendant admitted that he had sex with the woman but claimed that she participated willingly in a "consensual act of love". Senator Kennedy was among those who gave evidence, saying that he had heard no screams on the night of the alleged assault.

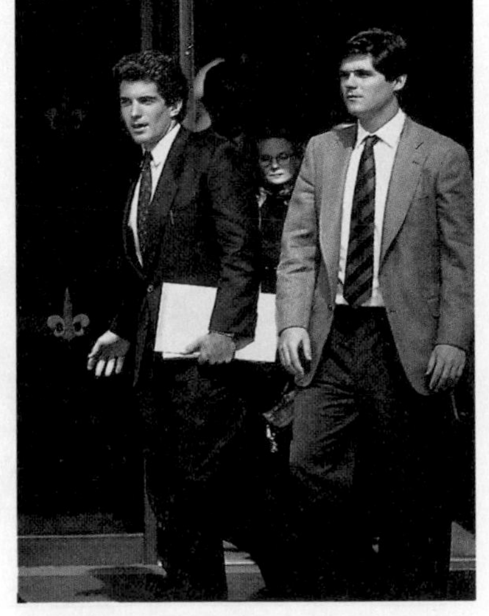

Smith (r): "woman consented".

Last Americans are freed from Lebanon

Dec 4. Terry Anderson, the American journalist who was the last and longest-held of the American hostages in Lebanon, is free. He will fly today to Germany where he will join two other US hostages, Joseph Cicippio and Alann Steen, who were released earlier this month. Anderson, who was captured on March 16, 1985, was reunited in Damascus today with his fiancee and their six-year-old daughter Sulome – a child he had never seen. The release of the three Americans leaves two Germans as the only Western hostages still being held in Lebanon.

Major claims victory at European summit

Dec 11. In the early hours of this morning European leaders reached an historic agreement on closer political union. The deal signed at Maastricht in the Netherlands sets 1999 as the deadline for a single currency, introduces majority voting into foreign policy and extends the powers of both the European Commission and the European parliament. Despite these moves to what the treaty calls "an ever closer union of peoples" the British Prime Minister, John Major, today hailed the result as "game, set and match" to Britain.

The British ministers claim three victories in the negotiations: the removal of the word "federal"; the right for Britain to take a later and separate decision on a single currency; and the removal of the "social chapter" from the treaty. It was the social chapter, covering working conditions, which was the greatest barrier to agreement in the two-day summit. Mr Major, facing party divisions at home, threatened to veto the entire treaty if it were not removed, arguing that controls on wages and working hours would harm British industry.

Chancellor Kohl of Germany and Ruud Lubbers, the Dutch Prime Minister who chaired the meeting, finally proposed that Britain opt out of the social chapter, leaving the other 11 countries to adopt their own social measures. Opposition leaders in Britain said that Mr Major had condemned his country to the "slow lane" in a two-tier Europe in order to maintain his party's unity.

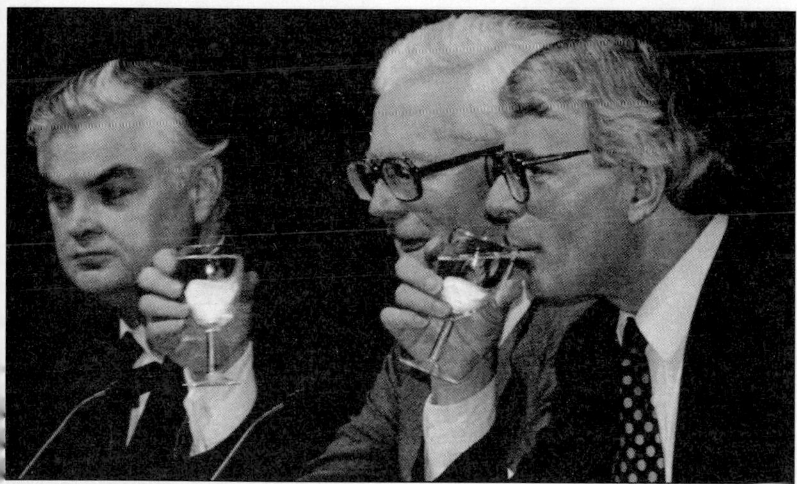

Premier John Major (r) drinks to victory with his ministerial colleagues.

Maxwell's empire collapses in chaos

Dec 7. The international business empire of Robert Maxwell lies in ruins barely a month after the publisher died mysteriously in the Atlantic. His major companies are in the hands of administrators and up for sale; his sons have resigned their directorships; and his transfers of more than £400 million from the Mirror Group pension fund are being investigated by the Serious Fraud Office. The transfers from the pension fund appear to have been intended to stave off the debt crisis which loomed as bankers sought repayment of loans which are estimated at £1.5 billion.

Interest rates add to economic gloom

Dec 19. An increase in German interest rates today capped a week of gloomy economic news for Britain, fuelling fears that the recession may drag on into 1992. Several European countries followed the Germans and by putting up their interest rates increased the pressure on sterling. The government will find it more difficult to lower interest rates to boost a flagging economy at a time when figures released this month show bankruptcies, unemployment and housing repossessions rising while manufacturing output, consumer confidence and exports are falling (→3/1/92).

Arts: Mozart, mega-opera and menace in the movies provide fun for the masses

A pop production of "Aida" with 600 singers transformed a sporting arena.

It was a year when "mega-opera" threatened to upstage grand opera. "Tosca" at London's Earl's Court and "Aida" at Birmingham's National Indoor Arena had casts of hundreds and circus-scale spectacle complete with animals. Opera as mass entertainment also took over the parks, with **Luciano Pavarotti** singing in the rain in Hyde Park and **Placido Domingo** performing in Windsor Great Park. While opera went pop, the Royal Opera House (where seats can now cost £100 plus) was briefly closed because of a pay dispute with musicians before resounding to cries of "Rubbish!" for its beachwear production of "Les Huguenots".

The English National Opera fared better with **Bryn Terfel**, a 25-year-old singer from Wales, acclaimed for his performance in Mozart's "Figaro's Wedding". Almost every opera written by Mozart from the age of 14 was performed in his bicentennial year, along with saturation coverage in concert halls, record catalogues and radio stations. There were even Mozart chocolates and ties.

In the cinema the honours went to **Kevin Costner**, scooping the Oscar pool with "Dances with Wolves" and enjoying a popular (if not critical) success as "Robin Hood: Prince of Thieves". Hollywood otherwise relied heavily on menace and murder in a year that produced "The Godfather Part III", "Terminator II" and "The Silence of the Lambs". One of the most original films was "Prospero's Books", adapted from "The Tempest" and directed by **Peter Greenaway**. This let **Sir John Gielgud** record his performance as Prospero in a year that saw the deaths of two titans of British stage and screen: **Peggy Ashcroft** and **David Lean**.

Of today's players **Fiona Shaw** offered a hypnotic "Hedda Gabler" and "Electra", **Juliet Stevenson** gave a devastating portrait of a torture victim in "Death and the Maiden", and **Nigel Hawthorne** illuminated **Alan Bennett's** "The Madness of George III". A revival of Jean Anouilh's "Becket" allowed **Derek Jacobi** and **Robert Lindsay** to shine, the latter also acclaimed for his role in "GBH", a TV drama by **Alan Bleasdale**. Even more watched, though, was "The Darling Buds of May", starring **David Jason**.

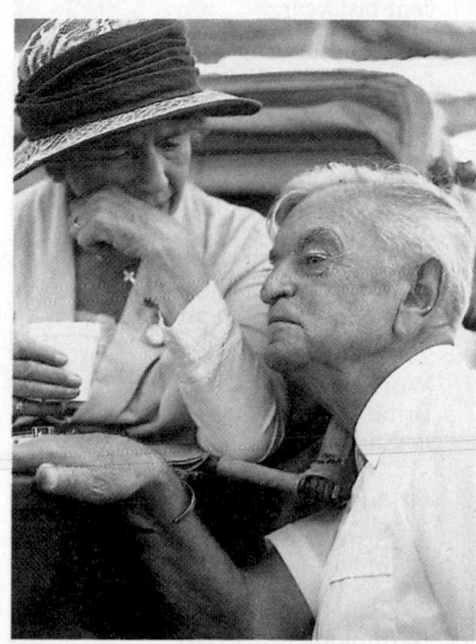

Farewell: greats of stage and screen, Peggy Ashcroft and David Lean.

1992

JANUARY

Su	Mo	Tu	We	Th	Fr	Sa
			1	2	3	4
5	6	7	8	9	10	11
12	13	14	15	16	17	18
19	20	21	22	23	24	25
26	27	28	29	30	31	

1. New York: Salvadoran government and guerrilla representatives sign a pact to end their 12-year civil war.

2. Moscow: State controls on food prices are lifted, causing sharp rises in the cost of bread, milk and meat (→ 10/2).

4. London: The first "Moslem parliament" is inaugurated, with the question of Moslem schools as its priority.

6. US: The Food and Drug Administration warns that silicone breast implants can be a health risk to women.

9. UK: Allison Halford, Britain's most senior policewoman, is suspended for misconduct.

14. London: The collapsed Bank of Credit and Commerce International is put into liquidation by the High Court.

17. New York: IBM announces a 1991 loss of £875 million, its first-ever annual loss.

20. France: An Air Inter Airbus crashes into a mountain near Strasbourg, killing 86 of the 96 people aboard.

21. New York: The UN orders Libya to hand over two Libyans linked to the bombing of Pan Am Flight 103 over Lockerbie.

22. London: HPI, the vehicle information bureau, reports that the number of stolen cars offered for sale rose by 300 per cent last year.

22. London: England agrees to reimburse the Baltic states for the 15.5 tons of gold, worth £250 million, sold in 1967.

29. London: The Department of Health says that cases of AIDS acquired through heterosexual intercourse increased by almost 50 per cent between 1990 and 1991.

29. London: A pressure group, Working for Childcare, says Britain's child care is the worst in Europe.

DEATHS

3. Australian actress Dame Judith Anderson (*10/2/1898).

23. British actor Freddie Bartholomew (*1924).

EC signals death of Yugoslav federation

Jan 15. The European Commission today signalled the end of Yugoslavia as one nation by recognising the independence of Croatia and Slovenia. The decision, made despite grave British and French reservations, is largely a result of strong German pressure.

Today's move came a week after Bosnian Serbs, led by Radovan Karadzic, created their own republic closely allied to Belgrade. Reaction from Belgrade, the Serbian capital, has, predictably, been angry. Foreign Minister Vladislav Jovanovic accused the EC of encouraging the break-up of the Yugoslav federation and said it risked "reaping a whirlwind" (→ 1/3).

Independence is feted by Croats.

Bleak prospects for Britain's economy

Jan 3. The harsh reality of the recession is being seen all round the country in ever-lengthening queues of men and women seeking work at unemployment offices. December's figure of 2,551,700 unemployed is certain to rise and experts predict the three million mark will be reached before the end of the year.

Prime Minister John Major has conceded that the Government had underestimated the length and the depth of the recesion. The Confederation of British Industry has warned that up to 73,000 manufacturing workers will lose their jobs in the first quarter of the year (→ 24/8).

Taoiseach bows out as economy falters

Jan 30. Charles Haughey, who has been Ireland's prime minister for eight of the last 12 years, today announced his retirement from politics. His party, Fianna Fail, is to present a new leader to Parliament next month, and Finance Minister Albert Reynolds is seen as the leading candidate for party leader and prime minister.

Haughey's decision comes in the wake of a scandal over the wiretapping of two journalists' telephones, although the 66-year-old premier has denied allegations he knew anything about it. Ireland's faltering economy, with unemployment at over 20 per cent, is seen as the main cause of his downfall (→ 11/2).

Jan 1. Boutros Boutros Ghali of Egypt, aged 69, takes over today as UN Secretary-General.

Major and Yeltsin agree weapons control

Handshakes and smiles mark the start of closer Anglo-Russian relations.

Jan 30. Boris Yeltsin and John Major stood outside 10 Downing Street today and said that the "ideological barriers" between Britain and Russia had fallen. Yeltsin said that Russian warheads would no longer be aimed at Britain. The two leaders signed a declaration committing their nations to cooperation on defence matters, including the restructuring of the former Soviet armed forces and the handling of surplus nuclear weapons. Yeltsin thanked Major for his support during last year's coup attempt, saying: "I can't hide the emotion I felt when he phoned me during some of the most difficult hours in Russia since the Second World War."

IRA murders seven

Jan 17. The IRA has made its worst attack in Northern Ireland since 1988: seven Protestant building workers were killed instantly, and seven others injured, when a bomb destroyed a van transporting them from a worksite at a British Army barracks near Omagh. It is not known if the workers were the intended target or not, but the IRA considers those who work for the British police and Army as "collaborators". Prime Minister John Major said the perpetrators would be prosecuted, adding that more troops would be sent to Ulster.

1992

FEBRUARY

Su	Mo	Tu	We	Th	Fr	Sa
						1
2	3	4	5	6	7	8
9	10	11	12	13	14	15
16	17	18	19	20	21	22
23	24	25	26	27	28	29

2. London: Labour leader Neil Kinnock denies allegations of a "Kremlin connection" during the 1980s (→ 13/4).

4. Venezuela: A coup attempt by rebel troops fails to topple President Carlos Perez (→ 27/11).

11. Dublin: Albert Reynolds is appointed Prime Minister by the Dail.

12. Ulan Bator: Mongolia's new constitution introduces a multi-party system.

15. Christchurch: The England XI beats New Zealand by 71 runs to finish their tour unbeaten with eight wins and three draws.

16. Berne: The Swiss vote against banning animals for medical and pharmaceutical experiments.

17. US: Jeffrey Dahmer is sentenced to life in prison for murdering 15 youths, mostly black homosexuals.

17. London: The Government announces plans to compensate who contracted the HIV virus through contaminated National Health blood.

19. Punjab: The ruling Congress Party wins local elections boycotted by Sikhs.

20. New York: The UN decides to send 16,000 troops to enforce the cease-fire in Cambodia.

23. France: As the Winter Olympics end in Albertville, Germany tops the medals table with a total of 26.

26. Dublin: Overturning a decision by a lower court, the Supreme Court rules that it is legal for a 14-year-old rape victim to travel to Britain for an abortion (→ 25/11).

26. Virginia: A group of Australian financiers and investors wins $27 million (£43 million) in the state lottery after buying seven million $1 tickets.

28. London: A terrorist bomb attack at London Bridge station injures 28 people.

DEATH

10. American author Alex Haley (*11/8/1921).

Food airlifted to Russia

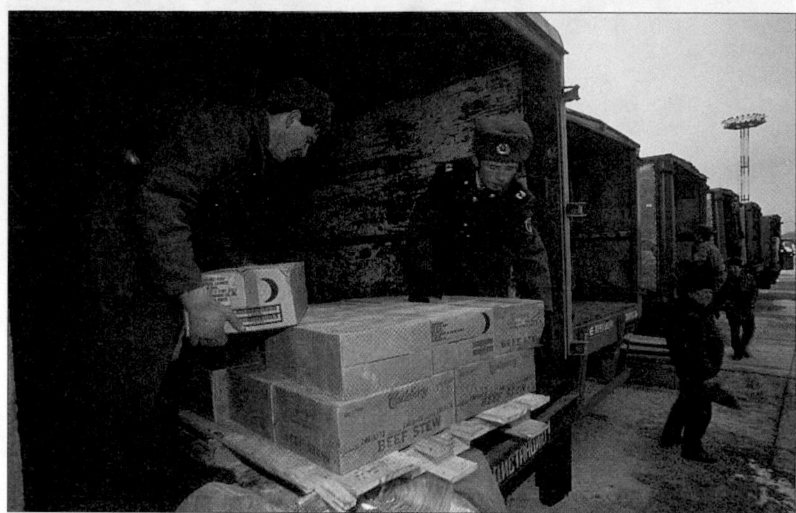
Russian troops begin unloading the badly-needed Western food supplies.

Feb 10. An international effort to send food and medical aid to cities of the former USSR got under way in earnest today. The first of 54 planned US and EC flights to Moscow and two dozen other cities took off from Frankfurt. The flights will carry more than 2,500 tons of surplus military food rations, mostly stock left over from the Gulf War, and pharmaceutical supplies. Russia and the newly independent republics are in the grip of winter and the shelves are bare. But unlike the Berlin airlift in 1949, the operation, called "Provide Hope" by the Pentagon, is not a long-term one. It is expected to last no more than three weeks and to cost approximately £160 million (→ 1/4).

The world's largest trade bloc is created

Feb 14. The 12 EC and seven European Free Trade Association nations have agreed to create the world's largest free trade zone. With a population of 380 million, the new European Economic Area will stretch from the Mediterranean Sea to the Arctic. Today's agreement comes into effect at the beginning of next year.

Ashdown admits to affair with secretary

Jane Ashdown stands by her man.

Feb 9. Having a love affair with your secretary could boost your political career. The standing of Paddy Ashdown, leader of the Liberal Democrats, has never been so high, following his admission that he had a relationship with his then secretary five years ago.

Ashdown's disclosure was made after the theft of notes about the affair from his solicitor's safe. Five days ago, the Liberal Democrat leader explained that with an election looming, he decided he must come clean. His wife Jane and MPs of all parties have rallied around him. Pollsters now say that his rating as a potential Prime Minister has risen by a stunning 13 per cent in the last week (→ 10/4).

Maastricht accord on EC cooperation

Feb 7. Foreign Secretary Douglas Hurd and his 11 EC colleagues today met in a small Dutch town to sign two crucial documents. They are the Treaty on European Union and the Maastricht Final Act. Together, these treaties commit the 12 European Community members to move closer to each other. Europeans will share common citizenship, economic and defence policies. But today's treaties only lay down broad outlines for European union. The details could be very difficult to thrash out. In Britain, doubts are already being expressed as to the wisdom of surrendering sovereignty to Brussels (→ 2/6).

US car giants skid into record losses

Feb 24. The year is off to a grim start for the US automobile industry. The world's biggest car manufacturer, General Motors, today announced a 1991 loss of £7.2 billion, a world record and the largest deficit in the Detroit firm's 84-year history.

This comes just 11 days after Ford, America's second largest manufacturer, reported a 1991 loss of £3.7 billion, the worst in its 89-year history. Much of this red ink is being blamed on Ford's overseas operations, which last year lost £1.5 billion. Job cuts are likely to follow at both Ford and GM.

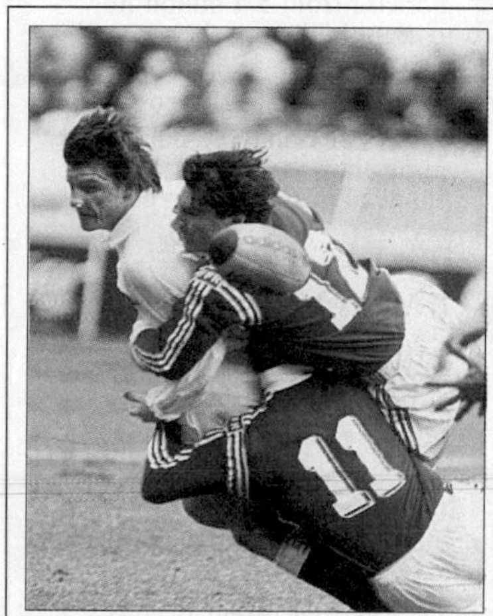
Feb 15. In the Five Nations championship, the England XV thrashes France by 31-13.

1992

MARCH

Su	Mo	Tu	We	Th	Fr	Sa
1	2	3	4	5	6	7
8	9	10	11	12	13	14
15	16	17	18	19	20	21
22	23	24	25	26	27	28
29	30	31				

1. Sarajevo: Bosnian Serb snipers open fire on civilians after a majority of the Moslem and ethnic Croatian communities vote in favour of Bosnia's independence (→30/5).

6. London: British Telecom announces 25,000 job cuts.

10. Tbilisi: Former Soviet Foreign Minister Eduard Shevardnadze is elected interim President of Georgia.

10. US: Governor Bill Clinton of Arkansas pulls ahead of rivals for the Democratic presidential nomination after winning eight primaries (→20/8).

12. Port Louis: Mauritius breaks its links with the British Crown, becoming a fully-fledged republic, but remains a member of the Commonwealth.

13. Turkey: An earthquake kills more than 1,000 people in eastern Turkey.

17. Buenos Aires: Ten people are killed in a suicide car bomb attack against the Israeli embassy.

19. London: Buckingham Palace confirms that the Duchess of York is seeking a divorce (→13/4).

21. New York: A British Airways Concorde loses parts of its rudder during flight.

21. Washington: The US Census Bureau predicts that the world's population will increase from 5.4 billion now to eight billion by the year 2020.

22. London: Olympia & York, owners of Canary Wharf, admit they are facing serious financial difficulties (→13/5).

DEATHS

1. Michael Havers, British lawyer and politician (*10/3/1923).

9. Former Israeli Prime Minister Menachem Begin (*16/8/1913).

11. Richard Brooks, American film writer and director (*18/5/1912).

23. Friedrich August (von) Hayek, British economist (*8/5/1899).

Voters approve South African reform plan

President Frederik de Klerk rallies support for his plan before the vote.

March 18. White South Africans voted in unprecedented numbers yesterday to say "Yes" to President de Klerk's plan for constitutional reforms giving legal equality to their black compatriots. De Klerk said the result had been "a landslide for the cause of peace and justice in the country". "Today", the 56-year-old President told cheering supporters last night, "we have closed the book on apartheid." Final results of the referendum show that 85.7 per cent of the white electorate went to the polls and that 68.7 per cent of them voted in favour of Mr de Klerk's proposed reforms (→26/11).

Charles for cheese

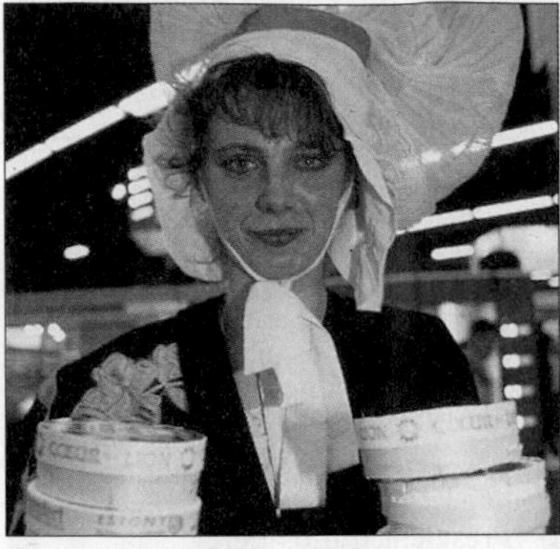
Camembert fit for a prince.

March 2. Smelly, runny French cheeses have found a new champion in the Prince of Wales. Prince Charles told a meeting in Paris today that "pettifogging" Eurocrats threatened to impose "soulless, mechanical" cheese production methods in the name of a "bacteriologically correct" society.

Mike Tyson gets six years for rape

March 26. The career of the world's youngest heavyweight champion ended in an Indianapolis courtroom today. Five years after winning the world title, Mike Tyson, aged 25, was sentenced to 10 years in jail, with four of them suspended, after being found guitly of one count of rape and two counts of criminal deviate conduct. Tyson was convicted for the rape of a Miss Black America contestant, Desiree Washington. The former champion will have to serve at least three years of his term.

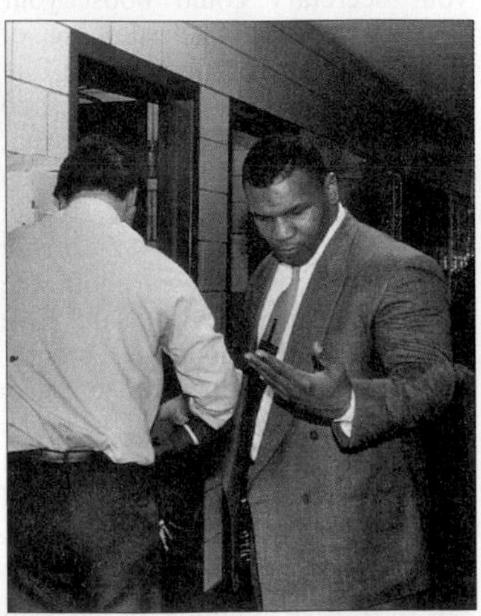
"Iron Mike" loses his toughest bout.

Mr Punch closes up after 150-year run

March 25. "Punch", the humorous magazine, is to close after 150 years of publication.

Once seen in every men's club and dentist's waiting room, it has not managed to adjust to modern trends. Its sales have fallen from 175,000 in the 1940s to just 33,000 and it has been losing about £2 million a year. Failing to find a buyer, its owners, United Newspapers, have decided it has had its day. Alan Coren, a former editor, said "there's no market for a magazine like 'Punch' anymore."

UK suffers its worst drought since 1745

March 26. Britain's water reserves are at their lowest level ever and are still dropping. It may not have felt like it at the time, but the last 20 years have seen much less rain than usual, and scientists fear that the drought – the worst since 1745 – could be an early sign of global warming.

Last winter was particularly dry, which means that unless it rains heavily soon 10 million Britons will face a hosepipe ban.

Pakistan victorious in World Cup final

March 25. Pakistan defeated England by 22 runs to win the World Cup in Melbourne. It was a personal triumph for the Pakistan captain, Imran Khan, who led his team through the month-long tournament. England, who played with great professionalism throughout, could not match Pakistan's fire. Pakistan scored 249 for 6 and England were 227 all out.

March 30. Jodie Foster and co-star Anthony Hopkins sweep the Oscars, winning five awards for "Silence of the Lambs".

1992

APRIL

Su	Mo	Tu	We	Th	Fr	Sa
			1	2	3	4
5	6	7	8	9	10	11
12	13	14	15	16	17	18
19	20	21	22	23	24	25
26	27	28	29	30		

1. Bonn: Britain and other Group of Seven nations agree on a £38.5-billion aid package for the former USSR.

2. Paris: Pierre Beregovoy replaces Edith Cresson as French Prime Minister.

4. London: In the University Boat Race, Oxford win for the sixth successive year, defeating Cambridge by 1.5 length.

6. Tirana: Sadi Berisha is elected Albania's first non-Communist President.

8. Libya: PLO leader Yassir Arafat survives a plane crash.

10. US: Former tennis star Arthur Ashe reveals he is HIV-positive (→6/2/93).

11. Wigan: Wigan beats Bradford Northern, 50-8, to win their third Rugby League championship.

12. France: Euro Disney, a £6.4-million amusement park, opens near Paris.

13. London: Neil Kinnock resigns as Labour leader (→18/7).

15. Libya: An air traffic embargo imposed by the UN to force Libya to hand over two suspected terrorist bombers goes into effect.

20. Seville: Expo 92, the first Universal Exposition in 22 years, opens.

22. Mexico: At least 200 people are killed by a gas explosion in Guadalajara.

29. Germany: The country is paralysed by a wave of strikes by public service workers.

29. US: A jury acquits four Los Angeles policemen accused of beating a young black man, Rodney King (→2/5).

DEATHS

6. Isaac Asimov, American science fiction writer (*2/1/1920).

19. Frankie Howerd, British comedian (*1912).

20. British comedian Benny Hill (*1924).→

23. Indian film director Satyajit Ray (*2/5/1921).

28. British artist Francis Bacon (*28/10/1909).

Conservatives win fourth straight election

Enthusiastic Tory supporters celebrate John Major's surprise victory.

April 10. The pollsters and pundits who predicted a Labour victory in yesterday's general election are eating their words. Unexpectedly, John Major has won a Tory majority of 21 seats, despite having fought a lacklustre campaign.

Appearing outside 10 Downing Street today, Mr Major vowed to lead the country out of recession. Meanwhile, Labour leader Neil Kinnock expressed disappointment at Labour's failure to block the Tories' fourth election victory since 1979. Many believe that Labour's poor showing is due to Mr Kinnock's plans to raise income tax. The Liberal Democrats, led by Paddy Ashdown, also suffered a setback, winning only 20 seats.

Tonight, the IRA marked the Tory victory by detonating a van loaded with 100 pounds of Semtex explosive in the heart of the City of London. The blast killed three people and injured 91 (→13).

'King Leer' is dead

April 20. Benny Hill, the comic genius who was loved worldwide, was found dead of a heart attack in his London home today. Known for his saucy sketches on the "Benny Hill Show", he was born in Southampton in 1924.

His show was seen in 80 countries.

Kabul in chaos as leader is ousted

April 28. An estimated 10,000 radical Moslem fighters, backed by at least 100 tanks, rolled into the battle-scarred Afghan capital today. They were led by rebel commander Ahmed Shah Masood, whose forces fought heavily for four days before capturing Kabul.

Masood's well-armed mujahedeen are now mopping up what remains of the forces of the rival Islamic Party, led by the Pakistan-based fundamentalist Gulbuddin Hekmatyar. The fall of Kabul has come just 10 days after the overthrow of Afghan President Najibullah. He has gone into hiding in Kabul after ruling the country for six years. Najibullah has been replaced by a shaky 51-member interim government headed by Sigbatullah Mojaddidi. The recent fighting in and around Kabul has left the city in chaos (→28/7).

Anne, Mark begin divorce proceedings

April 13. Buckingham Palace announced today that the Princess Royal has begun legal proceedings for a divorce from her husband of 18 years, Captain Mark Phillips. The couple, who have been legally separated for the last two-and-a-half years, are in agreement about the decision. Princess Anne will continue to live with their two children, Peter and Zara, at Gatcombe Park, and Captain Phillips will live at nearby Aston Farm, part of the estate given to them by the Queen. The "friendly" divorce has no effect on Anne's constitutional position as eighth in line to the throne (→7/6).

Big Bang theory is confirmed by NASA

April 23. Exited American scientists are claiming that they have finally found the Holy Grail of cosmology.

NASA's Cosmic Background Explorer, or COBE, satellite has found credible evidence of enormous, wispy clouds of matter near what could be the edge of the universe. These clouds explain how galaxies were produced after the Big Bang, the cosmic explosion scientists believe created the universe. The clouds date back 15 billion years, a mere 300,000 years after the Big Bang.

April 27. Betty Boothroyd is first woman in six centuries to be Speaker of House of Commons.

1992

MAY

Su	Mo	Tu	We	Th	Fr	Sa
					1	2
3	4	5	6	7	8	9
10	11	12	13	14	15	16
17	18	19	20	21	22	23
24	25	26	27	28	29	30
31						

3. Poland: Doctors adopt an ethical code which strongly limits a woman's right to have an abortion.

8. London: Due to the Cold War ending, MI5 will now focus on the IRA.

9. Wembley: Liverpool beat Sunderland, 2-0, to win the FA Cup.

11. Brussels: EC nations decide to recall their ambassadors from Belgrade.→

12. London: Plans are announced for a fifth terminal at Heathrow Airport.

12. Strasbourg: Queen Elizabeth tells the European Parliament she welcomes European integration.

13. Canada: Olympia & York files for bankruptcy as its debt surpasses £19 billion.

16. US: The yacht America[3] defeats the Italian entry, Il Moro di Venezia, to win the America's Cup.

17. Imola: British Formula One driver Nigel Mansell wins his fifth Grand Prix of the season (→ 16/8).

18. Oxford: A coroner's jury rules that American pilots are responsible for the "friendly fire" which killed nine British soldiers during the Gulf War.

27. Brussels: The EC forecasts 10 per cent unemployment for 1993.

28. London: David Platt becomes the most expensive football player, having been sold to an Italian club, Juventus, for £8 million.

30. New York: The UN Security Council votes to impose sanctions on Serbia in a bid to stop the Serbian offensive in Bosnia.

31. London: The unveiling by the Queen Mother of a statue of Marshal of the RAF Sir Arthur "Bomber" Harris is marred by demonstrators.

DEATHS

6. German-born American actress Marlene Dietrich (*27/12/1901).→

27. British journalist Peter Jenkins (*1934).

Los Angeles ravaged by race riots

May 2. An unseasy calm returned to a battered Los Angeles today, after two days of unprecedented urban violence.

Local authorities are now trying to estimate the cost of the race riots which have left 58 people dead and thousands injured. Simmering racial tensions exploded into an orgy of rioting, murder and looting two days ago. The violence began soon after an all-white jury acquitted four white policemen of savagely beating a young black man, Rodney King. The verdict outraged the city's black community and armed gangs of blacks quickly spread through the mainly-black neighbourhood of South Central. Whites and Koreans became targets and several were beaten to death. Shopkeepers, pedestrians and motorists were attacked and hundreds of buildings set on fire. Fire Department crews were repeatedly forced to flee by angry crowds. Police were unable to stop scores of shops being looted. Yesterday, President Bush was forced to call in the Army, and 5,000 soldiers and Marines are now on standby just outside city limits. A dawn-to-dusk curfew has been imposed on the city. The White House has promised £960 million in federal loans to help Los Angeles recover from America's deadliest riots this century.

Hatred and frustration come to the fore as blacks attack white-owned shops.

An Irish bishop has parental problems

May 8. Dr Eamonn Casey, Roman Catholic Bishop of Galway, has resigned for "personal reasons" following revelations that he is the father of a teenaged boy by Annie Murphy, a 44-year-old Irish woman now living in the US. Friends of the 65-year-old bishop say he plans to go to South America to work as a missionary.

The accused church leader resigns.

Judith Ward freed

May 11. Judith Ward, sentenced to life for the M62 coach bombing which killed 12 people in 1974, walked free from the London Court of Appeal today. The court ruled that her conviction was unsafe and unsatisfactory. Forensic evidence has been discredited and no reliance could be placed on her confession. She is the eighteenth person linked to IRA cases to be freed in recent appeals.

Anti-Mafia judge murdered in Sicily

May 23. Judge Giovanni Falcone, one of Italy's foremost anti-Mafia investigators, was killed when his car was blown up by a huge bomb near Palermo today.

The remote-control bomb had been placed in a drainage tunnel under the road. The judge's wife and several bodyguards were also killed. Judge Falcone, who had already been the target of a failed assassination attempt, had been instrumental in the arrest of more than 300 Mafia members.

Euro-corps is born

May 22. France and Germany today agreed to form a joint army corps of 35,000 to 45,000 troops. The new Euro-corps will be based near Strasbourg, near Germany's border, and will be ready for full deployment in three of four years. Paris and Bonn hope it will form the core of a larger corps, including units from other European nations. However, Britain has voiced opposition to the plan.

May 6. Mythical movie star Marlene Dietrich died today in her Paris appartment.

1992

JUNE

Su	Mo	Tu	We	Th	Fr	Sa
	1	2	3	4	5	6
7	8	9	10	11	12	13
14	15	16	17	18	19	20
21	22	23	24	25	26	27
28	29	30				

1. Moscow: President de Klerk of South Africa marks the end of 35 years of severed relations by visiting Russia.

2. Haiti: Conservative Marc Bazin is appointed premier.

5. Warsaw: Polish Peasants' Party leader Waldemar Pawlak is named Prime Minister.

8. Paris: Senior PLO official Atef Bsesio is assassinated during a routine trip to meet French officials.

10. London: A bomb blast in Victoria Street causes extensive damage.

11. Boston: The last survivor of the Titanic, Marjorie Robb, aged 103, dies.

12. Rio de Janeiro: At the Earth Summit, John Major announces that Britain will contribute £100 million to protect the environment.

12. Bordeaux: Queen Elizabeth ends a three-day state visit to France, her first in 20 years.

14. Falklands: Margaret Thatcher visits the islands to mark the 10th anniversary of the end of the war.

16. Beirut: Germans Heinrich Strubig and Thomas Kemptner, the last two Western hostages in the Middle East, are freed.

16. Philippines: Fidel Ramos is elected President.

24. London: Lloyd's announces a loss of £2.06 billion, the worst in its 300-year history.

24. Iles of Scilly: The Royal Navy intervenes in clashes between French and British fishing vessels.

26. Sweden: Denmark defeats Germany, 2-0, to win the European Football Championship.

30. London: Mrs Thatcher is introduced to the House of Lords as Baroness Thatcher.

DEATHS

3. Robert Morley, British actor (*26/5/1908).

23. John Spencer Churchill, British painter and sculptor (*31/5/1909).

Denmark's voters reject Maastricht treaty

June 2. Danish voters today dealt a body blow to the Maastricht treaty by voting against closer European union in a national referendum. The vote was close: 50.7 per cent against 49.3 per cent.

Unless all 12 EC members ratify the treaty it cannot take effect. Technically, the Danish vote means that the agreements on a single currency, a common foreign and security policy and moves towards a common defence strategy will not be put into operation. Reaction was mixed in London. Sir Leon Brittan, Britain's senior EC commissioner said he was disappointed, while Norman Tebbit said: "It is a good thing for the whole of Europe." His views reflect Tory unease about Maastricht. There are growing demands for a renegotiation of the treaty. September's French referendum is now vital. If the French vote "Non", then Maastricht is really dead (→20/9).

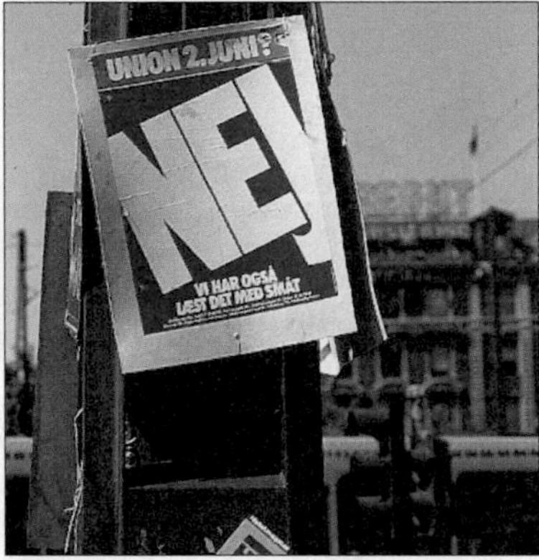

Danes' "Ne" wins by tiny margin.

Township massacre leaves dozens dead

June 17. A gang of 200 men armed with guns and pangas, or machetes, rampaged through a squatter camp 40 miles south of Johannesburg today, killing 39 people and wounding many more. Women and children died in the massacre.

Residents, supporters of the African National Congress, blamed the attack on members of the conservative Zulu Inkatha Freedom Party. The ANC leadership also accused the government of complicity, saying the attackers arrived in police vehicles. The government laid the blame on the ANC's campaign of mass protest, saying it had pushed the political temperature unacceptably high.

Diana suicide claim causes Court storm

June 7. The storm which has been looming over the royal family broke today with the publication of a book "Diana: Her True Story", by royal reporter Andrew Morton. In it he claims she has made five attempts to commit suicide in desperation over the uncaring attitude of Prince Charles.

The book is said to be based on information given to the author by Diana's friends. Prince Charles is portrayed throughout as a cold, unloving father and husband. Morton's biography, which makes it clear the royal marriage is a sham, is being condemned as an unforgiveable intrusion into the affairs of the royal family (→9/12).

Algerian President is gunned down

June 29. Mohammed Boudiaf, President of Algeria, was assassinated at a political rally in the city of Annaba, 280 miles east of Algiers, today. The assassin, wearing police uniform, was shot by the President's bodyguard.

Boudiaf, aged 73, was one of the historic leaders of the Algerian revolt against France. He returned from exile five months ago to help the military government in its fight against the Islamic Salvation Front, a powerful fundamentalist party. There is little doubt in government circles that the fundamentalists were responsible for the killing. Boudiaf's final words were: "We're all going to die."

Peace hopes surge after Rabin's win

June 23. New hope dawned for the Middle East peace process today with the election of Yitzhak Rabin, the Labour Party leader, as the new Prime Minister of Israel. His predecessor, Yitzhak Shamir, was a hardliner whose refusal to stop building Jewish settlements in the Occupied Territories brought delicate negotiations for Palestinian autonomy to a halt.

Rabin's election campaign was fought on a platform of compromise between the need for peace and Israel's security. He promised to curb Jewish settlement in the West Bank, Gaza Strip and Golan Heights. Arab leaders have welcomed today's results.

Andrew Morton's shocking book.

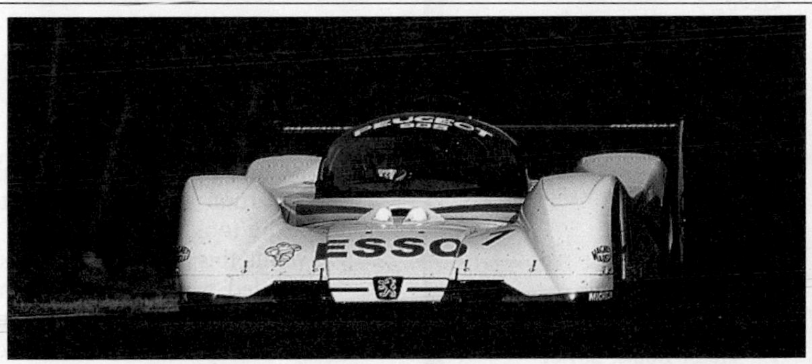

June 21. British racing drivers Derek Warwick and Mark Blundell, helped by Yannick Dalmas of France, win the Le Mans 24-Hour race with their Peugeot 905, at an average speed of 123.9 miles per hour. The Peugeot led the gruelling, 2,974-mile race from the second hour.

1992

JULY

Su	Mo	Tu	We	Th	Fr	Sa
			1	2	3	4
5	6	7	8	9	10	11
12	13	14	15	16	17	18
19	20	21	22	23	24	25
26	27	28	29	30	31	

1. Paris: France is chosen to organise the 1998 football World Cup.

2. Belfast: Police find the bodies of three men that the IRA killed for being informers.

3. Moldova: Moldovan President Mircea Snegur and Boris Yeltsin agree to seek an end to the bloody conflict between Russians and Moldovans.

5. Wimbledon: America's Andre Agassi wins the Men's finals; the Women's title is won by Steffi Graf of Germany.

6. France: Thousands of holidaymakers are stranded as French lorry drivers block roads in protest against a new driving licence system.

7. London: Sogo, the first Japanese department store in London, opens in Piccadilly.

8. London: South African cricket tour rebels have Test ban lifted because of changing political situation in South Africa.

8. Vienna: Thomas Klestil, aged 59, becomes President of Austria.

10. Miami: General Manuel Noriega of Panama is sentenced to 40 years in prison for drug-trafficking.

15. London: MPs give themselves a 40 per cent raise on their expense accounts.

16. India: Shankar Dayal Sharma is appointed President.

19. Scotland: Britain's Nick Faldo wins his third UK Golf Open.

25. London: The Government calls for an international conference to seek an end to the war in Bosnia-Herzegovina (→3/9).

28. Afghanistan: Women are no longer allowed to appear on television.

DEATHS

4. Aster Piazzolla, Argentinian composer (*3/3/1921).

19. Victor Louis, Soviet journalist (*5/2/1928).

31. Lord Cheshire, British war pilot (*7/9/1918).

UN forces in control of Sarajevo airport

Canadian UN troops open up Sarajevo airport for humanitarian aid flights.

July 2. Armoured vehicles of a Canadian infantry battalion brushed aside a Serb roadblock outside the besieged city of Sarajevo today and took up positions around the airport. It had taken the heavily-armed UN force three days to cover 180 miles. Colonel Michael Jones, commander of the battalion, had to threaten to open fire before drunken Serb officers agreed to let him pass. UN officials have now declared the airport ready to accept up to eight relief flights a day. Two landed this afternoon, one carrying French relief food and the other American-donated medicines. British and American aircraft will soon be joining the humanitarian airlift (→25).

Scotsman Smith takes over Labour

Smith, successor to Neil Kinnock.

July 18. John Smith scored a decisive victory over his only challenger, Bryan Gould, to become the 14th leader of the Labour Party. Margaret Beckett was elected deputy leader. Smith, former Shadow Chancellor, faces a formidable task to revive the party after Labour's election defeat and the resignation of Neil Kinnock.

Greenpeace decries whaling decision

July 3. Greenpeace said today that the virtual green light given to renewed whaling by the International Whaling Commission is a tragedy. At its annual meeting in Glasgow, 16 IWC member nations voted in favour of minke whale hunting. Eleven other members, including Britain, abstained, saying there is no way of killing whales humanely.

Vaclav Havel quits as federation splits

July 17. Vaclav Havel, Czechoslovakia's President, has resigned. The decision was announced after a proclamation of Slovak sovereignty by the Slovak parliament. This move is a step towards independence for Slovakia and a "velvet divorce" by the two members of the Federal Republic of Czechoslovakia (→1/1/93).

Luxury prison fails to keep drug lord in

July 22. Pablo Escobar, the most powerful and wealthy of South American drug lords, has escaped from a luxurious ranch-style prison just outside Medellin, the city that is the headquarters of his Colombian cocaine cartel. Escobar surrendered in June 1991 after being promised that he would not be extradited to the US.

Hong Kong's last governor moves in

July 9. Chris Patten, Hong Kong's new Governor issued a manifesto today as he took office.

He wants this British colony, due to be handed back to China at the end of his tenure, in July 1997, to have a more accessible and democratic government. Officials in Beijing have already lashed out at Patten's statement, claiming the Governor was intefering in China's internal affairs (→2/12).

July 25. The Summer Olympics open in a blaze of glory in Barcelona.

1992

AUGUST

Su	Mo	Tu	We	Th	Fr	Sa
						1
2	3	4	5	6	7	8
9	10	11	12	13	14	15
16	17	18	19	20	21	22
23	24	25	26	27	28	29
30	31					

3. Moscow: A Russian-Ukrainian accord is signed that places the Black Sea Fleet under joint command.

3. Paris: France ratifies the nuclear non-proliferation treaty.

6. Haiti: A wave of terrorist attacks leaves 10 people dead.

7. Rome: President Joaquim Chissano of Mozambique and Afonso Dhlakama, leader of the Renamo rebels, sign an agreement to end their 17-year civil war.

9. The Oval: Pakistan defeats England by 10 wickets to win the Fifth Test and the series.

12. US: Canada, Mexico and the US agree to create a three-nation free trade bloc.

18. London: Britain announces that 1,800 troops are ready to be sent to Bosnia to help UN relief efforts (→ 3/9).

20. Baghdad: Paul Ride, a Briton, is sentenced to seven years in prison for crossing the Iraqi border illegally.

20. US: Five weeks after Governor Bill Clinton of Arkansas won the Democratic nomination for the presidency, George Bush is nominated as the Republican candidate (→ 4/11).

24. London: The stock market suffers its biggest one-day fall in more than a year.

25. Florida: Hurricane Andrew sweeps through the Miami area, killing 15 people.

27. Iraq: USAF warplanes begin enforcing a "no-fly" zone in southern Iraq aimed at protecting Shiite Moslems.

29. Germany: Thousands of people demonstrate against a wave of racist attacks aimed at immigrants (→ 3/10)

DEATHS

4. Sir Edward Chilton, British Air Marshal (*1/11/1906).

9. Lord Devlin, former High Court judge (*25/11/1905).

14. John Sirica, American judge involved in the Watergate hearings (*19/3/1904).

18. John Sturges, American film director (*3/1/1911).

Serbian death camps stun the world

Aug 15. The apalling images of emaciated prisoners held in Serbian prison camps, chiefly in Bosnia, have shocked the world.

Rumours of brutality, murder and rape have now been confirmed by television pictures seen round the world. International Red Cross experts and British and US officials are denouncing the Serbs' policy of "ethnic cleansing", removing members of other ethnic communities from Serbian-dominated areas. A Red Cross report tells of "innocent civilians being arrested and subjected to inhumane treatment as part of a policy of forced population transfers carried out on a massive scale" (→ 18).

In Bosnia's camps, some victims of Serbia's "ethnic cleansing" policy.

Ex-USSR is still an Olympic superpower

Linford Christie surges across the finish line in a mere 9.96 seconds.

Aug 9. As the Olympic flame went out in Barcelona today, athletes of the Unified Team packed the 112 medals, including 45 golds, they won during the Games. The competitors from the former Soviet Union surprised many by reaping more medals than any other nation, despite the political turmoil that is wracking their homeland.

For Britain, the Summer Games were far from being a disappointment. Two exploits stand out: the first was the stunning performance by Linford Christie, who became the third Briton ever to win the 100 metres title, and, at 32, the oldest man ever to win the event. The second was Sally Gunnell's glorious victory in the 400 metres hurdles. Gunnell, aged 26, won the first British track gold medal since 1964.

Irish conflict claims its 3,000th victim

Aug 27. A grim milestone was reached in Northern Ireland today when Hugh McKibben, aged 19, became the 3,000th victim of the sectarian violence. The conflict has claimed a life every three days in the 23 years since John Gallagher, a 30-year-old Catholic, was shot dead by the now-disbanded B-Specials during riots in Armagh. McKibben's death is thought to stem from a dispute between rival factions of the Irish People's Liberation Army, a Republican splinter group. The security forces were not involved, and the IRA has denied any responsibility.

Fergie photo storm

Aug 20. A storm of protest broke out in Britain today following the publication by the "Daily Mirror" of revealing photographs of the Duchess of York.

A topless Fergie is pictured relaxing in private by a swimming pool in southern France with her American "financial adviser", 37-year-old John Bryan from Texas. In one photo, Bryan is shown sucking Fergie's toes. Buckingham Palace had tried and failed to block publication of the pictures. The Palace has also criticised the invasion of the royal family's privacy by reporters.

Aug 16. Britain's Nigel Mansell wins the Hungarian Grand Prix, thus becoming the Formula One champion of the world.

1992 Barcelona

Men's Athletics

100m
1. Christie GBR 9.96
2. Fredericks NAM 10.02
3. Mitchell USA 10.04

200m
1. Marsh USA 20.01
2. Fredericks NAM 20.13
3. Bates USA 20.38

400m
1. Watts USA 43.50
2. Lewis USA 44.21
3. Kitur KEN 44.24

800m
1. Tanui KEN 1:43.66
2. Kiprotich KEN 1:43.70
3. Gray USA 1:43.97

1500m
1. Cacho Ruiz SPA 3:40.12
2. El Basir MOR 3:40.62
3. Sulaiman QAT 3:40.69

5000m
1. Baumann GER 13:12.52
2. Bitok KEN 13:12.71
3. Bayisa ETH 13:13.03

10000m
1. Skah MOR 27:46.70
2. Chelimo KEN 27:47.72
3. Abebe ETH 28:00.07

110m Hurdles
1. McKoy CAN 13.12
2. Dees USA 13.24
3. Pierce USA 13.26

400m Hurdles
1. Young USA 46.78
2. Graham JAM 47.66
3. Akabusi GBR 47.82

3000m Steeple
1. Birir KEN 8:08.84
2. Sang KEN 8:09.55
3. Mutwol KEN 8:10.74

High Jump
1. Sotomayor CUB 2.34
2. Sjoeberg SWE 2.34
3. Partyka POL 2.34
Forsythe AUS 2.34
Conway USA 2.34

Long Jump
1. Lewis USA 8.67
2. Powell USA 8.64
3. Greene USA 8.34

Triple Jump
1. Conley USA 18.17
2. Simpkins USA 17.60
3. Rutherford BAH 17.36

Pole Vault
1. Tarassov CIS 5.80
2. Trandenkov CIS 5.80
3. Garcia Chico SPA 5.75

Shot Put
1. Stulce USA 21.70
2. Doehring USA 20.96
3. Lykho CIS 20.94

Hammer
1. Abduvaliev CIS 82.54
2. Astapkovitch CIS 81.96
3. Nikuline CIS 81.38

Discus Throw
1. Hubertas LIT 65.12
2. Schult GER 65.94
3. Moya Sandoval CUB 64.12

Javelin
1. Zelezny CZS 89.66
2. Raty FIN 86.60
3. Backley GBR 83.38

Decathlon
1. Zmelik CZS 8611 pts
2. Penalver SPA 8412 pts
3. Johnson USA 8309 pts

Marathon
1. Hwang Young-cho KOR 2 h 13:23
2. Morishita JAP 2 h 13:45
3. Freigang GER 2 h 14:00

4 x 100m Relay
1. USA 37.40 (Marsh, Burrell, Mitchell, Lewis)
2. NGA 37.98 (Kayode, Imoh, Adeniken, Ezinwa)
3. CUB 38 (Simon Gomez, Lamela Loaces, Isasi Gonzalez, Aguilera Ruiz)

4 x 400m Relay
1. USA 2:55.74 (Valmon, Watts, Johnson, Lewis)
2. CUB 2:59.51 (Martinez Despaigne, Herrera Ortiz, Tellez, Hernandez Prendez)
3. GBR 2:59.73 (Black, Grindley, Akabusi, Regis)

20 km Walk
1. Plaza Montero SPA 1 h 21:45
2. Leblanc CAN 1 h 22:05
3. De Benedictis ITA 1 h 23:11

Women's Athletics

100m
1. Devers USA 10.82
2. Cuthbert JAM 10.83
3. Privalova CIS 10.84

200m
1. Torrence USA 21.81
2. Cuthbert JAM 22.02
3. Ottey JAM 22.09

400m
1. Pérec FRA 48.83
2. Bryzgina CIS 49.05
3. Restrepo Gaviria COL 49.64

800m
1. Van Langen NET 1:55.54
2. Nurutdinova CIS 1:55.99
3. Quirot Moret CUB 1:56.80

1500m
1. Boulmerka ALG 3:55.30
2. Rogacheva CIS 3:56.91
3. Q. Yunxia CHN 3:57.08

3000m
1. Romanova CIS 8:46.04
2. Dorovskikh CIS 8:46.85
3. Chalmers CAN 8:47.22

10000m
1. Tulu ETH 31:6.02
2. Meyer SAF 31:11.75
3. Jennings USA 31:19.89

100m Hurdles
1. Patoulidou GRE 12.64
2. Martin USA 12.69
3. Donkova BUL 12.70

400m Hurdles
1. Gunnell GBR 53.23
2. Farmer-Patrick USA 53.69
3. Vickers USA 54.31

High Jump
1. Henkel GER 2.02
2. Astafei ROM 2.00
3. Quintero CUB 1.97

Long Jump
1. Drechsler GER 7.14
2. Kravets CIS 7.12
3. Joyner-Kersee USA 7.70

Shot Put
1. Kriveleva CIS 21.06
2. Huang CHN 20.47
3. Neimke GER 19.78

Discus Throw
1. Marten CUB 70.06
2. Khristova BUL 67.78
3. Costian AUS 66.24

Javelin
1. Renk GER 68.34
2. Shikolenko CIS 68.26
3. Forkel GER 66.86

Heptathlon
1. Joyner-Kersee USA 7044 pts
2. Belova CIS 6845 pts
3. Braun GBR 6649 pts

Marathon
1. Yegorova CIS 2 h 32:41
2. Arimori JAP 2 h 32:49
3. Moller NZE 2 h 33:59

4 x 100m Relay
1. USA 42.11 (Ashford, Jones, Guidry, Torrence)
2. CIS 42.16 (Bogoslovskaya, Malchugina, Trandenkova, Privalova)
3. NGA 42.81 (Utondu, Idehen, Opara Thompson, Onyali)

4 x 400m Relay
1. CIS 3:20.20 (Ruzina, Dzhigalova, Nazarova, Bryzgina)
2. USA 3:20.92 (Kaiser, Torrence, Miles, Stevens)
3. GBR 3:24.23 (Smith, Douglas, Stoute, Gunnell)

10 km Walk
1. Chen CHN 44.32
2. Nikolaeva CIS 44.33
3. Li CHN 44.41

Linford Christie of Britain.

Men's Rowing

Sculls
1. Lange GER 6:51.40
2. Chalupa CZS 6:52.93
3. Broniewski POL 6:56.82

Coxless Pairs
1. GBR 6:27.72 (Redgrave, Pinsent)
2. GER 6:32.68 (Hoeltzenbein, Von Ettinshausen)
3. SLO 6:33.43 (Cop, Zvegelj)

Double sculls
1. AUS 6:17.32 (Hawkins, Antonie Peter)
2. AUT 6:18.42 (Jonke, Zerbst)
3. NET 6:22.82 (Zwolle, Rienks)

Coxed Pairs
1. GBR 6:49.83 (Searle, Searle; coxswain: Herbert)
2. ITA 6:50.98 (Abbagnale, Abbagnale; coxswain: Di Capua)
3. ROM 6:51.58 (Popescu, Taga; coxswain: Raducanu)

Coxless Fours
1. AUS 5:55.04 (Cooper, McKay, Green, Tomkins)
2. USA 5:56.68 (Burden, McLaughlin, Bohrer, Manning)
3. SLO 5:58.24 (Klemencic, Mirjanic, Jansa, Mujkic)

Quadruple Sculls
1. GER 5:45.17 (Willms, Hajek, Volker, Steinbach)
2. NOR 5:47.09 (Bjonness, Thorsen, Undset, Saetersdal)
3. ITA 5:47.33 (Farina, Galtarossa, Corona, Soffici)

Coxed Fours
1. ROM 5:59.37 (Talapan, Ruican, Popescu, Taga, Raducanu)
2. GER 6:0.34 (Kellner, Brudel, Peters, Finger, Reiher)
3. POL 6:3.27 (Streich, Jankowski, Tomiak, Lasicki, Cieslak)

Eights
A. CAN 5:29.53
2. ROM 5:29.67
3. GER 5:31.00

Women's Rowing

Sculls
1. Lipa ROM 7:25.54
2. Bredael BEL 7:26.64
3. Lauman CAN 7:28.85

Coxless Pairs
1. CAN 7:6.22 (McLean, Heddle)
2. GER 7:7.96 (Werremeier, Schwerzmann)
3. USA 7:8.11 (Seaton, Pierson)

Double sculls
1. GER 6:49.00 (Koeppen, Boron)
2. ROM 6:51.47 (Cochelea, Lipa)
3. CHN 6:55.16 (Gu, Lu)

Coxless Fours
1. CAN 6:30.85 (Barnes, Taylor, Monroe, Worthington)
2. USA 6:31.86 (Donohoe, Eckert, Fuller, Feeney)
3. GER 6:32.33 (Frank, Mehl, Siech, Hohn)

Quadruple Sculls
1. GER 6:20.18
2. ROM 6:24.34
3. IOP 6:25.07

Eights
1. CAN 6:2.62
2. ROM 6:6.26
3. GER 6:7.80

Basketball

Men
1. United States – 2. Croatia – 3. Lithuania

Women
1. CIS – 2. China – 3. United States

Boxing

– 48 kg (Light Flyweight)
1. Marcelo Garcia CUB
2. Bojinov BUL
3. Velasco PHI
Quast GER

– 51 kg (Flyweight)
1. Chol Su Choi PRK
2. Gonzalez Sanchez CUB
3. Austin USA
Kovacs HUN

– 54 kg (Bantamweight)
1. Casamayor Johnson CUB
2. McCullough IRL
3. Sik Li PRK
Achik MOR

– 57 kg (Featherweight)
1. Tews GER
2. Reyes Lopez SPA
3. Soltani ALG
Paliani CIS

– 60 kg (Lightweight)
1. De La Hoya USA
2. Rudolph GER
3. Bayarsaikhan MON
Sik Hong-sung KOR

– 63.5 kg (Light Welterweight)
1. Vinent CUB
2. Leduc CAN
3. Goeran Kjall FIN
Doroftei ROM

– 67 kg (Welterweight)
1. Carruth IRL
2. Hernandez Sierra CUB
3. Chenglai THA
Santiago PUR

– 71 kg (Light Middleweight)
1. Lemus Garcia CUB
2. Delibas NET
3. Mizsei HUN
Reid GBR

– 75 kg (Middleweight)
1. Hernandez CUB
2. Byrd USA
3. Johnson CAN
Seng Bae-lee KOR

– 81 kg (Light Heavyweight)
1. May GER
2. Zaoulitchnyi CIS
3. Beres HUN
Bartnik POL

– 91 kg (Heavyweight)
1. Felix Savon Fabre CUB
2. Izonritei NGA
3. Tua NZE
Van Der Lijde NET

More than 91 kg (Super Heavyweight)
1. Balado Mendez CUB
2. Igbineghu NGA
3. Nielsen DEN
Aldinov Roussinov BUL

Men's Canoeing

Slalom C1
1. Pollert CZS 113.69 pts
2. Marriott GBR 116.48 pts
3. Avril FRA 117.18 pts

Slalom C2
1. Strausbaugh-Jacobi USA 122.41 pts
2. Simek-Rohan CZS 124.25 pts
3. Adisson-Forgues FRA 124.38 pts

Slalom K1
1. Ferrazzi ITA 106.89 pts
2. Curinier FRA 107.06 pts
3. Lettmann GER 108.52 pts

Kayak K1 (500m)
1. Kolehmainen FIN 1:40.34
2. Gyulay HUN 1:40.64
3. Holmann NOR 1:40.71

Kayak K2 (500m)
1. GER 1:28.27 (Bluhm, Gutsche)
2. POL 1:29.84 (Freimut, Kurpiewski)
3. ITA 1:30 (Rossi, Dreossi)

Canadian C1 (1000m)
1. Bulkhalov BUL
2. Klementjevs LAT
3. Zala HUN

Canadian C2 (1000m)
1. GER (Papke, Spelly)
2. DEN (Nielsson, Frederiksen)
3. FRA (Hoyer, Boivin)

Kayak K1 (1000m)
1. Robinson AUS
2. Holmann NOR
3. Barton USA

Kayak K2 (1000m)
1. GER (Bluhm, Gutsche)
2. SWE Olsson, Sundqvist)
3. POL (Kotowicz, Bialkowski)

Kayak K4 (1000m)
1. GER (Von Appen, Kegel, Reineck, Wohllebe)
2. HUN (Csipes, Gyulay, Fidel, Abraham)
3. AUS (Graham, Rowling, Wood, Andersson)

Women's Canoeing

Slalom K1
1. Micheler GER 126.41 pts
2. Woodward AUS 128.27 pts
3. Chiadek USA 131.75 pts

Kayak K1 (500m)
1. Schmidt GER 1:51.60
2. Koban HUN 1:51.96
3. Dylewska POL 1:52.36

Kayak K2 (500m)
1. GER 1:40.29 (Portwich, Von Seck)
2. SWE 1:40.41 (Gunnarsson, Andersson)
3. HUN 1:40.81 (Koban, Donusz)

Kayak K4 (500m)
1. HUN (Donusz, Czigany, Meszaros, Koban)
2. GER (Borchert, Schmidt, Von Seck, Portwich)
3. SWE (Olsson, Haglund, Rosenqvist, Andersson)

Men's Cycling

100 km Team Time Trial
1. GER 2 h 1:39 (B. Dittert, C. Meyer, U. Peschet, M. Rich)
2. ITA 2 h 2:39 (F. Anastasia, L. Colombo, G. Contri, A. Peron)
3. FRA 2 h 5:25 (H. Boussard, D. Faivre-Pierret, P. Gaumont, J. Harel)

Team Pursuit
1. Germany – 2. Australia – 3. Denmark

Speed
1. Fiedler GER
2. Neiwand AUS
3. Harnett CAN

1000m Sprint
1. Moreno SPA 1:3.342
2. Kelly AUS 1:4.288
3. Hartwell USA 1:4.753

4000m Individual Pursuit
1. Boardman GBR
2. Lehmann GER
3. Anderson NZE

Points Race
1. Lombardi ITA 44 pts
(50 km in 1 h 0:59.213. Average Speed: 49.190 km/h.)
2. Van Bon NET 43 pts
3. Mathy BEL 41 pts

Road Race
1. Casartelli ITA 4 h 35:21
(Average Speed: 42.360 km/h.)
2. Dekker NET 4 h 35:21
3. Ozols LAT 4 h 35:21

Women's Cycling

Individual Road Race
1. Rossner (GER) – 2. Watt (AUS) – 3. Twigg (USA)

Speed
1. Salumae (EST) – 2. Neumann (GER)
3. Haringa (NET)

Road Race
1. Watt AUS 81 km in 2 h 04:22
(Average Speed: 38.973 km/h.)
2. Longo-Ciprelli FRA 2 h 05:02
3. Knol NET 2 h 05:03

Equestrian Sports

Individual Jumping
1. Beerbaum GER "Classic Touch"
2. Raymakers NET "Ratina Z"
3. Dello Joio USA "Irish"

Jumping Team
1. NET 12 pts (Raymakers, "Ratina Z"; Tops, "Top Gun"; Lansink, "Egano")
2. AUT 16,75 pts (Muntzner, "Graf Grande"; Simon, "Apricot D"; Fruhmann, "Genius")
3. FRA 25,75 pts (Godignon "Quidam de Revel"; Bourdy, "Razzia du Poncel"; Robert, "Nonix"; Navet, "Quito de Baussy")

Individual Dressage
1. Uphoff GER "Rembrandt" 1626 pts
2. Werth GER "Gigolo" 1551 pts
3. Balkenhol GER "Goldstern" 1515 pts

Team Dressage
1. GER 5224 pts (Uphoff-"Rembrandt", Theodorescu-"Gruno x", Werth-"Gigolo")
2. NET 4742 pts (Van Grunsven-"Olympic Bonfire", Sanders-"Olympic Montreux", Bartels-"Olympic Courage")
3. USA 4643 pts

Grand Prix Individual Jumping
1. Ryan/"Kibach Tic Toc" AUS 70 pts
2. Blocker/"Feine Dame" GER 81.30 pts
3. Tait/"Messiah" NZE 87.60 pts

Grand Prix Team Jumping
1. AUS 288.80 pts (Rolton, Hoy, Ryan)
2. NZE 290.80 pts (Nicholson, Latta, Tait)
3. GER 300.30 pts (Baumann, Mysegaes, Ehrenbring, Blocker)

Men's Fencing

Individual Foil
1. Omnès FRA
2. Golubitski CIS
3. Gregory Gil CUB

Individual Sabre
1. Szabo HUN
2. Marin ITA
3. Lamour FRA

Individual Epée
1. Srecki FRA
2. Kolobkov CIS
3. Henry FRA

Team Foil
1. GER – 2. CUB – 3. POL

Team Sabre
1. CIS – 2. HUN – 3. FRA

Team Epée
1. GER – 2. HUN – 3. CIS

Women's Fencing

Individual Foil
1. Trillini ITA
2. Hui Feng CHN
3. Sadovskaia CIS

Team Foil
1. ITA – 2. GER – 3. ROM

Soccer

1. SPA – 2. POL – 3. GHA

Men's Gymnastics

All-round Individual Competition
1. Chtcherbo CIS
2. Misiutine CIS
3. Belenki CIS

Combined Exercises Team
1. CIS 585.450 pts (Chtcherbo, Belenki, Misiutine, Korobtchinski, Vorpaev, Charipov)
2. CHN 580.375 pts (X.-Li, C.-Li, Guo, J.-Li, D.-Li, G.-Li).
3. JAP 578.250 pts (Iketani, Hatakeda, Chinen, Nishikawa, Aihara, Matsunaga)

Horizontal Bar
1. Dimas USA 9.875 pts
2. Misiutine CIS 9.837 pts
3. Wecker GER 9.837 pts

Parallel Bars
1. Stcherbo CIS
2. JingLi CHN
3. Korobtchinski CIS
Linyao Guo CHN
Matsunaga JAP

Floor Exercises
1. Xiao Li CHN 9.925 pts
2. Misiutine CIS 9.787 pts
3. Iketani JAP 9.787 pts

Rings
1. Stcherbo CIS 9.937 pts
2. Li CHN 9.875 pts
3. Xiaosahuang Li CHN 9.862 pts
Wecker GER 9.862 pts

Pommel Horse
1. Stcherbo CIS 9.925 pts
Pae PRK 9.925 pts
3. Wecker GER 9.887 pts

Horse Vault
1. Chtcherbo CIS 9.856 pts
2. Misjoutine CIS 9.781 pts
3. Ok Ryul Yoo KOR 9.762 pts

1992  Barcelona

Women's Gymnastics

Individual Competition
1. Gutsu CIS 39.737 pts
2. Miller USA 39.725 pts
3. Milosovici ROM 39.687 pts

Team Competition
1. CIS 395.666 pts (Boginskaia, Lyssenko, Galierva, Gutsu, Grudneva, Tchussovitina)
2. ROM 395.079 pts (Bontas, Milosovici, Gogean, Hadarean, Neculita, Pasca)
3. USA 394.704 pts (Miller, Okino, Zmeskal, Strug, Dawes, Bruce)

Floor Exercices
1. Milosovici ROM 10 pts
2. Onodi HUN 9.950 pts
3. Gutsu CIS 9.912 pts
   Bontas ROM
   Miller USA

Horse Vault
1. Onodi HUN 9.925 pts
2. Milosovici ROM 9.925 pts
3. Lyssenko CIS 9.912 pts

Asymmetric Bars
1. Lu CHN 10 pts
2. Gutsu CIS 9.975 pts
3. Miller USA 9.962 pts

Beam
1. Lyssenko CIS 9.975 pts
2. Lu CHN 9.912 pts
3. Miller USA 9.912 pts

Rythmic Competition
1. Timoshenko CIS 59.037 pts
2. Pascual Garcia SPA 58.100 pts
3. Skaldina CIS 57.912 pts

Weightlifting

52 kg
1. Ivanov BUL 265 kg
2. Lin Qisheng CHN 262.5 kg
3. Ciharean ROM 252.5 kg

56 kg
1. Byung-kwan KOR 287.5 kg
2. Liu Shugin CHN 277.5 kg
3. Luo Jianming CHN 277.5 kg

– 60 kg
1. Suleymanoglu TUR 320 kg
2. Peshalov BUL 305 kg
3. Yingqiang CHN 295 kg

– 67.5 kg
1. Militossain CIS 337.5 kg
2. Yotov BUL 327.5 kg
3. Behm GER 320 kg

– 75 kg
1. Kassapu CIS 357.5 kg
2. Lara Rodriguez CUB 357.5 kg
3. Myong Nam PRK 352.5 kg

– 82.5 kg
1. Dimas GRE 370 kg (167.5 + 202.5)
2. Siemion POL 370 kg (165 + 205)
3. Bronze Medal not awarded.

90 kg
1. Kakhiachvili CIS 412.5 kg
2. Syrtsov CIS 412.5 kg
3. Wolczaniecki POL 392.5 kg

100 kg
1. Tregubov CIS 410 kg
2. Taimazov CIS 402.5 kg
3. Malak POL 400 kg

110 kg
1. Weller CIS 432 kg
2. Ahoev CIS 430 kg
3. Botev BUL 417.5 kg

+ 110 kg
1. Kurlovitch CIS 450 kg
2. Taranenko CIS 425 kg
3. Nerlinger GER 412.5 kg

Handball

Men
1. CIS – 2. SWE – 3. FRA

Women
1. KOR – 2. NOR – 3. CIS

Hockey Field

Men
1. GER – 2. AUS – 3. PAK

Women
1. SPA – 2. GER – 3. GBR

Men's Judo

Extra-Lightweight (less than 60 kg)
1. Gusseinov CIS
2. Yoon KOR
3. Koshino JAP
   Trautmann GER

Half-Lightweight (less than 65 kg)
1. Sampaio BRA
2. Csak HUN
3. Quellmalz GER
   Planas CUB

Lightweight (less than 71 kg)
1. Koga JAP
2. Hjtos HUN
3. Smaga ISR
   Chung KOR

Half-Middleweight (less than 78 kg)
1. Yoshida JAP
2. Morris USA
3. Byung-Joo KOR
   Damaisin FRA

Middleweight (less than 86 kg)
1. Legien POL
2. Tayot FRA
3. Gill CAN
   Okada JAP

Half-Heavyweight (less than 95 kg)
1. Kovacs HUN
2. Stevens GBR
3. Meijer NET
   Sergeev CIS

Heavyweight (more than 95 kg)
1. Khakhaleichvili CIS
2. Ogawa JAP
3. Douillet FRA
   Csosz HUN

Women's Judo

– 48 kg
1. Nowak FRA
2. Tamura JAP
3. Savon CUB
   Senyurt TUR

– 52 kg
1. Martinez SPA
2. Mizoguchi JAP
3. Rendle GBR
   Li CHN

– 56 kg
1. Blasco SPA
2. Fairbrother GBR
3. Tateno JAP
   Morales CUB

– 61 kg
1. Fleury FRA
2. Arad ISR
3. Zhang CHN
   Petrova CIS

– 66 kg
1. Reve CUB
2. Pierantozzi ITA
3. Rakels BEL
   Howey GBR

72 kg
1. Mi-Jung KOR
2. Tanabe JAP
3. Meignan FRA
   De Kok NET

+ 72 kg
1. Xiaoyan CHN
2. Rodriguez CUB
3. Lupino FRA
   Sakaue JAP

Greco-Roman Wrestling

Light-Flyweight (48 kg)
1. Kutcherenko CIS
2. Maenza ITA
3. Amita CUB

Flyweight (52 kg)
1. Ronningen NOR
2. Ter-Mkretchian CIS
3. Kyung Kap KOR

Bantamweight (57 kg)
1. Han-Bong KOR
2. Yildiz GER
3. Zetian CHN

Featherweight (62 kg)
1. Pirim (TUR) – 2. Martinov (CIS) – 3. Delis (CUB)

Lightweight (68 kg)
1. Repka HUN
2. Dugutchiev CIS
3. Smith USA

Welterweight (74 kg)
1. Iskandarian CIS
2. Tracz POL
3. Kornbakk SWE

Middleweight (82 kg)
1. Farkas HUN
2. Stepien POL
3. Turlykhanov CIS

Light Heavyweight (90 kg)
1. Bullmann GER
2. Basar TUR
3. Koguachvili CIS

Heavyweight (100 kg)
1. Perez CUB
2. Koslowski USA
3. Demiachkievitch CIS

Super Heavyweight (130 kg)
1. Karelin CIS
2. Johansson SWE
3. Grigoras ROM

Freestyle Wrestling

48 kg
1. Kim Il KOR
2. Jong Shin-kim KOR
3. Orudjov CIS

52 kg
1. Li (KOR) – 2. Jones (USA) – 3. Jordanov (BUL)

57 kg
1. Diaz PRK
2. Smal CIS
3. Sik Kim KOR

62 kg
1. Smith USA
2. Mohammadian IRA
3. Martinez CUB

68 kg
1. Fadzaev CIS
2. Dotchev Getzov BUL
3. Akkaishi JAP

74 kg
1. Jang Soon KOR
2. Monday USA
3. Azghadi GER

82 kg
1. Jackson USA
2. Jabraijlov CIS
3. Azghadi IRA

90 kg
1. Khadartsev CIS
2. Simsek TUR
3. Campbell USA

100 kg
1. Khabelov CIS
2. Balz GER
3. Kayali TUR

130 kg
1. Baumgartner USA
2. Thue CAN
3. Gobedjichvili CIS

Men's Swimming

50m Freestyle
1. Popov CIS 21.91
2. Biondi USA 22.09
3. Jager USA 22.30

100m Freestyle
1. Popov CIS 49.02
2. Borges BRA 49.43
3. Caron FRA 49.50

200m Freestyle
1. Sadovyi CIS 1:46.70
2. Holmertz SWE 1:46.86
3. Kasvio FIN 1:47.63

400m Freestyle
1. Sadovyi CIS 3:45.00
2. Perkins AUS 3:45.16
3. Holmertz SWE 3:46.77

1500m Freestyle
1. Perkins AUS 14:43.48
2. Housman AUS 14:55.29
3. Hoffmann GER 15:2.29

100m Backstroke
1. Tewksbury CAN 53.98
2. Rouse USA 54.04
3. Berkoff USA 54.78

200m Backstroke
1. Lopez Zubero SPA 1:58.47
2. Selkov CIS 1:58.87
3. Battistelli ITA 1:59.40

100m Butterfly
1. Morales USA 53.32
2. Szukala POL 53.35
3. Nesty SUR 53.41

200m Butterfly
1. Stewart USA 1:56.26
2. Loader NZE 1:57.93
3. Esposito FRA 1:58.51

100m Breaststroke
1. Diebel USA 1:1.50
2. Rozsa HUN 1:1.68
3. Rogers AUS 1:1.76

200m Breaststroke
1. Barrowman USA 2:10.16 (World Record)
2. Rozsa HUN 2:11.23
3. Gillingham GBR 2:11.29

200m Medley
1. Darnyi HUN 2:0.76
2. Burgess USA 2:0.97
3. Czene HUN 2:1

400m Medley
1. Darnyi HUN 4:14.23
2. Namesnik USA 4:15.57
3. Sacchi ITA 4:16.34

4 x 100m
1. USA 3:16.74 (Hudepohl, Biondi, Jager, Olsen)
2. CIS 3:17.56 (Khnykin, Prigoda, Bashkatov, Popov)
3. GER 3:17.90 (Troeger, Richter, Zesner, Pinger)

4 x 200m
1. CIS 7:11.95 (Lepikov, Pychnenko, Taianovitch, Sadovyi)
2. SWE 7:15.51 (Wallim, Holmertz, Werner, Frolander)
3. USA 7:16.23 (Hudepohl, Stewart, Olsen, Gjertsen)

4 x 100m Medley
1. USA 3:36.93 (Rousse, Diebel Morales, Olsen), World Record equaled
2. CIS 3:38.56 (Selkov, Ivanov Khnykine, Popov)
3. CAN 3:39.66 (Tewksbury, Cleveland, Gery, Clarke)

Women's Swimming

50m Freestyle
1. Yang CHN 24.79
2. Zhuang CHN 25.08
3. Martino USA 25.23

100m Freestyle
1. Zuhang CHN 54.64
2. Thompson USA 54.84
3. Van Almsick GER 54.94

200m Freestyle
1. Haislett USA 1:57.90
2. Van Almsick GER 1:58
3. Kieglas GER 1:59.67

400m Freestyle
1. Hase GER 4:7.18
2. Evans USA 4:7.37
3. Lewis AUS 4:11.22

800m Freestyle
1. Evans USA 8:25.52
2. Lewis AUS 8:30.34
3. Henke GER 8:30.99

100m Backstroke
1. Egerszegi HUN 1:0.68
2. Szabo HUN 1:1.14
3. Loveless USA 1:1.43

200m Backstroke
1. Egerszegi HUN 2:7.06
2. Hase GER 2:9.46
3. Stevenson AUS 2:10.20

100m Butterfly
1. Qian CHN 58.62
2. M. Ahmann-Leighton USA 58.74
3. Plewinski FRA 59.01

200m Butterfly
1. Sanders USA 2:8.67
2. Wang CHN 2:9.01
3. O'Neill AUS 2:9.03

100m Breaststroke
1. Rudkovskaia CIS 1:8
2. Nall USA 1:8.25
3. Riley AUS 1:9.25

200m Breaststroke
1. Iwasaki JAP 2:26.65
2. Lin CHN 2:26.85
3. Nall USA 2:26.88

200m Medley
1. Lin CHN 2:11.65 (World Record)
2. Sanders USA 2:11.91
3. Hunger GER 2:13.92

400m Medley
1. Egerszegi HUN 4:36.54
2. Li Lin CHN 4:36.73
3. Sanders USA 4:37.58

4 x 100m Freestyle
1. USA 3:39.46 (Haislett, Torres, Martino, Thompson)
2. CHN 3:41.60 (Zhuang, Lu, Yang, Le)
3. GER 3:41.60 (Van Almsick, Osygus, Hunger, Stellmach)

4 x 100m Medley
1. USA 4:2.54 (Loveless, Nall, Ahmann-Leighton, Thompson)
2. GER 4:5.19 (Hase, Doerries, Van Almsick, Hunger)
3. CIS 4:6.44 (Jivanevskaia, Rudkovskaia, Kiritchenko, Mechtcheriakova)

Men's Diving

Spring Board Diving 3 m
1. Lenzi USA 676.530 pts
2. Tan CAN 645.570 pts
3. Saoutin CIS 627.780 pts

Platform Diving
1. Shuwei Sun CHN 677.310 pts
2. Donie CIS 633.630 pts
3. Ni Xiong CHN 600.150 pts

Women's Diving

Spring Board Diving 3 m
1. Gao CHN 572.400 pts
2. Lachko CIS 514.140 pts
3. Baldus GER 503.070 pts

Platform Diving
1. Mingwia Fu CHN 461.430 pts
2. Mirochina CIS 411.630 pts
3. Clark USA 401.910 pts

Modern Pentathlon

Individual
1. Skrzypaszek POL 5559 pts
2. Mizser HUN 5446 pts
3. Zenovka CIS 5361 pts

Team
1. POL 16018 pts
2. CIS 15924 pts
3. ITA 15760 pts

Tennis

Men's Singles
1. Rosset SWI
2. Arrese SPA
3. Ivanisevic CRO
   Cherkasov CIS

Men's Doubles
1. Becker-Stich GER
2. Ferreira-Norval SAF
3. Ivanisevic-Prpic CRO
   Frana-Miniussi ARG

Women's Singles
1. Capriati USA
2. Graf GER
3. Sanchez SPA
   Fernandez USA

Table Tennis

Men's Singles
1. Waldner SWE
2. Gatien FRA
3. Ma Wenge CHN
   Taek Soo-kim KOR

Men's Doubles
1. Lu Lin-Wang Tao CHN
2. Fetzner-Roskopf GER
3. Kang Hee-Lee Chul KOR
   Kim Taek-Yo Nams KOR

Women's Singles
1. Deng Yaping CHN
2. Qiao Hong CHN
3. Hyun Jung KOR
   Li Bun PRK

Women's Doubles
1. Den Yaping-Qiao Hong CHN
2. Chen Zihe-Gao Jun CHN
3. Li Bun-Yu Sun PRK
   Hong Cha-Huyn Jung KOR

Men's Shooting

Rapid-Fire Pistol
1. Schumann GER 789 pts
2. Kuzmins LAT 785 pts
3. Vokhmianin CIS 786 pts

Free Pistol
1. Loukachik CIS 658 pts
2. Wang CHN 657 pts
3. Skanaker SWE 657 pts

Pistol, 10m
1. Wang Yifu CHN 684.8 pts
2. Pyjianov CIS 684.1 pts
3. Babii ROM 684.1 pts

Rifle, 10m
1. Fedkin CIS 593 pts
2. Badiou FRA 591 pts
3. Riederer GER 590 pts

Rifle, prone
1. Eun-Chul KOR 702.5 pts
2. Stenvaag NOR 701.4 pts
3. Pletikosic IOP 701.1 pts

Rifle, 3 x 40
1. Petikian CIS 1267.4 pts
2. Foth USA 1266.6 pts
3. Koba JAP 1265.9 pts

Moving Target
1. Jakosits GER 673 pts
2. Asrabaev CIS 672 pts
3. Racansky CZS 670 pts

Women's Shooting

Pistol, 10m
1. Logvinenko CIS 486.4 pts
2. Sekaric IOP 486.4 pts
3. Grusdeva BUL 481.6 pts

Pistol, 22 caliber
1. Logvinenko CIS 684 pts
2. Duihong Li CHN 680 pts
3. Munkhbayar MON 679 pts

Airgun
1. Kab-Soon Yeo KOR 498.2 pts
2. Letcheva BUL 495.3 pts
3. Binder BOS 495.1 pts

Rifle, 3 x 20
1. Meili USA 684.3 pts
2. Matova BUL 682.7 pts
3. Ksiazkiewicz POL 681.5 pts

Men's Archery

Individual
1. Flute FRA
2. Chung KOR
3. Terry GBR

Team
1. SPA – 2. FIN – 3. GBR

Women's Archery

Individual
1. Y. Cho (KOR) – 2. S. Kim (KOR)
3. Valeeva (CIS)

Team
1. KOR – 2. CHN – 3. CIS

Men's Yachting

Finn Class
1. SPA Garcia 33.40 pts
2. USA Ledbetter 54.70 pts
3. NZE Monk 64.70 pts

470 Class
1. SPA (Calafat, Sanchez) 50 pts
2. USA (Reeser, Burnham) 66.70 pts
3. EST (T. Toniste, N. Toniste) 68.70 pts

Flying Dutchman Class
1. SPA 29.70 pts
2. USA 32.70 pts
3. DEN 37.70 pts

Soling Class
1. DEN – 2. USA – 3. GBR

Tornado Class
1. FRA (Loday, Hénard) 40.40 pts
2. USA (Smyth, Notary) 42 pts
3. AUS (Booth, Forbes) 44.40 pts

Star Class
1. USA (Reynolds, Haenel) 31.40 pts
2. NZE (Davis, Cowie) 58.40 pts
3. CAN (McDonald, Jespersen) 62.70 pts

Windsurfing
1. David FRA
2. Gebhardt USA
3. Kleppich AUS

Women's Yachting

470 class
1. SPA (Zabell, Guerra) 30.70 pts
2. NZE (Egnot, Shearer) 39.70 pts
3. USA (Isler, Healy) 42.40 pts

Europ
1. NOR Andersen 48.70 pts
2. SPA Via Dufresne 57.40 pts
3. USA Trotman 62.70 pts

Windsurfing
1. NZE 47.80 pts
2. CHN 65.80 pts
3. NET 68.70 pts

Volleyball

Men
1. BRA – 2. NET – 3. USA

Women
1. CIS – 2. CUB – 3. USA

1992

SEPTEMBER

Su	Mo	Tu	We	Th	Fr	Sa
		1	2	3	4	5
6	7	8	9	10	11	12
13	14	15	16	17	18	19
20	21	22	23	24	25	26
27	28	29	30			

4. Bulgaria: Former Communist leader Todor Zhivkov is sentenced to seven years in prison for crimes committed during his 35 years in power.

7. Ciskei: At least 28 people are killed when soldiers fire on African National Congress marchers.

7. US: The first patient to receive a baboon liver transplant dies of a stroke.

12. US: The space shuttle Endeavour is launched; it carries the first married couple to go into space.

13. Monza: British driver Nigel Mansell announces his retirement from Formula One racing.

14. Pakistan: Three days of heavy rain claim 2,000 lives.

15. Strasbourg: The European Parliament celebrates its 40th anniversary.

16. Paris: President Mitterrand undergoes an operation for cancer.

20. France: In a referendum, 51 per cent of voters approve the Maastricht treaty (→2/12).

21. Vatican City: After a 130-year break, diplomatic relations are restored with Mexico.

23. Vietnam: General Le Duc Anh, a former Vietcong, is elected President.

25. US: A 12-year-old Florida boy wins a "divorce" from his biological parents, accused of having neglected him.

28. Germany: After protests from Britain, Bonn calls off celebrations to mark the 50th anniversary of the V-2 rocket.

29. Brazil: President Fernando Collor de Mello is impeached by Parliament on charges of financial impropriety.

30. London: The Royal Mint introduces a new, smaller 10-pence coin.

DEATHS

12. American film actor Anthony Perkins (*4/4/1932).

28. William Douglas-Home, British playwright (*3/6/1912).

End of the road for Shining Path leader

Abimael Guzman's guerrillas are responsible for the death of 25,000 people.

Sept 12. Abimael Guzman, the most wanted man in Peru, was arrested today in Lima. The former philosophy professor is the leader of the "Sendero Luminoso", or Shining Path, the Maoist guerrilla group he founded in 1970. The 57-year-old guerrilla leader faces charges of treason and a life sentence. He had been in hiding since 1980, when the Shining Path began its campaign of armed insurgency. The death toll left by the group has exceeded 25,000.

Minister Mellor resigns over sex scandal

David Mellor, a close friend of John Major, is dubbed "Minister for Fun".

Sept 24. Heritage Secretary David Mellor resigned today, blaming his departure on "a barrage of stories about me in tabloid newspapers". His problems began with the revelation in July of his affair with actress Antonia de Sancha. Then, a libel case brought by Mona Bauwens, daughter of a PLO official, against "The People" newspaper finished him off. Bauwens, who has invited the Mellor family to holiday with her in Spain, argued that "The People" had suggested she was not fit to be seen in decent company. The jury did not agree, and Mellor's wisdom in accepting a free holiday from Bauwens was so fiercely questioned that his resignation became inevitable.

UN plane is downed as peace talks open

Sept 3. All UN relief flights into Sarajevo were halted today after an Italian cargo plane was shot down by missile fire near the Bosnian capital. This was hardly a good omen for the first session of UN-sponsored international conference in Geneva today. The peace talks, aimed at putting a stop to fighting in Bosnia, are being held under the chairmanship of UN envoy Cyrus Vance and former British Foreign Secretary Lord Owen. Attending the Geneva talks are the leaders of Bosnia's Serb, Croat and Muslim communities. The conference will also focus on the return of refugees and closing down the Serb-run detention camps (→9/10).

Monetary chaos as sterling quits ERM

Sept 16. Bitter accusations were flying between London and Bonn today as Britain pulled out of the European exchange rate mechanism, or ERM, allowing sterling to float. The rift with Germany grew as London blamed Bonn's economic policies for the fall of the pound. Over the past few days, the Bank of England's battle against speculators is estimated to have cost Britain £15 billion. John Major has said Britain will not rejoin the ERM until the mechanism is run "in the interests of all".

Sept 20. British golfer Mark Roe wins the prestigious Lancome Trophy near Paris.

1992

OCTOBER

Su	Mo	Tu	We	Th	Fr	Sa
				1	2	3
4	5	6	7	8	9	10
11	12	13	14	15	16	17
18	19	20	21	22	23	24
25	26	27	28	29	30	31

2. Brazil: A riot in a Sao Paulo prison leaves 111 inmates dead.

6. Angola: UNITA guerrillas reject election results giving President Eduardo dos Santos a clear victory against rebel leader Jonas Savimbi.

9. New York: The UN imposes an air exclusion over Bosnia (→20/11).

11. Rumania: Ion Iliescu is elected President.

12. Cairo: An earthquake leaves nearly 400 people dead.

13. Germany: Police seize 4 4 pounds of uranium which originated in the former USSR.

13. London: The Booker Prize is awarded to Michael Ondaatje, for "The English Patient", and Barry Unsworth, for "Sacred Hunger".

16. Russia: A 100 per cent tariff on imported alcohol is imposed to protect domestic vodka producers.

21. Egypt: Islamic militants attack British tourists, killing one and wounding two.

22. Dresden: During a visit, Queen Elizabeth is jeered by anti-British demonstrators.

23. Paris: The former head of France's National Blood Transfusion Centre is sentenced to four years in prison for his role in the distribution of blood contaminated with the AIDS virus.

25. Egypt: Ceremonies are held at El Alamein to mark the 50th anniversary of the decisive World War II battle.

30. London: An IRA bomb attack near Downing Street causes minor damage.

31. Florida: British jockey Lester Piggott is injured during the Breeder's Cup Classic.

31. Vatican City: The Vatican admits Galileo was right in saying the Earth revolves around the Sun.

DEATHS

6. Denholm Elliott, British actor (*31/5/1922).

8. Willy Brandt, German statesman (*18/12/1913).

Furious miners force Major to back down

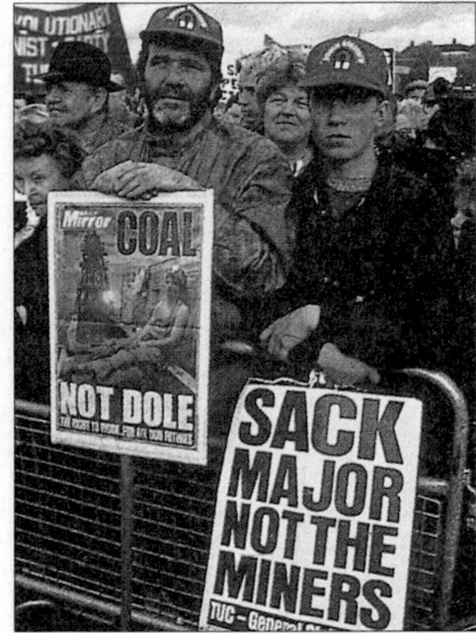

Uproar over the pit closures.

Oct 21. As tens of thousands of miners staged a protest march in London, John Major's government was forced to back down on proposed pit closures during a rowdy Commons debate tonight.

The Coal Board said eight days ago it planned to close 31 pits and make 30,000 miners redundant. Faced with howls of protest, the Government then said only 10 pits were to be closed. Tonight, as the protests continued to spread, Trade and Industry Minister, Michael Heseltine, retreated further. He told the packed House of Commons that a Government inquiry into the closures could save some of the 10 threatened pits.

West Indian gets Literature Nobel

Oct 8. Derek Walcott was awarded the Nobel Prize for Literature today. The poet and dramatist from Trinidad is the first Caribbean writer to receive the prize, worth £710,000 this year.

Derek Walcott is best known for "Omeros", which remakes the Homeric epics as the story of an itinerant West Indian. The 325-page poem, published two years ago, has sold tens of thousands of copies around the world. The Nobel Committee's choice of Walcott for the honour is especially significant in the year of the 500th anniversary of Christopher Columbus' landing in the West Indies.

Canada vote boosts Quebec separatists

Oct 26. Canada's voters today rejected a constitutional proposal which would have granted Quebec a special status within the federation. The referendum's result has placed the mostly French-speaking province firmly on the separatist path. The proposal, backed by Prime Minister Brian Mulroney, was an attempt to meet Quebec's demands for more autonomy within the nation's present constitutional framework. The national vote was 52.3 per cent "No". The province with the highest percentage of "No" votes was British Columbia with 67.9. The result in Quebec was 55.4 per cent "No".

Oct 4. A fully-loaded El Al Boeing 747-200F cargo plane crashes into a crowded housing complex minutes after taking off from Amsterdam's Schipol Airport, killing more than 70 people and injuring hundreds.

Racist violence in Germany spreads

Oct 3. Tens of thousands of Germans took to the streets today to protest against the wave of racist violence that has been sweeping the country.

For weeks, extreme-right thugs have been attacking foreign asylum seekers and hostels housing immigrants. Youths chanting Nazi slogans have beaten up immigrants, and petrol bombs have been thrown at hostels and businesses owned by foreigners. The police have been criticised for not acting decisively to put an end to the attacks. Nearly 1,000 racist incidents have occurred since last August (→23/11).

Neo-Nazi youths take to the streets.

Ambulance horror as computer fails

Oct 28. The failure of a brand new £1.5-million computerised system for directing emergency ambulance calls is alleged to have contributed to 20 deaths over the past seven days. The system was designed to allocate 999 calls more efficiently, but for 36 hours the service collapsed into chaos and had to revert to manual control.

This was the climax of months of dissatisfaction with the service. Government figures show that only 11 per cent of emergency calls in London are being answered within the required minimum time of 17 minutes. John Wilby, chief executive of the London Ambulance Service, announced today that he has offered his resignation.

1992

NOVEMBER

Su	Mo	Tu	We	Th	Fr	Sa
1	2	3	4	5	6	7
8	9	10	11	12	13	14
15	16	17	18	19	20	21
22	23	24	25	26	27	28
29	30					

2. Tehran: Iran increases the reward for killing British author Salman Rushdie.

9. London: The Renoir painting, "A Vase of Flowers", stolen from an art gallery five years ago, is recovered.

10. London: Russian President Boris Yeltsin invites Queen Elizabeth to visit Moscow.

10. London: John Major orders an inquiry into the "Iraqgate affair", the sale of equipment capable of boosting Iraq's military might.

13. Peru: An attempt to overthrow President Alberto Fujimori fails.

14. London: The England XV beats South Africa 33-16 at Twickenham in the first game between the two countries since 1984; sporting relations had been broken over apartheid.

16. Lithuania: Former Communist reformers, led by Algirdas Brazauskas, win a parliamentary majority.

20. Rome: NATO and Western European Union warships begin to enforce an embargo on Serbian shipping in the Adriatic (→29/12).

23. Australia: The government decides to allow homosexuals to join the military.

23. Germany: A Turkish woman and two girls aged 14 and 10 are burnt to death in a racist arson attack in the village of Mölln.

25. London: Agatha Christie's mystery, "The Mousetrap", celebrates its 40th anniversary in the West End. It has been seen by 9.5 million people.

26. South Africa: President Frederik de Klerk calls for elections for a non-racial government to be held by April 1994.

27. Venezuela: President Carlos Perez survives a new military coup attempt.

DEATHS

2. Hal Roach, American film producer and director (*1892).

7. Alexander Dubcek, Czechoslovak statesman (27/11/1921).

Clinton wins presidency

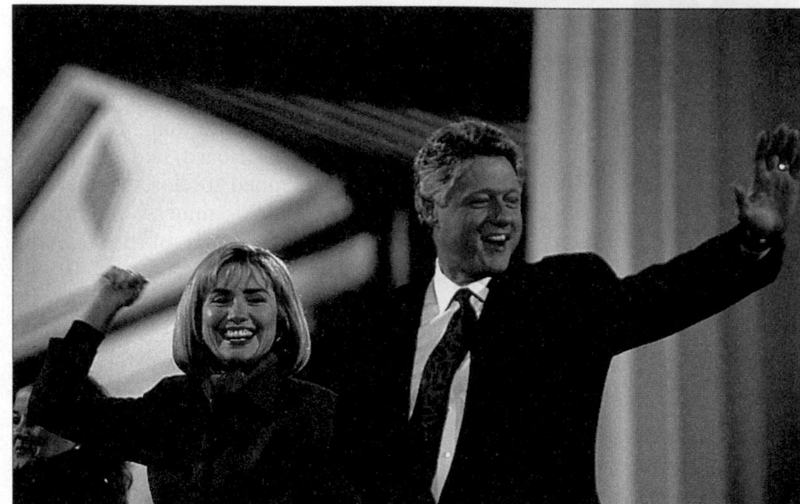

At 46, Bill Clinton is the first "baby-boomer" to reach the White House.

Nov 4. The results of yesterday's voting are in. The people of the US have chosen their 42nd President, Governor Bill Clinton of Arkansas. The chubby 46-year-old Democrat will be the first US President of the post-World War II generation.

Clinton received 43 per cent of the popular vote, well ahead of President George Bush's 38 per cent. A third candidate, the eccentric Texas billionnaire Ross Perot, received 19 per cent, the highest showing ever for an independent or third-party candidate. The Democrats also retained their majorities in the House of Representatives and the Senate. The President-elect has already begun to outline the priorities of his presidency. Creating new jobs, reducing the deficit and reforming the health-care system will be the primary domestic goals.

Clinton, thanking cheering supporters at his Little Rock, Arkansas, campaign headquarters, also revealed the international issues he will address. The new President wants to further global trade negotiations and peace talks between Israel and its Arab neighbours, complete arms agreements with Russia, aid the famine victims in Somalia and work toward an end to the war in the former republics of Yugoslavia (→20/1/93).

Women hail crucial General Synod vote

Nov 11. The Church of England today took a revolutionary step by voting, after 17 years of often bitter debate, to allow women to be ordained as priests. The motion gained the required two-thirds majority in the three houses of the General Synod by a mere five votes.

When the Archbishop of Canterbury, Dr George Carey, announced the result, men and women waiting outside the chamber wept, hugged and kissed each other in emotional scenes, hardly able to believe they had won their long struggle. It was not all joy, however. Traditionalists warned that the Church was on the brink of a schism.

Irish voters call for easier abortion law

Nov 25. Ireland's voters have approved a government proposal to allow women to travel abroad for abortions and have access to information on abortion services available elsewhere in the EC. Voters, however, turned down a proposal that abortion should be permitted when there is a substantial risk to the mother's life. This proposal's defeat reflects the fears of the pro-life lobby, who saw it as opening the way to abortion on demand.

Windsor Castle is badly damaged by a spectacular blaze

Nov 20. Windsor Castle, home of the royal family and the only royal residence in continuous use since the Norman Conquest, was badly damaged by fire today. Flames engulfed the State Apartments in the north-east corner of the Upper Quadrangle, destroying most of the roof and seriously weakening the structure. It is feared that the priceless collection of art treasures has been badly affected despite efforts by staff, who formed a human chain to pass paintings to safety, led by Prince Andrew. Tonight, as firemen are still damping down the fire, which apparently started in the Private Chapel, questions are being asked about who will provide the millions it will take to restore the castle (→11/2/93).

The seven-hour fire left Brunswick Tower and St. George's Hall in ruins.

1992

DECEMBER

Su	Mo	Tu	We	Th	Fr	Sa
		1	2	3	4	5
6	7	8	9	10	11	12
13	14	15	16	17	18	19
20	21	22	23	24	25	26
27	28	29	30	31		

2. Bonn: The Bundestag ratifies the Maastricht treaty.

2. Beijing: China threatens to set up its own shadow government in Hong Kong if Governor Patten goes ahead with democratic reforms.

3. Manchester: Two IRA bombs explode, injuring 64.

3. La Coruna: A Greek oil tanker runs aground, causing a major oil spill.

6. Geneva: Swiss voters reject a government plan to move towards EC membership.

7. UK: Thom Gunn wins the £10,000 Forward Poetry Prize.

10. Brussels: Britain, Italy, Germany and Spain agree to go ahead with a scaled-down version of the European Fighter Aircraft.

10. Stockholm: Nobel Prizes are awarded to Edmond Fischer and Edwin Kerbs (both US) for Medicine; Gary Becker (US) for Economics; Georges Charpak (France) for Physics; Rudolph Marcus (US) for Chemistry; Derek Walcott (Trinidad) for Literature; and in Oslo the Peace Prize to Rigoberta Menchu (Guatemala).

12. Indonesia: An earthquake kills 1,500 people.

23. UK: "The Sun" publishes a leaked copy of the Queen's Christmas speech.

29. Nairobi: President Daniel arap Moi wins Kenya's first multi-party elections in 26 years.

DEATHS

25. Helen Joseph, British-born South African anti-apartheid activist (*1905).

25. Monica Dickens, British author (*10/5/1915).

HITS OF 1992

The Days of Our Lives.

Tears in Heaven.

Why.

QUOTE OF THE YEAR

"Annus Horribilis."

Queen Elizabeth, on the 40th year of her reign. November 24.

Religious rioting sweeps India after Ayodhya mosque is razed

Dec 7. Religious riots are sweeping across India in the wake of the destruction of the ancient Babri Masjid mosque by rampaging Hindu fanatics in the northern Indian town of Ayodhya yesterday. More than 800 people have been killed and hundreds injured as Moslem and Hindu mobs stab, shoot and beat each other. The violence has thrown the government into chaos and has spilled into the neighbouring states of Pakistan and Bangladesh. The army has been called out to restore order in Bombay, where street battles have left 41 dead. The stock market has been closed down and parliament forced to adjourn.

Hindu militants use their bare hands to destroy the 16th-century mosque.

Bush sends Marines to Somalia for humanitarian aid mission

Not a Somali killer in sight: Marines in the unwelcome glare of publicity.

Dec 9. Heavily armed US Marines stormed ashore before dawn today ready to do battle with the Somali gunmen who have been holding the famine-stricken country to ransom. Much to their embarrassment, the Marines were instead confronted by the world's press.

The plan is to secure Mogadishu's airport and port areas so that food and medicine can be safely airlifted in to the thousands of Somalis dying of starvation. Once that goal has been achieved US and UN units will move out to the hinterland to distribute the relief aid and protect the supplies from Somalia's warlords.

Royal Family: Anne's wedding comes in wake of Di's separation

Charles and Diana pictured before the end of their fairy-tale marriage.

Dec 12. Today brought some good news at last for the royal family. The Princess Royal was married to Commander Tim Laurence during a private ceremony in the tiny stone church at Crathie, near Balmoral. It was a far cry indeed from Anne's first marriage, to Captain Mark Phillips, a full State occasion in Westminster Abbey.

Just three days ago, Buckingham Palace announced that the Prince and Princess of Wales are to separate after 11 years of marriage. The Palace made it clear that their decision had been reached amicably. There are no plans for divorce. Both Charles and Diana will continue to take part in bringing up their sons, William and Harry.

Anne's new husband, Commander Tim Laurence, is 37 years old.

West fails to deter Serbian nationalists

The two leaders agree the time has come to end the bloodshed in Bosnia.

Dec 29. Peace hopes in Yugoslavia suffered a setback today, barely nine days after John Major and George Bush met in Washington and sent a tough message to hardliners in Belgrade. Militant Serbian nationalists and Communists in Belgrade's parliament combined forces to topple a leading advocate of a negotiated settlement in the war-torn nation. Yugoslavia's moderate Prime Minister, Milan Panic, was unseated by a no-confidence vote. The clear winner of the trial of strength between moderates and nationalists is President Slobodan Milosevic, who routed Panic in fraud-ridden elections a week ago. Before Mr Major left Washington for a brief visit to British troops in Bosnia, he and the US President agreed on the need for a UN-backed "no-fly" zone over Bosnia to deter Serbian attacks (→2/1/93).

Australians to drop allegiance to Queen

Dec 17. Australian Prime Minister Paul Keating, well-known for his fervent republican views, announced today that in future new citizens will swear allegiance to Australia and not to Queen Elizabeth. He said the cabinet had decided to amend the Citizenship Act and the oath of allegiance to "better reflect contemporary Australia and its national aspirations". The existing oath, long a source of controversy, requires a pledge to be "faithful and bear true allegiance to Her Majesty Elizabeth II, Queen of Australia, her heirs and successors according to the law". Predictably, Australian monarchists, led by Lloyd Waddy, are protesting vociferously against the cabinet decision.

Yeltsin faces onslaught from hardliners

Russia's tough new Prime Minister.

Dec 23. President Boris Yeltsin is fighting for his political life as he tries to stop hardliners from derailing his reform policies. Ten days ago the Russian leader was forced to drop his reformist premier, Yegor Gaidar, and replace him with Viktor Chernomyrdin, a former Communist Party functionary and representative of the military-industrial complex. Today, Yeltsin barely managed to convince the new premier to keep reformers in the cabinet. Chernomyrdin agreed that reforms can continue, but he has warned Yeltsin not to go too far or too fast (→25/4/93).

Arts: a good year for hype and hoopla

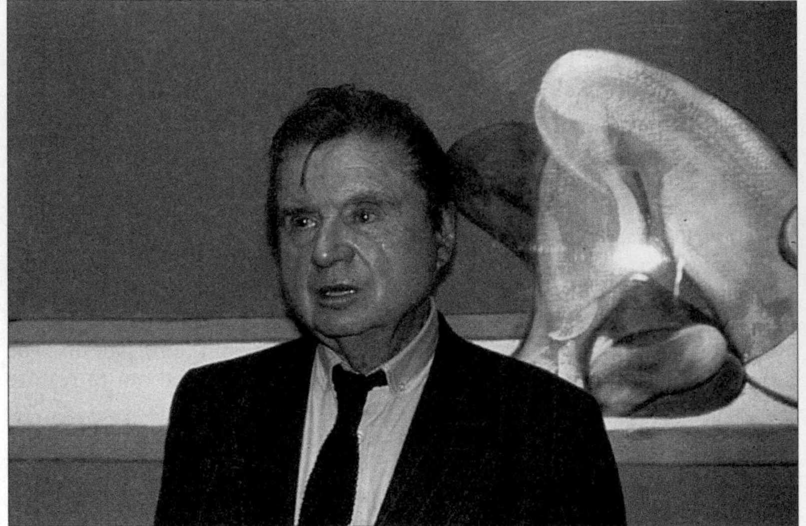

Francis Bacon, a giant of modern art, dies in Madrid at the age of 82.

Despite a grim, recession-ridden year, a few bright moments gave renewed hope that hype, smut and scandal would not remain the order of the day. Mega-hype came to London when **Madonna** launched "Sex", a photo-album of sexual exploration, and sold 100,000 copies in 12 hours. **Andrew Morton's** biography, "Diana: Her True Story", probably helped make 1992 an "Annus Horribilis" for the Queen. The posthumous publication of the poet **Philip Larkin's** "Letters" did little for his reputation.

In the theatre, **Kenneth Branagh** gave a brilliant performance as "Hamlet", while "Kiss of the Spider Woman", a musical dealing with torture and homosexuality, scored an astonishing success. The critics agreed that the year's worst offering was the musical "Which Witch", a Norwegian import. Cinemagoers saw **Daniel Day Lewis** give a splendidly macho performance in "The Last of the Mohicans", and **Gerard Depardieu** ham it up as Columbus in **Ridley Scott's** "1492". **Anthony Hopkins** hit the Hollywood big-time as "Hannibal the Cannibal" and was further rewarded with a knighthood. The musical event of the year was the collaboration between the BBC and Channel 4 to show the whole of "Tosca". In pop, **Elton John** became a super-nova by signing a £26-million deal with Time Warner, while **Sinead O'Connor** was booed off a New York stage during a tribute to **Bob Dylan**. It was a bad year for comedians: **Frankie Howerd** and **Benny Hill** died within a day of each other. The cinema lost **Marlene Dietrich**, **Robert Morley**, **Satyajit Ray** and the 100-year-old **Hal Roach,** among others.

The great Satyajit Ray.

Di loved McCartney's "Oratorio".

1993

JANUARY

Su	Mo	Tu	We	Th	Fr	Sa
					1	2
3	4	5	6	7	8	9
10	11	12	13	14	15	16
17	18	19	20	21	22	23
24	25	26	27	28	29	30
31						

2. Geneva: Lord Owen and Cyrus Vance present a peace plan based on the division of Bosnia into 10 autonomous provinces (→10/2).

3. London: Princess Margaret is admitted to hospital suffering from pneumonia.

3. Moscow: Presidents Bush and Yeltsin sign the START-2 Treaty calling for cuts in strategic nuclear weapons.

6. Buenos Aires: Foreign Secretary Douglas Hurd becomes the first British cabinet minister to visit Argentina since the 1982 Falklands war.

11. London: British Airways agrees to settle a libel suit filed by Virgin Atlantic Airways for a "dirty tricks" campaign.

12. Dublin: The Dail votes to confirm Albert Reynolds as head of a coalition government.

13. Iraq: US, British and French warplanes carry out air strikes in retaliation for Iraq's violations of UN resolutions.

13. Bosnia: Lance Corporal John Edwards of the Royal Welch Fusiliers becomes the first British soldier to be shot dead in Bosnia.

14. Baltic Sea: A Polish ferry capsizes, killing 48 people.

15. Shetlands: Oil from the wreck of the Braer is dispersed by wind and waves.

16. London: The England XV defeat France 16-15 in the Five Nations championship (→20/3).

20. Washington: Bill Clinton is inaugurated as 42nd President (→22/5).

31. Pasadena: The Dallas Cowboys beat the Buffalo Bills 52-17 to win Super Bowl XXVII.

DEATHS

6. Russian-born ballet dancer Rudolf Hametovich Nureyev (*17/3/1938).→

6. American jazz player John Birks (Dizzy) Gillespie (*10/21/1917).

20. American actress Audrey Hepburn (*4/5/1929).

Shetlands oil disaster

The stricken Braer was carrying more that 84,000 tonnes of light crude.

Jan 5. The Shetland Isles, one of Britain's richest wildlife areas, are facing an ecological disaster tonight. Pollution control crews are rushing to Quendale Bay, west of Sumburgh Head, where the Braer, an 89,000-ton tanker, is spewing its cargo of oil into the sea. The 17-year-old Liberian-registered ship ran aground in a 100mph gale after its engines lost power. The 34 Polish and Filipino crewmen have been taken off the tanker by rescue tugs and RAF helicopters. As the Braer is being pounded by huge waves and hurricane-force winds, experts of the Marine Pollution Control Unit are desperately trying to reach the wreck. So far, all attempts to set up booms to contain the oil have failed. Local conservationists say the oil-spill is threatening thousands of seabirds and otters who live on the remote southern tip of the Shetlands. However, officials are hoping that the strong winds and fierce seas will help break up the slick (→15/1).

EC's Single Market becomes a reality

Jan 1. The European Commission's grand design to create a Europe without frontiers finally came into being today. It consists of a Single Market stretching from the Arctic to the Mediterranean and from the Atlantic to the Oder, encompassing 375 million people generating £4.5 trillion.

Difficulties remain. Britain, Ireland, Denmark and Greece will still make travellers show passports in order to "fight terrorism". It has also been found impossible to write a business statute because of disagreements over the appointment of workers to company boards. Businessmen are complaining that the new documents are so complex that even the officials who will enforce them are confused.

A velvet divorce for Czechs and Slovaks

Jan 1. Czechoslovakia, born just 74 years ago, ceased to exist at midnight last night. As the new year began, the country's 15.6 million inhabitants became citizens of either Slovakia or the Czech Republic, known also by its traditional name of Czechland.

Unlike Yugoslavia, the split has been a remarkably peaceful and amicable one. Thousands of Czechs and Slovaks were out on the streets of Prague and Bratislava, the capitals of Europe's two newest independent nations, to celebrate what has been dubbed the "velvet divorce". The property of the former Czechoslovak federation is to be divided fairly, although the two new states will keep a common currency, the koruna.

Mafia boss caught

Jan 15. Sicily's carabinieri are rejoicing tonight, hours after scoring a spectacular coup in their fight against the Mafia.

Salvatore 'Toto' Riina, the "boss of bosses" of the Sicilian mob who evaded capture for 23 years, is spending his first night in a Palermo jail. The portly 62-year-old Mafioso is wanted in connection with more than 100 murders, including the assassination last year of Giovanni Falcone and Paolo Borsellino, both prominent anti-Mafia judges. Police arrested Riina and an unarmed bodyguard at a rush-hour road-block near Palermo as they sat in a Citroen sedan. Riina, said to be the most cunning and brutal of the Cosa Nostra's members, is to be transferred to a secret destination tomorrow.

Nintendo scare

Jan 14. Reports of several cases of epileptic fits caused by video games such as Nintendo's "Game Boy" have led the Government to call for an urgent inquiry.

In London, a spokesman for the Japanese company said Nintendo was planning to attach warnings against overindulgence to all its video games. This follows reports that teenagers both in Britain and abroad have suffered epileptic seizures after prolonged playing of video games. These were apparently prompted by repeated bursts of flickering lights.

Jan 6. Rudolf Nureyev, the great star of ballet who fled to the West in 1961, died of AIDS in a Paris hospital today at the age of 54.

1993

FEBRUARY

Su	Mo	Tu	We	Th	Fr	Sa
	1	2	3	4	5	6
7	8	9	10	11	12	13
14	15	16	17	18	19	20
21	22	23	24	25	26	27
28						

1. UK: Insurance companies put the value of a wife at £349 a week, up from £204 in 1981.

1. London: The Government outlines plans to privatise British Rail.

10. US: Washington agrees to send troops to Bosnia if needed to implement the Vance-Owen peace plan (→ 22).

10. Madagascar: Opposition leader Albert Zafy is elected President.

10. Hanoi: President Mitterrand says France's Indochina war was a mistake.

10. US: Ford posts record 1992 losses of $7.4 billion.

12. UK: Retail price inflation falls to 1.7 per cent, its lowest level in 25 years (→ 18/3).

14. Cyprus: Glafcos Clerides wins presidential elections.

17. Haiti: Up to 1,700 people are feared dead after a ferry capsizes and sinks.

22. New York: The UN votes to set up a tribunal to try war crimes committed in the former Yugoslavia (→ 1/3).

26. Los Angeles: British rock guitarist Eric Clapton wins six Grammy awards.

26. New York: Five people are killed by a bomb blast at the World Trade Center.

27. London: An IRA bomb attack injures 18 in Camden.

28. Texas: Six people are killed in a gun battle between federal agents and members of the Branch Davidian sect in Waco (→ 19/4).

DEATHS

5. Joseph Leo Mankiewicz, US film director (*11/2/1909).

5. Sidney Lewis Bernstein (Lord Bernstein), British businessman (*30/1/1899).

6. Arthur Robert Ashe, US tennis player (*10/7/1943).

20. Ferruccio Lamborghini, Italian car pioneer (*1917).

24. Bobby Moore, British footballer (*12/4/41).→

27. Lillian Diana Gish, US actress (*14/10/1896).

Two boys charged with toddler's murder

Video pictures record the moment when baby James Bulger is led away.

Feb 22. As a furious crowd screamed abuse, two 10-year-old Liverpool boys were driven away from South Sefton Youth Court under heavy police guard today.

They had just been arraigned on charges of kidnapping and murdering a local toddler. They are among the youngest children ever to be charged with murder in Britain. The killing of two-year-old James Bulger has caused shock and revulsion throughout the country, and there are mounting calls for tougher measures against young offenders. The child was enticed away 10 days ago while his mother was in a nearby butcher's shop in the New Strand shopping centre. His battered body was found four days later near a railway embankment in Walton, approximately three miles from the shopping centre. Pictures taken by security cameras at the centre show the toddler being led away by two youths. Both boys were formally charged on February 20, after being questioned by police for more that two days. Their identities are being kept secret.

Antarctic ordeal for two British trekkers

Polar heroes are happy to be back.

Feb 19. The two men are exhausted, emaciated, frost-bitten but exultant. Sir Ranulph Fiennes and Michael Stroud are back in Britain after a record-breaking hike across the frigid wastes of Antarctica. They have successfully completed the first unsupported crossing of the Antarctic ice shelf, a 1,345-mile trek that took them 95 days. Sir Ranulph, aged 48 and his 37-year-old partner had set out from the Weddell Sea last November. Using cross-country skis and sleds to carry their food and gear, they battled across the ice, sometimes walking up to 13 hours a day. But frostbite, infected feet, equipment failure and weight loss forced them to call off the last stage of their historic feat, undertaken to raise money for charity.

Queen Elizabeth II invites the taxman

Feb 11. The Queen is to join her subjects in paying full rates of income tax and capital gains tax on her private income. She is expected to pay a tax bill of £2 million on the annual income from her personal fortune, which is reliably estimated at some £50 million. She will also take over Civil List payments to junior members of the royal family.

Prime Minister John Major told the Commons today that the arrangement had been initiated by the Queen a year ago. There is little doubt, however, that her advisers were forced to make the move to stem growing public unease at the monarch's tax-exempt wealth at a time when Britain is groaning under the impact of the recession.

The only significant concession she has won is an exemption from inheritance tax on what she hands on to her successor. Mr Major said there could be no question of taxing assets such as royal palaces, Crown jewels and art treasures which the Queen owns as sovereign and not in a private capacity. She will also be able to claim almost all her working expenses, covering items such as staff uniforms and flower arrangements for official functions.

The agreement will also affect the Prince of Wales, whose Duchy of Cornwall income has been exempt. It will now be taxed with allowances for expenses.

Feb 24. Football legend Bobby Moore, who led England to victory in the 1966 World Cup, dies of cancer at the age of 51.

1993

MARCH

Su	Mo	Tu	We	Th	Fr	Sa
	1	2	3	4	5	6
7	8	9	10	11	12	13
14	15	16	17	18	19	20
21	22	23	24	25	26	27
28	29	30	31			

1. Bosnia: US Air Force planes begin to air-drop emergency aid to besieged Moslem enclaves (→16/4).

5. Canada: Sprinter Ben Johnson is banned for life after failing a drug test.

6. Angola: After a four-month battle that killed 10,000, UNITA rebels seize the key city of Huambo (→20/11/94).

7. Kabul: Rival Afghan leaders sign an accord to end months of fighting in the capital (→14/2/95).

8. Hampshire: A 1,400-year-old yew, the oldest tree in Britain, dies.

9. UK: Leading film stars, including Michael Caine, call for an end to film violence.

10. Indonesia: President Suharto, in power since 1965, is reelected for a fifth term.

10. UK: The Test and County Cricket Board lashes out at badly-dressed players with "designer stubble".

11. Pyongyang: North Korea pulls out of the nuclear Non-Proliferation Treaty.

12. US: Janet Reno is confirmed as the nation's first woman Attorney General.

14. US: A blizzard sweeps through East Coast states, leaving 115 dead.

18. UK: Unemployment figures show a drop, the first in nearly three years (→26/4).

20. Paris: France defeats Wales, 26-10, to win the Five Nations rugby championship.

24. Israel: Ezer Weizman is elected President.

24. S. Africa: President de Klerk says South Africa built six atomic bombs, but destroyed them after 1989.

27. London: Cambridge defeat Oxford in the 139th University Boat Race.

DEATHS

3. Albert Sabin, American virologist (*26/8/1906).

10. Cyril Northcote Parkinson, British historian and proponent of Parkinson's Law (*30/7/1909).

Hundreds killed in Bombay bombings

March 12. A devastating wave of car-bomb explosions killed up to 300 people and left hundreds of others injured today. The first blast ripped through Bombay's stock exchange, in the city's southern financial district. Minutes later, a dozen slightly less powerful explosions rocked the city, killing and maiming indiscriminately.

The bombing assault appears to have been a carefully-planned operation, although no one has yet claimed responsibility for the attacks. The devices were clearly meant to create maximum loss of life and damage to property. Today's tragic events have come just two months after bloody clashes between Hindus and Moslems in and around Bombay, which claimed nearly 600 lives.

Abortion foe strikes

March 11. A 47-year-old Florida doctor has been gunned down by an anti-abortion activist. Appearing in court today, Michael Griffin, aged 31, admitted killing Dr David Gunn outside an abortion clinic in Pensacola. Police believe it is the first time that "pro-lifers" have resorted to cold-blooded murder in their increasingly militant battle to prevent American women having abortions. Dr Gunn was married and had two children.

March 29. Emma Thompson wins the Oscar for best actress for her role in "Howard's End".

IRA admits to Warrington bomb carnage

Police and firemen sift through the bomb debris, looking for clues.

March 21. The IRA today claimed responsibility for yesterday's murderous bomb attacks in Warrington. The two lunchtime explosions at a crowded shopping center killed 4-year-old Jonathan Ball. Of the nearly 50 people injured, several are in serious condition, and one 12-year-old boy is critically ill. In a statement issued in Dublin today, the IRA said it regretted the "tragic consequences" of the blasts, but accused the police of failing to react to telephone warnings given before the explosions. The bombs sent shrapnel ripping through crowds doing last-minute Mother's Day shopping. Last night, John Major said: "The wickedness of this act defies belief." (→23/10/93).

Labour hangs on to power in Australia

March 13. Prime Minister Paul Keating, aged 49, has confounded his critics by leading Australia's Labour Party to victory in today's general elections. Despite being held responsible by many voters for the country's worst economic crisis since the 1930s, Keating defeated John Hewson, leader of the more conservative Liberal Party. Keating's success is largely due to his repeated attacks on Liberal Party proposals to introduce a 15 per cent value added tax (→1/4).

Socialists hammered in French elections

March 29. Still reeling from the humiliating defeat of his Socialist Party, President Francois Mitterrand today appointed a Gaullist former Finance Minister, Edouard Balladur, to head the government. Balladur takes over from the Socialist premier Pierre Beregovoy, who is said to be in a state of deep shock following his electoral rout. The conservatives have won a total of 484 seats in the 577-seat National Assembly. The Socialists won just 54 seats, their poorest showing since Mitterrand founded the party 20 years ago. The far-right National Front failed to get a single seat in the new Assembly, although it won 12.5 per cent of the vote (→1/5).

Edouard Balladur is 63 years old.

1993

APRIL

Su	Mo	Tu	We	Th	Fr	Sa
				1	2	3
4	5	6	7	8	9	10
11	12	13	14	15	16	17
18	19	20	21	22	23	24
25	26	27	28	29	30	

1. Canberra: One in seven Australians want their country to become a republic, a poll reveals.

6. Russia: An explosion damages a secret nuclear weapons complex in Siberia.

8. Germany: For the first time since 1945, German soldiers are given the go-ahead by the High Court to take part in combat missions abroad; they will join UN troops in Bosnia.

14. US: A young Illinois salesman wins $1 million after flinging a basketball through the hoop from about 75 feet.

16. Bosnia: The besieged Moslem town of Srebrenica falls to Serbian forces (→ 1/6).

18. London: Eamonn Martin of Britain wins the 13th London Marathon, his first such race.

20. France: Yachtsman Bruno Peyron completes his circumnavigation of the globe in 79 days, one less than the fictional Phileas Fogg.

21. Brazil: Voters reject a restoration of the country's 19th-century monarchy.

25. Russia: President Yeltsin wins a vote of confidence in a national referendum.

26. Rome: Carlo Ciampi is named Prime Minister.

27. Eritrea: Eritreans vote for independence from Ethiopia.

29. London: Buckingham Palace is to be open to tourists for a fee of £8 a head; the money will help pay for fire damage to Windsor Castle.

30. Hamburg: Tennis champion Monica Seles is stabbed during a match.

DEATHS

1. Lord (Solly) Zuckerman, British scientist (*1904).

4. Alfred Butts, American inventor of the board game Scrabble (*1900).

15. Leslie Charteris, American author (*12/5/1907).

17. Turgut Ozal, President of Turkey (*1927).

24. Oliver Tambo, South African politician (*1917).

Blaze ends Waco siege

Long-range cameras record the dramatic end of the long stand-off.

April 19. After a 51-day siege, FBI agents backed by armoured vehicles launched their assault just after dawn today. The modified tanks first punched holes through the walls of the fortified compound where David Koresh, leader of the apocalyptic Branch Davidian cult, and some 95 followers waited. As the world's media looked on, the tanks pumped CS gas into the buildings in the hope that the cult members would surrender. About noon, at least two people were seen lighting fires in various parts of the compound, near Waco, Texas. The blaze spread rapidly, engulfing the buildings as police and reporters watched helplessly. Only eight cult members, including two Britons, escaped from the self-inflicted inferno. Among the dead are at least 17 children. Koresh, aged 33, is believed to have shot himself.

SACP leader Chris Hani is gunned down

April 10. Chris Hani, a hero to thousands of black militants, was assassinated outside his Johannesburg home this morning. The 50-year-old head of the South African Communist Party was hit by several bullets as he was getting into his car. Police say they have arrested a suspect, Januzu Wallus, a Polish-born white rightist allegedly linked to racist organisations. Wallus emigrated to South Africa in 1981.

April 24. A huge IRA bomb rips through the City, killing a man and injuring 44. Damage is estimated at around £1 billion.

Recession is over, Lamont claims

April 26. Jubilant Cabinet ministers announced today the Britain's nearly three-year recession, the worst since the 1930s, is officially over. Chancellor Norman Lamont based his upbeat comments on figures just released which show that output grew by 0.6 per cent in the first quarter, after more than 30 months of stagnation. Economists, who are warning against complacency, say this spurt is due to increased exports after Britain's pull-out from the European exchange-rate mechanism last September (→ 27/5).

Steeplechase fiasco

April 3. The 1993 Grand National, the world's greatest steeplechase, ended in chaos today. Aintree officials have declared the race void, leaving in tears at least one jockey, John White, whose mount, Esha Ness, came in first. The trouble began when demonstrators ran onto the course seconds before the off. When calm was restored, a first attempt to raise the tapes ended in a false start. After a delay, there was a second attempt, but this turned into farce as the front runners carried on, believing that the shouts of officials trying to stop the race were those of protesters. The £75 million invested by the public in the race will have to be refunded.

EBRD chief Attali is called to account

An office fit for a prince?

April 18. It has been a bad week for Jacques Attali, a whiz-kid protege of President Mitterrand of France. The head of the City-based European Bank for Reconstruction and Development is increasingly under fire for lavish spending on the bank's new headquarters and an extravagant life-style. According to press reports, tons of Carrara marble and flashy sculptures have been brought in to outfit the offices of bank officials, while loans to Eastern Europe and the former USSR have been slow in coming. The cost of equipping the two-year-old bank's plush headquarters is said to have been about £200 million, about double the amount disbursed by the EBRD (→ 25/6).

1993

MAY

Su	Mo	Tu	We	Th	Fr	Sa
						1
2	3	4	5	6	7	8
9	10	11	12	13	14	15
16	17	18	19	20	21	22
23	24	25	26	27	28	29
30	31					

1. Sri Lanka: President Ranasinghe Premadasa is killed by a bomb in Colombo.

2. UK: Manchester United win the Football League trophy for the first time in 26 years.

4. UK: Businessman Asil Nadir jumps a £3.5 million bail and flees to Northern Cyprus (→ 24/6).

8. Sicily: Pope John Paul II condemns Mafia violence.

9. Paraguay: Juan Carlos Wasmosy wins the country's first multi-party elections for a civilian president.

10. Bangkok: A fire in a toy factory kills 220 people.

12. UK: The Home Office scraps the system of income-related fines just seven months after its introduction.

16. Turkey: Prime Minister Suleyman Demiral is named President (→ 13/6).

18. Denmark: In a second referendum, voters approve the Maastricht treaty.

21. Venezuala: President Andres Perez is removed from office for corruption.

24. Tibet: Violence breaks out during demonstrations against Chinese rule.

27. London: The Queen receives President Mary Robinson; it is the first meeting between the British and Irish heads of state since 1937.

27. Florence: A bomb blast outside the Uffizi Gallery kills five people and damages art treasures.

29. Germany: Five Turkish women are killed in a neo-Nazi arson attack.

DEATHS

1. Pierre Beregovoy, French politician (*23/12/1925).→

6. Ian Mikardo, British politician (*9/7/1908).

14. William Randolph Hearst, US press magnate (*27/1/1908).

27. Lord (Joseph) Gormley, British trade unionist (*5/7/1917).

Ex-French premier commits suicide

May 1. Pierre Beregovoy, France's former Socialist Prime Minister, shot himself with his bodyguard's gun today. The 67-year-old politician's body was found on the banks of the River Loire. Close friends say that Beregovoy, one of the rare working-class men to reach high office in France, had been traumatised by the Socialists' humiliating defeat in the March general elections. He was also extremely upset over allegations of financial impropriety. These stemmed from a £90,000 interest-free loan from a businessman friend who has been indicted for insider trading.

Hostage children rescued by police

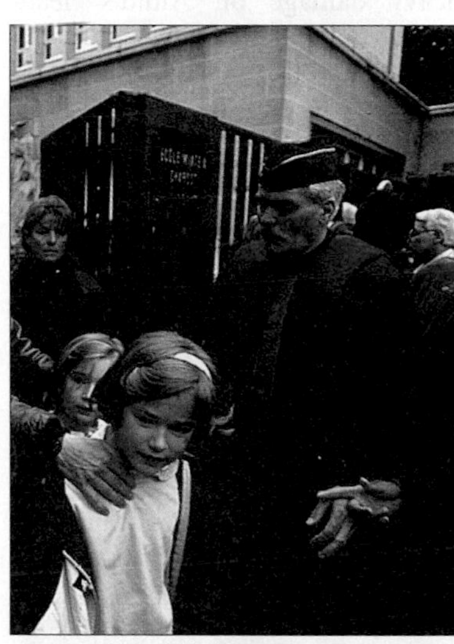

The terrified toddlers are freed.

May 15. Masked Paris police commandos burst into a booby-trapped classroom today, ending a two-day hostage drama with a hail of gunfire. They shot dead the "Human Bomb", as Eric Schmitt, an unemployed, divorced loner called himself. For 46 hours, police had waited for the hostage-taker, who had demanded a £12-million ransom, to fall asleep. His six remaining captives, girls aged three and four, were freed and rushed outside to their hysterical parents. Laurence Dreyfus, the young teacher who kept up the children's spirits during their long ordeal, has been made an immediate award of the Legion of Honour for her bravery.

Bill Clinton's $200 haircut makes waves

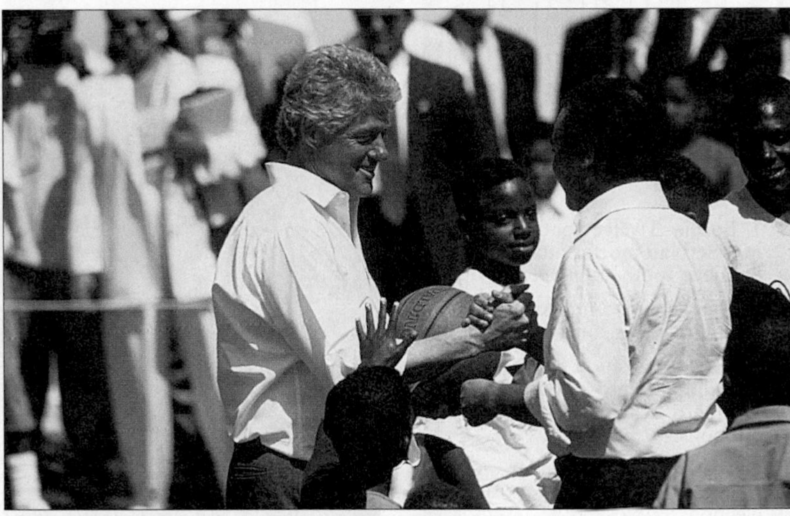

A desperate Bill Clinton tries to restore his battered 'street cred'.

May 22. "Hairgate", as the US press is calling the latest presidential blunder, may well prove to be the unkindest cut of all for Bill Clinton.

The case of the costly coiffure is rapidly turning into a White House nightmare. During a visit to Los Angeles four days ago, Clinton, who likes to be seen as a man of the people, summoned Cristophe, a top Beverly Hills hairdresser, for a $200 (£130) trim aboard Air Force One. Runways at the airport were closed to commercial traffic for 40 minutes while the presidential locks were shorn. This comes after a series of errors that have left Clinton looking like a stumbling amateur. Polls show that his approval rating has plunged to 36 per cent, a record low for a postwar US President. The Clinton presidency has been in trouble from day one. First there was the storm over homosexuals in the military. Then the White House was forced to withdraw several of its nominations to senior Admnistration positions, followed by the failure of Clinton's economic stimulus package. The President's plan to name a militant lesbian to a top post has caused outrage in Congress. Meanwhile, Clinton has failed to develop a coherent policy on Bosnia.

Chancellor Lamont dismissed by Major

May 27. In a sweeping reshuffle of his cabinet, John Major has today abruptly dismissed his Chancellor of the Exchequer.

The Home Secretary, Kenneth Clarke, aged 53, is to take over from Norman Lamont. The Prime Minister's move is seen as an attempt to restore public confidence in his government. Mr Lamont's dismissal came after humiliating Tory defeats in local elections and the Newbury by-election earlier this month. The Tory majority in Parliament has now dropped to just 20, and Mr Major's popularity is at an all-time low. The Government now awaits a statement from Mr Lamont with trepidation, fearing a scathing attack on Mr Major.

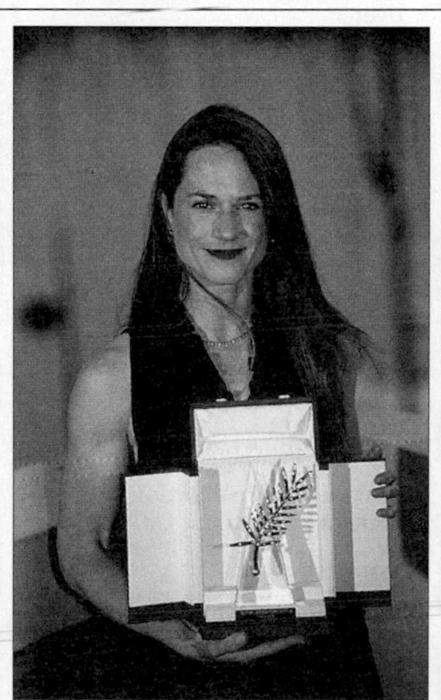

May 24. Holly Hunter, star of Jane Campion's "The Piano", which won the Golden Palm at the 1993 Cannes Film Festival.

1993

JUNE

Su	Mo	Tu	We	Th	Fr	Sa
		1	2	3	4	5
6	7	8	9	10	11	12
13	14	15	16	17	18	19
20	21	22	23	24	25	26
27	28	29	30			

1. Bosnia: Twelve youths die in a Serbian mortar attack on a Sarajevo football pitch (→17).

1. Guatemala: A military coup ousts President Jorge Elias.

6. Italy: Opposition groups, including the pro-autonomy Northern League, win local elections.

6. Spain: Socialist premier Felipe Gonzalez wins general elections.

7. US: Filmmaker Woody Allen loses a bitter child custody battle with Mia Farrow.

13. Iran: President Rafsanjani is re-elected for four years.

13. Cambodia: Prince Sihanouk is proclaimed head of state following UN-supervised elections in May.

17. Moscow: Russia and the Ukraine agree to divide evenly the disputed Black Sea Fleet.

18. France: The National Assembly approves a tough immigration law.

18. Tokyo: Premier Kiichi Miyazawa loses a vote of confidence in parliament.

18. Azerbaijan: President Elchibey flees Baku as rebel leader Geidar Aliyev takes over.

24. London: Britain announces sanctions against Nigeria after the cancellation of the July 12 presidential elections.

24. Europe: Kurdish separatists launch a series of violent anti-Turkish attacks.

25. London: EBRD president Jacques Attali resigns.

26. Baghdad: US forces launch a missile attack on Iraq's intelligence HQ, killing six people (→14/4/94).

30. London: Police announce an anti-terrorist cordon will be thrown around the City.

DEATHS

15. James Hunt, former British world motor racing champion (*29/8/1947).

19. Sir William Golding, British author (*19/9/1911).→

22. Patricia Nixon, former US First Lady (*16/3/1912).

UN forces get tough with Somali warlord

US AC-130 Spectre gunships fire down on General Aidid's headquarters.

June 17. UN ground troops, backed by US gunships and attack helicopters, launched a massive raid on the Mogadishu headquarters of Somalia's chief warlord, General Mohammed Farrah Aidid. The dawn operation, which left scores of Somali fighters and civilians dead, was a retaliatory strike at Aidid's forces following the killing of 23 Pakistani peacekeepers 12 days ago. Today's raid inflicted heavy damage on Aidid's headquarters, but failed to capture the warlord. UN forces are being criticised for the indiscriminate use of force in a densely populated sector of the Somali capital (→4/10).

Minister resigns as scandal rocks Tories

June 24. John Major stunned the House today by announcing the resignation of his junior minister for Northern Ireland. Michael Mates' downfall followed allegations over his links with the fugitive tycoon Asil Nadir. Nadir's flight to Cyprus last month has embroiled the Conservative Party in a scandal over the secret funding of the party. Revelations that Mr Mates had intervened on behalf of Nadir, who is wanted for 13 counts of fraud, are embarrassing the Tory hierarchy.

June 9. A Shinto wedding for Japan's future emperor, Crown Prince Naruhito, 33, and his Oxford-educated bride, 29-year-old Masako.

Women take helm in Canada, Turkey

June 13. Kim Campbell, aged 46, and 47-year-old Tansu Ciller today joined the exclusive club of women premiers. They became the first women ever to be appointed to head the Canadian and Turkish governments. Mrs Campbell, an outspoken Vancouver lawyer, was chosen by the Progressive Conservatives to replace Brian Mulroney as leader. In Ankara, Mrs Ciller, a former economics professor, was elected leader of the centre-right True Path Party, in succession to former premier Suleyman Demirel.

Bosnia plan 'dead'

June 17. Lord Owen was forced to admit today that months of UN and EC diplomacy aimed at bringing peace to Bosnia have failed utterly. Speaking in Geneva, Lord Owen conceded that his peace plan, based on the division of Bosnia into 10 semiautonomous provinces under a unified Bosnian state, had been "ripped up under our very eyes". He could only urge President Izetbegovic of Bosnia to accept the plan proposed by his victorious enemies, the Serb and Croat leaders, Presidents Milosevic and Tudjman. This calls for the partitioning of Bosnia into three ethnically homogenous states, with Bosnia's Moslems getting only 10 per cent of the total territory (→3/8).

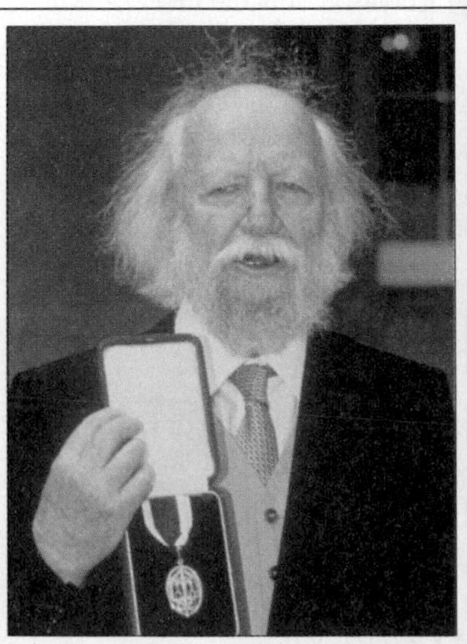

June 19. Sir William Golding, the celebrated author of "Lord of the Flies", dies near Truro, Cornwall, at the age of 81.

1993

JULY

Su	Mo	Tu	We	Th	Fr	Sa
				1	2	3
4	5	6	7	8	9	10
11	12	13	14	15	16	17
18	19	20	21	22	23	24
25	26	27	28	29	30	31

4. Wimbledon: Pete Sampras beats Jim Courier 7-6, 7-6, 3-6, 6-3 to win the men's singles championship; Steffi Graff won the women's singles title.

9. Tokyo: The G7 summit of industrialised nations agrees to the "biggest tariff reduction in history".

13. London: Andrew Lloyd Webber's musical version of "Sunset Boulevard" is a hit.

13. Moscow: Rolls-Royce opens its first showroom in Russia.

13. Brussels: The European Commission threatens to take Britain to court for flouting rules on drinking water quality.

18. Durham: Ian Botham, one of cricket's greatest all-rounders, announces his retirement.

20. Washington: Vincent Foster, a close Clinton friend and aide, commits suicide.

20. Washington: Mafia-busting federal judge Louis Freeh is appointed director of the FBI.

20. Milan: Raul Gardini, former head of the Ferruzzi Group, shoots himself; he is the second suicide victim of Italy's ongoing corruption scandals.

25. Cape Town: Black gunmen burst into an Anglican church and kill nine whites.

26. Headingly, Yorkshire: Graham Gooch resigns as England's cricket captain after Australia wins the Fourth Test.

26. Havana: Cuba celebrates the 40th anniversary of its revolution amid hints that President Fidel Castro is loosening the economic reins.

29. UK: The Tories lose the Christchurch by-election, a true-blue stronghold for 83 years, to the Liberal Democrats.

30. Nepal: Up to 1,700 people are feared dead after torrential rains.

DEATHS

25. Margaret, Duchess of Argyll, British socialite (*1/12/12).

26. General Matthew Ridgeway, US Army commander (*3/3/1895).

UK to comply with halt on bomb tests

July 3. Britain's plans to maintain the safety of its nuclear weapons were set back tonight when President Bill Clinton extended the ban on nuclear testing in the Nevada desert for another year.

Britain had hoped to keep a two-year window open for three explosions to test the safety devices on existing weapons but must now comply with the ban and rely on computer simulations to check the trigger mechanisms of its ageing Polaris warheads. The President said he hoped the ban would discourage other nations from developing nuclear weapons.

Secretive MI5 lifts the veil on its operations

Counterspy boss Stella Rimington.

July 16. Stella Rimington, the first woman head of MI5, broke new ground again today by meeting the press and revealing details of her organisation's work.

She refused to submit to cross-examination by the eager journalists but distributed a booklet, The Security Service, which gives MI5's address, its structure, a partial history, displays its coat of arms and discusses its role in the post-Soviet world. Rimington revealed herself as a cheerful and relaxed spy-master with a liking for chunky jewellery. She said the aim of her disclosures was to dispel "some of the more fanciful allegations" about her once-secret service.

UN warns of a vast migration problem

July 6. The United Nations Population Fund's annual report warns that migration "could become the human crisis of our era".

More people than ever before are leaving their homes and looking for better lives abroad. At least 100 million, about 2 per cent of the world's population, have emigrated. Most are economic migrants, but 17 million of them are estimated to be refugees. The classic circular pattern of migration, where people live and work for a while abroad, then return home, is gradually breaking down. Most now prefer to stay in their adopted countries.

Israeli raids prompt exodus in Lebanon

July 27. The main road to Beirut is jammed as some 150,000 people flee the heaviest bombardment of southern Lebanon since 1985. Israeli guns and aircraft are pounding villages in retaliation for rocket attacks on Israeli towns by pro-Iranian Hezbollah guerrillas. Major-General Herzl Bodinger, Israel's air force commander, said he was forcing the civilians to flee to put pressure on "Lebanese power brokers" to restrain Hezbollah. Prime Minister Yitzhak Rabin agrees: "If there is no quiet over here, there will be such disquiet in Lebanon they will not be able to live there."

Mystery bombings in Rome and Milan

July 27. Two powerful car bombs exploded in Rome and another in Milan today. Five people died and the Basilica of St John Lateran, built where Romulus and Remus were found, was severely damaged. Pope John Paul II visited the basilica and condemned the "vile attacks aimed at the heart of Rome". So far, no one has admitted responsibility for the bombings, the latest in a wave of terror aimed at cultural treasures. Some blame the Mafia, others the anti-corruption campaign. President Carlo Ciampi says they are "attempts to create disorder and panic to slow progress".

Jerusalem tribunal frees John Demjanjuk

New Soviet evidence set him free.

July 29. John Demjanjuk had his conviction for Nazi war crimes quashed and his sentence of death by hanging nullified today by the Israeli Supreme Court. The court said it had "gnawing doubts" that the Ukrainian-born former concentration camp guard was really the sadistic "Ivan the Terrible" who ran the gas chamber at Treblinka in which 870,000 Jews died.

Demjanjuk, who was extradited from the US in 1986 and convicted in Israel two years later, will now be freed. Holocaust survivors are furious. "Gentlemen, now all the Nazis can celebrate," said former Treblinka inmate Yosef Charni.

July 31. King Baudouin of the Belgians (*7/9/1930) dies.

1993

AUGUST

Su	Mo	Tu	We	Th	Fr	Sa
1	2	3	4	5	6	7
8	9	10	11	12	13	14
15	16	17	18	19	20	21
22	23	24	25	26	27	28
29	30	31				

1. London: England's women cricketers beat New Zealand to win the Women's World Cup.

3. Brussels: NATO prepares for possible air strikes against the Bosnian Serbs besieging Sarajevo (→9).

6. Tokyo: Morihiro Hosokawa, heir to a clan of feudal lords and leader of the Japan New Party, is elected Prime Minister.

8. London, New Hampshire: Nigel Mansell wins the New England 200 IndyCar race.

11. Ottawa: Canada lifts its 15-year-old embargo on humanitarian aid to Cuba.

11. London: The Department of Health says the number of people awaiting hospital treatment has risen to more than a million for the first time.

11. Cowes: The Admiral's Cup, the top prize in ocean racing, has been won by the unfancied German team.

15. Budapest: Damon Hill claims his first Formula One victory in the Hungarian Grand Prix.

18. Taiwan: The ruling Kuomintang re-elects President Lee Teng-hui as party leader.

19. Beirut: Eight Israeli soldiers are killed by bombs while out on patrol in southern Lebanon.

19. Stuttgart: Sally Gunnell wins the 400-metre hurdles in the record time of 52.74 seconds at the World Athletic Championships.

21. Algiers: Colonel Kasdi Merbah, former Algerian Prime Minister and security chief, is assassinated by extremists of the Islamic Salvation Front (→26/12/94).

23. London: England's cricketers win their first match since July 1992, beating Australia by 161 runs to win the Sixth Test.

30. New York: Briton Mark Nyman wins the World Scrabble Championship with the word "wet", worth 20 points.

DEATH

16 Stewart Granger, British-born film actor (*6/5/1913).

Flooding in the Midwest leaves a trail of death and destruction

Aug 1. The US has seen the worst flooding in its recorded history. Since early spring the Midwest has had an abnormal amount of rain and in late June the upper Mississippi River became unnavigable.

The mighty Mississippi and its tributaries burst their banks, sweeping away the levees and sandbag walls built to protect Midwest farms and towns. The devastation has been colossal. At least 50 people have died, the homes of 38,000 families have been damaged or destroyed, 20 million acres of farmland are under water, and the cost is estimated at $12 billion.

Some people regard the floods as "God's judgement on the people of America for their sinful ways".

It will take weeks of hard work for some communities to get back to normal.

Maastricht treaty is ratified by UK amid big monetary storm

Aug 2. The United Kingdom ratified the Maastricht treaty today, 20 months after it was negotiated. The final obstacle was removed when Lord Rees-Mogg, a bitter opponent of the treaty, abandoned his court case questioning its legality. The ratification, inscribed on vellum and signed by the Queen, had already been flown to Rome – where it all began – and as soon as the Rees-Mogg case ended, it was deposited with the Italian Foreign Ministry.

The irony is that after its politically divisive passage through parliament, many Euro-sceptics now see the treaty, in the words of the sacked Chancellor, Norman Lamont, "as a bit of a fossil".

While this was taking place, Jacques Delors, President of the European Commission, rose from his sickbed and summoned his commissioners for crisis talks on Europe's monetary chaos. Attacks by speculators on weak currencies have led to Britain suspending sterling's membership of the Exchange Rate Mechanism and to member governments negating the ERM by allowing currencies to move by 15 per cent on either side of their central rate. This move has curbed the speculators but called into question Delors's timetable for a single currency.

Injured Bosnian baby girl flown to London

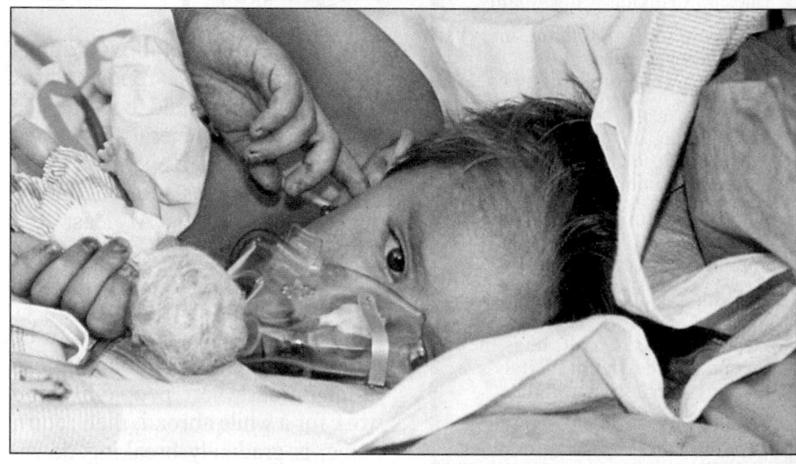

The 5-year-old Moslem victim of a Serb mortar attack which killed her mother.

Aug 9. Irma Hadzimuratovic, the desperately ill Bosnian child whose pitiful appearance on Britain's televison screens touched the heart of the nation, was flown out of the besieged capital, Sarajevo, yesterday and rushed to the Great Ormond Street children's hospital.

Irma, 5, suffered severe injuries in a mortar attack which killed her mother. She then developed meningitis and faced certain death in Sarajevo's shattered hospital, where her plight was filmed. Public outrage led Prime Minister John Major to intervene, and she was flown out by the RAF in horrendous weather. She remains very ill but her doctor says: "She is very brave and will not give in." All she can say is "pain everywhere". She is the frail symbol of Sarajevo's suffering (→9/11).

Aug 11. Scotsman Graeme Obree chalks up a record time of 4 mins 20.8 secs over 4,000 metres.

1993

SEPTEMBER

Su	Mo	Tu	We	Th	Fr	Sa
			1	2	3	4
5	6	7	8	9	10	11
12	13	14	15	16	17	18
19	20	21	22	23	24	25
26	27	28	29	30		

1. Tangier: Ffyona Campbell completes 10,000-mile walk across Africa from Cape Town.

5. Italy: Algerian Nourredine Morceli runs a world-record mile in 3 minutes, 44.39 seconds.

6. London: The Times drops its price from 45 pence to 30 pence.

6. London: The Archbishop of Canterbury condemns the public flogging of an Anglican bishop in Sudan; the bishop denied adultery but was found guilty by an Islamic court.

6. Zurich: UEFA bars the European champions, Olympique Marseille, from defending the title after Marseille players are accused of bribing opponents.

9. Jerusalem: Israel and the PLO agree to recognize each other (→13).

10. Paris: The Folies Bergères, forced to shut down last year, reopens.

14. Florida: Briton Gary Colley, touring Florida with his girlfriend, is killed by muggers; he is the ninth tourist to be murdered in the state in less than a year

16. Pittsburgh: British girl Laura Davis, 5, has seven major organs replaced in a 15-hour operation.

23. Monaco: The International Olympic Committee awards the 2000 Olympic Games to Sydney.

24. Manila: Former First Lady Imelda Marcos is sentenced to 18 years for corruption.

26. Sutton Coldfield: America's golfers retain the Ryder Cup, defeating Europe 15-13.

30. London: The Queen approves honorary knighthood for General Colin Powell, who retired yesterday as Chief of Staff of the US armed forces.

DEATHS

25. Bruno Pontecorvo, British nuclear scientist who defected to USSR (*22/8/1913).

27. Lieutenant General James Doolittle, American World War II hero (*14/12/1896).

Middle East: Shalom, salaam, peace

As President Clinton looks on, Israeli Prime Minister Yitzhak Rabin and PLO leader Yassir Arafat shake hands.

Sept 13 History was made today at 11.47am on the South Lawn of the White House when two bitter enemies shook hands. It was Yassir Arafat, Chairman of the PLO, who extended his hand to Israeli Prime Minister Yitzhak Rabin, who briefly hesitated, then took it. Two minutes earlier, on the desk used for the signing of the 1979 Israel-Egypt peace treaty, Shimon Peres, Israel's Foreign Minister and the PLO's Mahmoud Abbas signed an agreement providing for limited Palestinian autonomy in the Gaza Strip and the West Bank. President Clinton, whose foreign policy on Somalia, Bosnia and Haiti has been criticised as unfocused, is reaping the political benefits of today's accord. In his speech he hailed "the efforts of all who have laboured before us", thanking Norway's government, which brokered the secret talks between Israel and the PLO. The agreement gives the Palestinians a measure of self-rule immediately in Gaza, Jericho and some parts of the West Bank. Israeli withdrawal from Gaza and Jericho is scheduled to begin by December 13. The territories will be run by a Palestinian Council which should be elected by July 13 next year. The ultimate objective is a permanent peace accord to become effective by December 13, 1998. But much remains to be done to reach that goal – a country shared by Jews and Arabs in peace. It will not be easy, too much blood has been spilt. Already angry voices, both Israeli and Arab, have been raised against the agreement. Fanatics on both sides threaten renewed violence (→25/2/94).

Sihanouk returns to Cambodian throne

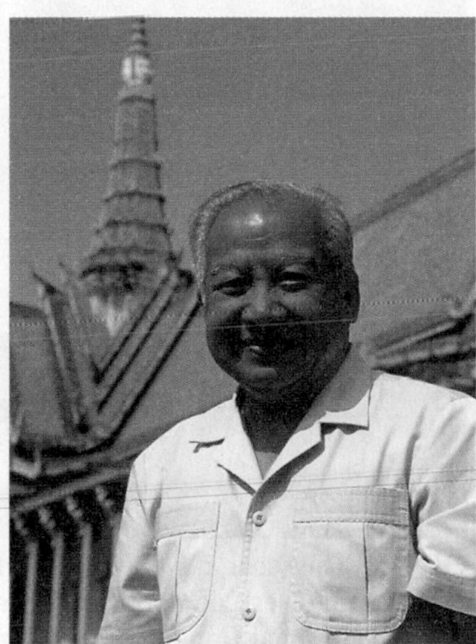

The prince abdicated 38 years ago.

Sept 24. Prince Norodom Sihanouk has returned to reign in Cambodia. The announcement of his restoration, made by his son, Prince Ranariddh, co-chairman of the interim coalition government, caused uproar in the constituent assembly. Some members claimed they had not been properly consulted, but the new constitutional monarchy was finally approved. The development was also an unpleasant surprise to the U.N. mission which, in May, supervised the country's first free elections in decades despite the boycott and violent opposition of the Khmer Rouge guerrillas, who continue their rebellion against the new government.

Sept 12. US actor Raymond Burr (*21/5/1917), better known as Perry Mason, dies of cancer.

1993

OCTOBER

Su	Mo	Tu	We	Th	Fr	Sa
					1	2
3	4	5	6	7	8	9
10	11	12	13	14	15	16
17	18	19	20	21	22	23
24	25	26	27	28	29	30
31						

3. Mogadishu: At least 12 US soldiers are killed and 78 wounded in a failed attempt to capture leaders of Somali warlord Mohammed Aidid's militia.

4. Strasbourg: Rumania becomes a member of the Council of Europe.

4. Cairo: President Mubarak is re-elected for a third six-year term.

4. Brussels: US General George Joulwan is appointed commander of NATO forces in Europe.

7. Stockholm: Toni Morrison becomes the first black American to win the Nobel Prize for Literature (→ 11)..

8. London: Viscount Lindley, son of Princess Margaret and the Earl of Snowdon, marries Serena Stanhope, granddaughter of the Earl of Stanhope.

8. New York: The UN lifts economic santions on South Africa (→ 22/12).

10. Athens: Veteran Socialist leader Andreas Papandreou, 74, is elected Premier.

11. Stockholm: Briton Richard Roberts and American Phillip Sharp share the Nobel Prize for Medicine (→ 15).

18. Poland: Waldemar Pawlak is appointed Premier by President Walesa.

20. The Hague: The Dutch government says it will ban the sale of cannabis to foreign tourists.

23. Belfast: An IRA bomb planted in a fish and chip shop in the Protestant Shankill Road kills nine people, including two girls aged 9 and 13 and one of the bombers (→ 30).

30. Londonderry: Ulster Freedom Fighters spray a pub in Greysteel with bullets, killing seven (→ 29/11).

DEATHS

7. Cyril Cusak, Irish actor (*26/11/1910).

24. Lord "Jo" Grimond, Liberal statesman (*29/7/13).

25. Vincent Price, American film actor (*27/5/11).

Yeltsin crushes hardliners' rebellion

Oct 4. The hardline rebellion against Boris Yeltsin was crushed today when the army swung its might behind the President, and in a day-long battle reduced the White House, the besieged parliament building, to a smouldering wreck, its walls holed by tank shells and blackened by smoke pouring from shattered windows. Dozens of people are feared dead in the hand-to-hand fighting that raged inside the building as Spetsnaz commandos took it over floor by floor. The end came when hundreds of delegates who had barricaded themselves inside the White House emerged under the guns of the soldiers. Some waved white flags, and others clasped their hands behind their heads as they walked dejectedly towards buses which carried them off to prison. Among the last to surrender were the leaders of the rebellion, Aleksander Rutskoi, the Vice President, and Ruslan Khasbulatov, the Speaker, who were driven off to the infamous Lefortovo prison.

Even after their capitulation, the sound of gunfire still echoes round Moscow as defiant snipers shoot from tall buildings and the tanks answer with their heavy machine guns. Muscovites are shocked by this battle in the capital. President Yeltsin has won this round, but he now finds himself perilously indebted to the army (→ 12/12).

Defenders of the parliament surrender after the assault by paratroopers.

Benazir Bhutto back in power in Pakistan

Oct 20. Benazir Bhutto, ousted from power three years ago, was sworn in today as Prime Minister of Pakistan for the second time. She won a convincing vote of confidence in the national assembly over her rival, Nawaz Sharif, to end the uncertainty which followed the inconclusive result of the general election on October 6. She outmanoeuvred Sharif by what he described as "horse-trading", gathering votes from the small parties and independents until she had accumulated 121 against Sharif's 72. Her Pakistan People's Party also seems set to win key elections in Punjab and Sind. Victory in these provinces will consolidate her power.

Oct 15. This year's Nobel Peace Prize is awarded jointly to President Frederik de Klerk of South Africa and Nelson Mandela, President of the African National Congress, for their work to end apartheid peacefully.

1993

NOVEMBER

Su	Mo	Tu	We	Th	Fr	Sa
	1	2	3	4	5	6
7	8	9	10	11	12	13
14	15	16	17	18	19	20
21	22	23	24	25	26	27
28	29	30				

2. Australia: Ireland's Vintage Crop, ridden by Michael Kinane, becomes the first European-trained horse to win the Melbourne Cup.

2. China: The US and China resume high-level military contacts, frozen since 1989.

2. Israel: Teddy Kollek is rejected by the voters after 28 years as Mayor of Jerusalem.

5. Strasbourg: Germany, France and Belgium inaugurate the Eurocorps, a joint military unit they hope will become the core of a future European army.

7. Adelaide: Brazil's Ayrton Senna wins the final race in the Formula One season; Alain Prost of France finishes second in the last race of his career.

8. Stockholm: Eight works by Picasso and Braque, worth £40 million, are stolen from a museum.

8. Los Angeles: British actress Joanne Whalley-Kilmer is chosen to play role of Scarlett O'Hara in a sequel to "Gone With the Wind".

9. Geneva: The UN says the number of refugees worldwide has risen from 2.5 million in 1973 to 19.7 million today.

11. New York: The UN imposes new sanctions on Libya for its refusal to hand over two suspects in the downing of Pan Am Flight 103 over Lockerbie.

17. France: The government says it will curb "sex tours" to Asia by Frenchmen.

22. New York: Britain wins six International Emmy Awards.

23. London: Graham Taylor, England's football manager, resigns.

29. London: Revelations that the government has been conducting secret negotiations with the IRA cause uproar in the House of Commons (→15/12).

DEATHS

12. Jill Tweedie, British columnist (*22/5/34).

22. Anthony Burgess, British author (*25/2/1917).

Croat artillery shells destroy Mostar's beautiful Ottoman bridge

Nov 9. The elegant 16th-century bridge built by Sultan Suleiman to link the east and west banks of the Bosnian town of Mostar was sent crashing into the Neretva River by a barrage of shells from Croatian guns today. Muslims who had tried to protect its slender single span with a pathetic barricade of tyres could only weep as the bridge, which has featured on a million postcards, was destroyed. Jerrie Hulme, a UN official in Bosnia, said the Croats pounded the bridge until there was nothing left. "It was certainly targeted, there's no doubt about it," said Hulme. "It wasn't a symbol of the Muslims or the Croats. It was a symbol of the whole city" (→19/12).

The 16th-century Stari Most, or Old Bridge, built across the Neretva River.

Penis case husband is acquitted in US

Nov 10. John Wayne Bobbitt, whose wife, Lorena, cut off part of his penis, was found not guilty of marital sexual assault in Manassas, Virginia, today by a jury of nine women and three men. His wife claimed he had raped her and that after he had fallen asleep she got a knife and sliced off his penis. "I sat up in this silent scream," he testified. The jury found there was not enough evidence to convict him of sexual assault. She will be tried for malicious wounding later (→21/1/94).

English World Cup hopes are dashed

Nov 17. England crashed out of the World Cup in utter ignominy tonight in Bologna when the longed-for miracle – a Dutch defeat in Poland – failed to materialise. The frantic English players did put seven goals past the amateurs of tiny San Marino, but that was only after the humiliation of allowing the weakest team in European international football to score barely 10 seconds into the match. This will probably mean the end of Graham Taylor as England's manager (→23).

Nov 4. Federico Fellini (*20/1/1920), tempestuous genius of the Italian cinema, who directed such self-indulgent masterpieces as "La Dolce Vita", "8 1/2" and "La Strada", lies in state in Rome's Studio 5 of Cinecitta studios, where Il Maestro made many of his films. He was buried today.

Boys found guilty of a toddler's murder

Nov 24. At the end of a harrowing trial, two 14-year-old boys, the youngest murderers in modern British legal history, have been ordered to be detained for "very, very many years" for killing two-year-old James Bulger. The boys lured James away from his mother while she was shopping. They then dragged him through Liverpool before beating and stoning him to death on a railway line. A number of people saw the weeping, bruised toddler but took no effective action.

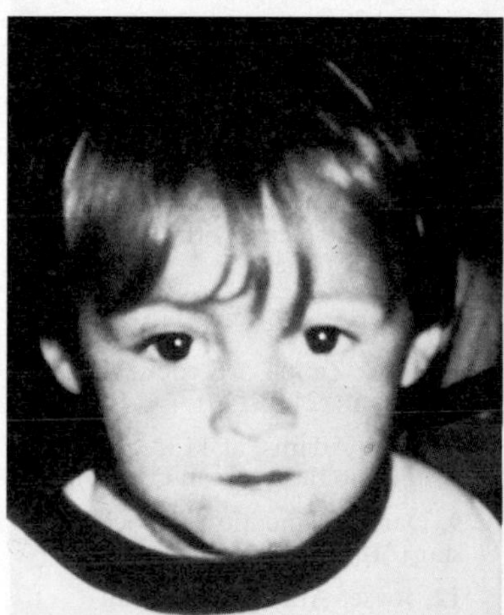

James Bulger was battered to death.

Throughout the trial the boys were known as Child A and Child B, but Judge Michael Morland gave permission today for their names, Jon Venables and Robert Thompson, to be revealed.

1993

DECEMBER

Su	Mo	Tu	We	Th	Fr	Sa
			1	2	3	4
5	6	7	8	9	10	11
12	13	14	15	16	17	18
19	20	21	22	23	24	25
26	27	28	29	30	31	

1. Paris: The obelisk in the Place de la Concorde is covered by a 22-metre condom to mark World AIDS Day.

2. Medellin: Colombian drug baron Pablo Escobar is trapped by the police and dies in hail of gunfire.

3. London: Princess Diana announces she is to withdraw from public life.

10. Houston: Spacewalking astronauts from the shuttle Endeavour repair the Hubble Space Telescope.

12. London: Olympic 100-metre champion Linford Christie is voted BBC Sports Personality of 1993.

15. Geneva: The Uruguay Round of GATT is signed after seven years of negotiations.

19. Belgrade: Serbia's President Slobodan Milosevic wins general elections (→ 5/1/94).

22. Johannesburg: The South African parliament votes itself out of existence in a move certain to lead to black majority rule (→ 28/3).

26. Berlin: Marlene Dietrich's grave is desecrated by neo-Nazis.

31. London: French Premier Edouard Balladur is named Man of the Year by the Financial Times.

DEATHS

4. Frank Zappa, US rock musician (*21/12/40).

8. Daisy Adams, at 113, Britain's oldest person (*1880).

9. Danny Blanchflower, soccer star (*10/2/26).

12. Jozsef Antall, Hungarian Prime Minister (*8/4/1932).

HITS OF 1993

Can't Help Falling in Love

If Ever I Lose My Faith in You

All That She Wants

That's the Way Love Goes

QUOTE OF THE YEAR

Shalom, salaam, peace

President Clinton, to Yassir Arafat and Yitzhak Rabin at the White House.

Northern Ireland peace pact is signed

Dec 15. John Major and Albert Reynolds, prime ministers of Britain and Ireland, today signed an historic declaration designed to bring peace to Northern Ireland. Standing in front of a Christmas tree in Downing Street, they urged the terrorists on both sides of the conflict to grasp the opportunity for peace, saying that another may not come their way soon. The declaration, agreed after much hard bargaining, holds out the prospect for Sinn Fein to join talks with London and Dublin on the future of Northern Ireland if the IRA renounces violence forever. It is now up to the men of violence, republican and loyalist, to choose war or peace (→ 11/1/94).

Premiers John Major and Albert Reynolds are appealing to the men of violence.

Australia's aborigines celebrate their victory over land rights

Aboriginal land rights were abolished by colonists more than 200 years ago.

Dec 22. Aborigines celebrated tonight after the Australian parliament passed the Native Title Bill confirming their right to claim for land lost when Europeans colonised Australia more than 200 years ago. Their victory was won when two members of the Green Party, who hold the balance of power in the Senate, voted for the bill, which could affect the ownership of a tenth of the country.

Prime Minister Paul Keating said the bill recognised the right of the indigenous people to their own soil, but opposition leader John Hewson warned that vital foreign investment would be endangered.

Russia's electorate opts for 'Mad Vlad'

Moscow, Sunday 12

The threat of fascism looms over Russia with the triumph of the ranting demagogue Vladimir Zhirinovsky and his misnamed Liberal Democratic Party in the elections for the new parliament. "Mad Vlad", derided as a buffoon and ignored by most foreign observers, won support from the working class and the frustrated military, who have gained nothing from Yeltsin's economic reforms, by promising free vodka, prosperity and an expansion of Russia so that the army could wash its feet in the Indian Ocean.

Arts in 1993: A good year for big money

Literature Nobel for Toni Morrison.

This was the year of the big bucks in the arts. A Turner landscape went to the Getty Museum for a record £11 million; Michelangelo's "The Holy Family on the Flight to Egypt" was sold for £4.18 million. **Steven Spielberg's** "Jurassic Park" took $81.7 million in its first week. The musical version of "Sunset Boulevard" opened to rave revues in London. Toni Morrison became the first black American to win the Nobel Prize for Literature. It was, alas, also a record year for the grim reaper: **Dizzy Gillespie, Audrey Hepburn, Lillian Gish, Sir William Golding, Myrna Loy** and **Federico Fellini** were among those who died.

1994

JANUARY

Su	Mo	Tu	We	Th	Fr	Sa
						1
2	3	4	5	6	7	8
9	10	11	12	13	14	15
16	17	18	19	20	21	22
23	24	25	26	27	28	29
30	31					

4. London: Torrential rain following the wettest December since 1979 causes havoc in southern England.

6. Detroit: America's ice queen, figure skater Nancy Kerrigan, is attacked at an ice rink by a man wielding a crowbar.

8. Mexico: The army prepares to attack Zapatista Army of National Liberation rebels after peasants seize five towns in Chiapas.

8. Sheffield: Jayne Torvill and Christopher Dean win the British ice-dancing championship with nine perfect sixes for their free-dance routine (→ 2/3).

11. Dublin: The Irish government lifts its long-standing broadcast ban on Sinn Fein (→ 1/2).

11. Brussels: NATO leaders endorse President Clinton's Partnership for Peace plan for closer political and military cooperation with former Communist-bloc countries (→ 22/6).

18. London: Prince Charles, who suffers from back problems, quits competitive polo.

21. Virginia: Lorena Bobbitt, who cut off part of her husband's penis, is found not guilty of malicious wounding by reason of insanity.

22. Headingley: Underdogs Castleford thrash Wigan 33-2 to win the rugby league Regal Trophy.

26. Sydney: An Asian student fires two blank shots from a starting pistol at the Prince of Wales.

29. Germany: Slalom champion Ulrike Maier dies in a 60mph crash when she hits soft snow on the Kandahar course.

DEATHS

5. Brian Johnston, cricket commentator (*24/6/1912).

13. Johan Holst, Norway's Foreign Minister and architect of last year's secret PLO-Israel talks (*29/11/1937).

22. Telly Savalas, US actor famous for his TV role as "Kojak" (*21/1/1924).

Major earthquake jolts Los Angeles before dawn, killing dozens

Jan 18. An earthquake measuring 6.6 on the Richter scale killed 34 people when it shook Los Angeles before dawn yesterday morning. It was not the feared "Big One" but it was big enough. With its epicentre in the commuter belt of San Fernando Valley at the city's northern limits, it crumbled motorways and destroyed bridges; water mains burst, and broken gas pipes spread flames through the area. The death toll would have been much higher if it had struck a few hours later, during the rush hour. Property damage has been estimated to exceed $7 billion, and the effects of the tremor are still being felt with aftershocks measuring 4.7 on the Richter scale causing further damage today. It could take this urban region with its 9 million people more than a year to repair the massive damage.

Broken gas and water mains cause havoc in several suburban neighbourhoods.

SAS hero Rose to lead UN forces in Bosnia

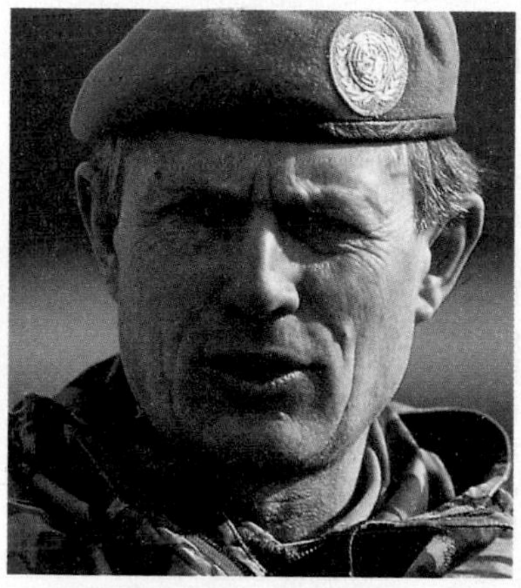

Jan 5. Lieutenant-General Sir Michael Rose, who master-minded the SAS assault on the occupied Iranian embassy in London and commanded the elite regiment, gun in hand, during the Falklands conflict, has been appointed to lead the United Nations peacekeeping force in Bosnia. Sir Michael, who is presently commanding the UK Field Army, is expected to take up his duties in Sarajevo before the end of the month. His reputation as a fighting leader promises a more vigorous pursuit of UN operations in Bosnia (→ 5/2).

The Duchess of Kent becomes a Catholic

Jan 14. The Duchess of Kent became the first member of the royal family to become a Roman Catholic in modern times tonight when she was received into the church in a private ceremony by Cardinal Hume, Archbishop of Westminster. Watched by her husband and their three children, who remain Anglicans, the duchess solemnly declared her belief in Catholic doctrine and was anointed with blessed oil by Cardinal Hume.

Major faces a new crisis

Jan 10. When John Major launched his "Back to Basics" campaign calling for a return to old-fashioned family values he could not have envisaged the disasters that were about to befall him.

Last week, he lost Tim Yeo, his Environment Minister, who resigned following the revelation that he had a love-child as the result of an extra-marital affair with Tory councillor Julia Stent. Yeo had been determined to hold onto his job but was forced into resignation when his South Suffolk constituency party called on him to reflect on the "widespread disappointment and criticism" over his affair. Now, the Prime Minister has lost the Earl of Caithness, who has resigned as aviation and shipping minister following the shotgun suicide of his wife. Westminster, a cruel gossip shop, is buzzing with rumours about these happenings and other tales of sexual and financial improprieties. Major has now called for an end to the moral witch hunt against Tories who have behaved foolishly. He said that Back to Basics is not about the sexual morality of individuals and denied he was "preaching" at single mothers. Meanwhile, the nation awaits the next scandal (→ 8/2).

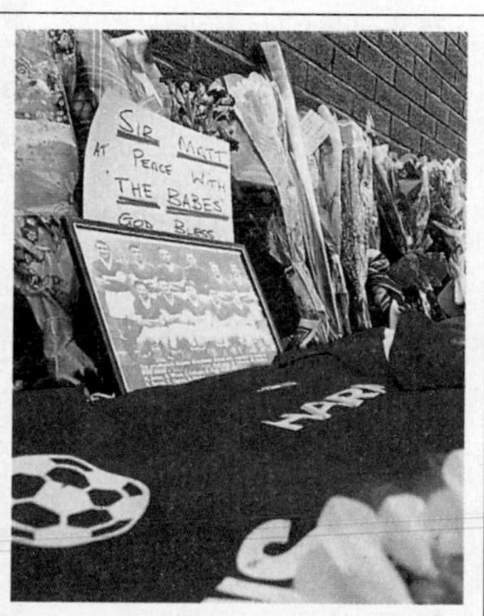

Jan 27. Thousands come to Old Trafford to mourn football manager Sir Matt Busby (*26/5/1926), who died a just week ago.

1994

FEBRUARY

Su	Mo	Tu	We	Th	Fr	Sa
		1	2	3	4	5
6	7	8	9	10	11	12
13	14	15	16	17	18	19
20	21	22	23	24	25	26
27	28					

1. London: The sale of Rover, the last British-owned car manufacturer, to the German firm BMW causes a huge political row.

1. London: The British government is outraged by adulation of Sinn Fein leader Gerry Adams on his visit to America (→ 13/3).

2. Egypt: An armed Islamic group tells foreigners to leave the country, warning of a "ferocious" campaign against the government.

6. Finland: Social Democrat Martii Ahtisaari is elected President.

8. London: Tory MP Stephen Milligan suffocates himself in a bizarre sexual act which goes wrong.

14. US: The three largest producers of silicone breast implants agree to pay $4.75 billion to women harmed by the implants.

22. Washington: Aldrich Hazen Ames, former head of the CIA's Soviet counter-intelligence branch, is charged with spying for the KGB (→ 28/4).

23. Britain: The decision by the Church of England to ordain women priests leads seven bishops and more than 700 clergy to announce their intention to become Roman Catholics.

25. London: Ian Holme ("Moonlight") and his wife Penelope Wilton ("Deep Blue Sea") are named best actor and actress in the London Critics' Drama Awards.

28. Bosnia: NATO fires its first shots in anger over Bosnia, shooting down four Serb warplanes which had bombed a Bosnian munitions factory (→ 18/3).

DEATHS

6. Joseph Cotten, American actor (*15/3/1905).

10. Mel Calman, British cartoonist (*19/5/1931).

24. Dinah Shore, American actress and singer (*1/3/1918).

27. Sir Harold Acton, British author and historian (*1905).

Artillery kills 68 in Sarajevo market

A shell landed in the city's crowded market, killing men, women and children.

Feb 5. There was carnage at Sarajevo's central market today when a single mortar bomb slaughtered 68 people and wounded nearly 200 others. The deadly attack came without warning, and the 120mm shell landed in the centre of the market crowded with weekend shoppers. The effect was devastating, with shrapnel slicing through the stalls. Sir Michael Rose, who commands the UN peacekeepers in Bosnia, said it was impossible to say where the shell came from, but the people of Sarajevo are in no doubt: It was the Serbs, their former neighbours, who now command the hills above the city. World leaders have swiftly condemned the massacre (→ 28).

The Bandit Queen of India is freed at last

Feb 18. Phoolan Devi, India's legendary Bandit Queen, has been released after spending 11 years in jail. A heroine to thousands of low caste Indians, she was born into the Mallah caste of fishermen, near the bottom of India's rigid social scale and became a bandit after she was gang-raped. She led her rural band in robbing and killing upper-caste Thakurs in revenge for the murder of her lover and acquired a Robin Hood image. Today, Phoolan Devi says she will "work for the upliftment of women and the downtrodden".

MPs vote for a lower gay age of consent

Feb 21. Gay-rights activists clashed with police outside parliament last night while an impassioned debate in the Commons ended with a lowering of the age of consent for homosexuals from 21 to 18.

The activists, keeping a candlelit vigil, became infuriated when they learnt that a somewhat more radical proposal to equalise the age of consent for homosexuals and heterosexuals had been turned down after Home Secretary Michael Howard argued there was a need to protect young men "from activities their lack of maturity might cause them to regret".

Jewish extremist causes Hebron bloodbath

Feb 25. A Jewish zealot, Dr Baruch Goldstein, shot down 30 Palestinian worshippers in the Ibrahim Mosque near the Tomb of the Patriarchs, holy to both Jew and Moslem, in Hebron today.

Goldstein, a member of a Jewish settlement, placed himself inside the door of the prayer room and opened fire with an automatic rifle on the kneeling worshippers. When he ran out of ammunition, the survivors beat him to death. Riots are raging throughout the Occupied Territories tonight, and it is feared the massacre will do great harm to the Middle East peace process (→ 1/7).

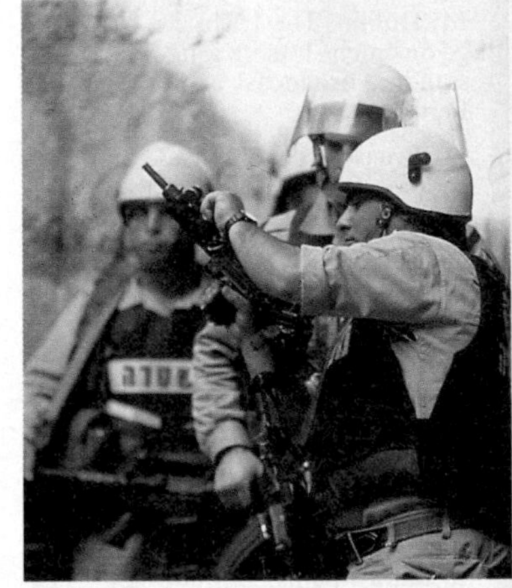

Police at the Tomb of the Patriarchs.

Feb 27. At the Lillehammer Winter Olympics, Diann Roffe-Steinrotter of New York wins her first Super-Giant gold. British athletes won only two bronze medals, one going to ice-dancers Jayne Torvill and Chris Dean.

1994

MARCH

Su	Mo	Tu	We	Th	Fr	Sa
		1	2	3	4	5
6	7	8	9	10	11	12
13	14	15	16	17	18	19
20	21	22	23	24	25	26
27	28	29	30	31		

2. Britain: Jayne Torvill and Christopher Dean, disappointed at only winning the bronze at the Lillehammer Olympics, retire from competitive skating.

4. London: David Spedding is named as head of MI6.

7. Moldova: In a referendum, more than 90 per cent of voters reject union with Rumania.

10. Gloucester: Frederick West is charged with the murder of eight women after their bodies are dug up in the garden of his "House of Horrors" (→28/4).

13. London: Heathrow is shut down for two hours after the third IRA mortar attack in five days; Gatwick is also closed because of bomb threats (→31/8).

13. London: The Chief of the Defence Staff, Sir Peter Harding, is forced to resign after newspaper revelations of his affair with the divorced wife of Sir Antony Buck, a former Navy minister.

18. Bosnia: Prime Minister John Major pays a visit to Sarajevo, inspects British troops and announces a £12 million aid package for the city (→14/5).

19. Twickenham: The Queen watches the 100th match between England and Wales; Wales loose 15-8 but win the Five Nations rugby championship.

26. London: Cambridge beat Oxford in the 140th University Boat Race.

27. Germany: Eurofighter 2000, built by Britain, Germany, Spain and Italy, makes a successful first test flight.

DEATHS

6. Melina Mercouri, Greek actress and politician (*18/10/1925).

9. Fernando Rey, Spanish film actor (*20/9/1917).

15. Mai Zetterling, Swedish actress and director (*24/5/1925).

28. Eugene Ionesco, foremost playwright of the Theatre of the Absurd (*26/11/1912).

Right-wing media tycoon Silvio Berlusconi wins elections in Italy

March 28. Silvio Berlusconi, the right-wing media baron, has scored a remarkable success in the Italian general election. His Forza Italia (Onward Italy) party has won 155 seats out of 315 in the Senate, just three short of an absolute majority.

He is also expected to benefit from the votes of the German-speaking minority in the South Tyrol. In the lower house, the alliance of Forza Italia, the Northern League and the neo-fascist National Alliance has a clear majority with 366 seats out of 630. This is a stunning victory for a man who entered politics only two months ago "to stop the left". The voters, disgusted with the corrupt old politicians, see him as a new broom (→22/12).

Some voters fear that his alliance with a neo-fascist party will cause turmoil.

Bullets fly in the streets of Johannesburg as black militants clash

Violence erupts between Zulus and ANC militants in the city's business district.

March 28. Battles raged today in Johannesburg between Zulus and African National Congress supporters, and at least 18 people have been killed. For the first time the violence of the settlements flared in the most important city and the commercial heart of the country. It started when snipers opened fire on Zulus marching in response to King Goodwill Zwelithini's call for a boycott of next month's elections. Crowds of angry Zulus, carrying their "traditional weapons" then massed outside two ANC offices where ANC guards fired into them. The two groups blamed each other for the bloodshed, adding that police did nothing to prevent the violence (→10/5).

A Mexican political leader assassinated

March 24. Luis Donaldo Colosio, candidate of Mexico's ruling Institutional Revolutionary Party (PRI) to succeed outgoing President Carlos Salinas de Gortari, was assassinated at an election rally in Tijuana yesterday. The powerful PRI has ruled Mexico for the last 65 years, and it was virtually certain that Colosio would have been the country's next President. Mario Aburto Martinez, arrested at the scene, is said to have confessed. The party met this morning to discuss choices for a replacement candidate (→22/8).

March 12. The Loch Ness monster is revealed as a hoax perpetrated by Marmaduke Wetherell, who used a toy submarine with a head and neck.

1994

APRIL

Su	Mo	Tu	We	Th	Fr	Sa
					1	2
3	4	5	6	7	8	9
10	11	12	13	14	15	16
17	18	19	20	21	22	23
24	25	26	27	28	29	30

1. Britain: VAT on gas and electricity goes into effect amid much criticism.

4. Iran: Television satellite dishes are banned.

7. Glasgow: Scenes from a criminal trial are broadcast for the first time.

8. Rome: The Pope celebrates Mass in the Sistine Chapel to mark the end of 14 years of restoration of Michelangelo's fresco "Christ the Judge, and the Virgin".

13. Barbados: England beat West Indies by 208 runs in the Fourth Test, the first time the West Indies have been beaten at home for 35 years, but they take the series.

14. Iraq: American fighters shoot down two of their own helicopters, killing 26 people.

14. Washington: The government approves the sale of female condoms.

20. Germany: Authorities say that Germans have replaced the French as the world's leading consumers of alcohol.

21. Belfast: Paul Hill, already released from prison as one of the Guildford Four, has another conviction, for the murder of a soldier, quashed.

24. Edinburgh: The England women's rugby union team beat the United States 38-23 to win the Women's World Cup.

26. Japan: A China Airlines Airbus A300 crashes, killing 262 people.

28. Gloucester: Rosemary West, wife of the alleged serial killer Frederick West, is charged with jointly murdering three of the victims (→ 1/1/95).

28. US: CIA traitor Aldrich Ames pleads guilty and gets life.

DEATHS

8. US rock singer Kurt Cobain (*20/2/1967).

15. John Curry, former British Olympic and world champion ice-skater (*9/9/1949).

26. Queen Zein, Queen Mother of Jordan (*2/8/1915).

30. Richard Scarry, US author (*1919).

Rwanda's killing fields

April 22. The stench of death pervades Kigali, the capital of Rwanda. Decomposing bodies are all around; the living have fled.

Nuns, priests and aid workers are among the victims. Eleven Belgian UN soldiers were killed in one incident. The Red Cross estimated yesterday that more than 100,000 people have been killed in two weeks of tribal slaughter following the death of President Habyarimana when his plane crashed – believed shot down – but nobody knows the real extent of the killing which has soaked every part of this lush and verdant land with blood. Now, it is feared starvation and disease will sweep through the makeshift refugee camps. Drugs, food and, especially, clean water are desperately needed. Even the small protection afforded by the UN force originally deployed to monitor peace accords between the Hutu government and the Tutsi rebels will end when, as expected, the Security Council votes to withdraw the force (→ 31/5).

Ex-President Nixon dies after a stroke

April 22. Richard Milhous Nixon (*9/1/1913), who had been in failing health, has died after a stroke. The former US President was probably modern America's most controversial politician. The Watergate scandal, which led to his resignation as President, seemed to confirm the Democrat view of him as a devious, vengeful and even paranoid politician. But his major foreign policy triumphs, especially the opening of relations with China, are widely praised, and his successors sought his advice in this field.

Batsman Brian Lara sets Test cricket record

April 18. The West Indies' left-handed batsman, Brian Lara, hooked English bowler Chris Lewis to the boundary just before lunch in St John's, Antigua, today to pass Sir Garfield Sobers's record Test score of 365 not out, made in Jamaica 36 years ago. Lara, one of a Trinidad family of 11 children, is only 24, and the way he is batting promises to break every record in the book. He was finally out for an amazing 375. Sir Garfield was one of the first to congratulate him.

April 1. Robin Knox-Johnston and his British and New Zealand crew smash the round-the-world record aboard their catamaran ENZA New Zealand.

Top quark is found after 20-year search

April 26. The Top quark, the missing link of the atom, has been found after a 20-year search. The physicists had already found Charm and Strange, Up, Down and Bottom, but Top, the sixth quark, remained elusive. Today, scientists at the Fermi National Accelerator Laboratory in Illinois presented evidence that Top exists.

Quarks, along with leptons, are the building blocks of matter. The evidence for Top, if confirmed, will complete the experimental proof of the Standard Model of theoretical physics, which for the last two decades has been accepted as the most viable theory to describe the atom and its structure. To hunt quarks, scientists create collisions between beams of protons and antiprotons racing round a four mile accelerator at the speed of light. It is in the traces left behind by the minute debris of these collisions that evidence of the quarks is found.

1994

MAY

Su	Mo	Tu	We	Th	Fr	Sa
1	2	3	4	5	6	7
8	9	10	11	12	13	14
15	16	17	18	19	20	21
22	23	24	25	26	27	28
29	30	31				

4. Copenhagen: Arsenal beat Parma 1-0 to win the European Cup Winner's Cup.

4. London: Prince Charles says the fashion of political correctness is destroying much of the fabric of society.

5. Singapore: American teenager Michael Fay gets four strokes of the cane for vandalism.

5. London: The Tories suffer a defeat in local elections, losing 429 council seats and control of 18 councils.

8. Milan: Canada win the World Ice Hockey Championship.

11. Frankfurt: The Bundesbank cuts interest rates to their lowest level in five years.

14. Wembley: Manchester United beat Chelsea 4-0 to win the FA Cup.

14. Sarajevo: President Izetbegovic rejects US and EU calls for a division of Bosnia that would give the Serbs 49 per cent of the territory (→27/8).

16. Vienna: Salman Rushdie is presented with Austria's prize for European literature.

16. Moscow: Armenia and Azerbaijan agree to a cease-fire in the disputed enclave of Nagorno-Karabakh.

18. UK: The British bobby's truncheon is to be replaced by the US-style side-handled baton.

23. Germany: Roman Herzog is appointed President.

25. New York: The UN lifts the arms embargo on South Africa (→20/7).

31. Rwanda: The death toll of the fighting between Tutsis and Hutus reaches 500,000.

DEATHS

8. Lady Victoria Wemyss (*27/2/1890), last surviving godchild of Queen Victoria.

12. John Smith, leader of the Labour Party (*13/9/1938).

24. John Wain, novelist, poet and critic (*14/3/1925).

30. Marcel Bich, French inventor of the Bic ball-point pen (*29/7/1914).

President Nelson Mandela sworn in

May 10. Nelson Mandela, who spent 27 years in jail as a prisoner of the apartheid regime, was inaugurated today as South Africa's first black President.

The historic ceremony, held in baking sunshine, was attended by the largest assembly of foreign dignitaries ever seen in Africa. The day, however, belonged to the tens of thousands of ordinary South Africans who danced and sang on the lawn of the Union Buildings and cheered as their new President said: "Let there be justice for all. Let there be peace for all. Let there be work, bread and salt for all. The time for the healing of the wounds has come" (→25).

South Africa's first black head of state shakes hands with Frederik de Klerk.

Queen Elizabeth and President Mitterrand inaugurate Chunnel

The Queen travelled through the tunnel to Coquelles for the historic ceremony.

May 6. After eight years of work and billions of pounds, a two-century-old dream became reality today when Queen Elizabeth and President François Mitterand cut red, white and blue ribbons to open the Channel Tunnel. The Queen, having first opened the Eurostar terminal at Waterloo, passed through the tunnel to Coquelles, where the trains of the two heads of state met nose to nose. After the ceremony, the Queen and the President sat in the royal Rolls Royce as it was brought to Folkestone on Le Shuttle. The tunnel, said the Queen, was a mixture of French elan and British pragmatism.

Racing champ Senna is killed in car crash

May 1. Ayrton Senna, the Brazilian Formula One driver, winner of 41 Grand Prix, idolised by the fans, died today when he spun off a curve during the San Marino Grand Prix at Imola and crashed into a concrete wall. He was just 34. Austrian driver Roland Ratzenberg met his death at nearly the same spot during a qualifying run yesterday. The motor-racing world is shattered by these deaths, and many are blaming the ban on active suspension and automatic driving aids introduced to make Formula One more of a "drivers' championship".

May 19. Jacqueline Kennedy Onassis (*28/7/1929) dies of cancer in her New York home.

Great Russian exile finally returns home

May 27. Alexander Solzhenitsyn, author in the great Russian tradition and survivor of the war, cancer and Stalin's death camps, came home today after 20 years of exile in America.

He went first to Magadan, the port of the Gulag Archipelago, where he paid tribute to Stalin's victims. Later, he told thousands gathered to greet him he never doubted communism was doomed. He said: "I know I am arriving in a Russia tormented, disheartened, in shock, changed beyond recognition and still searching for itself."

1994

JUNE

Su	Mo	Tu	We	Th	Fr	Sa
			1	2	3	4
5	6	7	8	9	10	11
12	13	14	15	16	17	18
19	20	21	22	23	24	25
26	27	28	29	30		

1. Epsom: Erhaab, ridden by Willie Carson, wins the 215th Derby.

2. Mull of Kintyre: A helicopter crash kills 25 of Britain's leading counter-terrorist experts.

2. Cairo: Colombia is chosen to head the non-aligned group of nations.

4. Kuwait: Six men are sentenced to death for plotting to assassinate former US President George Bush.

10. London: Soccer star Bobby Charlton is knighted by the Queen.

12. Switzerland: Voters reject government plans to provide United Nations peacekeeping troops.

15. London: Railway signalmen, striking over pay and productivity, bring misery to millions.

15. Rome: The Vatican and Israel establish full diplomatic relations.

16. US: The number of abortions performed in 1992 dropped to 1,529,000, the lowest level since 1979.

22. Washington: The Clinton administration halts its campaign for sanctions against North Korea after the country agrees to freeze its nuclear programme.

29. Japan: Tomiichi Murayama becomes Japan's first Socialist Prime Minister since 1948.

30. US: The prison population exceeds one million for the first time.

30. London: In an ITV documentary marking the 25th anniversary of his investiture, the Prince of Wales says he has no plans to divorce but insists he would not regard divorce as an impediment to becoming King.

DEATHS

4. Lord Thorneycroft, leading Tory politician (*29/7/1909).

7. Dennis Potter (*17/5/1935), television dramatist.

14. Henry Mancini, US composer and band leader (*16/4/1924).

Fundamentalists target Bangladesh author

June 4. With a warrant out for her arrest and Islamic fundamentalists calling for her death, Taslima Nasrin has gone underground.

Raised a Muslim, the 31-year-old Bangladeshi doctor and author has renounced her faith and denounced modern Islamic society as being oppressive of women. She is quoted in the press as saying the Koran should be thoroughly revised. "I'm not in favour of minor changes," she reportedly said; "It serves no purpose." This is blasphemy in the eyes of the fundamentalists and a further provocation from a woman who has written frankly about sex and criticised marriage (→10/8).

Taslima Nasrin is 31 years old.

Terrorists bomb peaceful march in Algiers

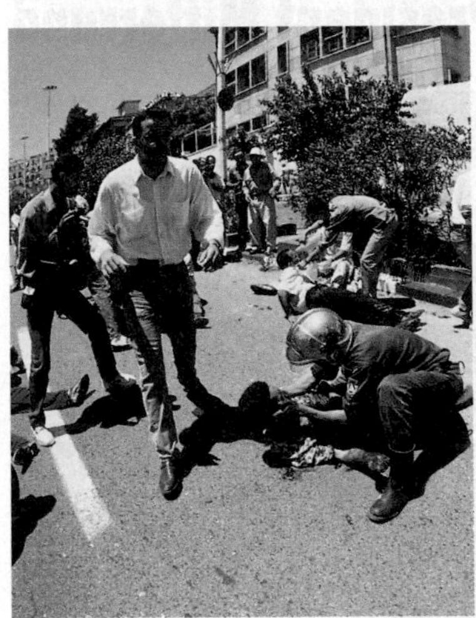

Reign of terror by Islamic extremists.

June 29. In the battle for Algeria, fought between the government and Islamic militants, there are those who oppose both sides. At noon today, 15,000 demonstrators gathered in Algiers to march peacefully in protest against both warring groups and to demand democracy. As the march began, there were two explosions, then gunfire; 64 people were wounded. When order was restored, the marchers, some bloodied, went on. The demonstration was held today, the second anniversary of the assassination of President Boudiaf, to demand an investigation into the hushed-up circumstances of his death (→26/12).

June 6. On the 50th anniversary of Operation Overlord, President Bill Clinton spends a quiet moment with three D-Day veterans in Normandy.

Millions watch fall of an American hero

June 17. A white Ford Bronco led a group of police cars and a fleet of TV-news helicopters across the motorways of Los Angeles County as thousands of people lined the roads and millions more watched on TV. In the Bronco was movie star and former football hero O.J. Simpson. He led the pack to his home and then gave himself up. Earlier today he had failed to appear for an agreed arraignment on charges of murdering his former wife Nicole and her friend Ronald Goldman who were savagely killed at her home last week.

Russia finally signs NATO peace accord

June 22. Russia today became the 21st of the former Warsaw Pact states to join NATO's Partnership for Peace programme, but only after weeks of hard bargaining to ensure Russia's status as a world power. The signing of the pact by Foreign Minister Andrei Kozyrev at a ceremony in NATO headquarters in Brussels was hailed by US Secretary of State Warren Christopher as a "dream which has animated this alliance and my country for more than four decades". However, hardline opposition to the pact with NATO continues in Moscow.

British veto wrecks crucial Euro-summit

June 25. A furious Jacques Delors accused John Major of wrecking the Euro-summit in Corfu today when Major vetoed the appointment of Jean-Luc Dehaene, the federalist Belgian Premier, to succeed Delors as President of the European Commission. Major, in defiant mood, used the veto despite being in a minority of one in opposing Dehaene at the end of the two-day summit. He says: "It was the right decision." Helmut Kohl, the German Chancellor, immediately called an emergency summit in Brussels on July 15. The search is now on for a compromise candidate acceptable to all 12 member states (→15/7).

1994

JULY

Su	Mo	Tu	We	Th	Fr	Sa
					1	2
3	4	5	6	7	8	9
10	11	12	13	14	15	16
17	18	19	20	21	22	23
24	25	26	27	28	29	30
31						

1. Geneva: The World Health Organization says that the number of AIDS cases worldwide has risen from 2.5 to 4 million over the past year.

3. Wimbledon: Pete Sampras retains his title, beating Goran Ivanisevic 7-6, 7-6, 6-0. In her last appearance at Wimbledon, Martina Navratilova is beaten in the final by Conchita Martinez, 6-4, 3-6,6-3.

7. Yemen: The government claims victory in a two-month civil war against secessionist forces.

12. Ukraine: An offer by industrialised nations of $200 million to shut down the Chernobyl nuclear reactors is rejected.

12. Westminster: Parliament is in uproar over accusations that two Tory MPs, Graham Riddick and David Tredinnick, were paid to ask "commercial" questons in the House.

15. Brussels: Luxembourg's Premier, Jacques Santer, is appointed President of the European Commission.

18. Buenos Aires: 96 people die when a bomb levels two buildings housing Jewish organisations.

20. London: South Africa is welcomed back into the Commonwealth.

24. Paris: Spanish cyclist Miguel Indurain wins the Tour de France.

25. Washington: Jordan's King Hussein and Israeli Prime Minister Yitzhak Rabin sign a declaration ending the 46-year state of war between their countries.

26. London: A car bomb badly damages the Israeli embassy, injuring 14.

DEATHS

20. Paul Delvaux, Belgian painter (*23/9/1897).

26. Terry Scott, British comedian (*4/5/1927).

31. Anne Shelton, the "Forces Favourite" (*10/11/1923).

31. Caitlin Thomas, widow of Welsh poet Dylan Thomas (*8/12/1913).

Yassir Arafat ends exile

July 1. Yassir Arafat crossed the Egyptian border into the Gaza Strip today, ending 27 years of exile from Palestine.

With tears in his eyes he kissed the ground then waved to his ecstatic supporters. His motorcade went on to the city of Gaza, where he addressed a cheering crowd of 10,000. He promised to help build a new homeland in the territories now coming under Palestinian self-rule and listed the holy places in Israeli-held territory where Palestinians would go to pray. He ended, predictably but controversially, with Jerusalem, which the Israelis insist will remain their undivided capital (→ 19/10).

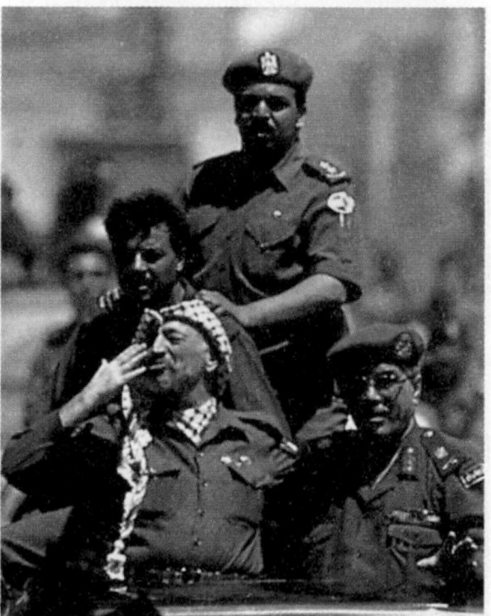

The PLO chief is back after 27 years.

Korean dictator Kim dies in Pyongyang

July 8. President Kim Il Sung of North Korea, the 20th century's longest-ruling dictator, died today, apparently of a heart attack, on the eve of crucial nuclear talks with the US. He was 82. He was the only leader North Korea has ever known, and he shut the country off from the rest of the world. It was he who started the Korean War in 1950 by invading the South, and when that ended in stalemate, he retreated behind a curtain of lies, pronouncing communism's victory in his fiefdom and his own virtues as the "Great Leader". His son, Kim Jong Il, has been groomed as his successor.

Brazilians win their fourth World Cup after disappointing final

July 17. The dazzling Brazilians won their fourth World Cup in Pasadena, California today, beating the equally talented Italians in the final of a competition hailed as a surprising success in the US. Two billion people around the world watched the final on TV. It was, however, a disappointing game and after two hours of unadventurous, scoreless play the match was settled by a penalty shootout. Italy's sweeper, Franco Baresi, blasted the first shot high over the bar. Both teams traded goals and agonising misses until, with the score at 3-2, Italy's Roberto Baggio repeated Baresi's mistake and Brazil had won.

Midfielder Dunga brandishes the trophy and leads his team for a victory lap.

Tony Blair wins race to lead Labour Party

July 21. Tony Blair has been elected leader of the Labour Party in a landslide, winning more than half the votes.

He easily beat John Prescott, who, in a separate vote, was elected deputy leader. Blair, at 41, is the party's youngest-ever leader. He is a modernist, far removed from the dinosaurs of old-fashioned socialism, and he regards his victory as a mandate to continue the reforms started by his predecessors, Neil Kinnock and John Smith, who died of a heart attack in May. In a speech tonight Blair told a triumphant meeting he would not rest until he had put Labour "in its rightful place – in government again".

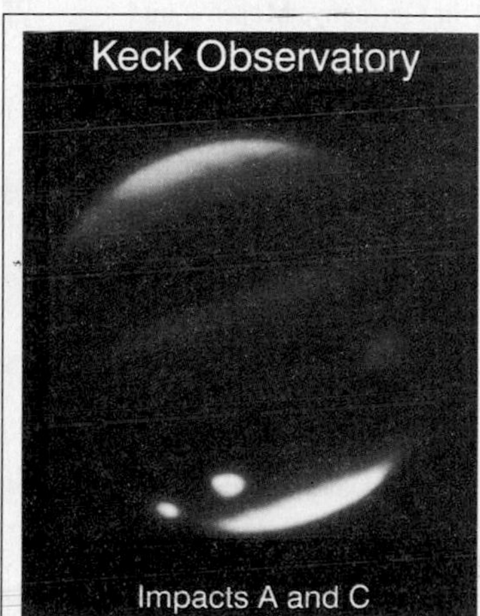

July 22. Star wars: Astronomers look on in awe as 21 fragments of a large comet, Shoemaker-Levy 9, crash into Jupiter, producing several gigantic fireballs.

1994

AUGUST

Su	Mo	Tu	We	Th	Fr	Sa
	1	2	3	4	5	6
7	8	9	10	11	12	13
14	15	16	17	18	19	20
21	22	23	24	25	26	27
28	29	30	31			

1. UK: A fire in Norwich Central Library destroys irreplaceable historic documents and more than 100,000 books.

1. New York: Lisa Marie Presley, daughter of Elvis, confirms rumors of her marriage to Michael Jackson.

2. Rome: The Vatican blames Italians' "selfishness" for the declining birthrate.

10. Sweden: Taslima Nasrin, under a death threat from Islamic fundamentalists, flees to safety from Bangladesh.

11. Grozny: Fearing a Russian military intervention, the Chechen leader, General Dzhokar Dudayev, orders full mobilisation (→ 11/12).

12. Helsinki: At the European Games, Linford Christie (100 metres), Steve Backley (javelin), Sally Gunnell (400 metres hurdles) and Colin Jackson (110 metres hurdles) win gold medals for Britain.

17. New York: The UN says the world's population will reach 8.5 billion by the year 2050.

17. Lesotho: Five people are killed in riots after King Letsie III dissolves the country's first democratically elected government in 23 years.

22. Moscow: After a rash of arrests of plutonium smugglers in Germany, Moscow and Bonn agree to work together to prevent smuggling of nuclear materials from Russia.

22. Mexico: Ernesto Zedillo Ponce de Leon, candidate of the ruling PRI party, is elected President.

29. London: For the first time shops open legally on a Sunday, and thousands of people respond enthusiastically throughout Britain.

31. Berlin: The last Russian troops leave Germany (→ 8/9).

DEATHS

11. Peter Cushing, British actor (*26/5/1913).

13. Manfred Worner, civilian head of NATO (*24/9/1934).

30. Lindsay Anderson, British film director (*17/4/1923).

Carlos the Jackal is hunted down at last

Aug 14. Carlos the Jackal, the world's most wanted terrorist, is being held under close guard in Paris's La Santé prison after being handed over to French agents by the Sudanese authorities. Born Illich Ramirez Sanchez, son of a Stalinist millionaire in Venezuela, he is wanted for at least 15 murders in France and faces a life sentence. His most notorious exploit was the occupation of OPEC headquarters in Vienna in 1975 when he kidnapped several Arab oil ministers.

Kurdish MPs on trial for separatist views

Aug 3. At the start of a treason trial which could damage Turkey's democratic credentials, the prosecution today demanded the death penalty for six Kurdish MPs. The MPs, stripped of their parliamentary immunity after Prime Minister Tansu Ciller said they were "traitors under the parliamentary roof", are accused of acting as the political wing of the PKK, the Kurdish separatist militants.

Serbs in Bosnia vote against peace plan

Aug 27. Bosnian Serbs, who voted this weekend on the latest international peace plan, have given it an emphatic thumbs down.

They refuse even to discuss a plan which involves surrendering territory won by force of arms. In doing so they are further humiliating Serbian President Slobodan Milosevic. He may cut the Bosnian Serbs adrift in revenge but, fiercely nationalistic, they remain defiant (→ 23/11).

Aug 14. Feelin' groovy: Some 350,000 people flock to Saugerties, in New York State, for the 25th anniversary of the original Woodstock concert.

IRA cease-fire lifts hopes for peace

Aug 31. After a quarter of a century of bombing and shooting and the deaths of more than 3,000 people, the IRA has announced a "complete cessation of military operations", and the way now seems open to a political settlement of this savage sectarian conflict.

Gerry Adams, President of Sinn Fein, who persuaded the IRA to accept the Downing Street Declaration, said: "We have taken a great step by removing the republican gun from Irish politics." Tonight there are triumphant celebrations in the Catholic areas of Belfast and Londonderry, where they scent an historic victory.

The reaction of the Protestant community is less ecstatic. Unionist hardliner Ian Paisley said the IRA's "war machine" could be turned on at any time, and there is much scepticism about the worth of the IRA's

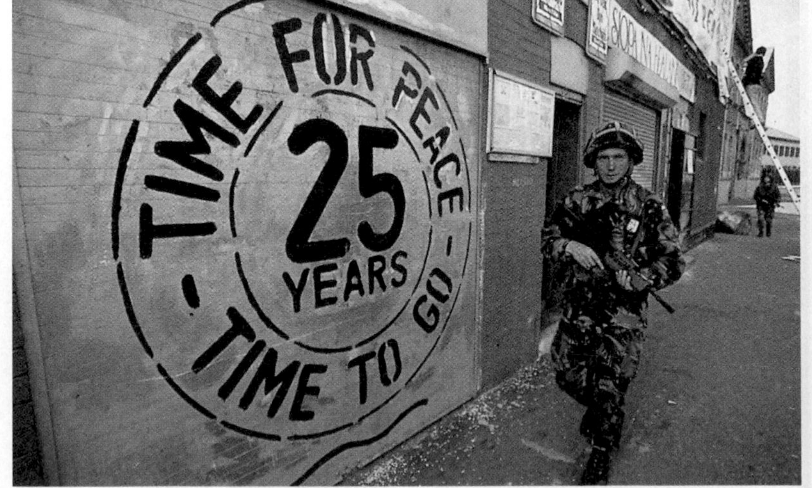

word. Prime Minister Major must convince the Loyalists that they have not been sold out in some secret deal. He was cautious tonight: "We are beyond the beginning, but we are not yet in sight of the end." Irish Prime Minister Albert Reynolds has no such doubts: "As far as we are concerned, the long nightmare is over" (→ 13/10).

1994

SEPTEMBER

Su	Mo	Tu	We	Th	Fr	Sa
				1	2	3
4	5	6	7	8	9	10
11	12	13	14	15	16	17
18	19	20	21	22	23	24
25	26	27	28	29	30	

6. Moscow: A government commission reports the Grand Duchess Anastasia was indeed murdered with the rest of the Russian royal family by the Bolsheviks in 1918.

8. Germany: The last Allied soldiers march through Berlin after spending 50 years guarding the city.

12. Paris: President Mitterrand appears on TV to explain his actions in working for Vichy and Marshal Petain during the war.

13. Washington: A mentally disturbed man dies when he crashes his light plane into the White House.

16. Alaska: A court orders Exxon to pay $5 billion to victims of the Exxon Valdez oil spill.

17. Arnhem: Thousands of Dutch people turn out to thank the "Red Devils" for their doomed attempt to take "The Bridge Too Far" 50 years ago.

18. London: Jean Simmons receives a BFI Fellowship in recognition of her distinguished career.

21. London: Gary Lineker, former England football captain, announces his retirement.

26. Brussels: Belgian Foreign Minister Willy Claes is appointed Secretary-General of NATO.

30. Shannon, Eire: Prime Minister Reynolds waits on the tarmac to meet Boris Yeltsin when his plane lands; the Russian President never gets off, flys on, and says on his arrival in Moscow that his aides failed to wake him from a nap.

DEATHS

2. Roy Castle, British comedian (*31/8/1932).

3. Billy Wright, former England football captain (*6/2/1924).

6. James Clavell, British author (*10/10/1924).

11. Jessica Tandy, US actress (*7/6/1909).

17. Sir Karl Popper, philosopher and author (*28/7/1902).

Baltic ferry tragedy claims 912 lives

Sept 28. The roll-on, roll-off ferry Estonia sank in heavy weather in the Baltic Sea early this morning, going down in minutes with terrible loss of life.

It is feared that 912 people have died. Survivors speak of water pouring through the bow doors before the 15,567-ton ferry capsized. An SOS signal sent at 12.20am said: "Mayday. Heavy list, 20 degrees, 30 degrees. Blackout." Five minutes later another message said: "We are sinking, the engines have stopped." Nothing more was heard from the stricken ship. She went down in 300 feet of bitterly cold water, and although ships raced to the rescue, there are only 141 survivors. There is no hope for anyone else.

The bow doors of the Estonia are suspected of having caused the disaster.

Demographic crisis talks held in Cairo

Sept 13. Against a background of bitter disputes about abortion, contraception and extra-marital sex, the United Nations conference on population ended here today with a 20-year plan to limit the world's population, promote the status of women and preserve the environment. Latin American and Moslem countries and the Vatican expressed reservations, but the conference was judged a success.

Panic as the plague breaks out in India

Sept 27. Pneumonic plague has struck the western Indian city of Surat, and some 300,000 people, their faces masked against the infection, have fled amid scenes of panic at bus and railway stations. The death toll here, where schools and public buildings have been closed, is put at 100. The first outbreak of plague in the state for 20 years has caught the authorities unprepared, and the fear is that the fleeing people will carry the disease to other parts of the country. Health services in Bombay, 100 miles to the south, have been put on full alert. Refugees will be examined, and anyone suspected of carrying the disease will be sent to isolation units.

Marines seize Haiti without firing a shot

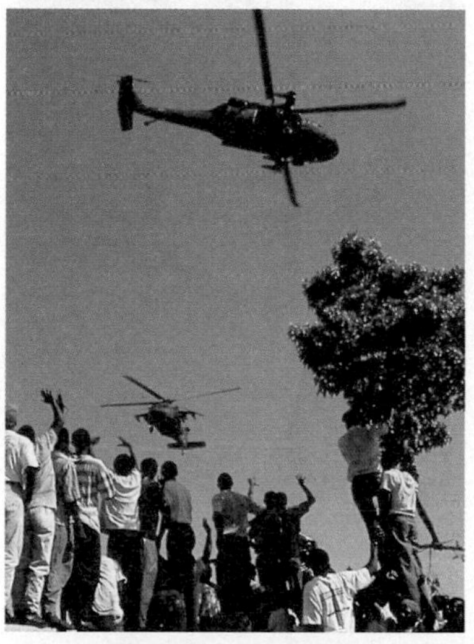

Haitians hope democracy will return.

Sept 19. Haiti is quiet tonight after US Marines took control without firing a shot under cover of helicopter loudspeakers blaring: "We're not at war. We're here to restore democracy and supply humanitarian aid." The peaceful invasion was brokered by a team led by former President Jimmy Carter which persuaded the military junta's leader, Raoul Cédras, to step down in an 11th hour agreement. The way is now clear for a return to the troubled island of President Jean-Bertrand Aristide, who was forced into exile by the junta three years ago. He faces the daunting task of rebuilding a country devastated by misrule and the UN's economic sanctions (→ 15/10).

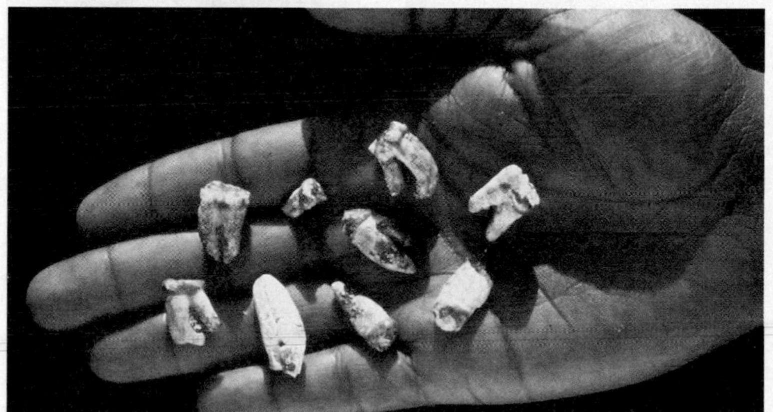

Sept 22. Fossils of a previously unknown human ancestor who lived about 4.5 million years ago and could well have been the "missing link" between apes and man have been found in the Middle Awash region of Ethiopia.

1994

OCTOBER

Su	Mo	Tu	We	Th	Fr	Sa
						1
2	3	4	5	6	7	8
9	10	11	12	13	14	15
16	17	18	19	20	21	22
23	24	25	26	27	28	29
30	31					

1. Koror: Palau, a group of islands east of the Philippines, becomes independent.

3. Brazil: Finance Minister Enrique Cardoso, an economic reformer, is elected President.

5. Wirral: Britain's oldest man, 109-year-old William Proctor, dies.

9. Austria: Jorg Haidar's far-right Freedom Party wins 22 per cent of the vote in parliamentary elections.

14. Oslo: The Nobel Peace Prize is won jointly by Yitzhak Rabin and Shimon Peres of Israel and Yassir Arafat of the PLO; the Literature prize goes to Kenzaburo Oe of Japan.

14. John o' Groats: Ffyona Campbell, the first woman to circle the globe on foot, completes her 11-year, 19,586-mile walk.

15. Port-au-Prince: President Jean-Bertrand Aristide returns to Haiti after three years in exile.

16. Virginia Water: South African golfer Ernie Els wins the World Match Play championship.

17. Tehran: Iran's production of caviar drops by 10 per cent for the third consecutive year due to pollution and poaching.

20. New York: The dollar falls to a two-year low against major currencies.

23. London: In his first visit to the mainland for 20 years, Sinn Fein leader Martin McGuinness warns that IRA violence could return if the peace process does not produce a satisfactory outcome (→ 9/12).

30. Rome: The Pope appoints 30 new cardinals, including the Archbishop of Glasgow, Tom Winning.

DEATHS

19. Martha Raye, American singer and dancer (*27/8/1916).

20. Sergei Bondarchuk, Ukrainian film director (*25/9/1920).

24. Alexander Shelepin, former head of the KGB (*18/8/1918).

31. Sir John Pope-Hennessey, art historian (*13/12/1913).

Mystery fire death of 50 sect members

Oct 5. Firefighters called to a farmhouse near the small Swiss village of Cheiry just after midnight found the bodies of 23 members of an apocalyptic cult, the Order of the Solar Temple. Clad in ceremonial robes, most had been shot, others had plastic bags over their heads. Later, another fire 100 miles away led to the discovery of the bodies of another 25 members of the cult. These deaths follow similar deaths of five cult members at Morin Heights near Montreal yesterday.

It is not yet clear if the deaths were mass suicide or murder. Cult leader Luc Jouret has vanished.

The Solar Temple guru Luc Jouret.

Elizabeth II makes historic visit to Russia

Oct 20. The Queen ended her mission to Russia today by inspecting the cathedral where her relative, the murdered Tsar Nicholas, is to be buried. It has been a successful visit despite an element of Russian chaos. The Queen did not meet as many ordinary Russians as she had wished, but neither has she been subjected to President Boris Yeltsin's bear-like hug. At a state banquet in the Kremlin, she told him: "You and I have spent most of our lives believing this evening could never happen. I hope you are as delighted as I am to be proved wrong. I am the first British sovereign to visit Moscow. You are the first President of an independent Russia."

The Queen and Yeltsin at the Bolshoi.

Loyalists announce cease-fire in Ulster

Oct 13. The three main loyalist terrorist groups in Northern Ireland announced a cease-fire today in Belfast to match that of the IRA, now seven weeks old.

This move by the loyalists, who have killed more than 900 people in 25 years of violence, has been greeted with enormous relief. Irish Prime Minister Albert Reynolds said it marked the "closure of a tragic chapter in our history", while John Major said it was "another very important part of the jigsaw falling into place." The government suggested there could be talks with Sinn Fein by Christmas (→ 23).

Suicide bomber kills 21 people in Israel

Oct 19. A suicide bomber blew up a bus in the centre of Tel Aviv today, killing 21 people and wounding 45 in the bloodiest terrorist attack in Israel for 16 years.

The fanatical Islamic movement Hamas said it was one of its "martyrs" who blew himself and the bus to pieces and threatened to carry out more suicide attacks on Jewish targets. The Israelis have reacted by imposing harsh security measures, sealing off Arab areas from the Jewish heartland. Premier Yitzhak Rabin, who cut short his visit to Britain to rush back to Jerusalem, blamed Iran for the bombing (→ 2/4/95).

Oct 20. Hollywood tough guy Burt Lancaster (*2/11/1913), star of films such as "The Leopard" and "Local Hero", dies in California.

Oct 26. Thousands of tonnes of crude oil spew out of a leaking Russian pipeline in the Arctic causing fears of a major environmental catastrophe.

1994

NOVEMBER

Su	Mo	Tu	We	Th	Fr	Sa
		1	2	3	4	5
6	7	8	9	10	11	12
13	14	15	16	17	18	19
20	21	22	23	24	25	26
27	28	29	30			

2. Cambodia: Three Western hostages have been murdered by the Khmer Rouge; Mark Slater, from Northampton, David Wilson from Australia and Frenchman Jean-Michel Braquet were abducted from a train three months ago.

3. London: The government drops plans for privatising the Post Office.

3. Paris: Paris Match reveals President François Mitterrand has a daughter by his mistress.

10. Sri Lanka: Prime Minister Chandrika Kumaratunga is elected President.

13. Massachusetts: A 79-year-old golfer drops dead after shooting his first-ever hole-in-one.

15. Jakarta: The 18 member nations of the Asia-Pacific Economic forum agree to create the world's largest free-trade zone by the year 2020.

16. Kiev: The Ukrainian parliament ratifies the Nuclear Nonproliferation Treaty.

21. Britain: Red Rum, the only horse to win the Grand National three times, is retired from public life at the age of 29.

23. Sarajevo: NATO fighters strike at Bosnian Serb SAM missile batteries; the Serbs continue their defiance pressing on with an attack on Bihac (→19/12).

28. Oslo: Norwegian voters say "nei" to the European Union in a referendum.

28. London: John Major wins a vital vote on increasing Britain's contributions to the EU, but eight Tories refuse to back the Bill and have the Whip withdrawn from them.

30. Indian Ocean: The Italian cruise liner Achille Lauro, hijacked by Palestinian terrorists in 1985, catches fire and sinks.

DEATHS

18. Cab Calloway, American jazz singer and bandleader (*23/12/1907).

29. Grand Ayatollah Mohammed Ali Araki, spiritual leader of the world's 100 million Shia Moslems (*1884).

Voters stun Bill Clinton

Nov 9. President Clinton was humiliated in yesterday's Congressional elections, with the Republicans winning control of both houses for the first time in 40 years.

In the Senate, 53 of the 100 seats are now Republican, and in the House, there are now 230 Republicans against 204 Democrats. Voters also turned out Democratic governors, including New York's Mario Cuomo, defeated by George Pataki. A majority of the statehouses are now Republican. The victors say the results are a rebuke by the voters to Bill Clinton. The President said today, "They sent us a clear message – I got it." He now faces a rough ride, especially from the combative Newt Gingrich, who is expected to be the next Speaker.

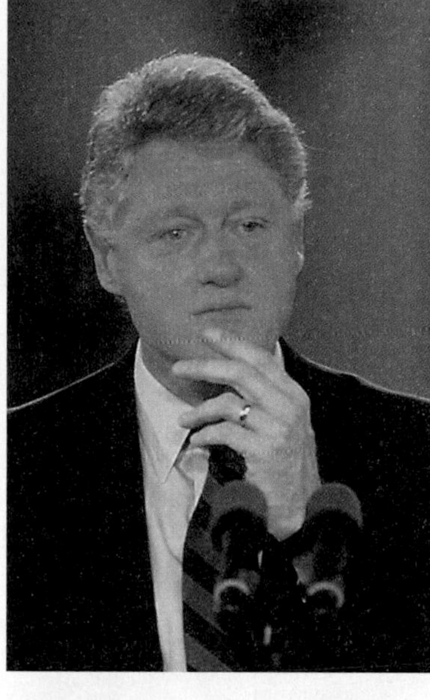

Dublin government falls amid turmoil

Nov 17. Ireland was again plunged into political turmoil today when Prime Minister Albert Reynolds resigned, saying it was "for the good of the nation". Reynolds had struggled for five days to save his government following the withdrawal of the Labour Party from the ruling coalition in protest against the appointment of Harry Whelehan, former Attorney General, as President of the High Court. Dick Spring, leader of the Labour Party, had objected to Whelehan's delay in extraditing a paedophile Roman Catholic priest to Northern Ireland. Dublin politics have a touch of farce about them, but this affair is serious; Reynolds's departure could harm the Irish peace process (→15/12).

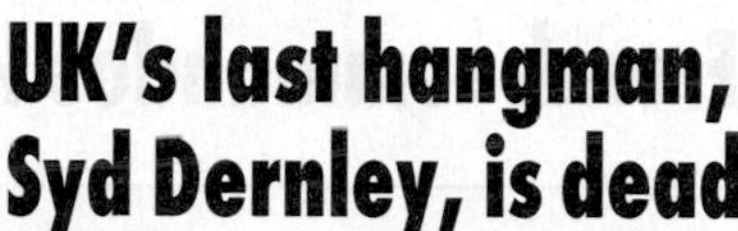

UK's last hangman, Syd Dernley, is dead

Nov 1. Syd Dernley, apprentice hangman to Albert Pierrepoint and Britain's last surviving executioner, died in Mansfield today. He was 73. A colliery welder, Dernley took part in the execution of 23 men, including Timothy Evans, who was posthumously pardoned. Dernley had a macabre sense of humour and boasted that he and Pierrepoint had carried out the fastest hanging on record, that of James Inglis. It took just seven seconds.

Millions chase first UK lottery jackpot

Nov 19. The winning numbers in Britain's first National Lottery came up in a TV extravaganza tonight as gambling fever seized the nation; but, much to the organisers' chagrin, no single ticket-holder claimed the jackpot.

Instead, the £15.8 million prize was shared by seven punters who selected the winning line. It is estimated that about 25 million people bought tickets, putting £45 million in the kitty.

A fragile peace pact is signed in Angola

Nov 20. UNITA rebels and the Angolan government signed a peace treaty under Zambian auspices in Lusaka today, but there are serious doubts that the civil war will really come to an end.

Fighting continues and UNITA leader Jonas Savimbi did not attend the signing ceremony. The rebels claimed he was unable to leave Angola because the airports in the areas they control are being bombarded by government forces.

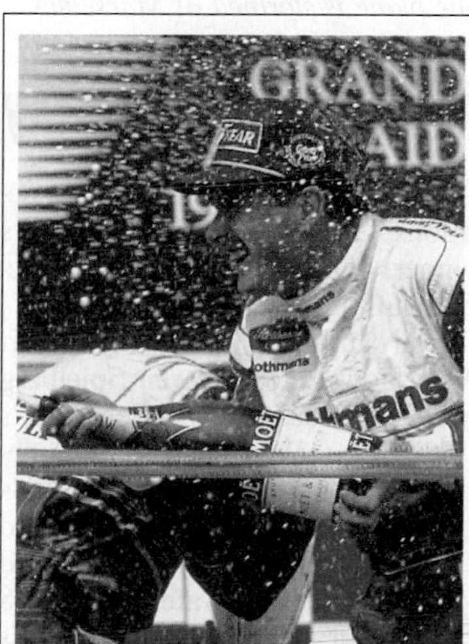

Nov 13. Nigel Mansell wins the Australian Grand Prix, but Michael Schumacher takes the Formula One world title on points.

Nov 5. By George! George Foreman, 45, beats Michael Moorer, 27, to regain the world heavyweight title he lost to Muhammed Ali 20 years ago.

1994

DECEMBER

Su	Mo	Tu	We	Th	Fr	Sa
				1	2	3
4	5	6	7	8	9	10
11	12	13	14	15	16	17
18	19	20	21	22	23	24
25	26	27	28	29	30	31

1. Paris: On World AIDS Day, delegates from 42 nations say that fighting the disease must be a political priority.

4. Moscow: Sweden wins the Davis Cup for the fifth time.

6. Windsor: The Queen allows a Canadian firm to prospect for oil in the grounds of Windsor castle.

9. Belfast: British officials meet representatives of Sinn Fein for their first formal talks in 22 years (→ 15/1/95).

13. Winhoek: President Sam Nujoma is re-elected.

15. Dublin: John Bruton is elected Taoiseach.

15. London: Diane Modahl, former 800 metres Commonwealth gold medalist, is banned for four years after failing drug tests.

20. Prague: Czech police say they have seized 6.6 pounds of smuggled weapons-grade uranium.

22. Brussels: Belgium, Germany, France, Portugal, Luxembourg, Spain and the Netherlands agree to end border controls in March 1995.

30. Israel: The Jewish Agency says that 78,000 immigrants, 66,000 of them from the former Soviet Union, settled in Israel this year.

31. Europe: At midnight Austria, Finland and Sweden join the European Union, bringing its membership to 15.

DEATHS

18. Lord Pitt, Labour politician (*3/10/1913).

20. Dean Rusk, US statesman (*9/2/1909).

24. John Osborne, actor and playwright (*12/12/1929).

HITS OF 1994

Parklife

Compliments on Your Kiss

Crazy for You

QUOTE OF THE YEAR

"You lived to tell the tale, did you?"

Prince Charles, to a man who said he had met Princess Diana.

Russian troops storm into Chechenia

Dec 11. Russian tanks and artillery rolled across the Chechen border today after two weeks of bombing had failed to bring the breakaway Russian territory to heel. President Yeltsin had made it plain that he would use force when the Chechen leader, General Dzhokar Dudayev, defeated an attempt to topple him by the Russian-backed opponents of his rule. Now it seems that Boris Yeltsin is following the old Soviet tactic of steam-rollering employed in Hungary and Czechoslovakia. He might find himself in difficulties, however, for the Chechens are fierce guerrilla warriors, and the Russian army is not the power it was. There are already reports of disaffection among the Russian conscripts sent into Chechenia (→ 24/1/95).

In Grozny, Chechen separatist fighters face Russian air and artillery attacks.

Carter negotiates a cease-fire in Bosnia

Dec 19. Former US President Jimmy Carter appears to have brought off a surprising coup. He emerged from several hours of talks in the Bosnian Serb stronghold of Pale today with an offer of a four-month cease-fire from the Serb leader Radovan Karadzic. Carter said the Serbs had "agreed to an immediate cease-fire and to negotiate a lasting cession of hostilities." He is due to return to Sarajevo tonight to present the Serb offer to the Bosnian government (→ 1/1/95).

French commandos kill Algerian hijackers

The plane is stormed at Marseilles.

Dec 26. French commandos have killed four Algerian Islamic fanatics who hijacked an Air France Airbus in Algiers on Christmas Eve.

The crowded A300 was flown to Marseilles after a 40-hour stand-off in Algiers during which the hijackers murdered three hostages. It is believed the hijackers' plan was to dive the plane into the heart of Paris, but the commandos stormed the jet, shot the terrorists and freed the 173 passengers. Thirteen passengers were injured in the shoot-out along with three crew members and nine of the police commandos.

Arts in 1994: a good year for controversy

Antonio Canova's "Three Graces".

The Booker Prize lived up to expectations with a splendid row over its winner, **James Kelman**, the Glaswegian author who uses the "F-word" liberally in his novel "How Late It Was, How Late". **Steven Spielberg** swept the Oscars with "Schindler's List". "Four Weddings and a Funeral" was a hit as was **Diana Rigg's** "Medea". The British Museum paid £1 million for the Tyndale bible, and computer king **Bill Gates** paid $30.8 million for Leonardo da Vinci's scientific treatise. The "Three Graces" was saved for the nation but **Elizabeth Esteve-Coll**, one of its saviours, resigned as director of the Victoria and Albert.

Silvio Berlusconi out as coalition falls

Dec 22. Italy is again in political crisis today following the resignation of Prime Minister Silvio Berlusconi, who threw in his hand rather than face a no-confidence vote.

President Oscar Scalfaro must decide whether to call new elections or appoint a Prime Minister to head a transitional government which would reform the electoral system before a new poll. Berlusconi, who will act as caretaker premier until the President has decided, wants spring elections, but his opponents want the system reformed before Italy votes again (→ 13/1/95).

1995

JANUARY

Su	Mo	Tu	We	Th	Fr	Sa
1	2	3	4	5	6	7
8	9	10	11	12	13	14
15	16	17	18	19	20	21
22	23	24	25	26	27	28
29	30	31				

1. Birmingham: Accused serial killer Frederick West, awaiting trial for the murder of 12 young women, is found hanged in his cell at Winson Green Prison.

1. Sarajevo: A four-month cease-fire goes into effect in Bosnia (→23).

1. Hawaii: Astronomers find the most distant known galaxy, some 15 billion light years away from Earth.

2. Belfast: The main debating chamber of Stormont, Northern Ireland's former parliament, is gutted by fire.

4. Washington: The mother of Republican House Speaker Newt Gingrich reveals in a television interview that her son once called Hillary Clinton "a bitch".

8. Sri Lanka: A truce between government forces and Tamil rebels goes into effect.

10. Madrid: Premier Felipe Gonzalez denies government involvement in the "dirty war" waged against Basque separatists in the 80s.

13. Rome: Former Treasury Minister Lamberto Dini is appointed Premier.

15. Belfast: British troops end daytime patrols (→22/2).

23. Sarajevo: Lt-Gen Sir Michael Rose is replaced by Lt-Gen Rupert Smith as commander of UN troops in Bosnia (→6/4).

27. Manchester: Eric Cantona, Manchester United's French forward, is barred for the rest of the season and fined £20,000 by his club for having attacked a fan who insulted him.

DEATHS

2. Mohammed Siad Barre, former President of Somalia (*c. 1914).

6. Joe Slovo, chairman of the South African Communist Party (*23/5/1926).

7. Harry Golombek, British chess grandmaster (*1/3/1911).

7. Larry Grayson, British comedian (*31/8/1923).

22. Rose Kennedy, matriarch of the Kennedy clan (*22/7/1890).

Thousands killed by Kobe earthquake

Jan 17. A devastating earthquake struck the city of Kobe, in Japan's industrial heartland, early this morning. It is feared that at least 4,000 people are dead. The 20-second shock rippled expressways and railway lines as if they were soft toffee. Supposedly earthquake-proof buildings collapsed into tangles of concrete and steel rods. Scores of fires, fed by fractured gas pipes, are raging out of control, and firefighters are hampered by blocked roads and broken water mains. After-shocks sent damaged buildings crashing on people trapped in the ruins of their homes. Whole areas have been reduced to ashes and rubble, and the authorities seem powerless in the face of this disaster.

Russians launch fierce attack on Grozny

Grozny's presidential palace in ruins.

Jan 24. Russian tanks and artillery opened up with their big guns on Grozny today after four days of relative quiet. Shells hammered into the broken streets of the Chechen capital as the Russian forces tried to block support reaching the guerrillas holed up in the rubble of the presidential palace.

The Chechen fighters are slipping through the streets in small parties to pick off Russian tanks that come too close to their positions. The Russians, for the most part, are content to keep out of harm's way and use their guns at long range to pound the city while they prepare their final assault (→24/3).

Clinton tries to solve Mexico's peso crisis

Jan 31. Bypassing Congressional opposition to his $40 billion plan to rescue Mexico's economy, US President Bill Clinton today vowed to create a $20 billion line of credit to help the country pay its growing foreign debt.

This emergency aid would be supplemented by a $30 billion line of credit from the IMF and the central banks of wealthy industrial nations. The Mexican financial crisis is seen as a threat to the stability of the US dollar and other major Western currencies. "We cannot risk further delay," stressed the President.

Peter Cook, genius of satire, dies at 57

Jan 9. Peter Cook, the anarchic satirist and comedian, died today of a gastro-intestinal haemorrhage, the result of a lifestyle which, he said, involved drinking "two large screwdrivers and smoking a packet of cigarettes for breakfast".

Cook became famous in 1959 in "Beyond the Fringe" with his great friend, Dudley Moore. "He had a verbal wit that was second to none," says Moore; "he lived his life as he wanted, on his own terms, which meant he led a great, extraordinary life." Peter Cook was 57.

Peru, Ecuador ready to open peace talks

Jan 31. Peru and Ecuador seem to be shadowboxing their way towards peace in their war over a remote patch of jungle. Ecuador announced today that it has accepted a cease-fire in order to allow time to seek a peaceful solution to the border dispute. Peru is dragging its heels but is expected to join in the cease-fire set up by the mediation of Argentina, Brazil, Chile and the United States. The Pope and other foreign leaders have also appealed for an end to an unexpected conflict which has cost dozens of lives (→17/2).

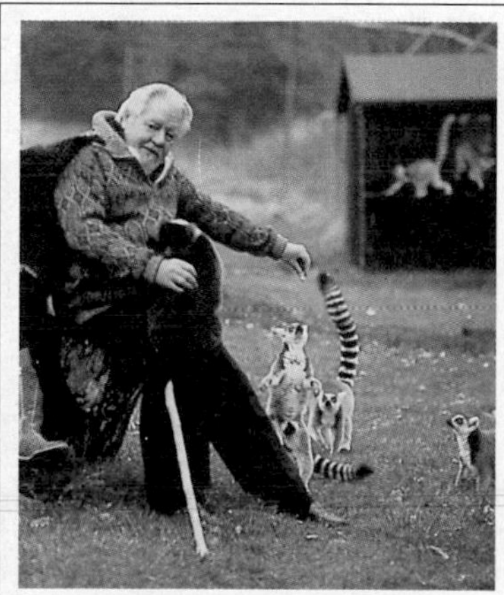

Jan 30. British writer, zoo pioneer and conservationist Gerald Durrell (*7/1/1925), author of more than 35 books, dies.

1995

FEBRUARY

Su	Mo	Tu	We	Th	Fr	Sa
			1	2	3	4
5	6	7	8	9	10	11
12	13	14	15	16	17	18
19	20	21	22	23	24	25
26	27	28				

1. Coventry: Jill Phipps, an animal-rights protester, dies when she falls under the wheels of a lorry carrying live calves for export.

2. Netherlands: A total of 240,000 people have been evacuated from eastern and central regions due to fears that flooding could destroy dikes.

7. London: Junior Scottish Industry Minister Allan Stewart resigns after accusations that he brandished a pickaxe during a confrontation with an anti-motorway protester.

7. Poland: Jozef Olesky is appointed Prime Minister.

9. Barbados: Frenchman Guy Delage arrives after having swum and drifted on a raft across the Atlantic.

9. Space: Michael Foale, a member of the shuttle Discovery's crew, becomes the first Briton to walk in space.

10. Alma Ata: A visibly unwell Boris Yeltsin attends a CIS summit.

13. Dresden: The Duke of Kent attends ceremonies marking the 50th anniversary of the Allied bombing of the city.

14. London: Oscar Wilde is admitted to Poets' Corner in Westminster Abbey.

17. Brasilia: Peru and Ecuador sign a formal cease-fire accord.

20. London: The rock group Blur wins four Brit Awards.

22. Paris: France asks the US to recall five Americans for spying.

22. Algiers: Nearly 100 inmates are killed by security forces during a prison riot.

26. Cambridge: Scientists reveal that an iceberg the size of Oxfordshire has broken away from Antarctica.

DEATHS

2. Fred Perry, British tennis player (*18/5/1909).

5. Patricia Highsmith, US thriller writer (*1/1/1921).

20. Robert Bolt, British playwright (*24/12/1933).

23. James Herriot, British author and vet (*3/10/1916).

London and Dublin present a plan for peace in Northern Ireland

Feb 22. British Prime Minister John Major and his Irish counterpart, John Bruton, presented their framework document for the future of Northern Ireland in Belfast today. Among its provisions are the establishment of a legislative assembly and an end to Dublin's constitutional claim to the province.

The document has received widespread support despite the predictably bitter reaction of the Ulster Unionists, who regard it as a "sell-out". Major promised the province would remain part of the UK as long as its people wished. He also urged them to read the document, "study it, talk about it, think of the prize at the end" (→9/3).

British and Irish leaders launch their crucial framework document in Belfast.

Ferocious Taleban fighters appear set to capture Afghan capital

Feb 14. Talebans, the "Students of Islam", a formidable army of young radicals which has stormed through a third of Afghanistan in only six months, is sitting just outside Kabul, the frightened capital, preparing for an assault which threatens to sweep away the government's garrison.

The young fighters, trained in Islamic schools in Pakistan, have already dealt with the powerful warlord, Gulbuddin Hekmatyar, who fled from his base at Charasyab, 15 miles from Kabul, leaving behind his clothes and personal papers. The white-turbanned Taleban fighters now aim to take control of the rest of the country.

The well armed Islamic guerrillas already control the mountains around Kabul.

RAF presents its first woman bomber pilot

Feb 21. Flight Lieutenant Jo Salter, of 617 "the Dambusters" squadron, showed off her flying skills today, taking off from Lossiemouth and easing her Tornado past a lumbering Hercules filled with pressmen.

Britain's first woman combat pilot, Salter, 26, rejected suggestions that frontline service-women lacked aggression: "I never feel fear, and I expect to go into combat when required like any other member of the armed forces." She has been trained, like her male counterparts, to manoeuvre her £20 million aircraft 20 metres above the waves to deliver long-range Sea Eagle missiles at enemy ships. She insists: "I'm just one of the boys."

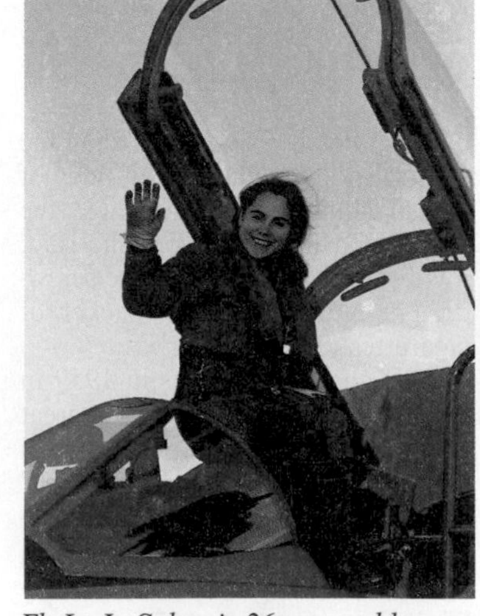

Flt Lt Jo Salter is 26 years old.

Feb 2. Blue-eyed, bald film villain Donald Pleasance (*5/10/1919), shown here in "Spare the Rod", dies near Nice, in France.

1995

MARCH

Su	Mo	Tu	We	Th	Fr	Sa
			1	2	3	4
5	6	7	8	9	10	11
12	13	14	15	16	17	18
19	20	21	22	23	24	25
26	27	28	29	30	31	

3. Westminster: The House of Commons votes in favour of banning all forms of hunting.

5. London: The Dutch group ING wins control of Barings for just £1.

6. London: Public Service and Science Minister Robert Hughes admits an extra-marital affair and resigns.

9. Belfast: During her first visit to Ulster since the IRA cease-fire, the Queen praises the "courage and compassion" of its people (→ 17).

10. London: A study says alcoholism has reached "pandemic proportions" in Russia.

11. Washington: Pentagon official John Deutch is appointed CIA director.

17. London: Sterling hits a record low against the German mark, at 2.1890.

17. Washington: Sinn Fein leader Gerry Adams attends a White House St Patrick's Day reception (→ 4/4).

18. Twickenham: England beat Scotland 24-12 to win the Five Nations rugby championship.

22. Kazakhstan: Russian cosmonaut Valeri Polyakov lands after a record 438 days in space.

24. Chechenia: Russian forces surround Achkhoi-Martan, one of the few rebel bases still operating (→ 10/5).

25. US: Former world heavyweight champion Mike Tyson is freed after serving a three-year sentence for rape.

26. Europe: Seven of the 15 EU states abolish border controls under the Schengen accord; the other states are due to follow, except for Britain, which insists on keeping its barriers.

DEATHS

13. Odette Hallowes, wartime heroine of the Special Operations Executive (*28/4/1912).

16. Lord Lovat, wartime commando leader (*9/7/1911).

17. Ronnie Kray, London underworld figure (*17/10/1933).

Young trader, accused of bankrupting Barings Bank, is detained

March 2. Nick Leeson, 28, the financial dealer whose multi-million pound gambles on the high-return, high-risk derivatives market in Singapore have bankrupted Barings Bank, was arrested at Frankfurt airport today when he arrived from Borneo. He and his wife had flown openly despite a week-long international manhunt during which they were rumoured to have fled Singapore aboard a luxury yacht.

He was apparently making his way to London, preferring to face a British court rather than stand trial in Singapore. It is still not certain what charges he will face, because it remains unclear how far his gambling was sanctioned by Barings.

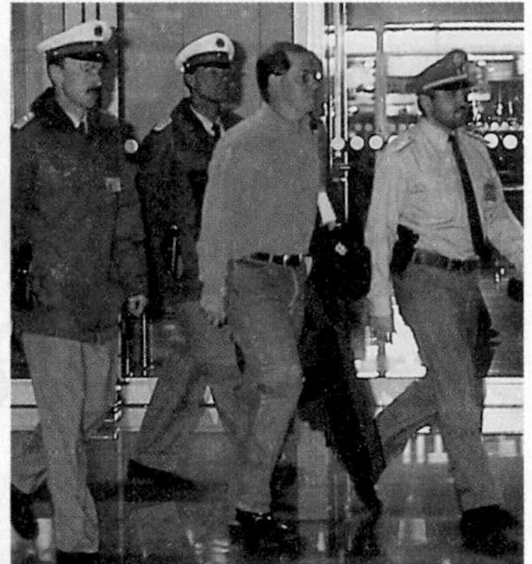

Nick Leeson at Frankfurt airport.

The results have been disastrous for the bank, one of Britain's oldest and most respected investment houses. It now seems likely it will be bought, along with its debts of £650 million, by the Dutch ING group. The price: just £1.

Barings was very much an upper-crust bank, with the Royal Family among its clients. The irony of it being brought down by a young man from a council house is exciting much comment (→ 5).

Sect blamed in Tokyo tube gas drama

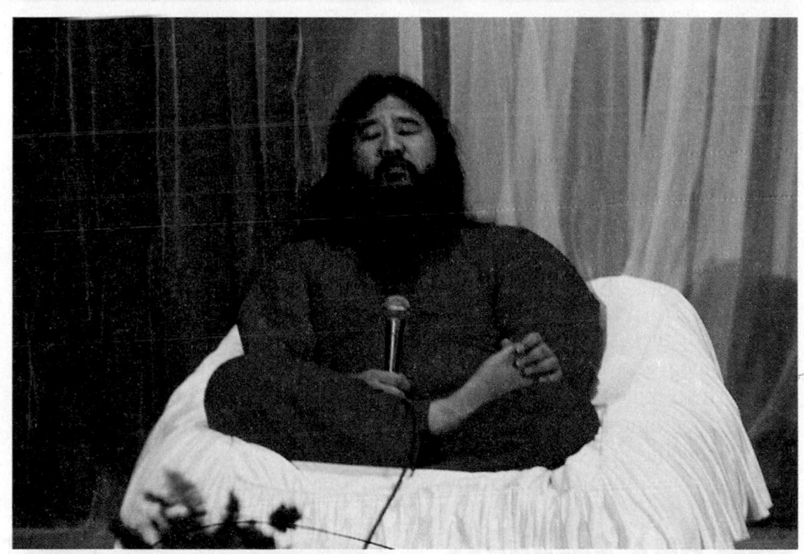

Police are searching for Shoko Asahara, guru of the Aum Supreme Truth sect.

March 21. Police raided the Tokyo headquarters of the Aum Shinrikyo (Supreme Truth) religious sect today searching for evidence to link the mysterious cult to the release yesterday of the deadly nerve gas Sarin on five trains in the Tokyo underground system.

The gas used in the horrific attack, which has so far killed eight people and affected over 4,000, was developed in Germany during the Second World War. It kills horribly within five minutes of a tiny amount being absorbed through the skin or the lungs. Suspicion centres on the Aum sect, which is led by Shoko Asahara and has thousands of members in Japan and Russia. Asahara is now believed to be in hiding (→ 16/5).

March 21. The Queen, on her first visit to South Africa since 1947, meets Archbishop Desmond Tutu at St George's Cathedral in Cape Town before attending a service held to mark the country's first Human Rights Day.

Turkey launches big raid against Kurds

March 20. Some 35,000 Turkish troops, supported by tanks and fighter-bombers, crossed the undefended border between Turkey and northern Iraq today in a major attempt to crush the separatist rebels of the Kurdistan Workers Party (PKK). A military spokesman confirmed that the army had penetrated 25 miles into Iraqi territory along a 130-mile front in pursuit of an estimated 2,800 PKK fighters. The rebels have been raiding into Turkey from their havens among the Kurdish refugees. The spokesman said: "We will not leave until the terrorists are wiped out."

1995

APRIL

Su	Mo	Tu	We	Th	Fr	Sa
						1
2	3	4	5	6	7	8
9	10	11	12	13	14	15
16	17	18	19	20	21	22
23	24	25	26	27	28	29
30						

2. London: Dionicio Ceron of Mexico wins the London marathon; the women's race is won by Malgorzata Sobaska of Poland.

2. Gaza: Kamal Kahil, a leader of the extremist Islamic group Hamas, is killed in a bomb explosion (→9/5).

4. London: Armed Forces Minister Nicholas Soames says that the RAF will end its nuclear capability in 1998.

4. Washington: John Major and Bill Clinton bury the hatchet as the US President expresses strong support for Major's approach to the Irish issue (→10/5).

6. Sydney: Australians celebrate the centenary of their unofficial anthem, "Waltzing Matilda".

6. Sarajevo: On the third anniversary of the outbreak of war in Bosnia, Prime Minister Haris Siladzic says: "We must be prepared to fight for 10 years" (→2/5).

6. Southampton: The Queen christens the Oriana, P&O's new luxury liner.

7. Edinburgh: In the Scottish local elections, only 81 Tory councillors are elected out of a total of more than 1,100.

8. Georgia: British-born Nicholas Ingram is executed for murder.

8. Aintree: Royal Athlete, a 40-1 outsider, wins the Grand National.

16. Tahiti: Marlon Brando's 25-year-old daughter, Cheyenne, commits suicide.

21. London: Lady Thatcher is appointed a Lady Companion of the Order of the Garter.

22. Rwanda: Hundreds of Hutu refugees are massacred by government troops in Kibeho camp.

30. Sheffield: Stephen Hendry wins the Embassy World Snooker Championship.

DEATHS

14. Kenny Everett, British comedian and disc jockey (*25/12/1944).

16. Arthur English, British comedian (*9/5/1919).

Terrorism hits Oklahoma

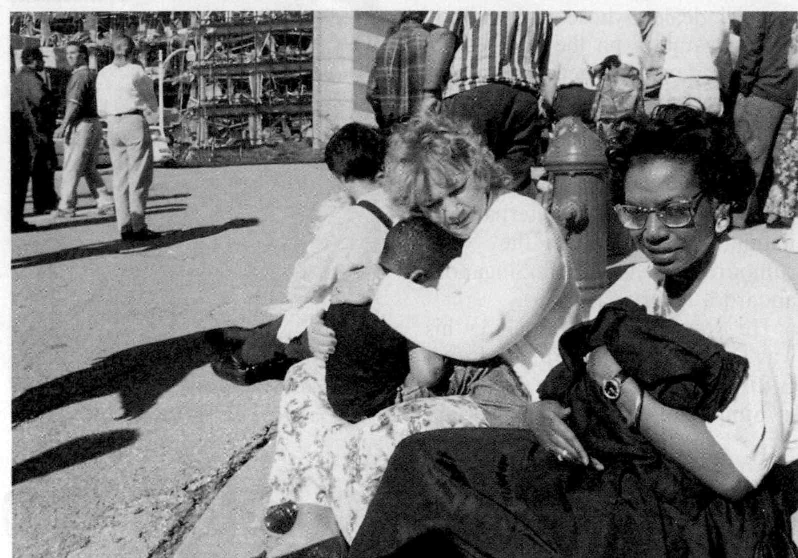

The huge bomb blast completely gutted Oklahoma City's federal building.

April 21. Americans, unused to bloody terrorist acts on their home turf, are still in a state of shock today, 48 hours after the worst bomb outrage the nation has ever known. As rescue teams continue to search the rubble of the federal building in Oklahoma City gutted by a huge car bomb, flags are flying at half mast throughout the US.

FBI agents investigating the attack, which killed more than 100 people, including 15 children, today announced the arrest of a key suspect. He was named as Timothy McVeigh, a 27-year-old former soldier with far-right political views. Investigators, who initially suspected that the bombing was linked to Middle East terrorists or the Colombian drug cartels, are now focusing on paramilitary "patriotic" US militia groups. These militias are often anti-Semitic and white-supremacist. The FBI believes that the slender, crew-cut McVeigh, who is refusing to cooperate with police and claims to be a "prisoner of war", was either directly involved with or influenced by these groups (→5/5).

Peter Wright, MI5's 'Spycatcher', dead

April 27. Peter Wright, the former senior MI5 officer and best-selling author of "Spycatcher", died in Tasmania today. He was born in Chesterfield on August 9, 1916. Wright, who had been living beyond the jurisdiction of British courts, caused a furore in 1986 when the Thatcher government launched a campaign to stop publication of his memoirs, which include revelations about illegal activities by MI5 in Britain. Peter Wright also remained convinced to his dying day that former MI5 head Sir Roger Hollis was a Soviet agent. The bid to ban his book ended ignominiously in 1988.

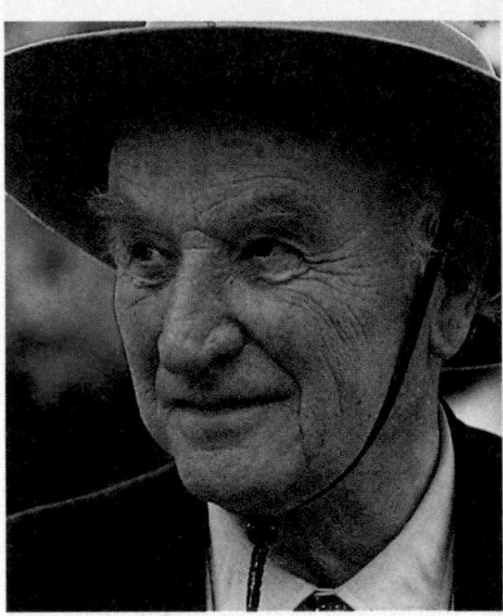

The controversial author was 78.

First DNA database inaugurated in UK

April 10. The world's first nationwide DNA database officially went into operation today. The computerised facility, based in Birmingham, was inaugurated by Home Secretary Michael Howard, who called it "the biggest breakthrough since fingerprinting". Under the new Criminal Justice Act, police will be able to forcibly take hair or saliva samples from anyone charged with a recordable offence. Up to five million of such records are expected to be stored in the database. A mass DNA testing operation is to begin tomorrow in Cardiff in an attempt to identify the man who raped and murdered 15-year-old Claire Hood. The killer left semen, and the police now have his genetic fingerprint.

April 25. The dream team: Fred Astaire dances with the graceful Ginger Rogers (*16/7/1911), who died today at her California home.

Clause Four victory for Labour's leader

April 29. Tony Blair has finally won the bitter six-month battle to scrap Clause Four of the Labour Party's constitution, which commits the party to state ownership of the means of production.

Delegates at a special Labour conference at Central Hall, in Westminster, voted 65 per cent in favour of rewriting the clause. Despite failing to win the backing of two of his party's largest affiliate unions, Unison and the transport workers, Blair managed to convince delegates to commit Labour to a mixed economy with a thriving private sector. A jubilant Tony Blair said after the vote: "Today a new Labour Party is being born. Our task now is nothing less than the rebirth of our nation."

1995

MAY

Su	Mo	Tu	We	Th	Fr	Sa
	1	2	3	4	5	6
7	8	9	10	11	12	13
14	15	16	17	18	19	20
21	22	23	24	25	26	27
28	29	30	31			

2. Croatia: As the UN-brokered four-month cease-fire expires, rebel Serb troops launch a major attack on Zagreb (→31).

4. Britain: The Tories are routed in local elections, taking control of only eight of the 346 councils at stake.

5. Oklahoma City: The final toll of the terrorist bombing is put at 167 dead.

9. Washington: Senator Robert Dole causes a furore by proposing that the US embassy in Israel be moved fom Tel Aviv to Jerusalem.

9. Moscow: John Major attends ceremonies marking the 50th anniversary of the end of the Great Patriotic War.

10. Moscow: President Yeltsin rejects a call by Bill Clinton that Russian troops pull out of Chechenia.

10. Belfast: The government holds the first ministerial talks with Sinn Fein in 23 years (→25).

11. London: Lord Nolan presents a report on the standards of public life aimed at cleaning up "sleaze" at Westminster.

13. Nepal: British climber Alison Hargreaves becomes the first woman to conquer Everest alone and without oxygen.

13. San Diego: New Zealand yacht Black Magic 1 routs Young America to win a 5-0 victory in the America's Cup.

14. Argentina: President Carlos Menem is re-elected.

15. Britain: In a survey, a large majority of officers reject the routine arming of police.

16. Japan: Shoko Asahara, guru of the Aum cult, is arrested.

26. South Africa: In the Rugby Union World Cup, Scottish captain Gavin Hastings scores a world record 44 points against the Ivory Coast.

28. Russia: A massive earthquake kills an estimated 2,000 people on Sakhalin Island.

31. Dublin: Prince Charles becomes the first member of the royal family to make an official visit to Ireland since 1911.

Crisis in Bosnia reaches a flashpoint

May 31. President Clinton took a reluctant but far-reaching step into the Bosnian quagmire today when he announced that he was prepared to offer NATO the "temporary use" of US ground troops in Bosnia. He has previously offered to send Marines to assist in a withdrawal of UN peacekeepers, but his commitment today to help in the "reconfiguration and strengthening" of UN forces has led him to the brink of involving US troops in any clash between NATO and the Serbs.

Meanwhile, John Major received the cautious support of Parliament for his decision to beef up Britain's forces in Bosnia after he told MPs that he would not give in to Serb blackmail. His statement came just days after Bosnian Serbs seized more than 350 UN peacekeepers and military observers, including 33 soldiers of the Royal Welch Fusiliers guarding the UN "safe haven" of Gorazde. London, Washington and Paris have reacted with outrage to the Serbs' decision to use 20 of these hostages as human shields, chained up at potential NATO targets. The US Navy has rushed a carrier group and 2,000 Marines to the Adriatic amid talk of a possible hostage rescue attempt.

Human shield: a UN peacekeeper.

Chirac's victory ends long Mitterrand era

May 8. Fourteen years of Socialist rule by François Mitterrand ended last night as Jacques Chirac won the French presidential election at his third attempt. The 78-year-old Mitterrand leaves office a dying man, marked by several scandals involving some of his associates and revelations of his wartime commitment to the Vichy government. Chirac, a right-wing Gaullist who has been mayor of Paris for 17 years, appeared at the Hôtel de Ville last night to tell his supporters that he would be president of "all the French".

Clinton urges IRA to heed Britain's calls

May 25. Bill Clinton took a political gamble by inviting Gerry Adams, the Sinn Fein leader, to the White House, but he showed signs of irritation today when he asked Adams to "begin to discuss the decommissioning of weapons." Addressing a conference on investment in Ireland, he insisted that the IRA and other groups had to abandon their guns for good. The conference was attended by Adams and Sir Patrick Mayhew, the Northern Ireland secretary, who shook hands with the Sinn Fein leader yesterday.

Deadly Ebola virus on rampage in Zaire

May 28. The virulent Ebola fever, which kills its victims within hours by destroying their internal organs, struck again today when an Italian nun, who had been caring for the sick, died at Kikwit, east of the Zairian capital, Kinshasa. She was the sixth nun to succumb, and her death brings the known number of casualties to 153. The Geneva-based World Health Organisation has announced, however, that the epidemic's most acute stage is over. Researchers are now trying to trace the source of this outbreak.

May 8. As more than 250,000 people cheer and sing "For She's a Jolly Good Fellow" and "Rule Britannia", the Queen Mum, flanked by the Queen and Princess Margaret, marks the 50th anniversary of VE-Day.

May 24. The Labour Party's four-time general election winner, Harold Wilson (*11/3/1916), dies.

General Index

This index provides rapid access to the information you seek. Each entry is followed by a date indicating the month and year of an event.

A

Abbado, Claudio 12/89
Abbas, Ferhat 8/46
Abbas, Mohammed 10/85
Abd al-Aziz, Sultan of Morocco 5/03, 8/08
Abdul Aziz, Saud ibn 10/62, 11/64, 2/69
Abdul Hamid II, Sultan of Turkey 7/08, 4/09
Abdullah, Emir of Iraq 5/41
Abdullah, King of Jordan 5/46, 5/48, 4/50, 7/51, 8/52, 5/53, 3/56
Abdullah, Mohammed bin ("Mad Mullah") 2/03
Abel, Rudolph 2/62
Abercrombie, Patrick 11/44
Abernathy, Ralph 3/56, 4/63, 4/68
Aberystwyth
- Welsh National Library 7/11
Abrahams, Harold 7/24, 12/81
Abruzzo, Ben 8/78
Abyssinia
- See also Ethiopia, World War II
- Haile Selassie (Ras Tafari) is crowned 11/30
- Selassie abolishes slavery 4/32
- Italians clash with Abyssinians, Wal Wal 12/34
- Italians bomb two villages 12/34
- Seeks arbitration with Italy; rejected 12/34
- France gives Italy free hand in new deal 1/35
- Asks League to stop Italian annexations 1/35
- Emperor Selassie wants peace 2/35
- Musters 80,000 troops, 12 planes 2/35
- Refuses to negotiate further with Italy 3/35
- Calls for special League meeting 5/35
- Selassie defies Italy; vows to fight 7/35
- Selassie: "Better to die for freedom ..." 7/35
- Kill 40 Italian troops in raid 7/35
- Geneva talks on conflict 8/35
- Selassie offers new concessions to Italy 8/35
- On war footing 8/35
- League appoints five-power committee to arbitrate in crisis 9/35
- Italy demands her disarmament 9/35
- Selassie refuses Italy privileges 9/35
- Invaded by Italy; loses Adowat and Adowa 10/35
- Selassie assembles tribal chiefs 10/35
- League embargoes Italy 10/35
- Confusion as Addis Ababa phone line cut 10/35
- Italy takes Tigre capital 11/35
- Many Italians killed on Sasa Baneh 11/35
- Britain rejects Hoare-Laval pact 12/35
- Italian bombers raze Daggha Bur 1/36
- Italian mustard gas breaks Geneva rules 4/36
- Italy wants vassal status 4/36
- Italy takes Dessye; attacks Addis Ababa 4/36
- Defeated at Mount Aradam, Emperor flees 5/36
- Italy announces annexation 5/36
- Dropped from the League 7/36
- Italy to issue "development bonds" 8/36
- League grants Abyssinia a seat 9/36
- Italians beat 3,000 rebels 2/37
- Italians execute Selassie's son-in-law 2/37
- Britain recognises Italy's annexation 5/38
- Return of Selassie reported 1/41
- South African troops occupy Addis Ababa 4/41
- Selassie enters Addis Ababa 5/41
- Italian viceroy surrenders 5/41
Acheampong, Ignatius 1/72
Acheson, Dean 1/49, 2/49, 5/49, 10/49, 1/50, 6/51
Ackroyd, Peter 12/90
Acton, Harold 2/94
Adair, Alan 8/50
Adam, Kenneth 2/66
Adamec, Ladislas 12/89
Adams, Bryan 10/91
Adams, Daisy 12/93
Adams, Gerry 2/78, 9/78, 10/82, 12/82, 11/83, 3/84, 8/94, 3/95
Adams, Walter 1/67, 3/67
Adams, Wayne 4/89
Adamson, George 8/89
Adamson, Joy 1/61, 1/80, 8/81
Adekunle, Benjamin 8/68
Adelstein, David 3/67, 1/69
Aden
- See also S. Arabian Federation-Yemen
- Anti-British strike breaks out 3/56
- British guards clash with Yemenis 4/56
- British troops, planes repel Yemenis 1/57
- Governor Luce calls state of emergency 5/58
- UK troops fire tear gas at rioters 9/62
Adenauer, Konrad 1/26, 5/49, 8/49, 5/50, 8/50, 1/51, 12/52, 4/53, 9/53, 5/55, 6/55, 9/55, 4/57, 5/57, 9/57, 4/59, 11/59, 1/60, 3/60, 11/61, 2/62, 1/63, 4/63, 10/63, 4/67
Adoula, Cyrille 8/61, 12/61, 1/63
Adulyadej, Bhumibol 6/46
Afghanistan
- British bomb Jellallabad and Kabul 4/19
- Treaty with Russia 2/21
- Independence recognised by Britain 11/21
- Telegraphic links with Britain 3/23
- Rebels attack Kabul; King Amanulla flees 12/28
- Modernising reforms spark mutiny, revolt 12/28
- King restores veil for women 1/29
- King Amanullah abdicates 1/29
- Rebel Nadir Khan becomes King 10/29
- Signs neutrality treaty with USSR 6/31
- Zahir Shah succeeds murdered King Nadir 11/33
- Non-aggression pact: Turkey, Iraq, Iran 12/35
- Admitted to UN 8/46
- Thousands greet Khrushchev 3/60
- Army-backed coup; republic proclaimed 4/73
- Army coup; President Daoud killed 4/78
- KGB involved in violent coup, Kabul 4/78
- Signs friendship treaty with USSR 12/78
- US ambassador shot dead 2/79
- USSR invades 12/79
- New leader Babrak Karmal 12/79
- 80,000 Soviets fighting army and mujahideen 1/80
- World conference condemns USSR invasion 1/80
- Carter to delay SALT over Afghanistan 1/80
- Martial law after rioting, Kabul 2/80
- Rebels attack Soviet convoys 2/80
- US wants Olympic boycott on Afghanistan 3/80
- Tass says Soviets are leaving 6/80
- USSR demands soldier from US embassy 9/80
- Salang Pass fire; hundreds die 11/82
- Bomb at Kabul airport kills 28 8/84
- Agrees timetable for Soviet withdrawal 3/88
- Soviet troops prepare to leave 5/88
- Last of Soviet troops leave after 10-year occupation 2/89
- Mujahedin guerrillas attack city of Jalalabad 3/89
- 15-week siege of Jalalabad ends 6/89
- Kabul falls to Masood's Moslem fighters 4/92
- Women are no longer allowed to appear on television 7/92
- Rival leaders sign accord to end fighting in capital 3/93
- Talebans set to capture Kabul 2/95
Aga Khan III 9/32, 9/35, 1/36, 6/48, 7/57
Aga Khan IV 7/57, 6/81, 6/86
Agar, John 9/45
Agassi, Andre 7/92
Agate, James 12/30, 12/44
Agca, Mehmet Ali 5/81, 7/81, 7/83, 12/83, 6/84, 6/85
Agello, Francesco 4/33
Agnew, Spiro 8/68, 11/68, 2/71, 8/73, 10/73, 4/81
Aguinaldo, Emilio 3/01, 2/64
Ahern, M.J. 2/38
Ahmad, Imam of Yemen 9/62
Ahmed Mirza, Sultan of Persia 7/09
Ahmed, Khandakar Mostaque 8/75
Ahmed, Manzur 5/81
Ahtisaari, Martii 2/94
Ahumada, Jorge 10/74, 3/80
Aidid, Mohammed Farrah 6/93
AIDS
- Immune system disease in homosexuals 12/81
- UK blood donors to be screened for AIDS 3/85
- 18-month-old UK boy dies of AIDS 4/85
- UK allots £1m to counter spread of AIDS 9/85
- WHO says AIDS has become an epidemic 9/85
- US actor Rock Hudson dies of AIDS 10/85
- UK government launches anti-AIDS drive 11/86
- 600 UK troops take test in Kenya 1/87
- Liberace, pianist, dies; AIDS suspected 2/87
- Currie: "Good Christians won't get AIDS" 2/87
- New UK campaign launched 5/87
- One a day dying in UK 8/87
- UK's new explicit anti-AIDS campaign 9/87
- Babies born infected in New York 1/88
- Pope appeals for help for sufferers 12/88
- 1,612 people died of AIDS by the end of 1989 1/90
- More than 3,000 Britons have fully-developed AIDS 3/90
- AIDS cases among heterosexuals have doubled in past year 4/90
- AIDS is main killer of women aged between 20 and 40 7/90
- Rise in heterosexual AIDS cases higher than any other group 10/90
- £42 million awarded to haemophiliacs contaminated with AIDS 12/90
- 40 million likely to have HIV virus by the year 2000 5/91
- Princess Diana attends funeral of friend who died of AIDS 8/91
- US basketball star Earvin "Magic" Johnson has AIDS 11/91
- Freddie Mercury of Queen dies of AIDS 11/91
- Dept of Health says heterosexual cases rose by 50 per cent 1/92
- HIV-virus victims contaminated by NH blood to be compensated 2/92
- Ex-tennis star Arthur Ashe admits being HIV-positive 4/92
- Ballet dancer, Rudolf Nureyev, dies of AIDS 1/93
- Giant condom in Paris for World AIDS Day 12/93
- Four million cases worldwide says World Health Organization 7/94
- World AIDS Day in Paris 12/94
Aimee, Anouk 4/32
Ainsworth, Laura 10/09
Airlines
- See also Aviation, Disasters (air)
- Belgian airline Sabena opens 5/23
- Imperial Airways formed 3/24
- Imperial gets Handley Page Hampstead 10/25
- Lufthansa is formed 1/26
- Cobham's flight portends African route 3/26
- First Imperial Airways service to India 12/26
- Pan Am employs male stewards 1/28
- In-flight film on Universal Air Line 2/29
- Three merge to form TWA 10/30
- Imperial starts route to central Africa 2/31
- Imperial's regular service to Cape Town 4/32
- Air France created 8/33
- Imperial flying-boat arrives in Cairo 2/37
- Imperial must share with British Airways 3/38
- Government criticises Imperial's record 3/38
- John Reith heads Imperial Airways 6/38
- Pan Am begins services to Europe 5/39
- Imperial Airways suspends bookings 9/39
- BOAC formed by merger of Imperial and BA 11/39
- Air France nationalised 4/45
- First civilian flights from Heathrow 1/46
- British European Airways created 8/46
- Commercial flights at Idlewild, New York 7/48
- BSAA to merge with BOAC 3/49
- TWA introduce "Tourist Class" 5/52
- UK air travel prices up 20 per cent 4/53
- German Lufthansa revived 4/55
- BEA fly London to Paris for £10 1/56
- BOAC's regular 707 Atlantic service 10/58
- Pan Am and TWA order supersonic planes 10/63
- Laker forms airline for cut-price tours 2/66
- British Airports Authority formed 4/66
- British Eagle ceases business 11/68
- All BOAC flights grounded by strike 3/69
- British Caledonian Airways named 9/71
- Airlines threaten Seoul boycott 12/71
- Pan Am and TWA scrap Concorde plans 1/73
- British Airways formed 3/74
- Carter approves Laker's "Skytrain" 6/77
- Laker's Skytrain undercuts big airlines 9/77
- Laker plans Australia service 9/77
- Laker Airlines collapses 2/82
- Fares go up after Laker collapse 2/82
- People's Express - transatlantic bargain 5/83
- First Virgin Atlantic flight leaves UK 6/84
- British Airways flotation 1/87
- British Airways to buy Caledonian 7/87
- Inquiry into BA's Caledonian takeover 8/87
- Fear of terrorist bombs hits air travel business 2/91
- Pan Am ceases operations after financial rescue plan fails 12/91
Aitken, W.M.
- See Beaverbrook
Akhromeyev, Sergei 12/88
Akihito, Emperor of Japan 1/89, 11/90
Akii-Bua, John 9/72
Al-Fayed brothers 4/87
Al-Ghashmi, Ahmed 6/78
Al-Majali, Habis 9/70
Al-Majid, Ali Hassabn 3/91
Al-Sabah, Sheikh Saad al-Jaber 8/90, 2/91, 3/91
Al-Sharaa, Farouk 10/91
Alain-Fournier, Henri 9/14, 12/18
Alaska
- See also USA
- US-UK commission to set frontier 1/03
- Commission sits 10/03
- Harding tours state 7/23
- US House approves statehood 5/58
- Whales stranded in ice 10/88
- Tanker spills 11 million gallons of oil off Alaskan coast 3/89
Albania
- See also World Wars I and II
- Italians bombard Point Medua 10/11
- Turkey grants Albania autonomy 8/12
- Declares independence from Turkey 11/12
- First cabinet revolt; Italians invade 12/12
- General Toptani calls for autonomy 5/13
- 3,000 occupy Dibra in Serbia 9/13
- Mobilises for war with Greece 4/14
- Essad Pasha deported 5/14
- Rebels besiege Durazzo; civil war looms 6/14
- Ahmed Zog crowns himself King Zog I 9/28
- Italian troops seize Tirana 4/39
- King Zog flees 4/39
- Revolt against Italian occupation 8/40
- Greeks capture Chimera 12/40
- 600 Italians die in clashes with rebels 12/42
- Italian troops start to withdraw 6/43
- Soviet troops cross border 9/44
- Yugoslav partisans cross border 9/44
- Allies recognise Hoxha government 11/44
- Zog ousted; people's republic declared 1/46
- Protests to US about UK mine-sweeping 11/46
- British plane shot down 1/58
- Death of ex-King Zog 4/61
- Eight Soviet submarines leave 6/61
- Banished from Soviet bloc 10/61
- USSR severs relations 12/61
- Says it will leave Warsaw Pact 9/69
- China cancels aid 7/78
- Premier Shehu killed in party shooting 1/82
- Death of Enver Hoxha 4/85
- Ramiz Alia to succeed Hoxha 5/85
- Serbs and Albanians clash 7/90
- 22-day general strike brings down hardline government 6/91
- Sadi Berisha is elected first non-Communist President 4/92
Albee, Edward 7/66
Albert, Archduke of Hungary 1/26
Albert, Duke of York 1/23
Albert, King of Belgium 11/06, 10/14, 12/14, 9/18, 8/20, 2/34
Alberto, Carlos 6/70
Alcock, John 6/19
Aldington, Lord (Toby) 11/89
Aldridge, John 11/89
Aldrin, Edwin (Buzz) 1/30, 11/66, 1/69, 7/69
Alekhine, Alexandre 11/27
Alexander I, King of Yugoslavia 6/03, 8/21, 1/29, 9/31, 10/34
Alexander, Harold 8/42, 6/44, 11/44, 4/45, 7/45, 6/69
Alexandra, Princess of Great Britain 10/60, 4/63, 2/64
Alexandra, Queen of Great Britain 11/05, 2/09, 3/20, 11/25
Alexei, Grand Duke of Russia 8/04, 4/18
Alfonsin, Raul 12/83, 4/87
Alfonso XIII, King of Spain 5/05, 5/06, 3/10, 4/13, 9/23, 6/26, 2/31, 4/31, 12/38, 2/41
Alfred, Duke of Edinburgh 7/00
Algeria
- See also France
- Special Algerian office created, France 4/05
- French repel Moor raid 4/08
- 300 die in severe floods 11/27
- 100 Jews, Arabs die after riots 8/34
- Royal Navy destroys French fleet 7/40
- End of resistance to Allies 11/42
- Giraud becomes French HC for N. Africa 12/42
- Giraud arrests 12 Vichy officials 12/42
- French HC for N. Africa, Darlan, is killed 12/42
- Giraud abolishes anti-semitic laws 3/43
- French provisional government set up 5/43
- De Gaulle to sack Vichy collaborators 6/43
- Giraud is C-in-C of Free French forces 6/43
- George VI arrives to meet Allies 6/43
- French Committee of Liberation set up 6/43
- Allies recognise CFLN 8/43
- De Gaulle opens Consultative Assembly 11/43
- Prov. government of France declared 5/44
- Independent Algerian republic proposed 8/46
- 1,000 feared dead in earthquake 9/54
- Ben Bella nationalists riot in Aures 11/54
- Plan to integrate Algeria with France 1/55
- 500 die in Constantine anti-French fight 8/55
- 100 killed in riot in Philippeville 8/55
- 26 die in rebel attacks 1/56
- Mollet talks with settlers, Arab FLN 2/56
- France airlifts troops to Algeria 3/56
- France dissolves Algerian parliament 4/56
- 19 French soldiers killed on mountain 5/56
- 100 French, 1,000 "loyal" Arabs killed 5/56
- Moslem leader Ali Chekkal killed 5/57
- Ten die in casino bomb blast 6/57
- J.F. Kennedy favours independence 7/57
- Morocco, Tunisia want end to conflict 11/57
- Settlers rebel against Arab deal 5/58
- Committee of Public Safety under Salan 5/58
- Settlers call for new French government 5/58
- Crisis brings de Gaulle to power 5/58
- De Gaulle confuses settlers with speech 6/58
- De Gaulle suggests amnesty to FLN 6/58
- Votes for negotiated settlement 9/58
- FLN fails to sabotage poll 9/58
- De Gaulle opposes torture 12/58
- UN rejects independence 12/58
- De Gaulle offers referendum 9/59
- Settlers dislike de Gaulle's compromise 9/59
- General Massu sacked; white uprising 1/60
- De Gaulle orders army to break revolt 1/60
- Michel Debre flies in; state of siege 1/60
- Settlers' revolt ends 2/60
- Offers Moslems a better deal 2/60
- De Gaulle visits 12/60
- De Gaulle favours self-determination 12/60
- France votes in favour of home rule 1/61
- Rebel French officers seize Algiers 4/61
- Rebels threaten to invade Paris 4/61
- De Gaulle orders blockade of Algeria 4/61
- Three-day cease-fire declared 5/61
- Troops kille 80 Moslem protesters 7/61
- France sentences coup leaders to death 7/61
- France ends cease-fire 8/61
- 86 die in riots 10/61
- Rebel leader Ben Bella on hunger strike 11/61
- More French troops to leave 12/61
- French kill 18 Moslem guerrillas 1/62
- 12 killed by bomb in Algiers 1/62
- OAS kills a dozen Algerians 2/62
- 40,000 French troops sent into Algiers 2/62
- De Gaulle pledges peace in Algeria 2/62
- De Gaulle orders troops to crush OAS 3/62
- OAS leader Jouhard arrested 3/62
- Raoul Salan arrested 4/62
- French referendum supports peace pacts 4/62
- Salan given life sentence in Paris 5/62
- 110 killed in OAS terror campaign 5/62
- European settlers evacuated 5/62
- OAS sets fire to oilfields 6/62
- Six OAS assassins arrested 6/62
- OAS terror campaign ends 6/62
- Independence proclaimed by France 7/62
- Algerians vote for independence 7/62
- 50 die in fighting 7/62
- Rebel leader Ben Bella returns 8/62
- Cease-fire between rival Moslem groups 9/62
- Ben Bella becomes first President 9/63
- French-owned land to be nationalised 10/63
- Moroccan troops launch fresh offensive 10/63
- Agrees to cease-fire with Morocco 10/63
- Agrees to end war with Morocco 2/64
- All French troops withdraw 6/64
- Army leader rebels against Ben Bella 7/64
- 100 die in bomb blast on ship 7/64
- Boumedienne ousts Ben Bella 6/65
- Tshombe's plane is hijacked 7/67
- Ordered to extradite Tshombe to Congo 7/67
- Moise Tshombe dies in jail 6/69
- Houari Boumedienne dies 12/78
- Colonel Chadli elected President 1/79
- Ben Bella freed after 14 years 7/79
- Quake kills 20,000 in El Asnam 10/80
- Plane flies US hostages out of Iran 1/81
- Hijacked Kuwaiti jumbo in Algiers 4/88
- Referendum on proposed reforms 10/88
- President Boudiaf is assassinated 6/92
- Former Prime Minister assassinated 8/93
- Demonstrations for democracy 6/94
- 100 killed in prison riots 2/95
Ali, Muhammad
- See Cassius Clay
Ali, Rashid 4/41
Alia, Ramiz 4/85
Aliyev, Geidar 6/93
Allen, Margaret 1/49
Allen, Woody 12/72, 12/77, 11/79, 6/93
Allenby, Edmund 12/17, 2/22
Allende, Isabel 9/88
Allende, Salvador 7/08, 9/70, 11/70, 11/72, 3/73, 6/73, 9/73
Alliluyeva, Olga 11/84, 4/86
Alliluyeva, Svetlana 3/67, 4/67, 11/84, 4/86
Allison, Frederick 11/31
Alon, Yigal 1/77
Altman, Robert 5/70
Altman, Sidney 12/89
Alton, David 3/79, 1/88, 5/88
Altwegg, Jeanette 2/52
Aly Khan 5/49
Amanullah, King of Afghanistan 12/28, 1/29
Ambler, Eric 6/09
Amer, Abdel Hakim 10/61
Amery, Julian 11/58
Amery, Leo 5/40
Ames, Aldrich Hazen 2/94, 4/94
Amin, Hafizullah 12/79
Amin, Idi 1/71, 2/71, 8/72, 9/72, 7/73, 12/73, 3/74, 6/74, 6/75, 7/75, 7/76, 2/77, 3/77, 8/78, 11/78, 3/79
Amis, Kingsley 4/22, 2/54, 12/54, 10/86, 12/86
Amis, Martin 12/87
Amkrah, Joseph 4/69
Amnesty International
- Report on Kuwait towards end of Gulf War 2/91
Amundsen, Roald 12/05, 9/06, 12/11, 5/26
Ananda, King of Siam 3/35
ANC (African National Congress)
- See South Africa
Anders, William 12/68
Andersen, Lale 8/72
Anderson, Judith 12/40, 1/92

Anderson, Lindsay 12/69, 8/94
Anderson, Marion 1/55
Anderson, Sulome 12/91
Anderson, Terry 12/91
Anderson, Willie 7/04, 8/58
Ando, Teruzo 2/36
Andre, Carl 2/76
Andress, Ursula 3/36, 5/63
Andretti, Mario 10/78
Andrew, Prince (Duke of York) 2/60, 11/78, 10/82, 3/86, 7/86
Andrews, Chapman 12/26
Andrews, Eamonn 8/55, 2/67, 11/87
Andrews, Julie 10/47, 11/48, 3/56, 4/58, 4/65
Andropov, Yuri 11/56, 4/73, 9/83, 11/83, 2/84
Angier, Carole 12/90
Angola
- Six die in nationalist unrest 2/61
- 500 whites killed in 5 weeks 4/61
- Portugal announces independence plans 8/74
- Portugal agrees independence; 13 year war 1/75
- Attempts for coalition government 1/75
- Civil war looms; whites flee 8/75
- Refugees pour into Luanda 8/75
- Gains independence from Portugal 11/75
- 40,000 die and million homeless in civil war 11/75
- MPLA in Luanda fights FNLA and UNITA 11/75
- Soviet advisers enter to help MPLA 11/75
- Cubans said to be backing MPLA 11/75
- South Africans said to be backing UNITA 11/75
- 128 UK mercenaries fly to Angola 1/76
- African summit on war 1/76
- Soviet MiGs join conflict 1/76
- Cuban-backed MPLA drive into south 2/76
- Savimbi's UNITA retreats 2/76
- 100,000 refugees south 2/76
- Four white mercenaries to be executed 6/76
- 13 white mercenaries on trial 6/76
- Mercenaries shot 7/76
- Guerrillas use as base to attack Zaire 3/77
- Rebels free 16 Britons 5/84
- Cuban troops to be withdrawn 8/88
- UNITA rebels reject election results 10/92
- UNITA rebels seize the city of Huambo 3/93
- UNITA and government sign peace treaty but doubts remain 11/94
Anh, Le Duc 9/92
Anne, Princess of Great Britain 8/50, 9/63, 3/66, 11/71, 3/73, 5/73, 8/73, 11/73, 3/74, 11/77, 12/85, 6/87, 8/89, 4/92, 12/92
Anne-Marie, Princess of Denmark 9/64
Annigoni, Pietro 6/10, 8/55
Anouilh, Jean 6/10
Anquetil, Jacques 7/62
Antall, Joszef 4/90, 12/93
Antarctic
- Amundsen beats Scott in race 12/11
- Scott arrives 1/12
- Richard Byrd flies over 11/29
- Becomes a science reserve 12/59
- 12 states sign hands-off treaty 12/59
- Nuclear tests and waste dumping banned 12/59
- British Antarctic Territory created 3/62
- Over 250 die in DC-10 crash 11/79
Antonescu, Ion 8/44
Antonioni, Michelangelo 12/67
Antonov, Sergei 7/83
Antuofermo, Vito 3/80
Aoun, Michel 3/89, 9/89
Apollinaire, Guillaume 9/11, 12/11, 12/17, 11/18
Appleton, Edward 12/47, 4/65
Aquino, Benigno 11/77, 8/83, 10/84, 1/85
Aquino, Corazon 8/83, 8/84, 12/85, 2/86, 11/86, 1/87, 8/87, 12/89
Arab League 8/90
Arabia
- See also Saudi Arabia, Turkey, Yemen
- Yemen in revolt 6/01
- Arab revolt against Ottomans 6/16
- Lawrence in pro-Arab revolt mission 10/16
- Emir Feisal's men destroy Turkish rail 9/18
- Ibn Saud's Wahabis enter Mecca, pledge 10/24
Arafat, Yassir 2/69, 2/70, 9/70, 1/73, 11/74, 3/79, 8/82, 9/82, 6/83, 11/83, 12/83, 5/85, 10/85, 10/86, 11/88, 1/89, 4/92, 9/93, 7/94, 10/94
Aragon, Dona Fabiola y 12/60
Aragon, Louis 12/20
Aramburu, Pedro 11/55
Arbuckle, Roscoe "Fatty" 9/20
Archaeology
- See Exploration & Archaeology
Archer, Jeffrey 12/76, 9/85, 10/86, 7/87, 5/89
Architecture
- Opening of dome of Sacre Coeur in Paris 6/00
- Liverpool cathedral begun 12/04
- Criminal Courts at Old Bailey opens 2/07
- New York's Singer Building is tallest 8/07
- County Hall begun, London 3/12
- Planned University Senate House, London 3/12
- Wellington monument, Hyde Park Corner 4/12
- Buckingham Palace Mall front redesigned 10/12
- Australia's Dominion House at Aldwych plan agreed 4/14
- King Edward VII Gallery, British Museum 5/14
- Lutyens' Cenotaph war memorial 7/19
- Imperial War Museum, Crystal Palace 6/20
- Royal Institute limits building height 3/22
- German royal emblems removed 3/22
- Imperial Stadium, Wembley, finished 10/22
- Le Corbusier publishes his ideas 12/23
- St Paul's bridge may harm Cathedral 8/24
- Bauhaus movement affects kitchen design 12/26
- Van der Rohe's German pavilion at show 5/29
- Lutyens resigns over Thames bridge fight 2/30
- London: bigger structures, wider streets 9/30
- Empire State Building, world's tallest 5/31
- Elizabeth Scott's Shakespeare Theatre 4/32
- Elliptical BBC building, Myers and Hart 5/32
- Austrian Adolf Loos dies 8/33
- Nazis shut down Berlin Bauhaus 12/33
- Battersea power station, Giles G. Scott 12/33
- Holden's designs for London Underground 12/34
- Paxton's Crystal Palace burns down 11/36
- Lutyens' plans for National Theatre 3/38
- Review of the 1930s 12/38
- Norwich City Hall; mixture of styles 12/38
- Neoclassical, Modern, Art Deco styles 12/38
- Daily Express Building, Fleet Street 12/38
- New Victoria Theatre cinema, Art Deco 12/38
- Hoover Factory in London, Wallis Gilbert 12/38
- De La Warr Pavilion, Bauhaus in Bexhill 12/38
- Viceroy's House, New Delhi, by Lutyens 12/38
- Influx of German and Russian refugees 12/38
- Lutyens is president of Royal Academy 12/38
- Death of Sir Edwin Lutyens 1/44
- R. Matthew builds Royal Festival Hall 5/51
- Hugh Casson's Festival of Britain work 5/51
- Basil Spence to design Coventry Cathedral 8/51
- Planned £55 million Barbican development 1/56
- Redeveloping St Paul's area, London 7/57
- Genius Frank Lloyd Wright dies 4/59
- Fine Art Commission blasts UK standards 12/59
- Reviews of high skyline 1950s styles 12/59
- Le Corbusier as an innovator 12/59
- Seagram Building: Johnson, van der Rohe 12/59
- UNESCO building: Breuer 12/59
- Brasilia, new capital by Costa, Niemeyer 12/59
- London planners to control high-rises 6/60
- Shell building near Thames 6/60
- Consecration of Coventry Cathedral 5/62
- Lasdun to design National Theatre 12/63
- Death of Le Corbusier 8/65
- Post Office Tower opens 10/65
- Centre Point skyscraper planned 8/66
- Cathedral of Christ the King, Liverpool 5/67
- German architect Walter Gropius dies 7/69
- Mies van der Rohe dies 8/69
- Work begins on National Theatre 11/69
- Lasdun's National Theatre opens 10/76
- Sir Basil Urwin Spence dies 11/76
- Pompidou Centre in Paris 2/77
- London's Barbican arts centre opens 3/82
- National Gallery extension design rejected 9/84
- Plans for Britain's biggest skyscraper 3/88
- Prince Charles attacks architects 10/88
- Architects hit back at Charles 11/88
- Charles resigns as patron in National Museum of Scotland row 8/91
Arden, Elizabeth 10/66
Arena, Dominic 7/69
Arens, Moshe 11/83, 1/91
Argentina
- Signs disarmament treaty with Chile 1/03
- Revolution breaks out 2/07
- Rejoices as Britain sinks German cruiser 12/14
- Cuts ties with Germany after spy scandal 9/17
- Loses first football World Cup to Uruguay 7/30
- Uriburu overthrows President Irigoyen 9/30
- Pan-American Peace Conference 12/36
- President Castillo ousted in coup 6/43
- Military junta under President Rawson 6/43
- Juan Peron becomes labour minister 6/43
- Declares war on Germany 3/45
- Peron to take over as leader 10/45
- Refuge to Nazis reported 2/46
- Peron becomes President 6/46
- Bernardo Houssay wins Medicine Nobel 12/47
- Warned by Britain over Falkland Islands 2/48
- UK protests 3/48
- Peronists win general election 3/48
- Army wants Eva Peron out of public life 2/49
- Deadlock in meat talks with Britain 1/51
- Eva Peron in hospital 11/51
- Juan Peron re-elected President 11/51
- Argentinians repel landing party on island 2/52
- Eva Peron dies of cancer at 33 7/52
- Six die in Peron rally bomb blast 4/53
- Peron re-elected; arrests opposition 4/54
- Divorce legalised 12/54
- Catholic Church is disestablished 5/55
- Peron exiles Catholic leaders 6/55
- 202 in uprising against Peron 6/55
- Students riot; army and navy revolt 9/55
- Peron overthrown; Lonardi is President 9/55
- Peron flees to Paraguay 9/55
- Pedro Aramburu ousts Lonardi 11/55
- Israel captures Nazi Eichmann 5/60
- Demands return of Eichmann from Israel 6/60
- Military coup overthrows Frondizi 3/62
- Restates claim to Falklands 9/65
- Stages raid of Falkland Islands 9/66
- President Ongania ousted in coup 6/70
- Luis Leloir wins Chemistry Nobel 12/70
- Premier Levingston toppled 3/71
- Juan Sanchez assassinated 4/72
- Abduction of a Fiat director 4/72
- Peron back after 17 years' exile 11/72
- UK businessman Lockwood kidnapped 6/73
- Peron re-elected President 9/73
- Campaign to regain Falklands launched 11/73
- Ransom to be paid for Exxon executive 12/73
- Isabel Peron takes control of government 6/74
- Juan Peron dies 7/74
- Isabel Peron becomes President 7/74
- Destroyer fires at UK research ship 2/76
- Isabel Peron overthrown in bloodless coup 3/76
- Military junta to tackle super-inflation 3/76
- USA cuts aid over human rights 2/77
- Wins World Cup 6/78
- Increasing links with Falklands 4/80
- Isabel Peron jailed 3/81
- Scrap merchants land on South Georgia 3/82
- Capture Falklands 4/82
- Celebrates unity in Buenos Aires 4/82
- Troops take South Georgia 4/82
- Mendez says "we recovered lost Malvinas" 4/82
- Forces leave UK exclusion zone 4/82
- USA imposes sanctions; backs UK 4/82
- Loses South Georgia to UK 4/82
- Fury at Belgrano loss 5/82
- UK invades Falklands 5/82
- Surrenders after losing Port Stanley 6/82
- Galtieri ousted from government and army 6/82
- EC lifts trade boycott 6/82
- Political party ban lifted 8/82
- UN wants talks on Falklands sovereignty 11/82
- Arrest of Galtieri ordered 4/83
- Frozen UK assets released 8/83
- Bignone pardons Isabel Peron 9/83
- Raul Alfonsin becomes civilian President 12/83
- Democracy restored 12/83
- Ex-President Videla jailed 12/85
- Wins World Cup 6/86
- Alfonsin stops army revolt by Rico 4/87
- 400,000 cheer Alfonsin; Erenu resigns 4/87
- Peronist Carlos Menem wins presidential elections 5/89
- More than 1,000 people arrested in food riots 5/89
- Full diplomatic relations with Britain re-established 2/90
- Suicide car bomb attack on Israeli Embassy kills 10 3/92
- Hurd is first cabinet minister to visit since Falklands war 1/93
- Bomb at buildings housing Jewish organisations kills 96 7/94
- President Menem re-elected 5/95
Argoud, Antoine 2/63, 12/63
Argov, Shlomo 6/82
Argyll, Margaret, Duchess of 7/93
Arias, Oscar 8/87
Arias, Roberto 4/59
Aristide, Jean-Bertrand 10/91, 10/94
Arlott, John 9/80, 12/91
Armstrong, Henry 12/12
Armstrong, Louis 7/00, 12/27, 6/30, 12/56, 12/58, 6/59, 7/71, 12/71, 9/91
Armstrong, Neil 8/30, 3/66, 1/69, 7/69
Armstrong, Patrick 10/89
Armstrong, Robert 11/86
Armstrong-Jones, Antony 2/60, 5/60, 10/61
Armstrong-Jones, Sarah 11/73
Arnim, Sixt von 5/43
Arnott, Penelope 8/80
Arnott, Richard 8/80
Arp, Jean 2/16, 12/20
Arroyo, Eduardo 2/37
Art
- See December survey and individual artists
Asanuma, Inejiro 10/60
Ashanti kingdom
- See Gold Coast
Ashcroft, Peggy 9/27, 5/30, 12/30, 12/35, 12/50, 12/52, 12/60, 12/64, 12/84, 5/89, 6/91
Ashdown, Jane 2/92
Ashdown, Paddy 7/88, 2/92, 4/92
Ashe, Arthur 7/75, 4/92, 2/93
Ashkenazy, Vladimir 4/63
Ashley, Laura 7/74, 9/85
Ashton, Frederick 9/04, 12/31, 12/70, 8/88
Ashwell, Paul 4/90
Asimov, Isaac 4/92
Askey, Arthur 11/82
Asquith, Anthony 11/02, 2/68
Asquith, Herbert Henry
- Suffragists' arch enemy 6/06
- Shouted down by militant suffragettes 11/07
- Becomes Prime Minister 4/08
- Introduces old age pensions 5/08
- Scraps Education Bill 12/08
- Wants action against Lords' powers 2/09
- Vows to take up Lords' challenge 9/09
- Lords throw out the budget 11/09
- Election campaign 12/09
- Stays in power with Labour support 2/10
- Urges King to create new peers 4/10
- Stays in power after election dead-heat 12/10
- King agrees to more Liberal peers 7/11
- Miners' minimum wages bill 3/12
- Introduces third Home Rule Bill 4/12
- Cat and Mouse Act 3/13
- Urged to reconsider Channel tunnel 8/13
- Suffragettes hurl themselves at his car 11/13
- Rejects compulsory military service 2/14
- Calls for 500,000 more to sign up 9/14
- Vows heavy economic pressure on Germany 3/15
- Remains as PM in coalition government 5/15
- Denies plans for conscription 7/15
- Seeks approval for £240 million war loan 2/16
- Meets Pope Benedict XV 4/16
- Recognises Czech provisional government 9/16
- Ousted by Lloyd George 12/16
- Attacks Lloyd George on conduct of war 5/18
- Loses seat in general election 12/18
- Returns to Parliament 2/20
- Urges free trade in election campaign 11/23
- Loses seat in general election 10/24
- Resigns as Liberal leader 10/26, 2/27
- Dies 2/28
Assad, Hafez 11/70, 9/73, 6/74, 6/83, 1/84, 5/85, 7/85
Astaire, Adele 12/26
Astaire, Fred 12/26, 11/33, 12/34, 12/35, 6/87
Astles, Bob 4/76
Aston, F.W. 12/22
Astor, Lord
- See Waldorf
Astor, Nancy 11/19, 5/64
Athenagoras, Patriarch 1/64
Athletics
- See also Olympic Games
- Pietri loses Marathon 7/08
- Thorpe, Olympic hero, stripped of medals 1/13
- Charles Paddock breaks 200 metres record 3/21
- Paddock runs 100 metres in 10.4 seconds 4/21
- Paavo Nurmi breaks 10,000 metres record 5/21
- L.T. Brown's high jump record 2/22
- First congress of Feminine Athletics 8/22
- Nurmi's new 1,500 metres record 6/24
- British Liddell and Abrahams win Olympics 7/24
- Charles Hoff breaks pole vault record 9/25
- Nurmi sets new 3,000 metres record 5/26
- Otto Peltzer breaks 1,500 metres record 9/26
- Lina Radke-Bratchsauer breaks 800 metres 8/27
- 4th Women's World Games; German triumph 8/34
- Jesse Owens breaks five records in a day 5/35
- Jesse Owens placed in US Olympic team 7/36
- Sydney Wooderson sets mile record, UK 8/37
- Wooderson runs half-mile in 1 minute, 49 8/38
- European Games, Oslo 8/46
- Bannister runs mile in 4 min. 1.48 sec. 3/50
- Britain wins 8 golds in European Games 8/50
- First Asian Games, New Delhi 3/51
- Chataway runs two miles in record time 6/52
- Jim Thorpe dies 3/53
- Chataway's new two-mile record 5/53
- Jim Peters runs marathon in record time 6/53
- Bannister and Chataway in mile relay record 8/53
- Bannister breaks four minute mile 5/54
- Commonwealth Games: Bannister wins mile 8/54
- Commonwealth Games: Peters collapses 8/54
- Bannister wins gold in European Games 8/54
- Chataway beats Soviet Kuts in 5,000 metres 10/54
- Bannister retires 12/54
- Kuts breaks 5,000-metre record 9/55
- Gordon Pirie smashes 5,000-metre record 6/56
- Ibbotson wins mile record for UK 7/57
- Herb Elliott breaks two mile records 8/58
- Armin Hary runs 100 metres in 10 seconds 6/60
- Peter Snell (NZ) sets new mile record 1/62
- Brumel: high-jump record of 7 ft. 5 ins. 7/62
- Pole vaulter Nikula (Finland) jumps 5m 2/63
- Henry Carr (US) runs 200m in 20.3 sec. 3/63
- Bob Hayes (US) sets 100 yards record 6/63
- Ron Clarke (Aus.) breaks 5,000m record 2/65
- Jim Ryun (US) sets new world mile record 7/66
- Jim Hines (US) sets new 100m record 6/68
- Board (UK) wins European Games 800m 9/69
- Lilian Board dies of cancer 12/70
- Finnish athlete Paavo Nurmi dies 10/73
- UK's Pascoe wins gold at European Champs 9/74
- UK's Jenkins wins European gold 9/74
- UK's Ovett wins European gold 9/74
- UK's Foster wins European gold 9/74
- UK's Thompson wins European gold 9/74
- John Walker breaks mile record 8/75
- Ovett wins 1,500 metres, European Championships 8/77
- Queen opens Commonwealth Games in Canada 8/78
- Daley Thompson wins decathlon 8/78
- Coe runs record mile in Oslo 7/79
- Coe breaks three middle distance records 8/79
- Coe wins mile, 1,500 and 800 metres 8/79
- Grete Waitz breaks 2.5 hour marathon 10/79
- Jesse Owens dies 3/80
- Ovett's new 1,500 metres record 8/80
- Coe beats Ovett's mile record 8/81
- David Moorcroft sets 5,000-metre record 7/82
- Daley Thompson wins European decathlon 9/82
- Michael Gratton wins London Marathon 4/83
- First World Championships 8/83
- Death of US actor-athlete Weissmuller 1/84
- South African Zola Budd to get UK passport 4/84
- US jogging champ Fixx dies 7/84
- UK's Steve Jones London Marathon 4/85
- Kristiansen wins women's London Marathon 4/85
- UK's Cram runs mile in 3 min. 46.32 sec. 7/85
- Zola Budd sets new 5,000m world record 8/85
- Steve Cram sets 2,000m world record 8/85
- Budd and Cowley: Commonwealth games ban 7/86
- Ben Johnson breaks 100-metre record 8/87
- Zola Budd returns to South Africa 5/88
- British male athletes win European Cup 8/89
- Mike Powell sets new record by leaping 8.95 metres 8/91
- Gunnell wins in record time at World Championships 8/93
- Nourredine Morceli runs mile in 3mn,44.39secs 9/93
- European Games medals for Britain 8/94
- Diane Modahl banned 12/94
Atkins, Humphrey 4/82
Atkins, Susan 12/69, 3/71
Atkinson, Rowan 12/79
Attall, Jacques 4/93, 6/93
Attenborough, David 3/65
Attenborough, Richard 8/23, 12/42, 11/52, 10/59, 12/69, 4/83, 12/83
Attlee, Clement
- Joins MacDonald's cabinet 5/30
- Succeeds Lansbury as Labour leader 10/35
- Attacks government on Franco recognition 2/39
- Questions conscription 4/39
- Deputy PM to Churchill 5/40
- Elected PM in Labour landslide victory 7/45
- Announces Japanese surrender; end of war 8/45
- Defends use of atomic bomb 8/45
- Announces austerity measures 8/45
- Promises Indian Home Rule 9/45
- Addresses first UN session in London 1/46
- Shows plans for independent India 5/46
- Angry at USA's Palestine statements 10/46
- Nationalises coal pits; gives warning 1/47
- Makes Mountbatten India's Viceroy 2/47
- Cabinet strain as rationing bites 6/47
- Makes Jinnah Governor of Pakistan 7/47
- Calls for "sacrifices" in austerity plan 8/47
- Promotes Stafford Cripps and Harold Wilson 9/47
- Chancellor Dalton quits 11/47
- Blasts "USSR imperialism" 1/48
- Bans radicals from Civil Service 3/48
- Welcomes National Health Service 7/48
- Sets up capital punishment commission 1/49
- Recognises Republic of Eire 5/49

- Moderation attacked by Bevanites 11/49
- Wins election with smaller majority 2/50
- Defeated on coal and petrol vote 3/50
- Commits Navy to help USA in Korea 6/50
- Rejects Hogg's plea to be MP 9/50
- Worried over Truman plans to use A-bomb 12/50
- Announces £4,700 million spending plan 1/51
- Accepts Bevan's resignation 4/51
- Cuts holiday for King's illness 9/51
- Opens Europe's largest oil refinery 9/51
- Calls October general election 9/51
- Loses election 10/51
- Attacks Bevan for "wrecking party" 10/52
- Leads Labour delegation to China 8/54
- Gaitskell is new party leader 12/55
- Takes seat in Lords 1/56
- Dies 10/67

Auchinleck, Claude 11/41, 6/42, 7/42, 6/43, 3/81
Auden, Wystan Hugh 2/07, 1/36, 2/56, 9/73
Augusta Victoria, ex-Kaiserin of Germany 4/21
Aung San Suu Kyi, Daw 10/91, 11/91
Auriol, Vincent 1/47, 5/47, 1/66
Aurora, Lieutenant-General 12/71
Aussem, Cilly 7/31
Austin, "Bunny" 7/38
Austin, Alfred 6/13
Austin, Hudson 10/83
Austin, Tracy 7/79
Australia
- See also World Wars I and II
- Earl of Hopetoun first Governor-General 7/00
- Royal approval of federal Australia 7/00
- First cabinet of new Commonwealth 12/00
- Barton first Prime Minister 1/01
- Tennyson, poet's son, made Governor 11/02
- Approves preferential trade with Britain 12/03
- Salvation Army buys land 7/05
- British New Guinea joins state 10/06
- Andrew Fisher is Labour Prime Minister 11/08
- Liberals lose elections to Labour 4/10
- Canberra becomes federal capital 3/13
- Australia House in London agreed on 4/14
- Troops in Gallipoli landings 4/15
- First Anzac Day, remembering Gallipoli 4/16
- Troops in Easter attack; Hindenburg line 4/17
- Referendum stops conscription 12/17
- Troops take Jericho in Mideast campaign 2/18
- Smith brothers fly from Britain 12/19
- Wireless conversation with England 6/24
- New tariffs favouring Britain 9/25
- Cobham touches down after 28,000 miles 10/26
- Self-governing Commonwealth dominion 11/26
- New Parliament House, Canberra 5/27
- James Scullin's Labour wins election 10/29
- Amy Johnson lands in Darwin 4/30
- Sydney Harbour Bridge joined 8/30
- "Buy British" drive; Prince's broadcast 11/31
- Labour government defeated 11/31
- Sydney Harbour Bridge opens 3/32
- Orient Line; £124 UK-Australia and back 5/34
- Protests against South Europe immigrants 8/37
- Jean Batten's record Australian flight 10/37
- Celebrates 150 years European settlement 1/38
- Duke of Kent is Governor-General 10/38
- Robert Menzies becomes PM 4/39
- Declares war on Germany 9/39
- Pledges aircraft and airmen for Allies 1/40
- Agrees with UK, USA on Pacific defence 11/40
- Signs Pacific pact with New Zealand 1/44
- Duke of Gloucester is Governor-General 1/45
- Currency devalued 9/49
- Refuses to recognise Communist China 10/49
- Biologist Burnet forms immunity theory 12/49
- Bill to ban Communists introduced 4/50
- Menzies compromises on Communist ban 6/50
- Forces to be sent to Korea 8/50
- Anzacs, UK troops repel China in Korea 5/51
- Defence pact with USA, New Zealand 9/51
- Field Marshal Slim is Governor-General 9/52
- First UK atomic bomb tested off Australia 10/52
- Large oilfield in North-West 12/53
- First visit by reigning monarch 2/54
- USSR diplomat Petrov seeks asylum 4/54
- Petrov warns that Tass press are spies 7/54
- 200 people die in New South Wales floods 3/55
- 44,000 homeless; 300,000 sheep drown 3/55
- Premier Menzies leads Suez inquiry team 8/56
- Hosts Olympic Games in Melbourne 11/56
- Herb Elliott breaks two mile records 8/58
- Herb Elliot wins Olympic 1,500 metres 9/60
- First issue of Oz magazine 4/63
- 85 die when destroyer Voyager sinks 2/64
- UK's Blue Streak missile launched 6/64
- 300,000 greet Beatles 6/64
- Donald Campbell - new land speed record 7/64
- Agrees on more aid for Malaysia 9/64
- Trans-Pacific journey by raft completed 9/64
- To mount drought relief in Africa 1/66
- Menzies resigns as PM 1/66
- Australian troops fly into Vietnam 4/66
- Opposition leader hurt in murder attempt 6/66
- Jack Brabham is world motor racing champ 9/66
- Alec Rose ends lone voyage from UK 12/67
- John McEwen becomes acting PM 12/67
- PM Harold Holt drowns in sea 12/67
- John Gorton becomes PM 1/68
- 33 die when West Gate Bridge collapses 10/70
- UK couple are first to row the Pacific 4/72
- Labour Party wins general election 12/72
- Aborigines granted the vote 11/73
- Patrick White wins Literature Nobel 12/73
- Police hold British MP John Stonehouse 12/74
- Cyclone shatters Darwin 12/74
- Stonehouse arrested; extradition warrant 3/75
- Papua New Guinea becomes independent 9/75
- Governor-General sacks Premier Whitlam 11/75
- Constitutional crisis on Whitlam budget 11/75
- Malcolm Fraser's Liberals win election 12/75
- 80 die in Sydney rail crash 1/77
- Packer wins cricket case in UK 11/77
- Robert Menzies dies 5/78
- Actress Merle Oberon dies 10/79
- Early days covered in Golding's "Rites" 12/80
- "Dingo Baby" murder trial; mother guilty 10/82
- 68 die in country's worst bush fires 2/83
- Hawke's Labour Party returns to power 3/83
- Wins America's Cup (sailing) 9/83
- "Dingo baby" mother freed from jail 2/86
- Queen signs bill to sever last UK ties 3/86
- UK cabinet secretary involved in Peter Wright case 11/86
- UK loses appeal against "Spycatcher" 9/87
- Country's first fatal earthquake kills 11 12/89
- Prime Minister Bob Hawke ousted by Paul Keating 12/91
- Government decides to allow homosexuals to join military 11/92
- To drop allegiance to Queen 12/92
- Paul Keating's Labour Party wins general elections 3/93
- Poll reveals one in seven Australians want a republic 4/93
- Aborigines celebrate Native Title Bill 12/93
- Centenary of "Waltzing Mathilda" 4/95

Austria
- See also World Wars I and II
- Strike by 5,000 miners 1/00
- Franz Josef dissolves parliament 9/00
- Fears of Russian troops in Balkans 8/01
- Restores relations with Mexico 9/01
- Triple Alliance renewed 6/02
- To supervise Macedonian reforms 12/02
- Army conscription decreed 2/03
- Dispute over universities 5/03
- Franz Josef wants more spent on army 5/04
- Universal suffrage 11/05
- 12,000 bakers strike; bread shortages 3/07
- Socialists gain in first free elections 5/07
- Triple Alliance renewed for further six years 7/07
- Women employed equally in universities 8/07
- Franz Josef's Diamond Jubilee 6/08
- Annexes Bosnia and Herzegovina 10/08
- Bans arms exports to Serbia 10/08
- Sends troops to Serbian border 11/08
- Resumes Balkans talks with Turkey 12/08
- Talks of Balkan "war of extermination" 2/09
- Czech nationalists disrupt parliament 2/09
- Rejects Russian mediation 3/09
- Accepts Serbian climbdown; less tension 3/09
- Bachelor tax to cure deficit 10/09
- English officers found guilty of spying 12/10
- Emperor orders Abdication Bill 4/12
- Prince Thun vetoes first woman MP 6/12
- Foreign Minister wants Balkans talks 8/12
- Renews Triple Alliance for six more years 12/12
- Premier Tisza and Pallaviani fight duel 8/13
- Triple Alliance affirmed; Italian doubts 9/13
- Forces Serbia to leave Albania 10/13
- Arms get budget priority; war looms 3/14
- Archduke Ferdinand shot dead 6/14
- Threat to invade Serbia over killing 7/14
- Declares war on Serbia; invades 7/14
- Foreign Minister Berchtold resigns 1/15
- Masaryk organises for Czech independence 11/15
- Emperor Franz Josef dies 11/16
- Emperor Karl suggests peace to France 3/17
- Welcomes Papal peace plan 9/17
- Emperor's peace offer to France 4/18
- Peace proposal rejected by US and Britain 9/18
- Emperor Karl abdicates; new republic 11/18
- Government will try war instigators 11/18
- Loses naval fleet to Italy 3/19
- Communist demonstration; eight die 6/19
- National Assembly will sign Versailles treaty 9/19
- Claims Kaiser urged Austria to start war 9/19
- Official end to war with Britain 7/20
- Admitted to League of Nations 12/20
- Declares bankruptcy 6/22
- Chancellor Seipel wounded by Socialists 6/24
- Troops halt Vienna workers' revolt; 89 die 7/27
- General strike; call on Chancellor to go 7/27
- Kaempfers acquitted of Communist murder 7/27
- Germans demand annexation 7/27
- Nazis protest Josephine Baker's visit 2/28
- Army bans "All Quiet on the Western Front" 8/29
- Steeruwitz resigns as Chancellor 9/29
- Schober new Chancellor; Nationalist help 9/29
- Socialists win poll; no Nazis, Red seats 11/30
- Nazis protest "All Quiet..." film 1/31
- Signs customs pact with Germany 3/31
- Leaves customs pact with Germany 8/31
- Pfrimer's right-wing coup attempt fails 9/31
- New Chancellor Dollfuss replaces Buresch 5/32
- Christian Socialists join Patriotic Bloc 5/32
- World Peace Conference opens in Vienna 9/32
- Chancellor Dollfuss bans Nazi meetings 5/33
- Nazis arrested; Dollfuss flies back 6/33
- Democracy is dead, says Dollfuss 9/33
- Cabinet resigns; Dollfuss is dictator 9/33
- Nazi leader Frauenfeld arrested 12/33
- First death sentence since republic 1/34
- Socialist uprising crushed 2/34
- Police machine-gun rebels; hundreds die 2/34
- Dollfuss arrests Vienna Mayor Karl Seitz 2/34
- Co-operation pact with Hungary and Italy 3/34
- Dollfuss bans jokes against him 3/34
- Dollfuss abolishes parliament 4/34
- Social Democrats in concentration camps 4/34
- Heimwehr crushes Dr Kaempel and Dr Foppa 4/34
- Nazis kill Dollfuss; coup fails 7/34
- Nazis arrested after Dollfuss murder 7/34
- Mussolini sends 40,000 troops to border 7/34
- Kurt von Schuschnigg is new Chancellor 7/34
- Germany wants Anschluss (union) 3/35
- Plans for bigger army; conscription 4/35
- Refuses sanctions on Italy 10/35
- Re-introduces military service 4/36
- Troops to border fearing German invasion 4/36
- Schuschnigg heads Fatherland Front 5/36
- Schuschnigg absorbs Fascists in Front 10/36
- Jewish psychoanalyst Freud flees Vienna 1/38
- Hitler tells Austria to free all Nazis 1/38
- Germany's Goering visits to set up pact 1/38
- Schuschnigg vows to defend independence 2/38
- Troops at Graz to stop Nazi march 2/38
- Schuschnigg calls for plebiscite 3/38
- Schuschnigg resigns; Seyss-Inquart rules 3/38
- "Reunification Act"; German Anschluss 3/38
- Jews must leave Austria, says Goering 3/38
- Leading Jews sent to Dachau camp 4/38
- Nazis seize Rothschild's Bank 4/38
- Plebiscite: 99 per cent favour Anschluss 4/38
- Compulsory physical exercise 5/38
- Only Aryans can marry 6/38
- Employers give Jews 14 days' notice 6/38
- Schuschnigg to be tried for treason 6/38
- Reich will pay off Austria's debts 7/38
- Reports of Jewish suicides 7/38
- Schuschnigg and others in Dachau camp 8/38
- Nazis purged; 135 die 11/38
- Nazis beat up Cardinal Innitzer 7/39
- New law completes German annexation 4/40
- Looted Nazi art hoard found in mine 4/45
- Vienna is liberated 4/45
- Karl Renner becomes Chancellor 4/45
- Daladier, Reynaud and others freed 5/45
- Composer Webern shot dead by US sentry 9/45
- Allies recognise Renner government 10/45
- Karl Renner becomes President 11/45
- Moderate People's Party wins election 11/45
- Wolfgang Pauli wins Physics Nobel 12/45
- Call for end to Allied occupation 10/46
- Communists dismissed from the government 11/47
- Exiled Hungarian opposition head arrives 2/49
- USSR vetoes entry to UN 9/49
- US naval attache Eugene Karp murdered 2/50
- Death of statesman Karl Renner 12/50
- Admitted to Council of Europe 4/55
- To be sovereign and neutral 5/55
- Belvedere Palace treaty ends occupation 5/55
- Herbert von Karajan directs Vienna Opera 6/56
- Troops fight Soviets chasing Hungarians 11/56
- Absorbs 100,000 Hungarian refugees 11/56
- Kennedy-Khrushchev summit 6/61
- Winter Olympics open in Innsbruck 1/64
- Ends dispute with Italy over South Tyrol 11/69
- Cardinal Mindszenty to live in Vienna 10/71
- Kurt Waldheim becomes UN chief 12/71
- Auschwitz designer Dejaco freed 3/72
- Palestinians attack train; take hostages 9/73
- Karl Lorenz wins Medicine Nobel 12/73
- Terrorists take 11 ministers hostage at oil summit 12/75
- Kreisky frees Palestinian terrorists 12/75
- Kurt von Schuschnigg dies 11/77
- Carter, Brezhnev sign SALT 2 arms treaty 6/79
- Premier Bruno Kreisky resigns 4/83
- Large quantities of toxic wine found 7/85
- Arab terrorist attack at Vienna airport 12/85
- Waldheim tops presidential ballot 5/86
- Kurt Waldheim elected President 6/86
- Pope welcomes President Waldheim 6/87
- Waldheim rides out storm over Nazi past 2/88
- Hungary opens border with Austria 9/89
- Thomas Klestil becomes President 7/92
- Joins the EU 12/94

Austro-Hungarian Empire
- See Austria, Hungary, World War I

Automobile Association
- Founded in Britain 6/05
- Complains about higher petrol price, UK 2/24
- Issues millionth badge 4/30

Automobile Club
- Reliability trials 9/02

Avebury, Lord 12/78
Avery, Oswald T. 1/44
Aviation
- See also Airlines, Disasters (air)
- First flight of Zeppelin airship 7/00
- Santos-Dumont crashes airship 7/01
- Santos-Dumont wins prize 10/01
- Airship "Pax" crashes 5/02
- Stanley Spencer's 30 mile airship flight 9/02
- Langley's heavier-than-air failure 10/03
- Wright brothers' first flight 12/03
- US Army rejects Wrights' plane 9/04
- Spelterini crosses Alps by balloon 9/04
- Cross-Channel balloon trip 2/05
- First motorised aeroplane flight in Europe 5/05
- Aeroplane on water floats experiment 6/05
- First aeroplane with tyres trial 3/06
- First hot-air balloon race in Britain 7/06
- First international hot-air balloon race 9/06
- First international balloon race ends 10/06
- Two Italians cross Alps in balloon 11/06
- Wright brothers demonstrate to Germans 4/07
- Louis Bleriot flies his monoplane 4/07
- Combination airship-plane crashes 6/07
- First US military air force set up 8/07
- UK's first military airship flies 9/07
- Bleriot flies plane "Libellule" 9/07
- German army buys Zeppelin airship 10/07
- First British public display of airship 10/07
- First vertical flight aeroplane, France 11/07
- Bleriot's plane crashes 12/07
- First circular flight in aeroplane 1/08
- Zeppelin plans passenger airship 1/08
- First passenger airplane flight 3/08
- New airship from Zeppelin 4/08
- Wright brothers test new steering gear 5/08
- Wright brothers patent "flying machine" 5/08
- Leon Delagrange makes record 5.5 mile flight 5/08
- Invention of "gyropter" 7/08
- First to die in aeroplane crash 9/08
- Wilbur Wright stays aloft for hour 10/08
- First international aviation show, Paris 12/08
- Commercial aeroplane manufacture 3/09
- First international aircraft exhibition 3/09
- Aerial League; for British supremacy 4/09
- Zeppelin crashes in tree after record 5/09
- Wright brothers win gold medal 5/09
- Bleriot makes first cross-Channel flight 7/09
- Latham's cross-Channel attempt fails 7/09
- Glenn Curtis wins 1st Gordon Bennett Cup 8/09
- International air meeting, Rheims 8/09
- Comte de Lambert flies over Eiffel Tower 10/09
- Air speed record, 55 mph 1/10
- Leon Delagrange dies in air crash 1/10
- First woman to get pilot's licence 3/10
- First air traffic conference 5/10
- Deutschland airship has paying customers 6/10
- First British victim, cross-Channel hero 7/10
- Air Battalion of Royal Engineers created 2/11
- First British airship wreck 5/11
- French Premier and minister die in crash 5/11
- First amphibious aeroplane flight, Issy 8/11
- First military use of aeroplanes 8/11
- World's first airmail service 9/11
- First aerial bombing, Tanguira Oasis 11/11
- Berry makes first parachute jump from plane 2/12
- Airships used in North African war 3/12
- First non-stop Paris-London flight 3/12
- UK's Royal Flying Corps established 4/12
- US Army Air Battalion 5/12
- Wilbur Wright dies 5/12
- Air mail service, London-Paris 8/12
- First all-metal aeroplane 11/12
- Strict air laws introduced in Britain 3/13
- Record double Channel crossing 4/13
- Cody killed in crash; endurance record 8/13
- Garros is first to fly the Mediterranean 9/13
- Bleriot performs first loop-the-loop 9/13
- First Paris-Berlin passenger flight 9/13
- Biggest Zeppelin flies, Germany 9/13
- 125-mph speed barrier broken 9/13
- New stunts every day; ten ride biplane 10/13
- Zeppelin L2 explodes; 28 die 10/13
- First French dirigible 1/14
- Igor Sikorsky's plane carries 17 passengers 2/14
- British planes bomb German airship sheds 9/14
- British plane downs German plane 10/14
- German Zeppelin bombs Norfolk; 20 die 1/15
- Austrians bomb Venice; few casualties 5/15
- Naval pilot bombs Zeppelin from air 6/15
- First all-metal aeroplane by Hugo Junkers 12/15
- First attempt at an air-drop 4/16
- British Air Board created 5/16
- William Boeing founds aero products firm 7/16
- German Zeppelin crew arrested in Essex 9/16
- US Army orders 375 new planes 10/16
- Count von Zeppelin dies 3/17
- German aeroplanes raid England; 76 die 5/17
- First aeroplane bombing of London 6/17
- German Gotha aeroplanes bomb Paris 2/18
- Red Baron, deadly German air ace, downed 4/18
- Royal Air Force formed 4/18
- First parachute drop from an aeroplane 7/18
- Allied aeroplanes machine-gun troops 8/18
- First London-Paris air service 2/19
- First public air service, Berlin-Leipzig 2/19
- Trial of British cross-Atlantic airship 3/19
- Wireless telephone for air pilots 3/19
- Aeroplanes used to crush Afghan invaders 4/19
- Helium instead of hydrogen in airships 4/19
- First UK commercial service, Manchester 4/19
- British fail in non-stop Atlantic flight 4/19
- Aviation opens once more to British civilians 5/19
- Plane crosses Atlantic Ocean in three stages 5/19
- First non-stop Atlantic flight 6/19
- First two-way Atlantic crossing by airship 7/19
- R-34 airship sets off to cross Atlantic 7/19
- Aeroplane helps arrest speeding motorist 7/19
- New record height, 34,610 feet 9/19
- End of Manchester-Stockport air service 9/19
- Japan to spend £30 million aviation development 10/19
- Smith brothers fly Britain-Australia 12/19
- Germany surrenders largest airship 7/20
- "Aerial Derby" wins race at speed of 153 mph 7/20
- US seaplane breaks distance speed record 1/21
- Two British passenger airships 1/21
- First proper helicopter flight 2/21
- World record parachute jump, 24,000 feet 3/21
- R-38, largest airship, flies in Bedford 6/21
- US flyers show aeroplanes can sink ships 7/21
- Sadi Lecointe sets record speed of 205 mph 9/21
- Civil Aviation Advisory Board, Britain 3/22
- First USA coast-to-coast under 24 hours 9/22
- New speed record, 217.5 mph 1/23
- MacReady and Kelley cross USA in 27 hours 5/23
- New speed record, 259 mph 11/23
- Imperial Air Transport Co planned 12/23
- Air service from Liverpool to Belfast 4/24
- Oehmichen's first 1km helicopter circuit 5/24
- Junkers and Ford discuss all-metal planes 6/24
- US Army aeroplanes fly round the world 9/24
- First three-engined plane by Handley Page 10/25
- Spanish "autogiro" tested at Farnborough 10/25
- UK government buys Hendon aerodrome 12/25

- Alan Cobham makes first return trip to Cape 3/26
- Airship and plane fly over Pole 5/26
- Cobham's record 28,000-mile round trip 10/26
- Cobham thinks seaplanes are the future 10/26
- Mario de Bernardi sets seaplane record 11/26
- Longest flight over sea 6/27
- Graf Zeppelin flies to USA in 111 hours 10/28
- All distance records broken by US plane 1/29
- Lindbergh made Federal Aviation Adviser 2/29
- Lindbergh and fiancee escape accident 2/29
- Nobile blamed for "Italia" airship crash 3/29
- 5,000 mile airmail service, Middle East 3/29
- Royal Air Force flies non-stop to India 4/29
- First UK municipal airport, Chat Moss 4/29
- Six-engined Dornier flying boat 7/29
- Graf Zeppelin circles earth in 21 days 7/29
- Hugo Eckener and 52 fly in Graf Zeppelin 7/29
- Waghorn reaches 350 mph in Supermarine 8/29
- Schneider Trophy won by Supermarine 9/29
- First rocket-powered aeroplane by von Opel 9/29
- Maiden voyage of UK airship R101 10/29
- R101: 52 passengers; dining saloon 10/29
- 16 parachutists jump together 11/29
- First solo flight to Australia by woman 4/30
- Johnson braves storms to reach Darwin 4/30
- Airship R101 makes first Atlantic flight 7/30
- R101 forced down by rain 10/30
- Spanish airman Franco in coup 12/30
- Inquiry blames R101 crash on gas leak 3/31
- Balloon height record by Piccard 5/31
- Waghorn dies after crash 5/31
- Mollison flies record 214 hours 8/31
- Stainforth flies Supermarine at 404 mph 9/31
- Amelia Earhart in record Atlantic flight 5/32
- Alberto Santos-Dumont dies 7/32
- Amy Johnson cuts 10 hours off record 11/32
- First flight over Everest 4/33
- Francesco Agello flies at 423.7 mph 4/33
- Howard Hughes reaches 347.5 mph 9/35
- Italians use bombers on Abyssinian towns 10/35
- Hurricane prototype makes first flight 11/35
- New balloon altitude record 11/35
- Douglas DC-3's maiden flight 12/35
- First viewing of Spitfire from Vickers 3/36
- Airship Hindenburg lands in USA 5/36
- Amy Johnson's record flight to Cape Town 5/36
- Maiden flight of Wellington bomber 6/36
- First commercial flight of Douglas DC-3 6/36
- Louis Bleriot dies 8/36
- Beryl Markham is first woman to fly Atlantic solo 9/36
- USSR "biggest air force", 7,000 planes 11/36
- Autogiro inventor Cierva dies in crash 12/36
- Guernica shows power of aerial bombing 4/37
- US's "Flying Fortress" Boeing bomber 4/37
- Hindenburg explodes in New Jersey 5/37
- Amelia Earhart disappears on flight 7/37
- Jean Batten's record Australian flight 10/37
- Warplane manufacture hampers airlines 3/38
- UK contract to buy 400 US planes 6/38
- Howard Hughes halves round-world record 7/38
- "Wrong-Way" Corrigan welcomed in New York 8/38
- Aircraft safety device: altimeter 10/38
- 42-passenger Ensign plane 10/38
- Hitler decorates US aviator Lindbergh 10/38
- Boeing Stratoliner (pressurised airliner) 12/38
- Fritz Wendel sets air record: 484.4 mph 4/39
- First jet flies in Germany 8/39
- Maiden flight of Mosquito fighter-bomber 3/40
- Messerschmitts over the Channel 7/40
- Spitfires and Hurricanes in action 8/40
- Battle of Britain 9/40
- Dornier 217 bombers play role in London Blitz 9/40
- Blenheims in action over Egypt 9/40
- Amy Johnson dies in Thames accident 1/41
- Stukas and Messerschmitts over Balkans 4/41
- Hess crashes his Messerschmitt in Scotland 5/41
- First flight of Gloster jet 5/41
- Russians fly Hurricanes and Spitfires 9/41
- Stukas over Leningrad 9/41
- Spitfires in RAF terror bombing campaign 3/42
- American B-25s bomb Tokyo 4/42
- Stukas in summer offensive on USSR 5/42
- RAF's latest bomber is Avro Lancaster 7/42
- Thunderbolt, new US fighter: 725 mph 12/42
- Mosquito fighter-bombers in Berlin raid 1/43
- Lancaster bombers in "Dambuster" raid 5/43
- Lancasters in Peenemunde Island raid 8/43
- Wellingtons in night precision bombing 11/43
- Lancasters and Halifaxes over Berlin 1/44
- Details of Gloster jet fighter revealed 1/44
- Flying Fortresses bomb Monte Cassino 2/44
- Spitfire being fitted with bigger engine 3/44
- Russian Stormvik bombers in Crimea 4/44
- Mosquitoes pinpoint and bomb one target 5/44
- US Super-Fortress B-29s over Japan 6/44
- US Mustangs, Lightnings, Thunderbolts 6/44
- Lancasters sink Tirpitz in fjord, Norway 11/44
- Lancasters in bombing of Dresden 2/45
- Liberator and Mitchell bombers in Burma 5/45
- Vampire jet fighter announced 6/45
- B-25 bomber hits Empire State Building 7/45
- RAF jet fighter flies at 540 mph 10/45
- First civilian flights from Heathrow 1/46
- US's Lockheed Constitution's maiden flight 11/46
- Bell XI plane breaks sound barrier, US 10/47
- Death of pioneer Orville Wright 1/48
- Vickers Viscount, first turbo-prop 7/48
- Dakotas, Globemasters, York aircraft 9/48
- Spitfires in attack on Hyderabad 9/48
- All Tudor IVs withdrawn in UK after crash 1/49
- XB-47 jet bomber in record flight, US 2/49
- Tudor IVs taken out of service, UK 3/49
- Maiden flight of first UK jet bomber 5/49
- First British escape by ejector seat 5/49
- De Havilland Comet makes its maiden flight 7/49
- Handley Page Hermes 8/49
- Avro 707 8/49
- Bell X-1 8/49
- Gloster Meteor in longest flight so far 8/49
- Maiden flight of Brabazon 9/49
- RAF retires last Lancaster bomber 3/50
- Canberra, UK's first jet bomber crosses Atlantic 2/51
- Valiant, first UK four-engined jet bomber 5/51
- Hawker Hunter's first flight 7/51
- New DC-6 airliner crashes in USA; 50 die 8/51
- First helicopter-borne assault 9/51
- Vickers Valiant atomic jet bomber crash 1/52
- US giant eight-engined YB-60 jet bomber 4/52
- Comet makes its first scheduled jet flight 5/52
- Prototype delta-wing Gloster GA-5 crash 6/52
- Canberra bomber flies Atlantic and back 8/52
- New Vulcan bombers in Royal Air Force 8/52
- Bristol Britannia makes its maiden flight 8/52
- New de Havilland fighter crashes, 26 die 9/52
- US Sabre jets patrol Korean "MiG Alley" 9/52
- First airliner to fly over North Pole 11/52
- BOAC grounds Stratocruisers 1/53
- Boeing's B-52 eight-engined jet bomber 7/53
- De Havilland Comet II 8/53
- 737 mph in Vickers Supermarine Swift jet 9/53
- Comets grounded after crash off Elba 1/54
- 50 changes to Comets; may fly again 2/54
- Comets grounded after Stromboli crash 4/54
- Farnborough centre to test Comet crashes 4/54
- Boeing unveils 707 aeroplane 5/54
- First flight of Boeing 707 7/54
- First flight of UK supersonic "Lightning" 8/54
- Rolls-Royce develop vertical power jet 9/54
- Metal fatigue is the cause of Comet jet crashes 10/54
- Swedish SAS flies over North Pole 11/54
- Vickers Valiant enters RAF 1/55
- Bristol Britannia with new turboprops 3/55
- New Hunter jet crashes at Farnborough 7/55
- Vickers-Armstrong turbo-prop Vanguards 10/55
- First vertical take-off plane, PD11 11/55
- First U-2 spy plane at RAF Lakenheath 4/56
- Manufacturer William E. Boeing dies 9/56
- Jet bomber Valiants, Canberras at Suez 10/56
- Vulcan bomber enters RAF service 2/57
- Viscount airliners grounded after crash 3/57
- Vickers plan new airliner VC-10 for BOAC 1/58
- Comet IV's maiden flight 4/58
- Henri Farman dies 7/58
- BOAC's regular Boeing 707 Atlantic trips 10/58
- Ice on wings caused Munich air crash 3/59
- Last Spitfire crashes 9/59
- Hawker Siddeley and de Havilland merge 12/59
- Comets, Vampires, Sea Vixens bought up 12/59
- UK plans for supersonic airliner 2/60
- Hawker P1127 vertical take-off jet 10/60
- De Havilland Trident jet makes its maiden flight 1/62
- UK and France sign Concorde deal 11/62
- First test flight of Boeing 727, US 2/63
- Maurice Farman dies 2/64
- Woman completes solo round-world flight 4/64
- First flight of 2,000-mph B-70 bomber, US 5/64
- First flight of supersonic TSR-2, UK 9/64
- TSR-2 flies faster than sound 2/65
- Death of pioneer Geoffrey de Havilland 5/65
- Many Starfighter crashes, West Germany 8/66
- Hawker Harrier shown at Farnborough 8/66
- Sea Vixens, Buccaneers, Hunters fight oil strike 3/67
- UK, France, W. Germany sign Airbus deal 9/67
- B-52s bomb North Vietnam 11/67
- Concorde 001 shown in France 12/67
- Galaxy - world's largest - from Lockheed 3/68
- Maiden flight of Boeing 747 2/69
- Maiden flight of Anglo-French Concorde 3/69
- Maiden flight of UK-built Concorde 002 4/69
- Handley Page goes into receivership 8/69
- Concorde 001 breaks sound barrier 10/69
- Concorde's first landing at Heathrow 9/70
- Rolls-Royce Co. calls in receiver 2/71
- Rolls-Royce aero activities nationalised 2/71
- Death of pioneer Igor Sikorsky 10/72
- Death of USSR pioneer Andrei Tupolev 12/72
- British Airways is formed 3/74
- UK-German-Italian combat aircraft 8/74
- Pentagon wants AWAC early-warning planes 1/75
- UK and France fly Concordes commercially 1/76
- British Aerospace formed 4/77
- Supersonic TU-144 airliner, USSR 11/77
- Balloon sets record Atlantic crossing 8/78
- Wilhelm Messerschmitt, engineer, dies 9/78
- DC-10 crashes in Chicago; worst US crash 5/79
- All DC-10s grounded after crash 5/79
- Designer Barnes Wallis dies 10/79
- First strike against nuclear power plant 6/81
- USA blocks F-16 fighters for Israel 7/81
- Microlight plane circles globe non-stop 12/86
- Last Bristol Blenheim crashes in UK 6/87
- Allied bombers flown more than 44,000 sorties in Gulf War 2/91
- 400 civilians killed in US Stealth bomber raid on Baghdad 2/91
- All 129 people onboard an SAS DC-9 survive crash 12/91
- BA Concorde loses parts of its rudder during flight 3/92
- Plans for fifth terminal at Heathrow Airport 5/92
- BA agrees to settle "dirty tricks" dispute with Virgin 1/93
- Eurofighter 2000 makes first test flight 3/94

Avon, Lord 1/65, 11/70
Ayala, Eusebio 2/36
Ayckbourn, Alan 3/77
Ayer, A.J. 6/89
Aylwin, Patricio 12/89
Azad Mulk, Regent of Persia 7/09
Azana, Manuel 10/31, 1/33, 6/33, 2/36, 3/36, 5/36, 2/39
Azerbaijan
- Riots in Baku leave more than 25 dead 1/90
- President Elchibey flees Baku as rebel leader takes over 6/93

Azhari, General 11/78
Azhari, Ismail 1/54
Aziz, Tariq 1/91
Azores
- Boeing 707 crashes, killing 144 2/89

B

Baader, Andreas 6/72, 4/77
Babel, Isaac 12/36
Babiuch, Edward 8/80
Bacall, Lauren 9/24
Bacon, Francis 10/09, 12/67, 6/77, 4/92
Baden, Max Prince of 11/29
Baden-Powell, Robert 6/00, 7/07, 5/10, 1/41
Bader, Douglas 9/82
Badoglio, Pietro 5/36, 12/40, 7/43, 9/43, 10/43, 11/43
Baekeland, Leo 12/09
Baer, Max 6/34
Baer, Richard 12/60
Baez, Joan 9/66, 10/67, 11/76
Bahomar, Mohammed Javad 8/81
Bahrain
- Becomes independent from Britain 8/71
- First commercial Concorde flight arrives 1/76

Bailey, David 8/65
Bailey, Emmanuel MacDonald 8/38
Bailey, Leonard L. 10/84
Bailey, Pearl 8/90
Bailey, Trevor 8/49, 8/53
Baird, John Logie 1/26, 1/38, 6/46
Baker, George 1/72
Baker, Howard 5/73
Baker, James 10/85, 1/91, 10/91, 12/91
Baker, Janet 8/33
Baker, Jim 11/88
Baker, Josephine 6/06, 10/25, 2/28, 2/29, 4/75
Baker, Kenneth 10/70, 5/86, 11/88
Bakhtiar, Shahpur 12/78, 7/80
Baklanov, Oleg 8/91
Baksi, Joe 4/47
Balch, Emily 12/46
Balcon, Michael 12/39, 12/49
Baldasare, Fred 7/62
Baldwin, Stanley 10/22, 4/23, 5/23, 11/23, 12/23, 1/26, 5/26, 12/26, 5/27, 7/27, 11/27, 5/29, 6/29, 8/31, 11/31, 11/33, 7/34, 2/35, 3/35, 5/35, 6/35, 10/35, 12/35, 7/36, 11/36, 5/37, 12/47
Balewa, Abubakar Tafawa 10/60, 1/66
Balfour, Arthur James 7/02, 10/02, 10/03, 1/06, 5/09, 8/09, 11/11, 11/17, 10/19, 4/22, 3/30
Bali
- 11,000 killed in volcanic eruption 3/63

Balkans
- See also Macedonia, World War I and II
- King Peter crowned in Belgrade 9/04
- Italy, France and Russia want congress 10/08
- Serbia votes against war with Austria 10/08
- 100,000 Montenegrin troops on Albania border 7/11
- Bulgarian-Turkish conflict scares Russia 9/12
- Balkan League surprises Turkish army 10/12
- Serbs and Bulgarians overwhelm Turkey 11/12
- Balkan League demands Turks out of Europe 11/12
- Turkey signs peace with all but Greece 12/12
- Peace talks founder; Turks attack Bulgarians 1/13
- Allies order Turks out of Adrianople 3/13
- Allies take Janina and Andrianople 3/13
- Turks take Chatalja; 4,000 die 3/13
- Montenegrins take Mt Tarabosh from Turks 4/13
- Montenegro takes Scutari; 8,000 killed 4/13
- Greece, Serbia break with Bulgaria 6/13
- Bulgarians and Serbs clash; undeclared war 6/13
- Bulgaria fights ex-allies; enters Serbia 7/13
- Treaty of Bucharest ends second war 8/13
- Turkey and Bulgaria settle frontier dispute 9/13
- Serbs persecute Bosnian Moslems 5/14
- Confederation under Serbian King Peter 11/18

Ball, Ian 3/74
Ball, Jonathan 3/93
Ball, Lucille 8/11, 4/89
Balla, Giacomo 12/12
Balladur, Edouard 12/93, 3/93
Ballard, Robert 7/86
Ballesteros, Severiano 7/79, 4/80, 4/83, 7/84, 7/88
Bamber, Jeremy 10/86
Banana, Canaan 4/80
Bancroft, Squire 4/26
Banda, Hastings 3/59, 8/61, 12/62, 2/63
Bandaranaike, Mrs Sirimavo 7/60, 5/70, 7/77
Bandaranaike, Solomon W.R. Dias 9/59
Bangladesh
- See also Pakistan
- Mujibur Rahman declares independence 3/71
- Pakistan civil war erupts 3/71
- West Pakistan army exacts bloody revenge 4/71
- Thousands killed in continuing violence 4/71
- Two million flee to India 5/71
- India seals border 6/71
- Western rock stars perform charity show for aid for refugees 8/71
- Recognised by India 12/71
- 300 children die in bombed orphanage 12/71
- Official government resigns 12/71
- Indian troops close on Dacca 12/71
- Mujibur Rahman becomes PM 1/72
- Recognised by USSR 1/72
- Recognised by Britain 2/72
- Friendship treaty with India 3/72
- Mujibur Rahman wins first election 3/73
- 10,000 babies being born each day 1/74
- Recognised by Pakistan 2/74
- Monsoon floods half the country 8/74
- Sheikh Mujibur Rahman killed by army 8/75
- Khandakar Ahmed becomes new ruler 8/75
- President Ziaur Rahman killed in coup bid 5/81
- 10,000 die in cyclone 5/85
- Cricket tour by England cancelled 1/86
- 80 killed in local election violence 2/88
- Tornado kills over 1,000 people 4/89
- Cyclone causes severe flooding 4/91
- West promises £12 million in relief after cyclone disaster 5/91
- Fundementalists target Taslima Nasrin 6/94

Bani-Sadr, Abol Hassan 11/79, 1/80, 2/80, 6/81, 7/81
Bank of Credit and Commerce (BCCI) 7/91, 1/92
Banks, Gordon 5/61, 10/72, 8/73
Bannister, Roger 3/50, 8/53, 5/54, 8/54, 12/54
Banting, Frederick 12/21
Bantock, Granville 9/46
Bao Dai, Emperor of Vietnam 3/49, 2/50, 4/54
Barankovics, Istvan 2/49
Barber, Anthony 2/65, 9/67, 7/70, 3/71, 11/71, 6/72, 12/73
Barber, Chris 12/59
Barber, David 11/87, 12/87
Barber, Samuel 1/81
Barbie, Klaus 1/72, 10/73, 1/83, 2/83, 8/83, 5/87, 7/87
Barbirolli, John 7/70
Bardeen, John 12/48
Bardot, Brigitte 9/34, 12/56, 6/59, 10/60, 7/66
Barenboim, Daniel 11/42, 2/76
Baridon, Silvio 4/45
Baring, Evelyn 1/53, 1/55
Barings Bank
- Bankrupted by Leeson's dealings; sold to ING group for £1 3/95

Barker, John 12/72
Barlach, Ernst 12/37
Barnacle, Nora 1/41
Barnard, Christiaan 12/67, 1/68, 7/71, 1/74
Barnardo, Thomas John 9/05
Barnato, Woolf 6/29
Barnes, Rosie 2/87
Barnett, Ross 9/62
Barrault, Jean-Louis 8/47
Barre, Mohammed Siad 1/95
Barre, Raymond 4/78
Barrett, Roger 7/26
Barrett, Vicky 8/63
Barrie, James 12/04, 9/08, 12/17, 4/29, 6/37
Barrow, Clyde 5/34
Barrow, Joe Louis 4/81
Barry, Marion 1/90
Barrymore, John 5/42
Barrymore, Lionel 11/54
Bart, Lionel 12/60
Barth, Karl 11/34
Barthes, Roland 3/80
Bartholdi, Frederic 10/04
Bartholomew, Freddie 1/92
Barthou, Louis 12/13, 10/34
Bartok, Bela 5/17, 9/45
Barton, Derek 12/69
Baruch, Bernard 2/47
Bary, Gerald 5/51
Baryshnikov, Mikhail 1/48, 6/74
Barzani, Mustafa al- 3/75
Baseball
- Red Sox's Babe Ruth bought for $125,000 1/20
- Babe Ruth hits record 60th home run 9/27
- First match broadcast on television 2/31

Basie, Count 8/04, 12/58, 4/84
Basinger, Kim 9/86
Baskt, Leon 12/24
Basutoland
- See also Lesotho
- Becomes independent; renamed Lesotho 10/66

Bateman, Henry 2/70
Bates, Ralph 3/91
Batista, Fulgencio 8/33, 3/52, 12/56, 3/58, 9/58, 1/59, 8/73
Batten, Jean 10/37
Battenberg, Prince Louis of 11/47
Baudouin I, King of Belgium 9/30, 7/51, 4/58, 6/60, 12/60, 7/93
Baudouin, Prince of Belgium 7/50, 8/50
Bauer, Hans 10/55
Bauwens, Mona 9/92
Bavadra, Timoci 5/87
Bavister, B.D. 2/69
Bax, Arnold 10/53
Baylis, Lilian 12/14
Bazin, Marc 6/92
Bazoft, Farzad 3/90
BBC
- See also Broadcasting
- John Reith is General Manager 12/22
- New London studios at Savoy Hill 5/23
- 7/6d to BBC from wireless licence 10/23
- Good reception of Imperial Exhibition 4/24
- Broadcasting for schools 4/24
- Reaches audience of 10 million 12/25
- Reith wants more news, education 12/25
- Controlled broadcasting with Commission 3/26
- Aim of political independence 3/26
- British Broadcasting Corporation in 1927 7/26
- First programmes as a Corporation 1/27
- Reith calls for responsible news 2/27
- Empire listeners hear cricket scores 5/27
- Rejects idea of trial television service 10/28
- Plans £500,000 Portland Place offices 11/28
- Conductor Beecham and BBC form orchestra 1/29
- Permanent orchestra under Adrian Boult 5/30
- New Empire-wide radio service 11/31
- First broadcast from Broadcasting House 3/32
- New headquarters open in Portland Place 5/32
- Henry Hall and the BBC Dance Orchestra 5/32
- Broadcasts to mark Elgar's 75th birthday 11/32
- First Empire broadcast from Daventry 12/32
- Study of public television service 4/34

- Plans first television service 2/35
- First women announcers: Bligh, Cowell 5/36
- First talking pictures on television 8/36
- Television broadcasts, Alexandra Palace 10/36
- Edward VIII announces abdication by radio 12/36
- Spanish, Portuguese, Arabic programmes planned 11/37
- Starts Arabic service 1/38
- Limited television service planned 1/38
- Names eight radio news readers 2/38
- Very High Frequency (VHF) tests succeed 2/38
- First game show: "Spelling Bee" 5/38
- Reith leaves to head Imperial Airways 6/38
- First film on television 9/38
- Lifts ban on conscientious objectors 3/41
- Promotes V for Victory campaign 7/41
- Radio main source of entertainment in UK 12/41
- Broadcasts in morse to French Resistance 3/42
- Overseas services on El Alamein victory 11/42
- Tells Europe of Beveridge Report 12/42
- To develop schools radio 2/44
- Postwar aim is television for all 4/44
- Introduces the Light Programme 7/45
- Begins broadcasts in Russian 3/46
- Third Programme introduced 9/46
- Most popular radio shows detailed 1/47
- Rules issued for "Dick Barton" serial 1/48
- First broadcast from Downing St 10/48
- To buy Shepherd's Bush studios 11/49
- Malcolm Sargent heads Symphony Orchestra 5/50
- To televise 100 sporting events a year 5/50
- First broadcast across the Channel 8/50
- Seven instead of 19 radio news readers 1/51
- No regional accents or women's voices 1/51
- Queen's first Christmas broadcast 12/52
- Television licences rise to £3 11/53
- Cult radio comedy: "The Goon Show" 12/53
- UK television linked to seven international TV companies 6/54
- Dimbleby turns down ITV offer 11/54
- Eamonn Andrews on TV's "This is Your Life" 8/55
- Countering the advent of ITV 9/55
- Colour television at Alexandra Palace 10/55
- Exclusive television rights to cricket 11/55
- "Tonight" programme on television 2/57
- Television programme: "The Sky at Night" 4/57
- Television's audiences overtake radio's 8/57
- Radio revamps to win back listeners 8/57
- Twice as many watch ITV as BBC TV 1/59
- Carleton-Greene is next Director-General 7/59
- Wants second TV channel 1/60
- Broadcaster Gilbert Harding dies 11/60
- "Children's Hour" to be dropped 2/61
- BBC2 proposed 6/62
- "That Was the Week ..." causes row 12/62
- Ends ban on sensitive subjects in comedy 1/63
- To scrap "What's My Line?" 7/63
- "That Was the Week That Was" taken off 12/63
- "Steptoe and Son" is top TV show 1/64
- BBC2 goes on the air 4/64
- David Attenborough heads BBC2 3/65
- Bans showing of "The War Game" 2/66
- Announces plans for colour TV 3/66
- First episode of "Till Death Us Do Part" 6/66
- "The Ken Dodd Show" proves popular 1/67
- Begins TV showing of "The Forsyte Saga" 1/67
- BBC2 begins regular colour broadcasting 7/67
- 17 ex-pirate DJs to join BBC radio 9/67
- Radios 1,2,3,4 begin broadcasting 9/67
- First local radio station - Leicester 11/67
- Popularity of "The Forsyte Saga" 12/68
- "The Dales" radio serial ends 4/69
- Kenneth Clark's "Civilisation" ends 5/69
- "Monty Python's Flying Circus" - a cult 12/70
- Death of broadcasting pioneer John Reith 6/71
- LBC breaks BBC's 50-year radio monopoly 10/73
- 500th episode of TV series "Z Cars" 5/74
- First TV transmission of Ceefax teletext 9/74
- "I, Claudius"; Graves adapted for TV 12/76
- Ian Trethowan becomes Director-General 12/76
- Permanent broadcasting of Commons 4/78
- Thatcher attacks BBC on terrorism 7/79
- "Tinker Tailor Soldier Spy" thriller shown on TV 12/79
- Musicians strike against cuts 6/80
- Musicians end two-month strike 7/80
- First black woman newsreader, Moira Stuart 8/81
- "Breakfast Time" goes on the air 1/83
- Christopher Hughes wins Mastermind quiz 5/83
- Buerk's TV report on Ethiopian famine 11/84
- Drops "Real Lives" documentary from TV 7/85
- Journalists strike over "Real Lives" ban 8/85
- Milne resigns as Director-General 1/87
- Police raid takes Zircon spy programme 2/87
- Michael Checkland is Director-General 2/87
- Whitehouse attacks "obscene" East Enders 4/87
- BBC unions start campaign of strikes in support of pay claim 5/89

Beach, Sylvia 12/22
Beamon, Bob 10/68, 8/91
Bean, Alan 11/69
Beardsley, Dick 3/81
Beatles 1/62, 2/63, 10/63, 11/63, 2/64, 6/64, 7/64, 2/65, 6/65, 7/65, 8/65, 10/65, 1/66, 12/66, 12/66, 6/67, 8/67, 8/67, 1/68, 10/68, 11/68, 3/69, 4/70, 12/70
Beaton, Cecil 1/04, 4/58, 1/80
Beatrice, Princess of Great Britain 10/44
Beatrix, Queen of the Netherlands 1/38, 1/65, 3/66, 1/80, 4/80
Beattie, Owen 11/84
Beatty, David 11/18, 3/36
Beaufre, Andre 8/56
Beaulieu, Priscilla 5/67
Beaverbrook, Lord 10/23, 3/31, 10/36, 12/36, 5/40, 8/40, 12/45, 6/53, 6/64
Becalli, Luigi 8/36
Bech, Harry 12/34
Bechstein, Carl 3/00
Bechuanaland
- See also Botswana
- Future of Seretse Khama in doubt 2/50
- Seretse Khama allowed to return 3/50
- Seretse Khama reunited with wife 4/50
- Khama is no longer Bamangwato chief 11/50
- UK bars Seretse Khama as chief of tribe 3/52
- Seretse Khama returns after exile 9/56
- Gains independence as Botswana 9/66

Beckenbauer, Franz 6/70, 7/74
Becker, Boris 7/85, 7/86, 7/88, 7/89, 7/90
Becker, Gary 12/92
Beckett, Joe 2/19
Beckett, John 5/40
Beckett, Samuel 1/53, 8/55, 12/57, 2/58, 3/70, 12/89
Beckmann, Max 6/19, 12/37, 12/50
Becquerel, Henri 6/01, 8/08
Bedell Smith 5/45
Bedser, Alec 9/58
Beecham, Joseph 12/14, 10/16
Beecham, Thomas 12/14, 6/16, 4/19, 1/29, 10/32, 12/32, 12/33, 3/37, 12/49, 3/61
Beeching, Richard 4/60, 3/61, 3/63, 12/64, 2/65
Beerbohm, Max 5/56
Begin, Menachem 8/13, 3/47, 5/77, 7/77, 11/77, 12/77, 4/78, 9/78, 12/78, 3/79, 4/79, 6/80, 6/81, 10/81, 12/81, 6/82, 9/82, 2/83, 8/83, 3/92
Begun, Joseph 2/87
Behan, Brendan 12/56, 3/64
Behring, Emil von 12/01
Beiderbecke, Bix 3/03, 12/27, 8/31
Belcher, John 10/48, 12/48
Belgian Congo
- See Congo (Belgian), World Wars I and II

Belgium
- Strikes and riots in mines 1/00
- Belgian arrested for threatening Prince 4/00
- World's first PR election 4/00
- Call for universal suffrage 4/01
- Strikes for electoral reform 6/02
- Attempt on Leopold II by anarchist 11/02
- King sets up board to check Congo cruelties 9/04
- Official's suicide after Congo report 3/05
- 39 nations join in Liege exhibition 4/05
- Prince Albert is new Congo sovereign 11/06
- Belgian state takes Congo from king 11/07
- Government to pay king for Congo 2/08
- Liberalisation of Congo announced 10/09
- Chemist Leo Baekeland creates Bakelite 12/09
- King Leopold II dies 12/09
- Fixes African frontiers with rivals 2/10
- Universal suffrage rejected 4/10
- Fire destroys World Exhibition stalls 8/10
- 215,000 march for universal suffrage 8/11
- Parliament rejects universal suffrage 2/13
- Strike grows to 400,000 4/13
- Bans boxing 8/13
- Liege and Brussels fall despite resistance 8/14
- Antwerp falls; government goes to France 10/14
- 7,000 face starvation 10/14
- Controlled by German Army; censorship 12/14
- Cardinal Mercier arrested; mass protests 1/15
- Anti-German demonstrations 9/16
- Cardinal Mercier protests deportations 10/16
- King Albert's 28 divisions fight Germans 9/18
- Seventh Olympic Games start at Antwerp 5/20
- End of Antwerp Olympic Games 8/20
- Cedes Rwanda to Britain 3/21
- Divided into French and Flemish provinces 7/21
- Edith Cavell betrayer sentenced to die 4/22
- Troops join French in occupying Ruhr 1/23
- 100,000 French-speakers' language protest 1/23
- Sabena airline formed 5/23
- 10 soldiers die in German bomb attack 6/23
- Rejects UK reparations committee offer 7/23
- Troops pull out of Ruhr towns 8/24
- Funeral of Cardinal Mercier 1/26
- New currency unit, Belga, launched 10/26
- Menin Gate memorial at Ypres unveiled 7/27
- Herge's Tintin cartoon in newspaper 1/29
- Attempt on Italian Crown Prince Umberto 10/29
- Henri Jaspar resigns over Flemish power 11/29
- Study customs union with Holland 6/32
- King Albert dies; Leopold III succeeds 2/34
- 42 miners and 17 rescuers die at Mons mine 5/34
- UK and France want anti-aggression pact 2/35
- Rexist fascists win 21 seats 5/36
- Eden warns Britain will defend Belgium 11/36
- Hitler guarantees her neutrality 1/37
- Hitler pledges to defend Belgium 10/37
- Japan rejects Brussels talks on China 10/37
- Neutrality restated 8/39
- Frontier defences fully manned 8/39
- War trade pact made with UK 4/40
- Germany invades 5/40
- Surrenders to Germany 5/40
- King Leopold III arrested 6/44
- Customs pact with Luxembourg and Holland 9/44
- Exiled government under Pierlot returns 9/44
- Signs economic pact with France 3/45
- Leopold III refuses to abdicate 6/45
- Leopold III's referendum call rejected 1/46
- Communists gain in national elections 2/46
- "Benelux" customs union effective 11/47
- Pact with France, UK and rest of Benelux 3/48
- Signs North Atlantic Treaty 4/49
- Death of Maurice Maeterlinck 5/49
- Exiled King rejects new abdication calls 2/50
- Votes for return of Leopold III 3/50
- Gaston Eyskens' government resigns 3/50
- King Leopold III returns from exile 7/50
- Socialist government resigns 7/50
- Leopold abdicates in favour of son 7/50
- Baudouin sworn in as Prince Regent 8/50
- King Leopold III will abdicate 6/51
- Leopold III abdicates 7/51
- King Baudouin I takes over 7/51
- Joins European Economic Community 3/57
- King opens World's Fair, Brussels 4/58
- 75 die in Congo riots; troops fly in 11/59
- Loses authority in Congo; Lumumba victory 5/60
- Gives Congo independence; Lumumba angry 6/60
- Hammarskjold says leave Congo 8/60
- Swedish replace Belgian forces in Congo 8/60
- Austerity policy starts fights and strikes 12/60
- Baudouin weds Dona Fabiola y Aragon 12/60
- King cuts short honeymoon because of riots 12/60
- 60 injured in anti-austerity protests 1/61
- Savage attack on Europeans in Congo 1/61
- Belgian paratroops fly into Congo 1/61
- 73 die in Boeing 707 crash near Brussels 2/61
- Lumumba dies mysteriously in Congo 2/61
- Pro-Lumumba and UN troops fight in Congo 2/61
- Federation of states agreed in Congo 3/61
- Congo army arrests Moise Tshombe 4/61
- Tshombe released in Congo 6/61
- Cyrille Adoula appointed Congo Premier 8/61
- UN crushes Katangan rebels in Congo 9/61
- Congo army attacks Katangan rebels 10/61
- Tshombe violates Congo cease-fire 11/61
- Tshombe and Kasavubu tied to Lumumba death 11/61
- Bodies of Italians sold in Congo market 11/61
- Tshombe gives up plans for Katangan state 12/61
- Supports UK entry to EEC 4/62
- Congo independence plan presented to UN 8/62
- Flemish protesters riot in Brussels 10/62
- Five acquitted of killing thalidomide baby 11/62
- Katangan rebels fight UN troops in Congo 12/62
- Tshombe flees Congo as UN troops advance 12/62
- Statue of "Mannekin Pis" stolen 1/63
- Katanga surrenders to Congo 1/63
- Tshombe put under house arrest, Congo 1/63
- Tshombe sworn in as Congo Premier 7/64
- Congo forces find 300 bodies in Bukavi 8/64
- European mercenaries aid Congo troops 8/64
- Belgian paratroops drop into Congo 11/64
- 2,000 Congo state troops attack rebels 11/64
- Congo rebels massacre 15 UK missionaries 12/64
- 322 die in department store fire 5/67
- Surrealist Rene Magritte dies 8/67
- Eddy Merckx becomes world cycling champ 8/67
- 63 killed in air crash 10/71
- Treaty of Brussels (EEC) signed 1/72
- Albert Claude wins Medicine Nobel 12/74
- Christian-Rene de Duve: Medicine Nobel 12/74
- Singer Jacques Brel dies 10/78
- Attempted assassination of General Haig 6/79
- Ship with nuclear cargo sinks off coast 8/84
- 41 die in Heysel football stadium riot 5/85
- Bans British soccer teams 5/85
- 200 die aboard Channel ferry, Zeebrugge 3/87
- Herald of Free Enterprise refloated 4/87
- Paul Vanden Boeynants is kidnapped 1/89
- Paul Vanden Boeynants is freed for a £1 million-ransom 2/89
- Soviet MiG-23 fighter crashes after flying pilotless 7/89

Bell, Alexander Graham 1/15, 8/22
Bell, Mary 12/68
Bell, Stuart 6/87
Bell, Vanessa 1/14, 3/41
Belloc, Hilaire Pierre 7/53
Bellow, Saul 12/76
Ben Bella, Mohammed Ahmed 11/54, 11/61, 7/62, 8/62, 9/63, 10/63, 3/64, 7/64, 6/65, 7/79
Ben Kheddah, Benyoussef 3/62, 7/62
Ben-Gurion, David 1/47, 5/48, 1/49, 2/51, 11/53, 11/55, 10/56, 2/57, 10/57, 11/59, 3/60, 5/60, 1/61, 6/63, 9/65, 12/73
Ben-Tzvi, Itzhak 12/52, 4/63
Benaud, Richie 2/59
Benes, Eduard 5/20, 9/21, 1/24, 9/29, 12/35, 8/38, 10/38, 12/43, 5/45, 9/47, 2/48, 6/48, 9/48
Benn, Anthony Wedgwood
- See Benn, Tony

Benn, Nigel 4/90
Benn, Tony 11/46, 2/55, 4/55, 10/60, 11/60, 11/60, 3/61, 5/61, 7/61, 5/63, 7/63, 6/64, 10/65, 7/66, 1/67, 6/71, 3/74, 3/75, 6/75, 8/75, 5/79, 9/81, 1/84, 3/84
Bennett, Alan 5/34, 12/61, 12/91
Bennett, Arnold 12/02, 12/08, 5/09, 12/28, 3/31
Bennett, D.C.T. 3/50
Bennett, Floyd 5/26
Bennett, Gareth 12/87
Bennett, James Gordon 5/18
Bennett, Jill 10/90
Bentley, Derek 12/52
Bentley, Dick 12/53
Bentley, Elizabeth 8/48
Bentley, Nicolas 8/78
Bentsen, Lloyd 11/88
Benz, Carl 4/29
Berall, John 11/69
Berbick, Trevor 11/86
Berchtold, Leopold 8/12, 1/15
Beregovoy, Pierre 4/92, 3/93, 5/93
Berenguer, Damaso 1/30, 2/30, 2/31, 4/31
Bergman, Ingmar 7/18, 12/58
Bergman, Ingrid 8/15, 12/42, 7/43, 12/46, 8/49, 6/60, 8/82
Bergson, Henri 1/41
Beria, Lavrenti 10/45, 3/53, 7/53, 8/53, 12/53
Berisha, Sadi 4/92
Berkeley, Busby 3/76
Berkeley, Lennox 9/54, 12/89
Berkowitz, David 5/78
Berlin
- See Germany

Berlin Wall 11/89, 12/89
Berlin, Irving 12/12, 12/35, 12/43, 12/47, 9/89
Berlin, Isaiah 6/09
Berliner, Emil 8/29
Berlinguer, Enrico 6/84
Berlusconi, Silvio 3/94, 12/94
Bermuda
- Governor Richard Sharples assassinated 3/73
- State of emergency declared 3/73
- 19 die when UK barque Marques sinks 6/84

Bern, Paul 9/32
Bernadotte, Folke 8/48, 9/48
Bernardi, Mario de 11/26
Bernhardt, Prince of the Netherlands 2/76, 8/76
Bernhardt, Sarah 6/02, 9/10, 3/12, 1/14, 11/15, 3/23
Bernhill, Jack 12/71
Bernstein, Carl 5/73, 8/73
Bernstein, Leonard 8/18, 12/61, 9/71, 12/74, 10/90
Bernstein, Sidney Lewis 2/93
Berri, Nabih 4/85, 5/85
Berruti, Livio 9/60
Berry, Anthony 10/84
Berry, Charles 12/68
Berry, Roger 2/90
Berteaux, Maurice 5/11
Besley, Campbell 2/14
Besse, Georges 11/86
Bessio, Atef 6/92
Best, Charles 12/21, 12/29
Best, George 5/68, 1/70, 8/71
Best, Keith 4/87, 9/87, 10/87
Bethlehem
- Catholics fight Greek Orthodox 1/05

Betjeman, John 12/58, 6/69, 10/72, 12/72, 5/84
Bettaney, Michael 4/84
Betterand, John 9/83
Betz, Pauline 7/46
Bevan, Aneurin 9/38, 4/39, 2/43, 1/46, 3/46, 1/48, 4/48, 7/48, 11/49, 1/51, 4/51, 3/52, 10/52, 11/52, 4/54, 9/54, 3/55, 5/55, 12/55, 10/56, 10/57, 7/58, 4/59, 7/60
Beveridge, William 3/26, 12/42, 3/63
Bevin, Ernest 10/35, 5/40, 3/41, 5/43, 12/43, 7/45, 8/45, 11/45, 12/45, 7/46, 4/47, 5/47, 6/47, 7/47, 12/47, 1/48, 3/48, 6/48, 3/49, 9/49, 3/51, 4/51
Bey, Talaat 1/13
Beyer, Elsie 2/48
Bhindranwale, Sant Jarnail Singh 6/84
Bhuller, Narinder Singh 6/84
Bhutan
- Premier Jigme Dorji assassinated 4/64
- Jigme Wangchuk escapes death attempt 7/65

Bhutto, Benazir 1/84, 4/86, 8/86, 11/88, 12/88, 11/89, 8/90, 10/93
Bhutto, Zulfikar Ali 9/65, 12/70, 12/71, 3/77, 4/77, 7/77, 3/78, 2/79, 4/79, 8/90
Biafra
- Announces its secession from Nigeria 5/67
- Nigerian government troops invade 7/67
- Europeans flee 7/67
- Federal troops take Enugu 10/67
- Nigerians mount major assault 8/68
- Red Cross can fly relief into Biafra 9/68
- 300 killed by bomb in market 2/69
- Evacuation of Umuahia town begins 4/69
- Federal troops capture Umuahia 4/69
- Nigeria bans Red Cross relief flights 6/69
- Nigeria eases air blockade 7/69
- 300,000 face famine in war zone 11/69
- Surrenders to Nigerian government 1/70
- Starvation, looting and rape reported 1/70

Bich, Marcel 5/94
Bidault, Georges 12/45, 4/47, 2/48, 10/49, 8/62, 3/63
Bielostock
- Fierce pogroms against Jews; many die 6/06

Biffen, John 11/78, 1/81
Big Bang
- See Space

Biggs, Ronald 4/64, 2/74, 5/74
Bignone, Reynaldo 4/83, 9/83
Bikila, Abebe 9/60, 10/64
Bikini Atoll 3/54
Biko, Steve 12/71, 9/77, 11/77, 12/77, 1/78
Bilk, Acker 12/59
Billiards and snooker
- Joe Davis and maximum break 1/55
- Steve Davis, 23, wins world championship 4/81
- Steve Davis regains world title 5/83
- Dennis Taylor becomes world champion 4/85
- Joe Johnson becomes world champion 5/86
- Stephen Hendry is youngest-ever snooker champion 4/90

Binet, Alfred 4/05
Bing, Rudolf 8/47
Bingham, David 1/72
Binyon, Laurence 12/18
Birch, Nigel 1/58
Birdseye, Clarence 6/30, 10/56
Birendra, King of Nepal 2/75
Birkenhead, Lord 5/26, 9/30
Birkin, H.R.S. 6/29
Birmingham
- British Industries Fair 2/27
- Debut: Peggy Ashcroft, Laurence Olivier 9/27
- New £1.5 million shopping centre 3/58
- Nine jailed for IRA bombing 5/75
- £45 million National Exhibition Centre 2/76
- Old Bailey rejects pub bombers' appeal 1/88
- West Midlands crime squad disbanded after corruption charges 8/89

Birmingham, Bishop of 10/47
Biro, Ladislao 11/46
Birrell, Augustine 4/16
Bishop, Maurice 3/79, 10/83, 11/83
Bishop, Michael 12/89
Bismarck, Otto von 5/42
Bitov, Oleg 1/84, 9/84
Black Hand Society
- Serbian group accused of Archduke's murder 6/14

Black Hundred
- Anti-Semitic group roaming Ukraine 11/05

Black, Christopher 8/83
Black, Douglas 6/84
Black, Hugo 10/37, 6/71
Blackburn, Tony 9/67
Blackett, Patrick 12/48
Blackmore, Richard 1/00
Blackpool
- Fire destroys Fun House 12/91

Blaiberg, Philip 8/69
Blair, Eric
- See George Orwell

Blair, Tony
- Elected leader of Labour Party 7/94
- Wins the Clause Four battle 4/95

Blake, George 4/61, 5/61, 10/66, 11/66

Blake, Peter 12/61
Blakelock, PC Keith 10/85, 3/87
Blakely, David 4/55
Blakey, Art 12/58
Blanchflower, Danny 2/61, 5/61, 12/93
Blanco, Luis 6/73
Bland, Colin 8/68
Blaney, Neil 5/70, 7/70
Blank, Theodor 11/55
Blankers-Koen, Fanny 8/48
Bleasdale, Alan 12/91
Bleriot, Louis 9/07, 12/07, 7/09, 9/13, 8/36
Bligh, Jasmine 5/36
Bliss, Arthur 11/53, 3/75
Blixen, Karen 11/37
Bloch, Dora 7/76
Blomberg, Werner von 1/33, 3/36, 1/38
Bloom, Claire 12/52
Bloom, Marshall 3/67
Blum, Leon 6/36, 1/38, 4/38, 10/41, 4/43, 5/45, 12/46, 1/47, 11/47, 3/50
Blundell, Mark 6/92
Blunden, Edward 12/18
Blunt, Anthony 11/79, 3/83
Blyth, Chay 8/71
Blyton, Enid 11/68, 12/83, 1/87
Boac
- See Airlines
Board, Lilian 9/69, 12/70
Boat Races
- Cambridge win; score now 40 wins each 3/29
- Cambridge win; first lead over Oxford 4/30
- Cambridge win for 10th consecutive time 4/33
- Cambridge win in record time 3/34
- Oxford win after 13 losses in a row 3/37
- Oxford boat sinks 3/51
- Cambridge win re-run by 12 lengths 3/51
- Oxford win in blizzard 3/52
- Oxford win 100th race 4/54
- Oxford win in record time 3/76
- Oxford win after Cambridge boat sinks 3/78
- Oxford win in closest finish 4/80
- Brown 1st woman to coax Oxford boat team 4/81
- Oxford win by eight lengths 4/81
- Oxford win in record time 3/84
- Oxford wins 136th race 3/90
- Oxford wins for the sixth successive year 4/92
- Cambridge wins 139th race 3/93
- Cambridge win the 140th 3/94
Bobbitt, John Wayne 11/93
Bobbitt, Lorena 1/94
Boccioni, Umberto 4/12, 12/12, 8/16, 12/18
Bodell, Jack 3/70
Boehme, Hans 5/45
Boeing
- See Aviation
Boeing, William Edward 7/16, 7/54, 9/56
Boell, Heinrich 2/74, 7/85
Boer War
- See Britain (Empire and Commomwealth), South Africa
Boesak, Allan 8/85
Boesky, Ivan 11/86, 12/86
Boeynants, Paul Vanden 1/89, 2/89
Bogarde, Dirk 12/56
Bogart, Humphrey 10/41, 12/42, 10/47, 3/52, 1/57
Bogdanov, Michael 3/82, 12/82
Bogrov, Mordkha 9/11
Bohlen, Count Krupp von 5/23
Bohm, Karl 8/81
Bohr, Niels 12/22, 11/62
Boito, Arrigo 6/18
Bokassa, Jean-Bedel 1/66, 12/77, 9/79, 10/79, 12/80
Bolan, Marc 9/77
Bolivia
- 80,000 Indians revolt against government 8/27
- Border fights with Uruguay; League plea 12/28
- Paraguay signs treaty to end dispute 9/29
- Ends 3-year Chaco dispute with Paraguay 6/35
- Coup ousts President Sorzano 5/36
- Che Guevara shot dead in jungle 10/67
- Right-wingers seize power in coup 8/71
- Barbie, "Butcher of Lyons", arrives 1/72
- Nazi Klaus Barbie freed from detention 10/73
- 102 die as Boeing crashes in main street 10/76
- Klaus Barbie arrested 1/83
- Klaus Barbie expelled 2/83
Bologna
- 84 die in station bomb blast 8/80
Bolsheviks
- See also Russia, USSR
- Birth of, led by Lenin 11/03
Bolt, Robert 2/95
Bomberg, David 12/14
Bomboko, Justin 4/61
Bonar Law, Andrew 11/11, 1/14, 12/16, 3/18, 1/19, 6/20, 3/21, 10/22, 11/22, 5/23, 10/23
Bond, Alan 9/83
Bond, Edward 12/66
Bondfield, Margaret 4/30, 6/53
Bonham-Carter, Mark 3/58, 4/67
Bonhoeffer, Dietrich 2/06
Bonington, Chris 8/62
Bonnard, Pierre 1/47
Bonner, Yelena 12/75, 4/76, 11/81, 12/81, 5/84, 8/84, 12/89
Bonnie and Clyde
- See Barrow and Parker
Bonomi, Ivanoe 6/44
Booker Prize
- P.H. Newby wins 12/69
- Bernice Rubens wins with "The Elected Member" 4/70
- John Berger wins 11/72
- Kingsley Amis: "The Old Devils" 10/86
- Won by Kazuo Ishiguro for "The Remains of the Day" 12/89
- Nigerian Ben Okri wins prize for "The Famished Road" 10/91
Boon, David 11/87
Boot, Jesse 6/31
Booth, Evangeline 9/34
Booth, William Bramwell 7/05, 8/05, 8/12, 1/29, 6/29
Boothroyd, Betty 4/92
Borden, Robert 9/11
Borg, Bjorn 6/56, 7/76, 7/78, 7/79, 7/80, 7/81, 1/83, 4/91
Borges, Jorge Luis 6/86
Borges, Tomas 9/78
Boris, King of Bulgaria 10/18, 6/23, 5/34, 8/43
Bork, Robert 10/73
Bormann, Frank 12/65, 12/68
Bormann, Martin 1/44, 10/46, 4/73
Borneo
- See also British North Borneo, Brunei
- Rich oil strike in jungle area 1/11
Borneo, British North
- Joins Federation of Malaysia 9/63
Borodin, Igor 6/14
Borotra, Jean 7/24, 7/26, 7/32
Borsellino, Paolo 1/93
Borzov, Valery 9/72
Bosanquet, Reginald 11/79
Bosch, Carl 12/31
Bosch, Juan 4/65
Bosnia
- See also Balkans, Yugoslavia
- Archduke Franz Ferdinand shot in Sarajevo 6/14
- Trial of Sarajevo conspirators 10/14
- Conspirators executed; except Princip 2/16
- Bosnian Serb snipers open fire on civilians in Sarajevo 3/92
- UN forces take control of Sarajevo airport 7/92
- Peace plan proposed over division of Bosnia 1/93
- John Edwards is first British soldier to be killed in Bosnia 1/93
- US Air Force drops emergency aid to trapped Bosnian Moslems 3/93
- Besieged Moslem town of Srebrenica falls to Serbian forces 4/93
- Serbian mortar attack kills 12 youths 6/93
- Peace plan fails 6/93
- Croats destroy Mostar Bridge 11/93
- NATO shoots down Serb warplanes 2/94
- 68 killed in Sarajevo market by mortar bomb 2/94
- Serbs say no to latest peace plan 8/94
- Serbs defiant despite NATO strike 11/94
- Jimmy Carter negotiates ceasefire 12/94
- Four-month cease-fire begins 1/95
- Lt. Gen. Rupert Smith replaces Rose as UN commander 1/95
- Premier says "prepare to fight for 10 years" 4/95
- New crisis as Serbs take peacekeepers hostage 5/95
Botha, Louis 2/07, 12/09, 4/10, 5/10, 6/10, 9/10, 1/14, 9/14, 11/14, 5/15, 8/19
Botha, Pieter Willem 9/78, 6/84, 12/84, 7/85, 8/85, 9/85, 6/86, 5/87, 2/89, 7/89, 8/89, 9/89, 5/90
Botha, Pik 5/86, 3/88
Botham, Ian 6/78, 7/81, 7/82, 11/85, 5/86, 3/90, 7/93
Botswana
- See also Bechuanaland
- Burton marries Taylor in village 10/75
- Sir Seretse Khama, President, dies 7/80
- Raided by South African forces 5/86
Bottomley, Horatio 5/22
Bottomley, Virginia 8/88
Botvinnik, Mikhail 5/51
Boudiaf, Mohammed 6/92
Boulez, Pierre 3/25
Boult, Adrian 5/30, 12/32, 4/40, 1/50, 5/50, 2/58
Boulting, Roy 12/42
Boumedienne, Houari 6/65, 12/78
Bourgeois, Leon 1/20, 9/25
Bourges-Manoury, Maurice 6/57
Bourguiba, Habib 6/55, 3/56, 7/57, 11/57, 2/58, 10/58, 1/63, 1/84, 11/87
Bourj al Barajneh 2/87
Boutros Ghali, Boutros 1/92
Bouvier, Jacqueline
- See Kennedy, Jacqueline
Bowbelle (dredger) 9/89
Bowden, Herbert 8/67
Bowen, Elizabeth 2/73
Bowes, Bill 6/32, 8/32
Bowes-Lyon, Elizabeth
- See also Elizabeth, Queen Mother 1/23, 4/23
Bowie, David 3/78
Boxer Rebellion
- See China
Boxer, Charles Mark Edward 7/88
Boxing
- Marquess of Queensberry dies 1/00
- Jeffries wins heavyweight crown 4/00
- Jeffries beats Fitzsimmons for title 7/02
- Jeffries retains heavyweight title 8/04
- Joe Bowker gains bantamweight title 10/04
- Jack Johnson wins heavyweight title 12/08
- Riots after Jack Johnson keeps title 7/10
- Charpentier's European heavyweight crown 6/13
- Banned in Belgium 8/13
- Carpentier beaten by Joe Jeanette, USA 3/14
- Jess Willard wins heavyweight crown 4/15
- Joe Beckett is British heavyweight champ 2/19
- Dempsey beats Willard for heavyweight title 7/19
- Triumph of "Manassa Mauler" Dempsey 7/19
- Dempsey beats Charpentier in four rounds 7/21
- Jack Dempsey beats Gibbons; keeps title 7/23
- Tunney beats Dempsey on points 9/26
- Tunney beats Dempsey; long count scandal 9/27
- Tunney keeps heavyweight crown 9/27
- Dempsey retires 2/28
- Heavyweight Schmeling beats Sharkey 6/30
- Sharkey beats heavyweight Scheling 6/32
- Carnera beats Sharkey, heavyweight title 6/33
- US heavyweight Max Baer beats Carnera 6/34
- UK heavyweight Petersen beaten by Neusel 2/35
- Championship bouts must be 15 rounds 2/35
- Joe Louis beats Braddock; new champion 6/37
- Joe Louis beats Britain's Tommy Farr 8/37
- Louis knocks out Schmeling in 1st round 6/38
- Len Harvey is world heavyweight champion 7/39
- US boxer Joe Louis to retire 10/42
- UK's Mills loses world title fight 5/46
- UK boxer Woodcock loses world title bout 4/47
- UK's Monaghan wins world flyweight title 3/48
- Joe Louis retains heavyweight title 6/48
- Mills wins light-heavyweight title 7/48
- Joe Louis announces his retirement 3/49
- Joey Maxim is light-heavyweight champion 1/50
- UK and Empire heavyweight champion: Gardner 11/50
- Sugar Ray Robinson becomes middleweight 2/51
- Robinson avenges his loss to La Motta 2/51
- Turpin wins Robinson's middleweight title 7/51
- Turpin loses return match to Robinson 9/51
- Marciano stops Joe Louis' comeback hopes 10/51
- Joe Louis retires a second time 10/51
- Marciano knocks out Walcott; keeps title 5/53
- Turpin wins back title; beats Humez 6/53
- Marciano knocks out LaStarza 9/53
- Olsen wins Turpin's middleweight title 10/53
- Marciano beats Charles; 47th victory 9/54
- Robinson regains middleweight title 12/55
- Rocky Marciano retires undefeated 4/56
- Robinson middleweight champion for fifth time 3/58
- Henry Cooper outpoints Zora Folley 10/58
- Cooper wins Empire heavyweight title 1/59
- Cooper's points win over Brian London 1/59
- Johansson wins heavyweight boxing title 6/59
- Johansson beats Patterson in third round 6/59
- Patterson beats Johansson; retakes title 6/60
- Three US Olympic golds, including Clay 9/60
- First professional bout for Cassius Clay 10/60
- UK's Downes wins world middleweight bout 7/61
- Sonny Liston is world heavyweight champ 9/62
- US Boxer Davey Moore dies after fight 3/63
- Henry Cooper floors Cassius Clay 6/63
- Clay is world heavyweight champion 2/64
- Freddie Mills found shot dead 7/65
- Cassius Clay beats Floyd Patterson 11/65
- Randy Turpin found shot dead 5/66
- Cassius Clay beats Henry Cooper 5/66
- McGowan is world flyweight champion 6/66
- Cassius Clay stripped of boxing title 4/67
- Rocky Marciano dies in plane crash 8/69
- Joe Frazier becomes heavyweight champion 2/70
- Cooper keeps British heavyweight title 3/70
- Cooper wins European heavyweight title 11/70
- Death of heavyweight Sonny Liston 1/71
- Bugner: European and Commonwealth titles 3/71
- Henry Cooper retires 3/71
- Muhammed Ali beats Joe Bugner 2/73
- Conteh takes world lightweight title 5/73
- Conteh wins light-heavyweight title 10/74
- Ali regains world heavyweight title 10/74
- Ali beats Frazier; regains title in Manila 9/75
- Ali beats Young to keep title 4/76
- Ali knocks out UK's Richard Dunn 5/76
- Ali beats Norton to keep title 9/76
- Ali keeps title by beating Shavers 9/77
- Leon Spinks beats Ali for world title 2/78
- Ali beats Spinks to win back title 9/78
- Muhammad Ali retires 6/79
- Minter wins world middleweight title 3/80
- Hagler beats Minter to win title 9/80
- Welsh boxer Owen dies after title fight 11/80
- Joe Louis dies 4/81
- Jack Dempsey dies 5/83
- McGuigan is world featherweight champion 6/85
- UK Honeyghan is welterweight champion 9/86
- Mike Tyson is world heavyweight champion 11/86
- Tyson beats Tucker; undisputed champion 8/87
- Honeyghan loses welterweight title 10/87
- Frank Bruno and Mike Tyson fight for heavyweight title 2/89
- James Douglas beats Mike Tyson in world heavyweight title 2/90
- Nigel Benn wins the world middleweight title 4/90
- Michael Watson faces brain surgery after collapsing in ring 9/91
- Mike Tyson is jailed for six years for rape 3/92
Boycott, Geoffrey 8/77, 9/78, 9/81, 12/81, 3/82, 10/83, 1/84, 9/86
Boyd, Patti 1/66
Boyd-Carpenter, John 5/52
Boyd-Orr, John 10/49
Boyer, Charles 8/78
Brabham, Jack 7/60, 8/66, 9/66, 10/70
Bradbury, Malcolm 12/75
Bradbury, Ray 8/20
Braddock, James J. 6/37
Bradford
- Rushdie's "Satanic Verses" is publicly burnt by Moslems 1/89
Bradford, Robert 11/81
Bradley, David 9/48
Bradley, Omar 9/44, 2/48, 5/51, 4/81
Bradman, Donald 1/30, 5/30, 7/30, 6/38, 8/48, 9/48
Brady, Ian 10/65, 4/66, 5/66, 8/87
Brady, Jim 3/81
Brailovsky, Alexander 9/20
Braine, John 12/59
Brambell, Wilfred 1/64
Branagh, Kenneth 12/83, 12/89, 12/92
Brancusi, Constantin 3/57
Brandenburg Gate 12/89
Brando, Marlon 4/24, 12/47, 12/53, 3/55, 12/59, 8/63, 12/72, 3/73
Brandt, Willy 12/13, 8/61, 2/63, 6/63, 8/65, 10/69, 3/70, 5/70, 9/72, 10/72, 11/72, 6/73, 5/74, 10/92
Brangwyn, Frank 6/56
Branson, Richard 6/86
Braque, Georges 10/05, 12/11, 12/46, 8/63
Brasher, Christopher 5/54, 11/56
Brattain, Walter 12/48
Brauchitsch, Walther von 8/39, 5/45
Braun, Eva 4/45, 10/55
Braun, Wernher von 2/58, 6/77
Brazauskas, Algirdas 11/92
Brazil
- See also World War II
- Signs Guyana arbitration with Britain 6/04
- Martial law follows riots 11/04
- Declares war on Germany; seizes ships 6/17
- Rebels take Sao Paulo; 250 die 7/24
- Leaves League of Nations 6/26
- Army coup leaders make Vargas President 10/30
- New leaders promise "reconciliation" 10/30
- Vargas dissolves congress 11/30
- 30,000 German Jews allowed to enter 6/39
- 21 Latin-American countries break with Axis 1/42
- Declares war on Germany 8/42
- Vargas faces corruption charges 8/54
- President Vargas commits suicide 8/54
- Margot Fonteyn reunited with husband 6/59
- Rhinoceros elected in Sao Paulo 10/59
- Brasilia, new capital by Costa and Niemeyer 12/59
- Brasilia made new capital 4/60
- Great Train Robber Ronald Biggs arrested 2/74
- Refuses Biggs' extradition 2/74
- Ronald Biggs freed from jail 5/74
- Train robber Biggs drinks on Navy ship 4/77
- Tancredo Neves elected President 1/85
- Neves dies on eve of inauguration 4/85
- Nazi Josef Mengele's body found 6/85
- 127 feared dead in floods 2/88
- John Major attends Earth Summit in Rio de Janeiro 6/92
- President Collor de Mello is impeached by parliament 9/92
- 111 prisoners die in Sao Paulo jail riot 10/92
- Voters reject restoration of monarchy 4/93
Brearley, Mike 7/81
Breasley, Scobie 6/64
Brecht, Bertolt 12/28, 2/33, 12/33, 4/41, 12/47, 8/56
Brede, Paul 5/32
Breedlove, Craig 8/63, 10/64
Brel, Jacques 4/29, 10/78
Bremer, Arthur 5/72, 8/72
Bremner, Billy 5/65, 9/75
Brenton, Howard 12/80
Bresson, Robert 9/07
Brest-Litovsk
- Gateway to Russia falls to Germans 8/15
- Site of German-Russian peace talks 12/17
Bretano, Otto von 9/01
Breton, Andre 12/20, 12/25, 9/66
Breuer, Marcel 12/26, 12/59
Brews, Sid 6/34
Brezhnev, Leonid
- Born 12/06
- Becomes head of state 5/60
- Succeeded by Mikoyan as Soviet President 7/64
- Ousts Khrushchev; becomes party leader 10/64
- Tries to heal Sino-Soviet split 11/64
- Calls for end to Indo-Pakistan conflict 9/65
- Opens 23rd Party Congress 3/66
- Calls for US to pull out of Vietnam 3/66
- Takes title of General Secretary 4/66
- Puts pressure on Czechoslovakia 7/68
- Signs pact with Nixon 5/72
- Improves relations with US during visit 6/73
- Meets Nixon in Moscow 6/74
- Reaches broad nuclear agreement with US 11/74
- Signs human rights pact in Helsinki 8/75
- Takes over as USSR President 6/77
- Agrees to defer neutron bomb production 4/78
- Signs SALT treaty 6/79
- Opens 22nd Olympic Games in Moscow 7/80
- Dies 11/82
Briand, Aristide 1/11, 3/13, 10/15, 11/15, 3/17, 1/21, 7/21, 11/25, 12/26, 7/29, 9/29, 10/29, 1/32, 3/32
Bridgeman, Percy 12/46
Bridges, Robert 7/13, 4/30
Bridgewater, Carl 9/78, 11/79
Briers, Richard 3/56
Briggs, Raymond 12/83
Brighton
- First nude bathing resort in Britain 8/79
Bristol
- Bath killer Smith sentenced to death 7/15
- Violent riots against unemployment 2/32
- Disturbances in St Pauls 1/82
Britain (Empire and Commonwealth)
- See also World Wars I and II
- Third Imperial Conference 6/02
- Tariff League for preferential trading 5/03
- Lyttleton new Colonial Secretary 10/03
- Convention 'yes' to coolies for colonies 5/04
- Survey shows Empire's extent and growth 3/06
- Fund to help Jamaican earthquake victims 1/07
- Meeting of colonial states' leaders 4/07
- Empire rallies round; offers armies 8/14
- 200,000 Empire troops died in war 11/18
- Two minutes' silence; Armistice memorial 11/19
- Winston Churchill is Colonial Secretary 2/21
- Rwanda ceded by Belgium 3/21
- Baldwin wants preferential trade 11/23
- Dominions can make foreign treaties 11/23
- Imperial Conference opens in London 10/26
- Conference unveils self-ruling dominions 11/26
- Chamberlain wants closer ties 9/27
- Airmail service for Middle East and India 3/29
- Imperial Conference, London 10/30
- Conference fails to agree on tariff terms 11/30
- Air route to central Africa 2/31
- Beaverbrook ends Empire Crusade movement 3/31
- "Buy British" drive in Australia 11/31
- New BBC Empire-wide radio service 11/31
- Tariff concession for Empire imports 2/32
- First Christmas Day royal broadcast 12/32
- World Economic Conference 6/33
- Malcolm MacDonald is Colonial Secretary 6/35
- Spanish rebels close Gibraltar frontier 8/36
- King George VI is crowned head of Empire 5/37
- John Gort heads Imperial General Staff 12/37
- King and Queen at Glasgow Empire Exhibition 5/38
- New plan to rule unified Palestine 10/38
- Duke of Kent becomes Australian Governor-General 10/38
- Duke of Windsor made Bahamas Governor 7/40
- Japanese assets frozen throughout Empire 7/41
- Duke of Windsor resigns as Bahamas Governor 3/45

- Alexander made Governor-General of Canada 7/45
- Premiers meet in London 4/46
- Warns Argentina over Falkland Islands 2/48
- Sends RN cruiser to Falklands 2/48
- Protests to Argentina over Deception Island 3/48
- Deadlock in meat talks with Argentina 1/51
- Argentinians repel landing party on island 2/52
- King George VI dies in sleep 2/52
- Queen Elizabeth II leads Commonwealth 2/52
- Slim is Australian Governor-General 9/52
- Elizabeth II is crowned in Westminster Abbey 6/53
- Troops sent to British Guiana 10/53
- Guiana constitution suspended; arrests 10/53
- Pakistan: Commonwealth Islamic republic 11/53
- Offers Malta new constitution 12/53
- Queen vows to devote life to Commonwealth ideal 12/53
- Queen opens New Zealand parliament 1/54
- Ex-British Guiana Premier Jagan jailed 4/54
- Anti-UK party wins British Honduras poll 4/54
- Commonwealth Games, Vancouver 8/54
- States accept Pakistan as republic 2/55
- Templar chief of Imperial General Staff 4/55
- Singapore independence talks fail 5/56
- Approval for Gold Coast independence 5/56
- Last British soldier leaves Suez Zone 6/56
- Furious at Egypt's seizure of Suez Canal 7/56
- Indian and New Zealand premiers honoured 7/56
- Canal talks with Egypt and France 8/56
- Expels two Egyptian diplomats 8/56
- Australian Premier's Suez inquiry team 8/56
- Troops in Cyprus to meet Suez crisis 8/56
- Nasser rejects Eden's 3-power Suez plan 9/56
- Eden and Lloyd get UK-French unity on Suez 9/56
- Gold Coast independence for March 1957 9/56
- Khama back in Bechuanaland after exile 9/56
- UK troops in toffee tin blast, Cyprus 9/56
- 15-nation Suez Canal Users' Association 10/56
- Warns Israel against action on Suez 10/56
- Anti-UK mobs attack whites in Kowloon 10/56
- Ultimatum expires; RAF planes bomb Suez 10/56
- Royal Marines capture Port Said 11/56
- Troops control Suez crowds as UN force moves in 11/56
- Will withdraw from Suez 12/56
- Possibility of Cyprus partition 12/56
- UK troops and planes in Aden repel Yemenis 1/57
- Egypt abrogates 1954 treaty with Britain 1/57
- Plans withdrawal from Jordan in six months 2/57
- Cyprus Governor rejects EOKA cease-fire 3/57
- Gold Coast becomes independent Ghana 3/57
- Releases Makarios from Seychelles 3/57
- Gives South Africa Simonstown naval base 4/57
- Cyprus state of emergency relaxed 4/57
- Grants Singapore self-government 4/57
- Jordan's King Hussein beats coup attempt 4/57
- South Africa drops British anthem 5/57
- London Commonwealth summit ends 6/57
- Commonwealth conference shows concern over Hungary 7/57
- British troops quell anti-sultan revolt 7/57
- Malaya declares independence 8/57
- 2,000 a week emigrate to Commonwealth 8/57
- Cyprus state of emergency revoked 8/57
- Troops take rebel Omani headquarters 8/57
- UN rejects motion opposing UK in Oman 8/57
- Pro-EOKA Cyprus protesters teargassed 10/57
- British West Indies Federation created 1/58
- Turks riot in Cyprus; 100 hurt, two die 1/58
- Malta's Mintoff resigns over UK aid cut 4/58
- Princess Margaret at Trinidad parliament 4/58
- Governor Laycock assumes power in Malta 4/58
- State of emergency in Malta 4/58
- Aden Governor calls state of emergency 5/58
- St Paul's altar is Empire War Memorial 5/58
- Official kills Pakistani Premier Sahib 5/58
- Cyprus peace plan rejected; riot, curfew 6/58
- Ceylon Tamils call for separate state 6/58
- UK paratrooopers come to help Jordan 7/58
- Empire Games, Cardiff 7/58
- Recognises Iraqi regime 8/58
- Grivas Cyprus cease-fire; Macmillan goes 8/58
- Attempt on UK army chief Kendrew, Cyprus 9/58
- New plan for Cyprus in pipeline 9/58
- Cypriots reject 7-year UK plan 10/58
- Renewed riots and attacks by Greeks and Turks in Cyprus 10/58
- UK troops leave Jordan 10/58
- Recognises Castro regime in Cuba 1/59
- Unfreezes Egyptian assets 1/59
- Southern Rhodesian state of emergency 2/59
- Cyprus deal: UK to end rule; keeps bases 2/59
- Egypt agrees with UK on Suez claims 2/59
- Cypriot EOKA accepts London agreement 3/59
- Bevan mocks Tories over Panama drama 4/59
- Labour blasts African policy in Commons 7/59
- 11 Mau Mau die in detention in Kenya 7/59
- Police shoot rioters, 51 die, Nyasaland 7/59
- Monckton studies Nyasaland and S. Rhodesia 9/59
- Queen vows independent Nigeria and Cyprus 10/59
- EFTA traders "no threat to Commonwealth" 11/59
- Kenyan state of emergency ends 11/59
- Makarios elected President in Cyprus 12/59
- Makarios praises EOKA, calls for peace 12/59
- Black Kenyans boycott constitution talks 1/60
- Macmillan gives "Winds of change" speech 2/60
- Kenyan conference accepts Macleod plan 2/60
- Defends "meddling"; warns of communism 2/60
- Nyasaland's Banda released from jail 4/60
- Commonwealth leaders attack apartheid 5/60
- Queen opens huge Kariba dam on Zambezi 5/60
- British Somaliland is independent 6/60
- Cyprus a republic under Makarios 8/60
- Ex-Governor Foot calls for peace, Cyprus 8/60
- Malayan state of emergency lifted 8/60
- Nigeria gets independence 10/60
- South African whites vote for republic 10/60
- Immigration curbs tightened 11/61
- Commonwealth Immigration Act becomes law 7/62
- Jamaica gains independence 8/62
- Trinidad and Tobago become independent 8/62
- Premiers oppose UK entry to EEC 9/62
- State of emergency in British Guyana 5/64
- Conference split on Vietnam and Rhodesia 6/65
- Argentina restates claim to Falklands 9/65
- Mauritius becomes independent 9/65
- Conference on Rhodesia 1/66
- Argentinians raid Falkland Islands 9/66
- Argentinian raid on Falklands abandoned 9/66
- Rhodesia leaves Commonwealth 12/66
- 61,377 Commonwealth immigrants in 1967 2/68
- Falklands' sovereignty to be preserved 3/68
- Commonwealth Immigrants Bill becomes law 3/68
- Lord Chalfont visits the Falklands 11/68
- Commonwealth fiancés immigration ban 1/69
- Invades Caribbean island of Anguilla 3/69
- Truce signed with rebel Anguillans 3/69
- Guyana Governor Rose killed in accident 11/69
- Tonga (SW Pacific) becomes independent 6/70
- Quebec rebels kidnap British diplomat 10/70
- Fiji becomes independent 10/70
- Quebec rebels free James Cross 12/70
- Commonwealth conference disagrees on arms for S. Africa 1/71
- Immigration Bill published 2/71
- Pakistan quits Commonwealth 1/72
- Bermuda Governor Sharples assassinated 3/73
- State of emergency in Bermuda 3/73
- Bahamas become independent 7/73
- Argentina in campaign to take Falklands 11/73
- Ends South African Simonstown naval deal 6/75
- Australian crisis over Whitlam budget 11/75
- Governor-General Kerr sacks Whitlam 11/75
- Rhodesian constitutional talks collapse 3/76
- Rhodesia announces multi-racial state 9/76
- Smith rejects Ivor Richard's proposals 1/77
- Commonwealth summit, London 6/77
- Seychelles leader Mancham ousted 6/77
- Commonwealth condemns S. Africa and Uganda 6/77
- Rhodesia accepts black majority rule 11/77
- Owen neutral on Rhodesian deal 2/78
- Absolute white rule ends in Rhodesia 3/78
- Solomon Islands get independence 7/78
- Rhodesian whites vote for black rule 1/79
- St Lucia gets independence 2/79
- Bishop ousts Gairy, Grenada 3/79
- Muzorewa is first black leader, Rhodesia 4/79
- Last British warships leave Malta 4/79
- Zimbabwe-Rhodesia, new name for Rhodesia 6/79
- Thatcher normalises ties with Zimbabwe 7/79
- Thatcher wants deal with Mugabe, Nkomo 8/79
- Commonwealth talks, Lusaka 8/79
- St Vincent and Grenada get independence 10/79
- Lancaster House: Zimbabwe is colony 12/79
- Argentine links with Falklands 4/80
- Last African colony Zimbabwe independent 4/80
- Spain to re-open Gibraltar border 4/80
- Spain halts siege of Gibraltar 1/82
- Argentinians land on Falklands 3/82
- Nuclear submarine Spartan to Atlantic 3/82
- Argentina takes Falklands; UK breaks ties 4/82
- Taskforce sets sail for South Atlantic 4/82
- Carrington resigns over Falklands 4/82
- Fears over 8,000-mile gap with Falklands 4/82
- 200-mile exclusion zone around islands 4/82
- Gives Canada constitutional sovereignty 4/82
- Helicopter crashes; first Briton to die 4/82
- Royal Marines recapture South Georgia 4/82
- British torpedoes sink Belgrano; hundreds die 5/82
- Threatens Argentinians 12 miles off coast 5/82
- Argentinians lose Port Stanley; surrender 6/82
- Falklands once more "under the crown" 6/82
- To return Argentinian prisoners 7/82
- Lifts 200-mile Falklands exclusion zone 7/82
- Thatcher discusses Hong Kong in China 9/82
- UN wants talks on Falklands sovereignty 11/82
- Spain-Gibraltar border re-opens 12/82
- Franks report on Falklands war issued 1/83
- Thatcher visits the Falklands 1/83
- Argentina releases frozen UK assets 8/83
- Angered by US invasion of Grenada 10/83
- US Marines invade Grenada 10/83
- Thatcher opposes S. Africa sanctions 10/85
- Agrees to voluntary S. Africa sanctions 8/86
- Rabuka makes Fiji republic 10/87
- Queen accepts Fiji Governor's resignation 10/87
- Full diplomatic relations with Argentina re-established 2/90
- Mauritius becomes republic, but remains part of Commonwealth 3/92
- Hong Kong's new Governor, Chris Patten, issues manifesto 7/92
- China threatens to set up own shadow government in Hong Kong 12/92
- Australia to drop allegiance to Queen 12/92

Britain (Irish policy)
- See also foreign affairs (Ireland)
- Irish call for uprising 1/00
- Ireland must stay British, says PM 5/01
- State of emergency in Dublin 9/02
- New deal for Irish tenants; report 1/03
- Chief Secretary resigns over policy 3/05
- 22 fewer MPs for Ireland 7/05
- Limited Home Rule Bill proposed 5/07
- Irish Council Bill abandoned 6/07
- Balfour warns of Irish disintegration 6/07
- Troops enter Ulster to quell unrest 7/07
- Four civilians shot by troops in Ulster 8/07
- High on election agenda 12/09
- Nationalists push Home Rule after poll 2/10
- Opposition to Home Rule at 30,000 rally 1/12
- Lords rejects Home Rule 1/12
- Third Irish Home Rule Bill proposed 4/12
- Home Rule passed; government relieved 5/12
- Home Rule Bill amended; Ulster excluded 6/12
- Ulster Orange Order cheers Tory speaker 7/12
- Home Rule rejected by 471,000 signatures 9/12
- Lords rejects Home Rule bill 1/13
- Proportional representation safeguards 1/13
- Bans arms sales to Ulster 12/13
- Bonar Law warns of Home Rule civil war 1/14
- Carson fails to exclude Ulster from bill 2/14
- King holds crisis meeting of Irish heads 7/14
- Buckingham Palace conference fails 7/14
- Home Rule shelved as World War looms 7/14
- Carson urges UVF to join army 9/14
- Tries to quell Dublin rebellion; curfew 4/16
- Ulster Unionists call for tougher action 4/16
- Seven rebels executed 5/16
- No conscription; Lord-Lieutenant resigns 5/16
- Martial law eased; Casement's trial 5/16
- Arms prohibition 7/16
- Wartime Home Rule plan excludes Ulster 5/17
- Police foil new Easter uprising plot 10/17
- Conscription introduced 3/18
- 500 Sinn Fein members arrested with de Valera 5/18
- British C-in-C resigns 5/18
- Government calls for 50,000 volunteers 6/18
- Home Rule postponed; conscription ended 6/18
- First meeting of Sinn Fein "parliament" 1/19
- Amnesty for Sinn Fein prisoners, including de Valera 4/19
- Rejects Sinn Fein role at peace talks 4/19
- Bans Sinn Fein parliament; Collins flees 9/19
- Six Sinn Fein prisoners escape 10/19
- Hunger strike prisoners not to be freed 11/19
- Partition and autonomy planned 12/19
- Nationalists object to partition plan 12/19
- 800 "special constables" raise tensions 3/20
- Ulster Unionists support British plan 3/20
- Home Rule Bill passed; Carson's warning 3/20
- Sinn Fein arson; 120 police stations burnt 4/20
- 89 Sinn Fein prisoners freed 4/20
- 40 hunger strikers freed; three policemen dead 5/20
- More troops called after 17 die in riots 6/20
- Call for emergency debate 6/20
- Roadblocks set up in Dublin 7/20
- New security bill; jury trials suspended 8/20
- No release for Cork hunger strike mayor 8/20
- Sinn Fein demands British withdrawal 9/20
- Riots after Cork mayor dies in prison 10/20
- 26 die in Bloody Sunday; reinforcements 11/20
- Sinn Fein founder Griffith arrested 11/20
- Martial law; army besieged, Cork and Kerry 12/20
- King signs partition bill 12/20
- British tanks in sealed Dublin, Cork 1/21
- IRA and army clash; 14 die 1/21
- Sinn Fein violence spreads to Glasgow 5/21
- Nominations for two parliaments' polls 5/21
- Sinn Feiners attack police families in London 5/21
- Lloyd George invites de Valera and Craig 5/21
- Truce after Mansion House surprise deal 7/21
- King meets Smuts to discuss problem 7/21
- London talks with Irish; Ulster pull out 7/21
- Jailed Sinn Fein MPs released 8/21
- De Valera rejects Dominion status 8/21
- Lloyd George cancels talks 9/21
- De Valera invited to Irish Treaty talks 9/21
- MPs back Lloyd George 10/21
- Irish Free State; divided dominion 12/21
- Six of Ulster provinces to stay in UK 12/21
- King wants Sinn Fein prisoners freed after treaty 12/21
- Irish parliament accepts treaty; dispute 1/22
- Prisoners' amnesty 1/22
- MPs back Irish Free State Bill 2/22
- Free State Act gets Royal Assent 3/22
- Ulster MP Twaddell killed by bomb 5/22
- Army chief Wilson killed by IRA, London 6/22
- Two sentenced to die for Wilson murder 7/22
- Irish Constitution Bill becomes law 12/22
- No border change, says Baldwin; deceit? 12/25
- King no longer sovereign of Ireland 11/26
- Eamon de Valera arrested in Belfast 2/29
- De Valera freed, exiled from Belfast 3/29
- Treaty future in doubt as de Valera wins 3/32
- De Valera to abolish Loyal Oath to King 3/32

Britain (Northern Ireland)
- Belfast refuses boundary commission 5/24
- Eamon de Valera arrested in Belfast 2/29
- De Valera released from jail and exiled 3/29
- Bermuda liner burns in Belfast dock 11/31
- Curfew after police kill jobs protester 10/32
- Prince opens Stormont parliament 11/32
- Nationalist MPs consider sitting in Dail 1/33
- Edward Carson, Ulster Unionist, dies 10/35
- Bomb near King and Queen in Belfast 7/37
- IRA bombs mainland cities 1/39
- IRA bombs London tube stations 2/39
- Suspected IRA fires in Coventry 2/39
- 20 IRA men jailed for bombings 3/39
- 19 hurt in IRA bomb raids in London 6/39
- Five IRA men jailed for 20 years 6/39
- Suspected IRA bomb blast in London 7/39
- IRA bomb kills five in Coventry 8/39
- Four more IRA men jailed for 20 years 10/39
- Three IRA bombs go off in Piccadilly 11/39
- IRA bombs go off at two London stations 11/39
- Two IRA men hanged in Birmingham 2/40
- IRA prisoners riot in Dartmoor 3/40
- IRA landmine kills six at Dublin Castle 4/40
- Huge mock invasion by British Army 6/41
- Police and IRA supporters clash in Belfast 9/42
- Two policemen shot dead by IRA in Belfast 9/42
- Four IRA men escape from Crumlin Road jail 1/43
- Five IRA men caught stealing arms 8/55
- Plot to attack Royal Navy bases foiled 3/57
- 63 IRA arrested in Ireland; Orange march 7/57
- Bomb kills policeman; 20 arrested 8/57
- IRA calls off 5-year violence campaign 2/62
- Irish terrorists to be freed 4/62
- O'Neill meets Irish PM Sean Lemass 1/65
- PM O'Neill bans UVF 6/66
- 100 Catholics injured in Londonderry riot 10/68
- Loyalists take over centre of Armagh 11/68
- Ulster police clash with rights marchers 1/69
- "B Specials" brought in to aid RUC 1/69
- Rev. Ian Paisley jailed for three months 1/69
- Terence O'Neill wins election 2/69
- Bernadette Devlin elected Mid-Ulster MP 4/69
- Rioting firebombers set Belfast ablaze 4/69
- UK troops to guard key installations 4/69
- 500 more troops sent to Northern Ireland 4/69
- O'Neill quits as PM 4/69
- James Chichester-Clark becomes PM 5/69
- Paisley freed in wide-ranging amnesty 5/69
- Sectarian violence kills five; injures many 8/69
- UK troops sent in to restore order 8/69
- Armoured cars crush Belfast barricades 8/69
- Army chief takes control of "B Specials" 8/69
- "B Specials" ordered to hand in arms 8/69
- Troops erect "peace wall" in Belfast 9/69
- 7000 troops are now in the province 9/69
- Army fires tear gas at Protestants 10/69
- "B Specials" to be disbanded 10/69
- Ulster Defence Regiment to be set up 11/69
- Bernadette Devlin jailed for six months 12/69
- Troops seal off Bogside, Londonderry 3/70
- Troops may kill petrol bombers 4/70
- Paisley wins Bannside by-election 4/70
- Devlin jailed after losing appeal 6/70
- Troops battle with IRA snipers in Belfast 7/70
- Biggest ever security operation 7/70
- Social and Democratic Labour Party formed 8/70
- Gerry Fitt to lead SDLP 8/70
- Army uses rubber bullets for first time 8/70
- Bernadette Devlin freed from jail 10/70
- Rioting in Belfast 10/70
- First British soldier killed in Ulster 2/71
- Two policemen die after Belfast shooting 2/71
- Chichester-Clark resigns as PM 3/71
- Brian Faulkner becomes PM 3/71
- Three soldiers shot dead 3/71
- Provisionals break from Official IRA 4/71
- 10 soldiers hurt in Londonderry riots 4/71
- IRA sinks RN launch in Baltimore, US 4/71
- One soldier killed; several hurt by bomb 5/71
- Worst Londonderry rioting for two years 7/71
- Seven explosions rock Belfast centre 7/71
- New emergency powers include internment 8/71
- 300 IRA suspects rounded up 8/71
- IRA reacts savagely to internment 8/71
- IRA threatens to bomb mainland 8/71
- Gunmen burn down 7000 Ulster homes 8/71
- Bomb destroys Crumlin Road prison gates 8/71
- Troubles claim 100th victim 9/71
- Official IRA condemns Provo pub bombing 9/71
- IRA bombs London's Post Office Tower 10/71
- Another 1,500 troops sent in 10/71
- Five shot dead by soldiers 10/71
- Report says Ulster suspects ill-treated 11/71
- Police to be armed with automatics 11/71
- IRA Christmas bombing campaign 12/71
- IRA kills Stormont Senator Jack Bernhill 12/71
- "Bloody Sunday" in Derry: 13 killed 1/72
- 55 hurt in Belfast store bomb 1/72
- Border gun battle between troops and IRA 1/72
- Seven die when IRA bombs Para HQ, Aldershot 2/72
- Civil rights march in Newry 2/72
- Inquiry into "Bloody Sunday" in Ulster 2/72
- Direct rule from Westminster imposed 3/72
- Ulster Unionists condemn direct rule 3/72
- Belfast bomb kills six shoppers; injures 146 3/72
- Army interrogation techniques criticised 3/72
- 100,000 Protestants in anti-direct rule demo 3/72
- Catholic women in pro-IRA demo, Belfast 4/72
- 23 explosions in one day 4/72
- Bloody Sunday report issued 4/72
- Rival vigilantes in Belfast battles 5/72
- Provos and troops agree to cease-fire 6/72
- Official IRA begins cease-fire 6/72
- Protestants erect barricades in Belfast 6/72
- Troops smash Ulster's no-go areas 7/72
- Whitelaw admits he met IRA leaders 7/72
- IRA abandons cease-fire 7/72
- 100th British soldier dies in province 7/72
- Troops clash with UDA for first time 8/72

- 400 Londonderry children attack troops 1/73
- Troops use plastic bullets in riots 1/73
- Ulster paralysed by general strike 2/73
- New IRA bombing campaign hits London 3/73
- Votes 90-1 in favour of staying in UK 3/73
- Trial without jury proposed 3/73
- Provo chief O'Connell at Easter rally 4/73
- Spate of tit-for-tat murders 6/73
- Police fire plastic bullets during riots 7/73
- First meeting of Ulster Assembly 7/73
- Two carrier-bag bombs explode in Solihull 8/73
- Police use plastic bullets 8/73
- Open verdict on Bloody Sunday victims 8/73
- Bomb blasts at two London stations 9/73
- Bomb kills disposal expert in Birmingham 9/73
- Power-sharing deal agreed 11/73
- Eight IRA men guilty of London car bombings 11/73
- 200th soldier killed in the province 11/73
- Sunningdale deal on a Council of Ireland 12/73
- Faulkner resigns as Unionist leader 1/74
- Protestants split on power-sharing deal 1/74
- Bomb rips apart troop bus on M62; 11 die 2/74
- Police seize Protestant arms caches 2/74
- IRA bomb injures ten in Buckinghamshire 2/74
- Two soldiers shot dead by police 3/74
- 1,000th victim of unrest dies 4/74
- Unionist general strike paralyses Ulster 5/74
- Ulster power-sharing toppled by strike 5/74
- IRA bomb damages Westminster Hall 6/74
- Price sisters end six-month hunger strike 6/74
- Bombs in Manchester and Birmingham 7/74
- Bomb explodes in Tower of London; one dies 7/74
- Judge and magistrate shot dead by IRA 9/74
- Rioters set fire to Maze prison 10/74
- Guildford pub bombs kill five, injuring 65 10/74
- Several IRA bomb blasts, central London 10/74
- 17 killed by IRA Birmingham pub bombs 11/74
- Judith Ward jailed for M62 bombing 11/74
- IRA terrorist McDade killed by own bomb 11/74
- Five arrested for Birmingham pub bombings 11/74
- Prevention of Terrorism Act becomes law 11/74
- Bloody Sunday victims to be compensated 12/74
- More IRA bombs in London 12/74
- IRA bombers attack Heath's London house 12/74
- IRA to restart bombing; Rees defiant 1/75
- Five London IRA bombs; 19 hurt, Manchester 1/75
- IRA man suspected of killing PC Tibble 2/75
- Nationalising Harland and Wolff shipyard 3/75
- Nine die and 79 injured in Belfast bomb blast 4/75
- IRA commander McMillan is shot dead 4/75
- Ulster Unionists win in Convention 5/75
- "Birmingham Six" assaulted in custody 7/75
- Three Dublin rockstars die in ambush 7/75
- Four-year-old killed; four die in barn raid 8/75
- Protestants kill 11 Catholics in revenge 10/75
- Merlyn Rees bans Ulster Volunteer Force 10/75
- Four Unionists blown up by own bomb 10/75
- Provisional Sinn Fein's McCusker killed 10/75
- IRA frees hostage Herrema after 36 days 11/75
- Convicted terrorists lose special status 11/75
- IRA bombs London restaurant; two die 11/75
- Ross McWhirter shot by Irish gunmen 11/75
- IRA gunmen take couple hostage in London 12/75
- IRA Balcombe Street siege ends, London 12/75
- First SAS units in South Armagh 1/76
- 15 die in sectarian violence, S. Armagh 1/76
- Gerry Fitt MP attacks SAS presence 1/76
- Rees dissolves Ulster Convention 3/76
- Ten die and 56 injured in violent weekend 5/76
- Corrigan starts women's peace movement 8/76
- 20,000 Protestants and Catholics at rally 8/76
- Gerry Fitt repels Republican crowd 8/76
- Third child dies from IRA hijacked car 8/76
- Ireland says UK practises torture 9/76
- Women's peace group founders attacked 10/76
- Sinn Fein vice-president Drumm killed 10/76
- Peace women march through London 11/76
- Ewart-Biggs widow among 30,000 marchers 11/76
- Corrigan and Williams win Nobel Peace Prize 12/76
- Seven IRA bombs in London's West End 1/77
- IRA bomb factory in Liverpool 2/77
- UK defends torture charges at Strasbourg 2/77
- IRA Balcombe St besiegers jailed for life 2/77
- 26 UVF members jailed 3/77
- Airey Neave wants Sinn Fein banned 4/77
- Paisley directs loyalist strike; troops sent in 5/77
- IRA says it killed "SAS officer" 5/77
- London police use Ulster shields 8/77
- £1 million bomb damage; Queen visits 8/77
- Peace Movement women win Nobel prize 10/77
- Car bomb kills UDR man and daughter 2/78
- 20 IRA suspects arrested for bombing 2/78
- Republican Gerry Adams charged 2/78
- Adams freed; "no IRA evidence" 9/78
- Maze Prison's deputy governor killed 11/78
- Operation Santa to foil IRA bombers 12/78
- Three soldiers shot dead 12/78
- Bombs in Bristol, Liverpool, Manchester 12/78
- Airey Neave MP killed by IRA bomb 3/79
- Bennett Committee - prison injuries 3/79
- Four police killed by IRA bomb 4/79
- Lord Mountbatten killed by IRA bomb 8/79
- 15 soldiers killed by Warrenpoint bomb 8/79
- Army's worst day in Ulster; shootings 8/79
- Pope calls for peace on Irish visit 9/79
- Desmond O'Hare arrested 10/79
- Irish police intercept IRA weapons 11/79
- Five soldiers die from bomb 12/79
- Peace woman Maguire dies 1/80
- Peace group founder Williams quits 2/80
- German industrialist's body found 3/80
- Seven hunger strikers ask for food 12/80
- End of political status campaigns 12/80
- IRA bomber escapes from Brixton Jail 12/80
- Loyalists shoot at ex-Ulster MP Devlin 1/81
- IRA man Bobby Sands on hunger strike 3/81
- Maze prisoners want war status 3/81
- Hunger-striker Bobby Sands wins election 4/81
- Clashes on 51st day of Sands' strike 4/81
- First De Lorean cars for New York 4/81
- Hunger-striker Bobby Sands dies 5/81
- Hunger-striker Francis Hughes dies 5/81
- Rioting follows hunger-strike deaths 5/81
- Mrs Thatcher rejects IRA "war status" 5/81
- Irish Premier Haughey blames Britain 5/81
- 5 soldiers die; plastic bullets kill 2 5/81
- Hunger-strikers O'Hara and McCreesh die 5/81
- New Irish Premier's vow on Ulster 6/81
- IRA men shoot way out of Belfast prison 6/81
- Eight "M60 case" prisoners on the loose 6/81
- Red Cross cannot end hunger strike 7/81
- Hunger-striker Joseph McDonnell dies 7/81
- Hunger-striker Martin Hurson dies 7/81
- Pro-IRA demonstration; 120 hurt 7/81
- Hunger-strikers Lynch and Doherty die 8/81
- Hunger-strikers McElwee and Devine die 8/81
- Sands's agent Owen Carron wins election 8/81
- Jim Prior is Ulster Secretary 9/81
- Hunger strikes end 10/81
- Marines chief Pringle hurt by car bomb 10/81
- Bomb expert dies in London's Oxford St 10/81
- Bradford, Unionist MP, shot dead by IRA 11/81
- Fitt says IRA wants civil war 11/81
- De Lorean sports cars in receivership 2/82
- IRA suspect Tuite escapes; re-arrested 3/82
- Two IRA bombs kill eight troops, London 7/82
- IRA bombs kill horses; bandstand carnage 7/82
- 41 troops, spectators hurt in IRA blasts 7/82
- De Lorean car plant closes; jobs go 10/82
- Sinn Fein's Adams and McGuinness elected 10/82
- SDLP and Sinn Fein boycott N.I. Assembly 11/82
- Four killed in three incidents 11/82
- Government blocks Sinn Fein visit to GLC 12/82
- 16 die in IRA's Ballykelly pub bombing 12/82
- Cardinal O'Fiaich, Thatcher on bombing 12/82
- "Supergrass" evidence jails IRA men 8/83
- Army officer charged with Belfast murder 8/83
- IRA arms consignment seized in France 8/83
- 134 IRA men break out of Maze prison 9/83
- Unionists pull out of Ulster Assembly 11/83
- Gerry Adams becomes Sinn Fein leader 11/83
- Gunmen kill three, hurt seven in Protestant chapel 11/83
- SAS shoot dead two IRA gunmen 12/83
- IRA bomb explodes outside Harrods 12/83
- Maze governor resigns after criticism 1/84
- Loyalists wound Sinn Fein leader Adams 3/84
- INLA leader McGlinchey arrested, Ireland 3/84
- McGlinchey extradited from Ireland 3/84
- De Lorean Co. accused of misusing funds 7/84
- Martin Galvin of Noraid visits Belfast 8/84
- One dies when police try to seize Galvin 8/84
- De Lorean acquitted of drugs charges in US 8/84
- IRA arms haul off Irish coast 9/84
- IRA bomb kills four at Tory conference, Brighton 10/84
- Nine RUC men die in IRA mortar attack 2/85
- Two IRA men jailed for bombing campaign 3/85
- IRA seaside bombing campaign foiled 6/85
- Patrick Magee charged with Brighton bomb 6/85
- BBC drops "Real Lives" documentary 7/85
- Journalists strike over "Real Lives" ban 8/85
- Dominic McGlinchey wins murder appeal 10/85
- Anglo-Irish Agreement signed 11/85
- Anglo-Irish pact: Unionist MPs resign 11/85
- First Anglo-Irish conference 12/85
- 38 police hurt in loyalist clashes 12/85
- Two escaped IRA men arrested in Netherlands 1/86
- 14 Unionists re-elected in by-elections 1/86
- Glenholmes extradition fails, Ireland 3/86
- Stalker taken off "shoot to kill" probe 6/86
- Magee gets eight life terms for IRA bombings 6/86
- Ulster Assembly dissolved 6/86
- Ian Paisley in struggle with police 6/86
- 100 injured in Orange Day clashes 7/86
- DU leader Robinson arrested in Ireland 8/86
- IRA suspect O'Reilly freed, Ireland 8/86
- Ulster MP Robinson fined for "invasion" 1/87
- IRA bomb injures 31 at UK German base 3/87
- Judge Gibson killed by bomb 4/87
- Eight IRA men die attacking RUC post 5/87
- Enoch Powell loses seat 6/87
- 11 killed in IRA Enniskillen bomb attack 11/87
- Secretary King dismisses IRA apology 11/87
- Remembrance Day parade wrecked by bomb 11/87
- Police cross border to arrest 40 IRA 11/87
- SAS shooting in Gibraltar, IRA response 3/88
- IRA kill British servicemen in Holland 5/88
- Six British soldiers die in N. Ireland 8/88
- Inquest on Gibraltar shooting by SAS 9/88
- Belgium will not extradite Patrick Ryan 11/88
- Irish refuse to extradite Patrick Ryan 12/88
- Belfast solicitor, Pat Finucane, is shot dead 2/89
- IRA bombs destroy Shropshire barracks 2/89
- IRA kills two Royal Ulster Constabulary officers 3/89
- 15-year-old boy dies from plastic-bullet wound during riots 8/89
- Loyalists claim security forces leaked information on IRA 8/89
- UDR members held pending inquiry into leaks on IRA suspects 10/89
- "Guilford Four" are freed 10/89
- IRA kills RAF corporal and his young child in West Germany 10/89
- Peter Brooke announces possible talks with Sinn Fein 11/89
- Two Australians killed in "error" by IRA near German border 5/90
- IRA attack in Lichfield leaves an army recruit dead 6/90
- IRA bomb Carlton Club 6/90
- Maguire family case referred to Court of Appeal 7/90
- IRA bomb explodes at London Stock Exchange 7/90
- Tory MP Ian Gow is killed by IRA car bomb 7/90
- IRA gunmen attack former governor of Gibraltar 9/90
- Police seize two IRA suspects near Stonehenge 10/90
- IRA attacks two border posts 10/90
- IRA bomb explodes at Victoria Station, killing one 2/91
- "Birmingham Six" murder convictions declared unsatisfactory 2/91
- IRA bomb attack on Downing Street 2/91
- Five Irishmen jailed in bid to smuggle Libyan arms to IRA 3/91
- "Birmingham Six" released from prison 3/91
- Unionists agree to Ulster peace talks 3/91
- Progress reported on bid to arrange all-party talks 5/91
- Three soldiers die in bomb explosion at army base 5/91
- Three suspected IRA terrorists shot dead in SAS ambush 6/91
- Court of Appeal overturns Maguires' conviction 6/91
- Political parties meet for formal discussions 6/91
- Loyalist paramilitaries call off cease-fire 7/91
- Sectarian violence claims seven lives in seven days 8/91
- Two Catholics persued by IRA seek sanctuary in cathedral 8/91
- Judith Ward's case is sent to the Court of Appeal 9/91
- Two IRA bombers blow themselves up near army band concert 11/91
- More troops are sent to Belfast 11/91
- Four people die in 12 hours of sectarian violence 12/91
- IRA makes its worst attack since 1988, killing seven 1/92
- London court frees Judith Ward 5/92
- Police find bodies of three murdered IRA informers 7/92
- Sectarian violence claims 3,000th victim 8/92
- IRA bombs injure 64 in Manchester 12/92
- IRA bomb injures 18 in Camden, London 2/93
- IRA claims responsibility for Warrington bomb attack 3/93
- IRA bomb rips through the City, killin one person 4/93
- Belfast chip shop bomb kills nine 10/93
- UFF kill seven in Greysteel pub 10/93
- Secret negotiations with IRA cause furore 11/93
- Peace pact signed 12/93
- Gerry Adams feted by US 2/94
- Paul Hill has murder conviction quashed 4/94
- IRA announces complete cessation of military operations 8/94
- Sinn Fein's McGuinness warns violence could return 10/94
- Loyalists announce Ulster ceasefire 10/94
- British officials talk to Sinn Fein 12/94
- Stormont gutted by fire 1/95
- End to daytime patrols in Belfast 1/95
- Queen's first visit since cease-fire 3/95
- Ministerial talks with Sinn Fein 5/95

Britain (education)

- Local councils take over schools 3/02
- Rhodes scholarships for non-British 4/02
- Hallies against church school reforms 10/02
- Liberals protest against Bill 11/02
- Lord Londonderry rules out school meals 9/05
- Protest against bill held at Albert Hall 5/06
- Committee recommends school meals 7/06
- Bill withdrawn 12/06
- Education Bill scrapped 12/08
- School-leaving age raised to 14 3/18
- Teachers want school-leaving age raised 4/27
- School-leaving age may rise to 15 10/35
- Education Bill; second reading 2/36
- Teaching value of fitness in schools 2/37
- Free schooling up to 16 advocated 7/43
- Radical education reform in new bill 2/44
- BBC says it will develop schools radio 2/44
- State will pay for 55% of education 1/45
- Needy university scholars to get grants 5/46
- General Certificate of Education appears 4/48
- Smuts is new Cambridge University chancellor 6/48
- Penson is first woman vice-chancellor 6/48
- "Comprehensive" school is planned 8/48
- Headmasters criticise GCE exams 1/52
- Florence Horsbrugh becomes first woman Tory minister 9/53
- Kidbrooke School; first comprehensive 9/54
- Burnham committee: equal teachers' pay 3/55
- Eton headmaster blasts comprehensives 1/56
- Children kept from school by Asian flu 9/57
- University numbers double since 1939 9/59
- New university at Canterbury announced 5/61
- New university at Colchester announced 5/61
- New university at Coventry announced 5/61
- Phonetic alphabet to be taught in test 7/61
- Rapid growth in higher education urged 10/63
- Overseas' students fees to go up 2/67
- LSE closed after student unrest 2/69
- Five male Oxford colleges to admit women 4/72
- Open University awards its first degrees 1/73
- Plans to phase out grammar schools 3/75
- Plans for single exam to replace Os and CSEs 10/78
- 1,000 schools close; no heating oil 2/79
- University grants cut 7/81
- New GCSE exams approved 6/84
- Oxford refuses Thatcher honorary degree 1/85
- 13-year-old gets Oxford maths first 7/85
- Plan to abolish ILEA 9/87
- Royal Assent given to Reform Bill 7/88
- Kenneth Baker on grammar testing 11/88
- University lecturers accept six per cent pay offer 6/89
- Teacher shortage causes hundreds of children to be sent home 9/89
- Leading British academic criticises Britain's schools 8/90

Britain (finance and economy)

- Hopes for tax cuts 3/00
- Cotton industry slump 9/00
- Call for restrictions 2/03
- Boer and Boxer wars took third of budget 4/03
- Tariff League for easier Empire trading 5/03
- Sugar imports banned 9/03
- Unions oppose tariff policy 9/03
- Balfour promises no tariff war 10/03
- Traders angry at tobacco tax 4/04
- Shipbuilders fear Japanese competition 12/07
- Empire trade boom continues 1/10
- Stalled budget costs Treasury 2/10
- Anger as high cotton prices cut demand 3/10
- Divorce too expensive for poor 3/10
- Minister gets cotton mills to re-open 10/10
- Population overtakes France; city growth 4/11
- Strikes lead to riots, food shortages 8/11
- Anglo-Chinese Bank formed 9/12
- Canada seeks to buy three dreadnoughts 12/12
- Oil interests safer after rail link abandoned 7/13
- Treaty with Turkey gives UK Arab oil 11/13
- Budget increases supertax 5/14
- Government buys Anglo-Persian oil share 5/14
- Large steamship companies amalgamate 5/14
- Hard conditions of women factory workers 7/14
- War sends jitters on Stock Exchange 8/14
- Government's £350 million War Loan 11/14
- Income tax to double in new War Budget 11/14
- Stock Exchange re-opens 1/15
- German U-boat blockade of British Isles starts 2/15
- War costs £2.1 million a day 5/15
- New war loan of £910 million 6/15
- 40,000 volunteers for munitions work 7/15
- Budget record boosts on taxes and duties 9/15
- Total budget revenue to be £387 million 9/15
- Stonehenge sold for a pittance 9/15
- Two million more women employed 1/16
- Asquith seeks £420 million war loan 2/16
- Paper and tobacco imports banned 2/16
- Wealthy should free servants for war effort 2/16
- Munitions strike halts vital production 3/16
- Britain to supply France with coal 5/16
- "Daylight saving time" to conserve coal 5/16
- Trade unionists protest at high food prices 8/16
- Government to control wheat supplies 10/16
- Highest ever bread price: flour shortage 10/16
- Food Controller to regulate consumption 11/16
- Money and securities contraband 11/16
- Food cartel inquiry; science research 12/16
- Call for huge war loan to meet debts 1/17
- Five million subscribe to war loan 2/17
- Women taxi drivers; non-military scheme 2/17
- War costing £7 million a day 7/17
- Bankers want decimalisation 11/17
- Westminster Bank arises out of merger 2/18
- New war loan of £600 million called for 3/18
- Coal, gas and electricity rationing 3/18
- Budget raises taxes and drops Penny Post 4/18
- State control of London Central Markets 5/18
- War loan of £500 million called for 6/18
- War loan of £700 million called for 8/18
- Hit by influenza-caused absenteeism 9/18
- First oil well, Hardstoft, Derbyshire 10/18
- Total war debts: £7,100 million 11/18
- National industrial conference 2/19
- National Industrial Council 4/19
- Sidney Webb wants coal nationalisation 4/19
- Coal commission pushes for nationalisation 6/19
- Coal price rise 7/19
- National debt almost £475 million 10/19
- Coal price cut 11/19
- Sugar ration cut after miners' strike 10/20
- Pound drops after miners' strike 10/20
- Severn Barrage electricity plant planned 11/20
- Coal rationing 4/21
- Geddes report urges spending cuts in pay 2/22
- Budget: lower income tax and postal charges 5/22
- First woman president of Co-operative 6/22
- Cadbury, chocolate king and visionary, dies 10/22
- Six million National Savings Certificates 10/22
- Cox's Bank merges with Lloyd's Bank 2/23
- Irish imposes 33.33 tax on British imports 3/23
- Federation of British Industries formed 6/23
- Sir Edward Hulton sells titles for £6m 10/23
- Agriculture subsidy plan 11/23
- Petrol two shillings a gallon; AA angry 2/24
- Bread price rises after dock strike 2/24

Britain (finance and economy)

- Milk price reduced 3/24
- Imperial Airways formed from four firms 3/24
- Imperial Exhibition 4/24
- Australia's new tariffs favour Britain 9/25
- Plan for national electricity "grid" 1/26
- Food Council wants standardised sales 2/26
- Kent coalfield development 2/26
- War footing in General Strike 5/26
- Three million tons of coal imported during strike 8/26
- Imperial Chemical Industries (ICI) formed 11/26
- Pit strike cost industry £300 million 11/26
- Coal restrictions end 12/26
- Strike depressed spending 1/27
- Cheque usage increases 1/27
- British Industries Fair in London 2/27
- Prices of bread and petrol drop 3/27
- Petrol cheapest since 1902 8/27
- Bus profits to subsidise tube losses 10/27
- Motor vehicle licence brings £17 million 10/27
- Air-dropped food for snowbound villages 12/27
- Cars for people on £400 a year 10/28
- First pound and ten-shilling notes 11/28
- Prince of Wales tours depressed North 1/29
- Food Council wants cheaper summer milk 3/29
- Coal price rises 10/29
- Wall Street Crash hits business 11/29
- Economic advisory council for government 1/30
- Changing fashions harm cotton industry 5/30
- London's building boom 9/30
- Empire fails to agree tariff terms 11/30
- Beaverbrook ends Empire Crusade movement 3/31
- Bank Governor's gold reserve warning 7/31
- European collapse causes sterling slide 8/31
- Leaves the gold standard; pound devalued 9/31
- Tight budget fails to stop run on pound 9/31
- Stock Exchange shuts; opens in two days 9/31
- Prince of Wales in "Buy British" drive 11/31
- EMI from His Master's Voice and Columbia 11/31
- 100 per cent duty on imports in new bill 11/31
- Chrysler to open British car factory 12/31
- Hoover Cleaners to build UK factory 1/32
- Ten per cent tariff on imports 2/32
- Import Duties Bill; UK drops free trade 2/32
- Government wants bonds to cover US debt 12/32
- Plan for centralised milk marketing 2/33
- Sainsbury's: butter at a shilling a pound 3/33
- World economic conference fails 7/33
- Butter at its cheapest ever 1/34
- Slimming craze hits British potato sales 3/34
- Egg price drops; farmers appeal 3/34
- Chamberlain talks of recovery 4/35
- Petrol costs 1/6d a gallon 4/35
- Air Force expansion: 22,000 new jobs 5/35
- New buoyancy seen in record Bank Holiday 8/35
- Mass production of gas masks 7/36
- Bread most expensive for six years 8/36
- £6 a week to keep above "poverty line" 9/36
- Jarrow march on London begins 10/36
- Keynes: public spending cures depression 12/36
- Every shipyard will work to capacity 2/37
- Petrol rises to 1/7d 2/37
- Orwell's portrait of gloom in "Wigan Pier" 3/37
- 824 millionaires; more people taxed 3/37
- Death duties bring in record £88 million 3/37
- Aircraft carrier: £3 million Ark Royal 4/37
- Defence Contribution Scheme forwarded 6/37
- Coal Commission planned in Coal Bill 11/37
- Coal, coke prices rise with shortages 2/38
- Whisky price rises to £1 15s 2/38
- Miss M.J. Ahern manages John Lewis 2/38
- Half Cardiff sold; biggest property deal 5/38
- Peaches at a penny each, oranges half penny 7/38
- Farms to get £26 million subsidy boost 11/38
- Farmers urged to dig for victory 5/39
- 1.5 million derelict acres to be sown 10/39
- Unemployment falls below one million 5/40
- Sweeping new price controls announced 1/41
- War is costing £11 million a day 2/41
- War budget raises income tax to 50 per cent 4/41
- War spending tops £9,050 million 3/42
- Takeover of coal mines announced 6/42
- J.M. Keynes made a peer 6/42
- Insurance companies attack Beveridge 12/42
- "Wings for Victory" savings campaign 3/43
- 100 per cent tax on luxuries 4/43
- Keynes publishes plan for world economy 4/43
- Savings made by clothes rationing 5/43
- Engineers call for "pay as you earn" tax 6/43
- Women's pay has risen by 80 per cent since 1938 7/43
- PAYE to be introduced 9/43
- Only one in ten get Christmas turkey 12/43
- PAYE taxation comes into force 4/44
- Income tax cut to 9d in pound 10/45
- Civil aviation to be nationalised 11/45
- Commons vote to accept massive US loan 12/45
- Commons vote for IMF and World Bank 12/45
- Wartime rations return 2/46
- London has only a week's supply of coal 2/46
- Police swoop on blackmarketeers 3/46
- Wages up 80 per cent since 1938 3/46
- First bananas since 1939 in London 3/46
- Plans to nationalise iron and steel 4/46
- Bread rationing introduced 5/46
- £937 million US loan to UK approved 7/46
- Not enough coal to get through winter 7/46
- Black market flourishing 8/46
- Forbes heads Iron and Steel Board 9/46
- Tourist Board to be set up 12/46
- Heathrow airport plans to expand 12/46
- 12 cotton mills close from fuel shortage 12/46
- Coal mines nationalised 1/47
- Rations reduced 1/47
- Steelworks close from coal shortage 1/47
- Hauliers vote to end strike 1/47
- 4 million idle from power cuts 2/47
- 800,000 return to work as crisis eases 3/47
- Flooding has serious economic results 4/47
- Use of coal and gas fires banned 4/47
- Food rations cut as crisis deepens 6/47
- Crisis austerity plan unveiled 8/47
- Princess Elizabeth to have no trousseau 8/47
- Sheffield steelworks close 9/47
- Export drive launched 9/47
- Gold reserves used to pay for imports 9/47
- Nationalisation programme suspended 9/47
- Midlands to have no power one day a week 9/47
- Women asked to avoid longer skirts 9/47
- Bacon ration cut 10/47
- Potatoes rationed to 3 lb. a week 11/47
- More meat, sugar and sweets for Christmas 11/47
- Railways nationalised 1/48
- Coal lost £5.44 million last quarter 1/48
- Cheese ration cut 3/48
- Electricity industry nationalised 4/48
- Tax imposed on investment income 4/48
- Motorists rationed to 90 miles a month 4/48
- Milk ration increased 4/48
- Extra clothing coupons made available 5/48
- Meat ration reduced 6/48
- National Health Service comes into being 7/48
- National Insurance comes into being 7/48
- Coal lost over £23 million last year 7/48
- Footwear rationing to end 7/48
- Rationing of furnishing fabrics to end 7/48
- Industrial red tape eased 11/48
- Jam rationing is to end 11/48
- Leading car makers to standardise parts 12/48
- Clothes rationing ends 3/49
- Budget pegs food subsidies 4/49
- Chocolate and sweet rationing ends 4/49
- Gas industry nationalised 5/49
- More rationing as crisis deepens 7/49
- London dock strike 7/49
- Tate and Lyle launch "Mr Cube" campaign 8/49
- Pound devalued by 30 per cent 9/49
- Milk ration cut 9/49
- Company profits tax raised to 30 per cent 9/49
- Cinema industry seeks government money 11/49
- Civil servants' pay frozen 2/50
- Petrol rationing ends 5/50
- Soap rationing ends 7/50
- First Sainsbury self-service store opens 7/50
- Arms production to be doubled 8/50
- NCB told to buy coal abroad 11/50
- Twopence off meat ration; worst shortage 1/51
- "Average UK housewife" works 15 hour day 7/51
- Austin raise car prices 8/51
- Attlee opens biggest oil refinery 9/51
- Revamped family Austin 7 at Motor Show 10/51
- "Kite Mark" standard replaces utility 3/52
- Cheese ration cut to an ounce a week 3/52
- State's £20 million textile orders 4/52
- Pharmacies to sell in metric weights 4/52
- Commons votes for women's equal pay 5/52
- Meat ration increases 5/52
- Tea rationing ends 10/52
- Sweet rationing ends 2/53
- Tractor makers Ferguson in Massey merger 8/53
- All rationing to end in 1954 11/53
- Meat rationing to end 2/54
- London Gold Market opens again 3/54
- Rationing ends; Smithfield meat boom 7/54
- Planned Scottish steel plant, Motherwell 7/54
- UK Atomic Energy Authority founded 8/54
- Loses half seatrade through dock strike 10/54
- British Petroleum formed 12/54
- West Indian immigrants seek jobs and homes 1/55
- Petrol up to 4/6d. a gallon 1/55
- 12 nuclear power stations planned 2/55
- End to purchase tax on non-woollen cloth 5/55
- Emergency Powers Act; direct food supply 5/55
- Biggest ever coal price rise 7/55
- Macmillan's tighter credit squeeze 2/56
- Macmillan pleads for wage restraint 2/56
- Duke of Edinburgh enterprise awards 2/56
- £103 million balance of payments deficit 3/56
- Macmillan introduces £1 premium bonds 4/56
- Self-service shops boost sales and thefts 5/56
- Modern stores threaten small shopkeepers 5/56
- Eden orders banks to keep credit squeeze 7/56
- First Premium Bonds go on sale 11/56
- Run on the pound during Suez crisis 11/56
- Asks US and Canada to waive interest 12/56
- IMF grants $1,300 million 12/56
- Egypt nationalises British banks 1/57
- UK wants new trade structure with EEC 3/57
- To treble nuclear energy by 1965 3/57
- Petrol rationing ends 5/57
- Macmillan celebrates buoyant economy 7/57
- Full employment 8/57
- 2,000 a week emigrate to Commonwealth 8/57
- Bank rate rises to 7 per cent 9/57
- Radioactive Windscale milk dumped 10/57
- Male civil servants get higher salary 1/58
- Bank rate cut to 6 per cent 3/58
- £1.5 million Birmingham shopping centre 3/58
- Dungeness is next nuclear power site 5/58
- Bank rate drops to 5 per cent 6/58
- Credit squeeze relaxed 7/58
- Midland Bank offers personal loans 8/58
- Bank rate falls to 4 per cent 11/58
- 36 coal pits to close 12/58
- Treasury drops all borrowing controls 2/59
- Unemployment at 620,728 2/59
- Filtered cigarette sales leap 5/59
- Mortgage rates drop to 5.5 per cent 5/59
- House of Fraser bids for Harrods 7/59
- Average weekly earnings: £13 2s 11d. 7/59
- Fraser beats Debenhams in Harrods bid 8/59
- Teenagers can spend £5 a week 8/59
- Barclays gets computer 8/59
- Coal Board to close up to 70 pits 8/59
- Falling cinema audiences: 91 sites close 9/59
- Royal Mint considers decimalisation 10/59
- Duty-free liquor at airports 11/59
- Joins EFTA free trade pact 11/59
- Planned £10 notes 11/59
- Aircraft merger worth £220 million 12/59
- £6 million to be spent on airliner 2/60
- New £1 note 3/60
- Last army intakes to learn trades 12/60
- To apply to join Common Market 7/61
- MPs vote in favour of joining EEC 8/61
- Britain formally applies for EEC entry 8/61
- Budget cuts purchase tax 4/62
- Share values fall by £1000 million 5/62
- National Incomes Commission announced 7/62
- Lyons Maid merges with two other firms 10/62
- Purchase tax on cars halved 11/62
- John Lewis, retail chain founder, dies 2/63
- American Express card launched in UK 9/63
- Average weekly wage is £16/4/11d 1/64
- First postwar £10 banknotes issued 2/64
- Import tax imposed 10/64
- Income tax up by 6 per cent to pay for pensions 11/64
- Loaned £1,080 million by 11 nations 11/64
- Death of Lord Marks of Marks & Spencer 12/64
- Whisky price war begins 2/65
- Japanese to enter UK saloon car racing 3/65
- Applies to IMF for £500 million loan 5/65
- Corporation tax to be introduced 6/65
- Squeeze on bank lending increased 2/66
- Decimal currency to be introduced in 1971 3/66
- Leslie O'Brien: Bank of England Governor 4/66
- Barclaycard, first UK credit card 6/66
- Pay and wages freeze imposed 7/66
- Bank rate raised to 7 per cent 7/66
- Price and wage freeze invoked 10/66
- Unemployment reaches 437,229 10/66
- Unofficial BMC stoppage ends 11/66
- US car firm Chrysler to take over Rootes 1/67
- Bank rate cut, ending sterling crisis 1/67
- Viyella closes two Lancs cotton mills 2/67
- Decimal Currency Bill published 3/67
- Pound reaches parity with dollar 4/67
- British Steel Corporation formed 7/67
- Pound devalued 14.3 per cent 11/67
- Credit squeeze to be tightened 11/67
- £250 million international credit given 11/67
- Port of London docks to be closed 1/68
- National Westminster Bank formed 1/68
- National Insurance payments raised 2/68
- Free secondary school milk abolished 2/68
- First decimal coins in circulation 4/68
- Promised $2000 million credit by 12 nations 7/68
- Big banks to close on Saturdays 9/68
- Lloyd's of London to admit women 2/69
- High-grade oil discovered in North Sea 6/69
- Fifty-pence coin comes into circulation 10/69
- Torrey Canyon owners pay £3 million 11/69
- Rolls-Royce seeks £50 million state loan 2/70
- Government lends Rolls-Royce £20 million 5/70
- National docks strike: troops stand by 7/70
- BP makes major oil find in North Sea 10/70
- Department of Trade and Industry created 10/70
- Strikes at highest level since 1926 11/70
- Decimal currency introduced 2/71
- Rolls-Royce calls in a receiver 2/71
- Rolls-Royce aero activities nationalised 2/71
- VAT to be introduced 3/71
- Upper Clyde shipbuilders liquidated 6/71
- Hire-purchase controls abolished 7/71
- 1d and 3d coins no longer legal tender 9/71
- £160 million provided to cut unemployment 11/71
- Queen's allowance to be doubled 12/71
- Signs treaty of entry to EEC 1/72
- Miners' strike begins 1/72
- Unemployment rises above a million 1/72
- Miners' strike causes power cuts 2/72
- State of emergency declared 2/72
- £6 pay increase for miners recommended 2/72
- Power cuts end after 20 days 3/72
- Travel firm Thomas Cook denationalised 5/72
- The pound is floated 6/72
- Nationwide dock strike begins 7/72
- Clydebank shipyard deal faces axe 8/72
- National dock strike called off 8/72
- Heath seeks pegs on prices and incomes 9/72
- Agreement ends Clydebank work-in 10/72
- Access credit cards introduced 10/72
- Pound at record low of $2.36 10/72
- 90-day freeze on prices and wages 11/72
- John Hicks wins Economics Nobel 12/72
- Joins EEC 1/73
- Phase II of pay and prices freeze 1/73
- Share values fall £4000m in a day 1/73
- Women allowed on Stock Exchange floor 2/73
- Gas workers begin nationwide strike 2/73
- Rail workers' strike begins 2/73
- Counter-inflation bill becomes law 3/73
- VAT introduced 4/73
- One-day TUC strike against pay restraint 5/73
- Fears of an oil crisis 8/73
- Japanese overtake British car sales 9/73
- OPEC raises oil prices by 70 per cent 10/73
- Phase III of pay policy announced 10/73
- Preparations made for petrol rationing 11/73
- Power workers begin industrial action 11/73
- Miners begin industrial action 11/73
- Goes onto a three-day week 12/73
- Crisis budget introduced 12/73
- Compulsory 50-mph speed limit imposed 12/73
- Arab funds withdrawn from banks 12/73
- Share values fall by £2000 million 12/73
- BP announces major North Sea oil find 1/74
- Miners' strike forces general election 2/74
- Petrol price rises; fourth time in year 2/74
- 81 per cent of miners vote for national strike 2/74
- Miners' strike ends 3/74
- Return to five-day week 3/74
- Burmah Oil finds Ninian field, North Sea 4/74
- Inflation reaches 16 per cent 6/74
- TUC and government in "social contract" 6/74
- State takes over Harland and Wolff 7/74
- Giant leisure group Court Line collapses 8/74
- Capital transfer tax to be introduced 8/74
- Wealth tax to be introduced 8/74
- FT share index falls below 200 8/74
- Keith Joseph backs monetarism 9/74
- Nurses get up to 58 per cent pay rises 9/74
- Inflation soars to 26 per cent 12/74
- Defence spending to be cut by £4700 million 12/74
- Friedrich von Hayek wins Economics Nobel 12/74
- Burmah Oil, UK's 2nd biggest, collapses 1/75
- £1,000 million wiped off shares 1/75
- Imperial Typewriters to close 1/75
- Wage inflation reaches 28.5 per cent 1/75
- Industry Bill; National Enterprise Board 1/75
- Coal prices to rise by 30 per cent 2/75
- Cabinet divided over EEC; majority for 3/75
- Electricity price up by a third 3/75
- Nationalising Harland and Wolff shipyard 3/75
- US Semi-Conductor buys Aston-Martin 4/75
- Pound sinks; inflation nears 22 per cent 5/75
- Nationalise shipbuilding and aircraft Bill 5/75
- First North Sea oil flows 6/75
- Inflation reaches 25 per cent 6/75
- Wilson sets wage freeze, price controls 7/75
- No more state money for motor cycle firm 7/75
- Healey's week's ultimatum on wages 7/75
- State takes over ailing British Leyland 8/75
- Queen opens first North Sea pipeline 11/75
- Asks IMF for £1,000 million 11/75
- Record number of bankruptcies in 1975 1/76
- Robert Woods loses £3 million in 4 months 1/76
- First time pound falls below $2 3/76
- Cambridge economists predict recession 3/76
- Biggest pit, Selby, Yorkshire, planned 4/76
- Inflation drops to 18.9 per cent 5/76
- Pound at new low of $1.71 6/76
- UK gets £3,000 million in foreign loans 6/76
- Two Arabs buy Dorchester Hotel 6/76
- Water rationing, forest fires, dry dams 8/76
- Applies for £2.3 billion from IMF 9/76
- Pound falls four cents 9/76
- Slater Walker Securities slumps 9/76
- Bank of England raises lending rate 10/76
- Building societies raise mortgage rates 10/76
- IMF approves £2,300 million loan to UK 1/77
- British Aerospace formed 4/77
- Laker's Skytrain undercuts big airlines 9/77
- Inflation drops to 11 per cent 9/77
- BL chief Dobson quits; Edwardes succeeds 10/77
- Swan Hunter shipyard loses order 11/77
- Unions accept BL "survival plan" 2/78
- Pay-breaching firms blacklisted 2/78
- Inflation falls below 10 per cent 2/78
- UK 16th oil state; million barrels daily 6/78
- UK will export oil in two years 6/78
- Shell and BP break Rhodesian sanctions 8/78
- TUC rejects incomes policy 10/78
- Will not join European Monetary System (EMS) 12/78
- Ends blacklist 12/78
- Food shortages from lorry strike 1/79
- Labour Party's union loose pay pact 2/79
- Thatcher plans lower taxes, union cuts 5/79
- MPs vote to sell nationalised industries 5/79
- Milk up to 15p 5/79
- Petrol price up to £1.22 a gallon 5/79
- Nigeria seizes BP assets 7/79
- Public cuts of £4,000 million planned 7/79
- France may not restrict UK lamb 9/79
- To outlaw "insider trading" 10/79
- Thatcher wants £1,000 million from EEC 11/79
- £3,500 million spending cuts 11/79
- Record mortgage rates of 15 per cent 11/79
- British Steel to axe 11,287 jobs 1/80
- Middle managers blast British Steel boss 2/80
- No more sixpences 2/80
- Thatcher withholds VAT to EEC 3/80
- Unemployment tops 1.5 million 4/80
- EEC cuts UK contribution to £250 million 5/80
- Ian MacGregor is chairman of British Steel 5/80
- Inflation up to 21.8 per cent 5/80
- "Insider dealing" to be banned 5/80
- Venice vow to cut oil consumption 6/80
- British Steel to close Consett 6/80
- Depression: 40,000 redundancies a week 7/80
- Orders fall off by 40 per cent 7/80
- Two million unemployed 8/80
- Howe cuts lending rate to 14 per cent 11/80
- Inflation down to 15.1 per cent 1/81
- Coal Board plans to close 50 pits 2/81
- Selling half of British Aerospace shares 2/81
- Unemployment reaches 2.5 million 4/81
- Rowland may buy Observer 6/81
- Community leaders: no work causes riots 7/81
- London's Royal Docks axed; 900 acres 9/81
- Second worst stock market fall 9/81
- Honda cars and British Leyland in link-up 11/81
- De Lorean sports cars in receivership 2/82
- Prior gives no more money to De Lorean 2/82
- Laker Airlines collapses; 6,000 stranded 2/82
- Offers to bail out Laker: too little 2/82
- Murdoch's News International takes control of Times 2/82
- Mercury's licence to compete with BT 2/82
- Barbican Centre costs £153 million 3/82
- 20p coin in circulation 6/82
- Britoil takes over from BNOC 8/82
- De Lorean car plant closes, jobs go 10/82
- Only 30 per cent of Britoil shares sold 11/82
- Pound slides; no government help 11/82
- Pound at record low of $1.5 1/83
- Habitat buys Heal's for £5 million 2/83
- £1 coin comes into circulation 4/83
- £500 million cut in public spending announced 7/83
- Halfpenny coin to be phased out 2/84

- Nissan to build pilot plant in UK 2/84
- Nationwide miners' strike begins 3/84
- Sealink to be sold to Sea Containers 7/84
- De Lorean Co accused of misusing funds 7/84
- Bank of England buys Johnson Matthey 10/84
- No more £1 notes to be issued 11/84
- British Telecom flotation 11/84
- Richard Stone wins Economics Nobel 12/84
- Trustee Savings Bank to be privatised 12/84
- Townsend Thoresen buys P& O ferries 1/85
- FT index breaks through 1000 points 1/85
- Pound falls below $1.10 2/85
- Miners end year-long strike 3/85
- House of Fraser bought by Al-Fayeds 3/85
- Receiver for TPD (Clive Sinclair firm) 10/85
- Habitat and British Home Stores to merge 11/85
- Channel Tunnel is given the go-ahead 1/86
- Amstrad buys Sinclair computer business 4/86
- Guinness wins Distillers takeover battle 4/86
- Partial ban on lamb slaughter: Chernobyl 6/86
- Nissan opens car factory in UK 9/86
- Four million apply for TSB shares 9/86
- "Big Bang" on London Stock Exchange 10/86
- £4.6 billion rise in public spending 11/86
- Tougher rules for insider share dealing 11/86
- Boesky confesses to insider dealing, US 11/86
- Share prices tumble 11/86
- Barclays to "disinvest" in S. Africa 11/86
- Guinness takeover of Distillers: inquiry 12/86
- Guinness shares plunge 12/86
- Flotation of British Gas 12/86
- Shock as Ronson repays Guinness loan 1/87
- Guinness City share bid scandal spreads 1/87
- Saunders quits Guinness over DTI inquiry 1/87
- British Airways flotation 1/87
- London broom cupboard house for £36,500 2/87
- City threat over Japan's closed markets 3/87
- Pound highest for four years 3/87
- UK go-ahead for Sizewell B nuclear plant 3/87
- Inquiry into Al-Fayed bid for Harrods 4/87
- Saunders charged with perverting justice 5/87
- Saunders quits as Guinness director 5/87
- Unemployment falls below three million 6/87
- Banker Collier fined for insider trading 7/87
- British Airways to buy Caledonian 7/87
- British Airways bid; monopoly inquiry 8/87
- Widening North-South gap in house prices 9/87
- Stock market disaster: £50 billion lost 10/87
- City asks Whitehall to stop BP flotation 10/87
- Accountant owes £1 million after crash 10/87
- Ronson charged with stealing £6 million 10/87
- Seelig charged with stealing £3 million 10/87
- Peter de Savary buys Land's End 11/87
- "Poll tax" planned for April 1990 11/87
- Wealth growing faster in the south 1/88
- British aerospace bids for Rover 3/88
- Interest rates up to 8 per cent 6/88
- £2.2 million trade deficit 8/88
- Rate of inflation rises 11/88
- Inflation rises to eight per cent 5/89
- Britain wants closer economic and monetary union in Europe 6/89
  Interest rates go up to 15 per cent 10/89
- Sale of water industry shares is 5.7 times over-subscribed 12/89
- Britain's trade deficit for 1989 was a record £20.31 billion 1/90
- Mortgage rates go up to 15.4 per cent 2/90
- Inflation rises to 8.1 per cent 4/90
- Government announces deficit of £1.8 billion for April 5/90
- Government announces near-record increase in inflation 5/90
- Inflation reaches 9.7 per cent 6/90
- Government unveils its proposed "hard Ecu" 6/90
- Petrol prices rise to 225.9p a gallon 8/90
- Inflation reaches 10.6 per cent 10/90
- Inflation reaches 10.9 per cent 10/90
- Petrol prices fall by 9.6p per gallon 10/90
- Recession hits retailers hard 12/90
- Unemployment hits two million 3/91
- Rise in VAT to reduce unpaid poll tax bills 3/91
- Bank of England Governor gets pay rise 5/91
- Bank of England orders closure of BCCI 7/91
- Local councils are said to have invested £30 million in BCCI 7/91
- Sheikh of Abu Dhabi deposits £50 m to help BCCI investors 7/91
- BCCI scandal continues 7/91
- Government claims worst of recession over 8/91
- Keith Prowse ticket agency collapses 9/91
- Annual rate of inflation drops by 4.7 per cent 9/91
- Queen's speech signals more money for public services 10/91
- Europe's raised interest rates put pressure on pound 12/91
- BCCI goes into liquidation 1/92
- Recession hits unemployment hard 1/92
- British Telecom announces 25,000 job losses 3/92
- Olympia & York admit serious financial difficulties 3/92
- Lloyd's announces worst loss in its 300-year history 6/92
- Stock market suffers biggest one-day fall 8/92
- Insurance companies put the value of a wife at £349 a week 2/93
- Retail price inflation falls to 1.7 per cent 2/93
- Figures show a drop in unemployment 3/93
- Cabinet ministers announce worst of recession is over 4/93
- Asil Nadir jumps bail and flees to Cyprus 5/93
- VAT on gas & electricity comes into effect 4/94
- Sunday shopping for the first time 8/94

Britain (foreign affairs, Africa)
- Boer War "threatens Empire" 1/00
- Lord Roberts heads British in Boer War 1/00
- Nigeria becomes British protectorate 1/00
- Government wins vote on war strategy 2/00
- Ladysmith relieved 2/00
- Rejects American role in war 3/00
- Mafeking relieved 6/00
- African boundaries agreed 2/01
- Boer camp conditions to be improved 4/01
- Fixes African borders with Italy 11/01
- Campbell-Bannerman condemns martial law 11/01
- German visit to Boer camps blocked 2/02
- Cecil John Rhodes dies 3/02
- Boer War ends 5/02
  Cruisers sent to Tetuan, North Africa 11/02
- General Manning marches on Somali Mullah 2/03
- General Morley occupies Kano 2/03
- Takes Sokoto; sultan flees 3/03
- Nigerian anti-white rule revolt 2/04
- Troops sent to quell Nigerian revolt 2/06
- Troops kill 60 Zulus in clashes 3/06
- Boer War compensation to be paid 3/06
- Commission condemns Boer War corruption 8/06
- South Africa Union bill second reading 7/09
- 12 colonial police killed 8/09
- Balfour warns on S. African black rights 8/09
- Egyptian Youth group wants Britain out 9/09
- Fixes African frontiers with rivals 2/10
- South Africa becomes a dominion 7/10
- Fears over German intentions in Morocco 7/11
- Declares Egypt a protectorate 12/14
- Troops sent to quell nationalist unrest 4/19
- Troops break up protest; ten die 11/19
- Grants constitution 11/19
- Troops disperse rioters; 23 die 5/21
- Milner report on future relations 5/21
- Allenby proclaims independence; unease 2/22
- King Fuad claims Sudan 5/22
- Crown takes over Southern Rhodesia 9/23
- Agrees to South Rhodesian autonomy 10/23
- South Africans oppose Union Jack 6/27
- King Fuad arrives on state visit 7/27
- South Africa: Union Jack compromise 10/27
- Treaty to evacuate troops from Egypt 8/29
- Nationalist Premier Nahas Pasha sacked 7/30
- Battleships sent to Egypt to quell anti-UK riots 7/30
- Egypt dissolves parliament and constitution 11/34
- Italy fights joint Abyssinian commission 12/34
- Anti-British Cairo riots; two die, 88 hurt 11/35
- Egyptian King restores 1923 constitution 12/35
- UK protests at Italian use of mustard gas 4/36
- New King Farouk of Egypt 4/36
- Haile Selassie arrives in exile 6/36
- Egyptian independence; protectorate ends 8/36
- Anglo-Egyptian treaty: Eden, Nahas Pasha 8/36
- Cairo ratifies treaty with Britain 11/36
- Egypt breaks 1936 alliance; riots flare 9/38
- Calls round-table talks on Palestine 11/38
- Talks on Palestine open 2/39
- Jan Smuts addresses UK Parliament 10/42
- Allies recognise Algeria-based CFLN 8/43
- Egypt agrees to plans for Nile dam 5/49
- East African groundnuts scheme 11/49
- Future of Seretse Khama in doubt 2/50
- Khama allowed to return to Bechuanaland 3/50
- Khama is no longer Bamangwato chief 11/50
- Farouk demands that UK quits Suez Canal 11/50
- East African groundnut scheme dropped 1/51
- Egypt rejects five-nation defence pact 10/51
- UK troops take Suez Canal Zone 10/51
- Halts arms exports to Egypt; Suez riots 10/51
- Biggest post-war airlift to Suez 11/51
- Egypt invites UN plebiscite on Suez 11/51
- Suez battles; 2,000 British evacuated 11/51
- Will leave Suez towns if terrorism ends 11/51
- Egyptian police backing guerrillas 12/51
- Seals off Suez town after fighting 12/51
- Farouk dismisses Nahas Pasha regime 1/52
- Capture Ismailia police; 46 die 1/52
- Cairo riots, 17 British die; looting 1/52
- Nkrumah black Africa's first premier 3/52
- Bars Khama as chief of Bamangwato tribe 3/52
- Farouk suspends parliament for month 3/52
- Offers Sudan limited self-rule 4/52
- Northern and Southern Rhodesia federation 5/52
- Neguib overthrows King Farouk in Egypt 7/52
- Curfew on Nairobi Mau Mau oath-takers 8/52
- Mau Mau spreads in "white highlands" 8/52
- Leaves Eritrea; now in Ethiopia union 9/52
- Kenyatta and 500 Mau Mau arrested in Kenya 10/52
- UK troops fly in; Kenya emergency 10/52
- Kenyatta charged with managing Mau Mau 11/52
- Closes 34 Kikuyu schools; fears Mau Mau 11/52
- Open Mau Mau rebellion; 2,000 arrested 11/52
- Kenya Governor: death penalty for oath 1/53
- Settlers demand tough action on Mau Mau 1/53
- Southern Rhodesia to join protectorates 2/53
- Troops kill 24 Mau Mau; capture 36 4/53
- Kenyatta sentenced to seven years, Kenya 4/53
- 1,000 Mau Mau suspects arrested, Nairobi 4/53
- New talks with Egypt on Suez Canal 4/53
- Second reading of Central African Federation bill 5/53
- Foreign Office removes UK families, Egypt 5/53
- Egypt: Republic under President Neguib 6/53
- 99 Mau Mau killed by British in Kenya 7/53
- £10 million aid plan for Kenya 12/53
- Neguib survives coup attempt, Egypt 2/54
- Seeking Mau Mau surrender; European fear 3/54
- New plan: 40,000 Kenya Mau Mau arrested 4/54
- Mau Mau burn down Treetops Hotel, Kenya 5/54
- To pull out 83,000 troops from Suez 7/54
- Right to re-activate base in trouble 7/54
- Nigeria's federal constitution 10/54
- Haile Selassie visits Britain 10/54
- Signs Suez Canal agreement with Egypt 10/54
- Baring's amnesty for Mau Mau, Kenya 1/55
- Humphrey Slade attacks amnesty 1/55
- Withdraws Mau Mau amnesty, Kenya 6/55
- Kabaka of Buganda returns to Uganda 7/55
- Kabaka of Buganda gives ministers powers 10/55
- 13,000 reported dead in Mau Mau activity 10/55
- Grants independence to Sudan 12/55
- Sudanese independence declared 1/56
- Gold Coast leaders call for independence 4/56
- Approval for Gold Coast independence 5/56
- Last British soldier leaves Suez Zone 6/56
- Refuses to fund Aswan Dam 7/56
- Nasser nationalises and seizes Suez Canal 7/56
- Furious at Egypt's seizure of Suez Canal 7/56
- Freezes Egyptian assets; arms embargo 7/56
- Canal talks with Egypt and France 8/56
- Khama back in Bechuanaland after exile 9/56
- Royal Marines capture Port Said, Egypt 11/56
- Egypt abrogates 1954 treaty with Britain 1/57
- Egypt nationalises British banks 1/57
- Gold Coast becomes independent Ghana 3/57
- Three Britons jailed as spies, Egypt; freed 6/57
- Turks riot in Cyprus; 100 hurt, two die 1/58
- Southern Rhodesian state of emergency 2/59
- Anti-British riots, Nyasaland 2/59
- Nyasaland rioting; Banda arrested 3/59
- 11 Mau Mau die in detention, Kenya 7/59
- Police shoot rioters, 51 die, Nyasaland 7/59
- Labour blasts African policy in Commons 7/59
- Southern Rhodesia commission 7/59
- Nyasaland and S. Rhodesian politics studied 9/59
- Queen's Speech: independent Nigeria 10/59
- Kenyan state of emergency ends 11/59
- Talks with Egypt's Nasser 12/59
- Black Kenyans boycott constitution talks 1/60
- Riots as Macmillan visits S. Rhodesia 1/60
- Macmillan gives "Winds of change" speech 2/60
- Kenyan conference accepts Macleod plan 2/60
- Defends "meddling", warns of communism 2/60
- Refuses to condemn South Africa at UN 4/60
- Nyasaland's Banda released from jail 4/60
- Queen opens huge Kariba dam on Zambezi 5/60
- Nyasaland state of emergency lifted 6/60
- British Somaliland is independent 6/60
- Macmillan meets Nasser at UN 9/60
- Nigeria gets independence 10/60
- South African whites vote for republic 10/60
- Troops in S. Rhodesian black townships 10/60
- UK-Nigeria defence pact; student protest 11/60
- Northern Rhodesian talks reach deadlock 2/61
- Lumumba murder protest, Belgian embassy 2/61
- South Africa to leave Commonwealth 3/61
- More Africans to vote in N. Rhodesia 6/61
- Nkrumah sacks UK C-in-C of Ghana army 9/61
- Tanganyika becomes independent 12/61
- Ends defence agreement with Nigeria 1/62
- Uganda becomes independent 10/62
- Nyasaland to be allowed to secede 12/62
- Nyasaland self-government begins 2/63
- Northern Rhodesia can secede 3/63
- Chief Enharo deported to Nigeria 5/63
- Effects of the "winds of change" 12/63
- Kenya becomes independent 12/63
- Zanzibar ceases to be protectorate 12/63
- Demo against jailing of Nelson Mandela 6/64
- Smith threatens Rhodesian UDI 6/64
- Nyasaland becomes independent Malawi 7/64
- Smith in talks on Rhodesian independence 9/64
- Arms embargo on South Africa 11/64
- Gambia becomes independent 2/65
- Rhodesia threatens to deport Africans 4/65
- Rhodesian Front Party wins election 5/65
- State of emergency in Rhodesia 5/65
  Smith issues Rhodesian UDI 11/65
- Imposes sanctions on Rhodesia 11/65
- Imposes oil sanctions on Rhodesia 12/65
- Offers military aid to Zambia 12/65
- Rejects military action against Rhodesia 1/66
- To mount drought-relief operations 1/66
- Three visiting MPs expelled from Rhodesia 1/66
- Queen commutes a Rhodesia death sentence 1/66
- Nearly all trade with Rhodesia banned 1/66
- Recognises new regime in Ghana 3/66
- RAF granted a base in Madagascar 3/66
- Oil-laden tanker intercepted, Mozambique 4/66
- Bechuanaland is independent (Botswana) 9/66
- Basutoland independence (Lesotho) 10/66
- Smith supporters demonstrate in London 11/66
- Smith rejects UK proposals to end row 12/66
- Rhodesia leaves Commonwealth 12/66
- Kenyan Asian immigrants flood into UK 2/68
- Rhodesia overturns reprieve of three blacks 3/68
- D'Oliveira out of S. Africa cricket tour 8/68
- Vorster bans MCC tour of South Africa 9/68
- Wilson and Smith in more abortive talks 10/68
- Exodus of Kenyan Asians to UK expected 1/69
- Wilson faces Biafra protest, W. Germany 2/69
- Censures Nigeria on Biafra relief 6/69
- Movement to stop arms to Nigeria 6/69
- Gibbs resigns as Rhodesia governor 6/69
- Springboks UK tour: apartheid protests 11/69
- Cricket tour of East Africa collapses 1/70
- Extra £5 million for Biafra refugees 1/70
- Rhodesia becomes a republic 3/70
- MCC cancels tour of South Africa 5/70
- UK recognises Amin regime in Uganda 2/71
- Uk to sell 7 helicopters to South Africa 2/71
- UK signs deal to end rift with Rhodesia 11/71
- BP's holdings in Libya nationalised 12/71
- Libya withdraws deposits from UK banks 12/71
- MPs approve Rhodesian settlement 12/71
- Libya is giving aid to IRA 6/72
- Amin to expel 50,000 Asians from Uganda 8/72
- Ugandan Asians arrive penniless in UK 9/72
- Idi Amin starts "Save Britain" fund 12/73
- Ends South African Simonstown naval deal 6/75
- 128 mercenaries fly to Angola 1/76
- Rhodesian constitutional talks collapse 3/76
- Thorpe alleges S. African smear plot 5/76
- Three UK mercenaries' death penalty, Angola 6/76
- Breaks diplomatic ties with Uganda 7/76
- Rhodesia announces multi-racial state 9/76
- Smith rejects Ivor Richard's proposals 1/77
- Archbishop Coggan condemns Ugandan death 2/77
- Owen on tour; talks to Smith 4/77
- Owen cautious over Rhodesian settlement 4/77
- Rhodesia accepts black majority rule 11/77
- Owen neutral on Rhodesian deal 2/78
- Twelve UK missionaries massacred, Rhodesia 6/78
- Shell and BP break Rhodesian sanctions 8/78
- Rhodesian whites vote for black rule 1/79
- Muzorewa is first black leader, Rhodesia 4/79
- Lule is new President of Uganda 4/79
- UK angry with Nigeria over assets-seizing 7/79
- Thatcher normalises ties with Zimbabwe 7/79
- Thatcher wants deal with Mugabe and Nkomo 8/79
- Commonwealth talks, Lusaka 8/79
- Lancaster House accord on Zimbabwe 12/79
- Soames's pressure frees Todd, Zimbabwe 2/80
- Last African colony Zimbabwe independent 4/80
- Mugabe speaks of Zimbabwe reconciliation 4/80
- Disasters Committee helps famine victims 6/80
- 650 pounds of cannabis, Moroccan embassy 6/80
- Gambia coup fails; SAS free hostages 8/81
- Athlete Zola Budd to get UK passport 4/84
- WPC Fletcher shot dead by Libyans 4/84
- 30 Libyan diplomats leave 4/84
- Angolan rebels free 16 Britons 5/84
- P.W. Botha visits UK 6/84
- Nigerian ex-minister Dikko kidnapped 7/84
- Dikko found in diplomatic bag 7/84
- Buerk's TV report on Ethiopian famine 11/84
- Huge public response to Ethiopian famine 11/84
- Band Aid record for Ethiopia 12/84
- Terry Waite frees Britons from Libya 2/85
- Leader of Dikko kidnap gang jailed 2/85
- Live Aid concert 7/85
- Live Aid appeal reaches £50 million 7/85
- Sudan famine aid appeal by Princess Anne 12/85
- US uses UK bases for Libya air strike 4/86
- Barclays to "disinvest" in S. Africa 11/86
- 600 UK troops have AIDS test in Kenya 1/87
- Gadaffi releases UK "spy" Maxwell 4/87
- UK announces sanctions against Nigeria 6/93

Britain (foreign affairs, Asia)
- See also foreign affairs (India)
- Treaty of alliance with Japan 1/02
- Shah visits Britain 8/02
- Neutral in Russo-Japanese War 2/04
- 300 Tibetans killed in attack on British 3/04
- Captures Tibetan capital 8/04
- Anglo-Tibet trade treaty 9/04
- Treaty with Japan to safeguard India 9/05
- First ambassador to Japan appointed 11/05
- Controls access to Tibet; foreigners out 4/06
- With Russia, tries to calm Persian unrest 1/10
- Troops land in Persia to protect interests 10/10
- Japanese Prince Hirohito on visit 5/21
- Afghanistan independence recognised 11/21
- UK proposes naval treaty to Japan 11/34
- No Japanese apology for wounding envoy 9/37
- Demands apology for Japanese tug attack 12/37
- Japan opposes British military movements 2/41
- Denounces Japan as an aggressor 7/41
- Japanese assets frozen throughout Empire 7/41
- Eden condemns Japanese torture of PoWs 1/44
- Troops take control of Hong Kong 9/45
- Troops take control of Singapore 9/45
- Allied troops mobilise in Java 10/45
- Indonesians at Surabaya told to yield 11/45
- RAF strikes in India, Ceylon, Singapore 1/46
- Burma becomes independent 1/48
- Rubber planters attacked in Malaya 6/48
- Malayan rebels wiped out 7/48
- India is republic within Commonwealth 4/49
- Hong Kong garrison to be reinforced 5/49
- 3,800 more UK troops arrive in Hong Kong 7/49
- Launches drive against Malayan rebels 11/49
- Governor in Sarawak stabbed by youth 12/49
- Recognises Bao Dai as Vietnam ruler 2/50
- Recognises royalist regime in Cambodia 2/50

- Recognises royalist regime in Laos 2/50
- Royal Navy to aid US in Korean War 6/50
- Decides to send troops to Korea 7/50
- Guy Russell appointed C-in-C Far East 9/50
- US and UK forces recapture Inchon, Korea 2/51
- Weather beats Commonwealth troops, Korea 8/51
- Malayan High Commissioner killed 10/51
- Cassels fears new Korean offensive 12/51
- Malayan rebels kill seven Highlanders 2/52
- Troops kill 22 Malayan insurgents 2/52
- 22 ex-Korean prisoners return 5/53
- 147 Gloucestershire men back from Korea 10/53
- Study plan for South-East Asian "NATO" 4/54
- China shoots down UK airliner; apology 7/54
- To give Malaya independence by 1957 2/56
- Anti-UK mobs attack whites in Kowloon 10/56
- Malaya declares independence 8/57
- Ceylon Tamils call for separate state 6/58
- Mrs Bandaranaike is Ceylon's new Premier 7/60
- Agrees on Federation of Malaysia 7/62
- Troops clash with rebels in Brunei 12/62
- Federation of Malaysia created 9/63
- Embassy in Cambodia wrecked 3/64
- Agrees on more aid for Malaysia 9/64
- Recognises Singapore 8/65
- Forces east of Suez to be withdrawn 7/67
- Disaster relief flown into Pakistan 11/70
- Emperor Hirohito of Japan visits 10/71
- Royal Navy's Far East Command ends 10/71
- Cuts ties with Taiwan 1/72
- Pakistan quits Commonwealth 1/72
- Recognises Bangladesh 2/72
- Two Pakistani terrorists shot dead, London 2/73
- Recognises Hanoi government 7/73
- 4,000 Vietnam refugees come to Hong Kong 5/75
- Mrs Thatcher praises Hua Kuo-feng in UK 10/79
- Sends marines to end New Hebrides revolt 6/80
- 200 Anglo-French marines end New Hebrides revolt 7/80
- Thatcher discusses Hong Kong in China 9/82
- Brunei becomes independent 1/84
- Kidnapped Indian diplomat found dead 2/84
- Hong Kong to be handed back to China in 1997 8/84
- Agrees Hong Kong deal with China 9/84
- Signs Hong Kong treaty with China 12/84
- Briton hanged in Malaysia for drugs 7/86
- City threat over Japan's closed markets 3/87
- Major criticises China's political prisoner record 9/91

Britain (foreign affairs, Europe)
- See also World Wars I and II
- Admiralty foregoes Gibraltar extension 6/01
- Customs treaty, Italy and Germany 5/03
- Accuses Belgium of Congo atrocities 2/04
- Forces Belgium to check Congo cruelties 9/04
- Triple Entente with Spain and France 6/07
- Papal Legate's visit 9/08
- Invited to join Balkans crisis congress 10/08
- Sends doctors to Italian quake victims 1/09
- Austria convicts British officers as spies 12/10
- Breaks diplomatic relations with Turkey 11/14
- Recognise state of Czechoslovakia 8/18
- Rejects Austrian peace proposal 9/18
- Official end to war with Austria 7/20
- Ex-Emperor Karl held on British ship 10/21
- Recognises Greek republic 4/24
- Italian King and Queen visit 5/24
- Austen Chamberlain meets Mussolini 4/29
- Signs commerce treaty with Rumania 8/30
- MacDonald justifies talks with Mussolini 3/33
- Churchill blames MacDonald for weakness 3/33
- Supports independent Austria 9/34
- Plans joint action against aggressors 2/35
- Hoare vacillates on Italian sanctions 10/35
- Hoare rules out military action on Italy 10/35
- League sanctions take effect 11/35
- Hoare-Laval pact allows Italy land 12/35
- Drops Italian sanctions 6/36
- Eden warns Britain will defend Belgium 11/36
- Blasts Spain over shelling of steamer 1/37
- Bans volunteers fighting in Spain 1/37
- Intellectuals flock to Spanish Civil War 2/37
- Eighteen English captured at Arganda 2/37
- UK, Italy, USSR, Germany halt aid to Spain 2/37
- Anglo-French patrols around Spain 6/37
- UK wants Mediterranean "piracy" talks 9/37
- Warship attacked by submarine, Spain 9/37
- Chamberlain to defend France and Belgium 3/38
- Chamberlain may defend Czechoslovakia 3/38
- Anglo-Italian pact signed 4/38
- Tries to loosen Italian links with Germany 4/38
- Anglo-Italian pact passed; Italy praised 5/38
- Recognises Abyssinian annexation 5/38
- London committee to evacuate volunteers 6/38
- John Simon warns on Czechoslovakia 8/38
- Chamberlain accepts German Sudeten deal 9/38
- Chamberlain: "Peace in our time" speech 9/38
- 11,000 Jews absorbed since 1933 11/38
- Chamberlain and Halifax visit Mussolini 1/39
- Recognises Franco 2/39
- Pledges to defend Poland 3/39
- Signs pact with France and Poland 4/39
- Pledges aid to Greece and Rumania 4/39
- Pledge to Poland reaffirmed 8/39
- Baltic and Med closed to merchant ships 8/39
- Signs mutual assistance pact with Turkey 10/39
- Signs finance pact with Spain 12/40
- Allies agree on UN war crimes commission 10/43
- Allies agree on Austrian independence 11/43
- Churchill agrees closer ties with Turkey 12/43
- Poles insist on recognition by USSR 1/44
- Simon defends bombing of Monte Cassino 2/44
- Poles reject Curzon Line as frontier 2/44
- Exiled Czechs sign convention with USSR 5/44
- Refuses to recognise Polish government 1/45
- Recognises Polish government 7/45
- "Iron Curtain" falls in Europe 7/45
- Bevin slams East European elections 8/45
- Churchill calls for united Europe 9/46
- Embassy in Rome wrecked by bombs 10/46
- Churchill leads United Europe rally 5/47
- Polish opposition leader in London 11/47
- Defence pact with France and Benelux 3/48
- Eight Czech exiles land at Manston, Kent 5/48
- MPs are against "Nenni" telegram inquiry 5/48
- Proposes "Council of Europe" 11/48
- Hungary jails Edgar Sanders for spying 2/50
- Czechoslovakia ends cultural agreement 5/50
- Montgomery is Eisenhower's deputy 3/51
- Police search for Burgess and MacLean 6/51
- Allies delay West German NATO membership 2/52
- Tito visits; first Communist head of state 3/53
- Eden for free elections in one Germany 1/54
- Refuses to recognise East German regime 1/54
- Pro-Cypriot march on embassy; 78 hurt 8/54
- Anti-British riots, Cyprus; 42 arrested 12/54
- Invites Greeks and Turks to Cyprus talks 6/55
- Aids Cypriot police in raids on EOKA 6/55
- Navy and Air Force patrol Cyprus; riots 6/55
- Cyprus talks with Turkey and Greece fail 9/55
- EOKA banned, Cyprus; commandos sent 9/55
- Anti-British general strike in Cyprus 9/55
- Fear Greek-Turkish clashes in Nicosia 9/55
- Cyprus riots; takes emergency powers 11/55
- Makarios defies British rule in Cyprus 11/55
- British form Home Guard, Cyprus 12/55
- Troops in Cyprus; Greek-Turkish violence 1/56
- Cyprus constitution plan: power-sharing 2/56
- Colonial Secretary Lennox-Boyd meets Makarios 2/56
- Jams Greek radio to Cyprus 3/56
- EOKA bomb threat to Governor Harding 3/56
- Greek riots, Cyprus; clash with Turks 3/56
- Deports Makarios on EOKA charge 3/56
- First UK civilian killed by EOKA, Cyprus 4/56
- £10,000 reward to catch Cypriot Grivas 5/56
- Hungarian refugees arrive in Britain 11/56
- Cyprus Governor rejects EOKA cease-fire 3/57
- UK wants new trade structure with EEC 3/57
- French delegates angry at UK out of EEC 3/57
- Macmillan and Adenauer discuss defence 5/57
- Pro-EOKA Cyprus protesters teargassed 10/57
- Albania shoots down British freight plane 1/58
- Malta's Mintoff resigns over UK aid cut 4/58
- Governor Laycock assumes power, Malta 4/58
- Cyprus peace plan rejected; riot, curfew 6/58
- Angry at Iceland's fishing limit 8/58
- Grivas Cyprus cease-fire; Macmillan goes 8/58
- Trawlers defy Icelandic fishing ban 9/58
- Icelandic gunboat boards trawler; beaten 9/58
- Renewed riots and attacks by Greeks and Turks 10/58
- Cypriots reject seven-year UK plan 10/58
- British kill EOKA leader Matsis, Cyprus 11/58
- Cyprus deal: Greek President, Turkish Vice-President 2/59
- Warns Iceland on Cod War shootings 5/59
- Iceland fires on Arctic Viking trawler 5/59
- Queen's Speech: independent Cyprus 10/59
- Joins EFTA free trade pact 11/59
- EFTA offers to absorb EEC and USSR 11/59
- Macmillan and Adenauer in talks 11/59
- Popular de Gaulle visits Britain 4/60
- Cyprus a republic under Makarios 8/60
- Iceland talks to end fishing dispute 10/60
- Malta to be given self-government 3/61
- Applies for entry to EEC 8/61
- British and US tanks face Soviet tanks along Berlin border 10/61
- Malta becomes fully independent 3/62
- French and Belgians support entry to EEC 4/62
- Turks walk out of Cyprus talks 1/64
- 1,500 troops flown to Cyprus 2/64
- UK troops involved in Cyprus fighting 3/64
- UK troops flown home from Cyprus 5/64
- Malta is independent Commonwealth member 9/64
- Cypriots demand removal of British bases 10/64
- Spain begins blockade of Gibraltar 2/65
- Queen makes visit to W. Germany 5/65
- De Gaulle rebuffs UK on EEC entry 5/67
- Reapplies for EEC membership 5/67
- Gibraltar votes to keep ties with UK 9/67
- Entry to EEC vetoed by de Gaulle 11/67
- Spain begins siege of Gibraltar 6/69
- Spain offers Gibraltarians nationality 7/69
- Three UK diplomats expelled from Poland 1/70
- Talks on EEC entry open 6/70
- Recognises Oder-Neisse line 11/70
- Terms for EEC entry agreed 6/71
- Malta ends ten-year defence pact with UK 6/71
- Anglo-Maltese defence talks collapse 7/71
- Commons votes in favour of EEC entry 10/71
- Signs treaty of entry to EEC 1/72
- Turks jail 14-year-old Briton for drugs 3/72
- Signs pact with Malta on military bases 3/72
- Terrorists kill three UK hostages in Turkey 3/72
- Icelandic gunboat sinks two UK trawlers 9/72
- Heath supports European Union 10/72
- Queen makes state visit to Yugoslavia 10/72
- Iceland boycotts British goods 10/72
- Joins EEC 1/73
- Super tug sent to protect fishing boats 1/73
- Icelandic gunboats fire at UK tug 3/73
- Icelandic gunboat fires on UK trawlers 4/73
- First RN action of Cod War 5/73
- UK embassy in Iceland stormed by rioters 5/73
- Icelandic gunboat engineer dies in clash 8/73
- Turks free London schoolboy from jail 5/74
- Callaghan clinches Cyprus peace deal 7/74
- Two thirds of UK vote to stay in EEC 6/75
- HMS Andromeda rammed by Icelandic boat 1/76
- Withdraws protecting ships near Iceland 1/76
- Iceland breaks relations; UK sends boat 2/76
- UK and Iceland sign end to third Cod War 6/76
- Jenkins leaves cabinet to head EEC 1/77
- Bomb found at UK army base 8/78
- Poison umbrella kills Bulgarian defector 9/78
- Bulgarian defector Simeonov dies, London 10/78
- Will not join European Monetary System (EMS) 12/78
- Sykes, UK ambassador to Holland, killed 3/79
- Last British warships leave Malta 4/79
- Poor one third poll in UK Euro elections 6/79
- Thatcher wants £1,000 million from EEC 11/79
- Thatcher withholds VAT to EEC 3/80
- Spain to re-open Gibraltar border 4/80
- EEC fails to solve UK contribution 4/80
- EEC cuts UK contribution to £250 million 5/80
- Thatcher still wants more from EEC 5/80
- French fishermen blockade UK ferries 8/80
- Spain halts siege of Gibraltar 1/82
- EEC bans Argentinian imports 4/82
- EEC wants ban on UK rubber bullets 5/82
- Blasts Poland's banning of Solidarity 10/82
- Spain-Gibraltar border re-opens 12/82
- Danish trawlers banned from UK waters 1/83
- Danish trawler captain Kirk arrested 1/83
- EEC summit collapses over UK budget 3/84
- UK diplomat Whitty shot dead in Athens 3/84
- 7 Cyprus servicemen on spying charges 4/84
- European Court condemns phone-tapping 8/84
- Franco ends siege of Gibraltar 2/85
- Seven acquitted in Cyprus secrets case 10/85
- Juan Carlos of Spain visits UK 4/86
- Thatcher refuses to pay more to EEC 6/87
- European passport to replace British 4/88
- European central bank plans rejected 6/88
- Thatcher visits Poland's Gdansk shipyard 11/88
- Dr Robert Runcie visits Pope John Paul II in Rome 9/89
- Four Allied powers sign German sovereignty treaty 9/90
- Britain to apply for ERM membership 10/90
- Thatcher vows to veto single European currency 10/90
- EC's demand to halt seven building projects angers Britain 10/91
- Agrees to reimburse Baltic states for gold sold in 1967 1/92
- Signs arms accord with Russia 1/92
- G7 agree on aid package for former USSR 4/92
- To send 1,800 troops to help UN relief efforts in Bosnia 8/92
- Russian President Yeltsin invites Queen Elizabeth to Moscow 11/92

Britain (foreign affairs, France)
- See also foreign affairs (Europe), World Wars I and II
- Global pact with France 4/04
- We will not help France, says Grey 3/11
- George V's visit wins French friendship 4/14
- Agrees on German war debts 11/20
- Lloyd George and Briand discuss disarmament 7/21
- Allied Supreme Council ended 1/22
- 20-year alliance signed 2/22
- Blames France for Ruhr occupation 1/23
- Blocks further occupation of Germany 11/23
- President Doumergue visits London 5/27
- Agrees ten-year non-aggression pact 5/33
- Joint pact to defend Czechoslovakia 4/38
- Royal visit to Paris 7/38
- Signs 50-year alliance with France 3/47
- UK and France ask World Court to settle Channel islands row 12/51
- Signs deal to build Concorde with France 11/62
- France ends no-passport trips by Britons 5/84
- Signs Channel Tunnel treaty with France 2/86
- France bans all British beef and live cattle imports 5/90
- Anglo-French "lamb war" stepped up 9/90

Britain (foreign affairs, Germany)
- See also foreign affairs (Europe), World Wars I and II
- Arbitration treaty with Germany 7/04
- Jubilation as Kaiser and King meet Mayor 11/07
- King meets Kaiser to calm tensions 8/08
- Kaiser's interview offends Britain 10/08
- Roberts warns Germany may invade 11/08
- Fears in Commons of German dreadnoughts 3/09
- War Minister Lord Haldane visits Germany 2/12
- Anglo-German talks fail; Navy buildup 7/12
- Pressurises Germany to give up rail link 7/13
- Grey's conciliation of Germany fails 7/14
- Warns Germany not to invade Belgium 8/14
- Declares war on Germany 8/14
- Fears of communism in famine-hit Germany 3/19
- German sailors sink fleet 6/19
- Lloyd George wants tough reparations 6/19
- Lloyd George tough on German reparations 2/21
- Troops occupy Dusseldorf to get debts 3/21
- Lloyd George's trade plan to get debts 3/21
- France rejects reparations mediation 7/23
- Accepts Dawes plan 4/24
- Joy at Locarno security pact outcome 10/25
- Troops leave Rhineland after seven years 1/26
- Officer predicts Germans will start war 11/27
- Wants League to review Austro-German pact 3/31
- Renews credits in light of falling mark 7/31
- Calls for new reparations 12/31
- MPs approve trade pact with Germany 5/33
- Agrees ten-year non-aggression pact 5/33
- TUC calls for boycott to protest against Nazism 5/33
- Italy attacks Nazism at League session 10/33
- Baldwin warns of re-arming dangers 11/33
- UK journalist on German treason charge 11/33
- Eden meets Hitler for "cordial" talks 2/34
- Warns against defaulting on reparations 4/34
- 20 per cent duty put on German goods 6/34
- Agrees on loan repayments 7/34
- First British troops leave Saar 2/35
- Hopes Germany will join East Europe security pact 3/35
- Eden, Simon hear demands on Berlin visit 3/35
- Anglo-German naval accord relaxes curbs 6/35
- Cautious approval of Rhineland invasion 3/36
- Ribbentrop is ambassador to Britain 8/36
- Ambassador Phipps witnesses Japan pact 11/36
- Eden warns on aid to Spanish rebels 12/36
- Government expels three German journalists 8/37
- Duke and Duchess of Windsor feted by Nazis 10/37
- Duke of Windsor visits housing and "model factory" 10/37
- Lord Halifax in Berlin over Sudetenland 11/37
- Chamberlain talks to Italian Ambassador 1/38
- Ambassador recalled from Berlin 8/38
- Chamberlain accepts German Sudeten deal 9/38
- Chamberlain denounces Hitler 3/39
- Ambassador to Berlin recalled 3/39
- Germany warned on use of force in Danzig 5/39
- Declares war on Germany 9/39
- Horrors of Nazi concentration camps 10/39
- Condemns Nazi atrocities 12/42
- Lord Haw Haw arrested in Germany 5/45
- Occupies assigned Berlin zone 7/45
- Agrees with US to merge occupation zones 5/47
- Agrees with US on control of Ruhr mines 9/47
- Berlin airlift begins 6/48
- Agrees on establishment of West Germany 4/49
- Berlin blockade ends 5/49
- Asks Germany to call off V-2 50th anniversary celebrations 9/92

Britain (foreign affairs, India)
- Aid for millions starving from drought 3/00
- India proclaims Edward as Emperor 1/03
- Promises more troops in India 7/03
- India Viceroy resigns in dispute over army 8/05
- Calcutta riots; Labour leader blamed 10/07
- Troops face Indian frontier men 4/08
- King hints at extending Indian democracy 11/08
- Indian local councils get more power 5/09
- Gandhi trade strike against security law 4/19
- Amristar massacre 4/19
- Congress chooses non-violent resistance 9/20
- Prince visits; mobs attack, cloth burnt 11/21
- Gandhi jailed six years for sedition 3/22
- Salt tax to balance budget; resentment 3/23
- National Congress; new civil disobedience 9/23
- Army move in on communal riots, Calcutta 4/26
- Commons sets up Simon Commission 11/27
- Parsee Communist MP opposes Commission 11/27
- Rioting as Simon Commission arrives 2/28
- Nationalists stop Communist expulsion 9/28
- British troops fire on Bombay rioters 2/29
- Royal Air Force flies non-stop to India 4/29
- Nehru wants revolt if no Dominion status 5/29
- Viceroy escapes bomb on train 12/29
- Congress demands independence; threatens 12/29
- Gandhi criticised for pro-Viceroy motion 1/30
- Nationalists suspected of Museum bomb 2/30
- Gandhi breaks Salt Law at Dandi beach 4/30
- Viceroy imposes anti-terrorism ordinance 4/30
- Gandhi arrested in Karadi 5/30
- Martial law in Sholapur; two police die 5/30
- Viceroy Irwin bans picketing and suborning 5/30
- Simon Commission recommends federation 6/30
- India House, Aldwych; King wants peace 7/30
- Round-table conference on India's future 11/30
- British Governor of Punjab wounded 12/30
- Churchill quits cabinet over policy 1/31
- Churchill favours princes over Gandhi 1/31
- Gandhi's first meeting with Lord Irving 2/31
- Highland Infantry quell Cawnpore rioting 3/31
- Viceroy: no salt tax if you end protests 3/31
- Bangalore riots; Punjab Governor wounded 7/31
- Gandhi in second Round Table conference 8/31
- Gandhi meets King George 11/31
- Gandhi wants foreign and military control 11/31
- Round Table talks end in failure 12/31
- Bengal Congress boycotts British goods 12/31
- Magistrate killed; police shoot rioters 12/31
- Congress disobedience; Gandhi arrested 1/32
- 100 Congress leaders arrested; boycotts 1/32
- Gandhi fast gets votes for Untouchables 9/32
- Richard A. Butler new Secretary for India 9/32
- Third Round Table conference ends 12/32
- To release Gandhi and 28,000 prisoners 12/32
- Commons backs India Federal Constitution 3/33

- Government of India Bill 2/35
- New bill gives limited home rule 2/35
- Troops fire at rioting Moslems; 27 die 3/35
- Troops patrol earthquake-hit Quetta 5/35
- Sixty Bombay rioters taken for flogging 10/36
- Government of India Act; constitution 4/37
- Burma separated from India 4/37
- Murder of O'Dwyer, ex-governor of Punjab 1/40
- Gandhi names Nehru as his successor 1/42
- India offered dominion status 3/42
- Indian Congress rejects British plan 4/42
- Nehru pledges "no surrender" to Axis 4/42
- Gandhi and 50 others arrested 8/42
- Wavell appointed Viceroy 6/43
- Auchinleck appointed C-in-C, India 6/43
- Nehru and other leaders freed by British 6/45
- Promises Home Rule for India 9/45
- Indian civil war looms 2/46
- Gandhi endorses Britain's "good faith" 4/46
- Plans for independent, united India 5/46
- Congress Party rejects independence plan 6/46
- Moslems in India prepare for civil war 7/46
- Thousands die in Hindu-Moslem riots 8/46
- Nehru heads provisional government, India 8/46
- Nehru's cabinet sworn in 9/46
- Moslems and Hindus dislike new Assembly 11/46
- Anglo-Indian talks end in failure 12/46
- Mountbatten appointed Viceroy 2/47
- Britain to quit India by June 1948 2/47
- Mountbatten in talks with Gandhi 3/47
- Hindu Moslem violence mounts 3/47
- MPs approve plan to quit India 3/47
- Troops sent to Amritsar 3/47
- 293 have died of violence in Punjab 3/47
- Troops sent in to quell riots in India 4/47
- Indian parliament counsels non-violence 4/47
- Agrees to partition of India 5/47
- Moslems and Hindus agree to partition 6/47
- Jinnah to be Governor-General of Pakistan 7/47
- Indian Independence Bill published 7/47
- Rule in India ends 8/47
- Mountbatten becomes Governor-General of India 8/47
- Ceylon becomes independent dominion 2/48
- Eight Gurkha battalions to join British Army 2/48
- Last troops leave India 2/48
- Mountbatten ends term as Governor-General of India 6/48
- Pakistan: Commonwealth Islamic republic 11/53
- East Pakistan minister sacked after call 5/54
- Pakistan called Islamic Republic 3/56
- Ceylon wants British bases removed 5/56
- Tamil asylum-seekers protest at expulsion 2/87
- Asks Gatting to apologise in cricket row 12/87

Britain (foreign affairs, Ireland)
- Trade threat over Loyal Oath decision 5/32
- Import duties approved on Irish goods 7/32
- Irish approve tariff reprisals on UK 7/32
- To buy more cattle and sell more coal 1/35
- Ireland drops allegiance to Crown; Eire 4/37
- Hopes for end of trade war 1/38
- De Valera holds two days' talks, London 1/38
- New Agreement: naval bases ceded back 4/38
- New Agreement: no coal duty, low tariffs 4/38
- New Agreement: Eire saves £140 million 4/38
- Recognises Ireland as a republic 5/49
- Pro-Ulster coalition beaten in Ireland 6/51
- Premiers of the two Irelands meet 1/65
- Embassy in Dublin burnt down 2/72
- Official IRA cease-fire declared, Ireland 5/72
- MI6 linked to bomb attacks in Dublin 8/73
- Three IRA men escape from jail in Dublin 10/73
- Sunningdale deal on a Council of Ireland 12/73
- Cosgrave concedes UK controls N. Ireland 3/74
- Dublin car bombs kill 23 in rush hour 5/74
- Ambassador Ewart-Biggs killed 7/76
- Ireland tells Court Britain practises torture 9/76
- Thatcher meets Fitzgerald: more links 11/81
- Ireland passes bill to seize IRA assets 2/85
- Anglo-Irish Agreement signed 11/85
- First Anglo-Irish conference 12/85
- Glenholmes extradition fails 3/86
- DU leader Robinson arrested in Ireland 8/86
- IRA suspect O'Reilly freed, Ireland 8/86
- London and Dublin present a plan for peace in Ulster 2/95

Britain (foreign affairs, Middle East)
- See also Palestine
- William Waldegrave meets PLO leader, Yassir Arafat 1/89
- Diplomatic relations with Iran resumed 9/90
- Edward Heath meets Saddam Hussein in Iraq for negotiations 10/90
- Heath obtains release of 33 British hostages from Iraq 10/90
- Another 15,000 British troops sent to the Gulf 11/90
- Resumes diplomatic links with Syria 11/90
- Iraq begins freeing foreign "human shield" hostages 12/90
- Eight Iraqi diplomats expelled from UK 1/91
- Operation Desert Storm is launched in the Gulf 1/91
- Allied tanks cross Saudi border 2/91
- Two Iraqi Republican Guards divisions surrounded by Allies 2/91
- Gulf War officially over 2/91
- Major outlines "safe haven" plan for Kurds in Iraq 4/91
- Beirut hostage Jackie Mann returns home 9/91
- Two Libyans suspected of Pan Am bombing over Lockerbie 11/91
- Terry Waite released after five years of captivity in Beirut 11/91
- US, British and French planes carry out air strikes on Iraq 1/93

Britain (foreign affairs, USA)
- See also World Wars I and II
- Agrees with US on Central American canal 11/01
- British and German ships bombard Venezuela 12/02
- King welcomes President Wilson 12/18
- Hoover meets MacDonald; war unthinkable 10/29
- Pays USA £27 million in gold for debts 12/32
- MacDonald and Roosevelt discuss recovery 4/33
- Stalls repayment of war debts to US 6/34
- Joseph Kennedy, Ambassador to London 12/37
- Contract to buy 400 planes 6/38
- First 25 F-86 Sabre jets arrive in Britain 8/38
- Gives leases on bases in Newfoundland 8/40
- Gives leases on bases in West Indies 8/40
- Joseph Kennedy quits as US envoy to UK 12/40
- Signs lease-lend pact with USA 3/41
- Agrees Atlantic Charter with USA 8/41
- Anglo-US loan agreement signed 12/45
- £937 million US loan approved 7/46
- Max Gardner, new US ambassador, dies 2/47
- Agrees with US on control of Ruhr mines 9/47
- Refuse to extradite Communist to US 5/49
- Asks US for A-bomb stockpile 1/50
- Washington embassy diplomats disappear 6/51
- Permission for Greenham Common air base 6/51
- Churchill allows USA to use UK bases 1/52
- USA doubles defence aid to Britain 3/52
- Eisenhower and Churchill: Potomac Agreement 6/54
- Anglo-American unity on peace, Potomac 6/54
- Dulles and Eden accept Vietnam partition 6/54
- Agreement on nuclear information 6/55
- First US U-2 spy plane at RAF Lakenheath 4/56
- Leaders restore links at Bermuda talks 3/57
- Dulles in London for disarmament talks 7/57
- Triumphant royal visit 10/57
- Lloyd and Macmillan in talks at White House 10/57
- To buy nuclear submarine plant 7/58
- Macmillan arrives for talks on Berlin 3/59
- Eisenhower and Macmillan: TV chat on issues 8/59
- Signs nuclear test ban treaty 3/60
- Macmillan allows US nuclear submarines 11/60
- US Nazi leader Rockwell ordered out 8/62
- To buy Polaris missiles from USA 12/62
- Signs Polaris deal with US 4/63
- Political leaders at Kennedy funeral 11/63
- Queen dedicates Runnymede field to JFK 5/65
- Nixon holds talks with Wilson in London 2/69
- Vietnam War protesters clash with police 1/70
- IRA sinks RN launch in Baltimore, US 4/71
- Jay, premier's son-in-law, is Ambassador 5/77
- Ex-premier Heath refuses ambassadorship 5/79
- Thatcher visits Reagan in Washington 2/81
- Reagan backs Britain over Argentina 4/82
- Reagan visits Britain; addresses parliament 6/82
- Bernadette McAliskey denied visa by US 6/83
- First cruise missiles arrive at Greenham 11/83
- Thatcher supports Star Wars 2/85
- Thatcher asks for end to US aid to IRA 2/85
- US uses British bases for Libya air strike 4/86
- US ratifies Anglo-US extradition treaty 7/86
- Labour's Kinnock meets Reagan 3/87

Britain (foreign affairs, USSR)
- See also World Wars I and II
- Government recognises USSR 2/24
- Trade agreement 8/24
- Foreign Office shows Zinoviev Letter 10/24
- Discover Argos papers, expels diplomats 5/27
- New government will restore ties 6/29
- Invitates USSR to resume relations 7/29
- Refuses Trotsky asylum 7/29
- Joins allies to stop Soviet grain dumping 3/31
- Ends trade treaty with USSR 10/32
- Protests at jailing of two UK engineers 4/33
- Ban on Soviet imports 4/33
- Eden and Litvinov discuss German rearmament 3/35
- Proposes pact with USSR 5/39
- Signs 20-year pact with USSR 5/42
- Stalingrad given sword of honour by UK 2/44
- BBC begins broadcasts in Russian 3/46
- Paris treaty talks 4/46
- Atom spy Nunn May jailed for ten years 5/46
- Bevin says "appeasement" is over 6/47
- Accuses USSR of duplicity over Germany 12/47
- Denounces Soviet imperialism 1/48
- Worries over missing Burgess and MacLean 6/51
- Burgess and MacLean suspected as spies 6/51
- Gromyko is Soviet ambassador to Britain 6/52
- Theory that Burgess and Maclean were warned 3/54
- Harold "Kim" Philby suspected third man 3/54
- Petrov says Burgess and Maclean are in USSR 4/54
- UK scientist Pontecorvo working in USSR 2/55
- Pontecorvo denies working on nuclear projects 3/55
- Admission: Burgess and MacLean were spies 9/55
- Protests at Khrushchev's attacks on policy 12/55
- Admits frogman spied on Soviet cruiser 5/56
- Crabb's body found; Soviet Navy cleared 6/57
- Macmillan in Moscow for arms talks 2/59
- To expand cultural and trade ties 2/59
- Selwyn Lloyd and Andrei Gromyko in talks 3/59
- Sending trade mission to Moscow 4/59
- Signs five-year trade pact 5/59
- Khrushchev disrupts Macmillan's UN speech 9/60
- Lonsdale and four others held for spying 1/61
- Signs technology and culture pact with USSR 1/61
- George Blake given 42 years for spying 5/61
- Soviet spy Robert Soblen deported 9/62
- Vassall charged under Official Secrets Act 9/62
- Soviet spy Vassall jailed for 18 years 10/62
- Briton Wynne arrested as spy in USSR 11/62
- Kim Philby has vanished from Lebanon 3/63
- Ashkenazy granted political asylum 4/63
- USSR gives Wynne eight years for spying 5/63
- Revealed that Philby was Third Man 7/63
- Physicist Martelli acquitted of spying 7/63
- Philby granted Soviet citizenship 7/63
- Traitor Guy Burgess reported dead, USSR 9/63
- Greville Wynne returns to UK in spy swap 4/64
- Squires, British officer, is working for USSR 6/65
- USSR jails Gerald Brooke for spying 7/65
- Kim Philby's OBE cancelled 8/65
- Harold Wilson visits USSR 7/66
- Double agent Blake escapes from jail, UK 10/66
- George Blake reported in East Berlin 11/66
- Kosygin visits UK 2/67
- Briton Brooke exchanged for two Russians 7/69
- Grants asylum to space expert Fedoseyev 6/71
- 90 Russians expelled for spying 9/71
- USSR expels five Britons, bars 13 more 10/71
- Bingham (RN) jailed for selling secrets 1/72
- Princess Anne visits USSR 8/73
- USSR attacks "Iron Lady" Mrs Thatcher 1/76
- USSR posters: "Cold War Witch" Thatcher 2/76
- Queen's art adviser Blunt was spy 11/79
- Blunt was fourth man after Burgess, MacLean and Philby 11/79
- UK Equestrian Federation boycotts Moscow Olympics 4/80
- UK salvagers with gold bars from ship 10/81
- Ex-spy Donald MacLean dies in Moscow 3/83
- Three alleged KGB agents expelled 4/83
- Soviet writer Bitov granted asylum 1/84
- Oleg Bitov says British agents kidnapped him 9/84
- Stalin's daughter returns to USSR 11/84
- Gorbachev visits Britain 12/84
- KGB head Gordievski defects 9/85
- Expels 31 Russians 9/85
- Warm Moscow welcome for Thatcher 3/87
- Thatcher-Gorbachev talks to end Cruise 3/87

Britain (health)
- See also Women
- Waterloo Hospital founded 10/03
- Aspirin on sale for first time 10/05
- Drink causes poverty, says Lloyd George 9/06
- Meningitis fears 2/07
- Doctors attack child smoking 8/07
- Florence Nightingale gets Order of Merit 11/07
- Florence Nightingale dies 8/10
- Doctors resist National Insurance 7/12
- Newman report highlights sick children 12/13
- Royal National Institute for the Blind 3/14
- Deaths exceed births, due to influenza 3/19
- Home Counties rabies: dogs muzzled 4/19
- 804 die from influenza in a week 1/22
- Sex education call from Birthrate Commission 4/23
- Health Ministry bans food preservatives 10/24
- 1,000 a week die from influenza 2/27
- BMA scared of a state medical service 7/27
- Lowest birthrate since 1860 9/27
- Lowest birth rate on record 1/28
- "Elastoplast" sticking plasters, Hull 10/28
- Birth rate is 85 per cent of death rate 4/29
- Peter Pan royalties sponsor hospital 4/29
- Nurses should get more pay: report 2/32
- "Iron lung" used for first time in UK 10/32
- Sherrington and Adrian win Medicine Nobel 12/32
- Call for improved hospital out-patients 1/33
- Doctors isolate influenza virus 7/33
- Report: healthier, but still slums, diet 9/33
- Slimming craze hits potato sales 3/34
- Gymnasia and slimming to music for women 10/35
- Midwives Bill: plan for national service 3/36
- League report: 30,000 drug addicts in Britain 5/36
- Nuffield's £2 million medical research 11/36
- £2 million national fitness campaign 2/37
- Oliver Stanley's aim: "lifelong fitness" 2/37
- Typhoid in London suburbs 11/37
- Housewife's suicide: "suburban neurosis" 6/38
- Dodds' new drug to ease menopause 12/38
- Women's League of Health and Beauty 6/39
- First successful use of penicillin 2/41
- "National health service" will be set up 4/43
- BMA opposes Beveridge plan 8/43
- Sharp rise in VD since start of war 10/43
- Plans for national health service 2/44
- Fleming, Chain, Florey: Medicine Nobel 12/45
- TB and VD are top targets of new NHS 1/46
- Three-year-old dies from banana overdose 2/46
- BMA sets up fund to fight NHS 3/46
- Bevan presents NHS proposals to MPs 3/46
- Penicillin is to be freely available 5/46
- BUPA founded 4/47
- Doctors threaten boycott of new NHS 1/48
- Doctors offered freedoms under NHS 4/48
- Over 10,000 doctors have joined NHS 6/48
- Dentists told not to join NHS 6/48
- First operation inside the heart 6/48
- National Health Service founded 7/48
- National Insurance comes into being 7/48
- Gaitskell charges for dentures and spectacles 4/51
- Labour resignations over charges 4/51
- "Rab" Butler announces new NHS charges 1/52
- 20,000 doctors to get backdated pay rise 3/52
- Ian Macleod Minister of Health 5/52
- Health service to prescribe fog masks 11/53
- Study finds smoking may cause cancer 2/54
- Tobacco companies deny cancer link 2/54
- Nine babies die in maternity ward fire 4/54
- Equal pay for women in the NHS 9/55
- Minister rejects anti-smoking campaign 5/56
- Calls for inquiry into child abuse 6/56
- Upset man threatens plastic surgeon 1/57
- Anti-smoking campaign launched 6/57
- Health minister rules out smoking bans 6/57
- Doctors worried about tranquilliser sales 7/57
- Myxomatosis in 11 counties 8/57
- Children killed by Asian flu and pneumonia 9/57
- Asian flu vaccine distributed 10/57
- Asian flu abating 11/57
- BMA says cigarettes cause lung cancer 1/58
- Church of England backs family planning 4/58
- More polio vaccinations 7/58
- Birth control pioneer Marie Stopes dies 10/58
- Warnings on overuse of sedatives 11/58
- Thalidomide drug causes birth defects 12/58
- Obesity bigger problem than malnutrition 1/59
- Leukaemia: Windscale nuclear plant links 1/59
- Bill to care for mentally ill 1/59
- BMA scandal over "chastity" book 3/59
- Health fears spur filter cigarette sales 5/59
- Hammersmith Hospital's spare organs bank 6/59
- Curbs on selling "pep pills" 1/60
- More venereal diseases among teenagers 2/60
- First NHS hearing aids 6/60
- Nye Bevan, NHS creator, dies - profile 7/60
- Contraceptive pill goes on sale 1/61
- Birth control pill available on NHS 12/61
- Six have died in smallpox outbreak 1/62
- Thalidomide research - Distillers to pay 9/62
- First successful kidney transplant 2/63
- Oral contraceptive on prescription 6/63
- Hodgkin and Huxley win Medicine Nobel 12/63
- 136 cases of typhoid in Aberdeen 4/64
- First Brook Advisory Centre opens 7/64
- Cigarette ads to be banned from TV 2/65
- Society for ... Unborn Children formed 1/67
- Pill carries "slight" thrombosis risk 4/67
- Petition against Abortion Bill 5/67
- Abortion Bill passes all Commons stages 7/67
- The Abortion Bill becomes law 10/67
- Ban on meat from foot and mouth nations 12/67
- First heart transplant 5/68
- First liver transplant 5/68
- First lung transplant 5/68
- First heart transplant patient dies 6/68
- Heroin addiction is "major emergency" 8/68
- Epidural promises painless childbirth 9/68
- Pregnancy Advisory Service launched 10/68
- First abortion clinic opens in London 10/68
- NHS charges to rise 5/69
- Two thalidomide boys win £33,600 7/69
- Rabid dog bites two people, Camberley 10/69
- Male sterilisation clinic to open 12/69
- 4,000 die of Hong Kong flu in one week 1/70
- 18 thalidomide children get £370,000 3/70
- First heart pacemaker 7/70
- 28 thalidomide children get £485,000 7/70
- World's first kidney and pancreatic transplant 1/72
- £3m made available for disabled children 11/72
- Kidney donor card scheme introduced 11/72
- Distillers offer £11.25m compensation 12/72
- Supermarkets boycott Distillers 1/73
- £20m settlement ends thalidomide case 7/73
- Free family planning for all on NHS 4/74
- State awards £5m to thalidomide victims 10/74
- Hospital pay rises up to 74 per cent 1/75
- Windscale workers die of leukaemia 1/75
- Overseas doctors in NHS must sit tests 3/75
- Radio-operated bleepers for doctors 4/75
- Half NHS pay beds closed 4/75
- Castle bows to union pressure on pay beds 4/75
- Unrefined fibre diet better for bowels 12/75
- Flour board attacks Burkitt and Trowell 12/75
- Abortion clinics to serve out-patients 1/76
- UK's only major women's hospital is to close 2/76
- World's first test-tube baby, Manchester 7/78
- Strikes - hospitals turn away patients 1/79
- Body scanner exports top £200 million 10/79
- Increase in prescription charges 11/79
- First test-tube twins are born 3/82
- Thatcher says: "NHS is safe with us" 10/82
- First heart and lung transplant 12/83
- Two million have stopped smoking recently 1/84
- Leukaemia threat in Sellafield area 6/84
- 11-day-old girl has heart transplant 7/84
- Baby with transplanted heart dies 8/84
- 22 die in Wakefield poisoning outbreak 9/84
- Two have died from AIDS after transfusions 11/84
- Contraceptive advice to under-16s banned 2/85
- Blood donors to be screened for AIDS 3/85
- Prescription charges raised to £2 3/85
- Youngest liver transplant patient dies 3/85
- 18-month-old boy dies of AIDS 4/85
- Cervical cancer screening programme 4/85
- 31 die in Legionnaire's disease outbreak 5/85
- Heart-graft patient Keith Castle dies 6/85
- Only one in three UK adults now smokes 9/85
- £1m allotted to counter spread of AIDS 9/85
- Government launches anti-AIDS campaign 11/86
- Currie: "Good Christians won't get AIDS" 2/87

- Prescription charges up 20p 3/87
- Law Lords agree to sterilising mental girl 4/87
- New AIDS campaign launched 5/87
- Dr Higgs' Cleveland child sex abuse case 6/87
- MP Stuart Bell accuses Higgs 6/87
- Parents take Higgs to court 6/87
- Six Cleveland children returned 7/87
- One a day dying from AIDS 8/87
- Cleveland child abuse inquiry 8/87
- New explicit anti-AIDS campaign 9/87
- Hole-in-heart baby waits five times for op 11/87
- Free dental and eye checkups scrapped 11/87
- Heart baby David Barber dies 12/87
- Manchester nurses strike over pay cuts 1/88
- Radical review of the NHS announced 1/88
- Nurses march on parliament 2/88
- Nurses offered 15 per cent pay rise 4/88
- Currie resigns after salmonella scare 12/88
- BMA backs campaign to cut working week of junior doctors 1/89
- Family doctors campaign against government NHS reforms 3/89
- 19,000 ambulance staff ban overtime in pay dispute 9/89
- Government to impose new contracts on GPs 10/89
- Police take over in ambulance dispute 10/89
- Ambulancemen begin ban on all but accidents and emergencies 11/89
- Army and RAF take over public ambulance duties in dispute 11/89
- Britain is hit with worst flu epidemic in 14 years 12/89
- Government gives £2.2 million for BSE research 1/90
- 50,000 rally to back ambulance workers 1/90
- Ambulance staff begin all-out strike in Merseyside 2/90
- Six-month ambulance dispute ends 2/90
- Nuclear workers may be advised to not have children 2/90
- More than 3,000 Britons have fully-developed AIDS 3/90
- MPs vote to reduce abortion time limit 4/90
- Ministry of agriculture confirms cat was suffering from BSE 5/90
- Government denies any risk of humans catching BSE 5/90
- BMA opposes proposals for hospitals to become self-governing 6/90
- Hospital waiting lists at their highest for six years 8/90
- Rise in heterosexual AIDS cases is higher than any group 10/90
- £42 million awarded to haemophiliacs contaminated with AIDS 12/90
- Fewer drivers fail Christmas period alcohol tests 1/91
- 10,000 NHS hospital beds prepared for Gulf War casualties 1/91
- Scientists say "mad cow" disease may last to end of decade 3/91
- Hospital "trusts" legislation comes into effect 3/91
- Further 99 hospitals and units to become self-governing 10/91
- Increase of 50 per cent in heterosexual AIDS cases 1/92
- HIV-virus victims contaminated by NH blood to be compensated 2/92
- Ambulance computer system fails, creating chaos 10/92
- Reports suggest video games can cause epileptic fits 1/93
- Waiting list now over a million 8/93

Britain (labour)
- Mining age limit raised 4/00
- Taff Vale dispute 9/01
- Miners' bill defeated 3/02
- Keir Hardie protests at Taff Vale decision 8/02
- "Peaceful picketing" legal 4/04
- TUC calls for eight-hour day 9/05
- Midlands jobless marchers in London 2/06
- Biggest ever TUC conference, Liverpool 9/06
- Labour MPs suggest general strike 10/07
- King announces medal for heroic miners 10/07
- Miners' Federation in Labour Committee 6/08
- End of Lancashire cotton strike 11/08
- Report demands Ministry of Labour 2/09
- Workers better off than Germans or French 3/09
- Government plans unemployment insurance 4/09
- Workers protest at Czar's visit 8/09
- Lords rules union political levy illegal 12/09
- Violent coal strikes over eight-hour day 1/10
- First labour exchanges open 2/10
- Railwaymen strike, Newcastle-on-Tyne 7/10
- 50,000 dockers fired; unions surprised 9/10
- Miners and cotton workers back striking dockers 9/10
- 60-hour week for shopworkers; Shops Bill 3/11
- Dockers want national strike for wages 6/11
- Welsh rail strike is riotous; nine die 7/11
- Shops Act; compulsory holiday 7/11
- Nationwide strikes; riots in North 8/11
- Industrial Council to settle disputes 10/11
- 300,000 cotton workers locked out 12/11
- Coal Miners Bill gives minimum wage 3/12
- Transport unions call for closed shop 5/12
- 10-week dock strike ends 7/12
- Osborne Judgement overturned 8/12
- Four shot as dockers return to work 8/12
- Board of Trade arbitration before strike 7/15
- Welsh miners strike; women want war work 7/15
- Miners' unions vote against conscription 1/16
- Commission for women's equal pay 9/18
- Railway workers get eight-hour day 12/18
- Glasgow strike for demobbed; violence 1/19
- Miners' union wants nationalisation 1/19
- 200,000 strike for shorter week 1/19
- Employer-union committee accepted 2/19
- Miners offered pay rise, coal commission 2/19
- Miners reject government offers 2/19
- Coal commission recommends pay rise 3/19
- Industrial conference "truce" 4/19
- Rejects a police trade union 4/19
- Labour Party for political strikes 6/19
- Police to strike over Police Bill 7/19
- Lloyd George hits rail strike conspiracy 9/19
- Rationing returns to counter rail strike 9/19
- Teachers want more pay; iron strike ends 10/19
- Sex Disqualification Removal Bill passed 12/19
- Sylvia Pankhurst jailed for dock action 10/20
- Emergency Powers Bill to beat strikes 10/20
- Unemployment at 927,000 1/21
- Unemployment tops million; new benefits 2/21
- Coal strike state of emergency 3/21
- Coal workers reject wage cuts 4/21
- Transport and railway unions abandon strike 4/21
- Unemployment reaches 2.2 million 6/21
- Unemployment falls 8/21
- Labour says jobless benefits are too low 10/21
- To spend £50 million on jobless relief 10/23
- National dock strike; TGWU pull out 2/24
- Council payment to dock strikers banned 6/24
- TUC threatens strikes over new war 9/24
- TUC votes against union amalgamation 9/25
- Miners angry at Commission wage cut plan 3/26
- National coal stoppage as subsidy ends 4/26
- Miners reject employers' wage cut offers 4/26
- Women's Guild demonstrates against strikes and lockouts 4/26
- General strike 5/26
- Bill sets longer hours for miners 7/26
- Government imports food; strike goes on 7/26
- Miners reopen talks to end strike 8/26
- TUC conference breaks up over miners 9/26
- 250,000 striking miners return to work 10/26
- 47 hurt in police-strikers clash, Wales 10/26
- Miners' leaders end strike 11/26
- Miners accept eight hours, local agreements 11/26
- 1.4 million jobless; wages depressed 1/27
- Government to cut postal workers' wages 1/27
- Bill to outlaw sympathy strikes 4/27
- Civil servants banned from unions by bill 5/27
- Baldwin snubs 200 jobless Welsh miners 11/27
- Labour needs Liberals to keep power 6/29
- Labour's priority: cutting unemployment 6/29
- Labour Party favours "contracting out" 10/29
- Unemployment tops 1.5 million 3/30
- Unions condemn government on unemployed 3/30
- Bondfield introduces 48-hour week bill 4/30
- Unionists protest at women in industry 6/30
- Government to borrow for unemployed 7/30
- Unemployment breaks two million barrier 8/30
- Commission proposes cut in dole 6/31
- Now 2.66 million unemployed 6/31
- May report calls for salary cuts 7/31
- Unemployment a record 2.71 million 7/31
- Bristol riots against unemployment 2/32
- Jobless means test protesters in clash 10/32
- 15,000 Trafalgar Square rally, 50 hurt 10/32
- Police pay cut by ten per cent in all 10/32
- Police clash with means test marchers 11/32
- Actors' union Equity adopts closed shop 11/32
- Glasgow unrest; jobless fight police 12/32
- 50,000 protest about unemployment, Hyde Park 2/33
- Unemployment falls to 2.44 million 7/33
- Unemployment down to two million 8/35
- Pay rises highest for ten years 1/36
- 68 per cent jobless in Jarrow; petition 10/36
- Jarrow jobless begin march to London 10/36
- Baldwin snubs Jarrow marchers 11/36
- King condemns unemployment, South Wales 11/36
- Committee suggests week's paid holiday 4/38
- All strikes banned 6/40
- British trade unionist Tom Mann dies 3/41
- TUC backs Beveridge Report 12/42
- Trade union leader John Burns dies 1/43
- Equity votes for theatres on Sundays 3/43
- All women must do part-time war work 5/43
- Engineers call for "pay as you earn" tax 6/43
- Troops take over from striking dockers 10/43
- "Bevin Boys" to work down mines 12/43
- Miners strike in South Wales 3/44
- Government and miners make four-year pact 3/44
- Troops unload ships in dock strike 10/45
- Dock strike ends 11/45
- Wages up 80% since 1938 3/46
- 12 cotton mills close from fuel shortage 12/46
- Road haulage workers strike 1/47
- Troops used to move food 1/47
- Coal mines nationalised 1/47
- Steelworks close from coal shortage 1/47
- Hauliers vote to end strike 1/47
- Four million idle from power cuts 2/47
- Welsh miners agree to work on Sundays 2/47
- 800,000 return to work as crisis eases 3/47
- Minister advocates more women in work 6/47
- South Yorkshire miners strike 9/47
- Sheffield steelworks close 9/47
- Order against "spivs and drones" issued 12/47
- Electricity industry nationalised 4/48
- Troops used in dock strike 6/48
- Gas industry nationalised 5/49
- London dock strike 7/49
- TGWU ban on Communists and Fascists 7/49
- Many cinema workers are losing jobs 11/49
- Civil servants' pay frozen 2/50
- Aneurin Bevan is new Minister for Labour 1/51
- Former unionist Bevin dies - profile 4/51
- Petrol tanker drivers strike 10/53
- Two million engineers in pay strike 12/53
- 51,000 port workers' overtime strike 10/54
- Monckton intervenes; dock strike ends 10/54
- Electricians' strike stops newspapers 3/55
- TGWU leader Deakin dies during speech 5/55
- Railwaymen strike over pay differentials 5/55
- Emergency powers to counter dock strike 5/55
- End of rail strike 6/55
- Communist unionists quit over Hungary 11/56
- National bus strike; picket violence 7/57
- Dockers' strike spreads 8/57
- Compulsory arbitration to end 10/58
- 15,000 BMC workers strike 1/59
- Cammell Laird shipyard chalk mark strike 4/59
- Job allocation fight; 2,000 laid off 4/59
- Electrical union ballot ruled invalid 6/61
- TUC expels Electrical Trades Union 9/61
- Industrial action causes power blackouts 1/63
- 4,000 jobless protest outside Parliament 3/63
- Dock strike: state of emergency 5/66
- Dock strike ends 7/66
- BMC lays off 7,000 workers 9/66
- Car strike closes all BMC factories 10/66
- Unemployment reaches 437,229 10/66
- Unofficial BMC stoppage ends 11/66
- NUR begins work to rule 6/68
- Ford women machinists' equal pay strike 6/68
- "In Place of Strife" white paper issued 1/69
- 1,600 Ford women workers win equal pay 2/69
- Pilots' strike grounds BOAC flights 3/69
- Sikh busmen allowed to wear turbans 4/69
- Bill to give women equal pay 2/70
- National docks strike: troops stand by 7/70
- Dockers vote to accept new pay offer 7/70
- Strikes at highest level since 1926 11/70
- Industrial Relations Court to be set up 12/70
- First postmen's strike 1/71
- Industrial Relations Bill - two one-day protests 3/71
- Postal strike ends 3/71
- Upper Clyde shipbuilders liquidated 6/71
- Joe Gormley becomes NUM president 6/71
- MPs approve Industrial Relations Bill 8/71
- Miners' strike begins 1/72
- Unemployment rises above a million 1/72
- Miners' strike causes power cuts 2/72
- £6 pay increase for miners recommended 2/72
- Power cuts end after 20 days 3/72
- TGWU fined under Industrial Relations Act 3/72
- Merseyside dockers to defy court ban 4/72
- TGWU fine quashed by appeal court 6/72
- Four dockers jailed for contempt 7/72
- Nationwide dock strike begins 7/72
- Clydebank shipyard deal faces axe 8/72
- National dock strike called off 8/72
- Heath seeks pegs on prices and incomes 9/72
- Agreement ends Clydebank work-in 10/72
- 90-day freeze on prices and wages 11/72
- Phase II of pay and prices freeze 1/73
- Gas workers begin nationwide strike 2/73
- Rail workers' strike begins 2/73
- Civil servants' strike begins 2/73
- One-day TUC strike against pay restraint 5/73
- TUC expels 20 unions 9/73
- Phase III of pay policy announced 10/73
- Firemen strike in Glasgow 10/73
- Power workers begin industrial action 11/73
- Miners begin industrial action 11/73
- Goes onto a three-day week 12/73
- Train drivers' strike cripples services 1/74
- Miners' strike forces general election 2/74
- 81% of miners vote for national strike 2/74
- Miners' strike ends 3/74
- Return to five-day week 3/74
- TUC and government in "social contract" 6/74
- Trade Union and Industrial Relations Act 7/74
- Nurses get up to 58% pay rises 9/74
- Hospital pay rises up to 74 per cent 1/75
- Miners accept 35 per cent pay rises 2/75
- Troops clear Glasgow refuse after strike 3/75
- Unemployment past the million mark 4/75
- More "hard-core" jobless; Healey warned 4/75
- Rail workers want 30 per cent more pay 4/75
- Unemployment at 1,147,633 7/75
- 1.25 million unemployed 8/75
- TUC votes to accept pay limits 9/75
- State-sponsored maternity pay 10/75
- Equal Pay Act; illegal to pay women less 12/75
- Sex Discrimination Act; curbs on adverts 12/75
- 27 railwaymen sacked over closed shop 4/76
- 1.5 million unemployed 8/76
- 40,000 strike over public sector cuts 11/76
- Report wants worker-directors on boards 1/77
- British Leyland will shut to end strike 2/77
- British Leyland ready to sack toolmakers 3/77
- 17 arrested at Grunwick plant; violence 6/77
- Social contract ends; wage claims rise 7/77
- Miners want £135 a week; Gormley opposes 7/77
- Unburied corpses as undertakers strike 10/77
- Parliament blacked out by strike 11/77
- Unions accept BL "survival plan" 2/78
- Unions reject new pay guidelines 7/78
- Bakers' strike ends after panic buying 11/78
- Industrial dispute stops The Times 11/78
- Lorry drivers' strike: shortages 1/79
- One-day rail strike 1/79
- Voluntary picketing code 1/79
- Public employees' strike hits hospitals 1/79
- Unions cannot control wildcat strikes 1/79
- Grave-diggers call off strike 2/79
- Lorry strike: oil shortage in schools 2/79
- Professor Clegg studies workers' pay 3/79
- Agreement at Times on settlement 10/79
- Miners reject 20 per cent pay rise 11/79
- More British women work than rest of Europe 1/80
- National steel strikes 1/80
- British Steel to axe 11,287 jobs 1/80
- Middle managers blast British Steel boss 2/80
- Steel strike called off 4/80
- Ian MacGregor is chairman of British Steel 5/80
- Tribunal rejects dismissed "Red Robbo" 5/80
- TUC's "Day of Action" 5/80
- BBC musicians strike against cuts 6/80
- British Steel to close Consett 6/80
- Unemployment at 1.6 million 6/80
- Depression: 40,000 redundancies a week 7/80
- BBC musicians end two-month strike 7/80
- Seven enterprise zones in jobless areas 7/80
- Two million unemployed 8/80
- Thatcher's coal promise; strike averted 2/81
- South Wales miners on unofficial strike 2/81
- People's March for Jobs blocked, London 5/81
- "Wrong" to sack non-union railwaymen 8/81
- 58,000 British Leyland workers strike 11/81
- Scargill elected Mines' Union president 12/81
- Unemployment tops three million mark 1/82
- Tebbit blames rise on weather 1/82
- Miners accept Coal Board's pay offer 1/82
- David Young heads Manpower Services Commission 2/82
- Sid Weighell quits as NUR leader 10/82
- Miners reject strike by 6:4 in ballot 11/82
- First national water strike ends 2/83
- Yorks and South Wales miners strike 2/83
- NUM calls national strike ballot 3/83
- Ian MacGregor becomes head of Coal Board 3/83
- Strike ballots to be made compulsory 7/83
- Many at GCHQ give up union rights 2/84
- Nationwide miners' strike begins 3/84
- Dean is first woman to head major union 3/84
- Notts miners to cross picket lines 4/84
- 100 arrested at Nottinghamshire and Derbyshire pits 4/84
- Scargill vetoes miners' national ballot 4/84
- Riot police battle with miners at Orgreave 5/84
- MacGregor-Scargill talks break down 5/84
- Scargill charged with obstruction 5/84
- 120 arrested in miners' protest, London 6/84
- Picketing miner killed by lorry 6/84
- Miners' strike violence at Maltby 9/84
- High Court rules pit strike unlawful 9/84
- High Court fines NUM and Scargill 10/84
- NACODS pit deputies vote to strike 10/84
- NACODS calls off threatened strike 10/84
- Court rules to sequestrate NUM assets 11/84
- North Wales NUM ends its strike 11/84
- Two miners charged with Wilkie murder 11/84
- Scargill fined for obstruction 12/84
- Nine striking miners jailed for arson 1/85
- Only 51% of miners remain on strike 2/85
- Miners end year-long strike 3/85
- Nissan and AUEW agree single-union deal 4/85
- Two miners jailed for David Wilkie murder 5/85
- Journalists strike over "Real Lives" ban 8/85
- Union of Democratic Mineworkers set up 10/85
- Life sentences on two miners commuted 10/85
- Pickets clash with police at Wapping 2/86
- SOGAT calls off Wapping picket 2/87
- Unemployment falls below three million 6/87
- Scargill seeks NUM re-election 11/87
- Ferry ports in chaos as strike continues 2/88
- P& O announce sacking of 2,300 strikers 3/88
- Ford abandons plans for plant in Dundee 3/88
- TUC fails to save Ford plant in Dundee 3/88
- Lorry drivers block P& O berths 5/88
- Postal strike escalates 9/88
- 2,400 jobs lost in Wearside 12/88
- North Sea oilfields closed in gales 12/88
- Wandsworth Prison warders walk out over new shift system 1/89
- BBC unions start campaign of strikes in support of pay claim 5/89
- Second national one-day rail strike 6/89
- Dockers begin strike over abolition scheme 7/89
- Rail workers stage fourth one-day strike 7/89
- Rail workers accept pay offer and call off strike campaign 7/89
- Three-week-old dock strike is called off 8/89
- Thousands go on 15-minute strike in support of ambulancemen 1/90
- NUM sues Arthur Scargill over allegedly missing funds 7/90
- Government forced to back down over pit closures 10/92
- Signalmen strike over pay 6/94

Britain (politics)
- Labour Party created 2/00
- Election called 9/00
- Queen Victoria dies 1/01
- New king opens his first parliament 2/01
- Lloyd George condemns Boer death rate 6/01
- Liberals divided over Boer War 7/01
- Factory Bill defeated 8/01
- Joseph Chamberlain attacks Germans 10/01
- Lord Rosebery splits Liberal Party 2/02
- Rosebery opposes Irish independence 2/02
- Textile workers call for votes for women 2/02
- Balfour becomes Prime Minister 7/02
- Trades Union Congress to back Labour MPs 9/02
- Irish MP explodes at Balfour in Commons 9/02
- Lord Salisbury dies 8/03
- Joseph Chamberlain resigns 9/03
- Cabinet reshuffle 10/03
- War Office to be reformed 11/03
- J. Chamberlain backs Empire trade 12/04
- Women's suffrage bill forced out 5/05
- Lord Rosebery wants Lords' power checked 10/05
- Suffragettes arrested and imprisoned 10/05
- Balfour out; Campbell-Bannerman in 12/05
- Violence stops Lloyd George's speech 1/06
- Balfour loses seat in general election 1/06
- Liberal election landslide on tariff issue 2/06
- Old age pension approved in principle 3/06
- Committee warns against "army of poor" 3/06
- Top suffragettes meet British Premier 6/06
- Premier tells suffragettes to be patient 6/06
- Commons agree on separate Welsh ministry 7/06
- Germany has model army, says Secretary 9/06
- Liberal reverses in council elections 11/06
- Keir Hardie's female emancipation bill 11/06
- Commons protest by suffragettes; arrests 2/07
- Lord Newton wants Lords reformed 5/07

- Pension bill's second reading 5/07
- First totally socialist MP 7/07
- Labour beats Liberals in Jarrow by-election 7/07
- Hardie says Britain runs India like Czar 9/07
- Labour losses in municipal elections 11/07
- Suffragettes drown out Asquith's speech 11/07
- Suffragettes raid six ministers' homes 1/08
- Emmeline Pankhurst tells of prison life 2/08
- Sir Henry Campbell-Bannerman dies 4/08
- Asquith is Premier; Churchill in cabinet 4/08
- New harbour at Dover for defence 10/08
- Asquith's pledge to cut jobless 10/08
- Asquith wants Lords' powers curbed 2/09
- Daylight saving bill debated 3/09
- Budget to boost rearmament 4/09
- Aerial League for British supremacy 4/09
- Radical "People's Budget"; taxes on rich 4/09
- Balfour's budget counter-attack 5/09
- Local Government Board debated; care of children 6/09
- Labour's Henderson takes on Lords 8/09
- Liberals clash with Lords over budget 9/09
- Lloyd George insults Lords 10/09
- Lords rejects budget; forces elections 11/09
- Parliament dissolved; budget is void 12/09
- Tories early lead in elections 1/10
- Liberals hold on, with Labour backing 2/10
- Asquith: if Lords vetoes, no budget 2/10
- Government must borrow due to no budget 3/10
- Bill to abolish Lords introduced 3/10
- Asquith wants new peers to swamp Lords 4/10
- Lloyd George wants women's suffrage 7/10
- Liberals and Tories in another election tie 12/10
- Ramsey MacDonald is new Labour leader 2/11
- Plans to build five more battleships 3/11
- Lords condemns "inadequate defence" 4/11
- Lords bill referendum amendment beaten 4/11
- Insurance Bill for the sick and jobless 5/11
- MPs to get salary, says Budget 5/11
- Pro-Lords Tories furious, suspend House 7/11
- Lords accepts Commons supremacy 8/11
- Churchill is First Sea Lord; new policy 10/11
- Women protest at Manhood Suffrage bill 11/11
- Maids and mistresses protest at Insurance bill 11/11
- Bonar Law new Tory leader 11/11
- Secrets Act rushed through Commons 11/11
- Royal assent and Insurance to Shops Bills 12/11
- Women's Enfranchisement Bill defeated 3/12
- Suffragettes smash London shop windows 3/12
- Wigan riots 4/12
- Seely is new War Minister after Haldane 6/12
- Franchise Bill: vote for all men over 21 6/12
- Franchise Bill is scrapped, too altered 1/13
- Ministers deny share scandal accusations 3/13
- Suffragette meetings banned 4/13
- Mrs Pankhurst found guilty of arson 4/13
- Commons rejects Franchise Bill 5/13
- Suffragette's Derby death unites women 6/13
- Lloyd George wants Lords abolished 7/13
- Churchill may resign over naval finance 1/14
- Joseph Chamberlain to retire 1/14
- Arms buildup "insanity": Lloyd George 1/14
- Asquith rejects compulsory army service 2/14
- Tory wins Bethnal Green by-election 2/14
- Welsh Church and Irish Home Rule Bills 3/14
- Bid to end Civil Service patronage 4/14
- Home Rule, Dogs and Welsh Church Bills read 4/14
- Budget increases supertax 5/14
- Commons rejects Scottish Home Rule 5/14
- Kitchener new Secretary for War; wary 8/14
- London crowds celebrate war declaration 8/14
- Emergency powers; wartime rule by decree 8/14
- Asquith calls for 500,000 volunteers 9/14
- Lloyd George heads munitions production 4/15
- Heavy increases in alcohol duty 4/15
- Asquith leads war coalition government 5/15
- Churchill demoted from Admiralty 5/15
- Protests force end of alcohol duty plan 5/15
- New Ministry of Munitions created 6/15
- National register of all adults to 65 6/15
- Government denies call-up plans 7/15
- Lloyd George appeals for TUC help in war 9/15
- Churchill resigns from government 11/15
- War cabinet debates war manpower shortage 11/15
- Commons votes for conscription 1/16
- Home Secretary resigns over conscription 1/16
- Herbert Samuel is new Home Secretary 1/16
- Not enough volunteers; now conscription 1/16
- Bill giving Parliament extra year passed 1/16
- Ministry of Blockade 2/16
- Restricted travel for aliens 3/16
- Military Service Act in force 3/16
- Rail tax dropped; split over conscripts 4/16
- Plan to conscript married men 5/16
- Lloyd George is War Secretary 7/16
- Asquith resigns; Lloyd George becomes Premier 12/16
- Bonar Law and Lloyd George oust Asquith 12/16
- Lloyd George's stirring war speech 1/17
- Commission blames Kitchener for Gallipoli 3/17
- Anger as U-boat torpedoes hospital ship 3/17
- Churchill returns as head of Air Board 6/17
- Commons votes to give wives over 30 vote 6/17
- Churchill is Minister of Munitions 7/17
- Lloyd George: "peace with German people" 7/17
- Lords debates "sale of peerships" 8/17
- Blocks Peace Conference visitors 8/17
- Rejects Papal peace plan 9/17
- Chequers, Prime Minister's country home 10/17
- Representation of People Act, more have vote 10/17
- Commons anti proportional representation 1/18
- Lord Rothermere heads Air Council 1/18
- Labour wants state ownership 2/18
- Military Services Bill gets Royal Assent 4/18
- Lloyd George beats off Asquith attack 5/18
- John Clines, Labour, new Food Controller 7/18
- Commons votes to allow women MPs 10/18
- Parliament dissolved; election pending 11/18
- Women vote in election for first time 12/18
- "Coupon Election"; Labour anti-Coalition 12/18
- Lloyd George's Coalition wins election 12/18
- Most cabinet posts taken by Tories 1/19
- Churchill is Secretary of State for War 1/19
- Ministries of Health and Transport proposed 2/19
- Welsh call for regional parliament 6/19
- Threats to dismiss striking policemen 7/19
- Lloyd George gets Order of Merit 8/19
- Police uncover Communist plot 8/19
- Lord Curzon is new Foreign Secretary 10/19
- Lloyd George anti mines nationalisation 10/19
- Federal devolution considered 10/19
- Nancy Astor is first woman to sit as MP 11/19
- Churchill plans volunteer army 2/20
- Asquith returned as MP for Paisley 2/20
- Communist Party; third International ties 7/20
- First Communist Party Congress 8/20
- Scotland rejects prohibition; big debate 12/20
- Unemployment Insurance Act amended 2/21
- Bonar Law resigns as Tory leader 3/21
- Austen Chamberlain new Tory leader 3/21
- Call for "Defence Units" to fight strike 4/21
- Islington council blasted for high rates 9/21
- Second woman to win seat, Louth by-election 9/21
- Socialist pioneer Hyndman dies 11/21
- Geddes report urges spending cuts in pay 2/22
- Balfour becomes Earl of Wittinghame 4/22
- Less hardship for divorced women in bill 5/22
- Chamberlain demands Turkish inquiry 5/22
- Coalition ends; Lloyd George ousted 10/22
- Andrew Bonar Law is new Prime Minister 10/22
- Parliament dissolved; election called 10/22
- Tories win overall election victory 11/22
- Labour Party becomes official Opposition 11/22
- Ramsay MacDonald is new Labour leader 11/22
- Labour loses in London borough elections 11/22
- Neville Chamberlain is Health Minister 3/23
- Baldwin's budget: 6d off income tax 4/23
- Bonar Law resigns; Baldwin new Premier 5/23
- Lord Curzon bypassed for Baldwin 5/23
- Oxford and Cambridge Bill: to get money 6/23
- Royal assent for Liquor, Housing and Oxford bills 7/23
- New scheme for unemployment relief 8/23
- Chamberlain is new Chancellor 8/23
- Andrew Bonar Law dies 10/23
- Baldwin calls snap election 11/23
- Baldwin seeks trade protection mandate 11/23
- Tory reverses in stalemate election 12/23
- Churchill loses seat 12/23
- Minority Labour government 1/24
- Churchill warns of Labour extremism 2/24
- Home Secretary Henderson wins seat 2/24
- Bill read on vote for women over 21 2/24
- Mosley applies to join Labour Party 3/24
- Labour's first defeat: Rent Restrictions 4/24
- Budget cuts tea and sugar taxes 4/24
- MacDonald accepts gift of car and shares 9/24
- Labour government falls over Campbell case 10/24
- Editor Campbell charged for strike piece 10/24
- Labour attacked for Soviet loans 10/24
- Tories win poll after Zinoviev Letter 10/24
- Labour rejects link-up with Communists 9/25
- 12 Communists arrested for sedition 10/25
- Communist trials condemned in parliament 12/25
- First widows' pensions paid out 1/26
- Coal Commission wants profit-sharing 3/26
- Coal Commission wants to end subsidy 3/26
- Central Electricity Board Bill 3/26
- General strike 5/26
- Communist papers published 6/26
- MP disrupt Coal Mines Bill in Lords 7/26
- Coal Mines Bill passed: longer hours set 7/26
- Sale of Food Bill follows Council ideas 7/26
- Asquith resigns as Liberal leader 10/26
- Government agrees to coal tribunal 11/26
- General Strike emergency powers ended 12/26
- Oswald Mosley wins Smethwick by-election 12/26
- Military moves in China criticised 1/27
- Compulsory quota of British films 3/27
- Trades Disputes Bill introduced 4/27
- Churchill budget: wine and tobacco taxes rise 4/27
- Labour furious at Trades Disputes Bill 5/27
- Trades Disputes Bill is passed 6/27
- Labour votes to nationalise mines 10/27
- Cook says unemployment is worst problem 11/27
- Commons rejects "popish" prayerbook 12/27
- Three Britons sentenced as Soviet spies 1/28
- Asquith, longest serving Premier, dies 2/28
- Herbert Henry Asquith: profile 2/28
- Mosley will not give up title 9/28
- Council of State acts for ill King 12/28
- First "green belt" is approved in UK 2/29
- Budget: 325-year-old tea duty abolished 4/29
- Ex-Premier Lord Rosebery dies: profile 5/29
- Stalemate election; Labour have most MPs 5/29
- Baldwin back in No 10; needs Liberals 5/29
- 13 women MPs; one is Megan Lloyd George 5/29
- MacDonald forms Labour cabinet 6/29
- Conservatives upset with Liberal tactics 6/29
- First woman minister: Margaret Bondfield 6/29
- Labour's priority: cutting unemployment 6/29
- Baldwin resigns rather than lose vote 6/29
- First King's Speech for Labour government 7/29
- Unemployment benefit to go up 7/29
- Ex-Liberal Attorney-General now Labour 7/29
- Labour dismantles strike bill 10/29
- Labour opts for fiscal orthodoxy 11/29
- J.H. Thomas announces £42 million public works 11/29
- Road Traffic Bill raising speed limit 11/29
- Offences of blasphemy and atheism to be abolished 1/30
- MPs oppose government's Thames bridge 2/30
- Blasphemy bill dropped 2/30
- Balfour dies: profile 3/30
- Poor Law Guardians abolished 4/30
- Budget: 6d on income tax, more surtax 4/30
- Mosley leaves cabinet over unemployment 5/30
- Clement Atlee becomes Employment Minister 5/30
- Liberals want electoral reform 5/30
- Liberal-Labour pact ends over reforms 5/30
- Emmanuel Shinwell is Secretary for Mines 6/30
- Tories want jobless benefit cut 6/30
- MPs vote for Naval Treaty 7/30
- Government pressured to boost economy 8/30
- Lord Birkenhead, Tory statesman, dies 9/30
- Stafford Cripps is Solicitor-General 9/30
- Air minister Thompson dies in R101 crash 10/30
- Mosley gains Labour executive seat 10/30
- MacDonald concedes electoral reform 12/30
- Mosley's public works manifesto 12/30
- Bill to relax picketing curbs 12/30
- Churchill quits cabinet over India 1/31
- Bill to end plural voting 1/31
- Education Bill defeated 1/31
- Reading for Trade Disputes Bill 1/31
- Mosley's New Party: "vitality, action" 2/31
- Government loses vote as Liberals desert 3/31
- Freedom in dress and politics go together 3/31
- Trevelyan resigns as Education Minister 3/31
- Trades Disputes Bill founders 3/31
- London Transport Bill to merge services 3/31
- Tory Duff Cooper wins by-election 3/31
- Sunday movies rumpus comes to parliament 4/31
- Budget: 2d a gallon on petrol 4/31
- Mosley's party splits vote; Tory wins 4/31
- Proposed cut in dole worries Labour MPs 6/31
- No new peers in Birthday Honours List 6/31
- Government will not cut dole after all 6/31
- May report suggests cuts of £96 million 7/31
- Chancellor Snowden seeks opposition help 7/31
- Labour MP McGovern expelled from Commons 7/31
- Coal Bill passed, setting miners' pay 7/31
- Civil service opens to women 7/31
- Labour falls; coalition takes over 8/31
- MPs desert MacDonald in financial crisis 8/31
- Cabinet and TUC oppose MacDonald cuts 8/31
- Samuel Home Secretary; Baldwin Lord President of Council 8/31
- Leaves the gold standard; pound devalued 9/31
- Sailors at Invergordon mutiny over cuts 9/31
- Snowden introduces exchange controls 9/31
- MacDonald gives home issues priority 9/31
- Mosley chased by Scottish socialists 9/31
- National Government beats Labour 10/31
- Biggest election landslide in history 10/31
- Mosley's New Party fails at poll 10/31
- Glasgow anti-emergency riots; 49 arrests 10/31
- New Liberal leader after Lloyd George 11/31
- Baldwin President of Council 11/31
- Neville Chamberlain is Chancellor 11/31
- Abnormal Importations Bill 11/31
- Bill to ban whipping of poor children 2/32
- Import Duties Bill; UK drops free trade 2/32
- Tory MP E. Marjoribanks shoots himself 4/32
- Budget: one new tax, fourpence on tea 4/32
- Four Free Trade ministers resign 9/32
- MacDonald isolated as Liberals quit 9/32
- Simon replaces Samuel in Liberal group 9/32
- Means test protesters clash with police 10/32
- Jobless rioters are funded by Moscow, claim 10/32
- Lansbury elected leader of Labour Party 10/32
- Mackenzie book breaches war "secrecy" 12/32
- Violence as Oxford votes against war 2/33
- Mosley meets Mussolini 4/33
- Fascists and Jews clash in London's West End 5/33
- Referendum planned; only Nazis on ballot 10/33
- Labour surprise win in East Fulham 10/33
- John Wilmot backs disarmament and more jobs 10/33
- Mosley and supporters stoned, Manchester 10/33
- Arms cutting dropped; Air Force boosted 11/33
- Labour makes big local election gains 11/33
- Mosley calls for dictatorship at rally 1/34
- Mosley Fascists adopt Italian black shirt 1/34
- Calls for tougher laws against Mosley 1/34
- MacDonald shuns 500 "hunger marchers" 2/34
- Labour rules London council for first time 3/34
- Budget: 6d off income tax; more benefits 4/34
- Fistfights at Mosley's Olympia rally 6/34
- Sir Kingsley Wood warns on Blackshirts 6/34
- 41 new Air Force squadrons planned 7/34
- Churchill wants stronger defences 11/34
- Churchill defeated on Indian bill 2/35
- Plans to treble size of Royal Air Force 5/35
- MacDonald quits; Baldwin Prime Minister 6/35
- National Government continues 6/35
- Lansbury resigns over war with Italy 10/35
- Ernest Bevin attacks Lansbury on war 10/35
- Labour leader Arthur Henderson dies 10/35
- Baldwin calls November election 10/35
- Tories win election convincingly 11/35
- National Labour wiped out in election 11/35
- Ramsay MacDonald and son lose seats 11/35
- Tories claim defence spending mandate 11/35
- Earl Jellicoe, World War I Admiral, dies 11/35
- Eden attacks unapologetic Hoare on pact 12/35
- Baldwin fires Hoare as Foreign Secretary 12/35
- King George V dies; Edward VIII succeeds 1/36
- Inskip is Defence Co-ordination Minister 3/36
- Budget: 3d in pound on income tax 4/36
- James Thomas resigns over budget leak 5/36
- Thomas found guilty of leak 6/36
- Baldwin adds £750,000 to dole budget 7/36
- Air Ministry plans reserve 8/36
- Jarrow marchers' petition for MPs 10/36
- 100,000 riot against Mosley Fascists 10/36
- Fighting Blackshirts in Cable Street 10/36
- Labour votes to stay neutral on Spain 10/36
- Baldwin snubs Jarrow marchers 11/36
- Marriage Bill widens grounds for divorce 11/36
- Labour loses 81 seats in local elections 11/36
- Public Order Bill published 11/36
- Premier Baldwin for Edward's abdication 12/36
- Edward VIII announces abdication, radio 12/36
- George VI becomes King 12/36
- Public Order Act curbs Mosley's party 1/37
- Air force gets extra pilots and personnel 1/37
- Chamberlain's £1,500 million arms spend 2/37
- Labour doubles London Council majority 3/37
- Minister's Bill to raise Premier's salary 3/37
- Austen Chamberlain dies 3/37
- Budget: 3d on income tax; profits tax 4/37
- King George VI is crowned head of Empire 5/37
- Chamberlain succeeds Baldwin as Premier 5/37
- Baldwin made an Earl 5/37
- Chamberlain stops defence profits tax 6/37
- Defence Contribution Scheme put forward 6/37
- Marriage Bill debate; Lords cut time 7/37
- Marriage Bill passed 7/37
- Ban on East End marches extended 8/37
- TUC votes for rearmament 9/37
- Stone knocks out Mosley, Liverpool rally 10/37
- 111 arrested for blocking Fascist march 10/37
- Government refuses to ban marches 10/37
- George VI opens his first parliament 10/37
- Ramsay MacDonald, ex-Labour leader, dies 11/37
- Ramsay MacDonald: profile 11/37
- Tributes to Ramsay MacDonald 11/37
- Vote for air-raid shelters in towns 11/37
- Plans for evacuation of London in war 11/37
- Coal Commission planned in Coal Bill 11/37
- To spend £106.5 million on defence 3/38
- Unity Mitford wears swastika at rally 4/38
- Budget: income tax raised to 5/6d 4/38
- Enquiry sought into air defences 5/38
- Anglo-Czech Bren gun enters service 6/38
- Pledge to double air defences 6/38
- 1,000 orders for Spitfire fighters 7/38
- MPs condemn Chamberlain Sudeten sellout 9/38
- Oxford by-election: Hogg beats Lindsay 10/38
- Oxford: fierce debate on appeasement 10/38
- Chamberlain defends appeasement in House 10/38
- National Register plans wartime jobs 12/38
- Cripps expelled from Labour Party 1/39
- Lords pass Bastardy Bill 2/39
- Defence spending to grow by £175 million 2/39
- Free air raid shelters for London 2/39
- Civil Defence Bill given second reading 4/39
- Conscription for men of 20 introduced 4/39
- Military Training Bill passed 5/39
- First military conscripts enrolled 6/39
- New defence borrowings of £500 million 7/39
- Free fresh milk for infants 7/39
- Chamberlain granted war powers 8/39
- 1.5 million children to be evacuated 8/39
- War raises income tax to 7/6d in pound 9/39
- First wartime regulations introduced 9/39
- Labour and Liberal parties support war 9/39
- Censorship department set up 10/39
- Prices of Food Bill introduced 10/39
- Unfinished pre-war legislation dropped 10/39
- Bigger family allowances for servicemen 11/39
- Oliver Stanley becomes War Secretary 1/40
- War budget introduces purchase tax 4/40
- H.A.L. Fisher dies 4/40
- Internment for Germans and Austrians 5/40
- Bill imposes death penalty for sabotage 5/40
- Churchill becomes Prime Minister 5/40
- Commons denounces UK bungling in Norway 5/40
- Coalition government formed 5/40
- Mosley and other UK Fascists detained 5/40
- Emergency Powers Act becomes law 5/40
- All strikes banned 6/40
- British Union of Fascists banned 7/40
- Trading in new cars banned 7/40
- 24 per cent tax on luxuries 7/40
- Beaverbrook appointed to war cabinet 8/40
- Chamberlain resigns from government 10/40
- Churchill elected leader of Tory Party 10/40
- Neville Chamberlain dies 11/40
- Eden becomes Foreign Secretary 12/40
- Halifax appointed Ambassador to USA 12/40
- Government closes Communist Daily Worker 1/41
- Sweeping new prices controls announced 1/41
- War budget raises income tax to 50% 4/41
- MPs meet in House of Lords 5/41
- Huge confidence vote for Churchill 1/42

Britain (politics)

- Jowitt heads reconstruction planning 3/42
- Daily Mirror threatened with suppression 3/42
- J.M. Keynes made a peer 6/42
- Churchill defeats Commons censure vote 7/42
- Government lifts ban on Daily Worker 8/42
- Boost promised to house building 11/42
- Morrison replaces Cripps in war cabinet 11/42
- Publication of Beveridge Report 12/42
- Insurance companies attack Beveridge 12/42
- Beveridge Report accepted in principle 2/43
- "National health service" will be set up 4/43
- 100% tax on luxuries 4/43
- Beatrice Webb dies 4/43
- All women must do part-time war work 5/43
- Engineers call for "pay as you earn" tax 6/43
- Women's pay has risen by 80% since 1938 7/43
- Communist organiser jailed for spying 7/43
- Free schooling up to 16 advocated 7/43
- BMA opposes Beveridge plan 8/43
- PAYE to be introduced 9/43
- Kingsley Wood, Chancellor, dies 9/43
- Troops take over from striking dockers 10/43
- Mosley released from jail 11/43
- "Bevin Boys" to work down mines 12/43
- Plans for national health service 2/44
- Radical education reform in new bill 2/44
- Miners strike in South Wales 3/44
- 300,000 houses to be built after the war 3/44
- Ban on marriage of women teachers lifted 3/44
- Government and miners make four-year pact 3/44
- PAYE taxation comes into force 4/44
- All foreign travel banned 4/44
- Plans for over three million homes revealed 7/44
- Jowitt made minister of social insurance 10/44
- Lloyd George retires from Parliament 12/44
- David Lloyd George dies 3/45
- Coalition government resigns 5/45
- Lord Haw Haw to be tried for treason 6/45
- Labour wins landslide in election 7/45
- Attlee becomes Prime Minister 7/45
- Attlee warns of need for austerity 8/45
- One million to be demobbed by 1946 8/45
- Labour MPs sing "The Red Flag" in Commons 8/45
- Press censorship ends 9/45
- Lord Haw Haw goes on trial 9/45
- Troops unload ships in dock strike 10/45
- Income tax cut to 9d in pound 10/45
- Civil aviation to be nationalised 11/45
- Dock strike ends 11/45
- Commons votes to accept massive US loan 12/45
- Commons votes for IMF and World Bank 12/45
- BMA sets up fund to fight NHS 3/46
- Single women may become diplomats 3/46
- Bevan presents NHS proposals to MPs 3/46
- Plans to nationalise iron and steel 4/46
- Plans to double number of scientists 5/46
- Lords debates "tidal wave" of divorce 11/46
- Commons votes to nationalise railways 12/46
- Commons votes to nationalise road haulage 12/46
- Commons vote to nationalise ports 12/46
- Montgomery made a Knight of the Garter 12/46
- Mountbatten made a Knight of the Garter 12/46
- Road haulage workers strike 1/47
- Troops used to move food 1/47
- Coal mines nationalised 1/47
- Electricity Bill published 1/47
- Hauliers vote to end strike 1/47
- Four million idle from power cuts 2/47
- Government acts to stem divorce flood 3/47
- 800,000 return to work as crisis eases 3/47
- Ban on midweek sport announced 3/47
- Use of coal and gas fires banned 4/47
- Gas to be nationalised by end of year 4/47
- Tories issue "industrial charter" 5/47
- Food rations cut as crisis deepens 6/47
- Minister advocates more women in work 6/47
- Crisis austerity plan unveiled 8/47
- Supplies and Services Bill introduced 8/47
- Harold Wilson joins the cabinet 8/47
- South Yorks miners strike 9/47
- Export drive launched 9/47
- Gold reserves used to pay for imports 9/47
- Nationalisation programme suspended 9/47
- Death of Sidney Webb 10/47
- Dalton resigns as Chancellor 11/47
- Plans outlined for rail nationalisation 11/47
- Stanley Baldwin dies 12/47
- Order against "spivs and drones" issued 12/47
- Doctors threaten boycott of new NHS 1/48
- Plural voting outlawed 1/48
- University seats abolished 1/48
- Railways nationalised 1/48
- Women's Service Bill passed 2/48
- Representation of the People Bill passed 2/48
- 86% of doctors vote against joining NHS 2/48
- Ban on radicals in civil service 3/48
- Political marches in London banned 3/48
- Electricity industry nationalised 4/48
- Motorists rationed to 90 miles a month 4/48
- MPs vote to suspend death penalty 4/48
- Doctors offered freedoms under NHS 4/48
- 20 "radical" civil servants suspended 5/48
- Dalton returns to cabinet 5/48
- Lords against death penalty suspension 6/48
- Over 10,000 doctors have joined NHS 6/48
- Dentists told not to join NHS 6/48
- State of emergency to tackle dock strike 6/48
- National Health Service comes into being 7/48
- National Insurance comes into being 7/48
- Lords reject compromise on hanging 7/48
- Duke of Edinburgh takes seat in Lords 7/48
- First State Opening since 1938 10/48
- Iron and Steel Bill published 10/48
- Industrial red tape eased 11/48
- National Service increased to 18 months 12/48
- John Belcher MP resigns in bribery probe 12/48
- Capital punishment commission set up 1/49
- Labour politician J.H. Thomas dies 1/49
- National Parks Bill published 3/49
- London marches banned for three months 3/49
- First national parks to be created 4/49
- Gas industry nationalised 5/49
- TGWU ban on Communists and Fascists 7/49
- Lords to admit peeresses in own right 7/49
- HMS Amethyst commander awarded DSO 8/49
- Pound devalued by 30% 9/49
- Labour soft-pedals on socialism 11/49
- Labour ideological battle rages 11/49
- Parliament Bill becomes law 11/49
- General election called 1/50
- Labour wins election; majority cut 2/50
- Attlee suffers first Commons defeat 3/50
- Arms production to be doubled 8/50
- Gaitskell replaces Cripps as Chancellor 10/50
- Scientist Pontecorvo missing - inquiry 10/50
- Restored House of Commons opens 10/50
- Scots Nats steal Coronation Stone 12/50
- Attlee to spend £4,700 million in three years 1/51
- Government beaten on shortages debate 3/51
- Seven years separation grounds for divorce 3/51
- Government withdraws divorce bill 4/51
- Ernest Bevin, Labour, dies; profile 4/51
- Ministers Bevan, Wilson, resign in anger 4/51
- Labour Left opposes NHS charges, defence 4/51
- Cost of Festival of Britain criticised 5/51
- Tories gain in local elections 5/51
- 75 Welsh protest at War Office's land purchase 8/51
- Attlee calls general election 9/51
- Castle ousts Shinwell on Labour committee 10/51
- General election: Churchill is Premier 10/51
- Narrow Tory win; Liberals just six seats 10/51
- Cabinet with Eden, Butler, Maxwell-Fyfe 10/51
- "Rab" Butler raises bank lending rate 11/51
- King George VI dies in sleep 2/52
- New monarch, Queen Elizabeth II 2/52
- Identity cards abolished 2/52
- Churchill announces British atomic bomb 2/52
- Revealed that Labour developed bomb secretly 2/52
- 57 Bevanites defy Labour on defence vote 3/52
- Budget: raises tax allowances 3/52
- Bank rate up; food subsidies cut 3/52
- Sir Stafford Cripps dies 4/52
- Labour wins 55 majority, London council 4/52
- Commons votes for women's equal pay 5/52
- Labour gains 609 borough seats 5/52
- Eden marries Churchill's niece Clarissa 8/52
- Bevanites oust Dalton and Morrison, on NEC 9/52
- Attlee blasts leftist Labour "wreckers" 10/52
- Morrison elected Labour deputy leader 11/52
- Murder trial: tightening firearms laws 12/52
- Budget: income tax down by sixpence 4/53
- Labour gains in municipal elections 5/53
- Churchill suffers partial stroke 6/53
- Margaret Bondfield, ex-minister, dies 6/53
- Labour MPs question Christie case 7/53
- MPs vote to keep death penalty 7/53
- Lords approve commercial TV channel 11/53
- UK atomic energy corporation planned 11/53
- Bill allows Prince Philip as Regent 11/53
- Tories fulfil housing pledge 12/53
- John Simon, statesman, dies 1/54
- Bill for Atomic Energy Authority 2/54
- Atomic Energy Authority approved 3/54
- Bevan leaves shadow cabinet over defence 4/54
- MPs vote for pay rise 5/54
- Government drops MPs' pay rise bill 6/54
- Rationing ends; books burnt in London 7/54
- Civil defence planned for H-bomb attack 7/54
- Television Bill gets Royal Assent 7/54
- Pensions rise to £2 a week 12/54
- Plane able to carry atomic bombs in RAF 1/55
- Women civil servants to get equal pay 1/55
- MPs vote to keep death penalty 2/55
- White paper confirms UK making H-bombs 2/55
- Lords refuse to allow Benn to renounce title 2/55
- Churchill resigns; Eden new Premier 4/55
- Eden calls election in two weeks 4/55
- Budget: sixpence off income tax 4/55
- Butler made Chancellor; Macmillan made Foreign Secretary 4/55
- Lords reject Benn's wish to lose title 4/55
- Biggest television press conference 5/55
- Eden wins big election mandate 5/55
- Labour right keeps shadow cabinet power 6/55
- Budget: purchase tax up on post and phones 10/55
- Housing subsidies and building cuts announced 10/55
- MP says Philby was a spy; retracts words 11/55
- Second reading of Clean Air Bill 11/55
- Attlee quits as Labour leader; to Lords 12/55
- Hugh Gaitskell is new Labour leader 12/55
- Cardiff becomes capital of Wales 12/55
- New anti-nuclear air raid warning scheme 1/56
- Home Guard unit refuses to disband 1/56
- Import and export of heroin is banned 1/56
- Macmillan's tighter credit squeeze 2/56
- MPs vote to abolish death penalty 2/56
- Gaitskell attacks Makarios deportation 3/56
- Budget: premium bonds with prizes 4/56
- Opposition blasts premium bonds as raffle 4/56
- Budget: tax relief on annuity payments 4/56
- Labour gains in municipal elections 5/56
- Death penalty for murders in prison 6/56
- Macmillan's spending cuts of £76 million 6/56
- Clean Air Bill is passed 7/56
- Lords votes to keep capital punishment 7/56
- Demonstrators call on Eden to resign 11/56
- Eden flies to Jamaica after Suez strain 11/56
- "Rab" Butler made acting Premier 11/56
- Communist Party members quit over Hungary 11/56
- Eden resigns; Harold Macmillan made Premier 1/57
- Labour's Gaitskell calls for election 1/57
- New Chancellor Peter Thorneycroft 1/57
- Eden resigns from parliament 1/57
- Plans to boost output of nuclear weapons 2/57
- US gives UK missiles and control warheads 3/57
- Last national call-up in 1960 4/57
- Diver Crabb found in harbour 6/57
- "Never had it so good" Macmillan speech 7/57
- Wolfenden report for adult homosexuality 9/57
- Paymaster General Maudling joins cabinet 9/57
- Bank rate rises to seven per cent 9/57
- Bevan leads Labour to accept H-bombs 10/57
- Lords reforms: life peers and women 10/57
- Improving Lords' day-to-day working 10/57
- Windscale inquiry talks of bad judgement 11/57
- Church backs Wolfenden homosexual report 11/57
- Government rejects Wolfenden report 12/57
- Windscale accident caused by insufficient staff 12/57
- Treasury trio resigns over spending 1/58
- Second reading of Life Peerages Bill 2/58
- US missiles for East Anglia and Yorkshire 2/58
- TUC calls for end to H-bomb testing 3/58
- First Liberal by-election win for 29 years 3/58
- Sufragette Christabel Pankhurst dies 3/58
- CND anti-bomb march on Aldermaston 4/58
- Budget cuts wine, cinema and purchase taxes 4/58
- Gaitskell and Bevan attack Mid-East policy 7/58
- Fourteen women life peers 7/58
- Donald Soper leads protest, Aldermaston 9/58
- First women peers take their seats 10/58
- Profumo, Amery and Fraser get junior posts 11/58
- George Brown loses shadow cabinet seat 11/58
- Protesters arrested at Swaffham base 12/58
- Profumo joins Foreign Office 1/59
- Budget: lower income and purchase taxes 4/59
- Shadow Chancellor Wilson blasts budget 4/59
- TV man Robin Day is Liberal candidate 4/59
- Churchill to stand for parliament at 85 4/59
- Tories' local election gains 5/59
- Labour's Morrison will retire 6/59
- Macmillan announces general election 9/59
- Summit stance key issue in election 9/59
- Huge Tory majority in election 10/59
- New MPs include Margaret Thatcher and Judith Hart 10/59
- Cabinet includes Heath and Marples 10/59
- Labour wary of nationalisation platform 10/59
- Peace Prize to UK MP Philip Noel-Baker 11/59
- Call for enquiry into police and public 11/59
- Edward Wood, Tory statesman, dies 12/59
- Mosleyites attack anti-apartheid rally 2/60
- Labour loses two by-elections 3/60
- Budget: twopence on cigarettes 4/60
- Government to scrap Blue Streak missiles 4/60
- Bill to curb Teddy Boys unopposed 5/60
- Lords wants Press Council "with teeth" 6/60
- Nye Bevan, Labour hero, dies; profile 7/60
- Home becomes Foreign Secretary with Heath as deputy 7/60
- Labour's Gaitskell loses nuclear vote 10/60
- Commission wants Greater London Council 10/60
- Wilson guns for Labour leader Gaitskell 10/60
- Bertrand Russell resigns as CND leader 10/60
- Benn is new Viscount Stansgate 11/60
- Michael Foot wins Bevan's old seat 11/60
- Benn tries to renounce title 11/60
- Last national service call-ups 12/60
- Labour withdraws whip from Michael Foot 3/61
- Commons disqualifies Viscount Stansgate 3/61
- 31 arrested in anti-nuclear protest 4/61
- Benn banned from Commons 5/61
- Benn wins Bristol by-election 5/61
- Macmillan orders security service review 5/61
- Lax security blamed for Lonsdale spies 6/61
- To ask to join Common Market 7/61
- Benn by-election victory quashed 7/61
- MPs vote in favour of joining EEC 8/61
- 850 arrested in huge CND demo 9/61
- Prominent nuclear protesters jailed 9/61
- Thatcher gets her first government job 10/61
- Immigration curbs tightened 11/61
- Macmillan attacked on Immigration Bill 11/61
- R.H. Tawney, political theorist, dies 1/62
- Six anti-nuclear protesters jailed 2/62
- Russell says atomic tests are "butchery" 2/62
- Bill curbing Commonwealth immigration 2/62
- Sensational Liberal win in by-election 3/62
- Clement Davies dies 3/62
- Budget cuts purchase tax 4/62
- Ban on Communists in Civil Service urged 4/62
- Spy chief Percy Sillitoe dies 4/62
- Tories lose control of 30 councils 5/62
- Macmillan sacks seven cabinet members 7/62
- Commonwealth Immigration Act becomes law 7/62
- Mosleyites march through London again 7/62
- National Incomes Commission announced 7/62
- Fascists in East End street battles 9/62
- Thomas Galbraith resigns from government 11/62
- "That Was the Week ..." causes row 12/62
- Hugh Gaitskell dies 1/63
- Industrial action causes power blackouts 1/63
- Two journalists jailed for contempt 2/63
- Plans to develop new nuclear weapon 2/63
- Profumo denies impropriety with Keeler 3/63
- Evidence grows that Philby was Third Man 3/63
- 4000 jobless protest outside Parliament 3/63
- Ministers cleared by Vassall tribunal 4/63
- 70,000 in Aldermaston nuclear protest 4/63
- 20 CND activists arrested 4/63
- Mandy Rice-Davies arrested 4/63
- Churchill announces his retirement 5/63
- Publication of Peerage Bill 5/63
- Lord Milford is first Communist peer 5/63
- Home Secretary admits to lying 5/63
- Profumo sex scandal; his resignation 6/63
- Revealed that Philby was Third Man 7/63
- 94 arrested in anti-Greek protest 7/63
- Ministry of Defence proposed 7/63
- Viscount Stansgate renounces his title 7/63
- Inquiry into Great Train Robbery ordered 8/63
- Macmillan blamed in Profumo report 9/63
- Macmillan resigns as PM 10/63
- Alec Douglas-Home becomes PM 10/63
- Lord Hailsham renounces his peerage 11/63
- Plans for Polaris fleet announced 2/64
- Admiralty is part of Ministry of Defence 3/64
- Labour wins first GLC elections 4/64
- Death of Nancy Astor MP 5/64
- General election called 9/64
- Labour wins general election 10/64
- Import tax imposed 10/64
- Income tax up by six per cent to pay for pensions 11/64
- MPs vote to abolish death penalty 12/64
- BR chief Beeching sacked 12/64
- Death of Churchill 1/65
- Michael Stewart becomes Foreign Secretary 1/65
- David Steel becomes youngest MP 3/65
- Racial hatred bill 4/65
- Bill to introduce metric system 5/65
- Corporation tax to be introduced 6/65
- Edward Heath becomes Tory leader 7/65
- Lords passes bill to end hanging 7/65
- Heath says he will take UK into EEC 10/65
- Russell protests at UK support for LBJ 10/65
- Sanctions imposed on Rhodesia after UDI 11/65
- Bill abolishing death penalty is law 11/65
- Race Relations Bill becomes law 11/65
- Wilson drops plans to nationalise steel 11/65
- Government reshuffle 12/65
- Breathalyser bill published 1/66
- BBC bans showing of "The War Game" 2/66
- Firms must reveal political donations 2/66
- Navy minister Mayhew resigns in protest 2/66
- General election called 2/66
- National Assistance to be abolished 3/66
- Ministry of Social Security to be set up 3/66
- Labour wins election with clear majority 4/66
- State Opening of Parliament televised 4/66
- Dock strike: state of emergency 5/66
- Inquiry into docks dispute announced 5/66
- Gwynfor Evans is first Welsh Nationalist MP 7/66
- Pay and wages freeze imposed 7/66
- Dock strike ends 7/66
- Cousins resigns as technology minister 7/66
- 31 arrested in anti-Vietnam demo 7/66
- Prices and Incomes Bill published 7/66
- TUC votes to back pay freeze 7/66
- George Brown becomes Foreign Secretary 8/66
- Price and wage freeze invoked 10/66
- Frank Cousins resigns as MP 12/66
- Grimond resigns as Liberal leader 1/67
- Thorpe becomes Liberal leader 1/67
- LSE demonstration against Rhodesian director 1/67
- 100 Labour MPs condemn Vietnam bombing 2/67
- Wilson in Torrey Canyon crisis meeting 3/67
- LSE students call off hunger strike 3/67
- Decimal Currency Bill published 3/67
- LSE students stage all-night sit-in 3/67
- Race Relations Board publishes report 4/67
- Tories win control of GLC 4/67
- Road Safety Bill (breathalyser) is law 5/67
- Powell calls UK the "sick man of Europe" 5/67
- Petition against Abortion Bill 5/67
- Abortion Bill passes all Commons stages 7/67
- Sexual Offences Bill becomes law 7/67
- Coal Board blamed for Aberfan disaster 8/67
- Anthony Barber becomes Tory chairman 9/67
- Clement Attlee dies 10/67
- Pound devalued 14.3 per cent 11/67
- Credit squeeze to be tightened 11/67
- Winifred Ewing elected as Scottish Nationalist MP 11/67
- Roy Jenkins becomes Chancellor 11/67
- James Callaghan becomes Home Secretary 11/67
- Tony O'Connor is first black headmaster 12/67
- Bill to reform divorce laws published 1/68
- Labour MPs rebel against spending cuts 1/68
- 24 rebel Labour MPs suspended 1/68
- Emergency bill to stem Asian immigration 2/68
- Bill to abolish stage censorship passed 2/68
- Violent anti-Vietnam war demonstration in London 3/68
- George Brown quits as Foreign Secretary 3/68
- Michael Stewart becomes Foreign Secretary 3/68
- Commonwealth Immigrants Bill becomes law 3/68
- Tories take three seats from Labour 3/68
- Enoch Powell foresees "river of blood" 4/68
- Powell sacked from shadow cabinet 4/68
- Rudi Dutschke shooting sparks unrest 4/68
- Employment and Productivity Dept formed 4/68
- Race Relations Bill published 4/68
- Students "sit in" at Hornsey college 5/68
- French student leader Cohn-Bendit visits 6/68
- Wilson announces plan to reform Lords 6/68
- David Owen is youngest government member 7/68

- Foreign and Commonwealth offices merge 10/68
- 250,000 in anti-Vietnam War demonstration, London 10/68
- Wilson reports on abortive Smith talks 10/68
- Another Powell warning on immigrants 10/68
- Judith Hart joins the government 10/68
- Race Relations Bill gets Royal Assent 10/68
- Bill to lower adulthood to 18 published 11/68
- Thatcher appointed to shadow transport 11/68
- Race Relations Act comes into force 11/68
- Trade Descriptions Act in force 11/68
- Powell forbidden to make Rhodesia speech 12/68
- Eleven-day sit-in at Bristol University 12/68
- Constantine is first black life peer 1/69
- Police and LSE students clash 1/69
- Student ringleaders banned from LSE 1/69
- Police battle with anti-apartheid marchers 1/69
- "In Place of Strife" white paper issued 1/69
- MPs condemn Wootton proposals on "pot" 1/69
- LSE closed "for immediate future" 2/69
- 1600 Ford women workers win equal pay 2/69
- Bernadette Devlin elected Mid-Ulster MP 4/69
- Callaghan ousted from inner cabinet 5/69
- "In Place of Strife" rebellion 5/69
- NHS charges to rise 5/69
- Sweeping Tory gains in borough elections 5/69
- Commons pass Divorce Reform Bill 6/69
- Powell promises immigrants' repatriation 6/69
- Industrial Relations Bill: penalties out 6/69
- Troops sent into Northern Ireland 8/69
- Prentice resigns as technology minister 10/69
- Divorce Reform Bill is passed 10/69
- Callaghan returns to inner cabinet 10/69
- Thatcher is shadow education spokesman 10/69
- Springboks' UK tour: apartheid protests 11/69
- Bernadette Devlin MP jailed for six months 12/69
- Lords consign death penalty to history 12/69
- 98 arrested at Springbok match, UK 12/69
- Bill to create earnings-based pensions 12/69
- Wolverhampton Council guilty of racism 12/69
- Anti-war protesters clash with police 1/70
- Age of majority reduced from 21 to 18 1/70
- Will Owen MP held for passing secrets 1/70
- Bill to give women equal pay 2/70
- 18-year-olds vote for first time 3/70
- Paisley wins Bannside by-election 4/70
- General election called 5/70
- Tories win surprise election victory 6/70
- Shinwell, 85, becomes life peer 6/70
- Alec Douglas-Home is Foreign Secretary 6/70
- Reginald Maudling is Home Secretary 6/70
- Iain Macleod is Chancellor 6/70
- Edward Heath becomes PM 6/70
- Chancellor Iain Macleod dies suddenly 7/70
- State of emergency - dock strike 7/70
- Social and Democratic Labour Party formed 8/70
- Gerry Fitt to lead SDLP 8/70
- George Brown awarded a peerage 8/70
- Department of Trade and Industry created 10/70
- Department of the Environment created 10/70
- Strikes at highest level since 1926 11/70
- Industrial Relations Court to be set up 12/70
- Angry Brigade bombs minister's house 1/71
- New divorce law comes into force 1/71
- Decimal currency introduced 2/71
- Rolls-Royce's aero activities nationalised 2/71
- Powell warns again of immigration perils 2/71
- Local government reorganisation plans 2/71
- Immigration Bill published 2/71
- VAT to be introduced 3/71
- Industrial Relations Bill: two one-day protests 3/71
- Angry Brigade sends letterbomb to Times 4/71
- Hundred Labour MPs declare EEC entry support 5/71
- Labour takes control of GLC 5/71
- Crossman blasts Queen's pay rise request 5/71
- Upper Clyde Shipbuilders liquidated 6/71
- Thatcher plans to ban free school milk 6/71
- Worst crisis in Northern Ireland since 1921 8/71
- IRA threaten to bomb mainland 8/71
- MPs approve Industrial Relations Bill 8/71
- Commons votes in favour of EEC entry 10/71
- Labour conference votes against EEC entry 10/71
- MPs approve Rhodesian settlement 12/71
- "Bloody Sunday" in Derry - 13 killed 1/72
- Signs treaty of entry to EEC 1/72
- Miners' strike begins 1/72
- Unemployment rises above a million 1/72
- Miners' strike causes power cuts 2/72
- Seven die when IRA bombs Para HQ, Aldershot 2/72
- State of emergency declared 2/72
- MPs pass bill to take UK into EEC 2/72
- £6 pay increase for miners recommended 2/72
- Inquiry into "Bloody Sunday" in Ulster 2/72
- Direct rule of Northern Ireland imposed 3/72
- Ulster Unionists condemn direct rule 3/72
- Jenkins resigns as Labour deputy leader 4/72
- Wilson supports call for EEC referendum 4/72
- Four Labour front-benchers resign over EEC 4/72
- Bloody Sunday report issued 4/72
- The pound is floated 6/72
- Maudling resigns as Home Secretary (Poulson) 7/72
- Poulson corruption inquiry set up 7/72
- Whitelaw admits he met IRA leaders 7/72
- Nationwide dock strike begins 7/72
- Dock strike called off 8/72
- Heath seeks pegs on prices and incomes 9/72
- End urged to Official Secrets Section II 9/72
- 90-day freeze on prices and wages 11/72
- Race Relations Act comes into force 11/72
- Joins EEC 1/73
- Phase II of pay and prices freeze 1/73
- 11 Clay Cross councillors surcharged 1/73
- Civil servants' strike begins 2/73
- New IRA bombing campaign hits London 3/73
- Counter-inflation bill becomes law 3/73
- Trials without jury proposed for Ulster 3/73
- Labour makes big local election gains 4/73
- Two ministers resign in sex scandal 5/73
- Liberals win Liverpool council control 5/73
- Heath condemns Lonrho's practices 5/73
- One-day TUC strike against pay restraint 5/73
- Inquiry into Lonrho announced 5/73
- Powell urges opposition to EEC 6/73
- Two carrier-bag bombs explode in Solihull 8/73
- Fire bombs at two West End stores 8/73
- Bomb blasts at two London stations 9/73
- Bomb kills disposal expert, Birmingham 9/73
- Phase III of pay policy announced 10/73
- Death of ex-MI5 chief Roger Hollis 10/73
- Power sharing deal agreed in Ulster 11/73
- Power workers begin industrial action 11/73
- Miners begin industrial action 11/73
- State of emergency declared 11/73
- Goes onto a three-day week 12/73
- Crisis budget introduced 12/73
- Sunningdale deal on a Council of Ireland 12/73
- "Who runs Britain?" election called 2/74
- Bomb rips apart troop bus on M62; 11 die 2/74
- IRA bomb injures ten in Buckinghamshire 2/74
- 81 per cent of miners vote for national strike 2/74
- Election results in no overall majority 3/74
- Liberals reject Heath's coalition offer 3/74
- Heath resigns 3/74
- Harold Wilson begins third term as PM 3/74
- Most of miners' demands granted 3/74
- Miners' strike ends 3/74
- Callaghan becomes Foreign Secretary 3/74
- Healey becomes Chancellor 3/74
- Return to five-day week 3/74
- Huge reorganisation of local government 4/74
- Wilson aides implicated in land deals 4/74
- Richard Crossman dies 4/74
- Unionist general strike paralyses Ulster 5/74
- Ulster power-sharing toppled by strike 5/74
- IRA bomb damages Westminster Hall 6/74
- Price sisters end six-month hunger strike 6/74
- Student dies in Red Lion Square disturbance 6/74
- TUC and government in "social contract" 6/74
- Bombs in Manchester and Birmingham 7/74
- Bomb explodes in Tower of London; one dies 7/74
- Trade Union and Industrial Relations Act 7/74
- Stirling launches anti-strike militia 8/74
- Keith Joseph backs monetarism 9/74
- Labour wins election with majority of three 10/74
- Documents stolen from Wilson's home 10/74
- Guildford pub bombs kill five; 65 injured 10/74
- Joseph: better birth control for poor 10/74
- Several IRA bomb blasts, central London 10/74
- State awards £5m to thalidomide victims 10/74
- 17 killed by IRA Birmingham pub bombs 11/74
- Judith Ward jailed for M62 bombing 11/74
- Rebel Clay Cross councillors reprieved 11/74
- IRA terrorist McDade killed by own bomb 11/74
- Five arrested for Birmingham pub bombings 11/74
- Prevention of Terrorism Act becomes law 11/74
- John Stonehouse MP turns up in Australia 12/74
- Inflation soars to 26 per cent 12/74
- Defence spending to be cut by £4700 million 12/74
- More IRA bombs in London 12/74
- "Bloody Sunday" victims to be compensated 12/74
- IRA bombers attack Heath's house 12/74
- Ulster Secretary Rees defies IRA bombing 1/75
- Referendum on EEC pending 1/75
- Industry Bill sets up National Enterprise Board 1/75
- Margaret Thatcher elected Tory leader 2/75
- Heath resigns after first ballot loss 2/75
- Plans nuclear power stations for Sizewell and Torness Point 2/75
- MPs approve £420,000 rise in Civil List 2/75
- Cabinet divided over EEC; majority for 3/75
- 105 South Vietnamese orphans arrive 4/75
- Wilson sacks Heffer over EEC 4/75
- Labour votes to leave EEC 4/75
- Fears of economy running out of control 5/75
- Bill to nationalise shipbuilding and aircraft industries 5/75
- Two thirds of UK vote to stay in EEC 6/75
- Referendum win for Tories 6/75
- First live broadcast of Commons 6/75
- Benn and Varley swap cabinet places 6/75
- Profumo made a CBE 6/75
- Peter Bottomley, Tory, wins by-election 6/75
- Wilson sets wage freeze and price controls 7/75
- Trade unions resent new law 7/75
- State takes over ailing British Leyland 8/75
- £1,400 million to rescue car industry 8/75
- Bombing attempt on Hugh Fraser, Tory MP 10/75
- Reappeared Stonehouse addresses Commons 10/75
- Campaigner Ross McWhirter shot by Irish 11/75
- Equal Pay Act; illegal to pay women less 12/75
- Sex Discrimination Act; curbs on adverts 12/75
- Labour's George Thomas is new Speaker 2/76
- Brown quits Labour over closed shop 3/76
- Harold Wilson resigns as Prime Minister 3/76
- Confusion over surprise resignation 3/76
- Foot beats Callaghan in first Labour ballot 3/76
- Callaghan is new Prime Minister 4/76
- Healey vows to halt inflation 4/76
- New Foreign Secretary Anthony Crosland 4/76
- Stonehouse quits Labour; majority of one 4/76
- Stonehouse joins English National Party 4/76
- Thorpe resigns as Liberal leader 5/76
- Wilson's Honours List outcry 5/76
- Honours for Goldsmith and Kagan 5/76
- Tory gains in local elections 5/76
- Commons suspended in disorder 5/76
- Steel chosen Liberal leader by members 7/76
- Special Drought Bill published 7/76
- Jailed Stonehouse resigns as MP 8/76
- "Save water" call to beat drought 8/76
- Howell is Minister of Drought 8/76
- Callaghan rules out tax cuts option 9/76
- Tories win Workington and Walsall elections 11/76
- Bill for Scottish and Welsh assemblies 11/76
- Fears over devolution emerge 12/76
- Labour power depends on devolutionists 12/76
- Nationalising aircraft and shipbuilding industries 12/76
- Anthony Eden, ex-Premier, dies: profile 1/77
- Jenkins leaves cabinet to head EEC 1/77
- Foreign Minister Crosland dies: profile 2/77
- David Owen is new Foreign Secretary 2/77
- Referenda planned on devolution 2/77
- Falkender admits making Honours List 2/77
- Tories win Westminster by-election 2/77
- Lib-Lab pact to save government 3/77
- Callaghan warns car-workers on dispute 3/77
- Budget: tax down 2p if union restraint 3/77
- Tories win by-election in Jenkins' seat 3/77
- Prices Commission to freeze prices 4/77
- Scandal of "nepotism" regarding Jay 5/77
- Queen indirectly criticises devolution 5/77
- Government ends social contract 7/77
- Healey prepares mini-budget with tax cut 7/77
- Liberals back pact with Labour 9/77
- Labour's Prentice seeks to join Tories 10/77
- Parliament blacked out by strike 11/77
- Clementine Churchill dies 12/77
- Thatcher speaks of "cultural swamping" 1/78
- Heath slams Thatcher's immigration talk 2/78
- Tories hire Saatchis' advertising agency 3/78
- Permanent BBC broadcasting of Commons 4/78
- Steel predicts end of Lib-Lab Pact 4/78
- Labour holds on in local elections 5/78
- Tories gain in London elections 5/78
- No compulsory metrication 5/78
- Labour beats Nationalists in Scottish seat 5/78
- Radio listeners shocked at parliament 6/78
- Freddie Laker is knighted 6/78
- TUC rejects Callaghan warning on policy 10/78
- Callaghan says it's "make or break" 11/78
- St John Stevas and Biffen in shadow cabinet 11/78
- Callaghan back from summit; denies chaos 1/79
- Pay deal ruined; opposition attacks 1/79
- Tories lead Labour by 20 per cent 2/79
- Shock at Commons carpark bomb; Neave killed 3/79
- Wales rejects mini-parliament 3/79
- Scotland narrowly for mini-parliament 3/79
- Devolution dies; blow to Callaghan 3/79
- Labour government falls on Commons vote 3/79
- Callaghan calls May election 3/79
- Liberals' by-election win; Labour crumble 3/79
- Tories win election with majority of 43 5/79
- Mrs Thatcher, first woman Prime Minister 5/79
- Thatcher promises economic changes 5/79
- Ex-premier Heath refuses ambassadorship 5/79
- Thorpe loses seat in election 5/79
- Howe, Chancellor; Carrington, Foreign 5/79
- William Whitelaw is Home Secretary 5/79
- MPs vote to sell nationalised industries 5/79
- Tory landslide in European elections 6/79
- Budget: tax cut by 3p, lower top rate 6/79
- Kinnock is shadow education spokesman 6/79
- Thatcher attacks BBC on terrorism 7/79
- Public cuts of £4,000 million planned 7/79
- Isle of Man: 1,000 years of parliament 7/79
- Labour chooses mandatory re-selection 10/79
- £3,500 million spending cuts planned 11/79
- Strikers' state benefits halved 2/80
- Underhill shows Militant plot in Labour 3/80
- Budget: tax allowances raised 3/80
- Budget: rises in petrol, drink, tobacco 3/80
- 400 march on Cruise site, East Anglia 4/80
- Cruise missiles based at Greenham 6/80
- Roy Jenkins hints at new centre party 6/80
- Fowler to sell off Sealink and BR hotels 7/80
- Seven enterprise zones in jobless areas 7/80
- Williams, Owen and Rodgers fight far left 7/80
- Thatcher: wage rises cause unemployment 8/80
- Callaghan resigns as Labour leader 10/80
- Labour extends leadership poll franchise 10/80
- Thatcher tells Party: "not for turning" 10/80
- Biggest nuclear protest in 20 years 10/80
- Michael Foot is new Labour leader 11/80
- Healey is deputy Labour leader 11/80
- Howe cuts lending rate to 14 per cent 11/80
- Oswald Mosley dies: profile 12/80
- 192 "quangos" axed by Thatcher 12/80
- Loyalists shoot at ex-Ulster MP Devlin 1/81
- "Gang of Four" breaks with Labour 1/81
- Social Democrats' Limehouse Declaration 1/81
- Biffen waives monopoly rule for Murdoch 1/81
- Thatcher sacks St John Stevas as Leader of House 1/81
- Francis Pym is new Leader of House 1/81
- Nationality Bill: three new categories 1/81
- Extra £900 million for British Leyland 1/81
- Coal Board plans to close 50 pits 2/81
- Thatcher's coal promise; strike averted 2/81
- Selling half of British Aerospace shares 2/81
- Thatcher outlines privatisation policy 2/81
- Williams resigns from Labour executive 2/81
- Gang of Four claim 100 sympathetic MPs 2/81
- Diplomat Hayman in paedophile trial 3/81
- Launch of Social Democratic Party (SDP) 3/81
- Hunger-striker Bobby Sands wins election 4/81
- Thatcher condemns Brixton violence 4/81
- Lord Scarman to lead Brixton inquiry 4/81
- Liberals and SDP plan electoral alliance 6/81
- Heseltine fact-finding on Merseyside 7/81
- Heseltine's plan to help Merseyside 8/81
- Healey beats Benn, deputy Labour leader 9/81
- Labour loses 16 councillors and MP to SDP 9/81
- Thatcher sacks three "wets" 9/81
- Cecil Parkinson is Tory chairman 9/81
- Liberals told: "Prepare for government" 9/81
- 150,000 protest about Cruise missiles, London 10/81
- Tebbit jobs policy: "On your bike" 10/81
- Liberal Pitt captures Croydon 10/81
- Scarman: race and police caused riots 11/81
- Bomb blast at Attorney General's home 11/81
- SDP's Williams wins Crosby from Tories 11/81
- Heseltine's £95 million for inner cities 12/81
- Unemployment tops three million mark 1/82
- Tory "wets" upset at unemployment total 1/82
- Scottish Solicitor-General Fairbairn quits 1/82
- David Young heads Manpower Services Commission 2/82
- Animal Liberation Front raids labs 2/82
- "Rab" Butler, statesman, dies 3/82
- SDP's Jenkins wins Hillhead by-election 3/82
- Argentina invades Falklands: UK at war 4/82
- Thatcher's "Rejoice!" speech, S. Georgia 4/82
- Ex-Labour SDP MP Mann loses seat 6/82
- Franks inquiry into Falklands War 7/82
- Britoil takes over from BNOC 8/82
- No government help for sliding pound 11/82
- Sinn Fein scandal puts GLC in jeopardy 12/82
- 20,000 women encircle Greenham Common 12/82
- Franks report on Falklands War issued 1/83
- Heseltine appointed Defence Secretary 1/83
- Thatcher visits the Falklands 1/83
- 2 letterbombs defused at 10 Downing St 3/83
- Ex-spy Anthony Blunt dies 3/83
- Ian MacGregor to be head of Coal Board 3/83
- 14-mile anti-nuclear human chain 4/83
- Heseltine condemns anti-nuclear protesters 4/83
- Labour backs unilateral disarmament 5/83
- Labour backs EEC withdrawal 5/83
- Callaghan attacks Labour defence plans 5/83
- Tories win general election 6/83
- 752 arrested at Upper Heyford protests 6/83
- Geoffrey Howe is Foreign Secretary 6/83
- Nigel Lawson becomes Chancellor 6/83
- Central Policy Review Staff scrapped 6/83
- Strike ballots to be made compulsory 7/83
- MacGregor becomes Coal Board chairman 9/83
- Arthur Scargill attacks Solidarity 9/83
- SDP votes against merger with Liberals 9/83
- Parkinson resigns over Keays affair 10/83
- Neil Kinnock becomes Labour Party leader 10/83
- Roy Hattersley is deputy Labour leader 10/83
- Over 250,000 march in CND rally 10/83
- Tories to abolish GLC and metropolitan counties 10/83
- First cruise missiles arrive at Greenham 11/83
- Greenham protest at Commons 11/83
- Women break into Greenham Common base 12/83
- Lords votes for experimental televising 12/83
- IRA bomb explodes outside Harrods 12/83
- Sarah Tisdall charged under Official Secrets Act 1/84
- Macmillan accepts a peerage 2/84
- Many at GCHQ give up union rights 2/84
- Sarah Tisdall jailed under Official Secrets Act 3/84
- Nationwide miners' strike begins 3/84
- Bailiffs clear main Greenham peace camp 4/84
- 100 arrested at Nottinghamshire and Derbyshire pits 4/84
- Scargill vetoes miners' national ballot 4/84
- Traitor Michael Bettaney jailed 4/84
- Riot police battle with miners at Orgreave 5/84
- Scargill charged with obstruction 5/84
- New law enables quicker divorces 6/84
- 120 arrested in miners' protest, London 6/84
- Ponting charged after Belgrano leak 8/84
- European Court condemns phone-tapping 8/84
- High Court grants Greenham eviction 9/84
- Miners' strike violence at Maltby 9/84
- High Court rules pit strike unlawful 9/84
- IRA bomb kills 4 at Tory conference, Brighton 10/84
- High Court fines NUM and Scargill 10/84
- Emmanuel Shinwell reaches 100th birthday 10/84
- Court rules to sequestrate NUM assets 11/84
- Macmillan makes maiden speech in Lords 11/84
- North Wales NUM ends its strike 11/84
- Jury acquits civil servant Clive Ponting 2/85
- 200 evicted from Molesworth Cruise base 2/85
- Miners end year-long strike 3/85
- Prescription charges raised to £2 3/85
- Bill to end GLC and metropolitan counties passed 3/85
- Bernie Grant is first black council head 4/85
- Alliance makes big gains in local polls 5/85
- New powers to combat mob violence 5/85
- IRA seaside bombing campaign foiled 6/85
- Lord George-Brown dies 6/85
- Local Government Bill becomes law 7/85
- Douglas Hurd becomes Home Secretary 9/85

- Labour councillors surcharged over rates 9/85
- Ian Gow resigns over Anglo-Irish pact 11/85
- MPs approve Anglo-Irish agreement 11/85
- Anglo-Irish pact: Unionist MPs resign 11/85
- Heseltine resigns over Westland affair 1/86
- Brittan resigns over Westland affair 1/86
- 14 Unionists re-elected in by-elections 1/86
- GLC and metropolitan counties abolished 3/86
- 81 councillors disqualified over rates 3/86
- Large local election gains for Labour 5/86
- Derek Hatton expelled from Labour Party 6/86
- Ulster Assembly dissolved 6/86
- Publication of Wright memoirs banned 7/86
- Archer resigns as Tory deputy chairman 10/86
- Archer denies sex allegations 10/86
- Cabinet secretary in Wright case, Australia 11/86
- Death of Harold Macmillan 12/86
- David Penhaligon MP killed in car crash 12/86
- Ulster MP Robinson fined for "invasion" 1/87
- Government clampdown on Zircon programme 2/87
- Anger at "police state" raid of BBC 2/87
- SDP Rosie Barnes wins Greenwich seat 2/87
- 47 Liverpool councillors sacked over rates 3/87
- Liberals control Liverpool; Hatton vow 3/87
- Taylor holds Truro for Liberals 3/87
- MPs vote against hanging 4/87
- Tory MP Best confesses BT share swindle 4/87
- Proctor MP charged with gross indecency 4/87
- Callaghan gets Order of the Garter 4/87
- Ex-MI5 boss Oldfield was homosexual 4/87
- Thatcher calls June 11 election 5/87
- Best arrested over Telecom shares 5/87
- Proctor admits sex with young men 5/87
- Thatcher wins historic third election 6/87
- Alliance disappointed with 24 seats 6/87
- Healey resigns from Labour front bench 6/87
- Enoch Powell loses seat 6/87
- Oxford refuses Thatcher honorary degree 7/87
- Callaghan and Jenkins get life peerages 7/87
- SDP votes to merge with Liberals 8/87
- Owen resigns as SDP leader 8/87
- Firearms law reform after Hungerford 8/87
- Maclennan new SDP leader; Owen breakaway 8/87
- Search for GCHQ mole after leaks 9/87
- Labour conference backs policy rethink 9/87
- MP Best jailed for share-cheating 9/87
- Lord Soames dies 9/87
- Meteorological Office blasted for poor forecast 10/87
- City asks Whitehall to stop BP flotation 10/87
- Court quashes Best's sentence 10/87
- Thatcher wants seven more years 10/87
- Opposition hits NHS over heart baby 11/87
- Agency calls yuppies Thatcher's children 11/87
- Brooke succeeds Tebbit as Tory chairman 11/87
- Planned reform of Official Secrets Act 11/87
- "Poll tax" planned for April 1990 11/87
- David Steel quits as Liberal leader 1/88
- Suppression of Windscale fire report 1/88
- Second reading of Alton's abortion bill 1/88
- Scargill re-elected as President of NUM 1/88
- Experimental televising of Commons 2/88
- Cooperation with Irish on terrorism 3/88
- Pubs to stay open all day 5/88
- Alton's abortion bill talked out 5/88
- Government fails to ban "Spycatcher" 6/88
- Tories keep Kensington in by-election 7/88
- Paddy Ashdown becomes leader of SLD 7/88
- Cuban ambassador and envoy expelled 9/88
- Lords reject "Spycatcher" ban 10/88
- Labour defy Kinnock at conference 10/88
- Right to remain silent to be abolished 10/88
- Shake-up of legal profession to go ahead 10/88
- Scottish nationalists win Govan 11/88
- Students demonstrate against loans 11/88
- Kinnock confirms Labour plan to drop nuclear disarmament 2/89
- Relatives of Lockerbie victims demand Channon's resignation 2/89
- Britain declared in breach of EC laws on drinking water 4/89
- Ulster Loyalists held for defence secrets-for-arms trading 4/89
- Prisoners end their three-day rooftop protest at Risley 5/89
- Three South African diplomats expelled from UK 5/89
- Margaret Thatcher celebrates ten years as Prime Minister 5/89
- Government refuses demand for haven for Hong Kong citizens 6/89
- Labour and Green Party share European election win 6/89
- Bill passed privatising water industry 7/89
- Thatcher faces row over cabinet reshuffle 7/89
- Report on Hillsborough disaster blames police action 8/89
- British ports ban import of toxic PCBs 8/89
- 300,000 people in Strathclyde have defaulted on poll tax 9/89
- Social Democrat Party is no longer national force 9/89
- Thatcher is alone in opposing sanctions against South Africa 10/89
- Nigel Lawson resigns as Chancellor of the Exchequer 10/89
- House of Commons proceedings televised for first time 11/89
- Government scraps plans for nuclear power plant sales 11/89
- Thatcher faces first leadership challenge within Tory Party 11/89
- Thatcher beats Meyer in Tory leadership poll 12/89
- Tory MPs split over Hong Kong policy 12/89
- Norman Fowler resigns 1/90
- House of Lords votes on human embryo experiments 2/90
- Labour backs income-related property tax to replace poll tax 2/90
- Poll shows 73 per cent of voters against poll tax 2/90
- Environmentalists attack government's new road proposal 2/90
- 18 Tory councillors resign over new poll tax rules 2/90
- Tory MP John Browne is suspended 2/90
- Tory-controlled Wandsworth has lowest poll tax 3/90
- Arthur Scargill accused of using NUM funds for personal use 3/90
- Police clash with rioters in Hackney during poll tax protest 3/90
- John Major delivers his first budget 3/90
- Labour wins Mid-Staffordshire by-elections 3/90
- Poll tax demonstration in London turns into riot 3/90
- Hong Kong Nationality Bill introduced 4/90
- Customs officers seize "supergun" bound for Iraq 4/90
- Makers of alleged supergun say 44 tubes are already in Iraq 4/90
- Tories suffer battering in local elections 5/90
- Animal rights activists confirm attack on vet with car bomb 6/90
- Baby injured in car bomb attack on animal researcher 6/90
- Government launches initiative to stop homelessness 6/90
- SDP no longer exists 6/90
- Nicholas Ridley resigns 7/90
- Tory MP, Ian Gow, is killed by IRA car bomb 7/90
- Figures show one Briton in five evading poll tax payment 8/90
- Academic blames Government cuts for bad education standards 8/90
- Liberal Democrats unveil new logo 9/90
- Edward Heath to go to Iraq in bid to free British hostages 10/90
- Liberal Democrats win former Tory seat in Eastbourne 10/90
- Government announces extra £1 a week child benefit 10/90
- Sir Geoffrey Howe resigns 11/90
- Polls show Tories would win more votes if led by Heseltine 11/90
- Major and Hurd announce candidature for Tory leadership 11/90
- Sir Geoffrey Howe delivers vehement resignation speech 11/90
- Michael Heseltine confirms candidacy for Tory leadership 11/90
- Margaret Thatcher decides to resign 11/90
- Norman Lamont warns Gulf War could cause increase in taxes 1/91
- John Major says poll tax will not be abolished 1/91
- Britain appeals to Allies for financial help for war 1/91
- Opinion polls put John Major as most popular premier 2/91
- Charter plans protecting citizens against corporate abuse 3/91
- Poll tax is ended 3/91
- British Army to lose quarter of manpower in government cuts 6/91
- House of Commons approves fighting dog bill 6/91
- Kinnock plans purge of Militants after by-election defeat 7/91
- Labour MP Terry Fields jailed for not paying his poll tax 7/91
- Police Federation calls for return of Riot Act 9/91
- Archbishop of Canterbury blames deprivation for riots 9/91
- Sir Allan Green resigns after incident in red light area 10/91
- Nicholas Ridley encourages people to vote anti-Europe 11/91
- Thatcher attacks Government over referendum refusal 11/91
- Shops open on Sudays to defy Sunday trading laws 12/91
- John Major hails victory at Maastricht summit 12/91
- First "Moslem parliament" inaugurated 1/92
- Pressure group says Britain's child care is worst in Europe 1/92
- Neil Kinnock denies "Kremlin connection" allegations 2/92
- Liberal Democrat leader admits to affair with secretary 2/92
- Neil Kinnock resigns as Labour leader 4/92
- Tories win fourth straight election 4/92
- MI5 to focus on IRA 5/92
- Mrs Thatcher introduced to the Lords as Baroness Thatcher 6/92
- MPs give themselves 40 per cent expense accounts raise 7/92
- Seeks international conference to end Bosnia-Herzegovina war 7/92
- Heritage Secretary, David Mellor, resigns after scandal 9/92
- Britain pulls out of ERM amid storm 9/92
- Major orders inquiry into "Iraqgate" affair 11/92
- Hurd is first cabinet minister to visit Argentina since war 1/93
- Government plans privatisation of British Rail 2/93
- Home Office scraps income-related fines system 5/93
- Junior minister, Michael Mates, resigns amid allegations 6/93
- Tories lose Christchurch 7/93
- MI5 lifts the veil 7/93
- Major faces "Back to Basics" crisis 1/94
- Age of consent for homosexuals lowered to 18 2/94
- Chief of Defence Staff forced to resign over love affair 3/94
- Tories lose control of 18 councils 5/94
- 2 MPs accused of being paid to ask commercial questions 7/94
- Tony Blair elected new leader of Labour Party 7/94
- Post Office privatisation off 11/94
- Major wins EU vote but suspends 8 Tories 11/94
- Commons in favour of ban on all hunting 3/95
- Blair wins battle to scrap Party's Clause Four 4/95
- Tories rejected in Scottish local elections 4/95
- Tories routed in local elections 5/95
- Lord Nolan presents "sleaze" report 5/95
- Police reject arming officers 5/95

British Army
- See also Royal Air Force, Royal Navy, World Wars I and II
- Germany is our model, says War Secretary 9/06
- New expeditionary force created 1/07
- Formation of Territorial Army by Haldane 4/08
- Military horse shortage 2/10
- Vickers machine gun introduced 11/12
- Field Marshal French resigns as Chief 3/14
- 70 officers resign over Ulster service 4/14
- Expeditionary force on alert; volunteers 8/14
- Asquith calls for 500,000 volunteers 9/14
- Field Marshal Roberts dies 11/14
- Stands at 720,000 men 1/15
- Special women's army battalion created 3/15
- Kitchener criticises slow arms delivery 5/15
- Kitchener's "New Army" proves itself 9/15
- War Office orders long boots 9/15
- Haig replaces French as first Army C-in-C 12/15
- Hands over to South African Union forces 12/21
- Army chief Wilson killed by IRA, London 6/22
- Commandeers food supply in General Strike 5/26
- Officer predicts Germans will start war 11/27
- Field Marshal Haig dies 1/28
- New armour piercing shell, ten-mile range 3/32
- New uniforms 1/33
- Allowed to keep 10,000 men in Suez zone 8/36
- Territorial Army size planned to double 3/39
- Reserves called up 8/39
- Women's Royal Army Corps formed from ATS 2/48
- WRAC incorporated 2/49
- Death of Archibald Wavell 5/50
- Carnarvon tank in trials 8/53
- Last national service call-ups 12/60
- Drops its colour bar 10/66
- Earl (Harold) Alexander of Tunis dies 6/69
- Death of Field Marshal William Slim 12/70
- Field Marshal Montgomery dies 3/76
- Death of Glubb Pasha 3/86
- 600 troops have AIDS test, Kenya 1/87
- Prince Edward resigns from Marines 1/87
- IRA bomb kills British soldier in Hanover 7/89
- IRA shoots soldier's wife by mistake in Dortmund 9/89
- IRA kills RAF corporal and his child 10/89
- Booby-trapped minibus explodes, killing army sergeant 5/90
- 7th Armoured Brigade prepares to leave for the Gulf 9/90
- US planes fire on British armoured vehicles in error; 9 die 2/91
- To lose quarter of manpower in government cuts 6/91

British East Africa
- See Kenya

British Guiana
- See Guiana, British

British Honduras
- 700 die in 100 mph winds 9/31
- Anti-British People's United Party win poll 4/54

British Medical Association
- See Britain (health)

British Nuclear Fuels (BNF)
- Nuclear workers may be advised to not have children 2/90

British Rail
- See Railways

British Somaliland
- See Somaliland

British Telecom
- Announces 25,000 job losses 3/92

Brittan, Leon 10/83, 5/85, 9/85, 1/86, 6/92

Britten, Benjamin 11/13, 12/38, 12/47, 5/52, 6/53, 10/54, 6/58, 12/62, 12/76

Broadcasting
- See also BBC, Television
- British Broadcasting Company formed 10/22
- First regular wireless news broadcast 11/22
- John Reith is BBC General Manager 12/22
- Ten shillings wireless licence suggested 10/23
- First transatlantic wireless to USA 11/23
- Six million hear Imperial Exhibition 4/24
- For schools by the BBC 4/24
- Newark, New Jersey, to Tokyo, Japan 4/24
- Diver broadcasts from North Sea bed 10/25
- Baird shows moving pictures by wireless 1/26
- British Broadcasting Corporation in 1927 7/26
- Three million have wireless sets, UK 2/27
- First Grand National on wireless 3/27
- Empire wireless listeners hear cricket 5/27
- Ramsay MacDonald on unemployment 6/29
- "Buy British" drive: Prince's broadcast 11/31
- Goebbels takes over German radio 2/33
- Daily broadcasts from Queen Mary liner 5/36
- Radio talks help Roosevelt win election 11/36
- Edward VIII announces abdication on radio 12/36
- BBC in Spanish, Portuguese and Arabic 11/37
- Very High Frequency (VHF) tests succeed 2/38
- Orson Welles' "War of the Worlds" panic 10/38
- Lord Haw Haw broadcasts from Germany 1/40
- On BBC de Gaulle urges French resistance 6/40
- Princess Elizabeth makes radio debut 10/40
- BBC lifts ban on conscientious objectors 3/41
- BBC promotes V for Victory campaign 7/41
- Radio main source of entertainment in UK 12/41
- BBC morse news to French Resistance 3/42
- "Midget" radios on sale in UK after war 1/44
- BBC says its postwar aim is TV for all 4/44
- UK comedian Tommy Handley dies 1/49
- "The War of the Worlds", Ecuador 2/49
- "Much Binding in the Marsh" 8/49
- Radio Free Europe heard in East Europe 5/51
- Cult UK radio comedy "The Goon Show" 12/53
- "Take It From Here": Muir and Norden 12/53
- "The Glums": Bentley, Whitfield, Edwards 12/53
- "Educating Archie" with Tony Hancock 12/53
- Television Bill sets up independent authority 3/54
- Thomas's "Under Milk Wood" radio play 12/54
- First ITV transmissions; advertisements 9/55
- Carleton-Greene made BBC Director-General 7/59
- Transistors replace valves in radios 8/59
- BBC "Children's Hour" to be dropped 2/61
- Radio Caroline starts up in North Sea 3/64
- Pirate Radio Atlanta goes on the air 5/64
- Radio Caroline and Radio Atlanta merge 7/64
- More listen to Radio Caroline than BBC 9/64
- UK National Viewers' and Listeners' Association 11/65
- UK broadcaster Richard Dimbleby dies 12/65
- Most pirate radio stations close 8/67
- Marine Broadcasting Act in force 8/67
- 17 ex-pirate DJs to join BBC radio 9/67
- BBC Radios 1,2,3 and 4 begin broadcasting 9/67
- Radio Leicester: first BBC local station 11/67
- Death of UK comedian Tony Hancock 6/68
- BBC serial "The Dales" to end 1/69
- BBC serial "The Dales" ends 4/69
- Britain approves 12 new local radio stations 11/69
- 60 commercial radio stations planned, UK 3/71
- British broadcasting pioneer John Reith dies 6/71
- London Broadcasting Company goes on air 10/73
- LBC breaks BBC's 50-year radio monopoly 10/73
- First live broadcast of Commons 6/75
- Radio listeners shocked at parliament 6/78
- John Arlott's last cricket commentary 9/80
- Radio Caroline returns to the air 8/83
- UK broadcaster Roy Plomley dies 5/85
- "Real Lives" ban: UK journalists strike 8/85
- UK broadcaster Huw Wheldon dies 3/86
- Baghdad Radio announces Iraqi army is leaving Kuwait 2/91

Brock, R.C. 6/48

Brockdorff-Rantzau, Ulrich 5/19, 6/19

Brockway, Fenner 4/83, 4/88

Broe, William 3/73

Bronowski, Jacob 8/74

Brook, Peter 12/46, 12/50, 12/62, 12/64, 12/66, 12/71, 12/89

Brooke, Alan 7/40, 11/41

Brooke, Edward 11/66

Brooke, Gerald 7/65, 7/69

Brooke, Henry 5/64

Brooke, Peter 11/87, 11/89, 3/91, 5/91, 6/91

Brooke, Rupert 4/15, 12/15, 12/18

Brookes, Norman 7/14

Brooks, Richard 3/92

Brooks, Tony 6/58, 9/58

Broome, David 7/70

Brough, Althea Louise 7/48, 7/49, 7/52, 7/54, 7/55

Brough, Peter 12/53

Brown, Arthur Whitten 6/19

Brown, Christy 9/81

Brown, Edmund 8/65

Brown, George 4/56, 11/58, 2/63, 5/64, 10/64, 8/66, 3/68, 6/70, 8/70, 3/76, 6/85

Brown, Kerrith 9/88

Brown, L.T. 2/22

Brown, Lesley 7/78

Brown, Louise 7/78

Brown, Sue 4/81

Browne, John 2/90

Browning, John Moses 11/26

Bruce, Lenny 6/64, 8/66

Bruges
- Falls to Germans 10/14

Brugnon, Jacques 7/32

Brumel, Valeri 7/62

Brundtland, Gro Harlem 2/81

Brunei
- British troops clash with rebels 12/62
- Becomes independent of Britain 1/84

Bruning, Heinrich 10/31, 1/32, 5/32

Bruno, Frank 2/89

Brusilov, Alexei 6/16

Brussels
- Fire destroys World Exhibition stalls 8/10
- King opens World's Fair 4/58

Bruton, John 2/95

Bryan, Charles 7/24

Bryan, John 8/92

Bryan, William Jennings 11/00, 11/08, 6/15, 7/25

Bryant, Margot 7/65

Bryant, P.C. 11/14

Brynner, Yul 10/85

Buchan, John (Lord Tweedsmuir) 2/40

Bucher, Roy 1/49

Buck, Pearl S. 3/73

Buckingham, John 4/67

Buckle, George 8/12

Buckley, Sheila 8/76

Buckner, Simon 6/45

Buckton, Ray 2/72

Budd, Zola 4/84, 8/84, 8/85, 7/86, 5/88

Budenny, Semyon 2/20, 8/20, 8/41

Budenz, Louis 8/48

Budge, Donald 7/37, 7/38

Bueno, Maria 7/59, 7/60

Buerk, Michael 11/84

Bugatti, Ettore 8/47

Bugner, Joe 3/71, 2/73

Buhari, Mohammed 1/84

Bujak, Zbigniew 5/86

Bukharin, Nikolai 11/28, 1/29, 2/29, 1/37, 3/38, 10/62

Bulganin, Nikolai 3/49, 2/55, 5/55, 7/55, 8/55, 4/56, 11/56, 1/58, 3/58, 2/75

Bulgaria
- See also World Wars I and II
- Turks massacre 50,000 9/03
- Calls on great powers to intervene 9/03
- Premier Petkov killed; Gudev succeeds 3/07
- Troops clash with peasants 4/07
- Turkey recognises independence 4/09
- Triple Alliance recognises independence 4/09
- Anti-Turkish pact with Greece 5/12
- Poised to attack Turkey over Macedonia 9/12
- Drives back Turkish troops with Serbia 10/12
- Besieges Adrianople in war with Turkey 11/12
- Signs armistice with Turkey 11/12
- Fights ex-allies and enters Serbia 7/13

- Forced to surrender spoils in new treaty 8/13
- Settles border dispute with Turkey 9/13
- Declares neutrality 11/14
- Wooed by Central Powers and Turkey 9/15
- Russia attacks; Allies blockade ports 10/15
- Surrenders after fierce attack 9/18
- King Ferdinand abdicates for son Boris 10/18
- Signs Treaty and recognises Yugoslavia 11/19
- Army coup; new Premier Professor Zankoff 6/23
- Ousted Premier Stambouliski thought shot 6/23
- 103 die in train crash 7/23
- Greeks invade; withdraw as League asks 10/25
- King Boris helps Fascist coup 5/34
- Diplomatic relations with USSR 8/34
- Accepts German occupation 2/41
- Signs non-aggression pact with Turkey 2/41
- Joins the Axis 3/41
- Germans complete military occupation 3/41
- Germans advance towards Greek border 3/41
- King Boris assassinated 8/43
- 400 reported killed in uprising 11/43
- Germans evacuate Sofia 11/43
- Told by Stalin to declare war on Germany 5/44
- Says it will quit war 8/44
- Declares war on Germany 9/44
- Left-wing government takes over 3/45
- Communist Fatherland Front wins election 11/45
- Referendum rejects monarchy 9/46
- Signs alliance treaty with Yugoslavia 8/47
- Agrarian party leader Petkov executed 9/47
- To cut church ties with foreign states 2/49
- Ends friendship pact with Yugoslavia 10/49
- Joins Warsaw Pact 5/55
- Premier Chervenkov forced out in purge 4/56
- Poison umbrella kills defector, London 9/78
- Second defector Simeonov dies, London 10/78
- Airline official linked to Pope shooting 11/82
- Thousands of persecuted Turks leave the country 6/89
- 100,000 rally in Sofia over reforms 11/89
- Plans to abolish Communist Party's political monopoly 12/89
- Coalition government takes over from Communist rule 2/90
- Petar Mladenov is elected President 4/90
- 20,000 protesters call for government's resignation 11/90
- Andrei Lukanov resigns as Prime Minister 11/90
- Todor Zhivkov is jailed for seven years 9/92

Bulger, James 2/93, 11/93
Buller, Redvers 2/00, 10/01
Bulow, Bernhard von 10/00, 1/08, 11/08
Bulow, Ferdinand von 7/09
Bunche, Ralph 10/48, 2/49
Bunge, R.G. 12/53
Bunuel, Luis 2/00, 7/83
Burchfield, Robert 12/86
Buresch, Karl 5/32
Burger, Warren 6/71, 7/74
Burgess, Anthony 2/17, 12/71, 12/80, 11/93
Burgess, Guy 6/51, 3/54, 4/54, 9/55, 11/55, 7/63, 9/63
Burgess, Thomas 9/11
Burke, Mike 2/67, 9/75
Burkitt, Denis 12/75
Burma
- Cyclone and tidal wave kill 1,200 5/26
- Pegu destroyed by earthquake; 6,000 die 5/30
- Simon Commission recommends separation 6/30
- Burma separated from India 4/37
- Premier U Aung San killed 7/47
- Becomes independent 1/48
- Round-up of Communist agitators 3/50
- State and companies form Burmah Oil 1/54
- General Ne Win ousts Premier U Nu 9/58
- Signs treaty with China 1/60
- U Thant becomes UN Secretary-General 11/61
- Army seizes power in coup 3/62
- Former UN Secretary-General U Thant dies 11/74
- Government imposes curfew in Rangoon 6/88
- Anti-government demonstrations 8/88
- Diplomats evacuated from Rangoon 9/88
- Army shoots 100 demonstrators in Rangoon 9/88
- Aung San Suu Kyi awarded Nobel Peace Prize 10/91
- Aung San Suu Kyi is critically ill on hunger strike 11/91
- Aung San Suu Kyi's sons collect Nobel Peace Prize 12/91

Burnet, Frank Macfarlane 12/49
Burnett, Frances Hodgson 10/24
Burns, John 1/43
Burr, Raymond 9/93
Burra, Edward John 10/76
Burrell, William 3/58
Burroughs, Edgar Rice 3/50
Burroughs, John 9/16
Burroughs, William 12/57
Burruni, Salvatore 6/66
Burton, Richard 12/53, 12/54, 12/55, 2/56, 3/64, 7/66, 12/67, 7/73, 10/75, 12/77, 8/84, 12/84
Burundi
- Hundreds killed in tribal uprising 5/72
- Thousands of Hutu tribesmen killed 6/72

Busby, Matt 2/58, 5/68, 6/68, 1/69, 1/94
Buscetta, Tommaso 2/86
Busch, Fritz 3/33, 12/33, 12/34
Busch, Wilhelm 1/08
Buses
- First long British bus service 8/00
- First closed-top double decker buses 4/09
- More motor-buses in London 5/11
- First electric trolley buses, Leeds 6/11
- Omnibus and Electric Underground to merge 1/12
- Big increase in deaths from buses 8/13
- First night bus services, London 8/20
- Allowed into Hyde Park 3/24
- Volunteers man transport in Strike 5/26
- Covered-top buses in London 8/27
- Six-wheeled bus on trial, London 9/27
- Britain may ban coaches over 60 mph 11/29
- National bus strike, Britain 7/57
- London trolleybuses taken out of service 5/62

Bush, Edwin 3/61
Bush, George
- Attends UN conference on China 10/71
- To run for presidency in 1980 5/79
- Chosen by Reagan as running-mate 7/80
- Together with Reagan, trounces President Carter in election 11/80
- Wins 59 per cent of vote 11/84
- Wins New Hampshire Republican primary 2/88
- Leads Republican presidential candidate race 3/88
- Set to become Dukakis's rival 4/88
- Chooses Dan Quayle as vice-presidential running-mate 8/88
- Wins second and final TV debate 10/88
- Elected President 11/88
- Sworn in as 41st President of the United States 1/89
- First visit to China as US President 2/89
- Cuts relations with Panama 9/89
- Announces $7.86 billion plan to finance war against drugs 9/89
- Elated at the news of the demolition of the Berlin Wall 11/89
- Announces end of Cold War 12/89
- US soldier's death triggers decision to invade Panama 12/89
- Thanks Syria for facilitating release of US hostage 4/90
- Agrees with Gorbachev on new arms cuts 6/90
- Warns Iraqis not to cross Kuwaiti border 8/90
- Meets King Hussein of Jordan 8/90
- United with Gorbachev on Iraq issue 9/90
- Says that there is no room for negotiated peace in Gulf 10/90
- Spends Thanksgiving Day with US troops in Saudi Arabia 11/90
- Seeks to open talks with Iraq 11/90
- Comes under pressure from Israel over Iraqi missile attacks 1/91
- Dismisses Saddam's peace offer as "cruel hoax" 2/91
- Orders Saddam Hussein to withdraw from Kuwait 2/91
- Publicly announces on television the end of the Gulf War 2/91
- Discusses tough cease-fire resolution with Major 3/91
- Suffers mild heart attack 5/91
- Signs START with President Gorbachev 8/91
- Angers Israel by refusing $10bn loan 9/91
- Participates in Middle East summit in Madrid 10/91
- Forced to call in army after Los Angeles race riots 5/92
- Nominated Republican presidential candidate 8/92
- Gains 38 per cent of presidential vote; loses election 11/92
- Signs START-2 Treaty with Yeltsin in Moscow 1/93

Busia, Kofi 1/72
Busoni, Ferruccio 7/24
Butcher, Lloyd 1/68
Bute, Marquess of 5/38
Butenandt, Adolf 12/39
Butler, M.A.H. 11/56
Butler, Richard Austen "Rab" 9/32, 2/44, 3/44, 1/45, 10/51, 11/51, 1/52, 4/55, 11/56, 1/57, 3/63, 10/63, 3/82
Butler, Samuel 6/02
Butlin, Billy 12/37, 6/80
Butterfield, Alexander 7/73
Butterworth, George 8/16
Butts, Alfred 4/93
Buxton, Angela 7/56
Byng, Viscount 7/29
Byrd, Richard 5/26, 3/57
Byrd, Robert 4/60
Byrne, James 4/72
Byrne, Roger 2/58
Byrne, William 5/73
Byrnes, James 12/45, 1/47

C

Caballero, Largo 5/37
Cadbury, George 10/22
Cadillac
- Company founded 8/01
- First car made and sold 10/02

Cadogan, Alexander 1/50
Cadorno, General 10/17
Cadwaladr, Dilys 8/53
Caetano, Marcello 9/68, 4/74
Cafferata, Superintendent 8/29
Cage, John 9/12, 12/66
Cagney, James 3/86
Cahill, Joe 8/71
Cahill, Patricia 7/90
Caillaux, Joseph 6/11, 3/14, 12/17, 1/18, 11/44
Caine, Michael 3/93
Caldwell, Erskine 12/03
Calfa, Marian 12/89
Calinescu, Armand 9/39
Callaghan, James 3/12, 2/63, 10/64, 3/66, 11/67, 5/68, 1/69, 5/69, 10/69, 5/70, 8/71, 3/74, 7/74, 3/76, 4/76, 9/76, 12/76, 5/77, 7/77, 10/78, 1/79, 2/79, 3/79, 10/80, 5/83, 4/87, 7/87
Callas, Maria 12/23, 11/52, 9/59, 12/59, 12/65, 9/77
Calles, Plutarco 2/26, 8/26
Calley, William 11/69, 11/70, 12/70, 3/71, 2/73
Callow, Simon 12/79
Calloway, Cab 11/94
Calman, Mel 2/94
Calmette, Gaston 3/14
Calvi, Roberto 6/82, 7/82, 6/83
Calvino, Italo 10/23
Calwell, Arthur 6/66
Camberabero, Didier 3/91
Cambodia
- Japanese troops begin to arrive 7/41
- Independence declared 3/45
- Thailand returns annexed areas 11/46
- Granted independence by France 12/48
- France recognises royalist regime 2/50
- UK and US recognise royalist regime 2/50
- King Sihanouk flees to Thailand 6/53
- King Sihanouk abdicates for father 3/55
- Sihanouk's party wins election 9/55
- Declares neutrality 11/57
- British embassy wrecked by protesters 3/64
- Eleven US prisoners to be freed 12/68
- Prince Sihanouk ousted in coup 3/70
- Appeals against invasion of territory 3/70
- Premier Lon Nol asks for US arms 3/70
- Nixon sends in US troops 4/70
- Declared a republic 10/70
- Rioters attack food markets seeking rice 9/72
- 20 die in failed attempt to kill Lon Nol 3/73
- Communists launch attack near Phnom Penh 6/73
- US bombing of Cambodia officially ends 8/73
- Convoy reaches besieged Phnom Penh 9/73
- Communists shell Phnom Penh 2/74
- Nixon promises aid to Lon Nol 2/74
- Khmer Rouge besiege capital Phnom Penh 1/75
- North Vietnamese sweep through Laos and Cambodia 1/75
- Communist Khmer Rouge conquers Phnom Penh 4/75
- Will Pol Pot hand over to Prince Norodom? 4/75
- Khmer Rouge threatens to hang ex-leaders 4/75
- Khmer Rouge kills thousands: reports 6/75
- Refugees tell of Pol Pot executions 7/75
- Townspeople forced onto fields, shackled 7/75
- Prince Sihanouk returns 9/75
- Pol Pot visits Hua Kuo-feng in China 9/77
- Wants aid, defence from China 9/77
- Breaks off relations with Vietnam 12/77
- 3,000 die in border clashes with Vietnam 1/78
- Vietnam crushes Khmer Rouge regime 1/79
- Heng Samrin is new pro-Hanoi leader 1/79
- Vietnamese attack along 200-mile front 1/79
- Hundreds of thousands died under Pol Pot 4/79
- New regime says Pol Pot killed three million 7/79
- Pol Pot sentenced to death for genocide 8/79
- Red Cross, UNICEF, to save two million 9/79
- Vietnamese hunting 30,000 Khmer troops 9/79
- Death of Lon Nol 11/85
- Vietnam is to withdraw its troops from Cambodia 4/89
- Vietnamese troops withdraw from Cambodia 9/89
- Prince Sihanouk is proclaimed head of state 6/93
- Sihanouk returns to throne 9/93
- Khmer Rouge murder 3 Western hostages 11/94

Cameron, James 2/58, 1/85
Cameroons
- Joins Free France 8/40
- 110 die in crash of British DC-7 3/62
- Gas from volcanic lake kills 1,500 8/86

Cammell and Laird
- Amalgamate 10/03

Camp David
- Sadat, Begin and Carter agree on peace 9/78

Campaign for Nuclear Disarmament (CND) 2/58, 4/58, 10/60, 10/81
Campbell, Donald 7/55, 11/55, 11/58, 5/59, 12/64, 1/67
Campbell, Duncan 2/87
Campbell, Ffyona 9/93, 10/94
Campbell, J. R. 10/24
Campbell, Kim 6/93
Campbell, Malcolm 2/27, 2/28, 2/31, 2/32, 3/33, 3/35, 9/35, 9/37, 12/41, 1/49, 7/60, 9/60
Campbell, Mrs Patrick 4/14, 4/40
Campbell, Patrick 11/80
Campbell, Roy 10/02
Campbell-Bannerman, Henry 7/01, 6/06, 4/08
Campion, Jane 5/93
Camus, Albert 11/13, 12/57, 1/60
Canada
- See also World Wars I and II
- Fires sweep Ottawa and Hull 4/00
- Liberal Laurier wins election 11/00
- 120 drown as steamer crashes off Canada 1/06
- Last British troops leave 5/06
- First radio broadcast 12/06
- 80 drown as bridge collapses, Quebec 8/07
- Votes to remain in Empire 2/11
- R.L. Borden is new Premier after polls 9/11
- Canadian born Bonar Law new Tory leader 11/11
- Premier wants three dreadnoughts 12/12
- Troops in Easter attack on Hindenburg line 4/17
- Anti-conscription riots; martial law 4/18
- Insulin isolated by Best and Banting 12/21
- 3,000 British to emigrate to Canada 8/24
- Customs scandal; Premier King resigns 6/26
- King's Liberals returned in polls 9/26
- Self-governing Commonwealth dominion 11/26
- 77 children die in Montreal theatre fire 1/27
- Breaks off relations with USSR 5/27
- Baldwin and Prince visit Diamond Jubilee 7/27
- Elected to League Council 9/27
- Britain rejects reciprocal tariff plan 11/30
- Mackenzie King record election majority 10/35
- UK breaks her 16-year ice hockey run 2/36
- King unveils Canadian War Memorial, Vimy 7/36
- Eskimoes complain of Arctic heatwave 7/38
- British King and Queen begin tour 5/39
- Declares war on Germany 9/39
- First Canadian troops arrive in Britain 12/39
- Canadian Air Force squadron arrives in Britain 2/40
- Free French take two islands from Canada 12/41
- Parliament votes for full conscription 7/42
- Breaks ties with Vichy France 11/42
- Churchill, Roosevelt and King hold summit 8/43
- Mountbatten to command Allies in SE Asia 8/43
- King's Liberal Party returned to power 6/45
- Alexander becomes Governor-General 7/45
- 47 alleged Soviet spies arrested 2/46
- Denies Russians have atomic secrets 2/47
- Truman is first US President to visit 6/47
- Signs North Atlantic Treaty 4/49
- 207 die in liner fire 9/49
- Refuses to recognise Communist China 10/49
- Death of Mackenzie King 7/50
- Princess Elizabeth and Prince Philip on tour 10/51
- Canadian liner gutted by fire, Liverpool 1/53
- Polio virus grown at Toronto University 4/54
- Commonwealth Games, Vancouver 8/54
- Diefenbaker's Conservatives in power 6/57
- Queen opens parliament 10/57
- End of work on St Lawrence Seaway 4/59
- Queen and Eisenhower inaugurate St Lawrence 6/59
- Viking remains found 11/63
- 118 die in plane crash 11/63
- Film stars Taylor and Burton marry 3/64
- Maple Leaf adopted as national flag 12/64
- To mount drought relief in Africa 1/66
- De Gaulle raises Free Quebec hopes 7/67
- De Gaulle's Quebec challenge dismissed 8/67
- Pierre Trudeau becomes Premier 4/68
- Trudeau's Liberals win election 6/68
- Jimi Hendrix arrested for heroin 5/69
- Trudeau gets tough with Quebec rebels 10/70
- Quebec rebels kidnap British envoy Cross 10/70
- Quebec rebels kidnap minister, Laporte 10/70
- Body of Pierre Laporte found 10/70
- Quebec rebels free James Cross 12/70
- Alleged killers of Laporte arrested 12/70
- Pierre Trudeau marries Margaret Sinclair 3/71
- Gerhard Erzberg wins Chemistry Nobel 12/71
- 22 killed in nightclub bomb blast 9/72
- USSR dancer Baryshnikov defects to West 6/74
- Trudeau's Liberals returned to power 7/74
- Pierre and Margaret Trudeau separate 5/77
- Trudeau to end nuclear weapons programme 5/78
- Commonwealth Games, Edmonton 8/78
- Joe Clark sworn in as Premier 6/79
- Ex-Premier John Diefenbaker dies 8/79
- Six US diplomats flee Iran embassy 1/80
- Iran angry at collusion with US envoys 1/80
- Trudeau re-elected 2/80
- Quebec votes against secession 5/80
- Ottawa summit gloom over inflation 7/81
- Britain gives constitutional sovereignty 4/82
- Trudeau quits as PM 2/84
- Endorses plans to combat world terrorism 6/84
- Brian Mulroney wins general election 9/84
- John Polanyi wins Chemistry Nobel 12/86
- Ben Johnson breaks 100 metres record 8/87
- Winter Olympics 2/88
- Fourteen women students are massacred in Montreal 12/89
- Indigenous Canadians to be given right to be self-governing 8/91
- Olympia & York file for bankruptcy 5/92
- Signs free trade bloc agreement with US and Mexico 8/92
- Voters reject proposal for special status for Quebec 10/92
- Kim Campbell becomes first woman Canadian premier 6/93
- Lifts Cuba embargo 8/93

Canary Islands
- 574 die in biggest air disaster ever 3/77
- Publishing tycoon, Robert Maxwell, found drowned 11/91
- Experts uncertain of cause of Robert Maxwell's death 11/91

Canberra
- Becomes federal capital of Australia 3/13
- New Australian Parliament House opened 5/27

Canessa, Roberto 12/72
Canetti, Elias 12/81
Cannes, Treaty of
- Allies defer German reparations 1/22

Canton
- See China

Cantona, Eric 1/95
Cantor, Eddy 10/64
Capablanca, Jose 3/21, 11/27
Capek, Karel 12/38
Capelle, Admiral von 3/16, 10/17
Capone, Al 9/26, 2/29, 5/29, 3/30, 6/30, 2/31, 6/31, 10/31, 3/32, 8/34, 1/47
Caporetto
- Germans smash Italian Second Army 10/17

Capote, Truman 12/66, 8/84
Carden, Sackville 2/15
Cardenas, Lazaro 8/35
Cardiff
- Riots break out on the Ely estate 8/91

Cardinale, Claudia 4/38
Cardoso, Enrique 10/94
Cardus, John Frederick Neville 2/75
Carey, George (Archbishop of Canterbury) 3/91, 9/91, 11/92
Carl Gustaf, King of Sweden 9/73
Carleton-Greene, Hugh 7/59, 12/63
Carlos (terrorist)
- Captured and handed over to France 7/75, 12/75, 8/94

Carlos I, King of Portugal 2/08
Carlos, John 10/68
Carlsen, Henrik 1/52
Carlson, Ingvar 3/86
Carmichael, Hoagy 12/81
Carmona, Antonio 2/27, 8/39
Carnahan, Mike 12/88
Carnegie Steel Corporation
- Shareholders fuel economy 11/09

Carnegie, Andrew 6/09, 8/13, 8/19
Carnegie, Dale 12/34
Carnera, Primo 6/33, 6/34
Carol II, King of Rumania 4/32, 4/34, 1/38, 9/40, 4/53
Caroline, Princess of Monaco 1/57
Caron, Leslie 7/31, 12/56
Carpenter, Malcolm Scott 5/62
Carpentier, Georges 3/14
Carr, Henry 3/63
Carr, Robert 1/71, 9/73
Carranza, Venustiano 7/14, 1/16, 5/20
Carrel, Alexis 6/35
Carreras, Jose 12/90
Carrero Blanco, Luis 12/73
Carriere, Eugene 3/06
Carrington, Lord (Peter) 4/63, 3/71, 8/73, 5/79, 7/79, 5/80, 4/82
Carron, Owen 8/81
Carrothers, William 12/30

Cars
- Automobile Club's 1,000-mile trial 4/00
- German front wheel drive patent 11/00
- First Mercedes 3/01
- H Fournier wins Paris-Berlin race 6/01
- French speed limit: 10 kph 7/01
- Cadillac company founded 8/01
- American Automobile Association created 3/02
- New speed record in France 4/02
- Renault wins first Paris-Vienna race 6/02
- Automobile Club reliability trials 9/02
- First Cadillac sold 10/02
- Six die in Paris-Madrid road race 5/03
- Ford Motor Company founded 6/03
- Daimler factory burns down 6/03
- Registrations and speed limits, UK 7/03
- First Model A Ford 7/03
- Henry Ford breaks record 1/04
- Founding of Rolls-Royce 5/04
- Cheaper and more reliable 9/04
- Biggest ever Motor Show in London 2/05
- Automobile Association founded 6/05
- Used in Salvation Army "crusade" 8/05
- New motor speed record, France and USA 1/06
- Prominent people protest at vehicle noise 8/06
- Henry Ford becomes president of company 10/06
- Peking-Paris race takes off 6/07
- Italian prince wins Peking-Paris race 8/07
- First all-steel cars 4/08
- Ford's first Model T; assembly line made 8/08
- TUC calls for car speed limits 9/08
- General Motors formed from Buick and Oldsmobile 9/08
- Model T, first with lefthand drive, sold 10/08
- International Motor Exhibition, London 11/08
- Motor car tax in budget on safety issue 5/09
- Automobile Association and Motor Union join 1/11
- Rolls-Royce commissions statuette design 2/11
- First Ford Model T made outside USA 10/11
- Chevrolet incorporated 11/11
- First Morris Oxford 3/13
- Hyde Park Corner gets 10 mph limit 5/13
- Ford uses moving assembly line, Michigan 10/13
- Henry Ford's workers will share profits 1/14
- Ford's millionth car 12/15
- Fun use of cars under war restrictions 2/16
- Ford's cheap touring car; garage sales 8/16
- Cheap cars stimulate rural economy, USA 8/16
- Sunday driving banned in half of USA 8/18
- Olympia Motor Show after six years 11/19
- London police get cars instead of horses 2/20
- £1 tax per horsepower, Britain 5/20
- Fuel Research Board says 750,000 by 1921 7/20
- British report on growing motor deaths 8/20
- British Transport Ministry introduces compulsory signals 10/20
- Nine million in USA 2/21
- Ford makes a million cars a year 4/21
- Wolseley sets 14 speed records 5/22
- 21 year old Lyons forms sidecar company 9/22
- Popular motoring boom, Britain 11/22
- New luxury Ford model 8/23
- UK Transport Ministry attacks billboards 10/23
- Petrol price rise threatens boom, UK 2/24
- Lords discusses need for driving tests 5/24
- Police warning to cyclists, London 7/24
- Olympia Motor Show; wide choice in price 9/25
- General Motors drops Austin bid 9/25
- Four months' jail for drunken drivers, UK 11/25
- First "motel" in California 12/25
- Cars are one third of US imports 5/26
- 20th Motor Show, Paris 10/26
- Morris Motors buys Wolseley Motors 2/27
- 15 millionth Model T 5/27
- Car length cut by law, UK 8/27
- 1.7 million vehicles; car replaces horse 10/27
- General Motors' $62 million dividend 11/27
- Ford Model A - successor to Model T 12/27
- Automatic gear change mechanism, UK 9/28
- Three a day die on London's roads 9/28
- Available to people on £400 a year 10/28
- 10,878 private cars in accidents, London 11/28
- Lords backs compulsory driving tests, UK 12/28
- General Motors buys German Opel firm 1/29
- Benz, internal combustion inventor, dies 4/29
- Mobile radios for Flying Squad cars 7/29
- Rover, Lanchester and Standard merge, UK 4/30
- A.A. issues millionth badge 4/30
- New Morris Minor, costing £215 8/30
- Highway Code drafted 12/30
- Bentley calls in the receiver 7/31
- Rolls-Royce buys Bentley Motors 11/31
- Chrysler to open British car factory 12/31
- US Automobile Club dissolved 1/32
- First UK three-letter number plates 8/32
- New Austin "Ten" 9/32
- Sir Frederick Royce of Rolls Royce dies 4/33
- New German car costing £61 displayed 3/34
- Two-seater "Opal" version Austin Seven 8/34
- 30 mph speed limit in built-up areas, UK 3/35
- Dipped headlights made compulsory, UK 7/35
- Andre Citroen, manufacturer, dies 7/35
- Stylish Jaguar SS unveiled at Motor Show 9/35
- 90 mph Jaguar for just £385; Ford V-8 9/35
- Rolls-Royce Phantom III sells for £1,850 10/35
- Hitler unveils Volkswagen "people's car" 2/36
- 2.58 million cars in UK; 17.5 per cent up 2/36
- First London Motor Show, Earl's Court 10/37
- Gearless, clutchless car tested, UK 8/38
- UK government bans trading in new cars 7/40
- Walter Chrysler dies 8/40
- "Jeep" launched for US Army 11/40
- Louis Chevrolet dies 6/41
- Ford Prefect and Anglia on sale, UK 11/46
- Henry Ford dies: profile 4/47
- Car designer Ettore Bugatti dies 8/47
- Austin unveils the A40 model, UK 10/47
- Compulsory inspection proposed, UK 10/47
- First postwar large-scale UK motor show 10/48
- Leading UK makers to standardise parts 12/48
- Rover produces first gas-turbine car 3/50
- Ford launches Consul and Zephyr ranges 7/50
- USA drive-in cinemas 6/51
- Austin raise car prices 8/51
- Streamlined German Porsche at Motor Show 10/51
- Revamped family Austin 7 at Motor Show 10/51
- Lord Nuffield resigns directorships 12/52
- Jaguar's success in Le Mans Grand Prix 6/53
- Ford's new Anglia and Prefect models 9/53
- Ford Popular cheapest four-cylinder car 10/53
- Austin A30 and Standard Eight in price war 10/53
- Flashing indicator lights 1/54
- Austin Cambridge: new model from BMC 9/54
- Moss wins race in Mercedes Benz 5/55
- MG's new sports model, the MG-A 9/55
- Rootes Motors takes over Singer Motors 12/55
- New Vauxhall Victor saloon 2/57
- New Vauxhall Cresta and Velox models 10/57
- BMC's Austin Healey Sprite sports car 5/58
- Bubble-cars from Isetta, Messerschmitt 10/58
- Daf's continuous variable gears 10/58
- USA style, long and low; Buick from GM 10/58
- British Motor Show, with runabouts 10/58
- 15,000 BMC workers strike 1/59
- BMC's new Mini, Austin and Morris types 8/59
- Stable, small Mini from Alec Issigonis 8/59
- Strike halts Mini production 9/59
- Rolls-Royce launches costly Phantom V 9/59
- Jaguar takes over Daimler for £3.5 million 6/60
- Armstrong Siddeley to end production 6/60
- Malcolm Campbell tests new Bluebird car 7/60
- Leyland to take over Standard-Triumph 12/60
- The millionth Morris Minor built in UK 1/61
- Jaguar E-Type, UK 3/61
- Death of Lord Nuffield (William Morris) 8/63
- Production of the millionth BMC "Mini" 2/65
- Japanese to enter UK saloon car racing 3/65
- Aston Martin presents the DB6 9/65
- BMC and Jaguar to merge, UK 7/66
- Jensen presents FF and Interceptor 10/66
- Rootes introduces the Hillman Hunter 11/66
- US car firm Chrysler to take over Rootes 1/67
- Rootes announces Sunbean Rapier 10/67
- British Leyland Motor Corporation formed 1/68
- Jaguar unveils the XJ6 9/68
- Ford unveils the Capri 1/69
- British Leyland announces Austin Maxi 4/69
- Production of Morris Minor to cease, UK 4/70
- Rover announces Range Rover 6/70
- Rolls-Royce calls in receiver 2/71
- German manufacturer Georg von Opel dies 8/71
- The MG sports car 3/72
- The Ford Granada 12/72
- Japanese overtake British car sales, UK 9/73
- State takes over ailing British Leyland 8/75
- Last Wolseley rolls off lines 9/75
- Four millionth Mini produced 11/76
- British Leyland will shut to end strike 2/77
- British Leyland ready to sack toolmakers 3/77
- Peugeot-Citroen buys Chrysler Europe 8/78
- British Leyland to end MGs 9/79
- BL to sell MG works at Abingdon 3/80
- Aston Martin-Lagonda to buy MG works 3/80
- UK industry hit: Lucas Industries, MG 7/80
- Extra £900 million for British Leyland 1/81
- First De Lorean cars for New York 4/81
- British Leyland closes plants 10/81
- Honda and British Leyland in link-up 11/81
- Honda-BL executive car, saving costs 11/81
- Prototype De Lorean sports car 11/81
- 58,000 British Leyland workers strike 11/81
- De Lorean sports cars in receivership 2/82
- De Lorean car plant closes 10/82
- BL Metro is UK's best-selling car 2/83
- De Lorean accused of misusing funds, UK 7/84
- Austin-Rover renamed Rover Group, UK 6/86
- Nissan opens car factory in UK 9/86
- US car giants, GM and Ford, make record losses 2/92
- Rolls Royce opens Moscow showroom 7/93
- Rover sold to BMW 2/94

Carson, Edward 9/12, 9/13, 2/14, 4/14, 7/14, 3/20, 6/21, 10/35
Carson, Violet 7/65
Carson, Willie 6/89
Carter, Elliot 12/08
Carter, Howard 11/22, 2/24
Carter, Jimmy 10/24, 12/74, 1/76, 7/76, 9/76, 10/76, 11/76, 1/77, 3/77, 4/77, 5/77, 7/77, 9/77, 12/77, 1/78, 4/78, 9/78, 10/78, 1/79, 3/79, 6/79, 6/79, 8/79, 9/79, 3/80, 8/80, 10/80, 11/80, 9/86, 12/94
Cartman, Billy 5/90
Cartwright, Tom 9/68
Caruso, Enrico 2/04, 4/09, 1/10, 12/10, 8/21
Carver, Howard 11/23
Casalini, Armando 9/24
Casals, Pablo 10/73
Casals, Rosie 9/70
Casement, Roger 3/04, 5/16, 6/16, 8/16
Casey, Eamonn 5/92
Casey, Lord 12/67
Cash, Pat 7/87
Cassels, Major-General 12/51
Cassidy, David 5/74
Casson, Hugh 5/51, 2/76, 12/84
Casters, Jacques 11/62
Castillo, Ramon 6/43
Castle, Barbara 10/51, 10/64, 12/65, 5/66, 7/67, 4/68, 1/69, 5/69, 2/70, 4/75
Castle, Keith 6/85
Castle, Roy 9/94
Castro, Cipriano 12/02
Castro, Fidel 8/27, 7/53, 11/56, 12/56, 2/57, 9/58, 11/58, 1/59, 2/59, 3/59, 4/59, 6/59, 7/59, 2/60, 9/60, 4/61, 5/61, 1/62, 10/62, 4/63, 4/65, 10/65, 10/67, 3/75, 5/75, 11/75, 6/84, 9/86
Catalonia
- See also Spain
- 1,000 die in revolt 8/09
- Autonomy recognised by Madrid 9/32
- Uprising crushed 10/34
Caulfield, Patrick 12/61
Cauthen, Steve 7/77
Cavell, Edith 10/15, 4/19
Cawley, Evonne (nee Goolagong) 7/51, 7/71, 7/72, 7/75, 7/76, 7/80
Ceausescu, Elena 12/89, 1/90
Ceausescu, Nicolae 1/18, 12/67, 11/89, 12/89, 1/90
Cech, Thomas 12/89
Cecil, Lord Robert 11/17, 12/37, 11/58
Cecile de Bourbon-Parma, Princess 1/70
Cela, Camilo Jose 12/89
Central Africa
- See also Central African Republic
- Becomes a French Union republic 12/58
Central African Empire
- See also Central African Republic
- Bokassa crowns himself emperor 12/77
- France pays for Bokassa coronation 12/77
- David Dacko overthrows Bokassa 9/79
Central African Federation
- See Rhodesia, Northern-Southern 00
Central African Republic
- See also Central African Empire
- Independent from France 7/60
- Bokassa takes office after coup 1/66
- Bokassa sentenced to death in absentia 12/80
Cerebotani, Luigi 10/06
Cermak, Anton 3/33
Cernik, Vladimir 7/49, 8/68
Ceron, Dionicio 4/95
Cerro, Luis Sanchez 4/33
Cespedes, Carlos de 8/33
Cevert, Francois 9/73
Ceylon
- See also Sri Lanka
- Bombed by Japanese 4/42
- Becomes independent 2/48
- Recognises Communist China 1/50
- Government wants British bases removed 5/56
- India's Tamils support Ceylon minority 6/58
- Tamils call for separate state 6/58
- Buddhist monk kills Premier Bandaranaike 9/59
- Bandaranaike first woman Premier ever 7/60
- Sri Lanka Freedom Party wins elections 7/60
- Mrs Bandaranaike re-elected PM 5/70
Cezanne, Paul 10/06, 12/06
Chaban-Delmas, Jacques 3/15, 6/69, 7/72
Chad
- Joins Free France 8/40
- Joins French Union as a republic 11/58
- Libya annexes northern strip of Chad 8/83
- France sends in men and arms 8/83
- US sends planes 8/83
Chadli, Benjedid 1/79
Chadwick, Florence 8/50, 10/55
Chadwick, James 12/32
Chaffee, Roger 1/67
Chagall, Marc 8/10, 9/64, 3/85, 12/85
Chaikovsky, Anastasia 2/28
Chain, Ernst 12/45
Chalfont, Lord 11/68
Chaliapin, Feodor 6/14, 12/14, 4/38
Chalmers, Len 5/61
Chamberlain, Austen 10/03, 1/19, 3/21, 5/22, 10/22, 5/23, 8/23, 10/25, 12/25, 5/27, 9/27, 4/32, 3/37
Chamberlain, Joseph 10/01, 5/03, 9/03, 7/04, 1/14
Chamberlain, Lindy 10/82, 2/86
Chamberlain, Neville 2/17, 3/23, 1/27, 6/30, 11/31, 4/34, 4/35, 11/35, 2/37, 5/37, 1/38, 3/38, 4/38, 5/38, 9/38, 10/38, 1/39, 2/39, 3/39, 4/39, 5/39, 7/39, 8/39, 9/39, 10/39, 2/40, 4/40, 5/40, 10/40, 11/40
Chambers, Dorothea 6/11, 7/13, 7/14, 7/19
Chambers, Whittaker 8/48, 12/48, 1/50
Chamorro, Violeta 2/90
Chamoun, Camille 7/58
Champion, Bob 4/81
Chan Chai-tong 4/31
Chandler, Raymond 3/59
Chanel, Gabrielle (Coco) 2/23, 1/71
Chaney, Lon 8/30
Chang Tso-lin 5/22, 6/27
Chang Tsung-kiang 3/27
Channel Tunnel
- Premier opposes Channel Tunnel bill 3/07
- Bill is withdrawn: "defence risk" 4/07
- Asquith urged to reconsider 8/13
- Government favours tunnel 3/19
- Government rejection 7/24
- Committee approves plan to build 3/30
- Suez Company resurrects idea 5/57
- Government drops plans 1/75
- More than 15,000 people protest at high-speed rail plans 2/89
- BR reveals Channel Tunnel link route 3/89
- Bans use of public money for project 3/89
- Sixth Briton to die building the tunnel 5/90
- Celebrations under the Channel as French and British meet 12/90
- Route to Stratford chosen for high-speed rail link 10/91
- Inaugurated by the Queen and President Mitterrand 5/94
Channon, Paul 10/87, 11/87, 1/89, 2/89
Chaplin, Charles 11/13, 6/17, 4/18, 4/19, 11/20, 9/21, 1/27, 8/27, 5/29, 6/33, 5/39, 12/40, 9/52, 10/52, 12/52, 4/53, 6/62, 1/75, 3/75, 12/77, 3/78, 5/78
Chaplin, Edward 6/87
Chaplin, Oona 4/53, 12/77
Chaplin, Ricky 1/90
Chapman, Colin 9/63
Chapman, Herbert 4/26
Chapman, Mark 12/80, 1/81, 8/81
Chapman, Percy 8/26
Chappell, Ian 5/77
Charles, Ezzard 10/38, 9/54
Charles, John 11/58
Charles, Prince of Wales 11/48, 12/48, 1/57, 7/58, 5/62, 6/63, 10/67, 2/69, 7/69, 2/70, 6/70, 11/70, 8/71, 6/74, 5/75, 8/78, 4/80, 9/80, 1/81, 2/81, 5/81, 7/81, 6/82, 7/82, 9/84, 5/86, 9/86, 3/88, 10/88, 11/88, 9/90, 12/90, 8/91, 3/92, 6/92, 12/92, 2/93
Charlton, Bobby 4/59, 6/62, 7/66, 5/68, 5/68, 6/94
Charpak, Georges 12/92
Charpentier, Georges 6/13, 7/21
Charteris, Leslie 4/93
Chataway, Christopher 6/52, 5/53, 8/53, 5/54, 10/54, 5/69
Chatwin, Bruce 12/89
Chautemps, Camille 2/30, 11/33, 1/34
Chechenia
- Russian troops and artillery roll across the border 12/94
- Russians launch fierce attack on Grozny 1/95
- Russians surround rebel base 3/95
Checkland, Michael 2/87
Chekhov, Anton 1/04, 7/04
Chekkal, Ali 5/57
Chen Tu-Hsiu 7/21
Chermayeff, Serge 12/38
Chernenko, Konstantin 9/11, 2/84, 4/84, 3/85
Chernomyrdin, Viktor 12/92
Chervenkov, Vulko 4/56
Chesebrough, Robert 9/33
Cheshire, Lord 7/92
Chess
- Capablanca and Lasker draw in championship 3/21
- Alekhine beats Capablanca, Buenos Aires 11/27
- Botvinnik keeps world title after draw 5/51
- Bobby Fischer beats Tigran Petrosian 10/71
- Fischer scores win against Spassky 7/72
- Bobby Fischer becomes world champion 9/72
- Bobby Fischer pulls out of Manila match 4/75
- Karpov, youngest champion by default 4/75
- Korchnoi seeks asylum in Netherlands 7/76
- Short is youngest chess challenger at 11 5/77
- Nigel Short, Korchnoi defeater, UK hope 5/77
- USSR champion Karpov beats Korchnoi 10/78
- Korchnoi claims Soviet mind tricks 10/78
- Karpov wins world championship, Italy 11/81
- World chess championship called off 2/85
- Kasparov becomes world champion 11/85
- Kasparov retains world championship 10/86
- Kasparov draws and wins against Karpov 12/87
- Soviet rebel holds onto title 12/87
Chesterton, Gilbert Keith 6/36
Chevalier, Maurice 12/30, 1/72
Chevrolet, Louis 6/41
Chiang Ching 9/76, 10/76, 1/81
Chiang Kai-shek
- See also China 9/26, 1/27, 3/27, 4/27, 6/27, 12/27, 9/28, 10/28, 7/29, 4/30, 9/30, 4/31, 6/35, 2/37, 9/37, 6/38, 10/38, 2/43, 11/43, 8/45, 2/46, 8/46, 10/46, 2/47, 7/47, 5/48, 10/48, 11/48, 1/49, 7/49, 12/49, 4/50, 7/50, 2/53, 9/54, 10/71, 4/75
Chicago
- Fines up to $100 for short skirts 5/21
Chichester, Francis 7/60, 6/64, 8/66, 1/67, 3/67, 5/67, 7/67, 8/72
Chichester-Clark, James 5/69, 9/69, 3/71
Chile
- Signs disarmament treaty with Argentina 1/03
- President Pedro Montt dies in Germany 8/10
- 30,000 reported killed in earthquake 1/39
- Declares war on Germany 2/45
- Gabriela Mistral wins Literature Nobel 12/45
- Salvador Allende elected President 9/70
- Attempt to murder army chief 10/70
- State of emergency declared 10/70
- Allende sworn in as President 11/70
- Pablo Neruda wins Literature Nobel 12/71
- Plane crash strands survivors in Andes 10/72
- Allende forms People's Front government 11/72
- Andes plane crash survivors ate the dead 12/72
- Evidence of anti-Allende plot by CIA 3/73
- Anti-Allende revolt crushed 6/73
- Salvador Allende killed in coup 9/73
- 2,000 feared dead after the coup 10/73
- Nixon admits CIA acted against Allende 3/76
- Referendum gives Pinochet eight more years 9/80
- Nationwide anti-Pinochet demos 6/83
- 17 killed in anti-Pinochet rioting 8/83
- Former President Allende's daughter returns 9/88
- General Pinochet loses election 10/88
- Patricio Aylwin is elected President 12/89
Chilton, Edward 8/92
China (Civil War)
- See also Formosa, Taiwan
- Civil war breaks out 6/21
- Rebel Manchurians driven from Peking 5/22
- President Yuan-Hung flees from Peking, caught 6/23
- British enter Shanghai during Civil War 9/24
- Northern leader flees as troops defect 10/24
- Chiang Kai-shek takes vital Hankow port 9/26
- Wu Pei-fu's northerners retreat 9/26
- Southern Reds take Wuchang and Hangyang 9/26
- British threatened in Shanghai and Hankow 1/27
- Chiang's nationalists move on Shanghai 1/27
- 2,000 British encircle Shanghai 2/27
- Chiang's men overrun Sunkiang 2/27
- Sun Chuang-fang's men flee to Shanghai 2/27
- Italians, French and Punjabis at Shanghai 2/27
- Chiang's Nationalists take Shanghai 3/27
- Warlords' troops crumble, Shanghai 3/27
- North retreats 3/27
- US and UK warships bomb Nanking 3/27
- Nationalists fight Red unions, Shanghai 4/27
- Chang Tso-lin unites three Northern armies 6/27
- Chiang Kai-shek regains Nanking command 8/27

- Chiang Kai-shek crushes Canton Red coup 12/27
- Northern warlord repels Chiang Kai-shek 4/30
- USSR-backed Red Army in Kuangsi province 4/30
- Communists attack Hankow 7/30
- Rebels split from Chiang; take Canton 4/31
- Rebels drive on Tientsin 7/31
- USA arranges truce in Manchuria war 11/31
- Chiang Kai-shek seals off Kiangsi Communists 10/34
- Mao Tse-tung leads 100,000 on Long March 10/34
- Long Marchers survive Nationalist attack 10/35
- Communists seize Tsitshar 4/46
- Communist-Nationalist civil war erupts 5/46
- Full-scale civil war breaks out 8/46
- Nationalists capture Kalgan 10/46
- Chiang slams US refusal to supply arms 2/47
- Chiang orders Nationalist mobilisation 7/47
- North China People's Government created 9/48
- Chiang has suffered many defeats in war 10/48
- Chiang acknowledges loss of Manchuria 10/48
- Communists cross Great Wall 11/48
- Communist troops take Peking 1/49
- Communists advance on Shanghai 4/49
- Shanghai falls to the Communists 5/49
- Nationalist defences in south crumbling 10/49
- Communists begin to occupy Canton 10/49
- Nationalists move to Formosa 12/49
- Nationalists halt Chinese mainland raids 6/50

China (foreign affairs)
- See also Korean War
- Foreign legations warn about Boxer sect 1/00
- Westerners to invade if rebels continue 4/00
- Foreigners flee from southern rebel takeover 4/00
- Sino-Russian clash on Manchurian railway 4/00
- 1,500 Europeans killed at Tientsin 7/00
- Allies storm Peking, relieve embassies 8/00
- "Punished" by Russia's Manchurian grip 9/00
- Anglo-German Open Door pact 10/00
- Yang-Tse waters international 10/00
- Allies protest at Manchuria deal 3/01
- Baulks at treaty with Russia 4/01
- End of Rebellion; Chinese concessions 9/01
- Independence set out in Anglo-Japanese treaty 1/02
- Manchurian Treaty with Russia 4/02
- Allies sign Tariff Protocol 8/02
- Commercial treaty with Britain 9/02
- Cannot pay Rebellion reparations 1/03
- Refuses to evacuate Manchuria 4/03
- Japanese spare Chinese in Mukden battle 3/05
- Forced to sign Tibet treaty with Britain 4/06
- Resumes control of Manchuria 4/07
- Trade and territory guarantee in treaty 7/07
- Treaty with Russia; USA protests 7/09
- Invades Tibet; Dalai Lama flees 2/10
- Foreign-owned buildings attacked 4/10
- Russia plans cross-desert railway 12/10
- Anglo-Chinese Bank formed 9/12
- 300 troops killed by Tibetan raid 1/13
- Mongolian independence; civil war flares 7/13
- Japanese marines land at Nanking 9/13
- Mongolia becomes protectorate 11/13
- Allies want China to join Entente 11/15
- Breaks diplomatic relations with Germany 3/17
- President declares war on Central Powers 8/17
- Offers 300,000 troops to Allies in West 9/17
- Admitted to League of Nations 12/20
- Mongolia independent Communist state 7/21
- Japan will hand back Shantung 2/22
- Peking protests at British troop presence 1/27
- Chiang Kai-Shek cuts relations with USSR 6/27
- Russians expelled from Shanghai 12/27
- Chiang expels Soviet advisers 10/28
- Signs tariff agreement with Britain 12/28
- Soviet troops retaliate for earlier raid 6/29
- Britain plans to rebuild Chinese navy 7/29
- USSR breaks off relations with China 7/29
- Troops fight with Russians over railway 7/29
- Chiang Kai-Shek war footing with USSR 7/29
- Clash with Soviets in Manchuria 8/29
- Retreat from heavy Russian attack 9/29
- Regain Chingkiang from British 11/29
- Japan invades Manchuria 11/29
- Railway border dispute with USSR ends 12/29
- Disbands anti-Bolshevik White Guards 12/29
- Japan attacks Chinese at Mukden, Manchuria 9/31
- Rejoices at Japan leaving League 2/33
- Japanese make Pu Yi Manchukuon Emperor 3/34
- Japan warns West: "Hands off China" 4/34
- Arrests three Japanese secret agents 6/35
- Forced to remove divisions from north 6/35
- Japan instals "friendly" Peking officers 6/35
- Japanese troops march into Peking 11/35
- Japanese set up Hopei state in north 11/35
- Japan attacks China from Manchukuo 7/37
- Clash with Japanese troops near Peking 7/37
- Non-aggression pact with USSR 8/37
- Japanese capture port of Swatow 6/39
- Chiang Kai-shek meets Western Allies 11/43
- Says United Nations will be set up 10/44
- Among 50 nations to sign UN charter 6/45
- Chiang offers Communists a peace plan 10/46
- US to boost marine force at Tsingtao 11/48
- 26 die when Communists shell UK warships 4/49
- Mao says USSR is China's true ally 6/49
- UK frigate Amethyst makes freedom dash 7/49
- Chiang appeals to US for aid 7/49
- Mao regime recognised by India 1/50
- Mao regime recognised by Pakistan 1/50
- Mao regime recognised by Ceylon 1/50
- US orders out its consular staff 1/50
- Chou En-lai has talks with Stalin, Moscow 1/50
- Signs friendship pact with USSR 2/50
- UK bans oil sales to China 7/50
- Mao's entry to UN rejected 8/50
- Threatens intervention in Korea 9/50
- Mao's troops march into Lhasa, Tibet 10/50
- Invades Tibet 10/50
- Enters Korean War 11/50
- Named as aggressor by United Nations 1/51
- General MacArthur wants to attack 3/51
- Attacks South Korea; UN forces retreat 4/51
- Chou En-Lai seizes UK oil company assets 4/51
- Allows Tibet religious freedom 5/51
- Controls Tibet army; wants minerals 5/51
- Stopped by Anzac and British troops south of Chunchon 5/51
- Occupies Lhasa, Tibet 9/51
- Says USA uses germ warfare in Manchuria 3/52
- 100,000 troops to Korea claimed 6/52
- US Guards kill 52 rioting Chinese POWs 10/52
- 30,000 troops invade South Korea 6/53
- US Senate bars China's entry to UN 6/53
- USA warns China not to aid Viet Minh 4/54

China may join Games; Taiwan withdraws 5/54
- Apologises for shooting down UK airliner 7/54
- Taiwan sinks eight Chinese gunboats 8/54
- UK Labour Party delegation visits China 8/54
- Bombs Nationalists on Quemoy Island 9/54
- Chou calls for Asian-Pacific peace pact 7/55
- USSR gives Port Arthur to China 10/55
- Chou En-lai goes to USSR for talks 1/57
- 65,000 die in Tibetan revolt 7/58
- Crushes Tibetan revolt; Dalai Lama flees 3/59
- Troops pursue Lama to border; fighting 3/59
- India warns not to attack Bhutan and Sikkim 8/59
- Not to join UN 9/59
- 17 Indian troops die in border clash 10/59
- Khrushchev visits Peking; meets Mao 10/59
- Chou En-lai wants talks with Nehru 12/59
- Signs treaty with Burma 1/60
- Absent from Communist leaders' meeting 2/60
- USSR's Krushchev attacks Mao 6/60
- Condemns USSR "revisionism" 6/60
- USSR's Pravda attacks China 10/60
- Party admits differences with Soviets 12/60
- USSR pledges to defend from attack 7/62
- U2 plane used by Taiwan shot down 9/62
- Heavy border fighting with Indians 10/62
- Wins border dispute with India 11/62
- Mao invites Khrushchev to visit 3/63
- Agrees to hold talks with USSR 5/63
- Split with USSR now complete 7/63
- UN votes against Chinese admission 10/63
- Purge of Soviet supporters 9/64
- Explodes her first A-bomb 10/64
- Chinese leaders meet Brezhnev 11/64
- Tension on Indian border 2/65
- Rejects Vietnam peace mission 6/65
- Pledges more aid to Ho Chi Minh 8/66
- Leadership denounced by USSR 11/66
- Anti-British protests in Peking 5/67
- Peking expels British diplomat 5/67
- Shanghai consulate closed 5/67
- Red Guards attack British envoys, Peking 8/67
- British envoys barred from leaving 8/67
- Chinese diplomats fight police in London 8/67
- In border clash with USSR 3/69
- Kosygin in talks with Chou En-lai 9/69
- Admitted to UN 10/71
- Mao in talks with Haile Selassie, Peking 10/71
- Delegates take their seats at UN 11/71
- UK appoints first ambassador to China 1/72
- Nixon visits; urges better relations 2/72
- Chiang dies; hopes for US recognition 4/75
- Mao not to receive foreign leaders 6/76
- Cambodia's Pol Pot visits Hua Kuo-feng 9/77
- Spanish King Juan Carlos visits 5/78
- Cancels aid to Vietnam 7/78
- Cancels aid to Albania 7/78
- Hua Kuo-feng visits Rumania 8/78
- Crosses into North Vietnam; "reprisals" 2/79
- Angry at Vietnam invading Cambodia 2/79
- Starts leaving Vietnam 3/79
- Mrs Thatcher praises Hua Kuo-feng, in Britain 10/79
- Tribute to Yugoslavia's late leader Tito 5/80
- Reagan to sell arms 6/81
- Thatcher discusses Hong Kong on visit 9/82
- Premier Zhao in talks with Reagan 1/84
- Reagan visits Beijing 4/84
- UK framework for handover of Hong Kong 8/84
- Agrees Hong Kong deal with UK 9/84
- Elizabeth II visits 10/86
- Six die in anti-Chinese riots, Tibet 10/87
- President Bush faces row over dissident on his first visit 2/89
- Threatens to set up own shadow government in Hong Kong 12/92
- Military contacts with US resumed 11/93

China (politics)
- Empress flees from Peking 8/00
- Rebellious officers sentenced 10/00
- Sun Yat-sen captures Mu-chan 10/00
- Leaders executed in public 2/01
- Southern rebellion spreading 3/02
- Kuomintang republicans founded 9/07
- Empress dies, foul play suspected 11/08
- Child Emperor Pu Yi comes to throne 12/08
- 100 die in mutiny 2/10
- Cities revolt against Empire; Sun Yat-sen rises 10/11
- Empire falls; Pu Yi grants constitution 10/11
- Imperial troops kill Republican, Nanking 11/11
- Sun Yat-sen chosen as President 12/11
- Republicans take Nanking, regent resigns 12/11
- Attempt to kill viceroy, Yuan Shi-kai 1/12
- Republic official; north-south split 2/12
- Yuan Shi-kai is effective dictator 2/12
- Martial law declared 3/12
- Yuan Shi-kai loses elections 1/13
- Opening of first parliament 4/13
- Martial law; unrest spreads to Peking 7/13
- Fierce fighting, Nanking and Canton 8/13
- Yuan Shi-kai elected President 10/13
- President Yuan Shi-kai dies 6/16
- Warrant for Sun Yat-sen's arrest 9/17
- Hsu Shi-chang becomes President 9/18
- Sun Yat-sen elected President 4/21
- Communist Party founded 6/21
- Chen Tu-hsiu Communist Party President 7/21
- 20,000 anti-British rioters in Shanghai 9/25
- 17 protesting students shot in Peking 3/26
- Attempted Communist coup in Canton 12/27
- US recognises Chiang Kai-shek government 9/28
- New constitution; President Chiang 10/28
- Chiang Kai-shek wants Henry Ford as aide 10/28
- Nationalist mutiny; martial law declared 3/29
- 12,000 mutinous troops looting towns 10/29
- Communists establish rural base, Kuangsi 4/30
- Yen Hsi-chan's Peking rebel government 9/30
- Chiang Kai-shek becomes Christian 9/30
- Deposed Pu Yi made Emperor of Manchukuo 3/32
- More than 100,000 died on Long March 10/35
- Mao's Communists to set up Soviet state 10/35
- Puppet state Hopei; new unrest, Chahar 11/35
- Chiang joins with Mao to fight Japanese 9/37
- Mao promises to dissolve Red army 9/37
- Mao and Chiang set up National Army 2/46
- Chiang Kai-shek re-elected President 5/48
- Chiang Kai-shek announces his retirement 1/49
- Mao elected chairman of People's Republic 9/49
- Proclaimed a Communist republic 10/49
- Chou En-lai appointed Premier 10/49
- Chiang orders Hainan Island evacuation 4/50
- First five-year plan 1/53
- Congress re-elects Mao President 9/54
- Compulsory military service 2/55
- Manchurian party boss Kao-kang dismissed 4/55
- Mao invites critics: "100 flowers bloom" 4/57
- Reforms to quell strikes and protests 4/57
- Liu Shao-chi to succeed Mao as head 4/59
- Mao stays head of party 4/59
- Ex-Emperor Pu Yi pardoned with 32 others 12/59
- Pu Yi: profile 12/59
- Mao proclaims cultural revolution 8/66
- Rebellion against Mao in Shanghai 1/67
- Mao accuses Liu Shao-chi of coup attempt 4/67
- Lin Piao chosen to succeed Mao 4/69
- Red Guards celebrate cultural revolution 4/69
- Reported that Lin Piao has died in crash 11/71
- Mao says Lin Piao died in air crash 7/72
- Ban on foreigners' travel within China 2/74
- Chou En-lai resigns as PM 9/74
- Premier Chou En-lai dies: profile 1/76
- Hua Kuo-feng acting Premier 2/76
- Chairman Mao dies 9/76
- Power struggle, radical versus moderate 9/76
- Mao's widow Chiang Ching arrested 10/76
- Hua Kuo-feng named as Mao's successor 10/76
- "Gang of Four" radicals condemned 10/76
- "Gang of Four" expelled from Party 7/77
- Teng Hsiao-ping rehabilitated 7/77
- People's Daily denounces Mao's Red Book 10/78
- Purge victims honoured 12/78
- Liu Shao-chi rehabilitated 2/80
- Hua resigns as Premier 9/80
- Chiang Ching guilty of anti-Party crimes 1/81
- Austerity measures; private business 2/81
- Hu Yaobang replaces Hua as chairman 6/81
- Some capitalist measures are introduced 10/84
- Huge student demos for democratic reform 12/86
- Hu Yaobang resigns as party leader 1/87
- Premier Zhao Ziyang replaces Hu 1/87
- Huge student demonstration, Beijing 1/87
- Deng Xiaoping retires as party secretary 11/87
- Army moves into Lhasa, Tibet 3/88
- Private enterprise to be allowed 4/88
- Soviet and Chinese Communist leaders meet 5/89
- Students lead protests in Tiananmen Square 5/89
- Martial law is declared in Beijing 5/89
- Leading reformers stripped of their posts 6/89
- Army massacres many during protests in Tiananmen Square 6/89
- Violence marks anniversary of Tiananmen Square massacre 6/90
- Han Dongfang is freed from jail 5/91
- Major criticises China's political prisoner record 9/91

China, Nationalist
- See Formosa, Taiwan

Chirac, Jacques 11/32, 5/74, 3/77, 3/86, 9/86, 4/88, 5/88, 5/95

Chirico, Giorgio di 12/25, 12/78

Chisholm, Shirley 11/68

Chissano, Joaquim 11/86, 8/92

Choltitz, Dietrich von 8/44

Chou En-lai 10/49, 1/50, 9/50, 11/50, 4/51, 7/55, 1/57, 12/59, 9/69, 2/72, 9/74, 1/76

Christian IX, King of Denmark 1/06

Christian X, King of Denmark 4/47

Christie, Agatha 12/21, 12/26, 11/52, 9/57, 1/76, 12/76, 11/92

Christie, John 12/34, 7/62

Christie, John Reginald 3/53, 4/53, 6/53, 10/66

Christie, Julie 9/65, 4/66, 12/67, 4/83

Christie, Linford 9/88, 1/90, 8/92, 12/93

Christo 12/85

Chrysler, Walter 8/40

Chu-teh 9/54

Chun Doo Hwan 11/88

Church of England
- Dr Randall Davidson, new Archbishop 2/03
- Police crush Protestant riots, Belfast 7/11
- Bishops vote for Lords reform 8/11
- Plans to disestablish Church of Wales 1/12
- Archbishop Canterbury attacks bad clergy 10/25
- Archbishop calls for peace in strike 5/26
- Book of Common Prayer revisions proposed 2/27
- Convocation approves prayerbook changes 3/27
- Archbishop Davidson called "popish" 4/27
- Approves Common Prayer revision 7/27
- Commons rejects "popish" prayerbook 12/27
- Prayerbook: wife no longer "obeys" man 12/27
- Approves amended Prayerbook 2/28
- Dr Lang blasts USSR religous persecution 2/30
- Archbishop of Canterbury discusses sex 4/30
- Archbishop Randall Davidson dies 5/30
- Cautious backing for birth control 8/30
- Old prayerbook preferred by buyers 9/30
- Naughty vicar in London love nest 3/32
- Rector of Stiffkey fights clergyman 6/32
- Rector of Stiffkey guilty of immorality 7/32
- Rector of Stiffkey defrocked 10/32
- Bishop Gordon of Jarrow backs marchers 10/36
- Archbishop supports easier divorce bill 11/36
- Archbishop Cosmo Lang advises abdication 12/36
- Archbishop Cosmo Lang leads Coronation 5/37
- Ex-Rector of Stiffkey mauled by lion 7/37
- Ends rule that women wear hats in church 11/42
- Church bells can be rung again 4/43
- Archbishops warn of "moral laxity" 10/43
- Temple, Archbishop of Canterbury, dies 10/44
- Fisher becomes Archbishop of Canterbury 1/45
- Victory service in Westminster Abbey 9/45
- Condemns divorce reforms 3/47
- Warns on sexual temptation at work 6/47
- Bishop of Birmingham rebuked 10/47
- Dr Fisher prays for King's recovery 9/51
- Elizabeth II is crowned in Westminster 6/53
- Princess Margaret and archbishop talk 10/55
- Arthur Ramsey is Archbishop of York 1/56
- Church blasts premium bonds "gambling" 4/56
- Remarried divorcees may take sacraments 5/57
- Bishop: working mothers "family enemy" 3/58
- Approves of family planning 4/58
- Archbishop Fisher says adultery is crime 11/59
- Pope meets Archbishop Fisher 12/60
- Ramsay becomes Archbishop of Canterbury 1/61
- Ramsay enthroned 6/61
- Consecration of Coventry Cathedral 5/62
- Religious belief remains strong 9/65
- Archbishop of Canterbury meets Pope 3/66
- Death of "Red Dean" Hewlett Johnson 10/66
- Ex-cricketer Sheppard is Bishop of Woolwich 2/69
- Geoffrey Fisher, former Archbishop of Canterbury, dies 9/72
- Ramsay to retire as Archbishop of Canterbury 3/74
- Coggan named as next Archbishop of Canterbury 5/74
- Donald Coggan new Archbishop of Canterbury 1/75
- Cardinal Heenan dies 11/75
- Archbishop Coggan condemns Ugandan death 2/77
- Dr Coggan to retire 6/79
- Robert Runcie becomes Archbishop of Canterbury 3/80
- Queen opens Synod; approves prayerbook 11/80
- Synod votes for women deacons 11/81
- Pope and Runcie pray at Canterbury 5/82
- Runcie comdemns war, Falklands memorial service 7/82
- David Jenkins becomes Bishop of Durham 7/84
- York Minister devastated by fire 7/84
- Bishop of Durham attacks UK social policies 10/84
- Terry Waite frees Britons from Libya 2/85
- Wilfred Wood is first black bishop in UK 4/85
- General Synod approves women deacons 7/85
- Waite secures UK hostage release, Beirut 11/86
- Envoy Terry Waite kidnapped in Beirut 1/87
- Synod votes for women's ordination 2/87
- Memorial service for Zeebrugge disaster 4/87
- Crockford's manual preface attacks Runcie 12/87
- Crockford author Bennett kills himself 12/87
- Plans for ordination of women 6/88
- Synod votes on ordination of women 7/88
- Anglican bishops vote for women priests 8/88
- Dr George Carey elected Archbishop of Canterbury 3/91
- Synod votes to allow ordination of women as priests 11/92
- Ordination of women drives Bishops to Catholicism 2/94

Church, Frank 3/73

Churchill, Clementine Ogilvy 12/77, 1/78

Churchill, Frank 1/38

Churchill, John Spencer 6/92

Churchill, Lady Jennie 6/21

Churchill, Randolph 2/33

Churchill, Winston
- Review of "Savrola", his first novel 2/00
- Doubts about Tariff League 5/03
- Joins Liberal cabinet after election 2/06
- Joins protest against vehicle noise 8/06
- Appointed Privy Councillor 4/07
- Joins Asquith's cabinet 4/08
- Engaged to Clementine Hozier 8/08
- England "best country for rich men" 1/09
- Defends Liberal budget against Lords 9/09
- Act in force, labour exchanges open 2/10
- Supports bill to abolish Lords 3/10
- Announces prison reform 7/10
- Mob prevents his polling day speech 12/10
- Orders the Sidney Street siege 1/11
- Home Secretary; supports Shops Bill 3/11
- Attacks strikers 8/11
- Made First Sea Lord; new policy planned 10/11
- Call to boost Royal Navy to face Germans 11/11
- Meets Irish nationalist leader Redmond 1/12
- Naval expansion "necessity for Britain" 2/12
- Pleased at Britain's Arab oil haul 11/13
- Threatens to resign over naval expenditure 1/14

- Has record naval budget to match Germany 3/14
- Called "Butcher of Belfast" by Carson 4/14
- Hopes Gallipoli landings will end Turkish involvement of war 4/15
- Demoted from Admiralty after disputes 5/15
- Resigns from government; goes to France 11/15
- Returns as head of Air Board 6/17
- Appointed Minister of Munitions 7/17
- Secretary of State for War 1/19
- Plans volunteer army 2/20
- Colonial Secretary 2/21
- Promises to abide by Balfour Declaration 3/21
- Mother, US-born Lady Jennie, dies 6/21
- Made Vice-President of National Liberal Council 1/22
- Loses seat in election 11/22
- Loses seat of West Leicester 12/23
- Douglas sentenced for libel 12/23
- Laments Socialist government 1/24
- Pleased with Irish border "settlement" 12/25
- Edits "Gazette"; papers banned in Strike 5/26
- Meets Mussolini in Italy 1/27
- Post-strike Budget: wine and tobacco duty rises 4/27
- Budget: 325-year-old tea duty abolished 4/29
- Tribute to Balfour 3/30
- Resigns from cabinet over India policy 1/31
- Blames MacDonald for weakness in talks 3/33
- Attack on Indian constitution plan fails 3/33
- "Never before so defenceless" speech 1/34
- Warns on weak defence, German rearmament 11/34
- Defeated as India gets limited home rule 2/35
- King Edward discusses affair 12/36
- Air raid shelters "indispensable" 11/37
- Criticises new Palestine constitution 2/39
- Supports plans for pact with USSR 5/39
- Made First Lord of the Admiralty 9/39
- Visits Supreme Allied War Council 2/40
- Becomes Prime Minister 5/40
- Meets Weygand at Tours 6/40
- Proposes union with France 6/40
- "This was their finest hour" speech 6/40
- Regrets loss of French lives in Algeria 7/40
- Signs alliance with de Gaulle 8/40
- Orders bombing of Berlin 8/40
- Speech on debt of many to "the Few" 8/40
- Promises aid to Greece 10/40
- Elected leader of the Tory Party 10/40
- Says: "We will not fail ..." 1/41
- Announces Yugoslav coup 3/41
- Announces German attack on Crete 5/41
- Promises to help USSR 6/41
- Agrees Atlantic Charter with Roosevelt 8/41
- Warns Japan against war with USA 11/41
- In personal correspondence with Stalin 12/41
- Talks with Roosevelt 12/41
- Gives V sign to US Congress 12/41
- Close relationship with Roosevelt 12/41
- Wins 462 majority in confidence vote 1/42
- Regrets fall of Singapore 2/42
- Worried by Indian civil disobedience 3/42
- Resents criticisms of war effort 3/42
- Signs 20-year pact with USSR 5/42
- Talks in Washington with Roosevelt 6/42
- Defeats Commons vote of censure 7/42
- Summit with Stalin in Moscow 8/42
- Attends Allied conference in Casablanca 1/43
- RAF presents wings on its 25th anniversary 4/43
- Says church bells can be rung again 4/43
- Talks with Roosevelt 5/43
- Historic address to US Congress 5/43
- In Quebec summit 8/43
- Proposes continuing Anglo-US cooperation 9/43
- Meets Stalin and Roosevelt in Teheran 11/43
- Meets Chiang Kai-shek in North Africa 11/43
- Says 700 U-boats have been destroyed 11/43
- Agrees closer ties with Turkey 12/43
- Announces D-Day landings 6/44
- Visits Eisenhower at his HQ 6/44
- Addresses Commons on V-1 bomb attacks on London 7/44
- Visits Allied HQ, Italy 8/44
- Turns Allied attention to Japan 9/44
- Talks with Stalin, Moscow 10/44
- Warning to Zionist gangsters 11/44
- Given freedom of Paris 11/44
- Tries to end Greek civil war 12/44
- Backs Stalin's planned Polish border 12/44
- At Yalta conference 2/45
- Cairo talks with Roosevelt on Japan 2/45
- Speaks about concentration camps 4/45
- Announces Victory in Europe 5/45
- Warns against USSR actions in E. Europe 5/45
- Resigns as Prime Minister 5/45
- Opens election campaign 6/45
- Says Allies sank 700 U-boats during war 6/45
- Leads Tories to defeat in election 7/45
- At Potsdam complains of "Iron Curtain" 7/45
- On dropping of atomic bombs on Japan 8/45
- On British part in "Manhattan Project" 8/45
- Backs Attlee on austerity 8/45
- Awarded Order of Merit 1/46
- In USA, says Iron Curtain has fallen 3/46
- Denounced by Pravda 3/46
- Objects to plan to withdraw from Egypt 5/46
- Calls for united Europe 9/46
- On Wavell's "dismissal" as India viceroy 2/47
- Leads United Europe rally 5/47
- Has hernia operation 6/47
- Publishes "The Gathering Storm" 10/48
- Publication of "Their Finest Hour" 6/49
- On Labour's narrow election win 2/50
- On Korean War 6/50
- Warns of a third world war 7/50
- Urges creation of European army 8/50
- Back as Prime Minister after poll win 10/51
- Promises to dismantle socialism 10/51
- Allows Truman to use UK bases at talks 1/52
- Announces British atomic bomb in House 2/52
- Niece Clarissa marries Anthony Eden 8/52
- Knight Companion of Order of the Garter 4/53
- Left side paralysed by stroke 6/53
- Wins Nobel Prize for Literature 12/53
- Recalls 1943 agreement with US on bomb 4/54
- Signs Potomac Agreement with Eisenhower 6/54
- Unhappy with Sutherland's portrait 11/54
- Angry at US Yalta accusations 3/55
- Resigns premiership at 80 4/55
- Wins Woodford seat 5/55
- Consulted over choice of Eden successor 1/57
- Gets Cross of Lorraine 11/58
- Burglars rob his home of £10,000 3/59
- Will stand for parliament at 85 4/59
- Awarded honorary US citizenship 4/63
- Annouces his retirement from Commons 5/63
- On the assassination of John F. Kennedy 11/63
- Makes last appearance in Commons 7/64
- Ninetieth birthday 11/64
- Dies 1/65

Ciampi, Carlo 4/93

Ciano, Galeazzo 3/03, 10/35, 10/36, 5/39, 3/40, 6/40, 2/43, 1/44

Cicippio, Joseph 8/89, 12/91

Cierva, Juan de la 12/36

Ciller, Tansu 6/93

Cinema
- See also Films
- Special effects in Melies's new film 5/02
- Judge says films need copyright 5/08
- Motion pictures employ 100,000 1/09
- First Hollywood film 3/10
- First talking motion pictures, Edison 8/10
- 80 die in cinema fire, Valencia 5/12
- British Censor of Films appointed 11/12
- Films banned from the Church by Pope 1/13
- Motion pictures "deprive brain power" 9/16
- Motion pictures are "essential industry" 8/18
- Stars form United Artists 4/19
- Mary Pickford marries Douglas Fairbanks 3/20
- Charlie Chaplin divorced 11/20
- "The Thief of Baghdad", with D. Fairbanks 3/24
- "Potemkin" and "Gold Rush" set new boundaries 12/25
- Valentino dies at 31 8/26
- Eastman Kodak working on colour film 8/26
- 50 die in cinema fire, Limerick, Ireland 9/26
- Novarro replaces Valentino as heartthrob 12/26
- "Movietone" synchronises sound with film 1/27
- Lita Grey sues Chaplin for divorce 1/27
- Compulsory quota of British films 3/27
- Garbo: love scenes on and off the screen 7/27
- Lita Grey wins Chaplin divorce, £825,000 8/27
- First talking film "The Jazz Singer" 10/27
- First sound news film "Fox Movietone" 10/27
- Walt Disney's Mickey Mouse in first film 9/28
- In-flight film on Universal Air Line 2/29
- First Academy Awards 5/29
- presented by Fairbanks 5/29
- Joan Crawford marries Douglas Fairbanks Jr 6/29
- 69 children die in Paisley cinema fire 12/29
- British censors change or reject 300 films 3/30
- First talkie with Greta Garbo 12/30
- Dietrich as "Blue Angel" cabaret singer 12/30
- Maurice Chevalier in English film 12/30
- First Hitchcock sound film "Blackmail" 12/30
- Milestone's "All Quiet ..." wins Academy 12/30
- Nazis protest at "All Quiet ..." in Vienna 1/31
- Chaplin's rapturous welcome in England 2/31
- Bill allows movies to be seen on Sundays 4/31
- Shirley Temple, four-year-old filmstar 7/32
- Rin tin tin, filmstar dog, dies 8/32
- First Venice Film Festival 8/32
- Film director Bern commits suicide 9/32
- Swimmer Johnny Weissmuller is new Tarzan 12/32
- Boris Karloff makes Frankenstein his own 12/32
- Comedy: Laurel and Hardy, Marx Brothers 12/32
- King sees first talkies 2/33
- "King Kong", triumph of special effects 3/33
- Dietrich trend: menswear for women 5/33
- Charlie Chaplin marries Paulette Goddard 6/33
- Dancer Fred Astaire on screen 11/33
- Film director Fritz Lang flees from Nazis 12/33
- Mary Pickford wants to divorce Fairbanks 12/33
- Germans ban "Catherine": Jewish actress 3/34
- Leni Riefenstahl films Nazi propaganda 9/34
- Distributors say cinemas may close in UK 11/34
- Mary Pickford divorces Douglas Fairbanks 1/35
- Gracie Fields' record £150,000 contract 2/35
- UK actor predicts colour film revolution 2/35
- Vivien Leigh signs £50,000 film contract 5/35
- Astaire-Rogers in "Top Hat" and "Roberta" 12/35
- Charlie Chaplin stars in his first talkie 2/36
- Television talking debut: film excerpts 8/36
- UK's Pinewood production studios open 9/36
- J. Arthur Rank's chain of Odeon cinemas 9/36
- Pinewood to rival Korda's Denham Studios 9/36
- UK cinema-goers spend £40 million a year 9/36
- Jean Harlow dies of kidney disease at 26 6/37
- Jean Harlow: profile 6/37
- Disney's "Snow White": long cartoon 1/38
- Greta Garbo becomes American citizen 2/38
- Riefenstahl's Olympics footage in Venice 12/38
- New Victoria Theatre cinema, Art Deco 12/38
- Sam Goldwyn controls United Artists 5/39
- Douglas Fairbanks Senior dies 12/39
- Shaw wins Academy Award for "Pygmalion" 12/39
- Vivien Leigh wins Academy Award 3/40
- Marlene Dietrich becomes US citizen 1/41
- Carole Lombard dies in air crash 1/42
- Cary Grant marries Barbara Hutton 7/42
- Errol Flynn cleared of rape charges 2/43
- UK actor and director Leslie Howard dies 6/43
- Shirley Temple marries John Agar 9/45
- Niven's wife dies after party accident 5/46
- Opening of first Cannes Film Festival 9/46
- UK's favourite stars: Mason and Lockwood 4/47
- Reagan warns against Hollywood witchhunt 10/47
- Rita Hayworth to divorce Orson Welles 10/47
- Inquiry into communism in Hollywood, US 10/47
- Ten Hollywood "reds" blacklisted 11/47
- Soviet director Eisenstein dies 2/48
- US director David Wark Griffith dies 7/48
- UK film "Oliver Twist" banned in Berlin 2/49
- US actor Mitchum jailed for pot smoking 2/49
- Olivier's "Hamlet" wins five Oscars 3/49
- Rita Hayworth marries Aly Khan 5/49
- Ingrid Bergman marries Roberto Rossellini 8/49
- TV taking over from cinema, UK 11/49
- Clark Gable marries Lady Ashley 12/49
- Drive-in cinemas in US number 2,200 12/50
- "The Third Man" wins an Oscar 3/51
- US drive-in cinemas 6/51
- Vivien Leigh wins Venice prize for "Streetcar" 9/51
- US critics name "Streetcar" film of year 12/51
- Elizabeth Taylor marries Michael Wilding 2/52
- "Singing in the Rain", film self-parody 3/52
- Oscars for Vivien Leigh and Humphrey Bogart 3/52
- Welles' "Othello" wins Cannes Grand Prix 5/52
- Chaplin investigated as "subversive" 9/52
- Mixed feelings about Chaplin's "Limelight" 12/52
- Kurosawa's debut in Japan 12/52
- Marilyn Monroe's debut in "Niagara" 12/52
- Lesser's three dimensional Stereocinema 1/53
- 20th Century Fox adopts Cinemascope 2/53
- Cinemascope: wide screen, stereo sound 2/53
- Vivien Leigh returns to UK with breakdown 3/53
- Chaplin called a Communist; shuns USA 4/53
- Marilyn Monroe and Jane Russell in film 7/53
- "Genevieve", car-based comedy 12/53
- Marlon Brando in "Julius Caesar" 12/53
- Jack Hawkins "most popular filmstar" 12/53
- Marilyn Monroe marries Joe DiMaggio 1/54
- Auguste Lumiere, French pioneer, dies 4/54
- Marilyn Monroe sues for divorce 10/54
- Brando and Grace Kelly win acting Oscars 3/55
- "On the Waterfront" Oscar for best film 3/55
- Three-dimensional films, special glasses 4/55
- Disneyland amusement park opens 7/55
- James Dean, actor, dies 9/55
- Alexander Korda, pioneer, dies 1/56
- Prince Rainier III to marry Grace Kelly 1/56
- Prince Rainier marries Grace Kelly 4/56
- Marilyn Monroe marries playwright Miller 6/56
- Actor Bela Lugosi dies 8/56
- "Rock Around the Clock" starts "riots" 9/56
- James Dean's last role in Ray's "Rebel" 12/56
- "Sex-kitten" Bardot in "Doctor at Sea" 12/56
- Singers Crosby and Sinatra with 12/56
- Armstrong and Grace Kelly in "High Society" 12/56
- Humphrey Bogart dies of cancer 1/57
- Erich von Stroheim, actor-director, dies 5/57
- Olivier and Monroe star in film 6/57
- Oliver Hardy of Laurel and Hardy dies 8/57
- "... River Kwai" wins three top UK awards 2/58
- "River Kwai" wins three Oscars 3/58
- Ronald Colman, British actor, dies 5/58
- Robert Donat, British actor, dies 6/58
- Bleak Swedish images from Bergman 12/58
- Tati, France's observant director-actor 12/58
- Cecil B. de Mille, top mogul, dies 1/59
- Profile of de Mille, creator of 70 films 1/59
- David Niven and Wendy Hiller win Oscars 4/59
- Brigitte Bardot marries Jacques Charrier 6/59
- Rank shows falling audience; TV's impact 9/59
- Swashbuckling Flynn dies: profile 10/59
- Attenborough and others' Allied group 10/59
- "Ben Hur" wins record 11 Oscars 11/59
- New Wave - Resnais and Truffaut 12/59
- Hitchcock's "Psycho" thrills audience 6/60
- Ingrid Bergman splits with Rossellini 6/60
- Bardot leaves hospital after suicide bid 10/60
- Heart-throb Clark Gable dies 11/60
- Director Mack Sennett dies 11/60
- Vivien Leigh divorces Olivier 12/60
- Gary Cooper dies 5/61
- Loren and Ponti to face bigamy charges 6/62
- Twentieth Century Fox scraps Monroe film 6/62
- Marilyn Monroe found dead in LA home 8/62
- Actor and director Charles Laughton dies 12/62
- Jean Cocteau dies, France 12/63
- Death of US actor Alan Ladd 1/64
- Peter Sellers marries Britt Ekland 2/64
- Liz Taylor and Richard Burton marry 3/64
- Death of US actor Peter Lorre 3/64
- Poitier is first black to win an Oscar 4/64
- Premiere of Beatles' first film 7/64
- Harpo Marx dies 9/64
- US actor Eddy Cantor dies 10/64
- Death of comedian Stan Laurel 2/65
- Julie Andrews wins Oscar in film debut 4/65
- Catherine Deneuve marries David Bailey 8/65
- Hedy Lamarr arrested for shoplifting, US 1/66
- Comic Buster Keaton dies 2/66
- Sophia Loren marries Carlo Ponti 4/66
- Brigitte Bardot marries Guenther Sachs 7/66
- Mia Farrow marries Frank Sinatra 7/66
- Death of US actor Montgomery Clift 7/66
- Death of Walt Disney 12/66
- Death of US actor Spencer Tracy 6/67
- Death of US actress Jayne Mansfield 6/67
- Death of actress Vivien Leigh 7/67
- Sharon Tate marries Roman Polanski 1/68
- Death of UK director Anthony Asquith 2/68
- Death of actor Boris Karloff 2/69
- Katherine Hepburn wins record third Oscar 4/69
- Judy Garland found dead in London flat 6/69
- Sharon Tate killed in Hollywood massacre 8/69
- Vanessa Redgrave wins Cannes award for "Isadora" 12/69
- Maggie Smith wins Oscar for "... Jean Brodie" 12/69
- Police seize Warhol film "Flesh", UK 2/70
- John Wayne wins Oscar for "True Grit" 4/70
- Death of US actor Harold Lloyd 3/71
- Death of French actor Maurice Chevalier 1/72
- Death of US actor Edward G. Robinson 1/73
- Marlon Brando rejects Oscar 3/73
- Taylor and Burton have separated 7/73
- Death of US actress Betty Grable 7/73
- Death of Kung Fu star Bruce Lee 7/73
- Death of US director John Ford 8/73
- Death of US producer Samuel Goldwyn 1/74
- "The Sting" wins seven Oscars 4/74
- UK actress Glenda Jackson wins Oscar 4/74
- Italian director Vittorio de Sica dies 11/74
- Charlie Chaplin knighted 3/75
- Susan Hayward, actress, dies 3/75
- Jodie Foster is child prostitute in film 2/76
- Howard Hughes, tycoon, dies 4/76
- Carol Reed, director, dies 4/76
- Fritz Lang, director, dies 8/76
- Peter Finch, actor, dies 1/77
- "Rocky" gets Oscar for best film 3/77
- Joan Crawford, US actress, dies 5/77
- Roberto Rossellini, director, dies 6/77
- Comedian Groucho Marx dies 8/77
- Director Polanski on underage sex charge 9/77
- Ken Russell's "Valentino" with Nureyev 10/77
- Charlie Chaplin dies 12/77
- "Star Wars", most successful film ever 12/77
- Spielberg's "Close Encounters" sci-fi 12/77
- "Annie Hall", Woody Allen comic romance 12/77
- Finch's best actor award for "Network" 12/77
- Year of "Equus", "Rocky", "Night Fever" 12/77
- Robbers steal Chaplin's coffin 3/78
- Chaplin's coffin found reburied 5/78
- "A Little Night Music", Elizabeth Taylor 12/78
- Jean Renoir, French director, dies 2/79
- Girlfriend sues Lee Marvin for palimony 3/79
- Mary Pickford, US actress, dies 5/79
- John Wayne, actor, dies 6/79
- Actress Jean Seberg dies 9/79
- Merle Oberon, actress, dies 10/79
- Three strong Vietnam films 12/79
- Alfred Hitchcock dies 4/80
- "Kramer vs Kramer" wins Oscar 4/80
- Guinness' award for lifetime achievement 4/80
- Comedian Peter Sellers dies 7/80
- Ex-actor Reagan runs for President 7/80
- McQueen, tough actor, dies 11/80
- US actress Mae West dies 11/80
- Greene novel adapted, "The Human Factor" 12/80
- Grass novel adapted, "The Tin Drum" 12/80
- De Niro wins Oscar for "Raging Bull" 4/81
- Sissy Spacek wins Oscar 4/81
- French director Abel Gance dies 11/81
- William Holden dies 11/81
- Natalie Wood dies 11/81
- "Chariots of Fire", UK Olympic legend 12/81
- "The French Lieutenant's Woman", Pinter 12/81
- Polanski adapts Hardy's "Tess" for film 12/81
- Puttnam's "Chariots of Fire" wins Oscar 3/82
- Jane Fonda accepts Oscar on behalf of her father 3/82
- Austrian actress Romy Schneider dies 5/82
- German director Rainer Fassbinder dies 6/82
- Actress Ingrid Bergman dies: profile 8/82
- Henry Fonda dies after receiving first Oscar 8/82
- Princess Grace dies: profile 9/82
- Meryl Streep in "Sophie's Choice" 11/82
- French director-actor Jacques Tati dies 11/82
- Spielberg's "ET" thrills UK children 12/82
- Jacques Tati: profile 12/82
- US director George Cukor dies 1/83
- "Gandhi" wins eight Oscars 4/83
- US actress Gloria Swanson dies 4/83
- Death of UK actor David Niven 7/83
- Spanish director Luis Bunuel dies 7/83
- Death of US actor/athlete Weissmuller 1/84
- Death of US actor Jackie Coogan 3/84
- US actor Jack Nicholson wins Oscar 4/84
- Shirley MacLaine wins an Oscar 4/84
- Death of UK actress Diana Dors 5/84
- US director Joseph Losey dies 6/84
- Death of UK actor James Mason 7/84
- Death of UK actor Richard Burton 8/84
- French director Francois Truffaut dies 10/84
- "Amadeus" wins eight Oscars 3/85
- Ben Kingsley wins Oscar for "Gandhi" 3/85
- Murdoch buys 50 per cent of 20th Century Fox 4/85
- Murdoch buys all of 20th Century Fox 9/85
- Death of actor-director Orson Welles 10/85
- US actor Rock Hudson dies of AIDS 10/85
- US actor Yul Brynner dies 10/85
- Death of US actor James Cagney 3/86
- US director Otto Preminger dies 4/86
- British actress Anna Neagle dies 6/86
- US actor Cary Grant dies 11/86
- Danny Kaye dies: profile 3/87
- Rita Hayworth dies 5/87
- Fred Astaire dies: profile 6/87
- Director John Huston dies 8/87
- Actor Lee Marvin dies 8/87
- British actor Trevor Howard dies 1/88
- Lord Oliver dies 7/89
- Bette Davis dies 10/89
- Sir Anthony Quayle dies 10/89
- Daniel Day Lewis wins Oscar for role in "My Left Foot" 3/90

- Greta Garbo dies 4/90
- Sammy Davis Jr dies 5/90
- Rex Harrison dies 6/90
- Margaret Lockwood dies 7/90
- Director Sir David Lean dies 4/91
- Dame Peggy Ashcroft dies 6/91
- Actor Bernard Miles dies 6/91
- British film stars call for an end to violence in films 3/93
- Emma Thompson wins Oscar for best actress in "Howard's End" 3/93
- Jane Campion's "The Piano" wins Golden Palm at Cannes 5/93
- Woody Allen loses child custody battle with Mia Farrow 6/93
- Actor Vincent Price dies 10/93

Citrine, Walter 5/26
Citroen, Andre 7/35
Claes, Willy 9/94
Clair, Rene 12/30
Clapton, Eric 8/71, 2/93
Clark, Barney 12/82, 3/83
Clark, J.J. 9/52
Clark, Jim 6/63, 9/63, 5/65, 6/65, 5/66, 10/66, 6/67, 10/67, 4/68
Clark, Joe 6/79
Clark, Kenneth 9/33, 8/54, 2/69, 5/69, 5/83, 3/85, 12/87
Clark, Mark 6/44, 7/53, 4/84
Clarke, Kenneth 11/89, 5/93
Clarke, Mike 12/88
Clarke, Ron 2/65
Clausen, George 12/18
Clavell, James 9/94
Clay, Cassius 1/42, 8/55, 9/60, 10/60, 6/63, 2/64, 5/65, 11/65, 5/66, 4/67, 8/67, 9/75, 4/76, 5/76, 9/76, 9/77, 2/78, 9/78, 6/79
Cleese, John 12/70, 12/75, 12/76, 12/79
Clemenceau, Georges 10/06, 7/09, 1/19, 2/19, 6/19, 10/19, 1/20, 1/23, 11/29
Clerides, Glafcos 7/74, 2/93
Cleveland
Child abuse inquiry 8/87
Cleveland, Grover 6/08
Clifford, Miles 3/48
Clift, Montgomery 7/66
Clifton Brown 8/45
Cline, Frank "Slippery" 5/29
Clines, John 7/18
Clinton, Bill
- Pulls ahead of rivals in Democratic presidential nomination 3/92
- To compete against Bush for presidency 8/92
- Elected 42nd President of the United States 11/92
- Inaugurated as President of the United States 1/93
- Causes chaos at an airport while stopping for a haircut 5/93
- Extends ban on nuclear tests in Nevada 7/93
- At D-Day anniversary in Normandy 6/94
- Humiliated in Congressional elections 11/94
- Vows to help Mexico pay its debts 1/95
- Urges IRA to decommission arms 5/95

Clough, Brian 10/73, 2/79
Clough, Ian 8/62
Clowes, Peter 6/88
Coal Creek 2/04
Coard, Bernard 10/83, 12/83
Coase, Roland 12/91
Cobain, Kurt 4/94
Cobb, John 9/38, 9/47, 9/52
Cobham, Alan 3/26, 10/26
Cobral, Donald Reid 4/65
Coca-Cola
- Britons get their first taste 8/00

Cochet, Henri 7/27, 7/29, 7/32
Cochran, Eddy 10/38
Cochrane, Ray 6/88
Cockcroft, John 12/31, 12/32, 9/67
Cockerell, Christopher 5/58, 4/59
Cocteau, Jean 12/17, 5/27, 10/63, 12/63
Cody, Samuel 8/13
Cody, William 1/17
Coe, Sebastian 9/56, 7/79, 8/79, 7/80, 8/81, 8/84
Coggan, Donald (Archbishop) 5/74, 1/75, 2/77, 6/79
Coghlan, Mary 7/87
Cohn-Bendit, Daniel 5/68, 6/68, 4/69
Colby, William 11/75
Cole, Lester 11/47
Cole, Nat King 4/56, 2/65
Coleman, Ornette 12/58
Coleridge, Peter 3/88
Coleridge-Taylor, Samuel 9/12
Colette 12/20
Colley, George 11/66, 8/79
Collier, Geoffrey 7/87
Collins, Canon 9/61
Collins, General 1/51
Collins, Joan 12/87
Collins, Michael 9/19, 11/20, 12/21, 1/22, 4/22, 7/22, 8/22
Collins, Michael 7/69
Collins, Morris 4/47
Collins, Peter 8/58
Collins, William Alexander Roy 9/76
Collor de Mello, Fernando 9/92
Colman, Ronald 5/29, 5/58

Colombia
- Invades Venezuela 8/01
- Liberals surrender to Panama Governor 11/01
- Rebels defeat government 9/02
- Rival generals in revolt near Panama 10/02
- Signs canal treaty with USA 1/03
- Rejects canal treaty 8/03
- Independent of Panama 1/09
- Pope begins visit to Latin America 8/68
- England soccer captain held for theft 5/70
- Bobby Moore found not guilty of theft 8/70
- "A Hundred Years of Solitude", Gabriel Marquez 12/77
- Gabriel Marquez wins Nobel Prize 12/82
- 50 die after 27-hour siege in Bogota 11/85
- 20,000 killed in mudslide 11/85
- Terrorist car bombs kill 39 5/90
- Drug lord, Pablo Escobar, escapes from prison 7/92

Colosio, Luis Donaldo 3/94
Coltrane, John 9/26, 12/58, 7/67
Colyer, Ken 12/59
Comaneci, Nadia 7/76, 11/89
Comintern
- Russian leaders want European revolution 3/19
- Alleged source of Zinoviev Letter 10/24

Common Market
- See European Community

Commonwealth Games
- Two Welsh weightlifters lose medals after using drugs 1/90

Commonwealth of Independent States
- (Previously USSR)
- Founded 12/91
- State controls on food prices are lifted 1/92
- G7 agree on aid package for former USSR 4/92

Communications
- See Post and Telecommunications

Communist Party (Britain)
- Daily Worker newspaper closed 1/41
- UK government lifts ban on Daily Worker 8/42
- Organiser Springhall jailed for spying 7/43
- Lord Milford is first Communist peer 5/63
- On jailing of Daniel and Sinyavsky 2/66

Compton, Denis 8/37, 6/38, 9/47, 6/52, 8/53
Compton, Edmund 4/67, 11/71
Compton-Burnett, Ivy 9/69
Computers
- See Science and Technology

Conan Doyle, Arthur 12/02, 3/05, 7/30
Condylis, Georgios 8/26
Confederation of British Industry
- Warns that 73,000 manufacturing workers may lose their jobs 1/92

Congo
- See also Congo Belgian, Zaire
- President Kasavubu, Premier Lumumba 6/60
- Katanga secedes under Tshombe 7/60
- Army mutinies against Lumumba 7/60
- Mutiny crushed; white officers sacked 7/60
- Belgian and UN troops file in; whites flee 7/60
- UN chief Hammarskjold arrives 7/60
- Tshombe's Katangan men oppose UN forces 8/60
- Hammarskjold tells Belgium to leave 8/60
- Swedish replace Belgian forces 8/60
- Lumumba calls six months' martial law 8/60
- Sacked Lumumba invades Katanga 9/60
- Colonel Mobutu sacks Kasavubu; third regime 9/60
- Army fights UN troops over Ghana envoy 11/60
- Lumumba escapes from army 11/60
- Lumumba arrested after three-day manhunt 12/60
- Lumumba troops beat up 1,000 whites 12/60
- Savage attack on Europeans 1/61
- Belgian paratroops fly in 1/61
- Patrice Lumumba has died mysteriously 2/61
- Pro-Lumumba and UN troops fight 2/61
- Leaders agree on federation of states 3/61
- Army arrests Moise Tshombe 4/61
- Tshombe released 6/61
- Cyrille Adoula appointed Premier 8/61
- UN crushes Katangan rebels 9/61
- Army offensive against Katangan rebels 10/61
- Tshombe violates cease-fire 11/61
- Tshombe and Kasavubu tied to Lumumba death 11/61
- Bodies of Italian troops sold in market 11/61
- Tshombe gives up plans for new state 12/61
- Independence plan presented to UN 8/62
- Katangan rebels fight UN troops 12/62
- Tshombe flees as UN troops advance 12/62
- Tshombe announces Katanga surrender 1/63
- Tshombe put under house arrest 1/63
- Tshombe sworn in as Premier 7/64
- State forces find 300 bodies in Bukavi 8/64
- European mercenaries aid state troops 8/64
- Belgian paratroops swoop on Stanleyville 11/64
- 2,000 government troops attack rebels 11/64
- Rebels massacre 15 British missionaries 12/64
- Tshombe's party wins election 3/65
- Mobutu heads another army coup 11/65
- Four former ministers sentenced to death 5/66
- Leopoldville renamed Kinshasa 6/66
- Tshombe sentenced to death in absentia 3/67
- Moise Tshombe dies in Algerian jail 6/69
- Changes its name to Zaire 10/71

Congo Reform Association
- Founded 3/04

Congo, Belgian
- See also Congo and Zaire
- King Leopold keeps Congo for himself 7/01
- Reported massacres 12/03
- Stanley, tracer of Congo's course, dies 5/04
- King sets board to check Congo cruelties 9/04
- Vice governor kills himself after report 3/05
- Prince Albert is new Congo sovereign 11/06
- France sides with Britain against Belgium 5/07
- Belgian state takes Congo from king 11/07
- Belgium announces liberalisation 10/09
- Patrice Lumumba founds MNC Nationalists 10/58
- National Movement splits 7/59
- Nationalist Lumumba arrested after riots 11/59
- 75 die in unrest; black police as target 11/59
- Lumumba allowed to speak in public 3/60
- 14 die in unrest; martial law 3/60
- Lumumba controls large areas 5/60
- Independence from Belgium 6/60
- Lumumba blasts Belgian "racist" legacy 6/60
- Congo, Democratic Republic of 6/60

Congo, French
- Joins French Union as a republic 11/50
- Belgians flee from across the border 7/60
- Independent from France 7/60

Conlon, Gerard 10/89
Connally, John 11/63
Connaught, Duke of 1/21
Conner, Dennis 9/83, 2/87
Connery, Sean 8/30, 5/63, 6/89
Connolly, James 5/16
Connolly, Maureen "Little Mo" 9/51, 7/52, 7/53, 7/54, 2/55, 6/69
Connors, Jimmy 7/74, 7/75, 7/78, 7/82, 7/84
Conrad, Charles 11/69
Conrad, Joseph 12/02, 12/15, 8/24
Conroy, John 10/42
Conservative Party (Britain)
- See Britain (politics)

Constantine I, King of Greece 3/13, 9/15, 8/16, 9/16, 6/17, 10/20, 12/20, 9/22, 1/23
Constantine II, King of Greece 3/64, 9/64, 8/65, 4/67, 12/67, 2/81
Constantine, Learie 1/69
Conteh, John 5/73, 10/74
Contenet, Henri 10/02
Coogan, Jackie 3/84
Cook, Arthur James 12/26, 11/27
Cook, Frederick A. 9/09
Cook, Peter 12/61, 4/62, 1/95
Cook, Sylvia 4/72
Cook, Thomas 5/38
Coolidge, Calvin 11/19, 6/20, 3/21, 8/23, 9/23, 11/23, 3/24, 4/24, 7/24, 1/27, 8/27, 12/27, 1/28, 1/33
Cooper, Ashley 7/57, 7/58
Cooper, Charlotte 7/00
Cooper, Duff 6/19, 3/31, 10/38
Cooper, Gary 7/43, 5/61
Cooper, Gordon 5/63
Cooper, Henry 10/58, 1/59, 6/63, 5/66, 3/70, 11/70, 3/71
Cooper, Joyce 2/31
Cooper, Roger 4/91
Cooper, Tommy 2/84
Copland, Aaron 6/42, 10/44, 12/90
Coplon, Judith 6/49
Coppola, Francis Ford 12/72, 12/79
Corbett, Harry 12/89
Corbett, Harry H. 1/64
Corbett, James 4/00
Coren, Alan 3/92
Corey, Elias James 12/90
Cori, Carl 12/47
Cori, Gerty 12/47
Cornell, George 3/69
Cornu, Paul 11/07
Corrigan, Douglas 8/38
Corrigan, Mairead 8/76, 10/77
Cosgrave, Liam 12/73, 3/74, 6/77
Cosgrave, William T. 8/27, 9/27, 10/27, 11/65
Costa Gomez, Francisco da 9/74
Costa Rica
- Warned not to invade Nicaragua by US 6/19
- Helps draft Central American peace plan 1/84
- Signs Central America peace plan 8/87
- Arias proposals basis for Guatemala plan 8/87

Costa, Alfonso 12/17
Costa, Lucio 12/59
Costello, John 2/48, 6/51, 6/54, 1/76
Costello, Lou 3/59
Costelloe, Seamus 10/77
Costner, Kevin 10/91, 12/91
Cotten, Joseph 12/49, 2/94
Cotton, Bill 4/87
Cotton, Henry 6/33, 6/34, 7/37, 7/48
Cotton, Kim 1/85
Coty, Rene 5/58, 12/58
Coubertin, Pierre de 9/25, 9/37
Council of Europe
- First meeting 8/49
- Rumania becomes a member 10/93

Courreges, Andre 11/65
Courrieres
- 1,200 die in mine explosion 3/06

Court, Margaret (nee Smith) 7/42, 6/62, 7/63, 7/65, 7/70, 9/70, 7/71
Courtauld, Samuel 3/32
Courtneidge, Cicely 12/38
Cousins, Frank 7/66, 12/66
Cousins, Robin 1/80
Couve de Murville, Maurice 7/68, 4/69
Coward, Noel 12/23, 12/30, 10/31, 12/31, 8/32, 2/34, 7/41, 12/45, 9/52, 3/73
Cowdrey, Colin 7/91
Cowell, Elizabeth 5/36
Cowley, Annette 7/86
Cox, Archibald 10/73
Cox, James M. 7/20
Coyle, Marian 11/75
Cozette, Philippe 12/90
Crabb, Buster 5/56, 6/57
Craig, Christopher 12/52
Craig, James 5/21
Craig, William 10/68, 9/71
Cram, Steve 8/83, 8/84, 7/85, 8/85, 9/87, 9/88
Cramm, Gottfried von 6/35, 7/37
Cranborne, Lord 4/42
Cranko, John 6/73
Crawford, Hasely 7/76
Crawford, Jack 7/34
Crawford, Joan 6/29, 5/77
Crawford, Marion 12/49
Craxi, Bettino 8/83, 10/85
Creech-Jones, Arthur 8/47
Creek, Hilary 12/72
Cremer, William 12/03
Crenshaw, Ben 9/87
Cresson, Edith 5/91, 4/92
Crete
- Declares independence from Turkey 10/08
- Four powers meet to settle problems 8/09
- Union with Greece pledged; violence 5/10

Crick, Francis 4/53, 12/62
Cricket
- See also Sport
- Record test innings by R.E. Forster 12/03
- England beat Australia in Test - just 1/08
- W.G. Grace's final season 8/08
- W.G. Grace, "finest player", dies 10/15
- Australia crushes England in fifth Test 3/21
- England beat Australia in final Test 8/21
- Russell's record century in South Africa 2/23
- Jack Hobbs's 100th century 5/23
- England regain Ashes after 14 years 8/26
- England win by 289 runs in fifth Test 8/26
- Hobbs breaks Lord's record with 316 runs 8/26
- Lancashire win county championships 8/26
- Australia: Victoria score 1,107 runs 12/26
- BBC's Empire listeners hear scores 5/27
- England get record 636 against Australia 12/28
- England win third Test against Australia 1/29
- England win fourth Test by 12 runs 2/29
- Australia win last Test; England retain Ashes 3/29
- Don Bradman scores record 452 an innings 1/30
- Bradman scores 1,000 runs in England 5/30
- Gloucester's record 627 for two against Oxford 5/30
- Bradman scores record 334 runs against England 7/30
- Bradman scores most in a day at Test 7/30
- Hobbs beats Grace's run aggregate record 8/30
- Australia win the Ashes 8/30
- England win first Test against India 6/32
- Test: pace bowling from Voce and Nissar 6/32
- Hobbs protests at Bowes's high-head bowling 8/32
- England's "bodyline" bowlers upset Test 1/33
- England win third Test in Adelaide 1/33
- Larwood and Voce "bodyline" restricts runs 1/33
- England win the Ashes 2/33
- Australia win fifth Test by 562 runs 8/34
- Jack Hobbs retires at 54: profile 2/35
- Derbyshire are county cricket champions 8/36
- Australia win fifth Test; retain Ashes 3/37
- Yorkshire beats Hampshire in county finals 8/37
- New generation emerges: Compton, Hutton 8/37
- England draw with Australia 6/38
- Denis Compton's first Test century 6/38
- Bradman scores 100 in 73 minutes 6/38
- Australia win fourth Test and Ashes 7/38
- England beat Australia by huge margin 8/38
- Batsman Len Hutton gets record 364 runs 8/38
- England level series at the Oval 8/38
- Denis Compton makes 3,816 runs in season 9/47
- Compton makes 18 centuries in season 9/47
- Don Bradman in last Test match 8/48
- Don Bradman retires 9/48
- Yorkshire and Middlesex tie for CCC 8/49
- Trevor Bailey: ten wickets in an innings 8/49
- England win fifth Test against Australia 2/51
- Len Hutton scores his 100th century 7/51
- Compton hits 100th century 6/52
- Surrey win county championship 8/52
- Yorkshire's Trueman best young cricketer 9/52
- Arthur Wilson's record ten catches 5/53
- Hutton, first professional to lead England 6/53
- England win back Ashes after 20 years 8/53
- Truman, Laker and Lock bowling for England 8/53
- Compton, Edrich, Bailey and Hutton batting 8/53
- Surrey win county championship 9/53
- Surrey win county championship for third time 8/54
- Len Hutton is honorary member of MCC 5/55
- England win Test series against South Africa 8/55
- Surrey wins county championships for fourth time 8/55
- BBC given exclusive television rights 11/55
- MCC insults Pakistani umpire, apologises 3/56
- Jim Laker's 10 for 88 against Australia 5/56
- Len Hutton is knighted in Birthday Honours 5/56
- Laker takes 19 wickets in Test Match 7/56
- Best bowling figures in top class match 7/56
- Pakistan against West Indies, longest innings 1/57
West Indies Sobers scores 365 not out 3/58
- Pakistani Mohammad's longest innings 3/58
- Douglas Jardine dies 6/58
- Surrey win county championship for seventh time 9/58
- Benaud's Australians win back Ashes 2/59
- Yorkshire win county championship 9/59
- England player boycotts South Africa 4/60
- Australia and West Indies Test tie; a first 12/60
- Joe Solomon stops an Australian victory 12/60
- Hampshire win county championship 9/61
- India win Test series against England 1/62
- England win Test series against Pakistan 2/62
Gentlemen-Players match to end at Lord's 6/62
- England win Test series against New Zealand 3/63
- West Indies win Test series against England 8/63
- Sussex win first one-day final, UK 9/63
- Yorkshire are county cricket champions 9/66
- Yorkshire CC refuses to tour Rhodesia 9/67
- Titmus (England) loses toes in accident 2/68
- D'Oliveira dropped from S. Africa tour 8/68
- UK refuses entry to S. African cricketer 8/68
- Vorster bans MCC tour of South Africa 9/68
- Fred Truman (England) retires 11/68
- D'Oliveira gets OBE 6/69
- England tour of East Africa collapses 1/70
- MCC cancels tour of South Africa 5/70
- India have first ever victory in Britain 8/71
- Death of UK cricketer Wilfred Rhodes 7/73
- Queen knights Gary Sobers, Barbados 2/75
- West Indies win first World Cup 6/75
- West Indies beat Australia by 17 runs 6/75
- Australian bowler Gilmour's six for 14 6/75
- Viv Richards' five run-outs 6/75
- Streaking at Lord's 8/75
- Edmonds takes five Australian wickets for 17 8/75
- Test abandoned after pitch is ruined 8/75
- Richards' West Indies beat England 8/76
- Richards' batting score of 291 8/76
- Packer's pirate cricket team, Australia 5/77
- Chappell and Greig to lead Packer teams 5/77
- International body to ban Packer players 7/77
- Tony Greig sacked as England captain 7/77
- Boycott scores his hundredth century 8/77
- Boycott defies Australian pace bowling 8/77
- Packer takes UK authorities to court 8/77
- Packer wins case in High Court; unbanned 11/77
- H.W. Sutcliffe dies 1/78
- Police fire over spectators at Test match, Jamaica 5/78
- Botham's batting and bowling beat Pakistan 6/78
- Gower's first century against New Zealand 7/78
- Boycott sacked as Yorkshire captain 9/78
- Essex are county champions for first time 8/79
- John Arlott's last commentary 9/80
- Botham leads England to beat Australia 7/81
- Botham scores 149; Willis takes eight 7/81
- Botham quits as England captain 7/81
- Boycott suspended for remarks 9/81
- Boycott sets record for Test match runs 12/81
- Illegal tour of South Africa by 12 2/82
- Rebel S. Africa tourers banned for three years 3/82

- India and Pakistan tours rescued? 3/82
- Botham scores 208 against India 7/82
- England beat Australia by three runs 12/82
- Australia regain Ashes 1/83
- Yorkshire CC sacks Geoff Boycott 10/83
- Yorks CC decides not to sack Boycott 1/84
- Viv Richards: one-day innings record 5/84
- England's tour of Bangladesh cancelled 1/86
- English cricketer Jim Laker dies 4/86
- Botham (England) banned for pot smoking 5/86
- Yorkshire CC sacks Geoffrey Boycott 9/86
- Australia win World Cup against England 11/87
- Australia beat Pakistan; England beat India 11/87
- Gatting-Pakistani umpire in public row 12/87
- Graeme Hick scores 405 not out 5/88
- Mike Gatting sacked as cricket captain 6/88
- India to refuse half the English team visas 9/88
- Worcestershire win county championship 9/88
- Australia win second Test at Lord's 6/89
- Worcestershire win County Cricket title 8/89
- English cricketers cause controversy over South African tour 8/89
- British rebel cricketers face riots in Bloemfontein 1/90
- Hadlee becomes first cricketer to take 400 Test wickets 2/90
- England finally beat West Indies 3/90
- England lose Test series 2-1 to West Indies 4/90
- Middlesex beat Sussex to win County championship 9/90
- England win Test match against West Indies 6/91
- Yorkshire breaks tradition by allowing outsiders to play 7/91
- England win final Test against West Indies 8/91
- Pakistan defeats England in World Cup in Melbourne 3/92
- South African cricket rebels have Test ban lifted 7/92
- Pakistan beats England to win fifth Test and series 8/92
- Cricket Board criticizes badly-dressed players 3/93
- Botham announces retirement 7/93
- Gooch resigns as England captain 7/93
- England's Women win Women's World Cup 8/93
- England win first match since July 1992 8/93
- England takes W. Indies to first home defeat for 35 years 4/94
- W. Indies batsman Lara beats record score, out for 375 4/94

Crime
- Child murderess Williams hanged 3/00
- Idolised in "The Great Train Robbery" 6/03
- Massive postal fraud, USA 11/03
- Chicago fire; arrests for manslaughter 12/03
- Chicago fire, mayor blamed 1/04
- New York ship disaster; owners negligent 6/04
- 70,000 fingerprints at Scotland Yard 9/04
- Wife murderer Johann Koch executed, US 2/06
- Caruso fined for sexual harassment 11/06
- British Court of Appeal bill 4/07
- Standard Oil's huge payback to Roosevelt 9/07
- Russian robbery chase, London: three die 1/09
- French murderers publicly guillotined 1/09
- Madame Popova arrested for 300 murders 3/09
- American doctor's wife vanishes, London 1/10
- Radio helps catch murderer Crippen 7/10
- Dr Crippen sentenced to be hanged 10/10
- Robbers kill three policemen, London 12/10
- Russian Jew murdered on Clapham Common 1/11
- Sidney Street siege, three anarchists killed 1/11
- Stinie Morrison convicted of murder 1/11
- Russian "Poison Doctor" admits 40 killed 2/11
- Morrison, Buron's killer, will not be hanged 4/11
- "Mona Lisa" stolen from the Louvre 8/11
- German officer tried for spying, Britain 8/11
- Poet arrested for Mona Lisa theft 9/11
- Naples gangsters guilty of murder 7/12
- Lloyd George's villa wrecked by bomb 2/13
- British ministers in Marconi share deals 3/13
- Mrs Pankhurst found guilty of arson 4/13
- Minister resigns over Marconi scandal 4/13
- Suffragette bomb found in St. Paul's Cathedral 5/13
- Suffragettes guilty of "conspiracy" 6/13
- Mona Lisa recovered; four arrested 12/13
- French minister's wife kills editor 3/14
- Suffragette Mansell jailed for vandalism 5/14
- Mme Caillaux acquitted of editor's death 7/14
- Bath triple killer sentenced to death 7/15
- Buying drinks' rounds is now an offence 10/15
- Conservative "Globe" censored, London 11/15
- Diplomat Casement tried for treason 5/16
- Sir Roger Casement found guilty gets death penalty 6/16
- Darlington ex-MP tried for spying 6/16
- Roger Casement hanged in London 8/16
- Mata Hari gets death sentence for spying 7/17
- Mata Hari executed 10/17
- Czar and family murdered, Ekaterinburg 7/18
- Body of Luxembourg discovered 6/19
- Six Sinn Fein prisoners escape 10/19
- Film comedian Arbuckle on murder charge 9/20
- Bomb kills 30 and injures 300 on Wall Street 9/20
- Russian Brailovsky arrested for bomb 9/20
- Former Dublin Castle keeper murdered 4/21
- Sacco, Vanzetti found guilty of murder 7/21
- First German war criminal sentenced 10/21
- French "Bluebeard" to die for 11 murders 12/21
- "Fatty" Arbuckle acquitted of murder 4/22
- Edith Cavell's betrayer sentenced to die 4/22
- Liberal MP Bottomley on fraud charges 5/22
- London Metropolitan Police Commissioner poisoned 11/22
- Edith Thompson to die for husband murder 12/22
- Mrs Ellis murdered and daughter kidnapped, India 4/23
- Bandits take 150 rail passengers, China 5/23
- Count Krupp von Bohlen sentenced to 15 years 5/23
- Saragosa Archbishop Soldevila murdered 6/23
- Prussian state executioner kills himself 1/24
- First execution by gas chamber, USA 2/24
- Rich Chicago boys killed for "thrills" 5/24
- 12 UK Communists arrested for sedition 10/25
- Woolworth heiress robbed of $750,000, US 10/25
- New York giant liquor ring smashed 12/25
- 200 Mafia leaders arrested, Sicily 2/26
- Four Constables stolen from Royal Academy 3/26
- Prince von Windischgraetz is forger 5/26
- Capone headquarters machine-gunned 9/26
- Mae West jailed for stage indecency 4/27
- Sacco and Vanzetti get death penalty, US 4/27
- Crazy man destroys US school; 42 die 5/27
- Sacco and Vanzetti are executed 8/27
- Baltimore mayor's house bombed 8/27
- Bootleg whisky kills 518 in a year 10/28
- Poisonous liquor sellers up for murder 10/28
- Al Capone's Valentine's Day massacre of nine 2/29
- Chicago gunmen impersonate police 2/29
- Capone jailed for first time on gun charge 5/29
- Al Capone released from prison 3/30
- Capone arrested on perjury charge 6/30
- Judge Patten orders Capone's arrest 2/31
- Capone faces 5,000 prohibition offences 6/31
- Arthur Flegenheimer's tax evasion charge 6/31
- "Legs" Diamond gets four years for liquor crime 8/31
- Capone jailed for 11 years on tax charge 10/31
- "Legs" Diamond shot dead in Albany 12/31
- Dartmoor Prison revolt, 76 hurt, UK 1/32
- Dartmoor governor saved by murderer 1/32
- Lindbergh's baby kidnapped; huge manhunt 3/32
- Capone offers reward for Lindbergh baby 3/32
- Naughty vicar in London love nest 3/32
- Five arrested for Pennine trespassing 4/32
- Body of Lindbergh's baby found in wood 5/32
- Money serial numbers to get baby-killer 5/32
- 23 Dartmoor convicts get revolt sentence 5/32
- Rector of Stiffkey guilty of immorality 7/32
- Doumer assassin Gorguloff death sentence 7/32
- Compton Mackenzie fined on secrets charge 1/33
- Zingara shoots at President Roosevelt 2/33
- Lubbe confesses to Reichstag fire 9/33
- Lubbe gets death penalty for fire 12/33
- French fraud artist Stavisky commits suicide 1/34
- Murderer Dillinger escapes police trap 3/34
- Bonnie and Clyde murder 12; rob banks 5/34
- Bonnie and Clyde killed in police ambush 5/34
- Dillinger kills policeman in bank raid 6/34
- Dillinger killed in Chicago: profile 7/34
- Hauptmann arrested in Lindbergh baby case 9/34
- Hauptmann gets death for baby murder 2/35
- Louisiana Senator Huey Long shot dead 9/35
- 20 accused in Stavisky trial, France 11/35
- 13 "Trotskyites" executed, USSR 2/37
- Spy Klaus Fuchs loses UK citizenship 2/38
- Capone moved to Terminal Island prison 1/39
- Al Capone dies, US 1/47
- Nuremberg inquiry into Katyn Forest massacre 4/52
- Thieves attack postmen and steal £200,000 5/52
- French trial of 25 SS in Oradour killing 1/53
- Bentley hanged despite 200 MPs' pleas 1/53
- Oradour SS trial ends; death penalties 2/53
- Assembly pardons 11 Frenchmen, Oradour 2/53
- Christie's wife Ethel among corpses 3/53
- Christie gets death sentence for four murders 6/53
- Rosenbergs executed; first to die in US for spying 6/53
- Scotland Yard uses television in hunt 10/53
- Ruth Ellis accussed of murdering lover 4/55
- U-2 pilot Powers sentenced for spying 8/60
- US Mafia chief Luciano dies in Italy 1/62
- James Hanratty hanged for A6 murder, UK 4/62
- Profumo sex scandal, UK 6/63
- Great Train Robbery, UK 8/63
- 12 UK train robbers get total of 307 years 4/64
- UK Moors murders: Hindley and Brady charged 10/65
- UK Moors murderers sentenced to life 5/66
- Thalidomide firm charged in W. Germany 3/67
- "Last Exit to Brooklyn" obscenity trial 4/67
- 11-year-old Mary Bell gets life term, UK 12/68
- Kray twins get life terms for murder, UK 3/69
- Manson convicted for Tate murders, US 1/71
- Manson "family" sentenced to death, US 3/71
- Six Watergate burglars sentenced, US 11/73
- John Poulson jailed for corruption, UK 3/74
- Nine jailed for IRA Birmingham bombing 5/75
- Hills guilty of treason for blaming Amin 6/75
- Amin pardons Hills after world pressure 7/75
- Kidnapped Patty Hearst on robbery charge 9/75
- Eight jailed for record bank robbery 11/76
- Thomas McMahon jailed for Mountbatten bomb 11/79
- Sardinian bandits free Schild girl 3/80
- Agca jailed for life for shooting Pope 7/81
- £25m Brinks-Mat gold bullion robbery, UK 11/83
- UK traitor Michael Bettaney jailed 4/84
- McDonald's killer massacres 20, US 7/84
- De Lorean acquitted of drugs charges, US 8/84
- Demjanjuk tried for war crimes, Israel 2/87
- 338 convicted in Palermo Mafia trial 12/87
- Peter Clowes arrested 6/88
- Policeman shot dead in bank hold-up 12/88
- Five school-children shot dead by gunman in California 1/89
- British woman murdered in Kenyan game park 10/89
- Man kills 22 in restaurant in Texas 10/91
- US Jeffrey Dahmer gets life for killing 15 youths 2/92
- Mafia kills Judge Giovanni Falcone 5/92
- Two young boys are charged with murder of two-year-old boy 2/93
- US doctor gunned down by anti-abortionist activist 3/93
- At least 17 die as 51-day siege by cult members ends in Waco 4/93
- Man holds children hostage in Paris school 5/93
- Briton murdered by muggers in Florida 9/93
- Eight works by Picasso and Braque stolen in Sweden 11/93
- Two boys sentenced for Jamie Bulger murder 11/93
- Bodies in "House of Horrors" - Fred West faces 8 charges 3/94
- Trial scenes broadcast for first time from Glasgow 4/94
- Fred West's wife jointly charged on three counts 4/94
- British police truncheon to be replaced 5/94
- Fred West found hanged in his prison cell 1/95
- UK has world's first national DNA database 4/95
- British-born man executed for murder in Georgia 4/95

Crippen, Hawley Harvey 7/10
Cripps, Stafford 1/39, 3/42, 5/42, 11/42, 4/46, 9/47, 7/49, 9/49, 10/50, 4/52
Crisp, Quentin 12/76
Cristiani, Alfredo 3/89
Cristophe (hairdresser) 5/93
Croatia
- Independence recognised by EC 1/92
- Attack on Zagreb ends four-month cease-fire 5/95

Crompton, Richmal 1/69
Cronin, Archibald Joseph 1/81
Cronje, Piet 2/00, 2/11
Crosby, Bing 5/04, 12/27, 4/41, 12/43, 2/46, 7/50, 12/56, 10/77
Croskery, Douglas 8/90
Crosland, Anthony 4/76, 2/77
Cross, J.H. 9/63
Cross, James 10/70, 12/70
Crossman, Richard 10/52, 10/64, 5/71, 4/74
Crowe, Colin 10/71
Cruyff, Johan 7/74, 6/78
Cruz, Joachim 8/84
Cruz, Ramon 12/72
Crystal Palace
- Paxton's edifice burns down; huge crowds 11/36

Cuba
- American law limits economy 3/01
- USA ends occupation 2/04
- USA steps in after President Palma goes 9/06
- US troops arrive to quell unrest 10/06
- Elections under US supervision 8/08
- US marines invade to protect "interests" 5/12
- Declares war on Germany 4/17
- Pan-American Conference in Havana 1/28
- Machado's martial law to stop revolt 8/31
- Fighting in Havana 8/31
- Riots; Batista ousts Machado 8/33
- New President Carlos de Cespedes 8/33
- Army foils "Communist plot" 7/35
- Elected to UN Security Council 10/48
- Trade pact with Britain 8/51
- Batista ousts President Socarras 3/52
- Rebels attack army bases; 55 killed 7/53
- Fidel Castro arrested 7/53
- Castro rebels attack police stations 11/56
- President Batista says Castro is dead 12/56
- Castro is alive, waging jungle warfare 2/57
- Urban sabotage; Batista police torture 2/57
- Rebels seize racing driver Fangio; freed 2/58
- Batista suspends constitution in war 3/58
- 40 die in Havana riots 4/58
- Castro launches offensive from mountains 9/58
- Guevara leads rebel brigade 9/58
- Castro frees 25 hijacked people 11/58
- Batista's sons flee 12/58
- Castro's guerillas take power 1/59
- Rebels overwhelm Batista base, Columbia 1/59
- Batista flees to Dominican Republic 1/59
- UK recognises Castro regime 1/59
- Castro takes oath as Premier 2/59
- Castro will not side with US 3/59
- Castro denies being a Red on US tour 4/59
- Vows to uphold mutual defence treaty 4/59
- Invaders of Panama surrender 5/59
- Agraian reforms 5/59
- Castro's land reforms worry USA 6/59
- Five cabinet ministers resign 6/59
- Says US is meddling by giving asylum 7/59
- Castro ousts Urrutia; becomes President 7/59
- Che Guevara heads national bank 11/59
- 104 government enemies jailed 2/60
- Castro nationalises private businesses 2/60
- Khrushchev backs Cuba to expel US troops 7/60
- Blamed for unrest by Nicaragua and Guatemala 11/60
- US breaks off diplomatic relations 1/61
- Cuban exiles invade Cuba at Bay of Pigs 4/61
- Proclaimed a socialist nation 5/61
- Elections abolished 5/61
- First successfully hijacked plane lands 12/61
- Pope excommunicates Castro 1/62
- US imposes embargo on Cuban imports 2/62
- 1,179 Bay of Pigs invaders given 30 years 4/62
- US-based exiles stage sea raid 8/62
- Cuban missile crisis 10/62
- US imposes arms blockade 10/62
- Kennedy says all missile bases destroyed 11/62
- US lifts blockade 11/62
- 1,113 exiles ransomed for $53 million 12/62
- Claims to have broken two US spy rings 1/63
- Cuban MiGs fire rockets at US boat 2/63
- Castro denounces US aid to Dominica 4/65
- Castro says that Guevara has left Cuba 10/65
- Che Guevara shot dead in Bolivian jungle 10/67
- Former dictator Batista dies in exile 8/73
- Proof of CIA plot to kill Castro 5/75
- Senate shows CIA plotted to kill Castro 11/75
- 15,000 Cuban troops back MPLA in Angola 2/76
- Zaire breaks ties after Shaba attack 4/77
- Castro frees 22 jailed Americans 6/84
- Branded a terrorist state by Reagan 7/85
- Troops to be withdrawn from Angola 8/88
- Signs treaty for withdrawal from Angola 12/88
- Revolution's 40th anniversary 7/93
- Canada lifts its embargo 8/93

Cukor, George 1/83
Cummings, Edward Estin 9/62
Cunard Line
- Price cutting battle with White Line 1/08
- Germany sinks Lusitania; 1,400 die 5/15
- Old Mauretania breaks crossing record 8/24

Cunhal, Alvaro 4/75
Cunningham, Alan 2/41, 1/47, 5/48
Cunningham, Glenn 8/36
Cunningham, John 7/49
Cuno, Wilhelm 11/22, 1/23, 8/23
Cuomo, Mario 7/84, 12/91
Curie, Marie 9/10, 1/11, 12/11, 7/34
Curie, Pierre 4/06
Curran, Peter 7/07
Curren, Kevin 7/85
Currie, Edwina 9/86, 2/87, 12/88
Curry, Don 9/86
Curry, John 1/76, 2/76, 3/76, 4/94
Curtis, Charles 11/28
Curtis, Tony 4/70
Curtiss, Glenn 8/09
Curzon, Lord (George Nathaniel) 2/01, 8/05, 10/19, 1/20, 9/22, 5/23, 3/25
Cusack, Cyril 10/93
Cushing, Peter 8/94
Cuthbert, Betty 11/56
Cutting, Pauline 2/87
Cycling
- Henri Contenet breaks speed record 10/02
- "Tour de France" announced 1/03
- Garin wins his second Tour de France 7/04
- Cornet declared winner of Tour de France 11/04
- European race starts 3/09
- Frenchman Garrigou wins Tour de France 7/11
- Anquetil wins his third Tour de France 7/62
- Tommy Simpson (UK) dies during Tour de France 7/67
- Eddy Merckx becomes world champion 8/67
- Greg LeMond (US) wins Tour de France 7/86
- Irishman Roche wins Tour de France 7/87
- Indurain wins Tour de France 7/94

Cyprus
- Riots; UK commissioner's house burnt 10/31
- Bishop of Kyrenia arrested 10/31
- Pro-Cypriot march on UK embassy; 78 hurt 8/54
- Rioters clamour for union with Greece 12/54
- British arrest 42 in Nicosia and Limassol 12/54
- Turks hit at Greek-owned shops 12/54
- Bomb attacks on British troops 6/55
- Police seize arms in raid on EOKA centres 6/55
- UK invites Greeks and Turks to crisis talks 6/55
- Britain outlaws EOKA guerrillas 9/55
- Mob sacks British Institute, Nicosia 9/55
- UK, Greek and Turkish talks break up 9/55
- UK troops take Nicosia police station 9/55
- Police fight rioters in Nicosia and Lacarna 11/55
- State of emergency after five UK troops die 11/55
- Archbishop Makarios defies Britain 11/55
- British in Cyprus form Home Guard 12/55
- Bombing campaign; arrests of Communists 12/55
- First murder of Turk by EOKA terrorists 1/56
- UK troops capture eight EOKA men and arms 1/56
- Makarios holds secret talks with Harding 1/56
- Makarios goodwill message to Turkish Mufti 2/56
- Bombings continue; power-sharing plan 2/56
- EOKA bomb threat to Governor Harding 3/56
- UK jams Greek radio to Cyprus 3/56
- Greeks riot; clash with Turks in streets 3/56
- British deport Makarios on EOKA charge 3/56
- First UK civilian killed by EOKA 4/56
- All over the age of 12 to carry identity cards 5/56
- £10,000 reward to catch EOKA's Grivas 5/56
- Bomb kills US vice-consul 6/56
- Constitution, prelude to independence 7/56
- Turkish Premier wants Britain to stay 7/56
- UK troops hurt in toffee tin blast 9/56
- Grivas diary buried by EOKA men 9/56
- Possibility of partition 12/56
- Greece rejects new NATO peace plan 3/57
- Governor rejects EOKA cease-fire offer 3/57
- State of emergency relaxed 4/57
- State of emergency revoked 8/57
- Pro-EOKA protesters are teargassed 10/57
- Turks riot in Nicosia; 100 hurt, two die 1/58
- Governor Foot back from Ankara talks 1/58
- UK peace plan rejected; riots and curfew 6/58
- Fears of communal Greek-Turk warfare 6/58
- 31 die in week of violence 7/58
- Eight die in one day 7/58
- EOKA boss Grivas orders cease-fire 8/58
- Macmillan leaves after peace mission 8/58
- Britain holds 2,000 Greek EOKA suspects 8/58
- Grivas calls off truce 9/58
- EOKA renews attacks on Britons and informers 10/58
- Turkish youths riot in Nicosia 10/58
- Greeks and Turks reject seven-year British plan 10/58
- British kill EOKA leader Matsis 11/58
- Peace deal: Greek President, Turkish Vice-President 2/59

- Peace deal: end to British rule; keeps bases 2/59
- British deal rules out Enosis with Greece 2/59
- 12 die in air crash; Turkish Premier survives 2/59
- Makarios welcomed back to Cyprus 3/59
- EOKA accepts London agreement 3/59
- Grivas flies to Greece 3/59
- Queen promises independence 10/59
- Makarios elected President by landslide 12/59
- Makarios praises EOKA "heroes" 12/59
- Republic under Makarios and Dr Kutchuk 8/60
- Ex-Governor Foot calls for peace 8/60
- Queen meets Makarios 1/61
- Applies to join Commonwealth 2/61
- Pacts with Britain, Greece and Turkey in danger 1/64
- Turks walk out of Cyprus talks, London 1/64
- 21 killed when Greeks and Turks clash 2/64
- 1,500 British troops flown in 2/64
- United Nations troops fly in 3/64
- UK troops become involved in fighting 3/64
- UK peacekeeping troops flown home 5/64
- Turkish planes raid northern Cyprus 8/64
- LBJ calls for truce 8/64
- Turks and Greeks accept cease-fire 8/64
- Greeks end food blockade 8/64
- 15,000 demand removal of UK bases 10/64
- Makarios escapes assassination attempt 3/70
- Makarios re-elected President 2/73
- Coup by Greek officers in National Guard 7/74
- Turks invade north of island 7/74
- Turks and Greeks fight 7/74
- Turks and Greeks sign peace deal, Geneva 7/74
- New constitution agreed 7/74
- Turks halt UN relief convoys 7/74
- Greeks flee as Turks invade Famagusta 8/74
- Mass Turkish grave uncovered 9/74
- Makarios returns 12/74
- Denktash declares Turkish Cyprus 2/75
- Archbishop Makarios dies of heart attack 8/77
- 15 Egyptians die trying to free hostages 2/78
- Turkish Republic of Cyprus declared 11/83
- UK charges seven servicemen with spying 4/84
- Briton who joined PLO gets life term 12/85
- Hijacked Kuwaiti jumbo lands at Larnaca 4/88
- Glafcos Clerides wins presidential elections 2/93

Czech Republic (Czechland)
- Czechs and Slovaks split, creating two new nations 1/93

Czechoslovakia
- See also Slovakia and Czech Republic (Czechland)
- Masaryk calls for Czech independence 11/15
- Asquith and Poincare hail "Czechoslovakia" 9/16
- Masaryk sentenced to death in absentia 12/16
- Czech Legion joins right to fight Russia 6/18
- US recognises Czech National Council 7/18
- UK recognises state of Czechoslovakia 8/18
- Formally recognised by US 9/18
- Republic officially proclaimed 10/18
- Masaryk is first President 11/18
- President Masaryk, Foreign Minister Benes 5/20
- Eduard Benes becomes Premier 9/21
- Alliance with France 1/24
- Czech is official language 2/26
- Tomas Masaryk re-elected President 5/27
- Masaryk elected President for fourth time 5/34
- Germany wants Sudetenland 3/35
- Nazi gains in elections 5/35
- Illicit arms arrive in embargoed Italy 11/35
- President Masaryk resigns 12/35
- Eduard Benes elected successor 12/35
- Ex-President Tomas Masaryk dies 9/37
- Lord Halifax discusses Germany's demands 11/37
- Chamberlain may defend Czechoslovakia 3/38
- Premier Hodza: We will defend ourselves 3/38
- Joint Anglo-French defence pact 4/38
- 40,000 troops to Austro-German border 5/38
- All Czechs aged up to 60 for defence training 5/38
- Czech-British Bren gun enters service 6/38
- German Sudeten Party gains in elections 6/38
- UK Chancellor Simon warns Germany 8/38
- Czech airliner crashes, Germany; 13 die 8/38
- Sudeten Germans talk to President Benes 8/38
- Sudeten mass rallies for German union 9/38
- Martial law in Sudetenland; Hodza appeal 9/38
- Accepts UK-French plan to cede Sudetenland 9/38
- Jan Syrovy replaces Hodza; mobilisation 9/38
- Hitler calls for four-power conference 9/38
- Munich agreement; Czechs absent from talks 9/38
- Benes offers Sudetens self-government 9/38
- Germans take Sudetenland; Benes resigns 10/38
- Poland annexes Teschen in Czech Silesia 10/38
- Hungarians want to annex southern region 10/38
- Hungarians reject Czech proposals 10/38
- Anger at "abandonment" by France and UK 10/38
- Henlein Nazis accompany Hitler march 10/38
- Loses Ruthenia and Slovakia to Hungary 11/38
- Germans march into Bohemia 3/39
- Hungarians occupy Ruthenia 3/39
- Bohemia-Moravia made German protectorate 3/39
- Nazis enter Prague 3/39
- Slovakia Premier Tiso sacked 3/39
- Gestapo executes Czech students 11/39
- Jews ordered to cease economic activities 2/40
- Slovakia joins the Axis 11/40
- Heydrich wounded; state of emergency 5/42
- Heidrich dies from wounds 6/42
- Nazi massacre in village of Lidice 6/42
- Exiled leader Benes signs pact with USSR 12/43
- German troops enter Slovakia 3/44
- Exiled Czechs sign convention with USSR 5/44
- Russians sweep across border 10/44
- Eduard Benes returns to Prague 5/45
- Soviet troops liberate Prague 5/45
- Cedes Carpathian Ruthenia to USSR 6/45
- Germans and Hungarians deprived of citizenship 8/45
- Communists win general election 5/46
- Rejects Marshall aid plan 7/47
- 142 arrested in plot to murder Benes 9/47
- Communists take over in Slovakia 1/48
- Communist coup 2/48
- Masaryk dies after falling out of window 3/48
- Adopts Soviet-style constitution 5/48
- Benes resigns as President; Gottwald takes over 6/48
- Mindszenty held for anti-government plot 12/48
- Bishops accuse government of persecution 6/49
- Ends friendship pact with Yugoslavia 10/49
- Church marriages no longer recognised 11/49
- Ends cultural agreement with UK 5/50
- Penal codes on USSR model introduced 6/50
- 25 flee to West on runaway train 9/51
- President Klement Gottwald dies 3/53
- Joins Warsaw Pact 5/55
- Zapotocky dies; Novotny becomes President 11/57
- Novotny re-elected President 11/64
- Alexander Dubcek becomes Premier 1/68
- Press censorship relaxed 3/68
- Former secret police head arrested 3/68
- Novotny resigns as President 3/68
- Soviet troops move up to Czech border 5/68
- Kosygin in talks with Dubcek 5/68
- Russian tanks mass on Czech border 7/68
- Dubcek in talks with Warsaw Pact leaders 7/68
- Russian tanks roll into Prague 8/68
- Tito visits Prague 8/68
- Dubcek signs 20-year pact with Rumania 8/68
- Warsaw Pact tanks cross the border 8/68
- One-hour strike in protest at invasion 8/68
- Censorship imposed; meetings banned 9/68
- Foreign Minister Halek resigns 9/68
- More press curbs 10/68
- Warsaw Pact troops to stay in country 10/68
- Huge demonstration against Soviet occupation 10/68
- Soviet flags burned; battles with police 11/68
- Students occupy Prague university 11/68
- Student Jan Palach sets fire to himself 1/69
- Jan Zajic burns himself to death 2/69
- Czechs beat USSR at ice hockey, Sweden 3/69
- USSR "normalisation" campaign 4/69
- Dubcek sacked as Communist Party leader 4/69
- Gustav Husak installed as leader 4/69
- Over 1,000 detained in two days 5/69
- Prague protests on invasion anniversary 8/69
- Soviet tanks enter Prague 8/69
- Dubcek ousted from Communist praesidium 9/69
- Ban on travel to the West 10/69
- Dubcek made ambassador to Turkey 12/69
- Dubcek suspended from Communist Party 3/70
- Signs friendship treaty with USSR 5/70
- Dubcek expelled from Communist Party 6/70
- Tennis star Navratilova defects to USA 9/75
- Charter 77 academics make rights charter 1/77
- Dissidents arrested over civil rights 1/77
- Dissident Potocka interrogated; dies 3/77
- Vladimir Remek is first spaceman from neither USSR or US 3/78
- Jaroslav Seifert wins Literature Nobel 12/84
- Navratilova plays tennis in native land 7/86
- Freedom demonstrations in Prague 10/88
- Dubcek attacks Soviet repression 11/88
- Demonstrators mar May Day in Prague 5/89
- Dissident Vaclav Havel is freed from prison 5/89
- Police violence against demonstrators 11/89
- General strike develops into anti-Communist victory 11/89
- Alexander Dubcek returns to Prague 11/89
- Marian Calfa replaces Ladislas Adamec as premier 12/89
- Gustav Husak resigns as President 12/89
- Vaclav Havel becomes new President 12/89
- Vaclav Havel is re-elected as President 7/90
- President Vaclav Havel resigns 7/92
- Czechs and Slovaks split, creating two new nations 1/93

D

Dacca 5/02
Dachau
- First concentration camp opened 3/33

Dacko, David 9/79
Dacre, Lord
- See Trevor-Roper Hugh

Dahl, Roald 12/90
Dahmer, Jeffrey 7/91, 2/92
Dahomey
- Becomes a French Union republic 12/58

Dail (Irish parliament)
- See Ireland

Daily Illustrated Mirror
- Colour photographs in a newspaper 3/04

Daily Mirror (newspaper)
- Journalist fired over Israeli spy scandal 10/91
- Owner, Robert Maxwell, found drowned near Canary Islands 11/91

Daimler
- See Cars

Daimler, Gottlieb 3/00
Daladier, Edouard 1/33, 10/33, 2/34, 4/38, 9/38, 3/39, 10/39, 2/40, 3/40, 8/40, 10/41, 4/43, 5/45, 10/70
Dalai Lama
- See also Tibet 2/40, 10/50, 12/50, 5/51, 7/58, 3/59, 4/59, 10/89, 12/89

Daley, Richard 8/68
Dalglish, Kenny 5/78, 4/89
Dali, Salvador 5/04, 12/36, 12/56, 1/89
Dalmas, Yannick 6/92
Dalton, Hugh 10/45, 6/47, 8/47, 9/47, 11/47, 5/48, 9/52
Dalyell, Tam 6/62, 8/84
Damascus
- Falls to Lawrence and Arab horsemen 10/18

Dana, Mufti Mehmed 2/56
Da Nang
- Falls to North Vietnamese 3/75

Dance
- Cakewalk craze 6/00
- "Danses-Idylles", Isadora Duncan 5/03
- Mata Hari's success 5/05
- "Obscene" Isadora Duncan banned 1/06
- Diaghilev's Ballets Russes in Paris 5/09
- "Les Sylphides" performed by Ballets Russes 6/09
- Choreography, costume and decor sensations by Ballets Russes 12/09
- Ballets Russes' new season includes "Firebird" 6/10
- Tamara Karsavina dances leading role in "Firebird" 12/10
- First performance of "Daphnis et Chloe" ballet 4/11
- First performance of Stravinsky's "Petrushka" 6/11
- "Petrushka" is a success 12/11
- Nijinsky dances in "L'Apres Midi d'un Faune" 5/12
- Ballets Russes performs "Daphnis et Chloe" in Paris 6/12
- Anna Pavlova dances celebrated "Dying Swan" 12/12
- "Firebird" and "Petrushka" come to Britain 2/13
- Isadora Duncan cancels performances after children's deaths 4/13
- Nijinsky dances in Debussy's "Jeux" 5/13
- Premiere of "The Rite of Spring" 5/13
- Kaiser orders army not to dance tango 11/13
- Wild rhythms of "Rite" excite Paris 12/13
- Drury Lane season of Russian ballet with Karsavina 12/14
- Ballets Russes perform "Parade"; music by Satie 5/17
- Premiere of "The Wooden Prince"; music by Bartok 5/17
- "Parade" inspired by Cocteau's circus ballet 12/17
- "A Soldier's Tale", Stravinsky 9/18
- "La Boutique Fantasque"; Leonid Massine 12/19
- "The Three-Cornered Hat"; Manuel de Falla 12/19
- Valentino: dancer turned filmstar 10/21
- Marathon dancing, US; injuries reported 4/23
- Dancing Masters condemn tango and foxtrot 5/23
- Ballets Russes perform "Les Noces"; music by Stravinsky 6/23
- America's Charleston overwhelms Britain 9/25
- Josephine Baker in "La Revue Negre" 10/25
- Isadora Duncan's death: profile 9/27
- Ida Rubinstein dances to Ravel's "Balero" 12/28
- Sergei Diaghilev dies: profile 7/29
- Anna Pavlova dies: profile 1/31
- "Job", Ralph Vaughan Williams 12/31
- De Valois's company transfers to Sadler's Wells 12/31
- "The Rio Grande" by Frederick Ashton 12/31
- Walton's "Facade" danced by Markova 12/31
- Ballroom dancing inspires lower-heeled shoes 10/35
- "Romeo and Juliet": Prokofiev ballet 12/35
- Margot Fonteyn's winning "Giselle" 1/37
- "Rodeo" by Aaron Copland 6/42
- Copland's "Appalachian Spring", US 10/44
- "The Red Shoes" (film) 12/49
- Death of Vaslav Nijinsky 4/50
- Bolshoi Ballet's first visit to London 12/56
- Royal Ballet formed at Sadler's Wells 1/57
- Margot Fonteyn jailed; Panama coup drama 4/59
- Fonteyn reunited with husband, Dr Arias 6/59
- Margot Fonteyn dances "Ondine" 12/59
- Rudolf Nureyev defects in Paris 6/61
- Fonteyn and Nureyev: "Romeo and Juliet" 12/65
- Death of US dancer Ruth St. Denis 7/68
- London Contemporary Dance Company 9/69
- Natalia Makarova defects to West 9/70
- Ashton retires from Royal Ballet 12/70
- Kenneth Macmillan becomes head of Royal Ballet 12/70
- British dancer John Cranko dies 6/73
- USSR Kirov Ballet stars, the Panovs, defect 6/74
- USSR dancer Baryshnikov defects to West 6/74
- Fred Astaire dies: profile 6/87
- Dame Margot Fonteyn dies 2/91

Daniel, Yuri 2/66
Daniloff, Nicholas 9/86
D'Annunzio, Gabriele 9/19, 12/20, 3/24, 3/38
Danzig
- Allies and Germany sign Free City treaty 4/19
- Freedom of movement to and from Poland 2/27
- Poland signs greater use treaty 8/33
- Police seize Jewish bank deposits 11/37
- Britain warns Germany on use of force 5/39
- Germany steps up activities 7/39
- 2,000 Nazi guards arrive from Germany 7/39
- Captured by Russians 3/45

D'Aosta, Duke 5/41
Daoud, Abu 1/77
Darcy, Eamonn 9/87
Dardanelles
- See World War I

Dario, Ruben 2/06
Darlan, Jean 11/42, 12/42
Darnard, Joseph 10/45
Darvall, Denise 12/67
Das, Ram 4/30
Da Silva, Ernesto 6/76
Daugherty, Harry M. 3/24
Davey, Timothy 3/72, 5/74
Davidson, George 7/08
Davidson, Harold 3/32, 10/32, 7/37
Davidson, Randall 2/03, 5/30
Davies, Beryl 5/53
Davies, Clement 10/38, 3/62
Davies, Franklin 6/76
Davies, John 6/71
Davies, Laura 7/87
Davies, Lynn 10/64
Davies, Marion 8/51
Davies, Mark 6/91
Davies, Stanley Clinton 3/78
Davis, Angela 6/72
Davis, Bette 4/08, 10/89
Davis, Colin 12/68
Davis, Dwight 2/00
Davis, George 8/75, 9/77, 7/78
Davis, James 12/61
Davis, Joe 1/55
Davis, John 7/24
Davis, Laura 9/93
Davis, Miles 5/26, 12/58, 12/74, 9/91
Davis, Nicholas 10/91
Davis, Sammy, Jr 5/90
Davis, Steve 4/81, 5/83
Davison, Emily 6/13
Davison, Ian 12/85
Davydova, Yelena 7/80
Dawes, Charles 12/25
Dawes, William 11/23, 4/24
Day Lewis, Cecil 2/38, 1/68, 5/72
Day Lewis, Daniel 3/90, 12/92
Day, Robin 4/59, 10/59
Dayan, Moshe 5/15, 1/58, 6/67, 7/67, 3/69, 2/73, 6/73, 5/74, 6/81
Dead Sea Scrolls 2/60
Deakin, Arthur 5/55
Dean, Brenda 3/84
Dean, Christopher 2/81, 2/84, 1/94, 3/94
Dean, James 2/30, 9/55, 10/55, 12/56, 12/59
Dean, John 4/73, 6/73, 8/74
Deat, Marcel 11/33
De Beauvoir, Simone 1/08, 12/49, 4/86
De Bono, Emilio 10/35
Debray, Regis 10/67
Debre, Michel 12/58, 1/60, 2/62, 4/62
Debs, Eugene 11/12, 10/26
Debussy, Claude 2/10, 5/13, 3/18
Decker, Mary 8/83, 8/84
De Cuellar, Javier Perez 9/90, 1/91, 8/91
De Falla, Manuel 12/19, 11/46
Deferre, Gaston 4/69
De Forest, Lee 12/06
Degas, Edgar 9/17
De Gaspari, Alcide 6/46, 2/47
De Gaulle, Charles
- In UK, urges French Resistance 6/40
- Signs alliance with Churchill 8/40
- Lands in Senegal with Free French troops 9/40
- Abandons attack on Dakar 9/40
- Free French enter French Somaliland 4/41
- French provisional government in exile 9/41
- Calls for national strike in France 10/41
- Free France forces renamed "Fighting France" 7/42
- Urges France on to victory 11/42
- At Allied conference in Casablanca 1/43
- Sets up provisional government in Algiers 5/43
- Insists on dismissal of all Vichy collaborators 6/43
- Sets up French Committee of Liberation 6/43
- Allies recognise Algeria-based CFLN 8/43
- Sets up Consultative Assembly 9/43
- Opens Consultative Assembly, Algiers 11/43
- Becomes head of Free French forces 4/44
- Plans for French provisional government 6/44
- Visits liberated areas of France 6/44
- Proclaims Fourth French Republic 8/44
- Government is recognised by Allies 10/44
- Seeks French occupation zone in Germany 11/44
- Signs alliance treaty with Stalin 12/44
- Nationalises Renault factories 1/45
- Nationalises Air France 4/45
- Reasserts power in Syria and Lebanon 5/45
- Reprieves Petain from death sentence 8/45
- Elected President of provisional government 11/45
- Forms new cabinet; includes Communists 11/45
- Resigns; announces his retirement 1/46
- Calls for general election 10/47
- Calls for new constitution 10/47
- Attacks European Defence Community 2/53
- Recalled as French PM; Algerian crisis 5/58
- France approves his new constitution 9/58
- UNR wins 198 seats in National Assembly 11/58
- Elected President 12/58
- Inaugurated as President 1/59
- Offers Algeria a referendum 9/59
- Granted emergency powers for one year 2/60
- Visits Britain 4/60
- Attends Big Four talks in Paris 5/60
- Algerian visit provokes mixed reception 12/60
- Receives mandate for Algerian home rule 1/61
- Calls on French to rout Algerian rebels 4/61
- Orders blockade of Algeria 4/61
- Opposes UK bid to join Common Market 7/61
- Survives attempt on his life by Salan 9/61
- Arrives in London for talks with Macmillan 11/61
- More French troops to leave Algeria 12/61
- Security crackdown on OAS terrorists 1/62
- Relying on army loyalty in Algiers 2/62
- Pledges to bring peace to Algeria 2/62
- Meets Adenauer on European unity 2/62
- Orders troops to crush OAS 3/62
- Proclaims independence of Algeria 7/62
- Escapes another attempt on his life 8/62
- Plans to change French constitution 8/62
- Gaullists win National Assembly majority 11/62
- Talks over British entry to EEC end in deadlock 12/62
- Dashes Britain's EEC hopes 1/63
- Rejects US offer of Polaris 1/63
- Political and military pact with Adenauer 1/63
- Police foil assassination attempt 2/63
- Will not sign test ban treaty 8/63
- In talks with Ben Bella 3/64
- Pays tribute to Churchill 1/65
- Condemns US involvement in Vietnam 4/65
- Meets Harold Wilson for Vietnam talks 4/65
- Condemns US intervention in SE Asia 6/65

- Condemns US involvement in Latin America 6/65
- Says France will leave NATO 9/65
- To stand for re-election 11/65
- Re-elected President with low majority 12/65
- Offers Ho Chi Minh aid to end war 2/66
- Launches France's first nuclear sub 3/67
- Rebuffs Wilson on British entry to EEC 5/67
- Raises hopes of Quebec separatists 7/67
- Visits Poland 9/67
- Vetoes Britain's entry to EEC 11/67
- Faces crisis caused by riots and strikes 5/68
- Tells France he will not quit 5/68
- Takes measures to counter unrest 5/68
- Calls general election 5/68
- Landslide win in election 6/68
- Bans open-air demonstrations 6/68
- Resigns after referendum defeat 4/69
- Dies 11/70

De Gennes, Pierre-Gilles 12/91
De Grey, Roger 12/84
De Havilland
- (See Aircraft)

De Havilland, Geoffrey 5/65
Dehmelt, Hans 12/89
Dejaco, Walter 3/72
Dejoie, Louis 7/58
De Klerk, Frederik W. 2/89, 9/89, 2/90, 5/90, 2/91, 3/92, 6/92, 11/92, 3/93, 10/93
De la Billiere, Peter 2/91
Delage, Guy 2/95
Delagrange, Leon 5/08, 1/10
Delaney, Shelagh 12/59
Delany, Ron 7/57
Delcasse, Paul Theophile 4/04, 7/09
Delegado, Alfredo 12/72
Delgado, Pedro 7/88
Delius, Frederick 2/10, 12/14, 6/34, 12/34
Dell, Christian 12/26
Dell, Edmund 1/68
Delors, Jacques 7/88, 6/90, 6/94
De Lorean, John 4/81, 10/81, 11/81, 2/82, 10/82, 8/84, 9/85, 12/86
Delvaux, Paul 7/94
De Mille, Cecil B. 4/27
Demirel, Suleyman 3/71, 5/93, 6/93
Demjanjuk, John 2/86, 2/87, 4/88, 7/93
Dempsey, Jack 7/19, 7/21, 7/23, 9/26, 9/27, 2/28, 5/83
Demtu, Ras Desta 2/37
Dench, Judi 5/89, 12/89
Deneuve, Catherine 10/43, 8/65
De Nicola, Enrico 6/46
Deng Xiaoping 7/77, 12/86, 11/87, 5/89, 6/89
Denikin, Anton 10/19, 2/20
De Niro, Robert 4/79, 12/79, 4/81
Denktash, Rauf 1/58, 2/75, 11/83
Denmark
- See also World War II
- King Christian IX dies 1/06
- Universal suffrage for taxpayers over 25 4/08
- Corporal punishment abolished 3/11
- Defence league with Dutch, Swedes and Swiss 6/14
- Grants Iceland independence 12/18
- Abandons gold standard 9/31
- The Hague declares Greenland Danish 4/33
- Jenny Kammersgaad is first to swim Baltic 7/38
- Non-aggression pact signed with Germany 5/39
- Reaffirms neutrality 1/40
- Protests at sinking of neutral ships 2/40
- Invaded by Germany 4/40
- War trade pact made with Britain 4/40
- Britain occupies Iceland and Faroes 5/40
- Joins Axis 11/41
- Johannes Jensen wins Literature Nobel 12/44
- King Christian X dies 4/47
- 150 die when liner hits mine 6/48
- Agrees to join NATO 3/49
- Signs North Atlantic Treaty 4/49
- Currency devalued 9/49
- Death of nuclear physicist Niels Bohr 11/62
- Six-day "Sex Fair" in Copenhagen 11/69
- Talks on EEC entry open 6/70
- Signs treaty of entry to EEC 1/72
- King Frederik IX dies 1/72
- Margrethe becomes Queen 1/72
- Referendum goes in favour of EEC entry 10/72
- Joins EEC 1/73
- Danish trawlers banned from UK waters 1/83
- UK arrests Danish trawler captain Kirk 1/83
- Unknown Mozart symphony found 2/83
- Niels Jerne wins Medicine Nobel 12/84
- Danes vote "No" to Maastricht treaty 6/92
- Voters approve of Maastricht treaty in second referendum 5/93

Denning, Lord 9/63, 2/80, 9/82
Depardieu, Gerard 12/48, 12/90, 12/92
Depth records
- Two UK divers reach 1,000 ft underwater 12/62

Derain, Andre 10/05, 9/54
De Rivera, Miguel Primo 9/23
Dernley, Syd 11/94
Derry, John 9/52
Desai, Morarji 1/66, 3/77
De Salvo, Albert 2/67
De Sancha, Antonia 9/92
Deschanel, Paul 1/20, 5/20, 9/20, 4/22
Desert Storm, Operation 1/91, 2/91
De Sica, Vittorio 7/02, 11/74
De Stempel, Susan 4/90
Deutch, John 3/95
Deutschland III (liner) 6/00
De Valera, Eamon 7/17, 3/18, 5/18, 4/19, 5/21, 7/21, 8/21, 9/21, 1/22, 5/23, 7/24, 8/27, 9/27, 3/29, 3/32, 4/32, 1/33, 7/37, 1/38, 4/38, 5/38, 6/39, 6/43, 3/44, 6/44, 2/48, 6/51, 3/57, 7/57, 1/59, 6/59, 6/66, 6/73, 8/75
De Valois, Ninette 12/31
De Vlaminck, Maurice 10/05
Devi, Phoolan 2/94
Devlin, Bernadette
- See also McAliskey Bernadette 4/69, 12/69, 6/70, 10/70, 1/72

Devlin, Lord 8/92
De Vries, Hugo 3/00
De Vries, William 12/82
Dewar, Donald 4/78
De Wet, Christiaan 11/14
Dewey, John 4/37
Dewey, Thomas 11/44, 11/48, 3/71
De Windt, Harry 8/02
Dexter, Ted 6/62
Dhlakama, Afonso 8/92
Diaghilev, Serge P. 5/09, 12/09, 6/10, 6/12, 7/29, 8/29
Diamond, Jack "Legs" 12/31
Diana, Princess of Wales 9/80, 2/81, 6/82, 9/84, 5/86, 7/91, 8/91, 6/92, 12/92
Diaz, Adolfo 11/26
Diaz, Felix 2/13
Diaz, Porfirio 4/11, 5/11, 6/11, 7/15
Dibah, Farah 12/59
Dibrowa, P.T. 6/53
Dickens, Monica 12/92
Dickson, William 6/52
Didrikson, Mildred "Babe" 8/32
Diefenbaker, John 6/57, 8/79
Diem, Ngo Dinh 4/61, 6/63, 9/63, 11/63
Diesel, Rudolf 9/13
Dietl, Eduard 4/40
Dietrich, Marlene 4/30, 12/30, 5/33, 1/41, 12/43, 5/92
Dietrich, Sepp 12/44
Dikko, Umari 7/84, 2/85
Dillinger, John 3/34, 6/34, 7/34
Dillon, James 2/48
DiMaggio, Joe 11/14, 1/54, 10/54, 8/62
Dimbleby, Richard 8/50, 11/54, 12/65
Dimitrov, Georgi 8/35
Dini, Lamberto 1/95
Dinizulu, King of the Zulus 12/07
Dinkins, David 11/89
Dinnyes, Lajos 6/47
Dior, Christian 1/05, 6/47, 8/47, 3/55, 10/57, 3/62
Dirac, Paul 12/30
Disasters (air)
- Bleriot's plane crashes 12/07
- Airship explodes at show, killing one 8/08
- Zeppelin L2 explodes; 28 die 10/13
- Airship ZR II explodes, Hull; 42 die 8/21
- London-Paris aeroplanes collide; six die 4/22
- Ross Smith, England-Australia hero, dies 4/22
- Airship Shenandoah crashes; 14 die 9/25
- Crash over Kent; seven die 10/26
- Seven die as airliner crashes in Channel 6/29
- Air crash kills 14, UK 12/36
- Hindenburg airship explodes; 33 die, US 5/37
- Czech airliner crashes, Germany; 13 die 8/38
- 14 die in Jersey crash 11/38
- Amy Johnson dies in Thames accident 1/41
- 22 die in TWA crash, USA 1/42
- Duke of Kent killed in air crash 8/42
- Polish PM Sikorski killed in air crash 7/43
- Orde Wingate killed in air crash, Burma 3/44
- Glenn Miller disappears over Channel 12/44
- B-25 bomber hits Empire State Building 7/45
- 21 die in London-Paris crash 9/46
- 49 die in crash in Newfoundland 9/46
- 16 die in crash in Portugal 2/47
- 38 die in DC-4 crash at LaGuardia, USA 5/47
- UK minister Wilson hurt in air accident 7/47
- 15 die in DC-4 crash near Paris 1/48
- 31 die in Tudor IV crash in Atlantic 2/48
- 19 die in DC-9 crash, UK 3/48
- 15 die in mid-air collision over Berlin 4/48
- 30 killed in crash at Shannon, Ireland 4/48
- 39 die in UK's worst crash for decades 7/48
- 34 die in KLM crash, Ayrshire, UK 10/48
- 20 die on Tudor IV, West Indies 1/49
- Italy's football team killed in crash 5/49
- 54 die in Puerto Rico 6/49
- 24 die in Yorkshire crash of BEA DC-3, UK 8/49
- 12 die when two bombers collide, UK 9/49
- 48 die when plane crashes near Azores 10/49
- Series of crashes kill 142 in one month 11/49
- 80 killed in world's worst crash, UK 3/50
- 28 die in crash at Mill Hill, London 10/50
- 28 die in fog crash at Heathrow airport 10/50
- 58 die when Canadian plane crashes, Alps 11/50
- DC-6 airliner crashes in US, 50 die 8/51
- 44 die as KLM plane crashes in Frankfurt 3/52
- 26 die in supersonic plane crash, UK 9/52
- 84 die as transporter crashes, US 12/52
- 43 die in UK Comet airliner crash, India 5/53
- 129 US troops die in crash near Tokyo 6/53
- 35 die as BOAC Comet crashes off Elba 1/54
- Third Comet crash kills 21 off Stromboli 4/54
- 28 die as KLM plane crashes in Ireland 9/54
- Metal fatigue caused Comet jet crashes 10/54
- 26 die on Italian Airways crash, US 12/54
- 28 die as Stratocruiser crashes, UK 12/54
- 26 die in BOAC airliner crash, Nigeria 6/56
- BEA Viscount crashes in Manchester, killing 22 3/57
- 31 die in troop plane crash, Hampshire 5/57
- 43 die in Isle of Wight crash, UK 11/57
- UK football team killed in Munich crash 2/58
- 35 killed near Bolton, UK 2/58
- 49 die as planes collide, Nevada, USA 4/58
- Dutch plane crashes off Ireland, 99 die 8/58
- Cyprus: 12 die; Turkish premier survives 2/59
- 68 die on TWA airliner, Italy 6/59
- 73 die in Boeing 707 crash near Brussels 2/61
- Six die in cable car accident, France 8/61
- Dag Hammarskjoeld dies in air crash 9/61
- 86 die in Shannon airport crash, Ireland 9/61
- 93 die in New York crash 3/62
- 110 die in British DC-7 crash, Cameroons 3/62
- 130 die in Boeing 707 crash, France 6/62
- 112 die in West Indies crash 6/62
- 67 die in crash, Turkey 2/63
- 36 Britons die in Pyrenees crash 9/63
- 118 die in Montreal crash 11/63
- 84 die in crash in Italian Alps 2/64
- 74 die in Philippines crash 5/64
- 44 die in Rome crash 11/64
- 30 die in Kansas crash 1/65
- 26 die in Jersey crash 4/65
- 36 die in Heathrow airport crash 10/65
- US H-bomb missing after mid-air crash 1/66
- 117 die in Mont Blanc crash 1/66
- 133 killed in crash, Japan 2/66
- 130 die in crash, Japan 3/66
- 92 die in Yugoslavia crash 8/66
- 18 die when jet crashes into motel, US 3/67
- 160 die in two holiday plane crashes 6/67
- 66 die in Mediterranean crash 10/67
- 37 die in crash near London 11/67
- US nuclear-bomb plane crashes, Greenland 1/68
- USSR astronaut Gagarin dies in crash 3/68
- 122 die in South African crash 4/68
- 48 die in West Germany crash 8/68
- 55 Nigerian troops killed in crash 9/68
- 50 die in crash near Gatwick, UK 1/69
- Boxer Rocky Marciano dies in plane crash 8/69
- 87 die in Nigeria crash 11/69
- 112 holidaymakers die in Spain crash 7/70
- 99 die in Peru plane crash 8/70
- 162 die in worst recorded crash, Japan 7/71
- 63 killed in Belgium crash 10/71
- 115 die in DC-8 crash, Italy 5/72
- 119 die in crash at Heathrow 6/72
- 156 die in East Berlin plane crash 8/72
- Crash kills Prince William of Gloucester, UK 8/72
- Private plane crash kills 22, California 9/72
- Chile crash strands survivors in Andes 10/72
- 170 die in USSR's worst air disaster 10/72
- Andes plane crash survivors ate the dead 12/72
- 155 die in Canary Islands crash 12/72
- 180 die in Nigeria crash 1/73
- 68 die in plane collision, France 3/73
- 105 Britons die in Swiss plane crash 4/73
- USSR supersonic airliner explodes, Paris 6/73
- 121 die in Paris crash 7/73
- 344 die in DC-10 crash outside Paris 3/74
- Over 100 die in Bali plane crash 4/74
- 100 die in Leningrad crash 4/74
- 88 die in Greece crash 9/74
- 140 Vietnamese orphans die on way to USA 4/75
- 109 die at Kennedy Airport, New York 6/75
- 188 die as Boeing 707 crashes, Morocco 8/75
- 82 die as Lebanese plane crashes, Saudi 1/76
- 176 die in mid-air collision, Yugoslavia 9/76
- 102 die as Boeing crashes in Bolivia 10/76
- 574 die in jumbo collision, Canaries 3/77
- KLM and Pan Am in worst ever air crash 3/77
- KLM 747 had not been cleared for takeoff 3/77
- Hijacked Malaysian plane crashes; 100 die 12/77
- 213 die as Air India jumbo explodes 1/78
- Rebels down Air Rhodesia plane; 58 die 9/78
- 150 die in mid-air collision, San Diego 9/78
- Light plane pilot error causes crash 9/78
- 202 die in Icelandic Airways crash, Sri Lanka 11/78
- Rhodesian rebels down airliner; 59 die 2/79
- DC-10 crashes, Chicago; 273 die 5/79
- 150 die in Soviet mid-air crash 8/79
- 160 Mecca pilgrims die in airliner blast 11/79
- 257 die as DC-10 crashes, Antarctic 11/79
- 146 die as Boeing 727 crashes, Tenerife 4/80
- 301 die on Tristar, Riyadh, Saudi Arabia 8/80
- 178 die aboard Yugoslav DC-9 12/81
- 78 die in icy crash, Washington, USA 1/82
- 119 die in Ecuador 7/83
- 20 die in UK's worst helicopter crash 7/83
- 180 die in Madrid crash 11/83
- 93 die in Madrid airport plane collision 12/83
- 13 die in crash at Uttoxeter, UK 8/84
- 150 die in crash near Bilbao, Spain 2/85
- 55 killed in Manchester plane fire, UK 8/85
- 517 killed in crash near Tokyo 8/85
- 140 killed in crash at Dallas-Fort Worth 8/85
- 166 killed in Mexico crash 3/86
- 67 killed in mid-air collision, US 8/86
- 45 die in UK oil rig helicopter crash 11/86
- 183 die on US-bound flight, Poland 5/87
- 160 die as airliner hits Indian Ocean 11/87
- 33 die at West German air show 8/88
- Pan American jumbo crashes on Lockerbie 12/88
- Hunt begins for Lockerbie bombers 12/88
- British Midlands jet crashes on motorway, killing 40 1/89
- Engine error revealed in British Midland 737 crash 1/89
- Boeing 707 crashes in Azores, killing 144 2/89
- Boeing 747 door blows off in mid-air; 16 passengers die 2/89
- Relatives of Lockerbie victims demand Channon's resignation 2/89
- Pan Am admits alert on type of bomb used in Lockerbie crash 3/89
- Soviet MiG-23 fighter crashes after flying pilotless 7/89
- United Airlines DC-10 crashes in Iowa, killing 107 7/89
- Pan Am pays compensation to Lockerbie victims' families 5/90
- BA pilot sucked out of cockpit after windscreen blows out 7/90
- US A-10s fire on British armoured vehicles in error; 9 die 2/91
- USAF blames air controller for British troop deaths in Gulf 5/91
- Air Inter Airbus crashes near Strasbourg, killing 86 1/92
- Libya ordered to hand over men linked to Lockerbie bombing 1/92
- El Al Boeing 747-200F crashes into houses near Amsterdam 10/92
- China Airlines Airbus crashes in Japan, 262 killed 4/94
- Helicopter crash kills 25 UK counter-terrorism experts 6/94

Disasters (earthquakes)
- Earthquake kills 300 in Mexico 1/02
- Earthquake destroys Turkish town 3/02
- Earthquake kills 4,000 in Turkestan 12/02
- Van, Turkey, kills 860 4/03
- 2,000 die in Constantinople quake 5/03
- Earthquake kills 10,000, India 4/05
- Thousands die in Calabria, Italy 9/05
- Quake destroys San Francisco 4/06
- Hundreds die in Chilean earthquake 8/06
- Hundreds die in Jamaican earthquake 1/07
- Messina quake, tidal wave, 75,000 die 12/08
- Messina death toll rises to 200,000 1/09
- Earthquake kills 500 in Nicaragua 5/10
- 100 die in Mexico City 6/11
- 700 die in Southern California 10/11
- 162 die in Catania, Italy 5/14
- 2,500 die in Turkey 10/14
- Central Italy, 29,000 die 1/15
- Guatemala City 12/17
- 500 die and 200,000 left homeless, Italy 9/20
- Chile, 1,000 die 11/22
- 20,000 die in five Persian villages 6/23
- 300,000 die and 2.5 million homeless in Tokyo 9/23
- 600 die in south Yugoslavia 2/27
- 26 die in Palestine 7/27
- 100 die in Madeira earthquake 3/29
- 3,000 die in Persian earthquake 5/29
- 6,000 die, Pegu city destroyed, Burma 5/30
- 3,000 die, 6,000 injured in Naples 7/30
- 300 die in Mishioma, Japan 11/30
- 1,100 die in Managua, Nicaragua 3/31
- 2,000 die in Bihar, India; relief plan 1/34
- 2,000 die on Formosa, off China 4/35
- 20,000 die in Baluchistan, India 5/35
- 23 killed in Venice, Italy 10/36
- 200 die in El Salvador 12/36
- 30,000 reported killed in Chile 1/39
- 1,500 die in three earthquakes in Iran 1/50
- 1,000 die in Orleansville, Algeria 9/54
- 2,000 die in Iran quakes 12/57
- 1,000 die in Agadir, Morocco 3/60
- 1,500 die in Lar, Iran 4/60
- 20,000 die in Iran's worst earthquake 9/62
- 300 die in Libya 2/63
- 1,000 die in Yugoslav village of Skopje 7/63
- At least 11,000 killed in Iran 9/68
- 10,000 killed in Nicaragua 12/72
- At least 500 die in Mexico 8/73
- 20,000 feared dead in China 5/74
- 4,700 killed in Pakistan 12/74
- 12,000 die in Guatemala 2/76
- 2,000 die, 80,000 homeless, north Italy 5/76
- Hundreds die in Tangshan quake, China 7/76
- 6,000 die in Turkey near Soviet border 11/76
- Hundreds die, Rumania 3/77
- 20,000 feared dead in Iran 9/78
- 20,000 die in El Asnam, Algeria 10/80
- 3,000 die in southern Italy 11/80
- 2,000 killed in Turkey 10/83
- 2,000 killed in Mexico 9/85
- Scores killed in San Salvador 8/86
- 500 die on Indian border with Nepal 8/88
- 1,000 feared dead in China 11/88
- Over 100,000 feared dead in Armenia 12/88
- Earthquake hits Soviet Central Asia, killing over 1,000 1/89
- Earthquake hits San Francisco, killing 273 10/89
- Australia's first fatal earthquake kills 11 12/89
- Earthquake devastates northern Iran; 40,000 feared dead 6/90
- Earthquake devastates eastern Turkey, killing over 1,000 3/92
- Earthquake leaves nearly 400 dead in Cairo 10/92
- 1,500 die in Indonesia 12/92
- Los Angeles earthquake causes death and damage 1/94
- At least 4000 feared dead in Kobe 1/95
- 2,000 killed on Russia's Sakhalin Island 5/95

Disasters (engineering)
- Ten die at World Exhibition 4/00
- 80 drown as bridge collapses, Quebec 8/07
- Canada's Civic Dam bursts 5/08
- Birkenhead dam bursts; 11 die 3/09
- Niagara Falls bridge collapses, 47 die 6/12
- Theatre collapses, killing 107 in Washington 1/22
- Collapse of Ronan Point tower block, UK 5/68
- 33 die when bridge collapses, Australia 10/70
- 96 die when Puerto Rico hotel collapses 1/87

Disasters (epidemics)
- 50 a day die from influenza in London 1/00
- Bubonic plague in Glasgow 8/00
- Disease claims 7,000 dead British in Boer War 12/00
- Arsenic in beer hits Liverpool and Manchester 12/00
- Dr Koch says rats cause plague 7/01
- Smallpox in London 9/01
- Measles claims thousands in Boer camps 11/01
- Almost 3,000 suffer smallpox in London 1/02
- Mosquitoes carry yellow fever; discovery 2/02
- Imperial Vaccination League, London 8/02
- 26,000 die from cholera, Egypt 9/02
- 32,000 reported dead in Egyptian cholera epidemic 10/02
- 900 a day die of cholera in Teheran 7/04
- Persian cholera claims 40,000 8/04
- Cattle immunised against tuberculosis 6/06
- Warning of tuberculosis in bad milk 7/06
- Meningitis in Glasgow, Edinburgh and Belfast 2/07
- 3,000 Russians die from cholera 9/08
- Thousands die each week from cholera 8/10
- 30,000 die of cholera, Italy 9/11
- Foot-and-mouth blights Yorkshire and Surrey 7/12
- Cholera spreads in Balkans and Rumania 9/13
- Newman report highlights sick children 12/13
- Austrian troops suffer dysentery 9/14
- Smallpox in north Germany 6/17
- Influenza delays Allied attack 7/18
- Spanish influenza spreads 7/18
- Spanish influenza hits Britain, killing millions 9/18
- Schools close; 2,225 a week die, London 10/18
- UK deaths exceed births due to flu 3/19
- Home Counties rabies; dogs muzzled 4/19
- Typhoid kills thousands in Poland 2/20
- Typhus and cholera in famine-ravaged Russia 8/21
- 804 die from influenza in week, Britain 1/22
- Foot and mouth disease, Britain 2/22
- Smallpox among Turks' Greek prisoners 2/23
- Plague claims 8,000 in India 4/23
- Cholera spreads to Tokyo quake victims 9/23
- 73,500 diseased animals killed, Britain 12/23
- 25,000 die in Punjab plague, India 4/24
- Bubonic plague in Portugal 1/27
- 1,000 British die a week from influenza 2/27
- Farmers warned of foot and mouth, UK 6/31
- First vaccine against yellow fever 4/32
- Influenza sweeps Europe 1/33
- Typhoid in London suburbs 11/37

- UK children hit by Asian flu and pneumonia 9/57
- Asian flu abating, UK 11/57
- 136 cases of typhoid in Aberdeen, UK 4/64
- Foot and mouth, UK 11/67
- Hong Kong flu kills 4,000 in one week, UK 1/70
- Cholera epidemic in West Bengal 6/71
- 10,000 at risk from smallpox, India 6/74
- Smallpox wiped out, says WHO 5/80
- 31 die in Legionnaire's outbreak, UK 5/85
- WHO says AIDS has become an epidemic 9/85
- Cholera epidemic breaks out among Vietnamese boat people 9/89
- Britain is hit with worst flu epidemic in 14 years 12/89
- Pneumonic plague breaks out in Surat, India 9/94
- Ebola fever kills at least 153 in Zaire 5/95

Disasters (explosions)
- See also Disasters (mining)
- 90 die in explosion at RAF bomb dump, UK 11/44
- Three killed in rocket test in Bucks, UK 11/47
- Flixborough chemical plant explodes, UK 6/74
- 188 die in Spanish campsite explosion 7/78
- Nine die at Abbeystead pumping station, UK 5/84
- Soviet naval arsenal destroyed by blast 6/84
- 260 killed by gas explosion, Mexico 11/84
- 8 die in Putney gas explosion, London 1/85
- 200 die in gas explosion in Guadalajara 4/92
- Oklahoma City bomb kills more than 100 including 15 children 4/95

Disasters (famine)
- Millions of Indians starve after drought 3/00
- Russia's worst famine since 1891 9/05
- Four million Chinese may be starving 12/06
- Some 20 million starve in Russian famine 4/07
- Nine million starve in Japan 1/14
- 7,000 wartorn Belgians face starvation 10/14
- Grips wartorn Russia, leads to revolt 3/17
- Central Europe and Germany; Allies send aid 3/19
- Worsens in China; reports of children being sold for food 11/20
- 18 million starve in Russia 8/21
- 33 million estimated starving, Russia 1/22
- Seven million starving in USSR 10/24
- Four million starving beggars, China 1/28
- Two million starved to death, China 1/30
- 100,000 feared dead in Ethiopia 11/73
- Ten million face famine in East Africa 6/80
- 20 million at risk in China 11/88
- Seven million Sudanese threatened by famine 3/91
- Millions threatened by starvation and civil war in Ethiopia 3/91

Disasters (fire)
- See also Disasters (mining)
- Fire at Buckingham Palace 3/00
- 12,000 homeless in Canadian fires 4/00
- Barbican blaze, London 4/02
- 51 die in mental hospital fire, Britain 1/03
- 84 die in Paris Metro 8/03
- Chicago Iroquois Theatre, 578 die 12/03
- 12,000 destitute after Norway blaze 1/04
- 39 die in Glasgow lodging-house 11/05
- Fire destroys World Exhibition stalls 8/10
- Constantinople ruined 2/11
- 80 die in cinema, Valencia 5/12
- 15,000 homeless in Philippines 4/21
- Petrograd Opera House burns; many die 5/23
- 50 die in cinema fire, Limerick, Ireland 9/26
- 77 children die in Montreal theatre fire 1/27
- 200 feared dead in Madrid Theatre 9/28
- 69 children die in Scottish cinema fire 12/29
- Church burns in Rumania; over 100 die 4/30
- 1,500 die in Hakodate, Japan 3/34
- London's Crystal Palace burns down 11/36
- 500 die at Texas school 3/37
- Petrol blaze at Avonmouth, Britain 9/38
- Destructive fire kills 74 in Marseilles 10/38
- New Zealand Avenue, London, destroyed 6/39
- Hotel fire in Atlanta kills 137 12/46
- 80 killed in Berlin dance hall fire 2/47
- 714 die in Texas City, USA 4/47
- 207 die in liner fire, Canada 9/49
- 90 die in Chicago school 12/58
- Leicester Rolls-Royce factory 8/59
- 322 die in Brussels department store 5/67
- 22 die in Shrewsbury hospital, UK 2/68
- 20 die in Glasgow warehouse fire, UK 11/68
- Maltings concert hall destroyed, UK 6/69
- 146 die in dance hall fire, Grenoble 11/70
- 156 die in hotel fire, Seoul 12/71
- Liner Queen Elizabeth destroyed by fire 1/72
- 118 die in store fire, Japan 5/72
- 50 die at holiday centre, Isle of Man 5/73
- 88 die in hotel fire, South Korea 11/74
- 377 die in Iran cinema fire caused by extremists 8/78
- 37 die in London nightclub blazes 8/80
- 49 die and 130 injured in Dublin disco on St Valentine's Day 2/81
- USSR, Afghan troops die in Salang Pass 11/82
- 64 die in theatre fire, Turin 2/83
- 68 die in bush fires, Australia 2/83
- 83 die in disco fire, Madrid 12/83
- York Minster devastated by fire, UK 7/84
- 30 die in King's Cross underground blaze 11/87
- Fire in New York disco kills 87 3/90
- Fire in toy factory kills 220 people in Bangkok 5/93

Disasters (floods)
- 50 die in UK floods and gales 12/00
- 2,000 die in floods, China 4/08
- 1,500 die in Monterrey, Mexico 8/09
- Paris devastated; art treasures in peril 1/10
- 1,000 die in Hungary 6/10
- 800 die in Japan 8/10
- 100,000 die along Yangtse-kiang, China 9/11
- Thames overflows; Windsor Castle cut off 1/15
- Storms wreck Zuyder Zee dam, Netherlands 1/16
- 500 feared dead, Colorado 6/21
- Villages destroyed in south India 7/24
- 50,000 feared dead, China 8/24
- North Wales dam bursts; 20 die 11/25
- 200 die and 15,000 left homeless, Poland 9/27
- 150 die in New England floods, USA 11/27
- 300 die in Algeria 11/27
- 14 die in Thames flood; artworks ruined 1/28
- 200 die in south-west France 3/30
- Sulphurous waters in Monghyr, India 1/34
- 227 die in Japan 7/35
- 1,000 die when Oveda dam bursts, Italy 8/35
- Ohio River floods kill 135 and leave 750,000 homeless 1/37
- Yellow River, China; worst since 1885 6/38

300 killed in Hawaii 4/46
- Lynmouth, north Devon, 36 feared dead 8/52
- 283 drown in British coastal floods 2/53
- 1,000 die after dykes burst, Netherlands 2/53
- 1,000 die as tidal waves hit Greek Isles 8/53
- Worst floods in Central Europe; 27 die 7/54
- 200 people and 300,000 sheep die, Australia 3/55

300 die in French Riviera floods as dam bursts 12/59
- Quakes and floods kill 96 in Japan 5/60
- 145 killed when dam bursts near Kiev 3/61
- 278 die in Hamburg 2/62
- 323 die in Barcelona 9/62
- 3,000 die in dam burst, Italy 10/63
- 500 die in floods and landslides, Haiti 11/63
- 1,000 die when reservoir bursts, India 9/64
- Florence flood destroys masterpieces 11/66
- Over 100 die in Italy 11/68
- 150,000 die in East Pakistan 11/70
- 356 die in the Philippines 8/72
- 500 die in Spain 10/73
- Monsoon floods half of Bangladesh 8/74
- 260 die after dam bursts, Italy 7/85
- 127 killed in Brazil 2/88
- At least 250 people die in China 8/88
- 1.5 million homeless in Sudan 8/88
- Millions made homeless in Bangladesh 9/88
- Cyclone causes severe flooding in Bangladesh 4/91
- Three days of heavy rain claim 2,000 lives in Pakistan 9/92
- Up to 1700 dead after torrential rains in Nepal 7/93
- US Midwest devastated as Mississippi bursts its banks 8/93
- Rain causes havoc in S. England 1/94

Disasters (heat and cold)
- Heatwave kills 652 in USA 7/11
- 2,500 London children die in heatwave 8/11
- Heatwave kills 206 in US Mid-West 7/34
- 34 die in freezing weather, Europe 2/86
- 700 die in Greek heatwave 7/87
- Heatwave hits Britain; hosepipe ban 7/89
- UK suffers worst drought since 1745 3/92

Disasters (hurricanes)
- Hurricane in Texas destroys cotton crop 9/00
- UK gales claim almost 200 lives 11/01
- Indian tornado kills 416 5/02
- Sicilian tornado kills hundreds 9/02
- 100 die in Gainsville, Georgia, US 6/03
- 30,000 destitute in Philippines typhoon 11/04
- 10,000 feared dead in Tahiti typhoon 2/06
- Hong Kong typhoon kills hundreds 9/06
- Typhoon sweeps Japan; hundreds die 9/12
- 200 die in tornado, Minnesota 6/19
- 140 killed in south US 4/20
- 300 die in Colorado, USA 6/24
- 80 feared dead in Virgin Islands 9/24
- Burma cyclone and tidal wave kills 1,200 5/26
- 1,500 die in Florida, US; many homeless 9/26
- 175 die in Luzon, Philippines 11/26
- 10,000 homeless in Siberia, USSR 8/27
- Five-minute tornado kills 69, US 9/27
- 50 die when storm hits Lancashire 10/27
- More than 200 killed in Florida, US 9/28
- 300 die on West Indian island Guadeloupe 9/28
- 19 drown at sea, seven die on land, UK 12/29
- Typhoon destroys 14 Filipino towns 1/30
- 700 die in winds, British Honduras 9/31
- 23 die in US southern states 2/34
- Typhoon kills 1,500 in Japan 9/34
- 26 die and 150 injured in Mississippi 4/35
- 200 die in Florida 9/35
- Typhoon hits Philippines; 109 die 10/36
- 226 die in Tokyo typhoon, Japan 10/38
- 41 die in Arkansas, US 1/49
- 250 killed, 300,000 injured, Japan 9/50
- 132 die in Jamaica 8/51
- 200 die in American Mid-West 3/52
- Winds and high tides kill 280 in UK 2/53
- 118 die as Hazel hits US 10/54
- 29 die in Mississippi, US 2/55
- 2,000 die in Chinese typhoon 8/56
- 3,300 die in Madagascar 3/59
- Thousands die in East Pakistan 10/60
- At least 11 die in gales, UK 2/62
- 10,000 die in East Pakistan 5/63
- 4,000 die in Haiti 10/63
- 7,000 die in Ceylon and Madras 12/64
- Over 10,000 die in East Pakistan 5/65
- Seven die in Britain 11/65
- 174 die in Japan 9/66
- 20 die in Scotland 1/68
- 800 die in Philippines 10/70
- 150,000 die in Pakistan 11/70
- Hundreds feared dead in Mozambique 1/71
- 5,000 killed in India 11/71
- Cyclone Fifi kills 10,000, Honduras 9/74
- Darwin, Australia, shattered by cyclone 12/74
- Eloise causes devastation, West Indies 9/75
- Hurricane David kills 1,000, West Indies 9/79
- Hurricane Frederick hits US; evacuation 9/79
- Six die in Britain 1/84
- 1,000 die in the Philippines 9/84
- 10,000 die in Bangladesh 5/85
- Winds kill 17 and cause £300 million worth damage, UK 10/87
- Hurricane Gilbert, West Indies 9/88
- Cyclone in Bangladesh kills over 1,200 12/88
- Tornado kills up to 1,000 in Bangladesh 4/89
- Hurricane Hugo hits American coast 9/89
- Gale-force winds kill 46 in the UK 1/90
- Thirteen people die in Britain in 100-mph winds 1/91
- Hurricane Andrew hits Miami area, killing 15 8/92
- Blizzards sweep through the US, killing 115 3/93

Disasters (industrial)
- Ten die in South African explosion 4/00
- Manchester factory blast kills 12 1/01
- 200 die in German chemical factory blast 4/01
- 16 die in Woolwich Arsenal explosion 6/03
- 400 die when Madrid reservoir collapses 4/05
- US town Fontanet destroyed in explosion 10/07
- 21 die in Liverpool mill explosion 11/11
- 50 die in factory fire, Britain 7/13
- Ammunition freight cars blast kills 26 7/16
- Munitions works explosion kills 69, London 1/17
- Arms factory blast in Lancashire kills 41 6/17
- Arms factory blast in Midlands kills 100 7/18
- BASF chemical works blast kills 574 in Germany 9/21
- 20 die and 100 injured in New Jersey blast 3/24
- French gunpowder factory blast kills 40 11/36
- Windscale nuclear pile closed after fire 10/57
- 60 die from smog in London 12/62
- Seveso evacuated in chemical scare 7/76
- Executives jailed for Seveso disaster 9/83
- Bhopal gas leak kills at least 2,000 12/84
- Gas from lake kills 1,500, Cameroons 8/86
- Massive pesticide pollution of Rhine 11/86
- Explosion on Piper Alpha oil rig 7/88
- Red Adair boards Piper Alpha 7/88
- Arctic pipeline leaks thousands of tonnes of Russian crude 10/94

Disasters (landslides)
- Austrian landslide kills 700 9/02
- 40 die in Lyons landslide, France 11/30
- Norwegian landslide kills 57 4/34
- Landslide destroys seven Indian villages 9/36
- Over 3,000 die in Peru 1/62
- 500 die in floods and landslides, Haiti 11/63
- 20,000 killed in mudslide, Colombia 11/85

Disasters (mining)
- 200 die in Utah coal mine explosion 4/00
- 78 buried in Welsh pit blasts 5/01
- 100 die in Wollongong, Australia 8/02
- 200 buried alive, US 1/04
- 32 die in South Wales 3/05
- 124 die in Glamorgan pit 7/05
- 1,200 die in explosion, France 3/06
- 25 die in Durham pit 9/06
- 164 die in Saarbrucken blast, Germany 12/06
- 471 die in Japanese pit 7/07
- Ten die in Norton Hill pit explosion 4/08
- 228 die in Russian pit 7/08
- 73 trapped in Lancashire pit 8/08
- 360 die in pit explosion, Hamm, Germany 11/08
- 105 die in pit explosion, West Virginia 1/09
- Up to 350 die in Lancashire pit 12/10
- 87 killed in colliery explosion 7/12
- 120 die, Westphalia, Germany 8/12
- 418 trapped in Welsh pit explosion 10/13
- Seven die, 46 injured, Sheffield 12/23
- Oklahoma blast; 65 die 1/26
- 53 feared dead in Ebbw Vale; 150 trapped 3/27
- 21 die in pit blast, Pittsburgh 3/29
- 26 die in Whitehaven pit blast, Britain 1/31
- 42 die in Bentley Colliery explosion 11/31
- Pit cage crashes into water killing 19 in Lancashire 10/32
- Pit explosion in Edge Green kills 25 11/32
- 42 miners and 17 rescuers die in Mons blasts 5/34
- 262 die in Gresford mine blast, Wrexham 9/34
- 57 die in Wharncliffe Woodmoor pit blast 8/36
- 35 die in pit explosion near Dunfermline 10/39
- Nine miners die in explosion, Barnsley, UK 5/47
- 111 miners trapped after pit blast, UK 8/47
- 80 killed in colliery fire, Derbyshire 9/50
- 13 miners die in Ayrshire, UK 9/50
- 83 feared dead in Easington, Durham 5/51
- 47 miners trapped in Glasgow colliery 9/59
- 28 die in Six Bells, Monmouthshire 6/60
- Over 400 miners die in the Saar 2/62
- 616 die in Japanese mining and rail disaster 11/63
- 250 die in pit explosion, Japan 6/65
- Aberfan coal tip disaster kills 144, UK 10/66
- 64 die in mine explosion, South Africa 11/69
- 422 miners die in explosion, Rhodesia 6/72
- 372 miners die in blast, Bihar, India 12/75
- 62 miners die in explosion, Japan 5/85
- 177 miners die in fire, South Africa 9/86

Disasters (nuclear)
- Windscale nuclear pile closes after fire 10/57
- Windscale leaks cause leukaemia 1/59
- Radioactive leak at Windscale 8/70
- Windcale workers die of leukaemia 1/75

Three Mile Island nuclear leak, USA 3/79
- Chernobyl nuclear reactor explosion 4/86
- Fear of meltdown at Chernobyl reactor 5/86
- An explosion damages nuclear weapons complex in Siberia 4/93

Disasters (rail)
- 17 die in Paris-Madrid crash 11/00
- 15 die in Glasgow crash 7/03
- 128 die as bridge collapses, Colorado 8/04
- 62 die in Tennessee 9/04
- Seven die in Barnsley 1/05
- 23 die in Liverpool 7/05
- 27 die near Salisbury, Britain 7/06
- 12 die on London-Scotland express train 9/06
- 19 die in Shrewsbury crash 10/07
- First Underground accident, 22 injured 9/12
- 15 die as train hits bridge, Lancashire 9/12
- 150 troops at Drama, Balkans 5/13
- 14 die in northern England crash 9/13
- Worst British crash; 158 die, Scotland 5/15
- 14 die and 50 injured in South Shields crash 12/15
- 17 die in British collision 1/21
- Lourdes train crash kills 20 pilgrims 8/22
- Paris-Strasbourg express crash; 27 die 2/23
- 103 die in Bulgarian crash 7/23
- 19 die in Paris-Le Havre crash 7/26
- 260 die in Yugoslavian crash 10/27
- 68 die in Moscow crash 1/32
- 190 die as express trains collide, Meaux 12/33
- 250 die in San Salvador train explosion 3/34
- 14 die in Welwyn Garden City, UK 6/35
- 34 die and 92 injured in Glasgow blizzard crash 12/37
- 68 die in high-speed train crash, Spain 9/38
- 30 die in Hertfordshire train crash, UK 9/45
- 15 die in crash in Staffordshire, UK 1/46
- 18 die in crash in Balby, UK 8/47
- 31 die in train crash, Croydon, UK 10/47
- 21 die in crash near Berwick, UK 10/47
- 5 die in London fog crash 11/47
- 24 die in crash at Winsford, UK 4/48
- 81 die in crash at Patna, India 5/50
- 75 die in collision on Long Island, US 11/50
- 14 die on express coach, Doncaster 3/51
- 112 die as three trains crash, UK 10/52
- Huge rescue operation; 50 foot smoke 10/52
- Worst UK crash since 1915 10/52
- 300 die in canyon crash, Mexico 4/55
- Ten die and 99 injured in Didcot crash, UK 11/55
- 12 die in Barnes fire, Britain 12/55
- 173 die in crash, Jamaica 9/57
- 92 die in Lewisham crash, South London 12/57
- Ten die and 80 injured in Dagenham crash 1/58
- Six killed and 116 injured in Blackpool, UK 7/61
- 93 killed in collision in Netherlands 1/62
- 616 die in Japanese mining and rail disaster 11/63
- 53 die in crash at Hither Green, London 11/67
- 147 killed, 700 injured in Mexico crash 10/72
- 150 die in Yugoslavia crash 9/74
- 38 die in Moorgate underground crash, UK 2/75
- Underground crash at Moorgate kills 35 2/75
- 80 die in Sydney crash 1/77
- Many die as Italian trains collide 4/78
- 11 die on sleeper train, UK 7/78
- 17 die and 51 injured in express crash, Ireland 8/80
- 13 die when two trains collide in Ireland 8/83
- 13 die in crash near Falkirk, UK 7/84
- 390 killed in Ethiopia 1/85
- 21 die when train hits bus, Israel 6/85
- 150 die in collision, Portugal 9/85
- 36 feared dead in Clapham crash 12/88
- Five people die in crash at Purley, Surrey 3/89
- Two people die in crash in Glasgow 3/89

Gas blast causes USSR's worst rail disaster, killing 800 6/89
- Inquest jury verdict on 1988 Clapham train crash 9/90

Disasters (road)
- 28 die in bus accident, Tennessee, US 2/58
- 13 children die in French coach crash 8/64
- 16 die in Durham bus crash, UK 8/69
- Ten die and 60 injured in series of UK crashes 9/71
- Seven die in multiple crash on M1, UK 11/71
- 32 die on coach in UK's worst road accident 5/75
- 46 children die in coach crash, France 7/82
- Nine die in multiple M6 crash, UK 2/85
- 17 RAF men die in bus crash near Munich 2/85
- 13 die in UK's worst motorway accident 10/85
- 13 die in M4 crash, UK 6/86
- 30 die in tanker lorry crash, West Germany 7/87
- Eleven British tourists die in a coach crash in France 6/90

Disasters (sea)
- New Royal yacht capsizes 1/00
- 11 killed as British steamer collides with boats 7/00
- 128 die as steamer sinks in US 2/01
- Royal yacht wrecked; King has lucky escape 5/01
- Lusitania wrecked off Canada 6/01
- 59 die in torpedo boat wreck off Grimsby 9/01
- Tidal wave kills thousands in Polynesia 1/03
- 100 die when Liban sinks, Marseilles 6/03
- Nelson's HMS Victory rammed 10/03
- British submarine sinks; 11 crew drowned 3/04
- Up to 1,000 die in paddleship fire, NY 6/04
- 700 Scandinavians die in Norge wreck 6/04
- 23 drown off Land's End 3/05
- 14 drown as submarine sinks, Plymouth 6/05
- Japanese steamer hits British ship; 127 die 8/05
- 544 die as Japanese flagship sinks 9/05
- 128 die as steamer wrecked off St Malo 11/05
- 120 drown as steamer wrecked off Canada 1/06
- Tidal wave kills 200, Colombia 2/06
- 200 die in wreck of the Sirio off Spain 8/06
- 1,500 die, Dutch East Indies tidal wave 1/07
- 144 drown on steamer Berlin 2/07
- 118 die as French battleship explodes 3/07
- 100 feared dead in wreck off France 5/07
- Mauretania runs aground 12/07
- Mount Temple wrecked off Nova Scotia 12/07
- 35 die as British destroyer hits cruiser 4/08
- 20 drown as barque sinks off South Wales 8/08
- Tidal wave kills 1,000, Italy 10/10
- River barge sinks; 300 die, Russia 12/10
- P& O liner founders; Princess on board 12/11
- 14 die in submarine accident, Isle of Wight 2/12
- Titanic sinks; 1,500 die 4/12
- 165 missing as ship hits mine off Turkey 5/12
- French navy submarine sinks, 24 drown 6/12
- Submarine hits liner; 14 die 10/12
- Missing submarine near Whitesand, UK 1/14
- HMS Bulwark blows up in port; 700 die 11/14
- Germany sinks liner Lusitania; 1,400 die 5/15
- Auxiliary ship Irene explodes; 270 die 5/15
- Liner Ancona torpedoed; 208 die 11/15
- Submarines collide, killing 103, Britain 1/18
- Ships collide off Scotland; 430 die 10/18
- 200 drown on yacht Stornoway, Scotland 1/19
- Spanish liner Valbanera sinks; 500 die 9/19
- Steamer wrecked, English Channel; 35 die 1/20
- Bismarck, largest liner, burns 10/20

- Santa Isabel sinks, killing 160, Spain 1/21
- Submarine K5 sinks; 56 crew die 1/21
- Steamer wrecked in China Sea; 862 die 3/21
- Steamer Rowan sinks off Scotland; 36 die 10/21
- Liner Egypt sinks; 102 die 5/22
- 23 die in seven US destroyers wreck 9/23
- US submarine S-51 sinks; 37 die 9/25
- M-1 submarine sinks in Channel; 60 die 11/25
- 3,000 die in tidal wave, Kiu-Siu, Japan 9/27
- 37 die when liner rams ferry, Australia 11/27
- 43 die as French submarine hits steamer 10/28
- More than 100 die as Vestris sinks, US 11/28
- Submarines collide in Irish Sea; 24 die 7/29
- Navy tug sinks off Ushant; 23 die 1/30
- Liner hits aircraft carrier; 30 die 4/31
- Six of 20 Hong Kong submarine crew saved 6/31
- 350 die as Loire River boat sinks 6/31
- 55 feared dead on Royal Navy submarine 1/32
- 49 killed as submarine sinks off France 4/32
- Japanese torpedo boat capsizes; 100 die 3/34
- Finnish ship Johanna Thorden sinks; 30 die 1/37
- 71 die when submarine HMS Thetis sinks 6/39
- 69 die when sub Phenix sinks, Indochina 6/39
- HMS Thetis lifted from sea bed 7/39
- 300 die when ship hits mine in Greece 1/47
- 20 die in liner blast, Belfast 9/47
- 150 die when liner hits mine in Denmark 6/48
- 75 feared dead as UK submarine vanishes 4/51
- 128 die in Princess Victoria ferry crash 1/53
- Ferry sinks as doors burst open; inquiry 1/53
- Inquest: sunken ferry left doors open 2/53
- Turkish submarine collides with ship; 97 die 4/53
- 1,700 drown on capsized ferry, Japan 9/54
- 13 die on submarine HMS Sidon 6/55
- 220 die when ferry sinks, Turkey 3/58
- 27 die in North Sea gales 12/59
- 150 die in fire on liner, Persian Gulf 4/61
- 129 die when US sub sinks in Atlantic 4/63
- 117 die in fire on liner Lakonia 12/63
- 85 die when destroyer sinks in Australia 2/64
- 13 die when North Sea oil rig collapses 12/65
- 11 die when pleasure boat wrecked, UK 7/66
- 31 die when Cornish pleasure boat sinks 8/66
- 280 die when ferry sinks, Greece 12/66
- Wreck of oil tanker Torrey Canyon, UK 3/67
- Accidents have killed 60 Hull trawlermen 2/68
- 200 die when ferry capsizes, NZ 3/68
- 56 US sailors killed in South China Sea 6/69
- Sub HMS Artemis sinks at Portsmouth, UK 7/71
- 25 die in fire aboard Greek liner 8/71
- 63 die when UK ship sinks, Argentina 5/72
- Deepest undersea rescue frees two from sub 9/73
- 17 die in Tasmanian ship ramming 1/75
- North Sea oil rig blows up, huge slick 4/77
- 100 oil platform workers rescued 4/77
- Vietnamese "boat people" killed at sea 12/77
- Amoco Cadiz tanker splits off UK coast 3/78
- Oil tanker explodes; 49 die, Ireland 1/79
- 750 die in tidal wave, Indonesia 7/79
- 14 yachtsmen die in Fastnet sailing race 8/79
- North sea oil rig collapses; 100 die 3/80
- Storms sink Phillips' Alexander Kielland 3/80
- 13 die aboard helicopter in North Sea 8/81
- 16 die in Cornish lifeboat rescue bid 12/81
- 500 die when Nile steamer sinks 5/83
- 100 die in USSR when ship rams bridge 6/83
- Tanker fire pollutes S. African coast 8/83
- 17 die when freighter sinks off Guernsey 1/84
- 19 die when UK barque sinks off Bermuda 6/84
- Ship with nuclear cargo sinks, Belgium 8/84
- 34 die when two tankers explode, Spain 5/85
- Wreck of the Titanic located 9/85
- Rivets blamed for sinking of Titanic 7/86
- 400 die when liner sinks in Black Sea 9/86
- 200 die aboard Herald Channel ferry 3/87
- 1,500 die as ferry sinks, Philippines 12/87
- 14 missing after Greek cruiser sinks 10/88
- Tanker spills 11 million gallons of oil off coast of Alaska 3/89
- Soviet submarine catches fire and sinks, killing 42 4/89
- Gun turret blows up on US battleship Iowa, killing 47 4/89
- Cruiser and tug collide on Danube, killing 162 9/89
- Party boat collides with dredger on Thames; 60 feared dead 9/89
- Ferry on its way to Denmark catches fire, killing 150 4/90
- 400 people feared dead as Egyptian ferry sinks in Red Sea 12/91
- Polish ferry capsizes in Baltic Sea, killing 48 1/93
- Oil from wreck of Braer is dispersed by wind and waves 1/93
- Over 1,700 feared dead when a ferry capsizes 2/93
- Ferry Estonia sinks. 912 dead 9/94

Disasters (sporting)
- Stand collapses at football; 20 die 4/02
- Six die in Paris-Madrid road race 5/03
- Averted disaster at overcrowded Wembley 4/23
- 22 die at Grand Prix d'Europe motor race 9/28
- 33 die at football match, UK 3/46
- 80 die when three Le Mans cars crash 6/55
- 14 die in Mille Miglia motor race crash 5/57
- Two die as Indianapolis 500 tower crashes 6/60
- Two UK drivers die in Belgian Grand Prix 6/60
- 13 killed at Italian Grand Prix 9/61
- 320 die in soccer riot, Peru 5/64
- Donald Campbell dies in Bluebird, UK 1/67
- UK's Tommy Simpson dies during Tour de France 7/67
- Jim Clark (UK) dies in motor race crash 4/68
- Racing driver Jochen Rindt dies in crash 9/70
- 66 die at Ibrox Park football match, UK 1/71
- 42 skiers die in cable car, Italy 3/76
- 24 die in football stampede, Greece 2/81
- Over 50 die in Bradford stadium fire, UK 5/85
- 41 die in Heysel stadium riot, Brussels 5/85
- Football supporters crushed to death at Hillsborough stadium 4/89
- Hillsborough disaster claims its 95th victim 4/89
- Fourteen Liverpool fans jailed for Heysel disaster 4/89

Disasters (volcanoes)
- Volcano destroys Martinique capital; 30,000 die 5/02
- Volcano devastates island off Sicily 3/06
- Mount Vesuvius erupts; hundreds dead 4/06
- Mount Etna erupts, Italy 3/10
- Mount Etna erupts, destroying villages 11/28
- 11,000 die in Mount Agung eruption, Bali 3/63
- Mount St Helen's erupts; eight die, USA 5/80

Disney, Walt 1/38, 11/40, 12/40, 10/41, 7/55, 12/66
Di Stefano, Alfredo 5/60
Dix, Otto 12/37, 7/69
Djakova 2/04
Djibouti
- Independence, last French African colony 6/77

Djilas, Milovan 1/54, 5/62
Dlamini, Sam 9/84
Dobbie, William 4/42
Dobbs, Henry 11/21
Doblin, Alfred 6/57
Dobson, Frank 7/63
Dobson, Richard 10/77
Docherty, Tommy 12/72
Docummun, Elie 12/02
Dodd, Ken 12/66, 7/89
Dodds, E.C. 12/38
Doe, Samuel 7/90, 9/90
Doenitz, Karl 4/41, 4/45, 11/45, 12/80
Dogs
- Scotland Yard to start using dogs 5/38
- 11-year-old girl killed by pet rottweilers 5/89
- Four-year-old girl savaged by pet dogs 5/89
- American pit bull terriers face import ban 5/91
- House of Commons approves fighting dog bill 6/91
- Two-year-old girl savaged by rottweiler 8/91
- Fighting dogs must be muzzled 8/91

Doheny, Edward L. 10/23
Doherty, Hugh 7/02
Doherty, Laurence 6/06
Doherty, Reginald 6/06
Dole, Robert 2/88, 4/88, 11/88, 5/95
D'Oliveira, Basil 8/68, 9/68, 6/69
Dollfuss, Engelbert 5/32, 5/33, 6/33, 8/33, 9/33, 2/34, 3/34, 4/34, 7/34
Domagk, Gerhard 12/32, 12/39, 4/64
Domingo, Placido 12/90
Dominican Republic
- Force by Roosevelt to repay creditors 12/04
- Batista flees from Cuba 1/59
- Military junta seizes power 4/65
- US troops go to aid of new regime 4/65
- Truce signed in civil war 5/65
- All US Marines withdrawn 6/65

Don, Kaye 7/31
Donat, Robert 12/39, 3/40, 6/58
Donges, Theophilus 5/51
Donnegan, Lonnie 12/57, 12/59
Donoghue, Steven 6/23, 11/37
Doolittle, James 9/22, 4/42, 9/93
Dora-Kaplan, Fanya 8/18
Dorji, Jigme 4/64
Dors, Diana 5/84
Dorsey, Jimmy 6/57
Dorsey, Tommy 12/27, 11/56
Dos Passos, John 9/70
Douglas, Alfred 12/23
Douglas, James "Buster" 2/90
Douglas, Melvyn 2/40
Douglas, William O. 7/44
Douglas-Home, Alec (Lord Home)
- Reforms in Lords; women to become peers 10/57
- Becomes Foreign Secretary 7/60
- Welcomes end of Cuban missile crisis 10/62
- Comments on signing of test ban treaty 8/63
- Becomes Tory leader 10/63
- Renounces his six titles 10/63
- Becomes PM 10/63
- Attends Kennedy's funeral 11/63
- Elected to House of Commons 11/63
- Attends Nehru's funeral 5/64
- Announces general election 9/64
- Leads Tories to defeat in election 10/64
- Resigns as Tory leader 7/65
- Becomes Foreign Secretary 6/70
- Expels 90 Russians from UK for spying 9/71
- Signs deal to end rift with Rhodesia 11/71

Douglas-Home, William 9/92
Douglass, Dorothea 7/06
Doumer, Paul 5/32
Doumergue, Gaston 12/13, 6/24, 5/27, 2/34, 11/34, 6/37
Dowding, Hugh 2/70
Dowell, Anthony 12/70
Downes, Terry 7/61
Downey, Lesley Ann 10/65, 5/66
Dozier, James 1/82
Draga, Queen of Serbia 6/03
Drake, Ted 12/35
Drakin, Alfred 4/10
Dreyfus Case 6/00, 9/00, 4/03, 3/04, 7/06, 8/06, 10/06, 7/07, 6/08, 7/11, 7/35
Dreyfus, Alfred
- See Dreyfus Case

Dreyfus, Laurence 5/93
Drinkwater, John 9/27
Drobny, Jaroslav 7/49, 7/52, 6/53, 7/54
Drugs
- Cocaine and heroin enter US from Germany 11/21
- Increasing use by young women: warning 2/26
- Ingeniously smuggled into Britain 7/27
- Cocaine disguised as "Fujitsu" 7/27
- League report: 30,000 addicts in Britain 5/36
- Young British girls smoke Indian hemp 8/51
- 700 arrests for marijuana trade, Jamaica 7/52
- Import and export of heroin is banned 1/56
- Warnings on overuse of sedatives 11/58
- Thalidomide drug causes birth defects 12/58
- Curbs on selling "pep pills" 1/60
- Olympic cyclist dies after drug-taking 9/60
- Overdose may have killed Presley 8/77
- Singer Sid Vicious dies of overdose 2/79
- Japan deports ex-Beatle on drugs charge 1/80
- 650 pounds of cannabis, Morocco embassy 6/80
- DeLorean arrested for cocaine 10/82
- Southampton cocaine haul: £51 million 11/87
- US announces $7.86 billion plan to finance war against drugs 9/89
- Manuel Noriega charged with drug-trafficking 1/90
- Mayor of New York, Marion Barry, is arrested for crack 1/90
- Two Welsh weightlifters lose medals after using drugs 1/90
- British customs officials seize 116lbs of heroin 3/90
- Two British girls arrested in Bangkok for smuggling drugs 7/90
- British girl given 25 years for drug-trafficking in Thailand 12/90
- General Noriega goes on trial in Miami for drug-trafficking 7/92
- Drug lord, Pablo Escobar, escapes from prison 7/92
- Holland to ban sale of cannabis to tourists 10/93
- Colombian drugs baron Escobar killed by police 12/93

Drumm, Maire 10/76
Duarte, Jose Napolean 3/80
Dubcek, Alexander 11/21, 1/68, 3/68, 5/68, 7/68, 8/68, 4/69, 9/69, 12/69, 3/70, 6/70, 11/88, 11/89, 12/89, 11/92
Du Bois, W.E.B. 5/10
Dubrovolsky, Georgi 6/71
Dubs, Adolph 2/79
Duca, Ion 12/33
Du Cann, Edward 9/67
Duchamp, Marcel 12/11
Duddy, John 8/66
Duffy, Seamus 8/89
Dufy, Raoul 3/53, 12/55
Dugan, Michael 9/90
Dugdale, Bridget Rose 6/74
Dukakis, Michael 3/87, 4/88, 7/88, 10/88, 11/88
Dukas, Paul 5/35
Duke, David 10/91
Dukes, Alan 3/86
Dulles, Allen 11/63
Dulles, John Foster 11/52, 5/53, 4/54, 6/54, 10/55, 11/55, 8/56, 9/56, 10/56, 11/56, 7/57, 10/57, 3/58, 4/59, 5/59
Du Maurier, Daphne 5/07, 6/69, 4/89
Dunant, Jean Henri 12/01, 10/10
Dunaway, Faye 3/77
Duncan, George 5/22
Duncan, Isadora 5/03, 1/06, 4/13, 9/27
Dunlop, John Boyd 10/21
Dunn, Richard 5/76
Dunne, Lawrence 5/49
Du Plessis, W.C. 10/55
Dupont, Clifford 4/70
Du Pre, Jacqueline 2/76, 10/87
Dupuis, Hector 6/65
Durant, William Crapo 9/08
Durante, Jimmy 1/80
Durrell, Gerald 1/95
Durrell, Lawrence 2/12, 12/90
Dutch East Indies
- See also Indonesia, Netherlands
- Dutch kill 541 Achinese 4/04
- Javanese Nationalists rebel; fight Dutch 11/26
- Sukarno founds Indonesian Nationalists 6/27
- Java Man may be humans' "missing link" 12/27
- Nationalists go to war with Dutch 10/45
- Allied troops mobilise in Java 10/45
- Indonesians at Surabaya told to yield 11/45
- Republic of Indonesia declared 11/45
- Sukarno calls for war on Dutch 6/46
- Dutch fight Indonesian Nationalists 7/47
- UN arranges cease-fire 8/47
- Martial law declared 9/48
- Dutch seize Jogjakarta and Madiun 12/48
- Dutch troops withdraw from Jakarta 6/49
- United States of Indonesia recognised 11/49

Dutschke, Rudi 4/68
Duvalier, Francois (Papa Doc) 9/57, 7/58, 5/63, 6/64, 4/71
Duvalier, Jean-Claude (Baby Doc) 4/71, 2/86
Dvorak, Antonin 5/04
Dyer, George 12/67
Dylan, Bob 5/41, 9/61, 8/63, 6/66, 12/66, 8/69, 12/92
Dyson, Terry 5/61

E

Eager, Vince 12/59
Eagleton, Thomas 7/72
Earhart, Amelia 5/32
Earp, Wyatt 1/29
Easdale, Brian 12/49
Eastland, Senator 5/54
Eastman, George 10/01, 10/14, 3/32
Eastman, Linda 3/69
Eastwood, Clint 4/30, 4/86
Eberle, Gertrude 8/26
Ebert, Carl 12/34
Ebert, Friedrich 11/18, 2/19, 3/20, 9/23, 2/25
Ecology
- American buffalo saved 8/02
- Aswan dam improves irrigation in Egypt 12/02
- US side of Niagara Falls runs dry 3/03
- Plant-searchers die on Alps 10/03
- Britain's first "garden city" 12/03
- Call for smokeless London 3/04
- Opening of Richmond Park 3/04
- Russo-Japanese treaty protects seals 7/07
- Roosevelt calls for conservation meeting 2/09
- Largest oceanographic museum, Monaco 3/10
- National Trust's long lease on Exmoor 2/17
- British Forestry Commission plants trees 1/18
- UK Transport Ministry attacks billboards 10/23
- Lord Ripon donates Fountains Abbey 10/23
- Hickory wood shortage; steel golf clubs 1/27
- First "green belt" is approved in UK 2/29
- Idea of National Parks 10/29
- Hikers arrested for Pennine trespassing 4/32
- Civilian Conservation Corps; US New Deal 6/33
- New and Epping Forests burn in heatwave 9/33
- London Council proposes a "green belt" 4/37
- Atomic tests in Nevada desert; no danger 1/51
- Dartmoor is a national park 8/51
- Eight British areas are nature reserves 5/52
- Hydrogen bomb test; island disappears 11/52
- Smog masks on prescription for the ill 11/53
- BMA wants action on smog pollution 11/53
- Myxomatosis destroys rabbits in UK 7/54
- National Trust buys Fair Isle 9/54
- Atomic waste is a health risk, WHO 1/55
- "Smokeless zone" London from October 3/55
- Britain's Clean Air Bill passed 7/55
- Myxomatosis in 11 UK counties 8/57
- Parts of Surrey deemed nature areas 5/58
- Leukaemia: Windscale nuclear plant links 1/59
- M1 motorway changed to save forest 8/59
- Rhinoceros elected in Sao Paulo 10/59
- Antarctic becomes a science reserve 12/59
- Commission blasts nuclear plants 12/59
- Dutch elm disease spreading, UK 8/75
- 6.5 million UK elms killed by disease 10/75
- Milan suburb evacuated in chemical scare 7/76
- Dioxin pollution, Seveso; 250 affected 7/76
- Seveso women's abortions 8/76
- UNESCO fund to save polluted Acropolis 1/77
- North Sea oil slick "worst pollution" 4/77
- Kenyatta bans big game hunting 5/77
- Economist Schumacher dies: profile 9/77
- Sweden passes law against aerosol sprays 1/78
- Amoco Cadiz tanker 220,000 ton oil slick 3/78
- Greenpeace stops seal cull 10/78
- Three Mile Island nuclear leak, US 3/79
- Panda gives birth in captivity, Mexico 8/80
- Zoo tiger kills two keepers, UK 9/80
- Anti-vivisectionists attack scientists 1/81
- Scientists warn of greenhouse effect 3/84
- Ship with nuclear cargo sinks, Belgium 8/84
- US-Canadian study of acid rain agreed 3/85
- Greenpeace ship sunk in mystery NZ blast 7/85
- Rainbow Warrior: sunk by French agents 9/85
- Two Rainbow Warrior saboteurs jailed in NZ 11/85
- Chernobyl nuclear reactor explosion 4/86
- Fear of meltdown at Chernobyl reactor 5/86
- Chernobyl report blames technicians 8/86
- Massive pesticide pollution of Rhine 11/86
- UK nuclear waste to be dumped on seabed 5/87
- 70 nations vow to save ozone, Montreal 9/87
- Conference freezes use of chemicals 9/87
- Rare Kew Gardens trees lost in storm 10/87
- Peter de Savary buys Land's End 11/87
- "Greenhouse effect" and depletion of ozone layer problems 12/87
- Karin B leaves Nigeria for Italy 7/88
- Seal disease spreads to British waters 8/88
- Karin B turned away from England 8/88
- Special ecology feature 12/88
- Population grows by 80 million a year 12/88
- Destruction of rain forests 12/88
- Six species destroyed each hour 12/88
- International Union for Conservation 12/88
- Symbol of panda and satellite pictures 12/88
- EC members agrees to ban use of chlorofluorocarbons by 1999 3/89
- Joseph Hazelwood, captain of Exxon Valdez, is fired 3/89
- 11-million gallon oil slick threatens Alaskan sea wildlife 3/89
- British ports ban import of toxic PCBs 8/89
- Oil leak in the Mersey threatens birdlife 8/89
- 103-nation conference votes for global ban on ivory trading 10/89
- Nuclear workers may be advised to not have children 2/90
- Iraq's act of "environmental terrorism" 1/91
- Iraqi forces begin deliberately burning Kuwaiti oilfields 2/91
- More than 150 Kuwaiti oil wells have been set on fire 2/91
- Kuwait's burning oil wells could affect human health 3/91
- Census predicts world's population will rise to 8 billion 3/92
- International Whaling Commission to allow renewed whaling 7/92
- Greek oil tanker runs aground off La Coruna 12/92
- Tanker spills oil into the sea surrounding the Shetlands 1/93
- 1,400-year-old yew tree dies in Britain 3/93
- Huge iceberg breaks away from Antarctica 2/95

Economy (world)
- American election issue 11/00
- International monetary conference 7/03
- Port Arthur opened after Russians leave 11/03
- Australia approves preferential trade 12/03
- Shares tumble as Italy attacks Turks 9/11
- Diamond price falls; South African boom 3/27
- International Economic Conference opens 5/27
- International talks on depression 11/30
- Allies act to stop Soviet grain dumping 3/31
- Hoover wants war debts suspended 6/31
- New York bankers agree £60 million loan 8/31
- Scandinavian Benelux economic alliance 2/32
- World Bank wants return to gold standard 7/32
- World Economic Conference, London 6/33
- Conference plans to stabilise currencies 6/33
- Conference fails to agree on anything 7/33
- International Monetary Fund created 12/45
- IMF grants $1,300 million to UK economy 12/56
- BP and Shell quit Israel with Arab pressure 7/57
- Half world's population is underfed 10/57
- World Banks warns of "poverty gap" 5/59

- Britain applies for £500m IMF loan 5/65
- Foreign exchange markets close worldwide 2/73
- OPEC raises oil prices by 70% 10/73
- OPEC agrees on 10 per cent oil price rise 1/75
- Britain asks IMF for £1,000 million 11/75
- Seven industrial states pledge action 5/77
- Four-nation summit, Guadeloupe 1/79
- Fears of oil price-fuelled inflation 12/79
- Seven industrial nations to cut oil use 6/80
- Ottawa summit gloom over inflation 7/81
- World Bank sets up fund for Africa 2/85
- Venice summit; leaders back growth 6/87
- Wall Street shares suffer second biggest fall on record 10/89
- Talks avert US-Europe trade war 12/90
- Biggest fall of shares on Wall Street for two years 11/91
- European countries put up interest rates 12/91
- IBM announces loss of £875 million 1/92
- 12 EC and 7 EFTA nations create world's largest trade bloc 2/92
- US car giants, GM and Ford, make record losses 2/92
- EC forecasts 10 per cent unemployment for 1993 5/92
- Ford posts record loss of $7.4 billion for 1992 2/93
- Head of EBRD, Jacques Attali, charged with extravagance 4/93
- Bundesbank interest rates lowest for 5 years 5/94
- Mexico's crisis threatens stability of Western currencies 1/95

Ecuador
- Declares war on Germany 2/45
- Mob burns radio station in Quito 2/49
- President Monray overthrown in coup 7/63
- 119 die when plane flies into mountain 7/83
- Moving towards peace with Peru 1/95
- Cease-fire signed with Peru 2/95

Edberg, Stefan 7/88, 7/89, 7/90
Eddery, Pat 6/90
Ede, Chuter 3/46
Eden, Anthony
- Defends MacDonald-Mussolini talks 3/33
- Meets Hitler 2/34
- Meets Litvinov in Moscow 3/35
- Becomes Foreign Secretary 12/35
- Makes first major speech as Foreign Secretary 2/36
- Signs Anglo-Egyptian treaty 8/36
- Warns Germany: UK will defend Belgium 11/36
- Resigns over Italian appeasement 2/38
- Backs Lindsay against Hogg, Oxford 10/38
- Supports alliance with USSR 5/39
- Recalled as Dominions Secretary 9/39
- War Minister: calls for volunteers 7/40
- Becomes Foreign Secretary 12/40
- Condemns Nazi atrocities against Jews 12/42
- Condemns Japanese torture of troops 1/44
- Back from Potsdam; Tories lose election 7/45
- Supports Middle East withdrawal 12/45
- Condemns railways nationalisation 12/46
- Receives letter bomb 6/47
- Foreign Secretary in Churchill's cabinet 10/51
- Marries Churchill's niece, Clarissa 8/52
- Wants all-German elections 1/54
- Discusses Indochina with US 6/54
- Succeeds Churchill as Prime Minister 4/55
- Wins general election 5/55
- Attends East-West summit in Geneva 7/55
- Meets Eisenhower for talks, US 1/56
- Awarded Order of the Garter 6/56
- Orders bank credit squeeze 7/56
- Warns Nasser over Suez Canal seizure 7/56
- Suez talks; Eden threatens to use force 8/56
- Joint stance with France on Suez 9/56
- Orders Egypt and Israel to withdraw 11/56
- Anglo-French forces bomb Suez 11/56
- US and UN force Suez pullout 12/56
- Strained by crisis; Jamaican holiday 12/56
- Resigns as PM owing to ill health 1/57
- Enters Boston clinic for liver disease 4/57
- Announces end of political life 6/57
- Dies 1/77

Edgar, David 12/80
Edgecombe, John 6/63
Edison, Thomas Alva 5/02, 2/08, 8/10, 5/13, 10/14, 10/27, 10/31
Edmonds, Phil 8/75
Edmondson, Adrian 12/83
Edrich, Bill 9/47, 8/53
Edward VII, King
- See also Royal Family (Britain) 4/05, 4/06, 8/06, 10/07, 11/07, 6/08, 2/09, 7/09, 8/09, 4/10, 5/10

Edward VIII, King
- See also Royal Family (Britain); Windsor, Duke of 1/36, 7/36, 8/36, 9/36, 11/36, 12/36

Edward, Prince of Great Britain 4/64, 11/73, 1/87
Edwardes, Michael 10/77, 2/78
Edwards, Duncan 2/58
Edwards, Gareth 3/79
Edwards, Jimmy 12/53
Edwards, John 1/93
Edwards, Margaret 11/56
Edwards, Robert 2/69, 7/78
Eggers, William van 4/44
Egypt
- See also World War II
- First Cairo-Khartoum through train 1/00
- Cholera kills 5,540 8/02
- 26,000 die from cholera 9/02
- Aswan dam completed on the Nile 12/02
- Anglo-French pact 4/04
- Tory MP rules out Egyptian autonomy 10/08
- Egyptian Youth group wants Britain out 9/09
- Discovery of tablet on Jerusalem's fall 7/10
- Discovery of pharaoh's tomb 10/10
- Kitchener is Consul-General 7/11
- Britain expels vessels from Suez Canal 10/14
- Declared a British protectorate 12/14
- Turkish Suez attack beaten off 2/15
- Attempted assassination on the Sultan 4/15
- British beat Turks in naval battle 8/16
- Nationalist Moslem women demonstrate 3/19
- Troops sent to quell nationalist unrest 4/19
- Police fire on nationalists; two die 10/19
- British troops break up protest; ten die 11/19
- Britain grants constitution 11/19
- British troops disperse rioters; 23 die 5/21
- Nationalists reject "independence fraud" 2/22
- Three English killed, Cairo 2/22
- Formal independence declared 3/22
- King Fuad claims Sudan 5/22
- Tutankhamun's tomb found after 30 years' hunt 11/22
- Earl of Carnavon dies from insect bite 4/23
- Carter finds Tutankhamun's second shrine 11/23
- Tutankhamun's sarcophagus found, Luxor 1/24
- Carter reveals Tutankhamun splendour 2/24
- King opens first parliament 3/24
- Premier Pasha escapes assassination 7/24
- Oldest surviving stone buildings found 9/24
- Tutenkhamun mummy uncovered 11/25
- Ancient tomb at Giza 3/26
- King Fuad visits Britain 7/27
- Women given limited divorce rights 3/29
- Treaty for evacuating British troops 8/29
- Nationalist Wafd Party wins election 12/29
- Parliament after 18 months' dictatorship 1/30
- UK sends battleships sent to quell riots 7/30
- Premier Nahas dismissed; riots in Cairo 7/30
- Friendship treaty with Iraq 4/31
- 23 die and 180 injured in election violence 5/31
- Abandons gold standard 9/31
- King dissolves parliament and constitution 11/34
- Anti-British Cairo riots; two die, 88 hurt 11/35
- King Fuad restores 1923 constitution 12/35
- King Fuad dies; 16-year Farouk succeeds 4/36
- Independence; British protectorate ends 8/36
- UK to control Suez Canal for 20 years 8/36
- Cairo ratifies treaty with Britain 11/36
- Nile floods; Cairo surrounded by water 8/38
- King Farouk declared Caliph 1/39
- French ships at Alexandria cannot leave 7/40
- Italian aircraft bomb Suez Canal 8/40
- Italian troops invade from Libya 9/40
- Lord Moyne, Middle East Resident, killed 11/44
- Stern Gang members killed Moyne 11/44
- Churchill and Roosevelt discuss Japan 2/45
- Declares war on Germany and Japan 2/45
- Premier Ahmed Maher Pasha shot dead 2/45
- Balfour Declaration anniversary riots 11/45
- Claims Palestine is Arab land 1/46
- UK troops open fire on Cairo rioters 2/46
- British troops to be withdrawn 5/46
- Bomb at British club in Alexandria 7/46
- Abdel Krim tells France to quit Morocco 5/47
- Foundation stone of Aswan Dam laid 3/48
- 25 die in Alexandria riots 4/48
- Troops ordered into Israel 5/48
- Attacks Jewish positions in Israel 7/48
- Signs truce with Israel 2/49
- Suez Canal Company admits Egyptian directors 3/49
- Agrees to UK plans for Nile dam, Uganda 5/49
- Currency devalued 9/49
- Signs security pacts with four nations 6/50
- Farouk demands that UK quits Suez Canal 11/50
- UK approves withdrawing troops from Suez 4/51
- Rescinds 1936 alliance with UK; riots 9/51
- Rejects five-nation defence pact and UK bases 10/51
- British troops take Suez Canal Zone 10/51
- Rioting at canal; UK halts arms exports 10/51
- UK's biggest postwar airlift to Suez 11/51
- Invites UN plebiscite on Suez 11/51
- Minister Pasha blames UK for Suez battle 11/51
- UK will leave towns if terrorism stops 11/51
- Take control of Ismailia 11/51
- 33 die and 60 injured in new Suez fighting 12/51
- Government and police back guerrillas 12/51
- British seal off Suez town 12/51
- British capture Ismailia; 46 die 1/52
- 12 Britons murdered in Cairo 1/52
- UK buildings and banks looted in Cairo 1/52
- Farouk dismisses Nahas Pasha regime 1/52
- Farouk suspends parliament for month 3/52
- Hussein Sirry Pasha is new Premier 7/52
- State of alert in Cairo 7/52
- Mohammed Neguib takes power in army coup 7/52
- Neguib deposes "corrupt" King Farouk 7/52
- Titles of Bey and Pasha abolished 7/52
- Neguib ousts Premier Aly Maher 9/52
- 25 officers arrested for plotting coup 1/53
- New talks with Britain on Suez Canal 4/53
- British families leave 5/53
- Neguib and Nasser depose King Fuad 6/53
- Republic under President Neguib 6/53
- 570 Moslem Brother extremists arrested 1/54
- Neguib ousted; swept back to power 2/54
- Pro-Neguib demonstrations; ten shot dead 2/54
- Neguib keeps power from parliament 3/54
- Nasser overthrows Neguib while in Sudan 4/54
- Neguib becomes figurehead President 4/54
- UK's 83,000 troops to leave Suez by 1956 7/54
- Success of Nasser's Suez policy 7/54
- Moslem Brother fires at Nasser and misses 10/54
- Crackdown planned after Alexandria shooting 10/54
- Signs Suez Canal agreement with Britain 10/54
- Nasser ousts Neguib; assumes powers 11/54
- Israel raids Gaza Strip; protests to UN 3/55
- Ends talks with Israel for peace in Gaza 8/55
- Clashes with Israel over Gaza; cease-fire 8/55
- Clashes with Israelis near El Auja, Sinai 10/55
- US in talks over financing Aswan Dam 11/55
- UK sells arms to Egypt and Israel 12/55
- Grants independence to Sudan 12/55
- Nasser assumes full powers 1/56
- Last British soldier leaves Suez Zone 6/56
- Soviet Foreign Minister talks to Nasser 6/56
- Nasser elected President 6/56
- US, UK and World Bank refuse funding for Dam 7/56
- Nasser nationalises and seizes Suez Canal 7/56
- Buys $200 million worth Communist arms 7/56
- Nasser will pay back Canal shareholders 7/56
- Canal talks with France and Britain 8/56
- Nasser boycotts London Suez conference 8/56
- Expels two British envoys for "spying" 8/56
- 22-nation conference creates Suez plan 8/56
- Nasser rejects US plan on Suez 9/56
- Nasser rejects Eden's three-power plan 9/56
- Suez talks in London: Users' Association 9/56
- British and French meet in Paris over Suez 9/56
- Canal Company pilots walk out; UN motion 9/56
- 15-nation Suez Canal Users' Association 10/56
- UK and France tell Egypt and Israel to withdraw from Canal 10/56
- Israelis cross into Sinai and approach Suez 10/56
- Nasser rejects ultimatum; UK bombs Suez 10/56
- UK Marines take Port Said after fighting 11/56
- French land at Port Fuad, move southward 11/56
- UN imposes cease-fire on UK-French attack 11/56
- Israeli troops control Gaza and Sinai 11/56
- UN forces take over Canal; crowds cheer 11/56
- Expels British, French and "Zionists" 11/56
- Anglo-French forces pull back from Suez 12/56
- Israel will not return Gaza 12/56
- UN salvage crews clear Suez Canal 1/57
- Abrogates 1954 treaty with Britain 1/57
- Nationalises British and French banks 1/57
- To keep Canal closed; pressure on Israel 2/57
- Nasser bars Canal to Israel 3/57
- Nasser appoints Gaza governor 3/57
- UN chief Hammarskjold talks with Nasser 3/57
- Jordan closes its embassy 6/57
- Three Britons jailed as spies; later freed 6/57
- Troops in Syria to stop Israel and Turkey 10/57
- Radio calls for King Hussein's death 11/57
- Anti-Western protests; Afro-Asian talks 12/57
- Joins Syria in United Arab Republic, UAR 2/58
- Nasser elected President of UAR 2/58
- Jordan's Hussein severs relations 7/58
- Defence pact, UAR and Iraq 7/58
- USSR to lend $100 million for Aswan Dam 10/58
- USSR agrees to give aid 12/58
- Nasser attacks Syrian Communists 12/58
- Britain unfreezes assets 1/59
- Agrees with UK on Suez claims 2/59
- Nasser talks with UK 12/59
- Nasser lays foundation of Aswan Dam 1/60
- Plan to move Abu Simbel approved 6/61
- UAR calls for UK to withdraw from Kuwait 7/61
- Syria declares independence of UAR 9/61
- State takeover of Shell and Anglo-Egyptian 3/64
- Course of Nile changed 5/64
- Appeal launched to rescue Nile treasures 5/64
- Congolese leader Tshombe held hostage 10/64
- UAR signs aid deal with East Germany 3/65
- King Farouk dies 3/65
- Nasser protests about Aden curfew 9/65
- UN to withdraw force from Israeli border 5/67
- To close Tiran Strait to Israeli ships 5/67
- UAR and Jordan sign military alliance 5/67
- Israel triumphant in Six-day War 6/67
- Nasser's resignation refused 6/67
- Arafat becomes head of PLO 2/69
- 32 Egyptians die in Israeli air raids 3/70
- Israeli bombers kill 30 children 4/70
- Aswan Dam is completed 7/70
- Nasser dies of heart attack 9/70
- Anwar Sadat becomes President 10/70
- 46 die during Nasser funeral 10/70
- Eight USSR troops died in missile-site raid 1/71
- Aswan High Dam opened 1/71
- Not to extend cease-fire with Israel 3/71
- Forms federation with Libya and Syria 4/71
- Sadat foils coup and purges opponents 5/71
- Signs 15-year friendship pact with USSR 5/71
- UAR reverts to the name Egypt 9/71
- Joins federation with Syria and Libya 9/71
- Cuts ties with Jordan 4/72
- Israeli and Egyptian warplanes clash 6/72
- Sadat orders USSR to withdraw advisers 7/72
- Federation with Libya planned 8/72
- Fights Israel in Yom Kippur war 10/73
- UN cease-fire ends Yom Kippur war 10/73
- Signs cease-fire agreement with Israel 11/73
- Fights Israel along Suez Canal line 11/73
- Military separation pact with Israel 1/74
- Israeli withdrawals from Suez west bank 1/74
- Sadat sacks editor Mohammed Heikal 2/74
- Restores diplomatic ties with US 2/74
- Refuses to return 40 planes to Libya 8/74
- 500 Egyptian troops arrested in Libya 8/74
- Reopens Suez Canal: Sadat peace gesture 6/75
- Sadat tells Ford of peace talk plan 6/75
- Sadat bans Soviet warships from ports 3/76
- Plane hijacked; 100 passengers freed 8/76
- 44 die in food riots; curfew 1/77
- Sadat tough on keeping Arab land 3/77
- Sadat arrives in USA for Carter talks 4/77
- Sadat orders end to war with Libya 7/77
- Sadat is first leader to visit Israel 11/77
- Sadat addresses Israeli Knesset: "peace" 11/77
- Sadat wants Middle East talks with US and USSR 11/77
- Carter offers to help Arab-Israeli pact 12/77
- Begin ready to return Sinai, he tells US 12/77
- Sadat and Begin, intense talks, Ismailia 12/77
- Severs ties with Syria, Libya and Algeria 12/77
- Carter and Sadat want Palestinian role 1/78
- Sadat threat over Israel's stance 1/78
- Sadat in Washington for talks 2/78
- Sadat accord with Begin, Camp David 9/78
- Shah arrives after fleeing Iran 1/79
- Signs peace treaty with US and Israel 3/79
- Sadat unhappy about Palestinian status 3/79
- Expelled from Arab League over Isreal 3/79
- Begin first Israeli Premier to visit Egypt 4/79
- Ex-Shah leaves Panama for Cairo 3/80
- Ex-Shah has lung operation 6/80
- Ex-Shah dies; Khomeini rejoices 7/80
- Sadat invites no leaders to Shah's funeral 7/80
- Begin meets Sadat, Sinai 6/81
- Sadat killed by fundamentalists 10/81
- Mubarak takes over as President 10/81
- Mubarak stands by Israeli treaty 10/81
- Parliament chooses Mubarak as president 11/81
- Sadat assassins on trial 11/81
- Five sentenced for Sadat murder 3/82
- Sadat's killers executed 4/82
- Regains Sinai from Israel 4/82
- 500 die when Nile steamer sinks 5/83
- Mubarak visits Jordan 10/84
- Arab terrorists attack bus, killing 15 Israelis 2/90
- Arab League demands Iraq's withdrawal from Kuwait 8/90
- 400 people feared dead as ferry sinks in Red Sea 12/91
- Earthquake leaves nearly 400 dead in Cairo 10/92
- Islamic militants attack British tourists 10/92
- Ceremonies held to mark 50th anniversary of El Alamein 10/92
- Mubarak re-elected for third six-year term 10/93
- Islamic group warns foreigners to leave 2/94

Ehrlich, Paul 8/15
Ehrlichman, John 4/73, 6/73, 8/74, 1/75, 2/75
Eichmann, Adolf 12/39, 5/60, 6/60, 4/61, 6/61, 8/61, 12/61, 5/62
Eicke, Theodor 7/34
Eiffel, Gustave 12/23
Einaudi, Luigi 5/48, 4/55
Einstein, Albert 4/55
Eisenhower, Dwight David 10/42, 3/69
Eisenhower, Mamie 9/55
Eisenstein, Sergei 12/25, 2/48
Eisler, Gerhart 5/49
Eisner, Kurt 2/19
Ekland, Britt 2/64
El Salvador
- With Honduras, repels Guatemalan invasion 7/06
- 250 die in San Salvador train explosion 3/34
- 200 die in earthquake 12/36
- El Salvador troops invade Honduras 7/69
- 100 killed in failed revolt 3/72
- Guerillas kidnap two UK bankers 12/78
- Police kill 24 outside cathedral 5/79
- 20,000 in anti-government funeral march 5/79
- Carlos Romero ousted in coup 10/79
- Reformist Archbishop Romero shot dead 3/80
- 20 killed at Romero's funeral 3/80
- Massacre: marchers blame rightists 3/80
- Leftists murdered; 20 more die 11/80
- US nuns and missionary killed 12/80
- Duarte returns to lead new junta 12/80
- Leftist guerrillas fire at army 12/80
- Martial law 1/81
- US Senate to cut aid if killings continue 4/81
- Soldiers arrested for US nuns' murder 5/81
- Reagan to send emergency aid 2/82
- Six soldiers charged with nuns' murders 2/82
- Helps draft Central American peace plan 1/84
- Ex-troops guilty of 1980 murder of nuns 5/84
- San Salvador earthquake kills scores 8/86
- Signs Central America peace plan 8/87
- Committed to amnesty and elections 8/87
- Right-wing Arena Party wins elections 3/89
- Over 650 die in guerilla attacks 11/89
- Government and guerrilla representatives sign peace pact 1/92

El-Said, Nuri 7/58
Elgar, Edward 3/04, 12/08, 5/11, 12/19, 5/24, 9/30, 11/32, 2/34, 12/34
Elgin, Lord 5/38
Elias, Jorge 6/93
Eliot T.S. (Thomas Stearns) 12/23, 12/35, 12/44, 12/48, 1/65, 12/81
Elizabeth (Queen Mother)
- See also Royal Family (Britain) 5/38, 4/59, 6/67, 4/87, 8/90, 5/92

Elizabeth, Princess (later Elizabeth II) 4/26, 5/35, 5/37, 10/40, 4/42, 12/44, 5/45, 6/47, 7/47, 8/47, 11/47, 4/48, 6/48, 11/48, 12/49, 8/50, 5/51, 6/51, 10/51, 1/52
Elizabeth II, Queen
- See also Royal Family (Britain) 5/37, 12/44, 5/45, 4/48, 2/52, 5/52, 11/52, 4/53, 6/53, 12/53, 1/54, 2/54, 5/54, 8/55, 1/56, 6/56, 10/57, 11/57, 3/58, 6/59, 8/59, 2/60, 1/61, 6/61, 10/61, 11/61, 3/64, 2/65, 5/65, 10/65, 11/65, 1/66, 9/66, 10/66, 3/67, 5/67, 6/67, 7/67, 9/67, 12/67, 7/68, 12/68, 3/69, 7/69, 11/71, 12/71, 6/72, 10/72, 3/73, 2/75, 3/75, 11/75, 10/76, 6/77, 7/79, 10/80, 1/81, 6/81, 7/81, 7/82, 3/83, 11/83, 2/86, 3/86, 10/86, 10/87, 5/89, 11/90, 7/91, 5/92, 6/92, 10/92, 11/92, 12/92, 2/93, 3/95, 3/95, 4/95

Ellington, Duke 12/27, 12/58, 9/71, 5/74, 12/74
Elliot, Walter 4/39
Elliott, Denholm 10/92
Elliott, Herb 8/58, 9/60
Elliott, Peter 1/90
Ellis, Jimmy 2/70
Ellis, Ruth 4/55, 6/55, 7/55
Ellsberg, Daniel 5/73
Ellsworth, Lincoln 5/26
Elsworth, David 4/88
Eluard, Paul 12/20, 11/52
Emburey, John 3/82, 8/89
Emerson, Roy 7/65
Empain, Edouard 1/78, 3/78
Endara, Guillermo 5/89, 12/89
Enescu, George 2/27
Engineering feats
- See Science and technology

English, Arthur 4/95
Enharo, Chief 5/63

Enrile, Juan Ponce 2/86, 11/86, 8/87
Ensslin, Gudrun 4/77
Epidemics
- See Disasters (epidemics)
Epstein, Brian 1/62, 10/65, 8/67
Epstein, Jacob 12/25, 12/34, 12/50, 8/59, 6/60, 5/62
Equatorial Guinea
- Dictator Nguema toppled in coup 8/79
- Nguema sentenced to death for genocide 9/79
Erenu, Hector Rios 4/87
Erhard, Ludwig 4/63, 10/63, 3/65, 8/65
Eritrea
- See Abyssinia, Ethiopia, World War II
Erlanger, Joseph 12/44
ERM (Exchange rate mechanism)
- See European Community
Ernst, Max 2/16, 12/20, 12/25, 4/76
Ernst, Richard 12/91
Ershad, Hossain Mohammed 5/85
Erskine, General 12/51
Ervin, Sam 5/73
Erzberger, Matthias 11/18, 8/21
Escobar, Pablo 7/92, 12/93
Eshkol, Levi 2/69
Esmond, Jill 1/40
Estlin, Edward 9/62
Estonia
- Capital Reval site of British Royal tour 6/08
- Declares independence from Russia 2/18
- Russia recognises independence 2/20
- Joins League of Nations 9/21
- Renews USSR friendship pact till 1945 4/34
- Votes to becomes part of USSR 7/40
- Germans capture capital, Tallin 8/41
- Parliament votes for independence from USSR 8/91
ETA
- See Spain; Catalonia
Ethiopia
- See also Abyssinia
- Eritrea joins federation 9/52
- Selassie grants liberal constitution 11/55
- Abebe Bikila wins Olympic marathon 9/60
- Coup collapses; Selassie returns 12/60
- Organisation of African Unity formed 5/63
- Elizabeth II makes tour 2/65
- Selassie talks with Mao in Peking 10/71
- 100,000 feared dead in famine 11/73
- First-ever general strike 3/74
- Haile Selassie overthrown in army coup 9/74
- Planes attack Eritrean rebels, Asmara 2/75
- Monarchy abolished 3/75
- Emperor Haile Selassie dies 8/75
- African summit on Angola in Addis Ababa 1/76
- US cuts aid over human rights record 2/77
- Somalis attack Harar 11/77
- Fights Somalis in Ogaden Desert 1/78
- USSR support after leaving Somalia 2/78
- Somalia prepares Ogaden invasion 2/78
- Crop failures, war, drought and famine 6/80
- EC grants £1.8 million famine aid 10/84
- Delivery of Western aid thwarted 11/84
- 25,000 Ethiopian Jews flown to Israel 1/85
- 390 killed in rail disaster 1/85
- Live Aid raises £50 million 7/85
- Millions threatened by starvation and civil war 3/91
- New government is formed called People's Revolutionary Front 5/91
- Eritrea votes for independence 4/93
Eubank, Chris 9/91
Euro Disney
- Opens near Paris 4/92
European Coal and Steel Community
- France, W. Germany, Italy and Benelux sign 3/51
- Inaugurated 8/52
European Community
- Six nations create Common Market, Rome 3/57
- UK wants new trade structure with EEC 3/57
- Free trade pact EFTA threatens EEC 11/59
- Britain will ask to join 7/61
- Britain formally applies for entry 8/61
- Agreement on common agricultural policy 1/62
- French and Belgians support UK entry 4/62
- De Gaulle dashes Britain's EC hopes 1/63
- Endorses UK's request to IMF for loan 5/65
- De Gaulle rebuffs Wilson on UK entry 5/67
- Britain reapplies for membership 5/67
- De Gaulle vetoes UK entry 11/67
- Members remove last customs barriers 7/68
- Talks open on entry of UK and Ireland 6/70
- Talks open on entry of Denmark and Norway 6/70
- Terms for UK entry agreed 6/71
- British MPs vote in favour of UK entry 10/71
- Treaty of Brussels signed 1/72
- Britain and Ireland sign treaty to join 1/72
- Norway and Denmark sign treaty to join 1/72
- Britain, Ireland and Denmark join 1/73
- UK announces referendum 1/75
- UK cabinet divided over whether to join 3/75
- UK Labour Party votes to leave EEC 4/75
- Two thirds of UK vote to stay in EEC 6/75
- Greece applies to join 6/75
- Jenkins to be President of Commission 7/76
- Jenkins leaves cabinet to head EEC 1/77
- Jenkins disputes Labour's policy 1/77
- Spain wants to join 7/77
- UK will not join European Monetary System 12/78
- Poor one third poll in UK European elections 6/79
- Socialists are largest group 6/79
- Rules France may not restrict UK lamb imports 9/79
- Thatcher wants £1,000 million rebate 11/79
- Prepared to give UK £350 million 11/79
- Thatcher withholds VAT payments 3/80
- Fails to solve UK contributions 4/80
- Cuts UK contribution to £250 million 5/80
- French fishermen blockade UK ferries 8/80
- Greece joins 1/81
- Threatens USSR over Poland martial law 2/82
- Greenland to pull out 2/82
- Bans Argentinian imports 4/82
- Eight nations continue Argentinian boycott 5/82
- Calls for ban on UK rubber bullets 5/82
- Lifts Argentinian trade boycott 6/82
- Protests at US Siberian pipeline ban 8/82
- Lifts sanctions on USSR 12/83
- Summit collapses over UK budget 3/84
- Grants £1.8m famine aid to Ethiopia 10/84
- Plans war against terrorism 6/85
- Sells surplus butter to USSR at 6p a pound 3/87
- Leaders attack UK for not paying more 6/87
- President says economic unity is on the way 7/88
- Thatcher attacks centralised government 9/88
- Agrees to ban use of chlorofluorocarbons by 1999 3/89
- Declares Britain in breach of laws on drinking water 4/89
- Britain wants closer economic and monetary union in Europe 6/89
- Labour and Green Party share European election win 6/89
- Agrees on urgent aid packages for Eastern Europe 11/89
- Commission modifies Social Chapter plans on workers' rights 11/89
- EC leaders vote 11-1 on changes to the Treaty of Rome 12/89
- Commission orders BAe to pay British government £33 million 6/90
- Sends $1 million aid package to quake hit northern Iran 6/90
- Britain isolated at summit over opposition to greater unity 6/90
- Iraqi military attaches expelled from member nations 9/90
- Britain to apply for ERM membership 10/90
- Thatcher vows to veto single European currency 10/90
- EC agrees to send food aid to USSR 12/90
- Talks avert US-Europe trade war 12/90
- Members agree to end sanctions against South Africa 4/91
- Leaves political and monetary union issue to next summit 6/91
- Threatens to halt aid if fighting continues in Yugoslavia 6/91
- Recognises independence of Baltic states 8/91
- Decision to send peace-keeping force to Yugoslavia deferred 9/91
- Shies sending peace-keeping force to Yugoslavia 9/91
- EC's demand to halt seven building projects angers Britain 10/91
- Ministers to recognise independence of Croatia and Slovenia 12/91
- Maastricht treaty signed 12/91
- Commission recognises independence of Croatia and Slovenia 1/92
- Members sign treaties for closer union; Maastricht accord 2/92
- EC nations to recall their ambassadors from Belgrade 5/92
- Queen Elizabeth welcomes European integration 5/92
- Denmark rejects Maastricht treaty 6/92
- European Parliament celebrates its 40th anniversary 9/92
- French vote "Yes" to Maastricht treaty in referendum 9/92
- Britain pulls out of ERM amid storm 9/92
- Begins enforcing shipping embargo on Serbia 11/92
- EC's Single Market comes into being 1/93
- Commission threatens UK over water quality 7/93
- UK ratifies Maastricht treaty amid monetary storm 8/93
- Major vetoes Delors' chosen successor 6/94
- Luxembourg's Jacques Santer is new President of EC 7/94
- Norway chooses not to join 11/94
- 7 mainland nations agree to end border controls 12/94
- Austria, Finland and Sweden join the Union 12/94
European Defence Community
- Attacked by de Gaulle 2/53
European Free Trade Association (EFTA)
- Formed with seven nations, including UK 11/59
- Offers to absorb Common Market 11/59
European Union
- Seven states abolish border controls 3/95
Evans, Arthur 7/41
Evans, Beryl 6/53
Evans, Charles 6/55
Evans, Edith 10/76
Evans, Edward 5/66
Evans, Gwynfor 7/66
Evans, Harold 1/67, 2/81
Evans, Hiram 6/23
Evans, Medgar 6/63
Evans, Timothy 3/53, 7/53, 8/65, 11/65, 10/66
Everest, Frank 8/49
Everett, Kenny 4/95
Evert, Chris 7/73, 7/74, 7/76, 7/79, 7/80, 7/81, 7/82, 7/84, 7/85
Evren, Kenan 9/80
Ewart-Biggs, Jane 11/76
Ewing, Maria 12/89
Ewing, Winifred 11/67
Exploration and Archaeology
- Gibbons traces course of Zambesi 8/00
- Harry de Windt finishes cross-world trek 8/02
- Stanley, tracer of Congo's course, dies 5/04
- Commander Perry sails for North Pole 7/05
- Amundsen discovers North Pole 12/05
- Amundsen completes North-West Passage 9/06
- Shackleton closest ever to South Pole 1/09
- Peary finally reaches North Pole 4/09
- Dr Cook says he got to Pole before Peary 9/09
- Captain Scott gets Terra Nova for trip 9/09
- Peary honoured for North Pole 10/09
- Cook disgraced after claim rejected 12/09
- South Pole explorer Shackleton knighted 12/09
- Captain Scott sails for South Pole 6/10
- British meet "pygmies" in East Indies 6/10
- Scott finds Amundsen near South Pole 3/11
- Amundsen wins South Pole race 12/11
- Scott arrives at South Pole in second place 1/12
- Professor first man to descend volcano 5/12
- Nelson's war stores found in Sardinia 2/13
- Captain Scott found dead in Antarctic 2/13
- Captain Besley finds Inca jungle ruins 2/14
- Robert Peary dies 2/20
- New statues found in Angkor, Cambodia 12/21
- Ernest Shackleton, Antarctic hero, dies 1/22
- Amundsen leaves for North Pole 6/22
- 26,000 feet up Mount Everest, new record 6/22
- Carter uncovers Tutankhamun's tomb 11/22
- Carter finds Tutankhamun's second shrine old statues 11/23
- Wall-paintings discovered in Tutankhamun's shrine 11/23
- Carter reveals Tutankhamun splendour 2/24
- Mallory and Irvine die on Mount Everest 6/24
- Remains of ancient civilisation found on Galapagos Islands 8/24
- Mallory may have climbed Everest 10/24
- Franco-US team find Saharan sea shells 10/25
- Five ancient Maya cities found 2/26
- Ancient tomb at Giza, Egypt 3/26
- Airship and plane fly over North Pole 5/26
- Archaeologist finds Saharan "Atlantis" 6/26
- Human remains and dinosaur eggs, Mongolia 12/26
- Prehistoric manicure set found in Iraq 3/27
- Genghis Khan tomb found, China 10/27
- Biblical Sodom "found" near Dead Sea 1/30
- Fridtjof Nansen, Arctic explorer, dies 5/30
- Million-year-old skull uncovered in China 7/30
- Ancient royal palace found at Ur 1/31
- Piccard first man to reach stratosphere 5/31
- Three Neanderthal skeletons in Palestine 5/32
- Atlantis ship finds life on ocean depths 10/33
- Belgian king in mountaineering accident 2/34
- 3,000-year-old archive, Jerusalem 3/35
- Ivan the Terrible's torture chamber found 7/35
- Oldest human ancestor found in Java 12/37
- Prehistoric cave-paintings, Dordogne 11/40
- Arthur Evans, excavator of Knossos, dies 7/41
- Stone Age fossils found in Kenya 5/44
- Mammoth skeletons unearthed in USA 5/47
- "The Kon-Tiki Expedition" published 3/50
- French expedition conquers Annapurna 6/50
- Himalayan "Yeti" discovered? 12/51
- Assault on Everest south face fails 5/53
- Hillary, Tensing conquer Mount Everest 6/53
- Hunt, Hillary knighted; Tensing's medal 7/53
- "Piltdown Man" skull is a hoax 11/53
- UK-led team to hunt for Yeti in Nepal 12/53
- Charles Evans climbs Kanchenjunga 6/55
- Admiral Richard Byrd dies 3/57
- Hillary beats Fuchs in South Pole race 1/58
- First overland crossing of Antarctica 3/58
- Roman mosaic at Sussex site 4/58
- Nautilus, first submarine under North Pole 8/58
- Richard Leakey shows prehistoric skulls 10/59
- Stonehenge not druid claim 12/59
- Ancient Hebrew biblical scrolls found 2/60
- Chinese claim to have climbed Everest north face 5/60
- Ten Stonehenge skeletons uncovered 9/60
- New find of fossil bones, Tanganyika 2/61
- 40 Biblical scrolls found in Judaea 4/61
- Evidence for Pilate's existence found 6/61
- Roman mosaics found at Fishbourne, UK 8/61
- Winter ascent of Matterhorn's north face 2/62
- 300-year-old skull dug up in Downing Street 3/62
- Bonington climbs Eiger north face 8/62
- Viking remains found in Canada 11/63
- Eiger North face conquered by direct route 3/66
- Matterhorn north face climbed in winter 2/67
- Oldest human skull found in Kenya 11/72
- Terracotta "army" found near Xian, China 7/75
- Haston and Scott climb south-west Everest 9/75
- Mike Burke dies up Everest 9/75
- Sir Robert Eric Mortimer Wheeler dies 7/76
- Mary Leakey finds ancient footprints 2/78
- Titanic sighted undersea 8/80
- David's palace found in Jerusalem 8/80
- Dinosaur remains found in clay pit, UK 7/83
- Death of Sherpa Tensing 5/86
- Biggest Iron Age burial site in UK 9/87
- No Loch Ness monster found 10/87
- Actors and archaeologists campaign to save Rose theatre 5/89
- Remains of Shakespeare's Globe theatre found 10/89
- Two British explorers make successful Antarctic trek 2/93
- Human fossils in Ethiopia may provide "missing link" 9/94
Exxon Shipping
- To take responsibility for oil slick off the coast of Alaska 3/89
- Must pay for Alaska oil spill 9/94
Eyre, Richard 12/83, 1/87
Eyskens, Gaston 3/50
Eyston, George 10/37, 9/38

F

Fabius, Laurent 7/84, 9/85
Facta, Luigi 10/22
Fagan, Michael 7/82
Fagg, Graham 12/90
Fahd, King of Saudi Arabia 6/82, 10/86
Fairbairn, Nicholas 1/82
Fairbank, Charles Warren 6/04
Fairbanks, Douglas 4/19, 3/20, 3/24, 5/29, 6/29, 12/33, 1/35, 5/39, 12/39
Fairfax, John 4/72
Fairley, Gordon 10/75
Fairley, Michael 2/85
Faisal, Emir of Iraq 4/39
Faith, Adam 1/65
Faithfull, Marianne 1/70
Falcone, Giovanni 5/92, 1/93
Faldo, Nick 7/87, 5/89, 4/90, 7/92
Falkenburg, Robert 7/48
Falkender, Lady (Marcia Williams) 5/76
Falkenhayn, Erich von 6/15, 8/16, 4/22
Falklands
- Royal Navy sinks four German cruisers 12/14
- Lord Chalfont visits 11/68
- Argentina increases links 4/80
- Argentinian scrap merchants land; fears 3/82
- Argentina captures islands 4/82
- 200-mile exclusion zone around islands 4/82
- UK Task Force sails from Plymouth; Argentina invades 4/82
- UK sink Belgrano; hundreds die 5/82
- Argentina sinks HMS Sheffield with Exocets 5/82
- QE2 requisitioned for Falklands 5/82
- UK beachhead, San Carlos; HMS Ardent sunk 5/82
- HMS Antelope sunk; Argentine planes downed 5/82
- Atlantic Conveyor sunk by Exocets 5/82
- UK troops land; victory at Goose Green 5/82
- UK forces advance on Port Stanley 5/82
- UK wins Port Stanley; Argentina surrenders 6/82
- Sir Gallahad and Sir Tristram hit at Fitzroy 6/82
- Franks inquiry into Falklands War 7/82
- UK lifts 200-mile exclusion zone 7/82
- 800 rewarded in Falklands honours list 10/82
- UN wants talks on Falklands sovereignty 11/82
- Thatcher visits the islands to mark 10th anniversary of war 6/92
Fall, Albert B. 10/23
Fallieres, Armand 1/05, 1/06, 7/07
Fanfani, Amintore 2/08
Fang Lizhi 2/89
Fangio, Juan 6/11, 7/51, 8/54, 2/58
Fantin-Latour, Henri 8/04
Farman, Henri 1/08, 3/08, 7/58
Farman, Maurice 2/64
Farouk, King of Egypt 4/36, 1/39, 3/48, 11/50, 1/52, 3/52, 7/52, 12/52, 3/65
Farr, Tommy 8/37
Farrell, Mairead 3/88
Farrow, Mia 7/66, 12/68, 6/93
Fashion and Fads
- Corsets out; knickerbockers in 11/00
- Pierre Lorillard, inventor of tuxedo, dies 7/01
- Corsets for sporting women 5/02
- The "Gibson Girl" look 12/03
- Patent leather shoes for less than 10 shillings 1/04
- First vegetarian organisation founded 1/05
- American-style store in London 3/09
- Ziegfeld Follies opens at New York's Jardin de Paris 6/11
- Paul Poiret's sensuous evening wear 1/12
- Latest fashion in tennis 6/12
- War on tight dresses; Modesty League, US 7/12
- Barbour clothing manufacturers founded 9/12
- US "Ragtime" comes to Britain 12/12
- Doctor analyses women's fashions 5/13
- Woman in split skirt arrested in London 7/13
- Kaiser orders army not to dance tango 11/13
- "Wigwam" hats all the rage in Paris 2/14
- War committee blasts extravagant dresses 3/16
- Suzanne Lenglen's daring tennis dress 7/19
- Latest wear for tango 5/20
- "Red Seal" artificial silk hosiery 3/21
- US police chief bans skirts too short 3/21
- Women with bare arms and short skirts to be fined in Chicago 5/21
- Evening dress by Worth 9/21
- Valentino causes a stir 10/21
- Women want styles to reflect new freedom 15/21
- "Oxford Bags" are latest men's fashion 5/22
- Plumes, veils and trains are back 6/22
- Coco Chanel creates new look 2/23
- Marathon dancing craze in US; injuries reported 4/23
- The royal wedding dress 4/23
- Dancing Masters condemn tango and foxtrot in Paris 5/23
- Wavy hair via cardboard tubes 10/23
- Extravagant French suits for women 3/24
- Nightclubbing is all the rage 5/24
- YWCA tells working women to "dress to succeed" 5/24
- Council of Catholic Women campaigns for dress modesty 7/24
- America's Charleston overwhelms Britain 9/25
- Medical officers praise hygienic values of modern fashions 7/26
- Oxford student magazine condemns "Bags" 1/27
- Shingling boosts hairdressers 5/27
- Long hair for women is out of date 9/27
- Beards and moustaches go out of fashion 9/27
- Longer skirts return according to dressmakers 1/28
- Women's Wear Exhibition opens in London 7/29
- Sun tan cruises 8/29
- Decline in petticoat demand hits cotton industry 5/30
- Colourful women's swimwear 6/30
- Hemline drops as dresses become more feminine 6/30
- National Union for Equal Citizenship condemns long skirts 3/31
- Pyjama suits on show at the British Industries Fair 5/32
- Backless gowns with capes for evenings 11/32
- More cheaper, ready-to-wear clothes 11/32
- Dietrich trend: menswear for women 5/33
- Prince of Wales backs women in shorts 3/34
- Women Wimbledon players may wear shorts 5/34
- Barker's grade one suits for four guineas 5/34
- Queen Mary's white Jubilee dress 5/35
- Gymnasia; slimming to music 10/35
- Lowest heels for years; Annual Shoe and Leather Fair 10/35
- Trend for pierced ears among the young 5/36
- Dazzling jewellery and dress; Coronation 5/37
- Sunbathing becomes more popular 8/37
- Men's summer wear slacks and shorts 7/38
- Women's League of Health and Beauty shows exercises are fun 6/39
- Introduction of coupons to buy clothes 7/41
- Women use beetroot juice for lipstick in cosmetic shortage 2/42
- Hemlines up; utility cloth introduced 3/42
- UK women have "bare legs for patriotism" 5/42
- Vatican bans women without stockings from St. Peter's 7/42
- Only grey or blue for school uniforms allowed to save on dye 1/43
- Clothes rationing is saving the country money 5/43
- Clothing restrictions lifted; end of "austerity suit" 2/44
- Jitterbug craze takes over Britain 5/46

- Black market nylons still flourishing 8/46
- Dior's "New Look" 6/47
- Dior's autumn collection; popular fabrics easier to find 8/47
- Extra clothing coupons available 5/48
- Clothes rationing abandoned 3/49
- Lace-trimmed panties shock Wimbledon 6/49
- Adolescents' free time spent at cinema and dancing 4/50
- Centenary of bowler hat 10/50
- US drive-in cinemas double in a year 12/50
- Shah's wife's wedding dress encrusted with diamonds 3/51
- Ultra-high stiletto heels on shoes 9/53
- Dior's "A" line dresses and wandering belts 3/55
- Dior "look" imitated in Britain 3/55
- 3-D films and glasses 4/55
- Teddy Boys arrested at dance-hall in Bath 5/55
- Women's blue jeans come to Britain 8/55
- Teddy Boy fashions 10/55
- "Rock Around the Clock" causes Teddy Boys to riot at cinemas 9/56
- Rock 'n' roll catchphrases spread 2/57
- Christian Dior dies 10/57
- Yves St. Laurent new fashion king 1/58
- New clean-cut home interiors 8/58
- Bubble-cars spark interest at British Motor Show 10/58
- British hula-hoop record 1/59
- Dior's red cabbage dress 3/59
- St. Laurent raises hemlines for young 7/59
- Chanel shows classic suits a la Hepburn 7/59
- Teenage culture - skiffle and rock 'n' roll 12/59
- Teddy Boy drainpipe trousers, draped jackets 12/59
- The motor-cyle look: Dean and Brando 12/59
- Yves St. Laurent starts his own business 1/62
- St. Laurent wins court case against Dior 3/62
- Mary Quant says Paris is "out of date" 1/64
- Mini skirts shock 11/65
- London is fashion capital of the world 12/66
- Pink hipster ... kaftans ... beads 12/66
- Biba department store opens in London 9/69
- "Maxi" and "midi" skirt lengths 10/69
- Coco Chanel dies, France 1/71
- Hot pants censure 4/71
- Topless women on Riviera told to cover up 7/71
- Micro skirts 11/71
- St. Laurent's "Le Look Anglais" 3/72
- Jeans 2/73
- French expert Elsa Schiaparelli dies 11/73
- Streaker at Twickenham, UK 4/74
- Laura Ashley opens first shop in US 7/74
- UK's latest pop idol: Boy George 1/84
- Pop singer Madonna influences fashion 9/85
- Death of Laura Ashley 9/85
- Homage to Dior's New Look 40 years on 1/87
- Agency reports new consumerist values 11/87
- French courturier, Guy Laroche, dies 2/89

Fassbinder, Rainer Werner 6/82
Fatima
- Virgin vision in Portuguese village 7/17

Faubus, Orval 9/57, 8/58, 8/59
Faulkner, Brian 2/69, 5/69, 3/71, 8/71, 3/72, 12/73, 1/74, 5/74
Faulkner, William 7/62
Faure, Edgar 2/52
Faure, Gabriel 11/24
Fawiz, Mohammad 5/71
Fawkes, Lindsay 8/56
Feather, Vic 2/69, 9/72, 11/72
Fechter, Peter 8/62
Fedoseyev, Anatol 6/71
Feisal, King of Iraq 8/21, 6/33, 9/33, 9/33, 5/53, 7/58
Feisal, King of Saudi Arabia 10/62, 11/64, 3/75
Feisal, King of Syria 10/18, 3/20, 7/20
Feldman, Marty 2/69
Fellini, Federico 1/20, 12/77, 11/93
Feminism
- See Women, Women's suffrage

Fenby, Eric 12/34
Feng Kua-Chang 8/17
Ferdinand, Foch 3/29
Ferdinand, King of Bulgaria 10/18
Ferdinand, King of Rumania 2/19, 11/26, 7/27, 6/30
Ferguson, Miriam "Ma" 7/26
Ferguson, Sarah 3/86, 7/86
Fermi, Enrico 8/01, 12/42, 11/54
Ferrari, Enzo 8/88
Ferraro, Geraldine 7/84, 11/84
Ferrer, Francisco 10/09
Ferrier, Kathleen 8/47, 10/53
Feuchtwanger, Leon 3/33
Feydeau, Georges 6/21, 12/21
Feynman, Richard Phillips 2/88
Field, Winston 4/64
Fields, Gracie 2/35, 1/38, 12/43, 9/79
Fields, Terry 7/91
Fields, William Claude (Dukenfield) 12/46
Fiennes, Ranulph 2/93
Fiji
- Becomes independent of Britain 10/70
- Colonel Rabuka leads anti-Indian coup 5/87
- Premier Bavadra arrested 5/87
- Governor-General Ganilau rejects coup 5/87
- Ganilau heads provisional government 5/87
- Rabuka in talks before republic 9/87
- Rabuka declares republic; Ganilau quits 10/87
- Queen must accept Ganilau's resignation 10/87

Films
- See also Cinema, December arts surveys
- "The Birth of a Nation", D.W. Griffith 3/15
- "The Tramp", with Charlie Chaplin 4/15
- "The Sheikh", starring Rudolph Valentino 10/21
- "Battleship Potempkin", Sergei Eisenstein 12/25
- "The Jazz Singer", first talkie, Johnson 10/27
- "Steamboat Willie", Mickey Mouse cartoon 9/28
- "The Terror", Edgar Wallace (all-talkie) 10/28
- First Marx Brothers' film: "The Cocoanuts" 5/29
- "Modern Times", with Charlie Chaplin 2/36
- "Snow White and the Seven Dwarfs" 1/38
- "Stagecoach", starring John Wayne 3/39
- "The Wizard of Oz", starring Judy Garland 8/39
- "Gone With the Wind" gets five Academy Awards 3/40
- "Fantasia" by Walt Disney 11/40
- "Citizen Kane", starring Orson Welles 4/41
- "Brief Encounter" wins Cannes prize 10/46
- Olivier's "Hamlet" wins five Oscars 3/49
- "A Streetcar Named Desire", starring Vivien Leigh 9/51
- "Singin' in the Rain", with Gene Kelly 3/52
- "Limelight", starring Charlie Chaplin 10/52
- Marilyn Monroe stars in "Gentlemen Prefer Blondes" 7/53
- "The Robe", using Cinemascope 9/53
- "Seven Brides for Seven Brothers" 7/54
- "Rebel Without a Cause", James Dean 9/55
- "Rock Around the Clock", with Bill Haley 9/56
- William Wyler's "Ben Hur", starring Charlton Heston 11/59
- "Lawrence of Arabia" wins seven Oscars 4/63
- Sean Connery stars in "From Russia With Love" 5/63
- "A Hard Day's Night", with the Beatles 7/64
- "Mary Poppins" wins five Oscars 4/65
- "My Fair Lady" wins eight Oscars 4/65
- Beatles' film: "Help!" 7/65
- "The Sound of Music" wins Oscar 4/66
- "A Man for All Seasons" wins six Oscars 4/67
- "M*A*S*H" wins Cannes prize 5/70
- "Valentino", starring Nureyev 10/77
- "Superman", with Christopher Reeve 6/78
- Richard Attenborough's "Gandhi" wins eight Oscars 4/83
- "Crocodile Dundee", with Paul Hogan 9/87
- "Silence of the Lambs" wins five Oscars 3/92

Finch, Peter 1/77, 3/77, 12/77
Finland
- See also World Wars I and II
- Russian as official language 6/02
- Czar abolishes "autonomy" 9/02
- Czar appoints Russian General Bobrikov as leader 3/03
- Governor-General Bobrikov is assassinated 6/04
- Prince Ivan Obolenski becomes new Governor 7/04
- Men and women over 24 get the vote 3/06
- First country in the world to elect women MPs 3/07
- Finnish Diet opens 5/07
- Kaiser meets Czar 6/09
- Finns exempt from Russian military service 10/09
- Russian Duma to abolish Finnish autonomy 6/10
- Proclaims independence from Russia 7/17
- Demands withdrawal of Russian troops 12/17
- Russia and Germany recognise independence 1/18
- Repels Russian Red Guards 5/18
- Peace treaty with Germany ratified 6/18
- Anti-Communist repressive measures 11/30
- Lifts ban on alcohol 1/32
- 1944 Olympics to be held in Helsinki 9/38
- Baltic fleet mobilised 10/39
- USSR tells Finnish troops to pull back 11/39
- Border clashes with Soviet troops 11/39
- Finns evacuate areas ceded to USSR 3/40
- Signs peace treaty with USSR 3/40
- Signs treaty with Germany 10/40
- Signs armistice with USSR 9/44
- Declares war on Germany 3/45
- Loses land under Paris peace treaties 2/47
- To experiment with collective farming 5/47
- Signs defence pact with USSR 4/48
- USSR vetoes entry to UN 9/49
- President opens Helsinki Olympic Games 7/52
- Urho Kekkonen elected President 2/56
- Sibelius, musical genius, dies 9/57
- Death of athlete Paavo Nurmi 10/73
- First World Athletics Championships 8/83
- Stray USSR missile found in Lake Inari 1/85
- Joins the EU 12/94

Finlay, Carlos 2/02
Finnbogadottir, Vigdis 6/80
Finnegan, Chris 5/73
Finney, Albert 3/56, 12/60, 10/76, 12/84
Finney, Tom 6/50, 4/57
Finucane, Pat 2/89
Fischer, Bobby 10/71, 7/72, 9/72, 4/75
Fischer, Edmond 12/92
Fischer, Edwin 1/60
Fischer, Emil 12/02
Fisher, Andrew 11/08, 4/10
Fisher, Geoffrey (Archbishop) 9/38, 1/45, 1/46, 3/47, 10/47, 6/53, 11/59, 12/60, 1/61, 9/72
Fisher, Herbert A.L. 3/18, 4/40
Fisher, John 6/04, 2/06, 10/14
Fitt, Gerry 8/70, 12/73, 1/76, 8/76, 9/79, 11/81, 7/83
FitzGerald, Garret 6/81, 11/81, 2/82, 11/85, 6/86, 1/87, 2/87
Fitzgerald, Ella 4/18
Fitzgerald, F. Scott 12/20, 12/25, 12/40
Fitzgerald, Michael 10/20
Fixx, James F. 7/84
Flanagan, Bud 10/68
Flanders, Michael 4/75
Flandin, Pierre 11/34, 6/35
Flegenheimer, Arthur "Dutch Schultz" 6/31
Fleitz, Beverly 7/55
Fleming, Alexander 9/28, 12/45, 3/55
Fleming, Anne 8/64
Fleming, Ian 5/08, 12/55, 5/63, 8/64
Fleming, John 10/04
Fleming, Victor 3/40
Fletcher, Frank 8/42
Fletcher, Yvonne 4/84
Florey, Howard 12/45
Flynn, Errol 2/43, 10/59
Foale, Michael 2/95
Foch, Ferdinand 9/14, 3/18, 11/18, 3/29
Folger, Abigail 8/69
Folies Bergère, Paris
- Closes after being open since 1869 12/92

Fonda, Henry 5/05, 3/82, 8/82
Fonda, Jane 12/37, 8/69, 12/78, 3/82
Fonda, Peter 12/69
Fontaine, Joan 12/40
Fontaine, Just 6/58
Fonteyn, Margot 1/37, 4/59, 6/59, 12/59, 12/65, 12/70, 2/91
Foot, Dingle 12/69
Foot, Hugh 1/58, 8/60
Foot, Michael 11/49, 2/58, 11/60, 3/61, 1/68, 11/71, 3/74, 3/76, 10/80, 11/80, 10/81, 6/83
Football (Britain)
- See also FA Cup winner, April or May most years
- Can footballers be considered workers? Injury dispute 11/09
- League resumes 11/18
- Chelsea win London "Victory Cup" 4/19
- Huddersfield Town win third League title 4/23
- Bolton Wanderers win FA Cup Final 4/26
- First cup tie under artificial light 2/30
- First match with numbered shirts 4/33
- Ted Drake scores record seven goals 12/35
- Joe Payne scores ten goals for Luton 4/36
- Baptists and traders attack football pools 4/38
- Bryn Jones record transfer fee of £13,000 8/38
- 59 matches cancelled because of weather 2/47
- Derby sign Billy Steel for record £15,000 5/47
- Arsenal win League a record seventh time 5/53
- Stanley Matthews wins his first FA Cup 5/53
- Newcastle in record tenth Cup Final 5/55
- First floodlit football match at Wembley 11/55
- Players want extra fee for televised games 3/56
- New Chelsea star: Jimmy Greaves 8/57
- Manchester United team in Munich air crash 2/58
- Spurs achieve League-Cup double 5/61
- Spurs win European Cup Winners' Cup 5/63
- Bristol players banned for bribe-taking 8/63
- John White of Spurs killed by lightning 7/64
- Stanley Matthews knighted 1/65
- Stanley Matthews retires 4/65
- Liverpool wins FA Cup for first time 5/65
- First substitute in Football League 8/65
- England beat Germany to win World Cup 7/66
- Alf Ramsay knighted; OBE for Bobby Moore 1/67
- Queen's Park Rangers win League Cup 3/67
- Celtic win European Cup 5/67
- Coventry manager Hill to move into TV 8/67
- Manchester United win European Cup 5/68
- Bobby Charlton scores 45th goal for England 5/68
- Matt Busby is knighted 6/68
- Manchester United manager Matt Busby resigns 1/69
- Soccer hooligans run riot on the tube 3/69
- George Best suspended 1/70
- England captain held for theft, Colombia 5/70
- Arsenal win FA Cup and League double 5/71
- Chelsea win European Cup Winners' Cup 5/71
- Best sent off in new referees' crackdown 8/71
- Chelsea achieve record European score 9/71
- Rangers win European Cup Winners' Cup 5/72
- Crash damages goalkeeper Banks' eyesight 10/72
- 180 arrested in soccer violence 8/73
- Derby team backs sacked manager, Clough 10/73
- Alf Ramsey sacked as England manager 5/74
- Don Revie becomes England manager 7/74
- Scottish captain banned after brawl 9/75
- Liverpool win League for record ninth time 5/76
- Liverpool win European Cup 5/77
- Scotland beat England; pitch vandalised 6/77
- Liverpool win European Cup, Wembley 5/78
- Trevor Francis, million-pound footballer 2/79
- Nottingham Forest win European Cup 5/79
- Nottingham Forest retain European Cup 5/80
- UK football fans riot at Turin match 6/80
- UEFA fines FA £8,000 for Turin riots 6/80
- Hundredth FA Cup Final 5/81
- Liverpool win third European Cup 5/81
- Pat Jennings in 1,000th top-class match 2/83
- Alcohol ban at some football grounds 4/85
- Over 50 die in Bradford stadium fire 5/85
- British fans riot in Heysel; 41 die 5/85
- UEFA bans UK clubs from Europe 6/85
- Popplewell report into football violence 1/86
- Rival fans battle on cross-Channel ferry 8/86
- 26 football hooligans arrested 1/87
- Celtic win the double 5/88
- 94 supporters die at Hillsborough during FA Cup semi-final 4/89
- Arsenal win football League by beating Liverpool 5/89
- Liverpool beat Everton 3-2 to win FA Cup 5/89
- Celtic beat Glasgow Rangers to win Scottish FA Cup 5/89
- English fans face ban on matches abroad 5/89
- Nottingham Forest keep the Littlewood's Cup 4/90
- Liverpool win League championship 4/90
- Aberdeen beat Celtic to win Scottish Cup Final 5/90
- Manchester United beat Crystal Palace 1-0 in FA Cup 5/90
- Plans announced to form new "super league" 4/91
- Tottenham beat Nottingham Forest in the FA Cup 5/91
- Motherwell beat Dundee United in Scottish Cup Final 5/91
- Liverpool beat Sunderland, 2-0, to win FA Cup 5/92
- Bobby Moore dies of cancer 2/93
- Manchester United win Football League trophy 5/93
- Graham Taylor resigns after World Cup humiliation of England 11/93
- Manchester United win FA Cup 5/94
- Man. Utd's Cantona banned for attack on fan 1/95

Football (international)
- First French teams to play in England 1/02
- England beat France, 15-0 11/06
- Russian police stop match as an illegal assembly 8/13
- France beat England in women's match 5/20
- Jules Rimet of FIFA announces World Cup 11/27
- Uruguay win first World Cup by 4-2 7/30
- Britain and most Europeans not in World Cup 7/30
- Italy beat Czechoslovakia in World Cup 6/34
- Italy's Sciavo is top World Cup scorer 6/34
- Britain beat Germany 6-3; Nazi salutes 5/38
- Italy win World Cup by 4-2 against Hungary 6/38
- Brazil's Leonidas top scorer in World Cup 6/38
- League football returns to post-war UK 9/46
- Air crash kills Italy's football team 5/49
- US beat UK in first round of World Cup 6/50
- Uruguay win World Cup 7/50
- First overseas team to win at Wembley 11/53
- Germany beat Hungary 3-2 for World Cup 7/54
- Rahn wins Cup for German underdogs 7/54
- "European Cup" set up by eight states 4/55
- Real Madrid win first European Cup 6/56
- Manchester United Munich air crash 2/58
- World Cup: France's Fontaine high scorer 6/58
- World Cup: Brazil beat Sweden in final 6/58
- Brazil's stars Garrincha and Pele 6/58
- Real Madrid win European Cup 6/59
- Real Madrid's fifth European Cup win 5/60
- Real beat Eintracht Frankfurt in Glasgow 5/60
- Brazil win World Cup in Chile 6/62
- England lose in World Cup quarter final 6/62
- Spurs (UK) win European Cup Winners' Cup 5/63
- Inter Milan win European Cup 5/64
- West Ham win European Cup Winners' Cup 5/65
- Eight soccer stars banned for drunkenness 10/65
- World Cup stolen in UK - found by dog 3/66
- England beat Germany to win World Cup 7/66
- Celtic win European Cup 5/67
- Manchester United win European Cup 5/68
- Pele (Brazil) scores his 1,000th goal 6/69
- Brazil win World Cup 6/70
- England beaten by West Germany in World Cup 6/70
- Chelsea win European Cup Winners' Cup 5/71
- Chelsea (UK) make record European score 9/71
- Rangers win European Cup Winners' Cup 5/72
- Ajax of Amsterdam win European Cup 5/72
- AC Milan win European Cup Winners' Cup 5/73
- Ajax Amsterdam win European Cup 5/73
- England beat Austria by 7-0 9/73
- Feyenoord win UEFA Cup 5/74
- West Germany win World Cup 7/74
- Pele signs $7 million Cosmos contract 6/75
- Liverpool win European Cup by 3-1 5/77
- England beat Luxembourg 10/77
- Liverpool win European Cup, Wembley 5/78
- Argentina beat Holland to win World Cup 6/78
- Brazil beat Italy to take third place 6/78
- Disappointment for MacLeod's Scots 6/78
- Nottingham Forest win European Cup 5/79
- Nottingham Forest retain European Cup 5/80
- UK fans riot at European match, Turin 6/80
- UEFA fines FA £8,000 for Turin riots 6/80
- Liverpool win third European Cup 5/81
- England beat Hungary; qualify for World Cup 11/81
- Barcelona buys Maradona for £5 million 5/82
- Italy wins World Cup against West Germany 7/82
- England fans riot in Luxembourg 11/83
- Liverpool win European Cup 5/84
- Naples to pay £1m for Diego Maradona 7/84
- 41 die in Heysel stadium riot, Brussels 5/85
- Belgium bans British teams 5/85
- UEFA bans English clubs from Europe 6/85
- Argentina wins World Cup 6/86
- Dutch win European Nation's championship 6/88
- Ireland beat England in Stuttgart 6/88
- England draws 0-0 with Poland in World Cup final 10/89
- Ireland and Scotland reach World Cup final 11/89
- England loses 2-1 to Italy in World Cup 7/90
- West Germany wins World Cup 7/90
- Lazio offers £6 million for Paul Gascoigne 3/91
- Manchester United win European Cup Winners' Cup 5/91
- England draw with Poland to qualify for European finals 11/91
- David Platt becomes the most expensive football player 5/92
- Denmark wins European football championship over Germany 6/92
- France is chosen to organise 1998 World Cup 7/92
- UEFA bars O.M. (Marseilles) 9/93
- Arsenal Win European Cupwinners Cup 5/94
- Brazil win World Cup 7/94

Forbes, Archibald 9/46
Forbes, Bryan 10/59
Forbes-Robertson, Johnston 11/37
Ford Motor company
- Reports record losses 2/92

Ford, Anna 2/78, 4/83, 12/83
Ford, Gerald 7/13
- Becomes US Vice-President 10/73
- Sworn in as Vice-President 12/73
- Sworn in as US President 8/74
- Pardons Nixon over Watergate scandal 9/74
- Broad nuclear agreement with Brezhnev 11/74
- Reaffirms commitments after Vietnam 4/75
- Talks to Sadat on Canal reopening 6/75
- Signs Helsinki pact with USSR 8/75
- Escapes two assassination bids 9/75
- Televised debate with Carter 9/76
- Gaffe over Eastern Europe 10/76
- Loses presidency to Jimmy Carter 11/76
- Acts in TV soap opera "Dynasty" 12/83

Ford, Guillermo 5/89
Ford, Harrison 6/89
Ford, Henry 6/03, 1/04, 10/06, 8/08, 1/14, 1/16, 7/18, 6/24, 10/28, 11/29, 4/47
Ford, John 3/39, 8/73
Ford, Robert 1/72
Foreman, George 10/74, 11/94

Forester, Cecil Scott 4/66
Forman, Milos 2/32, 12/84, 3/85
Formby, George 12/43, 3/61
Formosa
- See also Taiwan
- Nationalists halt Chinese mainland raids 6/50
- MacArthur talks with Chiang Kai-shek 7/50
- Truman says US will go after Korean War 8/50

Forster, E.M. (Edward Morgan) 6/70
Forster, Reginald Erskine 12/03
Forsyth, Bruce 1/68
Forsyth, Frederick 8/38, 12/73
Fosbury, Dick 10/68
Foster, Brendan 9/74, 7/76
Foster, Jodie 2/76, 3/92
Foster, Neil 8/89
Fowler, Norman 1/90
Fowler, William 12/83
Fowles, John 12/81
Fox, Dacre 3/15
Fox, Geoffrey 8/66
France (foreign affairs)
- See also Free French, World Wars I and II
- Shares out Africa with Italy 12/00
- Occupies Mytilene; makes Turkey pay 11/01
- Signs frontier treaty with Siam 10/02
- Secret pact with Italy over Africa 11/02
- Moroccan revolt; French troops on alert 5/03
- To "keep status quo" in Morocco 7/03
- Global pact with Britain 4/04
- Protests at Kaiser's visit to Morocco 3/05
- Conference to settle Moroccan question 1/06
- Moroccan conference ends; parties satisfied 3/06
- Takes Britain's side in Congo dispute 5/07
- French gunships shell Casablanca in revenge 8/07
- Repels Moorish raid into Algeria 4/08
- Backs Moroccan sultan who disavows jihad 9/08
- German treaty recognises French hegemony 2/09
- French Equatorial Africa formed from Congo 1/10
- Fears over German intentions in Morocco 7/11
- Settles Moroccan dispute with Germany 9/11
- Treaty divides Morocco 11/11
- Premier supports Russia in the Balkans 8/12
- Premier Poincare visits Russia 7/14
- Breaks off diplomatic relations with Turkey 11/14
- Indochinese troops play vital role in war 8/16
- Regains Alsace-Lorraine from Germans 12/18
- Wants frontier at Rhine 2/19
- Poincare wants a divided Germany; rejected 6/19
- MPs ratify Versailles treaty 10/19
- Troops enter Ruhr after German moves 4/20
- Creates Lebanon, with Beirut as capital 9/20
- Captures African state of Togo 9/20
- Agrees with Britain on German war debts 11/20
- Sets Syrian and Palestinian borders with UK 12/20
- Military and economic pact with Poland 2/21
- Mobilises to invade Ruhr 5/21
- 20-year alliance signed with Britain 2/22
- Problems of paying Britain war debts 7/22
- Clemenceau warns of German militarism 11/22
- Rejects German non-aggression pact offer 12/22
- Troops enter Essen over German debts default 1/23
- Fines disobedient industrialists in Ruhr 1/23
- Sends 100,000 troops into Ruhr 1/23
- Ruhr cordon to keep coal from Germany 2/23
- Occupies Rhine ports Mannheim and Karlsruhe 3/23
- General Weygand is Commissioner of Syria 4/23
- Troops seize Ruhr railways 6/23
- Alliance with Czechoslovakia 1/24
- Troops pull out of Ruhr towns 8/24
- Fails to agree with rebel Moroccans 4/26
- Forces defeat Krim's Moroccan rebels 5/26
- Forces bombard Damascus rebels; 600 die 5/26
- Plot to kill Spanish king in France 6/26
- Signs trade accord with Germany 8/26
- President Doumergue visits London 5/27
- Signs treaty with Yugoslavia; "Entente" 10/27
- Germany not to pay for French rebuilding 6/29
- Briand promises United Europe 9/29
- Walks out of naval talks 3/30
- Gives Syria constitution 5/30
- Troops leave Rhineland five years early 6/30
- International Colonial Exhibition, Paris 5/31
- Bank of France lends £25,000 to Bank of England 8/31
- Signs non-aggression treaty with USSR 8/31
- Calls for new German reparations 12/31
- Proposes international police force 2/32
- Loses border dispute with Switzerland 6/32
- Discusses its US debts with Britain 7/32
- Defaults on US debt repayment 12/32
- Agrees ten-year peace pact with UK and Germany 5/33
- Grants Trotsky asylum 7/33
- Laval and Mussolini settle frontiers 1/34
- Warns Germany on reparations defaulting 4/34
- Supports independent Austria 9/34
- Laval grants Italy Abyssinian rights 1/35
- Italy promises to stop Hitler in Austria 1/35
- League agrees to return Saar to Germany 1/35
- Plans joint action against aggressors 2/35
- Signs mutual defence pact with USSR 5/35
- Asks Britain to curb Italians in Africa 5/35
- Angry at Anglo-German naval accord 6/35
- Popular Front left alliance draws crowds 7/35
- Communists and Radicals to fight Fascism 7/35
- Fears upsetting Italy accord 10/35
- Germans occupy Rhineland; no resistance 3/36
- Calls for meeting of Locarno signatories 3/36
- Signs London Naval Treaty 3/36
- Drops Italian sanctions 6/36
- Will loan arms to Poland 8/36
- UK Pact with to defend Czechoslovakia 4/38
- Accepts Germany's Sudetenland annexation 9/38
- Calls up reserves; mans the Maginot line 9/38
- Captures Hao Binh in Vietnam 11/38
- Signs border pact with Germany 12/38
- Petain named as Ambassador to Spain 3/39
- Pledges to defend Poland 3/39
- Signs pact with Britain and Poland 4/39
- Pledges aid to Greece and Rumania 4/39
- Pledge to Poland reaffirmed 8/39
- Reserves called up; railways taken over 8/39
- Declares war on Germany 9/39
- Troops cross into Saarland 9/39
- Rejects Germany's peace overtures 10/39
- Signs mutual assistance pact with Turkey 10/39
- Petain breaks ties with Britain 7/40
- UK signs alliance with Free France in UK 8/40
- Napoleon II's ashes returned from Vienna 12/40
- Lebanon declares independence 11/43
- Churchill given freedom of Paris 11/44
- Signs alliance treaty with USSR 12/44
- Signs lend-lease deal with US 2/45
- Signs economic pact with Benelux nations 3/45
- Reasserts power in Syria and Lebanon 5/45
- Among 50 nations to sign UN charter 6/45
- UNESCO founded 11/45
- Plans with UK to quit Syria and Lebanon 12/45
- Recognises republic of Vietnam 3/46
- Four colonies becomes departments of France 3/46
- Big Four in treaty talks, Paris 4/46
- Paris peace treaties signed 2/47
- Signs 50-year alliance with Britain 3/47
- Big Four disagree on postwar settlement 4/47
- Told by Abdel Krim to quit Morocco 5/47
- In talks on Marshall aid plan 6/47
- Marshall aid plan splits Europeans 7/47
- Refuses entry to Jewish refugee ship 8/47
- Stern Gang bomb plot foiled 9/47
- Expresses concern at Czech coup 2/48
- Spain reopens border 2/48
- Signs pact with UK and Benelux countries 3/48
- North Atlantic pact agreed in principle 10/48
- Grants Cambodia independence 12/48
- Suez Canal Company admits Egyptian directors 3/49
- Recognises Bao Dai regime in Vietnam 3/49
- Signs North Atlantic Treaty 4/49
- Agrees on establishment of West Germany 4/49
- Berlin blockade ends 5/49
- Appeals for foreign wheat 6/49
- Laos becomes independent 7/49
- Proposes West European monetary union 9/49
- Protests at USSR's recognition of Ho 1/50
- Recognises Bao Dai regime in Vietnam 2/50
- Recognises royalist regime in Cambodia 2/50
- Recognises royalist regime in Laos 2/50
- Plans for federation of Europe 5/50
- Viet Minh attack French at Dong Khe 5/50
- Deportation of foreign Communists begins 9/50
- Troops repulse Viet Minh forces, killing 6,000 1/51
- Goes to Hague to settle islands dispute 12/51
- Allies delay West German NATO membership 2/52
- Tunisian riots; Premier Shenik arrested 3/52
- Wants UN action if China enters Viet War 4/52
- Facing all-out Viet Minh offensive 11/52
- Laos capital Pakseng falls to Viet Minh 4/53
- Viet Minh insurgents enter Mekong delta 5/53
- Paratroopers in Lang-Son, Indochina 7/53
- Deposes Moroccan Sultan Sidi Mohammed 8/53
- Navarre's paratroops take Dien Bien Phu 11/53
- Ready for Dien Bien Phu fight, Indochina 2/54
- Loses Dien Bien Phu, Indochina 5/54
- Mendes-France wants peace with Vietnam 6/54
- Sino-French pact ends Indochina War 7/54
- Tunisia offered autonomy 7/54
- Offers Morocco regional assemblies 8/54
- Pro-autonomy Mendes-France in Tunis 8/54
- Evacuates North Vietnam 10/54
- Unprepared for Algeria nationalist riots 11/54
- Mitterrand says troops to go to Algeria 11/54
- Approves West German rearmament and NATO membership 12/54
- Plans to integrate Algeria with France 1/55
- Backs Binh Xuyen group in Vietnam war 4/55
- Grants Tunisia internal autonomy 6/55
- Imposes martial law on Morocco after riot 7/55
- Wants Eastern bloc in Council of Europe 7/55
- Reform programme for Morocco 8/55
- Peace talks as 1,000 Moroccans die 8/55
- Rebels attack 25 targets; hundreds die 8/55
- Mollet attacked by settlers in Algeria 2/56
- Mollet: France will not abandon Algeria 2/56
- Grants Morocco independence 3/56
- Troops airlifted to Algeria 3/56
- Recognises Tunisian independence 3/56
- Last French troops leave Saigon 3/56
- Dissolves Algerian parliament 4/56
- Algeria FLN kills 1,000 Arabs and 100 French 5/56
- FLN hacks 19 soldiers to bits on mountain 5/56
- Canal talks with Egypt and Britain 8/56
- Ships requisitioned for Suez battle 8/56
- Troops to be stationed at Cyprus 8/56
- Mollet and Pineau in Suez talks with UK 9/56
- Nasser rejects ultimatum; Suez bombed 10/56
- Troops land at Port Fuad, Egypt; advance south 11/56
- Will withdraw from Suez 12/56
- Joins European Economic Community 3/57
- British Royal visit 4/57
- John Kennedy wants Algerian independence 7/57
- Bourguiba wants troops out of Tunisia 2/58
- Algerian settlers reject deal with Arabs 5/58
- Algerian Committee for Public Safety 5/58
- Settler Salan calls for new government 5/58
- General Lorillot talks to Algerian Salan 5/58
- De Gaulle suggests amnesty to FLN 6/58
- Francophone Africa vote to keep links 9/58
- Algeria votes for negotiated settlement 9/58
- Guinea declares independence 10/58
- Six African states join French Union 11/58
- Settlers vote for de Gaulle 12/58
- Five more French Union African republics 12/58
- De Gaulle offers Algeria referendum 9/59
- De Gaulle favours Algeria compromise 9/59
- UN bans French Saharan nuclear tests 11/59
- De Gaulle denies wanting to ruin NATO 12/59
- De Gaulle wants to break Algerian revolt 1/60
- Michel Debre flies to Algeria 1/60
- Settlers' revolt ends 2/60
- De Gaulle promises Moslems better deal 2/60
- Explodes A-bomb in Sahara 2/60
- De Gaulle visits Britain 4/60
- Refuses to condemn South Africa at UN 4/60
- Togoland gets independence 4/60
- Summit fails as USA will not apologise 5/60
- French Madagascar is independent 6/60
- Central African Republic independence 7/60
- French Congo gets independence 7/60
- De Gaulle visits Algeria 12/60
- French riot in Algeria; 123 die 12/60
- Explodes atomic device, Sahara 12/60
- Votes in favour of Algerian home rule 1/61
- Paris fears invasion by Algerian rebels 4/61
- De Gaulle orders blockade of Algeria 4/61
- 30-day cease-fire in Algeria declared 5/61
- Rudolf Nureyev defects to West 6/61
- Troops kill 80 Moslems in Algeria 7/61
- Algerian coup leaders sentenced to death 7/61
- End of cease-fire in Algeria 8/61
- De Gaulle survives attempt on his life 9/61
- Algerian unrest spreads to French cities 10/61
- 86 die in riots in Algeria 10/61
- More French troops to leave Algeria 12/61
- OAS explodes bombs in Paris 1/62
- Security crackdown on OAS terrorists 1/62
- French troops kill 18 Moslems in Algeria 1/62
- 12 killed by bomb in Algiers 1/62
- De Gaulle pledges peace in Algeria 2/62
- De Gaulle orders troops to crush OAS 3/62
- Boycotts East-West arms talks 3/62
- OAS leader Jouhard arrested in Algeria 3/62
- Salan arrested in Algiers 4/62
- Referendum supports Algerian peace pacts 4/62
- Government supports UK entry to EEC 4/62
- Salan given life sentence in Paris 5/62
- 110 die in OAS terror campaign, Algeria 5/62
- European settlers evacuated from Algeria 5/62
- OAS sets fire to Algerian oilfields 6/62
- Jouhard appeals for end to OAS campaign 6/62
- Six OAS assassins arrested 6/62
- OAS campaign in Algeria ends 6/62
- Proclaims independence of Algeria 7/62
- Algerians vote for independence 7/62
- De Gaulle escapes another death attempt 8/62
- Jouhard death sentence commuted to life 11/62
- Signs deal to build Concorde with UK 11/62
- To buy Polaris missiles from USA 12/62
- De Gaulle dashes Britain's EEC hopes 1/63
- De Gaulle rejects US's offer of Polaris 1/63
- Political and military pact with West Germany 1/63
- Withdraws from North Atlantic Fleet 6/63
- Will not sign test ban treaty 8/63
- Demonstrators protest at US involvement in Vietnam 4/65
- De Gaulle says France will leave NATO 9/65
- Offers Ho Chi Minh aid to end war 2/66
- Formally leaves NATO 6/66
- De Gaulle rebuffs UK on EEC entry 5/67
- De Gaulle raises Free Quebec hopes 7/67
- De Gaulle vetoes UK's entry to EEC 11/67
- Rene Cassin wins Nobel Peace Prize 12/68
- Withdraws from NATO command structure 4/69
- Cohn-Bendit deported to West Germany 4/69
- Embargo on jets to Israel upheld 7/69
- Pompidou gets hostile reception in Chicago 2/70
- Signs accord on Berlin's status 6/72
- Pompidou supports European Union 10/72
- US raid destroys French Embassy in Hanoi 10/72
- Black September seizes Saudi Embassy 9/73
- Israel withdraws envoy over Daoud case 1/77
- Independence for Djibouti 6/77
- Sponsors Central African Empire crowning 12/77
- Paras rescue Europeans in Zaire 5/78
- Shootout with Iraqi guards; two die 7/78
- Offers Iranian leader Khomeini asylum 10/78
- Attends four-nation Guadeloupe summit 1/79
- European Court rules France acting illegally over UK lamb 9/79
- Claims Bokassa gave Giscard diamonds 10/79
- 200 Anglo-French end New Hebrides revolt 7/80
- Fishermen blockade UK ferries 8/80
- Mitterrand committed to NATO 5/81
- Two policemen die in New Caledonia clashes 1/83
- 47 Soviet officials expelled for spying 4/83
- Sends men and arms to Chad 8/83
- IRA arms consignment seized in France 8/83
- 299 die in Shia kamikaze raids, Lebanon 10/83
- Beirut lorry bomb kills 17 French troops 12/83
- Peace-keeping force pulls out of Lebanon 2/84
- Ends no-passport trips by Britons 5/84
- Endorses plans to combat world terrorism 6/84
- Rainbow Warrior sunk: NZ holds two French 7/85
- Report clears government in Rainbow Warrior sinking 8/85
- Minister quits over Rainbow Warrior affair 9/85
- RW sinking: two French agents plead guilty 11/85
- Two Rainbow Warrior saboteurs jailed in NZ 11/85
- Signs Channel Tunnel treaty with UK 2/86
- Several Arab bombs explode in Paris 9/86
- Paris talks: USSR to destroy its chemical weapons 1/89
- Bans all British beef and live cattle imports 5/90
- Sends extra 4,000 troops to Saudi Arabia 9/90
- Four Allied powers sign German sovereignty treaty 9/90
- Anglo-French "lamb war" stepped up 9/90
- Offers Iraq compromise deal to avert war 1/91
- Five Irishmen jailed in bid to smuggle Libyan arms to IRA 3/91
- Winter Olympics held in Albertville ends 2/92
- Euro Disney opens near Paris 4/92
- Agrees to form joint army corps with Germany 5/92
- France is chosen to organise 1998 football World Cup 7/92
- Ratifies nuclear non-proliferation treaty 8/92
- US, British and French planes carry out air strikes on Iraq 1/93
- President Mitterrand says Indochina war was a mistake 2/93
- Government to curb "sex tours" to Asia 11/93
- Asks US to recall "spies" 2/95

France (politics)
- Jacques Chirac becomes President 5/95
- Radical Fallieres elected President 1/06
- Left bloc does well in elections 5/06
- Clemenceau succeeds Sarrien as premier 10/06
- Clemenceau wins majority in Deputies 6/07
- Left gains in Senate elections 1/09
- Clemenceau and cabinet resign 7/09
- Ernest Monis is new premier 3/11
- Joseph Caillaux is new premier 6/11
- Cabinet resigns; Poincare new premier 1/12
- Raymond Poincare becomes President 1/13
- Briand resigns as electoral reform fails 3/13
- Finance bill rejected; Doumergue premier 12/13
- Finance Minister Caillaux resigns 3/14
- Viviani forms national unity government 8/14
- Viviani resigns; Briand is new premier 10/15
- Briand's cabinet resigns 3/17
- Premier Clemenceau chairs peace talks 1/19
- Clemenceau to retire after elections 10/19
- Clemenceau's alliance wins elections 11/19
- Clemenceau's nationalist alliance wins general election 11/19
- Deschanel President, Millerand premier 1/20
- President Deschanel resigns; poll called 9/20
- Millerand elected President, Leygues premier 9/20
- Leygues government falls 1/21
- Briand becomes new PM 1/21
- Poincare beaten in poll; Left controls 5/24
- New President Doumergue; defeat for Left 6/24
- Poincare resigns, followed by Millerand 6/24
- Doumergue asks Herriot to form ministry 6/24
- Painleve resigns; Briand is new premier 11/25
- Franc fails; Poincare forms coalition 7/26
- Briand shares Nobel with Stresemann 12/26
- Poincare rules without Radicals 11/28
- Poincare resigns due to poor health 7/29
- New premier is Aristide Briand 7/29
- Briand's 11th government resigns 10/29
- Georges Clemenceau dies 11/29
- Italian Socialists in Riviera plot 1/30
- Andre Tardieu resigns as premier 2/30
- Tardieu returns as Chautemps fails 2/30
- Maginot line defences planned 9/30
- Pierre Laval forms government 1/31
- Marshal Joseph Joffre dies 1/31
- Briand resigns 1/32
- Andre Maginot, builder of the Line, dies 1/32
- Laval government falls over women's vote 2/32
- Painleve forms leftist government 2/32
- Aristide Briand, ex-premier, dies 3/32
- President Paul Doumer killed by rightist 5/32
- Albert Lebrun is chosen new President 5/32
- Left wins majority in national elections 5/32
- Right loses election, Herriot is premier 6/32
- Doumer's assassin, Gorguloff, gets death sentence 7/32
- Gorguloff guillotined 9/32
- Herriot resigns after government defeat 12/32
- Joseph Paul-Boncour forms new government 12/32
- Daladier becomes premier 1/33
- Daladier resigns as premier 10/33
- Sarraut forms leftist government 10/33
- Paul Painleve dies 10/33
- Marcel Deat founds new Socialist Party 11/33
- Sarraut resigns; Chautemps takes over 11/33
- Opposition sees cover-up in Stavisky case 1/34
- Colonial Secretary Dalimier resigns 1/34
- Chautemps resigns over Stavisky affair 1/34
- Daladier succeeds Chautemps 1/34
- Daladier resigns after two days of riots 2/34
- Ex-servicemen help topple Daladier 2/34
- Ex-President Doumergue is new premier 2/34
- Anti-Fascist manifesto signed by intellectuals 3/34
- Police find Trotsky plotting revolution 4/34
- Trotsky's political asylum cancelled 4/34
- Louis Barthou, Foreign Minister, killed 10/34
- Yugoslav king killed in Marseilles 10/34
- Raymond Poincare dies 10/34
- Flandin replaces Doumergue as premier 11/34
- Laval succeeds Flandin as premier 6/35
- Economic unrest: Brest, Paris, Le Havre 8/35
- 20 accused in Stavisky trial 11/35
- Sarraut succeeds Laval as premier 1/36
- Popular Front wins election 6/36
- Socialist Leon Blum is new premier 6/36
- Votes for budget to match German mility spending 2/37
- Gaston Doumergue dies 6/37

- Blum government falls; Chautemps premier 1/38
- Blum's budget defeated; he resigns 4/38
- Edouard Daladier takes over as premier 4/38
- Daladier empowered to rearm 4/38
- Daladier given full powers in crisis 3/39
- Communist Party dissolved by government 9/39
- Edouard Daladier resigns as premier 3/40
- Paul Reynaud becomes premier 3/40
- 36 Communist deputies jailed for five years 4/40
- Government moves to Tours 6/40
- Petain replaces Reynaud as premier 6/40
- Government moves to Bordeaux 6/40
- Petain's government moves to Vichy 7/40
- Allies recognise de Gaulle's government 10/44
- De Gaulle orders Resistance to disarm 10/44
- UK author P.G. Wodehouse arrested 11/44
- Joseph Caillaux dies 11/44
- Renault factories nationalised 1/45
- De Gaulle nationalises Air France 4/45
- Vichy police chief sentenced to death 4/45
- Petain arrested 4/45
- Daladier, Reynaud et al freed, Austria 5/45
- Laval handed to French forces 7/45
- Trial of Petain begins 7/45
- Petain sentenced to death but reprieved 8/45
- Laval executed 10/45
- Darnand, French Militia head, executed 10/45
- Left-wing parties win many seats 10/45
- De Gaulle elected President 11/45
- De Gaulle includes Communists in cabinet 11/45
- Five banks nationalised 12/45
- Bread riots in Paris and Rouen 1/46
- De Gaulle resigns, says he is retiring 1/46
- Coal mines nationalised 5/46
- Constitution of Fourth Republic approved 10/46
- Vincent Auriol elected President 1/47
- Blum resigns as premier 1/47
- Ramadier forms new cabinet 1/47
- Communist cabinet members sacked 5/47
- De Gaulle calls for new constitution 10/47
- Blum takes over as premier 11/47
- Robert Schuman becomes premier 11/47
- Death of Philippe Leclerc 11/47
- Saarland granted self-rule 1/48
- Franc devalued 1/48
- Andre Marie becomes premier 7/48
- Death of army commander Henri Giraud 3/49
- Georges Bidault becomes PM 10/49
- Strikes to be legalised 2/50
- Death of Leon Blum 3/50
- Police clash with Communist protesters 4/50
- Rene Pleven forms cabinet 7/50
- Former general and Vichy leader Petain dies 7/51
- Faure resigns; Paul Reynard new premier 2/52
- Pierre Mendes-France elected premier 6/54
- Mollet is new Socialist premier 2/56
- Mollet resigns after Assembly defeat 5/57
- Radical premier Bourges-Manoury 6/57
- Algerian crisis; de Gaulle made premier 5/58
- De Gaulle wants special powers and changes 5/58
- De Gaulle wins poll for a Fifth Republic 9/58
- De Gaulle given greater powers 9/58
- Fifth Republic officially declared 10/58
- De Gaulle's UNR wins 198 of 465 seats 11/58
- De Gaulle elected President by landslide 12/58
- Socialists join Gaullists 12/58
- Michel Debre to be new premier 12/58
- De Gaulle inaugurated President 1/59
- Senator Mitterrand avoids assassination 10/59
- Inquiry into Malpasset dam disaster 12/59
- New franc introduced 1/60
- De Gaulle gets emergency powers for a year 2/60
- Far right suffers election setbacks 6/61
- OAS explodes bombs in Paris 1/62
- Security crackdown on OAS terrorists 1/62
- Giscard d'Estaing is Finance Minister 1/62
- Eight die in protest over OAS in Paris 2/62
- General strike declared in Paris 2/62
- Georges Pompidou becomes premier 4/62
- Georges Bidault arrested 8/62
- De Gaulle plans to change constitution 8/62
- Votes for direct presidential elections 10/62
- Gaullists win National Assembly majority 11/62
- Plot to assassinate de Gaulle foiled 2/63
- OAS leader Argoud found injured in van 2/63
- Six OAS members sentenced to death 3/63
- Bidault seeks asylum in West Germany 3/63
- Statesman Robert Schumann dies 9/63
- OAS leader Argoud given life term 12/63
- Communist Party leader Thorez dies 7/64
- De Gaulle re-elected President 12/65
- Death of statesman Vincent Auriol 1/66
- Fierce student riots in Paris 5/68
- "The month of the barricades" 5/68
- Industrial action by ten million workers 5/68
- The franc plummets 5/68
- De Gaulle says he will not quit 5/68
- Measures taken to counter unrest 5/68
- General election called 5/68
- De Gaulle has landslide election win 6/68
- Open-air demonstrations banned 6/68
- Couve de Murville becomes premier 7/68
- De Gaulle suffers referendum defeat 4/69
- De Gaulle resigns 4/69
- Gaston Deferre is presidential candidate 4/69
- Georges Pompidou runs for President 4/69
- Georges Pompidou elected President 6/69
- Jacques Chaban-Delmas appointed premier 6/69
- Death of Edouard Daladier 10/70
- Death of de Gaulle 11/70
- Demonstrators and police fight in Paris 2/72
- Referendum approves enlarging EEC 4/72
- Mitterrand forms pact with Communists 6/72
- Chaban-Delmas resigns as PM 7/72
- Pierre Mauroy forms his second cabinet 4/73
- Pompidou dies of mysterious illness 4/74
- Valery Giscard d'Estaing is President 5/74
- Jacques Chirac becomes PM 5/74
- Andre Malraux dies 11/76
- Bomb at home of right-wing leader Le Pen 11/76
- Releases Black September man Daoud 1/77
- Chirac elected Mayor of Paris 3/77
- Students protest at beach oil pollution 3/78
- Barre forms new cabinet 4/78
- Pelletier, first Minister for Women 9/78
- Giscard leads Mitterrand in first ballot 4/81
- Mitterrand elected President 5/81
- End of 23 years' right-wing government 5/81
- Mitterrand wants nationalisation, taxes 5/81
- Socialists win Assembly elections 6/81
- Mitterrand abolishes guillotine 9/81
- Bank nationalisation starts 2/82
- Klaus Barbie charged and imprisoned 2/83
- Anti-nuclear human chain in Paris 10/83
- Laurent Fabius becomes PM 7/84
- Rainbow Warrior: Defence Minister resigns 9/85
- Mitterrand and Chirac: "cohabitation" 3/86
- Large election gains for National Front 3/86
- Several Arab bombs explode in Paris 9/86
- Tough new measures against terrorism 9/86
- Presidential election: Mitterrand leads 4/88
- Mitterrand re-elected President 5/88
- Bicentenary of the French Revolution 7/89
- Extra £450 million for education after student protests 11/90
- Edith Cresson becomes France's first woman Prime Minister 5/91
- Pierre Beregovoy replaces Edith Cresson as premier 4/92
- Lorry drivers block roads in protest against new licence 7/92
- President Mitterrand undergoes cancer operation 9/92
- 51 per cent voters approve Maastricht treaty in referendum 9/92
- Head of national blood transfusion centre is jailed 10/92
- Mitterrand's party suffers defeat in election 3/93
- Former Prime Minister Pierre Beregovoy commits suicide 5/93
- National Assembly approves of new immigration law 6/93
- Commandos kill Air France Airbus hi-jackers at Marseilles 12/94

France (science and technology)
- Madame Curie wins Nobel Physics Prize 12/03
- First vertical flight airplane 11/07
- Henri Becquerel, physicist, dies 8/08
- Marie Curie dies 7/34
- Lumiere's three-dimensional film, Paris 2/35
- First French atomic reactor starts up 12/48
- Accord signed for European space body 2/62
- Signs deal to build Concorde with UK 11/62
- To build Channel Tunnel with UK 2/64
- Death of aviation pioneer Maurice Farman 2/64
- First French satellite launched 11/65
- Jacob, Lwoff and Monod win Medicine Nobel 12/65
- Alfred Kastler wins Physics Nobel 12/66
- First nuclear sub launched 3/67
- Airbus deal with UK and West Germany 9/67
- Supersonic Concorde 001 on show to public 12/67
- Maiden flight of Anglo-French Concorde 3/69
- Concorde 001 breaks sound barrier 10/69
- Louis Neel wins Physics Nobel 12/70
- Tests H-bomb near Mururoa Atoll, Pacific 7/73

France, Anatole 10/24
Francis, Thomas 4/54
Francis, Trevor 2/79, 5/79
Franco, Francisco 12/30, 7/36, 8/36, 9/36, 10/36, 11/36, 2/37, 4/37, 5/37, 8/37, 10/37, 11/37, 1/38, 3/38, 4/38, 5/38, 7/38, 12/38, 1/39, 2/39, 3/39, 10/40, 9/42, 2/46, 3/46, 2/48, 2/49, 1/55, 11/55, 2/65, 10/66, 9/67, 6/69, 7/69, 6/73, 12/73, 7/74, 9/74, 9/75, 10/75, 11/75, 2/85
Franco, Joao 2/08
Franco, Ramon 12/30
Francombe, John 2/84
Franjieh, Suleiman 4/75
Frank, Anne 6/29, 3/45, 6/52
Frank, Hans 8/46, 10/46
Franklin, Aretha 3/42
Franks, Lord (Oliver) 9/72, 7/82, 1/83
Franz Ferdinand, Archduke of Austria 7/00, 6/14
Franz Josef, Emperor of Austro-Hungary 6/08, 11/16
Fraser, Angus 3/90
Fraser, Dawn 10/64
Fraser, Hugh 11/58, 8/59, 6/69, 10/75
Fraser, Malcolm 12/75
Fraser, Neale 7/58, 7/60
Fraser, Robert 5/67
Frauenfeld, Alfred 12/33
Frazier, Joe 2/70, 9/75
Frederik IX, King of Denmark 1/72
Frederika, Queen of Greece 2/81
Free French
- Troops enter French Somaliland 4/41
- De Gaulle creates government in exile 9/41
- De Gaulle seeks French national strike 10/41
- Forces take two islands off Canada 12/41
- Forces renamed "Fighting France" 7/42
- Troops take Oum-el-Araneb, Libya 1/43
- Troops merge with Monty's Eighth Army 1/43
- Troops help to take Tripoli 1/43
- Pro-Vichy French Guyana joins 3/43
- Provisional government set up in Algiers 5/43
- De Gaulle to sack Vichy collaborators 6/43
- Giraud is C in C of Free French forces 6/43
- French Committee of Liberation set up 6/43
- Allies recognise CFLN 8/43
- De Gaulle sets up Consultative Assembly 9/43
- De Gaulle opens Consultative Assembly 11/43
- Troops arrest Lebanese government 11/43
- Lebanese government released 11/43
- De Gaulle becomes head of armed forces 4/44
- Provisional government of France declared 5/44
- Participates in Allied invasion of South of France 8/44
- Allies recognise de Gaulle government 10/44

Freeh, Louis 7/93
Freeland, Ian 8/69, 9/69, 4/70
Freeman, John 4/51
French Guiana
- See Guiana, French

French, Dawn 12/83
French, Lord (John) 3/14, 8/14, 12/15, 12/19, 11/20, 5/25
Freud, Clement 7/87
Freud, Sigmund 10/00, 12/13, 12/25, 1/38, 9/39
Frick, Wilhelm 1/33, 2/33, 10/46
Friedman, Jerome 12/90
Friedman, Milton 12/76
Friedrich, Ernst 9/77
Friendly Islands
- See Tonga

Frisch, Max 5/11
Fritsch, Werner von 1/38
Fromm, Erich 3/00
Fromme, Lynette "Squeaky" 9/75
Frost, David 12/62, 2/67, 12/83
Frost, Robert 1/63
Fry, Charles Burgess 9/56
Fry, Christopher 12/50
Fry, Roger 1/14, 9/34
Fry, Shirley 7/51, 7/56
Frykowski, Voytec 8/69
Fuad, King of Egypt 2/22, 5/22, 3/24, 7/27, 12/35, 4/36
Fuchs, Klaus 2/50, 3/50, 2/51, 6/59, 1/88
Fuchs, Vivian 2/08, 1/58, 3/58
Fuentes, Miguel 3/63
Fujimori, Alberto 11/92
Fukuda, Takeo 12/76
Fulani empire
- Beaten by British at Sokoto 3/03

Funk, Casimir 11/67
Funk, Walther 12/38
Furtwangler, Wilhelm 11/54
Fury, Billy 12/59

G

G7
- See Group of Seven

Gable, Clark 2/01, 12/39, 12/49, 11/60
Gabon
- Joins French Union as a republic 11/58

Gabor, Denis 12/71
Gaddafi, Muammar 9/69, 11/69, 1/70, 12/71, 6/72, 8/72, 7/73, 1/74, 8/74, 3/79, 8/83, 9/84, 4/87, 1/89
Gaetjens, Larry 6/50
Gagarin, Yuri 3/34, 4/61, 5/61, 7/61, 3/68
Gaidar, Yegor 12/92
Gainsville
- 100 die in tornado 6/03

Gairy, Eric 3/79
Gaitskell, Hugh 9/38, 4/48, 10/50, 4/51, 5/55, 12/55, 3/56, 1/57, 7/58, 10/59, 11/59, 2/60, 10/60, 11/60, 11/61, 7/62, 1/63
Galapagos Islands
- Ancient civilisation remains found 8/24

Galbraith, Thomas 11/62, 4/63
Gale, George 9/70
Galenkov, Yuri 1/68
Gallagher, Eddie 11/75
Gallagher, John 8/92
Gallieni, Joseph 9/14
Gallipoli
- See also World War I
- Bulgarians kill 5,000 Turks in battle 2/13

Gallo, Robert 4/84
Gallup, George 9/01
Galsworthy, John 12/06, 11/32, 1/33, 12/68
Galtieri, Leopoldo 4/82, 6/82, 4/83
Galvin, Martin 8/84
Gambia
- Independence 2/65
- President Jarawa deposed in coup 7/81
- Coup fails as UK SAS free hostages 8/81

Gamelin, Maurice 10/39, 5/40, 8/40, 4/58
Gance, Abel 4/27, 11/81
Gandhi, Indira 11/17, 1/59, 2/59, 6/64, 1/66, 3/66, 10/66, 3/67, 11/70, 6/71, 11/71, 12/71, 5/74, 6/75, 9/76, 3/77, 10/77, 1/78, 12/78, 1/80, 6/80, 10/83, 5/84, 6/84, 10/84, 11/84, 1/86, 1/89
Gandhi, Mohandas (Mahatma)
- Begins civil disobedience, South Africa 3/07
- General Smuts frees Gandhi from prison 1/08
- Jailed for defying immigration law, Natal 11/13
- Returns to India from South Africa 11/15
- Starts trade strike against security law 4/19
- Congress chooses non-violent resistance 9/20
- Predicts "Sea of Blood" under British 12/20
- Leads Congress; protests at Duke's visit 1/21
- "Buy Indian" cloth drive; boycott plans 7/21
- Burns cloth in protest at Prince's visit 11/21
- Boycotts Prince's visit to Allahabad 12/21
- Pleads "guilty to sedition"; jailed 3/22
- Released from prison, Bombay 2/24
- Hunger strike against Hindu-Moslem clash 9/24
- Criticised in Lahore for Viceroy motion 1/30
- Independence motion passed, Lahore meet 1/30
- Begins 300-mile anti-tax march on sea 3/30
- Prepared to die defying salt tax 3/30
- Completes march, breaks Salt Law, Dandi 4/30
- Arrested in Karadi; supporters attacked 5/30
- "Victory gained by violence is ... defeat" 12/30
- Not satisfied with Round Table agreement 1/31
- Orders more civil disobedience 2/31
- First meeting with Viceroy Lord Irving 2/31
- In London for second Round Table talks 8/31
- Wants independence through partnership 9/31
- Meets King George V and Queen Mary, London 11/31
- Demands Indian foreign and military control 11/31
- Warned by Viceroy Willingdon on protests 12/31
- Arrested for Congress disobedience 1/32
- Hunger fast gets votes for Untouchables 9/32
- Gets one year's imprisonment 7/33
- Freed from hospital because of hunger strike 8/33
- Resigns leadership of All-India Congress 10/34
- Names Nehru as his successor 1/42
- Opposes dominion status plan for India 3/42
- Arrested with 50 other Congress leaders 8/42
- Begins 21-day fast 2/43
- Ends fast 3/43
- Endorses Britain's "good faith" 4/46
- Talks with Mountbatten, new viceroy 3/47
- Assassinated 1/48

Gandhi, Priyanka 5/91
Gandhi, Rahul 5/91
Gandhi, Rajiv 6/80, 10/84, 11/84, 12/84, 9/86, 10/86, 8/87, 4/88, 12/88, 11/89, 5/91
Gandhi, Sanjay 3/77, 6/80
Gandhi, Sonia 5/91
Ganilau, Ratu Sir Penaia 5/87, 10/87
Gapon, George 1/05, 4/06
Garbo, Greta 9/05, 10/26, 7/27, 12/30, 12/35, 2/40, 4/90
Gardiner, Alan 11/23
Gardner, Ava 1/90
Gardner, Jack 11/50
Gardner, Max 2/47
Gargan, Joseph 7/69
Garin, Maurice 7/04
Garland, Judy 6/22, 9/40, 8/63, 11/64, 4/65, 6/69, 6/87
Garretson, William 8/69
Garrison, Zina 7/90
Garros, Roland 9/13
Garson, Greer 12/42
Gascoigne, Paul 7/90, 3/91
Gascoyne-Cecil, Edgar 11/58
Gaspari, Cardinal 2/29
Gasser, Herbert 12/44
Gatling, Richard 2/03
GATT
- (General Agreement on Tariffs and Trade) 12/89
- (General Agreements on Tariff and Trade) 12/90
- Uruguay Round signed at last 12/93

Gatting, Mike 12/87, 6/88, 8/89, 1/90
Gatwick 6/58
Gaudier-Brzeska, Henri 12/14, 12/18
Gauguin, Paul 5/03
Gay, Hobart 9/50
Gaye, Marvin 4/84
Gbenye, Christophe 11/64
Geddes, Eric 2/22
Gee, Ethel 1/61
Geldenhuys, Mike 6/80
Geldof, Bob 12/84, 7/85, 5/86
Gemayel, Amin 9/82, 2/84, 3/84, 4/85
Gemayel, Bashir 8/82, 9/82
Geneen, Harold 3/73
General Agreement on Tariffs and Trade
- See GATT

General Motors Company
- See Cars

Genet, Jean 12/10, 4/86
Genoa, Conference of
- Allies plan to make Russia pay debts 5/22

George I, King of Greece 3/13
George II, King of Greece 9/22, 3/24, 11/35, 12/35, 4/41, 5/41, 9/46, 4/47
George V, King
- See also Royal Family (Britain) 5/10, 4/11, 6/11, 12/11, 4/14, 7/14, 12/14, 5/15, 10/15, 5/17, 6/17, 2/21, 6/21, 7/21, 11/28, 12/28, 7/29, 1/30, 9/31, 11/31, 7/32, 12/32, 6/33, 5/35, 1/36, 11/86

George VI, King
- See also Royal Family (Britain) 12/36, 2/37, 4/37, 5/37, 7/37, 10/37, 2/38, 5/38, 12/39, 6/40, 10/40, 4/42, 3/43, 6/43, 2/44, 6/44, 5/45, 6/45, 8/45, 1/46, 8/47, 4/48, 10/48, 11/48, 3/49, 8/49, 12/49, 10/50, 9/51, 2/52

George, Boy 1/84, 7/86
George, Charlie 5/71
George, Prince, Duke of Kent 8/34, 11/34
George, Stefan 12/33
Georges, Alphonse 10/34
Georgia
- Votes for independence from Soviet Union 4/91
- Eduard Shevardnadze elected interim President 3/92

Gerasimov, Gennady 10/88, 12/89
Gerassimov, Alexander 7/63
Germany
- See also World Wars I, II, Germany, East and Germany, West

Germany (foreign affairs)
- Ambassador murdered in China 6/00
- Colonies become protectorates 9/00
- Anglo-German Open Door pact on China 10/00
- Kaiser refuses to see Kruger 12/00
- Agrees African boundaries with Britain 2/01
- Criticises British Boer camps record 4/01
- To build Mid-east railway from Turkey 1/02
- Foreign Minister softens on Britain 3/02
- Kaiser ends Alsace-Lorraine dictatorship 5/02
- Triple Alliance renewed for 12 years 6/02
- Kaiser calls for "Germanisation" of Slavs 6/02
- Signs Chinese Tariff Protocol 8/02
- Nationalists want Poles suppressed 9/02
- Kaiser visits London 11/02
- 123 Germans killed in South-West Africa 1/04
- South-West African revolt spreads 10/04
- Trade treaty with Rumania 10/04
- Kaiser's visit to Morocco upsets French 3/05
- Pressurises Czar to end war 6/05
- Rules out talks on Morocco 6/05
- Imperial pact with Russia: anti-British 7/05
- Conference to settle Moroccan question 1/06
- Opposition to South-West Africa war 11/06
- Colonial committee demands expansion 1/07
- Triple Alliance with Austria and Italy renewed 7/07
- Kaiser calls for peace on London visit 11/07
- Edward VII meets Kaiser to calm tensions 8/08
- Kaiser's interview offends Britain 10/08
- Chancellor retracts Kaiser's interview 11/08
- Chancellor contradicts Earl Roberts 11/08
- Threatens USA with tariff war 1/10
- Fixes African frontiers with rivals 2/10
- Kaiser attends Edward VII's funeral 5/10
- Incident over Kiev pogrom painting 6/10
- Votes to increase army by 515,000 2/11
- Newspapers warn of French Moroccan moves 4/11
- Kaiser vetoes choice of US ambassador 6/11
- Fortifies Heligoland in North Sea 8/11
- Settles Moroccan dispute with France 9/11
- Treaty divides Morocco 11/11
- Haldane arrives; 15 battleships planned 2/12
- Wants "mutual neutrality" with Britain 7/12

- Renews Triple Alliance for six more years 12/12
- Britons pardoned for spying 5/13
- Forced to abandon rail link to Gulf 7/13
- Triple Alliance affirmed; Italian doubts 9/13
- Navy gets 14 new ships; war looms 3/14
- Kaiser reaffirms alliance with Austria 7/14
- Kaiser gives ultimatum to Russia 7/14
- Ignores British threat, invades Belgium 8/14
- Declares war on Russia, then France 8/14
- Britain and Serbia declare war on Germany 8/14
- Takes Brussels and threatens France 8/14
- Attacks Italian neutrality 8/14
- Loses Samoa and East Indies to New Zealand 8/14
- Businessmen want Poland, Ukraine and Baltic 6/15
- Accepts Lusitania liability 2/16
- Deployment dispute favours Hindenburg 8/16
- Attacks USA over citizens in air forces 9/16
- Proclaims independent Poland 11/16
- Chancellor rules out war with USA 3/17
- Helps Lenin back to Russia 4/17
- Agrees to Russian truce 11/17
- Recognises Finland and Ukraine independence 1/18
- Peace in the East, new power in West 3/18
- Allegedly offered Soviets millions 6/18
- Severs ties with Turkey 7/18
- Surrenders; must give up arms, transport 11/18
- Allies to occupy Rhineland 11/18
- 1,500,000 Allied prisoners freed 11/18
- Releases all prisoners 1/19
- Signs treaty after threat of occupation 6/19
- Fury at Versailles "cave-in" 6/19
- Allies demand ex-Kaiser's extradition 1/20
- Refuses Allies' war trial of 890 leaders 2/20
- Ex-Crown Prince offers himself for trial 2/20
- Ordered by the League to pay three billion marks a year 4/20
- Allies set reparations at £12,500 million 6/20
- Signs protocol on arms cuts 7/20
- Reichswehr minister refuses protocol 7/20
- France and Britain set war debts 11/20
- Plans giant armoured submarine 1/21
- Reparations at £10 billion over 42 years 1/21
- Allies divide Silesia between Poland and Germany 8/21
- Allies defer German reparations, Cannes 1/22
- Discusses Upper Silesia with Poles 2/22
- Rapallo economic treaty with Russia 4/22
- Barred from Genoa talks after Rapallo 4/22
- Reparation Commission partial moratorium 5/22
- Seeks to defer war debts 7/22
- Allies grant six-month reprieve 8/22
- Germany has defaulted, says committee 12/22
- France rejects non-aggression pact offer 12/22
- French occupy Ruhr to collect reparations 1/23
- France's Ruhr cordon to stop coal moving 2/23
- Dawes sets up international economic commission 11/23
- Agrees to Dawes Plan; new taxes, controls 4/24
- Excluded from Olympic Games 7/24
- Ten-nation conference on Dawes Plan 7/24
- Wishes to join League of Nations 9/24
- Invited to Locarno security conference 9/25
- Promises not to fight France, Locarno 10/25
- Reichstag approves Locarno agreement 11/25
- Refused a permanent League council seat 3/26
- Stresemann wants great power status back 4/26
- Signs trade accord with France 8/26
- League of Nations votes to admit Germany 9/26
- Allied military control ends 1/27
- Some want Austrian annexation after riot 7/27
- Joins International Arbitration Court 9/27
- British officer foresees new German war 11/27
- Trade pact with Poland 11/27
- Signs treaty with Lithuania over Memel 1/28
- Stresemann will not "barter" Rhineland 11/28
- Trotsky refused political asylum 4/29
- Young Plan: pay off war debts till 1988 6/29
- Germany not to pay for French rebuilding 6/29
- Last British Rhine troops quit Wiesbaden 12/29
- Ex-Chief of Staff in plot to topple Soviet regime 1/30
- French troops leave Rhineland early 6/30
- Hindenburg asks Hoover to suspend debts 6/31
- UK MPs approve trade pact with Germany 5/33
- Agrees ten-year peace pact with UK and France 5/33
- Closes Austrian border to non-Nazis 6/33
- Leaves the League over disarmament talks 10/33
- Ten-year non-aggression pact with Poland 1/34
- Denies French claims of re-arming 4/34
- Rejects mutual aid pact with USSR 6/34
- Britain agrees on loan repayments 7/34
- Two Americans seized as spies 11/34
- UK and France want anti-aggression pact 2/35
- Hitler supports mutual air defence pact 2/35
- Goering says 400,000 in army not enough 3/35
- Wants air and sea parity with UK and France 3/35
- Want Austrian Anschluss and united Prussia 3/35
- Wants to annex Sudeten Czechoslovakia 3/35
- Conscription response to "UK rearmament" 3/35
- Condemned by League Council for re-arming 4/35
- Tokyo rejects alliance with Germany 4/35
- Anglo-German naval accord relaxes curbs 6/35
- UK allows five battleships and 65 destroyers 6/35
- Germany officially leaves League 10/35
- Hitler offers UK air force limits 12/35
- Hitler warns League on Jewish issue 1/36
- Troops in Rhineland, defying Versailles 3/36
- Hitler proposes 25-year peace guarantee 3/36
- Austrians fear invasion; army at border 4/36
- Recognises Austria's independence 7/36
- Ribbentrop is ambassador to Britain 8/36
- Hitler's Condor legion will help Franco 10/36
- Agrees Victor Emmanuel rules Abyssinia 10/36
- Hitler and Italy's Count Ciano draft pact 10/36
- Anti-Communist Axis with Italy 11/36
- 5,000 Germans at Cadiz to help Franco 12/36
- Spain releases German freighter after protest 12/36
- Seizes Spanish ship in retaliation 1/37
- Offers non-intervention pact on Spain 1/37
- Belgian and Dutch neutrality guaranteed 1/37
- Ribbentrop's Nazi salute to King George 2/37
- UK, Italy, USSR and Germany say "no" to Spain aid 2/37
- Air force bombs Spanish town of Guernica 4/37
- Hindenburg airship explodes, 33 die, USA 5/37
- Deutschland battleship bombed by Spanish 5/37
- Germans bomb Almeria, avenging warship 5/37
- Leaves non-intervention cordon of Spain 5/37
- Opposes UK-French patrols around Spain 6/37
- Expels "Times" journalist 8/37
- Hitler wants colonies and "living space" 9/37
- Duke and Duchess of Windsor feted by Nazis 10/37
- Robert Ley and Adolf Hitler meet Duke 10/37
- Hitler pledges to defend Belgium 10/37
- Anti-Communist pact with Italy and Japan 11/37
- Von Ribbentrop is foreign minister 1/38
- Hitler tells Austria to free all Nazis 1/38
- Goering visits Austria to set up pact 1/38
- Hitler's plea for Czech and Austrian Germans 2/38
- Schuschnigg overthrown; Austria reunited 3/38
- Hitler marches into Vienna: big welcome 3/38
- Jews must leave Austria, says Goering 3/38
- Angry at UK's interest in Czechoslovakia 3/38
- German Sudeten Party gains in elections 6/38
- Reich will pay off Austria's debts 7/38
- UK Chancellor Simon warns on Czech case 8/38
- Sudeten Nazis foment disorder in region 9/38
- Munich talks: wins Sudetenland annexation 9/38
- Hitler marches into occupied Sudetenland 10/38
- Hitler's "Great German future" speech 10/38
- German diplomat von Rath shot by Jew 11/38
- Signs border pact with France 12/38
- Memel Germans want to join Reich 12/38
- Germany wants a pro-Fascist Pope 2/39
- Germans march into Bohemia 3/39
- Bohemia-Moravia made German protectorate 3/39
- British ambassador to Berlin recalled 3/39
- Memel (Lithuania) ceded to Germany 3/39
- Hitler tears up 1934 naval pact with UK 4/39
- Hitler denounces UK-France-Poland pact 4/39
- Non-aggression pact signed with Denmark 5/39
- Signs Pact of Steel with Italy 5/39
- Hitler guarantees Yugoslav frontiers 6/39
- Several hundred Polish Jews deported 6/39
- 2,000 Nazi guards sent to Danzig 7/39
- Polish border in Upper Silesia closed 8/39
- Hitler demands Danzig and Polish corridor 8/39
- Signs non-aggression pact with USSR 8/39
- Invasion of Poland 9/39
- French troops cross into Saarland 9/39
- Two Britons arrested; attempt on Hitler 11/39
- Signs pact with Japan 9/40
- Expels US consuls 6/41
- Mass Polish grave found at Katyn, USSR 3/43
- Italy declares war on Germany 10/43
- Troops enter Hungary and Slovakia 3/44
- Breaks off relations with Turkey 8/44
- Nazis shoot German commanders in Poland 2/45
- Surrenders to the Allies 4/45
- Russians dismantle arms factories 10/46
- UK and US agree on control of Ruhr mines 9/47
- Jewish refugees disembark at Hamburg 9/47
- USSR walks out of Allied talks on Berlin 3/48
- Begins airlifting food supplies to USSR 11/90
- Agrees to form joint army corps with France 5/92
- Calls off V-2 50th anniversary celebrations at UK's request 9/92
- Police seize uranium originating from former USSR 10/92
- German soldiers allowed to go into combat abroad 4/93
- Last Russian troops leave 8/94
- Last Allied soldiers march through Berlin 9/94

Germany (politics)
- Roman Herzog is new President 5/94
- Socialist election gains 6/03
- Universal suffrage in Baden 8/04
- Socialist rally attracts 250,000 1/06
- Anti-colonialist socialists lose in poll 1/07
- Socialist poll setback; Reichstag opens 2/07
- Chancellor rejects universal suffrage 1/08
- Law to unify Empire 5/08
- Councillor predicts airship invasions 10/08
- German naval growth to overtake Britain 3/09
- Millions in extra taxes 7/09
- Von Bulow resigns as Chancellor 7/09
- Kaiser pledges suffrage reform 1/10
- Socialists shot at suffrage protest 3/10
- 250,000 Socialists demonstrate 4/10
- Rosa Luxemburg attacked at congress 9/10
- 750,000 at Socialist Singer's funeral 2/11
- Socialists win quarter of election votes 1/12
- Chancellor rules out increased democracy 2/12
- Kaiser refuses to see Socialists 2/12
- Socialists' anti-war manifesto 3/13
- Peacetime army boosted; fear weak allies 6/13
- Socialists justify role in government 12/14
- Hindenburg is new Chief of Staff 8/16
- Liebknecht sentenced for peace protests 8/16
- 35 peace meetings in different cities 8/16
- New Chancellor Michaelis, first non-noble 7/17
- Kaiser backs Pope's peace plan 8/17
- Death penalty for mutinous sailors 8/17
- Spartacist strikes, martial law 1/18
- Berlin and Brandenburg in state of siege 9/18
- Hertling resigns as Chancellor 9/18
- Prince of Baden is new Chancellor 10/18
- Socialists declare republic in Bavaria 11/18
- Kaiser abdicates; republic declared 11/18
- Socialist Ebert heads new republic 11/18
- Nobles flee as revolt spreads 11/18
- Spartacists call for revolution 12/18
- Spartacist Communist revolt crushed 1/19
- Rightist Freikorps beats Berlin rebels 1/19
- Luxemburg and Liebknecht murdered 1/19
- Chancellor Ebert denounces Armistice 2/19
- Signs Armistice, gives up parts of Poland 2/19
- Bavarian premier murdered; Left revolts 2/19
- Exiled ex-Kaiser rejects trial 3/19
- Bavarian republic shaken by counter-coup 4/19
- Berlin troops enter Bavaria 4/19
- Two sentenced for Liebknecht murder 4/19
- Sailors sink fleet at Scapa Flow 6/19
- "Rhine Republic" declared 6/19
- Chancellor Scheidermann resigns 6/19
- Republic declared at Weimar 7/19
- Weimar gives President emergency powers 7/19
- Blockade lifted 7/19
- Troops crush Polish rising, Silesia 8/19
- Hitler addresses German Workers' Party 9/19
- Police machine-gun protesters, Reichstag 1/20
- Hitler's party blames Jews for defeat 2/20
- Monarchist coup fails, Berlin 3/20
- Bid to crush Ruhr revolt lets in French 4/20
- German Workers' Party becomes Nazi Party 4/20
- French occupy Frankfurt 4/20
- Rightist coup leader arrested, Stockholm 4/20
- Socialists told to obey Versailles treaty 6/20
- Does not disband security police or guard 7/20
- Reichstag fury at reparations bill 2/21
- Allied occupation to collect debts 3/21
- Upper Silesia votes to stay in Gemany 3/21
- Communist coup fails, Hamburg; 20 die 3/21
- Monarchist unrest at ex-Kaiserin funeral 4/21
- Pragmatism wins; reparations accepted 5/21
- Tax increases to pay for reparations 8/21
- Finance Minister killed by right-wingers 8/21
- Mark plummets; government resigns 10/21
- Royal emblems removed 3/22
- Foreign Minister Rathenau shot by right 6/22
- Nationalist arrested for Rathenau murder 7/22
- Chancellor Wirth challenges reparations 9/22
- New Chancellor Wilhelm Cuno 11/22
- 50,000 hear Hitler address Nazis, Munich 11/22
- Cuno calls for Ruhr "passive resistance" 1/23
- 20 die in Ruhr protests 1/23
- France occupies more of the Rhine 2/23
- French troops kill nine outside Krupp works 3/23
- Death penalty for Ruhr railway saboteurs 3/23
- Krupp's directors arrested for Essen riot 4/23
- Count Krupp von Bohlen gets 15 years 5/23
- French troops seize Ruhr railways 6/23
- Stresseman succeeds Cuno as Chancellor 8/23
- Bavaria's new dictator threatens Nazis 9/23
- Stresemann's conference to handle crises 9/23
- Ebert declares state of emergency 9/23
- Looting as French invade Rhineland 10/23
- Bavaria and Rhineland try to break away 10/23
- Hitler arrested after beer hall putsch 11/23
- Hitler's national revolution thwarted 11/23
- Reichsbank "new mark"; unions' demands 11/23
- Social Democrats resign from government 11/23
- Marx replaces Stresemann as Chancellor 11/23
- Rhineland Republic leader Heinz killed 1/24
- Hitler and Ludendorff tried for putsch 2/24
- Reichstag dissolved pending election 3/24
- Hitler given light sentence for putsch 4/24
- Conservative poll gains; left biggest 5/24
- Conservatives anti-Dawes; Marx resigns 5/24
- Marx's new government; Dawes plan passed 6/24
- Reichsbank independent of government 8/24
- Signs Dawes Plan; will pay war debts 8/24
- Dawes: French and Belgian troops pull out 8/24
- New Union flag 8/24
- 180,000 allowed to return to Ruhr 9/24
- Kaiser's family claim rejected 9/24
- Thalmann heads Communist Party 9/25
- Foundation of Nazi SS "protection squad" 11/25
- Dr Luther resigns as Chancellor 12/25
- British leave Rhineland after seven years 1/26
- Hohenzollerns owe millions in taxes 4/26
- Luther resigns, Marx is new Chancellor 5/26
- Road rules unified 6/26
- First congress of reconstituted Nazis 7/26
- Big Nazi rally in Nuremburg 8/26
- Stresemann bolstered by League success 9/26
- Goebbels heads Berlin Nazi Party 11/26
- Stresemann shares Nobel with Briand 12/26
- Marx upholds Weimar Constitution 2/27
- Bavarian ban on Hitler speeches lifted 3/27
- Nazi-Communist street clashes 3/27
- First Nazi Party meeting in Berlin 5/27
- Reichstag members in scuffle 7/27
- Hindenburg says "We did not start War" 9/27
- Prussia lifts ban on Hitler speaking 9/28
- Communist mass attacks on Berlin police 5/29
- Government lacks majority; world slump 5/29
- Nazis and Stahlhelm reject Young Plan 6/29
- Bomb at Reichstag, no injuries 9/29
- Gustav Stresemann dies 10/29
- New Foreign Minister Julius Curtius 10/29
- Prince Max van Baden dies 11/29
- Nazis win Bavarian municipal elections 12/29
- Admiral von Tirpitz dies 3/30
- Reichstag approves Young Plan 3/30
- Hindenburg's budget by decree 7/30
- Nazis come second in Reichstag elections 9/30
- Socialists largest party; Communists third 9/30
- Hitler barred from taking Reichstag seat 9/30
- Moderates let down Chancellor Bruening 9/30
- Ex-Kaiser wins libel case against paper 9/30
- Hitler denounces peace treaties 9/30
- Nazi Reichstag MPs break law on uniforms 10/30
- Nazis win in Bremen municipal poll 11/30
- Nazis call for withdrawal from League 2/31
- Nazi and Nationalist anti-Bruning pact 10/31
- Brunswick Nazi-Communist fight; 100 hurt 10/31
- Nazis win in Hesse 11/31
- Hitler claims to be a Democrat 12/31
- Bruning says Germany cannot repay 1/32
- Hindenburg to seek re-election 2/32
- Hitler to run for President 2/32
- Hitler granted German citizenship 2/32
- No clear majority for Hindenburg in poll 3/32
- Hindenburg wins presidency on second poll 4/32
- Nazi SS and SA paramilitary units banned 4/32
- Nazis lead in four state elections, Prussia 4/32
- Chancellor Bruning resigns 5/32
- Von Papen asked to form new government 5/32
- Von Papen's cabinet; Nazis excluded 6/32
- Reichstag dissolved before election 6/32
- Ban on SS and SA lifted after Hitler pledge 6/32
- Nazis double seats; become biggest party 7/32
- Communists gain Social Democrat seats 7/32
- 15 die in Nazi-Communist clashes, Berlin 7/32
- Von Papen sacks Prussia's Socialist premier 7/32
- War Minister von Schleicher's rearm call 7/32
- Death penalty for "political terrorism" 8/32
- Hitler refuses post of Vice-Chancellor 8/32
- Nazis riot after murder trial 8/32
- Nazi Goering becomes Reichstag President 8/32
- Von Papen and Hindenburg block Hitler at top 8/32
- Von Papen threatens to close Reichstag 9/32
- Presidential rule in Prussia planned 10/32
- Schools to teach Article 231 of Versailles treaty 10/32
- Nazis lose two million votes and 34 seats 11/32
- Business gives Nazi funds to Nationalists 11/32
- Von Papen resigns as government fails 11/32
- Von Schleicher is new Chancellor 12/32
- Communists and Nazis fight in Reichstag 12/32
- Hitler is made Chancellor in new cabinet 1/33
- Nazi fights; von Schleicher resigns 1/33
- Hindenburg and von Papen try to use Hitler 1/33
- Hitler curbs left-wing parties and press 2/33
- Nazi SS and SA usurp Prussian police 2/33
- Reichstag burns; Dutchman Lubbe arrested 2/33
- Nazis blame Communists for fire; Decree 2/33
- Goering raids Prussian Communists 2/33
- 68 die in election campaign; Frick warns 2/33
- Nazis close Bavarian parliament 3/33
- Hindenburg favours Nazi flag 3/33
- Hitler proclaims the Third Reich 3/33
- Nazis' first concentration camp, Dachau 3/33
- Enabling Act: Hitler rules by decree 3/33
- Nazis fail to get poll majority 3/33
- Foreigners need permits to leave Germany 4/33
- "Un-German" books burnt in schools 5/33
- Union leaders and Socialists arrested 5/33
- Unions banned; "mixed marriages" banned 5/33
- Nazis win Danzig; seize Communist goods 5/33
- Nazis ban parties; absorb Nationalists 6/33
- Baldur von Schirach sets up Hitler Youth 6/33
- Bernhard Rust writes Nazi school course 6/33
- Race council; Jews banned from Olympics 6/33
- Hindenburg bars Nazi head of Lutherans 6/33
- Only Nazis can be German citizens 7/33
- Jews herded to 64 concentration camps 8/33
- Lubbe "confesses" to Reichstag fire 9/33
- Ex-Hitler ally Ludendorff outlawed 9/33
- Nazis get 95 per cent plebiscite support 11/33
- Hindenburg urges Hitler vote 11/33
- Monarchist groups stifled; coup fears 11/33
- Nazis want to abolish women's vote 12/33
- Hitler keeps Hindenburg as President 12/33
- Reichstag adjourns after 12 minutes 12/33
- Lubbe gets death penalty for Reichstag fire 12/33
- Sterilisation law comes into effect 1/34
- Attack on Freemasons 1/34
- Millions swear Hitler allegiance 2/34

- Hitler bans Carnegie Endowment for Peace 4/34
- People's Court treason trials; no appeal 5/34
- Trial of 111 Communists 5/34
- Night of the Long Knives; Nazis purge SA 6/34
- Nazis kill ex-Chancellor von Schleicher 6/34
- Storm Trooper purge appeases army brass 6/34
- Hitler pre-empts Roehm's "coup" attempt 6/34
- Flags at half-mast for Versailles Day 6/34
- Himmler's SS guard concentration camps 7/34
- Eicke's brutal Dachau camp rules 7/34
- SS replace purged SA Storm Troopers 7/34
- Vice-chancellor von Papen resigns 7/34
- Hindenburg dies; Hitler becomes Fuehrer 8/34
- Hitler gets 90 per cent of vote as head of state 8/34
- Hitler Supreme Commander of Armed Forces 8/34
- Job scheme favours unemployed fathers 8/34
- Adolf Wagner: "Reich for 1,000 years" 9/34
- 700,000 greet Hitler at Nuremberg rally 9/34
- Army three times the allowed size 10/34
- 90 per cent of Saar vote to be reunited 1/35
- States to lose powers 1/35
- Two women beheaded for spying 2/35
- Introduces conscription 3/35
- Goering creates Luftwaffe air force 3/35
- Nazis win 60 per cent of Danzig votes 4/35
- Restricted sales of English newspapers 4/35
- Nazis declare war on "church enemies" 4/35
- Orders 12 submarines, defying Versailles 4/35
- Navy to build 28 submarines, two cruisers 7/35
- Berlin Jews beaten; anti-Semitic police 7/35
- Hitler bans German-Jewish marriages 8/35
- Signs exclude Jews from public places 8/35
- Goering takes over television service 8/35
- Swastika on national flag 8/35
- Anti-Semitic Nuremberg decrees 9/35
- Jews lose citizenship, jobs and pensions 9/35
- Hitler creates Reich's General Staff 10/35
- All men up to 45 are called reservists 11/35
- Jewish doctors made to resign 12/35
- 99 per cent approval in plebiscite 3/36
- Non-voters sacked 4/36
- Himmler is head of Reich police force 6/36
- Biggest army manoeuvres since 1914 9/36
- Starts building aircraft carriers 11/36
- Bans acceptance of Nobel Prizes 1/37
- Deports 2,000 "dangerous criminals" 3/37
- Nazis hold "Degenerate Art" exhibition 7/37
- Himmler reorganises concentration camps 8/37
- New Buchenwald camp for Jews and "enemies" 8/37
- Biggest ever Nuremberg Nazi rally 9/37
- Million attend Hitler-Mussolini rally 9/37
- Duke visits German houses and model factory 10/37
- American predicts German Jewry extinction 10/37
- Non-Nazi parents lose children to state 11/37
- Compulsory Nazi education from birth 11/37
- Police seize Jews' bank deposits, Danzig 11/37
- Field Marshal Erich von Ludendorff dies 12/37
- Hitler sacks Generals Blomberg and Fritsch 1/38
- 40 top army officers moved or sacked 1/38
- 3,000 inmates at Sachsenhausen death camp 3/38
- Children forbidden to speak to Jews 6/38
- Jews must hand in passports 10/38
- Expels Jews to Poland 10/38
- "Crystal Night" - mass attacks on Jews 11/38
- 7,000 Jewish shops and synagogues looted 11/38
- Goebbels' propaganda stirs up violence 11/38
- Jews told to leave Munich or go to camps 11/38
- Hitler fines Jews billion marks for Rath 11/38
- Jews expelled from colleges 11/38
- Special property tax for Jews 11/38
- Lindbergh plans to live in Germany 11/38
- Walther Funk confiscates Jewish property 12/38
- New law to ban Jews from all trades 12/38
- Hitler reopens Reichstag 1/39
- Bans against Jews in Berlin 1/39
- Women under 25 must do Reich service 1/39
- Church leaders punished 1/39
- More persecution of Jews in Berlin 2/39
- Jews drafted to work for Reich 3/39
- Jews ordered to join "Union of Jews" 7/39
- Proposes wearing of Star of David by Jews 10/39
- Horrors of concentration camps revealed 10/39
- Hitler escapes bomb in Munich 11/39
- Mass deportations of Jews begin 12/39
- New law completes annexation of Austria 4/40
- Karl Hausofer, friend of Hess, arrested 5/41
- Jews ordered to wear Star of David 9/41
- Von Brauchitsch resigns as army C-in-C 12/41
- Hitler becomes army C-in-C 12/41
- Nazis agree on "Final Solution" 1/42
- Deportations to Auschwitz begin 3/42
- Captive French General Giraud escapes 4/42
- European Jews killed by Nazis: one million 6/42
- All remaining Jewish schools closed 6/42
- 50,000 Jews slaughtered in Warsaw ghetto 9/42
- Purge of Nazi Party 10/42
- Himmler becomes Interior Minister 10/42
- All people 16-65 ordered to mobilise 1/43
- Saboteurs blow up bridges on River Oder 3/43
- State of emergency declared in Ruhr 5/43
- Goebbels says Berlin is "free of Jews" 6/43
- One million evacuated from Berlin 8/43
- Hitler's chancellery hit in air raid 1/44
- Hitler orders enlistment of children over the age of 10 1/44
- Nazis plan to breed Aryan elite 1/44
- Hitler suspends all laws in Berlin 4/44
- Goebbels becomes dictator of Berlin 4/44
- Hitler escapes assassination attempt 7/44
- Hunt for generals in plot against Hitler 7/44
- Eight executed for plot against Hitler 8/44
- Seven more generals die for Hitler plot 9/44
- Rommel commits suicide 10/44
- Hitler forms Home Guard for Germany 10/44
- Cut in food rations announced 10/44
- Himmler given control of German Army 11/44
- Food riots break out 1/45
- "Werewolves" kill German collaborators 3/45
- Kesselring is German commander in west 3/45
- Hitler kills himself in Berlin bunker 4/45
- Gates of Nazi death camps open 4/45
- Doenitz succeeds Hitler 4/45
- Country is crushed by defeat 5/45
- Goering gives himself up to Allies 5/45
- Bolcon razed to the ground 5/45
- Himmler kills himself in Allied custody 5/45
- "Lord Haw Haw" arrested 5/45
- Death of Goebbels 5/45
- First German troops demobbed 6/45
- Allied leaders sign occupation pact 6/45
- Russians find Hitler's body 6/45
- Ribbentrop captured by British 6/45
- Allies occupy assigned zones in Berlin 7/45
- Allied troops in victory parade, Berlin 7/45
- Soviet officers receive British awards 7/45
- Allies can fraternise with German women 7/45
- Big Three arrive for Potsdam conference 7/45
- Goering and Hess on trial for war crimes 8/45
- Nazi leaders go on trial at Nuremberg 11/45
- Kramer, "Butcher of Belsen", is to die 11/45
- A third copy of Hitler's will found 1/46
- Polish Jews leave Soviet Berlin sector 1/46
- 58 Matthausen camp guards are to die 4/46
- Himmler's deputy Pohl arrested 5/46
- Ten top Nazis executed at Nuremberg 10/46
- First free election in Berlin since 1932 10/46
- Hundreds of hidden Nazis rounded up 2/47
- Wives of top Nazis arrested 5/47
- USSR stops traffic to Berlin 4/48
- Deutschmark is to replace Reichsmark 6/48
- Establishment of West Germany agreed 4/49
- Constitution for West Germany agreed 4/49
- Federal Republic of Germany created 5/49
- German Democratic Republic created 10/49
- President of the Bundestag resigns 11/88
- Talks on German reunification 3/90
- Becomes reunified 10/90
- First elections held after reunification; Kohl is Chancellor 12/90
- Country paralysed by public service workers' strikes 4/92
- Thousands demonstrate against wave of racist attacks 8/92
- Germans protest against another wave of racist violence 10/92
- Turkish immigrants killed in racist attack 11/92
- Bundestag ratifies the Maastricht treaty 12/92
- Neo-Nazi arson attack kills five Turkish women 5/93

Germany, East
- Wilhelm Pieck becomes President 10/49
- Otto Grotewohl becomes PM 10/49
- 124,245 cross from East to West 12/49
- Signs treaty on Oder-Neisse line 6/50
- Rights of Sudeten Germans curtailed 6/50
- Million Berliners in anti-US protest 8/51
- Rejects UN free election request 1/52
- 16,000 flee in past month 8/52
- Food shortage crisis in Communist Berlin 5/53
- USSR tanks crush Berlin worker uprising 6/53
- Premier Grotewohl blames foreign agents 6/53
- Martial law lifted in East Berlin 7/53
- Security minister sacked 7/53
- Will cease reparations to USSR 8/53
- Eden for free elections in united state 1/54
- Molotov rejects Eden's plan 1/54
- 300,000 Eastern refugees in West 1/54
- Message from missing Westerner Otto John 7/54
- Joins Warsaw Pact 5/55
- Bulganin rejects free German elections 7/55
- Otto John flees back to west 12/55
- Claims that 19,000 were freed from jail 6/56
- Playwright Brecht dies 8/56
- Big Four meet to discuss united Germany 5/59
- Spy Fuchs freed; will go to East Germany 6/59
- Farms collectivised; refugees flee 4/60
- Closes Berlin's border with West 8/60
- Ulbricht is head of state, not president 9/60
- All public memorials to Stalin removed 11/61
- Tank traps built along Berlin Wall 11/61
- Russians block US troop convoy 11/63
- Amnesty for 10,000 political prisoners 10/64
- Signs aid deal with Egypt 3/65
- East and West German leaders meet 3/70
- Talks with West Germany end in stalemate 5/70
- Erich Honecker becomes General Secretary 5/71
- 156 die in East Berlin plane crash 8/72
- 171 political prisoners freed 11/72
- To normalise relations with West Germany 11/72
- To be admitted to UN Security Council 6/73
- Walter Ulbricht dies 8/73
- Family crosses in balloon 9/79
- Honecker's first visit to West Germany 9/87
- Emigration to the West demonstration broken up by police 9/89
- Erich Honecker is ousted 10/89
- Million-strong protest is held 11/89
- Entire cabinet resigns 11/89
- New politburo is appointed 11/89
- Million East Berliners visit the West 11/89
- Berlin Wall is torn down 11/89
- Egon Krenz is ousted 12/89
- Kohl is first West German Chancellor to visit East Germany 12/89
- Mob sacks secret police headquarters in East Berlin 1/90
- West and East German leaders' accord on economic union 4/90
- Deutschmark is official currency of East and West Germany 7/90
- MPs choose date for reunification of Germany 8/90
- Four Allied powers sign German sovereignty treaty 9/90
- Unifies with West Germany 10/90

Germany, West
- USSR denounces West German state 10/49
- 124,245 have crossed from East to West 12/49
- To join Council of Europe 5/50
- Plans relations with Israel 8/52
- To pay Israel £293 million for war dead 9/52
- Saarland votes against becoming part of West Germany 11/52
- Adenauer rejects Saar referendum 12/52
- Adenauer talks with Eisenhower 4/53
- Admitted to NATO without nuclear arms 10/54
- France approves rearmament, in NATO 12/54
- Adenauer invited to Soviet talks 6/55
- Adenauer in talks with USSR 9/55
- Establishes relations with USSR 9/55
- Seven Hungarians seek asylum after hijacking 7/56
- Joins European Economic Community 3/57
- Macmillan and Adenauer discuss defence 5/57
- Adenauer will not talk to East 4/59
- Big Four meet to discuss united Germany 5/59
- First meeting of German and Israeli leaders 3/60
- Strain to assimilate Eastern refugees 4/60
- Brandt asks US to act against East Germany 8/61
- Adenauer and de Gaulle in talks 2/62
- Political and military pact with France 1/63
- Anti-Gaullist Bidault seeks asylum 3/63
- To seek diplomatic relations with Israel 3/65
- Establishes relations with Israel 5/65
- Nine Arab states break diplomatic ties 5/65
- Queen Elizabeth visits 5/65
- Wilson faces Biafra protest during visit 2/69
- Cohn-Bendit deported from France 4/69
- Arabs attack El Al airliner, Munich 2/70
- East and West German leaders meet 3/70
- Ambassador murdered in Guatemala 4/70
- Talks with East Germany end in stalemate 5/70
- Non-aggression pact with USSR 8/70
- Reconciliation treaty with Poland 11/70
- Willy Brandt wins Peace Nobel 12/71
- Pays $3m ransom for Aden hostages 2/72
- Arabs massacre Israelis, Munich Olympics 9/72
- Brandt negotiates with Arab terrorists 9/72
- Brandt supports European Union 10/72
- Gives in to Black September demands 10/72
- To normalise relations with East Germany 11/72
- Willy Brandt visits Israel 6/73
- To be admitted to UN Security Council 6/73
- Rebukes US for Yom Kippur actions 10/73
- Israeli Premier Rabin visits 7/75
- Attends four-nation Guadeloupe summit 1/79
- Boycotts Moscow Olympics on Afghanistan 7/80
- Endorses plans to combat world terrorism 6/84
- Reagan visits Bitburg war cemetery 5/85
- Ex-counter-intelligence head was a spy 8/85
- Honecker arrives on first visit to Federal Republic 9/87
- Gorbachev meets Chancellor Kohl to sign Bonn declaration 6/89
- 7,000 East Germans refugees arrive 10/89
- Million East Berliners visit the West 11/89
- Terrorist bomb kills Deutsche Bank head, Alfred Herrhausen 11/89
- Berlin Wall is torn down 11/89
- Kohl is first West German Chancellor to visit East Germany 12/89
- West and East German leaders' accord on economic union 4/90
- Deutschmark is official currency of East and West Germany 7/90
- Four Allied powers sign German sovereignty treaty 9/90
- Unifies with East Germany 10/90

Geronimo, Apache Chief 2/09
Gershwin, George 2/18, 2/24, 12/26, 11/27, 12/28, 1/29, 9/30, 9/35, 12/35, 7/37
Gerson 6/70
Getty, Jean Paul 6/76
Getty, John Paul III 12/73
Ghana
- See also Gold Coast
- Independence, Nkrumah "casts off chains" 3/57
- Nkrumah inspires people with great past 3/57
- Signs union agreement with Guinea 11/58
- All Africa People's Conference 2/59
- Nkrumah takes over as army C-in-C 9/61
- Nkrumah arrests 50 opposition leaders 10/61
- Visit by Elizabeth II 11/61
- Nkrumah jointly wins Lenin Peace Prize 4/62
- Nkrumah escapes assassination attempt 8/62
- Nkrumah escapes another attempt on life 9/62
- Nkrumah overthrown in his absence 2/66
- Nkrumah: "President of Ghana and Guinea" 3/66
- Severs ties with Guinea 3/66
- New regime recognised by UK and US 3/66
- Junta head Amkrah resigns 4/69
- Acheampong seizes power in coup 1/72
- Kwame Nkrumah dies 4/72
- Rawlings' second coup, New Year's Eve 12/81
- 70 troops die as Limann is overthrown 12/81

Ghavam, Ahmad 7/52
Ghazi, King of Iraq 9/33
Ghent
- Falls to Germans 10/14

Ghotbzadegh, Sadegh 1/80, 9/82
Giacometti, Alberto 1/66
Giap, General 10/52, 2/54, 10/54
Gibb, Maurice 2/69
Gibbs, Humphrey 11/65, 6/69
Gibraltar
- First armed convoy leaves for Britain 6/17
- Spanish rebels close frontier 8/36
- Spain begins creeping blockade 2/65
- Votes to keep ties with UK 9/67
- Wilson and Smith talk aboard Fearless 10/68
- Spain begins siege 6/69
- Spain agrees to re-open border 4/80
- Spain halts siege; new deal with UK 1/82
- Border opens after 13 years 12/82
- End of siege of Gibraltar 2/85
- SAS shoot IRA trio 3/88

Gibson, Althea 7/57, 7/58
Gibson, Guy 5/43
Gibson, Maurice 4/87
Gibson, Violet 4/26
Gide, Andre 3/34, 12/47, 2/51
Gielgud, John 4/04, 4/30, 12/30, 12/35, 7/39, 12/44, 12/50, 12/53, 12/81, 12/91
Gierek, Edward 1/13, 12/70, 10/77, 9/80, 12/81
Gigli, Beniamino 11/57
Gil, Emilio Portes 9/28, 11/28, 2/29, 4/29
Gilbert, John 7/27, 12/30
Gilbert, Wallis 12/38
Gilbert, William Schwenk 5/11
Giles, Frank 2/81
Gill, Eric 5/32
Gillespie, Dizzy 10/17, 9/91, 1/93
Gillette 12/01
Gillick, Victoria 7/83, 10/85
Gillman, J.E. 11/01
Gilmore, Gary 1/77
Gilmour, Ian 1/82
Ginsberg, Allen 6/26, 12/57
Ginsburg, Alexander 1/68, 7/78
Giraud, Henri 4/42, 12/42, 12/42, 1/43, 2/43, 3/43, 5/43, 6/43, 4/44, 3/49
Girl Guides
- Founded as sister group to Boy Scouts 5/10

Giscard d'Estaing, Valery 2/26, 1/62, 5/74, 12/77, 1/79, 10/79, 4/81, 5/81
Gish, Lillian Diana 2/93
Gizenga, Antoine 1/61
Gizikis, Phaeton 7/74
Gladstone, Henry 10/08
Gladstone, Herbert 11/09
Glazunov, Alexander 3/36
Glemp, Josef 12/81, 8/82
Glenholmes, Evelyn 3/86
Glenn, John 7/21, 2/62
Gloucester, Duke of
- See Royal Family (Britain)

Glubb, John (Glubb Pasha) 3/86
Goa
- Portuguese kill 12 Goan passive marchers 8/55

Gobat, Charles 12/02
Gobbi, Tito 3/84
Goddard, Paulette 6/33
Goddard, Robert 3/26
Godfree, Kitty 7/26
Godse, Nathuram 1/48, 11/49
Goebbels, Josef 11/26, 4/32, 2/33, 3/33, 8/36, 11/38, 1/42, 1/43, 4/43, 6/43, 8/43, 4/44, 7/44, 10/44, 4/45, 5/45
Goerdler, Karl 8/44
Goering, Hermann 8/32, 1/33, 2/33, 3/33, 9/33, 1/34, 4/34, 3/35, 4/36, 1/38, 3/38, 5/39, 7/40, 8/40, 9/40, 11/40, 1/43, 4/45, 4/45, 5/45, 8/45, 11/45, 10/46
Goethals, George 10/13, 1/14
Goetz, Bernhard 1/85, 6/87
Goga, Octavian 1/38
Gold Coast
- Ashanti rebels attack fort 4/00
- Britain annexes Ashanti kingdom 9/01
- First parliament opened in Accra 2/38
- Africans given majority in legislature 3/46
- Kwame Nkrumah, first African premier 3/52
- Profile of anti-colonial fighter Nkrumah 3/52
- Leaders call for independent Ghana 4/56
- Colonial Secretary approves independence 5/56
- Independence set for March 1957 9/56
- Becomes independent state of Ghana 3/57

Gold, Harry 3/51
Gold, Jack 12/76
Goldberg, Abraham 8/82
Golding, Alan 10/68
Golding, Ernest 1/39
Golding, William 9/11, 10/54, 12/54, 10/80, 12/80, 12/83, 6/93
Goldman, Emma 5/09
Goldsmith, James 5/76, 7/76, 4/81, 7/83
Goldwater, Barry 1/09, 3/62, 1/64, 7/64, 11/64
Goldwyn, Samuel 5/39, 1/74
Golf
- Harry Vardon becomes champion 2/00
- Harry Vardon wins his fourth Open 6/03
- Jack White wins Open, lowest ever score 6/04
- Willie Anderson wins Open 7/04
- Vardon wins after eight lean years 6/11
- George Duncan's record round, St. Andrew's 5/22
- Amateur Jones wins Open tournament, UK 6/26
- Duncan prophesies steel club 1/27
- America wins first Ryder Cup tournament 6/27
- US amateur Bobby Jones wins Open 7/27
- Americans win Walker Cup trophy 5/30
- Bobby Jones wins third British Open 6/30
- Bobby Jones wins "impossible" Grand Slam 9/30
- Bobby Jones retires 11/30
- Gene Sarazen wins Open 6/32
- Briton Henry Cotton wins Open 6/34
- Harry Vardon dies 3/37
- Henry Cotton wins British Open for second time 7/37
- Henry Cotton wins British Open 7/48
- Bobby Locke wins British Open 7/49, 7/50
- Max Faulkner wins British Open 7/51
- Peter Thompson's record round of 62 7/51
- US's Ben Hogan wins British Open 7/53
- Peter Thomson, 24, wins British Open 7/54
- Arnold Palmer wins Amateur Championship 8/54
- Arnold Palmer wins US Masters 4/58
- Australia's Thomson wins Open for fourth time 7/58
- Gary Player wins US Masters by a stroke 4/61
- Jack Nicklaus wins British Open 7/66
- Jacklin wins major US tournament 3/68
- Gary Player wins British Open 7/68
- Tony Jacklin wins British Open 7/69
- Tony Jacklin wins US Open 6/70
- Jack Nicklaus wins British Open 7/70
- British golfers win Walker Cup 5/71
- Lee Trevino wins British Open 7/71
- US golfer Bobby Jones dies 12/71
- Jack Nicklaus wins US Open 6/72
- Lee Trevino wins British Open 7/72
- Gary Player wins British Open 7/74
- US's Tom Watson wins British Open 7/75
- Ryder Cup opened to Europeans 5/78
- Nicklaus wins third Open championship 7/78
- Ballesteros, 22, wins British Open 7/79
- Ballesteros, youngest Masters winner 4/80

- Tom Watson wins British Open by a stroke 7/82
- Ballesteros is US Masters champion 4/83
- Tom Watson wins his fifth British Open 7/83
- Seve Ballesteros wins British Open 7/84
- Sandy Lyle wins British Open 7/85
- Europe wins Ryder Cup 9/85
- Greg Norman wins British Open 7/86
- UK's Laura Davies wins US Women's Open 7/87
- UK's Nick Faldo wins British Open 7/87
- Darcy's put saves Ryder Cup for Europe 9/87
- Seve Ballesteros wins British Open 7/88
- Ireland wins Dunhill Cup 10/88
- Nick Faldo wins US Masters championship 5/89
- Europe draws with US in Ryder Cup 9/89
- Nick Faldo wins US Masters 4/90
- Ian Woosnam wins US Masters 4/91
- Hale Irwin wins Ryder Cup 9/91
- Nick Faldo wins UK Golf Open 7/92
- Mark Roe wins Lancome Trophy 9/92
- America retain Ryder Cup 9/93

Golitzin, Prince Dimitri 1/17
Gollan, John 2/66
Gollancz, Victor 2/67
Golombek, Harry 1/95
Gomaa, Sharawy 5/71
Gomes da Costa, Manuel 5/26
Gompers, Samuel 9/18
Gomulka, Wladyslaw 2/05, 9/48, 10/51, 4/56, 8/56, 10/56, 11/56, 1/57, 5/57, 12/70, 2/71, 9/82
Gonne, Maud 1/39
Gonzales, Pancho 6/69
Gonzalez, Felipe 10/82, 3/86, 10/89, 6/93
Gooch, Graham 3/82, 11/87, 3/90, 7/93
Goodhew, Duncan 7/80
Goodman, Benny 5/09, 12/35, 5/62, 6/86
Goolagong, Evonne
- See Cawley 7/80

Goon Show
- See Milligan, Secombe, Sellers

Goossens, Eugene 6/62
Gorbachev, Mikhail
- Born 3/31
- Visits Britain 12/84
- Becomes new Soviet leader 3/85
- Announces 10-month freeze in medium-range missile deployment 4/85
- Meets with Reagan for talks in Geneva 11/85
- Proposes 15-year timetable to eliminate nuclear arms 1/86
- Sends New Years's greetings to Reagan 1/86
- Attacks wasted Brezhnev years at Congress 2/86
- Attends Star Wars summit 10/86
- Frees dissident Andrei Sakharov 12/86
- Calls for greater democracy 1/87
- Pardons 140 dissidents 2/87
- Meets with Thatcher 3/87
- Makes new offer on arms cuts 4/87
- Fires critical party boss 11/87
- Signs missile treaty 12/87
- Sacks Boris Yeltsin 2/88
- Rehabilitates 21 "un-persons" 2/88
- Says he will sign Geneva peace accord 4/88
- Welcomes Reagan on his Soviet tour 5/88
- Retires President Andrei Gromyko 9/88
- Promises to free all political prisoners 10/88
- Faces ethnic unrest in Baltic states 11/88
- Slashes Red Army troops 12/88
- Gives warning to Communist Party 1/89
- Criticised by Yeltsin for being slow in reforms 3/89
- Purges top ranks of Communist Party 4/89
- Invites Queen Elizabeth II to visit Moscow 5/89
- Meets with Chinese leader Deng Xiaoping 5/89
- Elected President 5/89
- Signs Bonn declaration 6/89
- Faces mounting ethnic unrest 8/89
- Advises Erich Honecker to heed "impulses" of the times 10/89
- Announces end of Cold War 12/89
- Threatens to resign during a row at a meeting 12/89
- Re-establishes firm rule in Azerbaijan after insurrection 1/90
- Elected Executive President of USSR 3/90
- Rules out Soviet support for a unified Germany in NATO 4/90
- Humiliated as crowds jeer at him during May Day celebrations 5/90
- Polls confirm Gorbachev's major rival is Boris Yeltsin 5/90
- Agrees with Bush on new arms cuts 6/90
- Guarantees safety of perestroika 7/90
- United with Bush on Iraq issue 9/90
- Soviet parliament votes to give President new powers 10/90
- Wins increased powers after emergency debate 11/90
- To collect Peace Prize 12/90
- Shevardnadze, disgruntled with Gorbachev's reforms, resigns 12/90
- Accused of dictatorship by Boris Yeltsin 2/91
- Agrees with Yeltsin on election timetable 4/91
- Pleads with the West not to set conditions for helping USSR 6/91
- Likely to clash with newly-elected Russian President Yeltsin 6/91
- First Soviet leader to attend G7 economic summit 7/91
- Toppled by coup; under house arrest 8/91
- On his way back to Moscow after coup collapses 8/91
- Forced by Yeltsin to read out list of coup supporters 8/91
- Struggles to retain role for a central government 8/91
- Signs START with President Bush 8/91
- Participates in Middle East summit in Madrid 10/91
- Resigns from office 12/91

Gorbachev, Raisa
- Cuts short US trip to visit Armenian quake victims 12/84

Gordievski, Oleg 9/85
Gordimer, Nadine 10/91, 12/91
Gordon, Aloysius ("Lucky") 8/63, 12/63
Gordon, Rev. J.G. 10/36
Gordon, Richard 11/69
Gordon-Walker, Patrick 2/50, 3/50, 1/65
Gore, Arthur 7/01, 7/26
Gore, Spencer 12/11
Gorky, Maxim 12/02, 1/05, 11/09, 5/29, 6/36, 12/36
Gormley, Joe 6/71, 7/77, 2/81, 5/93
Gorse, George 1/62
Gorst, Eldon 10/08
Gort, Viscount (John) 12/37, 9/39, 5/40
Gorton, John 1/68
Gottlieb, Adolph 3/03
Gottwald, Klement 7/47, 2/48, 6/48, 3/53
Gould, Bryan 2/89
Gould, Glenn 10/82
Gouraud, Henri 7/20
Gow, Ian 11/85, 7/90
Gower, David 7/78, 3/90
Gowon, Yakubu 8/66, 5/67, 7/67, 8/68, 9/68, 7/69, 7/75
Grable, Betty 7/73
Grace, Princess of Monaco (nee Kelly) 3/55, 1/56, 4/56, 12/56, 1/57, 3/62, 9/82
Grace, William Gilbert 8/08, 10/15
Gracey, Douglas 1/49
Grade, Michael 11/87
Graf, Steffi 7/87, 6/88, 7/88, 9/88, 7/89, 7/91, 7/92, 7/93
Graft, Michael 6/86
Graham, Billy 2/54, 3/54, 5/54, 4/55
Graham, Winston 3/62
Grahame, Kenneth 12/08
Grainger, Percy 2/61
Granados, Enrique 12/18
Grand National
- See Horse-racing

Granger, Stewart 5/13, 8/93
Granjo, Antonio 10/21
Grant, Alexander 9/24
Grant, Bernie 4/85
Grant, Cary 1/04, 7/42, 12/46, 11/86
Grass, Günther 10/27, 12/80
Graves, Alvin C. 5/51
Graves, Robert 12/18, 12/29, 9/36, 2/61, 12/76, 12/85
Gray, Patrick 4/73
Grayson, Larry 1/95
Grayson, Victor 7/07
Graziani, Rodolfo 10/35, 2/41, 5/50
Greaves, Jimmy 8/57
Greece
- See also World Wars I and II
- Prince George to rule Crete 4/00
- Crete opts for Greek union 4/05
- Premier Delyannis killed in Athens 6/05
- Crete wants to join Greece 10/08
- Military fight parliament for power 12/09
- Crete pledges union; violence erupts 5/10
- Anti-Turkish pact with Bulgaria 5/12
- Mobilises troops against Montenegro 6/12
- Demonstrations against Turkish rule 9/12
- Wants Turkish compensation, Samos affair 9/12
- Routs Turks at Sarandaporos 10/12
- 62 Cretan deputies cheered in parliament 10/12
- Attacks Salonika, "unites" with Samos 11/12
- Refuses to sign general peace with Turks 12/12
- King George assassinated in Salonika 3/13
- Duke of Sparta is new King Constantine I 3/13
- Attacked by Bulgarians along with Serbia 7/13
- Pro-Allies premier Venizelos resigns 10/15
- Venizelos returns with Allied support 10/16
- King orders army to intercept rebels 11/16
- Allies force king to abdicate 6/17
- Premier wounded in Paris shooting 8/20
- Venizelos beaten at polls; resigns 11/20
- Referendum calls for return of king 12/20
- King Constantine returns 12/20
- King Constantine resigns after defeats 9/22
- Loses commander, seeks Turkish armistice 9/22
- Signs Mudania Treaty, leaves Thrace 10/22
- Five ex-cabinet ministers executed 11/22
- Ex-King Constantine I dies 1/23
- Accepts million refugees; saturated 2/23
- Agrees on peace talks with Turkey 5/23
- New republican government 2/24
- King George II democratically deposed 3/24
- Admiral Konduriotis plans referendum 3/24
- Referendum agrees to abolish monarchy 4/24
- Expels 50,000 Armenians 7/24
- Greeks expelled from Turkey; arrests 10/24
- Invades Bulgaria; withdraws as League asks 10/25
- Kondylis overthrows Pangalos in coup 8/26
- Twelve soldiers killed in shooting accident 7/29
- Parliament elects A. Zaimis president 12/29
- Signs treaty of friendship with Turkey 9/30
- First Balkan Congress 10/30
- Venizelos resigns as premier 5/32
- New government under Papanastasiou 5/32
- Balkan Pact: Rumania, Yugoslavia and Turkey 2/34
- Italians bomb Rhodes; ten die 4/34
- Prince George of Britain to marry Marina of Greece 8/34
- Venizelos fails in coup attempt; retires 3/35
- Popular reception for Kondylis victory 3/35
- Assembly votes for monarchy 10/35
- King George II returns to throne 11/35
- Kondylis maintains power in monarchy 11/35
- King's amnesty for republican rebels 12/35
- Britain and France pledge aid 4/39
- Italy invades 10/40
- King George abandons Athens for Crete 4/41
- Government abandons Athens for Crete 4/41
- King George flees from Crete to Egypt 5/41
- Rival partisans fight each other 10/44
- Civil war breaks out 12/44
- Churchill tries to end civil war 12/44
- UK forces oppose communist revolt 5/45
- Monarchists win election 3/46
- Vote approves restoration of monarchy 9/46
- Civil war looms 9/46
- King George II returns from exile 9/46
- Greek troops and Macedonian rebels fight 11/46
- 300 die when ship hits mine 1/47
- Gains land under Paris peace treaties 2/47
- King George II dies 4/47
- 2,500 alleged communist plotters arrested 7/47
- Communists attack in Thrace and Macedonia 3/49
- Joins Council of Europe 8/49
- Communist rebels under Markos defeated 8/49
- Civil war ends 10/49
- Invited to join NATO 9/51
- Friendship treaty with Turks and Yugoslavs 3/53
- 1,000 die as tidal waves hit Ionian Isles 8/53
- Pro-Cypriot march on UK embassy; 78 hurt 8/54
- Demands Cypriot autonomy; UN shelves it 12/54
- Talks with Turkey and UK on Cyprus fail 9/55
- Premier Papagos dies; Karamanlis new man 10/55
- King Paul supports Makarios 4/56
- Rejects new NATO Cyprus peace plan 3/57
- Karamanlis welcomes Makarios 4/57
- Premier Karamanlis resigns 3/58
- UK Cyprus deal rules out Enosis 2/59
- Maria Callas splits with husband 9/59
- Hundreds of political prisoners freed 11/63
- Giorgos Seferis wins Literature Nobel 12/63
- George Papandreou wins election 2/64
- King Paul I dies; Constantine succeeds 3/64
- King Constantine marries 9/64
- Anti-monarchist demonstration in Athens 8/65
- 280 die when ferry sinks in storm 12/66
- Army colonels seize power in coup 4/67
- Martial law and curfew imposed 4/67
- King's counter-coup attempt fails 12/67
- King Constantine flees to Rome 12/67
- Jackie Kennedy marries Aristotle Onassis 10/68
- 350 prisoners released 4/70
- Monarchy abolished; republic proclaimed 6/73
- Arab terrorists kill three, hurt 55, Athens 8/73
- Martial law ended 8/73
- Army coup puts colonels in power 11/73
- 9 die in riots; martial law imposed 11/73
- Rule of the colonels ended by civilians 7/74
- Karamanlis returns from exile 7/74
- Andreas Papandreou returns from exile 8/74
- 88 die in plane crash 9/74
- Karamanlis wins election 11/74
- Votes to become a republic 12/74
- Applies to join EEC 6/75
- Papadopoulos death sentence commuted 8/75
- Karamanlis wants pact with Turkey 4/76
- Palestinians hijack Air France Airbus 6/76
- UNESCO fund to save polluted Acropolis 1/77
- Prima donna Maria Callas dies 9/77
- Joins the EEC 1/81
- 24 die in football stampede, Athens 2/81
- Ex-King Constantine returns for mother's funeral 2/81
- Papandreou's Pasok comes to power 10/81
- UK diplomat Kenneth Whitty shot dead 3/84
- Bomb explodes on plane in mid-air 4/86
- 700 die in heatwave; hospitals crammed 7/87
- Terrorists open fire on ferry 7/88
- Election defeat for Pasok Party; Papandreou offers to resign 6/89
- Andreas Papandreou tried on fraud charges 9/89
- Paul Ashwell arrested for transporting tubing to Iraq 4/90

Green, Allan 10/91
Green, Hughie 9/55
Greenaway, Peter 12/91
Greene, Graham 10/04, 11/31, 12/32, 12/40, 12/49, 7/59, 12/73, 12/80, 4/91
Greenfield, John 12/72
Greenglass, Harry 3/51
Greenland
- The Hague declares Greenland Danish 4/33
- Occupied by US 4/41
- Crash of US B-52 carrying nuclear bombs 1/68
- Votes to pull out of EEC 2/82
- Papandreou elected Premier 10/93

Greenpeace
- See Ecology

Greenson, Ralph 8/62
Greenwood, Arthur 3/39
Greenwood, Ron 6/80
Greenwood, Walter 12/33
Greer, Germaine 1/39, 12/70
Gregory, Augusta 1/39
Gregsten, Michael 2/62
Greig, Tony 5/77, 7/77, 11/77
Grenada
- Coup ousts Prime Minister Gairy 3/79
- New premier Bishop appeals for calm 3/79
- Independent of Britain 10/79
- Army murders PM Bishop and seizes power 10/83
- US Marines invade 10/83
- US troops find 100 bodies, including Bishop's 11/83

Grenfell, Julian 12/15
Grey, Lita 1/27, 8/27
Grey, Viscount (Edward) 3/11, 4/14, 7/14, 12/14, 9/33
Greyhound racing
- First UK track at Belle Vue 7/26
- Wembley Stadium sold for greyhound races 8/27
- Three venues in a year; sport catches on 12/27
- Call for betting to be banned 1/33

Grieg, Edvard Hagerup 9/07
Grier, Roosevelt 6/68
Griffin, Michael 3/93
Griffith, Arthur 11/20, 1/22, 8/22
Griffith, David Wark 3/10, 3/15, 4/19, 7/48
Griffith-Joyner, Florence 9/88
Griffiths, John 6/69
Grigg, John 12/55
Grigson, Jane 3/90
Grimond, Jo 7/13, 3/62, 11/63, 1/67, 7/83, 10/93
Grinham, Judy 11/56
Gris, Jean 12/11
Grissom, Virgil "Gus" 7/61, 1/67
Grivas, George 3/56, 5/56, 8/58, 9/58, 3/59
Groce, Cherry 9/85, 1/87
Groener, General 11/18
Groesz, Jozsef 6/51
Gromov, Boris 2/89
Gromyko, Andrei 7/09, 9/38, 8/43, 3/47, 7/47, 5/48, 3/49, 6/52, 3/59, 10/72, 4/73, 10/78, 1/82, 7/85, 9/88, 4/89, 7/89
Gronchi, Giovanni 4/55
Gropius, Walter 12/26, 12/38, 7/69
Grossmith, George and Weedon 12/12
Grosz, George 12/20, 12/37, 7/59
Grotewohl, Otto 10/49, 6/53
Group of Seven
- Gorbachev is first Soviet leader to attend G7 summit 7/91
- G7 agrees "biggest tariff reduction in history" 7/93

Grove, George 5/00
Groves, Leslie L. 8/45
Grumiaux, Arthur 10/86
Grundy, Bill 12/76
Grunshi, Alhaji 11/14
Grunwick
- Picket violence at dispute 6/77

Gsovsky, Tatiana 2/01
Guadeloupe
- Hurricane kills 300 on island 9/28
- Becomes department of France 3/46
- Four-nation summit 1/79

Guardian Angels 2/89
Guatemala
- Defeated in war; signs treaty 7/06
- Blames Cuba for unrest 11/60
- Coup overthrows Miguel Fuentes 3/63
- Miguel Asturias wins Literature Nobel 12/67
- West German ambassador murdered 4/70
- 12,000 die in earthquake 2/76
- Helps draft Central American peace plan 1/84
- Signs Central American peace plan 8/87
- Military coup ousts President Elias 6/93

Gudev, Joseph 3/07
Guernica
- New autonomous Basque region 10/36
- Destruction of Basque town by German air force 4/37

Guevara, Ernesto "Che" 6/28, 9/58, 11/59, 10/65, 10/67
Guiana, British
- See also Guyana
- Arbitration agreement, Britain-Brazil 6/04
- UK sends warships to quell feared coup 10/53
- Constitution suspended 10/53
- People's Progressive Party internments 10/53
- Ex-premier Dr Jagan jailed 4/54
- State of emergency; UK troops fly in 5/64

Guiana, French
- Joins the Free French 3/43
- Becomes department of France 3/46
- European rocket launches two satellites 6/81

Guillaume, Gunther 5/74, 12/75
Guinea
- Rejects closer links with France 9/58
- Sekou Toure declares independence 10/58
- Signs union agreement with Ghana 11/58
- President Sekou Toure steps down 3/66
- Nkrumah: "President of Ghana and Guinea" 3/66
- New Ghanaian regime severs ties 3/66

Guinness scandal
- Three businessmen found guilty 8/90
- Sir Jack Lyons fined £4 million 9/90

Guinness, Alec 4/14, 12/46, 12/48, 12/49, 12/53, 12/57, 3/58, 1/59, 12/79, 4/80, 12/81
Guinness, Jennifer 4/86
Gulbenkian, Calouste 7/55
Gulf War
- See Iran, Iraq

Gullit, Ruud 6/88
Gummer, Cordelia 5/90
Gummer, John Selwyn 9/83, 2/87, 5/90
Gunn, David 3/93
Gunn, Thom 12/92
Gunnell, Sally 8/92, 8/93
Gurney, Henry 10/51
Gustav V, King of Sweden 10/50
Gustav VI Adolf, King of Sweden 9/73
Guston, Philip 6/80
Guthrie, Tyrone 12/50, 6/51
Guyana
- 913 die in Jonestown cult mass suicide 11/78
- Congressman Ryan killed near Jonestown 11/78
- Jim Jones: US do-gooder turned dictator 11/78

Guzman, Abimael 9/92
Gyngell, Bruce 10/91

H

Haakon VII, King of Norway 4/40, 9/57
Haavelmo, Trygve 12/89
Habash, George 2/69, 9/90
Habib, Philip 7/83
Habre, Hissen 8/83
Hadad, Wadi 5/72
Hadlee, Richard 2/90
Hadzimuratovic, Irma 8/93
Haeberle, Ron 11/69
Hagen, Jean 3/52
Hagen, Walter 6/27
Haggard, H. Rider 5/25
Hagler, Marvin 9/80
Hahn, Otto 1/39, 12/44, 8/45, 7/68
Haig, Alexander 12/24, 6/79, 3/81, 1/82, 4/82, 6/82
Haig, Earl (Douglas) 12/15, 7/16, 6/17, 8/17, 4/18, 9/19, 1/28
Hailsham, Lord
- See Hogg, Quintin

Hailwood, Mike 3/81
Hain, Peter 5/70, 10/75, 4/76
Hairdressing
- See Fashion and Fads

Haise, Fred 4/70
Haiti
- "Papa Doc" Duvalier wins presidency 9/57
- "Papa Doc" crushes coup; kills leaders 7/58
- Duvalier to rule by decree for six months 7/58
- Martial law declared 5/63
- 4,000 die in hurricane 10/63
- 500 die in floods and landslides 11/63
- "Papa Doc" Duvalier is President for life 6/64
- "Papa Doc" Duvalier dies 4/71
- "Baby Doc" Duvalier becomes President 4/71
- Riots as "Baby Doc" is thrown out 2/86
- Presidential election cancelled 11/87
- Military coup forces President to flee 10/91
- Conservative Marc Bazin is appointed premier 6/92
- Wave of terrorist attacks leaves 10 dead 8/92
- Over 1,700 feared dead when a ferry capsizes 2/93
- US Marines prepare way for return of exiled President 9/94
- President Aristide returns 10/94

Haitink, Bernard 11/67
Halasan, Teresa 11/83
Halberg, Murray 9/60
Haldane, John 12/64
Haldane, Richard Burdon 9/06, 4/08, 2/12, 6/12, 8/28
Haldeman, Harold Robbins ("Bob" 4/73, 6/73, 1/75, 2/75
Halek, Jiri 9/68
Haley, Alex 2/92
Haley, Bill 4/54, 9/56, 2/57, 12/57, 12/59, 2/81
Halford, Allison 1/92
Halifax, Lord (Edward Wood) 11/37, 1/39, 5/40, 12/40, 12/59
Hall, Fawn 7/87
Hall, Henry 5/32
Hall, Peter 8/55, 12/56, 12/59, 12/60, 12/64, 1/68, 10/76, 12/79, 12/81, 1/87
Hall, Radclyffe 12/28
Halley's Comet
– See Space
Halliwell, Kenneth 9/67
Hallowes, Odette 3/95
Halsbury, Lord 12/09
Halsey, William 7/45
Hamburg
– Communist coup fails; 20 die 3/21
Hamel, Gustav 4/13
Hamilton, Duke of 5/41
Hamilton, Richard 12/61
Hamilton-Grant, David 2/84
Hammani, Said 1/78
Hammarskjold, Dag 3/53, 3/57, 9/57, 7/60, 9/60, 9/61, 10/61
Hammer, Armand 12/90
Hammerstein, Oscar 12/47
Hammett, Dashiell 7/51, 1/61
Hampson, Tommy 8/32
Han Dongfang 5/91
Hancock, Michael 6/84
Hancock, Tony 12/53, 10/64, 6/68
Hand, Dorothy 7/59
Handley, Tommy 12/41, 1/49
Hani, Chris 4/93
Hankey, Maurice 3/43
Hanratty, James 1/62, 2/62, 4/62
Hanson, Irene 11/69
Hanson, John 11/69
Hara Kei, Takashi 11/21
Harbin, Wayne 8/72, 10/72
Hard, Darlene 7/57
Hardie, F.M. 2/33
Hardie, Keir 2/00, 4/06, 11/06, 3/07, 6/08, 7/08, 8/11, 7/14, 9/15
Harding, Gilbert Charles 11/60
Harding, John 8/50, 11/55, 1/56, 3/56
Harding, Peter 3/94
Harding, Warren Gamaliel 6/20, 9/20, 11/20, 3/21, 4/21, 6/21, 11/21, 2/23, 3/23, 5/23, 7/23, 8/23
Hardinge, Lord, Viceroy of India 4/14
Hardwick, Ben 3/85
Hardwicke, Cedric 2/35
Hardy, Oliver 12/32, 8/57
Hardy, Richard 8/33
Hardy, Thomas 2/14, 3/26, 1/28
Hare, John 3/08
Harger, H.N. 12/38
Hargreaves, Alison 5/95
Hargreaves, Roger 9/88
Harlech, Lord (David) 1/85
Harlow, Jean 6/37
Harmsworth, Esmond 12/36
Harmsworth, Harold
– See Rothermere, Lord
Harper, Ashley 8/82
Harries, Karl 4/10
Harriman, Averell 2/46, 9/46, 7/63, 5/68, 7/86
Harriman, Edward Henry 9/09
Harris, Arthur "Bomber" 5/42, 7/42, 8/43, 11/43, 2/45, 8/45, 4/84, 5/92
Harris, Barbara 9/88, 2/89
Harris, Emily 10/78
Harris, Jean 3/80
Harris, Joel Chandler 7/08
Harris, Wilfred 6/10
Harris, William 10/78
Harrison, Benjamin 3/01
Harrison, George 10/63, 10/65, 1/66, 3/69, 12/70, 8/71
Harrison, Rex (Reginald Carey) 8/46, 3/56, 4/58, 12/63, 4/65, 6/90
Harroun, Ray 5/11
Hart, Doris 7/51, 7/53
Hart, Gary 3/84, 5/87
Hart, Judith 7/67, 10/68
Hart, Lorenz 4/37, 11/43
Hart, Watson 5/32
Hartlepool
– Shelled by German warships 12/14
Hartmann, Karl Amadeus 8/05
Hartnell, Norman 11/47
Hartree, Douglas 2/46
Hartung, Hans 9/04
Harty, Herbert Hamilton 2/41
Harty, Russell 6/88
Harvey, Laurence 12/59
Harvey, Len 7/39
Harwood, Ronald 12/84
Hary, Armin 6/60, 9/60
Hasek, Jaroslav 1/23
Hasenfus, Eugene 10/86
Hashem, Ibrahim 4/57
Haslam, Robert 10/85
Hassan II, King of Morocco 2/61, 7/71, 8/72, 1/73, 10/75, 11/75
Hassan, Abu 1/79
Hassan, Joshua 6/69
Hastings, Gavin 5/95
Haston, Dougal 2/67, 9/75
Hattersley, Roy 10/83
Hatton, Derek 6/86, 3/87
Haug, Thorlief 1/24
Haughey, Charles 5/70, 10/70, 5/81, 2/82, 11/82, 2/87, 3/87, 6/89, 7/89, 10/90, 1/92
Hauptmann, Bruno 9/34, 1/35, 2/35, 6/35, 10/35, 4/36
Hauptmann, Gerhart 6/46
Hausofer, Karl 5/41
Havel, Vaclav 5/89, 11/89, 12/89, 7/90, 7/92
Havenstein, Rudolf 6/23
Havers, Michael 8/80, 11/81, 3/86, 3/92
Haw Haw, Lord (William Joyce) 1/40, 5/45, 6/45, 9/45
Hawaii
– Becomes American territory 4/00
– Statehood approved 3/59
Hawke, Bob 3/83, 12/91
Hawkins, Coleman 11/04, 12/27
Hawkins, Jack 12/53, 10/59, 2/66
Hawthorn, Mike 10/58, 1/59
Hawthorne, Nigel 12/91
Hayek, Friedrich August (von) 12/74, 3/92
Hayes, Bob 6/63
Hayman, Peter 3/81
Hays, Ann 5/70
Hayward, Susan 3/75
Hayworth, Rita 10/47, 6/48, 5/49, 5/87
Hazell, Heidi 9/09
Hazelwood, Joseph 3/89
Head, Christopher 8/66
Healey, Denis 10/61, 10/73, 12/73, 3/74, 12/74, 4/75, 7/75, 9/75, 4/76, 9/76, 7/77, 10/80, 11/80, 9/81, 6/87
Hearst, Patricia 2/74, 4/74, 9/75, 3/76, 5/77, 4/78, 10/78, 1/79, 2/79
Hearst, William Randolph 10/09, 8/51, 5/93
Heath, Edward
– Elected Oxford Union librarian 2/38
– Leads student Tories against appeasement 10/38
– Minister in Macmillan cabinet 10/59
– Becomes deputy to Foreign Minister 7/60
– To conduct Common Market negotiations 7/61
– Elected Tory leader 7/65
– Says he will take UK into EEC 10/65
– On Rhodesian oil sanctions 12/65
– Reshuffles shadow cabinet 4/66
– Sacks Powell from shadow cabinet 4/68
– Appoints Thatcher to shadow transport 11/68
– Thatcher made shadow education spokesman 10/69
– Aboard Morning Cloud 12/69
– Becomes Prime Minister 6/70
– Shaken by Iain Macleod's death 7/70
– Declares state of emergency: dock strike 7/70
– Creates two new ministries 10/70
– Attends de Gaulle's funeral 11/70
– Says country is sick of wildcat disputes 12/70
– In EEC talks with Pompidou 5/71
– Leads UK to Admiral's Cup win 8/71
– In talks with Jack Lynch 9/71
– Attends signing of Treaty of Brussels 1/72
– Imposes direct rule in Northern Ireland 3/72
– Vows to aid boy held in Turkish jail 3/72
– Calls for pegs on prices and incomes 9/72
– Gives views on proposed European union 10/72
– Puts 90-day freeze on prices and wages 11/72
– Condemns Lonhro's practices 5/73
– Announces Phase III of his pay policy 10/73
– Puts Britain on three-day week 12/73
– Sunningdale deal on a Council of Ireland 12/73
– Calls election on "Who runs Britain?" 2/74
– Election results in no overall majority 3/74
– Loses general election 10/74
– Bomb explodes close to him in London 10/74
– House attacked by IRA bombers 12/74
– Leadership battle with Thatcher 1/75
– Resigns after first ballot defeat 2/75
– Kept out of Thatcher cabinet 5/79
– Attacks Thatcher on unemployment 1/82
– Announces he is going to Iraq to plead release of hostages 10/90
– Meets with Saddam Hussein in Baghdad 10/90
– Manages to obtain release of 33 hostages held in Iraq 10/90
Heathcoat Amory, Derick 4/58, 11/59
Heathrow Airport
– Customs men intercept nuclear weapons bound for Iraq 3/90
– First planeload of women and children from Iraq lands 9/90
– Heathrow suffers third IRA mortar attack in five days 3/94
Hecht, Ben 5/29
Heckler, Margaret 4/84
Heenan, John Carmel 11/75
Heffer, Eric 4/75, 9/75
Hegedus, Andras 4/55
Heide, Wolff 7/26
Heidemann, Gerd 5/83
Heifetz, Jascha 2/01, 12/87
Heikal, Mohammed 2/74
Heineken, Alfred 11/83
Heines, Edmund 6/34
Heisenberg, Werner 12/27
Hekmatyar, Gulbuddin 4/92
Helicopters
– See Aviation
Helldorf, Wolf von 7/35
Heller, Joseph 5/23, 12/61
Hellman, Lillian 12/78, 6/84
Helpmann, Robert 1/37, 12/49
Hemery, David 10/68
Hemingway, Ernest 12/29, 12/37, 10/40, 5/53, 12/54, 7/61
Hemmings, David 12/67
Henderson, Arthur 8/09, 2/18, 2/19, 2/24, 8/31, 10/35
Henderson, Cornell 8/65
Henderson, Fletcher 12/27, 12/35
Henderson, Gregory 11/66
Henderson, Ian 12/64
Henderson, Nevile 8/38
Hendrix, Jimi 12/67, 5/69, 9/70
Hendry, Stephen 4/90, 4/95
Heng Samrin 1/79, 8/79
Henlein, Konrad 9/38, 10/38
Henrey, Bobby 12/49
Henry William, Duke of Gloucester 6/74
Henry, Mr Justice 8/90
Henry, Prince 9/84
Hepburn, Audrey 5/29, 3/54, 7/59, 1/93
Hepburn, Katharine 11/09, 12/40, 6/67, 4/69
Hepworth, Barbara 1/03, 5/75
Herbert, Alan (A.P.) 11/36
Herbison, Margaret 7/67
Herge (Georges Remi) 5/07, 1/29
Herrema, Tiede 10/75, 11/75
Herrera, Rodolfo 5/20
Herrhausen, Alfred 11/89
Herriot, Edouard 6/24, 6/32, 7/32, 12/32, 10/42, 8/44
Herriot, James 2/95
Hersh, Seymour 5/70, 12/70, 10/91
Hertling, Georg von 9/18
Hertogh, Bertha 12/50
Hertzog, James Barrie 4/10, 9/10, 11/25, 10/27, 6/29, 5/33
Herzl, Theodor 8/03, 7/04
Herzog, Chaim 3/83
Herzog, Roman 5/94
Heseltine, Michael 7/81, 8/81, 9/81, 12/81, 1/83, 4/83, 11/83, 1/86, 11/90, 3/91, 10/92
Hess, Myra 12/39
Hess, Rudolf 11/23, 5/41, 8/45, 11/45, 1/46, 8/46, 10/46, 8/87
Hess, Victor Francis 12/11
Hesse, Hermann 12/46, 8/62
Heston, Charlton 11/59
Heusinger, Lieutenant-General 11/55
Hewish, Antony 12/74
Hewson, John 3/93
Heydrich, Reinhard 3/04, 1/42, 5/42, 6/42, 10/46
Heyer, Georgette 7/74
Heyerdahl, Thor 10/14, 3/50
Hick, Graeme 5/88
Hicks, John 12/72
Higgs, Marietta 6/87
Highsmith, Patricia 2/95
Hill, Albert 8/20
Hill, Benny 4/92
Hill, Damon 8/93
Hill, Dave 6/70
Hill, Graham 4/62, 5/66, 5/68, 10/68, 11/68, 5/69, 7/75, 11/75
Hill, Jimmy 8/67
Hill, Norman 11/21
Hill, Paul 10/89, 4/94
Hillary, Edmund 6/53, 1/58
Hiller, Wendy 12/33, 12/39, 4/59
Hillery, Patrick 12/76
Hills, Denis 6/75, 7/75
Himmler, Heinrich 10/00, 7/34, 6/36, 11/36, 8/37, 11/39, 3/40, 1/42, 6/42, 9/42, 10/42, 2/43, 4/43, 7/44, 11/44, 2/45, 4/45, 5/45
Hinckley, John 3/81, 8/01, 6/82, 8/82
Hindawi, Nezar 4/86, 10/86
Hindemith, Paul 12/33, 12/38, 12/63
Hindenburg, Paul von 8/14, 11/14, 8/15, 8/16, 11/18, 9/27, 7/30, 6/31, 2/32, 3/32, 4/32, 8/32, 1/33, 6/33, 11/33, 12/33, 8/34
Hindley, Myra 10/65, 4/66, 5/66, 11/86, 7/87
Hinds, Alfred 6/58
Hines, Jim 6/68
Hiranuma, Baron 1/39
Hirohito, Emperor of Japan 4/01, 5/21, 11/21, 12/23, 12/26, 11/28, 10/41, 12/41, 8/45, 9/45, 6/46, 11/46, 2/50, 10/71, 1/89, 11/90
Hislop, Ian 5/89
Hiss, Alger 8/48, 12/48, 6/49, 7/49, 1/50, 11/54
Hitchcock, Alfred 12/30, 12/40, 12/46, 6/60, 3/62, 3/63, 4/80
Hitler, Adolf
– Addresses German Workers' Party 9/19
– Blasts Versailles and Jews; wants Third Reich 2/20
– German Workers' Party becomes Nazi Party 4/20
– Voted President of Nazi Party 7/21
– Addresses 50,000 Nazis, Munich 11/22
– Attacks Versailles at first Nazi congress 1/23
– Bavarian crackdown; rallies continue 9/23
– Attacks Weimar Republic at Nuremberg 9/23
– Arrested after Munich beer hall putsch 11/23
– Tried for failed putsch, Munich 2/24
– Given light sentence for putsch 4/24
– Paroled: writes book in jail 12/24
– Promises to shun violence 2/25
– Publishes "Mein Kampf" 7/25
– Bavarian ban on his speeches is lifted 3/27
– Holds first Nazi Party meeting in Berlin 5/27
– Nazi salute and "heil" catch on 11/27
– Prussia lifts ban on Hitler speaking 9/28
– Nazis come second in Reichstag elections 9/30
– Barred from seat because of his Austrian citizenship 9/30
– Denounces peace treaties; wants big army 9/30
– Pact with Hugenburg to defeat Bruning 10/31
– Tells UK and US papers: "I am a democrat" 12/31
– To run for President against Hindenburg 2/32
– Granted German citizenship 2/32
– Fails to win presidency; gets 13 million votes 4/32
– Nazis double seats, become biggest party 7/32
– Refuses vice-chancellorship under von Papen 8/32
– Upset by Hindenburg and von Papen block 8/32
– Claims providence chose him for mission 9/32
– Refuses chancellorship despite poor poll 11/32
– Made Chancellor in new cabinet 1/33
– Banker von Schroeder helps him to power 1/33
– Uses Reichstag fire to get strong decree 2/33
– Proclaims the Third Reich 3/33
– Enabling Act: Hitler rules by decree 3/33
– Still needs Centre and Nationalist support 3/33
– Orders roundup of Jews; shop boycott 3/33
– Bans all opposition parties 6/33
– Drops anti-Catholic acts after concordat 7/33
– Radio speech: equality, not arms our aim 10/33
– Claims huge plebiscite mandate 11/33
– Keeps Hindenburg as President 12/33
– Meets UK's Eden for "cordial" talks 2/34
– Millions swear allegiance, Berlin 2/34
– Creates Nazi-dominated People's Court 5/34
– Personal hand in Storm Trooper purge 6/34
– Meets Mussolini for first time, Venice 6/34
– Rejects mutual aid pact with USSR 6/34
– Does not disown Austrian Nazi assassins 7/34
– Becomes "Fuehrer" after Hindenburg dies 8/34
– 90 per cent vote for Hitler as head of state 8/34
– 700,000 greet him at Nuremberg rally 9/34
– Pleased with Saar vote to be reunited 1/35
– Fails to stop adverse League resolution 4/35
– World broadcast: peace, yet rearmament 5/35
– Uses double to foil assassins, claim 6/35
– Orders swastika on national flag 8/35
– Announces anti-Semitic Nuremberg decrees 9/35
– Declares all men up to 45 reservists 11/35
– Tells League not to interfere with Nazi treatment of Jews 1/36
– Wants to recover lost colonies 1/36
– Launches Volkswagen, the "people's car" 2/36
– Authorises Rhineland occupation 3/36
– Recognises Italy's Abyssinian occupation 7/36
– Opens Berlin Olympics 8/36
– Embarrassed by Owens' Olympics success 8/36
– Sends Condor legion to help Franco 10/36
– Drafts Italian pact with Count Ciano 10/36
– Recognises Franco's forces in Spain 11/36
– Signs Axis pacts with Italy and Japan 11/36
– Patches up feud with Ludendorff 3/37
– German planes bomb Guernica 4/37
– Ready to talk on arms reductions 4/37
– To "take measures" after ship's bombing 5/37
– Calls for German colonies and living space 9/37
– Meets Duke and Duchess of Windsor 10/37
– Threatens sterilisation of "insane artists" 12/37
– Sacks Generals Blomberg and Fritsch 1/38
– Wants Czech and Austrian Germans autonomous 2/38
– Marches into Vienna after Anschluss 3/38
– Now ruler of 74 million "Germans" 3/38
– Becomes ruler of Austria 3/38
– Votes in unanimous Anschluss plebiscite 4/38
– Meets Mussolini: "lasting friendship" 5/38
– Makes his birthplace, Braunau, a city 5/38
– Attacks exiled German artists' show 7/38
– Calls four-power talks on Czech crisis 9/38
– Wins Sudeten secession; warns of power 9/38
– Crosses into Eger, Czechoslovakia 10/38
– "Great German future" Sudetenland speech 10/38
– Decorates American aviator Lindbergh 10/38
– Reopens Reichstag 1/39
– Denounced by Chamberlain 3/39
– Enters Prague 3/39
– Bohemia-Moravia made German protectorate 3/39
– Seeks Slovakia and Ruthenia independence 3/39
– Tears up 1934 naval treaty with Britain 4/39
– Denounces Britain-France-Poland pact 4/39
– Signs pact with Mussolini 5/39
– Guarantees Yugoslav frontiers 6/39
– Designs on Danzig 7/39
– Demands Danzig and Polish corridor 8/39
– Non-aggression pact with USSR 8/39
– Invades Poland 9/39
– Says he wants peace with UK and France 10/39
– Escapes bomb in Munich 11/39
– Spends Christmas with troops 12/39
– Orders scuttling of Graf Spee in Uruguay 12/39
– Allows Unity Mitford to return to UK 1/40
– Orders total sea war by U-boats 2/40
– Meets Mussolini at Brenner Pass 3/40
– Bans peace negotiations with USA 3/40
– Accepts French surrender 6/40
– Furious at British bombing of Berlin 8/40
– Begins Blitz on London 9/40
– Signs pact with Japan 9/40
– Meets Franco on Franco-Spanish border 10/40
– Warns Greece to end war with Italy 2/41
– Gives Yugoslavia ultimatum to join Axis 3/41
– Secret talks with Vichy leaders 5/41
– His deputy, Hess, crashes in Scotland 5/41
– Breaks pact and invades USSR 6/41
– Nears gates of Moscow 10/41
– Declares war on US 12/41
– Becomes C-in-C of army 12/41
– Meets Mussolini, Salzburg 4/42
– Orders all Germans aged 16-65 to mobilise 1/43
– Talks with Mussolini on North Africa 4/43
– Orders enlistment of all German children over the age of 10 1/44
– Suspends all laws in Berlin 4/44
– Makes Goebbels dictator of Berlin 4/44
– Escapes assassination attempt 7/44
– Eight executed for attempt on his life 8/44
– Forms Home Guard for Germany 10/44
– Rails against Treaty of Versailles 1/45
– Takes refuge in fortress beneath Berlin Chancellery 4/45
– Kills himself in Berlin bunker 4/45
– His body is found under Chancellery 6/45
– Suicide confirmed by pilot 10/55
Hitler, William 3/39
Hitrec, Hrvoje 7/91
Hives, Gareth 1/90
Ho Chi Minh 9/41, 1/46, 3/46, 12/46, 1/47, 1/50, 2/50, 5/50, 10/54, 2/66, 12/67, 9/69
Ho Ying-chin 4/49
Hoad, Lew 7/56, 7/57
Hoare, "Mad Mike" 12/81, 1/82, 7/82
Hoare, Samuel 1/27, 6/35, 10/35, 12/35
Hobbs, Jack 5/23, 8/26, 8/30, 8/32, 2/35
Hobson, John 10/62
Hockney, David 7/37, 12/61, 12/74
Hod, Mordechai 8/78
Hodgkin, Dorothy 10/64
Hodgkinson, Simon 3/91
Hodza, Milan 3/38, 9/38
Hoess, Rudolph 5/46
Hoff, Charles 9/25
Hoffa, James 3/64
Hoffman, Dustin 8/37, 12/69, 12/79, 12/89
Hoffmansthal, Hugo von 7/29
Hoffnung, Gerard 9/59
Hogan, Ben 7/53
Hogan, Paul 9/87
Hogg, Quintin (Lord Hailsham) 2/33, 10/38, 9/50, 7/63, 11/63, 12/63, 1/82
Hohenburg, Duchess of 6/14
Hoisington, Elizabeth 5/70
Holden, Charles 12/34, 12/38
Holden, William 3/54, 11/81
Holland, Sidney 7/56
Holliday, Billie 4/15, 7/59
Hollies, Eric 8/48
Hollis, Roger 10/73, 3/81
Holly, Buddy 2/59
Holman Hunt, William 9/10
Holme, Ian 2/94
Holmes, David 6/79
Holst, Gustav 12/19, 5/34, 12/34
Holst, Johan 1/94
Holt, Harold 12/67
Home, Lord
– See Douglas-Home, Alec
Honasan, Gregorio 8/87

Honduras
- Repels Guatemalan invasion; peace treaty 7/06
- Military coup overthrows Morales 10/63
- Invaded by El Salvador 7/69
- Army topples President Ramon Cruz 12/72
- Cyclone Fifi kills 10,000 9/74
- Helps draft Central American peace plan 1/84
- US helicopters used to ferry Honduran troops 12/86
- Signs Central America peace plan 8/87

Honecker, Erich 8/12, 5/71, 9/87, 10/89
Honeger, Arthur 11/55
Honeyghan, Lloyd 9/86, 10/87
Hong Kong
- See also World War II
- Sole UK naval base on Chinese coast 10/02
- Typhoon kills hundreds 9/06
- Big heroin haul by British officials 7/27
- Falls to Japanese 12/41
- British troops take control 9/45
- British to reinforce Hong Kong garrison 5/49
- 3,800 more British troops arrive 7/49
- UK infantry to join UN forces in Korea 8/50
- Anti-UK mobs attack whites in Kowloon 10/56
- Fence erected against Chinese immigrants 5/62
- Four die in police clashes with Communists 7/67
- Liner Queen Elizabeth destroyed by fire 1/72
- 4,000 Vietnam refugees rescued from ship 5/75
- Thatcher discusses issue on China visit 9/82
- UK framework for handover to China 8/84
- Britain and China agree on deal 9/84
- Britain and China sign Hong Kong treaty 12/84
- Shares crash owing to student massacre in China 6/89
- Britain refuses demand for haven for Hong Kong citizens 6/89
- Cholera epidemic among Vietnamese boat people 9/89
- Vietnamese boat people deportation threats spark riots 11/89
- Start of repatriation of Vietnamese boat people programme 12/89
- British government introduces Hong Kong Nationality Bill 4/90
- Britain agrees to return 60,000 boat people to Vietnam 10/91
- Boat people struggle against police 11/91

Hong Kong Nationality Bill 4/90
Hoover, Herbert 8/17, 9/17, 10/17, 2/21, 1/28, 11/28, 3/29, 11/29, 12/30, 6/31, 1/32, 6/32, 8/32, 1/33, 6/36, 2/37, 10/64
Hoover, J. Edgar 11/66, 5/72
Hopcraft, Arthur 12/79
Hope, Bob 5/05, 4/41, 2/46, 4/65
Hopkins, Anthony 12/85, 3/92, 12/92
Hopkins, Gowland 12/06
Hopkins, Harry 6/42
Hopper, Dennis 12/69
Hopson, Donald 8/67
Horder, Lord 1/48
Hore-Belisha, Leslie 3/35, 3/39, 10/39, 1/40
Hornby, Frank 9/36
Horne, Kenneth 8/49
Horowitz, Vladimir 10/04, 10/30, 4/86, 11/89
Horsbrugh, Florence 9/53
Horse-racing
- See also Derby winner (May-June most years), National winner (March-April)
- Jockey Club to continue races in war 3/15
- Ally Sloper wins Grand National 3/15
- Pommern wins "New Derby" 6/15
- Vermouth wins Grand National, Gatwick 3/16
- Fifinella wins "New Derby" 5/16
- Gray Crusader wins delayed New Derby 7/17
- Papyrus wins Derby; Donoghue's third win 6/23
- First Grand National to be broadcast 3/27
- Call Boy wins Derby - BBC live broadcast 6/27
- First women-only horse race, Newmarket 10/27
- First all-electric Totalisator 4/30
- Aga Khan's horses in four places, St. Leger 9/32
- Jockey Gordon Richards breaks record, UK 11/32
- Aga Khan's Bahram wins St. Leger; treble 9/35
- Golden Miller wins Cheltenham Gold Cup 3/36
- Jockey Steve Donoghue retires 11/37
- Jockey Club cancels the Derby 1/40
- First wartime race meeting at Ascot 5/43
- Photo-finish cameras on racecourses 7/46
- Photo-finish camera used first time, UK 4/47
- 12-year-old Lester Piggott wins race 8/48
- Gordon Richard's 200th winner of season 10/51
- Irish stud buys Tulyar for record sum 2/53
- G. Richards wins his first Derby on Pinza 6/53
- Gordon Richards is first jockey knighted 6/53
- RSPCA wants safer Grand National 4/54
- Lester Piggott youngest Derby winner 6/54
- First US-bred horse to win Derby 6/54
- Gordon Richards retires 8/54
- Queen Mother's Devon Loch slips in race 3/56
- Piggott suspended 6/59
- Jockey Manny Mercer dies at Ascot 9/59
- Piggott's 1,000th win 9/60
- Arkle wins third Cheltenham Gold Cup 3/66
- First woman allowed to train racehorses 7/66
- Foinavon wins Grand National at 100-1 4/67
- Suspended by foot and mouth epidemic 11/67
- Racehorse Arkle dies, UK 5/70
- 100 striking stable-boys disrupt Ascot 6/75
- Stable-boys end 11-week strike; new pay deal 7/75
- Red Rum's Grand National hat trick 4/77
- First woman in Grand National 4/77
- Piggott's eighth Derby win on Minstrel 6/77
- Steve Cauthen, 17, to ride in UK 7/77
- Red Rum to retire 3/78
- Cancer victim Champion wins National 4/81
- Shergar wins Derby by record margin 6/81
- Derby winner Shergar kidnapped, Ireland 2/83
- First woman trainer to win National 4/83
- Piggott wins his record ninth Derby 6/83
- John Francome rides his 1,000th winner 2/84
- Jockey Club approves Sunday racing 9/87
- Piggott jailed: £3 million tax evasion 10/87
- Desert Orchid wins at Cheltenham 3/89
- Little Polveir wins the Grand National 4/89
- Nashwan wins the Derby 6/89
- Mr Frisk wins Grand National in record time 4/90
- Quest for Fame wins the Derby 6/90
- Seagram wins Grand National 4/91
- Generous wins Ever Ready Derby 6/91
- Lester Piggott is injured during Breeders' Cup Classic 10/92
- Aintree officials declare Grand National race void 4/93
- Vintage Crop first European horse to win Melbourne Cup 11/93
- Red Rum retires from public life 11/94
- Royal Athlete wins Grand National 4/95

Horthy, Miklos 2/20, 3/20, 10/44, 2/57
Horton, Max 7/36
Horwood, William 11/22
Hoskins, Bob 12/86
Hotson, Ernest 7/31
Houdini, Harry (Ernst Weiss) 10/26
Houghton, Henry 1/61
Hounsfield, Godfrey 10/79
Housman, Alfred Edward 4/36
Houssay, Bernardo 12/47
Houston, John 8/06
Hove, Robert 4/79
Hoveida, Amir 4/79
Howard, Ebenezer 12/03
Howard, Leslie 12/39, 12/42, 6/43
Howard, Trevor Wallace 1/88
Howe, Geoffrey 2/75, 5/79, 11/80, 1/82, 11/82, 6/83, 2/84, 8/84, 9/84, 3/88, 7/89, 11/90
Howe, Juliet Ward 10/10
Howell, Denis 3/61, 10/74, 8/76
Howerd, Frankie 4/92
Howes, Robert 3/88
Hoxha, Enver 10/08, 11/44, 1/82, 4/85
Hozier, Clementine 8/08
Hrawi, Elias 11/89
Hsu Shi-chang 9/18
Hu Guofeng
- See Hua Kuo-feng

Hu Yaobang 6/81, 1/87, 4/89
Hua Kuo-fen
- See Hua Kuo-feng

Hua Kuo-feng 2/76, 10/76, 9/77, 10/79, 9/80
Huber, Francis 2/10
Hubermann, Bronislaw 6/47
Huberty, Oliver 7/84
Huddleston, Trevor 6/55
Hudson, Rock 7/85, 10/85
Huerta, Adolfo de la 6/20, 7/20
Huerta, Victoriano 2/13, 8/13, 10/13, 11/13, 5/14, 7/14
Hugenburg, Alfred 10/31
Hughes, Charles Evans 6/16, 10/16
Hughes, Christopher 5/83
Hughes, Francis 5/81
Hughes, Howard 12/05, 9/35, 7/38, 3/72, 12/72, 4/76
Hughes, Robert 3/95
Hughes, Simon 2/83
Hughes, Ted 8/30, 12/84
Hulanicki, Barbara 12/66, 9/69
Hulce, Tom 12/84
Hull, Cordell 12/41, 12/45
Hull, William 5/62
Hulton, Edward 10/23, 5/25
Hume, Basil 2/76, 11/76
Humez, Charles 6/53
Humperdinck, Engelbert 9/21
Humperdinck, Engelbert (Gerry Dorsey) 12/67
Humphrey, Hubert 1/60, 5/60, 9/64, 11/64, 4/67, 4/68, 8/68, 11/68, 6/72, 8/77, 1/78
Hungary
- See also Austria, World Wars I and II
- Jews and students clash in Budapest 4/01
- Riots after railway strike 4/04
- Parliament building wrecked 12/04
- Nationalists begin tax boycott 6/05
- Hungarian taught in Rumanian schools 8/09
- Ministers assaulted in parliament 3/10
- Police clash with workers; many die 5/12
- Premier resigns after parliament fight 6/13
- Prisoners freed for lack of food 8/17
- Mihaly Karoly wants early peace 9/17
- Expels Jews and takes away their assets 8/18
- Independent from Habsburg Empire 10/18
- First ruler, Michael Karolyi, liberal 11/18
- Bela Kun leads Communist revolt 2/19
- Former President Karolyi arrested 3/19
- Kun's Soviet regiments desert 4/19
- Communist regime surrenders to Allies 4/19
- Rumanians overthrow Kun's Red Republic 8/19
- New rulers recognise Versailles treaty 8/19
- New ruler, Archduke Josef, resigns 8/19
- First universal suffrage elections 1/20
- Monarchy restored; Miklos Horthy regent 2/20
- Parliament dissolved; Horthy is dictator 3/20
- Cut to quarter size by Treaty of Trianon 6/20
- Emperor Karl fails in comeback bid 10/21
- Parliament deposes Habsburg dynasty 11/21
- First Socialists elected 6/22
- Fascist prince arrested for forgery 1/26
- Fascist leader Archduke Albert resigns 1/26
- Prince von Windischgraetz is forger 5/26
- 70 arrested for "Communist plot" 2/27
- Anti-Hungarian riots near Rumania and border 12/27
- Co-operation pact with Austria and Italy 3/34
- Accused of helping murder Yugoslav king 11/34
- Refuses sanctions on Italy 10/35
- Demands southern Czechoslovakian territory 10/38
- Rejects Czechoslovakian proposals 10/38
- Annexes Ruthenia and Slovakia from Czechs 11/38
- Occupies Ruthenia 3/39
- Joins Axis 11/40
- Premier Teleki commits suicide 4/41
- Germans begin occupation 3/44
- Germans begin deporting Jews 4/44
- Told by Stalin to declare war on Germany 5/44
- Horthy government ousted by pro-Nazis 10/44
- Soviet tanks enter Budapest 11/44
- Budapest now in Russian hands 1/45
- Declares war on Germany 1/45
- Composer Bela Bartok dies 9/45
- Jozsef Mindszenty named as Primate 10/45
- Martial law declared 10/45
- Federal republic declared; King ousted 11/45
- Declared a republic 1/46
- Loses land under Paris peace treaties 2/47
- Premier Nagy exiled in coup 6/47
- Premier Dinnyes promises free elections 6/47
- Opposition voters disenfranchised 8/47
- Communists win election 9/47
- President Tildy resigns 7/48
- 1,000 are fleeing the country each month 11/48
- Mindszenty jailed for life for treason 2/49
- Declared a people's republic 2/49
- Ends friendship pact with Yugoslavia 9/49
- Sanders and Vogeler jailed for spying 2/50
- Penal codes on USSR model introduced 6/50
- University theology departments closed 6/50
- New purge of non-Communists 8/50
- To release US spy Vogeler 4/51
- Archbishop jailed for "plotting" 6/51
- Matyas Rakosi appointed premier 8/52
- Offers exchange of Cold War prisoners 2/53
- UK "spy" Edgar Sanders freed 8/53
- Premier Nagy sacked; Hegedus takes over 4/55
- Joins Warsaw Pact 5/55
- Cardinal Mindszenty released from jail 7/55
- Seven Hungarian hijackers seek German asylum 7/56
- Pro-Stalin premier Rakosi resigns 7/56
- Anti-Soviet revolt; people fight tanks 10/56
- Troops join rebels; 3,000 feared dead 10/56
- Premier Nagy wants USSR troops out 10/56
- Nagy calls for democratic reform 10/56
- Rebels hold southern Baranja province 10/56
- Reports of Soviet army on German border 10/56
- Rebels release Cardinal Mindszenty 10/56
- Mindszenty blesses "glorious victory" 10/56
- Nagy says they will quit Warsaw Pact 11/56
- UN tells USSR to leave 11/56
- 1,000 tanks invade; USSR takes Budapest 11/56
- Last radio broadcast, newspaper dispatch 11/56
- Janos Kadar appointed premier 11/56
- More than 100,000 refugees go to Austria 11/56
- New strikes and fighting break out 12/56
- Martial law crushes last resisters 12/56
- Regent from 1920 to 1944 dies 2/57
- Three rebel leaders get death sentence 4/57
- Regime dissolves Writers' Association 4/57
- Commonwealth conference shows concern 7/57
- Former premier Nagy is executed 6/58
- USA, Yugoslavia and Poland slam Nagy's execution 6/58
- Kadar purges 25 Stalinists 8/62
- 500 political prisoners freed 4/63
- Death of composer Zoltan Kodaly 3/67
- Eastern Bloc leaders meet in Budapest 3/69
- Death of philosopher Gyorgy Lukacs 6/71
- Cardinal Mindszenty dies 5/75
- March for liberal reforms 3/87
- Law allows formation of political parties 1/89
- Rally calls for democracy and withdrawal of Soviet troops 3/89
- Troops begin destruction of border fence with Austria 5/89
- Janos Kadar is removed from all powerful posts 5/89
- Five executed leaders of 1956 uprising are reburied 6/89
- Exodus of 20,000 East Germans to West is approved 8/89
- Opens border with Austria 9/89
- Communist leaders vote to become Social Democrats 10/89
- Birth of a new republic 10/89
- Red Army leaves after 45 years of occupation 1/90
- Communists lose to Democratic Forum in election 4/90

Hunt, Howard 9/72, 5/73
Hunt, James 10/76, 6/93
Hunt, Kevin 1/89
Hunt, Lord (John) 6/53, 1/70
Hunt, Martita 12/30
Hunt, Rex 4/82
Hunt, Roger 5/65
Hunt, William Holman
- See Holman Hunt

Hunter, Holly 5/93
Hunton, Alphaeus 7/51
Huntziger, Charles 6/40, 11/41
Huong, Tran Van 11/64
Hurd, Douglas 9/80, 9/84, 9/85, 1/87, 7/89, 10/89, 12/89, 11/90, 5/91, 2/92, 1/93
Hurson, Martin 7/81
Hurst, Geoff 7/66
Hurt, John 12/76, 12/80
Husak, Gustav 1/12, 4/69, 12/89
Hussein, Grand Sheriff of Mecca 6/16
Hussein, King of Jordan 4/57, 11/57, 6/58, 7/58, 5/61, 4/63, 9/70, 9/73, 4/77, 5/84, 8/90, 1/91, 7/94
Hussein, Saddam 7/82, 7/83, 3/90, 4/90, 7/90, 8/90, 9/90, 10/90, 12/90, 1/91, 2/91, 3/91, 5/91, 12/91
Huston, John 10/41, 8/62, 8/87
Hutchinson, John 12/63
Hutchinson, Miller Reese 11/01
Hutton, Barbara 7/42
Hutton, Len 8/37, 8/38, 7/51, 8/53, 5/55, 5/56, 6/62
Hutton, Leonard 9/90
Huxley, Aldous 12/28, 12/32, 11/63
Huxley, Elspeth 1/53
Huxley, Julian Sorell 12/41, 2/75
Hyde, Douglas 4/38
Hyderabad, Nizam of 9/48, 2/49
Hyndman, Henry Mayers 11/21

I

Ibar, Jose Manuel 11/70
Ibarruri, Dolores (La Passionara) 5/77, 11/89
Ibbotson, Derek 7/57
IBM
- Announces loss of £875 million for 1991 1/92

Ibsen, Henrik 5/06
Ice hockey
- See Winter sports

Ice skating
- See Winter sports

Iceland
- Gets independence from Denmark 12/18
- War trade pact made with UK 4/40
- Occupied by British troops 5/40
- Bombed by Luftwaffe 2/41
- German ship seized with documents on "Enigma" coding machine 5/41
- Occupied by US forces 7/41
- Becomes independent 6/44
- Admitted to UN 8/46
- Signs North Atlantic Treaty 4/49
- Joins Council of Europe 8/49
- Parliament wants US troops to leave 3/56
- Declares fishing limit; Britain angry 8/58
- UK trawlers defy Icelandic fishing ban 9/58
- UK warns Iceland on Cod War shootings 5/59
- Talks with UK to end fishing dispute 10/60
- A new island is born off south coast 11/63
- World court bans fishing zone extension 8/72
- Gunboat sinks two UK trawlers in North Sea 9/72
- Boycott of British goods announced 10/72
- 7,000 evacuated as volcano erupts 1/73
- Gunboats fire at UK tug 3/73
- Gunboat fires on UK trawlers 4/73
- First Royal Navy action of Cod War 5/73
- British Embassy stormed by rioters 5/73
- Gunboat engineer dies in clash with RN 8/73
- Gunboat rams HMS Andromeda 1/76
- UK withdraws protecting ships 1/76
- Breaks relations with UK 2/76
- Vigdis Finnbogadottir becomes first woman premier 6/80
- Reagan-Gorbachev talks scuppered by SDI 10/86

Idris, King of Libya 12/51, 9/69
Ileo, Joseph 9/60
Iliescu, Ion 1/90, 5/90
Imbert, Peter 12/75
Inayatullah, King of Afghanistan 1/29
Inchcape, Lord 11/13
India
- See also Britain (foreign affairs), Kashmir

India (foreign affairs)
- Viceroy accepts Kaiser's famine aid 4/00
- British troops face frontier tribesmen 4/08
- Darjeeling welcomes Tibet's Dalai Lama 3/10
- Troops help fight off Turks at Suez 2/15
- Expeditionary Force defeated at Kut 4/16
- 60,000 men lost in World War I 11/18
- British troops beat Afghan invaders 4/19
- Indian troops memorial, France 10/27
- Burma separated from India in new Act 4/37
- Nehru pledges "no surrender" to Axis 4/42
- Calls for freedom of Indochina 9/45
- Accused by Pakistan of armed aggression 1/48
- Accepts UN mediation in Pakistan dispute 1/48
- Eight Gurkha battalions to join British Army 2/48
- Last British troops leave 2/48
- Recognises Communist China 1/50
- Offers help to get Korean War truce 3/51
- Pandit Nehru urges Indochina truce 2/54
- Nehru wants end to nuclear weapons race 4/54
- Cuts tariff on British imports 5/55
- Nehru demands Goa from Portugal 8/55
- Nehru breaks off relations with Portugal 8/55
- Refuses plan for international Suez Zone 8/56
- Kashmir joins, defying UN ruling 1/57
- Madras Tamils support Ceylon minority 6/58
- Tibetan exiles in India lead revolt 7/58
- Scared of China, no action over Tibet 7/58
- Gives Tibet's Dalai Lama sanctuary 4/59
- Warm welcome for Dalai in Silguri 4/59
- Nehru to talk with Dalai Lama 4/59
- Warns China not to attack Bhutan and Sikkim 8/59
- 17 troops die in border clash with China 10/59
- Chou En-lai wants talks with Nehru 12/59
- Heavy border fighting with Chinese 10/62
- China wins border dispute 11/62
- Pope visits 12/64
- Tension on Chinese border 2/65
- Clashes with Pakistan troops in Kashmir 8/65
- Launches full-scale invasion of Pakistan 9/65
- At war with Pakistan over Kashmir 9/65
- Pakistanis bomb Bombay 9/65
- Conference of "non-aligned" nations 10/66
- Appeals for Bangladeshi refugee aid 5/71
- Seals border with Bangladesh 6/71
- Pakistan army kills 95 troops in clash 8/71
- 20-year defence pact with USSR 8/71
- New border clashes with Pakistan 11/71
- Mrs Gandhi visits US for talks 11/71
- 90 Indian troops die in Pakistan clashes 11/71
- Defeats Pakistan in two-week war 12/71
- Recognises Bangladesh 12/71
- Pakistan breaks off relations 12/71
- Friendship treaty with Bangladesh 3/72
- To withdraw troops occuping Pakistan 7/72
- Annexes kingdom of Sikkim 4/73
- Pact to repatriate Pakistani POWs 4/74
- Gandhi proposes new ties with Pakistan 4/76
- Seychelles plotters hijack Indian plane 12/81
- Kidnapped Indian diplomat found dead, UK 2/84
- Sri Lankan guard hits visiting Gandhi 8/87
- Troops fight Tamil rebels, Sri Lanka 10/87
- Rajiv Gandhi closes border with Pakistan 4/88
- Signs nuclear agreement with Pakistan 12/88

India (politics)
- 27 rioters shot dead at Vizagapatam 4/00
- Troops readied for Chinese unrest 10/00
- Viceroy creates new frontier province 2/01
- Proclaims Edward VII Emperor 1/03
- Lord Curzon resigns as Viceroy in dispute 8/05
- Riots in Rawalpindi and Punjab 5/07
- Troops enter Lahore to quell unrest 5/07
- Labour criticises British policy 9/07
- Calcutta riots; Labour leader blamed 10/07
- Meetings banned 10/07
- First Indian National Congress splits 12/07
- Four shot dead in rioting 3/08

- Anarchist plot uncovered 5/08
- King hints at extending Indian democracy 11/08
- Hindu-Moslem riots in Calcutta 1/09
- Local councils get more power 5/09
- Assassination attempt on Viceroy 11/09
- Meetings ban extended; anarchists rife 1/10
- Press censorship 2/10
- British officials murdered, Sadiya 4/11
- King George V crowned Emperor of India 12/11
- Bomb thrown at Governor-General; survives 12/12
- Death penalty for rebel leader Govindgar 2/14
- Gandhi returns from South Africa 11/15
- Troops massacre protesters, Amritsar 4/19
- Gandhi trade strike against security law 4/19
- Martial law, Peshawar 4/19
- Gandhi's Congress chooses non-violence 9/20
- Duke to open parliament; riots flare 1/21
- Duke of Connaught opens legislature 2/21
- Gandhi's "Buy Indian" cloth campaign 7/21
- Riots on Malabar coast; over 1,000 die 8/21
- Gandhi burns cloth in protest at Prince's visit 11/21
- 16 Gurkha troops killed by rebels 11/21
- Mass boycott greets Prince in Calcutta 12/21
- Riot at Chauri Chaura; 22 police die 2/22
- Congress suspends civil disobedience campaign 2/22
- Gandhi jailed for six years for sedition 3/22
- Salt tax to balance budget; resentment 3/23
- National Congress new civil disobedience campaign 9/23
- Gandhi released from prison, Bombay 2/24
- Gandhi on hunger strike in protest against clashes 9/24
- Riots, Kohat: 20 Hindus and 11 Moslems die 9/24
- Hindu-Moslem riots sweep Calcutta 4/26
- Women can be elected to public office 5/26
- Hindu-Moslem riots in Rawalpindi 6/26
- Sectarian riot at Hindu festival 10/26
- Status unchanged at Imperial Conference 11/26
- Moslem-Sikh riots, Lahore; 14 die 5/27
- 15 die in Hindu-Moslem riot, Nagpur 9/27
- Rioting as Simon Commission arrives 2/28
- Nationalists stop Communist expulsion 9/28
- 100 die in Hindu-Moslem riots, Bombay 2/29
- Curfew after Hindu-Moslem riots, Bombay 5/29
- Nehru wants revolt if India does not get dominion status 5/29
- Gandhi made Congress President; declines offer 8/29
- All-India National Congress held in Lahore 12/29
- Viceroy escapes bomb on train 12/29
- Congress demands independence 12/29
- Gandhi criticised for pro-Viceroy motion 1/30
- Mock "Independence Day" celebrated 1/30
- Gandhi's independence motion passed 1/30
- Nationalists suspected of Museum bomb 2/30
- First "Untouchable" to win council seat 2/30
- Congress starts boycott of salt tax 2/30
- Gandhi's 300-mile anti-tax march to sea 3/30
- Gandhi breaks Salt Law at Dandi beach 4/30
- Crowds hail Gandhi after 300-mile march 4/30
- Police raid Congress headquarters 4/30
- Viceroy imposes anti-terrorism ordinance 4/30
- Gandhi jailed; Mrs Naidu leads campaign 5/30
- 2,500 Gandhi backers beaten, Dharasana 5/30
- Viceroy Irwin bans picketing and suborning 5/30
- Simon Commission recommends federation 6/30
- India House, London; King wants peace 7/30
- Martial law in Peshawar 8/30
- Round Table conference on India's future 11/30
- Equality for "Untouchables" proposed 11/30
- British Governor of Punjab wounded 12/30
- Gandhi released from prison 1/31
- Gandhi orders more civil disobedience 2/31
- Hindus attack Moslem shopkeepers in riot 3/31
- Viceroy hints at conditional end to tax 3/31
- Bangalore riots; Punjab Governor wounded 7/31
- Gandhi in second Round Table conference 8/31
- 19 die in anti-Hindu rioting, Kashmir 9/31
- Gandhi wants India equal and free 9/31
- Gandhi meets King George V 11/31
- Gandhi wants India to control foreign and military affairs 11/31
- Powers to suppress Bengali terrorism 11/31
- Round Table talks end in failure 12/31
- Bengal Congress boycotts British goods 12/31
- Viceroy warns Gandhi; Nehru and Khan arrested 12/31
- Congress disobedience; Gandhi arrested 1/32
- 100 Congress leaders arrested; boycotts 1/32
- Gandhi hunger fast over "Untouchables" issue 9/32
- Poona Pact extends "Untouchables" vote 9/32
- R.A. Butler becomes new Secretary for India 9/32
- Third Round Table conference 11/32
- UK releases Gandhi and 28,000 prisoners 12/32
- Gandhi gets one year's imprisonment 7/33
- Gandhi released from hospital, Poona 8/33
- Gandhi resigns leadership of Congress 10/34
- Congress wins almost half seats in poll 11/34
- Government of India Bill; some home rule 2/35
- Troops fire at rioting Moslems; 27 die 3/35
- Ten die as troops fire at Moslem rioters 7/35
- Jawaharlal Nehru is Congress President 2/36
- Five days' rioting in Bombay; 60 die 10/36
- Government of India Act, constitution 4/37
- 29 die in clashes, north-west frontier 4/37
- 26 die in Mysore riots 4/38
- Gandhi names Nehru as his successor 1/42
- Britain offers dominion status to India 3/42
- National Congress rejects British plan 4/42
- Gandhi and 50 others arrested 8/42
- Gandhi begins 21-day fast 2/43
- Nationwide prayers for Gandhi 2/43
- Gandhi ends fast 3/43
- Wavell appointed viceroy 6/43
- Nehru and other leaders freed by British 6/45
- Britain promises Home Rule 9/45
- Seeks freedom of India, Burma, Malaya 9/45
- Civil war looms 2/46
- Gandhi endorses Britain's "good faith" 4/46
- Britain plans independent, united India 5/46
- Congress Party rejects independence plan 6/46
- Moslems prepare for civil war 7/46
- Thousands die in Hindu-Moslem riots 8/46
- Nehru appointed head of provisional government 8/46
- Nehru's cabinet sworn in 9/46
- Moslems and Hindus dislike new Assembly 11/46
- Anglo-Indian talks end in failure 12/46
- Mountbatten appointed Viceroy 2/47
- Britain to quit India by June 1948 2/47
- Mountbatten arrives; talks with Gandhi 3/47
- Hindu-Moslem violence mounts 3/47
- British MPs approve plan to quit 3/47
- 293 have died by violence in Punjab 3/47
- Troops sent to Amritsar 3/47
- Troops sent in to quell riots 4/47
- New parliament appeals for non-violence 4/47
- Britain decides on partition of India 5/47
- Moslems and Hindus agree to partition 6/47
- Jinnah to be Governor-General of Pakistan 7/47
- Indian Independence Bill published, UK 7/47
- British rule ends 8/47
- Mountbatten becomes Governor-General of India 8/47
- 10,000 have died in Punjab border fights 8/47
- 1,200 Moslems massacred on Punjab border 8/47
- Kashmir agrees to join India 10/47
- Referendum on Kashmir border to be held 11/47
- Last Moslem refugees cross into Pakistan 12/47
- Troops and guerrillas clash in Kashmir 12/47
- Gandhi assassinated 1/48
- Godse identified as Gandhi's assassin 1/48
- Riots erupt after Gandhi's death 1/48
- Private armies banned 2/48
- Rajagopalachari becomes Governor-General 6/48
- Rebel kingdom of Hyderabad surrenders 9/48
- Cease-fire in Kashmir 1/49
- Nizam of Hyderabad's land nationalised 2/49
- Becomes a republic within Commonwealth 4/49
- Currency devalued 9/49
- Godse hanged for Gandhi's murder 11/49
- New constitution approved 11/49
- Proclaimed a republic 1/50
- With Pakistan, makes minorities' pledge 4/50
- Portuguese kill 12 Goan passive marchers 8/55
- Nehru's daughter, Mrs Gandhi, is up for presidency 1/59
- Indira Gandhi is President of Congress 2/59
- Mrs Gandhi seen as party peacemaker 2/59
- Sikhs demand own state; 783 arrested 6/60
- Troops take back Goa after 400 years 12/61
- Congress Party wins general election 3/62
- Numerous Moslems killed in clashes with Hindus 5/62
- State of emergency declared 10/62
- 200 die in Hindu-Moslem riots, Calcutta 1/64
- Nehru dies 5/64
- Gulzarilal Nanda becomes temporary PM 5/64
- Lal Bahadur Shastri becomes PM 6/64
- PM Lal Shastri dies 1/66
- Indira Gandhi becomes PM 1/66
- Indira Gandhi re-elected as PM 3/67
- Maharajahs' privileges abolished 9/70
- Gandhi supporters win state elections 3/72
- Gandhi found guilty of election fraud 6/75
- Gandhi barred from office for six years 6/75
- Mrs Gandhi and son Sanjay lose seats 3/77
- Morarji Desai's Janata advances in polls 3/77
- Mrs Gandhi arrested for corruption 10/77
- Mrs Gandhi expelled from Congress Party 1/78
- MPs vote to jail Mrs Gandhi 12/78
- Week of mourning for Mountbatten 8/79
- Mrs Gandhi wins general election 1/80
- Gandhi's heir, Sanjay, dies in plane crash 6/80
- Over 600 Moslem refugees massacred 2/83
- Mrs Gandhi sacks Punjab state government 10/83
- Hindu-Moslem clashes in Bombay 5/84
- Troops storm Sikh Golden Temple 6/84
- Sikh leader Bhindranwale killed 6/84
- Army launches offensive against Sikhs 6/84
- Indira Gandhi shot dead by bodyguards 10/84
- Rajiv Gandhi sworn in as PM 10/84
- Torn by riots as Rajiv takes power 11/84
- Indira Gandhi is cremated 11/84
- Rajiv Gandhi wins general election 12/84
- 59 die in Sikh extremist attack 5/85
- Sikh bomb destroys plane over Irish Sea 6/85
- Sikh leader Longowal murdered 8/85
- Three Sikhs to die for Gandhi murder 1/86
- Leader of Golden Temple attack shot dead 8/86
- Rajiv Gandhi escapes attempt on life 10/86
- Sikh extremists kill 24 on Punjab bus 11/86
- Sikhs abandon Golden Temple siege 5/88
- Troops thwart Tamil coup in Maldives 11/88
- Two Sikhs are hanged for murder of Indira Gandhi 1/89
- Salman Rushdie's "Satanic Verses" is banned 1/09
- Prime Minister Rajiv Gandhi faces defeat in general election 11/89
- V.P. Singh becomes Prime Minister 12/89
- Prime Minister V.P. Singh resigns 11/90
- Funeral of Rajiv Gandhi killed by suicide bomber 5/91
- Ruling Congress Party wins elections despite Sikh boycott 2/92
- Shankar Dayal Sharma is appointed President 7/92
- Religious riots break out between Moslems and Hindus 12/92
- Series of bombs kill 300 in Bombay 3/93
- Phoolan Devi "Bandit Queen" released from jail 2/94

Indochina
- See also Vietnam
- British arrest Communist Ho Chi Minh 6/31
- French capture Hao Binh 11/38
- 69 die when French sub Phenix sinks 6/39
- Japanese invade Tonkin 9/40
- Japanese troops move into Saigon 7/41
- Vichy grants Japan use of military bases 7/41
- Ho Chi Minh forms the Viet Minh 9/41
- Vietnamese People's Army formed 12/44
- Independence of Vietnam declared 3/45
- Cambodia declares independence 3/45
- Cease-fire between Vietnamese and French 10/45
- Viet Minh attack French north of Tonkin 1/51
- French repulse Viet Minh, kill 6,000 1/51
- Viet Minh attack Tonkin 12/51
- French move to smash Viet Minh, Tay Ninh 4/52
- France wants UN action if China joins war 4/52
- Laos capital Pakseng falls to Viet Minh 4/53
- Viet Minh cross into Mekong delta 5/53
- French paratroopers in Lang-Son 7/53
- French paratroops take Dien Bien Phu 11/53
- Navarre surprises Viet Minh; new base 11/53
- Viet Minh at Mekong next to Thailand 12/53
- French prepare for Dien Bien Phu battle 2/54
- India's Nehru urges Indochina truce 2/54
- President warns against US in Indochina 2/54
- Crucial Dien Bien Phu battle begins 3/54
- Dulles warns China not to aid Vietnamese 4/54
- Viet Minh capture Dien Bien Phu 5/54
- Vietnam conference, Geneva 5/54
- Viet Minh reject France; want freedom 5/54
- Sino-French pact ends war 7/54
- Vietnam divided along 17th Parallel 7/54

Indonesia
- See also Dutch East Indies and The Netherlands
- Java now under Dutch control 1/49
- US tells Dutch to pull out 1/49
- UN demands Dutch withdrawal 1/49
- United States of Indonesia recognised 11/49
- Sukarno becomes first President 12/49
- Cuts political ties with Netherlands 8/54
- Bandung talks: 29 "non-aligned" states 4/55
- President Sukarno hails new Third World 4/55
- President Sukarno escapes assassination 11/57
- Sukarno calls boycott of Dutch business 12/57
- Netherlands bars entry to citizens 12/57
- Expels all Dutch nationals 12/57
- Treaty of friendship with Malaya 4/59
- Attempt on Sukarno's life fails 5/62
- Dutch to cede western New Guinea 8/62
- UN takes control of west New Guinea 10/62
- State seizes UK tea and rubber estates 5/64
- Lands paratroops in Malaysia 9/64
- Sukarno says Indonesia will quit UN 1/65
- All UN offices closed 1/65
- First Indonesian rocket launched 8/65
- Sukarno survives attempted coup 10/65
- Sukarno hands over power to army 3/66
- Ends bush warfare with Malaysia 8/66
- Sukarno hands over power to Suharto 2/67
- Death of Ahmed Sukarno 6/70
- Over 100 die in Bali plane crash 4/74
- Moluccan secessionists storm embassy 12/75
- Seizes Portuguese Timor capital Dili 12/75
- 750 die in tidal wave, Lomblen 7/79
- 1,500 die in earthquake 12/92
- President Suharto is reelected President 3/93

Indurain, Miguel 7/94
Inge, William 6/73
Ingrams, Richard 7/76
Innitzer, Theodor 4/38, 7/39
Inonu, Ismet 12/43, 2/64
Inskip, Thomas 12/27, 3/36
International Monetary Fund
- See Economy (world)

Inukai, Ki 5/32
Ionesco, Eugene 12/60, 3/94
IRA
- See Britain (Northern Ireland)

Iran
- See also Persia, World War II
- Changes name from Persia 12/34
- Non-aggression pact with Turkey, Iraq and Afghanistan 12/35
- Shah's new wife shows off wedding dress 2/38
- British and Soviet troops invade 8/41
- Shah abdicates 9/41
- Mohammed Reza Pahlavi becomes Shah 9/41
- USSR withdraws troops 3/46
- USSR is to get 51 per cent of Iranian oil 4/46
- Soviet troops have departed 5/46
- Shah wounded in assassination attempt 2/49
- 1,500 die in three earthquakes 1/50
- Religious extremist kills PM Razmara 3/51
- Martial law declared, Teheran 3/51
- Education minister Zanganeh shot at 3/51
- Majlis votes to nationalise oil industry 3/51
- Shah appoints Hussein Ala new premier 3/51
- Abadan oil riots; eight Britons killed 4/51
- Strikes in Abadan and Bandur; martial la 4/51
- Mossadegh says seize assets 4/51
- 50,000 demonstrate for nationalisation 5/51
- Warned by UK against seizing oil assets 5/51
- UK oil workers reject nationalisation 6/51
- Oil workers prepare for evacuation 6/51
- Nine die in anti-British riots 7/51
- Talks with Britain on oil dispute 8/51
- Talks fail; UK and Indian workers must go 8/51
- Majlis backs Mossadegh's talks rejection 8/51
- Troops seize Abadan oil refinery 9/51
- Britons flee Abadan refinery 10/51
- Shah approves of nationalisation 10/51
- 10,000 police and students clash, Tehran 12/51
- Denounces 1857 friendship treaty with UK 1/52
- Ahmad Ghavam replaces premier Mossadegh 7/52
- Riots restore Mossadegh 7/52
- Fresh talks with UK to end oil dispute 9/52
- Severs ties with Britain 10/52
- Mossadegh's new offer to UK 11/52
- Army topples Mossadegh; Shah returns 8/53
- Appeals for international financial aid 8/53
- General Zahedi wants to try Mossadegh 8/53
- US gives $45 million grant 9/53
- Government attacks Tudeh Communist Party 10/53
- Restores relations with Britain 11/53
- Shah calls general election 12/53
- Oil nationalisation compensation agreed 8/54
- British Petroleum: 40 per cent Iran oil 12/54
- 2,000 die in earthquakes 12/57
- Shah divorces wife, Princess Soraya 3/58
- Shah marries Farah Dibah 12/59
- 1,500 die in Lar earthquake 4/60
- 20,000 die in earthquake 9/62
- Riots follow arrest of Khomeini, Tehran 6/63
- Martial law declared in Tehran 6/63
- Attempt on Shah's life fails 4/65
- Death of statesman Mohammed Mossadegh 3/67
- Coronation of the Shah 10/67
- At least 11,000 killed in earthquakes 9/68
- OPEC threatens to increase oil prices 2/71
- Iraq expels thousands of Iranians 12/71
- OPEC doubles price of oil 12/73
- 70 die in Iraqi border clashes 2/74
- Border deal with Iraq to crush Kurds 3/75
- Anti-Shah riots, Qum; 60 die 1/78
- Religious riot against Shah, Tehran 5/78
- 377 die in cinema fire caused by extremists 8/78
- Shah imposes martial law on 12 cities 9/78
- Shi'ites attack police; 58 die 9/78
- Leftists, Moslems oppose "modernisation" 9/78
- 20,000 feared dead from earthquake 9/78
- Iraq expels religious leader Khomeini 10/78
- Strikes stop oil production 10/78
- Premier Sharif-Emami resigns after riots 11/78
- Tehran mob rule; talk of Soviet threat 11/78
- New Premier General Azhari 11/78
- Shah bans religious marches 11/78
- Millions march peacefully against Shah 12/78
- Sanjhabi and Khomeini supporters in march 12/78
- Opposition leader Bakhtiar is premier 12/78
- Khomeini supporters drive out Shah 1/79
- Troops kill 35 1/79
- Ayatollah Khomeini returns 2/79
- Crowds cheer as Ayatollah claims power 2/79
- Four generals killed 2/79
- Kurds clash with Khomeini group; 100 die 2/79
- Tehran women protest against Islamic strictures 3/79
- Cease-fire after clashes with Kurds 3/79
- Khomeini rejects democracy 3/79
- Khomeini declares Islamic republic 4/79
- Ex-premier Hoveida executed 4/79
- Crisis starts UK petrol panic 5/79
- Nationalises private industry; amnesty 7/79
- Khomeini bans broadcast music 7/79
- 18 Kurds executed; fighting continues 8/79
- Exiled Shah treated for cancer, New York 10/79
- Khalkhali calls on Moslems to kill Shah 10/79
- Takes 100 US embassy hostages 11/79
- Embassy crowds demand USA return Shah 11/79
- Khomeini frees women and black hostages 11/79
- US warned not to invade 11/79
- Bani-Sadr calls foreign debts void 11/79
- Khomeini made absolute ruler 12/79
- Ex-Shah leaves for Panama 12/79
- Rebels fight in Baluchistan 12/79
- Up to $40 per oil barrel 12/79
- Six US envoys flee from Canadian Embassy 1/80
- Angry at Canada's help with US envoys 1/80
- Waldheim cancels trip after rebuff 1/80
- Abol Hassan Bani-Sadr is premier 1/80
- New President Bani-Sadr's powers 2/80
- Khomeini backs US hostage takers 3/80
- US Commission will not condemn Shah 3/80
- Ex-Shah leaves Panama for Cairo 3/80
- US hostage rescue ends in desert crash 4/80
- Khomeini condemns US "stupidity" 4/80
- Pro-Arab besiegers kill Abbas Lavasani 5/80
- UK forces free London embassy hostages 5/80
- Ex-Shah's father's tomb smashed 5/80
- Ex-Shah dies; Khomeini rejoices 7/80
- Women angry about Islamic dress 7/80
- Hostage Richard Queen released 7/80
- Attempt on ex-premier Bakhtiar 7/80
- 56 Iranians arrested near US Embassy, UK 8/80
- Iraq attacks oil plants 9/80
- Revokes 1975 border treaty with Iraq 9/80
- UK deports students and closes embassy 9/80
- Khomeini's conditions to free hostages 11/80
- Releases US hostages 1/81
- Bani-Sadr sacked; impeachment trial 6/81
- 72 politicians killed in bomb blast 6/81
- Bani-Sadr flees to France 7/81
- Premier Bahomar and President Rejai killed 8/81
- Ayatollah blasts "Islamic deviants" 8/81
- 149 "leftist militants" executed 9/81
- Four military chiefs die in crash 9/81
- Iranians killed by own bomb, London 12/81
- Ex-minister Ghobzadegh guilty of "plot" 9/82
- Tehran bomb blast; 60 die 10/82
- Expels 18 alleged Soviet spies 5/83
- Bans Tudeh Party (Communist) 5/83
- Arab League condemns Iran's aggression 5/84
- Attacks oil tanker off Saudi Arabia 5/84
- Branded a terrorist state by Reagan 7/85
- "Irangate" row erupts in US 11/86
- Reagan "regrets" Iran arms deal 1/87
- British diplomat beaten up 5/87
- UK expels six Iranian envoys 6/87
- Scores of pilgrims die in Mecca riots 7/87
- US ships find eight Gulf mines 9/87

- US intercepts Iran Ajr, minelaying ship 9/87
- Attacks US-flagged tanker; US hits back 10/87
- 54 men die in Iraqi attack 3/88
- Iraq attacks Iran's Larak oil terminal 5/88
- Iraq takes Basra Island 5/88
- US warship guns down Airbus in Gulf 7/88
- Cease-fire in Gulf War 8/88
- Khomeini orders death of British author, Salman Rushdie 2/89
- Britain and EC members withdraw envoys over Rushdie affair 2/89
- Funeral of Ayatollah Khomeini 6/89
- Hashemi Rafsanjani wins presidential election 7/89
- Earthquake hits northern Iran, killing 40,000 6/90
- Ends ten-year conflict with Iraq 8/90
- Calls for joint international effort to clear up oil spills 1/91
- British businessman is released from jail 4/91
- Reward for killing author Salman Rushdie is increased 11/92
- President Rafsanjani is re-elected for four years 6/93
- TV satellite dishes banned 4/94
- Caviar production down 10 percent 10/94

Iraq
- See also World War II
- Emir Feisal is crowned King 8/21
- Treaty of alliance with Britain 10/22
- League settlement on Turkish border question 12/25
- Anglo-Turkish accord over border 6/26
- Prehistoric manicure set found 3/27
- First oil strike, Kirkuk 10/27
- Independence recognised by Britain 6/30
- Ancient royal palace found at Ur 1/31
- Friendship treaty with Egypt 4/31
- Mandate ends, independent; joins League 10/32
- King Feisal visits UK 6/33
- Border clash; 600 Kurds and Syrians die 8/33
- King Feisal dies; new King Ghazi 9/33
- Non-aggression pact with Turkey, Iran and Afghanistan 12/35
- Pro-Western Kemalists win coup 10/36
- Leader General Bakr Sidki Pasha killed 8/37
- King killed in accident 4/39
- Ex-premier Rashid Ali seizes power 4/41
- British troops cross the border 4/41
- Emir Abdullah is new leader 5/41
- Signs alliance with Britain 1/48
- Attacks Jewish positions in Israel 7/48
- Ten die in anti-Western riots 11/52
- Demonstrations against pact with Allies 3/56
- Agrees to unite with Jordan; US approves 2/58
- Nasserite army coup; King and premier die 7/58
- Britain recognises new regime 8/58
- Jordan's Hussein dissolves union 8/58
- Renounces US military aid 6/59
- Claims Kuwait 6/61
- Hundreds killed in fighting between the army and Kurds 4/62
- 200 die in fighting between rival Kurds 5/62
- Army rebels seize power and kill Kassim 2/63
- Military coup 11/63
- Two British banks nationalised 7/64
- Thousands of Iranians are expelled 12/71
- Nationalises Iraq Petroleum Co. (London) 6/72
- 70 die in Iranian border clashes 2/74
- Border deal with Iran to crush Kurds 3/75
- Army attacks Barzani's mountain Kurds 3/75
- Shoots two French security men, Paris 7/78
- Expels Iranian religious leader Khomeini 10/78
- Police kill terrorists, British Embassy 6/80
- Attacks Iran oil plants 9/80
- Iran revokes 1975 border treaty 9/80
- Nuclear power plant bombed by Israelis 6/81
- Iraqi Exocets hit US frigate Stark 5/87
- Attacks Iranian oil terminal 3/88
- Mustard-gas attacks on Kurdish villages 4/88
- Launches new attack on Iran 7/88
- Cease-fire in Gulf War 8/88
- Army displays new missiles 1/90
- Iranian-born British journalist found guilty of spying 3/90
- British journalist, Farzad Bazoft, is hanged 3/90
- British nurse, Daphne Parish, jailed for 15 years 3/90
- Hussein's chemical weapons retaliation threat against Israel 4/90
- President Hussein denies that Iraq has nuclear capability 7/90
- Jailed British nurse, Daphne Parish, is freed 7/90
- Saddam Hussein sends 30,000 troops to Iraq-Kuwait border 7/90
- Saudi forces on full alert as Iraqis breach neutral zone 8/90
- President Bush warns Iraqis not to cross Kuwaiti border 8/90
- Jordan closes its border with Iraq 8/90
- Hussein says Western women and children hostages free to go 8/90
- Iraqi forces invade Kuwait 8/90
- Arab League demands Iraq's withdrawal from Kuwait 8/90
- Ends ten-year conflict with Iran 8/90
- Western hostages shown on Iraqi TV 8/90
- 40 foreign diplomats are expelled 9/90
- Arab-Western tension mounts over invasion 9/90
- UN vote on air embargo and naval blockade against Iraq 9/90
- Edward Heath meets Saddam Hussein for negotiations 10/90
- Edward Heath obtains release of 33 Britons held hostage 10/90
- Western hostages to be released little by little 11/90
- UN gives ultimatum for withdrawal from Kuwait 11/90
- Saddam refuses to meet US officials before January 12 12/90
- Begins freeing foreign "human shield" hostages 12/90
- Foreign diplomats leave as war looms 1/91
- Last-minute talks between US and Iraq to avert war fail 1/91
- Operation Desert Storm is launched 1/91
- Allied heavy bombing raid hits Baghdad 1/91
- Iraqi Scud missiles hit Tel Aviv and Haifa 1/91
- Saddam Hussein's peace offer dismissed by West 2/91
- Iraqi forces begin burning Kuwaiti oilfields 2/91
- 400 civilians killed in US Stealth bomber raid 2/91
- Two Iraqi Republican Guards divisions surrounded by Allies 2/91
- Baghdad Radio announces Iraqi army is leaving Kuwait 2/91
- Saddam Hussein releases several prisoners of war 3/91
- Kurdish families flee to mountains 3/91
- Saddam defies Allies and moves his police into Kurdish areas 4/91
- Allied troops to prepare camps for Kurds in northern Iraq 4/91
- Allied forces leave 7/91
- Besieged UN nuclear inspectors allowed to leave after a week 9/91
- Briton jailed for seven years for illegally crossing border 8/92
- USAF planes begin enforcing "no-fly" zone in southern Iraq 8/92
- US, British and French warplanes carry out air strikes 1/93
- US forces launch missile attack on intelligence HQ; six die 6/93

Ireland
- See also Britain (Irish policy, Northern Ireland)
- Nationalist call to rise against Britain 1/00
- Queen Victoria visits Dublin 4/00
- Ireland must stay British, says PM 5/01
- League wants American links 1/02
- State of emergency 4/02
- Anti-British demonstrations 9/02
- Irish MP explodes at Balfour in Commons 10/02
- New deal for tenants 1/03
- Redmond demands Home Rule 2/04
- Chief Secretary resigns over policy 3/05
- Storms and floods 8/05
- Home Rule on Parliament's agenda 2/07
- Nationalists oppose limited autonomy 5/07
- Four civilians shot by troops, Ulster 8/07
- Police crush Protestant riots, Belfast 7/11
- Ulster Unionists reject Home Rule 9/11
- Ulster Unionists rally against Liberals 1/12
- 240,000 rally against Home Rule, Belfast 4/12
- Home Rule Bill amended; Ulster excluded 6/12
- Ulster Orange Order cheers Tory speaker 7/12
- Anti-Home Rule Covenant led by Carson 9/12
- Unrest as police shoot Loyalist, Ulster 8/13
- Carson claims 150,000 Loyalist "troops" 9/13
- Ulster Unionist "provisional government" 9/13
- Ulster Volunteer Force marches on Balmoral 9/13
- Ulster businessmen refuse to pay tax 11/13
- Ulster Volunteer Force prepares for war 2/14
- London rally protests at army Ulster duty 4/14
- Ammunition landed for UVF 4/14
- Police seize anti-enlistment papers 12/14
- Rebels declare republic in Dublin 4/16
- British troops fight rebels; 11 killed 4/16
- All seven rebels executed 5/16
- Martial law eased; Casement's trial 5/16
- 794 civilians and 521 police die in unrest 5/16
- Ulster Unionists support partition 6/16
- Irish Nationalists blast partition plan 7/16
- Nationalists resist conscription 10/16
- Wartime Home Rule plan excludes Ulster 5/17
- Sinn Fein's de Valera wins by-election 7/17
- Police foil new Easter Uprising plot 10/17
- Widespread lawlessness 2/18
- Police and Sinn Fein clash over meeting 3/18
- Revolt against conscription 4/18
- Home Rule postponed; conscription ended 6/18
- First woman elected to Parliament 12/18
- First meeting of Sinn Fein "parliament" 1/19
- De Valera back; seeks peace talks role 4/19
- Serious Sinn Fein rioting 8/19
- Britain outlaws Sinn Fein "parliament" 9/19
- Policeman killed by Sinn Fein 11/19
- Partition and autonomy planned 12/19
- Attempt on Lord French, Lord-Lieutenant 12/19
- Cork and Limerick support Sinn Fein 1/20
- 800 "special constables" raise tensions 3/20
- Ulster Unionists support British plan 3/20
- Magistrate murdered by Sinn Feiners 3/20
- Women picket UK Embassy in US, demanding freedom for Ireland 4/20
- Sinn Fein arson destroys 120 police stations 4/20
- 40 hunger strikers freed; three police dead 5/20
- Sinn Fein fight Unionists, Londonderry 5/20
- More troops called after 17 die in riots 6/20
- Riots in Ulster; five die 6/20
- More troops in Londonderry after riots 6/20
- Fierce rioting in Belfast; 14 die 7/20
- Catholics riot against troops, Belfast 8/20
- Irish Republicans murder seven policemen 8/20
- 11 die and 40 hurt in Belfast unrest 8/20
- US dockers refuse British ships as Ireland protest 9/20
- Police arrest Countess Markiewicz 9/20
- Sinn Fein demands British withdrawal 9/20
- Riots after Cork mayor dies in prison 10/20
- Cork city hall bombed 10/20
- IRA kills two soldiers and three policemen 10/20
- Hunger striker, Michael Fitzgerald, dies 10/20
- Seven police killed in revenge for hanged Sinn Feiner 10/20
- Bloody Sunday: IRA kills 14 soldiers 11/20
- 12 die at football match 11/20
- Sinn Fein disrupts Armistice Day 11/20
- Sinn Fein founder, Griffith, arrested 11/20
- IRA kills 15 army cadets 11/20
- Martial law declared, Cork and Kerry 12/20
- British tanks in Dublin; city sealed 1/21
- IRA and army clash; 14 die 1/21
- Police murdered; houses burnt in revenge 2/21
- Army kills eight Sinn Feiners 2/21
- Sinn Fein kills soldier in hospital 2/21
- First woman to die in Sinn Fein violence 4/21
- Nominations for two parliaments' polls 5/21
- Sinn Fein wins 124 out of 128 South seats 5/21
- Ulster Unionists 40 seats; Craig premier 5/21
- George V opens Northern Ireland parliament 6/21
- Truce after Mansion House surprise deal 7/21
- Jailed Sinn Fein MPs released 8/21
- De Valera rejects dominion status 8/21
- Dail backs de Valera's rejection 8/21
- Riots in East Belfast; ten die 11/21
- Irish Free State: divided dominion 12/21
- Council to determine reunification 12/21
- Six Ulster provinces to stay in UK 12/21
- Dail Eireann parliament accepts treaty 1/22
- De Valera refuses presidency of the Dail 1/22
- First President Arthur Griffith, premier Michael Collins 1/22
- Army shoots at protesters; two die 1/22
- IRA kills four policemen in N. Ireland 2/22
- IRA attacks "B Special" police; three die 3/22
- Collins warns of civil war 4/22
- IRA seizes jail; murders Brigadier-General 4/22
- Sinn Fein banned in six counties 5/22
- MP Twaddell killed by bomb 5/22
- First general election 6/22
- Pro-Treaty party wins convincingly 6/22
- Troops force IRA to surrender law courts 6/22
- Last rebels surrender 7/22
- Collins leads Irish Army Council 7/22
- Troops capture Limerick and Waterford 7/22
- Republicans spring 105 prisoners 7/22
- Michael Collins assassinated in Cork 8/22
- Dail President Arthur Griffith dies 8/22
- Rebels beaten in Dublin; destroy cable 8/22
- Dail approves Free State constitution 9/22
- Amnesty offer for arms surrender 10/22
- Irish Dail member, Sean Hales, murdered 12/22
- Bill passed; last British troops leave 12/22
- One third tax on British goods 3/23
- Head of Irregulars, Liam Lynch, dies 4/23
- De Valera orders Irregulars to give up 5/23
- Government wins majority in first election 9/23
- Admitted to League of Nations 9/23
- Poet William B. Yeats wins Nobel Prize for Literature 12/23
- Eamon de Valera and others released 7/24
- No border change, says Baldwin 12/25
- 50 die in cinema fire, Limerick 9/26
- King no longer sovereign 11/26
- O'Casey Easter Rising play starts riot 12/26
- Vice-President O'Higgins assassinated 7/27
- Fears of civil war after O'Higgins death 7/27
- President Cosgrave barely wins Dail vote 8/27
- Fianna Fail forced back into Dail 8/27
- New clampdown after O'Higgins killing 8/27
- Cosgrave wins rowdy election 9/27
- De Valera's Fianna Fail is strong opposition 9/27
- Cosgrave re-elected President 10/27
- President warns political trial jurors 3/29
- Submarines collide in Irish Sea, 24 die 7/29
- 12 groups, including IRA, are banned 10/31
- De Valera wins polls; needs Labour help 3/32
- IRA pressurises de Valera on Treaty 3/32
- De Valera to abolish Loyal Oath to King 3/32
- Dail MPs drop loyalty oath to King 4/32
- UK trade threat over Loyal Oath decision 5/32
- UK import duties approved on Irish goods 7/32
- Senate approves tariff reprisals on UK 7/32
- De Valera gets majority of one 1/33
- Hardliners force de Valera on partition 1/33
- De Valera blasts IRA and Blue Shirts 8/33
- Ex-police chief leads 40,000 Blue Shirts 8/33
- Dail votes to abolish Senate 5/34
- Ex-IRA leader recruits "Citizens' Army" 8/34
- To sell more cattle and buy UK coal 1/35
- New constitution: no allegiance to Crown; renamed Eire 4/37
- Eamon de Valera re-elected President 7/37
- New constitution in force 12/37
- De Valera in London talks; hope for pact 1/38
- Britain hopes for end of trade war 1/38
- New Agreement with UK: naval bases 4/38
- Removal of British coal duty 4/38
- Tariffs easied; big savings 4/38
- Douglas Hyde is first President 4/38
- De Valera calls election 5/38
- Election victory for Fianna Fail party 6/38
- Poet W.B. Yeats dies 1/39
- IRA outlawed 6/39
- IRA landmine kills six, Dublin Castle 4/40
- German bombs fall on neutral Ireland 1/41
- Claims US landings violate neutrality 1/42
- De Valera loses majority 6/43
- Blockaded by Britain for fear of spies 3/44
- Refuses to expel enemy envoys 3/44
- Fianna Fail wins overall majority 6/44
- De Valera ends 16-year premiership 2/48
- John Costello becomes PM 2/48
- Refuses to join NATO while Ireland is divided 2/49
- Becomes a republic 4/49
- Recognised by Britain as a republic 5/49
- Currency devalued 9/49
- De Valera beats Costello to become new premier 6/51
- 128 die in Princess Victoria ferry crash 1/53
- Costello's Fine Gael forms government 6/54
- 28 die in Dutch airliner river crash 9/54
- De Valera wins general election 3/57
- State of emergency declared 7/57
- 63 IRA members arrested at Curragh 7/57
- Fianna Fail angry at no end to partition 7/57
- Dutch plane crashes off Ireland; 99 die 8/58
- De Valera seeks presidency 1/59
- De Valera becomes figurehead President 6/59
- 16 die in crash at Shannon Airport 9/61
- Fianna Fail wins election; majority lost 10/61
- Conor Cruise O'Brien sacked from UN 12/61
- President Kennedy visits 6/63
- Writer Sean O'Casey dies 9/64
- PM Sean Lemass meets Terence O'Neill 1/65
- W.T. Cosgrave, first President, dies 11/65
- IRA bomb destroys Nelson Column, Dublin 3/66
- Eamon de Valera is back as President 6/66
- Jack Lynch becomes PM 11/66
- Samuel Beckett wins Literature Nobel 12/69
- Two ex-ministers named in arms case 5/70
- Talks on EEC entry open 6/70
- Neil Blaney cleared of gun-running 7/70
- Charles Haughey acquitted of gun-running 10/70
- Lynch condemns internment in Northern Ireland 8/71
- Signs treaty of entry to EEC 1/72
- British Embassy in Dublin burnt down 2/72
- Referendum approves EEC entry 5/72
- Official IRA declares a cease-fire 5/72
- Provo leader MacStiofain arrested 11/72
- IRA and police in hospital shoot-out 11/72
- Two die in Dublin bomb blasts 12/72
- Joins EEC 1/73
- Fine Gael-Labour coalition wins election 3/73
- IRA chief MacStiofain freed from jail 4/73
- Surplus butter sold cheaply to the poor 4/73
- De Valera resigns as President 6/73
- Troops and police make mass arrests 7/73
- MI6 linked to bomb attacks in Dublin 8/73
- Helicopter plucks three IRA men from jail 10/73
- Sunningdale deal on a Council of Ireland 12/73
- Cosgrave concedes UK controls N. Ireland 3/74
- Paintings worth £8 million stolen 4/74
- Dublin car bombs kill 23 in rush hour 5/74
- Art-theft gang wants Price sisters freed 5/74
- Rose Dugdale jailed for art theft 6/74
- Ex-minister Sean MacBride: Nobel Peace 10/74
- IRA prisoners end hunger strike 2/75
- De Valera, Irish pioneer, dies 8/75
- Refuses to free IRA for kidnapped man 10/75
- Police vigil at kidnap house 10/75
- John Costello dies 1/76
- Dr Patrick Hillery is president 12/76
- Lynch's Fianna Fail wins election 6/77
- Cosgrave resigns as premier 6/77
- Ex-IRA chief Costelloe murdered 10/77
- Oil tanker explodes, 49 die, Bantry Bay 1/79
- Lord Mountbatten killed by IRA bomb 8/79
- Cardinal O'Fiaich slams IRA murder 8/79
- Two arrested for Mountbatten bomb 8/79
- Pope visits; calls for peace 9/79
- £500,000 in weapons for IRA seized 11/79
- Trial of Mountbatten bombers 11/79
- Thomas McMahon jailed for Mountbatten bomb 11/79
- 17 die, 51 hurt, as train jumps rails 8/80
- 49 die, Dublin disco, St. Valentine's Day 2/81
- Dr Garret Fitzgerald is new premier 6/81
- Fine Gael-Labour coalition 6/81
- Fitzgerald stresses Northern Ireland 6/81
- Thatcher meets Fitzgerald: more links 11/81
- Coalition collapses over taxes 1/82
- Haughey, premier in a hung Dail 2/82
- Haughey government falls after Dail vote 11/82
- Derby winner Shergar kidnapped 2/83
- INLA leader McGlinchey arrested 3/84
- McGlinchey extradited to Northern Ireland 3/84
- IRA arms haul off Irish coast 9/84
- Bill to seize IRA assets passed 2/85
- Shop sales of contraceptives legalised 2/85
- Sikh bomb destroys plane over Irish Sea 6/85
- Virgin Mary statue seen to move 8/85
- Fitzgerald signs Anglo-Irish Agreement 11/85
- First Anglo-Irish conference 12/85
- Glenholmes extradition fails 3/86
- Guinness heiress in week-long kidnap 4/86
- Divorce rejected in referendum 6/86
- Democratic Unionist Robinson arrested 8/86
- IRA suspect O'Reilly freed 8/86
- Fitzgerald's coalition collapses 1/87
- Haughey is premier for third time 2/87
- Outgoing Fitzgerald's pledge to UK deal 2/87
- Haughey vows to solve debt 2/87
- Haughey is made premier 3/87
- Cyclist Roche wins Tour de France 7/87
- Darcy's putt saves Ryder Cup for Europe 9/87
- 40 held in IRA arms swoop 11/87
- Fianna Fail loses seats in general election 6/89
- Charles Haughey resigns 6/89
- Charles Haughey retains post of Prime Minister 7/89
- Irish hostage Brian Keenan released in Beirut 8/90
- Prime Minister Haughey sacks his deputy, Brian Lenihan 10/90
- Mary Robinson becomes first woman President of Ireland 11/90
- Inquiry begins into business scandals linked to government 9/91
- Charles Haughey announces his retirement 1/92
- Finance Minister Albert Reynolds is possible PM candidate 1/92
- Albert Reynolds is appointed Prime Minister by the Dail 2/92
- 14-year-old rape victim may travel abroad to get abortion 2/92
- Roman Catholic bishop resigns after parental scandal 5/92
- Proposals to allow women to travel abroad for abortions 11/92
- Dail votes Albert Reynolds to head coalition government 1/93
- Dublin lifts broadcast ban on Sinn Fein 1/94
- Prime Minister Reynolds resigns "for the good of the nation" 11/94
- John Bruton elected Taoiseach 12/94
- Prince Charles visits 5/95

Irigoyen, Hipolito 9/30
Irons, Jeremy 12/81
Irvin, John 12/79
Irvine, Andrew 6/24
Irving, Clifford 3/72, 6/72
Irving, Henry 10/05
Irving, Lord 5/30, 2/31
Irwin, Hale 9/91
Irwin, James 7/71
Isaacs, Alick 1/80
Isaacs, George 6/47
Isaacs, Jeremy 9/80, 12/82, 11/87
Isaacs, Rufus 3/13
Isabel II, Queen of Spain 4/04
Isherwood, Christopher 8/04, 1/36, 12/39, 12/77, 12/86
Ishiguro, Kazuo 12/89

Islamic Conference Organisation
- Fails to back Iran in Rushdie affair 3/89

Israel
- See also Britain (foreign affairs), Palestine, Palestinians
- New state proclaimed 5/48
- David Ben-Gurion is first PM 5/48
- Opens doors to all Jewish immigrants 5/48
- Government recognised by US 5/48
- British high commissioner leaves 5/48
- Chaim Weizmann is first President 5/48
- Israel and Arab League agree to truce 6/48
- Egypt and Iraq attack Jewish positions 7/48
- Truce broken by attack in Jerusalem 8/48
- UN mediator Bernadotte killed in attack 9/48
- 200 terrorist suspects rounded up 9/48
- Stern Gang outlawed 9/48
- Irgun agrees to disband 9/48
- Israeli troops resume fighting 10/48
- Israelis shoot down five RAF planes 1/49
- Ben-Gurion's Mapai Party wins election 1/49
- Recognised by Britain 1/49
- Signs truce with Egypt 2/49
- Signs cease-fire with Jordan 3/49
- Voted into United Nations 5/49
- Currency devalued 9/49
- Capital moves to Jerusalem from Tel Aviv 12/49
- Ben-Gurion resigns 2/51
- Two villages occupied by Syrians 5/51
- Cease-fire with Syria; lasts three hours 5/51
- Weizmann elected President for second time 11/51
- Plans for relations with West Germany 8/52
- Arab League protests at West German moves 8/52
- West Germany pays £293 million restitution 9/52
- First President and pioneer Weizmann dies 11/52
- Itzhak Ben-Zvi is President 12/52
- Attacks three Jordanian villages; 56 die 10/53
- UK protests over Jordanian raids 10/53
- Ben-Gurion resigns; Sharett now premier 11/53
- 17 die in terrorist bus attack, Beersheba 3/54
- Raid on Egyptian Gaza Strip kills 42 3/55
- Sets neutral zone, Jerusalem, with Jordan 4/55
- Egypt ends Gaza peace talks 8/55
- Clashes with Egypt over Gaza; cease-fire 8/55
- Clashes with Egyptians near El Auja, Sinai 10/55
- Ben-Gurion forms new government 11/55
- US to sell arms to Isreal 11/55
- UK sells arms to Egypt and Israel 12/55
- Morocco blocks emigration to Israel 6/56
- Raids on Jordan; ten killed 9/56
- Condemns Egypt over Suez 9/56
- UK and France tell Egypt and Israel to leave 10/56
- Forces cross into Sinai, approach Suez 10/56
- 30,000 attack; 400,000 reserves mobilise 10/56
- US blames UK and France for "collusion" 10/56
- Troops control Gaza and Sinai 11/56
- UN resolution calls for troop withdrawal 11/56
- Minister Golda Meir says Gaza is Israeli 11/56
- Will not return Gaza to Egypt 12/56
- UN demands Gaza and Aqaba pull-out 1/57
- Clash with UN forces in Sinai 2/57
- Jerusalem protests against UN demands 2/57
- Rejects withdrawal demands 2/57
- Ben-Gurion wary of Egyptian interference 2/57
- Pulls out of Gaza and Aqaba 3/57
- Nasser bars Canal to Israel 3/57
- Saudi Arabia bars ships from Aqaba 4/57
- BP and Shell leave after Arab pressure 7/57
- Syria fears invasion; Egyptians enter 10/57
- Ben-Gurion and ministers hurt in bomb blast 10/57
- Dayan resigns as army chief 1/58
- Policemen jailed for killing 48 Arabs 10/58
- Ben-Gurion's Labour wins election 11/59
- Finds Biblical scrolls of ancient Hebrews 2/60
- Germany's Adenauer meets Ben-Gurion 3/60
- Captures Eichmann, holocaust architect 5/60
- Argentina demands return of Eichmann 6/60
- Ben-Gurion resigns as PM 1/61
- Eichmann admits role in Final Solution 4/61
- 40 Biblical scrolls found in Judaea 4/61
- Eichmann trial begins 4/61
- Evidence for Pilate's existence found 6/61
- Eichmann's trial ends 8/61
- Eichmann sentenced to death 12/61
- Fierce fighting on Syrian border 3/62
- Adolf Eichmann hanged 5/62
- President Itzhak Ben-Zvi dies 4/63
- Ben-Gurion resigns as PM 6/63
- Pope Paul VI visits the Holy Land 1/64
- Palestine Liberation Organisation formed 6/64
- To establish relations with West Germany 3/65
- Establishes relations with West Germany 5/65
- Ben-Gurion expelled from Mapai Party 9/65
- Shmuel Agnon wins Literature Nobel 12/66
- Triumphant in Six-day War against Arabs 6/67
- Moshe Dayan appointed defence minister 6/67
- Agrees to sign Gulf of Aqaba declaration 6/67
- USSR breaks ties 6/67
- Dayan announces annexation of Gaza 7/67
- Scheme to repatriate Arab refugees 8/67
- Death of statesman Levi Eshkol 2/69
- Golda Meir elected PM 3/69
- To keep territories captured in 1967 8/69
- Arabs attack El Al airliner, Munich 2/70
- Big Israeli-Syrian battle 4/70
- Eight Jewish children killed on school bus 5/70
- Troops withdraw from Lebanon after raid 5/70
- Army says it killed 11 Jordanian guerrillas 5/70
- Refuses to withdraw to pre-1967 borders 8/70
- Skeleton of crucified man found 1/71
- Troops cross border into Lebanon 2/71
- Egypt not to extend cease-fire 3/71
- Bars entry to 21 black Jewish Americans 10/71
- 350 Soviet Jews arrive 1/72
- Terrorists massacre 25, Tel Aviv Airport 5/72
- Troops storm hijacked jet and free 92 5/72
- Israeli and Egyptian warplanes clash 6/72
- Japanese terrorist jailed for massacre 7/72
- Israel downs Libyan airliner; 100 die 2/73
- To compensate for Libyan plane shootdown 2/73
- Brandt: first German Chancellor to visit 6/73
- 56 Arab prisoners freed in exchange deal 6/73
- Fights air battle with Syria 9/73
- Fights Egypt and Syria in Yom Kippur War 10/73
- US organises huge airlift of arms 10/73
- US cease-fire ends Yom Kippur War 10/73
- Signs cease-fire agreement with Egypt 11/73
- Fights Egypt along Suez Canal line 11/73
- Clashes with Syria on Golan Heights 12/73
- Death of statesman David Ben-Gurion 12/73
- Meir's Labour government re-elected 1/74
- Military separation pact with Egypt 1/74
- Begins withdrawals from Suez west bank 1/74
- Clashes with Syria in Golan Heights 3/74
- Golda Meir resigns as PM 4/74
- 18 die in Arab guerrilla raid 4/74
- Air battle with Syria 4/74
- Yitzhak Rabin heads Labour Party 4/74
- Arab-Israeli crossfire kills 16 children 5/74
- Six Arab terrorists captured 5/74
- Golan Heights truce signed with Syria 5/74
- Yitzhak Rabin becomes PM 6/74
- Sadat tells Ford of peace talk plan 6/75
- Jerusalem bomb; 13 die, 72 hurt 7/75
- Rabin visits West Germany 7/75
- Agrees to leave Sinai; Egypt deal 9/75
- Commandos free hijack hostages, Uganda 7/76
- Withdraws France envoy over Daoud case 1/77
- Premier Rabin talks with Carter, USA 3/77
- Premier Rabin resigns over bank account 4/77
- Shimon Peres takes over as premier 4/77
- Likud defeats Labour after 29 years 5/77
- Ex-terrorist Begin is Prime Minister 5/77
- New government has hawkish approach 5/77
- Begin backs West Bank "Judaea" settlement 7/77
- USA and UK angry at new West Bank policy 7/77
- Growing Arab protests on West Bank 7/77
- Proceeds with three settlements 8/77
- Sadat addresses Knesset; calls for peace 11/77
- Sadat is first Arab leader to visit 11/77
- Sadat wants Middle East talks with US and USSR 11/77
- Happy at peace; wary of making homeland 11/77
- Planes raid Lebanon, 68 killed 11/77
- Carter offers to help Arab-Israeli pact 12/77
- Begin ready to return Sinai, he tells US 12/77
- Sadat and Begin: intense talks, Ismailia 12/77
- Sadat's threat over Israel's stance 1/78
- 7,000 troops invade south Lebanon 3/78
- Sea raiders hijack Israeli buses; 37 die 3/78
- Syrian threat; Israel calls cease-fire 3/78
- To withdraw troops from Lebanon 4/78
- Begin talks to Carter, USA 4/78
- Invades "PLO base"; withdraws from Lebanon 6/78
- Two die in Arab attack on plane, London 8/78
- Reprisal raids on Lebanese PLO bases 8/78
- Begin accord with Sadat, Camp David 9/78
- Agrees to leave Sinai; accepts Arab rights 9/78
- Begin wants mutual defence treaty, Egypt 9/78
- First woman premier Golda Meir dies 12/78
- Begin collects Nobel Peace; Sadat absent 12/78
- Signs peace treaty with US and Egypt 3/79
- Begin insists on Jerusalem as capital 3/79
- Knesset approves peace treaty 3/79
- Begin first Israeli premier to visit Egypt 4/79
- New currency planned: the shekel 2/80
- Three bombs maim West Bank mayors 6/80
- Begin suffers heart attack 6/80
- David's Palace found in Jerusalem 8/80
- Shekel in circulation 9/80
- Bombs nuclear power plant in Iraq 6/81
- Dayan claims they can make A-bomb 6/81
- Begin meets Sadat, Sinai 6/81
- Jets bomb Beirut, 150 die 7/81
- USA blocks delivery of F-16 fighters 7/81
- Calls cease-fire with PLO, Lebanon 7/81
- New Egypt premier Mubarak keeps treaty 10/81
- Begin in Cairo for Sadat's funeral 10/81
- Plans to annex Golan Heights from Syria 12/81
- US condemns Golan moves 12/81
- Accepts UN peace-keeping force, Sinai 1/82
- Votes to pull out of Sinai 4/82
- Last army forces leave Sinai 4/82
- Army fights Jewish zealots, Yamit, Sinai 4/82
- Ambassador to UK, Argov, wounded by shot 6/82
- Jets bomb Lebanon to avenge London attack 6/82
- Land, sea and air invasion of Lebanon 6/82
- Approaches Beirut; battles at Tyre, Sidon 6/82
- Air battles with Syria; shoots down 61 6/82
- Gunboats, planes bomb Beirut; 120 die 7/82
- Bombs West Beirut; PLO and Arafat leave city 8/82
- National anger at Sabra and Chatila 9/82
- 300,000 protest; Peres challenges Begin 9/82
- Morocco's implicit recognition 9/82
- Sharon claims innocence over massacre 10/82
- Inquiry blames Sharon for camp killings 2/83
- Chaim Herzog elected President 3/83
- Plans to withdraw from parts of Lebanon 4/83
- Begin resigns as PM 8/83
- Yitzhak Shamir chosen as next PM 9/83
- Knesset confirms Shamir as PM 10/83
- Frees 5,000 Arabs for six Israeli soldiers 11/83
- Shimon Peres sworn in as PM 9/84
- 25,000 Ethiopian Jews flown to Israel 1/85
- 21 die when train hits bus 6/85
- Israeli air raid on PLO offices, Tunis 10/85
- John Demjanjuk extradited from US 2/86
- Wailing Wall grenade attack injures 70 10/86
- Peres hands over premiership to Shamir 10/86
- Holds nuclear technician kidnapped in UK 11/86
- Demjanjuk tried for war crimes 2/87
- 18 die in Arab West Bank unrest 12/87
- Christmas crackdown on rioters 12/87
- Takes tough line on Gaza uprising 1/88
- Jews on West Bank kill two Palestinians 2/88
- John Demjanjuk convicted as SS guard 4/88
- Likud party wins general election 11/88
- Accused of massacre in Nahhalin on the West Bank 4/89
- Man posing as soldier shoots seven Palestinian workers 5/90
- Reopens diplomatic relations with USSR 9/90
- Condemned by UN for Temple Mount killings 10/90
- 21 Palestinians shot dead by police 10/90
- Iraqi Scud missiles hit Tel Aviv and Haifa 1/91
- Puts pressure on Bush over Iraqi missile attacks 1/91
- Government agrees to attend Middle East peace talks 4/91
- Centre of new hostage deal 8/91
- Angered by Bush's refusal of $10bn loan 9/91
- Yitzhak Rabin is elected Prime Minister 6/92
- Ezer Weizman is elected President 3/93
- Demjanjuk's death sentence nullified 7/93
- Israel and PLO leaders shake hands at the White House 9/93
- 30 Palestinian worshippers shot in Mosque by Jewish zealot 2/94
- Full diplomatic relations with Vatican 6/94
- Yassir Arafat enters Gaza Strip ending 27 year exile 7/94
- Suicide bomber kills 21 in Tel Aviv 10/94
- 78,000 immigrants settled this year 12/94

Issigonis, Alexander Arnold Constantine
2/65, 10/88

Italian East Africa
- See also Italy, Somaliland 5/11
- Formed from Italian Somaliland, Eritrea 1/35
- Abyssinians kill 40 Italian troops 7/35

Italy
- See also World Wars I and II
- Leftist unrest closes parliament 4/00
- King Humbert I killed 7/00
- Shares out Africa with France 12/00
- Fixes African borders with Britain 11/01
- Minimum working age raised 3/02
- Triple Alliance renewed for 12 years 6/02
- Joins Anglo-German Venezuelan blockade 12/02
- Anti-Austrian riots 6/03
- Thousands die in Calabrian earthquake 9/05
- Mount Vesuvius erupts; hundreds dead 4/06
- Plot to kill King Victor Emmanuel found 6/06
- Reaffirms Triple Alliance 6/06
- Triple Alliance (with Germany and Austria) 7/07
- Garibaldi anniversary celebrations 7/07
- Kaiser visits Victor Emmanuel III 3/08
- About 75,000 die in Messina earthquake 12/08
- Asks Austria to pay for Balkan takeover 12/08
- Martial law in earthquake-hit south 1/09
- Stromboli volcano erupts after quake 1/09
- English, German and Russian monarchs talk 5/09
- Mount Etna erupts 3/10
- Tidal wave kills 1,000, Bay of Naples 10/10
- State life assurance scheme created 4/11
- Victor Emmanuel II monument unveiled 6/11
- Foreign minister limits African interests 6/11
- Army uses planes to spy on Turks 8/11
- Warships attack Turkish-occupied Tripoli 9/11
- 30,000 die of cholera 9/11
- Conquers Tripoli; imposes censorship 10/11
- Bombards Albanian town, Point Medua 10/11
- Occupies Benghazi, North Africa 10/11
- Annexes Tripolitania and Cyrenaica 11/11
- New discoveries at Pompeii 4/12
- Occupies Rhodes island 5/12
- Naples gangsters guilty of murder 7/12
- Gains Libya from Turkey by peace treaty 10/12
- Renews Triple Alliance for six more years 12/12
- Triple Alliance affirmed; Italian doubts 9/13
- 162 die in Catanian earthquake 5/14
- Neutrality attacked by Austria and Germany 8/14
- 29,000 die in earthquake 1/15
- Secret treaty with Allies upsets Germany 4/15
- Breaks with Austria over land claims 4/15
- Leaves Triple Alliance; declares war on Austria 5/15
- Declares war on Turkey 8/15
- Ancona liner torpedoed; 208 die 11/15
- Declares Albania a protectorate 6/17
- Defeated at Caporetto; 500,000 deserters 10/17
- Mussolini founds Fascist Party 3/19
- Takes over Austrian naval fleet 3/19
- Cities paralysed by general strike 12/19
- Bread price riots 6/20
- 500 die, 200,000 homeless in earthquake 9/20
- D'Annunzio surrenders Fiume to army 12/20
- Naples mourns at Caruso's funeral 8/21
- First International Sociology Conference 10/21
- Mussolini leads Fascists, gets finance 11/21
- New Pope Pius XI seeks peace with Italy 2/22
- Fascists take over Fiume 3/22
- Fascists fight Socialists 3/22
- Western Genoa conference; Rapallo Treaty 4/22
- Fascists capture Bologna and Modena 6/22
- Mussolini warns government on clampdown 7/22
- Fascists smash Communists; take Milan 8/22
- First Monza motor race; Bordino wins 9/22
- Fascists march on Rome; cabinet resigns 10/22
- King Victor Emmanuel allows Fascist rule 10/22
- Mussolini threatens to dissolve Chamber 11/22
- Mussolini arrests socialists 2/23
- May Day becomes Rome Founding Day 4/23
- Catholic Party resigns from government 4/23
- Mussolini approves women's suffrage bill 6/23
- "Italianisation" of ex-Austrian Tyrol 7/23
- Blocks more French occupation of Germany 11/23
- Pact with Yugoslavia's annexes Fiume 1/24
- Recognises USSR; commercial treaty 2/24
- D'Annunzio made Prince of Montenevoso 3/24
- Fascists sweep to victory in elections 4/24
- King and Queen visit Britain 5/24
- Socialist Matteotti claims poll-rigging 5/24
- Fascists kill Matteotti after revelation 6/24
- Communist shoots Fascist deputy Casalini 9/24
- Mussolini: Fascists "above parliament" 10/24
- Rome's first underground railway 9/25
- Mussolini bans all left-wing parties 11/25
- Liberals join Fascists; Freemasonry ban 11/25
- Mussolini answers only to king 12/25
- Mussolini premier and holds two posts 1/26
- Banned Communists gather in Lyons 1/26
- Mussolini to rule by decree 1/26
- 200 Mafia leaders arrested, Sicily 2/26
- Light sentence for Matteotti killers 3/26
- Senate abolishes strikes 3/26
- Mussolini shot by Violet Gibson 4/26
- Fascist leader Padovani dies in accident 6/26
- Working day gains extra hour 6/26
- Opposition banned; Fascists state party 10/26
- Women cannot hold public office 10/26
- Boy lynched after shooting at Mussolini 10/26
- Papal blessing for Mussolini 11/26
- Death penalty restored 11/26
- Vesuvius erupts 11/26
- Tax on bachelors 12/26
- "Fasces" adopted as national emblem 12/26
- Newspapers ban suicide and crime reports 1/28
- 100 Libyan tribesmen clash with Italians 1/28
- Trial by jury may be abolished 1/28
- 22 die at Milan's Grand Prix motor race 9/28
- Grand Fascist Council replaces Chamber 9/28
- Mount Etna erupts; threatens Catania 11/28
- Draining of Pontin marshes planned 12/28
- Mussolini makes pact with Pope 2/29
- Catholicism confirmed as national faith 2/29
- Mussolini claims 99 per cent vote Fascist 3/29
- King opens first all-Fascist parliament 4/29
- Mussolini bans "immoral" beauty contest 5/29
- Vatican state under Lateran Treaty 6/29
- Attempt on Italian Crown Prince Umberto 10/29
- Mussolini: "Too much talk of peace" 11/29
- Italian Socialists in Riviera plot 1/30
- Earthquake kills 3,000 in Naples 7/30
- Loading citizens caught plotting coup 11/30
- Toscanini punched for snubbing anthem 5/31
- Toscanini's passport withdrawn 5/31
- Mussolini suspends Catholic Action 5/31
- Toscanini's defiance wins friends 6/31
- Toscanini allowed to leave 6/31
- Fascists squeeze secret societies and Mafia 6/31
- Prizes for the biggest families 11/31
- Mussolini meets Pope; better relations 2/32
- Murder plot against Mussolini foiled 6/32
- First Venice Film Festival 8/32
- Ten-year peace pact, UK, France, Germany 5/33
- Anti-Nazi Toscanini refuses Bayreuth 6/33
- Mussolini meets Austrian leader Dollfuss 8/33
- Mussolini pledges aid to Austria 8/33
- Non-aggression pact with USSR 8/33
- Turin Shroud shown to 25,000 9/33
- Attacks Nazism at League session 10/33
- Co-operation pact with Hungary and Austria 3/34
- Mussolini urges German rearmament 3/34
- Mussolini cuts salaries 4/34
- Bombs Greek-ruled Rhodes island; ten die 4/34
- Parliament sheds its last powers 4/34
- Mussolini meets Hitler for first time, Venice 6/34
- Mussolini gets Fascist salute, World Cup 6/34
- Compulsory male military training 9/34
- Supports independent Austria 9/34
- Six-year-olds for pre-military training 10/34
- Teachers to wear Fascist uniform 11/34
- Pirandello wins Literature Nobel 12/34
- Clashes with Abyssinia at Wal Wal 12/34
- Hoping to avenge 1896 Abyssinia defeat 12/34
- Rejects Abyssinian call for arbitration 12/34
- Italian East Africa: Somaliland and Eritrea 1/35
- Forms Libya from three African colonies 1/35
- Promises to stop Hitler in Austria 1/35
- Troops and planes at Abyssinian border 1/35
- Mussolini dismisses entire cabinet 1/35
- Claims Abyssinia troops at Somali border 2/35
- Troops sail to Abyssinia on liners 2/35
- Promises to negotiate after League debate 2/35
- UK and France want anti-aggression pact 2/35
- Wants curbs on German rearmament 4/35
- 200,000 more mobilised for East Africa 5/35
- Abyssinia rejects "sphere of influence" 7/35
- 1,000 die when Oveda dam bursts 8/35
- Geneva talks on Abyssinia-Italy conflict 8/35
- Selassie offers new concessions to Italy 8/35
- Rejects Anglo-French plan for Abyssinia 8/35
- Settle dispute by arms, says Mussolini 8/35
- Truce pledge; then rejects League plan 9/35
- Demands Abyssinian disarmament 9/35

- Invades Abyssinia; takes Adowat and Adowa 10/35
- Defies threat of sanctions over Abyssinia 10/35
- 100,000 invade, plus Eritrean Askaris 10/35
- 40 million gather to hear Abyssinia news 10/35
- League sanctions take effect 11/35
- To quit League if sanctions continue 11/35
- Seize Tigre, capital of Makale 11/35
- Many Italians killed on Sasa Baneh 11/35
- Sanctions-busting: restricted food, cash 11/35
- Anti-British demonstrations, Rome 11/35
- Britain rejects Hoare-Laval pact 12/35
- Bombers raze Daggha Bur 1/36
- League threatens oil embargo 3/36
- Banks nationalised 3/36
- Mussolini to nationalise key industries 3/36
- Troops use mustard gas in Abyssinia 4/36
- Mussolini wants Abyssinian puppet state 4/36
- Occupies Dessye; prepare for Addis Ababa 4/36
- Italy wins six-month Abyssinian war 5/36
- Badoglio in Addis Ababa; wins Aradam 5/36
- Mussolini proclaims new empire after war 5/36
- Hitler recognises Abyssinian occupation 7/36
- To issue Abyssinian development bonds 8/36
- Hitler and Count Ciano draft pact 10/36
- 23 killed in Venice earthquake 10/36
- Anti-Communist Axis with Germany 11/36
- Forbids "mixed marriages" in Africa 1/37
- UK, Italy, USSR and Germany halt Spanish aid 2/37
- Italians beat 3,000 rebels, Addis Ababa 2/37
- Protests at UK's invitation to Selassie 2/37
- Leaves non-intervention cordon of Spain 5/37
- Mussolini warns Jews to "uphold Fascism" 5/37
- Guglielmo Marconi, radio pioneer, dies 7/37
- Mussolini at huge Berlin rally 9/37
- Mussolini speaks of peace and Empire 9/37
- Rejects, then joins, Nyon anti-piracy patrol 9/37
- Anti-Communist pact with Germany and Japan 11/37
- Leaves League of Nations 12/37
- Chamberlain talks to Italian Ambassador 1/38
- Troops adopt German-style goosestep 1/38
- Anglo-Italian pact signed 4/38
- UK parliament praises Italy after pact 5/38
- Promises UK to pull out of Spain 5/38
- Stromboli volcano erupts 5/38
- Curbs on Jewish books 7/38
- Foreign Jews barred; anti-Semitic papers 8/38
- Accepts Germany's Sudetenland annexation 9/38
- Jews rounded up, accused of treason 10/38
- Chamberlain and Halifax visit Mussolini 1/39
- Italian troops invade Albania 4/39
- Signs Pact of Steel with Germany 5/39
- Mussolini announces Italian neutrality 9/39
- Mussolini meets Hitler at Brenner Pass 3/40
- All males over 14 mobilised 4/40
- Declares war on Britain and France 6/40
- Signs pact with Japan 9/40
- Badoglio sacked as chief of staff 12/40
- Expels US consuls 6/41
- Mussolini becomes Foreign Minister 2/43
- State of emergency declared in south 5/43
- Mussolini deposed 7/43
- King Victor Emmanuel heads armed forces 7/43
- Badoglio becomes PM 7/43
- Badoglio declares martial law 7/43
- Badoglio asks Allies for peace terms 7/43
- Fascist Party abolished 7/43
- Political prisoners released 7/43
- Rome declared an open city 8/43
- Badoglio signs Armistice 9/43
- Germans rescue Mussolini from prison 9/43
- Germans occupy Rome 9/43
- Italians seize control of Sardinia 9/43
- Allies enter Naples 9/43
- Declares war on Germany 10/43
- Germans loot Rome of art treasures 10/43
- Allied advance held up at Monte Cassino 10/43
- Allies seize Isernia 11/43
- King Victor Emmanuel stripped of titles 11/43
- Canadians seize Adriatic port of Ortona 12/43
- Allied troops storm ashore at Anzio 1/44
- 18 sentenced to die for treason 1/44
- Nobile Ciano and four others executed 1/44
- Allies bomb Monte Cassino monastery 2/44
- Diplomatic relations with USSR restored 3/44
- Allies launch assault on Monte Cassino 3/44
- Allies take Monte Cassino 5/44
- Allies break German spine in Italy 5/44
- Rome falls to the Allies 6/44
- Victor Emmanuel abdicates 6/44
- Crown Prince Umberto becomes King 6/44
- Bonomi heads provisional government 6/44
- Allies take Perugia 6/44
- Elba surrenders to French troops 6/44
- Allies take Livorno and Ancona 7/44
- Churchill visits Allied HQ 8/44
- Allies take Florence 8/44
- Mussolini shot dead by partisans 4/45
- Germans in Italy surrender to Allies 4/45
- Allies take Milan and Venice 4/45
- King Victor Emmanuel III abdicates 5/46
- Votes to become a republic; King ousted 6/46
- Royalist riots in Rome, Naples, Pisa 6/46
- Republic of Italy declared 6/46
- Alcide de Gaspari becomes head of state 6/46
- Enrico de Nicola elected provisional President 6/46
- British Embassy in Rome wrecked by bombs 10/46
- Loses land under Paris peace treaties 2/47
- De Gaspari forms cabinet 2/47
- Car designer Ettore Bugatti dies 8/47
- Refuses to swap Trieste for Gorizia 3/48
- Luigi Einaudi elected President 5/48
- Signs North Atlantic Treaty 4/49
- Air crash kills Italy's football team 5/49
- USSR vetoes entry to UN 9/49
- Former Italian colonies are independent 11/49
- Wartime army chief Graziani jailed 5/50
- Recognises independence of Libya 12/51
- Education pioneer Maria Montessori dies 5/52
- Floods wreck 12 villages in the south 10/53
- UK and USA award Trieste; Yugoslavs angry 10/53
- 35 die as BOAC Comet crashes off Elba 1/54
- Toscanini's last concert, NBC Orchestra 4/54
- Inherits most of Trieste as Allies leave 10/54
- Gronchi succeeds Einaudi as President 4/55
- Arturo Toscanini dies 1/57
- Joins new European Economic Community 3/57
- 68 die on TWA airliner 6/59
- First Vatican synod held in Rome 1/60
- Rome hosts Olympic Games 8/60
- Livio Berruti wins Olympic 200 metres 9/60
- First Italian space rocket launched 1/61
- 13 killed at Italian Grand Prix 9/61
- US Mafia chief Luciano dies 1/62
- Loren and Ponti to face bigamy charges 6/62
- Mont Blanc tunnel completed 8/62
- Pope John XXIII travels by train 10/62
- 3,000 drown after Piave Valley dam bursts 10/63
- Giulio Natto wins Chemistry Nobel 12/63
- 84 die in Alps air crash 2/64
- Communists want independence from USSR 9/64
- 44 die in Rome air crash 11/64
- Mont Blanc tunnel opened 7/65
- Premier Aldo Moro forms new cabinet 2/66
- Florence flood destroys masterpieces 11/66
- Rudi Dutschke shooting sparks riots 4/68
- Over 100 die in floods 11/68
- Ends dispute with Austria over South Tyrol 11/69
- Terrorist bombings in Milan and Rome 12/69
- 100,000 in anti-Fascist march 11/71
- 115 die in DC-8 crash 5/72
- Black September attack oil pipeline 8/72
- Referendum approves keeping divorce laws 5/74
- 12 die in neo-Fascist attack on train 8/74
- 42 skiers die in cable car crash 3/76
- 2,000 die and 80,000 left homeless in earthquake 5/76
- Milan suburb evacuated in chemical scare 7/76
- 16 die in storms 10/77
- Red Brigade kidnap ex-premier Moro 3/78
- Christian Democrats reject deal for Moro 3/78
- Many die as Bologna trains collide 4/78
- Government appeals for Moro's life 4/78
- Parliament deadlock over kidnap deal 4/78
- Moro's body found in car, Rome 5/78
- Moro family funeral; anger at colleagues 5/78
- Hunt for Red Brigade kidnappers; arrests 5/78
- President Leone resigns over tax evasion 6/78
- Red Brigade trial: 29 jailed, 16 freed 6/78
- First Socialist President, Pertini 7/78
- "Christ's" Shroud of Turin displayed 8/78
- Kidnapped Schild girl freed, seven months on 3/80
- Sardinian Schild bandits in prison 3/80
- UK football fans riot at Turin match 6/80
- 84 die in Bologna station bomb blast 8/80
- Neo-Fascists claim Bologna bombing 8/80
- 3,000 die in southern earthquakes 11/80
- Vote for easier abortion laws 5/81
- Government resigns over freemasonry 5/81
- Troops storm flat to free US officer 1/82
- 63 charged with Moro kidnap and murder 4/82
- Sophia Loren jailed for tax evasion 5/82
- Banker Calvi found hanged in London 6/82
- Rome synagogue attacked; two-year-old dies 10/82
- 64 die in Turin theatre fire 2/83
- Mount Etna's lava flow diverted 5/83
- Agca says KGB tried to kill Pope 7/83
- Bettino Craxi becomes first Socialist PM 8/83
- Executives jailed for Seveso disaster 9/83
- Peace-keeping force pulls out of Lebanon 2/84
- Endorses plans to combat world terrorism 6/84
- Bulgarians alleged to have hired Acga 6/84
- Death of statesman Enrico Berlinguer 6/84
- Eight go on trial for trying to kill Pope 5/85
- Agca denies Pope plot charges 6/85
- 260 die after dam bursts 7/85
- Achille Lauro hijacker freed 10/85
- Craxi government falls 10/85
- Arab terrorist attack at Rome airport 12/85
- Biggest ever Mafia trial opens, Palermo 2/86
- Six cleared of plot to kill Pope 3/86
- Porn star Ilona Staller elected to parliament 7/87
- 338 convicted in Palermo Mafia trial 12/87
- Turin Shroud is mediaeval fake 10/88
- Thousands of Albanian refugees arrive seeking asylum 8/91
- Anti-Mafia Judge Giovanni Falcone is killed by bomb 5/92
- Sicilian Mafia boss, Salvatore Riina, is captured by police 1/93
- Carlo Ciampi becomes Prime Minister 4/93
- Bomb blast in Florence kills five 5/93
- Opposition groups win local elections 6/93
- Second suicide victim of corruption scandals 7/93
- Two car bombs explode in Rome and Milan 7/93
- Silvio Berlusconi wins General Election 3/94
- Mass in Sistine Chapel marks Michelangelo restoration 4/94
- Berlusconi's coalition collapses 12/94
- Lamberto Dini appointed Premier 1/95

Ito, Hirobumi, Prince of Japan 10/09
Ivanov, Eugene 6/63
Iveagh, Lord 11/27
Ives, Charles 5/54
Ivory Coast
- Francois Mitterrand opens Abidjan port 2/51
- Becomes a French Union republic 12/58
- Ojukwu granted political asylum 1/70
- Pope consecrates world's largest church 9/90

Iyad, Abu (Salah Khalaf) 1/91
Izetbegovic, Alija 6/93

J

Jablonski, Henryk 6/79
Jacklin, Tony 3/68, 7/69, 6/70, 9/85, 9/89
Jackson, Barry 12/46
Jackson, Derek 1/69
Jackson, Geoffrey 1/71, 9/71
Jackson, Glenda 12/64, 12/69, 4/74, 12/74
Jackson, Gordon 12/75
Jackson, Henry 6/79
Jackson, Jesse 10/41, 4/68, 1/84, 6/84, 3/88, 4/88
Jackson, Michael 8/58, 12/84, 7/88, 8/94
Jacob, Ian 7/59
Jacobi, Derek 8/57, 12/76, 12/91
Jacobs, Helen 7/34, 7/36, 7/38
Jacobsen, David 11/86
Jaeger, Andrea 7/83
Jagan, Dr 4/54
Jagger, Mick 8/65, 12/66, 5/67, 6/67, 7/67, 1/70, 5/71
Jagielski, Mieczyslaw 8/80
Jakes, Eileen 8/79
Jakes, Milos 11/89
Jamaica
- Earthquake hits Kingston, killing hundreds 1/07
- Governor Sweetenham resigns over quake 3/07
- 132 die in hurricane 8/51
- 700 arrests for marijuana trade 7/52
- Hundreds emigrate by sea to Britain 1/55
- Eden flies to Jamaica after Suez strain 11/56
- 173 die in rail crash 9/57
- Gains independence 8/62
- Manley's Labour Party wins election 3/72
- Seaga's Labour Party beats Manley 10/80
- Bob Marley, reggae apostle, dies 5/81
- Michael Manley wins landslide victory in elections 2/89

James, C.H. 12/38
James, Henry 7/15, 2/16, 12/16
James, Naomi 6/78
James, Roy 12/63
James, Sidney 4/76
James, William 12/16
Janacek, Leos 8/28
Jannings, Emil 12/30
Jansky, Karl 12/32

Japan
- See also China, World Wars I and II
- Worried about Russian fleet in Korea 3/00
- Japanese battleship made in Britain 11/00
- Treaty of alliance with Britain 1/02
- Signs Chinese Tariff Protocol 8/02
- Marines in Korea; tension with Russia 12/03
- Risks of war with Russia rise, Korea 1/04
- Russian fleet crippled by Japanese raid 2/04
- Woos Korea 2/04
- Surprising successes against Russians 3/04
- Beats Russians at Telissu; 2,000 die 6/04
- Japanese capture Liao-Yang with new arms 8/04
- Success over Russian fleet, Port Arthur 12/04
- Port Arthur surrenders to Japanese 1/05
- Overwhelms Russians at Mukden 3/05
- Crushing victory over Russian navy 5/05
- Treaty signed: gains in land and rights 9/05
- Riots against peace treaty 9/05
- Rice crop failure, spreading famine 11/05
- Treaty with Korea guarantees "dignity" 11/05
- 680,000 reported starving 12/05
- Plans to double navy's size by 1908 2/06
- Hands Manchuria back to China, withdraws 4/07
- Faces riots in Korea after Emperor abdicates 7/07
- Treaty with Russia gives China guarantee 7/07
- Occupies Korea 7/10
- Accepts Russia in Manchuria 7/10
- Officially annexes Korea 8/10
- 800 die in floods 8/10
- Agrees spheres of influence with Russia 8/12
- Nine million are starving 1/14
- Declares war on Germany 8/14
- Agrees to no separate peace with Germany 9/14
- Requisitions rice stocks to end riots 8/18
- To spend £30 million on aviation 10/19
- Prince Hirohito visits Britain 5/21
- Emperor is ill; Hirohito is made regent 11/21
- Reformist premier Hara Kei killed 11/21
- Pacific expansion curtailed by treaty 12/21
- To restore Shantung to China 2/22
- 300,000 die in worst earthquake, Tokyo 9/23
- Flooding and cholera claim quake survivors 9/23
- Martial law proclaimed; rebuilding begun 9/23
- Attempted assassination of Hirohito 12/23
- Hirohito succeeds late emperor Yoshihito 12/26
- 3,000 die in tidal wave, Kiu-Siu Island 9/27
- Hirohito crowned Emperor; pledges work 11/28
- Ratifies anti-war clause, Kellogg-Briand 6/29
- Invades Manchuria 11/29
- Premier Hamagushi killed by rightists 11/30
- 300 die in Mishioma earthquake 11/30
- Attacks Chinese at Mukden, Manchuria 9/31
- US arranges truce after Manchuria attack 11/31
- Abandons gold standard 12/31
- Captures Shanghai; active in north China 1/32
- Attempt on life of Emperor Hirohito 1/32
- Sets up puppet regime in Manchuria 2/32
- Deposed Pu-yi made Emperor of Manchukuo 3/32
- Withdraws from Shanghai after armistice 5/32
- Premier Inukai assassinated 5/32
- Slammed by League for breaking treaties 10/32
- Restores relations with USSR 12/32
- Rejects non-aggression pact with USSR 1/33
- Storms out of League of Nations 2/33
- Challenges China's sovereignty at League 2/33
- Leaves League of Nations 2/33
- Torpedo boat capsizes; 100 die 3/34
- 1,500 die in Hakodate fire 3/34
- Pu-yi installed as Emperor of Manchukuo 3/34
- Warns West: "Hands off China" 4/34
- Wants bigger navy and airforce 4/34
- Typhoon kills 1,500 in centre of country 9/34
- UK proposes equality for Japanese navy 11/34
- Rejects alliance with Germany 4/35
- Makes China remove northern divisions 6/35
- Installs "friendly" officials in Peking 6/35
- 227 die in floods 7/35
- Troops march into Peking 11/35
- Sets up northern Chinese Hopei state 11/35
- Demands naval parity with UK 12/35
- Captain Ando's army coup fails 2/36
- Post-coup fears of rightist government 2/36
- Signs Axis anti-Red pact with Germany 11/36
- Agreement with secret police of Germany 11/36
- Mao and Chiang cannot agree anti-Japan pact 2/37
- Attacks China from Manchukuo 7/37
- Clashes with Chinese troops near Peking 7/37
- Occupies Peking in Chinese War 8/37
- Bombs Shanghai; hundreds die 8/37
- Foreigners flee Shanghai 8/37
- Air raid wounds UK Ambassador to China 8/37
- No apology for wounding UK Ambassador 9/37
- Bombs Nationalist Nanking; 200 die 9/37
- League condemns invasion of China 9/37
- Chinese Communists and Nationalists unite 9/37
- Roosevelt condemns Japan over China 10/37
- New offensive in China; rejects talks 10/37
- Anti-Communist pact with Germany and Italy 11/37
- Takes Shanghai 11/37
- Recognises Franco's regime in Spain 12/37
- Occupies Nanking, China 12/37
- Sinks US Navy gunboat and two tankers, China 12/37
- Truce with USSR after border clashes 8/38
- Downs Chinese passenger plane; 19 die 8/38
- 226 die in Tokyo typhoon 10/38
- Tanks conquer Canton 10/38
- Hiranuma becomes premier 1/39
- Occupies Hainan Island, off China 2/39
- Captures port of Swatow, China 6/39
- Invades Tonkin, Indochina 9/40
- Signs pact with Germany and Italy 9/40
- Warns UK against movements in SE Asia 2/41
- Signs neutrality pact with USSR 4/41
- Granted use of Indochina military bases 7/41
- Freezes all British and US assets 7/41
- Troops advance into Thailand 7/41
- Troops occupy Cambodia and Indochina 7/41
- Konoye cabinet resigns 10/41
- Tojo succeeds Konoye as PM 10/41
- Relations with US deteriorate 11/41
- Attacks Pearl Harbor 12/41
- Declares war on US 12/41
- Foreign Minister Togo resigns 9/42
- Tojo becomes army chief of staff 2/44
- Tokyo devastated by fire bombing 3/45
- All Tokyo schools and universities are closed 3/45
- All over the age of six ordered to do war work 3/45
- Atomic bombs dropped on Hiroshima and Nagasaki 8/45
- Surrenders to the Allies 8/45
- Allied occupation begins 8/45
- Signs formal surrender 9/45
- Tojo fails in suicide attempt 9/45
- Propagandist Iva Togori arrested 9/45
- MacArthur orders arrest of Tojo 9/45
- Hirohito blames Tojo for Pearl Harbor 9/45
- Kijuro Shidehara becomes premier 10/45
- Women vote for first time in election 4/46
- Trial of Tojo begins 4/46
- Hirohito not to be tried as war criminal 6/46
- New constitution announced 11/46
- Allies allow "Rising Sun" flag to fly 5/47
- Tojo and 24 others convicted for war crimes 11/48
- Tojo and six others hanged 12/48
- US says USSR is inciting disorder 6/49
- US wants Hirohito tried as war criminal 2/50
- Typhoon kills 250, injures 300,000 9/50
- General MacArthur threatens to invade China 3/51
- Final peace treaty with 48 nations 9/51
- Loses empire; barred from re-arming 9/51
- US may station troops in Japan 9/51
- 49 states recognise Japanese sovereignty 4/52
- Re-opens relations with Nationalist China 8/52
- 129 US troops die in air crash, Tokyo 6/53
- Fishermen catch H-bomb radiation disease 3/54
- 1,700 drown on capsized ferry 9/54
- 25 Hiroshima victims go to US for surgery 5/55
- Barred from United Nations 12/55
- World's largest oil tanker launched 12/58
- Quakes and floods kill 96 5/60
- Riots against US treaty; one dies 6/60
- Rightist kills Socialist Asanuma 10/60
- 616 die in two disasters 11/63
- To enter UK saloon car races 3/65
- Establishes relations with South Korea 6/65
- 133 killed in air crash 2/66
- 130 die in air crash 3/66
- 174 die in typhoon 9/66
- Yukio Mishima commits hara-kiri 11/70
- 162 die in worst recorded plane crash 7/71
- Three die in anti-airport protests in Tokyo 9/71
- Hirohito visits Britain 10/71
- Winter Olympics open in Tokyo 2/72
- 118 die in department store fire 5/72
- Head of state Eisaku Sato resigns 6/72
- 10,000 commuters rampage in strike protest 3/73
- Seven Red Army people freed after threat 8/75
- Ex-premier Tanaka caught in Lockheed case 7/76
- Tanaka indicted on bribe charges 8/76
- Takeo Fukuda elected premier 12/76
- Protests at new international airport 5/78

- Paul McCartney deported on drugs charge 1/80
- Study shows passive smoking danger 1/81
- Honda cars and British Leyland in link-up 11/81
- Endorses plans to combat world terrorism 6/84
- 62 miners die in firedamp explosion 5/85
- 517 killed in air crash near Tokyo 8/85
- Seven-nation summit declares war on terror 5/86
- Nissan opens car plant in UK 9/86
- UK threat over Japan's closed markets 3/87
- Wall Street fall affects Japan 10/87
- Emperor Hirohito dies 1/89
- Prince Philip represents Britain at Hirohito's funeral 2/89
- Geisha publicly reveals affair with premier 6/89
- Sosuke Uno resigns after elections defeat 7/89
- Toshiki Kaifu becomes premier 8/89
- Liberal Democrats win general election 2/90
- Emperor Akihito enthroned 11/90
- Premier Miyazawa loses vote of confidence in parliament 6/93
- Crown Prince Naruhito marries Oxford-educated bride, Masako 6/93
- Morihiro Hosowaka is new Prime Minister 8/93
- Murayama is first Socialist Prime Minister since 1948 6/94
- Massive earthquake hits Kobe 1/95
- Sect blamed for Tokyo subway poison gas attack 3/95
- Cult guru Shoko Asahara arrested 5/95

Jarawa, Dawda 7/81
Jardine, Douglas 6/32, 1/33, 6/58
Jarry, Alfred 11/07
Jaruzelski, Wojciech 2/81, 10/81, 11/81, 12/81, 3/82, 7/83, 5/84, 11/88, 6/89, 7/89
Jason, David 12/91
Jaspar, Henri 11/29
Jassim, Latif 1/91
Jaworski, Leon 11/73, 2/74, 10/74
Jay, Peter 5/77, 3/83, 12/83
Jayawardene, Junius 7/77
Jazz
- See also Music (popular)
- Ellington, "jungle sound" jazz composer 12/27
- Louis Armstrong, master of the cornet 12/27
- Spirited blues from Rainey and Bessie Smith 12/27
- Henderson and saxophone soloist Hawkins 12/27
- White "symphonic jazz", Paul Whiteman 12/27
- Soloists: Beiderbecke, Teagarden, Dorsey 12/27
- Trumpeter Bix Beiderbecke dies 8/31
- Germany bans Jewish and black US jazz 10/35
- Benny Goodman's big band 12/35
- Fletcher Henderson arrangements 12/35
- Joe "King" Oliver dies 4/38
- "In the Mood", Glenn Miller 8/39
- Pianist "Jelly Roll" Morton dies 7/41
- US pianist "Fats" Waller dies 12/43
- Glenn Miller disappears over English Channel 12/44
- Guitarist, "Django" Reinhardt, dies 5/53
- Charlie Parker, saxophonist, dies 3/55
- Art Tatum and Tommy Dorsey die 11/56
- Louis Armstrong appears in "High Society" 12/56
- Jimmey Dorsey, band leader, dies 6/57
- New jazz at Newport from Miles Davis 12/58
- Bebop, Charlie Parker's legacy 12/58
- Free-style Monk, Coltrane and Coleman 12/58
- Classicists Basie, Armstrong and Ellington 12/58
- Piano geniuses Peterson and Lewis 12/58
- Armstrong suffers mild heart attack 6/59
- Billie Holliday, top blues singer, dies 7/59
- Students spawn "trad" jazz revival in UK 12/59
- UK's own Lyttleton, Colyer, Bilk and Barber 12/59
- US saxophonist John Coltrane dies 7/67
- Death of US musician Paul Whiteman 12/67
- Death of US trumpeter Louis Armstrong 7/71
- Duke Ellington gives concert in USSR 9/71
- US musician Duke Ellington dies 5/74
- Thelonius Monk, pianist, dies 2/82
- Death of Count Basie 4/84
- US clarinettist Benny Goodman dies 6/86
- Miles Davis dies 9/91

Jeanette, Joe 3/14
Jeannel, Rene 4/08
Jeanneret, C.E. 8/65
Jedrzejowska, Jadwiga 7/37
Jeffrey, Bill 6/50
Jeffries, Jim 4/00, 7/02, 8/04
Jellicoe, Earl (George) 10/44, 5/73
Jellicoe, Sir John (later Earl) 12/12, 8/14, 5/16, 11/35
Jenatzki, Camille 7/03
Jenkin, Patrick 9/84
Jenkins, David 9/74, 7/84, 9/84, 10/84
Jenkins, Peter 5/92
Jenkins, Roy 10/64, 12/65, 5/66, 4/67, 11/67, 7/70, 11/71, 4/72, 7/76, 1/77, 3/77, 1/81, 3/82, 7/82, 6/83, 7/87
Jenner, Bruce 7/76
Jenninger, Phillip 11/88
Jennings, Humphrey 12/42
Jennings, Pat 2/83
Jensen, Hans 2/73
Jensen, Johannes 12/44
Jensen, Knut 9/60
Jerome, Jerome K. 6/27
Jhabvala, Ruth Prawer 11/75, 12/75
Jibril, Ahmed 11/83
Jihad, Abu 4/88
Jimenez, Juan Ramon 5/58
Jimenez, Marcos Perez 1/58
Jinnah, Mohammed Ali 4/46, 7/46, 11/46, 5/47, 6/47, 7/47, 9/48
Joachim, Joseph 8/07
Jodl, Alfred 5/45, 10/46
Joffre, Joseph 7/11, 9/14, 9/15, 12/15, 2/16, 12/16, 1/31
Johansson, Ingemar 6/59, 6/60
John, Augustus 12/11, 7/38, 10/61
John, Elton 12/92
John, Otto 7/54, 12/55
Johnson, Amy 4/30, 5/36, 1/41
Johnson, Ben 8/87, 9/88, 3/93
Johnson, Daniel 7/67
Johnson, Donald 1/62
Johnson, Earvin "Magic" 11/91
Johnson, Hewlett 10/66
Johnson, Jack 12/08, 4/15
Johnson, Joe 5/86
Johnson, Lyndon B.
- Born 8/08
- Heads US Senate 11/54
- Calls for US to make advances in space 1/58
- Democratic nomination: beaten by Kennedy 7/60
- Sworn in as US President 11/63
- Confers with de Gaulle and Douglas-Home 11/63
- Says he will continue world peace effort 11/63
- Warren inquiry into Kennedy murder 11/63
- To wage "war against poverty" 1/64
- Urged to take control of Mississippi 6/64
- Signs sweeping Civil Rights Act 7/64
- Congress supports action in Vietnam 8/64
- Calls for Cyprus truce 8/64
- Signs anti-poverty bill 8/64
- Democratic candidate for presidency 9/64
- Landslide win in presidential election 11/64
- Pays tribute to Churchill 1/65
- Sworn in as 36th US President 1/65
- Sends Marines into Vietnam 3/65
- Talks with Martin Luther King 3/65
- Withdraws Marines from Dominica 6/65
- Sends another 50,000 troops to Vietnam 7/65
- Calls Watts a "disaster area" 8/65
- Welcomes refugees from Cuba 10/65
- Talks with South Vietnamese premier 2/66
- Holds talks with Indira Gandhi 3/66
- Urges firearms curbs 8/66
- Pays surprise visit to Vietnam 10/66
- Visits Seoul 11/66
- Undergoes surgery 11/66
- Announces inquiry into urban riots 7/67
- Authorises bombing targets in N. Vietnam 8/67
- Says war protests do not aid peace 11/67
- Visits Vietnam's Cam Ranh Bay 12/67
- Will not seek re-election as President 3/68
- To send up to 50,000 troops more to Vietnam 3/68
- Signs Civil Rights Bill 4/68
- To end some bombing of North Vietnam 5/68
- Warns USSR not to intervene in Rumania 8/68
- To halt bombing of North Vietnam 10/68
- Orders total end to North Vietnam bombing 11/68
- Dies 1/73

Johnson, Philip 12/59
Johnson, Rafer 6/68
Johnson, Tom 8/27
Johnson, William 7/23
Johnston, Brian 1/94
Johnston, Edward 12/34
Johnston, Willie 6/78
Jolson, Al 9/28, 10/50
Jones, A.G. 4/29
Jones, Allen 12/61
Jones, Ann 7/69
Jones, Bobby 6/26, 6/30, 9/30, 11/30, 12/71
Jones, Brian 5/67, 10/67, 12/67, 7/69
Jones, Bryn 8/38
Jones, Casey 4/00
Jones, Jim 11/78
Jones, Michael 7/92
Jones, Peter 4/90
Jones, Spike 5/64
Jones, Steve 4/85
Jones, Tom 12/67
Joplin, Janis 10/70
Joplin, Scott 4/17
Jordan
- See also Palestinians
- Expected to fight Israel 5/48
- Signs cease-fire with Israel 3/49
- Annexes Arab Palestine 4/50
- King Abdullah shot near Jerusalem mosque 7/51
- State of emergency; Emir Naif is Regent 7/51
- Schoolboy Hussein succeeds Talal as King 8/52
- King Hussein crowned 5/53
- 56 die as Israel attacks three villages 10/53
- Sets neutral zone, Jerusalem, with Israel 4/55
- Anti-US rioters burn American hospital 1/56
- King Hussein sacks Glubb Pasha from army 3/56
- Hussein bows to Nasser Arab nationalism 3/56
- Ten killed in Israeli raids 9/56
- UK plans to withdraw in six months 2/57
- King Hussein fires Premier Nabulsi 4/57
- King foils Nasser-style coup by Nuwar 4/57
- King confronts rebels personally 4/57
- Ibrahim Hashem forms pro-Western regime 4/57
- Martial law imposed 4/57
- Hussein flies to Saudi Arabia for talks 4/57
- Closes Cairo embassy 6/57
- Egyptian radio calls for Hussein's death 11/57
- Agrees to unite with Iraq; US approves 2/58
- UK promises Jordan paratroopers 6/58
- UK paratroopers come to help Hussein 7/58
- Hussein severs relations with UAR 7/58
- Fears Iraqi troops massing on border 7/58
- Dissolves union with Iraq 8/58
- Syria seals border 8/58
- UK paratroopers start leaving 10/58
- Last British troops leave 11/58
- Premier Majali assassinated with bomb 8/60
- Vote of no confidence in Hussein 4/63
- Hussein dissolves parliament 4/63
- Signs military alliance with UAR 5/67
- Israel triumphant in Six-day War 6/67
- Repatriation scheme for Arab refugees 8/67
- Israeli raiders blow up bridges 12/68
- Army attacks guerrillas in Amman 8/70
- Palestinians blow up three hijacked jets 9/70
- Truce between army and PLO 9/70
- PLO evicted from strongholds 9/70
- Hussein escapes assassination attempt 9/70
- Palestinian guerrillas control Irbid 9/70
- Army deports 384 Palestinian guerrillas 1/71
- Attack launched on Palestinian guerrillas 7/71
- Syria breaks off relations 8/71
- Ambassador to UK escapes attack, London 12/71
- Egypt cuts ties 4/72
- Palestinian prisoners freed in amnesty 9/73
- King Hussein in USA for peace talks 4/77
- Mubarak visits 10/84
- Closes its border with Iraq 8/90

Jordan, Colin 10/63
Jorden, William 9/78
Josef, Archduke of Hungary 8/19
Joseph, Helen 12/92
Joseph, Keith 11/72, 9/74, 10/74, 2/80, 1/81, 6/84, 5/86
Josephson, Brian 12/73
Jouhard, Edmond 4/61, 3/62, 5/62, 6/62, 11/62
Jouhaux, Leon 6/36
Joulwan, George 10/93
Jouret, Luc 10/94
Jouvet, Louis 8/47
Jovanovic, Vladislav 1/92
Jowitt, William 7/29, 3/42, 10/44
Joxe, Louis 3/62
Joyce, James 12/22, 1/41
Joyce, William
- See Haw-Haw, Lord 1/40

Juan Carlos, King of Spain 1/55, 7/69, 7/74, 10/75, 11/75, 8/76, 2/81, 4/86
Juantorena, Alberto 7/76
Juliana, Queen of the Netherlands 4/09, 10/47, 9/48, 12/49, 11/70, 2/76, 1/80
Jumblatt, Kamal 3/77
Jumblatt, Walid 12/82, 1/87
Jung, Carl Gustav 12/12, 6/61
Jungwirth, Stanislav 7/57
Junkers, Hugo 6/24

K

Kadar, Janos 5/12, 11/56, 12/56, 8/62, 5/89, 7/89
Kafka, Franz 6/24, 12/26
Kagan, Joseph 5/76
Kaganovitch, Lazar 7/57
Kahanamoku, Duke 7/22
Kahane, Meir 4/82
Kahil, Kamal 4/95
Kahr, Gustav von 11/23
Kaifu, Toshiki 8/89, 2/90
Kalinin, Mikhael 1/38
Kaltenbrunner, Ernst 10/46
Kamenev, Leon 1/24, 5/24, 10/32, 12/34, 8/36
Kamerlingh Onnes, Heike 12/11
Kammersgaad, Jenny 7/38
Kampuchea
- See Cambodia

Kandinsky, Wassily 12/10, 12/11, 12/26, 12/33, 12/44
Kania, Stanislaw 9/80, 11/80, 10/81
Kao-kang 4/55
Kaplan, Joseph 10/57
Kapp, Wolfgang 3/20, 4/20
Karadzic, Radovan 1/92
Karageorgevitch, Peter 6/03
Karajan, Herbert von 4/08, 6/56, 7/89
Karamanlis, Constantine 10/55, 4/57, 3/58, 7/74, 11/74
Karami, Rashid 9/75, 4/85, 6/87
Karas, Anton 12/49
Karl, Emperor of Austria-Hungary 3/17, 4/18, 11/18, 10/21, 4/22
Karloff, Boris 2/69
Karmal, Babrak 12/79
Karolyi, Mihaly 9/17, 11/18, 3/19
Karp, Eugene 2/50
Karpov, Anatoly 5/51, 4/75, 10/78, 11/81, 2/85, 11/85, 10/86, 12/87
Karsavina, Tamara 12/10, 12/14, 12/19
Kasavubu, Joseph 6/60, 9/60, 8/61, 11/65
Kashmir
- Cease-fire in India-Pakistan war 1/49
- Joins India, defying UN ruling 1/57
- Pakistani and Indian troops clash 8/65
- India and Pakistan in border war 9/65
- Police fire on crowds demonstrating for independence 1/90

Kashmir, Maharajah of 10/47
Kasparov, Gary 2/85, 11/85, 10/86, 12/87
Kassim, Abdul 2/63
Katz, Bernard 12/70
Kauffer, E. McKnight 12/34
Kaunda, Kenneth 1/64, 8/64
Kaye, Danny 1/13, 10/47, 3/87
Kazan, Ella 9/09
Kazantzakis, Nikos 10/57
Keating, Paul 12/91, 12/92, 3/93, 12/93
Keating, Tom 12/76, 2/79
Keaton, Buster 12/52, 2/66
Keaton, Diane 12/77, 11/79
Keayo, Sara 10/83
Kee, Robert 12/83
Keeler, Christine 3/63, 6/63, 7/63, 9/63, 12/63, 6/64
Keenan, Brian 8/90
Kefauver, Estes 8/56
Keightley, Charles 11/56
Keino, Kipchoge 9/72
Keir Hardie, James 9/15
Keitel, Wilhelm 5/45, 11/45, 10/46
Kekkonen, Urho 2/56
Keleman, Petrus 10/34
Keller, Helen 9/04, 8/12
Kelley, Oakley 5/23
Kellogg, Frank 12/29
Kellogg, William S. 2/06, 10/38, 10/51
Kelly, Eddie 5/71
Kelly, Gene 10/47, 3/52
Kelly, Gerard 1/86
Kelly, Grace
- See Grace, Princess of Monaco 11/29

Kemal Ataturk
- See Kemal, Mustafa

Kemal, Ismail 12/12
Kemal, Mustafa (Kemal Ataturk) 4/20, 8/20, 8/21, 9/22, 11/22, 10/23, 3/24, 8/26, 4/31, 5/31, 2/33, 11/34, 11/38
Kemp, Peter 2/37
Kempes, Mario 6/78
Kemptner, Thomas 6/92
Kemsley, Lord 12/52
Kendall, Henry 12/90
Kendrew, John 9/58, 12/62
Kennedy, Edward 3/62, 11/62, 11/64, 7/69, 4/70, 8/79, 3/80, 8/80, 12/85, 12/91
Kennedy, Jacqueline (nee Bouvier) 6/53, 9/53, 12/61, 11/63, 1/64, 5/65, 4/68, 10/68, 5/94
Kennedy, John F.
- Born 5/17
- Saves crew of his torpedo boat, Pacific 8/43
- Wins Massachusetts Senate seat 11/52
- Engaged to Jacqueline Bouvier 6/53
- Marries Jacqueline Bouvier: high society 9/53
- Profile: rising young politician 9/53
- In Senate after back surgery 5/55
- Starts bid for vice-presidency 6/56
- Favours Algerian independence 7/57
- Enters Democratic nomination race 1/60
- Nixon and Kennedy favourites after primary 3/60
- Byrd leads Democratic bid to stop him 4/60
- Humphrey leaves race after Kennedy wins 5/60
- Announces idea of "New Frontier" 7/60
- Chosen Democrat candidate with Johnson 7/60
- In first televised presidential debate 9/60
- Wins presidency narrowly 11/60
- Youngest President; wife expecting baby 11/60
- Sworn in as youngest US President 1/61
- Kissinger made national security adviser 2/61
- Increases money and arms for Laos 3/61
- Forms US Peace Corps 3/61
- On Bay of Pigs invasion 4/61
- Holds talks with Harold Macmillan 4/61
- Says US will put first man on moon 5/61
- Summit with Khrushchev in Vienna 6/61
- Briefs Macmillan on Khrushchev summit 6/61
- Calls for increased defence spending 7/61
- In talks with Macmillan 12/61
- Begins Latin American tour 12/61
- Announces more US aid for Vietnam 1/62
- Imposes embargo on Cuban imports 2/62
- Attacked by Barry Goldwater 3/62
- Atmospheric nuclear tests will resume 4/62
- Has talks with Macmillan 4/62
- To send forces to Thailand 5/62
- Given new powers in Cuban crisis 9/62
- Cuban missile crisis 10/62
- Imposes arms blockade of Cuba 10/62
- Says all Cuban missile bases destroyed 11/62
- Lifts blockade of Cuba 11/62
- Clinches deal to sell Polaris to UK 12/62
- Favours emergency phone link with USSR 12/62
- Delivers warning to Cuba 2/63
- Visited by Harold Wilson 4/63
- Gives Churchill honorary US citizenship 4/63
- Sends in troops to quell Alabama riot 5/63
- Praises civil rights demonstrators 5/63
- "Ich bin ein Berliner" speech 6/63
- Second son dies shortly after birth 8/63
- Addresses civil rights marchers 8/63
- Takes control of Alabama's National Guard 9/63
- Signs nuclear test ban treaty 10/63
- Shot dead in Dallas 11/63
- Warren Commission report published 9/64
- Queen Elizabeth dedicates memorial in his honour, UK 5/65
- Memorial unveiled in Dallas 6/70

Kennedy, Joseph 7/34, 12/37, 12/40, 11/69
Kennedy, Paddy 12/71
Kennedy, Robert 11/25, 4/63, 5/63, 0/64, 11/64, 6/65, 3/68, 5/68, 6/68, 4/69
Kennedy, Rose 1/95
Kent, Bruce 10/81, 10/83
Kent, Duke of 10/38, 8/42, 6/61
Kentridge, Sidney 12/77
Kenya
- See also Britain (foreign affairs, Africa)
- Nairobi chosen as capital 5/07
- Stone Age fossils found in Rift Valley 5/44
- Mau Mau take oath to expel whites 8/51
- Mau Mau spreads to Kikuyu in cities 8/51
- Princess Elizabeth leaves UK for tour 1/52
- Elizabeth hears of father's death 2/52
- Curfew on Nairobi Mau Mau oath-takers 8/52
- Chief Warahui denounces Mau Mau; killed 10/52
- UK troops fly in; state of emergency 10/52
- Jomo Kenyatta and 500 Mau Mau arrested 10/52
- 40 murders spawn European Home Guard 10/52
- Kenyatta charged with managing Mau Mau 11/52
- 34 Kikuyu schools closed by British 11/52
- Open Mau Mau rebellion; 2,000 arrested 11/52
- Governor Baring imposes death penalty for Mau Mau oath 1/53
- Settlers demand tough action on Mau Mau 1/53
- Settlers use Samburu to track Mau Mau 1/53
- Troops kill 24 Mau Mau and capture 36 4/53
- Kenyatta sentenced to seven years 4/53
- 1,000 Mau Mau suspects arrested, Nairobi 4/53
- Kikuyu territory sealed off 5/53
- 99 Mau Mau killed by British 7/53
- Britain offers £10 million aid plan 12/53
- Mau Mau's "General China" is captured 1/54
- Seeking Mau Mau surrender; European fear 3/54
- General China used to persuade surrender 3/54
- New plan: 40,000 Mau Mau arrested 4/54
- General China plan fails; intimidation 4/54
- 25,000 Kikuyu rounded up in Nairobi 5/54
- Mau Mau burn down Treetops Hotel 5/54
- Amnesty for Mau Mau; whites angry 1/55
- Mau Mau murder two English schoolboys 4/55
- Mau Mau amnesty withdrawn 6/55
- Nine Mau Mau activists get death sentence 6/55
- 13,000 reported dead in Mau Mau activity 10/55
- 11 Mau Mau detainees die in Hola Camp 7/59
- Richard Leakey finds prehistoric skulls 10/59
- State of emergency ends 11/59
- Africans boycott constitution talks 1/60
- Tom Mboya wins general election 2/61
- Africans agree to join government 4/61
- Kenyatta freed from British custody 8/61
- Kenyatta elected premier 5/63
- National Assembly opens 6/63
- Independence 12/63
- One-party state declared 11/64
- Becomes a republic 12/64
- Asians rush to emigrate to UK 2/68

- Asians' trading licences removed 1/69
- Asian exodus to Britain expected 1/69
- Oginga Odinga arrested 10/69
- Kenya People's Union banned 10/69
- Cancels matches on England's cricket tour 1/70
- Richard Leakey finds oldest human skull 11/72
- 27 die in bus station bomb blast 3/75
- Kenyatta bans big game hunting 5/77
- Jomo Kenyatta, pioneer, dies 8/78
- Author Joy Adamson killed 1/80
- Boycotts Moscow Olympics on Afghanistan 7/80
- Paul Ekai guilty of murdering Adamson 8/81
- Arap Moi crushes junior officer coup 8/82
- 10,000 attend women's rights conference 7/85
- 600 UK troops take AIDS test 1/87
- British woman murdered in game park 10/89
- Daniel arap Moi wins Kenya's first multi-party elections 12/92

Kenyatta, Jomo 10/52, 11/52, 4/53, 4/61, 7/61, 8/61, 5/63, 12/63, 12/64, 10/69, 5/77, 8/78
Kerans, John Simon 7/49, 8/49
Kerbs, Edwin 12/92
Kerensky, Alexander 3/17, 4/17, 7/17, 9/17, 11/17, 6/18, 2/30, 6/70
Kern, Jerome 12/27, 12/28, 12/35
Kerner, Otto 7/67
Kerouac, Jack 12/57, 10/69
Kerr, Bobby 5/73
Kerr, Deborah 12/56
Kerr, John 11/75, 3/91
Kerr, Malcolm 1/84
Kerrigan, Nancy 1/94
Kesselring, Albert 3/45
Keyes, Roger 5/40
Keynes, John Maynard 12/19, 11/29, 12/36, 6/42, 4/43, 4/46
Khachaturian, Aram 6/03, 12/48
Khaled, King of Saudi Arabia 3/75, 6/81, 6/82
Khaled, Leila 9/70
Khalidi, Hussein 11/47
Khalil, Mustafa 11/81
Khalkhali, Ayatollah 10/79
Khama, Seretse 2/50, 3/50, 11/50, 3/52, 7/80
Khamenei, Ali 6/89
Khan, Abdul Gaffar 12/31
Khan, Ali 10/38, 4/50
Khan, Ayub 8/65, 1/66, 3/69
Khan, Gulam Ishaq 8/90
Khan, Imran 3/92
Khan, Reza 2/21
Khan, Yahya 3/69
Khomeini, Ruhollah 6/63, 10/78, 12/78, 1/79, 2/79, 3/79, 4/79, 7/79, 12/79, 3/80, 11/80, 1/81, 6/81, 8/81, 7/82, 7/83, 2/89, 6/89
Khrushchev, Nikita
- Elected Moscow Party chief 3/35
- Replaces Malenkov as First Secretary 3/53
- Profile of K. at time of Stalin's death 3/53
- Elected First Secretary 9/53
- Ousts Malenkov and takes power 2/55
- Restores relations with Tito on visit 5/55
- Announces megaton H-bomb explosion 11/55
- Denounces Stalin at 20th Party Congress 3/56
- Visits UK; demands peaceful co-existence 4/56
- Warsaw talks on Polish and Hungarian unrest 10/56
- Foils coup by "anti-party group" 7/57
- Calls an end US aggression; first Sputnik 10/57
- Deposes Bulganin; now supreme power 3/58
- Backs Nasser; accepts UN summit 7/58
- Claims USSR leads in space race 1/59
- Proposes East-West summit on Berlin 2/59
- "Kitchen debate" with Nixon 7/59
- Diplomatic gaffes in US 9/59
- Wants Spring summit 12/59
- Welcomed on Afghan visit 3/60
- Announces shooting down of U-2 spy plane 5/60
- Denounces Mao as "another Stalin" 6/60
- Heckles Macmillan's speech at UN 9/60
- Quote on "politicians the same all over" 12/60
- Congratulates first man in space 4/61
- On Bay of Pigs invasion 4/61
- Summit with Kennedy in Vienna 6/61
- To increase military spending 7/61
- Banishes Albania from Soviet bloc 10/61
- Sees Benny Goodman concert 5/62
- Pledges to defend China from attack 7/62
- Threatens nuclear war if US attacks Cuba 9/62
- Cuban missile crisis 10/62
- Says USSR has 100 megaton A-bomb 1/63
- Invited by Mao to visit Peking 3/63
- Talks with Castro in Moscow 4/63
- Expresses pride in Tereshkova 6/63
- Split with China now complete 7/63
- On nuclear test ban treaty 8/63
- Dances with Tito in Yugoslavia 8/63
- Says USSR will not race US to the moon 10/63
- Accuses NATO of trying to occupy Cyprus 2/64
- With Nasser, changes course of Nile 5/64
- Admits USSR uses satellites for spying 5/64
- Ousted in Kremlin coup 10/64
- Makes first public appearance in year 6/66
- Dies 9/71

Kidd, Brian 5/68
Kiderlen-Waechter, Alfred von 12/12
Kiesinger, Kurt 12/66, 2/69
Kilbride, John 5/66
Killy, Jean-Claude 2/68
Kim Dae Jung 5/80, 9/80, 1/81, 12/87
Kim Il Sung 9/48, 6/51, 10/80, 7/94
Kim Jong Il 10/80
Kim Yung Sam 12/87
King, B.B. 9/25
King, Billie Jean (nee Moffit) 11/43, 6/62, 7/69, 7/70, 7/71, 7/72, 7/73, 7/74, 7/75, 7/79, 5/81
King, Cecil 1/64
King, Coretta Scott 4/68, 7/77
King, Ernest 6/42
King, Martin Luther 1/29, 3/56, 6/57, 9/58, 2/60, 3/60, 5/60, 7/62, 4/63, 5/63, 8/63, 9/63, 6/64, 7/64, 10/64, 12/64, 2/65, 3/65, 7/65, 6/66, 4/68, 3/69, 1/79
King, Rodney 4/92, 5/92
King, Tom 3/70, 9/85, 11/87, 9/89
King, William Mackenzie 6/26, 9/26, 8/43, 6/45, 7/50
Kingsley, Ben 4/83, 12/83, 3/85
Kinkaid, Thomas 10/44
Kinnock, Neil 6/79, 6/83, 7/83, 10/83, 11/84, 3/87, 6/87, 9/87, 7/88, 10/88, 12/88, 2/89, 6/89, 5/90, 5/91, 7/91, 2/92, 4/92
Kinsey, Alfred 12/48, 8/56
Kinski, Nastassia 12/81
Kipfer, Charles 5/31
Kipling, Rudyard 12/01, 10/02, 12/07, 12/20, 7/26, 1/36
Kirchner, Ernst Ludwig 12/37, 7/38
Kirk, Kent 1/83
Kirkman, Sidney 1/56
Kirkwall
- Nine children involved in sex abuse scandal 4/91

Kirov, Sergei 12/34
Kissinger, Henry 5/23, 2/61, 12/68, 2/72, 10/72, 12/72, 10/73, 4/74, 5/74, 6/74, 9/75, 9/76, 11/76
Kitaj, Roy 12/61
Kitchener, Horatio 5/02, 7/11, 8/14, 5/15, 11/15, 6/16, 3/17
Kitson, David 12/64
Klee, Paul 12/25, 12/26, 12/33, 6/40
Kleiber, Erich 12/33
Kleindienst, Richard 4/73
Klemperer, Otto 12/33
Klimt, Gustav 2/18
Kline, Franz 5/62
Kline, Lindsay 12/60
Klinghoffer, Leon 10/85
Klose, Margarete 8/02
Knatchbull-Hugessen, Hughe 8/37
Knievel, Evel 5/75
Knight, Laura 12/45, 7/70
Knight, Shirley 10/62
Knox, Frank 2/43
Knox-Johnston, Robin 4/69
Koch, Karl 8/37
Koch, Robert 12/05, 5/10
Kodaly, Zoltan 3/67
Kodes, Jan 7/73
Koestler, Arthur 9/05, 12/37, 3/83
Koestler, Cynthia 3/83
Kohl, Helmut 10/82, 3/83, 1/87, 10/88, 6/89, 11/89, 12/89, 6/90, 12/90, 12/91, 6/94
Kokoschka, Oskar 12/37, 2/80
Kokovtsev, Vladimir 9/11
Kolchak, Alexander 10/19, 2/20
Kolehmainen, Hannes 7/12, 8/20
Komarov, Vladimir 4/67
Konduriotis, Admiral 3/24
Kondylis, Georgios 3/35, 11/35
Kong Le 8/60
Koniev, Marshall 2/44, 2/45, 5/55
Konoye, Fumimaro 10/41
Koo, Wellington 6/45
Kooning, Wilhelm de 4/04
Kopechne, Mary Jo 7/69
Korbut, Olga 9/72
Korchnoi, Viktor 7/76, 5/77, 10/78
Korda, Alexander 9/36, 1/56
Korea
- See also Korea, North and South, and Korean War
- Russian fleet's arrival worries Japanese 3/00
- Japanese invade to quell rioting 12/03
- Risks of Russo-Japanese war, Korea 1/04
- Treaty gives Japanese exclusive rights 9/05
- Emperor abdicates; anti-Japanese riots 7/07
- Japanese control; Manchuria for Russia 7/10
- Officially annexed; Japanese clampdown 8/10
- To be partitioned by US and USSR 9/45
- Republic proclaimed in North Korea 2/48
- North claims jurisdiction over all Korea 5/48
- South claims jurisdiction over all Korea 5/48
- North Korea proclaims its independence 9/48

Korea, North
- See also Korea, Korean War
- Republic proclaimed 9/48
- Invades South Korea 6/50
- Accuses US of "barefaced aggression" 7/50
- Armistice signed; war is over 7/53
- United Nations Command leaves 8/54
- US "spy ship" Pueblo seized 1/68
- Refuses to release the Pueblo 2/68
- Crew of US spy ship Pueblo released 12/68
- Kim Jong Il to succeed father, Il Sung 10/80
- Three North Koreans die in UN troops clash 11/84
- Branded a terrorist state by Reagan 7/85
- Pulls out of nuclear Non-Proliferation Treaty 3/93
- President Kim Il Sung dies 7/94

Korea, South
- See also Korea, Korean War
- Republic of Korea proclaimed 9/48
- MacArthur arrives 10/48
- Entry to UN vetoed by USSR 4/49
- Last US combat troops leave 6/49
- Invaded by North Korea 6/50
- Syngman Rhee agrees to armistice 7/53
- Armistice signed; war is over 7/53
- MiG-15 fighter pilot surrenders to US 9/53
- United Nations Command leaves 8/54
- Syngman Rhee elected President 3/60
- Protests against rigged polls; 145 die 4/60
- Cabinet resigns; Syngman Rhee resigns 4/60
- President Po Sun Yun resigns 5/61
- Military coup 5/61
- Martial law declared in Seoul 6/64
- Establishes relations with Japan 6/65
- Syngman Rhee dies 7/65
- LBJ greeted at Seoul 11/66
- Sun Myung Moon marries 790 couples 10/70
- 156 die in hotel fire, Seoul 12/71
- Major airlines threaten Seoul boycott 12/71
- Martial law declared in Seoul 10/72
- President Park's wife shot by assassin 8/74
- 88 die in hotel fire 11/74
- President Park Chung Hee killed 10/79
- Army crushes Kwangju student revolt 5/80
- Protests against arrest of Kim Dae Jung 5/80
- Kim Dae Jung sentenced to death 9/80
- Death sentence on Kim Dae Jung commuted 1/81
- USSR shoots down Korean 747; 269 killed 9/83
- Four ministers killed in bomb blast 10/83
- Anti-government demonstrations in Seoul 5/86
- 35,000 police charge students 2/87
- More anti-regime protests 6/87
- Roh Tae Woo wins election 12/87
- Students riot against "rigged poll" 12/87
- Two Kims split Roh's opposition vote 12/87
- Students battle with police in Seoul 6/88
- Students demonstrate on eve of Olympics 8/88
- Olympic Games 9/88
- 24,000 police protect ex-president 11/88

Korean War
- North Korea invades South Korea 6/50
- Seoul falls to the North Koreans 6/50
- Americans badly mauled in first battle 7/50
- British troops arrive in Korea 8/50
- US attacks North Koreans at Chinju 8/50
- North Koreans make new assault on Taegu 8/50
- Hong Kong infantry to join UN forces 8/50
- UN troops land at Inchon 9/50
- North Koreans attack on 50-mile front 9/50
- US downs Soviet bomber 9/50
- Allies capture Suwon, south of Seoul 9/50
- UN forces recapture Seoul 9/50
- Syngman Rhee returns to Seoul 9/50
- UN troops reach 38th Parallel 9/50
- UN troops capture Pyongyang 10/50
- UN troops push through to Chinese border 10/50
- Chinese enter war 11/50
- Chinese launch assault across Yalu 11/50
- First ever combat between jet fighters 11/50
- Chinese eject UN from Manchurian border 11/50
- Chinese force retreat of UN forces 12/50
- Chinese capture Pyongyang 12/50
- UN forces suffer further setbacks 12/50
- North offensive with China on South 1/51
- China and North Korea invade on New Year's Day 1/51
- Seoul falls to Communists a second time 1/51
- US generals promise to "stay and fight" 1/51
- Wonju falls to Communists; UN fight back 1/51
- UN ships bombard Inchon 1/51
- Communist supply lines badly stretched 1/51
- Chinese cross 38th Parallel into South 1/51
- Chinese capture Seoul 1/51
- Chinese take Wonju with North Koreans 1/51
- Chinese named as aggressors by the UN 1/51
- UN forces push to ten miles outside Seoul 2/51
- South Koreans drive up coastal highway 2/51
- US and UK forces recapture Inchon 2/51
- UN forces take Anyang and Yongdungpo 2/51
- Communists resist outside Seoul 2/51
- South invades North with UN forces 3/51
- Communists surrender Seoul 3/51
- Lieutenant-General Ridgway replaces MacArthur 4/51
- Sacked MacArthur calls Truman "blind" 4/51
- Chinese attack over 50 miles; UN retreat 4/51
- Anzacs and UK repel Chinese, Chunchon 5/51
- Reports of Gloucesters' bravery at Imjin 5/51
- Marshall attacks MacArthur's aggression 5/51
- USSR delegate calls for cease-fire 6/51
- UN forces take Pyongyang 6/51
- Ridgway meets Communists at Kaesong 7/51
- US Admiral Joy and General Nam Il in talks 7/51
- Arranging North-South demilitarised zone 7/51
- Encouraging progress at talks 8/51
- Weather beats first Commonwealth Division 8/51
- Apologies for border incident 8/51
- Informal cease-fire along 38th Parallel 11/51
- Repatriation of prisoners is major obstacle 11/51
- Communists give list of 11,000 prisoners 12/51
- UN say 50,000 prisoners unaccounted for 12/51
- POW row sabotages truce talks; war fears 12/51
- Ridgway wants Red Cross in war camps 12/51
- Freed prisoners must not fight again 2/52
- UN planes down ten Communist MiG planes 4/52
- Ridgway gives Reds final armistice offer 5/52
- Allies bomb and napalm Suan; Red setback 5/52
- US troops kill 30 Red prisoners, Koje 6/52
- 100,000 Chinese troops on the way, claim 6/52
- North's hydro-electric plants bombed 6/52
- UN planes attack Pyongyang 8/52
- 160 US planes attack North Korea, near USSR 9/52
- US Sabre jets patrol "Mig Alley" 9/52
- US Guards kill 52 rioting Chinese PoWs 10/52
- Rocks thrown, bullets fired, Cheju Isle 10/52
- Eisenhower visits front 12/52
- UN and Korean prisoners swapped, Panmunjon 4/53
- Returned Allied prisoners "brainwashed"? 4/53
- 22 UK ex-prisoners return home 5/53
- 30,000 Chinese troops invade South 6/53
- South Korean Rhee agrees to armistice 7/53
- Armistice signed; war is over 7/53
- Truce terms: withdrawals and blockades end 7/53
- PoWs suffer lung disease 8/53

Koresh, David 4/93
Korn, Arthur 10/06
Kornilov, Lavr G. 9/17
Kosygin, Alexei 2/04, 10/64, 6/65, 1/66, 4/66, 7/66, 2/67, 5/68, 9/69, 3/70, 10/71, 10/80, 12/80
Kozlov, Peter 7/06, 10/27
Kramer, Jack 7/47
Kramer, Josef 11/45
Kratochvilova, Jarmila 8/83
Kraus, Werner 9/33
Kray, Charles 5/68, 3/69
Kray, Reginald 1/65, 4/65, 8/66, 5/68, 3/69
Kray, Ronald 1/65, 4/65, 8/66, 5/68, 3/69, 3/95
Kreisky, Bruno 1/11, 12/75, 4/83
Kreisler, Fritz 11/17, 6/27, 12/38
Krenek, Ernst 8/00
Krenwinkel, Patricia 12/69, 3/71
Krenz, Egon 10/89, 11/89, 12/89
Krim, Abdel 7/21, 9/21, 4/26, 5/26, 5/47, 2/63
Kristiansen, Ingrid 4/85, 8/85
Kroger, Helen 1/61
Kroger, Peter 1/61, 10/69
Kropotkin, Peter 2/21
Krosigk, Schwerin von 5/45
Kruchina, Nikolai 8/91
Kruger, Paul 3/00, 10/00, 7/04
Krupp, Friedrich 11/02
Kryuchkov, Vladimir 8/91
Ku Klux Klan
- See USA (race)

Kubrick, Stanley 7/28, 12/71
Kujau, Konrad 5/83
Kumaratunga, Chandrika 11/94
Kun, Bela 2/19, 8/19
Kunetiska, Vik 6/12
Kuropatkin, Aleksei 10/04, 3/05
Kurosawa, Akira 12/52
Kutchuk, Fadil 1/56, 8/60
Kuts, Vladimir 10/54, 9/55, 11/56
Kuwait
- Britain ends protectorate 6/61
- Claimed by Iraq 6/61
- British troops land 7/61
- Entry to UN vetoed by USSR 11/61
- Arab oil producers tighten embargo 11/73
- Arabs end hijack after killing 31 12/73
- Car bomb outside US embassy kills seven 12/83
- US plans to reflag Kuwaiti tankers, Gulf 7/87
- Kuwaiti jumbo hijacked 4/88
- Iraqi troops shoot dead British businessman 8/90
- Iraqi soldiers hold 82 Britons hostage 8/90
- Iraqi forces invade Kuwait 8/90
- Saddam annexes Kuwait into Iraq 8/90
- Thousands flee into Saudi Arabia 9/90
- Kuwaiti citizens offered Iraqi identity cards 11/90
- Operation Desert Storm is launched 1/91
- Iraq releases oil into sea to prevent Allies from landing 1/91
- Allied tanks cross Saudi border 2/91
- Baghdad Radio announces Iraqi army is leaving Kuwait 2/91
- Gulf War officially over 2/91
- Celebrates liberation 2/91
- Sheikh Jaber al-Sabah returns 3/91
- Six sentenced to death for Bush assassination plot 6/94

Kuznetsov, Vasily 9/68
Ky, Nguyen Cao 6/65, 2/66, 9/67
Kyprianos, Bishop of Kyrenia 3/56

L

LaBianca, Leon 12/69, 3/71, 3/71
Labour Party (Britain)
- See Britain (politics) and Britain (labour)

Lacoste, Rene 7/32, 2/63
Ladd, Alan 1/64
Lafargue, Paul 11/11
La Follette, Robert M. 6/12
Lagaillarde, Pierre 1/60
La Guardia, Fiorello 12/33, 9/47
Laing, R.D. 8/89
Laingen, Bruce 1/81
Laker, Freddie 2/66, 6/77, 9/77, 6/78, 2/82
Laker, Jim 8/53, 5/56, 7/56, 4/86
Lamarr, Hedy 11/15, 1/66
Lamb, Henry 12/11
Lambe, John 3/81
Lambert, Constant 12/31, 8/51
Lamborghini, Ferruccio 2/93
Lambros, Spiridon 10/16
Lambton, Antony 5/73
Lamont, Norman 1/91, 3/91, 4/93, 5/93
Lamour, Dorothy 4/41, 2/46
La Motta, Jake 2/51
Lamplugh, Suzy 7/86
Lancaster, Burt 11/13, 8/63, 6/81, 10/94
Land speed records
- Malcolm Campbell's Bluebird hits 174 mph 2/27
- Near disaster in Campbell record bid 2/27
- Segrave breaks the 200 mph barrier 3/27
- Campbell hits 206.3 mph, Daytona 2/28
- Frank Lockhart injured in attempt 2/28
- Major Segrave's Golden Arrow hits 231 mph 3/29
- Campbell achieves 245 mph in Blue Bird 2/31
- Campbell reaches 253.4 mph 2/32
- Campbell's Blue Bird hits 272 mph 3/33
- Campbell sets speed of 276.8 mph 3/35
- Campbell breaks 300 mph barrier 9/35
- Campbell survives burst tyre to succeed 9/35
- George Eyston overturns Cobb's record 9/38
- Briton John Cobb: 394 mph 9/47
- Malcolm Campbell dies in speed crash 1/49
- Donald Campbell tests new Bluebird car 7/60
- "Bluebird" crashes at 350 mph 9/60
- Craig Breedlove (US): 407.45 mph 8/63
- Donald Campbell (UK): 403.1 mph 7/64
- Craig Breedlove (US): 526.28 mph 10/64

Landon, Alfred 6/36
Landru, Henri "Bluebeard" 12/21
Landsbergis, Vitautas 3/90
Landsteiner, Karl 11/00
Landy, John 7/57
Lane, Allen 12/35, 11/60, 7/70
Lane, Elizabeth 10/62, 8/65
Lang, Cosmo (Archbishop) 12/36, 5/37
Lang, Fritz 1/26, 12/33, 8/76
Lang, Julia 12/50
Lange, David 8/89
Lange, Dorothea 8/36
Lange, Gunnar 11/59
Langer, Bernhard 9/91
Langley, Samuel 10/03
Langtry, Lillie 4/00, 6/02, 2/29
Lansbury, George 2/09, 9/21, 10/32, 10/35
Lansdorf, Hans 12/39
Lansing, Robert 6/15, 8/15
Lanza, Mario 10/59

Laos
- See also Indochina, Vietnam War
- Thailand returns annexed areas 11/46
- Independence 7/49
- France recognises royalist regime 2/50
- UK and US recognise royalist regime 2/50
- Communist revolt starts 7/59
- US denies bases 8/59
- Communist rebels Pathet Lao launch attack 9/59
- Captain Kong Le leads coup 8/60
- Prince Souvanna to rule; new neutrality 8/60
- Alleges North Vietnam invasion; calls UN 12/60
- US steps up military and financial aid 3/61
- Communist guerrillas capture Nam Tha 5/62
- Coalition government installed 7/62
- New leader in aid talks with US 7/62
- Army coup ousts Prince Phouma 4/64
- Attacked by North Vietnamese 12/67
- US escalates bombing raids 11/69
- US bombs Ho Chi Minh trail 3/70
- US plane with secret equipment shot down 12/70
- South Vietnamese attack 2/71
- Two sides sign pact aiming to end war 2/73
- US resumes bombing campaign 4/73
- North Vietnamese Army sweeps through 1/75

Laporte, Pierre 10/70
La Passionara
- See Ibarruri

Lapsley, John 3/67
Lara, Brian 4/94
Larionov, Michel 5/64
Larkin, Philip 12/71, 12/85, 12/92
La Rocca, Nick 12/19
Laroche, Baroness de 3/10
Laroche, Guy 2/89
Larsen, Jens 2/83
Larwood, Harold 1/33
Lasdun, Denys 12/63, 10/76
Lasker, Emanuel 3/21
LaStarza, Roland 9/53
Latvia
- See also USSR
- Joins League of Nations 9/21
- Karlis Ulmanic is new dictator 5/34
- Votes to becomes part of USSR 7/40
- Votes for independence from Moscow 5/89

Lauda, Niki 10/75, 10/77, 10/84
Lauder, Harry 12/12, 11/27, 2/50
Laughton, Charles 12/29, 9/36, 12/39, 12/47, 12/59, 12/62
Laurel, Stan 12/32, 8/57, 2/65
Laurence, Tim 12/92
Laval, Pierre 1/31, 2/32, 1/34, 1/35, 6/35, 12/35, 1/36, 7/40, 12/40, 8/41, 4/42, 6/42, 7/42, 8/42, 11/42, 8/44, 7/45, 10/45
Lavasani, Abbas 5/80
Laver, Rod 7/59, 7/60, 7/61, 7/62, 9/62, 7/68, 9/69
Law (international)
- See also United Nations
- International inquiry blames Russia for Dogger Bank incident 2/05
- Copyright breach by gramophone recordings 2/05
- Second International Peace Conference 6/07
- International High Court proposed 8/07
- The Hague ruling; powers must declare war 9/07
- International Court plan goes public 10/07
- Treaty guarantees North Sea status quo 4/08
- Germany against disarmament talks, The Hague 8/08
- Carnegie wants world disarmament talks 6/09
- Germany threatens all ships off the coast of Britain 2/15
- League decides on International Court of Justice 2/20
- Permanent Court of Justice, The Hague 2/22
- US to join International Court, The Hague 10/22
- Harding urges US membership of International Court 2/23
- Senate rejects International Court plan 3/23
- Senate says join International Court 1/26
- Germany joins International Arbitration 9/27
- 48 countries sign Geneva Convention 7/29
- Britain joins International Court 9/29
- The Hague questions Austro-German pact 5/31
- Before verdict, Austria leaves pact 8/31
- 60 nations at Geneva disarmament talks 2/32
- France wants international police force 2/32
- The Hague Court settles Franco-Swiss dispute 6/32
- The Hague declares Greenland Danish 4/33
- Britain and France to settle islands row 12/51
- Human Rights Court backs "Sunday Times" 4/79
- UK wrong to sack non-union railwaymen 8/81
- Strasbourg bans corporal punishment of children 2/82
- World court opposes US action, Nicaragua 5/84
- European Court condemns UK phone-tapping 8/84
- UK found guilty of immigration sex bias 5/85
- Reagan's aid to Contras ruled illegal 6/86
- "Yorkshire Ripper's" wife awarded £600,000 in libel suit 5/89
- Damages awarded to Sonia Sutcliffe is overturned on appeal 5/89
- Andreas Papandreou tried on fraud charges 9/89
- Lord Aldington awarded £1.5 million in libel case 11/89
- Three businessmen found guilty in Guinness scandal 8/90
- Winnie Mandela goes on trial for kidnapping 2/91
- "Birmingham Six" murder convictions declared unsatisfactory 2/91
- First man convicted in England of raping his wife 4/91
- William Kennedy Smith acquitted of rape 12/91
- Mike Tyson gets six years for rape 3/92
- Jury acquits Los Angeles policemen accused of beating youth 4/92
- US pilots found responsible for deaths of 9 British troops 5/92
- 12-year-old Florida boy wins divorce from parents 9/92

Lawler, R.H. 6/50
Lawler, Wallace 6/69
Lawrence, David Herbert 12/21, 7/29, 12/29, 3/30, 12/60
Lawrence, Ernest 12/39
Lawrence, Gemma 8/90
Lawrence, Gertrude 12/30
Lawrence, Pethick, Mr and Mrs 3/12
Lawrence, Ruth 7/85
Lawrence, Susan 9/21
Lawrence, Thomas Edward 6/16, 10/16, 10/18, 5/35, 7/35
Lawson, Nigel 9/70, 6/83, 7/83, 11/84, 11/86, 6/88, 11/88, 10/89
Lawther, Will 11/43
Laycock, Robert 4/58
Leach, Henry 4/82
League of Nations
- President Wilson moots peace league 5/16
- Wilson's speech; 27 states accept League 2/19
- Covenant to give small states autonomy 2/19
- Headquarters at Geneva, Switzerland 4/19
- Germany condemns League as pro-Allied 6/19
- Port of Fiume taken by poet d'Annunzio 9/19
- Wilson on pro-League peace tour of US 9/19
- First meeting; US boycott 1/20
- Council meets at St. James's Palace, London 2/20
- US Senate disagrees over membership 2/20
- Says Turkey must have no army 2/20
- Final attempt at US membership fails 3/20
- Restricts Turkey to Anatolia 3/20
- Gives Britain Palestine mandate 4/20
- Germany to pay three billion marks a year 4/20
- US Senate rejects Armenian mandate 5/20
- Britain rejects Armenian mandate 6/20
- Permanent Court of Justice, The Hague 6/20
- Candidate Harding wants US to join 9/20
- Approves Belgium's German annexations 9/20
- 41 nations at first full session 11/20
- Decides to help Armenia 11/20
- China and Austria admitted 12/20
- US President Harding rejects League 4/21
- Baltic states join 9/21
- To confirm British Palestine mandate 5/22
- Lloyd George proposes world disarmament 7/22
- Approve British Palestine and French Syria 7/22
- Nicaragua cannot afford membership 9/22
- Ireland is admitted 9/23
- Gives Memel to Lithuania 5/24
- Drafts anti-war protocol 9/24
- Germany wishes to join 9/24
- War outlawed using economic sanctions 10/24
- 47 members agree on compulsory arbitration 10/24
- Leon Bourgeois, first President, dies 9/25
- Forces Greeks to withdraw from Bulgaria 10/25
- Temporary settlement, Iraq-Turkey border 12/25
- German application 2/26
- Poland asks to join 2/26
- Refuses Germany permanent seat 3/26
- Brazil leaves; Spain also considers leaving 6/26
- Votes to admit Germany 9/26
- Rejects Spain's wish for permanent seat 9/26
- Spain leaves League 9/26
- To control German rearmament 1/27
- Canada elected to Council 9/27
- 23 members vote to accept Kellogg-Briand 9/28
- Peace plea in Uruguay-Bolivia fighting 12/28
- Britain ratifies anti-gas war protocol 4/29
- Briand speaks of united Europe at League 9/29
- Briand's utopian vision not shared 9/29
- Debates Saarland question 9/30
- Condemns Poland over German minority 1/31
- Nazis want Germany to withdraw 2/31
- Britain wants Austro-German pact review 3/31
- Fails to get Japanese to leave Manchuria 1/32
- Turkey becomes 56th member 7/32
- Japan blamed for breaking Chinese treaty 10/32
- Iraq is independent; joins League 10/32
- Japan storms out after Manchuria blame 2/33
- Jewish organisations ask League for aid 7/33
- USSR ready to join League, reports 5/34
- Council accepts USSR 9/34
- Italy rejects arbitration on Abyssinia 12/34
- Council ignores Abyssinia's request 1/35
- Decides to return Saar to Germany 1/35
- Debates Abyssinia issue 2/35
- Paraguay quits 2/35
- Condemns militarised Germany 4/35
- Abyssinia wants special League meeting 5/35
- Appoints five-power Abyssinian committee 9/35
- Grants Italy land and privileges in Abyssinia 9/35
- Arms embargo on Italy 10/35
- Germany officially leaves League 10/35
- Sanctions against Italy take effect 11/35
- Italy to quit if sanctions continue 11/35
- Threatens Italy with oil embargo 3/36
- Eden protests about Italian mustard gas 4/36
- Italians bombing Red Cross and civilians 4/36
- Haile Selassie's address; Italy angry 6/36
- Drops Abyssinia; stops Italian sanctions 7/36
- Grants Abyssinia a seat 9/36
- Condemns Japanese invasion of China 9/37
- Viscount Cecil wins Nobel Peace 12/37
- Italy leaves 12/37
- Spain leaves 5/39
- USSR expelled 12/39
- Replaced by United Nations 4/45
- Dissolved 4/46

Leakey, Louis 5/44, 2/61, 10/72
Leakey, Mary 2/78
Leakey, Richard 11/72
Lean, David 12/45, 12/46, 12/48, 12/49, 2/58, 4/66, 4/91
Leary, Timothy 8/67
Lebanon
- Created a state by France 9/20
- Druze rebels threaten Beirut 11/25
- Independence declared 11/43
- French troops arrest the government 11/43
- Government freed; President reinstated 11/43
- Declares war on Germany 2/45
- Signs security pact with Egypt 6/50
- World's longest pipeline completed 10/50
- US Sixth Fleet at Beirut 4/57
- Clashes with Syrian troops at border 9/57
- Wants US to stop UAR arms to rebels 6/58
- US troops land in Beirut to aid Chamoun 7/58
- 30 die in street clashes 9/58
- Last US troops leave 10/58
- 400 arrested in anti-government plot 1/62
- UK correspondent Kim Philby has vanished 3/63
- PLO and Lebanese agree on cease-fire 11/69
- Israelis withdraw after 32-hour raid 5/70
- PFLP hostages exchanged for Leila Khaled 9/70
- Israeli troops cross the border 2/71
- Top Syrians captured in Israeli raid 6/72
- Israelis bomb ten guerrilla bases 9/72
- Israelis attack guerrilla bases 10/72
- 40 die in Israeli raid 4/73
- Army and Palestinian guerrillas in civil war 5/73
- 16 die when Israel attacks refugee camps 6/74
- Christians fight Palestinians; 90 die 4/75
- President Franjieh fears a split army 4/75
- 40 die in Beirut street fighting 6/75
- Moslems fight Christians in Beirut 9/75
- Karami keeps army away from Palestinians 9/75
- Syria-sponsored peace accord 1/76
- Palestinians attack east Beirut 1/76
- Christians massacred in Damour 1/76
- Moslem troops desert army; want more say 1/76
- 30th cease-fire ends; artillery in Beirut 5/76
- Syrians and Moslems turn on Palestinians 6/76
- US envoy Francis Meloy and aide killed 6/76
- US evacuates 263 citizens 6/76
- Death toll at 40,000 8/76
- "Black September" leader Salameh is dead 10/76
- Druze leader Kamal Jumblatt assassinated 3/77
- Israeli planes raid; 68 killed 11/77
- 7,000 Israeli troops invade south 3/78
- UN troops at Litani River 3/78
- Israel to withdraw troops 4/78
- Israelis withdraw 6/78
- 22 die as Syrians clash with Christians 7/78
- Bomb kills Abu Hassan, Olympics suspect 1/79
- Israeli jets bomb Beirut; 150 die 7/81
- Israel calls cease-fire with PLO 7/81
- Bomb kills 50 in PLO Beirut office 10/81
- Israeli jets bomb after London attack 6/82
- Israel's land, sea and air invasion 6/82
- Israelis outside Beirut, tell PLO to go 6/82
- Israeli gunboats and planes bomb Beirut 7/82
- Israelis raid West Beirut for 11 hours 8/82
- PLO begin evacuation 8/82
- Christian Bashir Gemayel is President 8/82
- PLO leader Arafat leaves after 12 years 8/82
- Sabra and Chatila massacre of Palestinians 9/82
- President-elect Bashir Gemayel killed 9/82
- Amin Gemayel, Bashir's brother, sworn in 9/82
- Christians kill hundreds; Israel blamed 9/82
- US Marines act as Beirut peace-keepers 9/82
- UK, US, France and Italy send troops 12/82
- Druze leader Jumblatt escapes bomb 12/82
- US Embassy destroyed by car bomb 4/83
- Western forces are attacked in Beirut 8/83
- US troops return fire for first time 8/83
- 299 die in Shia kamikaze raids 10/83
- US Marines to remain 10/83
- Suicide bomber kills 39 Israeli troops 11/83
- PLO forced to evacuate 12/83
- Lorry bomb kills 15 French troops 12/83
- US University head murdered by gunmen 1/84
- Peace-keeping force pulls out 2/84
- Curfew imposed as civil war erupts 2/84
- 500 civilians evacuated 2/84
- Opposition leaders reject reconciliation 2/84
- Rebel army troops join Shi'ito and Druze 2/84
- USSR vetoes idea of UN force in Beirut 2/84
- Peace conference opens in Geneva 3/84
- Army tears down Green Line barricades 7/84
- 40 killed by Islamic suicide bomber 9/84
- US and UK ambassadors wounded 9/84
- Beirut car bomb kills 62 3/85
- 12 Israeli soldiers killed by lorry 3/85
- Shia Moslems win control of West Beirut 4/85
- Sunni PM Rashid Karami resigns 4/85
- New Shi'ite assault on refugee camps 5/85
- East Beirut car bomb kills over 50 5/85
- Shias free 39 TWA hostages after 16 days 6/85
- Beirut car bomb kills 52 6/85
- Beirut car bomb kills 50, injures 120 8/85
- Three British hostages murdered 4/86
- Terry Waite secures UK hostage release 11/86
- UK Church envoy Waite kidnapped, Beirut 1/87
- Shi'ites attack UN relief lorries 2/87
- Cutting reports starving Beirut camp 2/87
- Waite "under arrest" 2/87
- Syrians break Amal siege of Chatila camp 4/87
- 800 died in camps war since November 4/87
- Premier Karami killed by helicopter bomb 6/87
- Oxfam officials seized in Beirut 3/88
- Bomb explodes in Beirut, killing 54 4/88
- Israeli troops advance towards Syrian 5/88
- Amal and Hizbollah groups sign pact 1/89
- Four Palestinians killed in ambush on Israeli border 3/89
- General Aoun vows to drive Syrians out of Lebanon 3/89
- Christian areas suffer worst attacks in 14 years 4/89
- Jackie Mann is abducted 5/89
- Arab terrorists claim retaliation murder of US hostage 7/89
- Terrorists lift threat to kill hostage 8/89
- Cease-fire begins between Lebanese army and Syrians 8/89
- Gen. Michel Aoun abandons "war of liberation" against Syria 9/89
- President Moawad is assassinated 11/89
- Elias Hrawi becomes President 11/89
- Eleven children die in attack on school bus 4/90
- Second US hostage is freed 4/90
- Eleven people die in Israeli air raid 7/90
- Irish hostage Brian Keenan released 8/90
- Longest-held British captive, John McCarthy, is released 8/91
- Two Western hostages are released 11/91
- Terry Anderson is last of US hostages to be freed 12/91
- Last of Western hostages freed in Beirut 6/92
- 150,000 flee Israeli bombardment 7/93
- Israeli soldiers killed on patrol 8/93

Lebrun, Albert 5/32
Le Carre, John 12/79
Leclerc, Jacques 8/44
Leclerc, Philippe 1/43, 1/47, 11/47
Lecocq, Alexandre Charles 10/18
Lecointe, Sadi 1/23
Le Corbusier (Charles Jeanneret) 12/23, 12/38, 12/59, 8/65
Le Duc Tho 12/72, 1/73
Lee Bum Suk 10/83
Lee Kuan Yew 8/65
Lee, Bruce 7/73
Leeson, Nick 3/95
Leger, Fernand 10/12, 8/55, 12/55
Leguia, Augusto 8/30
Lehar, Franz 10/48
Lehmann, Rosamund 12/90
Leigh, Janet 6/60
Leigh, Vivien 11/13, 5/35, 12/39, 3/40, 9/51, 12/51, 3/52, 3/53, 12/60, 7/67, 7/89
Leigh-Pemberton, Robin 5/91
Lekhanya, Justin 1/86
Lemass, Sean 1/65
Lemieux, Robert 10/70
LeMond, Greg 7/86
Lendl, Ivan 7/86, 7/87
Lenglen, Suzanne 7/19, 7/20, 7/21, 7/22, 7/23, 2/26
Lenihan, Brian 10/90, 11/90
Lenin, Vladimir Ilyich
- Leads new Bolsheviks 11/03
- Returns to Russia in sealed train 4/17
- Wants Bolsheviks to rule Russia alone 6/17
- Uprising fails; Lenin flees to Finland 7/17
- Returns to Petrograd; plans uprising 10/17
- Overthrows Russian government, Petrograd 11/17
- Offers armistice to Austro-Germans 11/17
- Peace talks with Germany, opposed by Trotsky 12/17
- Consolidates power, dissolves Duma 1/18
- Wants peace at any cost; Trotsky opposes 2/18
- Red Army faces threats on all fronts 6/18
- Survives assassination attempt by Dora-Kaplan 8/18
- Calls for European revolution; Comintern 3/19
- Promises democratic parliament and to pay debts 2/20
- Survives assassination attempt 10/20
- Shocked by Kronstadt mutiny 2/21
- Allows private trade 3/21
- Appeals for Western famine aid 8/21
- Doctor's examination 3/22
- Suffers a stroke 5/22
- Rumours circulate that he is dying 1/23
- Says Stalin is rude and should go 1/23
- Massive stroke, quits; succession fears 3/23
- Dies after long illness 1/24

Lennon, John 10/63, 10/65, 8/67, 10/68, 11/68, 3/69, 4/70, 12/70, 12/80, 8/81
Lennox-Boyd, Alan 2/56, 7/59
Leonard, Graham 2/87
Leone, Giovanni 6/78
Leonev, Alexei 3/65, 7/75
Leonidas 6/38
Leopold II, King of Belgium 11/07, 2/08, 12/09
Leopold III, King of Belgium 9/01, 2/34, 5/40, 6/44, 6/45, 1/46, 2/50, 3/50, 7/50, 6/51, 7/51
Leopold, Nathan 5/24
Le Pen, Jean-Marie 11/76, 3/86, 5/88
Lerner, Alan P. 4/58
Leroux, Georges 9/15
Lesnevich, Gus 5/46, 7/48
Lesotho
- South African editor Woods flees here 1/78
- 41 die in South African raid on bases 12/82
- South Africa imposes a blockade 1/86
- Justin Lekhanya seizes power in coup 1/86
- Pope's visit marred by bus hijack 9/88
- Riots when King dissolves democratic government 8/94

Lessing, Doris 10/19, 3/50
Lester, Richard 7/64
Letchworth
- Britain's first "garden city" 12/03

Lettow Vorbeck, Paul von 11/14
Le Van Vien 4/55
Lever, Harold 4/72
Levi, Carlo 11/02
Levi-Strauss, Claude 11/08
Levin, Bernard 12/62
Levingston, Roberto 3/71
Lewanyika, Chief of the Barotse 8/14
Lewis, Carl 8/83, 8/84, 9/88, 8/91
Lewis, Hayley 1/90
Lewis, Jerry Lee 5/58
Lewis, John 11/40, 12/58, 2/63
Lewis, Sinclair 12/20, 1/51
Lewis, Thomas 11/09, 6/12
Lewis, Wyndham 12/11, 6/14, 12/14
Ley, Robert 6/33, 10/37
Leygues, Georges 9/20, 1/21
Lhote, Andre 1/62
Li Peng 6/89
Li Poa-Chen 3/27
Li Yuan-Hung 10/11, 6/23
Liberace 12/54, 6/59, 2/87
Liberal Party (Britain)
- See Britain (politics)

Liberia
- 13 ex-ministers killed by firing squad 4/80
- President Samuel Doe offers resignation 7/90
- US Marines rescue US citizens stranded in civil war 8/90
- President Samuel Doe is murdered 9/90

Libya
- France cedes it to Italy's influence 12/00
- Turkey cedes it to Italy, peace treaty 10/12
- 100 tribesmen clash with Italians 1/28
- Formed from Tripoli, Cyrenaica and Fezzan 1/35
- Granted independence by UN 11/50
- King proclaims independence with UN help 12/51
- 300 die in earthquake 2/63
- Gadaffi throws out king and takes power 9/69
- US recognises Gadaffi regime 9/69
- Gadaffi nationalises foreign banks 11/69
- Gadaffi becomes premier 1/70
- Joins federation with Syria and Egypt 9/71
- BP's holdings in Libya nationalised 12/71
- Withdraws all her deposits from UK banks 12/71
- Is giving aid to IRA 6/72
- Federation with Egypt planned 8/72
- Libyan airliner shot down by Israel 2/73
- Gadaffi withdraws his resignation 7/73
- Signs unification treaty with Tunisia 1/74
- Cairo refuses to return 40 planes 8/74
- 500 Egyptian troops arrested 8/74
- Japanese terrorists from Malaysia arrive 8/75
- US embassy attacked and burned 12/79
- Annexes northern strip of Chad 8/83
- WPC Fletcher killed by Libyans, London 4/84
- 30 Libyan diplomats leave UK 4/84
- Gadaffi has sent arms to Sandinistas 9/84
- Terry Waite frees Britons from Libya 2/85
- Branded a terrorist state by Reagan 7/85
- Clashes with US forces in Gulf of Sirte 3/86
- Suspected of planting bomb on TWA plane 4/86
- US launches air strike 4/86
- Gadaffi releases UK "spy" Maxwell 4/87
- US jets down two Libyan MiG-23 fighters off Libyan coast 1/89
- Severs links with IRA in bid to improve relations with UK 6/91
- Two Libyans suspected of Pan Am bombing over Lockerbie 11/91
- UN orders handing over of 2 men linked to Lockerbie bombing 1/92
- PLO leader Yassir Arafat survives plane crash 4/92
- UN imposes air traffic embargo 4/92
- UN imposes sanctions on Libya over Lockerbie suspects 11/93

Lichtenstein, Roy 12/62
Liddell Hart, Basil 1/70
Liddell, Eric 7/24, 12/81
Liddy, Gordon 9/72, 1/73, 4/73, 5/73
Lie, Trygve 1/46, 11/50, 11/52
Liebermann, Max 2/35
Liebknecht, Karl 10/07, 12/14, 5/16, 8/16, 11/18, 1/19, 4/19
Liebknecht, Wilhelm 8/00
Liechtenstein
- Refuses to give vote to women 2/71

Lifar, Serge 4/05
Ligachev, Yegor 11/87
Lill, John 6/70
Limann, Hilla 12/81
Lin Piao 4/69, 11/71, 7/72
Lincoln, Tribich 6/16
Lindbergh, Charles 2/02, 5/27, 6/27, 2/29, 3/32, 5/32, 8/32, 9/34, 2/35, 6/35, 10/38, 11/38, 1/39
Lindemann, Lionel 1/80
Lindsay, Alexander Dunlop 10/38
Lindsay, Hugh 3/88, 6/88
Lindsay, John 7/66, 7/67
Lindsay, Robert 12/91
Lindwall, Ray 8/48
Lineker, Gary 6/86, 9/94
Linklater, Eric 11/74
Linsengen, Alexander von 7/16
Lipchitz, Jacques 5/73
Lippmann, Gabriel 7/06
Lippmann, Walter 1/18, 12/74
Lipton, Marcus 11/55, 7/63
Lister, Joseph 2/12
Liston, Sonny 9/62, 2/64, 5/65, 1/71
Literature
- See December Surveys and individual writers

Lithuania
- Joins League of Nations 9/21
- League gives them Memel 5/24
- Claims Polish Vilna as capital 9/27
- Poland denies it will annex Lithuania 11/27
- Signs treaty with Germany over Memel 1/28
- Agrees to arbitration on Memel 1/28
- Dictator Voldemaras overthrown 9/29
- Renews USSR friendship pact till 1945 4/34
- Memel Germans want to join Reich 12/38
- Memel ceded to Germany 3/39
- Ceded Vilna by USSR 10/39
- Red Army invades 6/40
- Votes to becomes part of USSR 7/40
- Pro-independence party wins state's first free elections 3/90
- Seeks independence from USSR 3/90
- Soviet troops seize Lithuanian rebels 3/90
- Soviet troops open fire on unarmed civilians, killing 13 1/91
- Former Communist reformers win parliamentary majority 11/92

Litterick, Tom 4/75
Littlejohn, Keith 3/74
Littlejohn, Kenneth 8/73, 3/74
Littlewood, Joan 12/56, 12/59, 12/69
Litvinov, Maxim 9/18, 7/30, 10/33, 3/35, 4/35, 5/39, 11/41, 8/43, 12/51
Liu Shao-chi 4/59, 10/59, 4/67, 2/80
Liuzzo, Viola 12/65
Liverpool
- Mourns the victims of Hillsborough football disaster 4/89

Livingstone, Ken 5/81, 12/82
Ljunberg, Lars 12/83
Llano, Quipo del 7/36
Llewellyn, Roddy 2/78, 5/78
Lloyd George (Major) 5/55
Lloyd George, David
- Condemns Boer camp deaths, S. Africa 6/01
- Crowds stop his election rally speech 1/06
- Blasts drink and poverty link 9/06
- Call to destroy House of Lords power 1/07
- Approves Channel ferry plan 10/07
- Appointed Chancellor of the Exchequer 4/08
- Visits Germany and studies pension system 8/08
- Defends suffragettes against charges 10/08
- "People's Budget": taxes for pensions 4/09
- Mocks House of Lords 10/09
- Lords rejects budget; election called 11/09
- Backs women's suffrage 7/10
- Introduces Insurance Bill for ill 5/11
- Suffragette bomb his new house 2/13
- Condemns Europe's arms buildup 1/14
- Boosts supertax in budget 5/14
- Doubles income tax; announces War Loan 11/14
- Promises women equal pay for war work 3/15
- In charge of munitions; increases duties 4/15
- Munitions Minister; drops alcohol tax 5/15
- Calls for TUC war support 8/15
- Prime Minister - pact with Bonar Law 12/16
- Back from Rome talks; War Loan appeal 1/17
- Promises bill for votes for women over 30 3/17
- Condemns German "regime" 7/17
- Gets Chequers as country seat 10/17
- Fights off Asquith attack on war conduct 5/18
- Coalition triumph in "Coupon Election" 12/18
- Cabinet reshuffle; Tories get top posts 1/19
- Excludes Irish from peace talks 4/19
- Versailles: "Squeeze the German lemon" 6/19
- Attacks national rail strikers 8/19
- Announces Irish partition plan 12/19
- Receives French Grand Cross 1/20
- Calls on US to join League 7/20
- Gives ultimatum on German war debt 2/21
- Trade plan to force reparations 3/21
- Invites de Valera and Craig to talks 5/21
- Agrees Irish truce with de Valera 7/21
- Cancels Irish talks; restarted 9/21
- Offers Ireland Free State independence 12/21
- Ends Allied Supreme Council with France 1/22
- Ousted in Tory revolt; new election set 10/22
- Badly beaten in election; Tories rule 11/22
- Stalemate election; has balance of power 5/29
- Premier MacDonald keeps him out 6/29
- Calls for reflation after Wall Street 11/29
- Ends pact with Labour over voting reform 5/30
- Rejects Labour's Reform Bill clause 3/31
- Loses Liberal leadership to Samuel 11/31
- Helps fight heath fire 6/34
- Backs alliance with Russia 5/39
- Congratulations on 80th birthday 1/43
- Retires from Parliament 12/44
- Becomes Earl of Dwyfor 1/45
- Dies - tribute 3/45

Lloyd George, Frances 3/45
Lloyd George, Megan 5/29, 4/39, 3/45
Lloyd Webber, Andrew 12/78, 12/81
Lloyd, Clive 6/75
Lloyd, Frank 4/59
Lloyd, Geoffrey 11/37
Lloyd, Harold 3/71
Lloyd, Marie 12/12, 10/22
Lloyd, Selwyn 9/56, 11/56, 10/57, 3/59, 4/62, 7/62, 4/66
Lloyd, Sir Francis 11/15
Lloyd, W.L. 12/42
Locarno Pact
- Signatories condemn Rhineland occupation 3/36

Locarno, Conference of
- Germany invited 9/25
- Germany promises not to fight France 10/25
- Affirms Versailles borders for Rhineland 10/25
- Britain, France, Belgium and Germany sign 10/25
- German Reichstag approves agreement 11/25

Lock, Tony 8/53
Lock, Trevor 5/80
Locke, Bobby 7/49, 7/50
Lockerbie disaster
- See Disasters (air)

Lockhart, Frank 2/28
Lockwood, Charles 6/73
Lockwood, Margaret 7/90
Lockwood, Stuart 8/90
Lockwood, Virginia 4/47
Lodge, David 12/75
Lodge, Henry Cabot 3/20, 11/52
Loeb, Richard 5/24
Loesser, Frank 7/69
Loewe, Frederick 4/58
Loewe, Fritz 2/88
Lollobrigida, Gina 7/27
Lombard, Carole 1/42
Lon Nol 3/70, 3/73, 2/74, 11/85
Lonardi, Eduardo 9/55, 11/55
London
- Opening of the Hippodrome Theatre 1/00
- 50 a day die from influenza 1/00
- Underground "tube" opens to Bank 6/00
- Telephone system completed 11/01
- Barbican blaze; £1m damage 4/02
- Single dock authority 6/02
- King feeds poor Londoners 7/02
- Streets packed as Edward VII is crowned 8/02
- 82 acres of Earl's Court sold at auction 12/02
- Inquiry into traffic congestion 2/03
- Kew Bridge opened 5/03
- First electric trams 5/03
- Roman city walls discovered 10/03
- Russian Bolsheviks founded at a congress held by exiles 11/03
- Call for smokeless city 3/04
- 3,000 cabbies go on strike 5/04
- More people receive poor relief 11/04
- London's tube goes electric 12/04
- Biggest ever Motor Show in London 2/05
- Typhus outbreak in East End 2/05
- New County Council headquarters plan 4/05
- Electricity bill for the capital 7/05
- First motorised ambulance service: plan 12/05
- Thames burns as surface oil ignites 1/06
- Bakerloo underground line opens 3/06
- Vauxhall Bridge opens 5/06
- Warning of tuberculosis in bad milk 7/06
- "Noisy" buses banned; tram lobby at work 11/06
- Inquiry slams "extravagant" welfare of Poplar's poor 11/06
- Opening of the Piccadilly line 12/06
- Hampstead tube line 6/07
- First house in Hampstead Garden Suburb 10/07
- Anglo-French show at "White City" 5/08
- Rotherhithe Tunnel opened 6/08
- Fire in Moorgate tube 7/08
- Russian robbery chase, Tottenham; three die 1/09
- Opening of Victoria and Albert Museum 6/09
- Shelter for vagrants on the Embankment 11/09
- Labour suffers setbacks in municipal elections 11/09
- Cabbies asking for tips break the law 5/10
- Gas lamps replace electric 8/10
- Sidney Street siege; three anarchists killed 1/11
- City transport co-ordinated 5/11
- King gives fete for 100,000 children 6/11
- 50,000 troops to put down strike march 8/11
- Second most unhealthy city in the world 8/11
- 6,000 cabbies go on strike 11/11
- New London Opera House opens 11/11
- Lord Plymouth buys Crystal Palace 11/11
- Omnibus and Electric Underground to merge 1/12
- Deaths from cold: two per cent each week 2/12
- County Hall begun 3/12
- Plans for University Senate House 3/12
- Wellington monument, Hyde Park Corner 4/12
- Dock strikers march, Trafalgar Square 5/12
- First Underground accident; 22 injured 9/12
- Buckingham Palace Mall front redesigned 10/12
- Woolwich tunnel under Thames 10/12
- Two die in black fog 1/13
- Hyde Park Corner gets 10mph limit 5/13
- Lord Plymouth's gift of Crystal Palace to the nation 12/13
- Earl Grey's plan for Dominion House, Aldwych, approved 4/14
- King Edward VII Gallery, British Museum 5/14
- 300 Germans kept at Kensington Olympia 8/14
- Suffers first Zeppelin raid 5/15
- Attacks on Germans after sinking of Lusitania 5/15
- Women allowed to be bus and tram conductors 10/15
- Museums close for war 1/16
- Queen Mary opens Chelsea Hospital for Women 7/16
- Queen Mary opens women's extensions of School of Medicine 10/16
- First aeroplane bombing; 100 killed 6/17
- Policemen strike; prisoners in taxis 8/18
- 2,225 die in one week from influenza 10/18
- Victory Day: millions throng the streets 11/18
- First London-Paris air service 2/19
- Chelsea win "Victory Cup" football 4/19
- Inquiry into traffic problem 4/19
- Peace Thanksgiving service held at St. Paul's 7/19
- Lutyens' Cenotaph war memorial is unveiled in Whitehall 7/19
- Traffic Board proposed 7/19
- Labour win 14 of 28 boroughs 11/19
- Police get cars instead of horses 2/20
- Queen Alexandra unveils Cavell monument 3/20
- King opens Imperial War Museum housed at Crystal Palace 6/20
- Foreigners barred from council jobs 7/20
- First night bus services 8/20
- Metropolitan Police "Flying Squad" 9/20
- Police motor cycle patrols 4/21
- Protest over arrest of women councillors 9/21
- Poplar Council arrested for rates ban 9/21
- Islington Council blasted for high rates 9/21
- Sir Basil Thompson, police chief, retires 11/21
- Queen opens expanded Victoria Station 3/22
- Labour defeated in Boards of Guardians elections 4/22
- Rockefeller Foundation UK Hygiene School 4/22
- County Hall, new Council headquarters 7/22
- Telephone toll exchange system 9/22
- Port Authority, Tower Hill 10/22
- Imperial Stadium, Wembley 10/22
- Metropolitan Police Commissioner poisoned 11/22
- PC Storey and horse avert Wembley crush 4/23
- New BBC studios at Savoy Hill 5/23
- Tivoli "super-cinema" in Strand 9/23
- Imperial Exhibition 4/24
- Lords discuss proposal to build bridge by St. Paul's 5/24
- Master Builders' Association offers houses 5/24
- Tube strike collapses 6/24
- Prince of Wales at Wembley jamboree 8/24
- Arts Commission warns new bridge may harm St. Paul's 8/24
- Traffic lights in Piccadilly 9/25
- Labour gains in County Council elections 11/25
- Flooding in suburbs 2/26
- One-way traffic, Hyde Park Corner 3/26
- One-way traffic system, Trafalgar Square 4/26
- Circular traffic system, Piccadilly 7/26
- Northern Line extended to Morden 9/26
- Park Lane Hotel opens 1/27
- Plans for Waterloo and Lambeth bridges 5/27
- University buys Bloomsbury site 6/27
- Communist-Fascist clash, Hyde Park 6/27
- Pedestrian guiding signs, Oxford Street 8/27
- Six-wheeled bus on trial 9/27
- Bus profits to subsidise tube losses 10/27
- Public transport to be co-ordinated 10/27
- Hammersmith Council dustmen protest 11/27
- Holborn automatic telephone exchange 11/27
- Telephones: 52 new exchanges planned 1/28
- 14 die in Thames flood; artworks ruined 1/28
- Telephone lines cut by flood 1/28
- Old pub "Chained Swan" demolished 2/28
- Three a day die on roads 9/28
- City Corporation rejects St. Paul's bridge scheme 10/28
- 10,878 private cars in accidents 11/28
- BBC plans £500,000 Portland Place 11/28
- Piccadilly Circus Underground opens 12/28
- US-style traffic lights get go-ahead 5/29
- Mobile radios for Flying Squad cars 7/29
- Traffic lights reduce congestion 9/29
- Red buses chosen 10/29
- First public telephone boxes 12/29
- Five Power Naval Conference 1/30
- Lutyens resigns over new Thames bridge fight 2/30
- British Museum bomb; Indians suspected 2/30
- Police fight unemployed, East End 3/30
- Men and women bathe in Hyde Park Lido 6/30
- India House in Aldwych 7/30
- Building boom; wider streets, new houses 9/30
- Cambridge Theatre opens 9/30
- Plans to unite London Transport 10/30
- 30 injured by stampeding elephant 11/30
- Survey: better education, lower morals 11/30
- Opening of Adelphi Theatre 12/30
- First electric trolley buses 7/31
- Month of strikes and protests at pay cuts 9/31
- Floodlit buildings cause traffic chaos 9/31
- Labour wins only three out of 28 boroughs 11/31
- Courtauld Institute founded 3/32
- King George V opens Lambeth Bridge 7/32
- Street battles; jobless v. police 10/32
- 50,000 protest about unemployment, Hyde Park 2/33
- Mosley Fascists attacked over Jewish issue 4/33
- Installs a set of traffic lights a day 5/33
- London Passenger Transport Board created 7/33
- New bridges: Richmond, Chiswick, Hampton 7/33
- Tower skeletons are examined 11/33
- Battersea Power Station, Giles G. Scott 12/33
- Labour rules London Council for first time 3/34
- Herbert Morrison heads London Council 3/34
- Waterloo Bridge dismantled 6/34
- 18 arrested after clashes between Fascists and anti-Fascists 9/34
- Huge crowds for King's Silver Jubilee 5/35
- Leicester Square tube station 5/35
- Smithfield meat market strike 2/36
- Fighting Blackshirts in Cable Street 10/36
- Crystal Palace burns down; huge crowds 11/36
- Trams give way to trolley buses 11/36
- Margot Fonteyn's ballet debut 1/37
- Horse-drawn traffic banned from West End 1/37
- Labour doubles London Council majority 3/37
- London Council proposes a "green belt" 4/37
- One in four of total population lives in London area 4/37
- National Maritime Museum, Greenwich 4/37
- Ban on East End marches extended 8/37
- 111 arrested for blocking Fascist march 10/37
- Plans for evacuation and air raid shelters 11/37
- Scotland Yard uses dogs 5/38
- Underground crash; six die, 60 hurt 5/38
- Rush for gas masks as war fears grow 9/38
- Free air raid shelters to be provided 2/39
- New Zealand Avenue destroyed by fire 6/39
- Treasures removed from major museums 8/39
- Blitz begins 9/40
- Bomb destroys High Altar in St. Paul's 10/40
- Luftwaffe bombs City of London 12/40
- 100,000 bombs dropped in one night 4/41
- Bomb reduces chamber of House of Commons to rubble 5/41
- Tower of Westminster Abbey falls in; 1,400 civilians die 5/41
- British Museum damaged by incendiaries 5/41
- St. Paul's Cathedral bombed again 5/41
- 20,000 Londoners die in series of Blitz bombings 5/41
- MPs meet in House of Lords 5/41
- The new Waterloo Bridge opens 8/42
- St. Paul's service for victory in Tunisia 5/43
- LCC unveils plans for ring road 7/43
- Mass evacuation as V-1s fall on London 7/44
- V-2s terrorise London 9/44
- Evacuations suspended 9/44
- Lights switched on in some main streets 11/44
- "New towns" and "green belt" planned 12/44
- First boat train for five years leaves for Continent 1/45
- Partial blackout ends 4/45
- First civilian flights from Heathrow 1/46
- Has only a week's supply of coal 2/46
- Princess Elizabeth made City freeman 6/47
- Eros returns to Piccadilly Circus 6/47
- Political marches banned for three months 3/48
- Memorial to Roosevelt unveiled in Grosvenor Square 4/48
- Marches banned for three months 3/49
- Dock strike 7/49
- 64 die when sub sinks in Thames estuary 2/50
- Restored House of Commons opens 10/50
- Festival of Britain; new hopeful spirit 5/51
- First cadets at Metropolitan Police College, Hendon 6/51
- National Theatre founded 7/51
- Festival of Britain ends 9/51
- Crowds pay respects to late King George 2/52
- Labour wins majority of 55 on Council 4/52
- Londoners bid farewell to last tram 7/52
- 112 die as three trains crash, Harrow 10/52
- Eight die in Underground crash 4/53
- Elizabeth II is crowned in Westminster Abbey 6/53
- Billy Graham at Harringay arena 3/54
- Gold Market opens after 15 years 3/54
- 180,000 listen to Billy Graham, Wembley 5/54
- Rationing ends; Smithfield meat boom 7/54
- Kidbrooke School, first comprehensive 9/54
- Victoria to Walthamstow tube planned 2/55
- "Smokeless zone" from October 3/55
- Soho Fair, to improve image 7/55
- Planned £55 million Barbican development 1/56
- Plans for cultural "oasis" at Barbican 5/56

- Indian and New Zealand premiers honoured 7/56
- Plans to redevelop St. Paul's area 7/57
- 92 die in fogbound Lewisham rail crash 12/57
- Mayfair to get parking meters 2/58
- St. Paul's new altar is dedicated as Empire War Memorial 5/58
- Race riots in Notting Hill Gate 9/58
- Tube chiefs warn against strikes 1/59
- £50 million Victoria line underground 2/59
- Crime rate rises by 21 per cent in year 7/59
- House of Fraser buys up Harrods 8/59
- Floods cause chaos 8/59
- LSE recommends new Greater London body 10/59
- Thames flood barrier planned 3/60
- City planners to control high-rises 6/60
- Shell building near Thames 6/60
- "Travelator" on an underground 9/60
- Commission wants Greater London Council 10/60
- Last steam train on London Underground 10/61
- 300-foot blocks of flats for Hammersmith 12/61
- 300-year-old skull dug up in Downing Street 3/62
- Metropolitan Police set up frogman unit 4/62
- Fascists in East End street battles 9/62
- Hyde Park underpass opens 10/62
- 60 die from smog 12/62
- First automatic tube trains 3/63
- First ticket collecting machine on Underground 1/64
- Post Office Tower opens 10/65
- Three policemen shot dead 8/66
- Plans for Centre Point skyscraper 8/66
- Becomes fashion capital of world 12/66
- Queen Elizabeth Hall and Purcell Room open 3/67
- Tories win control of GLC 4/67
- Dartford Tunnel opens 8/67
- Port of London Docks to be closed 1/68
- US oil tycoon buys London Bridge 4/68
- Hayward Gallery opens 7/68
- First part of Victoria Line opens 9/68
- Queen opens Victoria tube line 3/69
- Soccer hooligans run riot on the tube 3/69
- Stolen paintings found on building site 7/69
- Karl Marx's grave disfigured 1/70
- Barbican Arts Centre given go-ahead 4/71
- London Bridge transported to Arizona 5/71
- Queen opens new London Bridge 3/73
- London Broadcasting Company goes on the air 10/73
- First big property deal by Arabs 7/74
- Bomb explodes in Tower of London; one dies 7/74
- Five IRA bombs go off 1/75
- Police find terrorist Carlos' safe house 7/75
- Hottest day for 35 years 8/75
- Bomb kills two and injures 63 at the Hilton Hotel 9/75
- IRA bomb restaurant; two die, 23 hurt 11/75
- IRA gunmen take couple hostage 12/75
- Two Arabs buy Dorchester Hotel 6/76
- Barbecues in Hyde Park: heatwave 8/76
- National Theatre on South Bank opens 10/76
- Seven IRA bombs in West End 1/77
- National Front clashes with anti-Nazis 4/77
- Seven-nation economic summit 5/77
- Tories to control Greater London Council 5/77
- Police riot shields at Lewisham rioting 8/77
- Council looks into power of Arab money 11/77
- Tories gain in local elections 5/78
- Operation Santa to foil IRA bombers 12/78
- Plans for reviving docklands 9/79
- SAS ends Iranian Embassy siege 5/80
- Fire damages Alexandra Palace 7/80
- Brixton riots: 213 arrested, 201 injured 4/81
- 80 hurt when skinheads fight Southall Asians 4/81
- People's March for Jobs blocked 5/81
- Labour wins GLC elections 5/81
- Ken Livingstone becomes leader of GLC 5/81
- 500 youths riot, Peckham 6/81
- Blank shots fired at Queen in Mall 6/81
- New unrest in Brixton 7/81
- Barbican arts centre opens 3/82
- Two IRA bombs kill eight, Hyde Park 7/82
- Government blocks Sinn Fein visit to GLC 12/82
- Thames Barrier raised for first time 2/83
- Michael Gratton wins London Marathon 4/83
- First wheel clamps introduced 5/83
- Some Metropolitan Police officers to carry automatics 4/84
- Thames Barrier inaugurated 5/84
- National Gallery extension design rejected 9/84
- Fire at Oxford Circus tube station 11/84
- Sultan of Brunei buys Dorchester Hotel 1/85
- Riots in Brixton after Groce shooting 9/85
- 246 injured in Tottenham riots 10/85
- PC Blakelock hacked to death in riots 10/85
- Riots in Peckham 10/85
- House prices rise 26.8 per cent in year 9/87
- Government plans to abolish ILEA 9/87
- Rare Kew Gardens trees lost in storm 10/87
- Stock market disaster - £50 billion lost 10/87
- 30 die in King's Cross underground blaze 11/87
- Nelson Mandela's birthday celebrated at Wembley Stadium 6/88
- Violence erupts at anti-Rushdie protest in Hyde Park 1/89
- Wandsworth Prison warders walk out over new shift system 1/89
- US subway Guardian Angels arrive to set up English branch 2/89
- Eight top V& A scholars are made redundant 2/89
- 15,000 protest against plans to build high-speed rail link 2/89
- Ayatollah Khomeini orders death of author Salman Rushdie 2/89
- Actors and archaeologists campaign to save Rose theatre 5/89
- Party boat collides with dredger on Thames; 60 feared dead 9/89
- Remains of Shakespeare's Globe theatre discovered 10/89
- Police take over in ambulance dispute 10/89
- 50,000 rally to back ambulance workers 1/90
- Wandsworth has lowest poll tax 3/90
- Police clash with rioters in Hackney during poll tax protest 3/90
- Poll tax demonstration turns into riot 3/90
- IRA bomb explodes at London Stock Exchange 7/90
- Islamic community rejects Rushdie's return to Islam 5/91
- Gay Rights demonstration in Trafalgar Square 6/91
- HPI reports rise in number of stolen cars on offer for sale 1/92
- Pressure group says Britain's child care is worst in Europe 1/92
- Terrorist bomb injures 28 at London Bridge station 2/92
- IRA marks Tory election win with bomb attack in the City 4/92
- Plans for fifth terminal at Heathrow Airport 5/92
- Bomb causes extensive damage in Victoria Street 6/92
- Japanses department store, Sogo, opens in Piccadilly 7/92
- Royal Mint introduces smaller 10-pence coin 9/92
- IRA bomb attack near Downing Street causes minor damage 10/92
- Stolen Renoir's "A Vase of Flowers" is recovered 11/92
- "The Mousetrap" celebrates 40th anniversary in the West End 11/92
- Eamonn Martin wins 13th London Marathon race 4/93
- Buckingham Palace is to be opened to the public 4/93
- Police announce anti-terrorist cordon around the City 6/93
- Car bomb damages Israeli Embassy 7/94

London Naval Conference
- See Royal Navy

London Zoo
- May be closed 4/91

London, Brian 1/59
London, Jack 12/03, 11/16, 12/16
Londonderry, Lord 9/13, 11/33
Long, Huey 11/34
Long, Lutz 8/36
Longford, Lord (Frank Pakenham) 9/72
Longowal, Harchang Singh 8/85
Lonsborough, Anita 9/60
Lonsdale, Gordon 1/61, 3/61, 4/64
Loos, Adolf 8/33
Lorca, Federico Garcia 8/36, 12/37
Loren, Sophia 9/34, 6/62, 4/66, 5/82
Lorentz, Hendrik 12/02
Lorenz, Konrad 11/03, 2/89
Lorenz, Peter 2/75, 3/75
Lorillard, Pierre 7/01
Lorillot, Henri 5/58
Lorimer, Peter 5/73
Lorre, Peter 6/04, 3/64

Los Angeles, California
- Jury acquits L.A. policemen accused of beating black youth 4/92
- Race riots erupt after acquittal of four policemen 5/92
- Huge earthquake causes death and damage 1/94

Losey, Joseph 6/84
Lossow, General von 11/23
Loubet, Emile 4/05, 5/05
Louganis, Greg 9/88
Louis, Joe 6/37, 8/37, 6/38, 10/42, 6/48, 3/49, 10/51, 4/81
Louis, Prince of Battenberg 12/12, 10/14
Louis, Victor 7/92
Lovat, Lord 3/95
Lovell, James 12/65, 11/66, 12/68, 4/70
Lovelock, Jack 8/36
Low, David 9/63
Lowry, L.S. (Laurence Stephen) 2/76
Lowry, Malcolm 7/09, 12/84
Loy, Myrna 12/93
Lu Yungh-S'ang 10/24
Lubbe, Marinus van der 2/33, 9/33, 1/34
Lubbers, Ruud 12/91
Lubbock, Eric 3/62
Lubitsch, Ernst 12/30, 2/40
Lubowski, Anton 9/89
Lucan, Lord 11/74, 6/75
Lucan, Veronica 11/74
Lucas, George 12/77
Luce, Richard 4/82
Luce, William 5/58
Luciano, Salvatore ("Lucky") 1/62
Lucy, Autherine 2/56
Ludendorff, Erich von 6/13, 8/14, 8/17, 3/18, 4/18, 7/18, 11/18, 11/23, 9/33, 3/37, 12/37
Luebke, Heinrich 7/59
Lugard, Frederick, Sir 3/03
Lugosi, Bela 8/56
Luis, Crown Prince of Portugal 2/08
Lukacs, Gyorgy 6/71
Lukanov, Andrei 11/90
Lukyanov, Anatoli 8/91
Lule, Yusuf 4/79
Lulu 2/69
Lumiere, Auguste 5/02, 6/07, 4/54
Lumiere, Louis 5/02, 6/07, 2/35
Lumumba, Patrice 10/58, 11/59, 3/60, 5/60, 6/60, 7/60, 8/60, 9/60, 11/60, 12/60, 1/61, 11/75
Luther, Hans 5/26
Luthuli, Albert 3/60, 12/60, 3/61, 7/67
Luttwitz, Baron 3/20
Lutyens, Edwin 7/19, 2/30, 3/38, 12/38, 1/44
Luwum, Janani 2/77

Luxembourg
- Becomes part of Germany 8/40
- Referendum on German annexation fails 10/41
- Customs pact with Belgium and Holland 9/44
- Signs economic pact with France 3/45
- "Benelux" customs union effective 11/47
- Pact with France, UK and rest of Benelux 3/48
- Joins new European Economic Community 3/57
- Gaston Thorn becomes PM 6/74
- English football fans riot 11/83

Luxemburg, Rosa 1/19, 6/19
Lydiard, Arthur 1/62
Lyle, Sandy 7/85
Lynch, David 12/90
Lynch, Jack 1/65, 11/66, 5/70, 10/70, 8/71, 9/71, 6/77
Lynch, Kelly 5/89
Lynch, Liam 4/23
Lynn, Vera 12/41, 12/44
Lyons, Jack 8/90, 9/90
Lyons, Joseph 4/39
Lyons, Mark 10/81
Lyons, William 9/22, 6/60
Lyttelton, Alfred 10/03
Lyttleton, Humphrey 12/59
Lytton, Constance 11/11

M

Maastricht treaty
- See European Community

MacArthur, Douglas 11/17, 9/35, 7/41, 12/41, 3/42, 9/42, 2/44, 4/44, 9/44, 10/44, 2/45, 8/45, 9/45, 10/48, 6/49, 6/50, 7/50, 9/50, 10/50, 11/50, 1/51, 3/51, 4/51, 5/51, 4/64, 1/89
MacBride, Sean 6/51, 10/74
MacDonald, James 7/88
MacDonald, James Ramsay 2/00, 2/11, 11/22, 5/23, 12/23, 1/24, 3/24, 9/24, 10/24, 5/29, 6/29, 1/30, 5/30, 12/30, 6/31, 7/31, 8/31, 9/32, 10/32, 4/33, 2/34, 6/35, 11/35, 11/37
MacDonald, Malcolm 11/35, 2/39, 7/39, 12/64
MacFarlane, Robert 7/83, 2/87
MacGregor, Ian 5/80, 3/83, 9/83, 3/84, 5/84, 9/84
MacInnes, Colin 12/59
MacLaine, Shirley 4/84
MacLeod, Ally 6/78
MacNamara, Robert 6/16
MacReady, John 5/23
MacStiofain, Sean 11/72, 4/73
MacSwiney, Tomas 8/20, 10/20
Macdonald, Jeanette 12/30

Macedonia
- See also Balkans, Bulgaria, Turkey and Yugoslavia
- Joint Russo-Austrian reform plan 12/02
- Italy and Austria help Turkey quell unrest 5/03
- Anarchy and death in Balkans 8/03
- Turks kill 50,000 Bulgarians 9/03
- Rebels sink Bulgarian steamer; 29 die 9/03
- Bulgarians kill 165 Moslem villagers 4/04
- Bulgaria demands its independence 9/12
- Turks driven out by Balkan League allies 10/12
- Victorious allies squabble over country 5/13
- Greece and Serbia break with Bulgaria 6/13

Machado, Bernardino 12/17
Machado, Gerardo 8/31, 8/33
Machel, Samora 3/76, 11/86
Mackay, Lord 5/89
Macke, August 9/14, 12/18
Mackensen, General von 8/15
Mackenzie, Compton 12/28, 10/32, 12/32, 12/49, 11/72, 12/72
Mackie, Philip 12/76
Maclean, Donald 6/51, 9/53, 3/54, 4/54, 9/55, 11/55, 7/63, 3/83
Maclennan, Ian 8/87
Maclennan, Mona 10/27
Maclennan, Robert 1/88
Macleod, Iain 5/52, 10/58, 2/60, 3/61, 10/63, 6/70, 7/70

Macmillan, Harold
- Allows council tenants to buy houses 8/52
- Says 300,000 houses were built in a year 12/53
- Plans to make house buying easier 5/54
- Becomes Foreign Secretary 4/55
- Attends Big Four meeting in Geneva 10/55
- As Chancellor, tightens credit squeeze 2/56
- Pleads for wage restraint 2/56
- Introduces premium bonds 4/56
- Announces £76 million spending cuts 6/56
- Made Prime Minister after Eden resigns 1/57
- Re-establishes confidence with US 3/57
- In European trade talks 3/57
- Discusses defence with Adenauer 5/57
- "We've never had it so good" speech 7/57
- Talks at White House 10/57
- Plays down three ministers' resignations 1/58
- Talks with Greece, Turkey and Cyprus 8/58
- Flies to Moscow for arms talks 2/59
- Launches World Refugee Year 6/59
- Southern Rhodesia commission 7/59
- Television discussion with Eisenhower 8/59
- Announces general election 9/59
- Huge Tory majority in election 10/59
- In talks with Adenauer 11/59
- Riots as he visits Southern Rhodesia 1/60
- "Wind of change" speech, Cape Town 2/60
- Signs nuclear test ban treaty with USA 3/60
- Deserts failing summit to meet de Gaulle 5/60
- In talks with Nasser at UN 9/60
- Allows US nuclear submarines 11/60
- Arrives in US for talks with Kennedy 4/61
- Promises review of security services 5/61
- Briefed by Kennedy on Khrushchev summit 6/61
- Announces UK bid to join Common Market 7/61
- Attacked on Immigration Bill 11/61
- In talks with de Gaulle 11/61
- In talks with Kennedy 12/61, 4/62
- Sacks seven cabinet members 7/62
- Announces National Incomes Commission 7/62
- Will sign test ban treaty with US and USSR 11/62
- Clinches deal to buy Polaris from USA 12/62
- Deadlock in EEC talks with de Gaulle 12/62
- Regards Profumo matter as closed 3/63
- Broken by Profumo affair 6/63
- Government admits Philby was "Third Man" 7/63
- Criticised for handling of Profumo Affair 9/63
- Resigns as PM 10/63
- "winds of change" speech effects on Africa 12/63
- Attends de Gaulle's funeral 11/70
- Accepts peerage on his 90th birthday 2/84
- Makes maiden speech in Lords 11/84
- Dies 12/86

Macmillan, Kenneth 12/65, 12/70
Macready, Neville 11/20, 7/21

Mad Mullah
- See Abdullah, Mohammed bin

Madagascar
- 3,300 die in hurricane 3/59
- Achieves independence from France 6/60
- RAF granted a patrol base 3/66
- Albert Zafy is elected President 2/93

Madeira
- 100 die in earthquake 3/29

Maderna, Bruno 11/73
Madero, Francisco 4/11, 7/11, 10/11, 2/13
Madonna 12/92
Maeterlinck, Maurice 3/11, 5/49
Magee, Patrick 6/85, 6/86

Magic Circle
- Lifts ban on women 9/91

Maginot, Andre 1/23, 1/32
Magloire, Paul 7/58
Magnani, Anna 3/08
Magritte, Rene 8/67
Magruder, Jeb Stuart 5/73
Maguire family 7/90
Maguire, Anne 1/80
Mahdi, Hadi al 4/70
Mahendra, King of Nepal 5/56
Maher, Aly 9/52
Mahfouz, Naguib 10/88
Mahidol, Ananda 6/46
Mahler, Gustav 1/08, 5/11, 12/11
Mailer, Norman 5/48, 12/57, 10/67, 12/68
Maillol, Aristide 9/44, 12/44
Maiman, Theodore 12/60
Majali, Hazza 8/60

Major, John
- Presents Ulster peace plan 2/95
- Buries the hatchet with Clinton 4/95
- Attends Russian commemoration event 5/95
- Becomes Foreign Secretary 7/89
- To succeed Nigel Lawson as Chancellor of the Exchequer 10/89
- Delivers his first budget 3/90
- Announces candidature for Tory leadership 11/90
- Replaces Margaret Thatcher as Prime Minister 11/90
- Says poll tax will not be abolished 1/91
- Put as most popular premier for years by opinion polls 2/91
- Escapes IRA bomb attack on Downing Street 2/91
- Outlines charter protecting citizens against corporate abuse 3/91
- Discusses tough cease-fire resolution with Bush 3/91
- Outlines "safe haven" plan for Kurds in Iraq 4/91
- Launches "citizen's charter" 7/91
- Criticises China's political prisoner record 9/91
- Announces that there is to be no general election next year 9/91
- Government attacked by Thatcher over referendum refusal 11/91
- Hails victory at Maastricht summit 12/91
- Concedes that Government has underestimated recession 1/92
- Signs arms accord with Russia 1/92
- Vows to send more troops to Ulster following bomb attack 1/92
- Vows to lead UK out of recession after Tory election win 4/92
- Says Britain will pay £100 million to protect environment 6/92
- Says UK will not rejoin ERM until mechanism is modified 9/92
- Orders inquiry into "Iraqgate" affair 11/92
- Announces that the Queen is to pay income tax 2/93
- Hits out at IRA's Warrington bomb attack 3/93
- Dismisses Mr Lamont 5/93
- Hits out at IRA's Warrington bomb attack 3/93
- Signs Ulster peace pact 12/93
- Accused of wrecking Euro-summit 6/94

Makarios III, Archbishop 8/13, 11/55, 1/56, 2/56, 3/56, 4/56, 7/56, 3/57, 12/59, 8/60, 1/61, 1/64, 3/70, 2/73, 12/74, 8/77
Makarova, Natalia 9/70
Malan, Daniel Francois 3/52, 10/54, 2/59
Malan, Douglas 5/48

Malawi
- See Nyasaland

Malaya
- See also Malaysia
- Rubber planters attacked 6/48
- British wipe out Malayan rebels 7/48
- British launch drive on Communist rebels 11/49
- UK High Commissioner Gurney killed 10/51
- Terrorism disrupts rubber plantations 11/51
- Insurgents kill seven Gordon Highlanders 2/52
- British kill 22 insurgents 2/52
- UK to give independence by 1957 2/56
- Independence declared, Kuala Lumpur 8/57
- Chief Minister Tengku Abdul Rahman 8/57
- Rahman denounces "Communist terrorists" 8/57
- Treaty of friendship with Indonesia 4/59
- State of emergency lifted 8/60
- UK agrees on Federation of Malaysia 7/62
- Joins Federation of Malaysia 9/63

Malaysia
- See also Malaya
- Federation of Malaysia created 9/63
- Martial law declared after riots 9/63
- Indonesian paratroops land 9/64
- State of emergency declared 9/64
- Singapore cuts links 8/65
- Ends bush warfare with Indonesia 8/66
- State of emergency in Selangor state 5/69
- Premier Tengku Abdul Rahman retires 8/70
- Abdul Razak becomes premier 9/70
- Japanese Embassy terrorists go to Libya 8/75
- Premier Abdul Razak dies in London 1/76
- Hijacked Malaysian plane crashes, 100 die 12/77
- Turns back Vietnamese refugees 6/79
- Two foreigners hanged under anti-drugs law 7/86

Malcolm X 5/25, 3/64, 2/65
Malcolm, Devon 3/90
Malcolm, Ian 6/02
Malenkov, Georgi 1/02, 3/53, 7/53, 8/53, 2/55, 7/57, 11/61

Mali
- Joins French Union as a republic 11/58

Malianos, Francisco Uryco 7/79
Malik, Jacob 1/50, 6/51
Mallory, George Leigh 6/22, 6/24, 10/24
Malone, Vivian 5/65
Malraux, Andre 9/01, 12/37, 2/62, 11/76

Malta
- See also World War II
- Protests at taxes and English language use 1/02
- British royal visit 4/07
- Premier Lord Strickland escapes killing 5/30
- Awarded George Cross by George VI 4/42
- Britain offers new constitution 12/53
- Premier Mintoff resigns over UK aid cut 4/58
- British Governor Laycock assumes power 4/58
- State of emergency declared 4/58
- Promised self-government 3/61
- Independence from Britain 10/61
- Becomes fully independent 3/62
- Referendum favours independence 5/64
- Is independent member of Commonwealth 9/64
- PM Olivier tells Britain to leave 1/67
- Mintoff's Socialists win election 6/71
- Scraps ten-year defence pact with Britain 6/71
- Anglo-Maltese defence talks collapse 7/71
- NATO removes its Mediterranean HQ 8/71
- UK signs seven-year pact on military bases 3/72
- Last British warships leave 4/79
- Dom Mintoff resigns as PM 12/84
- Palestinians hijack Egyptian airliner 11/85
- Commandos storm hijacked plane; 59 die 11/85

Mancham, James 6/77
Manchester
- Riot erupts in Strangeways Prison 4/90
- Last of the rebel prisoners evacuated from Strangeways 4/90
- IRA bombs injure 64 12/92

Manchukuo
- See also Manchuria
- Manchuria renamed Manchukuo by Japan 2/32
- Pu-yi installed as head of state 3/32
- Japanese appoint Pu-yi as Emperor 3/34
- Japan moves troops to Chinese border 11/35
- Japan attacks China from Manchukuo 7/37

Manchuria
- See also Manchukuo
- Sino-Russian treaty: troops to withdraw 4/02
- China refuses to evacuate 4/03
- Russian re-occupation 5/03
- UK and Japan call for Russian withdrawal 7/03
- Czar's effective annexation 8/03
- Chinese move in troops 11/03
- Russian minister warns off Japan 1/04
- Czar changes army there after setbacks 9/04
- Japanese kill 200,000 Russians, Mukden 3/05
- Russians evacuate at the end of war 9/05
- Japanese pull out; China resumes control 4/07
- Russia and Japan want "neutral" railway 1/10
- Russia gains free hand; Korea Japanese 7/10
- Kellogg-Briand Pact breached 8/29
- Sino-Russian railway border dispute ends 12/29
- Japan attacks Chinese at Mukden 9/31
- US arranges truce after Japanese attack 11/31
- Japan sets up puppet regime 2/32
- Renamed Manchukuo 2/32
- US accused of germ warfare 3/52

Mancini, Henry 6/94
Mandel, Georges 8/40, 4/43
Mandela, Nelson 5/61, 10/62, 11/62, 12/63, 4/64, 6/64, 7/78, 7/89, 1/90, 2/90, 5/90, 5/91,10/93, 5/94
Mandela, Winnie 3/71, 8/76, 12/76, 6/83, 5/87, 2/89, 1/90, 2/90, 2/91, 5/91
Mandelstam, Osip 12/36
Mandlikova, Hana 7/81, 7/86
Mangin, Gerald 6/18
Mankiewicz, Joseph Leo 2/93
Manley, Michael 3/72, 10/80, 2/89
Mann, Bruce Douglas 6/82
Mann, Heinrich 2/33, 3/50
Mann, Jackie 5/89, 9/91
Mann, Klaus 11/06
Mann, Thomas 12/29, 7/49, 8/55, 12/71
Mann, Tom 3/41
Mansell, Nigel 7/87, 7/91, 5/92, 8/92, 9/92,8/93, 11/94
Mansfield, Jayne 6/67
Mansfield, Katherine (Kathleen Murry) 1/23, 12/23
Manson, Charles 12/69, 8/70, 1/71, 3/71
Manstein, Erich von 5/45
Manteuffel, Hasso von 1/45
Manuel II, King of Portugal 10/10
Mao Tse-tung
- Attends Chinese Communist Party's first meeting 6/21
- Begins Long March, Kiangsi to Yenan 10/34
- Long March ends; 6,000 miles, 70,000 die 10/35
- Chiang Kai-shek rejects alliance 2/37
- Joins forces with Chiang against Japan 9/37
- Chungking talks to prevent civil war 8/45
- Forms National Army with Chiang Kai-shek 2/46
- Declares war on Nationalists after Japanese leave 8/46
- Wins in Manchuria; Chiang retreats 10/48
- Marches into Peking; takes Huai Hai 1/49
- Captures Shanghai after month-long siege 5/49
- Calls USSR a "true ally" 6/49
- Elected Chairman of People's Republic 9/49
- Proclaims Communist China; UK recognition 10/49
- US opposes new China at United Nations 1/50
- Recognises Ho Chi Minh's North Vietnam 1/50
- Signs friendship treaty with Stalin 2/50
- Secret pact with Ho Chi Minh 5/50
- Offers Tibet autonomy if it joins China 5/50
- Asks UN to ban US Navy off Formosa 8/50
- Re-elected Chairman; Chu-teh becomes deputy 9/54
- Dismisses Manchurian party boss Kao-kang 4/55
- Continues reform movement 4/57
- Remains head of Communist Party 4/59
- Talks with Khrushchev in Peking 10/59
- Condemns Khrushchev for "revisionism" 6/60
- Invites Khrushchev to Peking 3/63
- Suffers heart ailment 5/66
- Starts Cultural Revolution; red books 8/66
- Reports of anti-Mao revolt, Shanghai 1/67
- Accuses Liu Shao-chi of coup attempt 4/67
- Lin Piao designated successor 4/69
- Meets Haile Selassie in Peking 10/71
- Welcomes US President Nixon, Peking 2/72
- Claims Lin Piao died in air crash 7/72
- Loses deputy Chou En-lai 1/76
- No longer to meet foreign leaders 6/76
- Dies 9/76

Maradona, Diego 5/82, 7/84, 6/86
Marble, Alice 7/39
Marc, Franz 12/11, 12/18, 12/37
Marceau, Marcel 3/23
March, Fredric 12/35
Marciano, Rocky 10/38, 5/53, 9/53, 9/54, 4/56, 8/69
Marconi, Guglielmo 10/01, 12/01, 10/07, 2/14, 6/24, 8/32, 7/37
Marcos, Ferdinand 12/65, 1/73, 11/77, 6/83, 8/83, 9/83, 10/83, 8/84, 11/85, 2/86, 9/89
Marcos, Imelda 9/93
Marcus, Rudolph 12/92
Marcuse, Herbert 7/79
Mardian, Robert 2/75
Margai, Albert 1/66
Margaret, Princess of Great Britain
- See also Royal Family (Britain) 5/37, 10/40, 5/45, 12/49, 10/55, 2/57, 4/58, 4/59, 2/60, 5/60, 7/64, 3/76, 2/78, 5/78, 1/93

Margrethe, Queen of Denmark 1/72
Marie, Andre 7/48
Marie, Dowager Empress of Russia 10/28
Marina, Princess of Greece 8/34
Marjoribanks, Edward 4/32
Mark, Robert 6/76
Markham, Beryl 9/36
Markiewicz, Constance 12/18, 9/20
Markov, Georgi 9/78, 1/79
Markova, Alicia 12/10, 12/31
Markowitz, Harry 12/90
Marks, Lord (Simon) 12/64
Marley, Bob 5/81
Marlowe, Thomas 5/26
Marples, Ernest 7/59, 10/59, 4/66
Marquez, Gabriel Garcia 12/77
Marshall, George 6/44, 1/47, 3/47, 4/47, 6/47, 7/47, 9/47, 11/47, 1/48, 6/48, 7/48, 9/49, 5/51, 10/59
Marshall, Thurgood 6/67
Martelli, Giuseppe 7/63
Martin, Clifford 7/47
Martin, David 1/83
Martin, Eamonn 4/93
Martin, Mary 11/90
Martin, Millicent 12/62
Martinez, Conchita 7/94
Martinique
- Capital St Pierre destroyed by volcano 5/02
- Becomes department of France 3/46

Martov, Yuly 11/03
Marvin, Lee 3/79, 4/79, 8/87
Marvin, Michelle Triola 3/79
Marx Brothers 5/29, 12/32, 5/36
Marx, Groucho 8/77
Marx, Harpo 9/64
Marx, Wilhelm 11/23, 5/24, 6/24, 5/26
Mary, Princess
- See also Royal Family (Britain)

Mary, Queen
- See also Royal Family (Britain) 9/14, 3/21, 2/22, 11/31, 5/35, 6/36, 12/48, 2/52, 3/53

Masaryk, Jan 2/48, 3/48
Masaryk, Tomas 11/15, 12/16, 11/18, 5/20, 5/27, 5/34, 12/35, 9/37
Masefield, John 5/30, 5/67
Mason, James 5/09, 4/47, 12/49, 12/53, 7/84
Masood, Ahmed Shah 4/92
Masrayk, Jan 3/48
Mass Murders
- See Crime

Massenet, Jules 8/12
Massine, Leonid 12/19, 12/49
Massu, Jacques 1/60
Mastroianni, Marcello 9/24
Mata Hari (Margaretha Geertruida Zelle) 7/17, 10/17
Mates, Michael 6/93
Mathias, Bob 8/48
Matisse, Henri 10/05, 2/13, 12/46, 11/54, 12/55
Matsis, Kyriakos 11/58
Matteotti, Giacomo 5/24, 3/26
Matthew, Ken 10/64
Matthew, Robert 5/51
Matthews, Jessie 8/81
Matthews, Stanley 2/15, 5/53, 1/65, 4/65
Mature, Victor 1/59
Mau Mau
- See Kenya

Maude, Stanley 3/17
Maudling, Reginald 9/57, 12/62, 9/64, 7/65, 6/70, 7/72, 2/75
Maugham, William Somerset 9/09, 2/10, 12/15, 12/19, 6/54, 7/63, 12/65
Maurier, Gerald du 4/34
Mauritania
- Joins French Union as a republic 11/58
- Joins United Nations 10/61
- Admits defeat to Saharan Polisario army 8/79

Mauritius
- Becomes independent within Commonwealth 9/65
- Becomes independent of Britain 1/68
- 160 die as airliner hits Indian Ocean 11/87
- Breaks links with Crown, but remains part of Commonwealth 3/92

Maurois, Andre 10/67
Mauroy, Pierre 4/73
Maxim, Hiram 10/14, 11/16
Maxim, Joey 1/50
Maximilian, Prince of Baden 10/18, 11/18
Maxwell, Elisabeth 11/91
Maxwell, Philip 11/91
Maxwell, Robert 10/68, 1/69, 7/84, 10/91, 11/91
Maxwell-Fyfe, David 10/51
May Day demonstrations
- Demonstrators mar May Day in Prague, Berlin and Istanbul 5/89

May, Alan Nunn 5/46
May, Andrew 12/41
May, George 7/31
May, Peter 9/58, 2/59
Mayall, Rik 12/83
Mayer, Robert 1/85
Mayhew, Christopher 2/66
Mazowiecki, Tadeusz 8/89
M'Bow, Amadou-Mahtar 12/85
Mboya, Tom 2/61
McAdoo, William G. 7/20
McAliskey, Bernadette (nee Devlin) 1/81, 6/83
McArthur, Arthur 6/00
McAuliffe, Anthony 1/45
McAuliffe, Christa 1/86
McAvennie, Frank 5/88
McAvoy, Jock 7/39
McBride, Sean 1/88
McCann, Daniel 3/88
McCarthy, Eugene 3/68, 5/68, 6/68, 8/68
McCarthy, John 8/90, 8/91
McCarthy, Joseph 8/48, 2/50, 3/50, 11/53, 2/54, 3/54, 6/54, 12/54, 5/57
McCartney, Paul 10/63, 10/65, 3/69, 4/70, 12/70, 4/72, 12/77, 10/91
McCloy, John 11/63
McClure, Jessica 10/87
McCoist, Ally 11/89
McColgan, Liz 8/91
McCord, James 6/72, 1/73, 4/73, 5/73
McCowen, Alec 12/62
McCreesh, Ray 5/81
McCullough, Robert 4/68
McCusker, Seamus 10/75
McDade, James 11/74
McDermot, Frank 4/32
McDermott, Terry 5/77
McDivett, James 6/65
McDonald, Claude 11/05
McDonnell, Joseph 7/81
McEnroe, John 2/59, 7/80, 7/81, 7/82, 6/83, 7/83, 7/84
McEwan, Ian 12/83
McEwen, John 12/67
McFarlane, Brendan 1/86
McGahey, Mick 6/71
McGarvey, Danny 8/72
McGavigan, Annette 9/71
McGlinchey, Dominic 3/84, 10/85
McGoohan, Patrick 3/65
McGovern, George 8/68, 5/70, 1/71, 7/72, 10/72, 11/72
McGovern, John 7/31
McGowan, Cathy 9/65
McGowan, Walter 6/66
McGregor, Ken 7/51
McGuigan, Barry 6/85
McGuinness, Martin 10/82, 7/85
McKane, Kathleen 7/24
McKellen, Ian 12/84, 12/89
McKenna, Reginald 3/09, 9/15
McKenzie, Scott 12/67
McKibben, Hugh 8/92
McKinley, William 3/00, 6/00, 11/00, 9/01
McKinney, Joyce 4/78, 6/78
McLaren, Malcolm 12/76
McLuhan, Marshall 12/75
McMahon, George 7/36, 9/36
McMahon, Thomas 11/79
McMillan, Billy 4/75
McNamara, Robert 9/63
McNee, David 8/77, 4/81
McNee, Patrick 12/64
McParland, Peter 5/57
McQueen, Steve 12/65, 11/80
McStay, Terence 11/84
McVitie, Jack ("The Hat") 3/69
Mead, Margaret 11/78
Meadlo, Paul 11/69
Meccano
- inventor dies 9/36

Medawar, Peter 12/79
Medicine
- See also Britain (health) and Science and Technology
- X-ray cure for cancer claim 2/00
- Blood groups discovery 11/00
- Dr Koch says rats cause plague 7/01
- British Congress on Tuberculosis 7/01
- New mechanical hearing aid 11/01
- X-rays to treat breast cancer 11/01
- Vaccination for smallpox victims 1/02
- Mosquitoes carry yellow fever: discovery 2/02
- Compulsory smallpox vaccinations, Paris 2/02
- Sleeping pill acid patent, Germany 7/02
- Imperial Vaccination League, London 8/02
- Major Ross's Nobel for malaria work 12/02
- Porcelain to replace gold fillings 2/03
- Cataract operations 8/03
- Waterloo Hospital for Women and Children 10/03
- Electro-cardiograph 11/03
- Aspirin on sale in Britain 10/05
- Koch wins Nobel for finding tuberculosis bacillus 12/05
- Cattle immunised against tuberculosis 6/06
- Kidney transplants on animals 8/06
- Bad diet seen as major cause of diseases 12/06
- Dysentery serum discovered 4/07
- Warnings on tobacco addiction and cancer 8/07
- Florence Nightingale gets Order of Merit 11/07
- New York surgeons stitch heart together 4/08
- New tuberculosis serum 10/08
- No sick children in workhouses 6/09
- Auricular fibrillation of the heart 11/09
- X-rays help doctor remove nail from lung 2/10
- New drug for syphilis discovered by Dr Ehrlich 6/10
- New treatment for facial neuralgia 6/10
- Typhoid vaccination: Professor Vincent 6/10
- Florence Nightingale dies 8/10
- British doctor warns of more lunatics 9/10
- Cancer caused by virus, says Dr Rous 1/11
- Epsom salts cure tetanus, say doctors 2/11
- Infantile paralysis cause discovered 3/11
- Insurance Bill; workers' sickness scheme 5/11
- Fund says cancer may be inherited 11/11
- Cornea graft operations restore sight 1/12
- Joseph Lister, pioneer of antiseptics, dies 2/12
- Doctors condemn cocaine anaesthetics 6/12
- Electrocardiographic machine: Dr Lewis 6/12
- Heavy smoking causes heart blockages 6/12
- Deaf, dumb and blind Keller learns to sing 8/12
- Cancer microbe isolated, says Dr Odin 8/12
- Serum cure for tuberculosis 11/12
- US surgeon implants dog's brain in a man 2/13
- Typhus vaccine 4/13
- New diphtheria serum 4/13
- Cure for pellagra, claim 5/13
- Rabies virus isolated by Noguchi 9/13
- French Siamese twins separated 3/14
- Dr Paul Ehrlich, Nobel winner, dies 8/15
- UK wages government war on venereal disease 4/16
- X-ray photography of internal organs 9/16
- Drugs to combat syphilis in troops 10/16
- Dr Mary Scharlieb blames prostitutes for spread of VD 10/16
- First birth control clinic, New York 10/16
- First British woman doctor, Elizabeth Garrett Anderson, dies 12/17
- First UK birth control clinic opens 3/21
- Cancer incidences rise 3/21
- Eye transplants are carried out on fish 7/21
- First BCG tuberculosis vaccination 7/21
- Insulin isolated: hope for diabetics 12/21
- Rockefeller Foundation UK Hygiene School 4/22
- US drop in alcohol deaths since Prohibition 6/22
- Vitamin D stops rickets, discovery 6/22
- French scientists claim smoking is anti-bacterial 3/23
- Smokers absorb more nicotine 9/23
- Rabies bacillus isolated 1/24
- Health Ministry bans food preservatives 10/24
- Open heart surgery by Souttar, London 12/25
- Insulin cures diabetics, St. Bartholomew's 12/25
- Anti-tetanus serum, Pasteur Institute 1/26
- Smoking causes tongue cancer, says doctor 1/26
- Health risks of slimming, alcohol and drugs 2/26
- Plans to beat "cancer scourge" 1/27
- Treating cancer before it spreads, UK 1/27
- Tobacco exhibition says "no cancer risk" 4/27
- Distemper vaccine for animals 8/27
- Trichologists: short hair cures baldness 9/27
- Smoking causes most child deaths, claim 9/27
- Vitamin D can be made artificially 2/28
- Fleming discovers penicillin by accident 9/28
- "Elastoplast" sticking plasters, Hull 10/28
- First use of an "iron lung", Boston, US 10/28
- First radiotherapy congress, Paris 8/29
- Ageing population, says Health Ministry 8/29
- British drinking less 9/29
- Warm milk for schoolchildren 11/29
- Charles Best: heparin stops blood clots 12/29
- Prohibition leads to more drink deaths 1/30
- New polio immunisation claim 1/31
- Otto Warburg's Nobel for respiration 12/31
- First vaccine against yellow fever 4/32
- Vitamin C isolated 4/32
- Chamberlain chairs Tropical Medicine School 4/32
- Young drink, slim and smoke too much 7/32
- "Iron lung" used for first time in UK 10/32
- Dr Domagk finds a dye stops infections 12/32
- UK doctors isolate influenza virus 7/33
- X-ray couch 8/33
- Slimming craze causes slump in British potato sales 3/34
- Carrel keeps organs alive outside body 6/35
- Claim that Vitamin B-1 cures neuritis 6/35
- Disease virus crystallised for first time 6/35
- O.W. Stanley isolates pure viruses 12/35
- Vitamin E isolated - cure for sterility? 12/35
- Dodds' new drug to ease menopause 12/38
- First "drunkometer" tests drink-drivers 12/38
- First successful use of penicillin, UK 2/41
- Penicillin is saving many Allied lives 10/43
- Quinine, anti-malaria agent, synthesised 4/44
- First eye bank opens in New York 5/44
- New US research links smoking to cancer 10/46
- First operation inside the heart, UK 6/48
- Health Service comes into being, Britain 7/48
- Cause of sickle cell anaemia found 12/49
- Immunity theory by Australian biologist 12/49
- US man lives after "dying" twice 4/50
- First kidney transplant 6/50
- First use of artificial heart, US 3/52
- Operations and hormones change man's sex 12/52
- Dr Salk's successful polio vaccine 3/53
- Polio virus photographed 11/53
- Frederick Sanger analyses insulin 12/53
- Hope for diabetics with Sanger's find 12/53
- Woman impregnated with deep frozen sperm 12/53
- Study finds smoking may cause cancer 2/54
- Independent tests of polio vaccine, USA 4/54
- Alexander Fleming, Nobel winner, dies 3/55
- Tests show polio vaccine is effective 4/55
- UK call for inquiry into child abuse 6/56
- Smoking and cancer directly connected 6/57
- Asian flu vaccine distributed, Britain 10/57
- First internal heart pacemaker 10/58
- Birth control pioneer Marie Stopes dies 10/58
- Warnings on overuse of sedatives 11/58
- Thalidomide drug causes birth defects 12/58
- Hammersmith Hospital's spare organs bank 6/59
- Work towards kidney transplants 6/59
- First successful kidney transplant, UK 2/63
- First blood transfusion to unborn baby 9/63
- First successful heart transplant 12/67
- Epidural promises painless childbirth 9/68
- Human egg made fertile in test tube 2/69
- First heart pacemaker 7/70
- First heart and lungs transplant 7/71
- First kidney and pancreatic tissue graft 1/72
- Unrefined fibre diet better for bowels 12/75
- Uterine cancer fears with oestrogen 12/75
- World's first test-tube baby 7/78
- Steptoe fertilises eggs in test-tubes 7/78
- First fallopian tube transplant, UK 2/79
- Hounsfield's Nobel for CAT body scanner 10/79
- Harvard doctors synthesise interferon 1/80
- Genetic engineering creates virus killer 1/80
- Smallpox wiped out worldwide, says WHO 5/80
- Japan study shows passive smoking danger 1/81
- Immune system disease hits homosexuals 12/81
- Dista stops producing Opren 8/82
- Cautious approval for Opren drug 8/82
- DeVries gives Clark an artificial heart 12/82
- AIDS-causing virus is discovered 4/84

- Baby is given baboon's heart 10/84
- First heart, lungs and liver transplant 12/86
- Jewellery sale: £50 million for Pasteur Institute 12/87
- US FDA warns of danger of silicone breast implants 1/92
- $4.75 billion to silicone breast implant patients 2/94

Medina, Ernest 12/70, 9/71
Mehmet V, Sultan of Turkey 5/09
Mehmet VI, Sultan of Turkey 4/20
Meinhof, Ulrike 6/72, 11/74, 5/76
Meins, Holger 6/72
Meir, Golda 1/47, 11/56, 3/69, 5/70, 6/73, 1/74, 4/74, 12/78
Meirs, David 9/84
Meitner, Lise 1/39
Melba, Nellie 7/20, 10/25, 6/26, 2/31, 12/31
Melies, Georges 5/02
Mellor, David 9/92
Melly, George 9/61
Melrose, Stephen 5/90
Menchu, Rigoberta 12/92
Mendel, Gregor 3/00
Mendeleev, Dmitri 2/07
Mendelson, Anna 12/72
Mendelssohn, Erich 12/38
Menderes, Adnam 7/56, 2/59, 5/60, 9/61
Mendes-France, Pierre 6/54, 7/54
Mendez, Nicanor Costa 4/82, 6/82
Menem, Carlos 5/89
Mengelberg, Willem 3/51
Mengele, Josef 6/85
Menten, Peter 5/77
Menuhin, Yehudi 4/16, 2/27, 12/31, 2/87
Menzies, Robert 4/39, 4/50, 6/50, 8/50, 8/56, 1/66, 5/78
Mercader, Ramon 8/40
Mercer, Joe 8/90
Mercer, Johnny 6/76
Mercer, Manny 9/59
Mercier, Cardinal 12/14, 1/15, 10/16, 1/26
Merckx, Eddy 8/67
Mercouri, Melina 3/94
Mercury, Freddie 11/91
Meredith, George 5/09
Meredith, James 9/62, 10/62, 8/63, 6/66
Merman, Ethel 1/09
Merriam, William 3/73
Mesnel, Franck 3/91
Mesopotamia
- See also Iraq
- To be run by Britain after war 3/16
- 416 British troops die fighting rebels 10/20

Messerschmitt, Willy 9/78
Messiaen, Olivier 12/08
Meunier, Constantin 4/05
Mexico
- Restores relations with Austria 9/01
- Earthquake kills 300 in Mexico 1/02
- Supervises Central American peace treaty 7/06
- 1,500 die in Monterrey floods 8/09
- Rumours of imminent revolution 3/11
- President Diaz promises reforms 4/11
- US troops invade; rebel Madero holds on 4/11
- Diaz ousted by rebels; Madero in power 5/11
- 100 die in Mexico City earthquake 6/11
- After 45 years' rule, Diaz is exiled 6/11
- President Madero sets up liberal regime 7/11
- Madero elected President 10/11
- Madero is unable to quell Zapata's raids 10/11
- Madero deposed; shot dead for resisting 2/13
- General Victoriano Huerta becomes new President 2/13
- Huerta expels Americans; US arms boycott 8/13
- 350 US citizens held 9/13
- Huerta closes Congress and becomes dictator 10/13
- US ultimatum to Huerta; Villa leads rebellion 11/13
- Invaded by US Marines, Vera Cruz 4/14
- Huerta will resign if US pacifies state 5/14
- Huerta prepared to resign to get US peace 7/14
- Pancho Villa ends conflict with US 1/15
- Porfirio Diaz, former dictator, dies 7/15
- Villa's rebels kill 18 Americans 1/16
- US troops rout Villa's rebels; 30 killed 3/16
- Pancho Villa raids New Mexico; kills 17 3/16
- Asked by Germany to declare war on US 2/17
- Zapata killed by government troops 4/19
- US Cavalry kill bandits 8/19
- Rebel troops kill President Carranza 5/20
- Adolfo de la Huerta becomes President 6/20
- Pancho Villa, scourge of border, retires 7/20
- Rebels destroy railway, El Paso, Texas 2/22
- Revolutionary Pancho Villa shot dead 7/23
- Calles nationalises Church goods 2/26
- Five ancient Maya cities found 2/26
- President Calles in battle with clergy 8/26
- Calles rules out foreign mediation 8/26
- Calles rejects bishops' plea 8/26
- 100 die in Catholic revolt against government 1/27
- Rumblings over anti-clerical laws 3/27
- 14 shot for coup bid 10/27
- Emilio Gil succeeds Obregon as President 9/28
- Emilio Portes Gil sworn in as President 11/28
- Catholic rebels take Juarez town; 24 die 3/29
- US Air Force threatens to bomb rebels 4/29
- Four Americans hurt by rebel crossfire 4/29
- Accord with Church 6/29
- Pope condemns Mexican anti-clericalism 9/32
- Parliament expels Papal Legate 10/32
- Plot to kill President Cardenas foiled 8/35
- Women workers to get vote 9/35
- Grants Trotsky asylum 12/36
- Exiled Trotsky calls for Stalin's demise 4/37
- Trotsky injured in attack on home 5/40
- Trotsky assassinated in Mexico City 8/40
- Declares war on Axis 6/42
- Breaks ties with Vichy France 11/42
- Monard gets 20 years for killing Trotsky 4/43
- 300 die in train crash, Guadalajara 4/55
- Olympic Games open 10/68
- Student riot brutally put down 10/68
- 147 killed and 700 injured in train crash 10/72
- At least 500 die in earthquake 8/73
- 260 killed by gas plant explosion 11/84
- Earthquake kills 2,000 9/85
- 166 killed in air crash 3/86
- 200 die in gas explosion in Guadalajara 4/92
- Signs free trade bloc agreement with US and Canada 8/92
- Rebels sieze 5 towns in Chiapas 1/94
- Assassination of Luis Donaldo Colosio 3/94
- Ernesto Zedillo Ponce de Leon is new President 8/94

Meyer, Anthony 11/89, 12/89
Meyer, Barbadee 11/89
Mhatre, Ravindra 2/84
Michael, Grand Duke of Russia 3/17
Michael, King of Rumania 9/40, 8/44, 12/47, 3/48
Michael, Prince of Kent 6/78
Michaelis, Georg 7/17
Mies van der Rohe, Ludwig 12/26, 5/29, 12/33, 12/38, 12/59, 8/69
Mihai, Prince of Rumania 7/27
Mihailovich, Draja 3/46, 4/46, 7/46
Mikardo, Ian 5/93
Miki, Ryuki 7/34
Mikolajczyk, Stanislaw 1/47, 11/47
Mikoyan, Anastas 7/64, 12/65, 10/78
Milans del Bosch, Jaime 2/81
Milburn, Jackie 10/88
Miles, Bernard 12/42, 12/59
Milestone, Lewis 12/30
Miley, Bubber 12/27
Milford, Lord 5/63
Milford, T.R. 7/42
Milhaud, Darius 6/74
Milhench, Ronald 11/74
Mille, Cecil Blount de 1/59
Miller, Arthur 10/15, 6/56, 12/56, 5/57, 8/58, 8/62, 12/90
Miller, Glenn 3/04, 8/39, 12/43, 12/44
Miller, Henry 6/80
Miller, Joe 5/89
Miller, Jonathan 7/34, 6/55, 12/61
Miller, Max 5/63
Miller, Merton 12/90
Miller, Terry 7/50
Millerand, Alexandre 1/20, 9/20, 6/24
Milligan, Spike 12/53
Milligan, Stephen 2/94
Millikan, Robert 12/53
Mills, Freddie 5/46, 7/48, 1/50, 7/65
Mills, Jack 8/63
Mills, John 12/42
Milne, Alan Alexander 1/56
Milne, Alasdair 1/87
Milner, Alfred 1/01
Milosevic, Slobodan 11/88, 7/91, 12/92, 6/93, 12/93
Minchington, Lennie 11/76
Mindszenty, Josef 10/45, 12/48, 2/49, 7/55, 10/56, 9/71, 10/71, 5/75
Minkowski, Hermann 9/08
Minnelli, Liza 11/64
Minter, Alan 3/80, 9/80
Minto, Earl of 8/06
Mintoff, Dom 4/58, 6/71, 12/84
Mirbach-Harff, Wilhelm von 7/18
Miro, Joan 12/25, 12/37, 12/83
Mirror Group
- Scandal over £400 million transfers from pension fund 12/91

Mirza, Ahmed, Shah of Iran 10/25
Mishima, Yukio 1/25, 11/70
Mistral, Gabriela 12/45
Mitchell, John 1/71, 7/72, 5/73, 4/74, 1/75, 2/75, 1/79
Mitchell, Leslie 8/36
Mitchell, Margaret 11/00, 8/49
Mitchell, Reginald Joseph 12/42
Mitchell, Warren 11/66
Mitchell, William 7/21
Mitchum, Robert 8/17, 2/49
Mitford, Nancy 7/73, 12/73
Mitford, Unity 4/38, 1/40
Mitterrand, Francois 10/16, 11/54, 1/55, 10/59, 8/65, 12/65, 5/68, 6/72, 5/74, 4/81, 5/81, 9/81, 1/86, 2/86, 3/86, 7/86, 4/88, 5/88, 11/89, 6/90, 9/92, 2/93, 3/93, 4/93, 9/94, 11/94
Miyazawa, Kiichi 6/93
Mladenov, Petar 11/89, 4/90
Moawad, Rene 11/89
Mobutu, Joseph-Desire 9/60, 11/65
Mock, Geraldine 4/64
Modahl, Diane 12/94
Modigliani, Amedeo 1/20
Modrow, Hans 11/89, 12/89
Moffat, Alex 11/56
Mohammed Ali Mirza, Shah of Persia 1/07, 7/09
Mohammed V, King of Morocco 11/57, 2/61
Mohammed, Ali 10/09
Mohammed, Hanif 1/57
Mohammed, Muldi 4/03
Moi, Daniel Arap 8/82
Moi, Daniel arap 12/92
Mojaddidi, Sigbatullah 4/92
Mola, Emilio 6/37
Moldavia
- Soviet troops intervene in Moldavian-Gaugaz Turk clash 10/90
- See also Moldova

Moldova
- Presidents Snegur and Yeltsin agree to seek end to conflict 7/92

Molina, Tejero de 2/81
Mollet, Guy 2/56, 9/56, 5/57
Mollison, James A. 8/31
Molotov, Vyacheslav 1/31, 5/39, 8/39, 10/39, 8/40, 6/41, 5/42, 11/45, 12/45, 4/46, 4/47, 3/49, 1/54, 10/55, 6/56, 7/57, 8/57, 11/61, 4/64, 7/84, 11/86
Mommsen, Theodor 11/03
Momper, Walter 11/80
Monaco
- Rainier III sworn in as ruling prince 11/49
- Prince Rainier III to marry Grace Kelly 1/56
- Prince Rainier marries Grace Kelly 4/56
- Princess Grace has first child, Caroline 1/57
- Princess Grace dies in crash 9/82

Monaghan, Rinty 3/48
Monard, Jacques 4/43
Monckton, Lord (Walter) 10/54, 9/59
Mondale, Walter 7/76, 8/80, 11/80, 3/84, 7/84, 11/84
Mondrian, Piet 12/17, 2/44
Monet, Claude 5/04, 5/08, 12/19, 12/26
Mongolia
- Russian protectorate 12/11
- Independent; world's second Communist state 7/21
- Friendship treaty with Russia 11/21
- Human remains and dinosaur eggs found 12/26
- Molotov made Soviet ambassador 8/57
- Huge earthquake moves mountains 1/58
- Joins United Nations 10/61
- New constitution introduces multi-party system 2/92

Monis, Ernest 3/11, 5/11
Monk, Thelonius 12/58, 2/82
Monopolies Commission 2/89
Monray, Carlos 7/63
Monroe, Marilyn 6/26, 12/52, 1/53, 7/53, 1/54, 10/54, 6/55, 6/56, 12/56, 6/57, 6/62, 8/62
Montand, Yves 7/62
Montenegro
- See also Balkans, Yugoslavia
- Declares independence from Turkey 8/10
- Mobilises troops against Greece 6/12
- Declares war on Ottoman Empire 10/12

Montessori, Maria 5/52
Montgomery, Jim 5/73
Montgomery, Lucy Maude 12/09
Montgomery, Viscount (Bernard) 8/42, 10/42, 1/43, 7/43, 12/43, 6/44, 8/44, 12/44, 1/45, 3/45, 4/45, 5/45, 7/45, 12/45, 12/46, 3/51, 3/76
Montgomery-Massingberd, Archibald 11/27
Montini, Giovanni Battista 6/63
Montsarrat, Nicholas 12/51
Montt, Pedro 8/10
Moody, Helen (nee Wills) 2/26, 7/27, 7/29, 7/30, 7/32, 7/33, 7/34, 7/35, 7/38
Moon, Sun Myung 10/70, 5/82
Moorcroft, David 7/82
Moore, Ann 11/71
Moore, Bobby 7/66, 1/67, 5/70, 8/70, 2/93
Moore, Davey 3/63
Moore, Demi 12/90
Moore, Dudley 4/35, 12/61
Moore, Henry 12/45, 12/59, 8/86
Moore, Jeremy 6/82
Moore, John 11/83
Moore, Marianne 2/72
Moore, Roger 3/65
Moore, Sara Jane 9/75
Moorhouse, Adrian 9/88
Morales, Ramon 10/63
Moran, George ("Bugsy") 2/29
Moran, Gussie 6/49
Morandi, Giorgio 6/64
Moravia, Alberto 11/07, 12/90
Morceli, Nourredine 9/93
More, Kenneth 12/52
Moreau, Jeanne 1/62
Morecambe, Eric 12/74, 5/84
Morgan, Helen 11/74
Morgan, John Pierpont 12/09
Morley, Eric 10/78
Morley, John 6/92
Morley, Robert 6/37
Moro, Aldo 2/66, 3/78, 4/78, 5/78, 4/82
Morocco
- See also France (foreign affairs)
- France and Italy agree on Morocco 12/00
- Spanish invasion plans 12/02
- Pretender beats Sultan's troops 1/03
- Pretender repulsed 2/03
- Muldi Mohammed is new Sultan 4/03
- Rebels revolt; French troops on alert 5/03
- France and Spain to "keep status quo" 7/03
- Anglo-French pact 4/04
- Conference to determine German role 1/06
- Algeciras conference ends 3/06
- French occupy town after doctor's murder 3/07
- French bombard and invade Casablanca 8/07
- Fighting resumes after talks fail 9/07
- French repel Moorish raid into Algeria 4/08
- Sultan Abd-el Aziz flees; Mulai new head 8/08
- Treaty recognises French hegemony 2/09
- Sultan restricts Fez Jews 6/09
- Spanish defeat Moors 9/09
- Revolt against Europeans spreads 3/11
- French and allies march to help Sultan 4/11
- German gunboat sent to Agadir 7/11
- France and Germany settle their dispute 9/11
- Franco-German treaty divides country 11/11
- Becomes French protectorate, with Sultan 3/12
- Troops revolt against French rule 4/12
- Sultan Mulai Hafid abdicates 8/12
- French troops quell uprising 9/12
- Franco-Spanish spheres of influence pact 11/12
- Krim's rebels wipe out Spanish garrison 7/21
- Abdel Krim founds first Berber state 9/21
- Abdel Krim surrenders to Petain's forces 5/26
- Republicans kill 600 Moroccans, Spain 7/37
- Conference of Allies in Casablanca 1/43
- 24 Communist ex-deputies released 2/43
- Abdel Krim tells France to quit 5/47
- French depose Sultan Sidi Mohammed 8/53
- France offers regional assemblies 8/54
- Rioters want Sultan Sidi Mohammed back 8/54
- France imposes martial law after riots 7/55
- French prepare a reform programme 8/55
- Peace talks as 1,000 Moroccans die 8/55
- Granted independence by France 3/56
- Spanish Morocco granted independence 4/56
- Emigration to Israel blocked 6/56
- King Mohammed wants end to Algerian war 11/57
- 1,000 die in Agadir earthquake 3/60
- King Mohammed V dies 2/61
- Hassan II becomes King 2/61
- Statesman Abdel Krim dies 2/63
- Troops launch offensive against Algeria 10/63
- Agrees to cease-fire with Algeria 10/63
- Agrees to end war with Algeria 2/64
- King Hassan crushes coup attempt 7/71
- Failed coup attempt against King Hassan 8/72
- 13 executed for attempt on Hassan 1/73
- 188 die as Boeing 707 crashes 8/75
- King to lead 350,000 to claim Sahara 10/75
- King recalls 350,000 Sahara invaders 11/75
- Cannabis found in Moroccan Embassy in London 6/80
- Implicit recognition of Israel 9/82

Morozov, Platon 8/64
Morozova, Olga 7/74
Morrigan, Mairead 11/76
Morris, Desmond 10/67
Morris, Stuart 4/58
Morris, William
- See Nuffield, Lord

Morrison, Danny 12/82
Morrison, Herbert 3/34, 1/41, 3/42, 11/42, 11/43, 6/44, 7/45, 12/46, 11/49, 3/51, 5/51, 9/52, 11/52, 12/55, 6/59, 3/65
Morrison, Stinie 4/11
Morrison, Toni 10/93
Mortier, Madame Alfred 4/23
Mortimer, Angela 7/58, 7/61
Mortimer, John 12/79, 12/81
Morton, "Jelly Roll" 9/26, 7/41
Morton, Andrew 6/92, 12/92
Moscatelli, Cino 4/45
Moscicki, Ignac 6/26
Moser, Claus 8/90
Moses, Edwin 7/76, 9/88
Mosley, Oswald 11/29, 5/30, 10/30, 2/31, 3/31, 9/31, 12/31, 4/33, 10/33, 1/34, 6/34, 10/36, 10/37, 5/40, 11/43, 7/62, 12/80
Moss, Stirling 5/54, 5/55, 7/55, 5/56, 7/57, 9/57, 8/58, 10/58, 9/59, 4/60, 5/60, 5/61, 4/62
Mossadegh, Mohammed 4/51, 6/51, 8/51, 7/52, 10/52, 11/52, 8/53, 3/67
Motor racing
- See Motor sports

Motor sports
- Camille Jenatzki wins Gordon Bennett 7/03
- Thery wins Gordon Bennett 6/04
- First Le Mans circuit won by Szisz 6/06
- Peking-Paris race 6/07
- Italian prince wins Peking-Paris race 8/07
- American car wins intercontinental race 7/08
- Ray Harroun wins first Indianapolis 500 5/11
- Motor cycle breaks 100mph barrier 9/20
- First Monza race; Bordino wins 9/22
- First 24-hour Grand Prix, Le Mans 5/23
- Legache and Leonard win Grand Prix 5/23
- Nurburgring circuit opens, Germany 6/27
- Car kills 22 at Grand Prix, Milan 9/28
- First Monaco Grand Prix; won by Williams 4/29
- British Bentleys triumph at Le Mans 6/29
- Le Mans: Barnato and Birkin win 6/29
- British cars excel at Brooklands 5/30
- British cars in first four places, Le Mans 6/30
- Britain takes first 12 places, Brooklands 5/31
- Peter Walker wins Le Mans in Jaguar 6/51
- Argentinian Fangio wins Europe Grand Prix 7/51
- Jaguars' success in Le Mans Grand Prix 6/53
- Stirling Moss, Parnell win at Aintree 5/54
- Juan Fangio becomes world champion 8/54
- Moss, first Briton to win Mille Miglia 5/55
- 80 die when three Le Mans cars crash 6/55
- Le Mans Mercedes team surrenders medals 6/55
- Stirling Moss wins his first Grand Prix 7/55
- UK mopeds counter foreign competition 11/55
- Jaguar team wins Le Mans race 7/56
- 14 die in Mille Miglia crash, Italy 5/57
- Moss wins British Grand Prix, Aintree 7/57
- Moss wins Italian Grand Prix, Monza 9/57
- Cuban rebels seize Fangio; later freed 2/58
- Tony Brooks wins European Grand Prix 6/58
- Mike Hawthorn wins French Grand Prix 7/58
- UK's Collins dies in German Grand Prix 8/58
- Stirling Moss wins Portuguese Grand Prix 8/58
- Tony Brooks wins Italian Grand Prix 9/58
- First UK world champion, Mike Hawthorn 10/58
- Moss wins in Morocco; second in tournament 10/58
- Mike Hawthorn dies on road - profile 1/59
- Moss wins Italian Grand Prix 9/59
- Moss loses licence 4/60
- Stirling Moss wins Monaco Grand Prix 5/60
- Two die as Indianapolis 500 tower crashes 6/60
- Two drivers die in Belgian Grand Prix 6/60
- Jack Brabham wins French Grand Prix 7/60
- Stirling Moss wins Monaco GP 5/61
- Stirling Moss injured in crash 4/62
- Jim Clark wins Belgian Grand Prix 6/63
- Jim Clark is youngest world champion 9/63
- Japanese to enter UK saloon car racing 3/65
- Jim Clark wins Indianapolis 500 5/65
- Jim Clark wins French Grand Prix 6/65
- Jim Clark becomes world champion 8/65
- Graham Hill wins Indianapolis 500 5/66
- John Surtees wins Syracuse GP 5/66
- Jackie Stewart wins Monaco GP 5/66
- Jack Brabham wins German GP 8/66
- Jack Brabham becomes world champion 9/66
- Jim Clark wins US Grand Prix 10/66
- John Surtees wins Mexican Grand Prix 10/66
- A Mini Cooper wins Monte Carlo rally 1/67
- Jim Clark wins Dutch Grand Prix 6/67
- Jim Clark wins US Grand Prix 10/67
- Jim Clark killed in crash 4/68
- Graham Hill wins Monaco Grand Prix 5/68
- Britons take first three places in US GP 10/68
- Graham Hill becomes world champion 11/68
- Hill wins Monaco GP for fifth time 5/69
- Jackie Stewart is world champion 9/69
- Austrian driver Rindt killed in crash 9/70
- Rindt becomes world champ posthumously 10/70
- Jack Brabham retires 10/70
- Jackie Stewart wins Monaco Grand Prix 5/71
- Jackie Stewart keeps world championship 10/71
- Jackie Stewart retires 9/73
- Graham Hill retires 7/75
- Niki Lauda is world champion 10/75
- Graham Hill dies in plane crash 11/75
- Lauda badly burned in German Grand Prix 8/76
- UK's James Hunt wins championship 10/76
- Hunt's triumph at Japanese Grand Prix 10/76
- Lauda wins world championship 10/77
- Andretti, US, is Formula One champion 10/78
- Mark Thatcher missing in African rally 1/82
- Thatcher rescued in desert 1/82
- Niki Lauda becomes world champion 10/84
- Nigel Mansell wins British Grand Prix 7/87
- Ayrton Senna wins Fomula One championship 10/90
- Nigel Mansell wins British Grand Prix 7/91

- Nigel Mansell wins his fifth Grand Prix of the season 5/92
- British racing drivers win the Le Mans 24-Hour race 6/92
- Nigel Mansell wins the Hungarian Grand Prix 8/92
- Mansell announces his retirement from Formula One racing 9/92
- Mansell wins New England 200 Indycar 8/93
- Damon Hill's first F1 win 8/93
- Ayrton Senna wins final race of season 11/93
- Ayrton Senna dies after crashing at Imola 5/94
- Schumaker takes Formula 1 title 11/94

Mott, John 12/46
Moulin, Jean 3/43, 6/43, 7/43
Mountaineering
- See Exploration & Archaeology

Mountbatten, Louis 6/00, 3/22, 7/22, 4/42, 8/42, 12/42, 8/43, 9/45, 12/46, 2/47, 5/47, 6/47, 7/47, 8/47, 6/48, 10/51, 10/54, 5/64, 8/79, 9/79, 11/79
Mountjoy, Doug 4/81
Mousa, Sa'id 6/83
Mouskouri, Nana 10/34
Moyne, Lord 11/44
Moynihan, Berkeley 1/26, 1/27
Mozambique
- See also Portugal
- Oil-laden Greek tanker intercepted 4/66
- Hundreds feared dead in cyclone 1/71
- Portuguese army admits to massacre 8/73
- 100 die in two days of violence 9/74
- Frelimo transitional government in power 9/74
- 48 killed in racial violence 10/74
- Wins independence from Portugal 6/75
- President Machel adopts war footing 3/76
- Rhodesian commandos cross border 10/76
- Terror gang kills 27 Rhodesian Africans 12/76
- Rhodesians strike; kill 1,500 guerrillas 10/78
- 300 killed by Zimbabwe-Rhodesia troops 9/79
- Peace pact with South Africa 2/84
- Peace accord with South Africa signed 3/84
- President dies in plane crash, S. Africa 11/86
- Joaquim Chissano chosen as president 11/86
- President Chissano and Renamo rebel leader sign accord 8/92

Mubarak, Hosni 10/81, 11/81, 10/84, 10/93
Mueller, Gerd 6/70
Mugabe, Robert 11/77, 3/78, 6/78, 4/79, 8/79, 9/79, 12/79, 1/80, 3/80, 4/80, 2/82, 3/83, 9/86
Muggeridge, Malcolm 1/68, 12/90
Muhammed Ali 6/71, 2/73, 10/74
Muir, Frank 12/53
Muir, Karen 8/65
Mulai Hafid, Sultan of Morocco 8/08, 9/08, 8/12
Mulcahy, Richard 8/22, 2/48
Mulder, Connie 11/78, 1/79, 4/79
Mulgrew, Kevin 8/83
Muller, Hermann 12/46
Muller, Ludwig 1/34
Muller, Paul 12/48
Mulroney, Brian 9/84, 10/92, 6/93
Munch, Charles 11/68
Munch, Edvard 1/44
Mundt, Karl 8/48
Munnings, Alfred 4/49, 5/56
Munongo, Godefroid 2/61
Murayama, Tomiichi 6/94
Murders
- See Crime

Murdoch, Iris 7/19, 6/54
Murdoch, Richard 8/49
Murdoch, Rupert 3/31, 10/68, 1/69, 8/69, 9/69, 10/69, 2/70, 2/71, 3/71, 1/81, 2/81, 2/82, 4/85, 9/85, 12/85, 2/86, 4/86, 6/87, 2/89
Murphy, Ann Marie 4/86
Murphy, Annie 5/92
Murray, Archibald 3/17
Murray, Eunice 8/62
Murray, Gilbert 7/42
Murray, James 12/86
Murray, Joseph 12/90
Murray, Len 5/84, 5/84
Murrow, Edward R. 4/65
Museveni, Yoweri 1/86
Music
- See also individual composers; categories

Music (popular)
- See also Jazz, Pop Culture, and Hits of the Year (each
- December)
- "Watch Your Step", an Irving Berlin musical 12/14
- Dixieland Jazz at New York restaurant 1/17
- First jazz recording 3/17
- Scott Joplin, ragtime composer, dies 4/17
- Music hall hits in the trenches 9/17
- "Swanee" by George Gershwin 2/18
- Wartime songs turn from elation to irony 12/18
- Original Dixieland Jazz Band in London 12/19
- Churches blast jazz; Chicago new centre 1/22
- Music hall star Marie Lloyd dies 10/22
- Blues singer Bessie Smith: "Downhearted" 2/23
- Gershwin's "Rhapsody in Blue" 2/24
- "The Girl Friend" by Richard Rodgers 3/26
- "Jelly Roll" Morton's first recording 9/26
- The Astaires in "Lady Be Good" by Gershwin 12/26
- Gershwin's "Funny Face" 11/27
- Bing Crosby and Rhythm Boys sing jazz 12/27
- "Show Boat", Ziegfeld and Jerome Kern 12/27
- Paul Robeson sings in Kern's "Show Boat" 12/28
- "An American in Paris", George Gershwin 12/28
- "Strike Up The Band", George Gershwin 1/29
- Munich bans "indecent" Josephine Baker 2/29
- "Hot Chocolates" revue: "Ain't Misbehavin'" 6/30
- John Philip Sousa, "March King", dies 3/32
- Henry Hall and the BBC Dance Orchestra 5/32
- Brecht and Weill leave Germany 12/33
- US premiere of "Anything goes", Porter 11/34
- Gracie Fields lured onto silver screen 2/35
- Germany bans Jewish and black US jazz 10/35
- Gershwin's "Summertime" from "Porgy & Bess" is a hit 12/35
- UK premiere of "Anything Goes", Porter 12/35
- First "hit-parade" appears in "Billboard" magazine 1/36
- George Gershwin dies 7/37
- Blues singer, Bessie Smith, dies 9/37
- Vera Lynn is the "Forces' Sweetheart" 12/41
- "White Christmas" is a big hit 12/42
- US lyricist, Lorenz Hart, dies 11/43
- Gracie Fields performs at troop concerts 12/43
- George Formby appears at troop concerts 12/43
- Scots singer/comedian, Harry Lauder, dies 2/50
- Frank Sinatra makes London debut 7/50
- Death of US singer Al Jolson 10/50
- Frank Churchill's score for "Snow White" 1/51
- Ivor Novello, composer-actor, dies 3/51
- Hank Williams, country singer, dies 1/53
- Bill Haley and Comets' new rocking sound 4/54
- "That's All Right Mama", Elvis Presley 7/54
- "My Fair Lady", starring Julie Andrews and Rex Harrison 3/56
- Whites drag Nat King Cole off stage 4/56
- Elvis Presley appears on Ed Sullivan Show 9/56
- "Rock Around the Clock" starts riots 9/56
- Crosby and Sinatra appear in "High Society" 12/56
- Bill Haley and Comets come to London 2/57
- British rock 'n' rollers are a success 12/57
- Elvis Presley called up by US Army 12/57
- Elvis joins the Army 3/58
- Elvis sells 40 million records 3/58
- After two years on Broadway, "My Fair Lady" comes to Drury 4/58
- Jerry Lee Lewis cuts short UK tour 5/58
- Holly, Valens and Richardson die in plane crash 2/59
- Skiffle from the coffee bars: juke boxes 12/59
- "Oliver!", Bart's musical adaptation of Dickens novel 12/60
- Bob Dylan causes excitement in New York 9/61
- Beatles rejected by Decca 1/62
- "Please Please Me", Beatles' first LP 2/63
- Beatlemania takes hold of Britain 10/63
- Beatles at Royal Variety Performance, UK 11/63
- Death of US singer, Dinah Washington 12/63
- French singer, Edith Piaf, dies 12/63
- Radio Caroline starts in North Sea 3/64
- Rolling Stones shock Montreux Festival 4/64
- Pirate Radio Atlanta goes on the air, UK 5/64
- US band leader, Spike Jones, dies 5/64
- Radio Caroline and Radio Atlanta merge 7/64
- More listen to Radio Caroline than BBC 9/64
- "Ready, Steady, Go!" on UK television 10/64
- US composer Cole Porter dies 10/64
- US singer Nat King Cole dies 2/65
- Beatles awarded MBEs 6/65
- 55,000 attend Beatles concert at Shea Stadium 8/65
- "Ready, Steady, Go" is UK's popular TV programme 9/65
- Dusty Springfield is top UK woman singer 12/65
- Dylan plays with electric backing band 6/66
- Frank Sinatra marries Mia Farrow 7/66
- British rock rules the pop world 12/66
- Bob Dylan's UK tour 12/66
- The Monkees' fans run wild at Heathrow 2/67
- Sandie Shaw wins Eurovision Song Contest 4/67
- Elvis Presley marries Priscilla Beaulieu 5/67
- "Sergeant Pepper ...", Beatles 6/67
- Beatles manager, Brian Epstein, found dead 8/67
- Pirate radio stations banned, UK 8/67
- Lulu and Maurice Gibb marry, UK 2/69
- Rolling Stones play for free, Hyde Park 7/69
- Bob Dylan at Isle of Wight pop festival 8/69
- Rolling Stones play at Madison Square Garden 11/69
- The Who perform "Tommy" at Met, New York 6/70
- Second Isle of Wight pop festival 8/70
- Jimi Hendrix dies of overdose 9/70
- Janis Joplin dies of overdose 10/70
- Rock stars raise cash for Bangladesh 8/71
- Death of French singer Maurice Chevalier 1/72
- Death of German singer, Lale Andersen 8/72
- Scott Joplin's music in "The Sting" 12/73
- Mass hysteria at Cassidy concert, UK 5/74
- Josephine Baker dies 4/75
- Sinatra wins damages from BBC over Mafia 5/75
- Three Dublin rockstars die in ambush 7/75
- Working-class US rock from Springsteen 12/75
- Robeson, singer and black activist, dies 1/76
- Singer Johnny Mercer dies 6/76
- Punk rock group, Sex Pistols, disrupt TV show 12/76
- EMI sacks Sex Pistols 1/77
- Elvis Presley dies 8/77
- Marc Bolan, rock singer, dies 9/77
- Crooner Bing Crosby dies 10/77
- John Williams writes film score for "Star Wars" 12/77
- McCartney rules out Beatles' reunion 12/77
- Ex-Sex Pistol, Sid Vicious, charged with murder 10/78
- Jacques Brel, singer, dies 10/78
- "Evita", Rice and Lloyd Webber musical 12/78
- Sondheim's "Night Music" now a film 12/78
- Sid Vicious dies of overdose 2/79
- Japan deports McCartney on drugs charge 1/80
- Ex-Beatle John Lennon killed in New York 12/80
- Bill Haley, singer, dies 2/81
- Bob Marley, reggae apostle, dies 5/81
- Musical comedy star, Jessie Matthews, dies 8/81
- "Cats" - Lloyd Webber adapts Eliot poems 12/81
- Hoagy Carmichael, pianist, dies 12/81
- Advent of the compact disc 12/83
- Boy George is UK's latest pop idol 1/84
- Singer Marvin Gaye shot dead by father 4/84
- "Do They Know It's Christmas?" 12/84
- Michael Jackson's "Thriller" 12/84
- Wham! duo gives two concerts in China 4/85
- Live Aid concert 7/85
- Live Aid appeal reaches £50 million 7/85
- Michael Jackson's UK tour 7/88
- Songwriter Irving Berlin dies 9/89
- Bryan Adams sets 16-week record as number one in charts 10/91
- Freddie Mercury of Queen dies of AIDS 11/91
- Eric Clapton wins six Grammy awards 2/93
- Frank Zappa dies 12/93
- Woodstock's 25th anniversary concert 8/94
- Blur wins 4 Brits 2/95

Muskie, Edmund 11/68
Mussolini, Benito
- Watched by Swiss police: Marxist views 6/03
- Campaigns for Allies in his paper 4/15
- Founds Fascist Party 3/19
- Leads Fascists, rightist business backed 11/21
- Fascists take over Fiume 3/22
- Warns government on clampdown of Fascism 7/22
- Fascists smash Communists; take Milan 8/22
- Fascists enter Rome; take power 10/22
- Threatens to dissolve Chamber 11/22
- Arrests Socialists 2/23
- Turns May Day into Rome Founding Day 4/23
- Approves women's suffrage bill 6/23
- Annexes Fiume; dissolves parliament 1/24
- Fascists sweep to victory in elections 4/24
- Says Fascist Party is "above parliament" 10/24
- Bans all left-wing parties 11/25
- Answers only to King 12/25
- Creates Royal Academy of Italy 1/26
- Holds posts of premier, Foreign Minister and War Minister 1/26
- Power to rule by decree 1/26
- Survives shooting attack by Irishwoman, Violet Gibson 4/26
- "Italy must expand or suffocate" 7/26
- Assumes total power; opposition banned 10/26
- Boy lynched after shooting at Mussolini 10/26
- Pope gives blessing after shooting 11/26
- Meets Churchill in Italy 1/27
- Creates Vatican state; pact with Pope 2/29
- Claims 99 per cent vote Fascist in poll 3/29
- Meets British Foreign Secretary Chamberlain 4/29
- Bans "immoral" beauty contests 5/29
- Gives up seven cabinet posts 9/29
- Claims there is too much talk of peace 11/29
- Meets Pope Pius XI on Lateran Treaty Day 2/32
- Assassination plot foiled 6/32
- Talks with MacDonald blasted in London 3/33
- Meets British Fascist leader Mosley 4/33
- Meets Dollfuss; pledges aid to Austria 8/33
- Agrees to frontiers with France's Laval 1/34
- Cuts salaries and raises bachelors' taxes 4/34
- Watches Italy win the World Cup 6/34
- Meets Hitler for first time, Venice 6/34
- Rushes 40,000 troops to Austrian border 7/34
- Wants compulsory male military training 9/34
- Six-year-olds for pre-military training 10/34
- Hoping to avenge 1896 Abyssinia defeat 12/34
- Rejects League arbitration on Abyssinia 12/34
- Gets Laval's assurance on Abyssinia 1/35
- Dismisses entire cabinet 1/35
- Wants curbs on German rearmament 4/35
- Rejects Anglo-French plan for Abyssinia 8/35
- To settle Abyssinia dispute by arms 8/35
- Truce pledge; then rejects League plan 9/35
- Sons Bruno and Vittorio fly bombers 10/35
- "Solemn hour" speech on Abyssinia war 10/35
- Proclaims Abyssinian victory: new empire 5/36
- Announces anti-Communist Axis with Germany 11/36
- Warns Jews to "uphold Fascism or leave" 5/37
- Promises Franco support 6/37
- Boasts of empire and peace in Berlin speech 9/37
- Rejects Britain's "piracy" call 9/37
- UK parliament praises Italy after pact 5/38
- Meets Hitler: "lasting friendship" 5/38
- Chamberlain and Halifax visit 1/39
- Occupies and subjugates Albania 4/39
- Signs pact with Hitler 5/39
- Announces Italian neutrality 9/39
- Meets Hitler at Brenner Pass 3/40
- Orders mobilisation of all males over 14 4/40
- Asked by US to help halt war 4/40
- Declares war on Britain and France 6/40
- Talks with Ribbentrop on African colonies 9/40
- Italians defeated at Tobruk 1/41
- Declares southern Italy a war zone 2/41
- Admits capitulation of troops in Libya 2/41
- Italian offensive in Albania crushed 3/41
- Declares war on US 12/41
- Meets Hitler, Salzburg 4/42
- Assumes post of Foreign Minister 2/43
- Talks with Hitler on North Africa 4/43
- Says Italians have "African sickness" 5/43
- Deposed as Allies invade Italy 7/43
- Rescued by Germans from prison cell 9/43
- Shot dead by partisans 4/45

Mussolini, Bruno 10/35
Mussolini, Vittorio 10/35
Mussorgski, Modest 4/09
Muzaffar ad-Din, Shah of Persia 1/07
Muzorewa, Abel 10/76, 11/77, 2/78, 4/79, 5/79, 8/79, 9/79, 12/79
Myers, Val 5/32

N

Nabokov, Vladimir 12/55, 7/77
Nadar (Felix Tournachon) 3/10
Nader, Ralph 2/34
Nadir Khan, King of Afghanistan 10/29, 11/33
Nadir, Asil 5/93, 6/93
Nagle, Florence 7/66
Nagy, Imre 6/47, 8/53, 4/55, 10/56, 11/56, 6/58, 6/89
Naidu, Mrs Sarojini 5/30
Naipaul, Vidiadhar Surajprasad 8/32
Najibullah, Mohammad 4/92
Nakanishi, Mitsuko 6/89
Nam Il 7/51, 8/51
Namibia
- See also South West Africa
- S. Africans v. nationalists near Angola 5/80
- Five S. Africans and 81 guerrillas killed 5/80
- 216 SWAPO guerrillas killed in clash 8/82
- UN proposes truce to end fighting 4/89
- Senior white Swapo official is killed 9/89

Nanda, Gulzarilal 5/64
Nansen, Fridtjof 5/30
Napier, Oliver 12/73
Naruhito, Crown Prince of Japan 6/93
Narutowicz, Gabriel 12/22
Nash, John 12/18
Nash, Ogden 5/71
Nash, Paul 12/18, 12/45
Nasrin, Taslima 6/94, 8/94
Nasser, Gamal Abdel 1/18, 6/53, 2/54, 4/54, 7/54, 10/54, 11/54, 1/56, 6/56, 7/56, 8/56, 9/56, 10/56, 2/57, 3/57, 2/58, 7/58, 12/58, 12/59, 1/60, 9/60, 6/61, 7/62, 3/64, 4/64, 5/64, 9/65, 10/66, 5/67, 6/67, 9/70
Nastase, Ilie 7/49, 7/72, 7/73, 7/76, 7/78
Nation, Carry 6/11
National Lottery
- First draw as gambling fever seizes the nation 11/94

National Salvation Front (NSF)
- See Rumania

NATO
- Plans for NATO unveiled 3/49
- Twelve nations sign North Atlantic Treaty 4/49
- Defence Committee agrees to general plan 12/49
- Eight nations sign defence plan 1/50
- Plan adopted to strengthen state ties 5/50
- Adopts idea of European defence force 9/50
- Eisenhower appointed head of NATO forces 12/50
- Invites Greece and Turkey to join 9/51
- Allies delay West German membership 2/52
- Eisenhower wants to resign as chief 4/52
- New headquarters at Palais de Chaillot 4/52
- Eisenhower hands over to Ridgway 5/52
- Incorporates European Defence Community 8/52
- Allies reject USSR security proposal 2/54
- West Germany admitted; no nuclear arms 10/54
- Molotov wants NATO and Warsaw Pact ended 10/55
- New Cyprus peace plan; Greece rejects it 3/57
- First heads of government meeting 12/57
- Agrees to accept US nuclear missiles 12/57
- UK and Iceland fishing talks break down 8/58
- Queen opens conference 6/59
- De Gaulle denies wanting to ruin NATO 12/59
- France out of North Atlantic Fleet 6/63
- De Gaulle says France will leave 9/65
- Rusk says France not vital to NATO 4/66
- France formally leaves 6/66
- HQ to move from Paris to Brussels 10/66
- France withdraws from command structure 4/69
- Bomb explodes during talks in Portugal 6/71
- Mediterranean HQ removed from Malta 8/71
- Yom Kippur war causes split and crisis 10/73
- Anxiety over SALT 2 and USSR's SS-20s 6/79
- Attempted assassination of General Haig 6/79
- Cruise missiles to counter SS-20s 6/80
- Talks with Warsaw Pact on missile limits 11/81
- Spain joins 5/82
- 40th-birthday summit 5/89
- Agrees with Warsaw Pact countries to slash conventional arms 11/90
- Begins enforcing shipping embargo on Serbia 11/92
- Prepares air strikes against Bosnian Serbs 8/93
- US General Joulwan to command forces in Europe 10/93
- Clinton's Partnership for Peace plan endorsed 1/94
- NATO shoots down Serb warplanes over Bosnia 2/94
- Russia signs Partnership for Peace programme 6/94
- Civilian head Manfred Worner dies 8/94
- Willy Claes appointed Secretary General 9/94

Natta, Giulio 2/03
Navarre, Henri 11/53, 2/54
Navratilova, Martina 10/56, 9/75, 7/79, 7/82, 9/83, 7/84, 7/85, 7/86, 7/87, 7/88, 7/89, 7/90
Navy, British
- See Royal Navy

Nazli, Queen of Egypt 4/36
Ne Win 9/58
Neagle, Anna 6/69, 6/86
Neave, Airey 7/53, 4/77, 3/79
Neeskens, Johan 7/74
Neguib, Mohammed 7/52, 9/52, 6/53, 2/54, 4/54, 11/54
Neher, Erwin 12/91
Nehru, Jawaharlal Pandit 5/29, 12/31, 2/36, 1/42, 4/42, 4/46, 8/46, 9/46, 11/46, 6/47, 7/47, 11/47, 1/48, 4/50, 2/54, 4/54, 8/55, 7/56, 6/58, 1/59, 4/59, 12/59, 9/61, 3/62, 10/62, 5/64
Nemeth, Miklos 10/89
Neruda, Pablo 7/04, 12/71
Nesbit, Edith 5/24
Netanyahu, Benjamin 1/91

Netherlands
- See also World War II
- Troops kill 541 Achinese, Sumatra 4/04
- Treaty with Portugal over Timor 10/04
- Allies demand ex-Kaiser's extradition 1/20
- Refuses Allies' extradition demands 1/20
- Makes ex-Kaiser give up politics 3/20
- Javanese nationalist rebels fight Dutch 11/26
- Adalbert Smit forms a Nazi Party 12/31
- Scandinavian and Benelux economic alliance 2/32
- Studies customs union with Belgium 6/32
- Scientists achieve record low temperature 5/33
- Hitler guarantees neutrality 1/37
- Troops sent to German border 4/39
- Martial law declared 3/40
- War trade pact made with UK 4/40
- Troops put on alert along German border 4/40
- Germany invades 5/40
- Germans occupy The Hague 5/40
- Surrenders to Germany 5/40
- Germans seize Dutch works of art 2/43
- Germans declare martial law 5/43
- Customs pact with Belgium and Luxembourg 9/44
- Germans blow up a town hall, killing 135 11/44
- Signs economic pact with France 3/45
- Nationalist-Dutch war in East Indies 10/45
- Queen Wilhelmina to abdicate 10/47
- "Benelux" customs union effective 11/47
- Pact with France, UK and rest of Benelux 3/48
- Queen Wilhelmina abdicates 9/48
- Juliana becomes Queen 9/48
- Martial law declared, Dutch East Indies 9/48
- Dutch take Djakarta and Madiun, E. Indies 12/48
- UN demands withdrawal from Indonesia 1/49
- Signs North Atlantic Treaty 4/49
- Dutch troops withdraw from Jakarta 6/49
- United States of Indonesia recognised 11/49
- Ends rule over Dutch East Indies 12/49
- Anne Frank's diary published 6/52
- 1,000 die after dykes burst 2/53
- Cuts political ties with Indonesia 8/54
- Joins new European Economic Community 3/57
- Bars entry to Indonesians 12/57
- Indonesia expels all Dutch nationals 12/57
- Banks nationalised 1/58
- Dutch-born Verwoerd is S. African leader 9/58
- 93 killed in train collision 1/62
- UN takes control of west New Guinea 10/62
- Death of Queen Wilhelmina 11/62
- Princess Beatrix to marry a German 1/65
- Anti-German protest at Beatrix's wedding 3/66
- Rudi Dutschke shooting sparks riots 4/68
- Lennon and Ono "bed-in", Amsterdam 3/69
- Declares support for Israel (Yom Kippur) 10/73
- OPEC imposes oil embargo 10/73
- Feyenoord wins UEFA Cup 5/74
- OPEC ends oil boycott 7/74
- Fire outside Spanish Embassy 9/75
- Moluccans storm Indonesia Consulate 12/75
- Consulate siege ends peacefully after 15 days 12/75
- Moluccans hijack train and kill two 12/75
- Public shock at royal bribe-taking 2/76
- Chess star Korchnoi seeks asylum 7/76
- Prince Bernhardt resigns after bribes 8/76
- KLM 747 in crash 3/77
- Art dealer Menten tried for killing Jews 5/77
- South Moluccans hijack train with 161 5/77
- Marines storm besieged train; eight die 6/77
- Four school besiegers surrender 6/77
- Marines rescue 71 held by S. Moluccans 3/78
- Terrorists kill one, about to kill two 3/78
- UK Ambassador Sykes shot dead 3/79
- Queen Juliana to abdicate for Beatrix 1/80
- Queen Beatrix crowned; rioters clash 4/80
- Police free kidnapped brewer Heineken 11/83
- Simon van der Meer wins Physics Nobel 12/84
- Two escaped IRA men recaptured 1/86
- Christian Democrat-led coalition falls 5/89
- Two Australians killed in "error" by IRA near German border 5/90
- Flood fears cause mass evacuation 2/95

Neusel, Walter 2/35
Neves, Tancredo de Almeida 1/85, 4/85
Neveu, Ginette 10/49
Neville, John 2/56
Nevinson, Christopher Richard Wynne 12/18
New Caledonia
- Two policemen die in Melanesian clashes 1/83

New Hebrides
- UK to send marines to end revolt 6/80
- 200 Anglo-French end Espiritu revolt 7/80

New Zealand
- Fifth consecutive win for Progressives 11/02
- Court declares strikes illegal 9/07
- Gains autonomy from Britain as dominion 9/07
- Troops in Gallipoli landings 4/15
- First Anzac Day commemorates Gallipoli 4/16
- Self-governing Commonwealth dominion 11/26
- Pay cuts spark riots; hundreds hurt 4/32
- Jack Lovelock wins Olympic 1500 metres 8/36
- Declares war on Germany 9/39
- Role in World War II 9/39
- Signs Pacific pact with Australia 1/44
- Currency devalued 9/49
- Defence pact with US and Australia 9/51
- Queen opens parliament 1/54
- MPs vote to abolish death penalty 10/61
- First blood tranfusion to unborn baby 9/63
- Agrees on more aid for Malaysia 9/64
- 200 die when ferry capsizes 3/68
- Greenpeace ship sunk in mystery blast 7/85
- Rainbow Warrior sinking: Two French held 7/85
- Rainbow Warrior: sunk by French agents 9/85
- RW sinking: Two French agents plead guilty 11/85
- Two Rainbow Warrior saboteurs jailed 11/85
- Maori activists throw eggs at Queen 2/86
- Geoffrey Palmer succeeds David Lange as Prime Minister 8/89

Newby, Percy Howard 12/69
Newcombe, John 7/70, 7/71
Newfoundland
- Anglo-French pact ends old differences 4/04
- Reverts to direct British rule in crisis 12/33
- 49 die in air crash 9/46

Newman, George 12/13
Newman, Paul 1/25, 10/62, 12/73
Newton, Andrew 8/78
Ngo Dinh Diem 4/55, 5/55, 10/55, 1/56, 11/75
Ngo Dinh Nhu 9/63, 11/63
Nguema, Francisco 8/79, 9/79
Nguyen Van Vy 5/55
Niazi, "Tiger" 12/71
Nicaragua
- US Navy joins dispute with Costa Rica 3/00
- US Congress approves canal 4/00
- Sells US canal rights for $5 million 12/00
- Earthquake kills 500 near Cartago 5/10
- Jose Estrada's new government; US leaves 1/11
- Revolution crushed; four US troops die 10/12
- Declares war on Germany 5/18
- Cannot afford League membership 9/22
- President Diaz wants US to stop rebels 11/26
- UK sends warship to protect British interests 2/27
- Signs aid pact allowing US intervention 6/27
- Sandino attacks troops at Las Flores 9/27
- Five US Marines killed by Sandino rebels 1/28
- Hoover discusses rebels with Moncada 11/28
- 1,100 die in Managua earthquake 3/31
- Martial law in Managua; American is shot 4/31
- Sandinist rebels capture Puerto Cabezas 4/31
- US will withdraw by June 4/31
- Sandinistas fight troops, Lindo Lugar 9/32
- Martial law declared 8/33
- Guardsman Somoza kills Augusto Sandino 2/34
- Fears of a Somoza coup against Sacasa 2/34
- Anastasio Somoza elected President 12/36
- President Somoza dies of shooting wounds 9/56
- Somoza's son Luis takes over 9/56
- Blames Cuba for unrest 11/60
- Anastasio Somoza elected President 2/67
- Howard Hughes meets Somoza 3/72
- Earthquake kills 10,000 12/72
- Somoza becomes President 9/74
- Ten die in army-rebel clashes 2/78
- President Somoza to resign 9/78
- Sandinistas vow to topple regime 9/78
- 1,500 die in fighting; no Cuban aid 9/78
- US breaks off relations 2/79
- Somoza calls state of siege 6/79
- More opposition after TV report 6/79
- Somoza quits; Sandinistas take over 7/79
- 500,000 homeless after war 7/79
- Francisco Malianos temporary President 7/79
- Businessmen in US-backed junta 7/79
- Somoza killed in Paraguay 9/80
- Joy at Somoza's death; Sandinista denial 9/80
- Civil rights suspended; fears US attack 3/82
- Ortega plans defence from El Salvador 3/82
- Pope visits 3/83
- President Reagan sides with Contras 5/83
- US Congress votes to end aid to Contras 7/83
- Rebel aircraft bomb Managua 9/83
- US Senate vetoes mining of ports 4/84
- World Court rules against US action 5/84
- Gaddafi has sent arms to Sandinistas 9/84
- Daniel Ortega elected President 11/84
- US Congress rejects aid to Contras 4/85
- Reagan plans Sandinista trade embargo 4/85
- Branded a terrorist state by Reagan 7/85
- USAF plane shot down and pilot captured 10/86
- "Irangate" row erupts in US 11/86
- US Senate halts Contra aid 2/87
- Signs Central America peace plan 8/87
- Committed to amnesty and elections 8/87
- President offers cease-fire to Contras 1/88
- Ortega concedes victory to Violeta Chamorro in elections 2/90

Nichol, Lee 4/89
Nicholas II, Czar of Russia 7/02, 4/03, 12/04, 4/05, 7/05, 8/05, 10/05, 5/06, 11/07, 6/08, 7/09, 8/09, 2/13, 6/14, 7/14, 8/15, 9/15, 1/17, 3/17, 9/17, 5/18, 7/18
Nicholas, Grand Duke of Russia 11/22
Nicholson, Jack 12/69, 4/84
Nicklaus, Jack 1/40, 7/66, 7/70, 6/72, 7/79
Nidal, Abu 1/78, 7/91
Nielsen, Carl 11/02
Nielsen, Kurt 7/53, 7/55
Nielson, Donald 12/75, 7/76
Niemeyer, Oscar 12/59
Niemoeller, Martin 3/38, 5/45
Nietzsche, Friedrich 8/00
Niger
- Becomes a French Union republic 12/58

Nigeria
- See also Biafra
- Becomes British protectorate 1/00
- British beat rebel emirs 1/01
- General Morloy occupies Kano 2/03
- British enter Sokoto; sultan flees 3/03
- Uprising by "Silent Ones", Asaba 2/04
- British troops sent to quell revolt 2/06
- Twelve colonial police killed 8/09
- Britain orders "enemy" property sold 11/16
- Police kill 21 miners at colliery riot 6/50
- Federal constitution in effect 10/54
- Warm welcome for Queen; near-disaster 1/56
- 26 die in BOAC airliner crash 6/56
- Queen promises independence 10/59
- Gets independence; joins Commonwealth 10/60
- Premier Balewa lauds Princess Alexandra 10/60
- UK defence pact; students protest 11/60
- Ends defence agreement with Britain 1/62
- Republic proclaimed 10/63
- Nnamdi Azikiwe becomes first premier 10/63
- Politicians killed in army coup 1/66
- Commonwealth conference on Rhodesia 1/66
- Yakubu Gowon seizes power in coup 8/66
- Troops rampage in tribal riots 10/66
- Biafra announces its secession 5/67
- Government troops invade Biafra 7/67
- Biafran troops invade mid-western region 8/67
- Nigerians mount major assault on Biafra 8/68
- Red Cross can fly relief into Biafra 9/68
- 55 Nigerian troops killed in air crash 9/68
- Federal troops capture Umuahia, Biafra 4/69
- Bans Red Cross flights to Biafra 6/69
- Eases air blockade of Biafra 7/69
- 300,000 face famine in war zone 11/69
- 87 die in air crash 11/69
- Biafra surrenders 1/70
- 180 die when pilgrimage plane crashes 1/73
- General Gowon deposed while at summit 7/75
- Seizes BP assets over sanctions 7/79
- Expels all unskilled foreign workers 1/83
- General Buhari seizes power in coup 1/84
- President and politicians arrested 1/84
- 1,000 killed in religious riots 3/84
- Ex-minister Dikko kidnapped in London 7/84
- Wole Soyinka wins Literature Nobel 12/86

Nightingale, Florence 11/07, 3/08, 8/10
Nijinsky, Vaslav 5/09, 12/09, 12/11, 5/12, 5/13, 12/13, 4/50
Nikolayev, Andrian 8/62
Nikolayev, Leonid 12/34
Nikula, Penetti 2/63
Nilson, Dennis 2/83, 10/83
Nimitz, Chester 6/42, 2/44, 2/66
Nin, Anais 1/77
Nissar, Mohamed 6/32
Nivelle, Robert 12/16, 4/17
Niven, David 5/46, 4/59, 7/83
Nixon, Patricia 6/93
Nixon, Richard
- Born 1/13
- Eisenhower's running mate for presidency 7/52
- Refutes illegal political fund charges 9/52
- Youngest ever Vice-President 11/52
- Visits Eisenhower during his illness 9/55
- To seek vice-presidency again 4/56
- Chosen to run again for Vice-President 8/56
- Re-elected Vice-President 11/56
- Discusses race issues with King 6/57
- Visits Puerto Rico 5/58
- At US Memorial Chapel dedication, London 11/58
- Debates with Khrushchev at kitchen show 7/59
- Visits Poland after USSR 8/59
- Favourite of Republicans 12/59
- Primaries: Nixon and Kennedy favourites 3/60
- Chosen as Republican candidate 7/60
- First national televised debate 9/60
- Loses presidency narrowly 11/60
- Campaigns to become California Governor 9/62
- Arrives on visit to USSR 4/65
- To run for President 2/68
- Calls for US to scale down Vietnam role 8/68
- Wins Republican nomination 8/68
- Elected President 11/68
- Kissinger is national security adviser 12/68
- Sworn in as President 1/69
- Visits Wilson in London 2/69
- Signals intention to end Vietnam War 4/69
- Visits Rumania 8/69
- Orders B-52 raids on N. Vietnam to go on 9/69
- Sent letters about Mylai massacre 11/69
- Backs bombing of Ho Chi Minh trail, Laos 3/70
- In talks with Pompidou 3/70
- Sends US troops into Cambodia 4/70
- Deplores killing of anti-war students 5/70
- Promises to remove troops from Cambodia 5/70
- Declares Charles Manson guilty in gaffe 8/70
- Attends de Gaulle's funeral 11/70
- Warns USSR subs to keep away from Cuba 1/71
- Calley's Mylai guilt to be reviewed 4/71
- Vows to end US involvement in Vietnam 4/71
- To visit China 10/71
- Meets Tito in Washington 10/71
- 45,000 more troops to leave Vietnam 11/71
- Grants $5.5 billion for space shuttle 1/72
- To stand for re-election 1/72
- Visits China; urges better relations 2/72
- Steps up bombing of North Vietnam 4/72
- First visit to Moscow by a US President 5/72
- Signs nuclear pact with Brezhnev 5/72
- Withdraws US combat troops from Vietnam 8/72
- Renominated as Republican candidate 8/72
- Signs SALT agreement with USSR 10/72
- Wins presidential election landslide 11/72
- Orders halt to Hanoi bombing 12/72
- Announces cease-fire in Vietnam War 1/73
- Sworn in for second term 1/73
- Denies involvement in Watergate 4/73
- Admits White House cover-up of Watergate 5/73
- Implicated in Watergate cover-up 6/73
- Talks with Brezhnev in US 6/73
- Existence of Oval Office tapes revealed 7/73
- Refuses to hand over tapes 7/73
- Puts US forces on alert (Yom Kippur war) 10/73
- Requests $2,200m emergency aid for Israel 10/73
- Sacks Watergate prosecutor Cox 10/73
- Agrees to hand over Watergate tapes 10/73
- Names Jaworski as Watergate prosecutor 11/73
- Rejects court subpoenas for tapes 1/74
- Promises help to Lon Nol in Cambodia 2/74
- Refuses to surrender key tapes 2/74
- Grand jury says he knew of Watergate 3/74
- Threatened with impeachment 5/74
- Visits Belgium 6/74
- Announces resumption of ties with Syria 6/74
- Talks with Brezhnev in Moscow 6/74
- Ordered by court to deliver tapes 7/74
- Impeachment process begins 7/74
- Resigns 8/74
- Pardoned by Ford 9/74
- Aides guilty of Watergate cover-up 1/75
- Admits CIA plot in Chile 3/76
- Dies after a stroke 4/94

Nkomo, Joshua 2/59, 2/63, 4/63, 12/63, 6/64, 11/64, 9/75, 11/77, 9/78, 4/79, 8/79, 9/79, 12/79, 1/80, 3/80, 2/81, 2/82, 2/83, 3/83
Nkrumah, Kwame 9/09, 3/52, 9/61, 10/61, 11/61, 12/61, 4/62, 8/62, 9/62, 2/66, 3/66, 4/72
Nobel Prizes
- See December each year

Nobel, Alfred 12/01
Nobile, Umberto 5/26, 3/29
Noel-Baker, Philip 11/59
Nol, Lon 11/85
Nolan, Christopher 1/88
Nolan, Lord 5/95
Nolde, Emil 12/37, 4/56
Nomura, Kichisaburo 11/41, 12/41
Nordau, Max 4/20
Norden, Denis 12/53
Norgay, Tensing 5/86
Noriega, Manuel 5/89, 10/89, 12/89, 1/90, 7/92
Norman, Greg 7/86
Norman, Montague 8/31
Norrish, Ronald 12/67
North Korea
- See Korea, North

North Pole
- See Exploration

North, Andy 9/85
North, Oliver 11/86, 2/87, 7/87, 1/89, 5/89, 7/89
Northcliffe, Lord (Alfred Harmsworth) 3/08, 8/22
Northern Ireland
- See Britain (Northern Ireland)

Northrop, John 12/46
Norton, Ken 9/76
Norway
- See also World War II
- First vote for women; only in local elections 12/01
- No women's vote 12/03
- Declares independence from Sweden 6/05
- Referendum approves end of Swedish union 8/05
- Referendum chooses Danish king, Carl 11/05
- Edvard Grieg, nation's composer, dies 9/07
- Independence guaranteed by great powers 11/07
- Parliament to pay members 3/10
- Women get equal franchise with men 6/13
- Women win right to vote 4/16
- Protests to Germany over ship sinking 11/17
- Wins first place at Winter Games 2/24
- First Labour government elected 10/27
- Abandons gold standard 9/31
- Two towns fall into sea; 57 die 4/34
- Reaffirms neutrality 1/40
- 300 UK prisoners freed from German ship 2/40
- Protests at sinking of neutral ships 2/40
- Invaded by Germany 4/40
- King and government escape 4/40
- Quisling says he is head of government 4/40
- War trade pact made with UK 4/40
- Protests at mining of its waters 4/40
- Martial law declared in Oslo 9/41
- Quisling installed as puppet PM 2/42
- Quislingite Norway ends war with Germany 2/42
- All clergy resign 4/42
- State of emergency extended 10/42
- Quisling goes on trial 8/45
- Quisling sentenced to death for treason 9/45
- Quisling executed 10/45
- Trygve Lie is first UN Secretary-General 1/46
- European Games, Oslo 8/46
- Elected to UN Security Council 10/48
- Votes to join NATO 2/49
- Signs North Atlantic Treaty 4/49
- Currency devalued 9/49
- Winter Olympics begin at Oslo 2/52
- Troops spearhead UN Suez forces 11/56
- King Haakon VII dies; Olav V succeeds 9/57
- First internal heart pacemaker 10/58
- Talks on EEC entry open 6/70
- Signs treaty of entry to EEC 1/72
- Referendum vote goes against EEC entry 9/72
- Government resigns 9/72
- Grete Waitz breaks 2.5 hour marathon 10/79
- Brundtland, first woman Prime Minister 2/81

Norwich, Norfolk
- Library fire destroys irreplaceable documents 8/94

Nott, John 4/82, 1/83
Novarro, Ramon 12/26
Novello, Ivor 5/32, 12/39, 3/51, 12/51
Novotny, Antonin 11/57, 11/64, 1/68, 3/68
Nuclear weapons
- See Science

Nuffield, Lord (William Morris) 11/36, 10/37, 2/43, 12/52, 8/63
Numeiry, Gasfar al- 7/71
Nunn, Trevor 1/68
Nuremberg
- See also Germany, World War II
- Nazi leaders go on trial 11/45
- Hess ordered to stand trial 12/45
- Ribbentrop and Goering trial opens 12/45
- Hess asks to conduct his own defence 1/46
- Streicher suffers a mild heart attack 1/46
- Hess trial opens 2/46
- Goering takes blame for wartime actions 3/46
- Goering denies he knew of Final Solution 3/46
- Hess refuses to take witness stand 3/46
- Rosenberg tells why Jews must be killed 4/46
- Schirach opens his defence 5/46
- Speer begins his defence 6/46
- Hess's plea of insanity rejected 8/46
- Nazis experimented with germ warfare 8/46
- War crimes trial ends 8/46
- Tribunal begins to deliver judgements 9/46
- Ten top Nazis executed 10/46
- 12 Nazis sentenced to death 10/46
- Hess sentenced to life imprisonment 10/46
- Tribunal rejects clemency pleas 10/46
- Goering commits suicide 10/46
- Von Papen jailed for eight years 2/47

Nureyev, Rudolf 3/38, 6/61, 12/65, 12/70, 10/77, 1/93
Nurmi, Paavo 8/20, 5/21, 6/24, 7/24, 5/26, 10/73
Nuwar, Abu 4/57

Nyasaland
- Planned federation with two Rhodesias 5/52
- To join Northern and Southern Rhodesia 2/53
- Anti-British riots 2/59
- Rioting continues; Banda arrested 3/59
- 51 die in riots 7/59
- Lord Monckton studies constitution 9/59
- Dr Banda released from jail 4/60
- State of emergency lifted 6/60
- Hastings Banda wins general election 8/61
- To secede from Britain 12/62
- Self-government begins 2/63
- Hastings Banda is premier 2/63
- Becomes independent state of Malawi 7/64

Nyerere, Julius 9/60, 1/62
Nyers, Rezso 10/89
Nyman, Mark 8/93
Nzugwa, Chukwuma 1/66

O

Oakley, Annie 3/22, 11/26
Obeid, Abdul Karim 7/89, 8/91
Oberon, Merle 4/39, 10/79
Obolenski, Ivan 7/04
Obolensky, Alexander 1/36
Obote, Milton 2/66, 3/66, 12/69, 5/70, 1/71, 5/80, 7/85
Obree, Graeme 8/93
O'Brien, Conor Cruise 9/61, 12/61
O'Brien, Kate 8/74
O'Brien, Lawrence 6/72
O'Brien, Leslie 4/66
O'Brien, Tom 11/49
O'Carroll, Tom 3/81
O'Casey, Sean 12/26, 12/29, 9/64
O'Connell, David 4/73
O'Connor, Flannery 8/64
O'Connor, Sandra 7/81
O'Connor, Sinead 12/92
O'Connor, Tony 12/67
Odets, Clifford 7/06
Odin, Gaston 8/12
Odinga, Oginga 10/69
Odle, Robert 5/73
O'Duffy, Eoin 8/33
O'Dwyer, Michael 1/40
Oehmichen, Etienne 2/21, 5/24
Oerter, Al 10/64, 10/68
O'Fiaich, Tomas 8/79, 12/82, 5/90
Ogarkov, Nikolai 9/83
Ogdon, John 12/89
Ogilvy, Angus 4/63
O'Halloran, Michael 9/81
O'Hara, Patrick 5/81
O'Hare, Desmond 10/79
O'Higgins, Kevin 7/27
O'Higgins, Tom 6/66
Oistrakh, David 9/08, 10/74
Ojukwu, Odumegwu 5/67, 7/67, 4/69, 1/70
Okamato, Kozo 7/72
Okello, Tito 1/86
O'Kelly, Sean 4/19
Oklahoma City
- Bomb destroys federal building killing over 100 4/95
- Terrorist bomb: death toll is 167 5/95

Okri, Ben 10/91
Olav V, King of Norway 7/03, 9/57
Oldenburg, Claes 12/62
Oldfield, Maurice 3/81, 4/87
Olesky, Jozef 2/95
Oliver, Joseph ("King") 1/22, 4/38
Olivier, Borg 1/67
Olivier, Laurence 5/07, 9/27, 12/35, 4/39, 12/44, 12/46, 6/47, 3/49, 12/50, 12/51, 12/56, 4/57, 6/57, 12/59, 12/60, 8/62, 12/63, 12/64, 7/67, 6/70, 3/71, 10/76, 12/81, 12/83, 7/89
Olmedo, Alex 7/59
Olsen, Carl 10/53, 12/55
Olympia & York
- Files for bankruptcy 5/92

Olympic Games
- See also results each four years
- Open in Paris 4/00
- Women compete for first time 7/00
- Third Games open in St. Louis 7/04
- Return to Athens for tenth anniversary 4/06
- 21 sports, but technical disputes 7/08
- Opening of fifth Games, Stockholm 6/12
- 1916 Berlin Games cancelled 2/15
- Seventh start at Antwerp 5/20
- First Winter Games; rival Nordic Games 1/24
- Eighth Games, Paris; 42 nations present 7/24
- Founder Pierre de Courbertin retires 9/25
- Amsterdam Games 8/28
- International Committee recommends Berlin for 1936 5/30
- Open in Los Angeles 7/32
- Mildred Didrikson, USA, wins three golds 8/32
- Jews banned from 1936 Berlin Olympics 6/33
- 53 nations, 5,000 athletes; no boycott 8/36
- Hitler snubs Owens 8/36
- Founder Baron Pierre de Coubertin dies 9/37
- 1944 Games to be held in Helsinki 9/38
- Winter Olympics end, Switzerland 2/48
- Open in London 7/48
- East Germany turns down 1952 invitation 12/51
- Zatopek wins 5,000m, 10,000m and marathon 8/52
- China may join Games; Taiwan withdraws 5/54
- Open in Melbourne; first south of Equator 11/56
- Open in Rome; heatwave weather 8/60
- Bikila's gold is first for Africa 9/60
- Winter Olympics open in Innsbruck 1/64
- South Africa banned over apartheid 8/64
- Held in Tokyo - first Games in Asia 10/64
- East and West Germany to compete separately 10/65
- Killy wins three skiing golds 2/68
- Open in Mexico City 10/68
- US Black Power demo 10/68
- South Africa banned from 1972 Olympics 5/70
- Winter Olympics open in Tokyo 2/72
- IOC expels Rhodesia 8/72
- Open in Munich 8/72
- Mark Spitz wins seven swimming golds 9/72
- Palestinian massacre of Israelis 9/72
- Open in Montreal 7/76
- African states boycott over New Zealand 7/76
- UK rejects US boycott plea, Afghanistan 3/80
- Opens in Moscow; no US, Germany or Kenya 7/80
- Torvill and Dean win skating gold 2/84
- USSR to boycott Los Angeles Olympics 5/84
- Open in Los Angeles 7/84
- Winter Games in Canada 2/88
- Summer Games in South Korea 9/88
- Winter Olympics held in Albertville ends 2/92
- Summer Olympics open in Barcelona 7/92
- Ex-USSR tops the medals table in Barcelona 8/92
- The 2000 Games will be in Sydney 9/93
- Bronze for Torvill & Dean at Lillehammer 2/94

O'Malley, Des 7/89
Oman
- British troops quell anti-sultan revolt 7/57
- UK troops take rebel headquarters, Nizwa 8/57

Onassis, Aristotle 1/06, 9/59, 10/68, 3/75
Onassis, Christina 11/88
Onassis, Jacqueline
- See Jacqueline Kennedy

Ondaatje, Michael 10/92
O'Neill, "Tip" 3/81, 7/84
O'Neill, Eugene 10/31, 12/36, 11/53, 12/53, 5/57
O'Neill, Terence 1/65, 6/66, 2/69, 4/69
Ongania, Juan Carlos 6/70
Ono, Yoko 10/68, 3/69, 12/80
Onu, Ismet 11/38
Opel, Fritz von 9/29
Opel, Georg von 8/71
Opera
- See December Surveys and individual artists, composers

Oppenheimer, J. Robert 4/04, 8/45, 4/54, 6/54, 2/67
Oppenhoff, Karl 3/45
Orbison, Roy 12/88
O'Reilly, Gerard 8/86
Orff, Carl 3/82
Orlov, Yuri 5/78
Orozco, Jose 9/49
Orpen, William 12/18, 9/31
Ortega, Daniel 11/84, 9/86, 1/88, 2/90
Ortega, Humberto 3/82
Orton, Joe 12/66, 8/67
Orwell, George 6/03, 12/33, 3/37, 12/37, 12/38, 12/45, 6/49, 1/50
Osborne, John 12/29, 5/56, 4/57, 9/61, 12/64, 12/94
Osborne, Margaret 7/47
Oswald, Lee Harvey 11/63, 3/64, 9/64
O'Toole, Peter 12/60, 12/62, 12/63
Ottoman Empire
- See Turkey

Oueddei, Goukouni 8/83
Ovett, Steve 9/74, 8/77, 7/80, 8/80, 8/81
Owada, Masako 6/93
Owen, David 7/68, 4/72, 2/77, 4/77, 1/78, 2/78, 7/80, 1/81, 6/83, 6/87, 8/87, 1/88, 9/89, 6/90, 9/92, 1/93, 6/93
Owen, Johnny 11/80
Owen, Wilfred 11/18, 12/18, 12/62
Owen, Will 1/70
Owens, Jesse 9/13, 5/35, 7/36, 3/80
Ozal, Turgut 11/83, 6/88, 4/93

P

Paasikivi, Juho 7/52
Pacelli, Eugenio (Pope Pius XII) 7/33, 3/39, 10/58
Packer, Ann 10/64
Packer, Kerry 5/77, 7/77, 11/77
Paddock, Charles 3/21, 4/21
Paderewski, Ignacy 6/41
Padovani, Aurelio 6/26
Paes, Sidonio 12/17, 12/18
Page, Earle 4/39
Pahlavi, Ali Reza Khan, Shah of Persia 10/25, 4/26
Pahlavi, Mohammed Reza, Shah of Iran 10/19, 9/41, 2/49, 10/51, 12/53, 3/58, 12/59, 4/65, 10/67, 11/70, 5/78, 9/78, 12/78, 1/79, 10/79, 11/79, 12/79, 2/80, 3/80, 6/80, 7/80
Paice, Mervyn 7/47
Painleve, Paul 6/24, 2/32, 10/33
Paisley, Bob 5/77
Paisley, Ian 1/69, 2/69, 5/69, 4/70, 3/71, 1/74, 5/77, 6/86
Pakenham, Frank
- See Longford, Lord

Pakistan
- See also Bangladesh, Britain (foreign affairs), Kashmir
- Comes into being 8/47
- Government meets for the first time 8/47
- Rejects Kashmir's decision to join India 10/47
- Last Moslem refugees cross from India 12/47
- Accuses India of armed aggression 1/48
- Accepts UN mediation in India dispute 1/48
- Jinnah dies of heart attack 9/48
- Cease-fire in Kashmir 1/49
- Recognises Communist China 1/50
- With India, makes minorities' pledge 4/50
- Premier Ali Khan assassinated 10/51
- Islamic republic within Commonwealth 11/53
- East Pakistani minister sacked for demanding independence 5/54
- Accepted as a republic by Commonwealth 2/55
- Mohammed Ali resigns as premier 8/55
- Cricket: MCC insults umpire; apologises 3/56
- Declared an Islamic Republic 3/56
- Thousands die in hurricane and tidal wave 10/60
- 10,000 die in cyclone 5/63
- Over 10,000 die in cyclone 5/65
- Clashes with Indian troops in Kashmir 8/65
- At war with India over Kashmir 9/65
- Indian troops launch full-scale invasion 9/65
- President Ayub Khan resigns 3/69
- Army, under Yahya Khan, takes control 3/69
- 150,000 die in typhoon and tidal wave 11/70
- UK and US fly in relief supplies 11/70
- Bhutto becomes leader of West Pakistan 12/70
- Mujibur Rahman is leader of E. Pakistan 12/70
- Rahman declares Bangladesh independent 3/71
- Civil war erupts 3/71
- West Pakistan wreaks revenge on East 4/71
- Thousands killed in East Pakistan 4/71
- Two million flee from East to India 5/71
- Army kills 95 Indian troops in clash 8/71
- New border clashes with India 11/71
- 90 Indian troops die in border clashes 11/71
- Defeated by India in two-week war 12/71
- Breaks off relations with India 12/71
- Official government of East resigns 12/71
- Indian troops close on Dacca 12/71
- President Yahya Khan resigns 12/71
- Zulfikar Ali Bhutto becomes President 12/71
- Quits Commonwealth 1/72
- India to withdraw occupying troops 7/72
- Recognises Bangladesh 2/74
- India to repatriate 195 Pakistani PoWs 4/74
- 4,700 killed in earthquake 12/74
- India's Gandhi proposes new ties 4/76
- Bhutto wins elections 3/77
- Riots after poll-rigging claims 3/77
- Bhutto's martial law, Karachi and Lahore 4/77
- General strike by anti-Bhutto Alliance 4/77
- General Zia overthrows and arrests Bhutto 7/77
- Army rule after hundreds died in riots 7/77
- Bhutto sentenced to death for murder 3/78
- Bhutto appeals against sentence to Zia 3/78
- Court backs Bhutto death; USSR protests 2/79
- Zia introduces Islamic laws 2/79
- Bhutto granted stay of execution 2/79
- Ex-premier Bhutto is hanged 4/79
- Thousands protest Bhutto's death 4/79
- Mob storms US Embassy; troops rescue 11/79
- General Zia apologises to US 11/79
- Zia releases 54 opponents 3/81
- 101 Pakistan Airways hostages freed 3/81
- Benazir Bhutto freed from house arrest 1/84
- Benazir Bhutto returns 4/86
- Benazir Bhutto arrested 8/86
- Riots in several cities 8/86
- Commandos storm hijacked plane; 17 die 9/86
- Timetable for Soviets out of Afghanistan 3/88
- The President Zia ul-Huq dies 8/88
- 300 die in ethnic clashes 10/88
- Benazir Bhutto becomes Prime Minister 11/88
- Sign nuclear agreement with India 12/88
- Salman Rushdie's "Satanic Verses" is banned 1/89
- Benazir Bhutto narrowly survives no-confidence vote 11/89
- Bomb blast at Hyderabad kills more than 38 people 7/90
- Benazir Bhutto offered amnesty from corruption charges 8/90
- Prime Minister Benazir Bhutto is sacked 8/90
- Three days of heavy rain claim 2,000 lives 9/92
- Benazir Bhutto sworn in as Prime Minister 10/93

Pal, Satya 4/19
Palach, Jan 1/69
Palestine
- See also Britain (foreign affairs), Israel, Palestinians
- Druze massacre 100 8/10
- Turkish troops quell Arab unrest 12/10
- To be run by Britain after war 3/16
- British beat 20,000 Turks, Gaza 3/17
- Jews attacked by Moslems 5/17
- British take Beersheba; capture Turks 10/17
- Allenby wipes out Turks, Palestine 9/18
- British take Jaifa, Acre and Es-Salt 9/18
- League gives Britain mandate, San Remo 4/20
- Martial law as Jews and Arabs clash 4/20
- Arabs attack British troops 4/20
- Sets borders with Britain and France 12/20
- Vatican condemns Palestine mandate 5/22
- League approves British mandate 7/22
- Mandate begins 9/23
- 26 die in earthquake 7/27
- Earthquake in Nazareth 1/28
- Martial law as Jews and Arabs fight; 57 die 8/29
- Defence Corps stops Safed massacre 8/29
- Arabs attack Jews in Hebron 8/29
- First British casualties in Gaza 9/29
- Biblical Sodom "found" near Dead Sea 1/30
- Mandate White Paper criticised by Jews 10/30
- Three Neanderthal skeletons discovered 5/32
- 9,000 Arabs protest at Jewish immigration 10/33
- Twenty Jaffa Arab rioters killed by police 10/33
- 3,000 year old archive, Jerusalem 3/35
- Arab-Jewish rioting; 11 die, 50 hurt 4/36
- Abyssinia Emperor Haile Selassie arrives 5/36
- Arabs attack Jews, Mesha; Nablus strike 5/36
- Lines cut in Gaza; troops called in 5/36
- Arabs attack British convoy, Tulkarm 6/36
- RAF strafes Arab ambushers; ten die 6/36
- UK authorities ban planned Arab strike 9/36
- Royal Commission considers partition 6/37
- White Paper wants partition into thirds 7/37
- Planned mandate for Jerusalem and Bethlehem 7/37
- World Zionist Congress opposes partition 8/37
- Two UK officials killed; 100 Arabs held 9/37
- UK curbs Jewish immigration; resentment 10/37
- Arabs attack bus, Rosh Pinah, Jerusalem 10/37
- Syrian border closed; Jerusalem curfew 10/37
- Arabs blow up railway and fire on British 10/37
- Six Arabs and a Jew die in clashes 11/37
- Curfew after riots, Jerusalem 5/38
- Bomb attack on Arab cafe; 20 die 7/38
- Haifa market bomb blast; 43 die, 42 hurt 7/38
- Arabs stone Jews; two die 7/38
- Jews bomb Jerusalem mosque; ten die 7/38
- UK sailors cordon off Haifa after bomb 7/38
- 60 Arabs die in gun battle with British 10/38
- UK cabinet drops partition plan 10/38
- British impose martial law in Jerusalem 10/38
- Britain calls for round-table talks 11/38
- Palestine talks open in London 2/39
- 31 Arabs die in clashes with Jews 2/39
- Britain sets out new constitution 2/39
- London talks on Palestine end in failure 3/39
- Jewish women protest at British plan 5/39
- Illegal Jewish immigrants flooding in 7/39
- Land to be passed from Arabs to Jews 2/40
- Balfour Declaration anniversary riots 11/45
- Terrorists bomb four cities 12/45
- Jewish terrorists kill seven 4/46
- Anglo-US report recommends partition 5/46
- British troops stoned by Arabs 5/46
- Arabs refuse to discuss Anglo-US plan 5/46
- 30 Jewish terrorists jailed for 15 years 6/46
- Jewish terrorists kill two UK officers and kidnap three 6/46
- Zionists bomb King David Hotel 7/46
- Haganah arms cache found 7/46
- 379 alleged terrorists arrested 7/46
- British ban Jewish immigration 8/46
- Jewish Agency orders end to terrorism 9/46
- Jewish terrorists kill eight British troops 11/46
- Jews boycott British goods 11/46
- Bomb kills five British troops 12/46
- British families evacuated 1/47
- Haifa police station blown up 1/47
- Irgun rejects plea to end terrorism 1/47
- Evacuation of Britons begins 2/47
- Three Irgun members sentenced to death 2/47
- Martial law declared in Jewish areas 3/47
- Begin is top of British wanted list 3/47
- Jews blow up Tel Aviv barracks 4/47
- Zionists spring 251 from prison 5/47
- 5,000 Jews prevented from immigrating 7/47
- Weizmann asks for end to immigration ban 7/47
- Zionists hang two British soldiers 7/47
- 35 Zionist leaders detained 8/47
- Britain ready to leave Palestine 8/47
- Stern Gang bomb plot foiled by France 9/47
- Syrian troops mass on border 10/47
- US agrees to partition 10/47
- UN votes for partition 11/47
- First British troops leave 11/47
- Young Jews and Arabs called up to fight 12/47
- Death toll rises in Jewish-Arab clashes 1/48
- 28 UK soldiers die when train hits mine 2/48
- Jews blow up Arab quarter in Haifa 3/48
- Jewish Agency offices blown up 3/48
- Jewish forces agree to truce in Jaffa 4/48
- Jews massacre Arabs in Deir Yassin 4/48
- State of Israel is born 5/48
- British troops withdraw 5/48
- Jordan annexes Arab Palestine 4/50

Palestinians
- Yassir Arafat becomes PLO leader 2/69
- PLO agrees to cease-fire in Lebanon 11/69
- Arafat in Moscow talks 2/70
- PFLP blow up three hijacked jets, Jordan 9/70
- Leila Khaled exchanged for PLFP hostages 9/70
- PLO evicted from strongholds in Jordan 9/70
- Jordan expels 384 Palestinian guerrillas 1/71
- Massacre of Israelis at Munich Olympics 9/72
- Black September hijacks Boeing 727 10/72
- West Germany agrees to hijackers' terms 10/72
- Arafat re-elected PLO leader 1/73
- Gunmen shoot dead three diplomats in Sudan 3/73
- Guerillas in civil war with Lebanon army 5/73
- Terrorists seize Saudi Embassy in Paris 9/73
- Train attacked in Vienna and hostages are taken 9/73
- PLO recognised as sole legal representatives 11/73
- End Kuwait hijack after killing 31 12/73
- Yassir Arafat addresses UN 11/74
- Lebanese Christians fight Palestinians 4/75
- Lebanon's Karami keeps army out of war 9/75
- 70 hostages captured, including 11 oil ministers 12/75
- Austria gives in to terrorists 12/75
- East Beirut Christians attacked 1/76
- PLO does not accept Lebanese cease-fire 5/76
- "Black September" leader Salameh is dead 10/76
- French release Black September man Daoud 1/77
- Hijack 86-passenger plane to Mogadishu 10/77
- Carter favours West Bank homeland 12/77
- PLO London representative Hammami killed 1/78
- Carter and Sadat want Palestinian role 1/78
- Sadat's threat over Israel's stance 1/78
- 7,000 troops invade Lebanon; hit camps 3/78
- Sea raiders hijack Israeli buses; 37 die 3/78
- Syria vows to help against Israel 3/78
- Two die in Arab attack on plane, London 8/78
- Israel raids Lebanese PLO bases 8/78
- Begin to recognise rights, Camp David 9/78
- Demonstrators against Camp David, Oslo 12/78
- Bomb kills Abu Hassan, Olympics suspect 1/79
- Sadat unhappy about Palestinian status 3/79
- PLO's Arafat vows to eliminate Sadat 3/79
- Three bombs maim West Bank mayors 6/80
- Israel and PLO cease-fire, Lebanon 7/81
- Bomb kills 50 in PLO Beirut office 10/81
- Israelis at Beirut; tell PLO to leave 6/82
- Israel bombs their Beirut positions 7/82
- Defeated by Israelis; leave Beirut 8/82
- Arafat and PLO vow to continue struggle 8/82
- New Tunisian headquarters for Arafat 8/82
- Sabra and Chatila massacre, West Beirut 9/82
- Hundreds killed by Christian Phalangists 9/82
- Arafat meets Pope; "suffering people" 9/82
- PLO splits into rival warring factions 6/83
- Yassir Arafat expelled from Syria 6/83
- Israel frees 5,000 Arabs for six soldiers 11/83
- PLO forced to evacuate Lebanon 12/83
- PLO hijacks Achille Lauro cruise ship 10/85
- Israeli air raid on PLO offices, Tunis 10/85
- Egyptian airliner hijacked, Malta 11/85
- Terrorist attack at Rome airport 12/85
- Terrorist attack at Vienna airport 12/85

- PLO HQ to be moved to Yemen 10/86
- Amal blocks off Bourj al Barajneh camp 2/87
- Syrians break Amal siege of Chatila camp 4/87
- Cartoonist wounded in London shooting 7/87
- 18 die in Arab West Bank unrest 12/87
- Israeli crackdown on rioters, Christmas 12/87
- Israeli reaction to intifada uprising 1/88
- Two killed by Jews on West Bank 2/88
- Military commander of PLO murdered 4/88
- Yassir Arafat refused US entry visa 11/88
- US to open talks with Palestinians 12/88
- William Waldegrave meets PLO leader, Yassir Arafat 1/89
- PLO holds first formal talks with new US administration 3/89
- Guerrilla leader George Habash threatens support of Iraq 9/90
- 21 Palestinians shot dead by Israeli police 10/90
- PLO's deputy leader, Abu Iyad, is assassinated 1/91
- Not formally represented in Madrid Mid-East summit 11/91
- PLO leader, Yassir Arafat, survives plane crash 4/92
- PLO official, Atef Bessio, is assassinated in Paris 6/92
- PLO and Israeli leaders shake hands at White House 9/93

Palin, Michael 12/89
Palma, Estrada 9/06
Palma, Thomas 2/04
Palme, Olof 1/27, 10/69, 9/75, 9/76, 9/82, 2/86, 7/89, 10/89
Palmer, Arnold 9/29, 8/54, 4/58
Palmer, Geoffrey 0/09
Palmer, Samuel 12/76
Pan American
- Pays compensation to Lockerbie victims' families 5/90
- Ceases operations after financial rescue plan fails 12/91

Panama
- Founded; signs canal treaty with USA 11/03
- Engineer Goethals invited to be governor 1/14
- Declares war on Germany 4/17
- President Remon assassinated 1/55
- Nicaraguan President Somoza shot dead 9/56
- Ballerina Fonteyn jailed in coup drama 4/59
- Cuban invaders surrender 5/59
- To renegotiate Panama Canal Treaty with US 10/76
- US treaty gives Canal to Panama in 1999 9/77
- Ex-Shah leaves for Panama 12/79
- Ex-Shah leaves Panama for Cairo 3/80
- President Torrijos dies in plane crash 7/81
- Only vote against UK in UN on Falklands issue 4/82
- Demonstrators protest against ballot-rigging in elections 5/89
- Attempt to topple Noriega fails 10/89
- Manuel Noriega takes refuge in papal nunciature 12/89
- US troops invade and oust Noriega 12/89
- General Noriega goes on trial in Miami for drug-trafficking 7/92

Panama Canal
- Hay-Pauncefote Treaty on canal 2/01
- US Commission support 1/02
- US Congress buys French concession 6/02
- Rival generals in revolt near Panama 10/02
- Colombia rejects US offer 11/02
- US and Colombia sign treaty 1/03
- Senate ratifies treaty 3/03
- Colombian senate rejects treaty 8/03
- US warships sent in 11/03
- Work starts 5/04
- US buys French concession for $40m 11/04
- Inspected by President Roosevelt 11/06
- US Army will build it, says Roosevelt 2/07
- Engineer predicts £60 million costs 1/08
- President Wilson opens Canal 10/13
- Goethals invited to be Zone governor 1/14
- US, Panama to renegotiate treaty 10/76
- US treaty gives Canal to Panama in 1999 9/77
- Senate approves Canal treaty 4/78

Pangalos, Theodoros 8/26
Panic, Milan 12/92
Panitzki, Werner 8/66
Pankhurst, Christabel 10/05, 2/07, 6/08, 10/08, 11/11, 3/58
Pankhurst, Emmeline 10/03, 6/06, 10/08, 2/13, 10/13, 3/14, 5/14
Pankhurst, Sylvia 2/13, 7/13, 3/14, 10/20, 9/60
Panov, Valery 6/74
Panter, Noel 11/33
Papadopoulos, George 4/67, 4/70, 8/73, 11/73, 8/75
Papagos, Field Marshal 10/55
Papanastasiou, Andreas 5/32
Papandreou, Andreas 4/67, 8/74, 10/81, 6/89, 9/89, 10/93
Papandreou, George 2/64, 4/67
Papen, Franz von 5/32, 6/32, 7/32, 8/32, 9/32, 11/32, 1/33, 7/33, 7/34, 11/45, 2/47, 5/69

Papua New Guinea
- Becomes independent of Australia 9/75

Paraguay
- Bolivia signs treaty to end dispute 9/29
- Quits League of Nations 2/35
- Ends three-year Chaco dispute with Bolivia 6/35
- Rebels seize Asuncion; Ayala resigns 2/36
- First South American Fascist regime 3/36
- Declares war on Germany 2/45
- President Alfredo Stroessner re-elected 2/68
- Ex-Nicaraguan dictator Somoza killed 9/80
- Coup ousts dictator Alfredo Stroessner 2/89
- Juan Carlos Wasmosy wins first multi-party elections 5/93

Parish, Daphne 3/90, 7/90
Park Chung-hee 8/74
Parker, Alton B. 7/04
Parker, Bonnie 5/34
Parker, Charlie 8/20, 3/55, 12/58, 9/91
Parker, Dorothy 6/67
Parker, Tom 8/77
Parkinson, Cecil 11/70, 9/81, 9/83, 10/83
Parkinson, Cyril Northcote 3/93
Parkinson, Michael 12/83
Parkinson, Norman 2/90
Parks, Rosa 12/55
Parmoor, Lord 10/24
Parnell, Reg 5/54
Parnes, Tony 8/90
Parsons, William 8/45
Pascoe, Alan 9/74
Pasha, Ahmed Maher 2/45
Pasha, Bakr Sidki 8/37
Pasha, Essad 5/14
Pasha, Glubb
- See Glubb, John 3/56

Pasha, Hussein Sirry 7/52
Pasha, Khalil 4/16
Pasha, Nahas 8/36, 1/62
Pasha, Nokrashy 5/48
Pasha, Shefkat 1/13
Pasha, Sidky 2/46
Pasha, Zaghlol 7/24
Passayev, Victor 6/71
Pasey, Frederic 12/01
Pasternak, Boris 10/58, 12/58, 5/60
Patel, Praful 9/72
Patel, Vallabhai 1/32
Paterson, Jackie 3/40
Paton, Alan 1/03, 12/48
Patten, Chris 7/92, 12/92
Patten, Frank 2/31
Patterson, Floyd 6/59, 6/60, 9/62, 11/65
Patterson, Gerald 7/22
Patti, Adelina 9/19
Patton, George 8/44, 11/44, 12/44, 10/45, 12/45
Patty, "Budge" 6/53
Paul I, King of Greece 4/56, 3/64
Paul, Prince of Yugoslavia 3/41
Paul, Wolfgang 12/89
Paul-Boncour, Joseph 12/32
Pauli, Wolfgang 12/45
Pauling, Linus 2/01, 12/49, 12/62
Pavarotti, Luciano 12/90, 7/91
Pavese, Cesare 9/08, 8/50
Pavlov, Ivan 12/04, 2/36
Pavlov, Valentin 8/91
Pavlova, Anna 12/09, 12/12, 12/21, 1/31
Pavolini, Alessandro 4/45
Pawlak, Waldemar 6/92, 10/93
Paxton, Joseph 11/36
Payne, Cynthia 2/87
Paz, Octavio 12/90
Peach, Blair 4/79, 5/80
Peacock, Keith 8/65
Peake, Mervyn 11/68
Pearce, Padraic 4/16
Pearson, Arthur 1/08
Pearson, Lester 7/67, 8/67, 4/68
Peary, Robert Edwin 7/05, 4/09, 9/09, 2/16, 2/20
Peckinpah, Sam 12/84
Pedroza, Eusebio 6/85
Peel, John 9/67
Pegg, David 2/58
Peguy, Charles 12/18
Pele (Edson Arantes do Nascimento) 10/40, 6/58, 6/62, 7/66, 6/69, 6/75
Peled, Nejamin 9/73
Pelletier, Monique 9/78
Peltzer, Otto 9/26
Pender, Paul 7/61
Penderecki, Krzysztof 11/33
Penhaligon, David 3/77, 12/86
Penkovsky, Oleg 12/62, 5/63
Penrose, Roland 4/69, 7/69
Penson, Lillian 6/48
Peres, Shimon 8/23, 4/77, 5/77, 9/82, 9/84, 10/86, 11/88, 10/94
Perez, Andres 5/93
Perez, Carlos 2/92, 11/92
Perez, Garcia 6/86
Perkins, Anthony 6/60, 9/92
Peron, Eva 6/47, 8/47, 2/49, 11/51, 7/52
Peron, Isabel 6/74, 7/74, 3/76, 3/81, 9/83
Peron, Juan 6/43, 10/45, 6/46, 6/47, 2/49, 11/51, 4/53, 4/54, 6/55, 9/55, 11/72, 9/73, 7/74
Perot, Ross 11/92
Perry, Fred 7/31, 7/33, 9/33, 7/34, 9/34, 6/35, 7/35, 7/36, 9/36, 2/95
Pershing, John 3/16, 6/17, 7/19, 4/21, 7/48

Persia
- See also Iran
- Shah visits Britain 8/02
- Mohammad Ali becomes new Shah 1/07
- New shah has constitutional government 2/07
- Settles border dispute 2/08
- Shah survives assassination attempt 2/08
- Shah's army vents fury on reformists 6/08
- Shah reforms parliament 7/08
- Anglo-Persian Oil Company formed 4/09
- Shah accepts constitution idea 5/09
- Shah goes back on constitution and votes 6/09
- Nationalists overthrow Shah Mohammad Ali 7/09
- Russia and Britain step in to quell unrest 1/10
- British troops land to protect interests 10/10
- Britain buys Anglo-Persian oil share 5/14
- Britain and Russia form alliance 8/16
- Britain signs aid agreement 8/19
- Red Army invades from Caspian Sea 5/20
- General Reza Khan's coup reported 2/21
- Treaty with Russia 2/21
- 20,000 die in earthquakes 6/23
- Reza Khan Pahlavi deposes Shah Mirza 10/25
- Treaty with Britain extends oil contract 2/26
- Ex-trooper Reza Khan crowned Shah 4/26
- Signs non-aggression pact with USSR 10/27
- 3,000 die in earthquake, Khorassan area 5/29
- With Turks, attacks Kurds 8/30
- Ends 1901 oil concession to Britain 11/32
- Changes name to Iran 12/34

Pertini, Sandro 7/78
Peru
- Captain Besley finds Inca jungle ruins 2/14
- Breaks off relations with Germany 10/17
- President Leguia resigns after coup 8/30
- President Luis Cerro assassinated 4/33
- Declares war on Germany 2/45
- Over 3,000 die in landslide 1/62
- Army seizes power and arrests President 7/62
- 800 Communists arrested by junta 1/63
- 320 die in soccer riot 5/64
- 99 die in plane crash 8/70
- Eight newsmen killed in ambush 1/83
- President Perez escapes attempt on life 6/86
- Shining Path leader, Abimael Guzman, is arrested 9/92
- Attempt to overthrow President Fujimori fails 11/92
- Moving towards peace with Ecuador 1/95
- Cease-fire signed with Ecuador 2/95

Perutz, Max 12/62
Petacci, Clara 4/45
Petain, Henri Philippe 2/16, 4/17, 7/18, 5/26, 3/39, 6/40, 7/40, 10/40, 11/40, 12/40, 2/41, 3/41, 6/41, 7/41, 4/42, 11/43, 4/44, 5/44, 8/44, 4/45, 7/45, 8/45, 7/51
Peter II, King of Yugoslavia 10/34, 3/41, 8/45, 11/45
Peter, King of Serbia 10/15, 11/18
Peters, Jim 6/53, 8/54
Peters, John 1/91
Peters, Martin 7/66
Peters, Mary 9/72
Petersen, Jack 2/35
Peterson, Oscar 12/58
Petiot, Marcel 4/46
Petkov, Nicholas 3/07
Petkov, Nikola 9/47
Petra, Yvon 7/46
Petrosian, Tigran 10/71
Petrov, Vladimir 4/54, 7/54, 9/55
Pettersson, Christer 7/89, 10/89
Pettit, William 10/53
Peyron, Bruno 4/93
Pflimlin, Pierre 5/58
Pfrimer, Walter 9/31
Phat, Lam Van 9/64
Philby, Eleanor 3/63
Philby, Harold Adrian Russell (Kim) 3/54, 11/55, 3/63, 7/63, 8/65, 11/67, 12/67, 5/88
Philip, Prince, Duke of Edinburgh
- See also Royal Family (Britain) 3/47, 7/47, 11/47, 7/48, 10/51, 2/52, 11/53, 2/56, 10/57, 3/58, 11/63, 12/63, 9/66, 5/67, 11/69, 10/71, 6/72, 6/77, 12/82, 3/83, 10/86, 2/89

Philippines
- See also World Wars I and II
- America offers amnesty to rebels 6/00
- Rebels surrender 12/00
- Americans capture rebel leader Aguinaldo 3/01
- Rebel leader Tinio surrenders 4/01
- To be ruled by US commission 7/02
- General Wood beats rebels 11/03
- 30,000 destitute in Mindanao typhoon 11/04
- US troops and Moro tribesmen die in attack 5/05
- US Army boosted, fearing Chinese unrest 1/06
- Taft opens assembly; delays independence 10/07
- US Senate votes for independence 2/16
- 15,000 homeless after fire 4/21
- US President rules out independence 3/24
- 175 die in Luzon typhoon 11/26
- Total solar eclipse 5/29
- Typhoon destroys 14 towns 1/30
- Hoover vetoes Filipino independence bill 1/33
- Congress overrides Hoover Filipino veto 1/33
- US grants independence by 1945 3/34
- Quezon becomes President after elections 9/35
- US General MacArthur to organise army 9/35
- Quezon sworn in as first President 11/35
- Typhoon kills 109 10/36
- Japanese take Manila 1/42
- US leases air and naval bases 3/47
- Defence pact with US 4/52
- Eight nations sign defence pact 9/54
- Khrushchev thumps shoe at Filipino man 10/60
- UN delegate Sumulong: "USSR imperialism" 10/60
- Death of Emilio Aguinaldo 2/64
- 74 die in air crash 5/64
- Ferdinand Marcos becomes President 12/65
- 800 die in typhoon 10/70
- Knife-wielding man tries to attack Pope 11/70
- 356 die in floods 8/72
- Minister attacked; martial law declared 9/72
- Marcos extends his term of office 1/73
- Marcos's foe Aquino sentenced to death 11/77
- US reaffirms support for Marcos 6/83
- Benigno Aquino shot dead at airport 8/83
- Marcos accuses enemies of inciting panic 8/83
- Cory Aquino - husband's funeral speech 8/83
- Seven die in clashes with security forces 9/83
- Chief justice quits Aquino murder panel 9/83
- Marcos shuts newspaper critical of army 9/83
- Marcos announces new Aquino inquiry 10/83
- Anti-Marcos protests in Manila 11/83
- 900,000 in anti-Marcos protest 8/84
- 1,000 die in typhoon 9/84
- Aquino killing linked to armed forces 10/84
- 26 charged with Aquino murder 1/85
- Presidential election called 11/85
- Corazon Aquino to run for President 12/85
- Marcos declares he has won election 2/86
- US withdraws support for Marcos regime 2/86
- Marcos ousted by Corazon Aquino 2/86
- Over 30 die in election violence 2/86
- President Aquino forms cabinet 2/86
- Pro-Marcos coup attempt fails 7/86
- Defence Minister Enrile sacked 11/86
- Aquino quells pro-Marcos uprising 1/87
- Army rebels take radio station; evicted 1/87
- Coup leader Honasan in hiding 8/87
- 1,500 die as ferry sinks 12/87
- Rebel troops end bid to topple Aquino 12/89
- Government troops crush attempted coup 10/90
- Half a million people evacuated near Mount Pinatubo 6/91
- Fidel Ramos is elected President 6/92

Philipson, Mrs Hilton 6/23
Phillips, Mark 3/73, 5/73, 11/73, 3/74, 8/89, 4/92
Phillips, Peter 12/61
Phillips, Peter Mark Andrew 4/92
Phillips, Sam 12/68
Phillips, Zara Anne Elizabeth 4/92
Phipps, Eric 11/36
Phipps, Jill 2/95
Phouma, Prince of Laos 4/64
Piaf, Edith 12/15, 10/63, 12/63
Piano, Renzo 2/77
Piatakov, Grigori 1/37
Piazzolla, Aster 7/92
Picabia, Francis 2/16, 12/20, 1/22, 11/53, 12/53
Picasso, Pablo 3/07, 12/11, 2/13, 5/17, 12/17, 12/19, 10/25, 12/25, 12/37, 12/46, 3/61, 4/62, 4/67, 4/73
Piccard, Auguste 5/31, 3/62
Pick, Frank 12/34
Pickford, Mary 4/19, 3/20, 12/33, 1/35, 5/39, 5/79
Picot, Georges 3/16
Pieck, Wilhelm 10/49
Pierce, Stephen 12/38
Pierlot, Hubert 9/44
Piggott, Lester 8/48, 5/52, 6/54, 6/57, 6/59, 9/60, 6/70, 6/72, 6/76, 6/77, 6/83, 10/87, 10/92
Pigott-Smith, Tim 12/84
Pilsudski, Joseph 9/15, 7/17, 11/18, 12/22, 5/26, 6/26, 10/26, 2/27, 8/30, 5/35
Pinassilgo, Maria 7/79
Pincher, Chapman 3/81
Pindling, Lynden 7/73
Pineau, Christian 9/56
Pinero, Arthur 1/11
Pinkowski, Josef 8/80, 2/81
Pinochet, Augusto 9/80, 6/83, 10/88
Pinter, Harold 10/30, 5/58, 12/60, 12/81
Pintor, Lupe 11/80
Piper, John 12/45, 5/62
Pirandello, Luigi 12/22, 12/34, 12/36
Pirie, Gordon 6/56
Pissarro, Camille 11/03
Pissarro, Lucien 12/11
Pitman, Jenny 4/83
Pitt, Bill 10/81
Planck, Max 12/00, 6/29, 10/47
Planer, Nigel 12/83
Platt, David 7/90, 5/92
Player, Gary 4/61, 7/68, 7/74
Pleasance, Donald 2/95
Pleven, Rene 7/50, 1/51
PLO (Palestine Liberation Organisation)
- See Palestinians

Plomley, Roy 5/85
Plotz, Harry 4/13
Plowright, Joan 7/89
Po Sun Yun 5/61
Podgorny, Nikolai 12/65, 4/66, 11/70, 1/71, 6/77, 1/83
Pohl, Oswald 5/46
Poincare, Raymond 1/12, 8/12, 1/13, 7/14, 9/16, 6/19, 1/20, 1/22, 1/23, 10/23, 1/24, 5/24, 7/26, 7/29, 10/34
Poindexter, John 11/86, 7/87
Poitier, Sidney 3/55, 4/64
Pol Pot 1/75, 4/75, 7/75, 9/77, 1/79, 4/79, 7/79, 8/79, 9/79
Poland
- See also World War II
- Schools closed after anti-Russian protests 3/02
- Anti-Russian riots, troops mobilised 11/04
- Workers shoot at police; Warsaw looted 1/05
- Socialists meet in Geneva; agree tactics 5/05
- May Day protest; troops kill 100 5/05
- Anti-Semitic riots in Warsaw; many die 5/05
- General strike; state of emergency 8/05
- Strikes and curfew; school language win 10/05
- Attempt to kill Russian Governor-General 8/06
- Anti-Russian riots spread 8/06
- 100 Jews killed at authorities' instigation 9/06
- Pupils' anti-German language strike 10/06
- German-Vatican agreement on state education 9/07
- Russia threatens to sack rebel teachers 9/08
- Anti-Russian protests at ceremony 7/10
- Germany and Austria partition state in war 8/15
- Pilsudski launches freedom movement 9/15
- Proclaimed independent by Germany and Austria 11/16
- Germany deports a million Poles 12/16
- Provisional parliament 1/17
- Call for German and Austrian acceptance 5/17
- Pilsudski resigns from Council of State 7/17
- Central Powers accept new government 9/17
- Demonstrations over transfer to Ukraine 2/18
- UK, France and Italy accept independence 6/18
- Pilsudski is President with full powers 11/18
- 3,200 Jews reported killed at Lvov 12/18
- Germany surrenders territory 2/19
- Typhoid kills thousands 2/20
- Attacked by Russian Red Army 3/20
- Declares war on Russia; appeals for help 5/20
- Repels Russians from gates of Warsaw 8/20
- US warships in Danzig to counter Reds 8/20
- Takes 42,000 Russian prisoners 10/20
- Signs armistice with Russia at Riga 10/20
- Military and economic pact with France 2/21
- Allies divide Silesia between Poland and Germany 8/21
- Discusses Upper Silesia with Germans 2/22
- Absorbs Lithuanian city of Vilna 2/22
- Pilsudski resigns as president 12/22
- President Narutowicz killed after two days' rule 12/22
- Asks to join League 2/26
- Pilsudski leads military coup 5/26
- President Wojciechowski arrested 5/26
- Pilsudski given dictatorial powers 6/26
- New President Moscicki has few powers 6/26
- Pilsudski becomes premier 10/26
- Freedom of movement to and from Danzig 2/27
- 200 die and 15,000 homeless in Galician flood 9/27
- Vilna claimed by Lithuania as capital 9/27
- Trade pact with Germany 11/27
- Denies it plans to annex Lithuania 11/27
- Pilsudski is premier and war minister 8/30
- Signs friendship treaty with USSR 6/31
- Sign non-aggresion pact with USSR 1/32
- Defaults on US debt repayment 12/32
- Signs treaty with Free City of Danzig 8/33
- Discuss anti-German front with Rumania and USSR 9/33
- Ten-year non-aggression pact with Germany 1/34
- USSR and Poland non-aggression pact to 1945 5/34
- Frontier guarantee with USSR and Rumania 6/34
- Conscription for men and women 9/34

- Germany wants to abolish Polish Corridor 3/35
- President Marshal Pilsudski dies 5/35
- Frees 27,000 prisoners 1/36
- France will loan arms 8/36
- Annexes Teschen in Czech Silesia 10/38
- Accepts Jews expelled from Germany 10/38
- Ex-leader Gomulka arrested 10/38
- Britain pledges to defend Poland 3/39
- France pledges to defend Poland 3/39
- Signs pact with Britain and France 4/39
- Polish Jews deported from Germany 6/39
- Opposition to German designs on Danzig 7/39
- Troops rushed to border with Germany 8/39
- Reservists and men up to 40 called up 8/39
- Germany and USSR invade 9/39
- Troops evacuated as Warsaw surrenders 9/39
- Government flees to Lublin 9/39
- Government-in-exile set up in Paris 10/39
- Himmler orders camp built at Auschwitz 3/40
- 350,000 Jews are now in Warsaw ghetto 11/40
- Statesman Ignac Paderewski dies 6/41
- Deportations to Auschwitz begin 3/42
- 600,000 Jews in Warsaw ghetto 6/42
- 50,000 Jews slaughtered in Warsaw ghetto 9/42
- Jewish ghetto in Warsaw to be eliminated 2/43
- Seven villages razed and males massacred 3/43
- Jewish uprising in Warsaw ghetto 4/43
- Stalin says he wants strong, free Poland 5/43
- PM in exile, Sikorski, dies in air crash 7/43
- Jewish uprising in Bialystok ghetto 8/43
- Camp inmates used for medical trials 9/43
- USSR inquiry blames Germans for Katyn 1/44
- Exiled government rejects Curzon Line 2/44
- 47 Allied POWs shot after escape attempt 5/44
- Maidenek death camp found 8/44
- German tanks raze Warsaw 8/44
- Red Army discovers horror of Auschwitz 1/45
- UK refuses to recognise provisional government 1/45
- Warsaw falls to Soviet and Polish troops 1/45
- Nazis have shot German commanders 2/45
- Gates of Nazi death camps open 4/45
- UK and US recognise government 7/45
- Signs treaty with USSR fixing border 8/45
- 190,000 bodies of POWs found in Silesia 2/46
- Peasant Party says election was rigged 1/47
- Truman says Poland broke election pledge 2/47
- Condemned opposition leader is in London 11/47
- Communist leader Gomulka dismissed 9/48
- Asks US to recall its ambassador 3/49
- Ends friendship pact with Yugoslavia 9/49
- E. Germany signs Oder-Neisse line treaty 6/50
- Cardinal Stefan Wyszynski arrested 9/53
- Catholics march against Cardinal's arrest 10/53
- Ex-security boss Swiatlo gets US asylum 9/54
- Joins Warsaw Pact 5/55
- USSR releases ex-leader Gomulka 4/56
- 38 die in workers' riot, Poznan 6/56
- Police machinegun crowds; martial law 6/56
- Gomulka returns to Central Committee 8/56
- Gomulka elected premier; anti-USSR mood 10/56
- Khrushchev flies in for talks 10/56
- Cardinal Wyszynski freed 10/56
- Anti-Soviet, pro-Hungarian protests 10/56
- Demands restitution from USSR for Katyn 10/56
- Gomulka urges people to stop protesting 10/56
- Gomulka allows Soviet troops to stay 11/56
- National elections 1/57
- Asks USSR for aid 5/57
- Students riot against government 10/57
- US rejects Polish nuclear-free zone 5/58
- Protests at Hungary's execution of Nagy 6/58
- US Vice-President Nixon visits 8/59
- De Gaulle visits 9/67
- 300 arrested during riots 3/68
- Warsaw Pact leaders discuss Czech crisis 7/68
- Three British diplomats expelled 1/70
- Reconciliation pact with West Germany 11/70
- Anti-government riots over food prices 12/70
- Gomulka resigns 12/70
- Edward Gierek succeeds Gomulka 12/70
- Six killed in Gdansk riots 12/70
- Gierek pledges to freeze food prices 12/70
- Gomulka suspended from Communist CC 2/71
- Leader Gierek meets Cardinal Wyszynksi 10/77
- Pole is new Pope 10/78
- Two million greet visiting Pope 6/79
- Pope meets Cardinal Wyszynski, President 6/79
- Pope's tribute to the land and people 6/79
- Malinowski and Kozakiewicz win at Olympics 7/80
- Gdansk workers strike over dismissal 8/80
- Shipyard workers' 16-point manifesto 8/80
- Government talks to strikers 8/80
- Pinkowski replaces Babiuch as premier 8/80
- Walesa gets promises of free unions 8/80
- Jagielski promises less censorship 8/80
- Kania replaces Gierek as party leader 9/80
- Lech Walesa creates Solidarity union 9/80
- Catholic Church backs Solidarity 10/80
- State does not recognise Solidarity 10/80
- Kania says Solidarity abuses rights 11/80
- NATO warns USSR: stay out 12/80
- Soviet troops mass on borders 12/80
- Walesa condemns "irresponsible strikes" 12/80
- General Jaruzelski takes over as premier 2/81
- Solidarity's four-hour general strike 3/81
- Walesa blasts police treatment 3/81
- Warsaw Pact stops exercises 4/81
- Cardinal Wyszynski dies 5/81
- Communist Party leaders in crisis talks 6/81
- Million Solidarity members strike 8/81
- Solidarity's first national congress 9/81
- Pope supports free trade unions 9/81
- USSR slams "anti-Soviet" Solidarity 9/81
- USSR pressure; US union visit banned 9/81
- Jaruzelski new party leader after Kania 10/81
- National Alliance of party, church and union 11/81
- Martial law; 14,000 unionists jailed 12/81
- Seven killed in Silesian coalfields 12/81
- Cardinal Glemp wants peace; Gierek held 12/81
- Ambassador to US given asylum 12/81
- Food prices double; riots at Gdansk 1/82
- 200 arrested in Gdansk riots; curfew 1/82
- 3,500 arrested in new crackdown 2/82
- Jaruzelski in USSR for talks 3/82
- Martial law relaxed; prisoners freed 4/82
- New restrictions after May Day protests 5/82
- Government releases 1,227 detainees 7/82
- Protests against martial law, Warsaw 8/82
- Police use tear gas and water cannon in Gdansk 8/82
- Cardinal Glemp demands Walesa's release 8/82
- Gunmen seize embassy in Switzerland 9/82
- Ex-premier Gomulka dies 9/82
- Parliament outlaws Solidarity 10/82
- Party wants new union 10/82
- Solidarity stops mass protests 10/82
- Walesa writes to Jaruzelski; is freed 11/82
- Walesa warns on danger of mass protests 11/82
- Solidarity general strike fails 11/82
- Restoration of Solidarity sought, Gdansk 3/83
- Walesa returns to work at Lenin shipyard 4/83
- Pro-Solidarity May Day demonstration 5/83
- Pope, on visit, backs Polish freedoms 6/83
- Government warns Church off politics 6/83
- Martial law lifted 7/83
- Lech Walesa awarded Peace Nobel 10/83
- Signs economic pact with USSR 5/84
- Amnesty of 652 political prisoners 7/84
- Killing of Solidarity priest Popieluszko 10/84
- 200,000 attend Popieluszko funeral 11/84
- Four policemen on trial for Popieluszko murder 12/84
- Four policemen jailed for Popielusko murder 2/85
- Solidarity supporters clash with police 5/85
- Solidarity leader Bujak arrested 5/86
- 225 political prisoners freed 9/86
- 183 die on US-bound air flight 5/87
- Price increases lead to strikes 4/88
- Riot police smash strikes 5/88
- Lech Walesa calls for end to strikes 8/88
- Thatcher visits Gdansk shipyard 11/88
- Solidarity agrees to government terms to end ban on union 1/89
- Ban is lifted on Solidarity 5/89
- Solidarity wins 99 seats in new 100-seat senate 6/89
- Solidarity wins over Communists in elections 6/89
- Wojciech Jaruzelski elected President 7/89
- Elects non-Communist Prime Minister 8/89
- First cabinet for 40 years not dominated by Communists 9/89
- Lech Walesa wins landslide victory in presidential elections 12/90
- Doctors limit women's right to abortion 5/92
- Waldemar Pawlak is elected President 6/92
- Pawlak appointed Premier 10/93
- Jozef Olesky appointed Premier 2/95

Polanski, Roman 8/33, 1/68, 8/69, 9/77, 12/81
Polhill, Robert 4/90
Pollock, Jackson 1/12, 12/48, 8/56
Polly Peck group
- Police raid offices 9/90
- Goes into receivership with £1.3 billion debts 10/90

Pompidou, Georges 7/11, 4/62, 5/68, 7/68, 4/69, 6/69, 7/69, 2/70, 3/70, 11/70, 5/71, 10/72, 4/74
Pontecorvo, Bruno 10/50, 2/55, 3/55, 9/93
Ponti, Carlo 6/62, 4/66
Ponting, Clive 8/84, 2/85
Poole, Frederick 8/18
Poole, M.J. 7/70
Poole, Roger 11/89, 2/90
Pop culture
- See also Music (popular)
- 5,000 attend UK "Legalise Pot 1967" rally 7/67
- Festival of the Flower Children, UK 8/67
- Beatles meditate with Maharishi Yogi 8/67
- The year of flower power 12/67
- Beatles launch Apple boutique in London 1/68
- US musical "Hair" 12/68
- Lennon and Ono "bed-in" for peace 3/69
- Rolling Stones play for free, Hyde Park 7/69
- Isle of Wight pop festival 8/69
- 400,000 attend Woodstock festival, US 8/69
- Sharon Tate killed in Hollywood massacre 8/69
- Police storm peaceful Piccadilly squat 9/69
- Second Isle of Wight pop festival 8/70
- Hippies fight police at Windsor festival 8/74

Pope Benedict XV 9/14, 4/16, 8/17, 1/19, 5/20, 11/20, 1/22
Pope John Paul II 6/67, 10/78, 2/79, 6/79, 9/79, 10/79, 3/80, 5/80, 10/80, 11/80, 5/81, 6/81, 9/81, 5/82, 6/82, 9/82, 3/83, 6/83, 7/83, 12/83, 1/85, 8/85, 2/86, 6/87, 9/89, 9/90, 5/93
Pope John XXIII 10/58, 4/59, 1/60, 10/62, 5/63, 6/63
Pope John-Paul I 8/78, 9/78
Pope Leo XIII 7/03
Pope Paul VI 6/63, 8/63, 1/64, 11/64, 12/64, 1/65, 4/65, 10/65, 3/66, 6/67, 7/68, 8/68, 11/70, 9/71, 9/72, 6/78, 8/78
Pope Pius IX 11/26, 7/29
Pope Pius X 1/04, 2/06, 4/07, 7/07, 4/09, 9/10, 8/14
Pope Pius XI 12/22, 6/23, 3/24, 9/27, 2/29, 1/31, 5/31, 9/32, 5/35, 2/37, 2/39
Pope Pius XII 3/39, 10/45, 10/48, 2/49, 4/49, 7/49, 12/50, 1/54, 6/54, 10/58, 1/62
Pope-Hennessey, John 10/94
Pope-Hennessey, James 1/74
Popieluszko, Jerzy 10/84, 11/84, 2/85, 11/88
Popovitch, Pavel 8/62
Popper, Karl 9/94
Popplewell, Oliver 1/86
Porsche, Ferdinand 2/36, 1/51
Portago, Marquis de 5/57
Porter, Cole 11/34, 12/35, 10/64
Porter, Edwin 6/03
Porter, Eric 12/68
Porter, George 12/67
Porter, Rodney 12/72
Portugal
- Treaty with Holland over Timor 10/04
- King and Crown Prince assassinated 2/08
- Dictator Franco flees after King's death 2/08
- Monarchists win election 4/08
- Army overthrows King Manuel; many deaths 10/10
- New government bans monks and royal family 10/10
- Women's suffrage established 4/11
- New republic suppresses revolt 7/11
- Arriaga is first President of new republic 8/11
- Royalist peasant revolt crushed by army 10/11
- Machado overthrown in pro-German coup 12/17
- New President Paes, Premier Costa 12/17
- President Paes shot after year's rule 12/18
- Coup attempt kills Premier Granjo 10/21
- Gomes da Costa takes power in coup 5/26
- Bubonic plague outbreak 1/27
- Carmona crushes revolution; 200 die 2/27
- Salazar is new Fascist premier 7/32
- Leaves Spanish arms cordon 2/37
- President Carmona visits South Africa 8/39
- Grants Allies garrison on Azores 10/43
- US vetoes entry to UN 8/46
- 16 die in air crash 2/47
- Signs North Atlantic Treaty 4/49
- Antonio Moniz wins Medicine Nobel 12/49
- Oil boss Gulbenkian donates £300 million 7/55
- Shoots 12 Goan protesters; no to cession 8/55
- Queen and Prince Philip arrive 2/57
- Told by UN to reform Angola 4/61
- Indian troops take back Goa 12/61
- Remains colonial power in Africa 12/63
- Marcelo Caetano takes over as premier 9/68
- Former dictator Antonio Salazar dies 7/70
- Bomb explodes during NATO talks 6/71
- Army in Mozambique admits to massacre 8/73
- Spinola topples Caetano in coup 4/74
- Exiled Socialist Mario Soares returns 4/74
- Plans for Angolan independence 8/74
- West African colonies' independence pact 8/74
- Spinola forced out by young rebels 9/74
- Costa Gomez becomes President 9/74
- Agrees Angolan independence; 13 year war 1/75
- Spinola's right-wing coup quashed 3/75
- Soldiers set up dynamic Supreme Council 3/75
- Soares' Socialists win in free elections 4/75
- Mozambique wins independence 4/75
- Whites flee from Angola pre-independence 8/75
- Angola gains independence 11/75
- Socialist Mario Soares is premier 4/76
- Soares depends on minority Communists 4/76
- Pinassilgo is first woman premier 7/79
- Pope attacked near Shrine of Fatima 5/82
- Election makes Socialists largest party 4/83
- Seven die in Armenian terrorist action 7/83
- 150 die in train collision 9/85
- Mario Soares becomes President 2/86

Portuguese Timor
- See Timor

Post Office
- See Post and Telecommunications

Post and Telecommunications
- First book of stamps 4/00
- Public telephones in Paris 2/01
- First seaborne wireless telegraphy 6/01
- Marconi's wireless 10/01
- London's telephone system completed 11/01
- First cross-Atlantic wireless messages 12/01
- First parcel mail, Britain to America 8/02
- UK-Australia cable reaches Fiji 10/02
- Regular news service, London-New York 3/03
- Postcard craze in Britain 8/04
- Atlantic weather forecast by wireless 8/04
- Electric valve: basis of radio 10/04
- Post Office to send wireless telegrams to ships 12/04
- King lays new GPO's foundation stone 10/05
- First wireless conference adopts SOS 10/06
- Wireless messages travel 1,200 miles 12/06
- Marconi opens Canada-Ireland service 10/07
- US two cents post to UK announced 6/08
- GPO help employ jobless over Christmas 10/08
- Start of penny post to US 10/08
- Britain's telegraphic link with India 1/09
- German wireless without interference 5/09
- Marconi wins Nobel prize for wireless 12/09
- Caruso in first opera broadcast 1/10
- World's first airmail service 9/11
- GPO takes over National Telegraph Company 1/12
- Airmail service, London-Paris 8/12
- Ministers in Marconi telegraphy scandal 3/13
- Edison invents telephone recorder 5/13
- Marconi lights lamp by wireless 2/14
- British Post Office to run telephones 6/14
- Bell's longest ever telephone call 1/15
- Penny Post dropped in budget 4/18
- New York-Washington airmail service 5/18
- Wireless telephone for air pilots 3/19
- Airmail service to Amsterdam 7/20
- First advertised wireless broadcast 7/20
- Daily airmail San Francisco-New York 9/20
- Derby result broadcast by wireless 6/21
- Wireless entertainment by singer Scott 2/22
- First broadcast advertisement, USA 8/22
- Telephone inventor, Bell, dies 8/22
- British Broadcasting Company formed 10/22
- Telegraphic links with Afghanistan 3/23
- King sends himself telegram across world 4/24
- Wireless conversation with England 6/24
- Three out of five phones are American 1/26
- Cash-on-delivery parcel post 3/26
- Government wants to cut workers' wages 1/27
- 500,000 telephones in use, Britain 1/27
- Wireless link, Buenos Aires-Berlin 8/27
- UK's first automatic telephone exchange 11/27
- Compulsory worldwide radio arbitration 11/27
- London telephones: 52 new exchanges plan 1/28
- 1.6 million telephones in Britain 1/29
- First airmail from India arrives 4/29
- Mobile radios for Flying Squad cars 7/29
- Inventor of gramophone, Berliner, dies 8/29
- First public telephone boxes, London 12/29
- Edison, maker of 1,100 inventions, dies 10/31
- EMI from His Master's Voice and Columbia 11/31
- Marconi's first short-wave radio 8/32
- First telex operation, Berlin-Hamburg 10/33
- 800 million telephone calls in 1933, UK 1/34
- Long-distance phone calls cut to 3d rate 10/34
- Post Office's time-saving postal codes 11/34
- Speaking Clock voice found 6/35
- Speaking Clock service begins 7/36
- 130 million Edward VIII stamps sold 9/36
- New 12-sided threepenny bit 3/37
- Workers resent handling football pools 4/38
- Thieves attack postmen; steal £200,000 5/52
- IBM makes "Transceiver" using telephones 2/54
- New anti-nuclear air raid warning scheme 1/56
- TV detector to beat licence-dodgers 1/57
- Post Office - automatic trunk dialling 5/57
- Postcodes instead of addresses 11/57
- Stereo "High Fidelity" recordings 8/58
- Direct long distance telephone calls 12/58
- Jodrell Bank sends radio beams via moon 5/59
- Marples starts first post codes 7/59
- Radio telescope tracks 407,000 miles 3/60
- First "pay-on-answer" phone boxes, UK 5/61
- First Cosmos satellite launched, USSR 3/62
- Ariel, first UK satellite, launched 4/62
- Live transatlantic television: Telstar 7/62
- Second Telstar satellite launched, USA 5/63
- US satellite sends back moon pictures 7/64
- First USSR satellite, Molnya-1, launched 4/65
- Numbers-only phones to be adopted, UK 7/65
- Post Office Tower opened, UK 10/65
- France launches its first satellite 11/65
- First all-British satellite launched 5/67
- Radio-operated bleepers for the active 4/75
- End of Sunday collections 2/76
- Report wants post and telephones separate 7/77
- Post to be split from telephones 9/79
- British Telecom to scrap telegram 10/81
- Inland Telegram service ends 10/82
- Protests over BT destroying phone boxes 5/87

Poszgay, Imre 10/89
Potocka, Jan 3/77
Potter, Beatrix 12/02, 12/43
Potter, Dennis 6/94
Pottinger, George 2/74
Poulenc, Francis 12/20, 1/63
Poulson, John 7/72, 6/73, 10/73, 2/74, 3/74
Poulson, Norris 9/59
Pound, Ezra 12/23, 2/49, 12/50, 1/65, 11/72
Powell, Anthony 12/75
Powell, Brendan 4/88
Powell, Cecil 12/50
Powell, Colin 9/93
Powell, Enoch 1/58, 10/63, 7/65, 5/67, 4/68, 5/68, 10/68, 12/68, 6/69, 12/69, 2/71, 11/72, 6/73, 9/74, 6/87
Powell, Jody 3/80
Powell, Mike 8/91
Power, Tyrone 5/14, 5/46, 11/58
Powers, Gary 5/60, 8/60, 2/62
Pozzo, Vittorio 6/38
Prajadhipok, King of Siam 6/32, 10/34, 3/35
Pratt, David 4/60
Premadasa, Ranasinghe 1/89, 5/93
Preminger, Otto 12/06, 12/80, 4/86
Prentice, Reginald 10/69, 7/75, 10/77
Presley, Elvis 1/35, 7/54, 9/56, 12/57, 3/58, 12/59, 5/67, 8/77
Presley, Lisa Marie 8/94
Prestes, Julio 10/30
Preston, Peter 3/84
Prevert, Jacques 2/00, 4/77
Price, William 6/78
Priestley, John Boynton 2/33, 12/41, 12/46, 2/58, 12/77, 8/84
Prime, Geoffrey 7/82, 11/82
Princip, Gavrilo 6/14, 2/15
Pringle, Steuart 10/81
Prinz, Joachim 10/37
Prior, James 2/75, 9/81, 2/82, 11/83
Prison Officers' Association 1/89
Private Eye (magazine) 5/89, 10/89
Procter, Mike 11/77
Proctor, Harvey 4/87, 5/87
Proctor, William 10/94
Profumo, John 1/15, 11/58, 1/59, 3/63, 6/63, 11/71, 6/75
Prohibition
- See USA (politics)

Prokofiev, Sergei 12/35, 12/36, 2/48, 12/48, 3/53, 12/65
Proll, Astrid 9/78
Prost, Alain 2/55, 11/93
Proust, Marcel 11/13, 12/13, 11/22, 12/22, 12/27
Provide Hope, Operation 2/92
Prowse, Keith 9/91
Prudhomme, Sally 12/01
Pu Yi 12/08, 10/11, 3/32, 3/34, 12/59, 10/67
Puccini, Giacomo 12/10, 11/24
Puerto Rico
- 54 die in plane crash 6/49
- Puerto Ricans attempt to kill Truman, US 11/50
- Nixon arrives after hostile reception 5/58

Pugh, Arthur 5/26
Pugo, Boris 8/91
Pulitzer, Joseph 10/11
Punch (magazine)
- To stop publication after 150 years 3/92

Puskas, Ferenc 11/53, 5/60
Puttnam, David 3/82
Pym, Francis 3/61, 1/81, 4/82, 6/83

QR

Qatar
- Crown Prince seizes power in coup 2/72

Quaiton, Anthony 3/82
Quang Duc 6/63
Quant, Mary 1/64, 11/65, 4/66, 6/66, 12/66
Quarrie, Don 7/76
Quasimodo, Salvatore 8/01, 6/68
Quayle, Anthony 9/13, 10/89
Quayle, Dan 8/88, 11/88, 5/91
Queen, Richard 7/80

Queensberry, Marquess of 1/00
Queneau, Raymond 2/03
Quezon, Manuel 9/35
Quiller-Couch, Arthur 5/44
Quisling, Vidkun 4/40, 2/42, 8/45, 9/45, 10/45
Rabi, Isidor 12/44
Rabin, Yitzhak 4/74, 6/74, 3/77, 4/77, 1/88, 6/92, 9/93, 7/94, 10/94
Rabuka, Sitiveni 5/87, 9/87, 10/87
Rachman, Peter 6/63, 7/63
Rachmaninov, Sergey 11/09, 12/31, 11/34, 12/36, 3/43
Radcliffe, Lord 7/56
Radek, Karl 1/37
Radio
- See BBC, Broadcasting
Radke-Brachtsauer, Lina 8/27
Raeder, Erich 10/40
Rafsanjani, Ali Akbar Hashemi 6/89, 7/89, 6/90, 6/93
Rahman, Mujibur 12/70, 3/71, 4/71, 1/72, 3/73
Rahman, Tengku Abdul 8/57, 9/64, 8/65, 8/70
Rahman, Ziar 5/81
Rahmanthe, Mahabur 9/88
Railways
- First Cairo-Khartoum through train 1/00
- Sino-Russian clash on Manchurian railway 4/00
- Strikers blow up tramcar in St Louis 4/00
- Underground "tube" opens in London 6/00
- Opening of Paris metro underground 7/00
- Chinese line reopened 12/00
- Plans for 125mph Berlin line 2/01
- Germany to build line from Turkey 1/02
- Berlin underground 2/02
- Cape Town Beira line finished 10/02
- British South African Co. in Rhodesia 12/02
- First mainline electric train 3/04
- Record time London-Plymouth 4/04
- Trans-Siberian completed after 13 years 7/04
- New York underground opened 10/04
- London's first tube goes electric 12/04
- Trans-Siberian: official opening 1/05
- Bakerloo underground line opens, London 3/06
- First London-Dublin express train 8/06
- London's Piccadilly underground line 12/06
- Defence fears kill Channel Tunnel 4/07
- Experimental train reaches 98 mph 7/07
- Racial rail segregation, USA, banned 4/08
- Baghdad contract to build 500 mile line 6/08
- First entirely Chinese-built line 10/09
- St Gothard tunnel: Swiss, French and German 2/10
- Kissing banned in French stations 4/10
- Russia plans cross-desert railway, China 12/10
- Welsh strike turns riotous; nine die 7/11
- Largest station: Grand Central, New York 2/13
- Germany and Turkey give up link to Gulf 7/13
- 900 mile East African line inaugurated 2/14
- German lines help deploy 1.5m soldiers 8/14
- State control under new British Act 8/14
- Paris-Athens "Acropolis Express" 1/19
- Orient Express runs again 9/19
- US lines return to owners after war 3/20
- Trains packed for record Bank Holiday 8/21
- Queen opens rebuilt Victoria Station 3/22
- Bandits take 150 rail passengers, China 5/23
- Southern Railways goes electric 8/26
- Inefficient since Strike, say coal men 2/27
- Southern begins employee shares scheme 5/27
- Longest electric line in India 11/29
- Royal Commission: faster cheaper trains 1/31
- Royal Scot derailed; six die 3/31
- Cheltenham Flyer achieves 81.6 mph speed 6/32
- First electric express, London-Sussex 7/32
- Flying Scotsman reaches 97.5 mph 11/34
- London-Newcastle record 108 mph by steam 3/35
- Stalin opens 50-mile underground railway 4/35
- Silver Jubilee train's record 112 mph 9/35
- German passenger train achieves 124 mph 2/36
- Coronation Scot breaks record 7/37
- French Railways created 8/37
- Mallard's steam speed record of 126mph 7/38
- £1,240 million to electrify UK railways 1/55
- End of UK rail strike 6/55
- Overhead electrification planned 3/56
- British Rail abolishes Third Class 6/56
- BR announces loss of £16.5 million in 1956 6/57
- Plea to keep railway branches open, UK 10/57
- 92 die in fogbound Lewisham rail crash 12/57
- British Rail plans 230 station closures 5/59
- British Rail to raise fares 50 per cent 7/59
- Dr Beeching heads UK study of networks 4/60
- Savage cuts in UK's rail network planned 3/63
- First automatic tube trains in London 3/63
- Ticket collecting machine on London Underground 1/64
- Mass closure of rail lines announced, UK 3/64
- British Railways chief Beeching sacked 12/64
- British Rail network may be cut by half 2/65
- Queen opens Victoria tube line 3/69
- Sabotage marks new phase in Rhodesian war 4/76
- Fastest diesel service, HS-125, Britain 10/76
- Fowler to sell off Sealink and BR hotels 7/80
- 84 die in Bologna station bomb blast 8/80
- France's high speed TGV Paris-Lyons train 9/81
- Advanced Passenger Train revealed 12/81
- Advanced Passenger Train back in use 8/84
- High Speed Train in record London trip 9/85
- BR reveals plans for Channel Tunnel rail link 3/89
- BR puts off plans for new Channel Tunnel rail link 10/89
- BR denied permission to build high-speed rail link 12/90
- Fine snow blamed for failure of BR's new trains 2/91
- Route to Stratford chosen for high-speed rail link 10/91
- BR blames leaves on line for delays 11/91
- British government plans privatisation of British Rail 2/93
Rainier III, Prince of Monaco 11/49, 1/56, 4/56, 3/62
Rains, Claude 11/33, 5/67
Raison, Timothy 12/85
Rakosi, Matyas 8/52, 7/56
Ramadier, Paul 1/47, 11/47
Rambert, Marie 12/31
Ramee, Marie-Louise de la 1/08
Ramos, Fidel V. 2/86, 1/87, 6/92
Ramos, Sugar 3/63
Ramsamy, Sam 7/91
Ramsay, Jacqueline 6/91
Ramsay, Norman 12/89
Ramsey, Alf 7/66, 1/67, 5/74
Ramsey, Baron Arthur Michael 4/88
Ramsey, Michael (Archbishop) 5/40, 1/56, 1/61, 6/61, 3/66, 12/69, 3/74
Rana, Shakoor 12/87
Rance, Hubert 7/47
Rand, Mary 10/64
Rank, J. Arthur 9/36
Rankin, Jeannette 11/16, 5/73
Ransome, Arthur 6/67
Raphael, Frederick 12/67
Rappe, Virginia 9/20
Raskob, John J. 11/28
Raspe, Carl 6/72
Rasputin, Gregory 12/16
Rath, Ernst 11/38
Rathbone, Basil 7/67
Rathenau, Walter 6/22
Rattigan, Terence 12/52, 6/71, 11/77
Ratzenberg, Roland 5/94
Rauschenberg, Robert 12/66
Ravel, Maurice 5/04, 1/09, 4/11, 12/14, 1/15, 2/26, 12/28, 12/32, 12/37
Rawlings, Jerry 12/81
Rawson, Arturo 6/43
Ray, James Earl 4/68, 3/69, 6/77
Ray, Man 11/76
Ray, Nicholas 12/56
Ray, Satyajit 4/92
Ray, Ted 6/27
Rayburn, Sam 5/43
Raye, Martha 10/94
Razak, Abdul 8/66, 9/70, 1/76
Razmara, Ali 3/51
Read, A.C. 4/19
Reagan, Nancy 3/81, 5/88
Reagan, Ronald
- Born 2/11
- Warns against Hollywood witch-hunt 10/47
- Nominated as California Governor 6/66
- Elected Governor of California 11/66
- Sworn in as Californian Governor 1/67
- Urges escalation of Vietnam War 9/67
- Says he will run for President 8/68
- Republican presidential candidate 7/80
- In TV debate with Carter 10/80
- Becomes President of the United States 11/80
- Meets Thatcher for the first time 2/81
- Wounded in assassination attempt 3/81
- Agrees to sell arms to China 6/81
- Hinkley pleads not guilty to murder bid 8/81
- Military draft registration to continue 1/82
- Pledges support for UK over Falklands 4/82
- Rides with the Queen at Windsor 6/82
- Dubs USSR the "evil empire" 3/83
- Proposes "Star Wars" defence system 3/83
- Visited by Queen and Prince Philip 3/83
- Defends covert aid to Nicaraguan rebels 4/83
- Appeals for more aid to El Salvador 4/83
- Sides with Contra rebels in Nicaragua 5/83
- Orders US invasion of Grenada 10/83
- To keep US Marines in Lebanon 10/83
- In talks with Chinese premier Zhao 1/84
- To seek re-election 1/84
- Orders US forces out of Lebanon 2/84
- Visits Beijing 4/84
- Re-elected President 11/84
- Accepts Vietnam memorial 11/84
- Donald Regan made White House Chief of Staff 1/85
- Agrees to US-Canadian study of acid rain 3/85
- Congress rejects aid to Contras 4/85
- Plans trade embargo on Sandinista regime 4/85
- Visits Bitburg war cemetery, W. Germany 5/85
- Addresses European Parliament 5/85
- Declares war on terrorists 6/85
- Brands five nations as terrorist states 7/85
- Angry at Italy's freeing of hijacker 10/85
- Summit with Gorbachev in Geneva 11/85
- Sends New Year greetings to USSR 1/86
- Condemned by World Court on Contra aid 6/86
- S. Africa sanctions veto overridden 9/86
- Talks with Gorbachev scuppered by SDI 10/86
- "Irangate" row erupts 11/86
- Authorises US helicopters to ferry Honduran troops 12/86
- Regrets arms deal with Iran 1/87
- Criticised by "Irangate" inquiry 2/87
- Gorbachev makes new offer on arms cuts 4/87
- Protests at Iraqi attack on US ship 5/87
- Defends attacks on Iranian oil platforms 10/87
- Blamed in report for "Irangate" scandal 11/87
- Signs missile treaty with Gorbachev 12/87
- First visit to USSR 5/88
- Approves of Russian troop cuts 12/88
- Succeeded by George Bush as President 1/89
Red Cross
- Founder, Jean Henri Dunant, dies 10/10
- International Committee gets Nobel Prize 12/17
- International conference to limit war 4/21
- Wins Nobel Peace Prize 12/44
- Helps prisoner swap, Korea 4/53
- Wins Nobel Peace Prize 12/63
- Aid to two million Cambodians 9/79
- Swiss fail to end Ulster hunger strike 7/81
- Attack on Red Cross convoy in Yugoslavia 9/91
Redford, Robert 12/73, 12/85
Redgrave, Michael 12/63, 3/85, 12/85
Redgrave, Vanessa 1/37, 9/61, 3/68, 12/69, 12/78
Redmond, John 1/00
Redmond, William 1/12, 7/12
Redon, Odilon 7/16
Reed, Carol 12/49, 4/76
Reed, Frank 4/90
Reed, Walter 2/02
Rees, Merlyn 6/63, 1/75, 11/75, 3/76, 6/77
Rees, Roger 12/81
Rees-Mogg, William 1/67
Reeve, Ambrose 4/57
Reeve, Christopher 6/78
Regan, Donald 1/85, 2/87, 5/88
Reger, Max 5/16
Reid, Alec 3/88
Reid, Norman 12/76
Reinhardt, Jean-Baptiste "Django" 5/53
Reinhardt, Max 3/38, 10/41, 10/43
Reinkoff, William 10/46
Reisz, Karel 12/69
Reith, John 12/22, 12/25, 6/38, 12/49, 6/71
Rejai, Mohammed Ali 8/81
Remarque, Erich Maria 8/29, 12/29, 12/33, 9/70
Remek, Vladimir 3/78
Remon, Jose 1/55
Rene, Albert 6/77, 12/81
Renner, Karl 4/45, 10/45, 11/45, 12/50
Reno, Janet 3/93
Renoir, Jean 2/79
Renoir, Pierre August 12/19
Resnais, Alain 12/59
Revie, Don 5/65, 5/73, 7/74
Rexroth, Kenneth 12/57
Rey, Fernando 3/94
Reynaud, Paul 3/40, 6/40, 4/43, 5/45, 2/52
Reynolds, Albert 1/92, 2/92, 1/93, 12/93
Reynolds, Bruce 11/68
Reynolds, Sue 7/60
Rhee, Syngman 7/53, 3/60, 4/60, 7/65
Rhodes, Cecil John 2/00, 6/01, 3/02, 4/02
Rhodes, Wilfred 7/73
Rhodesia
- See also Rhodesia (Northern, Southern), Zambia, Zimbabwe
- Rich country to join SA, says Rhodes 6/01
- Report on "natives' work" 8/02
- Gold discovered 11/04
- White fury at no death penalty for black 1/11
- Crown takes over from Southern Rhodesia Company 9/23
- Britain agrees to autonomy 10/23
- Assembly meets first time; autonomy 5/24
- Harold Wilson says UDI would be treason 10/64
- Referendum backs Smith on independence 11/64
- Nkomo and 16 supporters freed from jail 11/64
- Threatens to deport Africans 4/65
- Rhodesian Front Party wins election 5/65
- State of emergency declared 5/65
- Smith poised for UDI 10/65
- Smith issues UDI 11/65
- Britain imposes economic sanctions 11/65
- Britain imposes oil sanctions 12/65
- Petrol rationing introduced 12/65
- Britain rejects military action 1/66
- Three visiting UK MPs jeered 1/66
- Three visiting MPs expelled 1/66
- Queen commutes a black's death sentence 1/66
- UK bans nearly all trade with Rhodesia 1/66
- Restrictions lifted on ex-PM Todd 10/66
- Smith supporters demonstrate in London 11/66
- Smith rejects UK proposals to end row 12/66
- UN to impose oil embargo 12/66
- Leaves the Commonwealth 12/66
- Ends Commonwealth tariff preferences 2/67
- Queen's reprieve of three blacks overturned 3/68
- Wilson and Smith in more abortive talks 10/68
- Humphrey Gibbs resigns as Governor 6/69
- Becomes a republic 3/70
- US to close its consulate 3/70
- Clifford Dupont is first President 4/70
- Smith in informal talks with Vorster 5/70
- Signs deal to end rift with Britain 11/71
- UK MPs approve Rhodesian settlement 12/71
- Former PM Garfield Todd arrested 1/72
- 422 miners die in pit explosion 6/72
- Expelled from Olympics 8/72
- Border with Zambia closed 1/73
- 270 kidnapped from Catholic mission school 7/73
- Smith and black nationalists agree truce 12/74
- ZANU leader Sithole arrested 3/75
- Police shoot 11 black demonstrators 6/75
- Black-white "railway talks" collapse 8/75
- Nkomo is President of UANC 9/75
- Mozambique seizes assets; talks collapse 3/76
- Rail sabotage; white reservists called up 4/76
- Mozambique-based guerrillas strike 4/76
- Former Premier Todd freed 6/76
- Multi-racial state announced by Smith 9/76
- Bishop Muzorewa returns from exile 10/76
- Conference begins; troops in Mozambique 10/76
- Gang kill 27 Africans who did not strike 12/76
- Highlands African women abducted 12/76
- Conference adjourned 12/76
- Smith rejects Ivor Richard's proposals 1/77
- 400 children kidnapped by guerrillas 1/77
- Guerrillas kill seven white missionaries 2/77
- Smith calls election 7/77
- 12 die in Salisbury bomb; 16 die at Umtali 8/77
- Smith wins election 8/77
- Smith accepts black majority rule 11/77
- Smith talks to Muzorewa and Sithole 11/77
- Nkomo and Mugabe left out of negotiations 11/77
- Deal for black rule; reserve white seats 2/78
- US blasts deal with no Mugabe, Nkomo 2/78
- Guerrillas reject "internal settlement" 3/78
- Mugabe's troops invade from east 3/78
- First three black ministers sworn in 3/78
- 12 UK missionaries massacred, Vumba 6/78
- Bingham says Shell and BP broke sanctions 8/78
- Rebels down airliner; 56 die 9/78
- Guerrillas kill eight air crash survivors 9/78
- Nkomo fighters enter Kariba area 9/78
- Smith in secret talks with Nkomo 9/78
- Martial law; 300 die in month 9/78
- Forces strike deep into Mozambique; kill 1,500 10/78
- Martial law in three quarters of country 11/78
- Whites vote for black rule constitution 1/79
- Guerrillas down airliner; 59 die 2/79
- UANC win election; Mugabe's denunciation 4/79
- Muzorewa elected first black Premier 4/79
- Muzorewa's spokesman Hove killed in Lusaka 4/79
- Troops destroy Nkomo's house 4/79
- Renamed Zimbabwe-Rhodesia 6/79
Rhodesia, Northern
- See also Zambia
- Barotse Chief offers Britain war support 8/14
- Planned federation with South and Nyasaland 5/52
- To join Southern Rhodesia and Nyasaland 2/53
- New constitution: white domination stays 9/53
- Queen opens huge Kariba dam on Zambezi 5/60
- Blacks refused more say in legislature 2/61
- London talks reach deadlock 2/61
- More Africans to have vote 6/61
- Dag Hammarskjoeld dies in air crash 9/61
- Britain will allow secession 3/63
- Kenneth Kaunda becomes first premier 1/64
- To be renamed Zambia 8/64
- Massacre of 150 by Lumpa church members 8/64
Rhodesia, Southern
- See also Rhodesian Zambia, Zimbabwe
- Planned federation with North and Nyasaland 5/52
- To fuse with Nyasaland, N. Rhodesia 2/53
- Central African Federation parliament 2/54
- Emergency after rail strike 6/54
- Premier Whitehead's state of emergency 2/59
- African nationalists rounded up 2/59
- Macmillan's review commission 7/59
- Lord Monckton studies constitution 9/59
- Riots as Macmillan visits Salisbury 1/60
- Troops surround black townships 10/60
- ZAPU banned 9/62
- Black nationalist leader Nkomo arrested 2/63
- Nkomo gets six months' hard labour 4/63
- Joshua Nkomo jailed 12/63
- Ian Smith becomes PM 4/64
- Smith threatens UDI from Britain 6/64
- Restrictions on Nkomo lifted 6/64
Rhoodie, Eschel 6/79
Rhys-Jones, Griff 12/79
Ribbentrop, Joachim von 6/35, 8/36, 2/37, 1/30, 5/39, 8/39, 10/39, 3/40, 5/40, 9/40, 5/41, 6/45, 11/45, 10/46
Ribicoff, Abraham 8/68
Ricardo, Ronna 8/63
Rice, Donna 5/87
Rice, Tim 12/72, 12/78
Rice-Davies, Marilyn (Mandy) 4/63, 6/63, 7/63
Richard, Cliff 12/59
Richard, Ivor 1/77
Richard, Keith 5/67, 6/67, 7/67
Richards, Gordon 11/32, 10/51, 6/53, 8/54
Richards, Vivian 6/75, 8/76, 5/84, 3/90
Richardson, Carole 10/89
Richardson, Elliot 4/73, 10/73
Richardson, George 2/14
Richardson, J.P. 2/59
Richardson, Mary 3/14
Richardson, Peter 12/83
Richardson, Ralph 5/30, 12/44, 10/46, 12/46, 1/47, 12/50, 10/83
Richter, Ian 11/91
Richter, Sviatoslav 3/15
Richthofen, Manfred von 4/18
Richthofen, Oswald von 4/01, 3/02
Rico, Aldo 4/87
Rida, Hassan 9/69
Ride, Paul 8/92
Ride, Sally 6/83
Ridenhour, Ronald 11/69
Rideout, Greta 12/78
Rideout, John 12/78
Ridgway, Matthew 4/51, 6/51, 12/51, 5/52, 7/93
Ridley, Nicholas 5/89, 7/90, 11/91
Riefenstahl, Leni 9/34, 12/38
Rigg, Diana 12/64
Riggs, Bobby 7/39
Riina, Salvatore "Toto" 1/93
Riley, Sidney George 6/27
Rilke, Rainer Maria 12/26
Rimington, Stella 7/93
Rimsky-Korsakov, Nikolai 6/08
Rin Tin Tin 8/32
Rindt, Jochen 9/69, 9/70, 10/70
Rippon, Angela 4/83, 12/83
Rippon, Geoffrey 6/71
Rivera, Diego 5/33, 11/57
Rivera, Jose Antonio Primo de 11/33, 11/36
Rivera, Miguel Primo de 8/26, 9/26, 1/30, 3/30
Rivett, Sandra 11/74, 6/75
Roach, Hal 11/92
Robb, Marjorie 6/92
Robberies
- See Crime
Robbins, Jerome 12/61
Robbins, Lord 10/63
Robens, Lord 10/66
Roberts, Frederick 1/00, 4/00, 11/14
Roberts, Margaret
- See Thatcher, Margaret
Roberts, Richard 10/93
Roberts, William 12/14, 12/18
Robertson Justice, James 7/75
Robertson, Brian 3/56
Robertson, Ian 5/66
Robertson, J.H. 9/28
Robertson, Pat 4/88
Robeson, Paul 12/28, 5/30, 12/30, 12/59, 1/76
Robey, George 12/12, 11/54
Robinson, "Red Robbo" 5/80
Robinson, Edward G. 1/73
Robinson, Heath 9/44
Robinson, Kenneth 2/65
Robinson, Mary 11/90, 5/93
Robinson, Peter 8/86, 1/87
Robinson, Robert 12/47
Robinson, Sugar Ray 2/51, 7/51, 9/51, 12/55, 3/58, 4/89
Rocard, Michel 5/88
Roche, Jean 5/68
Roche, Stephen 7/87
Rockefeller, John D. 11/07, 11/09, 9/16, 5/37, 12/46
Rockefeller, Nelson 5/33, 7/64, 6/65, 8/74, 12/74, 11/75, 1/79
Rockets
- See Space, Aviation

Rockwell, George 8/62, 8/67
Rodgers, Richard 6/02, 3/26, 12/47
Rodgers, William 4/62, 7/80, 1/81
Rodin, Auguste 11/17
Rodriguez, Francisco 9/89
Roe, Alliot Verdon 4/19
Roe, Erika 1/82
Roe, Mark 9/92
Roehm, Ernst 6/34
Roentgen, Wilhelm 12/01, 2/23
Roffe-Steinrotter, Diann 2/94
Roffey, Holly 7/84, 8/84
Rogers, Ginger 12/34, 12/35, 6/87, 4/95
Rogers, Richard 2/77
Rogers, Will 7/88
Rogstadt, Anna 3/11
Roh Tae Woo 12/87
Rohlfs, Roland 9/19
Rolling Stones 4/64, 12/66, 2/67, 5/67, 6/67, 7/67, 10/67, 12/67, 7/69, 11/69, 1/70, 5/71
Rolls Royce
- See Cars
Rolls, Charles Stewart 5/04, 7/10
Romano, Yosef 9/72
Rome, Treaty of
- EC leaders vote 11-1 on changes to the treaty 12/89
- Thatcher vows to veto single European currency 10/90
Romero, Carlos 10/79
Romero, Oscar Arnulfo (archbishop) 3/80
Rommel, Erwin 2/41, 4/41, 11/41, 1/42, 5/42, 6/42, 7/42, 8/42, 10/42, 2/43, 4/43, 5/44, 10/44
Romney, George 11/67
Roncalli, Angelo Giuseppe 6/63
Ronson, Gerald 1/87, 10/87, 8/90
Rooney, Mickey 9/40
Roosa, Stuart Allen 1/71
Roosevelt, Eleanor 11/36, 4/45, 11/62
Roosevelt, Franklin Delano
- Marries cousin Eleanor 3/05
- Surprise Democrat Vice-President nominee 7/20
- Elected Governor of New York State 11/28
- Letter bomb intercepted 4/29
- Wants to abolish prohibition 9/30
- Re-nominated as Governor 9/30
- Re-elected Democratic New York Governor 11/30
- Denies he seeks presidency 11/30
- Says he will run for President 1/32
- Nominated for President on fourth ballot 7/32
- Favours five-day week and aid for jobless 10/32
- Elected Democratic President by landslide 11/32
- Giuseppe Zingara shoots but misses 2/33
- 500,000 cheer President in Washington DC 3/33
- Unemployment pledge; repeals prohibition 3/33
- Meets MacDonald to discuss recovery 4/33
- Starts New Deal bills on farms and banking 4/33
- 13 New Deal acts in 100 days 6/33
- New moves to help poor and save banks 9/33
- Invites Litvinov to discuss recognition 10/33
- Calls for moderation as prohibition ends 12/33
- Helps end textile strike by 400,000 9/34
- Calls for inheritance tax 1/35
- Signs Social Security Bill 8/35
- Democrats' endorsement for next election 1/36
- Signs second Neutrality Bill 2/36
- Democrats choose him to run again 6/36
- Crushes Landon in election, 531 to eight 11/36
- "One-third of nation ill-housed ..." 1/37
- Wants to appoint new liberal Judges 2/37
- Shocked that liberal judge was Klansman 9/37
- Condemns Japan over aggression in China 10/37
- Condemns German anti-Semitism 11/38
- Declares US's neutrality 9/39
- Ends arms sales embargo 11/39
- Asks Mussolini to help halt war 4/40
- Criticises Italy's war declaration 6/40
- Democratic candidate for third term 7/40
- Supports UK action on French fleet 7/40
- Denies he plans to go to war 10/40
- Wins record third presidential term 11/40
- Says US is "arsenal of democracy" 12/40
- Inaugurated for third term 1/41
- Signs lease-lend pact with Britain 3/41
- Says US will occupy Greenland 4/41
- Orders freeze on German and Italian assets 6/41
- Calls Nazis "international outlaws" 6/41
- Pledges help to USSR 6/41
- Says US forces have landed in Iceland 7/41
- Bans certain fuel exports 8/41
- Arms to be sent to Axis enemies 8/41
- Agrees Atlantic Charter with Churchill 8/41
- US will do all possible to crush Hitler 9/41
- Appeals to Hirohito to avoid war 12/41
- Declares war on Japan, Germany and Italy 12/41
- Talks with Churchill; close relationship 12/41
- Presents biggest-ever budget estimate 1/42
- Price freeze on major domestic items 4/42
- Talks in Washington with Churchill 6/42
- Puts freeze on wages, rents and farm prices 10/42
- Attends Allied conference in Casablanca 1/43
- Says Allies should control Indochina 3/43
- Orders miners to continue working 4/43
- Discusses Keynes Plan for world economy 4/43
- On point of seizing mines 5/43
- Talks with Churchill 5/43
- Attends Quebec summit 8/43
- Meets Stalin and Churchill in Tehran 11/43
- Meets Chiang Kai-shek in North Africa 11/43
- Eisenhower to lead invasion of Europe 12/43
- Agrees closer ties with Turkey 12/43
- Visits Malta 12/43
- Asks Ireland to expel enemy envoys 3/44
- Gets Truman as running mate 7/44
- Agrees to run for fourth term 7/44
- Turns Allied attention to Japan 9/44
- Hopes for United Nations organisation 10/44
- Wins record fourth term as President 11/44
- Inaugurated for fourth term 1/45
- Attends Yalta conference 2/45
- Cairo talks with Churchill on Japan 2/45
- Dies on the eve of victory 4/45
- Exonerated from blame for Pearl Harbor 7/46
- Memorial unveiled in London 4/48
Roosevelt, Theodore
- Republican Vice-President candidate 6/00
- McKinley shot; Roosevelt is President 9/01
- Inivtes black man to the White House 10/01
- Settles coal strike 10/02
- Opens public offices to blacks 11/02
- Nominated for presidency 6/04
- Wins presidency, beating Parker 11/04
- Inaugurated with massive parade 3/05
- First President to leave US 11/06
- Committs army to build Panama Canal 2/07
- Standard Oil's campaign 9/07
- Warning on anti-Japanese laws 2/09
- Nominated as Independent "Bull Moose" 6/12
- Official Progressive candidate 8/12
- Shot and wounded, Milwaukee 10/12
- Loses election to Wilson 11/12
- Condems Lusitania sinking 5/15
- Dies 1/19
Roque, Jacqueline 3/61
Rose theatre 5/89
Rose, Alec 12/67, 7/68, 1/91
Rose, David 11/69
Rose, Michael 1/94
Rosebery, Lord (Archibald Primrose) 2/02, 5/29
Rosenberg, Alfred 4/46, 10/46
Rosenberg, Ethel 3/51, 4/51, 1/53, 6/53
Rosenberg, Isaac 12/18
Rosenberg, Julius 3/51, 4/51, 1/53, 6/53
Rosendahl, Heidi 9/72
Roser, Thomas 5/86
Rosewall, Ken 7/54, 7/56, 7/70, 7/74
Ross, Donald 5/68, 7/71
Ross, Ronald 12/02
Rossellini, Roberto 5/06, 8/49, 6/60, 6/77
Rossi, Paolo 7/82
Rostropovich, Mstislav 3/27, 10/70, 11/72
Rothermere, Lord (Harold Harmsworth) 10/23, 11/40
Rothko, Mark 9/03, 2/70
Rothschild, Baron 11/17, 4/38
Rothschild, Lord (Victor) 3/90
Rottee, Lucien 4/45
Roualt, Georges 10/05
Round, Dorothy 7/33, 7/34, 7/37
Rourke, Mickey 9/86
Rous, Francis Peyton 1/11
Rousseau, Henri 9/10, 12/10
Rowland, "Tiny" 6/81
Royal Air Force
- See also Aviation, World Wars I and II
- Formed from merger of RFC and RNAS 4/18
- Downs 4,102 German planes in year 6/18
- Trenchard's plan for permanent force 12/19
- 500 planes for home defence: plan 8/22
- To be boosted from 18 squadrons to 52 6/23
- Nine airmen die as flying-boat sinks 2/31
- Waghorn dies after crash: 42nd to do so 5/31
- Air Minister Londonderry announces boost 11/33
- 41 new squadrons planned to catch up with Europe 7/34
- European mutual air defence pact mooted 2/35
- White Paper calls for more aircraft 3/35
- Baldwin's plan: trebled in two years 5/35
- New heavy bombers, fast fighters and bases 5/35
- Officers die in Baluchistan earthquake 5/35
- 29,000 apply to join since new plan 5/35
- To grow at a squadron a week 1/36
- First viewing of Spitfire from Vickers 3/36
- Strafes Arab ambushers in Palestine 6/36
- Granted freedom of Egyptian air 8/36
- Air Ministry plans reserve 8/36
- Hits growth targets three months early 1/37
- £11 million for new aerodromes 3/38
- New recruitment drive 6/38
- 1,000 orders for Spitfire fighters 7/38
- Formation of Women's Auxiliary Air Force 7/39
- Reserves called up 8/39
- Bombs German fleet on Kiel Canal 9/39
- Reconnaissance flights over France 10/39
- Maiden flight of Mosquito fighter-bomber 3/40
- Bombs Berlin for first time 8/40
- Destroys many Luftwaffe planes 8/40
- Churchill makes speech on "the Few" 8/40
- Bombs Munich for first time 9/40
- Bombs Hamburg 9/40
- Bombs Italians as Egypt is invaded 9/40
- Makes heavy raids on Berlin and Hamburg 10/40
- Drops 2,000 bombs on Hamburg 11/40
- Launches attack in Western Desert 12/40
- Bombs Taranto and Naples 1/41
- Bombs Italian air bases in Libya 1/41
- Bombs Italian positions in Abyssinia 1/41
- Heavy raid on Tripoli 2/41
- Bombs enemy supply lines in Balkans 4/41
- Conduct in battle for Greece praised 4/41
- First flight of British jet, Gloster 5/41
- Says "radio-location" is UK's key weapon 6/41
- Unit arrives in USSR to aid air force 9/41
- First engagement in USSR 9/41
- Raid on German base at Aalesund, Norway 10/41
- In combined services raid on Norway 12/41
- Begins terror bombing campaign 3/42
- Heavy raid on Ruhr towns 3/42
- Bombs Baltic port of Rostock 4/42
- Devastates Cologne in one night 5/42
- Bombs U-boat yards in Danzig 7/42
- First daylight raid on Ruhr 7/42
- 100,000 bombs on Dusseldorf in one hour 9/42
- Hundredth raid on Bremen 9/42
- Biggest raid of war on Italy 10/42
- First daylight raid on Berlin 1/43
- Bombing of Germany's industrial centres 3/43
- Drops Jean Moulin into occupied France 3/43
- Presents Churchill with wings 4/43
- Bombs Stuttgart 4/43
- Bombs Berlin and three other cities 4/43
- Lays mines in Baltic 4/43
- "Dambuster" raid on the Ruhr 5/43
- Heaviest air raid so far, on Dortmund 5/43
- Heaviest raid yet, on Hamburg 7/43
- Bombs weapons base on Peenemunde Island 8/43
- Hamburg "wiped off the map" by air raid 8/43
- Threatens to bomb Berlin to nothing 11/43
- Wellingtons in night precision bombing 11/43
- Biggest ever bombing of Berlin 1/44
- Spitfire being fitted with bigger engine 3/44
- Drops 4,500 tons of bombs in one raid 4/44
- Makes first raid on Rumania 4/44
- Mosquitoes pinpoint and bomb one target 5/44
- D-Day landings in Normandy 6/44
- Sinks Tirpitz in Norwegian fjord 11/44
- Bombs Dresden 2/45
- Bombs Berlin 2/45
- Sinks Lutzow, last pocket battleship 4/45
- Announces new Vampire jet fighter 6/45
- Sir Arthur "Bomber" Harris to retire 8/45
- Jet fighter flies at record 540mph 10/45
- Gloster Meteor flies at record 606mph 11/45
- Strikes in India, Ceylon and Singapore 1/46
- Evacuates Britons from Palestine 2/47
- Women's Royal Air Force formed from WAAF 2/48
- Begins Berlin airlift 6/48
- Israelis shoot down five planes, Israel 1/49
- WRAF incorporated 2/49
- Retires last Lancaster bomber 3/50
- Valiant: first UK four-engined jet bomber 5/51
- Hawker Hunter's first flight 7/51
- Vickers Valiant atomic bomber jet crash 1/52
- William Dickson to lead Air Staff 6/52
- Prototype delta-wing Gloster GA-5 crash 6/52
- Canberra bomber flies Atlantic and back 8/52
- New four-engined Vulcan bombers 8/52
- Ex-chief "Bomber" Harris is knighted 1/53
- First supersonic fighters, 400 Sabres 1/53
- Duke of Edinburgh awarded his wings 5/53
- Vickers Valiant carrying atomic bombs 1/55
- First U-2 spy plane at RAF Lakenheath 4/56
- Valiants and Canberras bomb Cairo, Suez 10/56
- Vulcan bomber enters service 2/57
- First US-built Thor missiles in UK 9/58
- Granted a base in Madagascar 3/66
- Bombs Torrey Canyon wreck 3/67
- Death of Air Marshal William Tedder 6/67
- Death of Air Chief Marshal Dowding 2/70
- Prince Charles gets his wings 8/71
- Bombs Port Stanley, Falklands 5/82
- Airman Douglas Bader dies 9/82
- Death of Arthur "Bomber" Harris 4/84
- 17 RAF men die in bus crash near Munich 2/85
- IRA shoots soldier's wife by mistake in West Germany 9/89
- Tactic bombing of Iraqi airfields is abandoned 1/91
- British pilots tell of torture by Iraqi captors 8/91
- First woman combat pilot 2/95
- Will end its nuclear capability in 1998 4/95
Royal Family (Britain)
- See also under individual members
- New Royal yacht capsizes 1/00
- Fire at Buckingham Palace 3/00
- Man arrested for threatening Prince 4/00
- Prince's horse wins Derby 4/00
- Queen Victoria dies; Edward VII new king 1/01
- Royal yacht wrecked; King has lucky escape 5/01
- King's illness delays Coronation 6/02
- King feeds poor Londoners 7/02
- Edward VII crowned: first for 64 years 8/02
- India proclaims Edward as Emperor 1/03
- Edward visits France 5/03
- Edward's role in Anglo-French pact 4/04
- Edward becomes honorary Austrian officer 5/04
- King visits Morocco and Paris 4/05
- Prince and Princess of Wales visit India 10/05
- Queen's personal appeal for the jobless 11/05
- King visits Olympics and Vesuvius blast 4/06
- King visits nephew, the Kaiser, Kronberg 8/06
- Edward VII and Alexandra visit Paris 2/07
- Edward VII and Alexandra visit Malta 4/07
- Edward VII's new turbine yacht 5/07
- Prince of Wales is Wimbledon president 6/07
- Jubilation as Kaiser and King meet Lord Mayor 11/07
- Prince picnics with slum children 6/08
- Edward's cordial meeting with Czar 6/08
- Royal garden party snub to Labour leader 7/08
- Cullinan diamonds for Alexandra 11/08
- King and Queen visit Berlin 2/09
- King says science leads to prosperity 7/09
- Premier approaches King over new peers 4/10
- King Edward VII dies; George V succeeds 5/10
- New King's first address to the Empire 5/10
- Man imprisoned for libelling King 2/11
- King will not intervene on Lords' reform 4/11
- King and Queen open Festival of Empire 5/11
- George V and Kaiser reassert mutual friendship 5/11
- Queen Victoria memorial outside Palace 5/11
- George V's Coronation, Westminster Abbey 6/11
- George V guarantees Lords' reform 7/11
- Lords' reform bill gets royal assent 8/11
- George V, Emperor of India, shoots game 12/11
- Buckingham Palace facade redesigned 10/12
- King's horse kills suffragette Emily Davison 6/13
- King opens new RNIB headquarters 3/14
- George V's visit wins French friendship 4/14
- King criticised for Ulster partisanship 7/14
- Queen Mary starts "Work for Women" fund 9/14
- Prince of Wales becomes aide-de-camp to Sir John French 11/14
- King George V visits BEF and meets Belgian King 12/14
- Windsor Castle cut off by floods 1/15
- King bans drink at Buckingham Palace 4/15
- King strips Kaiser of Garter 5/15
- King injured in fall while inspecting troops 10/15
- King's proclamation: "eat less bread" 5/17
- German titles dropped 6/17
- Lords debates "sale of Birthday Honours" 8/17
- King and Queen make informal drive through Hyde Park 11/18
- George, first king to welcome President 12/18
- Prince of Wales becomes a freemason 4/19
- King's Speech: unemployment warning 2/21
- Queen is first woman to get Oxford degree 3/21
- Prince of Wales's Indian tour boycott 12/21
- Princess Mary marries Viscount Lascelles 2/22
- Heiress engaged to Lord Louis Mountbatten 3/22
- Louis Mountbatten marries Edwina Ashley 7/22
- Elizabeth Bowes-Lyon to marry Duke 1/23
- Duke of York and Lady Elizabeth marry 4/23
- Prince of Wales seeks bride 6/24
- Alexandra, King Edward's widow, dies 11/25
- Princess Elizabeth born to Duchess 4/26
- Wimbledon Jubilee: Prince of Wales plays 6/26
- King no longer sovereign of Ireland 11/26
- Duke and Duchess of York back from tour 6/27
- Baldwin and Prince visit Canada: Diamond Jubilee 7/27
- Dowager Russian Empress Marie dies 10/28
- King George V ill with congested lung 11/28
- Prince of Wales cuts short African visit 11/28
- Council of State acts for ill King 12/28
- Operation improves King's condition 12/28
- Prince of Wales tours depressed North 1/29
- First King's Speech for Labour government 7/29
- Prince of Wales avoids charging elephant 3/30
- King meets victorious Arsenal team 4/30
- Duchess of York has second daughter 8/30
- Prince of Wales promoted to Admiral 9/30
- No new peers in Birthday Honours List 6/31
- King takes pay cut of £50,000 9/31
- King George V and Queen Mary meet Gandhi 11/31
- "Buy British" drive: Prince's broadcast 11/31
- De Valera to abolish Loyal Oath to King 3/32
- Irish Dail drops loyalty oath to King 4/32
- Prince opens Stormont parliament 11/32
- First Christmas Day Empire broadcast 12/32
- Prince George to marry Marina of Greece 8/34
- Prince George marries Princess Marina 11/34
- King George and Queen Mary's Silver Jubilee 5/35
- King George V dies; Edward VIII succeeds 1/36
- Huge London funeral; 47 nations present 1/36
- Duchesses launch pierced ears trend 5/36
- Coronation set for May 1937 5/36
- Queen Mary welcomed in New York 6/36
- Journalist tries to kill King Edward 7/36
- Mrs Simpson divorces husband Ernest 10/36
- Beaverbrook's press silence on Simpson 10/36
- King condemns unemployment, South Wales 11/36
- Edward opens his first parliament 11/36
- King inspects Fleet 11/36
- Beaverbrook's press silence on Simpson 12/36
- Revealed: Mrs Simpson's affair with King 12/36
- Edward VIII wants to marry Mrs Simpson 12/36
- Premier Baldwin recommends abdication 12/36
- Edward VIII announces abdication on radio 12/36
- Younger brother George VI is new King 12/36
- Profile of King George VI, "Shy Bertie" 12/36
- King unveils memorial to George V 4/37
- King George VI is crowned with pomp 5/37
- Bomb near King and Queen, Belfast 7/37
- Duke and Duchess of Windsor feted by Nazis 10/37
- George VI opens his first parliament 10/37
- King gets ten per cent pay rise 2/38
- King and Queen at Glasgow Empire Exhibition 5/38
- Queen gets Scottish Order of the Thistle 5/38
- King George VI and Queen visit Paris 7/38
- King and Queen begin tour of Canada 5/39
- King and Queen begin tour of US 6/39
- George VI visits UK troops in France 12/39
- Princess Elizabeth makes radio debut 10/40
- Princess Elizabeth signs for war service 4/42
- Duke of Kent dies in air crash 8/42
- George VI has part-time munitions job 3/43
- George VI visits Allies in North Africa 6/43
- Princess Beatrice dies 10/44
- Gloucester is governor-general of Australia 1/45
- At Buckingham Palace on VE Day 5/45
- George VI pays tribute to Channel Isles 6/45
- Philip Mountbatten is naturalised Briton 3/47
- Princess Elizabeth made City freeman 6/47
- Princess Elizabeth announces engagement 7/47
- Princess Elizabeth to have no trousseau 8/47
- Princess Elizabeth marries 11/47
- Silver wedding of King and Queen 4/48
- Duke of Edinburgh takes seat in Lords 7/48
- Princess Elizabeth gives birth to son 11/48
- King cancels tour of Australia 11/48
- Princess Elizabeth's son christened 12/48
- George VI has foot operation 3/49
- Ex-royal governess reveals Palace secrets 12/49
- Princess Anne born 8/50
- King inaugurates Festival of Britain 5/51
- Princess Elizabeth stands in for father 6/51
- George VI has left lung removed 9/51
- Princess Elizabeth and Philip tour Canada 10/51
- Lord Mountbatten Mediterranean commander 10/51
- Princess Elizabeth leaves for Australia and Kenya 1/52
- Kenya: Princess Elizabeth hears of father's death; returns 2/52
- King George VI dies in his sleep 2/52
- George VI is buried in St. George's Chapel 2/52
- Duke of Windsor attends King's funeral 2/52

- To retain surname of Windsor 4/52
- Queen allows Britten to write Coronation opera 5/52
- Queen opens her first parliament 11/52
- Queen Mary dies 3/53
- Queen launches new yacht, Britannia 4/53
- Duke of Edinburgh gets his RAF wings 5/53
- Elizabeth II is crowned in Westminster Abbey 6/53
- Millions watch Coronation on television 6/53
- Bill allows Prince Philip as Regent 11/53
- Arthur Bliss, Master of Queen's Musick 11/53
- Queen vows to devote life to Commonwealth 12/53
- Australia welcomes Queen Elizabeth 2/54
- Queen returns from Commonwealth tour 5/54
- Queen's portrait draws record crowds 8/55
- Princess Margaret will not be marrying Townsend 10/55
- Queen's warm welcome in Nigeria 1/56
- Queen Mother's Devon Loch slips in race 3/56
- Queen Elizabeth II visits Sweden 6/56
- Prince Charles' first day at prep school 1/57
- Margaret's set uses rock 'n' roll catch-phrase 2/57
- Queen and Prince Philip visit Portugal 2/57
- Duchess of Kent in Ghana for independence ceremony 3/57
- Royals visit France 4/57
- Triumphant visit to US 10/57
- Queen opens Canadian parliament 10/57
- Queen ends presentations of debutantes 11/57
- First Queen's Christmas TV broadcast 12/57
- Last court presentation of debutantes 3/58
- Charles made Prince of Wales 7/58
- Queen dials UK's first direct trunk call 12/58
- Pope John meets Margaret and Queen Mother 4/59
- Queen opens NATO conference 6/59
- Queen inaugurates St Lawrence Seaway 6/59
- Queen expecting a third child 8/59
- Queen's head on banknotes 11/59
- Princess Margaret to marry commoner 2/60
- Descendants called Mountbatten-Windsor 2/60
- Queen gives birth to Prince Andrew 2/60
- Princess Margaret weds Armstrong-Jones 5/60
- Queen opens huge Kariba dam on Zambezi 5/60
- Duke of Kent marries Katherine Worsley 6/61
- Queen visits slums in the Gorbals 6/61
- Armstrong-Jones made Earl of Snowdon 10/61
- Prince Charles starts at Gordonstoun 5/62
- Princess Alexandra marries Angus Ogilvy 4/63
- 14-year-old Prince Charles buys a cherry brandy 6/63
- Princess Anne starts at Benenden school 9/63
- Prince Philip at Kennedy funeral 11/63
- Princess Alexandra gives birth to a son 2/64
- Elizabeth II gives birth to third son 3/64
- New Prince is named Edward 4/64
- Margaret at Beatles' film premiere 7/64
- Elizabeth II makes tour of Ethiopia 2/65
- Queen congratulates Francis Chichester 5/67
- Queen greets Duchess of Windsor 6/67
- Prince Charles starts at Cambridge 10/67
- Queen calls for racial tolerance 12/68
- Prince Charles acts in university revue 2/69
- Queen opens Victoria tube line 3/69
- Investiture of Prince of Wales 7/69
- Philip says royals may go into the red 11/69
- Prince Charles takes his Lords' seat 2/70
- Prince Charles to join Royal Navy 2/70
- Prince Charles gets a 2:2 in History 6/70
- Charles attends de Gaulle's funeral 11/70
- Crossman blasts Queen's pay rise request 5/71
- Prince Charles gets his wings 8/71
- Queen and Philip meet Emperor Hirohito 10/71
- Queen meets John Profumo 11/71
- Princess Anne named sportswoman of year 11/71
- Queen's allowance to be doubled 12/71
- Duke of Windsor dies 5/72
- Duke of Windsor buried at Frogmore 6/72
- Air crash kills Prince William of Gloucester 8/72
- Sterling University students hurl abuse at the Queen 10/72
- First state visit to Communist country 10/72
- Princess Anne denies romance 3/73
- Queen opens new London Bridge 3/73
- Engagement of Princess Anne announced 5/73
- Prince Charles at Bahamas independence ceremony 7/73
- Anne makes first royal visit to USSR 8/73
- Princess Anne marries Mark Phillips 11/73
- Princess Anne escapes kidnap attempt 3/74
- Prince Charles makes Lords' maiden speech 6/74
- Duke of Gloucester dies 6/74
- Queen knights Gary Sobers 2/75
- Queen knights Charlie Chaplin 3/75
- Charles is Master of Order of Garter 5/75
- Princess Margaret separates from Snowdon 3/76
- Queen arrives in Bicentennial US 7/76
- Queen opens Montreal Olympics 7/76
- Queen indirectly criticises devolution 5/77
- Jubilee week to celebrate Queen's 25 years of reign 6/77
- National jubilee bonfire-lighting 6/77
- Queen visits Northern Ireland 8/77
- Princess Anne has baby 11/77
- Anne's son christened Peter Mark Andrew 12/77
- Margaret in Mustique with Llewellyn 2/78
- Margaret seeks divorce from Snowdon 5/78
- Llewellyn denies plan to marry Margaret 5/78
- Pope bans Prince Michael's wedding in church 6/78
- Prince Michael weds Marie von Reibnitz 6/78
- Prince Andrew to join Royal Navy 11/78
- Queen visits Zambia 7/79
- Lord Mountbatten killed by IRA bomb 8/79
- Earl Mountbatten: profile 8/79
- Dowager Lady Brabourne dies of bomb wounds 8/79
- Queen's art adviser Blunt was spy 11/79
- Lady Diana Spencer, Charles' fiancee 9/80
- Queen visits Vatican; meets Pope 10/80
- Queen opens Synod; approves prayerbook 11/80
- Queen upset by press at Sandringham 1/81
- Prince Charles and Diana to marry 2/81
- Parcel bomb sent to Prince Charles 5/81
- Blank shots fired at Queen in Mall 6/81
- Prince Charles marries Lady Diana 7/81
- Profile of Charles and Diana 7/81
- Diana gives birth to son, William 6/82
- Intruder Fagan in Queen's bedroom 7/82
- Queen's bodyguard admits homosexuality 7/82
- Charles welcomes back Canberra liner 7/82
- Prince Andrew on holiday with Koo Stark 10/82
- Queen and Prince Philip visit Reagan 3/83
- Charles's view of National Gallery extension 9/84
- Princess of Wales gives birth to son, Henry 9/84
- Sudan famine aid appeal by Princess Anne 12/85
- Maori activists throw eggs at Queen, NZ 2/86
- Prince Andrew to marry Sarah Ferguson 3/86
- Duchess of Windsor dies 4/86
- Prince Andrew marries Sarah Ferguson 7/86
- Prince Charles admits talking to plants 9/86
- Queen visits China 10/86
- Secret report on George V's death 11/86
- Prince Edward resigns from Marines 1/87
- Queen Mother's cousins in mental home 4/87
- Princess Anne gets revived title 6/87
- Duchess's jewellery raises £31 million 12/87
- Prince Charles escapes avalanche 3/88
- Royal party blamed for avalanche 6/88
- Princess Beatrice is baptised 12/88
- Prince Philip attends Hirohito's funeral in Japan 2/89
- The Queen receives invitation from Gorbachev to visit Moscow 5/89
- Princess Anne and Captain Phillips to separate 8/89
- Queen inaugurates Glasgow as "cultural capital of Europe" 3/90
- Duchess of York gives birth to daughter, Eugenie Victoria 3/90
- Queen Mother celebrates 90th birthday 8/90
- Prince Charles undergoes hip-bone graft 9/90
- Prince William undergoes operation after golf club accident 6/91
- Queen's £6.6 million wealth dismissed as "exaggerated" 7/91
- Princess of Wales attends Pavarotti's Hyde Park concert 7/91
- Charles resigns as patron of National Museum of Scotland 8/91
- Princess Diana attends funeral of AIDS-victim friend 8/91
- Queen's speech signals more money for public services 10/91
- Biblical names more popular than those of the royals 11/91
- Queen quashes abdication rumours in Christmas broadcast 12/91
- Duchess of York seeks divorce 3/92
- Princess Anne begins divorce proceedings 4/92
- Queen Elizabeth welcomes European integration 5/92
- Queen Mother unveiling RAF statue causes demonstrations 5/92
- Queen ends three-day visit to France in Bordeaux 6/92
- Diana's biography causes scandal 6/92
- Duchess of York photos cause scandal 8/92
- Queen Elizabeth is jeered on visit to Dresden 10/92
- Fire badly damages Windsor Castle 11/92
- "The Sun" publishes leaked copy of Queen's Christmas speech 12/92
- Princess Anne marries Commander Tim Laurence 12/92
- Charles and Diana separate; there are no plans for divorce 12/92
- Princess Margaret enters hospital suffering from pneumonia 1/93
- The Queen is to pay income tax 2/93
- Buckingham Palace is to be opened to the public 4/93
- The Queen receives President Mary Robinso 5/93
- Viscount Lindley marries 10/93
- Princess Diana to withdraw from public life 12/93
- Prince Charles quits competitive polo 1/94
- Gun scare in Australia for Prince Charles 1/94
- Duchess of Kent becomes a Catholic 1/94
- Prince Charles criticises 'political correctness' 5/94
- Prince Charles says he has no plans to divorce 6/94
- Queen makes historic visit to Russia 10/94
- Queen allows oil prospecting at Windsor 12/94
- Duke of Kent attends Dresden commemoration ceremonies 2/95
- Prince Charles visits Ireland 5/95
- Queen Mother cheered at VE-Day anniversary celebrations 5/95

Royal Flying Corps
- Formed 4/12
- Reconnaissance developed 10/14
- New Zealand pilot bombs German Zeppelin 4/16
- Merges with RNAS to form RAF 4/18

Royal National Institute for the Blind
- New headquarters opened by King George 3/14

Royal Navy
- See also Britain (foreign affairs), Korean War, Shipping,
- World Wars I and II
- New base in the Firth of Forth 3/03
- Admiral Fisher, First Sea Lord 6/04
- Surrounds Russian Baltic Fleet 10/04
- Massive spending increase 3/05
- Press wants Navy to block German ships 7/05
- Well received in Yokohama, Japan 10/05
- HMS Dreadnought, biggest battleship 2/06
- Smaller budget announced 2/06
- Huge exercise includes mock port attacks 6/06
- HMS Dreadnought speed record 10/06
- Expecting less money 2/07
- Launch of HMS Bellerophon 7/07
- 35 die as destroyer hits cruiser 4/08
- Germans catching up 7/08
- New torpedo unveiled 7/08
- Indomitable sets record 8/08
- Fears Germany 8/08
- Sails to Aegean as Balkans crisis brews 10/08
- To get six more dreadnoughts 2/09
- Fears of German dreadnoughts overtaking 3/09
- Inspected by visiting Czar 8/09
- HMS Colossus, biggest battleship 4/10
- HMS Thunderer, dreadnought 2/11
- Plans to build five more battleships 3/11
- Churchill is First Sea Lord; new policy 10/11
- King George V, biggest ship, launched 10/11
- Boosts North Sea fleet after talks fail 7/12
- Review at Spithead 7/12
- HMS Audacious dreadnought launched, Cammell Laird 9/12
- HMS Iron Duke, most fully armed warship 10/12
- Prince Louis and Jellicoe are Sea Lords 12/12
- Estimates up by £16 million; more men 3/13
- HMS Elizabeth, first oil-driven battleship 10/13
- Churchill may resign over expenditure 1/14
- Record naval budget to match Germany 3/14
- Prepares for war 7/14
- Sir John Jellicoe is Supreme Admiral 8/14
- Prince Louis resigns as First Sea Lord 10/14
- Sinks four German destroyers off Holland 10/14
- Lord Fisher is new First Sea Lord 10/14
- Sinks four German cruisers off Falklands 12/14
- Sinks world's biggest cruiser, Blucher 1/15
- Battleship Formidable sunk by U-boat 1/15
- Launches a counter-blockade of Germany 3/15
- Naval General Service Medals awarded 8/15
- Churchill argues with admirals; resigns 11/15
- Heavy Jutland losses, but enemy retreat 5/16
- Accepts German Fleet's surrender, Forth 11/18
- On exercise while Germans scuttle fleet 6/19
- £157 million spent this year 12/19
- Submarine K5 sinks; 56 crew die 1/21
- Keeps four ports in Irish Free State 12/21
- UK and US agree to scrap eight battleships 2/30
- France and Japan block submarine ban 2/30
- France walks out of naval talks 3/30
- London Naval Treaty signed 4/30
- US, UK and Japan agree to naval limits 4/30
- France and Italy refuse naval treaty terms 4/30
- Limits to warships: London Naval Treaty 4/30
- MPs vote for Naval Treaty 7/30
- Sends battleships to quell Egyptian riots 7/30
- Invergordon 12,000 "mutiny" over pay 9/31
- Sent to protect foreigners in Shanghai 1/32
- 55 feared dead as submarine sinks 1/32
- New naval buildup planned 11/33
- White Paper wants more, stronger, warships 3/35
- Japan demands naval parity with Britain 12/35
- UK, US and France sign naval treaty 3/36
- Admiral David Beatty dies 3/36
- Warships patrol Spanish coast 7/36
- King inspects Fleet 11/36
- £50 million a year: highest spending since War 2/37
- 500,000 tons of ships ordered 2/37
- UK's first aircraft carrier, Ark Royal 4/37
- National Maritime Museum, Greenwich 4/37
- Eight die in HMS Hunter blast off Spain 5/37
- Warship attacked by submarine, Spain 9/37
- Japanese attack HMS Ladybird in China 12/37
- UK and US abandon naval treaty 4/38
- Chamberlain mobilises the Fleet 9/38
- Aircraft carrier Illustrious launched 4/39
- 71 die when submarine HMS Thetis sinks 6/39
- HMS Thetis lifted from sea bed 7/39
- King inspects Auxiliary Fleet 8/39
- Mobilisation 8/39
- HMS Courageous sunk with loss of 500 9/39
- Attacks German ship Graf Spee, Atlantic 12/39
- Destroyer HMS Daring is sunk 2/40
- Seizes seven Italian coal ships 3/40
- Mines Norwegian waters 4/40
- Destroys French fleet off Algeria 7/40
- Fleet Air Arm sinks seven Italian ships 11/40
- Destroys many Italian ships off Crete 3/41
- HMS Hood sunk by the Bismarck, Atlantic 5/41
- Ark Royal in Bismarck chase 5/41
- HMS Victorious in Bismarck chase 5/41
- Sinks German battleship Bismarck 5/41
- HMS Ark Royal sinks after torpedo attack 11/41
- Wipes out two Italian convoys in Med 11/41
- In combined services raid on Norway 12/41
- Escorts convoy to Malta 3/42
- Sinks German warship Scharnhorst 12/43
- D-Day landings in Normandy 6/44
- Rounds up remnants of German fleet 5/45
- Boards two Jewish immigrant ships in Med 1/48
- Cruiser sent to Falklands Islands 2/48
- HMS Amethyst makes freedom dash, China 7/49
- HMS Amethyst commander awarded DSO 8/49
- HMS Amethyst welcomed back to UK 11/49
- To aid US in South Korea 6/50
- Bans "snort" submarine breathing tubes 7/51
- Lord Mountbatten becomes Mediterranean commander 10/51
- Aircraft carrier HMS Hermes launched 2/53
- Mountbatten is First Sea Lord 10/54
- 13 die on submarine HMS Sidon 6/55
- Aircraft carrier Theseus leaves for Suez 8/56
- Plot to attack Northern Irish bases 3/57
- To buy US nuclear submarine plant 7/58
- Supports fishing boats off Iceland 8/58
- Wins back trawler boarded by Iceland 9/58
- First nuclear submarine, Dreadnought, launched 10/60
- Last national service call-ups 12/60
- Lax security blamed for Lonsdale spies 6/61
- Intercepts oil-laden tanker, Mozambique 4/66
- Launch of new nuclear submarine 9/66
- First Polaris missile tested 2/68
- Prince Charles to join 2/70
- IRA sinks RN launch in Baltimore, US 4/71
- Sub HMS Artemis sinks at Portsmouth; 3 sailors rescued 7/71
- Far East Command comes to an end 10/71
- Takes first action in Icelandic Cod War 5/73
- Prince Andrew to join 11/78
- HMS Hermes and HMS Invincible are loaded with planes 4/82
- Special Boat Squadron takes S. Georgia 4/82
- Loses Sheffield, Ardent and Coventry in war 5/82
- Thatcher refuses USA Gulf minesweepers 7/87
- IRA bomb kills 10 bandsmen at Royal Marines' School of Music 9/89
- Controversy over Wren found naked in another officer's cabin 6/91

Royce, Henry 5/04, 9/29, 4/33

Rubens, Bernice 4/70

Rubinstein, Artur 1/06, 12/82

Rubinstein, Ida 12/28

Ruby, Jack 11/63, 3/64, 9/64, 1/67

Ruckelshaus, William 10/73

Ruddock, Joan 10/83

Rudolph, Wilma 9/60

Ruffner, C.L. 1/51

Rugby
- England win first match against France 3/06
- England beat France at home 1/07
- England and France draw in International 1/22
- Scotland beat England in Calcutta Cup 3/26
- France beat England for the first time 4/27
- International board condemns scrummage 9/32
- England's first major win over New Zealand 1/36
- Obolensky scores England's winning tries 1/36
- England beat Scotland at Murrayfield 3/37
- Springboks UK tour: apartheid protests 11/69
- 98 arrested at Springbok match, UK 12/69
- Wales beat England for fourth time 3/79
- South African rugby tour of UK; protests 10/79
- Erika Roe streaks at England v Australia 1/82
- New Zealand win first World Cup 6/87
- France and Wales share title 3/88
- France win Five Nations' championship 3/89
- British Lions win rugby series in Australia 7/89
- Scotland beat England 13-7 at Murrayfield 3/90
- Wigan win the rugby League 4/90
- England win Five Nations' championship against France 3/91
- World Cup begins at Twickenham 10/91
- Australia beat England at Twickenham 11/91
- England beats France 31-13 in Five Nations' championship 2/92
- Wigan beats Bradford Northern, 50-8, in League championship 4/92
- England XV beats France in Five Nations championship 1/93
- France defeats Wales to win Five Nations championship 3/93
- Castleford thrash Wigan for Regal Trophy 1/94
- Wales loses to England but wins Five Nations 3/94
- England beats Scotland, wins the Five Nations 3/95
- Gavin Hastings scores record 44 points in World Cup 5/95

Rumania
- See also World Wars I and II
- Martial law declared 3/07
- Amnesty for 8,000 political prisoners 8/07
- Hungarian taught in Rumanian schools 8/09
- Mobilises and invades Bulgaria 7/13
- Declares war on Austria-Hungary 8/16
- Insurrection; King Ferdinand wounded 2/19
- Overthrows Hungary's Red Republic 8/19
- Allied pressure to sign Versailles treaty 11/19
- King Ferdinand suffers from cancer 11/26
- King Ferdinand dies; Mihai, aged five, succeeds 7/27
- Anti-Hungarian riots, Nagyvarad 12/27
- 30 die as a train on its way to Paris crashes 10/28
- Church fire, Costesti; more than 100 die 4/30
- Exiled Prince Carol recognised 6/30
- Signs commerce treaty with Britain 8/30
- King Carol's palace burnt down 4/32
- Discusses anti-German front with Poland and USSR 9/33
- Fascist kills liberal premier Ion Duca 12/33
- Balkan Pact with Greece, Yugoslavia and Turkey 2/34
- Plot to kill King Carol foiled 4/34
- Frontier guarantee with USSR and Poland 6/34
- Bans Jews from employing women under the age of 40 1/38
- Wants half a million Jews expelled 1/38
- King Carol ousts premier Goga 1/38
- Britain and France pledge aid 4/39
- Premier Calinescu murdered 9/39
- Russians invade Bukovina and Bessarabia 6/40
- King Carol abdicates in favour of son 9/40
- German and Italian troops invade 10/40
- Attempted Fascist coup fails 1/41
- Told by Stalin to declare war on Germany 5/44
- Armistice with USSR 8/44
- Declares war on Germany 8/44
- Left-wing government takes over 3/45
- Loses land under Paris peace treaties 2/47
- Signs friendship treaty with Yugoslavia 12/47
- King Michael forced to abdicate 12/47
- Ends friendship pact with Yugoslavia 10/49
- Former King Carol II dies 4/53
- Joins Warsaw Pact 5/55
- Warsaw Pact offers Vietnam volunteers 7/66
- Nicolae Ceausescu becomes premier 12/67
- Dubcek signs 20-year pact with Rumania 8/68
- Richard Nixon visits 8/69
- Gymnast Comaneci scores ten at Olympics 7/76
- Hundreds die in earthquake 3/77
- China's Hua Kuo-feng visits 8/78

- Gymnast Nadia Comaneci defects to Hungary 11/89
- Dictator Nicolae Ceausescu and his wife are executed 12/89
- Secret police abolished 1/90
- Opposition parties jostle to succeed Ceausescu 1/90
- Four leaders of the Ceausescu regime are jailed 2/90
- National Salvation Front wins in free elections 5/90
- Government busses in miners to quell opposition on streets 6/90
- Ion Iliescu is elected President 10/92

Runcie, Robert (Archbishop) 3/80, 7/81, 11/81, 5/82, 7/82, 7/84, 9/84, 2/87, 12/87, 9/89
Rundstedt, Gerd von 7/44, 12/44, 3/45, 5/45, 2/53
Runyon, Damon 12/46
Rushdie, Salman 1/89, 2/89, 5/91, 11/92, 5/94
Rushing, Jimmy 6/72
Rusk, Dean 8/61, 9/62, 8/63, 10/64, 4/66, 11/67, 1/68, 12/94
Ruskin, John 1/00
Russell, Bertrand 12/50, 2/58, 10/60, 9/61, 2/62, 10/62, 10/65, 2/70
Russell, Charles Taze 10/16
Russell, Guy 9/50
Russell, Jane 7/53
Russell, Ken 12/60, 12/69, 10/77
Russell, William F. 2/29
Russell, William Howard 2/07
Russia (foreign affairs)
- See now USSR until 12/91 0/23
- Fleet in Korea worries Japanese 3/00
- Sino-Russian clash on Manchurian railway 4/00
- Annexes parts of Manchuria 9/00
- Left out of Allies' Chinese policy 10/00
- Troop manoeuvres in Balkans 8/01
- Manchurian Treaty with China; troops out 4/02
- Russian official language in Finland 6/02
- To supervise Macedonian reforms 12/02
- Czar discusses problems with Franz Josef 9/03
- Russians beaten at Telissu; lose 2,000 6/04
- Russian governor of Finland killed 6/04
- Russia sinks British ship: crisis 7/04
- Liao-Yang defeat; General Keller killed 8/04
- Russians sink British North Sea trawlers 10/04
- Riots in Russian-ruled Poland 11/04
- Imperial pact with Germany: anti-British 7/05
- Anti-Russian riots in Poland 8/06
- Treaty with Japan gives China guarantee 7/07
- Discusses England and railway with Germany 8/07
- Soldiers jailed for Japanese surrender 12/07
- Settles Persian-Turkish border dispute 2/08
- British King meets Czar in Russia 6/08
- Will sack Polish rebel teachers 9/08
- Wants Serbia to drop claims for peace 2/09
- Treaty with China; USA protests 7/09
- Czar visits France 7/09
- UK workers protest at Czar's visit 8/09
- Duma to abolish Finnish autonomy 6/10
- Free hand in Manchuria agreed with Japan 7/10
- Suggests cross-desert railway line, China 12/10
- Mongolia becomes a protectorate 12/11
- Agrees spheres of influence with Japan 8/12
- France to support Russia in the Balkans 8/12
- Mobilises troops fearing Balkans conflict 9/12
- Czar condemns Bulgarian Balkan fighting 7/13
- German orders to naval shipyards banned 4/14
- Czar mobilises in support of Serbia 7/14
- Attacks East Prussia and Galicia 8/14
- Austria declares war; invades Poland 8/14
- Czar leaves for the front 10/14
- Breaks off diplomatic relations with Turkey 11/14
- Czar reveals pre-war peace proposals 1/15
- Wants access to Eastern Mediterranean 3/16
- Czar endorses Wilson's plans, free Poland 1/17
- Allied conference opens, Petrograd 1/17
- War to continue, but peace proposals too 5/17
- Lenin offers armistice to Austro-Germans 11/17
- Bolsheviks talk peace, Brest-Litovsk 12/17
- Recognises Finland and Ukraine independent 1/18
- Leaves Entente Allies 2/18
- Cedes Poland, Ukraine, Baltic and Caucasus 3/18
- Establishes diplomatic relations with Germany 4/18
- US severs ties 8/18
- Litvinov, ambassador to Britain, jailed 9/18
- Baltic states form defensive alliance 1/20
- Red Army invades from Caspian Sea 5/20
- Declares war on Poland 5/20
- Beaten from Warsaw; loses Novominsk 8/20
- Royal Air Force aids Polish resistance 8/20
- Poles claim to have taken 42,000 prisoners 10/20
- Signs armistice with Poland at Riga 10/20
- Treaties respecting Persia and Afghanistan 2/21
- Consuls banned from Afghanistan regions 11/21
- Rapallo economic treaty with Germany 4/22
- No recognition until debts paid, Genoa 5/22
- US and EC food airlifted to Moscow 2/92
- South African President de Klerk visits Moscow 6/92
- Black Sea Fleet accord is signed with the Ukraine 8/92
- Yeltsin and Bush sign START-2 Treaty in Moscow 1/93
- Agrees with Ukraine to divide Black Sea Fleet 6/93
- Queen Elizabeth II makes historic visit 10/94

Russia (politics)
- Plot to murder Czar uncovered 10/00
- 1,500 arrested in Odessa 4/01
- 30,000 students strike against curbs 2/02
- Bloody rioting in the south 7/02
- Cossacks attack Jewish socialists 6/03
- Lenin and Social Democrats meet 7/03
- Interior minister von Plehve killed 7/04
- Reserve soldiers disgruntled 10/04
- Students protest about war; call to democracy 11/04
- Czar promises reforms; tough on rioters 12/04
- Bloody Sunday: 500 strikers killed 1/05
- Assassin blows up Grand Duke in Moscow 2/05
- Gorky released; nobility urge reforms 2/05
- Nationwide protests after Mukden defeat 3/05
- Czar agrees to "consultative assembly" 3/05
- Governors of Ufa and Baku assassinated 5/05
- Red sailors seize battleship Potemkin 6/05
- Cossacks charge crowds; Czar cautious 6/05
- Ministers angry: pact harms French ties 7/05
- 6,000 killed in Odessa; Potemkin rebels give up 7/05
- Duma parliament created, but few powers 8/05
- Riots in Latvia; peace talks with Japan 8/05
- Zemstvo congress demands real assembly 9/05
- Duma begins, but general strike worsens 10/05
- Prisoners freed, but universities closed 11/05
- Kronstadt mutiny; martial law in Poland 11/05
- Congress of Soviets calls for democracy 12/05
- Army plot against Czar is revealed 12/05
- Revolutionaries capture Kiev fortress 12/05
- Failed student-worker revolt; many dead 12/05
- Crackdown in Moscow and the Balkans 1/06
- Mutiny in Sevastopol, Crimea 3/06
- Czar grants Duma some legislative power 3/06
- Peasants vote progressives in Duma poll 4/06
- Social Democrats murder Father Gapon 4/06
- Duma opens; anger over lack of amnesty 5/06
- Czar gives votes to all; redistributes land 5/06
- Mutinies: premier Stolypin condemned 6/06
- Duma closed; deputies demand tax boycott 7/06
- Premier Stolypin survives bomb attack 8/06
- 1,000 political figures exiled a day 10/06
- Trotsky exiled to Siberia 11/06
- Admiral Niebogatov tried for surrender 12/06
- Radicals gain in Duma elections 2/07
- New Duma met by 40,000 demonstrators 3/07
- Duma dissolved; socialists accused 6/07
- Compulsory school demands; trials open 8/07
- Third conservative Duma created 10/07
- New Duma says Czar "renounces autocracy" 11/07
- 167 Duma members jailed for manifesto 12/07
- Premier Komiakov resigns 12/08
- Gorky expelled from Revolutionary Party 11/09
- Government orders Jews to leave Kiev 5/10
- Students riot over corporal punishment 12/10
- Premier Stolypin resigns 3/11
- Stolypin shot dead at the opera 9/11
- Kokovtsev is new premier 9/11
- Plans to quadruple army's size 3/14
- Social Democrats expelled from Duma 5/14
- Czar takes personal control of army 9/15
- Trepov replaces Sturmer as premier 11/16
- Trepov resigns; Golitzin is new premier 1/17
- Czar abdicates after week's revolution 3/17
- Duma under Kerensky sides with revolution 3/17
- Lenin returns to Russia in sealed train 4/17
- Kerensky's economic and political reforms 4/17
- Peasants' Congress wants republic 5/17
- Ukraine declares independence 6/17
- Pan-Russian Congress of Soviets 6/17
- Soviets vote to abolish Duma 6/17
- Bolshevik uprising fails; Lenin flees 7/17
- Premier Kerensky recommitted to war 7/17
- Ex-Czar in Siberia, safe from Bolsheviks 9/17
- Kerensky sacks Kornilov and founds republic 9/17
- Grand dukes arrested for plotting coup 9/17
- Bolshevik coup; Kerensky ousted 11/17
- Red Army and Cheka security police force created 1/18
- Bolsheviks dissolve Duma 1/18
- Peace talks falter as Bolsheviks split 2/18
- Church-state separation proclaimed 2/18
- Moscow becomes the new capital 3/18
- Grand Duke heads counter-revolution push 4/18
- Military service reinstated 4/18
- Trial of ex-Czar ordered 5/18
- Georgia and Armenia declare independence 5/18
- Martial law in Moscow 5/18
- Bolshevik state attacked on all fronts 6/18
- Peace with Ukraine 6/18
- Ex-Czar and family executed by Ekaterinburg Cheka 7/18
- Congress wants socialist constitution 7/18
- German envoy shot by treaty opponents 7/18
- Provisional government in Siberia 7/18
- Whites, British bring martial law, north 8/18
- Red Army takes Kazan 8/18
- Lenin survives assassination attempt 8/18
- US troops rout Bolsheviks 2/19
- Bolsheviks' Comintern for world uprising 3/19
- Allies repel Red attack in north 4/19
- Pro-White Allies starve in south 4/19
- Red Army takes Crimea 4/19
- First Red Army surrenders to Ukrainians 4/19
- British sink Red ships, Kronstadt 6/19
- Whites hit Petrograd and Moscow; repelled 10/19
- Tukharchevsky's Reds push through Urals 10/19
- Admiral Kolchak stopped east of Moscow 10/19
- British Air Force tanks help Whites 10/19
- Denikin's Cossacks and Allies in disarray 2/20
- Red Army cavalry wins; Kolchak shot 2/20
- Reds capture Archangel 2/20
- Recognises independence of Estonia 2/20
- Lenin promises democratic parliament 2/20
- Red Army attacks Poland 3/20
- War ends when Whites beaten in Crimea 11/20
- Wrangel retreats under French protection 11/20
- Kronstadt sailors mutiny against Soviets 2/21
- Trotsky vindicated as private trade used 3/21
- Trotsky crushes Kronstadt mutiny 3/21
- All foreigners eligible for work 4/21
- Lenin appeals for Western famine aid 8/21
- Government admits 20 million starve 12/21
- Stalin is Party General Secretary 4/22
- Lenin suffers a stroke 5/22
- Lenin ill; three-man council governs 6/22
- Paris emigres name Grand Duke as Czar 11/22
- Union of Soviet Socialist Republics 12/22
- See now USSR until 12/91 0/23
- 100 per cent tariff imposed on imported alcohol 10/92
- Yeltsin fights for political life against hardliners 12/92
- President Yeltsin wins vote of confidence 4/93
- Yeltsin crushes rebellion, government building wrecked 10/93
- "Mad Vlad" triumphs in parliamentary elections 12/93
- Armenia and Azerbaijan agree to ceasefire 5/94
- Anastasia IS dead says report 9/94

Russon, Anthony 5/73
Rust, Bernhard 6/33
Rust, Mathias 5/87, 9/87
Rutan, Richard 12/86
Ruth, Babe 1/20, 9/27, 8/48
Rutherford, Ernest 11/08, 1/19, 10/37
Rutherford, Margaret 12/45, 5/72
Ruzicka, Leopold 12/39
Rwanda (Ruanda)
- Ceded to Britain by Belgium 3/21
- Thousands of Tutsi tribesmen massacred 2/64
- Red Cross estimate 100,000 killed in tribal slaughter 4/94
- Death toll reaches 500,000 5/94
- Government troops massacre Hutus in refugee camp 4/95

Ryan, Cornelius 11/74
Ryan, Leo 11/78
Ryan, Michael 8/87
Ryan, Patrick 5/68, 11/88, 12/88
Ryder, Lord 8/75
Rykov, Alexei 2/24, 2/29, 12/30, 3/38, 10/62
Ryle, Martin 12/74
Ryti, Risto 6/44
Ryun, Jim 7/66

S

Saar
- Votes for return to Germany 1/35
- League agrees to return 1/35
- Votes against joining West Germany 11/52
- Pro-German party wins elections 12/55
- Returns to West Germany 1/57

Saarinen, Eero 8/10
Saatchi and Saatchi 3/78
Sabatini, Gabriela 9/88
Sabin, Albert 3/93
Sabry, Ali 5/71
Sacasa, Juan 2/34
Sacco, Nicola 7/21, 4/27, 8/27
Sachs, Guenther 7/66
Sackville-West, Vita (Victoria) 6/62
Sadat, Anwar 12/18, 10/70, 1/71, 3/71, 5/71, 7/72, 8/72, 9/73, 2/74, 6/75, 3/76, 1/77, 3/77, 4/77, 11/77, 12/77, 1/78, 2/78, 9/78, 10/78, 12/78, 3/79, 7/80, 6/81, 10/81
Sagan, Francoise 6/35
Sahara
- See Spanish Sahara

Sahib, Khan 5/58
Saigon
- Falls to N. Vietnamese Communists 4/75

Sailing
- See also Disasters, Royal Navy, Shipping
- Columbia wins first America's Cup 9/01
- Clean sweep for US in America's Cup 10/01
- First powerboat race, in Ireland 7/03
- Reliance wins America's Cup 9/03
- Atlantic wins German Kaiser's Cup 5/05
- Cambridge beats Harvard in boat race 9/06
- University boat race: both boats sink 3/12
- Shamrock IV wins first round of America's Cup 7/20
- Resolute wins America's Cup 7/20
- US win America's Cup off Rhode Island 9/30
- US's Rainbow wins America's Cup 9/34
- Chichester sets Atlantic solo record 7/60
- Chichester crosses Atlantic in 30 days 6/64
- Chichester begins round-world voyage 8/66
- Francis Chichester to be knighted 1/67
- Sir Francis Chichester rounds Cape Horn 3/67
- Chichester ends sole round-world voyage 5/67
- Alec Rose ends lone UK-Australia voyage 12/67
- Alec Rose ends lone round-world voyage 7/68
- Alec Rose is knighted 7/68
- Knox-Johnson (UK) wins round-world race 4/69
- Heath leads UK to Admiral's Cup win 8/71
- Chay Blyth ends solo round-world voyage 8/71
- Death of Sir Francis Chichester 8/72
- Naomi James in round-the-world record 6/78
- 14 die in Fastnet race; 125 yachtsmen rescued 8/79
- Australia wins America's Cup 9/83
- 19 die when UK barque sinks off Bermuda 6/84
- 100 forced to retire from Fastnet race 8/85
- US Dennis Conner wins back America's Cup 2/87
- Yacht America wins America's Cup 5/92
- Bruno Peyron completes circumnavigation of globe in 79 days 4/93
- German team wins Admiral's Cup 8/93
- Knox-Johnston and ENZA smash record 4/94
- New Zealand's Black Magic 1 wins America's Cup 5/95

Saint Denis, Ruth 7/68
Saint Germain, Treaty of
- Creates Yugoslavia and Czechoslovakia 6/20

Saint Jean, Alfredo 6/82
Saint John, Ian 5/65
Saint Laurent, Yves 8/36, 1/58, 7/59, 9/61, 1/62, 3/62, 3/72
Saint Lucia
- Independent of Britain 2/79

Saint Petersburg
- Police clash with anti-government demo 12/04
- Bloody Sunday: 500 strikers killed 1/05
- Renamed Petrograd 8/14

Saint Vincent
- Independent of Britain 10/79

Saint-Exupery, Antoine de 6/00, 7/44
Saint-Laurent, Yves 8/36
Saint-Saens, Camille 11/13, 12/21
Sakharov, Andrei 5/21, 11/72, 3/73, 4/74, 10/75, 11/75, 4/76, 1/80, 11/81, 12/81, 5/84, 8/84, 12/86, 6/88, 10/88, 12/89
Saki 12/18
Sakman, Bert 12/91
Salameh, Ali Hassan 10/76
Salan, Raoul 5/58, 4/61, 7/61, 9/61, 2/62, 3/62, 4/62, 5/62
Salandra, Antonio 4/15
Salazar, Antonio de Oliveira 7/32, 9/68, 7/70
Salem, Elie 12/82
Salinger, J.D. 1/19, 12/51
Salisbury, Robert 3/00, 9/00, 10/00, 5/01, 7/02, 8/03
Salk, Jonas Edward 3/53, 4/54
Salter, Jo 2/95
Salvation Army
- First meeting 6/04
- British crusade 8/05
- Featured in Shaw play, "Major Barbara" 12/05
- Shelter for London's vagrants 11/09
- General William Booth dies 8/12
- General Bramwell Booth quells mutiny 1/29
- Commander Higgins replaces General Booth 2/29
- General Booth dies 6/29
- First woman general, Evangeline Booth 9/34

Sammons, Albert 8/57
Samphan, Khieu 4/75
Sampras, Pete 7/93, 7/94
Samuel, Herbert 3/13, 1/16, 3/26, 8/31, 11/31, 9/32
Samuel, Stuart 4/13
Samuelson, Victor 12/73
San Giuliano, Marquis di 6/11
Sanchez, Juan 4/72
Sanchez, Oscar Arias 12/87
Sanders, Edgar 2/50, 8/53
Sanderson, Tessa 8/84
Sandford, Jeremy 1/67
Sandino, Augusto 9/27, 1/28, 2/28, 2/34
Sands, Bobby 3/81, 4/81, 5/81
Sandys, Duncan 8/55, 2/60, 5/73
Saneyev, Viktor 7/80
Sanger, Frederick 12/53, 12/58, 10/80
Sanger, Margaret 10/16, 9/66
Sanjhabi, Karim 12/78
Sanjurjo, Jose 8/32, 7/36
Santayana, George 9/52
Santer, Jacques 7/94
Santos, Jose Eduardo dos 10/92
Santos-Dumont, Alberto 10/01, 6/07, 7/32
Sarawak
- UK Governor Stewart stabbed by youth 12/49
- Joins Federation of Malaysia 9/63

Sarazen, Gene 6/32
Sargeant, Marcus 6/81
Sargent, John 12/18, 4/25, 12/25
Sargent, Malcolm 6/47, 5/50
Saroyan, William 8/08
Sarraut, Albert 10/33, 1/36
Sarrien, Ferdinand 10/06
Sartre, Jean-Paul 6/05, 12/46, 10/64, 4/80, 4/86
Sassoon, Siegfried 12/18, 8/67
Sassoon, Vidal 1/64, 12/66
Satie, Erik 5/17, 12/17, 12/25
Sato, Eisaku 6/72
Sauckel, Fritz 11/45, 10/46
Saud, Ibn, Abdul Aziz
- See Abdul Aziz, Saud ibn

Saud, Ibn, King of Saudi Arabia 1/02, 10/24, 1/26, 3/26, 6/34, 11/53, 2/69
Saudi Arabia
- Ibn Saud crowned King 1/26
- Ibn Saud back from exile; beats Hussein 1/26
- UK hails Ibn Saud as Saudi Arabian King 3/26
- Britain recognises independence 5/27
- Captures Yemeni city of Hodeida 5/34
- Signs truce with Yemen in Jeddah 5/34
- Ibn Saud and Imam of Yemen sign treaty 6/34
- Declares war on Germany 3/45
- Says Palestine is Arab land 1/46
- Signs security pact with Egypt 6/50
- Aramco to share oil profits with Saudis 1/51
- King Ibn Saud dies 11/53
- Bars Israeli ships from Gulf of Aqaba 4/57
- Prince Feisal named as premier 10/62
- Feisal deposes Abdul Aziz 11/64
- Death of Abdul Aziz, Saud ibn 2/69
- Cuts oil supplies to US 8/73
- Yamani says UK oil supplies are safe 11/73
- King Faisal killed by nephew in palace 3/75
- Crown Prince Khalid succeeds to throne 3/75
- Faisal's assassin beheaded 6/75
- Carlos terrorists seize Sheikh Yamani 12/75
- 82 die as Lebanese airliner crashes 1/76
- Wanted only five per cent oil price rise 12/76
- UK's Owen apologises over execution 1/78
- Shi'ites capture Mecca mosque 11/79
- Troops recapture Mosque 11/79
- 160 Mecca pilgrims die in airliner blast 11/79
- 63 who seized mosque are executed 1/80
- UK "Death of a Princess" film starts row 4/80
- UK formally apologises 4/80
- UK's Carrington apologises over film 5/80
- Arnott and wife freed; may return 8/80
- 301 die on Tristar plane, Riyadh 8/80
- UK scandal over death of Helen Smith 8/80
- King Khaled visits London 6/81
- King Khaled dies; Prince Fahd becomes King 6/82
- Leeds inquest into nurse Helen Smith 8/82
- King Fahd sacks Sheikh Yamani 10/86
- Iranian pilgrims die in Mecca riots 7/87
- Salman Rushdie's "Satanic Verses" is banned 1/89

- ICO fails to back Iran in Rushdie affair 3/89
- Saudi forces on full alert as Iraqis breach neutral zone 8/90
- Thousands of Kuwaiti refugees flee into Saudi Arabia 9/90
- President Bush spends Thanksgiving Day with US troops 11/90
- Prince of Wales visits British troops 12/90
- Allied forces recapture border town of Khafji 1/91
- Iraqi Scud missiles hit Riyadh 1/91
- Allied tanks cross Saudi border 2/91
- Kuwait's exiled Crown Prince declares martial law 2/91

Saunders, Ernest 1/87, 5/87, 7/87, 8/90
Saunders, Jennifer 12/83
Savage, Sean 3/88
Savalas, Telly 12/74, 1/94
Savary, Peter de 11/87
Savimbi, Jonas 10/92
Savitt, Richard 7/51
Savundra, Emil 2/67
Sayers, Dorothy L. 12/41, 12/57
Scanlon, Hugh 11/67, 4/75
Scapa Flow
- German sailors sink fleet in defiant act 6/19

Scargill, Arthur 12/81, 3/83, 9/83, 4/84, 5/84, 9/84, 10/84, 11/84, 12/84, 3/85, 11/87, 1/88, 3/90, 7/90
Scarman, Lord 4/81, 11/81
Scarry, Richard 4/94
Schabowski, Gunter 11/89
Schacht, Hjalmar 5/45
Scharlieb, Mary 10/16
Scheckter, Jody 1/50
Scheldermann, Philipp 6/19
Schiaparelli, Elsa 11/73
Schidlof, Peter 8/87
Schlele, Egon 10/18
Schild, Annabel 3/80
Schild, Daphne 3/80
Schild, Rolf 3/80
Schirach, Baldur von 6/33, 5/46
Schirra, Walter 12/65
Schleicher, Kurt von 7/32, 12/32, 1/33, 6/34
Schlesinger, John 12/67
Schleyer, Hans Martin 9/77, 10/77
Schlieben, Karl von 6/44
Schmeling, Max 6/30, 6/32, 6/38, 5/41
Schmidt, Helmut 5/74, 1/79, 10/82
Schmitt, Eric 5/93
Schmoller, Gustav von 1/07
Schnabel, Artur 12/38, 8/47, 8/51
Schneider, Romy 9/38, 5/82
Schnitzler, Arthur 10/31, 12/33
Schoenberg, Arnold 12/33, 7/51, 12/65
Schranz, Karl 2/68
Schroeder, Fred 7/49
Schroeder, Kurt von 1/33
Schubert, Ingrid 11/77
Schultz, Phil Max 8/11
Schumacher, Ernst Friedrich "Fritz" 12/73, 9/77
Schumacher, Kurt 8/49, 8/52
Schumacher, Michael 11/94
Schuman Plan
- Creating Europe coal and steel community 6/52

Schuman, Robert 11/47, 5/50, 9/63
Schuman, William 8/10
Schumann, Maurice 4/11
Schuschnigg, Kurt von 7/34, 5/36, 10/36, 1/38, 6/38, 8/38, 5/45, 11/77
Schwarzenegger, Arnold 8/91
Schwarzkopf, Norman 2/91
Schweitzer, Albert 9/65
Schwitters, Kurt 12/20, 1/48
Science and Technology
- See also Medicine, Space, Television
- Dr Rowland discovers magnetism's cause 1/00
- Dutch de Vries rediscovers heredity laws 3/00
- New electrical insulation 8/00
- Max Planck's Quantum Theory unveiled 12/00
- Trams electrified in Portsmouth 4/01
- Becquerel discovers subatomic radiation 6/01
- First cross-Atlantic wireless messages 12/01
- Invention of electrical battery 5/02
- Siemens electric train reaches 125 mph 10/03
- Marie Curie wins Nobel for radioactivity 12/03
- First mainline electric train 3/04
- Cheaper and more reliable cars 9/04
- Electric valve, basis of radio 10/04
- Pavlov and dogs' "conditioned reflex" 12/04
- Einstein propounds Theory of Relativity 7/05
- Typewriter automatic carriage return 9/06
- First telegraph-transmitted pictures 10/06
- Wireless develops with triode invention 12/06
- Experimental train reaches 98 mph 7/07
- Solid helium produced, Netherlands 2/08
- Minkowski sees time as fourth dimension 9/08
- Rutherford detects atom 11/08
- Einstein shows quantum theory of life 11/08
- First "gyroscope" 11/08
- Rutherford's prize for particle physics 12/08
- Astronomers see new planet 1/09
- Oxygen on Mars, claim 9/09
- Tough Bakelite invented: Dr Baekeland 12/09
- Artificial rubber process 4/10
- First talking motion pictures: Edison 8/10
- Pure radium isolated: Madame Curie 9/10
- Kamerlingh Onnes finds superconductivity 12/11
- Radiation from outer space: Victor Hess 12/11
- US farmer instals petroleum cooker 5/12
- Continental drift theory: Alfred Wegener 12/12
- "Piltdown Man" discovered 12/12
- Edison invents telephone recorder 5/13
- Miners' electric safety lantern 10/14
- Einstein challenges Newton on gravity 12/15
- Braggs, father and son, work on X-rays 12/15
- Proactium discovered 1/17
- Rutherford splits the atom 1/19
- Solar eclipse confirms Einstein's theory 3/19
- Gravity bends light, Einstein theory proved 12/19
- Einstein says universe could be measured 1/21
- Pneumatic tyre inventor Dunlop dies 10/21
- Quantum photoelectric effect: Einstein 12/21
- Bohr explains electron orbits in atoms 12/22
- Aston and Snoddy win Nobels for isotopes 12/22
- Roentgen, X-ray pioneer, dies 2/23
- Mars atmosphere similar to earth's, claim 8/24
- Ancient civilisation, Galapagos Islands 8/24
- Astronomers estimate size of universe 8/27
- Rapid-computation machine, Massachusetts 10/27
- Heisenberg's "Uncertainty Principle" 12/27
- Java Man may be humans' "missing link" 12/27
- Professor Hill predicts artificial cells 9/28
- Einstein and Planck get Planck medals 6/29
- Big Bang theory of creation 12/29
- Einstein predicts expanding universe 12/29
- Tombaugh discovers planet Pluto: existence known from Uranus 2/30
- orbit 2/30
- X-rays show hidden Holbein painting 2/30
- Man on the moon by 2050, prediction 4/30
- Pluto accepted as new planet's name 5/30
- Quick-freezing for Birdseye frozen peas 6/30
- Nylon invented by Wallace Carrothers 12/30
- Paul Dirac discovers "anti-particles" 12/30
- Edison, maker of 1,100 inventions, dies 10/31
- Frederick Allison discovers halogen 11/31
- Better television definition 12/31
- High pressure reactions: Bosch and Bergius 12/31
- Einstein: Earth is 10 billion years old 10/32
- Atom-smashing Cockcroft and Watson 12/32
- Chadwick discovers the neutron 12/32
- Karl Jansky discovers interstellar radio 12/32
- Record low temperatures achieved 5/33
- Marie Curie, physics pioneer, dies 7/34
- Anderosterone, first artificial hormone 12/34
- Lindbergh invents pump-oxygenator 6/35
- Carrel keeps organs alive outside body 6/35
- Vitamin E isolated in California 8/35
- Radio device to spot planes: Watson-Watt 12/35
- Ivan Pavlov, physiologist, dies 2/36
- Guglielmo Marconi, radio pioneer, dies 7/37
- Atomic pioneer Rutherford dies 10/37
- Aircraft safety device: altimeter 10/38
- Discovery of nuclear fission 1/39
- "Radio-location" key weapon in air war 6/41
- First atomic chain reaction, US 12/42
- Radar and other equipment in U-boat war 5/43
- Properties of DNA identified 1/44
- DDT acts as anti-malarial insecticide 8/44
- Atomic bombs on Hiroshima and Nagasaki 8/45
- The secret of "radar" is disclosed, UK 8/45
- IBM introduces electronic calculator 2/46
- The Biro pen goes on sale 11/46
- US plane breaks the sound barrier 10/47
- Transistor invented 12/48
- Maiden flight of first jet airliner 7/49
- Einstein forms new theory of gravity 12/49
- Atom-smashing machine at Harwell, UK 12/49
- Berkelium, 93rd element, discovered 1/50
- Rover produces first gas-turbine car, UK 3/50
- ICI to manufacture "terylene" 11/50
- First hydrogen bomb tested in Pacific 5/51
- Ancient coelacanth fish found, S. Africa 12/52
- Crick and Watson discover DNA structure reproduction 4/53
- Waterproof nylon clothing used on Everest climb 6/53
- Farnborough centre to test Comet crashes 4/54
- IBM announce business computer 5/54
- Computer calculating speeds up 1000-fold 5/54
- Enrico Fermi, Italian physicist, dies 11/54
- Music "synthesiser" 1/55
- Albert Einstein dies 4/55
- West German scientists refuse nuclear work 4/57
- Jodrell Bank radio telescope 6/57
- USSR first in space with Sputnik 1 10/57
- Tests on space-dog for weightlessness 11/57
- Cockerell demonstrates the hovercraft 5/58
- Stereo "High Fidelity" recordings 8/58
- Satellite shows earth's radiation belts 12/58
- Silicon chip: electronic miniaturisation 12/58
- Harnessing the fusion power of H-bombs 12/58
- Space monkeys tested; return alive 5/59
- Antarctic made a "science reserve" 12/59
- First "hover-scooter", UK 11/60
- Laser light invented by Maiman, US 12/60
- Vertical take-off Hawker P1127 aircraft 12/60
- Subatomic "quarks" 12/60
- Live transatlantic television: Telstar 7/62
- Discovery of quasars 12/62
- Mariner II sends back pictures of Venus 12/62
- Genetic engineering in prospect 12/74
- Julian Huxley, scientist, dies - profile 2/75
- Radio-operated bleepers for the active 4/75
- "Cat's eyes" inventor Shaw dies 9/76
- Black hole in Scorpio constellation 6/78
- Hounsfield's Nobel for CAT body scanner 10/79
- Sanger wins second Nobel for DNA work 10/80
- Fibre optics on telephone networks 12/82
- Information systems, word processors 12/82
- Silicon chips for industrial computers 12/82
- Computers, from calculator to PC games 12/82
- Cheaper computers and videos: future links 12/82
- Advent of the compact disc 12/83
- Genetic fingerprinting used in UK 11/85
- High-temperature superconductors 12/86
- 1987 cut by one second 12/87
- £25 million Sky TV satellite network is launched 2/89
- First baboon liver-transplant patient dies 9/92
- Top quark found after 20 year search 4/94
- Astronomers find most distant known galaxy 1/95

Scilly, Isles of
- RN intervenes in clash between British and French trawlers 6/92

Scofield, Paul 12/50, 12/62, 12/67, 12/79
Scoon, Paul 11/83
Scorsese, Martin 2/76, 12/90
Scorza, Carlo 4/45
Scott, C.P. 1/32
Scott, David 3/66, 7/71
Scott, Doug 9/75
Scott, Elizabeth 4/32
Scott, George C. 4/70
Scott, Giles Gilbert 12/04, 12/33
Scott, Norah 2/22
Scott, Norman 3/76, 10/77, 6/78, 8/78, 12/78, 5/79
Scott, Paul 12/75, 12/84
Scott, Peter 8/89
Scott, Ridley 12/92
Scott, Robert Falcon 3/03, 9/09, 3/11, 12/11, 2/13
Scott, Terry 7/94
Scriabin, Alexander 4/15
Scudamore, Peter 4/89
Seaga, Edward 10/80
Seato
- South-East Treaty Organisation meets 2/55
- Forces may join US in opposing Laos 5/62

Seberg, Jean 9/79
Sebring, Jay 8/69
Secombe, Harry 12/53
Second World War
- See World War II

Sedgman, Frank 7/52
Seelig, Roger 1/87, 10/87
Segar, Elzie 7/29
Segovia, Andres 6/87
Segrave, Henry 3/27
Seimet, Henri 3/12
Sein Lwin 8/88
Seinkiewicz, Henryk 11/16
Seipel, Ignaz 6/24
Seitz, Karl 2/34
Selxas, Victor 7/53
Selassie, Haile, Emperor of Ethiopia 11/30, 4/32, 2/35, 7/35, 8/35, 9/35, 10/35, 5/36, 6/36, 2/37, 1/41, 3/41, 5/41, 10/54, 11/55, 12/60, 11/70, 10/71, 3/74, 9/74, 8/75
Selby, Hubert, Jr 7/68
Seles, Monica 4/93
Selfridge, Henry Gordon 5/47
Sellers, Peter 9/25, 12/53, 2/64, 10/64, 6/66, 7/80
Selznick, David O. 3/40
Senegal
- De Gaulle lands with Free French troops 9/40
- De Gaulle abandons attack on Dakar 9/40
- Joins French Union as a republic 11/58

Senna, Ayrton 10/90, 11/93, 5/94
Sennett, Mack 11/60
Serbia
- See also Austria, Yugoslavia
- Austria bans arms exports to Serbia 10/08
- Austria sends troops to border 11/08
- Demands return of annexed land in Austria 2/09
- Great power pressure to stop claims 3/09
- Joins Greek-Bulgarian anti-Turk alliance 7/12
- Joins Bulgaria in opposing Turkey 9/12
- Turkey invades; in turn invades Turkey 10/12
- Occupies Durazzo in war with Turkey 11/12
- Troops kill civilian Moslems 1/13
- Bulgaria invades 7/13
- Withdraws from Albania 10/13
- Blamed for Archduke's killing in Bosnia 6/14
- Assassination; no inquiry for Black Hand 6/14
- Vienna's war ultimatum surprise 7/14
- King Peter appeals for Allied help 10/15
- Becomes part of Yugoslavia 11/19
- UN Security Council votes to impose sanctions on Serbia 5/92

Serpell, David 1/83
Sevres, Treaty of
- Turkey loses 80 per cent of Empire 8/20

Sex Pistols 1/77
Seychelles
- See also Britain (Empire and Commonwealth)
- UK releases Makarios from island exile 3/57
- President Mancham ousted by leftists 6/77
- New leader Rene to kick out capitalists 6/77
- Mercenary coup plotters stopped at airport 12/81
- Hijacker-rebels jailed in South Africa 7/82

Seyss-Inquart, Arthur 3/38, 10/46
Shackleton, Ernest 3/03, 6/09, 1/22
Shaffer, Peter 7/58, 12/64, 12/77, 12/79
Shagari, Shehu 1/84
Shah of Persia-Iran
- See Pahlavi

Shamir, Yitzhak 9/83, 10/83, 9/84, 10/86, 11/88, 10/91, 6/92
Shanghai
- (See China)

Shankar, Ravi 8/71
Shankly, Bill 5/65
Shannon, Del 2/90
Sharett, Moshe 11/53
Sharif, Naraz 11/88
Sharif, Omar 4/66
Sharif-Emami, Jaffer 11/78
Sharkey, Jack 6/30, 6/32, 6/33
Sharma, Shankar Dayal 7/92
Sharman, Helen 5/91
Sharon, Ariel 10/82, 2/83, 1/85
Sharp, Phillip 10/93
Sharpe, William 12/90
Sharpeville
- Police kill 56 protesters 3/60

Sharples, Richard 3/73
Shastri, Lal Bahadur 6/64, 1/66
Shaver, Earnie 9/77
Shaw, Fiona 12/91
Shaw, George Bernard 4/04, 11/05, 12/05, 11/06, 12/06, 7/09, 8/09, 4/14, 12/19, 12/25, 11/26, 9/30, 7/31, 12/39, 11/50
Shaw, Percy 9/76
Shaw, Sandie 4/67
Shawcross, Hartley 5/46
Shazar, Zalman 3/69
Shcharansky, Anatoli 7/78, 2/86
Shearer, Moira 12/49
Sheehan, Olive 7/43
Sheffield Forgemasters
- Makers of seized "supergun" 4/90

Shehu, Mehmet 1/82
Shelepin, Alexander 4/75, 10/94
Shelton, Anne 7/94
Shelton, Harold 5/68
Sheng Shih-tsai 12/49
Shenik, Hamed 3/52
Shepard, Alan B. 11/23, 5/61
Shepard, E.H. 10/26
Shepilov, Dmitri 6/56
Sheppard, David 4/60, 2/69, 1/71
Sher, Anthony 12/84
Sherman, J.K. 12/53
Sherriff, Robert Cedric 12/29
Sherwood, Simon 3/89
Shevardnadze, Eduard 7/85, 9/90, 12/90, 7/91, 3/92
Shevchenko, Arkady 4/78
Shi'ite Moslems
- See Iran, Lebanon

Shidehara, Kijuro 10/45
Shinwell, Emmanuel 6/30, 11/35, 2/43, 7/46, 1/47, 4/47, 7/50, 10/51, 6/70, 10/84
Shipping
- See also Royal Navy and Sailing
- German liner speed record 6/00
- Weekly trips London to Paris 6/00
- Hay-Pauncefote Treaty on Panama Canal 2/01
- Daily transatlantic service 4/02
- Single dock authority in London mooted 6/02
- Launch of Cedric, largest ship 8/02
- Cammell and Laird amalgamate 10/03
- First ocean turbine steamer 8/04
- First underwater submarine journey 11/04
- Wireless telegrams to ships 12/04
- Largest turbine liner, Carmania, sails 11/05
- HMS Dreadnought, biggest battleship 2/06
- Largest, fastest liner, Lusitania, sails 6/06
- Launch of the Mauretania and Adriatic 9/06
- HMS Dreadnought's speed record 10/06
- Japan has world's biggest battleship 11/06
- First German U-boat submarine in service 12/06
- Lusitania completes 1,200 miles 8/07
- Lloyd George approves Channel ferry plan 10/07
- British and German liners battle for record 10/07
- Mauretania, world's biggest liner, sails 11/07
- British builders fear Japanese growth 12/07
- Price cutting battle, Cunard and White Line 1/08
- Liner price war ends; fares double 2/08
- Lusitania sets Atlantic record 5/08
- France to spend millions on new ships 6/09
- HMS Colossus, biggest British battleship 4/10
- 50,000 dockers fired in British strikes 9/10
- Launch of Olympic: biggest vessel afloat 10/10
- Launch of Titanic by White Star 5/11
- British dockers strike for better wages 6/11
- Titanic sinks in worst ever sea disaster 4/12
- Aquitania launched, biggest liner 4/13
- World's longest submarine, Cherbourg 5/13
- HMS Elizabeth, first oil-driven battleship 10/13
- White Star liner Britannic 2/14
- Kaiser launches biggest ship: Bismarck 6/14
- German mines threaten commercial traffic 9/14
- American anger at German naval blockade 2/15
- Turkish Suez attack beaten off 2/15
- Germany sinks Lusitania liner; 1,400 die 5/15
- President says US wants maritime freedom 7/15
- Ancona liner torpedoed; 208 die 11/15
- P& O liner Persia sunk by U-boat; 400 die 12/15
- US ships to stay neutral, but carry arms 2/17
- U-boat torpedoes hospital ship; 31 die 3/17
- Henry Ford's anti-submarine boat 7/18
- Dardanelles reopened as Turkey gives in 10/18
- Bismarck, largest liner, burns 10/20
- British fears of Turks at Dardanelles 9/22
- Supreme Court limits alcohol on ships 4/23
- Harwich to Zeebrugge boat train 4/24
- Old Mauretania breaks crossing record 8/24
- First oil-fired electric turbine liner 9/28
- UK and 17 others sign safety convention 6/29
- Record Atlantic crossing, Bremen liner 7/29
- MacDonald wants abolition of battleship 1/30
- Segrave killed during water speed record attempt 6/30
- Kaye Don's speedboat record of 110mph 7/31
- Illinois Waterway opens: Gulf-Lakes link 6/33
- Orient Line: £124 to Australia and back 5/34
- Cunard-White Star launch Queen Mary 9/34
- Queen Mary: biggest and safest ship 9/34
- Maiden voyage of Normandie 5/35
- Queen Mary runs aground, Clydeside 3/36
- Queen Mary's maiden voyage, Southampton 5/36
- Queen Mary: 1,840 passengers to New York 5/36
- UK to control Suez Canal for 20 years 8/36
- British liner holed by mine off Spain 2/37
- UK's first aircraft carrier: Ark Royal 4/37
- Normandie beats Queen Mary for Blue Riband 4/37
- Chinese torpedo Izumo, Japanese flagship 8/37
- Campbell breaks water speed record 9/37
- UK wants Mediterranean "piracy" talks 9/37
- Queen Mary sets cross-Atlantic records 8/38
- Largest liner launched, Queen Elizabeth 9/38
- Germany's first aircraft carrier 12/38
- Launch of German battleship Bismarck 2/39
- UK aircraft carrier Illustrious launched 4/39
- Liner Mauretania begins maiden voyage 6/39
- Queen Elizabeth on maiden voyage to USA 2/40
- Queen Elizabeth ends maiden voyage, USA 3/40
- Launch of USS Missouri, biggest warship 1/44
- The fourth HMS Ark Royal is launched 5/50
- First nuclear-powered submarine Nautilus 6/52
- United States crosses in record time 7/52
- John Cobb dies trying for water speed record 9/52
- Aircraft carrier: HMS Hermes 2/53
- Queen launches her new yacht, Britannia 4/53
- First nuclear-powered submarine launched 1/54
- Donald Campbell's water speed record 7/55
- Campbell sets new water speed record 11/55
- Magnate Sir William Burrell dies 3/58
- Cockerell's hovercraft: floating on air 5/58
- Nautilus, first submarine under North Pole 8/58

- Campbell's new record: 248.62 mph 11/58
- Largest oil tanker, Japan 12/58
- Iceland fires on Arctic Viking trawler 5/59
- Campbell's water speed record, 260 mph 5/59
- SS France: world's biggest liner 5/60
- First hovercraft enters service, UK 7/62
- Launch of UK's newest nuclear submarine 9/66
- Torrey Canyon wrecked off Cornish coast 3/67
- France launches first nuclear submarine 3/67
- Launch of QE2, Clydebank, UK 9/67
- Queen Mary ends last cruise 9/67
- Queen Mary leaves UK for last time 10/67
- Port of London Docks to be closed 1/68
- Maiden voyage of QE2 postponed 12/68
- QE2 sailings cancelled 1/69
- QE2 begins first commercial voyage 4/69
- QE2 arrives in New York 5/69
- P& O to cease passenger service to India 10/69
- Upper Clyde Shipbuilders liquidated, UK 6/71
- Liner Queen Elizabeth destroyed by fire 1/72
- Alleged that six bombs are aboard QE2 5/72
- Clydebank shipyard deal faces axe, UK 8/72
- Agreement ends Clydebank work-in, UK 10/72
- State takes over Harland and Wolff, UK 7/74
- Magnate Aristotle Onassis dies 3/75
- Swan Hunter shipyard loses order 11/77
- Athina B refloated after stranding, UK 2/80
- Titanic sighted under sea 8/80
- London's Royal Docks axed; 900 acres 9/81
- Task Force uses ships for scrapping 4/82
- QE2 requisitioned for Falklands 5/82
- Mary Rose raised from depths, UK 10/82
- Townsend Thoresen buys P& O ferries, UK 1/85
- Zeebrugge ferry capsizes 3/87
- US ships find eight Gulf mines 9/87

Shishekly, Adeeb 11/51
Shockley, William 12/48
Sholokhov, Mikhail 12/65
Shore, Dinah 2/94
Shore, Peter 8/74, 3/75
Short, Nigel 5/77
Shorthouse, John 8/85, 7/86
Shostakovich, Dmitri 9/06, 12/36, 12/42, 12/48, 8/75
Shrimpton, Jean 11/65
Shriver, Sargent 3/61, 8/72
Shultz, George 5/72, 6/82, 6/83, 2/88, 12/88
Shute, Nevil 1/60
Siam
- See also Thailand
- French sign frontier treaty 10/02
- Army coup ends 60-year absolute monarchy 6/32
- Civil servants join economic revolt 6/32
- King Prajadhipok promises to abdicate 10/34
- King abdicates as democracy plan fails 3/35
- Nine-year-old Prince Ananda is new King 3/35

Sibelius, Jean 12/21, 9/57
Sibley, Antoinette 12/70
Sickert, Walter 12/11
Sidi Mohammed Ben Youssef, Sultan 8/53, 8/54
Siedlice
- 100 Jews killed at authorities' instigation 9/06

Sieff, Joseph 12/73
Siegel, Ignaz 7/27
Siemens, Friedrich 4/04
Sienkiewicz, Henryk 11/16
Sierra Leone
- See also Britain (Africa) 0/-0
- Army seizes power in bloodless coup 3/67

Signoret, Simone 12/59
Sihanouk, Norodom 6/53, 3/55, 3/70, 4/75, 9/75, 9/89, 6/93, 9/93
Sikkim
- Annexed by India 4/73

Sikorski, Wladislaw 5/43, 7/43
Sikorsky, Igor 2/14, 10/72
Silcott, Winston 3/87, 11/91
Silesia
- To be divided between Poland and Germany 8/21

Silkin, Lewis 1/46
Silkwood, Karen 5/79, 8/86
Sillanpaa, Frans 12/39
Sillitoe, Alan 3/27, 12/60
Sillitoe, Percy 4/62
Silverman, Sidney 12/42
Silvestre, Fernandez 7/21
Sim, Alastair George Bell 8/76
Simenon, Georges 2/03, 9/89
Simeon, King of Bulgaria 9/46
Simeonov, Vladimir 10/78
Simmons, Jean 3/49, 9/94
Simmons, William 11/15
Simon, John 1/16, 11/27, 9/32, 3/35, 4/35, 6/37, 8/38, 7/39, 2/44, 1/54
Simonstown
- UK gives South Africa naval base 4/57
- UK and South Africa end naval agreement 6/75

Simpson, Ernest 12/36
Simpson, Lorraine 5/89
Simpson, O.J. 6/94
Simpson, Tommy 7/67
Simpson, Wallis
- See Windsor, Duchess of

Sinatra, Frank 12/15, 7/50, 12/56, 12/63, 7/66, 5/75
Sinclair, Archibald 1/42, 3/43
Sinclair, Clive 1/77, 6/83, 1/85, 3/85, 10/85, 4/86
Sinclair, Harry F. 10/23
Sinclair, Margaret 3/71
Sinclair, Upton 11/68
Singapore
- See also World War II
- Australian troops arrive 2/41
- More reinforcements land 4/41
- British troops take control 9/45
- "Jungle Girl" returned to Dutch parents 12/50
- Malay terrorists kill ten Moslems 12/52
- London independence talks fail 5/56
- Britain grants self-government 4/57
- 23 "Communist plotters" arrested 8/57
- Joins Federation of Malaysia 9/63
- Cuts links with Malaysia 8/65
- Commonwealth conference ends in disagreement 1/71
- Royal Navy's Far East Command ends 10/71
- US teenager caned for vandalism 5/94

Singer, Isaac Bashevis 7/04, 12/78
Singer, Paul 2/11
Singh, Devraj 1/48
Singh, Shanbeg 6/84
Singh, Vishwanath Pratap (V.P.) 12/89, 11/90
Singh, Zail 11/84
Sinha, Jag Mohan Lal 6/75
Sinha, Satyendra Prassano 1/19
Sinyavsky, Andrey 2/66
Siqueiros, David 1/74
Sirhan, Sirhan 6/68, 8/68, 2/69, 3/69, 4/69
Sirica, John 1/73, 4/73, 10/73, 8/92
Sisulu, Walter 7/63, 10/89
Sithole, Ndabaningi 3/75, 11/77
Sitwell, Edith 12/23, 6/54, 12/64
Sitwell, Osbert 12/23
Sitwell, Sacheverell 12/23
Skryabin, Alexander 4/15
Sky TV
- Satellite TV network launched 2/89
- Makes stars of Teenage Mutant Hero Turtles 10/90

Slade, Humphrey 1/55
Slater, Jim 3/79
Slessor, John 6/52
Slim, Field Marshal 9/52, 12/70
Slovakia
- See Czechoslovakia
- Czechs and Slovaks split, creating two new nations 1/93

Slovenia
- Independence recognised by EC 1/92

Slovo, Joe 1/95
Smart, William (Billy) 9/66
Smillie, Robert 10/20
Smirke, Charles 6/58
Smit, Adalbert 12/31
Smith, Al 11/28
Smith, Ben 2/46
Smith, Bessie 9/37
Smith, Bobby 5/61
Smith, Cyril 9/77
Smith, Dodie 12/39
Smith, Harvey 8/71
Smith, Helen 8/80, 12/82
Smith, Henry 8/03
Smith, Ian 2/63, 4/64, 6/64, 9/64, 10/64, 11/64, 10/65, 11/65, 12/66, 10/68, 5/70, 11/71, 1/72, 12/74, 9/76, 1/77, 4/77, 7/77, 8/77, 11/77, 2/78, 3/78, 9/78, 1/79, 9/79
Smith, John 5/94
Smith, Joseph 7/15
Smith, Joyce 3/81
Smith, Karyn 7/90, 12/90
Smith, Maggie 12/64, 12/69
Smith, Mel 12/79
Smith, Ross 4/22
Smith, Rupert 1/95
Smith, Stan 7/71, 7/72
Smith, T. Dan 10/73
Smith, Tom 3/35
Smith, Tommy 5/77
Smith, William Kennedy 5/91, 12/91
Smuts, Jan 2/02, 1/08, 11/14, 2/16, 4/18, 8/19, 2/21, 7/21, 6/24, 2/26, 12/28, 1/33, 5/33, 5/41, 10/42, 6/44, 6/45, 12/46, 5/48, 6/48, 6/50, 9/50
Smyth, Ethel 6/09, 5/44
Snagge, John 1/51
Snegur, Mircea 7/92
Sneh, Moshe 11/46
Snell, Peter 9/60, 1/62, 10/64
Snooker
- See Billiards and snooker

Snow, Charles Percy 12/70
Snow, Edgar 2/72
Snow, John 11/77
Snowden, Philip 7/31
Snowdon, Earl of 3/76, 5/78
Soames, Lord 12/79, 2/80, 9/87
Soares, Mario 4/74, 4/75, 4/76, 4/83, 2/86
Sobaska, Malgorzata 4/95
Sobers, Garfield 2/75
Sobhuza II, King of Swaziland 8/82
Soblen, Robert 9/62
Socarras, Carlos 3/52
Social Democratic Party (Britain)
- See Britain (politics)

Soddy, Frances 12/22
Sokolnikov, Gregori 1/37
Sokoto
- Taken by British; sultan flees 3/03

Solanis, Valeria 6/68
Solidarity
- See Poland

Solomon Islands
- See also World War II (Asia, Pacific)
- Independent from UK 7/78

Solomon, Joe 12/60
Solti, Georg 12/68
Solzhenitsyn, Alexander 11/18, 12/62, 12/68, 10/70, 12/70, 4/72, 8/72, 12/73, 2/74, 12/74, 5/94
Somalia
- See also Somaliland, Italian East Africa
- US Marines invade, bringing humanitarian aid 12/92
- UN troops launch raid on warlord's Mogadishu headquarters 6/93
- US troops killed in attempt to capture militia leaders 10/93

Somaliland
- See World War II
- Deputy commissioner killed 11/00
- British beat "Mad Mullah", reports 7/02
- Anglo-British moves against Mad Mullah 9/02
- Mad Mullah advances on British 11/02
- General Manning marches on Mad Mullah 2/03
- Falls to the Italians 8/40
- Achieves independence from Britain 6/60
- Joins Italian lands; new state Somalia 7/60

Somerfield, Stafford 1/69, 2/70
Somerville, James 7/40
Somme
- See also World War I, Western Front

Somoza, Anastasio 2/34, 12/36, 9/56, 2/67, 3/72, 9/74, 9/78, 6/79, 7/79, 9/80
Somoza, Luis 9/56
Son, Kitei 8/36
Sondheim, Stephen 3/30, 12/78
Soper, Donald 9/58
Sophia, Queen of Spain 11/75
Sopwith, Thomas 1/89
Soraya, Princess, Iran 3/58
Sorel, Albert 6/06
Sorzano, Terjado 5/36
Sotelo, Calvo 1/82
Sousa, John Philip 3/32
Soustelle, Jacques 8/55
South Africa
- General White repels Boer, attack Ladysmith 1/00
- Transvaal government talks to British 1/00
- British take Spion Kop under General Warren 1/00
- British government wins vote on war 2/00
- British invade Orange Free State 2/00
- Protests against war in London 2/00
- Lord Roberts takes Bloemfontein 3/00
- Britain rejects US mediation offer 3/00
- Britain rejects Boer peace offer 3/00
- Ten die in engineering explosion 4/00
- Mafeking relieved 6/00
- Roberts says war is over 9/00
- Paul Kruger flees 10/00
- Milner heads new provinces 1/01
- Peace conference fails 2/01
- Over 100,000 blacks and whites in camps 7/01
- Big gold find on Rand 8/01
- Cecil Rhodes dies 3/02
- Boers agree to surrender terms 4/02
- Boer War ends 5/02
- Tax on goldmine profits 6/02
- Basuto chief treason trial 7/02
- Cape martial law ends, gold rush in Transvaal 9/02
- Cape Town-Beira line finished 10/02
- Milner wants qualified black vote 5/03
- Transvaal loan oversubscribed 5/03
- Commission on "native question" 9/03
- Paul Kruger, Boer leader, dies 7/04
- Boers condemn new Transvaal constitution 4/05
- Boers angry at electoral laws 7/05
- British troops kill 60 Zulus in clashes 3/06
- Britain pays war damage compensation 3/06
- Troops called to quell Zulu revolt 4/06
- Troops kill 60 Zulus 5/06
- Zulu rebels surrender to British troops 7/06
- Transvaal gains "autonomy" 12/06
- General Louis Botha appointed premier 2/07
- Transvaal's anti-Asian law: Gandhi acts 3/07
- Orange Free State autonomy 7/07
- King of Zulus surrenders to British 12/07
- General Smuts frees Gandhi from prison 1/08
- De Beers mines close 7/08
- National Convention wants unified state 5/09
- Natal votes for union 6/09
- Union bill reading; blacks excluded 7/09
- Balfour warns of "danger" of black rights 8/09
- Herbert Gladstone becomes Governor-General 11/09
- Union proclaimed; Louis Botha premier 12/09
- South African Party formed 4/10
- General Botha first prime minister 5/10
- Botha wants closer ties with Britain 6/10
- Union becomes a dominion of the Empire 7/10
- Botha loses seat, but remains premier 9/10
- Death of Boer General Piet Cronje 2/11
- British troop presence reduced 11/12
- Premier Botha forms new cabinet 12/12
- Mine strike over after two days' rioting 7/13
- Indians killed protesting at Gandhi's arrest 11/13
- Botha deports leaders of general strike 1/14
- Martial law and army call-up after strike 1/14
- 600 blacks protest against racial discrimination 2/14
- Army takes Luderitzburg from Germany 9/14
- Premier Botha leads army in South West 9/14
- Botha crushes de Wet's pro-German rebels 11/14
- Smuts to command Allies, East Africa 2/16
- Botha dies; Jan Smuts new premier 8/19
- Smuts elected Prime Minister 2/21
- British Army hands over to Union forces 12/21
- Transvaal miners strike 1/22
- White miners riot; martial law declared 3/22
- Smuts loses seat; Nationalists win poll 6/24
- Premier Hertzog wants racial segregation 11/25
- Smuts condemns Colour Bar Bill 2/26
- First return air trip, London to Cape 3/26
- Liberal Senate rejects Colour Bar Bill 3/26
- 15,000 diamond seekers rush to new field 8/26
- Self-governing Commonwealth dominion 11/26
- 25,000 in diamond rush to Grasfontein 3/27
- Nationalists oppose Union Jack in flag 6/27
- Minister wants British not black miners 8/27
- Union Jack compromise in flag, Hertzog 10/27
- Smuts for women's vote in coming elections 12/28
- Bill for "coloureds" vote defeated 2/29
- Hertzog's Nationalists win election 6/29
- White women get the vote 5/30
- Regular air service, London to Cape Town 4/32
- Smuts calls for national cabinet 1/33
- Hertzog-Smuts coalition wins election 5/33
- Discovery of third biggest diamond 1/34
- Native Representation Act 4/36
- Blacks banned from office, "represented" 4/36
- President Carmona of Portugal visits 8/39
- Smuts is field marshal of British Empire 5/41
- Forbidden by UN to annex SW Africa 12/46
- Smuts says race equality does not work 12/46
- Smuts loses seat after 24 years 5/48
- Douglas Malan becomes premier 5/48
- "Cry, the Beloved Country", Alan Paton 12/48
- 105 die in Durban race riots 1/49
- Richest gold find yet 6/49
- Citizenship Bill approved 6/49
- Currency devalued 9/49
- Voortrekker Memorial unveiled 12/49
- Racial violence, Johannesburg townships 2/50
- Protest against racial legislation 5/50
- Smuts resigns as United Party leader 6/50
- Jan Smuts dies - profile 9/50
- Coloureds removed from voting register 5/51
- United Party votes for coloureds on roll 5/51
- Premier Malan overrules Supreme Court 3/52
- Government defies court, keeps poll bill 3/52
- Comet jet liner flies to Johannesburg 5/52
- MPs overule High Court ruling on bill 5/52
- Black and "non-whites" in defiance campaign 6/52
- Pass law defied; 150 arrested 6/52
- African National Congress people jailed 6/52
- High Court calls overruling bill null 8/52
- Police fire on rioters; 17 blacks die 11/52
- Two whites die, East London, Kimberley 11/52
- Ancient coelacanth fish found 12/52
- Premier Malan will retire 10/54
- Johannes Strydom is new Prime Minister 12/54
- African National Congress against evictions 1/55
- 60,000 blacks evicted from Sophiatown 2/55
- Group Areas Act makes Sophiatown "white" 2/55
- "Days of Prayer" protest-strikes 2/55
- Bandung conference condemns apartheid 4/55
- Police break up Congress mass protest 6/55
- Congress honours "fighters" Huddleston 6/55
- Storms out of United Nations Assembly 10/55
- Parliament removes "coloureds" from roll 2/56
- 140 arrested for alleged treason 12/56
- Church encourages race law defiance 4/57
- Cape Town University has black students 4/57
- Britain gives up Simonstown naval base 4/57
- Drops "God Save the Queen" as anthem 5/57
- African National Congress one-day strike 6/57
- Archbishop condemns apartheid 1/58
- National Party wins third election 4/58
- Premier J.G. Strijdom dies 8/58
- Hendrik Verwoerd is premier 9/58
- New hard-line race policy expected 9/58
- Dr Malan, statesman, dies 2/59
- 50,000 blacks in Cato Manor uprising 6/59
- Women lead attack on "slum clearance" 6/59
- White liberal MPs form Progressive Party 8/59
- Uproar at party's anti-apartheid views 1/60
- Macmillan gives "Winds of change" speech 2/60
- Verwoerd retorts: "Justice for whites" 2/60
- Police kill 56 protesters, Sharpeville 3/60
- Seven die, 209 injured, Langa township 3/60
- Pan-African Congress civil disobedience 3/60
- All black political groups banned 3/60
- ANC's Chief Luthuli starts pass-burning 3/60
- 30,000 blacks demand leaders' release 3/60
- Verwoerd shot at agricultural show 4/60
- Durban and Cape Town anti-apartheid riots 4/60
- Cases of police brutality, killings 4/60
- State of emergency extended 4/60
- Commonwealth leaders attack apartheid 5/60
- State of emergency lifted 8/60
- Whites vote for republic 10/60
- ANC leader Luthuli wins Nobel Peace Prize 12/60
- To leave the Commonwealth 2/61
- ANC treason trial dropped 3/61
- UN to censure South Africa for racism 4/61
- Nelson Mandela eludes police round-ups 5/61
- Declared a republic 5/61
- Luthuli receives Peace Nobel 10/61
- Again censured by UN 10/61
- Nationalists win whites-only election 10/61
- Mandela pleads not guilty to treason 10/62
- Nelson Mandela jailed for five years 11/62
- Ex-ANC leader Walter Sisulu arrested 7/63
- Mandela treason trial opens 12/63
- Mandela admits to planning sabotage 4/64
- Mandela sentenced to life for treason 6/64
- Banned from Olympics over apartheid 8/64
- Britain imposes arms embargo 11/64
- UK academic David Kitson jailed 12/64
- Singer Adam Faith cancels concerts 1/65
- Verwoerd's National Party wins election 3/66
- 3,000 Johannesburg students demonstrate 5/66
- PM Hendrik Verwoerd assassinated 9/66
- Vorster becomes PM 9/66
- Bill to abolish inter-racial politics 9/66
- Black leader Albert Luthuli dies 7/67
- First successful human heart transplant 12/67
- Second heart transplant operation 1/68
- 122 die in plane crash 4/68
- Vorster bans MCC tour of South Africa 9/68
- Heart-transplant patient Blaiberg dies 8/69
- 64 die in mine explosion 11/69
- Springboks UK tour: apartheid protests 11/69
- MCC cancels tour of South Africa 5/70
- Banned from 1972 Olympics 5/70
- UK to sell seven helicopters to S. Africa 2/71
- Winnie Mandela jailed for a year 3/71
- To allow international mixed-race sport 4/71
- First heart and lungs transplant 7/71
- Strike by 20,000 black workers 2/73
- 1,500 students expelled from university 6/73
- Racial segregation extended 10/73
- Ends Simonstown naval agreement with UK 6/75
- Thorpe alleges S. African smear plot 5/76
- Soweto blacks revolt over education 6/76
- 100 die in unrest; many children 6/76
- Troops fight Afrikaans language protesters 6/76
- New Zealand rugby ties: Olympic boycott 7/76
- Winnie Mandela arrested, among 20 blacks 8/76
- Unrest spreads to Cape Town; 29 killed 8/76
- Multi-racial international sports teams 9/76
- Forces Rhodesia's Smith to compromise 9/76
- 250,000 blacks in Cape Town strike 9/76
- Transkei is first "independent" homeland 10/76
- 26 die at Christmas; Winnie Mandela free 12/76
- British Foreign Secretary Owen visits 4/77
- Black leader Biko dies in detention 9/77
- 15,000 attend Biko's funeral 9/77
- 1,200 Biko mourners arrested 9/77
- Two papers and 18 organisations banned 10/77
- News editor Woods banned 10/77
- Vorster rejects black majority rule 10/77
- UN bans arms sales 11/77
- Police deny assaulting Biko 11/77

- Police cleared of Biko death by court 12/77
- Account of Biko treatment; medical neglect 12/77
- Dissident editor Woods swims to exile 1/78
- Woods' family in Lesotho; plans Biko book 1/78
- Information department disbanded 6/78
- Blocks Mandela's 60th birthday cards 7/78
- Prime Minister Vorster resigns 9/78
- P.W. Botha, "hawk", new Prime Minister 9/78
- Botha promises better race relations 9/78
- Information minister Mulder resigns 11/78
- Muldergate scandal: £37 million fund 11/78
- Connie Mulder quits parliament 1/79
- Mulder expelled from National Party 4/79
- President Vorster quits over funds scandal 6/79
- Minister Rhoodie disappears in scandal 6/79
- Nigeria seizes BP assets over sanctions 7/79
- Barbarians rugby tour of UK; protests 10/79
- Namibia-Angola clash; 81 killed 5/80
- Police arrest 52 protesting churchmen 5/80
- 42 die in Cape Town coloured unrest 6/80
- Police orders of "shoot to kill" 6/80
- Soweto: clashes at 1976 memorial 6/80
- Gives refuge to Seychelles coup plotters 12/81
- 45 Seychelles hijackers charged 1/82
- Geoff Boycott and 11 others on illegal tour 2/82
- Rebel UK cricketers banned for three years 3/82
- Treurnicht founds rightist Conservatives 3/82
- Seychelles hijackers jailed 7/82
- 216 SWAPO guerrillas killed in clash 8/82
- Raids Lesotho "guerrilla bases", 41 die 12/82
- Car bomb explodes outside air force HQ 5/83
- Winnie Mandela ban extended 6/83
- Spanish supertanker splits in two 8/83
- Death of John Vorster 9/83
- Whites vote for coloured power-sharing 11/83
- Peace pact with Mozambique 2/84
- Peace accord with Mozambique signed 3/84
- Athlete Zola Budd to get UK passport 4/84
- P.W. Botha begins tour of Europe 6/84
- New constitution comes into effect 9/84
- Rioting in five black townships 9/84
- Mob hacks Sharpeville mayor to death 9/84
- Desmond Tutu wins Nobel Peace Prize 10/84
- Eight die when police clash with squatters 2/85
- 17 blacks shot dead at Langa township 3/85
- Mixed-marriages ban to end 4/85
- First mixed marriage 6/85
- State of emergency in 30 districts 7/85
- Hundreds held under emergency laws 7/85
- Botha crushes hopes of reform 8/85
- US Congress votes to impose sanctions 8/85
- 40 die in riots 8/85
- Rev Allan Boesak arrested 8/85
- Tutu has little hope of peaceful change 8/85
- More killed in security force clashes 8/85
- Many "coloured" schools closed 9/85
- 15m blacks to have citizenship restored 9/85
- Severe restrictions on press reporting 11/85
- 13 blacks killed in Mamelodi township 11/85
- Shopping centre bomb kills six near Durban 12/85
- Imposes blockade on Lesotho 1/86
- Pro-South African coup in Lesotho 1/86
- Riots in Alexandra township 2/86
- Press barred from riot area 2/86
- Tutu calls for sanctions on South Africa 4/86
- Right-wing extremists halt Botha meeting 5/86
- 1.5 million blacks strike, Johannesburg 5/86
- Raids on Zambia, Zimbabwe and Botswana 5/86
- 30,000 expelled from Crossroads camp 5/86
- Nationwide state of emergency declared 6/86
- Hundreds of black activists rounded up 6/86
- Tutu protests to Botha about emergency 6/86
- Millions shun work on Soweto anniversary 6/86
- Police shoot 12 in fresh Soweto riots 8/86
- US Senate votes for sanctions 8/86
- Over 8,000 detained under emergency laws 8/86
- Tutu becomes Archbishop of Cape Town 9/86
- US Congress votes for sanctions 9/86
- 177 miners die in fire 9/86
- Press restrictions tightened 9/86
- Big US firms pull out 10/86
- Machel of Mozambique dies in plane crash 11/86
- Barclays Bank to "disinvest" 11/86
- Oil giant Esso to "disinvest" 12/86
- Envoy Worrall quits to fight government 1/87
- Tutu breaks laws by praying 4/87
- National Party keep power in elections 5/87
- Conservatives replace PFP as Opposition 5/87
- Million blacks strike during white poll 5/87
- Desmond Tutu arrested for demonstrating 2/88
- Botha says that Sharpeville Six must die 3/88
- Cease-fire agreed in Angola 8/88
- Nelson Mandela to hospital with TB 8/88
- Anti-apartheid campaigners sentenced 11/88
- Signs treaty for withdrawal from Angola 12/88
- F.W. de Klerk succeeds P.W. Botha as National Party leader 2/89
- Winnie Mandela's former bodyguards charged with murder 2/89
- P.W. Botha resigns from National Party 5/89
- President P.W. Botha visits Nelson Mandela in jail 7/89
- P.W. Botha resigns 8/89
- Biggest anti-apartheid march in 30 years takes place 9/89
- Ruling National Party wins 11th consecutive election 9/89
- Eight jailed nationalists are freed 10/89
- Winnie Mandela announces probable release of husband 1/90
- British rebel cricketers face riots in Bloemfontein 1/90
- De Klerk lifts ban on ANC 2/90
- Nelson Mandela is freed from prison 2/90
- Historic talks between Nelson Mandela and President de Klerk 5/90
- Over 150 die in township battles between Zulus and Xhosas 8/90
- At least 35 die in township clashes 9/90
- Government announces freedom for political prisoners 11/90
- Last of apartheid laws to be abolished 2/91
- Winnie Mandela goes on trial for kidnapping 2/91
- EC votes to end sanctions against South Africa 4/91
- Township battles kill more than 60 5/91
- Winnie Mandela gets six-year jail sentence for complicity 5/91
- Minister admits to funding Zulu Inkatha party 7/91
- Allowed to compete in international sport again 7/91
- White South Africans vote "Yes" to de Klerk's reforms 3/92
- Tribal township massacre near Johannesburg 6/92
- 28 die when soldiers fire on ANC marchers 9/92
- De Klerk calls elections for non-racial government 11/92
- De Klerk claims South Africa destroyed six atomic bombs 3/93
- SACP leader, Chris Hani, is assassinated 4/93
- Whites killed in church in Cape Town 7/93
- UN lifts economic sanctions 10/93
- Parliament votes itself out of existence 12/93
- Violence between ANC and Zulus in Johannesburg 3/94
- UN arms embargo on South Africa lifted 5/94
- President Nelson Mandela sworn in 5/94
- Welcomed back into Commonwealth 7/94
- The Queen on first visit since 1947 3/95

South Arabian Federation
- See also Yemen, Aden
- Grenade thrown at ministers in Aden 12/63
- State of emergency declared 12/63
- Extra UK troops flown into Aden 5/64
- UK soldier killed by grenade, Aden 3/65
- Aden constitution suspended 9/65
- Police use tear-gas to disperse students 10/65
- UK troops open fire on Aden rioters 3/67
- Three Arabs die in clashes with UK troops 4/67
- Nine Arab children killed by Aden landmine 4/67
- 18 Britons shot dead in police mutiny 6/67
- UK troops leave Aden after 128 years 11/67
- Republic of South Yemen formed 11/67

South Korea
- See Korea, South

South West Africa
- See also Namibia
- Herero tribesmen kill Germans in dispute 1/04
- Germans quell Herero revolt 2/04
- Hereros defeated near Waterberg 8/04
- Hottentot chief declares war on Germany 10/04
- Germans beat Hottentots at Warmbad 11/04
- German Socialists and centrists oppose funding of war 11/06
- Premier Botha leads army against Germans 9/14
- Botha takes German South West Africa 5/15
- Angolan refugees cross border 2/76

Southcott, Joanna 7/27

Southern Rhodesia
- See Rhodesia, Rhodesia, Southern

Souttar, Henry 12/25

Souvanna Phouma, Prince, Laos 8/60, 7/62

Soweto
- See South Africa

Spaak, Paul Henri 1/46, 11/49

Space
- See also Science and technology
- Solar eclipse seen in Britain 4/00
- Total eclipse of the sun 5/01
- Halley's Comet approaches earth 5/10
- First liquid fuel rocket: Robert Goddard 3/26
- Astronomer Royal mocks space travel 1/56
- US capable of intercontinental missiles 4/56
- US postpones satellite launch 5/57
- USSR first in space with Sputnik 1 10/57
- Sputnik monitored by BBC, US receivers 10/57
- Next Soviet satellite will carry animal 10/57
- Laika, first dog in space, USSR 11/57
- Sputnik 2 weighs six times heavier than Sputnik 1 11/57
- Tests on Laika the dog for weightlessness 11/57
- US Vanguard Rocket explodes in space bid 12/57
- Sputnik 1 breaks up on re-entry 1/58
- Senator Johnson: US must overtake USSR 1/58
- US calls for space warfare ban 1/58
- US's first satellite Explorer in orbit 2/58
- Jupiter C rocket designed by von Braun 2/58
- US Atlas rocket explodes: fifth failure 2/58
- Dulles says US is losing space race 3/58
- US plans civilian-controlled agency 4/58
- NASA is created, US 7/58
- Satellite shows earth's radiation belts 12/58
- US contract for manned capsule 1/59
- USSR Lunik passes moon; into solar orbit 1/59
- First craft to escape earth's gravity 1/59
- Khrushchev says USSR has the lead 1/59
- NASA picks ten for manned Mercury mission 4/59
- Go-ahead for UK space research 4/59
- US sends monkeys into space, return alive 5/59
- Space monkey Able dies 6/59
- USSR animals return from space 7/59
- USSR Lunik 2, first craft to hit moon 9/59
- Lunik collects data on radiation and matter 9/59
- Lunik 3 orbits the moon; pictures of dark side 10/59
- US monkey spends 55 days in space 12/59
- First meteorological satellite, Tiros 1 1/60
- Jodrell Bank telescope tracks Pioneer 5 3/60
- US satellite Tiros 1 sends back pictures 4/60
- USSR dogs in space retrieved safely 8/60
- First Italian space rocket launched 1/61
- Chimpanzee in space capsule flight 1/61
- "Interplanetary space station" launched 2/61
- USSR launches rocket containing dog 3/61
- USSR puts first man, Gagarin, into space 4/61
- Shepard is first American in space 5/61
- Kennedy says US will put man on moon 5/61
- Virgil Grissom is second US astronaut 7/61
- Gherman Titov is second Russian in orbit 8/61
- US puts Mercury capsule into orbit 9/61
- US rocket Ranger 3 strays off its path 1/62
- Glenn is first American to orbit earth 2/62
- European research body to be set up 2/62
- First Cosmos satellite launched, USSR 3/62
- Ariel, first UK satellite, launched 4/62
- US rocket Ranger IV crashes onto moon 4/62
- US's second orbital spaceflight 5/62
- Two Soviet cosmonauts orbit earth 8/62
- US launches Mariner II probe towards Venus 8/62
- Mariner II reveals solar winds 10/62
- USSR launches first rocket towards Mars 11/62
- Mariner II sends back pictures of Venus 12/62
- Second Telstar satellite launched, US 5/63
- US manned capsule orbits earth 22 times 5/63
- Tereshkova (USSR): first woman in space 6/63
- Launch of Echo C, US-USSR joint project 1/64
- US launches Saturn rocket 1/64
- US spacecraft crashes on moon 2/64
- NASA tests first efficient rocket engine 7/64
- US satellite sends back moon pictures 7/64
- First three-man spacecraft launched in USSR 10/64
- US and USSR probes launched for Mars 11/64
- USSR cosmonaut somersaults in space 3/65
- Ranger 9 launched, US 3/65
- First USSR communications satellite 4/65
- USSR launches Lunar V space station 5/65
- Lunar V fails to land on moon 5/65
- First US walk in space 6/65
- Mariner IV sends back Mars pictures 7/65
- First Indonesian rocket launched 8/65
- Gemini V capsule splashes down 8/65
- France launches its first satellite 11/65
- US astronauts rendezvous in space 12/65
- US astronauts in first space docking 3/66
- Soviet craft Lunar X orbits moon 4/66
- US unmanned space ship lands on moon 6/66
- US spacecraft Orbiter I orbits moon 8/66
- US Gemini 12 mission 11/66
- Fire kills three US astronauts on launchpad 1/67
- Vladimir Komarov killed in Soyuz crash 4/67
- First all-British satellite launched 5/67
- UK withdraws from European space project 4/68
- Three US astronauts orbit moon in Apollo 8 12/68
- Armstrong and Aldrin picked for moonshot 1/69
- US Mariner 6 launched on voyage to Mars 2/69
- First test of US lunar module 3/69
- Pictures of Venus from Venera 5 (USSR) 5/69
- Apollo 10 in moon-landing rehearsal (US) 5/69
- The first man sets foot on the moon 7/69
- Scientists have first look at moon rock 7/69
- USSR launches unmanned craft to moon 7/69
- Apollo 11 launched at Cape Kennedy 7/69
- US Mariner 6 sends back Mars close-ups 7/69
- US makes second moon landing 11/69
- Crippled Apollo 13 lands safely 4/70
- Soyuz 9 lands after 17 days in space 6/70
- US launches missile-detecting satellite 11/70
- US Apollo 14 mission to moon 1/71
- Apollo 14 lands on moon 2/71
- USSR puts manned Soyuz 10 into orbit 4/71
- Mariner 9 launched towards Mars 5/71
- Three Russian cosmonauts die in spaceship 6/71
- Two US astronauts go for drive on moon 7/71
- Apollo 15 splashes down safely 8/71
- Mariner 9 orbits Mars 11/71
- US allots $5.5 billion for space shuttle 1/72
- US Pioneer 10 craft launched to Jupiter 3/72
- Apollo 16 lands on moon 4/72
- Two Apollo 17 astronauts land on the moon 12/72
- US's Skylab orbits the earth 5/73
- Skylab's first crew launched into space 5/73
- Skylab astronauts fix broken panels 6/73
- Second Skylab crew end 59-day mission 9/73
- A third crew docks with Skylab 11/73
- US astronauts end 84-day orbit in Skylab 2/74
- Mariner 10 takes close-ups of Mercury 3/74
- USSR launches two-man craft into orbit 7/74
- USSR launches Soyuz 15 into orbit 8/74
- Cosmonauts travel to Salyut 4 station 5/75
- US Apollo joins USSR Soyuz in space 7/75
- Viking lands on Mars; takes pictures 7/76
- Maiden flight for US space shuttle 2/77
- Wernher von Braun, rocket pioneer, dies 6/77
- First space shuttle flight 8/77
- Voyager 2 launched for Jupiter 8/77
- Remek, first non-USA, non-USSR spaceman 3/78
- Voyager discovers rings around Jupiter 3/79
- Cosmonauts back after record 175 days 8/79
- 186 days in space aboard Salyut 6 10/80
- Voyager 1 finds Saturn's 15th moon 11/80
- First flight, Columbia reusable spacecraft 4/81
- European rocket launches two satellites 6/81
- Columbia space shuttle launched again 11/81
- Space shuttle Columbia's third flight 3/82
- Shuttle returns; launched satellite 11/82
- Sally Ride is first US woman in space 6/83
- US makes first untethered walk in space 2/84
- Maiden flight of space shuttle Discovery 9/84
- US space shuttle explodes, killing seven 1/86
- Report on Challenger disaster published 6/86
- Halley's Comet visible from earth 12/86
- Space probe takes pictures 12/86
- US back in the space race 9/88
- Spacecraft Voyager 2 transmits pictures of Neptune's moon 8/89
- Britain's first astronaut, Helen Sharman, returns to earth 5/91
- NASA's COBE satellite finds evidence of Big Bang 4/92
- Space shuttle Endeavour is launched 9/92
- Shuttle Endeavour astronauts repair Hubble 12/93
- Fragments of comet Shoemaker-Levy 9 crash into Jupiter 7/94
- First Briton to walk in space 2/95
- Cosmonaut back after record stay in space 3/95

Spacek, Sissy 4/81

Spain
- Rioters disrupt Madrid 4/00
- Carlists arrested 11/00
- Anti-Jesuit riots 2/01
- Plans to invade Morocco 12/02
- Student unrest 4/03
- Deaths in Catholic-Republican clashes 10/03
- 400 die when Madrid reservoir collapses 4/05
- Bomb thrown at king on his wedding day 5/06
- 200 die in wreck of the Sirio 8/06
- Martial law, Bilbao; nationwide strike 8/06
- Heavy floods in Malaga 9/07
- Backs Moroccan sultan who disavows jihad 9/08
- 1,000 die in Catalonian revolt 8/09
- Press wants censorship halt; Moors beaten 9/09
- Anarchists storm Paris embassy 10/09
- State of emergency lifted 11/09
- King Alfonso allows women in university 3/10
- King proclaims freedom of belief 6/10
- Striking miners start riot, Bilbao 7/10
- Rioting and general strike, Bilbao 9/10
- General strike, Valencia; martial law 9/11
- Martial law rescinded 10/11
- Severe floods; much death and damage 2/12
- 80 die in cinema fire, Valencia 5/12
- Attempt on King Alfonso XIII 4/13
- Martial law after food riots 3/19
- Communist Party founded 6/20
- Santa Isabel sinks; 160 drown 1/21
- Garrison wiped out by Moroccan rebels 7/21
- Saragosa Archbishop Soldevila murdered 6/23
- Army seizes power with king's approval 9/23
- New ruler de Rivera urged to fight Arabs 9/23
- Fail to agree with rebel Moroccans 4/26
- Attempt on Premier Primo de Rivera 8/26
- Wish for permanent League seat rejected 9/26
- Leaves League of Nations 9/26
- Referendum backs Premier Primo de Rivera 9/26
- 200 feared dead in Madrid theatre 9/28
- 43 die as French submarine hits steamer 10/28
- Universal Exhibition, Barcelona 5/29
- Primo de Rivera resigns 1/30
- Police fight students; Premier Berenguer 1/30
- Amnesty for political prisoners 2/30
- Berenguer government resigns 2/30
- Primo de Rivera: ex-premier, dies 3/30
- Ramon Franco fails in Republican coup 12/30
- Martial law re-imposed; King struggling 2/31
- General Berenguer resigns 2/31
- Police clash with Republicans in Madrid 2/31
- Admiral Aznar forms Royalist cabinet 2/31
- King abdicates; Republic declared 4/31
- Republicans win Cortes majority 4/31
- Berenguer jailed for embezzlement 4/31
- Riots break out 5/31
- Mob lynches Madrid ex-mayor 6/31
- Socialists win election 6/31
- First Republican Cortes, Madrid 7/31
- Catalonia chooses self-government 8/31
- President Zamora resigns; Azana replaces 10/31
- Legalises divorce 10/31
- Zamora elected first constitutional President 12/31
- Jesuits expelled, property confiscated 1/32
- Monarchist coup fails Sanjurjo arrested 8/32
- Abolishes death penalty 9/32
- Recognises Catalonian autonomy 9/32
- Martial law anarchists revolt in south 1/33
- Seville troops guard workers after bombs 1/33
- General strike, with bombings 5/33
- Premier Azana dismissed 6/33
- Right-wing parties make election gains 11/33
- Bid to kill Fascist leader de Rivera 11/33
- More than 100 die in Communist rebellion 12/33
- Saragossa anarchists call strike 4/34
- Government resigns; martial law 4/34
- Peasants strike in south 6/34
- Catalonia independence bid crushed 10/34
- Unions protest at Catholic party ministers 10/34
- National martial law; battle for Madrid 10/34
- Spanish troops in Morocco crush unrest 10/34
- Left-wing rulers free 30,000 prisoners 2/36
- President Azana's intellectual cabinet 2/36
- Communists angry at exclusion 2/36
- Army threatens Azana if violence goes on 3/36
- Parliament dismisses President Zamora 4/36
- Azana succeeds Zamora as president 5/36
- British consul Ernest Golding arrested 1/39
- Franco's troops enter Barcelona 1/39
- Nationalist troops occupy Minorca 2/39
- Manuel Azana abandons presidency claims 2/39
- Franco is recognised by Britain 2/39
- President Azana resigns 2/39

- US recognises Franco 3/39
- Petain named French ambassador to Spain 3/39
- Franco takes Madrid, ending Civil War 3/39
- Spanish Civil War officially ends 4/39
- Leaves League of Nations 5/39
- 53 executed after murder of police chief 8/39
- Finance pact signed with Britain 12/40
- Ex-King Alfonso XIII dies 2/41
- Franco takes full control of government 9/42
- Franco regime condemned by UN 2/46
- UN votes not to cut ties 6/46
- Regency Council created 3/47
- Reopens border with France 2/48
- US vetoes Spain's entry to UN 10/48
- Santayana, philosopher and author, dies 9/52
- Franco says Juan Carlos may be king 1/55
- Franco talks to Dulles over US relations 11/55
- Spanish Morocco granted independence 4/56
- Popular British holidays in Benidorm 6/57
- Coastal hotel economy boom 6/57
- Belgian King weds Dona Fabiola y Aragon 12/60
- 323 die in Barcelona floods 9/62
- Begins creeping blockade of Gibraltar 2/65
- Police beat up 100 priests in Barcelona 5/66
- Franco bans all Gibraltar traffic 10/66
- Gibraltar votes to keep ties with UK 9/67
- Begins siege of Gibraltar 6/69
- Franco names Juan Carlos as heir 7/69
- Offers Gibraltarians Spanish nationality 7/69
- 112 holidaymakers die in air crash 7/70
- 155 die in Canary Islands plane crash 12/72
- Luis Blanco appointed president 6/73
- Cellist Pablo Casals dies, Puerto Rico 10/73
- 500 die in floods 10/73
- PM Carrero Blanco killed by bomb 12/73
- Floats the peseta 1/74
- Franco hands over power to Juan Carlos 7/74
- Franco resumes control 9/74
- Basque terrorists to die by garrotting 8/75
- Kills Basque "guerrillas"; Europe protests 9/75
- Franco has heart attack 10/75
- Juan Carlos provisionally takes over 10/75
- To relinquish Spanish Sahara 11/75
- General Francisco Franco dies 11/75
- Juan Carlos is king; monarchy returns 11/75
- New king declares general amnesty 11/75
- Juan Carlos pardons political prisoners 8/76
- Communist "La Passionaria" returns at 81 5/77
- Democracy returns as Suarez wins poll 6/77
- Democratic Centre coalition will rule 6/77
- Wants to join EEC 7/77
- Juan Carlos visits China 5/78
- 188 die in campsite explosion 7/78
- New liberal constitution approved 10/78
- 12 officers arrested for coup plot 11/78
- Referendum endorses constitution 12/78
- Agrees to re-open Gibraltar border 4/80
- 48 children die in Basque school bombing 10/80
- Failure of right-wing Guardia Civil coup 2/81
- Molina takes cabinet and MPs hostage 2/81
- King's key role in crushing coup 2/81
- Madrid marchers for democracy 2/81
- Picasso's "Guernica" returns 9/81
- Halts siege of Gibraltar, after UK talks 1/82
- Joins NATO 5/82
- Three colonels tried for coup bid 10/82
- Socialists' landslide victory at polls 10/82
- Gonzalez, Europe's youngest premier 10/82
- Border with Gibraltar opens after 13 years 12/82
- 180 die in air crash 11/83
- 93 die in Madrid airport plane collision 12/83
- 83 die in disco fire 12/83
- Ends siege of Gibraltar 2/85
- 150 die in air crash near Bilbao 2/85
- 34 die when two oil tankers explode 5/85
- Referendum backs NATO membership 3/86
- King Juan Carlos visits UK 4/86
- ETA bomb kills three 6/86
- ETA bomb kills 15, Barcelona 6/87
- Socialists win third election victory 10/89
- Madrid hosts Middle East summit 10/91
- Expo 92 opens in Seville 4/92
- Summer Olympics opens in Barcelona 7/92
- Greek oil tanker runs aground off La Coruna 12/92
- Premier Felipe Gonzalez wins general elections 6/93
- Premier denies government was involved in "dirty war" 1/95

Spanish Sahara
- Moroccans claim land; King to lead army 10/75
- Spain to relinquish control 11/75
- King Hassan recalls 350,000 invaders 11/75
- Polisario beat Mauritanian army 8/79

Spanos, Nick 5/90
Spassky, Boris 10/71, 7/72, 9/72
Speaight, Robert 12/35
Speakes, Larry 12/81, 4/86
Speck, Richard 7/66
Spedding, David 3/94
Spee, Count Maximilian von 12/14
Speer, Albert 6/46, 9/81
Speidel, General 11/55
Spence, Basil 5/62, 11/76
Spence, Bill 8/51
Spencer, Earl 2/81
Spencer, Herbert 12/03
Spencer, Lady Diana
- See Diana, Princess of Wales

Spencer, Stanley 9/02, 12/45
Spencer, Winfield 12/36
Spender, Stephen 2/09, 3/55
Sperling, Gertrude 7/38
Sperling, Hilde 7/36
Spielberg, Steven 12/77, 12/82
Spinks, Leon 2/78, 9/78
Spinola, Antonio 4/74, 9/74
Spitz, Mark 8/72, 9/72, 7/76
Spock, Benjamin 1/68, 6/68, 7/68, 1/74
Spooner, William 8/30
Springfield, Dusty 12/65
Springhall, Douglas 7/43
Springsteen, Bruce 12/75, 5/85
Spungen, Nancy 10/78
Spurling, Hilary 12/90
Sputniks
- See Space

Sri Lanka
- See also Ceylon
- Jayawardene beats Bandaranaike at polls 7/77
- 202 die in Icelandic Airways crash 11/78
- 100 killed in race riots 7/83
- Over 100, mostly Tamils, die in ambush 12/84
- Security forces kill over 100 Tamils 6/85
- 20 killed by bomb at Columbo airport 5/86
- 50 killed by three Tamil separatist bombs 6/86
- UK asylum-seekers protest at repatriation 2/87
- Tamil bomb kills 105 in Colombo 4/87
- Air force bombs rebel Tamil bases 4/87
- Guard hits visiting Gandhi with gun 8/87
- Indian troops fight Tamil rebels, Jaffna 10/87
- Eelam Tigers fight Indian "peacekeepers" 10/87
- Ranasinghe Premadasa sworn in as President 1/89
- Ruling United National Party wins elections 2/89
- Tamil rebels massacre 144 Moslems 8/90
- President Ranasinghe Premadasa is killed by a bomb 5/93
- Chandrika Kumaratunga elected President 11/94
- Truce between government and Tamils 1/95

St. John Stevas, Norman 11/78, 1/81, 1/82
Stack, Tommy 4/77
Stael, Nicholas de 1/14
Stafford, Thomas 12/65, 7/75
Stainforth, George 9/31
Stakhanov, Alexis 9/35
Stalin's daughter
- See Alliluyeva, Svetlana

Stalin, Joseph
- Made Communist Party General Secretary 4/22
- His rudeness is criticised by Lenin 1/23
- Front-runner to succeed Lenin 3/23
- Criticised at Party Congress 4/23
- Becomes member of council to succeed Lenin 1/24
- Emerging as USSR's strongman 5/24
- Expels Trotsky from Communist Party 11/27
- First five-year economic plan 10/28
- Purges Trotsky supporters 11/28
- Expels Trotsky from USSR 2/29
- Makes all farms in USSR collectives 1/30
- Plans to wipe out rich farmers 3/30
- Justifies purges 6/30
- Meets George Bernard Shaw 7/31
- Purges Zinoviev, Kamenev and 20 others 10/32
- Threatens UK after it ends trade treaty 10/32
- Wife Nadya dies; suspected suicide 11/32
- "Pravda" attacks Lenin's widow for underating Stalin in book 5/34
- Personally interrogates Kirov assassin 12/34
- Initiates 100 summary executions 12/34
- Opens 50-mile underground railway 4/35
- Has 16 opponents killed for Kirov murder 8/36
- Leads state, party and Comintern 8/36
- Condemns Shostakovich opera "Lady Macbeth" 12/36
- Removes Old Bolsheviks with show trials 1/37
- Exiled Trotsky calls for Stalin's demise 4/37
- Purges army of eight generals, including Tukhachevsky 6/37
- 62 executed in latest purge 10/37
- Wary of British proposals for pact 5/39
- Non-aggression pact with Germany 8/39
- Renounces Finno-Soviet pact 11/39
- Sacks General Meretzkov 12/39
- Humiliated by Russo-Finnish Winter War 3/40
- Orders invasion of Lithuania 6/40
- Assumed to have ordered death of Trotsky 8/40
- Signs neutrality pact with Japan 4/41
- Sets up Committee of Defence 7/41
- Takes over as Soviet defence commissar 7/41
- Signs pact with exiled Polish government 7/41
- "Scorched earth" policy: blows up dam 8/41
- Declares state of siege in Moscow 10/41
- In direct correspondence with Churchill 12/41
- Signs 20-year pact with Britain 5/42
- Summit with Churchill in Moscow 8/42
- Breaks with Polish government-in-exile 4/43
- Says he wants strong, free Poland 5/43
- Dissolves Comintern 5/43
- Announces breaking of Leningrad siege 1/44
- Announces Soviet victory near Kiev 2/44
- Gives Eisenhower highest military award 2/44
- Says no Germans must escape in Crimea 4/44
- Tells Bulgaria to declare war on Germany 5/44
- Tells Rumania to declare war on Germany 5/44
- Tells Hungary to declare war on Germany 5/44
- Talks with Churchill, Moscow 10/44
- Signs alliance treaty with de Gaulle 12/44
- Attends Yalta conference 2/45
- US and UK to be kept out of Eastern Europe 5/45
- Attends Potsdam conference 7/45
- Declares war on Japan 8/45
- Orders drive to create Soviet A-bomb 10/45
- Announces new five-year plan 2/46
- Withdraws troops from Iran 3/46
- Summons Czech premier to Moscow 7/47
- In talks with Western envoys on Berlin 8/48
- Seeks more control over USSR satellites 1/49
- Decrees sweeping price cuts 2/49
- Appoints Gromyko Deputy Foreign Minister 3/49
- Sets up Communist German state 10/49
- Tells Tito to recall ambassador 10/49
- Talks with Chou En-lai 1/50
- Recognises Ho Chi Minh regime 1/50
- Formal alliance with Mao Tse-tung 2/50
- Refuses to intervene in Korean invasion 6/50
- Gives North Koreans arms, but no personnel 6/51
- Has nine doctors arrested for "plotting" 1/53
- Dies of brain haemorrhage, aged 73 3/53
- Denounced by Khrushchev in Congress speech 3/56

Stalin, Nadya Alliluyeva 11/32
Stalker, John 6/86, 8/86, 12/86
Staller, Ilona 7/87
Stallone, Sylvester 12/77
Stanford, Charles Villiers 3/24
Stanislavsky, Konstantin 8/38, 12/47
Stanley, Oliver 2/32, 2/37, 1/40
Stanley, Sir Henry Morton 5/04
Stanley, Wendell 12/46
Stans, Maurice 5/73, 4/74
Stansgate, Viscount
- See Benn, Tony

Stanwyck, Barbara 1/90
Starhemberg, Ernst von 5/36
Stark, Koo 10/82
Starr, Ringo 10/63, 2/65, 10/65, 12/70, 8/71
START (Strategic Arms Reduction Treaty) 8/91
Stauffenberg, Klaus von 7/44
Stavisky, Alexander 1/34
Stecher, Renate 9/72
Steel, Billy 5/47
Steel, David 3/65, 7/65, 7/76, 9/77, 4/78, 6/81, 9/81, 6/83, 6/87, 1/88
Steele, Tommy 12/57, 12/59, 12/67
Steen, Alann 12/91
Steiger, Rod 4/25
Stein, Gertrude 7/46
Steinbeck, John 2/02, 11/37, 12/39, 5/40, 12/62, 12/68
Steiner, Rudolph 3/25
Stephen, John 12/66
Stephen, Stainless 12/44
Stephenson, William 2/89
Steptoe, Patrick 2/69, 7/78
Sternberg, Josef von 4/30, 12/30
Sterry, Charlotte 7/02
Stettinus, Edward 6/45
Stevens, Robert 2/54
Stevenson, Adlai 2/00, 7/52, 8/56, 11/56, 6/59, 7/65
Stevenson, Juliet 12/91
Stevenson, Pamela 12/79
Stevenson, Teofilo 9/72, 7/80
Stewart, Allan 2/95
Stewart, Duncan 12/49
Stewart, Jackie 5/66, 10/68, 9/69, 5/71, 10/71, 9/73
Stewart, James 5/08
Stewart, Michael 1/65, 8/66, 3/68, 6/69
Stewart, Payne 7/85
Stewart-Smith, Geoffrey 6/70
Steyn, Marthinus 3/00
Steyrer, Kurt 6/86
Stich, Michael 7/91
Stillwell, "Vinegar Joe" 1/45
Stimson, Henry 7/29, 1/32, 6/44
Stirling, David 8/74
Stockhausen, Karlheinz 8/28, 12/67
Stockton, Earl of
- See Macmillan, Harold

Stokes, Lord 9/73
Stokes, Richard 8/51
Stokoe, Bob 5/73
Stokowski, Leopold 10/12, 11/34, 9/77
Stolypin, Peter 6/06, 8/06, 9/06, 6/07, 6/08, 3/11, 9/11
Stone, Oliver 12/87
Stonehouse, John 12/74, 3/75, 4/76, 8/76, 8/79, 4/88
Stopes, Marie 7/18, 3/21, 10/58
Stoph, Willi 3/70, 5/70
Stoppard, Tom 4/67, 12/80
Storrs, Ronald 10/16
Strachey, John 5/46, 1/47
Strachey, Lytton 12/21, 12/23, 12/32
Stratton, Eugene 12/12
Straus, Oskar 3/10
Strauss, Richard 11/01, 12/05, 1/09, 1/11, 12/11, 10/12, 10/15, 10/19, 7/33, 12/33, 6/35, 6/48, 9/49
Stravinsky, Igor 6/10, 12/10, 6/11, 12/11, 5/13, 12/13, 9/18, 6/23, 5/27, 12/30, 4/71
Streep, Meryl 6/49, 12/81, 11/82, 12/85
Streicher, Julius 8/35, 5/45, 11/45, 1/46, 10/46
Streisand, Barbra 4/42, 4/69
Stresemann, Gustav 8/23, 9/23, 11/23, 10/25, 4/26, 9/26, 12/26, 10/29
Strickland, Lord 5/30
Stride, John 12/60
Strijdom, Johannes 12/54, 8/58
Strindberg, August 12/01, 5/12
Strite, Charles 7/18
Stroessner, Alfredo 11/12, 2/68, 2/89
Stroheim, Erich von 5/57
Stroop, Juergen 4/43
Stroud, Michael 2/93
Strubig, Heinrich 6/92
Struther, Jan 12/39
Strutt, John 7/19
Stuart, Moira 8/81
Sturges, John 8/92
Sturmer, Boris 11/16
Suarez, Adolfo 6/77
Sudan
- See also Britain (Africa), Egypt
- First Cairo-Khartoum through train 1/00
- Egyptian King Fuad claims Sudan 5/22
- Last Italian troops expelled 2/41
- Britain offers limited self-rule 4/52
- Pro-Egyptian National Unionists win poll 11/53
- Ismail Azhari becomes first resident 1/54
- Britain and Egypt grant independence 12/55
- Independence declared, Khartoum 1/56
- Arab summit lifts oil embargo to West 9/67
- Government overthrown in army coup 5/69
- Coup leader Hadi al Mahdi killed 4/70
- Gasfar al-Numeiry restored to power 7/71
- Three diplomats shot dead by Black September 3/73
- Million refugees enter from five states 6/80
- Famine aid appeal launched by Princess Anne 12/85
- Seven million people threatened by famine 3/91
- Anglican bishop flogged for adultery 9/93

Suez Canal
- See Egypt

Suffragettes
- See Women, Women's Suffrage

Sugar, Alan 4/86
Suharto, Kemusu 2/67
Sukarno, Ahmed 6/01, 6/27, 11/45, 6/46, 9/48, 12/49, 4/55, 11/57, 12/57, 5/62, 1/65, 10/65, 3/66, 8/66, 2/67, 6/70
Sullivan, Arthur 11/00
Sullivan, Ed 9/56
Sullivan, Henry 8/23
Sulzberger, Arthur O. 6/71
Summerskill, Edith Clara 6/69
Sumner, James 12/46
Sumulong, Lorenzo 10/60
Sun Chuang-fang 3/27
Sun Yat-sen 9/07, 10/11, 12/11, 9/17, 5/22, 3/25
Sun, The (newspaper)
- Leaks copy of Queen's Christmas speech, causing a stir 12/92

Sunbathing
- See Fashion and Fads

Sunday Correspondent (newspaper)
- Makes its debut 9/89

Sung Cheh-yuan 6/35
Suramarit, Norodom, King of Cambodia 3/55
Surtees, John 5/66, 9/66, 10/66, 10/68
Suslapatov, Ivan 5/45
Suslov, Mikhail 4/66
Sutcliffe, Herbert William 1/78
Sutcliffe, Peter 1/81, 4/81, 5/81, 3/84, 5/89
Sutcliffe, Sonia 5/89, 10/89
Sutherland, Donald 12/77
Sutherland, Graham 12/45, 11/54, 5/62, 1/78, 2/80
Sutherland, Joan 12/59, 12/90
Sutherland, Tom 11/91
Sutton, May 6/05
Svendsen, Johann 6/11
Swaggart, Jimmy 2/88
Swanson, Gloria 4/83
Swayze, Patrick 12/90
Swaziland
- King Sobhuza II dies after 83 years' rule 8/82

Sweden
- Awards first Nobel Prizes 12/01
- Norwegians break away, reject king 6/05
- Opening of fifth Olympic Games, Stockholm 6/12
- German coup leader arrested, Stockholm 4/20
- Abolishes capital punishment 5/21
- Abandons gold standard 9/31
- Film star Greta Garbo becomes US citizen 2/38
- Pledges all possible aid to Finland 1/40
- Reaffirms neutrality 1/40
- Protests at sinking of neutral ships 2/40
- War trade pact made with UK 4/40
- Neutrality reaffirmed 4/40
- 4,200 British POWs exchanged for Germans 10/43
- Will bar entry to fleeing Nazis 9/44
- Admitted to UN 8/46
- Wins most golds in Winter Olympics 2/48
- Death of King Gustav V 10/50
- First airliner to fly over North Pole 11/52
- First publicised sex change, Christine 12/52
- Dag Hammarskjold new UN Secretary General 3/53
- Approves National Health System 10/54
- Queen Elizabeth II visits 6/56
- Joins EFTA free trade pact 11/59
- Swedes mourn Dag Hammarskjold 9/61
- Hammerskjold to get Peace Nobel 10/61
- Nelly Sachs wins Literature Nobel 12/66
- Traffic switches to driving on right 9/67
- Ragnar Granit wins Medicine Nobel 12/67
- Olof Palme elected PM 10/69
- Hannes Alfven wins Physics Nobel 12/70
- Ulf von Euler wins Medicine Nobel 12/70
- USSR denies visa to Nobel official 4/72
- Paul McCartney fined for importing pot 4/72
- Carl Gustaf becomes King 9/73
- Solzhenitsyn collects his Nobel Prize 12/74
- Baader-Meinhof blow up embassy; three die 4/75
- Palme calls Spanish "bloody murderers" 9/75
- Coalition defeats Palme's Socialists 9/76
- Passes law against aerosol sprays 1/78
- King's successor is to be oldest male or female child 11/79
- Soviet "spying" submarine stranded 10/81
- Submarine crew resist interrogation 10/81
- Releases Soviet submarine 11/81
- Ingrid Bergman, actress, dies 8/82
- Palme's Social Democrats regain power 9/82
- PM Olof Palme assassinated 2/86
- Ingvar Carlson elected PM 3/86
- Christer Pettersson is jailed for the murder of Olof Palme 7/89
- Conviction of Christer Pettersson is overturned on appeal 10/89
- All 129 people aboard an SAS DC-9 survive crash 12/91
- Joins the EU 12/94

Swiatlo, Josef 9/54
Swigert, John 4/70
Swimming
- See also Olympic Games pages
- Australian Kieran breaks mile record 8/05
- First Channel crossing in 36 years 9/11
- Weismuller swims 100 metres in a minute 7/22
- Sullivan swims Channel in 28 hours 8/23
- Tirbocchi swims Channel in 16.5 hours 8/23
- Eberle first woman across Channel: record 8/26
- Weissmuller sets three records 4/27
- Mona Maclennan admits Channel swim hoax 10/27
- Joyce Cooper sets 100 metres record 2/31
- Jenny Kammersgaad is first to swim Baltic 7/38
- Florence Chadwick: new Channel record 8/50
- Florence Chadwick in record Channel swim 10/55
- Fred Baldasare swims Channel underwater 7/62
- Karen Muir sets world backstroke record 8/65
- Mark Spitz, US, dominates Olympics 7/76
- Ashby Harper swims Channel at 65 8/82

Swinburne, Algernon Charles 4/09
Switzerland
- No election reforms 11/00
- Immigrant workers expelled after riots 10/02
- Simplon tunnel opened 4/05
- East European socialists join forces 5/05
- World conference wants child labour ban 9/08
- Red Cross founder Dunant dies 10/10
- International Peace Bureau wins Nobel 12/10
- Socialist pacifists at world conference 4/16
- Bars imported labour 1/21
- Turkey adopts their civil code 1/26
- Second Winter Olympics at St Moritz 2/28
- Wins border dispute with France, The Hague 6/32
- Fraud artist Stavisky in Swiss suicide 1/34
- Fascist Congress in Montreux 12/34
- Nazis barred from government 2/36
- Mobilisation under way 8/39
- General mobilisation ordered 11/39
- Instructions for mobilisation issued 4/40

- Irish author James Joyce dies in Zurich 1/41
- Premiere of Brecht's "Mother Courage" 4/41
- US bombs Schaffhausen in error 4/44
- Hermann Hesse wins Nobel for Literature 12/46
- Stones thrown at Eva Peron during visit 8/47
- Winter Olympics end 2/48
- Shelter for Chaplin 4/53
- Carl Gustav Jung dies 6/61
- Scientist Auguste Piccard dies 3/62
- Death of Hermann Hesse 8/62
- Opening of St Bernard tunnel to Italy 3/64
- Rolling Stones shock Montreux festival 4/64
- Death of architect Le Corbusier 8/65
- Death of sculptor Alberto Giacometti 1/66
- Eiger north face conquered by direct route 3/66
- Matterhorn north face climbed in winter 2/67
- Women win the vote 2/71
- 105 Britons die in Swiss plane crash 4/73
- Robbers steal Chaplin's coffin 3/78
- Longest road tunnel, Goschenen-Airolo 9/80
- Red Cross fails over Ulster hunger strike 7/81
- Gunmen seize Polish embassy; police hit 9/82
- Massive pesticide pollution of Rhine 11/86
- To compensate for Rhine pollution 11/86
- H. Rohrer wins Physics Nobel 12/86
- Swiss vote against banning animal experimentation 2/92
- Voters reject plan to join EC 12/92
- Referendum "NO" to providing UN peacekeepers 6/94
- Mystery fire death of 50 sect members 10/94

Sykes, Mark 3/16
Sykes, Richard 3/79
Synge, John Millington 6/07, 3/09
Syngman Rhee 5/48, 9/48, 7/50, 9/50, 7/65
Syria
- See World War II
- To be run by France after war 3/16
- Turks defeated; Emir Feisal is new king 10/18
- Proclaims independence from Turkey 3/20
- French crush anti-mandate revolt 7/20
- Sets borders with Britain and France 12/20
- French War chief Weygand is commissioner 4/23
- French bombard Damascus rebels; 600 die 5/26
- Granted own constitution by France 5/30
- Allies and Free French launch invasion 6/41
- Vichy French evacuate Damascus 6/41
- British Imperial troops take Damascus 6/41
- Declares war on Germany 2/45
- Cease-fire between French and Syrians 5/45
- Twelve die in synagogue bomb, Damascus 8/49
- Signs security pact with Egypt 6/50
- Crosses zone; occupies two Israeli villages 5/51
- Cease-fire with Israel; lasts three hours 5/51
- Adeeb Shishekly overthrows regime 11/51
- King Feisal II crowned 5/53
- Clashes with Lebanese troops at border 9/57
- Egyptian troops arrive to stop Israel 10/57
- Joins Egypt in United Arab Republic: UAR 2/58
- Seals border with Jordan 8/58
- Nasser attacks Syrian Communists 12/58
- Declares independence of UAR 9/61
- Egypt's pro-consul Amer arrested 10/61
- Army in revolt against Egyptian rule 10/61
- Military junta takes power in army coup 3/62
- Army seizes power in eighth coup since 1945 3/63
- 20 executed after coup attempt 7/63
- Israel triumphant in Six-day War 6/67
- Hafezal Assad seizes power 11/70
- President and premier arrested 11/70
- Breaks off relations with Jordan 8/71
- Joins federation with Libya and Egypt 9/71
- 50 killed in Israeli bombing raid 10/72
- Fights air battle with Israel 9/73
- Fights Israel in Yom Kippur war 10/73
- UN cease-fire ends Yom Kippur war 10/73
- First clashes with Israel on Golan Heights since cease-fire 12/73
- Sixth day of border clashes with Israel on Golan Heights 3/74
- Air battle with Israel 4/74
- Golan Heights truce signed with Israel 5/74
- Resumes diplomatic ties with US 6/74
- Sponsors Lebanon peace accord 1/76
- Encourages Palestinian assault on Beirut 1/76
- Assad sends 40,000 troops to Beirut 5/76
- Vows to help Palestinians against Israel 3/78
- Clashes with Christians, Lebanon; 22 die 7/78
- Israel plans to annex Golan Heights 12/81
- Air battles with Israel; shoots down 19 6/82
- PLO leader Arafat expelled 6/83
- Frees US airman shot down over Lebanon 1/84
- Not to withdraw troops from Lebanon 1/84
- UK expels three Syrian diplomats 5/86
- Three British diplomats expelled 5/86
- Nezar Hindawi jailed for bomb plot, UK 10/86
- Britain breaks off relations 10/86
- Breaks Amal siege of Chatila camp 4/87
- Resumes diplomatic links with Britain 11/90

Syrovy, Jan 9/38
Szisz, Ferenc 6/06
Szuros, Matyas 10/89

T

Taaffe, Pat 3/66
Taff Vale
- See Britain (labour)

Taft, Robert 11/40
Taft, William Howard 9/06, 6/08, 11/08, 11/09, 6/12, 11/12, 6/21, 10/21, 2/30, 3/30
Tagore, Rabindranath 8/41
Tahiti
- 10,000 feared dead in typhoon 2/06
- Joins Free France 8/40

Taimur, Said bin 7/70
Taiwan
- Reopens relations with Japan 8/52
- Eisenhower withdraws Seventh Fleet 1/53
- Chiang Kai-shek repudiates USSR pact 2/53
- China may join Games; Taiwan withdraws 5/54
- Nationalists sink eight Red gunboats 8/54
- Communists bomb Quemoy Island 9/54
- Nationalists bomb Tateng Island 9/54
- Expelled from UN 10/71
- UK cuts ties 1/72
- President Chiang Kai-shek dies 4/75

Tajikistan
- Earthquake hits Soviet Central Asia, killing over 1,000 1/89

Talal, King of Jordan 8/52
Tambo, Oliver 4/93
Tanaka, Kakuei 7/76
Tandy, Jessica 9/94
Tanganyika
- (See also Tanzania, Zanzibar)
- 900 mile railway inaugurated 2/14
- UK's plan to settle Jewish refugees 11/38
- Julius Nyerere, first premier 9/60
- Leakey makes new find of fossil bones 2/61
- Independence 12/61
- Nyerere resigns as President 1/62
- Act of union with Zanzibar announced 4/64

Tannenberg
- Hindenburg beats Russians; 300,000 men participate 8/14

Tanner, Beatrice
- See Campbell, Mrs Patrick

Tanner, Roscoe 7/79
Tanzania
- See also Tanganyika, Zanzibar
- Signs peace pact with Uganda 10/72
- Amin to annex part of Tanzania 11/78
- Mother Teresa unhurt in plane crash 10/86

Tardieu, Andre 2/30, 6/32
Tardieu, Jean 11/03
Targuist
- 290,000-Franco-Spanish force beats Krim 5/26

Tariff League
- Launched 5/03
- Chamberlain resigns to back Empire trade 9/03

Tarnower, Herman 3/80, 3/81
Tassigny, Jean de Lattre de 1/51
Tatchell, Peter 2/83
Tate, Harry 12/12
Tate, Sharon 1/68, 8/69, 12/69, 8/70, 1/71, 3/71
Tati, Jacques 10/07, 12/53, 12/58, 12/59, 11/82, 12/82
Tatum, Art 10/10, 11/56
Tauber, Richard 3/38
Taverne, Dick 3/62
Tawney, Richard Henry 1/62
Taylor, Alan John Percival 9/90
Taylor, Dennis 4/85
Taylor, Elizabeth 2/32, 2/52, 12/63, 3/64, 7/66, 4/67, 12/67, 7/73, 10/75, 12/78, 8/84, 12/87, 10/91
Taylor, Graham 11/93
Taylor, John 11/69
Taylor, Matthew 3/87
Taylor, Maxwell 9/63
Taylor, Richard 12/90
Taylor, Robert 10/47
Taylor, Roger 7/73
Taylor, Tommy 2/58
Teagarden, Jack 12/27
Tebbit, Margaret 10/84
Tebbit, Norman 1/79, 10/81, 1/82, 2/82, 7/83, 10/83, 2/84, 10/84, 9/85, 11/87, 12/89, 6/92
Tedder, Air Marshal (Arthur) 12/43, 6/67
Teddy Boys
- See Fashion and Fads

Teenage Mutant Hero Turtles 10/90
Tehran (Teheran)
- 900 a day die of cholera 7/04
- Churchill, Roosevelt and Stalin meet 11/43

Tekere, Edgar 8/80, 12/80
Teleki, Paul 4/41
Television
- See also BBC, Broadcasting, Firsts
- Baird shows moving pictures by wireless 1/26
- Anti-flutter device 2/28
- BBC rejects idea of trial service 10/28
- First full colour pictures, from Bell 6/29
- Bomb at Reichstag, no injuries 9/29
- First baseball broadcast 2/31
- Better definition 12/31
- All-electronic system by RCA 12/32
- Government study of public service 4/34
- BBC plans first service 2/35
- First high-definition service, Germany 3/35
- Leslie Mitchell first BBC announcer 6/36
- First talking pictures: BBC at Olympia 8/36
- Leslie Mitchell's television debut 8/36
- New sets on display; commercial rivalry 8/36
- Regular BBC broadcasts, Alexandra Palace 10/36
- Cheapest receiver costs 60 guineas 2/37
- GEC television set for under £50 8/37
- BBC's first opera, "Tristan and Isolde" 1/38
- Baird demonstrates large-screen set 1/38
- First film on television 9/38
- TV pioneer John Logie Baird dies, UK 6/46
- Colour TV system announced by RCA 8/49
- Taking over from cinema 11/49
- 100 sporting events a year to be on TV 5/50
- BBC makes cross-Channel broadcast 8/50
- Post-war UK spread from London base 10/51
- 35 million viewers watch Nevada A-bomb 4/52
- Accused Nixon's "Checkers" speech 9/52
- Queen says Coronation can appear 12/52
- Millions watch Coronation on television 6/53
- Olympia Radio Show: 27-inch set seen 9/53
- Commercial service planned 10/53
- White paper outlines TV on adverts 11/53
- Lords approve commercial TV channel 11/53
- Pope warns against television 1/54
- MPs support commercial channel 3/54
- "The Groves" serial rehearsed 4/54
- Britain linked up with seven states 6/54
- Television Bill gets royal assent 7/54
- Independent Television Authority set up 8/54
- Dimbleby turns down ITV offer 11/54
- Recorded maximum snooker break 1/55
- Eamonn Andrews appears on "This is Your Life", TV 8/55
- First ITV transmissions; advertisements 9/55
- "Double Your Money", with Hughie Green 9/55
- BBC colour television, Alexandra Palace 10/55
- First provincial ITV broadcasts 2/56
- Elementary video camera 4/56
- Elvis Presley on Ed Sullivan Show, US 9/56
- Evening broadcasts approved 12/56
- TV detector to beat licence-dodgers 1/57
- EEC signing seen by millions 3/57
- ITV's new comedy series, "The Army Game" 6/57
- Six million watch BBC and ITV each night 8/57
- "Reconstruction" starts Nottingham riot 9/58
- First televised opening of parliament 10/58
- 24.5 million UK households have sets 1/59
- Twice as many watch ITV as BBC TV 1/59
- Eisenhower and Macmillan chat on issues 8/59
- Causes falling cinema audiences 9/59
- BBC buys 20 US feature films 9/59
- Pope warns against watching 1/60
- Half UK population watch peak television 1/60
- BBC wants second channel 1/60
- Colour TV plans shelved, UK 6/60
- First US televised presidential debate 9/60
- BBC2 proposed 6/62
- First edition of "Police Five", UK 6/62
- BBC's "That Was the Week That Was" 11/62
- "That Was the Week That Was" causes row 12/62
- BBC to scrap "What's My Line?" 7/63
- "That Was the Week That Was" taken off 12/63
- "Steptoe and Son" is top show 1/64
- BBC2 goes on the air 4/64
- Takeaway TVs go on sale 8/64
- "Ready, Steady, Go!" goes on air 10/64
- Cigarette ads to be banned 2/65
- David Attenborough heads BBC2 3/65
- ITV's "Coronation Street" 7/65
- Most popular programme: "Coronation Street" 7/65
- Popularity of "Ready, Steady, Go" 9/65
- National Viewers' and Listeners' Assn 11/65
- Broadcaster Richard Dimbleby dies 12/65
- BBC bans showing of "The War Game" 2/66
- BBC announces plan for colour TV 3/66
- State Opening of Parliament televised 4/66
- First episode of "Till Death Us Do Part" 6/66
- Warren Mitchell named best TV actor 11/66
- Controversial play "Cathy Come Home" 1/67
- Popularity of BBC's "The Ken Dodd Show" 1/67
- David Frost interviews Emil Savundra 2/67
- BBC2 begins regular colour broadcasting 7/67
- ITV launches "News at Ten" 7/67
- Herbert Bowden appointed ITA chairman 8/67
- Popularity of "The Forsyte Saga" 12/68
- Marty Feldman is top TV personality 2/69
- BBC2 series "Civilisation" 2/69
- Kenneth Clark's "Civilisation" ends 5/69
- ITV makes first colour transmissions 9/69
- "Monty Python's Flying Circus", BBC 10/69
- 1,000th episode of "Coronation Street" 8/70
- "Monty Python's Flying Circus" - a cult 12/70
- Rupert Murdoch takes control of LWT 2/71
- LWT appoints new chief executive 3/71
- "Opportunity Knocks" most popular show 6/71
- First episode of "Colditz" 10/72
- 10.30 pm curfew on TV programmes 2/74
- 500th episode of BBC's "Z Cars" 5/74
- First transmissions of Ceefax Teletext 9/74
- "Kojak", with Telly Savalas 12/74
- "The Ascent of Man", Bronowski 12/74
- "Morecambe and Wise" 12/74
- Colour licence up to £18 1/75
- ITV blacked out by strike 5/75
- Popular TV series, "Upstairs, Downstairs", ends 12/75
- "Fawlty Towers", John Cleese comedy 12/75
- Ford and Carter in television debate 9/76
- "I, Claudius" adapted for TV 12/76
- Hurt wins prize for role in "The Naked Civil Servant" 12/76
- Last "Dixon of Dock Green", with Warner 12/76
- John Cleese is Basil in "Fawlty Towers" 12/76
- Punk rock group Sex Pistols disrupts TV show 12/76
- Sinclair's two inch screen TV set 1/77
- Licences up to £21 and £9 7/77
- Anna Ford, ITN's first woman newscaster 2/78
- ITV's "Upstairs, Downstairs": US award 4/78
- "Edward and Mrs Simpson" 12/78
- Bosanquet resigns from ITN 11/79
- Comedy, "Not the Nine O'Clock News" 12/79
- "Fawlty Towers"; "Rumpole of the Bailey" 12/79
- "Tinker Tailor Soldier Spy" thriller 12/79
- "Death of a Princess" sparks Saudi row 4/80
- ITN captures Iranian embassy siege live 5/80
- Isaacs to head fourth channel 9/80
- 80 million watch Reagan and Carter debate 10/80
- Dallas addicts ask "Who shot JR?" 11/80
- Southern and Westward TV lose franchises 12/80
- 700 million watch Charles marry Diana 7/81
- "Brideshead Revisited" adapted by Mortimer 12/81
- "Smiley's People", with Alec Guinness 12/81
- Licence up to £46 for colour, £15 black and white 12/81
- Three new ITV stations 1/82
- Go-ahead for satellite television 3/82
- Channel Four goes on the air 11/82
- Channel Four language angers Whitelaw 12/82
- BBC begins early morning television 1/83
- TV-am begins broadcasting 2/83
- Peter Jay resigns as TV-am chairman 3/83
- Rippon and Ford sacked from TV-am 4/83
- Christopher Hughes wins Mastermind quiz 5/83
- Lords votes for experimental televising 12/83
- "Film on Four", C4 12/83
- Alternative comedy in "Five Go Mad in Dorset" on C4 12/83
- Troubles of TV-am 12/83
- Gerald Ford in acting debut: "Dynasty" 12/83
- Buerk's report on Ethiopian famine 11/84
- "The Jewel in the Crown" 12/84
- BBC drops "Real Lives" documentary 7/85
- Journalists strike over "Real Lives" ban 8/85
- Whitehouse attacks "obscene" East Enders 4/87
- Michael Grade to head Channel Four 11/87
- US television evangelist confesses 2/88
- Controversial BBC Falklands film 5/88
- Three new channels announced in Britain 11/88
- £25 million Sky TV satellite network is launched 2/89
- House of Commons proceedings televised for first time 11/89
- Western hostages shown on Iraqi TV 8/90
- TV companies accused of being "used" by Iraqi propagandists 2/91
- Bush publicly announces on TV the end of the Gulf War 2/91
- Viewers watch in horror as planning officer is shot dead 6/91
- Four ITV companies to lose their licences 10/91
- Mikhail Gorbachev announces his resignation 12/91
- Trial of William Kennedy Smith televised live 12/91
- Joanne Whalley-Kilmer to play Scarlett O'Hara 11/93

Telissu
- Russians beaten at Telissu, lose 2,000 6/04

Tell, Wasfi 9/72
Teller, Edward 6/54
Templar, Gerald 4/55
Temple Black, Shirley
- See Temple, Shirley

Temple, Shirley 4/28, 7/32, 12/32, 12/35, 11/42, 9/45, 8/67
Temple, William (Archbishop) 10/44
Tenerife
- 146 die as Boeing 727 crashes 4/80

Teng Hsiao-ping
- See Deng Xiaoping

Tennessee
- Alcohol manufacture prohibited 1/09

Tenniel, John 6/01, 2/14
Tennis
- See also Wimbledon
- Davis Cup tournament created 2/00
- America wins Davis Cup doubles 8/00
- Champion Doherty brother to retire 6/06
- France wins Davis Cup for the first time 9/27
- France's "Four Musketeers" win Davis Cup 7/32
- British team wins Davis Cup 7/33
- Fred Perry wins US Open, first Briton since 1903 9/33
- Fred Perry keeps US championship 9/34
- Perry beats von Cramm in French match 6/35
- US offer for Perry to turn professional 7/36
- Britain wins Davis Cup fourth year in a row 7/36
- Perry first foreigner to win US tournament 9/36
- "Little Mo" Connolly to retire and marry 2/55
- Christine Truman, 17, wins Wightman Cup 6/58
- Rod Laver wins US title and Grand Slam 9/62
- Steel racquet goes on the market 2/63
- Smith is first Australian to win women's title at Wimbledon 7/63
- Australia wins Davis Cup for third year 12/66
- Amateur-professional distinction is out 12/67
- Virginia Wade (UK) is US open champion 9/68
- Rod Laver wins US Open and grand slam 9/69
- Margaret Court (Aus) wins grand slam 9/70
- Goolagong wins Wimbledon ladies' title 7/71
- US win Davis Cup 10/71
- Czech star Navratilova defects to USA 9/75
- Borg wins his fifth Wimbledon against McEnroe 7/80
- Billie Jean King admits lesbian affair 5/81
- McEnroe ends Borg's Wimbledon run 7/81
- Bjorn Borg retires from tennis 1/83
- Navratilova wins US Open championship 9/83
- Navratilova plays in Czechoslovakia 7/86
- Steffi Graf wins French Open 6/88
- Steffi Graf wins "Grand Slam" 9/88
- Steffi Graf beats Martina Navratilova at Wimbledon 7/89
- Boris Becker beats Stefan Edberg in the Men's final 7/89
- Stefan Edberg beats Boris Becker at Wimbledon 7/90
- Martina Navratilova wins record ninth Ladie's Singles title 7/90
- Bjorn Borg is beaten in his first comeback match 4/91
- Michael Stich wins Men's Singles at Wimbledon 7/91
- Steffi Graf wins Ladie's Singles at Wimbledon 7/91
- Agassi wins Men's finals; Graf wins Women's title 7/92
- Monica Seles is stabbed during a match 4/93
- Sampras and Graf are Wimbledon Singles champions 7/93
- Wimbledon Champions are Pete Sampras and Conchita Martinez 7/94
- Sweden win 5th Davis Cup 12/94
- Fred Perry dies 2/95

Tensing, Norgay 6/53, 5/86
Teresa, Mother 12/79, 11/83, 2/86, 10/86
Tereshkova, Valentina 6/63
Terfel, Bryn 12/91
Terre Blanche, Eugene 5/86
Terry, Ellen 12/28
Terry, Peter 9/90
Tetrazzini, Luisa 4/40
Tetuan 11/02
Teyte, Maggie 5/76
Thailand
- See also Siam
- Japanese troops advance into Thailand 7/41
- King Ananda Mahidol shot dead 6/46
- Bhumibol Adulyadej is new leader 6/46
- US vetoes entry to UN 8/46
- Returns annexed areas of Cambodia and Laos 11/46
- Cambodian King Sihanouk flees to Thailand 6/53
- Offers bases for fight against communism 5/54
- US to send forces in face of Laos threat 5/62
- Troops shoot 400 students 10/73
- Government resigns 10/73
- Army seizes power after clashes 10/76

- Two British girls arrested for drugs smuggling 7/90
- British girl sentenced to 25 years for drug trafficking 12/90

Thalidomide 4/79
Thalmann, Ernst 9/25
Thang, Ton Duc 9/69
Thant, Sithu U 1/09, 4/67, 11/74
Thatcher, Denis 10/84
Thatcher, Margaret
- Born 10/25
- President of Oxford University Tories 7/46
- Youngest candidate 10/51
- Elected for Conservatives 10/59
- First government job as PPS 10/61
- Appointed shadow transport minister 11/68
- Appointed shadow education spokesman 10/69
- Plans to ban free school milk 6/71
- Enters Tory leadership contest 1/75
- Elected Conservative Party leader 2/75
- Described as "Iron Lady" by USSR 1/76
- Denounces Lib-Lab pact 3/77
- On Britons' immigration fears 1/78
- Criticised by Heath for immigration remarks 2/78
- Criticises Labour pact with unions 2/79
- Demands dissolution of Parliament 3/79
- Becomes Prime Minister 5/79
- Moves to normalise Rhodesian relations 7/79
- Does U-turn on Rhodesia deal 8/79
- Praises Chinese Chairman Hua Kuo-feng 10/79
- Demands large EEC rebate 11/79
- Names Blunt as "fourth man" 11/79
- To halve state benefit to strikers 2/80
- Appeals for Olympic boycott 3/80
- Blames wage inflation for unemployment 8/80
- Says she is "not for turning" on economy 10/80
- Hears that IRA hunger strike has ended 12/80
- Sacks Norman St. John Stevas 1/81
- Steps up privatisation drive 2/81
- Does U-turn on miners' pay 2/81
- Condemns Brixton riots 4/81
- Denies political status to IRA prisoners 5/81
- Attends economic summit in Ottawa 7/81
- Sacks three "wets" 9/81
- Agrees to increase links with Ireland 11/81
- Faces strong criticism on economy 1/82
- On Argentinian invasion of Falklands 4/82
- British victory in Falklands War 6/82
- Condemns IRA pub bombing in Ulster 12/82
- Franks report on Falklands War issued 1/83
- Visits the Falklands 1/83
- Leads Tories to another election win 6/83
- Scraps Central Policy Review Staff 6/83
- Angered by US invasion of Grenada 10/83
- To abolish GLC and Metropolitan counties 10/83
- Sends goodwill message to Raul Alfonsin 12/83
- Heads action against world terrorism 6/84
- Escapes injury in Brighton hotel bomb explosion 10/84
- Refuses to drop Band Aid VAT bill 12/84
- Meets Gorbachev on his visit to UK 12/84
- Refused honorary degree by Oxford University 1/85
- Tells US Congress she supports Star Wars 2/85
- Appeals for US to end aid to IRA 2/85
- Claims victory over striking miners 3/85
- Condemns Heysel Stadium riot 5/85
- Leads EC war against terrorism 6/85
- Opposes sanctions against South Africa 10/85
- Signs Anglo-Irish agreement 11/85
- Gives go-ahead to Channel Tunnel 1/86
- The Westland affair 1/86
- Signs Channel Tunnel treaty with France 2/86
- Opposes once again sanctions on South Africa 7/86
- Agrees to voluntary S. Africa sanctions 8/86
- Opens Nissan car plant in Sunderland 9/86
- Warmly received in Moscow 3/87
- Calls general election 5/87
- Elected for third term as PM 6/87
- Refuses to send minesweepers to Gulf 7/87
- Claims highest amount ever being spent on NHS 11/87
- Ends African tour amidst Moslem protests 1/88
- Announces radical review of NHS 1/88
- Reject plans for European central bank 6/88
- Attacks centralised European government 9/88
- Visits Poland's Gdansk shipyard 11/88
- Views on Irish non-extradition of Patrick Ryan 12/88
- Claims a turning-point reached in Anglo-Soviet relations 5/89
- Celebrates ten years as Prime Minister 5/89
- Reffirms Britain wants closer economic union in Europe 6/89
- Row over cabinet reshuffle 7/89
- Remark upsets bicentenary celebrations of French Revolution 7/89
- Alone in opposing sanctions against South Africa 10/89
- Nigel Lawson resigns after row with Prime Minister 10/89
- Faces first leadership challenge within Tory Party 11/89
- Heralds news of demolition of the Berlin Wall 11/89
- Beats Meyer in Tory leadership poll 12/89
- Denies claim that Britain was isolated at EC summit 12/89
- Appeals to Saddam Hussein to spare British journalist's life 3/90
- Claims community charge is beginning to work 5/90
- Isolated at EC summit over opposition to greater unity 6/90
- Inflation higher than before Mrs Thatcher came to power 10/90
- Vows to veto single European currency 10/90
- Accused of having "nightmare vision" of Europe 11/90
- Decides to resign 11/90
- Leaves Downing Street 11/90
- Quoted as saying "It's a funny old world" 12/90
- Calls for action on Kurdish refugee problem in Iraq 4/91
- To retire as MP at next general election 6/91
- Sells memoirs for £2.5 million 10/91
- Apologises to axed ITV boss 10/91
- Attacks successor's government over referendum refusal 11/91
- Visits the Falklands to mark 10th anniversary of war 6/92
- Introduced to the House of Lords as Baroness Thatcher 6/92
- Appointed Lady Companion of the Order of the Garter 4/95

Thatcher, Mark 1/82
Theatre
- See December Surveys

Thieu, Nguyen Van 6/65, 9/67, 1/68, 10/71
Tho, Nguyen Huu 1/67
Thoma, Ritter von 11/42
Thomas, Alva Edison 10/31
Thomas, Caitlin 7/94
Thomas, Clarence 10/91
Thomas, David 7/58
Thomas, Donnall 12/90
Thomas, Dylan 10/14, 11/53, 12/54
Thomas, Edward 12/18
Thomas, George 10/66, 2/76, 6/83
Thomas, James H. 10/30, 5/36, 6/36, 1/49
Thompson, Basil 11/21
Thompson, Daley 7/58, 8/78, 7/80, 9/82, 8/83, 8/84, 9/87, 9/88
Thompson, Davina 12/86
Thompson, Don 9/60
Thompson, Edith 12/22
Thompson, Emma 12/89, 3/93
Thompson, Ian 9/74
Thompson, William 12/07
Thomson, George 9/65, 4/72
Thomson, Lord 2/62, 9/66, 10/80
Thomson, Peter 7/51, 7/54, 7/58
Thomson, Roy Herbert 8/76
Thorburn, Cliff 5/83
Thorez, Maurice 7/64
Thorn, Gaston 6/74
Thornburgh, Richard 3/79
Thorndike (Agnes), Sybil 5/30, 8/70, 6/76
Thorneycroft, Peter 1/57, 1/58, 6/94
Thorns, Sheila Ann 10/68
Thorpe, Caroline 6/70
Thorpe, Jeremy 10/59, 7/62, 1/67, 6/69, 3/72, 3/73, 3/74, 8/74, 3/76, 5/76, 10/77, 6/78, 8/78, 11/78, 12/78, 5/79, 6/79
Thorpe, Jim 7/12, 3/53
Three Mile Island 3/79
Thun, Prince of Bohemia 6/12
Thunberg, Clas 1/24
Thurber, James 11/61
Thuy, Xuan 5/68
Thwaite, Ann 12/90
Tibbets, Paul 8/45
Tibet
- See also China
- 300 Tibetans killed in attack on British 3/04
- British fight off Tibetans, Karo Pass 5/04
- British take Lhasa; Dalai Lama flees 8/04
- Anglo-Tibetan treaty gives UK trading posts 9/04
- Chinese take Lhasa; Dalai Lama flees 2/10
- Soldiers raid China, kill 300 troops 1/13
- Five-year-old Dalai Lama enthroned 2/40
- Mao offers regional autonomy 5/50
- Mao's troops march into Lhasa 10/50
- Chinese troops invade 10/50
- Dalai Lama flees 12/50
- Surrenders control of army to China 5/51
- Granted religious freedom; mining question 5/51
- Chinese occupy Lhasa 9/51
- 65,000 die in revolt against Chinese 7/58
- Rebels beat Chinese on highway to Lhasa 7/58
- Exiles in India lead revolt in east 7/58
- Dalai Lama flees as China crushes revolt 3/59
- Panchen Lama congratulates Peking 3/59
- India gives Dalai Lama sanctuary 4/59
- Six die in anti-Chinese riots 10/87
- Chinese army moves into Lhasa 3/88
- 16 die in riots marking 30th anniversary of uprising 3/89
- Violence breaks out during protests against Chinese rule 5/93

Tidal Cruises
- Party boat collides with dredger on Thames; 60 feared dead 9/89

Tidswell, Herbert 8/07
Tientsin 7/00
Tigre
- See also Abyssinia, Ethiopia
- Italians seize capital of Makale 11/35

Tigris
- British beat 60,000 Turks 1/16

Tilden, William (Bill) 7/20, 7/21, 7/30
Tildy, Zoltan 7/48
Tilley, Vesta 12/12
Timor
- Portuguese-Dutch treaty over island 10/04
- Indonesians seize capital Dili 12/75

Timoshenko, Semyon 3/40, 10/41, 12/41, 5/42
Tinbergen, Nikolaas 12/73
Tinling, Teddy 6/49
Tippett, Michael 1/55, 2/58, 12/90
Tirana
- Captured by Serbian troops 6/15

Tirbocchi, Enrique 8/23
Tirpitz, Alfred von 2/00, 6/00, 3/09, 3/14, 3/16, 3/30
Tisdall, Sarah 1/84, 3/84
Tiselius, Arne 12/48
Tiso, Joseph 3/39
Tisza, Istvan 8/13
Titanic
- Launch: biggest ship afloat 5/11
- Sinks on maiden voyage; 1,500 killed 4/12
- "Not enough lifeboats caused deaths" 4/12
- Inquiry opens; key questions missed 5/12
- US inquiry: verdict of negligence 5/12
- British inquiry finds captain guilty 7/12
- Last survivor, Marjorie Robb, aged 103, dies 6/92

Titmus, Fred 2/68
Tito, Josip Broz 10/41, 5/42, 11/42, 10/43, 12/43, 5/44, 6/44, 10/44, 3/45, 8/45, 11/45, 3/46, 4/46, 7/46, 3/48, 7/48, 8/49, 9/49, 10/49, 1/53, 3/53, 1/54, 5/55, 6/55, 4/63, 8/63, 10/66, 8/68, 7/71, 10/71, 9/76, 1/80, 2/80, 5/80
Titov, Gherman 8/61
Tixier-Vignancour 5/62
Tochangri 3/02
Todd, Garfield 10/66, 1/72, 6/76, 2/80
Todd, Judith 1/72
Togo
- France takes state 9/20
- Independent: Africa's smallest country 4/60
- Military coup 1/63

Togo, Heihachiro 3/04, 5/05
Togo, Shigenori 8/42
Togoland
- See Togo

Togori, Iva 9/45
Tojo, Hideki 10/41, 11/41, 12/41, 2/44, 9/45, 11/48, 12/48
Tolan, Eddie 8/32
Tolkien, J.R.R. 8/54, 9/73
Toller, Ernst 12/33
Tolstoy, Count Nikolai 11/89
Tolstoy, Leo 3/01, 11/10
Tomalin, Claire 12/90
Tombaugh, Clyde 2/06, 2/30
Tomkinson, Martin 1/69
Tonga
- British annexation 4/00
- Independence from Britain 6/70

Topolski, Feliks 8/89
Tornatore, Giuseppe 12/90
Torrance, Sam 9/85
Torrijos, Omar 7/81
Tortelier, Paul 12/90
Torvill, Jayne 2/81, 2/84, 1/94, 3/94
Toscanini, Arturo 12/10, 4/26, 6/30, 5/31, 6/33, 12/33, 12/37, 1/38, 4/54, 1/57
Toulouse-Lautrec, Henri de 9/01
Tour de France
- Announced 1/03
- Won by Maurice Garin 7/03
- Winner has failed earlier drugs test 7/88

Toure, Sekou 10/58
Tower, John 2/87, 3/89
Townsend, Peter 10/55
Townshend, Charles 4/16
Toynbee, Arnold Joseph 10/75
Toynbee, Philip 2/38
Trabert, Tony 7/55
Tracy, Edward 8/91
Tracy, Spencer 4/00, 6/67
Trade Unions
- See Britain (Labour)

Trakl, Georg 11/14
Tran Kim 3/45
Transjordan
- See also Jordan
- Britain recognises its independence 2/28
- Planned £2 million grant, White Paper 7/37
- Vichy planes bomb Amman 6/41
- Becomes independent kingdom: Jordan 5/46
- Renamed Hashemite Kingdom of Jordan 6/49

Transport
- See Aviation, Buses, Cars, Railways

Travers, Ben 12/25, 12/80
Travolta, John 12/77
Treboulsi, Omar 3/88
Tree, Herbert Beerbohm 4/14, 7/17
Trenchard, Hugh 4/18, 12/19
Trend, Lord 3/81
Trepov, Alexander 11/16, 1/17
Trestrail, Michael 7/82
Trethowan, Ian 12/76
Treurnicht, Andries 3/82
Trevaskis, Kennedy 12/63
Trevelyan, Charles 3/31
Trevelyan, George 8/28, 7/62
Trevelyan, Humphrey 10/56
Trevino, Lee 7/71, 7/72
Trevor-Roper, Hugh (Lord Dacre) 4/83
Trianon, Treaty of
- Treaty signed; Austro-Hungarian peace 6/20
- Cuts Hungary to a quarter of its old size 6/20

Trieste
- Awarded to Italy; Yugoslavia angry 10/53
- Allies leave; most goes to Italy 10/54

Trinder, Tommy 12/89
Trinidad
- Becomes an independent nation 8/62
- Crawford's Olympic sprinting gold 7/76

Trotha, Adolf von 11/04
Trotsky, Leon 11/06, 11/17, 12/17, 2/18, 6/18, 8/18, 10/19, 8/20, 3/21, 3/23, 5/24, 10/24, 10/26, 11/27, 12/27, 11/28, 1/29, 2/29, 7/29, 2/31, 10/32, 7/33, 4/34, 12/36, 1/37, 4/37, 5/40, 8/40
Trowell, Hubert 12/75
Trubshaw, Brian 4/69
Trudeau, Margaret 5/77
Trudeau, Pierre 4/68, 6/68, 10/70, 12/70, 3/71, 7/74, 5/77, 5/78, 2/80, 2/84
Trueman, Fred 9/52, 8/53, 11/68
Truffaut, Francois 2/32, 12/59, 1/62, 10/84
Trujillo, Rafael 11/75
Truman, Christine 6/58, 7/61
Truman, Harry S.
- Nomination as US Vice-President 7/44
- Becomes US President 4/45
- Attends signing of United Nations charter 6/45
- Attends Potsdam conference 7/45
- Orders dropping of A-bombs on Japan 8/45
- Announces Japanese surrender 8/45
- Promises wheat for Europe and Asia 4/46
- Urges more Jews in Palestine 10/46
- Claims Poland broke election pledge 2/47
- Begins crusade against world communism 3/47
- Condemns coup in Hungary 6/47
- Appeals for meatless days to help Europe 10/47
- Endorses Five Power Pact in Europe 3/48
- Recognises government of Israel 5/48
- Criticises US spy mania 8/48
- Wins presidential election 11/48
- Refuses four-power talks on Berlin 11/48
- Inaugurated as President 1/49
- Condemns jailing of Mindszenty, Hungary 2/49
- Says he would use A-bomb again 4/49
- Tries to calm anti-Communist hysteria 6/49
- Gives go-ahead for H-bomb 1/50
- No military aid to Nationalist Chinese 1/50
- Denounces McCarthy and two other senators 3/50
- Promises aid to South in Korean War 6/50
- US will leave Formosa after Korean War 8/50
- Wants to restrain MacArthur in Korea 10/50
- Says he hopes not to use A-bomb in Korea 12/50
- Declares state of emergency over Korea 12/50
- Commits US to Korean War 1/51
- Discusses Indochina with Premier Pleven 1/51
- Embarrassed by MacArthur's Chinese aims 3/51
- Fires Douglas MacArthur from all posts 4/51
- Senate inquiry into MacArthur sacking 5/51
- Ends Communist states' tariff privileges 8/51
- Gives reason as to why he dismissed MacArthur 12/51
- Churchill allows US to use UK bases 1/52
- Pulls out of presidential race 3/52
- Signs official end to Pacific War 4/52
- Immigration bill veto overridden 6/52
- NATO absorbs European Defence Community 8/52
- Calls Eisenhower "inept tool of unholy" 9/52
- Blames Eisenhower for Berlin affair 10/52
- Invites elected Eisenhower to talks 11/52
- McCarthy says Truman aided Communists 11/53
- Dies 12/72

Trump, Donald 3/91
Tsabari, Gad 9/72
Tsafendas, Demetrio 9/66
Tshombe, Moise 7/60, 8/60, 1/61, 2/61, 4/61, 6/61, 9/61, 11/61, 12/61, 12/62, 1/63, 7/64, 10/64, 3/65, 3/67, 7/67, 6/69
Tsiang, T.F. 1/50
Tsu-Hsi, Dowager Empress of China 11/08
Tsushima
- Japanese destroy Russian fleet 5/05

Tucker, Tony 8/87
Tudjman, Franjo 6/93
Tudor, General 11/20
Tuite, Gerard 12/80, 3/82
Tukharchevsky, General 10/19
Tunisia
- See also World War II
- Germans land forces in Tunis 11/42
- French arrest Premier Shenik after riots 3/52
- France offers autonomy 7/54
- Pro-autonomy Mendes-France in Tunis 8/54
- Bourguiba returns; internal autonomy 6/55
- Independent under Bourguiba 3/56
- Bourguiba ousts Bey; becomes President 7/57
- Bourguiba calls for end to Algerian war 11/57
- Bourguiba wants French troops out 2/58
- Bourguiba breaks off relations with UAR 10/58
- 13 to die for anti-Bourguiba plot 1/63
- Signs unification treaty with Libya 1/74
- New headquarters for Arafat 8/82
- 75 die in food riots 1/84
- Israeli air raid on PLO offices kills 50 10/85
- PLO HQ to be moved to Yemen 10/86
- Bourguiba deposed after 31 years 11/87
- William Waldegrave meets PLO leader Yassir Arafat 1/89
- PLO holds first formal talks with new US administration 3/89
- PLO's deputy leader, Abu Iyad, is assassinated 1/91

Tunney, Gene 9/26, 9/27
Tupolev, Andrei 12/72
Turkey
- See also World War I
- Troops rush to Bulgarian frontier 2/01
- Forced to pay compensation to France 11/01
- Troops mobilise against Macedonia 3/02
- Accepts Austro-Russian proposals 2/03
- 50,000 Bulgarians killed 9/03
- Agrees Balkan reforms 11/03
- Clashes with Albanians 2/04
- Embarrassment at Russian consul's murder 4/04
- 900 Armenians killed 5/04
- Crete opts for Greek union 4/05
- Moslems kill 170 Armenians 6/05
- Accused of inciting Armenians and Tartars 9/05
- Settles border dispute with Persia 2/08
- Samos islanders revolt; 150 die 5/08
- Contract to build 500 mile railway 6/08
- Young Turks' revolt restores constitution 7/08
- Reform proposals 8/08
- Crete declares independence 10/08
- Resumes Balkans talks with Austria 12/08
- First "reformed" parliament meets 12/08
- Accepts Austrian annexation payback 1/09
- Recognises Bulgaria's independence 4/09
- Sultan deposed by Young Turks 4/09
- 30,000 Armenians killed in pogroms 4/09
- New Sultan Mehmet V promises liberty 5/09
- Four powers meet to settle Crete crisis 8/09
- Parliament burns down 1/10
- Threatens Greece over breakaway Crete 2/10
- Turkey crushes 15,000 Albanian rebels 4/10
- Threatens war with Greece over Crete 7/10
- Montenegro declares independence 8/10
- Troops quell Arab unrest, Palestine 12/10
- Constantinople ruined by fire 2/11
- Italians attack Turkish-occupied Tripoli 9/11
- Italy takes Tripoli; Governor retreats 10/11
- Italy occupies Rhodes island 5/12
- Dardanelles re-open after Italian attack 5/12
- Abolishes martial law; frees prisoners 8/12
- Grants Albania limited autonomy 8/12
- Mobilisation to counter Bulgarian threat 9/12
- Concessions to provinces; fires on Greeks 9/12
- Retreat before Balkan League attacks 10/12
- Sultan concedes Libya to Italy 10/12
- Loses 40,000 men at Lule Burgas battle 11/12
- Suing for peace in Constantinople 11/12
- Signs peace with all but Greece 12/12
- Young Turks triumph; peace terms rejected 1/13
- Loses 5,000 in battle for Gallipoli 2/13
- Signs peace treaty; discord over Macedonia 5/13
- Grand Vizier assassinated 6/13
- Forced to abandon rail link to Gulf 7/13
- Regains Adrianople in wake of second war 8/13
- Settles border dispute with Bulgaria 9/13
- Treaty with Britain gives UK Arab oil 11/13
- Women admitted to universities 2/14
- Sultan orders general mobilisation 9/14
- 2,500 die in earthquake 10/14
- Attacks Russian Black Sea ports and fleet 10/14
- Russia, Britain and France break off relations 11/14
- Declares war on Allies 11/14
- Reports of a million Armenians killed 12/15
- Crown Prince Yussuf assassinated 2/16
- Allies plan its post-war dismemberment 3/16
- Arabs revolt in Mecca and Jeddah 6/16
- Reported to have killed 500,000 Armenians 8/16
- Heavy losses in Baghdad and Gaza 3/17
- Loses Jerusalem to Britain 12/17
- Armenian town wiped out by Moslems 3/18
- Germany severs ties 7/18

- Ottoman Empire loses Beirut and Damascus 10/18
- Surrenders; re-opens Dardanelles to ships 10/18
- 1.5 million Armenians killed 1/19
- Ex-ministers tried for atrocities 4/19
- Sultan's palace burns down 6/19
- Moslems kill 14,000 Armenians 3/20
- League restricts state to Anatolia 3/20
- Syria breaks away under King Feisal 3/20
- Allies in Constantinople after genocide 3/20
- Sultan ousted; Mustafa Kemal new leader 4/20
- Loses 80 per cent of Empire 8/20
- Kemal swears not to give up territory 8/20
- Hadjin seized; 10,000 Armenians killed 11/20
- Britain, France and Italy map out interests 11/20
- Swamped by 100,000 beaten White Russians 11/20
- Armenians killed in Kars and Alexandropol 2/21
- Kemal gets new powers as Greeks advance 8/21
- Fighting around Smyrna and Eskishar; unrest 8/21
- Chamberlain demands Turkish inquiry 5/22
- Attacks Greece 8/22
- Captures Smyrna from Greeks; 1,000 die 9/22
- Claims eastern Thrace; Allies accept 9/22
- Kemal halts attack on British, Chakal 10/22
- Treaty of Mudania; wins eastern Thrace 10/22
- Kemal abolishes monarchy 11/22
- Greek refugees in squalor, Scutari 2/23
- Ignores Lausanne Treaty and stays in Smyrna 2/23
- Peace talks 5/23
- To regain Aegean areas and Armenia: treaty 7/23
- British evacuate Istanbul 8/23
- Kemal is made President of new Turkish republic 10/23
- Caliphate ended; Moslem customs banned 3/24
- Expels Greeks; arrests 3,500 10/24
- League settlement; Iraqi border question 12/25
- Adopts Swiss civil code 1/26
- Accord with Britain over Iraqi borders 6/26
- Anti-Kemal plotters executed 8/26
- Adopts metric system and "day off" 1/29
- Exiled Trotsky arrives in Constantinople 2/29
- With Porsians, attacks Kurds 8/30
- Signs treaty of friendship with Greece 9/30
- Kemal's Republican Party wins landslide victory 4/31
- Kemal re-elected President by Assembly 5/31
- Becomes 56th member of League of Nations 7/32
- Kemal bans prayers and use of "Allah" 2/33
- Balkan Pact with Greece, Yugoslavia and Rumania 2/34
- Kemal orders Turks to adopt a surname 11/34
- Mustafa Kemal becomes Kemal Ataturk 11/34
- All inherited titles abolished 11/34
- Women get the vote 12/34
- Women vote in elections 2/35
- Non-aggression pact with Iraq, Iran and Afghans 12/35
- Dardanelles domain accepted, Montreaux 7/36
- Plans to conscript woman in wartime 1/37
- Kemal Ataturk dies; 20 die at lying in state 11/38
- Ismet Onu succeeds Ataturk as president 11/38
- Pact signed with France and Britain 10/39
- Signs non-aggression pact with Bulgaria 2/41
- Closes Dardanelles to foreign ships 3/41
- Refuses to join Axis 3/41
- Germany breaks off relations 8/44
- Declares war on Germany 2/45
- Joins Council of Europe 8/49
- Invited to join NATO 9/51
- Friendship treaty with Greeks and Yugoslavs 3/53
- Submarine collision; 97 feared dead 4/53
- Cypriot community welcomes talks 6/55
- Talks with Greece and UK on Cyprus fail 9/55
- Premier Menderes wants Britain in Cyprus 7/56
- Turks riot on Cyprus; two die, 100 injured 1/58
- 220 die when ferry sinks 3/58
- Premier Mendares signs Cyprus deal 2/59
- Cyprus air crash; 12 die, premier survives 2/59
- Three days' rioting; 3,000 arrested 4/60
- Regime closes universities 5/60
- Premier Menderes ousted in coup 5/60
- Ex-premier Menderes hanged 9/61
- US to remove its missile bases 11/62
- 67 die in plane crash 2/63
- Premier Demirel forced to resign by army 3/71
- 14-year-old Briton jailed for cannabis 3/72
- Terrorists kill three British hostages 3/72
- London schoolboy Davey freed from jail 5/74
- Turks invade northern Cyprus 7/74
- Signs Cyprus peace deal with Greeks 7/74
- Denktash declares Turkish Cyprus 2/75
- Bomb blast outside Spanish Embassy 9/75
- Greek premier wants pact with Turkey 4/76
- 6,000 die in quake near Soviet border 11/76
- General Evren heads army coup 9/80
- Evren ends strikes; arrests MPs 9/80
- Pope's attacker identified as Agca, an Armenian Turk 5/81
- Earthquake kills 2,000 10/83
- Turgut Ozal wins general election 11/83
- Arab gunmen kill 21 in synagogue 9/86
- Assassination attempt on Prime Minister 6/88
- Demonstrators mar May Day in Istanbul 5/89
- Government seeks UN aid for thousands of refugees from Iraq 4/91
- Earthquake devastates eastern Turkey, killing over 1,000 3/92
- Premier Suleyman Demiral becomes President 5/93
- Tansu Ciller becomes first woman Canadian premier 6/93
- Death sentences demanded for Kurdish MPs 8/94
- Its troops cross into Iraq to find and destroy Kurd rebels 3/95

Turner, Robert 9/06
Turpin, Randolph 7/51, 9/51, 6/53, 10/53, 5/66
Turtiainen, Arvo 9/04
Tushingham, Rita 12/59
Tutankhamun
- See Egypt

Tutu, Desmond 10/84, 12/84, 8/85, 4/86, 6/86, 0/86, 2/88
Twaddell, William 5/22
Twain, Mark (Samuel Langhorne Clemens) 4/06, 4/10
Tweedie, Jill 11/93
Twiggy 12/66, 7/68
Twomey, Seamus 10/73
Tyabji, Abbas 5/30
Tynan, Kenneth 2/47, 5/56, 7/70
Tyson, Mike 11/86, 8/87, 2/89, 2/90, 3/92, 3/95

U

U Aung San 7/47
Uganda
- See also Britain (foreign affairs, Africa)
- Ruled out as site of Jewish state 8/03
- Prince of Wales escapes charging elephant 3/30
- UK allows Kabaka of Buganda to return 7/55
- Kabaka of Buganda gives ministers powers 10/55
- Independence declared 10/62
- Army mutiny; British troops fly in 1/64
- Obote jails five ministers and takes power 2/66
- Obote abolishes post of President 3/66
- Obote is shot in the head 12/69
- Causes England to call off cricket tour 1/70
- All major industries nationalised 5/70
- Idi Amin takes power in coup 1/71
- Amin bans all political activity 1/71
- Amin releases 55 political prisoners 1/71
- Amin promotes himself to General 2/71
- Amin makes himself President 2/71
- State of emergency lifted 2/71
- Britain recognises Amin government 2/71
- Amin to expel 50,000 Asians to UK 8/72
- Asians flee Ugandan terror 9/72
- US halts $3 million loan to Uganda 9/72
- Repels invasion by exiles from Tanzania 9/72
- Signs peace pact with Tanzania 10/72
- 112 Peace Corps workers to be expelled 7/73
- Amin starts "Save Britain" fund 12/73
- Coup attempt against Amin fails 3/74
- 50 army officers killed in purge 3/74
- 250,000 alleged to have died under Amin 6/74
- Hills guilty of treason for blaming Amin 6/75
- Amin rejects Hills release appeal 6/75
- Amin pardons Hills after world pressure 7/75
- Bob Astles arrested for "rumours" 4/76
- Hijacked Airbus arrives in Entebbe 6/76
- Israeli commandos free Entebbe hostages 7/76
- Britain breaks diplomatic ties 7/76
- Archbishop Luwum killed in terror wave 2/77
- Amin quells army protests on tribalism 2/77
- Amnesty International accuses Amin of executing thousands 2/77
- Amin traps US citizens 2/77
- Amin tells Americans they can leave 3/77
- Prince Charles snubs Amin at funeral 8/78
- Fighting with Tanzania in west 10/78
- Amin to annex part of Tanzania 11/78
- Tanzanians attack Kampala 3/79
- Libyans aid Amin 3/79
- Idi Amin flees north; army mutinies 3/79
- Rebels take Kampala 4/79
- Amin overthrown; Yusuf Lule becomes President 4/79
- Lule demands "respect for life, rights" 4/79
- Ex-President Obote returns 5/80
- 500 die a day from famine, Karamoja 6/80
- Gets £300,000 from EEC for drugs 6/80
- Coup bid fails; 69 die 2/82
- Obote overthrown in bloodless coup 7/85
- Government troops fight rebel forces 1/86
- Yoweri Museveni takes power 1/86

Uhde, Fritz von 2/11
Ukraine
- Declares independence 6/17
- Russia and Germany recognise independence 1/18
- Peace with Russia 6/18
- 29,000 Jews killed in Ukraine 1/20
- 120 shot in Communist purge 7/27
- See USSR until 1991
- Refuses $200m to shut down Chernobyl 7/94
- Parliament ratifies Nuclear Nonproliferation Treaty 11/94

Ulanova, Galina 12/56
Ulbricht, Walter 9/60, 8/61, 5/71, 8/73
Ulm, Charles 10/33
Ulmanis, Karlis 5/34
Umberto I, King of Italy 7/00
Umberto II, King of Italy 6/44, 6/46
Unamuno, Miguel de 12/37
Underground railways
- See London, transport

Underwood, Derek 3/82
Underwood, Rory 3/91
Unification Church
- Sun Myung Moon marries 790 couples 10/70

United Arab Republic (UAR)
- See also Egypt
- Yemen joins 3/58
- Beirut asks US to halt flow of UAR arms to rebels 6/58
- Jordan's Hussein severs relations 7/58
- Defence pact with Iraq 7/58
- Tunisia breaks off relations 10/58
- USSR agrees to give aid 12/58

United Nations
- See also Korean War
- Created in San Francisco 4/45
- 50 nations sign World Security Charter 6/45
- UNESCO founded in Paris 11/45
- Sets up Atomic Energy Commission 1/46
- Trygve Lie is first Secretary-General 1/46
- First session of General Assembly 1/46
- Condemns Franco regime in Spain 2/46
- Votes not to cut ties with Spain 6/46
- USSR vetoes Thai and Portuguese entry 8/46
- Sweden, Iceland and Afghanistan admitted 8/46
- Offered site at Flushing Meadow, US 10/46
- Albania protests at UK mine-sweeping 11/46
- Rockefeller offers site on East River 12/46
- South Africa cannot annex S.W. Africa 12/46
- USSR may have atomic secrets 2/47
- Arabs appeal for independent Palestine 5/47
- USSR vetoes Balkan frontier commission 7/47
- Arranges truce in Indonesian crisis 8/47
- Britain ready to leave Palestine 8/47
- USSR accuses US of war-mongering 9/47
- Votes for partition of Palestine 11/47
- To mediate in India-Pakistan dispute 1/48
- Stunned by US recognition of Israel 5/48
- Gromyko resigns as USSR envoy 5/48
- Israel and Arab League agree to truce 6/48
- Israel mediator Bernadotte killed 9/48
- Calls for sanctions in Palestine 10/48
- US vetoes Spain's entry 10/48
- Norway elected to Security Council 10/48
- Cuba elected to Security Council 10/48
- Adopts declaration of human rights 12/48
- Cease-fire imposed in Kashmir 1/49
- Demands Dutch withdrawal from Indonesia 1/49
- Israel and Egypt sign truce 2/49
- USSR vetoes South Korea's entry 4/49
- Israel voted in 5/49
- USSR calls for ban on nuclear weapons 9/49
- USSR vetoes entry of four nations to UN 9/49
- UN flag hoisted over New York building 10/49
- Yugoslavia elected to Security Council 10/49
- Former Italian colonies are independent 11/49
- Members must reveal military capability 12/49
- USSR walks out in row over China 1/50
- Adopts plan to divide Jerusalem 4/50
- Urges aid to South Korea in Korean War 6/50
- Rejects Mao Tse-tung's entry 8/50
- USSR vetoes motion condemning N. Korea 9/50
- Lie re-elected as Secretary-General 11/50
- Grants independence to Libya 11/50
- Ships bombard Inchon, South Korea 1/51
- Troops fight Communists, Wonju, S. Korea 1/51
- Names China as aggressor in Korea 1/51
- UN forces take Anyang and Yongdungpo 2/51
- Invades North Korea with South Koreans 3/51
- UN forces take Pyongyang, North Korea 6/51
- Ridgway ready for cease-fire with Reds 6/51
- Encourages progress at Korean talks 8/51
- Resolution helps Libya to independence 12/51
- Angry at North Korean intransigence 12/51
- Requests free elections in East Germany 1/52
- First session in New York headquarters 2/52
- UN planes down ten Communist MiG planes 4/52
- Trygve Lie resigns as Secretary General 11/52
- Dag Hammarskjold new Secretary-General 3/53
- US Senate bars China's entry to UN 6/53
- Korean armistice signed; war is over 7/53
- Condemns Israeli raid on Jordan 11/53
- Command leaves Korea 8/54
- Shelves Greek demand for Cyprus autonomy 12/54
- Commissioner for Refugees wins Nobel Peace Prize 12/54
- Israel raids Gaza Strip; Egypt protests 3/55
- Apartheid criticised; South African exit 10/55
- Admits 16 new nations, but bars Japan and Mongolia 12/55
- Suez resolution brought before Security Council 9/56
- USSR vetoes UK-French Suez plan 10/56
- Calls cease-fire on UK-French Suez attack 11/56
- Prepares seven-nation force for Suez 11/56
- Tells USSR to leave Hungary 11/56
- Lloyd counters UK "collusion" charge 11/56
- Forces take over Canal from UK and France 11/56
- Salvage crews clear Suez Canal 1/57
- Demands Israeli pull-out from Gaza and Aqaba 1/57
- Hammarskjold talks with Nasser 3/57
- Rejects Arab motion blasting UK in Oman 8/57
- Hammarskjold re-elected Secretary 9/57
- Report suggests half world's population is underfed 10/57
- Rejects Algerian independence 12/58
- China not to join 9/59
- Bans French Saharan nuclear tests 11/59
- UN headquarters seen as architectural trend-setter 12/59
- Reports higher standards in USSR bloc 4/60
- Hammarskjold arrives in Congo 7/60
- Hammarskjold asks Belgium to leave Congo 8/60
- Khrushchev wants Hammarskjold fired 9/60
- Khruschev thumps desk during UK speech 9/60
- 15 new African nations admitted 9/60
- Khrushchev waves shoe at Philippine delegate during speech 10/60
- Troops fight Congo army over Ghana envoy 11/60
- Votes to censure South Africa for racism 4/61
- Tells Portugal to reform Angola 4/61
- Crushes Katangan rebels in Congo 9/61
- Dag Hammarskjold dies in air crash 9/61
- Censures South Africa again 10/61
- Mauritania and Mongolia join 10/61
- U Thant becomes Secretary-General 11/61
- Tshombe and Kasavubu tied to Lumumba death 11/61
- USSR vetoes Kuwait's entry 11/61
- Conor Cruise O'Brien sacked 12/61
- U Thant presents Congo independence plan 8/62
- Takes control of west New Guinea 10/62
- UN troops advance in Congo 12/62
- Tshombe announces surrender of Katanga 1/63
- Votes against admitting China 10/63
- Troops fly into Cyprus 3/64
- Report suggests world population is booming 8/64
- USSR tells US to halt Vietnam actions 8/64
- Turks and Greeks accept Cyprus cease-fire 8/64
- Sukarno says Indonesia will quit 1/65
- All UN offices in Indonesia closed 1/65
- Appeals for end to India-Pakistan war 9/65
- Argentina restates claim to Falklands 9/65
- Addressed by Pope 10/65
- Condemns Rhodesian UDI 11/65
- UNICEF awarded Nobel Peace Prize 12/65
- Says UN force cannot end Vietnam War 9/66
- Members requested to put oil embargo on Rhodesia 12/66
- U Thant calls for end to Vietnam War 4/67
- To withdraw force from Israeli border 5/67
- Israeli cease-fire ends Six-Day War 6/67
- Admits China and expels Taiwan 10/71
- Chinese delegates take their seats 11/71
- Kurt Waldheim becomes Secretary-General 12/71
- Security Council to admit East Germany 6/73
- Security Council to admit West Germany 6/73
- Cease-fire ends Yom Kippur war 10/73
- Relief convoys in Cyprus halted by Turks 7/74
- Addressed by Yassir Arafat 11/74
- Former Secretary-General U Thant dies 11/74
- US vetoes Vietnam's application to join 11/76
- Kurt Waldheim gets second term 12/76
- UNESCO fund to save polluted Acropolis 1/77
- Bans arms sales to South Africa 11/77
- UNICEF aid to two million Cambodians 9/79
- Lifts sanctions on Zimbabwe 12/79
- Waldheim cancels Iran trip after rebuff 1/80
- Waldheim commission on ex-Shah 2/80
- High Commissioner for Refugees wins Nobel 12/81
- Israel accepts Sinai peace-keeping force 1/82
- Backs UK's Falklands protest 4/82
- Calls for talks on Falklands sovereignty 11/82
- US vetoes Grenada resolution 10/83
- Arranges PLO evacuation of Lebanon 12/83
- USSR vetoes idea of UN force in Beirut 2/84
- US withdraws from UNESCO 1/85
- Britain pulls out of UNESCO 12/85
- Libyan leader demands emergency meeting of Security Council 1/89
- Proposes truce to end fighting in Namibia 4/89
- Votes to add air embargo to naval blockade against Iraq 9/90
- Condemns Israel for Temple Mount killings 10/90
- Gives Saddam Hussein ultimatum for withdrawal from Kuwait 11/90
- Iraq begins freeing foreign "human shield" hostages 12/90
- Tough cease-fire resolution after Gulf War 3/91
- "Safe havens" in Iraq end 7/91
- Besieged UN nuclear inspectors allowed to leave Iraq 9/91
- Butros Butros Ghali takes over as Secretary-General 1/92
- 16,000 troops to be sent to Cambodia to enforce cease-fire 2/92
- Imposes air traffic embargo on Libya 4/92
- Security Council votes to impose sanctions on Serbia 5/92
- UN forces take control of Sarajevo airport 7/92
- All UN relief flights to Sarajevo are halted 9/92
- Imposes air exclusion over Bosnia 10/92
- To set up tribunal to try war crimes committed in Yugoslavia 2/93
- UN ground troops launch raid on warlord's Mogadishu HQ 6/93
- Report warns on migration 7/93
- Economic sanctions on South Africa lifted 10/93
- 19.7 million refugees worldwide 11/93
- UN imposes sanctions on Libya over Lockerbie suspects 11/93
- SAS hero to head Bosnia peacekeepers 1/94
- UN arms embargo on South Africa lifted 5/94
- Population warning 8/94
- Disputes mar Cairo conference on population 9/94

Universal Exposition
- Expo 92 opens in Seville 4/92

Uno, Sosuke 6/89, 7/89
Unsworth, Barry 10/92
U Nu 9/58
Unwin, Stanley 10/68
Updike, John 12/68
Upper Volta
- Becomes a French Union republic 12/58

Urbanek, Karol 11/89
Uruguay
- Breaks off relations with Germany 10/17
- Border fights with Bolivia: League plea 12/28
- Germans scuttle warship Graf Spee 12/39
- Declares war on Germany 2/45
- British Ambassador kidnapped 1/71
- British Ambassador Jackson is freed 9/71
- Andes plane crash survivors eat the dead 12/72
- USA cuts aid over human rights issue 2/77

U Saw 7/47
US Federal Aviation Authority 2/89
Ushijama, Mitsuri 6/45
USA (foreign affairs)
- See also Vietnam War
- Signs Nicaraguan channel treaty with UK 2/00
- Senate approves International Court 2/00
- Cruisers sent to Central America 3/00
- Allies urge Chinese to suppress Boxers 4/00
- Congress gives go-ahead for building of Nicaraguan canal 5/00
- American amnesty offered to Filipino rebels 6/00
- Captures Filipino rebel leader Aguinaldo 3/01
- Platt amendment limiting Cuba 3/01
- Agrees with UK on Central American canal 11/01
- Commission supports Panama Canal 1/02
- Buys Panama Canal concession 6/02

USA (foreign affairs)

- To rule Philippines by commission 7/02
- Signs Chinese Tariff Protocol 8/02
- Signs canal treaty with Colombia 1/03
- Warships sent to Panama 11/03
- Ends Cuban occupation 2/04
- Neutral in Russo-Japanese War 2/04
- To police debtor South American states 12/04
- Supervises Central American peace treaty 7/06
- Adopts caretaker role in Cuba 9/06
- Roosevelt first President to leave US on official visit 11/06
- Protests at Sino-Russian treaty 7/09
- President chooses Pearl Harbor as base 11/09
- Troops leave Nicaragua 1/11
- Rushes troops to Mexican border 3/11
- Troops enter Mexico; rebels hold out 4/11
- US Marines invade Cuba 5/12
- Four troops die crushing Nicaraguan revolt 10/12
- Border clash with Mexico 3/13
- Boycotts arms to Mexico after expulsions 8/13
- President Wilson opens Panama Canal 10/13
- 500,000 men mobilised 11/13
- Gives Huerta ultimatum to resign 11/13
- Mexican arms embargo lifted 2/14
- Marines sieze Mexican port, Vera Cruz 4/14
- Pancho Villa ends Mexican border war 1/15
- Ship, William P. Frye, sunk by Germans 1/15
- Austrian ambassador recalled: spy plot 9/15
- Senate wants Philippines independence 2/16
- Troops rout Villa's rebels, 30 killed 3/16
- Wilson threatens Germany over U-boats 4/16
- President Wilson moots peace league 5/16
- War main election issue; Wilson attacked 10/16
- Army orders 375 new planes 10/16
- Wilson proposes peace terms in note 12/16
- Zimmerman telegram: Germany urges Mexico 2/17
- First to recognise post-Czarist Russia 3/17
- 26,000 more sailors enlisted 3/17
- US "Rainbow Division" arrives in Europe 11/17
- Protests at Russian armistice plan 12/17
- Declares war on Austria 12/17
- Wilson's 14-point post-war peace plan 1/18
- Wilson says no peace with autocrats 2/18
- 300,000 arrive at Front each month 7/18
- Wilson sends small force to White Russia 8/18
- Severs ties with Russia 8/18
- Rejects Austrian peace proposal 9/18
- Wilson's speech; 27 states accept League 2/19
- Troops rout Bolsheviks in Russia 2/19
- Warns Costa Rica not to invade Nicaragua 6/19
- Germans blame Wilson for ignoring plan 6/19
- Senate rejects Versailles treaty 11/19
- Boycotts first meeting of League 1/20
- US troops leave Vladivostok 2/20
- Sees Russian promises as propaganda 2/20
- US membership attempt fails 3/20
- Congress wants separate peace 4/20
- Senate rejects Armenian mandate 5/20
- Lloyd George appeals for US in League 7/20
- Send warships to Danzig 8/20
- Harding wants US to join League 9/20
- President Harding rejects League 4/21
- Officially ends war on Germany and Austria 7/21
- Famine aid for Russia 8/21
- Pacific talks with UK, France and Japan 10/21
- Pacific conference opens 11/21
- Harding wants more world conferences 11/21
- Four-power naval agreement to stop wars 12/21
- $20 million to help famine victims 12/21
- Washington conference outlaws U-boat war 1/22
- Washington conference outlaws gas warfare 1/22
- Mexican rebels destroy railway, El Paso 2/22
- Treaty protecting US citizens, Palestine 5/22
- Blames France for Ruhr occupation 1/23
- Harding urges approval of US joining International Court 2/23
- Senate rejects International Court plan 3/23
- New President offers to solve crisis 8/23
- Coolidge appeals for Tokyo relief fund 9/23
- Coolidge rules out Filipino independence 3/24
- $10 million in food for women and children 3/24
- Senate says join International Court 1/26
- Coolidge urges arms spending cut 5/26
- Ships sent to Hankow to prevent Communist attack 11/26
- Coolidge pledges to protect US citizens in China 1/27
- Nicaraguan pact allows US intervention 6/27
- Cruiser demands upset world naval talks 7/27
- Five Marines killed by Sandino rebels 1/28
- Sends another 1,000 Marines to Nicaragua 1/28
- Coolidge opens Pan-American Conference 1/28
- Recognises Chiang Kai-shek government 9/28
- Hoover arrives in Nicaragua to discuss rebel threat 11/28
- Air Force threatens to bomb Mexican rebels 4/29
- Four Americans hurt by Mexican rebels 4/29
- Reminds China and Soviets of peace pact 7/29
- Signs London Naval Treaty; accepts limits 4/30
- Fears trade with Brazil after coup 10/30
- Will withdraw from Nicaragua 4/31
- Hoover wants war debts suspended 6/31
- Federal Reserve lends £25,000,000 to the Bank of England 8/31
- Arranges truce in Manchuria war, China 11/31
- Fails to get Japanese to leave Manchuria 1/32
- Hoover sends infantry to Shanghai 1/32
- UK and France discuss their debts 7/32
- Roosevelt rejects Hoover's war debt plan 12/32
- Hoover vetoes Filipino independence bill 1/33
- Congress overrides Hoover's Filipino veto 1/33
- Considers recognising USSR 10/33
- Establishes diplomatic and trade relations with USSR 11/33
- Philippines to be given independence by 1945 3/34
- UK stalls repayment of war debts 6/34
- Two Americans seized as spies in Germany 11/34
- To close USSR consulate 2/35
- Neutrality Bill: no arms to war states 8/35
- Arms embargo on Italy under new act 10/35
- Second Neutrality Bill banning loans 2/36
- Signs London Naval Treaty 3/36
- Moves Embassy in Spain from Madrid to Valencia 11/36
- Pan-American Peace Conference, Argentina 12/36
- Bans volunteers fighting in Spain 1/37
- Roosevelt condemns Japan over China 10/37
- Duke of Windsor cancels trip 11/37
- Joseph Kennedy becomes Ambassador to London 12/37
- Brigadists defend Tortosa, Spain 4/38
- Drops London Naval Treaty; builds warships 4/38
- Roosevelt condemns German anti-Semitism 11/38
- Recognises Franco's regime 3/39
- British King and Queen begin visit 6/39
- Roosevelt declares neutrality 9/39
- Recognises Polish government-in-exile 10/39
- Rejects Hitler's plea for mediation 10/39
- Arms sales embargo ends 11/39
- Peace mission to Berlin fails 3/40
- Invasion of Denmark and Norway condemned 4/40
- Asks Mussolini to help halt war 4/40
- UK gives leases on bases in Newfoundland 8/40
- UK gives leases on bases in West Indies 8/40
- Roosevelt denies US plans to go to war 10/40
- Agrees with UK and Australia on Pacific defence 11/40
- Joseph Kennedy quits as envoy to UK 12/40
- Called "the arsenal of democracy" 12/40
- Signs lease-lend pact with Britain 3/41
- Occupies Greenland 4/41
- Envoys expelled from Paris 5/41
- First food ship arrives in UK 5/41
- German and Italian assets frozen 6/41
- Consuls expelled from Germany and Italy 6/41
- Pledges help to USSR 6/41
- Forces occupy Iceland 7/41
- Denounces Japan as an aggressor 7/41
- All Japanese assets abroad frozen 7/41
- MacArthur commands forces in Far East 7/41
- Certain fuel exports banned 8/41
- Arms to be sent to Axis enemies 8/41
- Agrees Atlantic Charter with Britain 8/41
- Destroyer Greer attacked by sub 9/41
- USS Reuben James attacked by U-boat 10/41
- Relations with Japan deteriorating 11/41
- Litvinov is Soviet ambassador 11/41
- Japanese attack Pearl Harbor 12/41
- Japan attacks US bases in Pacific 12/41
- Churchill gives V sign to Congress 12/41
- Declares war on Japan, Germany and Italy 12/41
- 26 countries affirm opposition to Axis 1/42
- Evacuation of 100,000 Japanese Americans 3/42
- Merchant ship sunk by sub on Mississippi 5/42
- Eisenhower heads forces in Europe 6/42
- Dutch Queen Wilhelmina at White House 8/42
- Vichy France severs relations 11/42
- Condemns Nazi atrocities 12/42
- Madame Chiang Kai-shek at Congress 2/43
- Cautiously welcomes Keynes plan 4/43
- United Nations Food Conference 6/43
- Gromyko becomes Soviet ambassador 8/43
- Roosevelt meets Stalin and Churchill 11/43
- Roosevelt meets Chiang Kai-shek 11/43
- Roosevelt agrees closer ties with Turkey 12/43
- Condemns Japanese torture of PoWs 1/44
- Roosevelt defends bombs on Monte Cassino 2/44
- Declares neutrality in USSR-Poland row 2/44
- Opening of Bretton Woods conference 6/44
- Bretton Woods economic conference ends 7/44
- Says United Nations will be set up 10/44
- Yalta conference 2/45
- Signs lend-lease deal with France 2/45
- Among 50 nations to sign UN charter 6/45
- "Iron Curtain" falls in Europe 7/45
- At Potsdam conference 7/45
- Occupies assigned Berlin zone 7/45
- Recognises Polish government 7/45
- Drops two atomic bombs on Japan 8/45
- US forces to occupy Japan 8/45
- To partition Korea with USSR 9/45
- Anglo-US loan agreement signed 12/45
- Harriman resigns as envoy to USSR 2/46
- Churchill says Iron Curtain has fallen 3/46
- Recognises Tito regime 4/46
- Large wheat supplies for Europe and Asia 4/46
- Paris treaty talks 4/46
- Report recommends Palestine partition 5/46
- £937 million loan to Britain approved 7/46
- Vetoes Thai and Portuguese entry to UN 8/46
- Offers UN a permanent site 10/46
- Wants Jewish immigration into Palestine 10/46
- Balch and Mott win Nobel Peace Prize 12/46
- Claims election in Poland was rigged 1/47
- Fears that USSR has atomic secrets 2/47
- Max Gardner, new ambassador to UK, dies 2/47
- Crusade against communism begins 3/47
- Leases Philippines air and naval bases 3/47
- Big Four disagree on postwar settlement 4/47
- Agrees with UK to merge German zones 5/47
- Truman condemns coup in Hungary 6/47
- George Marshall offers aid plan 6/47
- Marshall aid plan splits Europeans 7/47
- Urges USSR to take part in Korea talks 8/47
- Agrees with UK on control of Ruhr mines 9/47
- Interim aid plan for Europe announced 9/47
- Accused by USSR of war-mongering 9/47
- Agrees to partition of Palestine 10/47
- Friends Service Committee: Peace Nobel 12/47
- Atomic test at Eniwetock Atoll, Pacific 4/48
- Recognises government of Israel 5/48
- Berlin airlift begins 6/48
- Protests to USSR about Berlin blockade 7/48
- Vetoes Spain's entry to UN 10/48
- To boost marine force at Tsingtao, China 11/48
- Tells Dutch to pull out of Indonesia 1/49
- Condemns jailing of Mindszenty, Hungary 2/49
- Asked to recall Polish ambassador 3/49
- Signs North Atlantic Treaty 4/49
- Agrees on establishment of West Germany 4/49
- UK refuses to extradite communist 5/49
- Rejects German reparations claim by USSR 5/49
- Says USSR is inciting disorder in Japan 6/49
- Last US combat troops leave South Korea 6/49
- Tito asks US for loan 8/49
- Lends $20 million to Yugoslavia 9/49
- Refuses to recognise communist China 10/49
- Asked by UK for A-bomb stockpile 1/50
- No military aid to Nationalist Chinese 1/50
- Consular staff must leave mainland China 1/50
- Eight nations sign NATO defence plan 1/50
- Recognises Bao Dai as Vietnam ruler 2/50
- Recognises royalist regime in Laos 2/50
- Recognises royalist regime in Cambodia 2/50
- Hungary jails Robert Vogeler for spying 2/50
- Naval attache Karp murdered in Austria 2/50
- USSR shoots down bomber over Latvia 4/50
- Promises aid to South in Korean War 6/50
- Korean War 7/50
- Truman says no retreat on Korea 1/51
- General Collins wants more reinforcement 1/51
- US and UK forces recapture Inchon, Korea 2/51
- Rosenbergs "guilty" of spying for USSR 3/51
- MacArthur wants to destroy China regime 3/51
- Truman embarrassed by MacArthur ambition 3/51
- Douglas MacArthur fired for stirring war 4/51
- Lieutenant-General Ridgway replaces MacArthur, Korea 4/51
- Sacked MacArthur calls Truman "blind" 4/51
- Gens Bradley and Marshall blast MacArthur 5/51
- Senate inquiry into MacArthur sacking 5/51
- Acheson warns of serious UK spy trouble 6/51
- Admiral Joy in talks with North Korea 7/51
- Ends Communist states' tariff privileges 8/51
- Marines in first helicopter-borne assault 9/51
- Engineers official Japanese peace treaty 9/51
- To station troops in disarmed Japan 9/51
- Defence pact with Australia and New Zealand 9/51
- Security pact with Yugoslavia 11/51
- Allies delay West German NATO membership 2/52
- Senator McMahon praises new UK deterrent 2/52
- Uses germ warfare, Manchuria, claim 3/52
- Doubles defence aid to Britain 3/52
- Truman signs official end to Pacific War 4/52
- Defence pact with Philippines 4/52
- Troops kill 30 Red prisoners, Koje 6/52
- 160 planes attack North Korea, near USSR 9/52
- Guards kill 52 rioting Chinese PoWs 10/52
- Truman blames Eisenhower for Berlin 10/52
- John Foster Dulles Secretary of State 11/52
- Accuses USSR of arming Viet Minh 11/52
- Eisenhower talks peace with MacArthur 12/52
- Dulles warns of "domino effect" in East 5/53
- Fears Viet Minh successes in Indochina 5/53
- Third Infantry stops Chinese Korea attack 6/53
- Senate bars China's entry to UN 6/53
- General Clark welcomes Korean War's end 7/53
- $45 million grant to Iran 9/53
- Condemns Israeli raid on Jordan, UN 11/53
- President warns against US in Indochina 2/54
- Eisenhower talks Indochina with French 3/54
- Eisenhower anti-Red policy, Asia 3/54
- Bomb creator Oppenheimer "security risk" 4/54
- Dulles warns China not to aid Vietnamese 4/54
- Study plan for South-East Asian "NATO" 4/54
- Eisenhower and Churchill: Potomac Agreement 6/54
- Dulles and Eden accept Vietnam partition 6/54
- Indochina War ends; "victory for Reds"? 7/54
- Seventh Fleet to stop China invading Taiwan 8/54
- Two officers killed, Chinese Quemoy raid 9/54
- Polish security boss Swiatlo gets asylum 9/54
- Adenauer comes for talks with Eisenhower 6/55
- Agreement on exchange of nuclear information with UK 6/55
- Geneva summit with USSR, UK and France 7/55
- Franco and Dulles discuss Spanish relations 11/55
- To sell arms to Isreal 11/55
- Talks over financing Egypt's Aswan Dam 11/55
- Evacuates consul from North Vietnam 12/55
- Anti-US rioters burn US hospital, Jordan 1/56
- H-bomb dropped from plane, Bikini Atoll 5/56
- Bomb kills vice-consul in Cyprus 6/56
- Dulles plan to end Suez crisis 8/56
- Appeals to Israel to keep Suez peace 10/56
- Evacuates citizens from Israel and Egypt 10/56
- Anger at Anglo-French action on Suez 10/56
- Cash squeeze on UK forces Suez climbdown 11/56
- Condemns Soviet invasion of Hungary 11/56
- Ends cultural exchange with USSR 12/56
- Reports Israel is prepared to withdraw 2/57
- Restores links with UK at Bermuda talks 3/57
- US Sixth Fleet in Beirut 4/57
- Kennedy for Algerian independence 7/57
- Dulles in London for disarmament talks 7/57
- USSR unwilling to let US inspect bases 8/57
- Disappointed at USSR's space triumph 10/57
- Triumphant Royal visit 10/57
- Not to discuss missile control with USSR 10/57
- Bombs kill 18 Americans, South Vietnam 10/57
- Johnson: must overtake USSR in space 1/58
- Says USSR must join space warfare ban 1/58
- Puts first satellite Explorer in orbit 2/58
- Dulles says is losing space race 3/58
- Rejects Polish nuclear-free zone 5/58
- Nixon visits Puerto Rico 5/58
- Protests at Hungary's execution of Nagy 6/58
- Beirut wants US to stop arms to rebels 6/58
- Troops land in Beirut to aid Chamoun 7/58
- Propose UN summit with USSR 7/58
- Nautilus' trip poses war threat 8/58
- Troops leave Lebanon 10/58
- Nixon at London American Memorial Chapel 11/58
- UK, US and USSR make draft test ban treaty 12/58
- Castro visits; upholds defence treaty 4/59
- Dulles resigns through ill health 4/59
- John Foster Dulles dies - profile 5/59
- Fears of Cuban land reform 6/59
- Iraq renounces US military aid 6/59
- Khrushchev and Nixon debate at kitchen show 7/59
- Castro accuses of meddling 7/59
- Eisenhower and Macmillan: TV chat on issues 8/59
- Eisenhower gets warm welcome in Britain 8/59
- Plans for UK, USSR and France summit 8/59
- Denies Laos bases 8/59
- Eisenhower begins European tour, Berlin 8/59
- Khrushchev clashes with mayor on US tour 9/59
- Signs Antarctic "science reserve" treaty 12/59
- Withdraws support from S. Korea's Rhee 4/60
- USSR shoots down U-2; US denies spying 5/60
- Summit fails as US refuses to apologise 5/60
- 120 Air Force planes sent to south-east Asia 6/60
- Japanese riots against treaty; one dies 6/60
- U-2 pilot Powers indicted as spy, USSR 7/60
- Khrushchev backs Cuba to expel US troops 7/60
- Powers gets ten years for spying, USSR 8/60
- Assistant Secretary Wilcox angers USSR 10/60
- Breaks off diplomatic relations with Cuba 1/61
- Increases money and arms for Laos 3/61
- Cuban exiles invade Cuba at Bay of Pigs 4/61
- Agrees on more funding to South Vietnam 5/61
- Objects to building of Berlin Wall 8/61
- Wants atmospheric nuclear tests ban 9/61
- Faces Soviet tanks along Berlin border 10/61
- More advisers for South Vietnam 11/61
- Vietcong kills first US soldier 12/61
- More aid for Vietnam announced 1/62
- Walks out of nuclear test ban talks 1/62
- Imposes embargo on Cuban imports 2/62
- 1,179 Bay of Pigs invaders jailed, Cuba 4/62
- Atmospheric nuclear tests will resume 4/62
- Forces to be sent to Thailand 5/62
- In talks with new Laotian leader 7/62
- Kennedy given new powers in Cuban crisis 9/62
- Cuban missile crisis 10/62
- Imposes arms blockade of Cuba 10/62
- Says all Cuban missile bases destroyed 11/62
- Lifts blockade of Cuba 11/62
- Will remove missile bases from Turkey 11/62
- Agrees to sell Polaris missiles to UK 12/62
- Agrees to sell Polaris to France 12/62
- Linus Pauling wins Peace Nobel 12/62
- De Gaulle rejects offer of Polaris 1/63
- UK signs Polaris deal 4/63
- Tells Diem to redress Vietnam grievances 6/63
- Kennedy visits Berlin Wall 6/63
- Agrees to establish hot line with USSR 6/63
- Agrees to partial test ban treaty 7/63
- Signature of partial test ban treaty 8/63
- Hot line with Kremlin opens 8/63
- Worried by South Vietnam's hard line 9/63
- Recognises new South Vietnam government 11/63
- 5,000 advisers to be sent to Vietnam 7/64
- Congress supports LBJ's Vietnam actions 8/64
- Told by USSR to halt actions in Vietnam 8/64
- Wants Diego Garcia as military base 8/64
- Vietcong attacks US base at Bien Hoa 11/64
- Planes pound North Vietnam 2/65
- LBJ sends Marines into Vietnam 3/65
- Aids leaders of Dominican coup 4/65
- South Vietnam aid to be increased 4/65
- Marines withdrawn from Dominica 6/65
- Another 50,000 troops sent to Vietnam 7/65
- Johnson welcomes refugees from Cuba 10/65
- Recognises new regime in Ghana 3/66
- Rusk says France not vital to NATO 4/66
- LBJ pays surprise visit to Vietnam 10/66
- Svetlana Alliluyeva arrives 4/67
- LBJ authorises N. Vietnam bomb targets 8/67

- Rusk says Vietnam escalation inevitable 11/67
- Ho sends greeting to war protesters 12/67
- North Korea seizes "spy ship" Pueblo 1/68
- Nuclear-bomb plane crashes in Greenland 1/68
- North Korea refuses to free the Pueblo 2/68
- LBJ to send up to 50,000 more to Vietnam 3/68
- Ends some bombing of North Vietnam 5/68
- Talks on Vietnam peace deal in Paris 5/68
- 36 nations sign nuclear non-proliferation pact 7/68
- Nixon tells US to reduce Vietnam role 8/68
- To halt bombing of North Vietnam 10/68
- Orders total end to N. Vietnam bombing 11/68
- N. Korea frees crew of spy ship Pueblo 12/68
- Eleven US prisoners to be freed, Cambodia 12/68
- Nixon holds talks with Wilson in London 2/69
- Death toll in Vietnam exceeds Korea toll 4/69
- Nixon visits Rumania 8/69
- Recognises Gaddafi's regime in Libya 9/69
- Orders B-52 raids on N. Vietnam to go on 9/69
- US officer charged with Mylai massacre 11/69
- Bombing raids on Laos escalate 11/69
- Pompidou gets hostile reception, Chicago 2/70
- Bombs Ho Chi Minh trail, Laos 3/70
- To close its consulate in Rhodesia 3/70
- Cambodian premier asks for US arms 3/70
- Nixon sends US troops into Cambodia 4/70
- Disaster relief flown into Pakistan 11/70
- Norman Borlaug wins Peace Nobel 12/70
- Secret-equipment plane shot down, Laos 12/70
- Nixon warns USSR subs to avoid Cuba 1/71
- Calley found guilty of Mylai massacre 3/71
- US Senate blasted by Laos protest bomb 3/71
- Nixon vows to take US out of Vietnam 4/71
- IRA sinks RN launch in Baltimore, US 4/71
- Newspapers publish "Pentagon Papers" 6/71
- Policy on the two Chinas defeated at UN 10/71
- Israel bars 21 black Jewish Americans 10/71
- Nixon meets Tito in Washington 10/71
- Mrs Gandhi visits for talks 11/71
- 45,000 more US troops to leave Vietnam 11/71
- Resumes bombing of North Vietnam 12/71
- Nixon urges better relations in China 2/72
- Steps up bombing of North Vietnam 4/72
- Nixon and Brezhnev sign nuclear pact 5/72
- Signs accord on Berlin's status 6/72
- Science and technology pact with USSR 7/72
- Combat troops withdrawn from Vietnam 8/72
- Halts $3 million loan to Uganda 9/72
- Signs SALT agreement with USSR 10/72
- Kissinger says Vietnam peace is near 10/72
- Tries to force Hanoi into cease-fire 11/72
- Nixon orders halt to Hanoi bombing 12/72
- Vietnam War ceasefire agreed 1/73
- CIA "conspired to stop Allende" in Chile 3/73
- Resumes bombing of Laos 4/73
- Cambodia bombing funds to be cut off 5/73
- Nixon and Brezhnev in talks, US 6/73
- US court says Cambodia bombing must end 7/73
- Bombing of Cambodia officially ends 8/73
- Saudi Arabia cuts oil supplies to US 8/73
- US forces put on alert (Yom Kippur war) 10/73
- Huge airlift of arms for Israel 10/73
- OPEC imposes oil embargo on US 10/73
- Attacks Europe for Yom Kippur war stand 10/73
- Kissinger wins Nobel Peace Prize 10/73
- Nixon promises aid to Lon Nol, Cambodia 2/74
- Restores diplomatic ties with Egypt 2/74
- OPEC lifts oil embargo 3/74
- Kissinger mediates in Middle East 5/74
- Resumes diplomatic ties with Syria 6/74
- Nixon talks with Brezhnev in Moscow 6/74
- Prepares to evacuate Cambodia 1/75
- CIA planned to kill Castro, claim 3/75
- Ford says USA will honour commitments 4/75
- Evacuates Embassy in Saigon as Reds win 4/75
- Proof of CIA plot to kill Castro 5/75
- Apollo spacecraft joins USSR Soyuz 7/75
- Ford hopes Helsinki accord is sincere 8/75
- Senate finds CIA plotted against leaders 11/75
- CIA aimed at Castro, Lumumba and Trujillo 11/75
- CIA's Colby backs UNITA and FNLA in Angola 11/75
- Senate uncovers Dutch Lockheed scandal 2/76
- Nixon admits CIA acted against Allende 3/76
- Evacuates 263 from Beirut 6/76
- Envoy Francis Meloy killed in Lebanon 6/76
- Kissinger forces Rhodesia to compromise 9/76
- Vietnam says six missing US pilots are dead 9/76
- Ford's gaffe over Eastern Europe 10/76
- To renegotiate Panama Canal Treaty 10/76
- Talks with Vietnam in Paris 11/76
- Vetoes Vietnam's UN application 11/76
- Kissinger briefs President-elect Carter 11/76
- Cuts aid to Uruguay, Argentina and Ethiopia over human rights 2/77
- Amin traps US citizens in Uganda 2/77
- Israel's Rabin talks with Carter 3/77
- Carter calls for action at London summit 5/77
- Carter angered by Begin's West Bank policy 7/77
- Carter calls on Arabs to talk to Israel 7/77
- Treaty gives Canal to Panama by 1999 9/77
- Carter offers to help Arab-Israeli pact 12/77
- Carter flies to Poland and Saudi Arabia 12/77
- Carter: Jordan role in Palestinian case 12/77
- Begin tells Carter ready to return Sinai to Egypt 12/77
- Criticises new Rhodesia deal 2/78
- Somalis make secret approaches to US for military backing 2/78
- Soviet envoy at UN, Shevchenko, defects 4/78
- Senate approves Canal treaty 4/78
- Alleges Embassy in Moscow is bugged 6/78
- Plans for Sadat and Begin talks 8/78
- Forces Nicaragua's Somoza to resign 9/78
- Carter helps forge Egypt-Israel accord 9/78
- Gromyko and Carter discuss arms limits 10/78
- Congressman Ryan killed by Jones sect 11/78
- Attends four-nation Guadeloupe summit 1/79
- Breaks off relations with Nicaragua 2/79
- Sponsors Israel and Egypt peace treaty 3/79
- Carter and Brezhnev sign SALT 2 arms treaty 6/79
- Senator Jackson fights SALT 2 6/79
- USSR and US ceiling of 2,250 missiles 6/79
- Helps replace Somoza in Nicaragua 7/79
- Carter and Kennedy condemn Mountbatten bomb 8/79
- Exiled Shah treated for cancer, New York 10/79
- Embassy in Iran besieged; 100 hostages 11/79
- Iranian students protest at Shah in US 11/79
- Blacks and women released from Embassy in Iran 11/79
- Embassy in Pakistan stormed; police rescue 11/79
- Iran cancels foreign debts 11/79
- Embassy in Libya attacked and burned 12/79
- Six diplomats flee from Canada's Iranian embassy 1/80
- Carter to delay SALT over Afghanistan 1/80
- USA wants Olympic boycott on Afghanistan 3/80
- Khomeini backs US hostage takers 3/80
- Iran Commission will not condemn Shah 3/80
- Iran rescue bid ends in desert crash 4/80
- Carter takes responsibility for failure of hostage rescue 4/80
- Boycotts Moscow Olympics over Afghanistan issue 7/80
- One US hostage released in Tehran 7/80
- Neutral in Iran-Iraq war 9/80
- Nuns and missionary killed in El Salvador 12/80
- Suspends aid to El Salvador 12/80
- Iran releases US hostages 1/81
- Senate threatens to cut El Salvador aid 4/81
- Reagan to sell arms to China 6/81
- China deal angers USSR 6/81
- Blocks jet fighters to Israel 7/81
- Poland blocks visiting unionists 9/81
- Four US presidents pay tribute to Anwar Sadat 10/81
- Polish Ambassador given asylum 12/81
- Speakes condemns Israel's Golan moves 12/81
- Haig and Gromyko talk for eight hours 1/82
- Poor orders sink UK's De Lorean cars 2/82
- Reagan to send El Salvador emergency aid 2/82
- El Salvador soldiers on nun murder charge 2/82
- Threatens USSR over Poland martial law 2/82
- Ambassador to Nicaragua denies attack 3/82
- Haig to mediate in Falklands crisis 4/82
- Argentina and UK reject Haig plan 4/82
- Abandons Falklands neutrality, backs UK 4/82
- Reagan orders economic sanctions against Argentina 4/82
- Haig quits as Secretary; Shultz succeeds 6/82
- Reagan visits UK; addresses Parliament 6/82
- Bans companies from Siberian pipeline 8/82
- Marines to act as Beirut peace-keepers 9/82
- Demands Israelis and Syrians leave Lebanon 9/82
- To ease sanctions on pipeline 9/82
- UK women blockade Greenham Cruise base 12/82
- Reagan dubs USSR the "evil empire" 3/83
- Reagan proposes "Star Wars" system 3/83
- Embassy in Beirut destroyed by car bomb 4/83
- Reagan seeks more aid to El Salvador 4/83
- Reagan sides with Contras in Nicaragua 5/83
- Denies visa to Bernadette McAliskey 6/83
- Shultz reaffirms support for Marcos 6/83
- MacFarlane is roving Middle East envoy 7/83
- Congress votes to end aid to Contras 7/83
- Sends planes to Chad 8/83
- Admits protecting Barbie after the war 8/83
- Lifts ban on pipeline parts to USSR 8/83
- CIA denies Korean flight 007 was spying 9/83
- 299 die in Shia kamikaze raids, Lebanon 10/83
- US Marines invade Grenada 10/83
- US Marines to remain in Lebanon 10/83
- Vetoes UN resolution on Grenada 10/83
- Syria frees shot-down US airman 1/84
- Reagan in talks with Chinese premier 1/84
- Head of US University in Beirut murdered 1/84
- Peace-keeping force pulls out of Lebanon 2/84
- Senate vetoes mining of Nicaraguan ports 4/84
- Reagan visits Beijing 4/84
- World Court opposes US action, Nicaragua 5/84
- Endorses plans to combat world terrorism 6/84
- Martin Galvin of Noraid visits Belfast 8/84
- Ambassador in Beirut wounded 9/84
- Withdraws from UNESCO 1/85
- Time magazine cleared of Sharon libel 1/85
- UK PM Thatcher supports Star Wars 2/85
- Thatcher asks for end to US aid to IRA 2/85
- Congress rejects aid to Contras 4/85
- Reagan plans Sandinista trade embargo 4/85
- Reagan visits Bitburg war cemetery 5/85
- Reagan addresses European Parliament 5/85
- 39 US hostages held for 16 days, Beirut 6/85
- Live Aid concert 7/85
- Reagan brands five terrorist states 7/85
- Votes to impose sanctions on S. Africa 8/85
- American killed in Achille Lauro hijack 10/85
- Angry at Italy's freeing of hijacker 10/85
- Reagan-Gorbachev summit in Geneva 11/85
- Withdraws support for Marcos regime 2/86
- Marcos arrives in Hawaii 2/86
- John Demjanjuk extradited to Israel 2/86
- Clashes with Libya in Gulf of Sirte 3/86
- Bomb explodes in GI discotheque, Berlin 4/86
- Launches air strike against Libya 4/86
- Svetlana Alliluyeva returns to US 4/86
- Contra aid ruled illegal by World Court 6/86
- Anglo-US extradition treaty ratified 7/86
- Senate votes for S. Africa sanctions 8/86
- Zimbabwean minister insults US 9/86
- Stops aid to Zimbabwe 9/86
- USSR holds US journalist for spying 9/86
- USSR frees US journalist Daniloff 9/86
- Frees Soviet UN employee Zakharov 9/86
- Congress votes for S. Africa sanctions 9/86
- Big US firms pull out of South Africa 10/86
- Reagan-Gorbachev summit in Iceland 10/86
- Reagan sanctions veto overridden 10/86
- US pilot captured in Nicaragua 10/86
- "Irangate" row erupts 11/86
- US helicopters to ferry Honduran troops into Nicaragua 12/86
- Elie Wiesel wins Peace Nobel 12/86
- Esso to "disinvest" in South Africa 12/86
- Reagan "regrets" Iran arms deal 1/87
- Demjanjuk denies Nazi crimes 2/87
- Senate halts Contra aid 2/87
- Caution over Gorbachev's arms cut plans 4/87
- Iraqi jets hit frigate Stark, Gulf: 28 die; Reagan protests 5/87
- 28 die aboard Stark; Reagan protests 5/87
- Poindexter authorised funding for Contras 7/87
- North defends funds diversion 7/87
- Thatcher refuses US Gulf minesweepers 7/87
- Plans to reflag Kuwaiti tankers, Gulf 7/87
- Ships find eight Gulf mines 9/87
- Navy attacks Iranian oil platforms, Gulf 10/87
- Iran ship attacks US-flagged tanker 10/87
- Wall Street fall hits Japan and Britain 10/87
- Irangate report blames Reagan 11/87
- Reagan and Gorbachev sign missile treaty 12/87
- Reagan's first visit to USSR 5/88
- Refuse Yassir Arafat an entry visa 11/88
- US will open dialogue with PLO 12/88
- Bush makes his first visit to China as President 2/89
- PLO holds first formal talks with new US administration 3/89
- Cuts relations with Panama 9/89
- Bush and Gorbachev announce end of Cold War 12/89
- US troops invade Panama and oust Noriega 12/89
- Agrees with USSR on new arms cuts 6/90
- US Marines rescue US citizens stranded in Liberian civil war 8/90
- President Bush warns Iraqis not to cross Kuwaiti border 8/90
- US Marines intercept Iraqi freighter in the Gulf 9/90
- US Air Force chief of staff to be sacked over Iraq comments 9/90
- Four Allied powers sign German sovereignty treaty 9/90
- Bush says that there is no room for negotiated peace in Gulf 10/90
- President Bush spends Thanksgiving Day with US troops 11/90
- Bush seeks to open talks with Iraq 11/90
- Saddam refuses to meet US officials before January 12 12/90
- Talks avert US-Europe trade war 12/90
- Last-minute talks between US and Iraq to avert war fail 1/91
- Operation Desert Storm is launched in the Gulf 1/91
- Regards RAF's tactic bombing of Iraqi airfields as suicidal 1/91
- Bush under pressure from Israel over Iraqi missile attacks 1/91
- Bush dismisses Saddam's peace offer as "cruel hoax" 2/91
- Bush orders Saddam Hussein to withdraw from Kuwait 2/91
- 400 civilians killed in US Stealth bomber raid on Baghdad 2/91
- Two Iraqi Republican Guards divisions surrounded by Allies 2/91
- Gulf War officially over 2/91
- US hostage, Edward Tracy, freed in Lebanon 8/91
- Strategic Arms Reduction Treaty signed in Moscow 8/91
- Bush angers Israel by refusing $10bn loan 9/91
- Signs free trade bloc agreement with Canada and Mexico 8/92
- USAF planes begin enforcing "no-fly" zone in southern Iraq 8/92
- US Marines invade Somalia to bring humanitarian aid 12/92
- Bush and Yeltsin sign START-2 Treaty in Moscow 1/93
- US, British and French planes carry out air strikes on Iraq 1/93
- US agrees to send troops to Bosnia as part of peace plan 2/93
- US Air Force drops emergency aid to trapped Bosnian Moslems 3/93
- Military contacts resumed with China 11/93
- US fighters shoot down their own helicopters over Iraq 4/94
- Clinton Administration halts call for N. Korea sanctions 6/94
- King Hussein and Mr Rabin sign declaration in Washington 7/94
- US Marines in Haiti to clear way for President Aristide 9/94
- Dole proposes moving US Embassy from Tel Aviv to Jerusalem 5/95

USA (politics)

- Hawaii becomes American territory 4/00
- Republican McKinley elected President 11/00
- McKinley inaugurated 3/01
- McKinley killed; Roosevelt takes over 9/01
- President Roosevelt opposes colour bar 11/02
- Recognises Republic of Panama; canal treaty 11/03
- Republicans nominate Roosevelt and Warren 6/04
- Democrats nominate Judge Alton Parker 7/04
- President Roosevelt re-elected 11/04
- Crowds cheer Roosevelt's inauguration 3/05
- Elections: Republicans' victory avalanche 11/06
- Roosevelt wins Nobel Peace Prize 12/06
- Republicans nominate Taft 6/08
- Taft wins presidential election 11/08
- No direct election of senators 2/11
- US senators to be directly elected 6/11
- New Mexico becomes 47th state 1/12
- Arizona becomes 48th state 2/12
- Presidential candidates to show expenses 4/12
- Roosevelt goes independent; party splits 6/12
- Republicans choose Taft; drop Roosevelt 6/12
- Democrats nominate progressive Wilson 7/12
- New party, the Progressive: "Bull Moose" 8/12
- Democrat Wilson elected President 11/12
- Bull Moose pushes Republicans into third place 11/12
- Socialist gains in presidential election 11/12
- Federal income tax introduced 2/13
- Woodrow Wilson inaugurated 3/13
- Wilson asserts authority over Congress 4/13
- Navy chief Fiske resigns 4/13
- 17th Amendment comes into effect 5/13
- Roosevelt criticises US neutrality 11/14
- Wilson warns Germany over ship attacks 2/15
- State Department fury as Lusitania sinks 5/15
- Secretary of State resigns over war stand 6/15
- Inquiry into German spies 8/15
- Wilson to expand Army 10/15
- Wilson's defence plans 11/15
- German attaches dismissed 12/15
- Wilson wants standing army of 142,000 12/15
- War debate; Wilson says Navy is ready 1/16
- National Defense Act increases National Guard to 450,000 6/16
- Republicans nominate Charles E. Hughes 6/16
- Democrats renominate President Wilson 6/16
- Buys Danish Virgin Islands 8/16
- Wilson promises women vote 9/16
- War main election issue; Wilson attacked 10/16
- Wilson re-elected in close struggle 11/16
- First woman member of Congress 11/16
- Enters war; overwhelming Congress vote 4/17
- 91 German ships seized, New York 4/17
- Food, fuel and export controls 7/17
- Wilson rejects Pope's peace plan 8/17
- Wilson supports women's suffrage 10/17
- Senate votes for prohibition 12/17
- House votes for women's suffrage 1/18
- Wilson visits France and Britain 12/18
- Wilson has a nervous breakdown; ends tour 9/19
- Governor Coolidge re-elected 11/19
- 2,700 arrested in "Red Scare" 1/20
- House Democrats against compulsory army 2/20
- Senate disagrees over League compromise 2/20
- Women picket British Embassy over Irish issue 4/20
- Congressmen want Irish prisoners freed 5/20
- Republicans nominate Harding 6/20
- Disorder at Democratic Convention over Irish and Prohibition 6/20
- Democrats choose Cox and Franklin Roosevelt 7/20
- Wilson's Democratic nominee McAdoo fails 7/20
- 19th amendment: US women get to vote in federal elections 8/20
- Republican Harding convincingly elected 11/20
- Wilson wins Nobel Peace prize 12/20
- Wilson's last speech to Congress 12/20
- President Harding wants simple welcome 1/21
- Herbert Hoover is Commerce Secretary 2/21
- Harding and Coolidge sworn in 3/21
- Lynching bill blocked by Democrats 12/21
- Warren will run again 3/23
- Ku Klux Klan blasts foreign alliances 6/23
- Harding tours Alaska 7/23
- Harding ill with poisoning 7/23
- Coolidge succeeds Harding as President 8/23
- President Harding dies 8/23
- Ex-Minister Fall accused in oil scandal 10/23
- Senate committee finds oil deal swindle 10/23
- Coolidge to free political prisoners 11/23
- Coolidge bids for Republican nomination 12/23
- Ex-President Wilson reported ill 1/24
- Ex-President Wilson dies - profile 2/24
- Attorney-General resigns in oil scandal 3/24
- Coolidge sacks Senate-spying Daugherty 3/24
- Coolidge wins Republican nomination 4/24
- Coolidge wants to cut taxes and spending 6/24
- Democrats nominate Davis and Bryan 7/24
- Navy wants its own air force 9/25
- Coolidge warns against large air force 2/26
- Texas governor Miriam Ferguson resigns 7/26
- Socialist leader Debs dies 10/26
- Texas black voting ban overturned 3/27
- Coolidge calls for flood aid in south 5/27
- Coolidge will not run again 8/27
- Government takes Teapot Dome oil fields 10/27
- Coolidge and $1 billion naval expansion 12/27
- Coolidge will not run again 1/28
- Candidate Hoover will keep Prohibition 1/28
- Worries over Prohibition gangsters 10/28
- Herbert Hoover easily elected President 11/28
- Jovial Catholic Al Smith defeated 11/28
- Republican Hoover's deputy, C. Curtis 11/28
- New President want to "abolish poverty" 11/28
- Herbert Hoover inaugurated 3/29
- Wall Street slump 10/29
- Hoover wants funds for job creation 11/29
- William Taft, ex-President, dies 3/30
- Two unemployment protesters die in clash 3/30
- Police issue blacklist of "Communists" 3/30

USA (politics)

- Governor Roosevelt's unemployment board 3/30
- Re-elected Roosevelt denies presidency 11/30
- Democrats win control of House 11/30
- Hoover asks for $150 million for jobless 12/30
- Roosevelt will run for President 1/32
- States begin study of 20th Amendment: "lame duck" period 3/32
- Republicans renominate President Hoover 6/32
- Roosevelt nominated on fourth ballot 7/32
- Roosevelt champions Depression victims 7/32
- Hoover wants Prohibition abolished 8/32
- Roosevelt for five-day week and jobless aid 10/32
- Roosevelt elected President by landslide 11/32
- Roosevelt promises electorate "New Deal" 11/32
- Coolidge, 30th President, dies 1/33
- Zingara shoots at President Roosevelt 2/33
- 500,000 cheer Roosevelt in Washington, DC 3/33
- Emergency Congress session 3/33
- Roosevelt backs anti-Prohibition law 3/33
- Congress passes the Emergency Banking Act 3/33
- Roosevelt cuts $144 million off military spending 4/33
- Storm over RCA building's Marxist mural 5/33
- Prohibition ends; Utah last to ratify 12/33
- Republican La Guardia appointed New York Mayor 12/33
- $21 million for war veterans 1/34
- Senator Long wants Louisiana to secede 11/34
- Welfare for old, sick and unemployed 8/35
- Senator Huey Long killed by opponents 9/35
- Democrats endorse Roosevelt for election 1/36
- Senator Long's widow takes over 1/36
- Governor Landon is Republican candidate 6/36
- Democrats choose Roosevelt to run again 6/36
- Roosevelt's landslide re-election 11/36
- Roosevelt's hopeful inauguration speech 1/37
- Roosevelt attacks Supreme Court 2/37
- Hoover says Roosevelt is "court packing" 2/37
- Roosevelt's "liberal judge" was a Klansman 9/37
- Democrats lose 72 seats in Congress poll 11/38
- Roosevelt chosen as Democratic candidate 7/40
- Conscription for men 21 to 35 9/40
- Roosevelt wins third presidential term 11/40
- Roosevelt inaugurated for third term 1/41
- Biggest-ever budget estimate 1/42
- Price freeze on major domestic items 4/42
- Navy signs up its first ever black recruits 5/42
- Freeze on wages, rents and farm prices 10/42
- Coffee rationing begins 11/42
- Petrol rationing begins 12/42
- Shoe rationing introduced 2/43
- Coal strike called off 5/43
- Truman is Roosevelt's running mate 7/44
- Roosevelt agrees to run for fourth term 7/44
- Roosevelt wins record fourth term 11/44
- Roosevelt inaugurated for fourth term 1/45
- Roosevelt dies on eve of war victory 4/45
- Harry S. Truman sworn in as President 4/45
- First atomic bomb tests, New Mexico 7/45
- Japanese surrender announced 8/45
- Rationing of petrol and fuel oil ends 8/45
- Roosevelt not to blame for Pearl Harbor 7/46
- Harriman appointed Commerce Secretary 9/46
- Republicans win control of both Houses 11/46
- Congress televised for first time 1/47
- George Marshall is Secretary of State 1/47
- Ex-Mayor of New York, La Guardia, dies 9/47
- Reagan warns against Hollywood witchhunt 10/47
- Appeal for meatless days to help Europe 10/47
- Inquiry into communism in Hollywood 10/47
- Omar Bradley becomes US Army supremo 2/48
- Inquiries into Communist spy ring open 8/48
- Truman wins presidential election 11/48
- Kansas ends Prohibition 11/48
- Hiss accused of passing secrets to USSR 12/48
- Hiss indicted for perjury 12/48
- Dean Acheson is Secretary of State 1/49
- Truman inaugurated as President 1/49
- Ezra Pound wins Bollingen Poetry Prize 2/49
- Wave of anti-Communist hysteria 6/49
- Marshall becomes head of US Red Cross 9/49
- "Tokyo Rose" found guilty of treason 9/49
- "Tokyo Rose" jailed for ten years 10/49
- Alger Hiss jailed for perjury 1/50
- Joseph McCarthy starts anti-Red crusade 2/50
- Alaska to be admitted as 49th state 3/50
- Truman denounces McCarthy 3/50
- Truman survives assassination attempt 11/50
- State of emergency over Korean War 12/50
- Truman wants $60 million for defence 1/51
- Truman's Internal Security Commission 1/51
- President to be limited to two terms 2/51
- 22nd Amendment's opponents fear lame duck 2/51
- Eisenhower will run for Republicans 1/52
- Truman pulls out of presidential race 3/52
- Eisenhower wants to resign as NATO chief 4/52
- Congress passes immigration bill 6/52
- Eisenhower wins Republican nomination 7/52
- Nixon is Eisenhower's running mate 7/52
- Adlai Stevenson is Democratic candidate 7/52
- Stevenson: equal job rights for blacks 9/52
- Truman calls Eisenhower "inept tool" 9/52
- Nixon clears name in TV "Checkers" talk 9/52
- Chaplin investigated as "subversive" 9/52
- Eisenhower wins with largest vote 11/52
- Nixon is youngest ever Vice-President 11/52
- Republicans do less well in Senate poll 11/52
- John Kennedy beats Lodge, Massachusetts 11/52
- Eisenhower inaugurated 1/53
- Eisenhower rejects Rosenbergs' clemency 2/53
- Chaplin called a Communist; shuns US 4/53
- 5,000 vigil against Rosenberg execution 6/53
- McCarthy says Truman aided Communists 11/53
- Eisenhower wants 18-year-olds to vote 1/54
- McCarthy investigates Communists in the Army 2/54
- Army Secretary Stevens blasts McCarthy 2/54
- Eisenhower backs Stevens over McCarthy 2/54
- Senate votes $214,000 for McCarthy cause 2/54
- "Greatly increased" weapons production 4/54
- Supreme Court outlaws school segregation 5/54
- White South defies Court on segregation 5/54
- Oppenheimer found "loyal and discreet" 6/54
- McCarthy "finds" Communists in CIA 6/54
- Eisenhower blocks McCarthy on CIA 6/54
- Communist Party outlawed 8/54
- Lyndon Johnson heads Senate 11/54
- Congress condemns McCarthy 12/54
- Small Republican backlash over McCarthy 12/54
- Kennedy back in Senate after surgery 5/55
- Eisenhower suffers mild heart attack 9/55
- Eisenhower fit to run again, says doctor 2/56
- Nixon to seek vice-presidency again 4/56
- Kennedy's bid for vice-presidency 6/56
- Eisenhower will run for second term 7/56
- Hubert Humphrey to seek vice-presidency 7/56
- Eisenhower and Nixon are Republican candidates 8/56
- Eisenhower re-elected President 11/56
- Stevenson warns against Nixon; loses 11/56
- Miller convicted for not naming "Reds" 5/57
- Senator Joseph McCarthy dies 5/57
- Eisenhower suffers mild stroke 11/57
- Johnson: US must overtake USSR in space race 1/58
- House approves Alaskan statehood 5/58
- Arthur Miller's conviction overthrown 8/58
- Big Democratic gains in Congress 11/58
- Hawaii statehood approved 3/59
- Dulles resigns through ill health 4/59
- John Foster Dulles dies - profile 5/59
- Nuclear submarine with Polaris missiles 6/59
- Stevenson will not run again 6/59
- General George Marshall dies 10/59
- Rockefeller not to run for President 12/59
- Kennedy seeks Democratic nomination 1/60
- Nixon and Kennedy favourites after primary 3/60
- Byrd leads Democratic bid to stop Kennedy 4/60
- Kennedy hampered by Catholicism 4/60
- Humphrey leaves race after Kennedy wins 5/60
- Kennedy's "New Frontier" speech 7/60
- Kennedy and Johnson are Democrat candidates 7/60
- Nixon is Republican candidate 7/60
- First national televised debate: "draw" 9/60
- Debate: Kennedy calls Nixon "uncaring" 9/60
- Kennedy wins presidency narrowly 11/60
- Kennedy to use intellectuals 11/60
- Kennedy sworn in as youngest President 1/61
- Kissinger made national security adviser 2/61
- Kennedy forms Peace Corps 3/61
- Integrationists attacked in Alabama 5/61
- Kennedy calls for more defence spending 7/61
- Goldwater is darling of American right 3/62
- Martin Luther King jailed 7/62
- Southern college admits black student 9/62
- Riots follow college admission of black 9/62
- 200 arrested at Mississippi University riots 10/62
- Edward Kennedy elected to the Senate 11/62
- Death of Eleanor Roosevelt 11/62
- 187 anti-segregationists freed from jail 2/63
- Governor George Wallace to defy race law 4/63
- Martin Luther King arrested 4/63
- Race riot in Alabama: troops go in 5/63
- 1,000 arrested on Alabama rights march 5/63
- Wallace to defy court on race 6/63
- National Guards protect black students 6/63
- Civil rights leader Medgar Evans shot 6/63
- Riots in South following Evans shooting 6/63
- Luther King: "I have a dream" speech 8/63
- Biggest civil rights demo yet 8/63
- Black student Meredith receives diploma 8/63
- Four black girls killed by bomb in church 9/63
- Wallace orders high school sealed off 9/63
- Kennedy controls Alabama's National Guard 9/63
- 189 blacks arrested during rights demo 9/63
- John F. Kennedy shot dead in Dallas 11/63
- Lyndon Johnson sworn in as President 11/63
- Warren inquiry into Kennedy murder 11/63
- Goldwater is presidential candidate 1/64
- LBJ to wage "war against poverty" 1/64
- Jackie Kennedy thanks nation 1/64
- Malcolm X to form his own Moslem group 3/64
- General Douglas MacArthur dies 4/64
- Martin Luther King jailed 6/64
- Three rights workers missing after arrest 6/64
- Sailors to search for rights workers 6/64
- LBJ signs sweeping Civil Rights Act 7/64
- National Guard quell New York race riots 7/64
- Goldwater chosen as Republican candidate 7/64
- Bodies of three missing rights workers found 8/64
- Johnson signs anti-poverty bill 8/64
- Warren Commission report published 9/64
- Robert Kennedy to run for Senate 9/64
- Martin Luther King awarded Peace Nobel 10/64
- Two charged with murder of rights workers 10/64
- Herbert Hoover dies 10/64
- LBJ wins presidential landslide 11/64
- Robert and Edward Kennedy become senators 11/64
- Johnson sworn in as 36th President 1/65
- King jailed after race protest 2/65
- Malcolm X shot dead 2/65
- 25,000 on Alabama civil rights march 3/65
- First black graduates from Alabama University 5/65
- Death sentence abolished in NY State 6/65
- Luther King calls for end to Vietnam War 7/65
- Statesman Adlai Stevenson dies 7/65
- Race riots flare in Watts, Los Angeles 8/65
- Lurleen Wallace runs for Governor, Alabama 2/66
- Death of Admiral Chester Nimitz 2/66
- L. Wallace is Democratic candidate, Alabama 5/66
- 8,000 in anti-Vietnam demonstration 5/66
- Reagan nominated as California Governor 6/66
- Black student Meredith shot in back 6/66
- Race riots flare in several cities 7/66
- Black children taken to all-white school 9/66
- Reagan elected California Governor 11/66
- Edward Brooke is first black senator 11/66
- Reagan sworn in as California Governor 1/67
- Lurleen Wallace becomes Alabama Governor 1/67
- Cassius Clay stripped of boxing title 4/67
- Over 200,000 on anti-Vietnam demonstrations 4/67
- Clay indicted for refusing draft 5/67
- First black member of Supreme Court 6/67
- Race riots sweep through several cities 7/67
- Nazi George Rockwell shot dead 8/67
- Shirley Temple Black stands for Congress 8/67
- Reagan urges escalation of Vietnam War in order to end it 9/67
- Anti-war demonstration at Pentagon turns violent 10/67
- Singer Joan Baez arrested at demonstration 10/67
- LBJ says war protests do not aid peace 11/67
- Governor Romney (Michigan) to run for President 11/67
- Spock indicted for anti-draft activities 1/68
- Richard Nixon to run for President 2/68
- George Wallace to run for President 2/68
- Johnson not to stand for re-election 3/68
- Robert Kennedy to run for President 3/68
- Martin Luther King shot dead in Memphis 4/68
- Riots in major cities after King's death 4/68
- LBJ signs Civil Rights Bill 4/68
- Hubert Humphrey to run for President 4/68
- Poor People's March 5/68
- Robert Kennedy wins two primaries 5/68
- McCarthy beats Kennedy in Oregon primary 5/68
- Robert Kennedy fatally wounded by shots 6/68
- Sirhan Sirhan charged with Kennedy's death 6/68
- Spock found guilty on draft charges 6/68
- Westmoreland becomes Army Chief of Staff 7/68
- Spock jailed for draft offences 7/68
- Humphrey wins Democratic nomination 8/68
- Police run wild at Chicago convention 8/68
- Reagan says he will run for President 8/68
- Nixon wins Republican nomination 8/68
- Rioting in Watts district of LA 8/68
- Black Power demonstration at Mexico Olympics 10/68
- Richard Nixon elected President 11/68
- Spiro Agnew is Vice-President 11/68
- Chisholm is first black Representative 11/68
- Kissinger is national security adviser 12/68
- Nixon sworn in as President 1/69
- Ray jailed for 99 years for King's murder 3/69
- Death of Dwight D. Eisenhower 3/69
- Black students sit in at Cornell University 4/69
- Sirhan executed for Kennedy killing 4/69
- Eisenhower's funeral 4/69
- Riots close two New York universities 5/69
- Edward Kennedy: Chappaquiddick disaster 7/69
- E. Kennedy admits he left accident scene 7/69
- E. Kennedy not to run for President 7/69
- Millions protest against Vietnam War 10/69
- Joseph Kennedy dies 11/69
- Police shoot dead two Black Panthers 12/69
- Four states ordered to end segregation 12/69
- Whites attack buses carrying black children 3/70
- US Indians attack two forts near Seattle 3/70
- Seven shot dead in student rioting, Ohio 4/70
- Four anti-war students killed, Kent State University 5/70
- Six blacks die in racial violence, Georgia 5/70
- JFK memorial unveiled in Dallas 6/70
- First interracial wedding in Mississippi 8/70
- Kent State students burn draft cards 9/70
- Court-martial of William Calley begins 11/70
- McGovern pledges to pull out of Vietnam 1/71
- US Senate blasted by Laos protest bomb 3/71
- Death of politician Thomas Dewey 3/71
- 30,000 on Potomac anti-war demonstration 5/71
- Newspapers publish "Pentagon Papers" 6/71
- Wallace to run for President 8/71
- Nixon to stand for re-election 1/72
- Senate passes Equal Rights Amendment 3/72
- Statesman and judge James Byrne dies 4/72
- Wallace wounded in assassination attempt 5/72
- Death of J. Edgar Hoover 5/72
- George Shultz made Treasury Secretary 5/72
- Burglars caught in Watergate offices 6/72
- Angela Davis acquitted on several counts 6/72
- Eagleton out as McGovern's running mate 7/72
- Nixon campaign manager Mitchell resigns 7/72
- McGovern wins Democratic nomination 7/72
- Wallace shooting: Bremer gets 63 years 8/72
- Democrat Shriver runs for Vice-President 8/72
- Nixon chosen as Republican candidate 8/72
- Nixon re-elected President in landslide 11/72
- American Indians seize a federal office 11/72
- Harry S. Truman dies 12/72
- Lyndon B. Johnson dies 1/73
- Nixon sworn in for second term 1/73
- American Indians take ten hostages 2/73
- Marlon Brando rejects Oscar in protest 3/73
- Top Nixon aides quit over Watergate scandal 4/73
- Nixon denies involvement in Watergate 4/73
- Ellsberg escapes Pentagon Papers charges 5/73
- Senate begins Watergate hearings 5/73
- US Indians end Wounded Knee occupation 5/73
- Politician Jeanette Rankin dies 5/73
- States can censor obscene material 6/73
- Vice-President Agnew in bribery probe 8/73
- Nixon sacks Watergate prosecutor Cox 10/73
- Spiro Agnew resigns as Vice-President 10/73
- Gerald Ford becomes Vice-President 10/73
- Ford sworn in as Vice-President 12/73
- Symbionese Liberation Army seizes Patty Hearst 2/74
- Report says Nixon knew of Watergate 3/74
- Nixon threatened with impeachment 5/74
- Kissinger threatens to resign 6/74
- Nixon ordered by court to deliver tapes 7/74
- Nixon impeachment process begins 7/74
- Politician and judge Earl Warren dies 7/74
- Nixon resigns as President 8/74
- Gerald Ford sworn in as President 8/74
- Nelson Rockefeller is Vice-President 8/74
- Ehrlichman and Dean jailed 8/74
- Spectators attacked at US Indian trial 8/74
- Ford pardons Nixon 9/74
- Students hurt in racial fighting, Boston 10/74
- Jimmy Carter is presidential candidate 12/74
- Rockefeller sworn in as Vice-President 12/74
- Nixon aides guilty of Watergate cover-up 1/75
- Pentagon wants AWAC early-warning planes 1/75
- Four Nixon aides jailed for Watergate 2/75
- Ford to run again 7/75
- Two women try to kill Ford on two occasions 9/75
- Rockefeller not to run again 11/75
- Ronald Reagan to run for President 11/75
- Jimmy Carter leads in Democratic race 1/76
- Jimmy Carter wins Democratic nomination 7/76
- "Fritz" Mondale is Carter's running mate 7/76
- Jubilation at Bicentennial 7/76
- Ford wins Republican nomination 8/76
- Ford and Carter in television debate 9/76
- Ford's gaffe over Eastern Europe 10/76
- Jimmy Carter elected President 11/76
- Stigma of Nixon harms Ford; loses poll 11/76
- Carter inaugurated 1/77
- Humphrey suffers from cancer 8/77
- Hubert Humphrey, Democrat, dies 1/78
- Carter postpones US neutron bomb 4/78
- Carter praised for Camp David triumph 9/78
- Feminists upset at wife-rape verdict 12/78
- Carter wants King birthday as national holiday 1/79
- Nelson Rockefeller dies 1/79
- Three Mile Island nuclear leak, USA 3/79
- Three Mile Island crisis over 4/79
- All DC-10s grounded after crash 5/79
- Republican Bush to run for President 5/79
- Marcuse of the New Left dies 7/79
- Ban on DC-10s lifted 7/79
- Carter faints while jogging 9/79
- Death of Seberg, actress smeared by FBI 9/79
- Pope tours USA; statement with Carter 10/79
- Kennedy beats Carter in primary 3/80
- Ronald Reagan is Republican candidate 7/80
- Conservative Reagan chooses Bush as Vice-President 7/80
- Carter and Mondale are Democratic candidates 8/80
- Kennedy's rousing convention speech 8/80
- Reagan-Carter TV debate called draw 10/80
- Carter ridicules Reagan tax plans 10/80
- Reagan wins presidency by landslide 11/80
- Hostage crisis helps defeat Carter 11/80
- Republicans regain Senate control 11/80
- Jubilation as Iran hostages return 1/81
- Reagan inaugurated 1/81
- Reagan wounded in assassination bid 3/81
- Secretary Haig says he is "in control" 3/81
- Plans to cut 37,000 federal jobs 3/81
- Ex-Vice-President Agnew took bribes 4/81
- Reagan-shooter Hinckley pleads innocent 8/81
- Registration for military draft 1/82
- Shultz replaces Haig as Foreign Secretary 6/82
- Reagan proposes "Star Wars" system 3/83
- Congress votes to end aid to Contras 7/83
- Luther King's birthday made national holiday 10/83
- Reagan to seek re-election 1/84
- Gary Hart scores in Democratic primaries 3/84
- Mondale picks Ferraro as running mate 7/84
- Reagan re-elected President 11/84
- Reagan accepts Vietnam memorial 11/84
- Donald Regan made WH chief of staff 1/85
- Pentagon accepts "nuclear winter" theory 3/85
- Edward Kennedy not to run for President 12/85
- Clint Eastwood becomes Mayor of Carmel 4/86
- Averell Harriman dies 7/86
- "Irangate" row erupts 11/86
- Poindexter resigns as Security Adviser 11/86
- Oliver North sacked from Security staff 11/86
- Democrats win control of Senate 11/86
- Reagan "regrets" Iran arms deal 1/87
- Inquiry blasts Reagan for Iran mistakes 2/87

- Inquiry says North concealed information 2/87
- Iran suspect McFarlane attempts suicide 2/87
- Governor Dukakis enters presidency race 3/87
- Hart leaves presidential race over scandal 5/87
- Oliver North, new "patriotic hero" 7/87
- Irangate report blames Reagan 11/87
- Bush leads Dole in New Hampshire primary 2/88
- Bush leads Republican presidential race 3/88
- Jackson wins Michigan Democratic Caucus 3/88
- Dukakis heads for presidential candidacy 4/88
- Reagan takes astrologer's advice 5/88
- Dukakis accepts presidential candidacy 7/88
- Bush chooses running-mate, Dan Quayle 8/88
- First woman bishop elected 9/88
- Last TV debate between Dukakis and Bush 10/88
- George Bush elected president 11/88
- Air Force makes "Stealth" fighter public 11/88
- Conspiracy charges against Oliver North are dropped 1/89
- George Bush becomes 41st President of the United States 1/89
- Senate rejects nomination of John Tower as Defence Secretary 3/89
- Oliver North guilty of minor charges in Iran-Contra affair 5/89
- Jim Wright resigns after charges of financial corruption 5/89
- Oliver North gets suspended jail term and is fined 7/89
- New York elects its first black mayor 11/89
- Supreme Court judge nominee accused of sexual harassment 10/91
- Judge Thomas elected to Supreme Court despite sex charges 10/91
- KKK leader qualifies second round as Republican candidate 10/91
- New York Governor Mario Cuomo will not run for presidency 12/91
- Clinton leads in Democratic presidential nomination race 3/92
- Bush is nominated Republican presidential candidate 8/92
- Bill Clinton is elected 42nd President of the United States 11/92
- Bill Clinton is inaugurated President of the United States 1/93
- Janet Reno is nation's first woman Attorney General 3/93
- Polls show Clinton's rating has plunged 36 per cent 5/93
- Louis Freeh is director of FBI 7/93
- Former CIA officer Ames charged with spying for KGB 2/94
- Government approves sale of female condoms 4/94
- CIA traitor Ames gets life 4/94
- Prison population tops million for first time 6/94
- Gingrich's mother says Newt called Hillary "a bitch" 1/95
- Clinton defies Congress over aid to Mexico 1/95

USA (race)
- See also USA (politics)
- Black family lynched in Mississippi 8/01
- Booker T. Washington, black leader, dies 11/15
- 39 die in race riots 7/16
- 75 blacks murdered in riots 7/17
- Indian reservations opened for mining 11/19
- 30 police and two judges are Klansmen 3/23
- President appoints black customs officer 5/23
- Ku Klux Klan claims million members 6/23
- Martial law in Oklahoma to quell Klan 9/23
- Anti-Klan governor dropped from assembly 10/23
- Mob of 700 lynches two blacks, Texas 11/35
- Blacks boycott segregated Alabama buses 12/55
- Alabama University obliged to enrol blacks 2/56
- Whites attack Autherine Lucy, Alabama 2/56
- Montgomery bus segregation protests 2/56
- Supreme Court upholds segregation ban 3/56
- King vows to continue bus boycott 3/56
- Brown v. Board schools ruling extended 3/56
- Supreme Court calls bus race bar invalid 11/56
- Nixon discusses issues with King 6/57
- Injunction to end school segregation 9/57
- Arkansas Governor stops blacks at school 9/57
- Nine blacks enter Little Rock school 9/57
- Federal troops restrain whites at school 9/57
- Governor Faubus defies court on schools 8/58
- King arrested for "loitering" 9/58
- King fined for disobeying officer 9/58
- Governor closes four Little Rock schools 9/58
- Martin Luther King stabbed, Harlem 9/58
- Mixed-race boxing matches ban lifted 5/59
- Police guard blacks at a Little Rock school 8/59
- Governor Faubus backs racist protesters 8/59
- King arrested for tax perjury 2/60
- Blacks' anti-segregation march, Alabama 3/60
- King gets Eisenhower to admonish South 3/60
- Eisenhower orders Southern racial talks 3/60
- Ten die in worst race riot, Mississippi 4/60
- King acquitted of perjury 5/60

USSR
- See also Russia; Commonwealth of Independent States (CIS)

USSR (foreign affairs)
- USSR's envoy to Turkish talks killed by a Swiss 5/23
- Recognised by UK and Italy; trade treaty 2/24
- Denies British Zinoviev Letter claims 10/24
- Recognised by France 10/24
- Boycotts disarmament talks in Geneva 4/26
- Pilsudski leads successful coup in Poland; fears of war 6/26
- Britain cuts off relations: expels diplomats 5/27
- Ambassador to Poland is killed 6/27
- Signs Kellogg-Briand Pact 9/28
- Breaks off relations with China 7/29
- Border clashes between Soviet and Chinese troops 7/29
- Clashes in Manchuria; treaty broken 8/29
- Eastern Railway border dispute ends 12/29
- Supports Chinese Communists in rural area 4/30
- Signs friendship treaty with Poland 6/31
- Signs non-aggression pact with Poland 1/32
- Stalin threatens UK as trade treaty ends 10/32
- Restores relations with Japan 12/32
- Japan rejects non-aggression pact 1/33
- Two British engineers jailed for spying 4/33
- Soviet imports banned in Britain 4/33
- Non-aggression pact with Italy 8/33
- Plans anti-German front with Poland and Rumania 9/33
- Diplomatic and trade relations with USA 11/33
- Lithuania, Latvia and Estonia renew pacts 4/34
- New Poland non-aggression pact extended until 1945 5/34
- Izvestia says USSR ready to join League 5/34
- Frontier guarantee with Poland and Rumania 6/34
- Germany rejects mutual aid pact 6/34
- Diplomatic relations with Bulgaria 8/34
- US to close USSR consulate 2/35
- Joint communiqué on German rearmament 3/35
- Litvinov blasts German "revenge" policy 4/35
- Signs mutual defence pact with France 5/35
- To continue aiding Spanish Republicans 1/37
- UK, Italy, USSR and Germany halt aid to Spain 2/37
- Leaves Spanish arms cordon 2/37
- 15 Soviet bombers raid Cordoba, Spain 4/37
- Signs non-aggression pact with China 8/37
- Truce with Japan after border clashes 8/38
- Wary of Britain's proposals for pact 5/39
- Signs non-aggression pact with Germany 8/39
- Invasion of Poland 9/39
- Signs mutual aid pact with Latvia 10/39
- Signs pact ceding Vilna to Lithuania 10/39
- Molotov says USSR will remain neutral 10/39
- Stalin renounces Finno-Soviet pact 11/39
- Expelled from League of Nations 12/39
- Signs peace treaty with Finland 3/40
- Trotsky injured in Mexico City 5/40
- Red Army invades Lithuania 6/40
- Invades Bukovina and Bessarabia, Rumania 6/40
- Lithuania, Latvia and Estonia vote to become part of USSR 7/40
- Molotov reaffirms Soviet neutrality 8/40
- Stalin signs neutrality pact with Japan 4/41
- German troops invade USSR 6/41
- Concludes assistance pact with Britain 7/41
- Signs pact with exiled Polish government 7/41
- Litvinov appointed ambassador to USA 11/41
- Signs 20-year pact with Britain 5/42
- Condemns Nazi atrocities 12/42
- Mass Polish grave found at Katyn 3/43
- Stalin says he wants strong, free Poland 5/43
- Stain dissolves Comintern 5/43
- Gromyko becomes Soviet ambassador to US 8/43
- Stalin meets Roosevelt and Churchill 11/43
- Allies agree on closer military ties 11/43
- Allies agree on Austrian independence 11/43
- Benes signs pact with USSR 12/43
- Three Germans hanged for war crimes 12/43
- Refuses to negotiate over Polish border 1/44
- Inquiry blames Germans for Katyn outrage 1/44
- Stalingrad given sword of honour by UK 2/44
- Restores diplomatic relations with Italy 3/44
- Says United Nations will be set up 10/44
- Signs alliance treaty with France 12/44
- Big Three attend Yalta conference 2/45
- Bulgaria and Rumania fall under Kremlin control 3/45
- Plans to occupy half of Germany 6/45
- Among 50 nations to sign UN charter 6/45
- 12 war-exiled Polish leaders jailed 6/45
- Carpathian Ruthenia ceded by Czechs 6/45
- "Iron Curtain" falls in Europe 7/45
- Participates in Potsdam conference 7/45
- Occupies assigned Berlin zone 7/45
- Signs treaty with Poland fixing border 8/45
- To partition Korea with US 9/45
- Molotov says USSR will build its own A-bomb 11/45
- Allies agree on UN control of A-bombs 12/45
- Averell Harriman resigns as US envoy 2/46
- Admits spying in Canada 2/46
- "Pravda" denounces Churchill 3/46
- Withdraws troops from Iran 3/46
- To get 51% of Iranian oil over a period of 25 years 4/46
- Paris treaty talks 4/46
- US fears Soviets may possess atomic secrets 2/47
- Gains land under Paris peace treaties 2/47
- Claims US is seeking nuclear energy monopoly 3/47
- Big Four discuss future of Germany 3/47
- Claims to hold 890,532 German POWs 3/47
- Big Four disagree on post-war settlement 4/47
- Attends talks on Marshall aid plan 6/47
- Rejects Marshall aid plan 7/47
- Soviet UN delegate vetoes Balkan frontier commission 7/47
- Urged by US to take part in Korea talks 8/47
- Accuses US of war-mongering 9/47
- Accused by UK of duplicity over Germany 12/47
- UK denounces Soviet "new imperialism" 1/48
- Reported to be holding £42 million worth of German art 1/48
- Walks out of Allied talks on Berlin 3/48
- Signs defence pact with Finland 4/48
- Gromyko resigns as envoy to UN 5/48
- Urges overthrow of Tito 7/48
- US protests about Berlin blockade 7/48
- Drops call for nuclear weapons ban 10/48
- Refuses four-power talks on Berlin 11/48
- Stalin seeks more control of satellites 1/49
- Vetoes South Korea's entry to UN 4/49
- Calls for talks to end Berlin blockade 4/49
- Ends blockade of Berlin 5/49
- Mao claims USSR is China's true ally 6/49
- Soviet troops on Yugoslav frontier 8/49
- Denounces Tito's regime as "renegade" 8/49
- Tests first A-bomb 9/49
- Tito ends air and naval pact with USSR 9/49
- Vetoes entry of four nations to UN 9/49
- Ends assistance pact with Yugoslavia 9/49
- Recognises Communist China 10/49
- German Democratic Republic created 10/49
- Denounces West German state 10/49
- Yugoslavia told to recall ambassador 10/49
- Walks out of UN over China row 1/50
- Chou En-lai talks with Stalin, Moscow 1/50
- Recognises Ho Chi Minh regime 1/50
- Signs friendship pact with China 2/50
- Wants Hirohito tried as war criminal 2/50
- Shoots down US bomber over Latvia 4/50
- Korean War 6/50
- Vetoes UN motion condemning North Korea 9/50
- Malik calls for Korean cease-fire 6/51
- Gromyko claims Japan was too lightly punished 9/51
- Does not recognise Japan's sovereignty 4/52
- Gromyko is Soviet Ambassador to Britain 6/52
- Cuts off West Berlin with security belt 6/52
- Pact with Chiang Kai-shek repudiated 2/53
- Troops fire on people fleeing East Berlin 5/53
- Refuses Western aid to starving Berliners 5/53
- Malenkov announces USSR's hydrogen bomb 8/53
- East Germany will cease reparations 8/53
- Recognises Austrian Republic 9/53
- Rejects Eden's plans for united Germany 1/54
- Suggests Pan-European security pact 2/54
- UK scientist Pontecorvo working in USSR 2/55
- Bulganin signs Warsaw Pact agreement 5/55
- Khrushchev offers peace to Yugoslavia 5/55
- Proposes cuts in nuclear weapons 5/55
- Tito and Khrushchev sign normalising treaty 6/55
- Invites West Germany's Adenauer to talks 6/55
- Geneva summit with UK, US and France 7/55
- Bulganin rejects free German elections 7/55
- Bulganin rejects US inspection plan 8/55
- Planned escape of spies Burgess and MacLean 9/55
- Establishes relations with West Germany 9/55
- Molotov wants NATO and Warsaw Pact ended 10/55
- Gives Port Arthur to China 10/55
- Khrushchev attacks UK colonial policy 12/55
- Khrushchev blasts Stalin over Yugoslavia 3/56
- Khrushchev visits UK; calls for peace 4/56
- Releases Polish ex-leader Gomulka 4/56
- De-Stalinisation campaign 4/56
- Molotov resigns as Foreign Minister 6/56
- Minister Shepilov talks to Nasser 6/56
- Refuses plan for international Suez Zone 8/56
- Troops and tanks in Hungary to stop revolt 10/56
- Up to 3,000 die in Budapest violence 10/56
- Khrushchev attends Warsaw Polish talks 10/56
- Vetoes UN vote for UK-French Suez plan 10/56
- Bulganin's threat over UK's Suez action 11/56
- Hungary intends to leave Warsaw Pact 11/56
- UN tells USSR to leave Hungary 11/56
- Poland allows Soviet troops to stay 11/56
- Huge assault crushes Hungarian revolt 11/56
- Appoints Kadar to rule conquered Hungary 11/56
- Tries to seal off Hungary-Austria border 11/56
- Crushes new strikes in Hungary 12/56
- US ends cultural exchange programme 12/56
- China's Chou En-lai visits for talks 1/57
- Joint UK-US condemnation of repression 3/57
- Poland asks for aid 5/57
- Wants three-year nuclear test ban 6/57
- Unwilling to let US inspect military bases 8/57
- Molotov made Ambassador to Mongolia 8/57
- Urges European Socialists to end US and Turkish "agression" 10/57
- Bulganin wants big East-West talks 1/58
- Wants talks with West to end tests 5/58
- Wants US and UK troops to leave Middle East 7/58
- Manoeuvres near Turkish and Iranian borders 7/58
- Accepts UN summit 7/58
- To lend Egypt $100 million for Aswan Dam 10/58
- UK, US and USSR make draft test ban treaty 12/58
- Wants veto over international tests body 12/58
- Agrees to help United Arab Republic 12/58
- UK's Macmillan in Moscow for arms talks 2/59
- Wants East-West summit on Berlin 2/59
- Selwyn Lloyd and Andrei Gromyko in talks 3/59
- Signs five-year trade pact with UK 5/59
- Khrushchev and Nixon debate at kitchen show 7/59
- Khrushchev clashes with mayor on US tour 9/59
- Khrushchev begins talks on Berlin with US 9/59
- Khrushchev visits Peking; meets Mao 10/59
- Signs Antarctic "science reserve" treaty 12/59
- Khrushchev wants East-West summit 12/59
- Communist leaders' meeting; China absent 2/60
- US and UK prepare test ban proposals 3/60
- Khrushchev visits Afghanistan 3/60
- Khrushchev warns against "rebirth of German militarism" 3/60
- Shoots down US U-2 "spy plane" 5/60
- Says US wants to ruin summit talks 5/60
- Demands apology from US; wrecks summit 5/60
- Khrushchev attacks Mao 6/60
- US pilot Powers accused of spying 7/60
- Khrushchev backs Cuba to expel US troops 7/60
- Nuclear war "not inevitable" 7/60
- Gary Powers gets ten years for spying 8/60
- Powers confesses to spying 8/60
- Khrushchev wants UN chief Hammarskjold fired 9/60
- Khrushchev thumps desk during UN speech 9/60
- Khrushchev waves shoe at Philippine delegate during speech 10/60
- "Pravda" attacks China 10/60
- Party admits differences with Chinese 12/60
- Signs technology and culture pact with UK 1/61
- Cuban exiles invade Cuba at Bay of Pigs 4/61
- Rudolf Nureyev defects in Paris 6/61
- Relations with Albania worsening 6/61
- Berlin Wall erected 8/61
- Banishes Albania from Soviet bloc 10/61
- Faces Allied tanks along Berlin border 10/61
- Vetoes Kuwait's entry to UN 11/61
- Severs relations with Albania 12/61
- Picasso and Nkrumah: Lenin Peace Prize 4/62
- Pledges to defend China from attack 7/62
- Cuban missile crisis 10/62
- Accused of having Cuban missile sites 10/62
- Briton Greville Wynne arrested as a spy 11/62
- US lifts blockade of Cuba 11/62
- Oleg Penkovsky arrested in Wynne case 12/62
- Agrees to inspection of nuclear tests 1/63
- Greville Wynne charged with spying 4/63
- Castro arrives for talks with Khrushchev 4/63
- Greville Wynne given eight years for spying 5/63
- China agrees to hold talks 5/63
- Agrees to establish hot line with US 6/63
- Split with China now complete 7/63
- Agrees to partial test ban treaty 7/63
- Philby granted Soviet citizenship 7/63
- Signature of partial test ban treaty 8/63
- Hot line with White House opens 8/63
- British traitor Burgess reported dead 9/63
- Greville Wynne returns to UK in spy swap 4/64
- Khrushchev admits use of spy satellites 5/64
- Calls on US to halt Vietnam actions 8/64
- New leaders want world nuclear test ban 10/64
- Richard Nixon visits 4/65
- Rejects Vietnam peace mission 6/65
- UK officer Squires is working for USSR 6/65
- UK lecturer Brooke jailed for spying 7/65
- Brezhnev wants end to Indo-Pakistan war 9/65
- Calls for US to get out of Vietnam 3/66
- Harold Wilson visits 7/66
- Double agent Blake escapes from jail, UK 10/66
- Denounces Chinese leadership 11/66
- Kosygin visits UK 2/67
- Stalin's daughter defects to the West 3/67
- Svetlana Alliluyeva arrives in US 4/67
- Breaks ties with Israel 6/67
- Signs aid pact with North Vietnam 9/67
- Soviet troops move up to Czech border 5/68
- Russian tanks mass on Czech border 7/68
- 36 nations sign nuclear non-proliferation pact 7/68
- Russian tanks roll into Prague 8/68
- Dubcek in long talks with leaders 8/68
- LBJ warns against intervening in Rumania 8/68
- Czech censorship; ban on meetings 9/68
- Huge demonstration in Prague against occupation 10/68
- In border clash with China 3/69
- Briton Brooke exchanged for two Russians 7/69
- Kosygin in talks with Chou En-lai 9/69
- Albania to leave Warsaw Pact 9/69
- PLO leader Arafat in Moscow talks 2/70
- Friendship treaty with Czechoslovakia 5/70
- Non-aggression pact with West Germany 8/70
- Dancer Natalia Makarova defects to West 9/70
- Nixon warns USSR subs to avoid Cuba 1/71
- 40 nations ban seabed nuclear weapons 2/71
- Signs 15-year friendship pact with Egypt 5/71
- UK grants asylum to Anatol Fedoseyev 6/71
- 20-year defence pact with India 8/71
- UK expels 90 Russians for spying 9/71
- Expels five Britons and bars 13 more 10/71
- 350 Soviet Jews arrive in Israel 1/72
- Recognises Bangladesh 1/72
- Swedish Nobel official refused visa 4/72
- Nixon visits Moscow 5/72
- Nixon and Brezhnev sign nuclear pact 5/72
- Signs accord on Berlin's status 6/72
- Science and technology pact with US 7/72
- Ordered to withdraw advisers from Egypt 7/72
- Solzhenitsyn urges human rights crusade 8/72
- Signs SALT agreement with US 10/72
- Brezhnev talks with Nixon in US 6/73
- Princess Anne visits 8/73
- Panovs, ballet dancers, defect to West 6/74
- Dancer Baryshnikov defects to West 6/74
- Brezhnev talks with Nixon in Moscow 6/74
- Exiled Solzhenitsyn collects Nobel Prize 12/74
- US Apollo spacecraft joins Soyuz 7/75
- Signs Helsinki pact on rights and borders 8/75
- Recognises MPLA Angola regime; advisers 11/75
- Denies Sakharov visa to go to Oslo 11/75
- Attacks Mrs Thatcher 1/76

- Posters show Thatcher: "Cold War Witch" 2/76
- Egypt bans Soviet warships from ports 3/76
- Advisers expelled from Somalia 7/77
- KGB involved in violent Afghan coup 4/78
- UN envoy Shevchenko defects to US 4/78
- American Embassy claimed to be bugged 6/78
- Gromyko discusses arms limits with US 10/78
- Gromyko mocks Sadat and Begin's Peace Nobel 10/78
- 20-year friendship treaty, Afghanistan 12/78
- Protests at Bhutto's death sentence 2/79
- Brezhnev and Carter sign SALT 2 arms treaty 6/79
- Agrees a ceiling of 2,250 nuclear missiles with US 6/79
- Invades Afghanistan; instals Karmal 12/79
- Sakharov criticises Afghan invasion 1/80
- Brezhnev warns Afghan meddlers 2/80
- Tribute to Yugoslavia's late leader Tito 5/80
- Reports of troops out of Afghanistan 6/80
- "Pravda" denounces Polish strikers 8/80
- Neutral in Iran-Iraq war 9/80
- Demands soldier from US embassy, Kabul 9/80
- Troops mass on borders 12/80
- Stops Warsaw Pact exercises over Poland 4/81
- Angry over US-China arms deal 6/81
- Slams Solidarity union, Poland 9/81
- "Normal" army manoeuvres near Poland 9/81
- "Spying" submarine stranded in Sweden 10/81
- Haig and Gromyko talk for eight hours 1/82
- EEC and USA threats over Poland martial law 2/82
- Jaruzelski arrives for talks 3/82
- Dubbed the "evil empire" by Reagan 3/83
- Reagan proposes "Star Wars" system 3/83
- UK spy Donald MacLean dies 3/83
- UK expels three alleged KGB agents 4/83
- France expels 47 Soviet officials 4/83
- Iran expels 18 alleged Soviet spies 5/83
- KGB accused by Agca of attempted assassination of Pope 7/83
- US lifts ban on sale of pipeline parts 8/83
- Shoots down Korean Boeing 747; 269 die 9/83
- Rejects limits on missiles in Europe 9/83
- To increase sub missiles aimed at US 11/83
- EEC lifts sanctions 12/83
- UK grants asylum to Soviet writer Bitov 1/84
- Vetoes idea of UN force in Beirut 2/84
- To boycott Los Angeles Olympics 5/84
- Signs economic pact with Poland 5/84
- Bitov claims UK agents kidnapped him 9/84
- Svetlana Alliluyeva returns 11/84
- Gorbachev visits Britain 12/84
- Stray USSR missile found in Finnish lake 1/85
- Freezes deployment of some missiles 4/85
- London KGB head Gordievski defects 9/85
- Expels 31 Britons 9/85
- Reagan-Gorbachev summit in Geneva 11/85
- Svetlana Alliluyeva returns to US 4/86
- US journalist Daniloff held for spying 9/86
- Daniloff released 9/86
- US frees Soviet UN employee Zakharov 9/86
- Reagan-Gorbachev summit in Iceland 10/86
- Warm Moscow welcome for Thatcher 3/87
- Thatcher-Gorbachev talks to end Cruise 3/87
- Buys surplus butter from EEC 3/87
- Gorbachev may end short-range missiles 4/87
- West German defies Soviet air defences by flying into Moscow 5/87
- Military embarrassed by Rust's flight 5/87
- Reagan and Gorbachev sign missile treaty 12/87
- Soviet withdrawal from Afghanistan 4/88
- Reagan's first visit to USSR 5/88
- Moscow imposes direct rule on Nagorny Karabakh 1/89
- Paris talks: USSR to destroy its chemical weapons 1/89
- Soviet occupation of Afghanistan ends 2/89
- Eleven Britons expelled for spying 5/89
- Soviet and Chinese Communist leaders meet in Beijing 5/89
- Moldavia opens border with Rumania 5/89
- Gorbachev meets Chancellor Kohl to sign Bonn declaration 6/89
- Soviet troops intervene in Georgian-Ossetian clashes 1/90
- Riots in Azerbaijan capital leave more than 25 dead 1/90
- 40 die in ethnic clashes between Uzbeks and Kirghiz 6/90
- Agrees with USA on new arms cuts 6/90
- Lithuania suspends declaration of independence 6/90
- Reopens diplomatic relations with Israel 9/90
- Backs UN vote on air embargo and naval blockade against Iraq 9/90
- Four Allied powers sign German sovereignty treaty 9/90
- Soviet troops intervene in Moldavian-Gaugaz Turk clash 10/90
- Soviet troops storm police academy in Riga 1/91
- Strategic Arms Reduction Treaty signed in Moscow 8/91

USSR (politics)
- Rumours that Lenin is dying 1/23
- Lenin quits after stroke; succession fear 3/23
- Stalin criticised at 12th Party Congress 4/23
- Lenin, Russian Revolution's genius, dies 1/24
- Ruling trio: Stalin, Zinoviev, Kamenev 1/24
- Rykov succeeds Lenin as President 2/24
- Stalin plans to oust Trotsky 5/24
- Bomb in Lenin's tomb, report 9/24
- Revolt in Georgia 9/24
- Government quells Georgian revolt 9/24
- Trotsky leads Red Army in Georgia 10/24
- Voroshilov heads Red Army after Trotsky 11/25
- "Single country" communism 12/25
- Students' compulsory military training 1/26
- Zinoviev and Trotsky forced out of Committee 10/26
- Married couples are to receive identity cards 11/26
- Kerensky in US predicting downfall 3/27
- Executes 20 "British spies" 6/27
- 120 shot in Communist purge, Ukraine 7/27
- British TUC cuts links with USSR unions 9/27
- Nine "British spies" executed 9/27
- Three "British spies" executed 10/27
- Stalin expels Trotsky and Zinoviev from Party 11/27
- Trotsky and Zinoviev in anti-Stalin protest 11/27
- 15th Party Congress; Trotsky disgraced 12/27
- Stalin purges Kamenev and Zinoviev plus 28 1/28
- Trotsky exiled to Alma-Ata, near China 1/28
- New decree: counter-revolution a crime 1/28
- First Five-Year economic plan 10/28
- Trotsky supporters arrested by OGPU 11/28
- Stalin attacks Bukharin, Comintern chief 11/28
- Trotsky's secretary dies on hunger strike 11/28
- Bukharin resigns as head of Comintern 1/29
- OGPU arrests 400 Trotskyists for "plot" 1/29
- Trotsky ordered out of country 1/29
- Trotsky in Turkey; Stalin now anti-right 2/29
- Premier Alexei Rykov removed from office 2/29
- 1,600 Trotskyists exiled to Siberia 2/29
- Trotsky refused French political asylum 2/29
- Trotsky to give up politics 3/29
- Maxim Gorky on Congress executive 5/29
- Trotsky wants British asylum 6/29
- Bukharin expelled from Politburo 11/29
- Agents persecute rich kulak peasants 1/30
- Stalin strengthens control over peasants 1/30
- Churches closed; priests and nuns killed 2/30
- Estimated 40 kulaks a day are killed 2/30
- Stalin's vow: liquidate two million kulaks 3/30
- Kulaks defy state and burn houses; deported 3/30
- Peasants flee to Poland; fear state plan 3/30
- Stalin justifies purges at Party Congress 6/30
- 6,000 Trotskyists exiled or imprisoned 6/30
- Litvinov becomes Foreign Minister 7/30
- Ex-premier Rykov said to be purged 12/30
- Finnish claim 662,200 Soviet prisoners 1/31
- Trotsky stripped of citizenship 2/31
- Stalin announces second five-year plan 5/31
- Million march on May Day 5/32
- Stalin purges Zinoviev and Kamenev 10/32
- Stalin's wife dies; suspected suicide 11/32
- Emigration allowed for a big fee 11/32
- Two British engineers jailed for spying 4/33
- "Pravda" attacks Lenin's widow over Stalin 5/34
- OGPU abolished; new Internal Affairs 7/34
- Minor clergy, but not priests, given vote 10/34
- 12,000 exiled to Siberia 11/34
- Stalin aide Kirov murdered; Stalin starts purge 12/34
- 100 old Bolsheviks summarily executed 12/34
- Kamenev and Zinoviev sent into exile 12/34
- Nikolayev and 13 others shot for murder 12/34
- Claims Red Army is 940,000 strong 1/35
- Khrushchev elected Moscow Party chief 3/35
- Dimitrov heads Communist International 8/35
- Coal miner Stakhanov's production award 9/35
- Navy has grown fivefold in five years 12/35
- Ban on employing ex-Czarists lifted 5/36
- Show trials: Kamenev and Zinoviev executed 8/36
- Prosecutor Vishinsky condemns 16 to die 8/36
- Claims biggest air force: 7,000 planes 11/36
- Show trial courts purge 17 Trotskyists 1/37
- Propagandist Radek gets ten years' jail 1/37
- Ambassador Sokolnikov gets ten years' jail 1/37
- Piatakov, munitions chief, gets death penalty 1/37
- Bukharin sacked as Izvestia editor 1/37
- 13 Trotskyists executed 2/37
- Exiled Trotsky calls for Stalin's demise 4/37
- Trotsky predicts post-war capitalist USSR 4/37
- Eight generals and Tukhachevsky executed 6/37
- Generals accused of Fascist coup plot 6/37
- 36 more alleged spies executed 6/37
- 62 executed in latest purge 10/37
- Million at Revolution 20th anniversary 11/37
- Kalinin, President of Supreme Praesidium 1/38
- 21 top old Bolsheviks executed 3/38
- Litvinov replaced by Molotov 5/39
- Trotsky assassinated in Mexico City 8/40
- Stalin sets up Committee of Defence 7/41
- Stalin takes over as defence commissar 7/41
- Government moves to Kuibyshev 10/41
- Beria put in charge of drive for A-bomb 10/45
- Stalin announces new five-year plan 2/46
- Molotov ousted as Foreign Minister 3/49
- Andrei Vishinsky replaces Molotov 3/49
- Gromyko becomes deputy Foreign Minister 3/49
- Vasilevsky becomes head of armed forces 3/49
- Establishes Soviet Peace Prize 12/49
- Maxim Litvinov, statesman, dies 12/51
- Jewish doctors held for anti-Stalin plot 1/53
- Claims doctors took Zionist orders 1/53
- Attacks on Jews and Zionists 2/53
- Joseph Stalin dies 3/53
- Malenkov named premier and secretary 3/53
- Khrushchev replaces Malenkov as secretary 3/53
- Infighting at top: Politburo halved 3/53
- Nine doctors in plot freed; "an error" 4/53
- Secret police chief Beria on spy charge 7/53
- Malenkov purges secret police 7/53
- Khrushchev elected Party First Secretary 9/53
- Police Beria confesses "state crimes" 12/53
- Beria executed after secret trial 12/53
- Ukraine purged; warned of nationalism 1/54
- Khrushchev ousts Malenkov 2/55
- Nikolai Bulganin is new premier 2/55
- Khrushchev modifies Stalinism 2/55
- H-bomb-carrying rocket 12/55
- 20th Party Congress 2/56
- Khrushchev denounces Stalin at Congress 3/56
- Georgian rioting at anti-Stalin speech 3/56
- Molotov resigns as Foreign Minister 6/56
- Khrushchev foils "anti-Party" coup 7/57
- Kaganovitch, Molotov and Malenkov purged 7/57
- Zhukov dismissed as Defence Minister 10/57
- Marshal Zhukov loses Party position 11/57
- Khrushchev removes Premier Bulganin 3/58
- Khrushchev runs two posts, like Stalin 3/58
- Bulganin accused of "anti-party" actions 3/58
- Will cut armed forces by 1.2 million 1/60
- Living standards up, says UN report 4/60
- Brezhnev head of state after Voroshilov 5/60
- Missiles at Red Square parade, Moscow 11/60
- Military spending to be increased 7/61
- Stalin's body moved from Red Square tomb 10/61
- Lenin's mausoleum reopens 11/61
- Stalingrad renamed Volgograd 11/61
- Molotov, Malenkov and Kaganovich out of CP 11/61
- Bukharin and Rykov rehabilitated 10/62
- Oleg Penkovsky arrested in Wynne case 12/62
- Does not recognise Stalin anniversary 3/63
- Spy Oleg Penkovsky sentenced to death 5/63
- Briton Wynne given eight years for spying 5/63
- Philby granted Soviet citizenship 7/63
- Molotov expelled from Communist Party 4/64
- Jewish repression attacked in Geneva 7/64
- Mikoyan succeeds Brezhnev as President 7/64
- Khrushchev ousted by Brezhnev 10/64
- Zhukov rehabilitated 2/65
- Podgorny becomes head of state 12/65
- Daniel and Sinyavsky jailed for slander 2/66
- Brezhnev opens 23rd party congress 3/66
- Brezhnev becomes General Secretary 4/66
- Khrushchev seen in public after long gap 6/66
- Kim Philby gives first interview to West 11/67
- Philby hailed as hero of USSR 12/67
- Ginsburg and Galenkov jailed for slander 1/68
- Death of Kliment Voroshilov 12/69
- Death of Alexander Kerensky 6/70
- Solzhenitsyn wins Literature Nobel 10/70
- "Pravda" slams Solzhenitsyn 12/70
- Khrushchev dies 9/71
- Physicist Sakharov joins rights campaign 11/72
- Sakharov interviewed by KGB 3/73
- Gromyko and Andropov promoted to Politburo 4/73
- Solzhenitsyn exiled 2/74
- Sakharov urges leaders to renounce Marx 4/74
- Death of Marshal Georgi Zhukov 6/74
- Nikolai Bulganin dies 2/75
- Politburo fires ex-KGB chief Shelepin 4/75
- Dissident Sakharov wins Peace Nobel 10/75
- Sakharov and Bonner arrested for assault 4/76
- 45 Jews arrested for cultural symposium 12/76
- Several killed in Moscow bomb blast 1/77
- Podgorny sacked; Brezhnev is President 6/77
- Brezhnev will also stop nuclear bombs 4/78
- Dissident Orlov jailed for seven years 5/78
- Dissidents and refuseniks get hard labour 7/78
- Shcharansky gets 13 years' labour 7/78
- Anastas Mikoyan dies 10/78
- Brezhnev's ill health noticed at Vienna talks 6/79
- Sakharov exiled to Gorky 1/80
- Premier Kosygin resigns 10/80
- Alexei Kosygin, ex-premier, dies 12/80
- Sakharov and Bonner on hunger strike 11/81
- Sakharovs end hunger strike; demands met 12/81
- President Leonid Brezhnev dies - profile 11/82
- Yuri Andropov, ex-KGB boss, becomes President 11/82
- Nikolai Podgorny dies 1/83
- Yuri Andropov dies 2/84
- Chernenko becomes leader 2/84
- Chernenko elected President 4/84
- Andrei Sakharov on hunger strike 5/84
- To boycott Los Angeles Olympics 5/84
- Molotov reinstated as CP member 7/84
- Sakharov ends hunger strike 8/84
- Bonner joins husband in internal exile 8/84
- Konstantin Chernenko dies 3/85
- Gorbachev becomes General Secretary 3/85
- Eduard Shevardnadze becomes Foreign Minister 7/85
- Andrei Gromyko becomes President 7/85
- Gorbachev attacks wasted Brezhnev years 2/86
- Human rights activist Shcharansky freed 2/86
- Death of Vyacheslav Molotov 11/86
- Sakharov freed from internal exile 12/86
- Gorbachev wants more party democracy 1/87
- Introduction of perestroika and glasnost 1/87
- Gorbachev pardons 140 dissidents 2/87
- Jewish dissident Begun is freed 2/87
- Yeltsin, reformist Moscow leader, fired 11/87
- Yeltsin attacks number two in Kremlin, Yegor Ligachev 11/87
- Gorbachev rehabilitates "un-persons" 2/88
- Gorbachev sacks Boris Yeltsin 2/88
- Christian Armenian protests 2/88
- Withdrawal from Afghanistan: timetable 3/88
- Troops in Soviet Armenia and Azerbaijan 3/88
- Communist Party bosses sacked 5/88
- Andrei Sakharov calls for human rights 6/88
- Armenians vote to end strike 6/88
- Tanks sent into Armenia again 9/88
- Gorbachev retires President Gromyko 9/88
- Gorbachev will free political prisoners 10/88
- Latvians form Popular Front 10/88
- Estonia spurns Moscow's reforms 11/88
- Georgia calls for greater freedom 11/88
- Gorbachev will cut troops by 10 per cent 12/88
- Announces destruction of its chemical weapons during talks 1/89
- Gorbachev gives warning to Communist Party 1/89
- Communist leaders rejected in favour of reformers in polls 3/89
- Police clash with demonstrators in Georgia 4/89
- Gorbachev purges top ranks of the Communist Party 4/89
- Mikhail Gorbachev elected President 5/89
- Latvia votes for independence from Moscow 5/89
- Ethnic violence erupts in Uzbekistan; at least 100 die 6/89
- 180-mile chain marks 50th anniversary of Soviet-Nazi pact 8/89
- Gorbachev faces mounting ethnic unrest 8/89
- Gorbachev threatens to resign during row at a meeting 12/89
- Rule in Azerbaijan is re-established after insurrection 1/90
- Soviet Communist Party votes to abandon one-party rule 2/90
- First multi-party elections held since 1917 2/90
- Thousands of Soviet citizens rally to demand more reforms 2/90
- Gorbachev elected executive President of USSR 3/90
- Moscow imposes economic blockade on Lithuania 4/90
- Soviet support for a unified Germany in NATO ruled out 4/90
- Crowds jeer at Gorbachev during May Day celebrations 5/90
- Boris Yeltsin elected President of Russia 5/90
- Boris Yeltsin resigns from Communist Party 7/90
- Parliament votes to give President Gorbachev new powers 10/90
- Gorbachev wins increased powers after emergency debate 11/90
- Food rationing is introduced in Leningrad 12/90
- Gennady Yanayev elected Vice-President 12/90
- Eduard Shevardnadze resigns 12/90
- Thousands demonstrate outside Kremlin in support of Yeltsin 1/91
- Yeltsin accuses Gorbachev of dictatorship 2/91
- Latvians and Estonians vote for independence 3/91
- Gorbachev and Yeltsin agree on election timetable 4/91
- Boris Yeltsin becomes President of Russia 6/91
- Shevardnadze announces plans for new democratic movement 7/91
- Ukraine leads other republics in move to secede from Union 8/91
- Gorbachev toppled by coup 8/91
- Gorbachev on his way back to Moscow after coup collapses 8/91
- Thousands gather in Red Square to mourn victims of coup 8/91
- Nikolai Kruchina commits suicide after coup 8/91
- Parliament suspends all Communist activities 8/91
- Seven Soviet republics opt for independence 8/91
- 14 leading Soviet Communists to be tried over coup bid 8/91
- Gorbachev caught in power struggle 8/91
- Congress of People's Deputies votes to wind up USSR 9/91
- Ukraine votes for independence 12/91
- President Gorbachev resigns from office 12/91
- Soviet Union ends; Commonwealth of Independent States begins 12/91

Ustinov, Peter 4/21, 10/84
U Thant 11/61, 8/62, 1/63, 3/64, 8/65, 9/65, 9/66
Utrillo, Maurice 12/38, 11/55, 12/55
Uzbekistan
- Ethnic violence erupts; at least 100 die 6/89

V

Vadim, Roger 8/69
Vainio, Martti 8/84
Valachi, Joseph M. 9/63
Valadon, Suzanne 12/25, 12/38
Valens, Richie 2/59
Valentino, Rudolph 10/21, 7/26, 8/26, 12/26
Valparaiso
- Hundreds die in port earthquake 8/06

Van Allen, James 12/58
Van Basten, Marco 6/88
Van Fleet, James 11/38
Van Houten, Leslie 12/69, 3/71
Van Meegren, Hans 12/47
Van't Hoff, Jacobus Henricus 12/01
Vance, Cyrus 9/92, 1/93
Vandenberg, General 1/51
Vanderbilt, Gloria 10/34
Vanunu, Mordechai 10/86, 11/86
Vanzetti, Bartolomeo 7/21, 4/27, 8/27
Varda, Agnes 5/28
Vardon, Harry 2/00, 6/03, 6/11, 3/37
Varese, Edgar 11/65
Vargas, Getulio 10/30, 11/30, 6/39, 8/54
Varley, Eric 6/75
Varmus, Harold 12/89
Vasala, Pekka 9/72
Vasconcellos, Antonio de 9/89
Vasilevsky, Alexander 3/49
Vassall, William 9/62, 10/62, 11/62
Vatican City
- Diplomatic relations with Mexico are restored 9/92
- Vatican admits Galileo's theory was right 10/92

Vaughan Williams, Ralph 10/10, 12/14, 12/31, 4/48, 4/58, 8/58
Velayati, Ali Akbar 8/90
Velikhov, Yevgeny 5/86
Venezuela
- Invaded by Colombia 8/01
- President Castro beats rebels 10/02
- British lift blockade 2/03
- Blockade reparations 2/04
- Declares war on Germany 2/45
- Civilian coup ousts dictator Jimenez 1/58
- Kennedy begins Latin America tour 12/61
- Grandmother gives birth to quins 9/63
- Pope begins 12-day tour of South America 1/85
- Riots kill 200 in Caracas 3/89
- Rebel troop coup attempt fails to topple President Perez 2/92

- President Perez survives new military coup attempt 11/92
- President Perez is removed from office for corruption 5/93

Venizelos, Eleutherios 10/15, 8/16, 10/16, 6/17, 8/20, 11/20, 5/32, 3/35
Ver, Fabian 1/85
Verdi, Giuseppe 1/01, 12/01
Verdun
- See World War I (Western Front)

Vereeneging 5/02
Verne, Jules 3/05
Versailles, Treaty of
- First formal session of Peace Conference 1/19
- Germany must cut navy to 15,000 men 3/19
- Danzig to be a Free City 4/19
- German delegates arrive 5/19
- German delegate resigns rather than signs 5/19
- Germans sign; officially ending war 6/19
- German delegates stoned 6/19
- German reparation: 20 billion gold marks 6/19
- New Hungarian rulers recognise treaty 8/19
- Austrian National Assembly will sign 9/19
- French MPs ratify the treaty 10/19
- Rejected by US Senate over Article ten 11/19
- Allied pressure on Rumania to sign 11/19
- Bulgaria signs; recognises Yugoslavia 11/19
- Economist Keynes says disaster will come 12/19
- Wilson opposed; US will not ratify 3/20
- French enter Ruhr after German moves 4/20
- Geman Socialists told to obey treaty 6/20
- Germans fail to cut arms and drop air force 7/20
- Arms terms broken by Germany signing Treaty of Rapallo 4/22
- Attacked by Hitler who wins support 1/23

Verwoerd, Hendrik 9/58, 3/61, 3/66, 9/66
Vian, Boris 6/59
Vian, Philip 3/42
Vichy France
- See France, World War II

Vicious, Sid 10/78, 2/79
Vickers
- Machine gun introduced to British Army 11/12

Vickers, Arthur 4/21
Victor Emmanuel III, King of Italy 7/00, 6/06, 3/08, 10/22, 3/24, 4/29, 10/36, 7/43, 11/43, 6/44, 5/46
Victoria, Empress of Germany 8/01
Victoria, Queen of England
- See also Royal Family (Britain) 1/01

Vidal, Gore 12/68
Vidal, Mola 7/36, 8/36
Videla, Jorge 12/85
Vietnam
- See also Indochina
- Independence declared 3/45
- Ho Chi Minh wins election 1/46
- Recognised by France 3/46
- Ho Chi Minh elected President 3/46
- French proclaim martial law 12/46
- General Leclerc leaves 1/47
- Viet Minh mines kills seven French officers 2/49
- France recognises Bao Dai as ruler 3/49
- Mao recognises Ho Chi Minh regime 1/50
- USSR recognises Ho Chi Minh regime 1/50
- UK and US recognise Bao Dai as ruler 2/50
- France recognises Bao Dai regime 2/50
- Viet Minh attack French at Dong Khe 5/50
- Viet Minh occupy Dong Khe 9/50
- Viet Minh defeat French at Kaobang 10/50
- French abandon 250 miles of border zone 10/50
- Giap's Viet Minh Thai hills offensive 10/52
- US accuses USSR of arming Viet Minh 11/52
- General Giap prepares to besiege French forces 2/54
- US warns China not to aid Vietnamese 4/54
- Viet Minh capture Dien Bien Phu 5/54
- Vietnam conference, Geneva 5/54
- Dulles and Eden accept need for partition 6/54
- French premier Mendes-France wants peace 6/54
- Divided along 17th Parallel; truce terms 7/54
- US and Vietnam exchange POWs 2/73
- Says six missing US pilots were killed 9/76
- Begins talks with US in Paris 11/76
- USA vetoes Vietnam's application to join UN 11/76
- "Boat people" refugees ; many killed 12/77
- Western nations accept boat people 12/77
- Cambodia breaks off relations 12/77
- 3,000 Cambodians die in border clashes 1/78
- China cancels aid 7/78
- Crushes Cambodia's Khmer Rouge regime 1/79
- Chinese cross northern border; reprisals 2/79
- Chinese start withdrawing 3/79
- Reveals extent of Cambodian massacres 4/79
- Malaysia turns back refugees 6/79
- Vows to catch "genocidal" Pol Pot 8/79
- Hunting 30,000 Khmer army, Cambodia 9/79
- Scorns aid to Khmer-run regions 9/79
- To withdraw its troops from Cambodia 4/89
- Vietnamese troops withdraw from Cambodia 9/89
- Hong Kong starts repatriating Vietnamese boat people 12/89
- General Le Duc Anh is elected President 9/92

Vietnam War
- Kennedy considers US role 9/63
- LBJ sends US Marines into Da Nang 3/65
- Vietcong wreck US Embassy in Saigon 3/65
- US troops go into action for first time 6/65
- US sends another 50,000 troops 7/65
- US bombs friendly village by mistake 10/65
- Christmas truce agreed 12/65
- US launches offensive on "Iron Triangle" 1/66
- US planes resume bombing after pause 1/66
- De Gaulle offers Ho aid to end war 2/66
- Australian troops fly into Vietnam 4/66
- Americans evacuated from Da Nang 4/66
- US bombs hit Hanoi for first time 6/66
- US planes bomb demilitarised zone 7/66
- 20 US soldiers die in napalm mistake 8/66
- US bombs friendly village, killing 28 9/66
- LBJ pays surprise visit to Vietnam 10/66
- Vietcong shell Saigon 11/66
- US deaths in one week reach highest level 1/67
- US troops launch biggest assault so far 1/67
- US bombs first major industrial centre 3/67
- Three captured US pilots displayed in Hanoi 5/67
- LBJ authorises N. Vietnam bomb targets 8/67
- Hanoi rejects US peace talks offer 10/67
- US steps up bombing raids against North 11/67
- Vietcong launch Tet offensive 1/68
- Vietcong occupy US Embassy in Saigon 1/68
- US and S. Vietnamese recapture Hue 2/68
- LBJ to send in up to 50,000 more troops 3/68
- Talks on peace deal begin in Paris 5/68
- US reduces bombing of North Vietnam 5/68
- Bomb wounds Mayor of Saigon and seven officials 6/68
- US to halt bombing of North Vietnam 10/68
- LBJ orders total end to bombing of North 11/68
- US calls Tet truce 2/69
- US death toll exceeds that of Korean War 4/69
- Vietcong call three-day truce in Ho's memory 9/69
- US orders B-52 raids on North to continue 9/69
- Millions of Americans protest against war 10/69
- US officer charged with Mylai massacre 11/69
- Bomb wrecks Press Centre, Saigon 2/70
- US bombs Ho Chi Minh trail, Laos 3/70
- Mylai massacre - US Lt. Calley found guilty 3/71
- Nixon vows to end US involvement 4/71
- 15 die in Saigon nightclub bomb blast 9/71
- Medina cleared of all Mylai charges, US 9/71
- 45,000 more troops to leave Vietnam 11/71
- US resumes bombing of North Vietnam 12/71
- Intensive US bombing campaign of North 2/72
- North launches heavy attack on South 3/72
- US steps up bombing of North Vietnam 4/72
- Communists take part of Quangtri in South 4/72
- 150,000 evacuated as Communists near Hue 5/72
- US bombs Hanoi and other towns in North 5/72
- Martial law in South Vietnam 5/72
- US combat troops withdrawn from Vietnam 8/72
- Southern troops abandon Queson 8/72
- Kissinger says peace is near 10/72
- US raid destroys French Embassy in Hanoi 10/72
- US tries to force Hanoi into cease-fire 11/72
- First US B-52 bomber shot down 11/72
- Nixon orders halt to Hanoi bombing 12/72
- Cease-fire agreed at Paris peace talks 1/73

Vietnam, North
- See also Vietnam War
- Ho Chi Minh returns to Hanoi 10/54
- French evacuate Hanoi; Giap marches in 10/54
- US evacuates consul 12/55
- Laos alleges invasion; calls on UN 12/60
- Says China will defend her 2/64
- US destroyer fired on in Gulf of Tonkin 8/64
- US planes bomb North Vietnamese bases 8/64
- US and S. Vietnamese bomb N. Vietnam 2/65
- Rejects Commonwealth peace mission 6/65
- China pledges more aid to Ho Chi Minh 8/66
- Signs aid pact with USSR 9/67
- Hanoi rejects US peace talks offer 10/67
- Attacks Laos 12/67
- Ho sends greeting to US war protesters 12/67
- Talks on peace deal begin in Paris 5/68
- Ho Chi Minh dies 9/69
- Ton Duc Thang elected President 9/69
- Vietnam War cease-fire agreed 1/73
- Release of last US POWs 3/73
- Hanoi government recognised by UK 7/73
- Le Duc Tho refuses Nobel Peace Prize 10/73
- New truce and elections called for 3/74
- Army sweeps through S. Vietnam, Laos and Cambodia 1/75

Vietnam, South
- See also Vietnam War
- Refugees enter from North 10/54
- Civil war between Bao Dai and Binh Xuyen 4/55
- French back religious Binh Xuyen group 4/55
- Premier Ngo Dinh Diem sacks police chief 4/55
- Fighting in Saigon kills 160; Cholon burnt 4/55
- Ngo Dinh Diem foils coup by Van Vy 5/55
- Republic under Ngo Dinh Diem 10/55
- Ngo Dinh Diem wins first election 1/56
- Last French troops leave Saigon 3/56
- Bombs kill 18 Americans in Saigon 10/57
- Army clashes with Vietcong 10/60
- Loyalists crush coup 11/60
- Ngo Dinh Diem wins general election 4/61
- US agrees to give more cash and aid 5/61
- More US advisers to be sent 11/61
- Vietcong kill first US soldier 12/61
- US announces more aid and army units 1/62
- Unauthorised public meetings banned 5/62
- Vietcong shoot down five US helicopters 1/63
- Buddhist monk sets fire to himself in protest 6/63
- US tells Diem to redress grievances 6/63
- 100 Buddhist monks arrested 8/63
- 600 students arrested 8/63
- US worried by government's hard line 9/63
- Civilian leaders arrested 9/63
- Diem ousted in military coup 11/63
- US recognises new government 11/63
- Military coup overthrows Van Minh 1/64
- Vietcong rout state forces, Mekong delta 7/64
- US to send 5,000 advisers 7/64
- Coup attempt fails 9/64
- Saigon begins new attack on Vietcong 11/64
- Vietcong attack US base at Bien Hoa 11/64
- Martial law declared in Saigon 11/64
- Seven US troops die in Vietcong raid 2/65
- Nguyen Van Thieu becomes head of state 6/65
- Nguyen Cao Ky becomes premier 6/65
- Nguyen Van Thieu elected President 9/67
- Nguyen Cao Ky elected Vice-President 9/67
- US Marines held for murder of women 2/70
- US Marine is jailed for murder of 15 8/70
- Troops attack Laos 2/71
- Thieu re-elected President 10/71
- Martial law declared 5/72
- Vietnam War cease-fire agreed 1/73
- Last US troops depart 3/73
- 71 die when hijacker blows up plane 9/74
- North Vietnamese take Da Nang 3/75
- Refugees flee from North; Hue falls 3/75
- Communists take Qui Nhon, Nha Trang 4/75
- President Thieu resigns, attacking USA 4/75
- Britain closes Embassy in Saigon 4/75
- Surrenders to North; Saigon falls 4/75
- Thousands try to flee Saigon 4/75
- 105 Vietnamese orphans arrive in UK 4/75
- 140 orphans die in failed airlift to US 4/75

Viking Penguin (publishers) 2/89
Villa, Francisco "Pancho" 5/11, 11/13, 1/15, 1/16, 3/16, 7/20
Villa-Lobos, Heitor 11/59
Villiers, Charles 2/80
Vines, Henry 7/32
Viren, Lasse 9/72, 7/76
Virgo, Wallace 5/77
Virtanen, Ilmari 12/45
Visconti, Luchino 11/06, 12/71
Vishinsky, Andrei 8/36, 3/49, 9/49
Viviani, Rene 8/14, 10/15
Viz (magazine) 3/91
Vizagapatam 4/00
Vladivostock
- Japanese siege 2/05
- Army mutiny; hundreds die 11/05

Vlakfontein 7/00
Vlaminck, Maurice de 10/58
Vo Nguyen Giap 12/44
Voce, Bill 6/32, 1/33
Vogeler, Robert 2/50, 4/51
Voight, Jon 12/69, 12/79
Voikoff (Soviet Ambassador to Poland) 6/27
Voisin, Gabriel 6/05
Volcanoes
- See disasters (volcanoes)

Volkov, Vladislav 6/71
Volterra, Leon 6/49
Vonnegut, Kurt 12/70
Voroshilov, Kliment 11/25, 3/40, 9/41, 5/60, 12/69
Vorster, John 9/66, 9/68, 5/70, 4/71, 10/77, 6/79, 9/83

W

Waco
- Six people are killed in gun battle 2/93
- Blaze ends Waco siege 04/93

Waddington, David 4/90
Waddy, Lloyd 12/92
Wade, Virginia 9/68, 11/71, 7/77
Wagner, Adolf 9/34
Wagner, Siegfried 7/10
Wain, John 5/94
Waite, Terry 2/85, 11/86, 1/87, 2/87, 8/91, 11/91
Waitz, Grete 10/79, 4/83
Wakeham, John 10/84
Wakeham, Roberta 10/84
Walcott, Derek 10/92, 12/92
Walcott, Jersey Joe 6/48, 5/53
Waldegrave, William 1/89
Waldersee, Alfred von 8/00
Waldheim, Kurt 12/18, 12/71, 12/76, 1/80, 2/80, 3/80, 5/86, 6/86, 6/87, 2/88
Waldorf, Stephen 1/83, 10/83, 3/84
Waldorf, William (Lord Astor) 10/19
Walesa, Danuta 12/83
Walesa, Lech 8/80, 9/80, 12/80, 3/81, 8/82, 11/82, 4/83, 6/83, 10/83, 8/88, 11/88, 5/89, 6/89, 8/89, 12/90
Walker, Henry 9/34
Walker, John 8/75
Walker, Peter 6/51, 2/71, 9/73, 11/73
Walker, Walter 9/50
Wall, Max 5/90
Wallace, DeWitt 2/22, 3/81
Wallace, Edgar 10/27, 2/32
Wallace, George 4/63, 6/63, 9/63, 2/66, 2/68, 11/68, 8/71, 5/72
Wallace, Henry A. 7/44
Wallace, Irving 6/90
Wallace, Lila Bel 5/84
Wallace, Lurleen 2/66, 5/66, 1/67
Waller, "Fats" 5/04, 6/30, 12/43
Wallis, Barnes 11/44, 10/79
Wallus, Januzu 4/93
Walter, Bruno 12/38, 8/47, 2/62
Walters, Alan 10/89
Wolthour, Robert 8/01
Walton, Ernest 12/32
Walton, Janet 11/83
Walton, William 12/23, 10/31, 12/31, 12/44, 2/57, 3/83
Wangchuk, Jigme 7/65
Warburg, Otto 12/31
Ward Howe, Julia 10/10
Ward, John 10/89
Ward, Judith 11/74, 9/91, 5/92
Ward, Julie 10/89
Ward, Stephen 6/63, 7/63, 8/63, 12/63
Warhol, Andy 8/31, 12/62, 6/68, 2/70, 12/71, 2/87
Warneford, Reginald 6/15
Warner, Jack 6/65, 12/76
Warren, Earl 5/54, 11/63, 9/64, 7/74
Warsaw Pact
- Communist version of NATO; under Koniev 5/55
- USSR can station troops in satellites 5/55
- Yugoslavia left out 5/55
- Molotov wants NATO and Warsaw Pact ended 10/55
- Nagy says Hungary will leave Pact 11/56
- Invites West to sign nuclear weapons pact 11/76
- Stops exercises to calm Poland 4/81
- Talks with NATO on missile limits 11/81
- Gorbachev may end short-range missiles 4/87
- Agrees with NATO to slash conventional arms 11/90

Warwick, Derek 6/92
Washington, Booker T. 10/01, 3/11, 11/15
Washington, Desiree 3/92
Washington, Dinah 12/63
Washkansky, Louis 12/67
Wasmosy, Juan Carlos 5/93
Watergate
- See USA, (politics)

Waterhouse, Keith 12/60
Watkins, Peter 2/66
Watkinson, Harold 8/56
Watson, Charles (Tex) 12/69
Watson, Ernest 12/31
Watson, James D. 4/53
Watson, Michael 9/91
Watson, Tom 9/49, 7/82, 7/83
Watson, Willie 8/53
Watson-Watt, Robert 12/35
Watts, Nigel 11/89
Waugh, Benjamin 3/08
Waugh, Evelyn 10/03, 12/28, 12/32, 12/38, 12/45, 4/66
Wavell, Field Marshal (Lord) 7/39, 12/40, 1/41, 2/41, 1/42, 3/42, 6/43, 8/46, 2/47, 5/50
Wayne, John 3/39, 4/70, 6/79
Weather
- See Disasters

Weatherill, Bernard 6/83
Webb, Aston 10/12
Webb, Beatrice 2/09, 4/43
Webb, James 4/61
Webb, Sidney 4/19, 10/47
Webern, Anton von 9/45
Webster, Martin 10/79
Webster, Ronald 3/69
Wegener, Alfred 12/12
Weigel, Helene 12/56
Weighell, Sid 10/82
Weil, Andre 5/06
Weil, Simone 2/09
Weill, Kurt 3/00, 12/33, 4/50
Weimar
- New German democratic republic declared 7/19

Weinberg, Moshe 9/72
Weinberger, Caspar 8/17, 10/87
Weingartner, Felix 5/42
Weiss, Carl 9/35
Weiss, Peter 12/64
Weissmuller, Johnny 6/04, 7/22, 12/34, 1/84
Weizman, Ezer 3/93
Weizmann, Chaim 11/17, 2/18, 8/29, 10/30, 11/38, 7/47, 5/48, 11/52
Welbeck, Nathaniel 11/60
Weldon, Fay 9/33
Welensky, Roy 2/61, 12/62
Welles, Orson 5/15, 10/38, 12/38, 4/41, 10/47, 6/48, 12/49, 5/52, 10/85
Welles, Sumner 3/40
Wells, Alan 7/80
Wells, Billy 6/13
Wells, Herbert George 12/02, 10/09, 12/09, 4/10, 9/33, 5/34, 12/38, 8/46, 12/46
Wells, Peter 4/89
Wemyss, Lady Victoria 5/94
Wendel, Fritz 4/39
Wesker, Arnold 5/32, 9/61
West Africa, French
- Pro-Vichy West Africa joins Allies 11/42

West Indies
- See Britain (Empire and Commonwealth)

West, Frederick 6/68
West, Fred. 3/94, 1/95
West, Mae 4/27, 11/80
West, Nathanael 9/03
West, Rebecca 3/83
West, Rosemary 4/94
Westmoreland, William 2/68, 7/68
Weston, Gerry 2/72
Wetherell, Marmaduke 3/94
Weygand, Maxime 5/40, 6/40
Wheeler, Robert Eric Mortimer 7/76
Whelan, Bill 2/58
Wheldon, Huw 3/86
Whistler, James McNeill 7/03
Whitbread, Fatima 9/87
Whitby, David 8/63
White Star
- Launch of Olympic, biggest vessel afloat 10/10
- Launch of Titanic, biggest ship afloat 5/11
- Titanic sinks in worst ever sea disaster 4/12
- German U-boat sinks liner Arabic 8/15

White, Edward 6/65, 1/67
White, James 6/66
White, John 7/64, 4/93
Whitehead, Edgar 2/59, 9/62, 2/63
Whitehouse, Mary 11/65, 12/80, 12/82, 4/87
Whitelaw, William 3/72, 6/72, 7/72, 11/73, 2/75, 5/79, 12/82, 6/83, 1/88
Whiteman, Paul 12/27, 12/67
Whitfield, June 12/53
Whitlam, Gough 11/75
Whitman, Charles 8/66
Whitman, Slim 10/91
Whitney, John 8/66
Whittle, Frank 8/39, 5/41, 1/44
Whittle, Lesley 1/75, 3/75, 12/75, 7/76
Whitty, Kenneth 3/84
W.H. Smiths (bookshop) 1/89
Wilberforce, Lord 2/72
Wilby, John 10/92
Wilcox, Francis 10/60
Wilde, Marty 12/57, 12/59
Wilde, Oscar 11/00, 2/95
Wilder, Billy 6/06
Wilder, Thornton 12/75
Wilding, Anthony 7/11, 7/13, 7/14
Wilding, Michael 2/52
Wilhelm II, Kaiser of Germany 11/00, 3/05, 7/05, 8/06, 11/07, 3/08, 11/08, 2/09, 6/11, 2/12, 6/14, 7/14, 2/16, 7/17, 8/17, 4/18, 11/18, 3/19, 1/20, 3/20, 6/41
Wilhelmina, Queen of the Netherlands 5/40, 8/42, 10/47, 9/48, 11/62
Wilkie, David 7/76, 11/84, 5/85
Wilkie, Wendell 11/40
Wilkins, Maurice 12/62
Wilkinson, Ellen 10/36
Wilkinson, Geoffrey 12/73
Willard, Jess 4/15, 7/19
William Arthur Philip Louis, Prince 6/91
William, Duke of Gloucester
- See Royal Family (Britain)

Williams, Betty 11/76, 10/77, 2/80
Williams, Emlyn 12/39
Williams, Hank 1/53
Williams, J.P.R. 3/79
Williams, John 12/77
Williams, Kenneth 4/88
Williams, Owen 12/38
Williams, Shirley 7/80, 1/81, 6/81, 11/81
Williams, Tennessee 12/47, 5/48, 3/55, 10/62, 12/77, 2/83
Williams, William Carlos 3/63
Williamson, Henry 12/27
Williamson, Nicol 12/64
Willingdon, Viscount, (Viceroy of India) 12/31

Willis, Bob 7/81
Willis, Norman 9/84, 3/88
Willis, Ted 12/76
Willis, William 9/64
Willis, Helen
- See Moody, Helen
Wilmot, John 10/33
Wilson, Arthur 5/53
Wilson, Charlie 8/63, 8/64, 1/68
Wilson, Eric 9/89
Wilson, Harold
- Born 3/16
- Condemns Dior's hour-glass look 6/47
- injured in air accident 7/47
- Joins the cabinet as President of the Board of Trade 9/47
- Poverty speech 7/48
- Eases industrial red tape 11/48
- Announces end of clothes rationing 3/49
- Sets up Film Finance Corporation 12/49
- Resigns as President of Board of Trade 4/51
- Branded a Bevanite "wrecker" by Attlee 10/52
- Joins Labour shadow cabinet 4/54
- As shadow chancellor, attacks budget 4/59
- To run for Labour leadership 10/60
- Gaitskell beats off leadership challenge 11/60
- Elected leader of Labour Party 2/63
- Visits President Kennedy 4/63
- Accuses Macmillan over Profumo affair 6/63
- Denounces rent rackets 7/63
- "White heat of ... revolution" speech 10/63
- Attends Kennedy funeral 11/63
- Becomes Prime Minister 10/64
- Warns Ian Smith that UDI is treason 10/64
- Imposes import tax 10/64
- Pays tribute to Churchill 1/65
- Infuriates US over Vietnam issue 4/65
- Meets de Gaulle for Vietnam talks 4/65
- First Labour PM to meet Pope 4/65
- Pays tribut to late JFK 5/65
- Awards Beatles MBEs 6/65
- Suggests peace mission to Vietnam 6/65
- Claims Kashmir war is biggest threat to world peace 9/65
- Fails to head off Rhodesia's UDI 10/65
- Opens Post Office Tower 10/65
- Announces all ties with rebel Rhodesian UDI have been broken 11/65
- Imposes economic sanctions on Rhodesia 11/65
- Drops plans to nationalise steel 11/65
- Says UK has offered Zambia military aid 12/65
- Rejects military action against Rhodesia 1/66
- Calls general election 2/66
- Labour secures overall majority in general election 4/66
- Declares state of emergency over seamen's strike 5/66
- Names Communists involved in dock strike 6/66
- Imposes six-month pay freeze 7/66
- Tours industrial fair, Moscow 7/66
- Visits scene of Aberfan disaster 10/66
- Urges European economic build-up 11/66
- Attends talks with Ian Smith 12/66
- Crisis meeting on Torrey Canyon 3/67
- Rebuffed by de Gaulle on UK entry to EEC 5/67
- Congratulates Francis Chichester 5/67
- Explains 14.3% devaluation of pound 11/67
- Announces plan to reform Lords 6/68
- More talks with Smith, aboard Fearless 10/68
- Tells MPs of abortive talks with Smith 10/68
- Faces Biafra protest in West Germany 2/69
- Talks with Nixon in London 2/69
- Ousts Callaghan from inner cabinet 5/69
- Industrial Relations Bill: penalties out 6/69
- Voted "man of the decade" in poll 12/69
- Trip to US causes anger 1/70
- Leads Labour to defeat in election 6/70
- Supports Northern Ireland direct rule 3/72
- Supports Tory call for EEC referendum 4/72
- Appeals to miners to call off strike 2/74
- Begins third term as PM 3/74
- Labour wins election with majority of three 10/74
- Documents stolen from his London home 10/74
- Announces EEC referendum 1/75
- Prevents cabinet split on EEC referendum 3/75
- Sacks Industry Minister, Eric Heffer 4/75
- To limit pay rises by law 7/75
- Attends opening of North Sea oil pipeline 11/75
- Resigns as Prime Minister 3/76
- Receives life peerage 7/83
- Dies of Altzheimer's aged 79 5/95
Wilson, Henry 6/22
Wilson, Mary 9/70
Wilson, Matthew 2/14
Wilson, Mrs Woodrow 4/45
Wilson, Woodrow 7/12, 11/12, 3/13, 4/13, 10/13, 2/15, 5/15, 7/15, 8/15, 11/15, 12/15, 1/16, 5/16, 6/16, 9/16, 10/16, 11/16, 12/16, 8/17, 1/18, 2/18, 8/18, 12/18, 1/19, 9/19, 11/19, 12/19, 1/20, 3/20, 12/20, 1/24, 2/24, 11/44
Wilton, Penelope 2/94
Wimbledon
- See also results each July (except war years)
- First American lady to win, May Sutton 6/05
- Prince of Wales becomes first president 6/07
- More than 100 men participate 6/11
- Tournament suspended for war 1/15
- Opened at new site 6/22
- Suzanne Lenglen wins her fifth title 7/23
- Tournament introduces seeding system 6/24
- 50th Jubilee; Duke of York plays 6/26
- Sixth win for Helen Wills Moody in final 7/33
- Lady players may wear shorts 5/34
- Fred Perry wins men's; D. Round, ladies' 7/34
- Fred Perry, men's; Helen Moody, women's 7/35
- Helen Moody wins eighth title, v. Jacobs 7/38
- Americans win all five titles 7/38
- Shocked by Gussie Moran's lace panties 6/49
- Tournament's longest-ever set ends 31-29 7/50
- Droby beats Patty, longest men's singles 6/53
- Maureen Connolly wins for third time 7/54
- Althea Gibson wins ladies' title 7/57
- Two Britons reach ladies' final 7/61
- First Australian woman to win: Margaret Smith 7/63
- Amateur-professional distinction is out 12/67
- Rod Laver wins first open Wimbledon 7/68
- Billie Jean King wins third title in row 7/68
- Longest ever singles match 6/69
- Ann Jones wins ladies' title 7/69
- Top stars boycott 7/73
- Arthur Ashe beats Connors, men's title 7/75
- Centenary year celebrations 7/77
- Virginia Wade wins ladies' title for UK 7/77
- Nastase banned for bad behaviour 7/78
- McEnroe ends Borg's 41-win run 7/81
- Centenary year of ladies' championship 7/84
- Navratilova wins her fifth ladies' title 7/84
- Boris Becker, 17, is youngest champion 7/85
Wincott, Len 9/31
Windischgraetz, Prince von 5/26
Windsor, Barbara 4/65
Windsor, Duchess of 10/37, 6/67, 6/72, 4/86, 12/87
Windsor, Duke of
- See also Edward VIII, King; Royal Family (Britain) 10/37, 11/37, 3/45, 5/72, 6/72
Wingate, Orde 3/44
Winning, Tom 10/94
Wint, Arthur 8/48
Winter sports
- Speedskating Finn Thunberg wins five medals 1/24
- Winter Olympics, St Moritz, Switzerland 2/28
- UK's ice hockey gold at Winter Olympics 2/36
- Winter Olympics at Garmisch-Partenkirchen 2/36
- Winter Olympics begin at Oslo 2/52
- Winter Olympics in Cortina d'Ampezzo 1/56
- Winter Olympics, Squaw Valley, Idaho 2/60
- Czechs are world ice hockey champs 3/69
- John Curry wins skating, Innsbruck 2/76
- Robin Cousins wins European Championship 1/80
- Winter Olympics open at Lake Placid, USA 2/80
- Robin Cousins wins World Skating crown 3/80
- UK's Torvill and Dean win Euro skating title 2/81
- Torvill & Dean win British Championship with nine 6s 1/94
- Ulrike Maier dies in 60mph ski crash 1/94
- Torvill & Dean retire from competitive skating 3/94
- Canada wins World Ice Hockey Championship 5/94
Wirth, Joseph 9/22, 11/22
Wise, Ernie 12/74, 5/84
Witbooi, Hendrik 11/04
Witte, Sergei 10/05
Wittgenstein, Lutwig 4/51
Wodehouse, Pelham Grenville 11/25, 12/39, 7/41, 11/44, 1/75, 2/75, 12/75
Wojtyla, Karol
- See Pope John Paul II
Wolf, Hugo 2/03
Wolfenden, John 9/57
Wolff, Karl 4/45, 9/64
Wolfit, Donald 12/30, 12/44, 2/68
Wombwell, David 8/66
Women
- See also Women's Suffrage
- German women demand higher education 3/00
- First time in Olympic Games 7/00
- UK women's trade union meets 10/00
- First communal vote, Norway 12/01
- Feet-binding banned in China 2/02
- Textile workers call for votes for women 2/02
- Glasgow barmaids win ruling 5/02
- Prussia forbids political grouping 5/02
- Women obtain the vote in Connecticut elections 9/03
- Mrs Emmeline Pankhurst founds society 10/03
- Hospital for women opens in Waterloo 10/03
- Norwegian parliament blocks women's vote 12/03
- First woman to win Nobel prize: Marie Curie 12/03
- Pope attacks low-cut dresses 1/04
- Women's suffrage bill forced out, London 5/05
- First suffragettes to be imprisoned 10/05
- Bertha von Suttner wins Nobel Peace Prize 12/05
- Women participate in British election campaign 2/06
- Women over 24 get the vote in Finland 3/06
- Urged not to play "rough sports" 3/06
- Disrupt Parliament as motion is blocked 4/06
- Top suffragettes meet British premier 6/06
- Banned from "dangerous sport" in Britain 6/06
- Eleven Suffragettes jailed 10/06
- Keir Hardie's female emancipation bill 11/06
- Suffragettes on hunger strike 12/06
- Women's education under Persian shah 1/07
- Suffragettes clash with police; arrests 2/07
- Finns elect women MPs; first in world 3/07
- Hardie's bill is defeated 3/07
- Women's Labour League first conference 5/07
- Employed equally in Austrian universities 8/07
- German Women's Congress anti-militarism 8/07
- Suffragettes drown out Asquith's speech 11/07
- Pre-marital affidavits on good character 12/07
- Suffragettes raid six ministers' homes 1/08
- New York woman arrested for smoking 1/08
- Emmeline Pankhurst tells of prison life 2/08
- "Women's Parliament" meets 2/08
- Denmark chooses universal suffrage 4/08
- Automatic divorce law in France 6/08
- 200,000 support suffragettes at rally 6/08
- Barmaids banned, New Zealand 1/09
- Desertion not grounds for divorce 2/09
- Russian prosecutor stops woman barrister 11/09
- French law favours pregnant women 11/09
- Emancipated heroine in Shaw's play 12/09
- Divorce too expensive for poor, Britain 3/10
- First to get pilot's licence 3/10
- Spanish king allows women in university 3/10
- Calls for equality in divorce 6/10
- Rosa Luxemburg attacked at congress 9/10
- Julia Ward Howe, US suffragist, dies 10/10
- French Academie des Sciences snubs Marie Curie 1/11
- First in Norwegian Parliament 3/11
- Riot against food prices, France 9/11
- Protests against Manhood Suffrage Bill 11/11
- Madame Curie wins her second Nobel Prize 12/11
- Prince Thun vetoes Austrian woman MP 6/12
- Divorce Commission wants equal treatment 11/12
- Mrs Pankhurst charged with bomb attack 2/13
- Russian government bars women lawyers 2/13
- International Women's Peace Conference 4/13
- Why women dress up: view of a psychiatrist 5/13
- Emily Dawson, first woman magistrate, UK 6/13
- Woman in split skirt arrested in London 7/13
- Women are inferior, says Almroth Wright 10/13
- First woman to do aerial loop-the-loop 1/14
- Admitted to Turkish universities 2/14
- Mary Richardson slashes Velazquez art 3/14
- Problems of women factory workers, UK 7/14
- Queen starts war "Work for Women" fund 9/14
- Sewing guilds to make clothes for war 11/14
- Government wants war workers, equal pay 3/15
- Special army battalion created 3/15
- International Socialists call for peace 3/15
- Allowed to become bus and tram conductors 10/15
- Female factory workers double production 11/15
- First women fully employed on permanent staff, Scotland Yard 11/15
- Two million more employed in Britain 1/16
- 400,000 to till fields, plan 2/16
- British government promises equal pay 2/16
- Committee blasts "extravagant dresses" 3/16
- Women dockers strike over male prejudice 3/16
- To receive Military Medal 6/16
- Queen Mary opens South London Hospital for Women 7/16
- Dr Mary Scharlieb says prostitutes spread VD 10/16
- First birth control clinic, New York 10/16
- First woman member of US Congress 11/16
- 3.2 million work outside home, Britain 11/16
- Women taxi drivers; non-military scheme 2/17
- First women's battalion, Russia 6/17
- 200,000 work on land in wartime Britain 9/17
- Labour Party educates and organises women 10/17
- Dr Anderson, first UK woman doctor, dies 12/17
- Marie Stopes pioneers sex and birth control 7/18
- Million women factory-workers, USA 8/18
- London Underground strike for equal pay 8/18
- Revolutionary attacks Lenin; he survives 8/18
- Women railway workers settle dispute 9/18
- Commons votes to allow women MPs 10/18
- 100 women police patrols, London 11/18
- Vote for first time in UK election 12/18
- 17 women among election candidates; one elected 12/18
- Nationalist Moslem women protest, Egypt 3/19
- 1.2 million more worked during War 3/19
- Nancy Astor is first woman MP 11/19
- Sex Disqualification Removal Bill passed 12/19
- First woman bar student, Lincoln's Inn 12/19
- Women picket British Embassy in US over Irish problem 4/20
- France beat England at women's football 5/20
- Pope canonises Joan of Arc 5/20
- International Feminist Congress, Geneva 6/20
- First female jurors in Divorce Court, UK 1/21
- Unemployment benefits raised 2/21
- First UK birth control clinic opens 3/21
- Queen is first woman to get Oxford degree 3/21
- Shock at women's dress, free behaviour 5/21
- Fined for smoking, Washington, DC 6/21
- Eight million in paid employment, US 7/21
- British census shows more women than men 8/21
- Five women Poplar councillors arrested 9/21
- Second to win seat, Louth by-election 9/21
- Annie Oakley breaks shooting record 3/22
- Pope Pius XI attacks "immodest" dress 3/22
- Massachusetts public offices opened to all women 4/22
- Less hardship for divorced women in bill 5/22
- Dr Ivy Williams, first called to bar 5/22
- First woman president of Co-operative 6/22
- First congress, Feminine Athletics 8/22
- Women get equal citizenship rights, US 9/22
- Coco Chanel's new liberated fashions set trend 2/23
- Lords' coercion ruling, Britain 2/23
- Matrimonial Causes Bill; equal divorces 3/23
- First woman admitted to Academie Francaise 4/23
- First broadcast of BBC's "Woman's Hour" 5/23
- Mrs Hilton Philipson is third woman MP 6/23
- New law allows divorce of husbands for adultery 6/23
- First to practise at Old Bailey 2/24
- Late night working banned, US Court 3/24
- YWCA say "dress to succeed" 5/24
- Catholic women's group pro-modest dress 7/24
- Dr Russell warns of drugs and tobacco 2/26
- Irish woman, Violet Gibson, attempts to shoot Mussolini 4/26
- Guild wants no strikes or lockouts 4/26
- Can be elected to public office, India 6/26
- 100,000 in London peace march 6/26
- First to swim Channel, breaking a record 8/26
- Italian women cannot hold public office 10/26
- Short hair and "avant-garde" bobs are in 9/27
- First women-only horse race, Newmarket 10/27
- Hall's "Well of Loneliness" on lesbians 12/28
- Abolition of veil sparks Afghan revolt 12/28
- Given limited divorce rights in Egypt 3/29
- Thirteen elected in British general election 5/29
- First UK minister: Margaret Bondfield 6/29
- World Congress on Women's Work, Berlin 6/29
- Women civil servants agree to retire on marriage 1/30
- First to fly solo, Britain to Australia 4/30
- Trades unionists protest at "invasion" 6/30
- 476,041 women unemployed in Britain 8/30
- Feminists condemn new long skirt fashion 3/31
- Civil Service Royal Commission opens to women 7/31
- Elizabeth Scott's Shakespeare Theatre 4/32
- Mildred Didrikson breaks Olympic records 8/32
- Dietrich trend: menswear for women 5/33
- None in new Nazi Reichstag, Germany 11/33
- Women Wimbledon players may wear shorts 5/34
- Fourth Women's World Games; German triumph 8/34
- Polish conscription for men and women 9/34
- New trend: slimming exercises to music 10/35
- Laura Knight, first woman in Royal Academy 2/36
- First BBC women announcers 5/36
- Beryl Markham, first Atlantic women solo 9/36
- Marriage Bill widens grounds for divorce 11/36
- Turkey to conscript woman in wartime 1/37
- First women owner to win Derby 6/37
- Dodds' new drug to ease menopause 12/38
- Woman fellow at male Oxford college 5/39
- Women's League of Health and Beauty, UK 6/39
- Women's Auxiliary Air Force formed, UK 7/39
- Free fresh milk for nursing mothers, UK 7/39
- UK women arms workers demand equal pay 12/39
- Vichy: wives banned from public service 10/40
- 100,000 called on for war work, UK 3/41
- Call-up for unmarried women 20-30, UK 12/41
- Hats no longer compulsory in church, UK 11/42
- All women must do part-time war work, UK 5/43
- Pay in UK has risen by 80% since 1938 7/43
- Men to have housekeeping savings, UK 10/43
- Women teachers in UK allowed to marry 3/44
- UK women teachers to get same pay as men 3/44
- New homes in UK to be fit for housewives 7/44
- Queen Elizabeth praises war work, UK 12/44
- First GI brides leave UK for USA 1/46
- Single women may become diplomats, UK 3/46
- Vote for first time in Japanese election 4/46
- UK minister advocates more women in work 6/47
- UK women asked to avoid longer skirts 9/47
- Woman manager of Shakespeare Theatre, UK 2/48
- Women's Service Bill passed, UK 2/48
- Women's Royal Air Force formed, UK 2/48
- Women's Royal Army Corps formed, UK 2/48
- Penson is first UK woman vice-chancellor 6/48
- WRAF and WRAC incorporated in UK forces 2/49
- Lords to admit peeresses, UK 7/49
- Simone de Beauvoir's "The Second Sex" is published 12/49
- Banned from reading BBC news 1/51
- "Average UK housewife" works 15 hour day 7/51
- Education pioneer Maria Montessori dies 5/52
- Commons votes for women's equal pay 5/52
- Eva Peron dies, Argentina's heroine 7/52
- First woman to win Welsh Bardic Crown 8/53
- First Tory minister, F. Horsbrugh becomes Education Minister 9/53
- Equal pay for civil servants 1/55
- Burnham committee - equal teachers' pay 3/55
- UK Lords reforms: life peers and women 10/57
- Bishop: working mothers "family enemy" 3/58
- Christabel Pankhurst, suffragist, dies 3/58
- 14 women life peers 7/58
- Warnings on overuse of sedatives 11/58
- Black women lead Cato Manor unrest, South Africa 6/59
- New MPs Margaret Thatcher and Judith Hart 10/59
- Mrs Bandaranaike, first woman premier 7/60
- Suffragette Estelle Sylvia Pankurst dies 9/60
- Contraceptive pill goes on sale in UK 1/61
- First Mothercare shop opens, UK 9/61
- Birth control pill available on NHS, UK 12/61
- First woman judge in High Court' UK 10/62
- Tereshkova (USSR): first woman in space 6/63
- Oral contraceptive on prescription, UK 6/63
- Woman broadcaster reads TV news in Wales 8/63
- Woman completes solo round-world flight 4/64
- Death of Nancy Astor, first UK woman MP 5/64
- First Brook Advisory Centre opens, UK 7/64
- First woman High Court judge, UK 8/65
- First woman to train racehorses, UK 7/66
- Birth-control pioneer Margaret Sanger dies 9/66
- Twiggy is rising fashion star 12/66
- The Abortion Bill becomes law, UK 10/67
- Ford machinists' equal pay strike, UK 6/68
- Epidural promises painless childbirth 9/68

- First sextuplets born in Britain 10/68
- Pregnancy Advisory Service launched, UK 10/68
- First abortion clinic opens in London 10/68
- Human egg made fertile in test tube, UK 2/69
- Women workers at Ford (UK) win equal pay 2/69
- Lloyd's of London to admit women 2/69
- Irene Hanson gives birth to quins, UK 11/69
- Bill to give women equal pay, UK 2/70
- First women generals in US Army 5/70
- Methodists to admit women ministers, UK 6/70
- Missiles thrown at Miss World contest 11/70
- "The Female Eunuch" published 12/70
- Women win the vote in Switzerland 2/71
- Liechtenstein refuses women the vote 2/71
- UK's biggest women's lib march 3/71
- US Senate passes Equal Rights Amendment 3/72
- Male Oxford colleges to admit women, UK 4/72
- Allowed on UK Stock Exchange floor 2/73
- UK plans Equal Opportunities Commission 9/73
- Dalkon Shield IUD taken off market, US 5/74
- First as leader of a UK political party 2/75
- Two women try to kill Ford on two occasions 9/75
- State-sponsored maternity pay, UK 10/75
- International Women's Year ends 12/75
- Sex Discrimination Act, UK; employment 12/75
- Equal Pay Act, UK; equal opportunities 12/75
- UK's only big women's hospital to close 2/76
- Northern Irish women's peace movement 8/76
- First as Dartmouth Naval College cadets 9/76
- First as jockey in Grand National 4/77
- Red "La Passionaria" returns to Spain 5/77
- Peace Movement women win Nobel prize 10/77
- Naomi James in world sailing record 6/78
- Pelletier, first French Minister for Women 9/78
- Israel's woman premier, Golda Meir, dies 12/78
- US feminists upset at wife-rape verdict 12/78
- Tehran women protest at Islamic strictures 3/79
- International Women's Day protests 3/79
- Mrs Thatcher, first woman premier of UK 5/79
- First woman Prime Minister of Portugal 7/79
- Grete Waitz breaks 2.5 hour marathon 10/79
- Belfast peace woman Maguire dies 1/80
- More UK women work than rest of Europe 1/80
- Lung cancer kills many women in US 1/80
- Iceland's first woman premier 6/80
- Iranians protest about Islamic dress 7/80
- First Norwegian woman Prime Minister 2/81
- Brown first woman to cox Oxford boat team 4/81
- First woman Supreme Court Judge, O'Connor 7/81
- Church of England votes to admit women as deacons 11/81
- 20,000 women encircle Greenham Common against Cruise 12/82
- First woman trainer to win National, UK 4/83
- Sally Ride is first US woman in space 6/83
- First woman head of major union, UK 3/84
- Bailiffs clear main Greenham peace camp 4/84
- Geraldine Ferraro runs for US Vice-President 7/84
- UK High Court grants Greenham eviction 9/84
- Church of England approves women deacons 7/85
- 10,000 attend rights conference, Kenya 7/85
- Death of feminist Simone de Beauvoir 4/86
- UK synod votes for women's ordination 2/87
- US judge denies surrogate mother right of parenthood 3/87
- Plans for ordination of women published 6/88
- Synod votes to go ahead with plans to ordain women 7/88
- Anglican bishops vote on women priests 8/88
- First woman bishop elected in America 9/88
- Barbara Harris becomes first woman Anglican bishop 2/89
- Mary Robinson becomes first woman President of Ireland 11/90
- All-male Magic Circle lifts ban on women 9/91
- Betty Boothroyd, first Commons woman Speaker in 6 centuries 4/92
- Women are no longer allowed to appear on Afghan television 7/92
- C. of E. Synod votes to allow ordination of women priests 11/92

Women's suffrage
- See also Women
- WSPU founded by Mrs Pankhurst 10/03
- Pankhursts tried; Lloyd George witness 10/08
- Internation convention opens in London 4/09
- 120 arrested outside Downing Street 6/09
- Imprisoned suffragettes are force-fed 9/09
- Alleged brutality in prison investigated 10/09
- Suffragettes throw stones at Mayor's banquet 11/09
- Asquith mobbed by suffragettes 1/10
- George says Lords' reform has priority over female suffrage 7/10
- Julia Ward Howe, US activist, dies 10/10
- Massachusetts refuses women the vote 4/11
- Established by Portuguese court 4/11
- Five mile procession march in London 6/11
- Protest at male vote bill; 200 arrested 11/11
- British cabinet split 1/12
- 120 arrested for smashing shop windows 3/12
- Women's Enfranchisement Bill defeated 3/12
- Franchise Bill only for men over 21 6/12
- Male supporters evicted from meeting 6/12
- Suffragettes smash post office windows 6/12
- Irish Nationalist wounded in attack 7/12
- Feeling of betrayal as bill is scrapped 1/13
- Mrs Pankhurst charged with bomb attack 2/13
- Sylvia Pankhurst in jail hunger strike 2/13
- Suffragettes lock Labour Party delegates in conference hall 3/13
- New law to deal with hunger strikers; The Cat and Mouse Act 3/13
- Suffragettes attacked by London mobs 3/13
- Mrs Pankhurst found guilty of arson 4/13
- London poll rejection 5/13
- Bomb found in St. Paul's Cathedral 5/13
- Magistrate gets letter bomb 5/13
- Emily Davison killed by Derby horse 6/13
- Seven found guilty of "conspiracy" 6/13
- Norway gives women equal franchise 6/13
- Suffragettes foil police 7/13
- Bomb ministers' homes; attack Asquith 8/13
- Sir Almroth Wright's anti-suffrage book 10/13
- Emmeline Pankhurst deported from US 10/13
- Scottish women jump at Asquith's car 11/13
- Mrs Pankhurst arrested on return from US 12/13
- Protesters burn Scottish houses and church 2/14
- Suffragette, Mary Richardson, slashes Velazquez's "Venus" 3/14
- Pankhursts arrested, Richardson jailed 3/14
- Attacks on British Museum and Royal Academy 4/14
- Suffragettes throw bombs at church and Yarmouth pier 4/14
- Mrs Pankhurst among 57 Palace arrests 5/14
- Protest at Franchise Bill failure at Palace 5/14
- Protesters burn church, disrupt services 6/14
- Union offices raided; new arrests 6/14
- Jailed suffragettes get King's Amnesty 8/14
- 1,000 leave for French voluntary work 2/15
- Mrs Pankhurst welcomes Register of Women 3/15
- Women can do men's jobs, thanks to war 3/15
- Women win right to vote in Norway 4/16
- President Wilson promises women vote 9/16
- Bill to enfranchise women over 30 3/17
- Commons votes to give vote to wives over 30 6/17
- Representation of People Act 10/17
- Support from President Wilson, US 10/17
- US House of Representatives votes for female suffrage 1/18
- Representation Act: women over 30 vote 2/18
- Commons votes to allow women MPs 10/18
- Women vote for first time in UK election 12/18
- 17 women among candidates; one elected 12/18
- Nancy Astor is first woman MP 11/19
- 19th amendment US: women get federal vote 8/20
- Mussolini approves bill 6/23
- Bill read on vote for women over 21 2/24
- South African Jan Smuts campaigns for it 12/28
- UK poll has six million new women voters 5/29
- South African white women get the vote 5/30
- Laval government falls over women's vote 2/32
- German Nazis want to abolish it 12/33
- Turkish women get the vote 12/34
- Mexican women workers to get vote 9/35

Wood, Derek 3/88
Wood, Edward
- See Halifax

Wood, Henry 8/44
Wood, John 12/89
Wood, Kingsley 6/34, 9/39, 9/43
Wood, Natalie 11/81
Wood, Ray 5/57
Wood, Sydney 7/31
Wood, Wilfred 4/85
Woodcock, Bruce 4/47, 11/50
Wooderson, Sydney 8/37, 8/38
Woodfull, Bill 1/33
Woods, Donald 10/77, 1/78
Woods, Robert 1/76
Woods, Rose Mary 11/73
Woodward, Bob 5/73, 8/73
Woodward, Robert 4/44
Woodward, Sandy 5/82
Woolf, Leonard 12/23, 3/41
Woolf, Virginia 12/23, 12/25, 12/27, 3/41
Woolton, Lord 11/40, 1/41
Woosnam, Ian 4/91
Wootton, Lady 1/69
Worden, Alfred 7/71
World Bank
- See also Economy (World)
- Created 12/45

World Cup
- See Football, Cricket, Rugby

World Refugee Year
- Launched by Macmillan 6/59

World Trade Center
- Bomb blast kills five people 2/93

World War I (Africa)
- Louis Botha invades South West Africa 10/14
- Botha's forces crush pro-German rebels 11/14
- British drive Germans out of East Africa 11/14
- Indians and King's African Rifles, in Kenya 11/14
- British and French conquer Togoland 11/14
- Botha takes German South West Africa 5/15
- French and Belgians beat Germans, Cameroons 1/16
- Smuts to command Allies, East Africa 2/16
- Allied occupation of Cameroons complete 2/16
- Smuts drives Germans and Askari from Kenya 4/16
- British occupy Dar-es-Salaam 9/16

World War I (Asia, Pacific)
- New Zealanders take German-run Samoa 8/14
- Australians take German New Guinea port 9/14
- Russia invades Turkey's Armenia 11/14
- Britain annexes Cyprus 11/14
- Turkish Suez attack beaten off 2/15
- Japan scares China, then changes mind 5/15
- British beat 60,000 Turks, Tigris 1/16
- Russians beat Turks at Erzerum 1/16
- Britain and France plan Ottoman carve-up 3/16
- Russians take Bitlis, Kurdestan 3/16
- Allies bomb Constantinople 4/16
- Russia rejects Turkish armistice 4/16
- Turkish siege defeats British, Kut-el-Amara 4/16
- Empire troops repel Turks from Tigris 5/16
- Lawrence leads Arabians against Turks 6/16
- Arab independence: sea and trade links open 6/16
- Russians rout Turks at Erzinjan 7/16
- Britain and Russia allied with Persia 8/16
- Lawrence in anti-Turk revolt mission 10/16
- British capture Baghdad, Mesopotamia 3/17
- British beat 20,000 Turks, Gaza 3/17
- British take Beersheba, capture Turks 10/17
- British take Jaffa; Balfour Declaration 11/17
- British capture Jerusalem 12/17
- Australian troops take Jericho 2/18
- British oust Turks from River Euphrates 3/18
- US, British and Japanese storm Vladivostock 4/18
- Allenby wipes out Turks, Palestine 9/18
- British take Haifa, Acre, Es-Salt 9/18
- Arabs under Lawrence take Damascus 10/18
- British troops take Beirut and Sidon 10/18

World War I (Balkans)
- Bulgaria neutral 11/14
- Serb invade Albania and take Tirana 6/15
- Central Powers Turkey and lure Bulgaria 9/15
- Bulgaria mobilises and moves into Serbia 9/15
- Greece mobilises 9/15
- Russia attacks Bulgaria; Allies blockade 10/15
- Germans and Austrians direct Bulgarian army 10/15
- Allies land at Salonika to help Serbia 10/15
- Germans and Austrians direct Bulgarian army 10/15
- Bulgarians invade Serbia; cut Greek rail 10/15
- Central Powers control Serbia 11/15
- Austrians beat Montenegro; war resumes 1/16
- Austrians kill 9,000 Serb civilians 3/16
- Greece's ex-premier wants to back Allies 8/16
- Rumania declares war on Austria-Hungary 8/16
- Germany declares war on Rumania 8/16
- Rumania and Russia beat Germans at Dobrudja 9/16
- Greek King declares war on Bulgaria 9/16
- Serbs cross Albania to fight on own soil 9/16
- Allied offensive; French take Florina 9/16
- Rumanians beat Austrians, Orsova 9/16
- Allies occupy Athens; back Venizelos 10/16
- Germans take Braila from Rumanians 1/17
- Allies force Greek king to abdicate 6/17
- Bulgaria surrenders after fierce attack 9/18

World War I (Dardanelles)
- Royal Navy bombards Turkish forts 2/15
- Allies back Russia's claims to straits 3/15
- Allies land on Gallipoli; heavy losses 4/15
- British and French occupy Turkish forts 8/15
- Turks counterattack; disease takes toll 8/15
- British sink four Turkish transport ships 9/15
- Allies evacuate after heavy defeat 12/15
- Allies' indecision on Russian munitions 12/15
- Turks duped as 90,000 British and Anzacs go 12/15
- Commission partly blames Kitchener 3/17

World War I (Eastern Front)
- Russia attacks East Prussia, Galicia 8/14
- Germany and Austria invade Russian Poland 8/14
- Major Russian reverse at Tannenberg 8/14
- Russians rout Austrians at Lemberg 8/14
- Russians push back Austrians near Lvov 9/14
- Turkey attacks Russian ports and fleet 10/14
- Hindenburg becomes German Commander-in-Chief 11/14
- Russians advance on Konigsberg, Prussia 11/14
- Germans advance 40 miles from Warsaw 11/14
- Russians beat Germans on Polish front 11/14
- Germans take Lodz, Poland 12/14
- Turkish Ninth Army surrenders to Russia 1/15
- 800,000 Russians advance on East Prussia 1/15
- First use of tear gas, against Russians 1/15
- Russians enter Hungary and kill 30,000 2/15
- Germans take 100,000 Russian prisoners 2/15
- Russians defeat Germans at Prasnych 3/15
- Germans defeat Russians at Grodno 3/15
- Russians capture Memel on the Baltic 3/15
- Germans invade Russian Baltic provinces 4/15
- Austro-German force in Russian Galicia 5/15
- Austrians retake Lemberg from Russians 6/15
- Germans retake Przemysl from Russians 6/15
- Russians stop German advance, Lyublin 7/15
- Austro-Germans attack Warsaw 7/15
- Germans take Warsaw, Ivangorod and Kovno 8/15
- Germans take Brest-Litovsk; Russian loss 8/15
- Austria wants Poland and Galicia in Empire 8/15
- Russia rejects Austro-German peace offer 8/15
- Germany and Austria partition Poland 8/15
- Germans take Grodno, then Vilna 9/15
- Czar takes personal control of army 9/15
- Germans take Pinsk 12/15
- Russia turns tables on Austrians, Sokal 6/16
- Russians take 300,000 prisoners, Galicia 6/16
- Russians repel Austro-Germans over Lipa 7/16
- Germany deports a million Poles 12/16
- Russian offensive on Baltic 1/17
- Unbearable Russian losses; Czar falls 3/17
- Kerensky's Galician success; keeps power 7/17
- Russia stays in war; Germans fight back 7/17
- Germans drive Russians from Riga 9/17
- Russian army chief Kornilov dismissed 9/17
- Bolshevik Russia wants peace; to demobilise 11/17
- Germany, Austria and Russia agree to truce 11/17
- Brest-Litovsk talks: Germany and Russia 12/17
- Peace talks confusion; Russians invade 2/18
- Russia surrenders territory for peace 3/18
- British back White Russians, Archangel 8/18

World War I (Home Front)
- Defence of the Realm Act: emergency 8/14
- 300 Germans detained at London Olympia 8/14
- Asquith calls for 500,000 volunteers 9/14
- Aliens rounded up; Prince Louis resigns 10/14
- German internees riot, Isle of Man camp 11/14
- German warships shell towns; 100 die 12/14
- German Zeppelin bombs Norfolk; 20 die 1/15
- First Military Cross awards 1/15
- Clydeside armaments workers strike 2/15
- Navy seizes German cargo; ignores blockade 2/15
- King wants arms workers to cut drinking alcohol 4/15
- Liner Armenian sunk off Cornwall 6/15
- Government denies call-up plans 7/15
- U-boats sink four British steamships 7/15
- Naval General Service Medals awarded 8/15
- US gold shipment of £55 million arrives 8/15
- War Profits Tax included in new budget 9/15
- 600 Austrians and Germans interned, London 9/15
- Women factory workers produce twice as much as men 11/15
- Paper censored for anti-Kitchener piece 11/15
- War Cabinet debates manpower shortage 11/15
- Recruitment priority: unmarried men 11/15
- Commons votes for conscription 1/16
- Wealthy should free servants for war effort 2/16
- Tobacco and paper imports banned 2/16
- Peace Debate: MPs rebuked by Asquith 2/16
- Munitions strike leaders arrested, Clyde 3/16
- Spirits, motors and piano imports banned 3/16
- Zeppelin raids on eight counties 3/16
- New Zealand pilot bombs German Zeppelin 4/16
- Total war credit £2,382 million 5/16
- Women to receive Military Medal 6/16
- Lloyd George is made War Secretary 7/16
- Casement hanged in London for treason 8/16
- Zeppelin crew arrested in Essex 9/16
- One meatless day introduced 9/16
- 50,000 VD cases reported among soldiers 10/16
- Money and securities contraband 11/16
- Government to use vacant land for farming 11/16
- All men over 26 can be conscripted 12/16
- Call for huge war loan to meet debts 1/17
- US to lend £200 million 4/17
- King's proclamation: "eat less bread" 5/17
- German aeroplanes raid England: 76 die 5/17
- First aeroplane bombing, London: 100 die 6/17
- Churchill becomes Minister of Munitions 7/17
- 108 die in German air raids on Islands 9/17
- Zeppelin raid; four shot down 10/17
- Rationing increases; two meatless days 1/18
- Meat, butter and margarine rationing 2/18
- Conscription age up to 50; also Ireland 3/18
- Coal, gas and electricity rationing 3/18
- "Tank Week" raise millions for war effort 3/18
- Lloyd George defends war record 5/18
- General rationing 6/18

World War I (Italian Front)
- Italians fail to cross river; big losses 11/15
- Austria attacks Italy and South Tyrol 5/16
- Italian breakthrough at Trentino 6/16
- Italians take Gorizia 8/16
- New offensive at Trieste 9/16
- Italians take Monte Santo 8/17
- Italian army collapses, Caporetto 10/17
- Germans cross mountains; Italian soldiers desert 10/17
- Italians chase Austrians across Piave 6/18
- Austrians evacuate Italian land 10/18

World War I (Sea)
- Britain sinks cruisers off Heligoland 9/14
- Germany sinks British cruisers, Holland 9/14
- German mines claim British warships 9/14
- Britain sinks four German ships, Holland 10/14
- Australian cruiser sinks German, Sumatra 11/14
- Four German cruisers sunk off Falklands 12/14
- UK blocks Germans; sinks biggest cruiser 1/15
- HMS Formidable sunk by German U-boat 1/15
- Germans sink three UK merchant ships 1/15
- US ship, William P Frye, sunk by Germans 1/15
- German submarine threat to all ships off UK 2/15
- Britain sinks Dresden battleship 3/15
- Britain's counter-blockade of Germany 3/15
- HMS Bayano sinks off Scotland 3/15
- Germans sink trawlers, North Sea 4/15
- Austrian submarine sinks French cruiser 4/15
- Germany sinks Lusitania liner; 1,400 die 5/15
- Germans sink US merchant ships, Ireland 7/15
- U-boat sinks White Star liner Arabic 8/15
- P& O liner Persia sunk by U-boat; 400 die 12/15
- Kaiser orders increase in submarine war 2/16
- Portuguese seize four German ships 3/16
- Tirpitz hands Navy Ministry to Capelle 3/16
- Battle of Jutland; dreadnoughts clash 5/16
- British lose more, but Germans retreat 5/16
- Kitchener dies as cruiser hits mine 6/16
- British beat Turks off Port Said 8/16
- Ivernia liner sunk by U-boat; 153 die 1/17
- HMS Laurentic sunk by mine; 350 die 1/17
- US ships armed to meet submarine threat 2/17
- Laconia Cunard liner sunk; 30 die 2/17

- Germans step up U-boat attacks; 134 sunk 2/17
- US breaks with Germany after sinking of Housatonic 2/17
- Three US ships sunk without warning 3/17
- U-boat torpedoes hospital ship; 31 die 3/17
- 91 German ships seized, New York 4/17
- Germans sink two hospital ships; 75 die 4/17
- US ship sinks U-boat; first US shots 4/17
- UK transport ship torpedoed; 413 die 5/17
- British convoy system to dodge U-boats 6/17
- German naval chief resigns; mutiny 10/17
- British decoy raids fail; ship wrecked 5/18
- Nine ships sunk by U-boats 6/18
- Germans torpedo mailboat; 587 die 10/18
- Mutiny at Kiel heralds end of war 11/18
- German Fleet surrenders to Royal Navy 11/18

World War I (Western Front)

- Britain and Allies forced out of Mons 8/14
- Germany's 150 mile Belgian-French line 8/14
- French Lorraine thrust; retreat to Somme 8/14
- Joffre's Allies drive Germans from Marne 9/14
- 500,000 casualties in Marne trench fight 9/14
- Germans capture Rheims, Ghent and Lille 9/14
- Germans take Ghent, Bruges and Ostend 10/14
- Germans take Antwerp; Flanders trench warfare 10/14
- Antwerp falls; Belgian government flees 10/14
- British hold Ypres; fierce German raids 10/14
- Aerial bombing of Paris 10/14
- Stalemate; monotony in muddy trenches 11/14
- Christmas Day truce in the trenches 12/14
- King George V visits BEF and Belgian King 12/14
- French offensive in Champagne 2/15
- British take Neuve Chapelle; French lose 3/15
- British bomb Hoboken, Belgium 3/15
- British offensive, Ypres, to take hill 4/15
- French lose 69,000 to take wood 4/15
- Germans use gas; Allies unprepared 4/15
- French offensive from Meuse to Moselle 4/15
- Dunkirk shelled by Germans; panic 4/15
- French bomb German Crown Prince's quarters 5/15
- Second battle of Artois 5/15
- Naval pilot bombs Zeppelin from air 6/15
- Artois offensive halted 6/15
- British bombard German coastal positions 8/15
- Artois and Champagne offensives' stalemate 8/15
- French strike at Germans in Champagne 9/15
- British strike in Loos, Flanders 9/15
- Fears that Germans are reinforcing 9/15
- Briand wants Alsace; meets Kitchener 11/15
- General Joffre is French C-in-C 12/15
- Haig replaces French as first Army C-in-C 12/15
- Stalemate in the trenches 12/15
- Germans shock French with Verdun attack 2/16
- General Petain heads French Second Army 2/16
- French check Germans west of Verdun 3/16
- Germans attack along Meuse banks 5/16
- Russian Eastern threats divert Germans 6/16
- Germans' new Verdun offensive 6/16
- Somme offensive begins; thousands die 7/16
- 60,000 British casualties; French attack 7/16
- French take Fleury 8/16
- British use tanks against enemy, Somme 9/16
- Allies break Somme front 10/16
- Second Battle of Verdun; French success 10/16
- Germans abandon Verdun and Vaux 11/16
- Somme death toll is 1,150,000 11/16
- Christmas stalemate in trenches 12/16
- Nivelle replaces Joffre; Somme setback 12/16
- Internees over 45 to be exchanged 1/17
- British and Empire troops in Easter attack 4/17
- Allies achieve goals at Arras 4/17
- French attack fails; 100,000 casualties 4/17
- General Petain replaces Nivelle 4/17
- US sends 10,000 engineers to France 5/17
- Mutiny in French Army 5/17
- First US troops land in France 6/17
- Haig takes land south of Ypres 6/17
- Mata Hari sentenced to death on spy charges 7/17
- Germans break French lines, River Aisne 7/17
- Heaviest British assault; stuck in mud 8/17
- French breakthrough at Verdun 8/17
- Entertaining the troops in the trenches 9/17
- Germans bomb hospitals; China army offer 9/17
- British blockade Scandinavia and Holland 10/17
- First US shots of the war 10/17
- Fears of German attack if Russia leaves 11/17
- Canadians take Passchendaele 11/17
- US "Rainbow Division" arrives 11/17
- 45 die in Paris air raid 2/18
- Ferdinand Foch is C-in-C of Allies, France 3/18
- 75 die as German bomb hits Paris church 3/18
- Three million Germans assault France 3/18
- Red Baron, German air ace, killed, Somme 4/18
- Royal Air Force formed "for revenge" 4/18
- Allies lose 400,000 in three weeks; Haig call 4/18
- Amiens destroyed; Germans use mustard gas 5/18
- Germans take Soissons and threaten Rheims 5/18
- "Big Bertha" 420mm gun fires on Paris 6/18
- US Marines attack Chateau Thierry 6/18
- Counter-attack stops Germans near Paris 6/18
- British down 4,102 planes in a year 6/18
- Petain's elastic defence repels Germans 7/18
- 300,000 Americans arrive each month 7/18
- Allied commanders plan offensive in US 7/18
- Germans fail as 20 divisions hit Amiens 8/18
- French hold Champagne-Soissons 8/18
- 30,000 German prisoners; many surrender 8/18
- Allied breakthrough with Belgian backing 9/18
- Central Powers surrender; withdraw men 11/18

World War I (general)

- Serb kills Archduke Franz Ferdinand 6/14
- Austria declares war on Serbia; invades 7/14
- Czar mobilises in support of Serbia 7/14
- Kaiser backs Austria; threatens Russia 7/14
- Britain declares war on Germany 8/14
- Germany declares war on Russia and France 8/14
- Germany invades Belgium 8/14
- Austria declares war on Russia 8/14
- Serbia declares war on Germany 8/14
- Germany and Austria threaten neutral Italy 8/14
- Empire rallies around Britain in war 8/14
- Japan declares war on Germany 8/14
- UK, France and Russia agree no German peace 9/14
- Turkey declares war on Allies 11/14
- Germany has 578,000 Allied prisoners 12/14
- Italy opts for Allies over Germany 4/15
- Italy declares war on Austria 5/15
- Russia rejects Austro-German peace offer 8/15
- Italy declares war on Turkey 8/15
- President Wilson to expand US Army 10/15
- Germans shoot Nurse Cavell 10/15
- Allies ask China to join Entente 11/15
- Germany declares war on Portugal 3/16
- Allied Powers conference, Paris 3/16
- London Declaration abandoned 6/16
- Bulgaria declares war on Rumania 9/16
- Germany has spent £5 billion on war 1/17
- US declares war on Germany 4/17
- Austrians and Bulgarians consider peace 4/17
- Ten million Americans enrol for war 6/17
- China declares war on Central Powers 8/17
- Pro-German coup in Portugal 12/17
- US declares war on Austria 12/17
- Wilson's 14-point post-war peace plan 1/18
- Russia gives in to German peace demands 3/18
- Austrian peace plan rejected by US and UK 9/18
- Germany and Austria seek armistice 10/18
- Turkey surrenders; Dardanelles reopens 10/18
- Germany signs armistice and surrenders 11/18
- Austria signs armistice and surrenders 11/18
- End of costliest war; ten million dead 11/18
- Versailles Peace talks, end conscription call 12/18
- Germans sign Versailles treaty 6/19
- Unknown soldier buried in Westminster Abbey 11/20

World War II (Africa)

- British Somaliland falls to the Italians 8/40
- Four French colonies join Free France 8/40
- Italians invade Egypt from Libya 9/40
- Italy and Germany discuss colonies 9/40
- De Gaulle and Free French land in Senegal 9/40
- De Gaulle abandons attack on Dakar 9/40
- RAF bombs Italians invading Egypt 9/40
- 30,000 Italians captured in Egypt 12/40
- UK attacks Italians in Western Desert 12/40
- Commonwealth troops capture Tobruk 1/41
- Wavell's army reaches Libya 1/41
- Australian troops take Bardia in Libya 1/41
- RAF bombs Italian positions in Abyssinia 1/41
- 100,000 Italians so far taken prisoner 1/41
- Commonwealth troops advance in Eritrea 1/41
- Derna falls to Wavell's troops 1/41
- RAF carries out heavy raid on Tripoli 2/41
- UK and Commonwealth troops take Benghazi 2/41
- Last Italian troops expelled from Sudan 2/41
- Afrika Korps advance guard lands at Tripoli 2/41
- Allies take Mogadishu, Somaliland 2/41
- Haile Selassie's troops capture Burye 3/41
- Afrika Korps launches attack 3/41
- Allies recapture Berbera, Somaliland 3/41
- A last Italian stronghold in Libya falls 3/41
- Allies take Asmara, Eritrea 4/41
- British-led troops evacuate Benghazi 4/41
- South African troops occupy Addis Ababa 4/41
- Allied troops besieged at Tobruk 4/41
- Germans occupy Bardia 4/41
- Three Afrika Korps columns enter Egypt 4/41
- Free French enter French Somaliland 4/41
- Italians in Abyssinia surrender 5/41
- German boxer Schmeling killed in Egypt 5/41
- More Italians in Abyssinia surrender 6/41
- Italian general surrenders in Abyssinia 7/41
- Allies in new drive against Desert Rats 11/41
- S. African forces capture Vichy ships 11/41
- New Zealand troops take Bardia 11/41
- Germans and Italians take Benghazi 1/42
- Afrika Korps advances in Western Desert 1/42
- Rommel's offensive drives back Allies 5/42
- British land on Madagascar 5/42
- Diego Suarez, Madagascar, yields to UK 5/42
- Tobruk falls to Rommel's troops 6/42
- Auchinleck takes command of Eighth Army 6/42
- Eighth Army abandons Mersa Matruh, Egypt 6/42
- Rommel's advance halted at El Alamein 7/42
- Montgomery commands Eighth Army 8/42
- Rommel launches new offensive 8/42
- Madagascar falls to British advance 9/42
- Eighth Army seizes key posts, El Alamein 9/42
- Montgomery scores triumph at El Alamein 10/42
- Montgomery is victorious at El Alamein 11/42
- Germans land forces in Tunis 11/42
- Allies recapture Tobruk 11/42
- Pro-Vichy West Africa joins Allies 11/42
- US troops land in Vichy North Africa 11/42
- Axis troops withdraw in Tunisia 12/42
- Giraud, French HC for N. Africa, killed 12/42
- Free French troops take Oum-el-Araneb 1/43
- Free French troops merge with Eighth Army 1/43
- Conference of Allies in Casablanca 1/43
- Eighth Army crosses into Tunisia 1/43
- Allies take Tripoli 1/43
- US drives back Germans in Tunisia 2/43
- Germans take three towns in Tunisia 2/43
- Allies reverse Rommel's offensive 2/43
- Rommel evacuates Tunis 4/43
- Allies enter Tunis 5/43
- Organised Axis resistance ceases 5/43
- George VI visits Allies in North Africa 6/43
- Egypt declares war on Germany and Japan 2/45

World War II (Asia, Pacific)

- UK and Iraqi troops clash, Habbaniyah 5/41
- UK troops occupy Basra docks and airport 5/41
- British troops surround Baghdad 5/41
- British Imperial troops take Damascus 6/41
- UK and Vichy sign armistice in Syria 7/41
- British and Soviet troops invade Iran 8/41
- UK and Soviet troops enter Teheran 9/41
- Japan invades Malaya and Philippines 12/41
- Japan sinks two UK battleships 12/41
- Hong Kong falls to Japanese 12/41
- Massive Japanese offensive 12/41
- Japanese attack Pearl Harbor 12/41
- Japanese attack American bases 12/41
- US Wake and Guam islands fall to Japan 12/41
- Japanese take Manila 1/42
- Japanese land on Borneo and other islands 1/42
- Japanese bombing raids on Singapore 1/42
- Japanese lay siege to Singapore 1/42
- Japanese advance in Malaya 1/42
- Wavell heads Allied forces in SW Pacific 1/42
- Japan lands on New Guinea and Solomon Islands 1/42
- Singapore surrenders to the Japanese 2/42
- Java capitulates to Japanese 3/42
- MacArthur quits Philippines 3/42
- MacArthur succeeds Wavell as Allied chief 3/42
- Japanese bomb Ceylon 4/42
- Mountbatten heads Allies in SE Asia 4/42
- Main oilfields in Burma destroyed 4/42
- US bombs Tokyo 4/42
- Japanese take Bataan 4/42
- Japanese subs raid Sydney harbour 5/42
- Japanese take Mandalay in Burma 5/42
- 10,000 surrender to Japanese, Corregidor 5/42
- Japan and US wage Battle of Coral Sea 5/42
- Japanese shell Sydney and Newcastle 6/42
- US routs Japan in Battle of Midway 6/42
- Alexander becomes C-in-C Middle East 8/42
- US Marines land on Solomon Islands 8/42
- US forces raid Gilbert Islands 8/42
- Allied forces begin attack in New Guinea 9/42
- Two US destroyers sunk, Solomon Islands 10/42
- British push back Japanese in Burma 12/42
- Japanese in withdrawal from Guadalcanal 1/43
- Major US offensive on Guadalcanal 1/43
- Japan abandons Solomon Islands 2/43
- Japanese submarine torpedoes hospital ship 5/43
- US and Japanese clash near Bougainville 7/43
- Mountbatten is Supreme Allied Commander 8/43
- J.F. Kennedy saves torpedo boat crew 8/43
- Gilbert Islands fall to Allies 11/43
- Allies invade island of New Britain 12/43
- Australia and NZ sign Pacific pact 1/44
- Japanese torture of POWs reported 1/44
- Allies attack Marshall Islands 1/44
- US forces launch Pacific assault 2/44
- US shelling of Paramishu island 2/44
- US attacks bases on Guam and Marianas 2/44
- Orde Wingate killed in air crash, Burma 3/44
- Allies land behind Japanese lines, Burma 3/44
- Allies make second glider landing, Burma 4/44
- US forces land in New Guinea 4/44
- Allies land on Biak island 5/44
- US bombers reach Japanese mainland 6/44
- US bombs Marianas Islands 6/44
- US troops take Guam 7/44
- US forces attack Japanese near Manila 9/44
- MacArthur returns to the Philippines 10/44
- Japanese kamikaze pilots in action 10/44
- Heaviest US air raid, on Iwo Jima 12/44
- Allies begin drive to clear Burma Road 1/45
- US troops land on Luzon island 1/45
- US troops capture Manila and Corregidor 2/45
- Allies capture Iwo Jima 2/45
- British capture Meiktila in Burma 3/45
- Tokyo devastated by fire bombing 3/45
- US troops land on Okinawa island, Japan 4/45
- US Navy sinks Japanese warship Yamamoto 4/45
- British troops recapture Rangoon 5/45
- RN fights Japanese in Malacca Straits 5/45
- US forces take Okinawa 6/45
- Allies establish beachheads in Borneo 6/45
- Allies step up attack on Tokyo 7/45
- Allies at Potsdam tell Japan to yield 7/45
- Atomic bombs on Hiroshima and Nagasaki 8/45
- Japan surrenders to the Allies 8/45
- Kwang-tung Army surrenders to Russians 8/45
- Stalin declares war on Japan 8/45
- MacArthur made Supreme Allied Commander 8/45
- Russians occupy Harbin and Mukden 8/45
- Japan signs formal surrender 9/45
- Freed POWs tell of Japanese camp horrors 9/45

World War II (Eastern Europe)

- Warsaw surrenders to Germany 9/39
- Germany and USSR invade Poland 9/39
- Soviet and Finnish troops clash 11/39
- Stalin renounces Finno-Soviet pact 11/39
- USSR invades Finland 11/39
- Britain to send arms to Finland 12/39
- Stalin sacks General Meretzkov 12/39
- Finns claim to have pushed back Russians 12/39
- USSR launches new offensive in Finland 1/40
- Sweden pledges aid to Finland 1/40
- Finns humiliate the Red Army 1/40
- Soviet Army advances in Finland 2/40
- USSR presents Finland with peace terms 2/40
- First UK volunteers leave for Finland 2/40
- Finns evacuate areas ceded to USSR 3/40
- Finland signs peace treaty with USSR 3/40
- Russians invade Bukovina and Bessarabia 6/40
- Germans and Italians invade Rumania 10/40
- Hungary joins Axis 11/40
- Germans break pact and invade USSR 6/41
- Germans make great inroads in USSR 7/41
- First raid on Berlin by Soviet air force 8/41
- Germans take Soviet naval base, Nikolaev 8/41
- Red Army evacuates Novgorod 8/41
- Germans capture Tallin, Estonia 8/41
- Finns push Russians back to old frontier 8/41
- Red Army counter-offensive on Dnieper 8/41
- USSR blows up Lenin-Dnjeproges dam 8/41
- RAF unit arrives in USSR to aid air force 9/41
- UK to inform USSR about "radio-location" 9/41
- Kiev falls to the Germans 9/41
- Germans isolate Crimean peninsula 9/41
- RAF has first engagement in USSR 9/41
- Nazi noose tightens round Leningrad 9/41
- State of siege declared in Moscow 10/41
- Germans take Kharkhov, Ukraine 10/41
- German progress slowed by Soviet winter 11/41
- Simferopol, Crimean capital, falls 11/41
- Sevastopol falls to Germans and Rumanians 11/41
- German panzers suffer series of defeats 12/41
- Germans pushed back in Crimea 1/42
- Allied convoy reaches Murmansk 3/42
- Germans retreat from Kharkhov 4/42
- Russians foil Nazi summer offensive 5/42
- Red Army launches attack on Sevastopol 6/42
- US bombs Rumanian oilfields 6/42
- Germans launch offensive at Kursk 6/42
- Sevastopol falls to the Germans 7/42
- Germans take Voroshilovgrad 7/42
- Russians begin evacuation of Rostov 7/42
- Germans cross the River Don 8/42
- Germans take Novorossisk naval base 9/42
- Great war of attrition in Stalingrad 9/42
- Germans launch new attack on Stalingrad 10/42
- Germans are routed near Stalingrad 11/42
- Russians attack Germans on the Don 12/42
- Germans surrender in Stalingrad 1/43
- Soviet army breaks siege of Leningrad 1/43
- Russians take Voroshilovsk 1/43
- Russians free three Nazi-held cities 2/43
- Germans reoccupy Kharkhov 3/43
- Mass Polish grave found at Katyn, USSR 4/43
- Germans launch offensive in Kursk area 7/43
- US bombs oil bases at Ploesti, Rumania 7/43
- Russians capture key town of Orel 8/43
- Soviet Army advances into the Ukraine 8/43
- Germans quit Kharkhov 8/43
- Red Army recaptures Smolensk 9/43
- Russians enter suburbs of Kiev 9/43
- Red Army crosses the River Dnieper 10/43
- Kiev falls to the Russians 11/43
- Germans evacuate Sofia 11/43
- Three Germans hanged for war crimes, USSR 12/43
- Russians cross pre-war Polish border 1/44
- USSR inquiry blames Germans for Katyn 1/44
- Russians break German siege of Leningrad 1/44
- Red Army traps ten German divisions 2/44
- Stalingrad given Sword of Honour by UK 2/44
- Russians bomb Helsinki 2/44
- Red Army sweeps through Crimea 4/44
- Russians cross into Rumania 4/44
- Soviet army captures Simferopol 4/44
- RAF makes its first raid on Rumania 4/44
- 47 Allied POWs shot after escape attempt 5/44
- Soviet Army captures Sevastopol 5/44
- Russians open new offensive agains Finns 6/44
- Russians take Karelian port of Viipuri 6/44
- Red Army breaks German "Fatherland Line" 6/44
- Finland will continue fighting USSR 6/44
- Russians advance on Warsaw 7/44
- Minsk falls to the Russians 7/44
- Russians capture Vilna in Lithuania 7/44
- Soviets capture Lublin in Poland 7/44
- Soviet army captures Bucharest and its oil 8/44
- German tanks raze Warsaw 8/44
- Bulgaria says it will quit war 8/44
- Finland signs armistice with USSR 9/44
- Russians capture Tallinn in Estonia 9/44
- Russians enter Riga in Latvia 10/44
- Russians sweep across Czech border 10/44
- Soviet tanks enter Budapest 11/44
- Russians cross the Danube 11/44
- Red Army discovers horror of Auschwitz 1/45
- Budapest now in Russian hands 1/45
- Warsaw falls to Soviet and Polish troops 1/45
- Hungary declares war on Germany 1/45
- USSR advances into Germany from Poland 1/45
- Allied bombing devastates Dresden 2/45
- Russians capture Danzig 3/45
- Russians cross from Hungary to Austria 3/45
- Allies enter Berlin 4/45
- Hitler kills himself in Berlin bunker 4/45
- Vienna is liberated 4/45
- Germany surrenders to the Allies 5/45

World War II (Home Front)
- Blackout and other rules introduced 9/39
- ENSA formed 9/39
- Censorship department set up 10/39
- German air raid on Firth of Forth 10/39
- General call-up starts for men over 20 10/39
- Butter and bacon to be rationed 11/39
- First bombs dropped on British soil 11/39
- Germany mines dropped in Thames estuary 11/39
- First Canadian troops arrive in Britain 12/39
- Women arms workers demand equal pay 12/39
- Rationing extended to sugar and meat 12/39
- Two million more men called up 1/40
- Jockey Club cancels the Derby 1/40
- Unity Mitford returns to UK after suicide bid 1/40
- Women intensify equal pay campaign 1/40
- First food rationing comes into force 1/40
- Lord Haw Haw broadcasts from Germany 1/40
- Arrival of Canadian Air Force squadron 2/40
- Government launches anti-gossip campaign 2/40
- Meat rationing begins 3/40
- First UK civilian dies, in air raid 3/40
- Internment for Germans and Austrians 5/40
- Queen Wilhelmina arrives in exile 5/40
- Britain forms coalition government 5/40
- Australian and New Zealand troops arrive 6/40
- Biggest air raid shelter opens 6/40
- German bombers make first daylight raid 7/40
- Alan Brooke made C-in-C of home forces 7/40
- Home Guard formed 7/40
- Luftwaffe bombs London for first time 8/40
- Mass air raids over southern Britain 8/40
- Churchill makes speech on "the Few" 8/40
- Four French colonies join Free France 8/40
- Battle of Britain begins 9/40
- George Cross and George Medal introduced 9/40
- London Blitz begins 9/40
- Luftwaffe attacks provincial cities 11/40
- Coventry devastated in air raid 11/40
- Luftwaffe bombs City of London 12/40
- Churchill says: "We will not fail ..." 1/41
- Government issues "Blitz broth" recipe 2/41
- 100,000 women called on for war work 3/41
- New Blitz on south-east England 3/41
- 100,000 bombs on London in one night 4/41
- First US food ship arrives in UK 5/41
- Over 100,000 bombs on London in a night 5/41
- 1,400 killed in London in one night 5/41
- Bomb reduces House of Commons to rubble 5/41
- Tower of Westminster Abbey falls in 5/41
- British Museum damaged by incendiaries 5/41
- St. Paul's Cathedral hit again by bomb 5/41
- 20,000 Londoners dead in past few months 5/41
- Hull damaged by Blitz 5/41
- Many UK cities blitzed in recent months 5/41
- Hess crashes in Messerschmitt, Scotland 5/41
- Clothes coupons introduced 6/41
- BBC promotes "V for Victory" campaign 7/41
- Coal rationing begins 7/41
- P.G. Wodehouse accused of helping enemy 7/41
- Brooke is Chief of Imperial General Staff 11/41
- Scrap-metal collection to be quadrupled 12/41
- Unmarried women 20-30 to be called up 12/41
- Call-up age for men lowered 12/41
- Radio main source of entertainment in UK 12/41
- US troops land in Northern Ireland 1/42
- Effects of rationing 2/42
- Baking of white bread to be banned 3/42
- Fuel rationing to be introduced 3/42
- Princess Elizabeth signs up for war service 4/42
- Luftwaffe raids "Baedeker towns" 4/42
- Plans for fuel rationing postponed 5/42
- Big US contingent arrives in N. Ireland 5/42
- Takeover of coal mines announced 6/42
- Driving for pleasure is banned 7/42
- Canterbury devastated in reprisal raid 10/42
- 16-year-old John Conroy wins BEM 10/42
- British Jews in day of mourning 12/42
- 23 children killed when bomb hits school 1/43
- 178 die in air raid shelter accident 3/43
- George VI has part-time munitions job 3/43
- "Wings for Victory" savings campaign 3/43
- First wartime race meeting at Ascot 5/43
- All women must do part-time war work 5/43
- Savings made by clothes rationing 5/43
- Signposts to be returned to rural areas 6/43
- Only one in ten get Christmas turkey 12/43
- Clothing restrictions lifted 2/44
- The first V-1 bombs 6/44
- Mass evacuation as V-1s fall on London 7/44
- V-2s terrorise London 9/44
- Blackout ends in most of Britain 9/44
- Evacuations from London suspended 9/44
- Home Guard is "stood down" 11/44
- Queen praises women for war work 12/44
- Partial blackout of London ends 4/45
- Britain celebrates Victory in Europe 5/45
- Britain celebrates Victory in Japan 8/45

World War II (Mediterranean)
- Britain raids Libya 6/40
- Italian planes bomb Malta 6/40
- French ships at Alexandria cannot leave 7/40
- RN destroys French fleet at Algeria 7/40
- UK blockade of Europe and North Africa 7/40
- Italy invades Greece 10/40
- Greeks put Italian invaders to flight 11/40
- Fleet Air Arm sinks seven Italian ships 11/40
- Badoglio out as Italian chief of staff 12/40
- Greeks capture Chimera in Albania 12/40
- RAF bombs Taranto and Naples 1/41
- RAF bombs Italian bases in Libya 1/41
- Commonwealth troops capture Tobruk 1/41
- British bases in Malta bombed 1/41
- Southern Italy declared a war zone 2/41
- Greece warned to end war with Italy 2/41
- Turks close Dardanelles to foreign ships 3/41
- Italian offensive in Albania crushed 3/41
- Italians lose naval battle off Crete 3/41
- Coup ousts pro-Axis Yugoslav government 3/41
- Yugoslavia falls to Balkan Blitzkrieg 4/41
- Athens falls to the Germans 4/41
- Germans seize Canea, Crete 5/41
- Germans launch invasion of Crete 5/41
- UK and New Zealand troops leave Crete 6/41
- Soviet bombers to aid partisan Yugoslavs 10/41
- HMS Ark Royal sinks after torpedo attack 11/41
- RN wipes out two Italian convoys 11/41
- Malta suffers 1,000th air raid 11/41
- British convoy gets through to Malta 3/42
- George VI awards George Cross to Malta 4/42
- Germans in Yugoslavia to fight partisans 5/42
- German offensive on Malta ends 5/42
- Battle of the Convoys 6/42
- An Allied convoy reaches Malta 8/42
- RAF's biggest raid of the war on Italy 10/42
- French scuttle fleet in Toulon harbour 11/42
- Allies bomb Sicily 5/43
- State of emergency in southern Italy 5/43
- Allied planes attack Italian airfields 5/43
- US Air Force bombs Sardinia 5/43
- Italians start to withdraw from Albania 6/43
- Allies attack Pantelleria island (Italy) 6/43
- Allies capture Lampedusa island (Italy) 6/43
- Allies take Palermo in Sicily landing 7/43
- Allies bomb Rome 7/43
- Last Axis defences on Sicily crumble 8/43
- Allies bomb Rome, Turin and Milan 8/43
- Italy surrenders to the Allies 9/43
- Allies land at Salerno, near Naples 9/43
- Germans occupy Rome 9/43
- Italians seize control of Sardinia 9/43
- Allies enter Naples 9/43
- Corsica falls to French Resistance 10/43
- Penicillin is saving many Allied lives 10/43
- Allies held up at Monte Cassino, Italy 10/43
- Allies seize Isernia, Italy 11/43
- Roosevelt visits Malta and pays tribute 12/43
- Canadians seize Adriatic port of Ortona 12/43
- Allied troops storm ashore at Anzio 1/44
- Allies bomb Monte Cassino monastery 2/44
- Allies launch assault on Monte Cassino 3/44
- Allies take Monte Cassino, Italy 5/44
- Allies break German spine in Italy 5/44
- Rome falls to the Allies 6/44
- Elba surrenders to French troops 6/44
- Allies take Perugia, Italy 6/44
- Allies take Livorno and Ancona, Italy 7/44
- Allied forces land in South of France 8/44
- Churchill visits Allied HQ, Italy 8/44
- Allies take Florence 8/44
- Marseilles and Grenoble fall to Allies 8/44
- Red Army and Tito capture Belgrade 10/44
- British land in Greece 10/44
- British troops land on Crete 10/44
- British troops capture Salonika 11/44
- Alexander takes Supreme Allied Command 11/44
- Germans in Italy surrender to Allies 4/45
- Allies take Milan and Venice 4/45

World War II (Sea)
- HMS Courageous sunk with loss of 500 9/39
- UK liner Athenia sunk with loss of 112 9/39
- Allied blockade of German ports 9/39
- RAFs bomb German fleet on Kiel Canal 9/39
- UK battleship Royal Oak sunk, Scapa Flow 10/39
- Finland mobilises Baltic fleet 10/39
- U-boat war intensifies 10/39
- French steamer Louisiane sunk, Atlantic 10/39
- German ship Graf Spee scuttled, Uruguay 12/39
- Union Castle liner sunk by mine off UK 1/40
- German planes sink three ships, killing 35 1/40
- Destroyer HMS Daring is sunk 2/40
- Hitler orders total sea war by U-boats 2/40
- Three Scandinavian countries protest at sea war 2/40
- UK frees seven seized Italian coal ships 3/40
- German cruiser Bluecher sunk; 1,000 lost 4/40
- Royal Navy mines Norwegian waters 4/40
- British ship Lancastria sunk, France 6/40
- Luftwaffe attacks Channel shipping 7/40
- UK blockade of Europe and North Africa 7/40
- RN destroys French fleet at Algeria 7/40
- French ships in British ports seized 7/40
- French ships at Alexandria cannot leave 7/40
- Italian aircraft bomb Suez Canal 8/40
- German ship sunk in Baltic; 4,000 lost 9/40
- City of Benares sunk in Atlantic 9/40
- Battle for Atlantic control begins 10/40
- 11 German ships sunk off Norway 3/41
- HMS Hood sunk by the Bismarck, Atlantic 5/41
- RN sinks German battleship Bismarck 5/41
- Ark Royal in Bismarck chase 5/41
- HMS Victorious in Bismarck chase 5/41
- US destroyer Greer attacked by sub 9/41
- USS Reuben James attacked by U-boat 10/41
- HMS Ark Royal sinks after torpedo attack 11/41
- S. African forces capture Vichy ships 11/41
- RN wipes out two Italian convoys 11/41
- Japan sinks two UK battleships, Far East 12/41
- British convoy reaches Malta 3/42
- Allied convoy reaches Murmansk 3/42
- Arctic convoy PQ-17 destroyed by Germans 7/42
- Germans sink POW ship; 1,800 Italians die 9/42
- RAF lays mines in Baltic 4/43
- Allies turn tide in Atlantic U-boat war 5/43
- U-boats reported to have left Atlantic 6/43
- RAF bombs Peenemund Island weapons base 8/43
- U-boats return to Atlantic 10/43
- Allies torpedo the Tirpitz, Arctic 10/43
- Allies land on the Azores 10/43
- 700 U-boats have been destroyed so far 11/43
- RN sinks German warship Scharnhorst 12/43
- RAF sinks Tirpitz in Norwegian fjord 11/44
- Antwerp opened to Allied convoys 11/44
- RAF sinks Lutzow, last pocket battleship 4/45
- RN rounds up remnants of German fleet 5/45
- Convoy system ended for non-combat zones 5/45
- Allies sank 700 U-boats during war 6/45

World War II (Western Europe)
- French troops enter Saarland 9/39
- Polish government-in-exile in Paris 10/39
- France rejects Germany's peace overtures 10/39
- BEF sets up a casualty clearing station 10/39
- British troops now in France in strength 10/39
- Swiss order general mobilisation 11/39
- USSR tells Finnish troops to pull back 11/39
- George VI visits UK troops in France 12/39
- Hitler spends Christmas with his troops 12/39
- Germans advance north of Paris 1/40
- 300 UK prisoners freed from German ship 2/40
- Quisling says he is head of Norway 4/40
- British troops join battle for Norway 4/40
- Allies recapture Narvik, Norway 4/40
- Germany invades Belgium 5/40
- Germany invades Netherlands 5/40
- Britain occupies Iceland and Faroes 5/40
- Dutch forces ordered to stop fighting 5/40
- Germans occupy The Hague 5/40
- Maxime Weygand becomes Allied C-in-C 5/40
- Belgium and Netherlands surrender 5/40
- First British troops evacuate Dunkirk 5/40
- British bungle operations in Norway 5/40
- Germans encircle British on French coast 5/40
- Allies evacuated from Dunkirk 6/40
- Aerial bombing kills 45 in Paris 6/40
- Germans bomb Rhone valley and Marseilles 6/40
- Evacuation of Narvik completed 6/40
- French government moves to Tours 6/40
- Churchill meets Weygand at Tours 6/40
- Petain asks Germany for armistice 6/40
- De Gaulle forms "Free French" movement 6/40
- German troops given English phrasebooks 6/40
- Paris surrenders to the Germans 6/40
- Churchill proposes union with France 6/40
- In UK, de Gaulle urges French resistance 6/40
- Italy declares war on Britain and France 6/40
- Petain breaks ties with Britain 7/40
- Germans invade Channel Islands 7/40
- Alsace-Lorraine becomes part of Germany 8/40
- Luxembourg becomes part of Germany 8/40
- Churchill signs alliance with de Gaulle 8/40
- RAF bombs Berlin for first time 8/40
- RAF bombs Munich for first time 9/40
- France told to pay for occupying troops 9/40
- RAF bombs Hamburg 9/40
- RAF makes heavy raids on Berlin, Hamburg 10/40
- RAF drops 2,000 bombs on Hamburg 11/40
- German bombs fall on neutral Ireland 1/41
- German Enigma documents seized, Iceland 5/41
- Vichy France in secret talks with Hitler 5/41
- Rudolf Hess crashes in Scotland 5/41
- RAF says "radio-location" is key weapon 6/41
- All Britons must leave Vichy France 7/41
- Allies seize island of Spitzbergen 9/41
- Luxembourg referendum fails 10/41
- RAF raids German base in Norway 10/41
- Denmark joins Axis 11/41
- Free French take two Vichy islands off Canada 12/41
- First UK combined services raid, Norway 12/41
- First US troops set foot in Europe 1/42
- Germany and quislingite Norway end war 2/42
- RAF begins terror bombing campaign 3/42
- German radio-location centre destroyed 3/42
- BBC morse news to French resistance 3/42
- RAF in heavy raid on Ruhr towns 3/42
- UK marines storm U-boat base, St Nazaire 3/42
- Hitler meets Mussolini, Salzburg 4/42
- RAF bombs Baltic port of Rostock 4/42
- RAF devastates Cologne in one night 5/42
- Eisenhower heads US forces in Europe 6/42
- US bombs German air bases in Netherlands 7/42
- RAF bombs U-boat yards in Danzig 7/42
- RAF makes first daylight raid on Ruhr 7/42
- "Bomber" Harris to "scourge" Nazis 7/42
- Heavy Allied casualties in Dieppe raid 8/42
- UK and US bombers attack Rotterdam 8/42
- RAF bombs Dusseldorf 9/42
- 100th RAF raid on Bremen 9/42
- UK and USSR bomb Ploesti, Rumania 9/42
- Britain and Germany lock PoWs in chains 10/42
- French scuttle fleet in Toulon harbour 11/42
- Germany and Italy occupy Vichy France 11/42
- Allies' biggest daylight raid 12/42
- US bombs Wilhelmshaven and Emden 1/43
- All people 16-65 ordered to mobilise, Germany 1/43
- RAF makes first daylight raid on Berlin 1/43
- Bombing of Germany's industrial centres 3/43
- Germans reinforce Dutch coastal defences 4/43
- RAF bombs Stuttgart 4/43
- RAF bombs Berlin and three other cities 4/43
- Martial law imposed in Netherlands 5/43
- RAF's "Dambuster" raid on the Ruhr 5/43
- State of emergency declared in Ruhr 5/43
- RAF in heaviest air raid, on Dortmund 5/43
- Leslie Howard killed in shot-down plane 6/43
- RAF in heaviest raid yet, on Hamburg 7/43
- Hamburg "wiped off the map" by air raid 8/43
- 4,200 UK PoWs swapped for Germans, Sweden 10/43
- RAF says it will bomb Berlin to nothing 11/43
- Eisenhower to head invasion of Europe 12/43
- RAF's biggest ever bombing of Berlin 1/44
- Hitler's Chancellery hit in air raid 1/44
- Eisenhower takes over Supreme Command 1/44
- Britain blockades Ireland, fearing spies 3/44
- Eisenhower completes invasion plans 4/44
- US bombs Schaffhausen (Swiss) in error 4/44
- RAF drops 4,500 tons of bombs in one raid 4/44
- Rommel is appointed anti-invasion C-in-C 5/44
- D-Day: Allied landings in Normandy 6/44
- Cherbourg surrenders to the Allies 6/44
- Nazi massacre at Oradour-sur-Glane 6/44
- Allies seize two V-1 launch sites 6/44
- Allies drive Germans from Normandy 7/44
- Caen falls to the Allies 7/44
- Allies take Paris 8/44
- Germans leave Channel Islands 8/44
- Allies take Belgian cities including Brussels 9/44
- Germans on the run throughout Europe 9/44
- British paratroops cut off at Arnhem 9/44
- US First Army treads on German soil 9/44
- Calais falls to Allies 9/44
- Allies take first German city, Aachen 10/44
- Hitler forms Home Guard for Germany 10/44
- Patton's tanks enter Saarland 11/44
- French troops enter Strasbourg 11/44
- Germans fight back in Ardennes region 12/44
- Patton's troops reach Siegfried Line 12/44
- Allies winning Battle of the Bulge 1/45
- Montgomery is Supreme Allied Commander 1/45
- Allies close on Berlin 2/45
- US troops break through Siegfried Line 2/45
- Allies cross the Rhine 3/45
- Cologne falls to Allies 3/45
- Germans evacuate Peenemunde rocket base 3/45
- Biggest ever daylight air raid, Germany 3/45
- Allies enter Berlin 4/45
- Hitler kills himself in Berlin bunker 4/45
- Freed POWs reveal horrors of death camps 4/45
- Allies liberate Bergen-Belsen 4/45
- Allies liberate Buchenwald 4/45
- Nuremberg falls to the Allies 4/45
- Allies liberate Dachau 4/45
- Germany surrenders to the Allies 5/45
- Belsen razed to the ground 5/45

World War II (general)
- Germany and USSR invade Poland 9/39
- Britain declares war on Germany 9/39
- France declares war on Germany 9/39
- Australia declares war on Germany 9/39
- New Zealand declares war on Germany 9/39
- Canada declares war on Germany 9/39
- USSR says it will remain neutral 10/39
- Britain and France to buy arms from US 11/39
- Sweden, Norway and Denmark are neutral 1/40
- US peace mission to Berlin fails 3/40
- Finland signs peace treaty with USSR 3/40
- Mussolini meets Hitler at Brenner Pass 3/40
- UK and France agree on no separate peace 3/40
- Germany invades Denmark and Norway 4/40
- UK makes trade pacts with 6 countries 4/40
- Churchill becomes British PM 5/40
- Belgium and Netherlands surrender 5/40
- Paris surrenders to the Germans 6/40
- Molotov reaffirms Soviet neutrality 8/40
- Finland signs treaty with Germany 10/40
- Britain breaks off relations with Bulgaria 3/41
- Yugoslavia signs pact with Axis 3/41
- Yugoslavia capitulates to Germany 4/41
- Italians in Abyssinia surrender 5/41
- Germans break pact and invade USSR 6/41
- UK and USSR conclude assistance pact 7/41
- Exiled Polish government pact with USSR 7/41
- Nine exiled regimes adhere to Atlantic pact 9/41
- Japan declares war on US 12/41
- Britain declares war on Japan 12/41
- US declares war on Japan, Germany and Italy 12/41
- Britain declares war on Finland, Rumania and Hungary 12/41
- Italy and Germany declare war on USA 12/41
- Hitler becomes C-in-C of German Army 12/41
- 26 countries affirm opposition to Axis 1/42
- 21 American countries break with Axis 1/42
- First US troops set foot in Europe 1/42
- Singapore surrenders to the Japanese 2/42
- Germany and quislingite Norway end war 2/42
- Britain and USSR sign 20-year pact 5/42
- Churchill and Stalin have Moscow summit 8/42
- Brazil declares war on Germany 8/42
- Allies condemn Nazi atrocities 12/42
- Axis resistance in North Africa ends 5/43
- Mussolini deposed 7/43
- Italy surrenders to the Allies 9/43
- Italy declares war on Germany 10/43
- Rumania declares war on Germany 8/44
- Bulgaria declares war on Germany 9/44
- Finland signs armistice with USSR 9/44
- Hungary declares war on Germany 1/45
- Big Three attend Yalta conference 2/45
- Declarations of war against Germany 3/45
- Hitler kills himself in Berlin bunker 4/45
- Mussolini shot dead by partisans 4/45
- Germans in Italy surrender to Allies 4/45
- Gates of Nazi death camps open 4/45
- Germany surrenders to the Allies 5/45
- 55 million people died in the war 8/45
- Paris peace treaties signed 2/47

Worrall, Dennis 1/87
Worth, Harry 12/89
Wouk, Herman 12/51
Wrangel, Peter 5/28
Wright, Almroth 10/13
Wright, Billy 6/50, 9/94
Wright, Frank Lloyd 4/59
Wright, Jim 5/89
Wright, John Dickson 1/48
Wright, Orville 12/03, 9/04, 5/08, 8/08, 5/09, 1/48
Wright, Peter 7/86, 11/86, 10/88, 4/95

Wright, Wilbur 12/03, 9/04, 5/08, 10/08, 5/09, 5/12
Wu Pei-fu 5/22, 9/26
Wu, C.C. 12/27
Wyatt, Jane 10/47
Wyler, William 4/39, 11/59
Wyndham, John 3/69
Wynne, Greville 11/62, 12/62, 4/63, 5/63, 4/64
Wyszynski, Stefan (Cardinal) 8/01, 9/53, 10/56, 10/77, 10/78, 6/79, 10/80, 5/81

XYZ

Yaffe, Leib 3/48
Yagoda, Genrikh 3/38
Yahya Khan 12/71
Yamani, Ahmed Zaki (Sheikh) 11/73, 12/75, 10/86
Yanayev, Gennady 12/90, 8/91
Yazov, Dmitri 8/91
Yeager, Chuck 10/47, 6/48
Yeager, Jeana 12/86
Yeats, William Butler 11/05, 12/23, 12/26, 1/39
Yeltsin, Boris
- Sacked for criticising Gorbachev 11/87
- Wins seat with 90 per cent of vote in elections 3/89
- Elected President of Russia 5/90
- Resigns from Communist Party 7/90
- Thousands demonstrate outside Kremlin in support of Yeltsin 1/91
- Meets leaders of three Baltic states 1/91
- Accuses Gorbachev of dictatorship 2/91
- Agrees with Gorbachev on election timetable 4/91
- Becomes President of Russia 6/91
- Rallies to support Gorbachev after coup 8/91
- Popular resistance led by Yeltsin causes coup to collapse 8/91
- Forces Gorbachev to read out list of coup supporters 8/91
- Forces pace of founding of CIS 12/91
- Signs arms accord with Britain 1/92
- Agrees with Snegur to seek end to Moldovan-Russian conflict 7/92
- Invites Queen Elizabeth to Moscow 11/92
- Fights for political life against hardliners 12/92
- Signs START-2 Treaty with Bush in Moscow 1/93
- Wins vote of confidence in national referendum 4/93
- Crushes hardliner rebellion 10/93
- Sends troops into Chechenia 12/94
- Unwell at CIS summit 2/95
- Says "no" to Clinton on Chechenia 5/95

Yemen
- See also Aden, South Arabian Federation
- Saudis capture Hodeida 5/34
- Signs truce with Saudi Arabia in Jeddah 5/34
- Ibn Saud and Imam of Yemen sign treaty 6/34
- Signs security pact with Egypt 6/50
- UK troops and planes in Aden repel Yemenis 1/57
- South Yemen joins UAR 3/58
- Imam Ahmad assassinated 9/62
- Free Yemen Republic declared 9/62
- First Egyptian troops arrive 10/62
- Nasser vows to expel UK from Arab world 4/64
- Royalist-republican cease-fire 11/64
- People's Republic of South Yemen formed 11/67
- Arabs hijack Lufthansa Jumbo 2/72
- West Germany pays $3m ransom for hostages 2/72
- Arab gunman kills officials, London 4/77
- Over 1,000 evacuated from Aden 1/86
- Fierce fighting follows attemped coup 1/86
- PLO HQ to be moved from Tunis to Yemen 10/86
- Government claims victory in Civil War 7/94

Yemen, North
- See Yemen

Yemen, South
- See Yemen

Yen Hsi-Chan 4/30, 9/30, 12/49
Yermolov, Alexei 2/05
Yin Ju-Kang 11/35
Yogi, Maharishi Mahesh 8/67
York, Duchess of (Sarah Ferguson) 3/90, 3/92, 8/92
York, Eugenie Victoria of 3/90
Yoshiba, Shigeru 4/46
Yoshihito, Emperor of Japan 12/26
Young Plan
- Germany to pay off war debts by 1988 6/29
- Removes Allied controls on economy 6/29
- Germany not to pay for French rebuilding 6/29
- Bank for International Settlements 11/29

Young, Andrew 2/78
Young, Brigham 1/00
Young, David 2/82, 9/84, 9/85
Young, Hilton 10/33
Young, Jimmy 4/76
Young, Loretta 1/14
Young, Mark 12/41
Young, Owen 6/29
Ypres
- British hold despite fierce German raids 10/14
- Heavy losses as forces fight for Hill 60 4/15
- Germans use gas; Allies unprepared 4/15
- British launch third battle 8/17
- Ludendorff overruns Allied lines 4/18

Ysaye, Eugene 5/31
Yuan Shi-kai 10/11, 1/12, 2/12, 1/13, 10/13, 11/13, 6/16
Yudenich, Nikolai 10/19
Yugoslavia
- See also Austria, Bosnia, Serbia, World War II
- See also Croatia; Slovenia
- Recognised by Bulgaria 11/19
- New King Alexander 8/21
- Gives Fiume to Italy by treaty 1/24
- 600 die in southern earthquakes 2/27
- 260 die when train falls down ravine 10/27
- Signs treaty with France; new "Entente" 10/27
- King Alexander makes himself dictator 1/29
- Croatians demand autonomy; rejected 1/29
- King Alexander ends dictatorship 9/31
- Balkan Pact with Rumania, Greece and Turkey 2/34
- Croatian kills King Alexander in France 10/34
- Italy renews offer of pact 10/34
- Riots against Italians and Hungarians 10/34
- New King Peter is only ten years old 10/34
- Accuses Hungary of helping murder King 11/34
- King on Adriatic cruise with Mrs Simpson 8/36
- Security pact with US 11/38
- Hitler guarantees Yugoslav frontiers 6/39
- General mobilisation ordered 9/39
- Given ultimatum to join Axis 3/41
- Signs pact with Axis 3/41
- Coup ousts pro-Axis government 3/41
- Falls to Balkan Blitzkrieg 4/41
- Germans slaughter 700 in reprisal 7/42
- Bihacs falls to Tito's partisans 11/42
- Partisans advance along Dalmatian coast 9/43
- Italian troops join partisans 10/43
- Tito creates provisional government 12/43
- Partisans raid German posts in Zagreb 5/44
- Germans capture Tito's Bosnian HQ 5/44
- Tito and royalists form united front 6/44
- Red Army and Tito capture Belgrade 10/44
- Tito confirmed as undisputed leader 3/45
- Tito refuses to allow King Peter II to return 8/45
- Tito's National Front wins election 11/45
- Tito's opponent Mihailovich seized 3/46
- Tito regime recognised by US 4/46
- Mihailovich executed 7/46
- Signs alliance treaty with Bulgaria 8/47
- Signs friendship treaty with Rumania 12/47
- Exchanges Trieste for Gorizia with Italy 3/48
- USSR urges overthrow of Tito 7/48
- Soviet troops mobilise near frontier 8/49
- Tito asks US for loan 8/49
- USSR says Tito regime is "renegade" 8/49
- Tito ends air and naval pact with USSR 9/49
- US lends $20 million 9/49
- USSR ends mutual assistance pact 9/49
- Poland and Hungary end friendship pacts 9/49
- Rumania and Bulgaria end friendship pacts 10/49
- Czechoslovakia ends friendship pact 10/49
- Elected to UN Security Council 10/49
- Ambassador to USSR to be recalled 10/49
- Josip Tito elected President 1/53
- Maverick Tito continues "nonalignment" 1/53
- Tito discusses State-Church relations with Catholic bishops 1/53
- Tito visits Britain 3/53
- Friendship treaty with Turkey and Greece 3/53
- Angry at Italy's control of Trieste 10/53
- Trieste rioters smash US and UK embassies 10/53
- Tito sacks liberal rival Milovan Djilas 1/54
- Tito halts full democratisation 1/54
- Tito re-elected President 1/54
- Loses most of Trieste land to Italy 10/54
- Soviet Secretary Khrushchev visits 5/55
- "Different roads to socialism" speech 5/55
- Tito and Khrushchev sign normalising treaty 6/55
- Khrushchev blames Stalin for rift 3/56
- Protests at Hungary's execution of Nagy 6/58
- Ivo Andric wins Literature Nobel 12/61
- Vice-President Djilas jailed 5/62
- Tito made President for life 4/63
- Quake destroys town of Skopje 7/63
- Tito dances with Khrushchev 8/63
- 92 die when UK airliner crashes 8/66
- Tito visits Prague 8/68
- Tito re-elected for another five years 7/71
- Tito meets Nixon in Washington 10/71
- Queen Elizabeth arrives on state visit 10/72
- 150 die in train crash 9/74
- 176 die in mid-air plane collision 9/76
- Tito reported ill 9/76
- Tito's leg amputated 1/80
- Josip Tito dies 5/80
- Serbians demonstrate 9/88
- Workers besiege parliament in Belgrade 10/88
- Serbs demonstrate in Belgrade 11/88
- Government resigns after year of crisis 12/88
- Troops are sent to Kosovo 2/89
- Kosovo surrenders most of its autonomy to Serbia 3/89
- Communists vote to abandon one-party system 1/90
- Slovenia votes for independence 12/90
- Police fire on anti-Communist protesters in Belgrade 3/91
- Serbia calls up army reservists 5/91
- Civil war looms 6/91
- Serbian-led army rejects Slovenia's peace offer 7/91
- Peace meeting to be held in Dubrovnik 7/91
- Serbian and Croatian leaders agree to a cease-fire 8/91
- Fighting intensifies as civil war approaches 8/91
- Attack on Red Cross convoy 9/91
- Dubvronik under siege by Serb-dominated federal army 10/91
- 13th cease-fire is proclaimed 11/91
- Croatian city of Vukovar surrenders to Serbian-led army 11/91
- EC recognises independence of Croatia and Slovenia 1/92
- Serbian death camps revealed 8/92
- Peace hopes suffer setback 12/92
- See now each individual state 0/93

Yussuf Izzedin, Prince (Turkey) 2/16
Zafy, Albert 2/93
Zahedi, Fazollah 8/53
Zahir Shah, King of Afghanistan 11/33
Zaimis, Alexander 12/29
Zaire
- See also Belgian Congo, Congo
- Congo changes its name to Zaire 10/71
- CIA plot to kill Lumumba revealed 11/75
- Used as base by FNLA to attack MPLA, Angola 11/75
- Army in Shaba to stop invading Angolans 3/77
- Breaks ties with Cuba after Shaba attack 4/77
- 150 Europeans murdered in Kolwezi 5/78
- French and Belgian paras rescue Europeans 5/78
- Mobutu wants France to fight Katangans 5/78
- Pope starts African tour; Nine die in crowd 5/80

Zajic, Jan 2/69
Zakharov, Gennadi 9/86
Zambia
- See also Rhodesia and Northern Rhodesia
- Kaunda becomes President-elect 8/64
- Britain offers military aid 12/65
- To resume sending copper via Rhodesia 7/66
- Rhodesia closes border 1/73
- 38 die in Rhodesian raid 3/78
- Muzorewa spokesmen Hove killed in Lusaka 4/79
- Queen Elizabeth on visit 7/79
- Commonwealth talks on Zimbabwe, Lusaka 8/79
- Raided by South African forces 5/86

Zamora, Alcala 10/31, 12/31, 4/36
Zankoff, Alexander 6/23
Zanzibar
- See also Tanzania
- Afro-Shirazi Party wins elections 1/61
- Ceases to be British protectorate 12/63
- Nationalists overthrow Sultan's regime 1/64
- Republic proclaimed 1/64
- Act of union with Tanganyika announced 4/64

Zapata, Emiliano 5/11, 10/11, 4/19
Zapotocky, Antonin 11/57
Zatopek, Dana 8/52
Zatopek, Emil 8/48, 8/52, 8/68
Zec, Philip 3/42
Zeeman, Pieter 12/02
Zeffirelli, Franco 2/23, 12/60, 12/67
Zeller, Magnus 7/38
Zeppelin, Ferdinand von 7/00, 1/08, 4/08, 5/09, 6/10, 3/17
Zetterling, Mai 3/94
Zhao Ziyang 1/84, 1/87, 2/89, 5/89, 6/89
Zhdanov, Andrei 12/48
Zhirinovsky, Vladimir 12/93
Zhivkov, Todor 11/89, 12/89, 9/92
Zhukov, Georgi 12/41, 1/45, 2/45, 7/57, 10/57, 11/57, 2/65, 6/74
Zia ul-Haq, Mohammad 7/77, 3/78, 2/79, 11/79, 8/86, 8/88, 11/88, 8/90
Ziegfeld, Florenz 12/27
Zimbabwe
- See also Rhodesia and Rhodesia, Southern
- Zimbabwe-Rhodesia, new name for Rhodesia 6/79
- Thatcher normalises ties 7/79
- Thatcher wants deal with Mugabe and Nkomo 8/79
- UK prepares constitution and elections 8/79
- Muzorewa changes name to Zimbabwe 8/79
- 300 killed in raid on Mozambique 9/79
- Nkomo, Mugabe, Smith and Muzorewa in London 9/79
- Lancaster House accord: cease-fire 12/79
- Patriotic Front guerrillas return 12/79
- Nkomo and Mugabe return from exile 1/80
- Ex-premier Todd arrested for terrorism 2/80
- Elections begin 2/80
- Robert Mugabe elected President 3/80
- Nkomo leads small opposition as Home Affairs Minister 3/80
- Two whites in cabinet 3/80
- Canaan Banana is first President 4/80
- Independent as new republic 4/80
- Mugabe speaks of new harmony 4/80
- Minister Tekere on murder charge 8/80
- Tekere cleared of murder 12/80
- Mugabe's regular army fights Nkomo's rebels 2/81
- 300 die in Matabeleland; accusations 2/81
- Mugabe sacks Nkomo after arms cache find 2/82
- Nkomo "plotting coup"; businesses seized 2/82
- Salisbury becomes Harare 4/82
- Nkomo held by police 2/83
- Nkomo's house is ransacked 3/83
- Nkomo flees 3/83
- Raided by South African forces 5/86
- Minister delivers tirade against US 9/86
- US stops aid to Zimbabwe 9/86
- Mugabe hosts non-aligned summit 9/86
- Soames, last Rhodesia governor, dies 9/87
- Guerrillas kill 16 missionaries 11/87
- Mugabe apologises to Neil Kinnock 7/88

Zimmerman, Arthur 2/17
Zingara, Giuseppe 2/33
Zinneman, Fred 5/61
Zinoviev, Grigori 3/23, 1/24, 5/24, 10/26, 11/27, 10/32, 12/34, 8/36
Zionism
- See also Israel, Palestine
- Swiss Congress 12/01
- Clash over Uganda proposals 8/03
- Hertzl dies 7/04
- Vatican condemns "adherents", Palestine 5/22
- Accused Soviet doctors in "Zionist" plot 1/53
- Attacks on Jews and Zionists, USSR 2/53

Zircon
- Government clampdown on spy programme 2/87

Zita, (former) Empress of Austria 3/89
Zog I, King of Albania 9/28, 4/39, 1/46, 4/61
Zola, Emile 9/02
Zuckerman, Lord (Solly) 4/93
Zurbriggen, Pirmin 2/88
Zvereva, Natalia 6/88
Zweig, Arnold 12/33
Zweig, Stefan 12/33, 2/42

Photo credit

While every effort has been made to trace the copyright of the photographs and illustrations in this publication, there may be errors in the picture credits. If this is the case, we apologize and ask the copyright holder to contact us so that the errors can be rectified.

The following agency names have been abbreviated. For Bettmann, read Bettmann Archive, New York; for Chronicle, read Chronicle Communications Ltd, Farnborough; for Hulton, read Hulton Deutsch Picture Library; for Illustration, read L'Illustration, Sygma, Paris; for Keystone, read The Keystone Collection, London; for Mary Evans, read Mary Evans Picture Library; for Robert Opie, read Robert Opie Collection; for Sipa, read Sipa-Press, Paris; for Topham, read Topham Picture Library.

Credits are indicated by a page number and letters. T stands for Top, M for Middle, B for Bottom, L for Left, R for Right, X for Middle left, Y for Middle right. SPRD stands for Spread.

8 – sprd: NASA – Science Photo Library
10-11 – sprd: Charmet, Paris
12 – br: Mary Evans – tr: Topham Picture Library
13 – bl: Chronicle – tl: Popperfoto – br: Keystone
14 – tm: Mansell Collection – br: Mary Evans
15 – tr, mr: Mary Evans – bl: National Motor Museum, Beaulieu
16 – tr: Hulton – br: Mary Evans – bl: Pictorial History of Boxing
17 – bl: ET Archive – tm: Mansell Collection – br: Mary Evans – bm: Robert Opie
18 – bl: Chronicle – tl: Mary Evans
19 – tl: Olympic Records Book – tr: Topham
20 – bl: Bettmann – tr: Mary Evans – br: Topham
21 – tr: Mansell Collection – br: Robert Opie – tl: Topham
22 – tm, br: Hulton
23 – tr: Hulton – ml, br: Mary Evans
24 – tm, ml, bl: Mary Evans – br: Topham
25 – mm: Hulton – tm: Kobal Collection – br: Picturepoint – bm: Robert Opie
26 – bl: Chronicle – tr: Mary Evans
27 – tl: Illustration – br: Popperfoto – bl: Keystone
28 – tl: Illustration – br: Mary Evans – bl: Robert Opie
29 – tr: Mary Evans – br: National Motor Museum, Beaulieu
30 – bl, tm: Hulton
31 – ml: Robert Opie – tr: Royal Astronomical Society, London – br: Topham
32 – tl (C: Giraudon, Paris – mr: Hulton – bm: Roger Viollet, Paris
33 – bl: Marconi PLC – br: Robert Opie
34 – bm: Hulton – tr: Mary Evans
35 – br: Mary Evans – ml, bl: Popperfoto – tr: Robert Opie
36 – bl: Robert Opie – tl: Topham
37 – br: Hulton – mm: Marconi PLC – bl: Mary Evans – tm: Topham
38 – bl: Popperfoto
39 – br: Hulton – tr, bl: Topham
40 – br: Popperfoto – tl: Topham
41 – br: ET Archive – tl: Hulton
42 – tl: Charmet, Paris – br: Robert Opie – bl: Topham
43 – mr: Aldus Archive – tr: Charmet, Paris – br: Picturepoint – mm: Topham
44 – tl: Illustration – bl: Popperfoto – br: Topham
45 – br: Bettmann – tr: Topham
46 – tm, bl, mr: Hulton – br: Robert Opie
47 – tr, br: Mary Evans
48 – tr: Hulton – ml, bl: Illustration
49 – tm, mr: Hulton – br: Mary Evans – ml: Popperfoto
50 – tl: Mansell Collection – br: Topham
51 – br: Mary Evans – tl: Popperfoto
52 – tm: Bettmann – mr: EMI Music Publishing – br: Hulton
53 – tr, br: Hulton
54 – mr: Giraudon, Paris – tl, bl: Mary Evans
55 – mm: Ford Motor Co. – br: Kobal Collection – tr: Topham
56 – bl: Hulton – mr: Keystone – tl: Topham
57 – tm, br: Mary Evans – bl: Popperfoto
58 – mr: Chronicle – tr: Mary Evans – bl: Popperfoto
59 – bl: Mary Evans – tr: Tate Gallery
60 – tr: Bettmann – bl: Robert Opie
61 – tr, mr: Hulton – tm: Keystone – bl: Topham
62 – tm: Mary Evans – bm: Robert Opie
63 – br: Hulton – tm, bl: Mary Evans – mm: Topham
64 – tm: Edimedia – br: Illustration – bl: Robert Opie
65 – mm: Mary Evans – tr: Popperfoto – br: Robert Opie
66 – tl: Hulton – br: Mary Evans – tr: Keystone
67 – tr: Illustration – ml: Popperfoto – br: Robert Opie
68 – tl, mr: Hulton – bl: Popperfoto
69 – tm: Edimedia – bl: Hulton – br: Robert Opie
70 – tr: Bildarchiv Preussischer Kulturbesitz, Berlin tm: Topham
71 – mr, bl: Hulton – br: Metropolitan Police, London
72 – mr: John Frost Newspaper Archive – tl: Mary Evans – bl: Robert Opie
73 – bm: Edimedia – mr: Hulton – tl: Popperfoto
74 – bl: Archiv Fur Kunst U.G. – tl: David King Collection – bm: Hulton – mr: Robert Opie
75 – br: David King Collection – tr: Novosti Press Agency
76 – bl: Hulton – tr: Topham
77 – tm: David King Collection – br: Hulton – bm: Mary Evans – mm: Topham
78 – tr: Mary Evans – bl: Robert Opie
79 – bl: Chronicle – mm: Illustration – tm: Mary Evans – tl: Topham
80 – bl: Automobile Association – mr: Bettmann – tr: Hulton
81 – tl, bm, mr: Hulton
82 – bl: Popperfoto – br: Robert Opie – tl: Topham
83 – tr: Hulton – bl: Illustration – mr: Mary Evans
84 – tr: David King Collection – br: Westermann Verlag Braunschweig (Copyright Paris DACS)
85 – tl: Hulton – bl: Robert Opie
86 – tl: David King Collection – mr: Popperfoto – bl: Robert Opie
87 – tm: David King Collection – bm: Hulton – mr: Popperfoto
88 – bl: Mary Evans – tr: Topham
89 – tm: Mary Evans – mm, br: Topham
90 – br: Chronicle – tr: Topham
91 – ml, tr: Hulton
92 – tr: Bettmann – tl: Hulton – bl: Topham
93 – bl: Hulton – br: Robert Opie – ml: Topham
94 – br: Hulton – ml: Mary Evans
95 – tm: David King Collection – bm: Hulton – mr: Popperfoto
96 – bm: Mary Evans – mm: Press Association
97 – bl: Hulton – mr: Illustration – tl: Popperfoto
98 – tm: Bettmann – br: David King Collection – mr: Popperfoto
99 – mm: Mary Evans – br: Robert Opie – tm: Visual Arts
100 – mr: EMI Music Publishing – tm: Illustration – bm: Robert Opie
101 – ml: Hulton – tr: Mary Evans – br: Robert Opie
102 – br, bl: Hulton – tm: Visual Arts
103 – mm, br: Topham
104 – bl: Hulton – tl: Topham
105 – br: Hulton – tm: Mary Evans
106 – bl: Hulton – tm, br: Topham
107 – mm: Hulton – br: Mary Evans
108 – tm: Illustration – mm: Mary Evans
109 – bl: Illustration – br: Mary Evans – tm: Popperfoto – ml: Robert Opie
110 – br: Craig Dodd – tm: Hulton – bm: Topham
111 – mr: Illustrated London News – br: Illustration
112 – mm: Hulton – tr: Mary Evans – br: Robert Opie
113 – tr: Mary Evans – bm: Robert Opie
114 – br: Aldus Archive – tm, mm: Mary Evans
115 – tl, mr: Hulton – mm. Robert Opie
116 – bl: Mary Evans – tm, mr: Popperfoto
117 – bm: Illustration – mm: John Hillelson Agency – tr: Topham
118 – tl: Hulton
119 – mm, br, tr: Hulton
120 – tm: Hulton – bm: Illustration
121 – tm, ml, br: Mary Evans
122 – tm: Bettmann
123 – ml: Bettmann – mr, bm: Hulton – tm: Illustration
124 – mr: Hulton – tm: John Hillelson Agency – bm: Mary Evans
125 – tm, br: Hulton
126 – tr: Chronicle – mr: Mary Evans – bm: Popperfoto – tl: Topham
127 – tr: Hulton – tm, br: Mary Evans
128 – tr: Hulton – bm: Mary Evans – br: Robert Opie
129 – tr: John Hillelson Agency – tm, br: Mary Evans
130 – bl: Hulton – tr, br: Mary Evans – mm: Topham
131 – tr: Mary Evans – ml: Robert Opie – br: Topham
132 – bl, br: Hulton – tm: Mary Evans
133 – tm, mm: Mary Evans – br: Robert Opie Collecpion
134 – br, bl: Hulton
135 – bl: Hulton – br: Illustration – tl, tm, tr: Mary Evans
136 – 137 – sprd: Bildarchiv Preussicher Kulturbesitz, Berlin
138 – tm: Hulton – mr: Mary Evans – bm: Topham
139 – mm: Bettmann – br: Robert Opie – tr: Topham
140 – br: Bettmann – mm: Robert Opie
141 – tm, tr, br: Topham
142 – br: Hulton – tl: Mary Evans – mr: Popperfoto – bl: Robert Opie
143 – mr: Hulton – bl: Illustration – tr: Mary Evans
144 – br: Hulton – tm: Mary Evans
145 – br: Mary Evans – tr: St Paul's Cathedral, London – mm: Topham
146 – tm: John Hillelson Agency – bl: Mary Evans – br: Robert Opie
147 – tm: Illustration – bm, mr: Mary Evans
148 – bm: Bridgeman Art Library – br: Robert Opie – tm: Topham
149 – mr: Hulton – tr: Illustration
150 – mr: Hulton – tm: Mary Evans – bm: Topham
151 – mr: Chronicle – br: Hulton – tm: Mary Evans
152 – mr, bl: Hulton – tm: Popperfoto, Topham
153 – br: Hulton – tm: Mary Evans
154 – br, tr, bl: Hulton
155 – tr: Topham
156 – tm: David King Collection – bm: Hulton – mr: Mary Evans
157 – mm: Hulton – tr: Mary Evans – br: Robert Opie
158 – mm: Hulton – tr: Mary Evans – br: Robert Opie
159 – br: Chronicle
160 – tr: Anthony Shiel & Associates – mr: Hulton
161 – tm: ET Archive – br: Mary Evans – tr: Museum of London
162 – bm: Mary Evans – tm: Popperfoto
163 – tr: Hulton – bl: Mary Evans – tl: Popperfoto
164 – tr, br: Illustration – mr: Mary Evans
165 – mr: ET Archive – tm, bm: Hulton
166 – tm, bm: Mary Evans
167 – tm: Hulton – br: Mary Evans
168 – mm: Bettmann
169 – bm, br: Mary Evans
170 – bm: Chronicle – tm: Keystone
171 – tm, bl: Hulton – br: Robert Opie
172 – br: Imperial War Museum – tm: Topham
173 – bm: Mary Evans – tr: Visual Arts
174 – tm: Hulton – bm: John Hillelson Agency – mr: Ulster Museum
175 – tm: Hulton – mr: Illustration
176 – tr: Hulton – mm, br: Mary Evans
177 – mm, br: Mary Evans
178 – tr: Hulton – br: Illustration
179 – mm: Illustration – mr: Mary Evans – bm: Robert Opie
180 – mm: Hulton – br: Robert Opie
181 – tl: Hulton – bl: Popperfoto – mr: Robert Opie
182 – mr: Hulton – bl: Illustration – tl: Mary Evans
183 – tl, tr, br: Hulton
184 – bm: Mander and Mitchenson – tm: Popperfoto
185 – bm: Hulton – mr: Kharbine Tapabor, Paris – tl: Keystone
186 – bl: Chronicle – mr: Mary Evans – tl: Popperfoto
187 – tl, bl: Hulton – mr: Popperfoto
188 – tr, br: Hulton – mr: Robert Hunt
189 – br: Popperfoto – mr: Ulster Museum
190 – tl: Chronicle – bm: Robert Opie
191 – ml: Popperfoto – mr: Keystone
192 – bm: Chronicle – tm: David King Collection – br: Mary Evans
193 – bm: Chronicle – br: ET Archive – tm: Popperfoto
194 – bm: Chronicle – tm: Hulton – bl: Illustration
195 – br: Hulton – bm: Imperial War Museum – tm: John Hillelson Agency
196 – tm: Imperial War Museum – bm: Mary Evans – mr: Robert Hunt
197 – bm: Camera Press – tm: Robert Hunt
198 – br: Mary Evans – tr: Popperfoto
199 – mm: Hulton – tr: Imperial War Museum
200 – bm: Kobal Collection – tm, mr: Topham
201 – mr: Hulton – bm: Keystone – tm: Topham
202 – bl: Aldus Archive – tl: Hulton – mr: Imperial War Museum
203 – tm: Hulton – tl: Mary Evans – mr: Robert Hunt
204 – tm: David King Collection – bm: Mary Evans
205 – tr: David King Collection – br: Robert Opie – bl: Topham
206 – tr: Aldus Archive – br: Popperfoto
207 – br: Chronicle – tr: Popperfoto
208 – tm: Hulton – bl: Popperfoto – br: Robert Opie
209 – br: Aldus Archive – tm. Hulton – bl: Imperial War Museum
210 – br: Chronicle – tr: Robert Hunt
211 – bm, tr: Hulton – tl: Mary Evans – tm: Topham
212 – mm: Imperial War Museum – tm: Keystone
213 – tl: Hulton – br: Robert Opie
214 – br: Chronicle – ml: Hulton – tr: Imperial War Museum
215 – bl: Hulton – tl: Popperfoto
216 – bm: Chronicle – br: Popperfoto – tm: Topham
217 – tr: Imperial War Museum – ml: Popperfoto – br: Robert Opie
218 – tr, mr: Imperial War Museum
219 – tm: Popperfoto – bm: Topham
220 – tm: Illustration – bm: Imperial War Museum – br: Mary Evans
221 – tm, br: Hulton
222 – mm, tr: Popperfoto
223 – bm: Chronicle – mr: Hulton – tm: Imperial War Museum
224 – bm: Imperial War Museum – mr: Popperfoto – tm: Robert Opie
225 – bl: Chronicle – tl: ET Archive
226 – br: Illustration – tr: Popperfoto
227 – tl, br: Imperial War Museum – bm: Mary Evans
228 – br: ET Archive – tl: Illustration – bm: Keystone
229 – tr: ET Archive – mm: Topham
230 – tl, mm, mr: Popperfoto
231 – mr: Mary Evans – tl: Novosti Press Agency – bm: Topham
232 – bm: Aldus Archive – tl: Imperial War Museum
233 – tr, br: David King Collection – tl: Visual Arts
234 – mr: Chronicle – tl: Popperfoto
235 – tr: Bettmann – mr: David King Collection
236 – bl: Imperial War Museum – tm: Popperfoto
237 – tl, br: Imperial War Museum – tr: Mary Evans
238 – br: Hulton – tm: Mary Evans
239 – mr: ET Archive – bm: Robert Opie – tm: Keystone
240 – tm: Chronicle – mr: Mary Evans
241 – tl, mr: Popperfoto – bm: Topham
242 – mm: Imperial War Museum – tl: Popperfoto – br: Robert Opie
243 – tl, tr: Hulton
244 – br: Illustration – tr: Mary Evans – tm, bm: Topham
245 – tr: Illustration
246 – bm: Bettmann – tm: Popperfoto
247 – tm: Chronicle – br: Illustration – tm: Imperial War Museum
248 – bl: Chronicle – tr: Keystone
249 – bm: Illustration – tm: Popperfoto – mm: Topham
250 – tm: Imperial War Museum – br: Mary Evans – mm: Keystone
251 – br, bl, ml: Chronicle – tr: Illustration
252 – tm: Hulton – br: Illustration
253 – br: ET Archive – tl: Hulton – tr: Imperial War Museum – bl: Popperfoto
254 – mr: Mary Evans – tl, bm: Topham
255 – bl, br: Hulton – tm: Illustration
256 – tr: David King Collection – bl, br: Hulton
257 – ml: Popperfoto – mr: Topham
258 – mm: Chronicle – bl: David King Collection – tm: Topham
259 – tr, br: Popperfoto – bm: Robert Opie
260 – tm: Hulton – mm: Topham
261 – bl: Popperfoto – tm: Keystone – br: Topham
262 – mr, bm: Hulton – tm: Mary Evans
263 – br: Chronicle – tl: Mary Evans – tr: Keystone
264 – tm: Illustration
265 – bl: Illustration – tr: Topham – br: Visual Arts
266 – 267 – sprd: Bildarchiv Preussicher Kulturbesitz, Berlin
268 – tm: Gunn Brinson – bm: Hulton – mr: Visual Arts
269 – tr: David King Collection – bm: Hulton
270 – bm: Popperfoto
271 – tr, br: Mary Evans – tl: Keystone
272 – tr: Chronicle – bm: Popperfoto
273 – tm: Bettmann – bm: Marconi PLC
274 – tm, mr: Popperfoto – bm: Robert Opie
276 – mm: Hulton – mr: Mary Evans
277 – tl: Hulton – bm, mr: Popperfoto
278 – tm: Hulton – bm: Popperfoto
279 – tr: Hulton – mr: Mary Evans – tl: Popperfoto – br: Robert Opie
280 – tm: Mary Evans
281 – br: Cinémathèque Française – ml: Hulton – tr: Popperfoto
282 – tr, bm: Illustration
283 – tr: Hulton – tl: Mary Evans – bl: Robert Opie
284 – bl: Hulton – tm: Mary Evans
285 – bm: Mary Evans – br: Robert Opie
286 – mr: Bettmann – tm: Hulton – bl: Illustration
287 – tl: David King Collection – tr, br: Mary Evans
288 – mr: Hulton – tm: Illustration – bm: Mary Evans
289 – br: Robert Opie Collaction – tm: Topham
290 – tl: Hulton
291 – br: Illustration – tr: National Portrait Gallery, London – tm: Popperfoto
292 – bm: Mary Evans – mr: Popperfoto – tm: Topham
293 – tm, bm: Popperfoto – mr: Reader's Digest
294 – tm: Mary Evans
295 – bl: Mary Evans – br: Topham
296 – mr: Illustration – ml, tr: Popperfoto
297 – mm: Hulton – tr: Mary Evans
298 – mr: Hulton – bl: Mary Evans – tl: Popperfoto
299 – br, bm: Mary Evans – tm: Popperfoto
300 – tm, mr, bm: Popperfoto
301 – br: Aldus Archive – tm: Mary Evans – tr: Topham
302 – mr: Chronicle – tr: Popperfoto
303 – bm: Bettmann – ml: Keystone – tr: Topham
304 – mr: Gunn Brinson – bm: Illustration – tm: Popperfoto
305 – mr: Bettmann – bm: Popperfoto – tm: Keystone
306 – tm: Illustration – mr: Mary Evans – bm: Roger Viollet, Paris
307 – mm: Chronicle – tr: Keystone – bm: Topham
308 – br: Coles Collection – tr: Hulton – bm: Illustration
309 – tr: Popperfoto
310 – tm: Bettmann – bm: Hulton – mr: Popperfoto
311 – tr: Popperfoto – mr: Roger Viollet, Paris
312 – mm: Chronicle – tm: Hulton
313 – tl: Hulton – tr: Mary Evans – bl: Robert Opie – br: Keystone
314 – bm: David King Collection – tr: Topham
315 – tm, mr: Topham
316 – tl: Illustration – mr: Keystone
317 – bm: Mary Evans – tr: Popperfoto
318 – tl: Mary Evans – br: Keystone
319 – tl: Bettmann – bm: Mary Evans
320 – tl: Hulton – tm, br: Popperfoto – tr: Keystone
322 – tr: Gunn Brinson – bm: Popperfoto
323 – br: Hulton – tr: Illustration – ml: Mary Evans
324 – br: Hulton – ml, tr: Popperfoto
325 – tr, bm, br: Mary Evans – tm: Popperfoto
326 – tr: David King Collection – bm: Mary Evans
327 – mr: Mary Evans – bm: Robert Opie
328 – bl: Hulton – br: Robert Opie
329 – mm: Chronicle – bl: Hulton – tm, tr: Mary Evans – mr: Robert Opie
330 – tm, bm: Hulton – br: Popperfoto
331 – tm: Hulton – br: Mary Evans – bm: Topham
332 – br: Kodak Museum – tm: Popperfoto
333 – bm: Cinémathèque Française – tr: Hulton
334 – bm: Hulton – mr: Mary Evans – tl: Popperfoto – bl: Robert Opie
335 – tl, br: Hulton – tr: Keystone
336 – tl: Mary Evans – mr: Topham
337 – br: Kobal Collection – bl: Mander and Mitchenson – tr: National Portrait Gallery, London
338 – tr: Hulton – br: Mary Evans – bm: Popperfoto
339 – mr: Hulton – bm: Mary Evans – tm: Robert Opie
340 – tm: Hulton
341 – tr: John Hillelson Agency – tl, bl: Popperfoto – br: Robert Opie
342 – mr: Hulton – tr: Topham
343 – bl: Mary Evans – tl: Popperfoto – bm: Keystone
344 – bm: Popperfoto – tr: Keystone
345 – bm: Hulton – tm, mr: Mary Evans
346 – tm: Hulton – bm: Popperfoto
347 – bm: Hulton – tm, br: Mary Evans
348 – tm: Illustration – tr: Popperfoto – bm: Robert Opie
349 – br: Christian Dell – tl: Mary Evans – bl: National Gallery, London – tr: National Portrait Gallery, London – bm: Popperfoto
350 – tm: Popperfoto – br: Robert Opie
351 – tr: Hulton – bm: Popperfoto
352 – br: Hulton – tm: Popperfoto
353 – mm: Hulton – br: Robert Opie
354 – tm: Popperfoto
355 – mr: Hulton – bl: Keystone
356 – tm: Oesterr. Bundesverlag
357 – tr: Hulton – bl: Popperfoto
358 – tr: Hulton – tl: Popperfoto – bm: Robert Opie
359 – tr: Hulton – br: Popperfoto – bl: Robert Opie
360 – tl: Mary Evans – mr: Popperfoto
361 – br: Bettmann – tr: Hulton – bl: Robert Opie
362 – tm: Hulton – br: Illustration
363 – tm, tr: Hulton – br: Mary Evans – tl: Topham
364 – tm: Hulton – bm: Mary Evans
365 – tr: Hulton – bm: Mary Evans – tl: Topham
366 – tl, bl: Popperfoto
367 – mr: Mary Evans – tm: Keystone
368 – mr: Popperfoto – bm: Robert Opie – tr: Keystone
370 – bm: Hulton – tm: Science Photo Library
371 – bm: Hulton – tl, mr: Illustration
372 – bl: Hulton – tm: Illustration – mr: Popperfoto
373 – tm: Allsport – br: Illustration – tr: Popperfoto
374 – mr: Hulton – tm: Keystone – bm: Topham
375 – tm, br: Hulton
376 – mr: Hulton – bm: Mary Evans
377 – tr: Hulton – br: Labour Party – bl: Robert Opie
378 – tl: Kobal Collection – bm: Topham
379 – br: Mary Evans – tm: Keystone
380 – br: Kobal Collection – tm: Popperfoto
381 – tr: Hulton – br: Robert Opie – mm: Keystone
382 – tm: CJ Archive – bm: Robert Opie
383 – mm: Chronicle – tm: Popperfoto – mr: Topham
384 – tm: Popperfoto – bm: Topham
385 – br, tr: Popperfoto – bl: Robert Opie
386 – 387 – sprd: Westermann Verlag Buresch
388 – br: Mary Evans – tm: Popperfoto
389 – mr: Mary Evans – tm, mm: Popperfoto
390 – tr, bm: Popperfoto
391 – tm: Illustration – bl: Popperfoto – br: Robert Opie
392 – mm: Hulton – tr: Popperfoto – bl: Keystone
393 – bm: Mary Evans – tm: Popperfoto – br: Topham
394 – mr: Mary Evans – tm: Popperfoto
395 – tr: Popperfoto – br: Keystone
396 – tm: Hulton – bm: Popperfoto
397 – tl: Popperfoto – bm: Topham
398 – tl: Popperfoto – bl: Robert Opie – mr: Topham

399 – tr: Cinémathèque Française – tm: Hulton – bm: Popperfoto – br: Topham
400 – tm: Hulton – bm: Mary Evans
401 – tm: Hulton – bl: Mary Evans – br: Popperfoto
402 – br: Hulton – tr: Illustration – ml: Robert Opie
403 – bl: Hulton – mr: Popperfoto
404 – mr: Hulton – bl: Robert Opie
405 – br: Hulton – tr: John Hillelson Agency
406 – mr: Hulton – tr: Topham
407 – tr: Hulton – br: Popperfoto, Keystone
408 – tm: Mary Evans – bl: Robert Opie
409 – tr: Hulton – br: Mary Evans – tl, bm: Popperfoto
410 – br: Hulton – tm: Mary Evans
411 – mm: Chronicle – br: Hulton – tm: Mary Evans
412 – tm: Mary Evans – bl: Robert Opie – tr, br: Topham
413 – mm: Chronicle – tm: Popperfoto – mr: Robert Opie
414 – tm, br, bm: Hulton
415 – bm: ET Archive – tr: Hulton
416 – bl: Hulton – mm: Mary Evans – tr, br: Popperfoto
418 – mr: Gunn Brinson – bm: Robert Opie
419 – bl: Illustration – mr: Popperfoto – tl: Syndication International
420 – tl, mm: Hulton – bl: Popperfoto
421 – tm, br: Mary Evans – tm: Popperfoto – bl: Robert Opie
422 – tm: Mary Evans – bm: Keystone
423 – tl: Hulton – bm: Imperial War Museum
424 – tr: Topham
425 – mr: Illustration – tm: Popperfoto
426 – mm: Gunn Brinson – tl, tr: Popperfoto – br: Topham
427 – mr, bm: Popperfoto – tm: Topham
428 – tl: Imperial War Museum – mr: Popperfoto – bl: Robert Opie
429 – tr: Hulton – mm: Mary Evans – br: Popperfoto
430 – br: Illustration – tm: Popperfoto
431 – tm: Keystone – mr, bm: Topham
432 – bm: Mary Evans – mr: Popperfoto – tm: Topham
433 – tm: Popperfoto – br: Robert Opie
434 – mm: ET Archive – bm: Popperfoto
435 – bl: Aldus Archive – tr: Gunn Brinson – br: Hulton – tl: Popperfoto
436 – br: Robert Opie – tm: Topham
437 – tm: Keystone – bm: Topham
438 – mr: Hulton – bm: Robert Opie – tm: Topham
439 – tm, br: Popperfoto
440 – bl, br: Hulton – tm: Popperfoto
441 – tm, br: Keystone
442 – tr: Hulton – ml: Illustration – mr: Topham
443 – tr: Mary Evans – tl: Popperfoto – br: Robert Opie
444 – bm: Keystone
445 – tm: John Hillelson Agency – bm: Keystone – mr: Topham
446 – bm: Mary Evans – mr: Popperfoto
447 – tl: Chronicle – tr: Hulton – br: Topham
448 – tm: Illustration – bm: Robert Opie
449 – tr: Illustration – bm: Mary Evans – tl: Popperfoto
450 – tl: Illustration – br: Mary Evans
451 – tr: Topham
452 – mr: Hulton – tr: Popperfoto
453 – bl: Mary Evans – tm, mr: Popperfoto
454 – tm, bm: Illustration
455 – tr: Popperfoto – bl: Robert Opie – mr: Topham
456 – br: Robert Opie – tr: Topham
457 – tr: Chronicle – br: David King Collection – ml: Keystone
458 – tl: Popperfoto – tr: Keystone
459 – tm: Hulton – mr: Mary Evans – bm: Robert Opie
460 – ml: Hulton – br: Robert Opie
461 – tr: Cinémathèque Française – tl: Illustration – br: Kobal Collection
462 – tm: Popperfoto – br: Keystone
463 – bm: Cinémathèque Française – tm: Illustration
464 – tm: Popperfoto – bm: Topham
465 – bl: Hulton – tr: Topham
466 – mr: Mary Evans – tl: Popperfoto
467 – br: Chronicle – mr: Illustration – tr: Topham
468 – br: Mary Evans – ml: Robert Opie – tm: Topham
469 – br: Dorothea Lange Collection, The City of Oakland, Oa – tl: Popperfoto
470 – tm: John Hillelson Agency, Topham
471 – bm: Popperfoto
472 – tm: Popperfoto – br: Robert Opie
473 – tr: CJ Archive – br: Mary Evans
474 – tl, bm: Illustration – mr: Popperfoto
475 – tm: Hulton – bm: Popperfoto
476 – tr, br: Keystone
477 – tm: Popperfoto – bl: Keystone
478 – tl: Popperfoto – bm: Royal Opera House, London
479 – tm: John Hillelson Agency
480 – tm: Illustration – br: Robert Opie
481 – tm: Alfonso – bm: Popperfoto – bl: Topham
482 – tm, br: Popperfoto
483 – br: Popperfoto – tr: Keystone
484 – mm, tr: Hulton
485 – mm: Hulton – br: Mary Evans – tr: Topham
486 – tl: Topham
487 – tm, bm: Hulton – br: Robert Opie
488 – br: Popperfoto – tl: Keystone
489 – tl: John Hillelson Agency – bm: Robert Opie – tr: Topham
490 – bl: Popperfoto
491 – tr: ET Archive – bl: Robert Opie – bm, br: Topham
492 – tm: Illustration – bm: Popperfoto – mr: Keystone
493 – tm: Illustration – mr: Mary Evans
494 – mr: Gunn Brinson – tl: Keystone
495 – br: Gunn Brinson – tl: John Hillelson Agency
496 – tl, mr: Keystone
497 – tl, bl: Hulton – mr: Popperfoto
498 – tm: Hulton – bl: Mary Evans
499 – tl: Gunn Brinson – tr: Illustration – br: Topham
500 – bm: Mary Evans – tm: Keystone
501 – tr: Illustration – bm: Keystone
502 – mr: Chronicle – tl: Popperfoto
503 – bl: Hulton – br: Mary Evans – tr: Popperfoto
504 – tm, mm: Popperfoto
505 – tl, tr, bm: Architectural Press – br: Robert Opie
506 – mr: Hulton – tm: Illustration
507 – tm: Illustration – br: Popperfoto
508 – br: Chronicle – tr: Topham
509 – ml: Popperfoto – br: Robert Opie
510 – br: Cinémathèque Française – tl: Illustration
511 – tl: Illustration – br: Popperfoto
512 – br: Popperfoto – tm: Keystone
513 – tm: Hulton – mr: Mary Evans
514 – mm: Cine-Image – tr: Popperfoto
515 – tl: Illustration – tr: Popperfoto
516 – br: Chronicle – tr,mr: Popperfoto
517 – tr, mr: Popperfoto – ml: Keystone
518 – tm, mm: Popperfoto – bl: Topham
519 – br: Popperfoto – tm: Topham
520 – tm, br: Hulton
521 – bm: Cinémathèque Française – br: Kobal Collection – tm: Popperfoto
522 – 523 – sprd: Tate Gallery
524 – tr, bm: Popperfoto
525 – br: Cine-Image – tl: Imperial War Museum – bm: Popperfoto
526 – ml, mr: Mary Evans – tm: Popperfoto
527 – mr: Mary Evans – tm: Popperfoto
528 – tr: Keystone
529 – tr: Popperfoto
530 – tm, br, bl: Popperfoto
531 – br: Chronicle – tr: Popperfoto
532 – tr, bm: Popperfoto – br: Topham
533 – tr: Hulton – br: Keystone
534 – tm, tr: Hulton
535 – tr: Imperial War Museum
536 – mr: Gunn Brinson – tm: Popperfoto – bm: Topham
537 – tl, bm: Keystone
538 – tr: Keystone – br: Topham
539 – tm: Keystone – bm: Topham
540 – tr: Chronicle
541 – mr, bl: Hulton – tl: Popperfoto
542 – mm: Hulton – tm: Keystone
543 – tl: Popperfoto – tr: Topham
544 – mr: Hulton – tm: Popperfoto
545 – tl: Robert Opie – tr: Topham
546 – tm: Imperial War Museum
547 – ml: Hulton – br: Robert Opie – bm: Topham
548 – tm: Popperfoto – bm: Topham
549 – tl, tr, br: Popperfoto
550 – bm: Hulton – br: Keystone – tl: Topham
551 – tr, br: Keystone
552 – tl: Popperfoto – br: Robert Opie
553 – bm: Chronicle – tm: Magnum Photos Ltd.
554 – bm: Hulton – tm: Keystone
555 – tm, mr: Keystone
556 – tr: Popperfoto – bm: Robert Opie
557 – tm, mr: Topham
558 – tr: Hulton
559 – bm: Chronicle – tm: Topham
560 – tr: Kobal Collection – tl: Keystone – br: Topham
561 – tm: Popperfoto – br: Topham
562 – bm: CJ Archive – mr: Gunn Brinson – tl: Topham
563 – bm: Imperial War Museum – tr: Topham
564 – tl: Illustration – bl: Syndication International
565 – bl, br: Robert Opie – tm: Keystone
566 – tr: Magnum Photos Ltd. – bm: Popperfoto
567 – bl: Hulton – mr: Popperfoto
568 – tm, br: Topham
569 – br: Chronicle – tm: Keystone
570 – ml: Popperfoto – mr: Keystone
571 – br: Mary Evans – tm, bl: Popperfoto
572 – tr: Popperfoto – bm: Keystone
573 – bl: Chronicle – br: Robert Opie – tl: Topham
574 – bl: Cine-Image – mr: Imperial War Museum – tr: Topham
575 – tm: Magnum Photos Ltd. – br: Topham
576 – bl: Chronicle – tl: Imperial War Museum
577 – ml: Hulton – tr, br: Kobal Collection
578 – tm: Magnum Photos Ltd. – bm: Popperfoto
579 – br: JWT Archive – mm: Popperfoto
580 – br: Robert Opie – ml: Keystone
581 – ml, br: Popperfoto
582 – tl, tm: Keystone
583 – bm: Popperfoto
584 – tm: Chronicle – tl: Popperfoto – bm: Robert Opie
585 – bl, bm: Popperfoto – tm: Keystone
586 – tr: Magnum Photos Ltd. – br: Novosti Press Agency
587 – tm: Hulton – bm: Illustration
588 – mm: Imperial War Museum – br: Topham
589 – tm: Popperfoto – bm: Topham
590 – mm: John Hillelson Agency – br: Mary Evans
591 – tr: Popperfoto – tl: Keystone
592 – ml: Hulton – tm: Imperial War Museum – bm: Keystone
593 – tr: Hulton – bl: Robert Opie – bm: Keystone – tl: Topham
594 – tm: Chronicle – tr: Keystone
595 – br: Popperfoto – ml: Keystone
596 – tm, mr: Popperfoto
597 – bm: Chronicle – tm: Keystone
598 – br: Mary Evans – tr: Popperfoto
599 – br: Popperfoto – tr: Keystone, Keystone
600 – tm: Hulton – br: Keystone
601 – br: Popperfoto – tm: Keystone
602 – tr, br: John Hillelson Agency – bm: Topham
603 – tr: Chronicle – br: Topham
604 – tr, mm: Popperfoto
605 – tr: John Hillelson Agency – tm: Keystone
606 – tm: Imperial War Museum – bm: Keystone
607 – tr, br: John Hillelson Agency
608 – bm: Chronicle – tm: Magnum Photos Ltd.
609 – br: Mary Evans – tl: Keystone
610 – br: Hulton – tr: Popperfoto – tl: Keystone
611 – tr: Hulton – mr: Keystone
612 – bm: Popperfoto – tm: Keystone
613 – tm: Hulton – bm: Keystone
614 – tm: Chronicle – tr: Imperial War Museum
615 – tr: Cinémathèque Française – br: Popperfoto – ml: Keystone
616 – br: Imperial War Museum èv tm: John Hillelson Agency
617 – tr, br: Popperfoto
618 – tm, ml: Hulton
619 – mm: Popperfoto – tm: Keystone – mr: Topham
620 – tr: Magnum Photos Ltd. – br: Keystone
621 – tl, bl, tr: Popperfoto
622 – tr: Popperfoto – tl: Topham
623 – bl: Popperfoto – tr: Keystone – br: Topham
624 – tr: Gunn Brinson – br: Imperial War Museum
625 – tr: CJ Archive – tl: Hulton
626 – tm: Popperfoto – bm: Keystone
627 – tl: Chronicle – bm: John Hillelson Agency
628 – br: Hulton
629 – tl, bm: Popperfoto
630 – tr: Popperfoto – br: Keystone
631 – tl: Hulton – br: Popperfoto
632 – tm: Popperfoto – br: Robert Opie
633 – br, ml, bl: Chronicle – tr: Magnum Photos Ltd.
634 – tm, bm: Popperfoto
635 – tm: Hulton – bm: Robert Opie – mr: Keystone
636 – tm: Popperfoto
637 – tr: Kobal Collection – br: Popperfoto – ml: Keystone
638 – br: Hulton – tm: Topham
639 – br: Mary Evans – tr: Keystone
640 – ml, tr: Keystone
641 – tr: Hulton – ml: Illustration
642 – tm: Chronicle – ml: Keystone
643 – mr, bl: Popperfoto
644 – tl: Keystone
645 – tl: Popperfoto – br, bl: Keystone
646 – tl: Illustration – bm, br: Robert Opie
647 – br: Chronicle – tr: Keystone
648 – mm: Illustration – br: Robert Opie
649 – br: Cinémathèque Française – tr: Popperfoto
650 – tm: Illustration – br: Keystone
651 – bm: Illustration – tl: Popperfoto – br: Keystone
652 – bm: Hulton – tl: Illustration
653 – br: Popperfoto – tm: Keystone
654 – br: Illustration – tm: Keystone
655 – br: Chronicle
656 – bl: Gunn Brinson – br: Popperfoto – tr: Topham
657 – tl: Popperfoto – br: Topham
658 – tl, bm, br: Popperfoto
659 – tm, ml: Popperfoto – br: Topham
660 – tm, br: Popperfoto
661 – mr: Popperfoto – bm: Keystone – tl: Topham
662 – tm: Illustration – bm: Popperfoto
663 – mr: Illustration – tl, bm: Popperfoto
664 – tm: Popperfoto
665 – tl, br, tr: Popperfoto
666 – br: Popperfoto – tr: Keystone
667 – br: Mary Evans – tm, bm: Popperfoto
668 – tr: Hulton – br: Popperfoto
669 – tm: Hulton – br: Mary Evans
670 – tm, br: Popperfoto
671 – tr: Chronicle – bm: Hulton – br: Popperfoto
672 – tr: Bettmann – br: Cine-Image – tl: Hulton
673 – mr, bl: Illustration – tl: Popperfoto
674 – tm: Hulton – mm: Keystone
675 – tm, ml: Popperfoto – bm: Topham
676 – bl: Popperfoto – mm: Keystone
677 – mm: Popperfoto
678 – tm, br: Popperfoto
679 – br: Hulton – tm: Illustration
680 – tm: Popperfoto – bm: Topham
681 – br: Hulton – tr: Popperfoto – bl: Keystone – tm: Topham
682 – br: Hulton – tm: Popperfoto
683 – mm: Popperfoto – br: Robert Opie
684 – mm: Illustration – tr: Popperfoto
685 – tm, br: Popperfoto
686 – br: Illustration – tm: Keystone
687 – mr, bm: Popperfoto – bl: Keystone
688 – tm: Popperfoto – mr, bm: Keystone
689 – tm, br: Popperfoto
690 – tr: Popperfoto
691 – bl, tr: Popperfoto – br: Robert Opie
692 – br: Chronicle – tl: Keystone
693 – br: Robert Opie – tm: Topham
694 – bm: Hulton – tm: Illustration
695 – tr, bl, br: Kobal Collection
696 – 697 – sprd: Museum Fernand Leger (Copyright ACS 1988)
698 – tm: Illustration – mr: Topham
699 – mm: Hulton – br: Mary Evans
700 – tl: Popperfoto – mr: Keystone
701 – tr, bl: Hulton – tl: Popperfoto
702 – br: Illustration – tr: Popperfoto – bl: Robert Opie
703 – tr, bm: Popperfoto
704 – mr: Popperfoto – bm: Robert Opie
705 – tr: Chronicle – tl: Keystone
706 – tm: Popperfoto
707 – tr, br: Hulton
708 – tl, bl: Keystone – br: Topham
709 – tl, bm, tr: Popperfoto
710 – tl: Topham
711 – bl, tr: Hulton – tm, br: Popperfoto
712 – br: Chronicle – tr: Popperfoto
713 – tm: Popperfoto – br: Robert Opie
714 – tl, mr: Popperfoto – bl: Topham
715 – br: Popperfoto – ml: Keystone
716 – tm, br: Popperfoto – bl: Keystone
717 – mm: Popperfoto – br: Robert Opie
718 – tr, br: Hulton – tl, bm: Popperfoto – mr: Topham
719 – br: Hulton – tm: Popperfoto
720 – tm, br: Keystone
721 – tm: Popperfoto – br: Keystone
722 – bm: Popperfoto
723 – tm, bm: Popperfoto
724 – tm: Topham
725 – tl, tr, bl: Popperfoto
726 – tm, br: Popperfoto
727 – tr: Keystone – br: Topham
728 – br: Cinémathèque Française – bl: Popperfoto – tr: Topham
729 – mm: Illustration – br: Popperfoto
730 – tr: Popperfoto – br: Robert Opie – bl: Topham
731 – tm, bm, br: Popperfoto
732 – tr: Keystone
733 – mm: Illustration
734 – tm: Illustration – br: Popperfoto
735 – tm: Illustration – bm: Popperfoto
736 – br: Illustration – tr: Popperfoto
737 – tl, mr: Popperfoto
738 – bm: Popperfoto – tm: Keystone
739 – br: Popperfoto – tr, tl: Keystone
740 – tm, br: Popperfoto
741 – tm: Hulton – tr: Popperfoto
742 – tr, bm: Popperfoto
743 – mr, bl: Popperfoto – tm: Keystone
744 – tr: Popperfoto – bm: Robert Opie – tl: Keystone
745 – mr: Keystone – ml: Topham
746 – br: Popperfoto – tr: Keystone, – tl: Topham
747 – tr: Jacques Legrand SA, Paris
748 – tr: Popperfoto – mr: Topham
749 – br: Popperfoto – ml: Keystone
750 – tm, bm: Hulton
751 – bl: Hulton – tl: Popperfoto – br: Robert Opie
752 – tl, bm: Popperfoto – br: Robert Opie
753 – bl: Hulton – tr, br: Popperfoto
754 – tm: Popperfoto
755 – br, bl: Popperfoto – tm: Keystone
756 – br, tm: Hulton
757 – br: Hulton – tm: Popperfoto
758 – tl: Popperfoto – bm: Robert Opie
759 – tr: Chronicle – tl: Keystone – mr: Topham
760 – bm: Topham
761 – mm, bl: Popperfoto – br: Keystone
762 – tr: Popperfoto – bl: Robert Opie – br: Keystone
763 – br: Cine-Image – tm: Keystone
764 – tl, tr: Popperfoto
765 – br: Cinémathèque Française – tm: Popperfoto
766 – tm: Hulton – bm: Popperfoto
767 – mr: Hulton – tl: Popperfoto
768 – br: Popperfoto – bl, tr: Keystone
769 – mr, bm: Hulton – tm: Keystone – tl: Topham
770 – tr: Popperfoto – mm: Keystone
771 – tm: Hulton – br: Topham
772 – tl, mr: Popperfoto
773 – tr: Bridgeman Art Library – ml: Popperfoto
774 – tl: Popperfoto – bl: Robert Opie – bm: Keystone
775 – ml: Kobal Collection – tm: Robert Opie – mr: Keystone
776 – tm, bl: Popperfoto – tr: Keystone
777 – bl: Popperfoto – tr: Keystone
778 – tl: Popperfoto
779 – br: Illustration – tr: Tate Gallery – tm: Keystone – ml: Topham
780 – tm, bm: Popperfoto
781 – tm: Hulton – mr, bm: Keystone
782 – tr: Popperfoto – bm: Topham
783 – tl: Associated Press – tr: Keystone – bl, bm, br: Topham
784 – tm, mr: Popperfoto
785 – br: Hulton – tm: Popperfoto
786 – tm: Associated Press – br: Keystone
787 – tr: Keystone – br: Topham
788 – tm: Hulton – br: Robert Opie
789 – tm, bm: Popperfoto
790 – tr: John Hillelson Agency
791 – tr: Hulton – ml: Popperfoto
792 – tl: Popperfoto
793 – bl: Chronicle – tl: Hulton – tr: Keystone
794 – tm, bm: Keystone
795 – tm: Associated Press – mm: Hulton
796 – tm: Popperfoto – bl: Topham
798 – tr: Cine-Image – tm: Popperfoto – br: Keystone
799 – tm: Hulton – mr: Popperfoto
800 – tm: Hulton
801 – tm: Popperfoto – bl: Robert Opie – br: Syndication International
802 – br: Robert Opie – bm: Keystone – tm: Topham
803 – bm: Robert Opie
804 – tm: Keystone – br: Topham
805 – tr: Cinémathèque Française – mm, br: Keystone
806 – tm: Associated Press – mr: Popperfoto
807 – bm: Popperfoto – tr: Topham
808 – tm, bm: Popperfoto – ml: Keystone
809 – tr: Cine-Image – bl: Cinémathèque Française – tl: Keystone – bl: Topham
810 – br: Popperfoto – tm: Keystone
811 – tr, bm, br: Popperfoto
812 – tr: Popperfoto – bl: Robert Opie – br: Keystone
813 – bm: Hulton – ml: Popperfoto – tr: Topham
814 – tr, bm: Popperfoto
815 – tm, mr: Popperfoto – bm: Topham
816 – tr: Popperfoto – mr: Keystone
817 – mm, mr: Popperfoto
818 – bl: Popperfoto – tr: Topham
819 – tm: Popperfoto – br: Robert Opie
820 – br: Keystone – tr: Topham
821 – bm: Popperfoto – tm: Keystone – mr: Topham
822 – bm: Robert Opie
823 – br: Hulton – tl: Popperfoto
824 – tr: Hulton – br: Popperfoto
825 – tl: Popperfoto – bm: Robert Opie – mr: Topham
826 – tm: Popperfoto – mm: Keystone
827 – tl, tr, bm: Popperfoto
828 – tm, mr, bl: Topham
829 – bm: Popperfoto – br: Robert Opie – tm: Topham
830 – tm, bm: Topham
831 – tm: Popperfoto – bm: Robert Opie
832 – br: Hulton – tm: Popperfoto
833 – br: Robert Opie – tl: Keystone – bm: Topham
834 – tr: Popperfoto – br: Robert Opie – tl: Keystone
835 – br: Cinémathèque Française – tm, tr, bl: Popperfoto
836 – tm: Chronicle – br: Popperfoto
837 – tm: Popperfoto – bm: Sipa
838 – tr: Kobal Collection – br, bm: Popperfoto
839 – tl, tr, br: Popperfoto
840 – 841 – sprd: Andy Warhol – The Bridgeman Art Library (c DACS 88)
842 – bm: Robert Opie – tr, tm: Keystone
843 – mm: Popperfoto – tr: Topham
844 – tr, br: Popperfoto
845 – tl: Keystone – mr: Topham
846 – mr, bl: Popperfoto – tl: Topham
847 – mr: Popperfoto – tr: Keystone
848 – bl: Popperfoto – mr: Topham
849 – tm: Popperfoto – tl: Sipa – br, bl: Topham
850 – tm: Popperfoto – bm, mr: Topham
851 – tl: Popperfoto – br: Robert Opie – tr: Topham
852 – tm: Popperfoto – bm: Popperfoto – mm: Popperfoto
854 – tm: Hulton – bm: Topham
855 – mr, bl: Popperfoto – tm: Topham
856 – tl: Popperfoto – bm: Robert Opie – mr: Topham
857 – bm: Popperfoto èv tl: Topham
858 – tm: Hulton – br: Popperfoto
859 – bl, mr: Popperfoto – tm: Keystone
860 – bm: Cinémathèque Française – ml, mr: Popperfoto
861 – br: Sipa – tl: Keystone – bl: Topham
862 – tm: Popperfoto – bm: Sipa
863 – tr: Popperfoto – tl, br: Sipa – bl: Topham
864 – br: Popperfoto – tm, mr: Topham
865 – tr: Popperfoto – tl, bm: Keystone
866 – tl, bm: Popperfoto
867 – br: Hulton – tl: Popperfoto – mm: Topham
868 – tr: Popperfoto – ml: Topham
869 – ml: Popperfoto – bl: Robert Opie – tl: Keystone
870 – br: Popperfoto – tl: Topham
871 – br: Robert Opie – tl: Sipa – tr: Topham
872 – tr: Popperfoto – br: Popperfoto
873 – bl: Kobal Collection – tm, tr, bl: Popperfoto
874 – mm: Popperfoto – tr: Topham
875 – bl: Merseybeat Liverpool – tm, tr: Keystone – br: Topham
876 – bl: Robert Opie – tr, mr: Keystone – tl: Topham
877 – tm, br: Keystone – br: Keystone
878 – tm, bm: Popperfoto – mr: Keystone
879 – mr: Bridgeman Art Library – tm, bm: Popperfoto
880 – tm, mr: Popperfoto – bl: Keystone
881 – tl: Popperfoto – tr: Keystone
882 – tm: Sipa – bl, br: Keystone

883 – mr: Popperfoto – tl: Topham
884 – mm: Keystone – tm: Topham
885 – tm: Popperfoto – bl: Robert Opie – br: Keystone
886 – tr: Popperfoto – mr: Keystone
887 – bl: Kobal Collection – mm, tr: Keystone
888 – tr: Hulton – tl: Topham
889 – tm, br: Popperfoto – ml: Topham
890 – br: Associated Press – tr: Keystone
891 – ml, tr: Popperfoto – br: Robert Opie
892 – tl, mr: Popperfoto – tr: Topham
893 – tm: Hulton – tr: Popperfoto – bl: Sipa
894 – mr: Cinémathèque Française – tl: Hulton – bl: Popperfoto
895 – mr: Associated Press – tl: Popperfoto
896 – tr: Camera Press – br: Hulton – tm, bl: Topham
897 – br: Hulton – tr: Popperfoto – tl, bl: Keystone
898 – tl: Camera Press – br: Popperfoto – bl: Keystone
899 – tr: Associated Press – tl: Popperfoto – bm: Topham
900 – br: Hulton – tr: Topham
901 – br: Keystone – tr: Topham
902 – bm: Hulton – tm, br: Popperfoto
903 – tm: Hulton – br: Popperfoto – tm: Keystone
904 – tr: Hulton – br: Keystone
905 – tm, bl, br: Colorific!
906 – tm: Popperfoto
907 – tm: Keystone
908 – bm: Chronicle
909 – br: Cinémathèque Française – tr: Sipa – tl: Topham
910 – tm: Popperfoto – br: Syndication International – mr: Topham
911 – tm: Popperfoto – br: Keystone
912 – tm: Magnum Photos Ltd. – br: Popperfoto – bm: Topham
913 – tm: Hulton – tr, br: Popperfoto
914 – tr, bm: Popperfoto
915 – mm, br: Keystone
916 – bm: Popperfoto – br: Keystone – tm: Topham
917 – tr: Popperfoto – tl, bl: Keystone
918 – tm: Chronicle – bm: Topham
919 – mr, bm: Popperfoto – tm: Topham
920 – tr: Keystone – bm: Theatre Museum, London
921 – bm: Hulton – br: Robert Opie – tr: Keystone
922 – tm: Popperfoto – bm: Keystone
923 – mr: Keystone – tr: Topham
924 – tm, mm: Topham
925 – br: Camera Press – tl, bl: Popperfoto – tr: Shakespeare Centre
926 – tr, br: Popperfoto
927 – br: Hulton – tl: Pacemaker Press – bm: Robert Opie
928 – tm, bl: Topham
929 – tm: Associated Press – bl: Hulton – br: Topham
930 – tm: Hulton – mr, bm: Keystone
931 – tm, br: Popperfoto
932 – tm: Popperfoto – mr: Robert Opie
933 – tl, tr: Popperfoto – bl: Keystone
934 – bm: Popperfoto – tl, br: Keystone
935 – tl, bm: Hulton – tr: Popperfoto – br: Topham
936 – mm: Popperfoto – tr, br: Topham
937 – tr: Hulton – tl, bl: Popperfoto
938 – bm: Hulton – tl: Keystone
939 – mr: Hulton – tl: Popperfoto – bm: Keystone
940 – tr: Popperfoto – tm, bl: Topham
941 – br: Cinémathèque Française – mm: Science Photo Library – tr, bm: Keystone
942 – tm, mm, br: Popperfoto
943 – mr: Hulton – bm: Popperfoto – tl: Topham
944 – tr, br: Keystone
945 – bl: Popperfoto – br: Sipa – tr: Keystone
946 – mr: Hulton – tm, bl: Popperfoto
947 – tl, tm, mr: Popperfoto – bl: Topham
948 – bm: Popperfoto – tl: Topham
949 – tm, mr: Hulton – bl: Popperfoto
950 – bl: Chronicle – tr, br: Popperfoto
951 – tr, mr: Sipa
952 – bl: Hulton – tr: Popperfoto – br: Keystone – tl: Topham
953 – tm, tr: Popperfoto – bm: Topham
954 – bm: Keystone – tm: Topham
955 – tm: Popperfoto – bm: Science Photo Library – mr: Keystone
956 – tm: Popperfoto – bm: Keystone
957 – bl: Popperfoto – tm, br: Topham
958 – br: Keystone – tm: Topham
959 – tl, tr, mm: Popperfoto – br: Robert Opie
960 – br: Hulton – tr: Keystone
961 – tl: Hulton – tr: Sipa – bm: Topham
962 – tm, bl, br: Popperfoto
963 – tm, br: Popperfoto – bm: Keystone
964 – tl: Hulton – tr: Popperfoto – bl: Topham
965 – tr, br: Popperfoto – bl: Sipa
966 – bl: Hulton – tl, tr: Topham
967 – ml: Chronicle – br: Hulton – tr: Popperfoto
968 – ml: Hulton – mr: Popperfoto, Keystone
969 – br: Hulton – bm: Popperfoto – tl: Topham
970 – tm, br: Popperfoto
971 – mm: Chronicle – tm: Hulton – br: Keystone
972 – br: Hulton – tm, mm: Popperfoto
973 – br: Bridgeman Art Library – tl: Topham
974 – tr, br: Popperfoto
975 – ml: Robert Opie – tm: Sipa – mr: Keystone
976 – tl: Associated Press – bm: Popperfoto
977 – tr: Hulton – tl, br: Keystone – tl: Topham
978 – tm: Associated Press – tr, br: Popperfoto
979 – ml: Hulton – tr: Topham
980 – bl, br: Magnum Photos Ltd. – tm: Topham
981 – tm: Frank Spooner/Gamma – bl: Magnum Photos Ltd. – mr: Popperfoto
982 – ml: Popperfoto – tm: Topham
983 – tl: Frank Spooner/Gamma – bm, mr: Popperfoto
984 – tr: Frank Spooner/Gamma – ml: Keystone – bm: Topham
985 – tr, bl: Magnum Photos Ltd. – br: Topham
986 – bl, tr: Keystone – br: Topham
987 – br: Sipa – tm: Keystone
988 – mm: Popperfoto – tr: Topham
989 – mm: Popperfoto
990 – tm: Popperfoto – bm: Sport and General
991 – tr: Cinémathèque Française – tl: Popperfoto – br: Topham
992 – tm: Popperfoto – br: Sipa
993 – tm: Hulton – bl: Popperfoto – mr: Sipa
994 – tm, bm, bl: Popperfoto
995 – tl, tr, br: Popperfoto
996 – mr: Popperfoto – tm, bm: Topham
997 – tl, br: Popperfoto
998 – bm: Popperfoto – tm: Keystone
999 – bm: Hulton – tm: Magnum Photos Ltd. – br: Topham
1000 – tr: Popperfoto
1001 – bl: Popperfoto – ml: Science Photo Library – tl: Sygma, Paris – mr: Keystone
1002 – tm, tr, bl: Popperfoto – br: Keystone
1003 – tr, br: Popperfoto
1004 – bl: Magnum Photos Ltd. – tm, tr: Popperfopo
1005 – bl, mr: Popperfoto – tl: Keystone
1006 – mr: Hulton tm, bm: Popperfoto
1007 – tm, br: Popperfoto
1008 – tm, br: Popperfoto
1009 br, tr: Cinémathèque Française – tl, mm: Popperfoto
1010 – 1011 – sprd: David Hockney – The Bridgeman Art Library
1012 – br: Popperfoto – tm: Keystone
1013 – mr: Chronicle – tm: Topham
1014 – br: Hulton – tr: Popperfoto
1015 – bl: Cinématheque Française – tr: Topham
1016 – tr: Hulton – tl: Popperfoto – br: Keystone
1017 – br: Hulton – tl: Popperfoto
1018 – tm, mr, bl: Popperfoto
1019 – tl: Hulton – tr, mm: Popperfoto – br: Keystone
1020 – bm: Hulton – tr, br: Popperfoto
1021 – tl, bm: Popperfoto
1022 – mm: Magnum Photos Ltd. – tr, br: Popperfoto
1023 – tr: Popperfoto – ml: Keystone
1024 – tl: Magnum Photos Ltd. – bm: Popperfoto – tr: Keystone
1025 – bm: Hulton – tr: Kobal Collection – mm: Popperfoto
1026 – tm, bm: Popperfoto – br: Keystone
1027 – tm, bl: Popperfoto – mr: Robert Opie – tl: Keystone
1028 – tl, bm: Popperfoto
1029 – tm, bm: Popperfoto – ml: Keystone
1030 – tr, bm: Popperfoto
1031 – bl: Hulton – tl, tr, br: Popperfoto
1032 – bm: Hulton – tr: Popperfoto
1033 – br: Popperfoto – tr: Science Photo Library
1034 – tr, bm: Popperfoto
1035 – tm: Popperfoto – bl, mr: Keystone
1036 – tm, bm: Popperfoto
1037 – ml: Popperfoto – tr: Sipa – br: Topham
1038 – tm, br: Popperfoto
1039 – tl: Associated Press – bm: Topham
1040 èv mr: Hulton – tr: Magnum Photos Ltd. – bm: Popperfoto
1041 – mr: Hulton – tm, ml: Popperfoto
1042 – tl: Hulton – bm: Popperfoto
1043 – tm, bl: Popperfoto – br: Robert Opie
1044 bm: Popperfoto – tr: Sipa – mr: Keystone
1045 – br: Hulton – mm: Popperfoto – tm: Keystone
1046 – tl, tr: Popperfoto – bm: Keystone
1047 – bl: Associated Press – tm: Keystone
1048 – mr: Popperfoto – tm: Keystone – mm: Topham
1049 – tm: Colorific! – br: Popperfoto
1050 – bm: Popperfoto – br: Keystone – tr: Topham
1051 – tm, tr, br: Keystone
1052 – mm: Topham
1053 – mm: Popperfoto
1054 – bm: Hulton – tr: Sipa
1055 – br: Sipa – tm: Keystone
1056 – tr: Hulton èv br: Popperfoto
1057 – br: Cinémathèque Française – tl: Popperfoto – tr: Sygma, Paris
1058 – br: Hulton – tm: Popperfoto
1059 – bm: Magnum Photos Ltd. – tm: Popperfoto – br: Topham
1060 – bm: Associated Press – mr: Hulton – tm: Keystone
1061 – tm, tr, mm: Keystone
1062 – br: Sygma, Paris – tm: Keystone – bm: Topham
1063 – mr: Hulton – bm: Keystone – tl: Topham
1064 – tl: Popperfoto – bm: Keystone
1065 – mm: Hulton – br: Keystone – tr: Topham
1066 – bl: Popperfoto – tl, mm: Keystone
1067 – bm: Hulton – tm, ml: Keystone
1068 – tr: Magnum Photos Ltd. – br: Keystone
1069 – tm: Associated Press – bm: Keystone
1070 – tr: Popperfoto – bl: Keystone
1071 – tl, bm: Popperfoto – mr: Sygma, Paris
1072 – tr: Popperfoto – mr: Sygma, Paris – bm: Keystone
1073 – br: Cinémathèque Française – bl: Hulton – tm: Keystone – tr: Topham
1074 – tm, mr: Popperfoto
1075 – tl: Hulton – mr: Popperfoto
1076 – tm, bm: Popperfoto – mr: Keystone
1077 – bm: Syndication International – tm: Keystone – tr: Topham
1078 – tm, bm, mr: Popperfoto
1079 – tl: Sipa – tr: Keystone – br: Topham
1080 – ml: Hulton – mr: Popperfoto
1081 – ml: Popperfoto – tr: Sipa – tm, bm: Keystone
1082 – tm: Popperfoto – bl: Topham
1083 – mr: Hulton – tm: Sipa – bl: Sygma, Paris
1084 – tl: Hulton – mr: Topham
1085 – bm: Hulton – mm: Sygma, Paris – tl: Keystone
1086 – bm: Popperfoto – tm, mr: Sipa
1087 – tm: Hulton – bm: Popperfoto – mr: Keystone
1088 – tr: Popperfoto – br: Keystone – mr: Topham
1089 – bm: Sipa – tm, mr: Keystone
1090 – tl, br: Sipa
1091 – mm: Frank Spooner/Gamma – tm: Hulton
1092 – tm: Topham
1093 – tm: Hulton – br: Popperfoto – tl: Sipa – bl: Topham
1094 – tm: Popperfoto – mr: Keystone – bl: Topham
1095 – mm: Popperfoto – tl: Topham
1096 – tr: Popperfoto – br: Topham
1097 – br: Hulton – tm: Sipa – ml: Topham
1098 – tr, bm, tm: Popperfoto
1099 – tr, br: Keystone
1100 – tl: Cinémathèque Française – br: Rex Features
1101 – tl, bm: Popperfoto – tr: Sipa
1102 – tm: Sipa – mr, bm: Keystone
1103 – br: Sipa – tl, tr: Keystone
1104 – tl, br: Popperfoto – mm: Keystone
1105 – mr: Sipa – tl: Keystone
1106 – tm, bl: Hulton – mr: Popperfoto
1107 – tl: Frank Spooner/Gamma – bl: Hulton – mr: Sipa
1108 – bl, mr: Popperfoto – tm: Topham
1109 – mr: Popperfoto – tm: Sipa – bl: Keystone
1110 – mm: Popperfoto – tm: Sygma, Paris – br: Topham
1111 – tm: Topham
1112 – tm, br: Keystone
1113 – mr: Chronicle – bl: Popperfoto – tm: Keystone
1114 – tl: Keystone – mr: Topham
1115 – tl, tr: Sipa – bl: Topham
1116 – tm, ml, mr: Popperfoto
1117 – tl, br: Popperfoto – tr: Sipa – bl: Topham
1118 – bm: Hulton – mm: Popperfoto – tm: Topham
1119 – tr: Popperfoto – tm: Sipa – br: Topham
1120 – tm: Frank Spooner/Gamma – mr: Hulton
1121 – tm, mr: Sygma, Paris – br: Keystone
1122 – bm: Hulton – tm: Popperfoto – mr, mm: Sipa
1123 – bl: Kobal Collection – tl: Popperfoto – mr: Sipa
1124 – tm: Popperfoto – tl, bm: Keystone
1125 – bl: Popperfoto – tm: Sipa – br: Topham
1126 – mr: Popperfoto – tm: Sipa – bm: Keystone
1127 – tm: Popperfoto – br: Keystone
1128 – br: Kobal Collection – tm: Topham
1129 – bm: Popperfoto – tm: Sipa
1130 – bm: Frank Spooner/Gamma – br: Hulton – tm: Popperfoto
1131 – br: Cinémathèque Française – tr: Kobal Collection – tl: Sipa – bl: Keystone
1132 – tm: Hulton
1133 – br: Sipa – ml: Topham
1134 – br: Popperfoto – tm, mm: Sipa
1135 – mr: Frank Spooner/Gamma – tm: Popperfoto
1136 – tl: Frank Spooner/Gamma – bl: Topham
1137 – bl: Hulton – br: Kobal Collection – tr: Topham
1138 – mr, bm: Sygma, Paris – tm: Keystone
1139 – bm: Popperfoto – tm: Sipa
1140 – tr: Hulton – br: Sipa
1141 – tr: Popperfoto – mm: Sipa
1142 – br: Sipa – tm: Sygma, Paris
1143 – tr: Frank Spooner/Gamma – tl: Sipa
1144 – bm: Sipa – tr: Keystone
1145 – br: Kobal Collection – bl: Sipa – tl, tr: Keystone
1146 – br: Sipa – tm: Keystone
1147 – tl: Popperfoto – tr: Sipa – bl: Sygma, Paris
1148 – tl: Sipa – bm, mr: Keystone
1149 – tr: Hulton – ml: Topham
1150 – mm, tr, br: Sipa
1151 – tr: Hulton – ml: Sygma, Paris
1152 – mr: Popperfoto – tl: Sygma, Paris
1153 – mm: Frank Spooner/Gamma – tm: Sipa
1154 – mr: Popperfoto – bm: Sipa – tm: Sygma, Paris
1155 – tr: Popperfoto – tl: Sipa – br: Keystone
1156 – bm: Popperfoto – tm: Topham
1157 – bm: Frank Spooner/Gamma – br: Sipa – tm: Topham
1158 – tr, bl: Popperfoto – tl: Sipa
1159 – tr: Sipa – ml: Keystone
1160 – tr, bl: Sipa – tm: Keystone
1161 – tr: Kobal Collection – tm: Popperfoto – tl: Rex Features – br: Sipa
1162 – 1163 – sprd: Sichov/Sipa-Press
1164 – mr: Hulton – tm: Sygma, Paris – bm: Topham
1165 – tl: Sygma, Paris – mr: Keystone
1166 – bm: Hulton – mr: Sipa – tl: Keystone
1167 – tl, mr: Sygma, Paris
1168 – tr: Popperfoto – bm: Sipa
1169 – ml: Sygma, Paris – tr, mr: Topham
1170 – bm: Hulton – tl: Impact Photos
1171 – bm: Sipa – tm: Sygma, Paris
1172 – tl, mr: Popperfoto
1173 – br: Popperfoto – tl: Sipa – tr: Keystone
1174 – mm: Rex Features
1175 – mm: Keystone
1176 – tm: Frank Spooner/Gamma – br: Sipa
1177 – br: Hulton – tm: Sipa, Sygma, Paris
1178 – bl, mr: Popperfoto – tm: Sygma, Paris
1179 – tr: Rex Features – tl: Sygma, Paris – br: Topham
1180 – mr: Hulton – bl: Sipa – tm: Sygma, Paris
1181 – tr: Hulton – tl: Popperfoto – br: Keystone
1182 – tm: Sygma, Paris – bm: Keystone – mr: Topham
1183 – mr: Sygma, Paris – tl: Keystone – mm: Topham
1184 – br: Sipa – tm: Topham
1185 – br: Popperfoto – tr: Topham
1186 – mm: Popperfoto – tr: Keystone – br: Topham
1187 – mm: Network Photographers – br: Popperfoto – tm: Topham
1188 – tr, br: Keystone
1189 – br: Cinémathèque Française – mm: Sipa – tl: Sygma, Paris
1190 – tl, mr: Popperfoto
1191 – bm: Sygma, Paris – pm: Keystone
1192 – tl: Network Photographers – bm: Sygma, Paris – mr: Keystone
1193 – tl, br: Topham
1194 – bm: Sipa – tm: Sygma, Paris
1195 – tm: Pacemaker Press – mm: Keystone – br: Topham
1196 – mm: Rex Features – br: Topham
1197 – br: Chris Davies – tr: Kobal Collection – bl: Keystone – tl: Topham
1198 – tm: Network Photographers – bm: Popperfoto – br: Keystone
1199 – mm: Network Photographers
1200 – mr, bm: Popperfoto – tm: Topham
1201 – tr: Frank Spooner/Gamma – br: Popperfoto
1202 – br: Popperfoto – bm: Sygma, Paris – tl: Topham
1203 – tl: Chronicle – br: Sipa – bl: Topham
1204 – mr: Frank Spooner/Gamma – tr: Popperfoto – br: Keystone
1205 – tl: Chronicle – mr: Sipa – tr: Topham
1206 – bm: Sipa – mr: Sygma, Paris – tm: Topham
1207 – tl: Hulton – bl: Sygma, Paris – mr: Topham
1208 – bm: Sygma, Paris – tm: Topham
1209 – br: Sipa – tl, tm, bl: Sygma, Paris
1210 – tm, bm: Sygma, Paris – mr: Topham
1211 – bl: Sipa – tl, tm: Sygma, Paris
1212 – br: Cinémathèque Française – bm: Sygma, Paris, Topham
1213 – bm: Frank Spooner/Gamma – tm: Network Photographers – br: Sipa
1214 – tr: Frank Spooner/Gamma – br: Popperfoto – tl: Sygma, Paris
1215 – tl, bl: Science Photo Library – tr, br: Sygma, Paris
1216 – tm: Sipa
1217 – tr: Popperfoto – ml, br: Sygma, Paris
1218 – ml, mr: Popperfoto
1219 – tl: Network Photographers – bl: Topham
1220 – tl: Frank Spooner/Gamma – bl: Sipa – tr: Sygma, Paris
1221 – bl: Sipa – tm: Sygma, Paris èv br: Topham
1222 – ml: Hulton – tm: Sipa
1223 – bm: Frank Spooner/Gamma – mr: Sipa – tm, ml: Topham
1224 – mr: Sipa – br: Sygma, Paris – tr: Topham
1225 – tm: Sipa – br: Sygma, Paris
1226 – bl: Associated Press – tm, br: Hulton – mm: Sipa
1227 – tm: Sygma, Paris – bm: Topham
1228 – ml: Popperfoto – mr: Topham
1229 – tr: Rex Features – br: Sipa – tl: Sygma, Paris – bl: Topham
1230 – bm: Sipa – tm: Topham
1231 – tm: Sipa – mm, bl: Sygma, Paris – mr: Topham
1232 – tr: Network Photographers – mm: Popperfoto – bm: Topham
1233 – mr: Popperfoto – bm: Sipa – tm: Sygma, Paris
1234 – tr: Network Photographers
1235 – bm: Popperfoto – br: Sipa – tm: Keystone
1236 – tm: Sygma, Paris – bm: Topham
1237 – mr: Sipa – tl: Topham
1238 – tl, mr: Popperfoto – bm: Sygma, Paris
1239 – tl, br, bl: Sipa – tr: Sygma, Paris
1240 – mm: Sipa
1242 – mm, br: Sipa
1243 – tr: Network Photographers – mr: Topham
1244 – tl: Frank Spooner/Gamma – mm: Sipa – bm: Topham
1245 – tr: Network Photographers – bl: Popperfoto – tl: Sygma, Paris
1246 – bl: Frank Spooner/Gamma – tr: Sygma, Paris
1247 – br: Cinémathèqua Française – bl: Popperfopo – tr: Sipa – tl: Sygma, Paris
1248 – tm: Rex Features – bl: Sipa – mm: Topham
1249 – br: Network Photographers – tm: Sipa
1250 – tm: Sipa – br: Sygma, Paris
1251 – tm, bm: Sipa
1252 – ml: Rex Features
1253 – ml, br: Sipa – tr: The Observer/E. McCabe
1254 – tm: Sipa – br: Sygma, Paris
1255 – bl: Popperfoto – tr: Sipa – tl: Sygma, Paris
1256 – bl: Popperfoto – tl: Topham
1257 – ml: Popperfoto – br: Sipa – tr: Topham
1258 – tl, bl: Sygma, Paris
1259 – tr: Network Photographers – tm: Popperfoto – bl: Sipa – br: Sygma, Paris
1260 – mr: Sipa – tm, bm: Sygma, Paris
1261 – br: Hulton – tr: Popperfoto – mr: Sygma, Paris
1262 èv tr: Sipa – tm: Sygma, Paris
1263 – tm: Popperfoto – ml, tr: Sygma, Paris
1264 – tm: Sipa – tl, bl: Sygma, Paris
1265 – mm: Sipa – tl, mr: Sygma, Paris
1266 – tr: Sipa – bl: Sygma, Paris
1267 – bl: Frank Spooner/Gamma – tm, br: Sygma, Paris
1268 – tl: Novosti Press Agency – bm, br: Sygma, Paris
1269 – bl: Sipa – tl, tr: Sygma, Paris
1270 – bm: Sygma, Paris – tl: Topham
1271 – tm: Sipa – mr: Sygma, Paris – bl: Topham
1272 – br: Cinémathèque Française – ml: Sipa – tm: Topham
1273 – tl: Frank Spooner/Gamma – bm: Network Photographers
1274 – mr: Popperfoto – tl: Sygma, Paris – bm: Topham
1275 – mr: Network Photographers – tm: Popperfoto – bl: Topham
1276 – br: Frank Spooner/Gamma – tm, mm: Sygma, Paris
1277 – tr: Popperfoto – bl: Rex Features – tl: Sygma, Paris – br: Topham
1278 – tm, br: Sygma, Paris
1279 – bm: Popperfoto – tl, mr: Sipa
1280 – tl: Sipa – bm: Sygma, Paris
1281 – tr: Popperfoto – br: Sygma, Paris
1282 – tl: Popperfoto – br: Rex Features – tr: Sygma, Paris
1283 – tl, mr, bl: Sygma, Paris
1284 – tm: Chronicle – bl: Sipa – mm: Sygma, Paris
1285 – mm: Popperfoto – bl: Sipa – tr: Topham
1286 – mr: Popperfoto – tm: Sipa – ml: Sygma, Paris – bm: Topham
1287 – mr, bm: Sygma, Paris – tm: Topham
1288 – br: Sipa – tm: Sygma, Paris
1289 – tr: Popperfoto – mr: Topham
1290 – tm: Chronicle – bl: Sipa – br: Sygma, Paris – tl: Topham
1291 – tm, bm: Pacemaker Press
1292 – tl: Rex Features, Sipa – br: Sipa
1293 – tr: National Theatre, London – br: Sygma, Paris
1294 – tm: Rex Features
1295 – mr: Popperfoto – bl: Rex Features – tm: Topham
1296 – tm: Pacemaker Press – bm: Rex Features
1297 – bl: Allsport – tr: Topham
1298 – ml, bl: Rex Features – tr: Topham
1299 – bm: Rex Features – tr: Topham
1300 – tm: Chronicle – bm: Topham
1301 – br: Allsport – ml: Rex Features – tr: Topham
130 : Allsport
1304 – tr, mm, br: Rex Features
1305 – bm: Rex Features – tr: Topham
1306 – br: Chronicle – tm: Popperfoto – bm: Rex Feapures
1307 – br: Popperfoto – tr: Topham
1308 – br: Chronicle – tl, tr: Topham
1309 – br: Rex Features – tl, mm: Topham
1310 – mr: Sipa – tm, bm: Topham/Associated Press
1311 – tl: Empics Nottingham – mr: Rex Features
1312 – tm, mr, bm: Rex Features
1313 – br: Allsport – bl: Sipa – tm: Topham/Associated Press
1314 – br: Rex Features – tr: Topham
1315 – tl, mr: Rex Features – bl: Topham/Associated Press
1316 – bm: Popperfoto – tl: Rex Features
1317 – br: Rex Features – tl: Topham/Associated Press
1318 – tr: Popperfoto – ml: Rex Features
1319 – bl: Allsport – tm: Popperfoto – mr: Science Photo Library/NASA
1320 – ml: Popperfoto – br: Topham/Associated Press
1321 – br: Allsport – tr: Popperfoto – br: Topham/Associated Press
1322 – tx, mm: Rex Features – ty, tr: Topham
1323 – mr: Popperfoto – tr, tl, bl: Rex Features
1324 – bm: Allsport – tm: Popperfoto – mr: Rex Features
1325 – tm: Rex Features
1326 – tm, mm, bl: Rex Features
1327 – tr, mm: Rex Features

1328 – mm, br: Popperfoto
1329 – br: BBC Enterprises/J. Cahrrington – tr: Kobal Collection – tl: Topham/Associated Press
1330-1331 – sprd: Skyvisual/Sipa-Image
1332 – tr: Rex Features – ml: Topham/Associated Press
1333 – tr: Popperfoto – ml: Rex Features
1334 – tr: Rex Features – tl: Topham/Associated Press
1335 – mr: Popperfoto/AFP – tl, bl: Rex Features
1336 – br: Franck Spooner Pictures – tl: Popperfoto
1337 – bl: Popperfoto/AFP – mr: Press Association/Topham – tl: Rex Features
1338 – tr: Popperfoto/AFP – ml: Press Association/Topham – br: Ronald Grant Archive
1339 – tm: Allsport – br: Rex Features
1340 – bl, br: Rex Features – tl, tr: Topham/Associated Press
1341 – tr: Chronicle – ml: Popperfoto/AFP – mr: Topham/Associated Press
1342 – br: Allsport – tr: Topham/Associated Press
1343 – br: Allsport – ml: Rex Features – tr: Topham/Associated Press
1344 – tm: Popperfoto/AFP – ml: Topham/Associated Press
1345 – tr: Popperfoto/AFP – bm: Press Association/Topham – ml: Rex Features
1346 – tl, mr: Rex Features – ml: Topham/Associated Press
1347 – br: Channel Four – tr: Rex Features – tl: Topham
1348 – tr, bm: Rex Features
1349 – ml, br: Rex Features
1350 – bm: Chronicle – mm: Franck Spooner Pictures – tm: Rex Features
1351 – tl: Popperfoto – bl: Rex Features – br: Viz
1352 – bm: Franck Spooner Pictures – tm: Rex Features
1353 – tm: Associated Press/Topham – bm: Chronicle – mr: Topham
1354 – bm: Popperfoto – tm: Rex Features
1355 – bl: Associated Press – tm: Chronicle – br: Rex Features
1356 – tl: Rex Features – br: Topham
1357 – tr, bm: Popperfoto
1358 – bm: Chronicle – mm: Popperfoto – tm: Rex Features
1359 – tm: Rex Features – bl: Allsport – br: Kobal Collection
1360 – mr: Associated Press – bl: Popperfoto – tm: Rex Features
1361 – mr: Associated Press – tm, br: Rex Features
1362 – mm: Chronicle – tl, br: Rex Features
1363 – tl, bm: Popperfoto – tr: Rex Features
1364 – tl: Associated Press – tr: Popperfoto – bm: Rex Features
1365 – tr: Opera International – ml: Popperfoto – br: Ronald Grant Archive
1366 – tm, mr, bl: Sipa
1367 – bl: Rex Features/Sipa-Press – br: Sipa Sport – tm: Sipa
1368 – tm, tr, bl, br: Sipa
1369 – tm, bl: Sipa
1370 – tr, bl, br: Sipa
1371 – br: Sipa Sport – tm, bl, br: Sipa
1372 – tm, tr, br: Sipa
1373 – ml: Sipa Sport – tr: Sipa
1374 – mm: Sipa Sport
1375 – tm: Sipa Sport
1376 – ml: Rex Features/Sipa-Press – br: Sipa Sport – tm: Sipa
1377 – mr, br, tl: Sipa
1378 – br: Rex Features/Sipa-Press – tm: Sipa
1379 – br: Rex Features/Sipa-Press – tr, ml, bl: Sipa
1380 – tl, tr, br, mr, bl: Sipa
1381 – tl, br: Sipa
1382 – tl, bl, br: Sipa
1383 – tr, bl, br, mr: Sipa
1384 – tl, bl: Sipa
1385 – tr, ml, br: Sipa
1386 – tl, bl, br: Sipa
1387 – tm: Rex Features/Sipa-Press – bl, br: Sipa
1388 – mr: Rex Features/Sipa-Press – tr: Sipa – br: Colorsport/Sipa-Sport
1389 – t, br, bl: Sipa
1390 – t, b: Sipa
1391 – mr: Mercury Press/Sipa-Press – tr, bm: Sipa
1392 – bm, mm, tr: Sipa
1393 – br: Times/Rex Features/Sipa-Press – tr, ml: Sipa
1394 – tl, mr: Sipa – br: Sipa-Sport
1395 – tr, mm, br: Sipa
1396 – tm, mr, bm: Sipa
1397 – tr: Sipa – mm: QA Photos – br: Hulton Deutsch/Sipa-Press
1398 – tm, ml, bm: Sipa
1399 – tm: Sipa – mr: Action Images/Sipa-Press – br: NASA/Sipa-Press – bl: Rex Features/Sipa-Press
1400 – tl, mr, br: Sipa
1401 – mm, br: Sipa – tr: Pica Press/Sipa-Press
1402 – tr, ml: Sipa – bl: Rex Features/Sipa-Press – br: Alpha Diffusion/Sipa-Press
1403 – tm, br: Sipa – bl: Sipa-Sport
1404 – tr: Alpha Diffusion/Sipa-Press – mm: Gamma/LCI/TF1 – bl: Rex Features/Sipa-Press
1405 – tr, ml, br: Sipa
1406 – tr: Photocall/Sipa-Press – br: Rex Features/Sipa-Press – mr, bm: Sipa
1407 – tm: West Pool/Sipa-Press – bm: Rex Features/Sipa-Press – mm: East News/Sipa-Press
1408 – tm: Edmund Evening News/Sipa-Press – mr, bm: Sipa
1409 – tm: Sipa – bm, br: Rex Features/Sipa-Press

Olympics Abbreviations

AFG Afghanistan
ALG Algeria
ANT Antilles
ARG Argentina
ARS Saudi Arabia
AUS Australia
AUT Austria
BAH Bahamas
BAR Barbados
BEL Belgium
BER Bermuda
BIR Burma
BOH Bohemia
BRA Brazil
BUL Bulgaria
CAF Central Africa Republic
CAN Canada
CEY Ceylon
CGO Congo Republic
CHI Chile
CHN China
CIV Ivory Coast
CMR Cameroon
COL Colombia
CRC Costa Rica
CUB Cuba
DEN Denmark
DOM Dominican Republic
ECU Equador
EGY Egypt
ESP Spain
EST Estonia
ETH Ethiopia
FIJ Fiji
FIN Finland
FRA France
FRG Federal Republic of Germany
GAB Gabon
GBR Great Britain
GDR German Democratic Republic
GER Germany
GHA Ghana
GRE Greece
GUA Guatemala
GUI Guinea
GUY Guyana
HAI Haiti
HBR British Honduras
HKG Hong Kong
HOL Netherlands
HON Honduras
HUN Hungary
INA Indonesia
IND India
IRL Ireland
IRN Iran
IRQ Iraq
ISL Iceland
ISR Israel
ITA Italy
JAM Jamaica
JPN Japan
KEN Kenya
KHM Cambodia
KOR South Korea
KUW Kuwait
LBA Libya
LBR Liberia
LES Lesotho
LIB Lebanon
LIE Liechtenstein
LIT Lithuania
LUX Luxembourg
MAD Madagascar
MAL Malaysia
MAR Morocco
MEX Mexico
MGL Mongolia
MLI Mali
MLT Malta
MON Monaco
NBO North Borneo
NCA Nicaragua
NEP Nepal
NIG Nigeria
NOR Norway
NZL New Zealand
PAK Pakistan
PAN Panama
PAR Paraguay
PER Peru
PHI Philippines
POL Poland
POR Portugal
PRK North Korea
PUR Puerto Rico
RHO Rhodesia
ROM Rumania
RUS Russia
SAA Sarre
SAF South Africa
SAL El Salvador
SEN Senegal
SIN Singapore
SLE Sierra Leone
SMR San Marino
SUD Sudan
SUI Switzerland
SUR Surinam
SWE Sweden
SYR Syria
TAI Taiwan (Formosa)
TAN Tanzania
TCA Tchad
TCH Czechoslovakia
THA Thailand
TNG Tanganyika
TRI Trinidad and Tobago
TUN Tunisia
TUR Turkey
UGA Uganda
URS Soviet Union
URU Uruguay
USA United States of America
VEN Venezuela
VNM Vietnam
VOL Upper Volta (Burkina Faso)
YUG Yugoslavia
ZAI Zaire
ZAM Zambia

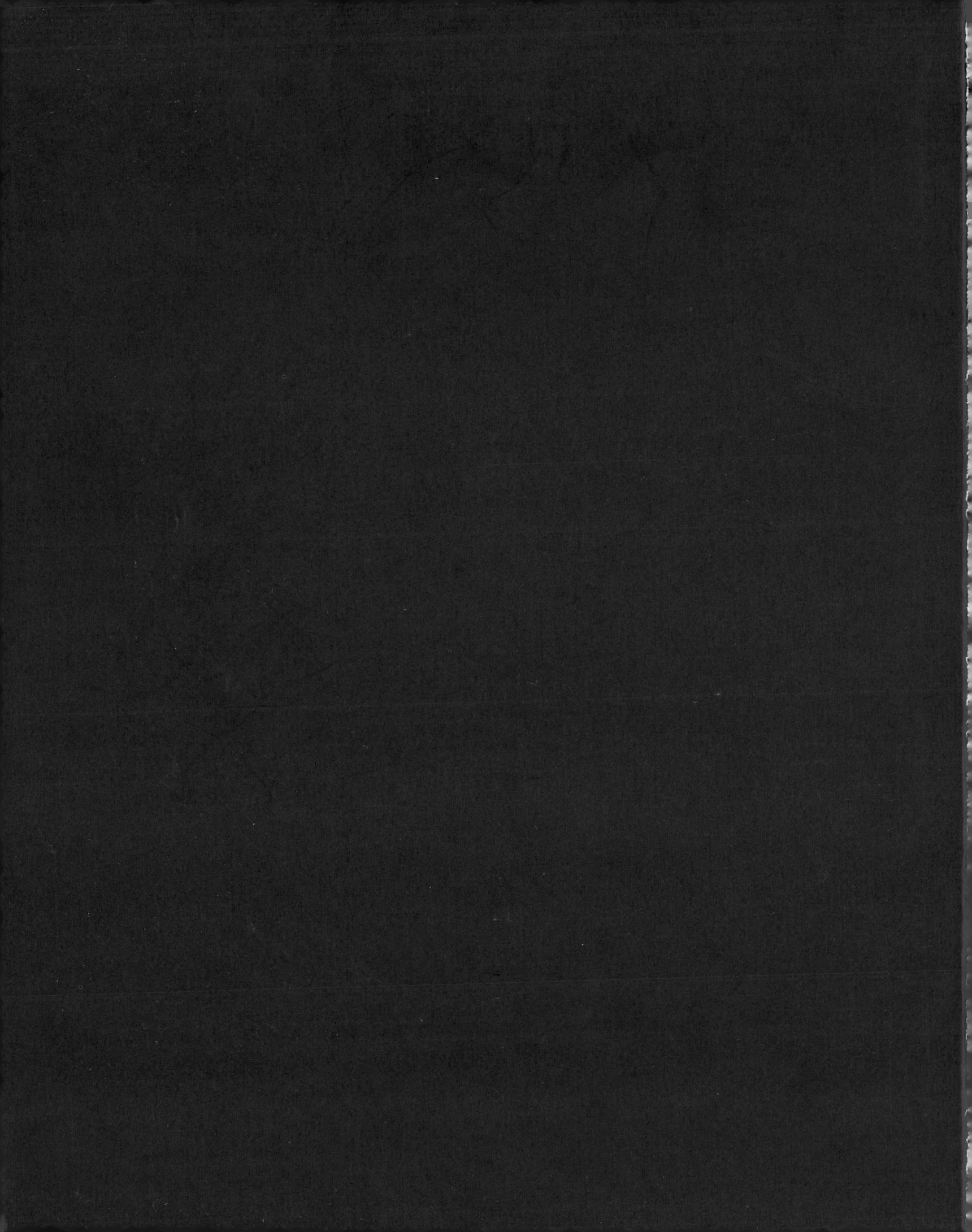